The Baseball Encyclopedia®

The Baseball Encyclopedia®

TENTH EDITION • REVISED, UPDATED, AND EXPANDED

The Complete and Definitive Record of Major League Baseball

Macmillan • USA

TENTH EDITION
EDITORIAL AND RESEARCH STAFF
Jeanine Bucek, Editorial Director
Traci Cothran
Bill Deane
Bob Kerler
Maria Massey
Bob Tiemann
Richard Topp
Ken Samelson, Statistical Director

Special thanks to Frank J. Williams, John Kovach, John Holway, Dick Clark, and the Society for American Baseball Research.

Macmillan
A Simon & Schuster Macmillan Company
1633 Broadway
New York, NY 10019

Macmillan is a registered trademark of Macmillan, Inc.

A catalogue record is available from
the Library of Congress

ISBN 0-02-860815-1 (book)
ISBN 0-02-861435-6 (book with CD-ROM)

Macmillan books are available at special discounts for bulk purchases for sales promotions, premiums, fund-raising, or educational use. For details, contact:

Special Sales Director
Macmillan Books
1633 Broadway
New York, NY 10019

Tenth Edition 1996

10 9 8 7 6 5 4 3 2 1

Printed in the United States of America

Contents

Preface

Part of the enduring beauty and charm of the game of baseball is that its history spans generation upon generation, a history of one generation handing down the tradition and legacy of the national pastime to the next generation.

And in a sense, the enduring beauty and charm of *The Baseball Encyclopedia* follows in that same path, because the *Encyclopedia* represents not just the work of a few dedicated baseball researchers and historians, but rather the passing along of a torch that keeps the flame of baseball lore and legend alive.

In keeping with that tradition, it is incumbent upon us, the editorial staff at Macmillan, to acknowledge the efforts of all baseball fans all over the world who breathe life into the *Encyclopedia* and keep its rich legacy growing. Whether it's used for a definite purpose, such as to check on a player's batting average or a pitcher's shutouts, or merely for a leisurely stroll to find unusual nicknames, the *Encyclopedia* has been with us since 1969, and is now in its tenth edition.

The People Who Made the Encyclopedia Happen

As mentioned, the *Encyclopedia* represents the efforts of baseball fans everywhere, but there are certain individuals whose special efforts made the *Encyclopedia* come together.

Back in the late 1960s, two of baseball's finest historians were called upon to help put the *Encyclopedia* together. One was Lee Allen, the historian of the Baseball Hall of Fame in Cooperstown, New York, and the other was John Tattersall, an executive with a steamship firm in Philadelphia. Both men marveled at the idea of a complete reference work. Allen—long known as "the walking encyclopedia of baseball"—specialized in accumulating facts about the players. He had spent thirty years collecting the largest baseball demographic file in the country. A lot of that time had been spent visiting state record bureaus, speaking to ballplayers, corresponding with the descendants of ballplayers long dead, and even pursuing leads to graveyards to look at burial markers in search of birth and death dates.

Lee Allen suffered a fatal heart attack on May 20, 1969, and did not live to see the final product of his efforts, the culmination of a lifelong dream. Historian, columnist, reporter, and author, Lee was one of our foremost authorities on baseball.

Tattersall's forty-year plunge into nineteenth-century baseball history made him an expert on that period. The original material he gathered over the years was housed in a basement library that contained boxes of the sports sections of different newspapers from the early 1900s through the 1960s, a wide assortment of baseball publications, and a collection of scrapbooks from 1876 through 1900. There were box scores of every major league game played during that time, neatly preserved by year and league. By using these books, Tattersall was able to construct day-by-day playing records, which helped him to find or reconfirm past statistical achievements. The contribution of Allen and Tattersall and their invaluable collections really got the project off the ground.

A Word on Methodology and Historical Accuracy

The Baseball Encyclopedia is, and always has been, a work in progress. As such, it is the stated purpose of Macmillan's editorial staff to continue to make the *Encyclopedia* as accurate as possible. Unlike some other baseball recordkeepers, Macmillan does not recognize a statute of limitations on truth and accuracy when it comes to baseball records.

In our search for the truth, we constantly check all of our internal records and doublecheck all entries to verify the accuracy of the statistics and demographic records.

Occasionally, we discover a discrepancy in our records. The vast majority of these occur due to typographical errors in our recordkeeping devices. When such a discrepancy is discovered, we go back through our computerized database to find the source of the error and correct it. The forefathers of *The Baseball Encyclopedia* were clever enough to have written into the original database a verification program that insists that all batting, pitching, and fielding records add up, much in the way that a box score can be balanced at the end of a game.

This doublechecking program, known at Macmillan as the vertical edit, has been in use since 1969 when the first *Encyclopedia* was published. In 1988 and 1989, the editorial staff of the *Encyclopedia* did an extensive review of the vertical editing process and found some internal recordkeeping errors that were corrected in the eighth edition of *The Baseball Encyclopedia*. One of the most-discussed statistical corrections was that to the record of Honus Wagner. In 1969, when the first *Encyclopedia* was published, Wagner's lifetime batting average was calculated to be .327. That was based upon all of the research completed for the first edition of the *Encyclopedia*. Yet in the ensuing years, Wagner's records were inexplicably altered to reflect additional hits that our database has no record of. (Remember, if hits are added to the database, the vertical edit insists that a specific pitcher be charged with those hits.) Indeed, no matter how many times the vertical edit was run by Macmillan, the computerized printouts kept pointing to an unbalanced lifetime batting record for Honus Wagner.

Over the years, because of these added unexplained hits,

Wagner's lifetime batting average grew to .329. But when the eighth edition of the *Encyclopedia* was being prepared, since there was no statistical record of these extra Wagner hits nor was there any historical paper trail to explain why these extra hits had crept into his record, they were eliminated from Wagner's record. Sure enough, once the extra hits had been erased, the vertical edit came into balance. Furthermore, Wagner's lifetime batting average reverted to .327—the very same batting average that he had when the first edition of the *Encyclopedia* had been published in 1969. This change was made strictly by the Macmillan editorial staff, and was done based upon the vertical edit process, which serves as a balancing tool in our research.

This is not to suggest that statistical changes are not made to the *Encyclopedia*. Indeed, we do make changes to the book, but we make them only when they can first be verified and balanced in accordance with the scoring rules of major league baseball.

The History of Balancing the Database

When the first edition of the *Encyclopedia* was put together in the late 1960s, it was a given that some existing records would be called into question. Therefore, it became necessary to get official sanction for the project from baseball. Indeed, the presidents of both the American and National leagues enthusiastically put their stamp of approval on the project after hearing the plan.

In their presentation to the presidents, the *Encyclopedia* researchers showed how the old, hand-posted records would be transferred into a computerized database. The researchers knew that there were literally millions of entries to be entered into the database, and that such a project would probably involve some clerical mistakes. Building the vertical edit process into the database ensured that these clerical errors would be caught when each year's data was tabulated and balanced.

Further, in order to verify the research findings and set up guidelines never before established for this kind of historical work, a Special Records Committee was formed to discuss and vote upon the issues in question. The group consisted of representatives from the commissioner's office and both league offices, as well as representatives from the Hall of Fame and the Baseball Writer's Association of America. (The names of the committee members along with their rulings can be found in Appendix B.)

The actual material entered into the database consisted of baseball's official records—documents that record a man's day-to-day playing performance. Along with these microfilmed records were hundreds of reels of microfilmed newspapers from the early 1870s until 1920—the collection of baseball historians Lee Allen and John Tattersall—and baseball's trade papers, which included *The Sporting News*, *The Sporting Times*, and *The Sporting Life*. A basic file was established that contained the names of every man who had played major league baseball, along with the years he played and his team affiliations. Once this information was gathered and fed into the computer, rosters for each year, league, and team were produced. These rosters served as forms for entering the information. This meant that no player's yearly record would be missed. It was also a method for eliminating players included on the roster by mistake. If, for instance, a man played for New York in the National League in 1917 and was erroneously placed on the roster of the 1917 New York American League club, the mistake would be caught when the yearly information was entered from the source material.

To complete the information on the roster forms, baseball's official record sheets were the first source used. These data were supplemented by information researched from newspapers. For the years when official record sheets did not exist, they were produced, for the first time, after careful study of over 19,000 games. This was accomplished by transcribing data from newspaper box scores and stories to obtain the necessary day-by-day tallies. The best sources for the information were usually the local newspapers of the city where the game was played and the city of the visiting team.

Sometimes, however, as many as ten sources were checked to re-create a game and accurately determine such items as runs batted in and earned runs. If necessary, researchers traveled to cities and small towns and spent days in libraries and historical societies digging through the newspaper stacks. It was a gigantic puzzle, with the pieces falling slowly into place.

While the search for statistical information was being conducted, research on the demographic file was also in progress. This involved checking a player's height, weight, batting and throwing style, birth, death, relatives in the major leagues, nicknames, and managerial information. This sometimes led to the discovery of "phantoms," men who were originally included on baseball's all-time list because of typographical errors in the box scores. At the same time, "new" men were found, men who may have only pinch hit or pinch run and were never included in a box score.

The last important step of the research phase began when the statistical information from the roster was fed into the computer. Certain checksthe vertical editwere built into the system to ensure the accuracy of the final records. For example, if a team's hits did not equal the hits of the individuals on the team, a message was printed along with the information and the item in question. Only when this statistical dilemma was balanced would the vertical edit let the materials pass through. To this day, the vertical edit remains a feature of the Macmillan fact-checking process.

Macmillan's Baseball Historical Committee

Commencing with the ninth edition of the *Encyclopedia*, published in 1993, and continuing with this tenth edition, Macmillan has assembled a blue-ribbon panel of noted baseball historians to aid us in our search for accuracy. This panel includes Bill Deane, former Senior Research Associate at the National Baseball Hall of Fame in Cooperstown, New York; Dr. George Kirsch, professor of history at Manhattan College; and Bill James, the best-selling baseball author.

Macmillan has submitted to this panel a number of historical anomalies and has abided by their decisions on such matters. Again, only questions of historical accuracy have been addressed by the committee; internal vertical editing discrepancies have been handled by Macmillan.

If you have any questions regarding the statistical or demographic content of *The Baseball Encyclopedia*, submit them in writing, with complete historical documentation, to Ken Samelson, The Baseball Encyclopedia, Macmillan Books, 1633 Broadway, New York, NY 10019.

A List of Significant Challenges

A number of challenges to the Encyclopedia were presented during 1993–95. Only those challenges that carried substantial written documentation were reviewed by the Macmillan Baseball Historical Committee. Only those challenges that were accepted unanimously by the committee as historically legitimate and accurate have been entered into the *Encyclopedia*'s permanent record. Several of the challenges were originally printed in *The Baseball Records Update,* which was prepared by the Records Committee of The Society for American Baseball Research and published in 1993.

(1)Challenges to the pitching records of Walter Johnson

In 1912, there was a game on August 5 between Washington and Chicago (American League) in which Johnson pitched. According to Frank Williams, Johnson should have been ruled the winning pitcher in that game instead of Carl Cashion. Johnson entered a 7–7 game in the bottom of the eighth inning, pitched 2 1/3 scoreless innings and finished the game, while driving in the winning run in the top of the tenth inning. The official records credit the victory to Cashion, who pitched 5 1/3 innings in relief of starter Bob Groom, who lasted 2 1/3 innings. Interestingly, in 1912 Johnson became the first American League pitcher to win 16 consecutive games, a streak that lasted from July 3 to August 23 and included the August 5 victory. Williams felt that "it was probably a simple clerical error that resulted in the official sheets showing Cashion as the winner." Williams also pointed out that an additional inning pitched should be added to Johnson's record in 1912. On September 2 of that year, Johnson pitched 10 innings in a complete-game loss to Philadelphia, but the official sheets credited him with only 9 innings pitched. Adding a victory to Johnson's 1912 record gives him a 33–12 season record, and his lifetime win total becomes 417, instead of the 416 that was listed previously. As for Cashion, Macmillan had already showed him with a correct record of 10–6, rather than the 11–6 listed on the day-to-day sheets. In addition, Johnson now has 369 innings pitched for 1912.

(2)Challenges to the batting records of Roger Maris

On July 5, 1961, Roger Maris of the New York Yankees was credited with 2 RBI in a game against the Cleveland Indians at Yankee Stadium. Research by Ron Rakowski showed Maris should have been credited only with 1 RBI. The play in question came in the third inning. Tony Kubek was on first base when Maris singled to right field, sending Kubek to third base. Cleveland's right fielder Willie Kirkland attempted to throw out Kubek at third, but Kubek slid in ahead of the throw. Third baseman Bubba Phillips then threw to first base, trying to get Maris rounding the bag. The throw went into the stands and Kubek was awarded home plate on the play, with Maris advancing to third. Maris was given 2 RBI on the official scoresheet, having hit a solo home run in the seventh inning. He should not have been given an RBI on the third-inning play. According to the official records, Maris led the American League in 1961 with 142 RBI. Subtracting 1 now leaves him tied with Baltimore's Jim Gentile with 141.

(3) Challenges to the batting records of Herman Long

The original ICI records contained errors in Long's batting records with Boston of the National League in 1892, which were found by Frank Williams. Long should be given an additional RBI, making his season total 78. On June 14 against Cincinnati, the ICI sheet gave Long a home run and 1 RBI, but his home run came with a man on base.

(4)Challenges to the batting records of Roger Connor

On June 2, 1890, Connor, playing for New York of the Player's League, had a home run and 1 RBI against Boston, according to research by Frank Williams, not a single and RBI as shown on the ICI sheet. His league-leading home-run total changes from 13 to 14.

(5)Challenges to the batting records of Harry Stovey

Stovey, a member of Boston of the Player's League in 1890, had an error on his ICI sheet for that season. For the September 20 game at Chicago, Stovey was given a triple and no RBI on his ICI sheet, but he should instead be given credit for a home run and an RBI for his third-inning homer off Silver King, according to Frank Williams's research. His corrected 1890 totals are 11 triples, 12 home runs, and 83 RBI.

(6)Challenges to the batting records of Dan Brouthers

On July 4, 1891, Brouthers, playing for Boston of the American Association, homered against Columbus. The ICI sheet gives him a 2-run homer and 2 RBI, but Frank Williams found that the home run came with 2 men on base, increasing his RBI total to 109 for 1891.

(7)Challenges to the batting records of Mike Tiernan

Tiernan had been credited with a home run and 1 RBI on the ICI sheet for New York in a National League contest against Brooklyn on October 3, 1891. Pete Palmer found that Tiernan had a single and RBI in that game, so his home-run total drops to 16.

(8)Challenges to the batting records of Bobby Lowe

On May 11, 1893, Lowe, playing for Boston of the National League, hit a grand slam home run, giving him 4 RBI in a game at Brooklyn. Pete Palmer found that the ICI sheet gave him the 4 RBI, but with a single instead of home run. Lowe's correct home-run total for 1893 is 14.

(9)Challenges to the pitching records of the 1914 Boston Braves

Frank Williams found two errors on the official National League pitching sheets for Boston in 1914. On August 8, two pitchers, Dick Rudolph and Paul Strand, each received credit for Boston's victory over Cincinnati. According to Frank Williams, Strand should keep his victory, and 1 should be deducted from Rudolph's total. Rudolph left the game behind 3–0 and was relieved by Strand, who pitched the final two innings as Boston rallied for a 4–3 win. Rudolph should have a win deducted, making his record 26–10.

The second error concerned the second game of a double-header at Brooklyn on October 5. The Braves won 9–5, but no pitcher was credited with the victory. Tom Hughes, the starting pitcher, went 8 innings, and was pinch hit for in the ninth, when Boston rallied for 5 runs to overcome a 5–4 deficit and win 9–5. Hughes should get credit for the victory, making his record 2–0.

(10)Challenges to the batting records of Hardy Richardson

Frank Williams made corrections to Richardson's ICI sheets for 1890 and 1891. Richardson played for Boston in the Player's League in 1890, and the ICI sheets gave him 2 singles, a double, and 2 RBI on April 26 against New York. The correct totals are 1 single, a double, a home run, and 4 RBI. He had run-scoring singles in the second and seventh, and he slammed a 2-run home run off Ed Crane in the sixth inning.

On May 22 against Pittsburgh, Richardson was given a single, a double, and 3 RBI, but he should instead receive credit for a double, 1 home run, and 3 RBI. Richardson hit a 2-run homer in the second inning against Al Maul, and his double scored a run in the fifth inning. On June 5 against Philadelphia, he should receive an additional RBI, as his second-inning home run was listed as a 2-run homer, but it was hit with 2 runners on base, giving him 3, not 2, RBI for that game. His 1890 totals should be adjusted to 13 home runs and 146 RBI.

Richardson was a member of Boston's American Association team in 1891. In the August 18 game against Baltimore, Richardson was given credit for a home run and 3 RBI, but his home run came with the bases loaded in the second inning, and he should receive an additional RBI, making his 1891 total 52.

A Special Word of Thanks

There are a group of people who made this book happen and I'd like to take this opportunity to thank them for their time, energy, hard work, and devotion to making the *Encyclopedia* as great a baseball statistical reference as it can be.

Although there have been ten editions in its history, the *Encyclopedia,* in the form of its database, is never finished. It's an ongoing project that is tended, maintained, and cared for by its Statistical Director, Ken Samelson. Ken has made the Eighth, Ninth, and now the Tenth editions books, of which we are incredibly proud. His job is to know the game of baseball, pure and simple, and to present that game's facts and figures in the most accurate and definitive way. Ken is the keeper of the flame.

On the editorial side, we were wonderfully assisted by Macmillan publisher Natalie Chapman; Traci Cothran; Bill Deane; John Holway and Dick Clark on the Negro Leagues; Bob Tiemann for the Home/Road Performance section; and John Dewan, Steve Moyer, and Dave Mundo of Stats, Inc.

For the production work on the *Encyclopedia,* we would like to thank Richard Fusco of Simon and Schuster, George Yates of Yates Engineering Systems, Tony Luca of Finite Matters, Laurie Barnett, Scott Cook, Maria Massey, David Frost, Michele Laseau, Mohammed Al-Jabr, Barry Wolborsky, Jen McGlashan, Josh Berger, Barry Rogers, Ben Torter, and Hilary Smith.

For the people who contribute their efforts to *The Baseball Encyclopedia,* it truly is a labor of love. But we would also like to thank the fans who have expressed their love for the game by writing us and making the *Encyclopedia* the choice for their enjoyment of our national pastime. Thanks for making our tenth edition possible.

—Jeanine Bucek
Editorial Director

PART ONE

Introduction

America's Game: A Brief History of Baseball

America's Game: A Brief History of Baseball

David Q. Voigt

Organized baseball emerged at a time when the American nation was transforming from an agrarian to an urban industrial society. By the 1840s games were being played in northeastern towns and cities where early forms of baseball supplied a necessary recreational outlet for young men and boys. As a field sport the game of baseball had no sire, and debunking scholars have relegated the fable of the game's purported 1839 invention by the young West Point cadet Abner Doubleday to the historical dustbin. Indeed, American baseball developed out of informal bat and ball games, such as rounders and town ball, and with some infusions from English cricket, a game that was formally organized in the eighteenth century.

In 1845 the evolving game of baseball reached a stable equilibrium when the New York Knickerbocker Club published a version of the game inspired by one of its members, Alexander J. Cartwright. Cartwright's version included the familiar diamond-shaped infield with bases set ninety feet apart, a forty-five-foot pitching distance, and nine-man teams playing under such rules as three outs to end a team's inning at bat and three strikes as one way to put a batter out. Once published, this version of the game caught on and eclipsed competing forms. But continuing modifications over the years pose a reminder that American baseball is a constantly evolving sport.

During the 1850s popular enthusiasm for baseball inspired a veritable mania in the northeastern sections of America. As organized clubs and players proliferated, the growing numbers of spectators prompted clubs to charge admission prices and to compete with each other for the services of good players. In 1858 the newly organized National Association of Base Ball Players (NABBP) attempted to impose its authority and its definition of amateurism on the various clubs. By 1860, sixty clubs were enrolled as members of the association. But if the association succeeded in standardizing playing rules and equipment, it failed to regulate championship play or to halt the growing trend of teams paying players for their services.

But ineffective leadership failed to stunt the game's sturdy growth. Nor did the Civil War; converts were won over to the game among soldiers of both armies who played and watched games at camp sites during the war years. And on the northern home front strong teams like the Brooklyn Excelsiors and Brooklyn Atlantics continued to attract enthusiastic fans, some of whom followed the Atlantics as the team posted undefeated seasons in 1864 and 1865.

As the war ended a second baseball mania swept the land. No longer a regional pastime, the game burst its bounds by 1867 as over 100 of the 300 member clubs of the association hailed from midwestern towns and cities. And fueling the latest boom were the writings of Henry Chadwick, who was already acclaimed as the "Father of the Game." A tireless reporter of games, Chadwick designed a box score, edited guidebooks, published a history of the game in 1867, and served on the association's playing rules committee. The doughty Chadwick continued to serve the game for forty years.

The 1870s

Although still lacking a formal league organization or set playing schedules, by the end of the 1860s baseball was widely touted as America's "national game." As fans flocked to playing fields of the organized clubs, whose membership rolls included gentlemanly patrons, many willingly paid to see exciting games played by teams that now employed deceptive underhand pitching and defensive and offensive teamwork. By 1869 the best players were being paid in various ways, a trend that the amateur leaders of the NABBP viewed with alarm. And when the Cincinnati Red Stockings that year opted to field an openly all-salaried team under player-manager Harry Wright, the Reds' undefeated record of that season (which continued until the early part of the 1870 campaign) boosted the cause of professional baseball supporters. Although the Reds returned no profits to their joint-stock-company investors, their bold course of action inspired imitators and ignited the smoldering dispute between amateurs and professionals in NABBP councils to full flame by the end of the 1870 season.

In 1870 the hostilities between these factions so disrupted the association's annual meeting that the amateurs staged a walkout. But the professionals retaliated by forming their own league in March of 1871. That coup destroyed the amateur association and marked the beginnings of major league baseball in America. Thereafter the professional major leagues dominated organized baseball by effecting changes in rules and style of play.

As the first professional major league, the National Association of Professional Base Ball Players (NAPBBP) lasted five seasons and was controlled by the players, who enjoyed freedom of contract and a powerful voice in its councils. Although most member clubs were financed by profit-minded investors, player salaries came first. But with attendance averaging fewer than 3,000 a game, most clubs lost money. Disenchanted investors blamed those losses on the players, whose excessive freedoms led to such chronic abuses as contract jumping, poor discipline, and shady dealings with gamblers.

The NAPBBP also suffered from serious organizational problems. Like its amateur predecessor, whose playing rules and organizational structure were carried on, the NAPBBP lacked a fixed playing schedule of games. Instead, each team was required to play each rival five times a season with playing dates arranged by correspondence. Each season's championship pennant went to the team with the most victories, but seldom did a team meet its full quota of games. And the league's easy entrance policy allowed any team to enter by paying a ten-dollar entry fee, a system that led to frequent dropouts by outclassed teams. Moreover, there were endless disputes over playing dates, ticket pricing, the division of gate receipts, and poor officiating by volunteer umpires. Worse still, the league lacked competitive balance, a perennial problem that would plague major league baseball until the 1980s. At this time four of the NAPBBP's five pennants were won by the Boston Red Stockings.

Nevertheless the NAPBBP popularized professional baseball in America. Large crowds often flocked to the wooden parks to watch contending teams like the Boston Reds, which hosted 70,000 home fans in 1875. By then Boston's budget was $35,000, and manager Harry Wright's innovations in equipment procurement, training of players, park administration, and even his profitless 1874 baseball junket to Britain set standards for future promoters. At this time Wright was justly acclaimed as the "Father of Professional Baseball." And the short-lived NAPBBP, which Wright helped to found, furnished spectators with sprightly games and heroic players to worship. Expanded newspaper coverage and annual guides edited by Chadwick also stirred public interest in the professional game, which moved to a higher level of organization in 1876.

That year Chicago promoter William A. Hulbert staged a coup that replaced the player-controlled NAPBBP with a league dominated by club owners. Membership in the newly established National League of Professional Base Ball Clubs was limited to well-financed joint-stock company clubs from cities with populations of at least 75,000. The eight-team NL was organized along east-west lines, with each team holding monopoly rights to its territory. But the enfranchised clubs had to abide by Hulbert's moral code, which barred liquor sales, gamblers, and Sunday games. Until a fixed playing schedule was in place in 1877, teams in 1876 were ordered to play each rival ten times or face expulsion. Players were subjected to tight disciplinary codes and were bound to teams by rigid contracts. And Hulbert's chief lieutenant, Albert G. Spalding, was contracted to supply the league's official balls and to publish its guidebook.

But the NL's first four seasons sorely tested the resolve of its promoters. Attendance was low; in 1879 the champion Providence team drew only 42,000 spectators at home. Flagging profits forced austerity measures that kept player salaries below those of the 1875 Boston Reds. Moreover, at the close of the 1876 season the NL lost its two most lucrative sites when the Philadelphia and New York teams were expelled for failing to play their quota of games. And the following year the six-team NL suffered a major scandal when gamblers bribed four Louisville players to throw the pennant. For that outrage the players were barred from the NL for life and the Louisville club was replaced by Milwaukee. On yet another front in 1877, the NL faced stiff competition from the rival International Association, but when that league folded in 1879, NL control over organized baseball was secured. By then the NL was once again an eight-team circuit and its teams fielded the best players in the land. And to keep star players in their fold, NL owners in 1879 inserted reserve clauses in their playing contracts. At first players viewed reservation as a status symbol but when the practice was extended to all player contracts in 1883, players viewed the practice as an infringement on their freedom of contract. The reserve clause became a perennial bone of contention between players and owners.

The 1880s

During the prosperous years of the 1880s the gathering storm of player unrest was lightly regarded by owners. Buoyed by national prosperity, NL attendance and profits improved during the early years and took wing during the latter years of the decade. And as the NL prospered, interlopers formed competing major leagues to cash in on the boom. In 1882 the American Association took the field with a seductive formula of twenty-five-cent admission prices, optional liquor sales, and Sunday games. That formula and raids on NL playing rosters made the AA's campaign a success. In response hard-pressed NL officials extended major league recognition to the AA provided that roster raids ceased and the circuit accepted the reserve clause system. This was done and under the National Agreement of 1883 the AA was recognized as a major league and the two majors extended their sway over the minor leagues. And in 1884 the two majors crushed a third rival, the Union Association, which sought to lure major league players by opposing the reserve clause.

Over the years 1885–89 professional baseball enjoyed a prosperous golden age under the dual major league system. But constant tensions marked the relations between the two leagues. On the playing field the rivalry was fought out in annual postseason championship encounters, which the NL dominated after 1886. But the AA more than held its own at the turnstiles, especially in St. Louis where promoter Chris Von der Ahe hosted large crowds with sideshows, liquor sales, Sunday games, and four consecutive pennants won by his Browns. However, in 1889 the AA's Brooklyn Bridegrooms set the nineteenth-century attendance record by hosting over 300,000 spectators at home. That year attendance at major league games peaked at over 2 million admissions and some clubs counted profits of $100,000 and more. By then both leagues had upped their playing schedules to 140 games.

During this brief golden age fans thronged to larger wooden parks where they saw livelier games that resulted in part from a spate of rule changes. Some changes were shortlived, like the 1887 rule counting bases on balls as hits that produced twenty .400 hitters. But for that year such records were official and latter-day statisticians violated historical canons by revamping them. Meanwhile, by 1889 the game's development had been speeded by more permanent changes, such as extending the pitching distance to fifty feet, permitting overhand pitching, adopting a single strike zone, and establishing the four-ball and three-strike rule. By then, too, a pair of weekly journals, *The Sporting News* and *Sporting Life,* with columns wholly devoted to baseball, sated the growing public appetite for baseball news, as did telegraphed reports of scores and electric board displays of games in progress posted at telegraph offices. Journalistic coverage included complete accounts of games, the deeds of star players like King Kelly, Cap Anson, Tip O'Neill, and Dan Brouthers, incidents of fans abusing the professional umpires, and unique events like promoter Spalding's world baseball tour of 1888–89 or Ernest Thayer's poem, "Casey at the Bat." But the big story of the decade recounted the sale of Mike "King" Kelly to the NL Boston club for the astonishing price of $10,000. Kelly was the most celebrated player of this decade, and his diamond exploits and colorful antics also made him an enduring folk hero.

As the game of the 1880s prospered, so to a much lesser degree did its players, whose salaries averaged $2,000 with superstars like Kelly earning $5,000 and more. But by decade's end only white players played in the majors; reflecting widening patterns of racial segregation in the nation, major and minor league clubs excluded black players, who took to playing in segregated leagues until 1946. But white major leaguers of the times chafed under such impositions as the reserve clause, uncompensated player sales by teams, harsh disciplinary rules, and a threatened salary ceiling. In 1885 disgruntled NL players joined the Brotherhood of Professional Base Ball Players founded by John M. Ward, a star player and a lawyer. Under Ward's leadership the brotherhood in 1887 sought recognition as a collective bargaining agency. And when the owners refused to budge on the reserve clause and salary ceiling issues, Ward persuaded the brotherhood, whose ranks included most NL and many AA players, to field a rival major league in 1890. With financial backers secured, the Players' National League of Baseball Clubs promised its men fair shares of power and profits with long-term contracts as their antidote to the hated reserve clause.

The 1890s

The bitter and costly Players' League War of 1890 ended major league baseball's brief golden age. With most of the star players in its fold, the PL opened play with eight well-stocked teams planted in seven NL cities. In head-to-head competition with the NL on most playing dates, the PL outdrew the NL and the hopelessly outclassed AA. Financial losses savaged all three leagues. However, Spalding headed a well-financed NL war committee that forced the tremulous PL backers to sue for peace at the end of the season. The forsaken PL players were allowed to return to their former clubs without penalties, but within five years most ex-PL players no longer played in the major leagues.

Hard after this struggle, the NL and AA fought another baseball war in 1891 that was precipitated by disputes over the reassignments of PL players. When the AA pulled out of the National Agreement, a season-long struggle ended with the collapse of the AA. In the aftermath the NL annexed four AA teams and bought off the others at a cost of $130,000.

From 1892 to 1899 the single, twelve-team National League dominated major league baseball. In those years the owners styled themselves as magnates, pridefully comparing their monopoly "Big League" to the great economic trusts raised up by American captains of industry. But the big league failed to match the old dual major leagues in attendance and profits. For this failure such external factors as the nation's economic recession and the 1898 Spanish-American War were cited, but internally the league's competitive imbalance counted for more. In these years Boston, Baltimore, and Brooklyn teams outclassed all others, leaving scant cash and glory for the also-rans.

Efforts aimed at boosting attendance, such as staging postseason Temple Cup matches, increasing the playing schedule to 154 games, or attempting a split-season format in 1892, were failures. So were two abortive "syndicate" experiments, each involving single ownership of two major league clubs in 1899. That year another proposal aimed at pooling all players and receipts and redistributing the players among teams each new season. In rejecting this "baseball trust" scheme, the repentant owners voted instead to drop the four weakest teams and return to an eight-club format in 1900. This move saddled the owners with a hefty debt incurred by buying out the discarded teams; thus the big league that was born in debt in 1892 died in debt in 1900.

During this wayward era player salaries lagged well behind 1889 standards. With the collapse of the players' union the victorious owners imposed a salary cap, limiting salaries to a maximum of $2,400. Moreover, stricter disciplinary standards were laid on, including the unenforceable "brush rules" that threatened to banish players for such offenses as swearing and rowdy play. At this time rowdy tactics like brawling, umpire-baiting, bench-jockeying, and interfering with opposing players were widely used by aggressive teams like the Baltimore Orioles and Cleveland Spiders. Such tactics won games and excited fans and, when toned down, became a familiar part of the diamond drama. Likewise, bigger gloves and improved catcher's equipment made for better defensive play. And in this era two competing styles of offensive play, the "slugging" style and the "scientific" style, vied for acceptance. The slugging style was fostered by the 1893 rule that increased the pitching distance to its present length of sixty feet six inches and replaced the pitching box with a rubber slab atop a mound. Until pitchers adapted, sluggers feasted and set long-lasting batting and homer marks. But by the end of the decade the scientific style, with its emphasis on bunting, stealing, the hit and run, and sacrificing, had become the dominant offensive style, and it remained so for the next twenty seasons.

In other ways the game continued to grow and evolve. Ballpark fans were tempted with concessionary items like hot dogs and soda pop. Opponents of Sunday games mounted a long and ultimately unsuccessful campaign to bar such games. In these years a rash of ballpark fires led to stricter safety codes that soon forced the replacement of wooden parks. And in this era professional baseball continued to expand in the minor leagues and among the flourishing black leagues. And prospects for continuing growth followed the spread of the game to Latin America and Japan.

From 1900 through World War I

As the twentieth century opened, major league baseball entered an era of expansion marked by unprecedented prosperity and stability. In 1900 the eight-team NL still reigned as the only major league, but that year Western League president Byron "Ban" Johnson mounted a challenge. Angered by NL draft policies, Johnson sought parity with the NL. That year he renamed his circuit the American League; his clubs occupied some of the abandoned NL sites and signed some surplus NL players. When the AL prospered, Johnson demanded major league recognition for his American League and launched a classic baseball war. In 1901 AL clubs occupied Philadelphia and Boston and enticed NL stars to jump to the new league. After two years of strife, NL owners, who faced a serious crisis of leadership, sued for peace. The National Agreement of 1903 recognized the AL as a major league and returned the major league game to the dual major league format of the 1880s. Under the 1903 agreement the NL and AL functioned as separate but equal major leagues; however, a three-member national commission was empowered to settle disputes and keep peace between the two leagues. The two league presidents and Cincinnati owner Garry Herrmann headed the National Commission, which successfully governed the game for seventeen years, during which time the two leagues respected each other's territories and playing rosters, agreed on playing rules and playing schedules, reclassified the minor leagues, and staged increasingly popular and profitable World Series matches.

The 1903 settlement ushered in a long period of stability for major league baseball. After the AL planted a team in New York City in 1903, both leagues retained the same teams for 50 years. During those years, except for the years of 1918–19, each league's teams played 154 games a season.

Rising attendance, averaging over 7 million fans a season from 1907 to 1909, translated into profits that underscored the game's growing popularity. With no serious challenge from rival pro sports, baseball benefited from increasing coverage from big-city newspapers and from books, magazines, and films. Such coverage boosted public adulation of stars like Ty Cobb, Honus Wagner, Nap Lajoie, Walter Johnson, Christy Mathewson, and other heroes of the "deadball era," as the pitching-dominated, "scientific" style of play came to be called. Trick deliveries like the spitball and various scuffed-ball tactics made for pitching dominance. Other innovations included improved offensive and defensive team tactics, equipment changes such as more efficient gloves, and rule changes such as restricting the size of pitching mounds and assigning two umpires to work each game. All contributed to the game's growing popularity. So did the game's enduring hymn, "Take Me Out to the Ball Game," written at this time, and the presence of American presidents at opening-day games and World Series matches. By 1910 owner optimism over the game's prospects inspired a park-building boom thatreplaced wooden parks with capacious concrete-and-steel edifices. The building boom climaxed with the construction of Yankee Stadium in 1923, and most of these privately financed parks served until a new building boom began in the 1950s.

However, chronic problems of competitive imbalance and unequal distribution of attendance and revenues persisted. In this era the Giants and Cubs captured the lion's share of attendance and championships in the NL as did the Boston, Detroit, and Philadelphia clubs of the AL. Moreover, player salaries rose slowly, averaging $2,500 by 1910 with a few superstars getting $12,000 and more marginal players getting less than $1,000. Widespread discontent over salaries and the reserve clause prompted players in 1900 and again in 1912 to organize for reforms, but both movements were quashed by the owners and the national commission.

For their part, owners faced troubles of their own from the three major crises that affected the game over the years 1914–20. The troubles began with the Federal League War of 1914–15. A well-financed incursion by promoters of a rival major league, the invasion dropped annual attendance at NL and AL games below 5 million in those years. In 1915 the FL folded, but a dispute over the terms of the settlement prompted one Federal League club to sue major league baseball for monopoly practices. In 1922 the case reached the Supreme Court, which ruled that the game was a sport and not subject to the laws of interstate commerce.

Soon after the FL war came the crisis of World War I. The total war effort drafted players for service and forced the majors to reduce playing schedules in 1918–19. Combined with a raging influenza epidemic, such restrictions reduced total attendance to 3 million in 1918.

Yet another crisis followed just as attendance rebounded to 6.5 million in the shortened playing season of 1919. That year the World Series was blighted by gamblers who bribed eight Chicago White Sox players to throw games to the victorious Cincinnati Reds. When news of the scandal broke in 1920, the furor it caused led to the suspension of the accused players and the fall of the national commission. In place of that ruling body, federal judge Kenesaw M. Landis was named sole commissioner of the game and empowered to act on his own volition to defend the integrity of the game. Although Landis banished the eight accused ""Black Sox" players for life and later barred a few other players for consorting with gamblers, he failed to halt the long-established practice of betting on major league games. Such activity by players and managers is deeply rooted in baseball history. Among other incidents, Chicago manager Cap Anson bet on his team's games in the 1890s, contending teams often bribed rival teams to play harder against other contenders, and stars like Rube Waddell, Hal Chase, Ty Cobb, Tris Speaker, and Joe Wood were accused of betting or game fixing. Of those named, four (Anson, Waddell, Cobb, and Speaker) were later enshrined in the game's Hall of Fame.

Ironically, the furor over the 1919 World Series fix failed to affect attendance, which rose to a record 9.1 million in 1920. Had the owners known of the coming boom, they likely would not have granted Commissioner Landis such sweeping powers. Certainly none of the commissioners who succeeded Landis, who died in 1944, were granted such powers.

The 1920s

Meanwhile big league baseball's stock soared during the 1920s. Externally, national prosperity enabled Americans to spend nearly $5 billion a year on recreational pursuits in 1929. Such monies fostered the growth of other sports in which fans doted on the deeds of such heroes as Bobby Jones, Bill Tilden, Red Grange, Jack Dempsey, and Gene Tunney. Yet none of these champions matched the adulation heaped on baseball superstar Babe Ruth. In 1920 Ruth smote 54 homers, a record feat that drew a million fans to New York Yankees games and easily justified the record price Yankees owners spent to acquire the slugger from the Boston Red Sox.

Over the years 1920–31 Ruth won ten AL homer titles and he personified the new slugging style of play. Abetted in part by a ban on trick pitches and by the widespread use of lively cork-centered balls that were frequently replaced during games (and retained by souvenir-seeking fans when hit into the stands), the "big bang" became the perennially dominant offensive style. During the 1920s NL sluggers outhomered their AL counterparts, but hitters in both leagues set enduring records. Thus NL star Rogers Hornsby averaged .400 over a five-year period, while on four occasions AL star Harry Heilmann topped .390. The hitting frenzy peaked in 1930 when NL hitters averaged above .300.

That fans welcomed the batting assaults was evidenced at the turnstiles. During the 1920s annual attendance at major league games averaged about 9 million with a record 10.1 million admissions counted in 1930. Legalized Sunday games spurred attendance and radio broadcasts of World Series games won new fans, but most clubs refused to allow radio broadcasts of regular-season games. Moreover, expanding newspaper and magazine coverage supplied fans with plenteous information on teams and players. At this time baseball writers tended to use a highly romanticized, gee-whiz style of coverage that lionized players, especially Ruth, who became the most photographed and recognized American of the decade.

In retrospect the 1920s stand out as the game's second golden age. Annual revenues topped those of the 1900–20 era by 40 percent and player salaries averaged $7,000 by 1930. However, such figures were distorted by competitive imbalance. In this era the AL Yankees won six pennants and an inordinate share of attendance and revenues. In the NL the Giants won four consecutive pennants and outdrew all others at the gate. And the average player salary was dwarfed by Ruth's $80,000 salary of 1930.

Along with the new offensive style of play other innovations marked the game's continuing evolution. There was the bright promise of radio and films as new revenue sources, with the latter now serving as a useful training device. At St. Louis, Cardinal general manager Branch Rickey's farm system was revolutionizing the recruitment and training of young talent in the minors. Acquiring a network of minor league teams, Rickey-stocked them with young players whose steady development enabled the poor-drawing Cardinals to win pennants and profit by the sales of surplus players. Yet another revolution of the decade occurred outside organized baseball when promoter Rube Foster launched the Negro National League in 1920. Along with similar ventures by other promoters, the black majors enabled stars like pitchers Bullet Joe Rogan, Smokey Joe Williams, and Satchel Paige to display their formidable talents along with such hitting virtuosos as Pop Lloyd and Oscar Charleston. Such worthies continued to be shunned by white major and minor league teams; yet in time, when the walls of racial discrimination were finally razed, the wealth of black playing talent and their fans would revitalize major league baseball.

The 1930s

Reformists were battering at those walls in the 1930s, but their pleas made little headway during that depression-wracked decade. As the Great Depression idled millions of American workers, attendance at major league games hit a low point of 6.3 million in 1933. Recovering slowly thereafter, annual attendance still did not surpass the 1930 mark as late as 1940.

During the worst years of the Depression, from 1932 to 1934, most major league clubs lost money, especially the NL Braves and Phillies and the AL Athletics, Browns, and Senators. So did the players, whose salaries were sharply slashed; by 1933 salaries averaged $6,000, and in 1940 they still lagged behind the 1929 peak of $7,500.

To weather the storm, poorer clubs like the Phillies and Athletics sold star players, but such medicine had the side effect of worsening attendance for the sellers. The talent-rich Cardinals compensated for poor attendance by selling surplus players from their vast farm system and retaining the best to stay in contention. But such financial disparities among clubs worsened the chronic problem of competitive imbalance. In this decade the AL Yankees won four world titles in as many tries, and in the NL the Giants, Cardinals, and Cubs dominated the campaigns.

To attract more fans promoters turned to night baseball, a rejected innovation of the 1880s but by now a proven success as demonstrated by the black majors and at the minor league level. In 1935 Cincinnati general manager Larry MacPhail successfully staged night games in the NL. By 1940 most major league clubs followed suit, setting a trend that within a few decades transformed the game into a mainly nocturnal spectacle. In like manner clubs increasingly sold radio broadcasting rights, fostering a trend that would later transform the game into an electronic media event. For now, owners welcomed the windfall, which amounted to 7.3 percent of major league revenues by 1939. At this time, too, owners wrung money from fans by expanded concession sales, especially beer sales, revived after the failure of national prohibition, which halted such sales during the 1920s.

Scarcely touched by innovation was the game itself as teams of the 1930s continued to ply big-bang offensives in games now officiated by three-man umpire crews. As the game's towering hero Ruth faded from the scene, soon after his legendary feat of supposedly calling his homer shot in the 1932 World Series, new heroes emerged as worthy successors. Among them were pitcher Johnny Vander Meer (who hurled two consecutive no-hit games in 1938), Joe DiMaggio (who batted safely in 56 games in 1941), and Ted Williams (whose .406 batting mark of 1941 was the last .400 batting effort to this day).

In 1939 major league baseball's image as the national pastime was burnished by season-long celebrations of the game's mythical centennial birth date. At Cooperstown, New York, the purported site of the game's 1839 invention, the Baseball Hall of Fame was formally opened in June and the first five immortal players were enshrined. It attracted 25,000 visitors that year and now hosts more than 250,000 pilgrims annually.

World War II

Rebounding from the Depression, major league baseball enjoyed profitable seasons in 1940–41 when the game was rocked by the crisis of World War II. As the nation mounted its total war effort against the Axis powers, some 500 major leaguers and 3,500 minor league players were called to the colors along with 11 million other Americans. The manpower drain affected major league attendance, which fell to 8.8 million in 1942 and to a nadir of 7.7 million the following year. The accompanying financial losses hit poorer clubs hard and one, the NL Phillies, went bankrupt in 1943, but soon fell into the hands of a wealthy backer.

Although given a "green light" to continue play by President Roosevelt, major league teams had to cope with shortages of players, equipment, and accommodations. For a time night games were curtailed, but they were revived when government officials decided that such games provided useful recreation for war workers. But the biggest problem promoters faced was the scarcity of able players. To cope, clubs recruited draft rejects, and those too old or too young to serve; some clubs turned to Latin America, where a virtually untapped pool of players existed. During the war years fifty Latin American players appeared in various lineups. However, another promising pool of talent, the black majors, remained off limits; owners rejected promoter Bill Veeck's 1943 bid to buy the bankrupt Phillies, which Veeck proposed to stock with black players. Thus major league clubs muddled through the war years by fielding teams of below-average playing skills. At this time, government-imposed wage freezes helped to hold player salaries to an average of $6,400 and widespread resentment among players made them receptive to postwar union movements.

Meanwhile major league owners won plaudits for supporting the war effort with bond sales, free admissions to servicemen, and donations of equipment and radio broadcasts of games to the armed forces. Moreover, most owners profited when attendance rebounded to 8.7 million in 1944 and then posted a record 10.8 million admissions in 1945. By then the war was over, but its aftermath unleashed pent-up demands for higher wages andracial equality in the land. In 1946 these and other tremors shook major league baseball as the game entered its postwar era.

The Postwar Era

Baseball's postwar era (1946–60) confronted owners and players with vexing problems caused by changing social conditions. Indeed, the era was barely underway when owners were forced to grapple with problems of racial integration and player unionism. Of the two, it was the former that immediately transformed the game as black activists, backed by federal and state antidiscrimination laws, demanded an end to segregation in organized baseball. Although most major league owners resisted integration, their position was crumbling. Until his death in 1944 Commissioner Landis opposed integration, but his successor, Commissioner A. B. Chandler, favored the cause. Thus while opponents feared to voice their opposition, Brooklyn Dodgers president Branch Rickey decided to force the issue. In 1945 Rickey signed black player Jackie Robinson to a Dodgers contract and assigned him to the club's Montreal farm team. After leading the International League in hitting in 1946, Robinson joined the NL Dodgers in 1947 and won Rookie of the Year honors. Robinson's successful debut and that of Larry Doby, who became the first AL black player that year, opened the doors to other black Americans and Latin Americans whose performances validated Rickey's bold experiment. In the NL, where most blacks played during this era, black stars won seven Most Valuable Player awards during the 1950s. However, the integration of organized baseball did not end racial discrimination practices. Nor were black promoters fairly compensated for the loss of players, which also led to the demise of the black majors in 1950.

Although the crisis caused by the game's integration was short-lived, that of player unionism confronted major league owners with an enduring and chronically festering problem. In 1946 cumulative grievances nursed by players, including many returning war veterans, led to the formation of the American Baseball Guild. Although the guild folded that year, the players won such concessions as a pension plan (funded by national radio and television revenues), a minimum salary, pay for spring training, and the right to negotiate further through elected player representatives. Among these gains, the pension plan was the most portentous and when owners sought to abolish the system in 1953, the players retaliated by forming the permanent Major League Players Association. That year the MLPA managed to confirm all previous concessions, including the continuation of the pension system. But the MLPA later languished as an ineffective company union until 1966, when under Marvin Miller's leadership it became a formidable labor organization.

Meanwhile on another front of the 1946 labor struggle, several players were blacklisted by Commissioner Chandler for violating reserve clauses in their contracts by joining an outlaw Mexican league. In opposing that sanction, player Danny Gardella filed suit and when his case reached a federal circuit court, tremulous owners settled out of court. However, Gardella's challenge prompted congressional investigations into major league baseball's monopoly practices. Although no punitive legislation resulted, the future of the reserve clause was clouded. Some owners blamed Chandler for precipitating the investigation and also faulted him for acting against their wishes by supporting racial integration and the players' pension movement. As a result Chandler was forced to resign in 1951. Thereafter, commissioners became figureheads for the owners, who wielded power. Until his death in 1979, Walter O'Malley of the Dodgers was a most important decision maker in owner councils.

Crises notwithstanding, major league baseball flourished during the postwar era. Stimulated by national prosperity, attendance topped 18 million in 1946 and peaked at 21.3 million in 1948. The increasing number of night games was a catalyst for this upsurge, with every club but the Chicago Cubs staging such games. At the same time Cleveland owner Bill Veeck demonstrated new ways of attracting crowds with his imaginative promotional schemes, including giveaways. In 1948 the AL champion Indians set a record by hosting over 2 million fans.

Unfortunately the boom of the late 1940s burst in the 1950s when annual attendance failed to reach 20 million. For this reversal, such factors as population shifts away from major league cities, suburban growth, deteriorating parks in rundown neighborhoods, competition from rival sports, and the popularity of television were cited. Internally, competitive imbalance was a major factor; during the years 1947–60 the AL Yankees won eleven pennants and the NL Dodgers won seven.

By the 1950s financial losses forced the owners of the NL Braves and the AL Athletics and Browns to sell to new owners, who were permitted to relocate these clubs to more promising sites. In 1953 the NL Braves became the first breakaway franchise in half a century by moving to Milwaukee. Over the next two years the AL Browns reincarnated as the Baltimore Orioles and the Athletics relocated to Kansas City. And in 1958 the NL Dodgers and Giants stunned their fans by moving to the flourishing West Coast cities of Los Angeles and San Francisco.

At the same time the popular television medium was transforming the game. Although TV broadcasts of games were blamed for flagging attendance, the medium pumped new revenues into team coffers. From $2.3 million in 1950, annual TV revenue rose to $12 million by 1960. However, much of this money was unevenly distributed because such revenues derived mainly from local TV contracts. But all clubs shared equally in increasing revenue from national TV networks, which vied with one another to purchase rights to televise World Series games, All-Star games, and selected seasonal games. Thus increasing TV revenues helped boost franchise values to figures that dwarfed the 1945 sale of the Yankees for $2.5 million. Yet few observers of this era envisioned a time when ever-increasing TV monies would also boost player salaries to undreamed-of heights.

At this time player salaries rose modestly, keeping pace with the dollar's continuing inflation. By the late 1950s, 75 percent of player salaries ranged from $10,000 to $25,000 with $100,000 checks going to five superstars (Joe DiMaggio, Ted Williams, Stan Musial, Mickey Mantle, and Willie Mays). However, salaries were being pushed upward by talent scarcity caused by declining numbers of minor leagues and by rival sports competing for top athletes. As a result teams of this era engaged in costly bidding wars that made high-priced "bonus babies" of promising rookies. Other replacements came from dwindling numbers of black professionals and to a greater extent from Latin American recruits. But the chronic shortage of talent was ending the longstanding practice of free-enterprise scouting and forcing owners to seek other solutions to the problem. At this time the flourishing Little League baseball movement introduced thousands of youngsters to the game, but fewer youth and adult leagues made it difficult to sustain the enthusiasm of youngsters for the game.

Meanwhile big league players continued to play the slugging game, with NL hitters averaging 1,100 homers a season during the 1950s. Whippier bats, protective helmets, and the strategy of platooning hitters bolstered offenses, but more efficient gloves boosted defenses, and varied deliveries, including the effective slider, enabled pitchers to better cope with the hitters. Moreover, teams now deployed better-trained relief pitchers to quell batting rallies. The increased use of specialized role performers also had teams using more coaches and improving their training techniques.

A new park-building boom began in this era as breakaway clubs occupied new, publicly financed ballparks. More commodious than the idiosyncratic parks that had served fans for half a century, the new parks were located closer to suburban population centers and were more accessible to automobiles. And a rule of 1959 ordained that all new parks constructed after that year must conform to minimum 325-foot distances from home plate to the right- and left-field fences.

The 1960s

The 1959 rule calling for standardized playing fields was linked with a larger plan calling for the major leagues to expand to twenty teams. When this plan was implemented by the AL in 1961 and by the NL in 1962, major league baseball embarked upon the first phase of its expansion era. Although expansion was inspired in part by professional football's profitable example, the precipitating cause was the threat from a rival major league, the Continental League, to field teams in baseball-hungry urban areas. In defusing that threat, major league owners voted to add two new teams to each league and to increase the playing schedule to 162 games.

For its part the NL occupied Houston and New York, while the AL took on Washington and Los Angeles clubs. The NL's choice of New York quelled protests arising from that city's loss of the Giants and Dodgers in 1958. Similarly the AL's reoccupation of Washington was prompted by threats of lawsuits arising over the 1961 move by the original Washington Senators to Minnesota. The first round of expansion cost each new club owner $2 million for his franchise plus additional spending for the purchase of players picked from a pool of surplus players made available by an expansion draft procedure. Thus arrayed, the AL played its first season under the ten-team format in 1961 with the NL following suit in 1962.

But the first expansion ventures of 1961–68 fell short of expectations. Three franchise relocations of these years, including the NL Milwaukee Braves' move to Atlanta and moves by the AL's Kansas City Athletics to Oakland and Los Angeles Angels to nearby Anaheim, indicated dissatisfaction with the format. The format also aggravated the competitive imbalance problem. Ten teams competing in each league made for too many losers, both on the field of play and at the turnstiles. The situation was worsened by dominant teams like the AL Yankees, winners of five consecutive pennants through 1964, and by the Dodgers and Cardinals winning all six races in the NL in 1963–68. As a result annual attendance was disappointing. The era's best attendance mark, 25 million, bettered that of 1960 by little more than 5 million and by 1968 total attendance sagged to 23 million. Moreover, NL attendance of this era surpassed that of the AL by 15 million, an anomaly attributed to the NL's newer parks and better choices of expansion sites. In these years six of the eight new parks built housed NL clubs, including Houston's all-weather Astrodome with its artificial turf playing surface. Today ten major league teams play home games on artificial surfaces.

The NL also enjoyed batting superiority, but these were lackluster years for all hitters. Dominant pitching, backed by increasingly effective relief corps (whose stars now competed for annual Fireman of the Year honors), produced a hitting famine that by 1968 held hitters to a century-low .237 average. Although NL sluggers Willie Mays and Hank Aaron hit homers at a pace that threatened to topple Ruth's lifetime mark of 714 blows, most hitters were throttled by the dominant pitching of aces like Sandy Koufax, Bob Gibson, and Denny McLain. To restore balance, rules makers in 1969 lowered pitching mounds and shortened strike zones.

Yet if players' bats were relatively silent, their demands for reforms were effectively voiced. Reflecting the social climate of this frenzied decade, which had protestors of all stripes clamoring for reforms, including demonstrating for an end to the Vietnam War and sometimes rioting in the streets, major league players battled for improved salaries, pension benefits, and working conditions. To revive their moribund union, players in 1966 chose the experienced labor organizer Marvin Miller to head the MLPA. In short order Miller united the players and invoked federal labor laws to force owners to bargain with the association. Such negotiations produced formal labor contracts (known as basic agreements) in 1967 and 1970, which boosted pension benefits and minimum salaries. By the end of the 1960s player salaries averaged $20,000 and those of twenty stars topped $100,000. Moreover, in 1966 Dodgers pitchers Sandy Koufax and Don Drysdale set a precedent by using a lawyer in their contract negotiations that season. Within a few years all players won the right to use agents in salary negotiations. Even umpires gained a measure of power when their organization, the Major League Umpires Association, won recognition as a bargaining agency.

Helping to strengthen the players' bargaining position at this time was the continuing problem of talent scarcity. As the number of minor leagues continued to shrink, alarmed owners adopted a player development plan to save these vital nurseries of talent. Under this 1962 plan each major league club was required to subsidize at least five minor league teams of various classes. As a further step the owners in 1965 established annual free-agent (rookie) drafts of high school and college players. This equal sharing of annual crops of young players was accomplished by pooling the talent and allowing each team to choose in an order based on a team's finish in the previous year's standings. A dramatic departure from past practices, the rookie drafts ended free-enterprise scouting in the United States, but not in foreign lands such as the productive Latin American countries.

At this time worried owners benefited from increasing television revenues, which helped meet the expense of rising salaries and player development programs. By 1967 annual TV monies totaled $25 million with no signs of abating. Thus when major league owners embarked on a new expansion course in 1969, TV revenue played a vital part in the success of the venture.

The 1970s

By replacing the unwieldy ten-club format with a new expansion plan that would add two clubs to each league and subdivide each league into six-team Eastern and Western divisions, major league owners of 1969 hit upon a successful format. The new format retained the 162-game playing schedule, but added a postseason, best-of-five-games League Championship Series, which pitted each season's divisional winners in a test to determine the annual league champions. A proven success in professional football, which at this time rivaled big league baseball in popularity, divisional play in big league baseball also focused fan attention on divisional races where winning teams were rewarded with pennants.

In implementing the plan in 1969 the AL added the Kansas City Royals and Seattle Pilots, with the NL taking on the Montreal Expos (the first foreign franchise in major league history) and the San Diego Padres. A new AL franchise now cost $5.6 million with an NL franchise pegged at $10 million. Each owner spent additional money to stock teams from player cullings made available in another expansion draft.

Once underway the wisdom of this venture was demonstrated by rising attendance figures. From 30 million annual admissions in the early 1970s, annual attendance rose to 43 million by 1980. To be sure, the early years were plagued with glitches, especially for the outclassed AL where shaky franchises, flagging attendance, and poor offensive performance continued. Thus after one season of play, the AL's Seattle owner was forced to sell his club to Milwaukee interests. The Milwaukee move provided a more stable franchise and also quashed a lawsuit against the NL for its earlier abandonment of that city. But by quitting Seattle and by allowing the unstable Washington Senators to move to Arlington, Texas, in 1972, the AL now faced similar suits. While the Washington protest was defused by the vague promise of a future franchise, the Seattle suit was headed off by the AL's unilateral expansion move of 1977. That year the AL added two new clubs, the Seattle Mariners and the Toronto Blue Jays, whose new owners paid $6 million each for their franchises. This unilateral expansion made the AL a fourteen-team circuit with seven teams arrayed in each division. The 162-game schedule was retained, but annual matchups between teams were necessarily skewed. Nevertheless, the bold move stabilized the AL, whose annual attendance thenceforth surpassed that of the NL.

By then another unilateral move by the AL was boosting its annual offensive figures above those of the NL. This was accomplished in 1973 by the adoption, over NL protests, of a designated hitter rule allowing a batter to hit in place of a pitcher. To this day the AL use of the DH rule remains controversial. But at this time the two leagues settled an argument over the use of designated hitters in World Series play by restricting its use to alternate years. (A recent modification of this rule limits its use to World Series games played in AL parks.) Although the NL still refuses to adopt the rule, nearly twenty years of using designated hitters attests to its popularity among offense-minded AL fans.

Meanwhile, if owners expected the new divisional format to solve the chronic problem of competitive imbalance, such hopes were misplaced. Over the years 1969–80 most divisional races were dominated by the same two teams. In the AL East the Orioles and Yankees won most of these as did the Athletics and Kansas City Royals in the West. And in the NL the Phillies and Pirates dominated in the East with the Reds and Dodgers ruling in the West.

At least the booming attendance of these years demonstrated that such imbalance posed no barrier to the game's dynamic growth. In this decade new park construction and the refurbishing of old parks like Yankee Stadium helped the AL match the NL's parks and gain parity in attendance. Moreover, attendance everywhere was boosted by the use of promotional schemes such as free gift days, more varied concession items for sale, cavorting team mascots, sideshows, and enhanced season-ticket sales. Thus promoters now regarded a million admissions a year as a must, while the lordly Dodgers topped all others by drawing over 2 million fans a year.

At the same time surging TV revenues accounted for 30 percent of major league baseball's gross revenues of $500 million in 1980. Such revenues raised the value of franchises so that the Red Sox and Mets went for $16 million and $20 million respectively when sold to new buyers, while the Dodgers and Yankees were valued at an estimated $50 million each. Certainly TV played an important part in the rising values of clubs. By 1980 network contracts for World Series, League Championship Series, All-Star games, and other selected games provided each owner with $1.8 million a year; local TV revenues were also growing at a fast pace. However, TV interests altered the game by persuading ownersto schedule mostly night games, including World Series con-tests. And because improving technology now afforded TV fans a better view of a game than ballpark fans, clubs responded by erecting large TV screens at parks. Thus, ball games increasingly became entertainment spectacles, a trend that some observers blamed for the increasing episodes of crowd violence that forced clubs in these years to beef up their security staffs.

Indeed, many episodes of crowd violence targeted players, who were now cast as highly paid celebrities. TV exposure made players more visible and more onstage. Clad in colorful uniforms, many players sported facial hair, most were more assertive, and some like Jim Bouton wrote controversial, best-selling books that probed deeply into the private lives of players.

For players such unprecedented freedom was accompanied by mind-boggling salaries. Average player salaries soared from $25,000 in 1970 to $185,000 by 1980, with pitcher Nolan Ryan becoming the first million-dollar-a-year player. Although TV revenue provided the wherewithal for gains that boosted top payrolls from $1 million in 1970 to $9 million in 1980, it was the negotiating skills of MLPA director Marvin Miller that wrung the money from the owners. In this decade Miller negotiated three basic agreements that vastly benefited the players. The 1970 agreement won players the right to use agents in salary negotiations; the 1973 agreement, which followed after the players staged a thirteen-day strike in 1972, won players the right to seek binding arbitration in salary disputes. The passage of time soon demonstrated the significance of that concession. But its portent was overshadowed in 1975 by an arbitration panel's decision that pitchers Andy Messersmith and Dave McNally, each of whom played a full season without a contract, were free agents. When upheld by a federal court, it was apparent that this Seitz decision (named for arbitrator Peter Seitz) applied to all players and thus seemed to circumvent the reserve clause.

In 1976 the Seitz decision became the front of battle in negotiations over a new basic agreement. After staging an abortive lockout of spring training camps, the owners returned to the bargaining table where a compromise was reached. This latest agreement allowed six-year veterans to become free agents who could sell their services anew in annual re-entry drafts. And when some owners bid high salaries for the services of some free agents, these rates were soon matched by binding awards from arbitration panels acting under procedures established in 1973.

Still there was no gainsaying the claim that the fortune-favored stars of this era earned their inflation-eroded salaries. Among the record setters, slugger Hank Aaron broke Ruth's lifetime homer record of 714 in 1974; hitting dervish Pete Rose tied Willie Keeler's NL mark by hitting safely in 44 consecutive games in 1978 and continued his assault on Cobb's lifetime mark of 4,191 hits; base-stealer Lou Brock broke Cobb's lifetime mark of 892 steals in 1977; and pitcher Nolan Ryan broke Walter Johnson's lifetime record of 3,508 strike-outs in 1983.

The 1980s

The skyrocketing player salaries of the 1970s incurred the wrath of owners, who determined to halt the trend. Thus the opening of the decade of the 1980s saw owners and players marshaling their forces for a renewed battle in a continuing power struggle.

When a cooling-off period failed to produce a new basic agreement, the 1981 season was gutted by a player strike that lasted from mid-June to the end of July. The strike was provoked by owner demands for a ceiling on salaries and for compensation ""in kind" for players lost by clubs in annual re-entry drafts. In rejecting such givebacks, the players struck for fifty days and forced the cancellation of as many games. With both sides bloodied financially, a settlement was reached whereby the owners lost their demand for a salary cap, but won compensation for lost free agents by receiving either a minor league player or a major leaguer chosen from a pool of cullings from the rosters of all the clubs. In the wake of the great strike, a confusing split-season format was arranged in hopes of salvaging the playing season. However, the quixotic scheme failed to stimulate attendance, which fell to 26 million.

But fears of a continuing baseball recession were dispelled by three prosperous seasons that followed the 1981 debacle. Bucking the faltering national economy of those years, annual attendance averaged better than 40 million and average player salaries rose to $300,000 by 1984, with thirty stars joining the millionaire ranks.

Baseball was riding the same wave of prosperity when the expiring basic agreement renewed the struggle in 1985. Once again the owners demanded a salary cap and they also sought to limit the salary arbitration procedure, which they blamed for the soaring salary trend. When no agreement was reached, the players struck in August, but the walkout lasted only two days. With neither side wanting a reprise of the 1981 attrition, a new agreement was reached in which the players agreed to extend the eligibility period for salary arbitration to three years. For their part the owners dropped the salary cap demand and sweetened the pension fund so that a ten-year veteran of the major leagues could expect a pension of $91,000 a year.

Although the new basic agreement extended through the 1989 season, its peace was marred by such owner ploys as reducing playing rosters to twenty-four men and boycotting the free agent markets of 1985–86. The boycott prompted a grievance suit by the MLPA that resulted in a 1989 arbitrator's ruling that the owners were guilty of collusion and must pay $10.5 million in damages to the affected players. The two sides also locked horns over the issue of drug abuse. Reflecting the national epidemic of illegal drug use by Americans, many players were numbered among the estimated 20 million violators in the country. Early in the decade some players were caught and jailed, and in 1986 six admitted users testified under immunity at a Pittsburgh trial of an accused drug dealer. When these witnesses implicated other players as users, Commissioner Peter Ueberroth penalized those accused and sought to make all players submit to drug testing. But the MLPA successfull-yargued that drug testing be negotiated as part of a formal labor agreement.

An unprecedented spate of competitive balance made for hotly contested division races throughout the 1980s. Over the years 1981–88, eleven different teams won divisional titles in the AL. And if domination by the Dodgers and Cardinals made the NL less balanced, still ten different teams won divisional races, including the Cubs, who had been pennantless since 1945.

Among the splendid performers of this era, Pete Rose of the Reds broke Cobb's total hit record in 1985. In 1982 Rickey Henderson of the Athletics set a new seasonal mark by stealing 130 bases. And among the pitching aces, forty-two-year-old Nolan Ryan, still firing ninety-mile-per-hour fastballs, recorded his 5,000th strikeout in 1989.

The 1990s

The decade of the 1990s has been a turbulent one for baseball, with developments off the field overshadowing the feats on the diamond. During the 1992 season, Commissioner Fay Vincent, under pressure from major league owners, offered his resignation. The owners disagreed with Vincent's position that the commissioner should involve himself in labor negotiations with the players. Since Vincent's departure, the position of commissioner has remained vacant, with Milwaukee Brewer owner Bud Selig serving as acting commissioner.

With player salaries rising to an average of over $1 million a year, and hurt by a less-than-lucrative television deal, team owners sought to control spending by negotiating with the players a salary cap and revenue sharing as part of a new labor agreement. The players rejected the proposal in the summer of 1994 and, unable to reach a collective-bargaining agreement with the owners, went on strike in mid-August with a month and a half remaining in what had been an exciting season, the first in a new three-division format in each league. The counteroffer by the players called for a luxury tax on the highest-spending teams.

A month after the strike began, the owners canceled the World Series for the first time in ninety years. With no settlement in sight, the owners implemented a new system on their own, including a salary cap, elimination of salary arbitration, and modified free-agent requirements. The players countered by filing an unfair labor practice charge with the National Labor Relations Board. As spring training approached in 1995, the owners voted to employ replacement players for the strikers. These replacement players were mostly members of minor league farm clubs and former major leaguers. One team, the Baltimore Orioles, refused to field a team of replacement players. Spring training exhibition games were played using the replacements, and the owners planned to start the season with those players. However, the strike came to an end the day before the scheduled start of the season when federal judge Sonia Sotomayor ruled for the players and issued an injunction against the owners, ordering them to drop their self-imposed salary cap system, while restoring the terms of the previous collective-bargaining agreement. Opening day was pushed back to late April, and the 1995 season was shortened to 144 games.

The game itself produced several shining moments. In 1993, two new expansion teams joined the National League, the Florida Marlins and Colorado Rockies, and Colorado qualified for a playoff spot in only its third season. Two more teams, the Arizona Diamondbacks and Tampa Bay Devil Rays, are scheduled to bring the major leagues to thirty teams in 1998. Beautiful new "old-time" style ballparks in Baltimore, Cleveland, Texas, and Colorado opened, with several more slated to be built in coming seasons. The Toronto Blue Jays won back-to-back World Series in 1992 and 1993, becoming the first repeat winners since 1978, and the first team from outside the United States to win the Series. The Atlanta Braves, who dropped consecutive World Series in 1991 and 1992, and lost in the playoffs in 1993, put those defeats behind them in 1995 when they captured the world championship. The Braves became the first franchise to win the Series in three cities—Boston in 1914, Milwaukee in 1957, and Atlanta in 1995. A new round of divisional playoffs was played for the first time in 1995, with one wild-card team in each league joining the division winners.

Individual accomplishments were many. George Brett, Robin Yount, Dave Winfield, and Eddie Murray all joined the 3,000-hit club. Rickey Henderson broke Lou Brock's all-time stolen base record and Nolan Ryan threw his record seventh no-hitter in separate games on the same day in 1991. Greg Maddux won an unprecedented four consecutive Cy Young Awards. And, in 1995, Cal Ripken, Jr., broke Lou Gehrig's longstanding iron-man record of 2,130 consecutive games played.

PART TWO

Special Achievements

Most Valuable Player Awards
League Championship
Series, World Series,
and All-Star Game
Most Valuable Players
Rookie of the Year Award
Cy Young Award
Gold Glove Award
Triple Crown Winners
Manager of the Year Award
Consecutive Games Played
No-Hit Games
Baseball Hall of Fame
The Commissioners of Baseball

Special Achievements

Most Valuable Player Award

From 1911 through 1914, an automobile was presented to the player adjudged to be the most outstanding in his respective league. Thus the short-lived Chalmers Award was born. This award lasted four years.

The practice of selecting the league's Most Valuable Player actually began in 1922 when a special committee named George Sisler of the St. Louis Browns as the American League's Most Valuable Player. It was not until two years later, 1924, that the National League decided to join and Dazzy Vance, Brooklyn's flame-throwing right-hander, was chosen his league's MVP. This selection by committee process prevailed until 1930 when, for some reason, it simply faded away and there were no selections that year. A portent of what was to come actually surfaced in 1929 when the American League Selection Committee failed to make a selection.

The responsibility of selecting the respective leagues' most valuable players was turned over to the Baseball Writers Association of America (BBWAA) in 1931, and this able body of baseball writers has continued ever since. The first selections made were Robert "Lefty" Grove of the Philadelphia Athletics in the American League and Frankie Frisch of the St. Louis Cardinals in the National League. The only player ever to be selected MVP in both leagues is Frank Robinson, who won the honor in the National League in 1961 with Cincinnati and in the American League in 1966 with Baltimore.

League Championship Series, World Series, and All-Star Game Most Valuable Players

The Most Valuable Player Award in the American League Championship Series is officially called the "Leland S. MacPhail, Jr. Award," and the trophy is a large pewter tray. It was first given in 1980. The National League Championship Series Most Valuable Player receives a sterling silver platter. That award was first presented in 1977.

The World Series Most Valuable Player Award was first awarded in 1955, and the recipient is selected by a media panel at the World Series. The All-Star Most Valuable Player Award was started in 1962.

Rookie of the Year Award

The Rookie of the Year Award did not come into being until 1947, and again it was the Baseball Writers Association that did the voting. The first two years saw a combined selection, with Jackie Robinson of the Brooklyn Dodgers named in 1947 andAlvin Dark of the Boston Braves in 1948. Separate league selections began in 1949 with Roy Sievers of the St. Louis Browns in the American League and Don Newcombe of the Brooklyn Dodgers in the National. The Dodgers, with fifteen selections, and the Yankees, with seven, lead their respective leagues in boasting the most rookie winners.

Cy Young Award

The Cy Young Award, honoring the best pitcher in baseball, was the brainchild of Ford Frick. The former commissioner of baseball, disturbed to find that voters generally tended to pay more attention to players in the lineup every day, as opposed to pitchers who appeared every fourth or fifth day, concluded there should be a separate award for pitchers. Consequently, in 1956, he inaugurated the Cy Young Award and turned this project over to the BBWAA. Frick's choice of Cy Young was based on two important statistics—Young is baseball's biggest winner, with 511 victories, and is the only pitcher in history to win 200 or more games in both leagues.

Don Newcombe of the Brooklyn Dodgers was the first Cy Young Award winner. The year was 1956. The selection of a single pitcher as baseball's best lasted through 1966, when Los Angeles' Sandy Koufax won the honor for the third time in four years. In 1967, acceding to a petition from the BBWAA, General William Eckert, successor to Ford Frick as baseball commissioner, decreed that hereafter each league would have its own Cy Young Award winner. Jim Lonborg of Boston and Mike McCormick of San Francisco were the first to share that honor. The year 1969 produced the only tie for top honors when Mike Cuellar of Baltimore and Denny McLain of Detroit were deadlocked for first place in the American League. In 1981, Fernando Valenzuela became the first rookie to win the award. In 1982, Steve Carlton became the first four-time Cy Young Award winner, and Greg Maddux won four consecutive Cy Young Awards from 1993 to 1995. Tom Seaver, Jim Palmer, Sandy Koufax and Roger Clemens have won three each.

Gold Glove Award

Each year, the top defensive player at his position is selected by the individual league's managers and coaches. He is not necessarily the player with the highest fielding percentage at his position.

Triple Crown Winners

In 120 National League and 95 American League seasons, there have been only fourteen players, all but two since the turn of the century, who have led their respective leagues in the three major offensive departments—batting, home runs, and RBI. Only two players—Rogers Hornsby of the 1922 and 1925 St. Louis Cardinals and Ted Williams of the 1942 and 1947 Boston Red Sox—have accomplished it twice. Although the American League is twenty-five years younger than the National, it has had eight Triple Crown winners compared to six for its older rival. Two of the National League's six came before the twentieth century. Paul Hines of Providence won the batting, home run, and RBI titles in 1878, and Hugh Duffy of the Boston Nationals captured the coveted prize in 1894. Napoleon Lajoie of the 1901 Philadelphia Athletics, with a .422 batting average, 14 home runs, and 125 RBI, was the first American League Triple Crown winner.

Manager of the Year Award

The top manager for the American and National leagues respectively is selected at the end of each season by the Baseball Writers Association of America (BBWAA).

Consecutive Games Played

This listing consists of those "iron men" who played the most consecutive games without interruptions.

No-Hit Games

In 1991, the commissioner's office established new scoring guidelines for no-hit games. Under those guidelines, a pitcher must pitch at least nine innings and pitch a complete game and allow no hits in order to qualify as having pitched a no-hit game.

Combined no-hitters. If a game is completed after at least nine full innings without any hit being given up and more than one pitcher has pitched in the game for the team not allowing any hits, this game shall be deemed a no-hitter and shall be identified as a combined no-hitter.

No-hitters of less than nine innings. If a game is ruled to be complete but less than nine innings have been played and no hits have been given up, that game shall not be an official no-hitter but rather shall be identified separately as a game composed of a certain number of no-hit innings.

No-hitters broken up in extra innings. Games that are completed after more than nine full innings during which no hits were given up by a pitcher until after the ninth inning shall not be no-hitters but shall be identified as "games by pitchers who pitched nine or more hitless innings."

These same rules shall apply to perfect games.

In this edition of *The Baseball Encyclopedia,* the traditional listing of no-hit games has been divided into appropriate sections and noted according to the new criteria.

Baseball Hall of Fame

Baseball's Hall of Fame was founded in 1936 when five of the game's immortals were enshrined. These Hall of Fame pioneers were Babe Ruth, Ty Cobb, Honus Wagner, Christy Mathewson, and Walter Johnson. The special committee appointed by Commissioner Kenesaw Mountain Landis followed up its original selections by electing Napoleon Lajoie, Tris Speaker, and Cy Young to the Hall of Fame the following year. The committee also honored five others for meritorious service as field managers and baseball executives. The National Baseball Hall of Fame was established in Cooperstown, New York, in 1939. Several years later, the voting was turned over to the Baseball Writers Association of America, which was obliged to follow specified guidelines. These included that a player needs ten years of major league experience to qualify and 75 percent of the votes to be elected. No player is eligible for election until he has been retired for a minimum of five years.

In addition to the BBWAA, a Special Veterans Committee of twelve was established to consider players in the nineteenth century. Its scope has since been expanded to include eligible players retired for a minimum of twenty-five years. A third body, a ten-man Special Committee on the Negro Leagues, was authorized in 1971 to consider players of the old Negro leagues. Through 1996 a total of 226 players, managers, umpires, and executives have been inducted into the Hall of Fame.

MOST VALUABLE PLAYERS

CHALMERS

Year	NATIONAL LEAGUE	Year	AMERICAN LEAGUE
1911	Frank Schulte, Chicago (OF)	1911	Ty Cobb, Detroit (OF)
1912	Larry Doyle, New York (2B)	1912	Tris Speaker, Boston (OF)
1913	Jake Daubert, Brooklyn (1B)	1913	Walter Johnson, Washington (P)
1914	Johnny Evers, Boston (2B)	1914	Eddie Collins, Philadelphia (2B)

LEAGUE

Year	NATIONAL LEAGUE	Year	AMERICAN LEAGUE
1922	No Selection	1922	George Sisler, St. Louis (1B)
1923	No Selection	1923	Babe Ruth, New York (OF)
1924	Dazzy Vance, Brooklyn (P)	1924	Walter Johnson, Washington (P)
1925	Rogers Hornsby, St. Louis (2B)	1925	Roger Peckinpaugh, Washington (SS)
1926	Bob O'Farrell, St. Louis (C)	1926	George Burns, Cleveland (1B)
1927	Paul Waner, Pittsburgh (OF)	1927	Lou Gehrig, New York (1B)
1928	Jim Bottomley, St. Louis (1B)	1928	Mickey Cochrane, Philadelphia (C)
1929	Rogers Hornsby, Chicago (2B)	1929	No Selection

BASEBALL WRITERS ASSOCIATION OF AMERICA

Year	NATIONAL LEAGUE	Year	AMERICAN LEAGUE
1931	Frankie Frisch, St. Louis (2B)	1931	Lefty Grove, Philadelphia (P)
1932	Chuck Klein, Philadelphia (OF)	1932	Jimmie Foxx, Philadelphia (1B)
1933	Carl Hubbell, New York (P)	1933	Jimmie Foxx, Philadelphia (1B)
1934	Dizzy Dean, St. Louis (P)	1934	Mickey Cochrane, Detroit (C)
1935	Gabby Hartnett, Chicago (C)	1935	Hank Greenberg, Detroit (1B)
1936	Carl Hubbell, New York (P)	1936	Lou Gehrig, New York (1B)
1937	Joe Medwick, St. Louis (OF)	1937	Charlie Gehringer, Detroit (2B)
1938	Ernie Lombardi, Cincinnati (C)	1938	Jimmie Foxx, Boston (1B)
1939	Bucky Walters, Cincinnati (P)	1939	Joe DiMaggio, New York (OF)
1940	Frank McCormick, Cincinnati (1B)	1940	Hank Greenberg, Detroit (OF)
1941	Dolf Camilli, Brooklyn (1B)	1941	Joe DiMaggio, New York (OF)
1942	Mort Cooper, St. Louis (P)	1942	Joe Gordon, New York (2B)
1943	Stan Musial, St. Louis (OF)	1943	Spud Chandler, New York (2B)
1944	Marty Marion, St. Louis (SS)	1944	Hal Newhouser, Detroit (P)
1945	Phil Cavarretta, Chicago (1B)	1945	Hal Newhouser, Detroit (P)
1946	Stan Musial, St. Louis (1B)	1946	Ted Williams, Boston (OF)
1947	Bob Elliott, Boston (3B)	1947	Joe DiMaggio, New York (OF)
1948	Stan Musial, St. Louis (OF)	1948	Lou Boudreau, Cleveland (SS)
1949	Jackie Robinson, Brooklyn (2B)	1949	Ted Williams, Boston (OF)
1950	Jim Konstanty, Philadelphia (P)	1950	Phil Rizzuto, New York (SS)
1951	Roy Campanella, Brooklyn (C)	1951	Yogi Berra, New York (C)
1952	Hank Sauer, Chicago (OF)	1952	Bobby Shantz, Philadelphia (P)
1953	Roy Campanella, Brooklyn (C)	1953	Al Rosen, Cleveland (3B)
1954	Willie Mays, New York (OF)	1954	Yogi Berra, New York (C)
1955	Roy Campanella, Brooklyn (C)	1955	Yogi Berra, New York (C)

Year	NATIONAL LEAGUE	Year	AMERICAN LEAGUE
1956	Don Newcombe, Brooklyn (P)	1956	Mickey Mantle, New York (OF)
1957	Hank Aaron, Milwaukee (OF)	1957	Mickey Mantle, New York (OF)
1958	Ernie Banks, Chicago (SS)	1958	Jackie Jensen, Boston (OF)
1959	Ernie Banks, Chicago (SS)	1959	Nellie Fox, Chicago (2B)
1960	Dick Groat, Pittsburgh (SS)	1960	Roger Maris, New York (OF)
1961	Frank Robinson, Cincinnati (OF)	1961	Roger Maris, New York (OF)
1962	Maury Wills, Los Angeles (SS)	1962	Mickey Mantle, New York (OF)
1963	Sandy Koufax, Los Angeles (P)	1963	Elston Howard, New York (C)
1964	Ken Boyer, St. Louis (3B)	1964	Brooks Robinson, Baltimore (3B)
1965	Willie Mays, San Francisco (OF)	1965	Zoilo Versalles, Minnesota (SS)
1966	Roberto Clemente, Pittsburgh (OF)	1966	Frank Robinson, Baltimore (OF)
1967	Orlando Cepeda, St. Louis (1B)	1967	Carl Yastrzemski, Boston (OF)
1968	Bob Gibson, St. Louis (P)	1968	Denny McLain, Detroit (P)
1969	Willie McCovey, San Francisco (1B)	1969	Harmon Killebrew, Minnesota (3B)
1970	Johnny Bench, Cincinnati (C)	1970	Boog Powell, Baltimore (1B)
1971	Joe Torre, St. Louis (3B)	1971	Vida Blue, Oakland (P)
1972	Johnny Bench, Cincinnati (C)	1972	Dick Allen, Chicago (1B)
1973	Pete Rose, Cincinnati (OF)	1973	Reggie Jackson, Oakland (OF)
1974	Steve Garvey, Los Angeles (1B)	1974	Jeff Burroughs, Texas (OF)
1975	Joe Morgan, Cincinnati (2B)	1975	Fred Lynn, Boston (OF)
1976	Joe Morgan, Cincinnati (2B)	1976	Thurman Munson, New York (C)
1977	George Foster, Cincinnati (OF)	1977	Rod Carew, Minnesota (1B)
1978	Dave Parker, Pittsburgh (OF)	1978	Jim Rice, Boston (OF)
1979	Keith Hernandez, St. Louis (1B) Willie Stargell, Pittsburgh (1B)	1979	Don Baylor, California (DH)
1980	Mike Schmidt, Philadelphia (3B)	1980	George Brett, Kansas City (3B)
1981	Mike Schmidt, Philadelphia (3B)	1981	Rollie Fingers, Milwaukee (P)
1982	Dale Murphy, Atlanta (OF)	1982	Robin Yount, Milwaukee (SS)
1983	Dale Murphy, Atlanta (OF)	1983	Cal Ripken, Baltimore (SS)
1984	Ryne Sandberg, Chicago (2B)	1984	Willie Hernandez, Detroit (P)
1985	Willie McGee, St. Louis (OF)	1985	Don Mattingly, New York (1B)
1986	Mike Schmidt, Philadelphia (3B)	1986	Roger Clemens, Boston (P)
1987	Andre Dawson, Chicago (OF)	1987	George Bell, Toronto (OF)
1988	Kirk Gibson, Los Angeles (OF)	1988	Jose Canseco, Oakland (OF)
1989	Kevin Mitchell, San Francisco (OF)	1989	Robin Yount, Milwaukee (OF)
1990	Barry Bonds, Pittsburgh (OF)	1990	Rickey Henderson, Oakland (OF)
1991	Terry Pendleton, Atlanta (3B)	1991	Cal Ripken, Baltimore (SS)
1992	Barry Bonds, Pittsburgh (OF)	1992	Dennis Eckersley, Oakland (P)
1993	Barry Bonds, San Francisco (OF)	1993	Frank Thomas, Chicago (1B)
1994	Jeff Bagwell, Houston (1B)	1994	Frank Thomas, Chicago (1B)
1995	Barry Larkin, Cincinnati (SS)	1995	Mo Vaughn, Boston (1B)

LEAGUE CHAMPIONSHIP SERIES MOST VALUABLE PLAYERS

NATIONAL LEAGUE	YEAR	AMERICAN LEAGUE
Dusty Baker, Los Angeles	1977	—
Steve Garvey, Los Angeles	1978	—
Willie Stargell, Pittsburgh	1979	—
Manny Trillo, Philadelphia	1980	Frank White, Kansas City
Burt Hooton, Los Angeles	1981	Graig Nettles, New York
Darrell Porter, St. Louis	1982	Fred Lynn, California
Gary Matthews, Philadelphia	1983	Mike Boddicker, Baltimore
Steve Garvey, San Diego	1984	Kirk Gibson, Detroit
Ozzie Smith, St. Louis	1985	George Brett, Kansas City
Mike Scott, Houston	1986	Marty Barrett, Boston
Jeff Leonard, San Francisco	1987	Gary Gaetti, Minnesota
Orel Hershiser, Los Angeles	1988	Dennis Eckersley, Oakland
Will Clark, San Francisco	1989	Rickey Henderson, Oakland
Rob Dibble, Randy Myers, Cincinnati	1990	Dave Stewart, Oakland
Steve Avery, Atlanta	1991	Kirby Puckett, Minnesota
John Smoltz, Atlanta	1992	Roberto Alomar, Toronto
Curt Schilling, Philadelphia	1993	Dave Stewart, Toronto
No series	1994	No series
Mike Devereaux, Atlanta	1995	Orel Hershiser, Cleveland

WORLD SERIES MOST VALUABLE PLAYERS

1955	Johnny Podres, Brooklyn	1976	Johnny Bench, Cincinnati
1956	Don Larsen, New York (AL)	1977	Reggie Jackson, New York (AL)
1957	Lew Burdette, Milwaukee	1978	Bucky Dent, New York (AL)
1958	Bob Turley, New York (AL)	1979	Willie Stargell, Pittsburgh
1959	Larry Sherry, Los Angeles	1980	Mike Schmidt, Philadelphia
1960	Bobby Richardson, New York (AL)	1981	Ron Cey, Pedro Guerrero, Steve Yeager, Los Angeles
1961	Whitey Ford, New York (AL)		
1962	Ralph Terry, New York (AL)	1982	Darrell Porter, St. Louis
1963	Sandy Koufax, Los Angeles	1983	Rick Dempsey, Baltimore
1964	Bob Gibson, St. Louis	1984	Alan Trammell, Detroit
1965	Sandy Koufax, Los Angeles	1985	Bret Saberhagen, Kansas City
1966	Frank Robinson, Baltimore	1986	Ray Knight, New York (NL)
1967	Bob Gibson, St. Louis	1987	Frank Viola, Minnesota
1968	Mickey Lolich, Detroit	1988	Orel Hershiser, Los Angeles
1969	Donn Clendenon, New York (NL)	1989	Dave Stewart, Oakland
1970	Brooks Robinson, Baltimore	1990	Jose Rijo, Cincinnati
1971	Roberto Clemente, Pittsburgh	1991	Jack Morris, Minnesota
1972	Gene Tenace, Oakland	1992	Pat Borders, Toronto
1973	Reggie Jackson, Oakland	1993	Paul Molitor, Toronto
1974	Rollie Fingers, Oakland	1994	No series
1975	Pete Rose, Cincinnati	1995	Tom Glavine, Atlanta

ALL-STAR GAME MOST VALUABLE PLAYERS

ARCH WARD MEMORIAL AWARD

1962(1)	Maury Wills	Los Angeles	NL
1962(2)	Leon Wagner	Los Angeles	AL
1963	Willie Mays	San Francisco	NL
1964	Johnny Callison	Philadelphia	NL
1965	Juan Marichal	San Francisco	NL
1966	Brooks Robinson	Baltimore	AL
1967	Tony Perez	Cincinnati	NL
1968	Willie Mays	San Francisco	NL
1969	Willie McCovey	San Francisco	NL

COMMISSIONER'S TROPHY

1970	Carl Yastrzemski	Boston	AL
1971	Frank Robinson	Baltimore	AL
1972	Joe Morgan	Cincinnati	NL
1973	Bobby Bonds	San Francisco	NL
1974	Steve Garvey	Los Angeles	NL
1975	Bill Madlock	Chicago	NL
	Jon Matlack	New York	NL
1976	George Foster	Cincinnati	NL
1977	Don Sutton	Los Angeles	NL
1978	Steve Garvey	Los Angeles	NL
1979	Dave Parker	Pittsburgh	NL
1980	Ken Griffey	Cincinnati	NL
1981	Gary Carter	Montreal	NL
1982	Dave Concepcion	Cincinnati	NL
1983	Fred Lynn	California	AL
1984	Gary Carter	Montreal	NL

ARCH WARD MEMORIAL AWARD

1985	LaMarr Hoyt	San Diego	NL
1986	Roger Clemens	Boston	AL
1987	Tim Raines	Montreal	NL
1988	Terry Steinbach	Oakland	AL
1989	Bo Jackson	Kansas City	AL
1990	Julio Franco	Texas	AL
1991	Cal Ripken	Baltimore	AL
1992	Ken Griffey, Jr.	Seattle	AL
1993	Kirby Puckett	Minnesota	AL
1994	Fred McGriff	Atlanta	NL
1995	Jeff Conine	Florida	NL

ROOKIE OF THE YEAR

(one selection 1947–48)

NATIONAL LEAGUE		AMERICAN LEAGUE	
1947	Jackie Robinson, Brooklyn (1B)		—
1948	Alvin Dark, Boston (SS)		—
1949	Don Newcombe, Brooklyn (P)	1949	Roy Sievers, St. Louis (OF)
1950	Sam Jethroe, Boston (OF)	1950	Walt Dropo, Boston (1B)
1951	Willie Mays, New York (OF)	1951	Gil McDougald, New York (3B)
1952	Joe Black, Brooklyn (P)	1952	Harry Byrd, Philadelphia (P)
1953	Junior Gilliam, Brooklyn (2B)	1953	Harvey Kuenn, Detroit (SS)
1954	Wally Moon, St. Louis (OF)	1954	Bob Grim, New York (P)
1955	Bill Virdon, St. Louis (OF)	1955	Herb Score, Cleveland (P)
1956	Frank Robinson, Cincinnati (OF)	1956	Luis Aparicio, Chicago (SS)
1957	Jack Sanford, Philadelphia (P)	1957	Tony Kubek, New York (SS)
1958	Orlando Cepeda, San Francisco (1B)	1958	Albie Pearson, Washington (OF)
1959	Willie McCovey, San Francisco (1B)	1959	Bob Allison, Washington (OF)
1960	Frank Howard, Los Angeles (OF)	1960	Ron Hansen, Baltimore (SS)
1961	Billy Williams, Chicago (OF)	1961	Don Schwall, Boston (P)
1962	Ken Hubbs, Chicago (2B)	1962	Tom Tresh, New York (SS)
1963	Pete Rose, Cincinnati (2B)	1963	Gary Peters, Chicago (P)
1964	Richie Allen, Philadelphia (3B)	1964	Tony Oliva, Minnesota (OF)
1965	Jim Lefebvre, Los Angeles (2B)	1965	Curt Blefary, Baltimore (OF)
1966	Tommy Helms, Cincinnati (2B)	1966	Tommie Agee, Chicago (OF)
1967	Tom Seaver, New York (P)	1967	Rod Carew, Minnesota (2B)
1968	Johnny Bench, Cincinnati (C)	1968	Stan Bahnsen, New York (P)
1969	Ted Sizemore, Los Angeles (2B)	1969	Lou Piniella, Kansas City (OF)
1970	Carl Morton, Montreal (P)	1970	Thurman Munson, New York (C)
1971	Earl Williams, Atlanta (C)	1971	Chris Chambliss, Cleveland (1B)
1972	Jon Matlack, New York (P)	1972	Carlton Fisk, Boston (C)

NATIONAL LEAGUE		AMERICAN LEAGUE	
1973	Gary Matthews, San Francisco (OF)	1973	Al Bumbry, Baltimore (OF)
1974	Bake McBride, St. Louis (OF)	1974	Mike Hargrove, Texas (1B)
1975	John Montefusco, San Francisco (P)	1975	Fred Lynn, Boston (OF)
1976	Pat Zachry, Cincinnati (P)	1976	Mark Fidrych, Detroit (P)
	Butch Metzger, San Diego (P)		
1977	Andre Dawson, Montreal (OF)	1977	Eddie Murray, Baltimore (DH)
1978	Bob Horner, Atlanta (3B)	1978	Lou Whitaker, Detroit (2B)
1979	Rick Sutcliffe, Los Angeles (P)	1979	Alfredo Griffin, Toronto (SS)
			John Castino, Minnesota (3B)
1980	Steve Howe, Los Angeles (P)	1980	Joe Charboneau, Cleveland (OF)
1981	Fernando Valenzuela, Los Angeles (P)	1981	Dave Righetti, New York (P)
1982	Steve Sax, Los Angeles (2B)	1982	Cal Ripken, Baltimore (SS)
1983	Darryl Strawberry, New York (OF)	1983	Ron Kittle, Chicago (OF)
1984	Dwight Gooden, New York (P)	1984	Alvin Davis, Seattle (1B)
1985	Vince Coleman, St. Louis (OF)	1985	Ozzie Guillen, Chicago (SS)
1986	Todd Worrell, St. Louis (P)	1986	Jose Canseco, Oakland (OF)
1987	Benito Santiago, San Diego (C)	1987	Mark McGwire, Oakland (1B)
1988	Chris Sabo, Cincinnati (3B)	1988	Walt Weiss, Oakland (SS)
1989	Jerome Walton, Chicago (OF)	1989	Gregg Olson, Baltimore (P)
1990	David Justice, Atlanta (OF)	1990	Sandy Alomar, Jr., Cleveland (C)
1991	Jeff Bagwell, Houston (1B)	1991	Chuck Knoblauch, Minnesota (2B)
1992	Eric Karros, Los Angeles (1B)	1992	Pat Listach, Milwaukee (SS)
1993	Mike Piazza, Los Angeles (C)	1993	Tim Salmon, California (OF)
1994	Raul Mondesi, Los Angeles (OF)	1994	Bob Hamelin, Kansas City (DH)
1995	Hideo Nomo, Los Angeles (P)	1995	Marty Cordova, Minnesota (OF)

CY YOUNG AWARD WINNERS

(one selection 1956–66)

NATIONAL LEAGUE

1956	Don Newcombe, Brooklyn (RH)
1957	Warren Spahn, Milwaukee (LH)
1960	Vernon Law, Pittsburgh (RH)
1962	Don Drysdale, Los Angeles (RH)
1963	Sandy Koufax, Los Angeles (LH)
1965	Sandy Koufax, Los Angeles (LH)
1966	Sandy Koufax, Los Angeles (LH)
1967	Mike McCormick, San Francisco (LH)
1968	Bob Gibson, St. Louis (RH)
1969	Tom Seaver, New York (RH)
1970	Bob Gibson, St. Louis (RH)
1971	Ferguson Jenkins, Chicago (RH)
1972	Steve Carlton, Philadelphia (LH)
1973	Tom Seaver, New York (RH)
1974	Mike Marshall, Los Angeles (RH)
1975	Tom Seaver, New York (RH)
1976	Randy Jones, San Diego (LH)
1977	Steve Carlton, Philadelphia (LH)

AMERICAN LEAGUE

1958	Bob Turley, New York (RH)
1959	Early Wynn, Chicago (RH)
1961	Whitey Ford, New York (LH)
1964	Dean Chance, Los Angeles (RH)
1967	Jim Lonborg, Boston (RH)
1968	Denny McLain, Detroit (RH)
1969	Mike Cuellar, Baltimore (LH)
	Denny McLain, Detroit (RH)
1970	Jim Perry, Minnesota (RH)
1971	Vida Blue, Oakland (LH)
1972	Gaylord Perry, Cleveland (RH)
1973	Jim Palmer, Baltimore (RH)
1974	Jim (Catfish) Hunter, Oakland (RH)
1975	Jim Palmer, Baltimore (RH)
1976	Jim Palmer, Baltimore (RH)
1977	Sparky Lyle, New York (LH)
1978	Ron Guidry, New York (LH)
1979	Mike Flanagan, Baltimore (LH)

NATIONAL LEAGUE

1978	Gaylord Perry, San Diego (RH)
1979	Bruce Sutter, Chicago (RH)
1980	Steve Carlton, Philadelphia (LH)
1981	Fernando Valenzuela, Los Angeles (LH)
1982	Steve Carlton, Philadelphia (LH)
1983	John Denny, Philadelphia (RH)
1984	Rick Sutcliffe, Chicago (RH)
1985	Dwight Gooden, New York (RH)
1986	Mike Scott, Houston (RH)
1987	Steve Bedrosian, Philadelphia (RH)
1988	Orel Hershiser, Los Angeles (RH)
1989	Mark Davis, San Diego (LH)
1990	Doug Drabek, Pittsburgh (RH)
1991	Tom Glavine, Atlanta (LH)
1992	Greg Maddux, Chicago (RH)
1993	Greg Maddux, Atlanta (RH)
1994	Greg Maddux, Atlanta (RH)
1995	Greg Maddux, Atlanta (RH)

AMERICAN LEAGUE

1980	Steve Stone, Baltimore (RH)
1981	Rollie Fingers, Milwaukee (RH)
1982	Pete Vuckovich, Milwaukee (RH)
1983	LaMarr Hoyt, Chicago (RH)
1984	Willie Hernandez, Detroit (LH)
1985	Bret Saberhagen, Kansas City (RH)
1986	Roger Clemens, Boston (RH)
1987	Roger Clemens, Boston (RH)
1988	Frank Viola, Minnesota (LH)
1989	Bret Saberhagen, Kansas City (RH)
1990	Bob Welch, Oakland (RH)
1991	Roger Clemens, Boston (RH)
1992	Dennis Eckersley, Oakland (RH)
1993	Jack McDowell, Chicago (RH)
1994	David Cone, Kansas City (RH)
1995	Randy Johnson, Seattle (LH)

GOLD GLOVE AWARD WINNERS

COMBINED SELECTION

1957	P	Bobby Shantz, New York (AL)
	C	Sherm Lollar, Chicago (AL)
	1B	Gil Hodges, Brooklyn
	2B	Nellie Fox, Chicago (AL)
	3B	Frank Malzone, Boston
	SS	Roy McMillan, Cincinnati
	LF	Minnie Minoso, Chicago (AL)
	CF	Willie Mays, New York (NL)
	RF	Al Kaline, Detroit

		AMERICAN LEAGUE		NATIONAL LEAGUE
1958	P	Bobby Shantz, New York	P	Harvey Haddix, Cincinnati
	C	Sherm Lollar, Chicago	C	Del Crandall, Milwaukee
	1B	Vic Power, Cleveland	1B	Gil Hodges, Los Angeles
	2B	Frank Bolling, Detroit	2B	Bill Mazeroski, Pittsburgh
	3B	Frank Malzone, Boston	3B	Ken Boyer, St. Louis
	SS	Luis Aparicio, Chicago	SS	Roy McMillan, Cincinnati
	LF	Norm Siebern, New York	LF	Frank Robinson, Cincinnati
	CF	Jimmy Piersall, Boston	CF	Willie Mays, San Francisco
	RF	Al Kaline, Detroit	RF	Hank Aaron, Milwaukee
1959	P	Bobby Shantz, New York	P	Harvey Haddix, Pittsburgh
	C	Sherm Lollar, Chicago	C	Del Crandall, Milwaukee
	1B	Vic Power, Cleveland	1B	Gil Hodges, Los Angeles
	2B	Nellie Fox, Chicago	2B	Charlie Neal, Los Angeles
	3B	Frank Malzone, Boston	3B	Ken Boyer, St. Louis
	SS	Luis Aparicio, Chicago	SS	Roy McMillan, Cincinnati
	LF	Minnie Minoso, Cleveland	LF	Jackie Brandt, San Francisco
	CF	Al Kaline, Detroit	CF	Willie Mays, San Francisco
	RF	Jackie Jensen, Boston	RF	Hank Aaron, Milwaukee
1960	P	Bobby Shantz, New York	P	Harvey Haddix, Pittsburgh
	C	Earl Battey, Washington	C	Del Crandall, Milwaukee
	1B	Vic Power, Cleveland	1B	Bill White, St. Louis
	2B	Nellie Fox, Chicago	2B	Bill Mazeroski, Pittsburgh
	3B	Brooks Robinson, Baltimore	3B	Ken Boyer, St. Louis
	SS	Luis Aparicio, Chicago	SS	Ernie Banks, Chicago
	LF	Minnie Minoso, Chicago	LF	Wally Moon, Los Angeles
	CF	Jim Landis, Chicago	CF	Willie Mays, San Francisco
	RF	Roger Maris, New York	RF	Hank Aaron, Milwaukee

		AMERICAN LEAGUE		NATIONAL LEAGUE
1961	P	Frank Lary, Detroit	P	Bobby Shantz, Pittsburgh
	C	Earl Battey, Chicago	C	John Roseboro, Los Angeles
	1B	Vic Power, Cleveland	1B	Bill White, St. Louis
	2B	Bobby Richardson, New York	2B	Bill Mazeroski, Pittsburgh
	3B	Brooks Robinson, Baltimore	3B	Ken Boyer, St. Louis
	SS	Luis Aparicio, Chicago	SS	Maury Wills, Los Angeles
	OF	Al Kaline, Detroit	OF	Willie Mays, San Francisco
	OF	Jimmy Piersall, Cleveland	OF	Roberto Clemente, Pittsburgh
	OF	Jim Landis, Chicago	OF	Vada Pinson, Cincinnati
1962	P	Jim Kaat, Minnesota	P	Bobby Shantz, St. Louis
	C	Earl Battey, Minnesota	C	Del Crandall, Milwaukee
	1B	Vic Power, Minnesota	1B	Bill White, St. Louis
	2B	Bobby Richardson, New York	2B	Ken Hubbs, Chicago
	3B	Brooks Robinson, Baltimore	3B	Jim Davenport, San Francisco
	SS	Luis Aparicio, Chicago	SS	Maury Wills, Los Angeles
	OF	Jim Landis, Chicago	OF	Willie Mays, San Francisco
	OF	Mickey Mantle, New York	OF	Roberto Clemente, Pittsburgh
	OF	Al Kaline, Detroit	OF	Bill Virdon, Pittsburgh
1963	P	Jim Kaat, Minnesota	P	Bobby Shantz, St. Louis
	C	Elston Howard, New York	C	Johnny Edwards, Cincinnati
	1B	Vic Power, Minnesota	1B	Bill White, St. Louis
	2B	Bobby Richardson, New York	2B	Bill Mazeroski, Pittsburgh
	3B	Brooks Robinson, Baltimore	3B	Ken Boyer, St. Louis
	SS	Zoilo Versalles, Minnesota	SS	Bobby Wine, Philadelphia
	OF	Al Kaline, Detroit	OF	Willie Mays, San Francisco
	OF	Carl Yastrzemski, Boston	OF	Roberto Clemente, Pittsburgh
	OF	Jim Landis, Chicago	OF	Curt Flood, St. Louis
1964	P	Jim Kaat, Minnesota	P	Bobby Shantz, Philadelphia
	C	Elston Howard, New York	C	Johnny Edwards, Cincinnati
	1B	Vic Power, Los Angeles	1B	Bill White, St. Louis
	2B	Bobby Richardson, New York	2B	Bill Mazeroski, Pittsburgh
	3B	Brooks Robinson, Baltimore	3B	Ron Santo, Chicago
	SS	Luis Aparicio, Baltimore	SS	Ruben Amaro, Philadelphia
	OF	Al Kaline, Detroit	OF	Willie Mays, San Francisco
	OF	Jim Landis, Chicago	OF	Roberto Clemente, Pittsburgh
	OF	Vic Davalillo, Cleveland	OF	Curt Flood, St. Louis
		AMERICAN LEAGUE		**NATIONAL LEAGUE**
1965	P	Jim Kaat, Minnesota	P	Bob Gibson, St. Louis

GOLD GLOVE AWARD WINNERS *cont.*

		AMERICAN LEAGUE *cont.*		**NATIONAL LEAGUE** *cont.*
	C	Bill Freehan, Detroit	C	Joe Torre, Milwaukee
	1B	Joe Pepitone, New York	1B	Bill White, St. Louis
	2B	Bobby Richardson, New York	2B	Bill Mazeroski, Pittsburgh
	3B	Brooks Robinson, Baltimore	3B	Ron Santo, Chicago
	SS	Zoilo Versalles, Minnesota	SS	Leo Cardenas, Cincinnati
	OF	Al Kaline, Detroit	OF	Willie Mays, San Francisco
	OF	Tom Tresh, New York	OF	Roberto Clemente, Pittsburgh
	OF	Carl Yastrzemski, Boston	OF	Curt Flood, St. Louis
1966	P	Jim Kaat, Minnesota	P	Bob Gibson, St. Louis
	C	Bill Freehan, Detroit	C	John Roseboro, Los Angeles
	1B	Joe Pepitone, New York	1B	Bill White, Philadelphia
	2B	Bobby Knoop, California	2B	Bill Mazeroski, Pittsburgh
	3B	Brooks Robinson, Baltimore	3B	Ron Santo, Chicago
	SS	Luis Aparicio, Baltimore	SS	Gene Alley, Pittsburgh
	OF	Al Kaline, Detroit	OF	Willie Mays, San Francisco
	OF	Tommie Agee, Chicago	OF	Curt Flood, St. Louis
	OF	Tony Oliva, Minnesota	OF	Roberto Clemente, Pittsburgh
1967	P	Jim Kaat, Minnesota	P	Bob Gibson, St. Louis
	C	Bill Freehan, Detroit	C	Randy Hundley, Chicago
	1B	George Scott, Boston	1B	Wes Parker, Los Angeles
	2B	Bobby Knoop, California	2B	Bill Mazeroski, Pittsburgh
	3B	Brooks Robinson, Baltimore	3B	Ron Santo, Chicago
	SS	Jim Fregosi, California	SS	Gene Alley, Pittsburgh
	OF	Carl Yastrzemski, Boston	OF	Roberto Clemente, Pittsburgh
	OF	Paul Blair, Baltimore	OF	Curt Flood, St. Louis
	OF	Al Kaline, Detroit	OF	Willie Mays, San Francisco
1968	P	Jim Kaat, Minnesota	P	Bob Gibson, St. Louis
	C	Bill Freehan, Detroit	C	Johnny Bench, Cincinnati
	1B	George Scott, Boston	1B	Wes Parker, Los Angeles
	2B	Bobby Knoop, California	2B	Glenn Beckert, Chicago
	3B	Brooks Robinson, Baltimore	3B	Ron Santo, Chicago
	SS	Luis Aparicio, Chicago	SS	Dal Maxvill, St. Louis
	OF	Mickey Stanley, Detroit	OF	Willie Mays, San Francisco
	OF	Carl Yastrzemski, Boston	OF	Roberto Clemente, Pittsburgh
	OF	Reggie Smith, Boston	OF	Curt Flood, St. Louis
1969	P	Jim Kaat, Minnesota	P	Bob Gibson, St. Louis
	C	Bill Freehan, Detroit	C	Johnny Bench, Cincinnati
	1B	Joe Pepitone, New York	1B	Wes Parker, Los Angeles
	2B	Dave Johnson, Baltimore	2B	Felix Millan, Atlanta
	3B	Brooks Robinson, Baltimore	3B	Clete Boyer, Atlanta
	SS	Mark Belanger, Baltimore	SS	Don Kessinger, Chicago
	OF	Paul Blair, Baltimore	OF	Roberto Clemente, Pittsburgh
	OF	Mickey Stanley, Detroit	OF	Curt Flood, St. Louis
	OF	Carl Yastrzemski, Boston	OF	Pete Rose, Cincinnati
1970	P	Jim Kaat, Minnesota	P	Bob Gibson, St. Louis
	C	Ray Fosse, Cleveland	C	Johnny Bench, Cincinnati
	1B	Jim Spencer, California	1B	Wes Parker, Los Angeles
	2B	Dave Johnson, Baltimore	2B	Tommy Helms, Cincinnati
	3B	Brooks Robinson, Baltimore	3B	Doug Rader, Houston
	SS	Luis Aparicio, Chicago	SS	Don Kessinger, Chicago
	OF	Mickey Stanley, Detroit	OF	Roberto Clemente, Pittsburgh
	OF	Paul Blair, Baltimore	OF	Tommie Agee, New York
	OF	Ken Berry, Chicago	OF	Pete Rose, Cincinnati
1971	P	Jim Kaat, Minnesota	P	Bob Gibson, St. Louis
	C	Ray Fosse, Cleveland	C	Johnny Bench, Cincinnati
	1B	George Scott, Boston	1B	Wes Parker, Los Angeles
	2B	Dave Johnson, Baltimore	2B	Tommy Helms, Cincinnati
	3B	Brooks Robinson, Baltimore	3B	Doug Rader, Houston
	SS	Mark Belanger, Baltimore	SS	Bud Harrelson, New York
	OF	Paul Blair, Baltimore	OF	Roberto Clemente, Pittsburgh
	OF	Amos Otis, Kansas City	OF	Bobby Bonds, San Francisco
	OF	Carl Yastrzemski, Boston	OF	Willie Davis, Los Angeles
1972	P	Jim Kaat, Minnesota	P	Bob Gibson, St. Louis
	C	Carlton Fisk, Boston	C	Johnny Bench, Cincinnati
	1B	George Scott, Milwaukee	1B	Wes Parker, Los Angeles
	2B	Doug Griffin, Boston	2B	Felix Millan, Atlanta
	3B	Brooks Robinson, Baltimore	3B	Doug Rader, Houston
	SS	Ed Brinkman, Detroit	SS	Larry Bowa, Philadelphia
	OF	Paul Blair, Baltimore	OF	Roberto Clemente, Pittsburgh
	OF	Bobby Murcer, New York	OF	Cesar Cedeno, Houston
	OF	Ken Berry, California	OF	Willie Davis, Los Angeles

		AMERICAN LEAGUE *cont.*		**NATIONAL LEAGUE** *cont.*
1973	P	Jim Kaat, Chicago	P	Bob Gibson, St. Louis
	C	Thurman Munson, New York	C	Johnny Bench, Cincinnati
	1B	George Scott, Milwaukee	1B	Mike Jorgensen, Montreal
	2B	Bobby Grich, Baltimore	2B	Joe Morgan, Cincinnati
	3B	Brooks Robinson, Baltimore	3B	Doug Rader, Houston
	SS	Mark Belanger, Baltimore	SS	Roger Metzger, Houston
	OF	Paul Blair, Baltimore	OF	Bobby Bonds, San Francisco
	OF	Amos Otis, Kansas City	OF	Cesar Cedeno, Houston
	OF	Mickey Stanley, Detroit	OF	Willie Davis, Los Angeles
1974	P	Jim Kaat, Chicago	P	Andy Messersmith, Los Angeles
	C	Thurman Munson, New York	C	Johnny Bench, Cincinnati
	1B	George Scott, Milwaukee	1B	Steve Garvey, Los Angeles
	2B	Bobby Grich, Baltimore	2B	Joe Morgan, Cincinnati
	3B	Brooks Robinson, Baltimore	3B	Doug Rader, Houston
	SS	Mark Belanger, Baltimore	SS	Dave Concepcion, Cincinnati
	OF	Paul Blair, Baltimore	OF	Cesar Cedeno, Houston
	OF	Amos Otis, Kansas City	OF	Cesar Geronimo, Cincinnati
	OF	Joe Rudi, Oakland	OF	Bobby Bonds, San Francisco
1975	P	Jim Kaat, Chicago	P	Andy Messersmith, Los Angeles
	C	Thurman Munson, New York	C	Johnny Bench, Cincinnati
	1B	George Scott, Milwaukee	1B	Steve Garvey, Los Angeles
	2B	Bobby Grich, Baltimore	2B	Joe Morgan, Cincinnati
	3B	Brooks Robinson, Baltimore	3B	Ken Reitz, St. Louis
	SS	Mark Belanger, Baltimore	SS	Dave Concepcion, Cincinnati
	OF	Paul Blair, Baltimore	OF	Cesar Cedeno, Houston
	OF	Joe Rudi, Oakland	OF	Cesar Geronimo, Cincinnati
	OF	Fred Lynn, Boston	OF	Garry Maddox, Philadelphia
1976	P	Jim Palmer, Baltimore	P	Jim Kaat, Philadelphia
	C	Jim Sundberg, Texas	C	Johnny Bench, Cincinnati
	1B	George Scott, Milwaukee	1B	Steve Garvey, Los Angeles
	2B	Bobby Grich, Baltimore	2B	Joe Morgan, Cincinnati
	3B	Aurelio Rodriguez, Detroit	3B	Mike Schmidt, Philadelphia
	SS	Mark Belanger, Baltimore	SS	Dave Concepcion, Cincinnati
	OF	Joe Rudi, Oakland	OF	Cesar Cedeno, Houston
	OF	Dwight Evans, Boston	OF	Cesar Geronimo, Cincinnati
	OF	Rick Manning, Cleveland	OF	Garry Maddox, Philadelphia
1977	P	Jim Palmer, Baltimore	P	Jim Kaat, Philadelphia
	C	Jim Sundberg, Texas	C	Johnny Bench, Cincinnati
	1B	Jim Spencer, Chicago	1B	Steve Garvey, Los Angeles
	2B	Frank White, Kansas City	2B	Joe Morgan, Cincinnati
	3B	Graig Nettles, New York	3B	Mike Schmidt, Philadelphia
	SS	Mark Belanger, Baltimore	SS	Dave Concepcion, Cincinnati
	OF	Juan Beniquez, Texas	OF	Cesar Geronimo, Cincinnati
	OF	Carl Yastrzemski, Boston	OF	Garry Maddox, Philadelphia
	OF	Al Cowens, Kansas City	OF	Dave Parker, Pittsburgh
1978	P	Jim Palmer, Baltimore	P	Phil Niekro, Atlanta
	C	Jim Sundberg, Texas	C	Bob Boone, Philadelphia
	1B	Chris Chambliss, New York	1B	Keith Hernandez, St. Louis
	2B	Frank White, Kansas City	2B	Davey Lopes, Los Angeles
	3B	Graig Nettles, New York	3B	Mike Schmidt, Philadelphia
	SS	Mark Belanger, Baltimore	SS	Larry Bowa, Philadelphia
	OF	Fred Lynn, Boston	OF	Garry Maddox, Philadelphia
	OF	Dwight Evans, Boston	OF	Dave Parker, Pittsburgh
	OF	Rick Miller, California	OF	Ellis Valentine, Montreal
1979	P	Jim Palmer, Baltimore	P	Phil Niekro, Atlanta
	C	Jim Sundberg, Texas	C	Bob Boone, Philadelphia
	1B	Cecil Cooper, Milwaukee	1B	Keith Hernandez, St. Louis
	2B	Frank White, Kansas City	2B	Manny Trillo, Philadelphia
	3B	Buddy Bell, Texas	3B	Mike Schmidt, Philadelphia
	SS	Rick Burleson, Boston	SS	Dave Concepcion, Cincinnati
	OF	Dwight Evans, Boston	OF	Garry Maddox, Philadelphia
	OF	Sixto Lezcano, Milwaukee	OF	Dave Parker, Pittsburgh
	OF	Fred Lynn, Boston	OF	Dave Winfield, San Diego
1980	P	Mike Norris, Oakland	P	Phil Niekro, Atlanta
	C	Jim Sundberg, Texas	C	Gary Carter, Montreal
	1B	Cecil Cooper, Milwaukee	1B	Keith Hernandez, St. Louis
	2B	Frank White, Kansas City	2B	Doug Flynn, New York
	3B	Buddy Bell, Texas	3B	Mike Schmidt, Philadelphia
	SS	Alan Trammell, Detroit	SS	Ozzie Smith, San Diego
	OF	Fred Lynn, Boston	OF	Andre Dawson, Montreal
	OF	Dwayne Murphy, Oakland	OF	Garry Maddox, Philadelphia
	OF	Willie Wilson, Kansas City	OF	Dave Winfield, San Diego

GOLD GLOVE AWARD WINNERS *cont.*

Year		**AMERICAN LEAGUE** *cont.*		**NATIONAL LEAGUE** *cont.*
1981	P	Mike Norris, Oakland	P	Steve Carlton, Philadelphia
	C	Jim Sundberg, Texas	C	Gary Carter, Montreal
	1B	Mike Squires, Chicago	1B	Keith Hernandez, St. Louis
	2B	Frank White, Kansas City	2B	Manny Trillo, Philadelphia
	3B	Buddy Bell, Texas	3B	Mike Schmidt, Philadelphia
	SS	Alan Trammell, Detroit	SS	Ozzie Smith, San Diego
	OF	Dwayne Murphy, Oakland	OF	Andre Dawson, Montreal
	OF	Dwight Evans, Boston	OF	Garry Maddox, Philadelphia
	OF	Rickey Henderson, Oakland	OF	Dusty Baker, Los Angeles
1982	P	Ron Guidry, New York	P	Phil Niekro, Atlanta
	C	Bob Boone, California	C	Gary Carter, Montreal
	1B	Eddie Murray, Baltimore	1B	Keith Hernandez, St. Louis
	2B	Frank White, Kansas City	2B	Manny Trillo, Philadelphia
	3B	Buddy Bell, Texas	3B	Mike Schmidt, Philadelphia
	SS	Robin Yount, Milwaukee	SS	Ozzie Smith, St. Louis
	OF	Dwight Evans, Boston	OF	Andre Dawson, Montreal
	OF	Dave Winfield, New York	OF	Dale Murphy, Atlanta
	OF	Dwayne Murphy, Oakland	OF	Garry Maddox, Philadelphia
1983	P	Ron Guidry, New York	P	Phil Niekro, Atlanta
	C	Lance Parrish, Detroit	C	Tony Pena, Pittsburgh
	1B	Eddie Murray, Baltimore	1B	Keith Hernandez, St. Louis/New York
	2B	Lou Whitaker, Detroit	2B	Ryne Sandberg, Chicago
	3B	Buddy Bell, Texas	3B	Mike Schmidt, Philadelphia
	SS	Alan Trammell, Detroit	SS	Ozzie Smith, St. Louis
	OF	Dwight Evans, Boston	OF	Andre Dawson, Montreal
	OF	Dave Winfield, New York	OF	Dale Murphy, Atlanta
	OF	Dwayne Murphy, Oakland	OF	Willie McGee, St. Louis
1984	P	Ron Guidry, New York	P	Joaquin Andujar, St. Louis
	C	Lance Parrish, Detroit	C	Tony Pena, Pittsburgh
	1B	Eddie Murray, Baltimore	1B	Keith Hernandez, New York
	2B	Lou Whitaker, Detroit	2B	Ryne Sandberg, Chicago
	3B	Buddy Bell, Texas	3B	Mike Schmidt, Philadelphia
	SS	Alan Trammell, Detroit	SS	Ozzie Smith, St. Louis
	OF	Dwight Evans, Boston	OF	Dale Murphy, Atlanta
	OF	Dave Winfield, New York	OF	Bob Dernier, Chicago
	OF	Dwayne Murphy, Oakland	OF	Andre Dawson, Montreal
1985	P	Ron Guidry, New York	P	Rick Reuschel, Pittsburgh
	C	Lance Parrish, Detroit	C	Tony Pena, Pittsburgh
	1B	Don Mattingly, New York	1B	Keith Hernandez, New York
	2B	Lou Whitaker, Detroit	2B	Ryne Sandberg, Chicago
	3B	George Brett, Kansas City	3B	Tim Wallach, Montreal
	SS	Alfredo Griffin, Oakland	SS	Ozzie Smith, St. Louis
	OF	Gary Pettis, California	OF	Willie McGee, St. Louis
	OF	Dave Winfield, New York	OF	Andre Dawson, Montreal
	OF	Dwight Evans, Boston	OF	Dale Murphy, Atlanta
	OF	Dwayne Murphy, Oakland		
1986	P	Ron Guidry, New York	P	Fernando Valenzuela, Los Angeles
	C	Bob Boone, California	C	Jody Davis, Chicago
	1B	Don Mattingly, New York	1B	Keith Hernandez, New York
	2B	Frank White, Kansas City	2B	Ryne Sandberg, Chicago
	3B	Gary Gaetti, Minnesota	3B	Mike Schmidt, Philadelphia
	SS	Tony Fernandez, Toronto	SS	Ozzie Smith, St. Louis
	OF	Jesse Barfield, Toronto	OF	Dale Murphy, Atlanta
	OF	Kirby Puckett, Minnesota	OF	Willie McGee, St. Louis
	OF	Gary Pettis, California	OF	Tony Gwynn, San Diego
1987	P	Mark Langston, Seattle	P	Rick Reuschel, San Francisco
	C	Bob Boone, California	C	Mike LaValliere, Pittsburgh
	1B	Don Mattingly, New York	1B	Keith Hernandez, New York
	2B	Frank White, Kansas City	2B	Ryne Sandberg, Chicago
	3B	Gary Gaetti, Minnesota	3B	Terry Pendleton, St. Louis
	SS	Tony Fernandez, Toronto	SS	Ozzie Smith, St. Louis
	OF	Jesse Barfield, Toronto	OF	Eric Davis, Cincinnati
	OF	Kirby Puckett, Minnesota	OF	Andre Dawson, Chicago
	OF	Dave Winfield, New York	OF	Tony Gwynn, San Diego

Year		**AMERICAN LEAGUE** *cont.*		**NATIONAL LEAGUE** *cont.*
1988	P	Mark Langston, Seattle	P	Orel Hershiser, Los Angeles
	C	Bob Boone, California	C	Benito Santiago, San Diego
	1B	Don Mattingly, New York	1B	Keith Hernandez, New York
	2B	Harold Reynolds, Seattle	2B	Ryne Sandberg, Chicago
	3B	Gary Gaetti, Minnesota	3B	Tim Wallach, Montreal
	SS	Tony Fernandez, Toronto	SS	Ozzie Smith, St. Louis
	OF	Devon White, California	OF	Andre Dawson, Chicago
	OF	Gary Pettis, California	OF	Eric Davis, Cincinnati
	OF	Kirby Puckett, Minnesota	OF	Andy Van Slyke, Pittsburgh
1989	P	Bret Saberhagen, Kansas City	P	Ron Darling, New York
	C	Bob Boone, Kansas City	C	Benito Santiago, San Diego
	1B	Don Mattingly, New York	1B	Andres Galarraga, Montreal
	2B	Harold Reynolds, Seattle	2B	Ryne Sandberg, Chicago
	3B	Gary Gaetti, Minnesota	3B	Terry Pendleton, St. Louis
	SS	Tony Fernandez, Toronto	SS	Ozzie Smith, St. Louis
	OF	Devon White, California	OF	Andy Van Slyke, Pittsburgh
	OF	Gary Pettis, Detroit	OF	Eric Davis, Cincinnati
	OF	Kirby Puckett, Minnesota	OF	Tony Gwynn, San Diego
1990	P	Mike Boddicker, Boston	P	Greg Maddux, Chicago
	C	Sandy Alomar, Jr., Cleveland	C	Benito Santiago, San Diego
	1B	Mark McGwire, Oakland	1B	Andres Galarraga, Montreal
	2B	Harold Reynolds, Seattle	2B	Ryne Sandberg, Chicago
	3B	Kelly Gruber, Toronto	3B	Tim Wallach, Montreal
	SS	Ozzie Guillen, Chicago	SS	Ozzie Smith, St. Louis
	OF	Gary Pettis, Texas	OF	Andy Van Slyke, Pittsburgh
	OF	Ellis Burks, Boston	OF	Tony Gwynn, San Diego
	OF	Ken Griffey, Jr., Seattle	OF	Barry Bonds, Pittsburgh
1991	P	Mark Langston, California	P	Greg Maddux, Chicago
	C	Tony Pena, Boston	C	Tom Pagnozzi, St. Louis
	1B	Don Mattingly, New York	1B	Will Clark, San Francisco
	2B	Roberto Alomar, Toronto	2B	Ryne Sandberg, Chicago
	3B	Robin Ventura, Chicago	3B	Matt Williams, San Francisco
	SS	Cal Ripken, Baltimore	SS	Ozzie Smith, St. Louis
	OF	Ken Griffey, Jr., Seattle	OF	Andy Van Slyke, Pittsburgh
	OF	Devon White, Toronto	OF	Barry Bonds, Pittsburgh
	OF	Kirby Puckett, Minnesota	OF	Tony Gwynn, San Diego
1992	P	Mark Langston, California	P	Greg Maddux, Chicago
	C	Ivan Rodriguez, Texas	C	Tom Pagnozzi, St. Louis
	1B	Don Mattingly, New York	1B	Mark Grace, Chicago
	2B	Roberto Alomar, Toronto	2B	Jose Lind, Pittsburgh
	3B	Robin Ventura, Chicago	3B	Terry Pendleton, Atlanta
	SS	Cal Ripken, Baltimore	SS	Ozzie Smith, St. Louis
	OF	Ken Griffey, Jr., Seattle	OF	Barry Bonds, Pittsburgh
	OF	Devon White, Toronto	OF	Larry Walker, Montreal
	OF	Kirby Puckett, Minnesota	OF	Andy Van Slyke, Pittsburgh
1993	P	Mark Langston, California	P	Greg Maddux, Atlanta
	C	Ivan Rodriguez, Texas	C	Kirt Manwaring, San Francisco
	1B	Don Mattingly, New York	1B	Mark Grace, Chicago
	2B	Roberto Alomar, Toronto	2B	Robby Thompson, San Francisco
	3B	Robin Ventura, Chicago	3B	Matt Williams, San Francisco
	SS	Omar Vizquel, Seattle	SS	Jay Bell, Pittsburgh
	OF	Ken Griffey, Jr., Seattle	OF	Barry Bonds, San Francisco
	OF	Kenny Lofton, Cleveland	OF	Marquis Grissom, Montreal
	OF	Devon White, Toronto	OF	Larry Walker, Montreal
1994	P	Mark Langston, California	P	Greg Maddux, Atlanta
	C	Ivan Rodriguez, Texas	C	Tom Pagnozzi, St. Louis
	1B	Don Mattingly, New York	1B	Jeff Bagwell, Houston
	2B	Roberto Alomar, Toronto	2B	Craig Biggio, Houston
	3B	Wade Boggs, New York	3B	Matt Williams, San Francisco
	SS	Omar Vizquel, Cleveland	SS	Barry Larkin, Cincinnati
	OF	Ken Griffey, Jr., Seattle	OF	Barry Bonds, San Francisco
	OF	Kenny Lofton, Cleveland	OF	Marquis Grissom, Montreal
	OF	Devon White, Toronto	OF	Darren Lewis, San Francisco
1995	P	Mark Langston, California	P	Greg Maddux, Atlanta
	C	Ivan Rodriguez, Texas	C	Charles Johnson, Florida
	1B	J.T. Snow, California	1B	Mark Grace, Chicago
	2B	Roberto Alomar, Toronto	2B	Craig Biggio, Houston
	3B	Wade Boggs, New York	3B	Ken Caminiti, San Diego
	SS	Omar Vizquel, Cleveland	SS	Barry Larkin, Cincinnati
	OF	Ken Griffey, Jr., Seattle	OF	Steve Finley, San Diego
	OF	Kenny Lofton, Cleveland	OF	Marquis Grissom, Atlanta
	OF	Devon White, Toronto	OF	Raul Modesi, Los Angeles

TRIPLE CROWN WINNERS

NATIONAL LEAGUE

Paul Hines, Providence 1878
Hugh Duffy, Boston 1894
Heinie Zimmerman, Chicago 1912
Rogers Hornsby, St. Louis 1922
Rogers Hornsby, St. Louis 1925
Chuck Klein, Philadelphia 1933
Joe Medwick, St. Louis 1937

AMERICAN LEAGUE

Napoleon Lajoie, Philadelphia 1901
Ty Cobb, Detroit 1909
Jimmie Foxx, Philadelphia 1933
Lou Gehrig, New York 1934
Ted Williams, Boston 1942
Ted Williams, Boston 1947
Mickey Mantle, New York 1956
Frank Robinson, Baltimore 1966
Carl Yastrzemski, Boston 1967

MANAGER OF THE YEAR AWARD WINNERS

NATIONAL LEAGUE

1983	Tommy Lasorda, Los Angeles
1984	Jim Frey, Chicago
1985	Whitey Herzog, St. Louis
1986	Hal Lanier, Houston
1987	Buck Rodgers, Montreal
1988	Tommy Lasorda, Los Angeles
1989	Don Zimmer, Chicago
1990	Jim Leyland, Pittsburgh
1991	Bobby Cox, Atlanta
1992	Jim Leyland, Pittsburgh
1993	Dusty Baker, San Francisco
1994	Felipe Alou, Montreal
1995	Don Baylor, Colorado

AMERICAN LEAGUE

1983	Tony LaRussa, Chicago
1984	Sparky Anderson, Detroit
1985	Bobby Cox, Toronto
1986	John McNamara, Boston
1987	Sparky Anderson, Detroit
1988	Tony LaRussa, Oakland
1989	Frank Robinson, Baltimore
1990	Jeff Torborg, Chicago
1991	Tom Kelly, Minnesota
1992	Tony LaRussa, Oakland
1993	Gene Lamont, Chicago
1994	Buck Showalter, New York
1995	Lou Piniella, Seattle

CONSECUTIVE GAMES PLAYED

(500 or more games)

Cal Ripken	2153*	Dale Murphy	740	Aaron Ward	565
Lou Gehrig	2130	Richie Ashburn	730	Candy LaChance	540
Everett Scott	1307	Ernie Banks	717	Buck Freeman	535
Steve Garvey	1207	Earl Averill	673	Fred Luderus	533
Billy Williams	1117	Frank McCormick	652	Clyde Milan	512
Joe Sewell	1103	Sandy Alomar	648	Charlie Gehringer	511
Stan Musial	895	Eddie Brown	618	Vada Pinson	508
Eddie Yost	829	Roy McMillan	598	Joe Carter	507
Gus Suhr	822	George Pinckney	577	Charlie Gehringer	504
Nellie Fox	798	Steve Brodie	574	Omar Moreno	503
Pete Rose	745				

**Streak in progress at the end of the 1995 season.*

NO-HIT GAMES

(9 innings or more)

NATIONAL LEAGUE

1876	July 15	George W. Bradley, St.L. vs Har. 2-0
1880	June 12	John Richmond, Wor. vs Cle. 1-0 (perfect game)
	June 17	John M. Ward, Pro. vs Buf. 5-0 (perfect game)
	Aug. 19	Larry Corcoran, Chi. vs Bos. 6-0
	Aug. 20	Jim Galvin, Buf. at Wor. 1-0
1882	Sep. 20	Larry Corcoran, Chi. vs Wor. 5-0
1883	July 25	Charles Radbourn, Pro. at Cle. 8-0
	Sep. 13	Hugh Daily, Cle. at Phi. 1-0
1884	June 27	Larry Corcoran, Chi. vs Pro. 6-0
	Aug. 4	Jim Galvin, Buf. at Det. 18-0
1885	July 27	John Clarkson, Chi. vs Pro. 6-0
	Aug. 29	Charles Ferguson, Phi. vs Pro. 1-0
1891	July 31	Amos Rusie, N.Y. vs Bkn. 6-0
	Sep. 22	Tom Lovett, Bkn. vs N.Y. 4-0
1892	Aug. 6	John Stivetts, Bos. vs Bkn. 11-0
	Aug. 22	Alex Sanders, Lou. vs Bal. 6-2
	Oct. 15	Bumpus Jones, Cin. vs Pit. 7-1 (First major league game)
1893	Aug. 16	Bill Hawke, Bal. vs Was. 5-0
1897	Sep. 18	Cy Young, Cle. vs Cin. 6-0
1898	Apr. 22	Ted Breitenstein, Cin. vs Pit. 11-0
	Apr. 22	Jim Hughes, Bal. vs Bos. 8-0
	July 8	Frank Donahue, Phi. vs Bos. 5-0
	Aug. 21	Walter Thornton, Chi. vs Bkn. 2-0
1899	May 25	Deacon Phillippe, Lou. vs N.Y. 7-0
	Aug. 7	Vic Willis, Bos. vs Was. 7-1
1900	July 12	Frank Hahn, Cin. vs Phi. 4-0
1901	July 15	Christy Mathewson, N.Y. at St.L. 5-0
1903	Sep. 18	Chick Fraser, Phi. at Chi. 10-0
1905	June 13	Christy Mathewson, N.Y. at Chi. 1-0
1906	May 1	John Lush, Phi. at Bkn. 1-0
	July 20	Mal Eason, Bkn. at St.L. 2-0

NATIONAL LEAGUE cont.

1907	May 8	Frank Pfeffer, Bos. vs Cin. 6-0
	Sep. 20	Nick Maddox, Pit. vs Bkn. 2-1
1908	July 4	George Wiltse, N.Y. vs Phi. 1-0 (10 innings)
	Sep. 5	Nap Rucker, Bkn. vs Bos. 6-0
1912	Sep. 6	Jeff Tesreau, N.Y. at Phi. 3-0
1914	Sep. 9	George Davis, Bos. vs Phi. 7-0
1915	Apr. 15	Rube Marquard, N.Y. vs Bkn. 2-0
	Aug. 31	Jimmy Lavender, Chi. at N.Y. 2-0
1916	June 16	Tom Hughes, Bos. vs Pit. 2-0
1917	May 2	Fred Toney, Cin. at Chi. 1-0 (10 innings)
1919	May 11	Hod Eller, Cin. at St.L. 6-0
1922	May 7	Jesse Barnes, N.Y. vs Phi. 6-0
1924	July 17	Jesse Haines, St.L. vs Bos. 5-0
1925	Sep. 13	Dazzy Vance, Bkn. vs Phi. 10-1
1929	May 8	Carl Hubbell, N.Y. vs Pit. 11-0
1934	Sep. 21	Paul Dean, St.L. vs Bkn. 3-0
1938	June 11	Johnny Vander Meer, Cin. vs Bos. 3-0
	June 15	Johnny Vander Meer, Cin. at Bkn. 6-0
1940	Apr. 30	Tex Carleton, Bkn. at Cin. 3-0
1941	Aug. 30	Lon Warneke, St.L. at Cin. 2-0
1944	Apr. 27	Jim Tobin, Bos. vs Bkn. 2-0
	May 15	Clyde Shoun, Cin. vs Bos. 1-0
1946	Apr. 23	Ed Head, Bkn. vs Bos. 5-0
1947	June 18	Ewell Blackwell, Cin. vs Bos. 6-0
1948	Sep. 9	Rex Barney, Bkn. at N.Y. 2-0
1950	Aug. 11	Vern Bickford, Bos. vs Bkn. 7-0
1951	May 6	Cliff Chambers, Pit. at Bos. 3-0
1952	June 19	Carl Erskine, Bkn. vs Chi. 5-0
1954	June 12	Jim Wilson, Mil. vs Phi. 2-0
1955	May 12	Sam Jones, Chi. vs Pit. 4-0
1956	May 12	Carl Erskine, Bkn. vs N.Y. 3-0

NO-HIT GAMES *cont.*

(9 innings or more)

NATIONAL LEAGUE *cont.*

	Sep. 25	Sal Maglie, Bkn. vs Phi. 5-0
1960	May 15	Don Cardwell, Chi. vs St.L. 4-0
	Aug. 18	Lew Burdette, Mil. vs Phi. 1-0
	Sep. 15	Warren Spahn, Mil. vs Phi. 4-0
1961	Apr. 28	Warren Spahn, Mil. vs S.F. 1-0
1962	June 30	Sandy Koufax, L.A. vs N.Y. 5-0
1963	May 11	Sandy Koufax, L.A. vs S.F. 8-0
	May 17	Don Nottebart, Hou. vs Phi. 4-1
	June 15	Juan Marichal, S.F. vs Hou. 1-0
1964	Apr. 23	Ken Johnson, Hou. vs Cin. 0-1
	June 4	Sandy Koufax, L.A. at Phi. 3-0
	June 21	Jim Bunning, Phi. at N.Y. 6-0 (perfect game)
1965	Aug. 19	Jim Maloney, Cin. at Chi. 1-0 (10 innings)
	Sep. 9	Sandy Koufax, L.A. vs Chi. 1-0 (perfect game)
1967	June 18	Don Wilson, Hou. vs Atl. 2-0
1968	July 29	George Culver, Cin. at Phi. 6-1
	Sep. 17	Gaylord Perry, S.F. vs St.L. 1-0
	Sep. 18	Ray Washburn, St.L. at S.F. 2-0
1969	Apr. 17	Bill Stoneman, Mon. at Phi. 7-0
	Apr. 30	Jim Maloney, Cin. vs Hou. 10-0
	May 1	Don Wilson, Hou. at Cin. 4-0
	Aug. 19	Ken Holtzman, Chi. vs Atl. 3-0
	Sep. 20	Bob Moose, Pit. at N.Y. 4-0
1970	June 12	Dock Ellis, Pit. at S.D. 2-0
	July 20	Bill Singer, L.A. vs Phi. 5-0
1971	June 3	Ken Holtzman, Chi. at Cin. 1-0
	June 23	Rick Wise, Phi. at Cin. 4-0
	Aug. 14	Bob Gibson, St.L. at Pit. 11-0
1972	Apr. 16	Burt Hooton, Chi. vs Phi. 4-0
	Sep. 2	Milt Pappas, Chi. vs S.D. 8-0
	Oct. 2	Bill Stoneman, Mon. vs N.Y. 7-0
1973	Aug. 5	Phil Niekro, Atl. vs S.D. 9-0
1975	Aug. 24	Ed Halicki, S.F. vs N.Y. 6-0
1976	July 9	Larry Dierker, Hou. vs Mon. 6-0
	Aug. 9	John Candelaria, Pit. vs L.A. 2-0
	Sep. 29	John Montefusco, S.F. vs Atl. 9-0
1978	Apr. 16	Bob Forsch, St.L. vs Phi. 5-0
	June 16	Tom Seaver, Cin. vs St.L. 4-0
1979	Apr. 7	Ken Forsch, Hou. vs Atl. 6-0
1980	June 27	Jerry Reuss, L.A. at S.F. 8-0
1981	May 10	Charlie Lea, Mon. vs S.F. 4-0
	Sep. 26	Nolan Ryan, Hou. vs L.A. 5-0
1983	Sep. 26	Bob Forsch, St.L. vs Mon. 3-0
1986	Sep. 25	Mike Scott, Hou. vs S.F. 2-0
1988	Sep. 16	Tom Browning, Cin. vs L.A. 1-0 (perfect game)
1990	Jun. 29	Fernando Valenzuela, L.A. vs St.L. 6-0
	Aug. 15	Terry Mulholland, Phi. vs S.F. 6-0
1991	May 23	Tommy Greene, Phi. at Mon. 2-0
	July 28	Dennis Martinez, Mon. at L.A. 2-0 (perfect game)
	Sep. 11	Kent Mercker (6), Mark Wohlers (2) & Alejandro Pena (1), Atl. vs S.D. 1-0 (combined no-hitter)
1992	Aug. 17	Kevin Gross, L.A. vs S.F. 2-0
1993	Sep. 8	Darryl Kile, Hou. vs N.Y. 7–1
1994	Apr. 8	Kent Mercker, Atl. at L.A. 6–0
1995	July 14	Ramon Martinez, L.A. vs Fla. 7–0

AMERICAN LEAGUE

1902	Sep. 20	Jimmy Callahan, Chi. vs Det. 3-0
1904	May 5	Cy Young, Bos. vs Phi. 3-0 (perfect game)
	Aug. 17	Jesse Tannehill, Bos. vs Chi. 6-0
1905	July 22	Weldon Henley, Phi. at St.L. 6-0
	Sep. 6	Frank Smith, Chi. at Det. 15-0
	Sep. 27	Bill Dinneen, Bos. vs Chi. 2-0
1908	June 30	Cy Young, Bos. at N.Y. 8-0
	Sep. 18	Bob Rhoades, Cle. vs Bos. 2-0
	Sep. 20	Frank Smith, Chi. vs Phi. 1-0

AMERICAN LEAGUE *cont.*

	Oct. 2	Addie Joss, Cle. vs Chi. 1-0 (perfect game)
1910	Apr. 20	Addie Joss, Cle. at Chi. 1-0
	May 12	Chief Bender, Phi. vs Cle. 4-0
1911	July 29	Joe Wood, Bos. vs St.L. 5-0
	Aug. 27	Ed Walsh, Chi. vs Bos. 5-0
1912	July 4	George Mullin, Det. vs St.L. 7-0
	Aug. 30	Earl Hamilton, St.L. at Det. 5-1
1914	May 31	Joe Benz, Chi. vs Cle. 6-1
1916	June 21	George Foster, Bos. vs N.Y. 2-0
	Aug. 26	Joe Bush, Phi. vs Cle. 5-0
	Aug. 30	Hub Leonard, Bos. vs St.L. 4-0
1917	Apr. 14	Ed Cicotte, Chi. at St.L. 11-0
	Apr. 24	George Mogridge, N.Y. at Bos. 2-1
	May 5	Ernie Koob, St.L. vs Chi. 1-0
	May 6	Bob Groom, St.L. vs Chi. 3-0
	June 23	Babe Ruth (0) and Ernie Shore (9), Bos. vs Was. 4-0 (combined no-hitter)
1918	June 3	Hub Leonard, Bos. at Det. 5-0
1919	Sep. 10	Ray Caldwell, Cle. at N.Y. 3-0
1920	July 1	Walter Johnson, Was. at Bos. 1-0
1922	Apr. 30	Charlie Robertson, Chi. at Det. 2-0 (perfect game)
1923	Sep. 4	Sam Jones, N.Y. at Phi. 2-0
	Sep. 7	Howard Ehmke, Bos. at Phi. 4-0
1926	Aug. 21	Ted Lyons, Chi. at Bos. 6-0
1931	Apr. 29	Wes Ferrell, Cle. vs St.L. 9-0
	Aug. 8	Bob Burke, Was. vs Bos. 5-0
1935	Aug. 31	Vern Kennedy, Chi. vs Cle. 5-0
1937	June 1	Bill Dietrich, Chi. vs St.L. 8-0
1938	Aug. 27	Monte Pearson, N.Y. vs Cle. 13-0
1940	Apr. 16	Bob Feller, Cle. at Chi. 1-0 (opening day)
1945	Sep. 9	Dick Fowler, Phi. vs St.L. 1-0
1946	Apr. 30	Bob Feller, Cle. at N.Y. 1-0
1947	July 10	Don Black, Cle. vs Phi. 3-0
	Sep. 3	Bill McCahan, Phi. vs Was. 3-0
1948	June 30	Bob Lemon, Cle. at Det. 2-0
1951	July 1	Bob Feller, Cle. vs Det. 2-1
	July 12	Allie Reynolds, N.Y. at Cle. 1-0
	Sep. 28	Allie Reynolds, N.Y. vs Bos. 8-0
1952	May 15	Virgil Trucks, Det. vs Was. 1-0
	Aug. 25	Virgil Trucks, Det. at N.Y. 1-0
1953	May 6	Bobo Holloman, St.L. vs Phi. 6-0 (first major league start)
1956	July 14	Mel Parnell, Bos. vs Chi. 4-0
	Oct. 8	Don Larsen, N.Y. vs Bkn. 2-0 (perfect World Series game)
1957	Aug. 20	Bob Keegan, Chi. vs Was. 6-0
1958	July 20	Jim Bunning, Det. at Bos. 3-0
	Sep. 2	Hoyt Wilhelm, Bal. vs N.Y. 1-0
1962	May 5	Bo Belinsky, L.A. vs Bal. 2-0
	June 26	Earl Wilson, Bos. vs L.A. 2-0
	Aug. 1	Bill Monbouquette, Bos. at Chi. 1-0
	Aug. 26	Jack Kralick, Min. vs K.C. 1-0
1965	Sep. 16	Dave Morehead, Bos. vs Cle. 2-0
1966	June 10	Sonny Siebert, Cle. vs Was. 2-0
1967	Apr. 30	Steve Barber ($8\frac{2}{3}$) and Stu Miller ($\frac{1}{3}$), Bal. vs Det. 1-2 (combined no-hitter)
	Aug. 25	Dean Chance, Min. at Cle. 2-1
	Sep. 10	Joel Horlen, Chi. vs Det. 6-0
1968	Apr. 27	Tom Phoebus, Bal. vs Bos. 6-0
	May 8	Jim Hunter, Oak. vs Min. 4-0 (perfect game)
1969	Aug. 13	Jim Palmer, Bal. vs Oak. 8-0
1970	July 3	Clyde Wright, Cal. vs Oak. 4-0
	Sep. 21	Vida Blue, Oak. vs Min. 6-0
1973	Apr. 27	Steve Busby, K.C. at Det. 3-0
	May 15	Nolan Ryan, Cal. at K.C. 3-0
	July 15	Nolan Ryan, Cal. at Det. 6-0
	July 30	Jim Bibby, Tex. at Oak. 6-0
1974	June 19	Steve Busby, K.C. at Mil. 2-0
	July 19	Dick Bosman, Cle. vs Oak. 4-0

NO-HIT GAMES *cont.*

(9 innings or more)

AMERICAN LEAGUE *cont.*

	Sep. 28	Nolan Ryan, Cal. vs Min. 4-0
1975	June 1	Nolan Ryan, Cal. vs Bal. 1-0
	Sep. 28	Blue (5), Abbott & Lindblad (1), Fingers (2), Oak. vs Cal. 5-0 (combined no-hitter)
1976	July 28	John Odom (5) and Francisco Barrios (4), Chi. at Oak. 2-1 (combined no-hitter)
1977	May 14	Jim Colborn, K.C. vs Tex. 6-0
	May 30	Dennis Eckersley, Cle. vs Cal. 1-0
	Sep. 22	Bert Blyleven, Tex. at Cal. 6-0
1981	May 15	Len Barker, Cle. vs Tor. 3-0 (perfect game)
1983	July 4	Dave Righetti, N.Y. vs Bos. 4-0
	Sep. 9	Mike Warren, Oak. vs Chi. 3-0
1984	Apr. 7	Jack Morris, Det. at Chi. 4-0
	Sep. 30	Mike Witt, Cal. at Tex. 1-0 (perfect game)
1986	Sep. 19	Joe Cowley, Chi. at Cal. 7-1
1987	Apr. 15	Juan Nieves, Mil. at Bal. 7-0
1990	Apr. 11	Mark Langston (7) and Mike Witt (2), Cal. vs Sea. 1-0 (combined no-hitter)
	Jun. 2	Randy Johnson, Sea. vs Det. 2-0
	Jun. 11	Nolan Ryan, Tex. at Oak. 5-0
	Jun. 29	Dave Stewart, Oak. at Tor. 5-0
	Sep. 2	Dave Stieb, Tor. at Cle. 3-0
1991	May 1	Nolan Ryan, Tex. vs Tor. 3-0
	July 13	Bob Milacki (6), Mike Flanagan (1), Mark Williamson (1) & Gregg Olson (1), Bal. at Oak. 2-0 (combined no-hitter)
	Aug. 11	Wilson Alvarez, Chi. at Bal. 7-0
	Aug. 26	Bret Saberhagen, K.C. vs Chi. 7-0
1993	Apr. 22	Chris Bosio, Sea. vs. Bos. 7-0
	Sep. 4	Jim Abbott, N.Y. vs. Cle. 4-0
1994	Apr. 27	Scott Erickson, Min. vs. Mil. 6-0
	Jul. 28	Kenny Rogers, Tex. vs. Cal. 4-0 (perfect game)

AMERICAN ASSOCIATION

1882	Sep. 11	Tony Mullane, Lou. at Cin. 2-0

AMERICAN ASSOCIATION *cont.*

	Sep. 19	Guy Hecker, Lou. at Pit. 3-1
1884	May 24	Al Atkinson, Phi. vs Pit. 10-1
	May 29	Ed Morris, Col. at Pit. 5-0
	Jun. 5	Frank Mountain, Col. at Was. 12-0
	Oct. 4	Sam Kimber, Bkn. vs Tol. 0-0 (11 innings, game called due to darkness)
1886	May 1	Al Atkinson, Phi. vs N.Y. 3-2
	July 24	Bill Terry, Bkn. vs St.L. 1-0
	Oct. 6	Matt Kilroy, Bal. at Pit. 6-0
1888	May 27	Bill Terry, Bkn. vs Lou. 4-0
	June 6	Henry Porter, K.C. at Bal. 4-0
	July 26	Ed Seward, Phi. vs Cin. 12-2
	July 31	Gus Weyhing, Phi. vs K.C. 4-0
1890	Sep. 15	Ledell Titcomb, Roc. vs Syr. 7-0
1891	Oct. 4	Ted Breitenstein, St.L. vs Lou. 8-0 (first major league start)

FEDERAL LEAGUE

1914	Sep. 19	Ed Lafitte, Bkn. vs K.C. 6-2
1915	Apr. 24	Frank Allen, Pit. vs St.L. 2-0
	May 15	Claude Hendrix, Chi. vs Pit. 10-0
	Aug. 16	Miles Main, K.C. vs Buf. 5-0
	Sep. 7	Art Davenport, St.L. vs Cin. 3-0

UNION ASSOCIATION

1884	Aug. 26	Dick Burns, Cin. at K.C. 3-1
	Sep. 28	Ed Cushman, Mil. vs Was. 5-0

NATIONAL ASSOCIATION

1875	July 28	Joe Borden, Phi. vs Chi. 4-0

NO-HIT GAMES BROKEN UP IN EXTRA INNINGS

NATIONAL LEAGUE

1904	Jun. 11	Bob Wicker, Chi. at N.Y. 1-0 (hit in 10th; won in 12th)
1906	Aug. 1	Harry McIntire, Bkn. vs Pit. 0-1 (hit in 11th; lost in 13th)
1909	Apr. 15	Red Ames, N.Y. vs Bkn. 0-3 (hit in 10th, lost in 13th)
1917	May 2	Hippo Vaughn, Chi. vs Cin. 0-1 (hit in 10th; lost in 10th)
1956	May 26	John Klippstein (7), Hersh Freeman (1), Joe Black (2.1) Cin. at Mil. 1-2 (hit in 10th, lost in 11th)
1959	May 26	Harvey Haddix, Pit. at Mil. 0-1 (hit in 13th; lost in 13th)
1965	Jun. 14	Jim Maloney, Cin. vs N.Y. 0-1 (hit in 11th; lost in 11th)

NATIONAL LEAGUE *cont.*

1991	July 26	Mark Gardner, Mon. at L.A. 0-1 (hit in 10th; lost in 10th)
1995	Jun. 3	Pedro Martinez, Mon. at S.D. 1-0 (hit in 10th; won in 10th)

AMERICAN LEAGUE

1901	May 9	Earl Moore, Cle. vs Chi. 2-4 (hit in 10th; lost in 10th)
1910	Aug. 30	Tom Hughes, N.Y. vs Cle. 0-5 (hit in 10th; lost in 11th)
1914	May 14	Jim Scott, Chi. at Was. 0-1 (hit in 10th; lost in 10th)
1934	Sep. 18	Bobo Newsom, St.L. vs Bos. 1-2 (hit in 10th; lost in 10th)

NO HITS ALLOWED, LESS THAN 9 INNINGS

NATIONAL LEAGUE

1884	Oct. 1	Charlie Getzien (6), Det. vs Phi. 1-0
1885	Oct. 7	Dupee Shaw (5), Pro. vs Buf. 4-0
1888	Jun. 21	George Van Haltren (6), Chi. vs Pit. 1-0
	Sep. 27	Cannonball Crane (7), N.Y. vs Was. 3-0
1892	Oct. 15	Jack Stivetts (5), Bos. at Was. 4-0
1893	Sep. 23	Icebox Chamberlain (7), Cin. vs Bos. 6-0
1894	Jun. 2	Ed Stein (6), Bkn. vs Chi. 1-0
1903	Sep. 14	Red Ames (5), N.Y. at St.L. 5-0
1906	Aug. 24	Jake Weimer (7), Cin. vs Bkn. 1-0
	Sep. 24	Stoney McGlynn (7), St.L. at Bkn. 1-1
	Sep. 26	Lefty Leifield (6), Pit. at Phi. 8-0
1907	Aug. 11	Ed Karger (7), St.L. vs Bos. 4-0 (7 perfect innings)
	Aug. 23	Howie Camnitz (5), Pit. at N.Y. 1-0
1908	Aug. 6	Johnny Lush (6), St.L. at Bkn. 2-0
1910	July 31	King Cole (7), Chi. at St.L. 4-0
1937	Aug. 27	Fred Frankhouse (8) Bkn. vs Cin. 5-0
1944	Jun. 22	Jim Tobin (5), Bos. vs Phi. 7-0
1959	Jun. 12	Mike McCormick (5), S.F. at Phi. 3-0
	Sep. 26	Sam Jones (7), S.F. at St.L. 4-0
1984	Apr. 21	David Palmer (5), Mon. at St.L. 4-0 (5 perfect innings)

AMERICAN LEAGUE

1905	Aug. 15	Rube Waddell (5), Phi. vs St.L. 2-0

AMERICAN LEAGUE *cont.*

1906	Aug. 29	Jimmy Dygert (3), Rube Waddell (2), Phi. vs Chi. 4-3
1907	May 26	Ed Walsh (5), Chi. vs N.Y. 8-1
	Oct. 5	Rube Vickers (5), Phi. vs Was. 4-0 (5 perfect innings)
1912	Aug. 20	Jay Cashion (6), Was. vs Cle. 2-0
1924	Aug. 25	Walter Johnson (7), Was. vs St.L. 2-0
1940	Aug. 5	John Whitehead (6), St.L. vs Det. 4-0
1967	Aug. 6	Dean Chance (5), Min. vs Bos. 2-0 (5 perfect innings)
1990	July 1	Andy Hawkins (8), N.Y. at Chi. 0-4 (9 inning game)
	July 12	Melido Perez (6), Chi. at N.Y. 8-0
1992	Apr. 12	Matt Young (8), Bos. at Cle. 1-2 (9 inning game)

AMERICAN ASSOCIATION

1884	May 6	Larry McKeon (6), Ind. at Cin. 0-0
1889	July 29	Matt Kilroy (7), Bal. vs St.L. 0-0
1890	Sep. 23	George Nichol (7), St.L. vs Pit. 21-2
	Oct. 12	Hank Gastright (8), Col. vs Tol. 6-0

UNION ASSOCIATION

1884	Aug. 21	Charlie Gagus (8), Was. vs Wil. 12-1
	Oct. 5	Charlie Sweeney (2), Henry Boyle (3), St.L. vs St.P. 0-1

PLAYERS' LEAGUE

1890	Jun. 21	Silver King (8), Chi. vs Bkn. 0-1

BASEBALL HALL OF FAME

PLAYER	Position	Career Dates	Year Selected
Henry Aaron	OF	1954–1976	1982
Grover Alexander	P	1911–1930	1938
Cap Anson	1B	1876–1897	1939
Luis Aparicio	SS	1956–1973	1984
Luke Appling	SS	1930–1950	1964
Richie Ashburn	OF	1948–1962	1995
Earl Averill	OF	1929–1941	1975
J. Frank Baker	3B	1908–1922	955
Dave Bancroft	SS	1915–1930	1971
Ernie Banks	SS-1B	1953–1971	1977
Jake Beckley	1B	1888–1907	1971
James "Cool Papa" Bell*	OF		1974
Johnny Bench	C	1967–1983	1989
Chief Bender	P	1903–1925	1953
Yogi Berra	C	1946–1965	1972
Jim Bottomley	1B	1922–1937	1974
Lou Boudreau	SS	1938–1952	1970
Roger Bresnahan	C	1897–1915	1945
Lou Brock	OF	1961–1979	1985
Dan Brouthers	1B	1879–1904	1945
Mordecai Brown	P	1903–1916	1949
Jim Bunning	P	1955–1971	1996
Jesse Burkett	OF	1890–1905	1946
Roy Campanella	C	1948–1957	1969
Rod Carew	1B-2B	1967–1985	1991
Max Carey	OF	1910–1929	1961
Steve Carlton	P	1965–1988	1994
Frank Chance	1B	1898–1914	1946
Oscar Charleston*	OF		1976
Jack Chesbro	P	1899–1909	1946
Fred Clarke	OF	1894–1915	1945
John Clarkson	P	1882–1894	1963
Roberto Clemente	OF	1955–1972	1973
Ty Cobb	OF	1905–1928	1936
Mickey Cochrane	C	1925–1937	1947
Eddie Collins	2B	1906–1930	1939
Jimmy Collins	3B	1895–1908	1945
Earle Combs	OF	1924–1935	1970
Roger Connor	1B	1880–1897	1976
Stan Coveleski	P	1912–1928	1969
Sam Crawford	OF	1899–1917	1957
Joe Cronin	SS	1926–1945	1956
Candy Cummings	P	1872–1877	1939
Kiki Cuyler	OF	1921–1938	1968
Ray Dandridge*	3B		1987
Leon Day *	P		1995
Dizzy Dean	P	1930–1947	1953
Ed Delahanty	OF	1888–1903	1945
Bill Dickey	C	1928–1946	1954
Martin DiHigo*	P		1977
Joe DiMaggio	OF	1936–1951	1955
Bobby Doerr	2B	1937–1951	1986
Don Drysdale	P	1956–1969	1984
Hugh Duffy	OF	1888–1906	1945
Johnny Evers	2B	1902–1929	1939
Buck Ewing	C	1880–1897	1946
Red Faber	P	1914–1933	1964
Bob Feller	P	1936–1956	1962
Rick Ferrell	C	1929–1947	1984
Rollie Fingers	P	1968–1985	1992
Elmer Flick	OF	1898–1910	1963
Whitey Ford	P	1950–1967	1974
Bill Foster*	P		1996
Jimmie Foxx	1B	1925–1945	1951
Frankie Frisch	2B	1919–1937	1947
Pud Galvin	P	1879–1892	1965
Lou Gehrig	1B	1923–1939	1939
Charlie Gehringer	2B	1924–1942	1949
Bob Gibson	P	1959–1975	1981
Josh Gibson*	C		1972
Lefty Gomez	P	1930–1943	1972
Goose Goslin	OF	1921–1938	1968
Hank Greenberg	1B	1930–1947	1956
Burleigh Grimes	P	1916–1934	1964
Lefty Grove	P	1925–1941	1947
Chick Hafey	OF	1924–1937	1971
Jesse Haines	P	1918–1937	1970
Billy Hamilton	OF	1888–1901	1961
Gabby Hartnett	C	1922–1941	1955
Harry Heilmann	OF	1914–1932	1952
Billy Herman	2B	1931–1947	1975
Harry Hooper	OF	1909–1925	1971
Rogers Hornsby	2B	1915–1937	1942
Waite Hoyt	P	1918–1938	1969
Carl Hubbell	P	1928–1943	1947
Catfish Hunter	P	1965–1979	1987
Monte Irvin*	OF	1949–1956	1973
Reggie Jackson	OF	1967–1987	1993
Travis Jackson	SS	1922–1936	1982
Ferguson Jenkins	P	1965–1983	1991
Hugh Jennings	SS	1891–1918	1945
Judy Johnson*	3B		1975
Walter Johnson	P	1907–1927	1936
Addie Joss	P	1902–1910	1978
Al Kaline	OF	1953–1974	1980
Tim Keefe	P	1880–1893	1964
Willie Keeler	OF	1892–1910	1939
George Kell	3B	1943–1957	1983
Joe Kelley	OF	1891–1908	1971
George Kelly	1B	1915–1932	1973
King Kelly	C	1878–1893	1945
Harmon Killebrew	1B-3B	1954–1975	1984
Ralph Kiner	OF	1946–1955	1975
Chuck Klein	OF	1928–1944	1980
Sandy Koufax	P	1955–1966	1972
Nap Lajoie	2B	1896–1916	1937
Tony Lazzeri	2B	1926–1939	1991
Bob Lemon	P	1941–1958	1976
Buck Leonard*	1B		1972
Fred Lindstrom	3B	1924–1936	1976
John Henry Lloyd*	SS-1B		1977
Ernie Lombardi	C	1931–1947	1986
Ted Lyons	P	1923–1946	1955
Mickey Mantle	OF	1951–1968	1974
Heinie Manush	OF	1923–1939	1964
Rabbit Maranville	SS-2B	1912–1935	1954
Juan Marichal	P	1960–1975	1983
Rube Marquard	P	1908–1925	1971
Eddie Mathews	3B	1952–1968	1978
Christy Mathewson	P	1900–1916	1936
Willie Mays	OF	1951–1973	1979
Tommy McCarthy	OF	1884–1896	1946
Willie McCovey	1B	1959–1980	1986
Joe McGinnity	P	1899–1908	1946
Joe Medwick	OF	1932–1948	1968
Johnny Mize	1B	1936–1953	1981
Joe Morgan	2B	1963–1984	1990
Stan Musial	OF-1B	1941–1963	1969
Hal Newhouser	P	1939–1955	1992
Kid Nichols	P	1890–1906	1949
Jim O'Rourke	OF	1876–1904	1945
Mel Ott	OF	1926–1947	1951
Satchel Paige*	P	1948–1965	1971
Jim Palmer	P	1965–1984	1990
Herb Pennock	P	1912–1934	1948
Gaylord Perry	P	1962–1983	1991
Eddie Plank	P	1901–1917	1946
Hoss Radbourn	P	1880–1891	1939
Pee Wee Reese	SS	1940–1958	1984
Sam Rice	OF	1915–1935	1963
Eppa Rixey	P	1912–1933	1963
Phil Rizzuto	SS	1941–1956	1994
Robin Roberts	P	1948–1966	1976
Brooks Robinson	3B	1955–1977	1983
Frank Robinson	OF	1956–1976	1982
Jackie Robinson	2B	1947–1956	1962
Edd Roush	OF	1913–1931	1962
Red Ruffing	P	1924–1947	1967
Amos Rusie	P	1889–1901	1977
Babe Ruth	OF	1914–1935	1936
Ray Schalk	C	1912–1929	1955
Mike Schmidt	3B	1972–1989	1995
Red Schoendienst	2B	1945–1963	1989
Tom Seaver	P	1967–1986	1992
Joe Sewell	SS	1920–1933	1977
Al Simmons	OF	1924–1944	1953
George Sisler	1B	1915–1930	1939
Enos Slaughter	OF	1938–1959	1985
Duke Snider	OF	1947–1964	1980
Warren Spahn	P	1942–1965	1973
Al Spalding	P	1871–1878	1939
Tris Speaker	OF	1907–1928	1937
Willie Stargell	OF-1B	1962–1982	1988
Bill Terry	1B	1923–1936	1954
Sam Thompson	OF	1885–1906	1974
Joe Tinker	SS	1902–1916	1946
Pie Traynor	3B	1920–1937	1948
Dazzy Vance	P	1915–1935	1955
Arky Vaughan	SS	1932–1948	1985
Rube Waddell	P	1897–1910	1946
Honus Wagner	SS	1897–1917	1936
Bobby Wallace	SS	1894–1918	1953
Ed Walsh	P	1904–1917	1946
Lloyd Waner	OF	1927–1945	1967
Paul Waner	OF	1926–1945	1952
Monte Ward	2B-P	1878–1894	1964
Mickey Welch	P	1880–1892	1973
Zach Wheat	OF	1909–1927	1959

Career Dates indicate first and last appearances in the majors.
*Elected on the basis of his career in the Negro leagues.

BASEBALL HALL OF FAME *cont.*

Hoyt Wilhelm	P	1952–1972	1985
Billy Williams	OF	1959–1976	1987
Ted Williams	OF	1939–1960	1966
Vic Willis	P	1898–1910	1995
Hack Wilson	OF	1923–1934	1979
Early Wynn	P	1939–1963	1972
Carl Yastrzemski	OF	1961–1983	1989
Cy Young	P	1890–1911	1937
Ross Youngs	OF	1917–1926	1972

MANAGER	**Year Selected**
Walt Alston	1983
Charles Comiskey	1939
Clark Griffith	1946
Ned Hanlon	1996
Bucky Harris	1975
Miller Huggins	1964
Al Lopez	1977
Connie Mack	1937
Joe McCarthy	1957
John McGraw	1937
Bill McKechnie	1962
Wilbert Robinson	1945
Casey Stengel	1966
Earl Weaver	1996
George Wright	1937
Harry Wright	1953
Leo Durocher	1994

SELECTED FOR MERITORIOUS SERVICE

Al Barlick (Umpire)
Edward Barrow (Manager-Executive)
Morgan G. Bulkeley (Executive)
Alexander J. Cartwright (Executive)
Henry Chadwick (Writer-Statistician)
Happy Chandler (Commissioner-Executive)
John "Jocko" Conlan (Umpire)
Thomas Connolly (Umpire)
William G. Evans (Umpire-Executive)
Andrew "Rube" Foster (Player-Executive)
Ford C. Frick (Commissioner-Executive)
Warren Giles (Executive)
William Harridge (Executive)
Cal Hubbard (Umpire)
B. Bancroft Johnson (Executive)
William Klem (Umpire)
Kenesaw M. Landis (Commissioner)
Bill McGowan (Umpire)
Larry S. MacPhail (Executive)
W. Branch Rickey (Manager-Executive)
Bill Veeck (Executive)
George M. Weiss (Executive)
Tom Yawkey (Executive)

THE COMMISSIONERS OF BASEBALL

Judge Kenesaw Mountain Landis	Elected November 12, 1920. Served until his death on November 25, 1944.
A. B. "Happy" Chandler	Elected April 24, 1945. Served until July 15, 1951.
Ford Frick	Elected September 20, 1951. Served until November 16, 1965.
General William Eckert	Elected November 17, 1965. Served until December 20,1968.
Bowie Kuhn	Elected February 4, 1969. Served until September 30, 1984.
Peter V. Ueberroth	Elected March 3, 1984, took office October 1, 1984, andserved through March 31, 1989.
A. Bartlett Giamatti	Elected September 8, 1988, took office April 1, 1989, and served until his death on September 1, 1989.
Francis T. Vincent, Jr.	Appointed Acting Commissioner September 2, 1989; elected Commissioner September 13, 1989. Served until September 7, 1992.

PART THREE

All-Time Leaders

Individual Batting, Single Season
Individual Pitching, Single Season
Individual Fielding, Single Season
Individual Batting, Lifetime
Individual Pitching, Lifetime
Individual Fielding, Lifetime
World Series Lifetime Leaders
League Championship Lifetime Leaders

All-Time Leaders

The All-Time Leaders section provides information on individual all-time single season and lifetime leaders for all major leagues from 1876 through today. Included for all the various categories are leaders in batting, fielding, and pitching.

Much of the information has never been compiled, especially for the period 1876 through 1919. For certain other years some statistics are still missing or incomplete.

When teams in this section are listed by an abbreviation of the city or area in which the team played, the abbreviations are as follows:

ALT	Altoona	MON	Montreal
ATL	Atlanta	NWK	Newark
BAL	Baltimore	NY	New York
BKN	Brooklyn	OAK	Oakland
BOS	Boston	PHI	Philadelphia
BUF	Buffalo	PIT	Pittsburgh
CAL	California	PRO	Providence
CHI	Chicago	RIC	Richmond
CIN	Cincinnati	ROC	Rochester
CLE	Cleveland	SD	San Diego
CLR	Colorado	SEA	Seattle
COL	Columbus	SF	San Francisco
DET	Detroit	STL	St. Louis
FLA	Florida	STP	St. Paul
HAR	Hartford	SYR	Syracuse
HOU	Houston	TEX	Texas
IND	Indianapolis	TOL	Toledo
KC	Kansas City	TOR	Toronto
LA	Los Angeles	TRO	Troy
LOU	Louisville	WAS	Washington
MIL	Milwaukee	WIL	Wilmington
MIN	Minnesota	WOR	Worcester

Individual All-Time Single Season Leaders

The top 20 men are shown in batting and base running, the top 15 in pitching and relief pitching. If required by ties, 1 additional player is shown. If ties would require more than 1 additional man to be shown, none of the last tied group is included. All the information is self-explanatory, with the possible exception of Home Run Percentage, which is the number of home runs per 100 times at bat.

Stolen Bases. As shown here, stolen bases start in 1898. Although stolen bases were first considered a statistical item in 1886, they were known as "bases advanced," which credited a stolen base to a man taking an extra base on another player's hit or out, until 1898.

Pitching Categories. Pitching information appears for two separate periods: 1876 through 1892; 1893 through today, except for relief pitching information, which is shown only from 1893. The reason for these separate categories is that the pitching rubber was not moved to its present distance of 60 feet 6 inches until 1893.

Estimated Earned Run Averages (applies to all parts of this section). Any time an earned run average appears in italics it indicates that not all the earned runs allowed by the pitcher are known, and the information had to be estimated. For example, it is known that a team allowed 560 runs in 112 games. Of these games, it is known that in 90 of them the team allowed 420 runs of which 315 or 75% were earned. One man pitched $207\frac{2}{3}$ innings in 40 games and allowed 134 runs. In 35 of these games, it is known that he allowed 118 runs of which 83 were earned. By multiplying the team's known ratio of earned runs to total runs (75%) by the pitcher's 16 (134 minus 118) remaining runs allowed, a figure of 12 additional estimated earned runs is calculated. This means that the pitcher allowed an estimated total of 95 earned runs in $207\frac{2}{3}$ innings for an estimated earned run average of 4.12. In all cases at least 50% of the runs allowed by the team were "known" as a basis for estimating earned run averages.

League Leader Qualifications. Throughout baseball there have been different rules used to determine the minimum appearances necessary to qualify for league leader in categories concerning averages (Batting Average, Earned Run Average, etc.). For the rules and the years they were in effect, see Appendix C.

Individual Lifetime Leaders

The ranking of the batting, base running, pitching, and fielding leaders is based on calculation to 5 decimal points, although no more than the first 3 decimal points are shown. Players with identical ranking (through 5 decimal points) are listed with the same rank number. The following minimum criteria were used to establish the lifetime leaders:

Batting

Batting average, all players .300, 4,000 times at bat

Slugging average, .500, 4,000 at bat

Total bases, 4,000

Games played, 2,000

At bats, 9,000

Hits, 2,000

Doubles, 400

Triples, 150

Home runs, 300

Home run percentage, top 35 players, 4,000 at bat

Extra base hits, 800

Runs batted in, 1,000

RBI per game, top 35 players, 4,000 at bat

Runs, 1,000

Runs per game, top 35 players, 4,000 at bat

Bases on balls, 1,000

Bases on balls average, top 35 players, 4,000 at bat

Stolen bases, 300

Pinch hits, 50

Pinch hit batting average, top 35 players, 150 pinch hit at bat

Fewest strikeouts per at bat, top 35 players, 4,000 at bat

Most strikeouts per at bat, top 35 players, 4,000 at bat

Strikeouts, 1,000

Pitching

Wins, 200 or more

Winning percentage, top 35 players, 1,500 innings pitched

Earned run average, 2.50, 1,500 innings pitched

Games, 500

Completed games, 300

Innings pitched, 3,500

Strikeouts, 1,500

Strikeouts per nine innings, top 35 players, 1,500 innings

Shutouts, 30

Fewest hits per nine innings, top 35 players, 1,500 innings

Most bases on balls, top 35 players

Fewest bases on balls per nine innings, top 35 players, 1,500 innings

Most losses, top 35 players

Relief Pitching

Wins, 50

Winning percentage, top 35 players, 500 innings pitched

Saves, 75

Wins plus saves, 125

Games, 400

Fielding

The top 15 players in each category are shown for each position. A minimum of 1,000 games played at the indicated position is required, except for pitchers, where 1,500 innings or more pitched is the criterion.

INDIVIDUAL BATTING (SINGLE SEASON)

BATTING AVERAGE

1.	Hugh Duffy, 1894	.440
2.	Tip O'Neill, 1887	.435
3.	Ross Barnes, 1876	.429
4.	Willie Keeler, 1897	.424
5.	Rogers Hornsby, 1924	.424
6.	Nap Lajoie, 1901	.422
7.	George Sisler, 1922	.420
8.	Ty Cobb, 1911	.420
9.	Tuck Turner, 1894	.416
10.	Fred Dunlap, 1884	.412
11.	Ty Cobb, 1912	.410
12.	Ed Delahanty, 1899	.410
13.	Jesse Burkett, 1896	.410
14.	Jesse Burkett, 1895	.409
15.	Joe Jackson, 1911	.408
16.	Sam Thompson, 1894	.407
17.	George Sisler, 1920	.407
18.	Ed Delahanty, 1894	.407
19.	Ted Williams, 1941	.406
20.	Billy Hamilton, 1894	.404

AT BATS

1.	Willie Wilson, 1980	705
2.	Juan Samuel, 1984	701
3.	Dave Cash, 1975	699
4.	Matty Alou, 1969	698
5.	Woody Jensen, 1936	696
6.	Omar Moreno, 1979	695
6.	Maury Wills, 1962	695
8.	Bobby Richardson, 1962	692
9.	Kirby Puckett, 1985	691
10.	Lou Brock, 1967	689
10.	Sandy Alomar, 1971	689
12.	Dave Cash, 1974	687
12.	Tony Fernandez, 1986	687
14.	Horace Clarke, 1970	686
15.	Joe Moore, 1935	681
15.	Lloyd Waner, 1931	681
17.	Pete Rose, 1973	680
17.	Kirby Puckett, 1986	680
17.	Frank Taveras, 1979	680

TRIPLES

1.	Owen Wilson, 1912	36
2.	Dave Orr, 1886	31
2.	Heinie Reitz, 1894	31
4.	Perry Werden, 1893	29
5.	Harry Davis, 1897	28
6.	George Davis, 1893	27
6.	Sam Thompson, 1894	27
6.	Jimmy Williams, 1899	27
9.	Kiki Cuyler, 1925	26
9.	Joe Jackson, 1912	26
9.	Sam Crawford, 1914	26
9.	George Treadway, 1894	26
9.	Long John Reilly, 1890	26
14.	Tommy Long, 1915	25
14.	Larry Doyle, 1911	25
14.	Roger Connor, 1894	25
14.	Sam Crawford, 1903	25
14.	Buck Freeman, 1899	25
19.	Ty Cobb, 1911	24
19.	Ed McKean, 1893	24

EXTRA BASE HITS

1.	Babe Ruth, 1921	119
2.	Lou Gehrig, 1927	117
3.	Chuck Klein, 1930	107
4.	Chuck Klein, 1932	103
4.	Stan Musial, 1948	103
4.	Albert Belle, 1995	103
4.	Hank Greenberg, 1937	103
8.	Rogers Hornsby, 1922	102
9.	Lou Gehrig, 1930	100
9.	Jimmie Foxx, 1932	100
11.	Babe Ruth, 1920	99
11.	Babe Ruth, 1923	99
11.	Hank Greenberg, 1940	99
14.	Hank Greenberg, 1935	98
15.	Babe Ruth, 1927	97
15.	Joe Medwick, 1937	97
15.	Hack Wilson, 1930	97
18.	Hal Trosky, 1936	96
18.	Joe DiMaggio, 1937	96
18.	Hank Greenberg, 1934	96

SLUGGING AVERAGE

1.	Babe Ruth, 1920	.847
2.	Babe Ruth, 1921	.846
3.	Babe Ruth, 1927	.772
4.	Lou Gehrig, 1927	.765
5.	Babe Ruth, 1923	.764
6.	Rogers Hornsby, 1925	.756
7.	Jeff Bagwell, 1994	.750
8.	Jimmie Foxx, 1932	.749
9.	Babe Ruth, 1924	.739
10.	Babe Ruth, 1926	.737
11.	Ted Williams, 1941	.735
12.	Babe Ruth, 1930	.732
13.	Ted Williams, 1957	.731
14.	Frank Thomas, 1994	.729
15.	Hack Wilson, 1930	.723
16.	Rogers Hornsby, 1922	.722
17.	Lou Gehrig, 1930	.721
18.	Albert Belle, 1994	.714
19.	Babe Ruth, 1928	.709
20.	Al Simmons, 1930	.708

HITS

1.	George Sisler, 1920	257
2.	Bill Terry, 1930	254
2.	Lefty O'Doul, 1929	254
4.	Al Simmons, 1925	253
5.	Chuck Klein, 1930	250
5.	Rogers Hornsby, 1922	250
7.	Ty Cobb, 1911	248
8.	George Sisler, 1922	246
9.	Babe Herman, 1930	241
9.	Heinie Manush, 1928	241
11.	Wade Boggs, 1985	240
11.	Jesse Burkett, 1896	240
13.	Rod Carew, 1977	239
13.	Willie Keeler, 1897	239
15.	Ed Delahanty, 1899	238
15.	Don Mattingly, 1986	238
17.	Hugh Duffy, 1894	237
17.	Paul Waner, 1927	237
17.	Joe Medwick, 1937	237
17.	Harry Heilmann, 1921	237

HOME RUNS

1.	Roger Maris, 1961	61
2.	Babe Ruth, 1927	60
3.	Babe Ruth, 1921	59
4.	Jimmie Foxx, 1932	58
4.	Hank Greenberg, 1938	58
6.	Hack Wilson, 1930	56
7.	Babe Ruth, 1920	54
7.	Babe Ruth, 1928	54
7.	Ralph Kiner, 1949	54
7.	Mickey Mantle, 1961	54
11.	Willie Mays, 1965	52
11.	George Foster, 1977	52
11.	Mickey Mantle, 1956	52
14.	Ralph Kiner, 1947	51
14.	Willie Mays, 1955	51
14.	Johnny Mize, 1947	51
14.	Cecil Fielder, 1990	51
18.	Jimmie Foxx, 1938	50
18.	Albert Belle, 1995	50

RUNS BATTED IN

1.	Hack Wilson, 1930	190
2.	Lou Gehrig, 1931	184
3.	Hank Greenberg, 1937	183
4.	Lou Gehrig, 1927	175
4.	Jimmie Foxx, 1938	175
6.	Lou Gehrig, 1930	174
7.	Babe Ruth, 1921	171
8.	Chuck Klein, 1930	170
8.	Hank Greenberg, 1935	170
10.	Jimmie Foxx, 1932	169
11.	Joe DiMaggio, 1937	167
12.	Sam Thompson, 1887	166
13.	Lou Gehrig, 1934	165
13.	Al Simmons, 1930	165
13.	Sam Thompson, 1895	165
16.	Babe Ruth, 1927	164
17.	Babe Ruth, 1931	163
17.	Jimmie Foxx, 1933	163
19.	Hal Trosky, 1936	162

TOTAL BASES

1.	Babe Ruth, 1921	457
2.	Rogers Hornsby, 1922	450
3.	Lou Gehrig, 1927	447
4.	Chuck Klein, 1930	445
5.	Jimmie Foxx, 1932	438
6.	Stan Musial, 1948	429
7.	Hack Wilson, 1930	423
8.	Chuck Klein, 1932	420
9.	Lou Gehrig, 1930	419
10.	Joe DiMaggio, 1937	418
11.	Babe Ruth, 1927	417
12.	Babe Herman, 1930	416
13.	Lou Gehrig, 1931	410
14.	Lou Gehrig, 1934	409
14.	Rogers Hornsby, 1929	409
16.	Jim Rice, 1978	406
16.	Joe Medwick, 1937	406
18.	Hal Trosky, 1936	405
18.	Chuck Klein, 1929	405
20.	Lou Gehrig, 1936	403
20.	Jimmie Foxx, 1933	403

DOUBLES

1.	Earl Webb, 1931	67
2.	Joe Medwick, 1936	64
2.	George Burns, 1926	64
4.	Hank Greenberg, 1934	63
5.	Paul Waner, 1932	62
6.	Charlie Gehringer, 1936	60
7.	Chuck Klein, 1930	59
7.	Tris Speaker, 1923	59
9.	Billy Herman, 1935	57
9.	Billy Herman, 1936	57
11.	George Kell, 1950	56
11.	Joe Medwick, 1937	56
13.	Gee Walker, 1936	55
13.	Ed Delahanty, 1899	55
15.	Hal McRae, 1977	54
15.	John Olerud, 1993	54
17.	Al Simmons, 1926	53
17.	Paul Waner, 1936	53
17.	Stan Musial, 1953	53
17.	Tris Speaker, 1912	53
17.	Don Mattingly, 1986	53

HOME RUN PERCENTAGE

1.	Babe Ruth, 1920	11.8
2.	Babe Ruth, 1927	11.1
3.	Babe Ruth, 1921	10.9
4.	Mickey Mantle, 1961	10.5
5.	Hank Greenberg, 1938	10.4
6.	Roger Maris, 1961	10.3
7.	Babe Ruth, 1928	10.1
8.	Jimmie Foxx, 1932	9.9
9.	Ralph Kiner, 1949	9.8
10.	Mickey Mantle, 1956	9.8
11.	Jeff Bagwell, 1994	9.8
12.	Kevin Mitchell, 1994	9.7
13.	Matt Williams, 1994	9.7
14.	Hack Wilson, 1930	9.6
15.	Frank Thomas, 1994	9.5
16.	Babe Ruth, 1926	9.5
16.	Hank Aaron, 1971	9.5
18.	Jim Gentile, 1961	9.5
19.	Barry Bonds, 1994	9.5
20.	Babe Ruth, 1930	9.5

RUNS BATTED IN PER GAME

1.	Sam Thompson, 1895	1.39
2.	Sam Thompson, 1894	1.38
3.	Sam Thompson, 1887	1.31
4.	Hack Wilson, 1930	1.23
5.	Al Simmons, 1930	1.20
6.	Cap Anson, 1894	1.19
7.	Hank Greenberg, 1937	1.19
8.	Lou Gehrig, 1931	1.19
9.	Cap Anson, 1886	1.18
10.	Jimmie Foxx, 1938	1.17
11.	Hugh Duffy, 1894	1.16
12.	Dave Orr, 1890	1.16
13.	Ed Delahanty, 1894	1.15
14.	Babe Ruth, 1929	1.14
15.	Lou Gehrig, 1930	1.13
16.	Lou Gehrig, 1927	1.13
17.	Babe Ruth, 1921	1.13
18.	Babe Ruth, 1931	1.12
19.	Hardy Richardson, 1890	1.12
20.	Hank Greenberg, 1935	1.12

INDIVIDUAL BATTING (SINGLE SEASON), *cont.*

RUNS

1.	Billy Hamilton, 1894	192
2.	Tom Brown, 1891	177
2.	Babe Ruth, 1921	177
4.	Lou Gehrig, 1936	167
4.	Tip O'Neill, 1887	167
6.	Billy Hamilton, 1895	166
7.	Joe Kelley, 1894	165
7.	Willie Keeler, 1894	165
9.	Babe Ruth, 1928	163
9.	Lou Gehrig, 1931	163
9.	Arlie Latham, 1887	163
12.	Willie Keeler, 1895	162
13.	Hugh Duffy, 1890	161
14.	Hugh Duffy, 1894	160
14.	Fred Dunlap, 1884	160
14.	Jesse Burkett, 1896	160
17.	Hughie Jennings, 1895	159
18.	Babe Ruth, 1920	158
18.	Babe Ruth, 1927	158
18.	Bobby Lowe, 1894	158
18.	Chuck Klein, 1930	158

STOLEN BASES

1.	Rickey Henderson, 1982	130
2.	Lou Brock, 1974	118
3.	Vince Coleman, 1985	110
4.	Vince Coleman, 1987	109
5.	Rickey Henderson, 1983	108
6.	Vince Coleman, 1986	107
7.	Maury Wills, 1962	104
8.	Rickey Henderson, 1980	100
9.	Ron LeFlore, 1980	97
10.	Ty Cobb, 1915	96
10.	Omar Moreno, 1980	96
12.	Maury Wills, 1965	94
13.	Rickey Henderson, 1988	93
14.	Tim Raines, 1983	90
15.	Clyde Milan, 1912	88
16.	Rickey Henderson, 1986	87
17.	Ty Cobb, 1911	83
17.	Willie Wilson, 1979	83
19.	Bob Bescher, 1911	81
19.	Vince Coleman, 1988	81
19.	Eddie Collins, 1910	81

PINCH HIT BATTING AVERAGE

1.	Ed Kranepool, 1974	.486
2.	Smead Jolley, 1931	.467
3.	Frenchy Bordagaray, 1938	.465
4.	Gates Brown, 1968	.462
5.	Rick Miller, 1983	.457
6.	Jose Pagan, 1969	.452
7.	Elmer Valo, 1955	.452
8.	Randy Bush, 1986	.433
8.	Ted Easterly, 1912	.433
8.	Milt Thompson, 1985	.433
11.	Joe Cronin, 1943	.429
11.	Don Dillard, 1961	.429
13.	Candy Maldonado, 1986	.425
14.	Bob Bowman, 1958	.419
14.	Dick Williams, 1962	.419
14.	Richie Ashburn, 1962	.419
17.	Carl Taylor, 1969	.415
17.	Merritt Ranew, 1963	.415
19.	Bob Hansen, 1974	.412
19.	Kurt Bevacqua, 1983	.412

PINCH HITS

1.	John Vander Wal, 1995	28
2.	Jose Morales, 1976	25
3.	Rusty Staub, 1983	24
3.	Gerald Perry, 1993	24
3.	Dave Philley, 1961	24
3.	Vic Davalillo, 1970	24
7.	Sam Leslie, 1932	22
7.	Peanuts Lowrey, 1953	22
7.	Wallace Johnson, 1988	22
7.	Red Schoendienst, 1962	22
11.	Smoky Burgess, 1966	21
11.	Merv Rettenmund, 1977	21
13.	Ed Coleman, 1936	20
13.	Doc Miller, 1913	20
13.	Thad Bosley, 1985	20
13.	Ken Boswell, 1976	20
13.	Joe Frazier, 1954	20
13.	Jerry Turner, 1978	20
13.	Smoky Burgess, 1965	20
13.	Chris Chambliss, 1986	20
13.	Frenchy Bordagaray, 1938	20

RUNS PER GAME

1.	Ross Barnes, 1876	1.91
2.	Fred Dunlap, 1884	1.58
3.	Billy Hamilton, 1894	1.47
4.	George Gore, 1890	1.42
5.	Billy Hamilton, 1895	1.35
6.	Tip O'Neill, 1887	1.35
7.	Billy Hamilton, 1893	1.34
8.	Herman Long, 1894	1.32
9.	King Kelly, 1886	1.31
10.	Tom Brown, 1891	1.29
11.	Ed Delahanty, 1894	1.29
12.	Ed Delahanty, 1895	1.28
13.	Hugh Duffy, 1894	1.28
14.	Joe Kelley, 1894	1.28
14.	Willie Keeler, 1894	1.28
16.	George Gore, 1886	1.27
17.	John McGraw, 1894	1.26
18.	Dan Brouthers, 1887	1.24
19.	Willie Keeler, 1895	1.24
20.	Bill Dahlen, 1894	1.23

BASES ON BALLS

1.	Babe Ruth, 1923	170
2.	Ted Williams, 1947	162
2.	Ted Williams, 1949	162
4.	Ted Williams, 1946	156
5.	Eddie Yost, 1956	151
6.	Eddie Joost, 1949	149
7.	Babe Ruth, 1920	148
7.	Jimmy Wynn, 1969	148
7.	Eddie Stanky, 1945	148
10.	Jimmy Sheckard, 1911	147
11.	Mickey Mantle, 1957	146
12.	Ted Williams, 1941	145
12.	Ted Williams, 1942	145
12.	Harmon Killebrew, 1969	145
15.	Babe Ruth, 1921	144
15.	Babe Ruth, 1926	144
15.	Eddie Stanky, 1950	144
15.	Ted Williams, 1951	144
19.	Babe Ruth, 1924	142
20.	Eddie Yost, 1950	141

STRIKEOUTS

1.	Bobby Bonds, 1970	189
2.	Bobby Bonds, 1969	187
3.	Rob Deer, 1987	186
4.	Pete Incaviglia, 1986	185
5.	Cecil Fielder, 1990	182
6.	Mike Schmidt, 1975	180
7.	Rob Deer, 1986	179
8.	Rob Deer, 1991	175
8.	Jose Canseco, 1986	175
8.	Gorman Thomas, 1979	175
8.	Dave Nicholson, 1963	175
12.	Bo Jackson, 1989	172
12.	Jim Presley, 1986	172
14.	Reggie Jackson, 1968	171
15.	Gorman Thomas, 1980	170
16.	Rob Deer, 1993	169
16.	Andres Galarraga, 1990	169
18.	Juan Samuel, 1984	168
18.	Pete Incaviglia, 1987	168

INDIVIDUAL PITCHING (SINGLE SEASON)

WINS

1.	Jack Chesbro, 1904	41
2.	Ed Walsh, 1908	40
3.	Christy Mathewson, 1908	37
4.	Amos Rusie, 1894	36
4.	Frank Killen, 1893	36
4.	Walter Johnson, 1913	36
7.	Cy Young, 1895	35
7.	Joe McGinnity, 1904	35
9.	Cy Young, 1893	34
9.	Kid Nichols, 1893	34
9.	Smoky Joe Wood, 1912	34

BASES ON BALLS

1.	Amos Rusie, 1893	52
2.	Jack Chesbro, 1904	51
3.	Amos Rusie, 1894	50
3.	Pink Hawley, 1895	50
3.	Frank Killen, 1896	50
3.	Ted Breitenstein, 1894	50
3.	Ted Breitenstein, 1895	50
8.	Ed Walsh, 1908	49
8.	Wilbur Wood, 1972	49
10.	Wilbur Wood, 1973	48
10.	Frank Killen, 1893	48
10.	Joe McGinnity, 1903	48
10.	Jouett Meekin, 1894	48
14.	Cy Young, 1894	47
14.	Amos Rusie, 1895	47
14.	Jack Taylor, 1898	47

STRIKEOUTS PER 9 INNINGS

1.	Randy Johnson, 1995	12.35
2.	Nolan Ryan, 1987	11.48
3.	Dwight Gooden, 1984	11.39
4.	Nolan Ryan, 1989	11.32
5.	Hideo Nomo, 1995	11.10
6.	Randy Johnson, 1993	10.86
7.	Sam McDowell, 1965	10.71
8.	Randy Johnson, 1994	10.67
9.	Nolan Ryan, 1973	10.57
10.	Nolan Ryan, 1991	10.56
11.	Sandy Koufax, 1962	10.55
12.	Nolan Ryan, 1972	10.43
13.	Sam McDowell, 1966	10.42
14.	Nolan Ryan, 1976	10.36
15.	Randy Johnson, 1992	10.31

BASES ON BALLS PER 9 INNINGS

1.	Babe Adams, 1920	0.62
2.	Christy Mathewson, 1913	0.62
3.	Bret Saberhagen, 1994	0.66
4.	Christy Mathewson, 1914	0.66
5.	Cy Young, 1904	0.69
6.	Red Lucas, 1933	0.74
7.	Bob Tewksbury, 1992	0.77
8.	Cy Young, 1906	0.78
9.	Babe Adams, 1919	0.79
10.	Babe Adams, 1922	0.79
11.	Slim Sallee, 1919	0.79
12.	Slim Sallee, 1918	0.82
13.	Addie Joss, 1908	0.83
14.	Cy Young, 1905	0.84
15.	Bob Tewksbury, 1993	0.84

WINNING PERCENTAGE

1.	Roy Face, 1959	.947
2.	Johnny Allen, 1937	.938
3.	Greg Maddux, 1995	.905
4.	Randy Johnson, 1995	.900
5.	Ron Guidry, 1978	.893
6.	Freddie Fitzsimmons, 1940	.889
7.	Lefty Grove, 1931	.886
8.	Bob Stanley, 1978	.882
9.	Preacher Roe, 1951	.880
10.	Tom Seaver, 1981	.875
11.	Smoky Joe Wood, 1912	.872
12.	David Cone, 1988	.870
13.	Orel Hershiser, 1985	.864
14.	Whitey Ford, 1961	.862
14.	Wild Bill Donovan, 1907	.862

COMPLETE GAMES

1.	Amos Rusie, 1893	50
2.	Jack Chesbro, 1904	48
3.	Ted Breitenstein, 1894	46
3.	Ted Breitenstein, 1895	46
5.	Amos Rusie, 1894	45
5.	Vic Willis, 1902	45
7.	Cy Young, 1894	44
7.	Pink Hawley, 1895	44
7.	Kid Nichols, 1893	44
7.	Frank Killen, 1896	44
7.	Joe McGinnity, 1903	44

SHUTOUTS

1.	Grover Alexander, 1916	16
2.	Bob Gibson, 1968	13
2.	Jack Coombs, 1910	13
4.	Grover Alexander, 1915	12
4.	Christy Mathewson, 1908	12
6.	Ed Walsh, 1908	11
6.	Dean Chance, 1964	11
6.	Sandy Koufax, 1963	11
6.	Walter Johnson, 1913	11

LOSSES

1.	Red Donahue, 1897	35
2.	Jim Hughey, 1899	30
2.	Ted Breitenstein, 1895	30
4.	Bill Hart, 1896	29
4.	Vic Willis, 1905	29
4.	Jack Taylor, 1898	29
7.	Duke Esper, 1893	28
7.	Still Bill Hill, 1896	28
9.	Bill Hart, 1897	27
9.	George Bell, 1910	27
9.	Bill Carrick, 1899	27
9.	Chick Fraser, 1896	27
9.	Dummy Taylor, 1901	27
9.	Paul Derringer, 1933	27
9.	Willie Sudhoff, 1898	27

EARNED RUN AVERAGE

1.	Dutch Leonard, 1914	1.01
2.	Three Finger Brown, 1906	1.04
3.	Walter Johnson, 1913	1.09
4.	Bob Gibson, 1968	1.12
5.	Christy Mathewson, 1909	1.14
6.	Jack Pfiester, 1907	1.15
7.	Addie Joss, 1908	1.16
8.	Carl Lundgren, 1907	1.17
9.	Grover Alexander, 1915	1.22
10.	Cy Young, 1908	1.26
11.	Ed Walsh, 1910	1.27
12.	Walter Johnson, 1918	1.27
13.	Christy Mathewson, 1905	1.27
14.	Jack Coombs, 1910	1.30
15.	Three Finger Brown, 1909	1.31

INNINGS PITCHED

1.	Amos Rusie, 1893	482
2.	Ed Walsh, 1908	464
3.	Jack Chesbro, 1904	455
4.	Ted Breitenstein, 1894	447
5.	Amos Rusie, 1894	444
5.	Pink Hawley, 1895	444
7.	Joe McGinnity, 1903	434
8.	Frank Killen, 1896	432
9.	Ted Breitenstein, 1895	430
10.	Kid Nichols, 1893	425
11.	Cy Young, 1893	423
12.	Ed Walsh, 1907	422
13.	Frank Killen, 1893	416
14.	Cy Young, 1896	414
15.	Vic Willis, 1902	410

HITS PER 9 INNINGS

1.	Nolan Ryan, 1972	5.26
2.	Luis Tiant, 1968	5.30
3.	Nolan Ryan, 1991	5.31
4.	Ed Reulbach, 1906	5.33
5.	Jim Hearn, 1950	5.64
6.	Carl Lundgren, 1907	5.65
7.	Dutch Leonard, 1914	5.70
8.	Sid Fernandez, 1985	5.71
9.	Tommy Byrne, 1949	5.74
10.	Dave McNally, 1968	5.77
11.	Sandy Koufax, 1965	5.79
12.	Russ Ford, 1910	5.83
13.	Hideo Nomo, 1995	5.83
14.	Al Downing, 1963	5.84
15.	Herb Score, 1956	5.85

GAMES

1.	Mike Marshall, 1974	106
2.	Kent Tekulve, 1979	94
3.	Mike Marshall, 1973	92
4.	Kent Tekulve, 1978	91
5.	Kent Tekulve, 1987	90
5.	Wayne Granger, 1969	90
5.	Mike Marshall, 1979	90
8.	Mark Eichhorn, 1987	89
9.	Wilbur Wood, 1968	88
10.	Rob Murphy, 1987	87
11.	Kent Tekulve, 1982	85
11.	Frank Williams, 1987	85
11.	Mitch Williams, 1987	85

STRIKEOUTS

1.	Nolan Ryan, 1973	383
2.	Sandy Koufax, 1965	382
3.	Nolan Ryan, 1974	367
4.	Rube Waddell, 1904	349
5.	Bob Feller, 1946	348
6.	Nolan Ryan, 1977	341
7.	Nolan Ryan, 1972	329
8.	Nolan Ryan, 1976	327
9.	Sam McDowell, 1965	325
10.	Sandy Koufax, 1966	317
11.	J. R. Richard, 1979	313
11.	Walter Johnson, 1910	313
13.	Steve Carlton, 1972	310
14.	Randy Johnson, 1993	308
14.	Mickey Lolich, 1971	308

BASES ON BALLS

1.	Amos Rusie, 1893	218
2.	Cy Seymour, 1898	213
3.	Bob Feller, 1938	208
4.	Nolan Ryan, 1977	204
5.	Nolan Ryan, 1974	202
6.	Amos Rusie, 1894	200
7.	Bob Feller, 1941	194
8.	Bobo Newsom, 1938	192
9.	Ted Breitenstein, 1894	191
10.	Tony Mullane, 1893	189
11.	Kid Gleason, 1893	187
12.	Sam Jones, 1955	185
13.	Nolan Ryan, 1976	183
14.	Bob Harmon, 1911	181
14.	Bob Turley, 1954	181
14.	Willie McGill, 1893	181

INDIVIDUAL RELIEF PITCHING (SINGLE SEASON)

RELIEF WINS

1.	Roy Face, 1959	18
2.	John Hiller, 1974	17
2.	Bill Campbell, 1976	17
4.	Tom Johnson, 1977	16
4.	Dick Radatz, 1964	16
4.	Jim Konstanty, 1950	16
4.	Ron Perranoski, 1963	16
8.	Mace Brown, 1938	15
8.	Luis Arroyo, 1961	15
8.	Dale Murray, 1975	15
8.	Dick Radatz, 1963	15
8.	Eddie Fisher, 1965	15
8.	Hoyt Wilhelm, 1952	15
8.	Mike Marshall, 1974	15

WINNING PERCENTAGE

1.	Bob Grim, 1954	1.000
1.	Joe Pate, 1926	1.000
1.	Nig Cuppy, 1894	1.000
1.	Emil Kush, 1946	1.000
1.	Dennis Lamp, 1985	1.000
1.	Lew Burdette, 1953	1.000
1.	Frank DiPino, 1989	1.000
1.	Charlie Root, 1937	1.000
1.	Rube Waddell, 1905	1.000
1.	Grant Jackson, 1973	1.000
1.	George Mullin, 1914	1.000
1.	Sandy Consuegra, 1954	1.000
13.	Roy Face, 1959	.947
14.	Phil Regan, 1966	.933
15.	Eddie Yuhas, 1952	.917

SAVES

1.	Bobby Thigpen, 1990	57
2.	Randy Myers, 1993	53
3.	Dennis Eckersley, 1992	51
4.	Rod Beck, 1993	48
4.	Dennis Eckersley, 1990	48
6.	Lee Smith, 1991	47
7.	Jose Mesa, 1995	46
7.	Lee Smith, 1993	46
7.	Bryan Harvey, 1991	46
7.	Dave Righetti, 1986	46
11.	Duane Ward, 1993	45
11.	Bryan Harvey, 1993	45
11.	Bruce Sutter, 1984	45
11.	Jeff Montgomery, 1993	45
11.	Dan Quisenberry, 1983	45
11.	Dennis Eckersley, 1988	45

WINS PLUS SAVES

1.	Bobby Thigpen, 1990	61
2.	Dennis Eckersley, 1992	58
3.	Randy Myers, 1993	55
4.	Dave Righetti, 1986	54
5.	Lee Smith, 1991	53
6.	John Wetteland, 1993	52
6.	Jeff Montgomery, 1993	52
6.	Dennis Eckersley, 1990	52
9.	Rod Beck, 1993	51
10.	Bruce Sutter, 1984	50
10.	Dan Quisenberry, 1983	50
10.	Dan Quisenberry, 1984	50
13.	Jose Mesa, 1995	49
13.	Dennis Eckersley, 1988	49

GAMES

1.	Mike Marshall, 1974	106
2.	Kent Tekulve, 1979	94
3.	Mike Marshall, 1973	92
4.	Kent Tekulve, 1978	91
5.	Kent Tekulve, 1987	90
5.	Wayne Granger, 1969	90
7.	Mark Eichhorn, 1987	89
7.	Mike Marshall, 1979	89
9.	Rob Murphy, 1987	87
10.	Wilbur Wood, 1968	86
11.	Kent Tekulve, 1982	85
11.	Frank Williams, 1987	85

LOSSES

1.	Gene Garber, 1979	16
2.	John Hiller, 1974	14
2.	Mike Marshall, 1975	14
2.	Mike Marshall, 1979	14
2.	Darold Knowles, 1970	14
6.	Wilbur Wood, 1970	13
6.	Skip Lockwood, 1978	13
6.	Rollie Fingers, 1978	13

INDIVIDUAL PITCHING BEFORE 1893 (SINGLE SEASON)

WINS

1.	Old Hoss Radbourn, 1884	60
2.	John Clarkson, 1885	53
3.	Guy Hecker, 1884	52
4.	John Clarkson, 1889	49
4.	Old Hoss Radbourn, 1883	49
6.	Charlie Buffinton, 1884	48
7.	Monte Ward, 1879	47
7.	Al Spalding, 1876	47
9.	Pud Galvin, 1883	46
9.	Pud Galvin, 1884	46
9.	Matt Kilroy, 1887	46

WINNING PERCENTAGE

1.	Fred Goldsmith, 1880	.875
2.	Old Hoss Radbourn, 1884	.833
3.	Jocko Flynn, 1886	.800
3.	Mickey Welch, 1885	.800
5.	Bob Caruthers, 1889	.784
6.	Al Spalding, 1876	.783
7.	Jack Manning, 1876	.783
8.	Will White, 1882	.769
8.	Charlie Ferguson, 1886	.769
10.	John Clarkson, 1885	.768

EARNED RUN AVERAGE

1.	Tim Keefe, 1880	0.86
2.	Denny Driscoll, 1882	*1.21*
3.	George Bradley, 1876	1.23
4.	Guy Hecker, 1882	*1.30*
5.	George Bradley, 1880	1.38
6.	Old Hoss Radbourn, 1884	*1.38*
7.	Monte Ward, 1878	1.51
8.	Harry McCormick, 1882	*1.52*
9.	Will White, 1882	*1.54*
10.	Jim Devlin, 1876	1.56

GAMES

1.	Pud Galvin, 1883	76
1.	Guy Hecker, 1884	76
1.	Will White, 1879	76
1.	Old Hoss Radbourn, 1883	76
5.	Bill Hutchinson, 1892	75
5.	Old Hoss Radbourn, 1884	75
7.	Lee Richmond, 1880	74
7.	Jim McCormick, 1880	74
9.	John Clarkson, 1889	73
10.	Pud Galvin, 1884	72

COMPLETE GAMES

1.	Will White, 1879	75
2.	Old Hoss Radbourn, 1884	73
3.	Pud Galvin, 1883	72
3.	Guy Hecker, 1884	72
3.	Jim McCormick, 1880	72
6.	Pud Galvin, 1884	71
7.	Tim Keefe, 1883	68
7.	John Clarkson, 1885	68
7.	John Clarkson, 1889	68
10.	Bill Hutchinson, 1892	67

INNINGS PITCHED

1.	Will White, 1879	680
2.	Old Hoss Radbourn, 1884	679
3.	Guy Hecker, 1884	671
4.	Jim McCormick, 1880	658
5.	Pud Galvin, 1883	656
6.	Pud Galvin, 1884	636
7.	Old Hoss Radbourn, 1883	632
8.	Bill Hutchinson, 1892	627
9.	John Clarkson, 1885	623
10.	Jim Devlin, 1876	622

STRIKEOUTS

1.	Matt Kilroy, 1886	513
2.	Toad Ramsey, 1886	499
3.	One Arm Daily, 1884	483
4.	Dupee Shaw, 1884	451
5.	Old Hoss Radbourn, 1884	441
6.	Charlie Buffinton, 1884	417
7.	Guy Hecker, 1884	385
8.	Bill Sweeney, 1884	374
9.	Pud Galvin, 1884	369
10.	Mark Baldwin, 1889	368

STRIKEOUTS PER 9 INNINGS

1.	One Arm Daily, 1884	8.68
2.	Matt Kilroy, 1886	7.92
3.	Charlie Geggus, 1884	7.92
4.	John Clarkson, 1884	7.78
5.	Toad Ramsey, 1886	7.63
6.	Dupee Shaw, 1884	7.47
7.	Jim Whitney, 1884	7.23
8.	Mike Dorgan, 1884	7.17
9.	James Burke, 1884	7.13
10.	Hardie Henderson, 1884	7.09

SHUTOUTS

1.	George Bradley, 1876	16
2.	Ed Morris, 1886	12
2.	Pud Galvin, 1884	12
4.	Tommy Bond, 1879	11
4.	Dave Foutz, 1886	11
4.	Old Hoss Radbourn, 1884	11
7.	John Clarkson, 1885	10
7.	Jim McCormick, 1884	10
9.	Cy Young, 1892	9
9.	Tommy Bond, 1878	9
9.	George Derby, 1881	9

HITS PER 9 INNINGS

1.	Tim Keefe, 1880	6.09
2.	Jim Handiboe, 1886	6.47
3.	Guy Hecker, 1882	6.49
4.	Tim Keefe, 1888	6.55
5.	Charlie Sweeney, 1884	6.59
6.	Adonis Terry, 1888	6.69
7.	Silver King, 1888	6.72
8.	Tim Keefe, 1885	6.72
9.	Frank Knauss, 1890	6.73
10.	Ed Seward, 1888	6.73

BASES ON BALLS PER 9 INNINGS

1.	George Zettlein, 1876	.23
2.	Cherokee Fisher, 1876	.24
3.	George Bradley, 1880	.28
4.	Tommy Bond, 1876	.29
5.	Tommy Bond, 1879	.39
6.	Bobby Mathews, 1876	.42
7.	Guy Hecker, 1882	.43
8.	Al Spalding, 1876	.44
9.	Pud Galvin, 1879	.47
10.	George Bradley, 1879	.48

LOSSES

1.	John Coleman, 1883	48
2.	Will White, 1880	42
3.	Larry McKeon, 1884	41
4.	Jim McCormick, 1879	40
4.	George Bradley, 1879	40
6.	Kid Carsey, 1891	37
6.	George Cobb, 1892	37
6.	Henry Porter, 1888	37
9.	Stump Wiedman, 1886	36
9.	Bill Hutchinson, 1892	36

INDIVIDUAL FIELDING (SINGLE SEASON)

PUTOUTS

FIRST BASE	1.	Jiggs Donahue, 1907	1846
	2.	George Kelly, 1920	1759
	3.	Phil Todt, 1926	1755
	4.	Wally Pipp, 1926	1710
	5.	Jiggs Donahue, 1906	1697
	6.	Candy LaChance, 1904	1691
	7.	Tom Jones, 1907	1687
	8.	Ernie Banks, 1965	1682
	9.	Wally Pipp, 1922	1667
	10.	Lou Gehrig, 1927	1662
SECOND BASE	1.	Bid McPhee, 1886	529
	2.	Bobby Grich, 1974	484
	3.	Bucky Harris, 1922	479
	4.	Nellie Fox, 1956	478
	5.	Lou Bierbauer, 1889	472
	6.	Billy Herman, 1933	466
	7.	Cub Stricker, 1887	461
	8.	Buddy Myer, 1935	460
	9.	Bill Sweeney, 1912	459
	9.	Bill Wambsganss, 1924	459
THIRD BASE	1.	Denny Lyons, 1887	255
	2.	Jimmy Collins, 1900	251
	2.	Jimmy Williams, 1899	251
	4.	Willie Kamm, 1928	243
	4.	Jimmy Collins, 1898	243
	6.	Willie Kamm, 1927	236
	7.	Frank Baker, 1913	233
	8.	Bill Coughlin, 1901	232
	9.	Ernie Courtney, 1905	229
	10.	Jimmy Austin, 1911	228
SHORTSTOP	1.	Donie Bush, 1914	425
	1.	Hughie Jennings, 1895	425
	3.	Rabbit Maranville, 1914	407
	4.	Eddie Miller, 1940	405
	4.	Dave Bancroft, 1922	405
	6.	Monte Cross, 1898	404
	7.	Dave Bancroft, 1921	396
	8.	Mickey Doolan, 1906	395
	9.	Buck Weaver, 1913	392
	10.	Buck Herzog, 1915	391
	10.	Rabbit Maranville, 1915	391
OUTFIELD	1.	Taylor Douthit, 1928	547
	2.	Richie Ashburn, 1951	538
	3.	Richie Ashburn, 1949	514
	4.	Chet Lemon, 1977	512
	5.	Dwayne Murphy, 1980	507
	6.	Dom DiMaggio, 1948	503
	6.	Richie Ashburn, 1956	503
	8.	Richie Ashburn, 1957	502
	9.	Richie Ashburn, 1953	496
	10.	Richie Ashburn, 1958	495
CATCHER	1.	Johnny Edwards, 1969	1135
	2.	Johnny Edwards, 1963	1008
	3.	Darren Daulton, 1993	981
	4.	Randy Hundley, 1969	978
	5.	Tony Pena, 1983	976
	6.	Bill Freehan, 1968	971
	7.	Gary Carter, 1985	956
	8.	Gary Carter, 1982	954
	9.	Bill Freehan, 1967	950
	10.	Johnny Bench, 1968	942
PITCHER	1.	Dave Foutz, 1886	57
	2.	Tony Mullane, 1882	54
	3.	Guy Hecker, 1884	50
	3.	George Bradley, 1876	50
	5.	Mike Boddicker, 1984	49
	6.	Larry Corcoran, 1884	47
	7.	Al Spalding, 1876	45
	7.	Ted Breitenstein, 1895	45
	9.	Jim Devlin, 1876	44
	9.	Dave Foutz, 1887	44
	9.	Bill Hutchinson, 1890	44

ASSISTS

FIRST BASE	1.	Bill Buckner, 1985	184
	2.	Mark Grace, 1990	180
	3.	Mark Grace, 1991	167
	4.	Sid Bream, 1986	166
	5.	Bill Buckner, 1983	161
	6.	Bill Buckner, 1982	159
	7.	Bill Buckner, 1986	157
	8.	Mickey Vernon, 1949	155
	9.	Fred Tenney, 1905	152
	9.	Eddie Murray, 1985	152
SECOND BASE	1.	Frankie Frisch, 1927	641
	2.	Hughie Critz, 1926	588
	3.	Rogers Hornsby, 1927	582
	4.	Oscar Melillo, 1930	572
	5.	Ryne Sandberg, 1983	571
	6.	Rabbit Maranville, 1924	568
	7.	Frank Parkinson, 1922	562
	8.	Tony Cuccinello, 1936	559
	9.	Johnny Hodapp, 1930	557
	10.	Lou Bierbauer, 1892	555
THIRD BASE	1.	Graig Nettles, 1971	412
	2.	Graig Nettles, 1973	410
	2.	Brooks Robinson, 1974	410
	4.	Harlond Clift, 1937	405
	4.	Brooks Robinson, 1967	405
	6.	Mike Schmidt, 1974	404
	7.	Doug DeCinces, 1982	399
	8.	Buddy Bell, 1982	396
	8.	Clete Boyer, 1962	396
	8.	Mike Schmidt, 1977	396
SHORTSTOP	1.	Ozzie Smith, 1980	621
	2.	Glenn Wright, 1924	601
	3.	Dave Bancroft, 1920	598
	4.	Tommy Thevenow, 1926	597
	5.	Ivan DeJesus, 1977	595
	6.	Cal Ripken, 1984	583
	7.	Whitey Wietelmann, 1943	581
	8.	Dave Bancroft, 1922	579
	9.	Rabbit Maranville, 1914	574
	10.	Don Kessinger, 1968	573
OUTFIELD	1.	Orator Shaffer, 1879	50
	2.	Hugh Nicol, 1884	48
	3.	Hardy Richardson, 1881	45
	4.	Chuck Klein, 1930	44
	4.	Tommy McCarthy, 1888	44
	6.	Jimmy Bannon, 1894	43
	6.	Charlie Duffee, 1889	43
	8.	Jim Fogarty, 1889	42
	9.	Jim Lillie, 1884	41
	9.	Orator Shaffer, 1883	41
CATCHER	1.	Bill Rariden, 1915	238
	2.	Bill Rariden, 1914	215
	3.	Pat Moran, 1903	214
	4.	Art Wilson, 1914	212
	4.	Oscar Stanage, 1911	212
	6.	Gabby Street, 1909	210
	7.	Frank Snyder, 1915	204
	8.	George Gibson, 1910	203
	9.	Bill Bergen, 1909	202
	9.	Claude Berry, 1914	202
PITCHER	1.	Ed Walsh, 1907	227
	2.	Will White, 1882	223
	3.	Ed Walsh, 1908	190
	4.	Harry Howell, 1905	178
	5.	Tony Mullane, 1882	177
	6.	John Clarkson, 1885	174
	7.	John Clarkson, 1889	172
	8.	Matt Kilroy, 1887	167
	9.	Jack Chesbro, 1904	166
	10.	George Mullin, 1904	163

FIELDING AVERAGE

FIRST BASE	1.	Steve Garvey, 1984	1.000
	2.	Stuffy McInnis, 1921	.999
	3.	Frank McCormick, 1946	.999
	4.	Steve Garvey, 1981	.999
	5.	Jim Spencer, 1973	.999
	6.	Wes Parker, 1968	.999
	7.	Eddie Murray, 1981	.999
	8.	Hal Morris, 1992	.999
	9.	Jim Spencer, 1976	.998
	10.	Jim Spencer, 1981	.998
SECOND BASE	1.	Bobby Grich, 1985	.997
	2.	Jose Oquendo, 1990	.996
	3.	Ryne Sandberg, 1991	.995
	4.	Jody Reed, 1994	.995
	5.	Rob Wilfong, 1980	.995
	6.	Bobby Grich, 1973	.995
	7.	Frank White, 1988	.994
	8.	Mark Lemke, 1994	.994
	9.	Jose Oquendo, 1989	.994
	10.	Bret Boone, 1995	.994
THIRD BASE	1.	Tony Fernandez, 1994	.991
	2.	Don Money, 1974	.989
	3.	Hank Majeski, 1947	.988
	4.	Aurelio Rodriguez, 1978	.987
	5.	Willie Kamm, 1933	.984
	6.	Steve Buechele, 1991	.983
	7.	George Kell, 1946	.983
	8.	Heinie Groh, 1924	.983
	9.	Carney Lansford, 1979	.983
	10.	Gary Gaetti, 1994	.982
SHORTSTOP	1.	Cal Ripken, 1990	.996
	2.	Tony Fernandez, 1989	.992
	3.	Larry Bowa, 1979	.991
	4.	Ed Brinkman, 1972	.990
	5.	Cal Ripken, 1989	.990
	6.	Spike Owen, 1990	.989
	7.	Omar Vizquel, 1992	.989
	8.	Cal Ripken, 1995	.989
	9.	Tony Fernandez, 1990	.989
	10.	Dick Schofield, 1992	.988
OUTFIELD		Many players tied with1.000	
CATCHER	1.	Yogi Berra, 1958	1.000
	1.	Pete Daley, 1957	1.000
	1.	Rick Cerone, 1988	1.000
	1.	Buddy Rosar, 1946	1.000
	1.	Lou Berberet, 1957	1.000
	6.	Tom Pagnozzi, 1992	.999
	7.	Joe Azcue, 1967	.999
	8.	Wes Westrum, 1950	.999
	9.	Terry Steinbach, 1994	.998
	10.	Thurman Munson, 1971	.998
	10.	Mike LaValliere, 1991	.998
PITCHER		Many players tied with1.000	

INDIVIDUAL FIELDING (SINGLE SEASON), *cont.*

TOTAL CHANCES

FIRST BASE

1.	Jiggs Donahue, 1907	1998
2.	Phil Todt, 1926	1903
3.	George Kelly, 1920	1873
4.	Jiggs Donahue, 1906	1837
5.	Tom Jones, 1907	1821
6.	Wally Pipp, 1926	1817
7.	Ernie Banks, 1965	1790
8.	Jiggs Donahue, 1905	1780
9.	Earl Sheely, 1921	1778
10.	Fred Tenney, 1908	1769

SECOND BASE

1.	Frankie Frisch, 1927	1059
2.	Bid McPhee, 1886	1058
3.	Burgess Whitehead, 1936	1026
4.	Nap Lajoie, 1908	1025
5.	Billy Herman, 1933	1023
6.	Oscar Melillo, 1931	1003
7.	Jimmy Dykes, 1921	1002
8.	Gerry Priddy, 1950	1001
9.	Bucky Harris, 1922	992
10.	Fred Pfeffer, 1889	991

THIRD BASE

1.	Jimmy Williams, 1899	671
2.	Bill Shindle, 1892	660
3.	Tommy Leach, 1904	643
4.	Harlond Clift, 1937	637
5.	Bill Shindle, 1889	636
6.	Jimmy Collins, 1899	629
7.	Charlie Reilly, 1890	626
8.	Arlie Latham, 1891	622
9.	Jimmy Collins, 1900	620
10.	Jimmy Collins, 1898	617

SHORTSTOP

1.	Dave Bancroft, 1922	1046
1.	Rabbit Maranville, 1914	1046
3.	Donie Bush, 1914	1027
4.	Tommy Thevenow, 1926	1013
5.	Dave Bancroft, 1920	1005
6.	Donie Bush, 1911	1003
6.	Monte Cross, 1898	1003
6.	Heinie Wagner, 1908	1003
9.	George McBride, 1908	992
10.	Monte Cross, 1899	989

OUTFIELD

1.	Taylor Douthit, 1928	566
2.	Richie Ashburn, 1951	560
3.	Richie Ashburn, 1949	538
4.	Chet Lemon, 1977	536
5.	Richie Ashburn, 1957	527
6.	Dom DiMaggio, 1948	526
7.	Dwayne Murphy, 1980	525
8.	Richie Ashburn, 1956	523
9.	Richie Ashburn, 1953	519
10.	Lloyd Waner, 1931	515

CATCHER

1.	Johnny Edwards, 1969	1221
2.	Johnny Edwards, 1963	1101
3.	Tony Pena, 1983	1075
4.	Gary Carter, 1982	1068
5.	Randy Hundley, 1969	1065
6.	Darren Daulton, 1993	1057
7.	Johnny Bench, 1968	1053
8.	Bill Freehan, 1968	1050
9.	Tony Pena, 1985	1034
10.	Gary Carter, 1985	1031

PITCHER

1.	Ed Walsh, 1907	266
2.	Will White, 1882	257
3.	Tony Mullane, 1882	241
4.	Tim Keefe, 1883	238
5.	Ed Walsh, 1908	237
6.	John Clarkson, 1889	235
7.	Matt Kilroy, 1887	224
8.	John Clarkson, 1885	220
9.	Harry Howell, 1905	206
10.	Guy Hecker, 1884	205

TOTAL CHANCES/GAME

FIRST BASE

1.	Joe Gerhardt, 1876	13.3
2.	Jiggs Donahue, 1907	12.7
3.	Frank Isbell, 1909	12.7
4.	Gene Paulette, 1917	12.6
5.	Cap Anson, 1879	12.6
6.	Oscar Walker, 1879	12.6
7.	Joe Start, 1878	12.5
8.	Tim Murnane, 1878	12.5
9.	Joe Start, 1879	12.5
10.	Jake Goodman, 1878	12.4

SECOND BASE

1.	Thorny Hawkes, 1879	8.4
2.	Chick Fulmer, 1879	8.3
3.	Jack Burdock, 1878	8.3
4.	Ed Somerville, 1876	8.3
5.	Joe Gerhardt, 1877	8.1
6.	Fred Pfeffer, 1884	8.1
7.	Davy Force, 1881	8.1
8.	Jack Burdock, 1879	7.9
9.	Joe Quest, 1878	7.8
10.	Pop Smith, 1885	7.7

THIRD BASE

1.	Al Nichols, 1876	5.8
2.	Bob Ferguson, 1877	5.6
3.	Arthur Irwin, 1882	5.4
4.	Jumbo Davis, 1888	5.1
5.	John Shetzline, 1882	5.1
6.	Billy Alvord, 1891	5.0
7.	Cap Anson, 1876	5.0
8.	Bill Shindle, 1892	4.9
9.	Jack Gleason, 1882	4.9
10.	Bill Bradley, 1900	4.9

SHORTSTOP

1.	Herman Long, 1889	7.3
2.	Hughie Jennings, 1895	7.2
3.	Dave Bancroft, 1918	7.1
4.	Phil Tomney, 1889	7.1
5.	George Davis, 1899	7.1
6.	Hughie Jennings, 1896	7.1
7.	Hughie Jennings, 1897	7.0
8.	Bobby Wallace, 1901	7.0
9.	Monte Cross, 1897	7.0
10.	Bill Dahlen, 1895	6.9

OUTFIELD

1.	Fred Treacey, 1876	4.4
2.	Redleg Snyder, 1876	3.8
3.	Charley Jones, 1877	3.8
4.	Taylor Douthit, 1928	3.7
5.	Mike Mansell, 1879	3.6
6.	Richie Ashburn, 1951	3.6
7.	Chet Lemon, 1977	3.6
8.	Thurman Tucker, 1944	3.6
9.	Kirby Puckett, 1984	3.6
10.	Irv Noren, 1951	3.5

CATCHER

1.	Bill Holbert, 1883	10.6
2.	Sam Trott, 1884	10.4
3.	Bill Holbert, 1884	9.7
4.	Jocko Milligan, 1884	9.4
5.	Mert Hackett, 1884	9.4
6.	Barney Gilligan, 1884	9.3
7.	Mike Hines, 1883	9.3
8.	Fatty Briody, 1884	9.2
9.	George Baker, 1884	9.0
10.	Jocko Milligan, 1885	8.8

PITCHER

1.	Harry Howell, 1905	5.4
2.	Harry Howell, 1904	5.1
3.	Harry Arundel, 1882	5.1
4.	Will White, 1882	4.8
5.	Ed Walsh, 1907	4.8
6.	George Mullin, 1904	4.5
7.	Tony Mullane, 1882	4.4
8.	Red Donahue, 1902	4.4
9.	Nick Altrock, 1905	4.4
10.	Harry Howell, 1906	4.3

DOUBLE PLAYS

FIRST BASE

1.	Ferris Fain, 1949	194
2.	Ferris Fain, 1950	192
3.	Donn Clendenon, 1966	182
4.	Ron Jackson, 1979	175
5.	Gil Hodges, 1951	171
6.	Mickey Vernon, 1949	168
7.	Ted Kluszewski, 1954	166
8.	Rudy York, 1944	163
9.	Rod Carew, 1977	161
9.	Donn Clendenon, 1965	161

SECOND BASE

1.	Bill Mazeroski, 1966	161
2.	Gerry Priddy, 1950	150
3.	Bill Mazeroski, 1961	144
4.	Dave Cash, 1974	141
4.	Nellie Fox, 1957	141
6.	Buddy Myer, 1935	138
6.	Carlos Baerga, 1992	138
6.	Bill Mazeroski, 1962	138
9.	Jerry Coleman, 1950	137
9.	Jackie Robinson, 1951	137
9.	Red Schoendienst, 1954	137

THIRD BASE

1.	Graig Nettles, 1971	54
2.	Harlond Clift, 1937	50
3.	Paul Molitor, 1982	48
3.	Johnny Pesky, 1949	48
5.	Sammy Hale, 1927	46
5.	Clete Boyer, 1965	46
5.	Gary Gaetti, 1983	46
8.	Eddie Yost, 1950	45
8.	Darrell Evans, 1974	45
8.	Frank Malzone, 1961	45

SHORTSTOP

1.	Rick Burleson, 1980	147
2.	Roy Smalley, 1979	144
3.	Bobby Wine, 1970	137
4.	Lou Boudreau, 1944	134
5.	Spike Owen, 1986	133
6.	Rafael Ramirez, 1982	130
7.	Roy McMillan, 1954	129
8.	Hod Ford, 1928	128
8.	Gene Alley, 1966	128
8.	Vern Stephens, 1949	128

OUTFIELD

1.	Happy Felsch, 1919	15
2.	Jimmy Sheckard, 1899	14
3.	Tom Brown, 1893	13

CATCHER

1.	Steve O'Neill, 1916	36
2.	Frankie Hayes, 1945	29
3.	Yogi Berra, 1951	25
3.	Ray Schalk, 1916	25
5.	Jack Lapp, 1915	23
5.	Tom Haller, 1968	23
5.	Muddy Ruel, 1924	23
8.	Bob O'Farrell, 1922	22
8.	Steve O'Neill, 1914	22
10.	Wes Westrum, 1950	21
10.	Gabby Hartnett, 1927	21

PITCHER

1.	Bob Lemon, 1953	15
2.	Curt Davis, 1934	12
2.	Randy Jones, 1976	12
2.	Eddie Rommel, 1924	12
5.	Art Nehf, 1920	11
5.	Gene Bearden, 1948	11
5.	Burleigh Grimes, 1925	11

INDIVIDUAL BATTING (LIFETIME)

BATTING AVERAGE

1.	Ty Cobb	.367
2.	Rogers Hornsby	.358
3.	Joe Jackson	.356
4.	Ed Delahanty	.346
5.	Tris Speaker	.345
6.	Billy Hamilton	.345
7.	Ted Williams	.344
8.	Willie Keeler	.343
9.	Dan Brouthers	.342
10.	Babe Ruth	.342
11.	Harry Heilmann	.342
12.	Pete Browning	.341
13.	Bill Terry	.341
14.	George Sisler	.340
15.	Lou Gehrig	.340
16.	Jesse Burkett	.339
17.	Nap Lajoie	.338
18.	Tony Gwynn	.336
19.	Riggs Stephenson	.336
20.	Wade Boggs	.334
21.	Al Simmons	.334
22.	Paul Waner	.333
23.	Eddie Collins	.333
24.	Stan Musial	.331
25.	Sam Thompson	.331
26.	Heinie Manush	.330
27.	Cap Anson	.329
28.	Rod Carew	.328
29.	Honus Wagner	.327
30.	Tip O'Neill	.326
31.	Jimmie Foxx	.325
32.	Earle Combs	.325
33.	Joe DiMaggio	.325
34.	Babe Herman	.324
35.	Hugh Duffy	.324
36.	Joe Medwick	.324
37.	Edd Roush	.323
38.	Sam Rice	.322
39.	Ross Youngs	.322
40.	Kiki Cuyler	.321
41.	Charlie Gehringer	.320
42.	Chuck Klein	.320
43.	Pie Traynor	.320
44.	Mickey Cochrane	.320
45.	Ken Williams	.319
46.	Kirby Puckett	.318
47.	Earl Averill	.318
48.	Arky Vaughan	.318
49.	Roberto Clemente	.317
50.	Chick Hafey	.317
51.	Joe Kelley	.317
52.	Zack Wheat	.317
53.	Roger Connor	.317
54.	Lloyd Waner	.316
55.	George Van Haltren	.316
56.	Frankie Frisch	.316
57.	Goose Goslin	.316
58.	Bibb Falk	.314
59.	Cecil Travis	.314
60.	Hank Greenberg	.313
61.	Elmer Flick	.313
62.	Jack Fournier	.313
63.	Hughie Jennings	.313
64.	Bill Dickey	.313
65.	Fred Clarke	.312
66.	Johnny Mize	.312
67.	Joe Sewell	.312
68.	Barney McCosky	.312
69.	Bing Miller	.312
70.	Freddie Lindstrom	.311
71.	Jackie Robinson	.311
72.	Baby Doll Jacobson	.311
73.	Rip Radcliff	.311
74.	Ginger Beaumont	.311
75.	Mike Tiernan	.311
76.	Denny Lyons	.310
77.	Irish Meusel	.310
78.	Luke Appling	.310
79.	Elmer Smith	.310
80.	Bobby Veach	.310
81.	Jim O'Rourke	.310
82.	John Stone	.310
83.	Jim Bottomley	.310
84.	Sam Crawford	.309
85.	Bob Meusel	.309
86.	Jack Tobin	.309
87.	Spud Davis	.308
88.	Richie Ashburn	.308
89.	Jake Beckley	.308
90.	King Kelly	.308
91.	Stuffy McInnis	.308
92.	Don Mattingly	.307
93.	Joe Vosmik	.307
94.	Frank Baker	.307
95.	George Burns	.307
96.	Matty Alou	.307
97.	Hack Wilson	.307
98.	Johnny Pesky	.307
99.	George Kell	.306
100.	Dixie Walker	.306
101.	Jimmy Ryan	.306
102.	Chick Stahl	.306
103.	Cupid Childs	.306
104.	Ernie Lombardi	.306
105.	Mark Grace	.306
106.	Ralph Garr	.306
107.	Paul Molitor	.305
108.	Hank Aaron	.305
109.	George Brett	.305
110.	Bill Madlock	.305
111.	Billy Herman	.304
112.	Tony Oliva	.304
113.	Mel Ott	.304
114.	Curt Walker	.304
115.	Cy Seymour	.304
116.	Deacon White	.303
117.	Mike Greenwell	.303
118.	Charlie Jamieson	.303
119.	Jake Daubert	.303
120.	Al Oliver	.303
121.	Henry Larkin	.303
122.	Buck Ewing	.303
123.	Steve Brodie	.303
124.	Pete Rose	.303
125.	Buddy Myer	.303
126.	Harvey Kuenn	.303
127.	Hal Trosky	.302
128.	Ed McKean	.302
129.	George Grantham	.302
130.	Ben Chapman	.302
131.	Carl Reynolds	.302
132.	Tommy Holmes	.302
133.	Will Clark	.302
134.	Willie Mays	.302
135.	Joe Cronin	.301
136.	Stan Hack	.301
137.	Julio Franco	.301
138.	George Gore	.301
139.	Paul Hines	.301
140.	Oyster Burns	.300
141.	Wally Berger	.300
142.	Pedro Guerrero	.300
143.	Ethan Allen	.300
144.	Enos Slaughter	.300
145.	Patsy Donovan	.300
146.	Earl Sheely	.300
147.	Billy Goodman	.300
148.	Rafael Palmeiro	.300

SLUGGING AVERAGE

1.	Babe Ruth	.690
2.	Ted Williams	.634
3.	Lou Gehrig	.632
4.	Jimmie Foxx	.609
5.	Hank Greenberg	.605
6.	Joe DiMaggio	.579
7.	Rogers Hornsby	.577
8.	Johnny Mize	.562
9.	Stan Musial	.559
10.	Willie Mays	.557
11.	Mickey Mantle	.557
12.	Hank Aaron	.555
13.	Ralph Kiner	.548
14.	Hack Wilson	.545
15.	Chuck Klein	.543
16.	Barry Bonds	.541
17.	Duke Snider	.540
18.	Frank Robinson	.537
19.	Fred McGriff	.535
20.	Al Simmons	.535
21.	Dick Allen	.534
22.	Earl Averill	.533
23.	Mel Ott	.533
24.	Babe Herman	.532
25.	Ken Williams	.531
26.	Willie Stargell	.529
27.	Mike Schmidt	.527
28.	Chick Hafey	.526
29.	Hal Trosky	.522
29.	Wally Berger	.522
31.	Harry Heilmann	.520
32.	Dan Brouthers	.519
33.	Joe Jackson	.518
34.	Jose Canseco	.515
35.	Willie McCovey	.515
36.	Ty Cobb	.513
37.	Eddie Mathews	.509
38.	Jeff Heath	.509
39.	Harmon Killebrew	.509
40.	Bob Johnson	.506
41.	Bill Terry	.506
42.	Ed Delahanty	.505
43.	Sam Thompson	.505
44.	Darryl Strawberry	.505
45.	Joe Medwick	.505
46.	Jim Rice	.502
47.	Tris Speaker	.500
48.	Jim Bottomley	.500
49.	Goose Goslin	.500
50.	Roy Campanella	.500
51.	Ernie Banks	.500

TOTAL BASES

1.	Hank Aaron	6856
2.	Stan Musial	6134
3.	Willie Mays	6066
4.	Ty Cobb	5863
5.	Babe Ruth	5793
6.	Pete Rose	5752
7.	Carl Yastrzemski	5539
8.	Frank Robinson	5373
9.	Dave Winfield	5221
10.	Eddie Murray	5108
11.	Tris Speaker	5103
12.	Lou Gehrig	5059
13.	George Brett	5044
14.	Mel Ott	5041
15.	Jimmie Foxx	4956
16.	Ted Williams	4884
17.	Honus Wagner	4868
18.	Al Kaline	4852
19.	Reggie Jackson	4834
20.	Andre Dawson	4763
21.	Robin Yount	4730
22.	Rogers Hornsby	4712
23.	Ernie Banks	4706
24.	Al Simmons	4685
25.	Billy Williams	4599
26.	Tony Perez	4532
27.	Mickey Mantle	4511
28.	Roberto Clemente	4492
29.	Nap Lajoie	4473
30.	Paul Waner	4471
31.	Dave Parker	4405
32.	Mike Schmidt	4404
33.	Eddie Mathews	4349
34.	Sam Crawford	4335
35.	Goose Goslin	4325
36.	Brooks Robinson	4270
37.	Eddie Collins	4266
38.	Vada Pinson	4264
39.	Charlie Gehringer	4257
40.	Lou Brock	4238
41.	Dwight Evans	4230
42.	Willie McCovey	4219
43.	Willie Stargell	4190
44.	Rusty Staub	4185
45.	Jake Beckley	4155
46.	Harmon Killebrew	4143
47.	Jim Rice	4129
48.	Paul Molitor	4119
49.	Zack Wheat	4100
50.	Al Oliver	4083
51.	Cap Anson	4064
52.	Harry Heilmann	4053

GAMES

1.	Pete Rose	3562
2.	Carl Yastrzemski	3308
3.	Hank Aaron	3298
4.	Ty Cobb	3034
5.	Stan Musial	3026
6.	Willie Mays	2992
7.	Dave Winfield	2973
8.	Rusty Staub	2951
9.	Brooks Robinson	2896
10.	Robin Yount	2856
11.	Al Kaline	2834
12.	Eddie Collins	2826
13.	Reggie Jackson	2820
14.	Eddie Murray	2819
15.	Frank Robinson	2808
16.	Tris Speaker	2789
16.	Honus Wagner	2789
18.	Tony Perez	2777
19.	Mel Ott	2734
20.	George Brett	2707
21.	Graig Nettles	2700
22.	Darrell Evans	2687
23.	Rabbit Maranville	2670
24.	Joe Morgan	2649
25.	Lou Brock	2616
26.	Dwight Evans	2606
27.	Luis Aparicio	2599
28.	Willie McCovey	2588
29.	Andre Dawson	2585
30.	Paul Waner	2549
31.	Ernie Banks	2528
32.	Bill Buckner	2517
32.	Sam Crawford	2517
34.	Babe Ruth	2503
35.	Carlton Fisk	2499
36.	Ozzie Smith	2491
37.	Billy Williams	2488
37.	Dave Concepcion	2488
39.	Nap Lajoie	2479
40.	Max Carey	2476
41.	Rod Carew	2469
41.	Vada Pinson	2469
43.	Dave Parker	2466
44.	Ted Simmons	2456
45.	Bill Dahlen	2443
46.	Ron Fairly	2442
47.	Harmon Killebrew	2435
48.	Roberto Clemente	2433
49.	Willie Davis	2429
50.	Luke Appling	2422
51.	Zack Wheat	2410
52.	Mickey Vernon	2409
53.	Buddy Bell	2405
54.	Sam Rice	2404
54.	Mike Schmidt	2404
56.	Mickey Mantle	2401
57.	Lou Whitaker	2390
58.	Eddie Mathews	2388
59.	Jake Beckley	2386
60.	Bobby Wallace	2383
61.	Enos Slaughter	2380
62.	George Davis	2376
63.	Al Oliver	2368
64.	Nellie Fox	2367

INDIVIDUAL BATTING (LIFETIME), *cont.*

65. Willie Stargell 2360
66. Jose Cruz 2353
67. Brian Downing 2344
68. Steve Garvey 2332
69. Bert Campaneris 2328
70. Frank White 2324

71. Charlie Gehringer 2323
72. Jimmie Foxx 2317
73. Frankie Frisch 2311
74. Harry Hooper 2308
75. Gary Carter 2296
76. Don Baylor 2292
76. Ted Williams 2292
78. Goose Goslin 2287
79. Jimmy Dykes 2282
80. Cap Anson 2276

81. Lave Cross 2275
82. Bob Boone 2264
83. Paul Molitor 2261
84. Chris Speier 2260
85. Rogers Hornsby 2259
86. Larry Bowa 2247
87. Fred Clarke 2244
88. Ron Santo 2243
89. Doc Cramer 2239
90. Alan Trammell 2227

91. Cal Ripken 2218
92. Red Schoendienst 2216
93. Al Simmons 2215
94. Joe Torre 2209
95. Willie Randolph 2202
96. Tommy Corcoran 2200
97. Tony Taylor 2195
98. Rickey Henderson 2192
99. Richie Ashburn 2189
100. Harold Baines 2183

101. Bill Russell 2181
102. Dale Murphy 2180
103. Chris Chambliss 2173
104. Joe Judge 2171
105. Pee Wee Reese 2166
106. Lou Gehrig 2164
106. Charlie Grimm 2164
108. Bill Mazeroski 2163
109. Johnny Bench 2158
110. Toby Harrah 2155

110. Tommy Leach 2155
112. Willie Wilson 2154
113. Harry Heilmann 2146
114. Duke Snider 2143
115. Bid McPhee 2137
116. Stuffy McInnis 2128
117. Joe Cronin 2124
117. Orlando Cepeda 2124
119. Willie Keeler 2122
120. Jimmy Sheckard 2121

121. Yogi Berra 2120
122. Tim Wallach 2110
123. Eddie Yost 2109
124. Joe Kuhel 2104
125. Ken Griffey 2097
126. Roy McMillan 2093
127. Jim Rice 2089
127. Norm Cash 2089
129. Keith Hernandez 2088
130. Sherry Magee 2085

131. Hal McRae 2084
132. Ed Konetchy 2083
133. Felipe Alou 2082
133. Ken Singleton 2082
135. Garry Templeton 2079
136. Don Kessinger 2078
137. Brett Butler 2074
138. Ron Cey 2073
139. Lee May 2071
139. Gil Hodges 2071

141. Jesse Burkett 2070
142. George Sisler 2055
143. Tim Raines 2053
144. George Hendrick 2048
145. Boog Powell 2042
146. Dusty Baker 2039
147. Ken Boyer 2034
147. George Scott 2034
149. Gary Matthews 2033
150. Phil Cavarretta 2030

151. Willie Horton 2028
152. Sal Bando 2019
153. Jose Cardenal 2017
153. Aurelio Rodriguez 2017
155. Dick Bartell 2016
155. Mark Belanger 2016
157. Jake Daubert 2014
158. Jimmy Ryan 2012
158. Wally Moses 2012
158. Roger Peckinpaugh 2012

161. Heinie Manush 2009
162. Bobby Grich 2008
163. Cesar Cedeno 2006
164. Cy Williams 2002

AT BATS

1. Pete Rose 14053
2. Hank Aaron 12364
3. Carl Yastrzemski 11988
4. Ty Cobb 11429
5. Robin Yount 11008
6. Dave Winfield 11003
7. Stan Musial 10972
8. Willie Mays 10881
9. Brooks Robinson 10654
10. Eddie Murray 10603

11. Honus Wagner 10441
12. George Brett 10349
13. Lou Brock 10332
14. Luis Aparicio 10230
15. Tris Speaker 10197
16. Al Kaline 10116
17. Rabbit Maranville 10078
18. Frank Robinson 10006
19. Eddie Collins 9951
20. Andre Dawson 9869

21. Reggie Jackson 9864
22. Tony Perez 9778
23. Rusty Staub 9720
24. Vada Pinson 9645
25. Nap Lajoie 9592
26. Sam Crawford 9580
27. Jake Beckley 9527
28. Paul Waner 9459
29. Mel Ott 9456
30. Roberto Clemente 9454

31. Ernie Banks 9421
32. Bill Buckner 9397
33. Max Carey 9363
34. Dave Parker 9358
35. Billy Williams 9350
36. Rod Carew 9315
37. Joe Morgan 9277
38. Sam Rice 9269
39. Nellie Fox 9232
40. Willie Davis 9174

41. Ozzie Smith 9169
42. Doc Cramer 9140
43. Paul Molitor 9135
44. Frankie Frisch 9112
45. Cap Anson 9108
46. Zack Wheat 9106
47. Lave Cross 9064
48. Al Oliver 9049
49. George Davis 9035
50. Bill Dahlen 9033

HITS

1. Pete Rose 4256
2. Ty Cobb 4191
3. Hank Aaron 3771
4. Stan Musial 3630
5. Tris Speaker 3514
6. Carl Yastrzemski 3419
7. Honus Wagner 3418
8. Eddie Collins 3313
9. Willie Mays 3283
10. Nap Lajoie 3244

11. George Brett 3154
12. Paul Waner 3152
13. Robin Yount 3142
14. Dave Winfield 3110
15. Eddie Murray 3071
16. Rod Carew 3053
17. Lou Brock 3023
18. Al Kaline 3007
19. Cap Anson 3000
19. Roberto Clemente 3000

21. Sam Rice 2987
22. Sam Crawford 2964
23. Willie Keeler 2945
24. Frank Robinson 2943
25. Jake Beckley 2931
26. Rogers Hornsby 2930
27. Al Simmons 2927
28. Zack Wheat 2884
29. Frankie Frisch 2880
30. Mel Ott 2876

31. Babe Ruth 2873
32. Jesse Burkett 2853
33. Brooks Robinson 2848
34. Charlie Gehringer 2839
35. George Sisler 2812
36. Paul Molitor 2789
37. Andre Dawson 2758
38. Vada Pinson 2757
39. Luke Appling 2749
40. Al Oliver 2743

41. Goose Goslin 2735
42. Tony Perez 2732
43. Lou Gehrig 2721
44. Rusty Staub 2716
45. Bill Buckner 2715
46. Dave Parker 2712
47. Billy Williams 2711
48. Doc Cramer 2705
49. Luis Aparicio 2677
50. Fred Clarke 2675

51. Max Carey 2665
51. George Davis 2665
53. Nellie Fox 2663
54. Harry Heilmann 2660
55. Ted Williams 2654
56. Jimmie Foxx 2646
57. Lave Cross 2644
58. Rabbit Maranville 2605
59. Steve Garvey 2599
60. Ed Delahanty 2597

61. Reggie Jackson 2584
62. Ernie Banks 2583
63. Richie Ashburn 2574
64. Willie Davis 2561
65. Wade Boggs 2541
66. George Van Haltren 2536
67. Heinie Manush 2524
68. Joe Morgan 2517
69. Buddy Bell 2514
70. Jimmy Ryan 2500

71. Mickey Vernon 2495
72. Ted Simmons 2472
73. Joe Medwick 2471
74. Roger Connor 2467
75. Harry Hooper 2466
76. Lloyd Waner 2459
77. Bill Dahlen 2455
78. Jim Rice 2452
79. Red Schoendienst 2449
80. Dwight Evans 2446

81. Pie Traynor 2416
82. Mickey Mantle 2415
83. Stuffy McInnis 2406
84. Tony Gwynn 2401
85. Ozzie Smith 2396
86. Enos Slaughter 2383
87. Edd Roush 2376
88. Cal Ripken 2371
89. Lou Whitaker 2369
90. Carlton Fisk 2356

91. Joe Judge 2352
92. Orlando Cepeda 2351
93. Billy Herman 2345
94. Joe Torre 2342
95. Rickey Henderson 2338
96. Jake Daubert 2326
96. Dave Concepcion 2326
98. Alan Trammell 2320
99. Eddie Mathews 2315
100. Jim Bottomley 2313

101. Jim O'Rourke 2304
101. Kirby Puckett 2304
103. Bobby Wallace 2303
104. Kiki Cuyler 2299
104. Charlie Grimm 2299
106. Dan Brouthers 2296
107. Tim Raines 2295
108. Joe Cronin 2285
109. Hugh Duffy 2284
110. Harold Baines 2271

111. Jimmy Dykes 2256
112. Ron Santo 2254
113. Jose Cruz 2251
113. Tommy Corcoran 2251
115. Bid McPhee 2249
115. Bert Campaneris 2249
117. Patsy Donovan 2246
118. Brett Butler 2243
119. Mike Schmidt 2234
120. Willie Stargell 2232

121. Fred Tenney 2231
122. Joe Sewell 2226
123. Graig Nettles 2225
124. Darrell Evans 2223
125. Joe Kelley 2222
126. Joe DiMaggio 2214
127. Joe Kuhel 2212
128. Willie McCovey 2211
129. Willie Randolph 2210
130. Willie Wilson 2207

131. Stan Hack 2193
131. Bill Terry 2193
133. Cecil Cooper 2192
134. Larry Bowa 2191
135. Keith Hernandez 2182
136. Pee Wee Reese 2170
137. Sherry Magee 2169
138. Dick Bartell 2165
139. Billy Hamilton 2160
140. Hal Chase 2158

141. Don Mattingly 2153
142. Yogi Berra 2150
143. Ed Konetchy 2148
144. Tommy Leach 2144
145. Ken Boyer 2143
145. Ken Griffey 2143
147. Dick Groat 2138
147. Wally Moses 2138
149. Don Baylor 2135
150. Maury Wills 2134

151. Ryne Sandberg 2133
152. Buddy Myer 2131
153. Herman Long 2130
154. Tommy Davis 2121
155. Duke Snider 2116
156. Dale Murphy 2111
157. Chris Chambliss 2109
158. Monte Ward 2105
159. Arky Vaughan 2103
160. Felipe Alou 2101

161. Clyde Milan 2100
162. Brian Downing 2099
163. Garry Templeton 2096
164. Gary Carter 2092
164. Harvey Kuenn 2092
166. Hal McRae 2091
167. Alvin Dark 2089
168. Cesar Cedeno 2087
168. Jimmy Sheckard 2087
170. Harmon Killebrew 2086

171. Ed McKean 2083

INDIVIDUAL BATTING (LIFETIME), *cont.*

172.	George Burns	2077
173.	Chuck Klein	2076
174.	Carney Lansford	2074
175.	Bobby Veach	2064
175.	Dixie Walker	2064
177.	Del Ennis	2063
178.	Bob Elliott	2061
179.	George Kell	2054
180.	Bob Johnson	2051
181.	Johnny Bench	2048
182.	Dummy Hoy	2042
182.	Bobby Doerr	2042
184.	Jack Glasscock	2040
185.	Lee May	2031
186.	Ken Singleton	2029
187.	Amos Otis	2020
187.	Earl Averill	2020
187.	Reggie Smith	2020
190.	George Burns	2018
191.	Bill Mazeroski	2016
192.	Johnny Mize	2011
192.	Gary Matthews	2011
194.	Bill Madlock	2008
195.	Tony Taylor	2007
196.	Frank White	2006
197.	Dave Bancroft	2004
198.	Tim Wallach	2003

DOUBLES

1.	Tris Speaker	792
2.	Pete Rose	746
3.	Stan Musial	725
4.	Ty Cobb	724
5.	George Brett	665
6.	Nap Lajoie	658
7.	Carl Yastrzemski	646
8.	Honus Wagner	643
9.	Hank Aaron	624
10.	Paul Waner	603
11.	Robin Yount	583
12.	Charlie Gehringer	574
13.	Harry Heilmann	542
14.	Rogers Hornsby	541
15.	Joe Medwick	540
15.	Dave Winfield	540
17.	Al Simmons	539
18.	Lou Gehrig	535
19.	Eddie Murray	532
20.	Al Oliver	529
21.	Cap Anson	528
21.	Frank Robinson	528
23.	Dave Parker	526
24.	Ted Williams	525
25.	Willie Mays	523
25.	Ed Delahanty	523
27.	Joe Cronin	515
28.	Babe Ruth	506
29.	Tony Perez	505
30.	Paul Molitor	503
31.	Andre Dawson	501
32.	Goose Goslin	500
33.	Rusty Staub	499
34.	Al Kaline	498
34.	Bill Buckner	498
36.	Sam Rice	497
37.	Heinie Manush	491
38.	Mickey Vernon	490
39.	Wade Boggs	489
40.	Mel Ott	488
41.	Lou Brock	486
41.	Billy Herman	486
43.	Vada Pinson	485
44.	Hal McRae	484
45.	Ted Simmons	483
45.	Dwight Evans	483
47.	Brooks Robinson	482
48.	Zack Wheat	476
48.	Jake Beckley	476
50.	Frankie Frisch	466
51.	Jim Bottomley	465
52.	Reggie Jackson	463
53.	Dan Brouthers	460
54.	Jimmie Foxx	458
54.	Sam Crawford	458
56.	Jimmy Dykes	453
56.	George Davis	453
58.	Jimmy Ryan	451
59.	Joe Morgan	449
60.	Cal Ripken	447
61.	Rod Carew	445
62.	George Burns	444
63.	Dick Bartell	442
63.	Don Mattingly	442
65.	Roger Connor	441
66.	Luke Appling	440
66.	Steve Garvey	440
66.	Roberto Clemente	440
69.	Eddie Collins	438
70.	Joe Sewell	436
70.	Cesar Cedeno	436
72.	Wally Moses	435
73.	Billy Williams	434
74.	Joe Judge	433
75.	Red Schoendienst	427
76.	Keith Hernandez	426
77.	Buddy Bell	425
77.	Sherry Magee	425
77.	George Sisler	425
80.	Willie Stargell	423
81.	Tim Wallach	422
82.	Carlton Fisk	421
83.	Lou Whitaker	420
84.	Max Carey	419
85.	Orlando Cepeda	417
86.	Cecil Cooper	415
87.	Bill Dahlen	414
87.	Jim O'Rourke	414
87.	Kirby Puckett	414
90.	Enos Slaughter	413
91.	Joe Kuhel	412
92.	Lave Cross	411
93.	Alan Trammell	410
94.	Mike Schmidt	408
95.	Ernie Banks	407
95.	Ben Chapman	407
95.	Frank White	407
98.	Earl Averill	401
98.	Marty McManus	401

TRIPLES

1.	Sam Crawford	311
2.	Ty Cobb	297
3.	Honus Wagner	252
4.	Jake Beckley	242
5.	Roger Connor	233
6.	Tris Speaker	223
7.	Fred Clarke	220
8.	Dan Brouthers	205
9.	Joe Kelley	194
10.	Paul Waner	190
11.	Bid McPhee	188
12.	Eddie Collins	187
13.	Ed Delahanty	185
14.	Sam Rice	184
15.	Jesse Burkett	183
16.	Edd Roush	182
17.	Ed Konetchy	181
18.	Buck Ewing	178
19.	Stan Musial	177
19.	Rabbit Maranville	177
21.	Harry Stovey	174
22.	Goose Goslin	173
23.	Zack Wheat	172
23.	Tommy Leach	172
25.	Rogers Hornsby	169
26.	Joe Jackson	168
27.	Elmer Flick	166
27.	Sherry Magee	166
27.	Roberto Clemente	166
30.	Jake Daubert	165
31.	Pie Traynor	164
31.	George Sisler	164
33.	Bill Dahlen	163
34.	Lou Gehrig	162
34.	George Davis	162
34.	Mike Tiernan	162
34.	George Van Haltren	162
38.	Nap Lajoie	161
39.	Harry Hooper	160
39.	Sam Thompson	160
39.	Heinie Manush	160
42.	Max Carey	159
42.	Joe Judge	159
44.	Ed McKean	158
45.	Jimmy Ryan	157
45.	Kiki Cuyler	157
47.	Tommy Corcoran	155
48.	Earle Combs	154
49.	Bobby Wallace	153
50.	Jim Bottomley	151
50.	Harry Heilmann	151
52.	Willie Keeler	150
53.	Al Simmons	149
53.	Kip Selbach	149
55.	Wally Pipp	148
55.	Enos Slaughter	148
57.	Bobby Veach	147
57.	Willie Wilson	147
59.	Charlie Gehringer	146
60.	Harry Davis	145
61.	Lou Brock	141

HOME RUNS

1.	Hank Aaron	755
2.	Babe Ruth	714
3.	Willie Mays	660
4.	Frank Robinson	586
5.	Harmon Killebrew	573
6.	Reggie Jackson	563
7.	Mike Schmidt	548
8.	Mickey Mantle	536
9.	Jimmie Foxx	534
10.	Ted Williams	521
10.	Willie McCovey	521
12.	Ernie Banks	512
12.	Eddie Mathews	512
14.	Mel Ott	511
15.	Lou Gehrig	493
16.	Eddie Murray	479
17.	Stan Musial	475
17.	Willie Stargell	475
19.	Dave Winfield	465
20.	Carl Yastrzemski	452
21.	Dave Kingman	442
22.	Andre Dawson	436
23.	Billy Williams	426
24.	Darrell Evans	414
25.	Duke Snider	407
26.	Al Kaline	399
27.	Dale Murphy	398
28.	Graig Nettles	390
29.	Johnny Bench	389
30.	Dwight Evans	385
31.	Jim Rice	382
31.	Frank Howard	382
33.	Tony Perez	379
33.	Orlando Cepeda	379
35.	Norm Cash	377
36.	Carlton Fisk	376
37.	Rocky Colavito	374
38.	Gil Hodges	370
39.	Ralph Kiner	369
40.	Joe DiMaggio	361
41.	Johnny Mize	359
42.	Yogi Berra	358
43.	Lee May	354
44.	Dick Allen	351
45.	George Foster	348
46.	Ron Santo	342
47.	Jack Clark	340
48.	Dave Parker	339
48.	Boog Powell	339
50.	Don Baylor	338
51.	Joe Adcock	336
52.	Bobby Bonds	332
53.	Hank Greenberg	331
54.	Joe Carter	327
54.	Cal Ripken	327
56.	Willie Horton	325
57.	Gary Carter	324
57.	Lance Parrish	324
59.	Roy Sievers	318
60.	George Brett	317
61.	Ron Cey	316
62.	Reggie Smith	314
63.	Al Simmons	307
63.	Greg Luzinski	307
65.	Fred Lynn	306
66.	Harold Baines	301
66.	Rogers Hornsby	301
68.	Chuck Klein	300
68.	Jose Canseco	300

HOME RUN PERCENTAGE

1.	Babe Ruth	8.5
2.	Ralph Kiner	7.1
3.	Harmon Killebrew	7.0
4.	Ted Williams	6.8
5.	Dave Kingman	6.6
6.	Mickey Mantle	6.6
7.	Jimmie Foxx	6.6
8.	Mike Schmidt	6.6
9.	Fred McGriff	6.4
10.	Hank Greenberg	6.4
11.	Jose Canseco	6.4
12.	Willie McCovey	6.4
13.	Lou Gehrig	6.2
14.	Darryl Strawberry	6.1
15.	Hank Aaron	6.1
16.	Willie Mays	6.1
17.	Hank Sauer	6.0
18.	Eddie Mathews	6.0
19.	Willie Stargell	6.0
20.	Frank Howard	5.9
21.	Frank Robinson	5.9
22.	Barry Bonds	5.8
23.	Roy Campanella	5.8
24.	Rocky Colavito	5.8
25.	Gus Zernial	5.7
26.	Gorman Thomas	5.7
27.	Reggie Jackson	5.7
28.	Duke Snider	5.7
29.	Norm Cash	5.6
30.	Johnny Mize	5.6
31.	Dick Allen	5.5
32.	Ernie Banks	5.4
33.	Mel Ott	5.4
34.	Roger Maris	5.4
35.	Joe DiMaggio	5.3

EXTRA BASE HITS

1.	Hank Aaron	1477
2.	Stan Musial	1377
3.	Babe Ruth	1356
4.	Willie Mays	1323
5.	Lou Gehrig	1190
6.	Frank Robinson	1186
7.	Carl Yastrzemski	1157
8.	Ty Cobb	1139
9.	Tris Speaker	1132
10.	George Brett	1119
11.	Jimmie Foxx	1117
11.	Ted Williams	1117
13.	Dave Winfield	1093
14.	Reggie Jackson	1075
15.	Mel Ott	1071
16.	Eddie Murray	1045
17.	Pete Rose	1041
18.	Andre Dawson	1035
19.	Mike Schmidt	1015

INDIVIDUAL BATTING (LIFETIME), *cont.*

20.	Rogers Hornsby	1011
21.	Ernie Banks	1009
22.	Honus Wagner	996
23.	Al Simmons	995
24.	Al Kaline	972
25.	Tony Perez	963
26.	Robin Yount	960
27.	Willie Stargell	953
28.	Mickey Mantle	952
29.	Billy Williams	948
30.	Dwight Evans	941
31.	Dave Parker	940
32.	Eddie Mathews	938
33.	Goose Goslin	921
34.	Willie McCovey	920
35.	Paul Waner	905
36.	Charlie Gehringer	904
37.	Nap Lajoie	902
38.	Harmon Killebrew	887
39.	Joe DiMaggio	881
40.	Harry Heilmann	876
41.	Vada Pinson	868
42.	Sam Crawford	866
43.	Joe Medwick	858
44.	Duke Snider	850
45.	Roberto Clemente	846
46.	Carlton Fisk	844
47.	Rusty Staub	838
48.	Jim Bottomley	835
49.	Jim Rice	834
50.	Al Oliver	825
51.	Orlando Cepeda	823
52.	Brooks Robinson	818
53.	Cal Ripken	816
54.	Joe Morgan	813
55.	Roger Connor	811
55.	Paul Molitor	811
57.	Johnny Mize	809
58.	Ed Delahanty	808
59.	Jake Beckley	806
60.	Joe Cronin	803

RUNS BATTED IN

1.	Hank Aaron	2297
2.	Babe Ruth	2211
3.	Lou Gehrig	1990
4.	Ty Cobb	1961
5.	Stan Musial	1951
6.	Jimmie Foxx	1921
7.	Willie Mays	1903
8.	Mel Ott	1861
9.	Carl Yastrzemski	1844
10.	Ted Williams	1839
11.	Dave Winfield	1833
12.	Al Simmons	1827
13.	Eddie Murray	1820
14.	Frank Robinson	1812
15.	Honus Wagner	1732
16.	Cap Anson	1715
17.	Reggie Jackson	1702
18.	Tony Perez	1652
19.	Ernie Banks	1636
20.	Goose Goslin	1609
21.	Nap Lajoie	1599
22.	George Brett	1595
22.	Mike Schmidt	1595
24.	Rogers Hornsby	1584
24.	Harmon Killebrew	1584
26.	Al Kaline	1583
27.	Andre Dawson	1577
28.	Jake Beckley	1575
29.	Tris Speaker	1559
30.	Willie McCovey	1555
31.	Harry Heilmann	1551
32.	Willie Stargell	1540
33.	Joe DiMaggio	1537
34.	Sam Crawford	1525
35.	Mickey Mantle	1509
36.	Dave Parker	1493
37.	Billy Williams	1475
38.	Rusty Staub	1466
39.	Ed Delahanty	1464
40.	Eddie Mathews	1453
41.	Jim Rice	1451
42.	George Davis	1435
43.	Yogi Berra	1430
44.	Charlie Gehringer	1427
45.	Joe Cronin	1424
46.	Jim Bottomley	1422
47.	Robin Yount	1406
48.	Ted Simmons	1389
49.	Dwight Evans	1384
50.	Joe Medwick	1383
51.	Johnny Bench	1376
52.	Orlando Cepeda	1365
53.	Brooks Robinson	1357
54.	Darrell Evans	1354
55.	Lave Cross	1345
56.	Johnny Mize	1337
57.	Duke Snider	1333
58.	Ron Santo	1331
59.	Carlton Fisk	1330
60.	Al Oliver	1326
61.	Pete Rose	1314
61.	Graig Nettles	1314
63.	Mickey Vernon	1311
64.	Paul Waner	1309
65.	Steve Garvey	1308
66.	Roberto Clemente	1305
67.	Enos Slaughter	1304
68.	Eddie Collins	1300
69.	Hugh Duffy	1299
69.	Sam Thompson	1299
71.	Del Ennis	1284
72.	Bob Johnson	1283
73.	Don Baylor	1276
73.	Hank Greenberg	1276
75.	Gil Hodges	1274
76.	Pie Traynor	1273
77.	Cal Ripken	1267
78.	Dale Murphy	1266
79.	Zack Wheat	1261
79.	Harold Baines	1261
81.	Bobby Doerr	1247
82.	Lee May	1244
82.	Frankie Frisch	1244
84.	George Foster	1239
85.	Bill Dahlen	1233
86.	Gary Carter	1225
87.	Dave Kingman	1210
88.	Bill Dickey	1209
89.	Bill Buckner	1208
90.	Chuck Klein	1202
91.	Bob Elliott	1195
92.	Joe Kelley	1194
93.	Tony Lazzeri	1191
94.	Boog Powell	1187
95.	Joe Torre	1185
96.	Sherry Magee	1182
97.	Jack Clark	1180
98.	Gabby Hartnett	1179
99.	Vic Wertz	1178
100.	George Sisler	1175
101.	Vern Stephens	1174
102.	Joe Carter	1173
102.	Heinie Manush	1173
104.	Vada Pinson	1170
105.	Bobby Veach	1166
106.	Earl Averill	1165
107.	Willie Horton	1163
108.	Rocky Colavito	1159
109.	Rudy York	1152
110.	Roy Sievers	1147
111.	Ken Boyer	1141
112.	Ron Cey	1139
113.	Tommy Corcoran	1135
114.	Joe Morgan	1133
115.	Greg Luzinski	1128
116.	Roger Connor	1125
116.	Cecil Cooper	1125
118.	Joe Adcock	1122
119.	Bobby Wallace	1121
120.	Dick Allen	1119
120.	Frank Howard	1119
122.	Luke Appling	1116
123.	Fred Lynn	1111
123.	George Hendrick	1111
125.	Buddy Bell	1106
126.	Norm Cash	1103
127.	Chili Davis	1100
128.	Don Mattingly	1099
129.	Hal McRae	1097
130.	Jimmy Ryan	1093
131.	Reggie Smith	1092
132.	Kent Hrbek	1086
133.	Kirby Puckett	1085
134.	Lou Whitaker	1084
135.	Tim Wallach	1083
136.	Sam Rice	1078
136.	Bill Terry	1078
136.	Charlie Grimm	1078
139.	Jose Cruz	1077
140.	Gary Gaetti	1075
140.	Pinky Higgins	1075
142.	Brian Downing	1073
143.	Jimmy Dykes	1071
143.	Keith Hernandez	1071
145.	Ed McKean	1070
145.	Lance Parrish	1070
147.	Bob Meusel	1067
148.	Kiki Cuyler	1065
148.	Ken Singleton	1065
150.	Hack Wilson	1062
151.	Stuffy McInnis	1060
152.	Carl Furillo	1058
152.	Dan Brouthers	1058
154.	Herman Long	1053
154.	Willie Davis	1053
156.	Tommy Davis	1052
157.	Joe Sewell	1051
157.	George Scott	1051
159.	Joe Kuhel	1049
160.	Ron Fairly	1044
161.	Bobby Murcer	1043
162.	Sal Bando	1039
163.	Joe Judge	1037
164.	Paul Molitor	1036
165.	Ted Kluszewski	1028
166.	Bobby Thomson	1026
167.	Bobby Bonds	1024
168.	Dixie Walker	1023
168.	Minnie Minoso	1023
170.	George Kelly	1020
171.	Rod Carew	1015
171.	Fred Clarke	1015
171.	Ralph Kiner	1015
174.	George Van Haltren	1014
175.	Dusty Baker	1013
175.	Frank Baker	1013
177.	Hal Trosky	1012
178.	Amos Otis	1007
179.	Cy Williams	1005
180.	George Bell	1002

RUNS BATTED IN PER GAME

1.	Sam Thompson	.92
2.	Lou Gehrig	.92
3.	Hank Greenberg	.92
4.	Joe DiMaggio	.89
5.	Babe Ruth	.88
6.	Jimmie Foxx	.83
7.	Al Simmons	.82
8.	Ted Williams	.80
9.	Ed Delahanty	.80
10.	Hack Wilson	.79
11.	Jose Canseco	.76
12.	Bob Meusel	.76
13.	Cap Anson	.75
14.	Hal Trosky	.75
15.	Hugh Duffy	.75
16.	Harry Heilmann	.72
17.	Rudy York	.72
18.	Jim Bottomley	.71
19.	Johnny Mize	.71
20.	Roy Campanella	.70
21.	Goose Goslin	.70
22.	Rogers Hornsby	.70
23.	Earl Averill	.70
24.	Joe Medwick	.70
25.	Hank Aaron	.70
26.	Jim Rice	.69
27.	Ralph Kiner	.69
28.	Bob Johnson	.69
29.	Chuck Klein	.69
30.	Tony Lazzeri	.68
31.	Vern Stephens	.68
32.	Mel Ott	.68
33.	Bill Dickey	.68
34.	Del Ennis	.67
35.	Yogi Berra	.67

RUNS

1.	Ty Cobb	2245
2.	Babe Ruth	2174
2.	Hank Aaron	2174
4.	Pete Rose	2165
5.	Willie Mays	2062
6.	Stan Musial	1949
7.	Lou Gehrig	1888
8.	Tris Speaker	1882
9.	Mel Ott	1859
10.	Frank Robinson	1829
11.	Eddie Collins	1820
12.	Carl Yastrzemski	1816
13.	Ted Williams	1798
14.	Charlie Gehringer	1774
15.	Jimmie Foxx	1751
16.	Honus Wagner	1735
17.	Cap Anson	1719
17.	Willie Keeler	1719
17.	Rickey Henderson	1719
20.	Jesse Burkett	1718
21.	Billy Hamilton	1688
22.	Bid McPhee	1678
23.	Mickey Mantle	1677
24.	Dave Winfield	1669
25.	Joe Morgan	1650
26.	Jimmy Ryan	1642
27.	George Van Haltren	1639
28.	Robin Yount	1632
29.	Paul Waner	1626
30.	Al Kaline	1622
31.	Fred Clarke	1621
32.	Roger Connor	1620
33.	Lou Brock	1610
34.	Jake Beckley	1600
35.	Ed Delahanty	1599
36.	Bill Dahlen	1589
37.	George Brett	1583
38.	Rogers Hornsby	1579
39.	Hugh Duffy	1555
40.	Reggie Jackson	1551
41.	Max Carey	1545
41.	Paul Molitor	1545
41.	Eddie Murray	1545
44.	George Davis	1540
45.	Frankie Frisch	1532
46.	Dan Brouthers	1523
47.	Tom Brown	1521
48.	Sam Rice	1515
49.	Eddie Mathews	1509
50.	Al Simmons	1507
51.	Mike Schmidt	1506
52.	Nap Lajoie	1503
53.	Harry Stovey	1492
54.	Goose Goslin	1483
55.	Arlie Latham	1478
56.	Dwight Evans	1470
57.	Herman Long	1456
58.	Jim O'Rourke	1446
59.	Harry Hooper	1429
60.	Rod Carew	1424

INDIVIDUAL BATTING (LIFETIME), *cont.*

60.	Dummy Hoy	1424
62.	Joe Kelley	1423
63.	Roberto Clemente	1416
64.	Billy Williams	1410
65.	Monte Ward	1408
66.	Mike Griffin	1406
67.	Sam Crawford	1393
68.	Joe DiMaggio	1390
69.	Lou Whitaker	1386
70.	Tim Raines	1374
71.	Andre Dawson	1367
72.	Vada Pinson	1366
73.	Doc Cramer	1357
73.	King Kelly	1357
75.	Tommy Leach	1355
76.	Darrell Evans	1344
77.	Pee Wee Reese	1338
78.	Luis Aparicio	1335
79.	Lave Cross	1333
80.	George Gore	1327
81.	Richie Ashburn	1322
82.	Luke Appling	1319
83.	Patsy Donovan	1318
84.	Mike Tiernan	1313
85.	Ernie Banks	1305
85.	Kiki Cuyler	1305
87.	Jimmy Sheckard	1296
88.	Harry Heilmann	1291
89.	Zack Wheat	1289
90.	Wade Boggs	1287
90.	Heinie Manush	1287
92.	Brett Butler	1285
93.	George Sisler	1284
94.	Harmon Killebrew	1283
95.	Donie Bush	1280
96.	Nellie Fox	1279
97.	Carlton Fisk	1276
98.	Fred Tenney	1275
99.	Tony Perez	1272
99.	Cal Ripken	1272
99.	Dave Parker	1272
102.	Duke Snider	1259
103.	Bobby Bonds	1258
104.	Sam Thompson	1256
105.	Rabbit Maranville	1255
106.	Jim Rice	1249
107.	Enos Slaughter	1247
108.	Stan Hack	1239
108.	Bob Johnson	1239
108.	Willie Randolph	1239
111.	Joe Kuhel	1236
111.	Don Baylor	1236
113.	Joe Cronin	1233
114.	Brooks Robinson	1232
115.	Willie McCovey	1229
116.	Ed McKean	1227
117.	Earl Averill	1224
118.	Red Schoendienst	1223
119.	Ozzie Smith	1221
120.	Willie Davis	1217
121.	Eddie Yost	1215
121.	Alan Trammell	1215
123.	Cupid Childs	1214
124.	Lloyd Waner	1201
125.	Joe Medwick	1198
126.	Dale Murphy	1197
127.	Mickey Vernon	1196
128.	Willie Stargell	1195
129.	Graig Nettles	1193
130.	Al Oliver	1189
130.	Rusty Staub	1189
132.	George Burns	1188
132.	Brian Downing	1188
134.	Earle Combs	1186
135.	Joe Judge	1184
135.	Fielder Jones	1184
135.	Tommy Corcoran	1184
138.	Pie Traynor	1183
139.	Bert Campaneris	1181
140.	Ryne Sandberg	1179
141.	Jim Bottomley	1177
142.	Yogi Berra	1175
143.	Buddy Myer	1174
144.	Arky Vaughan	1173
145.	Willie Wilson	1169
146.	Chuck Klein	1168
147.	Jim Gilliam	1163
147.	Billy Herman	1163
147.	Jack Glasscock	1163
150.	Lu Blue	1151
151.	Buddy Bell	1150
152.	Ben Chapman	1144
153.	Steve Garvey	1143
154.	Joe Sewell	1141
155.	Ron Santo	1138
156.	Minnie Minoso	1136
157.	Bobby Lowe	1131
157.	Orlando Cepeda	1131
159.	Dick Bartell	1130
160.	Buck Ewing	1129
160.	Ken Griffey	1129
162.	Wally Moses	1124
162.	Keith Hernandez	1124
164.	Reggie Smith	1123
165.	Bill Terry	1120
165.	Hardy Richardson	1120
167.	Jack Clark	1118
167.	Johnny Mize	1118
169.	Jake Daubert	1117
170.	Toby Harrah	1115
171.	Sherry Magee	1112
172.	Jimmy Dykes	1108
173.	Gil Hodges	1105
173.	Jimmy Wynn	1105
175.	Ken Boyer	1104
176.	Edd Roush	1099
176.	Dick Allen	1099
178.	Bobby Doerr	1094
178.	Fred Pfeffer	1094
180.	Amos Otis	1092
181.	Johnny Bench	1091
182.	Cesar Cedeno	1084
182.	Tommy Tucker	1084
184.	Paul Hines	1083
184.	Gary Matthews	1083
186.	Bill Buckner	1077
187.	Ted Simmons	1074
188.	Tony Gwynn	1073
189.	Billy Nash	1072
190.	Kirby Puckett	1071
191.	Harlond Clift	1070
192.	Maury Wills	1067
193.	Tommy McCarthy	1066
194.	Alvin Dark	1064
194.	Bob Elliott	1064
194.	Kip Selbach	1064
197.	Fred Lynn	1063
198.	Charlie Jamieson	1062
199.	Bobby Wallace	1059
200.	Jimmy Collins	1055
201.	Hank Greenberg	1051
202.	Dave Bancroft	1048
203.	Norm Cash	1046
203.	Dom DiMaggio	1046
205.	Mickey Cochrane	1041
206.	Dixie Walker	1037
207.	Jose Cruz	1036
208.	Bobby Grich	1033
208.	Harold Baines	1033
210.	Chili Davis	1026
211.	Gary Carter	1025
212.	John McGraw	1024
212.	Cy Williams	1024
214.	Davey Lopes	1023
215.	Tom Daly	1022
216.	Kid Gleason	1020
217.	Cecil Cooper	1012
218.	Roy Thomas	1010
219.	Marty McManus	1008
220.	Don Mattingly	1007
220.	Carney Lansford	1007
222.	Frankie Crosetti	1006
222.	Roger Peckinpaugh	1006
224.	Tony Taylor	1005
225.	Augie Galan	1004
225.	Clyde Milan	1004
227.	Vern Stephens	1001

RUNS PER GAME

1.	Billy Hamilton	1.06
2.	George Gore	1.01
3.	Harry Stovey	1.00
4.	King Kelly	.93
5.	Mike Griffin	.93
6.	Dan Brouthers	.91
7.	Arlie Latham	.91
8.	Hugh Duffy	.90
9.	Sam Thompson	.89
10.	Mike Tiernan	.89
11.	Lou Gehrig	.87
12.	Ed Delahanty	.87
13.	Babe Ruth	.87
14.	Buck Ewing	.86
15.	Abner Dalrymple	.85
16.	Tom Brown	.85
17.	Hardy Richardson	.84
18.	Tommy McCarthy	.84
19.	Tip O'Neill	.84
20.	Denny Lyons	.83
21.	Jesse Burkett	.83
22.	Cupid Childs	.83
23.	Curt Welch	.83
24.	George Van Haltren	.83
25.	Jimmy Ryan	.82
26.	Earle Combs	.82
27.	Jim O'Rourke	.82
28.	Roger Connor	.81
29.	Willie Keeler	.81
30.	Pete Browning	.81
31.	Red Rolfe	.80
32.	Joe DiMaggio	.80
33.	Dummy Hoy	.79
34.	Long John Reilly	.79
35.	Bid McPhee	.79

BASES ON BALLS

1.	Babe Ruth	2056
2.	Ted Williams	2019
3.	Joe Morgan	1865
4.	Carl Yastrzemski	1845
5.	Mickey Mantle	1734
6.	Mel Ott	1708
7.	Eddie Yost	1614
8.	Darrell Evans	1605
9.	Stan Musial	1599
10.	Pete Rose	1566
11.	Harmon Killebrew	1559
12.	Rickey Henderson	1550
13.	Lou Gehrig	1508
14.	Mike Schmidt	1507
15.	Eddie Collins	1503
16.	Willie Mays	1463
17.	Jimmie Foxx	1452
18.	Eddie Mathews	1444
19.	Frank Robinson	1420
20.	Hank Aaron	1402
21.	Dwight Evans	1391
22.	Tris Speaker	1381
23.	Reggie Jackson	1375
24.	Willie McCovey	1345
25.	Luke Appling	1302
26.	Al Kaline	1277
27.	Ken Singleton	1263
28.	Jack Clark	1262
29.	Eddie Murray	1257
30.	Rusty Staub	1255
31.	Ty Cobb	1249
32.	Willie Randolph	1243
33.	Jimmy Wynn	1224
34.	Dave Winfield	1216
35.	Wade Boggs	1213
36.	Pee Wee Reese	1210
37.	Richie Ashburn	1198
38.	Lou Whitaker	1197
38.	Brian Downing	1197
40.	Billy Hamilton	1187
41.	Charlie Gehringer	1185
42.	Donie Bush	1158
43.	Max Bishop	1153
43.	Toby Harrah	1153
45.	Harry Hooper	1136
46.	Jimmy Sheckard	1135
47.	Tim Raines	1134
48.	Ron Santo	1108
49.	George Brett	1096
50.	Lu Blue	1092
50.	Stan Hack	1092
52.	Paul Waner	1091
53.	Graig Nettles	1088
54.	Bobby Grich	1087
55.	Brett Butler	1078
56.	Bob Johnson	1073
57.	Harlond Clift	1070
57.	Keith Hernandez	1070
59.	Bill Dahlen	1064
60.	Joe Cronin	1059
61.	Ron Fairly	1052
62.	Ozzie Smith	1047
63.	Billy Williams	1045
64.	Norm Cash	1043
65.	Roy Thomas	1042
66.	Eddie Joost	1041
67.	Max Carey	1040
68.	Rogers Hornsby	1038
69.	Jim Gilliam	1036
70.	Sal Bando	1031
71.	Jesse Burkett	1029
72.	Enos Slaughter	1019
73.	Rod Carew	1018
74.	Ron Cey	1012
75.	Ralph Kiner	1011
76.	Dummy Hoy	1002
76.	Roger Connor	1002
76.	Miller Huggins	1002
79.	Boog Powell	1001

BASE ON BALLS AVERAGE

1.	Ted Williams	.208
2.	Max Bishop	.204
3.	Babe Ruth	.197
4.	Eddie Stanky	.188
5.	Gene Tenace	.183
6.	Eddie Yost	.180
7.	Mickey Mantle	.176
8.	Mickey Tettleton	.170
9.	Joe Morgan	.167
10.	Earl Torgeson	.165
11.	Roy Thomas	.164
12.	Ralph Kiner	.163
13.	Rickey Henderson	.161
14.	Harmon Killebrew	.161
15.	Billy Hamilton	.159
16.	Lou Gehrig	.159
17.	Elmer Valo	.158
18.	Harlond Clift	.157
19.	Eddie Joost	.157
20.	Barry Bonds	.156
21.	Lu Blue	.156
22.	Jack Clark	.156
23.	Jimmy Wynn	.155
24.	Mel Ott	.153
25.	Mike Schmidt	.153
26.	Miller Huggins	.153
27.	Darrell Evans	.152
28.	Jimmie Foxx	.151
29.	Dolf Camilli	.150
30.	Cupid Childs	.150
31.	Ken Singleton	.149
32.	Elbie Fletcher	.149
33.	Mike Hargrove	.148
34.	Topsy Hartsel	.147
35.	Dwayne Murphy	.146

INDIVIDUAL BATTING (LIFETIME), *cont.*

STOLEN BASES

1.	Rickey Henderson	1149
2.	Lou Brock	938
3.	Ty Cobb	892
4.	Tim Raines	777
5.	Eddie Collins	743
6.	Vince Coleman	740
7.	Max Carey	738
8.	Honus Wagner	703
9.	Joe Morgan	689
10.	Willie Wilson	668
11.	Bert Campaneris	649
12.	Maury Wills	586
13.	Ozzie Smith	573
14.	Davey Lopes	557
15.	Cesar Cedeno	550
16.	Brett Butler	535
17.	Luis Aparicio	506
18.	Clyde Milan	495
19.	Omar Moreno	487
20.	Paul Molitor	466
21.	Bobby Bonds	461
22.	Jimmy Sheckard	460
23.	Ron LeFlore	455
24.	Steve Sax	444
24.	Otis Nixon	444
26.	Sherry Magee	441
27.	Tris Speaker	433
28.	Bob Bescher	428
29.	Frankie Frisch	419
30.	Tommy Harper	408
31.	Frank Chance	405
32.	Donie Bush	403
33.	Willie Davis	398
34.	Billy North	395
34.	Dave Collins	395
36.	Freddie Patek	385
37.	George Burns	383
38.	Sam Mertes	377
39.	Harry Hooper	375
39.	George Sisler	375
41.	Lonnie Smith	370
42.	Juan Samuel	369
43.	Sam Crawford	366
44.	Hal Chase	363
45.	Tommy Leach	361
46.	Nap Lajoie	355
47.	Gary Pettis	354
48.	Rod Carew	353
49.	Sam Rice	351
50.	Fred Clarke	350
51.	George Case	349
52.	Julio Cruz	343
53.	Amos Otis	341
54.	Barry Bonds	340
55.	Willie Mays	338
56.	Joe Tinker	336
57.	Elmer Flick	334
58.	Jose Cardenal	329
59.	Kiki Cuyler	328
60.	Mookie Wilson	327
61.	Willie McGee	325
61.	Ryne Sandberg	325
63.	Johnny Evers	324
63.	Miller Huggins	324
65.	Gary Redus	322
66.	Red Murray	321
66.	Dave Concepcion	321
68.	Larry Bowa	318
69.	Jose Cruz	317
70.	Hans Lobert	316
71.	Andre Dawson	314
72.	Buck Herzog	312
72.	Claudell Washington	312
74.	Eric Davis	306
75.	Vada Pinson	305
76.	Larry Doyle	300
76.	Frank Taveras	300

PINCH HITS

1.	Manny Mota	150
2.	Smoky Burgess	145
3.	Greg Gross	143
4.	Jose Morales	123
5.	Jerry Lynch	116
6.	Red Lucas	114
7.	Steve Braun	113
8.	Terry Crowley	108
8.	Denny Walling	108
10.	Gates Brown	107
11.	Mike Lum	103
12.	Jim Dwyer	100
12.	Rusty Staub	100
14.	Gerald Perry	95
14.	Vic Davalillo	95
14.	Larry Biittner	95
17.	Jerry Hairston	94
18.	Dave Philley	93
18.	Joel Youngblood	93
20.	Jay Johnstone	92
21.	Elmer Valo	90
21.	Ed Kranepool	90
23.	Dave Collins	85
24.	Jesus Alou	82
24.	Thad Bosley	82
24.	Tim McCarver	82
24.	Kurt Bevacqua	82
28.	Kevin Bass	81
28.	Dalton Jones	81
28.	Tito Francona	81
31.	Tom Hutton	79
31.	Milt Thompson	79
33.	Gary Varsho	78
33.	Wallace Johnson	78
35.	Enos Slaughter	77
36.	George Crowe	76
36.	Lee Mazzilli	76
36.	Harry Spilman	76
36.	Bob Fothergill	76
40.	Randy Bush	74
41.	Jerry Turner	73
42.	Mike Jorgensen	72
43.	Ken Griffey	71
43.	Dave Bergman	71
43.	Dwight Smith	71
43.	Jimmy Stewart	71
43.	Ed Kirkpatrick	71
48.	Dane Iorg	69
48.	Bob Skinner	69
50.	Ron Fairly	68
50.	Cliff Johnson	68
50.	Champ Summers	68
53.	Oscar Gamble	67
54.	Ken Boswell	66
54.	Bob Johnson	66
54.	Ernie Lombardi	66
54.	Willie McCovey	66
54.	Merv Rettenmund	66
59.	Lee Lacy	65
59.	Jim Wohlford	65
59.	Gene Woodling	65
62.	Jim King	63
62.	Tommy Davis	63
62.	Tony Taylor	63
62.	Julio Becquer	63
62.	Mitch Webster	63
67.	Bob Hale	62
67.	Vic Wertz	62
67.	Bob Bailey	62
67.	Danny Heep	62
67.	Peanuts Lowrey	62
72.	Mike Vail	61
72.	Terry Puhl	61
72.	Mike Aldrete	61
75.	Ty Cline	60
75.	Chris Gwynn	60
75.	Bill Buckner	60
78.	Sam Leslie	59
78.	Russ Nixon	59
78.	Gene Clines	59
78.	Cito Gaston	59
78.	Ron Northey	59
78.	Duke Snider	59
78.	Johnny Grubb	59
78.	Rance Mulliniks	59
86.	Red Ruffing	58
86.	Tom Paciorek	58
88.	Lee Maye	57
88.	Ham Hyatt	57
88.	Max Venable	57
88.	Wes Covington	57
88.	John Cangelosi	57
93.	Jose Pagan	56
93.	Walker Cooper	56
93.	Mickey Hatcher	56
93.	Fred Whitfield	56
93.	Charlie Maxwell	56
93.	John Vander Wal	56
93.	Herm Winningham	56
93.	Red Schoendienst	56
101.	Bob Cerv	55
101.	Dusty Rhodes	55
101.	Phil Gagliano	55
101.	Richie Hebner	55
101.	Earl Torgeson	55
101.	Len Gabrielson	55
101.	Jerry Mumphrey	55
101.	Billy Sullivan	55
101.	John Lowenstein	55
101.	Willie Stargell	55
111.	Del Unser	54
111.	Debs Garms	54
111.	Rick Miller	54
111.	Willie Smith	54
111.	Candy Maldonado	54
111.	Frenchy Bordagaray	54
117.	Lenny Green	53
117.	Johnny Mize	53
117.	Scot Thompson	53
117.	Ted Kluszewski	53
121.	Irv Noren	52
121.	Dave Hansen	52
121.	Jamie Quirk	52
121.	Larry Stahl	52
121.	Walt Williams	52
121.	Dom Dallessandro	52
127.	Pat Kelly	51
127.	Hal McRae	51
127.	Glenn Adams	51
127.	John Milner	51
127.	Lenny Harris	51
127.	Dick Williams	51
127.	Harvey Hendrick	51
127.	Terry Whitfield	51
135.	Tim Flannery	50
135.	Jose Cardenal	50

PINCH HIT BATTING AVERAGE

1.	Tommy Davis	.320
2.	Frenchy Bordagaray	.312
3.	Frankie Baumholtz	.307
4.	Sid Bream	.306
5.	Red Schoendienst	.303
6.	Bob Fothergill	.300
7.	Dave Philley	.299
8.	Manny Mota	.297
9.	Ted Easterly	.296
10.	Harvey Hendrick	.295
11.	Larry Herndon	.294
12.	Rance Mulliniks	.292
13.	Terry Puhl	.289
14.	Manny Sanguillen	.287
15.	Dave Hansen	.287
16.	Ricky Jordan	.287
17.	Smoky Burgess	.286
18.	Rick Miller	.286
19.	Mark Carreon	.285
20.	Johnny Mize	.283
21.	Ken Griffey	.282
22.	John Vander Wal	.281
23.	Bubba Morton	.281
23.	Jeff Treadway	.281
25.	Steve Braun	.281
26.	Kevin Bass	.280
27.	Don Mueller	.280
28.	Milt Thompson	.280
29.	Rusty Staub	.279
30.	Mickey Vernon	.279
31.	Ron Hassey	.279
32.	Herm Winningham	.279
33.	Dwight Smith	.278
34.	Thad Bosley	.278
35.	Gene Woodling	.278

FEWEST STRIKEOUTS PER AT BAT

1.	Joe Sewell	.016
2.	Willie Keeler	.019
3.	Lloyd Waner	.023
4.	Nellie Fox	.023
5.	Tommy Holmes	.024
6.	Lave Cross	.028
7.	Tris Speaker	.028
8.	Stuffy McInnis	.028
9.	Andy High	.030
10.	Sam Rice	.030
10.	Doggie Miller	.030
12.	Frankie Frisch	.030
13.	Jack Glasscock	.031
14.	Lou Bierbauer	.032
15.	Edd Roush	.032
16.	Charlie Comiskey	.033
17.	Frank McCormick	.033
18.	Don Mueller	.033
19.	Cap Anson	.034
20.	Billy Southworth	.034
21.	Jack Tobin	.034
22.	Rip Radcliff	.035
23.	Dan Brouthers	.036
24.	Ed McKean	.036
25.	Jack McCarthy	.036
26.	Pie Traynor	.037
27.	Patsy Donovan	.038
28.	Doc Cramer	.038
29.	Fielder Jones	.038
30.	Sam Thompson	.038
31.	Cupid Childs	.039
32.	Steve Brodie	.039
33.	Eddie Collins	.039
34.	Carson Bigbee	.039
35.	Hank Severeid	.039

MOST STRIKEOUTS PER AT BAT

1.	Gorman Thomas	.286
2.	Mickey Tettleton	.278
3.	Dave Kingman	.272
4.	Danny Tartabull	.271
5.	Jose Canseco	.269
6.	Reggie Jackson	.263
7.	Jesse Barfield	.259
8.	Bobby Bonds	.249
9.	Rick Monday	.247
10.	Dick Allen	.246
11.	Donn Clendenon	.245
12.	Willie Stargell	.244
13.	Darryl Strawberry	.244
14.	Andres Galarraga	.242
15.	Woodie Held	.235
16.	Tony Armas	.233
17.	Juan Samuel	.232
18.	Greg Luzinski	.230
19.	Gene Tenace	.227
20.	Fred McGriff	.226
21.	Mike Schmidt	.225
22.	Frank Howard	.225
23.	Larry Hisle	.224
24.	Deron Johnson	.222
25.	Kirk Gibson	.222

INDIVIDUAL BATTING (LIFETIME), *cont.*

26. Dale Murphy .220
27. Dwayne Murphy .219
28. Lance Parrish .216
29. Dave Henderson .215
30. Jimmy Wynn .214

31. Howard Johnson .213
32. Devon White .212
33. Mickey Mantle .211
34. Jack Clark .210
35. Candy Maldonado .210

STRIKEOUTS

1. Reggie Jackson 2597
2. Willie Stargell 1936
3. Mike Schmidt 1883
4. Tony Perez 1867
5. Dave Kingman 1816
6. Bobby Bonds 1757
7. Dale Murphy 1748
8. Lou Brock 1730
9. Mickey Mantle 1710
10. Harmon Killebrew 1699

11. Dwight Evans 1697
12. Dave Winfield 1686
13. Lee May 1570
14. Dick Allen 1556
15. Willie McCovey 1550
16. Dave Parker 1537
17. Frank Robinson 1532
18. Lance Parrish 1527
19. Willie Mays 1526
20. Rick Monday 1513

21. Andre Dawson 1496
22. Greg Luzinski 1495
23. Eddie Mathews 1487
24. Frank Howard 1460
25. Jack Clark 1441
26. Jimmy Wynn 1427
27. Jim Rice 1423
28. George Foster 1419
29. George Scott 1418
30. Darrell Evans 1410

31. Eddie Murray 1403
32. Carl Yastrzemski 1393
33. Carlton Fisk 1386
34. Chili Davis 1385
35. Hank Aaron 1383
36. Rob Deer 1379
37. Larry Parrish 1359
38. Robin Yount 1350
39. Ron Santo 1343
40. Gorman Thomas 1339

41. Juan Samuel 1336
42. Babe Ruth 1330
43. Deron Johnson 1318
44. Willie Horton 1313
45. Jimmie Foxx 1311
46. Gary Gaetti 1301
47. Kirk Gibson 1285
48. Bobby Grich 1278
48. Johnny Bench 1278
50. Jose Canseco 1267

51. Claudell Washington 1266
52. Ken Singleton 1246
53. Duke Snider 1237
54. Ernie Banks 1236
55. Ron Cey 1235
56. Jesse Barfield 1234
57. Danny Tartabull 1230
57. Roberto Clemente 1230
59. Tim Wallach 1228
60. Boog Powell 1226

61. Graig Nettles 1209
62. Tony Armas 1201
63. Vada Pinson 1196
64. Tom Brunansky 1187
65. Dave Concepcion 1186
66. Darryl Strawberry 1182
67. Andres Galarraga 1171
68. Orlando Cepeda 1169
69. Harold Baines 1163
70. Mickey Tettleton 1158
71. Willie Wilson 1144
72. Pete Rose 1143
73. Bert Campaneris 1142
74. Donn Clendenon 1140
75. Gil Hodges 1137
76. Leo Cardenas 1135
76. Lloyd Moseby 1135
76. Jeff Burroughs 1135
79. Pete Incaviglia 1132
80. Bob Bailey 1126

80. Brian Downing 1126
82. Gary Matthews 1125
83. Fred Lynn 1117
84. Joe Carter 1115
85. Tony Phillips 1105
85. Dave Henderson 1105
87. Rickey Henderson 1101
88. Lou Whitaker 1099
89. Jim Fregosi 1097
90. Joe Torre 1094

91. Garry Templeton 1092
92. Norm Cash 1091
93. Tony Taylor 1083
94. Tommy Harper 1080
95. Don Baylor 1068
96. Johnny Callison 1064
97. Andy Van Slyke 1063
98. Joe Adcock 1059
99. Paul Molitor 1058
100. Doug Rader 1055

101. Howard Johnson 1053
102. Ryne Sandberg 1050
103. Devon White 1047
104. Billy Williams 1046
105. Frank White 1035
106. Bob Allison 1033
107. Jose Cruz 1031
108. Reggie Smith 1030
109. Rod Carew 1028
110. Darrell Porter 1025

111. Chet Lemon 1024
112. Al Kaline 1020
113. Fred McGriff 1019
114. Ken Boyer 1017
115. Joe Morgan 1015
116. George Hendrick 1013
117. Keith Hernandez 1012
118. Larry Doby 1011
119. Willie McGee 1010
120. Amos Otis 1008

121. Hubie Brooks 1005
122. Steve Garvey 1003
123. Jeffrey Leonard 1000

INDIVIDUAL PITCHING (LIFETIME)

WINS

1.	Cy Young	511
2.	Walter Johnson	417
3.	Grover Alexander	373
3.	Christy Mathewson	373
5.	Warren Spahn	363
6.	Pud Galvin	361
6.	Kid Nichols	361
8.	Tim Keefe	342
9.	Steve Carlton	329
10.	Eddie Plank	326
10.	John Clarkson	326
12.	Nolan Ryan	324
12.	Don Sutton	324
14.	Phil Niekro	318
15.	Gaylord Perry	314
16.	Tom Seaver	311
16.	Old Hoss Radbourn	311
18.	Mickey Welch	308
19.	Early Wynn	300
19.	Lefty Grove	300
21.	Tommy John	288
22.	Bert Blyleven	287
23.	Robin Roberts	286
24.	Tony Mullane	284
24.	Ferguson Jenkins	284
26.	Jim Kaat	283
27.	Red Ruffing	273
28.	Burleigh Grimes	270
29.	Jim Palmer	268
30.	Bob Feller	266
30.	Eppa Rixey	266
32.	Jim McCormick	265
33.	Gus Weyhing	264
34.	Ted Lyons	260
35.	Red Faber	254
35.	Jack Morris	254
37.	Carl Hubbell	253
38.	Bob Gibson	251
39.	Vic Willis	249
40.	Jack Quinn	247
40.	Joe McGinnity	247
42.	Amos Rusie	245
42.	Jack Powell	245
44.	Juan Marichal	243
45.	Herb Pennock	240
45.	Frank Tanana	240
47.	Three Finger Brown	239
48.	Waite Hoyt	237
48.	Clark Griffith	237
50.	Whitey Ford	236
51.	Charlie Buffinton	233
52.	Dennis Martinez	231
53.	Luis Tiant	229
53.	Will White	229
53.	Sad Sam Jones	229
56.	George Mullin	228
57.	Jim Bunning	224
57.	Catfish Hunter	224
59.	Mel Harder	223
59.	Paul Derringer	223
61.	Hooks Dauss	222
61.	Jerry Koosman	222
63.	Joe Niekro	221
64.	Jerry Reuss	220
65.	Bob Caruthers	218
65.	Earl Whitehill	218
67.	Mickey Lolich	217
67.	Freddie Fitzsimmons	217
69.	Wilbur Cooper	216
69.	Charlie Hough	216
71.	Jim Perry	215
71.	Stan Coveleski	215
73.	Rick Reuschel	214
74.	Chief Bender	212
75.	Bob Welch	211
75.	Bobo Newsom	211
75.	Billy Pierce	211
78.	Jesse Haines	210
79.	Vida Blue	209
79.	Milt Pappas	209
79.	Don Drysdale	209
82.	Eddie Cicotte	208
83.	Bob Lemon	207
83.	Carl Mays	207
83.	Hal Newhouser	207
86.	Lew Burdette	203
86.	Jack Stivetts	203
88.	Al Orth	202
88.	Silver King	202
90.	Charlie Root	201
90.	Rube Marquard	201
92.	George Uhle	200

WINNING PERCENTAGE

1.	Bob Caruthers	.692
2.	Dave Foutz	.690
3.	Whitey Ford	.690
4.	Lefty Grove	.680
5.	Vic Raschi	.667
6.	Larry Corcoran	.665
7.	Christy Mathewson	.665
8.	Sam Leever	.658
9.	Sal Maglie	.657
10.	Sandy Koufax	.655
11.	Johnny Allen	.654
12.	Ron Guidry	.651
13.	Roger Clemens	.650
14.	Lefty Gomez	.649
15.	Three Finger Brown	.649
16.	Dwight Gooden	.649
17.	John Clarkson	.648
18.	Dizzy Dean	.644
19.	Grover Alexander	.642
20.	Deacon Phillippe	.639
21.	Jim Palmer	.638
22.	Kid Nichols	.634
23.	Joe McGinnity	.632
24.	Juan Marichal	.631
25.	Ed Reulbach	.631
26.	Mort Cooper	.631
27.	Allie Reynolds	.630
28.	Jesse Tannehill	.629
29.	Ray Kremer	.627
30.	Eddie Plank	.627
31.	Tommy Bond	.627
32.	Chief Bender	.625
33.	Don Newcombe	.623
34.	David Cone	.623
35.	Nig Cuppy	.623

EARNED RUN AVERAGE

1.	Ed Walsh	1.82
2.	Addie Joss	1.88
3.	Three Finger Brown	2.06
4.	Monte Ward	2.10
5.	Christy Mathewson	2.13
6.	Rube Waddell	2.16
7.	Walter Johnson	2.17
8.	Orval Overall	2.24
9.	Tommy Bond	2.25
10.	Will White	2.28
11.	Ed Reulbach	2.28
12.	Jim Scott	2.32
13.	Eddie Plank	2.34
14.	Larry Corcoran	2.36
15.	Eddie Cicotte	2.37
16.	George McQuillan	2.38
17.	Ed Killian	2.38
18.	Doc White	2.38
19.	Nap Rucker	2.42
20.	Jeff Tesreau	2.43
21.	Jim McCormick	2.43
22.	Terry Larkin	2.43
23.	Chief Bender	2.46
24.	Hooks Wiltse	2.47
25.	Sam Leever	2.47
26.	Lefty Leifield	2.47
27.	Hippo Vaughn	2.49
28.	Bob Ewing	2.49

GAMES

1.	Hoyt Wilhelm	1070
2.	Kent Tekulve	1050
3.	Goose Gossage	1002
4.	Lindy McDaniel	987
5.	Rollie Fingers	944
6.	Lee Smith	943
7.	Gene Garber	931
8.	Cy Young	906
9.	Dennis Eckersley	901
10.	Sparky Lyle	899
11.	Jim Kaat	898
12.	Jeff Reardon	880
13.	Don McMahon	874
14.	Phil Niekro	864
15.	Charlie Hough	858
16.	Roy Face	848
17.	Tug McGraw	824
18.	Jesse Orosco	819
19.	Nolan Ryan	807
20.	Walter Johnson	801
21.	Gaylord Perry	777
22.	Don Sutton	774
23.	Darold Knowles	765
24.	Tommy John	760
25.	Jack Quinn	755
26.	Ron Reed	751
27.	Warren Spahn	750
28.	Gary Lavelle	745
28.	Tom Burgmeier	745
30.	Guillermo Hernandez	744
31.	Steve Carlton	741
32.	Ron Perranoski	737
33.	Ron Kline	736
34.	Rick Honeycutt	734
35.	Steve Bedrosian	732
36.	Clay Carroll	731
37.	Mike Marshall	723
38.	Dave Righetti	718
39.	Johnny Klippstein	711
40.	Greg Minton	710
41.	Stu Miller	704
42.	Greg Harris	703
43.	Joe Niekro	702
44.	Bill Campbell	700
45.	Larry Andersen	699
46.	Bob McClure	698
47.	Pud Galvin	697
48.	Craig Lefferts	696
48.	Grover Alexander	696
50.	Bob Miller	694
51.	Eppa Rixey	692
51.	Bert Blyleven	692
51.	Grant Jackson	692
54.	Early Wynn	691
55.	Eddie Fisher	690
56.	Roger McDowell	682
57.	Ted Abernathy	681
58.	Robin Roberts	676
59.	Waite Hoyt	674
59.	Dan Quisenberry	674
61.	Red Faber	669
62.	Dave Giusti	668
63.	Ferguson Jenkins	664
64.	John Franco	661
64.	Bruce Sutter	661
66.	Tom Seaver	656
67.	Paul Lindblad	655
68.	Wilbur Wood	651
69.	Dave LaRoche	647
69.	Sad Sam Jones	647
71.	Tom Henke	642
72.	Gerry Staley	640
72.	Dutch Leonard	640
74.	Dennis Lamp	639
74.	Diego Segui	639
76.	Frank Tanana	638
77.	Bob Stanley	637
78.	Christy Mathewson	635
79.	Charlie Root	632
80.	Jim Perry	630
81.	Jerry Reuss	628
82.	Lew Burdette	626
83.	Murry Dickson	625
83.	Woodie Fryman	625
85.	Red Ruffing	624
86.	Eddie Plank	623
87.	Paul Assenmacher	622
88.	Kid Nichols	620
88.	Dick Tidrow	620
90.	Danny Darwin	618
91.	Herb Pennock	617
91.	Burleigh Grimes	617
93.	Lefty Grove	616
94.	Terry Forster	614
95.	Jerry Koosman	612
95.	Mitch Williams	612
97.	Dennis Martinez	610
98.	Dave Smith	609
99.	Mark Davis	605
100.	Bob Friend	602
100.	Al Worthington	602
102.	Elias Sosa	601
103.	Tim Keefe	600
103.	Bobo Newsom	600
103.	John Candelaria	600
106.	Rob Murphy	597
107.	Ted Lyons	594
108.	Pedro Borbon	593
109.	Jim Bunning	591
110.	Dick Farrell	590
111.	Moe Drabowsky	589
112.	Mickey Lolich	586
113.	Billy Pierce	585
114.	Doug Bair	584
114.	Jim Brewer	584
116.	Mel Harder	582
116.	Pedro Ramos	582
118.	Paul Derringer	579
119.	Jack Powell	578
120.	Bob Locker	576
121.	Stan Bahnsen	574
122.	Luis Tiant	573
123.	Mudcat Grant	571
124.	Bob Feller	570
124.	Larry French	570
126.	Curt Simmons	569
127.	Jay Howell	568
128.	Ted Power	564
128.	Mickey Welch	564
130.	Ray Sadecki	563
131.	Doyle Alexander	561
132.	Jim Palmer	558
132.	Larry Jackson	558
134.	Jack Russell	557
134.	Rick Reuschel	557
136.	Dan Spillner	556
137.	Jesse Haines	555
137.	Tony Mullane	555
139.	Jim Gott	554
140.	Phil Regan	551
140.	Firpo Marberry	551
142.	Dolf Luque	550
142.	Mike Jackson	550
144.	Jack Morris	549
145.	Tippy Martinez	546
146.	John Hiller	545
146.	Al Hrabosky	545
148.	Rube Walberg	544
149.	Tom Hume	543
149.	Juan Agosto	543
149.	Randy Myers	543
152.	Guy Bush	542
152.	Syl Johnson	542
154.	Claude Osteen	541
154.	Earl Whitehill	541
156.	Mark Eichhorn	539
157.	Hooks Dauss	538
157.	Gus Weyhing	538
159.	Bobby Shantz	537
160.	Rube Marquard	536

INDIVIDUAL PITCHING (LIFETIME), *cont.*

161.	Rudy May	535
161.	Carl Hubbell	535
163.	Dan Plesac	534
163.	Jeff Russell	534
163.	Randy Moffitt	534
166.	Red Ames	533
166.	Tom Zachary	533
168.	John Clarkson	531
169.	Camilo Pascual	529
170.	Bob Gibson	528
170.	Bump Hadley	528
170.	Old Hoss Radbourn	528
173.	Bill Henry	527
174.	Doug Jones	526
174.	Joe Nuxhall	526
174.	Mike Flanagan	526
177.	Don Robinson	524
178.	Dave Stewart	523
179.	Ken Forsch	521
179.	Dizzy Trout	521
181.	Milt Pappas	520
182.	Gary Bell	519
182.	Dick Drago	519
184.	Dale Murray	518
184.	Don Drysdale	518
186.	Wilbur Cooper	517
186.	Virgil Trucks	517
188.	Frank Linzy	516
189.	Frank DiPino	514
189.	Bill Sherdel	514
191.	Vic Willis	513
191.	Clem Labine	513
191.	George Uhle	513
191.	Freddie Fitzsimmons	513
195.	Mike Henneman	512
196.	Steve Farr	509
197.	Harry Gumbert	508
198.	Bob Welch	506
198.	Rick Wise	506
200.	Billy Hoeft	505
201.	Turk Lown	504
201.	Dan Schatzeder	504
203.	Joe Boever	503
204.	Vida Blue	502
204.	Eddie Cicotte	502
206.	Chris Short	501
207.	Eddie Rommel	500
207.	Catfish Hunter	500

COMPLETE GAMES

1.	Cy Young	750
2.	Pud Galvin	639
3.	Tim Keefe	557
4.	Kid Nichols	533
5.	Walter Johnson	531
6.	Mickey Welch	525
7.	Old Hoss Radbourn	489
8.	John Clarkson	485
9.	Tony Mullane	468
10.	Jim McCormick	466
11.	Gus Weyhing	448
12.	Grover Alexander	438
13.	Christy Mathewson	435
14.	Jack Powell	422
15.	Eddie Plank	412
16.	Will White	394
17.	Amos Rusie	392
18.	Vic Willis	388
19.	Warren Spahn	382
20.	Jim Whitney	377
21.	Adonis Terry	368
22.	Ted Lyons	356
23.	George Mullin	353
24.	Charlie Buffinton	351
25.	Chick Fraser	342
26.	Clark Griffith	337
27.	Red Ruffing	335
28.	Silver King	329
29.	Al Orth	324
30.	Bill Hutchinson	321
31.	Guy Hecker	314
31.	Joe McGinnity	314
31.	Burleigh Grimes	314
34.	Red Donahue	312
35.	Bill Dinneen	306
36.	Robin Roberts	305
37.	Gaylord Perry	303
38.	Lefty Grove	300
38.	Ted Breitenstein	300

INNINGS PITCHED

1.	Cy Young	7356
2.	Pud Galvin	5941
3.	Walter Johnson	5924
4.	Phil Niekro	5403
5.	Nolan Ryan	5387
6.	Gaylord Perry	5351
7.	Don Sutton	5280
8.	Warren Spahn	5244
9.	Steve Carlton	5217
10.	Grover Alexander	5190
11.	Kid Nichols	5070
12.	Tim Keefe	5061
13.	Bert Blyleven	4970
14.	Mickey Welch	4802
15.	Tom Seaver	4783
16.	Christy Mathewson	4782
17.	Tommy John	4708
18.	Robin Roberts	4689
19.	Early Wynn	4564
20.	John Clarkson	4536
21.	Old Hoss Radbourn	4535
22.	Tony Mullane	4531
23.	Jim Kaat	4528
24.	Eddie Plank	4506
25.	Ferguson Jenkins	4500
26.	Eppa Rixey	4495
27.	Jack Powell	4388
28.	Red Ruffing	4344
29.	Gus Weyhing	4324
30.	Jim McCormick	4276
31.	Frank Tanana	4188
32.	Burleigh Grimes	4180
33.	Ted Lyons	4161
34.	Red Faber	4088
35.	Vic Willis	3996
36.	Jim Palmer	3948
37.	Lefty Grove	3941
38.	Jack Quinn	3935
39.	Bob Gibson	3885
40.	Sad Sam Jones	3883
41.	Jerry Koosman	3839
42.	Bob Feller	3827
43.	Jack Morris	3825
44.	Charlie Hough	3799
45.	Amos Rusie	3770
46.	Waite Hoyt	3763
47.	Jim Bunning	3760
48.	Bobo Newsom	3759
49.	Dennis Martinez	3748
50.	George Mullin	3687
51.	Jerry Reuss	3669
52.	Paul Derringer	3645
53.	Mickey Lolich	3639
54.	Bob Friend	3611
55.	Carl Hubbell	3589
56.	Joe Niekro	3585
57.	Earl Whitehill	3566
58.	Herb Pennock	3558
59.	Rick Reuschel	3550
60.	Will White	3543
61.	Adonis Terry	3523
62.	Juan Marichal	3509

STRIKEOUTS

1.	Nolan Ryan	5714
2.	Steve Carlton	4136
3.	Bert Blyleven	3701
4.	Tom Seaver	3640
5.	Don Sutton	3574
6.	Gaylord Perry	3534
7.	Walter Johnson	3508
8.	Phil Niekro	3342
9.	Ferguson Jenkins	3192
10.	Bob Gibson	3117
11.	Jim Bunning	2855
12.	Mickey Lolich	2832
13.	Cy Young	2803
14.	Frank Tanana	2773
15.	Warren Spahn	2583
16.	Bob Feller	2581
17.	Jerry Koosman	2556
18.	Tim Keefe	2527
19.	Christy Mathewson	2502
20.	Don Drysdale	2486
21.	Jack Morris	2478
22.	Jim Kaat	2461
23.	Sam McDowell	2453
24.	Luis Tiant	2416
25.	Sandy Koufax	2396
26.	Charlie Hough	2363
27.	Robin Roberts	2357
28.	Early Wynn	2334
29.	Roger Clemens	2333
30.	Rube Waddell	2316
31.	Juan Marichal	2303
32.	Dennis Eckersley	2285
33.	Lefty Grove	2266
34.	Mark Langston	2252
35.	Eddie Plank	2246
36.	Tommy John	2245
37.	Jim Palmer	2212
38.	Grover Alexander	2199
39.	Vida Blue	2175
40.	Camilo Pascual	2167
41.	Bobo Newsom	2082
42.	Dazzy Vance	2045
43.	Dennis Martinez	2022
44.	Rick Reuschel	2015
45.	Catfish Hunter	2012
46.	Billy Pierce	1999
47.	Red Ruffing	1987
48.	John Clarkson	1978
49.	Bob Welch	1969
50.	Whitey Ford	1956
51.	Amos Rusie	1934
52.	Fernando Valenzuela	1918
53.	Jerry Reuss	1907
54.	Kid Nichols	1877
55.	Dwight Gooden	1875
56.	Mickey Welch	1850
57.	Old Hoss Radbourn	1830
58.	Frank Viola	1826
59.	Tony Mullane	1803
60.	Pud Galvin	1799
61.	Hal Newhouser	1796
62.	Ron Guidry	1778
63.	Rudy May	1760
64.	Joe Niekro	1747
65.	David Cone	1741
65.	Dave Stewart	1741
67.	Ed Walsh	1736
68.	Bob Friend	1734
69.	Joe Coleman	1728
69.	Milt Pappas	1728
71.	Floyd Bannister	1723
72.	Chief Bender	1711
73.	Larry Jackson	1709
74.	Jim McCormick	1704
75.	Bob Veale	1703
76.	Red Ames	1702
77.	Charlie Buffinton	1700
78.	Curt Simmons	1697
79.	Bruce Hurst	1689
80.	Rick Sutcliffe	1679
81.	Carl Hubbell	1678
82.	Tommy Bridges	1674
83.	Danny Darwin	1673
83.	John Candelaria	1673
85.	Mike Moore	1667
86.	Gus Weyhing	1665
87.	Sid Fernandez	1663
88.	Vic Willis	1651
89.	Rick Wise	1647
90.	Dave Stieb	1642
91.	Al Downing	1639
92.	Mike Cuellar	1632
93.	Kevin Gross	1629
93.	Chris Short	1629
95.	Andy Messersmith	1625
96.	Randy Johnson	1624
97.	Jack Powell	1621
97.	Steve Rogers	1621
99.	Ray Sadecki	1614
100.	Claude Osteen	1612
101.	Hoyt Wilhelm	1610
102.	Jim Maloney	1605
103.	Scott Sanderson	1604
104.	Ken Holtzman	1601
105.	Jose DeLeon	1594
106.	Rube Marquard	1593
107.	Ron Darling	1590
108.	Woodie Fryman	1587
109.	Jim Perry	1576
110.	Harvey Haddix	1575
111.	Jim Whitney	1571
112.	Jose Rijo	1556
113.	Adonis Terry	1555
114.	Orel Hershiser	1554
115.	Wild Bill Donovan	1552
116.	Dean Chance	1534
116.	Virgil Trucks	1534
118.	Doyle Alexander	1528
119.	Juan Pizarro	1522
120.	Jon Matlack	1516
121.	Toad Ramsey	1515
121.	Bill Singer	1515
123.	Dave McNally	1512
123.	Sonny Siebert	1512
123.	Burleigh Grimes	1512
126.	Bret Saberhagen	1510
127.	Paul Derringer	1507
128.	Goose Gossage	1502

STRIKEOUTS PER 9 INNINGS

1.	Nolan Ryan	9.55
2.	Sandy Koufax	9.28
3.	Sam McDowell	8.86
4.	J. R. Richard	8.37
5.	Sid Fernandez	8.32
6.	Roger Clemens	8.29
7.	David Cone	8.15
8.	Bob Veale	7.96
9.	Jose Rijo	7.84
10.	Jim Maloney	7.81
11.	Dwight Gooden	7.78
12.	Bobby Witt	7.72
13.	Mark Langston	7.65
14.	Jose DeLeon	7.56
15.	Mario Soto	7.54
16.	Sam Jones	7.54
17.	Goose Gossage	7.47
18.	John Smoltz	7.27
19.	Bob Gibson	7.22
20.	Steve Carlton	7.14
21.	Rube Waddell	7.04
22.	Mickey Lolich	7.00
23.	Rollie Fingers	6.87
24.	Tom Seaver	6.85
25.	Jim Bunning	6.83
26.	Juan Pizarro	6.73
27.	Bobby Bolin	6.71
28.	Chuck Finley	6.71
29.	Bert Blyleven	6.70
30.	Ray Culp	6.69
31.	Ron Guidry	6.69
32.	Stan Williams	6.66
33.	Camilo Pascual	6.66
34.	Bob Turley	6.65
35.	Don Wilson	6.60

INDIVIDUAL PITCHING (LIFETIME), *cont.*

SHUTOUTS

1.	Walter Johnson	110
2.	Grover Alexander	90
3.	Christy Mathewson	80
4.	Cy Young	76
5.	Eddie Plank	69
6.	Warren Spahn	63
7.	Nolan Ryan	61
7.	Tom Seaver	61
9.	Bert Blyleven	60
10.	Don Sutton	58
11.	Ed Walsh	57
11.	Pud Galvin	57
13.	Bob Gibson	56
13.	Three Finger Brown	56
15.	Steve Carlton	55
16.	Jim Palmer	53
16.	Gaylord Perry	53
18.	Juan Marichal	52
19.	Vic Willis	50
19.	Rube Waddell	50
21.	Luis Tiant	49
21.	Early Wynn	49
21.	Don Drysdale	49
21.	Ferguson Jenkins	49
25.	Kid Nichols	48
25.	Red Ruffing	48
27.	Babe Adams	47
27.	Jack Powell	47
29.	Doc White	46
29.	Bob Feller	46
29.	Tommy John	46
29.	Addie Joss	46
33.	Whitey Ford	45
33.	Phil Niekro	45
33.	Robin Roberts	45
36.	Milt Pappas	43
37.	Bucky Walters	42
37.	Catfish Hunter	42
39.	Chief Bender	41
39.	Hippo Vaughn	41
39.	Mickey Welch	41
39.	Mickey Lolich	41
43.	Tim Keefe	40
43.	Jim Bunning	40
43.	Ed Reulbach	40
43.	Larry French	40
43.	Sandy Koufax	40
43.	Claude Osteen	40
43.	Mel Stottlemyre	40
50.	Sam Leever	39
50.	Eppa Rixey	39
50.	Jerry Reuss	39
53.	Nap Rucker	38
53.	Billy Pierce	38
53.	Stan Coveleski	38
56.	Vida Blue	37
56.	Steve Rogers	37
56.	John Clarkson	37
56.	Larry Jackson	37
60.	Bill Doak	36
60.	Bob Friend	36
60.	Will White	36
60.	Mike Cuellar	36
60.	Carl Hubbell	36
60.	Curt Simmons	36
60.	Roger Clemens	36
60.	Wilbur Cooper	36
60.	Sad Sam Jones	36
60.	Camilo Pascual	36
60.	Allie Reynolds	36
71.	Joe Bush	35
71.	Tommy Bond	35
71.	Jack Coombs	35
71.	Lefty Grove	35
71.	Jack Chesbro	35
71.	Herb Pennock	35
71.	Eddie Cicotte	35
71.	George Mullin	35
71.	Virgil Trucks	35
71.	Burleigh Grimes	35
71.	Wild Bill Donovan	35
71.	Old Hoss Radbourn	35
83.	Earl Moore	34
83.	Frank Tanana	34
83.	Jesse Tannehill	34
86.	Dean Chance	33
86.	Mort Cooper	33
86.	Bob Shawkey	33
86.	Lew Burdette	33
86.	Dave McNally	33
86.	Tommy Bridges	33
86.	Jerry Koosman	33
86.	Dutch Leonard	33
86.	Jim McCormick	33
86.	Hal Newhouser	33
96.	Jim Perry	32
96.	Lefty Tyler	32
96.	Joe McGinnity	32
96.	Paul Derringer	32
96.	Lefty Leifield	32
101.	Al Orth	31
101.	Jim Kaat	31
101.	Bob Lemon	31
101.	Bobo Newsom	31
101.	Lon Warneke	31
101.	Ken Holtzman	31
101.	Charlie Buffinton	31
101.	Ken Raffensberger	31
101.	Fernando Valenzuela	31
110.	Art Nehf	30
110.	Red Faber	30
110.	Rick Wise	30
110.	Amos Rusie	30
110.	Dave Stieb	30
110.	Bob Knepper	30
110.	Jim Maloney	30
110.	Jon Matlack	30
110.	Dazzy Vance	30
110.	Tony Mullane	30
110.	Dutch Leonard	30
110.	Rube Marquard	30
110.	Orval Overall	30
110.	Johnny Vander Meer	30

HITS PER 9 INNINGS

1.	Nolan Ryan	6.55
2.	Sandy Koufax	6.79
3.	Sid Fernandez	6.84
4.	J. R. Richard	6.88
5.	Andy Messersmith	6.94
6.	Hoyt Wilhelm	7.02
7.	Sam McDowell	7.03
8.	Ed Walsh	7.12
9.	Bob Turley	7.18
10.	Orval Overall	7.22
11.	Jeff Tesreau	7.24
12.	Ed Reulbach	7.24
13.	Mario Soto	7.26
14.	Addie Joss	7.30
15.	Jose DeLeon	7.38
16.	Jim Maloney	7.39
17.	David Cone	7.44
18.	Goose Gossage	7.45
19.	Tom Seaver	7.47
20.	Walter Johnson	7.48
21.	Rube Waddell	7.48
22.	Bob Gibson	7.60
23.	Roger Clemens	7.61
24.	Don Wilson	7.61
25.	Jim Palmer	7.63
26.	Larry Cheney	7.68
27.	Three Finger Brown	7.68
28.	Sam Jones	7.68
29.	Bob Feller	7.69
30.	Johnny Vander Meer	7.69
31.	Catfish Hunter	7.72
32.	Al Downing	7.72
33.	Charlie Hough	7.78
34.	Bobby Bolin	7.79
34.	Stan Williams	7.79

BASES ON BALLS

1.	Nolan Ryan	2795
2.	Steve Carlton	1833
3.	Phil Niekro	1809
4.	Early Wynn	1775
5.	Bob Feller	1764
6.	Bobo Newsom	1732
7.	Amos Rusie	1704
8.	Charlie Hough	1665
9.	Gus Weyhing	1566
10.	Red Ruffing	1541
11.	Bump Hadley	1442
12.	Warren Spahn	1434
13.	Earl Whitehill	1431
14.	Tony Mullane	1408
15.	Sad Sam Jones	1396
16.	Tom Seaver	1390
16.	Jack Morris	1390
18.	Gaylord Perry	1379
19.	Mike Torrez	1371
20.	Walter Johnson	1355
21.	Don Sutton	1343
22.	Bob Gibson	1336
23.	Chick Fraser	1332
24.	Bert Blyleven	1322
25.	Sam McDowell	1312
26.	Jim Palmer	1311
27.	Mark Baldwin	1307
28.	Adonis Terry	1301
29.	Mickey Welch	1297
30.	Burleigh Grimes	1295
31.	Kid Nichols	1272
32.	Joe Bush	1263
33.	Joe Niekro	1262
34.	Allie Reynolds	1261
35.	Tommy John	1259

BASES ON BALLS PER 9 INNINGS

1.	Tommy Bond	.58
2.	George Bradley	.67
3.	Terry Larkin	.71
4.	Monte Ward	.92
5.	Fred Goldsmith	.96
6.	Jim Whitney	1.06
7.	Bobby Mathews	1.11
8.	Pud Galvin	1.13
9.	Deacon Phillippe	1.25
10.	Will White	1.26
11.	Babe Adams	1.29
12.	Jack Lynch	1.39
13.	Addie Joss	1.43
14.	Cy Young	1.49
15.	Guy Hecker	1.51
16.	Lee Richmond	1.53
17.	Jesse Tannehill	1.56
18.	Jim McCormick	1.58
19.	Christy Mathewson	1.59
20.	Red Lucas	1.61
21.	Nick Altrock	1.62
22.	Grover Alexander	1.65
23.	Jumbo McGinnis	1.65
24.	Ernie Bonham	1.67
25.	Ed Morris	1.67
26.	Noodles Hahn	1.69
27.	Bret Saberhagen	1.70
28.	Charlie Ferguson	1.72
29.	Fritz Peterson	1.73
30.	Robin Roberts	1.73
31.	Old Hoss Radbourn	1.74
32.	Dick Rudolph	1.77
33.	Al Orth	1.77
34.	Stump Wiedman	1.78
35.	Pete Donohue	1.80

LOSSES

1.	Cy Young	316
2.	Pud Galvin	308
3.	Nolan Ryan	292
4.	Walter Johnson	279
5.	Phil Niekro	274
6.	Gaylord Perry	265
7.	Jack Powell	257
8.	Don Sutton	256
9.	Eppa Rixey	251
10.	Bert Blyleven	250
11.	Warren Spahn	245
11.	Robin Roberts	245
13.	Early Wynn	244
13.	Steve Carlton	244
15.	Jim Kaat	237
16.	Frank Tanana	236
17.	Gus Weyhing	233
18.	Tommy John	231
19.	Ted Lyons	230
19.	Bob Friend	230
21.	Ferguson Jenkins	226
22.	Tim Keefe	225
22.	Red Ruffing	225
24.	Bobo Newsom	222
25.	Tony Mullane	220
26.	Jack Quinn	217
26.	Sad Sam Jones	217
28.	Charlie Hough	216
29.	Chick Fraser	214
30.	Red Faber	213
30.	Jim McCormick	213
32.	Paul Derringer	212
32.	Burleigh Grimes	212
34.	Mickey Welch	209
34.	Jerry Koosman	209

RELIEF WINS

1.	Hoyt Wilhelm	124
2.	Lindy McDaniel	119
3.	Goose Gossage	115
4.	Rollie Fingers	107
5.	Sparky Lyle	99
6.	Roy Face	96
7.	Gene Garber	94
7.	Kent Tekulve	94
9.	Mike Marshall	92
10.	Don McMahon	90
11.	Tug McGraw	89
12.	Clay Carroll	88
13.	Bob Stanley	85
14.	Gary Lavelle	80
14.	Bill Campbell	80
16.	Stu Miller	79
16.	Tom Burgmeier	79
16.	Ron Perranoski	79
19.	Jeff Reardon	73
19.	Johnny Murphy	73
21.	John Hiller	72
22.	Dick Hall	71
22.	Mark Clear	71
22.	Jesse Orosco	71
25.	Guillermo Hernandez	70
26.	Pedro Borbon	69
26.	Roger McDowell	69
28.	Lee Smith	68
28.	John Franco	68
28.	Bruce Sutter	68
31.	Steve Bedrosian	65
32.	Al Hrabosky	64
33.	Clem Labine	63
33.	Darold Knowles	63
35.	Jim Brewer	62
35.	Frank Linzy	62
35.	Dick Farrell	62
35.	Eddie Fisher	62
35.	Dave LaRoche	62
35.	Grant Jackson	62
35.	Paul Lindblad	62
42.	Joe Heving	60

INDIVIDUAL PITCHING (LIFETIME), *cont.*

43.	Elias Sosa	59
43.	Johnny Klippstein	59
45.	Phil Regan	58
45.	Aurelio Lopez	58
47.	Mace Brown	57
47.	Bob Locker	57
47.	Ted Abernathy	57
47.	Mike Henneman	57
51.	Greg Minton	56
51.	Gerry Staley	56
51.	Dan Quisenberry	56
54.	Dave Giusti	55
54.	Tippy Martinez	55
56.	Ron Reed	54
56.	Ron Kline	54
56.	Jack Quinn	54
56.	Al Worthington	54
60.	Doug Bair	53
60.	Dave Smith	53
60.	Dale Murray	53
60.	Firpo Marberry	53
64.	Jay Howell	52
64.	Ed Roebuck	52
64.	Dick Radatz	52
64.	Sammy Stewart	52
68.	Hugh Casey	51
68.	Eddie Rommel	51
68.	Jim Konstanty	51
71.	Jim Kern	50
71.	Dick Tidrow	50
71.	Jeff Parrett	50

RELIEF WINNING PERCENTAGE

1.	Hugh Casey	.708
2.	Guy Bush	.683
3.	Doug Bird	.677
4.	Grant Jackson	.653
5.	Pedro Borbon	.651
6.	Mace Brown	.648
7.	Al Hrabosky	.646
8.	Eddie Rommel	.646
9.	Al Brazle	.641
10.	Danny Darwin	.636
11.	Hooks Dauss	.635
12.	Johnny Murphy	.635
13.	Ed Roebuck	.634
14.	Dick Hall	.634
15.	Joe Heving	.632
15.	Eric Plunk	.632
17.	Aurelio Lopez	.630
18.	Mark Williamson	.625
19.	Clyde Shoun	.621
20.	Mike Henneman	.620
21.	Charlie Root	.618
22.	Juan Berenguer	.615
23.	Harry Gumbert	.611
24.	Jack Quinn	.607
25.	Tom Burgmeier	.598
26.	Dave Giusti	.598
27.	Sammy Stewart	.598
28.	Dennis Eckersley	.597
29.	Mark Clear	.597
30.	Johnny Klippstein	.596
31.	Ellis Kinder	.595
32.	Bob Locker	.594
33.	Jim Konstanty	.593
34.	Tim Burke	.593
35.	Phil Regan	.592

SAVES

1.	Lee Smith	471
2.	Jeff Reardon	367
3.	Rollie Fingers	341
4.	Dennis Eckersley	323
5.	Tom Henke	311
6.	Goose Gossage	310
7.	Bruce Sutter	300
8.	John Franco	295
9.	Dave Righetti	252
10.	Dan Quisenberry	244
11.	Randy Myers	243
12.	Doug Jones	239
13.	Sparky Lyle	238
14.	Hoyt Wilhelm	227
15.	Gene Garber	218
15.	Jeff Montgomery	218
17.	Dave Smith	216
18.	Rick Aguilera	211
19.	Bobby Thigpen	201
20.	Roy Face	193
21.	Mitch Williams	192
22.	Mike Marshall	188
23.	Kent Tekulve	184
23.	Steve Bedrosian	184
25.	Jeff Russell	183
26.	Tug McGraw	180
27.	Ron Perranoski	179
28.	Bryan Harvey	177
28.	Todd Worrell	177
30.	Lindy McDaniel	172
31.	Gregg Olson	164
32.	Mike Henneman	162
33.	Jay Howell	155
33.	Roger McDowell	155
35.	Stu Miller	154
36.	Don McMahon	153
37.	Greg Minton	150
38.	Ted Abernathy	148
39.	Guillermo Hernandez	147
40.	Dave Giusti	145
41.	Clay Carroll	143
41.	Darold Knowles	143
43.	Dan Plesac	137
43.	John Wetteland	137
45.	Gary Lavelle	136
46.	Jesse Orosco	133
47.	Jim Brewer	132
47.	Steve Farr	132
47.	Bob Stanley	132
50.	Ron Davis	130
51.	Rod Beck	127
51.	Terry Forster	127
53.	Dave LaRoche	126
53.	Bill Campbell	126
55.	John Hiller	125
56.	Jack Aker	123
57.	Dick Radatz	122
58.	Duane Ward	121
59.	Tippy Martinez	115
60.	Frank Linzy	111
61.	Al Worthington	110
62.	Fred Gladding	109
63.	Ron Kline	108
63.	Wayne Granger	108
65.	Johnny Murphy	107
66.	Bill Caudill	106
67.	Ron Reed	103
67.	John Wyatt	103
69.	Tim Burke	102
69.	Ellis Kinder	102
69.	Tom Burgmeier	102
72.	Craig Lefferts	101
72.	Firpo Marberry	101
74.	Joe Hoerner	99
75.	Mike Schooler	98
76.	Al Hrabosky	97
76.	Tom Niedenfuer	97
78.	Mark Davis	96
78.	Clem Labine	96
78.	Randy Moffitt	96
78.	Roberto Hernandez	96
82.	Bob Locker	95
83.	Aurelio Lopez	93
84.	Tom Hume	92
84.	Phil Regan	92
86.	Jim Gott	91
87.	Bill Henry	90
87.	Steve Howe	90
89.	Rob Dibble	89
89.	Donnie Moore	89
91.	Jim Kern	88
92.	Ken Sanders	86
92.	Cecil Upshaw	86
94.	Jeff Brantley	85
95.	Joe Sambito	84
96.	Mark Clear	83
96.	Elias Sosa	83
96.	Dick Farrell	83
96.	Claude Raymond	83
100.	Don Aase	82
100.	Larry Sherry	82
102.	Doug Bair	81
102.	Eddie Fisher	81
104.	Eddie Watt	80
104.	Pedro Borbon	80
106.	Grant Jackson	79
107.	Al Holland	78
108.	Joe Page	76
108.	Tim Stoddard	76
110.	Ed Farmer	75
110.	Neil Allen	75

WINS PLUS SAVES

1.	Lee Smith	539
2.	Rollie Fingers	448
3.	Jeff Reardon	440
4.	Goose Gossage	425
5.	Bruce Sutter	368
6.	Dennis Eckersley	366
7.	John Franco	363
8.	Tom Henke	352
9.	Hoyt Wilhelm	351
10.	Sparky Lyle	337
11.	Gene Garber	312
12.	Dan Quisenberry	300
13.	Dave Righetti	298
14.	Lindy McDaniel	291
15.	Roy Face	289
16.	Mike Marshall	280
17.	Doug Jones	279
18.	Kent Tekulve	278
19.	Randy Myers	275
20.	Tug McGraw	269
20.	Dave Smith	269
22.	Ron Perranoski	258
23.	Jeff Montgomery	256
24.	Steve Bedrosian	249
25.	Don McMahon	243
26.	Rick Aguilera	238
27.	Mitch Williams	237
28.	Stu Miller	233
29.	Bobby Thigpen	232
30.	Clay Carroll	231
31.	Roger McDowell	224
32.	Todd Worrell	221
33.	Mike Henneman	219
34.	Bob Stanley	217
34.	Guillermo Hernandez	217
36.	Gary Lavelle	216
37.	Jeff Russell	214
38.	Jay Howell	207
39.	Greg Minton	206
39.	Bill Campbell	206
39.	Darold Knowles	206
42.	Ted Abernathy	205
43.	Jesse Orosco	204
44.	Dave Giusti	200
45.	John Hiller	197
46.	Jim Brewer	194
46.	Bryan Harvey	194
48.	Dave LaRoche	188
49.	Gregg Olson	184
50.	Tom Burgmeier	181
51.	Johnny Murphy	180
52.	Ron Davis	177
53.	Dick Radatz	174
53.	Terry Forster	174
55.	Frank Linzy	173
56.	Dan Plesac	171
57.	Jack Aker	170
57.	Steve Farr	170
57.	Tippy Martinez	170
60.	Al Worthington	164
61.	Ron Kline	162
62.	Al Hrabosky	161
62.	John Wetteland	161
64.	Clem Labine	159
65.	Ron Reed	157
65.	Fred Gladding	157
67.	Mark Clear	154
67.	Firpo Marberry	154
69.	Duane Ward	153
70.	Bob Locker	152
71.	Aurelio Lopez	151
72.	Tim Burke	150
72.	Phil Regan	150
74.	Pedro Borbon	149
75.	Ellis Kinder	146
76.	Dick Farrell	145
77.	Eddie Fisher	143
77.	Wayne Granger	143
77.	Craig Lefferts	143
80.	Elias Sosa	142
80.	John Wyatt	142
82.	Rod Beck	141
82.	Grant Jackson	141
84.	Bill Caudill	140
85.	Dick Hall	139
85.	Randy Moffitt	139
87.	Jim Kern	138
87.	Joe Hoerner	138
89.	Steve Howe	137
90.	Doug Bair	134
91.	Tom Hume	133
91.	Tom Niedenfuer	133
93.	Donnie Moore	132
94.	Mark Davis	130
95.	Larry Sherry	129
96.	Paul Lindblad	126
97.	Jim Konstanty	125
97.	Claude Raymond	125
97.	Johnny Klippstein	125

RELIEF GAMES

1.	Kent Tekulve	1050
2.	Hoyt Wilhelm	1018
3.	Goose Gossage	965
4.	Lee Smith	937
5.	Gene Garber	922
6.	Lindy McDaniel	913
7.	Rollie Fingers	907
8.	Sparky Lyle	899
9.	Jeff Reardon	880
10.	Don McMahon	872
11.	Roy Face	821
12.	Jesse Orosco	815
13.	Tug McGraw	785
14.	Darold Knowles	757
15.	Gary Lavelle	742
15.	Tom Burgmeier	742
17.	Ron Perranoski	736
18.	Guillermo Hernandez	733
19.	Greg Minton	703
19.	Clay Carroll	703
21.	Mike Marshall	699
22.	Larry Andersen	698
23.	Bill Campbell	691
24.	Steve Bedrosian	686
25.	Roger McDowell	680
26.	Dan Quisenberry	674
27.	John Franco	661
27.	Bruce Sutter	661
29.	Craig Lefferts	651
30.	Ted Abernathy	647
31.	Tom Henke	642
32.	Dave LaRoche	632
33.	Dave Righetti	629
34.	Eddie Fisher	627
35.	Bob McClure	625

INDIVIDUAL PITCHING (LIFETIME), *cont.*

36.	Paul Lindblad	623
37.	Paul Assenmacher	621
38.	Stu Miller	611
39.	Grant Jackson	609
39.	Mitch Williams	609
41.	Dave Smith	608
42.	Greg Harris	605
43.	Elias Sosa	598
44.	Rob Murphy	597
45.	Bob Miller	595
46.	Pedro Borbon	589
47.	Doug Bair	579
48.	Bob Locker	576
49.	Terry Forster	575
50.	Bob Stanley	552
51.	Jim Brewer	549
51.	Johnny Klippstein	549
53.	Jay Howell	547
54.	Al Hrabosky	544
54.	Tippy Martinez	544
56.	Mike Jackson	543
57.	Juan Agosto	541
58.	Dennis Eckersley	540
59.	Dave Giusti	535
60.	Ron Kline	533
60.	Randy Moffitt	533
60.	Al Worthington	533
63.	Mark Eichhorn	532
64.	Randy Myers	531
65.	Doug Jones	522
66.	Mark Davis	520
66.	Dan Plesac	520
68.	Dale Murray	517
69.	Ron Reed	515
70.	Frank Linzy	514
71.	Mike Henneman	512
72.	Frank DiPino	508
73.	Joe Boever	503
74.	John Hiller	502
75.	Tim Burke	496
76.	Jack Aker	495
77.	Joe Hoerner	493
78.	Jeff Montgomery	491
79.	Tom Hume	488
80.	Tim Stoddard	485
81.	Tom Niedenfuer	484
82.	Bill Henry	483
83.	Dick Tidrow	482
84.	Ron Davis	481
84.	Steve Farr	481
86.	Mark Clear	480
86.	Todd Worrell	480
88.	Ted Power	479
89.	Dennis Lamp	476
90.	Clem Labine	475
91.	Ron Taylor	474
92.	Steve Howe	472
93.	Diego Segui	468
94.	Rick Honeycutt	466
95.	Duane Ward	460
96.	Ed Roebuck	459
97.	Jim Gott	458
98.	Jack Baldschun	457
99.	Joe Sambito	456
99.	Dick Farrell	456
101.	Turk Lown	455
101.	Jeff Russell	455
103.	Gerry Staley	454
104.	Wayne Granger	451
105.	Aurelio Lopez	450
106.	Fred Gladding	449
107.	Bobby Thigpen	448
108.	Phil Regan	446
109.	Chuck Crim	443
110.	Claude Raymond	442
111.	Jim Acker	435
111.	Don Elston	435
111.	Moe Drabowsky	435
114.	Dan Spillner	433
115.	Eric Plunk	431
116.	Jeff Parrett	429
117.	Alejandro Pena	427
118.	John Wyatt	426
119.	Gene Nelson	425
120.	Dick Hall	421
120.	Bill Caudill	421
122.	Sid Monge	418
122.	Charlie Hough	418
124.	George Frazier	415
125.	Edwin Nunez	413
126.	Donnie Moore	412
127.	Dave Tomlin	408
128.	Ken Sanders	407
129.	Steve Hamilton	404
130.	Jim Kern	402
131.	Larry Sherry	400

INDIVIDUAL FIELDING (LIFETIME)

GAMES

1B	1.	Eddie Murray	2412
	2.	Jake Beckley	2377
	3.	Mickey Vernon	2237
	4.	Lou Gehrig	2136
	5.	Charlie Grimm	2129
	6.	Joe Judge	2084
	7.	Ed Konetchy	2071
	8.	Steve Garvey	2061
	9.	Cap Anson	2058
	10.	Joe Kuhel	2057
	11.	Willie McCovey	2045
	12.	Keith Hernandez	2014
	13.	Jake Daubert	2001
	14.	Stuffy McInnis	1995
	15.	George Sisler	1970
2B	1.	Eddie Collins	2650
	2.	Joe Morgan	2527
	3.	Lou Whitaker	2308
	4.	Nellie Fox	2295
	5.	Charlie Gehringer	2206
	6.	Willie Randolph	2152
	7.	Frank White	2150
	8.	Bid McPhee	2125
	9.	Bill Mazeroski	2094
	10.	Nap Lajoie	2036
	11.	Bobby Doerr	1852
	12.	Red Schoendienst	1834
	13.	Billy Herman	1829
	14.	Frankie Frisch	1775
	15.	Bobby Grich	1765
3B	1.	Brooks Robinson	2870
	2.	Graig Nettles	2412
	3.	Mike Schmidt	2212
	4.	Buddy Bell	2186
	5.	Eddie Mathews	2181
	6.	Ron Santo	2130
	7.	Eddie Yost	2008
	8.	Ron Cey	1989
	9.	Aurelio Rodriguez	1983
	10.	Tim Wallach	1963
	11.	Sal Bando	1896
	12.	Pie Traynor	1864
	13.	Wade Boggs	1863
	14.	Stan Hack	1836
	15.	Gary Gaetti	1817
SS	1.	Luis Aparicio	2581
	2.	Ozzie Smith	2459
	3.	Larry Bowa	2222
	4.	Luke Appling	2218
	5.	Dave Concepcion	2178
	6.	Rabbit Maranville	2154
	7.	Cal Ripken	2141
	8.	Bill Dahlen	2132
	9.	Bert Campaneris	2097
	10.	Alan Trammell	2096
	11.	Tommy Corcoran	2073
	12.	Roy McMillan	2028
	13.	Pee Wee Reese	2014
	14.	Roger Peckinpaugh	1983
	15.	Garry Templeton	1964
OF	1.	Ty Cobb	2933
	2.	Willie Mays	2843
	3.	Hank Aaron	2760
	4.	Tris Speaker	2700
	5.	Lou Brock	2507
	6.	Al Kaline	2488
	7.	Dave Winfield	2469
	8.	Max Carey	2422
	9.	Vada Pinson	2403
	10.	Roberto Clemente	2370
	11.	Zack Wheat	2350
	12.	Willie Davis	2323
	13.	Andre Dawson	2317
	14.	Mel Ott	2313
	15.	Sam Crawford	2297
C	1.	Carlton Fisk	2226
	2.	Bob Boone	2225
	3.	Gary Carter	2056
	4.	Jim Sundberg	1927
	5.	Al Lopez	1918
	6.	Tony Pena	1845
	7.	Lance Parrish	1818
	8.	Rick Ferrell	1806
	9.	Gabby Hartnett	1790
	10.	Ted Simmons	1771
	11.	Johnny Bench	1742
	12.	Ray Schalk	1726
	13.	Bill Dickey	1712
	14.	Yogi Berra	1696
	15.	Rick Dempsey	1633
P	1.	Hoyt Wilhelm	1070
	2.	Kent Tekulve	1050
	3.	Goose Gossage	1001
	4.	Lindy McDaniel	987
	5.	Rollie Fingers	944
	6.	Lee Smith	943
	7.	Gene Garber	931
	8.	Cy Young	906
	9.	Dennis Eckersley	901
	10.	Sparky Lyle	899
	11.	Jim Kaat	898
	12.	Jeff Reardon	880
	13.	Don McMahon	874
	14.	Phil Niekro	864
	15.	Charlie Hough	858

FIELDING AVERAGE

1B	1.	Steve Garvey	.996
	2.	Don Mattingly	.996
	3.	Wes Parker	.996
	4.	Dan Driessen	.995
	5.	Jim Spencer	.995
	6.	Frank McCormick	.995
	7.	Rafael Palmeiro	.994
	8.	Mark Grace	.994
	9.	Keith Hernandez	.994
	10.	Vic Power	.994
	10.	Kent Hrbek	.994
	12.	Joe Adcock	.994
	13.	Wally Joyner	.994
	14.	Mark McGwire	.994
	15.	Pete O'Brien	.994
2B	1.	Ryne Sandberg	.990
	2.	Tommy Herr	.989
	3.	Jose Lind	.988
	4.	Jim Gantner	.985
	5.	Frank White	.984
	6.	Bobby Grich	.984
	7.	Lou Whitaker	.984
	8.	Jerry Lumpe	.984
	9.	Cookie Rojas	.984
	10.	Dave Cash	.984
	11.	Nellie Fox	.984
	12.	Tommy Helms	.983
	13.	Robby Thompson	.983
	14.	Dick Green	.983
	15.	Bill Doran	.983
3B	1.	Brooks Robinson	.971
	2.	Ken Reitz	.970
	3.	George Kell	.969
	4.	Steve Buechele	.968
	5.	Don Money	.968
	6.	Don Wert	.968
	7.	Willie Kamm	.967
	8.	Heinie Groh	.967
	9.	Carney Lansford	.966
	10.	Clete Boyer	.965
	11.	Ken Oberkfell	.965
	12.	Ken Keltner	.965
	13.	Jim Davenport	.964
	14.	Buddy Bell	.964
	15.	Aurelio Rodriguez	.964
SS	1.	Larry Bowa	.980
	2.	Tony Fernandez	.980
	3.	Cal Ripken	.979
	4.	Ozzie Smith	.978
	5.	Spike Owen	.977
	6.	Alan Trammell	.977
	7.	Mark Belanger	.977
	8.	Dick Schofield	.976
	9.	Bucky Dent	.976
	10.	Roger Metzger	.976
	11.	Ozzie Guillen	.974
	12.	Barry Larkin	.974
	13.	Greg Gagne	.973
	14.	Jay Bell	.973
	15.	Tim Foli	.973
OF	1.	Terry Puhl	.993
	2.	Brett Butler	.992
	3.	Pete Rose	.991
	4.	Amos Otis	.991
	5.	Joe Rudi	.991
	6.	Mickey Stanley	.991
	7.	Robin Yount	.990
	8.	Jimmy Piersall	.990
	9.	Ken Berry	.989
	9.	Jim Landis	.989
	11.	Paul O'Neill	.989
	12.	Tommy Holmes	.989
	13.	Kirby Puckett	.989
	14.	Gene Woodling	.989
	15.	Cesar Geronimo	.988
C	1.	Bill Freehan	.993
	2.	Elston Howard	.993
	3.	Jim Sundberg	.993
	4.	Sherm Lollar	.992
	5.	Tom Haller	.992
	5.	Johnny Edwards	.992
	7.	Lance Parrish	.991
	8.	Jerry Grote	.991
	9.	Ernie Whitt	.991
	10.	Gary Carter	.991
	11.	Johnny Bench	.990
	12.	Randy Hundley	.990
	13.	Tony Pena	.990
	14.	Rick Cerone	.990
	15.	Earl Battey	.990
P	1.	Don Mossi	.990
	2.	Gary Nolan	.990
	3.	Rick Rhoden	.989
	4.	Lon Warneke	.988
	5.	Jim Wilson	.988
	6.	Woodie Fryman	.988
	7.	Larry Gura	.986
	8.	Grover Alexander	.985
	9.	General Crowder	.984
	10.	Bill Monbouquette	.984
	11.	Harry Brecheen	.983
	12.	Rick Wise	.982
	13.	Red Lucas	.981
	14.	Ron Guidry	.981
	15.	Bob Smith	.981

PUTOUTS

1B	1.	Jake Beckley	23709
	2.	Ed Konetchy	21361
	3.	Eddie Murray	21243
	4.	Cap Anson	20761
	5.	Charlie Grimm	20711
	6.	Stuffy McInnis	20119
	7.	Mickey Vernon	19808
	8.	Jake Daubert	19634
	9.	Lou Gehrig	19510
	10.	Joe Kuhel	19386
	11.	Joe Judge	19277
	12.	Steve Garvey	18844
	13.	George Sisler	18814
	14.	Wally Pipp	18779
	15.	Jim Bottomley	18337
2B	1.	Bid McPhee	6545
	2.	Eddie Collins	6526
	3.	Nellie Fox	6090
	4.	Joe Morgan	5742
	5.	Nap Lajoie	5407
	6.	Charlie Gehringer	5369
	7.	Bill Mazeroski	4974
	8.	Bobby Doerr	4928
	9.	Willie Randolph	4859
	10.	Billy Herman	4780
	11.	Lou Whitaker	4770
	12.	Frank White	4739
	13.	Fred Pfeffer	4711
	14.	Red Schoendienst	4616
	15.	Frankie Frisch	4348
3B	1.	Brooks Robinson	2697
	2.	Jimmy Collins	2372
	3.	Eddie Yost	2356
	4.	Lave Cross	2304
	5.	Pie Traynor	2291
	6.	Billy Nash	2219
	7.	Frank Baker	2154
	8.	Willie Kamm	2151
	9.	Eddie Mathews	2049
	10.	Willie Jones	2045
	11.	Jimmy Austin	2042
	12.	Arlie Latham	1975
	13.	Ron Santo	1955
	14.	Stan Hack	1944
	15.	Graig Nettles	1898
SS	1.	Rabbit Maranville	5139
	2.	Bill Dahlen	4850
	3.	Dave Bancroft	4623
	4.	Honus Wagner	4576
	5.	Tommy Corcoran	4550
	6.	Luis Aparicio	4548
	7.	Luke Appling	4398
	8.	Herman Long	4219
	9.	Ozzie Smith	4160
	10.	Bobby Wallace	4142
	11.	Pee Wee Reese	4040
	12.	Donie Bush	4038
	13.	Monte Cross	3974
	14.	Roger Peckinpaugh	3919
	15.	Dick Bartell	3872
OF	1.	Willie Mays	7095
	2.	Tris Speaker	6791
	3.	Max Carey	6363
	4.	Ty Cobb	6361
	5.	Richie Ashburn	6089
	6.	Hank Aaron	5539
	7.	Willie Davis	5449
	8.	Doc Cramer	5412
	9.	Andre Dawson	5152
	10.	Vada Pinson	5097
	11.	Rickey Henderson	5081
	12.	Willie Wilson	5060
	13.	Brett Butler	5059
	14.	Al Kaline	5035
	15.	Zack Wheat	4996
C	1.	Gary Carter	11785
	2.	Carlton Fisk	11369
	3.	Bob Boone	11260
	4.	Tony Pena	10685
	5.	Bill Freehan	9941
	6.	Jim Sundberg	9767
	7.	Lance Parrish	9647
	8.	Johnny Roseboro	9291
	9.	Johnny Bench	9249
	10.	Johnny Edwards	8925
	11.	Ted Simmons	8906
	12.	Yogi Berra	8711
	13.	Mike Scioscia	8335
	14.	Tim McCarver	8206
	15.	Jerry Grote	8081
P	1.	Jack Morris	387
	2.	Phil Niekro	386
	3.	Ferguson Jenkins	363
	4.	Gaylord Perry	349
	5.	Don Sutton	334
	6.	Tom Seaver	328
	6.	Rick Reuschel	328
	8.	Tony Mullane	327
	9.	Pud Galvin	324
	10.	Robin Roberts	316
	11.	Chick Fraser	315
	12.	Kid Nichols	311
	13.	Dennis Martinez	297
	14.	Jim Palmer	292
	15.	Bob Gibson	291
	15.	Juan Marichal	291

PUTOUTS/GAME

1B	1.	Tom Jones	10.5
	2.	Candy LaChance	10.5
	3.	George Stovall	10.4
	4.	George Kelly	10.4
	5.	Wally Pipp	10.3
	6.	Ed Konetchy	10.3
	7.	Bill Phillips	10.2
	8.	Walter Holke	10.2
	9.	Charlie Comiskey	10.1
	10.	Long John Reilly	10.1
	11.	George Burns	10.1
	12.	Cap Anson	10.1
	13.	Stuffy McInnis	10.1
	14.	Bill Terry	10.1
	15.	Hal Chase	10.0
2B	1.	Bid McPhee	3.1
	2.	Fred Pfeffer	3.1

INDIVIDUAL FIELDING (LIFETIME), *cont.*

	3.	Cub Stricker	3.0
	4.	Gerry Priddy	2.7
	5.	Lou Bierbauer	2.7
	6.	Bucky Harris	2.7
	7.	Bobby Doerr	2.7
	8.	Cupid Childs	2.7
	9.	Nap Lajoie	2.7
	10.	Nellie Fox	2.7
	11.	Eddie Stanky	2.6
	12.	Billy Herman	2.6
	13.	Oscar Melillo	2.6
	14.	Buddy Myer	2.6
	15.	Joe Quinn	2.5
3B	1.	Jerry Denny	1.6
	2.	Denny Lyons	1.5
	3.	Billy Nash	1.5
	4.	Bill Shindle	1.4
	5.	Jimmy Austin	1.4
	6.	Jimmy Collins	1.4
	7.	Frank Baker	1.4
	8.	Hick Carpenter	1.4
	9.	Lave Cross	1.3
	10.	Hans Lobert	1.3
	11.	Willie Kamm	1.3
	12.	Harry Steinfeldt	1.3
	13.	Bobby Byrne	1.3
	14.	Willie Jones	1.3
	15.	George Pinckney	1.3
SS	1.	Dave Bancroft	2.5
	2.	Honus Wagner	2.4
	3.	Rabbit Maranville	2.4
	4.	Monte Cross	2.4
	5.	Herman Long	2.4
	6.	George Davis	2.3
	7.	Dick Bartell	2.3
	8.	Bill Dahlen	2.3
	9.	Bobby Wallace	2.3
	10.	Ivy Olson	2.3
	11.	George McBride	2.2
	12.	Mickey Doolan	2.2
	13.	Tommy Corcoran	2.2
	14.	Doc Lavan	2.2
	15.	Travis Jackson	2.2
OF	1.	Taylor Douthit	3.0
	2.	Richie Ashburn	2.9
	3.	Mike Kreevich	2.8
	4.	Dwayne Murphy	2.8
	5.	Dom DiMaggio	2.8
	6.	Sammy West	2.7
	7.	Sam Chapman	2.7
	8.	Devon White	2.7
	9.	Fred Schulte	2.7
	10.	Lloyd Waner	2.7
	11.	Billy North	2.6
	12.	Garry Maddox	2.6
	13.	Robin Yount	2.6
	14.	Vince DiMaggio	2.6
	15.	Max Carey	2.6
C	1.	Johnny Edwards	6.4
	2.	Johnny Roseboro	6.3
	3.	Bill Freehan	6.3
	4.	Jerry Grote	6.0
	5.	Mike Scioscia	6.0
	6.	Tim McCarver	5.9
	7.	Tom Haller	5.8
	8.	Tony Pena	5.8
	9.	Gary Carter	5.7
	10.	Earl Battey	5.7
	11.	Elston Howard	5.7
	12.	Randy Hundley	5.6
	13.	Clay Dalrymple	5.5
	14.	Roy Campanella	5.5
	15.	Benito Santiago	5.5
P	1.	Greg Maddux	.9
	2.	Dave Foutz	.8
	3.	Nick Altrock	.8
	4.	Chick Fraser	.7
	5.	Doug Drabek	.7
	6.	Mike Boddicker	.7
	7.	Carl Morton	.7
	8.	Jack Morris	.7
	9.	Dan Petry	.7
	10.	Orel Hershiser	.7
	11.	Mel Stottlemyre	.7
	12.	Nixey Callahan	.7
	13.	Ted Breitenstein	.6
	14.	Dave Stieb	.6
	15.	Dwight Gooden	.6

ASSISTS

1B	1.	Eddie Murray	1864
	2.	Keith Hernandez	1682
	3.	George Sisler	1528
	4.	Mickey Vernon	1448
	5.	Fred Tenney	1363
	6.	Bill Buckner	1351
	6.	Chris Chambliss	1351
	8.	Norm Cash	1317
	9.	Jake Beckley	1315
	10.	Joe Judge	1300
	11.	Ed Konetchy	1292
	12.	Gil Hodges	1281
	13.	Stuffy McInnis	1238
	14.	Jimmie Foxx	1222
	14.	Willie McCovey	1222
2B	1.	Eddie Collins	7630
	2.	Charlie Gehringer	7068
	3.	Joe Morgan	6967
	4.	Bid McPhee	6905
	5.	Bill Mazeroski	6685
	6.	Lou Whitaker	6652
	7.	Nellie Fox	6373
	8.	Willie Randolph	6336
	9.	Nap Lajoie	6259
	10.	Frank White	6246
	11.	Frankie Frisch	6026
	12.	Bobby Doerr	5710
	13.	Billy Herman	5681
	14.	Ryne Sandberg	5645
	15.	Bobby Grich	5381
3B	1.	Brooks Robinson	6205
	2.	Graig Nettles	5299
	3.	Mike Schmidt	5045
	4.	Buddy Bell	4925
	5.	Ron Santo	4581
	6.	Eddie Mathews	4323
	7.	Aurelio Rodriguez	4150
	8.	Ron Cey	4018
	9.	Tim Wallach	3843
	10.	Sal Bando	3720
	11.	Gary Gaetti	3705
	12.	Lave Cross	3703
	13.	Jimmy Collins	3702
	14.	George Brett	3674
	15.	Wade Boggs	3672
SS	1.	Ozzie Smith	8213
	2.	Luis Aparicio	8016
	3.	Bill Dahlen	7500
	4.	Rabbit Maranville	7354
	5.	Luke Appling	7218
	6.	Tommy Corcoran	7106
	7.	Larry Bowa	6857
	8.	Dave Concepcion	6594
	9.	Dave Bancroft	6561
	10.	Cal Ripken	6510
	11.	Roger Peckinpaugh	6334
	12.	Bobby Wallace	6303
	13.	Don Kessinger	6212
	14.	Roy McMillan	6191
	15.	Germany Smith	6154
OF	1.	Tris Speaker	448
	2.	Ty Cobb	392
	3.	Jimmy Ryan	375
	4.	Tom Brown	348
	4.	George Van Haltren	348
	6.	Harry Hooper	344
	7.	Max Carey	339
	8.	Jimmy Sheckard	307
	9.	Clyde Milan	294
	10.	Orator Shaffer	289
	11.	King Kelly	287
	12.	Sam Thompson	283
	13.	Sam Rice	278
	14.	Dummy Hoy	273
	15.	Jesse Burkett	270
C	1.	Deacon McGuire	1859
	2.	Ray Schalk	1811
	3.	Steve O'Neill	1698
	4.	Red Dooin	1590
	5.	Chief Zimmer	1580
	6.	Johnny Kling	1552
	7.	Ivy Wingo	1487
	8.	Wilbert Robinson	1454
	9.	Bill Bergen	1444
	10.	Duke Farrell	1417
	10.	Wally Schang	1417
	12.	George Gibson	1386
	13.	Oscar Stanage	1379
	14.	Mal Kittridge	1363
	15.	Lou Criger	1342
P	1.	Cy Young	2013
	2.	Christy Mathewson	1503
	3.	Grover Alexander	1419
	4.	Pud Galvin	1390
	5.	Walter Johnson	1348
	6.	Burleigh Grimes	1252
	7.	George Mullin	1244
	8.	Jack Quinn	1240
	9.	Ed Walsh	1210
	10.	Eppa Rixey	1195
	11.	John Clarkson	1143
	12.	Carl Mays	1138
	13.	Hooks Dauss	1128
	14.	Vic Willis	1124
	15.	Red Faber	1108
	15.	Eddie Plank	1108

ASSISTS/GAME

1B	1.	Mark Grace	.9
	2.	Bill Buckner	.9
	3.	Keith Hernandez	.8
	4.	Ferris Fain	.8
	5.	Vic Power	.8
	6.	Wally Joyner	.8
	7.	George Sisler	.8
	8.	Eddie Murray	.8
	9.	Pete O'Brien	.8
	10.	Rafael Palmeiro	.8
	11.	Rudy York	.8
	12.	Fred Tenney	.8
	13.	Mike Hargrove	.7
	14.	Dick Stuart	.7
	15.	Willie Upshaw	.7
2B	1.	Hughie Critz	3.5
	2.	Frankie Frisch	3.4
	3.	Oscar Melillo	3.4
	4.	Lou Bierbauer	3.3
	5.	Glenn Hubbard	3.3
	6.	Fred Pfeffer	3.3
	7.	Rogers Hornsby	3.3
	8.	Ryne Sandberg	3.3
	9.	Bid McPhee	3.2
	10.	Tony Cuccinello	3.2
	11.	Cupid Childs	3.2
	12.	Charlie Gehringer	3.2
	13.	Bill Mazeroski	3.2
	14.	Bobby Lowe	3.2
	15.	Max Bishop	3.1
3B	1.	Mike Schmidt	2.3
	2.	Bill Shindle	2.3
	3.	Arlie Latham	2.3
	4.	Buddy Bell	2.3
	5.	Clete Boyer	2.2
	6.	Terry Pendleton	2.2
	7.	Jimmy Collins	2.2
	8.	Graig Nettles	2.2
	9.	George Brett	2.2
	10.	Darrell Evans	2.2
	11.	Brooks Robinson	2.2
	12.	Lave Cross	2.2
	13.	Ron Santo	2.2
	14.	Doug Rader	2.1
	15.	Billy Nash	2.1
SS	1.	Germany Smith	3.7
	2.	Art Fletcher	3.6
	3.	Bill Dahlen	3.5
	4.	Dave Bancroft	3.5
	5.	Bones Ely	3.5
	6.	Travis Jackson	3.5
	7.	George Davis	3.5
	8.	Jack Glasscock	3.5
	9.	Bobby Wallace	3.5
	10.	Tommy Corcoran	3.4
	11.	Herman Long	3.4
	12.	Rabbit Maranville	3.4
	13.	Freddy Parent	3.4
	14.	Joe Tinker	3.4
	15.	Ozzie Smith	3.3
OF	1.	Tommy McCarthy	.2
	2.	Chicken Wolf	.2
	3.	Pop Corkhill	.2
	4.	Sam Thompson	.2
	5.	Tom Brown	.2
	6.	Curt Welch	.2
	7.	Jimmy Ryan	.2
	8.	George Van Haltren	.2
	9.	George Gore	.2
	10.	Ed Delahanty	.2
	11.	Paul Hines	.2
	12.	Joe Hornung	.2
	13.	Ned Hanlon	.2
	14.	Tris Speaker	.2
	15.	Tilly Walker	.2
C	1.	Duke Farrell	1.4
	2.	Red Dooin	1.3
	3.	Johnny Kling	1.3
	4.	Bill Killefer	1.3
	5.	Oscar Stanage	1.3
	6.	Chief Zimmer	1.3
	7.	Jack Warner	1.3
	8.	Ivy Wingo	1.2
	9.	Billy Sullivan	1.2
	10.	George Gibson	1.2
	11.	Deacon McGuire	1.2
	12.	Mal Kittridge	1.1
	13.	Steve O'Neill	1.1
	14.	Wilbert Robinson	1.1
	15.	Frank Snyder	1.1
P	1.	Addie Joss	3.0
	2.	Harry Howell	2.8
	3.	Ed Walsh	2.8
	4.	Nick Altrock	2.8
	5.	Willie Sudhoff	2.7
	6.	Nixey Callahan	2.6
	7.	George Mullin	2.5
	8.	Ed Willett	2.5
	9.	Barney Pelty	2.5
	10.	Red Donahue	2.5
	11.	Bill Bernhard	2.4
	12.	Jack Taylor	2.4
	13.	Christy Mathewson	2.4
	14.	Bob Rhoads	2.3
	15.	Jesse Tannehill	2.3

CHANCES

1B	1.	Jake Beckley	25505
	2.	Eddie Murray	23274
	3.	Ed Konetchy	22877
	4.	Cap Anson	22299
	5.	Charlie Grimm	22087
	6.	Stuffy McInnis	21517
	7.	Mickey Vernon	21467
	8.	Jake Daubert	20943
	9.	Lou Gehrig	20790
	10.	Joe Kuhel	20722
	11.	Joe Judge	20719
	12.	George Sisler	20611
	13.	Wally Pipp	20099
	14.	Steve Garvey	19951
	15.	Keith Hernandez	19706
2B	1.	Eddie Collins	14591
	2.	Bid McPhee	14241
	3.	Joe Morgan	12953
	4.	Charlie Gehringer	12746
	5.	Nellie Fox	12672
	6.	Nap Lajoie	12117
	7.	Bill Mazeroski	11863
	8.	Lou Whitaker	11611
	9.	Willie Randolph	11429
	10.	Frank White	11163
	11.	Bobby Doerr	10852
	12.	Billy Herman	10815
	13.	Fred Pfeffer	10672
	14.	Frankie Frisch	10654
	15.	Red Schoendienst	10029
3B	1.	Brooks Robinson	9165
	2.	Graig Nettles	7492
	3.	Buddy Bell	6979
	4.	Mike Schmidt	6949
	5.	Ron Santo	6853

INDIVIDUAL FIELDING (LIFETIME), *cont.*

	6. Eddie Mathews	6665
	7. Jimmy Collins	6539
	8. Lave Cross	6401
	9. Arlie Latham	6342
	10. Eddie Yost	6285
	11. Pie Traynor	6140
	12. Billy Nash	5952
	13. Aurelio Rodriguez	5894
	14. Ron Cey	5741
	15. Stan Hack	5684
SS	1. Bill Dahlen	13325
	2. Rabbit Maranville	13124
	3. Luis Aparicio	12930
	4. Ozzie Smith	12646
	5. Tommy Corcoran	12612
	6. Luke Appling	12259
	7. Dave Bancroft	11844
	8. Herman Long	11419
	9. Honus Wagner	11292
	10. Bobby Wallace	11130
	11. Donie Bush	10846
	12. Roger Peckinpaugh	10806
	13. Dave Concepcion	10575
	14. Larry Bowa	10382
	15. Pee Wee Reese	10319
OF	1. Tris Speaker	7461
	2. Willie Mays	7431
	3. Ty Cobb	7024
	4. Max Carey	6937
	5. Richie Ashburn	6377
	6. Hank Aaron	5857
	7. Willie Davis	5719
	8. Doc Cramer	5702
	9. Zack Wheat	5411
	10. Andre Dawson	5401
	11. Vada Pinson	5370
	12. Fred Clarke	5300
	12. Rickey Henderson	5300
	14. Al Kaline	5278
	15. Paul Waner	5254
C	1. Gary Carter	13109
	2. Bob Boone	12612
	3. Carlton Fisk	12572
	4. Tony Pena	11803
	5. Jim Sundberg	10855
	6. Bill Freehan	10734
	7. Lance Parrish	10721
	8. Johnny Bench	10196
	9. Johnny Roseboro	10073
	10. Ted Simmons	9951
	11. Johnny Edwards	9710
	12. Yogi Berra	9619
	13. Deacon McGuire	9291
	14. Mike Scioscia	9186
	15. Ray Schalk	9157
P	1. Cy Young	2388
	2. Pud Galvin	1875
	3. Christy Mathewson	1836
	4. Walter Johnson	1679
	5. Grover Alexander	1633
	6. George Mullin	1555
	7. Burleigh Grimes	1548
	8. Tim Keefe	1531
	9. John Clarkson	1526
	10. Ed Walsh	1499
	11. Tony Mullane	1496
	12. Vic Willis	1456
	13. Jack Quinn	1451
	14. Kid Nichols	1409
	15. Eddie Plank	1377

CHANCES/GAME

1B	1. Tom Jones	11.4
	2. George Stovall	11.3
	3. George Kelly	11.1
	4. Wally Pipp	11.0
	5. Ed Konetchy	11.0
	6. Candy LaChance	11.0
	7. George Burns	10.9
	8. Bill Terry	10.9
	9. Fred Tenney	10.9
	10. Hal Chase	10.8
	11. Cap Anson	10.8
	12. Walter Holke	10.8
	13. Bill Phillips	10.8
	14. Charlie Comiskey	10.8
	15. Stuffy McInnis	10.8
2B	1. Fred Pfeffer	6.9
	2. Bid McPhee	6.7
	3. Cub Stricker	6.6
	4. Lou Bierbauer	6.5
	5. Cupid Childs	6.3
	6. Oscar Melillo	6.2
	7. Hughie Critz	6.1
	8. Bobby Lowe	6.0
	9. Frankie Frisch	6.0
	10. Bucky Harris	6.0
	11. Nap Lajoie	6.0
	12. Gerry Priddy	5.9
	13. Billy Herman	5.9
	14. Bobby Doerr	5.9
	15. Hobe Ferris	5.8
3B	1. Jerry Denny	4.2
	2. Bill Shindle	4.1
	3. Billy Nash	4.1
	4. Arlie Latham	4.0
	5. Denny Lyons	4.0
	6. Jimmy Collins	3.9
	7. Hick Carpenter	3.8
	8. Jimmy Austin	3.7
	9. Lave Cross	3.7
	10. Frank Baker	3.6
	11. Bill Bradley	3.6
	12. Harry Steinfeldt	3.6
	13. George Pinckney	3.6
	14. Doc Casey	3.5
	15. Art Devlin	3.5
SS	1. Herman Long	6.4
	2. Dave Bancroft	6.3
	3. Bill Dahlen	6.3
	4. George Davis	6.2
	5. Bobby Wallace	6.1
	6. Rabbit Maranville	6.1
	7. Tommy Corcoran	6.1
	8. Monte Cross	6.1
	9. Bones Ely	6.1
	10. Honus Wagner	6.0
	11. Germany Smith	6.0
	12. Travis Jackson	6.0
	13. Art Fletcher	5.9
	14. Joe Tinker	5.9
	15. Dick Bartell	5.8
OF	1. Taylor Douthit	3.2
	2. Richie Ashburn	3.0
	3. Dom DiMaggio	3.0
	4. Mike Kreevich	2.9
	5. Dwayne Murphy	2.9
	6. Sam Chapman	2.9
	7. Sammy West	2.9
	8. Max Carey	2.9
	9. Fred Schulte	2.8
	10. Devon White	2.8
	11. Lloyd Waner	2.8
	12. Vince DiMaggio	2.8
	13. Joe DiMaggio	2.8
	14. Tris Speaker	2.8
	15. Billy North	2.8
C	1. Johnny Edwards	7.0
	2. Johnny Roseboro	6.8
	3. Bill Freehan	6.8
	4. Mike Scioscia	6.6
	5. Jerry Grote	6.5
	6. Tim McCarver	6.4
	7. Tony Pena	6.4
	8. Gary Carter	6.4
	9. Tom Haller	6.3
	10. Bill Killefer	6.3
	11. Earl Battey	6.2
	12. Johnny Kling	6.2
	13. Clay Dalrymple	6.2
	14. Benito Santiago	6.2
	15. Randy Hundley	6.2
P	1. Nick Altrock	3.7
	2. Addie Joss	3.6
	3. Harry Howell	3.6
	4. Ed Walsh	3.5
	5. Nixey Callahan	3.5
	6. Willie Sudhoff	3.3
	7. George Mullin	3.2
	8. Barney Pelty	3.2
	9. Chick Fraser	3.1
	10. Ed Willett	3.0
	11. Red Donahue	2.9
	12. Bill Bernhard	2.9
	13. Jack Taylor	2.9
	14. Doc White	2.9
	15. Bert Cunningham	2.9

DOUBLE PLAYS

1B	1. Mickey Vernon	2044
	2. Eddie Murray	2033
	3. Joe Kuhel	1769
	4. Charlie Grimm	1733
	5. Chris Chambliss	1687
	6. Keith Hernandez	1654
	7. Gil Hodges	1614
	8. Lou Gehrig	1574
	9. Jim Bottomley	1560
	10. Jimmie Foxx	1528
	10. Steve Garvey	1528
	12. Joe Judge	1500
	12. Don Mattingly	1500
	14. George Scott	1480
	15. George Sisler	1467
2B	1. Bill Mazeroski	1706
	2. Nellie Fox	1619
	3. Willie Randolph	1547
	4. Lou Whitaker	1527
	5. Bobby Doerr	1507
	6. Joe Morgan	1505
	7. Charlie Gehringer	1444
	8. Frank White	1381
	9. Red Schoendienst	1363
	10. Bobby Grich	1302
	11. Eddie Collins	1215
	12. Bid McPhee	1186
	13. Billy Herman	1183
	14. Joe Gordon	1160
	15. Frankie Frisch	1060
3B	1. Brooks Robinson	618
	2. Graig Nettles	470
	3. Mike Schmidt	450
	4. Buddy Bell	430
	5. Aurelio Rodriguez	408
	6. Ron Santo	395
	7. Gary Gaetti	394
	8. Eddie Mathews	369
	9. Wade Boggs	357
	10. Ken Boyer	355
	11. Sal Bando	345
	11. Eddie Yost	345
	13. Doug DeCinces	331
	14. Ron Cey	315
	14. Clete Boyer	315
SS	1. Luis Aparicio	1553
	2. Ozzie Smith	1551
	3. Cal Ripken	1453
	4. Luke Appling	1424
	5. Roy McMillan	1304
	6. Alan Trammell	1291
	7. Dave Concepcion	1290
	8. Larry Bowa	1265
	9. Pee Wee Reese	1246
	10. Dick Groat	1237
	11. Phil Rizzuto	1217
	12. Bert Campaneris	1186
	13. Rabbit Maranville	1183
	14. Lou Boudreau	1180
	15. Don Kessinger	1170
OF	1. Tris Speaker	139
	2. Ty Cobb	107
	3. Max Carey	86
	4. Tom Brown	85
	5. Harry Hooper	81
	5. Jimmy Sheckard	81
	7. Mike Griffin	75
	8. Dummy Hoy	72
	9. Jimmy Ryan	71
	10. Fielder Jones	70
	11. Patsy Donovan	69
	12. Sam Rice	67
	13. George Van Haltren	64
	14. Jesse Burkett	62
	15. Sam Thompson	61
C	1. Ray Schalk	221
	2. Yogi Berra	175
	2. Steve O'Neill	175
	4. Gabby Hartnett	173
	5. Bob Boone	154
	6. Jimmie Wilson	153
	7. Gary Carter	149
	7. Wally Schang	149
	9. Carlton Fisk	148
	10. Jim Sundberg	144
	11. Rollie Hemsley	143
	12. Deacon McGuire	142
	13. Ivy Wingo	141
	14. Tony Pena	139
	14. Rick Ferrell	139
P	1. Phil Niekro	83
	2. Warren Spahn	82
	3. Freddie Fitzsimmons	79
	4. Bob Lemon	78
	5. Bucky Walters	76
	6. Burleigh Grimes	74
	7. Walter Johnson	72
	8. Tommy John	69
	9. Jim Kaat	65
	10. Dizzy Trout	63
	11. Gaylord Perry	58
	12. Ted Lyons	57
	13. Carl Mays	56
	14. Eppa Rixey	55
	14. Lew Burdette	55
	14. Don Drysdale	55

WORLD SERIES BATTING (LIFETIME)

BATTING AVERAGE

1.	Paul Molitor	.418
1.	Pepper Martin	.418
3.	Hal McRae	.400
4.	Lou Brock	.391
5.	Thurman Munson	.373
6.	George Brett	.373
7.	Hank Aaron	.364
8.	Frank Baker	.363
9.	Roberto Clemente	.362
10.	Lou Gehrig	.361
11.	Reggie Jackson	.357
12.	Carl Yastrzemski	.352
13.	Earle Combs	.350
14.	Stan Hack	.348
15.	Roberto Alomar	.347

TOTAL BASES

1.	Mickey Mantle	123
2.	Yogi Berra	117
3.	Babe Ruth	96
4.	Lou Gehrig	87
5.	Joe DiMaggio	84
6.	Duke Snider	79
7.	Hank Bauer	75
8.	Frankie Frisch	74
8.	Reggie Jackson	74
10.	Gil McDougald	72
11.	Bill Skowron	69
12.	Elston Howard	66
13.	Goose Goslin	63
14.	Pee Wee Reese	59
15.	Lou Brock	57

HOME RUNS

1.	Mickey Mantle	18
2.	Babe Ruth	15
3.	Yogi Berra	12
4.	Duke Snider	11
5.	Lou Gehrig	10
5.	Reggie Jackson	10
7.	Joe DiMaggio	8
7.	Bill Skowron	8
7.	Frank Robinson	8
10.	Hank Bauer	7
10.	Goose Goslin	7
10.	Gil McDougald	7
13.	Al Simmons	6
13.	Len Dykstra	6
13.	Roger Maris	6
13.	Reggie Smith	6

BASES ON BALLS

1.	Mickey Mantle	43
2.	Babe Ruth	33
3.	Yogi Berra	32
4.	Phil Rizzuto	30
5.	Lou Gehrig	26
6.	Mickey Cochrane	25
7.	Jim Gilliam	23
8.	Jackie Robinson	21
9.	Gil McDougald	20
10.	Joe DiMaggio	19
10.	Gene Woodling	19
12.	Roger Maris	18
12.	Pee Wee Reese	18
14.	Gil Hodges	17
14.	Gene Tenace	17
14.	Ross Youngs	17

SLUGGING AVERAGE

1.	Reggie Jackson	.755
2.	Babe Ruth	.744
3.	Lou Gehrig	.731
4.	Len Dykstra	.700
5.	Al Simmons	.658
6.	Lou Brock	.655
7.	Paul Molitor	.636
7.	Pepper Martin	.636
9.	Hank Greenberg	.624
10.	Charlie Keller	.611
11.	Jimmie Foxx	.609
12.	Rickey Henderson	.607
13.	Dave Henderson	.606
14.	Hank Aaron	.600
15.	Joe Carter	.596

HITS

1.	Yogi Berra	71
2.	Mickey Mantle	59
3.	Frankie Frisch	58
4.	Joe DiMaggio	54
5.	Hank Bauer	46
5.	Pee Wee Reese	46
7.	Phil Rizzuto	45
7.	Gil McDougald	45
9.	Lou Gehrig	43
10.	Babe Ruth	42
10.	Eddie Collins	42
10.	Elston Howard	42
13.	Bobby Richardson	40
14.	Bill Skowron	39
15.	Duke Snider	38

HOME RUN PERCENTAGE

1.	Len Dykstra	12.0
2.	Babe Ruth	11.6
3.	Reggie Jackson	10.2
4.	Frank Robinson	8.7
5.	Joe Carter	8.5
6.	Lou Gehrig	8.4
7.	Duke Snider	8.3
8.	Al Simmons	8.2
8.	Reggie Smith	8.2
10.	Mickey Mantle	7.8
11.	Gene Tenace	7.0
11.	Steve Yeager	7.0
13.	Charlie Keller	6.9
14.	Don Buford	6.9
15.	Jose Canseco	6.7

STOLEN BASES

1.	Lou Brock	14
1.	Eddie Collins	14
3.	Davey Lopes	10
3.	Frank Chance	10
3.	Phil Rizzuto	10
6.	Honus Wagner	9
6.	Frankie Frisch	9
8.	Johnny Evers	8
9.	Joe Morgan	7
9.	Pepper Martin	7
9.	Roberto Alomar	7
9.	Rickey Henderson	7

GAMES

1.	Yogi Berra	75
2.	Mickey Mantle	65
3.	Elston Howard	54
4.	Hank Bauer	53
4.	Gil McDougald	53
6.	Phil Rizzuto	52
7.	Joe DiMaggio	51
8.	Frankie Frisch	50
9.	Pee Wee Reese	44
10.	Babe Ruth	41
10.	Roger Maris	41
12.	Carl Furillo	40
13.	Gil Hodges	39
13.	Jim Gilliam	39
13.	Bill Skowron	39

DOUBLES

1.	Yogi Berra	10
1.	Frankie Frisch	10
3.	Pete Fox	9
3.	Jack Barry	9
3.	Carl Furillo	9
6.	Lou Gehrig	8
6.	Duke Snider	8
6.	Lonnie Smith	8

RUNS BATTED IN

1.	Mickey Mantle	40
2.	Yogi Berra	39
3.	Lou Gehrig	35
4.	Babe Ruth	33
5.	Joe DiMaggio	30
6.	Bill Skowron	29
7.	Duke Snider	26
8.	Hank Bauer	24
8.	Bill Dickey	24
8.	Gil McDougald	24
8.	Reggie Jackson	24
12.	Hank Greenberg	22
13.	Gil Hodges	21
14.	Tony Lazzeri	19
14.	Billy Martin	19
14.	Elston Howard	19

STRIKEOUTS

1.	Mickey Mantle	54
2.	Elston Howard	37
3.	Duke Snider	33
4.	Babe Ruth	30
5.	Gil McDougald	29
6.	Bill Skowron	26
7.	Hank Bauer	25
8.	Bob Meusel	24
8.	Reggie Jackson	24
10.	Tony Kubek	23
10.	Joe DiMaggio	23
10.	George Kelly	23
10.	Frank Robinson	23

AT BATS

1.	Yogi Berra	259
2.	Mickey Mantle	230
3.	Joe DiMaggio	199
4.	Frankie Frisch	197
5.	Gil McDougald	190
6.	Hank Bauer	188
7.	Phil Rizzuto	183
8.	Elston Howard	171
9.	Pee Wee Reese	169
10.	Roger Maris	152
11.	Jim Gilliam	147
12.	Tony Kubek	146
13.	Bill Dickey	145
14.	Jackie Robinson	137
15.	Duke Snider	133
15.	Bill Skowron	133

TRIPLES

1.	Tommy Leach	4
1.	Tris Speaker	4
1.	Billy Johnson	4
4.	Hank Bauer	3
4.	Lou Gehrig	3
4.	Mark Lemke	3
4.	Bob Meusel	3
4.	Bobby Brown	3
4.	Dan Gladden	3
4.	Chick Stahl	3
4.	Buck Freeman	3
4.	Billy Martin	3
4.	Tim McCarver	3
4.	Freddy Parent	3
4.	Frankie Frisch	3
4.	Dave Concepcion	3

RUNS

1.	Mickey Mantle	42
2.	Yogi Berra	41
3.	Babe Ruth	37
4.	Lou Gehrig	30
5.	Joe DiMaggio	27
6.	Roger Maris	26
7.	Elston Howard	25
8.	Gil McDougald	23
9.	Jackie Robinson	22
10.	Hank Bauer	21
10.	Duke Snider	21
10.	Phil Rizzuto	21
10.	Gene Woodling	21
10.	Reggie Jackson	21
15.	Eddie Collins	20
15.	Pee Wee Reese	20

WORLD SERIES PITCHING (LIFETIME)

WINS

1.	Whitey Ford	10
2.	Bob Gibson	7
2.	Red Ruffing	7
2.	Allie Reynolds	7
5.	Waite Hoyt	6
5.	Lefty Gomez	6
5.	Chief Bender	6
8.	Vic Raschi	5
8.	Jack Coombs	5
8.	Herb Pennock	5
8.	Catfish Hunter	5
8.	Christy Mathewson	5
8.	Three Finger Brown	5

GAMES STARTED

1.	Whitey Ford	22
2.	Waite Hoyt	11
2.	Christy Mathewson	11
4.	Red Ruffing	10
4.	Chief Bender	10
6.	Art Nehf	9
6.	Bob Gibson	9
6.	Catfish Hunter	9
6.	Allie Reynolds	9
10.	Jim Palmer	8
10.	Vic Raschi	8
10.	Don Sutton	8
10.	Bob Turley	8
10.	Dave Stewart	8
10.	Rube Marquard	8
10.	George Earnshaw	8

STRIKEOUTS

1.	Whitey Ford	94
2.	Bob Gibson	92
3.	Allie Reynolds	62
4.	Red Ruffing	61
4.	Sandy Koufax	61
6.	Chief Bender	59
7.	George Earnshaw	56
8.	Waite Hoyt	49
9.	Christy Mathewson	48
10.	Bob Turley	46
11.	Jim Palmer	44
12.	Vic Raschi	43
13.	Jack Morris	40
14.	Don Gullett	37
15.	Lefty Grove	36
15.	Don Drysdale	36

BASES ON BALLS

1.	Whitey Ford	34
2.	Art Nehf	32
2.	Allie Reynolds	32
4.	Jim Palmer	31
5.	Bob Turley	29
6.	Red Ruffing	27
6.	Paul Derringer	27
8.	Don Gullett	26
8.	Burleigh Grimes	26
10.	Vic Raschi	25
11.	Carl Erskine	24
12.	Dave Stewart	23
12.	Bill Hallahan	23
14.	Waite Hoyt	22
15.	Jack Coombs	21
15.	Chief Bender	21

WINNING PERCENTAGE

1.	Babe Ruth	1.000
1.	Babe Adams	1.000
1.	Luis Tiant	1.000
1.	Jack Coombs	1.000
1.	Lefty Gomez	1.000
1.	Ed Reulbach	1.000
1.	John Smoltz	1.000
1.	Tom Zachary	1.000
1.	Jesse Barnes	1.000
1.	Herb Pennock	1.000
1.	Jerry Koosman	1.000
1.	Mickey Lolich	1.000
1.	Monte Pearson	1.000
1.	George Pipgras	1.000
1.	Jack Billingham	1.000

COMPLETE GAMES

1.	Christy Mathewson	10
2.	Chief Bender	9
3.	Bob Gibson	8
4.	Whitey Ford	7
4.	Red Ruffing	7
6.	Art Nehf	6
6.	Waite Hoyt	6
6.	Eddie Plank	6
6.	George Mullin	6

MOST STRIKEOUTS PER 9 INNINGS

1.	Bob Gibson	10.22
2.	Sandy Koufax	9.63
3.	Steve Carlton	9.09
4.	Danny Cox	8.69
5.	Roger Craig	8.54
6.	Orel Hershiser	8.44
7.	Jesse Barnes	8.20
8.	Don Drysdale	8.17
9.	Tom Seaver	8.10
9.	John Smoltz	8.10
11.	George Earnshaw	8.04
12.	Bob Turley	7.71
13.	Ron Guidry	7.31
14.	Allie Reynolds	7.22
15.	Bill Dinneen	7.20

FEWEST BASES ON BALLS PER 9 INNINGS

1.	Schoolboy Rowe	.39
2.	Deacon Phillippe	.72
3.	Christy Mathewson	.89
4.	Red Faber	1.00
5.	Lefty Grove	1.05
6.	Cy Young	1.06
6.	Scott McGregor	1.06
8.	Ralph Terry	1.17
9.	Carl Mays	1.26
10.	Herb Pennock	1.30
11.	Eddie Cicotte	1.41
12.	Lew Burdette	1.46
13.	Stan Coveleski	1.52
14.	Slim Sallee	1.57
15.	Dizzy Dean	1.57

EARNED RUN AVERAGE

1.	Jack Billingham	.36
2.	Harry Brecheen	.83
3.	Babe Ruth	.87
4.	Sherry Smith	.89
5.	Sandy Koufax	.95
6.	Hippo Vaughn	1.00
7.	Monte Pearson	1.01
8.	Christy Mathewson	1.15
9.	Babe Adams	1.29
10.	Eddie Plank	1.32
11.	Rollie Fingers	1.35
12.	Bill Hallahan	1.36
13.	Orval Overall	1.58
14.	George Earnshaw	1.58
15.	Cy Young	1.59

INNINGS PITCHED

1.	Whitey Ford	146
2.	Christy Mathewson	102
3.	Red Ruffing	86
4.	Chief Bender	85
5.	Waite Hoyt	84
6.	Bob Gibson	81
7.	Art Nehf	79
8.	Allie Reynolds	77
9.	Jim Palmer	65
10.	Catfish Hunter	63
10.	George Earnshaw	63
12.	Joe Bush	61
13.	Vic Raschi	60
14.	Rube Marquard	59
15.	George Mullin	58
15.	Three Finger Brown	58

SHUTOUTS

1.	Christy Mathewson	4
2.	Whitey Ford	3
2.	Three Finger Brown	3
4.	Art Nehf	2
4.	Bob Gibson	2
4.	Lew Burdette	2
4.	Bill Dinneen	2
4.	Sandy Koufax	2
4.	Bill Hallahan	2
4.	Allie Reynolds	2

LOSSES

1.	Whitey Ford	8
2.	Joe Bush	5
2.	Eddie Plank	5
2.	Rube Marquard	5
2.	Schoolboy Rowe	5
2.	Christy Mathewson	5

GAMES

1.	Whitey Ford	22
2.	Rollie Fingers	16
3.	Bob Turley	15
3.	Allie Reynolds	15
5.	Clay Carroll	14
6.	Clem Labine	13
7.	Art Nehf	12
7.	Waite Hoyt	12
7.	Catfish Hunter	12
10.	Vic Raschi	11
10.	Carl Erskine	11
10.	Rube Marquard	11
10.	Paul Derringer	11
10.	Christy Mathewson	11

SAVES

1.	Rollie Fingers	6
2.	Johnny Murphy	4
2.	Allie Reynolds	4
4.	Roy Face	3
4.	Tug McGraw	3
4.	Herb Pennock	3
4.	Kent Tekulve	3
4.	Todd Worrell	3
4.	Will McEnaney	3
4.	Firpo Marberry	3

FEWEST HITS PER 9 INNINGS

1.	Orel Hershiser	4.22
2.	Tom Glavine	4.47
3.	Jesse Barnes	4.78
4.	Monte Pearson	4.79
5.	Jack Billingham	4.97
6.	Sherry Smith	5.04
7.	Jerry Koosman	5.47
8.	Babe Ruth	5.52
9.	George Earnshaw	5.60
10.	Ron Guidry	5.63
11.	Hippo Vaughn	5.67
12.	Sandy Koufax	5.68
13.	Art Nehf	5.70
14.	Eddie Plank	5.93
15.	Don Larsen	6.00
15.	Lefty Tyler	6.00

LEAGUE CHAMPIONSHIP BATTING (LIFETIME)

BATTING AVERAGE

1.	Will Clark	.489
2.	Devon White	.392
3.	Roberto Alomar	.391
4.	Mickey Rivers	.386
5.	Pete Rose	.381
6.	Dusty Baker	.371
7.	Steve Garvey	.356
8.	Tim Raines	.354
9.	Ozzie Smith	.351
10.	Brooks Robinson	.348
11.	George Brett	.340
12.	Thurman Munson	.339
13.	Bill Russell	.337
14.	Fred McGriff	.333
14.	Tony Fernandez	.333

TOTAL BASES

1.	George Brett	75
2.	Pete Rose	63
3.	Reggie Jackson	62
4.	Steve Garvey	61
5.	Johnny Bench	44
6.	Greg Luzinski	43
7.	Graig Nettles	42
7.	Terry Pendleton	42
9.	Ron Cey	41
9.	Don Baylor	41
9.	Richie Hebner	41
12.	Sal Bando	39
12.	Len Dykstra	39
12.	Rickey Henderson	39
15.	Will Clark	38
15.	Devon White	38

HOME RUNS

1.	George Brett	9
2.	Steve Garvey	8
3.	Reggie Jackson	6
4.	Sal Bando	5
4.	Johnny Bench	5
4.	Greg Luzinski	5
4.	Gary Matthews	5
4.	Graig Nettles	5

BASES ON BALLS

1.	Joe Morgan	23
2.	Reggie Jackson	17
2.	Rickey Henderson	17
4.	Darrell Porter	16
5.	Barry Bonds	14
5.	David Justice	14
7.	Ron Cey	13
7.	Gene Tenace	13
9.	Don Baylor	11
9.	Mark Lemke	11
9.	Len Dykstra	11
9.	George Brett	11
9.	Keith Hernandez	11

SLUGGING AVERAGE

1.	Will Clark	.844
2.	George Brett	.728
3.	Steve Garvey	.678
4.	Len Dykstra	.629
5.	Dusty Baker	.597
6.	Boog Powell	.592
7.	Greg Luzinski	.589
8.	Kirby Puckett	.556
9.	Pete Rose	.534
10.	Johnny Bench	.530
11.	Sal Bando	.527
12.	Brooks Robinson	.522
13.	Dave Henderson	.520
14.	Devon White	.514
15.	Roberto Alomar	.507

HITS

1.	Pete Rose	45
2.	Reggie Jackson	37
3.	George Brett	35
4.	Steve Garvey	32
5.	Terry Pendleton	30
6.	Devon White	29
7.	Bill Russell	28
8.	Roberto Alomar	27
9.	Bob Boone	26
9.	Don Baylor	26
11.	Richie Hebner	25
11.	Carney Lansford	25
13.	Brooks Robinson	24
13.	Rickey Henderson	24
15.	Hal McRae	23
15.	Dusty Baker	23

HOME RUN PERCENTAGE

1.	Steve Garvey	8.9
2.	George Brett	8.7
3.	Boog Powell	8.2
4.	Greg Luzinski	6.8
5.	Kirk Gibson	6.8
6.	Sal Bando	6.8
7.	Will Clark	6.7
7.	Kirby Puckett	6.7
9.	Len Dykstra	6.5
10.	Pat Sheridan	6.1
11.	Johnny Bench	6.0
12.	Dave Henderson	6.0
13.	Eddie Murray	5.9
13.	Graig Nettles	5.9
15.	Darryl Strawberry	5.8

STOLEN BASES

1.	Rickey Henderson	16
2.	Roberto Alomar	11
3.	Davey Lopes	9
4.	Ron Gant	8
4.	Amos Otis	8
4.	Joe Morgan	8
4.	Willie Wilson	8
8.	Steve Sax	6
8.	Barry Bonds	6
8.	Kirk Gibson	6
8.	Vince Coleman	6
8.	Bert Campaneris	6
13.	Ken Griffey	5
13.	Kenny Lofton	5
13.	Tony Fernandez	5

GAMES

1.	Reggie Jackson	45
2.	Terry Pendleton	32
3.	Hal McRae	28
3.	Pete Rose	28
3.	Don Baylor	28
6.	Bob Boone	27
6.	Joe Morgan	27
6.	George Brett	27
9.	Frank White	26
9.	Lonnie Smith	26
9.	Richie Hebner	26
12.	Paul Blair	25
12.	Andy Van Slyke	25
12.	Candy Maldonado	25

DOUBLES

1.	Ron Cey	7
1.	Hal McRae	7
1.	Pete Rose	7
1.	Mike Schmidt	7
1.	Richie Hebner	7
1.	Reggie Jackson	7
7.	Roy White	6
7.	Fred McGriff	6
7.	Doug DeCinces	6
7.	Greg Luzinski	6
7.	Andy Van Slyke	6
7.	Brooks Robinson	6

RUNS BATTED IN

1.	Steve Garvey	21
2.	Reggie Jackson	20
3.	George Brett	19
3.	Graig Nettles	19
5.	Don Baylor	17
6.	Al Oliver	15
7.	Ron Cey	14
7.	Terry Pendleton	14
9.	Ron Gant	13
9.	Tony Perez	13
9.	Dusty Baker	13
9.	David Justice	13
9.	Gary Matthews	13

STRIKEOUTS

1.	Reggie Jackson	41
2.	Cesar Geronimo	24
3.	Bobby Grich	22
4.	Ron Gant	20
4.	Greg Luzinski	20
6.	Willie Stargell	19
7.	Willie McGee	18
7.	Mike Marshall	18
7.	Andy Van Slyke	18
10.	Jay Bell	17
10.	Hal McRae	17
10.	Paul Blair	17
10.	Mariano Duncan	17
10.	Candy Maldonado	17
10.	Darryl Strawberry	17

AT BATS

1.	Reggie Jackson	163
2.	Terry Pendleton	129
3.	Pete Rose	118
4.	George Brett	103
5.	Don Baylor	96
5.	Joe Morgan	96
7.	Ron Gant	92
8.	Rickey Henderson	91
9.	Steve Garvey	90
10.	Andy Van Slyke	89
11.	Hal McRae	88
11.	Bobby Grich	88
11.	Richie Hebner	88
14.	Frank White	87
15.	Graig Nettles	85

TRIPLES

1.	George Brett	4
2.	Willie McGee	3
2.	Mariano Duncan	3
4.	Jose Lind	2
4.	Davey Lopes	2
4.	Ozzie Smith	2
4.	Johnny Bench	2
4.	Kenny Lofton	2
4.	Luis Salazar	2
4.	Andy Van Slyke	2
4.	Terry Pendleton	2
4.	Rickey Henderson	2

RUNS

1.	George Brett	22
2.	Rickey Henderson	18
3.	Pete Rose	17
4.	Reggie Jackson	16
5.	Steve Garvey	15
5.	Willie McGee	15
7.	Ron Cey	14
7.	Ron Gant	14
7.	Len Dykstra	14
10.	Don Baylor	13
11.	Joe Morgan	12
11.	Dusty Baker	12
11.	Devon White	12
11.	Fred McGriff	12
11.	David Justice	12
11.	Terry Pendleton	12

LEAGUE CHAMPIONSHIP PITCHING (LIFETIME)

WINS

1.	Dave Stewart	8
2.	Juan Guzman	5
3.	Tommy John	4
3.	Jim Palmer	4
3.	Don Sutton	4
3.	Steve Avery	4
3.	Bruce Kison	4
3.	John Smoltz	4
3.	Steve Carlton	4
3.	Orel Hershiser	4
3.	Catfish Hunter	4

WINNING PERCENTAGE

1.	Gary Nolan	1.000
1.	Juan Guzman	1.000
1.	Bruce Kison	1.000
1.	Dave Stewart	1.000
1.	Orel Hershiser	1.000
1.	Paul Splittorff	1.000
7.	Tommy John	.800
7.	Jim Palmer	.800
7.	Don Sutton	.800
7.	Steve Avery	.800
7.	John Smoltz	.800
12.	Tim Belcher	.750
12.	Danny Jackson	.750
12.	Fernando Valenzuela	.750

EARNED RUN AVERAGE

1.	Bruce Kison	1.21
2.	Gary Nolan	1.35
3.	Orel Hershiser	1.83
4.	Danny Cox	1.84
5.	Fernando Valenzuela	1.95
6.	Jim Palmer	1.96
7.	Don Sutton	2.02
7.	John Smoltz	2.02
9.	Dave Stewart	2.03
10.	Dwight Gooden	2.04
11.	Doug Drabek	2.05
12.	Ken Holtzman	2.06
13.	Tommy John	2.08
14.	John Candelaria	2.13
15.	Juan Guzman	2.27

GAMES

1.	Tug McGraw	15
1.	Rick Honeycutt	15
1.	Dennis Eckersley	15
4.	Mark Wohlers	14
5.	Ron Reed	13
5.	Dave Giusti	13
5.	Alejandro Pena	13
8.	Tom Henke	12
9.	Duane Ward	11
9.	Rollie Fingers	11
11.	Bob Welch	10
11.	Don Gullett	10
11.	Pedro Borbon	10
11.	Dave Stewart	10
11.	Catfish Hunter	10
11.	Warren Brusstar	10

GAMES STARTED

1.	Dave Stewart	10
1.	Catfish Hunter	10
3.	Steve Carlton	8
4.	Tommy John	7
4.	Jim Palmer	7
4.	Doug Drabek	7
4.	John Smoltz	7
4.	Orel Hershiser	7
9.	Don Sutton	6
9.	Don Gullett	6
9.	Jack Morris	6
9.	Mike Cuellar	6
9.	Dennis Leonard	6

COMPLETE GAMES

1.	Jim Palmer	5
2.	Tommy John	3
2.	Catfish Hunter	3
4.	Danny Cox	2
4.	Mike Scott	2
4.	Don Sutton	2
4.	Doug Drabek	2
4.	Bruce Hurst	2
4.	Jack Morris	2
4.	Mike Cuellar	2
4.	Ken Holtzman	2
4.	Dave McNally	2
4.	Tim Wakefield	2
4.	Mike Boddicker	2
4.	Orel Hershiser	2
4.	Dennis Leonard	2

INNINGS PITCHED

1.	Dave Stewart	75
2.	Catfish Hunter	69
3.	Jim Palmer	60
4.	Steve Carlton	54
4.	Orel Hershiser	54
6.	Don Sutton	49
6.	John Smoltz	49
8.	Tommy John	48
8.	Doug Drabek	48
10.	Mike Cuellar	44
11.	Steve Avery	43
12.	Nolan Ryan	41
12.	Don Gullett	41
12.	Jack Morris	41
15.	Dave McNally	40

SAVES

1.	Dennis Eckersley	10
2.	Tug McGraw	5
3.	Ken Dayley	4
3.	Dave Giusti	4
3.	Alejandro Pena	4
6.	Tom Henke	3
6.	Duane Ward	3
6.	Randy Myers	3
6.	Jeff Reardon	3
6.	Rick Aguilera	3
6.	Goose Gossage	3
6.	Steve Bedrosian	3

STRIKEOUTS

1.	Jim Palmer	46
1.	Nolan Ryan	46
1.	John Smoltz	46
4.	Dave Stewart	39
4.	Steve Carlton	39
6.	Catfish Hunter	37
7.	Steve Avery	36
8.	Orel Hershiser	35
9.	Doug Drabek	33
10.	Don Sutton	30
10.	Dave McNally	30
12.	Roger Clemens	29
12.	Dwight Gooden	29
14.	Dave Stieb	28
14.	Mike Cuellar	28
14.	Fernando Valenzuela	28

MOST STRIKEOUTS PER 9 INNINGS

1.	Nolan Ryan	10.02
2.	John Candelaria	8.88
3.	John Smoltz	8.45
4.	Dave Stieb	7.96
5.	Steve Avery	7.48
6.	Dwight Gooden	7.39
7.	Tug McGraw	7.33
8.	Bruce Kison	7.28
9.	Vida Blue	7.18
10.	Roger Clemens	6.99
11.	Jim Palmer	6.94
12.	Bob Welch	6.82
12.	Tom Seaver	6.82
14.	Fernando Valenzuela	6.81
15.	Dave McNally	6.69

SHUTOUTS

1.	Vida Blue	1
1.	Danny Cox	1
1.	Ray Burris	1
1.	Bob Forsch	1
1.	Tommy John	1
1.	Jim Palmer	1
1.	Mike Scott	1
1.	Don Sutton	1
1.	Joe Coleman	1
1.	Jon Matlack	1
1.	John Smoltz	1
1.	Ken Holtzman	1
1.	Dave McNally	1
1.	Dave Dravecky	1
1.	Danny Jackson	1
1.	Mike Boddicker	1
1.	Orel Hershiser	1

FEWEST HITS PER 9 INNINGS

1.	Bruce Kison	4.55
2.	Bob Walk	6.17
2.	Ken Holtzman	6.17
4.	Dave Stewart	6.21
5.	Dave McNally	6.47
6.	Dave Stieb	6.54
7.	Mike Cuellar	6.55
8.	Dwight Gooden	6.62
9.	John Candelaria	6.75
10.	Don Sutton	6.80
11.	Fernando Valenzuela	6.81
12.	Juan Guzman	6.82
13.	Steve Avery	6.85
14.	Don Gullett	6.86
15.	Jim Palmer	6.94

BASES ON BALLS

1.	Steve Carlton	28
2.	Dave Stewart	25
3.	John Smoltz	20
4.	Jim Palmer	19
4.	Mike Cuellar	19
4.	Fernando Valenzuela	19
7.	Juan Guzman	18
7.	Catfish Hunter	18
9.	Jerry Reuss	17
10.	Tug McGraw	16
10.	Dave Stieb	16
10.	Steve Avery	16
10.	Orel Hershiser	16
14.	Bob Welch	15
14.	Tommy John	15
14.	Dave McNally	15

FEWEST BASES ON BALLS PER 9 INNINGS

1.	Don Sutton	1.29
2.	Ken Holtzman	1.54
3.	Larry Gura	1.61
4.	Bruce Hurst	1.93
5.	Nolan Ryan	1.96
6.	Dennis Leonard	2.01
7.	Vida Blue	2.30
8.	Catfish Hunter	2.34
9.	Gary Nolan	2.36
10.	Paul Splittorff	2.43
11.	John Tudor	2.45
12.	Doug Drabek	2.61
13.	Don Gullett	2.66
14.	Orel Hershiser	2.67
15.	Tom Glavine	2.80

LOSSES

1.	Jerry Reuss	7
2.	Doug Drabek	5
3.	Tom Glavine	4
3.	Doyle Alexander	4
5.	Zane Smith	3
5.	Dave Stieb	3
5.	Gene Garber	3
5.	Don Gullett	3
5.	Ken Holtzman	3
5.	Catfish Hunter	3
5.	Dennis Leonard	3
5.	Todd Stottlemyre	3
5.	Charlie Leibrandt	3

PART FOUR

Lifetime Major League Team Rosters

National League
American League
American Association
Union Association
Players League
Federal League

Lifetime Major League Team Rosters

This section provides complete lifetime team rosters for every major league team. The list also shows the movement of each team as well as the various names under which the team played. Each man's name is shown together with the years he played for that team. If his career with the team was interrupted and he then returned, that date is also shown. Team managers are listed at the end of each team's roster. An asterisk next to the manager's name indicates that he was a player-manager.

National League

ATLANTA Braves 1966–95
Moved from MILWAUKEE Braves

Hank Aaron	1966–74
Tommie Aaron	1968–71
Ted Abernathy	1966
Jim Acker	1986–89
Jack Aker	1974
Jay Aldrich	1989
Doyle Alexander	1980, 1986–87
Sandy Alomar	1966
Felipe Alou	1966–69
Jose Alvarez	1981–82, 1988–89
Bob Aspromonte	1969–70
Brian Asselstine	1976–81
Paul Assenmacher	1986–89
Al Autry	1976
Steve Avery	1990–95
Dusty Baker	1968–75
Lee Bales	1966
Steve Barber	1970–72
Len Barker	1983–85
Bob Beall	1975, 1978–79
Mike Beard	1974–77
Steve Bedrosian	1981–85, 1993–95
Rick Behenna	1983
Mike Bell	1990–91
Rafael Belliard	1991–95
Rob Belloir	1975–78
Bruce Benedict	1978–89
Juan Berenguer	1991–92
Geronimo Berroa	1989–90
Damon Berryhill	1991–93
Mike Bielecki	1991–92, 1994
Kevin Blankenship	1988
Larvell Blanks	1972–75, 1980
Wade Blasingame	1966–67
Jeff Blauser	1987–95
Terry Blocker	1988–89
Joe Boever	1987–90
Tommy Boggs	1978–83
Frank Bolling	1966
Barry Bonnell	1977–79
Pedro Borbon	1992–93, 1995
Jim Bouton	1978
Clete Boyer	1967–71
Larry Bradford	1977, 1979–81
Sid Bream	1991–93
Jim Breazeale	1969, 1971–72
Jim Britton	1967–69
Tony Brizzolara	1979, 1983–84
Oscar Brown	1969–73
Jarvis Brown	1994
Bob Bruce	1967
Jeff Burroughs	1977–80
Brett Butler	1981–83
Francisco Cabrera	1989–93
Rick Camp	1976–78, 1980–85
Dave Campbell	1977–78
Buzz Capra	1974–77
Ramon Caraballo	1993
Don Cardwell	1970
Clay Carroll	1966–68
Rico Carty	1966–67, 1969–70, 1972
Chuck Cary	1987–88
Paul Casanova	1972–74
Vinny Castilla	1991–92
Tony Castillo	1989–91
Wayne Causey	1968
Orlando Cepeda	1969–72
Rick Cerone	1985
Chris Chambliss	1980–86
Darrel Chaney	1976–79
Dave Cheadle	1973
Jim Clancy	1991
Terry Clark	1995
Marty Clary	1987, 1989–90
Ty Cline	1966–67
Tony Cloninger	1966–68
Brad Clontz	1995
Al Closter	1973
Kevin Coffman	1987–88
Don Collins	1977
Gary Cooper	1980
Vic Correll	1974–77
Joe Cowley	1982
Bruce Dal Canton	1975–76
Mike Davey	1977–78
Ted Davidson	1968
Mark Davis	1992
Jody Davis	1988–90
Trench Davis	1987
Ken Dayley	1982–84
Mike de la Hoz	1966–67
Jeff Dedmon	1983–87
Drew Denson	1989
Mike Devereaux	1995
Adrian Devine	1973, 1975–76, 1978–79
Carlos Diaz	1982
Bob Didier	1969–72
Dick Dietz	1973
Pat Dobson	1973
Paul Doyle	1969
Jamie Easterly	1974–79
Gary Eave	1988–89
Mike Eden	1976
Juan Eichelberger	1988
Mark Eichhorn	1989
Nick Esasky	1990
Darrell Evans	1969–76, 1989
Pete Falcone	1983–84
Hank Fischer	1966
Mike Fischlin	1987
Wenty Ford	1973
Terry Forster	1983–85
Leo Foster	1971, 1973–74
Tito Francona	1967–69
Jimmy Freeman	1972–73
Marvin Freeman	1990–93
Pepe Frias	1979
Danny Frisella	1973–74
John Fuller	1974
Dave Gallagher	1994
Ron Gant	1987–93
Gene Garber	1978–87
Damaso Garcia	1988
Ralph Garr	1969–75
Adrian Garrett	1966
Gil Garrido	1968–72
Cito Gaston	1967, 1975–78
Aubrey Gatewood	1970
Gary Geiger	1966–67
Gary Gentry	1973–75
Rod Gilbreath	1972–78
Ed Giovanola	1995
Tom Glavine	1987–95
Chuck Goggin	1973
Luis Gomez	1980–81
Tony Gonzalez	1969–70
Ed Goodson	1975
Mark Grant	1990
Tommy Greene	1989–90
Tommy Gregg	1988–92
Ken Griffey	1986–88
Marquis Grissom	1995
Skip Guinn	1968
Jimmie Hall	1970
Albert Hall	1981, 1983–88
Preston Hanna	1975–82
Jim Hardin	1972
Steve Hargan	1977
Terry Harper	1980–86
Roric Harrison	1973–75
Tom Hausman	1982
Mike Heath	1991
Danny Heep	1991
Ken Henderson	1976
Dwayne Henry	1989–90
Ron Herbel	1971
Angel Hermoso	1967
Ramon Hernandez	1967
John Herrnstein	1966
Joe Hesketh	1990
Garry Hill	1969
Milt Hill	1994
Herb Hippauf	1966
Joe Hoerner	1972–73
Bob Horner	1978–86
Tom House	1971–75
Larry Howard	1973
Jay Howell	1993
Al Hrabosky	1980–82
Walt Hriniak	1968–69
Glenn Hubbard	1978–87
Brian Hunter	1991–93
Alexis Infante	1990
Sonny Jackson	1968–74
Brook Jacoby	1981, 1983
Dion James	1987–89
Pat Jarvis	1966–72
Larry Jaster	1970, 1972
Joey Jay	1966
German Jimenez	1988
Davey Johnson	1973–74
Deron Johnson	1968
Ken Johnson	1966–69
Bob Johnson	1968
Bob Johnson	1977
Randy Johnson	1982–84
Joe Johnson	1985–86
Mack Jones	1966–67
Chipper Jones	1993, 1995
Mike Jorgensen	1983–84
David Justice	1989–95
Dick Kelley	1966–68
Tom Kelley	1971–73
Roberto Kelly	1994
Mike Kelly	1994–95
Marty Keough	1966
Charlie Kerfeld	1990
Rick Kester	1968–70
Hal King	1970–71
Ryan Klesko	1992–95
Ron Kline	1970
Steve Kline	1977
Brad Komminsk	1983–86
George Kopacz	1966
Brian Kowitz	1995
Lew Krausse	1974
Jimmy Kremers	1990
Frank LaCorte	1975–79
Lee Lacy	1976
Tony LaRussa	1971
Charlie Leibrandt	1990–92
Denny Lemaster	1966–67
Mark Lemke	1988–95
Max Leon	1973–78
Derek Lilliquist	1989–90
Rufino Linares	1981–82, 1984
Javier Lopez	1992–95
Rick Luecken	1990
Mike Lum	1967–75, 1979–81
Steve Lyons	1992
Mike Macha	1979
Jerry Maddox	1978
Greg Maddux	1993–95
Mickey Mahler	1977–79
Rick Mahler	1979–88, 1991
Kelly Mann	1989–90
Paul Marak	1990
Mike Marshall	1976–77
Marty Martinez	1967–68
Eddie Mathews	1966
Gary Matthews	1977–80
Rick Matula	1979–81
Larry Maxie	1969
Dave May	1975–76
Darrell May	1995
Oddibe McDowell	1989–90
Fred McGriff	1993–95
Denny McLain	1972
Bo McLaughlin	1979
Joey McLaughlin	1977, 1979
Greg McMichael	1993–95
Craig McMurtry	1983–86
Mike McQueen	1969–72
Larry McWilliams	1978–82, 1987
Denis Menke	1966–67
Kent Mercker	1989–95
Andy Messersmith	1976–77
Felix Millan	1966–72
Norm Miller	1973–74
Stu Miller	1968
Eddie Miller	1978–81
Keith Mitchell	1991
John Mizerock	1989
Willie Montanez	1976–77
John Montefusco	1981
Donnie Moore	1982–84
Junior Moore	1976–77
Mike Mordecai	1994–95
Omar Moreno	1986
Roger Moret	1976
Jim Morrison	1988
Carl Morton	1973–76
Darryl Motley	1986–87
Dale Murphy	1976–90
Matt Murray	1995
Ivan Murrell	1974
Bill Nahorodny	1980–81
Jim Nash	1970–72
Julio Navarro	1970
Gary Neibauer	1969–73
Graig Nettles	1987
Rod Nichols	1995
Dave Nicholson	1967
Dave Nied	1992
Phil Niekro	1966–83, 1987
Joe Niekro	1973–74
Melvin Nieves	1992
Otis Nixon	1991–93
Joe Nolan	1975, 1977–80
Johnny Oates	1973–75
Ken Oberkfell	1984–88
Charlie O'Brien	1994–95
Billy O'Dell	1966
Blue Moon Odom	1975
Rowland Office	1972, 1974–79
Jose Oliva	1994–95
Gene Oliver	1966–67
Chi Chi Olivo	1966
Gregg Olson	1994
Greg Olson	1990–93
Ed Olwine	1986–88
Randy O'Neal	1987
Larry Owen	1981–83, 1985
Tom Paciorek	1976–78
Mike Page	1968
David Palmer	1986–87
Jim Panther	1973
Milt Pappas	1968–70
Jeff Parrett	1990–91
Mike Payne	1984
Bill Pecota	1993–94
Alejandro Pena	1991–92, 1995
Terry Pendleton	1991–94
Joe Pepitone	1973
Marty Perez	1971–76
Pascual Perez	1982–85
Eddie Perez	1995
Gaylord Perry	1981
Gerald Perry	1983–89
Dan Petry	1991
Jack Pierce	1973–74
Biff Pocoroba	1975–83
Luis Polonia	1995
Bob Porter	1982
Jim Presley	1990
Bob Priddy	1969–71
Charlie Puleo	1986–89
Johnny Rabb	1985
Ed Rakow	1967
Rafael Ramirez	1980–87
Claude Raymond	1967–69
Jeff Reardon	1992
Ron Reed	1966–75
Armando Reynoso	1991–92
Rusty Richards	1989–90
Jay Ritchie	1966–67
Ben Rivera	1992
Bill Robinson	1966
Craig Robinson	1974–77
Pat Rockett	1976–78
Gary Roenicke	1987–88
Ed Romero	1989
Victor Rosario	1990
Rico Rossy	1991
Jerry Royster	1976–84, 1988
Chico Ruiz	1978, 1980
Paul Runge	1981, 1983–88
John Russell	1989
Dick Ruthven	1976–78
Ray Sadecki	1975
Eddie Sadowski	1966
Billy Sample	1986
Deion Sanders	1991–94
Al Santorini	1968
Jason Schmidt	1995
Dan Schneider	1966
Ron Schueler	1972–73
Dave Schuler	1985
Don Schwall	1966–67

Mike Sharperson	1995
Steve Shields	1985–86
Ted Simmons	1986–88
Matt Sinatro	1981–84
Doug Sisk	1990–91
Craig Skok	1978–79
Hank Small	1978
Lonnie Smith	1988–92
Ken Smith	1981–83
Zane Smith	1984–89
Pete Smith	1987–93
Dwight Smith	1995
John Smoltz	1988–95
Eddie Solomon	1977–79
Elias Sosa	1975–76
Cliff Speck	1986
Charlie Spikes	1979–80
Randy St. Claire	1991–92
Marv Staehle	1971
Mike Stanton	1989–95
George Stone	1967–72
Bruce Sutter	1985–86, 1988
Tony Tarasco	1993–94
Frank Tepedino	1973–74
Duane Theiss	1977–78
Tom Thobe	1995
Lee Thomas	1966
Andres Thomas	1985–90
Mike Thompson	1974–75
Milt Thompson	1984–85
Bob Tillman	1968–70
Joe Torre	1966–68
Pablo Torrealba	1975–76
Jeff Treadway	1989–92
Alex Trevino	1984
Bob Uecker	1967
Arnie Umbach	1966
Cecil Upshaw	1966–69, 1971–73
Sandy Valdespino	1968
Sergio Valdez	1989–90
Pete Varney	1976
Jim Vatcher	1990
Charlie Vaughan	1966, 1969
Freddie Velazquez	1973
Zoilo Versalles	1971
Ozzie Virgil	1986–88
Terrell Wade	1995
Bob Walk	1981–83
Duane Ward	1986
Claudell Washington	1981–86
Bob Watson	1982–84
Jim Wessinger	1979
Jeff Wetherby	1989
Larry Whisenton	1978–79, 1981–82
Ed Whited	1989
Ernie Whitt	1990
Hoyt Wilhelm	1969–71
Jerry Willard	1991–92
Earl Williams	1970–72, 1975–76
Mark Wohlers	1991–95
Brad Woodall	1994–95
Woody Woodward	1966–68
Jimmy Wynn	1976
Steve Ziem	1987
Paul Zuvella	1982–85

Managers

Vern Benson	1977
Bobby Bragan	1966
Dave Bristol	1976–77
Bobby Cox	1978–81, 1990–95
Eddie Haas	1985
Lum Harris	1968–72
Billy Hitchcock	1966–67
Clyde King	1974–75
Eddie Mathews	1972–74
Russ Nixon	1988–90
Connie Ryan	1975
Ken Silvestri	1967
Chuck Tanner	1986–88
Joe Torre	1982–84
Ted Turner	1977
Bobby Wine	1985

BALTIMORE Orioles 1892–99
Moved from American Association

Doc Amole	1897
Kirtley Baker	1893–94
Art Ball	1898
George Blackburn	1897
Frank Bonner	1894–95
Frank Bowerman	1895–98
Steve Brodie	1893–96, 1898–99
Dan Brouthers	1894–95
Stub Brown	1893–94
Willard Brown	1893
Charlie Buffinton	1892
Scoops Carey	1895
Boileryard Clarke	1893–98
Dad Clarkson	1895–96
George Cobb	1892
Dick Cogan	1897
Joe Corbett	1896–97
Pat Crisham	1899
Monte Cross	1892
Sun Daly	1892
Gene DeMontreville	1898–99
Jim Donnelly	1896
Jack Doyle	1896–97
Harry Ely	1892
Duke Esper	1894–96
Alex Ferson	1892
Frank Foreman	1892
Dave Fultz	1899
Pete Gilbert	1892
Bill Gilbert	1892
Bob Gilks	1893
Kid Gleason	1894–95
John Godar	1892
Joe Gunson	1892
Jocko Halligan	1892
Charlie Harris	1899
Bill Hawke	1893–94
Egyptian Healy	1892
George Hemming	1894–96
Tom Hess	1892
Mike Heydon	1898
Still Bill Hill	1899
Bill Hoffer	1895–98
Ducky Holmes	1898–99
Jack Horner	1894
Harry Howell	1899
Jim Hughes	1898
Bert Inks	1894
Hughie Jennings	1893–99
Bill Johnson	1892
Willie Keeler	1894–98
Bill Keister	1896, 1899
Joe Kelley	1892–98
Bill Kissinger	1895
Frank Kitson	1898–99
Bill Kling	1892
Candy LaChance	1899
Jim Long	1893
George Magoon	1899
Al Maul	1897–98
Dan McGann	1898
Joe McGinnity	1899
John McGraw	1892–99
Doc McJames	1898
Kit McKenna	1899
Sadie McMahon	1892–96
Edgar McNabb	1893
Ralph Miller	1899
Jocko Milligan	1893
Tony Mullane	1893–94
Jerry Nops	1896–99
John O'Brien	1899
Tom O'Brien	1897–98
Tim O'Rourke	1892–93
John Pickett	1892
Arlie Pond	1895–98
Joe Quinn	1896–98
Heinie Reitz	1893–97
Wilbert Robinson	1892–99
Bobby Rothermel	1899
John Ryan	1899
Crazy Schmit	1892–93
Jimmy Sheckard	1899
Bill Shindle	1892–93
George Shoch	1892
Broadway Aleck Smith	1899
Jake Stenzel	1897–98
George Stephens	1892
Otis Stocksdale	1896
Harry Stovey	1892–93
Cub Stricker	1892
Sy Sutcliffe	1892
Harry Taylor	1893
Adonis Terry	1892
George Treadway	1893
George Van Haltren	1892
Tom Vickery	1892
Jack Wadsworth	1893
Piggy Ward	1892–93
Curt Welch	1892
Lew Whistler	1892
Henry Wilson	1898
George Wood	1892

Managers

Ned Hanlon	1892–98
*John McGraw	1899
*George Van Haltren	1892
John Waltz	1892

BOSTON Braves 1876–1952
Known as Red Caps 1876–82
Beaneaters 1883–1906
Doves 1907–10
Rustlers 1911
Bees 1936–40
Moved to MILWAUKEE Braves

Ed Abbaticchio	1903–05, 1910
Bob Addis	1950–51
Morrie Aderholt	1945
Bill Akers	1932
Frank Allen	1916–17
Myron Allen	1886
Bob Allen	1897
Bill Anderson	1925
Nate Andrews	1943–45
Stan Andrews	1939–40
Bill Annis	1884
Johnny Antonelli	1948–50
Tom Asmussen	1907
Harry Aubrey	1903
Chick Autry	1909
Earl Averill	1941
Johnny Babich	1936
Bill Bagwell	1923
Gene Bailey	1919–20
Fred Bailey	1916–17
Harvey Bailey	1899–1900
Mike Balas	1938
Jim Ball	1907–08
Dave Bancroft	1924–27
Bill Banks	1895–96
Jimmy Bannon	1894–96
Walter Barbare	1921–22
Frank Barberich	1907
George Barclay	1904–05
Red Barkley	1939
Jesse Barnes	1915–17, 1923–25
Ross Barnes	1881
Virgil Barnes	1928
George Barnicle	1939–41
Red Barrett	1943–45, 1947–49
Frank Barrett	1946
Johnny Barrett	1946
Marty Barrett	1884
Dick Barrett	1934
Red Barron	1929
Shad Barry	1900–01
Joe Batchelder	1923–25
Johnny Bates	1906–09
Ginger Beaumont	1907–09
Johnny Beazley	1947–49
Fred Beck	1909–10
Beals Becker	1908–09
Les Bell	1928–29
Ray Benge	1936
Charlie Bennett	1889–93
Larry Benton	1923–27, 1935
Marty Bergen	1896–99
Wally Berger	1930–37
John Bergh	1880
Ray Berres	1940–41
Huck Betts	1932–35
Vern Bickford	1948–52
Earl Blackburn	1915–16
Lena Blackburne	1919
Al Blanche	1935–36
Tony Boeckel	1919–23
Ray Boggs	1928
Tommy Bond	1877–81
Frank Bonner	1903
Al Bool	1931
Joe Borden	1876
Jake Boultes	1907–09
Frank Bowerman	1908
Buzz Boyle	1929–30
Foghorn Bradley	1876
Bob Brady	1946
Bill Brady	1912
King Brady	1912
Dave Brain	1906–07
Ed Brandt	1928–35
Kitty Bransfield	1898
Garland Braxton	1921–22
Buster Bray	1941
Al Bridwell	1906–07, 1911–12
Steve Brodie	1890–91
Siggy Broskie	1940
Dan Brouthers	1889
Buster Brown	1909–13
Drummond Brown	1913
Eddie Brown	1926–28
Fred Brown	1901–02
Lew Brown	1876–77, 1883
Bob Brown	1930–36
Sam Brown	1906–07
Tom Brown	1888–89
George Browne	1908
Bill Brubaker	1943
Bob Brush	1907
Charlie Brynan	1891
Art Bues	1913
Charlie Buffinton	1882–86
Lew Burdette	1951–52
Jack Burdock	1878–88
Pete Burg	1910
Dan Burke	1892
Frank Burke	1907
Billy Burke	1910–11
Joe Burns	1943
Paul Burris	1948, 1950, 1952
Dick Burrus	1925–28
Guy Bush	1936–37
Art Butler	1911
Bill Calhoun	1913
Joe Callahan	1939–40
Hank Camelli	1947
John Cameron	1906
Vin Campbell	1912
Hugh Canavan	1918
Rip Cannell	1904–05
Ben Cantwell	1928–36
Pat Capri	1944
Ben Cardoni	1943–45
Eddie Carnett	1941
Pat Carney	1901–04
Dixie Carroll	1919
Cliff Carroll	1893
Ted Cather	1914–15
Red Causey	1919
Chet Chadbourne	1918

Rome Chambers	1900
Tiny Chaplin	1936
Larry Chappell	1916–17
Bill Chappelle	1908–09
Buster Chatham	1930–31
Larry Cheney	1919
Bob Chipman	1950–52
Lloyd Christenbury	1919–22
Earl Clark	1927–33
Josh Clarke	1911
Boileryard Clarke	1899–1900
Dad Clarkson	1892
Buzz Clarkson	1952
John Clarkson	1888–92
Bill Clarkson	1928–29
Chet Clemens	1939, 1944
Jack Clements	1900
Otis Clymer	1913
Gene Cocreham	1913–15
Jack Coffey	1909
Dick Coffman	1940
Ed Cogswell	1879
Dave Cole	1950–52
Bill Coliver	1885
Cyril Collins	1913–14
Jimmy Collins	1895–1900
Zip Collins	1915–17
Pat Collins	1929
Bill Collins	1910–11
Pete Compton	1915–16
Clint Conatser	1948–49
Gene Conley	1952
Art Conlon	1923
Frank Connaughton	1894, 1906
Joe Connolly	1913–16
John Connor	1884
Joe Connor	1900
Dick Conway	1887–88
Rip Conway	1918
Duff Cooley	1901–04
Jimmy Cooney	1928
Johnny Cooney	1921–26, 1928–30, 1938–42
Bill Cooney	1909–10
Mort Cooper	1945–47
Walker Cooper	1950–52
Joe Coscarart	1935–36
Ensign Cottrell	1914
Ernie Courtney	1902
Dee Cousineau	1923–25
Sam Covington	1917
Bill Coyle	1893
Charlie Cozart	1945
Del Crandall	1949–50
Doc Crandall	1918
Fred Crolius	1901
Bill Cronin	1928–31
George Crowe	1952
Bill Crowley	1881, 1884
Walt Cruise	1919–23
Cal Crum	1917–18
Dick Crutcher	1914–15
Tony Cuccinello	1936–40, 1942–43
Dick Culler	1944–47
Jack Cummings	1929
Bruce Cunningham	1929–32
Bill Cunningham	1924
Nig Cuppy	1900
Sam Curran	1902
Cliff Curtis	1909–11
Jack Cusick	1952
John Dagenhard	1943
Bill Dahlen	1908–09
Babe Dahlgren	1941
Con Daily	1886–87
Bill Daley	1889
Joe Daly	1892
Bill Dam	1909
Jack Daniels	1952
Alvin Dark	1946, 1948–49
George Davis	1913–15
Daisy Davis	1884–85
Charlie Deal	1913–14
Pat Dealey	1885–86
Pat Deasley	1881–82
Jim Delahanty	1904–05
Art Delaney	1928–29
Al Demaree	1919
Frank Demaree	1941–42
Gene DeMontreville	1901–02
Rube Dessau	1907
Ducky Detweiler	1942

Art Devlin	1912–13
Rex DeVogt	1913
Josh Devore	1914
Charlie Dexter	1902–03
Walt Dickson	1912–13
Ernie Diehl	1906, 1909
George Diehl	1942–43
Steve Dignan	1880
Vince DiMaggio	1937–38
Bill Dinneen	1900–01
Jack Dittmer	1952
Cozy Dolan	1895–96, 1905–06
Art Doll	1935–36, 1938
Mike Donlin	1911
Ed Donnelly	1911–12
Blix Donnelly	1951
Patsy Donovan	1890
Dick Donovan	1950–52
Bill Donovan	1942–43
Gus Dorner	1906–09
Bill Dreesen	1931
Bob Dresser	1902
Frank Drews	1944–45
John Dudra	1941
Hugh Duffy	1892–1900
Joe Dugan	1929
Oscar Dugey	1913–14
Bill Dunlap	1929–30
Tom Earley	1938–42, 1945
Mal Eason	1902
Eddie Eayrs	1920–21
Foster Edwards	1925–28
Dick Egan	1915–16
Rowdy Elliott	1910
Glenn Elliott	1947–49
Jumbo Elliott	1934
Bob Elliott	1947–51
Bob Emmerich	1923
Gil English	1937–38
Dick Errickson	1938–42
George Estock	1951
Buck Etchison	1943–44
Chick Evans	1909–10
Johnny Evers	1914–17, 1929
Ed Fallenstin	1933
Doc Farrell	1927–29
Kerby Farrell	1943
Gus Felix	1923–25
George Ferguson	1908–11
Nanny Fernandez	1942, 1946–47
Wes Ferrell	1941
Lou Fette	1937–40, 1945
Dana Fillingim	1918–23
Tom Fisher	1904
Ed Fitzpatrick	1915–17
Patsy Flaherty	1907–08, 1911
Elbie Fletcher	1934–35, 1937–39, 1949
Curry Foley	1879–80
Gene Ford	1936
Hod Ford	1919–23, 1932–33
Jack Fournier	1927
John Fox	1881
Fred Frankhouse	1930–35, 1939
Chick Fraser	1905
Vic Frasier	1937
Buck Freeman	1900
Howard Freigau	1928
Charlie Frisbee	1899
Sam Frock	1907, 1910–11
Frank Gabler	1937–38
Gil Gallagher	1922
Daff Gammons	1901
Charlie Ganzel	1889–97
Debs Garms	1937–39
Jim Garry	1893
Hank Gastright	1893
Doc Gautreau	1925–28
Dinty Gearin	1924
Phil Geier	1904
Joe Genewich	1922–28
Lefty George	1918
Ben Geraghty	1943–44
Lefty Gervais	1913
Gus Getz	1909–10
Charlie Getzien	1890–91
Frank Gibson	1921–27
Larry Gilbert	1914–15
Carden Gillenwater	1945–46
Billy Ging	1899
Roland Gladu	1944

Ed Glenn	1888
Al Glossop	1940
Hal Goldsmith	1926–28
Mike Gonzalez	1912
Gene Good	1906
Ralph Good	1910
Wilbur Good	1910–11
Sid Gordon	1950–52
Hank Gowdy	1911–17, 1919–23, 1929–30
Peaches Graham	1908–11
Kyle Graham	1924–26
Sid Graves	1927
Kent Greenfield	1927–29
Ed Gremminger	1902–03
Buddy Gremp	1940–42
Hank Griffin	1911–12
Tommy Griffith	1913–14
Burleigh Grimes	1930
George Grossart	1901
Tom Gunning	1884–86
Dick Gyselman	1933–34
Mert Hackett	1883–85
Walter Hackett	1885
Mickey Haefner	1950
Hal Haid	1931
Dad Hale	1902
Bob Hall	1949–50
Billy Hamilton	1896–1901
Jack Hannifin	1908
Lew Hardie	1890
Pinky Hargrave	1932–33
Dick Harley	1905
George Harper	1929
Joe Harrington	1895–96
Dave Harris	1925, 1928
Roy Hartsfield	1950–52
Mickey Haslin	1936
Buddy Hassett	1939–41
Bill Hawes	1879
Marv Hawley	1894
Bunny Hearn	1918, 1920
Bunny Hearn	1926–29
Jeff Heath	1948–49
Heinie Heltzel	1943
Don Hendrickson	1945–46
Snake Henry	1922
John Henry	1918
Billy Herman	1946
Al Hermann	1923
Frank Hershey	1905
Buck Herzog	1910–11, 1918–19
Otto Hess	1912–15
Joe Heving	1945
Jim Hickey	1942, 1944
Mike Hickey	1899
Piano Legs Hickman	1897–99
Bill Higgins	1888
Andy High	1925–27
Mike Hines	1883–85, 1888
Paul Hines	1890
John Hinton	1901
Jim Hitchcock	1938
Ralph Hodgin	1939
George Hodson	1894
Stew Hofferth	1944–46
Izzy Hoffman	1907
Shanty Hogan	1925–27, 1933–35
Brad Hogg	1911–12
Bobby Hogue	1948–51
Walter Holke	1919–22
Dutch Holland	1932–33
Bonnie Hollingsworth	1928
Tommy Holmes	1942–50
Abie Hood	1925
Dick Hoover	1952
Johnny Hopp	1946–47
Rogers Hornsby	1928
Joe Hornung	1881–88
Pete Hotaling	1882
Sadie Houck	1879–80
Ben Houser	1911–12
Del Howard	1906–07
Otto Huber	1939
Tom Hughes	1914–18
Harry Hulihan	1922
Bill Hunnefield	1931
Jerry Hurley	1889
Warren Huston	1944
Johnny Hutchings	1941–42, 1944–46
Ira Hutchinson	1937–38, 1944–45

Scotty Ingerton	1911
Fred Jacklitsch	1917
George Jackson	1911–13
Bernie James	1929–30
Bill James	1913–15, 1919
Al Javery	1940–46
George Jeffcoat	1943
Virgil Jester	1952
Sam Jethroe	1950–52
Art Johnson	1940–42
Ernie Johnson	1950, 1952
Roy Johnson	1937–38
Si Johnson	1946–47
Jimmy Johnston	1926
Dick Johnston	1885–89
Johnny Jones	1920
Ken Jones	1930
Percy Jones	1929
Sheldon Jones	1952
Bill Jones	1911
Charley Jones	1879–80
Eddie Joost	1943, 1945
Buck Jordan	1932–36
Al Kaiser	1911–12
Ike Kamp	1924–25
Tom Kane	1938
Andy Karl	1947
Ray Keating	1919
Bill Keister	1898
Joe Kelley	1891, 1908
Bob Kelly	1918
Joe Kelly	1917–19
King Kelly	1887–89, 1891–92
Art Kenney	1938
Buddy Kerr	1950–51
Hod Kibbie	1925
John Kiley	1891
Frank Killen	1899
Jay Kirke	1911–13
Mal Kittridge	1901–03
Billy Klaus	1952
Johnny Kling	1911–12
Fred Klobedanz	1896–99, 1902
Stan Klopp	1944
Billy Klusman	1888
Clyde Kluttz	1942–45
Elmer Knetzer	1916
Jack Knight	1927
Fritz Knothe	1932–33
Joe Knotts	1907
Ed Konetchy	1916–18
Jim Konstanty	1946
Larry Kopf	1922–23
Fabian Kowalik	1936
Clarence Kraft	1914
Rube Kroh	1912
Charlie Kuhns	1899
Hi Ladd	1898
Fred Lake	1891, 1897
Al Lakeman	1949
Frank LaManna	1940–42
Henry Lampe	1894
Hunter Lane	1924
Walt Lanfranconi	1947
Johnny Lanning	1936–39, 1947
Gene Lansing	1922
Swede Larsen	1936
Bill Lauterborn	1904–05
Al Lawson	1890
Bob Lawson	1901
Freddy Leach	1932
Jack Leary	1880
Hal Lee	1933–36
Bill Lee	1945–46
Lou Legett	1929
Andy Leonard	1876–78
Dixie Leverett	1929
Ted Lewis	1896–1900
Fred Lewis	1881
Bill Lewis	1935–36
Vive Lindaman	1906–09
Ernie Lindemann	1907
Walt Linden	1950
Carl Lindquist	1943–44
Danny Litwhiler	1946–48
Mickey Livingston	1949
Bobby Loane	1940
Johnny Logan	1951–52
Bob Logan	1945
Ernie Lombardi	1942

Herman Long	1890–1902
Red Long	1902
Al Lopez	1936–40
Bris Lord	1913
Tom Lovett	1894
Fletcher Low	1915
Bobby Lowe	1890–1901
Red Lucas	1924–25
Dolf Luque	1914–15
Billy Lush	1901–02
Al Lyons	1948
Danny MacFayden	1935–39, 1943
Joe Mack	1945
Max Macon	1944, 1947
Harry MacPherson	1944
Kid Madden	1887–89
Bunny Madden	1906
Sherry Magee	1915–17
Harl Maggert	1938
Freddie Maguire	1929–31
Mike Mahoney	1897
Willard Mains	1896
Hank Majeski	1939, 1941
John Malarkey	1902–03
Les Mallon	1934–35
Charlie Maloney	1908
Leo Mangum	1932–35
Les Mann	1913–14, 1919–20, 1924–27
Jimmy Manning	1884–85
Jack Manning	1876, 1878
Don Manno	1940–41
Dick Manville	1950
Rabbit Maranville	1912–20, 1929–33, 1935
Rube Marquard	1922–25
Luis Marquez	1951
Bill Marriott	1925
Willard Marshall	1950–52
Doc Marshall	1904
Marty Martel	1910
Jack Martin	1914
Ray Martin	1943, 1947–48
Bill Martin	1914
Phil Masi	1939–49
Roy Massey	1918
Mike Massey	1917
Joe Mathes	1916
Eddie Mathews	1952
Bobby Mathews	1881–82
Al Mattern	1908–12
Joe Matthews	1922
Gene Mauch	1950–51
Eddie Mayo	1937–38
Bill McAfee	1931
Gene McAuliffe	1904
Dick McBride	1876
Johnny McCarthy	1943, 1946
Tommy McCarthy	1885, 1892–95
Tom McCarthy	1908–09
Bill McCarthy	1905
Bill McCarthy	1906
Jeff McCleskey	1913
Jim McCloskey	1936
Hal McClure	1882
Frank McCormick	1947–48
Mike McCormick	1946–48
Tom McCreery	1903
Tex McDonald	1913
Ed McDonald	1911–12
Frank McElyea	1942
Dan McGann	1896, 1908
Chippy McGarr	1890
Dan McGee	1934
Tim McGinley	1876
Frank McGowan	1937
Stuffy McInnis	1923–24
Bill McKechnie	1913
Ralph McLeod	1938
Marty McManus	1934
Dinny McNamara	1927–28
Tim McNamara	1922–25
Ed McNichol	1904
Hugh McQuillan	1918–22, 1927
Bill McTigue	1911–12
Joe Medwick	1945
Jouett Meekin	1899
Bill Merritt	1893–94, 1899
Chief Meyers	1917
Eddie Miller	1939–42
Frank Miller	1922–23
Doc Miller	1910–12
Art Mills	1927–28
George Mogridge	1926–27
Al Montgomery	1941
Gene Moore	1936–38, 1940–41
Eddie Moore	1926–28
Randy Moore	1930–35
Hiker Moran	1938–39
Herbie Moran	1908–10, 1914–15
Pat Moran	1901–05
Forrest More	1909
Cy Morgan	1921–22
Gene Moriarity	1884
Ed Moriarty	1935
Jim Moroney	1906
John Morrill	1876–88
Guy Morrison	1927–28
Ray Moss	1931
Joe Mowry	1933–35
Heinie Mueller	1928–29
Ray Mueller	1935–38, 1951
Joe Muich	1924
Dick Mulligan	1946–47
Tim Murnane	1876–77
Dave Murphy	1905
Frank Murphy	1901
Buzz Murphy	1918
Jim Murray	1914
Amby Murray	1936
Danny Murtaugh	1947
Hap Myers	1913
Billy Nash	1885–89, 1891–95
Tom Needham	1904–07
Art Nehf	1915–19
Tommy Neill	1946–47
Bernie Neis	1925–26
Tom Nelson	1945
Johnny Neun	1930–31
Kid Nichols	1890–1901
Chet Nichols	1951
Tricky Nichols	1876
Fred Nicholson	1921–22
Butch Nieman	1943–45
Johnny Niggeling	1938, 1946
Al Nixon	1921–23
Lou North	1924
Jake Northrop	1918–19
Wynn Noyes	1913
Dizzy Nutter	1919
Charlie Nyce	1895
Ken O'Dea	1946
Dave Odom	1943
Joe Oeschger	1919–23
Joe Ogrodowski	1925
Kid O'Hara	1904
Dan O'Leary	1880
Luis Olmo	1950–51
Mickey O'Neil	1919–25
Jack O'Neill	1906
Jess Orndorff	1907
Frank O'Rourke	1912
Jim O'Rourke	1876–78, 1880
John O'Rourke	1879–80
Tom O'Rourke	1887–88
Wayne Osborne	1936
Jimmy Outlaw	1939
Don Padgett	1946
Ernie Padgett	1923–25
Phil Paine	1951
Emilio Palmero	1928
Bill Parks	1876
Jiggs Parson	1910–11
Charlie Parsons	1886
Red Peery	1929
Henry Peploski	1929
Hub Perdue	1911–14
Big Jeff Pfeffer	1906–08, 1911
Damon Phillips	1944
Eddie Phillips	1924
Wiley Piatt	1903
Charlie Pick	1919–20
Dave Pickett	1898
Clarence Pickrel	1934
Al Piechota	1940–41
Al Pierotti	1920–21
Togie Pittinger	1900–04
Hugh Poland	1943–44, 1946
Tom Poorman	1885–86
Bill Posedel	1939–41, 1946
Nels Potter	1948–49
Ray Powell	1917–24
Phil Powers	1880
Mel Preibisch	1940–41
Jim Prendergast	1948
Hub Pruett	1932
Blondie Purcell	1885
Ewald Pyle	1945
Bill Quarles	1893
Jack Quinn	1913
Joe Quinn	1888–89, 1891–92
Paddy Quinn	1881
Old Hoss Radbourn	1886–89
Paul Radford	1883
Pat Ragan	1915–19
Bill Ramsey	1945
Newt Randall	1907
Bill Rariden	1909–13
Johnny Rawlings	1917–20
Irv Ray	1888–89
Fred Raymer	1904–05
Bill Reed	1952
Wally Rehg	1917–18
Earl Reid	1946
Bobby Reis	1936–38
Tommy Reis	1938
Pete Reiser	1949–50
Ed Reulbach	1916–17
Flint Rhem	1934–35
Billy Rhiel	1930
Woody Rich	1944
Hardy Richardson	1889
Lance Richbourg	1927–31
Lew Richie	1909–10
John Richmond	1880–81
Lee Richmond	1879
Joe Rickert	1901
Marv Rickert	1948–49
Art Rico	1916–17
Harry Riconda	1926
Johnny Riddle	1937–38
Joe Riggert	1919
Jimmy Riley	1910
Claude Ritchey	1907–09
Skippy Roberge	1941–42, 1946
Charlie Robertson	1927–28
Gene Robertson	1929–30
Red Rollings	1930
George Rooks	1891
Steve Roser	1946
Jack Roser	1922
Chet Ross	1939–44
Bama Rowell	1939–41, 1946–47
Ed Rowen	1882
Norm Roy	1950
Dick Rudolph	1913–20, 1922–23, 1927
Jim Russell	1948–49
Babe Ruth	1935
Connie Ryan	1943–44, 1946–50
Cyclone Ryan	1891
John Ryan	1894–96
Rosy Ryan	1925–26
Johnny Sain	1942, 1946–51
Bill Salkeld	1948–49
Manny Salvo	1940–43
Ray Sanders	1946, 1949
Mike Sandlock	1942, 1944
Ed Sauer	1949
Les Scarsella	1940
Sid Schacht	1951
Hal Schacker	1945
Harry Schafer	1876–78
Al Schellhase	1890
Butch Schmidt	1913–15
Hank Schreiber	1917
Wes Schulmerich	1931–33
Jack Schulte	1906
Johnny Schulte	1932
Joe Schultz	1912–13
Bill Schuster	1939
Art Schwind	1912
Jack Scott	1917, 1919–21
Socks Seibold	1929–33
Rube Sellers	1910
Frank Sexton	1895
Cy Seymour	1913
Joe Shannon	1915
Red Shannon	1915
Bud Sharpe	1905, 1910
Al Shaw	1909
Marty Shay	1924
Dave Shean	1909–10, 1912
Earl Sheely	1931
Steve Shemo	1944–45
Bill Sherdel	1930–32
Art Shires	1932
Milt Shoffner	1937–39
Clyde Shoun	1947–49
Vince Shupe	1945
Oscar Siemer	1925–26
Al Simmons	1939
Hosea Siner	1909
Elmer Singleton	1945–46
George Sisler	1928–30
Sibby Sisti	1939–42, 1946–52
Jimmy Slagle	1901
Edgar Smith	1883
Pop Smith	1889–90
Earl Smith	1923–24
Elmer Smith	1901
Fred Smith	1913
Harry Smith	1908, 1910
Stub Smith	1898
Red Smith	1914–19
Jimmy Smith	1918
Jack Smith	1926–29
Bob Smith	1923–30, 1933–37
Tom Smith	1894
Fred Snodgrass	1915–16
Pop Snyder	1878–79, 1881
Pete Sommers	1888
Billy Southworth	1921–23
Bill Sowders	1888–89
Warren Spahn	1942, 1946–52
Chet Spencer	1906
Ed Sperber	1924
Al Spohrer	1928–35
Harry Spratt	1911–12
Ebba St. Claire	1951–52
General Stafford	1898–99
Chick Stahl	1897–1900
Harry Staley	1891–94
Eddie Stanky	1948–49
Joe Stanley	1903–04
Charlie Starr	1909
Ray Starr	1933
Harry Steinfeldt	1911
Fred Stem	1908–09
Bill Stemmeyer	1885–87
Casey Stengel	1924–25
Joe Stewart	1904
Jack Stivetts	1892–98
Otis Stocksdale	1895
Allyn Stout	1943
Harry Stovey	1891–92
Paul Strand	1913–15
Gabby Street	1905
Oscar Streit	1899
Nick Strincevich	1940–41
Joe Stripp	1938
Allie Strobel	1905–06
Dutch Stryker	1924
George Stultz	1894
Bobby Sturgeon	1948
Andy Sullivan	1904
Denny Sullivan	1880
Jim Sullivan	1891, 1895–97
John Sullivan	1920
Joe Sullivan	1939–41
Marty Sullivan	1890–91
Mike Sullivan	1898–99
Billy Sullivan	1899–1900
Max Surkont	1950–52
Butch Sutcliffe	1938
Ezra Sutton	1877–88
Bill Sweeney	1907–13
Bill Swift	1940
John Taber	1890
Roy Talcott	1943
Pop Tate	1885–88
Eddie Taylor	1926
Zack Taylor	1926–29
Fred Tenney	1894–1907, 1911
Zeb Terry	1918
Tommy Thevenow	1937
Bert Thiel	1952
Herb Thomas	1924–25, 1927
Roy Thomas	1909
Walt Thomas	1908
Don Thompson	1949
Fuller Thompson	1911
Tommy Thompson	1933–36
Bob Thorpe	1952
Jim Thorpe	1919
Cotton Tierney	1924

John Titus	1912–13
Jim Tobin	1940–45
Earl Torgeson	1947–52
Red Torphy	1920
Lou Tost	1942–43
Clay Touchstone	1928–29
Ira Townsend	1920–21
Leo Townsend	1920–21
Walt Tragesser	1913, 1915–19
Sam Trott	1880
Tommy Tucker	1890–97
Tom Tuckey	1908–09
Jim Turner	1937–39
George Twombly	1917
Fred Tyler	1914
Lefty Tyler	1910–17
Johnnie Tyler	1934–35
Jim Tyng	1879

Mike Ulisney	1945
Bill Upham	1918
Luke Urban	1927–28
Billy Urbanski	1931–36

Bill Van Dyke	1893
Bill Vargus	1925–26
Al Veigel	1939
Emil Verban	1950
Lee Viau	1892
Bill Voiselle	1947–49
Jake Volz	1905
Hon Von Fricken	1890
Phil Voyles	1929

Bill Wagner	1918
Murray Wall	1950
Lefty Wallace	1942, 1945–46
Norm Wallen	1945
Ed Walsh	1917
Joe Walsh	1938
Bucky Walters	1931–32, 1950
Lloyd Waner	1941
Paul Waner	1941–42
Jack Warner	1895
Rabbit Warstler	1936–40
Link Wasem	1937
Mule Watson	1920–23
Hal Weafer	1936
Orlie Weaver	1911
Roy Weir	1936–39
Jimmy Welsh	1925–27, 1929–30
Stan Wentzel	1945
Johnny Wertz	1926–29
Frank West	1894
Max West	1938–42, 1946
Oscar Westerberg	1907
Bert Whaling	1913–15
Bobby Wheelock	1887
Tom Whelan	1920
Pete Whisenant	1952
Bob Whitcher	1945
Ernie White	1946–48
Deacon White	1877
Jack White	1904
Kirby White	1909–10
Sam White	1919
Steve White	1912
Will White	1877
Gil Whitehouse	1912
Gurdon Whiteley	1885
Pinky Whitney	1933–36
Frank Whitney	1876
Jim Whitney	1881–85
Possum Whitted	1914
Al Wickland	1918
Whitey Wietelmann	1939–46
Claude Wilborn	1940
Kaiser Wilhelm	1904–05
Joe Wilhoit	1916–17
Earl Williams	1928
Ace Williams	1940, 1946
Pop Williams	1903
Vic Willis	1898–1905
Art Wilson	1918–20
Charlie Wilson	1931
Frank Wilson	1924–26
Zeke Wilson	1895
Jim Wilson	1951–52
Nick Wise	1888
Sam Wise	1882–88
Roy Witherup	1906
Harry Wolverton	1905
Sid Womack	1926
George Woodend	1944
Chuck Workman	1943–46
Red Worthington	1931–34
Al Wright	1933
Ab Wright	1944
George Wright	1876–78, 1880–81
Ed Wright	1945–48
Sam Wright	1876, 1881

George Yeager	1896–99
Jim Yeargin	1922, 1924
Cy Young	1911
Harley Young	1908
Herman Young	1911
Irv Young	1905–08

Tom Zachary	1930–34
Guy Zinn	1913

Managers

*Dave Bancroft	1924–27
Del Bissonette	1945
Frank Bowerman	1909
Al Buckenberger	1902–04
*Jack Burdock	1883
Bob Coleman	1943–45
Johnny Cooney	1949
Judge Fuchs	1929
Charlie Grimm	1952
Jim Hart	1889
Tommy Holmes	1951–52
*Rogers Hornsby	1928
*Joe Kelley	1908
*King Kelly	1887
*Johnny Kling	1912
Fred Lake	1910
Bill McKechnie	1930–37
Fred Mitchell	1921–23
*John Morrill	1882–88
Dick Rudolph	1924
Frank Selee	1890–1901
Jack Slattery	1928
Harry Smith	1909
Billy Southworth	1946–51
George Stallings	1913–20
Casey Stengel	1938–43
*Fred Tenney	1905–07, 1911
Harry Wright	1876–81

BROOKLYN Dodgers
1890–1957

Moved from American Association
Known as Bridegrooms 1890–98
Superbas 1899–1910
Robins 1914–31
Moved to LOS ANGELES Dodgers

Bert Abbey	1895–96
Cal Abrams	1949–52
Morrie Aderholt	1944–45
Eddie Ainsmith	1923
Raleigh Aitchison	1911, 1914–15
Ed Albosta	1941
Frank Allen	1912–14
Horace Allen	1919
Johnny Allen	1941–43
Mel Almada	1939
Whitey Alperman	1906–09
Sandy Amoros	1952, 1954–57
Ferrell Anderson	1946
John Anderson	1894–99
Stan Andrews	1944–45
Pat Ankenman	1943–44
Bill Antonello	1953
Ed Appleton	1915–16
Jimmy Archer	1918

Charlie Babb	1904–05
Johnny Babich	1934–35
Sweetbreads Bailey	1921
Gene Bailey	1923–24
Doug Baird	1919–20
Tom Baker	1935–37
Lady Baldwin	1890
Win Ballou	1929
Dave Bancroft	1928–29
Dan Bankhead	1947, 1950–51
Jack Banta	1947–50
Turner Barber	1923
Cy Barger	1910–12
Red Barkley	1943
Jesse Barnes	1926–27
Rex Barney	1943, 1946–50
Bob Barr	1935
Bob Barrett	1927
Boyd Bartley	1943
Al Bashang	1918
Eddie Basinski	1944–45
Emil Batch	1904–07
Erve Beck	1899
Boom-Boom Beck	1933–34
Hank Behrman	1946–48
Wayne Belardi	1950, 1953
George Bell	1907–11
Ray Benge	1933–35
Moe Berg	1923
Bill Bergen	1904–11
Ray Berres	1934, 1936
Don Bessent	1955–57
Ralph Birkofer	1937
Del Bissonette	1928–31, 1933
Joe Black	1952–55
Clarence Blethen	1929
Lu Blue	1933
George Boehler	1926
Sammy Bohne	1926
Jack Bolling	1944
Frank Bonner	1896
Ike Boone	1930, 1932
Frenchy Bordagaray	1935–36, 1942–45
Bob Borkowski	1955
Buzz Boyle	1933–35
Gib Brack	1937–38
Joe Bradshaw	1929
Bobby Bragan	1943–44, 1947–48
Ralph Branca	1944–53, 1956
Ed Brandt	1936
Rube Bressler	1928–31
Rocky Bridges	1951–52
Matt Broderick	1903
Dan Brouthers	1892–93
Eddie Brown	1924–25
Elmer Brown	1913–15
John Brown	1897
Lindsay Brown	1937
Lloyd Brown	1925
Mace Brown	1941
Tommy Brown	1944–45, 1947–51
George Browne	1911
Pete Browning	1894
Jim Bucher	1934–37
Cy Buker	1945
Al Burch	1907–11
Jack Burdock	1891
Sandy Burk	1910–12
Oyster Burns	1890–95
Buster Burrell	1895–97
Doc Bushong	1890
Max Butcher	1936–38
John Butler	1906–07
Johnny Butler	1926–27

Leon Cadore	1915–23
Bruce Caldwell	1932
Leo Callahan	1913
Dolf Camilli	1938–43
Roy Campanella	1948–57
Al Campanis	1943
Gilly Campbell	1938
Jimmy Canavan	1897
Guy Cantrell	1925, 1927
Ben Cantwell	1937
Max Carey	1926–29
Tex Carleton	1940
Ownie Carroll	1933–34
Kid Carsey	1901
Bob Caruthers	1890–91
Hugh Casey	1939–42, 1946–48
Doc Casey	1899–1900, 1906–07
Pete Cassidy	1899
Tom Catterson	1908–09
Ed Chandler	1947
Glenn Chapman	1934
Ben Chapman	1944–45
Larry Cheney	1915–19
Paul Chervinko	1937–38
Bob Chipman	1941–44
Gino Cimoli	1956–57
George Cisar	1937
Moose Clabaugh	1926
Bud Clancy	1932
Bob Clark	1890
Watty Clark	1927–37
Wally Clement	1909
Alta Cohen	1931–32
Hub Collins	1890–92
Bill Collins	1913
Jackie Collum	1957
Jack Coombs	1915–18
Johnny Cooney	1935–37, 1943–44
Claude Corbitt	1945
Tommy Corcoran	1892–96
Chuck Corgan	1925, 1927
Pop Corkhill	1890
Pete Coscarart	1938–41
Bob Coulson	1910–11
Dick Cox	1925–26
Billy Cox	1948–54
George Crable	1910
Roger Craig	1955–57
Cannonball Crane	1893
Sam Crane	1922
Claude Crocker	1944–45
John Cronin	1895, 1904
Lave Cross	1900
Bill Crouch	1939
Tony Cuccinello	1932–35
Roy Cullenbine	1940
Nick Cullop	1929
Cliff Curtis	1912–13
George Cutshaw	1912–17
Kiki Cuyler	1938

Bill Dahlen	1899–1903
Babe Dahlgren	1942
Con Daily	1891–95
Jud Daley	1911–12
Jack Dalton	1910, 1914
Tom Daly	1890–96, 1898–1901
Jake Daniel	1937
Fats Dantonio	1944–45
Cliff Dapper	1942
Bob Darnell	1954, 1956
Dan Daub	1893–97
Jake Daubert	1910–18
Bill Davidson	1910–11
Lefty Davis	1901
Curt Davis	1940–46
Pea Ridge Day	1931
Lindsay Deal	1939
Hank DeBerry	1922–30
Art Decatur	1922–25
Artie Dede	1916
Raoul Dedeaux	1935
Pat Deisel	1902
Wheezer Dell	1915–17
Bert Delmas	1933
Don Demeter	1956
Gene DeMontreville	1900
Eddie Dent	1909, 1911–12
Rube Dessau	1910
Leo Dickerman	1923–24
Pop Dillon	1904
Bill Doak	1924, 1927–28
John Dobbs	1903–05
George Dockins	1947
Cozy Dolan	1901–02
Patsy Donovan	1890
Wild Bill Donovan	1899–1902
Mickey Doolan	1918
Jack Doscher	1903–06
John Douglas	1945
Phil Douglas	1915
Snooks Dowd	1926
Red Downey	1909
Red Downs	1912
Jack Doyle	1903–04
Carl Doyle	1939–40
Tom Drake	1941
Don Drysdale	1956–57
Clise Dudley	1929–30
Jack Dunn	1897–1900
Joe Dunn	1908–09
Bull Durham	1904
Dick Durning	1917–18
Leo Durocher	1938–40
Red Durrett	1944–45

Billy Earle	1894
George Earnshaw	1935–36
Mal Eason	1905–06
Eddie Eayrs	1921
Ox Eckhardt	1936
Bruce Edwards	1946–51
Dick Egan	1914
Rube Ehrhardt	1924–28
Harry Eisenstat	1935–37

Kid Elberfeld	1914
Rowdy Elliott	1920
Jumbo Elliott	1925, 1927–30
Don Elston	1957
Bones Ely	1891
Woody English	1937–38
Gil English	1944
Johnny Enzmann	1914
Al Epperly	1950
Carl Erskine	1948–57
Tex Erwin	1910–14
Dude Esterbrook	1891
Roy Evans	1902–03
Red Evans	1939
Bunny Fabrique	1916–17
George Fallon	1937
Alex Farmer	1908
Duke Farrell	1899–1902
Jim Faulkner	1930
Gus Felix	1926–27
Alex Ferguson	1929
Chico Fernandez	1956
Wes Ferrell	1940
Lou Fette	1940
Chick Fewster	1926
Pembroke Finlayson	1908–09
Mickey Finn	1930–32
Bill Fischer	1913–14
Chauncey Fisher	1897
Bob Fisher	1912–13
Freddie Fitzsimmons	1937–43
Tom Fitzsimmons	1919
Sam Fletcher	1909
Tim Flood	1902–03
Wes Flowers	1940, 1944
Jake Flowers	1927–31, 1933
Hod Ford	1925
Jack Fournier	1923–26
Dave Foutz	1890–95
Fred Frankhouse	1936–38
Jack Franklin	1944
Herman Franks	1940–41
Johnny Frederick	1929–34
Howard Freigau	1928
Larry French	1941–42
Ray French	1923
Lonny Frey	1933–36
Charlie Fuchs	1944
Nig Fuller	1902
Carl Furillo	1946–57
John Gaddy	1938
Augie Galan	1941–46
Joe Gallagher	1940
Phil Gallivan	1931
Ned Garvin	1902–04
Welcome Gaston	1898–99
Hank Gastright	1894
Frank Gatins	1901
Sid Gautreaux	1936
Jim Gentile	1957
Greek George	1938
Ben Geraghty	1936
Doc Gessler	1903–06
Gus Getz	1914–16
Charlie Gilbert	1940
Pete Gilbert	1894
Wally Gilbert	1928–31
Carden Gillenwater	1943
Jim Gilliam	1953–57
Al Gionfriddo	1947
Tony Giuliani	1940–41
Al Glossop	1943
John Gochnaur	1901
Johnny Gooch	1928
Ray Gordinier	1921–22
Jack Graham	1946
Harvey Green	1935
Nelson Greene	1924–25
Kent Greenfield	1929
Hal Gregg	1943–47
Mike Griffin	1891–98
Bert Griffith	1922–23
Tommy Griffith	1919–25
John Grim	1895–99
Burleigh Grimes	1918–26
Dan Griner	1918
Lee Grissom	1940–41
Ad Gumbert	1895–96
Bert Haas	1937
George Haddock	1892–93
Johnny Hall	1948
Bob Hall	1905
Bill Hall	1913
Bill Hallman	1898
Luke Hamlin	1937–41
Pat Hannifan	1897
F. C. Hansford	1898
Charlie Hargreaves	1923–28
George Harper	1896
Harry Harper	1923
Joe Harris	1928
Bill Harris	1957
Bill Hart	1892
Bill Hart	1943–45
Chris Hartje	1939
Buddy Hassett	1936–38
Gil Hatfield	1893
Ray Hathaway	1945
Joe Hatten	1946–51
Chris Haughey	1943
Phil Haugstad	1947–48, 1951
Ray Hayworth	1938–39, 1944–45
Ed Head	1940, 1942–44, 1946
Hugh Hearne	1901–03
Mike Hechinger	1913
Jake Hehl	1918
Fred Heimach	1930–33
Henry Heitmann	1918
George Hemming	1891
Harvey Hendrick	1927–30
Lafayette Henion	1919
Weldon Henley	1907
Butch Henline	1927–29
Dutch Henry	1923–24
Roy Henshaw	1937
Babe Herman	1926–31, 1945
Billy Herman	1941–43, 1946
Gene Hermanski	1943, 1946–51
Art Herring	1934, 1944–46
Marty Herrmann	1918
Jim Hickman	1916–19
Kirby Higbe	1941–43, 1946–47
Bob Higgins	1911–12
Andy High	1922–25
George Hildebrand	1902
Still Bill Hill	1899
Hunkey Hines	1895
Don Hoak	1954–55
Oris Hockett	1938–39
Gil Hodges	1943, 1947–57
Bert Hogg	1934
Al Hollingsworth	1939
Bonnie Hollingsworth	1924
Jim Holmes	1908
Tommy Holmes	1952
Wally Hood	1920–21
Johnny Hopp	1949
Lefty Hopper	1898
Elmer Horton	1898
Ed Householder	1903
Harry Howell	1898, 1900
Dixie Howell	1955–56
Waite Hoyt	1932, 1937–38
Bill Hubbell	1925
Johnny Hudson	1936–40
Ed Hug	1903
Jim Hughes	1899, 1901–02
Jim Hughes	1952–56
Mickey Hughes	1890
John Hummel	1905–15
Al Humphrey	1911
Bernie Hungling	1922–23
George Hunter	1909–10
Pat Hurley	1907
Joe Hutcheson	1933
Ira Hutchinson	1939
Roy Hutson	1925
Bert Inks	1891–92
Charlie Irwin	1901–02
Fred Jacklitsch	1903–04
Randy Jackson	1956–57
Merwin Jacobson	1926–27
Hal Janvrin	1921–22
Roy Jarvis	1944
George Jeffcoat	1936–37, 1939
Hughie Jennings	1899–1900, 1903
Jimmy Johnston	1916–25
Fred Johnston	1924
Art Jones	1932
Fielder Jones	1896–1900
Binky Jones	1924
Oscar Jones	1903–05
Dutch Jordan	1903–04
Jimmy Jordan	1933–36
Tim Jordan	1906–09
Spider Jorgensen	1947–50
Bill Joyce	1892
Joe Judge	1933
Alex Kampouris	1941–43
John Karst	1915
Willie Keeler	1893, 1899–1902
Chet Kehn	1942
John Kelleher	1916
Frank Kellert	1955
Joe Kelley	1899–1901
George Kelly	1932
Bob Kennedy	1957
Brickyard Kennedy	1892–1901
Maury Kent	1912–13
Pete Kilduff	1919–21
Newt Kimball	1940–43
Clyde King	1944–45, 1947–48, 1951–52
Tom Kinslow	1891–94
Fred Kipp	1957
Enos Kirkpatrick	1912–13
Frank Kitson	1900–02
Joe Klugmann	1924
Elmer Klumpp	1937
Elmer Knetzer	1909–12
Hub Knolls	1906
Barney Koch	1944
Len Koenecke	1934–35
Ed Konetchy	1919–21
Jim Korwan	1894
Sandy Koufax	1955–57
Joe Koukalik	1904
Lou Koupal	1928–29
Ernie Koy	1938–40
Charlie Kress	1954
Ernie Krueger	1917–21
Abe Kruger	1908
Joe Kustus	1909
Clem Labine	1950–57
Candy LaChance	1893–98
Frank Lamanske	1935
Bill Lamar	1920–21
Wayne LaMaster	1938
Joe Landrum	1950, 1952
Lyn Lary	1939
Tom Lasorda	1954–55
Tacks Latimer	1902
Cookie Lavagetto	1937–41, 1946–47
Tony Lazzeri	1939
Bill Leard	1917
Hal Lee	1930
Ken Lehman	1952, 1956–57
Larry LeJeune	1911
Steve Lembo	1950, 1952
Ed Lennox	1909–10
Dutch Leonard	1933–36
Sam Leslie	1933–35
Phil Lewis	1905–08
Jim Lindsey	1937
Freddie Lindstrom	1936
Mickey Livingston	1951
Billy Loes	1950, 1952–56
Dick Loftus	1924–25
Bob Logan	1935
Bill Lohrman	1943–44
Ernie Lombardi	1931
Vic Lombardi	1945–47
Tom Long	1924
Al Lopez	1928, 1930–35
Charlie Loudenslager	1904
Tom Lovett	1890–91, 1893
Ray Lucas	1933–34
Con Lucid	1894–95
Harry Lumley	1904–10
Don Lund	1947–48
Dolf Luque	1930–31
Ed MacGamwell	1905
Max Macon	1940, 1942–43
Lee Magee	1919
Sal Maglie	1956–57
George Magoon	1898
Duster Mails	1915–16
Charlie Malay	1905
Tony Malinosky	1937
Mal Mallette	1950
Lew Malone	1919
Billy Maloney	1906–08
Al Mamaux	1918–23
Gus Mancuso	1940
Heinie Manush	1937–38
Rabbit Maranville	1926
Rube Marquard	1915–20
Bill Marriott	1926–27
Buck Marrow	1937–38
Doc Marshall	1909
Morrie Martin	1949
Earl Mattingly	1931
Gene Mauch	1944, 1948
Al Maul	1899
Carmen Mauro	1953
Bill McCabe	1920
Gene McCann	1901–02
Bill McCarren	1923
Jack McCarthy	1906–07
Johnny McCarthy	1934–35
Tommy McCarthy	1896
Lew McCarty	1913–16
Mike McCormick	1904
Mike McCormick	1949
Walt McCreedie	1903
Tom McCreery	1901–03
Danny McDevitt	1957
Sandy McDougal	1895
Pryor McElveen	1909–11
Dan McFarlan	1899
Chappie McFarland	1906
Dan McGann	1899
Joe McGinnity	1900
Pat McGlothin	1949–50
Bob McGraw	1925–27
Deacon McGuire	1899–1901
Harry McIntire	1905–09
Doc McJames	1899, 1901
Kit McKenna	1898
Ed McLane	1907
Cal McLish	1944, 1946
Sadie McMahon	1897
John McMakin	1902
Frank McManus	1903
Tommy McMillan	1908–10
Doug McWeeny	1926–29
Joe Medwick	1940–43, 1946
Rube Melton	1943–44, 1946–47
Fred Merkle	1916–17
Irish Meusel	1927
Benny Meyer	1913
Leo Meyer	1909
Russ Meyer	1953–55
Chief Meyers	1916–17
Glenn Mickens	1953
Eddie Miksis	1944, 1946–51
Johnny Miljus	1917, 1920–21
Fred Miller	1910
Hack Miller	1916
Otto Miller	1910–22
Ralph Miller	1898
Walt Miller	1911
Wally Millies	1934
Bob Milliken	1953–54
Buster Mills	1935
Paul Minner	1946, 1948–49
Clarence Mitchell	1918–22
Fred Mitchell	1904–05
Johnny Mitchell	1924–25
Dale Mitchell	1956
George Mohart	1920–21
Dee Moore	1943
Gene Moore	1939–40
Eddie Moore	1929–30
Randy Moore	1936–37
Ray Moore	1952–53
Cy Moore	1929–32
Herbie Moran	1912–13
Eddie Morgan	1937
Bobby Morgan	1950, 1952–53
Johnny Morrison	1929–30
Walt Moryn	1954–55
Ray Moss	1926–31
Earl Mossor	1951
Glen Moulder	1946
Ray Mowe	1913
Mike Mowrey	1916–17
Billy Mullen	1923
Joe Mulvey	1895
Van Lingle Mungo	1931–41
Les Munns	1934–35
Simmy Murch	1908
Jim Murray	1922
Hy Myers	1909, 1911, 1914–22

Sam Nahem	1938
Charlie Neal	1956–57
Ron Negray	1952
Bernie Neis	1920–24
Rocky Nelson	1952, 1956
Don Newcombe	1949–51, 1954–57
Bobo Newsom	1929–30, 1942–43
Doc Newton	1901–02
Otho Nitcholas	1945
Al Nixon	1915–16, 1918
Jerry Nops	1900
Hub Northen	1911–12
John O'Brien	1891
Darby O'Brien	1890–92
Whitey Ock	1935
Lefty O'Doul	1931–33
Luis Olmo	1943–45, 1949
Ivy Olson	1915–24
Ollie O'Mara	1914–16, 1918–19
Mickey O'Neil	1926
Joe Oeschger	1925
Curly Onis	1935
Joe Orengo	1943
Frank O'Rourke	1917–18
Tiny Osborne	1924–25
Charlie Osgood	1944
Fritz Ostermueller	1943–44
Chink Outen	1933
Mickey Owen	1941–45
Red Owens	1905
Don Padgett	1946
Andy Pafko	1951–52
Phil Page	1934
Erv Palica	1947–51, 1953–54
Art Parks	1937, 1939
Jay Partridge	1927–28
Jim Pastorius	1906–09
Harry Pattee	1908
Jimmy Pattison	1929
Harley Payne	1896–98
Johnny Peacock	1945
Charlie Perkins	1934
Jim Peterson	1937
Jesse Petty	1925–28
Jeff Pfeffer	1913–21
George Pfister	1941
Lee Pfund	1945
Ed Phelps	1912–13
Babe Phelps	1935–41
Ray Phelps	1930–32
Val Picinich	1929–33
Joe Pignatano	1957
George Pinckney	1890–91
Ed Pipgras	1932
Norman Plitt	1918, 1927
Bud Podbielan	1949–52
Johnny Podres	1953–55, 1957
Boots Poffenberger	1939
Nick Polly	1937
Ed Poole	1904
Bill Posedel	1938
Sam Post	1922
Dykes Potter	1938
Bill Pounds	1903
Tot Pressnell	1938–40
Jack Quinn	1931–32
Steve Rachunok	1940
Marv Rackley	1947–49
Jack Radtke	1936
Pat Ragan	1911–15
Bob Ramazzotti	1946, 1948–49
Willie Ramsdell	1947–48, 1950
Phil Reardon	1906
Harry Redmond	1909
Pee Wee Reese	1940–42, 1946–57
Bill Reidy	1899, 1903–04
Bobby Reis	1931–32, 1935
Pete Reiser	1940–42, 1946–48
Doc Reisling	1904–05
Ed Reulbach	1913–14
Billy Rhiel	1929
Paul Richards	1932
Danny Richardson	1893
Harry Riconda	1928
Joe Riggert	1914
Lew Riggs	1941–42, 1946
Jimmy Ripple	1939–40
Lew Ritter	1902–08
Johnny Rizzo	1942
Jim Roberts	1924–25
Dick Robertson	1918
Jackie Robinson	1947–56
Lou Rochelli	1944
Preacher Roe	1948–54
Ed Roebuck	1955–57
Oscar Roettger	1927
Lee Rogers	1938
Packy Rogers	1938
Stan Rojek	1946–47
Jim Romano	1950
Johnny Roseboro	1957
Goody Rosen	1937–39, 1944–46
Max Rosenfeld	1931–33
Don Ross	1940
Schoolboy Rowe	1942
Jean Pierre Roy	1946
Luther Roy	1929
Nap Rucker	1907–16
Ernie Rudolph	1945
Dutch Ruether	1921–24
Andy Rush	1925
Jim Russell	1950–51
John Russell	1917–18
Johnny Rutherford	1952
Jack Ryan	1911
John Ryan	1898
Rosy Ryan	1933
Mike Sandlock	1945–46
Bill Sayles	1943
Doc Scanlan	1904–07, 1909–11
Bill Schardt	1911–12
Al Scheer	1913
Dutch Schliebner	1923
Ray Schmandt	1918–22
Henry Schmidt	1903
Johnny Schmitz	1951–52
Charlie Schmutz	1914–15
Frank Schneiberg	1910
Paul Schreiber	1922–23
Howie Schultz	1943–47
Joe Schultz	1915
Ferdie Schupp	1921
Tom Seats	1945
Jimmy Sebring	1909
Elmer Sexauer	1948
George Sharrott	1893–94
Joe Shaute	1931–33
Merv Shea	1938
Jimmy Sheckard	1897–98, 1900–05
Jack Sheehan	1920–21
Tommy Sheehan	1908
Red Sheridan	1918, 1920
Vince Sherlock	1935
Bill Shindle	1894–98
George Shoch	1893–97
Harry Shriver	1922–23
George Shuba	1948, 1950, 1952–55
Dick Siebert	1932, 1936
Fred Sington	1938–39
Frank Skaff	1935
Gordon Slade	1930–32
Dwain Sloat	1948
Broadway Aleck Smith	1897–1900
Tony Smith	1910–11
George Smith	1918, 1923
Germany Smith	1890, 1897
Hap Smith	1910
Red Smith	1911–14
Sherry Smith	1915–17, 1919–22
Red Smyth	1915–17
Harry Smythe	1934
Duke Snider	1947–57
Jack Snyder	1917
Andy Sommerville	1894
Denny Sothern	1931
Roy Spencer	1937–38
Karl Spooner	1954–55
Eddie Stack	1912–13
Tuck Stainback	1938–39
George Stallings	1890
Jerry Standaert	1926
Eddie Stanky	1944–47
Dolly Stark	1910–12
Jigger Statz	1927–28
Elmer Steele	1911
Bill Steele	1914
Farmer Steelman	1900–01
Ed Stein	1892–96, 1898
Casey Stengel	1912–17
Ed Stevens	1945–47
Stuffy Stewart	1923
Milt Stock	1924–26
Harry Stovey	1893
Sammy Strang	1903–04
Elmer Stricklett	1905–07
Joe Stripp	1932–37
Dutch Stryker	1926
Clyde Sukeforth	1932–34, 1945
Billy Sullivan	1942
Tom Sunkel	1944
Bill Swift	1941
Vito Tamulis	1938–41
Tommy Tatum	1941, 1947
Danny Taylor	1932–36
Harry Taylor	1946–48
Zack Taylor	1920–25, 1935
Chuck Templeton	1955–56
Joe Tepsic	1946
Adonis Terry	1890–91
Wayne Terwilliger	1951
Grant Thatcher	1903–04
Henry Thielman	1903
Fay Thomas	1932
Ray Thomas	1938
Tim Thompson	1954
Don Thompson	1951, 1953–54
Fresco Thompson	1931
Hank Thormahlen	1925
Sloppy Thurston	1930–33
Cotton Tierney	1925
Al Todd	1939
Bert Tooley	1911–12
George Treadway	1894–95
Nick Tremark	1934–36
Overton Tremper	1927–28
Tommy Tucker	1898
Ty Tyson	1928
Fred Underwood	1894
Rene Valdez	1957
Elmer Valo	1957
Chris Van Cuyk	1950–52
Johnny Van Cuyk	1947–49
Dazzy Vance	1922–32, 1935
Arky Vaughan	1942–43, 1947–48
Rube Vickers	1903
Joe Vosmik	1940–41
Paul Wachtel	1917
Ben Wade	1952–54
Butts Wagner	1898
Bull Wagner	1913–14
Rube Walker	1951–57
Dixie Walker	1939–47
Mysterious Walker	1913
Joe Wall	1902
Lloyd Waner	1944
Paul Waner	1941, 1943–44
Chuck Ward	1918–22
Rube Ward	1902
Monte Ward	1891–92
Preston Ward	1948
Jack Warner	1929–31
Tommy Warren	1944
Jimmy Wasdell	1940–41
George Watkins	1936
Les Webber	1942–46
John Wells	1944
Max West	1928–29
Gus Weyhing	1900
Mack Wheat	1915–19
Zack Wheat	1909–26
Ed Wheeler	1902
Bill White	1945
Jesse Whiting	1906–07
Dick Whitman	1946–49
Kemp Wicker	1941
Kaiser Wilhelm	1908–10
Leon Williams	1926
Dick Williams	1951–54
Woody Williams	1938
Eddie Wilson	1936–37
Tex Wilson	1924
Hack Wilson	1932–34
Jim Winford	1938
Lave Winham	1902
Tom Winsett	1936–38
Hank Winston	1936
Whitey Witt	1926
Pete Wojey	1954
Clarence Wright	1901
Glenn Wright	1929–33
Zeke Wrigley	1899
Frank Wurm	1944
Whit Wyatt	1939–44
Ad Yale	1905
Rube Yarrison	1924
Joe Yeager	1898–1900
Earl Yingling	1912–13
Chink Zachary	1944
Tom Zachary	1934–36
Don Zimmer	1954–57
Eddie Zimmerman	1911
Bill Zimmerman	1915

Managers

Walter Alston	1954–57
Billy Barnie	1897–98
Ray Blades	1948
Max Carey	1932–33
Bill Dahlen	1910–13
Patsy Donovan	1906–08
Chuck Dressen	1951–53
*Leo Durocher	1939–46, 1948
Charlie Ebbets	1898
*Dave Foutz	1893–96
*Mike Griffin	1898
Burleigh Grimes	1937–38
Ned Hanlon	1899–1905
*Harry Lumley	1909
Bill McGunnigle	1890
Wilbert Robinson	1914–31
Burt Shotton	1947–50
Casey Stengel	1934–36
Clyde Sukeforth	1947
*Monte Ward	1891–92

BUFFALO Bisons 1879–85

Dan Brouthers	1881–85
James Burke	1882–83
Scrappy Carroll	1885
John Clapp	1879
Chub Collins	1884
John Connor	1885
Pete Conway	1885
Ed Coughlin	1884
Cannonball Crane	1885
Bill Crowley	1879–80, 1885
Ed Cushman	1883
One Arm Daily	1882
Dell Darling	1883
George Derby	1883
Buttercup Dickerson	1885
Tom Dolan	1882
Denny Driscoll	1880, 1885
Dave Eggler	1879, 1883–85
Bones Ely	1884
Dude Esterbrook	1880
Fisher	1885
Curry Foley	1881–83
Davy Force	1879–85
Chick Fulmer	1879–80
Pud Galvin	1879–85
Art Hagan	1883–84
Gil Hatfield	1885
Moxie Hengle	1885
Joe Hornung	1879–80
Tom Kearns	1880
Jim Keenan	1880
Doc Kennedy	1883
Arlie Latham	1880
Steve Libby	1879
Jim Lillie	1883–85
Jack Lynch	1881
Denny Mack	1880
Jack Manning	1881
Jim McCauley	1885

Jim McDonald	1885
Bill McGunnigle	1879–80
John Morrissey	1881
Mike Moynahan	1880
George Myers	1884–85
Jim O'Rourke	1881–84
Johnny Peters	1881
Dick Phelan	1885
Tom Poorman	1880
Blondie Purcell	1881–82
Old Hoss Radbourn	1880
Hardy Richardson	1879–85
Charles Ritter	1885
Jack Rowe	1879–85
Billy Serad	1884–85
Orator Shaffer	1883
Pop Smith	1881
Joe Staples	1885
Dan Stearns	1880, 1885
Tony Suck	1883
Sleeper Sullivan	1881
Ed Swartwood	1881
Oscar Walker	1879–80
Deacon White	1881–85
Stump Wiedman	1880
Fred Wood	1885
Pete Wood	1885

Managers

Jack Chapman	1885
*John Clapp	1879
Sam Crane	1880
*Pud Galvin	1885
*Jim O'Rourke	1881–84

CHICAGO Cubs 1876–1995
Known as White Stockings 1876–89
Colts 1890–97
Orphans 1898–1901

Bert Abbey	1893–95
Ted Abernathy	1965–66, 1969–70
Cliff Aberson	1947–49
Johnny Abrego	1985
Jimmy Adair	1931
Red Adams	1946
Sparky Adams	1922–27
Karl Adams	1915
Bobby Adams	1957–59
Mike Adams	1976–77
Terry Adams	1995
Bob Addis	1952–53
Bob Addy	1876
Dewey Adkins	1949
Hank Aguirre	1969–70
Jack Aker	1972–73
Dale Alderson	1943–44
Vic Aldridge	1917–18, 1922–24
Grover Alexander	1918–26
Matt Alexander	1973–74
Nick Allen	1916
Ethan Allen	1936
Milo Allison	1913
Porfi Altamirano	1984
George Altman	1959–62, 1965–67
Joey Amalfitano	1964–66
Vincente Amor	1955
Bob Anderson	1957–62
John Andre	1955
Jim Andrews	1890
Fred Andrus	1876, 1884
Tom Angley	1929
Cap Anson	1876–97
Jimmy Archer	1909–16
Jose Arcia	1968
Alex Arias	1992
Jim Asbell	1938
Richie Ashburn	1960–61
Ken Aspromonte	1963
Paul Assenmacher	1989–93
Toby Atwell	1952–53
Earl Averill	1959–60
Fred Baczewski	1953
Ed Baecht	1931–32
Sweetbreads Bailey	1919–21
Ed Bailey	1965
Gene Baker	1953–57
Tom Baker	1963
Mark Baldwin	1887–88
Jay Baller	1985–87
Tony Balsamo	1962
Ernie Banks	1953–71
Willie Banks	1994–95
Turner Barber	1917–22
Steve Barber	1970
Ross Barnes	1876–77
Cuno Barragan	1961–63
Bob Barrett	1924–25
Dick Barrett	1943
Shad Barry	1904–05
Dick Bartell	1939
Vince Barton	1931–32
Charlie Bastian	1889
Johnny Bates	1914
Russ Bauers	1946
Frank Baumann	1965
Frankie Baumholtz	1949, 1951–55
Jose Bautista	1993–94
Tommy Beals	1880
Dave Beard	1985
Ginger Beaumont	1910
Clyde Beck	1926–30
Heinz Becker	1943, 1945
Glenn Beckert	1965–73
Fred Beebe	1906
Les Bell	1930–31
George Bell	1991
Butch Benton	1982
Joe Berry	1942
Damon Berryhill	1987–91
Dick Bertell	1960–65, 1967
Oscar Bielaski	1876
Mike Bielecki	1988–91
Larry Biittner	1976–80
Steve Bilko	1954
Doug Bird	1981–82
Bill Bishop	1889
Hi Bithorn	1942–43, 1946
Tim Blackwell	1978–81
Rick Bladt	1969
Footsie Blair	1929–31
Sheriff Blake	1924–31
Kevin Blankenship	1988–90
Cy Block	1942, 1945–46
Randy Bobb	1968–69
John Boccabella	1963–68
Jim Bolger	1955, 1957–58
Bobby Bonds	1981
Julio Bonetti	1940
Bill Bonham	1971–77
Zeke Bonura	1940
George Borchers	1888
Rich Bordi	1983–84
Bob Borkowski	1950–51
Steve Boros	1963
Hank Borowy	1945–48
Shawn Boskie	1990–94
Thad Bosley	1983–86
Derek Botelho	1985
John Bottarini	1937
Ed Bouchee	1960–61
Pat Bourque	1971–73
Larry Bowa	1982–85
Bob Bowman	1942
Bill Bowman	1891
George Bradley	1877
Bill Bradley	1899–1900
Kitty Bransfield	1911
Danny Breeden	1971
Hal Breeden	1971
Bill Brennan	1993
Roger Bresnahan	1900, 1913–15
Herb Brett	1924–25
Jim Brewer	1960–63
Charlie Brewster	1944
Al Bridwell	1913
Buttons Briggs	1896–98, 1904–05
Johnny Briggs	1956–58
Dan Briggs	1982
Jim Brillheart	1927
Leon Brinkopf	1952
Pete Broberg	1977
Lou Brock	1961–64
Ernie Broglio	1964–66
Herman Bronkie	1914
Mandy Brooks	1925–26
Jim Brosnan	1954, 1956–58
Joe Brown	1884
Lew Brown	1879
Three Finger Brown	1904–12, 1916
Ray Brown	1909
Tommy Brown	1952–53
Jumbo Brown	1925
Jophrey Brown	1968
Byron Browne	1965–67
George Browne	1909
Mike Brumley	1987
Warren Brusstar	1983–85
Clay Bryant	1935–40
Don Bryant	1966
Charlie Brynan	1888
Bill Buckner	1977–84
Steve Buechele	1992–95
Art Bues	1914
Bob Buhl	1962–66
Scott Bullett	1995
Jim Bullinger	1992–95
Freddie Burdette	1962–64
Lew Burdette	1964–65
Smoky Burgess	1949, 1951
Leo Burke	1963–65
Tom Burns	1880–91
Ray Burris	1973–79
John Burrows	1943–44
Ellis Burton	1963–65
Dick Burwell	1960–61
Guy Bush	1923–34
Johnny Butler	1928
John Buzhardt	1958–59
Marty Callaghan	1922–23
Nixey Callahan	1897–1900
Johnny Callison	1970–71
Dick Calmus	1967
Dolf Camilli	1933–34
Llewellan Camp	1893–94
Kid Camp	1894
Ron Campbell	1964, 1966
Gilly Campbell	1933
Joe Campbell	1967
Bill Campbell	1982–83
Jimmy Canavan	1892
Chris Cannizzaro	1971
Mike Capel	1988
Doug Capilla	1979–81
Jose Cardenal	1972–77
Don Cardwell	1960–62
Tex Carleton	1935–38
Don Carlsen	1948
Hal Carlson	1927–30
Bill Carney	1904
Bob Carpenter	1947
Cliff Carroll	1890–91
Al Carson	1910
Paul Carter	1916–20
Joe Carter	1983
Rico Carty	1973
Bob Caruthers	1893
Hugh Casey	1935
Doc Casey	1903–05
Larry Casian	1995
John Cassidy	1878
Frank Castillo	1991–95
Bill Caudill	1979–81
Phil Cavarretta	1934–51
Art Ceccarelli	1959–60
Ron Cey	1983–86
Cliff Chambers	1948
Frank Chance	1898–1910
Harry Chapman	1912
Virgil Cheeves	1920–23
Larry Cheney	1911–15
Cupid Childs	1900–01
Pete Childs	1901
Bob Chipman	1944–49
Harry Chiti	1950–52, 1955–56
Steve Christmas	1986
Loyd Christopher	1945
Bubba Church	1953–55
Len Church	1966
John Churry	1924–27
Fred Clark	1902
Dave Clark	1990
Henry Clarke	1898
Sumpter Clarke	1920
Tommy Clarke	1918
Dad Clarke	1888
John Clarkson	1884–87
Fritz Clausen	1893–94
Clem Clemens	1916
Doug Clemens	1964–65
Ty Cline	1966
Gene Clines	1977–78
Billy Clingman	1900
Otis Clymer	1913
Andy Coakley	1908–09
Kevin Coffman	1990
Dick Cogan	1899
Hy Cohen	1955
Jim Colborn	1969–71
Dave Cole	1954
King Cole	1909–12
Joe Coleman	1976
Ripper Collins	1937–38
Phil Collins	1923
Bob Collins	1940
Bill Collins	1911
Jackie Collum	1957
Jorge Comellas	1945
Clint Compton	1972
Bunk Congalton	1902
Fritz Connally	1983
Jim Connor	1892, 1897–99
Chuck Connors	1951
Bill Connors	1966
Jim Cook	1903
Jimmy Cooney	1926–27
Jimmy Cooney	1890–92
Wilbur Cooper	1925–26
Mort Cooper	1949
Walker Cooper	1954–55
Larry Corcoran	1880–85
Mike Corcoran	1884
Red Corriden	1913–15
Frank Corridon	1904
Jim Cosman	1970
Harvey Cotter	1924
Dick Cotter	1912
Henry Cotto	1984
Ensign Cottrell	1912
Roscoe Coughlin	1890
Wes Covington	1966
Billy Cowan	1963–64
Larry Cox	1978, 1982
Chuck Crim	1994
Harry Croft	1901
George Crosby	1884
Ken Crosby	1975–76
Jeff Cross	1948
Hector Cruz	1978, 1981–82
Dick Culler	1948
Ray Culp	1967
Bert Cunningham	1900–01
Doc Curley	1899
Clarence Currie	1903
Cliff Curtis	1911
Jack Curtis	1961–62
Jack Cusick	1951
Kiki Cuyler	1928–35
Mike Cvengros	1929
Bill Dahlen	1891–98
Babe Dahlgren	1941–42
Con Daily	1896
Dom Dallessandro	1940–44, 1946–47
Abner Dalrymple	1879–86
Tom Daly	1918–21
Tom Daly	1887–88
Kal Daniels	1992
Alvin Dark	1958–59
Dell Darling	1887–89
Bobby Darwin	1977
Doug Dascenzo	1988–92
Bill Davidson	1909
Brock Davis	1970–71
Curt Davis	1936–37
Tommy Davis	1970, 1972
Jim Davis	1954–56
Ron Davis	1986–87
Steve Davis	1979
Jody Davis	1981–88
Andre Dawson	1987–92
Boots Day	1970
Brian Dayett	1985–87
Charlie Deal	1916–21
Dizzy Dean	1938–41
Wayland Dean	1927
George Decker	1892–97
Joe Decker	1969–72
Ivan DeJesus	1977–81
Bobby Del Greco	1957
Jim Delahanty	1901
Fred Demarais	1890
Al Demaree	1917

Frank Demaree	1932–33, 1935–38
Harry DeMiller	1892
Gene DeMontreville	1899
Roger Denzer	1897
Bob Dernier	1984–87
Claud Derrick	1914
Paul Derringer	1943–45
Tom Dettore	1974–76
Charlie Dexter	1900–02
Mike Diaz	1983
Lance Dickson	1990
Steve Dillard	1979–81
Pickles Dillhoefer	1917
Miguel Dilone	1979
Frank DiPino	1986–88
Alec Distaso	1969
John Dobbs	1902–03
Jess Dobernic	1948–49
John Dolan	1895
Cozy Dolan	1900–01
Tom Dolan	1879
Tim Donahue	1895–1900
Ed Donnelly	1959
Frank Donnelly	1893
Mickey Doolan	1916
Jack Doscher	1903
Herm Doscher	1879
Phil Douglas	1915, 1917–19
Taylor Douthit	1933
Dave Dowling	1966
Tom Downey	1912
Red Downs	1912
Jim Doyle	1911
Jack Doyle	1901
Larry Doyle	1916–17
Moe Drabowsky	1956–60
Sammy Drake	1960–61
Solly Drake	1956
Paddy Driscoll	1917
Dick Drott	1957–61
Monk Dubiel	1949–52
Hugh Duffy	1888–89
Nick Dumovich	1923
Jim Dunegan	1970
Sam Dungan	1892–94, 1900
Ron Dunn	1974–75
Shawon Dunston	1985–95
Kid Durbin	1907–08
Leon Durham	1981–88
Frank Dwyer	1888–89
Don Eaddy	1959
Bad Bill Eagan	1893
Howard Earl	1890
Arnold Earley	1966
Mal Eason	1900–02
Roy Easterwood	1944
Rawly Eastwick	1981
Vallie Eaves	1941–42
Dennis Eckersley	1984–86
Charlie Eden	1877
Tom Edens	1995
Bruce Edwards	1951–52
Hank Edwards	1949–50
Dave Eggler	1877
Ed Eiteljorge	1890
Lee Elia	1968
Pete Elko	1943–44
Allen Elliott	1923–24
Carter Elliott	1921
Rowdy Elliott	1916–18
Jim Ellis	1967
Dick Ellsworth	1958, 1960–66
Don Elston	1953, 1957–64
Steve Engel	1985
Woody English	1927–36
Al Epperly	1938
Paul Erickson	1941–48
Frank Ernaga	1957
Dick Errickson	1942
Chuck Estrada	1966
Uel Eubanks	1922
Bill Everitt	1895–1900
Johnny Evers	1902–13
Jim Fanning	1954–57
Carmen Fanzone	1971–74
Duke Farrell	1888–89
Doc Farrell	1930
Darcy Fast	1968
Bill Faul	1965–66
Vern Fear	1952
Marv Felderman	1942

John Felske	1968
Charlie Ferguson	1901
Bob Ferguson	1878
Frank Fernandez	1971–72
Jesus Figueroa	1980
Tom Filer	1982
Bill Fischer	1916
Bob Fisher	1914–15
Cherokee Fisher	1877
Howie Fitzgerald	1922, 1924
Max Flack	1916–22
John Flavin	1964
Bill Fleming	1942–44, 1946
Scott Fletcher	1981–82
Silver Flint	1879–89
Jesse Flores	1942
John Fluhrer	1915
George Flynn	1896
Jocko Flynn	1886–87
Gene Fodge	1958
Dee Fondy	1951–57
Ray Fontenot	1985–86
Barry Foote	1979–81
Elmer Foster	1890–91
Kevin Foster	1994–95
Bill Foxen	1910–11
Jimmie Foxx	1942, 1944
Ken Frailing	1974–76
Ossie France	1890
Matt Franco	1995
Terry Francona	1986
Chick Fraser	1907–09
George Frazier	1984–86
Buck Freeman	1921–22
Hersh Freeman	1958
Mark Freeman	1960
Howard Freigau	1925–27
Larry French	1935–41
Lonny Frey	1937, 1947
Barney Friberg	1919–20, 1922–25
Danny Friend	1895–98
Owen Friend	1955
Woodie Fryman	1978
Oscar Fuhr	1921
Fred Fussell	1922–23
Len Gabrielson	1964–65
Phil Gagliano	1970
Augie Galan	1934–41
Oscar Gamble	1969
Bill Gannon	1901
John Ganzel	1900
Joe Garagiola	1953–54
Bob Garbark	1938–39
Rich Garces	1995
Jim Gardner	1902
Rob Gardner	1967
Mike Garman	1976
Adrian Garrett	1973–75
Ned Garvin	1899–1900
Charlie Gassaway	1944
Ed Gastfield	1885
Chippy Gaw	1920
Dave Geisel	1978–79, 1981
Emil Geiss	1887
Greek George	1941
Dave Gerard	1962
George Gerberman	1962
Dick Gernert	1960
Doc Gessler	1906
Bob Gibson	1890
Norm Gigon	1967
Charlie Gilbert	1941–43, 1946
Johnny Gill	1936
Paul Gillespie	1942, 1944–45
Joe Girardi	1989–92
Dave Giusti	1977
Fred Glade	1902
Jim Gleeson	1939–40
Bob Glenalvin	1890, 1893
Ed Glenn	1902
John Glenn	1876–77
Al Glossop	1946
John Goetz	1960
Fred Goldsmith	1880–84
Walt Golvin	1922
Mike Gonzalez	1925–29
Luis Gonzalez	1995
Wilbur Good	1911–15
Ival Goodman	1943–44
Mike Gordon	1977–78
George Gore	1879–86
Hank Gornicki	1941

John Goryl	1957–59
Goose Gossage	1988
Billy Grabarkewitz	1974
Earl Grace	1929, 1931
Mark Grace	1988–95
Peaches Graham	1903, 1911
Alex Grammas	1962–63
Henry Grampp	1927, 1929
Tom Grant	1983
George Grantham	1922–24
Joe Graves	1926
Danny Green	1898–1901
Lee Gregory	1964
Hank Griffin	1911
Mike Griffin	1981
Clark Griffith	1893–1900
Frank Griffith	1892
Tommy Griffith	1925
Denver Grigsby	1923–25
Burleigh Grimes	1932–33
Ray Grimes	1921–24
Charlie Grimm	1925–34
Greg Gross	1977–78
Ernie Groth	1904
Marv Gudat	1932
Ad Gumbert	1888–89, 1891–92
Dave Gumpert	1985–86
Larry Gura	1970–73, 1985
Frankie Gustine	1949
Charlie Guth	1880
Jose Guzman	1993–94
Eddie Haas	1957
Stan Hack	1932–47
Warren Hacker	1948–56
Casey Hageman	1914
Rip Hagerman	1909
John Hairston	1969
Jimmie Hall	1969–70
Mel Hall	1981–84
Drew Hall	1986–88
Jimmy Hallinan	1877–78
Steve Hamilton	1972
Ralph Hamner	1947–49
Bill Hands	1966–72
Todd Haney	1994–95
Frank Hankinson	1878–79
Bill Hanlon	1903
Ollie Hanson	1921
Ed Hanyzewski	1942–46
Bill Harbidge	1878–79
Lew Hardie	1886
Bud Hardin	1952
Alex Hardy	1902–03
Jack Hardy	1907
Alan Hargesheimer	1983
Bubbles Hargrave	1913–15
Mike Harkey	1988, 1990–93
Dick Harley	1903
Jack Harper	1906
Ray Harrell	1939
Vic Harris	1974–75
Chuck Hartenstein	1966–68
Gabby Hartnett	1922–39
Topsy Hartsel	1901
Jeff Hartsock	1992
Ervin Harvey	1900
Ron Hassey	1984
Billy Hatcher	1984–85
Joe Hatten	1951–52
Grady Hatton	1960
Jack Hayden	1908
Bill Hayes	1980–81
Egyptian Healy	1889
Bill Heath	1969
Cliff Heathcote	1922–30
Richie Hebner	1984–85
Mike Hechinger	1912
Jim Hegan	1960
Al Heist	1960–61
Rollie Hemsley	1931–32
Ken Henderson	1979–80
Steve Henderson	1981–82
Bob Hendley	1965–67
Harvey Hendrick	1933
Jack Hendricks	1902
Ellie Hendricks	1972
Claude Hendrix	1916–20
George Hennessey	1945
Bill Henry	1958–59
Roy Henshaw	1933, 1935–36
Babe Herman	1933–34
Billy Herman	1931–41

Gene Hermanski	1951–53
Sal Hernandez	1942–43
Ramon Hernandez	1968, 1976–77
Guillermo Hernandez	1977–83
Jose Hernandez	1994–95
Tom Hernon	1897
LeRoy Herrmann	1932–33
John Herrnstein	1966
Buck Herzog	1919–20
Jack Hiatt	1970
John Hibbard	1884
Greg Hibbard	1993
Bryan Hickerson	1995
Ed Hickey	1901
Jim Hickman	1968–73
Kirby Higbe	1937–39
Irv Higginbotham	1909
R. E. Hildebrand	1902
Glenallen Hill	1993–94
Frank Hiller	1950–51
Dave Hillman	1955–59
Paul Hines	1876–77
Gene Hiser	1971–75
Don Hoak	1956
Glen Hobbie	1957–64
Billy Hoeft	1965–66
Larry Hoffman	1901
Guy Hoffman	1986
Solly Hofman	1904–12, 1916
Brad Hogg	1915
Ed Holley	1928
Jessie Hollins	1992
John Hollison	1892
Charlie Hollocher	1918–24
Billy Holm	1943–44
Fred Holmes	1904
Ken Holtzman	1965–71, 1978–79
Marty Honan	1890–91
Burt Hooton	1971–75
Trader Horne	1929
Rogers Hornsby	1929, 1931
Tim Hosley	1975
John Houseman	1894
Del Howard	1907–09
Cal Howe	1952
Jay Howell	1981
Mike Hubbard	1995
Ken Hubbs	1961–63
Johnny Hudson	1941
Joe Hughes	1902
Jim Hughes	1956
Roy Hughes	1944–45
Long Tom Hughes	1900–01
Terry Hughes	1970
Jim Hughey	1893
Bob Humphreys	1965
Bert Humphries	1913–15
Randy Hundley	1966–73, 1976–77
Herb Hunter	1916–17
Walter Huntzinger	1926
Don Hurst	1934
Ed Hutchinson	1890
Bill Hutchinson	1889–95
Herb Hutson	1974
Blaise Ilsley	1994
Monte Irvin	1956
Charlie Irwin	1893–95
Frank Isbell	1898
Larry Jackson	1963–66
Lou Jackson	1958
Randy Jackson	1950–55, 1959
Danny Jackson	1991–92
Darrin Jackson	1985, 1987–89
Tony Jacobs	1948
Mike Jacobs	1902
Elmer Jacobs	1924–25
Merwin Jacobson	1916
Paul Jaeckel	1964
Joe Jaeger	1920
Art Jahn	1925
Rick James	1967
Cleo James	1970–71, 1973
Hal Jeffcoat	1948–55
Frank Jelincich	1941
Ferguson Jenkins	1966–73, 1982–83
Doug Jennings	1993
Garry Jestadt	1971
Abe Johnson	1893
Ben Johnson	1959–60
Davey Johnson	1978
Don Johnson	1943–48

Ken Johnson	1969
Lou Johnson	1960, 1968
Howard Johnson	1995
Cliff Johnson	1980
Bill Johnson	1983–84
Jimmy Johnston	1914
Jay Johnstone	1982–84
Roy Joiner	1934–35
Davy Jones	1902–04
Percy Jones	1920–22, 1925–28
Sam Jones	1955–56
Sheldon Jones	1953
Charley Jones	1877
Clarence Jones	1967–68
Claude Jonnard	1929
Bill Jurges	1931–38, 1946–47
Mike Kahoe	1901–02, 1907
Al Kaiser	1911
Don Kaiser	1955–57
John Kane	1909–10
John Katoll	1898–99
Tony Kaufmann	1921–27
Ted Kearns	1924–25
Chick Keating	1913–15
Vic Keen	1921–25
John Kelleher	1921–23
Mick Kelleher	1976–80
Frank Kellert	1956
George Kelly	1930
Joe Kelly	1916
Joe Kelly	1926, 1928
King Kelly	1880–86
Bob Kelly	1951–53
Snapper Kennedy	1902
Ted Kennedy	1885
Junior Kennedy	1982–83
Marty Keough	1966
Matt Keough	1986
Don Kessinger	1964–75
Pete Kilduff	1917–19
Paul Kilgus	1989
Bill Killefer	1918–20
Frank Killen	1900
Matt Kilroy	1898
Newt Kimball	1937–38
Bruce Kimm	1979
Jerry Kindall	1956–58, 1960–61
Ralph Kiner	1953–54
Charlie King	1958–59
Jim King	1955–56
Dave Kingman	1978–80
Walt Kinzie	1884
Chris Kitsos	1954
Mal Kittridge	1890–97
Chuck Klein	1934–36
Johnny Kling	1900–08, 1910–11
Johnny Klippstein	1950–54
Joe Klugmann	1921–22
Joe Kmak	1995
Otto Knabe	1916
Pete Knisely	1914–15
Darold Knowles	1975–76
Mark Koenig	1932–33
Elmer Koestner	1914
Cal Koonce	1962–67
Jim Korwan	1897
Fabian Kowalik	1935–36
Joe Kraemer	1989–90
Randy Kramer	1990
Ken Kravec	1981–82
Mike Kreevich	1931
Jim Kremmel	1974
Bill Krieg	1885
Mickey Krietner	1943–44
Gus Krock	1888–89
Rube Kroh	1908–10
Chris Krug	1965–66
Marty Krug	1922
Mike Krukow	1976–81
Harvey Kuenn	1965–66
Jeff Kunkel	1992
Emil Kush	1941–42, 1946–49
Pete LaCock	1972–76
Doyle Lade	1946–50
Steve Lake	1983–86, 1993
Jack Lamabe	1968
Pete Lamer	1902
Dennis Lamp	1977–80
Les Lancaster	1987–91
Hobie Landrith	1956
Don Landrum	1962–65
Bill Landrum	1988
Ced Landrum	1991
Walt Lanfranconi	1941
Bill Lange	1893–99
Terry Larkin	1878–79
Dave LaRoche	1973–74
Vic LaRose	1968
Don Larsen	1967
Dan Larson	1982
Al Lary	1954, 1962
Chuck Lauer	1890
Jimmy Lavender	1912–16
Vance Law	1988–89
Tony Lazzeri	1938
Tommy Leach	1912–14
Fred Lear	1919
Hal Leathers	1920
Don Lee	1966
Tom Lee	1884
Bill Lee	1934–43, 1947
Craig Lefferts	1983
Hank Leiber	1939–41
Lefty Leifield	1912–13
Dick LeMay	1963
Dave Lemonds	1969
Bob Lennon	1957
Ed Lennox	1912
Dutch Leonard	1949–53
Roy Leslie	1917
Carlos Lezcano	1980–81
Gene Lillard	1936, 1939
Freddie Lindstrom	1935
Dick Littlefield	1957
Jack Littrell	1957
Mickey Livingston	1943, 1945–47
Hans Lobert	1905
Bob Locker	1973, 1975
Bob Logan	1937–38
Dale Long	1957–59
Bill Long	1990
Davey Lopes	1984–86
Grover Lowdermilk	1912
Bobby Lowe	1902–03
Turk Lown	1951–54, 1956–58
Peanuts Lowrey	1942–43, 1945–49
Pat Luby	1890–92
Fred Luderus	1909–10
Mike Lum	1981
Carl Lundgren	1902–09
Tom Lundstedt	1973–74
Henry Lynch	1893
Dummy Lynch	1948
Mike Lynch	1902
Thomas Lynch	1884
Ed Lynch	1986–87
Red Lynn	1944
Pop Lytle	1890
Ray Mack	1947
Bill Mack	1908
Steve Macko	1979–80
Len Madden	1912
Clarence Maddern	1946, 1948–49
Greg Maddux	1986–92
Bill Madlock	1974–76
Sal Madrid	1947
Lee Magee	1919
George Magoon	1899
Freddie Maguire	1928
Willard Mains	1888
George Maisel	1921–22
Mike Maksudian	1994
John Malarkey	1899
Candy Maldonado	1993
Pat Malone	1928–34
Billy Maloney	1905
Gus Mancuso	1939
Hal Manders	1946
Les Mann	1916–19
Dick Manville	1952
Rabbit Maranville	1925
Luis Marquez	1954
Gonzalo Marquez	1973–74
Bill Marriott	1917, 1920–21
Jim Marshall	1958–59
Doc Marshall	1908
Speed Martin	1918–22
Frank Martin	1898
J. C. Martin	1970–72
Morrie Martin	1959
Stu Martin	1943
Jerry Martin	1979–80
Mike Martin	1986
Carmelo Martinez	1983
Dave Martinez	1986–88
Joe Marty	1937–39
Randy Martz	1980–82
Mike Mason	1987
Gordon Massa	1957
Nelson Mathews	1960–63
Gary Matthews	1984–87
Bobby Mattick	1938–40
Gene Mauch	1948–49
Hal Mauck	1893
Carmen Mauro	1948, 1950–51
Jakie May	1931–32
Scott May	1991
Derrick May	1990–94
Ed Mayer	1957–58
Bill McAfee	1930
Jim McAnany	1961
Ike McAuley	1925
Algie McBride	1896
Bill McCabe	1918–19
Dutch McCall	1948
Alex McCarthy	1915–16
Jack McCarthy	1900, 1903–05
Jim McCauley	1885
Harry McChesney	1904
Bill McClellan	1878
Lloyd McClendon	1989–90
George McConnell	1914, 1916
Jim McCormick	1885–86
Barry McCormick	1896–1901
Clyde McCullough	1940–43, 1946–48, 1953–56
Lindy McDaniel	1963–65
Chuck McElroy	1991–93
Monte McFarland	1895–96
Willie McGill	1893–94
Dan McGinn	1972
Gus McGinnis	1893
Lynn McGlothen	1978–81
Harry McIntire	1910–12
Jim McKnight	1960, 1962
Polly McLarry	1915
Larry McLean	1903
Cal McLish	1949, 1951
Jimmy McMath	1968
Norm McMillan	1928–29
Brian McRae	1995
Cal McVey	1876–77
George Meakim	1892
Russ Meers	1941, 1946–47
Dave Meier	1988
Sam Mejias	1979
Jock Menefee	1900–03
Rudi Meoli	1978
Ron Meridith	1984–85
Fred Merkle	1917–20
Lloyd Merriman	1955
Bill Merritt	1891
Sam Mertes	1898–1900
Lennie Merullo	1941–47
Steve Mesner	1938–39
Catfish Metkovich	1953
Roger Metzger	1970
Alex Metzler	1925
Russ Meyer	1946–48, 1956
Ralph Michaels	1924–25
Ed Mickelson	1957
Pete Mikkelsen	1967–68
John Miklos	1944
Eddie Miksis	1951–56
Dakin Miller	1902
Ox Miller	1947
Hack Miller	1922–25
Bob Miller	1970–71
Ward Miller	1912–13
George Milstead	1924–26
Paul Minner	1950–56
Mike Mitchell	1913
George Mitterwald	1974–77
Bill Moisan	1953
Bob Molinaro	1982
Fritz Mollwitz	1913–14, 1916
Rick Monday	1972–76
Allan Montreuil	1972
George Moolic	1886
Charley Moore	1912
Earl Moore	1913
Johnny Moore	1929, 1931–32
Donnie Moore	1975, 1977–79
Jake Mooty	1940–43
Jerry Morales	1974–77, 1981–83
Pat Moran	1906–09
Bill Moran	1895
Seth Morehead	1959–60
Keith Moreland	1982–87
Bobby Morgan	1957
Vern Morgan	1954–55
Mike Morgan	1992–95
Moe Morhardt	1961
George Moriarty	1903–04
Jim Moroney	1912
Ed Morris	1922
Deacon Morrissey	1902
Walt Moryn	1956–60
Paul Moskau	1983
Jim Mosolf	1933
Mal Moss	1930
Jamie Moyer	1986–88
Phil Mudrock	1963
Eddie Mulligan	1915–16
Jerry Mumphrey	1986–88
Bob Muncrief	1949
Joe Munson	1925–26
Bobby Murcer	1977–79
Danny Murphy	1960–62
Tony Murray	1923
Jim Murray	1902
Red Murray	1915
Billy Myers	1941
Randy Myers	1993–95
Chris Nabholz	1995
Tom Nagle	1890–91
Buddy Napier	1918
Jaime Navarro	1995
Tom Needham	1909–14
Cal Neeman	1957–60
Art Nehf	1927–29
Lynn Nelson	1930, 1933–34
Dick Nen	1968
Joel Newkirk	1919–20
Charlie Newman	1892
Ray Newman	1971
Bobo Newsom	1932
Art Nichols	1898–1900
Dolan Nichols	1958
Bill Nicholson	1939–48
George Nicol	1891
Hugh Nicol	1881–82
Joe Niekro	1967–69
Al Nipper	1988
Paul Noce	1987
Dickie Noles	1982–84, 1987
Pete Noonan	1906
Wayne Nordhagen	1983
Irv Noren	1959–60
Fred Norman	1964, 1966–67
Billy North	1971–72
Ron Northey	1950
Don Nottebart	1969
Lou Novikoff	1941–44
Rube Novotney	1949
Jose Nunez	1990
Rich Nye	1966–69
Mike O'Berry	1980
John O'Brien	1893
Pete O'Brien	1890
Bucky O'Connor	1916
Ken O'Dea	1935–38
Bob O'Farrell	1915–25, 1934
Hal O'Hagen	1902
Gene Oliver	1968–69
Nate Oliver	1969
Barney Olsen	1941
Vern Olsen	1939–42, 1946
Jack O'Neill	1904–05
Emmett O'Neill	1946
Steve Ontiveros	1977–80
Jose Ortiz	1971
Bob Osborn	1925–27, 1929–30
Tiny Osborne	1922–24
John Ostrowski	1943–46
Reggie Otero	1945
Billy Ott	1962, 1964
Dave Otto	1994
Orval Overall	1906–10, 1913
Ernie Ovitz	1911
Mickey Owen	1949–51
Dave Owen	1983–85
Gene Packard	1916–17
Andy Pafko	1943–51
Vance Page	1938–41
Donn Pall	1994

Rafael Palmeiro	1986–88
Milt Pappas	1970–73
Erik Pappas	1991
Mark Parent	1994–95
Doc Parker	1893, 1895–96
Roy Parmelee	1937
Tom Parrott	1893
Jiggs Parrott	1892–95
Dode Paskert	1918–20
Claude Passeau	1939–47
Reggie Patterson	1983–85
Ken Patterson	1992
Mike Paul	1973–74
Dave Pavlas	1990–91
Ted Pawelek	1946
George Pearce	1912–16
Charlie Pechous	1916–17
Jorge Pedre	1992
Chick Pedroes	1902
Roberto Pena	1965–66
Ken Penner	1929
Joe Pepitone	1970–73
Mike Perez	1995
Yorkis Perez	1991
Harry Perkowski	1955
Jon Perlman	1985
Scott Perry	1916
Pat Perry	1988–89
Johnny Peters	1876–77, 1879
Bob Pettit	1887–88
Jesse Petty	1930
Big Jeff Pfeffer	1905, 1910
Fred Pfeffer	1883–89, 1891, 1896–97
Jack Pfiester	1906–11
Art Phelan	1913–15
Babe Phelps	1933–34
Adolfo Phillips	1966–69
Taylor Phillips	1958–59
Tom Phoebus	1972
Bill Phyle	1898–99
Charlie Pick	1918–19
Eddie Pick	1927
Jeff Pico	1988–90
Ray Pierce	1924
Andy Piercy	1881
Bill Piercy	1926
George Piktuzis	1956
Horacio Pina	1974
Pinky Pittenger	1925
Juan Pizarro	1970–73
Whitey Platt	1942–43
Dan Plesac	1993–94
Bill Plummer	1968
Tom Poholsky	1957
Howie Pollet	1953–55
Elmer Ponder	1921
Tom Poorman	1880
Paul Popovich	1966–67, 1969–73
Bob Porterfield	1959
Bill Powell	1912
Phil Powers	1878
Willie Prall	1975
Johnny Pramesa	1952
Todd Pratt	1995
Mike Prendergast	1916–17
Tot Pressnell	1941–42
Ray Prim	1943, 1945–46
Don Prince	1962
Mike Proly	1982–83
Ed Putman	1976, 1978
John Pyecha	1954
Shadow Pyle	1887
Jimmy Qualls	1969
Joe Quest	1879–82
Frank Quinn	1899
Joe Quinn	1877
Wimpy Quinn	1941
Luis Quinones	1987
Dick Radatz	1967
Dave Rader	1978
Ken Raffensberger	1940–41
Pat Ragan	1909
Chuck Rainey	1983–84
Bob Ramazzotti	1949–53
Domingo Ramos	1989–90
Willie Ramsdell	1952
Fernando Ramsey	1992
Newt Randall	1907
Lenny Randle	1980
Merritt Ranew	1963–64
Dennis Rasmussen	1992
Tommy Raub	1903
Bob Raudman	1966–67
Fred Raymer	1901
Frank Reberger	1968
Phil Regan	1968–72
Herm Reich	1949
Josh Reilly	1896
Hal Reilly	1919
Laurie Reis	1877–78
Ken Reitz	1981
Jack Remsen	1878–79
Laddie Renfroe	1991
Steve Renko	1976–77
Ed Reulbach	1905–13
Paul Reuschel	1975–78
Rick Reuschel	1972–81, 1983–84
Carl Reynolds	1937–39
Archie Reynolds	1968–70
Bob Rhoads	1902
Karl Rhodes	1993–95
Del Rice	1960
Hal Rice	1954
Len Rice	1945
Fred Richards	1951
Lance Richbourg	1932
Lew Richie	1910–13
Beryl Richmond	1933
Reggie Richter	1911
Marv Rickert	1942, 1946–47
George Riley	1979–80
Allen Ripley	1982
Roberto Rivera	1995
Mel Roach	1961
Skel Roach	1899
Fred Roat	1892
Kevin Roberson	1993–95
Robin Roberts	1966
Dave Roberts	1977–78
Daryl Robertson	1962
Dave Robertson	1919–21
Don Robertson	1954
Jeff Robinson	1992
Andre Rodgers	1961–64
Freddy Rodriguez	1958
Roberto Rodriguez	1970
Billy Rogell	1940
Dan Rohn	1983–84
Rolando Roomes	1988
Charlie Root	1926–41
Dave Rosello	1972–77
Gary Ross	1968–69
Jack Rowan	1911
Wade Rowdon	1987
Dave Rowe	1877
Luther Roy	1927
Vic Roznovsky	1964–65
Dutch Rudolph	1904
Ken Rudolph	1969–73
Dutch Ruether	1917
Bob Rush	1948–57
Rip Russell	1939–42
Jack Russell	1938–39
Dick Ruthven	1983–86
Jimmy Ryan	1885–89, 1891–1900
Vic Saier	1911–17
Luis Salazar	1989–92
Angel Salazar	1988
Rey Sanchez	1991–95
Ryne Sandberg	1982–94
Scott Sanderson	1984–89
Ron Santo	1960–73
Ed Sauer	1943–45
Hank Sauer	1949–55
Ted Savage	1967–68
Carl Sawatski	1950, 1953
Bob Scanlan	1991–93
Germany Schaefer	1901–02
Jimmie Schaffer	1963–64
Joe Schaffernoth	1959–61
Bob Scheffing	1941–42, 1946–50
Hank Schenz	1946–49
Morrie Schick	1917
Calvin Schiraldi	1988–89
Harry Schlafly	1902
Freddy Schmidt	1947
Johnny Schmitz	1941–42, 1946–51
Ed Schorr	1915
Paul Schramka	1953
Hank Schreiber	1926
Pop Schriver	1891–94
Al Schroll	1960
Art Schult	1959–60
Wildfire Schulte	1904–16
Johnny Schulte	1929
Barney Schultz	1961–63
Joe Schultz	1915
Bob Schultz	1951–53
Buddy Schultz	1975–76
Don Schulze	1983–84
Wayne Schurr	1964
Bill Schuster	1943–45
Rudy Schwenck	1909
Pete Scott	1926–27
Milt Scott	1882
Dick Scott	1964
Rodney Scott	1978
Gary Scott	1991–92
Tom Seaton	1916–17
Frank Secory	1944–46
Herman Segelke	1982
Kurt Seibert	1979
Dick Selma	1969
Mike Sember	1977–78
Manny Seoane	1978
Bill Serena	1949–54
Scott Servais	1995
Orator Shaffer	1879
Art Shamsky	1972
Red Shannon	1926
Bobby Shantz	1964
Bob Shaw	1967
Sam Shaw	1893
Marty Shay	1916
Al Shealy	1930
Dave Shean	1911
Jimmy Sheckard	1906–12
Tommy Shields	1993
Clyde Shoun	1935–37
Walter Signer	1943, 1945
Charlie Silvera	1957
Curt Simmons	1966–67
Duke Simpson	1953
Elmer Singleton	1957–59
Ted Sizemore	1979
Jimmy Slagle	1902–08
Cy Slapnicka	1911
Sterling Slaughter	1964
Dwain Sloat	1949
Heathcliff Slocumb	1991–93
Roy Smalley	1948–53
Broadway Aleck Smith	1904
Bobby Gene Smith	1962
Charlie Smith	1911–14
Harry Smith	1877
Earl Smith	1916
Paul Smith	1958
Bob Smith	1931–32
Riverboat Smith	1959
Willie Smith	1968–70
Dave Smith	1991–92
Lee Smith	1980–87
Dwight Smith	1989–93
Greg Smith	1989–90
Marcelino Solis	1958
Eddie Solomon	1975
Pete Sommers	1889
Rudy Sommers	1912
Lary Sorensen	1985
Sammy Sosa	1992–95
Al Spalding	1876–78
Al Spangler	1967–70
Bob Speake	1955, 1957
Chris Speier	1985–86
Rob Sperring	1974–76
Carl Spongberg	1908
Charlie Sprague	1887
Jack Spring	1964
Jim St. Vrain	1902
Eddie Stack	1913–14
Tuck Stainback	1934–37
Gale Staley	1925
Pete Standridge	1915
Eddie Stanky	1943–44
Joe Stanley	1909
Tom Stanton	1904
Ray Starr	1945
Joe Start	1878
Jigger Statz	1922–25
Ed Stauffer	1923
John Stedronsky	1879
Morrie Steevens	1962
Ed Stein	1890–91
Randy Stein	1982
Harry Steinfeldt	1906–10
Rick Stelmaszek	1974
Jake Stenzel	1890
Joe Stephenson	1944
Riggs Stephenson	1926–34
Johnny Stephenson	1967
Walter Stephenson	1935–36
Earl Stephenson	1971
Phil Stephenson	1989
Ace Stewart	1895
Tuffy Stewart	1913
Jimmy Stewart	1963–66
Mack Stewart	1944–45
Tim Stoddard	1984
Steve Stone	1974–76
Bill Stoneman	1967–68
Joe Strain	1981
Sammy Strang	1900, 1902
Doug Strange	1991–92
Scott Stratton	1894–95
Lou Stringer	1941–42, 1946
George Stueland	1921–23, 1925
Bobby Sturgeon	1940–42, 1946–47
Tanyon Sturtze	1995
John Sullivan	1921
Marty Sullivan	1887–88
Mike Sullivan	1890
Bill Sullivan	1878
Champ Summers	1975–76
Billy Sunday	1883–87
Jim Sundberg	1987–88
Sy Sutcliffe	1884–85
Rick Sutcliffe	1984–91
Bruce Sutter	1976–80
Dave Swartzbaugh	1995
Bill Sweeney	1907, 1914
Leo Sweetland	1931
Steve Swisher	1974–77
Jerry Tabb	1976
Pat Tabler	1981–82
Dale Talbot	1953–54
Chuck Tanner	1957–58
El Tappe	1954–56, 1958, 1960
Ted Tappe	1955
Bennie Tate	1934
Tony Taylor	1958–60
Chink Taylor	1925
Danny Taylor	1929–32
Harry Taylor	1932
Zack Taylor	1929–33
Jack Taylor	1898–1903, 1906–07
Sammy Taylor	1958–62
Bud Teachout	1930–31
Patsy Tebeau	1887
John Tener	1888–89
Adonis Terry	1894–97
Zeb Terry	1920–22
Wayne Terwilliger	1949–51
Bob Tewksbury	1987–88
Moe Thacker	1958, 1960–62
Frank Thomas	1960–61
Lee Thomas	1966–67
Red Thomas	1921
Scot Thompson	1978–83
Bobby Thomson	1958–59
Walter Thornton	1895–98
Andre Thornton	1973–76
Bob Thorpe	1955
Dick Tidrow	1979–82
Bobby Tiefenauer	1968
Ozzie Timmons	1995
Ben Tincup	1928
Joe Tinker	1902–12
Bud Tinning	1932–34
Al Todd	1940, 1943
Jim Todd	1974, 1977
Chick Tolson	1926–27, 1929–30
Ron Tompkins	1971
Fred Toney	1911–13
Hector Torres	1971
Paul Toth	1962–64
Steve Trachsel	1993–95
Jim Tracy	1980–81
Bill Traffley	1878
Bill Tremel	1954–56
Manny Trillo	1975–78, 1986–88
Cooker Triplett	1938
Steve Trout	1983–87
Harry Truby	1895–96
Pete Turgeon	1923
Ted Turner	1920
Babe Twombly	1920–21
Lefty Tyler	1918–21
Earl Tyree	1914

Jim Tyrone	1972, 1974–75
Wayne Tyrone	1976
Mike Tyson	1980–81
John Upham	1967–68
Mike Vail	1978–80
Vito Valentinetti	1956–57
George Van Haltren	1887–89
Ike Van Zandt	1904
Hy Vandenburg	1944–45
Johnny Vander Meer	1950
Andy Varga	1950–51
Gary Varsho	1988–90
Hippo Vaughn	1913–21
Emil Verban	1948–50
Randy Veres	1994
Joe Vernon	1912
Tom Veryzer	1983–84
Tom Vickery	1891
Hector Villanueva	1990–92
Jose Vizcaino	1991–93
Otto Vogel	1923–24
Bill Voiselle	1950
Rube Waddell	1901
Ben Wade	1948
Gale Wade	1955–56
Eddie Waitkus	1941, 1946–48
Charlie Waitt	1877
Matt Walbeck	1993
Rube Walker	1948–51
Harry Walker	1949
Roy Walker	1917–18
Chico Walker	1985–87, 1991–92
Mike Walker	1995
Jack Wallace	1915
Tye Waller	1981–82
Joe Wallis	1975–78
Lee Walls	1957–59
Tom Walsh	1906
Jerome Walton	1989–92
Preston Ward	1950, 1953
Dick Ward	1934
Chris Ward	1974
Lon Warneke	1930–36, 1942–43, 1945
Hooks Warner	1921
Jack Warner	1962–65
Rabbit Warstler	1940
Carl Warwick	1966
Doc Watson	1913
Eddie Watt	1975
Harry Weaver	1917–19
Jim Weaver	1934
Orlie Weaver	1910–11
Earl Webb	1927–28
Ramon Webster	1971
Mitch Webster	1988–89
Jake Weimer	1903–05
Lefty Weinert	1927–28
Butch Weis	1923–25
Johnny Welch	1926–28, 1931
Turk Wendell	1993–95
Rip Wheeler	1923–24
Pete Whisenant	1956
Elder White	1962
Deacon White	1876
Jerry White	1978
Earl Whitehill	1939
Bob Wicker	1903–06
Charlie Wiedemeyer	1934
Milt Wilcox	1975
Hoyt Wilhelm	1970
Harry Wilke	1927
Curtis Wilkerson	1989–90
Dean Wilkins	1989–90
Rick Wilkins	1991–95
Bob Will	1957–58, 1960–63
Art Williams	1902
Billy Williams	1959–74
Dewey Williams	1944–47
Cy Williams	1912–17
Otto Williams	1903–04
Pop Williams	1902–03
Wash Williams	1885
Mitch Williams	1989–90
Ned Williamson	1879–89
Jim Willis	1953–54
Bump Wills	1982
Walt Wilmot	1890–95
Art Wilson	1916–17
Hack Wilson	1926–31
Willie Wilson	1993–94
Steve Wilson	1989–91
Ed Winceniak	1956–57
Kettle Wirts	1921–23
Casey Wise	1957
Harry Wolfe	1917
Harry Wolter	1917
Harry Wolverton	1898–1900
Walt Woods	1898
Gary Woods	1982–85
Chuck Wortman	1916–18
Dave Wright	1897
Mel Wright	1960–61
Pat Wright	1890
Bob Wright	1915
Rick Wrona	1988–90
Marvell Wynne	1989–90
Hank Wyse	1942–47
George Yantz	1912
Eric Yelding	1993
Carroll Yerkes	1932–33
Steve Yerkes	1916
Tony York	1944
Lefty York	1921
Gus Yost	1893
Elmer Yoter	1927–28
Don Young	1965, 1969
Anthony Young	1994–95
Zip Zabel	1913–15
Geoff Zahn	1975–76
Eddie Zambrano	1993–94
Oscar Zamora	1974–76
Rollie Zeider	1916–18
Todd Zeile	1995
Bob Zick	1954
Don Zimmer	1960–61
Heinie Zimmerman	1907–16
Dutch Zwilling	1916

Managers

Joe Altobelli	1991
Joey Amalfitano	1979–81
*Cap Anson	1879–97
Lou Boudreau	1960
*Roger Bresnahan	1915
Tom Burns	1898–99
*Phil Cavarretta	1951–53
*Frank Chance	1905–12
Harry Craft	1961
Leo Durocher	1966–72
Lee Elia	1982–83
Jim Essian	1991
*Johnny Evers	1913, 1921
*Bob Ferguson	1878
*Silver Flint	1879
Charlie Fox	1983
Herman Franks	1977–79
Jim Frey	1984–86
Frankie Frisch	1949–51
George Gibson	1925
Preston Gomez	1980
*Charlie Grimm	1932–38, 1944–49, 1960
Stan Hack	1954–56
*Gabby Hartnett	1938–40
Vedie Himsl	1961
Rogers Hornsby	1930–32
Roy Johnson	1944
Bob Kennedy	1963–65
Bill Killefer	1921–25
Lou Klein	1961–62, 1965
Jim Lefebvre	1992–93
Whitey Lockman	1972–74
Tom Loftus	1900–01
Frank Lucchesi	1987
*Rabbit Maranville	1925
Jim Marshall	1974–76
Joe McCarthy	1926–30
Charlie Metro	1962
Gene Michael	1986–87
Fred Mitchell	1917–20
Hank O'Day	1914
Jim Riggleman	1995
Bob Scheffing	1957–59
Frank Selee	1902–05
*Al Spalding	1876–77
El Tappe	1961–62
Joe Tinker	1916
Tom Trebelhorn	1994
John Vukovich	1986
Jimmie Wilson	1941–44
Don Zimmer	1988–91

CINCINNATI Reds 1876–80
Known as Red Stockings 1876–77

Bob Addy	1877
Ross Barnes	1879
Amos Booth	1876–77, 1880
Mike Burke	1879
Hick Carpenter	1880
Bobby Clack	1876
John Clapp	1880
Candy Cummings	1877
Ned Cuthbert	1877
Dory Dean	1876
Buttercup Dickerson	1878–79
Sam Field	1876
Cherokee Fisher	1876
Will Foley	1876–77, 1879
Billy Geer	1878
Joe Gerhardt	1878–79
Charlie Gould	1876–77
Jimmy Hallinan	1877
Scott Hastings	1877
Nat Hicks	1877
Pete Hotaling	1879
Charley Jones	1876–78
King Kelly	1878–79
Henry Kessler	1876–77
Andy Leonard	1880
John Magner	1879
Jack Manning	1877, 1880
Mike Mansell	1880
Bobby Mathews	1877
Cal McVey	1878–79
Levi Meyerle	1877
George Miller	1877
Bobby Mitchell	1877–78
Jack Neagle	1879
Dave Pierson	1876
Lip Pike	1877–78
Blondie Purcell	1879–80
Billy Redmond	1877
Charlie Reilley	1880
Long John Reilly	1880
Johnny Ryan	1877
Lew Say	1880
Harry Smith	1877
Pop Smith	1880
Redleg Snyder	1876
Joe Sommer	1880
Chub Sullivan	1877–78
Charlie Sweasy	1876
Harry Wheeler	1879–80
Deacon White	1878–80
Will White	1878–80
Dale Williams	1876
Sam Wright	1880

Managers

*Bob Addy	1877
*John Clapp	1880
*Charlie Gould	1876
*Jack Manning	1877
*Cal McVey	1878–79
*Lip Pike	1877
*Deacon White	1879

CINCINNATI Reds 1890–1995
Moved from American Association
Known as Red Legs 1953–58

Ted Abernathy	1967–68
Cal Abrams	1952
George Abrams	1923
Joe Abreu	1942
Tom Acker	1956–59
Sparky Adams	1933–34
Karl Adams	1914
Bobby Adams	1946–55
Joe Adcock	1950–52
Troy Afenir	1992
Santo Alcala	1976–77
Chuck Aleno	1941–44
Nick Allen	1918–20
Ethan Allen	1926–30
Rafael Almeida	1911–13
Dave Altizer	1910–11
Rogelio Alvarez	1960, 1962
Red Ames	1913–15
Vincente Amor	1957
Harry Anderson	1960
Wingo Anderson	1910
Mike Anderson	1993
Nate Andrews	1946
Eric Anthony	1995
Pete Appleton	1927–28
Jimmy Archer	1918
Ed Armbrister	1973–77
Jack Armstrong	1988–91
Morrie Arnovich	1940
Jerry Arrigo	1965–69
Luis Arroyo	1959
Asby Asbjornson	1931–32
Ken Ash	1928–30
Rick Auerbach	1977–80
Chick Autry	1907, 1909
Jim Avrea	1950
Bobby Ayala	1992–93
Joe Azcue	1960
Fred Baczewski	1953–55
Jim Bagby	1912
Jim Bailey	1959
Ed Bailey	1953–61
King Bailey	1895
Bob Bailey	1976–77
Doug Bair	1978–81
Ernie Baker	1905
Bill Baker	1940–41
Bobby Balcena	1956
Jack Baldschun	1966–67
Kid Baldwin	1890
Frank Baldwin	1953
Mike Balenti	1911
Dick Baney	1973–74
Scott Bankhead	1992
Junie Barnes	1934
Skeeter Barnes	1983–84
German Barranca	1982
Red Barrett	1937–40
Jimmy Barrett	1899–1900, 1906
Shad Barry	1905–06
Bob Barton	1973
Johnny Bates	1911–14
Billy Bates	1990
Matt Batts	1955
Jim Baumer	1961
Frankie Baumholtz	1947–49
Harry Bay	1901–02
Dick Bayless	1908
Johnny Beall	1915–16
Ollie Beard	1890
Jim Beauchamp	1968–69
Clyde Beck	1931
Erve Beck	1902
Fred Beck	1911
Boom–Boom Beck	1945
Beals Becker	1913
Jake Beckley	1897–1903
Jim Beckman	1927–28
Fred Beebe	1910
Jodie Beeler	1944
Joe Beggs	1940–44, 1946–47
Jim Begley	1924
Mel Behney	1970
Tim Belcher	1992–93
Bo Belinsky	1970
Gus Bell	1953–61
Buddy Bell	1985–88
Freddie Benavides	1991–92
Johnny Bench	1967–83
Ray Benge	1938
Rube Benton	1910–15, 1923–25
Larry Benton	1930–34
Todd Benzinger	1989–91
Bruce Berenyi	1980–84
Bill Bergen	1901–03
Wally Berger	1938–39
Marty Berghammer	1913–14
Geronimo Berroa	1992

Damon Berryhill	1995
Bob Bescher	1908–13
Hal Betts	1913
Harry Biemiller	1925
Larry Biittner	1981–82
Dann Bilardello	1983–85
Steve Bilko	1958
Jack Billingham	1972–77
Tim Birtsas	1988–90
Joe Black	1955–56
Jim Blackburn	1948, 1951
Earl Blackburn	1912–13
Lena Blackburne	1918
Ewell Blackwell	1942, 1946–52
Paul Blair	1979
Ed Blake	1951–53
Link Blakely	1934
Fred Blank	1894
Cliff Blankenship	1905
Don Blasingame	1961–63
Steve Blateric	1971
Jimmy Bloodworth	1949–50
Jack Blott	1924
Otto Bluege	1933
Jim Bluejacket	1916
Len Boehmer	1967
Sammy Bohne	1921–26
Jim Bolger	1950, 1954
Tom Bolton	1992
Nino Bongiovanni	1938–39
Bill Bonham	1978–80
Bret Boone	1994–95
Pedro Borbon	1970–79
Frenchy Bordagaray	1939
Bob Borkowski	1952–55
Steve Boros	1964–65
Mel Bosser	1945
Jim Bottomley	1933–35
Joe Bowman	1945
Ray Boyd	1911
Buddy Bradford	1971
Scott Bradley	1992
Neal Brady	1925
Glenn Braggs	1990–92
Dave Brain	1908
Jeff Branson	1992–95
Jeff Brantley	1994–95
Angel Bravo	1970
Danny Breeden	1969
Ted Breitenstein	1897–1900
Don Brennan	1934–37
Lynn Brenton	1920–21
Rube Bressler	1917–27
Charlie Brewster	1943
Rocky Bridges	1953–57
Marshall Bridges	1960–61
Al Bridwell	1905
Harry Bright	1963
Gus Brittain	1937
Jim Brosnan	1959–63
Curly Brown	1915
Three Finger Brown	1913
Stub Brown	1897
Jumbo Brown	1937
Scott Brown	1981
Keith Brown	1988, 1990–92
Marty Brown	1988–89
Pete Browning	1891–92
Tom Browning	1984–94
Frank Bruggy	1925
Jacob Brumfield	1992–94
Bob Buchanan	1985
Dave Burba	1995
Smoky Burgess	1955–58
Eddie Burke	1892, 1895–97
Ken Burkhart	1948–49
George Burns	1922–24
Bill Burns	1910–11
Sheldon Burnside	1980
George Burpo	1946
Guy Bush	1945
Jack Bushelman	1909
Chris Bushing	1993
Sal Butera	1986–87
Bud Byerly	1950–52
Sammy Byrd	1935–36
Greg Cadaret	1993
Mike Caldwell	1977
Marty Callaghan	1928, 1930
Ray Callahan	1915
Archie Campbell	1930
Gilly Campbell	1935–37
Billy Campbell	1907–09
Jimmy Canavan	1893–94
Tom Cantwell	1909–10
Doug Capilla	1977–79
Bernie Carbo	1970–72
Leo Cardenas	1960–68
Don Carman	1991
Chet Carmichael	1909
Charlie Carr	1906
Hector Carrasco	1994–95
Clay Carroll	1968–75
Ownie Carroll	1930–32
Tom Carroll	1974–75
Arnold Carter	1944–45
Howard Carter	1926
Bob Caruthers	1893
Joe Cascarella	1937–38
Charlie Case	1901
Roy Castleton	1909–10
Keefe Cato	1983–84
Ike Caveney	1922–25
Cesar Cedeno	1982–85
Elio Chacon	1960–61
Icebox Chamberlain	1892–94
Darrel Chaney	1969–75
Calvin Chapman	1935–36
Bill Chappelle	1909
Chappy Charles	1909–10
Norm Charlton	1988–92
Hal Chase	1916–18
Charlie Chech	1905–06
Harry Chozen	1937
Cuckoo Christensen	1926–27
Steve Christmas	1983
Bubba Church	1952–53
Bob Clark	1891
Alan Clarke	1921
Tommy Clarke	1909–17
Dain Clay	1943–46
Ty Cline	1970–71
Billy Clingman	1890
Tony Cloninger	1968–71
Andy Coakley	1907–08
Jim Coates	1963
Al Cochran	1915
Jimmie Coker	1964–67
Gordy Coleman	1960–67
Percy Coleman	1898
Chuck Coles	1958
Darnell Coles	1992
Dave Collins	1978–81, 1987–89
Jackie Collum	1953–55
Jeff Combe	1980–81
Charlie Comiskey	1892–94
Adam Comorosky	1934–35
Jack Compton	1911
Dave Concepcion	1970–88
Snipe Conley	1918
Cliff Cook	1959–62
Dusty Cooke	1938
Walker Cooper	1949–50
Claude Corbitt	1946, 1948–49
Mickey Corcoran	1910
Tommy Corcoran	1897–1906
Pop Corkhill	1891
Pat Corrales	1968–72
Vic Correll	1978–80
Tim Costo	1992–93
Johnny Couch	1922–23
Bob Coulson	1908
Fritz Coumbe	1920–21
John Courtright	1995
Harry Coveleski	1910
Estel Crabtree	1931–32, 1943–44
Harry Craft	1937–42
Roger Craig	1965
Bill Cramer	1912
Cannonball Crane	1891
Sam Crane	1920–21
Pat Crawford	1930
Sam Crawford	1899–1902
Pete Cregan	1903
Walker Cress	1948–49
Tony Criscola	1944
Hughie Critz	1924–30
Ned Crompton	1910
John Cronin	1899
Ed Crosby	1973
Lem Cross	1893–94
Jack Crouch	1933
George Crowe	1956–58
Terry Crowley	1974–75
Hector Cruz	1979–80
Tony Cuccinello	1930–31
Mike Cuellar	1959
Manuel Cueto	1917–19
Nick Cullop	1930–31
George Culver	1968–69
Clarence Currie	1902
Jim Curtiss	1891
Kiki Cuyler	1935–37
Gene Dale	1915–16
Tom Daley	1908
Tom Daly	1903
Bill Dammann	1897–99
Bert Daniels	1914
Kal Daniels	1986–89
George Darby	1893
Pat Darcy	1974–76
Frank Dasso	1945–46
Dan Daub	1892
Jake Daubert	1919–24
Jack Daugherty	1993
Dave Davenport	1914
Ted Davidson	1965–68
Lefty Davis	1907
Dixie Davis	1912
Kiddo Davis	1937–38
Peaches Davis	1936–39
Spud Davis	1937–38
Wiley Davis	1896
Eric Davis	1984–91
Pea Ridge Day	1926
Tommy de la Cruz	1944
Snake Deal	1906
Charlie DeArmond	1903
Art DeFreitas	1978–79
Pat Deisel	1903
Mike Dejan	1940
Jim Delahanty	1906
Rich DeLucia	1994
John Denny	1986
Tony DePhillips	1943
Claud Derrick	1914
Paul Derringer	1933–42
Josh Devore	1913
Bo Diaz	1985–89
Rob Dibble	1988–93
Pedro Dibut	1924–25
Jim Dickson	1964
Vince DiMaggio	1939–40
Leo Dixon	1929
Bill Doak	1912
John Dobbs	1901–02
Jess Dobernic	1949
John Dodge	1913
Cozy Dolan	1909
John Dolan	1890
Cozy Dolan	1903–05
Ed Donalds	1912
Mike Donlin	1902–04
Pete Donohue	1921–30
Red Dooin	1915
Bill Doran	1990–92
Gus Dorner	1906
Brian Dorsett	1993–94
Jack Doscher	1908
Dutch Dotterer	1957–60
Phil Douglas	1914–15
Astyanax Douglass	1921, 1925
Taylor Douthit	1931–32
Tom Downey	1909–11
Tom Dowse	1892
Jim Doyle	1910
Slow Joe Doyle	1910
Moe Drabowsky	1962
Chuck Dressen	1925–31
Karl Drews	1954
Dan Driessen	1973–84
Walt Dropo	1958–59
Carl Druhot	1906
Jean Dubuc	1908–09
Jim Duffalo	1965
Charlie Duffee	1893
Frank Duffy	1970–71
Dan Dumoulin	1977–78
Pat Duncan	1919–24
Mariano Duncan	1989–91, 1995
Ryne Duren	1964
Leon Durham	1988
Bobby Durnbaugh	1957
Leo Durocher	1930–33
Jesse Duryea	1890–92
Frank Dwyer	1892–99
Jim Dyck	1956
Rawly Eastwick	1974–77
Al Eckert	1930–31
Joe Edelen	1981–82
Bruce Edwards	1956
Hank Edwards	1951–52
Jim Joe Edwards	1928
Johnny Edwards	1961–67
Sherman Edwards	1934
Dick Egan	1908–13
Red Ehret	1896–97
Rube Ehrhardt	1929
Jake Eisenhart	1944
Kid Elberfeld	1899
Roy Ellam	1909
Hod Eller	1917–21
Claude Elliott	1904
Sammy Ellis	1962, 1964–67
Frank Emmer	1916, 1926
Joe Engel	1917
Charlie English	1937
Del Ennis	1959
Eddie Erautt	1947–51, 1953
Hank Erickson	1935
Tex Erwin	1914
Nick Esasky	1983–88
Nino Escalera	1954
Jimmy Esmond	1911–12
Cecil Espy	1993
Bill Essick	1906–07
Bob Ewing	1902–09
Buck Ewing	1895–96
Pete Fahrer	1914
Frank Fanovich	1949
Buck Fausett	1944
Bob Ferguson	1944
Tony Fernandez	1994
Al Ferrara	1971
Steve Filipowicz	1948
Hank Fischer	1966
Chauncey Fisher	1894, 1896
Jack Fisher	1969
Maury Fisher	1955
Ray Fisher	1919–20
Bob Fisher	1916
Paul Fittery	1914
Wally Flager	1945
Sam Fletcher	1912
Curt Flood	1957
Carney Flynn	1894
Doug Flynn	1975–77
Lee Fohl	1903
Hank Foiles	1953, 1962–63
Tom Foley	1983–85
Dee Fondy	1958
Lew Fonseca	1921–24
Hod Ford	1926–31
Frank Foreman	1890–91, 1895–96
Brownie Foreman	1896
Tim Fortugno	1994
George Foster	1971–81
Steve Foster	1991–93
Henry Fournier	1894
Art Fowler	1954–57
Boob Fowler	1923–24
Howie Fox	1944–46, 1948–51
Bill Fox	1901
John Franco	1984–89
Terry Francona	1987
Chick Fraser	1906
Joe Frazier	1956
Roger Freed	1974
Hersh Freeman	1955–58
Gene Freese	1961–63
Tony Freitas	1934–36
Benny Frey	1929–36
Lonny Frey	1938–43, 1946
Jim Fridley	1958
John Frill	1912
Emil Frisk	1899
Art Fromme	1909–13
Woodie Fryman	1977
Phil Gagliano	1973–74
Joe Gaines	1960–62
Augie Galan	1947–48
Milt Galatzer	1939
Rich Gale	1983
Lee Gamble	1935, 1938–40
Ron Gant	1995
John Ganzel	1907–08
Leo Garcia	1987–88
Greg Garrett	1971

Harry Gaspar	1909–12
Hank Gastright	1896
Bob Geary	1921
Paul Gehrman	1937
Phil Geier	1900
Charley Gelbert	1937
Frank Genins	1892
Lefty George	1915
Ed Gerner	1919
Dick Gernert	1961
Cesar Geronimo	1972–80
Gus Getz	1917
Joe Gibbon	1971–72
Steve Gibralter	1995
Buddy Gilbert	1959
Wally Gilbert	1932
Haddie Gill	1923
John Gillespie	1922
Jim Gleeson	1941–42
Martin Glendon	1902
Norm Glockson	1914
Jot Goar	1898
Lonnie Goldstein	1943
Jesse Gonder	1963
Tony Gonzalez	1960
Mike Gonzalez	1914
Johnny Gooch	1929–30
Ival Goodman	1935–42
Marv Goodwin	1925
Glen Gorbous	1955
Keith Gordon	1993
Mike Grace	1978
Tiny Graham	1914
Alex Grammas	1956–58
Wayne Granger	1969–71
Eddie Grant	1911–13
George Grantham	1932–33
Jeff Gray	1988
Gene Green	1963
Gary Green	1992
Willie Greene	1992–95
Jim Greengrass	1952–55
Tommy Gregg	1993
Frank Gregory	1912
Bill Grey	1895–96
Ken Griffey	1973–81, 1988–90
Pat Griffin	1914
Mike Griffin	1989
Tommy Griffith	1915–18
Bob Grim	1960
Ross Grimsley	1971–73
Lee Grissom	1934–39
Heinie Groh	1913–21
Don Gross	1955–57
Kip Gross	1990–91
Matt Grott	1995
Marv Gudat	1929
Whitey Guese	1901
Witt Guise	1940
Brad Gulden	1984
Don Gullett	1970–76
Bill Gullickson	1986–87
Harry Gumbert	1944, 1946–49
Bert Haas	1942–43, 1946–47
Emil Haberer	1901, 1903, 1909
Warren Hacker	1957
Harvey Haddix	1958
Chick Hafey	1932–35, 1937
Bud Hafey	1939
Leo Hafford	1906
Joe Hague	1972–73
Noodles Hahn	1899–1905
Jesse Haines	1918
Charley Hall	1906–07
Tom Hall	1972–75
Bill Hallahan	1936–37
Jocko Halligan	1891–92
Chris Hammond	1990–92
Lee Handley	1936
Erik Hanson	1994
Bubbles Hargrave	1921–28
Dick Harley	1900–01
Chuck Harmon	1954–56
Jack Harper	1903–06
George Harper	1922–24
Tommy Harper	1962–67
Andy Harrington	1913
Jerry Harrington	1890–92
Bill Harris	1923–24
Greg Harris	1982–83
Lenny Harris	1988–89, 1994–95
Earl Harrist	1945

Frank Harter	1912–13
Topsy Hartsel	1900
Billy Hatcher	1990–92
Grady Hatton	1946–53
Phil Haugstad	1952
Pink Hawley	1898–99
Gene Hayden	1958
Ben Hayes	1982–83
Bob Hazle	1955
Mickey Heath	1931–32
Cliff Heathcote	1931
Chink Heileman	1901
Harry Heilmann	1930, 1932
Crese Heisman	1901–02
Tommy Helms	1965–71
George Hemming	1892
Rollie Hemsley	1933, 1942
Ken Henderson	1978–79
Joe Henderson	1976–77
Harvey Hendrick	1931–32
Bobby Henrich	1957–59
George Henry	1893
Bill Henry	1960–65
Dwayne Henry	1992–93
Ernie Herbert	1913
Babe Herman	1932, 1935–36
Xavier Hernandez	1995
Cesar Hernandez	1992–93
LeRoy Herrmann	1935
Willard Hershberger	1938–40
Buck Herzog	1914–16
Johnny Hetki	1945–48, 1950
Ed Heusser	1943–46
Andy High	1932–33
Whitey Hilcher	1931–32, 1935–36
Still Bill Hill	1898
Milt Hill	1991–93
Frank Hiller	1952
Dave Hillman	1962
Bill Hinchman	1905–06
Rich Hinton	1976
Roy Hitt	1907
Don Hoak	1957–58
Bill Hobbs	1913, 1916
Dick Hoblitzell	1908–14
Ed Hock	1924
Joe Hoerner	1977
Guy Hoffman	1987
Ken Hogan	1921
Marty Hogan	1894
George Hogriever	1895
Ken Holcombe	1948
Bill Holden	1914
Walter Holke	1925
Mul Holland	1926
Bug Holliday	1890–98
Al Hollingsworth	1935–38
Jay Hook	1957–61
Cy Hooker	1902–03
Bob Hooper	1955
Buster Hoover	1892
Hanson Horsey	1912
Frank House	1960
Paul Householder	1980–84
Fred Houtz	1899
Thomas Howard	1993–95
Dixie Howell	1949–52
Dixie Howell	1949
Jay Howell	1980
Dummy Hoy	1894–97, 1902
Jimmy Hudgens	1925–26
Miller Huggins	1904–09
Tommy Hughes	1948
Keith Hughes	1993
Emil Huhn	1916–17
Rudy Hulswitt	1908
Tom Hume	1977–85, 1987
Bert Humphries	1911–12
Ken Hunt	1961
Eddie Hunter	1933
Brian Hunter	1994–95
Clint Hurdle	1982
Pat Hurley	1901
Johnny Hutchings	1940–41
Bob Ingersoll	1914
Bert Inks	1896
Charlie Irwin	1896–1901
Ray Jablonski	1955–56
Al Jackson	1969
Danny Jackson	1988–90
Mike Jackson	1995

Art Jacobs	1939
Larry Jacobus	1918
Charlie James	1965
Larry Jansen	1956
Kevin Jarvis	1994–95
Julian Javier	1972
Joey Jay	1961–66
Hal Jeffcoat	1956–59
Stan Jefferson	1991
Reggie Jefferson	1991
Ollie Johns	1905
Alex Johnson	1968–69
Darrell Johnson	1961–62
Deron Johnson	1964–67
Chief Johnson	1913–14
Hank Johnson	1939
Ken Johnson	1961
Bob Johnson	1968
Si Johnson	1928–36
Syl Johnson	1934
Doc Johnston	1909
Bumpus Jones	1892–93
Mack Jones	1968
Sherman Jones	1961
Willie Jones	1959–61
Jeff Jones	1983
Tracy Jones	1986–88
Chris Jones	1991
Eddie Joost	1936–37, 1939–42
Buck Jordan	1937
Niles Jordan	1952
Pinky Jorgensen	1937
Frank Jude	1906
Howie Judson	1953–54
Joe Just	1944–45
Herb Juul	1911
Mike Kahoe	1895, 1899–1901
Jeff Kaiser	1993
Alex Kampouris	1934–38
John Kane	1907–08
Ed Karger	1909
Eddie Kasko	1959–63
Bob Katz	1944
Eddie Kazak	1952
Cactus Keck	1922–23
Bob Keefe	1911–12
Jim Keenan	1890–91
Frankie Kelleher	1942–43
Joe Kelley	1902–06
Alex Kellner	1958
Bill Kellogg	1914
Win Kellum	1904
George Kelly	1927–30
Bob Kelly	1953, 1958
Roberto Kelly	1993–94
Bill Kelso	1968
Dutch Kemner	1929
Vern Kennedy	1945
Bill Kennedy	1956–57
Junior Kennedy	1974, 1978–81
Marty Keough	1962–65
Jim Kern	1982
Dan Kerwin	1903
Keith Kessinger	1993
Red Killefer	1914–16
Wally Kimmick	1921–23
Silver King	1893
Clyde King	1953
Hal King	1973–74
Ed Kippert	1914
Clay Kirby	1974–75
Bobby Klaus	1964
Ollie Klee	1925
Ted Kleinhans	1934, 1937–38
Johnny Kling	1913
Johnny Klippstein	1955–58, 1962
Ted Kluszewski	1947–57
Frank Knauss	1892
Elmer Knetzer	1916–17
Alan Knicely	1983–85
Joe Knight	1890
Ray Knight	1974, 1977–81
Pete Knisely	1912
Brian Koelling	1993
Mark Koenig	1934
Elmer Koestner	1914
Ray Kolp	1927–34
Mike Konnick	1909–10
Jim Konstanty	1944
Larry Kopf	1916–17, 1919–21
Andy Kosco	1973–74
Ernie Koy	1941

Charlie Krause	1901
Wayne Krenchicki	1982–85
Charlie Kress	1947, 1949
Ernie Krueger	1925
Art Kruger	1907
Willie Kuehne	1892
Andy Kyle	1912
Mike LaCoss	1978–81
Al Lakeman	1942–46
Ray Lamanno	1941–42, 1946–48
Clay Lambert	1946–47
Pete Lamer	1907
Rafael Landestoy	1981–83
Hobie Landrith	1950–55
Bill Landrum	1986–87, 1993
Jerry Lane	1954–55
Don Lang	1938
Paul LaPalme	1956
Barry Larkin	1986–95
Harry LaRoss	1914
Arlie Latham	1890–95
Garland Lawing	1946
Tom Lawless	1982, 1984
Brooks Lawrence	1956–60
Tim Layana	1990–91
Tommy Leach	1915
King Lear	1914–15
Frank Leary	1907
Tim Leary	1989
Cliff Lee	1924
Bob Lee	1967–68
Terry Lee	1990–91
Charlie Leibrandt	1979–82
George Lerchen	1953
Brad Lesley	1982–84
Darren Lewis	1995
Mark Lewis	1995
Al Libke	1945–46
Jim Lindsey	1934
Hod Lisenbee	1945
Danny Litwhiler	1948–51
Bud Lively	1947–49
Wes Livengood	1939
Paddy Livingston	1906
Hans Lobert	1906–10
Bobby Locke	1965
Gene Locklear	1973
Whitey Lockman	1959–60
Bob Logan	1941
Howard Lohr	1914
Bill Lohrman	1944
Ernie Lombardi	1932–41
Baldy Louden	1916
George Lowe	1920
Turk Lown	1958
Peanuts Lowrey	1949–50
Red Lucas	1926–33
Larry Luebbers	1993
Eddie Lukon	1941, 1945–47
Mike Lum	1976–78
Dolf Luque	1918–29
Red Lutz	1922
Jerry Lynch	1957–63
Bob Mabe	1959
Danny MacFayden	1935
Scotti Madison	1989
Lee Magee	1918
Sherry Magee	1917–19
George Magoon	1901–03
Rick Mahler	1989–90
Dan Mahoney	1892
Bob Malloy	1943–44, 1946–47
Jim Maloney	1960–70
Billy Maloney	1902
Clyde Manion	1932–34
Cliff Markle	1921–22
Rube Marquard	1921
Bob Marquis	1953
Lefty Marr	1890–91
Armando Marsans	1911–14
Max Marshall	1942–44
Willard Marshall	1952–53
Bill Marshall	1934
Billy Martin	1960
Barney Martin	1953
Carmelo Martinez	1991
Dave Martinez	1992
Del Mason	1906–07
Bill Massey	1894
Bobby Mattick	1941–42
Jakie May	1924–30

Lee May	1966–71
Carl Mays	1924–28
Algie McBride	1898–1901
Swat McCabe	1909–10
Jack McCarthy	1893–94
Tom McCarthy	1908
Bill McCarthy	1907
Lloyd McClendon	1987–88
Harry McCluskey	1915
Billy McCool	1964–68
Frank McCormick	1934, 1937–45
Mike McCormick	1940–43, 1946
Barney McCosky	1951
Harry McCurdy	1934
Tex McDonald	1912–13
Chuck McElroy	1994–95
Will McEnaney	1974–76
Barney McFadden	1901
Herm McFarland	1898
Andy McGaffigan	1984–85
Willie McGill	1892
Dan McGinn	1968
Jim McGlothlin	1970–73
Howard McGraner	1912
Terry McGriff	1987–90
McGuire	1894
Harry McIntire	1913
Bill McKechnie	1916–17
Limb McKenry	1915–16
Kid McLaughlin	1914
Larry McLean	1906–12
Cal McLish	1960
Joe McManus	1913
Roy McMillan	1951–60
Tommy McMillan	1910
Hugh McMullen	1929
Bid McPhee	1890–99
Herb McQuaid	1923
Mike McQueen	1974
George McQuillan	1911
George McQuinn	1936
Hal McRae	1968, 1970–72
Doug McWeeny	1930
Rufe Meadows	1926
George Meakim	1892
Roy Meeker	1926
Sammy Meeks	1949–51
Bob Meinke	1910
Karl Meister	1913
Sam Mejias	1979–81
Dutch Mele	1937
Sam Mele	1955
Tony Menendez	1992
Denis Menke	1972–73
Lloyd Merriman	1949–51, 1954
Jim Merritt	1969–72
Bill Merritt	1894–95
Steve Mesner	1943–45
Bob Meusel	1930
Russ Meyer	1956
Ezra Midkiff	1909
Eddie Miksis	1958
Dusty Miller	1895–99
Eddie Miller	1936–37, 1943–47
Bob Miller	1962
Doc Miller	1914
Ward Miller	1909–10
Randy Milligan	1993
Eddie Milner	1981–86, 1988
Cotton Minahan	1907
Rudy Minarcin	1955
Gino Minutelli	1990–91
Roy Mitchell	1918–19
Clarence Mitchell	1916–17
Mike Mitchell	1907–12
Kevin Mitchell	1993–94
Mike Modak	1945
Fritz Mollwitz	1914–16
Jeff Montgomery	1987
Dee Moore	1936–37
Gene Moore	1931
Gene Moore	1912
Johnny Moore	1933–34
Whitey Moore	1936–42
Jake Mooty	1936–37
Herbie Moran	1914
Dan Morejon	1958
Cy Morgan	1913
Joe Morgan	1972–79
Bill Moriarty	1909
Hal Morris	1990–95
Jack Morrissey	1902–03
Jo–Jo Morrissey	1932–33
Earl Moseley	1916
Paul Moskau	1977–81
Howie Moss	1946
Frank Motz	1893–94
Mike Mowrey	1905–09
Ray Mueller	1943–44, 1946–49
Tony Mullane	1890–93
Connie Murphy	1893–94
Morg Murphy	1892–95
Rob Murphy	1985–88
Dale Murray	1977–78
Hy Myers	1925
Billy Myers	1935–40
Randy Myers	1990–91

Pete Naktenis	1939
Buddy Napier	1920–21
Charlie Neal	1963
Greasy Neale	1916–22, 1924
Art Nehf	1926–27
Red Nelson	1913
Emmett Nelson	1935–36
Roger Nelson	1973–74
Ernie Nevel	1953
Don Newcombe	1958–60
Doc Newton	1900–01
Chet Nichols	1964
Hugh Nicol	1890
Al Niehaus	1925
Bert Niehoff	1913–14
Jack Niemes	1943
Johnny Niggeling	1939
C. J. Nitkowski	1995
Gary Nolan	1967–73, 1975–77
Joe Nolan	1980–81
John Noriega	1969–70
Fred Norman	1973–79
Ron Northey	1950
Don Nottebart	1966–67
Howie Nunn	1961–62
Joe Nuxhall	1944, 1952–60, 1962–66

Rebel Oakes	1909
Mike O'Berry	1981–82
Pete O'Brien	1901
Fred Odwell	1904–07
Ron Oester	1978–90
Jack Ogden	1931–32
Joe Oliver	1989–94
Ivy Olson	1915
Tip O'Neill	1892
Mike O'Neill	1907
Peaches O'Neill	1904
Paul O'Neill	1985, 1987–92
Pat Osburn	1974
Claude Osteen	1957, 1959–61
Darrell Osteen	1965–67
Jim O'Toole	1958–66
Marty O'Toole	1908
Jimmy Outlaw	1937
Orval Overall	1905–06
Bob Owchinko	1984
Jim Owens	1963
Eric Owens	1995

Pat Pacillo	1987–88
Gene Packard	1912–13
Stan Palys	1955–56
Milt Pappas	1966–68
Kelly Paris	1983
Doc Parker	1901
Dave Parker	1984–87
Tom Parrott	1893–95
Camilo Pascual	1969
Dode Paskert	1907–10, 1921
Frank Pastore	1979–85
Claire Patterson	1909
Si Pauxtis	1909
Don Pavletich	1962–68
Jim Pearce	1954–55
Ducky Pearce	1908–09
Monte Pearson	1941
Steve Pegues	1994
Heinie Peitz	1896–1904
Eddie Pellagrini	1952
Orlando Pena	1958–60
Jose Pena	1969
Jim Pendleton	1959
Brad Pennington	1995
Tony Perez	1964–76, 1984–86
Harry Perkowski	1947, 1949–54
Scott Perry	1917
Pat Perry	1987–88
Kent Peterson	1944, 1947–51
Ted Petoskey	1934–35
Bill Pfann	1894
Art Phelan	1910, 1912
Ed Phelps	1905–06
Damon Phillips	1942
Bill Phillips	1895, 1899–1903
Val Picinich	1926–28
Eddie Pick	1923–24
Mario Picone	1954
Tony Piet	1934–35
Herman Pillette	1917
Babe Pinelli	1922–27
Vada Pinson	1958–68
Wally Pipp	1926–28
Pinky Pittenger	1927–29
Bill Plummer	1970–77
Bud Podbielan	1952–55, 1957
Hugh Poland	1947
Ken Polivka	1947
Harlin Pool	1934–35
Ed Poole	1902–03
Mark Portugal	1995
Wally Post	1949, 1951–57, 1960–63
Bill Powell	1913
Ross Powell	1993
Ted Power	1983–87, 1991
Johnny Powers	1959
Johnny Pramesa	1949–51
Joe Price	1980–86
Doc Prothro	1926
Bill Prough	1912
Tim Pugh	1992–95
Charlie Puleo	1983–84
Pid Purdy	1927–29
Bob Purkey	1958–64
Harlan Pyle	1928

Mel Queen	1964–69
Jack Quinn	1933
Joe Quinn	1900
Luis Quinones	1988–91

Charlie Rabe	1957–58
Old Hoss Radbourn	1891
Ken Raffensberger	1947–54
Pat Ragan	1909
Chucho Ramos	1944
Pedro Ramos	1969
Willie Ramsdell	1950–51
Bill Rariden	1919–20
Dennis Rasmussen	1987–88
Morrie Rath	1919–20
Johnny Rawlings	1914
Rip Reagan	1903
Jeff Reardon	1993
Gary Redus	1982–85
Jeff Reed	1988–92
Rick Reed	1995
Mike Regan	1917–19
Wally Rehg	1919
Long John Reilly	1890–91
Mike Remlinger	1995
Merv Rettenmund	1974–75
George Rettger	1892
Jerry Reuss	1987
Billy Rhines	1890–92, 1895–97
Charlie Rhodes	1908
Dennis Ribant	1969
Harry Rice	1933
Len Rice	1944
Duane Richards	1960
Nolen Richardson	1938–39
Jeff Richardson	1989
Beryl Richmond	1934
Elmer Riddle	1939–45, 1947
Johnny Riddle	1941, 1944–45
Steve Ridzik	1955
Lew Riggs	1935–40
Jose Rijo	1988–95
Jimmy Ring	1917–20
Jimmy Ripple	1940–41
Claude Ritchey	1897
Jay Ritchie	1968
Eppa Rixey	1921–33
Johnny Rizzo	1940
Tommy Robello	1933
Bip Roberts	1992–93
Dick Robertson	1913
Rabbit Robinson	1910
Floyd Robinson	1967
Frank Robinson	1956–65
Ron Robinson	1984–90
Bill Rodgers	1915–16
Rosario Rodriguez	1989–90
Ron Roenicke	1988
Mike Roesler	1989
Wally Roettger	1931–33
Clint Rogge	1921
Cookie Rojas	1962
Rolando Roomes	1989–90
John Roper	1993–95
Pete Rose	1963–78, 1984–86
Cliff Ross	1954
Joe Rossi	1952
Frank Roth	1909–10
Edd Roush	1916–26, 1931
Jack Rowan	1908–10, 1913–14
Wade Rowdon	1984–86
Sonny Ruberto	1972
Don Rudolph	1959
Dutch Ruether	1917–20
Johnny Ruffin	1993–95
Chico Ruiz	1964–69
Tom Runnells	1985–86
Amos Rusie	1901
Scott Ruskin	1992–93
Jeff Russell	1983–84
Connie Ryan	1950–51

Chris Sabo	1988–93
Slim Sallee	1919–20
Juan Samuel	1993
Gus Sanberg	1923–24
Raul Sanchez	1957, 1960
Roy Sanders	1917
Deion Sanders	1994–95
Reggie Sanders	1991–95
Mo Sanford	1991
Benito Santiago	1995
Manny Sarmiento	1976–79
Hank Sauer	1941–42, 1945, 1948–49
Ted Savage	1969
Ralph Savidge	1908–09
Moe Savransky	1954
Pat Scantlebury	1956
Les Scarsella	1935–37
Jimmie Schaffer	1968
Bob Scheffing	1950–51
Richie Scheinblum	1973
Bill Scherrer	1982–84, 1987
Admiral Schlei	1904–08
Bob Schmidt	1961
Willard Schmidt	1958–59
Johnny Schmitz	1952
Pete Schneider	1914–18
Karl Schnell	1922–23
Gene Schott	1935–38
Pete Schourek	1994–95
Barney Schreiber	1911
Hank Schreiber	1919
Pop Schriver	1897
Wes Schulmerich	1934
Art Schult	1956–57
Howie Schultz	1948
Joe Schultz	1925
Mike Schultz	1947
Al Schulz	1916
Dick Scott	1901
Ed Scott	1900
Jack Scott	1922
Everett Scott	1926
Donnie Scott	1991
Scott Scudder	1989–91
Tom Seaver	1977–82
Bob Sebra	1989
Jimmy Sebring	1904–05
Frank Secory	1942
Charlie See	1919–21
Kip Selbach	1899
Andy Seminick	1952–55
Scott Service	1993–94
Hank Severeid	1911–13
Socks Seybold	1899
Cy Seymour	1902–06
Art Shamsky	1965–67
Wally Shaner	1929
Joe Shaute	1934
Dave Shean	1917
Jimmy Sheckard	1913
Tom Sheehan	1924–25
Jimmy Shevlin	1932, 1934
Bob Shirley	1982
Ivey Shiver	1934
Milt Shoffner	1939–40
Eddie Shokes	1946

Bill Short	1969
Chick Shorten	1924
Clyde Shoun	1942–44, 1946–47
Eddie Sicking	1920
Johnny Siegle	1905–06
Candy Sierra	1988
Frank Sigafoos	1931
Al Silvera	1955
Al Simmons	1939
Dick Simpson	1966–67
Wayne Simpson	1970–72
Bert Sincock	1908
Dick Sipek	1945
Dave Sisler	1962
Dick Sisler	1952
Dave Skaugstad	1957
Bob Skinner	1963–64
Gordon Slade	1934–35
Walt Slagle	1910
Mike Slattery	1891
John Smiley	1993–95
Elmer Smith	1898–1900
Elmer Smith	1925
Frank Smith	1911–12
Frank Smith	1950–54, 1956
Fred Smith	1907
George Smith	1918
Germany Smith	1891–96
Hal Smith	1964
Harry Smith	1917–18
Jimmy Smith	1919
Chick Smith	1913
Jud Smith	1893
Milt Smith	1955
Paul Smith	1916
Bob Smith	1933
Willie Smith	1971
Mike Smith	1984–86
Pete Smith	1995
Homer Smoot	1906
Van Snider	1988–89
Mario Soto	1977–88
Bob Spade	1907–10
Daryl Spencer	1963
Harry Spies	1895
Harry Spilman	1979–81
Jerry Spradlin	1993–94
Ed Sprague	1971–73
Brad Springer	1926
Randy St. Claire	1988
Larry Stahl	1973
Gerry Staley	1955
Virgil Stallcup	1947–52
Oscar Stanage	1906
Ray Starr	1941–43
Justin Stein	1938
Harry Steinfeldt	1898–1905
Jake Stenzel	1899
Clarence Stephens	1891–92
Jimmy Stewart	1969–71
Mark Stewart	1913
Kurt Stillwell	1986–87
Archie Stimmel	1900–02
Lee Stine	1936
Rocky Stone	1943
Allyn Stout	1933–34
Gabby Street	1904–05
Ed Strelecki	1931
Joe Stripp	1928–31
John Stuper	1985
Lena Styles	1930–31
George Suggs	1910–13
Clyde Sukeforth	1927–31
Mike Sullivan	1892–93
Tom Sullivan	1925
Billy Sullivan	1935
Scott Sullivan	1995
Champ Summers	1977–79
Glenn Sutko	1990–91
Jack Sutthoff	1901, 1903–04
Evar Swanson	1929–30
Dazzy Swartz	1920
Greg Swindell	1992
Len Swormstedt	1901–02
Joe Szekely	1953
Jesse Tannehill	1894, 1911
Tommy Tatum	1947
Eddie Taubensee	1994–95
Ben Taylor	1912
Joe Taylor	1957
Jack Taylor	1899

Sammy Taylor	1963
Kent Tekulve	1989
Johnny Temple	1952–59
Scott Terry	1986
Jack Theis	1920
Tommy Thevenow	1936
Henry Thielman	1902
Frank Thomas	1959
Junior Thompson	1939–42
Jim Thorpe	1917
Bob Thurman	1955–58
Jay Tibbs	1984–85
Eddie Tiemeyer	1906
Joe Tinker	1913
Eric Tipton	1942–45
Bobby Tolan	1969–70, 1972–73
Fred Toliver	1984
Dave Tomlin	1972–73, 1978–80
Chuck Tompkins	1912
Fred Toney	1915–18
Angel Torres	1977
Bill Tozer	1908
Jeff Treadway	1987–88
Alex Trevino	1982–84, 1990
Manny Trillo	1989
John Tsitouris	1962–68
Greg Tubbs	1993
Jim Turner	1940–42
Twink Twining	1916
George Twombly	1914–16
Ted Uhlaender	1972
Maury Uhler	1914
George Ulrich	1893
Al Unser	1945
Bob Usher	1946–47, 1950–51
Mike Vail	1981–82
Corky Valentine	1954–55
Dave Van Gorder	1982, 1984–86
Dazzy Vance	1934
Johnny Vander Meer	1937–43, 1946–49
Gary Varsho	1993
Farmer Vaughn	1892–99
Max Venable	1985–87
Lee Viau	1890
Rube Vickers	1902
Frank Viola	1995
Clyde Vollmer	1942, 1946–48
Jake Volz	1908
Fritz Von Kolnitz	1914–15
Rip Vowinkel	1905
John Vukovich	1975
Joe Wagner	1915
Kermit Wahl	1944–45, 1947
Mysterious Walker	1910
Gee Walker	1942–45
Harry Walker	1949
Hub Walker	1936–37
Tom Walker	1904–05
Curt Walker	1924–30
Duane Walker	1982–85
Lee Walls	1960
Ken Walters	1963
Bucky Walters	1938–47
Jerome Walton	1994–95
Lloyd Waner	1941
Pee Wee Wanninger	1927
Piggy Ward	1893
Jay Ward	1970
Ray Washburn	1970
Jim Weaver	1938–39
Herm Wehmeier	1945, 1947–54
Jake Weimer	1906–08
Phil Weintraub	1937
Curt Welch	1892
David Wells	1995
Chris Welsh	1986
Bill Werber	1939–41
Don Werner	1975–78, 1980
Max West	1946
Dick West	1939–42
Wally Westlake	1952
Gus Weyhing	1901
Pete Whisenant	1957–59, 1961
Jack White	1927–28
Jo–Jo White	1944
Fred Whitfield	1968–69
Bill Whitrock	1894
Kevin Wickander	1993
Bob Wicker	1906
Al Wickland	1913

Ted Wieand	1958, 1960
Jimmy Wiggs	1903
Bill Wight	1958
Milt Wilcox	1970–71
Dewey Williams	1948
Denny Williams	1921
Ken Williams	1915–16
Woody Williams	1943–45
Dallas Williams	1983
Frank Williams	1987–88
Carl Willis	1984–86
Ted Wills	1962
Jimmie Wilson	1939–40
Dan Wilson	1992–93
Nigel Wilson	1995
Ivy Wingo	1915–26, 1929
Herm Winningham	1988–91
Whitey Wistert	1934
Ray Wolf	1927
Harry Wolter	1907
George Wood	1892
Harry Wood	1903
Jake Wood	1967
Bob Wood	1898–1900
Orville Woodruff	1904, 1910
Woody Woodward	1968–71
Ralph Works	1912–13
Al Worthington	1963–64
Craig Worthington	1995
Rick Wrona	1992
Johnny Wyrostek	1948–52
Biff Wysong	1930–32
Earl Yingling	1914
Del Young	1909
Pep Young	1941
Babe Young	1947–48
Joel Youngblood	1976, 1989
Pat Zachry	1976–77
Paul Zahniser	1929
Dom Zanni	1963, 1965–66
Benny Zientara	1941, 1946–48
Don Zimmer	1962
Jerry Zimmerman	1961
Billy Zitzmann	1919, 1925–29
George Zuverink	1954

Managers

Bob Allen	1900
Sparky Anderson	1970–78
Frank Bancroft	1902
Dave Bristol	1966–69
Earle Brucker	1952
Donie Bush	1933
*Charlie Comiskey	1892–94
Chuck Dressen	1934–37
Jimmy Dykes	1958
*Buck Ewing	1895–99
*John Ganzel	1908
Hank Gowdy	1946
Clark Griffith	1909–11
*Heinie Groh	1918
Ned Hanlon	1906–07
Don Heffner	1966
Tommy Helms	1988–89
Jack Hendricks	1924–29
*Buck Herzog	1914–16
Rogers Hornsby	1952–53
Dan Howley	1930–32
Fred Hutchinson	1959–64
Davey Johnson	1993–95
*Joe Kelley	1902–05
Tom Loftus	1890–91
Christy Mathewson	1916–18
Bill McKechnie	1938–46
John McNamara	1979–82
Bid McPhee	1901–02
Buster Mills	1953
Pat Moran	1919–23
Johnny Neun	1947–48
Russ Nixon	1982–83
Hank O'Day	1912
Bob O'Farrell	1934
Tony Perez	1993
Lou Piniella	1990–92
Vern Rapp	1984
*Pete Rose	1984–89
Luke Sewell	1949–52
Burt Shotton	1934
Dick Sisler	1964–65
Mayo Smith	1959

Birdie Tebbetts	1954–58
*Joe Tinker	1913
Bobby Wallace	1937
Bucky Walters	1948–49
*Ivy Wingo	1916

CLEVELAND Blues 1879–84

Jack Allen	1879
Joe Ardner	1884
George Bradley	1881–83
Fatty Briody	1882–84
Cal Broughton	1883
Ernie Burch	1884
Doc Bushong	1883–84
Charlie Cady	1883
Tom Carey	1879
John Clapp	1881
Bill Crowley	1883
One Arm Daily	1883
Herm Doscher	1881–82
Fred Dunlap	1880–83
John Dwyer	1882
Charlie Eden	1879
Dude Esterbrook	1882
Jake Evans	1883–84
George Fisher	1884
Gid Gardner	1880
Barney Gilligan	1879–80
Pit Gilman	1884
Jack Glasscock	1879–84
Fred Gunkle	1879
Al Hall	1880
Frank Hankinson	1880
Ned Hanlon	1880
John Harkins	1884
John Henry	1884
Hickey Hoffman	1879
Pete Hotaling	1880, 1883–84
Lem Hunter	1883
Kick Kelly	1882
Rudy Kemmler	1881
Doc Kennedy	1879–82
Jim McCormick	1879–84
Mike McGeary	1880
Bill McGunnigle	1882
Bobby Mitchell	1879
Sam Moffett	1884
Jerry Moore	1884
Mike Moynahan	1881, 1884
Mike Muldoon	1882–84
Willie Murphy	1884
The Only Nolan	1881
Bill Phillips	1879–84
George Pinckney	1884
Phil Powers	1881
Blondie Purcell	1881
Jack Remsen	1881
John Richmond	1882
Billy Riley	1879
Dave Rowe	1882
Will Sawyer	1883
Orator Shaffer	1880–82
Pop Smith	1881
Germany Smith	1884
Bill Smith	1884
Len Stockwell	1879
George Strief	1879, 1884
Billy Taylor	1881
John Tilley	1882
Fred Warner	1879
Harry Wheeler	1880
Gurdon Whiteley	1884
Julius Willigrod	1882
Tom York	1883

Managers

Frank Bancroft	1883
*John Clapp	1881
*Fred Dunlap	1882
Charlie Hackett	1884
*Jim McCormick	1879–80, 1882
Mike McGeary	1881

CLEVELAND Spiders 1889–99

Moved from American Association
Moved to ST. LOUIS Cardinals (merged)

Pete Allen	1893
Billy Alvord	1891, 1893
Joe Ardner	1890
Jersey Bakely	1889
Frank Bates	1898–99
Eb Beatin	1889–91
Ed Beecher	1898
Ira Belden	1897
Harry Blake	1894–98
Frank Boyd	1893
George Bristow	1899
Charlie Brown	1897
Jimmy Burke	1898
Jesse Burkett	1891–98
Kid Carsey	1899
Icebox Chamberlain	1896
Cupid Childs	1891–98
Henry Clarke	1897
John Clarkson	1892–94
Jack Clements	1899
Harry Colliflower	1899
Bill Collins	1891
Fred Cooke	1897
Lou Criger	1896–98
Lave Cross	1899
Nig Cuppy	1892–98
Vince Dailey	1890
Joe Daly	1891
George Davies	1892–93
George Davis	1890–92
Tom Delahanty	1896
Bill Delaney	1890
Jerry Denny	1891
Fred Donovan	1895
Tommy Dowd	1899
Tom Dowse	1890
Jack Doyle	1891–92
Jim Duncan	1899
Buck Ewing	1893–94
Jay Faatz	1889
Chauncey Fisher	1893–94
Fred Frank	1898
Chick Fraser	1898
Bill Garfield	1890
Dale Gear	1896–97
Charlie Getzien	1891
Bob Gilks	1889–90
Jim Gilman	1893
Ed Gremminger	1895
Frank Griffith	1894
Henry Gruber	1889, 1891
Joe Gunson	1893
Dick Harley	1899
Jack Harper	1899
Charlie Hastings	1893
Emmett Heidrick	1898
Charlie Hemphill	1899
Still Bill Hill	1899
Jim Hughey	1899
Spud Johnson	1891
Cowboy Jones	1898
George Kelb	1898
Henry Killeen	1891
Frank Knauss	1891, 1894
Phil Knell	1895
Charlie Knepper	1899
Eddie Kolb	1899
Otto Krueger	1899
Ezra Lincoln	1890
Harry Lochhead	1899
Pat Lyons	1890
Bill Lyston	1894
Harry Maupin	1899
Jimmy McAleer	1889, 1891–98
Sport McAllister	1896–99
Pete McBride	1898
Mike McDermott	1897
Ed McFarland	1893
Chippy McGarr	1893–96
Ed McKean	1889–98
Tony Mullane	1894
Darby O'Brien	1889
Jack O'Connor	1892–98
Tom O'Meara	1895–96
John Pappalau	1897
Charlie Parsons	1890
Charlie Petty	1894
Ollie Pickering	1897
Jack Powell	1897–98
Joe Quinn	1899
Paul Radford	1889
George Rettger	1892
John Scheible	1893
Crazy Schmit	1899
Ossee Schreckengost	1898–99
Ed Seward	1891
John Shearon	1891, 1896
Will Smalley	1890
Edgar Smith	1890
Pop Snyder	1889
Louis Sockalexis	1897–99
Joe Sommer	1890
Pete Sommers	1890
Charlie Sprague	1889
John Stafford	1893
Jack Stivetts	1899
Len Stockwell	1890
Cub Stricker	1889
Willie Sudhoff	1899
Joe Sugden	1899
Marty Sullivan	1891
Mike Sullivan	1894–95
Suter Sullivan	1899
Sy Sutcliffe	1889
Pussy Tebeau	1895
White Wings Tebeau	1894–95
Patsy Tebeau	1889, 1891–98
Tommy Tucker	1899
Larry Twitchell	1889
Peek-A-Boo Veach	1890
Lee Viau	1890–92
Jake Virtue	1890–94
Jack Wadsworth	1890
Bobby Wallace	1894–98
Buck West	1890
Tom Williams	1892–93
Zeke Wilson	1895–98
Highball Wilson	1899
Rasty Wright	1890
Cy Young	1890–98
Charlie Ziegler	1899
Chief Zimmer	1889–99

Managers

*Lave Cross	1899
Bob Leadley	1890–91
Tom Loftus	1889
*Joe Quinn	1899
Gus Schmelz	1890
*Patsy Tebeau	1891–98

COLORADO Rockies 1993–95

Juan Acevedo	1995
Scott Aldred	1993
Andy Ashby	1993
Roger Bailey	1995
Jason Bates	1995
Freddie Benavides	1993
Dante Bichette	1993–95
Willie Blair	1993–94
Daryl Boston	1993
Kent Bottenfield	1993–94
Jorge Brito	1995
Ellis Burks	1994–95
Pedro Castellano	1993, 1995
Vinny Castilla	1993–95
Jerald Clark	1993
Alex Cole	1993
Craig Counsell	1995
Jim Czajkowski	1994
Scott Fredrickson	1993
Marvin Freeman	1994–95
Jay Gainer	1993
Andres Galarraga	1993–95
Joe Girardi	1993–95
Joe Grahe	1995
Mark Grant	1993
Mike Harkey	1994
Greg Harris	1993–94
Charlie Hayes	1993–94
Butch Henry	1993
Bryan Hickerson	1995
Darren Holmes	1993–95
Trenidad Hubbard	1994–95
Bruce Hurst	1993
Howard Johnson	1994
Chris Jones	1993–94
Mike Kingery	1994–95
Mark Knudson	1993
Curtis Leskanic	1993–95
Nelson Liriano	1993–94
Quinton McCracken	1995
Roberto Mejia	1993–95
Marcus Moore	1993–94
Mike Munoz	1993–95
Dale Murphy	1993
Dave Nied	1993–95
Matt Nokes	1995
Omar Olivares	1995
Jayhawk Owens	1993–95
Lance Painter	1993–95
Jeff Parrett	1993
Harvey Pulliam	1995
Steve Reed	1993–95
Bryan Rekar	1995
Armando Reynoso	1993–95
Kevin Ritz	1994–95
Bruce Ruffin	1993–95
Bret Saberhagen	1995
A. J. Sager	1995
Mo Sanford	1993
Scott Service	1993
Danny Sheaffer	1993–94
Keith Shepherd	1993
Bryn Smith	1993
Bill Swift	1995
Jim Tatum	1993, 1995
Mark Thompson	1994–95
Ty Van Burkleo	1994
John Vander Wal	1994–95
Larry Walker	1995
Bruce Walton	1994
Gary Wayne	1993
Eric Wedge	1993
Walt Weiss	1994–95
Gerald Young	1993
Eric Young	1993–95

Managers

Don Baylor	1993–95

DETROIT Wolverines 1881–88

Lady Baldwin	1885–88
Eb Beatin	1887–88
Dave Beatle	1884
Charlie Bennett	1881–88
George Bradley	1881
Frank Brill	1884
Fatty Briody	1887
Cal Broughton	1888
Dan Brouthers	1886–88
Lew Brown	1881
George Bryant	1885
Harry Buker	1884
Turk Burke	1887
Dick Burns	1883
Count Campau	1888
Dan Casey	1885
Bob Casey	1882
Chub Collins	1885
Pete Conway	1886–88
Frank Cox	1884
Sam Crane	1885–86
Harry Decker	1886
George Derby	1881–82
Jim Donnelly	1885
Jerry Dorgan	1885
Mike Dorgan	1881
Fred Dunlap	1886–87
Joe Farrell	1882–84
Will Foley	1881
Tom Forster	1882
Charlie Ganzel	1886–88
Ed Gastfield	1884–85
Bill Geiss	1884
Joe Gerhardt	1881
Charlie Getzien	1884–88
Tom Gillen	1886
Barney Gilligan	1888
Henry Gruber	1887–88
Ben Guiney	1883–84
Jim Halpin	1885
Ned Hanlon	1881–88
Sadie Houck	1881, 1883
Jumping Jack Jones	1883
Frank Jones	1884
Henry Jones	1884
Tom Kearns	1882, 1884
Nat Kellogg	1885
Walt Kinzie	1882
Lon Knight	1881–82
Sam LaRoque	1888
Jack Leary	1881
Dickie Lowe	1884
Henry Luff	1882
Jimmy Manning	1885–87
Tom Mansell	1883
Jack McGeachy	1886
Mike McGeary	1882
Deacon McGuire	1885, 1888
Frank McIntyre	1883
Mox McQuery	1885
Frank Meinke	1884–85
Jerry Moore	1885
Gene Moriarity	1885
John Morrissey	1882
Frank Mountain	1881
Mike Moynahan	1881
Tony Mullane	1881
Parson Nicholson	1888
Dan O'Leary	1881
Frank Olin	1885
Marr Phillips	1885
Martin Powell	1881–83
Walter Prince	1884
Joe Quest	1883, 1885
George Radbourn	1883
Charlie Reilley	1881
Hardy Richardson	1886–88

Frank Ringo	1885
Yank Robinson	1882
Jack Rowe	1886–88
Ed Santry	1884
Ted Scheffler	1888
Frank Scheibeck	1888
Milt Scott	1884–85
Dupee Shaw	1883–84
Bill Shindle	1886–87
Phenomenal Smith	1886
Bill Smith	1886
Dan Stearns	1881
Sy Sutcliffe	1888
Billy Taylor	1881
Sam Thompson	1885–88
Sam Trott	1881–83
Dasher Troy	1881–82
Larry Twitchell	1886–88
Wallie Walker	1884
Joe Weber	1884
Jake Wells	1888
Deacon White	1886–88
Will White	1881
Art Whitney	1881–82
Stump Wiedman	1881–85, 1887
Julius Willigrod	1882
Sam Wise	1881
Fred Wood	1884
George Wood	1881–85
Chief Zimmer	1884

Managers

Frank Bancroft	1881–82
Jack Chapman	1883–84
Bob Leadley	1888
Charlie Morton	1885
Bill Watkins	1885–88

FLORIDA Marlins 1993–95

Kurt Abbott	1994–95
Luis Aquino	1993–94
Alex Arias	1993–95
Jack Armstrong	1993
Willie Banks	1995
Bret Barberie	1993–94
Geronimo Berroa	1993
Ryan Bowen	1993–95
Greg Briley	1993
Jerry Browne	1994–95
John Burkett	1995
Cris Carpenter	1993
Chuck Carr	1993–95
Matias Carrillo	1993–94
Greg Colbrunn	1994–95
Jeff Conine	1993–95
Jim Corsi	1993
Henry Cotto	1993
Andre Dawson	1995
Steve Decker	1993, 1995
Orestes Destrade	1993–94
Mario Diaz	1994–95
Brian Drahman	1994
Matt Dunbar	1995
Carl Everett	1993–94
Monty Fariss	1993
Junior Felix	1993
Willie Fraser	1994
Rich Garces	1995
Mark Gardner	1994–95
Tommy Gregg	1995
Buddy Groom	1995
Chris Hammond	1993–95
Bryan Harvey	1993–95
Jeremy Hernandez	1994–95
Trevor Hoffman	1993
Charlie Hough	1993–94
Mike Jeffcoat	1994
Charles Johnson	1994–95
John Johnstone	1993–95
Joe Klink	1993
Richie Lewis	1993–95
Mitch Lyden	1993
Dave Magadan	1993–94
Matt Mantei	1995
Terry Mathews	1994–95
Bob McClure	1993
Terry McGriff	1993
Kurt Miller	1994
Russ Morman	1994–95
Rob Murphy	1995
Jeff Mutis	1994
Mike Myers	1995
Bob Natal	1993–95
Robb Nen	1993–95
Greg O'Halloran	1994
Alejandro Pena	1995
Terry Pendleton	1995
Yorkis Perez	1994–95
Gus Polidor	1993
Scott Pose	1993
Jay Powell	1995
Pat Rapp	1993–95
Rick Renteria	1993–94
Rich Rodriguez	1993
Benito Santiago	1993–94
Rich Scheid	1994–95
Gary Sheffield	1993–95
Aaron Small	1995
Jesus Tavarez	1994–95
Ron Tingley	1994
Matt Turner	1993
Marc Valdes	1995
Quilvio Veras	1995
Randy Veres	1995
Dave Weathers	1993–95
Walt Weiss	1993
Darrell Whitmore	1993–95
Nigel Wilson	1993
Bobby Witt	1995
Eddie Zosky	1995

Managers

Rene Lachemann	1993–95

HARTFORD Dark Blues 1876–77

Doug Allison	1876–77
John Bass	1877
Tommy Bond	1876
Josh Bunce	1877
Jack Burdock	1876–77
Tom Carey	1876–77
John Cassidy	1876–77
Candy Cummings	1876
Bob Ferguson	1876–77
Bill Harbidge	1876–77
Dick Higham	1876
Jim Holdsworth	1877
Terry Larkin	1877
John Maloney	1877
Everett Mills	1876
Jay Pike	1877
Jack Remsen	1876
Joe Start	1877
Oak Taylor	187
Tom York	1876–77

Managers

*Bob Ferguson	1876–77

HOUSTON Astros 1962–95
Known as Colt .45s 1962–64

Dave Adlesh	1963–68
Troy Afenir	1987
Tommie Agee	1973
Juan Agosto	1987–90, 1993
Jesus Alou	1969–73, 1978–79
Joey Amalfitano	1962
Larry Andersen	1986–90
John Anderson	1962
Rob Andrews	1975–76
Joaquin Andujar	1976–81, 1988
Eric Anthony	1989–93
Don Arlich	1965–66
Alan Ashby	1979–89
Bob Aspromonte	1962–68
Jeff Bagwell	1991–95
Mark Bailey	1984–88
Reggie Baldwin	1978–79
Jeff Baldwin	1990
Lee Bales	1967
Alan Bannister	1984
Floyd Bannister	1977–78
Mike Barlow	1976
Kevin Bass	1982–89, 1993–94
John Bateman	1963–68
Rafael Batista	1973
Jim Beauchamp	1964–65, 1970
Bo Belinsky	1967
Buddy Bell	1988
Eric Bell	1993
Derek Bell	1995
Dave Bergman	1978–81
Dale Berra	1987
Buddy Biancalana	1987
Craig Biggio	1988–95
Jack Billingham	1969–71
George Bjorkman	1983
Willie Blair	1992
Wade Blasingame	1967–72
Curt Blefary	1969
Bruce Bochy	1978–80
Joe Boever	1992
Walt Bond	1964–65
Danny Boone	1982
Pat Borders	1995
Ken Boswell	1975–77
Jim Bouton	1969–70
Ryan Bowen	1991–92
Don Bradey	1964
Ron Brand	1965–68
Jackie Brandt	1967
Sid Bream	1994
Doug Brocail	1995
Hal Brown	1963–64
Ollie Brown	1974
Byron Browne	1968
Pidge Browne	1962
Bob Bruce	1962–66
Mike Brumley	1993, 1995
George Brunet	1962–63
Don Bryant	1969–70
Don Buddin	1962
Eric Bullock	1985–86
Jim Busby	1962
Ray Busse	1971, 1973–74
John Buzhardt	1967–68
Enos Cabell	1975–80, 1984–85
Craig Cacek	1977
Jeff Calhoun	1984–86
Ernie Camacho	1988
Ken Caminiti	1987–94
Jim Campbell	1962–63
Dave Campbell	1973–74
Casey Candaele	1988, 1990–93
John Cangelosi	1995
Joe Cannon	1977–78
Jose Cano	1989
Mike Capel	1991
George Cappuzzello	1982
Conrad Cardinal	1963
Frank Carpin	1966
Cesar Cedeno	1970–81
Andujar Cedeno	1990–94
Bob Cerv	1962
Rocky Childress	1987–88
Rich Chiles	1971–72, 1976
Al Cicotte	1962
Jim Clancy	1989–91
Terry Clark	1990
Nate Colbert	1968
Ron Cook	1970–71
Danny Coombs	1963–69
Gary Cooper	1991
Jim Corsi	1991
Mike Cosgrove	1972–76
Willie Crawford	1977
Jim Crawford	1973, 1975
Jose Cruz	1975–87
Mike Cuellar	1965–68
George Culver	1970–72
Jay Dahl	1963
Danny Darwin	1986–90
Jack Daugherty	1993
Jerry DaVanon	1975–76
Mark Davidson	1989–91
Brock Davis	1963–64, 1966
Tommy Davis	1969–70
Ron Davis	1962, 1966–68
Glenn Davis	1984–90
Bill Dawley	1983–85
Ramon de los Santos	1974
Jim Deshaies	1985–91
Jim Dickson	1963
Larry Dierker	1964–76
Jack DiLauro	1970
Frank DiPino	1982–86
Benny Distefano	1992
Tom Dixon	1977–79
Chris Donnels	1993–95
Bill Doran	1982–90
Jim Dougherty	1995
Doug Drabek	1993–95
Cameron Drew	1988
Dan Driessen	1986
Dick Drott	1962–63
Keith Drumright	1978
Tom Dukes	1967–68
Arnold Earley	1967
Mike Easler	1973
Tom Edens	1993–94
Johnny Edwards	1969–74
Dave Eilers	1967
Tony Eusebio	1991, 1994–95
Dick Farrell	1962–67
Ernie Fazio	1962–63
Mike Felder	1994
Bobby Fenwick	1972
Joe Ferguson	1977–78
Steve Finley	1991–94
Mike Fischlin	1977–78, 1980
John Fishel	1988
Brian Fisher	1990
Bob Forsch	1988–89
Ken Forsch	1970–80
Nellie Fox	1964–65
Gene Freese	1966
Jim Fuller	1977
Tom Funk	1986
Joe Gaines	1964–66
Ty Gainey	1985–87
Bob Gallagher	1973–74
Kiko Garcia	1981–82
Art Gardner	1975, 1977
Chris Gardner	1991
Phil Garner	1981–87
Rich Gedman	1990
Gary Geiger	1969–70
Jim Gentile	1965–66
Dick Gernert	1962
Cesar Geronimo	1969–71
Joe Gibbon	1972
Hal Gilson	1968
Dave Giusti	1962, 1964–68

Fred Gladding	1968–73
Jerry Goff	1995
Jim Golden	1962–63
Julio Gonzalez	1977–80
Luis Gonzalez	1990–95
Billy Goodman	1962
Howie Goss	1963
Julio Gotay	1966–69
Wayne Granger	1975
Mark Grant	1993
Bill Greif	1971
Tom Griffin	1969–76
Greg Gross	1973–76, 1989
Jerry Grote	1963–64
Juan Guerrero	1992
Skip Guinn	1969, 1971
Bill Gullickson	1990
Ricky Gutierrez	1995
Mike Hampton	1994–95
Carroll Hardy	1963–64
Larry Hardy	1976
Pete Harnisch	1991–94
Buddy Harris	1970–71
Chuck Harrison	1965–67
Dean Hartgraves	1995
J. C. Hartman	1962–63
Billy Hatcher	1986–89
Bill Heath	1966–67
Jeff Heathcock	1983, 1985, 1987–88
Danny Heep	1979–82
Al Heist	1962
Tommy Helms	1972–75
Steve Henderson	1988
Mike Henneman	1995
Randy Hennis	1990
Bill Henry	1969
Dwayne Henry	1991
Butch Henry	1992
Manny Hernandez	1986–87
Xavier Hernandez	1990–93
Jose Herrera	1968
Ed Herrmann	1976–78
Steve Hertz	1964
Jack Hiatt	1971–72
Joe Hoerner	1963–64
John Hoffman	1964–65
Pat House	1967–68
Paul Householder	1987
Larry Howard	1970–73
Wilbur Howard	1974–78
Art Howe	1976–82
John Hudek	1994–95
Brian Hunter	1994–95
Pete Incaviglia	1992
Mike Ivie	1981
Sonny Jackson	1963–67
Chuck Jackson	1987–88
Chris James	1993
Alfredo Javier	1976
Ken Johnson	1962–65
Jerry Johnson	1974
Cliff Johnson	1972–77
Gordon Jones	1964–65
Doug Jones	1992–93
Chris Jones	1985
Jimmy Jones	1991–92
Chris Jones	1992
Todd Jones	1993–95
Jeff Juden	1991, 1993
Skip Jutze	1973–76
Eddie Kasko	1964–65
Mick Kelleher	1974
Russ Kemmerer	1962–63
Matt Keough	1986
Charlie Kerfeld	1985–87, 1990
Darryl Kile	1991–95
Hal King	1967–68
Bob Knepper	1981–89
Alan Knicely	1979, 1981–82
Ray Knight	1982–84
Mark Knudson	1985–86
Doug Konieczny	1973–75, 1977
Gary Kroll	1966
Frank LaCorte	1979–83
Mike LaCoss	1982–84
Pete Ladd	1979
Jack Lamabe	1965
Keith Lampard	1969–70
Rafael Landestoy	1978–81
Jim Landis	1967
Norm Larker	1962
Don Larsen	1964–65
Dan Larson	1976–77
Barry Latman	1966–67
Don Lee	1965–66
Denny Lemaster	1968–71
Mark Lemongello	1976–78
Jeffrey Leonard	1978–81
Bob Lillis	1962–67
Jim Lindeman	1993
Kenny Lofton	1991
Steve Lombardozzi	1989
Davey Lopes	1986–87
Aurelio Lopez	1986–87
Scott Loucks	1980–83
Ken MacKenzie	1965
Mike Madden	1983–86
Dave Magadan	1995
Jim Mahoney	1965
Rob Mallicoat	1987, 1991–92
Felix Mantilla	1966
Mike Marshall	1970
Marty Martinez	1969–71
Pedro Martinez	1995
Roger Mason	1989
Eddie Mathews	1967
Ron Mathis	1985, 1987
Lee May	1972–74
Milt May	1974–75
Derrick May	1995
John Mayberry	1968, 1970–71
Lee Maye	1965–66
Leon McFadden	1968–69
Terry McGriff	1990
Bo McLaughlin	1976–79
Mark McLemore	1991
Don McMahon	1962–63
Craig McMurtry	1995
Louie Meadows	1986, 1988–90
Dave Meads	1987–88
Roman Mejias	1962
Mike Mendoza	1979
Denis Menke	1968–71, 1974
Roger Metzger	1971–78
Brian Meyer	1988–90
Larry Milbourne	1974–76
Norm Miller	1965–73
Orlando Miller	1994–95
John Mizerock	1983, 1985–86
Randy Moffitt	1982
Rafael Montalvo	1986
Aurelio Monteagudo	1966
Omar Moreno	1983
Joe Morgan	1963–71, 1980
Andy Mota	1991
James Mouton	1994–95
Jerry Mumphrey	1983–85
Rob Murphy	1992
Ivan Murrell	1963–64, 1967–68
Mike Nagy	1974
Phil Nevin	1995
Carl Nichols	1989–91
Dave Nicholson	1966
Joe Niekro	1975–85
Randy Niemann	1979–80
Don Nottebart	1963–65
Ken Oberkfell	1990–91
Jim Obradovich	1978
Javier Ortiz	1990–91
Dan Osinski	1970
Claude Osteen	1974
Al Osuna	1990–93
Jim Owens	1964–67
John Paciorek	1963
Jim Pankovits	1984–88
Rick Parker	1993
Bert Pena	1981, 1983–87
Jim Pendleton	1962
Gene Pentz	1976–78
Joe Pepitone	1970
Roberto Petagine	1994
Joe Pittman	1981–82
Juan Pizarro	1973
Gordon Pladson	1979–82
Phil Plantier	1995
Aaron Pointer	1963, 1966–67
Mark Portugal	1989–93
Ross Powell	1994–95
Terry Puhl	1977–90
Luis Pujols	1977–83
Doug Rader	1967–75
Rafael Ramirez	1988–92
Merritt Ranew	1962
Jim Ray	1965–66, 1968–73
Larry Ray	1982
Claude Raymond	1964–67
Howie Reed	1967
Jerry Reuss	1972–73
Craig Reynolds	1979–89
Ronn Reynolds	1987
Shane Reynolds	1992–95
Rick Rhoden	1989
Karl Rhodes	1990–93
Frank Riccelli	1978–79
J. R. Richard	1971–80
Ernest Riles	1992
German Rivera	1985
Bert Roberge	1979–80, 1982
Dave Roberts	1962, 1964
Robin Roberts	1965–66
Dave Roberts	1972–75
Leon Roberts	1976–77
Dave Roberts	1981
Dave Rohde	1990–91
Gil Rondon	1976
Mark Ross	1982, 1984–85
Vern Ruhle	1978–84
Pete Runnels	1963–64
Nolan Ryan	1980–88
Joe Sambito	1976–82, 1984
Dan Schatzeder	1989–90
Rich Scheid	1992
Fred Scherman	1974–75
Curt Schilling	1991
Jay Schlueter	1971
Dan Schneider	1967, 1969
Mike Scott	1983–91
Tony Scott	1981–84
Carroll Sembera	1965–67
Scott Servais	1991–95
Jimmy Sexton	1978–79
Bobby Shantz	1962
Steve Shea	1968
Larry Sherry	1967
Craig Shipley	1995
Paul Siebert	1974–76
Mike Simms	1990–92, 1994–95
Dick Simpson	1968
Greg Sims	1966
Craig Smajstrla	1988
Hal Smith	1962–63
Dave Smith	1980–90
Billy Smith	1981
Julio Solano	1983–87
Jose Sosa	1975–76
Al Spangler	1962–65
Rob Sperring	1977
Harry Spilman	1981–85, 1988–89
Scipio Spinks	1969–71
Bobby Sprowl	1979–81
Andy Stankiewicz	1994–95
Mike Stanton	1975
Rusty Staub	1963–68
Jimmy Stewart	1972–73
Bob Stinson	1972
Dean Stone	1962
Franklin Stubbs	1990
Gary Sutherland	1972–73
Don Sutton	1981–82
Greg Swindell	1993–95
Jeff Tabaka	1995
Eddie Taubensee	1992–94
Don Taussig	1962
Alex Taveras	1976
Ron Taylor	1965–66
Johnny Temple	1962–63
Frank Thomas	1965
Lee Thomas	1968
Roy Thomas	1977
Derrel Thomas	1971
Milt Thompson	1994–95
Dickie Thon	1981–87
Otis Thornton	1973
George Throop	1979
Bobby Tiefenauer	1962
Jose Tolentino	1991
Tim Tolman	1981–85
Hector Torres	1968–70, 1973
Alex Trevino	1988–90
Gus Triandos	1965
Scooter Tucker	1992–93, 1995
Jim Umbricht	1962–63
Cecil Upshaw	1973
Jose Uribe	1993
Sandy Valdespino	1969
Glenn Vaughan	1963
David Veres	1994–95
Bruce Von Hoff	1965, 1967
Billy Wagner	1995
Tony Walker	1986
Donne Wall	1995
Tye Waller	1987
Denny Walling	1977–88
Danny Walton	1977
Dan Warthen	1978
Carl Warwick	1962–63
Ron Washington	1989
Bob Watkins	1969
Bob Watson	1967–79
Johnny Weekly	1962–64
Mike White	1963–65
Tom Wiedenbauer	1979
Tom Wieghaus	1984
Dean Wilkins	1991
Rick Wilkins	1995
George Williams	1962
Walt Williams	1964
Rick Williams	1978–79
Mitch Williams	1994
Brian Williams	1991–94
Ron Willis	1969
Don Wilson	1966–74
Gary Wilson	1979
Glenn Wilson	1989–90
Robbie Wine	1986–87
George Witt	1962
Dooley Womack	1969
Hal Woodeshick	1962–65
Gary Woods	1980–81
Jimmy Wynn	1963–73
Eric Yelding	1989–92
Larry Yellen	1963–64
Jim York	1972–75
Gerald Young	1987–92
Larry Yount	1971
Chris Zachary	1963–67
Oscar Zamora	1978

Managers

Terry Collins	1994–95
Harry Craft	1962–64
Leo Durocher	1972–73
Preston Gomez	1974–75
Lum Harris	1964–65
Grady Hatton	1966–68
Art Howe	1989–93
Hal Lanier	1986–88
Bob Lillis	1982–85
Salty Parker	1972
Bill Virdon	1975–82
Harry Walker	1968–72

INDIANAPOLIS Hoosiers 1878

John Clapp	1878
Art Croft	1878
Silver Flint	1878
Jimmy Hallinan	1878
Tom Healey	1878
Jim McCormick	1878
Russ McKelvy	1878
Candy Nelson	1878
The Only Nolan	1878
Joe Quest	1878
Orator Shaffer	1878
Fred Warner	1878
Ned Williamson	1878

Managers

*John Clapp	1878

INDIANAPOLIS
Hoosiers 1887–89
Moved from ST. LOUIS Maroons

Varney Anderson	1889
Ed Andrews	1889
Tug Arundel	1887
Charley Bassett	1887–89
Henry Boyle	1887–89
Tom Brown	1887
Dick Buckley	1888–89
Bill Burdick	1888–89
John Cahill	1887
Larry Corcoran	1887
Con Daily	1888–89
Jerry Denny	1887–89
Dude Esterbrook	1888
Jack Fanning	1889
Fast	1887
Jack Fee	1889
Gid Gardner	1887
Charlie Getzien	1889
Jack Glasscock	1887–89
Mert Hackett	1887
Egyptian Healy	1887–88
Paul Hines	1888–89
Henry Jackson	1887
Bill Johnson	1887
John Kirby	1887
Gus Krock	1889
Doc Leitner	1887
Jack McGeachy	1887–89
Sam Moffett	1887–88
Hank Morrison	1887
George Myers	1887–89
Mark Polhemus	1887
Amos Rusie	1889
Jumbo Schoeneck	1888–89
Otto Schomberg	1887–88
Emmett Seery	1887–89
Lev Shreve	1887–89
Pete Sommers	1889
John Sowders	1887
Marty Sullivan	1889
Pete Weckbecker	1889
Jim Whitney	1889

Managers

Frank Bancroft	1889
Watch Burnham	1887
Horace Fogel	1887
*Jack Glasscock	1889
Harry Spence	1888
Fred Thomas	1887

KANSAS CITY Cowboys 1886

George Baker	1886
Charley Bassett	1886
Fatty Briody	1886
Pete Conway	1886
Jim Donnelly	1886
Dan Dugdale	1886
Mert Hackett	1886
Silver King	1886
Jim Lillie	1886
Larry McKeon	1886
Mox McQuery	1886
Al Myers	1886
Paul Radford	1886
Frank Ringo	1886
Dave Rowe	1886
Jim Whitney	1886
Stump Wiedman	1886

Managers

*Dave Rowe	1886

LOS ANGELES Dodgers
1958–95
Moved from BROOKLYN Dodgers

Don Aase	1990
Hank Aguirre	1968
Luis Alcaraz	1967–68
Doyle Alexander	1971
Dick Allen	1971
Orlando Alvarez	1974
Ed Amelung	1984, 1986
Sandy Amoros	1960
Dave Anderson	1983–89, 1992
Billy Ashley	1992–95
Bob Aspromonte	1960–61
Pedro Astacio	1992–95
Rick Auerbach	1974–76
Bob Bailey	1967–68
Bob Bailor	1984–85
Dusty Baker	1976–83
Willie Banks	1995
Jim Barbieri	1966
Brian Barnes	1994
Jim Baxes	1959
Billy Bean	1989
Joe Beckwith	1979–80, 1982–83, 1986
Mark Belanger	1982
Tim Belcher	1987–91
Todd Benzinger	1992
Don Bessent	1958
Steve Bilko	1958
Jack Billingham	1968
Babe Birrer	1958
Rafael Bournigal	1992–94
Ken Boyer	1968–69
Mark Bradley	1981–82
Sid Bream	1983–85
Marv Breeding	1963
Tom Brennan	1985
Bill Brennan	1988
Ken Brett	1979
Jim Brewer	1964–75
Tony Brewer	1984
Greg Brock	1982–86
Hubie Brooks	1990
Jerry Brooks	1993
Bruce Brubaker	1967
Jim Bruske	1995
Ralph Bryant	1985–87
Bill Buckner	1970–76
Jim Bunning	1969
Glenn Burke	1976–78
Larry Burright	1962
Mike Busch	1995
Brett Butler	1991–95
Enos Cabell	1985–86
Dick Calmus	1963
Doug Camilli	1960–64
Jim Campanis	1966–68
John Candelaria	1991–92
Tom Candiotti	1992–95
Chris Cannizzaro	1972–73
Andy Carey	1962
Gary Carter	1991
Bobby Castillo	1977–81, 1985
Juan Castro	1995
Cesar Cedeno	1986
Roger Cedeno	1995
Ron Cey	1972–82
Mike Christopher	1991
Chuck Churn	1959
Gino Cimoli	1958
Rocky Colavito	1968
Jackie Collum	1958
Dennis Cook	1990–91
Wes Covington	1966
Roger Craig	1958–61
Willie Crawford	1964–65, 1967–75
Tim Crews	1987–92
Don Crow	1982
Henry Cruz	1975–76
George Culver	1973
John Cummings	1995
Omar Daal	1993–95
Kal Daniels	1989–92
Bobby Darwin	1969, 1971
Vic Davalillo	1977–80
Tommy Davis	1960–66
Willie Davis	1960–73
Ron Davis	1987
Mike Davis	1988–89
Eric Davis	1992–93
Tommy Dean	1967
Ivan DeJesus	1974–76
Don Demeter	1958–61
Rick Dempsey	1988–90
Delino DeShields	1994–95
John DeSilva	1993
Mike Devereaux	1987–88
Carlos Diaz	1984–86
Dick Dietz	1972
Al Downing	1971–77
Sally Drake	1959
Darren Dreifort	1994
Don Drysdale	1958–69
John Duffie	1967
Mariano Duncan	1985–87, 1989
Dick Egan	1967
Joey Eischen	1995
Carl Erskine	1958–59
Cecil Espy	1983
Chuck Essegian	1959–60
Jim Fairey	1968
Ron Fairly	1958–69
Dick Farrell	1961
Joe Ferguson	1970–76, 1978–81
Sid Fernandez	1983
Al Ferrara	1963, 1965–68
Jack Fimple	1983–84, 1986
Jeff Fischer	1989
Darrin Fletcher	1989–90
Chad Fonville	1995
Terry Forster	1978–82
Alan Foster	1967–70
Art Fowler	1959
Pepe Frias	1980–81
Carl Furillo	1958–60
Len Gabrielson	1967–70
Balvino Galvez	1986
Karim Garcia	1995
Mike Garman	1977–78
Phil Garner	1987
Steve Garvey	1970–82
Jim Gentile	1958
Bob Giallombardo	1958
Kirk Gibson	1988–90
Jim Gilliam	1958–66
Jim Golden	1960–61
Dave Goltz	1980–82
Jose Gonzalez	1985–91
Ed Goodson	1976–77
Tom Goodwin	1991–93
Jim Gott	1990–94
Billy Grabarkewitz	1969–72
Mudcat Grant	1968
Dick Gray	1958–59
Alfredo Griffin	1988–91
Derrell Griffith	1963–66
Kevin Gross	1991–94
Kip Gross	1992–93
Jerry Grote	1977–78, 1981
Pedro Guerrero	1978–88
Brad Gulden	1978
Mark Guthrie	1995
Chris Gwynn	1987–91, 1994–95
John Hale	1974–77
Tom Haller	1968–71
Jeff Hamilton	1986–91
Gerald Hannahs	1978–79
Greg Hansell	1995
Dave Hansen	1990–95
Tim Harkness	1961–62
Bill Harris	1959
Lenny Harris	1989–93
Mike Hartley	1989–91
Mickey Hatcher	1979–80, 1987–90
Brad Havens	1987–88
Danny Heep	1987–88
Enzo Hernandez	1978
Carlos Hernandez	1990–95
Orel Hershiser	1983–94
Greg Heydeman	1973
Jim Hickman	1967
Shawn Hillegas	1987–88
Gil Hodges	1958–61
Glenn Hoffman	1987
Todd Hollandsworth	1995
Darren Holmes	1990
Brian Holton	1985–88
Rick Honeycutt	1983–87
Burt Hooton	1975–84
Gail Hopkins	1974
Ricky Horton	1988–89
Charlie Hough	1970–80
Frank Howard	1958–64
Steve Howe	1980–83, 1985
Jay Howell	1988–92
Ken Howell	1984–88
Rex Hudson	1974
Mike Huff	1989
Ron Hunt	1967
Willard Hunter	1962
Tom Hutton	1966, 1969
Garey Ingram	1994–95
Randy Jackson	1958
Cleo James	1968
Stan Javier	1990–92
Jack Jenkins	1969
Tommy John	1972–74, 1976–78
Lou Johnson	1965–67
Jay Johnstone	1980–81
Von Joshua	1969–71, 1973–74, 1979
Eric Karros	1991–95
Mike Kekich	1965, 1968
Roberto Kelly	1995
John Kennedy	1965–66
Fred Kipp	1958–59
Johnny Klippstein	1958–59
Andy Kosco	1969–70
Sandy Koufax	1958–66
Bill Krueger	1987–88
Clem Labine	1958–60
Lee Lacy	1972–78
Lerrin LaGrow	1979
Ray Lamb	1969–70
Rafael Landestoy	1977, 1983–84
Ken Landreaux	1981–87
Tito Landrum	1987
Norm Larker	1958–61
Rudy Law	1978, 1980
Tim Leary	1987–89
Bob Lee	1967
Leron Lee	1975–76
Jim Lefebvre	1965–72
Don LeJohn	1965
Jeffrey Leonard	1977
Dennis Lewallyn	1975–79
Bob Lillis	1958–61
Davey Lopes	1972–81
Luis Lopez	1990
Barry Lyons	1990–91
Jim Lyttle	1976
Mike Maddux	1990
Bill Madlock	1985–87
Candy Maldonado	1981–85
Juan Marichal	1975
Mike Marshall	1974–76
Mike Marshall	1981–89
Teddy Martinez	1977–79
Ramon Martinez	1988–95
Pedro Martinez	1992–93
Len Matuszek	1985–87
Ralph Mauriello	1958
Al McBean	1969–70
Terry McDermott	1972
Danny McDevitt	1958–60
Roger McDowell	1991–94
Ken McMullen	1962–64, 1973–75

Orlando Mercado 1987
Andy Messersmith 1973–75, 1979
Gene Michael 1967
Pete Mikkelsen 1969–72
Don Miles 1958
John Miller 1969
Larry Miller 1964
Bob Miller 1963–67
Lemmie Miller 1984
Bobby Mitchell 1980–81
Joe Moeller 1962, 1964, 1966–71
Rick Monday 1977–84
Raul Mondesi 1993–95
Wally Moon 1959–65
Gary Moore 1970
Jose Morales 1983
Mike Morgan 1989–91
Manny Mota 1969–77, 1979
Mike Munoz 1989–90
Noe Munoz 1995
Rob Murphy 1995
Eddie Murray 1989–91

Charlie Neal 1958–61
Ron Negray 1958
Jim Neidlinger 1990
Dick Nen 1963
Don Newcombe 1958
Rod Nichols 1993
Tom Niedenfuer 1981–87
Hideo Nomo 1995
Fred Norman 1970
Billy North 1978

Johnny Oates 1977–79
Bob O'Brien 1971
Jose Offerman 1990–95
Bob Ojeda 1991–92
Nate Oliver 1963–67
Al Oliver 1985
Jesse Orosco 1988
Jorge Orta 1982
Phil Ortega 1960–64
Claude Osteen 1965–73
Al Osuna 1994
Antonio Osuna 1995

Tom Paciorek 1970–75
Ed Palmquist 1960–61
Chan Ho Park 1994–95
Wes Parker 1964–72
Rick Parker 1995
Jose Parra 1995
Camilo Pascual 1970
Kevin Pasley 1974, 1976–77
Dave Patterson 1979
Stu Pederson 1985
Jose Pena 1970–72
Alejandro Pena 1981–89
Jack Perconte 1980–81
Ron Perranoski 1961–67, 1972
Pat Perry 1990
Mike Piazza 1992–95
Joe Pignatano 1958–60
Johnny Podres 1958–66
Jim Poole 1990
Paul Popovich 1968–69
Boog Powell 1977
Paul Ray Powell 1973, 1975
Dennis Powell 1985–86
Ted Power 1981–82
Tom Prince 1994–95
John Purdin 1964–65, 1968–69
Eddie Pye 1994–95

Ed Rakow 1960
Mike Ramsey 1985
Mike Ramsey 1987
Willie Randolph 1989–90
Doug Rau 1972–79
Lance Rautzhan 1977–79
Howie Reed 1964–66
Jody Reed 1993
Pee Wee Reese 1958
Phil Regan 1966–68
Rip Repulski 1959–60
Jerry Reuss 1979–87
Gilberto Reyes 1983–85, 1987–88
R. J. Reynolds 1983–85
Rick Rhoden 1974–78
Pete Richert 1962–64, 1972–73
German Rivera 1983–84
Earl Robinson 1958
Frank Robinson 1972

Sergio Robles 1976
Rich Rodas 1983–84
Ellie Rodriguez 1976
Henry Rodriguez 1992–95
Felix Rodriguez 1995
Ed Roebuck 1958, 1960–63
Ron Roenicke 1981–83
Vicente Romo 1968, 1982
Johnny Roseboro 1958–67
Ken Rowe 1963
Jerry Royster 1973–75
Bill Russell 1969–86

Juan Samuel 1990–92
Ted Savage 1968
Jack Savage 1987
Steve Sax 1981–88
Dave Sax 1982–83
Dick Schofield 1966–67
Dick Schofield 1995
Mike Scioscia 1980–92
Dick Scott 1963
Rudy Seanez 1994–95
Ray Searage 1989–90
Larry See 1986
Dave Sells 1975
Greg Shanahan 1973–74
Mike Sharperson 1987–93
John Shelby 1987–90
Larry Sherry 1958–63
Norm Sherry 1959–62
Craig Shipley 1986–87
Bart Shirley 1964, 1966, 1968
Steve Shirley 1982
Joe Simpson 1975–78
Duke Sims 1971–72
Bill Singer 1964–72
Ted Sizemore 1969–70, 1976
Bill Skowron 1963
Charley Smith 1960–61
Jack Smith 1962–63
Reggie Smith 1976–81
Dick Smith 1965
Greg Smith 1991
Duke Snider 1958–62
Gene Snyder 1959
Cory Snyder 1993–94
Eddie Solomon 1973–74
Elias Sosa 1976–77
Daryl Spencer 1961–63
Don Stanhouse 1980
Jerry Stephenson 1970
Dave Stewart 1978, 1981–83
Bob Stinson 1969–70
Mike Strahler 1970–72
Darryl Strawberry 1991–93
Dick Stuart 1966
Franklin Stubbs 1984–89
Bill Sudakis 1968–71
Rick Sutcliffe 1976, 1978–81
Don Sutton 1966–80, 1988

Kevin Tapani 1995
Alex Taveras 1982–83
Derrel Thomas 1979–83
Gary Thomasson 1979–80
Jeff Torborg 1964–70
Dick Tracewski 1962–65
Brian Traxler 1990
Jeff Treadway 1994–95
Alex Trevino 1986–87
Rick Trlicek 1993
John Tudor 1988–89

Mike Vail 1984
Ismael Valdes 1994–95
Bobby Valentine 1971–72
Fernando Valenzuela 1980–90
Hector Valle 1965
Elmer Valo 1958
Sandy Vance 1970–71
Ed Vande Berg 1986
Zoilo Versalles 1968
Jose Vizcaino 1989–90

Rube Walker 1958
Stan Wall 1975–77
Tim Wallach 1993–95
Lee Walls 1962–64
David Walsh 1990
Carl Warwick 1961
Ron Washington 1977
Gary Wayne 1994
Hank Webb 1977

Mitch Webster 1991–95
Gary Weiss 1981
Bob Welch 1978–87
Brad Wellman 1987
Terry Wells 1990
Johnny Werhas 1964–65
John Wetteland 1989–91
Myron White 1978
Larry White 1983–84
Terry Whitfield 1984–86
Hoyt Wilhelm 1971–72
Nick Willhite 1963–66
Stan Williams 1958–62
Reggie Williams 1985–87
Reggie Williams 1995
Todd Williams 1995
Maury Wills 1959–66, 1969–72
Bob Wilson 1958
Steve Wilson 1991–93
Gordie Windhorn 1961
Tracy Woodson 1987–89
Todd Worrell 1993–95
Ricky Wright 1982–83
Jimmy Wynn 1974–75

Steve Yeager 1972–85
Matt Young 1987
Eric Young 1992

Pat Zachry 1983–84
Geoff Zahn 1973–75
Don Zimmer 1958–59, 1963

Managers

Walter Alston 1958–76
Tom Lasorda 1976–95

LOUISVILLE Grays 1876–77

Art Allison 1876

George Bechtel 1876

Jack Carbine 1876
Jim Clinton 1876
Dan Collins 1876
Bill Craver 1877
Bill Crowley 1877

Jim Devlin 1876–77

Chick Fulmer 1876

Joe Gerhardt 1876–77

Bill Hague 1876–77
John Haldeman 1877
George Hall 1877
Scott Hastings 1876
Bill Holbert 1876

Flip Lafferty 1877
Juice Latham 1877
Harry Little 1877

Al Nichols 1877

Frank Pearce 1876

Johnny Ryan 1876

Orator Shaffer 1877
Pop Snyder 1876–77
Ed Somerville 1876

Managers

Jack Chapman 1876–77

LOUISVILLE Colonels 1892–99

Moved from American Association
Moved to PITTSBURGH Pirates (merged)

Nick Altrock 1898

Charley Bassett 1892
George Borchers 1895
Eddie Boyle 1896
Kitty Brashear 1899
Grant Briggs 1895
Dan Brouthers 1895
Tom Brown 1892–94
Willard Brown 1893–94
Pete Browning 1892–93
Hercules Burnett 1895
Dick Butler 1897
Burley Byers 1899

Scoops Carey 1898
Pete Cassidy 1896
Bill Childers 1895
Bob Clark 1893
Bill Clark 1897
Fred Clarke 1894–99
Josh Clarke 1898
Dad Clarke 1897–98
Fritz Clausen 1892–93, 1896
Billy Clingman 1896–99
Jimmy Collins 1895
Henry Cote 1894–95
Jack Crooks 1896
Bert Cunningham 1895–99

Harry Davis 1898
George Decker 1898–99
Tom Delahanty 1897
Jerry Denny 1893–94
Charlie Dexter 1896–99
Joe Dolan 1896–97
Jack Dooms 1892
Pete Dowling 1897–99
Tom Dowse 1892
Sam Dungan 1894

Billy Earle 1894
Red Ehret 1898
Charlie Emig 1896
Frank Eustace 1896
Roy Evans 1897

Clay Fauver 1899
John Fitzgerald 1892
Pat Flaherty 1894
Patsy Flaherty 1899
Chick Fraser 1896–98
Larry Freund 1896

Tom Gettinger 1895
Pete Gilbert 1894
Jack Glasscock 1895
John Grim 1892–94
Billy Gumbert 1893

Irv Hach 1897
Jerry Harrington 1893
Topsy Hartsel 1898–99
Bill Hassamaer 1895–96
Gil Hatfield 1895
Egyptian Healy 1892
George Hemming 1892–94, 1897
Art Herman 1896–97
Still Bill Hill 1896–97
Ducky Holmes 1895–97
Dummy Hoy 1898–99
Rudy Hulswitt 1899

Bert Inks 1894–95

Hughie Jennings 1892–93
Abbie Johnson 1896–97
Alex Jones 1892
Jim Jones 1897

Mike Kelley 1899
Billie Kemmer 1895
Fred Ketcham 1899
Matt Kilroy 1893–94
Tom Kinslow 1896
Mal Kittridge 1898–99
Bill Kling 1895
Phil Knell 1894–95
Joe Kostal 1896
Willie Kuehne 1892

Fred Lake 1894
Bob Langsford 1899
Tacks Latimer 1899
Tommy Leach 1898–99
Pat Luby 1895
Con Lucid 1893
Luke Lutenberg 1894

Bill Magee	1897–99
Lou Mahaffey	1898
Frank Martin	1897
Barry McCormick	1895
Tom McCreery	1895–97
Mike McDermott	1895–96
Alex McFarlan	1892
Dan McFarlan	1895
Herm McFarland	1896
Ambrose McGann	1895
George Meakim	1895
Jouett Meekin	1892
Jock Menefee	1893–94
Bill Merritt	1892
Tom Messitt	1899
Burt Miller	1897
Doggie Miller	1896
Dan Minnehan	1895
Tom Morrison	1895–96
Doc Nance	1897–98
George Nicol	1894
John O'Brien	1895–96
Tim O'Rourke	1893–94
Bill Peppers	1894
Fred Pfeffer	1892–95
Deacon Phillippe	1899
Ollie Pickering	1896–97
George Pinckney	1893
Mike Powers	1898–99
Walt Preston	1895
Billy Rhines	1893
Bill Rhodes	1893
Danny Richardson	1894
John Richter	1898
Claude Ritchey	1898–99
Jim Rogers	1896–97
Ben Sanders	1892
Ossee Schreckengost	1897
Emmett Seery	1892
Frank Shannon	1896
Frank Shugart	1895
Heinie Smith	1897–98
Ollie Smith	1894
Tom Smith	1896
Cooney Snyder	1898
Harry Spies	1895
General Stafford	1897–98
Farmer Steelman	1899
Tom Stouch	1898
Sammy Strang	1896
Scott Stratton	1892–94
Dan Sweeney	1895
Harry Taylor	1892
Wally Taylor	1898
Frank Todd	1898
George Treadway	1896
Mike Trost	1895
Larry Twitchell	1893–94
Lee Viau	1892
Rube Waddell	1897, 1899
Jack Wadsworth	1894–95
Honus Wagner	1897–99
Jack Warner	1895–96
Farmer Weaver	1892–94
Curt Welch	1893
Tub Welch	1895
Perry Werden	1897
Gus Weyhing	1895–96
Lew Whistler	1892–93
Bill Whitrock	1893–94
Harry Wilhelm	1899
Dave Wills	1899
Bill Wilson	1897–98
Walt Woods	1899
Joe Wright	1895–96
Fred Zahner	1894–95
Chief Zimmer	1899

Managers

Billy Barnie	1893–94
Jack Chapman	1892
*Fred Clarke	1897–99
John McCloskey	1895–96
Bill McGunnigle	1896
*Fred Pfeffer	1892
*Jim Rogers	1897

MILWAUKEE Cream Citys 1878

Charlie Bennett	1878
Frank Bliss	1878
George Creamer	1878
Abner Dalrymple	1878
Joe Ellick	1878
Will Foley	1878
Mike Golden	1878
Jake Goodman	1878
Bill Holbert	1878
Alamazoo Jennings	1878
Jake Knowdell	1878
Bill Morgan	1878
Johnny Peters	1878
Billy Redmond	1878
Sam Weaver	1878

Managers

Jack Chapman	1878

MILWAUKEE Braves 1953–65
Moved from BOSTON Braves
Moved to ATLANTA Braves

Hank Aaron	1954–65
Tommie Aaron	1962–63, 1965
Joe Adcock	1953–62
Sandy Alomar	1964–65
Felipe Alou	1964–65
Johnny Antonelli	1953, 1961
Ken Aspromonte	1962
Toby Atwell	1956
Bobby Avila	1959
Ed Bailey	1964
Jim Beauchamp	1965
Howie Bedell	1962
Gus Bell	1962
Vern Bickford	1953
Ethan Blackaby	1962, 1964
Johnny Blanchard	1965
Wade Blasingame	1963–65
Frank Bolling	1961–65
Ray Boone	1959–60
Bob Boyd	1961
John Braun	1964
George Brunet	1960–61
Bill Bruton	1953–60
Bob Buhl	1953–62
Lew Burdette	1953–63
Paul Burris	1953
Cecil Butler	1962, 1964
Sammy Calderone	1954
Clay Carroll	1964–65
Rico Carty	1964–65
Gino Cimoli	1961
Ty Cline	1963–65
Tony Cloninger	1961–65
Dave Cole	1953
Dick Cole	1957
Gene Conley	1954–58
Jim Constable	1962
Walker Cooper	1953
Chuck Cottier	1959–60
Wes Covington	1956–61
Billy Cowan	1965
Del Crandall	1953–63
Ray Crone	1954–57
George Crowe	1953, 1955
Jack Curtis	1962
Alvin Dark	1960
Mike de la Hoz	1964–65
John DeMerit	1957–59, 1961
Don Dillard	1963, 1965
Jack Dittmer	1953–56
Moe Drabowsky	1961
John Edelman	1955
Dave Eilers	1964–65
Hank Fischer	1962–65
Terry Fox	1960
Frank Funk	1963
Len Gabrielson	1960, 1963–64
Bob Giggie	1959–60
Jesse Gonder	1965
Sid Gordon	1953
Charlie Gorin	1954–55
Eddie Haas	1958, 1960
Harry Hanebrink	1953, 1957–58
Bob Hartman	1959
Bob Hazle	1957–58
Bob Hendley	1961–63
Earl Hersh	1956
Billy Hoeft	1964
Joey Jay	1953–55, 1957–60
Virgil Jester	1953
Ernie Johnson	1953–58
Ken Johnson	1965
Lou Johnson	1962
Dave Jolly	1953–57
Mack Jones	1961–63, 1965
Nippy Jones	1957
Dick Kelley	1964–65
Lou Klimchock	1963–65
Gary Kolb	1964–65
Joe Koppe	1958
Dave Koslo	1954–55
Mike Krsnich	1960, 1962
Norm Larker	1963
Frank Lary	1964
Charlie Lau	1960–61
Denny Lemaster	1962–65
Don Liddle	1953
Dick Littlefield	1958
Johnny Logan	1953–61
Stan Lopata	1959–60
Ken MacKenzie	1960–61
Bobby Malkmus	1957
Felix Mantilla	1956–61
Eddie Mathews	1953–65
Lee Maye	1959–65
Don McMahon	1957–62
Roy McMillan	1961–64
Denis Menke	1962–65
Catfish Metkovich	1954
Seth Morehead	1961
Joe Morgan	1959
Bubba Morton	1963
Red Murff	1956–57
Chet Nichols	1954–56
Phil Niekro	1964–65
Don Nottebart	1960–62
Johnny O'Brien	1959
Danny O'Connell	1954–57
Billy O'Dell	1965
Gene Oliver	1963–65
Chi Chi Olivo	1961, 1964–65
Dan Osinski	1965
Andy Pafko	1953–59
Phil Paine	1954–57
Jim Pendleton	1953–56
Taylor Phillips	1956–57
Ron Piche	1960–63
Jim Pisoni	1959
Juan Pizarro	1957–60
Billy Queen	1954
Merritt Ranew	1964
Claude Raymond	1961–63
Del Rice	1955–59
Mel Roach	1953–54, 1957–61
Humberto Robinson	1955–56, 1958
Phil Roof	1961, 1964
Bob Roselli	1955–56
Bob Rush	1958–60
Bob Sadowski	1963–65
Amado Samuel	1962–63
Carl Sawatski	1957–58
Dan Schneider	1963–64
Red Schoendienst	1957–60
Bob Shaw	1962–63
Ray Shearer	1957
Sibby Sisti	1953
Enos Slaughter	1959
Lou Sleater	1956
Roy Smalley	1954
Jack Smith	1964
Bill Southworth	1964
Warren Spahn	1953–64
Al Spangler	1959–61
Ebba St. Claire	1953
Max Surkont	1953
Chuck Tanner	1955–57
Bennie Taylor	1955
Hawk Taylor	1957–58, 1961–63
Frank Thomas	1961, 1965
Bobby Thomson	1954–57
Bob Thorpe	1953
Bobby Tiefenauer	1963–65
Frank Torre	1956–60
Joe Torre	1961–65
Bob Trowbridge	1956–59
Bob Uecker	1962–63
Arnie Umbach	1964
Roberto Vargas	1955
Mickey Vernon	1959
Charlie White	1954–55
Sammy White	1961
Carl Willey	1958–62
Jim Wilson	1953–54
Casey Wise	1958–59
Woody Woodward	1963–65

Managers

Bobby Bragan	1963–65
Chuck Dressen	1960–61
Charlie Grimm	1953–56
Fred Haney	1956–59
Birdie Tebbetts	1961–62

MONTREAL Expos 1969–95

Santo Alcala	1977
Scott Aldred	1993
Mike Aldrete	1989–90
Bernie Allen	1973
Bill Almon	1980
Felipe Alou	1973
Moises Alou	1990, 1992–95
Tavo Alvarez	1995
Scott Anderson	1990
Shane Andrews	1995
Luis Aquino	1995
Bill Atkinson	1976–79
Stan Bahnsen	1977–81
Bob Bailey	1969–75
Bret Barberie	1991–92
Greg Bargar	1983–84
Skeeter Barnes	1985
Brian Barnes	1990–93
Tim Barrett	1988
Randy Bass	1979
John Bateman	1969–72
Juan Bell	1994
Freddie Benavides	1994
Yamil Benitez	1995
Tony Bernazard	1979–80
Sean Berry	1992–95
Larry Biittner	1974–76
Dann Bilardello	1986
Tim Blackwell	1977, 1982–83
Dennis Blair	1974–76
John Boccabella	1969–73
Frank Bolick	1993
Don Bosch	1969
Kent Bottenfield	1992–93
Denis Boucher	1993–94

Oil Can Boyd	1990–91
Ron Brand	1969–71
Hal Breeden	1972–75
Fred Breining	1984
Dan Briggs	1981
Jim Britton	1971
Hubie Brooks	1985–89
Jackie Brown	1977
Curt Brown	1986–87
Curt Brown	1973
Eric Bullock	1991
Tim Burke	1985–91
Ray Burris	1981–83
Sal Butera	1984–85
Ivan Calderon	1991–92
Bill Campbell	1987
Casey Candaele	1986–88
John Candelaria	1989
Don Carrithers	1974–76
Gary Carter	1974–84, 1992
Dave Cash	1977–79
Craig Caskey	1973
Rick Cerone	1992
Archi Cianfrocco	1992–93
Donn Clendenon	1969
Ty Cline	1969
Rich Coggins	1975
Nate Colbert	1975–76
Greg Colbrunn	1992–93
Kevin Collins	1969
Wil Cordero	1992–95
Reid Cornelius	1995
John Costello	1990
Jim Cox	1973–76
Warren Cromartie	1974, 1976–83
Terry Crowley	1983
John D'Acquisto	1980
Ron Darling	1991
Jack Daugherty	1987
Willie Davis	1974
Andre Dawson	1976–86
Boots Day	1970–74
Jose DeLeon	1995
Don DeMola	1974–75
Delino DeShields	1990–93
Bill Dillman	1970
Miguel Dilone	1984–85
Tom Dixon	1983
John Dopson	1985, 1988
Dan Driessen	1984–85
Hal Dues	1977–78, 1980
Steve Dunning	1976
Jim Dwyer	1975–76
Duffy Dyer	1979
Joey Eischen	1994
Dave Engle	1987–88
Rick Engle	1981
Terry Enyart	1974
Bryan Eversgerd	1995
Roy Face	1969
Jim Fairey	1969–72
Ron Fairly	1969–74
Howard Farmer	1990
Jeff Fassero	1991–95
Jeff Fischer	1987
Mike Fitzgerald	1985–91
Darrin Fletcher	1992–95
Cliff Floyd	1993–95
Doug Flynn	1982–85
Tom Foley	1986–92, 1995
Tim Foli	1972–77
Chad Fonville	1995
Barry Foote	1974–77
Terry Francona	1981–85
Willie Fraser	1995
Lou Frazier	1993–95
Roger Freed	1976
Steve Frey	1989–91
Pepe Frias	1973–78
Doug Frobel	1985
Jerry Fry	1978
Woodie Fryman	1975–76, 1978–83
Mike Fuentes	1984
Andres Galarraga	1985–91
Damaso Garcia	1989
Mike Gardiner	1993
Mark Gardner	1989–92
Jeff Gardner	1994
Mike Garman	1978
Wayne Garrett	1976–78
Mike Gates	1981–82
Bob Gebhard	1974
Brett Gideon	1989–90
Joe Gilbert	1972–73
Ed Glynn	1985
Jerry Goff	1990
Rene Gonzales	1984, 1986
Tom Gorman	1981–82
Jim Gosger	1970–71
Wayne Granger	1976
Mudcat Grant	1969
Dick Grapenthin	1983–85
Ross Grimsley	1978–80
Marquis Grissom	1989–94
Kevin Gross	1989–90
Mark Grudzielanek	1995
Brad Gulden	1982
Bill Gullickson	1979–85
Rich Hacker	1971
Don Hahn	1969–70
Drew Hall	1990
Chris Haney	1991–92
Todd Haney	1992
Gerald Hannahs	1976–77
Greg Harris	1984, 1995
Gene Harris	1989
Ron Hassey	1991
Heath Haynes	1994
Neal Heaton	1987–88
Rod Henderson	1994
Butch Henry	1993–95
Ubaldo Heredia	1987
Gil Heredia	1992–95
Angel Hermoso	1969–70
Jose Herrera	1969
Ed Herrmann	1978
Joe Hesketh	1984–90
Jack Hiatt	1970
Ken Hill	1992–94
Fred Holdsworth	1977–78
Brian Holman	1988–89
Dave Hostetler	1981
Rex Hudler	1988–89
Terry Humphrey	1971–74
Ron Hunt	1971–74
Randy Hunt	1986
Jonathan Hurst	1992
Jeff Huson	1988–89
Tom Hutton	1978–81
Grant Jackson	1981
Bob James	1978–79, 1982–84
Pat Jarvis	1973
Larry Jaster	1969
Garry Jestadt	1969
Ken Johnson	1970
Tony Johnson	1981
Wallace Johnson	1981–82, 1984, 1986–90
Ron Johnson	1984
Roy Johnson	1982, 1984–85
Larry Johnson	1975–76
Randy Johnson	1988–89
Mack Jones	1969–71
Tracy Jones	1988
Barry Jones	1991
Jimmy Jones	1993
Mike Jorgensen	1972–77
Joe Keener	1976
Roberto Kelly	1995
Joe Kerrigan	1976–77
Clay Kirby	1976
Darold Knowles	1978
Wayne Krenchicki	1986
Bill Krueger	1992
Coco Laboy	1969–73
Tim Laker	1992–93, 1995
Larry Landreth	1976–77
Bill Landrum	1992
Chip Lang	1975–76
Mark Langston	1989
Mike Lansing	1993–95
Bill Laskey	1985
Vance Law	1985–87
Tom Lawless	1984
Charlie Lea	1980–84, 1987
Bill Lee	1979–82
Ron LeFlore	1980
Dave Leiper	1995
Denny Lemaster	1972
Randy Lerch	1982–83
Larry Lintz	1973–75
Bryan Little	1982–84
Bill Long	1991
Brian Looney	1993–94
Gary Lucas	1984–85
Urbano Lugo	1989
Steve Lyons	1992
Jim Lyttle	1973–76
Ken Macha	1979–80
Pete Mackanin	1975–77
Mickey Mahler	1985
Rick Mahler	1991
Bob Malloy	1990
Pepe Mangual	1972–76
Fred Manrique	1985
Jerry Manuel	1980–81
Leo Marentette	1969
Oreste Marrero	1993
Mike Marshall	1970–73
Dennis Martinez	1986–93
Dave Martinez	1988–91
Pedro Martinez	1994–95
Clyde Mashore	1970–73
Jim Mason	1979
Rudy May	1978–79
Matt Maysey	1992
Ernie McAnally	1971–74
Tim McCarver	1972
Bob McClure	1986–88
Dave McDonald	1971
Will McEnaney	1977
Andy McGaffigan	1984, 1986–89
Dan McGinn	1969–71
Tim McIntosh	1993
Dave McNally	1975
Sam Mejias	1977–78
Orlando Mercado	1990
Randy Miller	1978
Randy Milligan	1994
Brad Mills	1980–83
John Milner	1981–82
Dale Mohorcic	1990
John Montague	1973–75
Willie Montanez	1980–81
Charlie Montoyo	1993
Balor Moore	1970, 1972–74
Billy Moore	1986
Jose Morales	1974–77
Carl Morton	1969–72
Manny Mota	1969
Dale Murray	1974–76, 1979–80
Chris Nabholz	1990–93
Bob Natal	1992
Graig Nettles	1988
Al Newman	1985–86
Reid Nichols	1987
Steve Nicosia	1985
Tom Nieto	1986
Otis Nixon	1988–90
Junior Noboa	1989–91
Fred Norman	1980
Dan Norman	1982
Nelson Norman	1987
Jim Northrup	1974
Rich Nye	1970
Mike O'Berry	1985
Jack O'Connor	1985
John O'Donoghue	1970–71
Rowland Office	1980–82
Al Oliver	1982–83
Tom O'Malley	1988
Bob Owchinko	1986
Spike Owen	1989–92
David Palmer	1978–80, 1982, 1984–85
Stan Papi	1977–78
Johnny Paredes	1988, 1990
Jeff Parrett	1986–88
Larry Parrish	1974–81
Bob Pate	1980–81
Tony Perez	1977–79
Pascual Perez	1987–89
Carlos Perez	1995
Marty Pevey	1989
Adolfo Phillips	1969–70
Mike Phillips	1981–83
Doug Piatt	1991
Gerry Pirtle	1978
Alonzo Powell	1987
Curtis Pride	1993, 1995
Jimmy Qualls	1970
Dick Radatz	1969
Tim Raines	1980–90
Bobby Ramos	1978, 1980–81, 1983–84
Mike Ramsey	1984
Steve Ratzer	1980–81
Claude Raymond	1969–71
Randy Ready	1993
Jeff Reardon	1981–86
Bob Reece	1978
Howie Reed	1969–71
Jeff Reed	1987–88
Darren Reed	1992
Steve Renko	1969–76
Gilberto Reyes	1989, 1991
Bob Reynolds	1969
Nikco Riesgo	1991
George Riley	1986
Bill Risley	1992–93
Bombo Rivera	1975–76
Luis Rivera	1986–88
Bert Roberge	1985–86
Jerry Robertson	1969
Henry Rodriguez	1995
Gary Roenicke	1976
Steve Rogers	1973–85
Mel Rojas	1990–95
Tom Romano	1987
Gene Roof	1983
Rolando Roomes	1990
Pat Rooney	1981
Jorge Roque	1973
Pete Rose	1984
Kirk Rueter	1993–95
Scott Ruskin	1990–91
Angel Salazar	1983–84
Bill Sampen	1990–92
Scott Sanderson	1978–83
F. P. Santangelo	1995
Nelson Santovenia	1987–91
Rich Sauveur	1988
Pat Scanlon	1974–76
Dan Schatzeder	1977–79, 1982–86
Fred Scherman	1975–76
Dave Schmidt	1990–91
Curt Schmidt	1995
Rodney Scott	1976, 1979–82
Mickey Scott	1973
Tony Scott	1973–75, 1984
Tim Scott	1993–95
Bob Sebra	1986–87
David Segui	1995
Carroll Sembera	1969–70
Scott Service	1992
Don Shaw	1969
Jeff Shaw	1993–95
Steve Shea	1969
Razor Shines	1983–85, 1987
Joe Siddall	1993, 1995
Dave Silvestri	1995
Doug Simons	1992
Ken Singleton	1972–74
Chris Smith	1981
Bryn Smith	1981–89
Zane Smith	1989–90
Mike Smith	1988
Tony Solaita	1979
Lary Sorensen	1987
Elias Sosa	1979–81
Joe Sparma	1970
Tim Spehr	1993–95
Chris Speier	1977–84
Randy St. Claire	1984–88
Marv Staehle	1969–70
Matt Stairs	1992–93
Don Stanhouse	1975–77
Rusty Staub	1969–71, 1979
John Stefero	1987
Mike Stenhouse	1983–84
Bob Stinson	1973–74
Bill Stoneman	1969–73
John Strohmayer	1970–73
Gary Sutherland	1969–71
Stan Swanson	1971
Ron Swoboda	1971
John Tamargo	1979–80
Tony Tarasco	1995

Frank Taveras	1982
Chuck Taylor	1973–76
Wil Tejada	1986, 1988
Jeff Terpko	1977
J. J. Thobe	1995
Derrel Thomas	1984
Jason Thompson	1986
Scot Thompson	1985
Rich Thompson	1989–90
Andre Thornton	1976
Jay Tibbs	1986–87
Dave Tomlin	1982, 1986
Hector Torres	1972
Mike Torrez	1971–74
Jeff Treadway	1995
Manny Trillo	1983
Wayne Twitchell	1977–78
Del Unser	1976–78
Ugueth Urbina	1995
Mike Vail	1983
Sergio Valdez	1986, 1992–93
Ellis Valentine	1975–81
John Vander Wal	1991–93
Max Venable	1984
Dave Wainhouse	1991
Tom Walker	1972–74, 1977
Larry Walker	1989–94
Tim Wallach	1980–92
Bruce Walton	1993
Dan Warthen	1975–77
U. L. Washington	1985
Gary Waslewski	1969–70
Mitch Webster	1985–88
Lenny Webster	1994
Mike Wegener	1969–70
Chris Welsh	1983
John Wetteland	1992–94
Jerry White	1974–83
Derrick White	1993
Rondell White	1993–95
Gabe White	1994–95
Fred Whitfield	1970
Floyd Wicker	1969
Tom Wieghaus	1981, 1983
Jerry Willard	1992
Earl Williams	1976
Kenny Williams	1991
Maury Wills	1969
Bobby Wine	1969–72
Herm Winningham	1985–88
Jim Wohlford	1983–86
Ted Wood	1993
Ron Woods	1971–74
George Wright	1986
Ned Yost	1985
Floyd Youmans	1985–88
Pete Young	1992–93
Joel Youngblood	1982

Managers

Felipe Alou	1992–95
Jim Fanning	1981–82, 1984
Charlie Fox	1976
Karl Kuehl	1976
Gene Mauch	1969–75
Buck Rodgers	1985–91
Tom Runnells	1991–92
Bill Virdon	1983–84
Dick Williams	1977–81

NEW YORK Mutuals 1876

George Bechtel	1876
Eddie Booth	1876
Bill Craver	1876
George Fair	1876
Davy Force	1876
Jimmy Hallinan	1876
John Hatfield	1876
Mike Hayes	1876
George Heubel	1876
Nat Hicks	1876
Jim Holdsworth	1876
Terry Larkin	1876
John Maloney	1876
Bobby Mathews	1876
John McGuinness	1876
Al Nichols	1876
Neal Phelps	1876
George Seward	1876
Jim Shanley	1876
Joe Start	1876
Fred Treacey	1876
Pete Treacey	1876
Bob Valentine	1876
Billy West	1876

Managers

*Bill Craver	1876

NEW YORK Giants 1883–1957

Moved from TROY Trojans
Known as Gothams 1883–84
Moved to SAN FRANCISCO Giants

Woody Abernathy	1946–47
Ace Adams	1941–46
Eddie Ainsmith	1924
Vic Aldridge	1928
Ethan Allen	1930–32
Johnny Allen	1943–44
Myron Allen	1883
Joey Amalfitano	1954–55
Red Ames	1903–13
Fred Anderson	1916–18
Hub Andrews	1947–48
Nate Andrews	1946
Johnny Antonelli	1954–57
Morrie Arnovich	1941, 1946
Bill Ayers	1947
Charlie Babb	1903
Charlie Babington	1915
Lore Bader	1912
Loren Bain	1945
Al Baird	1917, 1919
Doug Baird	1920
Howard Baker	1915
Tom Baker	1937–38
Harry Baldwin	1924–25
Mark Baldwin	1893
George Bamberger	1951–52
Hal Bamberger	1948
Dave Bancroft	1920–23, 1930
Tom Bannon	1895–96
Curt Barclay	1957
Babe Barna	1941–43
Jesse Barnes	1918–23
Virgil Barnes	1919–20, 1922–28
Bob Barr	1891
Shad Barry	1908
Dick Bartell	1935–38, 1941–43, 1946
Bob Barthelson	1944
Bill Bartley	1903
Charley Bassett	1890–92
Larry Battam	1895
Joe Bean	1902
Des Beatty	1914
Buck Becannon	1887
Beals Becker	1910–12
Marty Becker	1915
Jake Beckley	1896–97
Roy Beecher	1907–08
Joe Beggs	1947–48
Ed Begley	1884
Gene Begley	1886
Hank Behrman	1949
Hi Bell	1932–34
Jack Bentley	1923–27
Rube Benton	1915–21
Larry Benton	1927–30
Wally Berger	1937–38
Jack Berly	1931
Curt Bernard	1900–01
Ray Berres	1942–45
Joe Berry	1921–22
Bob Bescher	1914
Rae Blaemire	1941
Buddy Blattner	1946–48
Bob Blewett	1902
Clint Blume	1922–23
Hank Boney	1927
Zeke Bonura	1939
Andy Boswell	1895
Chick Bowen	1919
Cy Bowen	1896
Frank Bowerman	1900–07
Joe Bowman	1934
Bob Bowman	1941
Roger Bowman	1949, 1951–52
Jim Boyle	1926
Jack Boyle	1892
Vic Bradford	1943
Dave Brain	1908
Fred Brainerd	1914–16
Jackie Brandt	1956
Don Brennan	1937
Roger Bresnahan	1902–08
Ed Bressoud	1956–57
Jack Brewer	1944–46
Al Bridwell	1908–11
Steve Brodie	1902
Ken Brondell	1944
Dan Brouthers	1904
Eddie Brown	1920–21
Jim Brown	1884
Jumbo Brown	1937–41
Willard Brown	1887–89
George Browne	1902–07
Garland Buckeye	1928
Dick Buckley	1890–91
Mike Budnick	1946–47
Charlie Buelow	1901
Eddie Burke	1892–95
Frank Burke	1906
John Burke	1902
Jesse Burkett	1890
George Burns	1911–21
Oyster Burns	1895
Pete Burnside	1955, 1957
Buster Burrell	1891
Joe Bush	1927
Frank Butler	1895
Leon Cadore	1924
Sammy Calderone	1950, 1953
Red Callahan	1902
Sal Campfield	1896
Ben Cantwell	1927–28, 1937
John Carden	1946
Roger Carey	1887
Bob Carpenter	1940–42, 1946–47
Bill Carrick	1898–1900
Kid Carsey	1899
Blackie Carter	1925–26
Ed Caskin	1883–84, 1886
Slick Castleman	1934–39
Foster Castleman	1954–57
Red Causey	1918–19, 1921–22
Leon Chagnon	1935
Tiny Chaplin	1928, 1930–31
Hal Chase	1919
Ken Chase	1943
Virgil Cheeves	1927
Lou Chiozza	1937–39
Bill Cissell	1938
Roy Clark	1902
Willie Clark	1895–97
Watty Clark	1933–34
Archie Clarke	1890–91
Dad Clarke	1894–97
Boileryard Clarke	1905
Dad Clarkson	1891
Bill Clarkson	1927–28
Elmer Cleveland	1888
Gil Coan	1955
Dick Coffman	1936–39
Dick Cogan	1900
Andy Cohen	1926, 1928–29
Tom Colcolough	1899
Pete Compton	1918
Frank Connaughton	1896
Bill Connelly	1952–53
Joe Connolly	1921
Roger Connor	1883–89, 1891, 1893–94
Jim Constable	1956–57
Sandy Consuegra	1957
Jack Conway	1948
Bobby Coombs	1943
Jimmy Cooney	1919
Claude Cooper	1913
Mort Cooper	1947
Walker Cooper	1946–49
Larry Corcoran	1885–86
Tommy Corcoran	1907
Al Corwin	1951–55
Roscoe Coughlin	1891
Dick Cramer	1883
Doc Crandall	1908–13
Cannonball Crane	1888–89, 1892–93
Sam Crane	1890
Pat Crawford	1929–30
Pete Cregan	1899
Hughie Critz	1930–35
Ray Crone	1957
John Cronin	1902–03
Buddy Crump	1924
Al Cuccinello	1935
Tony Cuccinello	1940
Dick Culler	1949
Jack Cummings	1926–29
Bill Cunningham	1921–23
Harry Curtis	1907
Mike Cvengros	1922
Bill Dahlen	1904–07
Ed Daily	1890
George Daly	1909
Harry Danning	1933–42
Alvin Dark	1950–56
Claude Davenport	1920
George Davies	1893
Chick Davies	1925–26
George Davis	1893–1901, 1903
Kiddo Davis	1933, 1935–37
Harry Davis	1895–96
Ira Davis	1899
Jim Davis	1957
John Davis	1941
Paul Dean	1940–41
Wayland Dean	1924–25
Pat Deasley	1885–87
Dummy Deegan	1901
Bill DeKoning	1945
Jim Delahanty	1902
Al Demaree	1912–14, 1917–18
Frank Demaree	1939–41
Jerry Denny	1890–91
Roger Denzer	1901
Jim Devine	1886
Mickey Devine	1925
Art Devlin	1904–11
Jim Devlin	1886
Josh Devore	1908–13
Al DeVormer	1927
Johnny Dickshot	1939
Walt Dickson	1910
Chuck Diering	1952
Vince DiMaggio	1946
Ed Doheny	1895–1901
Red Donahue	1893
Mike Donlin	1904–06, 1908, 1911
Jim Donnelly	1897
Pete Donohue	1930–31
Red Dooin	1915–16
Mickey Doolan	1916
Mike Dorgan	1883–87
Phil Douglas	1919–22
Jack Doyle	1892–95, 1898–1900, 1902
Larry Doyle	1907–16, 1918–20
Clem Dreisewerd	1948
Chuck Dressen	1933
Louis Drucke	1909–12
Jean Dubuc	1919
Jack Dunn	1902–04
Andy Dunning	1891
Bull Durham	1908–09
Ben Dyer	1914–15
Hugh East	1941–43
Claude Elliott	1904–05
Bob Elliott	1952
Slim Emmerich	1945–46
Charlie English	1936
Gil English	1931–32
Eric Erickson	1914
Paul Erickson	1948
Dude Esterbrook	1885–86, 1890
Roy Evans	1902

Steve Evans	1908
Hoot Evers	1954
John Ewing	1891
Buck Ewing	1883–89, 1891–92
Duke Farrell	1894–96
Doc Farrell	1925–27, 1929
Jim Faulkner	1927–28
Charlie Faust	1911
Harry Feldman	1941–46
Harry Felix	1901
George Ferguson	1906–07
Jocko Fields	1892
Steve Filipowicz	1944–45
Bill Finley	1886
Rube Fischer	1941, 1943–46
Leo Fishel	1899
Chauncey Fisher	1901
Don Fisher	1945
Matty Fitzgerald	1906–07
Freddie Fitzsimmons	1925–37
Tom Fleming	1899
Art Fletcher	1909–20
Paul Florence	1926
Carney Flynn	1896
Frank Foreman	1893
Pop Foster	1898–1900
Elmer Foster	1888–89
Charlie Fox	1942
Herman Franks	1949
Lonny Frey	1948
Charlie Frisbee	1900
Frankie Frisch	1919–26
Art Fromme	1913–15
Shorty Fuller	1892–96
Chick Fullis	1929–32
Frank Gabler	1935–37
Augie Galan	1949
John Ganzel	1901
Joe Garagiola	1954
Al Gardella	1945
Danny Gardella	1944–45
Billy Gardner	1954–55
Willie Garoni	1899
Alex Gaston	1920–23
Lloyd Gearhart	1947
Dinty Gearin	1923–24
Johnny Gee	1944–46
Joe Genewich	1928–30
Bill George	1887–89
Oscar Georgy	1938
Joe Gerhardt	1885–87
Les German	1893–96
Al Gettel	1951
Charlie Gettig	1896–99
George Gibson	1917–18
Sam Gibson	1932
Paul Giel	1954–55
Tookie Gilbert	1950, 1953
Jack Gilbert	1898
Billy Gilbert	1903–06
Pete Gillespie	1883–87
Jim Gladd	1946
Jack Glasscock	1890–91
Kid Gleason	1896–1900
Ed Glenn	1898
Al Glossop	1939–40
Ruben Gomez	1953–57
Mike Gonzalez	1919–21
Sid Gordon	1941–43, 1946–49, 1955
George Gore	1887–89, 1891–92
Tom Gorman	1939
Ted Goulait	1912
Hank Gowdy	1910–11, 1923–25
Mike Grady	1898–1900
Moonlight Graham	1905
Jack Graham	1946
Eddie Grant	1913–15
George Grantham	1934
Mickey Grasso	1946, 1955
Kent Greenfield	1924–27
Hal Gregg	1952
Pug Griffin	1920
Sandy Griffin	1884
Burleigh Grimes	1927
Roy Grimes	1920
Marv Grissom	1946, 1953–57
Heinie Groh	1912–13, 1922–26
Tom Grubbs	1920
Harry Gumbert	1935–41

Bert Haas	1949
Bump Hadley	1941
Bill Haeffner	1928
Tom Hafey	1939
Odell Hale	1941
Bob Hall	1905
Jack Hallett	1948
Sam Hamby	1926–27
Frank Hankinson	1883–84
Jack Hannifin	1906–08
Andy Hansen	1944–45, 1947–50
Scott Hardesty	1899
Red Hardy	1951
George Harper	1927–28
Ray Harrell	1945
Gail Harris	1955–57
Jack Harshman	1948, 1950, 1952
Grover Hartley	1911–13, 1924–26
Chick Hartley	1902
Fred Hartman	1898–99
Gabby Hartnett	1941
Clint Hartung	1947–52
Mickey Haslin	1937–38
Gil Hatfield	1887–89
George Hausmann	1944–45, 1949
Pink Hawley	1900
Ray Hayworth	1939
Francis Healy	1930–32
Bunny Hearn	1913
Jim Hearn	1950–56
Bud Heine	1921
Ed Hemingway	1917
Ed Hendricks	1910
Jack Hendricks	1902
Dutch Henry	1927–29
John Henry	1890
Fred Herbert	1915
Buck Herzog	1908–09, 1911–13, 1916–17
Larry Hesterfer	1901
Joe Heving	1930–31
Piano Legs Hickman	1900–01
Kirby Higbe	1949–50
Mahlon Higbee	1922
Carmen Hill	1922
Frank Hiller	1953
Bobby Hofman	1949, 1952–56
Shanty Hogan	1928–32
Walter Holke	1914, 1916–18
Mul Holland	1927
Ducky Holmes	1897
Rogers Hornsby	1927
Joe Hornung	1890
Shorty Howe	1890, 1893
Bill Howerton	1952
Waite Hoyt	1918, 1932
Carl Hubbell	1928–43
Bill Hubbell	1919–20
Willis Hudlin	1940
Johnny Hudson	1945
Al Huenke	1914
John Humphries	1883–84
Bill Hunnefield	1931
Herb Hunter	1916
Walter Huntzinger	1923–25
Hooks Iott	1947
Monte Irvin	1949–55
Ray Jablonski	1957
Jim Jackson	1902
Travis Jackson	1922–36
Merwin Jacobson	1915
Art Jahn	1928
Bernie James	1933
Larry Jansen	1947–54
Tex Jeanes	1927
Art Johnson	1927
Elmer Johnson	1914
Fred Johnson	1922–23
Youngy Johnson	1899
Jimmy Johnston	1926
Roy Joiner	1940
Bumpus Jones	1893
Gordon Jones	1957
Jim Jones	1901–02
Johnny Jones	1919
Sheldon Jones	1946–51
Claude Jonnard	1921–24
Buck Jordan	1929
Spider Jorgensen	1950–51
Bob Joyce	1946

Bill Joyce	1896–98
Ralph Judd	1929–30
Bill Jurges	1939–45
Alex Kampouris	1938–39
Ray Katt	1952–57
Benny Kauff	1916–20
Tony Kaufmann	1929
Tim Keefe	1885–89, 1891
Willie Keeler	1892–93, 1910
Duke Kelleher	1916
George Kelly	1915–17, 1919–26
King Kelly	1893
Monte Kennedy	1946–53
Brickyard Kennedy	1902
Buddy Kerr	1943–49
Pete Kilduff	1917
Silver King	1892–93
Lee King	1919–22
Bob Kinsella	1919–20
Kinsler	1893
LaRue Kirby	1912
Jay Kirke	1918
Al Klawitter	1909–10
Joe Klinger	1927
Clyde Kluttz	1945–46
Frank Knauss	1895
Jimmy Knowles	1892
Brad Kocher	1915–16
Pip Koehler	1925
Len Koenecke	1932
Mark Koenig	1935–36
Alex Konikowski	1948, 1951, 1954
Wally Kopf	1921
Dave Koslo	1941–42, 1946–53
Jack Kramer	1950–51
Tex Kraus	1946
Red Kress	1946
Ernie Krueger	1917
Joe Lafata	1947, 1949
Dick Lajeskie	1946
Max Lanier	1952–53
Arlie Latham	1909
Tacks Latimer	1898
Billy Lauder	1902–03
Garland Lawing	1946
Les Layton	1948
Tony Lazzeri	1939
Freddy Leach	1929–31
Fred Lear	1920
Roy Lee	1945
Thornton Lee	1948
Al LeFevre	1920
Hank Leiber	1933–38, 1942
Dummy Leitner	1901
Bob Lennon	1956
Sam Leslie	1929, 1931–33, 1936–38
Don Liddle	1954–56
Freddie Lindstrom	1924–32
Dick Littlefield	1956
Mickey Livingston	1947–49
Jake Livingstone	1901
Hans Lobert	1915–17
Whitey Lockman	1945, 1948–57
Lucky Lohrke	1947–51
Bill Lohrman	1937–43
Ernie Lombardi	1943–47
Lou Lombardo	1948
Loughran	1884
Hugh Luby	1944
Red Lucas	1923
Ray Lucas	1929–31
Dolf Luque	1932–35
Mike Lynch	1907
Red Lynn	1939–40
Denny Lyons	1892
Harry Lyons	1889, 1892–93
Waddy MacPhee	1922
Ed Madjeski	1937
Bill Magee	1901–02
Sal Maglie	1945, 1950–55
Freddie Maguire	1922–23
Jack Maguire	1950–51
Jim Mahady	1921
Bill Malarkey	1908
Joe Malay	1933
Jim Mallory	1945
Gus Mancuso	1933–38, 1942–44
Jim Mangan	1956
Leo Mangum	1928

Charlie Manlove	1884
Les Mann	1927–28
Firpo Marberry	1936
Joe Margoneri	1956–57
Rube Marquard	1908–15
Doc Marshall	1929–32
Willard Marshall	1942, 1946–49
Doc Marshall	1904, 1906
Frank Martin	1899
Joe Martin	1936
Christy Mathewson	1900–16
Henry Mathewson	1906–07
Mike Mattimore	1887
Al Maul	1901
Ernie Maun	1924
Bert Maxwell	1911
Buster Maynard	1940, 1942–43, 1946
Eddie Mayo	1936
Carl Mays	1929
Willie Mays	1951–52, 1954–57
Algie McBride	1901
Windy McCall	1954–57
Johnny McCarthy	1936–41, 1948
Lew McCarty	1916–20
Moose McCormick	1904, 1908–09, 1912–13
Mike McCormick	1956–57
Tom McCreery	1897–98
Jim McDonald	1902
Dan McGann	1902–07
Bill McGee	1941–42
Joe McGinnity	1902–08
Mickey McGowan	1948
Bill McKechnie	1916
Alex McKinnon	1884
Art McLarney	1932
Larry McLean	1913–15
Jack McMahon	1892–93
George McMillan	1890
Hugh McMullen	1925–26
Tim McNamara	1926
Frank McPartlin	1899
Hugh McQuillan	1922–27
Charlie Mead	1943–45
Joe Medwick	1943–45
Jouett Meekin	1894–99
Cliff Melton	1937–44
Jock Menefee	1898
Win Mercer	1900
Fred Merkle	1907–16
Howard Merritt	1913
Sam Mertes	1903–06
Irish Meusel	1921–26
Chief Meyers	1909–15
Jim Middleton	1917
Jim Miller	1901
Ken Miller	1944
Roscoe Miller	1902–03
Stu Miller	1957
Jocko Milligan	1893
Billy Milligan	1904
Willie Mills	1901
Pete Milne	1948–49
Clarence Mitchell	1930–32
Johnny Mize	1942, 1946–49
John Monroe	1921
Ray Monzant	1954–57
Jim Mooney	1931–32
Al Moore	1925–26
Euel Moore	1935
Eddie Moore	1932
Joe Moore	1930–41
Bill Morrell	1930–31
Howie Moss	1942
Heinie Mueller	1926–27
Don Mueller	1948–57
Ray Mueller	1949–50
Van Lingle Mungo	1942–43, 1945
Danny Murphy	1900–01
Danny Murphy	1892
Frank Murphy	1901
Pat Murphy	1887–90
Bob Murphy	1890
Yale Murphy	1894–95, 1897
Red Murray	1909–15, 1917
George Myatt	1938–39
Glenn Myatt	1935
Offa Neal	1905
Tom Needham	1908
Art Nehf	1919–26
Candy Nelson	1887
Ray Nelson	1901

Charlie Newman	1892
Bobo Newsom	1948
Chet Nichols	1928
Roy Nichols	1944
Bert Niehoff	1918
Ray Noble	1951–53
Tom O'Brien	1899
Walter Ockey	1944
Danny O'Connell	1957
Jimmy O'Connell	1923–24
Hank O'Day	1889
Ken O'Dea	1939–41
Lefty O'Doul	1928, 1933–34
Joe Oeschger	1919, 1924
Bob O'Farrell	1928–32
Jack Ogden	1918
Hal O'Hagen	1902
Bill O'Hara	1909
Mickey O'Neil	1927
Tip O'Neill	1883
John O'Neill	1899, 1902
Jack Onslow	1917
Joe Orengo	1941, 1943
Jim O'Rourke	1885–89, 1891–92, 1904
Tom O'Rourke	1890
Dave Orr	1883
Marty O'Toole	1914
Mel Ott	1926–45
Henry Oxley	1884
Emilio Palmero	1915–16
Roy Parmelee	1929–35
Pat Patterson	1921
Gene Paulette	1911
Homer Peel	1933–34
Pol Perritt	1915–21
Charlie Petty	1893
Fred Pfeffer	1896
Monte Pfyl	1907
John Phillips	1945
Bill Phyle	1901
Mario Picone	1947, 1952, 1954
Gracie Pierce	1883
Sandy Piez	1914
Jess Pike	1946
Emil Planeta	1931
Norman Plitt	1927
Ray Poat	1947–49
Joe Poetz	1926
Hugh Poland	1943
Lou Polli	1944
Ned Porter	1926–27
Joe Price	1928
Hub Pruett	1930
John Puhl	1898–99
Ewald Pyle	1944–45
Pat Ragan	1919
John Rainey	1887
Goldie Rapp	1921
Bill Rariden	1916–18
Johnny Rawlings	1921–22
Bugs Raymond	1909–11
Andy Reese	1927–30
Joe Regan	1898
Bill Reidy	1896
Nap Reyes	1943–45, 1950
Bobby Rhawn	1947–49
Dusty Rhodes	1952–57
Paul Richards	1933–35
Hardy Richardson	1892
Danny Richardson	1884–89, 1891
Steve Ridzik	1956–57
Bill Rigney	1946–53
Jimmy Ring	1926
Jimmy Ripple	1936–39
Hank Ritter	1914–16
John Roach	1887
Dave Robertson	1912, 1914–17, 1922
Jack Robinson	1902
Andre Rodgers	1957
Eric Rodin	1954
Jose Rodriguez	1917–18
Wally Roettger	1930
Goody Rosen	1946
Harry Rosenberg	1930
George Ross	1918
Frank Rosso	1944
Edd Roush	1916, 1927–29
Johnny Rucker	1940–41, 1943–46
Dick Rudolph	1910–11
Rudy Rufer	1949–50

Amos Rusie	1890–95, 1897–98
Connie Ryan	1942
Blondy Ryan	1933–34, 1937–38
Rosy Ryan	1919–24
Slim Sallee	1916–18, 1920–21
Jack Salveson	1933–34
Manny Salvo	1939
Ron Samford	1954
Bill Sarni	1956
Hank Sauer	1957
Bill Sayles	1943
Frank Scalzi	1939
Mort Scanlan	1890
Ray Schalk	1929
Bobby Schang	1915
Rube Schauer	1913–16
Mike Schemer	1945
Admiral Schlei	1909–10
Crazy Schmit	1893
Red Schoendienst	1956–57
Hank Schreiber	1921
Pop Schriver	1895
Hal Schumacher	1931–42, 1946
Ferdie Schupp	1913–19
Jack Scott	1922–23, 1925–26, 1928–29
Doc Sechrist	1899
Bob Seeds	1938–40
Kip Selbach	1900–01
Frank Seward	1943–44
Cy Seymour	1896–1900, 1906–10
Tillie Shafer	1909–10, 1912–13
Spike Shannon	1906–08
John Sharrott	1890–92
Danny Shay	1907
Red Shea	1921–22
Jim Sheehan	1936
Tommy Sheehan	1900
Ralph Shinners	1922–23
Ernie Shore	1912
Bill Shores	1933
Eddie Sicking	1918–20
Seth Sigsby	1893
Mike Slattery	1888–89
Scottie Slayback	1926
Bruce Sloan	1944
Broadway Aleck Smith	1901, 1906
Al Smith	1934–37
Al Smith	1926
Earl Smith	1919–23
Elmer Smith	1900
Mike Smith	1926
George Smith	1916–19
Heinie Smith	1901–02
Harry Smith	1914–15
Jimmy Smith	1917
Red Smith	1927
Fred Snodgrass	1908–15
Colonel Snover	1919
Frank Snyder	1919–26
Moe Solomon	1923
Pete Sommers	1890
Don Songer	1927
Billy Southworth	1924–26
Tully Sparks	1902
Daryl Spencer	1952–53, 1956–57
George Spencer	1950–55
Glenn Spencer	1933
Roy Spencer	1936
Vern Spencer	1920
Al Spohrer	1928
Ebba St. Claire	1954
General Stafford	1893–97
Eddie Stanky	1950–51
Ray Starr	1933
Jigger Statz	1919–20
Bob Steele	1918–19
Casey Stengel	1921–23
Joe Stephenson	1943
Glen Stewart	1940
Milt Stock	1913–14
Allyn Stout	1935
Sammy Strang	1901, 1905–08
Sailor Stroud	1915–16
Bill Stuart	1899
Mike Sullivan	1891, 1896–97
Tom Sunkel	1941–43
Max Surkont	1956–57
Bill Swaback	1887
Ad Swigler	1917

Zack Taylor	1927
Jack Taylor	1891
Dummy Taylor	1900–08
Bill Taylor	1954–56
Jim Tennant	1929
Fred Tenney	1908–09
Bill Terry	1923–36
Wayne Terwilliger	1955–56
Jeff Tesreau	1912–18
Henry Thielman	1902
Fay Thomas	1927
Herb Thomas	1927
Valmy Thomas	1957
Junior Thompson	1946–47
Hank Thompson	1949–56
Fresco Thompson	1926
Bobby Thomson	1946–53, 1957
Jim Thorpe	1913–15, 1917–19
Mike Tiernan	1887–99
Cannonball Titcomb	1887–89
Andy Tomasic	1949
Fred Toney	1918–22
Red Tramback	1940
Red Treadway	1944–45
Ken Trinkle	1943, 1946–48
Dasher Troy	1883
Ty Tyson	1926–27
George Uhle	1933
George Ulrich	1896
George Van Haltren	1894–1903
Ike Van Zandt	1901
Hy Vandenburg	1937–40
Art Veltman	1928–29
Johnny Vergez	1931–34
Ozzie Virgil	1956–57
Bill Voiselle	1942–47
Ham Wade	1907
Heinie Wagner	1902
Rube Walberg	1923
Frank Walker	1925
Curt Walker	1920–21
Bill Walker	1927–32
Joe Wall	1901–02
Red Waller	1909
Monte Ward	1883–89, 1893–94
Jack Warner	1896–1901, 1903–04
Bennie Warren	1946–47
Libe Washburn	1902
George Watkins	1934
Mule Watson	1923–24
Roy Weatherly	1950
Red Webb	1948–49
Jake Weimer	1909
Phil Weintraub	1933–35, 1937, 1944–45
Mickey Welch	1883–92
Jimmy Welsh	1928–29
Lew Wendell	1915
Bill Werber	1942
Huyler Westervelt	1894
Wes Westrum	1947–57
Lew Whistler	1890–91
Fuzz White	1947
Bill White	1956
Burgess Whitehead	1936–37, 1939–41
Art Whitney	1888–89
Stump Wiedman	1887–88
Hoyt Wilhelm	1952–56
Joe Wilhoit	1917–18
Davey Williams	1949, 1951–55
Walt Wilmot	1897–98
Art Wilson	1909–13
Artie Wilson	1951
Parke Wilson	1893–99
Ted Wilson	1952, 1956
Hack Wilson	1923–25
Hooks Wiltse	1904–14
Jesse Winters	1919–20
John Wisner	1925–26
Mickey Witek	1940–43, 1946–47
Johnnie Wittig	1938–39, 1941, 1943
Pete Woodruff	1899
Al Worthington	1953–54, 1956–57
Roy Wright	1956
Russ Wrightstone	1928
Zeke Wrigley	1899
George Yeager	1902
Babe Young	1939–42, 1946
Ross Youngs	1917–26
Sal Yvars	1947–53

Adrian Zabala	1945, 1949
Elmer Zacher	1910
Dave Zearfoss	1896–98
Heinie Zimmerman	1916–19
Roy Zimmerman	1945
Walt Zink	1921

Managers

Cap Anson	1898
John Clapp	1883
*George Davis	1895, 1900–01
John Day	1899
*Jack Doyle	1895
Leo Durocher	1948–55
Buck Ewing	1900
Horace Fogel	1902
Fred Hoey	1899
*Rogers Hornsby	1927
Arthur Irwin	1896
Hughie Jennings	1924–25
*Bill Joyce	1896–98
John McGraw	1902–32
Jim Mutrie	1885–91
*Mel Ott	1942–48
Pat Powers	1892
Jim Price	1884
Bill Rigney	1956–57
*Heinie Smith	1902
*Bill Terry	1932–41
*Monte Ward	1884, 1893–94
Harvey Watkins	1895

NEW YORK Mets 1962–95

Don Aase	1989
Tommie Agee	1968–72
Rick Aguilera	1985–89
Jack Aker	1974
Edgardo Alfonzo	1995
Neil Allen	1979–83
Bill Almon	1980, 1987
Sandy Alomar	1967
Jesus Alou	1975
George Altman	1964
Luis Alvarado	1977
Craig Anderson	1962–64
Rick Anderson	1986
Bob Apodaca	1973–77
Jerry Arrigo	1966
Richie Ashburn	1962
Tucker Ashford	1983
Bob Aspromonte	1971
Benny Ayala	1974, 1976
Wally Backman	1980–88
Kevin Baez	1990, 1992–93
Bob Bailor	1981–83
Billy Baldwin	1976
Rick Baldwin	1975–77
Lute Barnes	1972
Jeff Barry	1995
Kevin Bass	1992
Ed Bauta	1963–64
Billy Beane	1984–85
Larry Bearnarth	1963–66
Blaine Beatty	1989, 1991
Jim Beauchamp	1972–73
Gus Bell	1962
Dennis Bennett	1967
Butch Benton	1978, 1980
Juan Berenguer	1978–80
Bruce Berenyi	1984–86
Dwight Bernard	1978–79
Yogi Berra	1965
Jim Bethke	1965
Mike Birkbeck	1992, 1995
Mike Bishop	1983
Terry Blocker	1985
Bruce Bochy	1982
Tim Bogar	1993–95
Bruce Boisclair	1974, 1976–79
Danny Boitano	1981
Mark Bomback	1980
Bobby Bonilla	1992–95
Don Bosch	1967–68
Daryl Boston	1990–92
Ken Boswell	1967–74
Ed Bouchee	1962
Larry Bowa	1985
Ken Boyer	1966–67

Mark Bradley	1983
Ed Bressoud	1966
Rico Brogna	1994–95
Hubie Brooks	1980–84, 1991
Terry Bross	1991
Leon Brown	1976
Kevin Brown	1990
Mike Bruhert	1978
Jerry Buchek	1967–68
Damon Buford	1995
Tim Burke	1991–92
Jeromy Burnitz	1993–94
Larry Burright	1963–64
Ray Burris	1979–80
Brett Butler	1995
Paul Byrd	1995
John Candelaria	1987
John Cangelosi	1994
Chris Cannizzaro	1962–65
Buzz Capra	1971–73
Jose Cardenal	1979–80
Don Cardwell	1967–70
Duke Carmel	1963
Chuck Carr	1990–91
Mark Carreon	1987–91
Gary Carter	1985–89
Tony Castillo	1991
Juan Castillo	1994
Alberto Castillo	1995
Rick Cerone	1991
Elio Chacon	1962
Dean Chance	1970
Kelvin Chapman	1979, 1984–85
Ed Charles	1967–69
Rich Chiles	1973
Harry Chiti	1962
John Christensen	1984–85
Joe Christopher	1962–65
Galen Cisco	1962–65
Donn Clendenon	1969–71
Gene Clines	1975
Choo Choo Coleman	1962–63, 1966
Vince Coleman	1991–93
Kevin Collins	1965, 1967–69
David Cone	1987–92
Bill Connors	1967–68
Cliff Cook	1962–63
Tim Corcoran	1986
Mardie Cornejo	1978
Reid Cornelius	1995
Billy Cowan	1965
Roger Craig	1962–63
Jerry Cram	1974–75
Mike Cubbage	1981
Ron Darling	1983–91
Ray Daviault	1962
Tommy Davis	1967
John DeMerit	1962
Bill Denehy	1967
Mark Dewey	1992
Carlos Diaz	1982–83
Mario Diaz	1990
Jack DiLauro	1969
Steve Dillon	1963–64
Jerry DiPoto	1995
Chris Donnels	1991–92
D. J. Dozier	1992
Sammy Drake	1962
Mike Draper	1993
Jim Dwyer	1976
Duffy Dyer	1968–74
Len Dykstra	1985–89
Tom Edens	1987
Dave Eilers	1965–66
Larry Elliot	1964, 1966
Dock Ellis	1979
Kevin Elster	1986–92
Nino Espinosa	1974–78
Chuck Estrada	1967
Francisco Estrada	1971
Carl Everett	1995
Pete Falcone	1979–82
Chico Fernandez	1963
Sid Fernandez	1984–93
Tony Fernandez	1993
Sergio Ferrer	1978–79
Tom Filer	1992
Jack Fisher	1964–67
Mike Fitzgerald	1983–84
Shaun Fitzmaurice	1966
Don Florence	1995
Gil Flores	1978–79
Doug Flynn	1977–81
Tim Foli	1970–71, 1978–79
Rich Folkers	1970
Larry Foss	1962
George Foster	1982–86
Leo Foster	1976–77
Joe Foy	1970
John Franco	1990–95
Jim Fregosi	1972–73
Bob Friend	1966
Danny Frisella	1967–72
Brent Gaff	1982–84
Bob Gallagher	1975
Dave Gallagher	1992–93
Ron Gardenhire	1981–85
Rob Gardner	1965–66
Wes Gardner	1984–85
Jeff Gardner	1991
Wayne Garrett	1969–76
Rod Gaspar	1969–70
Gary Gentry	1969–72
John Gibbons	1984, 1986
Bob Gibson	1987
Paul Gibson	1992–93
Brian Giles	1981–83
Joe Ginsberg	1962
Ed Glynn	1979–80
Jesse Gonder	1963–65
Dwight Gooden	1984–94
Greg Goossen	1965–68
Tom Gorman	1982–85
Jim Gosger	1969, 1973–74
Mauro Gozzo	1993–94
Wayne Graham	1964
Bill Graham	1967
Pumpsie Green	1963
Dallas Green	1966
Kenny Greer	1993
Tom Grieve	1978
Jerry Grote	1966–77
Joe Grzenda	1967
Lee Guetterman	1992
Eric Gunderson	1994–95
Don Hahn	1971–74
Tom Hall	1975–76
Jack Hamilton	1966–67
Ike Hampton	1974
Shawn Hare	1994
Tim Harkness	1963–64
Pete Harnisch	1995
Bud Harrelson	1965–77
Greg Harris	1981
Andy Hassler	1979
Tom Hausman	1978–82
Ed Hearn	1986
Richie Hebner	1979
Danny Heep	1983–86
Jack Heidemann	1975–76
Bob Heise	1967–69
Ken Henderson	1978
Steve Henderson	1977–80
Bob Hendley	1967
Phil Hennigan	1973
Doug Henry	1995
Bill Hepler	1966
Ron Herbel	1970
Keith Hernandez	1983–89
Manny Hernandez	1989
Tommy Herr	1990–91
Rick Herrscher	1962
Jim Hickman	1962–66
Joe Hicks	1963
Chuck Hiller	1965–67
Dave Hillman	1962
Eric Hillman	1992–94
Jerry Hinsley	1964, 1967
Gil Hodges	1962–63
Ron Hodges	1973–84
Scott Holman	1980, 1982–83
Jay Hook	1962–64
Wayne Housie	1993
Mike Howard	1981–83
Pat Howell	1992
Jesse Hudson	1969
Keith Hughes	1990
Todd Hundley	1990–95
Ron Hunt	1963–66
Willard Hunter	1962, 1964
Clint Hurdle	1983, 1985, 1987
Jonathan Hurst	1994
Butch Huskey	1993, 1995
Jeff Innis	1987–93
Jason Isringhausen	1995
Al Jackson	1962–65, 1968–69
Roy Lee Jackson	1977–80
Darrin Jackson	1993
Jason Jacome	1994–95
Gregg Jefferies	1988–91
Stan Jefferson	1986
Chris Jelic	1990
Bob Johnson	1967
Bob Johnson	1969
Howard Johnson	1985–93
Cleon Jones	1963, 1965–75
Sherman Jones	1962
Ross Jones	1984
Randy Jones	1981–82
Barry Jones	1992
Chris Jones	1995
Bobby Jones	1993–95
Mike Jorgensen	1968, 1970–71, 1980–83
Jeff Kaiser	1993
Rod Kanehl	1962–64
Jeff Kent	1992–95
Dave Kingman	1975–77, 1981–83
Bobby Klaus	1964–65
Jay Kleven	1976
Ray Knight	1984–86
Kevin Kobel	1978–80
Gary Kolb	1965
Cal Koonce	1967–70
Jerry Koosman	1967–78
Ed Kranepool	1962–79
Gary Kroll	1964–65
Clem Labine	1962
Jack Lamabe	1967
Hobie Landrith	1962
Ced Landrum	1993
Frank Lary	1964–65
Bill Latham	1985
Terry Leach	1981–82, 1985–89
Tim Leary	1981, 1983–84
Aaron Ledesma	1995
Johnny Lewis	1965–67
Dave Liddell	1990
Jim Lindeman	1994
Doug Linton	1994
Phil Linz	1967–68
Ron Locke	1964
Skip Lockwood	1975–79
Mickey Lolich	1976
Phil Lombardi	1989
Kevin Lomon	1995
Al Luplow	1966–67
Ed Lynch	1980–86
Barry Lyons	1986–90
Julio Machado	1989–90
Ken MacKenzie	1962–63
Elliott Maddox	1978–80
Mike Maddux	1993–94
Dave Magadan	1986–92
Pepe Mangual	1976–77
Phil Mankowski	1980, 1982
Felix Mantilla	1962
Josias Manzanillo	1993–95
Jim Marshall	1962
Dave Marshall	1970–72
Mike Marshall	1981
Mike Marshall	1990
J. C. Martin	1968–69
Jerry Martin	1984
Teddy Martinez	1970–74
Roger Mason	1994
Jon Matlack	1971–77
Jerry May	1973
Willie Mays	1972–73
Lee Mazzilli	1976–81, 1986–89
Jim McAndrew	1968–73
Bob McClure	1988
Rodney McCray	1992
Terry McDaniel	1991
Roger McDowell	1985–89
Tug McGraw	1965–67, 1969–74
Jeff McKnight	1989, 1992–94
Roy McMillan	1964–66
Kevin McReynolds	1987–91, 1994
Doc Medich	1977
Orlando Mercado	1990
Butch Metzger	1978
Felix Millan	1973–77
Larry Miller	1965–66
Bob Miller	1962
Bob Miller	1962, 1973–74
Dyar Miller	1980–81
Keith Miller	1987–91
John Milner	1971–77
Blas Minor	1995
Kevin Mitchell	1984, 1986
John Mitchell	1986–89
Vinegar Bend Mizell	1962
Dave Mlicki	1995
Herb Moford	1962
Willie Montanez	1978–79
Joe Moock	1967
Tommy Moore	1972–73
Bob Moorhead	1962, 1965
Jerry Morales	1980
Al Moran	1963–64
Jose Moreno	1980
Billy Murphy	1966
Dale Murray	1978–79
Eddie Murray	1992–93
Dennis Musgraves	1965
Jeff Musselman	1989–90
Randy Myers	1985–89
Bob Myrick	1976–78
Danny Napoleon	1965–66
Tito Navarro	1993
Charlie Neal	1962–63
Randy Niemann	1985–86
Junior Noboa	1992
Joe Nolan	1972
Dan Norman	1977–80
Edwin Nunez	1988
Charlie O'Brien	1990–93
Alex Ochoa	1995
Bob Ojeda	1986–90
Tom O'Malley	1989–90
Jose Oquendo	1983–84
Jesse Orosco	1979, 1981–87
Joe Orsulak	1993–95
Junior Ortiz	1983–84
Brian Ostrosser	1973
Ricky Otero	1995
Amos Otis	1967, 1969
Rick Ownbey	1982–83
John Pacella	1977, 1979–80
Tom Paciorek	1985
Harry Parker	1973–75
Rick Parker	1994
Tom Parsons	1964–65
Bill Pecota	1992
Al Pedrique	1987
Brock Pemberton	1974
Alejandro Pena	1990–91
Robert Person	1995
Bobby Pfeil	1969
Mike Phillips	1975–77
Jimmy Piersall	1963
Joe Pignatano	1962
Grover Powell	1963
Rich Puig	1974
Charlie Puleo	1981–82
Bill Pulsipher	1995
Gary Rajsich	1982–83
Mario Ramirez	1980
Lenny Randle	1977–78
Willie Randolph	1992
Bob Rauch	1972
Jeff Reardon	1979–81
Darren Reed	1990
Mike Remlinger	1994–95
Hal Reniff	1967
Tommie Reynolds	1967
Ronn Reynolds	1982–83, 1985
Dennis Ribant	1964–66
Gordie Richardson	1965–66
Luis Rivera	1994
Dave Roberts	1981
Les Rohr	1967–69
Luis Rosado	1977, 1980
Don Rose	1971
Don Rowe	1963
Dick Rusteck	1966
Nolan Ryan	1966, 1968–71

Bret Saberhagen	1992–95
Ray Sadecki	1970–74, 1977
Joe Sambito	1985
Amado Samuel	1964
Juan Samuel	1989
Ken Sanders	1975–76
Rafael Santana	1984–87
Mackey Sasser	1988–92
Doug Saunders	1993
Rich Sauveur	1991
Mac Scarce	1975
Jimmie Schaffer	1965
Dan Schatzeder	1990
Calvin Schiraldi	1984–85
Al Schmelz	1967
Dave Schneck	1972–74
Dick Schofield	1992
Pete Schourek	1991–93
Ted Schreiber	1963
Don Schulze	1987
Mike Scott	1979–82
Ray Searage	1981
Tom Seaver	1967–77, 1983
David Segui	1994–95
Dick Selma	1965–68
Frank Seminara	1994
Art Shamsky	1968–71
Bob Shaw	1966–67
Don Shaw	1967–68
Norm Sherry	1963
Craig Shipley	1989
Bart Shirley	1967
Bill Short	1968
Paul Siebert	1977–78
Doug Simons	1991
Ken Singleton	1970–71
Doug Sisk	1982–87
Bobby Gene Smith	1962
Charley Smith	1964–65
Dick Smith	1963–64
Pete Smith	1994
Duke Snider	1963
Warren Spahn	1965
Bill Spiers	1995
Larry Stahl	1967–68
Roy Staiger	1975–77
Tracy Stallard	1963–64
Leroy Stanton	1970–71
Rusty Staub	1972–75, 1981–85
John Stearns	1975–82, 1984
Johnny Stephenson	1964–66
Randy Sterling	1974
Kelly Stinnett	1994–95
George Stone	1973–75
Darryl Strawberry	1983–90
John Strohmayer	1973–74
Brent Strom	1972
Dick Stuart	1966
Tom Sturdivant	1964
Bill Sudakis	1972
John Sullivan	1967
Darrell Sutherland	1964–66
Craig Swan	1973–84
Ron Swoboda	1965–70
Pat Tabler	1990
Frank Tanana	1993
Kevin Tapani	1989
Randy Tate	1975
Frank Taveras	1979–81
Hawk Taylor	1964–67
Ron Taylor	1967–71
Sammy Taylor	1962–63
Chuck Taylor	1972
Dave Telgheder	1993–95
Garry Templeton	1991
Walt Terrell	1982–84
Ralph Terry	1966–67
Tim Teufel	1986–91
George Theodore	1973–74
Frank Thomas	1962–64
Ryan Thompson	1992–95
Lou Thornton	1989–90
Marv Throneberry	1962–63
Dick Tidrow	1984
Rusty Tillman	1982
Jackson Todd	1977
Joe Torre	1975–77
Mike Torrez	1983–84
Kelvin Torve	1990–91
Alex Trevino	1978–81, 1990
Wayne Twitchell	1979
Del Unser	1975–76
Mike Vail	1975–77
Bobby Valentine	1977–78
Ellis Valentine	1981–82
Julio Valera	1990–91
Tom Veryzer	1982
Fernando Vina	1994
Frank Viola	1989–91
Joe Vitko	1992
Jose Vizcaino	1994–95
Bill Wakefield	1964
Chico Walker	1992–93
Pete Walker	1995
Gene Walter	1987–88
Claudell Washington	1980
Hank Webb	1972–76
Al Weis	1968–71
David West	1988–89
Mickey Weston	1993
Wally Whitehurst	1989–92
Carl Willey	1963–65
Nick Willhite	1967
Charlie Williams	1971
Mookie Wilson	1980–89
Herm Winningham	1984
Gene Woodling	1962
Billy Wynne	1967
Anthony Young	1991–93
Joel Youngblood	1977–82
Pat Zachry	1977–82
Don Zimmer	1962

Managers

George Bamberger	1982–83
Yogi Berra	1972–75
Mike Cubbage	1991
Joe Frazier	1976–77
Dallas Green	1993–95
Bud Harrelson	1990–91
Gil Hodges	1968–71
Frank Howard	1983
Davey Johnson	1984–90
Roy McMillan	1975
Salty Parker	1967
Casey Stengel	1962–65
Jeff Torborg	1992–93
*Joe Torre	1977–81
Wes Westrum	1965–67

PHILADELPHIA Athletics 1876

John Bergh	1876
Doc Bushong	1876
William Coon	1876
Pete Curren	1876
Dave Eggler	1876
Wes Fisler	1876
Davy Force	1876
Bill Fouser	1876
George Hall	1876
Lon Knight	1876
Flip Lafferty	1876
Fergy Malone	1876
Levi Meyerle	1876
John Mullen	1876
Lou Paul	1876
Neal Phelps	1876
Ed Ritterson	1876
Ezra Sutton	1876
Jim Ward	1876
Fred Warner	1876
George Zettlein	1876

Managers

Al Wright	1876

PHILADELPHIA Phillies 1883–1995
Moved from WORCESTOR Ruby Legs
Known as Quakers 1883–89
Blue Jays 1944–45

Ed Abbaticchio	1897–98
Fred Abbott	1905
Kyle Abbott	1992, 1995
Cy Acosta	1975
Buster Adams	1943–45, 1947
Bert Adams	1915–19
Bob Adams	1931–32
Jim Adduci	1989
Luis Aguayo	1980–88
Darrel Akerfelds	1990–91
Jack Albright	1947
Grover Alexander	1911–17, 1930
Ethan Allen	1934–36
Dick Allen	1963–69, 1975–76
Bob Allen	1937
Bob Allen	1890–94
Hezekiah Allen	1884
Bill Almon	1988
Porfi Altamirano	1982–83
Ruben Amaro	1960–65
Ruben Amaro	1992–93
Red Ames	1919
Larry Andersen	1983–86, 1993–94
Dave Anderson	1889–90
Sparky Anderson	1959
Harry Anderson	1957–60
John Anderson	1958
Mike Anderson	1971–75, 1979
Ed Andrews	1884–89
Stan Andrews	1945
Fred Andrews	1976–77
Bill Andrus	1937
Joe Antolick	1944
John Antonelli	1945
Buzz Arlett	1931
Morrie Arnovich	1936–40
Richie Ashburn	1948–59
Andy Ashby	1991–92
Dick Attreau	1926–27
Bill Atwood	1936–40
Earl Averill	1963
Ramon Aviles	1979–81
Bob Ayrault	1992–93
Wally Backman	1991–92
Ed Baecht	1926–28
Stan Bahnsen	1982
Doug Bair	1987
Doug Baird	1919
Floyd Baker	1954–55
Jack Baldschun	1961–65
Henry Baldwin	1927
Jay Baller	1982, 1992
Dave Bancroft	1915–20
Alan Bannister	1974–75
Salome Barojas	1988
Dick Barrett	1943–45
Tom Barrett	1988–89
Shad Barry	1901–04
Tom Barry	1904
Rich Barry	1969
Dick Bartell	1931–34
Walt Bashore	1936
Charlie Bastian	1885–88, 1891
John Bateman	1972
Bud Bates	1939
Johnny Bates	1909–10
Del Bates	1970
Kim Batiste	1991–94
Stan Baumgartner	1914–16, 1921–22
Frankie Baumholtz	1956
Ernie Beam	1895
Fred Beck	1911
Boom–Boom Beck	1939–43
Beals Becker	1913–15
Bob Becker	1897–98
Steve Bedrosian	1986–89
Fred Beebe	1911
Petie Behan	1921–23
Bo Belinsky	1965–66
Juan Bell	1992–93
Chief Bender	1916–17
Art Benedict	1883
Ray Benge	1928–32, 1936
Stan Benjamin	1939–42
Dave Bennett	1964
Dennis Bennett	1962–64
Joe Bennett	1923
Jack Bentley	1926
Stan Benton	1922
Wally Berger	1940
Jack Berly	1932–33
Bill Bernhard	1899–1900
Joe Berry	1902
Lefty Bertrand	1936
Huck Betts	1920–25
Charlie Bicknell	1948–49
Doug Bird	1979
Jim Bishop	1923–24
Jeff Bittiger	1986
Jim Bivin	1935
Lena Blackburne	1919
Tim Blackwell	1976–77
Sheriff Blake	1931
Cy Blanton	1940–42
Johnny Blatnik	1948–50
Buddy Blattner	1949
Marv Blaylock	1955–57
Jimmy Bloodworth	1950–51
Joe Boever	1990–91
Danny Boitano	1978
Ed Boland	1934–35
Stew Bolen	1931–32
Jim Bolger	1959
Jack Bolling	1939
Rod Booker	1990–91
Bob Boone	1972–81
John Boozer	1962–64, 1966–69
Toby Borland	1994–95
Hank Borowy	1949–50
Rick Bosetti	1976
Shawn Boskie	1994
Ricky Bottalico	1994–95
Ed Bouchee	1956–60
Larry Bowa	1970–81
Joe Bowman	1935–36
Bob Bowman	1955–59
Sumner Bowman	1890
Jack Boyle	1893–98
Jack Boyle	1912
Gib Brack	1938–39
John Brackenridge	1904
Phil Bradley	1988
King Brady	1905
Bobby Bragan	1940–42
Art Bramhall	1935
Darrell Brandon	1971–73
Jackie Brandt	1966–67
Kitty Bransfield	1905–11
Cliff Brantley	1991–92
Roy Brashear	1903
Alonzo Breitenstein	1883
Ad Brennan	1910–13
Rube Bressler	1932
Ken Brett	1973
Charlie Brewster	1943
Fred Brickell	1930–33
John Briggs	1964–71
Brad Brink	1992–93
Bill Brinker	1912
John Brittin	1950–51
Dan Brouthers	1896
Buster Brown	1907–09
Lloyd Brown	1940
Ollie Brown	1974–77
Paul Brown	1961–63, 1968
Tommy Brown	1951–52
Willard Brown	1891
Byron Browne	1970–72
George Browne	1901–02, 1912
Earl Browne	1937–38
Frank Bruggy	1921
Roy Bruner	1939–41
Warren Brusstar	1977–82
Dick Buckley	1894–95
Charlie Buffinton	1887–89
Bob Buhl	1966–67
Eric Bullock	1989
Jim Bunning	1964–67, 1970–71
Fred Burchell	1903
Lew Burdette	1965
Smoky Burgess	1952–55
Bill Burich	1942, 1946

Mack Burk	1956
Elmer Burkart	1936–39
Eddie Burke	1890
Bobby Burke	1937
Ed Burns	1913–18
George Burns	1925
Bill Burns	1911
Al Burris	1894
Paul Busby	1941, 1943
Joe Buskey	1926
Mike Buskey	1977
Max Butcher	1938–39
Charlie Butler	1933
John Buzhardt	1960–61
Bobby Byrne	1913–17
Marty Bystrom	1980–84
Putsy Caballero	1944–45, 1947–52
Hick Cady	1919
Earl Caldwell	1928
Ralph Caldwell	1904–05
Jeff Calhoun	1987–88
Nixey Callahan	1894
Leo Callahan	1919
Johnny Callison	1960–69
Dolf Camilli	1934–37
Howie Camnitz	1913
Bill Campbell	1984
Sil Campusano	1990–91
Milo Candini	1950–51
Mike Cantwell	1919–20
Ralph Capron	1913
Jose Cardenal	1978–79
Don Cardwell	1957–60
Jim Carlin	1941
Hal Carlson	1924–27
Steve Carlton	1972–86
Don Carman	1983–90
Amalio Carreno	1991
Kid Carsey	1892–97
Andy Carter	1994–95
Dan Casey	1886–89
Dave Cash	1974–76
Ed Cassian	1891
Braulio Castillo	1991–92
John Castle	1910
Danny Cater	1964
Red Causey	1920–21
John Cavanaugh	1919
George Chalmers	1910–16
Wes Chamberlain	1990–94
Billy Champion	1969–72
Darrin Chapin	1992
Norm Charlton	1995
Harry Cheek	1910
Larry Cheney	1919
Mitch Chetkovich	1945
Rocky Childress	1985–86
Cupid Childs	1888
Pete Childs	1902
Pearce Chiles	1899–1900
Dino Chiozza	1935
Lou Chiozza	1934–36
Larry Christenson	1973–83
Bubba Church	1950–52
Ted Cieslak	1944
Bud Clancy	1934
Cap Clark	1938
Mel Clark	1951–55
Nig Clarke	1919
Bill Clay	1902
Danny Clay	1988
Doug Clemens	1966–68
Wally Clement	1908
Jack Clements	1884–97
Dave Coble	1939
Dick Coffman	1945
Alta Cohen	1933
Jimmie Coker	1958, 1960–61
Dave Cole	1955
Choo Choo Coleman	1961
John Coleman	1890
John Coleman	1883–84
Hap Collard	1930
Phil Collins	1929–35
Larry Colton	1968
Pat Combs	1989–92
Steve Comer	1983
Jim Command	1954
Mike Compton	1970
Dick Conger	1943
Gene Conley	1959–60
Bob Conley	1958

Bert Conn	1898, 1900–01
Gene Connell	1931
Roger Connor	1892
Jerry Connors	1892
Billy Consolo	1962
Bill Conway	1884
Paul Cook	1884
Dennis Cook	1989–90
Duff Cooley	1896–99
Jimmy Cooney	1927
Claude Cooper	1916–17
Gene Corbett	1936–38
Tim Corcoran	1983–85
Pat Corrales	1965
Frank Corridon	1904–05, 1907–09
Ed Cotter	1926
Dick Cotter	1911
Johnny Couch	1923–25
Ernie Courtney	1905–08
Harry Coveleski	1907–09
Chet Covington	1944
Wes Covington	1961–65
Billy Cowan	1967
Joe Cowley	1987
Danny Cox	1991–92
Larry Cox	1973–75
Roger Craig	1966
Gavvy Cravath	1912–19
Larry Crawford	1937
Glenn Crawford	1945
Ches Crist	1906
Leo Cristante	1951
Harry Croft	1899
Lave Cross	1892–97
Monte Cross	1898–1901
Bill Crouch	1941
John Crowley	1884
Roy Crumpler	1925
Todd Cruz	1978
Benny Culp	1942–44
Ray Culp	1963–66
Bill Culp	1910
George Culver	1973–74
Tony Curry	1960–61
Cliff Curtis	1911–12
Tony Cusick	1884–87
Babe Dahlgren	1943
Sam Dailey	1929
Ed Daily	1885–87
Clay Dalrymple	1960–68
Fred Daniels	1945
Alvin Dark	1960
George Darrow	1934
Darren Daulton	1983, 1985–95
Curt Davis	1934–36
Dixie Davis	1918
Kiddo Davis	1932, 1934
Jacke Davis	1962
Spud Davis	1928–33, 1938–39
Dick Davis	1981–82
Mark Davis	1980–81, 1993
Bill Dawley	1988
Bill Day	1889–90
Wayland Dean	1926–27
Art Decatur	1925–27
Harry Decker	1889–90
Pep Deininger	1908–09
Ivan DeJesus	1982–84
Jose DeJesus	1990–91
Bobby Del Greco	1960–61, 1965
Garton Del Savio	1943
Ed Delahanty	1888–89, 1891–1901
Tom Delahanty	1894
Jose DeLeon	1992–93
Eddie Delker	1932–33
Al Demaree	1915–16
Don Demeter	1961–63
Tod Dennehey	1923
Jerry Denny	1891
John Denny	1982–85
Mike DePangher	1884
Bob Dernier	1980–83, 1988–89
Jim Deshaies	1995
Mickey Devine	1918
Jim Devlin	1887
Josh Devore	1913–14
Bo Diaz	1982–85
Murry Dickson	1954–56
Bill Dietrick	1927–28
Dutch Dietz	1943
Gordon Dillard	1989
Pickles Dillhoefer	1918

Vince DiMaggio	1945–46
Kerry Dineen	1978
Vance Dinges	1945–46
Ron Diorio	1973–74
John Dodge	1912–13
Cozy Dolan	1912–13
Joe Dolan	1899–1901
She Donahue	1904
Red Donahue	1898–1901
Deacon Donahue	1943–44
Blix Donnelly	1946–50
Joe Donohue	1891
Jerry Donovan	1906
Red Dooin	1902–12
Mickey Doolan	1905–13
Klondike Douglass	1898–1904
Tommy Dowd	1897
Ken Dowell	1987
Tom Downey	1912
Dave Downs	1972
Tom Dowse	1892
Conny Doyle	1883
Jack Doyle	1904
Denny Doyle	1970–73
Solly Drake	1959
Karl Drews	1951–54
Monk Dubiel	1948
Clise Dudley	1931–32
Gus Dugas	1933
Oscar Dugey	1915–17
Bill Duggleby	1898, 1901–07
Vern Duncan	1913
Mariano Duncan	1992–95
Lee Dunham	1926
Davey Dunkle	1897–98
Jack Dunn	1900–01
Ryne Duren	1963–65
George Durning	1925
Len Dykstra	1989–95
Mike Easler	1987
Rawly Eastwick	1978–79
Tom Edens	1994
Doc Edwards	1970
Jim Eisenreich	1993–95
Kid Elberfeld	1898
Hal Elliott	1929–32
Jumbo Elliott	1931–34
Ben Ellis	1896
Dick Ellsworth	1967
Kevin Elster	1995
Cal Emery	1963
Spoke Emery	1924
Del Ennis	1946–56
Johnny Enzmann	1920
Don Erickson	1958
Paul Erickson	1948
Duke Esper	1890–92
Nino Espinosa	1979–81
Chuck Essegian	1958
Jim Essian	1973–75
Nick Etten	1941–42, 1947
Johnny Evers	1917
Bob Ewing	1910–11
George Eyrich	1943
Rags Faircloth	1919
Ed Fallenstin	1931
Jack Fanning	1894
Ed Farmer	1974, 1982–83
Sid Farrar	1883–89
Jack Farrell	1886
Dick Farrell	1956–61, 1967–69
Eddie Feinberg	1938–39
Harry Felix	1902
Charlie Ferguson	1884–87
Alex Ferguson	1927–29
Bob Ferguson	1883
Chico Fernandez	1957–59
Sid Fernandez	1995
Don Ferrarese	1961–62
John Fick	1944
Jocko Fields	1891
Jack Fifield	1897–99
Frank Figgemeier	1894
Sam File	1940
Dana Fillingim	1925
Bob Finley	1943–44
Mickey Finn	1933
Happy Finneran	1912–13
Steve Fireovid	1984
Ike Fisher	1898
Paul Fittery	1917

Mike Fitzgerald	1918
Wally Flager	1945
Patsy Flaherty	1910
Tom Fleming	1902, 1904
Art Fletcher	1920, 1922
Darrin Fletcher	1990–91
Paul Fletcher	1993, 1995
Elmer Flick	1898–1901
Hilly Flitcraft	1942
Kevin Flora	1995
Ben Flowers	1956
Jim Fogarty	1884–89
Tom Foley	1985–86
Lew Fonseca	1925
Barry Foote	1977–78
Hod Ford	1924
Curt Ford	1989–90
Gary Fortune	1916, 1918
Kevin Foster	1993
Henry Fox	1902
Howie Fox	1952
Terry Fox	1966
Bill Foxen	1908–10
Jimmie Foxx	1945
Julio Franco	1982
Tito Francona	1967
Chick Fraser	1899–1900, 1902–04
Ed Freed	1942
Roger Freed	1971–72
Marvin Freeman	1986, 1988–90
Gene Freese	1959
Steve Frey	1995
Barney Friberg	1925–32
Fred Frink	1934
Ben Froelich	1909
Todd Frohwirth	1987–90
Charlie Frye	1940
Woodie Fryman	1968–72
Charlie Fuchs	1943
Chick Fullis	1933–34
Dave Fultz	1898–99
Len Gabrielson	1939
Bill Gallagher	1896
Bill Gallagher	1883
Dave Gallagher	1995
Bert Gallia	1920
Oscar Gamble	1970–72
Bob Gandy	1916
Charlie Ganzel	1885–86
Gene Garber	1974–78
Kiko Garcia	1983–85
Art Gardiner	1923
Gid Gardner	1888
Ned Garvin	1896
Phil Geier	1896–97
Al Gerheauser	1943–44
Tony Ghelfi	1983
Charlie Gilbert	1946–47
Sam Gillen	1897
Charlie Girard	1910
Buck Gladman	1883
Tommy Glaviano	1953
Whitey Glazner	1923–24
Kid Gleason	1888–91, 1903–08
Al Glossop	1942
Bill Glynn	1949
Bill Goeckel	1899
Mike Goliat	1949–51
Chile Gomez	1935–36
Ruben Gomez	1959–60, 1967
Tony Gonzalez	1960–68
Orlando Gonzalez	1978
Wilbur Good	1916
Glen Gorbous	1955–56
Howie Gorman	1937
Tom Gorman	1986
Joe Gormley	1891
Nick Goulish	1945
Billy Grabarkewitz	1973–74
Reggie Grabowski	1932–34
Earl Grace	1936–37
Mike Grace	1995
Mike Grady	1894–97
Peaches Graham	1912
Wayne Graham	1963
Eddie Grant	1907–10
Jim Grant	1923
Lou Grasmick	1948
Don Grate	1945–46
Lew Graulich	1891
John Gray	1958
Dallas Green	1960–64, 1967

Tyler Green	1993, 1995
June Greene	1928–29
Willie Greene	1902
Tommy Greene	1990–95
Jim Greengrass	1955–56
Bob Greenwood	1954–55
Bill Grey	1890–91
John Grim	1888
Ray Grimes	1926
Jason Grimsley	1989–91
Lee Grissom	1941
Dick Groat	1966–67
Em Gross	1883
Kevin Gross	1983–88
Greg Gross	1979–88
Jeff Grotewold	1992
Ad Gumbert	1896
Tom Gunning	1887
Jackie Gutierrez	1988

Bert Haas	1948
Warren Hacker	1957–58
Harvey Haddix	1956–57
George Haddock	1894
Bud Hafey	1939
Art Hagan	1883
Don Hahn	1975
Jim Haislip	1913
Bert Hall	1911
Dick Hall	1967–68
Bob Hall	1904
Bill Hallahan	1938
Bill Hallman	1888–89, 1892–97, 1901–03
Earl Hamilton	1924
Jack Hamilton	1962–63
Billy Hamilton	1890–95
Granny Hamner	1944–59
Garvin Hamner	1945
Ray Hamrick	1943–44
Lee Handley	1947
Harry Hanebrink	1959
Andy Hansen	1951–53
Snipe Hansen	1930, 1932–35
Bill Harbidge	1883
Lew Hardie	1884
Bill Harman	1941
Chuck Harmon	1957
Terry Harmon	1969–77
George Harper	1894
George Harper	1924–26
Ray Harrell	1939
Bud Harrelson	1978–79
Herb Harris	1936
Greg Harris	1988–89
Gene Harris	1995
Mike Hartley	1991–92
Ray Hartranft	1913
Don Hasenmayer	1945–46
Mickey Haslin	1933–36
Billy Hatcher	1994
Chicken Hawks	1925
Von Hayes	1983–91
Charlie Hayes	1989–91, 1995
Ralph Head	1923
Jim Hearn	1957–59
Cliff Heathcote	1932
Richie Hebner	1977–78
Jim Hegan	1958–59
Ken Heintzelman	1947–52
Heinie Heltzel	1944
Ed Hemingway	1918
Rollie Hemsley	1946–47
Solly Hemus	1956–58
Hardie Henderson	1883
Harvey Hendrick	1934
Butch Henline	1921–26
George Hennessey	1942
Fritz Henrich	1924
Jim Henry	1939
Ray Herbert	1965–66
Jesus Hernaiz	1974
Guillermo Hernandez	1983
Tommy Herr	1989–90
Pancho Herrera	1958, 1960–61
John Herrnstein	1962–66
Ed Heusser	1938, 1948
Kirby Higbe	1939–40
Andy High	1934
John Hiland	1885
Tom Hilgendorf	1975
Chuck Hiller	1967
Pat Hilly	1914
Charlie Hilsey	1883
Larry Hisle	1968–71
Don Hoak	1963
Harry Hoch	1908
Bert Hodge	1942
Eli Hodkey	1946
George Hodson	1895
Joe Hoerner	1970–72, 1975
Frank Hoerst	1940–42, 1946–47
Bill Hoffman	1939
Brad Hogg	1918–19
Bill Hohman	1927
Joe Holden	1934–35
Walter Holke	1923–25
Al Holland	1983–85
Ed Holley	1932–34
Al Hollingsworth	1938–39
Dave Hollins	1990–95
Stan Hollmig	1949–50
Jim Holloway	1929
Buster Hoover	1884
Marty Hopkins	1934
Ken Howell	1989–90
Dan Howley	1913
Bill Hubbell	1920–25
Clarence Huber	1925–26
Charles Hudson	1983–86
Roy Hughes	1939, 1946
Tommy Hughes	1941–42, 1946–47
Keith Hughes	1987
Billy Hulen	1896
Rudy Hulswitt	1902–04
Tom Hume	1986–87
Bert Humphries	1910–11
John Humphries	1946
Don Hurst	1928–34
Harry Huston	1906
Jim Hutto	1970
Tom Hutton	1972–77

Ham Iburg	1902
Doc Imlay	1913
Pete Incaviglia	1993–94
Bert Inks	1896
Dane Iorg	1977
Hal Irelan	1914
Arthur Irwin	1886–89
Orlando Isales	1980

Fred Jacklitsch	1900–02, 1907–10
Grant Jackson	1965–70
John Jackson	1933
Larry Jackson	1966–68
Mike Jackson	1970
Danny Jackson	1993–94
Mike Jackson	1986–87
Ken Jackson	1987
Elmer Jacobs	1914, 1918–19
Art Jahn	1928
Jeff James	1968–69
Chris James	1986–89
Stan Javier	1992
Gregg Jefferies	1995
Irv Jeffries	1934
Greg Jelks	1987
Steve Jeltz	1983–89
Ferguson Jenkins	1965–66
Hughie Jennings	1901–02
Alex Johnson	1964–65
Charlie Johnson	1908
Darrell Johnson	1961
Davey Johnson	1977–78
Deron Johnson	1969–73
Louis Johnson	1894
Ken Johnson	1950–51
Si Johnson	1940–43, 1946
Syl Johnson	1934–40
Youngy Johnson	1897
Jerry Johnson	1968–69
Jay Johnstone	1974–78
Alex Jones	1894
Dale Jones	1941
Broadway Jones	1923
Nippy Jones	1952
Willie Jones	1947–59
Doug Jones	1994
Barry Jones	1992
Ron Jones	1988–90
Bubber Jonnard	1926–27, 1935
Buck Jordan	1938
Charlie Jordan	1896
Niles Jordan	1951
Ricky Jordan	1988–94
Kevin Jordan	1995
Orville Jorgens	1935–37
Rick Joseph	1967–70
Oscar Judd	1945–48
Jeff Juden	1994–95
George Jumonville	1940–41
Al Jurisich	1946–47

Jim Kaat	1976–79
Mike Kahoe	1905
Harry Kane	1905–06
Erv Kantlehner	1916
Joe Kappel	1884
Andy Karl	1943–46
Ryan Karp	1995
Tony Kaufmann	1927
Ted Kazanski	1953–58
Chick Keating	1926
Tim Keefe	1891–93
Ed Keegan	1959, 1962
Jim Keenan	1920–21
Harry Keener	1896
Bill Keister	1903
Hal Kelleher	1935–38
Charlie Kelly	1883
Mike Kelly	1926
Bill Kelly	1928
Kick Kelly	1883
Al Kenders	1961
John Kennedy	1957
Vern Kennedy	1944–45
Bill Kerksieck	1939
Jim Kern	1984
Bill Killefer	1911–17
Mike Kilroy	1891
Newt Kimball	1943
Wally Kimmick	1925–26
Lee King	1921–22
Thornton Kipper	1953–55
Billy Klaus	1962–63
Chuck Klein	1928–33, 1936–41, 1943–44
Ted Kleinhans	1934
Red Kleinow	1911
Bill Kling	1891
Johnny Klippstein	1963–64
Otto Knabe	1907–13
Phil Knell	1892
Alan Knicely	1985
Jack Knight	1925–26
Joe Knight	1884
George Knothe	1932
Fritz Knothe	1933
Darold Knowles	1966
Dick Koecher	1946–48
Pete Koegel	1971–72
Ed Konetchy	1921
Jim Konstanty	1948–54
Jerry Koosman	1984–85
Joe Koppe	1959–61
Fred Koster	1931
Lou Koupal	1929–30
Fabian Kowalik	1936
Ernie Koy	1942
Joe Kracher	1939
Tex Kraus	1943, 1945
Gary Kroll	1964
Otto Krueger	1905
Henry Krug	1902
John Kruk	1989–94
Mike Krukow	1982
Jack Kucek	1979
Harvey Kuenn	1966
Bob Kuzava	1955

Lerrin LaGrow	1980
Nap Lajoie	1896–1900
Steve Lake	1989–92
Al Lakeman	1947–48
Wayne LaMaster	1937–38
Gene Lambert	1941–42
Henry Lampe	1895
Don Landrum	1957
Tom Lanning	1938
Andy Lapihuska	1942–43
Dave LaPoint	1991
Ralph LaPointe	1947
Dan Larson	1978–81
Billy Lauder	1898–99
Mike LaValliere	1984
Jimmy Lavender	1917
Bill Laxton	1970
Freddy Leach	1923–28
Dan Leahy	1896
Bevo LeBourveau	1919–22
Cliff Lee	1921–24
Hal Lee	1931–33
Bill Lee	1943–45
Joe Lefebvre	1983–84, 1986
Greg Legg	1986–87
Ken Lehman	1961
Clarence Lehr	1911
Jim Lemon	1963
Ed Lennon	1928
Sid Leon	1945
Dutch Leonard	1947–48
Ted Lepcio	1960
Randy Lerch	1975–80, 1986
Walt Lerian	1928–29
Barry Lersch	1969–73
Roy Leslie	1922
Charlie Letchas	1939, 1944, 1946
Jesse Levan	1947
Fred Lewis	1883
Burt Lewis	1924
Sixto Lezcano	1983–84
Mike Lieberthal	1994–95
Johnny Lindell	1953
Jim Lindeman	1991–92
Doug Lindsey	1991, 1993
Phil Linz	1966–67
Frank Linzy	1974
Angelo LiPetri	1956, 1958
Tom Lipp	1897
Joe Lis	1970–72
Ad Liska	1932–33
Danny Litwhiler	1940–43
Mickey Livingston	1941–43
Mike Loan	1912
Hans Lobert	1911–14
Don Lock	1967–69
Bobby Locke	1962–64
Lucky Lohrke	1952–53
Bill Lohrman	1934
Jim Lonborg	1973–79
Herman Long	1904
Tony Longmire	1993–95
Joe Lonnett	1956–59
Stan Lopata	1948–58
Art Lopatka	1946
Marcelino Lopez	1963
Carlton Lord	1923
Larry Loughlin	1967
Lynn Lovenguth	1955
Jay Loviglio	1980
Peanuts Lowrey	1955
Fritz Lucas	1935
Con Lucid	1895–96
Lou Lucier	1944–45
Fred Luderus	1910–20
Al Lukens	1894
Tony Lupien	1944–45
Johnny Lush	1904–07
Greg Luzinski	1970–80
Sparky Lyle	1980–82
Tom Lynch	1884–85
Harry Lyons	1887
Terry Lyons	1929

Harvey MacDonald	1928
Pete Mackanin	1978–79
Tom Madden	1911
Garry Maddox	1975–86
Mike Maddux	1986–89
Art Madison	1895
Alex Madrid	1988–89
Sherry Magee	1904–14
Bill Magee	1899, 1902
Art Mahaffey	1960–65
Art Mahan	1940
Billy Maharg	1916
Alex Main	1918
Cy Malis	1934
Bobby Malkmus	1960–62
Les Mallon	1931–32
Chuck Malone	1990
Gus Mancuso	1945
George Mangus	1912
Jack Manning	1883–85
Jeff Manto	1993
Hal Marnie	1940–42
Tom Marsh	1992, 1994–95
Rube Marshall	1912–14
Doc Marshall	1904
Marty Martel	1909
Hersh Martin	1937–40

Jack Martin	1914
Jerry Martin	1974–78
Renie Martin	1984
Carmelo Martinez	1990
Joe Marty	1939–41
Hank Mason	1958, 1960
Roger Mason	1993–94
Walt Masters	1937
Paul Masterson	1940–42
Greg Mathews	1992
Henry Matteson	1914
Gary Matthews	1981–83
Dale Matthewson	1943–44
Len Matuszek	1981–84
Al Maul	1887, 1900
Ernie Maun	1926
Dick Mauney	1945–47
Tim Mauser	1991, 1993
Pinky May	1939–43
Ed Mayer	1890–91
Erskine Mayer	1912–18
Paddy Mayes	1911
Jackie Mayo	1948–53
Mel Mazzera	1940
Bake McBride	1977–81
Tommy McCarthy	1886–87
Tim McCarver	1970–72, 1975–80
Al McCauley	1890
Bill McClellan	1883–84
John McCloskey	1906–07
Don McCormack	1980–81
Frank McCormick	1946–47
Moose McCormick	1908
Harry McCurdy	1930–33
Ed McDonough	1909–10
Roger McDowell	1989–91
Jim McElroy	1884
Chuck McElroy	1989–90
Barney McFadden	1902
Ed McFarland	1897–1901
Jack McFetridge	1890, 1903
Patsy McGaffigan	1917–18
Willie McGill	1895–96
Gus McGinnis	1893
Tug McGraw	1975–84
Bob McGraw	1928–29
Deacon McGuire	1886–88
Rogers McKee	1943–44
Barney McLaughlin	1887
Warren McLaughlin	1900, 1903
Jim McLeod	1933
Cal McLish	1962–64
John McPherson	1904
George McQuillan	1907–10, 1915–16
Larry McWilliams	1989
Lee Meadows	1919–23
Louie Meadows	1990
Francisco Melendez	1984, 1986
Rube Melton	1941–42
Rudi Meoli	1979
Sam Mertes	1896
Lenny Metz	1923–25
Irish Meusel	1918–21
Benny Meyer	1925
Jack Meyer	1955–61
Russ Meyer	1949–52
Bob Micelotta	1954–55
Larry Milbourne	1983
Eddie Miller	1948–49
Elmer Miller	1929
Kohly Miller	1897
Dots Miller	1920–21
Cyclone Miller	1884
Red Miller	1923
Ralph Miller	1920–21
Bob Miller	1949–58
Doc Miller	1912–13
Russ Miller	1927–28
Stu Miller	1956
Keith Miller	1988–89
Joe Millette	1992–93
Wally Millies	1939–41
John Milligan	1928–31
Al Milnar	1946
Michael Mimbs	1995
Clarence Mitchell	1923–28
Fred Mitchell	1903–04
Johnny Mokan	1922–27
Fred Mollenkamp	1914
Al Monchak	1940
Don Money	1968–72
Sid Monge	1982–83
John Monroe	1921
John Montague	1975
Willie Montanez	1970–75, 1982
Rene Monteagudo	1945
Dee Moore	1943, 1946
Earl Moore	1908–13
Euel Moore	1934–36
Johnny Moore	1934–37
Cy Moore	1933–34
Brad Moore	1988, 1990
Pat Moran	1910–12, 1914
Mickey Morandini	1990–95
Seth Morehead	1957–59
Keith Moreland	1978–81
Harry Morelock	1891–92
Lew Moren	1907–10
Joe Morgan	1960
Joe Morgan	1983
Bobby Morgan	1954–57
Jim Moroney	1910
John Morris	1966
John Morris	1991
Jim Morrison	1977–78
Sparrow Morton	1884
Walter Moser	1906
Bitsy Mott	1945
Frank Motz	1890
Ron Mrozinski	1954–55
Emmett Mueller	1938–41
Hugh Mulcahy	1935–40, 1945–46
Terry Mulholland	1989–93
Moon Mullen	1944
Dick Mulligan	1946
Joe Mulvey	1883–89, 1892
Manny Muniz	1971
Scott Munninghoff	1980
Bobby Munoz	1994–95
Red Munson	1905
Con Murphy	1884
Ed Murphy	1898
Ed Murphy	1942
Dummy Murphy	1914
Morg Murphy	1898, 1900
Dale Murphy	1990–92
Dwayne Murphy	1989
Pat Murray	1919
Tom Murray	1894
Danny Murtaugh	1941–43, 1946
Barney Mussill	1944
Bert Myers	1900
Al Myers	1885, 1889–91
Bill Nagel	1941
Sam Nahem	1942, 1948
Bill Nahorodny	1976
Jim Nash	1972
Billy Nash	1896–98
Earl Naylor	1942–43
Jack Neagle	1883
Greasy Neale	1921
Cal Neeman	1960–61
Ron Negray	1955–56
Gary Neibauer	1972
Al Neiger	1960
Red Nelson	1912–13
Tom Newell	1987
Skeeter Newsome	1946–47
Gus Niarhos	1954–55
Kid Nichols	1905–06
Chet Nichols	1930–32
Frank Nicholson	1912
Bill Nicholson	1949–53
Bert Niehoff	1915–17
Tom Nieto	1989–90
Al Nixon	1926–28
The Only Nolan	1885
Dickie Noles	1979–81, 1990
Jerry Nops	1896
Leo Norris	1936–37
Ron Northey	1942–44, 1946–47
Lou Novikoff	1946
Prince Oana	1934
Johnny Oates	1975–76
Mickey O'Brien	1923
Frank O'Connor	1893
Harry O'Donnell	1927
Lefty O'Doul	1929–30
Joe Oeschger	1914–19, 1924
Bob Oldis	1962–63
Omar Olivares	1995
Gene Oliver	1967
Al Oliver	1984
Skinny O'Neal	1925, 1927
Randy O'Neal	1989
John O'Neil	1946
Steve Ontiveros	1989–90
Al Orth	1895–1901
Fred Osborn	1907–09
Jim Owens	1955–56, 1958–62
Red Owens	1899
Gene Packard	1919
Tom Padden	1943
Don Padgett	1947–48
Jose Pagan	1973
Donn Pall	1993
Lowell Palmer	1969–71
David Palmer	1988
Stan Palys	1953–55
Al Pardo	1988–89
Dixie Parker	1923
Frank Parkinson	1921–24
Jeff Parrett	1989–90
Sam Parrilla	1970
Lance Parrish	1987–88
Dode Paskert	1911–17
Mike Pasquella	1919
Claude Passeau	1936–39
Gene Paulette	1919–20
Johnny Peacock	1944–45
Frank Pearce	1933–35
Harry Pearce	1917–19
Ike Pearson	1939–42, 1946
Homer Peel	1929
Julio Peguero	1992
Eddie Pellagrini	1951
Roberto Pena	1968
Paul Penson	1954
Luis Peraza	1969
Tony Perez	1983
Bill Peterman	1942
John Peters	1921–22
Kent Peterson	1952–53
Leon Pettit	1937
Pretzels Pezzullo	1935–36
Bobby Pfeil	1971
Dave Philley	1958–60
Adolfo Phillips	1964–66
Buz Phillips	1930
Taylor Phillips	1959–60
Wiley Piatt	1898–1900
Nick Picciuto	1945
Clarence Pickrel	1933
Ty Pickup	1918
Ray Pierce	1925–26
Duane Pillette	1956
Horacio Pina	1978
Lerton Pinto	1922, 1924
Jim Pirie	1883
Alex Pitko	1938
Togie Pittinger	1905–07
Walter Plock	1891
Johnny Podgajny	1940–43
John Poff	1979
Jennings Poindexter	1939
Hugh Poland	1947
Al Porto	1948
Lou Possehl	1946–48, 1951–52
Wally Post	1958–60
Jake Powell	1945
Vic Power	1964
Les Powers	1939
Todd Pratt	1992–94
Mike Prendergast	1918–19
Ray Prim	1935
Mike Proly	1981
Hub Pruett	1927–28
Troy Puckett	1911
Blondie Purcell	1883–84
Jesse Purnell	1904
Shadow Pyle	1884
Tom Qualters	1953, 1957–58
Paul Quantrill	1994–95
Tom Quinlan	1994
John Quinn	1911
Don Rader	1921
Dave Rader	1979
Ken Raffensberger	1943–47
Al Raffo	1969
Pat Ragan	1923
Frank Ragland	1933
Pete Rambo	1926
Pedro Ramos	1967
Goldie Rapp	1921–23
Shane Rawley	1984–88
Johnny Rawlings	1920–21
Lou Raymond	1919
Randy Ready	1989–91, 1994–95
Art Rebel	1938
Gary Redus	1986
Milt Reed	1913–14
Ron Reed	1976–83
Jerry Reed	1981–82
Scott Reid	1969–70
Charlie Reilly	1892–95
Tommy Reis	1938
Butch Rementer	1904
Jack Remsen	1884
Tony Rensa	1930–31
Rip Repulski	1957–58
Ken Reynolds	1970–72
Ronn Reynolds	1986
Flint Rhem	1932–33
Chuck Ricci	1995
Bob Rice	1926
Ken Richardson	1946
Lance Richbourg	1921
Pete Richert	1974
Lew Richie	1906–09
Steve Ridzik	1950, 1952–55, 1966
Lee Riley	1944
Jimmy Ring	1921–25, 1928
Frank Ringo	1883–84
Charlie Ripple	1944–46
Wally Ritchie	1987–88, 1991–92
Hank Ritter	1912
Ben Rivera	1992–94
Eppa Rixey	1912–17, 1919–20
Johnny Rizzo	1940–41
Mel Roach	1962
Robin Roberts	1948–61
Dave Roberts	1982
Humberto Robinson	1959–60
Bill Robinson	1972–74, 1982–83
Don Robinson	1992
Craig Robinson	1972–73
Freddy Rodriguez	1959
Ed Roebuck	1964–66
Ron Roenicke	1986–87
Mike Rogodzinski	1973–75
Saul Rogovin	1955–57
Cookie Rojas	1963–69
Pete Rose	1979–83
Bob Ross	1956
Frank Roth	1903–04
Jack Rowan	1911
Schoolboy Rowe	1943, 1946–49
Bama Rowell	1948
Charlie Roy	1906
Luther Roy	1929
Vic Roznovsky	1969
Art Ruble	1934
Dave Rucker	1985–86
Bruce Ruffin	1986–91
John Russell	1984–88
Dick Ruthven	1973–75, 1978–83
Mark Ryal	1989
Connie Ryan	1952–53
Blondy Ryan	1935
Mike Ryan	1968–73
Bob Sadowski	1961
Solly Salisbury	1902
Manny Salvo	1943
Juan Samuel	1983–89
Alejandro Sanchez	1982–83
Heinie Sand	1923–28
Ryne Sandberg	1981
Ben Sanders	1888–89
Jack Sanford	1956–58
Ed Sanicki	1949, 1951
Kevin Saucier	1978–80
Jim Savage	1912
Ted Savage	1962
Carl Sawatski	1958–59
Phil Saylor	1891
Frank Scanlan	1909
Mac Scarce	1972–74
Russ Scarritt	1932
Steve Scarsone	1992
Jimmie Schaffer	1966–67
Gene Schall	1995
Charley Schanz	1944–47
George Scharein	1937–40
Dan Schatzeder	1986–87
John Scheible	1894
Danny Schell	1954

Bill Scherrer	1988
Dutch Schesler	1931
Lou Schettler	1910
Curt Schilling	1992–95
Freddy Schmidt	1947
Mike Schmidt	1972–89
Gene Schott	1939
Pop Schriver	1888–90
Al Schroll	1959
Rick Schu	1984–87, 1991
Ron Schueler	1974–76
Wes Schulmerich	1933–34
Wildfire Schulte	1917
Johnny Schulte	1928
Ham Schulte	1940
Howie Schultz	1947–48
Joe Schultz	1924–25
John Schultze	1891
Jack Scott	1927
LeGrant Scott	1939
Lefty Scott	1945
Steve Searcy	1991–92
Tom Seaton	1912–13
Bob Sebra	1988–89
Duke Sedgwick	1921
Kevin Sefcik	1995
Dick Selma	1970–73
Andy Seminick	1943–51, 1955–57
Ray Semproch	1958–59
Paul Sentell	1906–07
Manny Seoane	1977
Scott Service	1988
Bobby Shantz	1964
John Sharrott	1893
Nap Shea	1902
Merv Shea	1944
Dave Shean	1908–09
Charlie Sheerin	1936
Keith Shepherd	1992
Monk Sherlock	1930
Ben Shields	1931
Jim Shilling	1939
Bill Shindle	1891
Dave Shipanoff	1985
Costen Shockley	1964
Chris Short	1959–72
Frank Shugart	1897
Toots Shultz	1911–12
Harry Shuman	1944
Eddie Sicking	1919
Roy Sievers	1962–64
Tripp Sigman	1929–30
Ken Silvestri	1949–51
Curt Simmons	1947–50, 1952–60
Wayne Simpson	1975
John Singleton	1922
Dick Sisler	1948–51
Pete Sivess	1936–38
Ed Sixsmith	1884
Ted Sizemore	1977–78
Jimmy Slagle	1900–01
Barney Slaughter	1910
Heathcliff Slocumb	1994–95
Roy Smalley	1955–58
Al Smith	1938–39
Bobby Gene Smith	1960–61
Charley Smith	1961
Edgar Smith	1883
George Smith	1919–22
Jake Smith	1911
Jimmy Smith	1921–22
Phenomenal Smith	1890–91
Tom Smith	1895
Bill Smith	1962
Lonnie Smith	1978–81
Lefty Smoll	1940
Harry Smythe	1929–30
Bill Sorrell	1965
Denny Sothern	1926, 1928–30
Dick Spalding	1927
Tully Sparks	1897, 1903–10
Byron Speece	1930
Tubby Spencer	1911
Stan Sperry	1936
Hal Spindel	1945–46
Jim Spotts	1930
Homer Spragins	1947
Jack Spring	1955
Russ Springer	1995
Dennis Springer	1995
Charlie Sproull	1945
Eddie Stack	1910–11
Tuck Stainback	1938
Charley Stanceu	1946
Buck Stanley	1911
John Stearns	1974
Morrie Steevens	1964–65
Justin Stein	1938
Gene Steinbrenner	1912
Ray Steineder	1924
Casey Stengel	1920–21
Dummy Stephenson	1892
Walter Stephenson	1937
Bobby Stevens	1931
Glen Stewart	1943–44
Neb Stewart	1940
Dave Stewart	1985–86
Milt Stock	1915–18
Kevin Stocker	1993–95
Ron Stone	1969–72
Gene Stone	1969
Jeff Stone	1983–87
Lil Stoner	1931
Ray Stoviak	1938
John Strike	1886
Nick Strincevich	1948
Dick Stuart	1965
Paul Stuffel	1950, 1952–53
George Stutz	1926
Gus Suhr	1939–40
Ernie Sulik	1936
Frank Sullivan	1961–62
John Sullivan	1968
Joe Sullivan	1894–96
Tom Sullivan	1922
Billy Sunday	1890
Rich Surhoff	1985
George Susce	1929
Gary Sutherland	1966–68
Jack Sutthoff	1904–05
Dale Sveum	1992
Leo Sweetland	1927–30
Lefty Taber	1926–27
Jim Tabor	1946–47
Doug Taitt	1931
Vito Tamulis	1941
Fred Tauby	1937
Tony Taylor	1960–71, 1974–76
Jack Taylor	1892–97
Kent Tekulve	1985–88
Bob Terlecki	1972
Tommy Thevenow	1929–30
Bobby Thigpen	1993
Dick Thoenen	1967
Tommy Thomas	1935
Frank Thomas	1964–65
Roy Thomas	1899–1908, 1910–11
Valmy Thomas	1959
Bill Thomas	1902
Derrel Thomas	1985
Erskine Thomason	1974
Jocko Thompson	1948–51
Fresco Thompson	1927–30
Sam Thompson	1889–98
Milt Thompson	1986–88, 1993–94
Dickie Thon	1989–91
John Thornton	1891–92
Cotton Tierney	1923
Ben Tincup	1914–15, 1918
Cannonball Titcomb	1886
John Titus	1903–12
Al Todd	1932–35
Bobby Tolan	1976–77
Fred Toliver	1985–87
Earl Torgeson	1953–55
Frank Torre	1962–63
Cesar Tovar	1973
Jack Townsend	1901
Walt Tragesser	1919–20
Gus Triandos	1964–65
Manny Trillo	1979–82
Ken Trinkle	1949
Coaker Triplett	1943–45
Tuck Turner	1893–96
Shane Turner	1988
Wayne Twitchell	1971–77
Jim Tyng	1888
Bob Uecker	1966–67
Dutch Ulrich	1925–27
Tom Underwood	1974–77
Del Unser	1973–74, 1979–82
Gene Vadeboncoeur	1884
Fernando Valenzuela	1994
Elmer Valo	1956, 1961
Deacon Van Buren	1904
Ben Van Dyke	1909
Andy Van Slyke	1995
Gary Varsho	1995
Jim Vatcher	1990
Emil Verban	1946–48
Joe Verbanic	1966
Al Verdel	1944
Johnny Vergez	1935–36
Tom Vickery	1890, 1893
Bob Vines	1925
Bill Vinton	1884–85
Ozzie Virgil	1980–85
Cy Vorhees	1902
George Vukovich	1980–82
John Vukovich	1970–71, 1976, 1979–81
Woodie Wagenhorst	1888
Gary Wagner	1965–69
Hal Wagner	1948–49
Eddie Waitkus	1949–53, 1955
Charlie Waitt	1883
Ed Walczak	1945
Bob Walk	1980
Harry Walker	1947–48
Marty Walker	1928
Curt Walker	1921–24
Doc Wallace	1919
Huck Wallace	1912
Dave Wallace	1973–74
Mike Wallace	1973–74
Lee Walls	1960–61
Augie Walsh	1927–28
John Walsh	1903
Jimmy Walsh	1910–13
Ken Walters	1960–61
Bucky Walters	1934–38
Lloyd Waner	1942
Piggy Ward	1883, 1889
Joe Ward	1906, 1909–10
Fred Warner	1883
Jack Warner	1933
Bennie Warren	1939–42
Dan Warthen	1977
Jimmy Wasdell	1943–46
Libe Washburn	1903
Buck Washer	1905
Ed Watkins	1902
George Watkins	1935–36
Dave Watkins	1969
Milt Watson	1918–19
Eddie Watt	1974
Frank Watt	1931
Cliff Watwood	1939
Bill Webb	1943
Lenny Webster	1995
Herm Wehmeier	1954–56
Dave Wehrmeister	1984
Lefty Weinert	1919–24
Phil Weintraub	1938
Bud Weiser	1915–16
Harry Welchonce	1911
Bob Wells	1994
Lew Wendell	1924–26
Fred Wenz	1970
David West	1993–95
Mickey Weston	1992
Gus Weyhing	1892–95
Mack Wheat	1920–21
George Wheeler	1896–99
C. B. White	1883
Deke White	1895
Doc White	1901–02
Sammy White	1962
Bill White	1966–68
Mark Whiten	1995
Jesse Whiting	1902
Dick Whitman	1950–51
Pinky Whitney	1928–33, 1936–39
Bill Whitrock	1896
Possum Whitted	1915–19
Del Wilber	1951
Cy Williams	1918–30
George Williams	1961
Pop Williams	1903
Mitch Williams	1991–93
Mike Williams	1992–95
Hugh Willingham	1931
Claude Willoughby	1925–30
Maxie Wilson	1940
Jimmie Wilson	1923–28, 1934–36
Hack Wilson	1934
Billy Wilson	1969–73
Glenn Wilson	1984–87
Hal Wiltse	1931
Bobby Wine	1960, 1962–68
Jesse Winters	1921–23
Rick Wise	1964, 1966–71
Frank Withrow	1920, 1922
John Wockenfuss	1984–85
Andy Woehr	1923–24
Bill Wolfe	1902
Abe Wolstenholme	1883
Harry Wolverton	1900–04
George Wood	1886–89
Pete Wood	1889
Jim Woods	1960–61
Frank Woodward	1918–19
Russ Wrightstone	1920–28
Whit Wyatt	1945
Johnny Wyrostek	1946–47, 1952–54
Rusty Yarnall	1926
Joe Yingling	1894
Floyd Youmans	1989
Del Young	1937–40
Dick Young	1951–52
Bobby Young	1958
Mike Young	1988
Tom Zachary	1936
Pat Zachry	1985
Charlie Ziegler	1900

Managers

*Bob Allen	1890
Ben Chapman	1945–48
*Jack Clements	1890
Andy Cohen	1960
Dusty Cooke	1948
Jack Coombs	1919
Pat Corrales	1982–83
*Gavvy Cravath	1919–20
Wild Bill Donovan	1921
*Red Dooin	1910–14
Hugh Duffy	1904–06
Lee Elia	1987–88
John Felske	1985–87
*Bob Ferguson	1883
Freddie Fitzsimmons	1943–45
Art Fletcher	1923–26
Jim Fregosi	1991–95
Dallas Green	1979–81
Bucky Harris	1943
Arthur Irwin	1894–95
Nick Leyva	1989–91
Hans Lobert	1938, 1942
Frank Lucchesi	1970–72
Gene Mauch	1960–68
Stuffy McInnis	1927
Terry Moore	1954
Pat Moran	1915–18
Billy Murray	1907–09
George Myatt	1968–69
*Billy Nash	1896
Steve O'Neill	1952–54
Paul Owens	1972, 1983–84
Danny Ozark	1973–79
Doc Prothro	1939–41
*Blondie Purcell	1883
Al Reach	1890
Eddie Sawyer	1948–52, 1958–60
Bill Shettsline	1898–1902
Burt Shotton	1928–33
Bob Skinner	1968–69
Mayo Smith	1955–58
George Stallings	1897–98
John Vukovich	1988
Kaiser Wilhelm	1921–22
*Jimmie Wilson	1934–38
Harry Wright	1884–93
Chief Zimmer	1903

PITTSBURGH Pirates 1887–1995

Known as Alleghenys 1887–90

Ed Abbaticchio	1907–10
Cal Abrams	1953–54
Bill Abstein	1906, 1909
Ed Acosta	1970
Babe Adams	1907, 1909–16, 1918–26

Sparky Adams	1928–29
Spencer Adams	1923
Ed Albosta	1946
Vic Aldridge	1925–27
Gary Alexander	1981
Matt Alexander	1979–81
Gene Alley	1963–73
Gair Allie	1954
Bill Almon	1985–87
Matty Alou	1966–70
Moises Alou	1990
Jesse Altenburg	1916–17
Alf Anderson	1941–42
Goat Anderson	1907
Dave Anderson	1890
Jimmy Archer	1904, 1918
Tony Armas	1976
Luis Arroyo	1956–57
Toby Atwell	1953–56
Rich Aude	1993, 1995
Dave Augustine	1973–74

Wally Backman	1990
Jim Bagby	1947
Jim Bagby	1923
Ed Bahr	1946–47
Bob Bailey	1962–66
Doug Bair	1976, 1989–90
Doug Baird	1915–17
Gene Baker	1957–58, 1960–61
Kirtley Baker	1890
Bill Baker	1941–43, 1946
Mark Baldwin	1891–93
Jeff Ballard	1993–94
Walter Barbare	1919–20
Jap Barbeau	1909
Dave Barbee	1932
Sam Barkley	1887
Eppie Barnes	1923–24
Ed Barney	1915–16
Clyde Barnhart	1920–28
Vic Barnhart	1944–45
Dick Barone	1960
Frank Barrett	1950
Johnny Barrett	1942–46
Dick Bartell	1927–30
Les Bartholomew	1928
Tony Bartirome	1952
Monty Basgall	1948–49, 1951
Eddie Basinski	1947
Miguel Batista	1992
Russ Bauers	1936–41
Ross Baumgarten	1982
Alex Beam	1889
Ted Beard	1948–52
Ginger Beaumont	1899–1906
Boom–Boom Beck	1945
Beals Becker	1908
Jake Beckley	1888–89, 1891–96
Andy Bednar	1930–31
Harry Beecher	1887
Hank Behrman	1947
Stan Belinda	1989–93
Bo Belinsky	1969
Gus Bell	1950–52
Fern Bell	1939
Bill Bell	1952, 1955
Jay Bell	1989–95
Rafael Belliard	1982–90
Fred Bennett	1931
Johnny Berardino	1950, 1952
Clarence Berger	1914
Tun Berger	1890–91
Carlos Bernier	1953
Dale Berra	1977–84
Ray Berres	1937–40
Kurt Bevacqua	1974, 1980–81
Jim Bibby	1978–81, 1983
Mike Bielecki	1984–87
Lou Bierbauer	1891–96
Carson Bigbee	1916–26
Lyle Bigbee	1921
Dann Bilardello	1989–90
Ralph Birkofer	1933–36
Bill Bishop	1887
Ron Blackburn	1958–59
Earl Blackburn	1912
Fred Blackwell	1917–19
Sheriff Blake	1920
Homer Blankenship	1928
Cy Blanton	1934–39
Steve Blass	1964, 1966–74
Jimmy Bloodworth	1947
Bert Blyleven	1978–80
Eddie Bockman	1948–49
Tony Boeckel	1917, 1919
George Boehler	1923
Pat Bohen	1914
Barry Bonds	1986–92
Ernie Bonham	1947–49
Bobby Bonilla	1986–91
Everitt Booe	1913
Al Bool	1930
Luke Boone	1918
Frank Bork	1964
Hank Borowy	1950
Don Bosch	1966
Frank Bowerman	1898–99
Joe Bowman	1937–41
Roger Bowman	1953, 1955
Sumner Bowman	1890
Doe Boyland	1978
Eddie Boyle	1896
King Brady	1906–07
Dave Brain	1905
Erv Brame	1928–32
Ron Brand	1963
Chick Brandom	1908–09
Ed Brandt	1937–38
Bill Brandt	1941–43
Kitty Bransfield	1901–04
Sid Bream	1985–90
Sam Brenegan	1914
Bill Brenzel	1932
Ken Brett	1974–75
Fred Brickell	1926–30
Bunny Brief	1917
Harry Bright	1958–59
Nellie Briles	1971–73
Chuck Brinkman	1974
Gil Britton	1913
Steve Brodie	1897–98
Frank Brosseau	1969, 1971
Tony Brottem	1921
Jimmy Brown	1946
Mace Brown	1935–41
Myrl Brown	1922
Tom Brown	1887
Mike Brown	1985–86
Earl Browne	1935–36
Pete Browning	1891
Bill Brubaker	1932–40
Jacob Brumfield	1995
George Brunet	1970
Steve Brye	1978
Steve Buechele	1991–92
Scott Bullett	1991, 1993
Jim Bunning	1968–69
Smoky Burgess	1959–64
Eddie Burke	1890
Jimmy Burke	1901–02
Bill Burwell	1928
Guy Bush	1935–36
Joe Bush	1926–27
Max Butcher	1939–45
Art Butler	1912–13
Tom Butters	1962–65
Bobby Byrne	1909–13

Ernie Camacho	1981
Fred Cambria	1970
Hank Camelli	1943–46
Harry Camnitz	1909
Howie Camnitz	1904, 1906–13
Kid Camp	1892
Vin Campbell	1910–11
Marc Campbell	1907
John Candelaria	1975–85, 1993
John Cangelosi	1987–90
Chris Cannizzaro	1968
Don Cardwell	1963–66
Max Carey	1910–26
Bobby Cargo	1892
Fred Carisch	1903–06
Don Carlsen	1951–52
Hal Carlson	1917–23
Paul Carpenter	1916
Frank Carpin	1965
Lew Carr	1901
Clay Carroll	1978
Fred Carroll	1887–89, 1891
Cliff Carroll	1888
Steve Carter	1989–90
Charlie Case	1904–06
Hugh Casey	1949
Dave Cash	1969–73
Harry Cassady	1904
Pete Castiglione	1947–53
Buster Caton	1917–20
Leon Chagnon	1929–30, 1932–34
Cliff Chambers	1949–51
Tom Cheney	1960–61
Jack Chesbro	1899–1902
Bob Chesnes	1948–50
Jason Christiansen	1995
Joe Christopher	1959–61
Chuck Churn	1957
Gino Cimoli	1960–61
Bill Clancy	1905
Willie Clark	1898–99
Dave Clark	1992–95
Fred Clarke	1900–11
Nig Clarke	1920
Stu Clarke	1929–30
Bill Clemensen	1939, 1941, 1946
Roberto Clemente	1955–72
Ed Clements	1890
Pat Clements	1985–86
Donn Clendenon	1961–68
Elmer Cleveland	1888
Gene Clines	1970–74
Billy Clingman	1895
Otis Clymer	1905–07
Tom Colcolough	1893–95
King Cole	1912
Dick Cole	1951, 1953–56
Alex Cole	1992
Victor Cole	1992
John Coleman	1887–88, 1890
Joe Coleman	1979
Bob Coleman	1913–14
Darnell Coles	1987–88
Ripper Collins	1941
Zip Collins	1914–15
Frank Colman	1942–46
Dick Colpaert	1970
Adam Comorosky	1926–33
Pete Compton	1916
Ralph Comstock	1918
Onix Concepcion	1987
Dick Conger	1941–42
Wid Conroy	1902
Pete Conway	1889
Joe Conzelman	1913–15
Dale Coogan	1950
Steve Cooke	1992–94
Duff Cooley	1900
Wilbur Cooper	1912–24
Walker Cooper	1954
John Corcoran	1895
Pop Corkhill	1891–92
Pete Coscarart	1942–46
Dan Costello	1914–16
Ensign Cottrell	1911
Billy Cox	1941, 1946–47
Danny Cox	1992
Del Crandall	1965
Sam Crane	1890
Fred Crolius	1902
John Cronin	1898
Joe Cronin	1926–27
Monte Cross	1894–95
Victor Cruz	1981
Cookie Cuccurullo	1943–45
Bud Culloton	1925–26
Midre Cummings	1993–95
Gene Curtis	1903
Harv Cushman	1902
George Cutshaw	1918–21
Kiki Cuyler	1921, 1923–27
Mike Cvengros	1927

Babe Dahlgren	1944–45
Bruce Dal Canton	1967–70
Abner Dalrymple	1887–88
Bennie Daniels	1957–60
Pete Daniels	1890
Vic Davalillo	1971–73
Lefty Davis	1901–02
Harry Davis	1896–98
Brandy Davis	1952–53
Ron Davis	1969
Spud Davis	1940–41, 1944–45
Dick Davis	1982
Butch Davis	1987
Trench Davis	1985–86
Joe Dawson	1927–29
Bill Day	1890
Adam DeBus	1917
Harry Decker	1890
Bobby Del Greco	1952, 1956
Tom Delahanty	1896
Jose DeLeon	1983–86
Larry Demery	1974–77
Gene DeMontreville	1894
Con Dempsey	1951
Orestes Destrade	1988
Tom Dettore	1973
Mark Dewey	1993–94
Mike Diaz	1986–88
Johnny Dickshot	1936–38
Murry Dickson	1949–53
Ernie Diehl	1903–04
Dutch Dietz	1940–43
Bob Dillinger	1950–51
Pop Dillon	1899–1900
Miguel Dilone	1974–77
Vince DiMaggio	1940–44
Benny Distefano	1984, 1986, 1988–89
Ona Dodd	1912
Ed Doheny	1901–03
Cozy Dolan	1913
Jiggs Donahue	1900–01
Mike Donlin	1912
Jim Donnelly	1897
Lino Donoso	1955–56
Patsy Donovan	1892–99
Jerry Dorsey	1911
Whammy Douglas	1957
Skip Dowd	1910
Doug Drabek	1987–92
Tim Drummond	1987
Clise Dudley	1933
Bernie Duffy	1913
Gus Dugas	1930, 1932
Bill Duggleby	1907
Pat Duncan	1915
Fred Dunlap	1888–90
Jim Dunn	1952
Mike Dunne	1987–89
Andy Dunning	1889
Erv Dusak	1951–52
Jerry Dybzinski	1985
Duffy Dyer	1975–78
Mike Dyer	1994–95

Truck Eagan	1901
Bad Bill Eagan	1898
Billy Earle	1892–93
Mike Easler	1977, 1979–83
Logan Easley	1987, 1989
John Easton	1894
Eddie Eayrs	1913
Stump Edington	1912
Mike Edwards	1977
Red Ehret	1892–94
Roy Ellam	1918
Larry Elliot	1962
Bob Elliott	1939–46
Dock Ellis	1968–75, 1979
Bones Ely	1896–1901
Angelo Encarnacion	1995
Charlie Engle	1930
Jewel Ens	1922–25
Aubrey Epps	1935
John Ericks	1995
Ralph Erickson	1929–30
Duke Esper	1890, 1892
Cecil Espy	1991–92
Bill Evans	1916–17, 1919

Roy Face	1953, 1955–68
Hector Fajardo	1991
Cy Falkenberg	1903
Stan Fansler	1986
Jack Farmer	1916
Bill Farmer	1888
Duke Farrell	1892
Felix Fermin	1987–88
Ed Fernandes	1940
Nanny Fernandez	1950
Jack Ferry	1910–13
Jocko Fields	1887–89, 1891
Hal Finney	1931–34, 1936
Bill Fischer	1916–17
Harry Fisher	1952
Brian Fisher	1987–89
Ed Fitz Gerald	1948–53
Ira Flagstead	1929–30
Patsy Flaherty	1900, 1904–05
Steamer Flanagan	1905
Les Fleming	1949

Elbie Fletcher	1939–43, 1946–47
Don Flinn	1917
John Flynn	1910–11
Lee Fohl	1902
Hank Foiles	1956–59
Tom Foley	1993–94
Tim Foli	1979–81, 1985
Dee Fondy	1957
Jim Foor	1973
Brownie Foreman	1895–96
Terry Forster	1977
Larry Foss	1961
Paddy Fox	1899
Earl Francis	1960–64
Gene Freese	1955–58, 1964–65
George Freese	1955
Jim Fregosi	1977–78
Larry French	1929–34
Bob Friend	1951–65
Doug Frobel	1982–85
Sam Frock	1909–10
Woodie Fryman	1966–67
Fred Fussell	1928–29
Ken Gables	1945–47
Pud Galvin	1887–89, 1891–92
Bob Ganley	1905–06
Gussie Gannon	1895
John Ganzel	1898
Joe Garagiola	1951–53
Mike Garber	1956
Gene Garber	1969–70, 1972
Miguel Garcia	1987–89
Carlos Garcia	1990–95
Freddy Garcia	1995
Harry Gardner	1911–12
Jim Gardner	1895, 1897–99
Bill Garfield	1889
Debs Garms	1940–41
Phil Garner	1977–81
Cito Gaston	1978
Hank Gastright	1893
Huck Geary	1942–43
Johnny Gee	1939, 1941, 1943–44
John Gelnar	1964, 1967
Frank Genins	1895
Wally Gerber	1914–15
Al Gerheauser	1945–46
Lou Gertenrich	1903
Gus Getz	1918
Joe Gibbon	1960–65, 1969–70
Bob Gibson	1890
George Gibson	1905–16
Kirk Gibson	1992
Brett Gideon	1987
Paul Giel	1959–60
Harry Gilbert	1890
John Gilbert	1890
Jack Gilbert	1904
Warren Gill	1908
Sam Gillen	1893
Len Gilmore	1944
Al Gionfriddo	1944–46
Dave Giusti	1970–76
Jack Glasscock	1893–94
Whitey Glazner	1920–23
Bill Gleason	1916–17
Jerry Don Gleaton	1992
Jot Goar	1896
Jerry Goff	1993–94
Chuck Goggin	1972–73
Jesse Gonder	1966–67
Fernando Gonzalez	1972–73, 1977–78
Denny Gonzalez	1984–85, 1987–88
Jose Gonzalez	1991
Johnny Gooch	1921–28
Sid Gordon	1954–55
Hank Gornicki	1942–43, 1946
Howie Goss	1962
Goose Gossage	1977
Julio Gotay	1963
Jim Gott	1987–89, 1995
Earl Grace	1931–35
George Grant	1931
Mudcat Grant	1970–71
George Grantham	1925–31
Charlie Gray	1890
Chummy Gray	1899
Reddy Gray	1890, 1893
Stan Gray	1912
Freddie Green	1959–61, 1964
Chris Green	1984
Hank Greenberg	1947
Hal Gregg	1948–50
Tommy Gregg	1987–88
Reddy Grey	1903
Bill Grey	1898
Tom Griffin	1982
Burleigh Grimes	1916–17, 1928–29, 1934
Charlie Grimm	1919–24
Dick Groat	1952, 1955–62
Heinie Groh	1927
Don Gross	1958–60
Howdie Grossklos	1930–32
Al Grunwald	1955
Cecilio Guante	1982–86
Ben Guintini	1946
Ad Gumbert	1893–94
Harry Gumbert	1949–50
Billy Gumbert	1890, 1892
Frankie Gustine	1939–48
Mule Haas	1925
Harvey Haddix	1959–63
Bill Haeffner	1920
Bud Hafey	1935–36
Jerry Hairston	1977
Dick Hall	1952–57, 1959
Bob Hall	1953
Bill Hall	1954, 1956, 1958
Albert Hall	1989
Jack Hallett	1942–43, 1946
Newt Halliday	1916
Bill Hallman	1906–07
Earl Hamilton	1918–23
Dave Hamilton	1978
Ken Hamlin	1957, 1959
Luke Hamlin	1942
Jack Hammond	1922
Lee Hancock	1995
Lee Handley	1937–41, 1944–46
Ned Hanlon	1889, 1891
Charlie Hargreaves	1928–30
Bob Harmon	1914–16, 1918
Brian Harper	1982–84
Terry Harper	1987
Ray Harrell	1940
Joe Harris	1927–28
Bill Harris	1931–34
Bill Hart	1895, 1898
Chuck Hartenstein	1969–70
Fred Hartman	1894
Andy Hassler	1980
Charlie Hastings	1896–98
Billy Hatcher	1989
Pink Hawley	1895–97
Charlie Heard	1890
Neal Heaton	1989–91
Wally Hebert	1943
Richie Hebner	1969–76, 1982–83
Guy Hecker	1890
Ken Heintzelman	1937–42, 1946–47
Tommy Helms	1976
Ducky Hemp	1890
Rollie Hemsley	1928–31
Hardie Henderson	1888
George Hendrick	1985
Claude Hendrix	1911–13
Gail Henley	1954
Bill Henry	1968
Babe Herman	1935
Gene Hermanski	1953
Jackie Hernandez	1971–73
Ramon Hernandez	1971–76
Art Herring	1947
Johnny Hetki	1953–54
Jake Hewitt	1895
John Heyner	1890
Kirby Higbe	1947–49
Carmen Hill	1915–16, 1918–19, 1926–29
Homer Hillebrand	1905–06, 1908
Chuck Hiller	1968
Mack Hillis	1928
Bill Hinchman	1915–18
Paul Hines	1890
Don Hoak	1959–62
Bill Hoffer	1898–99
Jesse Hoffmeister	1897
Solly Hofman	1903, 1912–13
Cal Hogue	1952–54
Al Holland	1977, 1985
Ed Holley	1934
Bonnie Hollingsworth	1922
John Hope	1993–95
Mike Hopkins	1902
Johnny Hopp	1948–50
Jim Hopper	1946
Elmer Horton	1896
Dave Hostetler	1988
Del Howard	1905
Lee Howard	1946–47
Art Howe	1974–75
Dixie Howell	1947
Bill Howerton	1951–52
Waite Hoyt	1933–37
Bill Hughes	1921
Jim Hughey	1896–97
Mark Huismann	1990–91
Newt Hunter	1911
Brian Hunter	1994
Bert Husting	1900
Ham Hyatt	1909–10, 1912–14
Al Jackson	1959, 1961
Charlie Jackson	1917
Grant Jackson	1977–82
Danny Jackson	1992
Spook Jacobs	1956
Elmer Jacobs	1916–18
Vic Janowicz	1953–54
Roy Jarvis	1946–47
Jesse Jefferson	1980
Woody Jensen	1931–39
John Jeter	1969–70
Sam Jethroe	1954
Manny Jimenez	1967–68
Juan Jimenez	1974
Houston Jimenez	1987
Lloyd Johnson	1934
Bob Johnson	1971–73
Dave Johnson	1987
Mark Johnson	1995
Rex Johnston	1964
Doc Johnston	1915–16
Joel Johnston	1993–94
Alex Jones	1889
Cobe Jones	1928–29
Percy Jones	1930
Odell Jones	1975, 1977–78, 1981
Tim Jones	1977
Barry Jones	1986–88
Baldy Jones	1890
Bubber Jonnard	1922
Harry Jordan	1894–95
Mike Jordan	1890
Walt Judnich	1949
Red Juelich	1939
Ken Jungels	1942
Jack Kading	1910
Jake Kafora	1913–14
Frank Kalin	1940
Jim Kane	1908
Erv Kantlehner	1914–16
Ed Karger	1906
Bill Keen	1911
Mickey Keliher	1911
Joe Kelley	1891–92
George Kelly	1917
Herb Kelly	1914–15
Bob Kelly	1914
Joe Kelly	1914
Bill Kelly	1911–13
Billy Kelsey	1907
John Kelty	1890
Steve Kemp	1985–86
Brickyard Kennedy	1903
Sam Khalifa	1985–87
Pat Kilhullen	1914
Frank Killen	1893–98
Ralph Kiner	1946–53
Silver King	1891
Lee King	1916–18
Nellie King	1954–57
Jeff King	1989–95
Ed Kinsella	1905
Tom Kinslow	1895
Bob Kipper	1985–91
Ed Kirkpatrick	1974–77
Bruce Kison	1971–79
Chuck Klein	1939
Ron Kline	1952, 1955–59, 1968–69
Bob Klinger	1938–43
Ted Kluszewski	1958–59
Clyde Kluttz	1947–48
Otto Knabe	1905, 1916
Phil Knell	1888, 1894
Cliff Knox	1924
Nick Koback	1953–55
Gary Kolb	1968–69
Fred Kommers	1913
Ed Konetchy	1914
Dennis Konuszewski	1995
George Kopacz	1970
Clem Koshorek	1952
Bill Koski	1951
Lou Koupal	1925–26
Randy Kramer	1988–90
Danny Kravitz	1956–60
Ray Krawczyk	1984–86
Ray Kremer	1924–33
Otto Krueger	1903–04
Al Krumm	1889
Willie Kuehne	1887–89
Charlie Kuhns	1897
Earl Kunz	1923
Bob Kuzava	1957
Clem Labine	1960–61
Lee Lacy	1979–84
Fred Lake	1898
Bud Lally	1891
Jack Lamabe	1962
John Lamb	1970–71, 1973
Dennis Lamp	1992
Dick Lanahan	1940–41
Bill Landrum	1989–91
Marty Lang	1930
Rick Langford	1976
Johnny Lanning	1940–43, 1945–46
Paul LaPalme	1951–54
Dave LaPoint	1988
Sam LaRoque	1890–91
Tacks Latimer	1900
Chuck Lauer	1889
Cookie Lavagetto	1934–36
Mike LaValliere	1987–93
Vern Law	1950–51, 1954–67
Vance Law	1980–81
Al Lawson	1890
Herman Layne	1927
Tommy Leach	1900–12, 1918
Tom Leahy	1897
Cliff Lee	1919–20
Watty Lee	1904
Mark Lee	1980–81
Sam Leever	1898–1910
Lefty Leifield	1905–12
Ed Leip	1940–41
Larry LeJeune	1915
Johnnie LeMaster	1985
Joe Leonard	1914
Don Leppert	1961–62
Sixto Lezcano	1985
Jon Lieber	1994–95
Jose Lind	1987–92
Johnny Lindell	1953
Freddie Lindstrom	1933–34
Bob Linton	1929
Nelson Liriano	1995
Scott Little	1989
Dick Littlefield	1954–56
Abel Lizotte	1896
Esteban Loaiza	1995
Hans Lobert	1903
Johnny Logan	1961–63
Al Lois	1978
Vic Lombardi	1948–50
Dale Long	1951, 1955–57
Bob Long	1981
Al Lopez	1940–46
Scott Loucks	1985
Red Lucas	1934–38
Frank Luce	1923
Bill Luhrsen	1913
Del Lundgren	1924
Al Luplow	1967
Jerry Lynch	1954–56, 1963–66
Mike Lynch	1904–07
Al Lyons	1947
Denny Lyons	1893–94, 1896–97
Pop Lytle	1890
Bill MacDonald	1950, 1953
Danny MacFayden	1940
Ken Macha	1974, 1977–78
Connie Mack	1891–94
Morris Madden	1988–89
Nick Maddox	1907–10
Mike Maddux	1995
Art Madison	1899

Bill Madlock	1979–85
Harl Maggert	1907
Jack Maguire	1951
Roy Mahaffey	1926–27
Mickey Mahler	1980
Woody Main	1948, 1950, 1952–53
Al Mamaux	1913–17
Jim Mangan	1952, 1954
Angel Mangual	1969
Lou Manske	1906
Heinie Manush	1939
Ravelo Manzanillo	1994–95
Rabbit Maranville	1921–24
Lou Marone	1969–70
Luis Marquez	1954
Joe Marshall	1903
Jim Marshall	1962
Paul Martin	1955
Stu Martin	1941–42
Al Martin	1992–95
Jose Martinez	1969–70
Carmelo Martinez	1990–91
Phil Masi	1949
Roger Mason	1991–92
Jim Mattox	1922–23
Gene Mauch	1947
Al Maul	1888–89, 1891
Dal Maxvill	1973–74
Bert Maxwell	1906
Jerry May	1964–70
Buckshot May	1924
Milt May	1971–73, 1983–84
Erskine Mayer	1918–19
Bill Mazeroski	1956–72
Lee Mazzilli	1983–86
Dixie McArthur	1914
Ike McAuley	1914–16
Al McBean	1961–68, 1970
George McBride	1905
Windy McCall	1950
Alex McCarthy	1910–17
Jack McCarthy	1898–99
Tom McCarthy	1908
Lloyd McClendon	1990–94
Moose McCormick	1904
Jim McCormick	1887
Tom McCreery	1898–1900
Clyde McCullough	1949–52
Jeff McCurry	1995
Sam McDowell	1975
Will McEnaney	1978
Chappie McFarland	1906
Orlando McFarlane	1962, 1964
Frank McGinn	1890
Irish McIlveen	1906
Stuffy McInnis	1925–26
Bill McKechnie	1907, 1910–12, 1918, 1920
Jim McKee	1972–73
Alex McKinnon	1887
Warren McLaughlin	1902
Cal McLish	1947–48
Jack McMahan	1956
Jerry McNertney	1973
George McQuillan	1913–15
Pete McShannic	1888
Larry McWilliams	1982–86
Johnny Meador	1920
Lee Meadows	1923–29
Doc Medich	1976
Scott Medvin	1988–89
Jouett Meekin	1900
Dutch Meier	1906
Heinie Meine	1929–34
Roman Mejias	1955, 1957–59, 1961
Mario Mendoza	1974–78
Jock Menefee	1892, 1894–95
Tony Menendez	1993
Ed Mensor	1912–14
Orlando Merced	1990–95
Jack Mercer	1910
George Merritt	1901–03
Bill Merritt	1894–97
Jack Merson	1951–52
Catfish Metkovich	1951–53
Dan Miceli	1993–95
Gene Michael	1966
Pete Mikkelsen	1966–67
Johnny Miljus	1927–28
Frank Miller	1916–19
Doggie Miller	1887–93
Jake Miller	1922
Dots Miller	1909–13
Ray Miller	1917
Bob Miller	1971–72
Roscoe Miller	1904
Ward Miller	1909
Bill Miller	1902
Paul Miller	1991–93
Randy Milligan	1988
John Milner	1978–82
Blas Minor	1992–94
Jim Minshall	1974–75
Mike Mitchell	1913–14
Vinegar Bend Mizell	1960–62
Danny Moeller	1907–08
Dennis Moeller	1993
Johnny Mokan	1921–22
Fritz Mollwitz	1917–19
Willie Montanez	1981–82
Felipe Montemayor	1953, 1955
Gene Moore	1909–10
George Moore	1905
Eddie Moore	1923–26
Bob Moose	1967–76
Sam Moran	1895
Ramon Morel	1995
Lew Moren	1903–04
Omar Moreno	1975–82
John Morlan	1973–74
Ed Morris	1887–89
Johnny Morrison	1920–27
Phil Morrison	1921
Jim Morrison	1982–87
Walt Moryn	1961
Paul Moskau	1982
Jim Mosolf	1929–31
Manny Mota	1963–68
Mike Mowrey	1914
Ray Mueller	1939–40, 1950
Walter Mueller	1922–24, 1926
Joe Muir	1951–52
Hugh Mulcahy	1947
Eddie Mulligan	1928
Bob Muncrief	1949
George Munger	1952, 1956
Eddie Murphy	1926
Leo Murphy	1915
Morg Murphy	1898
Danny Murtaugh	1948–51
Judge Nagle	1911
Steve Nagy	1947
Cholly Naranjo	1956
Pete Naton	1953
Denny Neagle	1992–95
Jim Nealon	1906–07
Ron Necciai	1952
Cal Neeman	1962
Cy Neighbors	1908
Rocky Nelson	1951, 1959–61
Jim Nelson	1970–71
John Newell	1891
Sam Nichol	1888
Chet Nichols	1926–27
Fred Nicholson	1919–20
Ovid Nicholson	1912
George Nicol	1894
Steve Nicosia	1978–83
Al Niehaus	1925
Randy Niemann	1982–83
Billy Niles	1895
Junior Noboa	1994
Wayne Nordhagen	1982
Nelson Norman	1982
Ken Oberkfell	1988–89
Eddie O'Brien	1953, 1955–58
John O'Brien	1899
Johnny O'Brien	1953, 1955–57
Ray O'Brien	1916
Tommy O'Brien	1943–45
Tom O'Brien	1898, 1900
Danny O'Connell	1950, 1953
John O'Connell	1928–29
Jack O'Connor	1900–02
Paddy O'Connor	1908–10
Billy O'Dell	1966–67
George O'Donnell	1954
Red Oldham	1925–26
Bob Oldis	1960–61
Bob Oliver	1965
Al Oliver	1968–77
Diomedes Olivo	1960, 1962
Tony Ordenana	1943
Joe Orsulak	1983–86
Junior Ortiz	1982–83, 1985–89
Bob Osborn	1931
Fred Osborne	1890
Wayne Osborne	1935
Fritz Ostermueller	1944–48
Bill Otey	1907
Amos Otis	1984
Marty O'Toole	1911–14
Ed Ott	1974–80
Dave Otto	1993
Bob Owchinko	1983
Dick Padden	1896–98
Tom Padden	1932–37
Jose Pagan	1965–72
Dave Pagan	1977
Joe Page	1954
Jim Pagliaroni	1963–67
Vicente Palacios	1987–88, 1990–92
Frank Papish	1950
Mark Parent	1995
Jay Parker	1899
Dave Parker	1973–83
Steve Parris	1995
Lance Parrish	1994
Tom Parsons	1963
Claude Passeau	1935
Freddie Patek	1968–70
Daryl Patterson	1974
Bob Patterson	1986–87, 1989–92
Harley Payne	1899
Al Pedrique	1987–88
Red Peery	1927
Steve Pegues	1994–95
Heinie Peitz	1905–06
Eddie Pellagrini	1953–54
Orlando Pena	1970
Tony Pena	1980–86
Alejandro Pena	1994
Hipolito Pena	1986–87
Jim Pendleton	1957
William Pennyfeather	1992–94
Laurin Pepper	1954–57
George Perez	1958
Pascual Perez	1980–81
Hardy Peterson	1955, 1957–59
Mark Petkovsek	1993
Paul Pettit	1951, 1953
Jesse Petty	1929–30
Jeff Pfeffer	1924
Jack Pfiester	1903–04
Ed Phelps	1902–04, 1906–08
Babe Phelps	1942
Deacon Phillippe	1900–11
Eddie Phillips	1931
Jack Phillips	1949–52
Bill Phillips	1890
Val Picinich	1933
Bill Pierro	1950
Tony Piet	1931–33
Jake Pitler	1917–18
Juan Pizarro	1967–68, 1974
Elmo Plaskett	1962–63
Dan Plesac	1995
Ray Poat	1949
Johnny Podgajny	1943
Howie Pollet	1951–53, 1956
Elmer Ponder	1917, 1919–21
Ed Poole	1900–02
Paul Popovich	1974–75
Bob Porterfield	1958–59
Bill Powell	1909–10
Ross Powell	1995
Ted Power	1990
Johnny Powers	1955–58
Bob Priddy	1962, 1964
Tom Prince	1987–93
Buddy Pritchard	1957
Alfonso Pulido	1983–84
Bob Purkey	1954–57, 1966
Mel Queen	1947–48, 1950–52
Rey Quinones	1989
Marv Rackley	1949
Drew Rader	1921
Jack Rafter	1904
Pep Rambert	1939–40
Pedro Ramos	1969
Dick Rand	1957
Willie Randolph	1975
Johnny Rawlings	1923, 1925–26
Johnny Ray	1981–87
Curt Raydon	1958
Harry Raymond	1892
Joe Redfield	1991
Gary Redus	1988–92
Rick Reed	1988–91
Bill Regan	1931
Wally Rehg	1912
Arch Reilly	1917
Charlie Reilly	1891
Pete Reiser	1951
Heinie Reitz	1899
Ken Reitz	1982
Rick Renteria	1986
Xavier Rescigno	1943–45
Dino Restelli	1949, 1951
Rick Reuschel	1985–87
Jerry Reuss	1974–78, 1990
Craig Reynolds	1975–76
R. J. Reynolds	1985–90
Bobby Rhawn	1949
Billy Rhines	1898–99
Rick Rhoden	1979–86
Hal Rhyne	1926–27
Dennis Ribant	1967
Hal Rice	1953–54
Jeff Richardson	1991
Joe Rickert	1898
Marv Rickert	1950
Dave Ricketts	1970
Harry Riconda	1929
Elmer Riddle	1948–49
Johnny Riddle	1948
Cully Rikard	1941–42, 1947
Claude Ritchey	1900–06
Jim Ritz	1894
Johnny Rizzo	1938–40
Fred Roat	1890
Curt Roberts	1954–56
Dave Roberts	1966
Dave Roberts	1979–80
Dave Robertson	1921
Bob Robertson	1967, 1969–76
Rich Robertson	1993–94
Hank Robinson	1911–13
Bill Robinson	1975–82
Don Robinson	1978–87
Jeff Robinson	1987–89
Jeff Robinson	1992
Chick Robitaille	1904–05
Andre Rodgers	1965–67
Bill Rodgers	1944
Ruben Rodriguez	1986, 1988
Rosario Rodriguez	1991
Preacher Roe	1944–47
Mike Roesler	1990
Wally Roettger	1934
Ray Rohwer	1921–22
Stan Rojek	1948–51
Enrique Romo	1979–82
Jim Rooker	1973–80
Zeke Rosebraugh	1898–99
Mark Ross	1987, 1990
Jack Rothfuss	1897
Phil Routcliffe	1890
Jack Rowe	1889
Al Rubeling	1943–44
Dave Rucker	1988
Scott Ruskin	1990
Reb Russell	1922–23
Jim Russell	1942–47
Mark Ryal	1990
Mike Ryan	1974
Jim Sadowski	1974
Tom Saffell	1949–51, 1955
Vic Saier	1919
Freddy Sale	1924
Ed Sales	1890
Bill Salkeld	1945–47
Jack Saltzgaver	1945
Jack Salveson	1935
Roger Samuels	1989
Roy Sanders	1918
Mike Sandlock	1953
Charlie Sands	1971
Manny Sanguillen	1967, 1969–76, 1978–80
Ben Sankey	1929–31
Manny Sarmiento	1982–83
Mackey Sasser	1987, 1995
Rich Sauveur	1986
Ted Savage	1963
Doc Scanlan	1903–04
Bobby Schang	1914–15

Fritz Scheeren	1914–15
Frank Scheibeck	1894
John Scheneberg	1913
Hank Schenz	1950–51
Walter Schmidt	1916–24
Crazy Schmit	1890
Dick Schofield	1958–65
Pop Schriver	1898–1900
Wildfire Schulte	1916–17
Fred Schulte	1936–37
Joe Schultz	1939–40
Joe Schultz	1916
Bob Schultz	1953
Bill Schuster	1937
Don Schwall	1963–66
Pete Scott	1928
Jack Scott	1916
Rod Scurry	1980–85
Jimmy Sebring	1902–04
Sonny Senerchia	1952
Rip Sewell	1938–49
Spike Shannon	1908
Bobby Shantz	1961
Bud Sharpe	1910
Ben Shaw	1918
Tom Sheehan	1925–26
Tommy Sheehan	1906–07
Earl Sheely	1929
Jim Shellenback	1966–67, 1969
Ben Shelton	1993
Jack Shepard	1953–56
Bill Short	1967
Brian Shouse	1993
Frank Shugart	1891–93
Harry Shuman	1942–43
Eddie Sicking	1927
Paddy Siglin	1914–16
Mike Simon	1909–13
Harry Simpson	1959
Elmer Singleton	1947–48
Tommie Sisk	1962–68
Bill Skiff	1921
Bob Skinner	1954, 1956–63
Cy Slapnicka	1918
Phil Slattery	1915
Don Slaught	1990–95
John Smiley	1986–91
Pop Smith	1887–89
Earl Smith	1955
Earl Smith	1924–28
Elmer Smith	1892–97, 1901
Heinie Smith	1899
Hal Smith	1932–35
Hal Smith	1965
Hal Smith	1960–61
Harry Smith	1902–07
Jimmy Smith	1916
Phenomenal Smith	1890
Jud Smith	1896, 1901
Bull Smith	1904
Paul Smith	1953, 1957
Dick Smith	1951–55
Bob Smith	1957–59
Sherry Smith	1911–12
Syd Smith	1914
Vinnie Smith	1941, 1946
Red Smith	1917–18
Lonnie Smith	1993
Jimmy Smith	1982
Zane Smith	1990–94
Mike Smith	1989
Frank Smykal	1916
Eddie Solomon	1980–82
Don Songer	1924–27
Denny Sothern	1930
Billy Southworth	1918–20
Bill Sowders	1889–90
Tully Sparks	1899
Glenn Spencer	1928, 1930–32
Roy Spencer	1925–27
George Spriggs	1965, 1967
Ed Spurney	1891
Harry Staley	1888–89, 1891
Tom Stankard	1904
Willie Stargell	1962–82
Charlie Starr	1908
Ray Starr	1944–45
Elmer Steele	1910–11
Bob Steele	1917–18
Fred Steere	1894
Bill Steinecke	1931
Ray Steineder	1923–24
Casey Stengel	1918–19
Rennie Stennett	1971–79
Jake Stenzel	1892–96
Ed Stevens	1948–50
R C Stevens	1958–60
Bud Stewart	1941–42
Stuffy Stewart	1922
Arnie Stone	1923–24
Lil Stoner	1930
Alan Storke	1906–09
Scott Stratton	1891
George Strickland	1950–52
Nick Strincevich	1941–42, 1944–48
Jim Stroner	1929
Steamboat Struss	1934
Dick Stuart	1958–62
Bill Stuart	1895
Tom Sturdivant	1961–63
Jim Suchecki	1952
Joe Sugden	1893–97
Gus Suhr	1930–39
John Sullivan	1908
Joe Sullivan	1941
Billy Sullivan	1947
Homer Summa	1920
Billy Sunday	1888–90
Max Surkont	1954–56
George Susce	1939
Harry Swacina	1907–08
Red Swanson	1955–57
Ed Swartwood	1892
Jeff Sweeney	1919
Hank Sweeney	1944
Steve Swetonic	1929–33
Bill Swift	1932–39
Oad Swigart	1939–40
Jeff Tabaka	1994
Jesse Tannehill	1897–1902
Al Tate	1946
Walt Tauscher	1928
Frank Taveras	1972, 1974–79
Carl Taylor	1968–69, 1971
Dorn Taylor	1987, 1989
Kent Tekulve	1974–85
Gene Tenace	1983
Walt Terrell	1990
Adonis Terry	1892–94
Zeb Terry	1919
Tommy Thevenow	1931–35, 1938
Jake Thies	1954–55
Frank Thomas	1951–58
Roy Thomas	1908
Gus Thompson	1903
Fresco Thompson	1925
Bill Thompson	1892
Jason Thompson	1981–85
Luis Tiant	1981
Jay Tibbs	1990
Cotton Tierney	1920–23
Jack Tising	1936
Jim Tobin	1937–39
Al Todd	1936–38
Bobby Tolan	1977
Fred Toliver	1993
Andy Tomberlin	1993
Dave Tomlin	1983, 1985
Randy Tomlin	1990–94
Lou Tost	1947
Pie Traynor	1920–35
Joe Trimble	1957
Fred Truax	1890
Harry Truby	1896
John Tudor	1984
Lee Tunnell	1982–85
Earl Turner	1948, 1950
Terry Turner	1901
Elmer Tutwiler	1928
Jim Umbricht	1959–61
Bob Vail	1908
George Van Haltren	1892–93
Maurice Van Robays	1939–43, 1946
Andy Van Slyke	1987–94
Dazzy Vance	1915
Hedi Vargas	1982, 1984
Gary Varsho	1991–92, 1994
Arky Vaughan	1932–41
Peek-A-Boo Veach	1890
Bob Veale	1962–72
Bucky Veil	1903–04
Art Veltman	1934
Jim Viox	1912–16
Bill Virdon	1956–65, 1968
Ozzie Virgil	1965
Joe Vitelli	1944
Charlie Wacker	1909
Rube Waddell	1900–01
Ben Wade	1955
Honus Wagner	1900–17
Bill Wagner	1914–17
Paul Wagner	1992–95
Tim Wakefield	1992–93
Bob Walk	1984–93
Dixie Walker	1948–49
Luke Walker	1965–66, 1968–73
Jim Wallace	1905
Lee Walls	1952, 1956–57
Connie Walsh	1907
Junior Walsh	1946, 1948–51
Bernie Walter	1930
Reggie Walton	1982
Lloyd Waner	1927–41, 1944–45
Paul Waner	1926–40
Chuck Ward	1917
Piggy Ward	1891
Preston Ward	1953–56
Ed Warner	1912
Hooks Warner	1916–17, 1919
Bill Warwick	1921
Jimmy Wasdell	1942
U. L. Washington	1986–87
Fred Waters	1955–56
Mule Watson	1920
Jim Waugh	1952–53
Art Weaver	1903
Jim Weaver	1935–37
Farmer Weaver	1894
Lefty Webb	1910
Billy Webb	1917
Mitch Webster	1991
John Wehner	1991–95
Johnny Welch	1936
Bill Werle	1949–52
Max West	1948
Wally Westlake	1947–51
Gus Weyhing	1895
Rip Wheeler	1921–22
Deacon White	1889
Kirby White	1910–11
Rick White	1994–95
Burgess Whitehead	1946
Art Whitney	1887
Ed Whitson	1977–79
Possum Whitted	1919–21
Dave Wickersham	1968
Whitey Wietelmann	1947
Kaiser Wilhelm	1903
Joe Wilhoit	1917
Curtis Wilkerson	1991
Lefty Wilkie	1941–42, 1946
Ted Wilks	1951–52
Don Williams	1958–59
Jimmy Williams	1899–1900
Vic Willis	1906–09
Claude Willoughby	1931
Maury Wills	1967–68
Art Wilson	1916
Grady Wilson	1948
Owen Wilson	1908–13
Mike Wilson	1921
Bill Wilson	1890
Glenn Wilson	1988–89, 1993
Gary Wilson	1995
Snake Wiltse	1901
Bill Windle	1928–29
Lave Winham	1903
Jim Winn	1983–86
Roy Wise	1944
John Wisner	1919–20
Dave Wissman	1964
George Witt	1957–61
Ed Wolfe	1952
Harry Wolfe	1917
Roger Wolff	1947
Harry Wolter	1907
Tony Womack	1993–94
Spades Wood	1930–31
Roy Wood	1913
Wilbur Wood	1964–65
Fred Woodcock	1892
Gene Woodling	1947
Walt Woods	1900
Chuck Workman	1946
Ron Wotus	1983–84
Dave Wright	1895
Glenn Wright	1924–28
Joe Wright	1896
Marvell Wynne	1983–85
Johnny Wyrostek	1942–43
Henry Yaik	1888
Emil Yde	1924–27
George Yeager	1901
Chief Yellowhorse	1921–22
Len Yochim	1951, 1954
Mike York	1990
Harley Young	1908
Irv Young	1908
Pep Young	1933–40
Kevin Young	1992–95
Henry Youngman	1890
Chris Zachary	1973
Frankie Zak	1944–46
Jeff Zaske	1984
George Ziegler	1890
Chief Zimmer	1900–02
Jimmy Zinn	1920–22
Richie Zisk	1971–76
Billy Zitzmann	1919

Managers

Hugo Bezdek	1917–19
Bobby Bragan	1956–57
Al Buckenberger	1892–94
Tom Burns	1892
Bill Burwell	1947
Donie Bush	1927–29
Nixey Callahan	1916–17
*Fred Clarke	1900–15
Spud Davis	1946
*Patsy Donovan	1897, 1899
*Fred Dunlap	1889
Jewel Ens	1929–31
Frankie Frisch	1940–46
George Gibson	1920–22, 1932–34
Alex Grammas	1969
Fred Haney	1953–55
*Ned Hanlon	1889, 1891
*Guy Hecker	1890
Billy Herman	1947
Jim Leyland	1986–95
*Connie Mack	1894–96
Bill McGunnigle	1891
Bill McKechnie	1922–26
Billy Meyer	1948–52
Danny Murtaugh	1957–64, 1967, 1970–71, 1973–76
Horace Phillips	1887–89
Larry Shepard	1968–69
Chuck Tanner	1977–85
*Pie Traynor	1934–39
Bill Virdon	1972–73
*Honus Wagner	1917
Harry Walker	1965–67
Bill Watkins	1898–99

PROVIDENCE Grays 1878–85

Doug Allison	1878–79
Bill Andrus	1885
Harry Arundel	1884
Charley Bassett	1884–85
George Bradley	1880
Lew Brown	1878–79, 1881
Tom Carey	1878
Cliff Carroll	1882–85
John Cassidy	1883
John Cattanach	1884
Ed Conley	1884
Fred Corey	1878
Cannonball Crane	1885
Con Daily	1885
Jerry Denny	1881–85
Mike Dorgan	1880
Jack Farrell	1879–85
Cherokee Fisher	1878
John Foley	1885
Barney Gilligan	1881–85
Em Gross	1879–81

Bill Hague	1878–79
Charlie Hallstrom	1885
Tom Healey	1878
Dick Higham	1878
Mike Hines	1885
Paul Hines	1878–85
Sadie Houck	1880
Arthur Irwin	1883–85
Rudy Kemmler	1879
Sam Kimber	1885
Lon Knight	1885
Denny Lyons	1885
Tim Manning	1882, 1885
Bobby Mathews	1879, 1881
Bill McClellan	1881
Jim McCormick	1885
Mike McGeary	1879
Cyclone Miller	1884
Joe Mulvey	1883
Tim Murnane	1878
Miah Murray	1884
Henry Myers	1881
Sandy Nava	1882–84
Tricky Nichols	1878
Dan O'Leary	1879
Jim O'Rourke	1879
Johnny Peters	1880
Lip Pike	1878
Old Hoss Radbourn	1881–85
Paul Radford	1884–85
Charlie Reilley	1882
Lee Richmond	1883
Ed Seward	1885
Dupee Shaw	1885
Edgar Smith	1883, 1885
Joe Start	1879–85
Bill Stellberger	1885
Denny Sullivan	1879
Charlie Sweasy	1878
Charlie Sweeney	1882–84
Dasher Troy	1882
Monte Ward	1878–82
John Ward	1885
Harry Wheeler	1878
Bill White	1879
Art Whitney	1882
George Wright	1879, 1882
Tom York	1878–82

Managers

Frank Bancroft	1884–85
*Mike Dorgan	1880
*Jack Farrell	1881
Mike McGeary	1880
*Monte Ward	1880
*George Wright	1879
Harry Wright	1882–83
*Tom York	1878, 1881

SAN DIEGO Padres 1969–95

Shawn Abner	1987–91
Ed Acosta	1971–72
Mike Aldrete	1991
Bill Almon	1974–79
Roberto Alomar	1988–90
Sandy Alomar	1989
Matty Alou	1974
Larry Andersen	1991–92
Dwain Anderson	1973
Jose Arcia	1969–70
Steve Arlin	1969–74
Mike Armstrong	1980–81
Randy Asadoor	1986
Andy Ashby	1993–95
Tucker Ashford	1976–78
Brad Ausmus	1993–95
Oscar Azocar	1991–92
Chuck Baker	1978, 1980
Jack Baldschun	1969–70
Marty Barrett	1991
Bob Barton	1970–72, 1974
Randy Bass	1980–82
Billy Bean	1993–95
Glenn Beckert	1974–75
Derek Bell	1993–94
Andy Benes	1989–95
Vic Bernal	1977
Andres Berumen	1995
Jim Beswick	1978
Kurt Bevacqua	1979–80, 1982–85
Dann Bilardello	1991–92
Dennis Blair	1980
Willie Blair	1995
Curt Blefary	1972
Doug Bochtler	1995
Bruce Bochy	1983–87
Ricky Bones	1991
Juan Bonilla	1981–83
Greg Booker	1983–89
Danny Boone	1981–82
Angel Bravo	1971
Dan Briggs	1979
Doug Brocail	1992–94
Ollie Brown	1969–72
Bobby Brown	1983–85
Chris Brown	1987–88
Jarvis Brown	1993
Al Bumbry	1985
Randell Byers	1987–88
Mike Caldwell	1971–73
Ken Caminiti	1995
Dave Campbell	1970–73
Mike Campbell	1994
Chris Cannizzaro	1969–71, 1974
Joe Carter	1990
Dave Cash	1980
Tony Castillo	1978
Andujar Cedeno	1995
Mike Champion	1976–78
Floyd Chiffer	1982–84
Archi Cianfrocco	1993–95
Jack Clark	1989–90
Jerald Clark	1988–92
Phil Clark	1993–95
Horace Clarke	1974
Pat Clements	1989–92
Nate Colbert	1969–74
Keith Comstock	1987–88
Scott Coolbaugh	1991
Danny Coombs	1970–71
Joey Cora	1987, 1989–90
Mike Corkins	1969–74
Pat Corrales	1972–73
John Costello	1991
Mike Couchee	1983
John Curtis	1980–82
John D'Acquisto	1977–80
Paul Dade	1979–80
Jerry DaVanon	1969
Bill Davis	1969
Willie Davis	1976
Mark Davis	1987–89, 1993–94
Storm Davis	1987
Jerry Davis	1983, 1985
Bob Davis	1973, 1975–78
John Davis	1990
Tommy Dean	1969–71
Marty Decker	1983
Luis DeLeon	1982–85
Jim Deshaies	1992
Miguel Dilone	1985
Glenn Dishman	1995
Pat Dobson	1970
Brian Dorsett	1991
Paul Doyle	1970
Dave Dravecky	1982–87
Tom Dukes	1969–70
Mike Dunne	1990
Mike Dupree	1976
Dave Edwards	1981–82
Juan Eichelberger	1978–82
Dave Eiland	1992–93
Randy Elliott	1972, 1974
Donnie Elliott	1994–95
Mark Ettles	1993
Barry Evans	1978–81
Leon Everitt	1969
Bill Fahey	1979–80
Paul Faries	1990–92
Tony Fernandez	1991–92
Al Ferrara	1969–71
Rollie Fingers	1977–80
Steve Finley	1995
Steve Fireovid	1981, 1983
Tim Flannery	1979–89
Bryce Florie	1994–95
Rich Folkers	1975–76
Alan Foster	1975–76
Jay Franklin	1971
Dave Freisleben	1974–78
Danny Frisella	1975
Tito Fuentes	1975–76
Oscar Gamble	1978
Ralph Garcia	1972, 1974
Wes Gardner	1991
Jeff Gardner	1992–93
Steve Garvey	1983–87
Rod Gaspar	1971, 1974
Cito Gaston	1969–74
Bob Geren	1993
Allen Gerhardt	1974
Joe Goddard	1972
Pat Gomez	1993
Tony Gonzalez	1969
Fernando Gonzalez	1978–79
Tom Gorman	1987
Goose Gossage	1984–87
Mark Grant	1987–90
Gary Green	1986, 1989
Brian Greer	1979
Bill Greif	1972–76
Tom Griffin	1976–77
Mike Griffin	1982
Johnny Grubb	1972–76
Ricky Gutierrez	1993–94
Doug Gwosdz	1981–84
Tony Gwynn	1982–95
Don Hahn	1975
Joey Hamilton	1994–95
Atlee Hammaker	1990–91
Larry Hardy	1974–75
Mike Hargrove	1979
Greg Harris	1984
Greg Harris	1988–93
Gene Harris	1992–94
Andy Hawkins	1982–88
Ray Hayward	1986–87
George Hendrick	1977–78
Ron Herbel	1970
Dustin Hermanson	1995
Enzo Hernandez	1971–77
Jeremy Hernandez	1991–93
Kevin Higgins	1993
Dave Hilton	1972–75
George Hinshaw	1982–83
Trevor Hoffman	1993–95
Ray Holbert	1994–95
Thomas Howard	1990–91
Jack Howell	1991
LaMarr Hoyt	1985–86
Walt Hriniak	1969
Randy Hundley	1975
Steve Huntz	1970, 1975
Bruce Hurst	1989–93
Tim Hyers	1994–95
Dane Iorg	1986
Mike Ivie	1971, 1974–77
Roy Lee Jackson	1985
Darrin Jackson	1989–92
Chris James	1989
Stan Jefferson	1987–88
Garry Jestadt	1971–72
John Jeter	1971–72
Jerry Johnson	1975–76
Mike Johnson	1974
Brian Johnson	1994–95
Jay Johnstone	1979
Ruppert Jones	1981–83
Randy Jones	1973–80
Jimmy Jones	1986–88
Von Joshua	1980
Dick Kelley	1969, 1971
Van Kelly	1969–70
Fred Kendall	1969–76, 1979–80
Terry Kennedy	1981–86
Mike Kilkenny	1972
Dave Kingman	1977
Dennis Kinney	1978–80
Clay Kirby	1969–73
Marc Kroon	1995
Bill Krueger	1994–95
Chris Krug	1969
John Kruk	1986–89
Ted Kubiak	1975–76
Fred Kuhaulua	1981
Tom Lampkin	1990–92
Rick Lancellotti	1982
Joe Lansford	1982–83
Dave LaPoint	1986
Bill Laxton	1971, 1974
Leron Lee	1971–73
Mark Lee	1978–79
Joe Lefebvre	1981–83
Craig Lefferts	1984–87, 1990–92
Dave Leiper	1987–89
Jim Lewis	1991
Sixto Lezcano	1982–83
Francisco Libran	1969
Derek Lilliquist	1990–91
John Littlefield	1981
Scott Livingstone	1994–95
Keith Lockhart	1994
Gene Locklear	1973–76
Mickey Lolich	1978–79
Tim Lollar	1981–84
Luis Lopez	1993–94
Gary Lucas	1980–83
Fred Lynn	1990
Shane Mack	1987–88
Mike Maddux	1991–92
Jerry Manuel	1982
Dave Marshall	1973
Carmelo Martinez	1984–89
Pedro Martinez	1993–94
Jose Martinez	1994
Don Mason	1971–73
Roger Mason	1993
Tim Mauser	1993–95
Jim McAndrew	1974
Al McBean	1969
Billy McCool	1969
Willie McCovey	1974–76
Lance McCullers	1985–88
Ray McDavid	1994–95
Fred McGriff	1991–93
Joe McIntosh	1974–75
Kevin McReynolds	1983–86
Luis Melendez	1976–77
Jose Melendez	1991–92
Butch Metzger	1975–77
Bob Miller	1971, 1973
Eddie Miller	1984
Kevin Mitchell	1987
Sid Monge	1983–84
Willie Montanez	1980
John Montefusco	1982–83
Rich Morales	1973–74
Jerry Morales	1969–73
Keith Moreland	1988
Jose Moreno	1981
Gerry Moses	1975
Jose Mota	1991
Jerry Mumphrey	1980
Steve Mura	1978–81
Dan Murphy	1989
Ivan Murrell	1969–73
Randy Myers	1992
Rob Nelson	1987–89
Graig Nettles	1984–86
Marc Newfield	1995
Joe Niekro	1969
Melvin Nieves	1993–95
Eric Nolte	1987–89, 1991
Fred Norman	1971–73
Jerry Nyman	1970
Bob Owchinko	1976–79
Mike Pagliarulo	1989–90
Lowell Palmer	1974
Mark Parent	1986–90
Bob Patterson	1985
Roberto Pena	1969
Broderick Perkins	1978–82
Sam Perlozzo	1979

Gaylord Perry 1978–79
Roberto Petagine 1995
Adam Peterson 1991
Gary Pettis 1992
Mike Phillips 1981
Tom Phoebus 1971–72
Joe Pittman 1982
Phil Plantier 1993–95
Johnny Podres 1969
Jim Presley 1991
Tim Pyznarski 1986

Doug Rader 1976–77
Mario Ramirez 1981–85
Eric Rasmussen 1978–80
Dennis Rasmussen 1983, 1988–91
Randy Ready 1986–89
Frank Reberger 1969
Jody Reed 1995
Merv Rettenmund 1976–77
Don Reynolds 1978–79
Ken Reynolds 1976
Ronn Reynolds 1990
Gene Richards 1977–83
Dave Roberts 1969–71
Dave Roberts 1972–75, 1977–78
Bip Roberts 1986, 1988–91, 1994–95
Dave Robinson 1970
Rafael Robles 1969–70, 1972
Aurelio Rodriguez 1980
Roberto Rodriguez 1970
Edwin Rodriguez 1983
Rich Rodriguez 1990–93
Ron Roenicke 1984
Vicente Romo 1973–74
Steve Rosenberg 1991
Gary Ross 1969–74
Jerry Royster 1985–86
Sonny Ruberto 1969

A. J. Sager 1994
Luis Salazar 1980–84, 1987, 1989
Scott Sanders 1993–95
Benito Santiago 1986–92
Al Santorini 1969–71
Rick Sawyer 1976–77
Pat Scanlon 1977
Mark Schaeffer 1972
Calvin Schiraldi 1989–90
Don Schulze 1989
John Scott 1974–75
Tim Scott 1991–93
Rudy Seanez 1993
Dick Selma 1969
Frank Seminara 1992–93
Al Severinsen 1971–72
Dick Sharon 1975
Gary Sheffield 1992–93
Darrell Sherman 1993
Craig Shipley 1991–94
Bob Shirley 1977–80
Eric Show 1981–90
Sonny Siebert 1975
Paul Siebert 1977
Candy Sierra 1988
Steve Simpson 1972
John Sipin 1969
Tommie Sisk 1969
Ron Slocum 1969–71
Ozzie Smith 1978–81
Frank Snook 1973
Elias Sosa 1983
Ed Spiezio 1969–72
Dan Spillner 1974–78
George Stablein 1980
Larry Stahl 1969–72
Fred Stanley 1972
Dave Staton 1993–94
James Steels 1987
Phil Stephenson 1989–90, 1992
Kurt Stillwell 1992–93
Craig Stimac 1980
Tim Stoddard 1985–86
Bob Stoddard 1986
Brent Strom 1975–77
Champ Summers 1984
Gary Sutherland 1977
Rick Sweet 1978
Steve Swisher 1981–82

Jeff Tabaka 1994–95
Ron Taylor 1972
Kerry Taylor 1993–94

Tom Tellmann 1979–80
Garry Templeton 1982–91
Gene Tenace 1977–80
Walt Terrell 1989
Tim Teufel 1991–93
Derrel Thomas 1972–74, 1978
Dickie Thon 1988
Mark Thurmond 1983–86
Ron Tingley 1982
Bobby Tolan 1974–75, 1979
Fred Toliver 1989
Dave Tomlin 1974–77
Hector Torres 1975–76
Rich Troedson 1973–74
Jerry Turner 1974–81, 1983

John Urrea 1981

Rafael Valdez 1990
Bobby Valentine 1975–77
Fernando Valenzuela 1995
Jim Vatcher 1991–92
Guillermo Velasquez 1992–93
Ron Villone 1995
Ed Vosberg 1986

Gene Walter 1985–86
Dan Walters 1992–93
Kevin Ward 1991–92
Mark Wasinger 1986
Ramon Webster 1970
Dave Wehrmeister 1976–78
Chris Welsh 1981–83
Wally Whitehurst 1993–94
Ed Whitson 1983–84, 1986–91
Alan Wiggins 1981–85
Mark Wiley 1978
Jim Wilhelm 1978–79
Jim Williams 1969–70
Bernie Williams 1974
Eddie Williams 1990, 1994–95
Brian Williams 1995
Ron Willis 1970
Earl Wilson 1970
Dave Winfield 1973–80
Rick Wise 1980–82
Ed Wojna 1985–87
Tim Worrell 1993–95
Marvell Wynne 1986–89

Managers

Bruce Bochy 1995
Steve Boros 1986
Larry Bowa 1987–88
Jerry Coleman 1980
Roger Craig 1978–79
Alvin Dark 1977
Preston Gomez 1969–72
Frank Howard 1981
Jack McKeon 1988–90
John McNamara 1974–77
Greg Riddoch 1990–92
Jim Riggleman 1992–94
Bob Skinner 1977
Dick Williams 1982–85
Don Zimmer 1972–73

SAN FRANCISCO Giants 1958–95

Moved from NEW YORK Giants

Glenn Adams 1975–76
Ricky Adams 1985
Mike Aldrete 1986–88
Doyle Alexander 1981
Gary Alexander 1975–77
Andy Allanson 1993
Felipe Alou 1958–63
Jesus Alou 1963–68
Matty Alou 1960–65
Joey Amalfitano 1960–61, 1963
Dave Anderson 1990–91
Rob Andrews 1977–79
Johnny Antonelli 1958–60
Luis Aquino 1995
Chris Arnold 1971–76
Rich Aurilia 1995

Ed Bailey 1961–63, 1965
Mark Bailey 1990, 1992
Dusty Baker 1984
Steve Barber 1974
Curt Barclay 1958–59
Jim Barr 1971–78, 1982–83
Jose Barrios 1982
Bob Barton 1965–69
Shawn Barton 1995
Kevin Bass 1990–92
Bill Bathe 1989–90
Jose Bautista 1995
Rod Beck 1991–95
Steve Bedrosian 1989–90
Marvin Benard 1995
Mike Benjamin 1989–95
Todd Benzinger 1993–95
Juan Berenguer 1986
Dave Bergman 1981–83
Dick Bertell 1965
Bud Black 1991–94
Damaso Blanco 1972–73
Don Blasingame 1960
Vida Blue 1978–81, 1985–86
John Boccabella 1974
Randy Bockus 1986–88
Carl Boles 1962
Bobby Bolin 1961–69
Bobby Bonds 1968–74
Barry Bonds 1993–95
Greg Booker 1990
Pedro Borbon 1979
Bill Bordley 1980
Kent Bottenfield 1994
Chris Bourjos 1980
Ernie Bowman 1961–63
Tom Bradley 1973–75
Jackie Brandt 1958–59
Jeff Brantley 1988–93
Fred Breining 1980–83
Bob Brenly 1981–89
Ed Bressoud 1958–61
Jamie Brewington 1995
Brad Brink 1994
Terry Bross 1993
Ollie Brown 1965–68
Jake Brown 1975
Chris Brown 1984–87
Greg Brummett 1993
Ron Bryant 1967, 1969–74
Dave Burba 1992–95
Bob Burda 1965–66, 1969–70
Enrique Burgos 1995
John Burkett 1987, 1990–94
Pete Burnside 1958
Brett Butler 1988–90
Bud Byerly 1959–60

Enos Cabell 1981
Mike Caldwell 1974–76
Mark Calvert 1983–84
Ernie Camacho 1989–90
Jose Cardenal 1963–64
Steve Carlton 1986
Mark Carreon 1993–95
Don Carrithers 1970–73
Gary Carter 1990
Larry Carter 1992
Orlando Cepeda 1958–66
Nestor Chavez 1967
Don Choate 1960
Mike Chris 1982–83
Jack Clark 1975–84
Will Clark 1986–93
Royce Clayton 1991–95
Ty Cline 1967–68
Jimmie Coker 1963
Craig Colbert 1992–93
Joe Coleman 1979
Darnell Coles 1991
Keith Comstock 1987
Jim Constable 1958, 1963
Dennis Cook 1988–89
Jeff Cornell 1984
Terry Cornutt 1977–78
Del Crandall 1964
Ray Crone 1958
Hector Cruz 1978–79
John Cumberland 1970–72
John Curtis 1977–79

John D'Acquisto 1973–76
Jim Davenport 1958–70
Ron Davis 1988
Mark Davis 1983–87
Chili Davis 1981–87
Mike Davison 1969–70
Steve Decker 1990–92
Rob Deer 1984–85
Ivan DeJesus 1987
Mark Dempsey 1982
Jim Deshaies 1993
Mark Dewey 1990, 1995
Dick Dietz 1966–71
Kelly Downs 1986–92
Dave Dravecky 1987–89
Rob Dressler 1975–76
Dan Driessen 1985–86
Jim Duffalo 1961–65
Frank Duffy 1971
Jim Dwyer 1978

Randy Elliott 1977
Angel Escobar 1988
Dick Estelle 1964–65
Shawn Estes 1995
Bobby Etheridge 1967, 1969
Darrell Evans 1976–83

Pete Falcone 1975
Rikkert Faneyte 1993–95
Paul Faries 1993
Bob Farley 1961
Bill Faul 1970
Mike Felder 1991–92
Jim Finigan 1958
Eddie Fisher 1959–61
Jack Fisher 1963
John Fitzgerald 1958
Tim Foli 1977
George Foster 1969–71
Alan Fowlkes 1982
Steve Frey 1994–95
Tito Fuentes 1965–67, 1969–74

Len Gabrielson 1965–66
Rich Gale 1982
Alan Gallagher 1970–73
Bob Garibaldi 1962–63, 1966, 1969
Phil Garner 1988
Scott Garrelts 1982–91
Gil Garrido 1964
Joe Gibbon 1966–69
Russ Gibson 1970–72
Paul Giel 1958
Dan Gladden 1983–86
Ruben Gomez 1958
Randy Gomez 1984
Pat Gomez 1994–95
Ed Goodson 1970–75
Goose Gossage 1989
Jim Gott 1985–87
Mark Grant 1984, 1986–87
David Green 1985
Kenny Greer 1995
Tom Griffin 1979–81
Marv Grissom 1958
Dick Groat 1967
Brad Gulden 1986
Eric Gunderson 1990–91
Cesar Gutierrez 1967, 1969

Ed Halicki 1974–80
Tom Haller 1961–67
Steve Hamilton 1971
Atlee Hammaker 1982–85, 1987–90
Bill Hands 1965
Alan Hargesheimer 1980–81
John Harrell 1969
Vic Harris 1977–78
Jim Ray Hart 1963–73
Charlie Hayes 1988–89
Fran Healy 1971–72
Dave Heaverlo 1975–77
Jim Hegan 1959
Tom Heintzelman 1978
Bob Heise 1970–71
Ken Henderson 1965–72
Dave Henderson 1987
Bob Hendley 1964–65
Bill Henry 1965–68
Chuck Hensley 1986
Ron Herbel 1963–69
Gil Heredia 1991–92
Larry Herndon 1976–81
Tommy Herr 1991
Jack Hiatt 1965–69
Bryan Hickerson 1991–94
Marc Hill 1975–80

Glenallen Hill	1995
Chuck Hiller	1961–65
Billy Hoeft	1963, 1966
Al Holland	1979–82
Chris Hook	1995
Steve Hosey	1992–93
Jim Howarth	1971–74
Randy Hundley	1964–65
Ron Hunt	1968–70
Mike Ivie	1978–81
Ray Jablonski	1958
Mike Jackson	1992–94
Skip James	1977–78
Chris James	1992
Mike Jeffcoat	1985
Don Johnson	1958
Frank Johnson	1966–71
Jerry Johnson	1970–72
Wallace Johnson	1983
Jim Johnson	1970
Erik Johnson	1993–94
Greg Johnston	1979
Gordon Jones	1958–59
Sam Jones	1959–61
Sherman Jones	1960
Tracy Jones	1989
Von Joshua	1975–76
Ed Jurak	1989
Bob Kearney	1979
Terry Kennedy	1989–91
Jim King	1958
Mike Kingery	1990–91
Dave Kingman	1971–74
Brian Kingman	1983
Willie Kirkland	1958–60
Ron Kline	1969
Bob Knepper	1976–80, 1989–90
Brad Komminsk	1990
Mike Krukow	1983–89
Harvey Kuenn	1961–65
Duane Kuiper	1982–84
Randy Kutcher	1986–87
Bob Lacey	1984
Mike LaCoss	1986–91
Mike Laga	1989–90
Tom Lampkin	1995
Rick Lancellotti	1986
Hobie Landrith	1959–61
Don Landrum	1966
Hal Lanier	1964–71
Dave LaPoint	1985
Norm Larker	1963
Pat Larkin	1983
Don Larsen	1962–64
Bill Laskey	1982–86
Gary Lavelle	1974–84
Tim Layana	1993
Rick Leach	1990
Craig Lefferts	1987–89
Mark Leiter	1995
Johnnie LeMaster	1975–85
Dick LeMay	1961–62
Jeffrey Leonard	1981–88
Mark Leonard	1990–92, 1994–95
Randy Lerch	1983–84
Darren Lewis	1991–95
Frank Linzy	1963, 1965–70
Dennis Littlejohn	1978–80
Greg Litton	1989–92
Whitey Lockman	1958
Billy Loes	1960–61
Dale Long	1960
Ken MacKenzie	1964
Garry Maddox	1972–75
Bill Madlock	1977–79
Candy Maldonado	1986–89
Kirt Manwaring	1987–95
Georges Maranda	1960
Juan Marichal	1960–73
Jim Marshall	1960–61
Dave Marshall	1968–69
Jerry Martin	1981
Renie Martin	1982–84
Dave Martinez	1993–94
Don Mason	1966–70
Roger Mason	1985–87
Gary Matthews	1972–76
Milt May	1980–83

Willie Mays	1958–72
Randy McCament	1989–90
Roger McCardell	1959
David McCarty	1995
Paul McClellan	1990–91
Mike McCormick	1958–62, 1967–70
Willie McCovey	1959–73, 1977–80
Lindy McDaniel	1966–68
Sam McDowell	1972–73
Andy McGaffigan	1982–83, 1990
Willie McGee	1991–94
Lynn McGlothen	1977–78
Don McMahon	1969–74
Jim McNamara	1992–93
Francisco Melendez	1987–88
Bob Melvin	1986–88
Tony Menendez	1994
Luis Mercedes	1993
Butch Metzger	1974
Roger Metzger	1978–80
Stu Miller	1958–62
Bruce Miller	1973–76
Eddie Milner	1987
Greg Minton	1975–87
Steve Mintz	1995
Gino Minutelli	1993
Kevin Mitchell	1987–91
Randy Moffitt	1972–81
Bill Monbouquette	1968
Willie Montanez	1975–76
John Montefusco	1974–80
Rich Monteleone	1994
Ray Monzant	1958, 1960
Bob Moore	1985
Joe Morgan	1981–82
John Morris	1972–74
Manny Mota	1962
Billy Muffett	1959
Terry Mulholland	1986, 1988–89, 1995
Fran Mullins	1984
Masanori Murakami	1964–65
Bobby Murcer	1975–76
Rich Murray	1980, 1983
Phil Nastu	1978–80
Steve Nicosia	1983–84
Bob Nieman	1962
Donell Nixon	1988–89
Matt Nokes	1985
Billy North	1979–81
Rafael Novoa	1990
Ken Oberkfell	1989
Danny O'Connell	1958–59
Billy O'Dell	1960–64
Nate Oliver	1968
Al Oliver	1984
Francisco Oliveras	1990–92
Tom O'Malley	1982–84
Randy O'Neal	1990
Steve Ontiveros	1973–76
John Orsino	1961–62
Phil Ouellette	1986
Jose Pagan	1959–65
Rick Parker	1990–91
John Patterson	1992, 1994–95
Jim Pena	1992
Marty Perez	1976
Tony Perezchica	1988, 1990–91
Jon Perlman	1987
Gaylord Perry	1962–71
Cap Peterson	1962–66
Joe Pettini	1980–83
Dave Philley	1960
Dick Phillips	1962
Mike Phillips	1973–75
J. R. Phillips	1993–95
Billy Pierce	1962–64
Joe Pignatano	1962
Skip Pitlock	1970
Joe Pittman	1984
Eddie Plank	1978–79
Mark Portugal	1994–95
John Pregenzer	1963–64
Joe Price	1987–89
Bob Priddy	1965–66
Ron Pruitt	1982
Miguel Puente	1970
Luis Quinones	1986
Dan Quisenberry	1990

Johnny Rabb	1982–84
Dave Rader	1971–76
Gary Rajsich	1985
Jeff Ransom	1981–83
Pat Rapp	1992
Frank Reberger	1970–72
Glenn Redmon	1974
Jeff Reed	1993–95
Steve Reed	1992
Jessie Reid	1987
Ken Reitz	1976
Mike Remlinger	1991
Marshall Renfroe	1959
Rick Reuschel	1987–91
Frank Riccelli	1976
Gene Richards	1984
Dave Righetti	1991–93
Ernest Riles	1988–90
George Riley	1984
Allen Ripley	1980–81
Dave Roberts	1979
Rich Robertson	1966–71
Don Robinson	1987–91
Craig Robinson	1975–76
Jeff Robinson	1984–87
Andre Rodgers	1958–60
Rick Rodriguez	1990
Ron Roenicke	1985
Kevin Rogers	1992–94
John Roper	1995
Jimmy Rosario	1971–72
Don Rose	1974
Joe Rosselli	1995
Mike Rowland	1980–81
Ken Rudolph	1974, 1977
Ray Sadecki	1966–69
Mike Sadek	1973, 1975–81
Roger Samuels	1988
Alejandro Sanchez	1984
Deion Sanders	1995
Scott Sanderson	1993
Jack Sanford	1959–65
Andres Santana	1990
Mackey Sasser	1987
Hank Sauer	1958–59
Steve Scarsone	1993–95
Dan Schatzeder	1982
Bob Schmidt	1958–61
Dick Schofield	1965–66
Bob Schroder	1965–68
Jose Segura	1991
Scott Service	1995
Bob Shaw	1964–66
Pat Sheridan	1989
Joe Shipley	1958–60
Norm Siebern	1967
Reggie Smith	1982
Billy Smith	1981
Chris Smith	1983
Duke Snider	1964
Cory Snyder	1992
Lary Sorensen	1988
Bill Sorrell	1967
Elias Sosa	1972–74
Warren Spahn	1965
Bob Speake	1958
Horace Speed	1975
Chris Speier	1971–77, 1987–89
Daryl Spencer	1958–59
Harry Spilman	1986–88
Al Stanek	1963
James Steels	1989
Jeff Stember	1980
Rennie Stennett	1980–81
Johnny Stephenson	1969–70
Steve Stone	1971–72
Joe Strain	1979–80
Darryl Strawberry	1994
Guy Sularz	1980–83
Champ Summers	1982–83
Russ Swan	1989–90
Bill Swift	1992–94
John Tamargo	1978–79
Stu Tate	1989
Don Taussig	1958
Bob Taylor	1970
Nick Testa	1958
Valmy Thomas	1958
Derrel Thomas	1975–77
Gary Thomasson	1972–77
Scot Thompson	1984–85

Robby Thompson	1986–95
Mark Thurmond	1990
Rusty Tillman	1988
Tommy Toms	1975–77
Salomon Torres	1993–95
Alex Trevino	1985
Manny Trillo	1984–85
Bob Tufts	1981
Jose Uribe	1985–92
Mike Vail	1983
Sergio Valdez	1995
Carlos Valdez	1995
William VanLandingham	1994–95
Max Venable	1979–83
Ozzie Virgil	1966
Ed Vosberg	1990
Leon Wagner	1958–59, 1969
Colin Ward	1985
Mark Wasinger	1987–88
Jim Weaver	1989
Brad Wellman	1982–86
Steve Whitaker	1970
Bill White	1958
Terry Whitfield	1977–80
Ed Whitson	1979–81
Floyd Wicker	1971
Rob Wilfong	1987
Bernie Williams	1970–72
Charlie Williams	1972–78
Frank Williams	1984–86
Matt Williams	1987–95
Jim Willoughby	1971–74
Neil Wilson	1960
Trevor Wilson	1988–93, 1995
Jim Wohlford	1980–82
Ted Wood	1991–92
Mike Woodard	1985–87
Al Worthington	1958–59
Joel Youngblood	1983–88
Dom Zanni	1958–59, 1961

Managers

Joe Altobelli	1977–79
Dusty Baker	1993–95
Dave Bristol	1979–80
Roger Craig	1985–92
Alvin Dark	1961–64
Jim Davenport	1985
Charlie Fox	1970–74
Herman Franks	1965–68
Clyde King	1969–70
Danny Ozark	1984
Bill Rigney	1958–60, 1976
Frank Robinson	1981–84
Tom Sheehan	1960
Wes Westrum	1974–75

ST. LOUIS Brown Stockings 1876–77

Joe Battin	1876–77
Joe Blong	1876–77
George Bradley	1876
John Clapp	1876–77
Art Croft	1877
Ned Cuthbert	1876
Dutch Dehlman	1876–77
Mike Dorgan	1877
Davy Force	1877
Jack Gleason	1877
Leonidas Lee	1877
Harry Little	1877
Tom Loftus	1877
Denny Mack	1876
Mike McGeary	1876–77
Ed McKenna	1877
T. E. Newell	1877
Tricky Nichols	1877

Dickey Pearce 1876–77
Lip Pike 1876

Jack Remsen 1877

Managers

Mase Graffen 1876
George McManus 1876–77

ST. LOUIS Maroons 1885–86
Moved to INDIANAPOLIS Hoosiers

Billy Alvord 1885

George Baker 1885
Al Bauers 1886
Henry Boyle 1885–86
Jim Brennan 1885
Fatty Briody 1885
Dick Burns 1885

John Cahill 1886
Ed Caskin 1885
Red Connally 1886
Sam Crane 1886

One Arm Daily 1885
Jerry Denny 1886
Tom Dolan 1885–86
Fred Dunlap 1885–86

Joe Fogarty 1885

Jack Glasscock 1885–86
Jack Gleason 1885
Frank Graves 1886

Egyptian Healy 1885–86

John Kirby 1885–86
Charlie Krehmeyer 1885

Fred Lewis 1885

George Mappes 1886
Jack McGeachy 1886
Alex McKinnon 1885–86
Trick McSorley 1885
Joe Murphy 1886
George Myers 1886

Palmer 1885
Lou Pelouze 1886
Dick Phelan 1885

Joe Quinn 1885–86

Jerry Reardon 1886
Dave Rowe 1885

Emmett Seery 1885–86
Orator Shaffer 1885
Sy Sutcliffe 1885
Charlie Sweeney 1885–86
Rooney Sweeney 1885

Managers

*Fred Dunlap 1885
*Alex McKinnon 1885
Gus Schmelz 1886

ST. LOUIS Cardinals 1892–1995
Known as Browns 1892–98
Perfectos 1899

Ody Abbott 1910
Ted Abernathy 1970
Babe Adams 1906
Sparky Adams 1930–33
Buster Adams 1943, 1945–46
Joe Adams 1902
Jim Adduci 1983
Henry Adkinson 1895
Tommie Agee 1973
Juan Agosto 1991–92
Eddie Ainsmith 1921–23
Gibson Alba 1988
Cy Alberts 1910
Grover Alexander 1926–29
Luis Alicea 1988, 1991–94
Ethan Allen 1933
Dick Allen 1970
Neil Allen 1983–85
Ron Allen 1972
Matty Alou 1971–73
Tom Alston 1954–57
Walter Alston 1936
George Altman 1963
Luis Alvarado 1974, 1976
Brant Alyea 1972
Ruben Amaro 1958
Red Ames 1915–19
Ferrell Anderson 1953
George Anderson 1918
John Anderson 1962
Craig Anderson 1961
Dwain Anderson 1972–73
Mike Anderson 1976–77
Nate Andrews 1937, 1939
John Andrews 1973
Joaquin Andujar 1981–85
Pat Ankenman 1936
John Antonelli 1944–45
Harry Arndt 1905–07
Scott Arnold 1988
Rene Arocha 1993–95
Luis Arroyo 1955
Rudy Arroyo 1971
Dennis Aust 1965–66
Benny Ayala 1977

Les Backman 1909–10
Bill Bailey 1921–22
Cory Bailey 1995
Doug Bair 1981–83, 1985
Doug Baird 1917–19
Dave Bakenhaster 1964
Bill Baker 1948–49
Steve Baker 1983
Ollie Baldwin 1908
Art Ball 1894
Jimmy Bannon 1893
Jap Barbeau 1909–10
Brian Barber 1995
George Barclay 1902–04
Ray Bare 1972, 1974
Clyde Barfoot 1922–23
Greg Bargar 1986
Mike Barlow 1975
Frank Barnes 1957–58, 1960
Skeeter Barnes 1987
Red Barrett 1945–46
Frank Barrett 1939
Shad Barry 1906–08
Dave Bartosch 1945
Richard Batchelor 1993
Frank Bates 1899
Allen Battle 1995
Ed Bauta 1960–63
John Baxter 1907
Johnny Beall 1918
Ralph Beard 1954
Jim Beauchamp 1970–71
Johnny Beazley 1941–42, 1946
Zinn Beck 1913–16
Jake Beckley 1904–07
Bill Beckmann 1942
Fred Beebe 1906–09
Ed Beecher 1897
Clarence Beers 1948
Hi Bell 1924, 1926–27, 1929–30
Les Bell 1923–27
David Bell 1995
Joe Benes 1931
Alan Benes 1995
Pug Bennett 1906–07
Vern Benson 1951–52
Sid Benton 1922
Augie Bergamo 1944–45
Jack Berly 1924
Joe Bernard 1909
Frank Bertaina 1970
Harry Berte 1903
Bob Bescher 1915–17
Frank Betcher 1910
Hal Betts 1903
Bruno Betzel 1914–18
Jim Bibby 1972–73
Lou Bierbauer 1897–98
Steve Bilko 1949–54
Dick Billings 1974
Frank Bird 1892
Ray Blades 1922–28, 1930–32
Harry Blake 1899
Sheriff Blake 1937
Coonie Blank 1909
Don Blasingame 1955–59
Johnny Blatnik 1950
Buddy Blattner 1942
Gary Blaylock 1959
Bob Blaylock 1956, 1959
Jack Bliss 1908–12
Clyde Bloomfield 1963
Charlie Boardman 1915
Joe Boever 1985–86
Sammy Bohne 1916
Dick Bokelmann 1951–53
Bill Bolden 1919
Don Bollweg 1950–51
Bobby Bonds 1980
Frank Bonner 1895
Rod Booker 1987–89
Pedro Borbon 1980
Frenchy Bordagaray 1937–38
Rick Bosetti 1977
Jim Bottomley 1922–32
Bob Bowman 1939–40
Cloyd Boyer 1949–52
Ken Boyer 1955–65
Buddy Bradford 1975
Terry Bradshaw 1995
Dave Brain 1903–05
Harvey Branch 1962
Jackie Brandt 1956
Roy Brashear 1902
Joe Bratcher 1924
Steve Braun 1981–85
Al Brazle 1943, 1946–54
Harry Brecheen 1940, 1943–52
Ted Breitenstein 1892–96, 1901
Herb Bremer 1937–39
Roger Bresnahan 1909–11
Rube Bressler 1932
Ed Bressoud 1967
Rod Brewer 1990–93
Rocky Bridges 1960
Marshall Bridges 1959–60
Grant Briggs 1892
Nellie Briles 1965–70
Ed Brinkman 1975
John Brock 1917–18
Lou Brock 1964–79
Steve Brodie 1892–93
Ernie Broglio 1959–64
Herman Bronkie 1918
Jim Brosnan 1958–59
Tony Brottem 1916, 1918
Buster Brown 1905–07
Don Brown 1915
Jimmy Brown 1937–43
Three Finger Brown 1903
Tom Brown 1895
Willard Brown 1894
Byron Browne 1969
Cal Browning 1960
Pete Browning 1894
Glenn Brummer 1981–84
Tom Brunansky 1988–90
George Brunet 1971
Tom Bruno 1978–79
Ron Bryant 1975
Johnny Bucha 1948, 1950
Jerry Buchek 1961, 1963–66
Jim Bucher 1938
Gary Buckels 1994
Dick Buckley 1892–94
Fritz Buelow 1899–1900
Nels Burbrink 1955
Al Burch 1906–07
Bob Burda 1962, 1971
Lew Burdette 1963–64
Tom Burgess 1954
Sandy Burk 1912–13
Jimmy Burke 1899, 1903–05
Leo Burke 1963
Jesse Burkett 1899–1901
Ken Burkhart 1945–48
Jack Burnett 1907
Ed Burns 1912
Farmer Burns 1901
Todd Burns 1993
Ray Burris 1986
Ellis Burton 1958, 1960
Guy Bush 1938
Ray Busse 1973
Art Butler 1914–16
John Butler 1904
Johnny Butler 1929
Bud Byerly 1943–45
Bill Byers 1904
Bobby Byrne 1907–09

Al Cabrera 1913
John Calhoun 1902
Jim Callahan 1898
Wes Callahan 1913
Ernie Camacho 1990
Harry Camnitz 1911
Llewellan Camp 1892
Billy Campbell 1905
Dave Campbell 1973
Bill Campbell 1985
Sal Campisi 1969–70
Chris Cannizzaro 1960–61
Ozzie Canseco 1992–93
Doug Capilla 1976–77
Ramon Caraballo 1995
Bernie Carbo 1972–73, 1979
Jose Cardenal 1970–71
Tex Carleton 1932–34
Steve Carlton 1965–71
Duke Carmel 1959–60, 1963
Hick Carpenter 1892
Cris Carpenter 1988–92
Chuck Carr 1992
Clay Carroll 1977
Cliff Carroll 1892
Kid Carsey 1897–98
Bob Caruthers 1892
Pete Castiglione 1953–54
Danny Cater 1975
Ted Cather 1912–14
Cesar Cedeno 1985
Orlando Cepeda 1966–68
Cliff Chambers 1951–53
John Chambers 1937
Bill Chambers 1910
Charlie Chant 1976
Chappy Charles 1908–09
Tom Cheney 1957, 1959
Cupid Childs 1899
Pete Childs 1901
Nels Chittum 1958
Bob Chlupsa 1970–71
Larry Ciaffone 1951
Al Cicotte 1961
Gino Cimoli 1959
Frank Cimorelli 1994
Ralph Citarella 1983–84
Doug Clarey 1976
Danny Clark 1927
Jim Clark 1911
Mike Clark 1952–53
Phil Clark 1958–59
Jack Clark 1985–87
Mark Clark 1991–92
Josh Clarke 1905
Stan Clarke 1990
Dad Clarkson 1893–95
Doug Clemens 1960–64
Jack Clements 1898
Verne Clemons 1919–24
Lance Clemons 1972
Donn Clendenon 1972
Reggie Cleveland 1969–73
Tony Cloninger 1972
Ed Clough 1924–26
Dick Cole 1951
John Coleman 1895
Percy Coleman 1897
Vince Coleman 1985–90
Darnell Coles 1995
Ripper Collins 1931–36
Phil Collins 1935
Dave Collins 1990
Collins 1892
Jackie Collum 1951–53, 1956
Bob Coluccio 1978
Joe Connor 1895
Roger Connor 1894–97
Tim Conroy 1986–87
Ed Conwell 1911
Scott Coolbaugh 1994
Duff Cooley 1893–96
Jimmy Cooney 1924–25
Mort Cooper 1938–45
Walker Cooper 1940–45, 1956–57

Scott Cooper	1995
Mays Copeland	1935
Joe Corbett	1904
Roy Corhan	1916
Rheal Cormier	1991–94
Pat Corrales	1966
Frank Corridon	1910
Jim Cosman	1966–67
John Costello	1988–90
Tom Coulter	1969
John Coveney	1903
Bill Cox	1936
Danny Cox	1983–88
Estel Crabtree	1933, 1941
Roger Craig	1964
Doc Crandall	1913
Pat Crawford	1933–34
Forrest Crawford	1906–07
Glenn Crawford	1945
Willie Crawford	1976
Doug Creek	1995
Jack Creel	1945
Bernie Creger	1947
Creepy Crespi	1938–42
Lou Criger	1899–1900
Jack Crimian	1951–52
Tripp Cromer	1993–95
Jack Crooks	1892–93, 1898
Ed Crosby	1970, 1972–73
Jeff Cross	1942, 1946–47
Lave Cross	1898–1900
Monte Cross	1896–97
Bill Crouch	1941, 1945
George Crowe	1959–60
Walt Cruise	1914, 1916–19
Gene Crumling	1945
Jose Cruz	1970–74
Tommy Cruz	1973
Hector Cruz	1973, 1975–77
Mike Cuellar	1964
George Culver	1970
John Cumberland	1972
Joe Cunningham	1954, 1956–61
Ray Cunningham	1931–32
Nig Cuppy	1899
Clarence Currie	1902–03
Murphy Currie	1916
John Curtis	1974–76
John D'Acquisto	1977
Gene Dale	1911–12
Jack Damaska	1963
Pete Daniels	1898
Rolla Daringer	1914–15
Alvin Dark	1956–58
Vic Davalillo	1969–70
Jerry DaVanon	1969–70, 1974, 1977
Curt Davis	1938–40
Kiddo Davis	1934
Jim Davis	1957
Ron Davis	1968
Spud Davis	1928, 1934–36
Willie Davis	1975
Bill Dawley	1987
Pea Ridge Day	1924–25
Boots Day	1969
Ken Dayley	1984–90
Cot Deal	1950, 1954
Dizzy Dean	1930, 1932–37
Paul Dean	1934–39
Doug DeCinces	1987
George Decker	1898
Tony DeFate	1917
Rube DeGroff	1905–06
Ivan DeJesus	1985
Bobby Del Greco	1956
Joe Delahanty	1907–09
Bill DeLancey	1932, 1934–35, 1940
Art Delaney	1924
Luis DeLeon	1981
Jose DeLeon	1988–92
Eddie Delker	1929, 1931–32
Wheezer Dell	1912
Rich DeLucia	1995
Frank Demaree	1943
Lee DeMontreville	1903
Don Dennis	1965–66
John Denny	1974–79
Paul Derringer	1931–33
Joe DeSa	1980
Leo Dickerman	1924–25
Murry Dickson	1939–40, 1942–43,
	1946–48, 1956–57
Chuck Diering	1947–51
Larry Dierker	1977
Pat Dillard	1900
Pickles Dillhoefer	1919–21
Mike Dimmel	1979
Frank DiPino	1989–90, 1992
Dutch Distel	1918
Steve Dixon	1993–94
Bill Doak	1913–24, 1929
George Dockins	1945
Cozy Dolan	1914–15
John Dolan	1893
She Donahue	1904
Red Donahue	1895–97
Mike Donlin	1899–1900
Jim Donnelly	1898
Blix Donnelly	1944–46
Patsy Donovan	1900–03
Klondike Douglass	1896–97
Taylor Douthit	1923–31
Tommy Dowd	1893–98
Dave Dowling	1964
Carl Doyle	1940
Jeff Doyle	1983
Moe Drabowsky	1971–72
Lee Dressen	1914
Rob Dressler	1978
Dan Driessen	1987
Carl Druhot	1906–07
Bob Duliba	1959–60, 1962
Taylor Duncan	1977
Wiley Dunham	1902
Grant Dunlap	1953
Jack Dunleavy	1903–05
Joe Durham	1959
Leon Durham	1980, 1989
Don Durham	1972
Leo Durocher	1933–37
Erv Dusak	1941–42, 1946–48,
	1950–51
Frank Dwyer	1892
Jim Dwyer	1973–75, 1977–78
Eddie Dyer	1922–27
Bill Earley	1986
George Earnshaw	1936
John Easton	1892
Rawly Eastwick	1977
Al Eckert	1935
Joe Edelen	1981
Johnny Edwards	1968
Wish Egan	1905–06
Red Ehret	1895
Harry Elliott	1953, 1955
Rube Ellis	1909–12
Jim Ellis	1969
Bones Ely	1893–95
Bill Endicott	1946
Del Ennis	1957–58
Charlie Enwright	1909
Hal Epps	1938, 1940
Eddie Erautt	1953
Duke Esper	1897–98
Chuck Essegian	1959
Roy Evans	1897
Steve Evans	1909–13
Bryan Eversgerd	1994
Bob Ewing	1912
Reuben Ewing	1921
Fred Fagin	1895
Ron Fairly	1975–76
Pete Falcone	1976–78
George Fallon	1943–45
Harry Fanok	1963–64
Doc Farrell	1930
John Farrell	1902–05
Jack Faszholz	1953
Bobby Fenwick	1973
Joe Ferguson	1976
Don Ferrarese	1962
Bien Figueroa	1992
Mike Fiore	1972
Sam Fishburn	1919
Chauncey Fisher	1901
Eddie Fisher	1973
Showboat Fisher	1930
Bob Fisher	1918–19
Mike Fitzgerald	1988
Max Flack	1922–25
Tom Flanigan	1958
Curt Flood	1958–69
Tim Flood	1899
Ben Flowers	1955–56
Jake Flowers	1923, 1926, 1931–32
Rich Folkers	1972–74
Hod Ford	1932
Curt Ford	1985–88
Bob Forsch	1974–88
Tony Fossas	1995
Alan Foster	1973–74
Jack Fournier	1920–22
Jesse Fowler	1924
Earl Francis	1965
Tito Francona	1965–66
Charlie Frank	1893–94
Fred Frankhouse	1927–30
Herman Franks	1939
John Frascatore	1994–95
Willie Fraser	1991
Joe Frazier	1954–56
George Frazier	1978–80
Roger Freed	1977–79
Gene Freese	1958
Howard Freigau	1922–25
Benny Frey	1932
Frankie Frisch	1927–36
Danny Frisella	1976
Art Fromme	1906–08
John Fulgham	1979–80
Chick Fullis	1934, 1936
Les Fusselman	1952–53
Phil Gagliano	1963–70
Del Gainer	1922
Fred Gaiser	1908
Andres Galarraga	1992
Bad News Galloway	1912
Pud Galvin	1892
Joe Gannon	1898
Joe Garagiola	1946–51
Glenn Gardner	1945
Art Garibaldi	1936
Mike Garman	1974–75
Debs Garms	1943–45
Wayne Garrett	1978
Rich Gedman	1991–92
Charley Gelbert	1929–32, 1935–36
Frank Genins	1892
Al Gettel	1955
Charlie Getzien	1892
Rube Geyer	1910–13
Ray Giannelli	1995
Bob Gibson	1959–75
Billy Gilbert	1908–09
George Gilham	1920
Frank Gilhooley	1911–12
Bernard Gilkey	1990–95
Carden Gillenwater	1940
George Gillpatrick	1898
Hal Gilson	1968
Dave Giusti	1969
Jack Glasscock	1892–93
Tommy Glaviano	1949–52
Kid Gleason	1892–94
Bob Glenn	1920
Harry Glenn	1915
John Glenn	1960
Danny Godby	1974
Roy Golden	1910–11
Hal Goldsmith	1929
Mike Gonzalez	1915–18, 1924–25,
	1931–32
Julio Gonzalez	1981–82
Bill Goodenough	1893
Marv Goodwin	1917, 1919–22
Hank Gornicki	1941
Julio Gotay	1960–62
Al Grabowski	1929–30
Mike Grady	1897, 1904–06
Alex Grammas	1954–56, 1959–62
Wayne Granger	1968, 1973
Mudcat Grant	1969
Mark Grater	1991
Dick Gray	1959–60
Bill Greason	1954
Gene Green	1957–59
David Green	1981–84, 1987
Bill Greif	1976
Tim Griesenbeck	1920
Tom Grieve	1979
Sandy Griffin	1893
Bob Grim	1960
Burleigh Grimes	1930–31, 1933–34
John Grimes	1897
Charlie Grimm	1918
Dan Griner	1912–16
Marv Grissom	1959
Dick Groat	1963–65
Johnny Grodzicki	1941, 1946–47
Joe Grzenda	1972
Pedro Guerrero	1988–92
Mario Guerrero	1975
Lee Guetterman	1993
Harry Gumbert	1941–44
Joe Gunson	1893
Don Gutteridge	1936–40
Santiago Guzman	1969–72
Bob Habenicht	1951
John Habyan	1994–95
Jim Hackett	1902–03
Harvey Haddix	1952–56
Chick Hafey	1924–31
Casey Hageman	1914
Kevin Hagen	1983–84
Joe Hague	1968–72
Fred Hahn	1952
Don Hahn	1975
Hal Haid	1928–30
Ed Haigh	1892
Jesse Haines	1920–37
Charley Hall	1916
Russ Hall	1898
Bill Hallahan	1925–26, 1929–36
Bill Hallman	1897
Dave Hamilton	1978
Fred Haney	1929
Larry Haney	1973
Dick Harley	1897–98
Chuck Harmon	1956–57
Bob Harmon	1909–13
Jack Harper	1900–01
George Harper	1928
Brian Harper	1985
Ray Harrell	1935, 1937–38
Vic Harris	1976
Bill Hart	1896–97
Chuck Hartenstein	1970
Fred Hartman	1897, 1902
Andy Hassler	1984–85
Grady Hatton	1956
Arnold Hauser	1910–13
Bill Hawke	1892–93
Pink Hawley	1892–94
Doc Hazleton	1902
Francis Healy	1934
Bunny Hearn	1910–11
Jim Hearn	1947–50
Mike Heath	1986
Cliff Heathcote	1918–22
Jack Heidemann	1974
Emmett Heidrick	1899–1901
Don Heinkel	1989
Tom Heintzelman	1973–74
Clarence Heise	1934
Bob Heise	1974
Scott Hemond	1995
Charlie Hemphill	1899
Solly Hemus	1949–55
Harvey Hendrick	1932
George Hendrick	1978–84
Tom Henke	1995
Roy Henshaw	1938
Keith Hernandez	1974–83
Larry Herndon	1974
Tommy Herr	1979–88
Neal Hertweck	1952
Ed Heusser	1935–36
Mike Heydon	1901
Jim Hickman	1974
Jim Hicks	1969
Irv Higginbotham	1906, 1908–09
Dennis Higgins	1971–72
Thomas Higgins	1909–10
Andy High	1928–31
Palmer Hildebrand	1913
Tom Hilgendorf	1969–70
Carmen Hill	1929–30
Hugh Hill	1904
Marc Hill	1973–74
Ken Hill	1988–91, 1995
Howard Hilton	1990
Jack Himes	1905–06
Bruce Hitt	1917
Glen Hobbie	1964
Ed Hock	1920
Art Hoelskoetter	1905–08
Joe Hoerner	1966–69
Marty Hogan	1894–95
Mul Holland	1929
Ed Holly	1906–07
Wattie Holm	1924–29, 1932

Ducky Holmes	1906
Ducky Holmes	1898
Don Hood	1980
Sis Hopkins	1907
Johnny Hopp	1939–45
Bill Hopper	1913–14
Bob Horner	1988
Rogers Hornsby	1915–26, 1933
Oscar Horstmann	1917–19
Ricky Horton	1984–87, 1989–90
Paul Householder	1984
John Houseman	1897
Earl Howard	1918
Doug Howard	1975
Art Howe	1984–85
Roland Howell	1912
Bill Howerton	1949–51
Al Hrabosky	1970–77
Jimmy Hudgens	1923
Rex Hudler	1990–92
Charles Hudson	1972
Frank Huelsman	1897
Miller Huggins	1910–15
Dick Hughes	1966–68
Tom Hughes	1959
Terry Hughes	1973
Jim Hughey	1898, 1900
Tim Hulett	1995
Rudy Hulswitt	1909–10
Bob Humphreys	1963–64
Ben Hunt	1913
Joel Hunt	1931–32
Ron Hunt	1974
Randy Hunt	1985
Herb Hunter	1921
Steve Huntz	1967, 1969
Walter Huntzinger	1926
Clint Hurdle	1986
Ira Hutchinson	1940–41
Bill Hutchinson	1897
Ham Hyatt	1915
Pat Hynes	1903
Dane Iorg	1977–84
Ray Jablonski	1953–54, 1959
Al Jackson	1966–67
Larry Jackson	1955–62
Mike Jackson	1971
Danny Jackson	1995
Tony Jacobs	1955
Elmer Jacobs	1919–20
Bert James	1909
Charlie James	1960–64
Hal Janvrin	1919–21
Hi Jasper	1916
Larry Jaster	1965–68
Julian Javier	1960–71
Hal Jeffcoat	1959
Gregg Jefferies	1993–94
Adam Johnson	1918
Alex Johnson	1966–67
Darrell Johnson	1960
Ken Johnson	1947–50
Bob Johnson	1969
Si Johnson	1936–38
Syl Johnson	1926–33
Billy Johnson	1951–53
Jerry Johnson	1970
Lance Johnson	1987
Cowboy Jones	1899–1901
Gordon Jones	1954–56
Howie Jones	1921
Red Jones	1940
Sam Jones	1957–58, 1963
Nippy Jones	1946–51
Tim Jones	1988–93
Bubber Jonnard	1929
Brian Jordan	1992–95
Mike Jorgensen	1984–85
Felix Jose	1990–92
Lyle Judy	1935
Al Jurisich	1944–45
Skip Jutze	1972
Jim Kaat	1980–83
Ed Karger	1906–08
Eddie Kasko	1957–58
Ray Katt	1956, 1958–59
Tony Kaufmann	1927–28, 1930–31, 1935
Marty Kavanagh	1918
Eddie Kazak	1948–52
Bob Keely	1944–45

Vic Keen	1926–27
Jeff Keener	1982–83
Bill Keister	1900
John Kelleher	1912
Mick Kelleher	1972–73, 1975
Alex Kellner	1959
Win Kellum	1905
John Kelly	1907
Bill Kelly	1910
Jim Kennedy	1970
Terry Kennedy	1978–80
Matt Keough	1985
Kurt Kepshire	1984–86
George Kernek	1965–66
Don Kessinger	1976–77
Paul Kilgus	1993
Newt Kimball	1940
Hal Kime	1920
Wally Kimmick	1919
Ellis Kinder	1956
Charlie King	1959
Jim King	1957
Lynn King	1935–36, 1939
Walt Kinlock	1895
Tom Kinslow	1898
Matt Kinzer	1989
Mike Kircher	1920–21
Bill Kissinger	1895–97
Lou Klein	1943, 1945–46, 1949
Nub Kleinke	1935, 1937
Ron Kline	1960
Rudy Kling	1902
Clyde Klutz	1946
Alan Knicely	1986
Jack Knight	1922
Mike Knode	1920
Darold Knowles	1979–80
Will Koenigsmark	1919
Gary Kolb	1960, 1962–63
Ed Konetchy	1907–13
Jim Konstanty	1956
George Kopshaw	1923
Ernie Koy	1940–41
Lew Krausse	1973
Kurt Krieger	1949, 1951
Howie Krist	1937–38, 1941–43, 1946
Otto Krueger	1900–02
Ted Kubiak	1971
Willie Kuehne	1892
Ryan Kurosaki	1975
Whitey Kurowski	1941–49
Bob Kuzava	1957
Mike Laga	1986–88
Lerrin LaGrow	1976
Jeff Lahti	1982–86
Eddie Lake	1939–41
Steve Lake	1986–88
Bud Lally	1897
Jack Lamabe	1967
Fred Lamline	1915
Les Lancaster	1993
Hobie Landrith	1957–58
Don Landrum	1960–62
Tito Landrum	1980–87
Don Lang	1948
Max Lanier	1938–46, 1949–51
Ray Lankford	1990–95
Paul LaPalme	1955–56
Dave LaPoint	1981–84, 1987
Ralph LaPointe	1948
Bob Larmore	1918
Lyn Lary	1939
Don Lassetter	1957
Mike LaValliere	1985–86
Doc Lavan	1919–24
Tom Lawless	1985–88
Brooks Lawrence	1954–55
Tom Leahy	1905
Leron Lee	1969–71
Manny Lee	1995
Jim Lentine	1978–80
Leonard	1892
Barry Lersch	1974
Roy Leslie	1919
Dan Lewandowski	1951
Johnny Lewis	1964
Bill Lewis	1933
Sixto Lezcano	1981
Don Liddle	1956
Gene Lillard	1940
Bob Lillis	1961
Johnny Lindell	1950

Jim Lindeman	1986–89
Jim Lindsey	1929–34
Royce Lint	1954
Larry Lintz	1975
Frank Linzy	1970–71
Mark Littell	1978–82
Jeff Little	1980
Dick Littlefield	1956
John Littlefield	1980
Carlisle Littlejohn	1927–28
Danny Litwhiler	1943–44
Paddy Livingston	1917
Bobby Locke	1962
Whitey Lockman	1956
Bill Lohrman	1942
Jeoff Long	1964
Tommy Long	1915–17
Art Lopatka	1945
Aurelio Lopez	1978
Joe Lotz	1916
Lynn Lovenguth	1957
John Lovett	1903
Grover Lowdermilk	1909, 1911
Lou Lowdermilk	1911–12
Peanuts Lowrey	1950–54
Con Lucid	1897
Bill Ludwig	1908
Memo Luna	1954
Ernie Lush	1910
Johnny Lush	1907–10
Denny Lyons	1895
George Lyons	1920
Hersh Lyons	1941
Bill Lyons	1983–84
Bob Mabe	1958
John Mabry	1994–95
Ken MacKenzie	1963
Johnny Mackinson	1955
Lonnie Maclin	1993
Max Macon	1938
Lee Magee	1911–14
Bill Magee	1901
Sal Maglie	1958
Joe Magrane	1987–90, 1992–93
Art Mahaffey	1966
Mike Mahoney	1898
Duster Mails	1925–26
Jim Mallory	1945
Gus Mancuso	1928, 1930–32, 1941–42
Les Mann	1921–23
Fred Manrique	1986
Rabbit Maranville	1927–28
Walt Marbet	1913
Marty Marion	1940–50
Roger Maris	1967–68
Fred Marolewski	1953
Charlie Marshall	1941
Joe Marshall	1906
Doc Marshall	1906–08
Freddie Martin	1946, 1949–50
Pepper Martin	1928, 1931–40, 1944
Morrie Martin	1957–58
Stu Martin	1936–40
John Martin	1980–83
Marty Martinez	1972
Silvio Martinez	1978–81
Teddy Martinez	1975
Ernie Mason	1894
Greg Mathews	1986–88, 1990
T. J. Mathews	1995
Wally Mattick	1918
Gene Mauch	1952
Harry Maupin	1898
Dal Maxvill	1962–72
Jakie May	1917–21
Jack McAdams	1911
Ike McAuley	1917
George McBride	1905–06
Pete McBride	1899
Bake McBride	1973–77
Joe McCarthy	1906
Lew McCarty	1920
Tim McCarver	1959–61, 1963–69, 1973–74
Pat McCauley	1893
Bob McClure	1991–92
Billy McCool	1970
Jim McCormick	1892
Harry McCurdy	1922–23
Lindy McDaniel	1955–62
Von McDaniel	1957–58
Mickey McDermott	1961

Mike McDermott	1897
Sandy McDougal	1905
John McDougal	1895–96
Will McEnaney	1979
Guy McFadden	1895
Chappie McFarland	1902–06
Ed McFarland	1896–97
Dan McGann	1900–01
Bill McGee	1935–41
Willie McGee	1982–90
Dan McGeehan	1911
Jim McGinley	1904–05
Lynn McGlothen	1974–76
Stoney McGlynn	1906–08
John McGraw	1900
Bob McGraw	1927
Terry McGriff	1994
Mark McGrillis	1892
Austin McHenry	1918–22
Otto McIvor	1911
Ed McKean	1899
Ralph McLaurin	1908
Larry McLean	1904, 1913
Jerry McNertney	1971–72
Larry McWilliams	1988
Lee Meadows	1915–19
Joe Medwick	1932–40, 1947–48
Sam Mejias	1976
Luis Melendez	1970–76
Steve Melter	1909
Ted Menze	1918
John Mercer	1912
Lloyd Merritt	1957
Sam Mertes	1906
Steve Mesner	1941
Butch Metzger	1977
Ed Mickelson	1950
Larry Miggins	1952
Pete Mikkelsen	1968
Eddie Miksis	1957
Dusty Miller	1899
Charlie Miller	1913–14
Eddie Miller	1950
Elmer Miller	1912
Kohly Miller	1892
Doggie Miller	1894–95
Dots Miller	1914–17, 1919
Bob Miller	1957, 1959–61
Stu Miller	1952–54, 1956
Buster Mills	1934
Larry Milton	1903
Minnie Minoso	1962
Clarence Mitchell	1928–30
Johnny Mize	1936–41
Vinegar Bend Mizell	1952–53, 1956–60
Herb Moford	1955
Fritz Mollwitz	1919
Wally Moon	1954–58
Jim Mooney	1933–34
Gene Moore	1933–34
Whitey Moore	1942
Randy Moore	1937
Terry Moore	1935–42, 1946–48
Donnie Moore	1980
Tommy Moore	1975
Jerry Morales	1978
Charley Moran	1903, 1908
Bill Moran	1892
Forrest More	1909
Eddie Morgan	1936
Bobby Morgan	1956
Mike Morgan	1995
Gene Moriarity	1892
Walter Morris	1908
John Morris	1986–90
Hap Morse	1911
Walt Moryn	1960–61
Mike Mowrey	1909–13
Jamie Moyer	1991
Heinie Mueller	1920–26
Billy Muffett	1957–58
Jerry Mumphrey	1974–79
George Munger	1943–44, 1946–52
Les Munns	1936
Steve Mura	1982
Simmy Murch	1904–05
Tim Murchison	1917
Wilbur Murdoch	1908
Ed Murphy	1901–03
Howard Murphy	1909
John Murphy	1902
Mike Murphy	1912
Morg Murphy	1896–97

Tom Murphy	1973
Rob Murphy	1993–94
Red Murray	1906–08
Stan Musial	1941–44, 1946–63
Bert Myers	1896
Hy Myers	1923–24
Lynn Myers	1938–39
Mike Nagy	1973
Sam Nahem	1941
Sam Narron	1935, 1942–43
Ken Nash	1914
Mike Naymick	1944
Rocky Nelson	1949–51, 1956
Mel Nelson	1960, 1968–69
Art Nichols	1901–03
Charlie Niebergall	1921, 1923–24
Tom Niedenfuer	1990
Dick Niehaus	1913–15
Bert Niehoff	1918
Bob Nieman	1960–61
Tom Nieto	1984–85
Tom Niland	1896
Pete Noonan	1906–07
Irv Noren	1957–59
Fred Norman	1970–71
Lou North	1917, 1920–24
Ron Northey	1947–49
Joe Nossek	1969
Howie Nunn	1959
Rich Nye	1970
Rebel Oakes	1910–13
Ken Oberkfell	1977–84
Johnny O'Brien	1958
Dan O'Brien	1978–79
Jack O'Connor	1899–1900
Paddy O'Connor	1914
Ken O'Dea	1942–46
Bob O'Farrell	1925–28, 1933, 1935
Brusie Ogrodowski	1936–37
Tom O'Hara	1906–07
Bill O'Hara	1910
Charley O'Leary	1913
Jose Oliva	1995
Ed Olivares	1960–61
Omar Olivares	1990–94
Gene Oliver	1959, 1961–63
Diomedes Olivo	1963
Al Olmsted	1980
Randy O'Neal	1987–88
Dennie O'Neill	1893
Jack O'Neill	1902–03
Mike O'Neill	1901–04
Jose Oquendo	1986–95
Joe Orengo	1939–40
Patsy O'Rourke	1908
Tim O'Rourke	1894
Ernie Orsatti	1927–35
Donovan Osborne	1992–93, 1995
Claude Osteen	1974
Champ Osteen	1908–09
Joe Otten	1895
Jim Otten	1980–81
Mickey Owen	1937–40
Rick Ownbey	1984, 1986
Gene Packard	1917–18
Dick Padden	1901
Don Padgett	1937–41
Tom Pagnozzi	1987–95
Phil Paine	1958
Vicente Palacios	1994–95
Lowell Palmer	1972
Al Papai	1948, 1950
Stan Papi	1974
Erik Pappas	1993–94
Freddy Parent	1899
Kelly Paris	1982
Roy Parker	1919
Harry Parker	1970–71, 1975
Roy Parmelee	1936
Jeff Parrett	1995
Tom Parrott	1896
Stan Partenheimer	1945
Daryl Patterson	1971
Harry Patton	1910
Gene Paulette	1917–19
Gil Paulsen	1925
George Paynter	1894
George Pearce	1917
Frank Pears	1893
Alex Pearson	1902

Homer Peel	1927, 1930
Charlie Peete	1956
Heinie Peitz	1892–95, 1913
Joe Peitz	1894
Orlando Pena	1973–74
Tony Pena	1987–89
Geronimo Pena	1990–95
Terry Pendleton	1984–90
Ray Pepper	1932–33
Hub Perdue	1914–15
Mike Perez	1990–94
Pol Perritt	1912–14
Gerald Perry	1991–95
Pat Perry	1985–87
Bill Pertica	1921–23
Steve Peters	1987–88
Mark Petkovsek	1995
Jeff Pfeffer	1921–24
Ed Phelps	1909–10
Mike Phillips	1977–80
Bill Phyle	1906
Ron Piche	1966
Charlie Pickett	1910
George Pinckney	1892
Vada Pinson	1969
Cotton Pippen	1936
Tim Plodinec	1972
Tom Poholsky	1950–51, 1954–56
Howie Pollet	1941–43, 1946–51
Bill Popp	1902
J. W. Porter	1959
Darrell Porter	1981–85
Nels Potter	1936
Mike Potter	1976–77
Jack Powell	1899–1901
Ted Power	1989
Joe Presko	1951–54
Mike Proly	1976
George Puccinelli	1930, 1932
Bob Purkey	1965
Ambrose Puttmann	1906
Finners Quinlan	1913
Joe Quinn	1893–96, 1898, 1900
Jamie Quirk	1983
Dan Quisenberry	1988–89
Roy Radebaugh	1911
Dave Rader	1977
Ken Raffensberger	1939
Gary Rajsich	1984
John Raleigh	1909–10
Milt Ramirez	1970–71
Mike Ramsey	1978, 1980–84
Dick Rand	1953, 1955
Vic Raschi	1954–55
Eric Rasmussen	1975–78, 1982–83
Tommy Raub	1906
Floyd Rayford	1983
Bugs Raymond	1907–08
Art Rebel	1945
Phil Redding	1912–13
Ron Reed	1975
Bill Reeder	1949
Jimmy Reese	1932
Tom Reilly	1908–09
Art Reinhart	1919, 1925–28
Jack Reis	1911
Ken Reitz	1972–75, 1977–80
Bob Repass	1939
Rip Repulski	1953–56
Jerry Reuss	1969–71
Bob Reynolds	1971
Ken Reynolds	1975
Flint Rhem	1924–28, 1930–32, 1934, 1936
Bob Rhoads	1903
Charlie Rhodes	1906, 1908–09
Dennis Ribant	1969
Del Rice	1945–55, 1960
Hal Rice	1948–52
Lee Richard	1976
Gordie Richardson	1964
Bill Richardson	1901
Pete Richert	1974
Don Richmond	1951
Dave Ricketts	1963, 1965, 1967–69
Dick Ricketts	1959
John Ricks	1894
Elmer Rieger	1910
Joe Riggert	1914
Andy Rincon	1980–82
Jimmy Ring	1927

Tink Riviere	1921
Skipper Roberts	1913
Hank Robinson	1914–15
Wilbert Robinson	1900
Jack Roche	1914–15, 1917
Rich Rodriguez	1994–95
Preacher Roe	1938
Wally Roettger	1927–29, 1931
Cookie Rojas	1970
Stan Rojek	1951
Ray Rolling	1912
Johnny Romano	1967
John Romonosky	1953
Marc Ronan	1993
Gene Roof	1981–83
Jorge Roque	1970–72
Jack Rothrock	1934–35
Stan Royer	1991–94
Dave Rucker	1983–84
Ken Rudolph	1975–76
Jack Russell	1940
Paul Russell	1894
John Ryan	1895
John Ryan	1901–03
Mike Ryba	1935–38
Chris Sabo	1995
Ray Sadecki	1960–66, 1975
Bob Sadowski	1960
Mark Salas	1984
Slim Sallee	1908–16
Ike Samuls	1895
Orlando Sanchez	1981–83
Ray Sanders	1942–45
War Sanders	1903–04
Rafael Santana	1983
Al Santorini	1971–73
Bill Sarni	1951–52, 1954–56
Ed Sauer	1949
Hank Sauer	1956
Ted Savage	1965–66
Carl Sawatski	1960–63
Jimmie Schaffer	1961–62
Bobby Schang	1927
Bob Scheffing	1951
Carl Scheib	1954
Bill Schindler	1920
Freddy Schmidt	1944, 1946–47
Walter Schmidt	1925
Willard Schmidt	1952–53, 1955–57
Red Schoendienst	1945–56, 1961–62
Dick Schofield	1953–58, 1968, 1971
Ossee Schreckengost	1899
Pop Schriver	1901
Heinie Schuble	1927, 1936
Johnny Schulte	1927
Barney Schultz	1955, 1963–65
Joe Schultz	1919–24
Buddy Schultz	1977–79
Walt Schulz	1920
Ferdie Schupp	1919–21
Lou Scoffic	1936
George Scott	1920
Tony Scott	1977–81
Kim Seaman	1979–80
Diego Segui	1972–73
Epp Sell	1922–23
Carey Selph	1929
Walter Sessi	1941
Jimmy Sexton	1983
Mike Shannon	1962–70
Wally Shannon	1959–60
Spike Shannon	1904–06
Bobby Shantz	1962–64
Al Shaw	1907–09
Don Shaw	1971–72
Danny Shay	1904–05
Gerry Shea	1905
Danny Sheaffer	1995
Jimmy Sheckard	1913
Biff Sheehan	1895–96
Ray Shepardson	1924
Bill Sherdel	1918–30, 1932
Tim Sherrill	1990–91
Charlie Shields	1907
Vince Shields	1924
Ralph Shinners	1925
Bob Shirley	1981
Burt Shotton	1919–22
Clyde Shoun	1938–42
Frank Shugart	1893–94
Dick Siebert	1937
Sonny Siebert	1974

Curt Simmons	1960–66
Ted Simmons	1968–80
Dick Simpson	1968
Dick Sisler	1946–47, 1952–53
Ted Sizemore	1971–75
Bob Skinner	1964–65
Gordon Slade	1933
Jack Slattery	1906
Enos Slaughter	1938–42, 1946–53
Bobby Gene Smith	1957–59, 1962
Charley Smith	1966
Earl Smith	1928–30
Frank Smith	1955
Fred Smith	1917
Germany Smith	1898
Hal Smith	1956–61
Jack Smith	1915–25
Jud Smith	1893
Reggie Smith	1974–76
Bob Smith	1957
Tom Smith	1898
Wally Smith	1911–12
Bill Smith	1958–59
Keith Smith	1979–80
Ozzie Smith	1982–95
Lonnie Smith	1982–85
Lee Smith	1990–93
Bryn Smith	1990–92
Willie Smith	1994
Homer Smoot	1902–06
Red Smyth	1917–18
Frank Snyder	1912–19, 1927
Ray Soff	1986–87
Eddie Solomon	1976
Lary Sorensen	1981
Elias Sosa	1975
Allen Sothoron	1924–26
Billy Southworth	1926–27
Chris Speier	1984
Daryl Spencer	1960–61
Ed Spiezio	1965–68
Scipio Spinks	1972–73
Ed Sprague	1973
Jack Spring	1964
Joe Sprinz	1933
Tuck Stainback	1938
Gerry Staley	1947–54
Harry Staley	1895
Tracy Stallard	1965–66
Virgil Stallcup	1952
Pete Standridge	1911
Harry Stanton	1900
Ray Starr	1932
Bob Steele	1916–17
Bill Steele	1910–14
Bill Stein	1972–73
Jake Stenzel	1898–99
Ray Stephens	1990–91
Bobby Stephenson	1955
Stuffy Stewart	1916–17
Bob Stinson	1971
Chuck Stobbs	1958
Milt Stock	1919–23
Dean Stone	1959
Tige Stone	1923
Alan Storke	1909
Allyn Stout	1931–33
Joe Stripp	1938
Johnny Stuart	1922–25
John Stuper	1982–84
Willie Sudhoff	1897–1901
Joe Sugden	1898
Harry Sullivan	1909
Joe Sullivan	1896
Suter Sullivan	1898
Kid Summers	1893
Tom Sunkel	1937, 1939
Max Surkont	1956
Rick Sutcliffe	1994
Gary Sutherland	1978
Bruce Sutter	1981–84
Jack Sutthoff	1899
Johnny Sutton	1977
Mark Sweeney	1995
Charlie Swindells	1904
Steve Swisher	1978–80
Bob Sykes	1979–81
John Tamargo	1976–78
Lee Tate	1958–59
Don Taussig	1961
Rube Taylor	1903
Joe Taylor	1958

Jack Taylor	1898
Jack Taylor	1904–06
Ron Taylor	1963–65
Carl Taylor	1970
Chuck Taylor	1969–71
Bud Teachout	1932
Patsy Tebeau	1899
Garry Templeton	1976–81
Gene Tenace	1981–82
Greg Terlecky	1975
Scott Terry	1987–91
Dick Terwilliger	1932
Bob Tewksbury	1989–94
Moe Thacker	1963
Tommy Thevenow	1924–28
Jake Thielman	1905–06
Tom Thomas	1899–1900
Roy Thomas	1978–80
Gus Thompson	1906
Mike Thompson	1973–74
Milt Thompson	1989–92
John Thornton	1892
Bobby Tiefenauer	1952, 1955, 1961
Bud Tinning	1935
Bobby Tolan	1965–68
Fred Toney	1923
Specs Toporcer	1921–28
Joe Torre	1969–74
Mike Torrez	1967–71
Paul Toth	1962
Harry Trekell	1913
Coaker Triplett	1941–43
Bill Trotter	1944
Tommy Tucker	1898
John Tudor	1985–88, 1990
Oscar Tuero	1918–20
Lee Tunnell	1987
Tuck Turner	1896–98
Old Hoss Twineham	1893–94
Mike Tyson	1972–79
Bob Uecker	1964–65
Tom Underwood	1977
Jack Urban	1959
Tom Urbani	1993–95
Jose Uribe	1984
John Urrea	1977–80
Lou Ury	1903
Benny Valenzuela	1958
Bill Van Dyke	1892
Jay Van Noy	1951
Andy Van Slyke	1983–86
Dazzy Vance	1933–34
Emil Verban	1944–45
Johnny Vergez	1936
Ernie Vick	1922, 1924–26
Hector Villanueva	1993
Bob Vines	1924
Bill Virdon	1955–56
Dave Von Ohlen	1983–84
Bill Voss	1972
Pete Vuckovich	1978–80
Ben Wade	1954
Leon Wagner	1960
Harry Walker	1940–43, 1946–47, 1950–51
Roy Walker	1921–22
Joe Walker	1923
Bill Walker	1933–36
Duane Walker	1988
Tom Walker	1976
Bobby Wallace	1899–1901, 1917–18
Mike Wallace	1975–76
Tye Waller	1980
Denny Walling	1988–90
Dick Ward	1935
Cy Warmoth	1916
Lon Warneke	1937–42
Jack Warner	1905
Carl Warwick	1961–62, 1964–65
Bill Warwick	1925–26
Ray Washburn	1961–69
Gary Waslewski	1969
Steve Waterbury	1976
George Watkins	1930–33
Milt Watson	1916–17
Allen Watson	1993–95
Art Weaver	1902–03
Skeeter Webb	1932
Herm Wehmeier	1956–58
Bob Weiland	1937–40
Perry Werden	1892–93
Bill Werle	1952
Wally Westlake	1951–52
Gus Weyhing	1900
Dick Wheeler	1918
Pete Whisenant	1955
Lew Whistler	1893
Ade White	1937
Ernie White	1940–43
Hal White	1953–54
Bill White	1959–65, 1969
Jerry White	1986
Burgess Whitehead	1933–35
Mark Whiten	1993–94
Fred Whitfield	1962
Possum Whitted	1912–14
Bob Wicker	1901–03
Bill Wight	1958
Fred Wigington	1923
Del Wilber	1946–49
Hoyt Wilhelm	1957
Denney Wilie	1911–12
Ted Wilks	1944–51
Jimy Williams	1966–67
Otto Williams	1902–03
Steamboat Williams	1914, 1916
Stan Williams	1971
Joe Willis	1911–13
Ron Willis	1966–69
Vic Willis	1910
Charlie Wilson	1932–33, 1935
Zeke Wilson	1899
Jimmie Wilson	1928–33
Owen Wilson	1914–16
Craig Wilson	1989–92
Jim Winford	1932, 1934–37
Ivy Wingo	1911–14
Tom Winsett	1935
Rick Wise	1972–73
Corky Withrow	1963
Chicken Wolf	1892
Harry Wolter	1907
John Wood	1896
Gene Woodburn	1911–12
Hal Woodeshick	1965–67
Tracy Woodson	1992–93
Frank Woodward	1919
Floyd Wooldridge	1955
Todd Worrell	1985–89, 1992
Mel Wright	1954–55
Stan Yerkes	1901–03
Ray Yochim	1948–49
Cy Young	1899–1900
Joe Young	1892
Pep Young	1945
Babe Young	1948
Bobby Young	1948
Gerald Young	1994
Joel Youngblood	1977
Eddie Yuhas	1952–53
Sal Yvars	1953–54
Chris Zachary	1971
Elmer Zacher	1910
George Zackert	1911–12
Dave Zearfoss	1904–05
Todd Zeile	1989–95
Bart Zeller	1970
Eddie Zimmerman	1906
Ed Zmich	1910–11

Managers

Ray Blades	1939–40
Ken Boyer	1978–80
*Roger Bresnahan	1909–12
Al Buckenberger	1895
*Jimmy Burke	1905
*Bob Caruthers	1892
*Roger Connor	1896
*Jack Crooks	1892
Harry Diddlebock	1896
*Patsy Donovan	1901–03
*Tommy Dowd	1896–97
Eddie Dyer	1946–50
*Frankie Frisch	1933–38
*Jack Glasscock	1892
Mike Gonzalez	1938, 1940
George Gore	1892
Stan Hack	1958
*Bill Hallman	1897
Louie Heilbroner	1900
Solly Hemus	1959–61
Jack Hendricks	1918
Whitey Herzog	1980–90
*Rogers Hornsby	1925–26
*Miller Huggins	1913–17
Tim Hurst	1898
Fred Hutchinson	1956–58
Mike Jorgensen	1995
Johnny Keane	1961–64
Jack Krol	1978, 1980
Arlie Latham	1896
Marty Marion	1951
John McCloskey	1906–08
Bill McKechnie	1928–29
*Doggie Miller	1894
*Kid Nichols	1904–05
Hugh Nicol	1897
*Bob O'Farrell	1927
Lew Phelan	1895
*Joe Quinn	1895
Vern Rapp	1977–78
Branch Rickey	1919–25
Matt Robison	1905
Red Schoendienst	1965–76, 1980, 1990
Billy Southworth	1929, 1940–45
Eddie Stanky	1952–55
Gabby Street	1929–33
Cub Stricker	1892
*Patsy Tebeau	1899–1900
Joe Torre	1990–95
Chris Von Der Ahe	1895–97
Harry Walker	1955
Bill Watkins	1893

SYRACUSE Stars 1879

George Adams	1879
Jack Allen	1879
Hick Carpenter	1879
George Creamer	1879
Frank Decker	1879
Mike Dorgan	1879
Jack Farrell	1879
Bill Holbert	1879
Honest John Kelly	1879
Jimmy Macullar	1879
Mike Mansell	1879
Tom Mansell	1879
Harry McCormick	1879
John McGuinness	1879
Charlie Osterhout	1879
Blondie Purcell	1879
John Richmond	1879
Red Woodhead	1879

Managers

*Mike Dorgan	1879
*Bill Holbert	1879
*Jimmy Macullar	1879

TROY Trojans 1879–82
Moved to NEW YORK Giants

Charlie Ahearn	1880
George Bradley	1879
Fatty Briody	1880
Dan Brouthers	1879–80
Ed Caskin	1879–81
John Cassidy	1879–82
Aaron Clapp	1879
Ed Cogswell	1880
Roger Connor	1880–82
Buttercup Dickerson	1880
Herm Doscher	1879
Jim Egan	1882
Jake Evans	1879–81
Buck Ewing	1880–82
Bob Ferguson	1879–82
Gid Gardner	1879
Pete Gillespie	1880–82
Fred Goldsmith	1879
Fred Haley	1880
Al Hall	1879
Frank Hankinson	1881
Bill Harbidge	1880, 1882
Thorny Hawkes	1879
Dick Higham	1880
Bill Holbert	1879–82
Jim Holdsworth	1882
Tim Keefe	1880–82
Honest John Kelly	1879
Terry Larkin	1880
Mike Lawlor	1880
Tom Mansell	1879
Pat McManus	1879
Frank Mountain	1880
Candy Nelson	1879
Fred Pfeffer	1882
Charlie Reilley	1879
Chief Roseman	1882
Harry Salisbury	1879
John Shoupe	1879
John Smith	1882
Joe Straub	1880
Sandy Taylor	1879
Bill Tobin	1880
Mickey Welch	1880–82

Managers

*Bob Ferguson	1879–82
Horace Phillips	1879

WASHINGTON Statesmen 1886–89

Tug Arundel	1888
Phil Baker	1886
Jim Banning	1888–89
Bob Barr	1886
Harry Beecher	1889
Jack Carney	1889
Cliff Carroll	1886–87
Spider Clark	1889
Harry Clarke	1889
Larry Corcoran	1886
Cannonball Crane	1886
Sam Crane	1887
Ed Daily	1887–88
One Arm Daily	1886
Tom Daly	1889
Pat Dealey	1887
Pat Deasley	1888
Harry Decker	1886
Jim Donnelly	1887–89
Hi Ebright	1889
Jack Farrell	1886–87
Alex Ferson	1889
Davy Force	1886
John Fox	1886
Shorty Fuller	1888
Ed Fuller	1886
Jim Gallagher	1886
Gid Gardner	1888

Barney Gilligan	1886–87
Frank Gilmore	1886–88
Buck Gladman	1886
Walt Goldsby	1886
John Greening	1888
George Haddock	1888–89
Jack Hayes	1886
Egyptian Healy	1889
John Henry	1886
Paul Hines	1886–87
Sadie Houck	1886
Dummy Hoy	1888–89
Arthur Irwin	1889
John Irwin	1887–89
Joyce	1886
George Keefe	1886–89
Tom Kinslow	1886
Jimmy Knowles	1886
Bill Krieg	1886–87
Gus Krock	1889
Connie Mack	1886–89
Tony Madigan	1886
Art McCoy	1889
John McGlone	1886
John Morrill	1889
Miah Murray	1888
Al Myers	1887–89
Jerry O'Brien	1887
Billy O'Brien	1887–89
Hank O'Day	1886–89
Dave Oldfield	1886
John Riddle	1889
Dupee Shaw	1886–88
George Shoch	1886–89
Joe Start	1886
Mike Sullivan	1889
Pete Sweeney	1888–89
John Thornton	1889
Perry Werden	1888
Ed Whiting	1886
Jim Whitney	1887–88
Wild Bill Widner	1888
Walt Wilmot	1888–89
George Winkelman	1886
Sam Wise	1889
Bill Wise	1886
Bill Wright	1887
Joe Yingling	1886

Managers

John Gaffney	1886–87
Walter Hewett	1888
*Arthur Irwin	1889
*John Morrill	1889
Mike Scanlon	1886
Ted Sullivan	1888

WASHINGTON Senators 1892–99
Moved from American Association

Bert Abbey	1892
Charlie Abbey	1893–97
Doc Amole	1898
Varney Anderson	1894–96
John Anderson	1898
Charlie Atherton	1899
Kirtley Baker	1898–99
Shad Barry	1899
Tun Berger	1892
Frank Bonner	1899
Andy Boswell	1895
Jake Boyd	1894–96
Roger Bresnahan	1897
Tom Brown	1895–97
Ed Buckingham	1895
Dick Butler	1899
Count Campau	1894
Charlie Carr	1898
Kid Carsey	1899
Ed Cartwright	1894–97
Doc Casey	1898–99
Pete Cassidy	1899
Dan Coogan	1895
Jimmy Cooney	1892
Joe Corbett	1895
Bill Coughlin	1899
Jack Crooks	1895–96
Harry Davis	1898–99
George Decker	1899
Gene DeMontreville	1895–97
Bill Dinneen	1898–99
John Dolan	1892
Patsy Donovan	1892
Wild Bill Donovan	1898
Tommy Dowd	1892
Tom Dowse	1892
Jack Doyle	1898
Jake Drauby	1892
Charlie Duffee	1892
Dan Dugdale	1894
Jim Duncan	1899
Davey Dunkle	1899
Jesse Duryea	1892–93
Bill Eagle	1898
Rip Egan	1894
Duke Esper	1893–94
Roy Evans	1898–99
Duke Farrell	1893, 1896–99
Jim Field	1898
Jack Fifield	1899
Carney Flynn	1896
Frank Foreman	1892
Bill Fox	1897
Buck Freeman	1898–99
Hank Gastright	1892
Frank Gatins	1898
Les German	1896–97
Jake Gettman	1897–99
Jack Gilbert	1898
John Gilroy	1895–96
Jack Glasscock	1895
Ed Glenn	1898
John Graff	1893
George Haddock	1894
Bill Hassamaer	1894–95
Lefty Herring	1899
Mike Heydon	1899
Dummy Hoy	1892–93
Billy Hulen	1899
Bert Inks	1892
Alex Jones	1892
Bill Joyce	1894–96
Frank Killen	1892, 1898–99
Matt Kilroy	1892
Silver King	1896–97
Tom Kinslow	1898
Mal Kittridge	1899
Phil Knell	1892
Henry Larkin	1892–93
Arlie Latham	1899
Tom Leahy	1897–98
Bill Leith	1899
Billy Lush	1895–97
Bill Magee	1899
Dan Mahoney	1895
John Malarkey	1894–96
Al Maul	1893–97
Bill McCauley	1895
Pat McCauley	1896
Dan McFarlan	1899
Dan McGann	1899
Deacon McGuire	1892–99
Bob McHale	1898
Doc McJames	1895–97
Frank McManus	1899
Marty McQuaid	1898
Jouett Meekin	1892–93
Win Mercer	1894–99
Kohly Miller	1892
Jocko Milligan	1892
Kid Mohler	1894
Carlton Molesworth	1895
Joe Mulvey	1893
Bert Myers	1898
Parson Nicholson	1895
Elisha Norton	1896–97
John O'Brien	1896–97
Jack O'Brien	1899
Hal O'Hagen	1892
Jim O'Rourke	1893
Tim O'Rourke	1894
Dick Padden	1899
Charlie Petty	1894
Dan Potts	1892
Mike Powers	1899
Oscar Purner	1895
Paul Radford	1892–94
Harry Raymond	1892
Charlie Reilly	1897
Heinie Reitz	1898
Hardy Richardson	1892
Danny Richardson	1892
Dorsey Riddlemoser	1899
Mike Roach	1899
Yank Robinson	1892
Jim Rogers	1896
Frank Scheibeck	1894–95, 1899
Kip Selbach	1894–98
Frank Shannon	1892
Jimmy Slagle	1899
Harvey Smith	1896
Jud Smith	1898
General Stafford	1899
Joe Stanley	1897
George Stephens	1893–94
Otis Stocksdale	1893–95
Cub Stricker	1893
Joe Sullivan	1893–94
Mike Sullivan	1894
Jack Sutthoff	1898
Cy Swaim	1897–98
White Wings Tebeau	1894
Tommy Tucker	1897
Larry Twitchell	1892
George Ulrich	1892
Butts Wagner	1898
Piggy Ward	1894
Charlie Weber	1898
Gus Weyhing	1898–99
Pop Williams	1898
Sam Wise	1893
Phil Wisner	1895
Joe Woerlin	1895
Zeke Wrigley	1896–98
Bill Wynne	1894

Managers

Billy Barnie	1892
*Tom Brown	1897–98
*Jack Doyle	1898
Arthur Irwin	1892, 1898–99
*Deacon McGuire	1898
*Jim O'Rourke	1893
*Danny Richardson	1892
Gus Schmelz	1894–97

WORCESTOR Ruby Legs 1880–82
Moved to PHILADELPHIA Phillies

Charlie Bennett	1880
Doc Bushong	1880–82
Hick Carpenter	1881
John Clarkson	1882
Jim Clinton	1882
Ed Cogswell	1882
Fred Corey	1880–82
George Creamer	1880–82
Buttercup Dickerson	1880–81
Steve Dignan	1880
Jerry Dorgan	1880
Mike Dorgan	1881
Joe Ellick	1880
Jake Evans	1882
Marty Flaherty	1881
Billy Geer	1880
Jim Halpin	1882
Jack Hayes	1882
Pete Hotaling	1881
Arthur Irwin	1880–82
John Irwin	1882
Lon Knight	1880
Fred Mann	1882
Harry McCormick	1881
Bill McGunnigle	1880
Frank McLaughlin	1882
Ed Merrill	1882
Frank Mountain	1882
Candy Nelson	1881
Tricky Nichols	1880
Tom O'Brien	1882
Dan O'Leary	1882
Lip Pike	1881
Paddy Quinn	1881
Charlie Reilley	1881
Lee Richmond	1880–82
John Smith	1882
Pop Smith	1881
Harry Stovey	1880–82
Asa Stratton	1881
Chub Sullivan	1880
Billy Taylor	1881
Bill Tobin	1880
Art Whitney	1880
George Wood	1880

Managers

Frank Bancroft	1880
Tommy Bond	1882
Freeman Brown	1882
Jack Chapman	1882
*Mike Dorgan	1881
*Harry Stovey	1881

American League

BALTIMORE Orioles 1901–02
Moved to NEW YORK Highlanders

Harry Arndt	1902
Roger Bresnahan	1901–02
Steve Brodie	1901
Ike Butler	1902
Ernie Courtney	1902
John Cronin	1902
Pop Dillon	1902
Mike Donlin	1901
Lew Drill	1902
Jack Dunn	1901
Frank Foreman	1901–02
Frank Foutz	1901
Billy Gilbert	1902
Dad Hale	1902
Burt Hart	1901
Crese Heisman	1902
Harry Howell	1901–02
Long Tom Hughes	190

Jim Jackson	1901
Tom Jones	1902
Slats Jordan	1901–02
Bill Karns	1901
John Katoll	1902
Bill Keister	1901
Joe Kelley	1902
Tacks Latimer	1901
Bob Lawson	1902
Jimmy Mathison	1902
Sport McAllister	1902
Herm McFarland	1902
Dan McGann	1902
Joe McGinnity	1901–02
John McGraw	1901
Bill Mellor	1902
Jerry Nops	1901
Andy Oyler	1902
George Prentiss	1902
Wilbert Robinson	1901–02
George Rohe	1901
Ernie Ross	1902
Crazy Schmit	1901
Kip Selbach	1902
Cy Seymour	1901–02
Jimmy Sheckard	1902
Charlie Shields	1902
Broadway Aleck Smith	1902
Chappie Snodgrass	1901
Jack Thoney	1902
Jimmy Williams	1901–02
Snake Wiltse	1902
George Yeager	1902
Stan Yerkes	1901

Managers

*John McGraw	1901–02
*Wilbert Robinson	1902

BALTIMORE Orioles 1954–95
Moved from ST. LOUIS Browns

Don Aase	1985–88
Cal Abrams	1954–55
Jerry Adair	1958–66
Bobby Adams	1956
Mike Adamson	1967–69
Jay Aldrich	1990
Bob Alexander	1955
Doyle Alexander	1972–76
Manny Alexander	1992–93, 1995
John Anderson	1960
Mike Anderson	1978
Brady Anderson	1988–95
Luis Aparicio	1963–67
Tony Arnold	1986–87
Bobby Avila	1959
Benny Ayala	1979–84
Bob Bailor	1975–76
Harold Baines	1993–95
Frank Baker	1973–74
Jeff Ballard	1987–91
George Bamberger	1959
Steve Barber	1960–67
Bret Barberie	1995
Ray Barker	1960
Ed Barnowski	1965–66
Kevin Bass	1995
Jose Bautista	1988–91
Don Baylor	1970–75
Charlie Beamon	1956–58
Fred Beene	1968–70
Mark Belanger	1965–81
Eric Bell	1985–87
Juan Bell	1989–91
Juan Beniquez	1986
Armando Benitez	1994–95
Neil Berry	1954
Frank Bertaina	1964–67, 1969
Fred Besana	1956
Vern Bickford	1954
Babe Birrer	1956
Paul Blair	1964–76
Curt Blefary	1965–68
Mike Blyzka	1954
Mike Boddicker	1980–88
Tom Bolton	1994
Juan Bonilla	1986
Bobby Bonilla	1995
Bob Bonner	1980–83
Danny Boone	1990
Rich Bordi	1986
Joe Borowski	1995
Dave Boswell	1971
Sam Bowens	1963–67
Bob Boyd	1956–60
Gene Brabender	1966–68
Phil Bradley	1989–90
Jackie Brandt	1960–65
Marv Breeding	1960–62
Jim Brideweser	1954, 1957
Nellie Briles	1977–78
Hal Brown	1955–62
Dick Brown	1963–65
Larry Brown	1973
Mark Brown	1984
Kevin Brown	1995
Marty Brown	1990
Jarvis Brown	1995
George Brunet	1963
Don Buford	1968–72
Damon Buford	1993–95
Al Bumbry	1972–84
Wally Bunker	1963–68
Leo Burke	1958–59
Rick Burleson	1987
Pete Burnside	1963
Jim Busby	1957–58, 1960–61
John Buzhardt	1967
Harry Byrd	1955
Enos Cabell	1972–74
Paul Carey	1993
Chico Carrasquel	1959
Camilo Carreon	1966
Foster Castleman	1958
Wayne Causey	1955–57
Art Ceccarelli	1957
Bob Chakales	1954
Tony Chevez	1977
Tom Chism	1979
Gino Cimoli	1964
Terry Clark	1995
Pat Clements	1992
Gil Coan	1954–55
Rich Coggins	1972–74
Joe Coleman	1954–55
Rip Coleman	1959–60
Fritz Connally	1985
Sandy Consuegra	1956–57
Mike Cook	1993
Doug Corbett	1987
Mark Corey	1979–81
Clint Courtney	1954, 1960–61
Billy Cox	1955
Dave Criscione	1977
Terry Crowley	1969–73, 1976–82
Todd Cruz	1983–84
Mike Cuellar	1969–76
Angie Dagres	1955
Clay Dalrymple	1969–71
Rich Dauer	1976–85
Jerry DaVanon	1971
Tommy Davis	1972–75
Storm Davis	1982–86, 1992
Butch Davis	1988–89
Glenn Davis	1991–93
Francisco de la Rosa	1991
Doug DeCinces	1973–81
Jim Dedrick	1995
Luis DeLeon	1987
Ike Delock	1963
Rick Dempsey	1976–86, 1992
John DeSilva	1995
Cesar Devarez	1995
Mike Devereaux	1989–94
Chuck Diering	1954–56
Gordon Dillard	1988
Bill Dillman	1967
Mike Dimmel	1977–78
Ken Dixon	1984–87
Pat Dobson	1971–72
Tom Dodd	1986
Harry Dorish	1955–56
Moe Drabowsky	1966–68, 1970
Dick Drago	1977
Walt Dropo	1959–61
Tom Dukes	1971
Dave Duncan	1975–76
Ryne Duren	1954
Joe Durham	1954, 1957
Jim Dwyer	1981–88
Jim Dyck	1955–56
Mark Eichhorn	1994
Mike Epstein	1966–67
Scott Erickson	1995
Chuck Estrada	1960–64
Andy Etchebarren	1962, 1965–75
Dwight Evans	1991
Hoot Evers	1955–56
Ed Farmer	1977
Chico Fernandez	1968
Sid Fernandez	1994–95
Don Ferrarese	1955–57
Jim Finigan	1959
Steve Finley	1989–90
Mike Fiore	1968
Eddie Fisher	1966–67
Jack Fisher	1959–62
Tom Fisher	1967
Mike Flanagan	1975–87, 1991–92
John Flinn	1978–79, 1982
Bobby Floyd	1968–70
Hank Foiles	1961
Dan Ford	1982–85
Dave Ford	1978–81
Mike Fornieles	1956–57
Howie Fox	1954
Tito Francona	1956–57
Joe Frazier	1956
Roger Freed	1970
Jim Fridley	1954
Todd Frohwirth	1991–93
Jim Fuller	1973–74
Joe Gaines	1963–64
Dave Gallagher	1990
Chico Garcia	1954
Kiko Garcia	1976–80
Billy Gardner	1956–59
Wayne Garland	1973–76
Tommy Gastall	1955–56
Jim Gentile	1960–63
Ken Gerhart	1986–88
Paul Gilliford	1967
Joe Ginsberg	1956–60
Leo Gomez	1990–95
Rene Gonzales	1987–90
Billy Goodman	1957
Curtis Goodwin	1995
Dan Graham	1980–81
Ted Gray	1955
Gene Green	1960
Lenny Green	1957–59, 1964
Bobby Grich	1970–76
Mike Griffin	1987
Ross Grimsley	1974–77, 1982
Wayne Gross	1984–85
Glenn Gulliver	1982–83
Jackie Gutierrez	1986–87
John Habyan	1985–88
Harvey Haddix	1964–65
Bob Hale	1955–59
Dick Hall	1961–66, 1969–71
Jeffrey Hammonds	1993–95
Larry Haney	1966–68
Ron Hansen	1958–62
Jim Hardin	1967–71
Larry Harlow	1975, 1977–79
Pete Harnisch	1988–90
Tommy Harper	1976
Gene Harris	1995
Bob Harrison	1955–56
Roric Harrison	1972
Jack Harshman	1958–59
Mike Hart	1987
Mike Hartley	1995
Paul Hartzell	1980
Grady Hatton	1956
Brad Havens	1985–86
Jimmy Haynes	1995
Drungo Hazewood	1980
Jay Heard	1954
Mel Held	1956
Woodie Held	1966–67
Ellie Hendricks	1968–76, 1978–79
Leo Hernandez	1983, 1985
Whitey Herzog	1961–62
Kevin Hickey	1989–91
Billy Hoeft	1959–62
Chris Hoiles	1989–95
Fred Holdsworth	1976–77
Brian Holton	1989–90
Ken Holtzman	1976
Don Hood	1973–74
Sam Horn	1990–92
Art Houtteman	1957
Bruce Howard	1968
Rex Hudler	1986
Phil Huffman	1985
Keith Hughes	1988
Mark Huismann	1989
Tim Hulett	1989–94
Billy Hunter	1954
Dave Huppert	1983
Jeff Huson	1995
Jim Hutto	1975
Dick Hyde	1961
Grant Jackson	1971–76
Lou Jackson	1964
Reggie Jackson	1976
Ron Jackson	1984
Jesse Jefferson	1973–75
Stan Jefferson	1989–90
Connie Johnson	1956–58
Darrell Johnson	1962
Davey Johnson	1965–72
Don Johnson	1955
Ernie Johnson	1959
Bob Johnson	1963–66
Dave Johnson	1974–75
Dave Johnson	1989–91
Gordon Jones	1960–61
Sam Jones	1964
Odell Jones	1986
Doug Jones	1995
Ricky Jones	1986
Stacy Jones	1991
George Kell	1956–57
Frank Kellert	1954
Pat Kelly	1977–80
Bob Kennedy	1954–55
Terry Kennedy	1987–88
Joe Kerrigan	1978, 1980
Paul Kilgus	1991
Mike Kinnunen	1986–87
Willie Kirkland	1964
Ron Kittle	1990
Billy Klaus	1959–60
Scott Klingenbeck	1994–95
Ray Knight	1987
Darold Knowles	1965
Dick Kokos	1954
Brad Komminsk	1990
Dave Koslo	1954
Wayne Krenchicki	1979–81
Lou Kretlow	1954–55
Rick Krivda	1995
Dick Kryhoski	1954
Bob Kuzava	1954–55
Lee Lacy	1985–87
Hobie Landrith	1962–63
Tito Landrum	1983, 1988
Don Larsen	1954, 1965
Charlie Lau	1961–65
Mark Lee	1995
Craig Lefferts	1992
Jim Lehew	1961–62
Ken Lehman	1957–58
Don Lenhardt	1954
Mark Leonard	1993
Dave Leonhard	1967–72
Don Leppert	1955
Richie Lewis	1992
Dick Littlefield	1954
Charlie Locke	1955
Whitey Lockman	1959
Billy Loes	1956–59
Ed Lopat	1955
Marcelino Lopez	1967, 1969–70
Carlos Lopez	1978

John Lowenstein	1979–85
Steve Luebber	1981
Dick Luebke	1962
Fred Lynn	1985–88
Bob Mabe	1960
Elliott Maddox	1977
Hank Majeski	1955
Jeff Manto	1995
Roger Marquis	1955
Freddie Marsh	1955–56
Jim Marshall	1958
Morrie Martin	1956
Tippy Martinez	1976–86
Dennis Martinez	1976–86
Chito Martinez	1991–93
Tom Matchick	1972
Lee May	1975–80
Rudy May	1976–77
Dave May	1967–70
Mike McCormick	1963–64
Jim McDonald	1955
Ben McDonald	1989–95
Kevin McGehee	1993
Scott McGregor	1976–88
Mickey McGuire	1962, 1967
Jeff McKnight	1990–91
Mark McLemore	1992–94
Dave McNally	1962–74
Sam Mele	1954
Francisco Melendez	1989
Bob Melvin	1989–91
Luis Mercedes	1991–93
Jose Mesa	1987, 1990–92
Eddie Miksis	1958
Bob Milacki	1988–92
John Miller	1962–63, 1965–67
Stu Miller	1963–67
Bill Miller	1955
Dyar Miller	1975–77
Randy Miller	1977
Randy Milligan	1989–92
Alan Mills	1992–95
Paul Mirabella	1983
Willie Miranda	1955–59
Paul Mitchell	1975
John Mitchell	1990
Ron Moeller	1956, 1958
Bob Molinaro	1979
Ray Moore	1955–57
Andres Mora	1976–78
Jose Morales	1981
Keith Moreland	1989
Mike Morgan	1988
Dan Morogiello	1983
John Morris	1968
Les Moss	1954–55
Curt Motton	1967–71, 1973–74
Jamie Moyer	1993–95
Ray Murray	1954
Eddie Murray	1977–88
Tony Muser	1975–77
Mike Mussina	1991–95
Buster Narum	1963
Bob Nelson	1955–57
Roger Nelson	1968
Carl Nichols	1986–88
Dave Nicholson	1960, 1962
Tom Niedenfuer	1987–88
Bob Nieman	1956–59
Donell Nixon	1990
Matt Nokes	1995
Joe Nolan	1982–85
Dickie Noles	1988
Tim Nordbrook	1974–76
Jim Northrup	1974–75
Johnny Oates	1970, 1972
Sherman Obando	1993, 1995
Jack O'Connor	1987
Billy O'Dell	1954, 1956–59
John O'Donoghue	1968
John O'Donoghue	1993
Chuck Oertel	1958
Bob Oliver	1974
Gregg Olson	1988–93
Tom O'Malley	1985–86
Mike Oquist	1993–95
Jesse Orosco	1995
John Orsino	1963–65
Joe Orsulak	1988–92
John Pacella	1984
Dave Pagan	1976
Mike Pagliarulo	1993
Erv Palica	1955–56
Rafael Palmeiro	1994–95
Jim Palmer	1965–67, 1969–84
John Papa	1961–62
Milt Pappas	1957–65
Al Pardo	1985–86
Mark Parent	1992–93
Kelly Paris	1985–86
Mike Parrott	1977
Tom Patton	1957
Albie Pearson	1959–60
Orlando Pena	1971, 1973
Brad Pennington	1993–95
Oswald Peraza	1988
Buddy Peterson	1957
Dave Philley	1955–56, 1960–61
Tom Phoebus	1966–70
Al Pilarcik	1957–60
Duane Pillette	1954–55
Jim Poole	1991–94
Dave Pope	1955–56
Arnie Portocarrero	1958–60
Boog Powell	1961–74
Johnny Powers	1960
Carl Powis	1957
Joe Price	1990
Jim Pyburn	1955–57
Art Quirk	1962
Jamie Quirk	1989
Allan Ramirez	1983
Floyd Rayford	1980, 1982, 1984–87
Mike Reinbach	1974
Merv Rettenmund	1968–73
Bob Reynolds	1972–75
Harold Reynolds	1993
Arthur Rhodes	1991–95
Del Rice	1960
Pete Richert	1967–71
Jeff Rineer	1979
Cal Ripken	1981–95
Billy Ripken	1987–92
Robin Roberts	1962–65
Brooks Robinson	1955–77
Earl Robinson	1961–62, 1964
Frank Robinson	1966–71
Jeff Robinson	1991
Sergio Robles	1972–73
Aurelio Rodriguez	1983
Vic Rodriguez	1984
Gary Roenicke	1978–85
Saul Rogovin	1955
Wade Rowdon	1988
Ken Rowe	1964–65
Willie Royster	1981
Vic Roznovsky	1966–67
Ken Rudolph	1977
Chris Sabo	1994
Lenn Sakata	1980–85
Chico Salmon	1969–72
Orlando Sanchez	1984
Bob Saverine	1962–64
Steve Scarsone	1992
Art Schallock	1955
Bill Scherrer	1988
Curt Schilling	1988–90
Dave Schmidt	1987–89
Johnny Schmitz	1956
Jeff Schneider	1981
Rick Schu	1988–89
Mickey Scott	1972–73
Kal Segrist	1955
David Segui	1990–93
Al Severinsen	1969
Larry Sheets	1984–89
John Shelby	1981–87
Barry Shetrone	1959, 1961–62
Tom Shopay	1971–72, 1975–77
Bill Short	1962, 1966
Norm Siebern	1964–65
Nelson Simmons	1987
Ken Singleton	1975–84
Doug Sisk	1988
Dave Skaggs	1977–80
Lou Sleater	1958
Al Smith	1963
Hal Smith	1955–56
Nate Smith	1962
Billy Smith	1977–79
Lonnie Smith	1993–94
Lee Smith	1994
Roy Smith	1991
Dwight Smith	1994
Mike Smith	1989–90
Mark Smith	1994–95
Nate Snell	1984–86
Russ Snyder	1961–67
Don Stanhouse	1978–79, 1982
Pete Stanicek	1987–88
Herm Starrette	1963–65
John Stefero	1983, 1986
Gene Stephens	1960–61
Vern Stephens	1954–55
Earl Stephenson	1977–78
Sammy Stewart	1978–85
Royle Stillman	1975–76
Wes Stock	1959–64
Tim Stoddard	1978–83
Dean Stone	1963
Steve Stone	1979–81
Jeff Stone	1988
Marlin Stuart	1954
Gordie Sundin	1956
Rick Sutcliffe	1992–93
Bill Swaggerty	1983–86
Jeff Tackett	1991–94
Willie Tasby	1958–60
Joe Taylor	1958–59
Dorn Taylor	1990
Anthony Telford	1990–91, 1993
Johnny Temple	1962
Mickey Tettleton	1988–90
Valmy Thomas	1960
Bobby Thomson	1960
Marv Throneberry	1961–62
Mark Thurmond	1988–89
Jay Tibbs	1988–90
Mike Torrez	1975
Jim Traber	1984, 1986, 1988–89
Gus Triandos	1955–62
Dizzy Trout	1957
Bob Turley	1954
Shane Turner	1991
Tom Underwood	1984
Fred Valentine	1959, 1963, 1968
Fernando Valenzuela	1993
Dave Van Gorder	1987
Andy Van Slyke	1995
Dave Vineyard	1964
Jack Voigt	1993–95
Eddie Waitkus	1954–55
Jerry Walker	1957–60
Greg Walker	1990
Pete Ward	1962
Carl Warwick	1965
Ron Washington	1987
Eddie Watt	1966–73
Don Welchel	1982–83
George Werley	1956
Vic Wertz	1954
Wally Westlake	1955
Mickey Weston	1989–90
Ernie Whitt	1991
Alan Wiggins	1985–87
Bill Wight	1955–57
Hoyt Wilhelm	1958–62
Dick Williams	1956–58, 1961–62
Earl Williams	1973–74
Dallas Williams	1981
Mark Williamson	1987–94
Jim Wilson	1955–56
Gene Woodling	1955, 1958–60
Craig Worthington	1988–91
Bobby Young	1954–55
Mike Young	1982–87
Greg Zaun	1995
Frank Zupo	1957–58, 1961
George Zuverink	1955–59

Managers

Joe Altobelli	1983–85
Hank Bauer	1964–68
Jimmy Dykes	1954
Lum Harris	1961
Billy Hitchcock	1962–63
Johnny Oates	1991–94
Phil Regan	1995
Paul Richards	1955–61
Cal Ripken	1985, 1987–88
Frank Robinson	1988–91
Earl Weaver	1968–82, 1985–86

BOSTON Red Sox 1901–95
Known as Somersets 1901–02
Pilgrims 1903–06

Don Aase	1977
Jerry Adair	1967–68
Bob Adams	1925
Doc Adkins	1902
Harry Agganis	1954–55
Sam Agnew	1916–18
Rick Aguilera	1995
Dale Alexander	1932–33
Luis Alicea	1995
Gary Allenson	1979–84
Mel Almada	1933–37
Nick Altrock	1902–03
Luis Alvarado	1968–70
Larry Andersen	1990
Fred Anderson	1909, 1913
Brady Anderson	1988
Ernie Andres	1946
Kim Andrew	1975
Ivy Andrews	1932–33
Mike Andrews	1966–70
Luis Aparicio	1971–73
Luis Aponte	1980–83
Pete Appleton	1932
Frank Arellanes	1908–10
Tony Armas	1983–86
Charlie Armbruster	1905–07
Asby Asbjornson	1928–29
Ken Aspromonte	1957–58
Jim Atkins	1950, 1952
Eldon Auker	1939
Doyle Aulds	1947
Bobby Avila	1959
Ramon Aviles	1977
Joe Azcue	1969
Lore Bader	1917–18
Jim Bagby	1938–40, 1946
Gene Bailey	1920
Bob Bailey	1978
Cory Bailey	1993–94
Al Baker	1938
Floyd Baker	1953–54
Tracy Baker	1911
Jack Baker	1976–77
Neal Ball	1912–13
Scott Bankhead	1993–94
Walter Barbare	1918
Frank Barberich	1910
Brian Bark	1995
Babe Barna	1943
Steve Barr	1974–75
Frank Barrett	1944–45
Jimmy Barrett	1907–08
Bob Barrett	1929
Bill Barrett	1929–30
Marty Barrett	1982–90
Tom Barrett	1992
Ed Barry	1905–07
Jack Barry	1915–17, 1919
Matt Batts	1947–51
Frank Baumann	1955–59
Don Baylor	1986–87
Bill Bayne	1929–30
Hugh Bedient	1912–14
Stan Belinda	1995
Gary Bell	1967–68
Juan Bell	1995
Juan Beniquez	1971–72, 1974–75
Dennis Bennett	1965–67
Frank Bennett	1927–28
Al Benton	1952
Todd Benzinger	1987–88
Lou Berberet	1958
Moe Berg	1935–39
Boze Berger	1939
Charlie Berry	1928–32
Damon Berryhill	1994
Hal Bevan	1952
Charlie Beville	1901
Elliott Bigelow	1929

Jack Billingham	1980
Doug Bird	1983
John Bischoff	1925–26
Max Bishop	1934–35
Dave Black	1923
Tim Blackwell	1974–75
Clarence Blethen	1923
Greg Blosser	1993–94
Mike Boddicker	1988–90
Larry Boerner	1932
Wade Boggs	1982–92
Bobby Bolin	1970–73
Milt Bolling	1952–56
Tom Bolton	1987–92
Ike Boone	1923–25
Ray Boone	1960
Tom Borland	1960–61
Lou Boudreau	1951
Sam Bowen	1977–78, 1980
Stew Bowers	1935–36
Joe Bowman	1944–45
Ted Bowsfield	1958–60
Oil Can Boyd	1982–89
Herb Bradley	1927–29
Hugh Bradley	1910–12
Cliff Brady	1920
King Brady	1908
Darrell Brandon	1966–68
Fritz Bratschi	1926
Ed Bressoud	1962–65
Ken Brett	1967, 1969–71
Tom Brewer	1954–61
Ralph Brickner	1952
Jim Brillheart	1931
Dick Brodowski	1952, 1955
Jack Brohamer	1978–80
Hal Brown	1953–55
Lloyd Brown	1933
Mace Brown	1942–43, 1946
Mike Brown	1982–86
Mike Brumley	1991
Tom Brunansky	1990–92, 1994
Jim Bucher	1944–45
Bill Buckner	1984–87, 1990
Don Buddin	1956, 1958–61
Fred Burchell	1907–09
Bob Burda	1972
Tom Burgmeier	1978–82
Jesse Burkett	1905
Ellis Burks	1987–92
Rick Burleson	1974–80
George Burns	1922–23
Jim Burton	1975, 1977
Jim Busby	1959–60
Joe Bush	1918–21
Jack Bushelman	1911–12
Frank Bushey	1927, 1930
Bill Butland	1940, 1942, 1946–47
Bud Byerly	1958
Jim Byrd	1993

Hick Cady	1912–17
Ivan Calderon	1993
Earl Caldwell	1948
Ray Caldwell	1919
Dolf Camilli	1945
Paul Campbell	1942, 1946
Bill Campbell	1977–81
Jose Canseco	1995
Bernie Carbo	1974–78
Tom Carey	1939–42, 1946
Walter Carlisle	1908
Swede Carlstrom	1911
Cleo Carlyle	1927
Roy Carlyle	1925–26
Bill Carrigan	1906, 1908–14
Ed Carroll	1929
Jerry Casale	1958–60
Joe Cascarella	1935–36
Danny Cater	1972–74
Rex Cecil	1944–45
Orlando Cepeda	1973
Rick Cerone	1988–89
Chet Chadbourne	1906–07
Bob Chakales	1957
Wes Chamberlain	1994–95
Esty Chaney	1913
Ed Chaplin	1920–22
Ben Chapman	1937–38
Pete Charton	1964
Ken Chase	1942–43
Charlie Chech	1909
Jack Chesbro	1909
Nels Chittum	1959–60
Joe Christopher	1966
Loyd Christopher	1945
Joe Cicero	1929–30
Eddie Cicotte	1908–12
Galen Cisco	1961–62, 1967
Bill Cissell	1934
Danny Clark	1924
Otie Clark	1945
Jack Clark	1991–92
Mark Clear	1981–85
Roger Clemens	1984–95
Lance Clemons	1974
Reggie Cleveland	1974–78
Tex Clevenger	1954
Lu Clinton	1960–64
Bill Clowers	1926
George Cochran	1918
Jack Coffey	1918
Dave Coleman	1977
Rip Collins	1922
Jimmy Collins	1901–05, 1907
Shano Collins	1921–25
Ray Collins	1909–15
Merrill Combs	1947, 1949
Ralph Comstock	1915
Bunk Congalton	1907
Tony Conigliaro	1964–67, 1969–70, 1975
Billy Conigliaro	1969–71
Gene Conley	1961–63
Bud Connolly	1925
Ed Connolly	1964
Ed Connolly	1929–32
Joe Connolly	1924
Bill Conroy	1942–44
Billy Consolo	1953–59
Dusty Cooke	1933–36
Jimmy Cooney	1917
Guy Cooper	1914–15
Cecil Cooper	1971–76
Scott Cooper	1991–94
Rheal Cormier	1995
Vic Correll	1972
Marlan Coughtry	1960
Fritz Coumbe	1914
Ted Cox	1977
Doc Cramer	1936–40
Gavvy Cravath	1908
Steve Crawford	1980–82, 1984–87
Pat Creeden	1931
Bob Cremins	1927
Lou Criger	1901–08
Joe Cronin	1935–44
Zach Crouch	1988
Leon Culberson	1943–47
Ray Culp	1968–73
Nig Cuppy	1901
Steve Curry	1988
John Curtis	1970–73

Babe Dahlgren	1935–36
Pete Daley	1955–59
Dom Dallessandro	1937
Babe Danzig	1909
Bobby Darwin	1976–77
Danny Darwin	1991–94
Andre Dawson	1993–94
Cot Deal	1947–48
Rob Deer	1993
Pep Deininger	1902
Ike Delock	1952–53, 1955–63
Don Demeter	1966–67
Brian Denman	1982
Sam Dente	1947
Jim Derrick	1970
Gene Desautels	1937–40
Mel Deutsch	1946
Mickey Devine	1920
Hal Deviney	1920
Al DeVormer	1923
Bo Diaz	1977
George Dickey	1935–36
Emerson Dickman	1936, 1938–41
Bob Didier	1974
Steve Dillard	1975–77
Dom DiMaggio	1940–42, 1946–52
Bill Dinneen	1902–07
Bob DiPietro	1951
Ray Dobens	1929
Joe Dobson	1941–43, 1946–50, 1954
Sam Dodge	1921–22
Pat Dodson	1986–88
Bobby Doerr	1937–44, 1946–51
John Donahue	1923
Pat Donahue	1908–10
Chris Donnels	1995
Pete Donohue	1932
John Dopson	1989–93
Tom Doran	1904–06
Harry Dorish	1947–49, 1956
Jim Dorsey	1984–85
Patsy Dougherty	1902–04
Tommy Dowd	1901
Danny Doyle	1943
Denny Doyle	1975–77
Dick Drago	1974–75, 1978–80
Clem Dreisewerd	1944–46
Walt Dropo	1949–52
Jean Dubuc	1918
Frank Duffy	1978–79
Joe Dugan	1922
Bob Duliba	1965
George Dumont	1919
Ed Durham	1929–32
Cedric Durst	1930
Jim Dwyer	1979–80

Arnold Earley	1960–65
Mike Easler	1984–85
Dennis Eckersley	1978–84
Elmer Eggert	1927
Howard Ehmke	1923–26
Hack Eibel	1920
Dick Ellsworth	1968–69
Steve Ellsworth	1988
Clyde Engle	1910–14
Nick Esasky	1989
Vaughn Eshelman	1995
Al Evans	1951
Bill Evans	1951
Dwight Evans	1972–90
Hoot Evers	1952–54
Homer Ezzell	1924–25

Carmen Fanzone	1970
Steve Farr	1994
Duke Farrell	1903–05
Doc Farrell	1935
Alex Ferguson	1922–25
Rick Ferrell	1933–37
Wes Ferrell	1934–37
Hobe Ferris	1901–07
Boo Ferriss	1945–50
Chick Fewster	1922–23
Joel Finch	1979
Tom Fine	1947
Lou Finney	1939–42, 1944
Gar Finnvold	1994
Mike Fiore	1970–71
Hank Fischer	1966–67
Carlton Fisk	1969, 1971–80
Howie Fitzgerald	1926
Ira Flagstead	1923–29
John Flaherty	1992–93
Al Flair	1941
Bill Fleming	1940–41
Scott Fletcher	1993–94
Ben Flowers	1951, 1953
Happy Foreman	1926
Frank Foreman	1901
Mike Fornieles	1957–63
Gary Fortune	1920
Tony Fossas	1991–94
Eddie Foster	1920–22
Rube Foster	1913–17
Bob Fothergill	1933
Boob Fowler	1926
Pete Fox	1941–45
Jimmie Foxx	1936–42
Joe Foy	1966–68
Ray Francis	1925
Hersh Freeman	1952–53, 1955
John Freeman	1927
Buck Freeman	1901–07
Charlie French	1909–10
Barney Friberg	1933
Owen Friend	1955
Todd Frohwirth	1994
Oscar Fuhr	1924–25
Frank Fuller	1923
Curt Fullerton	1921–25, 1933

Fabian Gaffke	1936–38
Phil Gagliano	1971–72
Del Gainer	1914–17, 1919
Rich Gale	1984
Denny Galehouse	1939–40, 1947–49
Ed Gallagher	1932
Bob Garbark	1945
Mike Gardiner	1991–92
Billy Gardner	1962–63
Larry Gardner	1908–17
Wes Gardner	1986–90
Mike Garman	1969, 1971–73
Cliff Garrison	1928
Ford Garrison	1943–44
Alex Gaston	1926, 1929
Milt Gaston	1929–31
Rich Gedman	1980–90
Gary Geiger	1959–65
Charley Gelbert	1940
Wally Gerber	1928–29
Dick Gernert	1952–59
Doc Gessler	1908–09
Chappie Geygan	1924–26
Joe Giannini	1911
Norwood Gibson	1903–06
Russ Gibson	1967–69
Andy Gilbert	1942, 1946
Don Gile	1959–62
Frank Gilhooley	1919
Bob Gillespie	1950
Grant Gillis	1929
Joe Ginsberg	1961
Ralph Glaze	1906–08
Harry Gleason	1901–03
Joe Glenn	1940
John Godwin	1905–06
Chuck Goggin	1974
Joe Gonzales	1937
Eusebio Gonzalez	1918
Johnny Gooch	1933
Billy Goodman	1947–56
Jim Gosger	1963, 1965–66
Skinny Graham	1934–35
Charlie Graham	1906
Lee Graham	1983
Dave Gray	1964
Jeff Gray	1990–91
Pumpsie Green	1959–62
Lenny Green	1965–66
Mike Greenwell	1985–95
Vean Gregg	1914–16
Marty Griffin	1928
Doug Griffin	1971–77
Guido Grilli	1966
Ray Grimes	1920
Moose Grimshaw	1905–07
Marv Grissom	1953
Turkey Gross	1925
Lefty Grove	1934–41
Mike Guerra	1951
Mario Guerrero	1973–74
Bob Guindon	1964
Randy Gumpert	1952
Eric Gunderson	1995
Hy Gunning	1911
Jackie Gutierrez	1983–85
Don Gutteridge	1946–47

Casey Hageman	1911–12
Odell Hale	1941
Ray Haley	1915
Charley Hall	1909–13
Garry Hancock	1978, 1980–82
Fred Haney	1926–27
Erik Hanson	1995
Carroll Hardy	1960–62
Harry Harper	1920
Tommy Harper	1972–74
Billy Harrell	1961
Ken Harrelson	1967–69
Joe Harris	1922–25
Joe Harris	1905–07
Mickey Harris	1940–41, 1946–49
Bill Harris	1938
Greg Harris	1989–94
Slim Harriss	1926–28
Jack Harshman	1959
Chuck Hartenstein	1970
Grover Hartley	1927
Mike Hartley	1995
Charlie Hartman	1908
Bill Haselman	1995
Herb Hash	1940–41
Andy Hassler	1978–79
Billy Hatcher	1992–94
Fred Hatfield	1950–52
Scott Hatteberg	1995

Grady Hatton	1954–55
Clem Hausmann	1944–45
Jack Hayden	1906
Frankie Hayes	1947
Ed Hearn	1910
Danny Heep	1989–90
Bob Heffner	1963–65
Randy Heflin	1945–46
Fred Heimach	1926
Bob Heise	1975–76
Tommy Helms	1977
Charlie Hemphill	1901
Dave Henderson	1986–87
Tim Hendryx	1920–21
Olaf Henriksen	1911–16
Jim Henry	1936–37
Bill Henry	1952–55
Ramon Hernandez	1977
Mike Herrera	1925–26
Tom Herrin	1954
Joe Hesketh	1990–94
Eric Hetzel	1989–90
Johnnie Heving	1924–25, 1928–30
Joe Heving	1938–40
Piano Legs Hickman	1902
Pinky Higgins	1937–38, 1946
Hob Hiller	1920
Dave Hillman	1960–61
Gordie Hinkle	1934
Paul Hinrichs	1951
Harley Hisner	1951
Billy Hitchcock	1948–49
Dick Hoblitzell	1914–18
Butch Hobson	1975–80
George Hockette	1934–35
Johnny Hodapp	1933
Mel Hoderlein	1951
Billy Hoeft	1959
John Hoey	1906–08
Glenn Hoffman	1980–87
Fred Hofmann	1927–28
Ken Holcombe	1953
Dave Hollins	1995
Billy Holm	1945
Harry Hooper	1909–20
Sam Horn	1987–89
Tony Horton	1964–67
Dwayne Hosey	1995
Tom House	1976–77
Wayne Housie	1991
Elston Howard	1967–68
Paul Howard	1909
Chris Howard	1994
Les Howe	1923–24
Peter Hoy	1992
Waite Hoyt	1919–20
Sid Hudson	1952–54
Joe Hudson	1995
Ed Hughes	1905–06
Long Tom Hughes	1902–03
Terry Hughes	1974
Tex Hughson	1941–44, 1946–49
Bill Humphrey	1938
Ben Hunt	1910
Herb Hunter	1920
Buddy Hunter	1971, 1973, 1975
Tom Hurd	1954–56
Bruce Hurst	1980–88
Bert Husting	1902
Daryl Irvine	1990–92
Ron Jackson	1960
Beany Jacobson	1907
Baby Doll Jacobson	1926–27
Charlie Jamerson	1924
Bill James	1919
Chris James	1995
Hal Janvrin	1911, 1913–17
Ray Jarvis	1969–70
Reggie Jefferson	1995
Ferguson Jenkins	1976–77
Tom Jenkins	1925–26
Jackie Jensen	1954–59, 1961
Adam Johnson	1914
Deron Johnson	1974–76
Earl Johnson	1940–41, 1946–50
Hank Johnson	1933–35
Bob Johnson	1944–45
Roy Johnson	1932–35
Vic Johnson	1944–45
John Henry Johnson	1983–84
Joel Johnston	1995
Smead Jolley	1932–33
Charlie Jones	1901
Dalton Jones	1964–69
Jake Jones	1947–48
Sad Sam Jones	1916–21
Rick Jones	1976
Eddie Joost	1955
Duane Josephson	1971–72
Oscar Judd	1941–45
Joe Judge	1933–34
Ed Jurak	1982–85
Rudy Kallio	1925
Ed Karger	1909–11
Andy Karl	1943
Marty Karow	1927
Benn Karr	1920–22
Eddie Kasko	1966
George Kell	1952–54
Al Kellett	1924
Red Kellett	1934
Win Kellum	1901
Ed Kelly	1914
Ken Keltner	1950
Russ Kemmerer	1954–55, 1957
Fred Kendall	1978
John Kennedy	1970–74
Bill Kennedy	1953
Marty Keough	1957–60
Dana Kiecker	1990–91
Joe Kiefer	1925–26
Leo Kiely	1951, 1954–56, 1958–59
Jack Killilay	1911
Ellis Kinder	1948–55
Walt Kinney	1918
Bruce Kison	1985
Billy Klaus	1955–58
Red Kleinow	1910–11
Bob Kline	1930–33
Ron Kline	1969
Bob Klinger	1946–47
John Knight	1907
Hal Kolstad	1962–63
Cal Koonce	1970–71
Andy Kosco	1972
Jack Kramer	1948–49
Lew Krausse	1972
Rick Kreuger	1975–77
Rube Kroh	1906–07
John Kroner	1935–36
Marty Krug	1912
Randy Kutcher	1988–90
Candy LaChance	1902–05
Ty LaForest	1945
Roger LaFrancois	1982
Joe Lahoud	1968–71
Eddie Lake	1943–45
Jack Lamabe	1963–65
Bill Lamar	1919
Dennis Lamp	1988–91
Rick Lancellotti	1990
Jim Landis	1967
Bill Landis	1967–69
Carney Lansford	1981–82
Frank LaPorte	1908
John LaRose	1978
Lyn Lary	1934
Johnny Lazor	1943–46
Dud Lee	1924–26
Bill Lee	1969–78
Bill Lefebvre	1938–39
Lou Legett	1933–34
Regis Leheny	1932
Paul Lehner	1952
Nemo Leibold	1921–23
John Leister	1987, 1990
Don Lenhardt	1952, 1954
Dutch Leonard	1913–18
Ted Lepcio	1952–59
Dutch Lerchen	1910
Louis LeRoy	1910
Ted Lewis	1901
Duffy Lewis	1910–17
Jack Lewis	1911
John Lickert	1981
Derek Lilliquist	1995
Johnny Lipon	1952–53
Hod Lisenbee	1929–32
Dick Littlefield	1950
Greg Litton	1994
Don Lock	1969
Skip Lockwood	1980
George Loepp	1928
Tim Lollar	1985–86
Jim Lonborg	1965–71
Walt Lonergan	1911
Brian Looney	1995
Harry Lord	1907–10
Johnny Lucas	1931
Joe Lucey	1925
Lou Lucier	1943–44
Del Lundgren	1926–27
Tony Lupien	1940, 1942–43
Sparky Lyle	1967–71
Walt Lynch	1922
Fred Lynn	1974–80
Steve Lyons	1985–86, 1991–93
Mike Macfarlane	1995
Danny MacFayden	1926–32
Bill MacLeod	1962
Keith MacWhorter	1980
Tom Madden	1909–11
Mike Maddux	1995
Pete Magrini	1966
Ron Mahay	1995
Chris Mahoney	1910
Jim Mahoney	1959
Jerry Mallett	1959
Paul Maloy	1913
Frank Malzone	1955–65
Felix Mantilla	1963–65
Heinie Manush	1936
Josias Manzanillo	1991
Phil Marchildon	1950
Johnny Marcum	1936–38
Juan Marichal	1974
Ollie Marquardt	1931
Mike Marshall	1990–91
Babe Martin	1948–49
John Marzano	1987–92
Walt Masterson	1949–52
Tom Matchick	1970
Bill Matthews	1909
Gene Mauch	1956–57
Charlie Maxwell	1950–52, 1954
Wally Mayer	1917–18
Chick Maynard	1922
Carl Mays	1915–19
Dick McAuliffe	1974–75
Tom McBride	1943–47
Dick McCabe	1918
Windy McCall	1948–49
Emmett McCann	1926
Tom McCarthy	1985
Tim McCarver	1974–75
Amby McConnell	1908–10
Mickey McDermott	1948–53
Jim McDonald	1950
Ed McFarland	1908
Ed McGah	1946–47
Willie McGee	1995
Lynn McGlothen	1972–73
Art McGovern	1905
Bob McGraw	1919
Jim McHale	1908
Marty McHale	1910–11, 1916
Stuffy McInnis	1918–21
Archie McKain	1937–38
Jud McLaughlin	1931–33
Larry McLean	1901
Don McMahon	1966–67
Doc McMahon	1908
Marty McManus	1931–33
Norm McMillan	1923
Eric McNair	1936–38
Mike McNally	1915–17, 1919–20
Gordon McNaughton	1932
Jeff McNeely	1993
Norm McNeil	1919
Roman Mejias	1963–64
Sam Mele	1947–49, 1954–55
Jose Melendez	1993–94
Oscar Melillo	1935–37
Bob Melvin	1993
Mike Menosky	1920–23
Mike Meola	1933, 1936
Andy Merchant	1975–76
Spike Merena	1934
Jack Merson	1953
Catfish Metkovich	1943–46
Russ Meyer	1957
John Michaels	1932
Dick Midkiff	1938
Dee Miles	1943
Bing Miller	1935–36
Elmer Miller	1922
Hack Miller	1918
Otto Miller	1930–31
Rick Miller	1971–77, 1981–85
Buster Mills	1937
Dick Mills	1970
Rudy Minarcin	1956–57
Nate Minchey	1993–94
Fred Mitchell	1901–02
Johnny Mitchell	1922–23
Charlie Mitchell	1984–85
Herb Moford	1959
Vince Molyneaux	1918
Bill Monbouquette	1958–65
Freddie Moncewicz	1928
Bob Montgomery	1970–79
Bill Moore	1926–27
Wilcy Moore	1931–32
Dave Morehead	1963–68
Roger Moret	1970–75
Ed Morgan	1934
Cy Morgan	1907–09
Red Morgan	1906
Ed Morris	1928–31
Deacon Morrissey	1901
Kevin Morton	1991
Earl Moseley	1913
Walter Moser	1911
Gerry Moses	1968–70
Wally Moses	1946–48
Doc Moskiman	1910
Les Moss	1951
Gordy Mueller	1950
Billy Muffett	1960–62
Freddie Muller	1933–34
Joe Mulligan	1934
Frank Mulroney	1930
Bill Mundy	1913
Johnny Murphy	1947
Walter Murphy	1931
Tom Murphy	1976–77
Rob Murphy	1989–90
George Murray	1923–24
Matt Murray	1995
Tony Muser	1969
Paul Musser	1919
Alex Mustaikis	1940
Buddy Myer	1927–28
Elmer Myers	1920–22
Hap Myers	1910–11
Chris Nabholz	1994
Tim Naehring	1990–95
Judge Nagle	1911
Mike Nagy	1969–72
Bill Narleski	1929–30
Ernie Neitzke	1921
Hal Neubauer	1925
Don Newhauser	1972–74
Jeff Newman	1983–84
Bobo Newsom	1937
Skeeter Newsome	1941–45
Dick Newsome	1941–43
Gus Niarhos	1952–53
Chet Nichols	1960–63
Reid Nichols	1980–85
Al Niemiec	1934
Harry Niles	1908–10
Al Nipper	1983–87
Merlin Nippert	1962
Russ Nixon	1960–65, 1968
Willard Nixon	1950–58
Otis Nixon	1994
Red Nonnenkamp	1938–39
Chet Nourse	1909
Les Nunamaker	1911–14
Frank Oberlin	1906–07
Mike O'Berry	1979
Jack O'Brien	1903
Tommy O'Brien	1949–50
Buck O'Brien	1911–13
Syd O'Brien	1969
Lefty O'Doul	1923
Ben Oglivie	1971–73
Bob Ojeda	1980–85
Len Okrie	1952
Troy O'Leary	1995
Gene Oliver	1968
Tom Oliver	1930–33
Hank Olmsted	1905
Karl Olson	1951, 1953–55

Marv Olson	1931–33
Ted Olson	1936–38
Emmett O'Neill	1943–45
Steve O'Neill	1924
Bill O'Neill	1904
George Orme	1920
Frank O'Rourke	1922
Luis Ortiz	1993–94
Dan Osinski	1966–67
Harry Ostdiek	1908
Fritz Ostermueller	1934–40
Mickey Owen	1954
Marv Owen	1940
Spike Owen	1986–88
Frank Owens	1905
Jim Pagliaroni	1955, 1960–62
Mike Palm	1948
Jim Pankovits	1990
Al Papai	1950
Larry Pape	1909, 1911–12
Stan Papi	1979–80
Freddy Parent	1901–07
Mel Parnell	1947–56
Larry Parrish	1988
Roy Partee	1943–44, 1946–47
Stan Partenheimer	1944
Ben Paschal	1920
Casey Patten	1908
Hank Patterson	1932
Marty Pattin	1972–73
Don Pavletich	1970–71
Mike Paxton	1977
Johnny Peacock	1937–44
Eddie Pellagrini	1946–47
Tony Pena	1990–93
Alejandro Pena	1995
Herb Pennock	1915–17, 1919–22, 1934
Tony Perez	1980–82
Jack Perrin	1921
Bill Pertica	1918
Johnny Pesky	1942, 1946–52
Gary Peters	1970–72
Bob Peterson	1906–07
Rico Petrocelli	1963, 1965–76
Dan Petry	1991
Dave Philley	1962
Ed Phillips	1970
Val Picinich	1923–25
Urbane Pickering	1931–32
Jeff Pierce	1995
Bill Piercy	1922–24
Jimmy Piersall	1950, 1952–58
George Pipgras	1933–35
Pinky Pittenger	1921–23
Juan Pizarro	1968–69
Phil Plantier	1990–92
Herb Plews	1959
Jeff Plympton	1991
Jennings Poindexter	1936
Dick Pole	1973–76
Nick Polly	1945
Ralph Pond	1910
Tom Poquette	1979, 1981
Dick Porter	1934
Bob Porterfield	1956–58
Nels Potter	1941
Ken Poulsen	1967
Del Pratt	1921–22
Larry Pratt	1914
George Prentiss	1901–02
Joe Price	1989
Doc Prothro	1925
Tex Pruiett	1907–08
Billy Purtell	1910–11
Frankie Pytlak	1941, 1945–46
Paul Quantrill	1992–94
Frank Quinn	1949–50
Jack Quinn	1922–25
Rey Quinones	1986
Carlos Quintana	1988–91, 1993
Dick Radatz	1962–66
Dave Rader	1980
Chuck Rainey	1979–82
Jeff Reardon	1990–92
Johnny Reder	1932
Jerry Reed	1990
Jody Reed	1987–92
Bobby Reeves	1929–31
Bill Regan	1926–30
Wally Rehg	1913–15
Dick Reichle	1922–23
Win Remmerswaal	1979–80
Jerry Remy	1978–84
Steve Renko	1979–80
Bill Renna	1958–59
Rip Repulski	1960–61
Carl Reynolds	1934–35
Gordon Rhodes	1932–35
Karl Rhodes	1995
Hal Rhyne	1929–32
Jim Rice	1974–89
Woody Rich	1939–41
Jeff Richardson	1993
Al Richter	1951, 1953
Joe Riggert	1911
Topper Rigney	1926–27
Ernest Riles	1993
Walt Ripley	1935
Allen Ripley	1978–79
Pop Rising	1905
Jay Ritchie	1964–65
Luis Rivera	1989–93
Billy Jo Robidoux	1990
Aaron Robinson	1951
Floyd Robinson	1968
Jack Robinson	1949
Mike Rochford	1988–90
Bill Rodgers	1915
Carlos Rodriguez	1994–95
Frank Rodriguez	1995
Steve Rodriguez	1995
Billy Rogell	1925, 1927–28
Lee Rogers	1938
Garry Roggenburk	1966, 1968–69
Billy Rohr	1967
Red Rollings	1927–28
Ed Romero	1986–89
Kevin Romine	1985–91
Vicente Romo	1969–70
Buddy Rosar	1950–51
Si Rosenthal	1925–26
Buster Ross	1924–26
Braggo Roth	1919
Jack Rothrock	1925–32
Rich Rowland	1994–95
Stan Royer	1994
Joe Rudi	1981
Muddy Ruel	1921–22, 1931
Red Ruffing	1924–30
Pete Runnels	1958–62
Allan Russell	1919–22
Rip Russell	1946–47
Jack Russell	1926–32, 1936
Jeff Russell	1993–94
Babe Ruth	1914–19
Jack Ryan	1909
Jack Ryan	1929
Mike Ryan	1964–67
Ken Ryan	1992–95
Mike Ryba	1941–46
Gene Rye	1931
Eddie Sadowski	1960
Bob Sadowski	1966
Joe Sambito	1986–87
Ken Sanders	1966
Jose Santiago	1966–70
Tom Satriano	1969–70
Dave Sax	1985–87
Bill Sayles	1939
Ray Scarborough	1951–52
Russ Scarritt	1929–31
Wally Schang	1918–20
Charley Schanz	1950
Bob Scherbarth	1950
Chuck Schilling	1961–65
Calvin Schiraldi	1986–87
Biff Schlitzer	1909
George Schmees	1952
Dave Schmidt	1981
Johnny Schmitz	1956
Dick Schofield	1969–70
Ossee Schreckengost	1901
Al Schroll	1958–59
Don Schwall	1961–62
George Scott	1966–71, 1977–79
Everett Scott	1914–21
Tom Seaver	1986
Bob Seeds	1933–34
Diego Segui	1974–75
Kip Selbach	1904–06
Aaron Sele	1993–95
Jeff Sellers	1985–88
Merle Settlemire	1928
Wally Shaner	1926–27
Howard Shanks	1923–24
Red Shannon	1919
Al Shaw	1907
John Shea	1928
Merv Shea	1933
Danny Sheaffer	1987
Dave Shean	1918–19
Rollie Sheldon	1966
Keith Shepherd	1995
Ben Shields	1930
Strick Shofner	1947
Ernie Shore	1914–17
Bill Short	1966
Chick Shorten	1915–17
Terry Shumpert	1995
Norm Siebern	1967–68
Sonny Siebert	1969–73
Al Simmons	1943
Pat Simmons	1928–29
Dave Sisler	1956–59
Ted Sizemore	1979–80
Camp Skinner	1923
Craig Skok	1973
Jack Slattery	1901
Steve Slayton	1928
Charlie Small	1930
Broadway Aleck Smith	1903
Al Smith	1964
Charlie Smith	1909–11
Doug Smith	1912
Eddie Smith	1947
Elmer Smith	1922
Frank Smith	1910–11
George Smith	1966
George Smith	1930
John Smith	1931
Paddy Smith	1920
Pete Smith	1962–63
Reggie Smith	1966–73
Bob Smith	1955
Riverboat Smith	1958
Lee Smith	1988–90
Zane Smith	1995
Mike Smithson	1988–89
Wally Snell	1913
Moose Solters	1934–35
Rudy Sommers	1926–27
Allen Sothoron	1921
Bill Spanswick	1964
Tully Sparks	1902
Tris Speaker	1907–15
Stan Spence	1940–41, 1948–49
Tubby Spencer	1909
Andy Spognardi	1932
Jack Spring	1957
Bobby Sprowl	1978
Chick Stahl	1901–06
Jake Stahl	1903, 1908–10, 1912
Matt Stairs	1995
Tracy Stallard	1960–62
Jerry Standaert	1929
Lee Stange	1966–70
Bob Stanley	1977–89
John Stansbury	1918
Mike Stanton	1995
Dave Stapleton	1980–86
Jigger Statz	1920
Elmer Steele	1907–09
Ben Steiner	1945–46
Red Steiner	1945
Mike Stenhouse	1986
Gene Stephens	1952–53, 1955–60
Vern Stephens	1948–52
Jerry Stephenson	1963, 1965–68
Sammy Stewart	1986
Dick Stigman	1966
Carl Stimson	1923
Chuck Stobbs	1947–51
Al Stokes	1925–26
Dean Stone	1957
Jeff Stone	1989–90
Howie Storie	1931–32
Lou Stringer	1948–50
Amos Strunk	1918–19
Dick Stuart	1963–64
George Stumpf	1931–33
Tom Sturdivant	1960
Jim Suchecki	1950
Denny Sullivan	1907–08
Frank Sullivan	1953–60
Haywood Sullivan	1955, 1957, 1959–60
Marc Sullivan	1982, 1984–87
Carl Sumner	1928
Jeff Suppan	1995
George Susce	1955–58
Bill Swanson	1914
Bill Sweeney	1930–31
Len Swormstedt	1906
Jim Tabor	1938–44
Doug Taitt	1928–29
Frank Tanana	1981
Jesse Tannehill	1904–08
Arlie Tarbert	1927–28
Jose Tartabull	1966–68
LaSchelle Tarver	1986
Willie Tasby	1960
Bennie Tate	1932
Ken Tatum	1971–73
Harry Taylor	1950–52
Scott Taylor	1992–93
Birdie Tebbetts	1947–50
Yank Terry	1940, 1942–45
Jake Thielman	1908
Tommy Thomas	1937
Blaine Thomas	1911
Pinch Thomas	1912–17
Fred Thomas	1918
George Thomas	1966–71
Lee Thomas	1964–65
Bobby Thomson	1960
Jack Thoney	1908–09
Hank Thormahlen	1921
Faye Throneberry	1952, 1955–56
Luis Tiant	1971–78
Bob Tillman	1962–67
Lee Tinsley	1994–95
Johnny Tobin	1945
Jack Tobin	1926–27
Phil Todt	1924–30
Andy Tomberlin	1994
Tony Tonneman	1911
Mike Torrez	1978–82
John Trautwein	1988
Joe Trimble	1955
Rick Trlicek	1994
Dizzy Trout	1952
Frank Truesdale	1918
Mike Trujillo	1985–86
John Tudor	1979–83
Bob Turley	1963
Tommy Umphlett	1953
Bob Unglaub	1904–05, 1907–08
Tex Vache	1925
Julio Valdez	1980–83
Sergio Valdez	1994
John Valentin	1992–95
Dave Valle	1994
Al Van Camp	1931–32
Ben Van Dyke	1912
Hy Vandenburg	1935
Tim VanEgmond	1994–95
Mo Vaughn	1991–95
Bobby Veach	1924–25
Bob Veale	1972–74
Mickey Vernon	1956–57
Sammy Vick	1921
Frank Viola	1992–94
Ossie Vitt	1919–21
Clyde Vollmer	1950–52
Jake Volz	1901
Joe Vosmik	1938–39
Jake Wade	1939
Heinie Wagner	1906–13, 1915–16, 1918
Charlie Wagner	1938–42, 1946
Gary Wagner	1969–70
Hal Wagner	1944, 1946–47
Tim Wakefield	1995
Rube Walberg	1934–37
Tilly Walker	1916–17
Chico Walker	1980–81, 1983–84
Murray Wall	1957–59
Jimmy Walsh	1916–17
Roxy Walters	1919–23
Fred Walters	1945
Bucky Walters	1933–34
Bill Wambsganss	1924–25
Pee Wee Wanninger	1927
Jack Warner	1902
Rabbit Warstler	1930–33
Gary Waslewski	1967–68

Bob Watson	1979
Cliff Watwood	1932–33
Monte Weaver	1939
Earl Webb	1930–32
Ray Webster	1960
Eric Wedge	1991–92, 1994
Bob Weiland	1932–34
Frank Welch	1927
Herb Welch	1925
Johnny Welch	1932–36
Tony Welzer	1926–27
Fred Wenz	1968–69
Bill Werber	1933–36
Bill Werle	1953–54
Vic Wertz	1959–61
Sammy White	1951–59
George Whiteman	1907, 1918
Mark Whiten	1995
Ernie Whitt	1976
Al Widmar	1947
Bill Wight	1951–52
Del Wilber	1952–54
Joe Wilhoit	1919
Buff Williams	1911
Dave Williams	1902
Dib Williams	1935
Denny Williams	1924–25, 1928
Ken Williams	1928–29
Dick Williams	1963–64
Stan Williams	1972
Ted Williams	1939–42, 1946–60
Dana Williams	1989
Jim Willoughby	1975–77
Ted Wills	1959–62
Archie Wilson	1952
Duane Wilson	1958
Earl Wilson	1959–60, 1962–66
Squanto Wilson	1914
Jim Wilson	1945–46
Gary Wilson	1902
Jack Wilson	1935–41
John Wilson	1927–28
Les Wilson	1911
Hal Wiltse	1926–28
Ted Wingfield	1924–27
George Winn	1919
Herm Winningham	1992
Tom Winsett	1931, 1933
George Winter	1901–08
Clarence Winters	1924
Rick Wise	1974–77
Johnnie Wittig	1949
Larry Wolfe	1979–80
Harry Wolter	1909
Smoky Joe Wood	1908–15
Joe Wood	1944
Ken Wood	1952
Wilbur Wood	1961–64
Pinky Woods	1943–45
John Woods	1924
Rob Woodward	1985–88
Hoge Workman	1924
Al Worthington	1960
Tom Wright	1950–51
Jim Wright	1978–79
John Wyatt	1966–68
John Wyckoff	1916–18
Carl Yastrzemski	1961–83
Steve Yerkes	1909, 1911–14
Rudy York	1946–47
Cy Young	1901–06, 1908
Matt Young	1991–92
Paul Zahniser	1925–26
Al Zarilla	1949–50, 1952–53
Norm Zauchin	1951, 1955–57
Matt Zeiser	1914
Bill Zuber	1946–47
Bob Zupcic	1991–94

Managers

Del Baker	1960
Ed Barrow	1918–20
*Jack Barry	1917
Lou Boudreau	1952–54
*Bill Carrigan	1913–16, 1927–29
Frank Chance	1923
*Jimmy Collins	1901–06
Shano Collins	1931–32
*Joe Cronin	1935–47
Patsy Donovan	1910–11
Hugh Duffy	1921–22
Lee Fohl	1924–26
Bucky Harris	1934
Billy Herman	1964–66
Pinky Higgins	1955–62
Butch Hobson	1992–94
Ralph Houk	1981–84
George Huff	1907
Darrell Johnson	1974–76
Bill Jurges	1959–60
Eddie Kasko	1970–73
Kevin Kennedy	1995
Fred Lake	1908–09
Joe McCarthy	1948–50
Deacon McGuire	1907–08
*Marty McManus	1932–33
John McNamara	1985–88
Joe Morgan	1988–91
Steve O'Neill	1950–51
Johnny Pesky	1963–64, 1980
Eddie Popowski	1969, 1973
Pete Runnels	1966
*Chick Stahl	1906
*Jake Stahl	1912–13
*Bob Unglaub	1907
Heinie Wagner	1930
Dick Williams	1967–69
Rudy York	1959
*Cy Young	1907
Don Zimmer	1976–80

CALIFORNIA Angels 1965–95
Moved from LOS ANGELES Angels

Don Aase	1978–82, 1984
Jim Abbott	1989–92, 1995
Kyle Abbott	1991
Shawn Abner	1991
Ricky Adams	1982–83
Joe Adcock	1966
Willie Aikens	1977, 1979
Mike Aldrete	1995
Andy Allanson	1995
Lloyd Allen	1969–73
Bob Allietta	1975
Sandy Alomar	1969–74
Orlando Alvarez	1976
Ruben Amaro	1969
Ruben Amaro	1991
Jim Anderson	1978–79
Kent Anderson	1989–90
Brian Anderson	1993–95
Garret Anderson	1994–95
Tony Armas	1987–89
Joe Azcue	1969–70, 1972
Stan Bahnsen	1982
Scott Bailes	1990–92
John Balaz	1974–75
Floyd Bannister	1991
Steve Barber	1972–73
Mike Barlow	1977–79
Jim Barr	1979–80
Don Baylor	1977–82
Chris Beasley	1991
Juan Beniquez	1981–85
Dennis Bennett	1968
Erik Bennett	1995
Ken Berry	1971–73
Dante Bichette	1988–90
Mike Bielecki	1995
Steve Blateric	1975
Bert Blyleven	1989–90, 1992
Bruce Bochte	1974–77
Bobby Bonds	1976–77
Bob Boone	1982–88
Pedro Borbon	1969
Shawn Boskie	1995
Thad Bosley	1977, 1988
Lyman Bostock	1978
Ralph Botting	1979–80
Tom Bradley	1969–70
Brian Brady	1989
Ken Brett	1977–78
Jim Brewer	1975–76
Dan Briggs	1975–77
Bobby Brooks	1973
Hubie Brooks	1992
Randy Brown	1969–70
Curt Brown	1983
Mike Brown	1983–85, 1988
Steve Brown	1983–84
Tom Brunansky	1981
George Brunet	1966–69
T. R. Bryden	1986
Bill Buckner	1987–88
DeWayne Buice	1987–88
Lew Burdette	1966–67
Tom Burgmeier	1968
Rick Burleson	1981–83, 1986
Mike Butcher	1992–95
Bert Campaneris	1979–81
John Candelaria	1985–87
John Caneira	1977–78
Jose Cardenal	1966–67
Leo Cardenas	1972
Rod Carew	1979–85
Wayne Causey	1968
Ray Chadwick	1986
Dave Chalk	1973–78
Bob Chance	1969
Dean Chance	1966
Bruce Christensen	1971
Pete Cimino	1967–68
Rickey Clark	1967–69, 1971–72
Bobby Clark	1979–83
Terry Clark	1988–89
Mark Clear	1979–80, 1990
Pat Clements	1985
Stan Cliburn	1980
Stewart Cliburn	1984–85, 1988
Bobby Coachman	1990
Jim Coates	1966–67
Chris Coletta	1972
Dave Collins	1975–76
Tony Conigliaro	1971
Mike Cook	1986–88
Doug Corbett	1982–86
Sherman Corbett	1988–90
Rod Correia	1993–95
Chuck Cottier	1968–69
Billy Cowan	1969–71
Al Cowens	1980
Terry Cox	1970
Chuck Crim	1992–93
Chris Cron	1991
Todd Cruz	1980
Mike Cuellar	1977
John Cumberland	1974
John Curtis	1982–84
Chad Curtis	1992–94
John D'Acquisto	1981
Paul Dade	1975–76
Mark Dalesandro	1994–95
Vic Davalillo	1968–69
Jerry DaVanon	1973
Tommy Davis	1976
Willie Davis	1979
Chili Davis	1988–90, 1993–95
Alvin Davis	1992
Bob Davis	1981
Doug Davis	1988
Mark Davis	1991
Doug DeCinces	1982–87
Frank DiMichele	1988
Gary DiSarcina	1989–95
Chuck Dobson	1974–75
John Doherty	1974–75
Tom Donohue	1979–80
John Dopson	1994
Brian Dorsett	1988
Jim Dorsey	1980
Brian Downing	1978–90
Paul Doyle	1970, 1972
Denny Doyle	1974–75
Dick Drago	1976–77
Rob Ducey	1992
Tom Dukes	1972
Steve Dunning	1976
Mike Easler	1976
Damion Easley	1992–95
Steve Eddy	1979
Ken Edenfield	1995
Jim Edmonds	1993–95
Dick Egan	1966
Tom Egan	1966–70, 1974–75
Mark Eichhorn	1990–92
Sammy Ellis	1968
Jim Eppard	1987–89
Mike Epstein	1973–74
Andy Etchebarren	1975–77
Jorge Fabregas	1994–95
Ron Fairly	1978
John Farrell	1993–94
Junior Felix	1991–92
Joe Ferguson	1981–83
Bob Ferris	1979–80
Mike Fetters	1989–91
Ed Figueroa	1974–75
Jack Fimple	1987
Chuck Finley	1986–95
Todd Fischer	1986
Eddie Fisher	1969–72
Mike Fitzgerald	1992
Al Fitzmorris	1978
Kevin Flora	1991, 1995
Gil Flores	1977
Tim Foli	1982–83
Dan Ford	1979–81
Ken Forsch	1981–84, 1986
Terry Forster	1986
Tim Fortugno	1992
Alan Foster	1972
Alan Fowlkes	1985
Willie Fraser	1986–90
Jim Fregosi	1966–71
Steve Frey	1992–93
Dave Frost	1978–81
Len Gabrielson	1967
Gary Gaetti	1991–93
Alan Gallagher	1973
Dave Gallagher	1991, 1995
Miguel Garcia	1987
Ralph Garr	1979–80
Adrian Garrett	1975–76
Greg Garrett	1970
Vern Geishert	1969
Craig Gerber	1985
Bill Gilbreth	1974
Dave Goltz	1982–83
Rene Gonzales	1992–93, 1995
Larry Gonzales	1993
Tony Gonzalez	1970–71
Jose Gonzalez	1992
Danny Goodwin	1975, 1977–78
Billy Grabarkewitz	1973
Joe Grahe	1990–94
Bobby Grich	1977–86
Tom Griffin	1978
Doug Griffin	1970
Kelly Gruber	1993
Mario Guerrero	1976–77
John Habyan	1995
Ed Halicki	1980
Jimmie Hall	1967–68
Jack Hamilton	1967–68
Ike Hampton	1975–79
Rich Hand	1973
Mike Harkey	1995
Larry Harlow	1979–81
Tommy Harper	1975
Brian Harper	1979, 1981
Bill Harrelson	1968
John Harris	1979–81
Paul Hartzell	1976–78
Bryan Harvey	1987–92
Andy Hassler	1971, 1973–76, 1980–83
Hilly Hathaway	1992–93
Von Hayes	1992
Bob Heffner	1968
Bob Heise	1974
Woodie Held	1967–68
George Hendrick	1985–88
Jackie Hernandez	1966
Ed Herrmann	1976
Jack Hiatt	1972
Jim Hicks	1969
Donnie Hill	1990–91
Chuck Hinton	1968
Butch Hobson	1981
Chuck Hockenbery	1975
Glenn Hoffman	1989
Al Holland	1985
Mark Holzemer	1993, 1995
Doug Howard	1972–74
Jack Howell	1985–91
Rex Hudler	1994–95
Charles Hudson	1975
Terry Humphrey	1976–79
Reggie Jackson	1982–86
Ron Jackson	1975–78, 1982–84
Bo Jackson	1994
Mike James	1995
Stan Javier	1993

Jesse Jefferson	1981
Tommy John	1982–85
Alex Johnson	1970–71
Lou Johnson	1969
Jay Johnstone	1966–70
Bobby Jones	1976–77
Ruppert Jones	1985–87
Wally Joyner	1986–91
Curt Kaufman	1984
Steve Kealey	1968–70
Pat Keedy	1985
Mick Kelleher	1982
Bill Kelso	1966–67
Dave Kingman	1977
Bob Kipper	1985
Ed Kirkpatrick	1966–68
Don Kirkwood	1974–77
Bruce Kison	1980–84
Chris Knapp	1978–80
Bobby Knoop	1966–69
Andy Kosco	1972
Ray Krawczyk	1988
Gil Kubski	1980
Fred Kuhaulua	1977
Art Kusnyer	1971–73
Bob Lacey	1983
Frank LaCorte	1984
Joe Lahoud	1974–76
Ken Landreaux	1977–78
Dick Lange	1972–75
Mark Langston	1990–95
Carney Lansford	1978–80
Dave LaRoche	1970–71, 1977–80
Fred Lasher	1971
Jack Lazorko	1987–88
Bob Lee	1966
Craig Lefferts	1994
Phil Leftwich	1993–94
Mark Leiter	1994
Dave Lemanczyk	1980
Scott Lewis	1990–94
Rufino Linares	1985
Jose Lind	1995
Doug Linton	1993
Winston Llenas	1968–69, 1972–75
Bobby Locke	1967–68
Skip Lockwood	1974
Marcelino Lopez	1966–67
Ramon Lopez	1966
Carlos Lopez	1976
Andrew Lorraine	1994
Vance Lovelace	1988–89
Torey Lovullo	1993
Steve Lubratich	1981, 1983
Gary Lucas	1986–87
Urbano Lugo	1985–88
Fred Lynn	1981–84
Barry Lyons	1991
Dave Machemer	1978
Tony Mack	1985
Joe Magrane	1993–94
Mickey Mahler	1981–82
Jim Maloney	1971
Frank Malzone	1966
Mike Marshall	1991
Fred Martinez	1980–81
Carlos Martinez	1995
Rudy May	1969–74
Carlos May	1977
Kirk McCaskill	1985–91
Bob McClure	1989–91
Tom McCraw	1973–74
Orlando McFarlane	1967–68
Jim McGlothlin	1966–69
Byron McLaughlin	1983
Mark McLemore	1986–90
Ken McMullen	1970–72
Bill Melton	1976
Rudi Meoli	1973–75
Andy Messersmith	1968–72
Mike Miley	1975–76
Dyar Miller	1977–79
Rick Miller	1978–80
Darrell Miller	1984–88
Don Mincher	1967–68
Greg Minton	1987–90
Sid Monge	1975–77
John Montague	1979–80
Willie Montanez	1966
Aurelio Monteagudo	1973

Rich Monteleone	1988–89, 1995
Donnie Moore	1985–88
Balor Moore	1977
Jose Moreno	1982
Angel Moreno	1981–82
John Morris	1992
Bubba Morton	1966–69
Gerry Moses	1971
Curt Motton	1972
Rance Mulliniks	1977–79
Tom Murphy	1968–72
Greg Myers	1992–95
Jerry Narron	1983–86
Gene Nelson	1993
Morris Nettles	1974–75
Fred Newman	1966–67
Jerry Nielsen	1993
Junior Noboa	1988
Gary Nolan	1977
Tim Nordbrook	1976
Ken Oberkfell	1992
Mike O'Berry	1983
Syd O'Brien	1971–72
Bob Oliver	1972–74
Phil Ortega	1969
John Orton	1989–93
Ed Ott	1981
Mike Overy	1976
Spike Owen	1994–95
Ray Oyler	1970
Joe Pactwa	1975
Orlando Palmeiro	1995
Billy Parker	1971–73
Dave Parker	1991
Lance Parrish	1989–92
Freddie Patek	1980–81
Bob Patterson	1994–95
Ken Patterson	1993–94
Marty Pattin	1968
Albie Pearson	1966
Orlando Pena	1974–75
Troy Percival	1995
Marty Perez	1969–70
Eduardo Perez	1993–95
Ron Perranoski	1973
Dan Petry	1988–89
Gary Pettis	1982–87
Tony Phillips	1995
Rob Picciolo	1984
Jimmy Piersall	1966–67
Horacio Pina	1974
Vada Pinson	1972–73
Gus Polidor	1985–88
Luis Polonia	1990–93
Bob Priddy	1969
Mel Queen	1970–72
Luis Quintana	1974–75
Orlando Ramirez	1974–77, 1979
Domingo Ramos	1988
Doug Rau	1981
Johnny Ray	1987–90
Barry Raziano	1974
Joe Redfield	1988
Howie Reed	1966
Rick Reichardt	1966–70
Jerry Remy	1975–77
Steve Renko	1981–82
Roger Repoz	1967–71
Merv Rettenmund	1978–80
Jerry Reuss	1987
Tommie Reynolds	1970–71
Archie Reynolds	1971
Harold Reynolds	1994
Jeff Richardson	1990
Mickey Rivers	1970–75
Frank Robinson	1973–74
Don Robinson	1992
Jeff Robinson	1991
Buck Rodgers	1966–69
Aurelio Rodriguez	1967–70
Ellie Rodriguez	1974–75
Minnie Rojas	1966–68
Ron Romanick	1984–86
Don Rose	1972
Bobby Rose	1989–92
Gary Ross	1975–77
Jorge Rubio	1966–67
Joe Rudi	1977–80

Vern Ruhle	1986
Chico Ruiz	1970–71
Mark Ryal	1986–87
Nolan Ryan	1972–79
Tim Salmon	1992–95
Bill Sampen	1994
Luis Sanchez	1981–85
Ken Sanders	1974
Scott Sanderson	1993, 1995
Charlie Sands	1973–74
Jack Sanford	1966–67
Tom Satriano	1966–69
Paul Schaal	1966–68, 1974
Richie Scheinblum	1973–74
Dick Schofield	1983–92, 1995
Bill Schroeder	1989–90
Rick Schu	1990
Dave Schuler	1979–80
Jeff Schwarz	1994
Daryl Sconiers	1981–85
Mickey Scott	1975–77
Darryl Scott	1993
Dave Sells	1972–75
Dick Selma	1974
Harvey Shank	1970
Larry Sherry	1968
Norm Siebern	1966
Tom Silverio	1970–72
Curt Simmons	1967
Wayne Simpson	1977
Bill Singer	1973–75
Dave Skaggs	1980
Bill Skowron	1967
Jim Slaton	1984–86
Willie Smith	1966
Billy Smith	1975–76
Lee Smith	1995
Dave Smith	1984–85
Dwight Smith	1994
J. T. Snow	1993–95
Luis Sojo	1991–92
Tony Solaita	1976–78
Al Spangler	1966
Jim Spencer	1968–73
Russ Springer	1993–95
Leroy Stanton	1972–76
Ricky Steirer	1982–84
Rick Stelmaszek	1973
Johnny Stephenson	1971–73
Lee Stevens	1990–92
Kurt Stillwell	1993
Bill Stoneman	1974
Dick Stuart	1969
Bill Sudakis	1975
Ed Sukla	1966
Don Sutton	1985–87
Craig Swan	1984
Paul Swingle	1993
Frank Tanana	1973–80
Jarvis Tatum	1968–70
Ken Tatum	1969–70
Hawk Taylor	1967
Derrel Thomas	1984
Jason Thompson	1980
Dickie Thon	1979–80
Luis Tiant	1982
Ron Tingley	1989–93
Jeff Torborg	1971–73
Rusty Torres	1976–77
Bill Travers	1981, 1983
Bobby Trevino	1968
Ken Turner	1967
Chris Turner	1993–95
Bobby Valentine	1973–75
Ellis Valentine	1983
Fernando Valenzuela	1991
Julio Valera	1992–93
Ty Van Burkleo	1993
Max Venable	1989–91
John Verhoeven	1976–77
Charlie Vinson	1966
Bill Voss	1969–70
Jim Walewander	1993
Chico Walker	1988
Tom Walker	1977
Don Wallace	1967
Jerome Walton	1993
Jackie Warner	1966
Greg Washburn	1969

Claudell Washington	1989–90
Jim Weaver	1967–68
Johnny Werhas	1967
Gary Wheelock	1976
Devon White	1985–90
Dan Whitmer	1980
Rob Wilfong	1982–86
Hoyt Wilhelm	1969
Nick Willhite	1967
Mitch Williams	1995
Reggie Williams	1992
Terry Wilshusen	1973
Tack Wilson	1987
Dave Winfield	1990–91
Mike Witt	1981–90
Wally Wolf	1969–70
Clyde Wright	1966–73
Butch Wynegar	1987–88
Billy Wynne	1971
Cliff Young	1990–91
Geoff Zahn	1981–85

Managers

Jim Fregosi	1978–81
Dave Garcia	1977–78
Whitey Herzog	1974
Bobby Knoop	1994
Marcel Lachemann	1994–95
Gene Mauch	1981–82, 1985–87
John McNamara	1983–84
Lefty Phillips	1969–71
Doug Rader	1989–91
Del Rice	1972
Bill Rigney	1966–69
Buck Rodgers	1991–94
Cookie Rojas	1988
Norm Sherry	1976–77
Larry Stubing	1988
John Wathan	1992
Dick Williams	1974–76
Bobby Winkles	1973–74

CHICAGO White Sox 1901–95
Known as White Stockings 1901–03

Jim Abbott	1995
Shawn Abner	1992
Cal Abrams	1956
Fritz Ackley	1963–64
Jose Acosta	1922
Cy Acosta	1972–74
Jerry Adair	1966–67
Herb Adams	1948–50
Bobby Adams	1955
Doug Adams	1969
Grady Adkins	1928–29
Tommie Agee	1965–67
Juan Agosto	1981–86
Scotty Alcock	1914
Hank Allen	1972–73
Dick Allen	1972–74
Lloyd Allen	1974–75
Neil Allen	1986–87
Bill Almon	1981–82
Luis Aloma	1950–53
Sandy Alomar	1967–69
Dave Altizer	1909
Nick Altrock	1903–09
Luis Alvarado	1971–74
Wilson Alvarez	1991–95
Hal Anderson	1932
John Anderson	1908
Larry Anderson	1977
Mike Andrews	1971–73
Luis Andujar	1995
Luis Aparicio	1956–62, 1968–70
Pete Appleton	1940–42
Luke Appling	1930–43, 1945–50
Maurice Archdeacon	1923–25
Rudy Arias	1959
Charlie Armbruster	1907
Jerry Arrigo	1970
Ken Ash	1925
Paul Assenmacher	1994
Jake Atz	1907–09
Martin Autry	1929–30
Earl Averill	1960

Stan Bahnsen	1972–75
Harold Baines	1980–89
Floyd Baker	1945–51
Howard Baker	1914
Jesse Baker	1911
Dave Baldwin	1973
James Baldwin	1995
Alan Bannister	1976–80
Floyd Bannister	1983–87
Charlie Barnabe	1927–28
Red Barnes	1930
Bob Barnes	1924
Rich Barnes	1982
Salome Barojas	1982–84
Bill Barrett	1923–28
Francisco Barrios	1974, 1976–81
Cuke Barrows	1909–12
Les Bartholomew	1932
Earl Battey	1955–59
Jim Battle	1927
Matt Batts	1954
Frank Baumann	1960–64
Jim Baumer	1949
Ross Baumgarten	1978–81
Johnny Beall	1913
Ted Beard	1957–58
Gene Bearden	1953
Ollie Bejma	1939
Tim Belcher	1993
Gary Bell	1969
Ralph Bell	1912
Kevin Bell	1976–80
George Bell	1992–93
Esteban Beltre	1991–92
Chief Bender	1925
Bugs Bennett	1921
Joe Benz	1911–19
Jason Bere	1993–95
Moe Berg	1926–30
Joe Berger	1913–14
Boze Berger	1937–38
Marty Berghammer	1911
Tony Bernazard	1981–83
Denny Berran	1912
Ken Berry	1962–70
Charlie Berry	1932–33
Claude Berry	1904
Neil Berry	1953
Mike Bertotti	1995
Charlie Biggs	1932
John Bischoff	1925
Hi Bithorn	1947
Jeff Bittiger	1988–89
Bill Black	1924
Babe Blackburn	1921
Lena Blackburne	1910, 1912, 1914–15, 1927
George Blackerby	1928
Ossie Blanco	1970
Homer Blankenship	1922–23
Ted Blankenship	1922–30
Bruno Block	1910–12
Ron Blomberg	1978
Lu Blue	1931–32
Milt Bocek	1933–34
Ping Bodie	1911–14
Bob Boken	1934
Greg Bollo	1965–66
Rodney Bolton	1993, 1995
Bobby Bonds	1978
Bobby Bonilla	1986
Zeke Bonura	1934–37
Buddy Booker	1968
Ike Boone	1927
Ray Boone	1958–59
Frenchy Bordagaray	1934
Glenn Borgmann	1980
Babe Borton	1912–13
Thad Bosley	1978–80
Daryl Boston	1984–90
Billy Bowers	1949
Grant Bowler	1931–32
Emmett Bowles	1922
Red Bowser	1910
Bob Boyd	1951, 1953–54
Ken Boyer	1967–68
Harry Boyles	1938–39
Buddy Bradford	1966–70, 1972–76
Fred Bradley	1948–49
Tom Bradley	1971–72
Phil Bradley	1990
Scott Bradley	1986
Doug Brady	1995
Dave Brain	1901
Fritz Bratschi	1921
Angel Bravo	1969
Garland Braxton	1930–31
Jim Breazeale	1978
Tom Brennan	1984
Jim Breton	1913–15
Ken Brett	1976–77
Alan Brice	1961
Jim Brideweser	1955–56
Bunny Brief	1915
Chuck Brinkman	1969–74
Jack Brohamer	1976–77
Jim Brosnan	1963
Clint Brown	1936–40
Hal Brown	1951–52
Joe Brown	1927
Dick Brown	1960
George Browne	1910
Jack Bruner	1949–50
Warren Brusstar	1982
Don Buford	1963–67
Smoky Burgess	1965–66
Jimmy Burke	1901
Ellis Burks	1993
Joe Burns	1924
Bill Burns	1909–10
Britt Burns	1978–85
Jim Busby	1950–52, 1955
John Buzhardt	1962–67
Harry Byrd	1955–56
Jerry Byrne	1929
Bobby Byrne	1917
Tommy Byrne	1953
Leon Cadore	1923
Sugar Cain	1936–38
Bob Cain	1949–51
George Caithamer	1934
Ivan Calderon	1986–90, 1993
Earl Caldwell	1945–48
Nixey Callahan	1901–05, 1911–12
Johnny Callison	1958–59
Mike Cameron	1995
Bruce Campbell	1930–32
John Cangelosi	1985–86
Pat Caraway	1930–32
Andy Carey	1961
Cisco Carlos	1967–69
Steve Carlton	1986
Eddie Carnett	1944
Alex Carrasquel	1949
Chico Carrasquel	1950–55
Camilo Carreon	1959–64
Clay Carroll	1976–77
Jeff Carter	1991
Chuck Cary	1993
Norm Cash	1958–59
Vince Castino	1943–45
Paul Castner	1923
Danny Cater	1965–66
Wayne Causey	1966–68
Phil Cavarretta	1954–55
Bob Chakales	1955
Bill Chamberlain	1932
Joe Chamberlain	1934
Ben Chapman	1941
Harry Chappas	1978–80
Larry Chappell	1913–14
Hal Chase	1913–14
Italo Chelini	1935–37
Felix Chouinard	1910–11
Chief Chouneau	1910
Bob Christian	1969–70
Steve Christmas	1984
Loyd Christopher	1947
Eddie Cicotte	1912–20
Bill Cissell	1928–32
Ralph Citarella	1987
Bud Clancy	1924, 1926–30
Allie Clark	1953
Pep Clark	1903
Bryan Clark	1986–87
Grey Clarke	1944
Gil Coan	1955
Dave Cochrane	1986
Rich Coggins	1976
Rocky Colavito	1967
Mike Colbern	1978–79
Bert Cole	1927
Willis Cole	1909–10
Ray Coleman	1951–52
Eddie Collins	1915–26
Shano Collins	1910–20
Bob Coluccio	1975, 1977
Ramon Conde	1962
Jocko Conlan	1934–35
Sarge Connally	1921, 1923–29
Bill Connelly	1950
Merv Connors	1937–38
Sandy Consuegra	1953–56
Nardi Contreras	1980
Dennis Cook	1994
Cecil Coombs	1914
Joey Cora	1991–94
Ed Corey	1918
Roy Corhan	1911
Ed Correa	1985
Clint Courtney	1955
Henry Courtney	1922
Wes Covington	1961
Joe Cowley	1986
Ernie Cox	1922
George Cox	1928
Les Cox	1926
Bill Cox	1937–38
Jim Crabb	1912
Rodney Craig	1986
Gavvy Cravath	1909
Jerry Crider	1970
Chris Cron	1992
Buck Crouse	1923–30
Henry Cruz	1977–78
Julio Cruz	1983–86
Todd Cruz	1980
Tommy Cruz	1977
Tony Cuccinello	1943–45
Charlie Cuellar	1950
Tim Cullen	1968
Dick Culler	1943
Joe Cunningham	1962–64
Guy Curtright	1943–46
Mike Cvengros	1923–25
Pete Daglia	1932
Jerry Dahlke	1956
Bruce Dal Canton	1977
Tom Daly	1913–15
Tom Daly	1902–03
Dave Danforth	1916–19
Wally Dashiell	1924
Lum Davenport	1921–24
Dixie Davis	1915
George Davis	1902, 1904–09
Tommy Davis	1968
Ike Davis	1924–25
Joel Davis	1985–88
John Davis	1988–89
Bill Dawley	1986
Joe De Maestri	1951
Dave DeBusschere	1962–63
Mike DeGerick	1961–62
Jose DeLeon	1986–87, 1993–95
Flame Delhi	1912
Jim Delsing	1948, 1956
Ray Demmitt	1914–15
Drew Denson	1993
Bucky Dent	1973–76
Sam Dente	1952–53
Jim Derrington	1956–57
Joe DeSa	1985
Mike Devereaux	1995
Bernie DeViveiros	1924
Al DeVormer	1918
Mike Diaz	1988
Rob Dibble	1995
George Dickey	1941–42, 1946–47
Johnny Dickshot	1944–45
Bill Dietrich	1936–46
Steve Dillard	1982
Bob Dillinger	1951
Miguel Dilone	1983
John Dobb	1924
Jess Dobernic	1939
Joe Dobson	1951–53
Larry Doby	1956–57, 1959
Cozy Dolan	1903
Jiggs Donahue	1904–09
Dick Donovan	1955–60
Harry Dorish	1951–55
Charlie Dorman	1923
Richard Dotson	1979–87, 1989
Patsy Dougherty	1906–11
Tom Dougherty	1904
Phil Douglas	1912
Brian Downing	1973–77
Moe Drabowsky	1972
Brian Drahman	1991–93
Tom Drees	1991
Walt Dropo	1955–58
Larry Duff	1922
Dan Dugan	1928–29
Gus Dundon	1904–06
Davey Dunkle	1903
Mike Dunne	1992
Frank Dupee	1901
Ed Durham	1933
Jimmy Durham	1902
Ray Durham	1995
Jerry Dybzinski	1983–84
Jimmy Dykes	1933–37
George Earnshaw	1934–35
Ted Easterly	1912–13
Vallie Eaves	1939–40
Don Eddy	1970–71
Mike Eden	1978
Paul Edmondson	1969
Hank Edwards	1952
Jim Joe Edwards	1925–26
Wayne Edwards	1989–91
Tom Egan	1971–72
Fred Eichrodt	1931
Lee Elia	1966
Bob Elliott	1953
Sammy Ellis	1969
Roy Elsh	1923–25
Slim Embrey	1923
Charlie English	1932–33
Del Ennis	1959
George Enright	1976
Mutz Ens	1912
Joe Erautt	1950–51
Ernesto Escarrega	1982
Sammy Esposito	1952, 1955–62
Mark Esser	1979
Jim Essian	1976–77, 1981
Red Evans	1936
Art Evans	1932
Bill Evans	1949
Johnny Evers	1922
Sam Ewing	1973, 1976
Red Faber	1914–33
Ferris Fain	1953–54
Bibb Falk	1920–28
Bob Fallon	1984–85
Bob Farley	1962
Ed Farmer	1979–81
Kerby Farrell	1945
Bill Fehring	1934
Happy Felsch	1915–20
Hod Fenner	1921
Ed Fernandes	1946
Alex Fernandez	1990–95
Don Ferrarese	1960
Clarence Fieber	1932
Lou Fiene	1906–09
Pete Filson	1986
Steve Fireovid	1985
Carl Fischer	1935
Bill Fischer	1956–58
Eddie Fisher	1962–66, 1972–73
Jack Fisher	1968
Carlton Fisk	1981–93
Patsy Flaherty	1903–04
Tom Flanigan	1954
John Flannery	1977
Ray Flaskamper	1927
Scott Fletcher	1983–85, 1989–91
Marv Foley	1978–80, 1982
Lew Fonseca	1931
Gene Ford	1938
Happy Foreman	1924
Mike Fornieles	1953–56
Terry Forster	1971–76
Tim Fortugno	1995
Pop Foster	1901
George Foster	1986
Bob Fothergill	1930–32
Jack Fournier	1912–16
Nellie Fox	1950–63
Ken Frailing	1972–73
Julio Franco	1994
Tito Francona	1958
Vic Frasier	1931–33, 1939
Gene Freese	1960, 1965–66
Jake Freeze	1925
Charlie French	1910

Ray French	1924
Dave Frost	1977
Liz Funk	1932–33

Frank Gabler	1938
Dave Gallagher	1988–90
Phil Gallivan	1932, 1934
Oscar Gamble	1977, 1985
Chick Gandil	1910, 1917–19
Mike Garcia	1960
Ramon Garcia	1991
Lou Garland	1931
Ralph Garr	1976–79
Hank Garrity	1931
Ned Garvin	1902
Milt Gaston	1932–34
Joe Gates	1978–79
Pete Gebrian	1947
Jim Geddes	1972–73
Johnny Gerlach	1938–39
Al Gettel	1948–49
George Gick	1937–38
Mark Gilbert	1985
Brian Giles	1986
Claral Gillenwater	1923
Bob Gillespie	1947–48
Joe Ginsberg	1960–61
Kid Gleason	1912
Jerry Don Gleaton	1984–85
Bill Gogolewski	1975
Gordon Goldsberry	1949–51
Wilbur Good	1918
John Goodell	1928
Billy Goodman	1958–61
Jim Goodwin	1948
Goose Gossage	1972–76
Johnny Grabowski	1924–26
Roy Graham	1922–23
Wayne Granger	1974
Jimmy Grant	1942–43
Ted Gray	1955
Lorenzo Gray	1982–83
Craig Grebeck	1990–95
Danny Green	1902–05
Paul Gregory	1932–33
Ross Grimsley	1951
Marv Grissom	1952
Ernie Groth	1949
Johnny Groth	1954–55
Orval Grove	1940–49
Frank Grube	1931–33, 1935–36
Ozzie Guillen	1985–95
Tom Gulley	1926
Randy Gumpert	1948–51

Bert Haas	1951
Mule Haas	1933–37
Warren Hacker	1961
Bump Hadley	1932
Mickey Haefner	1949–50
Ed Hahn	1906–10
Hal Haid	1933
Sam Hairston	1951
Jerry Hairston	1973–77, 1981–87, 1989
Joe Hall	1994
Jack Hallett	1940–41
Bill Hallman	1903
Jack Hamilton	1969
Steve Hamilton	1970
Dave Hamilton	1975–77
Atlee Hammaker	1994–95
Ralph Hamner	1946
Fred Hancock	1949
Ron Hansen	1963–69
Don Hanski	1943–44
John Happenny	1923
Jack Hardy	1989
Dave Harris	1930
Spence Harris	1925–26
Earl Harrist	1947–48, 1953
Jack Harshman	1954–57
Hub Hart	1905–07
Fred Hartman	1901
Ervin Harvey	1901
Ziggy Hasbrook	1916–17
Ron Hassey	1986–87
Fred Hatfield	1956–57
Grady Hatton	1954
Frankie Hayes	1946
Jackie Hayes	1932–40
Joe Haynes	1941–48
Spencer Heath	1920
Val Heim	1942

Woodie Held	1968–69
Scott Hemond	1992
Frank Hemphill	1906
Ken Henderson	1973–75
Joe Henderson	1974
Butch Henline	1930–31
Dutch Henry	1929–30
Ray Herbert	1961–64
Rudy Hernandez	1972
Roberto Hernandez	1991–95
Art Herring	1939
Ed Herrmann	1967, 1969–74
Mike Hershberger	1961–64, 1971
Joe Heving	1933–34
Mike Heydon	1904
Greg Hibbard	1989–92
Kevin Hickey	1981–83
Piano Legs Hickman	1907
Jim Hicks	1965–66
Joe Hicks	1959–60
Bill Higdon	1949
Dennis Higgins	1966–67
Donnie Hill	1987–88
Marc Hill	1981–86
Shawn Hillegas	1988–90
Rich Hinton	1971, 1975, 1978–79
Myril Hoag	1941–42, 1944
Oris Hockett	1945
Johnny Hodapp	1932
Shovel Hodge	1920–22
Ralph Hodgin	1943–44, 1946–48
Dutch Hoffman	1929
Guy Hoffman	1979–80, 1983
Ken Holcombe	1950–52
Al Hollingsworth	1946
Ducky Holmes	1903–05
Harry Hooper	1921–25
Marty Hopkins	1934–35
Gail Hopkins	1968–70
Joe Horlen	1961–71
Ricky Horton	1988
Ken Hottman	1971
Charlie Hough	1991–92
Joe Hovlik	1911
Bruce Howard	1963–67
Fred Howard	1979
Chris Howard	1993
Dixie Howell	1955–58
Dann Howitt	1994
Dummy Hoy	1901
LaMarr Hoyt	1979–84
Hal Hudson	1952–53
Frank Huelsman	1904
Mike Huff	1991–93
Ed Hughes	1902
Jim Hughes	1957
Tim Hulett	1983–87
John Humphries	1941–45
Bill Hunnefield	1926–30
Steve Huntz	1971
Ira Hutchinson	1933

Frank Isbell	1901–09

Joe Jackson	1915–20
Ron Jackson	1954–59
Darrin Jackson	1994
Bo Jackson	1991, 1993
Otto Jacobs	1918
Elmer Jacobs	1927
Pat Jacquez	1971
Bill James	1919
Bob James	1985–87
Gerry Janeski	1970
Hi Jasper	1914–15
Jesse Jefferson	1975–76
Irv Jeffries	1930–31
John Jenkins	1922
Joe Jenkins	1919
John Jeter	1973
Shawn Jeter	1992
Tommy John	1965–71
Pete Johns	1915
Connie Johnson	1953, 1955–56
Darrell Johnson	1952
Deron Johnson	1975
Don Johnson	1954
Ellis Johnson	1912, 1915
Ernie Johnson	1912, 1921–23
Johnny Johnson	1945
Stan Johnson	1960
Bart Johnson	1969–74, 1976–77
Lamar Johnson	1974–81

Randy Johnson	1980
Larry Johnson	1978
Lance Johnson	1988–95
Dane Johnson	1994
Jimmy Johnston	1911
Jay Johnstone	1971–72
Stan Jok	1954–55
Smead Jolley	1930–32
Cleon Jones	1976
Davy Jones	1913
Fielder Jones	1901–08
Deacon Jones	1962–63
Jake Jones	1941–42, 1946–47
Sad Sam Jones	1932–35
Tex Jones	1911
Steve Jones	1967
Al Jones	1983–85
Barry Jones	1988–90, 1993
Bubber Jonnard	1920
Rip Jordan	1912
Tom Jordan	1944, 1946
Duane Josephson	1965–70
Ted Jourdan	1917–18, 1920
Mike Joyce	1962–63
Howie Judson	1948–52

Jim Kaat	1973–75
Willie Kamm	1923–31
Johnny Kane	1925
Matt Karchner	1995
Ron Karkovice	1986–95
John Katoll	1901–02
Steve Kealey	1971–73
Pat Keedy	1987
Bob Keegan	1953–58
George Kell	1954–56
Red Kelly	1910
Pat Kelly	1971–76
Russ Kemmerer	1960–62
Steve Kemp	1982
Vern Kennedy	1934–37
Bob Kennedy	1939–42, 1946–48, 1955–56
Bill Kennedy	1952
Dick Kenworthy	1962, 1966–68
Gus Keriazakos	1950
Jim Kern	1982–83
John Kerr	1929–31
Dickie Kerr	1919–21, 1925
Don Kessinger	1977–79
Brian Keyser	1995
Joe Kiefer	1920
Bruce Kimm	1980
Chad Kimsey	1932–33
Ellis Kinder	1956–57
Jim King	1967
Eric King	1989–90
Harry Kinzy	1934
Don Kirkwood	1977
Joe Kirrene	1950, 1954
Ron Kittle	1982–86, 1989–91
Hugo Klaerner	1934
Fred Klages	1966–67
Ed Klepfer	1915
Eddie Klieman	1949
Joe Klinger	1930
Ted Kluszewski	1959–60
Chris Knapp	1975–77
Bill Knickerbocker	1941
Bobby Knoop	1969–70
Jack Knott	1938–40
Don Kolloway	1940–43, 1946–49
Jerry Koosman	1981–83
Fabian Kowalik	1932
Al Kozar	1950
Ken Kravec	1975–80
Mike Kreevich	1935–41
Ralph Kreitz	1911
Charlie Kress	1949–50
Red Kress	1932–34
Lou Kretlow	1950–53
Frank Kreutzer	1962–64
Rocky Krsnich	1949, 1952–53
John Kruk	1995
Jack Kucek	1974–79
Joe Kuhel	1938–43, 1946
Walt Kuhn	1912–14
Rusty Kuntz	1979–83
Art Kusnyer	1970
Jerry Kutzler	1990
Bob Kuzava	1949–50

Lerrin LaGrow	1977–79
Jack Lamabe	1966–67
Fred Lamline	1912
Dennis Lamp	1981–83
Ken Landenberger	1952
Jim Landis	1957–64
Jesse Landrum	1938
Dick Lane	1949
Frank Lange	1910–13
Paul LaPalme	1956–57
Dave LaPoint	1987–88
Jack Lapp	1916
Don Larsen	1961
Frank Lary	1965
Bill Lathrop	1913–14
Barry Latman	1957–59
Mike LaValliere	1993–95
Rudy Law	1982–85
Vance Law	1982–84
Bob Lawrence	1924
Danny Lazar	1968–69
Terry Leach	1992–93
Thornton Lee	1937–47
George Lees	1921
Ron LeFlore	1981–82
Paul Lehner	1951
Nemo Leibold	1915–20
Elmer Leifer	1921
Dummy Leitner	1902
Jim Lemon	1963
Chet Lemon	1975–81
Dave Lemonds	1972
Don Lenhardt	1951
Eddie Leon	1973–74
Rudy Leopold	1928
Ted Lepcio	1961
Dixie Leverett	1922–24, 1926
Bill Lindsey	1987
Doug Lindsey	1993
Charlie Lindstrom	1958
Bryan Little	1985–86
Dick Littlefield	1951
Bob Locker	1965–69
Dario Lodigiani	1941–42, 1946
Ron Lolich	1971
Sherm Lollar	1952–63
Tim Lollar	1985
Jim Long	1922
Jeoff Long	1964
Bill Long	1985, 1987–90
Dean Look	1961
Ed Lopat	1944–47
Harry Lord	1910–14
Andrew Lorraine	1995
Jay Loviglio	1981–82
Grover Lowdermilk	1919–20
Turk Lown	1958–62
Tony Lupien	1948
Greg Luzinski	1981–84
Sparky Lyle	1982
Byrd Lynn	1916–20
Ted Lyons	1923–42
Steve Lyons	1986–90
Barry Lyons	1995
Jim Lyttle	1972

Frank Mack	1922–23, 1925
Ed Madjeski	1934
Jim Magnuson	1970–71
George Magoon	1903
Bob Mahoney	1951
Hank Majeski	1950–51
Jule Mallonee	1925
Eddie Malone	1949–50
Gordon Maltzberger	1943–44, 1946–47
Carl Manda	1914
Leo Mangum	1924–25
Johnny Mann	1928
Fred Manrique	1987–89
Moxie Manuel	1908
Ravelo Manzanillo	1988
Johnny Marcum	1939
Dick Marlowe	1956
Isidro Marquez	1995
Freddie Marsh	1953–54
Willard Marshall	1954–55
J. C. Martin	1959–67
Morrie Martin	1954–56
Norberto Martin	1993–95
Silvio Martinez	1977
Dave Martinez	1995
Carlos Martinez	1988–90
Randy Martz	1983

Phil Masi	1950–52
John Matias	1970
Wally Mattick	1912–13
Mark Mauldin	1934
Charlie Maxwell	1962–63
Carlos May	1968–76
Milt May	1979
Lee Maye	1971
Erskine Mayer	1919
Wally Mayer	1911–12, 1914–15
John McAleese	1901
Jim McAnany	1958–59
Pryor McBee	1926
Ken McBride	1959–60
Dick McCabe	1922
Brian McCall	1962–63
Tom McCarthy	1988–89
Kirk McCaskill	1992–95
Harvey McClellan	1919–24
Amby McConnell	1910–11
Mike McCormick	1950
Tom McCraw	1963–70
Rodney McCray	1990–91
Harry McCurdy	1926–28
Jim McDonald	1956–58
Jack McDowell	1987–88, 1990–94
Ed McFarland	1902–07
Herm McFarland	1901–02
Ed McGhee	1950, 1954–55
Lynn McGlothen	1981
Jim McGlothlin	1973
Tom McGuire	1919
Stover McIlwain	1957–58
Matty McIntyre	1911–12
Hal McKain	1929–32
Joel McKeon	1986–87
Rich McKinney	1970–71
Cal McLish	1961
Sam McMackin	1902
Don McMahon	1967–68
Fred McMullin	1916–20
Eric McNair	1939–40
Jerry McNertney	1964, 1966–68
Doug McWeeny	1921–22, 1924
Sam Mele	1952–53
Paul Meloan	1910–11
Bill Melton	1968–75
Bob Melvin	1994
Sam Mertes	1901–02
Matt Merullo	1989, 1991–93
Bobby Messenger	1909–11
Catfish Metkovich	1949
Bill Metzig	1944
Alex Metzler	1927–30
George Meyer	1938
Billy Meyer	1913
Cass Michaels	1943–50, 1954
John Michaelson	1921
Frank Miller	1913
Bob Miller	1970
Jake Miller	1933
Minnie Minoso	1951–57, 1960–61, 1964, 1976
Willie Miranda	1952
Roy Mitchell	1918
George Mogridge	1911–12
Bob Molinaro	1977–78, 1980–81
Rich Moloney	1970
Larry Monroe	1976
Aurelio Monteagudo	1967
Barry Moore	1970
Jim Moore	1930–32
Jimmy Moore	1930
Randy Moore	1927–28
Ray Moore	1958–60
Junior Moore	1978–80
Rich Morales	1967–73
Carl Moran	1974
Ray Morehart	1924, 1926
George Moriarty	1916
Russ Morman	1986, 1988–89
Jim Morrison	1979–82
Jo–Jo Morrissey	1936
Gerry Moses	1975
Wally Moses	1942–46
Les Moss	1955–57
Don Mossi	1964
Johnny Mostil	1918, 1921–29
Glen Moulder	1948
Lyle Mouton	1995
Don Mueller	1958
Bill Mueller	1942, 1945
Greg Mulleavy	1930, 1932
Charlie Mullen	1910–11
Eddie Mulligan	1921–22
Fran Mullins	1980
Dominic Mulrenan	1921
Steve Mura	1983
Danny Murphy	1969–70
Eddie Murphy	1915–20
George Murray	1933
Tony Muser	1971–75
Bill Nagel	1945
Bill Nahorodny	1977–79
Frank Naleway	1924
Cotton Nash	1967
Bernie Neis	1927
Andy Nelson	1908
Roger Nelson	1967
Gene Nelson	1984–86
Jack Ness	1916
Dan Neumeier	1972
Warren Newson	1991–95
Gus Niarhos	1950–51
Don Nicholas	1952, 1954
Reid Nichols	1985–86
Dave Nicholson	1963–65
Scott Nielsen	1987
Bob Nieman	1955–56
Randy Niemann	1984
Tim Nordbrook	1977
Wayne Nordhagen	1976–81
Bill Norman	1931–32
Ron Northey	1955–56
Wynn Noyes	1919
Jerry Nyman	1968–69
Nyls Nyman	1974–76
Chris Nyman	1982–83
Buck O'Brien	1913
Syd O'Brien	1970
Blue Moon Odom	1976
Fred Olmstead	1908–11
Tom O'Malley	1984
Emmett O'Neill	1946
Bill O'Neill	1906
Joe Orengo	1945
Jorge Orta	1972–79
Jose Ortiz	1969–70
Danny Osborn	1975
Dan Osinski	1969
Claude Osteen	1975
John Ostrowski	1949–50
Jim O'Toole	1967
Denny O'Toole	1969–73
Jim Otten	1974–76
Frank Owen	1903–09
Marv Owen	1938–39
Frank Owens	1909
Tom Paciorek	1982–85
Donn Pall	1988–93
Al Papai	1955
Frank Papish	1945–48
Freddy Parent	1908–11
Kelly Paris	1988
Casey Parsons	1983
Johnny Pasek	1934
Dan Pasqua	1988–94
Ham Patterson	1909
Roy Patterson	1901–07
Reggie Patterson	1981
Ken Patterson	1988–91
Don Pavletich	1969
John Pawlowski	1987–88
Fred Payne	1909–11
George Payne	1920
Ike Pearson	1948
Roger Peckinpaugh	1927
Elmer Pence	1922
Russ Pence	1921
Jack Perconte	1986
Melido Perez	1988–91
John Perkovich	1950
Len Perme	1942, 1946
Stan Perzanowski	1971, 1974
Gary Peters	1959–69
Rube Peters	1912
Buddy Peterson	1955
Adam Peterson	1987–90
Ray Phelps	1935–36
Dave Philley	1941, 1946–51, 1956–57
Bubba Phillips	1956–59
Taylor Phillips	1963
Wiley Piatt	1901–02
Billy Pierce	1949–61
Marino Pieretti	1948–49
Tony Piet	1935–37
Al Pilarcik	1961
Babe Pinelli	1918
Skip Pitlock	1974–75
Juan Pizarro	1961–66
Whitey Platt	1946
Howie Pollet	1956
John Pomorski	1934
Irv Porter	1914
Bob Poser	1932
Bob Priddy	1968–69
Red Proctor	1923
Mike Proly	1978–80
Ron Pruitt	1980
Greg Pryor	1978–81
Pid Purdy	1926
Billy Purtell	1908–10
Jimmy Qualls	1972
Tom Qualters	1958
Lee Quillen	1906–07
Finners Quinlan	1915
Jack Quinn	1918
Jamie Quirk	1984
Rip Radcliff	1934–39
Don Rader	1913
Scott Radinsky	1990–93, 1995
Pat Ragan	1919
Tim Raines	1991–95
Jim Randall	1988
Earl Rapp	1949
Morrie Rath	1912–13
Fred Rath	1968–69
Claude Raymond	1959
Buck Redfern	1928–29
Gary Redus	1987–88
Ron Reed	1984
Phil Regan	1972
Rick Reichardt	1971–73
Barney Reilly	1909
Steve Renko	1977
Tony Rensa	1937–39
Jerry Reuss	1988–89
Carl Reynolds	1927–31
Danny Reynolds	1945
Bobby Rhawn	1949
Hal Rhyne	1933
Dennis Ribant	1968
Lee Richard	1971–72, 1974–75
Marv Rickert	1950
Johnny Riddle	1930
Dave Righetti	1995
Johnny Rigney	1937–42, 1946–47
Swede Risberg	1917–20
Jim Rivera	1952–60
Tink Riviere	1925
Bert Roberge	1984
Charlie Robertson	1919, 1922–25
Billy Jo Robidoux	1989
Aaron Robinson	1948
Floyd Robinson	1960–66
Eddie Robinson	1950–52
Dewey Robinson	1979–81
Les Rock	1936
Hec Rodriguez	1952
Aurelio Rodriguez	1982–83
Saul Rogovin	1951–53
George Rohe	1905–07
Johnny Romano	1958–59, 1965–66
Vicente Romo	1971–72
Gil Rondon	1979
Phil Roof	1976
Bob Roselli	1961–62
Lou Rosenberg	1923
Steve Rosenberg	1988–90
Larry Rosenthal	1936–41
Buck Ross	1941–45
Marv Rotblatt	1948, 1950–51
Frank Roth	1906
Braggo Roth	1914–15
Jack Rothrock	1932
Virle Rounsaville	1970
Edd Roush	1913
Jerry Royster	1987
Don Rudolph	1957–59
Muddy Ruel	1934
Scott Ruffcorn	1993–95
Red Ruffing	1947
Bob Rush	1960
Reb Russell	1913–19
John Russell	1921–22
Mark Ryal	1985
Connie Ryan	1953
Blondy Ryan	1930
Chris Sabo	1995
Bob Sadowski	1962
Olmedo Saenz	1994
Mark Salas	1988
Luis Salazar	1985–86
Bill Salkeld	1950
Jack Salveson	1935
Scott Sanderson	1994
Ron Santo	1974
Nelson Santovenia	1992
Carl Sawatski	1954
Steve Sax	1992–93
Jerry Scala	1948–50
Randy Scarbery	1979–80
Ray Scarborough	1950
Jeff Schaefer	1989
Jimmie Schaffer	1965
Roy Schalk	1944–45
Ray Schalk	1912–26
Biff Schaller	1913
Norm Schlueter	1938–39
Dave Schmidt	1986
Ossee Schreckengost	1908
Hank Schreiber	1914
Ron Schueler	1978–79
Webb Schultz	1924
Ferdie Schupp	1922
Jeff Schwarz	1993–94
Jim Scoggins	1913
Herb Score	1960–62
Jim Scott	1909–17
Everett Scott	1926
Ray Searage	1986–87
Tom Seaver	1984–86
Don Secrist	1969–70
Bob Seeds	1932
Pat Seerey	1948–49
Jose Segura	1988–89
Rick Seilheimer	1980
Carey Selph	1932
Luke Sewell	1935–38
Bill Sharp	1973–75
Al Shaw	1908
Bob Shaw	1958–61
Jeff Shaw	1995
Merv Shea	1934–37
Earl Sheely	1921–27
Bud Sheely	1951–53
Frank Shellenback	1918–19
Joe Shipley	1963
Art Shires	1928–30
Bill Shores	1936
Dave Short	1941
Clyde Shoun	1949
Frank Shugart	1901
Roy Sievers	1960–61
Frank Sigafoos	1929
Ken Silvestri	1939–40
Al Sima	1954
Bill Simas	1995
Al Simmons	1933–35
Mel Simons	1931–32
Harry Simpson	1959
Mike Sirotka	1995
Tommie Sisk	1970
Jim Siwy	1982, 1984
Bud Sketchley	1942
Joel Skinner	1983–86
Lou Skizas	1959
John Skopec	1901
Bill Skowron	1964–66
Jack Slattery	1903
Roy Smalley	1984
Joe Smaza	1946
Al Smith	1958–62
Art Smith	1932
Charley Smith	1962–64
Pop Boy Smith	1913
Eddie Smith	1939–43, 1946–47
Ernie Smith	1930
Frank Smith	1904–10
Harry Smith	1912
Bob Smith	1913
Chris Snopek	1995
Russ Snyder	1968
Cory Snyder	1991
Eric Soderholm	1977–79
Eddie Solomon	1982

Moose Solters	1940–41, 1943
Sammy Sosa	1989–91
Steve Souchock	1949
Floyd Speer	1943–44
Bob Spence	1969–71
Jim Spencer	1976–77
Tom Spencer	1978
Ed Spiezio	1972
Dan Spillner	1984–85
Mike Squires	1975, 1977–84
Marv Staehle	1966–67
Gerry Staley	1956–61
Lee Stange	1970
Joe Stanka	1959
Mike Stanton	1985
Matt Stark	1990
Milt Steengrafe	1924, 1926
Dave Stegman	1983–84
Bill Stein	1974–76
Hank Steinbacher	1937–39
Gene Stephens	1963–64
Vern Stephens	1953, 1955
Joe Stephenson	1947
Bud Stewart	1951–54
Frank Stewart	1927
Jimmy Stewart	1967
Dave Stieb	1993
Royle Stillman	1977
Lee Stine	1934–35
Chuck Stobbs	1952
Tim Stoddard	1975
Dean Stone	1962
Steve Stone	1973, 1977–78
John Stoneham	1933
Dick Strahs	1954
Sammy Strang	1902
Monty Stratton	1934–38
Elmer Stricklett	1904
Jake Striker	1960
Ed Stroud	1966–67, 1971
Amos Strunk	1920–23
George Stumpf	1936
Joe Sugden	1901
John Sullivan	1919
Billy Sullivan	1931–33
Billy Sullivan	1901–12, 1914
Max Surkont	1949
Rube Suter	1909
Leo Sutherland	1980–81
Dale Sveum	1992
Evar Swanson	1932–34
Karl Swanson	1928
Augie Swentor	1922
Bill Swift	1943
Doug Taitt	1929
Fred Talbot	1963–64
Leo Tankersley	1925
Lee Tannehill	1903–12
Bruce Tanner	1985
Bennie Tate	1930–32
Ken Tatum	1974
Fred Tauby	1935
Wiley Taylor	1912
Zeb Terry	1916–17
Bobby Thigpen	1986–93
Tommy Thomas	1926–32
Leo Thomas	1952
Frank Thomas	1990–95
Larry Thomas	1995
Lee Thompson	1921
Tommy Thompson	1938
Sloppy Thurston	1923–26
Dick Tidrow	1983
Verle Tiefenthaler	1962
Les Tietje	1933–36
Ron Tingley	1994
Joe Tipton	1949
Wayne Tolleson	1986
Earl Torgeson	1957–61
Pablo Torrealba	1978–79
Rusty Torres	1978–79
Clay Touchstone	1945
Babe Towne	1906
Chris Tremie	1995
Mike Tresh	1938–48
Hal Trosky	1958
Hal Trosky	1944, 1946
Steve Trout	1978–82
Virgil Trucks	1953–55
Thurman Tucker	1942–44, 1946–47
Tom Turner	1940–44
Jerry Turner	1981
Cy Twombly	1921
Frenchy Uhalt	1934
Bob Uhl	1938
Charlie Uhlir	1934
Cecil Upshaw	1975
Vito Valentinetti	1954
Joe Vance	1935
Pete Varney	1973–76
Art Veltman	1926
Robin Ventura	1989–95
John Verhoeven	1977
Rube Vinson	1906
Fritz Von Kolnitz	1916
Bill Voss	1965–68
Pete Vuckovich	1975–76
Jake Wade	1942–44
Leon Wagner	1968
Don Wakamatsu	1991
Dixie Walker	1936–37
Gee Walker	1938–39
Greg Walker	1982–90
Jack Wallaesa	1947–48
Ed Walsh	1928–30, 1932
Ed Walsh	1904–16
Steve Wapnick	1991
Aaron Ward	1927
Pete Ward	1963–69
George Washington	1935–36
Claudell Washington	1978–80
Cliff Watwood	1929–32
Bob Way	1927
Art Weaver	1908
Floyd Weaver	1970
Buck Weaver	1912–20
Earl Webb	1933
Skeeter Webb	1940–44
Biggs Wehde	1930–31
Dave Wehrmeister	1985
Ralph Weigel	1948
Ed Weiland	1940, 1942
Bob Weiland	1928–31
Al Weis	1962–67
Mike Welday	1907, 1909
Leo Wells	1942, 1946
Sammy West	1942
Don Wheeler	1949
Ed White	1955
Doc White	1903–13
John Whitehead	1935–39
Frank Whitman	1946, 1948
Al Widmar	1952
Jack Wieneke	1921
Bill Wight	1948–50
Randy Wiles	1977
Hoyt Wilhelm	1963–68
Roy Wilkinson	1919–22
Jerry Willard	1990
Lefty Williams	1916–20
Walt Williams	1967–72
Eddie Williams	1989
Kenny Williams	1986–88
Al Williamson	1928
Hugh Willingham	1930
Carl Willis	1988
Jim Willoughby	1978
Ted Wills	1965
Kid Willson	1927
Ted Wilson	1952
Jim Wilson	1956–58
Red Wilson	1951–54
Roy Wilson	1928
Bill Wilson	1950, 1953–54
Jim Winn	1987
Kettle Wirts	1924
Archie Wise	1932
Polly Wolfe	1914
Mellie Wolfgang	1914–18
Wilbur Wood	1967–78
Mike Woodard	1988
Frank Woodward	1923
Rich Wortham	1978–80
Al Worthington	1960
Ceylon Wright	1916
Glenn Wright	1935
Taffy Wright	1940–42, 1946–48
Tom Wright	1952–53
Rick Wrona	1993
Whit Wyatt	1933–36
Early Wynn	1958–62
Billy Wynne	1968–70
Hugh Yancy	1972, 1974, 1976
George Yankowski	1949
Yam Yaryan	1921–22
Rudy York	1947
Irv Young	1910–11
Dom Zanni	1962–63
Al Zarilla	1951–52
Rollie Zeider	1910–13
Gus Zernial	1949–51
Richie Zisk	1977
Bob Zupcic	1994
Dutch Zwilling	1910

Managers

Bill Adair	1970
Terry Bevington	1995
Lena Blackburne	1928–29
Donie Bush	1930–31
*Nixey Callahan	1903–04, 1912–14
*Eddie Collins	1924–26
Red Corriden	1950
Larry Doby	1978
Hugh Duffy	1910–11
*Jimmy Dykes	1934–46
Johnny Evers	1924
Lew Fonseca	1932–34
Jim Fregosi	1986–88
Kid Gleason	1919–23
*Clark Griffith	1901–02
Don Gutteridge	1969–70
*Fielder Jones	1904–08
*Don Kessinger	1979
Gene Lamont	1992–95
Tony LaRussa	1979–86
Bob Lemon	1977–78
Al Lopez	1957–65, 1968–69
Ted Lyons	1946–48
Marty Marion	1954–56
Les Moss	1968
Jack Onslow	1949–50
Doug Rader	1986
Paul Richards	1951–54, 1976
Pants Rowland	1915–18
Ray Schalk	1927–28
Eddie Stanky	1966–68
*Billy Sullivan	1909
Chuck Tanner	1970–75
Jeff Torborg	1989–91
Ed Walsh	1924

CLEVELAND Indians 1901–95
Known as Blues 1901–04
Naps 1905–14

Fred Abbott	1903–04
Paul Abbott	1993
Al Aber	1950, 1953
Bill Abernathie	1952
Ted Abernathy	1963–64
Harry Ables	1909
Bert Adams	1910–12
Joe Adcock	1963
Tommie Agee	1962–64
Luis Aguayo	1989
Hank Aguirre	1955–57
Darrel Akerfelds	1987
Mike Aldrete	1991
Hugh Alexander	1937
Bob Alexander	1957
Gary Alexander	1978–80
Andy Allanson	1986–89
Johnny Allen	1936–40
Bob Allen	1961–63, 1966–67
Neil Allen	1989
Rod Allen	1988
Milo Allison	1916–17
Beau Allred	1989–91
Sandy Alomar	1990–95
Dell Alston	1979–80
Dave Altizer	1908
Joe Altobelli	1955, 1957
Luis Alvarado	1974
Max Alvis	1962–69
Ruben Amaro	1994–95
Larry Andersen	1975, 1977, 1979
Dwain Anderson	1974
Bud Anderson	1982–83
Ivy Andrews	1937
Nate Andrews	1940–41
Johnny Antonelli	1961
Luis Aponte	1984
Pete Appleton	1930–32
Steve Arlin	1974
Mike Armstrong	1987
Jack Armstrong	1992
Brad Arnsberg	1992
Alan Ashby	1973–76
Ken Aspromonte	1960–62
Paul Assenmacher	1995
Keith Atherton	1989
Rick Austin	1970–71
Martin Autry	1926–28
Earl Averill	1956, 1958
Earl Averill	1929–39
Bobby Avila	1949–58
Benny Ayala	1985
Dick Aylward	1953
Joe Azcue	1963–69
Carlos Baerga	1990–95
Jim Bagby	1941–45
Jim Bagby	1916–22
Scott Bailes	1986–89
Steve Bailey	1967–68
Bock Baker	1901
Howard Baker	1912
Frank Baker	1969, 1971
Neal Ball	1909–12
Mark Ballinger	1971
Chris Bando	1981–88
George Banks	1964–65
Alan Bannister	1980–83
Walter Barbare	1914–16
Jap Barbeau	1905–06
Ray Barker	1965
Len Barker	1979–83
Jeff Barkley	1984–85
Rich Barnes	1983
Brian Barnes	1994
Les Barnhart	1928, 1930
Jim Baskette	1911–13
Johnny Bassler	1913–14
Ray Bates	1913
Jim Baxes	1959
Harry Bay	1902–07
Bill Bayne	1928
Belve Bean	1930–31, 1933–35
Gene Bearden	1947–50
Kevin Bearse	1990
Erve Beck	1901
George Beck	1914
Heinz Becker	1946
Joe Becker	1936–37
Gene Bedford	1925
Phil Bedgood	1922–23
Fred Beebe	1916
Fred Beene	1974–75
Rick Behenna	1983–85
Gary Bell	1958–67
Beau Bell	1940–41
Buddy Bell	1972–78
Eric Bell	1991–92
Jay Bell	1986–88
David Bell	1995
Albert Belle	1989–95
Harry Bemis	1902–10
Ray Benge	1925–26
Stan Benjamin	1945
Henry Benn	1914
Al Benton	1949–50
Butch Benton	1985
Johnny Berardino	1948–50, 1952
Moe Berg	1931, 1934
Heinie Berger	1907–10
Boze Berger	1932, 1935–36
Al Bergman	1916
Tony Bernazard	1984–87
Bill Bernhard	1902–07
Ken Berry	1975
Joe Berry	1946
Bob Bescher	1918
Kurt Bevacqua	1971–72
Jim Bibby	1975–77
Mike Bielecki	1993
Josh Billings	1913–18
Steve Biras	1944
Joe Birmingham	1906–12
Lloyd Bishop	1914
Rivington Bisland	1914
Don Black	1946–48

Bud Black	1988–90, 1995
George Blaeholder	1936
Willie Blair	1991
Ossie Blanco	1974
Fred Blanding	1910–14
Larvell Blanks	1976–78
Bert Blyleven	1981–85
Bruce Bochte	1977
Eddie Bockman	1947
Joe Boehling	1916–17, 1920
John Bohnet	1982
Joe Boley	1932
Cecil Bolton	1928
Walt Bond	1960–62
Bobby Bonds	1979
Frank Bonner	1902
Bill Bonness	1944
Buddy Booker	1966
Red Booles	1909
Danny Boone	1922–23
Ray Boone	1948–53
Dick Bosman	1973–75
Harley Boss	1933
Denis Boucher	1991–92
Lou Boudreau	1938–50
Abe Bowman	1914–15
Ted Bowsfield	1960
Gary Boyd	1969
Jack Bracken	1901
Buddy Bradford	1970–71
Jack Bradley	1916
Bill Bradley	1901–10
Dick Braggins	1901
Ad Brennan	1918
Tom Brennan	1981–83
Bert Brenner	1912
Lynn Brenton	1913, 1915
Bill Brenzel	1934–35
Charlie Brewster	1946
Rocky Bridges	1960
Johnny Briggs	1959–60
Dan Briggs	1978
Lou Brissie	1951–53
Johnny Broaca	1939
Dick Brodowski	1958–59
Jack Brohamer	1972–75, 1980
Herman Bronkie	1910–12
Tom Brookens	1990
Frank Brower	1923–24
Clint Brown	1928–35, 1941–42
Lloyd Brown	1934–37
Dick Brown	1957–59
Jumbo Brown	1927–28
Larry Brown	1963–71
Jackie Brown	1975–76
Jerry Browne	1989–91
Garland Buckeye	1925–28
Fritz Buelow	1904–06
Larry Burchart	1969
Johnny Burnett	1927–34
Jeromy Burnitz	1995
George Burns	1920–21, 1924–28
Ellis Burton	1963
Jim Busby	1956–57
Tom Buskey	1974–77
Hank Butcher	1911–12
John Butcher	1986
Bill Butler	1972
Brett Butler	1984–87
Joe Caffie	1956–57
Ben Caffyn	1906
Wayne Cage	1978–79
Bruce Caldwell	1928
Ray Caldwell	1919–21
Dave Callahan	1910–11
Paul Calvert	1942–45
Ernie Camacho	1983–87
Lou Camilli	1969–72
Bruce Campbell	1935–39
Soup Campbell	1940–41
Card Camper	1977
Tom Candiotti	1986–91
Bernie Carbo	1978
Jose Cardenal	1968–69
Leo Cardenas	1973
Fred Carisch	1912–14
Steve Carlton	1987
Eddie Carnett	1945
Charlie Carr	1904–05
Chico Carrasquel	1956–58
Camilo Carreon	1965
Kit Carson	1934–35
Paul Carter	1914–15
Joe Carter	1984–89
Rico Carty	1974–77
George Case	1946
Larry Casian	1994
Carmen Castillo	1982–88
Pete Center	1942–43, 1945–46
Ed Cermak	1901
Rick Cerone	1975–76
Bob Chakales	1951–54
Chris Chambliss	1971–74
Bob Chance	1963–64
Dean Chance	1970
Ray Chapman	1912–20
Sam Chapman	1951
Ben Chapman	1939–40
Joe Charboneau	1980–82
Charlie Chech	1908
Virgil Cheeves	1924
Russ Christopher	1948
Mike Christopher	1992–93
Chuck Churn	1958
Al Cicotte	1959
Al Cihocki	1945
Bill Cissell	1932–33
Uke Clanton	1922
Allie Clark	1948–51
Ginger Clark	1902
Bob Clark	1920–21
Watty Clark	1924
Jim Clark	1971
Bryan Clark	1985
Dave Clark	1986–89
Mark Clark	1993–95
Nig Clarke	1905–10
Josh Clarke	1908–09
Sumpter Clarke	1923–24
Walter Clarkson	1907–08
Ty Cline	1960–62
Billy Clingman	1903
Lu Clinton	1965
David Clyde	1978–79
Chris Codiroli	1988
Rocky Colavito	1955–59, 1965–67
Vince Colbert	1970–72
Bert Cole	1925
Alex Cole	1990–92
Gordy Coleman	1959
Bob Coleman	1916
Allan Collamore	1914–15
Hap Collard	1927–28
Don Collins	1980
Jackie Collum	1962
Merrill Combs	1951–52
Steve Comer	1984
Bunk Congalton	1905–07
Sarge Connally	1931–34
Bruce Connatser	1931–32
Ed Connolly	1967
Joe Connolly	1922–23
Joe Connor	1901
Jim Constable	1958
Jack Conway	1941, 1946–47
Herb Conyers	1950
Dennis Cook	1992–93, 1995
Fritz Coumbe	1914–19
Stan Coveleski	1916–24
Ted Cox	1978–79
Howard Craghead	1931, 1933
Rodney Craig	1982
Del Crandall	1966
Keith Creel	1985
Bill Cristall	1901
Ed Crosby	1974–76
Frank Cross	1901
Victor Cruz	1979–80
Roy Cullenbine	1943–45
Nick Cullop	1927
Nick Cullop	1913–14
Wil Culmer	1983
George Culver	1966–67
Jack Curtis	1963
Al Cypert	1914
Paul Dade	1977–79
Bill Dailey	1961–62
Pete Dalena	1989
Bud Daley	1955–57
Tom Daly	1916
Lee Dashner	1913
Vic Davalillo	1963–68
Homer Davidson	1908
Bill Davis	1966
Steve Davis	1989
Joe Dawson	1924
Mike de la Hoz	1960–63
Chubby Dean	1941–43
Hank DeBerry	1916–17
Jeff Dedmon	1988
Frank Delahanty	1907
Don Demeter	1967
Steve Demeter	1960
Ben DeMott	1910–11
Rick Dempsey	1987
Otto Denning	1942–43
John Denny	1980–82
Sam Dente	1954–55
Shorty Des Jardien	1916
Gene Desautels	1941–43, 1945
George Detore	1930–31
Jim Devlin	1944
Bo Diaz	1978–81
George Dickerson	1917
Don Dillard	1960–62
Harley Dillinger	1914
Miguel Dilone	1980–83
Jerry DiPoto	1993–94
Walt Doane	1909–10
Joe Dobson	1939–40
Pat Dobson	1976–77
Larry Doby	1947–55, 1958
Frank Doljack	1943
Red Donahue	1903–05
Pat Donahue	1910
Pete Donohue	1931
Mike Donovan	1904
Dick Donovan	1962–65
Tom Donovan	1901
Bill Doran	1922
Red Dorman	1928
Gus Dorner	1902–03
Cal Dorsett	1940–41, 1947
Brian Dorsett	1987
Pete Dowling	1901
Logan Drake	1922–24
Tom Drake	1939
Frank Duffy	1972–77
Dave Duncan	1973–74
George Dunlop	1913–14
Steve Dunning	1970–73
Jerry Dybzinski	1980–82
Truck Eagan	1901
Luke Easter	1949–53
Ted Easterly	1909–12
Jamie Easterly	1983–87
Dennis Eckersley	1975–77
George Edmondson	1922–24
Eddie Edmonson	1913
Hank Edwards	1941–43, 1946–49
Doc Edwards	1962–63
Jim Joe Edwards	1922–25
Harry Eells	1906
Ben Egan	1914–15
Bruce Egloff	1991
Hack Eibel	1912
Juan Eichelberger	1983
Fred Eichrodt	1925–27
Harry Eisenstat	1939–42
Frank Ellerbe	1924
Bruce Ellingsen	1974
John Ellis	1973–75
George Ellison	1920
Dick Ellsworth	1969–70
Red Embree	1941–42, 1944–47
Alan Embree	1992, 1995
Joe Engel	1919
Clyde Engle	1916
Johnny Enzmann	1918–19
Jim Eschen	1915
Jose Escobar	1991
Alvaro Espinoza	1993–95
Chuck Essegian	1961–62
Jim Essian	1983
Ferd Eunick	1917
Joe Evans	1915–22
Hoot Evers	1955
Tony Faeth	1919–20
Red Fahr	1951
Ferris Fain	1955
Bibb Falk	1929–31
Cy Falkenberg	1908–11, 1913
Harry Fanwell	1910
Jack Farmer	1918
Ed Farmer	1971–73
Steve Farr	1984, 1994
John Farrell	1987–90, 1995
Bob Feller	1936–41, 1945–56
Felix Fermin	1989–93
Don Ferrarese	1958–59
Wes Ferrell	1927–33
Tom Ferrick	1942, 1946
Cy Ferry	1905
Chick Fewster	1924–25
Dan Firova	1988
Carl Fischer	1937
Mike Fischlin	1981–85
Gus Fisher	1911
Eddie Fisher	1968
Ed Fitz Gerald	1959
Paul Fitzke	1924
Al Fitzmorris	1977–78
Ray Flanigan	1946
Les Fleming	1941–42, 1945–47
Elmer Flick	1902–10
Jesse Flores	1950
Hank Foiles	1953, 1955–56, 1960
Lew Fonseca	1927–31
Ted Ford	1970–71, 1973
Ray Fosse	1967–72, 1976–77
Slim Foster	1908
Alan Foster	1971
Roy Foster	1970–72
Julio Franco	1983–88
Tito Francona	1959–64
Terry Francona	1988
Joe Frazier	1947
George Frazier	1984
Vern Freiburger	1941
Dave Freisleben	1978
Jim Fridley	1952
Owen Friend	1953
Buck Frierson	1941
Doug Frobel	1987
Jay Fry	1923
Vern Fuller	1966–70
Frank Funk	1960–62
Fabian Gaffke	1941–42
Milt Galatzer	1933–36
Denny Galehouse	1934–38
Shorty Gallagher	1901
Jackie Gallagher	1923
Dave Gallagher	1987
Oscar Gamble	1973–75
Chick Gandil	1916
Bob Garbark	1934–35
Mike Garcia	1948–59
Ray Gardner	1929–30
Rob Gardner	1968
Larry Gardner	1919–24
Wayne Garland	1977–81
Clarence Garrett	1915
Charlie Gassaway	1946
Gary Geiger	1958
Frank Genins	1901
Jim Gentile	1966
Greek George	1935–36
Lefty George	1912
George Gerken	1927–28
Al Gettel	1947–48
Gus Getz	1918
Gus Gil	1967
Brian Giles	1995
Johnny Gill	1927
Tinsley Ginn	1914
Joe Ginsberg	1953–54
Luke Glavenich	1913
Jim Gleeson	1936
Martin Glendon	1903
Sal Gliatto	1930
Bill Glynn	1952–54
Ed Glynn	1981–83
John Gochnaur	1902–03
Bill Gogolewski	1974
Jonah Goldman	1928, 1930–31
Ruben Gomez	1962
Rene Gonzales	1994
Pedro Gonzalez	1965–67
Orlando Gonzalez	1976
Denny Gonzalez	1989
Jose Gonzalez	1991
Wilbur Good	1908–09
Joe Gordon	1947–50
Don Gordon	1987–88
Al Gould	1916–17
Mauro Gozzo	1990–91
Rod Graber	1958

Peaches Graham	1902
Tommy Gramly	1968
Jack Graney	1908, 1910–22
Eddie Grant	1905
George Grant	1927–29
Jimmy Grant	1943–44
Mudcat Grant	1958–64
Mickey Grasso	1954
John Gray	1957
Ted Gray	1955
Gary Gray	1980
Gene Green	1962–63
Dave Gregg	1913
Vean Gregg	1911–14
Alfredo Griffin	1976–78
Art Griggs	1911–12
Bob Grim	1960
Oscar Grimes	1938–42
Ross Grimsley	1980
Jason Grimsley	1993–95
Steve Gromek	1941–53
Bob Groom	1918
Ernie Groth	1947–48
Harvey Grubb	1912
Johnny Grubb	1977–78
Cecilio Guante	1990
Lou Guisto	1916–17, 1921–23
Tom Gulley	1923–24
Red Gunkel	1916
Rip Hagerman	1914–16
Odell Hale	1931, 1933–40
Bob Hale	1960
Jimmie Hall	1968–69
Russ Hall	1901
Mel Hall	1984–88
John Halla	1905
Bill Hallman	1901
Al Halt	1918
Doc Hamann	1922
Jack Hamilton	1969
Steve Hamilton	1961
Jack Hammond	1915, 1922
Granny Hamner	1959
Rich Hand	1970–71
Mel Harder	1928–47
Carroll Hardy	1958–60
Jack Hardy	1903
Steve Hargan	1965–72
Mike Hargrove	1979–85
Specs Harkness	1910–11
Tommy Harper	1968
Toby Harrah	1979–83
Billy Harrell	1955, 1957–58
Ken Harrelson	1969–71
Charlie Harris	1951
Joe Harris	1917, 1919
Mickey Harris	1952
Billy Harris	1968
Roric Harrison	1975
Jack Harshman	1959–60
Oscar Harstad	1915
Bill Hart	1901
Bruce Hartford	1914
Grover Hartley	1929–30
Bob Hartman	1962
Luther Harvel	1928
Ervin Harvey	1901–02
Ron Hassey	1978–84
Fred Hatfield	1958
Art Haugher	1912
Joe Hauser	1929
Brad Havens	1988–89
Wynn Hawkins	1960–62
Howie Haworth	1915
Frankie Hayes	1945–46
Von Hayes	1981–82
Jeff Heath	1936–45
Neal Heaton	1982–86
Mike Hedlund	1965, 1968
Bob Heffner	1966
Jim Hegan	1941–42, 1946–57
Jack Heidemann	1969–72, 1974
Woodie Held	1958–64
Hank Helf	1938, 1940
Russ Heman	1961
Charlie Hemphill	1902
Rollie Hemsley	1938–41
Bernie Henderson	1921
Harvey Hendrick	1925
George Hendrick	1973–76
Tim Hendryx	1911–12
Dave Hengel	1989

Phil Hennigan	1969–72
Earl Henry	1944–45
Angel Hermoso	1974
Keith Hernandez	1990
Jose Hernandez	1992
Jeremy Hernandez	1993
Orel Hershiser	1995
Otto Hess	1902, 1904–08
Joe Heving	1937–38, 1941–44
John Hickey	1904
Piano Legs Hickman	1902–04, 1908
Dennis Higgins	1970
Bob Higgins	1909
Mark Higgins	1989
Oral Hildebrand	1931–36
Tom Hilgendorf	1972–74
Herbert Hill	1915
Ken Hill	1995
Glenallen Hill	1991–93
Shawn Hillegas	1991
Harry Hinchman	1907
Bill Hinchman	1907–09
Chuck Hinton	1965–67, 1969–71
Tommy Hinzo	1987, 1989
Myril Hoag	1944–45
Oris Hockett	1941–44
Johnny Hodapp	1925–32
Gomer Hodge	1971
Bill Hoffer	1901
Tex Hoffman	1915
Harry Hogan	1901
Eddie Hohnhorst	1910, 1912
Dutch Holland	1934
Ken Holloway	1929–30
Don Hood	1975–79
Bob Hooper	1953–54
Sam Horn	1993
Tony Horton	1967–70
Willie Horton	1978
Dave Hoskins	1953–54
Art Houtteman	1953–57
Ivon Howard	1916–17
Doug Howard	1976
Thomas Howard	1992–93
Dixie Howell	1940
Dick Howser	1963–66
Willis Hudlin	1926–40
Mike Huff	1991
Roy Hughes	1935–37
Mark Huismann	1987
John Humphries	1938–40
Bill Hunnefield	1931
Billy Hunter	1958
Bill Hunter	1912
Happy Iott	1903
Tommy Irwin	1938
Jim Jackson	1905–06
Joe Jackson	1910–15
Randy Jackson	1958–59
Mike Jackson	1973
Baby Doll Jacobson	1927
Brook Jacoby	1984–92
Lefty James	1912–14
Bill James	1911–12
Dion James	1989–90
Chris James	1990–91
Charlie Jamieson	1919–32
Hi Jasper	1919
Tex Jeanes	1921–22
Mike Jeffcoat	1983–85
Stan Jefferson	1990
Reggie Jefferson	1991–93
John Jeter	1974
Houston Jimenez	1988
Tommy John	1963–64
Alex Johnson	1972
Lou Johnson	1968
Vic Johnson	1946
Jerry Johnson	1973
Bob Johnson	1974
Cliff Johnson	1979–80
Larry Johnson	1972
Doc Johnston	1912–14, 1918–21
Hal Jones	1961–62
Sam Jones	1951–52
Sad Sam Jones	1914–15
Willie Jones	1959
Doug Jones	1986–91
Tom Jordan	1946
Scott Jordan	1988
Addie Joss	1902–10

Walt Judnich	1948
Ken Jungels	1937–38, 1940–41
Ike Kahdot	1922
Nick Kahl	1905
George Kahler	1910–14
Bob Kaiser	1971
Jeff Kaiser	1987–90
Willie Kamm	1931–35
Paul Kardow	1936
Benn Karr	1925–27
Marty Kavanagh	1916–18
Pat Keedy	1989
Dave Keefe	1922
Mike Kekich	1973
Tom Kelley	1964–67
Bob Kelly	1958
Pat Kelly	1981
Ken Keltner	1937–44, 1946–49
Fred Kendall	1977
Vern Kennedy	1942–44
Bob Kennedy	1948–54
Bill Kennedy	1948
Jerry Kenney	1973
Marty Keough	1960
Jim Kern	1974–78, 1986
Jack Kibble	1912
Mike Kilkenny	1972–73
Ed Killian	1903
Jerry Kindall	1962–64
Ralph Kiner	1955
Jim King	1967
Eric King	1991
Dennis Kinney	1978
Wayne Kirby	1991–95
Jay Kirke	1914–15
Willie Kirkland	1961–63
Harry Kirsch	1910
Garland Kiser	1991
Ron Kittle	1988
Mal Kittridge	1906
Hal Kleine	1944–45
Ed Klepfer	1915–17, 1919
Eddie Klieman	1943–48
Lou Klimchock	1968–70
Steve Kline	1974
Johnny Klippstein	1960
Joe Klugmann	1925
Cotton Knaupp	1910–11
Bill Knickerbocker	1933–36
Ray Knode	1923–26
Elmer Koestner	1910
Brad Komminsk	1989
Larry Kopf	1913
Joe Krakauskas	1941–42, 1946
Jack Kralick	1963–67
Tom Kramer	1991, 1993
Gene Krapp	1911–12
Harry Krause	1912
Rick Kreuger	1978
Gary Kroll	1969
John Kroner	1937–38
Ernie Krueger	1913
Art Kruger	1910
Jack Kubiszyn	1961–62
Harvey Kuenn	1960
Bub Kuhn	1924
Kenny Kuhn	1955–57
Duane Kuiper	1974–81
Hal Kurtz	1968
Bob Kuzava	1946–47
Bob Lacey	1981
Candy LaChance	1901
Guy Lacy	1926
Nap Lajoie	1902–14
Ray Lamb	1971–73
Otis Lambeth	1916–18
Tom Lampkin	1988
Grover Land	1908, 1910–11, 1913
Jim Landis	1966
Sam Langford	1927–28
Dave LaRoche	1975–77
Lyn Lary	1937–39
Fred Lasher	1970
Bill Laskey	1988
Barry Latman	1960–63
Bill Lattimore	1908
Ron Law	1969
Jim Lawrence	1963
Roxie Lawson	1930–31
Bill Laxton	1977
Emil Leber	1905

Cliff Lee	1925–26
Mike Lee	1960
Thornton Lee	1933–36
Leron Lee	1974–75
Gene Leek	1959
Paul Lehner	1951
Norm Lehr	1926
Nemo Leibold	1913–15
Dummy Leitner	1902
Jack Lelivelt	1914
Johnnie LeMaster	1985
Jim Lemon	1950, 1953
Bob Lemon	1941–42, 1946–58
Eddie Leon	1968–72
Joe Leonard	1916
Jesse Levis	1992–93, 1995
Dutch Levsen	1923–28
Dennis Lewallyn	1981–82
Mark Lewis	1991–94
Glenn Liebhardt	1906–09
Derek Lilliquist	1992–94
Carl Lind	1927–30
Lymie Linde	1947–48
Bill Lindsay	1911
Jim Lindsey	1922, 1924
Fred Link	1910
Larry Lintz	1978
Bob Lipski	1963
Joe Lis	1974–76
Pete Lister	1907
Larry Littleton	1981
Paddy Livingston	1901, 1912
Bobby Locke	1959–61
Stu Locklin	1955–56
Kenny Lofton	1992–95
Howard Lohr	1916
Ron Lolich	1972–73
Sherm Lollar	1946
Al Lopez	1947
Marcelino Lopez	1972
Luis Lopez	1991
Albie Lopez	1993–95
Bris Lord	1909–10
Grover Lowdermilk	1916
John Lowenstein	1970–77
Gordon Lund	1967
Jack Lundbom	1902
Harry Lunte	1919–20
Al Luplow	1961–65
Billy Lush	1904
Rube Lutzke	1923–27
Russ Lyon	1944
Chuck Machemehl	1971
Ray Mack	1938–44, 1946
Felix Mackiewicz	1945–47
Clarence Maddern	1951
Ever Magallanes	1991
Sal Maglie	1955–56
Tom Magrann	1989
Jim Mahoney	1962
Duster Mails	1920–22
Hank Majeski	1952–55
Candy Maldonado	1990, 1993–94
Rick Manning	1975–83
Jeff Manto	1990–91
Roger Maris	1957–58
Billy Martin	1959
Morrie Martin	1958
Tony Martinez	1963–64, 1966
Dennis Martinez	1994–95
Carlos Martinez	1991–93
Carl Mathias	1960
Lee Maye	1967–69
Bake McBride	1982–83
Ralph McCabe	1946
Jack McCarthy	1901–03
Barney McCosky	1951–52
Tom McCraw	1972, 1974–75
Frank McCrea	1925
Jim McDonnell	1943–45
Sam McDowell	1961–71
Oddibe McDowell	1989
Jim McGuire	1901
Deacon McGuire	1908
Marty McHale	1916
Stuffy McInnis	1922
Hal McKain	1927
Mark McLemore	1990
Cal McLish	1956–59
Don McMahon	1964–66
Harry McNeal	1901
Pat McNulty	1922, 1924–27

George McQuillan	1918
Luis Medina	1988–89, 1991
Sam Mele	1956
Bill Melton	1977
Matt Merullo	1994
Jose Mesa	1992–95
Bud Messenger	1924
Dewey Metivier	1922–24
Catfish Metkovich	1947
Dutch Meyer	1945–46
John Middleton	1922
Bob Milacki	1993
Larry Milbourne	1982
Johnny Miljus	1928–29
Ed Miller	1918
Ray Miller	1917
Bob Miller	1970
Jake Miller	1924–31
Randy Milligan	1993
Jack Mills	1911
Buster Mills	1942, 1946
Frank Mills	1914
Al Milnar	1936, 1938–43
Steve Mingori	1970–73
Minnie Minoso	1949, 1951, 1958–59
Dale Mitchell	1946–56
Willie Mitchell	1909–16
Dave Mlicki	1992–93
Danny Moeller	1916
Blas Monaco	1937
Sid Monge	1977–81
Ed Montague	1928, 1930–32
Leo Moon	1932
Barry Moore	1970
Earl Moore	1901–07
Eddie Moore	1934
Jim Moore	1928–29
Andres Mora	1980
Billy Moran	1958–59, 1964–65
Ed Morgan	1928–33
Joe Morgan	1960–61
Jeff Moronko	1984
Jack Morris	1994
Guy Morton	1914–24
Gerry Moses	1972
Howie Moss	1946
Don Mossi	1954–58
Fran Mullins	1986
Bob Muncrief	1948
Tim Murchison	1920
Ray Murray	1950–51
Eddie Murray	1994–95
Jeff Mutis	1991–93
Glenn Myatt	1923–35
Elmer Myers	1919–20
Chris Nabholz	1994
Lou Nagelsen	1912
Russ Nagelson	1969–70
Charles Nagy	1990–95
Bill Nahorodny	1982
Hal Naragon	1951, 1954–57, 1959
Ray Narleski	1954–58
Ken Nash	1912
Mike Naymick	1939–40, 1943–44
Cal Neeman	1963
Jim Neher	1912
Bernie Neis	1927
Rocky Nelson	1954
Dave Nelson	1968–69
Graig Nettles	1970–72
Milo Netzel	1909
Don Newcombe	1960
Hal Newhouser	1954–55
Simon Nicholls	1910
Rod Nichols	1988–92
Dick Niehaus	1920
Phil Niekro	1986–87
Milt Nielsen	1949
Bob Nieman	1961
Harry Niles	1910
Rabbit Nill	1907–08
Al Nipper	1990
Ron Nischwitz	1963
Russ Nixon	1957–60
Otis Nixon	1984–87
Junior Noboa	1984, 1987
Dickie Noles	1986
Jim Norris	1977–79
Les Nunamaker	1919–22
Jack O'Brien	1901
Pete O'Brien	1907
Pete O'Brien	1989
Paul O'Dea	1944–45
Ted Odenwald	1921–22
Blue Moon Odom	1975
John O'Donoghue	1966–67
Bryan Oelkers	1986
Chad Ogea	1994–95
Hal O'Hagen	1902
Bob Ojeda	1993
Steve Olin	1989–92
Dave Oliver	1977
Ivy Olson	1911–14
Gregg Olson	1995
Steve O'Neill	1911–23
Eddie Onslow	1918
Jesse Orosco	1989–91
Jorge Orta	1980–81
Junior Ortiz	1992–93
Harry Ostdiek	1904
Harry Otis	1909
Dave Otto	1991–92
Johnny Oulliber	1933
Bob Owchinko	1980
Ernie Padgett	1926–27
Karl Pagel	1981–83
Pat Paige	1911
Satchel Paige	1948–49
Lowell Palmer	1972
Frank Papish	1949
Harry Parker	1976
Lance Parrish	1993
Casey Parsons	1987
Camilo Pascual	1971
Mike Paul	1968–71
Stan Pawloski	1955
Mike Paxton	1978–80
Alex Pearson	1903
Monte Pearson	1932–35
Hal Peck	1947–49
Roger Peckinpaugh	1910, 1912–13
Orlando Pena	1967
Tony Pena	1994–95
Ken Penner	1916
Jack Perconte	1982–83
Tony Perezchica	1991–92
Broderick Perkins	1983–84
Jon Perlman	1988
Bill Perrin	1934
George Perring	1908–10
Gaylord Perry	1972–75
Jim Perry	1959–63, 1974–75
Herbert Perry	1994–95
John Peters	1918
Rusty Peters	1940–44, 1946
Cap Peterson	1969
Fritz Peterson	1974–76
Jesse Petty	1921
Larry Pezold	1914
Ken Phelps	1990
Dave Philley	1954–55
Adolfo Phillips	1972
Eddie Phillips	1935
Bubba Phillips	1960–62
Tom Phillips	1919
Ollie Pickering	1901–02
Marino Pieretti	1950
Jimmy Piersall	1959–61
Horacio Pina	1968–69
Lou Piniella	1968
Vada Pinson	1970–71
Stan Pitula	1957
Juan Pizarro	1969
Eric Plunk	1992–95
Ray Poat	1942–44
Bud Podbielan	1959
Johnny Podgajny	1946
Lou Polchow	1902
Jim Poole	1995
Dave Pope	1952, 1954–56
J. W. Porter	1958
Dick Porter	1929–34
Wally Post	1964
Nellie Pott	1922
Bill Pounds	1903
Boog Powell	1975–76
Vic Power	1958–61
Ted Power	1992–93
Mike Powers	1932–33
Johnny Powers	1960
Jackie Price	1946
Ron Pruitt	1976–81
Frankie Pytlak	1932–40
Jamie Quirk	1984
Joe Rabbitt	1922
Dick Radatz	1966–67
Tom Raftery	1909
Tom Ragland	1973
Eric Raich	1975–76
Larry Raines	1957–58
Manny Ramirez	1993–95
Pedro Ramos	1962–64
Domingo Ramos	1988
Morrie Rath	1910
Jerry Reed	1982–83, 1985
Rudy Regalado	1954–56
Herm Reich	1949
Duke Reilley	1909
Art Reinholz	1928
Pete Reiser	1952
Bugs Reisigl	1911
Paul Reuschel	1978–79
Allie Reynolds	1942–46
Bob Reynolds	1975
Bob Rhoads	1903–09
Kevin Rhomberg	1982–84
Sam Rice	1934
Denny Riddleberger	1972
Steve Ridzik	1958
Billy Ripken	1995
Reggie Ritter	1986–87
Jim Rittwage	1970
Joe Roa	1995
Frank Robinson	1974–75
Humberto Robinson	1959
Eddie Robinson	1942, 1946–48, 1957
Mickey Rocco	1943–46
Bill Rodgers	1915
Rick Rodriguez	1988
Dave Rohde	1992
Dan Rohn	1986
Billy Rohr	1968
Rich Rollins	1970
Jose Roman	1984–86
Johnny Romano	1960–64
Ramon Romero	1984–85
Vicente Romo	1968–69
Phil Roof	1965
Buddy Rosar	1943–44
Dave Rosello	1979–81
Al Rosen	1947–56
Larry Rosenthal	1941
Don Ross	1945–46
Claude Rossman	1904, 1906
Braggo Roth	1915–18
Bob Rothel	1945
Luther Roy	1924–25
Dick Rozek	1950–52
Don Rudolph	1962
Vern Ruhle	1985
Jack Russell	1932
Jeff Russell	1994
Hank Ruszkowski	1944–45, 1947
Jim Rutherford	1910
Jack Ryan	1908
Bud Ryan	1912–13
Mark Salas	1989
Chico Salmon	1964–68
Jack Salveson	1943, 1945
Ken Sanders	1973–74
Rafael Santana	1990
Jose Santiago	1954–55
Germany Schaefer	1918
Joe Schaffernoth	1961
Dan Schatzeder	1988
Frank Scheibeck	1901
Richie Scheinblum	1967–69
Norm Schlueter	1944
Ossee Schreckengost	1902
Ken Schrom	1986–87
Don Schulze	1984–86
Bill Schwartz	1904
Herb Score	1955–59
Ed Scott	1901
Scott Scudder	1992–93
Rudy Seanez	1989–91
Bob Seeds	1930–32, 1934
Pat Seerey	1943–48
Ted Sepkowski	1942, 1946–47
Luke Sewell	1921–32, 1939
Joe Sewell	1920–30
Gordon Seyfried	1963–64
Wally Shaner	1923
Joe Shaute	1922–30
Jeff Shaw	1990–92
Danny Shay	1901
Danny Sheaffer	1989
Pete Shields	1915
Jim Shilling	1939
Ginger Shinault	1921–22
Bill Shipke	1906
Milt Shoffner	1929–31
Paul Shuey	1994–95
Sonny Siebert	1964–69
Harry Simpson	1951–53
Duke Sims	1964–70
Carl Sitton	1909
Joe Skalski	1989
Joel Skinner	1989–91
Jack Slattery	1903
Heathcliff Slocumb	1993
Al Smith	1940–45
Al Smith	1953–57, 1964
Charlie Smith	1902
Pop Boy Smith	1916–17
Clay Smith	1938
Elmer Smith	1914–17, 1919–21
Riverboat Smith	1959
Sherry Smith	1922–27
Syd Smith	1910–11
Willie Smith	1967–68
Roy Smith	1984–85
Tommy Smith	1973–76
Russ Snyder	1968–69
Cory Snyder	1986–90
Moose Solters	1937–39
Lary Sorensen	1982–83
Chick Sorrells	1922
Paul Sorrento	1992–95
Allen Sothoron	1921–22
Billy Southworth	1913, 1915
Tris Speaker	1916–26
Byron Speece	1925–26
Horace Speed	1978–79
Roy Spencer	1933–34
Charlie Spikes	1973–77
Dan Spillner	1978–84
Jack Spring	1965
Steve Springer	1990
Joe Sprinz	1930–31
Freddy Spurgeon	1924–27
Lee Stange	1964–66
Fred Stanley	1971–72
Mike Stanton	1980–81
Dolly Stark	1909
George Starnagle	1902
Bill Steen	1912–15
Red Steiner	1945
Bryan Stephens	1947
Riggs Stephenson	1921–25
Lefty Stewart	1935
Sammy Stewart	1987
Dick Stigman	1960–61
Snuffy Stirnweiss	1951–52
Tim Stoddard	1989
George Stovall	1904–11
Jesse Stovall	1903
Oscar Streit	1902
George Strickland	1952–57, 1959–60
Jim Strickland	1975
Jake Striker	1959
Brent Strom	1973
Floyd Stromme	1939
Ken Suarez	1968–69, 1971
Charley Suche	1938
Bill Sudakis	1975
Denny Sullivan	1908–09
Jim Sullivan	1923
Lefty Sullivan	1939
Billy Sullivan	1936–37
Homer Summa	1922–28
George Susce	1941–44
Rick Sutcliffe	1982–84
Darrell Sutherland	1968
Russ Swan	1994
Josh Swindell	1911
Greg Swindell	1986–91
Pat Tabler	1983–88
Chuck Tanner	1959–60
Willie Tasby	1962–63
Eddie Taubensee	1991
Julian Tavarez	1993–95
Jackie Tavener	1929
Dummy Taylor	1902
Ron Taylor	1962
Sammy Taylor	1963

Birdie Tebbetts	1951–52
Al Tedrow	1914
Johnny Temple	1960–61
Ralph Terry	1965
Jake Thielman	1907–08
Carl Thomas	1960
Pinch Thomas	1918–21
Fay Thomas	1931
Valmy Thomas	1961
Stan Thomas	1976
Gorman Thomas	1983
Art Thomason	1910
Jim Thome	1991–95
Rich Thompson	1985
Jack Thoney	1902–03
Andre Thornton	1977–79, 1981–87
Luis Tiant	1964–69
Dick Tidrow	1972–74
Bobby Tiefenauer	1960, 1965, 1967
Tom Timmerman	1973–74
Ron Tingley	1988
Joe Tipton	1948, 1952–53
Chick Tolson	1925
Dick Tomanek	1953–54, 1957–58
Red Torkelson	1917
Rusty Torres	1973–74
Jack Townsend	1906
Jeff Treadway	1993
Mike Tresh	1949
Manny Trillo	1983
Hal Trosky	1933–41
Quincy Trouppe	1952
Ollie Tucker	1928
Thurman Tucker	1948–50
Scooter Tucker	1995
Eddie Turchin	1943
Terry Turner	1904–18
Matt Turner	1994
Dave Tyriver	1962
Ted Uhlaender	1970–71
George Uhle	1919–28, 1936
Jerry Ujdur	1984
Willie Underhill	1927–28
Del Unser	1972
Jerry Upp	1909
Cecil Upshaw	1974
Willie Upshaw	1988
Bob Usher	1957
Dutch Ussat	1925, 1927
Mike Vail	1978
Sergio Valdez	1990–91
Efrain Valdez	1990–91
Vito Valentinetti	1957
Elmer Valo	1959
Al Van Camp	1928
Ed Vande Berg	1987
Johnny Vander Meer	1951
Dike Varney	1902
Moses Vasbinder	1902
Otto Velez	1983
Mickey Vernon	1949–50, 1958
Zoilo Versalles	1969
Tom Veryzer	1978–81
Jose Vidal	1966–68
Rube Vinson	1904–05
Omar Vizquel	1994–95
Dave Von Ohlen	1985
Joe Vosmik	1930–36
George Vukovich	1983–85
Tom Waddell	1984–85, 1987
Leon Wagner	1964–68
Rick Waits	1975–83
Howard Wakefield	1905, 1907
Ed Walker	1902–03
Mysterious Walker	1912
Gee Walker	1941
Roy Walker	1912, 1915
Jerry Walker	1963–64
Mike Walker	1988, 1990–91
Roxy Walters	1924–25
Bill Wambsganss	1914–23
Aaron Ward	1928
Preston Ward	1956–58
Colby Ward	1990
Turner Ward	1990–91
Curt Wardle	1985
Jimmy Wasdell	1946
Ron Washington	1988
Frank Wayenberg	1924
Roy Weatherly	1936–42
Floyd Weaver	1962, 1965
Skeeter Webb	1938–39
Les Webber	1946, 1948
Ray Webster	1959
Mitch Webster	1990–91
Ralph Weigel	1946
Dick Weik	1950
Bob Weiland	1934
Elmer Weingartner	1945
Butch Wensloff	1948
Vic Wertz	1954–58
Bill Wertz	1993–94
Hi West	1905, 1911
Wally Westlake	1952–55
Gus Weyhing	1901
Ed Wheeler	1945
Pete Whisenant	1960
Earl Whitehill	1937–38
Mark Whiten	1991–92
Fred Whitfield	1963–67
Ed Whitson	1982
Kevin Wickander	1989–90, 1992–93
Bill Wight	1953, 1955
Sandy Wihtol	1979–80, 1982
Milt Wilcox	1972–74
Hoyt Wilhelm	1957–58
Denney Wilie	1915
Eric Wilkins	1979
Roy Wilkinson	1918
Ted Wilks	1952–53
Jerry Willard	1984–85
Buff Williams	1918
Pap Williams	1945
Dick Williams	1957
Stan Williams	1965, 1967–69
Walt Williams	1973
Reggie Williams	1988
Eddie Williams	1986–88
Les Willis	1947
Frank Wills	1986–87
Art Wilson	1921
Red Wilson	1960
Jim Wilson	1985
Fred Winchell	1909
Ralph Winegarner	1930, 1932, 1934–36
Dave Winfield	1995
George Winn	1922–23
Rick Wise	1978–79
Ed Wojna	1989
Ernie Wolf	1912
Roger Wolff	1947
Smoky Joe Wood	1917–22
Bob Wood	1901–02
Roy Wood	1914–15
Hal Woodeshick	1958
Gene Woodling	1943, 1946, 1955–57
Chuck Workman	1938
Craig Worthington	1992
Ab Wright	1935
Clarence Wright	1902–03
Lucky Wright	1909
Whit Wyatt	1937
Joe Wyatt	1924
Early Wynn	1949–57, 1963
George Yeager	1901
Rich Yett	1986–89
Earl Yingling	1911
Mike York	1991
Elmer Yoter	1924
Cy Young	1909–11
Bobby Young	1955
Mike Young	1989
Matt Young	1993
Cliff Young	1993
Carl Yowell	1924–25
Jimmy Zinn	1929
Sam Zoldak	1948–50
Bill Zuber	1936, 1938–40
Paul Zuvella	1988–89
George Zuverink	1951–52

Managers

Joe Adcock	1967
Bill Armour	1902–04
Ken Aspromonte	1972–74
*Joe Birmingham	1912–15
*Lou Boudreau	1942–50
*Bill Bradley	1905
Bobby Bragan	1958
Pat Corrales	1983–87
Alvin Dark	1968–71
Harry Davis	1912
Jimmy Dykes	1960–61
Doc Edwards	1987–89
Bibb Falk	1933
Kerby Farrell	1957
Mike Ferraro	1983
Lee Fohl	1915–19
Dave Garcia	1979–82
Joe Gordon	1958–60
Mel Harder	1961–62
Mike Hargrove	1991–95
John Hart	1989
Walter Johnson	1933–35
*Nap Lajoie	1905–09
Johnny Lipon	1971
Al Lopez	1951–56
Jimmy McAleer	1901
Jack McCallister	1927
Mel McGaha	1962
Deacon McGuire	1909–11
John McNamara	1990–91
Steve O'Neill	1935–37
Roger Peckinpaugh	1928–33, 1941
*Frank Robinson	1975–77
*Tris Speaker	1919–26
*George Stovall	1911
George Strickland	1964, 1966
Birdie Tebbetts	1963–66
Jeff Torborg	1977–79
Ossie Vitt	1938–40
Jo–Jo White	1960

DETROIT Tigers 1901–95

Glenn Abbott	1983–84
Al Aber	1953–57
Bob Adams	1977
Hank Aguirre	1958–67
Pat Ahearne	1995
Eddie Ainsmith	1919–21
Bill Akers	1929–31
Scott Aldred	1990–92
Dale Alexander	1929–32
Doyle Alexander	1987–89
Andy Allanson	1991
Rod Allen	1984
Ernie Alten	1920
George Alusik	1958, 1961
Luis Alvarado	1977
Sandy Amoros	1960
Bob Anderson	1963
Jimmy Archer	1907
Harry Arndt	1902
Fernando Arroyo	1975, 1977–79
Eldon Auker	1933–38
Earl Averill	1939–40
Doc Ayers	1919–21
Bill Bailey	1918
Howard Bailey	1981–83
Doug Bair	1983–85
Del Baker	1914–16
Steve Baker	1978–79
Doug Baker	1984–87
Billy Baldwin	1975
Chris Bando	1988
Ray Bare	1975–77
Clyde Barfoot	1926
Frank Barnes	1929
Sam Barnes	1921
Skeeter Barnes	1991–94
Jimmy Barrett	1901–05
Dick Bartell	1940–41
Al Bashang	1912
Johnny Bassler	1921–27
Matt Batts	1952–54
Paddy Baumann	1911–14
Harry Baumgartner	1920
John Baumgartner	1953
Danny Bautista	1993–95
Billy Bean	1987–89
Billy Beane	1988
Dave Beard	1989
Gene Bearden	1951
Erve Beck	1902
Boom–Boom Beck	1944
Heinie Beckendorf	1909–10
Wayne Belardi	1954, 1956
Tim Belcher	1994
Beau Bell	1939
Al Benton	1938–42, 1945–48
Lou Berberet	1959–60
Juan Berenguer	1982–85
Dave Bergman	1984–92
Sean Bergman	1993–95
Tony Bernazard	1991
Johnny Bero	1948
Neil Berry	1948–52
Reno Bertoia	1953–58, 1961–62
Monte Beville	1904
Steve Bilko	1960
Jack Billingham	1978–80
Haskell Billings	1927–29
Babe Birrer	1955
Bill Black	1952, 1955–56
Ike Blessitt	1972
Ben Blomdahl	1995
Jimmy Bloodworth	1942–43, 1946
Lu Blue	1921–27
Randy Bockus	1989
George Boehler	1912–16
Joe Boever	1993–95
John Bogart	1920
Brian Bohanon	1995
Bernie Boland	1915–20
Frank Bolling	1954, 1956–60
Milt Bolling	1958
Cliff Bolton	1937
Tom Bolton	1993
Danny Boone	1921
Ray Boone	1953–58
Red Borom	1944–45
Steve Boros	1957–58, 1961–62
Hank Borowy	1950–51
Dave Boswell	1971
Jim Brady	1956
Ralph Branca	1953–54
Jim BridewesER	1956
Rocky Bridges	1959–60
Tommy Bridges	1930–43, 1945–46
Ed Brinkman	1971–74
Rico Brogna	1992
Ike Brookens	1975
Tom Brookens	1979–88
Lou Brower	1931
Dick Brown	1961–62
Gates Brown	1963–74
Ike Brown	1969–74
Darrell Brown	1981
Chris Brown	1989
Frank Browning	1910
Bob Bruce	1959–61
Andy Bruckmiller	1905
Mike Brumley	1989
Arlo Brunsberg	1966
Bill Bruton	1961–64
Johnny Bucha	1953
Don Buddin	1962
Fritz Buelow	1901–04
George Bullard	1954
Jim Bunning	1955–63
Les Burke	1923–26
George Burns	1914–17
Jack Burns	1936
John Burns	1903–04
Joe Burns	1913
Bill Burns	1912
Pete Burnside	1959–60
Sheldon Burnside	1978–79
Donie Bush	1908–21
Sal Butera	1983
Harry Byrd	1957
Enos Cabell	1982–83
Greg Cadaret	1994
Bob Cain	1951
Les Cain	1968, 1970–72
Paul Calvert	1950–51
Bruce Campbell	1940–41
Paul Campbell	1948–49
Dave Campbell	1967–69
Bill Campbell	1986
Guy Cantrell	1930
George Cappuzzello	1981
Fred Carisch	1923
Charlie Carr	1903–04
Mark Carreon	1992
Ownie Carroll	1925, 1927–30
Frank Carswell	1953
Chuck Cary	1985–86
Jerry Casale	1961–62
Doc Casey	1901–02
Joe Casey	1909–11

Norm Cash	1960–74
Ron Cash	1973–74
George Caster	1945–46
Marty Castillo	1981–85
Pug Cavet	1911, 1914–15
John Cerutti	1991
Dean Chance	1971
Harry Chiti	1960–61
Mike Chris	1979
Neil Chrisley	1959–60
Bob Christian	1968
Mark Christman	1938–39
Mike Christopher	1995
Al Cicotte	1958
Eddie Cicotte	1905
Dave Claire	1920
Danny Clark	1922
Mel Clark	1957
Phil Clark	1992
Tony Clark	1995
Nig Clarke	1905
Rufe Clarke	1923–24
Al Clauss	1913
Flea Clifton	1934–37
Ty Cobb	1905–26
Mickey Cochrane	1934–35
Jack Coffey	1918
Slick Coffman	1937–39
Rocky Colavito	1960–63
Nate Colbert	1975
Bert Cole	1921–25
Joe Coleman	1955
Joe Coleman	1971–76
Darnell Coles	1986–87, 1990
Orlin Collier	1931
Rip Collins	1923–27
Kevin Collins	1970–71
Dave Collins	1986
Wayne Comer	1967–68, 1972
Ralph Comstock	1913
Dick Conger	1940
Red Conkwright	1920
Bill Connelly	1950
Earl Cook	1941
Duff Cooley	1905
Jack Coombs	1920
Wilbur Cooper	1926
Tim Corcoran	1977–80
Red Corriden	1912
Chuck Cottier	1961
Johnny Couch	1917
Bill Coughlin	1904–08
Ernie Courtney	1903
Harry Coveleski	1914–18
Tex Covington	1911–12
Al Cowens	1980–81
Red Cox	1920
Doc Cramer	1942–48
Sam Crawford	1903–17
Jim Crawford	1976–78
Jack Crimian	1957
Leo Cristante	1955
Davey Crockett	1901
John Cronin	1901–02
Frank Croucher	1939–41
General Crowder	1934–36
Roy Crumpler	1920
Roy Cullenbine	1938–39, 1945–47
George Cunningham	1916–19, 1921
Jim Curry	1918
Chad Curtis	1995
George Cutshaw	1922–23
Milt Cuyler	1990–95
Jack Dalton	1916
Mike Dalton	1991
Chuck Daniel	1957
Jeff Datz	1989
Hooks Dauss	1912–26
Jerry Davie	1959
Harry Davis	1932–33
Woody Davis	1938
Storm Davis	1993–94
Eric Davis	1993–94
Luis de los Santos	1991
Charlie Deal	1912–13
Rob Deer	1991–93
John Deering	1903
Tony DeFate	1917
Ivan DeJesus	1988
Mark DeJohn	1982
Jim Delahanty	1909–12
Jim Delsing	1952–56
Don Demeter	1964–66
Steve Demeter	1959
Bill Denehy	1971
Gene Desautels	1930–33
John DeSilva	1993
Bernie DeViveiros	1927
Bob Didier	1973
Steve Dillard	1978
Pop Dillon	1901–02
George Disch	1905
Jack Dittmer	1957
Pat Dobson	1967–69
Larry Doby	1959
John Doherty	1992–95
Frank Doljack	1930–34
Red Donahue	1906
Jim Donohue	1961
Dick Donovan	1954
Wild Bill Donovan	1903–12, 1918
Tom Doran	1905
Red Downs	1907–08
Jess Doyle	1925–27
Delos Drake	1911
Lee Dressen	1918
Lew Drill	1904–05
Walt Dropo	1952–54
Brian Dubois	1989–90
Jean Dubuc	1912–16
Joe Dugan	1931
Bob Dustal	1963
Ben Dyer	1916–19
Duffy Dyer	1980–81
Scott Earl	1984
Mal Eason	1903
Paul Easterling	1928, 1930
Zeb Eaton	1944–45
Wish Egan	1902
Dick Egan	1963–64
Howard Ehmke	1916–17, 1919–22
Harry Eisenstat	1938–39
Kid Elberfeld	1901–03
Heinie Elder	1913
Babe Ellison	1916–20
Dave Engle	1986
Gil English	1936–37
Eric Erickson	1916, 1918–19
Hal Erickson	1953
Tex Erwin	1907
John Eubank	1905–07
Darrell Evans	1984–88
Hoot Evers	1941, 1946–51, 1954
Roy Face	1968
Bill Fahey	1981–83
Ferris Fain	1955
Bob Farley	1962
Ed Farmer	1973
Bill Faul	1962–64
Al Federoff	1951–52
Junior Felix	1994
Jack Feller	1958
Chico Fernandez	1960–63
Cy Ferry	1904
Mark Fidrych	1976–80
Cecil Fielder	1990–95
Bruce Fields	1986
Jim Finigan	1957
Happy Finneran	1918
Carl Fischer	1933–35
Bill Fischer	1958, 1960–61
Fritz Fisher	1964
Ed Fisher	1902
Ira Flagstead	1917, 1919–22
John Flaherty	1994–95
Les Fleming	1939
Tom Fletcher	1962
Van Fletcher	1955
Scott Fletcher	1995
Ben Flowers	1955
Bubba Floyd	1944
Doug Flynn	1985
Hank Foiles	1960
Jim Foor	1971–72
Gene Ford	1905
Larry Foster	1963
Bob Fothergill	1922–30
Steve Foucault	1977–78
Pete Fox	1933–40
Terry Fox	1961–66
Paul Foytack	1953, 1955–63
Ray Francis	1923
Tito Francona	1958
Murray Franklin	1941–42
Vic Frasier	1933–34
Bill Freehan	1961, 1963–76
Cy Fried	1920
Owen Friend	1953
Emil Frisk	1901
Bill Froats	1955
Woodie Fryman	1972–74
Travis Fryman	1990–95
Charlie Fuchs	1942
Tito Fuentes	1977
Frank Fuller	1915–16
Liz Funk	1930
Chick Gagnon	1922
Del Gainer	1909, 1911–14
Dan Gakeler	1991
Doug Gallagher	1962
Chick Galloway	1928
John Gamble	1972
Barbaro Garbey	1984–85
Pedro Garcia	1976
Mike Gardiner	1993–95
Ned Garver	1952–56
Charlie Gehringer	1924–42
Charley Gelbert	1937
Rufe Gentry	1943–44, 1946–48
Dick Gernert	1960
Doc Gessler	1903
Frank Gibson	1913
Sam Gibson	1926–28
Kirk Gibson	1979–87, 1993–95
Paul Gibson	1988–91
Floyd Giebell	1939–41
Bill Gilbreth	1971–72
George Gill	1937–39
Bob Gillespie	1944
Joe Ginsberg	1948, 1950–53
Dan Gladden	1992–93
Fred Gladding	1961–67
John Glaiser	1920
Kid Gleason	1901–02
Jerry Don Gleaton	1990–91
Ed Glynn	1975–78
Greg Gohr	1993–95
Izzy Goldstein	1932
Purnal Goldy	1962
Chris Gomez	1993–95
Julio Gonzalez	1983
Dan Gonzalez	1979–80
Johnny Gorsica	1940–44, 1946–47
Goose Goslin	1934–37
Johnny Grabowski	1931
Kyle Graham	1929
Bill Graham	1966
Mark Grater	1993
Ted Gray	1946, 1948–54
Lenny Green	1967–68
Hank Greenberg	1933–41, 1945–46
Willie Greene	1903
Al Greene	1979
Ed Gremminger	1904
Art Griggs	1918
Steve Grilli	1975–77
Marv Grissom	1949
Steve Gromek	1953–57
Buddy Groom	1992–95
Johnny Groth	1946–52, 1957–60
Charlie Grover	1913
Johnny Grubb	1983–87
Joe Grzenda	1961
Bill Gullickson	1991–94
Dave Gumpert	1982–83
Cesar Gutierrez	1969–71
Dave Haas	1991–93
Sammy Hale	1920
Charley Hall	1918
Herb Hall	1918
Marc Hall	1913–14
Joe Hall	1995
Tom Haller	1972
Earl Hamilton	1916
Jack Hamilton	1964–65
Luke Hamlin	1933–34
Fred Haney	1922–25
Don Hankins	1927
Jim Hannan	1971
Charlie Harding	1913
Shawn Hare	1991–92
Pinky Hargrave	1928–30
Dick Harley	1902
George Harper	1916–18
Brian Harper	1986
Terry Harper	1987
Gail Harris	1958–60
Bob Harris	1938–39
Bob Harris	1941–43
Gene Harris	1994
Earl Harrist	1953
Fred Hatfield	1952–56
Clyde Hatter	1935, 1937
Brad Havens	1989
Ray Hayworth	1926, 1929–38
Bob Hazle	1958
Bill Heath	1967
Mike Heath	1986–90
Richie Hebner	1980–82
Don Heffner	1944
Jim Hegan	1958
Harry Heilmann	1914, 1916–29
Don Heinkel	1988
Mike Henneman	1987–95
Les Hennessy	1913
Dwayne Henry	1995
Roy Henshaw	1942–44
Ray Herbert	1950–51, 1953–54
Babe Herman	1937
Guillermo Hernandez	1984–89
Larry Herndon	1982–88
Art Herring	1929–33
Whitey Herzog	1963
Gus Hetling	1906
Piano Legs Hickman	1904–05
Buddy Hicks	1956
Pinky Higgins	1939–44, 1946
Bobby Higginson	1995
Ed High	1901
Hugh High	1913–14
John Hiller	1965–70, 1972–80
Billy Hitchcock	1942, 1946, 1953
Billy Hoeft	1952–59
Chief Hogsett	1929–36, 1944
Fred Holdsworth	1972–74
Carl Holling	1921–22
Ken Holloway	1922–28
Shawn Holman	1989
Ducky Holmes	1901–02
Vern Holtgrave	1965
Joe Hoover	1943–45
Johnny Hopp	1952
Willie Horton	1963–77
Tim Hosley	1970–71
Gene Host	1956
Chuck Hostetler	1944–45
Frank House	1950–51, 1954–57, 1961
Fred House	1913
Art Houtteman	1945–50, 1952–53
Frank Howard	1972–73
Waite Hoyt	1930–31
Clarence Huber	1920–21
Charles Hudson	1989
Frank Huelsman	1904
Tom Hughes	1930
Mark Huismann	1988
Terry Humphrey	1975
Bob Humphreys	1962
Fred Hutchinson	1939–40, 1946–51
Gary Ignasiak	1973
Pete Incaviglia	1991
Riccardo Ingram	1994
Ed Irvin	1912
Mike Ivie	1982–83
Charlie Jackson	1905
Ron Jackson	1981
Baby Doll Jacobson	1915
Charlie Jaeger	1904
Bill James	1915–19
Art James	1975
Bob James	1982–83
Paul Jata	1972
Bill Jensen	1912
Augie Johns	1926–27
Alex Johnson	1976
Earl Johnson	1951
Ken Johnson	1952
Roy Johnson	1929–32
Syl Johnson	1922–25
Howard Johnson	1982–84
Dave Johnson	1993
Alex Jones	1903
Deacon Jones	1916–18
Dalton Jones	1970–71
Davy Jones	1906–12

Elijah Jones	1907, 1909
Ken Jones	1924
Bob Jones	1917–25
Sam Jones	1962
Tom Jones	1909–10
Ruppert Jones	1984
Lynn Jones	1979–83
Tracy Jones	1989–90
Milt Jordan	1953
Walt Justis	1905

Jeff Kaiser	1991
Al Kaline	1953–74
Rudy Kallio	1918–19
Harry Kane	1903
Marty Kavanagh	1914–16, 1918
George Kell	1946–52
Mick Kelleher	1981–82
Charlie Keller	1950–51
Bryan Kelly	1986–87
Steve Kemp	1977–81
Vern Kennedy	1938–39
Bob Kennedy	1956
John Kerr	1923–24
John Kiely	1991–93
Mike Kilkenny	1969–72
Red Killefer	1907–09
Ed Killian	1904–10
Bruce Kimm	1976–77
Chad Kimsey	1936
Charlie King	1954–56
Eric King	1986–88, 1992
Dennis Kinney	1981
Matt Kinzer	1990
Jay Kirke	1910
Rube Kisinger	1902–03
Frank Kitson	1903–05
Al Klawitter	1913
Ron Kline	1961–62
Johnny Klippstein	1967
Rudy Kneisch	1926
Ray Knight	1988
John Knox	1972–75
Kurt Knudsen	1992–94
Alan Koch	1963–64
Brad Kocher	1912
Mark Koenig	1930–31
Don Kolloway	1949–52
Howie Koplitz	1961–62
George Korince	1966–67
Frank Kostro	1962–63
Wayne Krenchicki	1983
Charlie Kress	1954
Red Kress	1939–40
Lou Kretlow	1946, 1948–49
Chad Kreuter	1992–94
Bill Krueger	1993–94
Dick Kryhoski	1950–51
Harvey Kuenn	1952–59
Rusty Kuntz	1984–85

Chet Laabs	1937–39
Clem Labine	1960
Ed Lafitte	1909, 1911–12
Mike Laga	1982–86
Lerrin LaGrow	1970, 1972–75
Eddie Lake	1946–50
Joe Lake	1912–13
Al Lakeman	1954
Gene Lamont	1970–72, 1974–75
Les Lancaster	1992
Jim Landis	1967
Marv Lane	1971–74, 1976
Dave LaPoint	1986
Steve Larkin	1934
Frank Lary	1954–64
Fred Lasher	1967–70
Chick Lathers	1910–11
Charlie Lau	1956, 1958–59
Bill Lawrence	1932
Roxie Lawson	1933, 1935–39
Bill Laxton	1976
Jack Lazorko	1986
Rick Leach	1981–83
Razor Ledbetter	1915
Don Lee	1957–58
Ron LeFlore	1974–79
Bill Leinhauser	1912
Mark Leiter	1991–93
Bill Lelivelt	1909–10
Dave Lemanczyk	1973–76
Chet Lemon	1982–90
Don Lenhardt	1952
Jim Lentine	1980
Dutch Leonard	1919–21, 1924–25
Ted Lepcio	1959
Pete LePine	1902
George Lerchen	1952
Don Leshnock	1972
Jose Lima	1994–95
Jim Lindeman	1990
Pinky Lindsay	1905–06
Johnny Lipon	1942, 1946, 1948–52
Felipe Lira	1995
Dick Littlefield	1952
Jack Lively	1911
Scott Livingstone	1991–94
Harry Lochhead	1901
Bob Logan	1937
Mickey Lolich	1963–75
Herman Long	1903
Aurelio Lopez	1979–85
Lefty Lorenzen	1913
Art Loudell	1910
Baldy Louden	1912–13
Slim Love	1919–20
Torey Lovullo	1988–89
Grover Lowdermilk	1915–16
Bobby Lowe	1904–07
Dwight Lowry	1984, 1986–87
Willie Ludolph	1924
Urbano Lugo	1990
Jerry Lumpe	1964–67
Don Lund	1952–54
Scott Lusader	1987–90
Billy Lush	1903
Red Lynn	1939
Fred Lynn	1988–89

Duke Maas	1955–57
Frank MacCormick	1976
Bob MacDonald	1993
Dave Machemer	1979
Morris Madden	1987
Elliott Maddox	1970
Dave Madison	1952–53
Scotti Madison	1985–86
Bill Madlock	1987
Billy Maharg	1912
Mickey Mahler	1985
Bob Maier	1945
Alex Main	1914
George Maisel	1916
Tom Makowski	1975
Herm Malloy	1907–08
Harry Malmberg	1955
Hal Manders	1941–42, 1946
Clyde Manion	1920–24, 1926
Phil Mankowski	1976–79
Jerry Manuel	1975–76
Heinie Manush	1923–27
Cliff Mapes	1952
Firpo Marberry	1933–35
Leo Marentette	1965
Dick Marlowe	1951–56
Buck Marrow	1932
Mike Marshall	1967
Billy Martin	1958
John Martin	1983
Roger Mason	1984
Walt Masterson	1956
Tom Matchick	1967–69
Eddie Mathews	1967–68
Brian Maxcy	1995
Charlie Maxwell	1955–62
Milt May	1976–79
Eddie Mayo	1944–48
Sport McAllister	1901–03
Dick McAuliffe	1960–73
Arch McCarthy	1902
Barney McCosky	1939–42, 1946
Benny McCoy	1938–39
Ed McCreery	1914
Lance McCullers	1990
Red McDermott	1912
Mickey McDermott	1958
Orlando McFarlane	1966
Jim McGarr	1912
Dan McGarvey	1912
Pat McGehee	1912
Deacon McGuire	1902–03, 1912
John McHale	1945, 1947
Matty McIntyre	1904–10
Archie McKain	1939–41
Red McKee	1913–16
Denny McLain	1963–70
Pat McLaughlin	1937, 1945
Wayne McLeland	1951–52
Sam McMackin	1902
Don McMahon	1968–69
Frank McManus	1904
Marty McManus	1927–31
Fred McMullin	1914
Eric McNair	1941–42
Norm McRae	1969–70
Bill McTigue	1916
Rusty Meacham	1991
Pat Meaney	1912
Phil Meeler	1972
Bob Melvin	1985
Orlando Mercado	1987
Win Mercer	1902
Herm Merritt	1921
Scat Metha	1940
Charlie Metro	1943–44
Dutch Meyer	1940–42
Dan Meyer	1974–76
Gene Michael	1975
Jim Middleton	1921
Ed Mierkowicz	1945, 1947–48
Hack Miller	1944–45
Bob Miller	1953–56
Bob Miller	1973
Roscoe Miller	1901–02
Eddie Miller	1982
Clarence Mitchell	1911
Willie Mitchell	1916–19
Herb Moford	1958
John Mohardt	1922
Bob Molinaro	1975, 1983
Bill Monbouquette	1966–67
Sid Monge	1984
Manny Montejo	1961
Anse Moore	1946
Jackie Moore	1965
Roy Moore	1922–23
Bill Moore	1925
Mike Moore	1993–95
Jake Mooty	1944
Jerry Morales	1979
Harry Moran	1912
Keith Moreland	1989
Chet Morgan	1935, 1938
Tom Morgan	1958–60
George Moriarty	1909–15
Jack Morris	1977–90
Bill Morrisette	1920
Jim Morrison	1987–88
Bubba Morton	1961–63
Lloyd Moseby	1990–91
Gerry Moses	1974
John Moses	1991
Don Mossi	1959–63
Les Mueller	1941, 1945
Billy Mullen	1926
George Mullin	1902–13
Pat Mullin	1940–41, 1946–53
Mike Munoz	1991–93
John Murphy	1903
Dwayne Murphy	1988
Glenn Myatt	1936
Mike Myers	1995

Russ Nagelson	1970
Doc Nance	1901
Ray Narleski	1959
Julio Navarro	1964–66
Bots Nekola	1933
Lynn Nelson	1940
Jack Ness	1911
Jim Nettles	1974
Johnny Neun	1925–28
Phil Nevin	1995
Hal Newhouser	1939–53
Bobo Newsom	1939–41
Simon Nicholls	1903
Fred Nicholson	1917
Joe Niekro	1970–72
Bob Nieman	1953–54
Ron Nischwitz	1961–62, 1965
C. J. Nitkowski	1995
Matt Nokes	1986–90
Dickie Noles	1987
Lou North	1913
Jim Northrup	1964–74
Randy Nosek	1989–90
Edwin Nunez	1989–90
Prince Oana	1943, 1945
John O'Connell	1902
Ben Oglivie	1974–77
Frank Okrie	1920
Red Oldham	1914–15, 1920–22
Charley O'Leary	1904–12
Ole Olsen	1922–23
Karl Olson	1957
Ollie O'Mara	1912
Randy O'Neal	1984–86
Eddie Onslow	1912–13
Jack Onslow	1912
Joe Orengo	1944
Frank O'Rourke	1924–26
Joe Orrell	1943–45
Bobo Osborne	1957, 1959, 1961–62
Jimmy Outlaw	1943–48
Stubby Overmire	1943–49
Frank Owen	1901
Marv Owen	1931, 1933–37
Ray Oyler	1965–68

John Pacella	1986
Phil Page	1928–30
David Palmer	1989
Stan Papi	1980–81
Johnny Paredes	1990–91
Salty Parker	1936
Clay Parker	1990
Slicker Parks	1921
Lance Parrish	1977–86
Dixie Parsons	1939, 1942–43
Steve Partenheimer	1913
Johnny Pasek	1933
Larry Pashnick	1982–83
Bob Patrick	1941–42
Daryl Patterson	1968–71
Fred Payne	1906–08
Marv Peasley	1910
Al Pedrique	1989
Rudy Pemberton	1995
Orlando Pena	1965–67
Ramon Pena	1989
Shannon Penn	1995
Gene Pentz	1975
Pepper Peploski	1913
Don Pepper	1966
Hub Pernoll	1910, 1912
Ron Perranoski	1971–72
Pol Perritt	1921
Boyd Perry	1941
Clay Perry	1908
Jim Perry	1973
Hank Perry	1912
Johnny Pesky	1952–53
John Peters	1915
Ricky Peters	1979–81
Dan Petry	1979–87, 1990–91
Gary Pettis	1988–89, 1992
Dave Philley	1957
Red Phillips	1934, 1936
Eddie Phillips	1929
Jack Phillips	1955–56
Bubba Phillips	1955, 1963–64
Tony Phillips	1990–94
Billy Pierce	1945, 1948
Jack Pierce	1975
Tony Piet	1938
Herman Pillette	1922–24
Babe Pinelli	1920
Wally Pipp	1913
Cotton Pippen	1939–40
Chris Pittaro	1985
Al Platte	1913
Johnny Podres	1966–67
Boots Poffenberger	1937–38
J. W. Porter	1955–57
Lew Post	1902
Ray Powell	1913
Ted Power	1988
Del Pratt	1923–24
Joe Presko	1957–58
Jim Price	1967–71
Gerry Priddy	1950–53
Jim Proctor	1959
Augie Prudhomme	1929
Billy Purtell	1914
Ed Putman	1979

George Quellich	1931

Dick Radatz	1969
Rip Radcliff	1941–43

Ed Rakow	1964–65
Jim Ray	1974
Bugs Raymond	1904
Wayne Redmond	1965
Bob Reed	1969–70
Rich Reese	1973
Phil Regan	1960–65
Frank Reiber	1933, 1935–36
Alex Remneas	1912
Erwin Renfer	1913
Tony Rensa	1930
Ross Reynolds	1914–15
Bob Reynolds	1975
Billy Rhiel	1932–33
Dennis Ribant	1968
Harry Rice	1928–30
Paul Richards	1943–46
Nolen Richardson	1929, 1931–32
Rob Richie	1989
Hank Riebe	1942, 1947–49
Topper Rigney	1922–25
Kevin Ritz	1989–92
Mike Roarke	1961–64
Bruce Robbins	1979–80
Dave Roberts	1976–77
Leon Roberts	1974–75
Jerry Robertson	1970
Aaron Robinson	1949–51
Rabbit Robinson	1904
Eddie Robinson	1957
Jeff Robinson	1987–90
Aurelio Rodriguez	1971–79
Steve Rodriguez	1995
Joe Rogalski	1938
Billy Rogell	1930–39
Saul Rogovin	1949–51
Bill Roman	1964–65
Ed Romero	1990
Henri Rondeau	1913
Jim Rooker	1968
Don Ross	1938, 1942–45
Claude Rossman	1907–09
Larry Rothschild	1981–82
Jack Rowan	1906
Schoolboy Rowe	1933–42
Rich Rowland	1990–93
Dave Rozema	1977–84
Art Ruble	1927
Dave Rucker	1981–83
Muddy Ruel	1931–32
Vern Ruhle	1974–77
Jack Russell	1937
Mark Salas	1990–91
Luis Salazar	1988
Ron Samford	1955, 1957
Juan Samuel	1994–95
Joe Samuels	1930
Alejandro Sanchez	1985
Reggie Sanders	1974
Joe Sargent	1921
Kevin Saucier	1981–82
Dennis Saunders	1970
Ray Scarborough	1953
Germany Schaefer	1905–09
Biff Schaller	1911
Wally Schang	1931
Dan Schatzeder	1980–81
Frank Scheibeck	1906
Fred Scherman	1969–73
Bill Scherrer	1984–86
Lou Schiappacasse	1902
Boss Schmidt	1906–11
Rick Schu	1989
Heinie Schuble	1929, 1932–35
Barney Schultz	1959
Bob Schultz	1955
Mike Schwabe	1989–90
Chuck Scrivener	1975–77
Johnnie Seale	1964–65
Steve Searcy	1988–91
Tom Seats	1940
Chuck Seelbach	1971–74
Ray Semproch	1960
Rip Sewell	1932
Dick Sharon	1973–74
Al Shaw	1901
Bob Shaw	1957–58
Merv Shea	1927–29, 1939
Larry Sheets	1990
John Shelby	1990–91
Hugh Shelley	1935
Pat Sheridan	1986–89

Larry Sherry	1964–67
Jimmy Shevlin	1930
Ivey Shiver	1931
Ron Shoop	1959
Chick Shorten	1919–21
Ed Siever	1901–02, 1906–08
Frank Sigafoos	1929
Al Simmons	1936
Hack Simmons	1910
Nelson Simmons	1984–85
Duke Sims	1972–73
Matt Sinatro	1989
Dave Sisler	1959–60
Dave Skeels	1910
Lou Skizas	1958
John Skopec	1903
Jim Slaton	1978, 1986
Bill Slayback	1972–74
Lou Sleater	1957–58
Jim Small	1955–57
Jack Smith	1912
Clay Smith	1940
Heinie Smith	1903
George Smith	1963–65
George Smith	1926–29
Bob Smith	1959
Rufus Smith	1927
Willie Smith	1963
Nate Snell	1987
Clint Sodowsky	1995
Vic Sorrell	1928–37
Elias Sosa	1982
Steve Souchock	1951–54
Joe Sparma	1964–69
George Speer	1909
Tubby Spencer	1916–18
George Spencer	1958, 1960
Charlie Spikes	1978
Harry Spilman	1986
Tuck Stainback	1940–41
Gerry Staley	1961
Oscar Stanage	1909–20, 1925
Mickey Stanley	1964–78
Joe Staton	1972–73
Rusty Staub	1976–79
Bill Steen	1915
Dave Stegman	1978–80
Todd Steverson	1995
Lefty Stewart	1921
Phil Stidham	1994
Bob Stoddard	1985
John Stone	1928–33
Lil Stoner	1922, 1924–29
Jesse Stovall	1904
Mike Strahler	1973
Bob Strampe	1972
Doug Strange	1989
Walt Streuli	1954–56
Sailor Stroud	1910
Marlin Stuart	1949–52
Franklin Stubbs	1995
Jim Stump	1957, 1959
Tom Sturdivant	1963
Joe Sugden	1912
George Suggs	1908–09
Jack Sullivan	1944
Charlie Sullivan	1928, 1930–31
John Sullivan	1905
John Sullivan	1963–65
Joe Sullivan	1935–36
Russ Sullivan	1951–53
Billy Sullivan	1940–41
Billy Sullivan	1916
Ed Summers	1908–12
Champ Summers	1979–81
George Susce	1932
George Susce	1958–59
Gary Sutherland	1974–76
Suds Sutherland	1921
Bill Sweeney	1928
Bob Swift	1944–53
Bob Sykes	1977–78
Ken Szotkiewicz	1970
Frank Tanana	1985–92
Jackie Tavener	1921, 1925–28
Tony Taylor	1971–73
Bennie Taylor	1952
Wiley Taylor	1911
Bill Taylor	1957–58
Gary Taylor	1969
Bruce Taylor	1977–79
Birdie Tebbetts	1936–42, 1946–47

Walt Terrell	1985–88, 1990–92
John Terry	1902
Mickey Tettleton	1991–94
Frosty Thomas	1905
George Thomas	1957–58, 1961, 1963–65
Ira Thomas	1908
Bud Thomas	1939–41
Tim Thompson	1958
Sam Thompson	1906
Jason Thompson	1976–80
Gary Thurman	1993
Mark Thurmond	1986–87
Tom Timmerman	1969–73
Ron Tingley	1995
Dave Tobik	1978–82
Jim Tobin	1945
Tim Tolman	1986–87
Earl Torgeson	1955–57
Dick Tracewski	1966–69
Alan Trammell	1977–95
Al Travers	1912
Tom Tresh	1969
Gus Triandos	1963
Dizzy Trout	1939–52
Bun Troy	1912
Virgil Trucks	1941–43, 1945–52, 1956
Mike Trujillo	1988–89
John Tsitouris	1957
Jerry Turner	1982
Bill Tuttle	1952, 1954–57
Guy Tutwiler	1911, 1913
Bob Uhl	1940
George Uhle	1929–33
Jerry Ujdur	1980–83
Pat Underwood	1979–80, 1982–83
Al Unser	1942–44
Vito Valentinetti	1958
Elam Vangilder	1928–29
Bobby Veach	1912–23
Coot Veal	1958–60, 1963
Lou Vedder	1920
Tom Veryzer	1973–77
George Vico	1948–49
Ozzie Virgil	1958, 1960–61
Ossie Vitt	1912–18
Jake Wade	1936–38
Hal Wagner	1947–48
Mark Wagner	1976–80
Dick Wakefield	1941, 1943–44, 1946–49
Jim Walewander	1987–88
Frank Walker	1918
Dixie Walker	1938–39
Gee Walker	1931–37
Hub Walker	1931, 1935, 1945
Luke Walker	1974
Tom Walker	1975
Jim Walkup	1939
Jim Walkup	1927
Jim Walsh	1921
Steve Wapnick	1990
Hap Ward	1912
Gary Ward	1989–90
Jon Warden	1968
Jack Warner	1905–06
Jack Warner	1925–28
Johnny Watson	1930
Roger Weaver	1980
Jim Weaver	1985
Earl Webb	1932–33
Skeeter Webb	1945–47
Herm Wehmeier	1958
Dick Weik	1953–54
Milt Welch	1945
Ed Wells	1923–27
David Wells	1993–95
Don Wert	1963–70
Vic Wertz	1947–52, 1962
Charlie Wheatley	1912
Jack Whillock	1971
Lou Whitaker	1977–95
Hal White	1941–43, 1946–52
Jo–Jo White	1932–38
Derrick White	1995
Earl Whitehill	1923–32
Sean Whiteside	1995
Kevin Wickander	1995
Dave Wickersham	1964–67
Jimmy Wiggs	1905–06
Bill Wight	1952–53
Milt Wilcox	1977–85

Ed Willett	1906–13
Lefty Williams	1913–14
Johnny Williams	1914
Frank Williams	1989
Kenny Williams	1989–90
Carl Willis	1984
Earl Wilson	1966–70
Squanto Wilson	1911
Jack Wilson	1942
Red Wilson	1954–60
Walter Wilson	1945
Mutt Wilson	1920
Glenn Wilson	1982–83
Al Wingo	1924–28
George Winter	1908
Hughie Wise	1930
Casey Wise	1960
John Wockenfuss	1974–83
Pete Wojey	1956–57
Jake Wood	1961–67
Joe Wood	1943
Bob Wood	1904–05
Larry Woodall	1920–28
Hal Woodeshick	1956, 1961
Ron Woods	1969
Ralph Works	1909–12
Yats Wuestling	1929–30
John Wyatt	1968
Whit Wyatt	1929–33
Emil Yde	1929
Joe Yeager	1901–03
Archie Yelle	1917–19
Tom Yewcic	1957
Rudy York	1934, 1937–45
Eddie Yost	1959–60
Ralph Young	1915–21
Kip Young	1978–79
John Young	1971
Chris Zachary	1972
Carl Zamloch	1913
Bill Zepp	1971
Gus Zernial	1958–59
George Zuverink	1954–55

Managers

Sparky Anderson	1979–95
Bill Armour	1905–06
Del Baker	1933, 1936–42
Ed Barrow	1903–04
*Ty Cobb	1921–26
*Mickey Cochrane	1934–38
Chuck Dressen	1963–66
Frank Dwyer	1902
Jimmy Dykes	1959–60
Joe Gordon	1960
Bucky Harris	1929–33, 1955–56
Billy Hitchcock	1960
Ralph Houk	1974–78
Fred Hutchinson	1952–54
Hughie Jennings	1907–20
*Bobby Lowe	1904
Billy Martin	1971–73
George Moriarty	1927–28
Les Moss	1979
Bill Norman	1958–59
Steve O'Neill	1943–48
Red Rolfe	1949–52
Bob Scheffing	1961–63
Joe Schultz	1973
Frank Skaff	1966
Mayo Smith	1967–70
George Stallings	1901
Bob Swift	1965–66
Jack Tighe	1957–58
Dick Tracewski	1979

KANSAS CITY Athletics 1955–67

Moved from PHILADELPHIA Athletics
Moved to OAKLAND Athletics

Al Aber	1957
Jack Aker	1964–67
George Alusik	1962–64
Jim Archer	1961–62
Joe Astroth	1955–56
Joe Azcue	1962–63

Sal Bando	1966–67
Norm Bass	1961–63
Hank Bauer	1960
Mike Baxes	1956, 1958
Zeke Bella	1959
Reno Bertoia	1961
Hal Bevan	1955
Charlie Bishop	1955
Ewell Blackwell	1955
Ed Blake	1957
Johnny Blanchard	1965
Gil Blanco	1966
Don Blasingame	1966
Ray Blemker	1960
Chet Boak	1960
Don Bollweg	1955
Ray Boone	1959
Hoss Bowlin	1967
Ted Bowsfield	1963–64
Bob Boyd	1961
Clete Boyer	1955–57
Cloyd Boyer	1955
Bill Bradford	1956
Johnny Briggs	1960
George Brunet	1956–57, 1959–60
Billy Bryan	1961–66
Wally Burnette	1956–58
Moe Burtschy	1955–56
Don Buschhorn	1965
Bert Campaneris	1964–67
Andy Carey	1960–61
Chico Carrasquel	1958
Tommy Carroll	1959
Danny Cater	1966–67
Wayne Causey	1961–66
Art Ceccarelli	1955–56
Bob Cerv	1957–60
Ed Charles	1962–67
Ossie Chavarria	1966–67
Harry Chiti	1958–60
Gino Cimoli	1962–64
Frank Cipriani	1961
Lu Clinton	1965
Rocky Colavito	1964
Rip Coleman	1957, 1959
Billy Consolo	1962
Marlan Coughtry	1962
Wes Covington	1961
Glenn Cox	1955–58
Walter Craddock	1955–56, 1958
Jack Crimian	1956
Bud Daley	1958–61
Pete Daley	1960
Bob Davis	1958, 1960
Joe De Maestri	1955–59
Bobby Del Greco	1961–63
Jim Delsing	1960
Jim Dickson	1965–66
Murry Dickson	1958–59
Art Ditmar	1955–56, 1961–62
Sonny Dixon	1955
Chuck Dobson	1966–67
John Donaldson	1966–67
Moe Drabowsky	1962–65
Jim Duckworth	1966
Bob Duliba	1967
Dave Duncan	1964, 1967
Ryne Duren	1957
Carl Duser	1956, 1958
Bill Edgerton	1966–67
Doc Edwards	1963–65
Sammy Esposito	1963
Chuck Essegian	1961, 1963
Ernie Fazio	1966
Jim Finigan	1955–56
Bill Fischer	1961–63
Hank Foiles	1960
Mark Freeman	1959
Marion Fricano	1955
Ned Garver	1957–60
Jim Gentile	1964–65
Alex George	1955
Paul Giel	1961
Bob Giggie	1960, 1962
Joe Ginsberg	1956
Tom Gorman	1955–59
Jim Gosger	1966–67
Milt Graff	1957–58
John Gray	1955
Dick Green	1963–67
Guido Grilli	1966
Bob Grim	1958–59, 1962
Johnny Groth	1956–57
Al Grunwald	1959
Joe Grzenda	1964, 1966
Kent Hadley	1958–59
Dick Hall	1960
Ken Hamlin	1960
Granny Hamner	1962
Vern Handrahan	1964, 1966
Jay Hankins	1961, 1963
Ken Harrelson	1963–67
Bill Harrington	1955–56
Tom Harrison	1965
Woodie Held	1957–58
Ray Herbert	1955, 1958–61
Troy Herriage	1956
Mike Hershberger	1965–67
Whitey Herzog	1958–60
Jess Hickman	1965–66
Dave Hill	1957
Gene Host	1957
Frank House	1958–59
Dick Howser	1961–63
Billy Hunter	1957–58
Catfish Hunter	1965–67
Ray Jablonski	1959–60
Reggie Jackson	1967
Spook Jacobs	1955–56
Manny Jimenez	1962–64, 1966
Deron Johnson	1961–62
Ken Johnson	1958–61
Bob Johnson	1960
Stan Johnson	1961
Gordon Jones	1962
Rick Joseph	1964
Dick Joyce	1965
Ed Keegan	1961
Alex Kellner	1955–58
Gus Keriazakos	1955
Bill Kern	1962
Leo Kiely	1960
Evans Killeen	1959
Bill Kirk	1961
Lou Klimchock	1958–61
Lew Krausse	1961, 1964–67
Danny Kravitz	1960
Lou Kretlow	1956
Dick Kryhoski	1955
Ted Kubiak	1967
Johnny Kucks	1959–60
John Kume	1955
Bill Kunkel	1961–62
Marty Kutyna	1959–60
Rene Lachemann	1965–66
Jim Landis	1965
Bill Landis	1963
Don Larsen	1960–61
Tony LaRussa	1963
Tom Lasorda	1956
Charlie Lau	1963–64
George Lauzerique	1967
Paul Lindblad	1965–67
Jack Littrell	1955
Skip Lockwood	1965
Hector Lopez	1955–59
Pete Lovrich	1963
Jerry Lumpe	1959–63
Duke Maas	1958
Eric MacKenzie	1955
Gordon MacKenzie	1961
Roger Maris	1958–59
Billy Martin	1957
Hector Martinez	1963
Bob Martyn	1957–58
Nelson Mathews	1964–65
Mickey McDermott	1957, 1961
Danny McDevitt	1962
Jack McMahan	1956
Jim McManus	1960
Dave Melton	1956, 1958
Bob Meyer	1964
Russ Meyer	1959
Rick Monday	1966–67
Aurelio Monteagudo	1963–66
Joe Morgan	1959
Tom Morgan	1957
Don Mossi	1965
Jim Nash	1966–67
Irv Noren	1957
Fred Norman	1962–63
Joe Nossek	1966–67
Joe Nuxhall	1961
Blue Moon Odom	1964–67
John O'Donoghue	1963–65
Dan Osinski	1962
Satchel Paige	1965
Orlando Pena	1962–65
Dan Pfister	1961–64
Tony Pierce	1967
Joe Pignatano	1961
Al Pilarcik	1956, 1961
Jim Pisoni	1956–57
Don Plarski	1955
Rance Pless	1956
Arnie Portocarrero	1955–57
Leo Posada	1960–62
Vic Power	1955–58
Bobby Prescott	1961
Hal Raether	1957
Ed Rakow	1961–63
Vic Raschi	1955
Howie Reed	1958–60
Bill Renna	1955–56
Roger Repoz	1966–67
Tommie Reynolds	1963–65
Jim Rivera	1961
Jim Robertson	1955
Eddie Robinson	1956
Roberto Rodriguez	1967
Phil Roof	1966–67
Santiago Rosario	1965
Joe Rudi	1967
Tom Saffell	1955
Johnny Sain	1955
Ken Sanders	1964, 1966
Jack Sanford	1967
Jose Santiago	1956
Jose Santiago	1963–65
Randy Schwartz	1965–66
Jerry Schypinski	1955
Diego Segui	1962–65, 1967
Bobby Shantz	1955–56
Billy Shantz	1955
Bob Shaw	1961
Rollie Sheldon	1965–66
Charlie Shoemaker	1961–62, 1964
Norm Siebern	1960–63
Harry Simpson	1955–59
Lou Skizas	1956–57
Enos Slaughter	1955–56
Lou Sleater	1955
Jim Small	1958
Hal Smith	1956–59
Russ Snyder	1959–60
Bob Spicer	1955–56
Bill Stafford	1966–67
Larry Stahl	1964–66
Gerry Staley	1961
Gene Stephens	1961
Bill Stewart	1955
Wes Stock	1964–67
Ron Stone	1966
Tom Sturdivant	1959, 1963–64
Ken Suarez	1966–67
Pete Suder	1955
Haywood Sullivan	1961–63
Fred Talbot	1965–66
Tim Talton	1966–67
Jose Tartabull	1962–66
Harry Taylor	1957
Ralph Terry	1957–59, 1966
Wayne Terwilliger	1959–60
Dave Thies	1963
Tim Thompson	1956–57
Marv Throneberry	1960–61
Dick Tomanek	1958–59
Ron Tompkins	1965
Rupe Toppin	1962
Bob Trice	1955
Bob Trowbridge	1960
Virgil Trucks	1957–58
John Tsitouris	1958–60
Bill Tuttle	1958–61
Jack Urban	1957–58
Elmer Valo	1955–56
Ozzie Van Brabant	1955
Ozzie Virgil	1961
Jerry Walker	1961–62
Preston Ward	1958–59
Ramon Webster	1967
Lee Wheat	1955
Dave Wickersham	1960–63
Don Williams	1962
George Williams	1964
Dick Williams	1959–60
Dale Willis	1963
Bill Wilson	1955
Gordie Windhorn	1962
John Wojcik	1962–64
John Wyatt	1961–66
Gus Zernial	1955–57

Managers

Luke Appling	1967
Hank Bauer	1961–62
Lou Boudreau	1955–57
Harry Craft	1957–59
Alvin Dark	1966–67
Bob Elliott	1960
Joe Gordon	1961
Ed Lopat	1963–64
Mel McGaha	1964–65
Haywood Sullivan	1965

KANSAS CITY Royals 1969–95

Ted Abernathy	1970–72
Jerry Adair	1969–70
Willie Aikens	1980–83
Luis Alcaraz	1969–70
Rick Anderson	1987–88
Scott Anderson	1995
Norm Angelini	1972–73
Kevin Appier	1989–95
Luis Aquino	1988–92
Mike Armstrong	1982–83
Tucker Ashford	1984
Steve Balboni	1984–88
Jay Baller	1990
Scott Bankhead	1986
Floyd Bannister	1988–89
German Barranca	1979
Joe Beckwith	1984–85
Stan Belinda	1993–94
Terry Bell	1986
Juan Beniquez	1987
Todd Benzinger	1991
Juan Berenguer	1981, 1992
Sean Berry	1990–91
Kurt Bevacqua	1973–74
Buddy Biancalana	1982–87
Doug Bird	1973–78
Bud Black	1982–88
Vida Blue	1982–83
Mike Boddicker	1991–92
Bob Boone	1989–90
Pat Borders	1995
Thad Bosley	1987–88
Derek Botelho	1982
Steve Braun	1978–80
Ken Brett	1980–81
George Brett	1973–93
Mike Brewer	1986
Billy Brewer	1993–95
Nellie Briles	1974–75
Hubie Brooks	1993–94
Tom Browning	1995
Tom Bruno	1976
Bob Buchanan	1989
Bill Buckner	1988–89
Melvin Bunch	1995
Wally Bunker	1969–71
Tom Burgmeier	1969–73
Enrique Burgos	1993
Steve Busby	1972–76, 1978–80
Bill Butler	1969–71

Edgar Caceres	1995
Greg Cadaret	1993
Jim Campanis	1969–70
Jim Campbell	1990
Nick Capra	1988
Jose Cardenal	1980
Manny Castillo	1980
Bill Castro	1982–83
Orlando Cepeda	1974
Dave Chalk	1980–81
Craig Chamberlain	1979–80
Gary Christenson	1979–80
Galen Cisco	1969
Dave Clark	1991
Stan Clarke	1989
Lance Clemons	1971
Chris Codiroli	1990
Jim Colborn	1977–78
Stu Cole	1991
Vince Coleman	1994–95
Onix Concepcion	1980–85
David Cone	1986, 1993–94
Jeff Conine	1990, 1992
Jim Converse	1995
Brent Cookson	1995
Archie Corbin	1991
Al Cowens	1974–79
Jerry Cram	1969, 1976
Steve Crawford	1989–91
Keith Creel	1982–83
Dave Cripe	1978
Warren Cromartie	1991
Todd Cruz	1979
Bruce Dal Canton	1971–75
Johnny Damon	1995
Tommy Davis	1976
Mark Davis	1990–92
Storm Davis	1990–91
Butch Davis	1983–84
John Davis	1987
Luis de los Santos	1988–89
Jose DeJesus	1988–89, 1994
Bucky Dent	1984
Bob Detherage	1980
Frank DiPino	1993
Richard Dotson	1990
Moe Drabowsky	1969–70
Dick Drago	1969–73
Rawly Eastwick	1980
Craig Eaton	1979
Jim Eisenreich	1987–92
Luis Encarnacion	1990
Steve Farr	1985–90
Tony Ferreira	1985
Pete Filson	1990
Mike Fiore	1969–70
Al Fitzmorris	1969–76
Dave Fleming	1995
Bobby Floyd	1970–74
Steve Foucault	1978
Joe Foy	1969
Dave Frost	1982
Gary Gaetti	1993–95
Greg Gagne	1993–95
Rich Gale	1978–81
Gene Garber	1973–74, 1987–88
Danny Garcia	1981
Wes Gardner	1991
Mark Gardner	1993
Jim Gaudet	1978–79
Cesar Geronimo	1981–83
Kirk Gibson	1991
Jerry Don Gleaton	1987–89
Fernando Gonzalez	1974
Tom Goodwin	1994–95
Tom Gordon	1988–95
Jeff Granger	1993–94
Jerry Grote	1981
Jeff Grotewold	1995
Mark Gubicza	1984–95
Dave Gumpert	1987
Larry Gura	1976–85
Chris Gwynn	1992–93
John Habyan	1993
Tom Hall	1976–77
Bob Hamelin	1993–95
Atlee Hammaker	1981

Steve Hammond	1982
Chris Haney	1992–95
Ron Hansen	1972
Alan Hargesheimer	1986
Billy Harris	1969
Chuck Harrison	1969, 1971
Andy Hassler	1976–78
Fran Healy	1969, 1973–76
Ed Hearn	1987–88
Kelly Heath	1982
Neal Heaton	1992
Mike Hedlund	1969–72
Bob Hegman	1985
Bob Heise	1977
Dave Henderson	1994
Jackie Hernandez	1969–70
Phil Hiatt	1993, 1995
Joe Hoerner	1973–74
Don Hood	1982–83
Gail Hopkins	1971–73
Steve Hovley	1972–73
Dave Howard	1991–95
Al Hrabosky	1978–79
Rick Huisman	1995
Mark Huismann	1983–86
Clint Hurdle	1977–81
Dane Iorg	1984–85
Tim Ireland	1981–82
Grant Jackson	1982
Mike Jackson	1972–73
Danny Jackson	1983–87
Bo Jackson	1986–90
Jason Jacome	1995
Chris James	1995
Gregg Jefferies	1992
Steve Jeltz	1990
Bob Johnson	1970
Ron Johnson	1982–83
Randy Johnson	1986
Joel Johnston	1991–92
Steve Jones	1969
Ruppert Jones	1976
Lynn Jones	1984–86
Mike Jones	1980–81, 1984–85
Ross Jones	1987
Felix Jose	1993–95
Wally Joyner	1992–95
Greg Keatley	1981
Pat Kelly	1969–70
Joe Keough	1969–72
Harmon Killebrew	1975
Mike Kingery	1986
Ed Kirkpatrick	1969–73
Bobby Knoop	1971–72
Kevin Koslofski	1992–94
Art Kusnyer	1978
Pete LaCock	1977–80
Mike LaCoss	1985
Joe Lahoud	1977–78
Gary Lance	1977
Rudy Law	1986
Terry Leach	1989
Mark Lee	1988
Dave Leeper	1984–85
Charlie Leibrandt	1984–89
Dennis Leonard	1974–83, 1985–86
Jose Lind	1993–95
Doug Linton	1995
Nelson Liriano	1991
Mark Littell	1973, 1975–77
Keith Lockhart	1995
Aurelio Lopez	1974
Rick Luecken	1989
Mike Macfarlane	1987–94
Scotti Madison	1987–88
Mike Magnante	1991–95
Carlos Maldonado	1990–91
Keith Marshall	1973
Jerry Martin	1982–83
Renie Martin	1979–81
Buck Martinez	1969–71, 1973–77
Carmelo Martinez	1991
Gary Martz	1975
Tom Matchick	1970
Jerry May	1971–73
Lee May	1981–82
John Mayberry	1972–77
Brent Mayne	1990–95

Bob McClure	1975–76
Mike McCormick	1971
Lindy McDaniel	1974–75
Andy McGaffigan	1990–91
Randy McGilberry	1977–78
Russ McGinnis	1995
Hal McRae	1973–87
Brian McRae	1990–94
Kevin McReynolds	1992–93
Larry McWilliams	1989–90
Rusty Meacham	1992–95
Bob Melvin	1992
Henry Mercedes	1995
Bob Milacki	1994
Keith Miller	1992–95
Steve Mingori	1973–79
Dennis Moeller	1992
Aurelio Monteagudo	1970
Monty Montgomery	1971–72
Jeff Montgomery	1988–95
Bobby Moore	1991
Dave Morehead	1969–70
Omar Moreno	1985
Russ Morman	1990–91
Jose Mota	1995
Darryl Motley	1981, 1983–86
Rance Mulliniks	1980–81
Tom Murphy	1972
Roger Nelson	1969–72, 1976
Dave Nelson	1976–77
Jim Nettles	1979
Les Norman	1995
Scott Northey	1969
Jon Nunnally	1995
Bob Oliver	1969–72
Gregg Olson	1995
Jorge Orta	1984–87
Don O'Riley	1969–70
Frank Ortenzio	1973
Amos Otis	1970–83
Larry Owen	1987–88
Dave Owen	1988
Dennis Paepke	1969, 1971–72, 1974
Rey Palacios	1988–90
Bill Paschall	1978–79, 1981
Cliff Pastornicky	1983
Freddie Patek	1971–79
Marty Pattin	1974–80
Bill Pecota	1986–91
Jorge Pedre	1991
Melido Perez	1987
Gaylord Perry	1983
Gerald Perry	1990
Ken Phelps	1980–81
Hipolito Pichardo	1992–95
Eddie Pierce	1992
Lou Piniella	1969–73
Vada Pinson	1974–75
Jim Pittsley	1995
Tom Poquette	1973, 1976–79, 1982
Darrell Porter	1977–80
Ted Power	1988
Greg Pryor	1982–86
Terry Puhl	1991
Luis Pujols	1984
Harvey Pulliam	1991–93
Jamie Quirk	1975–76, 1978–82, 1985–88
Dan Quisenberry	1979–88
Joe Randa	1995
Eric Rasmussen	1983
Dennis Rasmussen	1992–93, 1995
Barry Raziano	1973
Rick Reed	1992–93
Rick Reichardt	1973
Steve Renko	1983
Fred Rico	1969
Juan Rios	1969
Bombo Rivera	1982
Leon Roberts	1983–84
Ellie Rodriguez	1969–70
Ed Rodriguez	1979
Cookie Rojas	1970–77
Jim Rooker	1969–72
Rico Rossy	1992–93
Mark Ryal	1982

Bret Saberhagen	1984–91
Ray Sadecki	1975–76
Angel Salazar	1986–87
Bill Sampen	1992–93
Juan Samuel	1992, 1995
Orlando Sanchez	1984
Israel Sanchez	1988, 1990
Ken Sanders	1976
Nelson Santovenia	1993
Rich Sauveur	1992
Ted Savage	1971
Paul Schaal	1969–74
Jeff Schattinger	1981
Dan Schatzeder	1991
Richie Scheinblum	1972, 1974
Jeff Schulz	1989–90
George Scott	1979
Rodney Scott	1975
Jim Scranton	1984–85
Kevin Seitzer	1986–91
Rich Severson	1970–71
Pat Sheridan	1981, 1983–85
Steve Shields	1986
Steve Shifflett	1992
Bob Shirley	1987
Terry Shumpert	1990–94
Luis Silverio	1978
Joe Simpson	1983
Wayne Simpson	1973
Don Slaught	1982–84
Lonnie Smith	1985–87
Daryl Smith	1990
Tony Solaita	1974–76
Bill Sorrell	1970
Tim Spehr	1991
Paul Splittorff	1970–84
George Spriggs	1969–70
Kurt Stillwell	1988–91
Bob Stinson	1975–76
Bob Stoddard	1987
Mel Stottlemyre	1990
Chris Stynes	1995
Jim Sundberg	1985–86
Mike Sweeney	1995
Pat Tabler	1988–90
Danny Tartabull	1987–91
Hawk Taylor	1969–70
Carl Taylor	1971–73
Dwight Taylor	1986
Jerry Terrell	1978–80
George Throop	1975, 1977–79
Gary Thurman	1987–92
Rusty Torres	1980
Dilson Torres	1995
Michael Tucker	1995
Bob Tufts	1982–83
Jeff Twitty	1980
Sandy Valdespino	1971
Joe Vitiello	1995
Hector Wagner	1990–91
U. L. Washington	1977–84
John Wathan	1976–85
Brad Wellman	1988–89
Dennis Werth	1982
Frank White	1973–90
Dave Wickersham	1969
Curtis Wilkerson	1992–93
Frank Wills	1983–84
Willie Wilson	1976–90
Craig Wilson	1993
Matt Winters	1989
Jim Wohlford	1972–76
Ken Wright	1970–73
Jim Wright	1981–82
Jim York	1970–71
Curt Young	1992
Chris Zachary	1969
Joe Zdeb	1977–79
Paul Zuvella	1991

Managers

Bob Boone	1995
Mike Ferraro	1986
Jim Frey	1980–81
Billy Gardner	1987
Joe Gordon	1969
Whitey Herzog	1975–79

Dick Howser	1981–86
Bob Lemon	1970–72
Jack McKeon	1973–75
Hal McRae	1991–94
Charlie Metro	1970
Bob Schaefer	1991
John Wathan	1987–91

LOS ANGELES Angels 1961–64
Moved to CALIFORNIA Angels

Joe Adcock	1964
Dan Ardell	1961
Ken Aspromonte	1961
Earl Averill	1961–62
Julio Becquer	1961
Bo Belinsky	1962–64
Steve Bilko	1961–62
Bob Botz	1962
Ted Bowsfield	1961–62
Fritzie Brickell	1961
Rocky Bridges	1961
George Brunet	1964
Tom Burgess	1962
Leo Burke	1962
Jerry Casale	1961
Bob Cerv	1961
Dean Chance	1961–64
Tex Clevenger	1961
Lu Clinton	1964
Billy Consolo	1962
Marlan Coughtry	1962
Bobby Darwin	1962
Charlie Dees	1963–64
Jim Donohue	1961–62
Bob Duliba	1963–64
Ryne Duren	1961–62
Hank Foiles	1963
Art Fowler	1961–64
Paul Foytack	1963–64
Jim Fregosi	1961–64
Ned Garver	1961
Aubrey Gatewood	1963–64
Eli Grba	1961–63
Lenny Green	1964
Ken Hamlin	1961
Russ Heman	1961
Jack Hiatt	1964
Ken Hunt	1961–63
Johnny James	1961
Lou Johnson	1961
Bill Kelso	1964
Ed Kirkpatrick	1962–64
Ron Kline	1961
Ted Kluszewski	1961
Bobby Knoop	1964
Joe Koppe	1961–64
Frank Kostro	1963
Barry Latman	1964
Don Lee	1962–64
Mike Lee	1963
Bob Lee	1964
Gene Leek	1961–62
Frank Leja	1962
Ken McBride	1961–64
Bob Meyer	1964
Ron Moeller	1961, 1963
Billy Moran	1961–64
Tom Morgan	1961–63
Julio Navarro	1962–64
Mel Nelson	1963
Fred Newman	1962–64
Joe Nuxhall	1962
Dan Osinski	1962–64
Albie Pearson	1961–64
Bob Perry	1963–64
Jimmy Piersall	1963–64
Vic Power	1964
Rick Reichardt	1964
Del Rice	1961
Buck Rodgers	1961–64
Eddie Sadowski	1961–63
Bob Sadowski	1963
Tom Satriano	1961–64
Paul Schaal	1964
Ray Semproch	1961
Dick Simpson	1962, 1964
Willie Smith	1964
Jack Spring	1961–64
Bob Sprout	1961
Ed Sukla	1964
Chuck Tanner	1961–62
George Thomas	1961–63
Lee Thomas	1961–64
Faye Throneberry	1961
Felix Torres	1962–64
Bob Turley	1963
Leon Wagner	1961–63
Gordie Windhorn	1962
George Witt	1962
Eddie Yost	1961–62

Managers

Bill Rigney	1961–64

MILWAUKEE Brewers 1901
Moved to ST. LOUIS Browns

John Anderson	1901
George Bone	1901
Ed Bruyette	1901
Jimmy Burke	1901
John Butler	1901
Joe Connor	1901
Wid Conroy	1901
Jiggs Donahue	1901
Pete Dowling	1901
Hugh Duffy	1901
Bill Friel	1901
Ned Garvin	1901
Phil Geier	1901
Lou Gertenrich	1901
Billy Gilbert	1901
Bill Hallman	1901
Pink Hawley	1901
George Hogriever	1901
Bert Husting	1901
Davy Jones	1901
Tom Leahy	1901
Billy Maloney	1901
George McBride	1901
Bill Reidy	1901
Tully Sparks	1901
Irv Waldron	1901

Managers

*Hugh Duffy	1901

MILWAUKEE Brewers 1970–95
Moved from SEATTLE Pilots

Hank Aaron	1975–76
Jim Adduci	1986, 1988
Jay Aldrich	1987, 1989
Andy Allanson	1992
Hank Allen	1970
Felipe Alou	1974
Max Alvis	1970
Larry Anderson	1974–75
Rick Auerbach	1971–73
Don August	1988–91
Jerry Augustine	1975–84
Rick Austin	1975–76
Jim Austin	1991–93
Joe Azcue	1972
Dave Baldwin	1970
Sal Bando	1977–81
Len Barker	1987
Kevin Bass	1982
Billy Bates	1989–90
Gary Beare	1976–77
Larry Bearnarth	1971
Andy Beene	1983–84
Jerry Bell	1971–74
Juan Bell	1993
Dwight Bernard	1981–82
Ken Berry	1974
Kurt Bevacqua	1975–76
Tommy Bianco	1975
Dante Bichette	1991–92
Mike Birkbeck	1986–89
Mike Boddicker	1993
Danny Boitano	1979–80
Bobby Bolin	1970
Mark Bomback	1978
Ricky Bones	1992–95
Chris Bosio	1986–92
Thad Bosley	1981
Steve Bowling	1976
Gene Brabender	1970
Glenn Braggs	1986–90
Ken Brett	1972
John Briggs	1971–75
Pete Broberg	1975–76
Greg Brock	1987–91
Jeff Bronkey	1994–95
Mark Brouhard	1980–85
Ollie Brown	1972–73
Kevin Brown	1990–91
Bruce Brubaker	1970
Tom Brunansky	1993–94
Steve Brye	1977
Bob Burda	1970
Ray Burris	1985, 1987
Mike Caldwell	1977–84
George Canale	1989–91
Tom Candiotti	1983–84
Mike Capel	1990
Bernie Carbo	1976
Jose Cardenal	1971
Matias Carrillo	1991
Juan Castillo	1986–89
Bill Castro	1974–80
Rick Cerone	1986
Billy Champion	1973–76
Mark Ciardi	1987
Jeff Cirillo	1994–95
Ron Clark	1972
Bobby Clark	1984–85
Mark Clear	1986–88
Reggie Cleveland	1979–81
Bryan Clutterbuck	1986, 1989
Jaime Cocanower	1983–86
Jim Colborn	1972–76
Bob Coluccio	1973–75
Wayne Comer	1970
Billy Conigliaro	1972
Cecil Cooper	1977–87
Barry Cort	1977
Chuck Crim	1987–91
Lafayette Currence	1975
Bobby Darwin	1975–76
Danny Darwin	1985–86
Brock Davis	1972
Dick Davis	1977–80
Rob Deer	1986–90
Rick Dempsey	1991
Edgar Diaz	1986, 1990
Alex Diaz	1992–94
Rob Dibble	1995
Frank DiPino	1981
Bill Doran	1993
Al Downing	1970
Jamie Easterly	1981–83
Tom Edens	1990
Marshall Edwards	1981–83
Cal Eldred	1991–95
Rob Ellis	1971, 1974–75
Dick Ellsworth	1970–71
Narciso Elvira	1990
Dave Engle	1989
Andy Etchebarren	1978
Ed Farmer	1978
Mike Felder	1985–90
John Felske	1972–73
Mike Ferraro	1972
Mike Fetters	1992–95
Tom Filer	1988–90
Rollie Fingers	1981–82, 1984–85
Scott Fletcher	1992
John Flinn	1980
Rich Folkers	1977
Tony Fossas	1989–90
Ray Fosse	1979
Tito Francona	1970
Terry Francona	1989–90
LaVel Freeman	1989
Danny Frisella	1976
Bob Galasso	1979
Jim Gantner	1976–92
Pedro Garcia	1973–76
Rob Gardner	1973
John Gelnar	1970–71
Chris George	1991
Bob Gibson	1983–86
Gus Gil	1970–71
Brian Giles	1985
Brian Givens	1995
Greg Goossen	1970
Moose Haas	1976–85
Darryl Hamilton	1988, 1990–95
Larry Haney	1977–78
Jim Hannan	1971
Bob Hansen	1974, 1976
Tommy Harper	1970–71
Brian Harper	1994
Vic Harris	1980
Paul Hartzell	1984
Tom Hausman	1975–76
Neal Heaton	1992
Mike Hegan	1970–71, 1974–77
Jack Heidemann	1976–77
Bob Heise	1971–73
Doug Henry	1991–94
Mike Hershberger	1970
Ted Higuera	1985–91, 1993–94
Sam Hinds	1977
Larry Hisle	1978–82
Fred Holdsworth	1980
Darren Holmes	1991–92
Paul Householder	1985–86
Steve Hovley	1970
Wilbur Howard	1973
Roy Howell	1981–84
David Hulse	1995
Bob Humphreys	1970
Jim Hunter	1991
Dave Huppert	1985
Mike Ignasiak	1991, 1993–95
John Jaha	1992–95
Dion James	1983–85
Deron Johnson	1974
John Henry Johnson	1986–87
Tim Johnson	1973–78
Odell Jones	1988
Doug Jones	1982
Von Joshua	1976–77
Scott Karl	1995
Buster Keeton	1980–81
John Kennedy	1970
Jim Kern	1984–85
Steve Kiefer	1986–88
Mark Kiefer	1993–95
Ed Kirkpatrick	1977
Joe Kmak	1993
Mark Knudson	1986–91
Kevin Kobel	1973–74, 1976
Pete Koegel	1970–71
Brad Komminsk	1987
Andy Kosco	1971
Lew Krausse	1970–71
Ray Krawczyk	1989
Bill Krueger	1989–90
Ted Kubiak	1970–71
Art Kusnyer	1976

Pete Ladd	1982–85
Joe Lahoud	1972–73
Tom Lampkin	1993
Dave LaPoint	1980
George Lauzerique	1970
Jack Lazorko	1984
Tim Leary	1985–86
Mark Lee	1990–91
Jeffrey Leonard	1988
Randy Lerch	1981–82
Brad Lesley	1985
Sixto Lezcano	1974–80
Jack Lind	1974–75
Frank Linzy	1972–73
Pat Listach	1992–95
Graeme Lloyd	1993–95
Bob Locker	1970
Skip Lockwood	1970–73
Doug Loman	1984–85
Jim Lonborg	1972
Marcelino Lopez	1971
Mark Loretta	1995
Willie Lozado	1984
Julio Machado	1990–91
Alex Madrid	1987
Candy Maldonado	1991
Carlos Maldonado	1993
Rick Manning	1983–87
Josias Manzanillo	1993
Buck Martinez	1978–80
Tom Matchick	1971
Mike Matheny	1994–95
Dave May	1970–74, 1978
Derrick May	1995
Matt Maysey	1993
Jamie McAndrew	1995
Bob McClure	1977–86
Tim McIntosh	1990–93
Ken McMullen	1977
Jerry McNertney	1970
Doc Medich	1982
Jose Mercedes	1994–95
Bob Meyer	1970
Joey Meyer	1988–89
Matt Mieske	1993–95
Roger Miller	1974
Paul Mirabella	1987–90
Angel Miranda	1993–95
Paul Mitchell	1979–80
Bobby Mitchell	1971, 1973–75
Paul Molitor	1978–92
Don Money	1973–83
Donnie Moore	1981
Charlie Moore	1973–86
John Morris	1970–71
Curt Motton	1972
Willie Mueller	1978, 1981
Tom Murphy	1974–76
Tony Muser	1978
Jaime Navarro	1989–94
Ray Newman	1972–73
Juan Nieves	1986–88
Dave Nilsson	1992–95
Tim Nordbrook	1978–79
Rafael Novoa	1993
Edwin Nunez	1991–92
Syd O'Brien	1972
Charlie O'Brien	1987–90
John O'Donoghue	1970
Ben Oglivie	1978–86
Jim Olander	1991
Troy O'Leary	1993–94
Joe Oliver	1995
Jesse Orosco	1992–94
Pat Osburn	1975
Jim Paciorek	1987
Dave Parker	1990
Bill Parsons	1971–73
Marty Pattin	1970–71
Roberto Pena	1970–71
Jeff Peterek	1989
Ray Peters	1970
Rob Picciolo	1982–83
Dan Plesac	1986–92
John Poff	1980
Gus Polidor	1989–90
Carlos Ponce	1985
Darrell Porter	1971–76

Chuck Porter	1981–85
Dennis Powell	1990
Jamie Quirk	1977
Willie Randolph	1991
Paul Ratliff	1971–72
Lance Rautzhan	1979
Randy Ready	1983–86
Jody Reed	1994
Kevin Reimer	1993
Andy Replogle	1978–79
Jerry Reuss	1989
Alberto Reyes	1995
Tommie Reynolds	1972
Archie Reynolds	1972
Bob Reynolds	1971
Ken Reynolds	1973
Ron Rightnowar	1995
Ernest Riles	1985–88
Sid Roberson	1995
Billy Jo Robidoux	1985–88
Ron Robinson	1990–92
Ellie Rodriguez	1971–73
Ed Rodriguez	1973–78
Rich Rollins	1970
Ed Romero	1977, 1980–85, 1989
Phil Roof	1970–71
Jimmy Rosario	1976
Bruce Ruffin	1992
Gary Ryerson	1972–73
Ray Sadecki	1976
Lenn Sakata	1977–79
Ken Sanders	1970–72
Ted Savage	1970–71
Bob Scanlan	1994–95
Dick Schofield	1971
Bill Schroeder	1983–88
George Scott	1972–76
Ray Searage	1984–86
Bob Sebra	1990
Kevin Seitzer	1992–95
Dick Selma	1974
Bill Sharp	1975–76
Gary Sheffield	1988–91
Bob Sheldon	1974–75, 1977
Chris Short	1973
Ted Simmons	1981–85
Duane Singleton	1994–95
Bob Skube	1982–83
Jim Slaton	1971–77, 1979–83
Joe Slusarski	1995
Bernie Smith	1970–71
Russ Snyder	1970
Lary Sorensen	1977–80
Steve Sparks	1995
Bill Spiers	1989–94
Ed Sprague	1973–76
Steve Stanicek	1987
Fred Stanley	1970
Dave Stapleton	1987–88
Randy Stein	1978
Earl Stephenson	1972
Franklin Stubbs	1991–92
William Suero	1992–93
Jim Sundberg	1984
B. J. Surhoff	1987–95
Gary Sutherland	1976
Don Sutton	1982–84
Dale Sveum	1986–88, 1990–91
Jim Tatum	1992
Chuck Taylor	1972
Tom Tellmann	1983–84
Frank Tepedino	1971
Ron Theobald	1971–72
Danny Thomas	1976–77
Gorman Thomas	1973–76, 1978–83, 1986
Mike Thomas	1995
Dickie Thon	1993
Bill Travers	1974–80
Wayne Twitchell	1970
Tim Unroe	1995
Sandy Valdespino	1970
Jose Valentin	1992–95
Dave Valle	1994
Greg Vaughn	1989–95
Carlos Velazquez	1973
Randy Veres	1989–90
Fernando Vina	1995

Bill Voss	1971–72
Pete Vuckovich	1981–83, 1985–86
John Vukovich	1973–74
Rick Waits	1983–85
Danny Walton	1970–71
Turner Ward	1994–95
Floyd Weaver	1971
Bill Wegman	1985–95
Kevin Wickander	1995
Floyd Wicker	1970
Jim Wohlford	1977–79
Clyde Wright	1974
Rick Wrona	1994
Jimmy Wynn	1977
Al Yates	1971
Ned Yost	1980–83
Mike Young	1988
Robin Yount	1974–93
Jeff Yurak	1978

Managers

George Bamberger	1978–80, 1985–86
Dave Bristol	1970–72
Del Crandall	1972–75
Phil Garner	1992–95
Alex Grammas	1976–77
Harvey Kuenn	1975, 1982–83
Rene Lachemann	1984
Roy McMillan	1972
Buck Rodgers	1980–82
Tom Trebelhorn	1986–91

MINNESOTA Twins 1961–95
Moved from WASHINGTON Senators

Paul Abbott	1990–92
Glenn Adams	1977–81
Mike Adams	1972–73
Juan Agosto	1986
Rick Aguilera	1989–95
Vic Albury	1973–76
Bernie Allen	1962–66
Bob Allison	1961–70
Joe Altobelli	1961
Brant Alyea	1970–71
Allan Anderson	1986–91
Jerry Arrigo	1961–64
Fernando Arroyo	1980–82
Keith Atherton	1986–88
Wally Backman	1989
Mike Bacsik	1979–80
Chuck Baker	1981
Doug Baker	1988–90
Eddie Bane	1973, 1975–76
George Banks	1962–63
Willie Banks	1991–93
Steve Barber	1970–71
Randy Bass	1977
Earl Battey	1961–67
Don Baylor	1987
Billy Beane	1986–87
Rich Becker	1993–95
Julio Becquer	1961
Steve Bedrosian	1991
Juan Berenguer	1987–90
Reno Bertoia	1961
Karl Best	1988
Bill Bethea	1964
Jeff Bittiger	1987
Clyde Bloomfield	1964
Bert Blyleven	1970–76, 1985–88
Walt Bond	1967
Joe Bonikowski	1962
Greg Booker	1989
Glenn Borgmann	1972–79
Paul Boris	1982
Lyman Bostock	1975–77
Dave Boswell	1964–70
Pat Bourque	1974
Darrell Brandon	1969
Steve Braun	1971–76
Ken Brett	1979
John Briggs	1975
Bernardo Brito	1992–93, 1995
Darrell Brown	1983–84
Mark Brown	1985
Jarvis Brown	1991–92
Fred Bruckbauer	1961

J. T. Bruett	1992–93
Greg Brummett	1993
Tom Brunansky	1982–88
Steve Brye	1970–76
Terry Bulling	1977
Eric Bullock	1988
Tom Burgmeier	1974–77
Dennis Burtt	1985–86
Randy Bush	1982–93
John Butcher	1984–86
Sal Butera	1980–82, 1987
Bill Butler	1974–75, 1977
Bill Campbell	1973–76
Kevin Campbell	1994–95
Sal Campisi	1971
John Candelaria	1990
Leo Cardenas	1969–71
Rod Carew	1967–78
Steve Carlton	1987–88
Don Carrithers	1977
Larry Casian	1990–94
Bobby Castillo	1982–84
Carmen Castillo	1989–91
John Castino	1979–84
Dean Chance	1967–69
Rich Chiles	1977–78
John Christensen	1988
Pete Cimino	1965–66
Ron Clark	1966–69
Jerald Clark	1995
Alex Cole	1994–95
Jackie Collum	1962
Keith Comstock	1984
Billy Consolo	1961
Mike Cook	1989
Ron Coomer	1995
Don Cooper	1981–82
Doug Corbett	1980–82
Ray Corbin	1971–75
Tim Corcoran	1981
Marty Cordova	1995
Jerry Crider	1969
Mike Cubbage	1976–80
Berto Cueto	1961
Bill Dailey	1963–64
Bobby Darwin	1972–75
Andre David	1984
Mark Davidson	1986–88
Ron Davis	1982–86
Chili Davis	1991–92
Joe Decker	1973–76
Rick Dempsey	1969–72
Jim Deshaies	1993–94
Dan Dobbek	1961
Jim Donohue	1962
Gary Dotter	1961, 1963–64
Tim Drummond	1989–90
Steve Dunn	1994–95
Jim Dwyer	1988–90
Mike Dyer	1989
Tom Edens	1991–92
Dave Edwards	1978–80
Jim Eisenreich	1982–84
Dave Engle	1981–85
Roger Erickson	1978–82
Scott Erickson	1990–95
Alvaro Espinoza	1984–86
Frank Eufemia	1985
Len Faedo	1980–84
Terry Felton	1979–82
Sergio Ferrer	1974–75
Dan Fife	1973–74
Pete Filson	1982–86
Bill Fischer	1964
Ray Fontenot	1986
Dan Ford	1975–78
Mike Fornieles	1963
Jerry Fosnow	1964–65
George Frazier	1986–87
Mark Funderburk	1981, 1985
Gary Gaetti	1981–90
Greg Gagne	1983, 1985–92
Keith Garagozzo	1994
Rich Garces	1990, 1993
Billy Gardner	1961
Bob Gebhard	1971–72
Paul Giel	1961
Dan Gladden	1987–91

Dave Goltz	1972–79
Ruben Gomez	1962
Luis Gomez	1974–77
German Gonzalez	1988–89
Danny Goodwin	1979–81
Bob Gorinski	1977
John Goryl	1962–64
Mauro Gozzo	1992
Dan Graham	1979
Wayne Granger	1972
Mudcat Grant	1964–67
Lenny Green	1961–64
Joe Grzenda	1969
Eddie Guardado	1993–95
Bucky Guth	1972
Mark Guthrie	1989–95
Chip Hale	1989–90, 1993–95
Jimmie Hall	1963–66
Tom Hall	1968–71
Pete Hamm	1970–71
Bill Hands	1973–74
Carroll Hardy	1967
Brian Harper	1988–93
Greg Harris	1995
Roric Harrison	1978
Mike Hart	1984
Mike Hartley	1993
Paul Hartzell	1979
Mickey Hatcher	1981–86
Brad Havens	1981–83
LaTroy Hawkins	1995
Hal Haydel	1970–71
Neal Heaton	1986
Ron Henry	1961, 1964
Jackie Hernandez	1967–68
Tommy Herr	1988
Herman Hill	1969–70
Donnie Hill	1992
Larry Hisle	1973–77
Jack Hobbs	1981
Denny Hocking	1993–95
Ed Hodge	1984
Jeff Holly	1977–79
Jim Holt	1968–74
Vince Horsman	1995
Steve Howe	1985
Kent Hrbek	1981–94
Jim Hughes	1974–77
Randy Hundley	1974
Riccardo Ingram	1995
Hank Izquierdo	1967
Ron Jackson	1979–81
Roy Lee Jackson	1986
Darrell Jackson	1978–82
Lamar Jacobs	1961
Houston Jimenez	1983–84
Dave Johnson	1977–78
Tom Johnson	1974–78
Randy Johnson	1982
Greg Johnston	1980–81
Terry Jorgensen	1989, 1992–93
Jim Kaat	1961–73
Ron Keller	1966, 1968
Pat Kelly	1968
Tom Kelly	1975
Harmon Killebrew	1961–74
Jerry Kindall	1964–65
Mike Kinnunen	1980
Bob Kipper	1992
Tom Klawitter	1985
Ron Kline	1967
Scott Klingenbeck	1995
Joe Klink	1987
Johnny Klippstein	1964–66
Chuck Knoblauch	1991–95
Jerry Koosman	1979–81
Andy Kosco	1965–67
Frank Kostro	1964–65, 1967–68
Jack Kralick	1961–63
Bill Krueger	1992
Rusty Kuntz	1983
Craig Kusick	1973–79
Ken Landreaux	1979–80
Gene Larkin	1987–93
Dave LaRoche	1972
Fred Lasher	1963
Bill Latham	1986
Tim Laudner	1981–89
Matt Lawton	1995
Charlie Lea	1988
Terry Leach	1990–91
Don Lee	1961–62
Derek Lee	1993
Scott Leius	1990–95
Jim Lemon	1961–63
Ted Lepcio	1961
Jim Lewis	1983
Nelson Liriano	1990
Joe Lis	1973–74
Jeff Little	1982
Steve Lombardozzi	1985–88
Bruce Look	1968
Dwight Lowry	1988
Steve Luebber	1971–72, 1976
Tom Lundstedt	1975
Rick Lysander	1983–85
Kevin Maas	1995
Shane Mack	1990–94
Pete Mackanin	1980–81
Pat Mahomes	1992–95
Mike Maksudian	1993
Jim Manning	1962
Fred Manrique	1990
Chuck Manuel	1969–72
Georges Maranda	1962
Mike Marshall	1978–80
Billy Martin	1961
Marty Martinez	1962
Tippy Martinez	1988
Mike Mason	1988
Dan Masteller	1995
Joe McCabe	1964
David McCarty	1993–95
Danny McDevitt	1961
Dave McKay	1975–76
Pat Meares	1993–95
Dave Meier	1984–85
Minnie Mendoza	1970
Orlando Mercado	1989
Brett Merriman	1993–94
Jim Merritt	1965–68
Matt Merullo	1995
Larry Milbourne	1982
Bob Miller	1968–69
Don Mincher	1961–66
Bobby Mitchell	1982–83
George Mitterwald	1966, 1968–73
Danny Monzon	1972–73
Ray Moore	1961–63
Jose Morales	1978–80
Danny Morris	1968–69
Jack Morris	1991
John Moses	1988–90
Pedro Munoz	1990–95
Oscar Munoz	1995
Hal Naragon	1961–62
Cotton Nash	1969–70
Denny Neagle	1991
Mel Nelson	1965, 1967
Graig Nettles	1968–69
Jim Nettles	1970–72
Al Newman	1987–91
Joe Niekro	1987–88
Randy Niemann	1987
Chuck Nieson	1964
Tom Nieto	1987–88
Russ Nixon	1966–67
Tom Norton	1972
Willie Norwood	1977–80
Joe Nossek	1964–66
Jack O'Connor	1981–84
Bryan Oelkers	1983
Tony Oliva	1962, 1964–76
Francisco Oliveras	1989
Jim Ollom	1966–67
Greg Olson	1989
Junior Ortiz	1990–91
John Pacella	1982
Mike Pagliarulo	1991–93
Ed Palmquist	1961
Derek Parks	1992–94
Jose Parra	1995
Camilo Pascual	1961–66
Larry Pashnick	1984
Frank Pastore	1986
Mike Pazik	1975–77
Sam Perlozzo	1977
Ron Perranoski	1968–71
Jim Perry	1963–72
Stan Perzanowski	1978
Jay Pettibone	1983
Chris Pittaro	1986–87
Bill Pleis	1961–66
Mike Poepping	1975
Mark Portugal	1985–88
Wally Post	1963
Hosken Powell	1978–81
Paul Ray Powell	1971
Vic Power	1962–64
Kirby Puckett	1984–95
Carlos Pulido	1994
Pat Putnam	1984
Frank Quilici	1965, 1967–70
Luis Quinones	1992
Brian Raabe	1995
Brad Radke	1995
Pedro Ramos	1961
Bob Randall	1976–80
Paul Ratliff	1963, 1970–71
Shane Rawley	1989
Jeff Reardon	1987–89
Jeff Reboulet	1992–95
Pete Redfern	1976–82
Jeff Reed	1984–86
Darren Reed	1992
Rich Reese	1964–65, 1967–73
Rick Renick	1968–72
Bombo Rivera	1978–80
Rich Robertson	1995
Vic Rodriguez	1989
Frank Rodriguez	1995
Garry Roggenburk	1963, 1965–66
Jim Roland	1962–64, 1966–68
Rich Rollins	1961–68
Phil Roof	1971–76
Johnny Roseboro	1968–69
Ted Sadowski	1961–62
Mark Salas	1985–87
Alejandro Sanchez	1986
Ken Sanders	1973
Mo Sanford	1995
Jack Savage	1990
Mac Scarce	1978
Dan Schatzeder	1987–88
Al Schroll	1961
Ken Schrom	1983–85
Ron Schueler	1977
Erik Schullstrom	1994–95
Gary Serum	1977–79
John Sevcik	1965
Jim Shellenback	1977
Steve Shields	1989
Garland Shifflett	1964
Dwight Siebler	1963–67
Bill Singer	1976
Roy Smalley	1976–82, 1985–87
John Smiley	1992
Ray Smith	1981–83
Roy Smith	1986–90
Mike Smithson	1984–87
Jimmy Snyder	1961–62, 1964
Eric Soderholm	1971–75
Rick Sofield	1979–81
Paul Sorrento	1989–91
Chris Speier	1984
Randy St. Claire	1989
Scott Stahoviak	1993, 1995
Kevin Stanfield	1979
Lee Stange	1961–64
Mike Stenhouse	1985
Buzz Stephen	1968
Dave Stevens	1994–95
Dick Stigman	1962–65
Chuck Stobbs	1961
Les Straker	1987–88
Jim Strickland	1971–73
Frank Sullivan	1962–63
Johnny Sutton	1978
Kevin Tapani	1989–95
Jerry Terrell	1973–77
Tim Teufel	1983–85
Greg Thayer	1978
George Thomas	1971
Danny Thompson	1970–76
Paul Thormodsgard	1977–79
Luis Tiant	1970
Tom Tischinski	1969–71
Fred Toliver	1988–89
Kelvin Torve	1988
Cesar Tovar	1965–72
Mike Trombley	1992–95
George Tsamis	1993
Lee Tunnell	1989
Bill Tuttle	1961–63
Ted Uhlaender	1965–69
Scott Ullger	1983
Sandy Valdespino	1965–67
Jose Valdivielso	1961
Elmer Valo	1961
Jesus Vega	1979–80, 1982
John Verhoeven	1980–81
Zoilo Versalles	1961–67
Bob Veselic	1980–81
Frank Viola	1982–89
Matt Walbeck	1994–95
Charley Walters	1969
Mike Walters	1983–84
Danny Walton	1973, 1975
Jay Ward	1963–64
Gary Ward	1979–83
Curt Wardle	1984–85
Ron Washington	1981–86
Scott Watkins	1995
Gary Wayne	1989–92
Lenny Webster	1989–93
Boomer Wells	1982
Vic Wertz	1963
David West	1989–92
Pete Whisenant	1961
Bill Whitby	1964
Len Whitehouse	1983–85
Mark Wiley	1975
Rob Wilfong	1977–82
Stan Williams	1970–71
Don Williams	1963
Al Williams	1980–84
Carl Willis	1991–95
Tack Wilson	1983
Dave Winfield	1993–94
Jim Winn	1988
Larry Wolfe	1977–78
Al Woods	1986
Dick Woodson	1969–70, 1972–74
Al Worthington	1964–69
Butch Wynegar	1976–82
Rich Yett	1985, 1990
Geoff Zahn	1977–80
Bill Zepp	1969–70
Jerry Zimmerman	1962–68

Managers

Cal Ermer	1967–68
Billy Gardner	1981–85
John Goryl	1980–81
Tom Kelly	1986–95
Cookie Lavagetto	1961
Billy Martin	1969
Gene Mauch	1976–80
Sam Mele	1961–67
Ray Miller	1985–86
Frank Quilici	1972–75
Bill Rigney	1970–72

NEW YORK Yankees 1903–95
Moved from BALTIMORE Orioles
Known as Highlanders 1903–12

Jim Abbott	1993–94
Harry Ables	1911
Spencer Adams	1926
Doc Adkins	1903
Steve Adkins	1990
Luis Aguayo	1988
Jack Aker	1969–72
Walt Alexander	1915–17
Doyle Alexander	1976, 1982–83
Bernie Allen	1972–73
Johnny Allen	1932–35
Neil Allen	1985, 1987–88
Sandy Alomar	1974–76
Felipe Alou	1971–73
Matty Alou	1973

Dell Alston	1977
Ruben Amaro	1966–68
John Anderson	1904–05
Rick Anderson	1979
Ivy Andrews	1931–32, 1937–38
Pete Appleton	1933
Angel Aragon	1914, 1916–17
Rugger Ardizoia	1947
Mike Armstrong	1984–86
Brad Arnsberg	1986–87
Luis Arroyo	1960–63
Tucker Ashford	1981
Paul Assenmacher	1993
Joe Ausanio	1994–95
Jimmy Austin	1909–10
Martin Autry	1924
Oscar Azocar	1990
Loren Babe	1952–53
Stan Bahnsen	1966, 1968–71
Bill Bailey	1911
Frank Baker	1916–19, 1921–22
Frank Baker	1970–71
Steve Balboni	1981–83, 1989–90
Neal Ball	1907–09
Scott Bankhead	1995
Steve Barber	1967–68
Jesse Barfield	1989–92
Cy Barger	1906–07
Ray Barker	1965–67
Frank Barnes	1930
Honey Barnes	1926
Ed Barney	1915
George Batten	1912
Hank Bauer	1948–59
Paddy Baumann	1915–17
Don Baylor	1983–85
Walter Beall	1924–27
Jim Beattie	1978–79
Rich Beck	1965
Zinn Beck	1918
Fred Beene	1972–74
Joe Beggs	1938
John Bell	1907
Zeke Bella	1957
Benny Bengough	1923–30
Juan Beniquez	1979
Lou Berberet	1954–55
Dave Bergman	1975, 1977
Walter Bernhardt	1918
Juan Bernhardt	1976
Yogi Berra	1946–63
Dale Berra	1985–86
Bill Bevens	1944–47
Monte Beville	1903–04
Harry Billiard	1908
Doug Bird	1980–81
Ewell Blackwell	1952–53
Rick Bladt	1975
Paul Blair	1977–80
Walter Blair	1907–11
Johnny Blanchard	1955, 1959–65
Gil Blanco	1965
Wade Blasingame	1972
Steve Blateric	1972
Gary Blaylock	1959
Curt Blefary	1970–71
Elmer Bliss	1903–04
Ron Blomberg	1969, 1971–76
Mike Blowers	1989–91
Eddie Bockman	1946
Ping Bodie	1918–21
Len Boehmer	1969, 1971
Brian Boehringer	1995
Wade Boggs	1993–95
Don Bollweg	1953
Bobby Bonds	1975
Ernie Bonham	1940–46
Juan Bonilla	1985, 1987
Luke Boone	1913–16
Frenchy Bordagaray	1941
Rich Bordi	1985, 1987
Hank Borowy	1942–45
Babe Borton	1913
Daryl Boston	1994
Jim Bouton	1962–68
Clete Boyer	1959–66
Scott Bradley	1984–85
Neal Brady	1915, 1917
Ralph Branca	1954
Norm Branch	1941–42
Marshall Brant	1980
Garland Braxton	1925–26
Don Brennan	1933
Jim Brenneman	1965
Ken Brett	1976
Marv Breuer	1939–43
Fritzie Brickell	1958–59
Jim Brideweser	1951–53
Marshall Bridges	1962–63
Harry Bright	1963–64
Ed Brinkman	1975
Johnny Broaca	1934–37
Lew Brockett	1907, 1909, 1911
Jim Bronstad	1959
Tom Brookens	1989
Bob Brower	1989
Boardwalk Brown	1914–15
Hal Brown	1962
Bobby Brown	1946–52, 1954
Jumbo Brown	1932–33, 1935–36
Bobby Brown	1979–81
Curt Brown	1984
Billy Bryan	1966–67
Jess Buckles	1916
Jay Buhner	1987–88
Bill Burbach	1969–71
Lew Burdette	1950
Tim Burke	1992
George Burns	1928
Alex Burr	1914
Ray Burris	1979
Joe Bush	1922–24
Tom Buskey	1973–74
Ralph Buxton	1949
Joe Buzas	1945
Harry Byrd	1954
Sammy Byrd	1929–34
Tommy Byrne	1943, 1946–51, 1954–57
Marty Bystrom	1984–85
Greg Cadaret	1989–92
Charlie Caldwell	1925
Ray Caldwell	1910–18
Johnny Callison	1972–73
Howie Camp	1917
Bert Campaneris	1983
Archie Campbell	1928
John Candelaria	1988–89
Mike Cantwell	1916
Andy Carey	1952–60
Roy Carlyle	1926
Duke Carmel	1965
Ownie Carroll	1930
Dick Carroll	1909
Tommy Carroll	1955–56
Chuck Cary	1989–91
Hugh Casey	1949
Roy Castleton	1907
Bill Castro	1981
Danny Cater	1970–71
Rick Cerone	1980–84, 1987, 1990
Bob Cerv	1951–52, 1954–56, 1960–62
Chris Chambliss	1974–79
Spud Chandler	1937–47
Les Channell	1910
Darrin Chapin	1991
Ben Chapman	1930–36
Mike Chartak	1940
Hal Chase	1905–13
Jack Chesbro	1903–09
Clay Christiansen	1984
Al Cicotte	1957
Allie Clark	1947
George Clark	1913
Jack Clark	1988
Horace Clarke	1965–74
Walter Clarkson	1904–07
Ken Clay	1977–79
Pat Clements	1987–88
Tex Clevenger	1961–62
Lu Clinton	1966–67
Al Closter	1971–72
Andy Coakley	1911
Jim Coates	1956, 1959–62
Jim Cockman	1905
Rich Coggins	1975–76
Rocky Colavito	1968
King Cole	1914–15
Curt Coleman	1912
Jerry Coleman	1949–57
Rip Coleman	1955–56
Rip Collins	1920–21
Joe Collins	1949–57
Orth Collins	1904
Bob Collins	1944
Pat Collins	1926–28
Dave Collins	1982
Frank Colman	1946–47
Loyd Colson	1970
Earle Combs	1924–35
David Cone	1995
Tom Connelly	1921
Joe Connor	1905
Wid Conroy	1903–08
Doc Cook	1913–16
Andy Cook	1993
Dusty Cooke	1930–31
Johnny Cooney	1944
Phil Cooney	1905
Guy Cooper	1914
Don Cooper	1985
Henry Cotto	1985–87
Ensign Cottrell	1915
Clint Courtney	1951
Ernie Courtney	1903
Stan Coveleski	1928
Billy Cowan	1969
Joe Cowley	1984–85
Casey Cox	1972–73
Bobby Cox	1968–69
Birdie Cree	1908–15
Lou Criger	1910
Herb Crompton	1945
Frankie Crosetti	1932–48
Jose Cruz	1988
Jack Cullen	1962, 1965–66
Roy Cullenbine	1942
Nick Cullop	1916–17
John Cumberland	1968–70
Jim Curry	1911
Fred Curtis	1905
Babe Dahlgren	1938–40
Bud Daley	1961–64
Tom Daley	1914–15
Bert Daniels	1910–13
Bobby Davidson	1989
Lefty Davis	1903
George Davis	1912
Kiddo Davis	1926
Ron Davis	1978–81
Russ Davis	1994–95
Brian Dayett	1983–84
Joe De Maestri	1960–61
John Deering	1903
Jim Deidel	1974
Ivan DeJesus	1986
Bobby Del Greco	1957–58
Frank Delahanty	1905–06, 1908
Jim Delsing	1949–50
Ray Demmitt	1909
Rick Dempsey	1973–76
Bucky Dent	1977–82
Claud Derrick	1913
Russ Derry	1944–45
Jim Deshaies	1984
Jimmie DeShong	1934–35
Orestes Destrade	1987
Charlie Devens	1932–34
Al DeVormer	1921–22
Bill Dickey	1928–43
Murry Dickson	1958
Joe DiMaggio	1936–42, 1946–51
Kerry Dineen	1975–76
Art Ditmar	1957–61
Sonny Dixon	1956
Pat Dobson	1973–75
Cozy Dolan	1911–12
Atley Donald	1938–45
Mike Donovan	1908
Brian Dorsett	1989–90
Richard Dotson	1988–89
Patsy Dougherty	1904–06
John Dowd	1912
Al Downing	1961–69
Jack Doyle	1905
Slow Joe Doyle	1906–10
Brian Doyle	1978–80
Doug Drabek	1986
Bill Drescher	1944–46
Karl Drews	1946–48
Monk Dubiel	1944–45
Joe Dugan	1922–28
Ryne Duren	1958–61
Leo Durocher	1928–29
Cedric Durst	1927–30
Mike Easler	1986–87
Rawly Eastwick	1978
Foster Edwards	1930
Doc Edwards	1965
Robert Eenhoorn	1994–95
Dave Eiland	1988–91, 1995
Kid Elberfeld	1903–07, 1909
Gene Elliott	1911
Dock Ellis	1976–77
John Ellis	1969–72
Kevin Elster	1994–95
Red Embree	1948
Clyde Engle	1909–10
Jack Enright	1917
Roger Erickson	1982–83
Juan Espino	1982–83, 1985–86
Alvaro Espinoza	1988–91
Nick Etten	1943–46
Barry Evans	1982
Steve Farr	1991–93
Doc Farrell	1932–33
Alex Ferguson	1918, 1921, 1925
Frank Fernandez	1967–69
Tony Fernandez	1995
Mike Ferraro	1966, 1968
Wes Ferrell	1938–39
Tom Ferrick	1950–51
Chick Fewster	1917–22
Ed Figueroa	1976–80
Pete Filson	1987
Happy Finneran	1918
Mike Fischlin	1986
Gus Fisher	1912
Ray Fisher	1910–17
Brian Fisher	1985–86
Mike Fitzgerald	1911
Tim Foli	1984
Ray Fontenot	1983–84
Barry Foote	1981–82
Whitey Ford	1950, 1953–67
Russ Ford	1909–13
Eddie Foster	1910
Jack Fournier	1918
Ray Francis	1925
George Frazier	1981–83
Mark Freeman	1959
Ray French	1920
Lonny Frey	1947
Bob Friend	1966
John Frill	1910
Bill Fulton	1987
Dave Fultz	1903–05
John Gabler	1959–60
Joe Gallagher	1939
Mike Gallego	1992–94
Oscar Gamble	1976, 1979–84
John Ganzel	1903–04
Mike Garbark	1944–45
Damaso Garcia	1978–79
Earl Gardner	1908–12
Rob Gardner	1970–72
Billy Gardner	1961–62
Ned Garvin	1904
Milt Gaston	1924
Mike Gazella	1923, 1926–28
Joe Gedeon	1916–17
Lou Gehrig	1923–39
Bob Geren	1988–91
Al Gettel	1945–46
Joe Giard	1927
Jake Gibbs	1962–71
Sam Gibson	1930
Paul Gibson	1993–94
Frank Gilhooley	1913–18
Fred Glade	1908
Frank Gleich	1919–20
Joe Glenn	1932–33, 1935–38
Lefty Gomez	1930–42
Jesse Gonder	1960
Pedro Gonzalez	1963–64
Fernando Gonzalez	1974
Wilbur Good	1905
Art Goodwin	1905
Joe Gordon	1938–43, 1946
Tom Gorman	1952–54
Goose Gossage	1978–83, 1989
Dick Gossett	1913–14
Larry Gowell	1972
Johnny Grabowski	1927–29
Wayne Granger	1973
Ted Gray	1955

Eli Grba	1959–60
Willie Greene	1903
Ken Griffey	1982–86
Mike Griffin	1979–81
Bob Grim	1954–58
Burleigh Grimes	1934
Oscar Grimes	1943–46
Lee Grissom	1940
Cecilio Guante	1987–88
Lee Guetterman	1988–92
Ron Guidry	1975–88
Brad Gulden	1979–80
Don Gullett	1977–78
Bill Gullickson	1987
Randy Gumpert	1946–48
Larry Gura	1974–75
John Habyan	1990–93
Bump Hadley	1936–40
Kent Hadley	1960
Ed Hahn	1905–06
Noodles Hahn	1906
Hinkey Haines	1923
George Halas	1919
Bob Hale	1961
Jimmie Hall	1969
Mel Hall	1989–92
Roger Hambright	1971
Steve Hamilton	1963–70
Mike Handiboe	1911
Jim Hanley	1913
Truck Hannah	1918–20
Ron Hansen	1970–71
Joe Hanson	1913
Jim Hardin	1971
Bubbles Hargrave	1930
Harry Harper	1921
Toby Harrah	1984
Joe Harris	1914
Greg Harris	1994
Jim Ray Hart	1973–74
Roy Hartzell	1911–16
Buddy Hassett	1942
Ron Hassey	1985–86
Andy Hawkins	1989–91
Chicken Hawks	1921
Charlie Hayes	1992
Fran Healy	1976–78
Mike Heath	1978
Neal Heaton	1993
Don Heffner	1934–37
Mike Hegan	1964, 1966–67, 1973–74
Fred Heimach	1928–29
Woodie Held	1954
Charlie Hemphill	1908–11
Rollie Hemsley	1942–44
Bill Henderson	1930
Rickey Henderson	1985–89
Harvey Hendrick	1923–24
Ellie Hendricks	1976–77
Tim Hendryx	1915–17
Tommy Henrich	1937–42, 1946–50
Bill Henry	1966
Leo Hernandez	1986
Xavier Hernandez	1994
Ed Herrmann	1975
Hugh High	1915–18
Oral Hildebrand	1939–40
Jesse Hill	1935
Shawn Hillegas	1992
Frank Hiller	1946, 1948–49
Mack Hillis	1924
Rich Hinton	1972
Sterling Hitchcock	1992–95
Myril Hoag	1931–32, 1934–38
Butch Hobson	1982
Red Hoff	1911–13
Danny Hoffman	1906–07
Solly Hofman	1916
Fred Hofmann	1919–25
Bill Hogg	1905–08
Bobby Hogue	1951–52
Ken Holcombe	1945
Bill Holden	1913–14
Al Holland	1986–87
Ken Holloway	1930
Fred Holmes	1903
Roger Holt	1980
Ken Holtzman	1976–78
Rick Honeycutt	1995
Wally Hood	1949
Don Hood	1979
Johnny Hopp	1950–52
Shags Horan	1924
Ralph Houk	1947–53
Elston Howard	1955–67
Steve Howe	1991–95
Harry Howell	1903
Jay Howell	1982–84
Dick Howser	1967–68
Waite Hoyt	1921–30
Rex Hudler	1984–85
Charles Hudson	1987–88
Long Tom Hughes	1904
Tom Hughes	1906–07, 1909–10
John Hummel	1918
Mike Humphreys	1991–93
Ken Hunt	1959–60
Billy Hunter	1955–56
Catfish Hunter	1975–79
Mark Hutton	1993–94
Ham Hyatt	1918
Fred Jacklitsch	1905
Grant Jackson	1976
Reggie Jackson	1977–81
Johnny James	1958, 1960–61
Dion James	1992–93, 1995
Stan Javier	1984
Domingo Jean	1993
Stan Jefferson	1989
Jackie Jensen	1950–52
Derek Jeter	1995
Elvio Jimenez	1964
Tommy John	1979–82, 1986–89
Alex Johnson	1974–75
Darrell Johnson	1957–58
Deron Johnson	1960–61
Don Johnson	1947, 1950
Ernie Johnson	1923–25
Hank Johnson	1925–26, 1928–32
Johnny Johnson	1944
Ken Johnson	1969
Otis Johnson	1911
Roy Johnson	1936–37
Billy Johnson	1943, 1946–51
Cliff Johnson	1977–79
Jeff Johnson	1991–93
Jay Johnstone	1978–79
Sad Sam Jones	1922–26
Ruppert Jones	1980
Gary Jones	1970–71
Darryl Jones	1979
Jimmy Jones	1989–90
Tim Jordan	1903
Arndt Jorgens	1929–39
Mike Jurewicz	1965
Jim Kaat	1979–80
Scott Kamieniecki	1991–95
Bob Kammeyer	1978–79
Bill Karlon	1930
Herb Karpel	1946
Benny Kauff	1912
Curt Kaufman	1982–83
Eddie Kearse	1942
Ray Keating	1912–16, 1918
Bob Keefe	1907
Willie Keeler	1903–09
Mike Kekich	1969–73
Charlie Keller	1939–43, 1945–49, 1952
Roberto Kelly	1987–92
Pat Kelly	1991–95
Steve Kemp	1983–84
John Kennedy	1967
Jerry Kenney	1967, 1969–72
Matt Keough	1983
Jimmy Key	1993–95
Steve Kiefer	1989
Henry Kingman	1914
Dave Kingman	1977
Fred Kipp	1960
Frank Kitson	1907
Ron Kittle	1986–87
Ted Kleinhans	1936
Red Kleinow	1904–10
Ed Klepfer	1911, 1913
Ron Klimkowski	1969–70, 1972
Steve Kline	1970–74
Mickey Klutts	1976–78
Bill Knickerbocker	1938–40
John Knight	1909–11, 1913
Mark Koenig	1925–30
Jim Konstanty	1954–56
Andy Kosco	1968
Steve Kraly	1953
Jack Kramer	1951
Ernie Krueger	1915
Dick Kryhoski	1949
Tony Kubek	1957–65
Johnny Kucks	1955–59
Bill Kunkel	1963
Bob Kuzava	1951–54
Joe Lake	1908–09
Bill Lamar	1917–19
Hal Lanier	1972–73
Dave LaPoint	1989–90
Frank LaPorte	1905–10
Dave LaRoche	1981–83
Don Larsen	1955–59
Lyn Lary	1929–34
Marcus Lawton	1989
Gene Layden	1915
Tony Lazzeri	1926–37
Tim Leary	1990–92
Joe Lefebvre	1980
Al Leiter	1987–89
Mark Leiter	1990
Frank Leja	1954–55
Jack Lelivelt	1912–13
Eddie Leon	1975
Louis LeRoy	1905–06
Ed Levy	1942, 1944
Duffy Lewis	1919–20
Jim Lewis	1982
Terry Ley	1971
Jim Leyritz	1990–95
Paul Lindblad	1978
Johnny Lindell	1942–50
Phil Linz	1962–65
Jack Little	1912
Bryan Little	1986
Clem Llewellyn	1922
Gene Locklear	1976–77
Sherm Lollar	1947–48
Tim Lollar	1980
Phil Lombardi	1986–87
Herman Long	1903
Dale Long	1960, 1962–63
Ed Lopat	1948–55
Art Lopez	1965
Hector Lopez	1959–66
Baldy Louden	1907
Slim Love	1916–18
Torey Lovullo	1991
Johnny Lucadello	1947
Joe Lucey	1920
Roy Luebbe	1925
Jerry Lumpe	1956–59
Scott Lusader	1991
Sparky Lyle	1972–78
Al Lyons	1944, 1946–47
Jim Lyttle	1969–71
Duke Maas	1958–61
Kevin Maas	1990–93
Bob MacDonald	1995
Danny MacFayden	1932–34
Elliott Maddox	1974–76
Dave Madison	1950
Lee Magee	1916–17
Sal Maglie	1957–58
Stubby Magner	1911
Jim Magnuson	1973
Fritz Maisel	1913–17
Hank Majeski	1946
Frank Makosky	1937
Pat Malone	1935–37
Pat Maloney	1912
Al Mamaux	1924
Rube Manning	1907–10
Mickey Mantle	1951–68
Josias Manzanillo	1995
Cliff Mapes	1948–51
Roger Maris	1960–66
Cliff Markle	1915–16, 1924
Jim Marquis	1925
Armando Marsans	1917–18
Cuddles Marshall	1946, 1948–49
Billy Martin	1950–53, 1955–57
Hersh Martin	1944–45
Jack Martin	1912
Tippy Martinez	1974–76
Jim Mason	1974–76
Vic Mata	1984–85
Don Mattingly	1982–95
Rudy May	1974–76, 1980–83
Carlos May	1976–77
John Mayberry	1982
Carl Mays	1919–23
Lee Mazzilli	1982
Larry McCall	1977–78
Joe McCarthy	1905
Pat McCauley	1903
Larry McClure	1910
George McConnell	1909, 1912–13
Mike McCormick	1970
Lance McCullers	1989–90
Lindy McDaniel	1968–73
Mickey McDermott	1956
Danny McDevitt	1961
Jim McDonald	1952–54
Dave McDonald	1969
Gil McDougald	1951–60
Sam McDowell	1973–74
Jack McDowell	1995
Lou McEvoy	1930–31
Herm McFarland	1903
Andy McGaffigan	1981
Lynn McGlothen	1982
Bob McGraw	1917–20
Deacon McGuire	1904–07
Marty McHale	1913–15
Irish McIlveen	1908
Bill McKechnie	1913
Rich McKinney	1972
Frank McManus	1904
Norm McMillan	1922
Tommy McMillan	1912
Mike McNally	1921–24
Herb McQuaid	1926
George McQuinn	1947–48
Bobby Meacham	1983–88
Charlie Meara	1914
Doc Medich	1972–75
Bob Melvin	1994
Fred Merkle	1925–26
Andy Messersmith	1978
Tom Metcalf	1963
Bud Metheny	1943–45
Hensley Meulens	1989–93
Bob Meusel	1920–29
Bob Meyer	1964
Gene Michael	1968–74
Ezra Midkiff	1912–13
Pete Mikkelsen	1964–65
Larry Milbourne	1981–83
Sam Militello	1992–93
Elmer Miller	1915–18, 1921–22
John Miller	1966
Bill Miller	1952–54
Buster Mills	1940
Alan Mills	1990–91
Mike Milosevich	1944–45
Paul Mirabella	1979
Willie Miranda	1953–54
Fred Mitchell	1910
Johnny Mitchell	1921–22
Bobby Mitchell	1970
Johnny Mize	1949–53
Kevin Mmahat	1989
George Mogridge	1915–20
Dale Mohorcic	1988–89
Fenton Mole	1949
Bill Monbouquette	1967–68
Ed Monroe	1917–18
Zack Monroe	1958–59
John Montefusco	1983–86
Rich Monteleone	1990–93
Archie Moore	1964–65
Earl Moore	1907
Wilcy Moore	1927–29, 1932–33
Ray Morehart	1927
Omar Moreno	1983–85
Tom Morgan	1951–52, 1954–56
Mike Morgan	1982
George Moriarty	1906–08
Jeff Moronko	1987
Hal Morris	1988–89
Ross Moschitto	1965, 1967
Gerry Moses	1973
Terry Mulholland	1994
Charlie Mullen	1914–16
Jerry Mumphrey	1981–83
Bob Muncrief	1951
Bobby Munoz	1993
Thurman Munson	1969–79
Bobby Murcer	1965–66, 1969–74, 1979–83
Johnny Murphy	1932, 1934–43, 1946
Rob Murphy	1994

George Murray	1922
Dale Murray	1983–85
Larry Murray	1974–76
Jerry Narron	1979
Bots Nekola	1929
Luke Nelson	1919
Gene Nelson	1981
Graig Nettles	1973–83
Tex Neuer	1907
Ernie Nevel	1950–51
Floyd Newkirk	1934
Bobo Newsom	1947
Doc Newton	1905–09
Gus Niarhos	1946, 1948–49
Phil Niekro	1984–85
Joe Niekro	1985–87
Scott Nielsen	1986, 1988–89
Jerry Nielsen	1992
Harry Niles	1908
Otis Nixon	1983
Matt Nokes	1990–94
Irv Noren	1952–56
Don Nottebart	1969
Les Nunamaker	1914–17
Johnny Oates	1980–81
Mike O'Berry	1984
Andy O'Connor	1908
Jack O'Connor	1903
Paddy O'Connor	1918
Heinie Odom	1925
Lefty O'Doul	1919–20, 1922
Rowland Office	1983
Bob Ojeda	1994
Rube Oldring	1905, 1916
Bob Oliver	1975
Steve O'Neill	1925
Paul O'Neill	1993–95
Queenie O'Rourke	1908
Al Orth	1904–09
Champ Osteen	1904
Joe Ostrowski	1950–52
Bill Otis	1912
Stubby Overmire	1951
Spike Owen	1993
John Pacella	1982
Del Paddock	1912
Dave Pagan	1973–76
Joe Page	1944–50
Mike Pagliarulo	1984–89
Donn Pall	1994
Clay Parker	1989–90
Ben Paschal	1924–29
Dan Pasqua	1985–87
Gil Patterson	1977
Mike Patterson	1981–82
Jeff Patterson	1995
Dave Pavlas	1995
Monte Pearson	1936–40
Roger Peckinpaugh	1913–21
Steve Peek	1941
Hipolito Pena	1988
Herb Pennock	1923–33
Joe Pepitone	1962–69
Marty Perez	1977
Pascual Perez	1990–91
Melido Perez	1992–95
Cy Perkins	1931
Cecil Perkins	1967
Gaylord Perry	1980
Fritz Peterson	1966–74
Andy Pettitte	1995
Ken Phelps	1988–89
Eddie Phillips	1932
Jack Phillips	1947–49
Cy Pieh	1913–15
Bill Piercy	1917, 1921
Duane Pillette	1949–50
Lou Piniella	1974–84
George Pipgras	1923–24, 1927–33
Wally Pipp	1915–25
Jim Pisoni	1959–60
Eric Plunk	1989–91
Luis Polonia	1989–90, 1994–95
Bob Porterfield	1948–51
Jorge Posada	1995
Jake Powell	1936–40
Jack Powell	1904–05
Mike Powers	1905
Del Pratt	1918–20
Gerry Priddy	1941–42
Johnnie Priest	1911
Alfonso Pulido	1986
Ambrose Puttmann	1903–05
Mel Queen	1942, 1944, 1946–47
Ed Quick	1903
Jack Quinn	1909–12, 1919–21
Jamie Quirk	1989
Dave Rajsich	1978
Pedro Ramos	1964–66
Domingo Ramos	1978
Bobby Ramos	1982
John Ramos	1991
Lenny Randle	1979
Willie Randolph	1976–88
Vic Raschi	1946–53
Dennis Rasmussen	1984–87
Shane Rawley	1982–84
Jeff Reardon	1994
Jack Reed	1961–63
Jimmy Reese	1930–31
Hal Reniff	1961–67
Bill Renna	1953
Tony Rensa	1933
Roger Repoz	1964–66
Rick Reuschel	1981
Dave Revering	1981–82
Allie Reynolds	1947–54
Bill Reynolds	1913–14
Rick Rhoden	1987–88
Gordon Rhodes	1929–32
Harry Rice	1930
Nolen Richardson	1935
Bobby Richardson	1955–66
Branch Rickey	1907
Dave Righetti	1979, 1981–90
Jose Rijo	1984
Mariano Rivera	1995
Ruben Rivera	1995
Mickey Rivers	1976–79
Phil Rizzuto	1941–42, 1946–56
Roxy Roach	1910–11
Dale Roberts	1967
Gene Robertson	1928–29
Andre Robertson	1981–85
Aaron Robinson	1945–47
Hank Robinson	1918
Eddie Robinson	1954–56
Bill Robinson	1967–69
Bruce Robinson	1979–80
Jeff Robinson	1990
Aurelio Rodriguez	1980–81
Ellie Rodriguez	1968
Edwin Rodriguez	1982
Carlos Rodriguez	1991
Gary Roenicke	1986
Oscar Roettger	1923–24
Jay Rogers	1914
Tom Rogers	1921
Jim Roland	1972
Red Rolfe	1931, 1934–42
Buddy Rosar	1939–42
Larry Rosenthal	1944
Steve Roser	1944–46
Braggo Roth	1921
Jerry Royster	1987
Muddy Ruel	1917–20
Dutch Ruether	1926–27
Red Ruffing	1930–42, 1945–46
Allan Russell	1915–19
Marius Russo	1939–43, 1946
Babe Ruth	1920–34
Blondy Ryan	1935
Rosy Ryan	1928
Johnny Sain	1951–55
Lenn Sakata	1987
Mark Salas	1987
Jack Saltzgaver	1932, 1934–37
Billy Sample	1985
Celerino Sanchez	1972–73
Roy Sanders	1918
Deion Sanders	1989–90
Scott Sanderson	1991–92
Fred Sanford	1949–51
Rafael Santana	1988
Don Savage	1944–45
Rick Sawyer	1974–75
Steve Sax	1989–91
Ray Scarborough	1952–53
Germany Schaefer	1916
Harry Schaeffer	1952
Roy Schalk	1932
Art Schallock	1951–55
Wally Schang	1921–25
Butch Schmidt	1909
Bob Schmidt	1965
Johnny Schmitz	1952–53
Pete Schneider	1919
Dick Schofield	1966
Paul Schreiber	1945
Al Schulz	1912–14
Don Schulze	1989
Bill Schwarz	1914
Pius Schwert	1914–15
George Scott	1979
Everett Scott	1922–25
Rodney Scott	1982
Rod Scurry	1985–86
Ken Sears	1943
Bob Seeds	1936
Kal Segrist	1952
George Selkirk	1934–42
Hank Severeid	1926
Joe Sewell	1931–33
Howard Shanks	1925
Bobby Shantz	1957–60
Billy Shantz	1960
Bob Shawkey	1915–27
Spec Shea	1947–49, 1951
Al Shealy	1928
George Shears	1912
Tom Sheehan	1921
Rollie Sheldon	1961–62, 1964–65
Skeeter Shelton	1915
Roy Sherid	1929–31
Pat Sheridan	1991
Dennis Sherrill	1978, 1980
Ben Shields	1924–25
Steve Shields	1988
Bob Shirley	1983–87
Urban Shocker	1916–17, 1925–28
Tom Shopay	1967, 1969
Ernie Shore	1919–20
Bill Short	1960
Norm Siebern	1956, 1958–59
Ruben Sierra	1995
Charlie Silvera	1948–56
Ken Silvestri	1941, 1946–47
Dave Silvestri	1992–95
Hack Simmons	1912
Harry Simpson	1957–58
Dick Simpson	1969
Duke Sims	1973–74
Bill Skiff	1926
Camp Skinner	1922
Joel Skinner	1986–88
Bill Skowron	1954–62
Roger Slagle	1979
Don Slaught	1988–89
Enos Slaughter	1954, 1956–59
Roy Smalley	1982–84
Walt Smallwood	1917, 1919
Charley Smith	1967–68
Elmer Smith	1922–23
Klondike Smith	1912
Joe Smith	1913
Lee Smith	1993
Keith Smith	1984–85
Harry Smythe	1934
J. T. Snow	1992
Eric Soderholm	1980
Tony Solaita	1968
Steve Souchock	1946, 1948
Jim Spencer	1978–81
Charlie Spikes	1972
Russ Springer	1992
Bill Stafford	1960–65
Jake Stahl	1908
Roy Staiger	1979
Tuck Stainback	1942–45
Gerry Staley	1955–56
Charley Stanceu	1941, 1946
Andy Stankiewicz	1992–93
Fred Stanley	1973–80
Mike Stanley	1992–95
Dick Starr	1947–48
Dutch Sterrett	1912–13
Lee Stine	1938
Snuffy Stirnweiss	1943–50
Tim Stoddard	1986–88
Mel Stottlemyre	1964–74
Hal Stowe	1960
Darryl Strawberry	1995
Gabby Street	1912
Marlin Stuart	1954
Bill Stumpf	1912–13
Tom Sturdivant	1955–59
Johnny Sturm	1941
Bill Sudakis	1974
Steve Sundra	1936, 1938–40
Jeff Sweeney	1908–15
Ron Swoboda	1971–73
Fred Talbot	1966–69
Vito Tamulis	1934–35
Frank Tanana	1993
Jesse Tannehill	1903
Danny Tartabull	1992–95
Zack Taylor	1934
Wade Taylor	1991
Frank Tepedino	1967, 1969–71
Walt Terrell	1989
Ralph Terry	1956–57, 1959–64
Dick Tettelbach	1955
Bob Tewksbury	1986–87
Ira Thomas	1906–07
Myles Thomas	1926–29
Stan Thomas	1977
Gary Thomasson	1978
Homer Thompson	1912
Tommy Thompson	1912
Jack Thoney	1904
Hank Thormahlen	1917–20
Marv Throneberry	1955, 1958–59
Luis Tiant	1979–80
Dick Tidrow	1974–79
Bobby Tiefenauer	1965
Eddie Tiemeyer	1909
Ray Tift	1907
Bob Tillman	1967
Thad Tillotson	1967–68
Dan Tipple	1915
Wayne Tolleson	1986–90
Earl Torgeson	1961
Rusty Torres	1971–72
Mike Torrez	1977
Cesar Tovar	1976
Tom Tresh	1961–69
Gus Triandos	1953–54
Steve Trout	1987
Virgil Trucks	1958
Frank Truesdale	1914
Bob Turley	1955–62
Jim Turner	1942–45
George Uhle	1933–34
Tom Underwood	1980–81
Bob Unglaub	1904
Cecil Upshaw	1974
Elmer Valo	1960
Russ Van Atta	1933–35
Dazzy Vance	1915, 1918
Joe Vance	1937–38
Hippo Vaughn	1908, 1910–12
Bobby Vaughn	1909
Bobby Veach	1925
Randy Velarde	1987–95
Otto Velez	1973–76
Joe Verbanic	1967–68, 1970
Frank Verdi	1953
Sammy Vick	1917–20
Jake Wade	1946
Jim Walewander	1990
Dixie Walker	1931, 1933–36
Mike Wallace	1974–75
Jimmy Walsh	1914
Joe Walsh	1910–11
Roxy Walters	1915–18
Danny Walton	1971
Jack Wanner	1909
Pee Wee Wanninger	1925
Aaron Ward	1917–26
Joe Ward	1909
Pete Ward	1970
Gary Ward	1987–89
Jack Warhop	1908–15
George Washburn	1941
Claudell Washington	1986–88, 1990
Gary Waslewski	1970–71
Bob Watson	1980–82
Roy Weatherly	1943
Jim Weaver	1931
Dave Wehrmeister	1981
Lefty Weinert	1931
Ed Wells	1929–32

Butch Wensloff	1943, 1947
Julie Wera	1927, 1929
Bill Werber	1930, 1933
Dennis Werth	1979–81
John Wetteland	1995
Stefan Wever	1982
Steve Whitaker	1966–68
Roy White	1965–79
George Whiteman	1913
Terry Whitfield	1974–76
Ed Whitson	1985–86
Kemp Wicker	1936–38
Al Wickland	1919
Bob Wickman	1992–95
Bob Wiesler	1951, 1954–55
Bill Wight	1946–47
Ted Wilborn	1980
Ed Wilkinson	1911
Harry Williams	1913–14
Jimmy Williams	1903–07
Bob Williams	1911–13
Stan Williams	1963–64
Walt Williams	1974–75
Bernie Williams	1991–95
Gerald Williams	1992–95
Archie Wilson	1951
Pete Wilson	1908–09
Ted Wilson	1956
Snake Wiltse	1903
Gordie Windhorn	1959
Dave Winfield	1981–88, 1990
Whitey Witt	1922–25
Mike Witt	1990–91, 1993
Bill Wolfe	1903–04
Harry Wolter	1910–13
Dooley Womack	1966–68
Gene Woodling	1949–54
Ron Woods	1969–71
Dick Woodson	1974
Hank Workman	1950
Ken Wright	1974
Yats Wuestling	1930
John Wyatt	1968
Butch Wynegar	1982–86
Jimmy Wynn	1977
Joe Yeager	1905–06
Jim York	1976
Ralph Young	1913
Curt Young	1992
Tom Zachary	1928–30
Jack Zalusky	1903
George Zeber	1977–78
Rollie Zeider	1913
Guy Zinn	1911–12
Bill Zuber	1943–46
Paul Zuvella	1986–87

Managers

Yogi Berra	1964, 1984–85
Frank Chance	1913–14
*Hal Chase	1910–11
Bucky Dent	1989–90
Bill Dickey	1946
Wild Bill Donovan	1915–17
Kid Elberfeld	1908
Art Fletcher	1929
Dallas Green	1989
*Clark Griffith	1903–08
Bucky Harris	1947–48
Ralph Houk	1961–63, 1966–73
Dick Howser	1978, 1980
Miller Huggins	1918–29
Johnny Keane	1965–66
Clyde King	1982
Bob Lemon	1978–79, 1981–82
Billy Martin	1975–79, 1983, 1985, 1988
Joe McCarthy	1931–46
Stump Merrill	1990–91
Gene Michael	1981–82
Johnny Neun	1946
*Roger Peckinpaugh	1914
Lou Piniella	1986–88
Bob Shawkey	1930
Buck Showalter	1992–95
George Stallings	1909–10
Casey Stengel	1949–60
Bill Virdon	1974–75
Harry Wolverton	1912

OAKLAND Athletics 1968–95
Moved from KANSAS CITY Athletics

Glenn Abbott	1973–76
Kurt Abbott	1993
Mark Acre	1994–95
Mike Adams	1978
Troy Afenir	1990–91
Jack Aker	1968
Darrel Akerfelds	1986
Mike Aldrete	1993–95
Gary Alexander	1978
Matt Alexander	1975–77
Dick Allen	1977
Dana Allison	1991
Bill Almon	1983–84
Felipe Alou	1970–71
Jesus Alou	1973–74
Matty Alou	1972
Dell Alston	1978
Brant Alyea	1972
Dwain Anderson	1971–72
Mike Andrews	1973
Joaquin Andujar	1986–87
Tony Armas	1977–82
Marcos Armas	1993
Larry Arndt	1989
Fernando Arroyo	1982, 1986
Keith Atherton	1983–86
Shooty Babitt	1981
Stan Bahnsen	1975–77
Harold Baines	1990–92
Doug Bair	1977, 1986
Dusty Baker	1985–86
Steve Baker	1982–83
Scott Baker	1995
Sal Bando	1968–76
Chris Bando	1989
Bill Bathe	1986
Chris Batton	1976
Don Baylor	1976, 1988
Billy Beane	1989
Dave Beard	1980–83
Kevin Bell	1982
Tony Bernazard	1987
Geronimo Berroa	1994–95
Jeff Bettendorf	1984
Tim Birtsas	1985–86
Joe Bitker	1990
Lance Blankenship	1988–93
Curt Blefary	1971–72
Vida Blue	1969–77
Bruce Bochte	1984–86
Joe Boever	1993
Warren Bogle	1968
Rich Bordi	1980–81, 1988
Mike Bordick	1990–95
Rick Bosetti	1981–82
Dick Bosman	1975–76
Pat Bourque	1973–74
Jim Bowie	1994
Bert Bradley	1983
Marshall Brant	1983
John Briscoe	1991–95
Pete Broberg	1978
Bobby Brooks	1969–70, 1972
Scott Brosius	1991–95
Ollie Brown	1972
Larry Brown	1971–72
Darrell Brown	1982
Jerry Browne	1992–93
Mike Brumley	1994
Derek Bryant	1979
Mark Budaska	1978, 1981
Tom Burgmeier	1983–84
Glenn Burke	1978–79
Todd Burns	1988–91
Ray Burris	1984
Jeff Burroughs	1982–84
Greg Cadaret	1987–89
Ben Callahan	1983
Ernie Camacho	1980
Bert Campaneris	1968–76
Kevin Campbell	1991–93
Jose Canseco	1985–92
Ozzie Canseco	1990
Rico Carty	1973, 1978
Danny Cater	1968–69
Bill Caudill	1984, 1987
Ron Cey	1987
Dave Chalk	1979
Charlie Chant	1975
Steve Chitren	1990–91
Darryl Cias	1983
Ron Clark	1972
Chris Codiroli	1982–87
Nate Colbert	1976
Joe Coleman	1977–78
Dave Collins	1985
Billy Conigliaro	1973
Tim Conroy	1978, 1982–85
Jim Corsi	1988–89, 1992, 1995
Jeff Cox	1980–81
Willie Crawford	1977
Fausto Cruz	1994–95
Tim Cullen	1972
John D'Acquisto	1982
Ron Darling	1991–95
Vic Davalillo	1973–74
Tommy Davis	1970–71
Mike Davis	1980–87
Storm Davis	1987–89, 1993
Bill Dawley	1989
Miguel Dilone	1978–79
Chuck Dobson	1968–71, 1973
John Donaldson	1968–70, 1974
Al Downing	1970
Kelly Downs	1992–93
Brian Doyle	1981
Tom Dozier	1986
Kirk Dressendorfer	1991
Jim Driscoll	1970
Keith Drumright	1981
Dave Duncan	1968–72
Taylor Duncan	1978
Steve Dunning	1977
Dennis Eckersley	1987–95
Chris Eddy	1995
Mike Edwards	1978–80
Randy Elliott	1980
Dock Ellis	1977
Mike Epstein	1971–72
Jim Essian	1978–80, 1984
Ron Fairly	1976
Ed Farmer	1983
Ramon Fermin	1995
Frank Fernandez	1970–71
Ed Figueroa	1981
Rollie Fingers	1968–76
Ray Fosse	1973–75
Eric Fox	1992–94
Tito Francona	1969–70
Tito Fuentes	1978
Mike Gallego	1985–91, 1995
Rob Gardner	1971, 1973
Phil Garner	1973–76
Adrian Garrett	1971–72
Brent Gates	1993–95
Jason Giambi	1995
Dave Giusti	1977
Orlando Gonzalez	1980
Danny Goodwin	1982
Jim Gosger	1968
Goose Gossage	1992–93
Billy Grabarkewitz	1975
Mudcat Grant	1970–71
Dick Green	1968–74
Alfredo Griffin	1985–87
Wayne Gross	1976–83, 1986
Mario Guerrero	1978–80
Johnny Guzman	1991–92
Moose Haas	1986–87
Dave Hamilton	1972–75, 1979–80
Garry Hancock	1983–84
Larry Haney	1969–70, 1972–76
Preston Hanna	1982
Mike Harkey	1995
Tommy Harper	1975
Brian Harper	1987, 1995
Reggie Harris	1990–91
Ron Hassey	1988–90
Andy Hawkins	1991
Mike Heath	1979–85
Dave Heaverlo	1978–79, 1981
Mike Hegan	1971–73
Gorman Heimueller	1983–84
Eric Helfand	1993–95
Scott Hemond	1990–94
Steve Henderson	1985–87
Rickey Henderson	1979–84, 1989–95
Dave Henderson	1988–93
George Hendrick	1971–72
Jose Herrera	1995
Mike Hershberger	1968–69
Donnie Hill	1983–86
Shawn Hillegas	1992–93
Jim Holt	1974–76
Ken Holtzman	1972–75
Rick Honeycutt	1987–93, 1995
Leon Hooten	1974
Don Hopkins	1975–76
Joe Horlen	1972
Vince Horsman	1992–94
Willie Horton	1978
Tim Hosley	1973–74, 1976–78, 1981
Steve Hovley	1970–71
Steve Howard	1990
Jay Howell	1985–87
Dann Howitt	1989–92
Glenn Hubbard	1988–89
Dave Hudgens	1983
Catfish Hunter	1968–74
Reggie Jackson	1968–75, 1987
Brook Jacoby	1991
Stan Javier	1986–90, 1994–95
Doug Jennings	1988–91
Miguel Jimenez	1993–94
Tommy John	1985
Doug Johns	1995
Deron Johnson	1973–74
Bob Johnson	1969–70
John Henry Johnson	1978–79
Cliff Johnson	1981–82
Jay Johnstone	1973
Jeff Jones	1980–84
Mike Jorgensen	1977
Felix Jose	1988–90
Ed Jurak	1988
Jeff Kaiser	1985
Steve Karsay	1993–94
Bob Kearney	1981–83
Joe Keough	1968
Matt Keough	1977–83
Steve Kiefer	1984–85
Mike Kilkenny	1972
Mike Kingery	1992
Dave Kingman	1984–86
Brian Kingman	1979–82
Dennis Kinney	1982
Ron Klimkowski	1971
Joe Klink	1990–91
Mickey Klutts	1979–82
Darold Knowles	1971–74
Brad Komminsk	1991
Lew Krausse	1968–69
Bill Krueger	1983–87
Ted Kubiak	1968–69, 1972–75
Bob Lacey	1977–80
Rene Lachemann	1968
Marcel Lachemann	1969–71
Dennis Lamp	1987
Rick Langford	1977–86
Carney Lansford	1983–92
Tony LaRussa	1970–71
George Lauzerique	1968–69
Gary Lavelle	1987
Vance Law	1991
Dave Leiper	1984, 1986–87, 1994–95
Johnnie LeMaster	1987
Allan Lewis	1968, 1970, 1972–73
Darren Lewis	1990
Paul Lindblad	1968–71, 1973–76
Larry Lintz	1976–77
Bob Locker	1970–72
Davey Lopes	1982–84
Scott Lydy	1993
Rick Lysander	1980
Sheldon Mallory	1977
Angel Mangual	1971–76
Fred Manrique	1991
Gonzalo Marquez	1972–73
Marty Martinez	1972
Teddy Martinez	1975
Francisco Matos	1994
Dal Maxvill	1972–75
Steve McCatty	1977–85
Willie McCovey	1976
Willie McGee	1990

Mark McGwire	1986–95
Dave McKay	1980–82
Rich McKinney	1973–75, 1977
Denny McLain	1972
Bo McLaughlin	1981–82
Byron McLaughlin	1982
Ken McMullen	1976
Rusty McNealy	1983
Bill McNulty	1969, 1972
Doc Medich	1977
Orlando Mercado	1988
Henry Mercedes	1992–93
Dan Meyer	1982–85
Scott Meyer	1978
Don Mincher	1970–72
Craig Minetto	1978–81
Paul Mitchell	1976–77
Craig Mitchell	1975–77
Mike Mohler	1993–95
Rick Monday	1968–71
Bill Mooneyham	1986
Kelvin Moore	1981–83
Mike Moore	1989–92
Jose Morales	1973
Joe Morgan	1984
Mike Morgan	1978–79
Steve Mura	1985
Dwayne Murphy	1978–87
Larry Murray	1977–79

Jim Nash	1968–69
Troy Neel	1992–94
Gene Nelson	1987–92
Rob Nelson	1986–87
Jim Nettles	1981
Jeff Newman	1976–82
Junior Noboa	1994
Mike Norris	1975–83, 1990
Billy North	1973–78
Joe Nossek	1969
Edwin Nunez	1993–94

Charlie O'Brien	1985
Blue Moon Odom	1968–75
Steve Ontiveros	1985–88, 1994–95
Darrell Osteen	1970
Dave Otto	1987–90
Bob Owchinko	1981–82

Mitchell Page	1977–83
Jim Pagliaroni	1968–69
Jim Panther	1971
Craig Paquette	1993–95
Dave Parker	1988–89
Jeff Parrett	1992
Bill Parsons	1974
Daryl Patterson	1971
Mike Patterson	1981
Roberto Pena	1970
Marty Perez	1977–78
Jim Perry	1975
Ricky Peters	1983, 1986
Ken Phelps	1989–90
Tony Phillips	1982–89
Steve Phoenix	1994–95
Rob Picciolo	1977–82, 1985
Tony Pierce	1968
Horacio Pina	1973
Gaylen Pitts	1974–75
Juan Pizarro	1969
Eric Plunk	1986–89
Luis Polonia	1987–89
Ariel Prieto	1995

Luis Quinones	1983
Jamie Quirk	1989–92

Mike Raczka	1992
Chuck Rainey	1984
Milt Ramirez	1979
Willie Randolph	1990
Randy Ready	1992
Steve Renko	1978
Todd Revenig	1992
Dave Revering	1978–81
Carlos Reyes	1994–95
Tommie Reynolds	1969
Dave Righetti	1994
Jose Rijo	1985–87
Ernest Riles	1991
Floyd Robinson	1968
Bruce Robinson	1978
Roberto Rodriguez	1970
Rick Rodriguez	1986–87
Jim Roland	1969–72
Phil Roof	1968–69
Joe Rudi	1968–76, 1982
Jeff Russell	1992

Lenn Sakata	1986
Alejandro Sanchez	1987
Ken Sanders	1968
Scott Sanderson	1990
Charlie Sands	1975
Tom Sandt	1975–76
Manny Sanguillen	1977
Steve Sax	1994
Jeff Schaefer	1994
Rodney Scott	1977
Dick Scott	1989
Diego Segui	1968, 1970–72
Kevin Seitzer	1993
Jimmy Sexton	1981–82
Jeff Shaver	1988
Don Shaw	1972
Eric Show	1991
Sonny Siebert	1975
Ruben Sierra	1992–95
Matt Sinatro	1987–88
Joe Slusarski	1991–93
Mark Smith	1983
Roger Smithberg	1993–94
Brian Snyder	1989
Lary Sorensen	1984
Elias Sosa	1978
Mark Souza	1980
Jim Spencer	1981–82
Ed Sprague	1968–69
Steve Staggs	1978
Fred Stanley	1981–82
Terry Steinbach	1986–95
Dave Stewart	1986–92, 1995
Todd Stottlemyre	1995
Champ Summers	1974
Don Sutton	1985
Dale Sveum	1993

Jerry Tabb	1977–78
Fred Talbot	1969–70
Jose Tartabull	1969–70
Danny Tartabull	1995
Bill Taylor	1994
Tom Tellmann	1985
Gene Tenace	1969–76
Mickey Tettleton	1984–87
Gary Thomasson	1978
Rusty Tillman	1986
Jim Todd	1975–76, 1979
Andy Tomberlin	1995
Pablo Torrealba	1977
Mike Torrez	1976–77, 1984
Cesar Tovar	1975–76
Manny Trillo	1973–74
Jim Tyrone	1977

Jim Umbarger	1977
Tom Underwood	1981–83

Todd Van Poppel	1991, 1993–95
Dave Von Ohlen	1986–87
Ed Vosberg	1994
Bill Voss	1972

Mark Wagner	1984
Denny Walling	1975–76
Joe Wallis	1978–79
Bruce Walton	1991–92
Mike Warren	1983–85
John Wasdin	1995
Claudell Washington	1974–76
Gary Waslewski	1972
Ramon Webster	1968–69, 1971
Walt Weiss	1987–92
Bob Welch	1988–94
Don Wengert	1995
Jerry Willard	1986–87
Billy Williams	1975–76
Mark Williams	1977
Earl Williams	1977
George Williams	1995
Willie Wilson	1991–92
Alan Wirth	1978–80
Ron Witmeyer	1991
Bobby Witt	1992–94
Steve Wojciechowski	1995
Dooley Womack	1970
Darrell Woodard	1978
Gary Woods	1976
Rich Wortham	1983
John Wyatt	1969

Curt Young	1983–91, 1993
Matt Young	1989
Ernie Young	1994–95

Managers

Hank Bauer	1969
Steve Boros	1983–84
Alvin Dark	1974–75
Bob Kennedy	1968
Tony LaRussa	1986–95
Jim Marshall	1979
Billy Martin	1980–82
Jack McKeon	1977–78
John McNamara	1969–70
Jackie Moore	1984–86
Jeff Newman	1986
Chuck Tanner	1976
Dick Williams	1971–73
Bobby Winkles	1977–78

PHILADELPHIA
Athletics 1901–54
Moved to KANSAS CITY Athletics

Tal Abernathy	1942–44
Merito Acosta	1918
Willie Adams	1918–19
Dick Adams	1947
Dick Adkins	1942
Bob Allen	1919
Wayne Ambler	1937–39
Walter Ancker	1915
Walter Anderson	1917, 1919
Elbert Andrews	1925
Fred Applegate	1904
Fred Archer	1936–37
Harry Armbruster	1906
George Armstrong	1946
Howard Armstrong	1911
Orie Arntzen	1943
Joe Astroth	1945–46, 1949–54
Tommy Atkins	1909–10

Loren Babe	1953
Johnny Babich	1940–41
Eddie Bacon	1917
Bill Bagwell	1925
Gene Bailey	1917
Bock Baker	1901
Frank Baker	1908–14
Neal Baker	1927
Bill Bankston	1915
Dave Barbee	1926
Babe Barna	1937–38
Scotty Barr	1908–09
Dick Barrett	1933
Bill Barrett	1921
Jack Barry	1908–15
Hardin Barry	1912
John Barthold	1904
Bill Bartley	1906–07
Irv Bartling	1938
Harry Barton	1905
Charlie Bates	1927
Ray Bates	1917
Lou Bauer	1918
Stan Baumgartner	1924–26
Bill Beckmann	1939–42
Chief Bender	1903–14
Vern Benson	1946
Al Benton	1934–35
Johnny Berger	1922
Bill Bernhard	1901–02
Charlie Berry	1925, 1934–36, 1938
Claude Berry	1906–07
Joe Berry	1944–46
Herman Besse	1940–43, 1946
Hal Bevan	1952
Hank Biasetti	1949
Lyle Bigbee	1920
George Binks	1947–48
Charlie Bishop	1952–54
Max Bishop	1924–33
Bill Bishop	1921
Don Black	1943–45
George Blaeholder	1935
Buddy Blair	1942
Bert Blue	1908
Charlie Boardman	1913–14
Ping Bodie	1917
Pat Bohen	1913
Joe Boley	1927–32
Don Bollweg	1954
Frank Bonner	1902
Danny Boone	1919
Henry Bostick	1915
Charlie Bowles	1943, 1945
Joe Bowman	1932
Dallas Bradshaw	1917
Al Brancato	1939–41, 1945
Dudley Branom	1927
Frank Brazill	1921–22
Bill Breckinridge	1929
Rube Bressler	1914–16
George Brickley	1913
Lou Brissie	1947–51
Art Brouthers	1906
Boardwalk Brown	1911–14
Don Brown	1916
Norm Brown	1943, 1946
Lou Bruce	1904
Earle Brucker	1948
Earle Brucker	1937–40
Frank Bruggy	1922–24
Red Bullock	1936
Bill Burgo	1943–44
Denny Burns	1923–24
George Burns	1918–20, 1929
Joe Burns	1944–45
John Burrows	1943
Dick Burrus	1919–20
Moe Burtschy	1950–51, 1954
Ed Busch	1943–45
Joe Bush	1912–17, 1928
Ralph Buxton	1938
Harry Byrd	1950, 1952–53
Jim Byrnes	1906

Sugar Cain	1932–35
Fred Caligiuri	1941–42
Frank Callaway	1921–22
Guy Cantrell	1927
Charlie Carr	1901
Doc Carroll	1916
Nick Carter	1908
Sol Carter	1931
Joe Cascarella	1934–35
George Caster	1934–35, 1937–40
Jim Castiglia	1942
Louis Castro	1902
John Caulfield	1946
Fred Chapman	1939–41
John Chapman	1924
Sam Chapman	1938–41, 1945–51
Russ Christopher	1942–47
Joe Cicero	1945
Ed Cihocki	1933
Lou Ciola	1943
Bill Cissell	1937
Allie Clark	1951–53
Gowell Claset	1933
Tom Clyde	1943
Andy Coakley	1902–06
Ty Cobb	1927–28
Mickey Cochrane	1925–33
Joe Coleman	1942, 1946–51, 1953
Ed Coleman	1932–35
Ray Coleman	1948
Allan Collamore	1911
Eddie Collins	1939, 1941–42
Eddie Collins	1906–14, 1927–28
Jimmy Collins	1907–08
Zip Collins	1921
Bob Cone	1915
Bill Connelly	1945
Bill Conroy	1935–37
Owen Conway	1915
Jack Coombs	1906–14
Bobby Coombs	1933
Pat Cooper	1946–47
Art Corcoran	1915
Ensign Cottrell	1913
Stan Coveleski	1912
Toots Coyne	1914
Jim Crabb	1912
George Craig	1907
Doc Cramer	1929–35
Sam Crane	1914–16
Jim Cronin	1929

Lave Cross	1901–05
Monte Cross	1902–07
Cap Crowell	1915–16
Woody Crowson	1945
Press Cruthers	1913–14
Dick Culler	1936
Mike Cunningham	1906
Jim Curry	1909

Tom Daley	1913–14
Bert Daly	1903
Harry Damrau	1915
Lee Daney	1928
Dave Danforth	1911–12
Buck Danner	1915
Claude Davidson	1918
Chick Davies	1914–15
Harry Davis	1901–11, 1913–15
Bud Davis	1915
Crash Davis	1940–42
Tod Davis	1949, 1951
Joe De Maestri	1953–54
Chubby Dean	1936–41
Billy DeMars	1948
Claud Derrick	1910–12
Russ Derry	1946
Gene Desautels	1946
Jimmie DeShong	1932
Bill Dietrich	1933–36, 1947–48
Bob Dillinger	1950
Art Ditmar	1954
Moxie Divis	1916
Sonny Dixon	1954
Joe Dolan	1901
Pat Donahue	1910
Snooks Dowd	1919
Carl Doyle	1935–36
Larry Drake	1945
Mike Driscoll	1916
Joe Dugan	1917–21
Bill Duggleby	1902
Jimmy Dygert	1905–10
Jimmy Dykes	1918–32

George Earnshaw	1928–33
Paul Easterling	1938
Vallie Eaves	1935
Harry Eccles	1915
Charlie Eckert	1919–20, 1922
Ralph Edwards	1915
Ben Egan	1908, 1912
Howard Ehmke	1926–30
Bones Ely	1901
Chester Emerson	1911
Charlie Engle	1925–26
Hal Epps	1944
Larry Eschen	1942
Bobby Estalella	1943–45, 1949
Nick Etten	1938–39
Art Ewoldt	1919

Everett Fagan	1943, 1946
Frank Fahey	1918
Howard Fahey	1912
Ferris Fain	1947–52
Jim Fairbank	1903–04
Cy Falkenberg	1917
Frank Fanovich	1953
Bill Ferrazzi	1935
Tom Ferrick	1941
Eddie Files	1908
Dana Fillingim	1915
Jim Finigan	1954
Herman Fink	1935–37
Lou Finney	1931, 1933–39
Jack Flater	1908
Elmer Flick	1902
Lew Flick	1943–44
Mort Flohr	1934
Jesse Flores	1943–47
Stu Flythe	1936
Dick Fowler	1941–42, 1945–52
Nellie Fox	1947–49
Jack Fox	1908
Jimmie Foxx	1925–35
Herman Franks	1947–48
Chick Fraser	1901
Harvey Freeman	1921
Tony Freitas	1932–33
Pat French	1917
Walter French	1923, 1925–29
Marion Fricano	1952–54
Charlie Fritz	1907
Harry Fritz	1913
Ollie Fuhrman	1922
Dot Fulghum	1921
Dave Fultz	1901–02

Augie Galan	1949
Chick Galloway	1919–27
Bob Ganley	1909
Joe Gantenbein	1939–40
Bob Garbark	1944
Larry Gardner	1918
Ford Garrison	1944–46
Charlie Gassaway	1945
Doc Gautreau	1925
Bob Geary	1918–19
Phil Geier	1901
Greek George	1945
Steve Gerkin	1945
Charlie Gibson	1924
Joe Giebel	1913
Tommy Giordano	1953
Tom Glass	1925
Lee Gooch	1917
John Gray	1954
Sam Gray	1924–27
Vean Gregg	1918
Bill Grevell	1919
Lee Griffeth	1946
Pug Griffin	1917
Ivy Griffin	1919–21
Oscar Grimes	1946
Charlie Grimm	1916
Lew Groh	1919
Lefty Grove	1925–33
Roy Grover	1916–17, 1919
Mike Guerra	1947–50
Ben Guintini	1950
Randy Gumpert	1936–38

Bruno Haas	1915
Mule Haas	1928–32, 1938
Bump Hadley	1941
Bill Haeffner	1915
Sammy Hale	1923–29
Ray Haley	1916–17
Irv Hall	1943–46
Tom Hamilton	1952–53
Luke Hamlin	1944
Buddy Hancken	1940
Gene Handley	1946–47
Jack Harper	1915
Slim Harrell	1912
Bill Harrington	1953
Lum Harris	1941–44, 1946
Charlie Harris	1948–49, 1951
Bob Harris	1942
Spence Harris	1930
Slim Harriss	1920–26
Topsy Hartsel	1902–11
Joe Hassler	1928–29
Gene Hasson	1937–38
Bob Hasty	1919–24
Joe Hauser	1922–24, 1926, 1928
Clem Hausmann	1949
Jack Hayden	1901
Frankie Hayes	1933–34, 1936–42, 1944–45
Tom Healy	1915–16
Don Heffner	1943
Fred Heimach	1920–26
Heinie Heitmuller	1909–10
Weldon Henley	1903–05
George Hesselbacher	1916
Ed Heusser	1940
Johnnie Heving	1931–32
Pinky Higgins	1930, 1933–36
Charlie High	1919–20
Red Hill	1917
Jesse Hill	1937
Ed Hilley	1903
Billy Hitchcock	1950–52
Danny Hoffman	1903–06
Happy Hogan	1911
Wally Holborow	1948
Ed Holmes	1918
Jim Holmes	1906
Red Holt	1925
Alex Hooks	1935
Bob Hooper	1950–52
Sam Hope	1907
Byron Houck	1912–14
Ben Houser	1910
Tex Hoyle	1952
Waite Hoyt	1931
Earl Huckleberry	1935
Jim Hulvey	1923
Carl Husta	1925
Bert Husting	1902
Warren Huston	1937

Joe Jackson	1908–09
Spook Jacobs	1954
Baby Doll Jacobson	1927
Charlie Jamieson	1917–18
Tom Jenkins	1926
Bill Jensen	1914
Adam Johnson	1941
Ellis Johnson	1917
Hank Johnson	1936
Paul Johnson	1920–21
Bob Johnson	1933–42
Roy Johnson	1918
Jing Johnson	1916–17, 1919, 1927–28
Bill Johnson	1916–17
Doc Johnston	1922
John Jones	1923, 1932
Eddie Joost	1947–53
Bob Joyce	1939

John Kalahan	1903
Bill Kalfass	1937
Dave Keefe	1917, 1919–21
Vic Keen	1918
Jim Keesey	1925, 1930
Skeeter Kell	1952
George Kell	1943–46
Al Kellett	1923
Harry Kelley	1936–38
Alex Kellner	1948–54
Walt Kellner	1952–53
Al Kellogg	1908
Ren Kelly	1923
Bill Kelly	1920
Ed Kenna	1902
Fred Ketcham	1901
Gus Ketchum	1922
Lee King	1916
Walt Kinney	1919–20, 1923
Mike Kircher	1919
Ernie Kish	1945
Lou Klein	1951
Eddie Klieman	1950
Bob Kline	1934
Lou Knerr	1945–46
Austin Knickerbocker	1947
Bill Knickerbocker	1942
John Knight	1905–07
Jack Knott	1941–42, 1946
Tom Knowlson	1915
Bill Knowlton	1920
Don Kolloway	1953
Bruce Konopka	1942, 1946
Larry Kopf	1914–15
Merlin Kopp	1918–19
Harry Krause	1908–12
Lew Krausse	1931–32
Mike Kreevich	1942
Johnny Kucab	1950–52
Bert Kuczynski	1943
John Kull	1909

Chet Laabs	1947
Ed Lagger	1934
Nap Lajoie	1901–02, 1915–16
Bill Lamar	1924–27
Les Lanning	1916
Jack Lapp	1908–15
Ed Larkin	1909
Billy Lauder	1901
Doc Lavan	1913
Otis Lawry	1916–17
Tom Leahy	1901
Fred Lear	1915
Bevo LeBourveau	1929
Paul Lehner	1950–51
Dummy Leitner	1901
Ed Lennox	1906
Elmer Leonard	1911
John Leovich	1941
Dutch Lieber	1935–36
Glenn Liebhardt	1930
Bill Lillard	1939–40
Lou Limmer	1951, 1954
Bob Lindemann	1901
Axel Lindstrom	1916
Hod Lisenbee	1936
Jack Littrell	1952, 1954
Paddy Livingston	1909–11
Harry Lochhead	1901
Dario Lodigiani	1938–39
Lep Long	1911
Pete Loos	1901
Bris Lord	1905–07, 1910–12
Sam Lowry	1942–43
Hugh Luby	1936

Earle Mack	1910–11, 1914
Felix Mackiewicz	1941–43
Johnny Mackinson	1953
Ed Madjeski	1932–34
Harl Maggert	1912
Roy Mahaffey	1930–35
Al Mahon	1930
Emil Mailho	1936
Jim Mains	1943
Hank Majeski	1946–49, 1951–52
Ben Mallonee	1921
Lew Malone	1915–16
Frank Manush	1908
Phil Marchildon	1940–42, 1945–49
Johnny Marcum	1933–35
Gene Markland	1950
Doc Martin	1908, 1911–12
Morrie Martin	1951–54
Pat Martin	1919–20
Wedo Martini	1935
Walt Masters	1939
Len Matarazzo	1952
Joe Mathes	1912
Wid Matthews	1923
Cloy Mattox	1929
Harry Matuzak	1934, 1936
Carmen Mauro	1953
Bert Maxwell	1908
Eddie Mayo	1943
Wickey McAvoy	1913–15, 1917–19
Bill McCahan	1946–49
Emmett McCann	1920–21
Sammy McConnell	1915
Barney McCosky	1946–48, 1950–51
Benny McCoy	1940–41
Les McCrabb	1939–42, 1950
Frank McCue	1922
Hank McDonald	1931, 1933
Lee McElwee	1916
Connie McGeehan	1903
Ed McGhee	1953–54
Bill McGhee	1944–45
John McGillen	1944
Frank McGowan	1922–23
Stuffy McInnis	1909–17
Matty McIntyre	1901
Tim McKeithan	1932–34
Bob McKinney	1901
Pat McLaughlin	1940
Eric McNair	1929–35, 1942
Bob McNamara	1939
John McPherson	1901
Jerry McQuaig	1934
George McQuinn	1946
Bill Meehan	1915
Roy Meeker	1923–24
Joe Mellana	1927
Charlie Metro	1944–45
Alex Metzler	1926
Billy Meyer	1916–17
Cass Michaels	1952–53
Carl Miles	1940
Dee Miles	1939–42
Bing Miller	1922–26, 1928–34
Rudy Miller	1929
Billy Milligan	1901
Bill Mills	1944
Ray Miner	1921
Fred Mitchell	1902
Ralph Mitterling	1916
Rinty Monahan	1953
Ferdie Moore	1914
Jimmy Moore	1930–31
Roy Moore	1920–22
Herbie Moran	1908
Dave Morey	1913
Cy Morgan	1909–12
Doyt Morris	1937
Bill Morrisette	1915–16
Bud Morse	1929
Wally Moses	1935–41, 1949–51
Charlie Moss	1934–36
Jim Mullin	1904

Jake Munch	1918
Danny Murphy	1902–13
Eddie Murphy	1912–15
Mike Murphy	1916
Morg Murphy	1901
Joe Murray	1950
Ray Murray	1951–53
Glenn Myatt	1920–21
Elmer Myers	1915–18
Joe Myers	1905
Jack Nabors	1915–17
Bill Nagel	1939
Pete Naktenis	1936
Rollie Naylor	1917, 1919–24
Lynn Nelson	1937–39
Bobo Newsom	1944–46, 1952–53
Skeeter Newsome	1935–39
Simon Nicholls	1906–09
Bill Nicholson	1936
Al Niemiec	1936
Pete Noonan	1904
Wynn Noyes	1917, 1919
Curly Ogden	1922–24
Jim Oglesby	1936
Rube Oldring	1906–16, 1918
Harry O'Neill	1939
Harry O'Neill	1922–23
Bill Orr	1913–14
Roberto Ortiz	1950
Ossie Orwoll	1928–29
Bill Oster	1954
Jack Owens	1935
Doc Ozmer	1923
Sam Page	1939
Eddie Palmer	1917
Joe Palmisano	1931
Tony Parisse	1943–44
Ace Parker	1937–38
Roy Parmelee	1939
Rube Parnham	1916–17
Joe Pate	1926–27
Bill Patton	1935
Hal Peck	1944–46
Jack Peerson	1935–36
Herb Pennock	1912–15
Bob Pepper	1915
Charlie Perkins	1930
Cy Perkins	1915, 1917–30
Scott Perry	1918–21
Rusty Peters	1936–38
Jim Peterson	1931, 1933
Monte Pfeffer	1913
Dave Philley	1951–53
Wiley Piatt	1901
Val Picinich	1916–17
Charlie Pick	1916
Ollie Pickering	1903–04
Bill Pierson	1918–19, 1924
Squiz Pillion	1915
Ed Pinnance	1903
Cotton Pippen	1939
Eddie Plank	1901–14
Jim Poole	1925–27
Jim Porter	1902
Arnie Portocarrero	1954
Nels Potter	1938–41, 1948
Vic Power	1954
Ike Powers	1927–28
Mike Powers	1901–09
Jim Pruett	1944–45
George Puccinelli	1936
Tad Quinn	1902–03
Jack Quinn	1925–30
Hal Raether	1954
Morrie Rath	1909–10
Carl Ray	1915–16
Al Reiss	1932
Jim Reninger	1938–39
Bill Renna	1954
Otto Rettig	1922
Gordon Rhodes	1936
Paul Richards	1935
Jack Richardson	1915–16
Ken Richardson	1942
Don Richmond	1941, 1946–47
Harry Riconda	1923–24
Bob Rinker	1950
Jimmy Ripple	1943
Ray Roberts	1919
Jim Robertson	1954
Sherry Robertson	1952
Eddie Robinson	1953
Ben Rochefort	1914
Oscar Roettger	1932
Tom Rogers	1919
Dutch Romberger	1954
Eddie Rommel	1920–32
Buddy Rosar	1945–49
Larry Rosenthal	1944–45
Buck Ross	1936–41
Braggo Roth	1919
Jack Rothrock	1937
Harland Rowe	1916
Chuck Rowland	1923
Emile Roy	1933
Dick Rozek	1953–54
Al Rubeling	1940–41
Joe Rullo	1943–44
Lefty Russell	1910–12
Mickey Rutner	1947
Roger Salmon	1912
Gus Salve	1908
Ed Samcoff	1951
Rusty Saunders	1927
Bob Savage	1942, 1946–48
Wally Schang	1913–17, 1930
Rube Schauer	1917
Heinie Scheer	1922–23
Carl Scheib	1943–45, 1947–54
Jim Schelle	1939
Red Schillings	1922
Biff Schlitzer	1908–09
Ossee Schreckengost	1902–08
Hack Schumann	1906
Socks Seibold	1915–17, 1919
Socks Seybold	1901–08
Bill Shanner	1920
Red Shannon	1917–20
Bobby Shantz	1949–54
Billy Shantz	1954
Ralph Sharman	1917
Shag Shaughnessy	1908
Bob Shawkey	1913–15
Red Shea	1918
Dave Shean	1906
Tom Sheehan	1915–16
Joe Sherman	1915
Tex Shirley	1941–42
Bill Shores	1928–31
Dick Siebert	1938–45
Frank Sigafoos	1926
Al Sima	1954
Al Simmons	1924–32, 1940–41, 1944
Frank Skaff	1943
John Slappey	1920
Dave Smith	1938–39
Eddie Smith	1936–39
Mayo Smith	1945
Harry Smith	1901
Red Smith	1925
Syd Smith	1908
Bernie Snyder	1935
Tris Speaker	1928
Stan Sperry	1938
Tuck Stainback	1946
George Staller	1943
Farmer Steelman	1901–02
Irv Stein	1932
Bill Stellbauer	1916
Art Stokes	1925
Paul Strand	1924
Amos Strunk	1908–17, 1919–20, 1924
Dean Sturgis	1914
Lena Styles	1919–21
Pete Suder	1941–43, 1946–54
Jim Sullivan	1921–22
Homer Summa	1929–30
Charlie Sweeney	1914
Bob Swift	1942–43
John Taff	1913
Arlas Taylor	1921
Joe Taylor	1954
Fred Thomas	1919–20
Ira Thomas	1909–15
Kite Thomas	1952–53
Bud Thomas	1937–39
Harry Thompson	1919
Shag Thompson	1914–16
Buck Thrasher	1916–17
Eric Tipton	1939–41
Joe Tipton	1950–52
Pat Tobin	1941
Phil Todt	1931
Bob Trice	1953–54
George Turbeville	1935–37
Terry Turner	1919
Tink Turner	1915
Jim Tyack	1943
Woody Upchurch	1935–36
Bill Upton	1954
Elmer Valo	1940–43, 1946–54
Ozzie Van Brabant	1954
Porter Vaughan	1940–41, 1946
Clarence Vaughn	1934
Al Veach	1935
Rube Vickers	1907–09
Rube Waddell	1902–07
Hal Wagner	1937–44
Kermit Wahl	1950–51
Rube Walberg	1923–33
Frank Walker	1920–21
Tilly Walker	1918–23
Johnny Walker	1919–21
Tom Walker	1902
Jack Wallaesa	1940, 1942, 1946
Jimmy Walsh	1912–16
Bill Wambsganss	1926
Rabbit Warstler	1934–36
Neal Watlington	1953
Mule Watson	1918–19
Harry Weaver	1915–16
Skeeter Webb	1948
Johnny Welaj	1943
Frank Welch	1919–26
Bob Wellman	1948, 1950
Bill Werber	1937–38
Buzz Wetzel	1927
Lee Wheat	1954
Zack Wheat	1927
Woody Wheaton	1943–44
Don White	1948–49
Jo–Jo White	1943–44
Walt Whittaker	1916
Spider Wilhelm	1953
Bobby Wilkins	1944–45
Al Williams	1937–38
Dib Williams	1930–35
Marsh Williams	1916
Lefty Willis	1925–27
Whitey Wilshere	1934–36
Highball Wilson	1902
Jim Wilson	1949
Jack Wilson	1934
Bill Wilson	1954
Snake Wiltse	1901–02
Al Wingo	1919
Ed Wingo	1920
Hank Winston	1933
Whitey Witt	1916–17, 1919–21
Lefty Wolf	1921
Chuck Wolfe	1923
Roger Wolff	1941–43
Doc Wood	1923
Fred Worden	1914
Ed Wright	1952
Taffy Wright	1949
John Wyckoff	1913–16
Hank Wyse	1950–51
George Yankowski	1942
Rube Yarrison	1922
Carroll Yerkes	1927–29
Lefty York	1919
Rudy York	1948
Ralph Young	1922
Eddie Yount	1937
Tom Zachary	1918
Joe Zapustas	1933
Gus Zernial	1951–54
Jimmy Zinn	1919
Sam Zoldak	1951–52

Managers

Jimmy Dykes	1951–53
Eddie Joost	1954
Connie Mack	1901–50
Earle Mack	1937, 1939

SEATTLE Pilots 1969
Moved to MILWAUKEE Brewers

Jack Aker	1969
Dick Baney	1969
Steve Barber	1969
Dick Bates	1969
Gary Bell	1969
Jim Bouton	1969
Gene Brabender	1969
Darrell Brandon	1969
George Brunet	1969
Ron Clark	1969
Wayne Comer	1969
Tommy Davis	1969
John Donaldson	1969
Bill Edgerton	1969
Mickey Fuentes	1969
John Gelnar	1969
Gus Gil	1969
Greg Goossen	1969
Jim Gosger	1969
Larry Haney	1969
Tommy Harper	1969
Mike Hegan	1969
Steve Hovley	1969
John Kennedy	1969
Bob Locker	1969
Skip Lockwood	1969
Gordon Lund	1969
Mike Marshall	1969
Jerry McNertney	1969
Bob Meyer	1969
Don Mincher	1969
John Morris	1969
John O'Donoghue	1969
Ray Oyler	1969
Jim Pagliaroni	1969
Marty Pattin	1969
Merritt Ranew	1969
Garry Roggenburk	1969
Rich Rollins	1969
Diego Segui	1969
Dick Simpson	1969
Fred Stanley	1969
Jerry Stephenson	1969
Fred Talbot	1969
Gary Timberlake	1969
Sandy Valdespino	1969
Freddie Velazquez	1969
Jose Vidal	1969
Danny Walton	1969
Steve Whitaker	1969
Billy Williams	1969
Dooley Womack	1969

Managers

Joe Schultz	1969

SEATTLE Mariners 1977–95

Glenn Abbott	1977–81, 1983
Jim Acker	1992
Juan Agosto	1992
Brian Allard	1981
Kim Allen	1980–81
Jamie Allen	1983
Rod Allen	1983
Rich Amaral	1991–95
Larry Andersen	1981–82
Jim Anderson	1980–81
Rick Anderson	1980
Eric Anthony	1994
Rick Auerbach	1981

Bobby Ayala	1994–95
Bob Ayrault	1993
Wally Backman	1993
Jose Baez	1977–78
Steve Balboni	1988
Scott Bankhead	1987–91
Floyd Bannister	1979–82
Salome Barojas	1984–85
Shawn Barton	1992
Charlie Beamon	1978–79
Dave Beard	1984
Jim Beattie	1980–86
Tim Belcher	1995
Andy Benes	1995
Juan Beniquez	1980
Tony Bernazard	1983
Juan Bernhardt	1977–78
Karl Best	1983–86
Bud Black	1981
Mike Blowers	1992–95
Bruce Bochte	1978–82
Barry Bonnell	1984–86
Bret Boone	1992–93
Rich Bordi	1982
Chris Bosio	1993–95
Shawn Boskie	1994
Thad Bosley	1982
Phil Bradley	1983–87
Scott Bradley	1986–92
Darren Bragg	1994–95
Roy Branch	1979
Mickey Brantley	1986–89
Steve Braun	1977–78
Greg Briley	1988–92
Tom Brown	1978
Bobby Brown	1982
Mike Brown	1986–87
Kevin Brown	1992
Mike Brumley	1990
Jay Buhner	1988–95
Terry Bulling	1981–83
Dave Burba	1990–91
Steve Burke	1977–78
Jeff Burroughs	1981
Ivan Calderon	1984–86
Mike Campbell	1987–89
Rafael Carmona	1995
Manny Castillo	1982–83
Bill Caudill	1982–83
Al Chambers	1983–84
Norm Charlton	1993, 1995
John Christensen	1987
Bryan Clark	1981–83, 1990
Stan Clarke	1987
Ken Clay	1981
Dave Cochrane	1989–92
Jim Colborn	1978
Vince Coleman	1995
Darnell Coles	1983–85, 1988–90
Dave Collins	1977
Keith Comstock	1989–91
Jim Converse	1993–95
Joey Cora	1995
Henry Cotto	1988–93
Al Cowens	1982–86
Ted Cox	1980
Larry Cox	1977, 1979–80
Rodney Craig	1979–80
Julio Cruz	1977–83
Todd Cruz	1982–83
John Cummings	1993–95
Jeff Darwin	1994
Alvin Davis	1984–91
Tim Davis	1994–95
Scott Davison	1995
Joe Decker	1979
Luis DeLeon	1989
Luis Delgado	1977
Rich DeLucia	1990–93
Mario Diaz	1987–89
Alex Diaz	1995
Dick Drago	1981
Rob Dressler	1979–80
Mike Dunne	1989
Gary Eave	1990
Dave Edler	1980–83
Joe Erardi	1977
Jim Essian	1982
Mike Felder	1993
Felix Fermin	1994–95
Bruce Fields	1988–89
Steve Fireovid	1986
Dan Firova	1981–82
Brian Fisher	1992
Dave Fleming	1991–95
Ray Fosse	1977
Steve Frey	1995
Bob Galasso	1977, 1981
Mike Gardiner	1990
Dave Geisel	1984–85
Brian Giles	1990
Jerry Don Gleaton	1981–82
George Glinatsis	1994
Goose Gossage	1994
Mark Grant	1992
Gary Gray	1981–82
Ken Griffey	1990–91
Ken Griffey	1989–95
Lee Guetterman	1984, 1986–87, 1995
Brad Gulden	1981
Eric Gunderson	1992
John Hale	1978–79
Mike Hampton	1993
Erik Hanson	1988–93
Tim Harikkala	1995
Gene Harris	1989–92
Bill Haselman	1992–94
Dave Heaverlo	1980
Bert Heffernan	1992
Steve Henderson	1983–84
Dave Henderson	1981–86
Dave Hengel	1986–88
Dwayne Henry	1993
Greg Hibbard	1994
Marc Hill	1980
Milt Hill	1994
Rich Hinton	1979
Brian Holman	1989–91
Brad Holman	1993
Rick Honeycutt	1977–80
Willie Horton	1979–80
Tom House	1977–78
Chris Howard	1991, 1993–94
Dann Howitt	1992–93
Mark Huismann	1986–87
Mike Jackson	1988–91
Reggie Jefferson	1994
Randy Johnson	1989–95
Odell Jones	1979
Rick Jones	1977–78
Ruppert Jones	1977–79
Ross Jones	1986
Tracy Jones	1990–91
Calvin Jones	1991–92
Skip Jutze	1977
Bob Kearney	1984–87
Mike Kekich	1977
Kevin King	1993–95
Mike Kingery	1987–89
Brent Knackert	1990
Randy Kramer	1992
Chad Kreuter	1995
Bill Krueger	1991, 1995
Pete Ladd	1986
Mark Langston	1984–89
Bill Laxton	1977
Jack Lazorko	1985
Tim Leary	1992–93
Patrick Lennon	1991–92
Jeffrey Leonard	1989–90
Jim Lewis	1979, 1985
Joe Lis	1977
Greg Litton	1993
Bob Long	1985
Carlos Lopez	1977
Vance Lovelace	1990
Torey Lovullo	1994
Frank MacCormick	1977
Quinn Mack	1994
Dave Magadan	1993
Jim Maler	1981–83
Edgar Martinez	1987–95
Tino Martinez	1990–95
Gary Matthews	1987
Bill McGuire	1988–89
Vance McHenry	1981–82
Byron McLaughlin	1977–80
Tommy McMillan	1977
Jim Mecir	1995
Doc Medich	1977
Scott Medvin	1990
Jose Melendez	1990
Mario Mendoza	1979–80
Orlando Mercado	1982–84
Dan Meyer	1977–81
Larry Milbourne	1977–80, 1984
Paul Mirabella	1984–86
Paul Mitchell	1977–79
Kevin Mitchell	1992
Keith Mitchell	1994
John Montague	1977–79
Rich Monteleone	1987
Mike Moore	1982–88
Tommy Moore	1977
Mike Morgan	1985–87
John Moses	1982–87, 1992
Rob Murphy	1991
Ron Musselman	1982
Bill Nahorodny	1984
Jerry Narron	1980–81, 1987
Gene Nelson	1982–83
Jamie Nelson	1983
Ricky Nelson	1983–86
Jeff Nelson	1992–95
Marc Newfield	1993–95
Warren Newson	1995
Tom Niedenfuer	1989
Donell Nixon	1987
Edwin Nunez	1982–88
Pete O'Brien	1990–93
Steve Ontiveros	1993
Spike Owen	1983–86
Tom Paciorek	1978–81
Dave Pagan	1977
Clay Parker	1987, 1992
Lance Parrish	1992
Mike Parrott	1978–81
Casey Parsons	1981
Kevin Pasley	1977–78
Jack Perconte	1984–85
Gaylord Perry	1982–83
Ken Phelps	1983–88
Greg Pirkl	1993–95
Erik Plantenberg	1993–94
Bill Plummer	1978
Dick Pole	1977–78
Dennis Powell	1987–90, 1992–93
Alonzo Powell	1991
Ted Power	1993
Arquimedez Pozo	1995
Jim Presley	1984–89
Pat Putnam	1983–84
Rey Quinones	1986–89
Johnny Rabb	1988
Domingo Ramos	1982–87
Lenny Randle	1981–82
Shane Rawley	1978–81
Jerry Reed	1986–90
Rick Renteria	1987–88
Dave Revering	1982
Craig Reynolds	1977–78
Harold Reynolds	1983–92
Pat Rice	1991
Bill Risley	1994–95
Dave Roberts	1980
Leon Roberts	1978–80
Bob Robertson	1978
Alex Rodriguez	1994–95
Ron Roenicke	1983
Enrique Romo	1977–78
Roger Salkeld	1993–94
Manny Sarmiento	1980
Mackey Sasser	1993–94
Jeff Schaefer	1990–92
Dave Schmidt	1992
Mike Schooler	1988–92
Donnie Scott	1985
Rod Scurry	1988
Diego Segui	1977
Paul Serna	1981–82
Jimmy Sexton	1977
Larry Sheets	1993
Steve Shields	1987
Zak Shinall	1993
Joe Simpson	1979–82
Matt Sinatro	1990–92
Tommy Smith	1977
Brick Smith	1987–88
Brian Snyder	1985
Luis Sojo	1994–95
Julio Solano	1988–89
Mike Stanton	1982–85
Leroy Stanton	1977–78
Randy Stein	1979, 1981
Bill Stein	1977–80
Bob Stinson	1977–80
Bob Stoddard	1981–84
Doug Strange	1995
Steve Stroughter	1982
Dale Sveum	1994
Russ Swan	1990–93
Rick Sweet	1982–83
Bill Swift	1985–86, 1988–91
Danny Tartabull	1984–86
Terry Taylor	1988
Bobby Thigpen	1994
Stan Thomas	1977
Roy Thomas	1983–85, 1987
Gorman Thomas	1984–86
Gary Thurman	1995
Lee Tinsley	1993
Dave Tobik	1985
Jim Todd	1978
Salomon Torres	1995
Steve Trout	1988–89
Mike Trujillo	1986–87
Brian Turang	1993–94
Shane Turner	1992
Wayne Twitchell	1979
Bobby Valentine	1979
Dave Valle	1984–93
Ed Vande Berg	1982–85
Rafael Vasquez	1979
Ron Villone	1995
Fernando Vina	1993
Omar Vizquel	1989–93
Dave Wainhouse	1993
Mike Walker	1992
Gene Walter	1988
Reggie Walton	1980–81
Jim Weaver	1987
Bob Wells	1994–95
Gary Wheelock	1977, 1980
Chris Widger	1995
Milt Wilcox	1986
Bill Wilkinson	1985, 1987–88
Jerry Willard	1994
Frank Wills	1985
Glenn Wilson	1988
Jim Wilson	1989
Dan Wilson	1994–95
Bob Wolcott	1995
Kerry Woodson	1992
Steve Yeager	1986
Matt Young	1983–86, 1990
Clint Zavaras	1989
Richie Zisk	1981–83

Managers

Chuck Cottier	1984–86
Del Crandall	1983–84
Darrell Johnson	1977–80
Rene Lachemann	1981–83
Jim Lefebvre	1989–91
Marty Martinez	1986
Lou Piniella	1993–95
Bill Plummer	1992
Jimmy Snyder	1988
Dick Williams	1986–88
Maury Wills	1980–81

ST. LOUIS Browns 1902–53

Moved from MILWAUKEE Brewers
Moved to BALTIMORE Orioles

Harry Ables	1905
Bill Abstein	1910
Willie Adams	1912–13

Spencer Adams	1927
Sam Agnew	1913–15
George Aiton	1912
Ed Albrecht	1949–50
Walt Alexander	1912–13, 1915
Ethan Allen	1937–38
Sled Allen	1910
Johnny Allen	1941
Mack Allison	1911–13
Mel Almada	1938–39
Andy Anderson	1948–49
John Anderson	1902–03
Ivy Andrews	1934–36
Pete Appleton	1942, 1945
George Archie	1941, 1946
Hank Arft	1948, 1950–52
Eldon Auker	1940–42
Jimmy Austin	1911–22, 1925–26, 1929

Art Bader	1904
Red Badgro	1929–30
Ed Baecht	1937
Grover Baichley	1914
Bill Bailey	1907–12
Floyd Baker	1943–44
Mike Balenti	1913
Win Ballou	1926–27
Red Barkley	1937
Ed Barnhart	1924
Matt Batts	1951
Russ Bauers	1950
George Baumgardner	1912–16
Bill Bayne	1919–24
Gene Bearden	1952
Boom–Boom Beck	1924, 1927–28
Ollie Bejma	1934–36
Beau Bell	1935–39
Benny Bengough	1931–32
Herschel Bennett	1923–27
Fred Bennett	1928
Bugs Bennett	1918, 1921
Johnny Berardino	1939–42, 1946–47, 1951
Johnny Bero	1951
Neil Berry	1953
Larry Bettencourt	1928, 1931–32
Jim Bilbrey	1949
Emil Bildilli	1937–41
Josh Billings	1919–23
George Binks	1948
Frank Biscan	1942, 1946, 1948
Rivington Bisland	1913
Jack Black	1911
George Blaeholder	1925, 1927–35
Sheriff Blake	1937
Bert Blue	1908
Lu Blue	1928–30
Mike Blyzka	1953
George Boehler	1920–21
Bernie Boland	1921
Charlie Bold	1914
Stew Bolen	1926–27
Julio Bonetti	1937–38
Babe Borton	1916
Jim Bottomley	1936
Benny Bowcock	1903
Tim Bowden	1914
Ray Boyd	1910
George Bradley	1946
Otis Brannan	1928–29
Garland Braxton	1931, 1933
Harry Brecheen	1953
Bunny Brief	1912–13
Herman Bronkie	1919, 1922
Curly Brown	1911–13
Elmer Brown	1911–12
Lloyd Brown	1933
Walter Brown	1947
Willard Brown	1947
Bill Brown	1912
Jack Bruner	1950
Jim Buchanan	1905
Fritz Buelow	1907
Pat Burke	1924
Jesse Burkett	1902–04
Johnny Burnett	1935
Jack Burns	1930–36
Bill Burwell	1920–21
Joe Bush	1925
Kid Butler	1907
Tommy Byrne	1951–52
Milt Byrnes	1943–45

Tom Cafego	1937
Sugar Cain	1935–36
Bob Cain	1952–53
Earl Caldwell	1935–37
Bruce Campbell	1932–34
Tom Carey	1935–37
George Caster	1941–45
Harry Chapman	1916
Mike Chartak	1942–44
Mark Christman	1939, 1943–46
Al Clancy	1911
Earl Clark	1934
Nig Clarke	1911
Ellis Clary	1943–45
Bob Clemens	1914
Verne Clemons	1916
Harlond Clift	1934–43
Herb Cobb	1929
Dick Coffman	1928–35
Slick Coffman	1940
Ed Cole	1938–39
Ed Coleman	1935–36
Ray Coleman	1947–48, 1950–52
Rip Collins	1929–31
Pat Collins	1919–24
Pete Compton	1911–13
Rollin Cook	1915
Bob Cooney	1931–32
Red Corriden	1910
Clint Courtney	1952–53
Sam Covington	1913
Bill Cox	1938–40
Doc Crandall	1916
Rufus Crawford	1952
Lou Criger	1909, 1912
Tony Criscola	1942–43
Joe Crisp	1910
Dode Criss	1908–11
Ned Crompton	1909
Frank Crossin	1912–14
Jack Crouch	1930–31, 1933
Bill Crouch	1910
General Crowder	1927–30
Roy Cullenbine	1940–42
Nick Cullop	1921
Perry Currin	1947
George Curry	1911

Babe Dahlgren	1946
John Daley	1912
Bill Dalrymple	1915
Dave Danforth	1922–25
Ike Danning	1928
Dave Davenport	1916–19
Dixie Davis	1920–26
Harry Davis	1937
Joe De Maestri	1952
Charlie Deal	1916
Dizzy Dean	1947
Paul Dean	1943
Joe DeBerry	1920–21
Shorty Dee	1915
Jim Delahanty	1907
Jim Delsing	1950–52
Frank Demaree	1944
Billy DeMars	1950–51
Ray Demmitt	1910, 1917–19
Gene DeMontreville	1904
Sam Dente	1948
Walt Devoy	1909
Bob Dillinger	1946–49
Bill Dinneen	1907–09
Leo Dixon	1925–27
Red Donahue	1902–03
Jiggs Donahue	1902
Len Dondero	1929
Harry Dorish	1950
Jess Doyle	1931
Clem Dreisewerd	1948
Karl Drews	1948–49
Jim Duggan	1911
Cedric Durst	1922–23, 1926
Jim Dyck	1951–53

Jake Early	1947
Carl East	1915
Hank Edwards	1953
George Elder	1949
Frank Ellerbe	1921–24
Jumbo Elliott	1923
Bob Elliott	1953
Verdo Elmore	1924
Red Embree	1949
Jack Enzenroth	1914
Hal Epps	1943–44
Bobby Estalella	1941
Oscar Estrada	1929
Joe Evans	1924–25
Roy Evans	1903
Homer Ezzell	1923

Chet Falk	1925–27
Cliff Fannin	1945–52
Stan Ferens	1942, 1946
Rick Ferrell	1929–33, 1941–43
Tom Ferrick	1946, 1949–50
Hobe Ferris	1908–09
Bill Fincher	1916
Tom Fine	1950
Lou Finney	1945–46
Carl Fischer	1932
Showboat Fisher	1932
Red Fisher	1910
Charlie Flanagan	1913
Eddie Foster	1922–23
Bill Friel	1902–03
Owen Friend	1949–50
John Frill	1912
Emil Frisk	1905
Charlie Fuchs	1943

Denny Galehouse	1941–44, 1946–47
Joe Gallagher	1939–40
Bert Gallia	1918–20
Debs Garms	1932–35
Ned Garver	1948–52
Milt Gaston	1925–27
Joe Gedeon	1918–20
Lefty George	1911
Wally Gerber	1917–28
Al Gerheauser	1948
Joe Giard	1925–26
Charlie Gibson	1905
George Gill	1939
Jack Gilligan	1909–10
Tony Giuliani	1936–37
Fred Glade	1904–07
Harry Gleason	1904–05
Bill Gleason	1921
Joe Glenn	1939
Gordon Goldsberry	1952
Mike Goliat	1951–52
Goose Goslin	1930–32
Claude Gouzzie	1903
Joe Grace	1938–41, 1946
Fred Graff	1913
Bert Graham	1910
Jack Graham	1949
Bill Grahame	1908–10
George Grant	1923–25
Pete Gray	1945
Sam Gray	1928–33
Howie Gregory	1911
Art Griggs	1909–10
Ed Grimes	1931–32
Bob Groom	1916–17
Johnny Groth	1953
Frank Grube	1934–35, 1941
Sig Gryska	1938–39
Ted Gullic	1930, 1933
Ernie Gust	1911
Frankie Gustine	1950
Don Gutteridge	1942–45

Bob Habenicht	1953
Bump Hadley	1932–34
Tom Hafey	1944
Hal Haid	1919
George Hale	1914, 1916–18
Sammy Hale	1930
Marc Hall	1910
Ed Hallinan	1911–12
Earl Hamilton	1911–17
Loy Hanning	1939, 1942
Snipe Hansen	1935
Pinky Hargrave	1925–26
Jack Harper	1902
Bill Harper	1911
Bob Harris	1939–42
Earl Harrist	1952
Sam Harshaney	1937–40
Grover Hartley	1916–17, 1934
Roy Hartzell	1906–10
Joe Hassler	1930
Ed Hawk	1911
Frankie Hayes	1942–43
Red Hayworth	1944–45
Jeff Heath	1946–47
Tommy Heath	1935, 1937–38
Wally Hebert	1931–33
Don Heffner	1938–43
Emmett Heidrick	1902–04, 1908
Hank Helf	1946
Ed Hemingway	1914
Charlie Hemphill	1902–04, 1906–07
Rollie Hemsley	1933–37
Tim Hendryx	1918
George Hennessey	1937
Dutch Henry	1921–22
Tito Herrera	1951
Johnny Hetki	1952
Oral Hildebrand	1937–38
Hunter Hill	1903–04
Billy Hitchcock	1947
Myril Hoag	1939–40
Harry Hoch	1914–15
Red Hoff	1915
Danny Hoffman	1908–11
Happy Hogan	1911–12
Chief Hogsett	1936–37
Bobby Hogue	1951–52
Ken Holcombe	1952
Al Hollingsworth	1942–46
Bobo Holloman	1953
Herm Holshouser	1930
Paul Hopkins	1929
Byron Houck	1918
Ivon Howard	1914–15
Harry Howell	1904–10
Willis Hudlin	1940, 1944
Hal Hudson	1952
Frank Huelsman	1904
Ben Huffman	1937
Roy Hughes	1938–39
Bernie Hungling	1930
Billy Hunter	1953
Pat Hynes	1904

Hooks Iott	1941, 1947

Beany Jacobson	1906–07
Baby Doll Jacobson	1915, 1917, 1919–26
Sig Jakucki	1936, 1944–45
Bill James	1914–15
Ray Jansen	1910
Heinie Jantzen	1912
Joe Jenkins	1914
Tom Jenkins	1929–32
Bill Jennings	1951
Pete Johns	1918
Chet Johnson	1946
Darrell Johnson	1952
Don Johnson	1950–51
Ernie Johnson	1916–18
Fred Johnson	1938–39
Johnny Johnston	1913
Charlie Jones	1908
Davy Jones	1902
Earl Jones	1945
Sad Sam Jones	1927
Tom Jones	1904–09
Claude Jonnard	1926
Walt Judnich	1940–42, 1946–47

Mike Kahoe	1902–04
Harry Kane	1902
Dick Kauffman	1914–15
Frank Kellert	1953
Vern Kennedy	1939–41
Bill Kennedy	1948–51
Duke Kenworthy	1917
Phil Ketter	1912
Bill Killefer	1909–10
Harry Kimberlin	1936–39
Chad Kimsey	1929–32
Ellis Kinder	1946–47
Ed Kinsella	1910
Nap Kloza	1931–32
Clyde Kluttz	1951
Bill Knickerbocker	1937
Jack Knott	1933–38
Ben Koehler	1905–06
Dick Kokos	1948–50, 1953
Ray Kolp	1921–24
Ernie Koob	1915–17, 1919
Lou Koupal	1937
Jack Kramer	1939–41, 1943–47
Mike Kreevich	1943–45
Red Kress	1927–32, 1938–39

Lou Kretlow	1950, 1953
Paul Krichell	1911–12
Dick Kryhoski	1952–53
Ed Kusel	1909
Joe Kutina	1911–12
Chet Laabs	1939–46
Joe Lake	1910–12
Al LaMacchia	1943, 1945–46
Lyman Lamb	1920–21
Bobby LaMotte	1925–26
Max Lanier	1953
Frank LaPorte	1911–12
Don Larsen	1953
Lyn Lary	1935–36, 1940
Bill Lasley	1924
Doc Lavan	1913–17
Roxie Lawson	1939–40
Pete Layden	1948
John Leary	1914–15
Dud Lee	1920–21
Bill Lee	1915–16
Paul Lehner	1946–49, 1951
Lefty Leifield	1918–20
Don Lenhardt	1950–53
Walt Leverenz	1913–15
Hod Leverette	1920
Jim Levey	1930–33
Glenn Liebhardt	1936, 1938
Fred Link	1910
Ed Linke	1938
Johnny Lipon	1953
Nig Lipscomb	1937
Dick Littlefield	1952–53
Sherm Lollar	1949–51
Dale Long	1951
Grover Lowdermilk	1915, 1917–19
Johnny Lucadello	1938–41, 1946
Don Lund	1948
Joe Lutz	1951
Adrian Lynch	1920
George Lyons	1924
Dave Madison	1952
Lee Magee	1917
Jack Maguire	1951
Roy Mahaffey	1936
Bob Mahoney	1951–52
Fritz Maisel	1918
George Maisel	1913
Alex Malloy	1910
Bob Malloy	1949
Billy Maloney	1902
Frank Mancuso	1944–46
Clyde Manion	1928–30
Ernie Manning	1914
Heinie Manush	1928–30
Rolla Mapel	1919
Cliff Mapes	1951
Johnny Marcum	1939
Marty Marion	1952
Duke Markell	1951
Armando Marsans	1916–17
Freddie Marsh	1951–52
Cuddles Marshall	1950
Babe Martin	1944–46, 1953
Speed Martin	1917
Joe Martin	1903
Wally Mayer	1919
Mel Mazzera	1935, 1938–39
Bill McAfee	1934
John McAleese	1909
Bill McAllester	1913
Tim McCabe	1915–18
Jerry McCarthy	1948
Barry McCormick	1902–03
Bill McCorry	1909
Hank McDonald	1933
Jim McDonald	1951
Joe McDonald	1910
Bill McGill	1907
Frank McGowan	1928–29
Archie McKain	1941, 1943
Reeve McKay	1915
Jim McLaughlin	1932
Marty McManus	1920–26
Norm McMillan	1924
Earl McNeely	1928–31
Glenn McQuillen	1938, 1941–42, 1946
George McQuinn	1938–45
Irv Medlinger	1949, 1951
Tommy Mee	1910
Heinie Meine	1922
Walt Meinert	1913
Oscar Melillo	1926–35
Paul Meloan	1911
Mike Meola	1936
Bobby Messenger	1914
Alex Metzler	1930
Cass Michaels	1952
Ed Mickelson	1953
Charlie Miller	1912
Bing Miller	1926–27
Ed Miller	1912, 1914
Ox Miller	1943, 1945–46
Otto Miller	1927
Ward Miller	1916–17
Bill Miller	1937
Buster Mills	1938
Lefty Mills	1934, 1937–40
Al Milnar	1943, 1946
Willie Miranda	1952–53
Roy Mitchell	1910–14
George Mogridge	1925
Vince Molyneaux	1917
Gene Moore	1944–45
Scrappy Moore	1917
Charlie Moran	1904–05
Cy Morgan	1903–05, 1907
Walter Moser	1911
Les Moss	1946–53
Glen Moulder	1947
Ollie Moulton	1911
Heinie Mueller	1935
Billy Mullen	1921, 1928
Bob Muncrief	1937, 1939, 1941–47
Ed Murray	1917
Jim Murray	1911
Hap Myers	1911
Doc Nance	1904
Buddy Napier	1912
Al Naples	1949
Bob Neighbors	1939
Red Nelson	1910–12
Otto Neu	1917
Ernie Nevers	1926–28
Maury Newlin	1940–41
Pat Newnam	1910–11
Bobo Newsom	1934–35, 1938–39, 1943
Bob Nieman	1951–52
Johnny Niggeling	1940–43
Harry Niles	1906–07
Lou Nordyke	1906
Hub Northen	1910
Les Nunamaker	1918
George O'Brien	1915
Pete O'Brien	1906
Jack O'Connor	1904, 1906–07
Jack Ogden	1928–29
Steve O'Neill	1927–28
Frank O'Rourke	1927–31
Fritz Ostermueller	1941–43
Joe Ostrowski	1948–50
Stubby Overmire	1950–52
Dick Padden	1902–05
Satchel Paige	1951–53
Emilio Palmero	1921
Al Papai	1949
Jim Park	1915–17
Pat Parker	1915
Roy Partee	1948
Ham Patterson	1909
Gene Paulette	1917
Eddie Pellagrini	1948–49
Barney Pelty	1903–12
Kewpie Pennington	1917
Ray Pepper	1934–36
Scott Perry	1915
Parson Perryman	1915
Rusty Peters	1947
Sid Peterson	1943
Jeff Pfeffer	1911
Tom Phillips	1915
Ollie Pickering	1907
Duane Pillette	1950–53
Jim Pisoni	1953
Eddie Plank	1916–17
Whitey Platt	1948–49
Lou Polli	1932
J. W. Porter	1952
Bob Poser	1935
Nels Potter	1943–48
Jack Powell	1902–03, 1905–12
Jack Powell	1913
Del Pratt	1912–17
Gerry Priddy	1948–49
Gibby Pruess	1920
Hub Pruett	1922–24
George Puccinelli	1934
Ewald Pyle	1939, 1942
Rip Radcliff	1940–41
Ribs Raney	1949–50
Earl Rapp	1951–52
Farmer Ray	1910
Tony Rego	1924–25
Bill Reidy	1902–03
Alex Remneas	1915
Carl Reynolds	1933
Harry Rice	1924–27
Ray Richmond	1920–21
Branch Rickey	1905–06
Jim Riley	1921
Jim Rivera	1952
Charlie Robertson	1926
Gene Robertson	1919, 1922–26
Ike Rockenfield	1905–06
Ed Roetz	1929
Tom Rogers	1917–19
Stan Rojek	1952
Charlie Root	1923
Chuck Rose	1909
Claude Rossman	1909
Frank Roth	1905
Dave Rowan	1911
Muddy Ruel	1915, 1933
Bill Rumler	1914, 1916–17
Dee Sanders	1945
Roy Sanders	1920
Fred Sanford	1943, 1946–48, 1951
Frank Saucier	1951
Bob Savage	1949
Ollie Sax	1928
Sid Schacht	1950–51
Wally Schang	1926–29
Art Scharein	1932–33
John Scheneberg	1920
Joe Schepner	1919
Dutch Schliebner	1923
Ray Schmandt	1915
George Schmees	1952
Pete Schmidt	1913
Fred Schulte	1927–32
Johnny Schulte	1923, 1932
Len Schulte	1945–46
Joe Schultz	1943–46
Blackie Schwamb	1948
Al Schweitzer	1908–11
Hal Schwenk	1913
Ken Sears	1946
Hank Severeid	1915–25
Doc Shanley	1912
Owen Shannon	1903
Merv Shea	1933
Charlie Shields	1902
Tex Shirley	1944–46
Urban Shocker	1918–24
Ray Shore	1946, 1948–49
Chick Shorten	1922
Burt Shotton	1909, 1911–17
John Shovlin	1919–20
Ed Siever	1903–04
Roy Sievers	1949–53
Eddie Silber	1937
Syl Simon	1924
Pete Sims	1915
George Sisler	1915–22, 1924–27
Lou Sleater	1950–52
Tod Sloan	1913, 1917, 1919
Earl Smith	1917–21
Ed Smith	1906
Syd Smith	1908
Wib Smith	1909
Henry Smoyer	1912
Charlie Snell	1912
Moose Solters	1935–36, 1939
Bill Sommers	1950
Allen Sothoron	1914–15, 1917–21
Clyde Southwick	1911
Bob Spade	1910
Stan Spence	1949
Tubby Spencer	1905–08
Hack Spencer	1912
Paul Speraw	1920
Hal Spindel	1939
Brad Springer	1925
Buck Stanton	1931
Charlie Starr	1905
Dick Starr	1949–51
Ed Stauffer	1925
Bryan Stephens	1948
Jim Stephens	1907–12
Vern Stephens	1941–47, 1953
Chuck Stevens	1941, 1946, 1948
Lefty Stewart	1927–32
Fred Stiely	1929–31
Rollie Stiles	1930–31, 1933
Snuffy Stirnweiss	1950
Dwight Stone	1913
George Stone	1905–10
Lin Storti	1930–33
George Stovall	1912–13
Alan Strange	1934–35, 1940–42
Ed Strelecki	1928–29
Phil Stremmel	1909–10
Bill Strickland	1937
Luke Stuart	1921
Marlin Stuart	1952–53
Guy Sturdy	1927–28
Jim Suchecki	1951
Willie Sudhoff	1902–05
Joe Sugden	1902–05
John Sullivan	1949
Billy Sullivan	1938–39
Steve Sundra	1942–44, 1946
George Susce	1940
Pinky Swander	1903
Bud Swartz	1947
Bob Swift	1940–42
Vito Tamulis	1938
Bennie Taylor	1951
Pete Taylor	1952
Wiley Taylor	1913–14
John Terry	1903
Tommy Thomas	1936–37
Fay Thomas	1935
Bud Thomas	1951
Leo Thomas	1950, 1952
Frank Thompson	1920
Hank Thompson	1947
Tommy Thompson	1939
Sloppy Thurston	1923
Les Tietje	1936–38
Johnny Tillman	1915
Jack Tobin	1916, 1918–25
Bill Trotter	1937–42
Virgil Trucks	1953
Frank Truesdale	1910
Bob Turley	1951, 1953
Tom Turner	1944
Tom Upton	1950–51
Russ Van Atta	1935–39
Ike Van Zandt	1905
Elam Vangilder	1919–27
Ollie Voigt	1924
Joe Vosmik	1937
Rube Waddell	1908–10
Frank Waddey	1931
Jake Wade	1939
Kermit Wahl	1951
Fred Walden	1912
Tilly Walker	1913–15
Ernie Walker	1913–15
Jim Walkup	1934–39
Bobby Wallace	1902–16
Dee Walsh	1913–15
Buzzy Wares	1913–14
Hal Warnock	1935
Art Weaver	1905
Jim Weaver	1934, 1938
Bob Weiland	1935
Carl Weilman	1912–17, 1919–20
Ed Wells	1933–34
Vic Wertz	1952–53
Sammy West	1933–38
Lefty West	1944–45
Buzz Wetzel	1920–21
Bill Whaley	1923
Hal White	1953
John Whitehead	1939–40, 1942
Al Widmar	1948, 1950–51
Gus Williams	1911–15
Jimmy Williams	1908–09
Ken Williams	1919–27

Joe Willis	1911
Frank Wilson	1928
Jim Wilson	1948
Hal Wiltse	1928
Ralph Winegarner	1949
Ernie Wingard	1924–27
Jerry Witte	1946–47
Ken Wood	1948–51
Clarence Wright	1903–04
Jim Wright	1927–28
Tom Wright	1952
Rasty Wright	1917–19, 1922–23
Joe Yeager	1907–08
Bobby Young	1951–53
Russ Young	1931
Tom Zachary	1926–27
Al Zarilla	1943–44, 1946–49, 1952
Sam Zoldak	1944–48

Managers

*Jimmy Austin	1913, 1918, 1923
Jim Bottomley	1937
Jimmy Burke	1918–20
Lee Fohl	1921–23
Fred Haney	1939–41
Rogers Hornsby	1933–37, 1952
Dan Howley	1927–29
Fielder Jones	1916–18
Bill Killefer	1930–33
*Marty Marion	1952–53
Jimmy McAleer	1902–09
Oscar Melillo	1938
Jack O'Connor	1910
Branch Rickey	1913–15
Muddy Ruel	1947
Luke Sewell	1941–46
*George Sisler	1924–26
Allen Sothoron	1933
*George Stovall	1912–13
Gabby Street	1938
Zack Taylor	1946, 1948–51
*Bobby Wallace	1911–12

TEXAS Rangers 1972–95
Moved from WASHINGTON Senators

Darrel Akerfelds	1989
Jose Alberro	1995
Doyle Alexander	1977–79
Gerald Alexander	1990–92
Brian Allard	1979–80
Lloyd Allen	1973–74
Sandy Alomar	1977–78
Wilson Alvarez	1989
Jim Anderson	1983–84
Scott Anderson	1987
Jack Armstrong	1994
Brad Arnsberg	1989–91
Tucker Ashford	1980
Doug Ault	1976
Bob Babcock	1979–81
Mike Bacsik	1975–77
Harold Baines	1989–90
Steve Balboni	1993
Alan Bannister	1984–85
Floyd Bannister	1992
John Barfield	1989–91
Len Barker	1976–78
Steve Barr	1976
Randy Bass	1982
Lew Beasley	1977
Kevin Belcher	1990
Buddy Bell	1979–85, 1989
Esteban Beltre	1994–95
Juan Beniquez	1976–78
Kurt Bevacqua	1977–78
Jim Bibby	1973–75, 1984
Larry Biittner	1972–73, 1983
Dick Billings	1972–74
Joe Bitker	1990–91
Larvell Blanks	1979
Bert Blyleven	1976–77
Terry Bogener	1982
Tommy Boggs	1976–77, 1985
Brian Bohanon	1990–94
Danny Boitano	1982
Bobby Bonds	1978
Thad Bosley	1989–90
Dick Bosman	1972–73
Oil Can Boyd	1991
Mark Brandenburg	1995
Nellie Briles	1976–77
Ed Brinkman	1975
Pete Broberg	1972–74
Jeff Bronkey	1993
Bob Brower	1986–88
Larry Brown	1974
Jackie Brown	1973–75
Kevin Brown	1986, 1988–94
Jerry Browne	1986–88
Duff Brumley	1994
Glenn Brummer	1985
Kevin Buckley	1984
Steve Buechele	1985–91, 1995
Todd Burns	1992–93
Jeff Burroughs	1972–76
Terry Burrows	1994–95
John Butcher	1980–83
Bert Campaneris	1977–79
Mike Campbell	1992
John Cangelosi	1992
Jose Canseco	1992–94
Nick Capra	1982–83, 1985, 1991
Leo Cardenas	1974–75
Don Carman	1992
Cris Carpenter	1993–94
Rico Carty	1973
Don Castle	1973
Jose Cecena	1988
Dave Chalk	1979
Scott Chiamparino	1990–92
Will Clark	1994–95
Ken Clay	1980
Reggie Cleveland	1978
Gene Clines	1976
David Clyde	1973–75
Cris Colon	1992
Steve Comer	1978–82
Glen Cook	1985
Dennis Cook	1995
Scott Coolbaugh	1989–90
Ed Correa	1986–87
Casey Cox	1972
Larry Cox	1981
Keith Creel	1987
Victor Cruz	1983
Mike Cubbage	1974–76
Bobby Cuellar	1977
Danny Darwin	1978–84, 1995
Doug Dascenzo	1993
Jack Daugherty	1989–92
Willie Davis	1975
Odie Davis	1980
Butch Davis	1993–94
Bucky Dent	1982–83
John Dettmer	1994–95
Adrian Devine	1977, 1980
Mario Diaz	1991–93
Brian Downing	1991–92
Steve Dreyer	1993–94
Jim Driscoll	1972
Rob Ducey	1993–94
Jan Dukes	1972
Tommy Dunbar	1983–85
Steve Dunning	1973–74
Dan Duran	1981
Don Durham	1973
Dock Ellis	1977–79
John Ellis	1976–81
Mike Epstein	1973
Cecil Espy	1987–90
Bill Fahey	1972, 1974–77
Hector Fajardo	1991, 1993–95
Monty Fariss	1991–92
Ed Farmer	1979
Jimmy Farr	1982
Ed Figueroa	1980
Steve Fireovid	1992
Scott Fletcher	1986–89
Doug Flynn	1982
Marv Foley	1984
Ted Ford	1972
Tony Fossas	1988
Steve Foucault	1973–76
Eric Fox	1995
Julio Franco	1989–93
Lou Frazier	1995
Jim Fregosi	1973–77
Pepe Frias	1980
Jeff Frye	1992, 1994–95
Oscar Gamble	1979
Barbaro Garbey	1988
Jim Gideon	1975
Benji Gil	1993, 1995
Jerry Don Gleaton	1979–80
Bill Gogolewski	1972–73
Juan Gonzalez	1989–95
Goose Gossage	1991
Gary Gray	1977–79
Gary Green	1990–91
Rusty Greer	1994–95
Tom Grieve	1972–77
Kevin Gross	1995
Johnny Grubb	1978–82
Cecilio Guante	1988–89
Jose Guzman	1985–88, 1991–92
Drew Hall	1989
Rich Hand	1972–73
Bill Hands	1974–75
Shawn Hare	1995
Steve Hargan	1974–77
Mike Hargrove	1974–78
Toby Harrah	1972–78, 1985–86
Bud Harrelson	1980
Greg Harris	1985–87
Vic Harris	1972–73
Donald Harris	1991–93
Mike Hart	1980
Bill Haselman	1990
Billy Hatcher	1995
Ray Hayward	1988
Rick Helling	1994–95
Ken Henderson	1977
Tom Henke	1982–84, 1993–94
Rick Henninger	1973
Dwayne Henry	1984–88
Wilson Heredia	1995
Jose Hernandez	1991
Rich Hinton	1972
Joe Hoerner	1976
Guy Hoffman	1988
Gary Holle	1979
Rick Honeycutt	1981–83, 1994
Burt Hooton	1985
John Hoover	1990
Sam Horn	1995
Willie Horton	1977
Dave Hostetler	1982–84
Charlie Hough	1980–90
Frank Howard	1972
Chris Howard	1995
Steve Howe	1987
Roy Howell	1974–77
Jay Howell	1994
Charles Hudson	1973
David Hulse	1992–94
Bruce Hurst	1994
James Hurst	1994
Jeff Huson	1990–93
Pete Incaviglia	1986–90
Chuck Jackson	1994
Chris James	1993–94
Gerry Janeski	1972
Mike Jeffcoat	1987–92
Ferguson Jenkins	1974–75, 1978–81
Alex Johnson	1973–74
Lamar Johnson	1982
John Henry Johnson	1979–81
Bobby Johnson	1981–83
Cliff Johnson	1985
Dalton Jones	1972
Bobby Jones	1974–75, 1981, 1983–86
Odell Jones	1983–84
Mike Jorgensen	1978–79
Don Kainer	1980
Mike Kekich	1975
Steve Kemp	1988
Jim Kern	1979–81
Paul Kilgus	1987–88
Hal King	1972
Ed Kirkpatrick	1977
Darold Knowles	1977
Jim Kremmel	1973
Chad Kreuter	1988–91
Ted Kubiak	1972
Jeff Kunkel	1984–90
Bob Lacey	1981
Al Lachowicz	1983
Joe Lahoud	1976
Steve Lawson	1972
Rick Leach	1989
Tim Leary	1994
Manny Lee	1993–94
Craig Lefferts	1993
Charlie Leibrandt	1993
Danilo Leon	1992
Dennis Lewallyn	1980
Paul Lindblad	1972, 1977–78
Rick Lisi	1981
Joe Lovitto	1972–75
John Lowenstein	1978
Mike Loynd	1986–87
Sparky Lyle	1979–80
Pete Mackanin	1973–74
Elliott Maddox	1972–73
Bill Madlock	1973
Greg Mahlberg	1978–79
Mickey Mahler	1986
Candy Maldonado	1995
Bob Malloy	1987
Ramon Manon	1990
Fred Manrique	1989
Barry Manuel	1991–92
Mike Marshall	1977
Marty Martinez	1972
John Marzano	1995
Jim Mason	1972–73, 1977–78
Mike Mason	1982–87
Terry Mathews	1991–92
Jon Matlack	1978–83
Rob Maurer	1991–92
Dave May	1977
Scott May	1988
Lee Mazzilli	1982
Larry McCall	1979
Lance McCullers	1992
Oddibe McDowell	1985–88, 1994
Roger McDowell	1995
Russ McGinnis	1992
Joey McLaughlin	1984
Mark McLemore	1995
Craig McMurtry	1988–90
Doc Medich	1978–82
Dave Meier	1987
Mario Mendoza	1981–82
Orlando Mercado	1986
Mark Mercer	1981
Ron Meridith	1986–87
Jim Merritt	1973–75
Gary Mielke	1987, 1989–90
Eddie Miller	1977
Don Mincher	1972
Paul Mirabella	1978, 1982
Dave Moates	1975–76
Dale Mohorcic	1986–88
Willie Montanez	1979
Tommy Moore	1975
Roger Moret	1977–78
Jamie Moyer	1989–90
Dale Murray	1985
Dave Nelson	1972–75
Gene Nelson	1993
Robb Nen	1993
Al Newman	1992
Chris Nichting	1995
Otis Nixon	1995
Dickie Noles	1984–85
Eric Nolte	1991
Nelson Norman	1978–81
Jim Norris	1980
Edwin Nunez	1992
Pete O'Brien	1982–88
Al Oliver	1978–81
Darren Oliver	1993–95
Tom O'Malley	1987
Junior Ortiz	1994
Luis Ortiz	1995
Tom Paciorek	1986–87
Mike Pagliarulo	1995
Rafael Palmeiro	1989–93
Dean Palmer	1989, 1991–95
Jim Panther	1972

Ken Pape	1976
Mark Parent	1991
Larry Parrish	1982–88
Bob Patterson	1993
Mike Paul	1972–73
Roger Pavlik	1992–95
Dan Peltier	1992–93
Gaylord Perry	1975–77, 1980
Stan Perzanowski	1975–76
Fritz Peterson	1976
Mark Petkovsek	1991
Geno Petralli	1985–93
Gary Pettis	1990–91
Horacio Pina	1972
John Poloni	1977
Jim Poole	1991
Tom Poquette	1981
Darrell Porter	1986–87
Ron Pruitt	1975
Greg Pryor	1976
Luis Pujols	1985
Pat Putnam	1977–82
Tom Ragland	1972
Dave Rajsich	1979–80
Lenny Randle	1972–76
Gary Redus	1993–94
Rick Reed	1993–94
Kevin Reimer	1988–92
Mike Richardt	1980, 1982–84
Billy Ripken	1993–94
Mickey Rivers	1979–84
Leon Roberts	1981–82
Dave Roberts	1979–80
Jeff Robinson	1992
Tom Robson	1974–75
Ivan Rodriguez	1991–95
Kenny Rogers	1989–95
Jim Roland	1972
Wayne Rosenthal	1991–92
Dave Rozema	1985–86
Jeff Russell	1985–92, 1995
John Russell	1990–93
Nolan Ryan	1989–93
Billy Sample	1978–84
Calvin Schiraldi	1991
Dave Schmidt	1981–85
Mike Schooler	1993
Donnie Scott	1983–84
Tony Scruggs	1991
Bob Sebra	1985
Larry See	1988
Jon Shave	1993
Jim Shellenback	1972–74
Sonny Siebert	1973
Ruben Sierra	1986–92
Duke Sims	1974
Bill Singer	1976
Craig Skok	1976
Don Slaught	1985–87
Roy Smalley	1975–76
Keith Smith	1977
Dan Smith	1992, 1994
Mike Smithson	1982–83
Eric Soderholm	1979
Sammy Sosa	1989
Jim Spencer	1973–75
Don Stanhouse	1972–74
Mike Stanley	1986–91
Rusty Staub	1980
James Steels	1988
Bill Stein	1981–85
Rick Stelmaszek	1973
Ray Stephens	1992
Dave Stewart	1983–85
Jeff Stone	1989
Doug Strange	1993–94
Ken Suarez	1972–73
Bill Sudakis	1973
Jim Sundberg	1974–83, 1988–89
Rich Surhoff	1985
Greg Tabor	1987
Frank Tanana	1982–85
Scott Taylor	1995
Jeff Terpko	1974, 1976
Mickey Tettleton	1995
Bob Tewksbury	1995
Stan Thomas	1974–75
Bobby Thompson	1978
Danny Thompson	1976
Dickie Thon	1992
Dave Tobik	1983–84
Wayne Tolleson	1981–85
Cesar Tovar	1974–75
Jim Umbarger	1975–78
Ellis Valentine	1985
Dave Valle	1995
Ed Vande Berg	1988
DeWayne Vaughn	1988
Jack Voigt	1995
Ed Vosberg	1995
Mark Wagner	1981–83
Rick Waits	1973
Duane Walker	1985
Mike Wallace	1977
Denny Walling	1991
Danny Walton	1980
Gary Ward	1984–86
Claudell Washington	1977–78
LaRue Washington	1978–79
Chris Welsh	1985
Don Werner	1981–82
Len Whitehouse	1981
Matt Whiteside	1992–95
Curtis Wilkerson	1983–88
Matt Williams	1985
Mitch Williams	1986–88
Bump Wills	1977–81
Paul Wilmet	1989
Steve Wilson	1988
Bobby Witt	1986–92, 1995
Craig Worthington	1995
Clyde Wright	1975
George Wright	1982–86
Ricky Wright	1983–86
Ned Yost	1984
Richie Zisk	1978–80

Managers

Pat Corrales	1978–80
Toby Harrah	1992
Whitey Herzog	1973
Billy Hunter	1977–78
Darrell Johnson	1982
Kevin Kennedy	1993–94
Frank Lucchesi	1975–77
Billy Martin	1973–75
Johnny Oates	1995
Doug Rader	1983–85
Connie Ryan	1977
Eddie Stanky	1977
Bobby Valentine	1985–92
Del Wilber	1973
Ted Williams	1972
Don Zimmer	1981–82

TORONTO Blue Jays 1977–95

Jim Acker	1983–86, 1989–91
Glenn Adams	1982
Willie Aikens	1984–85
Danny Ainge	1979–81
Butch Alberts	1978
Doyle Alexander	1983–86
Gary Allenson	1985
Roberto Alomar	1991–95
Luis Aquino	1986
Alan Ashby	1977–78
Doug Ault	1977–78, 1980
Bob Bailor	1977–80
Doug Bair	1988
Dave Baker	1982
Jesse Barfield	1981–89
Mike Barlow	1980–81
Kevin Batiste	1989
Howard Battle	1995
Charlie Beamon	1981
George Bell	1981, 1983–90
Derek Bell	1991–92
Juan Beniquez	1987–88
Juan Berenguer	1981
Bud Black	1990
Willie Blair	1990
Mark Bomback	1981–82
Barry Bonnell	1980–83
Pat Borders	1988–94
Rick Bosetti	1978–81
Denis Boucher	1991
Steve Bowling	1977
Steve Braun	1980
Bob Brenly	1989
Scott Brow	1993–94
Bobby Brown	1979
Tom Bruno	1977
DeWayne Buice	1989
Jeff Burroughs	1985
Tom Buskey	1978–80
Sal Butera	1988
Rob Butler	1993–94
Jeff Byrd	1977
Francisco Cabrera	1989
Greg Cadaret	1994
Sil Campusano	1988
Willie Canate	1993
John Candelaria	1990
Tom Candiotti	1991
Joe Cannon	1979–80
Giovanni Carrara	1995
Joe Carter	1991–95
Rico Carty	1978–79
Tony Castillo	1988–89, 1993–95
Bill Caudill	1985–86
Domingo Cedeno	1993–95
Rick Cerone	1977–79
John Cerutti	1985–90
Jim Clancy	1977–88
Bryan Clark	1984
Stan Clarke	1983, 1985–86
Joe Coleman	1978
Darnell Coles	1993–94
Dave Collins	1983–84
David Cone	1992, 1995
Don Cooper	1983
Brad Cornett	1994–95
Ted Cox	1981
Danny Cox	1993–95
Tim Crabtree	1995
Victor Cruz	1978
Steve Cummings	1989–90
Mike Darr	1977
Danny Darwin	1995
Dick Davis	1982
Steve Davis	1985–86
Bob Davis	1979–80
Ken Dayley	1991, 1993
Denny DeBarr	1977
Carlos Delgado	1993–95
Jeff DeWillis	1987
Carlos Diaz	1990
Rob Ducey	1987–92
Butch Edge	1979
Mark Eichhorn	1982, 1986–88, 1992–93
Nino Espinosa	1981
Sam Ewing	1977–78
Ron Fairly	1977
Junior Felix	1989–90
Tony Fernandez	1983–90, 1993
Cecil Fielder	1985–88
Tom Filer	1985
Mike Flanagan	1987–90
Huck Flener	1993
Willie Fraser	1991
Dave Freisleben	1979
Damaso Garcia	1980–86
Pedro Garcia	1977
Jerry Garvin	1977–82
Dave Geisel	1982–83
Ray Giannelli	1991
Tom Gilles	1990
Luis Gomez	1978–79
Rene Gonzales	1991
Alex Gonzalez	1994–95
Don Gordon	1986–87
Jim Gott	1982–84
Mauro Gozzo	1989
Shawn Green	1993–95
Alfredo Griffin	1979–84, 1992–93
Steve Grilli	1979
Kelly Gruber	1984–92
Juan Guzman	1991–95
Darren Hall	1994–95
Steve Hargan	1977
Chuck Hartenstein	1977
Jeff Hearron	1985–86
Rickey Henderson	1993
Tom Henke	1985–92
Pat Hentgen	1991–95
Pedro Hernandez	1979, 1982
Toby Hernandez	1984
Xavier Hernandez	1989
Glenallen Hill	1989–91
Paul Hodgson	1980
Vince Horsman	1991
Willie Horton	1978
Roy Howell	1977–80
Mike Huff	1994–95
Phil Huffman	1979
Edwin Hurtado	1995
Tom Hutton	1978
Alexis Infante	1987–89
Garth Iorg	1978, 1980–87
Roy Lee Jackson	1981–84
Darrin Jackson	1993
Jesse Jefferson	1977–80
Jerry Johnson	1977
Tony Johnson	1982
Cliff Johnson	1983–86
Joe Johnson	1986–87
Tim Johnson	1978–79
Ricardo Jordan	1995
Dale Kelly	1980
Jeff Kent	1992
Jimmy Key	1984–92
Paul Kilgus	1990
Don Kirkwood	1978
Mickey Klutts	1983
Randy Knorr	1991–95
Jack Kucek	1980
Craig Kusick	1979
Dennis Lamp	1984–86
Gary Lavelle	1985, 1987
Tom Lawless	1989–90
Rick Leach	1984–88
Luis Leal	1980–85
Manny Lee	1985–92
Al Leiter	1989–95
Dave Lemanczyk	1977–80
Mark Lemongello	1979
Doug Linton	1992–93
Nelson Liriano	1987–90
Steve Luebber	1979
Rick Luecken	1990
Bob MacDonald	1990–92
Ken Macha	1981
Mike Macha	1980
Mickey Mahler	1986
Mike Maksudian	1992
Candy Maldonado	1991–92, 1995
Fred Manrique	1981, 1984
Buck Martinez	1981–86
Domingo Martinez	1992–93
Sandy Martinez	1995
Jim Mason	1977
Len Matuszek	1985
John Mayberry	1978–82
Lee Mazzilli	1989
Fred McGriff	1986–90
Dave McKay	1977–79
Joey McLaughlin	1980–84
Paul Menhart	1995
Dyar Miller	1979
Brian Milner	1978
Paul Mirabella	1980–81
Randy Moffitt	1983
Paul Molitor	1993–95
Balor Moore	1978–80
Charlie Moore	1987
Mike Morgan	1983
Jack Morris	1992–93
Lloyd Moseby	1980–89
Rance Mulliniks	1982–92
Tom Murphy	1977–79
Dale Murray	1981–82
Ron Musselman	1984–85
Jeff Musselman	1986–89
Greg Myers	1987, 1989–92
Steve Nicosia	1985
Phil Niekro	1987
Tim Nordbrook	1977–78

Wayne Nordhagen	1982
Jose Nunez	1987–89
John Olerud	1989–95
Al Oliver	1985
Jorge Orta	1983
Dave Parker	1991
Lance Parrish	1995
Robert Perez	1994–95
Tomas Perez	1995
Geno Petralli	1982–84
Hosken Powell	1982–83
Tom Quinlan	1990, 1992
Doug Rader	1977
Domingo Ramos	1980
Dave Revering	1982
Dave Righetti	1994
Leon Roberts	1982
Bob Robertson	1979
Kenny Robinson	1995
Jimmy Rogers	1995
Phil Roof	1977
Mark Ross	1988
Alex Sanchez	1989
Dick Schofield	1993–94
Ken Schrom	1980, 1982
John Scott	1977
Steve Senteney	1982
Mike Sharperson	1987
Ron Shepherd	1984–86
Bill Singer	1977
Aaron Small	1994
Cory Snyder	1991
Luis Sojo	1990, 1993
Tony Solaita	1979
Paul Spoljaric	1994
Ed Sprague	1991–95
Randy St. Claire	1994
Steve Staggs	1977
Matt Stark	1987
Dave Stewart	1993–94
Shannon Stewart	1995
Dave Stieb	1979–92
Todd Stottlemyre	1988–94
Pat Tabler	1991–92
Lou Thornton	1985, 1987–88
Mike Timlin	1991–95
Jackson Todd	1979–81
Hector Torres	1977
Rick Trlicek	1992
Tom Underwood	1978–79
Willie Upshaw	1978, 1980–87
Otto Velez	1977–82
Ozzie Virgil	1989–90
Pete Vuckovich	1977
Dave Wallace	1978
Duane Ward	1986–93, 1995
Turner Ward	1991–93
Jeff Ware	1995
Dave Weathers	1991–92
Mitch Webster	1983–85
Boomer Wells	1981
David Wells	1987–92
Mickey Weston	1991
Devon White	1991–95
Mark Whiten	1990–91
Dan Whitmer	1981
Ernie Whitt	1977–78, 1980–89
Ted Wilborn	1979
Mark Wiley	1978
Matt Williams	1983
Kenny Williams	1990–91
Woody Williams	1993–95
Mike Willis	1977–81
Frank Wills	1988–91
Mookie Wilson	1989–91
Dave Winfield	1992
Gary Woods	1977–78
Al Woods	1977–82
Eddie Zosky	1991–92

Managers

Bobby Cox	1982–85
Cito Gaston	1989–95
Roy Hartsfield	1977–79
Bobby Mattick	1980–81
Gene Tenace	1991
Jimy Williams	1986–89

WASHINGTON Senators 1901–60
Known as Nationals 1901–56
Moved to MINNESOTA Twins

Ted Abernathy	1955–57, 1960
Merito Acosta	1913–16
Jose Acosta	1920–21
Rick Adams	1905
Spencer Adams	1925
Morrie Aderholt	1939–41
Dewey Adkins	1942–43
Sam Agnew	1919
Eddie Ainsmith	1910–18
Jerry Akers	1912
Joe Albanese	1958
Bob Allison	1958–60
Mel Almada	1937–38
Dave Altizer	1906–08
Nick Altrock	1909, 1912–15, 1918–19, 1924, 1929
Ossie Alvarez	1958
Red Anderson	1937, 1940–41
John Anderson	1905–07
Bill Andrus	1931
Pete Appleton	1936–39, 1945
George Archie	1941
Orville Armbrust	1934
Ken Aspromonte	1958–59
Jake Atz	1902
Doc Ayers	1913–19
Floyd Baker	1952–53
Jesse Baker	1919
Pelham Ballenger	1928
Win Ballou	1925
Turner Barber	1915–16
Bruce Barmes	1953
Red Barnes	1927–29
Bill Barrett	1930
Frank Barron	1914
Dick Bass	1939
Earl Battey	1960
Walter Beall	1929
Belve Bean	1935
Gene Bearden	1950–51
Heinie Beckendorf	1910
Charlie Becker	1911–12
Julio Becquer	1955, 1957–60
Allen Benson	1934
Jack Bentley	1913–16
Lou Berberet	1956–58
Moe Berg	1932–34
Johnny Berger	1927
Bob Berman	1918
Reno Bertoia	1959–60
Lou Bevil	1942
Harry Biemiller	1920
George Binks	1944–46
Red Bird	1921
Joe Black	1957
Cliff Blankenship	1907, 1909
Bruno Block	1907
Jimmy Bloodworth	1937, 1939–41
Ossie Bluege	1922–39
Joe Boehling	1912–16
Bob Boken	1933–34
Joe Bokina	1936
Ed Boland	1944
Milt Bolling	1957
Cliff Bolton	1931, 1933–36, 1941
Gus Bono	1920
Zeke Bonura	1938, 1940
Al Bool	1928
Harley Boss	1928–30
George Bradshaw	1952
Garland Braxton	1927–30
Ad Brennan	1918
Rocky Bridges	1957–58
Jim Brillheart	1922–23
Dick Brodowski	1956–57
Tony Brottem	1921
Frank Brower	1920–22
Alton Brown	1951
Lloyd Brown	1928–32
George Browne	1909–10
Garland Buckeye	1918
Bobby Burke	1927–35
Bill Burns	1908–09
Jim Busby	1952–55
Joe Bush	1926
Donie Bush	1921–22
Ed Butka	1943–44
Bud Byerly	1956–58
Tommy Byrne	1953
Paul Calvert	1949
Jack Calvo	1913, 1920
Archie Campbell	1929
Bruce Campbell	1942
John Campbell	1933
Frank Campos	1951–52
Milo Candini	1943–44, 1946–49
Scoops Carey	1902–03
Leon Carlson	1920
Lew Carpenter	1943
Alex Carrasquel	1939–45
Bill Carrick	1901–02
Scott Cary	1947
Joe Cascarella	1936–37
George Case	1937–45, 1947
Joe Casey	1918
Jay Cashion	1911–14
Harry Cassady	1905
Joe Cassidy	1904–05
Eli Cates	1908
Hardin Cathey	1942
Bob Chakales	1955–57
Ed Chapman	1933
Ben Chapman	1936–37, 1941
Mike Chartak	1942
Ken Chase	1936–41
Harry Child	1930
Walt Chipple	1945
Neil Chrisley	1957–58
Mark Christman	1947–49
Al Cicotte	1958
Jim Clark	1948
Webbo Clarke	1955
Boileryard Clarke	1901–04
Ellis Clary	1942–43
Joe Cleary	1945
Tex Clevenger	1956–60
Harlond Clift	1943–45
Billy Clingman	1901
Otis Clymer	1907–09
Gil Coan	1946–53
Dick Coffman	1927, 1932
Syd Cohen	1934, 1936–37
Orth Collins	1909
Merrill Combs	1950
Tom Connolly	1915
Wid Conroy	1909–11
Pep Conroy	1923
Billy Consolo	1959–60
Jim Constable	1958
Sandy Consuegra	1950–53
Pat Conway	1920
Charlie Conway	1911
Cal Cooper	1948
Henry Coppola	1935–36
Bill Coughlin	1901–04
Clint Courtney	1955–59
Henry Courtney	1919–22
Stan Coveleski	1925–27
Molly Craft	1916–19
Doc Cramer	1941
Sam Crane	1917
Gavvy Cravath	1909
Herb Crompton	1937
Joe Cronin	1928–34
Tom Crooke	1909–10
Lave Cross	1906–07
Frank Croucher	1942
General Crowder	1926–27, 1930–34
Ed Crowley	1928
Leon Culberson	1948
Roy Cullenbine	1942
Nick Cullop	1927
Bill Cunningham	1910–12
Bill Currie	1955
Vern Curtis	1943–44, 1946
Yo-Yo Davalillo	1953
Claude Davidson	1919
Ike Davis	1919
Rex Dawson	1913
Harry Dean	1941
Buddy Dear	1927
Ed Delahanty	1902–03
Jim Delahanty	1907–09
Juan Delis	1955
Gene DeMontreville	1903
Sam Dente	1949–51
Jimmie DeShong	1936–39
Bill Dietrich	1936
Roy Dietzel	1954
Jay Difani	1949
Reese Diggs	1934
Sonny Dixon	1953–54
Dan Dobbek	1959–60
Jiggs Donahue	1909
Tim Donahue	1902
Patsy Donovan	1904
Jack Doyle	1902
Buzz Dozier	1947, 1949
Larry Drake	1948
Lew Drill	1902–04
Tom Drohan	1913
Gus Dugas	1934
George Dumont	1915–18
Sam Dungan	1901
Davey Dunkle	1903–04
Bull Durham	1907
Jake Early	1939–43, 1946, 1948–49
Carl East	1924
Ed Edelen	1932
Sam Edmonston	1906–07
Bob Edmundson	1908
Bruce Edwards	1955
Kid Elberfeld	1910–11
Frank Ellerbe	1919–21
Bones Ely	1902
Joe Engel	1912–15, 1920
Russ Ennis	1926
Eric Erickson	1919–22
Cal Ermer	1947
Bobby Estalella	1935, 1939, 1942
Al Evans	1939–42, 1944–50
Joe Evans	1923
Bill Everitt	1901
Cy Falkenberg	1905–08
John Farrell	1901
Alex Ferguson	1925–26
Rick Ferrell	1937–41, 1944–45, 1947
Wes Ferrell	1937–38
Tom Ferrick	1947–48, 1951–52
Marc Filley	1934
Carl Fischer	1930–32, 1937
Bill Fischer	1958–60
Clarence Fisher	1919–20
Showboat Fisher	1923–24
Ed Fitz Gerald	1953–59
Ira Flagstead	1929
Angel Fleitas	1948
John Flynn	1912
Bill Forman	1909–10
Mike Fornieles	1952
George Foss	1921
Pop Foster	1901
Eddie Foster	1912–19
Ray Francis	1922
Jerry Freeman	1908–09
Skipper Friday	1923
Bob Friedrichs	1932
Chick Gagnon	1924
Nemo Gaines	1921
Stan Galle	1942
Bert Gallia	1912–17
Chick Gandil	1912–15
Bob Ganley	1907–09
Babe Ganzel	1927–28
Ramon Garcia	1948
Billy Gardner	1960
Milt Gaston	1928
Dale Gear	1901
Elmer Gedeon	1939
Joe Gedeon	1913–14
Henry Gehring	1907–08
Charley Gelbert	1939–40
Doc Gessler	1909–11
Al Gettel	1949
Patsy Gharrity	1916–17, 1919–23, 1930
Ed Gill	1919
Johnny Gill	1931, 1934
Carden Gillenwater	1948
Grant Gillis	1927–28
Tony Giuliani	1938–39, 1943
Joe Gleason	1920, 1922

Ed Goebel	1922
Chile Gomez	1942
Preston Gomez	1944
Lefty Gomez	1943
Vince Gonzales	1955
Julio Gonzalez	1949
Charlie Gooch	1929
Clyde Goodwin	1906
Marv Goodwin	1916
Ray Goolsby	1946
Goose Goslin	1921–30, 1933, 1938
Joe Grace	1946–47
Mike Grady	1901
Oscar Graham	1907
Mickey Grasso	1950–53
Milt Gray	1937
Dolly Gray	1909–11
Lenny Green	1959–60
Vean Gregg	1925
Bart Griffith	1924
Hal Griggs	1956–59
Connie Grob	1956
Bob Groom	1909–13
Harley Grossman	1952
Johnny Groth	1955
Roy Grover	1919
Mike Guerra	1937, 1944–46, 1951
Randy Gumpert	1952
Bump Hadley	1926–31, 1935
Mickey Haefner	1943–49
Dick Hahn	1940
Roy Hansen	1918
Harry Hardy	1905–06
Jack Hardy	1909–10
Pinky Hargrave	1923–25, 1930–31
Harry Harper	1913–19
Lum Harris	1947
Dave Harris	1930–34
Joe Harris	1925–26
Mickey Harris	1949–52
Spence Harris	1929
Bucky Harris	1919–28
Ben Harrison	1901
Earl Harrist	1948
Roy Hawes	1951
Jim Hayes	1935
Jackie Hayes	1927–31
Joe Haynes	1939–40, 1949–52
Jeff Heath	1946
Harry Hedgepath	1913
Jim Heise	1957
Frank Hemphill	1909
Jack Hendricks	1903
John Henry	1910–17
Phil Hensiek	1935
Evelio Hernandez	1956–57
Rudy Hernandez	1960
Walt Herrell	1911
Herb Herring	1912
Lefty Herring	1904
Whitey Herzog	1956–58
Mike Heydon	1905–07
Piano Legs Hickman	1905–07
Hunter Hill	1904–05
Jesse Hill	1936–37
Dutch Hinrichs	1910
Billy Hitchcock	1946
Lloyd Hittle	1949–50
Mel Hoderlein	1952–54
Izzy Hoffman	1904
Ray Hoffman	1942
Shanty Hogan	1936–37
Chief Hogsett	1938
Wally Holborow	1944–45
Sammy Holbrook	1935
Bill Hollahan	1920
Bill Holland	1939
Al Hollingsworth	1940
Bonnie Hollingsworth	1923
Ducky Holmes	1903
Paul Hopkins	1927, 1929
Bill Hopper	1915
Hick Hovlik	1918–19
Joe Hovlik	1909–10
Willis Hudlin	1940
Sid Hudson	1940–42, 1946–52
Frank Huelsman	1904–05
Long Tom Hughes	1904–09, 1911–13
Dick Hyde	1955, 1957–60
Bucky Jacobs	1937, 1939–40
Beany Jacobson	1904–05

Charlie Jamieson	1915–17
Hal Janvrin	1919
Tex Jeanes	1925–26
Jackie Jensen	1952–53
Don Johnson	1951–52
Ed Johnson	1920
Bob Johnson	1943
Walter Johnson	1907–27
Charlie Jones	1905–07
Dick Jones	1926–27
Sad Sam Jones	1928–31
Buck Jordan	1931
Rip Jordan	1919
Tim Jordan	1901
Ralph Judd	1927
Joe Judge	1915–32
Jim Kaat	1959–60
Mike Kahoe	1907–09
Alex Kampouris	1943
Bill Kay	1907
Burt Keeley	1908–09
Bill Keister	1902
Hal Keller	1950, 1952
Harry Kelley	1925–26, 1938–39
Bob Kelly	1909
Russ Kemmerer	1957–60
Ed Kenna	1928
Vern Kennedy	1941
Bill Kennedy	1942, 1946–47
Duke Kenworthy	1912
Gus Keriazakos	1954
John Kerr	1932–34
Harmon Killebrew	1954–60
Red Killefer	1909–10
Dick Kimble	1945
Wes Kingdon	1932
Frank Kitson	1906–07
Mal Kittridge	1903–06
Eddie Klieman	1949
Bobby Kline	1955
Bob Kline	1934
Elmer Klumpp	1934
Clyde Kluttz	1951–52
Lou Knerr	1947
John Knight	1912
Punch Knoll	1905
Joe Kohlman	1937–38
Merlin Kopp	1915
Steve Korcheck	1954–55, 1958–59
Al Kozar	1948–50
Joe Krakauskas	1937–40
Jack Kralick	1959–60
Mike Kreevich	1945
Red Kress	1934–36
Joe Kuhel	1930–37, 1944–46
Bob Kuzava	1950–51
Al Kvasnak	1942
Al LaMacchia	1946
Bobby LaMotte	1920–22
Dick Lanahan	1935, 1937
Doc Land	1929
Jerry Lane	1953
Sam Lanford	1907
Pete Lapan	1922
Frank LaPorte	1912–13
Lyn Lary	1935
Doc Lavan	1918
Hilly Layne	1941, 1944–45
Don Lee	1960
Watty Lee	1901–03
Bill Lefebvre	1943–44
Wade Lefler	1924
Nemo Leibold	1923–25
Ed Leip	1939
Jack Lelivelt	1909–11
Jim Lemon	1954–60
Dutch Leonard	1938–46
Joe Leonard	1916–17, 1919
Charlie Letchas	1941
Jesse Levan	1954
Duffy Lewis	1921
Buddy Lewis	1935–41, 1945–47, 1949
Ed Linke	1933–37
Hod Lisenbee	1927–28
Ad Liska	1929–31
Mickey Livingston	1938
Bobby Loane	1939
George Loepp	1930
Frank Loftus	1926
Tommy Long	1911
Slim Love	1913

Ralph Lumenti	1957–59
Charlie Luskey	1901
Lyle Luttrell	1956–57
Jim Lyle	1925
Jerry Lynn	1937
Ed Lyons	1947
Danny MacFayden	1941
Felix Mackiewicz	1947
Hector Maestri	1960
Bobby Malkmus	1958–59
Jim Mallory	1940
Frank Mancuso	1947
Moxie Manuel	1905
Heinie Manush	1930–35
Howard Maple	1932
Firpo Marberry	1923–32, 1936
Red Marion	1935, 1943
Connie Marrero	1950–54
Freddie Marsh	1952
Joe Martin	1903
Joe Martina	1924
Rogelio Martinez	1950
Del Mason	1904
Walt Masters	1931
Walt Masterson	1939–42, 1945–49, 1952–53
Henry Matteson	1918
Wid Matthews	1924–25
Carmen Mauro	1953
Sam Mayer	1915
Bill McAfee	1932–33
Tom McAvoy	1959
George McBride	1908–20
Tom McBride	1947–48
Alex McColl	1933–34
Mike McCormick	1951
Barry McCormick	1903–04
Paul McCullough	1929
Phil McCullough	1942
Mickey McDermott	1954–55
John McDonald	1907
Howie McFarland	1945
Tubby McGee	1925
Slim McGrew	1922–24
Vance McIlree	1921
Mac McLean	1935
Jim McLeod	1930, 1932
Mike McNally	1925
George McNamara	1922
Earl McNeely	1924–27
Sammy Meeks	1948
Sam Mele	1949–52
Mike Menosky	1916–17, 1919
Win Mercer	1901
Jim Mertz	1943
Irish Meusel	1914
Cass Michaels	1950–52
John Mihalic	1935–37
Horace Milan	1915, 1917
Clyde Milan	1907–21
Dee Miles	1935–36
Bing Miller	1921
Ox Miller	1943
Ralph Miller	1921
Ralph Miller	1924
Ronnie Miller	1941
Warren Miller	1909, 1911
Wally Millies	1936–37
John Milligan	1934
Don Mincher	1960
Don Minnick	1957
Willie Miranda	1951
Mike Mitchell	1914
Monroe Mitchell	1923
Danny Moeller	1912–16
George Mogridge	1921–25
Rene Monteagudo	1938, 1940, 1944
Carlos Moore	1930
Gene Moore	1942–43
Ray Moore	1960
Charlie Moran	1903–04
Roy Moran	1912
Julio Moreno	1950–53
Ray Morgan	1911–18
Tom Morgan	1960
Bill Morley	1913
Bill Morrell	1926
Charlie Moyer	1910
Dick Mulligan	1941
George Mullin	1913
Jim Mullin	1904–05
Buzz Murphy	1919

George Murray	1926–27
Bobby Murray	1923
Bill Murray	1917
Paul Musser	1912
Danny Musser	1932
George Myatt	1943–47
Buddy Myer	1925–27, 1929–41
Steve Nagy	1950
Hal Naragon	1959–60
Doug Neff	1914–15
Bobo Newsom	1935–37, 1942–43, 1946–47, 1952
Johnny Niggeling	1943–46
Rabbit Nill	1904–07
Irv Noren	1950–52
Frank Oberlin	1907, 1909–10
Jack O'Brien	1901
Pete O'Brien	1907
Tommy O'Brien	1950
Curly Ogden	1924–26
Joe Ohl	1909
Len Okrie	1948, 1950–51
Bob Oldis	1953–55
Karl Olson	1956–57
Mickey O'Neil	1927
Jim O'Neill	1920, 1923
Bill O'Neill	1904
Eddie Onslow	1927
Ernie Oravetz	1955–56
Frank O'Rourke	1920–21
Al Orth	1902–04
Baby Ortiz	1944
Roberto Ortiz	1941–44, 1949–50
Champ Osteen	1903
John Ostrowski	1950
Bill Otey	1910–11
Tom Padden	1943
Mike Palagyi	1939
Emilio Palmero	1926
Camilo Pascual	1954–60
Carlos Pascual	1950
Casey Patten	1901–08
Carlos Paula	1954–56
Jim Pearce	1949–50, 1953
Albie Pearson	1958–59
Roger Peckinpaugh	1922–26
Les Peden	1953
Barney Pelty	1912
Nig Perrine	1907
Johnny Pesky	1954
Leon Pettit	1935
Bill Phebus	1936–38
Eddie Phillips	1934
Tom Phillips	1921–22
Val Picinich	1918–22
Charlie Pick	1914
Ollie Pickering	1908
Marino Pieretti	1945–48
Alex Pitko	1939
Herb Plews	1956–59
Jimmy Pofahl	1940–42
Dan Porter	1951
J. W. Porter	1959
Bob Porterfield	1951–55
Squire Potter	1923
Jake Powell	1930, 1934–36, 1943–45
Bob Prichard	1939
Gerry Priddy	1943, 1946–47
Ray Prim	1933–34
Doc Prothro	1920, 1923–24
Spence Pumpelly	1925
Ewald Pyle	1943
Hal Quick	1939
Joe Quinn	1901
Frank Ragland	1932
Doc Ralston	1910
Pedro Ramos	1955–60
Earl Rapp	1952
Jack Redmond	1935
Stan Rees	1918
Bobby Reeves	1926–28
Doc Reisling	1909–10
Bob Repass	1942
Carl Reynolds	1932, 1936
Sam Rice	1915–33
Harry Rice	1931
Lance Richbourg	1924
Johnny Riddle	1937

Topper Rigney	1927
Jim Riley	1923
Roxy Roach	1912
Red Roberts	1943
Dick Robertson	1919
Sherry Robertson	1940–41, 1943, 1946–51
Rabbit Robinson	1903
Eddie Robinson	1949–50
Armando Roche	1945
Clay Roe	1923
Buck Rogers	1935
Tony Roig	1953, 1955–56
John Romonosky	1958–59
Henri Rondeau	1915–16
Bob Ross	1950–51
Braggo Roth	1920
Claude Rothgeb	1905
Muddy Ruel	1923–30
Dutch Ruether	1925–26
Pete Runnels	1951–57
Allan Russell	1923–25
Jack Russell	1933–36
Jimmy Ryan	1902–03
John Ryan	1912–13

Alex Sabo	1936–37
Frank Sacka	1951, 1953
Ted Sadowski	1960
Ron Samford	1959
Raul Sanchez	1952
Jack Sanford	1940–41, 1946
Fred Sanford	1951
Don Savidge	1929
Carl Sawyer	1915–16
Ray Scarborough	1942–43, 1946–50
Al Schacht	1919–21
Germany Schaefer	1909–14
Johnny Schaive	1958–60
Owen Scheetz	1943
Lefty Schegg	1912
Fred Schemanske	1923
Harry Schlafly	1906–07
Johnny Schmitz	1953–55
Jerry Schoonmaker	1955, 1957
Art Schult	1957
Wildfire Schulte	1918
Fred Schulte	1933–35
Everett Scott	1925
Jimmy Sebring	1909
Duke Sedgwick	1923
Kip Selbach	1903–04
Hank Severeid	1925–26
Luke Sewell	1933–34
Howard Shanks	1912–22
Warren Shannabrook	1906
Red Shannon	1920
Owen Shannon	1907
Shag Shaughnessy	1905
Jim Shaw	1913–21
Spec Shea	1952–55
Bert Shepard	1945
Fred Sherry	1911
Garland Shifflett	1957
Bill Shipke	1907–09
Art Shires	1930
Duke Shirey	1920
Mule Shirley	1924–25
Burt Shotton	1918
Roy Sievers	1954–59
Danny Silva	1919
Al Sima	1950–51, 1953
Al Simmons	1937–38
John Simmons	1949
Elmer Singleton	1950
Fred Sington	1934–37
George Sisler	1928
Jack Slattery	1909
Lou Sleater	1952
Tony Smith	1907
Carr Smith	1923–24
Charlie Smith	1906–09
Earl Smith	1921–22
Elmer Smith	1916–17
Wally Smith	1914
Jerry Snyder	1952–58
Bill Snyder	1919–20
Jock Somerlott	1910–11
Dick Spalding	1928
Tris Speaker	1927
Byron Speece	1924
Stan Spence	1942–44, 1946–47
Ben Spencer	1913
Roy Spencer	1929–32
Jack Spring	1958
Jake Stahl	1904–06
Joe Stanley	1902, 1905–06
Con Starkell	1906
Dick Starr	1951
Chick Starr	1935–36
Jim Stevens	1914
Bud Stewart	1948–50
Stuffy Stewart	1925–27, 1929
Bunky Stewart	1952–56
Lefty Stewart	1933–35
Chuck Stobbs	1953–60
Dick Stone	1945
Dean Stone	1953–57
John Stone	1934–38
Alan Strange	1935
Gabby Street	1908–11
Luis Suarez	1944
Willie Sudhoff	1906
Denny Sullivan	1905
John Sullivan	1942–44, 1947–48
Steve Sundra	1941–42
Pete Susko	1934
Dizzy Sutherland	1949

Jesse Tannehill	1908–09
Bennie Tate	1924–30
Hugh Tate	1905
Walt Tauscher	1931
Danny Taylor	1926
Fred Taylor	1950–52
Tommy Taylor	1924
Wayne Terwilliger	1953–54
Dick Tettelbach	1956–57
Jug Thesenga	1944
Tommy Thomas	1932–35
Lefty Thomas	1925–26
Claude Thomas	1916
Fred Thomas	1920
Kite Thomas	1953
Bud Thomas	1932–33, 1939
Myles Thomas	1929–30
Dave Thompson	1948–49
Harry Thompson	1919
Jack Thoney	1904
Faye Throneberry	1957–60
Lou Thuman	1939–40
Sloppy Thurston	1927
Joe Tipton	1954
Jack Tobin	1926
Hal Toenes	1947
Doc Tonkin	1907
Gil Torres	1940, 1944–46
Ricardo Torres	1920–22
Jack Townsend	1902–05
Cecil Travis	1933–41, 1945–47
Ray Treadaway	1930
Frank Trechock	1937
Bill Trotter	1942
Ollie Tucker	1927
Lucas Turk	1922
George Twombly	1919

Jimmy Uchrinsko	1926
Sandy Ullrich	1944–45
Tommy Umphlett	1954–55
Bob Unglaub	1908–10
Tom Upton	1952
Bob Usher	1957

Jose Valdivielso	1955–56, 1959–60
Vito Valentinetti	1958–59
Elmer Valo	1960
Clay Van Alstyne	1927–28
Buck Varner	1952
Fred Vaughn	1944–45
Hippo Vaughn	1912
Bobby Veach	1925
Vince Ventura	1945
Gene Verble	1951, 1953
Mickey Vernon	1939–43, 1946–48, 1950–55
Zoilo Versalles	1959–60
Clyde Vollmer	1948–50, 1953–54
Cy Vorhees	1902
Joe Vosmik	1944

Jake Wade	1946
Rip Wade	1923
Howard Wakefield	1906
Doc Waldbauer	1917
Irv Waldron	1901
Tilly Walker	1911–12
Dixie Walker	1909–12
Gee Walker	1940
Murray Wall	1959
Cy Warmoth	1922–23
Jack Warner	1906–08
Jimmy Wasdell	1937–40
Allie Watt	1920
Jim Weaver	1928
Monte Weaver	1931–38
Ralph Weigel	1949
Dick Weik	1948–50
Johnny Welaj	1939–41
Dick Welteroth	1948–50
Sammy West	1927–32, 1938–41
Pete Whisenant	1960
Steve White	1912
Earl Whitehill	1933–36
Charlie Whitehouse	1919
Bob Wiesler	1956–58
Buff Williams	1912–16
Mutt Williams	1913–14
Otto Williams	1906
Archie Wilson	1952
Maxie Wilson	1946
Highball Wilson	1903–04
Chink Wilson	1906
Jack Wilson	1942
John Wilson	1913
Tom Wilson	1914
Ed Wineapple	1929
Ted Wingfield	1923–24
Roy Witherup	1908–09
Bill Wolfe	1904–06
Roger Wolff	1944–46
Harry Wolverton	1902
Ken Wood	1952–53
Hal Woodeshick	1959–60
Frank Woodward	1921–22
Earl Wooten	1947–48
Taffy Wright	1938–39
Tom Wright	1954
Early Wynn	1939, 1941–44, 1946–48
Hank Wyse	1951

Earl Yingling	1918
Bill Yohe	1909
Eddie Yost	1944, 1946–58
Chief Youngblood	1922

Tom Zachary	1919–25, 1927–28
Paul Zahniser	1923–24
Jose Zardon	1945
Norm Zauchin	1958–59
Bill Zinser	1944
Bill Zuber	1941–42

Managers

Ossie Bluege	1943–47
Donie Bush	1923
Joe Cantillon	1907–09
*Joe Cronin	1933–34
*Patsy Donovan	1904
Chuck Dressen	1955–57
Clark Griffith	1912–20
*Bucky Harris	1924–28, 1935–42, 1950–54
Walter Johnson	1929–32
*Mal Kittridge	1904
Joe Kuhel	1948–49
Cookie Lavagetto	1957–60
Tom Loftus	1902–03
Jimmy Manning	1901
Jimmy McAleer	1910–11
George McBride	1921
Clyde Milan	1922
*Jake Stahl	1905–06

WASHINGTON Senators 1961–71

Moved to TEXAS Rangers

Bernie Allen	1967–71
Hank Allen	1966–70
Brant Alyea	1965, 1968–69

Bob Baird	1962–63
Dave Baldwin	1966–69
Frank Bertaina	1967–69
Larry Biittner	1971
Dick Billings	1968–71
Don Blasingame	1963–66
Chet Boak	1961
Dick Bosman	1966–71
Carl Bouldin	1961–64
Sam Bowens	1968–69
Marv Breeding	1963
Marshall Bridges	1964–65
Harry Bright	1961–62
Ed Brinkman	1961–70
Pete Broberg	1971
Jim Bronstad	1963–64
Tom Brown	1963
Jackie Brown	1970–71
Mike Brumley	1964–66
George Brunet	1970
Billy Bryan	1968
Pete Burnside	1961–63
Jeff Burroughs	1970–71

Doug Camilli	1965–67, 1969
Cisco Carlos	1969–70
Paul Casanova	1965–71
Bob Chance	1965–67
Tom Cheney	1961–64, 1966
Al Closter	1966
Jim Coates	1963
Frank Coggins	1967–68
Joe Coleman	1965–70
Wayne Comer	1970
Chuck Cottier	1961–64
Casey Cox	1966–71
Pete Craig	1964–66
Tim Cullen	1966–71
Joe Cunningham	1964–66

Pete Daley	1961
Bennie Daniels	1961–65
Bill Denehy	1968
Dick Donovan	1961
Dutch Dotterer	1961
Jim Duckworth	1963–66
Jan Dukes	1969–70
Ryne Duren	1965

Mike Epstein	1967–71

Bill Fahey	1971
Frank Fernandez	1971
Curt Flood	1971
Joe Foy	1971
Jim French	1965–71

John Gabler	1961
Mike Garcia	1961
Bill Gogolewski	1970–71
Greg Goossen	1970
Gene Green	1961
Freddie Green	1962
Dallas Green	1965
Tom Grieve	1970
Joe Grzenda	1970–71

Steve Hamilton	1962–63
Ken Hamlin	1962, 1965–66
Jim Hannan	1962–70
Ron Hansen	1968
Toby Harrah	1969, 1971
Ken Harrelson	1966–67
Bill Haywood	1968
Roy Heiser	1961
Woodie Held	1965
Rudy Hernandez	1961
Joe Hicks	1961–62
Dennis Higgins	1968–69
Chuck Hinton	1961–64
Ed Hobaugh	1961–63
Gary Holman	1968–69
Bruce Howard	1968
Frank Howard	1965–71
Bob Humphreys	1966–70
Ken Hunt	1963–64

Gerry Janeski	1971
Jack Jenkins	1962–63
Bob Johnson	1961–62
Steve Jones	1968

John Kennedy	1962–64
Marty Keough	1961
Jim King	1961–67
Willie Kirkland	1964–66
Billy Klaus	1961
Lou Klimchock	1963
Ron Kline	1963–66

Johnny Klippstein	1961
Darold Knowles	1967–71
Alan Koch	1964
Howie Koplitz	1964–66
Frank Kreutzer	1964–66, 1969
Marty Kutyna	1961–62
Hobie Landrith	1963
Don Leppert	1963–64
Paul Lindblad	1971
Dick Lines	1966–67
Don Lock	1962–66
Dale Long	1961–62
Don Loun	1964
Elliott Maddox	1971
Hector Maestri	1961
Jim Mahoney	1961
Gene Martin	1968
Jim Mason	1971
Carl Mathias	1961
Lee Maye	1969–70
Joe McCabe	1965
Joe McClain	1961–62
Mike McCormick	1965–66
Tom McCraw	1971
Denny McLain	1971
Ken McMullen	1965–70
Jim Miles	1968–69
Don Mincher	1971
Minnie Minoso	1963
Ron Moeller	1963
Barry Moore	1965–69
Buster Narum	1964–67
Cal Neeman	1963
Dave Nelson	1970–71
Dick Nen	1965–67, 1970
Dick Nold	1967
Danny O'Connell	1961–62
John Orsino	1966
Phil Ortega	1965–68
Bobo Osborne	1963
Claude Osteen	1961–64
Camilo Pascual	1967–69
Cap Peterson	1967–68
Dick Phillips	1963–64, 1966
Jimmy Piersall	1962–63
Horacio Pina	1970–71
Bob Priddy	1967
Art Quirk	1963
Tom Ragland	1971
Pedro Ramos	1970
Lenny Randle	1971
Rick Reichardt	1970
Ken Retzer	1961–64
Pete Richert	1965–67
Denny Riddleberger	1970–71
Steve Ridzik	1963–65
Ray Rippelmeyer	1962
Aurelio Rodriguez	1970
Ed Roebuck	1963–64
Johnny Roseboro	1970
Don Rudolph	1962–64
Bob Saverine	1966–67
Johnny Schaive	1962
Richie Scheinblum	1971
Bob Schmidt	1962–63
Gerry Schoen	1968
Diego Segui	1966
Jim Shellenback	1969–71
Roy Sievers	1964–65
Dave Sisler	1961
Bill Skowron	1964
Dick Smith	1969
Rick Stelmaszek	1971
Dave Stenhouse	1962–64
R C Stevens	1961
Ron Stillwell	1961–62
Ed Stroud	1967–70
Tom Sturdivant	1961
Dick Such	1970
Willie Tasby	1961–62
Mike Thompson	1971
Del Unser	1968–71
Fred Valentine	1964–68
Coot Veal	1961
Zoilo Versalles	1969
Don Wert	1971
Nick Willhite	1965
Hal Woodeshick	1961
Gene Woodling	1961–62
Don Zimmer	1963–65
Bud Zipfel	1961–62

Managers

Gil Hodges	1963–67
Jim Lemon	1968
Mickey Vernon	1961–63
Ted Williams	1969–71
Eddie Yost	1963

American Association

BALTIMORE Orioles 1882–91
Moved to National League

John Ake	1884
Doug Allison	1883
Jersey Bakely	1891
George Baker	1883
Norm Baker	1890
Phil Baker	1883
Ned Bligh	1886
Amos Booth	1882
George Bradley	1888
Cal Broughton	1883
Joe Brown	1885
Tom Brown	1882
Pat Burns	1884
Oyster Burns	1884–85, 1887–88
Frank Burt	1882
Bart Cantz	1888–89
Dennis Casey	1884–85
Monk Cline	1882
Jim Clinton	1883–84, 1886
Dick Conway	1886
Bill Conway	1886
Bert Cunningham	1888–89, 1891
Law Daniels	1887
Jumbo Davis	1886–87
Gene Derby	1885
Jim Devine	1883
Buttercup Dickerson	1884
Tom Dolan	1886
Joe Dowie	1889
Harry East	1882
Dave Eggler	1883
Bob Emslie	1883–85
Jake Evans	1885
Tom Evers	1882
Jack Farrell	1888–89
Joe Farrell	1886
Bill Farrell	1883
Jim Field	1885
Frank Foreman	1885, 1889
John Fox	1883
Chris Fulmer	1886–89
Bill Gallagher	1883
Gid Gardner	1883–85
Bill Gardner	1887
Emil Geis	1882
Les German	1890
Pete Gilbert	1890–91
George Goetz	1889
Walt Goldsby	1888
Fred Goldsmith	1884
Bill Greenwood	1887–88
Ed Greer	1885–86
Mike Griffin	1887–89
Lew Hardie	1891
John Harkins	1888
Jack Hayes	1887
Egyptian Healy	1891
Tony Hellman	1886
Hardie Henderson	1883–86
John Henry	1885
Belden Hill	1890
Will Holland	1889
Buster Hoover	1886
Joe Hornung	1889
Sadie Houck	1886
Charlie Householder	1882
Frank Houseman	1886
Charlie Ingraham	1883
Harry Jacoby	1882, 1885
Bill Johnson	1890–91
Bill Jones	1882
Ed Keating	1887
Kick Kelly	1883
John Kerins	1889
Matt Kilroy	1886–89
Mike Kilroy	1888
Ed Knouff	1886–87
Doc Landis	1882
Jack Leary	1882–83
Charlie Levis	1885
Dan Long	1890
Bill Loughlin	1883
Reddy Mack	1889–90
Jimmy Macullar	1884–86
Kid Madden	1891
Jack Manning	1886
Tim Manning	1883–85
George Mappes	1885
Jerry McCormick	1883
Tom McDermott	1885
Chippy McGarr	1889
Jumbo McGinnis	1886
John McGraw	1891
Joe McGuckin	1890
Jim McLaughlin	1884
Sadie McMahon	1890–91
Dusty Miller	1889
Mike Morrison	1890
Billy Mountjoy	1885
Mike Muldoon	1885–86
Henry Myers	1882
Sandy Nava	1885–86
Jack Neagle	1883
Tricky Nichols	1882
Jack O'Brien	1888
Tom O'Brien	1883, 1885
John O'Connell	1891
Pat O'Connell	1886
Dave Oldfield	1883
Mike O'Rourke	1890
John Peltz	1888
Gracie Pierce	1882
Abner Powell	1886
Tom Power	1890
Phil Powers	1885
Blondie Purcell	1886–88
Tom Quinn	1889
Irv Ray	1889–91
Billy Reid	1883
Wilbert Robinson	1890–91
Dave Rowe	1883
Jim Roxburgh	1884
John Russ	1882
Lew Say	1883
Nick Scharf	1882–83
Milt Scott	1886
Sam Shaw	1888
John Shetzline	1882
Bill Shindle	1888–89
Lev Shreve	1887
Bill Smiley	1882
Phenomenal Smith	1887–88
L. Smith	1882
Joe Sommer	1884–90
Len Sowders	1886
Dan Stearns	1883–85
Rooney Sweeney	1883
Pop Tate	1889–90
Billy Taylor	1886
John Tener	1885
George Townsend	1890–91
Bill Traffley	1884–86
Sam Trott	1884–85, 1887–88
Tommy Tucker	1887–89
George Van Haltren	1891
Joe Visner	1885
Charlie Waitt	1882
George Walker	1888
Oscar Walker	1885
Joe Walsh	1891
Curt Welch	1890–91
Perry Werden	1891
Shorty Wetzel	1885
Pat Whitaker	1888–89
Ed Whiting	1882
Sam Wise	1891
Bill Wise	1882
George Wood	1889
Tom York	1884–85
Zay	1886

Managers

Billy Barnie	1883–91
*Henry Myers	1882

BOSTON Reds 1891
Moved from Players League

Dan Brouthers	1891
Tom Brown	1891
Charlie Buffinton	1891
Tom Cotter	1891
Bill Daley	1891
Tim Donahue	1891
Tommy Dowd	1891
Hugh Duffy	1891
Duke Farrell	1891
John Fitzgerald	1891
Mike Flynn	1891
Clark Griffith	1891
George Haddock	1891
John Irwin	1891
Bill Joyce	1891
King Kelly	1891
Kid Madden	1891
Jack McGeachy	1891
Morg Murphy	1891
Darby O'Brien	1891
Frank Quinlan	1891
Paul Radford	1891
Hardy Richardson	1891
Cub Stricker	1891

Managers

Arthur Irwin	1891

BROOKLYN Trolley-Dodgers 1884–89
Known as Bridegrooms 1889
Moved to National League

Frank Bell	1885
Ike Benners	1884
Ernie Burch	1886–87
Jack Burdock	1888
Oyster Burns	1888–89
Doc Bushong	1888–89
Bob Caruthers	1888–89
John Cassidy	1884–85
Bob Clark	1886–89
Hub Collins	1888–89
Jim Conway	1884

John Corcoran	1884
Pop Corkhill	1888–89
Bert Cunningham	1887
Jerry Dorgan	1884
John Farrow	1884
Dave Foutz	1888–89
Billy Geer	1884
Bill Greenwood	1884
Ed Greer	1887
John Harkins	1885–87
Jack Hayes	1884–85
Hardie Henderson	1886–87
Mike Hines	1885
Bill Holbert	1888
Pete Hotaling	1885
Charlie Householder	1884
Mickey Hughes	1888–89
Charlie Jones	1884
Ed Kennedy	1886
Sam Kimber	1884
Jimmy Knowles	1884
Bill Krieg	1885
Tom Lovett	1889
Al Mays	1888
Jim McCauley	1886
Bill McClellan	1885–88
Jim McTamany	1885–87
George McVey	1885
Jack O'Brien	1887
Darby O'Brien	1888–89
Dave Oldfield	1885–86
Dave Orr	1888
Billy Otterson	1887
Jimmy Peoples	1885–88
Bill Phillips	1885–87
George Pinckney	1885–89
Henry Porter	1885–87
Paul Radford	1888
Jack Remsen	1884
Charlie Reynolds	1889
Charlie Robinson	1885
Chief Roseman	1887
Bill Schenck	1885
Pop Schriver	1886
Ed Silch	1888
Germany Smith	1885–89
Phenomenal Smith	1885
Joe Strauss	1886
Ed Swartwood	1885–87
Adonis Terry	1884–89
Steve Toole	1886–87
Joe Visner	1889
Oscar Walker	1884
Fred Warner	1884
Hickie Wilson	1884

Managers

Charlie Byrne	1885–87
Charlie Hackett	1885
Bill McGunnigle	1888–89
George Taylor	1884

BROOKLYN Gladiators 1890

Frank Bowes	1890
Hi Church	1890
Ed Daily	1890
Jumbo Davis	1890
Frank Fennelly	1890
Tom Ford	1890
Joe Gerhardt	1890
Jack Lynch	1890
Mike Mattimore	1890
Charlie McCullough	1890
Con Murphy	1890
Candy Nelson	1890
Billy O'Brien	1890
Pat O'Connell	1890
John Peltz	1890
Herman Pitz	1890
Jim Powers	1890
Fred Siefke	1890
Henry Simon	1890
Steve Toole	1890
Jim Toy	1890
Gus Williams	1890

Managers

Jim Kennedy	1890

CINCINNATI Red Stockings 1882–89
Moved to National League

Kid Baldwin	1885–89
Ollie Beard	1889
Frank Berkelbach	1884
Dan Bickham	1886
Ned Bligh	1888
Jack Boyle	1886
Hick Carpenter	1882–89
Jim Clinton	1885
Ted Conovar	1889
Pop Corkhill	1883–88
Ren Deagle	1883–84
Jesse Duryea	1889
Billy Earle	1889
Frank Fennelly	1884–88
Chick Fulmer	1882–84
Bug Holliday	1889
Bill Irwin	1886
Charley Jones	1883–87
Heinie Kappel	1887–88
Jim Keenan	1885–89
Rudy Kemmler	1882
Fred Lewis	1886
Henry Luff	1882
Jimmy Macullar	1882–83
Tom Mansell	1884
Lefty Marr	1886
Leech Maskrey	1886
Harry McCaffrey	1885
Harry McCormick	1882–83
Jumbo McGinnis	1887
Larry McKeon	1885–86
Bid McPhee	1882–89
George Miller	1884
Billy Mountjoy	1883–85
Tony Mullane	1886–89
Joe Murphy	1886
Hugh Nicol	1887–89
Jack O'Connor	1887–88
John Parsons	1884
George Pechiney	1885–86
Jimmy Peoples	1884–85
Charlie Petty	1889
Abner Powell	1886
Phil Powers	1882–85
Jerry Reardon	1886
Icicle Reeder	1884
Long John Reilly	1883–89
Lee Richmond	1886
Billy Serad	1887–88
Gus Shallix	1884–85
Mike Shea	1887
Elmer Smith	1886–89
Smith	1886
Pop Snyder	1882–86
Joe Sommer	1882–83
Dan Stearns	1882
Clarence Stephens	1886
Lou Sylvester	1886
White Wings Tebeau	1887–89
Tug Thompson	1882
Bill Tierney	1882
Bill Traffley	1883
Farmer Vaughn	1886
Lee Viau	1888–89
Mother Watson	1887
Podgie Weihe	1883
Buck West	1884
John Weyhing	1888
Harry Wheeler	1882
Will White	1882–86
Wild Bill Widner	1887
Jimmy Woulfe	1884

Managers

Ollie Caylor	1885–86
Gus Schmelz	1887–89
*Pop Snyder	1882–84
*Will White	1884

CINCINNATI Kellys 1891
Moved to MILWAUKEE Brewers

Ed Andrews	1891
Charlie Bastian	1891
Charlie Bell	1891
Joe Burke	1891
Jimmy Canavan	1891
Jack Carney	1891
Billy Clingman	1891
Cannonball Crane	1891
Frank Dwyer	1891
Jerry Hurley	1891
Dick Johnston	1891
Kid Keenan	1891
King Kelly	1891
Matt Kilroy	1891
Willard Mains	1891
Lefty Marr	1891
Willie McGill	1891
Yank Robinson	1891
Emmett Seery	1891
John Slagle	1891
Farmer Vaughn	1891
Art Whitney	1891
Wild Bill Widner	1891

Managers

*King Kelly	1891

CLEVELAND Blues 1887–88
Moved to National League

Gus Alberts	1888
Myron Allen	1887
Jersey Bakely	1888
Scrappy Carroll	1887
Billy Crowell	1887–88
One Arm Daily	1887
Jay Faatz	1888
Ed Flynn	1887
Bob Gilks	1887–88
Mike Goodfellow	1888
Ed Herr	1887
Eddie Hogan	1888
Pete Hotaling	1887–88
Ed Keas	1888
John Kirby	1887
Ed Knouff	1888
Fred Mann	1887
Bill McClellan	1888
John McGlone	1887–88
Deacon McGuire	1888
Ed McKean	1887–88
Mike Morrison	1887–88
John Munyan	1887
Doc Oberlander	1888
Darby O'Brien	1888
George Pechiney	1887
George Proeser	1888
Phil Reccius	1887
Charlie Reipschlager	1887
Jimmy Say	1887
Frank Scheibeck	1887
Henry Simon	1887
Pop Snyder	1887–88
Bill Stemmeyer	1888
Cub Stricker	1887–88
Charlie Sweeney	1887
Jim Toy	1887
Dick Van Zant	1888
Chief Zimmer	1887–88

Managers

Tom Loftus	1888
Jimmy Williams	1887–88

COLUMBUS Buckeyes 1883–84

Al Bauers	1884
Tom Brown	1883–84
John Cahill	1884
Fred Carroll	1884
Ed Dundon	1883–84
Jim Field	1883–84
Pete Fries	1883
Rudy Kemmler	1883–84
Willie Kuehne	1883–84
Fred Mann	1883–84
Tom Mansell	1884
Frank McIntyre	1883
Ed Morris	1884
Frank Mountain	1883–84
Gracie Pierce	1883
John Richmond	1883–84
Pop Schwartz	1883
Pop Smith	1883–84
Joe Straub	1883
Tom Sullivan	1884
John Valentine	1883
Harry Wheeler	1883

Managers

Horace Phillips	1883
Gus Schmelz	1884

COLUMBUS Buckeyes 1889–91

Mark Baldwin	1889
Ned Bligh	1889–90

Icebox Chamberlain 1890
Ed Clark 1891
Dad Clarke 1891
Elmer Cleveland 1891
Jack Crooks 1889–91

Ed Daily 1889
John Dolan 1891
Jim Donahue 1891
Jim Donnelly 1891
Tom Dowse 1891
Jack Doyle 1889–90
Charlie Duffee 1891

Henry Easterday 1889–90
John Easton 1889–91

Tom Ford 1890

Hank Gastright 1889–91
Bill George 1889
Bill Greenwood 1889

Spud Johnson 1889–90

Heinie Kappel 1889
Rudy Kemmler 1889
Frank Knauss 1890
Phil Knell 1891
Willie Kuehne 1891

Mickey Lehane 1890–91
Jack Leiper 1891
Bill Lyston 1891

Lefty Marr 1889
Al Mays 1889–90
Sparrow McCaffrey 1889
Jim McTamany 1889–91
John Munyan 1890

Sam Nichol 1890

Jack O'Connor 1889–91
Tim O'Rourke 1891
Dave Orr 1889

Jimmy Peoples 1889

Charlie Reilly 1889–90

Jack Sneed 1890–91
Jim Sullivan 1891

Larry Twitchell 1891

John Weyhing 1889
Bobby Wheelock 1890–91
Wild Bill Widner 1889–90

Managers

Al Buckenberger 1889–90
Gus Schmelz 1890–91
Pat Sullivan 1890

INDIANAPOLIS Hoosiers 1884

Jake Aydelott 1884

Bob Barr 1884
Marty Barrett 1884
Bob Blakiston 1884
Tommy Bond 1884
Bill Butler 1884

Pat Callahan 1884
Chub Collins 1884

Harry Decker 1884
Jim Donnelly 1884
Jerry Dorgan 1884

Pete Fries 1884

Jim Holdsworth 1884

Jim Keenan 1884
John Kerins 1884

Charlie Levis 1884
Marshall Locke 1884

Mac MacArthur 1884
Al McCauley 1884
Larry McKeon 1884
Ed Merrill 1884
Frank Monroe 1884
Gene Moriarity 1884
Jon Morrison 1884
George Mundinger 1884

John Peltz 1884
Marr Phillips 1884

Charlie Reising 1884
Charlie Robinson 1884

Jack Sneed 1884

Tug Thompson 1884
Jim Tray 1884

Bill Watkins 1884
Harry Weber 1884
Podgie Weihe 1884

Managers

Jim Gifford 1884
*Bill Watkins 1884

KANSAS CITY Cowboys 1888–89

Myron Allen 1888
Billy Alvord 1889

Sam Barkley 1888–89
John Bates 1889
Charlie Bell 1889
Red Bittmann 1889
Jim Brennan 1888
Fatty Briody 1888
Jim Burns 1888–89

Monk Cline 1888
Jim Conway 1889

Law Daniels 1888
Jumbo Davis 1888–89
Jim Donahue 1888–89

Henry Easterday 1888
Red Ehret 1888

Bill Fagan 1888

Ed Glenn 1888
Joe Gunson 1889

Frank Hafner 1888
Billy Hamilton 1888–89
Frank Hankinson 1888
Frank Hoffman 1888
Charlie Hoover 1888–89

Charley Jones 1888

John Kirby 1888

Steve Ladew 1889
Herman Long 1889

Jimmy Manning 1889
Mike Mattimore 1889
John McCarty 1889
Chippy McGarr 1889
Jim McTamany 1888

Frank Pears 1889
Bill Phillips 1888
John Pickett 1889
Henry Porter 1888–89

Charlie Reynolds 1889

John Sowders 1889
Dan Stearns 1889
Tom Sullivan 1888–89
Park Swartzel 1889

Steve Toole 1888

Managers

*Sam Barkley 1888
Dave Rowe 1888
Bill Watkins 1888–89

LOUISVILLE Colonels 1882–91
Known as Eclipse 1882–84
Moved to National League

Wally Andrews 1884, 1888

Norm Baker 1885
Ollie Beard 1891
Charlie Bell 1891
Ned Bligh 1890
Charlie Bohn 1882
George Boone 1891
Amos Booth 1882
Grant Briggs 1891
Lew Brown 1883
Pete Browning 1882–89
Hercules Burnett 1888

Tom Cahill 1891
Fred Carl 1889
Icebox Chamberlain 1886–88
Monk Cline 1884–85, 1891
Hub Collins 1886–88
John Connor 1885
Paul Cook 1886–89, 1891
Amos Cross 1885–87
Lave Cross 1887–88
Joe Crotty 1882, 1885
Billy Crowell 1888

Ed Daily 1890–91
Jack Darragh 1891
Ren Deagle 1884
Buttercup Dickerson 1884
Patsy Donovan 1891
John Doran 1891
Denny Driscoll 1884
John Dyler 1882

Henry Easterday 1890
Red Ehret 1889–91
Bones Ely 1886
Dude Esterbrook 1888
John Ewing 1888–89

Charlie Fisher 1889
John Fitzgerald 1891
Ed Flanagan 1889
Paddy Fox 1891
Ed Fusselbach 1888

John Galligan 1889
Mike Gaule 1889
Billy Geer 1885
Joe Gerhardt 1883–84, 1891
Jack Gleason 1883
Bill Gleason 1889
Herb Goodall 1890

Charlie Hamburg 1890
Guy Hecker 1882–89
John Heinzman 1886
Ducky Hemp 1887
Bill Hunter 1884

John Irwin 1891

Hughie Jennings 1891
Mickey Jones 1890
Jack Jones 1883

Ted Kennedy 1886
John Kerins 1885–89
Charlie Krehmeyer 1885
Willie Kuehne 1891

Sam LaRoque 1891
Juice Latham 1883–84
Jack Leary 1883
Jim Long 1891
Long 1888
Henry Luff 1883

Denny Mack 1882
Reddy Mack 1885–88

Harry Maskrey 1882
Leech Maskrey 1882–86
Al Mays 1885
Harry McCaffrey 1882
Mike McDermott 1889
Tom McLaughlin 1883–85
George Meakim 1890
Jouett Meekin 1891
Ed Merrill 1882
Joe Miller 1885
Tony Mullane 1882
Clarence Murphy 1886
Miah Murray 1885

Joe Neale 1886–87

Dan O'Connor 1890

Pat Pettee 1891
Dan Phelan 1890
Gracie Pierce 1882
Walter Prince 1883

Toad Ramsey 1885–89
Harry Raymond 1888–91
John Reccius 1882–83
Phil Reccius 1882–88
Nick Reeder 1891
Bill Robinson 1889
Chief Roseman 1890
John Ryan 1889–91

Jimmy Say 1882
Al Schellhase 1891
Bill Schenck 1882
Harry Scherer 1889
Dan Shannon 1889
Tim Shinnick 1890–91
Harry Smith 1889
Pop Smith 1882
Skyrocket Smith 1888
Ed Springer 1889
Len Stockwell 1884
Scott Stratton 1888–91
Joe Strauss 1885–86
John Strick 1882
Dan Sullivan 1882–85
Tom Sullivan 1886
Pete Sweeney 1890
Lou Sylvester 1886

Harry Taylor 1890–91
Tom Terrell 1886
Phil Tomney 1888–90
John Traffley 1889

Farmer Vaughn 1888–89
Peek-A-Boo Veach 1887

Sam Weaver 1883
Farmer Weaver 1888–91
Pete Weckbecker 1890
Jack Wentz 1891
Joe Werrick 1886–88
Bill White 1886–88
Ed Whiting 1883–84
George Winkelman 1883
Chicken Wolf 1882–91

Managers

Jack Chapman 1889–91
Mordecai Davidson 1888
Dude Esterbrook 1889
*Joe Gerhardt 1883
Jim Hart 1885–86
Honest John Kelly 1887–88
*John Kerins 1888
*Denny Mack 1882
*Dan Shannon 1889
Mike Walsh 1884
*Chicken Wolf 1889

MILWAUKEE Brewers 1891
Moved from CINCINNATI Kellys

Gus Alberts 1891

Eddie Burke 1891

Jimmy Canavan 1891
Jack Carney 1891

Abner Dalrymple	1891
George Davies	1891
Frank Dwyer	1891
Howard Earl	1891
John Grim	1891
Jim Hughey	1891
Frank Killen	1891
Tom Letcher	1891
Willard Mains	1891
Bob Pettit	1891
George Shoch	1891
Farmer Vaughn	1891

Managers

Charlie Cushman	1891

NEW YORK
Metropolitans 1883–87

Buck Becannon	1884–85
Ed Begley	1885
Steve Behel	1886
Steve Brady	1883–86
Harry Brooks	1886
Cal Broughton	1885
Hugh Collins	1887
Pete Connell	1886
Sam Crane	1883
Clarence Cross	1887
Dug Crothers	1885
Joe Crotty	1886
Ed Cushman	1885–87
Jim Donahue	1886–87
Dude Esterbrook	1883–84, 1887
Bill Fagan	1887
Tom Forster	1885–86
Elmer Foster	1886
Joe Gerhardt	1887
Charlie Hall	1887
Frank Hankinson	1885–87
Eddie Hogan	1887
Bill Holbert	1883–87
Sadie Houck	1887
Charley Jones	1887
Jones	1885
Tim Keefe	1883–84
Ed Kennedy	1883–85
Tom Kinslow	1887
Jimmy Knowles	1887
Jack Lynch	1883–87
Al Mays	1886–87
Tom McLaughlin	1886
George McMullen	1887
John Meister	1886–87
Jon Morrison	1887
Tony Murphy	1884
Candy Nelson	1883–87
Tom O'Brien	1887
Darby O'Brien	1887
Fred O'Neill	1887
John O'Rourke	1883
Dave Orr	1883–87
Henry Oxley	1884
Charlie Parsons	1887
Gracie Pierce	1884
Dick Pierson	1885
Lip Pike	1887
Paul Radford	1887
Joe Reilly	1885
Charlie Reipschlager	1883–86
Chief Roseman	1883–87
Cyclone Ryan	1887
John Shaffer	1886–87
Pete Sommers	1887
Dasher Troy	1884–85
Stump Wiedman	1887
Chief Zimmer	1886

Managers

Ollie Caylor	1887
Bob Ferguson	1886–87
Jim Gifford	1885–86
Jim Mutrie	1883–84
*Dave Orr	1887

PHILADELPHIA
Athletics 1882–90

Tug Arundel	1882
Al Atkinson	1884, 1886–87
Jake Aydelott	1886
Jersey Bakely	1883
Kid Baldwin	1890
George Bausewine	1889
Lou Bierbauer	1886–89
Jud Birchall	1882–84
Bill Blair	1888
Bob Blakiston	1882–84
George Bradley	1883, 1886
Jim Brennan	1889
Jim Brown	1886
Caffrey	1890
Sam Campbell	1890
Bart Cantz	1890
George Carman	1890
Bill Casey	1887
Fred Chapman	1887
Ed Clark	1886
John Coleman	1884–86, 1889
Bill Collins	1889–90
Ben Conroy	1890
Jim Conway	1885
Fred Corey	1883–85
George Crawford	1890
Lave Cross	1889
Bill Crowley	1883
Ed Cushman	1885
Joe Daly	1890
Jerry Dorgan	1882
Henry Easterday	1890
Bob Emslie	1885
Duke Esper	1890
Bill Farmer	1888
Bill Farrell	1882
Frank Fennelly	1888–89
Dennis Fitzgerald	1890
Ed Flanagan	1887
Elmer Foster	1884
Ed Fusselbach	1885
Bob Gamble	1888
Charlie Gessner	1886
Whitey Gibson	1888
Jack Gleason	1886
Bill Gleason	1888
Barney Graham	1889
Ed Green	1890
Bill Greenwood	1882
Ed Greer	1886–87
Tom Gunning	1888–89
Ed Halbriter	1882
Bill Hart	1886–87
Pete Hasney	1890
Horace Helmbold	1890
Charlie Hilsey	1884
Sadie Houck	1884–85
Al Hubbard	1883
Mickey Hughes	1890
Bill Hughes	1885
Jim Hyndman	1886
John Irwin	1886
Jumping Jack Jones	1883
Joe Kappel	1890
Bill Keinzil	1882
Charlie Kelly	1886
Ted Kennedy	1886
Lon Knight	1883–85
Ed Knouff	1885, 1889
Andy Knox	1890
Lackey	1890
Doc Landis	1882
Henry Larkin	1884–89
Juice Latham	1882
Tom Lovett	1885
Denny Lyons	1886–90
Macey	1890
Fred Mann	1882, 1887
John Mansell	1882
Mike Mansell	1884
Charlie Mason	1883
Bobby Mathews	1883–87
Mike Mattimore	1888–89
John McBride	1890
Chippy McGarr	1886–87
Sadie McMahon	1889–90
Henry Meyers	1890
Cyclone Miller	1886
Jocko Milligan	1884–87
Frank Mountain	1882
Mike Moynahan	1883–84
Jack O'Brien	1882–86, 1890
Ed O'Neill	1890
Ed Pabst	1890
Tom Poorman	1887–88
Martin Powell	1885
Bill Price	1890
Blondie Purcell	1885, 1888–90
Joe Quest	1886
Marshall Quinton	1885
Charlie Reynolds	1882
John Richmond	1882
John Riddle	1890
Frank Ringo	1884
Wilbert Robinson	1886–90
Chief Roseman	1887
Ed Rowen	1883–84
Jim Roxburgh	1887
Al Sauters	1890
Jimmy Say	1882
Lew Say	1882
Ed Seward	1887–90
Orator Shaffer	1885–86, 1890
Taylor Shaffer	1890
Frank Siffell	1884–85
Pop Smith	1882
Phenomenal Smith	1884–85, 1888–89
Rex Smith	1886
Charlie Snyder	1890
George Snyder	1882
Bob Stafford	1890
Charlie Stecher	1890
John Sterling	1890
Harry Stine	1890
Harry Stovey	1883–89
Joe Straub	1882
Cub Stricker	1882–85
George Strief	1885
Mike Sullivan	1888
Pete Sweeney	1890
Bill Sweeney	1882
Ham Sweigert	1890
Billy Taylor	1884–85, 1887
Cannonball Titcomb	1887
George Townsend	1887–88
Bill Vinton	1885
Sam Weaver	1882, 1886
Curt Welch	1888–90
Gus Weyhing	1887–89
Jim Whitney	1890
Frank Zinn	1888

Managers

Frank Bancroft	1887
*Lon Knight	1883–84
*Juice Latham	1882
Charlie Mason	1887
Bill Sharsig	1886, 1888–90
Lew Simmons	1886
*Harry Stovey	1885

PHILADELPHIA
Athletics 1891
Moved from Players League

Harry Beecher	1891
Sumner Bowman	1891
Will Callahan	1891
Icebox Chamberlain	1891
Bill Clymer	1891
Tommy Corcoran	1891
Pop Corkhill	1891
Lave Cross	1891
Pat Friel	1891
Bill Hallman	1891
Henry Larkin	1891
Bob Matthews	1891
Jack McGeachy	1891
Dave McKeough	1891
Jim McTamany	1891
George Meakim	1891
Jocko Milligan	1891
Joe Mulvey	1891
Ben Sanders	1891
Mike Sullivan	1891
Gus Weyhing	1891
George Wood	1891

Managers

Bill Sharsig	1891
*George Wood	1891

PITTSBURGH
Alleghenys 1882–86
Moved to National League

Gus Alberts	1884
Harry Arundel	1882
Norm Baker	1883
Sam Barkley	1886
Bob Barr	1883
Joe Battin	1882–84
Frank Beck	1884
Bill Bishop	1886
Wes Blogg	1883
Tom Brown	1885–86
Fred Carroll	1885–86
John Coleman	1886
Bill Colgan	1884
George Creamer	1883–84
Morrie Critchley	1882
Jim Dee	1884
Buttercup Dickerson	1883
Conny Doyle	1884
Denny Driscoll	1882–83
Charlie Eden	1884–85
Jay Faatz	1884
Jim Field	1885
Tom Forster	1884
John Fox	1884
Pud Galvin	1885–86
Ed Glenn	1886
Jake Goodman	1882

Jack Gorman	1884
Jim Gray	1884
Jim Handiboe	1886
Charlie Hautz	1884
Jack Hayes	1883–84
John Hofford	1885–86
Jim Keenan	1882
Rudy Kemmler	1882, 1885
Jimmy Knowles	1884
Willie Kuehne	1885–86
Chappy Lane	1882
Chuck Lauer	1884
Jack Leary	1882
Denny Mack	1883
Fred Mann	1885–86
Mike Mansell	1882–84
Jim McDonald	1884
Russ McKelvy	1882
Frank McLaughlin	1883
Pete Meegan	1885
Doggie Miller	1884–86
Bill Morgan	1882
Bill Morgan	1883
Ed Morris	1885–86
Charlie Morton	1882
Frank Mountain	1885–86
Jack Neagle	1883–84
Bill Nelson	1884
The Only Nolan	1883
Henry Oberbeck	1883
Hank O'Day	1885
Johnny Peters	1882–84
Marr Phillips	1885
Joe Quest	1884
Tom Quinn	1886
Billy Reid	1884
John Richmond	1885
Frank Ringo	1885–86
Harry Salisbury	1882
Otto Schomberg	1886
Milt Scott	1885
Jake Seymour	1882
Pop Smith	1885–86
Frank Smith	1884
Phenomenal Smith	1884
George Strief	1882
Dan Sullivan	1886
Fleury Sullivan	1884
Ed Swartwood	1882–84
Oak Taylor	1884
Billy Taylor	1882–83
Bill White	1884
Art Whitney	1884–86
Jimmy Woulfe	1884
Ren Wylie	1882

Managers

*Joe Battin	1883–84
Ormond Butler	1883
*George Creamer	1884
Bob Ferguson	1884
Denny McKnight	1884
Horace Phillips	1884–86
Al Pratt	1882–83

RICHMOND Virginians 1884

Wes Curry	1884
Ed Dugan	1884
Bill Dugan	1884
Ted Firth	1884
Ed Ford	1884
Ed Glenn	1884
Walt Goldsby	1884
John Hanna	1884
Dick Johnston	1884
Terry Larkin	1884
Mike Mansell	1884
Pete Meegan	1884
Bill Morgan	1884
Billy Nash	1884
Jim Powell	1884
Marshall Quinton	1884
Bill Schenck	1884
Andy Swan	1884
Wash Williams	1884

Managers

Felix Moses	1884

ROCHESTER 1890

Bob Barr	1890
Henry Blauvelt	1890
Dan Burke	1890
Will Callahan	1890
Jim Field	1890
John Fitzgerald	1890
Bill Greenwood	1890
Sandy Griffin	1890
John Grim	1890
Jimmy Knowles	1890
Harry Lyons	1890
Deacon McGuire	1890
Dave McKeough	1890
Bob Miller	1890
Tom O'Brien	1890
Marr Phillips	1890
Phil Reccius	1890
Ted Scheffler	1890
Leo Smith	1890
Cannonball Titcomb	1890

Managers

Pat Powers	1890

ST. LOUIS Browns 1882–91
Known as Brown Stockings 1882–83
Moved to National League

Jim Adams	1890
Nin Alexander	1884
Sam Barkley	1885
John Bellman	1889
Jack Boyle	1887–89, 1891
Ted Breitenstein	1891
Cal Broughton	1885
Ed Brown	1882
Joe Burke	1890
Harry Burrell	1891
Doc Bushong	1885–87
Count Campau	1890
Ed Cartwright	1890
Bob Caruthers	1884–87
Icebox Chamberlain	1888–90
Charlie Comiskey	1882–89, 1891
Paul Cook	1891
Gus Creely	1890
Morrie Critchley	1882
Joe Crotty	1882
Ned Cuthbert	1882–83
Dell Darling	1891
Jumbo Davis	1889–90
Daisy Davis	1884
Pat Deasley	1883–84
Frank Decker	1882
Jim Devlin	1888–89
Tom Dolan	1883–84, 1888
Jim Donnelly	1890
Bert Dorr	1882
John Doyle	1882
Mike Drissel	1885
Charlie Duffee	1889–90
Jesse Duryea	1891
Bad Bill Eagan	1891
Billy Earle	1890
John Easton	1891
John Ewing	1883
Dave Foutz	1884–87
Julie Freeman	1888
Shorty Fuller	1889–91
Harry Fuller	1891
Chick Fulmer	1884
Ed Fusselbach	1882
Tom Gettinger	1889–90
Jim Gill	1889
Jack Gleason	1882–83
Bill Gleason	1882–87
Walt Goldsby	1884
Mike Goodfellow	1887
Jack Gorman	1883
Clark Griffith	1891
Lou Harding	1886
Bob Hart	1890
Pat Hartnett	1890
Ed Herr	1888, 1890
Bill Higgins	1890
Charlie Hodnett	1883
Eddie Hogan	1882
Dummy Hoy	1891
Nat Hudson	1886–89
Jere Kane	1890
Rudy Kemmler	1886
John Kerins	1890
Silver King	1887–89
Walt Kinzie	1884
Billy Klusman	1890
Ed Knouff	1887–88
Charlie Krehmeyer	1884
Arlie Latham	1883–89
Johnny Lavin	1884
Fred Lewis	1883–84
Tom Loftus	1883
Denny Lyons	1891
Harry Lyons	1887–88
Tom Mansell	1883
Harry McCaffrey	1882–83
Tommy McCarthy	1888–91
Jim McCauley	1884
Chippy McGarr	1888
Willie McGill	1891
Jumbo McGinnis	1882–86
Marty McQuaid	1891
Trick McSorley	1886
Paul McSweeney	1891
Dad Meek	1889–90
Frank Millard	1890
Dusty Miller	1890
Jocko Milligan	1888–89
Bobby Mitchell	1882
Charlie Morton	1882
Tony Mullane	1883
John Munyan	1890–91
Joe Murphy	1886–87
Joe Neale	1890–91
George Nicol	1890
Hugh Nicol	1883–86
Henry Oberbeck	1883
Tip O'Neill	1884–89, 1891
Ed Pabst	1890
Joe Quest	1883–84
Toad Ramsey	1889–90
George Rettger	1891
John Ricks	1891
Yank Robinson	1885–89, 1891
Chief Roseman	1890
Jack Schappert	1882
John Schultz	1891
George Seward	1882
John Shoupe	1882
Bill Smiley	1882
Jack Stivetts	1889–91
George Strief	1883–84
Al Struve	1884
Dan Sullivan	1885
Sleeper Sullivan	1882–83
Pete Sweeney	1889–90
Lou Sylvester	1887
Mike Trost	1890
Joe Visner	1891
Oscar Walker	1882
Curt Welch	1885–87
Jake Wells	1890
Harry Wheeler	1884
Bill White	1888
Art Whitney	1891
Bill Whitrock	1890
Bill Zies	1891

Managers

*Count Campau	1890
*Charlie Comiskey	1883–89, 1891
*Ned Cuthbert	1882
Joe Gerhardt	1890
*Tommy McCarthy	1890
*Chief Roseman	1890
Ted Sullivan	1883
Jimmy Williams	1884

SYRACUSE Stars 1890

Joe Battin	1890
Grant Briggs	1890
Dan Burke	1890
Dan Casey	1890
Cupid Childs	1890
Pat Dealey	1890
Mike Dorgan	1890
Bones Ely	1890
Pat Friel	1890
Louis Graff	1890
Ducky Hemp	1890
Bill Higgins	1890
John Keefe	1890
Frank Keffer	1890
John Leighton	1890
Ezra Lincoln	1890
Toby Lyons	1890
Ed Mars	1890
Charlie McCullough	1890
Barney McLaughlin	1890
Mox McQuery	1890
Mike Morrison	1890
Tim O'Rourke	1890
Tom O'Rourke	1890
John Peltz	1890
Herman Pitz	1890
George Proeser	1890
Henry Simon	1890
Bill Sullivan	1890
Rasty Wright	1890

Managers

Wally Fessenden	1890
George Frazer	1890

TOLEDO Blue Stockings 1884

Tug Arundel 1884

Sam Barkley 1884
Ed Brown 1884
Sim Bullas 1884

Ed Kent 1884

Chappy Lane 1884

Deacon McGuire 1884
Trick McSorley 1884
George Meister 1884
Joe Miller 1884
Ed Miller 1884
Joe Moffett 1884
Charlie Morton 1884
Tony Mullane 1884

Hank O'Day 1884
Frank Olin 1884

Tom Poorman 1884

John Tilley 1884

Fleet Walker 1884
Welday Walker 1884
Curt Welch 1884

Managers

*Charlie Morton 1884

WASHINGTON 1884

Bob Barr 1884
Jack Beach 1884

Lyman Drake 1884

Tom Farley 1884
Frank Fennelly 1884

Alex Gardner 1884
Buck Gladman 1884
Walt Goldsby 1884

John Hamill 1884
John Hanna 1884
Thorny Hawkes 1884
John Humphries 1884

Jones 1884

John Kiley 1884
Sam King 1884

Bill Morgan 1884
Henry Mullin 1884
Willie Murphy 1884

Frank Olin 1884

Walter Prince 1884

Edgar Smith 1884
Andy Swan 1884

Ed Trumbull 1884

Wills 1884

Ed Yewell 1884

Managers

Bickerson 1884
Holly Hollingshead 1884

WASHINGTON Statesmen 1891
Moved to National League

Billy Alvord 1891

Jersey Bakely 1891
Harry Beecher 1891
Jim Burns 1891
Kid Carsey 1891
Ed Cassian 1891
Jim Curtiss 1891

Ed Daily 1891
Jumbo Davis 1891
Patsy Donovan 1891
Tommy Dowd 1891
Martin Duke 1891
Fred Dunlap 1891

Ed Eiteljorge 1891

Frank Foreman 1891
Buck Freeman 1891

Tom Hart 1891
Gil Hatfield 1891
Paul Hines 1891

George Keefe 1891

Pete Lohman 1891

Harry Mace 1891
Al McCauley 1891
Deacon McGuire 1891
Tom McLaughlin 1891
Mox McQuery 1891
Bob Miller 1891
Larry Murphy 1891
Miah Murray 1891

Bill Quarles 1891

Mike Slattery 1891
Will Smalley 1891
Pop Smith 1891
Sy Sutcliffe 1891

Joe Visner 1891

Managers

Sandy Griffin 1891
Dan Shannon 1891
Pop Snyder 1891
Sam Trott 1891

Union Association

ALTOONA 1884

Charlie Berry 1884
Jim Brown 1884

Pat Carroll 1884
Joe Connors 1884
Clarence Cross 1884

George Daisey 1884
Charlie Dougherty 1884

John Grady 1884

Frank Harris 1884

Harry Koons 1884

Jack Leary 1884

Charlie Manlove 1884
Jerry Moore 1884
John Murphy 1884

George Noftsker 1884

Frank Shaffer 1884
Germany Smith 1884

Managers

Ed Curtis 1884

BALTIMORE 1884

Al Atkinson 1884

Frank Bahret 1884
Joe Battin 1884
Frank Beck 1884
Pat Burns 1884

John Cuff 1884
Ned Cuthbert 1884

Jerry Dorsey 1884

Joe Ellick 1884

Ed Fusselbach 1884

Gid Gardner 1884
Bernie Graham 1884

Tom Lee 1884
Charlie Levis 1884

Chris McFarland 1884
Bill Morgan 1884
E. Morris 1884

John O'Brien 1884
Henry Oberbeck 1884

Dick Phelan 1884

Yank Robinson 1884
John Ryan 1884

Lew Say 1884
Jumbo Schoeneck 1884
Scott 1884
Emmett Seery 1884
Frank Shaffer 1884
Al Skinner 1884
Phenomenal Smith 1884
Smith 1884
Joe Stanley 1884
Tony Suck 1884
Rooney Sweeney 1884
Bill Sweeney 1884

Bill Tierney 1884

Harry Wheeler 1884

Managers

Bill Henderson 1884

BOSTON Reds 1884

Tommy Bond 1884
Lew Brown 1884
James Burke 1884
Frank Butler 1884

Ed Callahan 1884
Cannonball Crane 1884

Charlie Daniels 1884
Clarence Dow 1884

Joe Flynn 1884

Walter Hackett 1884

John Irwin 1884

Tommy McCarthy 1884
Jim McKeever 1884
Henry Mullin 1884
Tim Murnane 1884
Murphy 1884

Tom O'Brien 1884

Elias Peak 1884

Charlie Reilley 1884
John Rudderham 1884

Pat Scanlon 1884
Dupee Shaw 1884
Art Sladen 1884
Mike Slattery 1884

Fred Tenney 1884

Managers

*Tim Murnane 1884

CHICAGO Browns 1884
Moved to PITTSBURGH Stogies

Al Atkinson 1884

Charlie Baker 1884
Charlie Berry 1884
Frank Bishop 1884
Charlie Briggs 1884

Charlie Cady 1884
Phillip Corridan 1884
Dan Cronin 1884

One Arm Daily 1884

Joe Ellick 1884

Charlie Fisher 1884
Will Foley 1884
Frank Foreman 1884

Gid Gardner 1884
Bernie Graham 1884
Em Gross 1884

Moxie Hengle 1884
John Horan 1884
Charlie Householder 1884

Harry Koons 1884
Bill Krieg 1884

Jack Leary 1884

Steve Matthias 1884
Chippy McGarr 1884
Frank McLaughlin 1884
Cyclone Miller 1884

Richardson 1884

Jumbo Schoeneck 1884
Al Skinner 1884
Tony Suck 1884

Harry Wheeler 1884
Frank Wyman 1884

Managers

Ed Hengle 1884

CINCINNATI Outlaw Reds 1884

Charlie Barber 1884
George Bradley 1884
Fatty Briody 1884
Dick Burns 1884

Elmer Cleveland 1884
Sam Crane 1884
Joe Crotty 1884

John Ewing 1884

Jack Glasscock 1884

Bill Harbidge 1884
Bill Hawes 1884

Jack Jones 1884

Kick Kelly 1884
Ed Kennedy 1884

Jim McCormick 1884
Frank McLaughlin 1884
Mox McQuery 1884
Lew Meyers 1884

Dan O'Leary 1884

Martin Powell 1884

Fred Robinson 1884

Pop Schwartz 1884
Lou Sylvester 1884

Managers

*Sam Crane 1884
*Dan O'Leary 1884

KANSAS CITY Cowboys 1884

Nin Alexander 1884

Jersey Bakely 1884
Kid Baldwin 1884
Charlie Bastian 1884
Charlie Berry 1884
Bob Black 1884
Dick Blaisdell 1884

Charlie Cady 1884
Ed Callahan 1884
Jim Chatterton 1884
Joe Connors 1884
Clarence Cross 1884
Dug Crothers 1884
Jim Cudworth 1884

Jumbo Davis 1884
John Deasley 1884
Harry Decker 1884
Jim Donnelly 1884
Bill Dugan 1884
Ward Dwight 1884

Joe Ellick 1884

Charlie Fisher 1884
Frank Foreman 1884

Jack Gorman 1884

Ernie Hickman 1884
Bill Hutchinson 1884

John Kirby 1884
Krieger 1884

Henry Luff 1884

Barney McLaughlin 1884
Frank McLaughlin 1884

Henry Oberbeck 1884
Billy O'Brien 1884

Jimmy Say 1884
Lew Say 1884
Emmett Seery 1884
Frank Shaffer 1884
Joe Strauss 1884
George Strief 1884
Pat Sullivan 1884
Jerry Sweeney 1884

Jerry Turbidy 1884

Peek–A–Boo Veach 1884
Alex Voss 1884

Milt Whitehead 1884
Wills 1884
Frank Wyman 1884

Managers

Matt Porter 1884
Ted Sullivan 1884
Harry Wheeler 1884

MILWAUKEE Cream Citys 1884

Lady Baldwin 1884
Steve Behel 1884
George Bignell 1884
Cal Broughton 1884

Ed Cushman 1884

Anton Falch 1884

Tom Griffin 1884

Eddie Hogan 1884

Tom Morrissey 1884
Al Myers 1884

Henry Porter 1884

Tom Sexton 1884

Managers

Tom Loftus 1884

PHILADELPHIA Keystones 1884

Jersey Bakely 1884

Pat Carroll 1884
Jack Clements 1884
Clarence Cross 1884

Con Daily 1884
Dave Drew 1884

Henry Easterday 1884

Fisher 1884
Joe Flynn 1884
Elmer Foster 1884

Bill Gallagher 1884
Billy Geer 1884
Tom Gillen 1884

Buster Hoover 1884

Bill Johnson 1884
Bill Jones 1884

Bill Keinzil 1884

Henry Luff 1884

Al Maul 1884
Jerry McCormick 1884
John McGuinness 1884
Levi Meyerle 1884

John O'Donnell 1884

George Pattison 1884
Elias Peak 1884

Chris Rickley 1884

John Siegel 1884

Sam Weaver 1884

Managers

Fergy Malone 1884

PITTSBURGH Stogies 1884
Moved from CHICAGO Browns

Al Atkinson 1884

Charlie Baker 1884
Kid Baldwin 1884
Joe Battin 1884
Charlie Berry 1884

One Arm Daily 1884

Joe Ellick 1884

Gid Gardner 1884

Charlie Householder 1884

Bill Krieg 1884

Jumbo Schoeneck 1884
George Strief 1884
Tony Suck 1884

Harry Wheeler 1884

Managers

*Joe Battin 1884
*Joe Ellick 1884

ST. PAUL White Caps 1884

Bill Barnes 1884
Jim Brown 1884

Scrappy Carroll 1884

Pat Dealey 1884
Steve Dunn 1884

Lou Galvin 1884
Charlie Ganzel 1884

Moxie Hengle 1884

Billy O'Brien 1884

John Tilley 1884

Joe Werrick 1884

Managers

Andrew Thompson 1884

WASHINGTON Nationals 1884

Gus Alberts 1884

Phil Baker 1884
Al Bradley 1884

Chick Carroll 1884
Marty Creegan 1884

One Arm Daily 1884
John Deasley 1884
Dave Drew 1884

Tom Evers 1884
John Ewing 1884

Franklin 1884
Chris Fulmer 1884

Charlie Geggus 1884
Jim Green 1884
Joe Gunson 1884

Jim Halpin 1884
Bill Hughes 1884

Pop Joy 1884

Charlie Kalbfus 1884
Kick Kelly 1884

Terry Larkin 1884
Mike Lawlor 1884
Mickey Lehane 1884
Charlie Levis 1884
Milo Lockwood 1884

Jerry McCormick 1884
Jim McDonald 1884
Frank McKee 1884
Ed McKenna 1884
Jim McLaughlin 1884
McRemer 1884
Henry Moore 1884
P. Morris 1884
Mulligan 1884

Emory Nusz 1884

Frank Olin 1884

Maury Pierce 1884
Abner Powell 1884
Walter Prince 1884

Icicle Reeder 1884
William Rollinson 1884

Daniel Sheehan 1884
John Shoupe 1884

Fred Tenney 1884
Art Thompson 1884

Alex Voss 1884

John Ward 1884

Warren White 1884
Wiley 1884
Bill Wise 1884

Ed Yewell 1884

Managers

Mike Scanlon 1884

WILMINGTON Quicksteps 1884

Jersey Bakely 1884
Charlie Bastian 1884
Ike Benners 1884
Oyster Burns 1884

Dan Casey 1884
Dennis Casey 1884
John Cullen 1884
Tony Cusick 1884

George Fisher 1884

Tom Lynch 1884

Bill McCloskey 1884
Jim McElroy 1884
John Munce 1884
John Murphy 1884
Henry Myers 1884

The Only Nolan 1884

Jimmy Say 1884
Daniel Sheehan 1884
Redleg Snyder 1884

Fred Tenney 1884

Managers

Joe Simmons 1884

Players League

BOSTON Reds 1890
Moved to American Association

Dan Brouthers 1890
Tom Brown 1890

Bill Daley 1890

Ad Gumbert 1890

Arthur Irwin 1890

Dick Johnston 1890

King Kelly 1890
Matt Kilroy 1890

Kid Madden 1890
John Morrill 1890
Morg Murphy 1890

Billy Nash 1890

Joe Quinn 1890

Old Hoss Radbourn 1890
Hardy Richardson 1890

Harry Stovey 1890
Pop Swett 1890

Managers

*King Kelly 1890

BROOKLYN Wonders 1890
Known as Wonders 1890

Ed Andrews 1890

Lou Bierbauer 1890

Paul Cook 1890

Con Daily 1890

Jack Hayes 1890
George Hemming 1890

Bill Joyce 1890

Tom Kinslow 1890

Jack McGeachy 1890
Con Murphy 1890

Dave Orr 1890

Emmett Seery 1890
John Sowders 1890
Art Sunday 1890

George Van Haltren 1890

Monte Ward 1890
Gus Weyhing 1890

Managers

*Monte Ward 1890

BUFFALO Bisons 1890

Lady Baldwin 1890
Harry Beecher 1890
John Buckley 1890

Jack Carney 1890
Spider Clark 1890
Dan Cotter 1890
Bert Cunningham 1890

Al Doe 1890
Bill Duzen 1890

Alex Ferson 1890

Jim Gillespie 1890

George Haddock 1890
Jocko Halligan 1890
Dummy Hoy 1890

John Irwin 1890

George Keefe 1890
Gus Krock 1890

Lewis 1890

Connie Mack 1890

John Rainey 1890
Jack Rowe 1890

General Stafford 1890

Larry Twitchell 1890

Deacon White 1890
Sam Wise 1890

Managers

Jay Faatz 1890
*Jack Rowe 1890

CHICAGO Pirates 1890

Mark Baldwin 1890
Charlie Bartson 1890
Charlie Bastian 1890
Jack Boyle 1890

Charlie Comiskey 1890

Dell Darling 1890
Hugh Duffy 1890
Frank Dwyer 1890

Duke Farrell 1890

Silver King 1890

Arlie Latham 1890

Tip O'Neill 1890

Fred Pfeffer 1890

Jimmy Ryan 1890

Frank Shugart 1890

Ned Williamson 1890

Managers

*Charlie Comiskey 1890

CLEVELAND Infants 1890

Jersey Bakely 1890
Jim Brennan 1890
Pete Browning 1890
Budd 1890

Jack Carney 1890

Ed Delahanty 1890
Charlie Dewald 1890

Bill Gleason 1890
Henry Gruber 1890

George Hemming 1890

Henry Larkin 1890

Jimmy McAleer 1890
Willie McGill 1890

Darby O'Brien 1890

Paul Radford 1890

Pop Snyder 1890
Cub Stricker 1890
Neil Stynes 1890
Sy Sutcliffe 1890

Patsy Tebeau 1890
Larry Twitchell 1890

Managers

*Henry Larkin 1890
*Patsy Tebeau 1890

NEW YORK Giants 1890

Willard Brown 1890

Roger Connor 1890
Cannonball Crane 1890

Fred Dunlap 1890

John Ewing 1890
Buck Ewing 1890

George Gore 1890

Gil Hatfield 1890

Dick Johnston 1890

Tim Keefe 1890

Hank O'Day 1890
Jim O'Rourke 1890

Danny Richardson 1890

Dan Shannon 1890
Mike Slattery 1890

Farmer Vaughn 1890

Art Whitney 1890

Managers

*Buck Ewing 1890

PHILADELPHIA Quakers 1890
Moved to American Association

Charlie Buffinton 1890

Lave Cross 1890
Bert Cunningham 1890

Sid Farrar 1890
Jim Fogarty 1890

Mike Griffin 1890

Bill Hallman 1890
Bill Husted 1890

Phil Knell 1890

Jocko Milligan 1890
Joe Mulvey 1890

John Pickett 1890

Ben Sanders 1890
Dan Shannon 1890
Bill Shindle 1890

George Wood 1890

Managers

*Charlie Buffinton 1890
*Jim Fogarty 1890

PITTSBURGH Burghers 1890

Jake Beckley 1890

Fred Carroll 1890
Tommy Corcoran 1890

Al Doe 1890

Jocko Fields 1890

Pud Galvin 1890
Reddy Gray 1890

Ned Hanlon 1890
Jerry Hurley 1890

Willie Kuehne 1890

Al Maul 1890
Ed Morris 1890

Tom Quinn 1890

Yank Robinson 1890

Harry Staley 1890

John Tener 1890

Joe Visner 1890

Managers

*Ned Hanlon 1890

Federal League

BALTIMORE Terrapins 1914–15

Joe Agler 1915
John Allen 1914

Bill Bailey 1914–15
Johnny Bates 1914
Chief Bender 1915
Dave Black 1915
Medric Boucher 1914

Felix Chouinard 1914
Snipe Conley 1914–15
Ken Crawford 1915

Mickey Doolan 1914–15
Larry Douglas 1915
Vern Duncan 1914–15

Charlie Eakle 1915
Steve Evans 1915

Edward Forsyth 1915

John Gallagher 1915

Jim Hickman 1915
Vern Hughes 1914

Fred Jacklitsch 1914–15
Adam Johnson 1915

Doc Kerr 1914–15
Enos Kirkpatrick 1914–15
Otto Knabe 1914–15
Karl Kolseth 1915
Fred Kommers 1914

George LaClaire 1915
Frank Lobert 1914

Charlie Maisel 1915
Scott McCandless 1914–15
Benny Meyer 1914–15

Frank Owens 1915

Jack Quinn 1914–15

Wally Reinecker 1915
Jack Ridgway 1914
Harvey Russell 1914–15

Hack Simmons 1914–15
Frank Smith 1914–15
Jimmy Smith 1915
George Suggs 1914–15
Harry Swacina 1914–15

Tommy Vereker 1915

Jimmy Walsh 1914–15
Kaiser Wilhelm 1914–15

Charlie Young 1915
Ducky Yount 1914

Guy Zinn 1914–15

Managers

*Otto Knabe 1914–15

BROOKLYN Tip–Tops 1914–15

George Anderson 1914–15

Jim Bluejacket 1914–15
Hugh Bradley 1915
Three Finger Brown 1914

Esty Chaney 1914
Bill Chappelle 1914
Felix Chouinard 1914–15
Claude Cooper 1914–15

Jim Delahanty 1914–15

Steve Evans 1914–15

Cy Falkenberg 1915
Happy Finneran 1914–15

Ed Gagnier 1914–15
Art Griggs 1914–15

Al Halt 1914–15
Ty Helfrich 1915
Bill Herring 1915
Solly Hofman 1914
Byron Houck 1914
Dave Howard 1915

Earl Juul 1914

Frank Kane 1915
Benny Kauff 1915

Ed Lafitte	1914–15
Grover Land	1914–15
Lee Magee	1915
Dan Marion	1914–15
Bert Maxwell	1914
John McGraw	1914
Danny Murphy	1914–15
Hap Myers	1914–15
Frank Owens	1914
Rube Peters	1914
Larry Pratt	1915
Milt Reed	1915
Tom Seaton	1914–15
Al Shaw	1914
Mike Simon	1915
Frank Smith	1915
Fred Smith	1915
Harry Smith	1915
Rudy Sommers	1914
Al Tesch	1915
Bill Upham	1915
Joe Vernon	1914
Mysterious Walker	1915
Art Watson	1914–15
Rinaldo Williams	1914
Fin Wilson	1914–15
Hooks Wiltse	1915
Tex Wisterzil	1914–15
Dick Wright	1915

Managers

Bill Bradley	1914
John Ganzel	1915
*Lee Magee	1915

BUFFALO Blues 1914–15
Known as Buffeds 1914

Joe Agler	1914–15
Nick Allen	1914–15
Fred Anderson	1914–15
Hugh Bedient	1915
Walter Blair	1914–15
Luther Bonin	1914
Everitt Booe	1914
Hal Chase	1914–15
Bill Collins	1914
Jack Dalton	1915
Frank Delahanty	1914
Tom Downey	1914–15
Howard Ehmke	1915
Clyde Engle	1914–15
Russ Ford	1914–15
Ed Gagnier	1915
Charlie Hanford	1914
Solly Hofman	1915
Joe Houser	1914
Gene Krapp	1914–15
George LaClaire	1915
Ed Lafitte	1915
Art LaVigne	1914
Harry Lord	1915
Baldy Louden	1914–15
Rube Marshall	1915
Tex McDonald	1914–15
Benny Meyer	1915
Earl Moore	1914
Harry Moran	1914
Ed Porray	1914
Roxy Roach	1915
Biff Schlitzer	1914
Al Schulz	1914–15
Fred Smith	1914–15
Bob Smith	1914–15
Jack Snyder	1914
Art Watson	1915
Del Wertz	1914
Dan Woodman	1914–15
Del Young	1914–15

Managers

*Walter Blair	1915
*Harry Lord	1915
Harry Schlafly	1914–15

CHICAGO Whales 1914–15
Known as Chi–Feds 1914

Bill Bailey	1915
Fred Beck	1914–15
Dave Black	1914–15
Bruno Block	1914
Ad Brennan	1914–15
Three Finger Brown	1915
Clem Clemens	1914–15
Mickey Doolan	1915
Jack Farrell	1914–15
Bill Fischer	1915
Max Fiske	1914
Max Flack	1914–15
Harry Fritz	1914–15
Charlie Hanford	1915
Arnold Hauser	1915
Claude Hendrix	1914–15
Bill Jackson	1914–15
Adam Johnson	1914–15
Leo Kavanagh	1914
Erv Lange	1914
Les Mann	1915
George McConnell	1915
Tom McGuire	1914
Charlie Pechous	1915
Mike Prendergast	1914–15
Hans Rasmussen	1915
Babe Sherman	1914
Jimmy Smith	1914–15
Jimmy Stanley	1914
Joe Tinker	1914
Austin Walsh	1914
Doc Watson	1914
Joe Weiss	1915
Al Wickland	1914–15
Art Wilson	1914–15
Tex Wisterzil	1915
Rollie Zeider	1914–15
Dutch Zwilling	1914–15

Managers

*Joe Tinker	1914–15

INDIANAPOLIS Hoosiers 1914
Moved to NEWARK Peppers

Harry Billiard	1914
Everitt Booe	1914
Vin Campbell	1914
Charlie Carr	1914
Biddy Dolan	1914
Jimmy Esmond	1914
Cy Falkenberg	1914
Frank Harter	1914
Ed Henderson	1914
Al Kaiser	1914
George Kaiserling	1914
Benny Kauff	1914
Katsy Keifer	1914
Frank LaPorte	1914
Ralph McConnaughey	1914
Bill McKechnie	1914
Earl Moseley	1914
George Mullin	1914
Fred Ostendorf	1914
Bill Rariden	1914
Frank Rooney	1914
Edd Roush	1914
Al Scheer	1914
George Textor	1914
Carl Vandagrift	1914
Bill Warren	1914
Charlie Whitehouse	1914
Clarence Woods	1914

Managers

Bill Phillips	1914

KANSAS CITY Packers 1914–15

Dan Adams	1914–15
Babe Blackburn	1915
Bill Bradley	1915
Drummond Brown	1914–15
Chet Chadbourne	1914–15
Cad Coles	1914
Nick Cullop	1914–15
Cliff Daringer	1914
Ted Easterly	1914–15
Jack Enzenroth	1914–15
Ernie Gilmore	1914–15
Joe Gingras	1915
Pep Goodwin	1914–15
Ben Harris	1914–15
Pete Henning	1914–15
George Hogan	1914
Chief Johnson	1914–15
Duke Kenworthy	1914–15
Art Kruger	1914–15
Alex Main	1915
Gene Packard	1914–15
George Perring	1914–15
John Potts	1914
Johnny Rawlings	1914–15
Al Shaw	1915
Dwight Stone	1914
George Stovall	1914–15
Ducky Swan	1914
Walter Tappan	1914

Managers

*George Stovall	1914–15

NEWARK Peppers 1915
Moved from INDIANAPOLIS Hoosiers

Harry Billiard	1915
Hugh Bradley	1915
Chick Brandom	1915
Vin Campbell	1915
Jimmy Esmond	1915
Cy Falkenberg	1915
Emil Huhn	1915
George Kaiserling	1915
Frank LaPorte	1915
Bill McKechnie	1915
Rupert Mills	1915
Harry Moran	1915
Earl Moseley	1915
George Mullin	1915
Larry Pratt	1915
Bill Rariden	1915
Ted Reed	1915
Ed Reulbach	1915
Edd Roush	1915
Germany Schaefer	1915
Al Scheer	1915
Tom Seaton	1915
Johnny Strands	1915
George Textor	1915
Fred Trautman	1915
Bill Warren	1915
Charlie Whitehouse	1915
Gil Whitehouse	1915

Managers

*Bill McKechnie	1915
Bill Phillips	1915

PITTSBURGH Rebels 1914–15

Willie Adams	1914
Frank Allen	1914–15
Cy Barger	1914–15
Marty Berghammer	1915
Claude Berry	1914–15
Hugh Bradley	1914–15
Al Braithwood	1915
Sandy Burk	1915
Howie Camnitz	1914–15
Felix Chouinard	1914
Ralph Comstock	1915
Bob Coulson	1914
Frank Delahanty	1914–15
Walt Dickson	1914–15
Bunny Hearn	1915
Ed Henderson	1914
Ed Holly	1914–15
Davy Jones	1914–15
Bob Kelly	1915
Orie Kerlin	1915
Doc Kerr	1914
Elmer Knetzer	1914–15
Ed Konetchy	1915
George LaClaire	1914–15
Ed Lennox	1914–15
Jack Lewis	1914–15
Red Madden	1914
Ralph Mattis	1914
Tex McDonald	1914
Mike Menosky	1914–15
Johnny Miljus	1915
Mike Mowrey	1915
Paddy O'Connor	1915
Rebel Oakes	1914–15
Cy Rheam	1914–15
Skipper Roberts	1914
Clint Rogge	1915
Jim Savage	1914–15
Jim Scott	1914
Mysterious Walker	1914
Al Wickland	1915

Steve Yerkes	1914–15

Managers

Doc Gessler	1914
*Rebel Oakes	1914–15

ST. LOUIS Terriers 1914–15

Babe Borton	1915
Al Boucher	1914
Al Bridwell	1914–15
Harry Chapman	1914–15
Pete Compton	1915
Doc Crandall	1914–15
Manuel Cueto	1914
Dave Davenport	1914–15
Charlie Deal	1915
Delos Drake	1914–15
Bob Groom	1914–15
Grover Hartley	1914–15
Ernie Herbert	1914–15
Ernie Johnson	1915
Hank Keupper	1914
LaRue Kirby	1914–15
Fred Kommers	1914
Art Kores	1915
Armando Marsans	1914–15
Joe Mathes	1914
Hughie Miller	1914–15
Ward Miller	1914–15
John Misse	1914
Eddie Plank	1915
Mike Simon	1914
Jack Tobin	1914–15
Bobby Vaughn	1915
Jimmy Walsh	1915
Doc Watson	1914–15
Ted Welch	1914
Ed Willett	1914–15
Tex Wisterzil	1915

Managers

*Three Finger Brown	1914
Fielder Jones	1914–15

PART FIVE

The Teams and Their Players

Year-by-Year Order of Finish
The Lineups, Including Pitchers
Individual Batting, Pitching, and Fielding
The Managers
Team Statistics
League Leaders

The Teams and Their Players

The Teams and Their Players is a chronological listing of team standings, league leaders, basic team rosters, and player records for every major league from 1876 through today. This section, which serves as a cross-reference to the Player and Pitcher registers, makes it possible to find out such information as who played second base for the Brooklyn Dodgers in 1924, or who were the top pitchers for the Detroit Tigers in 1917. It also gives the yearly league leaders in many statistical categories and includes the names and records of the men who managed the teams. The information is presented on a year-by-year basis starting with the National League in 1876.

All information and abbreviations that may appear unfamiliar are explained in the sample format presented below. The National League team rosters of 1876 would normally appear first, but as an example to illustrate the information only the Chicago team is shown. They finished first in 1876, and all teams are presented in the order of final standing.

NATIONAL LEAGUE 1876

	POS	Player	AB	BA	HR	RBI	PO	A	E	DP	TC/G	FA	Pitcher	G	IP	W	L	SV	ERA
Chicago	1B	C. McVey	308	.347	1	53	485	10	21	21	9.4	.959	A. Spalding	61	529	**47**	13	0	1.75
W-52 L-14	2B	R. Barnes	322	**.429**	1	59	167	199	36	22	6.1	**.910**							
Al Spalding	SS	J. Peters	316	.351	1	47	95	193	21	**16**	4.7	**.932**							
	3B	C. Anson	309	.356	1	59	**135**	**147**	50	**8**	5.0	.849							
	RF	B. Addy	142	.282	0	16	46	6	13	0	2.0	.800							
	CF	P. Hines	305	.331	2	59	159	8	14	4	2.8	.923							
	LF	J. Glenn	276	.304	0	32	128	5	18	1	2.7	.881							
	C	D. White	303	.343	1	**60**	295	50	64	3	6.5	.844							
	P	A. Spalding	292	.312	0	44	45	92	7	**7**	2.4	.951							
	OF	O. Bielaski	139	.209	0	10	41	4	14	1	1.8	.763							

Roster Column Headings Information

POS	Fielding Position
AB	At Bats
BA	Batting Average
HR	Home Runs
RBI	Runs Batted In
PO	Putouts
A	Assists
E	Errors
DP	Double Plays
TC/G	Total Fielding Chances per Game
FA	Fielding Average
G	Games Pitched In
IP	Innings Pitched (rounded off to the nearest inning)
W	Wins
L	Losses
SV	Saves
ERA	Earned Run Average

Team Information Explanation

Directly beneath the city name is the team won and lost record and name of the man who managed the team. (Teams with more than one manager have the managers listed in the order of when they managed. The top listing would indicate the first manager.)

Multiple Team Players. If a man played for more than one team in the same year, the information shown is only his record for the indicated team.

Regulars. The men who appear first on the team roster are considered the regulars for that team at the positions indicated. There are several factors for determining regulars, of which "most games played at a position" and "most fielding chances at a position" are the two prime considerations. Fielding information applies only to the position indicated. For regular outfielders the fielding information is for all the outfield positions.

Substitutes. Appearing directly beneath the regulars are the substitutes for the team. Substitutes listed here must have a total of at least one at bat per scheduled game, or 20 or more runs batted in for the season. Substitutes are listed in order of most at bats, and can be someone who played most of the team's games as a regular, but not at one position. The rules for determining the listed positions of substitutes are as follows:

One Position Substitutes. If a man played at least 70% of his games in the field at one position, then he is listed only at that position, except for outfielders, where all three outfield positions are included under one category. Fielding information applies only to the position indicated.

Two Position Substitutes. If a man did not play at least 70% of his games in the field at one position, but did play more than 90% of his total games at two positions, then he is shown with a combination fielding position. For example, a player who has an "S2" shown in his position column played at least 90% of his games either at shortstop or at second base. These combinations are always indicated by the first letter or number of the position. Fielding information applies only to the two positions indicated. The position listed first is where the most games were played.

Utility Players. If a player has a "UT" shown in his position column, it means that he did not meet the above 70% or 90% requirement and is listed as a utility player. The fielding information is his total for all positions.

Pinch Hitters. Men who played less than 15 games in the field, but who had 20 runs batted in or more, are considered pinch hitters and are listed as "PH" and no fielding information is shown.

Total Fielding Chances per Game. This statistic is not shown for men who were two position substitutes or utility players, because total chances per game is only meaningful in reference to a specific fielding position.

Pitchers. A pitcher is included if he pitched 100 or more innings, or had ten decisions (a decision being a win, loss, or save). Pitchers are listed in order of innings pitched.

League Leader Qualifications (also applies to Yearly League Leaders Information). Throughout baseball, there have been different rules used to determine the minimum appearances necessary to qualify for league leader in categories concerning averages (Batting Average, Earned Run Average, etc.). For the rules and the years they were in effect, see Appendix C.

League Batting Leaders. Batting statistics that appear in boldfaced print indicate that the player led his league in a particular batting category. When there is a tie for league lead, the figures for all the men who tied are shown in boldface.

League Fielding Leaders. Fielding statistics that appear in boldfaced print indicate that the player led his league in a particular fielding category at his position. For the purpose of determining league leaders, all outfield positions are combined into one position. When there is a tie for league lead, the figures for all the men who tied are shown in boldface.

League Pitching Leaders. Pitching statistics that appear in boldfaced print indicate that the pitcher led his league in a particular pitching category. When there is a tie for league lead, the figures for all the men who tied are shown in boldface.

Traded League Leaders. An asterisk (*) next to a particular figure indicates that the player led the league that year in the particular statistical category, but since he played for more than one team, the figure does not necessarily represent his league leading total or average.

Unavailable Information. Any time a blank space is shown in a particular statistical column it indicates that the information was unavailable or incomplete. This, however, does not apply for *Total Chances per Game,* which is explained above.

Estimated Earned Run Averages (also applies to Yearly League Leaders Information). Any time an earned run average appears in italics it indicates that not all the earned runs allowed by the pitcher are known, and the information had to be estimated. For example, it is known that a pitcher's team allowed 560 runs in 112 games. Of these games, it is known that in 90 of them the team allowed 420 of which 315 or 75% were earned. One man is known to have pitched 207 2/3 innings in 40 games and allowed 134 runs. In 35 of these games it is known that he allowed 118 runs of which 83 were earned. By multiplying the team's known ratio of earned runs to total runs (75%) by the pitcher's 16 (134 minus 118) remaining runs allowed, a figure of 12 additional estimated earned runs is calculated. This means that the pitcher allowed an estimated total of 95 earned runs in 207 2/3 innings, for an estimated earned run average of 4.12. In all cases at least 50% of the runs allowed by the team were "known" as a basis for estimating earned run averages.

Yearly League Leaders Information

Appearing directly after the roster information are yearly league leaders. The categories generally include the top three and the top five players. However, there can be exceptions to the number of men included in the various categories if there are ties for a position. The exceptions if there are ties for any position other than first are explained below. The rule used for first place ties is that if more than six men tied for first (in a category that lists five), then the information in the categories shows only the number of players tied, along with the appropriate statistic. For categories of three, the most players that would be shown are four. The following is the list of categories included:

Batting and Base Running Leaders

Batting Average, Slugging Average. The top five players are shown. All ties are broken by carrying the average out to seven decimal places. If a tie still remains, then the players involved are considered tied but the man who had the most at bats is listed first. If required by ties, six players are shown. If ties would require more than six men to be shown, none of the last tied group are included.

Home Runs, Total Bases, Runs Batted In, Stolen Bases. The top five players are shown. If players are tied for a position, the man who had the fewest at bats is listed first. If required by ties, six players are shown. If ties would require more than six men to be shown, none of the last tied group are included.

Home Run Percentages (the number of home runs per 100 times at bat). The top four players are shown. All ties are broken by carrying the average out to seven decimal places. If a tie still remains, then the players involved are considered tied but the man that had the most at bats is listed first. If required by ties, five players are shown. However, if ties would require more than five men to be shown, none of the last tied group are included.

Runs Scored, Hits, Bases on Balls, Doubles, Triples. The top four players are shown. If players are tied for a position, the man who had the fewest at bats is listed first. If required by ties, five players are shown. If ties would require more than five men to be shown, none of the last tied group are included.

Pitching Leaders

Winning Percentage, Earned Run Average. The top five pitchers are shown. All ties are broken by carrying the average out to seven decimal places. If a tie still remains, then the pitchers involved are considered tied but the man who pitched the most innings is listed first. If required by ties, six pitchers are shown. If ties would require more than six men to be shown, none of the last tied group are included.

Wins, Strikeouts, Saves, Complete Games. The top five pitchers are shown. If pitchers are tied for a position in Wins or Strikeouts, the man who pitched the fewest innings is listed first. If pitchers are tied for a position in Saves, the man who pitched the fewest games in relief is listed first. If pitchers are tied for a position in Complete Games, the man who started the fewest games is listed first. If required by ties, six players are shown. If ties would require more than six men to be shown, none of the last tied group are included.

Fewest Hits per 9 Innings, Fewest Bases on Balls per 9 Innings, Most Strikeouts per 9 Innings. The top four pitchers are shown. All ties are broken by carrying the average out to seven decimal places. If a tie still remains, then the pitchers involved are considered tied but the man who pitched the most innings is listed first, except Most Strikeouts per 9 Innings. The man listed first in this category is the one who pitched the fewest innings. If required by ties, five pitchers are shown. If ties would require more than five men to be shown, none of the last tied group are included.

Games Pitched, Shutouts, Innings Pitched. The top four pitchers are shown. If pitchers are tied for a position in Games Pitched, the man who pitched the most innings is listed first. If pitchers are tied for a position in Shutouts, the man who started the fewest games is listed first. If pitchers are tied for a position in Innings Pitched, the man who pitched in the most games is listed first. If ties would require more than four men to be shown, none of the last tied group are included.

League Column Headings Information

								Batting						Fielding			Pitching					
		W	L	PCT	GB	R	OR	2B	3B	HR	BA	SA	SB	E	DP	FA	CG	BB	SO	ShO	SV	ERA
East	Detroit	86	70	.551		558	514	179	32	122	.237	.356	17	**96**	137	**.984**	46	465	952	11	33	2.96
	Boston	85	70	.548	0.5	**640**	620	**229**	**34**	124	.248	**.376**	66	130	141	.978	48	512	918	20	25	3.47
	Baltimore	80	74	.519	5	519	**430**	193	29	100	.229	.339	78	100	150	.983	**62**	**395**	788	20	21	**2.54**
	New York	79	76	.510	6.5	557	527	201	24	103	.249	.357	71	134	**179**	.978	35	419	625	19	39	3.05
	Cleveland	72	84	.462	14	472	519	187	18	91	.234	.330	49	116	157	.981	47	534	846	13	25	2.97
	Milwaukee	65	91	.417	21	493	595	167	22	88	.235	.328	64	139	145	.977	37	486	740	14	32	3.45
West	Oakland	93	62	.600		604	457	195	29	**134**	.240	.366	87	130	146	.979	42	418	862	**23**	**43**	2.58
	Chicago	87	67	.565	5.5	566	538	170	28	108	.238	.346	100	135	136	.977	36	431	936	14	42	3.12
	Minnesota	77	77	.500	15.5	537	535	182	31	93	.244	.344	53	159	133	.974	37	444	838	17	34	2.86
	Kansas City	76	78	.494	16.5	580	545	220	26	78	**.255**	.353	85	120	164	.980	44	405	801	16	28	3.24
	California	75	80	.484	18	454	533	171	26	78	.242	.330	57	114	135	.981	57	620	**1000**	18	16	3.06
	Texas	54	100	.351	38.5	461	628	166	17	56	.217	.290	**126**	166	147	.972	11	613	868	8	34	3.53
						6441	6441	2260	316	1175	.239	.343	853	1539	1770	.979	502	5742	10174	193	372	3.07

W	Wins
L	Loses
PCT	Winning Percentage
GB	Games Behind the League Leader
R	Runs Scored
OR	Opponets' Runs (Runs Scored Against)

Batting

2B	Doubles
3B	Triples
HR	Home Runs
BA	Batting Average
SA	Slugging Average
SB	Stolen Bases

Fielding

E	Errors
DP	Double Plays
FA	Fielding Average

Pitching

CG	Complete Games
BB	Bases on Balls
SO	Strikeouts
ShO	Shutouts
SV	Saves
ERA	Earned Run Average

League Leaders, Team Information. Statistics that appear in boldfaced print indicate that the team led the league that year in a particular statistical category. The leaders for opponents' runs, pitcher's bases on balls, and errors are the teams that allowed or committed the fewest of these. When there is a tie for league lead the figures for all teams that tied are shown in boldface.

Unavailable Information. Any time a blank space is shown in a particular statistical column, it indicates that the information is unavailable or incomplete.

Team Estimated Earned Run Averages. Any time an earned run average appears in italics, it indicates that not all the earned runs allowed by the team are known, and the information had to be estimated. For example, it is known that a team allowed 560 runs in 112 games. Of these games, it is known that in 90 of them the team allowed 460 runs of which 345 or 75% were earned. By applying this percentage to the 100 remaining runs, it is estimated that 75 of these runs were earned. Thus, the earned runs allowed by the pitching staff is calculated as 420 (345 known plus 75 estimated). Since the pitchers worked a total of 1,020 innings, the estimated team earned run average is 3.71. In all cases at least 50% of the runs allowed by the team were "known" as a basis for estimating earned run averages.

1981 Split Season.
The 1981 season was split into two halves as a result of the players' strike. The teams appear in order of their combined records for the two halves, and the managers' records as listed are also for the combined season. The standings for the two half-seasons appear below the combined standings and team statistics. The same applies to the 1892 National League season.

NATIONAL LEAGUE 1876

Chicago

W-52 L-14

Al Spalding

POS	Player	AB	BA	HR	RBI	PO	A	E	DP	TC/G	FA	Pitcher	G	IP	W	L	SV	ERA
1B	C. McVey	308	.347	1	53	485	10	21	21	9.4	.959	A. Spalding	61	529	**47**	13	0	1.75
2B	R. Barnes	322	**.429**	1	59	167	199	36	22	6.1	**.910**							
SS	J. Peters	316	.351	1	47	95	193	21	**16**	4.7	**.932**							
3B	C. Anson	309	.356	1	59	**135**	**147**	50	**8**	5.0	.849							
RF	B. Addy	142	.282	0	16	46	6	13	0	2.0	.800							
CF	P. Hines	305	.331	2	59	159	8	14	4	2.8	.923							
LF	J. Glenn	276	.304	0	32	128	5	18	1	2.7	.881							
C	D. White	303	.343	1	**60**	295	50	64	3	6.5	.844							
P	A. Spalding	292	.312	0	44	45	92	7	**7**	2.4	.951							
OF	O. Bielaski	139	.209	0	10	41	4	14	1	1.8	.763							

St. Louis

W-45 L-19

Mase Graffen
W-39 L-17

George McManus
W-6 L-2

POS	Player	AB	BA	HR	RBI	PO	A	E	DP	TC/G	FA	Pitcher	G	IP	W	L	SV	ERA
1B	D. Dehlman	245	.184	0	9	**750**	8	33	21	12.4	.958	G. Bradley	64	573	45	19	0	**1.23**
2B	M. McGeary	276	.261	0	30	132	180	39	16	6.3	.889							
SS	D. Mack	180	.217	1	7	42	114	20	6	4.3	.886							
3B	J. Battin	283	.300	0	46	115	145	40	**8**	4.8	**.867**							
RF	J. Blong	264	.235	0	30	64	13	9	2	1.4	.895							
CF	L. Pike	282	.323	1	50	82	13	11	5	1.7	.896							
LF	N. Cuthbert	283	.247	0	25	95	7	19	2	1.9	.843							
C	J. Clapp	298	.305	0	29	**333**	56	56	**5**	7.3	.874							
P	G. Bradley	265	.249	0	28	**50**	87	12	4	2.3	.919							
SS	D. Pearce	102	.206	0	10	23	87	12	6	5.3	.902							

Hartford

W-47 L-21

Bob Ferguson

POS	Player	AB	BA	HR	RBI	PO	A	E	DP	TC/G	FA	Pitcher	G	IP	W	L	SV	ERA
1B	E. Mills	254	.260	0	23	644	7	42	13	11.0	.939	T. Bond	45	408	31	13	0	1.68
2B	J. Burdock	309	.259	0	23	**211**	174	45	18	6.2	.895	C. Cummings	24	216	16	8	0	1.67
SS	T. Carey	289	.270	0	26	74	218	39	9	4.9	.882							
3B	B. Ferguson	310	.265	0	32	124	133	54	5	4.5	.826							
RF	D. Higham	312	.327	0	35	57	16	11	1	1.4	.869							
CF	J. Remsen	324	.275	1	30	177	12	24	5	3.1	.887							
LF	T. York	263	.259	1	39	153	8	18	1	2.7	.899							
C	D. Allison	163	.264	0	15	201	43	33	2	6.9	**.881**							
P	T. Bond	182	.275	0	21	25	93	15	0	**3.0**	.887							
C	B. Harbidge	106	.217	0	6	97	30	32	0	6.6	.799							
P	C. Cummings	105	.162	0	7	9	27	2	0	1.6	.947							

Boston

W-39 L-31

Harry Wright

POS	Player	AB	BA	HR	RBI	PO	A	E	DP	TC/G	FA	Pitcher	G	IP	W	L	SV	ERA
1B	T. Murnane	308	.282	2	34	689	5	**55**	**30**	11.5	.927	J. Borden	29	218	11	12	1	2.89
2B	J. Morrill	278	.263	0	26	105	117	37	18	7.0	.857	J. Manning	34	197	18	5	**5**	2.14
SS	G. Wright	**335**	.299	1	34	89	**251**	43	**16**	5.6	.888	F. Bradley	22	173	9	10	1	2.49
3B	H. Schafer	286	.252	0	35	122	146	63	**8**	4.7	.810							
RF	J. Manning	288	.264	2	25	73	7	23	0	1.8	.777							
CF	J. O'Rourke	312	.327	2	43	154	7	27	1	2.8	.856							
LF	A. Leonard	303	.281	0	27	68	6	6	2	2.3	.925							
C	L. Brown	195	.210	2	21	192	45	40	4	6.2	.856							
OF	F. Whitney	139	.237	0	15	73	8	18	4	2.9	.818							
PO	J. Borden	121	.207	0	7	20	34	29	0		.651							
P	F. Bradley	82	.232	0	8	10	24	2	0	1.6	.944							

Louisville

W-30 L-36

Jack Chapman

POS	Player	AB	BA	HR	RBI	PO	A	E	DP	TC/G	FA	Pitcher	G	IP	W	L	SV	ERA
1B	J. Gerhardt	292	.260	2	18	664	**13**	40	13	**13.3**	.944	J. Devlin	**68**	**622**	30	**35**	0	1.56
2B	E. Somerville	256	.188	0	14	210	**251**	**69**	22	**8.3**	.870							
SS	C. Fulmer	267	.273	1	29	83	209	47	12	5.1	.861							
3B	B. Hague	294	.265	1	22	67	89	51	5	3.1	.754							
RF	A. Allison	130	.208	0	10	34	11	12	1	2.5	.789							
CF	S. Hastings	283	.258	0	21	98	11	16	4	1.9	.872							
LF	J. Ryan	241	.253	1	18	131	1	17	1	2.3	.886							
C	P. Snyder	224	.196	1	9	249	**86**	67	2	7.3	.833							
P	J. Devlin	298	.315	0	28	44	**100**	9	4	2.3	.941							

New York

W-21 L-35

Bill Craver

POS	Player	AB	BA	HR	RBI	PO	A	E	DP	TC/G	FA	Pitcher	G	IP	W	L	SV	ERA
1B	J. Start	264	.277	0	21	547	10	21	11	10.3	**.964**	B. Mathews	56	516	21	34	0	2.86
2B	B. Craver	246	.224	0	22	95	84	41	7	5.2	.814							
SS	J. Hallinan	240	.279	2	36	45	172	**67**	7	5.7	.764							
3B	A. Nichols	212	.179	0	9	123	135	**73**	1	**5.8**	.779							
RF	E. Booth	228	.215	0	7	73	11	26	0	2.1	.764							
CF	J. Holdsworth	241	.266	0	19	109	10	13	1	2.7	.902							
LF	F. Treacey	256	.211	0	18	202	9	39	1	4.4	.844							
C	N. Hicks	188	.234	0	15	222	47	**94**	3	**8.1**	.741							
P	B. Mathews	218	.183	0	9	41	78	**28**	0	2.6	.810							

Philadelphia

W-14 L-45

Al Wright

POS	Player	AB	BA	HR	RBI	PO	A	E	DP	TC/G	FA	Pitcher	G	IP	W	L	SV	ERA
1B	E. Sutton	236	.297	1	31	324	11	31	6	12.6	.915	L. Knight	34	282	10	22	0	2.62
2B	W. Fisler	278	.288	1	30	45	65	22	7	6.3	.833	G. Zettlein	28	234	4	20	2	3.88
SS	D. Force	284	.232	0	17	108*	237	39	11	6.4*	.898							
3B	L. Meyerle	256	.340	0	34	84	101	49	4	4.8	.791							
RF	W. Coon	220	.227	0	22	43	8	16	1	2.3	.761							
CF	D. Eggler	174	.299	0	19	109	6	11	1	3.2	.913							
LF	G. Hall	268	.366	**5**	45	150	7	39	3	3.3	.801							
C	F. Malone	96	.229	0	6	78	30	31	0	6.9	.777							
UT	L. Knight	240	.250	0	24	156	48	40	10		.836							
P	G. Zettlein	128	.211	0	11	7	36	5	2	1.7	.896							
20	B. Fouser	89	.135	0	2	45	55	21	3		.826							

NATIONAL LEAGUE 1876, *cont.*

Cincinnati

W-9 L-56

Charlie Gould

POS	Player	AB	BA	HR	RBI	PO	A	E	DP	TC/G	FA
1B	C. Gould	258	.252	0	11	584	**13**	39	28	10.4	.939
2B	C. Sweasy	225	.204	0	10	167	158	51	**30**	6.8	.864
SS	H. Kessler	248	.258	0	11	57	118	47	11	4.8	.788
3B	W. Foley	221	.226	0	9	67	101	41	4	4.5	.804
RF	D. Pierson	233	.236	0	13	46	9	9	2	2.1	.859
CF	C. Jones	276	.286	4	38	151	11	27	2	3.0	.857
LF	R. Snyder	205	.151	0	12	168	6	37	1	3.8	.825
C	A. Booth	272	.261	0	14	77	29	38	3	6.0	.736
P	D. Dean	138	.261	0	4	22	38	13	2	2.4	.822
PO	C. Fisher	129	.248	0	4	31	28	13	0		.819
UT	B. Clack	118	.161	0	5	105	33	26	1		.841

Pitcher	G	IP	W	L	SV	ERA
D. Dean	30	263	4	26	0	3.73
C. Fisher	28	229	4	20	0	3.02

BATTING AND BASE RUNNING LEADERS

Batting Average

R. Barnes, CHI	.429
G. Hall, PHI	.366
C. Anson, CHI	.356
J. Peters, CHI	.351
C. McVey, CHI	.347

Slugging Average

R. Barnes, CHI	.590
G. Hall, PHI	.545
L. Pike, STL	.472
L. Meyerle, PHI	.449
C. Anson, CHI	.440

Home Runs

G. Hall, PHI	5
C. Jones, CIN	4

Total Bases

R. Barnes, CHI	190
G. Hall, PHI	146
C. Anson, CHI	136
P. Hines, CHI	134
L. Pike, STL	133
G. Wright, BOS	133

Runs Batted In

D. White, CHI	60
P. Hines, CHI	59
C. Anson, CHI	59
R. Barnes, CHI	59
C. McVey, CHI	53

Stolen Bases

(not available)

Hits

R. Barnes, CHI	138
J. Peters, CHI	111
C. Anson, CHI	110
C. McVey, CHI	107

Base on Balls

R. Barnes, CHI	20
J. O'Rourke, BOS	15
J. Burdock, HAR	13
J. Glenn, CHI	12
C. Anson, CHI	12

Home Run Percentage

G. Hall, PHI	1.9
C. Jones, CIN	1.4
L. Brown, BOS	1.0
J. Hallinan, NY	0.8

Runs

R. Barnes, CHI	126
G. Wright, BOS	72
J. Peters, CHI	70
D. White, CHI	66
J. Burdock, HAR	66

Doubles

P. Hines, CHI	21
D. Higham, HAR	21
R. Barnes, CHI	21
L. Pike, STL	19

Triples

R. Barnes, CHI	14
G. Hall, PHI	13
L. Pike, STL	10
L. Meyerle, PHI	8

PITCHING LEADERS

Winning Percentage

A. Spalding, CHI	.783
J. Manning, BOS	.783
T. Bond, HAR	.705
G. Bradley, STL	.703
J. Borden, BOS	.478

Earned Run Average

G. Bradley, STL	1.23
J. Devlin, LOU	1.56
C. Cummings, HAR	1.67
T. Bond, HAR	1.68
A. Spalding, CHI	1.75

Wins

A. Spalding, CHI	47
G. Bradley, STL	45
T. Bond, HAR	31
J. Devlin, LOU	30
B. Mathews, NY	21

Saves

J. Manning, BOS	5
C. McVey, CHI	2
G. Zettlein, PHI	2

Strikeouts

J. Devlin, LOU	122
G. Bradley, STL	103
T. Bond, HAR	88
A. Spalding, CHI	39
B. Mathews, NY	37

Complete Games

J. Devlin, LOU	66
G. Bradley, STL	63
B. Mathews, NY	55
A. Spalding, CHI	53
T. Bond, HAR	45

Fewest Hits/9 Innings

G. Bradley, STL	7.38
T. Bond, HAR	7.83
J. Devlin, LOU	8.19
C. Cummings, HAR	8.96

Shutouts

G. Bradley, STL	16
A. Spalding, CHI	8
T. Bond, HAR	6
C. Cummings, HAR	5
J. Devlin, LOU	5

Fewest Walks/9 Innings

G. Zettlein, PHI	0.23
C. Fisher, CIN	0.24
T. Bond, HAR	0.29
B. Mathews, NY	0.42

Most Strikeouts/9 Inn.

T. Bond, HAR	1.94
J. Devlin, LOU	1.77
G. Bradley, STL	1.62
J. Borden, BOS	1.40

Innings

J. Devlin, LOU	622
G. Bradley, STL	573
A. Spalding, CHI	529
B. Mathews, NY	516

Games Pitched

J. Devlin, LOU	68
G. Bradley, STL	64
A. Spalding, CHI	61
B. Mathews, NY	56

							Batting						Fielding			Pitching					
	W	L	PCT	GB	R	OR	2B	3B	HR	BA	SA	SB	E	DP	FA	CG	BB	SO	ShO	SV	ERA
Chicago	52	14	.788		**624**	257	**131**	32	7	**.337**	**.416**	0	282	33	.899	58	29	51	9	4	1.76
St. Louis	45	19	.703	6	386	**229**	73	27	2	.259	.313	0	**268**	33	**.902**	63	39	103	**16**	0	**1.22**
Hartford	47	21	.691	6	429	261	96	22	2	.267	.322	0	337	27	.888	**69**	27	114	11	0	1.67
Boston	39	31	.557	15	471	450	96	24	**9**	.266	.328	0	442	42	.860	49	104	77	3	**7**	2.51
Louisville	30	36	.455	22	280	344	68	14	6	.249	.294	0	397	44	.875	67	38	**125**	5	0	1.69
New York	21	35	.375	26	260	412	39	15	2	.227	.261	0	473	18	.825	56	**24**	37	2	0	2.94
Philadelphia	14	45	.237	34.5	378	534	79	**35**	7	.271	.342	0	456	32	.839	53	41	22	1	2	3.22
Cincinnati	9	56	.138	42.5	238	579	51	12	4	.234	.271	0	469	**45**	.841	57	34	60	0	0	3.62
					3066	3066	633	181	39	.264	.318	0	3124	274	.866	472	336	589	47	13	2.33

NATIONAL LEAGUE 1877

Boston

W-42 L-18

Harry Wright

POS	Player	AB	BA	HR	RBI	PO	A	E	DP	TC/G	FA
1B	D. White	266	**.387**	2	**49**	324	13	13	16	10.0	.963
2B	G. Wright	**290**	.276	0	35	171	209	**53**	28	7.5	.878
SS	E. Sutton	253	.292	0	39	66	91	21	8	4.9	.882
3B	J. Morrill	242	.302	0	28	33	43	12	1	2.9	.864
RF	H. Schafer	141	.277	0	13	17	1	11	0	1.3	.621
CF	J. O'Rourke	265	.362	0	23	112	9	22	0	2.4	.846
LF	A. Leonard	272	.287	0	27	79	5	12	2	2.6	.875
C	L. Brown	221	.253	1	31	**360**	67	**49**	5	**8.7**	.897
P	T. Bond	259	.228	0	30	29	104	9	**2**	2.4	.937
OF	T. Murnane	140	.279	1	15	39	5	10	2	1.8	.815

Pitcher	G	IP	W	L	SV	ERA
T. Bond	58	521	**40**	17	0	**2.11**

Louisville

W-35 L-25

Jack Chapman

POS	Player	AB	BA	HR	RBI	PO	A	E	DP	TC/G	FA
1B	J. Latham	278	.291	0	22	659	**24**	**36**	**28**	12.2	.950
2B	J. Gerhardt	250	.304	1	35	167	**244**	52	**30**	**8.1**	.888
SS	B. Craver	238	.265	0	29	71	175	26	15	4.8	.904
3B	B. Hague	263	.266	1	24	78	78	29	4	3.1	.843
RF	O. Shaffer	260	.285	3	34	121	21	28	1	2.8	.835
CF	B. Crowley	238	.282	1	23	109	20	23	2	2.6	.849
LF	G. Hall	269	.323	0	26	92	7	11	1	1.8	.900
C	P. Snyder	248	.258	2	28	292	**102**	39	**8**	7.1	**.910**
P	J. Devlin	268	.269	1	27	**30**	**110**	10	**2**	**2.5**	.933

Pitcher	G	IP	W	L	SV	ERA
J. Devlin	**61**	**559**	35	**25**	0	2.25

NATIONAL LEAGUE 1877, *cont.*

Hartford

W-31 L-27

Bob Ferguson

POS	Player	AB	BA	HR	RBI	PO	A	E	DP	TC/G	FA	Pitcher	G	IP	W	L	SV	ERA
1B	J. Start	271	.332	1	21	**704**	10	27	25	**12.4**	**.964**	T. Larkin	56	501	29	**25**	0	2.14
2B	J. Burdock	277	.260	0	9	**185**	189	40	25	7.5	**.903**							
SS	T. Carey	274	.255	1	20	49	203	**53**	11	5.1	.826							
3B	B. Ferguson	254	.256	0	35	**109**	**155**	**50**	6	**5.6**	.841							
RF	J. Cassidy	251	.378	0	27	41	16	22	2	1.4	.722							
CF	J. Holdsworth	260	.254	0	20	79	11	18	1	2.0	.833							
LF	T. York	237	.283	1	37	130	5	21	1	2.8	.865							
C	B. Harbidge	167	.222	0	8	143	27	23	2	6.0	.881							
P	T. Larkin	228	.228	1	18	26	89	**15**	0	2.3	.885							
C	D. Allison	115	.148	0	6	127	36	19	4	6.3	.896							

St. Louis

W-28 L-32

George McManus

POS	Player	AB	BA	HR	RBI	PO	A	E	DP	TC/G	FA	Pitcher	G	IP	W	L	SV	ERA
1B	D. Dehlman	119	.185	0	11	306	4	23	14	10.7	.931	T. Nichols	42	350	18	23	0	2.60
2B	M. McGeary	258	.252	0	20	125	140	35	12	7.7	.883	J. Blong	25	187	10	9	0	2.74
SS	D. Force	225	.262	0	22	75	160	22	9	5.1	**.914**							
3B	J. Battin	226	.199	1	22	58	77	29	6	5.1	.823							
RF	J. Blong	218	.216	0	13	60	6	13	0	2.0	.835							
CF	J. Remsen	123	.260	0	13	73	4	8	0	2.6	.906							
LF	M. Dorgan	266	.308	0	23	70	5	16	3	1.8	.824							
C	J. Clapp	255	.318	0	34	269	44	40	2	6.7	.887							
10	A. Croft	220	.232	0	27	338	10	22	10		.941							
P	T. Nichols	186	.167	0	9	14	62	4	1	1.9	.950							

Chicago

W-26 L-33

Al Spalding

POS	Player	AB	BA	HR	RBI	PO	A	E	DP	TC/G	FA	Pitcher	G	IP	W	L	SV	ERA
1B	A. Spalding	254	.256	0	35	472	21	21	23	11.4	.959	G. Bradley	50	394	18	23	0	3.31
2B	R. Barnes	92	.272	0	5	49	70	23	5	6.5	.838	C. McVey	17	92	4	8	**2**	4.50
SS	J. Peters	265	.317	0	41	**124**	**215**	45	**23**	**6.4**	.883							
3B	C. Anson	255	.337	0	32	74	77	20	**9**	4.3	**.883**							
RF	P. Hines	261	.280	0	23	75	4	19	1	2.0	.806							
CF	D. Eggler	136	.265	0	20	60	8	11	3	2.4	.861							
LF	J. Glenn	202	.228	0	20	66	7	4	1	2.1	.948							
C	C. McVey	266	.368	0	36	137	34	28	3	5.0	.859							
P	G. Bradley	214	.243	0	12	25	71	5	1	2.0	**.950**							
20	H. Smith	94	.202	0	3	47	32	18	2		.814							
OF	J. Hallinan	89	.281	0	11	27	1	7	1	1.8	.800							

Cincinnati

W-15 L-42

Lip Pike
W-3 L-11

Bob Addy
W-5 L-19

Jack Manning
W-7 L-12

POS	Player	AB	BA	HR	RBI	PO	A	E	DP	TC/G	FA	Pitcher	G	IP	W	L	SV	ERA
1B	C. Gould	91	.275	0	13	229	9	20	13	10.8	.922	C. Cummings	19	156	5	14	0	4.34
2B	J. Hallinan	73	.370	0	7	52	36	15	8	6.4	.854	B. Mathews	15	129	3	12	0	4.04
SS	J. Manning	252	.317	0	36	30	62	32	2	4.8	.742	B. Mitchell	12	100	6	5	0	3.51
3B	W. Foley	216	.190	0	18	94	130	44	**9**	4.8	.836							
RF	B. Addy	245	.278	0	31	74	17	22	5	2.0	.805							
CF	L. Pike	262	.298	**4**	23	79	10	22	1	2.9	.802							
LF	C. Jones	232	.310	2	36	133	14	28	2	3.8	.840							
C	S. Hastings	71	.141	0	3	63	24	23	1	5.5	.791							
UT	A. Booth	157	.172	0	13	77	101	36	6		.832							
S2	L. Meyerle	107	.327	0	15	54	86	24	5		.854							
P	C. Cummings	70	.200	0	4	6	31	3	0	2.1	.925							

BATTING AND BASE RUNNING LEADERS

Batting Average

D. White, BOS	.387
J. Cassidy, HAR	.378
C. McVey, CHI	.368
J. O'Rourke, BOS	.362
C. Anson, CHI	.337

Slugging Average

D. White, BOS	.545
C. Jones, CIN, CHI	.471
J. Cassidy, HAR	.458
C. McVey, CHI	.455
J. O'Rourke, BOS	.445

Home Runs

L. Pike, CIN	4
O. Shaffer, LOU	3
C. Jones, CIN, CHI	2
P. Snyder, LOU	2
D. White, BOS	2

Total Bases

D. White, BOS	145
C. McVey, CHI	121
J. O'Rourke, BOS	118
G. Hall, LOU	118
J. Cassidy, HAR	115

Runs Batted In

D. White, BOS	49
J. Peters, CHI	41
E. Sutton, BOS	39
C. Jones, CIN, CHI	38
T. York, HAR	37

Stolen Bases

(not available)

Hits

D. White, BOS	103
C. McVey, CHI	98
J. O'Rourke, BOS	96
J. Cassidy, HAR	95

Base on Balls

J. O'Rourke, BOS	20
C. Jones, CIN, CHI	15
A. Booth, CIN	12
G. Hall, LOU	12

Home Run Percentage

L. Pike, CIN	1.5
O. Shaffer, LOU	1.2
C. Jones, CIN, CHI	0.8
P. Snyder, LOU	0.8

Runs

J. O'Rourke, BOS	68
C. McVey, CHI	58
G. Wright, BOS	58
J. Start, HAR	55

Doubles

C. Anson, CHI	19
T. York, HAR	16
J. Manning, CIN	16
G. Hall, LOU	15
G. Wright, BOS	15

Triples

D. White, BOS	11
C. Jones, CIN, CHI	10
L. Brown, BOS	8
G. Hall, LOU	8

PITCHING LEADERS

Winning Percentage

T. Bond, BOS	.702
J. Devlin, LOU	.583
T. Larkin, HAR	.537
J. Blong, STL	.526
G. Bradley, CHI	.439
T. Nichols, STL	.439

Earned Run Average

T. Bond, BOS	2.11
T. Larkin, HAR	2.14
J. Devlin, LOU	2.25
T. Nichols, STL	2.60
J. Blong, STL	2.74

Wins

T. Bond, BOS	40
J. Devlin, LOU	35
T. Larkin, HAR	29
T. Nichols, STL	18
G. Bradley, CHI	18

Saves

C. McVey, CHI	2
J. Manning, CIN	1
A. Spalding, CHI	1

Strikeouts

T. Bond, BOS	170
J. Devlin, LOU	141
T. Larkin, HAR	96
T. Nichols, STL	80
G. Bradley, CHI	59

Complete Games

J. Devlin, LOU	61
T. Bond, BOS	58
T. Larkin, HAR	55
T. Nichols, STL	35
G. Bradley, CHI	35

Fewest Hits/9 Innings

T. Bond, BOS	9.16
T. Larkin, HAR	9.16
T. Nichols, STL	9.67
J. Blong, STL	9.75

Shutouts

T. Bond, BOS	6
T. Larkin, HAR	4
J. Devlin, LOU	4
G. Bradley, CHI	2

Fewest Walks/9 Innings

T. Bond, BOS	0.62
J. Devlin, LOU	0.66
C. Cummings, CIN	0.75
G. Bradley, CHI	0.89

Most Strikeouts/9 Inn.

B. Mitchell, CIN	3.69
T. Bond, BOS	2.94
J. Blong, STL	2.45
J. Devlin, LOU	2.27

Innings

J. Devlin, LOU	559
T. Bond, BOS	521
T. Larkin, HAR	501
G. Bradley, CHI	394

Games Pitched

J. Devlin, LOU	61
T. Bond, BOS	58
T. Larkin, HAR	56
G. Bradley, CHI	50

NATIONAL LEAGUE 1877, *cont.*

	W	L	PCT	GB	R	OR	Batting 2B	3B	HR	BA	SA	SB	Fielding E	DP	FA	Pitching CG	BB	SO	ShO	SV	ERA
Boston	42	18	.700		**419**	**263**	**91**	**37**	4	**.296**	**.370**	0	290	36	.889	**61**	**38**	**177**	**7**	0	**2.15**
Louisville	35	25	.583	7	339	288	75	36	**9**	.280	.354	0	**267**	37	**.904**	**61**	41	141	4	0	2.25
Hartford	31	27	.534	10	341	311	63	31	4	.270	.328	0	313	32	.885	59	56	99	4	0	2.32
St. Louis	28	32	.467	14	284	318	51	36	1	.244	.302	0	281	29	.892	52	92	132	1	0	2.66
Chicago	26	33	.441	15.5	366	375	79	30	0	.278	.340	0	313	**43**	.883	45	58	92	3	**3**	3.37
Cincinnati	15	42	.263	25.5	291	485	72	34	6	.255	.329	0	394	33	.852	48	61	85	1	1	4.19
					2040	2040	431	204	24	.270	.337	0	1858	210	.884	326	346	726	20	4	2.82

NATIONAL LEAGUE 1878

	POS	Player	AB	BA	HR	RBI	PO	A	E	DP	TC/G	FA	Pitcher	G	IP	W	L	SV	ERA
Boston	1B	J. Morrill	233	.240	0	23	606	22	28	**36**	11.1	.957	T. Bond	**59**	**533**	**40**	19	0	2.06
W-41 L-19	2B	J. Burdock	246	.260	0	25	**245**	**212**	41	**34**	**8.3**	**.918**							
Harry Wright	SS	G. Wright	267	.225	0	12	**72**	197	15	**24**	4.8	**.947**							
	3B	E. Sutton	239	.226	1	29	80	118	25	8	3.8	.888							
	RF	J. Manning	248	.254	0	23	61	9	23	1	1.6	.753							
	CF	J. O'Rourke	255	.278	1	29	102	15	19	4	2.4	.860							
	LF	A. Leonard	262	.260	0	16	65	8	21	1	1.6	.777							
	C	P. Snyder	226	.212	0	14	**344**	92	42	2	**8.2**	**.912**							
	P	T. Bond	236	.212	0	23	27	**117**	9	4	2.6	.941							
Cincinnati	1B	C. Sullivan	244	.258	0	20	680	**23**	18	33	11.8	**.975**	W. White	52	468	30	21	0	1.79
W-37 L-23	2B	J. Gerhardt	259	.297	0	28	159	206	38	26	6.7	.906							
Cal McVey	SS	B. Geer	237	.219	0	20	58	177	36	15	4.5	.867							
	3B	C. McVey	271	.306	2	28	78	106	**42**	6	3.7	.814							
	RF	K. Kelly	237	.283	0	27	51	24	23	2	2.1	.765							
	CF	L. Pike	145	.324	0	11	38	4	9	1	1.6	.824							
	LF	C. Jones	261	.310	3	39	120	9	15	1	2.4	.896							
	C	D. White	258	.314	0	29	262	66	33	4	7.5	.909							
	P	W. White	197	.142	0	9	13	90	15	2	2.3	.873							
	OF	B. Dickerson	123	.309	0	9	56	1	8	0	2.2	.877							
Providence	1B	T. Murnane	188	.239	0	14	543	22	36	25	12.5	.940	M. Ward	37	334	22	13	0	**1.51**
W-33 L-27	2B	C. Sweasy	212	.175	0	8	141	183	59	20	7.0	.846	T. Nichols	11	98	4	7	0	4.22
Tom York	SS	T. Carey	253	.237	0	24	56	207	38	8	4.9	.874							
	3B	B. Hague	250	.204	0	25	81	**177**	21	5	4.5	**.925**							
	RF	D. Higham	281	.320	1	29	76	27	24	4	2.0	.811							
	CF	P. Hines	257	**.358**	**4**	**50**	109	15	22	4	2.4	.849							
	LF	T. York	269	.309	1	26	89	14	15	3	1.9	.873							
	C	L. Brown	243	.305	1	43	232	84	43	**11**	8.0	.880							
	P	M. Ward	138	.196	1	15	23	74	15	4	**3.0**	.866							
	C	D. Allison	76	.289	0	7	96	27	12	1	7.1	.911							
Chicago	1B	J. Start	**285**	.351	1	27	**719**	13	33	28	**12.5**	.957	T. Larkin	56	506	29	26	0	2.24
W-30 L-30	2B	B. McClellan	205	.224	0	29	87	139	35	15	6.2	.866							
Bob Ferguson	SS	B. Ferguson	259	.351	0	39	71	**226**	**40**	17	**5.9**	.881							
	3B	F. Hankinson	240	.267	1	27	**94**	138	33	**9**	**4.6**	.875							
	RF	J. Cassidy	256	.266	0	29	89	30	28	6	2.5	.810							
	CF	J. Remsen	224	.232	1	19	103	14	7	5	2.2	.944							
	LF	C. Anson	261	.341	0	40	60	6	14	0	1.7	.825							
	C	B. Harbidge	240	.296	0	37	257	66	**45**	1	7.4	.878							
	P	T. Larkin	226	.288	0	32	19	90	**18**	0	2.3	.858							
	02	J. Hallinan	67	.284	0	2	26	14	12	1		.769							
Indianapolis	1B	A. Croft	222	.158	0	16	534	8	21	19	11.0	.963	T. Nolan	38	347	13	22	0	2.57
W-24 L-36	2B	J. Quest	278	.205	0	13	228	196	**60**	27	7.8	.876	J. McCormick	14	117	5	8	0	1.69
John Clapp	SS	F. Warner	165	.248	0	10	41	124	17	9	4.4	.907	T. Healey	11	89	6	4	1*	2.22
	3B	N. Williamson	250	.232	1	19	88	128	33	6	4.0	.867							
	RF	O. Shaffer	266	.338	0	30	105	28	25	2	2.5	.842							
	CF	R. McKelvy	253	.225	2	36	119	18	25	2	2.6	.846							
	LF	J. Clapp	263	.304	0	29	60	5	8	0	1.7	.890							
	C	S. Flint	254	.224	0	18	285	**102**	39	7	7.2	.908							
	P	T. Nolan	152	.243	0	16	19	80	11	**5**	2.9	.900							
	SS	C. Nelson	84	.131	0	5	19	50	13	1	4.3	.841							
Milwaukee	1B	J. Goodman	252	.246	1	27	693	12	**42**	15	12.4	.944	S. Weaver	45	383	12	**31**	0	1.95
W-15 L-45	2B	J. Peters	246	.309	0	22	97	136	40	14	8.0	.853	M. Golden	22	161	3	13	0	4.14
Jack Chapman	SS	B. Redmond	187	.230	0	21	31	97	35	5	4.2	.785							
	3B	W. Foley	229	.271	0	22	68	87	36	8	3.6	.812							
	RF	B. Holbert	173	.185	0	12	35	19	12	1	2.2	.818							
	CF	M. Golden	214	.206	0	20	50	9	12	2	1.8	.831							
	LF	A. Dalrymple	271	.354	0	15	128	11	28	3	2.7	.832							
	C	C. Bennett	184	.245	1	12	176	31	42	4	7.1	.831							
	UT	G. Creamer	193	.212	0	15	82	117	37	7		.843							
	P	S. Weaver	170	.200	0	3	**31**	78	16	1	2.8	.872							

NATIONAL LEAGUE 1878, *cont.*

BATTING AND BASE RUNNING LEADERS

Batting Average		Slugging Average		Home Runs	
P. Hines, PRO	.358	P. Hines, PRO	.486	P. Hines, PRO	4
A. Dalrymple, MIL	.354	T. York, PRO	.465	C. Jones, CIN	3
B. Ferguson, CHI	.351	O. Shaffer, IND	.455	R. McKelvy, IND	2
J. Start, CHI	.351	L. Brown, PRO	.453	C. McVey, CIN	2
C. Anson, CHI	.341	C. Jones, CIN	.441		

Total Bases		Runs Batted In		Stolen Bases	
P. Hines, PRO	125	P. Hines, PRO	50	(not available)	
T. York, PRO	125	L. Brown, PRO	43		
J. Start, CHI	125	C. Anson, CHI	40		
O. Shaffer, IND	121	B. Ferguson, CHI	39		
D. Higham, PRO	117	C. Jones, CIN	39		

Hits		Base on Balls		Home Run Percentage	
J. Start, CHI	100	J. Remsen, CHI	17	P. Hines, PRO	1.6
A. Dalrymple, MIL	96	T. Larkin, CHI	17	C. Jones, CIN	1.1
P. Hines, PRO	92	C. Anson, CHI	13	R. McKelvy, IND	0.8
B. Ferguson, CHI	91	J. Clapp, IND	13	C. McVey, CIN	0.7
		O. Shaffer, IND	13		

Runs		Doubles		Triples	
D. Higham, PRO	60	D. Higham, PRO	22	T. York, PRO	10
J. Start, CHI	58	L. Brown, PRO	21	J. O'Rourke, BOS	7
T. York, PRO	56	O. Shaffer, IND	19	C. Jones, CIN	7
C. Anson, CHI	55	T. York, PRO	19		

PITCHING LEADERS

Winning Percentage		Earned Run Average		Wins	
T. Bond, BOS	.678	M. Ward, PRO	1.51	T. Bond, BOS	40
M. Ward, PRO	.629	J. McCormick, IND	1.69	W. White, CIN	30
W. White, CIN	.588	W. White, CIN	1.79	T. Larkin, CHI	29
T. Larkin, CHI	.527	S. Weaver, MIL	1.95	M. Ward, PRO	22
T. Nolan, IND	.371	T. Bond, BOS	2.06	T. Nolan, IND	13

Saves		Strikeouts		Complete Games	
T. Healey, PRO, IND	1	T. Bond, BOS	182	T. Bond, BOS	57
		W. White, CIN	169	T. Larkin, CHI	56
		T. Larkin, CHI	163	W. White, CIN	52
		T. Nolan, IND	125	S. Weaver, MIL	39
		M. Ward, PRO	116	M. Ward, PRO	37
				T. Nolan, IND	37

Fewest Hits/9 Innings		Shutouts		Fewest Walks/9 Innings	
M. Ward, PRO	8.30	T. Bond, BOS	9	S. Weaver, MIL	0.49
S. Weaver, MIL	8.72	M. Ward, PRO	6	T. Larkin, CHI	0.55
T. Larkin, CHI	9.09	W. White, CIN	5	T. Bond, BOS	0.56
W. White, CIN	9.17			W. White, CIN	0.87

Most Strikeouts/9 Inn.		Innings		Games Pitched	
W. White, CIN	3.25	T. Bond, BOS	533	T. Bond, BOS	59
T. Nolan, IND	3.24	T. Larkin, CHI	506	T. Larkin, CHI	56
M. Ward, PRO	3.13	W. White, CIN	468	W. White, CIN	52
T. Bond, BOS	3.08	S. Weaver, MIL	383	S. Weaver, MIL	45

							Batting						Fielding			Pitching					
	W	L	PCT	GB	R	OR	2B	3B	HR	BA	SA	SB	E	DP	FA	CG	BB	SO	ShO	SV	ERA
Boston	41	19	.683		298	**241**	75	25	2	.241	.300	0	**228**	**48**	**.914**	58	38	184	**9**	0	2.32
Cincinnati	37	23	.617	4	333	281	67	22	5	.276	.331	0	269	37	.900	**61**	63	**220**	6	0	**1.84**
Providence	33	27	.550	8	353	337	**107**	**30**	**8**	.263	.346	0	311	42	.892	59	86	173	6	0	2.38
Chicago	30	30	.500	11	**371**	331	91	20	3	**.290**	**.350**	0	304	37	.891	**61**	**35**	175	1	0	2.37
Indianapolis	24	36	.400	17	293	328	76	15	3	.236	.286	0	290	37	.898	59	87	182	2	**1**	2.32
Milwaukee	15	45	.250	26	256	386	65	20	2	.250	.300	0	376	32	.866	54	55	147	1	0	2.60
					1904	1904	481	132	23	.259	.319	0	1778	233	.894	352	364	1081	25	1	2.31

NATIONAL LEAGUE 1879

Providence

W-59 L-25

George Wright

POS	Player	AB	BA	HR	RBI	PO	A	E	DP	TC/G	FA	Pitcher	G	IP	W	L	SV	ERA
1B	J. Start	317	.319	2	37	779	11	22	24	12.5	.973	M. Ward	70	587	**47**	17	**1**	2.15
2B	M. McGeary	374	.275	0	35	218	255	**62**	21	7.3	.884	B. Mathews	27	189	12	8	**1**	2.29
SS	G. Wright	388	.276	1	42	**96**	**319**	34	17	5.3	.924							
3B	B. Hague	209	.225	0	21	54	122	38	2	4.2	.822							
RF	J. O'Rourke	362	.348	1	46	51	11	17	2	1.4	.785							
CF	P. Hines	**409**	**.357**	2	52	146	24	26	3	2.3	.867							
LF	T. York	342	.310	1	50	114	9	14	2	1.7	.898							
C	L. Brown	229	.258	2	40	286	63	63*	5	8.6*	.847							
P	M. Ward	364	.286	2	41	31	134	11	2	2.5	.938							
PO	B. Mathews	173	.202	1	10	21	44	9	1		.878							
C	E. Gross	132	.348	0	24	152	39	22	1	7.1	.897							

Boston

W-54 L-30

Harry Wright

POS	Player	AB	BA	HR	RBI	PO	A	E	DP	TC/G	FA	Pitcher	G	IP	W	L	SV	ERA
1B	E. Cogswell	236	.322	1	18	539	10	19	24	11.6	.967	T. Bond	64	555	43	19	0	**1.96**
2B	J. Burdock	359	.240	0	36	**303**	300	59	43	7.9	.911	C. Foley	21	162	9	9	**1**	2.51
SS	E. Sutton	339	.248	0	34	53	167	29	15	4.9	.884							
3B	J. Morrill	348	.282	0	49	70	96	23	2	3.7	**.878**							
RF	S. Houck	356	.267	2	49	62	17	18	2	2.1	.814							
CF	J. O'Rourke	317	.341	6	**62**	147	10	21	2	2.5	.882							
LF	C. Jones	355	.315	**9**	**62**	162	20	13	1	2.3	.933							
C	P. Snyder	329	.237	2	35	**398**	**142**	44	**10**	7.3	**.925**							
P	T. Bond	257	.241	0	21	33	**144**	8	7	2.9	**.957**							
OF	B. Hawes	155	.200	0	9	38	10	10	2	1.7	.828							
PO	C. Foley	146	.315	0	17	13	28	12	0		.774							

Buffalo

W-46 L-32

John Clapp

POS	Player	AB	BA	HR	RBI	PO	A	E	DP	TC/G	FA	Pitcher	G	IP	W	L	SV	ERA
1B	O. Walker	287	.275	1	35	**828**	**30**	**49**	**52**	12.6	.946	P. Galvin	66	593	37	27	0	2.28
2B	C. Fulmer	306	.268	0	28	273	301	60	**46**	8.3	.905	B. McGunnigle	14	120	9	5	0	2.63
SS	D. Force	316	.209	0	8	74	264	26	**26**	4.7	**.929**							
3B	H. Richardson	336	.283	0	37	83	153	**44**	**13**	3.6	.843							
RF	B. Crowley	261	.287	0	30	62	14	18	4	2.2	.809							
CF	D. Eggler	317	.208	0	27	114	11	11	2	1.7	.919							
LF	J. Hornung	319	.266	0	38	129	12	26	1	2.2	.844							
C	J. Clapp	292	.264	1	36	286	60	36	4	6.1	.906							
P	P. Galvin	265	.249	0	27	35	141	**26**	**8**	3.1	.871							
OF	B. McGunnigle	171	.175	0	5	61	6	6	0	2.1	.918							

NATIONAL LEAGUE 1879, *cont.*

Team	POS	Player	AB	BA	HR	RBI	PO	A	E	DP	TC/G	FA	Pitcher	G	IP	W	L	SV	ERA
Chicago	1B	C. Anson	227	.317	0	34	620	8	16	26	**12.6**	**.975**	T. Larkin	58	513	31	23	0	2.44
	2B	J. Quest	334	.207	0	22	263	**331**	48	30	7.7	**.925**	F. Hankinson	26	231	15	10	0	2.50
	SS	J. Peters	379	.245	1	31	94	271	**71**	14	5.3	.837							
W-46 L-33	3B	N. Williamson	320	.294	1	36	**84**	**193**	41	**13**	**4.5**	.871							
	RF	O. Shaffer	316	.304	0	35	99	50	37	3	2.6	.801							
Cap Anson	CF	G. Gore	266	.263	0	32	93	9	15	0	2.2	.872							
W-41 L-21	LF	A. Dalrymple	333	.291	0	23	103	4	40	1	2.1	.728							
	C	S. Flint	324	.284	1	41	341	109	42	6	6.3	.915							
Silver Flint	P	T. Larkin	228	.219	0	18	10	79	8	1	1.7	.918							
W-5 L-12	UT	F. Hankinson	171	.181	0	8	42	87	14	1		.902							
	OF	J. Remsen	152	.217	0	8	52	4	9	1	2.1	.862							

Team	POS	Player	AB	BA	HR	RBI	PO	A	E	DP	TC/G	FA	Pitcher	G	IP	W	L	SV	ERA
Cincinnati	1B	C. McVey	354	.297	0	55	736	5	42	33	10.9	.946	W. White	**76**	**680**	43	31	0	1.99
	2B	J. Gerhardt	313	.198	1	39	191	192	39	23	7.7	.908							
	SS	R. Barnes	323	.266	1	30	93	211	48	14	**5.8**	.864							
W-43 L-37	3B	K. Kelly	345	.348	2	47	36	88	25	3	4.5	.832							
	RF	W. Foley	218	.211	0	25	38	9	8	0	2.2	.855							
Deacon White	CF	P. Hotaling	369	.279	1	27	118	16	25	2	2.3	.843							
W-9 L-9	LF	B. Dickerson	350	.291	2	57	144	9	38	1	2.4	.801							
	C	D. White	333	.330	1	52	307	92	44	3	7.5	.901							
Cal McVey	P	W. White	294	.136	0	17	20	114	20	0	2.0	.870							
W-34 L-28	UT	M. Burke	117	.222	0	8	36	62	32	3		.754							

Team	POS	Player	AB	BA	HR	RBI	PO	A	E	DP	TC/G	FA	Pitcher	G	IP	W	L	SV	ERA
Cleveland	1B	B. Phillips	365	.271	0	29	726	22	36	23	10.5	.954	J. McCormick	62	546	20	**40**	0	2.42
	2B	J. Glasscock	325	.209	0	29	201	208	36	18	6.7	.919	B. Mitchell	23	195	7	15	0	3.28
	SS	T. Carey	335	.239	0	32	79	263	54	13	4.9	.864							
	3B	F. Warner	316	.244	0	22	78	109	39	5	4.2	.827							
W-27 L-55	RF	C. Eden	353	.272	3	34	101	21	29	3	1.9	.808							
	CF	G. Strief	264	.174	0	15	104	8	10	0	2.2	.918							
Jim McCormick	LF	B. Riley	165	.145	0	9	79	12	16	1	2.5	.850							
	C	D. Kennedy	193	.290	1	18	277	50	40	2	8.0	.891							
	P	J. McCormick	282	.220	0	20	**39**	119	9	4	2.7	.946							
	CO	B. Gilligan	205	.171	0	11	179	47	36	0		.863							
	P	B. Mitchell	109	.147	0	6	11	24	14	0	2.1	.714							

Team	POS	Player	AB	BA	HR	RBI	PO	A	E	DP	TC/G	FA	Pitcher	G	IP	W	L	SV	ERA
Syracuse	1B	H. Carpenter	261	.203	0	20	298	10	17	12	9.6	.948	H. McCormick	54	457	18	33	0	2.99
	2B	J. Farrell	241	.303	1	22	162	186	52	16	7.4	.870	B. Purcell	22	180	4	15	0	3.76
	SS	J. Macullar	246	.211	0	13	61	111	27	9	5.4	.864							
W-22 L-48	3B	R. Woodhead	131	.160	0	2	52	51	27	4	3.8	.792							
	RF	B. Purcell	277	.260	0	24	64	4	20	0	1.9	.773							
Mike Dorgan	CF	J. Richmond	254	.213	1	23	76	7	12	1	2.7	.874							
W-17 L-26	LF	M. Mansell	242	.215	1	13	204	11	29	2	3.6	.881							
	C	B. Holbert	229	.201	0	21	277	64	39	4	6.8	.897							
Bill Holbert	UT	M. Dorgan	270	.267	1	17	275	60	46	10		.879							
W-0 L-1	P	H. McCormick	230	.222	1	21	13	68	8	0	1.6	.910							
Jimmy Macullar																			
W-5 L-21																			

Team	POS	Player	AB	BA	HR	RBI	PO	A	E	DP	TC/G	FA	Pitcher	G	IP	W	L	SV	ERA
Troy	1B	D. Brouthers	168	.274	4	17	406	6	33	11	12.0	.926	G. Bradley	54	487	13	**40**	0	2.85
	2B	T. Hawkes	250	.208	0	20	220	264	56	26	**8.4**	.896	H. Salisbury	10	89	4	6	0	2.22
	SS	E. Caskin	304	.257	0	21	42	169	23	10	5.6	.902							
W-19 L-56	3B	H. Doscher	191	.220	0	18	49	96	35	7	3.8	.806							
	RF	J. Evans	280	.232	0	17	153	30	24	4	2.9	.884							
Horace Phillips	CF	A. Hall	306	.258	0	14	126	18	27	3	2.6	.842							
W-12 L-34	LF	T. Mansell	177	.243	0	11	63	3	23	1	2.2	.742							
	C	C. Reilley	236	.229	0	19	231	49	43	2	6.6	.867							
Bob Ferguson	P	G. Bradley	251	.247	0	23	24	132	24	0	3.3	.867							
W-7 L-22	10	A. Clapp	146	.267	0	18	279	7	25	10		.920							
	3B	B. Ferguson	123	.252	0	4	29	55	20	5	4.3	.808							
	SS	C. Nelson	106	.264	0	10	37	89	25	8	6.3	.834							
	OF	S. Taylor	97	.216	0	8	37	2	12	0	2.1	.765							

BATTING AND BASE RUNNING LEADERS

Batting Average		**Slugging Average**		**Home Runs**	
P. Hines, PRO	.357	J. O'Rourke, BOS	.521	C. Jones, BOS	9
J. O'Rourke, PRO	.348	C. Jones, BOS	.510	J. O'Rourke, BOS	6
K. Kelly, CIN	.348	K. Kelly, CIN	.493	D. Brouthers, TRO	4
J. O'Rourke, BOS	.341	P. Hines, PRO	.482	C. Eden, CLE	3
D. White, CIN	.330	J. O'Rourke, PRO	.459		

Total Bases		**Runs Batted In**		**Stolen Bases**
P. Hines, PRO	197	J. O'Rourke, BOS	62	(not available)
C. Jones, BOS	181	C. Jones, BOS	62	
K. Kelly, CIN	170	B. Dickerson, CIN	57	
J. O'Rourke, PRO	166	C. McVey, CIN	55	
J. O'Rourke, BOS	165	D. White, CIN	52	
		P. Hines, PRO	52	

PITCHING LEADERS

Winning Percentage		**Earned Run Average**		**Wins**	
M. Ward, PRO	.734	T. Bond, BOS	1.96	M. Ward, PRO	47
T. Bond, BOS	.694	W. White, CIN	1.99	T. Bond, BOS	43
F. Hankinson, CHI	.600	M. Ward, PRO	2.15	W. White, CIN	43
B. Mathews, PRO	.600	P. Galvin, BUF	2.28	P. Galvin, BUF	37
W. White, CIN	.581	B. Mathews, PRO	2.29	T. Larkin, CHI	31

Saves		**Strikeouts**		**Complete Games**	
B. Mathews, PRO	1	M. Ward, PRO	239	W. White, CIN	75
C. Foley, BOS	1	W. White, CIN	232	P. Galvin, BUF	65
M. Ward, PRO	1	J. McCormick, CLE	197	J. McCormick, CLE	59
		T. Bond, BOS	155	T. Bond, BOS	59
		T. Larkin, CHI	142	M. Ward, PRO	58

NATIONAL LEAGUE 1879, *cont.*

BATTING AND BASE RUNNING LEADERS

Hits	
P. Hines, PRO	146
J. O'Rourke, PRO	126
K. Kelly, CIN	120
C. Jones, BOS	112

Base on Balls	
C. Jones, BOS	29
N. Williamson, CHI	24
T. York, PRO	19
R. Barnes, CIN	16
H. Richardson, BUF	16

Home Run Percentage	
C. Jones, BOS	2.5
J. O'Rourke, BOS	1.9
C. Eden, CLE	0.8
L. Brown, PRO, CHI	0.8

Runs	
C. Jones, BOS	85
P. Hines, PRO	81
G. Wright, PRO	79
K. Kelly, CIN	78

Doubles	
C. Eden, CLE	31
A. Dalrymple, CHI	25
T. York, PRO	25
P. Hines, PRO	25

Triples	
B. Dickerson, CIN	14
N. Williamson, CHI	13
K. Kelly, CIN	12
J. O'Rourke, BOS	11

PITCHING LEADERS

Fewest Hits/9 Innings	
B. McGunnigle, BUF	8.47
M. Ward, PRO	8.75
T. Bond, BOS	8.80
P. Galvin, BUF	8.88

Shutouts	
T. Bond, BOS	11
P. Galvin, BUF	6
H. McCormick, SYR	5
T. Larkin, CHI	4
W. White, CIN	4

Fewest Walks/9 Innings	
T. Bond, BOS	0.39
P. Galvin, BUF	0.47
G. Bradley, TRO	0.48
T. Larkin, CHI	0.53

Most Strikeouts/9 Inn.	
B. McGunnigle, BUF	4.65
B. Mathews, PRO	4.29
B. Mitchell, CLE	4.16
M. Ward, PRO	3.66

Innings	
W. White, CIN	680
P. Galvin, BUF	593
M. Ward, PRO	587
T. Bond, BOS	555

Games Pitched	
W. White, CIN	76
M. Ward, PRO	70
P. Galvin, BUF	66
T. Bond, BOS	64

	W	L	PCT	GB	R	OR	Batting 2B	3B	HR	BA	SA	SB	Fielding E	DP	FA	Pitching CG	BB	SO	ShO	SV	ERA
Providence	59	25	.702		**612**	355	142	**55**	12	**.296**	**.381**	0	382	41	.902	73	62	**329**	3	**2**	**2.18**
Boston	54	30	.643	5	562	**348**	138	51	**20**	.274	.368	0	**319**	58	**.913**	79	**46**	230	**13**	1	2.19
Buffalo	46	32	.590	10	394	365	105	54	2	.252	.328	0	331	**62**	.906	78	47	198	8	0	2.34
Chicago	46	33	.582	10.5	437	411	**167**	32	3	.259	.336	0	381	52	.900	**82**	57	211	6	0	2.46
Cincinnati	43	37	.538	14	485	464	127	53	8	.264	.347	0	454	48	.877	79	81	246	4	0	2.29
Cleveland	27	55	.329	31	322	461	116	29	4	.223	.285	0	406	42	.889	79	116	287	3	0	2.65
Syracuse	22	48	.314	30	276	462	61	19	5	.227	.270	0	398	37	.872	64	52	132	5	0	3.19
Troy	19	56	.253	35.5	321	543	102	24	4	.237	.294	0	460	44	.875	75	47	210	3	0	2.80
					3409	3409	958	317	58	.254	.326	0	3131	384	.892	609	508	1843	45	3	2.51

NATIONAL LEAGUE 1880

Chicago

W-67 L-17

Cap Anson

POS	Player	AB	BA	HR	RBI	PO	A	E	DP	TC/G	FA	Pitcher	G	IP	W	L	SV	ERA
1B	C. Anson	356	.337	1	**74**	833	15	20	28	10.7	**.977**	L. Corcoran	63	536	43	14	2	1.95
2B	J. Quest	300	.237	0	27	223	270	58	26	6.9	.895	F. Goldsmith	26	210	21	3	1	1.75
SS	T. Burns	333	.309	0	43	62	186	39	9	3.6	.864							
3B	N. Williamson	311	.251	0	31	83	143	27	5	4.0	**.893**							
RF	K. Kelly	344	.291	1	60	49	32	23	1	1.6	.779							
CF	G. Gore	322	**.360**	2	47	124	18	21	4	2.2	.871							
LF	A. Dalrymple	**382**	.330	0	36	157	19	29	4	2.4	.859							
C	S. Flint	284	.162	0	17	388	117	37	4	8.1	**.932**							
P	L. Corcoran	286	.231	0	25	34	122	7	2	2.6	.957							
PO	F. Goldsmith	142	.261	0	15	21	53	8	0		.902							

Providence

W-52 L-32

Mike McGeary
W-8 L-7

Monte Ward
W-18 L-13

Mike Dorgan
W-26 L-12

POS	Player	AB	BA	HR	RBI	PO	A	E	DP	TC/G	FA	Pitcher	G	IP	W	L	SV	ERA
1B	J. Start	345	.278	0	27	**954**	10	29	30	**12.1**	.971	M. Ward	70	595	40	23	1	1.74
2B	J. Farrell	339	.271	3	36	207	274	61	26	6.8	.887	G. Bradley	28	196	12	9	1	1.38
SS	J. Peters	359	.228	0	24	**111**	268	42	26	4.9	**.900**							
3B	G. Bradley	309	.227	0	23	71	**165**	40	8	**4.8**	.855							
RF	M. Dorgan	321	.246	0	31	96	25	20	4	1.8	.858							
CF	P. Hines	374	.307	3	35	148	17	13	7	2.4	.927							
LF	T. York	203	.212	0	18	94	5	7	1	2.0	.934							
C	E. Gross	347	.259	1	34	**429**	**126**	**86**	5	7.4	.866							
P	M. Ward	356	.228	0	27	**43**	133	3	1	2.6	.983							
OF	S. Houck	184	.201	1	22	86	10	14	0	2.2	.873							

Cleveland

W-47 L-37

Jim McCormick

POS	Player	AB	BA	HR	RBI	PO	A	E	DP	TC/G	FA	Pitcher	G	IP	W	L	SV	ERA
1B	B. Phillips	334	.254	1	36	842	25	33	**37**	10.6	.963	J. McCormick	**74**	**658**	**45**	28	0	1.85
2B	F. Dunlap	373	.276	4	30	252	**290**	53	**44**	7.0	.911							
SS	J. Glasscock	296	.243	0	27	107	252	44	21	5.2	.891							
3B	F. Hankinson	263	.209	1	19	68	89	29	7	3.3	.844							
RF	O. Shaffer	338	.266	0	21	128	35	18	5	2.2	.901							
CF	P. Hotaling	325	.240	0	41	115	14	15	4	1.8	.896							
LF	N. Hanlon	280	.246	0	32	135	9	35	4	2.6	.804							
C	D. Kennedy	250	.200	0	18	397	68	52	**9**	8.0	.899							
P	J. McCormick	289	.246	0	26	36	135	22	3	2.6	.886							
3B	M. McGeary	111	.252	0	3	37	49	11	4	3.3	.887							
C	B. Gilligan	99	.172	1	13	124	33	5	4	7.0	.969							

Troy

W-41 L-42

Bob Ferguson

POS	Player	AB	BA	HR	RBI	PO	A	E	DP	TC/G	FA	Pitcher	G	IP	W	L	SV	ERA
1B	E. Cogswell	209	.301	0	13	475	15	20	18	10.9	.961	M. Welch	65	574	34	30	0	2.54
2B	B. Ferguson	332	.262	0	22	294	255	58	38	7.4	.904	T. Keefe	12	105	6	6	0	**0.86**
SS	E. Caskin	333	.225	0	28	97	297	**51**	16	5.4	.885							
3B	R. Connor	340	.332	3	47	116	159	**60**	**10**	4.0	.821							
RF	J. Evans	180	.256	0	22	68	9	8	4	1.8	.906							
CF	J. Cassidy	352	.253	0	29	128	18	20	1	2.0	.880							
LF	P. Gillespie	346	.243	2	24	185	14	21	5	2.7	.905							
C	B. Holbert	212	.189	0	8	261	107	36	6	7.0	.911							
P	M. Welch	251	.287	0	27	35	86	21	4	2.2	.852							
1B	B. Tobin	136	.162	0	8	297	8	16	25	9.7	.950							
OF	B. Dickerson	119	.193	0	10	77	7	9	3	3.1	.903							

NATIONAL LEAGUE 1880, *cont.*

Worcestor

W-40 L-43

Frank Bancroft

POS	Player	AB	BA	HR	RBI	PO	A	E	DP	TC/G	FA
1B	C. Sullivan	166	.259	0	0	447	12	8	19	10.9	.983
2B	G. Creamer	306	.199	0	27	238	274	68	34	6.8	.883
SS	A. Irwin	352	.259	1	35	95	**339**	**51**	**27**	**5.9**	.895
3B	A. Whitney	302	.222	1	36	83	162	40	6	3.8	.860
RF	L. Knight	201	.239	0	21	47	22	11	1	1.6	.863
CF	H. Stovey	355	.265	**6**	28	68	6	12	1	1.9	.860
LF	G. Wood	327	.245	0	28	123	10	17	0	1.9	.887
C	C. Bennett	193	.228	0	18	280	45	31	3	7.7	.913
P	L. Richmond	309	.227	0	34	13	97	**23**	1	1.8	.827
C	D. Bushong	146	.171	0	19	261	76	30	6	9.2	.918
OP	F. Corey	138	.174	0	6	25	19	13	2		.772
OF	B. Dickerson	133	.293	0	20	48	4	9	2	2.0	.852

Pitcher	G	IP	W	L	SV	ERA
L. Richmond	**74**	591	32	32	**3**	2.15
F. Corey	25	148	8	9	2	2.43

Boston

W-40 L-44

Harry Wright

POS	Player	AB	BA	HR	RBI	PO	A	E	DP	TC/G	FA
1B	J. Morrill	342	.237	2	44	434	**26**	16	26	10.3	.966
2B	J. Burdock	356	.253	2	35	**328**	275	50	39	**7.6**	.923
SS	J. Richmond	129	.248	0	9	30	73	19	14	3.9	.844
3B	E. Sutton	288	.250	0	25	64	66	15	5	3.9	.897
RF	C. Foley	332	.292	2	31	35	6	8	1	1.4	.837
CF	J. O'Rourke	313	.275	3	36	156	19	26	0	2.5	.871
LF	C. Jones	280	.300	5	38	108	11	25	3	2.2	.826
C	P. Powers	126	.143	0	10	152	59	37	6	6.7	.851
UT	J. O'Rourke	363	.275	**6**	45	268	96	43	18		.894
PO	T. Bond	282	.220	0	24	60	152	16	8		.930
C	S. Trott	125	.208	0	9	170	56	27	0	7.0	.893

Pitcher	G	IP	W	L	SV	ERA
T. Bond	63	493	26	29	0	2.67
C. Foley	36	238	14	14	0	3.89

Buffalo

W-24 L-58

Sam Crane

POS	Player	AB	BA	HR	RBI	PO	A	E	DP	TC/G	FA
1B	D. Esterbrook	253	.241	0	35	463	17	31	20	10.9	.939
2B	D. Force	290	.169	0	17	163	206	24	27	7.4	**.939**
SS	M. Moynahan	100	.330	0	14	30	70	16	7	4.3	.862
3B	H. Richardson	343	.259	0	17	108	154	47	6	3.8	.848
RF	D. Stearns	104	.183	0	13	21	3	7	1	1.5	.774
CF	B. Crowley	354	.268	0	20	131	23	33	3	2.5	.824
LF	J. Hornung	342	.266	1	42	127	12	20	2	2.4	.874
C	J. Rowe	326	.252	1	36	231	56	33	3	5.3	.897
P	P. Galvin	241	.212	0	12	24	97	13	1	2.3	.903
10	O. Walker	126	.230	1	15	267	10	27	17		.911

Pitcher	G	IP	W	L	SV	ERA
P. Galvin	58	459	20	35	0	2.71
S. Wiedman	17	114	0	9	0	3.40
T. Poorman	11	85	1	8	1	4.13

Cincinnati

W-21 L-59

John Clapp

POS	Player	AB	BA	HR	RBI	PO	A	E	DP	TC/G	FA
1B	L. Reilly	272	.206	0	16	615	13	**35**	36	9.2	.947
2B	P. Smith	334	.207	0	27	282	243	**89**	32	7.4	.855
SS	L. Say	191	.199	0	15	54	164	44	11	5.5	.832
3B	H. Carpenter	300	.240	0	23	**136**	126	45	9	4.6	.853
RF	J. Manning	190	.216	2	17	59	12	18	1	1.9	.798
CF	B. Purcell	325	.292	1	24	78	14	21	1	2.1	.814
LF	M. Mansell	187	.193	2	12	147	13	25	5	3.5	.865
C	J. Clapp	323	.282	1	20	420	121	62	5	**8.3**	.897
P	W. White	207	.169	0	14	17	68	10	2	1.5	.895
OF	D. White	141	.298	0	7	36	9	16	1	1.8	.738
S3	A. Leonard	133	.211	1	17	29	75	21	4		.832
UT	C. Reilley	103	.204	0	9	68	16	14	0		.857
OF	J. Sommer	88	.182	0	6	38	4	4	1	2.1	.913

Pitcher	G	IP	W	L	SV	ERA
W. White	62	517	18	**42**	0	2.14
B. Purcell	25	196	3	17	0	3.21

BATTING AND BASE RUNNING LEADERS

Batting Average

G. Gore, CHI	.360
C. Anson, CHI	.337
R. Connor, TRO	.332
A. Dalrymple, CHI	.330
T. Burns, CHI	.309

Slugging Average

G. Gore, CHI	.463
R. Connor, TRO	.459
A. Dalrymple, CHI	.458
H. Stovey, WOR	.454
J. O'Rourke, BOS	.441

Home Runs

H. Stovey, WOR	6
J. O'Rourke, BOS	6
C. Jones, BOS	5
F. Dunlap, CLE	4

Total Bases

A. Dalrymple, CHI	175
H. Stovey, WOR	161
J. O'Rourke, BOS	160
F. Dunlap, CLE	160
R. Connor, TRO	156

Runs Batted In

C. Anson, CHI	74
K. Kelly, CHI	60
G. Gore, CHI	47
R. Connor, TRO	47
J. O'Rourke, BOS	45

Stolen Bases

(not available)

Hits

A. Dalrymple, CHI	126
C. Anson, CHI	120
G. Gore, CHI	116
P. Hines, PRO	115

Base on Balls

B. Ferguson, TRO	24
G. Gore, CHI	21
J. Clapp, CIN	21
J. O'Rourke, BOS	21

Home Run Percentage

C. Jones, BOS	1.8
H. Stovey, WOR	1.7
J. O'Rourke, BOS	1.7
F. Dunlap, CLE	1.1

Runs

A. Dalrymple, CHI	91
H. Stovey, WOR	76
K. Kelly, CHI	72
J. O'Rourke, BOS	71

Doubles

F. Dunlap, CLE	27
A. Dalrymple, CHI	25
C. Anson, CHI	24
G. Gore, CHI	23

Triples

H. Stovey, WOR	14
A. Dalrymple, CHI	12
J. Hornung, BUF	11
J. O'Rourke, BOS	11

PITCHING LEADERS

Winning Percentage

F. Goldsmith, CHI	.875
L. Corcoran, CHI	.754
M. Ward, PRO	.635
J. McCormick, CLE	.616
G. Bradley, PRO	.571

Earned Run Average

T. Keefe, TRO	0.86
G. Bradley, PRO	1.38
M. Ward, PRO	1.74
F. Goldsmith, CHI	1.75
J. McCormick, CLE	1.85

Wins

J. McCormick, CLE	45
L. Corcoran, CHI	43
M. Ward, PRO	40
M. Welch, TRO	34
L. Richmond, WOR	32

Saves

L. Richmond, WOR	3
L. Corcoran, CHI	2
F. Corey, WOR	2

Strikeouts

L. Corcoran, CHI	268
J. McCormick, CLE	260
L. Richmond, WOR	243
M. Ward, PRO	230
W. White, CIN	161

Complete Games

J. McCormick, CLE	72
M. Welch, TRO	64
M. Ward, PRO	59
W. White, CIN	58
L. Corcoran, CHI	57
L. Richmond, WOR	57

Fewest Hits/9 Innings

T. Keefe, TRO	6.09
L. Corcoran, CHI	6.78
G. Bradley, PRO	7.26
M. Ward, PRO	7.58

Shutouts

M. Ward, PRO	8
J. McCormick, CLE	7
P. Galvin, BUF	5
L. Richmond, WOR	5

Fewest Walks/9 Innings

G. Bradley, PRO	0.28
P. Galvin, BUF	0.63
M. Ward, PRO	0.68
F. Goldsmith, CHI	0.77

Most Strikeouts/9 Inn.

L. Corcoran, CHI	4.50
F. Goldsmith, CHI	3.85
L. Richmond, WOR	3.70
T. Keefe, TRO	3.69

Innings

J. McCormick, CLE	658
M. Ward, PRO	595
L. Richmond, WOR	591
M. Welch, TRO	574

Games Pitched

L. Richmond, WOR	74
J. McCormick, CLE	74
M. Ward, PRO	70
M. Welch, TRO	65

NATIONAL LEAGUE 1880, *cont.*

	W	L	PCT	GB	R	OR	Batting 2B	3B	HR	BA	SA	SB	Fielding E	DP	FA	Pitching CG	BB	SO	ShO	SV	ERA
Chicago	67	17	.798		**538**	317	**164**	39	4	**.279**	**.360**	0	**329**	41	**.911**	80	129	**367**	8	3	1.93
Providence	52	32	.619	15	419	**299**	114	34	8	.248	.313	0	357	53	.910	75	**51**	286	**13**	2	**1.64**
Cleveland	47	37	.560	20	387	337	130	**52**	7	.242	.327	0	330	52	.910	**83**	98	289	7	1	1.90
Troy	41	42	.494	25.5	392	438	114	37	5	.251	.319	0	366	**58**	.900	81	113	173	4	0	2.74
Worcestor	40	43	.482	26.5	412	370	129	**52**	8	.231	.316	0	355	49	.905	68	97	297	7	**5**	2.27
Boston	40	44	.476	27	416	456	134	41	**20**	.253	.343	0	367	54	.901	70	86	187	4	0	3.08
Buffalo	24	58	.293	42	331	502	104	37	3	.226	.289	0	408	55	.890	72	78	186	6	1	3.09
Cincinnati	21	59	.262	44	296	472	91	36	7	.224	.288	0	437	49	.877	79	88	208	3	0	2.44
					3191	3191	980	328	62	.244	.319	0	2949	411	.900	608	740	1993	52	12	2.39

NATIONAL LEAGUE 1881

Team	POS	Player	AB	BA	HR	RBI	PO	A	E	DP	TC/G	FA	Pitcher	G	IP	W	L	SV	ERA
Chicago	1B	C. Anson	343	**.399**	1	**82**	**892**	**43**	24	48	**11.4**	**.975**	L. Corcoran	45	397	**31**	14	0	2.31
W-56 L-28	2B	J. Quest	293	.246	1	26	238	249	37	28	6.8	.929	F. Goldsmith	39	330	24	13	0	2.59
Cap Anson	SS	T. Burns	342	.278	4	42	100	249	**52**	20	5.0	.870							
	3B	N. Williamson	343	.268	1	48	117	**194**	31	10	4.5	**.909**							
	RF	K. Kelly	353	.323	2	55	85	31	22	2	1.9	.841							
	CF	G. Gore	309	.298	1	44	146	21	24	3	2.7	.874							
	LF	A. Dalrymple	362	.323	1	37	143	14	31	1	2.3	.835							
	C	S. Flint	306	.310	1	34	319	92	27	6	5.5	.938							
	P	L. Corcoran	189	.222	0	9	29	63	11	0	2.3	.893							
	P	F. Goldsmith	158	.241	0	16	18	95	18	2	**3.4**	.863							
	OF	H. Nicol	108	.204	0	7	44	11	4	1	2.3	.932							
Providence	1B	J. Start	348	.328	0	29	837	17	33	50	11.2	.963	M. Ward	39	330	18	18	0	*2.13*
W-47 L-37	2B	J. Farrell	345	.238	5	36	214	**271**	**64**	40	6.7	.883	O. Radbourn	41	325	25	11	0	*2.43*
Jack Farrell	SS	B. McClellan	259	.166	0	16	59	147	35	18	4.8	.855	B. Mathews	14	102	4	8	0*	3.17
W-24 L-27	3B	J. Denny	320	.241	1	24	144	181	**62**	12	**4.6**	.840							
Tom York	RF	M. Ward	357	.244	0	53	64	14	9	0	2.2	.897							
W-23 L-10	CF	P. Hines	361	.285	2	31	178	14	22	2	2.7	.897							
	LF	T. York	316	.304	2	47	159	17	29	1	2.4	.859							
	C	E. Gross	182	.275	1	24	240	70	37	5	6.9	.893							
	UT	O. Radbourn	270	.219	0	28	57	121	30	8		.856							
	C	B. Gilligan	183	.219	0	20	184	41	17	9	6.7	.930							
Buffalo	1B	D. Brouthers	270	.319	**8**	45	321	11	17	17	11.6	.951	P. Galvin	56	474	29	24	0	*2.37*
W-45 L-38	2B	D. Force	278	.180	0	15	168	218	26	19	**8.1**	**.937**	J. Lynch	20	166	10	9	0	*3.59*
Jim O'Rourke	SS	J. Peters	229	.214	0	25	102	183	43	17	**6.2**	.869							
	3B	J. O'Rourke	348	.302	0	30	85	80	36	8	3.6	.821							
	RF	C. Foley	**375**	.256	1	25	79	14	24	5	2.1	.795							
	CF	H. Richardson	344	.291	2	53	179	45	21	3	3.1	.914							
	LF	D. White	319	.310	0	53	19	8	11	0	2.2	.711							
	C	J. Rowe	246	.333	1	43	187	39	25	5	5.5	.900							
	P	P. Galvin	236	.212	0	21	**36**	**123**	19	**7**	3.2	.893							
	C	S. Sullivan	121	.190	0	15	108	31	24	1	5.3	.853							
	OF	B. Purcell	113	.292	0	17	32	4	15	0	2.0	.706							
Detroit	1B	M. Powell	219	.338	1	38	513	17	31	47	10.2	.945	G. Derby	56	495	29	26	0	2.20
W-41 L-43	2B	J. Gerhardt	297	.242	0	36	259	242	51	**62**	7.0	.908	S. Wiedman	13	115	8	5	0	**1.80**
Frank Bancroft	SS	S. Houck	308	.279	1	36	88	241	50	**40**	5.1	.868							
	3B	A. Whitney	214	.182	0	9	73	141	38	10	4.3	.849							
	RF	L. Knight	340	.271	1	52	116	21	17	6	1.9	.890							
	CF	N. Hanlon	305	.279	2	28	141	15	18	4	2.4	.897							
	LF	G. Wood	337	.297	2	32	132	18	24	4	2.2	.862							
	C	C. Bennett	299	.301	7	64	**418**	85	20	6	**7.5**	**.962**							
	P	G. Derby	236	.186	0	12	25	97	9	4	2.3	.931							
	1B	L. Brown	108	.241	3	14	252	8	11	20	10.0	.959							
Troy	1B	R. Connor	367	.292	2	31	836	40	**46**	**51**	10.8	.950	T. Keefe	45	402	18	27	0	*3.25*
W-39 L-45	2B	B. Ferguson	339	.283	1	35	**263**	254	55	47	6.7	.904	M. Welch	40	368	21	18	0	*2.67*
Bob Ferguson	SS	E. Caskin	234	.226	0	21	85	205	30	18	5.1	.906							
	3B	F. Hankinson	321	.193	1	19	**151**	169	33	**21**	4.2	.907							
	RF	J. Evans	315	.241	0	28	145	31	14	5	2.3	.926							
	CF	J. Cassidy	370	.222	1	11	143	20	24	0	2.2	.872							
	LF	P. Gillespie	348	.276	0	41	180	16	14	5	2.5	.933							
	C	B. Ewing	272	.250	0	25	211	89	28	9	7.5	.915							
	C	B. Holbert	180	.272	0	14	201	69	24	**10**	6.8	.918							
	P	T. Keefe	152	.230	0	19	23	79	17	5	2.6	.857							
	P	M. Welch	148	.203	0	11	20	39	7	3	1.6	.894							
Boston	1B	J. Morrill	311	.289	1	39	743	37	25	32	10.9	.969	J. Whitney	**66**	**552**	**31**	**33**	0	*2.48*
W-38 L-45	2B	J. Burdock	282	.238	1	24	202	207	40	35	6.2	.911	J. Fox	17	124	6	8	0	*3.33*
Harry Wright	SS	R. Barnes	295	.271	0	17	91	214	**52**	17	5.7	.854							
	3B	E. Sutton	333	.291	0	31	114	157	38	10	3.8	.877							
	RF	F. Lewis	114	.219	0	9	35	6	8	1	1.8	.837							
	CF	B. Crowley	279	.254	0	31	130	17	20	5	2.3	.880							
	LF	J. Hornung	324	.241	2	25	198	19	12	5	2.8	.948							
	C	P. Snyder	219	.228	0	16	261	105	42	0	6.8	.897							
	P	J. Whitney	282	.255	0	32	19	99	**28**	3	2.2	.808							
	UT	P. Deasley	147	.238	0	8	159	48	21	6		.908							
	UT	J. Fox	118	.178	0	4	68	29	10	4		.907							
	OF	J. Richmond	98	.276	1	12	59	4	2	1	2.6	.969							

NATIONAL LEAGUE 1881, *cont.*

Cleveland

W-36 L-48

Mike McGeary
W-4 L-7

John Clapp
W-32 L-41

POS	Player	AB	BA	HR	RBI	PO	A	E	DP	TC/G	FA	Pitcher	G	IP	W	L	SV	ERA
1B	B. Phillips	357	.272	1	44	806	24	29	**51**	10.1	.966	J. McCormick	59	526	26	30	0	2.45
2B	F. Dunlap	351	.325	3	24	258	254	51	41	7.1	.909	T. Nolan	22	180	8	14	0	3.05
SS	J. Glasscock	335	.257	0	33	**105**	**274**	37	29	5.3	**.911**							
3B	G. Bradley	241	.249	2	18	78	76	24	6	3.7	.865							
RF	O. Shaffer	343	.257	1	34	122	24	20	4	2.0	.880							
CF	J. Remsen	172	.174	0	13	117	7	18	1	3.0	.873							
LF	M. Moynahan	135	.230	0	8	65	3	9	2	2.4	.883							
C	J. Clapp	261	.253	0	25	211	73	35	8	6.6	.890							
P	J. McCormick	309	.256	0	26	34	81	13	4	2.2	.898							
UT	T. Nolan	168	.244	0	18	32	37	9	2		.885							
C	D. Kennedy	150	.313	0	15	207	36	21	4	7.5	.920							
OF	B. Taylor	103	.243	0	12	51	4	9	1	2.8	.859							

Worcestor

W-32 L-50

Mike Dorgan
W-24 L-32

Harry Stovey
W-8 L-18

POS	Player	AB	BA	HR	RBI	PO	A	E	DP	TC/G	FA	Pitcher	G	IP	W	L	SV	ERA
1B	H. Stovey	341	.270	2	30	562	16	28	26	10.6	.954	L. Richmond	53	462	25	26	0	*3.39*
2B	G. Creamer	309	.207	0	25	230	248	51	39	6.6	.904	F. Corey	23	189	6	15	0	*3.72*
SS	A. Irwin	206	.267	0	24	50	155	36	11	4.8	.851							
3B	H. Carpenter	347	.216	2	31	141	172	56	14	4.4	.848							
RF	M. Dorgan	220	.277	0	18	41	7	7	1	2.4	.873							
CF	P. Hotaling	317	.309	1	35	142	21	26	2	2.6	.862							
LF	B. Dickerson	367	.316	1	31	153	28	22	6	2.5	.892							
C	D. Bushong	275	.233	0	21	368	**124**	**44**	**10**	7.1	.918							
P	L. Richmond	252	.250	0	28	18	100	8	3	2.4	.937							
UT	F. Corey	203	.222	0	10	55	71	15	3		.894							
SS	C. Nelson	103	.282	1	15	20	94	13	6	5.3	.898							

BATTING AND BASE RUNNING LEADERS

Batting Average	
C. Anson, CHI	.399
M. Powell, DET	.338
J. Rowe, BUF	.333
J. Start, PRO	.328
F. Dunlap, CLE	.325

Slugging Average	
D. Brouthers, BUF	.541
C. Anson, CHI	.510
J. Rowe, BUF	.480
C. Bennett, DET	.478
F. Dunlap, CLE	.444

Home Runs	
D. Brouthers, BUF	8
C. Bennett, DET	7
J. Farrell, PRO	5
T. Burns, CHI	4
L. Brown, DET, PRO	3
F. Dunlap, CLE	3

Total Bases	
C. Anson, CHI	175
F. Dunlap, CLE	156
K. Kelly, CHI	153
A. Dalrymple, CHI	150
B. Dickerson, WOR	149

Runs Batted In	
C. Anson, CHI	82
C. Bennett, DET	64
K. Kelly, CHI	55
D. White, BUF	53
H. Richardson, BUF	53
M. Ward, PRO	53

Stolen Bases	
(not available)	

Hits	
C. Anson, CHI	137
A. Dalrymple, CHI	117
B. Dickerson, WOR	116

Base on Balls	
J. Clapp, CLE	35
T. York, PRO	29
B. Ferguson, TRO	29
J. Farrell, PRO	29

Home Run Percentage	
D. Brouthers, BUF	3.0
C. Bennett, DET	2.3
J. Farrell, PRO	1.4
T. Burns, CHI	1.2

Runs	
G. Gore, CHI	86
K. Kelly, CHI	84
A. Dalrymple, CHI	72
J. O'Rourke, BUF	71

Doubles	
K. Kelly, CHI	27
P. Hines, PRO	27
H. Stovey, WOR	25
F. Dunlap, CLE	25

Triples	
J. Rowe, BUF	11
B. Phillips, CLE	10

PITCHING LEADERS

Winning Percentage	
O. Radbourn, PRO	.694
L. Corcoran, CHI	.689
F. Goldsmith, CHI	.649
P. Galvin, BUF	.547
M. Welch, TRO	.538

Earned Run Average	
S. Wiedman, DET	1.80
M. Ward, PRO	*2.13*
G. Derby, DET	2.20
L. Corcoran, CHI	2.31
P. Galvin, BUF	*2.37*

Wins	
L. Corcoran, CHI	31
J. Whitney, BOS	31
P. Galvin, BUF	29
G. Derby, DET	29
J. McCormick, CLE	26

Saves	
B. Mathews, PRO, BOS	2
J. Morrill, BOS	1

Strikeouts	
G. Derby, DET	212
J. McCormick, CLE	178
J. Whitney, BOS	162
L. Richmond, WOR	156
L. Corcoran, CHI	150

Complete Games	
J. McCormick, CLE	57
J. Whitney, BOS	57
G. Derby, DET	55
L. Richmond, WOR	50
P. Galvin, BUF	48

Fewest Hits/9 Innings	
J. McCormick, CLE	8.28
S. Wiedman, DET	8.45
O. Radbourn, PRO	8.55
L. Corcoran, CHI	8.62

Shutouts	
G. Derby, DET	9
J. Whitney, BOS	6
F. Goldsmith, CHI	5
P. Galvin, BUF	5

Fewest Walks/9 Innings	
P. Galvin, BUF	0.87
S. Wiedman, DET	0.94
F. Goldsmith, CHI	1.20
L. Richmond, WOR	1.32

Most Strikeouts/9 Inn.	
G. Derby, DET	3.86
L. Corcoran, CHI	3.40
M. Ward, PRO	3.25
O. Radbourn, PRO	3.24

Innings	
J. Whitney, BOS	552
J. McCormick, CLE	526
G. Derby, DET	495
P. Galvin, BUF	474

Games Pitched	
J. Whitney, BOS	66
J. McCormick, CLE	59
P. Galvin, BUF	56
G. Derby, DET	56

							Batting						Fielding			Pitching					
	W	L	PCT	GB	R	OR	2B	3B	HR	BA	SA	SB	E	DP	FA	CG	BB	SO	ShO	SV	ERA
Chicago	56	28	.667		**550**	**379**	**157**	36	12	**.295**	**.380**	0	**309**	54	.916	81	122	228	9	0	*2.43*
Providence	47	37	.560	9	447	426	144	37	11	.253	.335	0	390	66	.896	76	138	264	7	0	***2.40***
Buffalo	45	38	.542	10.5	440	447	**157**	50	12	.264	.361	0	408	48	.891	72	**89**	185	5	0	*2.84*
Detroit	41	43	.488	15	439	429	131	**53**	**17**	.260	.357	0	338	**80**	.905	83	137	**265**	**10**	0	*2.65*
Troy	39	45	.464	17	399	429	124	31	5	.248	.314	0	311	70	**.917**	**85**	159	207	8	0	*2.97*
Boston	38	45	.458	17.5	349	410	121	27	5	.251	.317	0	325	54	.909	72	143	199	6	**3**	*2.71*
Cleveland	36	48	.429	20	392	414	120	39	7	.255	.326	0	348	68	.904	82	126	240	2	0	*2.68*
Worcestor	32	50	.390	23	410	492	114	31	7	.253	.316	0	353	50	.903	80	120	196	5	0	*3.54*
					3426	3426	1068	304	76	.260	.338	0	2782	490	.905	631	1034	1784	52	3	*2.78*

NATIONAL LEAGUE 1882

Chicago

W-55 L-29

Cap Anson

POS	Player	AB	BA	HR	RBI	PO	A	E	DP	TC/G	FA	Pitcher	G	IP	W	L	SV	ERA
1B	C. Anson	348	.362	1	**83**	810	27	**45**	42	10.8	.949	F. Goldsmith	45	405	28	17	0	*2.42*
2B	T. Burns	355	.248	0	48	129	127	25	21	6.5	.911	L. Corcoran	39	356	27	12	0	**1.95**
SS	K. Kelly	377	.305	1	55	66	117	43	9	5.4	.810							
3B	N. Williamson	348	.282	3	60	108	**210**	43	**16**	4.3	**.881**							
RF	H. Nicol	186	.199	1	16	59	27	11	1	2.1	.887							
CF	G. Gore	367	.319	3	51	153	23	33	5	2.5	.842							
LF	A. Dalrymple	**397**	.295	1	36	185	8	27	4	2.6	.877							
C	S. Flint	331	.251	4	44	440	91	37	3	7.0	.935							
P	F. Goldsmith	183	.230	0	19	7	0	1	0	0.2	.875							
P	L. Corcoran	169	.207	1	24	0	0	0	0	0.0								
2B	J. Quest	159	.201	0	15	113	127	33	18	6.7	.879							

Providence

W-52 L-32

Harry Wright

POS	Player	AB	BA	HR	RBI	PO	A	E	DP	TC/G	FA	Pitcher	G	IP	W	L	SV	ERA
1B	J. Start	356	.329	0		**905**	21	25	54	**11.6**	.974	O. Radbourn	55	474	33	19	0	*2.09*
2B	J. Farrell	366	.254	2		212	283	**71**	41	6.7	.875	M. Ward	33	278	19	13	**1**	*2.59*
SS	G. Wright	185	.162	0		46	133	26	16	4.5	.873							
3B	J. Denny	329	.246	2		**136**	206	**55**	7	4.7	.861							
RF	M. Ward	355	.245	0		69	20	19	3	2.2	.824							
CF	P. Hines	379	.309	4		151	16	27	4	2.4	.861							
LF	T. York	321	.268	1		159	11	24	3	2.4	.876							
C	B. Gilligan	201	.224	0		287	82	27	8	7.3	.932							
PO	O. Radbourn	326	.239	1		71	97	16	4		.913							
C	S. Nava	97	.206	0		112	31	22	6	6.1	.867							

Boston

W-45 L-39

John Morrill

POS	Player	AB	BA	HR	RBI	PO	A	E	DP	TC/G	FA	Pitcher	G	IP	W	L	SV	ERA
1B	J. Morrill	349	.289	2	54	741	16	28	22	10.3	.964	J. Whitney	49	420	24	21	0	*2.64*
2B	J. Burdock	319	.238	0	27	223	256	35	28	6.2	**.932**	B. Mathews	34	285	19	15	0	*2.87*
SS	S. Wise	298	.221	4	34	84	197	49	13	4.6	.852							
3B	E. Sutton	319	.251	2	38	98	146	41	6	3.7	.856							
RF	E. Rowen	327	.248	1	43	47	7	7	2	1.3	.885							
CF	P. Hotaling	378	.259	0	28	150	16	26	5	2.3	.865							
LF	J. Hornung	388	.302	1	50	191	14	15	4	2.6	.932							
C	P. Deasley	264	.265	0	29	357	54	18	0	7.7	**.958**							
P	J. Whitney	251	.323	5	48	13	88	13	3	2.3	.886							
P	B. Mathews	169	.225	0	13	5	34	6	1	1.3	.867							

Buffalo

W-45 L-39

Jim O'Rourke

POS	Player	AB	BA	HR	RBI	PO	A	E	DP	TC/G	FA	Pitcher	G	IP	W	L	SV	ERA
1B	D. Brouthers	351	**.368**	6		882	19	24	35	11.0	**.974**	P. Galvin	52	445	28	23	0	*3.17*
2B	H. Richardson	354	.271	2		**275**	280	63	28	7.4	.898	O. Daily	29	256	15	14	0	*2.99*
SS	D. Force	278	.241	1		66	209	28	13	5.0	**.908**							
3B	D. White	337	.282	1		59	111	33	6	3.2	.837							
RF	C. Foley	341	.305	3		118	22	28	7	2.0	.833							
CF	J. O'Rourke	370	.281	2		140	15	24	3	2.2	.866							
LF	B. Purcell	380	.276	2		144	11	34	0	2.3	.820							
C	J. Rowe	308	.266	1		246	41	15	5	6.6	.950							
P	P. Galvin	206	.214	0		20	85	8	1	2.2	.929							
P	O. Daily	110	.164	0		1	28	4	0	1.1	.879							
C	T. Dolan	89	.157	0		70	26	6	1	5.7	.941							

Cleveland

W-42 L-40

Jim McCormick
W-0 L-4

Fred Dunlap
W-42 L-36

POS	Player	AB	BA	HR	RBI	PO	A	E	DP	TC/G	FA	Pitcher	G	IP	W	L	SV	ERA
1B	B. Phillips	335	.260	4	47	827	24	25	**55**	11.2	.971	J. McCormick	**68**	**596**	**36**	29	0	*2.37*
2B	F. Dunlap	364	.280	0	28	268	**297**	63	**62**	**7.5**	.900	G. Bradley	18	147	6	10	0	*3.73*
SS	J. Glasscock	358	.291	4	46	111	**311**	47	**40**	5.7	.900							
3B	M. Muldoon	341	.246	6	45	86	133	30	12	4.1	.880							
RF	O. Shaffer	313	.214	3	28	111	17	31	2	1.9	.805							
CF	J. Richmond	140	.171	0	11	65	12	7	0	2.0	.917							
LF	D. Esterbrook	179	.246	0	19	102	15	14	6	2.9	.893							
C	F. Briody	194	.258	0	13	251	89	37	6	7.1	.902							
P	J. McCormick	262	.218	2	15	**43**	**100**	13	1	2.3	.917							
UT	G. Bradley	115	.183	0	6	82	47	13	8		.908							
C	K. Kelly	104	.135	0	5	113	35	37	2	6.2	.800							
3B	H. Doscher	104	.240	0	10	33	45	13	2	4.1	.857							
OF	D. Rowe	97	.258	1	17	33	3	7	1	1.9	.837							

Detroit

W-42 L-41

Frank Bancroft

POS	Player	AB	BA	HR	RBI	PO	A	E	DP	TC/G	FA	Pitcher	G	IP	W	L	SV	ERA
1B	M. Powell	338	.240	1	29	680	14	44	27	9.2	.940	S. Wiedman	46	411	25	20	0	2.63
2B	D. Troy	152	.243	0	14	74	76	27	9	5.7	.847	G. Derby	40	362	17	20	0	3.26
SS	M. McGeary	133	.143	0	2	56	112	13	5	5.5	.928							
3B	J. Farrell	283	.247	1	24	50	65	26	8	3.4	.816							
RF	L. Knight	347	.207	0	24	112	25	21	2	1.9	.867							
CF	N. Hanlon	347	.231	5	38	194	19	27	8	2.9	.887							
LF	G. Wood	375	.269	**7**	29	161	14	23	8	2.4	.884							
C	C. Bennett	342	.301	5	51	**446**	70	30	8	**8.4**	.945							
P	S. Wiedman	193	.218	0	20	35	71	11	2	2.5	.906							
P	G. Derby	149	.195	0	8	19	69	4	1	2.3	**.957**							
UT	S. Trott	129	.240	0	12	207	53	33	6		.887							
3S	A. Whitney	115	.183	0	4	58	66	21	7		.855							

Troy

W-35 L-48

Bob Ferguson

POS	Player	AB	BA	HR	RBI	PO	A	E	DP	TC/G	FA	Pitcher	G	IP	W	L	SV	ERA
1B	J. Smith	149	.242	0	14	352	9	15	19	10.7	.960	T. Keefe	43	375	17	26	0	*2.50*
2B	B. Ferguson	319	.257	0	33	247	221	44	38	6.5	.914	M. Welch	33	281	14	16	0	*3.46*
SS	F. Pfeffer	330	.218	1	31	**161**	276	**73**	35	**6.1**	.857	J. Egan	12	100	4	6	0	*4.14*
3B	B. Ewing	328	.271	2	29	76	112	24	11	4.8	.887							
RF	C. Roseman	331	.236	1	43	107	21	22	6	1.8	.853							
CF	R. Connor	349	.330	4	42	52	2	11	0	2.7	.831							
LF	P. Gillespie	298	.275	2	32	144	9	32	1	2.5	.827							
C	B. Holbert	251	.183	0	23	247	**124**	45	**13**	7.2	.892							
P	T. Keefe	189	.228	1	19	32	89	11	4	3.1	.917							
P	M. Welch	151	.245	1	17	10	46	10	4	2.0	.848							
OF	B. Harbidge	123	.187	0	13	43	3	9	1	2.4	.836							
O3	J. Cassidy	121	.174	0	9	35	23	25	1		.699							
OP	J. Egan	115	.200	0	10	23	13	20	3		.643							

NATIONAL LEAGUE 1882, *cont.*

Worcestor

W-18 L-66

Freeman Brown
W-9 L-32

Tommy Bond
W-2 L-4

Jack Chapman
W-7 L-30

POS	Player	AB	BA	HR	RBI	PO	A	E	DP	TC/G	FA
1B	H. Stovey	360	.289	5	26	469	13	22	25	11.7	.956
2B	G. Creamer	286	.227	1	29	241	283	54	50	7.1	.907
SS	F. Corey	255	.247	0	29	29	76	19	5	4.8	.847
3B	A. Irwin	333	.219	0	30	84	147	45	8	**5.4**	.837
RF	J. Evans	334	.213	0	25	131	31	16	2	2.6	.910
CF	J. Hayes	326	.270	4	54	93	13	18	2	2.1	.855
LF	J. Clinton	98	.163	0	3	43	4	17	1	2.5	.734
C	D. Bushong	253	.158	1	15	308	101	**47**	8	6.6	.897
P	L. Richmond	228	.281	2	28	15	97	**14**	2	2.6	.889
OF	T. O'Brien	89	.202	0	7	41	4	12	0	2.8	.789
UT	F. Mountain	86	.233	2	6	29	23	7	3		.881

Pitcher	G	IP	W	L	SV	ERA
L. Richmond	48	411	14	**33**	0	*3.74*
F. Mountain	18	144	2	16	0	3.69
F. Corey	21	139	1	13	0	*3.56*

BATTING AND BASE RUNNING LEADERS

Batting Average

D. Brouthers, BUF	.368
C. Anson, CHI	.362
R. Connor, TRO	.330
J. Start, PRO	.329
J. Whitney, BOS	.323

Slugging Average

D. Brouthers, BUF	.547
R. Connor, TRO	.530
J. Whitney, BOS	.510
C. Anson, CHI	.500
P. Hines, PRO	.467

Home Runs

G. Wood, DET	7
M. Muldoon, CLE	6
D. Brouthers, BUF	6

Total Bases

D. Brouthers, BUF	192
R. Connor, TRO	185
P. Hines, PRO	177
C. Anson, CHI	174
A. Dalrymple, CHI	167

Runs Batted In

C. Anson, CHI	83
N. Williamson, CHI	60
K. Kelly, CHI	55
J. Hayes, WOR	54
J. Morrill, BOS	54

Stolen Bases

(not available)

Hits

D. Brouthers, BUF	129
C. Anson, CHI	126

Base on Balls

G. Gore, CHI	29
O. Shaffer, CLE	27
N. Williamson, CHI	27
N. Hanlon, DET	26

Home Run Percentage

J. Whitney, BOS	2.0
G. Wood, DET	1.9
M. Muldoon, CLE	1.8
D. Brouthers, BUF	1.7

Runs

G. Gore, CHI	99
A. Dalrymple, CHI	96
H. Stovey, WOR	90
K. Kelly, CHI	81

Doubles

K. Kelly, CHI	37
C. Anson, CHI	29
P. Hines, PRO	28
N. Williamson, CHI	27
J. Glasscock, CLE	27

Triples

R. Connor, TRO	18
F. Corey, WOR	12
G. Wood, DET	12

PITCHING LEADERS

Winning Percentage

L. Corcoran, CHI	.692
O. Radbourn, PRO	.635
F. Goldsmith, CHI	.622
M. Ward, PRO	.594
B. Mathews, BOS	.559

Earned Run Average

L. Corcoran, CHI	1.95
O. Radbourn, PRO	*2.09*
J. McCormick, CLE	*2.37*
F. Goldsmith, CHI	*2.42*
T. Keefe, TRO	*2.50*

Wins

J. McCormick, CLE	36
O. Radbourn, PRO	33
F. Goldsmith, CHI	28
P. Galvin, BUF	28
L. Corcoran, CHI	27

Saves

M. Ward, PRO	1

Strikeouts

O. Radbourn, PRO	201
J. McCormick, CLE	200
G. Derby, DET	182
J. Whitney, BOS	180
L. Corcoran, CHI	170

Complete Games

J. McCormick, CLE	65
O. Radbourn, PRO	51
P. Galvin, BUF	48
J. Whitney, BOS	46
F. Goldsmith, CHI	45

Fewest Hits/9 Innings

L. Corcoran, CHI	7.11
O. Radbourn, PRO	8.15
J. McCormick, CLE	8.31
F. Goldsmith, CHI	8.38

Shutouts

O. Radbourn, PRO	6
M. Welch, TRO	5

Fewest Walks/9 Innings

B. Mathews, BOS	0.69
P. Galvin, BUF	0.81
F. Goldsmith, CHI	0.84
S. Wiedman, DET	0.85

Most Strikeouts/9 Inn.

B. Mathews, BOS	4.83
G. Derby, DET	4.52
L. Corcoran, CHI	4.30
O. Daily, BUF	4.08

Innings

J. McCormick, CLE	596
O. Radbourn, PRO	474
P. Galvin, BUF	445
J. Whitney, BOS	420

Games Pitched

J. McCormick, CLE	68
O. Radbourn, PRO	55
P. Galvin, BUF	52
J. Whitney, BOS	49

	W	L	PCT	GB	R	OR	Batting					SB	Fielding			Pitching					ERA
							2B	3B	HR	BA	SA		E	DP	FA	CG	BB	SO	ShO	SV	
Chicago	55	29	.655		**604**	**353**	**209**	54	15	**.277**	**.389**	0	376	54	.898	**83**	102	279	7	0	**2.22**
Providence	52	32	.619	3	463	356	121	54	10	.250	.333	0	371	67	.901	80	87	273	**10**	**1**	*2.27*
Boston	45	39	.536	10	472	414	114	50	15	.264	.347	0	**314**	37	**.910**	81	**77**	352	4	0	*2.80*
Buffalo	45	39	.536	10	500	461	146	47	18	.274	.368	0	315	42	**.910**	79	114	287	3	0	*3.25*
Cleveland	42	40	.512	12	402	411	139	40	**20**	.238	.331	0	358	**71**	.905	81	132	232	4	0	*2.75*
Detroit	42	41	.506	12.5	407	488	117	44	**20**	.230	.315	0	396	44	.893	82	129	**354**	7	0	*2.98*
Troy	35	48	.422	19.5	430	522	116	**59**	12	.244	.333	0	432	70	.887	81	168	189	6	0	*3.08*
Worcestor	18	66	.214	37	379	652	109	57	16	.231	.322	0	468	66	.877	75	151	195	0	0	*3.75*
					3657	3657	1071	405	126	.251	.342	0	3030	451	.898	642	960	2161	41	1	*2.89*

AMERICAN ASSOCIATION 1882

Cincinnati

W-55 L-25

Pop Snyder

POS	Player	AB	BA	HR	RBI	PO	A	E	DP	TC/G	FA
1B	D. Stearns	214	.257	0		305	5	23	16	9.5	.931
2B	B. McPhee	311	.228	1		**274**	207	42	**36**	6.7	**.920**
SS	C. Fulmer	324	.281	0		130	243	43	14	5.3	.897
3B	H. Carpenter	351	.342	1		**137**	167	60	7	4.6	**.835**
RF	H. Wheeler	344	.250	1		94	11	25	1	2.0	.808
CF	J. Macullar	299	.234	0		141	13	13	2	2.1	.922
LF	J. Sommer	**354**	.288	1		188	9	16	2	2.7	.925
C	P. Snyder	309	.291	1		**358**	92	41	3	7.0	.916
P	W. White	207	.266	0		23	**223**	11	3	4.8	.957
1B	H. Luff	120	.233	0		266	7	23	12	11.0	.922
P	H. McCormick	93	.129	0		12	76	5	0	3.7	.946

Pitcher	G	IP	W	L	SV	ERA
W. White	54	**480**	**40**	12	0	*1.54*
H. McCormick	25	220	14	11	0	*1.52*

AMERICAN ASSOCIATION 1882, *cont.*

Team	POS	Player	AB	BA	HR	RBI	PO	A	E	DP	TC/G	FA	Pitcher	G	IP	W	L	SV	ERA
Philadelphia	1B	J. Latham	323	.285	0		792	12	23	28	11.2	**.972**	S. Weaver	42	371	26	15	0	*2.74*
W-41 L-34	2B	C. Stricker	272	.217	0		239	**251**	52	29	**7.5**	.904	B. Sweeney	20	170	9	11	0	*2.91*
Juice Latham	SS	L. Say	199	.226	1		69	192	40	7	6.1	.867							
	3B	F. Mann	121	.231	0		32	39	18	3	3.1	.798							
	RF	B. Blakiston	281	.228	0		52	13	11	0	2.0	.855							
	CF	J. Mansell	126	.238	0		49	4	14	0	2.2	.791							
	LF	J. Birchall	338	.263	0		134	14	24	0	2.3	.860							
	C	J. O'Brien	241	.303	3		205	66	22	1	6.5	**.925**							
	CO	J. Dorgan	181	.282	0		158	30	30	0		.862							
	P	S. Weaver	155	.232	0		16	127	9	1	3.6	.941							
	P	B. Sweeney	88	.159	0		9	51	6	0	3.3	.909							
	SS	J. Say	82	.207	0		31	76	14	10	5.5	.884							
Louisville	1B	G. Hecker	340	.276	3		689	**22**	**31**	**43**	11.2	.958	T. Mullane	**55**	460	30	24	0	*1.88*
W-42 L-38	2B	P. Browning	288	**.378**	5		157	127	35	19	7.6	.890	G. Hecker	13	104	6	6	0	*1.30*
Denny Mack	SS	D. Mack	264	.182	0		51	161	24	9	4.8	**.898**	J. Reccius	13	95	4	6	0	*3.03*
	3B	B. Schenck	231	.260	0		70	110	41	4	3.8	.814							
	RF	C. Wolf	318	.299	0		71	21	10	2	1.5	.902							
	CF	J. Reccius	266	.237	1		87	15	17	3	1.8	.857							
	LF	L. Maskrey	288	.226	0		136	11	16	1	2.1	.902							
	C	D. Sullivan	286	.273	0		294	95	54	3	**8.2**	.878							
	UT	T. Mullane	303	.257	0		187	191	24	10		.940							
	UT	J. Strick	110	.164	0		110	45	22	6		.876							
Pittsburgh	1B	C. Lane	214	.178	3		480	12	13	19	11.7	.974	H. Salisbury	38	335	20	18	0	*2.63*
W-39 L-39	2B	G. Strief	297	.195	2		241	200	40	28	6.2	.917	D. Driscoll	23	201	13	9	0	**1.21**
Al Pratt	SS	J. Peters	333	.288	0		90	280	49	21	5.4	.883	H. Arundel	14	120	4	10	0	*4.65*
	3B	J. Battin	133	.211	1		62	108	24	5	5.7	.876							
	RF	E. Swartwood	325	.329	5		99	9	29	2	1.9	.788							
	CF	J. Leary	257	.292	2		26	2	9	0	1.4	.757							
	LF	M. Mansell	347	.277	2		159	16	36	1	2.7	.829							
	C	B. Taylor	299	.281	4		116	40	25	0	6.7	.862							
	P	H. Salisbury	145	.152	0		10	96	11	1	3.1	.906							
	OF	C. Morton	103	.282	0		31	9	9	0	2.0	.816							
	C	R. Kemmler	99	.253	0		123	37	14	1	7.6	.920							
	C	J. Keenan	96	.219	1		142	21	17	3	8.2	.906							
	P	D. Driscoll	80	.138	1		4	50	7	1	2.7	.885							
St. Louis	1B	C. Comiskey	329	.243	1		**860**	14	30	25	**11.7**	.967	J. McGinnis	44	379	25	17	0	*2.47*
W-37 L-43	2B	B. Smiley	240	.212	0		145	155	39	20	5.9	.885	J. Schappert	15	128	8	7	0	*3.52*
Ned Cuthbert	SS	B. Gleason	347	.288	1		**131**	**294**	**85**	**23**	**6.5**	.833							
	3B	J. Gleason	331	.254	2		107	**168**	**83**	**11**	4.9	.768							
	RF	G. Seward	144	.215	0		40	12	15	1	1.9	.776							
	CF	O. Walker	318	.239	**7**		158	18	32	4	2.8	.846							
	LF	N. Cuthbert	233	.223	0		74	12	10	0	1.6	.896							
	C	S. Sullivan	188	.181	0		231	46	50	4	6.5	.847							
	P	J. McGinnis	203	.217	0		13	97	11	2	2.8	.909							
	UT	H. McCaffrey	153	.275	0		71	49	17	5		.876							
	UT	E. Fusselbach	136	.228	0		92	54	25	4		.854							
Baltimore	1B	C. Householder	307	.254	1		749	20	23	30	10.7	.971	D. Landis	42	341	11	27*	0	*3.33*
W-19 L-54	2B	G. Pierce	151	.199	0		123	99	57*	17	7.3	.796	T. Nichols	16	118	1	12	0	*5.02*
Henry Myers	SS	H. Myers	294	.180	0		66	257	70	15	5.8	.822	E. Geis	13	96	4	9	0	4.80
	3B	J. Shetzline	282	.220	0		91	121	53	9	**5.1**	.800							
	RF	T. Brown	181	.304	1		59	16	28	1	2.3	.728							
	CF	M. Cline	172	.221	0		78	16	20	1	2.9	.825							
	LF	C. Waitt	250	.156	0		142	11	22	2	2.4	.874							
	C	E. Whiting	308	.260	0		299	**108**	**81**	**6**	6.8	.834							
	P	D. Landis	175	.166	0		19	101	11*	2	3.1	.916							
	30	H. Jacoby	121	.174	1		46	59	26	3		.802							
	PO	T. Nichols	95	.158	0		26	36	13	0		.827							

BATTING AND BASE RUNNING LEADERS

Batting Average
P. Browning, LOU .378
H. Carpenter, CIN .342
E. Swartwood, PIT .329
J. O'Brien, PHI .303
C. Wolf, LOU .299

Slugging Average
P. Browning, LOU .510
E. Swartwood, PIT .498
B. Taylor, PIT .455
M. Mansell, PIT .438
H. Carpenter, CIN .422

Home Runs
O. Walker, STL 7
P. Browning, LOU 5
E. Swartwood, PIT 5
B. Taylor, PIT 4

Total Bases
E. Swartwood, PIT 162
M. Mansell, PIT 152
H. Carpenter, CIN 148
P. Browning, LOU 147
B. Taylor, PIT 136

Runs Batted In
(not available)

Stolen Bases
(not available)

Hits
H. Carpenter, CIN 120
P. Browning, LOU 109
E. Swartwood, PIT 107
J. Sommer, CIN 102

Base on Balls
J. Gleason, STL 27
P. Browning, LOU 26
J. Sommer, CIN 24
J. Reccius, LOU 23

Home Run Percentage
O. Walker, STL 2.2
P. Browning, LOU 1.7
E. Swartwood, PIT 1.5
C. Lane, PIT 1.4

PITCHING LEADERS

Winning Percentage
W. White, CIN .769
S. Weaver, PHI .634
J. McGinnis, STL .595
H. McCormick, CIN .560
T. Mullane, LOU .556

Earned Run Average
D. Driscoll, PIT *1.21*
G. Hecker, LOU *1.30*
H. McCormick, CIN *1.52*
W. White, CIN *1.54*
T. Mullane, LOU *1.88*

Wins
W. White, CIN 40
T. Mullane, LOU 30
S. Weaver, PHI 26
J. McGinnis, STL 25
H. Salisbury, PIT 20

Saves
E. Fusselbach, STL 1

Strikeouts
T. Mullane, LOU 170
H. Salisbury, PIT 135
J. McGinnis, STL 134
W. White, CIN 122
S. Weaver, PHI 104

Complete Games
W. White, CIN 52
T. Mullane, LOU 51
J. McGinnis, STL 42
S. Weaver, PHI 41
H. Salisbury, PIT 38

Fewest Hits/9 Innings
G. Hecker, LOU 6.49
H. McCormick, CIN 7.25
D. Driscoll, PIT 7.25
W. White, CIN 7.71

Shutouts
W. White, CIN 8
T. Mullane, LOU 5
H. McCormick, CIN 3
J. McGinnis, STL 3

Fewest Walks/9 Innings
G. Hecker, LOU 0.43
D. Driscoll, PIT 0.54
S. Weaver, PHI 0.85
H. Salisbury, PIT 0.99

AMERICAN ASSOCIATION 1882, *cont.*

BATTING AND BASE RUNNING LEADERS / **PITCHING LEADERS**

Runs		Doubles		Triples		Most Strikeouts/9 Inn.		Innings		Games Pitched	
E. Swartwood, PIT	86	E. Swartwood, PIT	18	M. Mansell, PIT	16	H. Salisbury, PIT	3.63	W. White, CIN	480	T. Mullane, LOU	55
J. Sommer, CIN	82	M. Mansell, PIT	18	B. Taylor, PIT	12	H. Arundel, PIT	3.53	T. Mullane, LOU	460	W. White, CIN	54
H. Carpenter, CIN	78	P. Browning, LOU	17	E. Swartwood, PIT	11	T. Mullane, LOU	3.32	J. McGinnis, STL	379	D. Landis, PHI, BAL	44
P. Browning, LOU	67	N. Cuthbert, STL	16	H. Wheeler, CIN	11	J. McGinnis, STL	3.18	S. Weaver, PHI	371	J. McGinnis, STL	44
		B. Taylor, PIT	16								

							Batting						Fielding			Pitching					
	W	L	PCT	GB	R	OR	2B	3B	HR	BA	SA	SB	E	DP	FA	CG	BB	SO	ShO	SV	ERA
Cincinnati	55	25	.688		**489**	**268**	95	47	5	**.264**	.332	0	**332**	41	**.907**	**77**	125	165	**11**	0	***1.67***
Philadelphia	41	34	.547	11.5	406	389	89	21	4	.244	.297	0	361	36	.895	72	99	190	2	0	*2.99*
Louisville	42	38	.525	13	443	352	**110**	28	9	.259	.328	0	385	**57**	.893	73	112	240	6	0	*2.08*
Pittsburgh	39	39	.500	15	428	418	**110**	**58**	**21**	.251	**.351**	0	397	40	.889	**77**	**82**	**252**	2	0	*2.87*
St. Louis	37	43	.463	18	399	496	87	41	11	.231	.302	0	446	41	.875	75	103	225	3	**1**	*2.95*
Baltimore	19	54	.260	32.5	273	515	60	24	4	.207	.254	0	490	41	.859	64	108	113	1	0	*3.87*
					2438	2438	551	219	54	.243	.311	0	2411	256	.886	438	629	1185	25	1	*2.74*

NATIONAL LEAGUE 1883

Boston

W-63 L-35

Jack Burdock
W-30 L-24

John Morrill
W-33 L-11

POS	Player	AB	BA	HR	RBI	PO	A	E	DP	TC/G	FA	Pitcher	G	IP	W	L	SV	ERA
1B	J. Morrill	404	.319	6	68	794	20	22	33	10.3	**.974**	J. Whitney	62	514	37	21	**2**	*2.24*
2B	J. Burdock	400	.330	5	**88**	224	290	44	39	5.8	.921	C. Buffinton	43	333	25	14	1	*3.03*
SS	S. Wise	406	.271	4	58	134	274	**88**	21	5.2	.823							
3B	E. Sutton	414	.324	3	73	120	152	42	14	3.4	.866							
RF	P. Radford	258	.205	0	14	86	16	20	2	1.7	.836							
CF	E. Smith	115	.217	0	16	54	3	6	3	2.1	.905							
LF	J. Hornung	**446**	.278	8	66	175	15	13	3	2.1	.936							
C	M. Hines	231	.225	0	16	**382**	103	62	5	**9.3**	.887							
PO	J. Whitney	409	.281	5	57	67	100	25	2		.870							
OP	C. Buffinton	341	.238	1	26	67	68	33	6		.804							
C	M. Hackett	179	.235	2	24	254	57	31	2	7.8	.909							

Chicago

W-59 L-39

Cap Anson

POS	Player	AB	BA	HR	RBI	PO	A	E	DP	TC/G	FA	Pitcher	G	IP	W	L	SV	ERA
1B	C. Anson	413	.308	0		1031	**41**	40	59	11.3	.964	L. Corcoran	56	474	34	20	0	*2.49*
2B	F. Pfeffer	371	.235	1		264	264	67	49	7.5	.887	F. Goldsmith	46	383	25	19	0	*3.15*
SS	T. Burns	405	.294	2		121	260	56	25	5.5	.872							
3B	N. Williamson	402	.276	2		111	**252**	**87**	**20**	**4.6**	.807							
RF	K. Kelly	428	.255	3		101	38	32	5	2.1	.813							
CF	G. Gore	392	.334	2		195	27	34	4	2.8	.867							
LF	A. Dalrymple	363	.298	2		149	12	34	3	2.4	.826							
C	S. Flint	332	.265	0		301	104	57	4	5.6	.877							
P	L. Corcoran	263	.209	0		**37**	88	13	3	2.5	.906							
P	F. Goldsmith	235	.221	1		23	86	17	3	2.7	.865							

Providence

W-58 L-40

Harry Wright

POS	Player	AB	BA	HR	RBI	PO	A	E	DP	TC/G	FA	Pitcher	G	IP	W	L	SV	ERA
1B	J. Start	370	.284	1		923	29	43	48	11.4	.957	O. Radbourn	**76**	632	**49**	25	1	*2.05*
2B	J. Farrell	420	.305	3		258	**365**	51	**51**	7.1	**.924**	C. Sweeney	20	147	7	7	0	*3.13*
SS	A. Irwin	406	.286	0		93	293	65	29	4.8	.856	L. Richmond	12	92	3	7	0	*3.33*
3B	J. Denny	393	.275	8		**178**	188	52	13	4.3	**.876**							
RF	J. Cassidy	366	.238	0		120	26	23	2	1.9	.864							
CF	P. Hines	442	.299	4		169	21	20	2	2.4	.905							
LF	C. Carroll	238	.265	1		109	11	13	4	2.3	.902							
C	B. Gilligan	263	.198	0		379	**108**	54	10	7.3	.900							
P	O. Radbourn	381	.283	3		33	**139**	15	3	2.5	.920							
OF	L. Richmond	194	.284	1		47	3	20	0	1.7	.714							
C	S. Nava	100	.240	0		98	41	32	4	6.3	.813							

Cleveland

W-55 L-42

Frank Bancroft

POS	Player	AB	BA	HR	RBI	PO	A	E	DP	TC/G	FA	Pitcher	G	IP	W	L	SV	ERA
1B	B. Phillips	382	.246	2		953	22	33	53	10.4	.967	O. Daily	45	379	23	19	1	*2.42*
2B	F. Dunlap	396	.326	4		**304**	290	58	49	7.0	.911	J. McCormick	43	342	28	12	1	**1.84**
SS	J. Glasscock	383	.287	0		134	313	38	28	5.2	**.922**	W. Sawyer	17	141	4	10	0	2.36
3B	M. Muldoon	378	.228	0		122	170	62	9	3.6	.825							
RF	J. Evans	332	.238	0		119	29	16	1	1.9	.902							
CF	P. Hotaling	417	.259	0		181	23	42	5	2.5	.829							
LF	T. York	381	.260	2		176	15	30	3	2.2	.864							
C	D. Bushong	215	.172	0		370	88	46	5	8.0	.909							
P	J. McCormick	157	.236	0		28	101	16	**4**	**3.4**	.890							
C	F. Briody	145	.234	0		171	46	24	5	7.3	.900							
P	O. Daily	142	.127	0		6	71	5	1	1.8	.939							

Buffalo

W-52 L-45

Jim O'Rourke

POS	Player	AB	BA	HR	RBI	PO	A	E	DP	TC/G	FA	Pitcher	G	IP	W	L	SV	ERA
1B	D. Brouthers	425	**.374**	3		**1040**	35	44	40	**11.5**	.961	P. Galvin	**76**	**656**	46	29	0	*2.72*
2B	H. Richardson	399	.311	1		289	344	68	33	**7.6**	.903	G. Derby	14	108	2	10	1	*5.85*
SS	D. Force	378	.217	0		79	240	42	22	4.6	.884							
3B	D. White	391	.292	0		84	128	54	8	3.5	.797							
RF	O. Shaffer	401	.292	0		182	41	36	3	2.7	.861							
CF	D. Eggler	153	.248	0		83	4	16	1	2.7	.845							
LF	J. O'Rourke	436	.328	1		89	8	15	0	1.8	.866							
C	J. Rowe	374	.278	1		234	50	32	3	6.4	.899							
P	P. Galvin	322	.220	1		20	127	10	**4**	2.1	.936							
OF	J. Lillie	201	.234	1		73	8	16	2	2.1	.835							
OF	C. Foley	111	.270	0		44	2	6	0	2.3	.885							

NATIONAL LEAGUE 1883, *cont.*

New York

W-46 L-50

John Clapp

POS	Player	AB	BA	HR	RBI	PO	A	E	DP	TC/G	FA	Pitcher	G	IP	W	L	SV	ERA
1B	R. Connor	409	.357	1		958	40	44	37	10.6	.958	M. Welch	54	426	25	23	0	*2.73*
2B	D. Troy	316	.215	0		187	226	57	23	6.4	.879	M. Ward	33	277	16	13	0	*2.70*
SS	E. Caskin	383	.238	1		146	250	67	14	5.7	.855	T. O'Neill	19	148	5	12	0	*4.07*
3B	F. Hankinson	337	.220	2		122	166	43	9	3.6	.870							
RF	M. Dorgan	261	.234	0		104	7	20	1	2.2	.847							
CF	M. Ward	380	.255	7		118	28	24	2	3.0	.859							
LF	P. Gillespie	411	.314	1		216	11	26	6	2.6	.897							
C	B. Ewing	376	.303	**10**		270	96	31	8	6.3	.922							
PO	M. Welch	320	.234	3		71	63	38	4		.779							
CO	J. Humphries	107	.112	0		84	31	26	0		.816							

Detroit

W-40 L-58

Jack Chapman

POS	Player	AB	BA	HR	RBI	PO	A	E	DP	TC/G	FA	Pitcher	G	IP	W	L	SV	ERA
1B	M. Powell	421	.273	1		995	32	**54**	**62**	10.7	.950	S. Wiedman	52	402	20	24	**2**	*3.53*
2B	S. Trott	295	.244	0		102	92	26	16	5.2	.882	D. Shaw	26	227	10	15	0	*2.50*
SS	S. Houck	416	.252	0		**162**	**328**	85	**36**	5.7	.852	D. Burns	17	128	2	12	0	*4.51*
3B	J. Farrell	444	.243	0		111	248	66	13	4.2	.845	J. Jones	12	93	6	5	0	*3.50*
RF	T. Mansell	131	.221	0		35	12	15	1	1.8	.758							
CF	N. Hanlon	413	.242	1		216	13	30	6	2.9	.884							
LF	G. Wood	441	.302	5		226	15	34	3	2.8	.876							
C	C. Bennett	371	.305	5		333	88	25	**11**	6.2	**.944**							
PO	S. Wiedman	313	.185	1		73	81	18	2		.895							
PO	D. Shaw	141	.206	0		21	50	7	5		.910							
OP	D. Burns	140	.186	0		22	32	14	2		.794							
2B	J. Quest	137	.234	0		114	112	26	25	6.8	.897							

Philadelphia

W-17 L-81

Bob Ferguson
W-4 L-13

Blondie Purcell
W-13 L-68

POS	Player	AB	BA	HR	RBI	PO	A	E	DP	TC/G	FA	Pitcher	G	IP	W	L	SV	ERA
1B	S. Farrar	377	.233	1		1038	31	39	45	11.2	.965	J. Coleman	65	538	12	**48**	0	*4.87*
2B	B. Ferguson	329	.258	0		261	287	**88**	38	7.4	.862	A. Hagan	17	137	1	14	0	*5.45*
SS	B. McClellan	326	.230	1		152	254	72	25	**6.1**	.849							
3B	F. Warner	141	.227	0		46	54	29	4	3.4	.775							
RF	J. Manning	420	.267	0		155	37	33	5	2.3	.853							
CF	F. Lewis	160	.250	0		84	8	21	1	3.0	.814							
LF	B. Purcell	425	.268	1		60	14	14	2	2.0	.841							
C	E. Gross	231	.307	1		207	70	**74**	1	6.4	.789							
PO	J. Coleman	354	.234	0		91	132	31	6		.878							
UT	B. Harbidge	280	.221	0		138	79	62	3		.778							
UT	F. Ringo	221	.190	0		197	98	64	9		.822							

BATTING AND BASE RUNNING LEADERS

Batting Average
D. Brouthers, BUF .374
R. Connor, NY .357
G. Gore, CHI .334
J. Burdock, BOS .330
J. O'Rourke, BUF .328

Slugging Average
D. Brouthers, BUF .572
J. Morrill, BOS .525
R. Connor, NY .506
E. Sutton, BOS .486
B. Ewing, NY .481

Home Runs
B. Ewing, NY 10
J. Denny, PRO 8
J. Hornung, BOS 8
M. Ward, NY 7
J. Morrill, BOS 6

Total Bases
D. Brouthers, BUF 243
J. Morrill, BOS 212
R. Connor, NY 207
E. Sutton, BOS 201
J. Hornung, BOS 199

Runs Batted In
J. Burdock, BOS 88
E. Sutton, BOS 73
J. Morrill, BOS 68
J. Hornung, BOS 66
S. Wise, BOS 58

Stolen Bases
(not available)

Hits
D. Brouthers, BUF 159
R. Connor, NY 146
J. O'Rourke, BUF 143
E. Sutton, BOS 134

Base on Balls
T. York, CLE 37
N. Hanlon, DET 34
M. Powell, DET 28
G. Gore, CHI 27
O. Shaffer, BUF 27

Home Run Percentage
B. Ewing, NY 2.7
J. Denny, PRO 2.0
M. Ward, NY 1.8
J. Hornung, BOS 1.8

Runs
J. Hornung, BOS 107
G. Gore, CHI 105
J. O'Rourke, BUF 102
E. Sutton, BOS 101

Doubles
N. Williamson, CHI 49
D. Brouthers, BUF 41
T. Burns, CHI 37
C. Anson, CHI 36

Triples
D. Brouthers, BUF 17
J. Morrill, BOS 16
R. Connor, NY 15
E. Sutton, BOS 15

PITCHING LEADERS

Winning Percentage
J. McCormick, CLE .700
O. Radbourn, PRO .662
C. Buffinton, BOS .641
J. Whitney, BOS .638
L. Corcoran, CHI .630

Earned Run Average
J. McCormick, CLE *1.84*
O. Radbourn, PRO *2.05*
J. Whitney, BOS *2.24*
W. Sawyer, CLE 2.36
O. Daily, CLE *2.42*

Wins
O. Radbourn, PRO 49
P. Galvin, BUF 46
J. Whitney, BOS 37
L. Corcoran, CHI 34
J. McCormick, CLE 28

Saves
S. Wiedman, DET 2
J. Whitney, BOS 2

Strikeouts
J. Whitney, BOS 345
O. Radbourn, PRO 315
P. Galvin, BUF 279
L. Corcoran, CHI 216
C. Buffinton, BOS 188

Complete Games
P. Galvin, BUF 72
O. Radbourn, PRO 66
J. Coleman, PHI 59
J. Whitney, BOS 54
L. Corcoran, CHI 51

Fewest Hits/9 Innings
W. Sawyer, CLE 7.60
O. Radbourn, PRO 8.01
J. McCormick, CLE 8.32
O. Daily, CLE 8.56

Shutouts
C. Buffinton, BOS 5
P. Galvin, BUF 5
O. Daily, CLE 4
M. Welch, NY 4
O. Radbourn, PRO 4

Fewest Walks/9 Innings
J. Whitney, BOS 0.61
P. Galvin, BUF 0.69
O. Radbourn, PRO 0.80
J. Coleman, PHI 0.80

Most Strikeouts/9 Inn.
J. Whitney, BOS 6.04
C. Buffinton, BOS 5.08
W. Sawyer, CLE 4.85
O. Radbourn, PRO 4.48

Innings
P. Galvin, BUF 656
O. Radbourn, PRO 632
J. Coleman, PHI 538
J. Whitney, BOS 514

Games Pitched
O. Radbourn, PRO 76
P. Galvin, BUF 76
J. Coleman, PHI 65
J. Whitney, BOS 62

							Batting						Fielding			Pitching					
	W	L	PCT	GB	R	OR	2B	3B	HR	BA	SA	SB	E	DP	FA	CG	BB	SO	ShO	SV	ERA
Boston	63	35	.643		669	456	209	**86**	**34**	.276	**.408**	0	409	58	.901	89	**90**	**538**	**6**	**3**	*2.55*
Chicago	59	39	.602	4	**679**	540	**277**	61	13	.273	.393	0	543	76	.879	91	123	299	5	1	*2.78*
Providence	58	40	.592	5	636	**436**	189	59	21	.272	.372	0	419	75	.903	88	111	376	4	1	*2.37*
Cleveland	55	42	.567	7.5	476	443	184	38	8	.246	.329	0	**389**	69	**.909**	**92**	217	402	5	2	***2.22***
Buffalo	52	45	.536	10.5	614	576	184	59	8	**.284**	.371	0	445	52	.896	90	101	362	5	2	*3.32*
New York	46	50	.479	16	530	577	138	69	25	.255	.355	0	468	52	.889	87	170	323	5	0	*2.94*
Detroit	40	58	.408	23	524	650	164	48	13	.250	.330	0	470	**77**	.893	89	184	324	5	2	*3.56*
Philadelphia	17	81	.173	46	437	887	181	47	4	.240	.320	0	639	62	.858	91	125	253	3	0	*5.33*
					4565	4565	1526	467	126	.262	.360	0	3782	521	.891	717	1121	2877	38	11	*3.13*

AMERICAN ASSOCIATION 1883

Team	POS	Player	AB	BA	HR	RBI	PO	A	E	DP	TC/G	FA	Pitcher	G	IP	W	L	SV	ERA
Philadelphia	1B	H. Stovey	421	.302	**14**		984	22	37	31	11.2	**.965**	B. Mathews	44	381	30	13	0	*2.46*
W-66 L-32	2B	C. Stricker	330	.273	1		253	223	**93**	23	6.5	.837	G. Bradley	26	214	16	7	0	*3.15*
Lon Knight	SS	M. Moynahan	400	.308	1		105	268	75	14	4.7	.833	F. Corey	18	148	10	7	0	*3.40*
	3B	G. Bradley	312	.234	1		46	106	43	6	4.4	.779							
	RF	L. Knight	429	.252	1		123	22	24	5	1.8	.858							
	CF	B. Blakiston	167	.246	0		51	5	10	0	1.8	.848							
	LF	J. Birchall	**449**	.241	1		168	22	45	0	2.4	.809							
	C	J. O'Brien	390	.290	0		301	58	51	3	7.1	.876							
	UT	F. Corey	298	.258	1		86	150	57	7		.805							
	C	E. Rowen	196	.219	0		266	52	54	2	8.5	.855							
	P	B. Mathews	167	.186	0		15	68	12	2	2.2	.874							
St. Louis	1B	C. Comiskey	401	.294	2		**1085**	20	43	49	**12.0**	.963	T. Mullane	53	461	35	15	**1**	*2.19*
W-65 L-33	2B	G. Strief	302	.225	1		205	214	47	28	7.0	.899	J. McGinnis	45	383	28	16	0	*2.33*
Ted Sullivan	SS	B. Gleason	425	.287	2		120	257	56	22	4.4	.871							
W-53 L-26	3B	A. Latham	406	.236	0		120	256	58	**14**	4.4	.866							
Charlie Comiskey	RF	H. Nicol	368	.288	0		133	31	15	4	2.1	.916							
W-12 L-7	CF	F. Lewis	209	.301	1		89	6	17	0	2.3	.848							
	LF	T. Dolan	295	.214	1		55	11	11	2	1.9	.857							
	C	P. Deasley	206	.257	0		301	59	27	6	6.9	**.930**							
	PO	T. Mullane	307	.225	0		58	104	25	5		.866							
	P	J. McGinnis	180	.200	0		14	80	21	3	2.6	.817							
	OF	T. Mansell	112	.402	0		32	1	9	0	1.5	.786							
Cincinnati	1B	L. Reilly	437	.311	9		959	19	40	**50**	10.4	.961	W. White	65	577	**43**	22	0	**2.09**
W-61 L-37	2B	B. McPhee	367	.245	2		**314**	**277**	46	**48**	6.6	**.928**	R. Deagle	18	148	10	8	0	*2.31*
Pop Snyder	SS	C. Fulmer	361	.258	5		**134**	243	60	**26**	4.8	.863	H. McCormick	15	129	8	6	0	*2.87*
	3B	H. Carpenter	436	.296	3		133	181	47	6	3.8	.870							
	RF	P. Corkhill	375	.216	2		162	10	13	0	2.2	.930							
	CF	C. Jones	391	.294	11		172	12	26	1	2.3	.876							
	LF	J. Sommer	413	.278	3		171	11	31	1	2.3	.854							
	C	P. Snyder	250	.256	0		283	71	31	4	6.8	.919							
	P	W. White	240	.225	0		23	106	23	1	2.3	.849							
	CO	P. Powers	114	.246	0		74	20	12	0		.887							
	C	B. Traffley	105	.200	0		121	33	27	2	6.2	.851							
New York	1B	S. Brady	432	.271	0		824	29	35	31	11.0	.961	T. Keefe	**68**	**619**	41	27	0	*2.41*
W-54 L-42	2B	S. Crane	349	.235	0		283	249	87	26	6.4	.859	J. Lynch	29	255	13	15	0	*4.09*
Jim Mutrie	SS	C. Nelson	417	.305	0		98	232	47	18	3.9	.875							
	3B	D. Esterbrook	407	.253	0		110	173	42	8	3.4	.871							
	RF	C. Roseman	398	.251	0		105	19	21	3	1.6	.855							
	CF	J. O'Rourke	315	.270	2		95	12	18	2	1.6	.856							
	LF	E. Kennedy	356	.219	2		112	10	16	0	1.5	.884							
	C	B. Holbert	299	.237	0		**527**	**138**	58	8	**10.6**	.920							
	P	T. Keefe	259	.220	0		31	**148**	**59**	3	**3.5**	.752							
	C	C. Reipschlager	145	.186	0		202	46	17	1	9.1	.936							
	P	J. Lynch	107	.187	0		18	46	20	0	2.9	.762							
Louisville	1B	J. Latham	368	.250	0		625	21	30	40	10.1	.956	G. Hecker	55	451	28	25	0	*3.33*
W-52 L-45	2B	J. Gerhardt	319	.263	0		278	263	56	42	7.7	.906	S. Weaver	46	419	24	20	0	*3.70*
Joe Gerhardt	SS	J. Leary	165	.188	3		62	106	38	11	5.2	.816							
	3B	J. Gleason	355	.296	2		83	107	49	6	2.9	.795							
	RF	C. Wolf	389	.262	1		157	29	23	6	2.7	.890							
	CF	L. Maskrey	361	.202	1		193	19	20	1	2.4	.914							
	LF	P. Browning	358	.338	2		94	5	16	1	2.4	.861							
	C	E. Whiting	240	.292	2		244	62	40	5	6.9	.884							
	UT	G. Hecker	322	.273	1		144	100	24	7		.910							
	P	S. Weaver	203	.192	0		21	81	6	3	2.3	**.944**							
	C	D. Sullivan	147	.211	0		149	34	21	2	6.4	.897							
	UT	T. McLaughlin	146	.192	0		105	72	27	8		.868							
Columbus	1B	J. Field	295	.254	1		781	10	52	44	11.1	.938	F. Mountain	59	503	26	**33**	0	*3.60*
W-32 L-65	2B	P. Smith	405	.262	4		250	247	62	38	**7.7**	.889	E. Dundon	20	167	3	16	0	*4.48*
Horace Phillips	SS	J. Richmond	385	.283	0		122	**304**	60	19	5.3	**.877**	J. Valentine	13	102	2	10	0	*3.53*
	3B	W. Kuehne	374	.227	1		61	133	39	11	3.4	.833							
	RF	T. Brown	420	.274	5		151	22	42	3	2.2	.805							
	CF	F. Mann	394	.249	1		124	16	24	4	2.0	.854							
	LF	H. Wheeler	371	.226	1		131	15	35	2	2.2	.807							
	C	R. Kemmler	318	.208	0		388	97	**71**	**10**	6.8	.872							
	P	F. Mountain	276	.217	3		31	105	24	3	2.7	.850							
	C1	J. Straub	100	.130	0		182	22	21	8		.907							
Pittsburgh	1B	E. Swartwood	413	**.356**	3		632	23	45	28	11.7	.936	D. Driscoll	41	336	18	21	0	*3.99*
W-31 L-67	2B	G. Creamer	369	.255	0		310	274	67	42	7.2	.897	B. Barr	26	203	6	18	**1**	*4.38*
Al Pratt	SS	D. Mack	224	.196	0		29	106	25	7	4.2	.844	B. Taylor	19	127	4	7	0	*5.39*
W-12 L-20	3B	J. Battin	388	.214	1		**151**	**258**	50	12	**4.7**	**.891**	J. Neagle	16	114	3	12	0	*5.84*
Ormond Butler	RF	B. Dickerson	355	.248	0		106	28	34	2	2.2	.798							
W-17 L-36	CF	B. Taylor	369	.260	2		49	10	20	0	2.1	.747							
Joe Battin	LF	M. Mansell	412	.257	3		186	11	26	1	2.3	.883							
W-2 L-11	C	J. Hayes	351	.262	3		277	70	34	2	6.1	.911							
	P	D. Driscoll	148	.182	0		14	99	14	2	3.1	.890							
	UT	B. Barr	142	.246	0		62	43	17	2		.861							
	UT	B. Morgan	114	.158	0		59	72	25	4		.840							
	SS	F. McLaughlin	114	.219	1		19	78	24	4	4.8	.802							
	PO	J. Neagle	101	.188	0		23	22	10	0		.818							

AMERICAN ASSOCIATION 1883, *cont.*

Baltimore

W-28 L-68

Billy Barnie

POS	Player	AB	BA	HR	RBI	PO	A	E	DP	TC/G	FA
1B	D. Stearns	382	.246	1		984	**38**	**57**	38	11.7	.947
2B	T. Manning	121	.215	0		105	106	20	8	6.6	.913
SS	L. Say	324	.256	1		76	241	**82**	13	**5.4**	.794
3B	J. McCormick	389	.262	0		138	196	**84**	10	4.5	.799
RF	D. Rowe	256	.313	0		70	5	19	0	1.9	.798
CF	D. Eggler	202	.188	0		92	6	9	1	2.0	.916
LF	J. Clinton	399	.313	0		158	18	33	2	2.3	.842
C	K. Kelly	202	.228	0		169	35	50	3	6.7	.803
P	H. Henderson	191	.162	1		23	59	22	3	2.3	.788*
OF	G. Gardner	161	.273	1		62	5	13	0	2.3	.837
2B	T. O'Brien	138	.268	0		77	93	36	8	7.1	.825
CO	P. Baker	121	.273	1		113	14	21	2		.858
C	R. Sweeney	101	.208	0		97	40	19	2	6.8	.878

Pitcher	G	IP	W	L	SV	ERA
H. Henderson	45	358	10	32	0	*4.02*
B. Emslie	24	201	9	13	0	*3.17*
J. Fox	20	165	6	13	0	*4.03*

BATTING AND BASE RUNNING LEADERS

Batting Average
E. Swartwood, PIT .356
P. Browning, LOU .338
J. Clinton, BAL .313
D. Rowe, BAL .313
L. Reilly, CIN .311

Slugging Average
H. Stovey, PHI .504
L. Reilly, CIN .485
E. Swartwood, PIT .475
C. Jones, CIN .473
P. Browning, LOU .458

Home Runs
H. Stovey, PHI 14
C. Jones, CIN 11
L. Reilly, CIN 9
C. Fulmer, CIN 5
T. Brown, COL 5

Total Bases
H. Stovey, PHI 212
L. Reilly, CIN 212
E. Swartwood, PIT 196
C. Jones, CIN 185
B. Gleason, STL 167

Runs Batted In
(not available)

Stolen Bases
(not available)

Hits
E. Swartwood, PIT 147
L. Reilly, CIN 136
H. Carpenter, CIN 129
C. Nelson, NY 127
H. Stovey, PHI 127

Base on Balls
D. Stearns, BAL 34
C. Nelson, NY 31
M. Moynahan, PHI 30
J. Gleason, STL, LOU 29

Home Run Percentage
H. Stovey, PHI 3.3
C. Jones, CIN 2.8
L. Reilly, CIN 2.1
C. Fulmer, CIN 1.4

Runs
H. Stovey, PHI 110
L. Reilly, CIN 103
H. Carpenter, CIN 99
L. Knight, PHI 98

Doubles
H. Stovey, PHI 31
E. Swartwood, PIT 24
J. Hayes, PIT 23
L. Knight, PHI 23

Triples
P. Smith, COL 17
W. Kuehne, COL 14
L. Reilly, CIN 14
F. Mann, COL 13
M. Mansell, PIT 13

PITCHING LEADERS

Winning Percentage
T. Mullane, STL .700
B. Mathews, PHI .698
G. Bradley, PHI .696
W. White, CIN .662
J. McGinnis, STL .636

Earned Run Average
W. White, CIN *2.09*
T. Mullane, STL *2.19*
R. Deagle, CIN *2.31*
J. McGinnis, STL *2.33*
T. Keefe, NY *2.41*

Wins
W. White, CIN 43
T. Keefe, NY 41
T. Mullane, STL 35
B. Mathews, PHI 30
J. McGinnis, STL 28
G. Hecker, LOU 28

Saves
B. Barr, PIT 1
T. Mullane, STL 1

Strikeouts
T. Keefe, NY 361
B. Mathews, PHI 203
T. Mullane, STL 191
F. Mountain, COL 159
G. Hecker, LOU 153

Complete Games
T. Keefe, NY 68
W. White, CIN 64
F. Mountain, COL 57
G. Hecker, LOU 53
T. Mullane, STL 49

Fewest Hits/9 Innings
T. Keefe, NY 7.07
T. Mullane, STL 7.27
W. White, CIN 7.38
J. McGinnis, STL 7.64

Shutouts
J. McGinnis, STL 6
W. White, CIN 6
T. Keefe, NY 5
S. Weaver, LOU 4
F. Mountain, COL 4

Fewest Walks/9 Innings
B. Mathews, PHI 0.73
S. Weaver, LOU 0.82
J. Lynch, NY 0.88
G. Bradley, PHI 0.92

Most Strikeouts/9 Inn.
T. Keefe, NY 5.25
B. Mathews, PHI 4.80
J. Lynch, NY 4.20
T. Mullane, STL 3.73

Innings
T. Keefe, NY 619
W. White, CIN 577
F. Mountain, COL 503
T. Mullane, STL 461

Games Pitched
T. Keefe, NY 68
W. White, CIN 65
F. Mountain, COL 59
G. Hecker, LOU 55

							Batting						Fielding				Pitching				
	W	L	PCT	GB	R	OR	2B	3B	HR	BA	SA	SB	E	DP	FA	CG	BB	SO	ShO	SV	ERA
Philadelphia	66	32	.673		**720**	547	**149**	50	20	**.262**	.345	0	584	40	.865	92	**95**	347	1	0	*2.87*
St. Louis	65	33	.663	1	549	409	118	46	7	.255	.321	0	388	62	**.909**	93	150	325	**9**	**1**	***2.23***
Cincinnati	61	37	.622	5	662	413	122	73	**35**	**.262**	**.364**	0	**383**	57	.905	96	168	213	8	0	*2.26*
New York	54	42	.563	11	498	**405**	111	58	6	.250	.319	0	439	45	.895	**97**	123	**480**	6	0	*2.90*
Louisville	52	45	.536	13.5	564	562	114	66	12	.251	.330	0	488	67	.884	96	110	269	7	0	*3.50*
Columbus	32	65	.330	33.5	476	659	101	**78**	16	.240	.326	0	540	**69**	.873	90	211	222	4	0	*3.97*
Pittsburgh	31	67	.316	35	525	728	120	58	13	.247	.323	0	506	55	.884	82	151	271	1	**1**	*4.62*
Baltimore	28	68	.292	37	471	742	125	49	5	.246	.314	0	624	44	.855	86	190	290	1	0	*4.08*
					4465	4465	960	478	114	.252	.330	0	3952	439	.884	732	1198	2417	37	2	*3.30*

NATIONAL LEAGUE 1884

Providence

W-84 L-28

Frank Bancroft

POS	Player	AB	BA	HR	RBI	PO	A	E	DP	TC/G	FA
1B	J. Start	381	.276	2		939	21	20	31	10.5	**.980**
2B	J. Farrell	469	.217	1		249	351	51	36	6.0	.922
SS	A. Irwin	404	.240	2		99	307	55	20	4.5	.881
3B	J. Denny	439	.248	6		144	168	45	5	3.6	.874
RF	P. Radford	355	.197	1		146	26	23	4	2.0	.882
CF	P. Hines	490	.302	3		202	20	26	5	2.3	.895
LF	C. Carroll	452	.261	3		206	11	23	1	2.1	.904
C	B. Gilligan	294	.245	1		**605**	94	54	7	9.3	.928
P	O. Radbourn	361	.230	1		21	119	17	1	2.1	.892
PO	C. Sweeney	168	.298	1		31	49	6	1		.930
C	S. Nava	116	.095	0		172	40	27	1	8.9	.887

Pitcher	G	IP	W	L	SV	ERA
O. Radbourn	**75**	**679**	**60**	12	1	**1.38**
C. Sweeney	27	221	17	8	1	*1.55*

NATIONAL LEAGUE 1884, *cont.*

Boston

W-73 L-38

John Morrill

POS	Player	AB	BA	HR	RBI	PO	A	E	DP	TC/G	FA	Pitcher	G	IP	W	L	SV	ERA
1B	J. Morrill	438	.260	3		953	34	30	33	11.2	.971	C. Buffinton	67	587	48	16	0	*2.15*
2B	J. Burdock	361	.269	6		183	278	39	23	5.7	**.922**	J. Whitney	41	336	23	14	0	*2.09*
SS	S. Wise	426	.214	4		156	307	61	16	4.9	.884							
3B	E. Sutton	468	.346	3		119	186	31	7	3.1	**.908**							
RF	B. Crowley	407	.270	6		125	22	22	5	1.6	.870							
CF	J. Manning	345	.241	2		115	15	18	2	2.0	.878							
LF	J. Hornung	518	.268	7		182	14	18	1	1.9	.916							
C	M. Hackett	268	.205	1		512	104	48	2	**9.4**	.928							
P	C. Buffinton	352	.267	1		40	118	9	2	2.5	.946							
UT	J. Whitney	270	.259	3		135	80	10	3		.956							
C	M. Hines	132	.174	0		255	64	28	7	9.9	.919							

Buffalo

W-64 L-47

Jim O'Rourke

POS	Player	AB	BA	HR	RBI	PO	A	E	DP	TC/G	FA	Pitcher	G	IP	W	L	SV	ERA
1B	D. Brouthers	398	.327	14		958	30	37	38	11.0	.964	P. Galvin	72	636	46	22	0	*1.99*
2B	H. Richardson	439	.301	6		191	243	50	18	6.8	.897	B. Serad	37	308	16	20	0	*4.27*
SS	D. Force	403	.206	0		110	312	48	21	4.5	**.898**							
3B	D. White	452	.325	5		113	198	66	11	3.5	.825							
RF	J. Lillie	471	.223	3		190	41	40	7	2.4	.852							
CF	D. Eggler	241	.195	0		104	14	15	1	2.1	.887							
LF	J. O'Rourke	467	.347	5		112	6	14	2	1.5	.894							
C	J. Rowe	400	.315	4		373	60	26	3	7.1	**.943**							
CO	G. Myers	325	.182	2		320	61	78	5		.830							
P	P. Galvin	274	.179	0		32	**154**	7	3	2.7	.964							
2B	C. Collins	169	.178	0		108	137	23	15	6.4	.914							
P	B. Serad	137	.175	0		4	57	14	1	2.0	.813							

Chicago

W-62 L-50

Cap Anson

POS	Player	AB	BA	HR	RBI	PO	A	E	DP	TC/G	FA	Pitcher	G	IP	W	L	SV	ERA
1B	C. Anson	475	.335	21		**1211**	40	**58**	**86**	**11.7**	.956	L. Corcoran	60	517	35	23	0	*2.40*
2B	F. Pfeffer	467	.289	25		**395**	**422**	**88**	**85**	**8.1**	.903	F. Goldsmith	21	188	9	11	0	*4.26*
SS	T. Burns	343	.245	7		99	254	68	21	5.3	.838	J. Clarkson	14	118	10	3	0	*2.14*
3B	N. Williamson	417	.278	**27**		121	**250**	60	**25**	4.4	.861							
RF	K. Kelly	452	**.354**	13		69	31	26	1	2.0	.794							
CF	G. Gore	422	.318	5		185	25	32	5	2.3	.868							
LF	A. Dalrymple	**521**	.309	22		176	18	26	5	2.0	.882							
C	S. Flint	279	.204	9		354	110	61	9	7.2	.884							
P	L. Corcoran	251	.243	1		**47**	132	**24**	5	3.4	.882							
OF	B. Sunday	176	.222	4		45	8	27	1	1.9	.662							

New York

W-62 L-50

Jim Price
W-56 L-42

Monte Ward
W-6 L-8

POS	Player	AB	BA	HR	RBI	PO	A	E	DP	TC/G	FA	Pitcher	G	IP	W	L	SV	ERA
1B	A. McKinnon	470	.272	4		1097	31	53	57	10.2	.955	M. Welch	65	557	39	21	0	*2.50*
2B	R. Connor	477	.317	4		230	205	71	30	7.6	.860	E. Begley	31	266	12	18	0	*4.16*
SS	E. Caskin	351	.231	2		121	278	53	**28**	4.7	.883	M. Dorgan	14	113	8	6	0	*3.50*
3B	F. Hankinson	389	.231	2		135	182	47	8	3.5	.871							
RF	M. Dorgan	341	.276	1		101	13	20	3	2.1	.851							
CF	M. Ward	482	.253	2		103	13	21	2	2.3	.847							
LF	P. Gillespie	413	.264	2		159	8	20	1	1.9	.893							
C	B. Ewing	382	.277	3		445	**127**	41	10	7.7	.933							
OF	D. Richardson	277	.253	1		77	20	10	3	1.9	.907							
P	M. Welch	249	.241	3		25	78	14	**6**	1.8	.880							
P	E. Begley	121	.182	0		16	46	9	2	2.3	.873							

Philadelphia

W-39 L-73

Harry Wright

POS	Player	AB	BA	HR	RBI	PO	A	E	DP	TC/G	FA	Pitcher	G	IP	W	L	SV	ERA
1B	S. Farrar	428	.245	1		1142	**42**	42	41	11.0	.966	C. Ferguson	50	417	21	25	1	*3.54*
2B	E. Andrews	420	.221	0		239	326	69	37	5.8	.891	B. Vinton	21	182	10	10	0	*2.23*
SS	B. McClellan	450	.258	3		**165**	**313**	**83**	22	5.1	.852	J. Coleman	21	154	5	15	0	*4.90*
3B	J. Mulvey	401	.229	2		**151**	216	**73**	20	**4.4**	.834	J. McElroy	13	111	1	12	0	*4.86*
RF	J. Manning	424	.271	5		140	26	30	7	1.9	.847							
CF	J. Fogarty	378	.212	1		193	12	19	3	2.9	.915							
LF	B. Purcell	428	.252	1		182	12	28	1	2.2	.874							
C	J. Crowley	168	.244	0		198	49	50	2	6.2	.832							
P	C. Ferguson	203	.246	0		23	72	12	4	2.1	.888							
OP	J. Coleman	171	.246	0		61	44	13	2		.890							

Cleveland

W-35 L-77

Charlie Hackett

POS	Player	AB	BA	HR	RBI	PO	A	E	DP	TC/G	FA	Pitcher	G	IP	W	L	SV	ERA
1B	B. Phillips	464	.276	3	**46**	1107	30	48	59	10.7	.959	J. Harkins	46	391	12	**32**	0	*3.68*
2B	G. Smith	291	.254	4	26	111	136	34	23	6.7	.879	J. McCormick	42	359	19	22	0	*2.86**
SS	J. Glasscock	281	.249	1	22	118	267	46	16	6.2*	.893	S. Moffett	24	198	3	19	0	*3.87*
3B	M. Muldoon	422	.239	2	38	126	204	66	15	3.6	.833							
RF	J. Evans	313	.259	1	39	136	19	14	3	2.2	.917							
CF	P. Hotaling	408	.243	3	27	174	23	35	5	2.3	.849							
LF	W. Murphy	168	.226	1	9	60	7	26	0	2.2	.720							
C	D. Bushong	203	.236	0	10	355	98	58	**11**	8.2	.886							
OP	S. Moffett	256	.184	0	14	78	65	23	2		.861							
P	J. Harkins	229	.205	0	20	15	81	17	3	2.5	.850							
P	J. McCormick	190	.263	0	23	18	67	0	4	2.0	1.000*							
C	F. Briody	148	.169	1	12	243	74	27	5	8.2	.922							
2S	G. Pinckney	144	.313	0	16	73	110	32	11		.851							
OF	E. Burch	124	.210	0	7	52	10	7	1	2.2	.899							

Detroit

W-28 L-84

Jack Chapman

POS	Player	AB	BA	HR	RBI	PO	A	E	DP	TC/G	FA	Pitcher	G	IP	W	L	SV	ERA
1B	M. Scott	438	.247	3		1120	26	38	37	10.8	.968	F. Meinke	35	289	8	23	0	*3.18*
2B	B. Geiss	283	.177	2		190	217	65	27	6.5	.862	D. Shaw	28	228	9	18	0	*3.04*
SS	F. Meinke	341	.164	6		57	146	39	16	4.7	.839	S. Wiedman	26	213	4	21	0	*3.72*
3B	J. Farrell	461	.226	3		126	198	61	12	3.5	.842	C. Getzien	17	147	5	12	0	*1.95*
RF	S. Wiedman	300	.163	0		76	12	16	2	2.0	.846	F. Brill	12	103	2	10	0	*5.50*
CF	N. Hanlon	450	.264	5		241	30	39	5	2.7	.874							
LF	G. Wood	473	.252	8		190	17	24	1	2.0	.896							
C	C. Bennett	337	.264	3		449	96	48	9	7.5	.919							
P	D. Shaw	136	.191	1		10	55	11	2	2.7	.855							
UT	H. Jones	129	.209	0		52	90	17	1		.893							

NATIONAL LEAGUE 1884, *cont.*

BATTING AND BASE RUNNING LEADERS

Batting Average	
K. Kelly, CHI	.354
J. O'Rourke, BUF	.347
E. Sutton, BOS	.346
C. Anson, CHI	.335
D. Brouthers, BUF	.327

Slugging Average	
D. Brouthers, BUF	.563
N. Williamson, CHI	.554
C. Anson, CHI	.543
K. Kelly, CHI	.524
F. Pfeffer, CHI	.514

Home Runs	
N. Williamson, CHI	27
F. Pfeffer, CHI	25
A. Dalrymple, CHI	22
C. Anson, CHI	21
D. Brouthers, BUF	14

Total Bases	
A. Dalrymple, CHI	263
C. Anson, CHI	258
F. Pfeffer, CHI	240
K. Kelly, CHI	237
N. Williamson, CHI	231

Runs Batted In	
B. Phillips, CLE	46
J. Evans, CLE	39
M. Muldoon, CLE	38
P. Hotaling, CLE	27
G. Smith, CLE	26

Stolen Bases	
(not available)	

Hits	
J. O'Rourke, BUF	162
E. Sutton, BOS	162
A. Dalrymple, CHI	161
K. Kelly, CHI	160

Base on Balls	
G. Gore, CHI	61
K. Kelly, CHI	46
P. Hines, PRO	44
N. Williamson, CHI	42

Home Run Percentage	
N. Williamson, CHI	6.5
F. Pfeffer, CHI	5.4
C. Anson, CHI	4.4
A. Dalrymple, CHI	4.2

Runs	
K. Kelly, CHI	120
J. O'Rourke, BUF	119
J. Hornung, BOS	119
A. Dalrymple, CHI	111

Doubles	
P. Hines, PRO	36
D. Brouthers, BUF	33
C. Anson, CHI	30
J. Manning, PHI	29

Triples	
B. Ewing, NY	20
D. Brouthers, BUF	15
J. Rowe, BUF	14
B. Phillips, CLE	12
A. McKinnon, NY	12

PITCHING LEADERS

Winning Percentage	
O. Radbourn, PRO	.833
C. Buffinton, BOS	.750
C. Sweeney, PRO	.680
P. Galvin, BUF	.676
M. Welch, NY	.650

Earned Run Average	
O. Radbourn, PRO	*1.38*
C. Sweeney, PRO	*1.55*
C. Getzien, DET	*1.95*
P. Galvin, BUF	*1.99*
J. Whitney, BOS	*2.09*

Wins	
O. Radbourn, PRO	60
C. Buffinton, BOS	48
P. Galvin, BUF	46
M. Welch, NY	39
L. Corcoran, CHI	35

Saves	
J. Morrill, BOS	2
C. Ferguson, PHI	1
J. O'Rourke, BUF	1
O. Radbourn, PRO	1
C. Sweeney, PRO	1

Strikeouts	
O. Radbourn, PRO	441
C. Buffinton, BOS	417
P. Galvin, BUF	369
M. Welch, NY	345
L. Corcoran, CHI	272

Complete Games	
O. Radbourn, PRO	73
P. Galvin, BUF	71
C. Buffinton, BOS	63
M. Welch, NY	62
L. Corcoran, CHI	57

Fewest Hits/9 Innings	
C. Sweeney, PRO	6.23
O. Radbourn, PRO	7.00
J. Clarkson, CHI	7.17
C. Getzien, DET	7.21

Shutouts	
P. Galvin, BUF	12
O. Radbourn, PRO	11
C. Buffinton, BOS	8
L. Corcoran, CHI	7

Fewest Walks/9 Innings	
J. Whitney, BOS	0.72
P. Galvin, BUF	0.89
C. Buffinton, BOS	1.17
C. Sweeney, PRO	1.18

Most Strikeouts/9 Inn.	
J. Clarkson, CHI	7.78
J. Whitney, BOS	7.23
M. Dorgan, NY	7.17
C. Getzien, DET	6.54

Innings	
O. Radbourn, PRO	679
P. Galvin, BUF	636
C. Buffinton, BOS	587
M. Welch, NY	557

Games Pitched	
O. Radbourn, PRO	75
P. Galvin, BUF	72
C. Buffinton, BOS	67
M. Welch, NY	65

							Batting						Fielding			Pitching					
	W	L	PCT	GB	R	OR	2B	3B	HR	BA	SA	SB	E	DP	FA	CG	BB	SO	ShO	SV	ERA
Providence	84	28	.750		665	**388**	153	43	21	.241	.315	0	398	50	.918	107	172	639	**16**	**2**	***1.59***
Boston	73	38	.658	10.5	684	468	**179**	60	36	.254	.351	0	**384**	46	**.922**	109	**135**	**742**	14	**2**	*2.47*
Buffalo	64	47	.577	19.5	700	626	163	**69**	39	.262	.361	0	462	71	.905	108	189	534	14	1	*2.95*
Chicago	62	50	.554	22	**834**	647	162	50	**142**	**.281**	**.446**	0	595	**107**	.886	106	231	472	9	0	*3.03*
New York	62	50	.554	22	693	623	148	67	24	.255	.341	0	514	69	.895	**111**	326	567	4	0	*3.12*
Philadelphia	39	73	.348	45	549	824	149	39	14	.234	.301	0	536	67	.888	106	254	411	3	1	*3.93*
Cleveland	35	77	.313	49	458	716	147	49	16	.237	.312	0	512	75	.897	107	269	482	7	0	*3.43*
Detroit	28	84	.250	56	445	736	114	47	31	.208	.284	0	549	60	.886	109	245	488	3	0	*3.38*
					5028	5028	1215	424	323	.246	.339	0	3950	545	.900	863	1821	4335	70	6	*2.99*

AMERICAN ASSOCIATION 1884

	POS	Player	AB	BA	HR	RBI	PO	A	E	DP	TC/G	FA	Pitcher	G	IP	W	L	SV	ERA
New York	1B	D. Orr	458	**.354**	9		1161	24	49	29	11.2	.960	T. Keefe	58	492	37	17	0	*2.29*
	2B	D. Troy	421	.264	2		224	314	74	25	5.7	.879	J. Lynch	54	487	37	15	0	*2.64*
	SS	C. Nelson	432	.255	1		113	292	56	16	4.2	.879							
W-75 L-32	3B	D. Esterbrook	477	.314	1		126	208	43	11	3.4	.886							
	RF	S. Brady	485	.252	0		154	26	16	1	1.8	.918							
Jim Mutrie	CF	C. Roseman	436	.298	4		157	12	22	0	1.8	.885							
	LF	E. Kennedy	378	.190	1		138	13	14	4	1.6	.915							
	C	B. Holbert	255	.208	0		374	**142**	**54**	7	9.7	.905							
	C	C. Reipschlager	233	.240	0		369	109	39	3	10.1	.925							
	P	T. Keefe	213	.235	3		18	95	30	2	2.5	.790							
	P	J. Lynch	195	.154	0		24	80	**37**	3	2.6	.738							

	POS	Player	AB	BA	HR	RBI	PO	A	E	DP	TC/G	FA	Pitcher	G	IP	W	L	SV	ERA
Columbus	1B	J. Field	417	.233	4		1150	27	52	58	11.7	.958	E. Morris	52	430	34	13	0	*2.18*
	2B	P. Smith	445	.238	6		324	**394**	75	55	7.3	.905	F. Mountain	42	361	23	17	**1**	*2.45*
	SS	J. Richmond	398	.251	3		96	306	62	26	4.4	.866	E. Dundon	11	81	6	4	0	*3.78*
W-69 L-39	3B	W. Kuehne	415	.236	5		117	218	46	13	3.5	.879							
	RF	T. Brown	451	.273	5		164	18	33	5	2.0	.847							
Gus Schmelz	CF	F. Mann	366	.276	7		120	12	22	2	1.6	.857							
	LF	J. Cahill	210	.219	0		62	8	13	0	1.5	.843							
	C	R. Kemmler	211	.199	0		268	77	36	3	6.6	.906							
	C	F. Carroll	252	.278	6		379	89	28	3	9.2	.944							
	P	F. Mountain	210	.238	4		14	88	9	0	2.6	.919							
	P	E. Morris	199	.186	0		19	88	23	3	2.5	.823							

	POS	Player	AB	BA	HR	RBI	PO	A	E	DP	TC/G	FA	Pitcher	G	IP	W	L	SV	ERA
Louisville	1B	J. Latham	308	.169	0		788	32	33	48	11.2	.961	G. Hecker	**76**	**671**	**52**	20	0	**1.80**
	2B	J. Gerhardt	404	.220	0		334	389	64	64	7.5	.919	P. Reccius	18	129	6	7	0	*2.71*
	SS	T. McLaughlin	335	.200	1		121	330	55	**34**	5.4	.891	D. Driscoll	13	102	6	6	0	*3.44*
W-68 L-40	3B	P. Browning	447	.336	4		79	66	35	4	3.5	.806	R. Deagle	12	87	4	6	0	*2.58*
	RF	C. Wolf	**486**	.300	3		173	26	26	4	2.2	.884							
Mike Walsh	CF	M. Cline	396	.290	2		143	25	24	1	2.1	.875							
	LF	L. Maskrey	412	.250	0		138	17	18	2	1.7	.896							
	C	D. Sullivan	247	.239	0		340	61	30	2	6.8	.930							
	P	G. Hecker	316	.297	4		**50**	**145**	10	3	2.7	.951							
	UT	P. Reccius	263	.240	3		56	147	31	7		.868							
	C	E. Whiting	157	.223	0		199	54	31	6	7.1	.891							

AMERICAN ASSOCIATION 1884, *cont.*

St. Louis

W-67 L-40

Jimmy Williams
W-51 L-33

Charlie Comiskey
W-16 L-7

POS	Player	AB	BA	HR	RBI	PO	A	E	DP	TC/G	FA	Pitcher	G	IP	W	L	SV	ERA
1B	C. Comiskey	460	.239	2		**1193**	38	40	56	**11.8**	.969	J. McGinnis	40	354	24	16	0	*2.84*
2B	J. Quest	310	.206	0		232	242	56	39	6.6	.894	D. Foutz	25	207	15	6	0	*2.18*
SS	B. Gleason	472	.269	1		119	316	67	23	4.6	.867	D. Davis	25	198	10	12	0	*2.90*
3B	A. Latham	474	.274	1		142	**302**	**70**	**16**	**4.7**	.864	T. O'Neill	17	141	11	4	0	*2.68*
RF	H. Nicol	442	.260	0		144	48	28	3	2.5	.873							
CF	F. Lewis	300	.323	0		118	15	23	1	2.1	.853							
LF	T. O'Neill	297	.276	3		67	6	17	1	1.4	.811							
C	P. Deasley	254	.205	0		428	120	48	3	7.9	.919							
OF	G. Strief	184	.201	2		50	5	10	0	1.5	.846							
P	J. McGinnis	146	.233	0		8	71	12	1	2.3	.868							
C	T. Dolan	137	.263	0		188	45	34	2	7.9	.873							
PO	D. Foutz	119	.227	0		26	45	6	6		.922							

Cincinnati

W-68 L-41

Will White
W-44 L-27

Pop Snyder
W-24 L-14

POS	Player	AB	BA	HR	RBI	PO	A	E	DP	TC/G	FA	Pitcher	G	IP	W	L	SV	ERA
1B	L. Reilly	448	.339	**11**		977	26	30	**60**	10.0	.971	W. White	52	456	34	18	0	*3.32*
2B	B. McPhee	450	.278	5		**415**	365	64	**74**	**7.5**	.924	B. Mountjoy	33	289	19	12	0	*2.93*
SS	J. Peoples	267	.169	0		54	140	40	19	5.0	.829	G. Shallix	23	200	11	10	0	*3.70*
3B	H. Carpenter	474	.255	4		**157**	168	44	**16**	3.4	.881							
RF	P. Corkhill	452	.274	4		169	29	14	5	2.3	.934							
CF	T. Mansell	266	.248	0		88	3	30	0	1.9	.752							
LF	C. Jones	472	.314	7		207	12	28	0	2.2	.887							
C	P. Snyder	268	.257	0		341	135	40	5	7.9	.922							
P	W. White	184	.190	1		8	72	18	2	1.9	.816							
OF	B. West	131	.244	0		46	1	10	0	1.7	.825							
C	P. Powers	130	.138	0		152	53	25	2	7.4	.891							
SS	F. Fennelly	122	.352	2		25	84	25	12	4.8	.813							
P	B. Mountjoy	119	.151	0		13	64	6	2	2.5	.928							
SS	C. Fulmer	114	.175	0		22	66	24	7	3.9	.786							

Baltimore

W-63 L-43

Billy Barnie

POS	Player	AB	BA	HR	RBI	PO	A	E	DP	TC/G	FA	Pitcher	G	IP	W	L	SV	ERA
1B	D. Stearns	396	.237	3		959	**48**	**54**	36	10.6	.949	B. Emslie	50	455	32	17	0	*2.75*
2B	T. Manning	341	.205	2		228	277	52	28	6.1	.907	H. Henderson	52	439	27	23	0	*2.62*
SS	J. Macullar	358	.204	4		119	317	67	23	4.7	.867							
3B	J. Sommer	479	.269	4		118	168	54	10	3.5	.841							
RF	G. Gardner	173	.214	2		62	12	12	0	2.2	.860							
CF	J. Clinton	433	.273	3		133	17	35	5	1.8	.811							
LF	T. York	314	.223	1		100	7	20	1	1.5	.843							
C	S. Trott	284	.257	2		**491**	87	43	**10**	**10.4**	.931							
C	B. Traffley	210	.176	0		321	57	30	6	8.7	.926							
P	H. Henderson	203	.227	0		27	78	22	3	2.4	.827							
P	B. Emslie	195	.190	0		27	83	22	0	2.6	.833							
OF	D. Casey	149	.248	3		48	5	6	2	1.6	.898							
O2	O. Burns	131	.298	6		49	34	13	2		.865							

Philadelphia

W-61 L-46

Lon Knight

POS	Player	AB	BA	HR	RBI	PO	A	E	DP	TC/G	FA	Pitcher	G	IP	W	L	SV	ERA
1B	H. Stovey	448	.326	10		1061	32	45	46	10.9	.960	B. Mathews	49	431	30	18	0	*3.32*
2B	C. Stricker	399	.231	1		280	257	**80**	40	5.8	.870	B. Taylor	30	260	18	12	0*	*2.53*
SS	S. Houck	472	.297	0		122	**379**	60	30	5.2	**.893**	A. Atkinson	22	184	11	11	0	*4.20*
3B	F. Corey	439	.276	5		121	209	42	10	3.6	**.887**							
RF	L. Knight	484	.271	1		158	36	19	6	2.0	.911							
CF	H. Larkin	326	.276	3		106	7	19	0	1.6	.856							
LF	J. Birchall	221	.258	0		81	7	17	1	2.0	.838							
C	J. Milligan	268	.287	3		474	100	37	5	9.4	**.939**							
P	B. Mathews	184	.185	0		8	78	25	1	2.3	.775							
C	J. O'Brien	138	.283	1		169	43	16	6	7.6	.930							
OF	B. Blakiston	128	.258	0		48	7	6	1	2.2	.902							
P	B. Taylor	111	.252	0		12	64	21	1	3.2	.784							

Toledo

W-46 L-58

Charlie Morton

POS	Player	AB	BA	HR	RBI	PO	A	E	DP	TC/G	FA	Pitcher	G	IP	W	L	SV	ERA
1B	C. Lane	215	.228	1		474	20	27	17	11.3	.948	T. Mullane	67	567	36	26	0	*2.52*
2B	S. Barkley	435	.306	1		318	358	51	46	7.1	.930	H. O'Day	41	327	9	28	**1**	*3.75*
SS	J. Miller	423	.239	1		125	320	70	26	4.9	.864							
3B	E. Brown	153	.176	0		41	54	22	1	3.0	.812							
RF	T. Poorman	382	.233	0		129	29	29	5	2.0	.845							
CF	C. Welch	425	.224	0		206	24	29	3	2.4	.888							
LF	F. Olin	86	.256	1		22	6	4	0	1.2	.875							
C	F. Walker	152	.263	0		220	70	37	4	8.0	.887							
UT	T. Mullane	352	.276	3		139	161	41	10		.880							
PO	H. O'Day	242	.211	0		38	90	17	2		.883							
UT	J. Moffett	204	.201	0		421	42	33	23		.933							
C	D. McGuire	151	.185	1		224	56	29	1	7.5	.906							
3B	G. Meister	119	.193	0		27	40	15	3	2.4	.817							
UT	C. Morton	111	.162	0		33	26	8	1		.881							

Brooklyn

W-40 L-64

George Taylor

POS	Player	AB	BA	HR	RBI	PO	A	E	DP	TC/G	FA	Pitcher	G	IP	W	L	SV	ERA
1B	C. Householder	273	.242	3		426	18	19	17	11.6	.959	A. Terry	57	485	20	35	0	*3.49*
2B	B. Greenwood	385	.216	3		230	300	59	40	6.4	.900	S. Kimber	40	352	17	20	0	*3.91*
SS	B. Geer	391	.210	0		176*	360	81*	34*	5.8*	.869	J. Conway	13	105	3	9	0	*4.44*
3B	F. Warner	352	.222	1		94	147	52	13	3.5	.823							
RF	J. Cassidy	433	.252	2		124	25	26	5	1.8	.851							
CF	J. Remsen	301	.223	3		152	7	15	2	2.1	.914							
LF	O. Walker	382	.270	2		87	12	15	0	1.9	.868							
C	J. Corcoran	185	.211	0		191	57	36	4	7.5	.873							
P	A. Terry	240	.233	0		32	81	34	0	2.6	.769							
OF	I. Benners	189	.201	1		64	1	13	0	1.6	.833							
1B	J. Knowles	153	.235	1		304	17	16	18	11.6	.953							
P	S. Kimber	138	.145	0		32	67	30	0	3.2	.767							

AMERICAN ASSOCIATION 1884, *cont.*

Richmond

W-12 L-30

Felix Moses

POS	Player	AB	BA	HR	RBI	PO	A	E	DP	TC/G	FA	Pitcher	G	IP	W	L	SV	ERA
1B	J. Powell	151	.245	0		380	18	24	15	10.3	.943	E. Dugan	20	166	5	14	0	*4.49*
2B	T. Larkin	139	.201	0		94	129	23	14	6.2	.907	P. Meegan	17	140	5	9	0	*4.37*
SS	B. Schenck	151	.205	3		32	121	30	8	4.6	.836							
3B	B. Nash	166	.199	1		77	87	34	8	4.4	.828							
RF	M. Mansell	113	.301	0		24	5	9	1	1.3	.763							
CF	D. Johnston	146	.281	2		86	10	15	3	3.0	.865							
LF	E. Glenn	175	.246	1		85	5	18	2	2.5	.833							
C	J. Hanna	67	.194	0		108	38	12	2	7.5	.924							
CO	M. Quinton	94	.234	0		62	20	12	3		.872							
P	E. Dugan	70	.114	0		13	23	13	0	2.5	.735							
P	P. Meegan	59	.136	0		6	34	9	0	2.9	.816							

Pittsburgh

W-30 L-78

Joe Battin
W-6 L-7

Denny McKnight
W-4 L-8

Bob Ferguson
W-11 L-31

George Creamer
W-0 L-8

Horace Phillips
W-9 L-24

POS	Player	AB	BA	HR	RBI	PO	A	E	DP	TC/G	FA	Pitcher	G	IP	W	L	SV	ERA
1B	J. Knowles	182	.231	0		499	15	21	20	11.6	.961	F. Sullivan	51	441	16	35	0	*4.20*
2B	G. Creamer	339	.183	0		308	336	43	47	7.0	**.937**	J. Neagle	38	326	11	26	0	*3.73*
SS	B. White	291	.227	0		58	185	58	12	5.0	.807							
3B	J. Battin	158	.177	0		53	95	13	4	3.7	.919							
RF	E. Swartwood	399	.288	0		109	22	32	2	2.1	.804							
CF	O. Taylor	152	.211	0		68	7	19	0	2.3	.798							
LF	D. Miller	347	.225	0		74	13	22	1	2.2	.798							
C	B. Colgan	161	.155	0		228	71	31	5	7.5	.906							
P	F. Sullivan	189	.153	0		24	90	24	2	2.7	.826							
P	J. Neagle	148	.149	0		19	57	24	1	2.6	.760							
30	J. McDonald	145	.159	0		43	38	19	2		.810							
SS	T. Forster	126	.222	0		45	103	17	8	5.9	.897							
C	J. Hayes	124	.226	0		135	30	16	2	7.5	.912							
OF	C. Eden	122	.270	1		40	4	14	0	1.9	.759							
1B	J. Faatz	112	.241	0		283	6	11	16	10.3	.963							

Indianapolis

W-29 L-78

Jim Gifford
W-25 L-60

Bill Watkins
W-4 L-18

POS	Player	AB	BA	HR	RBI	PO	A	E	DP	TC/G	FA	Pitcher	G	IP	W	L	SV	ERA
1B	J. Kerins	361	.216	6		887	41	27	20	11.0	**.972**	L. McKeon	61	512	18	**41**	0	*3.50*
2B	E. Merrill	196	.179	0		144	162	34	15	6.2	.900	B. Barr	16	132	3	11	0	4.99
SS	M. Phillips	413	.269	0		108	335	71	16	5.3	.862	J. Aydelott	12	106	5	7	0	*4.92*
3B	P. Callahan	258	.260	2		66	94	37	5	3.2	.812							
RF	P. Weihe	256	.254	4		90	14	17	2	2.1	.860							
CF	J. Morrison	182	.264	1		78	9	24	4	2.5	.784							
LF	J. Peltz	393	.219	3		155	16	38	1	2.0	.818							
C	J. Keenan	249	.293	3		399	71	39	5	8.6	.923							
P	L. McKeon	247	.215	0		35	124	20	1	2.9	.888							
OF	J. Dorgan	141	.298	0		37	9	12	1	2.0	.793							
2B	C. Collins	138	.225	0		97	105	26	10	6.0	.886							
UT	J. Donnelly	134	.254	0		33	62	21	2		.819							
32	B. Watkins	127	.205	0		44	57	14	4		.878							

Washington

W-12 L-51

Holly Hollingshead
W-12 L-50

Bickerson
W-0 L-1

POS	Player	AB	BA	HR	RBI	PO	A	E	DP	TC/G	FA	Pitcher	G	IP	W	L	SV	ERA
1B	W. Prince	166	.217	0		405	4	26	19	10.1	.940	B. Barr	32	281	9	23	0	3.45
2B	T. Hawkes	151	.278	0		124	103	20	10	6.5	.919	J. Hamill	19	157	2	17	0	*4.48*
SS	F. Fennelly	257	.292	2		88	215	48	14	5.8	.863	E. Trumbull	10	84	1	9	0	*4.71*
3B	B. Gladman	224	.156	1		62	90	39	5	3.6	.796							
RF	B. Morgan	162	.173	0		46	4	14	1	2.1	.781							
CF	H. Mullin	120	.142	0		47	6	8	0	1.8	.869							
LF	T. Farley	52	.212	0		24	2	4	1	2.1	.867							
C	J. Humphries	193	.176	0		198	52	31	6	8.0	.890							
P	B. Barr	135	.148	2		13	57	24	1	2.9	.745							

BATTING AND BASE RUNNING LEADERS

Batting Average

D. Orr, NY	.354
L. Reilly, CIN	.339
P. Browning, LOU	.336
H. Stovey, PHI	.326
F. Lewis, STL	.323

Slugging Average

L. Reilly, CIN	.551
H. Stovey, PHI	.545
D. Orr, NY	.539
F. Fennelly, WAS, CIN	.480
P. Browning, LOU	.472

Home Runs

L. Reilly, CIN	11
H. Stovey, PHI	10
D. Orr, NY	9
F. Mann, COL	7
C. Jones, CIN	7

Total Bases

L. Reilly, CIN	247
D. Orr, NY	247
H. Stovey, PHI	244
C. Jones, CIN	222
P. Browning, LOU	211

Runs Batted In

(not available)

Stolen Bases

(not available)

Hits

D. Orr, NY	162
L. Reilly, CIN	152
P. Browning, LOU	150
D. Esterbrook, NY	150

Base on Balls

C. Nelson, NY	74
B. Geer, BKN	38
C. Jones, CIN	37
J. Macullar, BAL	35
J. Richmond, COL	35

Home Run Percentage

L. Reilly, CIN	2.5
F. Carroll, COL	2.4
H. Stovey, PHI	2.2
D. Orr, NY	2.0

PITCHING LEADERS

Winning Percentage

E. Morris, COL	.723
G. Hecker, LOU	.722
D. Foutz, STL	.714
J. Lynch, NY	.712
T. Keefe, NY	.685

Earned Run Average

G. Hecker, LOU	*1.80*
D. Foutz, STL	*2.18*
E. Morris, COL	*2.18*
T. Keefe, NY	*2.29*
F. Mountain, COL	*2.45*

Wins

G. Hecker, LOU	52
J. Lynch, NY	37
T. Keefe, NY	37
T. Mullane, TOL	36
E. Morris, COL	34
W. White, CIN	34

Saves

O. Burns, BAL	1
F. Mountain, COL	1
H. O'Day, TOL	1

Strikeouts

G. Hecker, LOU	385
H. Henderson, BAL	346
T. Mullane, TOL	325
T. Keefe, NY	323
L. McKeon, IND	308

Complete Games

G. Hecker, LOU	72
T. Mullane, TOL	64
L. McKeon, IND	59
T. Keefe, NY	57
A. Terry, BKN	55

Fewest Hits/9 Innings

E. Morris, COL	7.02
G. Hecker, LOU	7.06
T. Keefe, NY	7.10
F. Mountain, COL	7.21

Shutouts

W. White, CIN	7
T. Mullane, TOL	7
G. Hecker, LOU	6

Fewest Walks/9 Innings

D. Driscoll, LOU	0.62
G. Hecker, LOU	0.75
J. Lynch, NY	0.78
E. Dugan, RIC	0.81

AMERICAN ASSOCIATION 1884, *cont.*

BATTING AND BASE RUNNING LEADERS

Runs

H. Stovey, PHI	124
C. Jones, CIN	117
A. Latham, STL	115
C. Nelson, NY	114
L. Reilly, CIN	114

Doubles

S. Barkley, TOL	39
P. Browning, LOU	33
D. Orr, NY	32
D. Esterbrook, NY	29

Triples

H. Stovey, PHI	23
L. Reilly, CIN	19
F. Mann, COL	18
J. Peltz, IND	17
C. Jones, CIN	17

Most Strikeouts/9 Inn.

H. Henderson, BAL	7.09
D. Davis, STL	6.49
E. Morris, COL	6.33
B. Mathews, PHI	5.98

PITCHING LEADERS

Innings

G. Hecker, LOU	671
T. Mullane, TOL	567
L. McKeon, IND	512
T. Keefe, NY	492

Games Pitched

G. Hecker, LOU	76
T. Mullane, TOL	67
L. McKeon, IND	61
T. Keefe, NY	58

	W	L	PCT	GB	R	OR	Batting 2B	3B	HR	BA	SA	SB	Fielding E	DP	FA	Pitching CG	BB	SO	ShO	SV	ERA
New York	75	32	.701		734	423	155	64	21	.262	.348	0	450	42	.905	**111**	119	611	9	0	2.46
Columbus	69	39	.639	6.5	585	459	107	96	**40**	.240	.351	0	433	74	.908	102	172	526	8	**1**	2.68
Louisville	68	40	.630	7.5	573	425	152	68	18	.254	.340	0	426	**84**	**.912**	101	97	470	6	0	**2.17**
St. Louis	67	40	.626	8	658	539	151	60	11	.249	.326	0	490	65	.900	99	172	477	8	0	2.67
Cincinnati	68	41	.624	8	**754**	512	109	98	34	.254	.353	0	430	82	.909	**111**	181	308	**11**	0	3.33
Baltimore	63	43	.594	11.5	636	515	133	84	30	.233	.335	0	459	61	.900	105	219	**635**	8	**1**	2.71
Philadelphia	61	46	.570	14	700	546	**167**	**100**	26	**.267**	**.379**	0	457	63	.901	105	127	530	5	0	3.40
Toledo	46	58	.442	27.5	463	571	153	48	8	.231	.305	0	469	67	.900	103	169	501	9	**1**	3.07
Brooklyn	40	64	.385	33.5	476	644	112	47	16	.225	.292	0	520	68	.889	105	163	378	6	0	3.79
Richmond	12	30	.286	30.5	194	**294**	40	33	7	.221	.308	0	**239**	27	.874	45	**52**	167	1	0	4.54
Pittsburgh	30	78	.278	45.5	406	725	105	50	2	.211	.268	0	524	71	.889	108	216	338	4	0	4.35
Indianapolis	29	78	.271	46	462	755	129	62	20	.234	.316	0	514	45	.889	107	199	479	2	0	4.21
Washington	12	51	.190	41	248	481	61	24	5	.200	.258	0	400	40	.858	62	110	235	3	0	4.00
					6889	6889	1574	834	238	.237	.321	0	5811	789	.895	1264	1996	5655	80	3	3.34

UNION ASSOCIATION 1884

St. Louis

W-94 L-19

Ted Sullivan
W-28 L-3

Fred Dunlap
W-66 L-16

POS	Player	AB	BA	HR	RBI	PO	A	E	DP	TC/G	FA	Pitcher	G	IP	W	L	SV	ERA
1B	J. Quinn	429	.270	0		1033	**33**	**62**	**55**	11.3	.945	C. Sweeney	33	271	24	7	0	1.83
2B	F. Dunlap	449	**.412**	**13**		**341**	**300**	51	**54**	**6.9**	**.926**	B. Taylor	33	263	25	4	4*	1.68
SS	M. Whitehead	393	.211	1		85	269	87	19*	4.7	.803	H. Boyle	19	150	15	3	1	1.74
3B	J. Gleason	395	.324	3		95	170	80	11	3.8	.768	P. Werden	16	141	12	1	0	1.97
RF	O. Shaffer	467	.360	2		110	24	20	3	1.5	.870	C. Hodnett	14	121	12	2	0	2.01
CF	D. Rowe	**485**	.293	3		146	15	9	5	1.8	.947							
LF	B. Dickerson	211	.365	0		65	12	9	2	2.0	.895							
C	G. Baker	317	.164	0		**435**	113	63	**11**	**9.0**	**.897**							
UT	H. Boyle	262	.260	4		85	49	19	7		.876							
UT	J. Brennan	231	.216	0		172	92	40	4		.868							
P	B. Taylor	186	.366	3		17	51	10	2	2.4	.872							
P	C. Sweeney	171	.316	1		23	76	6	4*	3.2	.943*							

Milwaukee

W-8 L-4

Tom Loftus

POS	Player	AB	BA	HR	RBI	PO	A	E	DP	TC/G	FA	Pitcher	G	IP	W	L	SV	ERA
1B	T. Griffin	41	.220	0		100	1	9	0	10.0	.918	H. Porter	6	51	3	3	0	3.00
2B	A. Myers	46	.326	0		26	30	10	1	5.5	.848	E. Cushman	4	36	4	0	0	1.00
SS	T. Sexton	47	.234	0		8	21	5	1	2.8	.853							
3B	T. Morrissey	47	.170	0		7	15	9	1	2.6	.710							
RF	E. Hogan	37	.081	0		16	9	6	1	2.8	.806							
CF	L. Baldwin	27	.222	0		6	1	2	1	1.8	.778							
LF	S. Behel	33	.242	0		4	1	0	0	0.6	1.000							
C	C. Broughton	39	.308	0		65	9	5	0	11.3	.937							
PO	H. Porter	40	.275	0		2	10	0	0		1.000							
OC	A. Falch	18	.111	0		16	8	3	0		.889							

Cincinnati

W-69 L-36

Dan O'Leary
W-20 L-15

Sam Crane
W-49 L-21

POS	Player	AB	BA	HR	RBI	PO	A	E	DP	TC/G	FA	Pitcher	G	IP	W	L	SV	ERA
1B	M. Powell	185	.319	1		463	11	30	19	11.7	.940	G. Bradley	41	342	25	15	0	2.71
2B	S. Crane	309	.233	1		224	217	73	27	6.4	.858	D. Burns	40	330	23	15	0	2.46
SS	J. Jones	272	.261	2		54	140	32	9	5.5	.858	J. McCormick	24	210	21	3	0	**1.54***
3B	C. Barber	204	.201	0		68	112	35	4	3.9	.837							
RF	B. Hawes	349	.278	4		74	7	17	0	1.7	.827							
CF	B. Harbidge	341	.279	2		101	24	13	2	1.7	.906							
LF	L. Sylvester	333	.267	2		110	23	35	2	2.1	.792							
C	K. Kelly	142	.282	1		210	60	42	3	8.4	.865							
OP	D. Burns	350	.306	4		87	81	26	1		.866							
UT	G. Bradley	226	.190	0		82	94	24	4		.880							
SS	J. Glasscock	172	.419	2		45	107	19	4	4.8*	.889							
OF	D. O'Leary	132	.258	1		48	8	9	0	2.0	.862							
1B	M. McQuery	132	.280	2		340	8	8	9	10.2	.978							
3B	E. Cleveland	115	.322	1		48	54	19	0	4.2	.843							

Baltimore

W-58 L-47

Bill Henderson

POS	Player	AB	BA	HR	RBI	PO	A	E	DP	TC/G	FA	Pitcher	G	IP	W	L	SV	ERA
1B	C. Levis	373	.228	6		923	24	45	33	11.4*	.955	B. Sweeney	**62**	**538**	**40**	21	0	2.59
2B	D. Phelan	402	.246	3		272	251	77	33	6.0	.872	T. Lee	15	122	5	8	0	3.39
SS	L. Say	339	.239	2		103*	234*	87*	16*	5.4*	.795							
3B	Y. Robinson	415	.267	2		98	163	53	10	**4.4**	**.831**							
RF	B. Graham	167	.269	0		60	10	16	2	2.2	.814							
CF	N. Cuthbert	168	.202	0		41	10	17	0	1.5	.750							
LF	E. Seery	463	.311	2		157	26	38	3	2.1	.828							
C	E. Fusselbach	303	.284	1		378	**137**	50	5	10.5	.912							
P	B. Sweeney	296	.240	0		25	**133**	**34**	3	3.1	.823							
CO	R. Sweeney	186	.226	0		218	60	35	1		.888							
OF	H. Oberbeck	125	.184	0		33	10	6	1	1.8	.878							

UNION ASSOCIATION 1884, *cont.*

Boston

W-58 L-51

Tim Murnane

POS	Player	AB	BA	HR	RBI	PO	A	E	DP	TC/G	FA	Pitcher	G	IP	W	L	SV	ERA
1B	T. Murnane	311	.235	0		588	7	31	8	9.9	.950	J. Burke	38	322	19	15	0	*2.85*
2B	T. O'Brien	449	.263	4		257	267	90	23	6.2	.853	D. Shaw	39	316	21	15	0	*1.77*
SS	W. Hackett	415	.243	1		126	294	71	12	4.8	**.855**	T. Bond	23	189	13	9	0	*3.00*
3B	J. Irwin	432	.234	1		117	**191**	**87**	7	3.8	.780							
RF	C. Crane	428	.285	12		74	21	20	3	2.0	.826							
CF	M. Slattery	413	.208	0		140	26	41	3	2.2	.802							
LF	F. Butler	255	.169	0		56	8	15	1	1.5	.810							
C	L. Brown	325	.231	1		414	117	50	6	10.8	.914							
OF	T. McCarthy	209	.215	0		39	11	13	1	1.3	.794							
P	J. Burke	184	.223	0		13	45	11	2	1.8	.841							
PO	T. Bond	162	.296	0		22	57	12	2		.868							
P	D. Shaw	153	.242	0		18	59	17	1	2.4	.819							

Chicago

W-34 L-39

Ed Hengle

POS	Player	AB	BA	HR	RBI	PO	A	E	DP	TC/G	FA	Pitcher	G	IP	W	L	SV	ERA
1B	J. Schoeneck	289	.325	2		714*	17	39	20	10.7	.949*	O. Daily	46	397	22	23	0	2.43
2B	M. Hengle	74	.203	0		40	39	15	2	4.9	.840							
SS	S. Matthias	142	.275	0		30	101	25	5	4.3	.840							
3B	W. Foley	71	.282	0		18	23	10	2	2.7	.804							
RF	J. Ellick	314	.255	0		43	13	6	1	1.1	.903							
CF	C. Briggs	182	.170	1		42	6	11	1	1.6	.814							
LF	C. Householder	244	.234	1		24	0	3	0	1.2	.889							
C	B. Krieg	240	.229	0		378	96	35	3	11.8	.931							
P	O. Daily	160	.244	0		9	89	19	2	2.5	.838							
UT	T. Suck	153	.144	0		146	68	35	2		.859							

Washington

W-47 L-65

Mike Scanlon

POS	Player	AB	BA	HR	RBI	PO	A	E	DP	TC/G	FA	Pitcher	G	IP	W	L	SV	ERA
1B	P. Baker	371	.288	1		309	12	15	13	8.6	.955	B. Wise	50	364	23	18	0	*3.04*
2B	T. Evers	427	.232	0		326	296	**94**	28	6.6	.869	A. Voss	27	186	5	14	0	*3.57*
SS	J. Halpin	168	.185	0		37	94	31	4	4.2	.809	C. Geggus	23	177	10	9	0	*2.54*
3B	J. McCormick	157	.217	0		42*	42	22	5*	2.8	.792	A. Powell	18	134	6	12	0	*3.43*
RF	B. Wise	339	.233	2		47	21	19	5	2.0	.782	M. Lockwood	11	68	1	9	0	*7.32*
CF	A. Powell	191	.283	0		39	3	6	0	1.6	.875							
LF	H. Moore	461	.336	1		134	16	33	4	1.7	.820							
C	C. Fulmer	181	.276	0		213	41	17	4	8.0	.937							
UT	A. Voss	245	.192	0		166	96	32	9		.891							
CO	J. Gunson	166	.139	0		237	59	33	0		.900							
PO	C. Geggus	154	.247	0		45	47	19	1		.829							
SS	J. Deasley	134	.216	0		26	86	22	7	4.3	.836							
1B	P. Joy	130	.215	0		331	7	12	14	9.7	.966							
OF	F. Tenney	119	.235	0		34	5	6	2	1.7	.867							
UT	E. McKenna	117	.188	0		124	46	35	5		.829							

Pittsburgh

W-7 L-11

Joe Battin

W-1 L-5

Joe Ellick

W-6 L-6

POS	Player	AB	BA	HR	RBI	PO	A	E	DP	TC/G	FA	Pitcher	G	IP	W	L	SV	ERA
1B	J. Schoeneck	77	.286	0		202*	7	4	7	11.8	.981*	O. Daily	10	88	5	4	0	2.45
2B	G. Strief	53	.208	0		34	33	7	1	4.9	.905	A. Atkinson	8	69	2	6	0	2.88
SS	J. Ellick	80	.162	0		13	43	5	3	3.4	.918							
3B	J. Battin	69	.188	0		31	48	8	3	4.8	.908							
RF	G. Gardner	64	.266	0		19	1	4	0	1.6	.833							
CF	H. Wheeler	73	.233	0		16	0	5	0	1.2	.762							
LF	C. Householder	66	.258	0		17	3	6	2	1.5	.769							
C	T. Suck	35	.171	0		71	17	11	2	9.9	.889							
C	B. Krieg	39	.359	0		51	19	5	0	8.3	.933							
P	O. Daily	36	.111	0		3	16	1	0	2.0	.950							
P	A. Atkinson	33	.121	0		0	20	4	1	3.0	.833							

Philadelphia

W-21 L-46

Fergy Malone

POS	Player	AB	BA	HR	RBI	PO	A	E	DP	TC/G	FA	Pitcher	G	IP	W	L	SV	ERA
1B	J. McGuinness	220	.236	0		550	12	24	19	12.2	.959	J. Bakely	39	345	14	25*	0	*4.47*
2B	E. Peak	215	.195	0		145	137	60	14	7.3	.825	S. Weaver	17	136	5	10	0	*5.76*
SS	H. Easterday	115	.243	0		35	98	19	6	5.4	.875							
3B	J. McCormick	295	.285	0		90*	116	48	8*	4.7	.811							
RF	J. Flynn	209	.249	4		41	8	14	3	1.5	.778							
CF	B. Keinzil	299	.254	0		87	18	31	2	2.0	.772							
LF	B. Hoover	275	.364	0		51	13	18	2	2.2	.780							
C	T. Gillen	116	.155	0		152	61	25	1	8.8	.895							
OC	J. Clements	177	.282	3		142	46	31	2		.858							
P	J. Bakely	167	.132	0		14	69	23	3*	2.7	.783							

St. Paul

W-2 L-6

Andrew Thompson

POS	Player	AB	BA	HR	RBI	PO	A	E	DP	TC/G	FA	Pitcher	G	IP	W	L	SV	ERA
1B	S. Dunn	32	.250	0		64	5	2	2	7.9	.972	J. Brown	6	36	1	4	0	3.75
2B	M. Hengle	33	.152	0		25	23	4	3	5.8	.923	L. Galvin	3	25	0	2	0	*2.88*
SS	J. Werrick	27	.074	0		8	26	11	0	5.0	.756							
3B	B. O'Brien	30	.233	0		7	14	4	0	3.1	.840							
RF	S. Carroll	31	.097	0		9	5	3	1	2.1	.824							
CF	B. Barnes	30	.200	0		8	0	3	1	1.4	.727							
LF	J. Tilley	26	.154	0		14	1	1	0	1.8	.938							
C	C. Ganzel	23	.217	0		36	7	2	0	7.5	.956							
P	J. Brown	16	.313	0		0	12	5	0	2.8	.706							
C	P. Dealey	15	.133	0		18	9	4	1	7.8	.871							
P	L. Galvin	9	.222	0		1	1	1	0	1.0	.667							

UNION ASSOCIATION 1884, *cont.*

Altoona

W-6 L-19

Ed Curtis

POS	Player	AB	BA	HR	RBI	PO	A	E	DP	TC/G	FA	Pitcher	G	IP	W	L	SV	ERA
1B	F. Harris	95	.263	0		169	8	11	1	11.1	.941	J. Murphy	14	112	5	6	0	3.87
2B	C. Dougherty	85	.259	0		47	41	15	2	6.4	.854	J. Brown	11	74	1	9	0	5.35
SS	G. Smith	108	.315	0		40	88	19	1	5.9	.871							
3B	H. Koons	78	.231	0		39	45	13	1	4.6	.866							
RF	J. Brown	88	.250	1		14	2	10	0	1.9	.615							
CF	J. Murphy	94	.149	0		11	4	4	2	1.9	.789							
LF	F. Shaffer	74	.284	0		22	2	3	0	1.6	.889							
C	J. Moore	80	.313	1		54	18	18	0	7.5	.800							
C	P. Carroll	49	.265	0		40	6	4	0	6.3	.920							
1B	J. Grady	36	.306	0		87	3	9	1	12.4	.909							
OP	J. Leary	33	.091	0		10	7	7	0		.708							
2B	C. Berry	25	.240	0		16	9	4	0	4.1	.862							
OC	G. Noftsker	25	.040	0		21	9	5	1		.857							

Kansas City

W-16 L-63

Harry Wheeler
W-0 L-4

Matt Porter
W-3 L-13

Ted Sullivan
W-13 L-46

POS	Player	AB	BA	HR	RBI	PO	A	E	DP	TC/G	FA	Pitcher	G	IP	W	L	SV	ERA
1B	J. Sweeney	129	.264	0		304	14	14	15	10.7	.958	E. Hickman	17	137	4	13	0	*4.52*
2B	C. Berry	118	.246	1		63	55	15	6	6.0	.887	B. Black	16	123	4	9	0	*3.22*
SS	C. Cross	93	.215	0		15	92	21	3	5.3	.836	P. Veach	12	104	3	9	0	*2.42*
3B	P. Sullivan	114	.193	1		31	35	20	5	4.1	.767							
RF	F. Shaffer	164	.171	0		51	12	19	0	2.0	.768							
CF	F. Wyman	124	.218	0		41	11	18	3	2.8	.743							
LF	B. McLaughlin	162	.228	0		21	11	10	4	1.8	.762							
C	K. Baldwin	191	.194	1		199	86	37	4	7.3	.885							
UT	B. Black	146	.247	1		58	50	20	4		.844							
1B	J. Gorman	137	.277	0		264	4	13	7	11.7	.954							
UT	F. McLaughlin	123	.228	1		55	50	30	4		.778							
10	J. Cudworth	116	.147	0		201	8	8	10		.963							

Wilmington

W-2 L-16

Joe Simmons

POS	Player	AB	BA	HR	RBI	PO	A	E	DP	TC/G	FA	Pitcher	G	IP	W	L	SV	ERA
1B	R. Snyder	52	.192	0		155	5	4	8	10.3	.976	J. Murphy	7	48	0	6	0	3.00
2B	C. Bastian	60	.200	2		37	61	10	3	6.8	.907	T. Nolan	5	40	1	4	0	*2.92*
SS	H. Myers	24	.125	0		6	15	3	0	4.8	.875							
3B	J. Say	59	.220	0		12	21	12	2	2.8	.733							
RF	J. Munce	21	.190	0		4	2	3	0	1.3	.667							
CF	G. Fisher	29	.069	0		9	0	2	0	1.8	.818							
LF	T. Lynch	58	.276	0		9	2	1	0	1.5	.917							
C	T. Cusick	34	.147	0		42	19	9	2	11.7	.871							
PO	T. Nolan	33	.273	0		5	11	1	0		.941							
UT	J. Murphy	31	.065	0		4	11	9	2		.625							
OS	J. Cullen	31	.194	0		9	8	9	0		.654							
OC	B. McCloskey	30	.100	0		38	7	13	1		.776							
OF	I. Benners	22	.045	0		8	1	3	1	2.0	.750							

BATTING AND BASE RUNNING LEADERS

Batting Average

F. Dunlap, STL	.412
O. Shaffer, STL	.360
H. Moore, WAS	.336
J. Gleason, STL	.324
E. Seery, BAL, KC	.313

Slugging Average

F. Dunlap, STL	.621
O. Shaffer, STL	.501
D. Burns, CIN	.457
C. Crane, BOS	.451
J. Gleason, STL	.433

Home Runs

F. Dunlap, STL	13
C. Crane, BOS	12
C. Levis, BAL, WAS	6

Total Bases

F. Dunlap, STL	279
O. Shaffer, STL	234
D. Rowe, STL	205
C. Crane, BOS	193
E. Seery, BAL, KC	192

Runs Batted In

(not available)

Stolen Bases

(not available)

Hits

F. Dunlap, STL	185
O. Shaffer, STL	168
H. Moore, WAS	155
E. Seery, BAL, KC	146

Base on Balls

Y. Robinson, BAL	37
O. Shaffer, STL	30
F. Dunlap, STL	29
B. Harbidge, CIN	25

Home Run Percentage

F. Dunlap, STL	2.9
C. Crane, BOS	2.8
C. Levis, BAL, WAS	1.6
B. Hawes, CIN	1.1

Runs

F. Dunlap, STL	160
O. Shaffer, STL	130
E. Seery, BAL, KC	115
Y. Robinson, BAL	101

Doubles

O. Shaffer, STL	40
F. Dunlap, STL	39
D. Rowe, STL	32
T. O'Brien, BOS	31

Triples

D. Burns, CIN	12
D. Rowe, STL	11
O. Shaffer, STL	10

PITCHING LEADERS

Winning Percentage

B. Taylor, STL	.862
C. Sweeney, STL	.774
B. Sweeney, BAL	.656
G. Bradley, CIN	.625
D. Burns, CIN	.605

Earned Run Average

J. McCormick, CIN	*1.54*
B. Taylor, STL	*1.68*
H. Boyle, STL	*1.74*
D. Shaw, BOS	*1.77*
C. Sweeney, STL	*1.83*

Wins

B. Sweeney, BAL	40
O. Daily, CHI, PIT, WAS	28
B. Taylor, STL	25
G. Bradley, CIN	25
C. Sweeney, STL	24

Saves

B. Taylor, STL	4
L. Brown, BOS	1
F. Dunlap, STL	1
L. Sylvester, CIN	1
H. Boyle, STL	1

Strikeouts

O. Daily, CHI, PIT, WAS	483
B. Sweeney, BAL	374
D. Shaw, BOS	309
B. Wise, WAS	268
J. Burke, BOS	255

Complete Games

B. Sweeney, BAL	58
O. Daily, CHI, PIT, WAS	56
J. Bakely, PHI, WIL, KC	43
G. Bradley, CIN	36
D. Shaw, BOS	35

Fewest Hits/9 Innings

J. McCormick, CIN	6.47
D. Shaw, BOS	6.47
C. Sweeney, STL	6.87
H. Boyle, STL	7.08

Shutouts

J. McCormick, CIN	7
D. Shaw, BOS	5
B. Wise, WAS	4
O. Daily, CHI, PIT, WAS	4
B. Sweeney, BAL	4

Fewest Walks/9 Innings

C. Sweeney, STL	0.43
J. McCormick, CIN	0.60
H. Boyle, STL	0.60
G. Bradley, CIN	0.61

Most Strikeouts/9 Inn.

D. Shaw, BOS	8.81
O. Daily, CHI, PIT, WAS	8.68
C. Geggus, WAS	7.92
J. Burke, BOS	7.13

Innings

B. Sweeney, BAL	538
O. Daily, CHI, PIT, WAS	501
J. Bakely, PHI, WIL, KC	395
B. Wise, WAS	364

Games Pitched

B. Sweeney, BAL	62
O. Daily, CHI, PIT, WAS	58
B. Wise, WAS	50
J. Bakely, PHI, WIL, KC	46

UNION ASSOCIATION 1884, *cont.*

							Batting						Fielding			Pitching					
	W	L	PCT	GB	R	OR	2B	3B	HR	BA	SA	SB	E	DP	FA	CG	BB	SO	ShO	SV	ERA
St. Louis	94	19	.832		**887**	429	**259**	41	**30**	**.292**	**.393**	0	554	**79**	.888	**104**	110	550	8	**6**	***1.95***
Milwaukee	8	4	.667	35.5	53	**34**	25	0	0	.223	.286	0	53	4	.892	12	**13**	139	3	0	*2.25*
Cincinnati	69	36	.657	21	703	466	118	**62**	27	.271	.357	0	532	45	.882	95	90	503	**11**	1	*2.39*
Baltimore	58	47	.552	32	662	627	150	26	17	.245	.310	0	616	53	.872	92	177	628	4	0	*3.01*
Boston	58	51	.532	34	636	558	168	32	19	.236	.309	0	633	39	.868	100	110	**753**	5	1	*2.70*
Chicago	34	39	.466	40	360	411	99	19	10	.234	.300	0	393	29	.875	68	111	560	4	0	*2.74*
Washington	47	65	.420	46.5	572	679	120	26	4	.237	.284	0	625	55	.869	94	168	684	5	0	*3.43*
Pittsburgh	7	11	.389	39.5	78	71	28	7	0	.218	.282	0	66	9	**.912**	18	26	119	1	0	*2.64*
Philadelphia	21	46	.313	50	414	545	108	35	7	.245	.324	0	501	36	.841	64	105	310	1	0	*4.63*
St. Paul	2	6	.250	39.5	24	57	13	1	0	.180	.235	0	**47**	6	.872	7	27	44	1	0	*3.17*
Altoona	6	19	.240	44	90	216	30	6	2	.248	.301	0	156	4	.862	20	52	93	0	0	*4.67*
Kansas City	16	63	.203	61	311	618	102	15	8	.199	.254	0	520	51	.861	70	127	334	0	0	*4.05*
Wilmington	2	16	.111	44.5	35	114	8	8	2	.175	.232	0	104	10	.860	15	18	113	0	0	*3.04*
					4825	4825	1228	278	126	.231	.297	0	4800	420	.873	759	1134	4830	43	8	*3.13*

NATIONAL LEAGUE 1885

Team	POS	Player	AB	BA	HR	RBI	PO	A	E	DP	TC/G	FA	Pitcher	G	IP	W	L	SV	ERA
Chicago	1B	C. Anson	464	.310	7	**114**	**1253**	39	**57**	62	**12.0**	.958	J. Clarkson	**70**	**623**	**53**	16	0	*1.85*
W-87 L-25	2B	F. Pfeffer	469	.241	6	71	**325**	**391**	**86**	**66**	**7.4**	.893	J. McCormick	24	215	20	4	0	*2.43*
Cap Anson	SS	T. Burns	445	.272	7	70	151	370	**96**	35	5.6	.844							
	3B	N. Williamson	407	.238	3	64	113	**258**	45	**18**	3.7	**.892**							
	RF	K. Kelly	438	.288	9	74	95	29	19	2	2.1	.867							
	CF	G. Gore	441	.313	5	51	204	17	29	2	2.3	.884							
	LF	A. Dalrymple	**492**	.274	**11**	58	180	16	27	2	2.0	.879							
	C	S. Flint	249	.209	1	19	**356**	100	36	2	7.2	**.927**							
	P	J. Clarkson	283	.216	4	31	26	**174**	**20**	**8**	3.1	.909							
	OF	B. Sunday	172	.256	2	20	46	6	11	2	1.4	.825							
New York	1B	R. Connor	455	**.371**	1		1178	**42**	31	**66**	11.4	.975	M. Welch	56	492	44	11	1	*1.66*
W-85 L-27	2B	J. Gerhardt	399	.155	0		314	352	65	59	6.5	.911	T. Keefe	46	398	32	13	0	**1.58**
Jim Mutrie	SS	M. Ward	446	.226	0		**167**	350	55	**36**	5.2	.904							
	3B	D. Esterbrook	359	.256	2		111	159	35	14	3.6	.885							
	RF	M. Dorgan	347	.326	0		142	11	16	4	1.9	.905							
	CF	J. O'Rourke	477	.300	5		162	10	11	0	1.6	.940							
	LF	P. Gillespie	420	.293	0		133	12	9	2	1.5	.942							
	C	B. Ewing	342	.304	6		337	**102**	39	8	7.6	.918							
	C	P. Deasley	207	.256	0		281	80	25	4	7.1	.935							
	P	M. Welch	199	.206	2		16	70	14	0	1.8	.860							
	UT	D. Richardson	198	.263	0		52	58	5	1		.957							
	P	T. Keefe	166	.163	0		**30**	80	13	0	2.7	.894							
Philadelphia	1B	S. Farrar	420	.245	3		1153	41	31	50	11.0	.975	E. Daily	50	440	26	23	0	2.21
W-56 L-54	2B	A. Myers	357	.204	1		201	287	64	31	5.9	.884	C. Ferguson	48	405	26	20	0	*2.22*
Harry Wright	SS	C. Bastian	389	.167	4		164	337	62	34	5.5	.890							
	3B	J. Mulvey	443	.269	6		**144**	201	**62**	12	3.8	.848							
	RF	J. Manning	445	.256	3		134	21	18	3	1.6	.896							
	CF	J. Fogarty	427	.232	0		227	26	16	5	3.1	.941							
	LF	E. Andrews	421	.266	0		175	11	16	1	2.0	.921							
	C	J. Clements	188	.191	1		181	47	28	2	6.2	.891							
	P	C. Ferguson	235	.306	1		27	87	9	3	2.6	.927							
	P	E. Daily	184	.207	1		11	87	12	2	2.2	.891							
	C	T. Cusick	141	.177	0		180	60	**57**	2	7.8	.808							
	C	C. Ganzel	125	.168	0		175	39	27	3	7.3	.888							
Providence	1B	J. Start	374	.275	0	41	1036	35	31	42	10.9	.972	O. Radbourn	49	446	28	21	0	*2.20*
W-53 L-57	2B	J. Farrell	257	.206	1	19	158	194	39	16	5.8	.900	D. Shaw	49	400	23	26	0	*2.57*
Frank Bancroft	SS	A. Irwin	218	.179	0	14	70	209	40	17	5.5	.875							
	3B	J. Denny	318	.223	3	25	128	157	43	10	**4.0**	.869							
	RF	P. Radford	371	.243	0	32	141	26	29	7	2.2	.852							
	CF	P. Hines	411	.270	1	35	199	18	34	3	2.7	.865							
	LF	C. Carroll	426	.232	1	40	207	10	28	2	2.4	.886							
	C	B. Gilligan	252	.214	0	12	305	84	**57**	**13**	6.9	.872							
	UT	C. Bassett	285	.144	0	16	141	248	39	24		.909							
	P	O. Radbourn	249	.233	0	22	18	115	9	7	2.9	.937							
	C	C. Daily	223	.260	0	19	220	70	41	8	6.9	.876							
	P	D. Shaw	165	.133	0	9	11	76	8	2	1.9	.916							
Boston	1B	J. Morrill	394	.226	4	44	952	32	31	53	11.0	.969	J. Whitney	51	441	18	**32**	0	*2.98*
W-46 L-66	2B	J. Burdock	169	.142	0	7	99	134	21	16	5.6	.917	C. Buffinton	51	434	22	27	0	*2.88*
John Morrill	SS	S. Wise	424	.283	4	46	135	270	67	29	**6.0**	.858	D. Davis	11	94	5	6	0	*4.29*
	3B	E. Sutton	457	.313	4	47	132	168	43	**18**	3.8	.875							
	RF	T. Poorman	227	.238	3	25	82	9	14	1	1.9	.867							
	CF	J. Manning	306	.206	2	27	164	21	21	3	2.5	.898							
	LF	T. McCarthy	148	.182	0	11	69	8	12	0	2.2	.865							
	C	T. Gunning	174	.184	0	15	252	68	45	4	7.6	.877							
	UT	C. Buffinton	338	.240	1	33	196	121	27	11		.922							
	PO	J. Whitney	290	.234	0	36	49	130	20	1		.899							
	OF	G. Whiteley	135	.185	1	7	42	8	14	2	2.0	.781							
	C	P. Dealey	130	.223	1	9	162	42	22	8	7.8	.903							
	2S	W. Hackett	125	.184	0	9	59	86	22	9		.868							
	C	M. Hackett	115	.183	0	4	194	53	27	6	8.1	.901							
	OF	D. Johnston	111	.234	1	23	40	8	9	2	2.2	.842							

NATIONAL LEAGUE 1885, *cont.*

Detroit

W-41 L-67

Charlie Morton
W-7 L-31

Bill Watkins
W-34 L-36

POS	Player	AB	BA	HR	RBI	PO	A	E	DP	TC/G	FA	Pitcher	G	IP	W	L	SV	ERA
1B	M. McQuery	278	.273	3	30	707	28	18	32	10.9	.976	S. Wiedman	38	330	14	24	0	*3.14*
2B	S. Crane	245	.192	2	20	179	197	38	21	6.1	.908	C. Getzien	37	330	12	25	0	*3.03*
SS	M. Phillips	139	.209	0	17	35	120	21	6	5.3	.881	L. Baldwin	21	179	11	9	1	*1.86*
3B	J. Donnelly	211	.232	1	22	73	102	31	3	3.7	.850	D. Casey	12	104	4	8	0	*3.29*
RF	S. Thompson	254	.303	7	44	84	24	14	0	2.0	.885							
CF	N. Hanlon	424	.302	1	29	220	19	38	2	2.6	.863							
LF	G. Wood	362	.290	5	28	112	11	16	1	2.0	.885							
C	C. Bennett	349	.269	5	60	347	87	38	10	**7.6**	.919							
2B	J. Quest	200	.195	0	21	107	122	26	10	6.5	.898							
OF	J. Dorgan	161	.286	0	24	55	5	10	2	1.8	.857							
OP	S. Wiedman	153	.157	1	14	5	2	7	1		.500							
1B	M. Scott	148	.264	0	12	394	18	14	17	11.2	.967							
P	C. Getzien	137	.212	0	16	17	66	8	0	2.5	.912							
PO	L. Baldwin	124	.242	0	18	29	44	10	1		.880							
C	D. McGuire	121	.190	0	9	249	52	26	2	10.5	.920							

Buffalo

W-38 L-74

Pud Galvin
W-7 L-17

Jack Chapman
W-31 L-57

POS	Player	AB	BA	HR	RBI	PO	A	E	DP	TC/G	FA	Pitcher	G	IP	W	L	SV	ERA
1B	D. Brouthers	407	.359	7	60	996	25	26	54	10.7	.975	P. Galvin	33	284	13	19	1	*4.09*
2B	D. Force	253	.225	0	17	113	134	33	23	6.7	.882	B. Serad	30	241	7	21	0	*4.10*
SS	J. Rowe	421	.290	2	51	71	186	51	26	4.7	.834	P. Conway	27	210	10	17	0	*4.67*
3B	D. White	404	.292	0	57	118	198	40	12	3.6	.888	P. Wood	24	199	8	15	0	*4.44*
RF	J. Lillie	430	.249	2	30	183	23	33	4	2.1	.862							
CF	H. Richardson	426	.319	6	44	120	6	14	2	2.9	.900							
LF	B. Crowley	344	.241	1	36	152	8	23	1	2.0	.874							
C	G. Myers	326	.206	0	19	305	95	45	4	6.4	.899							
P	P. Galvin	122	.189	1	10	17	83	13	3	3.4	.885							

St. Louis

W-36 L-72

Fred Dunlap
W-21 L-29

Alex McKinnon
W-6 L-32

Fred Dunlap
W-9 L-11

POS	Player	AB	BA	HR	RBI	PO	A	E	DP	TC/G	FA	Pitcher	G	IP	W	L	SV	ERA
1B	A. McKinnon	411	.294	1	44	1102	26	25	50	11.5	**.978**	H. Boyle	42	367	16	24	0	*2.75*
2B	F. Dunlap	423	.270	2	25	314	374	49	53	7.0	**.934**	C. Sweeney	35	275	11	21	0	*3.93*
SS	J. Glasscock	446	.280	1	40	156	**397**	50	33	5.5	**.917**	J. Kirby	14	129	5	8	0	3.55
3B	E. Caskin	262	.179	0	12	82	139	29	5	3.6	.884	O. Daily	11	91	3	8	0	*3.94*
RF	O. Shaffer	257	.195	0	18	106	28	12	0	2.1	.918							
CF	J. Quinn	343	.213	0	15	83	8	13	0	1.8	.875							
LF	E. Seery	216	.162	1	14	95	16	16	1	2.2	.874							
C	F. Briody	215	.195	1	17	243	83	39	3	6.1	.893							
OP	C. Sweeney	267	.206	0	24	81	67	27	3		.846							
PO	H. Boyle	258	.202	1	21	88	73	15	4		.915							
OF	F. Lewis	181	.293	1	27	71	18	4	2	2.1	.957							
C	G. Baker	131	.122	0	5	148	31	28	1	6.5	.865							

BATTING AND BASE RUNNING LEADERS

Batting Average

R. Connor, NY	.371
D. Brouthers, BUF	.359
M. Dorgan, NY	.326
H. Richardson, BUF	.319
G. Gore, CHI	.313

Slugging Average

D. Brouthers, BUF	.543
R. Connor, NY	.495
B. Ewing, NY	.471
C. Anson, CHI	.461
H. Richardson, BUF	.458

Home Runs

A. Dalrymple, CHI	11
K. Kelly, CHI	9
S. Thompson, DET	7
D. Brouthers, BUF	7
T. Burns, CHI	7
C. Anson, CHI	7

Total Bases

R. Connor, NY	225
D. Brouthers, BUF	221
A. Dalrymple, CHI	219
C. Anson, CHI	214
J. O'Rourke, NY	211

Runs Batted In

C. Anson, CHI	114
K. Kelly, CHI	74
F. Pfeffer, CHI	71
T. Burns, CHI	70
N. Williamson, CHI	64

Stolen Bases

(not available)

Hits

R. Connor, NY	169
D. Brouthers, BUF	146
C. Anson, CHI	144
E. Sutton, BOS	143
J. O'Rourke, NY	143

Base on Balls

N. Williamson, CHI	75
G. Gore, CHI	68
J. Morrill, BOS	64
R. Connor, NY	51

Home Run Percentage

A. Dalrymple, CHI	2.2
K. Kelly, CHI	2.1
B. Ewing, NY	1.8
D. Brouthers, BUF	1.7

Runs

K. Kelly, CHI	124
J. O'Rourke, NY	119
G. Gore, CHI	115
A. Dalrymple, CHI	109

Doubles

C. Anson, CHI	35
D. Brouthers, BUF	32
J. Rowe, BUF	28
A. Dalrymple, CHI	27

Triples

J. O'Rourke, NY	16
R. Connor, NY	15
C. Bennett, DET	13
G. Gore, CHI	13

PITCHING LEADERS

Winning Percentage

M. Welch, NY	.800
J. Clarkson, CHI	.768
J. McCormick, PRO, CHI	.750
T. Keefe, NY	.711
O. Radbourn, PRO	.571

Earned Run Average

T. Keefe, NY	*1.58*
M. Welch, NY	*1.66*
J. Clarkson, CHI	*1.85*
L. Baldwin, DET	*1.86*
O. Radbourn, PRO	*2.20*

Wins

J. Clarkson, CHI	53
M. Welch, NY	44
T. Keefe, NY	32
O. Radbourn, PRO	28
C. Ferguson, PHI	26
E. Daily, PHI	26

Saves

N. Williamson, CHI	2
F. Pfeffer, CHI	2
L. Baldwin, DET	1
P. Galvin, BUF	1
M. Welch, NY	1

Strikeouts

J. Clarkson, CHI	308
M. Welch, NY	258
C. Buffinton, BOS	242
T. Keefe, NY	230
J. Whitney, BOS	200

Complete Games

J. Clarkson, CHI	68
M. Welch, NY	55
J. Whitney, BOS	50
O. Radbourn, PRO	49
C. Buffinton, BOS	49
E. Daily, PHI	49

Fewest Hits/9 Innings

T. Keefe, NY	6.72
M. Welch, NY	6.80
L. Baldwin, DET	6.88
J. Clarkson, CHI	7.18

Shutouts

J. Clarkson, CHI	10
T. Keefe, NY	7
M. Welch, NY	7
D. Shaw, PRO	6
C. Buffinton, BOS	6

Fewest Walks/9 Innings

J. Whitney, BOS	0.75
P. Galvin, BUF	1.17
J. Clarkson, CHI	1.40
L. Baldwin, DET	1.41

Most Strikeouts/9 Inn.

D. Casey, DET	6.84
L. Baldwin, DET	6.78
T. Keefe, NY	5.20
C. Buffinton, BOS	5.01

Innings

J. Clarkson, CHI	623
M. Welch, NY	492
O. Radbourn, PRO	446
J. Whitney, BOS	441

Games Pitched

J. Clarkson, CHI	70
M. Welch, NY	56
C. Buffinton, BOS	51
J. Whitney, BOS	51

							Batting						Fielding			Pitching					
	W	L	PCT	GB	R	OR	2B	3B	HR	BA	SA	SB	E	DP	FA	CG	BB	SO	ShO	SV	ERA
Chicago	87	25	.777		**834**	470	**184**	74	**55**	.264	**.385**	0	496	80	.903	108	202	458	14	**4**	*2.23*
New York	85	27	.759	2	691	**370**	150	**82**	16	**.269**	.359	0	**331**	**85**	**.929**	109	266	**519**	**16**	1	***1.72***
Philadelphia	56	54	.509	30	513	511	156	35	20	.229	.302	0	447	66	.905	108	218	378	10	0	*2.39*
Providence	53	57	.482	33	442	531	114	30	6	.220	.272	0	459	70	.903	108	235	371	8	0	*2.71*
Boston	46	66	.411	41	528	589	144	53	22	.232	.312	0	478	79	.901	**111**	**188**	480	10	0	*3.03*
Detroit	41	67	.380	44	514	582	149	65	26	.243	.338	0	463	61	.901	105	224	475	6	1	*2.88*
Buffalo	38	74	.339	49	495	761	149	50	23	.251	.333	0	464	65	.901	107	234	320	4	1	*4.30*
St. Louis	36	72	.333	49	390	593	121	21	8	.221	.270	0	398	67	.916	107	278	337	4	0	*3.37*
					4407	4407	1167	410	176	.241	.321	0	3536	573	.907	863	1845	3338	72	7	*2.83*

AMERICAN ASSOCIATION 1885

St. Louis

W-79 L-33

Charlie Comiskey

POS	Player	AB	BA	HR	RBI	PO	A	E	DP	TC/G	FA	Pitcher	G	IP	W	L	SV	ERA
1B	C. Comiskey	340	.256	2		879	24	29	34	11.2	.969	B. Caruthers	53	482	**40**	13	0	**2.07**
2B	S. Barkley	418	.268	2		286	328	53	38	6.9	.921	D. Foutz	47	408	33	14	0	*2.63*
SS	B. Gleason	472	.252	3		115	303	63	18	4.3	.869	J. McGinnis	13	112	6	6	0	*3.38*
3B	A. Latham	485	.206	1		112	**217**	47	16	3.4	.875							
RF	H. Nicol	425	.207	0		213	33	31	2	2.5	.888							
CF	C. Welch	432	.271	2		236	25	15	5	2.5	.946							
LF	T. O'Neill	206	.350	3		83	6	12	1	1.9	.881							
C	D. Bushong	300	.267	0		**429**	**122**	40	10	7.0	.932							
UT	Y. Robinson	287	.261	0		155	76	32	7		.878							
P	D. Foutz	238	.248	0		24	104	14	3	3.0	.901							
P	B. Caruthers	222	.225	1		24	84	11	**4**	2.2	.908							

Cincinnati

W-63 L-49

Ollie Caylor

POS	Player	AB	BA	HR	RBI	PO	A	E	DP	TC/G	FA	Pitcher	G	IP	W	L	SV	ERA
1B	L. Reilly	482	.297	5		1034	22	41	**59**	10.3	.963	W. White	34	293	18	15	0	*3.53*
2B	B. McPhee	431	.265	0		339	354	47	**57**	6.7	**.936**	L. McKeon	33	290	20	13	0	*2.86*
SS	F. Fennelly	454	.273	10		151	359	74	**46**	5.2	.873	B. Mountjoy	17	154	10	7	0	*3.16*
3B	H. Carpenter	473	.277	2		**153**	191	56	**17**	3.6	.860	G. Pechiney	11	98	7	4	0	*2.02*
RF	P. Corkhill	440	.252	1		208	38	16	5	2.4	.939	G. Shallix	13	91	6	4	0	*3.25*
CF	J. Clinton	408	.238	0		215	14	32	4	2.5	.877							
LF	C. Jones	**487**	.322	4		214	22	29	6	2.4	.891							
C	P. Snyder	152	.237	1		185	64	34	3	7.4	.880							
C	J. Keenan	132	.265	1		164	37	16	1	6.6	.926							
UT	K. Baldwin	126	.135	1		142	37	34	4		.840							
P	L. McKeon	121	.165	0		18	41	1	0	1.8	.983							
P	W. White	118	.169	0		10	35	6	0	1.5	.882							

Pittsburgh

W-56 L-55

Horace Phillips

POS	Player	AB	BA	HR	RBI	PO	A	E	DP	TC/G	FA	Pitcher	G	IP	W	L	SV	ERA
1B	J. Field	209	.239	1		622	15*	23	33	11.8	.965	E. Morris	**63**	**581**	39	24	0	*2.35*
2B	P. Smith	453	.249	0		**372**	**384**	64	53	**7.7**	.922	P. Meegan	18	146	7	8	0	*3.39*
SS	A. Whitney	373	.233	0		95	219	28	21	4.6	**.918**	H. O'Day	12	103	5	7	0	*3.67*
3B	W. Kuehne	411	.226	0		102	187	45	14	3.4	.865	P. Galvin	11	88	3	7	0	*3.67*
RF	T. Brown	437	.307	4		186	21	43	2	2.3	.828							
CF	F. Mann	391	.253	0		157	10	17	2	1.9	.908							
LF	C. Eden	405	.254	0		111	7	27	2	1.5	.814							
C	F. Carroll	280	.268	0		328	99	38	3	7.8	.918							
P	E. Morris	237	.186	0		24	93	**20**	**4**	2.2	.854							
1B	M. Scott	210	.248	0		623	16	9	28	11.8	.986							
C	D. Miller	166	.163	0		177	49	27	4	7.7	.893							
SO	J. Richmond	131	.206	0		27	66	17	6		.845							

Philadelphia

W-55 L-57

Harry Stovey

POS	Player	AB	BA	HR	RBI	PO	A	E	DP	TC/G	FA	Pitcher	G	IP	W	L	SV	ERA
1B	H. Stovey	486	.315	**13**		877	**28**	31	47	11.4	.967	B. Mathews	48	422	30	17	0	*2.43*
2B	C. Stricker	398	.234	1		284	304	**81**	41	6.3	.879	T. Lovett	16	139	7	8	0	*3.70*
SS	S. Houck	388	.255	0		121	362	77	34	6.0	.863	E. Knouff	14	106	7	6	0	*3.65*
3B	F. Corey	384	.245	1		102	184	42	14	3.6	.872	E. Cushman	10	87	3	7	0	3.52
RF	J. Coleman	398	.299	2		128	23	28	5	1.9	.844							
CF	H. Larkin	453	.329	8		208	23	31	9	2.4	.882							
LF	B. Purcell	304	.296	0		78	13	15	1	1.6	.858							
C	J. Milligan	265	.268	2		419	84	35	**11**	**8.8**	.935							
UT	J. O'Brien	225	.267	2		276	95	38	10		.907							
P	B. Mathews	179	.168	0		7	67	10	1	1.8	.881							
UT	G. Strief	175	.274	0		62	82	19	10		.883							
OF	L. Knight	119	.210	0		49	9	5	3	2.2	.921							

Brooklyn

W-53 L-59

Charlie Hackett
W-15 L-22

Charlie Byrne
W-38 L-37

POS	Player	AB	BA	HR	RBI	PO	A	E	DP	TC/G	FA	Pitcher	G	IP	W	L	SV	ERA
1B	B. Phillips	391	.302	3		**1109**	24	32	40	**11.8**	**.973**	H. Porter	54	482	33	21	0	*2.78*
2B	G. Pinckney	447	.277	0		147	173	34	15	6.2	.904	J. Harkins	34	293	14	20	0	*3.75*
SS	G. Smith	419	.258	4		161	**455**	**81**	23	**6.5**	.884	A. Terry	25	209	6	17	1	*4.26*
3B	B. McClellan	464	.267	0		65	84	29	9	3.1	.837							
RF	J. Cassidy	221	.213	1		62	7	12	3	1.5	.852							
CF	P. Hotaling	370	.257	1		159	17	21	3	2.1	.893							
LF	E. Swartwood	399	.266	0		140	8	26	0	1.8	.851							
C	J. Hayes	137	.131	0		209	53	29	4	6.9	.900							
OP	A. Terry	264	.170	1		89	46	13	2		.912							
P	H. Porter	195	.205	0		13	93	7	0	2.1	.938							
P	J. Harkins	159	.264	1		**36**	63	16	0	**3.4**	.861							
C	J. Peoples	151	.199	1		173	57	27	3	6.9	.895							
OF	J. McTamany	131	.275	1		43	0	5	0	1.4	.896							

Louisville

W-53 L-59

Jim Hart

POS	Player	AB	BA	HR	RBI	PO	A	E	DP	TC/G	FA	Pitcher	G	IP	W	L	SV	ERA
1B	J. Kerins	456	.243	3		966	**28**	**56**	47	10.9	.947	G. Hecker	54	480	30	23	0	*2.17*
2B	T. McLaughlin	411	.212	2		320	266	78	43	7.1	.883	N. Baker	25	217	13	12	0	*3.40*
SS	J. Miller	339	.183	0		94	266	44	23	5.1	.891	A. Mays	17	150	6	11	0	*2.76*
3B	P. Reccius	402	.241	1		105	183	**59**	**17**	3.6	.830							
RF	C. Wolf	483	.292	1		180	19	18	4	2.0	.917							
CF	P. Browning	481	**.362**	9		214	20	26	4	2.3	.900							
LF	L. Maskrey	423	.229	1		169	9	20	2	1.8	.899							
C	J. Crotty	129	.155	0		190	51	21	2	6.9	.920							
P	G. Hecker	297	.273	2		30	**105**	10	1	2.7	.931							
C	A. Cross	130	.285	0		173	48	18	1	6.8	.925							

New York

W-44 L-64

Jim Gifford

POS	Player	AB	BA	HR	RBI	PO	A	E	DP	TC/G	FA	Pitcher	G	IP	W	L	SV	ERA
1B	D. Orr	444	.342	6		1089	20	39	48	10.7	.966	J. Lynch	44	379	23	21	0	*3.61*
2B	T. Forster	213	.221	0		127	143	29	21	5.8	.903	E. Cushman	22	191	8	14	0	2.78
SS	C. Nelson	420	.255	1		153	370	63	33	5.5	.892	D. Crothers	18	154	7	11	0	*5.08*
3B	F. Hankinson	362	.224	2		106	212	33	9	**3.7**	**.906**	E. Begley	15	115	4	9	0	*4.93*
RF	S. Brady	434	.295	3		178	10	26	3	2.0	.879	B. Becannon	10	85	2	8	0	*6.25*
CF	C. Roseman	410	.278	3		177	9	29	1	2.1	.865							
LF	E. Kennedy	349	.203	2		154	15	32	1	2.1	.841							
C	C. Reipschlager	268	.243	0		262	117	**52**	6	7.3	.879							
CO	B. Holbert	202	.173	0		250	85	34	5		.908							
2B	D. Troy	177	.220	2		124	103	35	17	6.2	.866							
P	J. Lynch	153	.196	0		11	34	4	0	1.1	.918							

AMERICAN ASSOCIATION 1885, *cont.*

Baltimore

W-41 L-68

Billy Barnie

POS	Player	AB	BA	HR	RBI	PO	A	E	DP	TC/G	FA
1B	D. Stearns	253	.186	1		605	19	17	35	10.2	.973
2B	T. Manning	157	.204	0		118	132	22	19	6.6	.919
SS	J. Macullar	320	.191	3		**175**	311	68	28	5.7	.877
3B	M. Muldoon	410	.251	2		103	184	43	16	3.3	.870
RF	E. Greer	211	.199	0		93	6	10	1	2.3	.908
CF	D. Casey	264	.288	3		100	10	24	0	2.1	.821
LF	J. Sommer	471	.251	1		230	14	21	2	2.5	.921
C	B. Traffley	254	.154	1		357	105	28	6	8.0	**.943**
UT	O. Burns	321	.231	5		121	83	27	12		.883
P	H. Henderson	229	.223	1		28	81	14	**4**	2.0	.886
2B	G. Gardner	170	.218	0		113	132	30	16	7.1	.891
1B	J. Field	144	.208	0		373	13*	15	15	10.6	.963

Pitcher	G	IP	W	L	SV	ERA
H. Henderson	61	539	25	**35**	0	*3.19*
B. Emslie	13	107	3	10	0	*4.28*
O. Burns	15	106	7	4	**3**	*3.58*

BATTING AND BASE RUNNING LEADERS

Batting Average

P. Browning, LOU	.362
D. Orr, NY	.342
H. Larkin, PHI	.329
C. Jones, CIN	.322
H. Stovey, PHI	.315

Slugging Average

D. Orr, NY	.543
P. Browning, LOU	.530
H. Larkin, PHI	.525
H. Stovey, PHI	.488
C. Jones, CIN	.456

Home Runs

H. Stovey, PHI	13
F. Fennelly, CIN	10
P. Browning, LOU	9
H. Larkin, PHI	8
D. Orr, NY	6

Total Bases

P. Browning, LOU	255
D. Orr, NY	241
H. Larkin, PHI	238
H. Stovey, PHI	237
C. Jones, CIN	222

Runs Batted In

(not available)

Stolen Bases

(not available)

Hits

P. Browning, LOU	174
C. Jones, CIN	157
H. Stovey, PHI	153
D. Orr, NY	152

Base on Balls

C. Nelson, NY	61
J. Macullar, BAL	49
P. Hotaling, BKN	49
H. Stovey, PHI	39

Home Run Percentage

H. Stovey, PHI	2.7
F. Fennelly, CIN	2.2
P. Browning, LOU	1.9
H. Larkin, PHI	1.8

Runs

H. Stovey, PHI	130
H. Larkin, PHI	114
C. Jones, CIN	108
C. Nelson, NY	98
P. Browning, LOU	98

Doubles

H. Larkin, PHI	37
P. Browning, LOU	34
D. Orr, NY	29
H. Stovey, PHI	27

Triples

D. Orr, NY	21
W. Kuehne, PIT	19
F. Fennelly, CIN	17
C. Wolf, LOU	17
C. Jones, CIN	17

PITCHING LEADERS

Winning Percentage

B. Caruthers, STL	.755
D. Foutz, STL	.702
B. Mathews, PHI	.638
E. Morris, PIT	.619
H. Porter, BKN	.611

Earned Run Average

B. Caruthers, STL	*2.07*
G. Hecker, LOU	*2.17*
E. Morris, PIT	*2.35*
B. Mathews, PHI	*2.43*
D. Foutz, STL	*2.63*

Wins

B. Caruthers, STL	40
E. Morris, PIT	39
D. Foutz, STL	33
H. Porter, BKN	33
B. Mathews, PHI	30
G. Hecker, LOU	30

Saves

O. Burns, BAL	3
P. Reccius, LOU	1
J. Sommer, BAL	1
A. Terry, BKN	1
P. Corkhill, CIN	1

Strikeouts

E. Morris, PIT	298
B. Mathews, PHI	286
H. Henderson, BAL	263
G. Hecker, LOU	209
H. Porter, BKN	197

Complete Games

E. Morris, PIT	63
H. Henderson, BAL	59
B. Caruthers, STL	53
H. Porter, BKN	53
G. Hecker, LOU	51

Fewest Hits/9 Innings

E. Morris, PIT	7.11
A. Mays, LOU	7.74
D. Foutz, STL	7.75
J. McGinnis, STL	7.88

Shutouts

E. Morris, PIT	7
B. Caruthers, STL	6
J. McGinnis, STL	3

Fewest Walks/9 Innings

J. Lynch, NY	1.00
G. Hecker, LOU	1.01
B. Caruthers, STL	1.06
B. Mathews, PHI	1.21

Most Strikeouts/9 Inn.

B. Mathews, PHI	6.09
E. Cushman, PHI, NY	5.50
E. Morris, PIT	4.62
H. Henderson, BAL	4.39

Innings

E. Morris, PIT	581
H. Henderson, BAL	539
B. Caruthers, STL	482
H. Porter, BKN	482

Games Pitched

E. Morris, PIT	63
H. Henderson, BAL	61
G. Hecker, LOU	54
H. Porter, BKN	54

							Batting						Fielding			Pitching					
	W	L	PCT	GB	R	OR	2B	3B	HR	BA	SA	SB	E	DP	FA	CG	BB	SO	ShO	SV	ERA
St. Louis	79	33	.705		677	**461**	132	57	14	.246	.319	0	**381**	64	**.920**	**111**	**168**	378	**11**	0	***2.43***
Cincinnati	63	49	.563	16	642	575	108	77	25	.258	.341	0	426	**86**	.910	102	250	330	7	1	*3.27*
Pittsburgh	56	55	.505	22.5	547	539	123	79	5	.240	.315	0	426	77	.912	104	201	454	8	0	*2.92*
Philadelphia	55	57	.491	24	**764**	691	**169**	77	**29**	**.265**	**.364**	0	483	79	.901	105	212	**506**	5	0	*3.22*
Brooklyn	53	59	.473	26	624	650	121	65	14	.245	.319	0	447	56	.908	110	211	436	3	1	*3.45*
Louisville	53	59	.473	26	564	598	126	**83**	19	.248	.336	0	466	75	.904	109	217	462	3	1	*2.68*
New York	44	64	.407	33	526	688	123	58	20	.247	.327	0	452	62	.901	103	204	408	2	0	*4.15*
Baltimore	41	68	.376	36.5	541	683	124	59	17	.219	.296	0	419	71	.909	104	222	395	2	**4**	*3.89*
					4885	4885	1026	555	143	.246	.327	0	3500	570	.908	848	1685	3369	41	7	*3.25*

NATIONAL LEAGUE 1886

Chicago

W-90 L-34

Cap Anson

POS	Player	AB	BA	HR	RBI	PO	A	E	DP	TC/G	FA
1B	C. Anson	504	.371	10	**147**	1188	**66**	**48**	**69**	10.4	.963
2B	F. Pfeffer	474	.264	7	95	**343**	340	**73**	**66**	6.4	.903
SS	N. Williamson	430	.216	6	58	**161**	355	**78**	36	4.9	.869
3B	T. Burns	445	.276	3	65	149	247	49	12	4.0	.890
RF	J. Ryan	327	.306	4	53	93	18	23	3	1.9	.828
CF	G. Gore	444	.304	6	63	184	20	29	4	2.0	.876
LF	A. Dalrymple	331	.233	3	26	126	15	7	1	1.8	.953
C	S. Flint	173	.202	1	13	300	93	**47**	2	8.1	.893
UT	K. Kelly	451	**.388**	4	79	387	141	59	11		.899
P	J. Clarkson	210	.233	3	23	19	**114**	**19**	3	2.8	.875
PO	J. Flynn	205	.200	4	19	34	59	9	2		.912
P	J. McCormick	174	.236	2	21	21	74	6	3	2.4	.941

Pitcher	G	IP	W	L	SV	ERA
J. Clarkson	55	467	35	17	0	2.41
J. McCormick	42	348	31	11	0	*2.82*
J. Flynn	32	257	24	6	1	2.24

NATIONAL LEAGUE 1886, *cont.*

Detroit

W-87 L-36

Bill Watkins

POS	Player	AB	BA	HR	RBI	PO	A	E	DP	TC/G	FA
1B	D. Brouthers	489	.370	**11**	72	1256	27	42	64	11.0	.968
2B	F. Dunlap	196	.286	4	37	118	162*	25	22	6.0*	.918
SS	J. Rowe	468	.303	6	87	86	310	54	26	4.1	.880
3B	D. White	491	.289	1	76	131	245	68	18	3.6	.847
RF	S. Thompson	503	.310	8	89	194	29	13	11	1.9	.945
CF	N. Hanlon	494	.235	4	60	205	18	17	4	1.9	.929
LF	H. Richardson	**538**	.351	**11**	61	131	21	17	1	2.1	.899
C	C. Bennett	235	.243	5	34	**425**	84	24	**13**	**7.7**	**.955**
C	C. Ganzel	213	.272	1	31	274	63	33	9	8.2	.911
P	L. Baldwin	204	.201	0	25	18	105	4	7	2.3	.969
2B	S. Crane	185	.141	1	12	104	111	23	19	6.3	.903
P	C. Getzien	165	.176	0	19	16	65	1	3	1.9	.988

Pitcher	G	IP	W	L	SV	ERA
L. Baldwin	56	487	**42**	13	0	*2.24*
C. Getzien	43	387	30	11	0	*3.03*
P. Conway	11	91	6	5	0	3.36

New York

W-75 L-44

Jim Mutrie

POS	Player	AB	BA	HR	RBI	PO	A	E	DP	TC/G	FA
1B	R. Connor	485	.355	7	71	1164	65	34	55	10.7	.973
2B	J. Gerhardt	426	.190	0	40	340	355	57	50	6.1	.924
SS	M. Ward	491	.273	2	81	91	369	69	36	4.3	.870
3B	D. Esterbrook	473	.264	3	43	148	219	43	9	3.3	**.895**
RF	M. Dorgan	442	.292	3	79	153	13	21	4	1.6	.888
CF	J. O'Rourke	440	.309	1	34	101	11	9	1	1.9	.926
LF	P. Gillespie	396	.273	0	58	121	6	14	0	1.5	.901
C	B. Ewing	275	.309	4	31	270	91	31	4	7.8	.921
OF	D. Richardson	237	.232	1	27	94	7	5	0	1.7	.953
P	M. Welch	213	.216	0	18	19	82	5	0	1.8	.953
P	T. Keefe	205	.171	1	20	29	107	15	3	2.4	.901
CO	P. Deasley	143	.266	0	17	167	42	21	4		.909

Pitcher	G	IP	W	L	SV	ERA
T. Keefe	**64**	**540**	**42**	20	0	*2.53*
M. Welch	59	500	33	22	0	*2.99*

Philadelphia

W-71 L-43

Harry Wright

POS	Player	AB	BA	HR	RBI	PO	A	E	DP	TC/G	FA
1B	S. Farrar	439	.248	5	50	1220	45	26	38	10.9	**.980**
2B	C. Bastian	373	.217	2	38	157	286	26	19	5.4	**.945**
SS	A. Irwin	373	.233	0	34	137	322	56	21	5.2	.891
3B	J. Mulvey	430	.267	2	53	99	191	40	2	3.1	.879
RF	J. Fogarty	280	.293	3	47	114	9	6	3	2.2	.953
CF	E. Andrews	437	.249	2	28	189	24	23	2	2.3	.903
LF	G. Wood	450	.273	4	50	148	13	17	2	1.8	.904
C	D. McGuire	167	.198	2	18	298	50	39	3	7.9	.899
OP	E. Daily	309	.227	4	50	98	70	27	3		.862
PO	C. Ferguson	261	.253	2	25	72	101	14	1		.925
C	J. Clements	185	.205	0	11	318	52	28	3	8.5	.930
P	D. Casey	151	.152	0	9	17	70	8	0	2.2	.916

Pitcher	G	IP	W	L	SV	ERA
C. Ferguson	48	396	30	9	**2**	*1.98*
D. Casey	44	369	24	18	0	*2.41*
E. Daily	27	218	16	9	0	3.06

Boston

W-56 L-61

John Morrill

POS	Player	AB	BA	HR	RBI	PO	A	E	DP	TC/G	FA
1B	S. Wise	387	.289	4	72	527	17	25	21	10.0	.956
2B	J. Burdock	221	.217	0	25	145	165	33	22	5.8	.904
SS	J. Morrill	430	.247	7	69	92	156	29	13	5.0	.895
3B	B. Nash	417	.281	1	45	137	177	50	9	4.0	.863
RF	T. Poorman	371	.261	3	41	145	21	18	6	1.9	.902
CF	D. Johnston	413	.240	1	57	243	29	33	4	2.8	.892
LF	J. Hornung	424	.257	2	40	187	12	11	1	2.2	.948
C	C. Daily	180	.239	0	21	264	55	31	5	7.1	.911
UT	E. Sutton	499	.277	3	48	181	204	56	19		.873
P	O. Radbourn	253	.237	2	22	**39**	107	12	**8**	2.7	.924
1P	C. Buffinton	176	.290	1	30	181	35	11	8		.952
P	B. Stemmeyer	148	.277	0	20	6	61	17	0	2.0	.798

Pitcher	G	IP	W	L	SV	ERA
O. Radbourn	58	509	27	31	0	*3.00*
B. Stemmeyer	41	349	22	18	0	*3.02*
C. Buffinton	18	151	7	10	0	4.59

St. Louis

W-43 L-79

Gus Schmelz

POS	Player	AB	BA	HR	RBI	PO	A	E	DP	TC/G	FA
1B	A. McKinnon	491	.301	8	72	1170	35	46	61	10.5	.963
2B	F. Dunlap	285	.267	3	32	215	231*	33	42	6.7*	.931
SS	J. Glasscock	486	.325	3	40	156	**392**	57	**43**	5.0	**.906**
3B	J. Denny	475	.257	9	62	**182**	**270**	53	**22**	**4.3**	.895
RF	J. Cahill	463	.199	1	32	166	34	31	5	1.9	.866
CF	J. Quinn	271	.232	1	21	89	13	12	1	2.4	.895
LF	E. Seery	453	.238	2	48	176	20	26	2	1.8	.883
C	G. Myers	295	.190	0	27	368	80	35	8	6.7	.928
OF	J. McGeachy	226	.204	2	24	88	15	14	3	2.1	.880
P	E. Healy	145	.097	0	5	6	62	4	2	1.7	.944
C	F. Graves	138	.152	0	9	223	76	39	3	8.2	.885
P	J. Kirby	136	.110	0	5	14	61	9	2	2.0	.893

Pitcher	G	IP	W	L	SV	ERA
E. Healy	43	354	17	23	0	*2.88*
J. Kirby	41	325	11	25	0	*3.30*
H. Boyle	25	210	9	15	0	**1.76**
C. Sweeney	11	93	5	6	0	4.16

Kansas City

W-30 L-91

Dave Rowe

POS	Player	AB	BA	HR	RBI	PO	A	E	DP	TC/G	FA
1B	M. McQuery	449	.247	4	38	**1295**	50	43	61	**11.4**	.969
2B	A. Myers	473	.277	4	51	298	384	65	50	6.3	.913
SS	C. Bassett	342	.260	2	32	120	277	51	25	**5.5**	.886
3B	J. Donnelly	438	.201	0	38	153	245	**73**	13	4.2	.845
RF	P. Radford	493	.229	0	20	125	29	19	5	1.9	.890
CF	D. Rowe	429	.240	3	57	154	11	29	2	2.2	.851
LF	J. Lillie	416	.175	0	22	199	30	30	3	2.3	.884
C	F. Briody	215	.237	0	29	258	95	31	4	7.1	.919
PO	J. Whitney	247	.239	2	23	38	116	15	6		.911
C	M. Hackett	230	.217	3	25	252	63	25	6	6.5	.926
OP	P. Conway	194	.242	1	18	56	39	18	3		.841
P	S. Wiedman	179	.168	0	7	25	106	9	5	2.7	.936

Pitcher	G	IP	W	L	SV	ERA
S. Wiedman	51	428	12	**36**	0	*4.52*
J. Whitney	46	393	12	32	0	*4.49*
P. Conway	23	180	5	15	0	5.75

NATIONAL LEAGUE 1886, *cont.*

Team	POS	Player	AB	BA	HR	RBI	PO	A	E	DP	TC/G	FA	Pitcher	G	IP	W	L	SV	ERA
Washington	1B	P. Baker	325	.222	1	34	567	13	20	29	10.7	.967	D. Shaw	45	386	13	31	0	*3.34*
	2B	J. Knowles	443	.212	3	35	196	224	47	32	7.5	.899	B. Barr	23	191	3	18	0	*4.30*
	SS	D. Force	242	.182	0	16	58	211	27	21	5.3	.909	T. Madigan	14	116	1	13	0	*5.06*
W-28 L-92	3B	B. Gladman	152	.138	1	15	53	74	26	8	3.5	.830							
	RF	C. Crane	292	.171	0	20	107	16	19	4	2.1	.866							
Mike Scanlon	CF	P. Hines	487	.312	9	56	167	19	21	1	2.3	.899							
W-13 L-67	LF	C. Carroll	433	.229	2	22	153	22	28	4	1.8	.862							
	C	B. Gilligan	273	.190	0	17	358	**101**	37	7	7.0	.925							
John Gaffney	SS	S. Houck	195	.215	0	14	58	159	36	9	5.0	.858							
W-15 L-25	2B	J. Farrell	171	.240	2	18	99	131	22	12	5.4	.913							
	P	D. Shaw	148	.088	0	6	13	70	3	1	1.9	.965							

BATTING AND BASE RUNNING LEADERS / PITCHING LEADERS

Batting Average		Slugging Average		Home Runs		Winning Percentage		Earned Run Average		Wins	
K. Kelly, CHI	.388	D. Brouthers, DET	.581	D. Brouthers, DET	11	J. Flynn, CHI	.800	H. Boyle, STL	1.76	L. Baldwin, DET	42
C. Anson, CHI	.371	C. Anson, CHI	.544	H. Richardson, DET	11	C. Ferguson, PHI	.769	C. Ferguson, PHI	*1.98*	T. Keefe, NY	42
D. Brouthers, DET	.370	R. Connor, NY	.540	C. Anson, CHI	10	L. Baldwin, DET	.764	L. Baldwin, DET	*2.24*	J. Clarkson, CHI	35
R. Connor, NY	.355	K. Kelly, CHI	.534	J. Denny, STL	9	J. McCormick, CHI	.738	J. Flynn, CHI	2.24	M. Welch, NY	33
H. Richardson, DET	.351	H. Richardson, DET	.504	P. Hines, WAS	9	C. Getzien, DET	.732	J. Clarkson, CHI	2.41	J. McCormick, CHI	31

Total Bases		Runs Batted In		Stolen Bases		Saves		Strikeouts		Complete Games	
D. Brouthers, DET	284	C. Anson, CHI	147	C. Anson, CHI	29	C. Ferguson, PHI	2	L. Baldwin, DET	323	T. Keefe, NY	62
C. Anson, CHI	274	F. Pfeffer, CHI	95			J. Devlin, NY	1	J. Clarkson, CHI	313	O. Radbourn, BOS	57
H. Richardson, DET	271	S. Thompson, DET	89			J. Ryan, CHI	1	T. Keefe, NY	291	M. Welch, NY	56
R. Connor, NY	262	J. Rowe, DET	87			N. Williamson, CHI	1	M. Welch, NY	272	L. Baldwin, DET	55
K. Kelly, CHI	241	M. Ward, NY	81			J. Flynn, CHI	1	B. Stemmeyer, BOS	239	J. Clarkson, CHI	50

Hits		Base on Balls		Home Run Percentage		Fewest Hits/9 Innings		Shutouts		Fewest Walks/9 Innings	
H. Richardson, DET	189	G. Gore, CHI	102	D. Brouthers, DET	2.2	L. Baldwin, DET	6.86	L. Baldwin, DET	7	J. Whitney, KC	1.26
C. Anson, CHI	187	K. Kelly, CHI	83	H. Richardson, DET	2.0	C. Ferguson, PHI	7.21	D. Casey, PHI	4	C. Ferguson, PHI	1.57
D. Brouthers, DET	181	N. Williamson, CHI	80	C. Anson, CHI	2.0	J. Flynn, CHI	7.25	C. Ferguson, PHI	4	J. Clarkson, CHI	1.66
K. Kelly, CHI	175	D. Brouthers, DET	66	J. Denny, STL	1.9	B. Stemmeyer, BOS	7.74			T. Keefe, NY	1.67

Runs		Doubles		Triples		Most Strikeouts/9 Inn.		Innings		Games Pitched	
K. Kelly, CHI	155	D. Brouthers, DET	40	R. Connor, NY	20	B. Stemmeyer, BOS	6.17	T. Keefe, NY	540	T. Keefe, NY	64
G. Gore, CHI	150	C. Anson, CHI	35	G. Wood, PHI	15	J. Clarkson, CHI	6.04	O. Radbourn, BOS	509	M. Welch, NY	59
D. Brouthers, DET	139	K. Kelly, CHI	32	D. Brouthers, DET	15	L. Baldwin, DET	5.97	M. Welch, NY	500	O. Radbourn, BOS	58
H. Richardson, DET	125	P. Hines, WAS	30	S. Thompson, DET	13	E. Healy, STL	5.42	L. Baldwin, DET	487	L. Baldwin, DET	56

							Batting						Fielding			Pitching					
	W	L	PCT	GB	R	OR	2B	3B	HR	BA	SA	SB	E	DP	FA	CG	BB	SO	ShO	SV	ERA
Chicago	90	34	.726		**900**	555	**198**	**87**	53	.279	**.401**	0	475	82	.912	116	262	**647**	8	**3**	*2.54*
Detroit	87	36	.707	2.5	829	538	176	80	**54**	**.280**	.391	0	373	82	**.928**	**122**	270	592	8	0	*2.85*
New York	75	44	.630	12.5	692	558	175	67	22	.269	.356	0	**359**	70	.927	119	278	582	3	1	*2.85*
Philadelphia	71	43	.623	14	621	**498**	145	66	26	.240	.327	0	393	46	.921	110	264	540	**10**	2	***2.45***
Boston	56	61	.479	30.5	657	661	151	59	24	.260	.341	0	457	63	.906	116	298	511	3	0	*3.24*
St. Louis	43	79	.352		547	712	183	46	30	.236	.321	0	452	**92**	.914	118	392	501	6	0	*3.27*
Kansas City	30	91	.248		494	872	177	48	19	.228	.306	0	482	79	.910	117	**246**	442	4	0	*4.85*
Washington	28	92	.233	1.5	445	791	135	51	23	.210	.285	0	458	69	.910	116	379	500	4	0	*4.30*
					5185	5185	1340	504	251	.250	.341	0	3449	583	.916	934	2389	4315	46	6	*3.29*

AMERICAN ASSOCIATION 1886

Team	POS	Player	AB	BA	HR	RBI	PO	A	E	DP	TC/G	FA	Pitcher	G	IP	W	L	SV	ERA
St. Louis	1B	C. Comiskey	578	.254	3		1156	49	31	67	10.1	.975	D. Foutz	59	504	**41**	16	**1**	**2.11**
	2B	Y. Robinson	481	.274	3		351	406	**95**	66	6.8	.888	B. Caruthers	44	387	30	14	0	*2.32*
	SS	B. Gleason	524	.269	0		128	352	83	37	4.5	.853	N. Hudson	29	234	16	10	**1**	*3.03*
W-93 L-46	3B	A. Latham	578	.301	1		138	284	**88**	22	3.8	.827	J. McGinnis	10	88	5	5	0	3.80
	RF	H. Nicol	253	.206	0		86	11	6	0	1.8	.942							
Charlie Comiskey	CF	C. Welch	563	.281	2		297	19	16	4	2.4	.952							
	LF	T. O'Neill	579	.328	3		279	14	23	4	2.3	.927							
	C	D. Bushong	386	.223	1		**647**	134	48	**14**	7.8	**.942**							
	UT	D. Foutz	414	.280	3		211	86	19	7		.940							
	PO	B. Caruthers	317	.334	4		67	75	18	5		.887							
	PO	N. Hudson	150	.233	0		31	36	6	1		.918							
Pittsburgh	1B	O. Schomberg	246	.272	1		702	6	25	34	10.2	.966	E. Morris	64	555	**41**	20	**1**	*2.45*
	2B	S. Barkley	478	.266	0		362	328	47	52	6.6	.936	P. Galvin	50	435	29	21	0	*2.67*
	SS	P. Smith	483	.217	2		132	356	57	28	5.6	**.895**	J. Handiboe	14	114	7	7	0	*3.32*
W-80 L-57	3B	A. Whitney	511	.239	0		120	209	34	17	3.8	**.906**							
	RF	T. Brown	460	.285	1		185	30	42	12	2.2	.837							
Horace Phillips	CF	F. Mann	440	.250	2		203	13	30	2	2.1	.878							
	LF	E. Glenn	277	.191	0		124	10	21	2	2.2	.865							
	C	F. Carroll	486	.288	5		435	87	45	8	8.1	.921							
	UT	W. Kuehne	481	.204	1		303	99	29	11		.933							
	C	D. Miller	317	.252	2		247	56	27	0	5.4	.918							
	P	E. Morris	227	.167	1		21	90	10	2	1.9	.917							
	P	P. Galvin	194	.253	0		22	101	8	3	2.6	.939							

AMERICAN ASSOCIATION 1886, *cont.*

Brooklyn

W-76 L-61

Charlie Byrne

POS	Player	AB	BA	HR	RBI	PO	A	E	DP	TC/G	FA	Pitcher	G	IP	W	L	SV	ERA
1B	B. Phillips	585	.274	0		1395	33	32	65	10.4	.978	H. Porter	48	424	27	19	0	*3.42*
2B	B. McClellan	595	.255	1		423	435	88	64	6.7	.907	J. Harkins	34	292	15	16	0	*3.60*
SS	G. Smith	426	.246	2		142	381	85	30	5.8	.860	A. Terry	34	288	18	16	0	*3.09*
3B	G. Pinckney	**597**	.261	0		**184**	234	69	17	3.5	.858	H. Henderson	14	124	10	4	0	2.90
RF	E. Swartwood	471	.280	3		189	32	29	4	2.0	.884	S. Toole	13	104	6	6	0	*4.41*
CF	J. McTamany	418	.254	2		215	27	29	5	2.4	.893							
LF	E. Burch	456	.261	2		142	10	20	3	1.5	.884							
C	J. Peoples	340	.218	3		379	145	**73**	6	**7.9**	.878							
UT	A. Terry	299	.237	2		99	117	35	3		.861							
UT	B. Clark	269	.216	0		246	106	64	11		.846							
P	H. Porter	184	.179	0		17	70	15	0	2.1	.853							
P	J. Harkins	142	.225	1		24	61	8	2	2.7	.914							

Louisville

W-66 L-70

Jim Hart

POS	Player	AB	BA	HR	RBI	PO	A	E	DP	TC/G	FA	Pitcher	G	IP	W	L	SV	ERA
1B	P. Cook	262	.206	0		420	13	25	21	10.7	.945	T. Ramsey	67	**589**	38	27	0	*2.45*
2B	R. Mack	483	.244	1		350	446	88	60	6.5	.900	G. Hecker	52	421	26	23	0	*2.87*
SS	B. White	557	.257	1		**212**	430	95	48	5.5	.871							
3B	J. Werrick	561	.250	3		162	257	72	9	3.6	.853							
RF	C. Wolf	545	.272	3		197	28	16	5	2.0	.934							
CF	P. Browning	467	**.340**	2		153	14	44	1	1.9	.791							
LF	J. Strauss	297	.215	1		95	19	19	0	1.8	.857							
C	J. Kerins	487	.269	4		487	**157**	46	12	10.6	.933							
UT	G. Hecker	343	.341	4		243	10	23	12		.917							
C1	A. Cross	283	.276	1		431	83	42	12		.924							
P	T. Ramsey	241	.241	0		14	78	23	1	1.7	.800							
OF	L. Sylvester	154	.227	0		54	9	6	3	1.5	.913							

Cincinnati

W-65 L-73

Ollie Caylor

POS	Player	AB	BA	HR	RBI	PO	A	E	DP	TC/G	FA	Pitcher	G	IP	W	L	SV	ERA
1B	L. Reilly	441	.265	4		1120	37	**40**	**80**	10.9	.967	T. Mullane	63	530	33	27	0	*3.70*
2B	B. McPhee	560	.266	**7**		**529**	**464**	65	**90**	**7.6**	**.939**	G. Pechiney	40	330	15	21	0	*4.14*
SS	F. Fennelly	497	.249	6		169	**485**	**117**	**54**	**5.8**	.848	L. McKeon	19	156	8	8	0	*5.08*
3B	H. Carpenter	458	.221	2		127	221	66	23	3.7	.841							
RF	P. Corkhill	540	.265	4		156	25	16	6	1.8	.919							
CF	F. Lewis	324	.318	2		126	11	18	1	2.0	.884							
LF	C. Jones	500	.270	5		217	23	33	1	2.1	.879							
C	K. Baldwin	315	.229	3		355	102	61	13	7.3	.882							
PO	T. Mullane	324	.225	0		80	108	20	8		.904							
C1	P. Snyder	220	.186	0		328	80	44	11		.903							
UT	J. Keenan	148	.270	3		220	54	24	6		.919							
P	G. Pechiney	144	.208	1		17	45	8	2	1.8	.886							

Philadelphia

W-63 L-72

Lew Simmons
W-41 L-55

Bill Sharsig
W-22 L-17

POS	Player	AB	BA	HR	RBI	PO	A	E	DP	TC/G	FA	Pitcher	G	IP	W	L	SV	ERA
1B	H. Stovey	489	.294	**7**		656	13	33	26	11.3	.953	A. Atkinson	45	397	25	17	0	*3.95*
2B	L. Bierbauer	522	.226	2		380	429	80	54	6.7	.910	B. Mathews	24	198	13	9	0	*3.96*
SS	C. McGarr	267	.266	2		109	231	60	25	5.6	.850	B. Hart	22	186	9	13	0	*3.19*
3B	J. Gleason	299	.187	1		85	150	60	19	3.8	.797	T. Kennedy	20	173	5	15	0	*4.53*
RF	J. Coleman	492	.246	0		183	27	33	6	2.1	.864	C. Miller	19	170	10	8	0	*2.97*
CF	E. Greer	264	.193	1		143	9	13	3	2.4	.921							
LF	H. Larkin	565	.319	2		264	21	44	2	2.4	.866							
C	W. Robinson	342	.202	1		265	109	45	12	6.9	.893							
UT	J. O'Brien	423	.253	0		426	170	70	26		.895							
C1	J. Milligan	301	.252	5		522	63	31	13		.950							
SS	J. Quest	150	.207	0		56	138	35	15	5.6	.847							
P	A. Atkinson	148	.122	0		21	59	7	1	1.9	.920							

New York

W-53 L-82

Jim Gifford
W-5 L-12

Bob Ferguson
W-48 L-70

POS	Player	AB	BA	HR	RBI	PO	A	E	DP	TC/G	FA	Pitcher	G	IP	W	L	SV	ERA
1B	D. Orr	571	.338	**7**		**1445**	34	28	62	**11.1**	**.981**	J. Lynch	51	433	20	30	0	*3.95*
2B	T. Forster	251	.195	1		152	193	42	26	6.2	.891	A. Mays	41	350	11	28	0	*3.39*
SS	C. Nelson	413	.225	0		103	216	54	17	5.1	.855	E. Cushman	38	326	17	20	0	*3.12*
3B	F. Hankinson	522	.241	2		181	**316**	72	**26**	**4.2**	.873							
RF	S. Brady	466	.240	0		169	25	38	1	1.9	.836							
CF	S. Behel	224	.205	0		84	7	15	0	1.8	.858							
LF	C. Roseman	559	.227	5		203	18	27	6	1.9	.891							
C	C. Reipschlager	232	.211	0		268	107	51	5	7.5	.880							
SS	T. McLaughlin	250	.136	0		93	203	38	11	5.3	.886							
2B	J. Meister	186	.237	2		130	121	26	18	6.2	.906							
OC	J. Donahue	186	.199	0		141	37	22	1		.890							
C	B. Holbert	171	.205	0		265	100	31	6	8.8	.922							
P	J. Lynch	169	.160	0		9	65	11	0	1.7	.871							

Baltimore

W-48 L-83

Billy Barnie

POS	Player	AB	BA	HR	RBI	PO	A	E	DP	TC/G	FA	Pitcher	G	IP	W	L	SV	ERA
1B	M. Scott	484	.190	2		1347	**59**	38	38	10.5	.974	M. Kilroy	**68**	583	29	**34**	0	*3.37*
2B	M. Muldoon	381	.199	0		136	184	31	18	6.2	.912	J. McGinnis	26	209	11	13	0	3.48
SS	J. Macullar	268	.205	0		115	208	56	19	4.6	.852	H. Henderson	19	171	3	15	0	4.62
3B	J. Davis	216	.194	1		82	114	35	6	3.8	.848							
RF	J. Manning	556	.223	1		165	16	23	3	1.5	.887							
CF	B. Hoover	157	.217	0		70	3	14	0	2.2	.839							
LF	J. Sommer	560	.209	1		186	12	22	4	2.3	.900							
C	C. Fulmer	270	.244	1		465	113	35	5	9.0	.943							
23	J. Farrell	301	.209	1		109	180	45	9		.865							
SS	S. Houck	260	.192	0		73	152	40	4	4.8	.849							
P	M. Kilroy	218	.174	0		32	**116**	**28**	1	2.6	.841							
OF	P. O'Connell	166	.181	0		57	4	17	0	1.9	.782							

BATTING AND BASE RUNNING LEADERS

Batting Average		Slugging Average		Home Runs	
P. Browning, LOU	.340	D. Orr, NY	.527	H. Stovey, PHI	7
D. Orr, NY	.338	B. Caruthers, STL	.527	B. McPhee, CIN	7
B. Caruthers, STL	.334	H. Larkin, PHI	.450	D. Orr, NY	7
T. O'Neill, STL	.328	P. Browning, LOU	.441	F. Fennelly, CIN	6
H. Larkin, PHI	.319	T. O'Neill, STL	.440		

PITCHING LEADERS

Winning Percentage		Earned Run Average		Wins	
D. Foutz, STL	.719	D. Foutz, STL	*2.11*	D. Foutz, STL	41
B. Caruthers, STL	.682	B. Caruthers, STL	*2.32*	E. Morris, PIT	41
E. Morris, PIT	.672	T. Ramsey, LOU	*2.45*	T. Ramsey, LOU	38
N. Hudson, STL	.615	E. Morris, PIT	*2.45*	T. Mullane, CIN	33
A. Atkinson, PHI	.595	P. Galvin, PIT	*2.67*	B. Caruthers, STL	30

AMERICAN ASSOCIATION 1886, *cont.*

BATTING AND BASE RUNNING LEADERS

Total Bases

D. Orr, NY	301
T. O'Neill, STL	255
H. Larkin, PHI	254
C. Welch, STL	221
B. McPhee, CIN	217

Runs Batted In

(not available)

Stolen Bases

(not available)

Hits

D. Orr, NY	193
T. O'Neill, STL	190
H. Larkin, PHI	180
A. Latham, STL	174

Base on Balls

E. Swartwood, BKN	70
G. Pinckney, BKN	70
R. Mack, LOU	68
J. Kerins, LOU	66

Home Run Percentage

H. Stovey, PHI	1.4
B. Caruthers, STL	1.3
B. McPhee, CIN	1.3
D. Orr, NY	1.2

Runs

A. Latham, STL	152
B. McPhee, CIN	139
H. Larkin, PHI	133
B. McClellan, BKN	131

Doubles

H. Larkin, PHI	36
B. McClellan, BKN	33
S. Barkley, PIT	32
C. Welch, STL	31

Triples

D. Orr, NY	31
W. Kuehne, PIT	17
F. Fennelly, CIN	17
J. Coleman, PHI, PIT	17

PITCHING LEADERS

Saves

B. Ely, LOU	1
E. Morris, PIT	1
J. Strauss, LOU	1
D. Foutz, STL	1
N. Hudson, STL	1

Strikeouts

M. Kilroy, BAL	513
T. Ramsey, LOU	499
E. Morris, PIT	326
D. Foutz, STL	283
T. Mullane, CIN	250

Complete Games

T. Ramsey, LOU	66
M. Kilroy, BAL	66
E. Morris, PIT	63
T. Mullane, CIN	55
D. Foutz, STL	55

Fewest Hits/9 Innings

J. Handiboe, PIT	6.47
T. Ramsey, LOU	6.83
M. Kilroy, BAL	7.35
E. Morris, PIT	7.37

Shutouts

E. Morris, PIT	12
D. Foutz, STL	11
A. Terry, BKN	5
M. Kilroy, BAL	5

Fewest Walks/9 Innings

P. Galvin, PIT	1.55
E. Morris, PIT	1.91
B. Caruthers, STL	2.00
J. McGinnis, STL, BAL	2.27

Most Strikeouts/9 Inn.

M. Kilroy, BAL	7.92
T. Ramsey, LOU	7.63
J. Handiboe, PIT	6.55
E. Morris, PIT	5.28

Innings

T. Ramsey, LOU	589
M. Kilroy, BAL	583
E. Morris, PIT	555
T. Mullane, CIN	530

Games Pitched

M. Kilroy, BAL	68
T. Ramsey, LOU	67
E. Morris, PIT	64
T. Mullane, CIN	63

							Batting						Fielding			Pitching					
	W	L	PCT	GB	R	OR	2B	3B	HR	BA	SA	SB	E	DP	FA	CG	BB	SO	ShO	SV	ERA
St. Louis	93	46	.669		**944**	**592**	**206**	85	20	**.273**	**.360**	0	494	96	.915	134	329	583	14	**2**	***2.52***
Pittsburgh	80	57	.584	12	810	647	187	96	15	.241	.329	0	**487**	90	**.917**	137	**299**	515	**15**	1	*2.84*
Brooklyn	76	61	.555	16	832	832	196	80	16	.250	.330	0	611	87	.900	**138**	464	540	6	0	*3.41*
Louisville	66	70	.485	25.5	833	805	182	88	20	.263	.348	0	593	89	.901	131	432	720	5	**2**	*3.07*
Cincinnati	65	73	.471	27.5	883	865	145	**97**	**40**	.249	.342	0	588	**122**	.904	129	481	495	3	0	*4.18*
Philadelphia	63	72	.467	28	772	942	192	82	21	.235	.321	0	637	99	.894	134	388	513	4	0	*3.98*
New York	53	82	.393	38	628	766	108	72	18	.224	.289	0	546	81	.907	134	386	559	5	0	*3.50*
Baltimore	48	83	.366	41	625	878	124	51	8	.204	.258	0	536	59	.908	134	403	**805**	5	0	*4.08*
					6327	6327	1340	651	158	.242	.322	0	4492	723	.906	1071	3182	4730	57	5	*3.45*

NATIONAL LEAGUE 1887

Detroit

W-79 L-45

Bill Watkins

POS	Player	AB	BA	HR	RBI	PO	A	E	DP	TC/G	FA
1B	D. Brouthers	500	.338	12	101	1141	35	38	67	9.9	.969
2B	F. Dunlap	272	.265	5	45	212	225	24	44	7.1	.948
SS	J. Rowe	537	.318	6	96	119	378	51	36	4.4	.907
3B	D. White	449	.303	3	75	133	225	**64**	18	4.0	.848
RF	S. Thompson	**545**	**.372**	11	**166**	217	24	24	7	2.1	.909
CF	N. Hanlon	471	.274	4	69	264	18	30	4	2.6	.904
LF	L. Twitchell	264	.333	0	51	84	4	13	1	1.9	.871
C	C. Ganzel	227	.260	0	20	275	71	33	5	7.4	.913
20	H. Richardson	543	.328	11	94	328	223	37	28		.937
C	C. Bennett	160	.244	3	20	197	57	13	9	5.9	.951
P	C. Getzien	156	.186	1	14	23	58	3	1	2.0	.964
C	F. Briody	128	.227	2	26	144	61	21	4	6.8	.907

Pitcher	G	IP	W	L	SV	ERA
C. Getzien	43	367	29	13	0	3.73
L. Baldwin	24	211	13	10	0	3.84
S. Wiedman	21	183	13	7	0	5.36
P. Conway	17	146	8	9	0	2.90
L. Twitchell	15	112	11	1	**1**	4.33

Philadelphia

W-75 L-48

Harry Wright

POS	Player	AB	BA	HR	RBI	PO	A	E	DP	TC/G	FA
1B	S. Farrar	443	.282	4	72	1149	46	28	55	10.5	.977
2B	B. McLaughlin	205	.220	1	26	106	156	36	15	6.0	.879
SS	A. Irwin	374	.254	2	56	178	301	58	30	5.4	.892
3B	J. Mulvey	474	.287	2	78	123	197	50	18	3.3	.865
RF	J. Fogarty	495	.261	8	50	273	39	27	9	2.8	.920
CF	E. Andrews	464	.325	4	67	203	18	24	1	2.5	.902
LF	G. Wood	491	.289	14	66	155	10	24	2	1.8	.873
C	J. Clements	246	.280	1	47	328	79	26	8	7.3	.940
UT	C. Buffinton	269	.268	1	46	124	93	23	8		.904
UT	C. Ferguson	264	.337	3	85	93	130	22	11		.910
2S	C. Bastian	221	.213	1	21	101	165	25	19		.914
P	D. Casey	164	.165	1	17	10	66	9	0	1.9	.894
C	D. McGuire	150	.307	2	23	214	52	35	6	7.3	.884

Pitcher	G	IP	W	L	SV	ERA
D. Casey	45	390	28	13	0	**2.86**
C. Buffinton	40	332	21	17	0	3.66
C. Ferguson	37	297	22	10	**1**	3.00

Chicago

W-71 L-50

Cap Anson

POS	Player	AB	BA	HR	RBI	PO	A	E	DP	TC/G	FA
1B	C. Anson	472	.347	7	102	1232	**70**	36	75	11.0	.973
2B	F. Pfeffer	479	.278	16	89	**393**	402	**72**	**68**	**7.0**	.917
SS	N. Williamson	439	.267	9	78	133	361	61	31	4.4	.890
3B	T. Burns	424	.264	3	60	168	246	61	**23**	4.4	.872
RF	B. Sunday	199	.291	3	32	78	4	25	2	2.1	.766
CF	J. Ryan	508	.285	11	74	164	33	33	7	1.9	.857
LF	M. Sullivan	472	.284	7	77	189	10	36	0	2.0	.847
C	T. Daly	256	.207	2	17	354	**148**	35	12	**8.4**	**.935**
P	J. Clarkson	215	.242	6	25	**34**	**125**	7	**5**	2.8	.958
C	S. Flint	187	.267	3	21	255	73	33	3	7.7	.909
OP	G. Van Haltren	172	.203	3	17	47	26	8	2		.901
OC	D. Darling	141	.319	3	20	132	45	23	3		.885
P	M. Baldwin	139	.187	4	17	7	45	6	0	1.5	.897
OF	B. Pettit	138	.261	2	12	34	8	5	0	1.5	.894

Pitcher	G	IP	W	L	SV	ERA
J. Clarkson	**60**	**523**	**38**	21	0	3.08
M. Baldwin	40	334	18	17	**1**	3.40
G. Van Haltren	20	161	11	7	**1**	3.86

NATIONAL LEAGUE 1887, *cont.*

New York

W-68 L-55

Jim Mutrie

POS	Player	AB	BA	HR	RBI	PO	A	E	DP	TC/G	FA	Pitcher	G	IP	W	L	SV	ERA
1B	R. Connor	471	.285	17	104	**1325**	44	10	67	10.9	**.993**	T. Keefe	56	479	35	19	0	3.10
2B	D. Richardson	450	.278	3	62	257	384	50	46	6.4	.928	M. Welch	40	346	22	15	0	3.36
SS	M. Ward	**545**	.338	1	53	**226**	469	61	53	5.9	**.919**	B. George	13	108	3	9	0	5.25
3B	B. Ewing	318	.305	6	44	76	101	28	6	4.0	.863							
RF	M. Dorgan	283	.258	0	34	128	6	20	0	2.2	.870							
CF	G. Gore	459	.290	1	49	221	20	30	7	2.4	.889							
LF	M. Tiernan	407	.287	10	62	150	10	25	3	1.8	.865							
C	W. Brown	170	.218	0	25	229	69	28	5	7.1	.914							
UT	J. O'Rourke	397	.285	3	88	248	127	48	7		.887							
OF	P. Gillespie	295	.264	3	37	91	14	6	1	1.5	**.946**							
P	T. Keefe	191	.220	2	23	17	102	**15**	1	2.4	.888							
P	M. Welch	148	.243	2	15	17	51	12	0	2.0	.850							
C	P. Deasley	118	.314	0	23	86	31	18	0	5.6	.867							

Boston

W-61 L-60

King Kelly
W-49 L-43

John Morrill
W-12 L-17

POS	Player	AB	BA	HR	RBI	PO	A	E	DP	TC/G	FA	Pitcher	G	IP	W	L	SV	ERA
1B	J. Morrill	504	.280	12	81	1231	50	21	**76**	10.3	.984	O. Radbourn	50	425	24	23	0	4.55
2B	J. Burdock	237	.257	0	29	117	188	41	34	5.3	.882	K. Madden	37	321	21	14	0	3.79
SS	S. Wise	467	.334	9	92	152	233	58	22	6.2	.869	D. Conway	26	222	9	15	0	4.66
3B	B. Nash	475	.295	7	94	**207**	242	59	19	4.3	.884	B. Stemmeyer	15	119	6	8	**1**	5.20
RF	K. Kelly	484	.322	8	63	78	11	15	2	1.7	.856							
CF	D. Johnston	507	.258	5	77	339	34	27	9	3.1	.933							
LF	J. Hornung	437	.270	5	49	192	23	15	3	2.3	.935							
C	P. Tate	231	.260	0	27	209	109	26	6	6.5	.924							
UT	E. Sutton	326	.304	3	46	178	234	58	12		.877							
P	O. Radbourn	175	.229	1	24	15	69	**15**	3	2.0	.848							
OS	B. Wheelock	166	.253	2	15	68	69	19	5		.878							
PO	D. Conway	145	.248	0	10	25	53	13	0		.857							
P	K. Madden	132	.242	1	10	4	59	13	1	2.1	.829							

Pittsburgh

W-55 L-69

Horace Phillips

POS	Player	AB	BA	HR	RBI	PO	A	E	DP	TC/G	FA	Pitcher	G	IP	W	L	SV	ERA
1B	S. Barkley	340	.224	1	35	552	15	12	24	10.9	.979	P. Galvin	49	441	28	21	0	3.29
2B	P. Smith	456	.215	2	54	225	298	49	32	6.4	.914	J. McCormick	36	322	13	23	0	4.30
SS	W. Kuehne	402	.299	1	41	136	310	59	29	5.5	.883	E. Morris	38	318	14	22	0	4.31
3B	A. Whitney	431	.260	0	51	166	237	33	13	3.7	**.924**							
RF	J. Coleman	475	.293	2	54	214	17	26	3	2.2	.899							
CF	T. Brown	192	.245	0	6	130	10	21	0	3.4	.870							
LF	A. Dalrymple	358	.212	2	31	184	14	22	1	2.4	.900							
C	D. Miller	342	.243	1	34	266	58	25	1	4.8	.928							
UT	F. Carroll	421	.328	6	54	451	56	62	9		.891							
1B	A. McKinnon	200	.340	1	30	483	25	12	27	10.8	.977							
P	P. Galvin	193	.212	2	22	22	123	11	2	**3.2**	.929							
OF	H. Beecher	169	.243	2	22	85	12	9	1	2.6	.915							
UT	J. Fields	164	.268	0	17	141	29	18	2		.904							
P	J. McCormick	136	.243	0	18	13	88	8	1	3.0	.927							
P	E. Morris	126	.198	0	10	5	52	5	1	1.6	.919							

Washington

W-46 L-76

John Gaffney

POS	Player	AB	BA	HR	RBI	PO	A	E	DP	TC/G	FA	Pitcher	G	IP	W	L	SV	ERA
1B	B. O'Brien	453	.278	**19**	73	1159	26	32	53	**11.7**	.974	J. Whitney	47	405	24	21	0	3.22
2B	A. Myers	362	.232	2	36	193	248	44	23	6.2	.909	H. O'Day	30	255	8	20	0	4.17
SS	J. Farrell	339	.221	0	41	91	156	35	14	5.9	.876	F. Gilmore	28	235	7	20	0	3.87
3B	J. Donnelly	425	.200	1	46	136	**275**	63	21	4.1	.867	D. Shaw	21	181	7	13	0	6.45
RF	E. Daily	311	.251	2	36	116	8	21	1	1.9	.855							
CF	P. Hines	478	.308	10	72	180	14	25	5	2.0	.886							
LF	C. Carroll	420	.248	4	37	146	19	18	6	1.8	.902							
C	C. Mack	314	.201	0	20	**391**	119	**53**	**15**	7.4	.906							
UT	P. Dealey	312	.272	1	18	171	105	34	9		.890							
OF	G. Shoch	264	.239	1	18	115	15	15	3	2.3	.897							
P	J. Whitney	201	.264	2	22	13	92	11	**5**	2.5	.905							

Indianapolis

W-37 L-89

Watch Burnham
W-6 L-22

Fred Thomas
W-11 L-18

Horace Fogel
W-20 L-49

POS	Player	AB	BA	HR	RBI	PO	A	E	DP	TC/G	FA	Pitcher	G	IP	W	L	SV	ERA
1B	O. Schomberg	419	.308	5	83	1216	28	**55**	**76**	11.6	.958	E. Healy	41	341	12	**29**	0	5.17
2B	C. Bassett	452	.230	1	47	273	**444**	53	62	6.5	**.931**	H. Boyle	38	328	13	24	0	3.65
SS	J. Glasscock	483	.294	0	40	211	**493**	**73**	**58**	**6.4**	.906	L. Shreve	14	122	5	9	0	4.72
3B	J. Denny	510	.324	11	97	201	262	58	21	**4.5**	.889							
RF	J. Cahill	263	.205	0	26	84	11	20	1	2.1	.826							
CF	J. McGeachy	405	.269	1	56	231	22	30	3	2.9	.894							
LF	E. Seery	465	.224	4	28	220	25	30	2	2.3	.891							
C	G. Myers	235	.217	1	20	176	58	18	8	5.0	.929							
C	T. Arundel	157	.197	0	13	153	64	34	5	6.0	.865							
C	M. Hackett	147	.238	2	10	128	52	12	4	4.8	.938							
P	H. Boyle	141	.191	2	13	11	41	5	2	1.5	.912							
OF	T. Brown	140	.179	2	9	58	7	15*	2	2.2	.813							
P	E. Healy	138	.174	3	14	7	51	12	0	1.7	.829							

BATTING AND BASE RUNNING LEADERS

Batting Average

S. Thompson, DET	.372
C. Anson, CHI	.347
D. Brouthers, DET	.338
M. Ward, NY	.338
S. Wise, BOS	.334

Slugging Average

S. Thompson, DET	.571
D. Brouthers, DET	.562
R. Connor, NY	.541
S. Wise, BOS	.522
C. Anson, CHI	.517

Home Runs

B. O'Brien, WAS	19
R. Connor, NY	17
F. Pfeffer, CHI	16
G. Wood, PHI	14
D. Brouthers, DET	12
J. Morrill, BOS	12

PITCHING LEADERS

Winning Percentage

C. Getzien, DET	.690
C. Ferguson, PHI	.688
D. Casey, PHI	.683
T. Keefe, NY	.648
J. Clarkson, CHI	.644

Earned Run Average

D. Casey, PHI	2.86
P. Conway, DET	2.90
C. Ferguson, PHI	3.00
J. Clarkson, CHI	3.08
T. Keefe, NY	3.10

Wins

J. Clarkson, CHI	38
T. Keefe, NY	35
C. Getzien, DET	29
D. Casey, PHI	28
P. Galvin, PIT	28

NATIONAL LEAGUE 1887, *cont.*

BATTING AND BASE RUNNING LEADERS

Total Bases	
S. Thompson, DET	311
D. Brouthers, DET	281
H. Richardson, DET	272
J. Denny, IND	256
R. Connor, NY	255

Runs Batted In	
S. Thompson, DET	166
R. Connor, NY	104
C. Anson, CHI	102
D. Brouthers, DET	101
J. Denny, IND	97

Stolen Bases	
M. Ward, NY	111
J. Fogarty, PHI	102
K. Kelly, BOS	84
N. Hanlon, DET	69
J. Glasscock, IND	62

Hits	
S. Thompson, DET	203
M. Ward, NY	184
H. Richardson, DET	178
J. Rowe, DET	171

Base on Balls	
J. Fogarty, PHI	82
R. Connor, NY	75
N. Williamson, CHI	73
E. Seery, IND	71
D. Brouthers, DET	71

Home Run Percentage	
B. O'Brien, WAS	4.2
R. Connor, NY	3.6
F. Pfeffer, CHI	3.3
G. Wood, PHI	2.9

Runs	
D. Brouthers, DET	153
J. Rowe, DET	135
H. Richardson, DET	131
K. Kelly, BOS	120

Doubles	
D. Brouthers, DET	36
K. Kelly, BOS	34
J. Denny, IND	34
C. Anson, CHI	33

Triples	
S. Thompson, DET	23
R. Connor, NY	22
D. Brouthers, DET	20
D. Johnston, BOS	20

PITCHING LEADERS

Saves	
8 tied with	1

Strikeouts	
J. Clarkson, CHI	237
T. Keefe, NY	186
M. Baldwin, CHI	164
C. Buffinton, PHI	160
J. Whitney, WAS	146

Complete Games	
J. Clarkson, CHI	56
T. Keefe, NY	54
O. Radbourn, BOS	48
P. Galvin, PIT	47
J. Whitney, WAS	46

Fewest Hits/9 Innings	
P. Conway, DET	8.14
T. Keefe, NY	8.40
D. Casey, PHI	8.69
M. Welch, NY	8.82

Shutouts	
D. Casey, PHI	4
K. Madden, BOS	3
E. Healy, IND	3
J. Whitney, WAS	3
P. Galvin, PIT	3

Fewest Walks/9 Innings	
J. Whitney, WAS	0.93
P. Galvin, PIT	1.37
C. Ferguson, PHI	1.42
J. Clarkson, CHI	1.58

Most Strikeouts/9 Inn.	
M. Baldwin, CHI	4.42
F. Gilmore, WAS	4.37
C. Buffinton, PHI	4.33
G. Van Haltren, CHI	4.25

Innings	
J. Clarkson, CHI	523
T. Keefe, NY	479
P. Galvin, PIT	441
O. Radbourn, BOS	425

Games Pitched	
J. Clarkson, CHI	60
T. Keefe, NY	56
O. Radbourn, BOS	50
P. Galvin, PIT	49

							Batting						Fielding			Pitching					
	W	L	PCT	GB	R	OR	2B	3B	HR	BA	SA	SB	E	DP	FA	CG	BB	SO	ShO	SV	ERA
Detroit	79	45	.637		**969**	714	**213**	**126**	59	**.299**	**.436**	267	**394**	92	**.925**	122	344	337	3	1	3.95
Philadelphia	75	48	.610	3.5	901	**702**	**213**	89	47	.274	.389	355	471	76	.912	119	305	435	**7**	1	3.47
Chicago	71	50	.587	6.5	813	716	178	98	**80**	.271	.412	382	472	99	.914	117	338	**510**	4	**3**	**3.46**
New York	68	55	.553	10.5	816	723	167	93	48	.279	.389	**415**	431	83	.921	123	373	412	5	1	3.57
Boston	61	60	.504	16.5	831	792	185	94	54	.277	.395	373	522	94	.905	123	396	254	4	1	4.41
Pittsburgh	55	69	.444	24	621	750	183	78	20	.258	.349	221	425	70	.921	123	**246**	248	4	0	4.12
Washington	46	76	.377	32	601	818	149	63	47	.242	.336	334	483	77	.910	**124**	299	396	4	0	4.19
Indianapolis	37	89	.294	43	628	965	162	70	33	.247	.339	334	479	**105**	.912	118	431	245	4	1	5.25
					6180	6180	1450	711	388	.268	.381	2681	3677	696	.915	969	2732	2837	35	8	4.05

AMERICAN ASSOCIATION 1887

St. Louis

W-95 L-40

Charlie Comiskey

POS	Player	AB	BA	HR	RBI	PO	A	E	DP	TC/G	FA	Pitcher	G	IP	W	L	SV	ERA
1B	C. Comiskey	538	.335	4		1135	**51**	29	60	10.5	.976	S. King	46	390	32	12	1	*3.78*
2B	Y. Robinson	430	.305	1		320	355	76	52	6.4	.899	B. Caruthers	39	341	29	9	0	*3.30*
SS	B. Gleason	598	.288	0		169	411	83	27	4.9	.875	D. Foutz	40	339	25	12	0	*3.87*
3B	A. Latham	**627**	.316	2		155	288	62	17	3.8	.877							
RF	B. Caruthers	364	.357	8		91	11	11	1	2.1	.903							
CF	C. Welch	544	.278	3		336	29	23	7	3.2	.941							
LF	T. O'Neill	517	**.435**	**14**		247	8	30	2	2.3	.895							
C	J. Boyle	350	.189	2		339	114	56	7	5.9	**.890**							
UT	D. Foutz	423	.357	4		282	65	23	11		.938							
P	S. King	222	.207	0		16	69	6	0	2.0	.934							
C	D. Bushong	201	.254	0		201	93	23	3	6.1	.927							

Cincinnati

W-81 L-54

Gus Schmelz

POS	Player	AB	BA	HR	RBI	PO	A	E	DP	TC/G	FA	Pitcher	G	IP	W	L	SV	ERA
1B	L. Reilly	551	.309	10		1267	33	26	**84**	10.4	.980	E. Smith	52	447	34	18	0	**2.94**
2B	B. McPhee	540	.289	2		442	**434**	72	**76**	**7.3**	.924	T. Mullane	48	416	31	17	0	***3.24***
SS	F. Fennelly	526	.266	8		161	421	**99**	31	5.1	.855	B. Serad	22	187	10	11	1	*4.08*
3B	H. Carpenter	498	.249	1		144	242	70	17	3.6	.846							
RF	H. Nicol	475	.215	1		194	20	19	1	1.9	.918							
CF	P. Corkhill	541	.311	5		310	29	17	7	2.8	.952							
LF	W. Tebeau	318	.296	4		175	14	24	2	2.5	.887							
C	K. Baldwin	388	.253	1		**381**	**165**	**79**	9	**6.5**	.874							
P	T. Mullane	199	.221	3		29	72	6	**5**	2.2	.944							
P	E. Smith	186	.253	0		7	67	13	2	1.7	.851							
C	J. Keenan	174	.253	0		161	67	20	8	6.5	.919							
OF	C. Jones	153	.314	2		74	7	9	2*	2.2	.900							

Baltimore

W-77 L-58

Billy Barnie

POS	Player	AB	BA	HR	RBI	PO	A	E	DP	TC/G	FA	Pitcher	G	IP	W	L	SV	ERA
1B	T. Tucker	524	.275	6		**1346**	50	**35**	49	**10.5**	.976	M. Kilroy	**69**	**589**	**46**	19	0	*3.07*
2B	B. Greenwood	495	.263	0		357	360	56	33	6.6	**.928**	P. Smith	58	491	25	30	0	*3.79*
SS	O. Burns	551	.341	9		136	245	72	20	4.6	.841							
3B	J. Davis	485	.309	8		91	199	61	7	**4.0**	.826							
RF	B. Purcell	567	.250	4		203	18	18	5	1.7	.925							
CF	M. Griffin	532	.301	3		256	13	22	1	2.1	.924							
LF	J. Sommer	463	.266	0		191	20	22	4	2.1	.906							
C	S. Trott	300	.257	0		373	102	44	6	7.5	.915							
P	M. Kilroy	239	.247	0		37	**167**	20	2	3.2	.911							
P	P. Smith	205	.234	1		9	108	20	1	2.4	.854							
C	C. Fulmer	201	.269	0		201	73	28	5	6.3	.907							
UT	L. Daniels	165	.248	0		188	44	45	5		.838							

AMERICAN ASSOCIATION 1887, *cont.*

Louisville

W-76 L-60

Honest John Kelly

POS	Player	AB	BA	HR	RBI	PO	A	E	DP	TC/G	FA
1B	J. Kerins	476	.294	5		695	18	22	26	9.9	.970
2B	R. Mack	478	.308	1		366	395	73	48	6.5	.912
SS	B. White	512	.252	2		**204**	**431**	96	**45**	5.5	.869
3B	J. Werrick	533	.285	7		153	286	**89**	12	3.9	.831
RF	C. Wolf	569	.281	1		207	27	15	5	1.9	.940
CF	P. Browning	547	.402	4		281	21	46	7	2.6	.868
LF	H. Collins	559	.290	1		192	19	27	1	2.2	.887
C	P. Cook	223	.247	0		220	95	29	4	6.3	.916
UT	G. Hecker	370	.319	4		429	82	29	27		.946
P	T. Ramsey	225	.191	0		7	88	**31**	0	1.9	.754
C	L. Cross	203	.266	0		251	66	31	7	7.9	.911

Pitcher	G	IP	W	L	SV	ERA
T. Ramsey	65	561	37	27	0	*3.43*
I. Chamberlain	36	309	18	16	0	*3.79*
G. Hecker	33	285	18	12	1	*4.16*

Philadelphia

W-64 L-69

Charlie Mason
W-38 L-40

Frank Bancroft
W-26 L-29

POS	Player	AB	BA	HR	RBI	PO	A	E	DP	TC/G	FA
1B	J. Milligan	377	.302	2		436	13	16	21	9.3	.966
2B	L. Bierbauer	530	.272	1		332	378	61	45	6.1	.921
SS	C. McGarr	536	.295	1		198	402	86	42	5.0	.875
3B	D. Lyons	570	.367	6		**255**	215	73	**29**	4.0	.866
RF	T. Poorman	585	.265	4		237	18	25	6	2.1	.911
CF	H. Stovey	497	.286	4		195	16	23	1	2.9	.902
LF	H. Larkin	497	.310	3		183	14	23	0	2.4	.895
C	W. Robinson	264	.227	1		281	137	46	9	6.9	.901
P	E. Seward	266	.188	5		21	79	11	1	2.0	.901
OF	F. Mann	229	.275	0		103	7	10	2	2.2	.917
P	G. Weyhing	209	.201	0		18	88	24	**5**	2.4	.815

Pitcher	G	IP	W	L	SV	ERA
E. Seward	55	471	25	25	0	*4.13*
G. Weyhing	55	466	26	28	0	*4.27*
A. Atkinson	15	125	6	8	0	*5.92*

Brooklyn

W-60 L-74

Charlie Byrne

POS	Player	AB	BA	HR	RBI	PO	A	E	DP	TC/G	FA
1B	B. Phillips	533	.266	2		1299	46	24	62	10.4	**.982**
2B	B. McClellan	548	.263	1		366	397	**105**	52	6.4	.879
SS	G. Smith	435	.294	4		157	387	70	23	**6.1**	**.886**
3B	G. Pinckney	580	.267	3		196	**290**	60	26	4.0	**.890**
RF	E. Swartwood	363	.253	1		129	23	30	5	2.0	.835
CF	J. McTamany	520	.258	1		281	32	28	8	2.5	.918
LF	E. Greer	327	.254	2		155	8	14	1	2.3	.921
C	J. Peoples	268	.254	1		226	106	59	3	6.9	.849
OP	A. Terry	352	.293	3		124	86	23	1		.901
OF	E. Burch	188	.293	2		90	8	11	1	2.2	.899
C	B. Clark	177	.266	0		197	66	40	7	6.7	.868
P	H. Porter	146	.199	1		8	66	12	1	2.2	.860

Pitcher	G	IP	W	L	SV	ERA
H. Porter	40	340	15	24	0	*4.21*
A. Terry	40	318	16	16	**3**	*4.02*
J. Harkins	24	199	10	14	0	*6.02*
S. Toole	24	194	14	10	0	*4.31*
H. Henderson	13	112	5	8	0	*3.95*

New York

W-44 L-89

Bob Ferguson
W-6 L-24

Dave Orr
W-3 L-5

Ollie Caylor
W-35 L-60

POS	Player	AB	BA	HR	RBI	PO	A	E	DP	TC/G	FA
1B	D. Orr	345	.368	2		806	28	27	41	10.6	.969
2B	J. Gerhardt	307	.221	0		288	271	65	48	7.4	.896
SS	P. Radford	486	.265	4		121	229	70	28	5.5	.833
3B	F. Hankinson	512	.268	1		161	276	69	26	4.0	.864
RF	C. Roseman	241	.228	0		99	6	16	2	2.1	.868
CF	C. Jones	247	.255	3		114	18	12	6	2.3	.917
LF	D. O'Brien	522	.301	5		244	20	25	4	2.4	.913
C	B. Holbert	255	.227	0		237	102	43	9	6.4	.887
OS	C. Nelson	257	.245	0		120	111	27	18		.895
P	A. Mays	221	.204	2		21	144	24	4	**3.6**	.873
C	J. Donahue	220	.282	1		208	90	42	3	6.7	.876
O2	J. Meister	158	.222	1		66	38	10	8		.912

Pitcher	G	IP	W	L	SV	ERA
A. Mays	52	441	17	**34**	0	*4.73*
E. Cushman	26	220	10	14	0	*5.97*
J. Lynch	21	187	7	14	0	*5.10*
J. Shaffer	13	112	2	11	0	*6.19*
S. Wiedman	12	97	4	8	0	*4.64*

Cleveland

W-39 L-92

Jimmy Williams

POS	Player	AB	BA	HR	RBI	PO	A	E	DP	TC/G	FA
1B	J. Toy	423	.222	1		707	30	19	54	9.2	.975
2B	C. Stricker	534	.264	2		**461**	365	80	61	7.2	.912
SS	E. McKean	539	.286	2		195	351	**99**	32	5.2	.847
3B	P. Reccius	229	.205	0		85	137	31	18	4.1	.877
RF	F. Mann	259	.309	2		112	11	17	4	2.2	.879
CF	P. Hotaling	505	.299	3		267	23	31	5	2.5	.903
LF	M. Allen	463	.276	4		222	22	29	6	2.4	.894
C	P. Snyder	282	.255	0		314	143	53	8	8.1	.896
C	C. Reipschlager	231	.212	0		196	105	43	9	7.2	.875
OF	S. Carroll	216	.199	0		79	7	16	1	1.9	.843
P	B. Crowell	156	.141	0		5	65	5	4	1.7	.933
P	M. Morrison	141	.191	0		14	109	11	4	3.3	.918

Pitcher	G	IP	W	L	SV	ERA
B. Crowell	45	389	14	31	0	*4.88*
M. Morrison	40	317	12	25	0	*4.92*
O. Daily	16	140	4	12	0	3.67
B. Gilks	13	108	7	5	0	*3.08*
G. Pechiney	10	86	1	9	0	*7.12*

BATTING AND BASE RUNNING LEADERS

Batting Average

T. O'Neill, STL	.435
P. Browning, LOU	.402
D. Orr, NY	.368
D. Lyons, PHI	.367
B. Caruthers, STL	.357

Slugging Average

T. O'Neill, STL	.691
B. Caruthers, STL	.547
P. Browning, LOU	.547
D. Lyons, PHI	.523
O. Burns, BAL	.519

Home Runs

T. O'Neill, STL	14
L. Reilly, CIN	10
O. Burns, BAL	9
B. Caruthers, STL	8
J. Davis, BAL	8
F. Fennelly, CIN	8

Total Bases

T. O'Neill, STL	357
P. Browning, LOU	299
D. Lyons, PHI	298
O. Burns, BAL	286
L. Reilly, CIN	263

Runs Batted In

(not available)

Stolen Bases

H. Nicol, CIN	138
A. Latham, STL	129
C. Comiskey, STL	117
P. Browning, LOU	103
B. McPhee, CIN	95

PITCHING LEADERS

Winning Percentage

B. Caruthers, STL	.763
S. King, STL	.727
M. Kilroy, BAL	.708
D. Foutz, STL	.676
E. Smith, CIN	.654

Earned Run Average

E. Smith, CIN	*2.94*
M. Kilroy, BAL	*3.07*
B. Gilks, CLE	*3.08*
T. Mullane, CIN	*3.24*
B. Caruthers, STL	*3.30*

Wins

M. Kilroy, BAL	46
T. Ramsey, LOU	37
E. Smith, CIN	34
S. King, STL	32
T. Mullane, CIN	31

Saves

A. Terry, BKN	3

Strikeouts

T. Ramsey, LOU	355
M. Kilroy, BAL	217
P. Smith, BAL	206
G. Weyhing, PHI	193
E. Smith, CIN	176

Complete Games

M. Kilroy, BAL	66
T. Ramsey, LOU	61
P. Smith, BAL	54
G. Weyhing, PHI	53
E. Seward, PHI	52

AMERICAN ASSOCIATION 1887, *cont.*

BATTING AND BASE RUNNING LEADERS

Hits		Base on Balls		Home Run Percentage	
T. O'Neill, STL	225	P. Radford, NY	106	T. O'Neill, STL	2.7
P. Browning, LOU	220	Y. Robinson, STL	92	B. Caruthers, STL	2.2
D. Lyons, PHI	209	H. Nicol, CIN	86	L. Reilly, CIN	1.8
A. Latham, STL	198	R. Mack, LOU	83	J. Davis, BAL	1.6

Runs		Doubles		Triples	
T. O'Neill, STL	167	T. O'Neill, STL	52	6 tied with	19
A. Latham, STL	163	D. Lyons, PHI	43		
M. Griffin, BAL	142	P. Browning, LOU	35		
T. Poorman, PHI	140	L. Reilly, CIN	35		
		A. Latham, STL	35		

PITCHING LEADERS

Fewest Hits/9 Innings		Shutouts		Fewest Walks/9 Innings	
E. Smith, CIN	8.05	T. Mullane, CIN	6	G. Hecker, LOU	1.58
E. Seward, PHI	8.51	M. Kilroy, BAL	6	B. Caruthers, STL	1.61
S. Toole, BKN	8.63	E. Seward, PHI	3	J. Lynch, NY	1.73
B. Gilks, CLE	8.67	E. Smith, CIN	3	D. Foutz, STL	2.39

Most Strikeouts/9 Inn.		Innings		Games Pitched	
T. Ramsey, LOU	5.70	M. Kilroy, BAL	589	M. Kilroy, BAL	69
M. Morrison, CLE	4.49	T. Ramsey, LOU	561	T. Ramsey, LOU	65
A. Terry, BKN	3.91	P. Smith, BAL	491	P. Smith, BAL	58
P. Smith, BAL	3.77	E. Seward, PHI	471	E. Seward, PHI	55
				G. Weyhing, PHI	55

							Batting						Fielding			Pitching					
	W	L	PCT	GB	R	OR	2B	3B	HR	BA	SA	SB	E	DP	FA	CG	BB	SO	ShO	SV	ERA
St. Louis	95	40	.704		**1131**	761	**261**	78	**39**	**.307**	**.413**	**581**	**485**	86	**.916**	132	**323**	334	6	2	*3.78*
Cincinnati	81	54	.600	14	892	**745**	179	**102**	37	.268	.371	527	488	**106**	.915	129	396	330	**11**	1	***3.59***
Baltimore	77	58	.570	18	975	861	202	100	31	.277	.380	545	558	66	.906	132	418	470	8	0	*3.87*
Louisville	76	60	.559	19.5	956	854	195	98	26	.289	.384	466	576	83	.903	**133**	357	**544**	3	1	*3.82*
Philadelphia	64	69	.481	30	893	890	231	84	29	.277	.375	476	528	95	.907	131	433	417	5	1	*4.59*
Brooklyn	60	74	.448	34.5	904	918	200	82	25	.261	.350	409	565	88	.904	132	454	332	3	**3**	*4.46*
New York	44	89	.331	50	754	1093	193	66	20	.248	.328	305	643	102	.893	132	406	316	1	0	*5.30*
Cleveland	39	92	.298	54	729	1112	178	77	14	.252	.332	355	589	97	.897	127	533	332	2	1	*4.99*
					7234	7234	1639	687	221	.272	.367	3664	4432	723	.905	1048	3320	3075	39	9	*4.30*

NATIONAL LEAGUE 1888

New York

W-84 L-47

Jim Mutrie

POS	Player	AB	BA	HR	RBI	PO	A	E	DP	TC/G	FA	Pitcher	G	IP	W	L	SV	ERA
1B	R. Connor	481	.291	14	71	1337	43	26	57	10.6	.982	T. Keefe	51	434	**35**	12	0	**1.74**
2B	D. Richardson	561	.226	8	61	321	423	46	43	5.9	**.942**	M. Welch	47	425	26	19	0	1.93
SS	M. Ward	510	.251	2	49	185	331	**86**	39	4.9	.857	C. Titcomb	23	197	14	8	0	2.24
3B	A. Whitney	328	.220	1	28	90	184	35	11	3.4	.887	C. Crane	12	93	5	6	1	2.43
RF	M. Tiernan	443	.293	9	52	174	16	8	2	1.8	.960							
CF	M. Slattery	391	.246	1	35	187	16	18	3	2.1	.919							
LF	J. O'Rourke	409	.274	4	50	130	13	6	1	1.7	.960							
C	B. Ewing	415	.306	6	58	480	143	35	**12**	**8.4**	.947							
OF	G. Gore	254	.220	2	17	88	4	18	0	1.7	.836							
P	T. Keefe	181	.127	2	8	29	79	10	1	2.3	.915							
P	M. Welch	169	.189	2	10	16	75	17	1	2.3	.843							

Chicago

W-77 L-58

Cap Anson

POS	Player	AB	BA	HR	RBI	PO	A	E	DP	TC/G	FA	Pitcher	G	IP	W	L	SV	ERA
1B	C. Anson	515	**.344**	12	**84**	1314	65	20	**85**	10.4	**.986**	G. Krock	39	340	25	14	0	2.44
2B	F. Pfeffer	517	.250	8	57	**421**	**457**	**65**	**78**	**7.0**	.931	M. Baldwin	30	251	13	15	0	2.76
SS	N. Williamson	452	.250	8	73	120	**375**	65	**48**	4.2	.884	G. Van Haltren	30	246	13	13	1	3.52
3B	T. Burns	483	.238	3	70	**194**	**273**	49	16	3.9	.905	J. Tener	12	102	7	5	0	2.74
RF	H. Duffy	298	.282	7	41	103	19	12	5	2.0	.910							
CF	J. Ryan	549	.332	**16**	64	217	34	35	5	2.2	.878							
LF	M. Sullivan	314	.236	7	39	114	13	10	7	1.8	.927							
C	T. Daly	219	.192	0	29	400	107	33	10	8.7	.939							
OP	G. Van Haltren	318	.283	4	34	98	62	17	0		.904							
CO	D. Farrell	241	.232	3	19	221	53	39	4		.875							
OF	B. Pettit	169	.254	4	23	46	8	4	3	1.3	.931							

Philadelphia

W-69 L-61

Harry Wright

POS	Player	AB	BA	HR	RBI	PO	A	E	DP	TC/G	FA	Pitcher	G	IP	W	L	SV	ERA
1B	S. Farrar	508	.244	1	53	1345	53	30	57	10.9	.979	C. Buffinton	46	400	28	17	0	1.91
2B	C. Bastian	275	.193	1	17	145	253	23	14	6.5	.945	D. Casey	33	286	14	18	0	3.15
SS	A. Irwin	448	.219	0	28	**204**	374	64	31	5.3	.900	B. Sanders	31	275	19	10	0	1.90
3B	J. Mulvey	398	.216	0	39	87	174	32	9	2.9	.891	K. Gleason	24	200	7	16	0	2.84
RF	J. Fogarty	454	.236	1	35	239	26	20	9	2.4	.930							
CF	E. Andrews	528	.239	3	44	210	23	25	5	2.1	.903							
LF	G. Wood	433	.229	6	15	175	15	20	3	2.0	.905							
C	J. Clements	326	.245	1	32	**494**	104	47	6	7.6	.927							
2B	E. Delahanty	290	.228	1	31	129	170	44	20	6.1	.872							
PO	B. Sanders	236	.246	1	25	55	79	9	1		.937							
P	C. Buffinton	160	.181	0	12	**31**	**122**	10	3	**3.5**	.939							
UT	P. Schriver	134	.194	1	23	156	63	36	3		.859							

Boston

W-70 L-64

John Morrill

POS	Player	AB	BA	HR	RBI	PO	A	E	DP	TC/G	FA	Pitcher	G	IP	W	L	SV	ERA
1B	J. Morrill	486	.198	4	39	**1398**	**72**	31	67	**11.3**	.979	J. Clarkson	54	**483**	33	20	0	2.76
2B	J. Quinn	156	.301	4	29	97	115	20	11	6.1	.914	B. Sowders	36	317	19	15	0	2.07
SS	S. Wise	417	.240	4	40	179	271	57	34	**5.7**	.888	O. Radbourn	24	207	7	16	0	2.87
3B	B. Nash	526	.283	4	75	139	250	37	**20**	4.1	**.913**	K. Madden	20	165	7	11	0	2.95
RF	T. Brown	420	.248	9	49	172	18	22	3	2.0	.896							
CF	D. Johnston	**585**	.296	12	68	286	30	36	3	2.6	.898							
LF	J. Hornung	431	.239	3	53	151	10	9	0	1.6	.947							
C	K. Kelly	440	.318	9	71	367	146	**54**	8	7.5	.905							
SS	I. Ray	206	.248	2	26	58	130	26	6	4.5	.879							
P	J. Clarkson	205	.195	1	17	22	117	**19**	3	2.9	.880							
C	P. Tate	148	.230	1	6	188	64	43	6	7.2	.854							

NATIONAL LEAGUE 1888, *cont.*

Team	POS	Player	AB	BA	HR	RBI	PO	A	E	DP	TC/G	FA	Pitcher	G	IP	W	L	SV	ERA
Detroit	1B	D. Brouthers	522	.307	9	66	1345	48	**42**	56	11.1	.971	C. Getzien	46	404	19	25	0	3.05
W-68 L-63	2B	H. Richardson	266	.289	7	32	173	185	29	21	6.7	.925	P. Conway	45	391	30	14	0	2.26
Bill Watkins	SS	J. Rowe	451	.277	2	74	133	312	72	24	4.9	.861	H. Gruber	27	240	11	14	0	2.29
W-49 L-44	3B	D. White	527	.298	4	71	146	244	**65**	19	3.6	.857	E. Beatin	12	107	5	7	0	2.86
Bob Leadley	RF	C. Campau	251	.203	1	18	101	10	8	3	1.7	.933							
W-19 L-19	CF	N. Hanlon	459	.266	5	39	230	7	21	3	2.4	.919							
	LF	L. Twitchell	524	.244	5	67	195	13	27	4	1.8	.885							
	C	C. Bennett	258	.264	5	29	424	94	18	10	7.3	**.966**							
	UT	C. Ganzel	386	.249	1	46	288	241	52	24		.910							
	OF	S. Thompson	238	.282	6	40	86	4	12	0	1.8	.882							
	UT	S. Sutcliffe	191	.257	0	23	172	127	39	13		.885							
	P	P. Conway	167	.275	3	23	10	96	7	4	2.5	.938							
	P	C. Getzien	167	.246	1	10	29	70	16	**5**	2.5	.861							
Pittsburgh	1B	J. Beckley	283	.343	0	27	744	19	16	38	11.0	.979	E. Morris	**55**	480	29	24	0	2.31
W-66 L-68	2B	F. Dunlap	321	.262	1	36	240	279	33	44	6.7	.940	P. Galvin	50	437	23	25	0	2.63
Horace Phillips	SS	P. Smith	481	.206	4	52	91	247	37	18	5.0	.901	H. Staley	25	207	12	12	0	2.69
	3B	W. Kuehne	524	.235	3	62	96	168	26	10	3.9	.910							
	RF	J. Coleman	438	.231	0	26	160	20	14	2	2.1	.928							
	CF	B. Sunday	505	.236	0	15	297	27	21	5	2.9	.939							
	LF	A. Dalrymple	227	.220	0	14	81	9	9	0	1.7	.909							
	C	D. Miller	404	.277	0	36	268	76	35	6	5.6	.908							
	CO	F. Carroll	366	.249	2	48	314	63	48	10		.887							
	1O	A. Maul	259	.208	0	31	449	16	14	22		.971							
	P	E. Morris	189	.101	0	6	20	106	8	3	2.4	**.940**							
	P	P. Galvin	175	.143	1	3	23	113	10	2	2.9	.932							
	OC	J. Fields	169	.195	1	15	103	22	23	2		.845							
Indianapolis	1B	D. Esterbrook	246	.220	0	17	628	20	16	32	10.9	.976	H. Boyle	37	323	15	22	0	3.26
W-50 L-85	2B	C. Bassett	481	.241	2	60	250	423	57	44	5.7	.922	E. Healy	37	321	12	24	0	3.89
Harry Spence	SS	J. Glasscock	442	.269	1	45	201	334	59	36	5.4	**.901**	L. Shreve	35	298	11	24	0	4.63
	3B	J. Denny	524	.261	12	63	158	214	44	14	**4.3**	.894	B. Burdick	20	176	10	10	0	2.81
	RF	J. McGeachy	452	.219	0	30	194	27	16	5	2.0	.932							
	CF	P. Hines	513	.281	4	58	255	13	26	3	2.4	.912							
	LF	E. Seery	500	.220	5	50	258	19	18	6	2.2	.939							
	C	D. Buckley	260	.273	5	22	213	60	31	5	6.0	.898							
	UT	G. Myers	248	.238	2	16	235	85	32	6		.909							
	C	C. Daily	202	.218	0	14	215	69	34	6	7.6	.893							
	1B	J. Schoeneck	169	.237	0	20	501	16	14	19	11.1	.974							
Washington	1B	B. O'Brien	528	.225	9	66	1272	38	33	55	10.2	.975	H. O'Day	46	403	16	**29**	0	3.10
W-48 L-86	2B	A. Myers	502	.207	2	46	271	399	60	37	5.5	.918	J. Whitney	39	325	18	21	0	3.05
Walter Hewett	SS	G. Shoch	317	.183	2	24	84	168	28	6	5.4	.900	W. Widner	13	115	5	7	0	2.82
W-10 L-29	3B	J. Donnelly	428	.201	0	23	126	230	51	15	3.5	.875	G. Keefe	13	114	6	7	0	2.84
Ted Sullivan	RF	E. Daily	453	.225	8	39	179	19	19	4	2.2	.912	F. Gilmore	12	96	1	9	0	6.59
W-38 L-57	CF	D. Hoy	503	.274	2	29	296	26	37	7	2.6	.897							
	LF	W. Wilmot	473	.224	4	43	260	19	41	4	2.7	.872							
	C	C. Mack	300	.187	3	29	361	**152**	47	8	7.1	.916							
	SS	S. Fuller	170	.182	0	12	67	140	38	14	5.2	.845							
	P	H. O'Day	166	.139	0	6	19	64	7	1	2.0	.922							
	P	J. Whitney	141	.170	1	17	15	67	11	2	2.4	.882							

BATTING AND BASE RUNNING LEADERS

Batting Average

C. Anson, CHI	.344
J. Ryan, CHI	.332
K. Kelly, BOS	.318
D. Brouthers, DET	.307
B. Ewing, NY	.306

Slugging Average

J. Ryan, CHI	.515
C. Anson, CHI	.499
R. Connor, NY	.480
K. Kelly, BOS	.480
D. Johnston, BOS	.472

Home Runs

J. Ryan, CHI	16
R. Connor, NY	14
C. Anson, CHI	12
J. Denny, IND	12
D. Johnston, BOS	12

Total Bases

J. Ryan, CHI	283
D. Johnston, BOS	276
C. Anson, CHI	257
D. Brouthers, DET	242
R. Connor, NY	231

Runs Batted In

C. Anson, CHI	84
B. Nash, BOS	75
J. Rowe, DET	74
N. Williamson, CHI	73

Stolen Bases

D. Hoy, WAS	82
E. Seery, IND	80
B. Sunday, PIT	71
F. Pfeffer, CHI	64
J. Ryan, CHI	60

Hits

J. Ryan, CHI	182
C. Anson, CHI	177
D. Johnston, BOS	173
D. Brouthers, DET	160

Base on Balls

R. Connor, NY	73
D. Hoy, WAS	69
D. Brouthers, DET	68
N. Williamson, CHI	65

Home Run Percentage

J. Ryan, CHI	2.9
R. Connor, NY	2.9
C. Anson, CHI	2.3
J. Denny, IND	2.3

Runs

D. Brouthers, DET	118
J. Ryan, CHI	115
D. Johnston, BOS	102
C. Anson, CHI	101

Doubles

D. Brouthers, DET	33
J. Ryan, CHI	33
D. Johnston, BOS	31
J. Denny, IND	27

Triples

D. Johnston, BOS	18
R. Connor, NY	17
B. Ewing, NY	15
B. Nash, BOS	15

PITCHING LEADERS

Winning Percentage

T. Keefe, NY	.745
P. Conway, DET	.682
B. Sanders, PHI	.655
G. Krock, CHI	.641
J. Clarkson, BOS	.623

Earned Run Average

T. Keefe, NY	1.74
B. Sanders, PHI	1.90
C. Buffinton, PHI	1.91
M. Welch, NY	1.93
B. Sowders, BOS	2.07

Wins

T. Keefe, NY	35
J. Clarkson, BOS	33
P. Conway, DET	30
E. Morris, PIT	29
C. Buffinton, PHI	28

Saves

G. Wood, PHI	2

Strikeouts

T. Keefe, NY	333
J. Clarkson, BOS	223
C. Getzien, DET	202
C. Buffinton, PHI	199
H. O'Day, WAS	186

Complete Games

E. Morris, PIT	54
J. Clarkson, BOS	53
T. Keefe, NY	51
P. Galvin, PIT	49
M. Welch, NY	47

Fewest Hits/9 Innings

T. Keefe, NY	6.55
C. Titcomb, NY	6.81
G. Keefe, WAS	6.87
M. Welch, NY	6.94

Shutouts

B. Sanders, PHI	8
T. Keefe, NY	8
C. Buffinton, PHI	6
P. Galvin, PIT	6

Fewest Walks/9 Innings

B. Sanders, PHI	1.08
P. Galvin, PIT	1.09
G. Krock, CHI	1.19
C. Getzien, DET	1.20

Most Strikeouts/9 Inn.

T. Keefe, NY	6.90
C. Titcomb, NY	5.89
M. Baldwin, CHI	5.63
G. Van Haltren, CHI	5.09

Innings

J. Clarkson, BOS	483
E. Morris, PIT	480
P. Galvin, PIT	437
T. Keefe, NY	434

Games Pitched

E. Morris, PIT	55
J. Clarkson, BOS	54
T. Keefe, NY	51
P. Galvin, PIT	50

NATIONAL LEAGUE 1888, *cont.*

	W	L	PCT	GB	R	OR	Batting 2B	3B	HR	BA	SA	SB	Fielding E	DP	FA	Pitching CG	BB	SO	ShO	SV	ERA
New York	84	47	.641		659	**479**	130	76	55	.242	.336	314	432	76	.924	**136**	308	**724**	**20**	**3**	**1.96**
Chicago	77	58	.570		**734**	659	147	**95**	**77**	.260	**.383**	287	417	**112**	**.927**	123	308	588	13	1	2.96
Philadelphia	69	61	.531	5.5	535	509	151	46	16	.225	.290	246	424	70	.923	125	196	519	16	**3**	2.38
Boston	70	64	.522	6.5	669	619	167	89	56	.245	.351	293	494	91	.917	134	269	484	7	0	2.61
Detroit	68	63	.519	7	721	629	177	71	52	**.263**	.361	193	463	83	.919	130	**183**	522	10	1	2.74
Pittsburgh	66	68	.493	10.5	534	580	150	49	14	.227	.289	287	**416**	88	**.927**	135	223	367	13	0	2.67
Indianapolis	50	85	.370	27	603	731	**180**	33	33	.238	.313	**350**	449	84	.921	132	308	388	6	0	3.81
Washington	48	86	.358	28.5	482	731	98	49	31	.208	.271	331	494	69	.912	133	298	406	6	0	3.54
					4937	4937	1200	508	334	.238	.324	2301	3589	673	.921	1048	2093	3998	91	8	2.83

AMERICAN ASSOCIATION 1888

	POS	Player	AB	BA	HR	RBI	PO	A	E	DP	TC/G	FA	Pitcher	G	IP	W	L	SV	ERA
St. Louis	1B	C. Comiskey	**576**	.273	6	83	1293	46	**42**	52	10.4	.970	S. King	**66**	**586**	**45**	21	0	**1.64**
W-92 L-43	2B	Y. Robinson	455	.231	3	53	197	256	53	18	5.0	.895	N. Hudson	39	333	25	10	0	2.54
Charlie Comiskey	SS	B. White	275	.175	2	30	132*	205	41	10	5.1	.892	I. Chamberlain	14	112	11	2	0	1.61
	3B	A. Latham	570	.265	2	31	178	287	62	19	4.0	.882	J. Devlin	11	90	6	5	0	3.19
	RF	T. McCarthy	511	.274	1	68	243	44	21	12	2.4	.932							
	CF	H. Lyons	499	.194	4	63	237	32	33	4	2.5	.891							
	LF	T. O'Neill	529	**.335**	5	98	231	8	16	1	2.0	.937							
	C	J. Boyle	257	.241	1	23	381	123	37	**11**	7.7	.932							
	C	J. Milligan	219	.251	5	37	317	85	25	**11**	7.4	.941							
	P	S. King	207	.208	1	14	32	119	12	**4**	2.5	.926							
	PO	N. Hudson	196	.255	2	28	72	55	9	4		.934							
	SO	E. Herr	172	.267	3	43	63	71	19	4		.876							
Brooklyn	1B	D. Orr	394	.305	1	59	976	44	22	41	10.5	.979	B. Caruthers	44	392	29	15	0	2.39
W-88 L-52	2B	J. Burdock	246	.122	1	8	172	223	42	23	6.2	.904	M. Hughes	40	363	25	13	0	2.13
Bill McGunnigle	SS	G. Smith	402	.214	3	61	155	352	94	29	**5.8**	.844	A. Terry	23	195	13	8	0	2.03
	3B	G. Pinckney	575	.271	4	52	189	234	48	14	3.3	.898	D. Foutz	23	176	12	7	0	2.51
	RF	D. Foutz	563	.277	3	99	115	13	15	3	1.8	.895	A. Mays	18	161	9	9	0	2.80
	CF	P. Radford	308	.218	2	29	180	22	12	2	2.4	.944							
	LF	D. O'Brien	532	.280	2	65	231	15	18	1	1.9	.932							
	C	D. Bushong	253	.209	0	16	347	105	42	8	7.2	.915							
	OP	B. Caruthers	335	.230	5	53	127	97	26	5		.896							
	2B	B. McClellan	278	.205	0	21	145	149	31	23	5.8	.905							
	SO	O. Burns	204	.284	2	25	72	98	31	6		.846							
	C	B. Clark	150	.240	1	20	197	61	36	6	8.2	.878							
Philadelphia	1B	H. Larkin	546	.269	7	101	1218	36	**42**	44	10.6	.968	E. Seward	57	519	35	19	0	2.01
W-81 L-52	2B	L. Bierbauer	535	.267	0	80	342	**399**	**68**	39	6.7	.916	G. Weyhing	47	404	28	18	0	2.25
Bill Sharsig	SS	B. Gleason	499	.224	0	61	112	370	80	32	4.6	.858	M. Mattimore	26	221	15	10	0	3.38
	3B	D. Lyons	456	.296	6	83	159	193	49	11	3.6	.878							
	RF	T. Poorman	383	.227	2	44	115	8	14	1	1.4	.898							
	CF	C. Welch	549	.282	1	61	272	23	15	6	2.3	.952							
	LF	H. Stovey	530	.287	9	65	204	12	13	4	1.9	.943							
	C	W. Robinson	254	.244	1	31	**428**	**143**	38	5	9.4	.938							
	P	E. Seward	225	.142	2	14	24	125	19	**4**	2.9	.887							
	P	G. Weyhing	184	.217	1	14	22	93	17	1	2.8	.871							
	C	G. Townsend	161	.155	0	12	225	76	31	2	7.9	.907							
	PO	M. Mattimore	142	.268	0	12	32	71	10	6		.912							
Cincinnati	1B	L. Reilly	527	.321	**13**	**103**	1264	42	31	**73**	11.4	.977	L. Viau	42	388	27	14	0	2.65
W-80 L-54	2B	B. McPhee	458	.240	4	51	369	365	47	**65**	**7.2**	**.940**	T. Mullane	44	380	26	16	**1**	2.84
Gus Schmelz	SS	F. Fennelly	448	.196	2	56	150	419*	94*	37*	5.9	.858	E. Smith	40	348	22	17	0	2.74
	3B	H. Carpenter	551	.267	3	67	142	286	66	15	3.6	.866							
	RF	H. Nicol	548	.239	1	35	188	17	9	4	1.7	.958							
	CF	P. Corkhill	490	.271	1	74	255	17	12	5	2.4	.958							
	LF	W. Tebeau	411	.229	3	51	195	20	21	3	2.0	.911							
	C	J. Keenan	313	.233	1	40	356	114	29	7	7.2	.942							
	C	K. Baldwin	271	.218	1	25	350	107	41	6	7.7	.918							
	P	T. Mullane	175	.251	1	16	22	81	13	1	2.6	.888							
	P	L. Viau	149	.087	0	8	18	78	9	0	2.5	.914							
	S2	H. Kappel	143	.259	1	15	47	89	38	9		.782							
Baltimore	1B	T. Tucker	520	.287	6	61	1354	**59**	36	64	11.2	.975	B. Cunningham	51	453	22	29	0	3.39
W-57 L-80	2B	B. Greenwood	409	.191	0	29	158	243	38	17	5.1	.913	M. Kilroy	40	321	17	21	0	4.04
Billy Barnie	SS	J. Farrell	398	.204	3	36	75	173	27	11	5.1	.902	P. Smith	35	292	14	19	0	3.61
	3B	B. Shindle	514	.208	1	53	**218**	**340**	47	26	4.5	**.922**							
	RF	B. Purcell	406	.236	2	39	145	9	16	3	1.7	.906							
	CF	M. Griffin	542	.256	0	46	274	27	20	6	2.3	.938							
	LF	O. Burns	325	.298	4	42	97	3	17	1	2.1	.855							
	C	C. Fulmer	166	.187	0	10	237	42	30	5	6.9	.903							
	OS	J. Sommer	297	.219	0	35	107	105	29	13		.880							
	UT	J. O'Brien	196	.224	0	18	286	43	26	9		.927							
	P	B. Cunningham	177	.186	1	9	20	106	**25**	3	3.0	.834							
	OF	W. Goldsby	165	.236	0	14	53	3	6	0	1.4	.903							
	P	M. Kilroy	145	.179	0	19	17	60	6	2	2.1	.928							
	C	S. Trott	108	.278	0	22	156	32	19	4	7.7	.908							

AMERICAN ASSOCIATION 1888, *cont.*

Cleveland

W-50 L-82

Jimmy Williams
W-20 L-44

Tom Loftus
W-30 L-38

POS	Player	AB	BA	HR	RBI	PO	A	E	DP	TC/G	FA
1B	J. Faatz	470	.264	0	51	1171	39	13	50	10.2	**.989**
2B	C. Stricker	493	.233	1	33	**387**	361	57	58	6.6	.929
SS	E. McKean	548	.299	6	68	120	240	36	13	5.1	.909
3B	G. Alberts	364	.206	1	48	68	103	20	9	3.9	.895
RF	E. Hogan	269	.227	0	24	104	8	13	1	1.6	.896
CF	P. Hotaling	403	.251	0	55	170	10	25	7	2.1	.878
LF	B. Gilks	484	.229	1	63	136	15	16	2	1.9	.904
C	C. Zimmer	212	.241	0	22	311	111	40	6	7.8	.913
OF	M. Goodfellow	269	.245	0	29	93	8	16	1	1.9	.863
C	P. Snyder	237	.215	0	14	308	130	**48**	**11**	8.4	.901
3B	J. McGlone	203	.182	1	22	70	93	44	5	4.3	.787
P	J. Bakely	194	.134	1	9	21	114	18	3	2.5	.882

Pitcher	G	IP	W	L	SV	ERA
J. Bakely	61	533	25	33	0	2.97
D. O'Brien	30	259	11	19	0	3.30
B. Crowell	18	151	5	13	0	5.79

Louisville

W-48 L-87

Honest John Kelly
W-10 L-29

Mordecai Davidson
W-1 L-2

John Kerins
W-3 L-4

Mordecai Davidson
W-34 L-52

POS	Player	AB	BA	HR	RBI	PO	A	E	DP	TC/G	FA
1B	S. Smith	206	.238	1	31	568	22	18	15	10.5	.970
2B	R. Mack	446	.217	3	34	307	344	67	35	6.4	.907
SS	B. White	198	.278	1	30	52*	130	41	5	5.9	.816
3B	J. Werrick	413	.215	0	51	96	170	62	9	3.7	.811
RF	C. Wolf	538	.286	0	67	113	19	17	4	1.8	.886
CF	P. Browning	383	.313	3	72	174	16	24	8	2.2	.888
LF	H. Collins	485	.307	2	50	175	20	24	6	2.7	.890
C	P. Cook	185	.184	0	13	221	81	35	7	6.4	.896
OC	J. Kerins	319	.235	2	41	308	65	47	5		.888
OP	S. Stratton	249	.257	1	29	66	70	17	1		.889
1P	G. Hecker	211	.227	0	29	305	57	25	12		.935
OC	F. Vaughn	189	.196	1	21	164	49	28	6		.884
C	L. Cross	181	.227	0	15	202	60	20	3	7.6	.929
P	T. Ramsey	142	.120	0	9	8	57	18	1	2.1	.783

Pitcher	G	IP	W	L	SV	ERA
T. Ramsey	40	342	8	30	0	3.42
S. Stratton	33	270	10	17	0	3.64
G. Hecker	26	223	8	17	0	3.39
I. Chamberlain	24	196	14	9	0	2.53
J. Ewing	21	191	8	13	0	2.83

Kansas City

W-43 L-89

Dave Rowe
W-14 L-36

Sam Barkley
W-21 L-36

Bill Watkins
W-8 L-17

POS	Player	AB	BA	HR	RBI	PO	A	E	DP	TC/G	FA
1B	B. Phillips	509	.236	1	56	**1476**	55	32	66	**12.1**	.980
2B	S. Barkley	482	.216	3	51	341	314	43	44	6.0	.938
SS	H. Easterday	401	.190	3	37	120	459	73	30	5.7	**.888**
3B	J. Davis	491	.267	3	61	155	334	**91**	**27**	**5.1**	.843
RF	M. Cline	293	.235	0	19	91	22	15	4	1.8	.883
CF	J. McTamany	516	.246	4	41	245	27	26	5	2.3	.913
LF	M. Allen	136	.213	0	10	72	9	6	1	2.5	.931
C	J. Donahue	337	.234	1	28	282	106	42	9	6.4	.902
OC	L. Daniels	218	.202	1	28	159	67	34	7		.869
P	H. Porter	195	.144	0	10	11	**133**	16	3	2.9	.900
UT	F. Hankinson	155	.174	1	20	72	84	18	12		.897

Pitcher	G	IP	W	L	SV	ERA
H. Porter	55	474	18	**37**	0	4.16
T. Sullivan	24	215	8	16	0	3.40
B. Fagan	17	142	5	11	0	5.69
F. Hoffman	12	104	3	9	0	2.77
S. Toole	12	92	5	6	0	6.68

BATTING AND BASE RUNNING LEADERS

Batting Average

T. O'Neill, STL	.335
L. Reilly, CIN	.321
P. Browning, LOU	.313
H. Collins, LOU, BKN	.307
D. Orr, BKN	.305

Slugging Average

L. Reilly, CIN	.501
H. Stovey, PHI	.460
T. O'Neill, STL	.446
P. Browning, LOU	.436
O. Burns, BAL, BKN	.435

Home Runs

L. Reilly, CIN	13
H. Stovey, PHI	9
H. Larkin, PHI	7

Total Bases

L. Reilly, CIN	264
H. Stovey, PHI	244
T. O'Neill, STL	236
E. McKean, CLE	233
O. Burns, BAL, BKN	230

Runs Batted In

L. Reilly, CIN	103
H. Larkin, PHI	101
D. Foutz, BKN	99
T. O'Neill, STL	98
P. Corkhill, CIN, BKN	93

Stolen Bases

A. Latham, STL	109
H. Nicol, CIN	103
C. Welch, PHI	95
T. McCarthy, STL	93
H. Stovey, PHI	87

Hits

T. O'Neill, STL	177
L. Reilly, CIN	169
E. McKean, CLE	164
H. Collins, LOU, BKN	162

Base on Balls

Y. Robinson, STL	116
F. Fennelly, CIN, PHI	72
J. McTamany, KC	67
H. Nicol, CIN	67

Home Run Percentage

L. Reilly, CIN	2.5
H. Stovey, PHI	1.7
B. Caruthers, BKN	1.5
D. Lyons, PHI	1.3

Runs

G. Pinckney, BKN	134
H. Collins, LOU, BKN	133
H. Stovey, PHI	127
C. Welch, PHI	125

Doubles

H. Collins, LOU, BKN	31
L. Reilly, CIN	28
C. Wolf, LOU	28
H. Larkin, PHI	28

Triples

H. Stovey, PHI	20
O. Burns, BAL, BKN	15
E. McKean, CLE	15
L. Reilly, CIN	14

PITCHING LEADERS

Winning Percentage

N. Hudson, STL	.714
I. Chamberlain, LOU, STL	.694
S. King, STL	.682
B. Caruthers, BKN	.659
L. Viau, CIN	.659

Earned Run Average

S. King, STL	1.64
E. Seward, PHI	2.01
A. Terry, BKN	2.03
M. Hughes, BKN	2.13
I. Chamberlain, LOU, STL	2.19

Wins

S. King, STL	45
E. Seward, PHI	35
B. Caruthers, BKN	29
G. Weyhing, PHI	28
L. Viau, CIN	27

Saves

P. Corkhill, CIN	1
B. Gilks, CLE	1
T. Mullane, CIN	1

Strikeouts

E. Seward, PHI	272
S. King, STL	258
T. Ramsey, LOU	228
J. Bakely, CLE	212
G. Weyhing, PHI	204

Complete Games

S. King, STL	64
J. Bakely, CLE	60
E. Seward, PHI	57
H. Porter, KC	53
B. Cunningham, BAL	50

Fewest Hits/9 Innings

A. Terry, BKN	6.69
S. King, STL	6.72
E. Seward, PHI	6.73
I. Chamberlain, LOU, STL	6.95

Shutouts

E. Seward, PHI	6
S. King, STL	6
N. Hudson, STL	5
E. Smith, CIN	5

Fewest Walks/9 Innings

S. King, STL	1.17
B. Caruthers, BKN	1.22
N. Hudson, STL	1.59
J. Ewing, LOU	1.60

Most Strikeouts/9 Inn.

A. Terry, BKN	6.37
T. Ramsey, LOU	5.99
I. Chamberlain, LOU, STL	5.14
P. Smith, BAL, PHI	4.90

Innings

S. King, STL	586
J. Bakely, CLE	533
E. Seward, PHI	519
H. Porter, KC	474

Games Pitched

S. King, STL	66
J. Bakely, CLE	61
E. Seward, PHI	57
H. Porter, KC	55

							Batting						Fielding			Pitching					
	W	L	PCT	GB	R	OR	2B	3B	HR	BA	SA	SB	E	DP	FA	CG	BB	SO	ShO	SV	ERA
St. Louis	92	43	.681		789	**501**	149	47	**36**	**.250**	.324	468	**430**	73	**.924**	132	**225**	517	12	0	**2.09**
Brooklyn	88	52	.629	6.5	758	584	172	70	25	.242	.321	334	507	88	.917	**138**	285	577	9	0	2.33
Philadelphia	81	52	.609	10	**827**	594	**183**	**89**	31	**.250**	**.344**	434	477	73	.918	133	324	596	**13**	0	2.41
Cincinnati	80	54	.597	11.5	745	628	132	82	32	.242	.323	**469**	458	**100**	.923	132	310	539	10	**2**	2.73
Baltimore	57	80	.416	36	653	779	162	70	18	.229	.306	326	461	88	.920	130	419	525	3	0	3.78
Cleveland	50	82	.379	40.5	651	839	128	59	12	.234	.295	353	490	87	.915	131	389	500	6	1	3.72
Louisville	48	87	.356	44	689	870	**183**	67	14	.241	.315	318	611	75	.900	133	281	**599**	6	0	3.25
Kansas City	43	89	.326	47.5	579	896	142	61	17	.218	.286	257	507	95	.914	128	401	381	4	0	4.29
					5691	5691	1251	545	185	.238	.314	2959	3941	679	.916	1057	2634	4234	63	3	3.07

NATIONAL LEAGUE 1889

New York

W-83 L-43

Jim Mutrie

POS	Player	AB	BA	HR	RBI	PO	A	E	DP	TC/G	FA
1B	R. Connor	496	.317	13	**130**	1265	32	30	68	10.1	.977
2B	D. Richardson	497	.280	7	100	332	416	53	60	6.4	.934
SS	M. Ward	479	.299	1	67	229	319	**68**	38	5.7	.890
3B	A. Whitney	473	.218	1	59	160	265	57	27	3.7	.882
RF	M. Tiernan	499	.335	11	73	179	19	23	2	1.8	.896
CF	G. Gore	488	.305	7	54	239	21	41	5	2.5	.864
LF	J. O'Rourke	502	.321	3	81	165	18	22	2	1.6	.893
C	B. Ewing	407	.327	4	87	**524**	**149**	45	**10**	**7.4**	.937
P	M. Welch	156	.192	0	12	13	59	4	2	1.7	.947
P	T. Keefe	149	.154	0	8	10	78	8	3	2.0	.917
C	W. Brown	139	.259	1	29	138	38	32	3	5.6	.846

Pitcher	G	IP	W	L	SV	ERA
M. Welch	45	375	27	12	2	3.02
T. Keefe	47	364	28	13	1	3.31
C. Crane	29	230	14	10	0	3.68
H. O'Day	10	78	9	1	0	4.27

Boston

W-83 L-45

Jim Hart

POS	Player	AB	BA	HR	RBI	PO	A	E	DP	TC/G	FA
1B	D. Brouthers	485	**.373**	7	118	1243	58	35	**78**	10.6	.974
2B	H. Richardson	536	.304	7	79	246	310	46	44	7.0	.924
SS	J. Quinn	444	.261	2	69	67	167	38	19	4.3	.860
3B	B. Nash	481	.274	3	76	205	274	50	25	4.1	.905
RF	K. Kelly	507	.294	9	78	155	24	32	4	1.9	.848
CF	D. Johnston	539	.228	5	67	267	22	26	6	2.4	.917
LF	T. Brown	362	.232	2	24	169	13	20	1	2.2	.901
C	C. Bennett	247	.231	4	28	419	74	23	9	6.3	**.955**
UT	C. Ganzel	275	.265	1	43	292	87	30	19		.927
P	J. Clarkson	262	.206	2	23	**36**	**172**	**27**	**8**	**3.2**	.885
SS	P. Smith	208	.260	0	32	121	170	36*	23	5.5	.890

Pitcher	G	IP	W	L	SV	ERA
J. Clarkson	**73**	**620**	**49**	19	1	**2.73**
O. Radbourn	33	277	20	11	0	3.67
K. Madden	22	178	10	10	1	4.40

Chicago

W-67 L-65

Cap Anson

POS	Player	AB	BA	HR	RBI	PO	A	E	DP	TC/G	FA
1B	C. Anson	518	.311	7	117	**1409**	**79**	27	73	**11.3**	**.982**
2B	F. Pfeffer	531	.228	7	77	**452**	**483**	56	**69**	**7.4**	.943
SS	N. Williamson	173	.237	1	30	48	130	33	7	4.5	.844
3B	T. Burns	525	.242	4	66	**225**	**301**	**72**	**30**	**4.4**	.880
RF	H. Duffy	**584**	.295	12	89	184	19	24	2	1.8	.894
CF	J. Ryan	576	.307	17	72	252	36	23	9	2.9	.926
LF	G. Van Haltren	543	.309	9	81	222	25	28	3	2.1	.898
C	D. Farrell	407	.248	11	75	344	119	46	3	6.7	.910
SS	C. Bastian	155	.135	0	10	63	153	19	9	5.2	.919
P	A. Gumbert	153	.288	7	29	17	44	6	1	2.2	.910
P	J. Tener	150	.273	1	19	22	69	7	1	2.8	.929

Pitcher	G	IP	W	L	SV	ERA
B. Hutchinson	37	318	16	17	0	3.54
J. Tener	35	287	15	15	0	3.64
F. Dwyer	32	276	16	13	0	3.59
A. Gumbert	31	246	16	13	0	3.62

Philadelphia

W-63 L-64

Harry Wright

POS	Player	AB	BA	HR	RBI	PO	A	E	DP	TC/G	FA
1B	S. Farrar	477	.268	3	58	1265	42	30	66	10.3	.978
2B	A. Myers	305	.269	0	28	192	261	78*	33	7.1	.853
SS	B. Hallman	462	.253	2	60	237	337	67	39	**6.0**	.895
3B	J. Mulvey	544	.289	6	77	165	284	54	20	3.9	.893
RF	S. Thompson	533	.296	**20**	111	173	19	21	7	1.7	.901
CF	J. Fogarty	499	.259	3	54	302	42	14	6	2.8	.961
LF	G. Wood	422	.251	5	53	164	9	16	1	2.1	.915
C	J. Clements	310	.284	4	35	380	77	42	7	6.4	.916
O2	E. Delahanty	246	.293	0	27	116	61	17	11		.912
C	P. Schriver	211	.265	1	19	233	76	27	4	7.0	.920
P	B. Sanders	169	.278	0	21	22	58	11	1	2.1	.879
P	C. Buffinton	154	.208	0	21	18	80	9	4	2.3	.916

Pitcher	G	IP	W	L	SV	ERA
C. Buffinton	47	380	28	16	0	3.24
B. Sanders	44	350	19	18	1	3.55
K. Gleason	29	205	9	15	1	5.58
D. Casey	20	153	6	10	0	3.77

Pittsburgh

W-61 L-71

Horace Phillips
W-28 L-43

Fred Dunlap
W-7 L-10

Ned Hanlon
W-26 L-18

POS	Player	AB	BA	HR	RBI	PO	A	E	DP	TC/G	FA
1B	J. Beckley	522	.301	9	97	1236	53	24	73	10.8	.982
2B	F. Dunlap	451	.235	2	65	342	393	39	51	6.4	**.950**
SS	J. Rowe	317	.259	2	32	108	228	39	26	5.0	.896
3B	W. Kuehne	390	.246	5	57	89	157	32	14	3.7	.885
RF	B. Sunday	321	.240	2	25	157	17	10	2	2.3	.946
CF	N. Hanlon	461	.239	2	37	277	18	26	2	2.8	.919
LF	A. Maul	257	.276	4	44	123	17	8	4	2.3	.946
C	D. Miller	422	.268	6	56	299	87	**48**	8	5.7	.889
CO	F. Carroll	318	.330	2	51	228	56	27	4		.913
OF	J. Fields	289	.311	2	43	97	7	17	2	2.0	.860
SS	P. Smith	258	.209	5	27	93	187	32*	21	5.4	.897
3B	D. White	225	.253	0	26	68	95	24	7	3.6	.872
P	H. Staley	186	.161	0	8	19	89	5	3	2.3	.956
P	P. Galvin	150	.187	0	16	20	72	11	6	2.5	.893

Pitcher	G	IP	W	L	SV	ERA
H. Staley	49	420	21	**26**	1	3.51
P. Galvin	41	341	23	16	0	4.17
E. Morris	21	170	6	13	0	4.13
B. Sowders	13	53	6	5	0*	7.35

Cleveland

W-61 L-72

Tom Loftus

POS	Player	AB	BA	HR	RBI	PO	A	E	DP	TC/G	FA
1B	J. Faatz	442	.231	2	38	1145	62	24	67	10.5	.981
2B	C. Stricker	566	.251	1	47	434	429	63	65	6.9	.932
SS	E. McKean	500	.318	4	75	206	398	62	42	5.5	.907
3B	P. Tebeau	521	.282	8	76	185	287	54	26	3.9	.897
RF	P. Radford	487	.238	1	46	205	24	14	6	1.8	.942
CF	J. McAleer	447	.235	1	35	247	29	13	9	2.6	.955
LF	L. Twitchell	549	.275	4	95	220	10	21	0	1.9	.916
C	C. Zimmer	259	.259	1	21	315	131	33	**10**	5.9	.931
UT	B. Gilks	210	.238	0	18	172	54	9	9		.962
C	S. Sutcliffe	161	.248	1	21	179	70	30	3	7.5	.892
P	D. O'Brien	140	.250	0	18	25	70	7	3	2.5	.931

Pitcher	G	IP	W	L	SV	ERA
D. O'Brien	41	347	22	17	0	4.15
E. Beatin	36	318	20	15	0	3.57
J. Bakely	36	304	12	22	0	2.96
H. Gruber	25	205	7	16	1	3.64

Indianapolis

W-59 L-75

Frank Bancroft
W-25 L-43

Jack Glasscock
W-34 L-32

POS	Player	AB	BA	HR	RBI	PO	A	E	DP	TC/G	FA
1B	P. Hines	486	.305	6	72	1090	57	**43**	66	10.9	.964
2B	C. Bassett	477	.245	4	68	322	451	52	67	6.5	.937
SS	J. Glasscock	582	.352	7	85	**246**	**478**	67	**60**	6.0	**.915**
3B	J. Denny	578	.282	18	112	199	276	45	12	4.2	**.913**
RF	J. McGeachy	532	.267	2	63	189	36	20	8	1.9	.918
CF	M. Sullivan	256	.285	4	35	133	9	14	4	2.4	.910
LF	E. Seery	526	.314	8	59	220	20	24	4	2.1	.909
C	D. Buckley	260	.258	8	41	182	53	33	2	4.9	.877
C	C. Daily	219	.251	0	26	225	49	35	1	6.1	.887
OF	E. Andrews	173	.306	0	22	67	10	10	1	2.2	.885
P	H. Boyle	155	.245	1	17	17	51	3	0	1.5	.958
OC	G. Myers	149	.195	0	12	106	36	18	1		.887

Pitcher	G	IP	W	L	SV	ERA
H. Boyle	46	379	21	23	0	3.92
C. Getzien	45	349	18	22	1	4.54
A. Rusie	33	225	12	10	0	5.32

NATIONAL LEAGUE 1889, *cont.*

Washington

W-41 L-83

John Morrill
W-13 L-38

Arthur Irwin
W-28 L-45

POS	Player	AB	BA	HR	RBI	PO	A	E	DP	TC/G	FA
1B	J. Carney	273	.231	1	29	521	16	24	29	10.6	.957
2B	S. Wise	472	.250	4	62	170	225	36	26	6.0	.916
SS	A. Irwin	313	.233	0	32	165	279	52	36	5.8	.895
3B	J. Irwin	228	.289	0	25	82	129	32	14	4.2	.868
RF	H. Beecher	179	.296	0	30	61	7	11	1	2.0	.861
CF	D. Hoy	507	.274	0	39	255	29	35	4	2.5	.890
LF	W. Wilmot	432	.289	9	57	232	22	20	4	2.5	.927
C	T. Daly	250	.300	1	40	268	86	32	5	6.8	.917
UT	C. Mack	386	.293	0	42	432	100	57	22		.903
3B	P. Sweeney	193	.228	1	23	67	83	37	6	4.0	.802
2B	A. Myers	176	.261	0	20	147	148	18*	26	6.8	.942
1B	J. Morrill	146	.185	2	16	369	18	8	15	9.9	.980
UT	S. Clark	145	.255	3	22	101	75	26	10		.871

Pitcher	G	IP	W	L	SV	ERA
A. Ferson	36	288	17	17	0	3.90
G. Haddock	33	276	11	19	0	4.20
G. Keefe	30	230	8	18	0	5.13
H. O'Day	13	108	2	10	0	4.33
E. Healy	13	101	1	11	0	6.24

BATTING AND BASE RUNNING LEADERS

Batting Average

D. Brouthers, BOS	.373
J. Glasscock, IND	.352
M. Tiernan, NY	.335
F. Carroll, PIT	.330
B. Ewing, NY	.327

Slugging Average

R. Connor, NY	.528
D. Brouthers, BOS	.507
M. Tiernan, NY	.501
J. Ryan, CHI	.498
S. Thompson, PHI	.492

Home Runs

S. Thompson, PHI	20
J. Denny, IND	18
J. Ryan, CHI	17
R. Connor, NY	13
H. Duffy, CHI	12

Total Bases

J. Ryan, CHI	287
J. Glasscock, IND	272
R. Connor, NY	262
S. Thompson, PHI	262
M. Tiernan, NY	250

Runs Batted In

R. Connor, NY	130
D. Brouthers, BOS	118
C. Anson, CHI	117
J. Denny, IND	112
S. Thompson, PHI	111

Stolen Bases

J. Fogarty, PHI	99
K. Kelly, BOS	68
T. Brown, BOS	63
M. Ward, NY	62
J. Glasscock, IND	57

Hits

J. Glasscock, IND	205
D. Brouthers, BOS	181
J. Ryan, CHI	177
H. Duffy, CHI	172

Base on Balls

M. Tiernan, NY	96
R. Connor, NY	93
P. Radford, CLE	91
C. Anson, CHI	86

Home Run Percentage

S. Thompson, PHI	3.8
J. Denny, IND	3.1
J. Ryan, CHI	3.0
D. Farrell, CHI	2.7

Runs

M. Tiernan, NY	147
H. Duffy, CHI	144
J. Ryan, CHI	140
G. Gore, NY	132

Doubles

K. Kelly, BOS	41
J. Glasscock, IND	40
J. O'Rourke, NY	36
S. Thompson, PHI	36

Triples

W. Wilmot, WAS	19
R. Connor, NY	17
J. Fogarty, PHI	17
M. Tiernan, NY	14
J. Ryan, CHI	14

PITCHING LEADERS

Winning Percentage

J. Clarkson, BOS	.721
M. Welch, NY	.692
T. Keefe, NY	.683
O. Radbourn, BOS	.645
C. Buffinton, PHI	.636

Earned Run Average

J. Clarkson, BOS	2.73
J. Bakely, CLE	2.96
M. Welch, NY	3.02
C. Buffinton, PHI	3.24
T. Keefe, NY	3.31

Wins

J. Clarkson, BOS	49
T. Keefe, NY	28
C. Buffinton, PHI	28
M. Welch, NY	27
P. Galvin, PIT	23

Saves

B. Sowders, BOS, PIT	3
B. Bishop, CHI	2
M. Welch, NY	2

Strikeouts

J. Clarkson, BOS	284
T. Keefe, NY	209
H. Staley, PIT	159
C. Buffinton, PHI	153
C. Getzien, IND	139

Complete Games

J. Clarkson, BOS	68
H. Staley, PIT	46
D. O'Brien, CLE	39
M. Welch, NY	39

Fewest Hits/9 Innings

T. Keefe, NY	7.66
M. Welch, NY	8.16
J. Clarkson, BOS	8.55
C. Crane, NY	8.65

Shutouts

J. Clarkson, BOS	8
P. Galvin, PIT	4

Fewest Walks/9 Innings

P. Galvin, PIT	2.06
H. Boyle, IND	2.26
O. Radbourn, BOS	2.34
F. Dwyer, CHI	2.35

Most Strikeouts/9 Inn.

T. Keefe, NY	5.17
C. Crane, NY	5.09
A. Rusie, IND	4.36
E. Healy, WAS, CHI	4.35

Innings

J. Clarkson, BOS	620
H. Staley, PIT	420
C. Buffinton, PHI	380
H. Boyle, IND	379

Games Pitched

J. Clarkson, BOS	73
H. Staley, PIT	49
C. Buffinton, PHI	47
T. Keefe, NY	47

							Batting						Fielding			Pitching					
	W	L	PCT	GB	R	OR	2B	3B	HR	BA	SA	SB	E	DP	FA	CG	BB	SO	ShO	SV	ERA
New York	83	43	.659		**935**	708	207	**77**	53	**.282**	**.394**	292	437	90	.920	118	523	**542**	6	3	3.47
Boston	83	45	.648		826	**626**	196	53	43	.270	.363	**331**	413	105	.926	121	413	497	**10**	**5**	**3.36**
Chicago	67	65	.508		867	814	184	66	**79**	.263	.377	243	463	91	.923	123	408	434	6	2	3.73
Philadelphia	63	64	.496	1.5	742	748	215	52	44	.266	.362	269	466	92	.915	106	428	443	4	2	4.00
Pittsburgh	61	71	.462	6	726	801	209	65	42	.253	.351	231	385	94	.931	125	**374**	345	5	1	4.51
Cleveland	61	72	.459	6.5	656	720	131	59	25	.250	.319	237	**365**	**108**	**.936**	**132**	519	435	6	1	3.66
Indianapolis	59	75	.440	9	819	894	**228**	35	62	.278	.377	252	420	102	.926	109	420	408	3	2	4.85
Washington	41	83	.331	22	632	892	151	57	25	.251	.329	232	519	91	.904	113	527	388	1	0	4.68
					6203	6203	1521	464	373	.264	.359	2087	3468	773	.923	947	3612	3492	41	16	4.03

AMERICAN ASSOCIATION 1889

Brooklyn

W-93 L-44

Bill McGunnigle

POS	Player	AB	BA	HR	RBI	PO	A	E	DP	TC/G	FA
1B	D. Foutz	553	.277	7	113	1371	33	30	65	10.7	.979
2B	H. Collins	560	.266	2	73	385	410	61	56	6.2	.929
SS	G. Smith	446	.231	3	53	182	417	67	37	5.6	.899
3B	G. Pinckney	545	.246	4	82	183	278	53	19	3.7	**.897**
RF	O. Burns	504	.304	5	100	139	23	14	5	1.6	.920
CF	P. Corkhill	537	.250	8	78	317	35	19	8	2.7	.949
LF	D. O'Brien	567	.300	5	80	255	14	28	5	2.2	.906
C	B. Clark	182	.275	0	22	275	86	**54**	4	7.8	.870
CO	J. Visner	295	.258	8	68	237	74	42	8		.881
P	B. Caruthers	172	.250	2	31	29	95	4	4	2.3	.969
P	A. Terry	160	.300	2	26	24	86	4	2	2.8	.965

Pitcher	G	IP	W	L	SV	ERA
B. Caruthers	56	445	**40**	11	1	3.13
A. Terry	41	326	22	15	0	3.29
T. Lovett	29	229	17	10	0	4.32
M. Hughes	20	153	9	8	0	4.35

AMERICAN ASSOCIATION 1889, *cont.*

St. Louis

W-90 L-45

Charlie Comiskey

POS	Player	AB	BA	HR	RBI	PO	A	E	DP	TC/G	FA
1B	C. Comiskey	587	.286	3	102	1225	45	39	71	9.8	.970
2B	Y. Robinson	452	.208	5	70	305	333	81	53	5.4	.887
SS	S. Fuller	517	.226	0	51	240	459	67	46	5.5	**.913**
3B	A. Latham	512	.246	4	49	197	249	59	22	4.4	.883
RF	T. McCarthy	**604**	.291	2	63	229	38	32	11	2.1	.893
CF	C. Duffee	509	.244	15	86	296	43	23	7	2.7	.936
LF	T. O'Neill	534	.335	9	110	264	12	19	3	2.2	.936
C	J. Boyle	347	.245	4	42	378	108	27	**11**	6.4	.947
C	J. Milligan	273	.366	12	76	370	105	34	7	7.7	.933
P	S. King	189	.228	0	30	19	91	5	2	2.1	.957
P	I. Chamberlain	171	.199	2	31	15	67	7	0	1.7	.921

Pitcher	G	IP	W	L	SV	ERA
S. King	56	458	33	17	1	3.14
I. Chamberlain	53	422	32	15	1	2.97
J. Stivetts	26	192	13	7	1	**2.25**

Philadelphia

W-75 L-58

Bill Sharsig

POS	Player	AB	BA	HR	RBI	PO	A	E	DP	TC/G	FA
1B	H. Larkin	516	.318	3	74	1230	37	35	**88**	9.9	.973
2B	L. Bierbauer	549	.304	7	105	**472**	406	55	80	**7.2**	.941
SS	F. Fennelly	513	.257	1	64	181	453	93	53	5.3	.872
3B	D. Lyons	510	.329	9	82	202	291	80	**29**	4.4	.860
RF	B. Purcell	507	.316	0	85	172	15	20	3	1.6	.903
CF	C. Welch	516	.271	0	39	282	29	26	10	2.7	.923
LF	H. Stovey	556	.308	**19**	**119**	287	38	37	9	2.6	.898
C	W. Robinson	264	.231	0	28	290	106	24	8	6.1	.943
C	L. Cross	199	.221	0	23	278	102	27	7	7.4	.934
P	G. Weyhing	191	.131	0	12	12	71	8	2	1.7	.912
P	E. Seward	143	.217	2	17	13	67	9	1	2.3	.899

Pitcher	G	IP	W	L	SV	ERA
G. Weyhing	54	449	30	21	0	2.95
E. Seward	39	320	21	15	0	3.97
S. McMahon	30	242	14	12	0	3.53

Cincinnati

W-76 L-63

Gus Schmelz

POS	Player	AB	BA	HR	RBI	PO	A	E	DP	TC/G	FA
1B	L. Reilly	427	.260	5	66	1143	30	19	76	10.9	**.984**
2B	B. McPhee	540	.269	5	57	429	**446**	50	**85**	6.9	**.946**
SS	O. Beard	558	.285	1	77	214	**537**	87	**63**	5.9	.896
3B	H. Carpenter	486	.261	0	63	143	207	69	18	3.5	.835
RF	H. Nicol	474	.255	2	58	168	22	17	4	1.8	.918
CF	B. Holliday	563	.321	**19**	104	234	29	22	6	2.1	.923
LF	W. Tebeau	496	.252	7	70	241	18	33	3	2.2	.887
C	J. Keenan	300	.287	6	60	319	91	16	**11**	6.5	.962
C	K. Baldwin	223	.247	1	34	274	89	35	5	7.2	.912
UT	T. Mullane	196	.296	0	29	78	80	22	10		.878
OC	B. Earle	169	.266	4	31	157	31	34	5		.847
P	J. Duryea	162	.272	0	17	15	80	11	1	2.0	.896
P	L. Viau	147	.143	0	9	9	61	4	2	1.6	.946

Pitcher	G	IP	W	L	SV	ERA
J. Duryea	53	401	32	19	1	2.56
L. Viau	47	373	22	20	1	3.79
T. Mullane	33	220	11	9	**5**	2.99
E. Smith	29	203	9	12	0	4.88

Baltimore

W-70 L-65

Billy Barnie

POS	Player	AB	BA	HR	RBI	PO	A	E	DP	TC/G	FA
1B	T. Tucker	527	**.372**	5	99	1144	45	44	63	10.0	.964
2B	R. Mack	519	.241	1	87	367	358	**83**	70	6.0	.897
SS	J. Farrell	157	.210	1	26	65	131	24	13	5.2	.891
3B	B. Shindle	567	.314	3	64	**225**	**323**	**88**	25	**4.6**	.862
RF	J. Sommer	386	.220	1	36	172	24	15	7	2.0	.929
CF	M. Griffin	531	.279	4	48	246	17	26	5	2.7	.910
LF	J. Hornung	533	.229	1	78	250	32	27	10	2.3	.913
C	P. Tate	253	.182	1	27	306	75	25	3	6.5	.938
P	M. Kilroy	208	.274	1	26	25	139	**17**	4	3.1	.906
C	T. Quinn	194	.175	1	15	290	81	30	10	7.3	.925
P	F. Foreman	181	.144	1	11	9	72	14	1	1.9	.853
SS	W. Holland	143	.189	0	16	37	102	24	9	4.2	.853

Pitcher	G	IP	W	L	SV	ERA
M. Kilroy	59	481	29	25	0	2.85
F. Foreman	51	414	23	21	0	3.52
B. Cunningham	39	279	16	19	1	4.87

Columbus

W-60 L-78

Al Buckenberger

POS	Player	AB	BA	HR	RBI	PO	A	E	DP	TC/G	FA
1B	D. Orr	560	.327	4	87	1291	**61**	23	64	10.3	.983
2B	B. Greenwood	414	.225	3	49	313	322	60	50	5.9	.914
SS	H. Easterday	324	.173	4	34	134	326	57	27	5.8	.890
3B	L. Marr	546	.306	1	75	111	151	44	13	4.6	.856
RF	S. Johnson	459	.283	2	79	75	12	12	2	1.4	.879
CF	J. McTamany	529	.276	4	52	247	28	30	8	2.2	.902
LF	E. Daily	578	.256	3	70	212	27	41	4	2.1	.854
C	J. O'Connor	398	.269	4	60	**423**	128	26	7	**6.9**	**.955**
P	M. Baldwin	208	.188	2	25	**33**	91	13	1	2.2	.905
3S	H. Kappel	173	.272	3	21	69	128	40	7		.831

Pitcher	G	IP	W	L	SV	ERA
M. Baldwin	**63**	**514**	27	**34**	1	3.61
W. Widner	41	294	12	20	1	5.20
H. Gastright	32	223	10	16	0	4.57
A. Mays	21	140	10	7	0	4.82

Kansas City

W-55 L-82

Bill Watkins

POS	Player	AB	BA	HR	RBI	PO	A	E	DP	TC/G	FA
1B	D. Stearns	560	.286	2	87	**1398**	56	**49**	75	**11.1**	.967
2B	S. Barkley	176	.284	0	23	90	103	16	20	5.1	.923
SS	H. Long	574	.275	3	60	**335**	479	**117**	55	**7.3**	.874
3B	J. Davis	241	.266	0	30	93	140	57	14	4.7	.803
RF	B. Hamilton	534	.301	3	77	202	20	37	6	1.9	.857
CF	J. Burns	579	.304	5	97	323	11	32	4	2.7	.913
LF	J. Manning	506	.204	3	68	119	20	11	2	2.2	.927
C	C. Hoover	258	.248	1	25	266	105	34	8	6.1	.916
UT	J. Donahue	252	.234	0	32	187	100	46	7		.862
UT	J. Pickett	201	.224	0	12	77	44	23	4		.840
UT	B. Alvord	186	.231	0	18	66	140	43	17		.827
P	P. Swartzel	174	.144	0	20	19	**145**	11	**6**	**3.6**	.937
P	J. Conway	149	.208	0	12	10	85	7	2	2.5	.931

Pitcher	G	IP	W	L	SV	ERA
P. Swartzel	48	410	19	27	1	4.32
J. Conway	41	335	19	19	0	3.25
J. Sowders	25	185	6	16	1	4.82
J. McCarty	15	120	8	6	0	3.91
T. Sullivan	10	87	2	8	0	5.67

AMERICAN ASSOCIATION 1889, *cont.*

Louisville

W-27 L-111

Dude Esterbrook
W-2 L-8

Chicken Wolf
W-14 L-51

Dan Shannon
W-10 L-46

Jack Chapman
W-1 L-6

POS	Player	AB	BA	HR	RBI	PO	A	E	DP	TC/G	FA
1B	G. Hecker	327	.284	1	36	609	23	20	43	10.0	.969
2B	D. Shannon	498	.257	4	48	307	391	69	59	6.3	.910
SS	P. Tomney	376	.213	4	38	229	454	114	57	7.1	.857
3B	H. Raymond	515	.239	0	47	206	261	60	23	4.1	.886
RF	C. Wolf	546	.291	3	57	159	16	10	2	2.1	.946
CF	F. Weaver	499	.291	0	60	249	30	25	4	2.5	.918
LF	P. Browning	324	.256	2	32	152	12	22	4	2.2	.882
C	P. Cook	286	.227	0	15	293	**138**	35	6	6.3	.925
UT	F. Vaughn	360	.239	3	45	441	121	51	18		.917
PO	R. Ehret	258	.252	1	31	36	101	22	3		.862
UT	S. Stratton	229	.288	4	34	198	57	21	15		.924

Pitcher	G	IP	W	L	SV	ERA
R. Ehret	45	364	10	29	0	4.80
J. Ewing	40	331	6	30	0	4.87
G. Hecker	19	151	5	13	0	5.59
T. Ramsey	18	140	1	16	0	5.59
S. Stratton	19	134	3	13	1	3.23

BATTING AND BASE RUNNING LEADERS

Batting Average	
T. Tucker, BAL	.372
T. O'Neill, STL	.335
D. Lyons, PHI	.329
D. Orr, COL	.327
B. Holliday, CIN	.321

Slugging Average	
H. Stovey, PHI	.525
B. Holliday, CIN	.497
T. Tucker, BAL	.484
T. O'Neill, STL	.478
D. Lyons, PHI	.469

Home Runs	
H. Stovey, PHI	19
B. Holliday, CIN	19
C. Duffee, STL	15
J. Milligan, STL	12
D. Lyons, PHI	9
T. O'Neill, STL	9

Total Bases	
H. Stovey, PHI	292
B. Holliday, CIN	280
T. Tucker, BAL	255
T. O'Neill, STL	255
D. Orr, COL	250

Runs Batted In	
H. Stovey, PHI	119
D. Foutz, BKN	113
T. O'Neill, STL	110
L. Bierbauer, PHI	105
B. Holliday, CIN	104

Stolen Bases	
B. Hamilton, KC	111
D. O'Brien, BKN	91
H. Long, KC	89
H. Nicol, CIN	80
A. Latham, STL	69

Hits	
T. Tucker, BAL	196
D. Orr, COL	183
B. Holliday, CIN	181
T. O'Neill, STL	179

Base on Balls	
Y. Robinson, STL	118
J. McTamany, COL	116
M. Griffin, BAL	91
B. Hamilton, KC	87
L. Marr, COL	87

Home Run Percentage	
H. Stovey, PHI	3.4
B. Holliday, CIN	3.4
C. Duffee, STL	2.9
J. Keenan, CIN	2.0

Runs	
M. Griffin, BAL	152
H. Stovey, PHI	152
D. O'Brien, BKN	146
B. Hamilton, KC	144

Doubles	
C. Welch, PHI	39
H. Stovey, PHI	38
D. Lyons, PHI	36
T. O'Neill, STL	33

Triples	
L. Marr, COL	15
M. Griffin, BAL	14
O. Beard, CIN	14

PITCHING LEADERS

Winning Percentage	
B. Caruthers, BKN	.784
I. Chamberlain, STL	.681
S. King, STL	.660
J. Stivetts, STL	.650
T. Lovett, BKN	.630

Earned Run Average	
J. Stivetts, STL	2.25
J. Duryea, CIN	2.56
M. Kilroy, BAL	2.85
G. Weyhing, PHI	2.95
I. Chamberlain, STL	2.97

Wins	
B. Caruthers, BKN	40
S. King, STL	33
J. Duryea, CIN	32
I. Chamberlain, STL	32
G. Weyhing, PHI	30

Saves	
T. Mullane, CIN	5

Strikeouts	
M. Baldwin, COL	368
M. Kilroy, BAL	217
G. Weyhing, PHI	213
I. Chamberlain, STL	202
S. King, STL	188

Complete Games	
M. Kilroy, BAL	55
M. Baldwin, COL	54
G. Weyhing, PHI	50
S. King, STL	47
B. Caruthers, BKN	46

Fewest Hits/9 Innings	
J. Stivetts, STL	7.18
G. Weyhing, PHI	7.66
A. Terry, BKN	7.87
F. Foreman, BAL	7.91

Shutouts	
B. Caruthers, BKN	7
M. Baldwin, COL	6
F. Foreman, BAL	5
M. Kilroy, BAL	5

Fewest Walks/9 Innings	
B. Caruthers, BKN	2.10
J. Conway, KC	2.42
S. King, STL	2.46
T. Lovett, BKN	2.55

Most Strikeouts/9 Inn.	
J. Stivetts, STL	6.71
M. Baldwin, COL	6.45
A. Terry, BKN	5.13
J. Sowders, KC	5.06

Innings	
M. Baldwin, COL	514
M. Kilroy, BAL	481
S. King, STL	458
G. Weyhing, PHI	449

Games Pitched	
M. Baldwin, COL	63
M. Kilroy, BAL	59
B. Caruthers, BKN	56
S. King, STL	56

	W	L	PCT	GB	R	OR	Batting						Fielding			Pitching					
							2B	3B	HR	BA	SA	SB	E	DP	FA	CG	BB	SO	ShO	SV	ERA
Brooklyn	93	44	.679		**995**	706	188	79	48	.263	.365	389	**421**	92	**.928**	120	**400**	471	**10**	1	3.61
St. Louis	90	45	.667	2	957	**680**	211	64	**58**	.266	.370	336	438	100	.925	121	413	**617**	7	3	**3.00**
Philadelphia	75	58	.564	16	880	787	**239**	65	43	**.275**	.377	252	465	120	.921	**130**	509	479	9	1	3.53
Cincinnati	76	63	.547	18	897	769	197	**96**	52	.270	**.382**	462	440	**121**	.926	114	475	562	3	**8**	3.50
Baltimore	70	65	.519	22	791	795	155	68	20	.254	.328	311	536	104	.907	128	424	540	**10**	1	3.56
Columbus	60	78	.435	33.5	779	924	171	95	36	.259	.356	304	497	92	.916	114	551	610	9	4	4.39
Kansas City	55	82	.401	38	852	1031	162	77	17	.254	.328	**472**	611	109	.900	128	457	447	0	2	4.36
Louisville	27	111	.196	66.5	632	1091	170	75	22	.252	.330	203	584	117	.907	127	475	451	2	1	4.81
					6783	6783	1493	619	296	.262	.354	2729	3992	855	.916	982	3704	4177	50	21	3.84

NATIONAL LEAGUE 1890

Brooklyn

W-86 L-43

Bill McGunnigle

POS	Player	AB	BA	HR	RBI	PO	A	E	DP	TC/G	FA
1B	D. Foutz	509	.303	5	98	1192	39	28	63	**11.1**	.978
2B	H. Collins	510	.278	3	69	298	420	42	56	5.9	.945
SS	G. Smith	481	.191	1	47	232	468	74	49	6.0	.904
3B	G. Pinckney	485	.309	7	83	179	222	29	15	3.4	.933
RF	O. Burns	472	.284	13	**128**	137	23	10	4	1.5	.941
CF	D. O'Brien	350	.314	2	63	176	14	8	2	2.3	.960
LF	P. Corkhill	204	.225	1	21	122	6	3	1	2.7	.977
C	T. Daly	292	.243	5	43	332	72	20	7	6.1	.953
OP	A. Terry	363	.278	4	59	123	79	19	6		.914
OP	B. Caruthers	238	.265	1	29	65	83	20	2		.881
P	T. Lovett	164	.201	1	20	10	79	10	3	2.3	.899
C	B. Clark	151	.219	0	15	164	40	40	5	5.8	.836

Pitcher	G	IP	W	L	SV	ERA
T. Lovett	44	372	30	11	0	2.78
A. Terry	46	370	26	16	0	2.94
B. Caruthers	37	300	23	11	0	3.09

NATIONAL LEAGUE 1890, *cont.*

Chicago

W-84 L-53

Cap Anson

POS	Player	AB	BA	HR	RBI	PO	A	E	DP	TC/G	FA	Pitcher	G	IP	W	L	SV	ERA
1B	C. Anson	504	.312	7	107	1345	**49**	31	61	10.6	.978	B. Hutchinson	**71**	**603**	**42**	25	**2**	2.70
2B	B. Glenalvin	250	.268	4	26	128	194	25	20	5.3	.928	P. Luby	34	268	20	9	1	3.19
SS	J. Cooney	574	.272	4	52	237	452	47	50	5.5	**.936**	E. Stein	20	161	12	6	0	3.81
3B	T. Burns	538	.277	6	86	188	290	54	25	3.8	.898	M. Sullivan	12	96	5	6	0	4.59
RF	J. Andrews	202	.188	3	17	80	10	10	1	1.9	.900	R. Coughlin	11	95	4	6	0	4.26
CF	W. Wilmot	571	.278	**14**	99	320	26	23	4	2.7	.938							
LF	C. Carroll	**582**	.285	7	65	265	28	20	7	2.3	.936							
C	M. Kittridge	333	.201	3	35	458	113	34	9	6.3	.944							
O2	H. Earl	384	.247	6	51	144	145	42	11		.873							
P	B. Hutchinson	261	.203	2	27	**44**	128	14	5	2.6	.925							
C	T. Nagle	144	.271	1	11	161	25	12	0	6.0	.939							
OF	E. Foster	105	.248	5	23	69	2	1	0	2.7	.986							

Philadelphia

W-78 L-54

Harry Wright
W-14 L-8

Jack Clements
W-13 L-6

Al Reach
W-4 L-7

Bob Allen
W-25 L-10

Harry Wright
W-22 L-23

POS	Player	AB	BA	HR	RBI	PO	A	E	DP	TC/G	FA	Pitcher	G	IP	W	L	SV	ERA
1B	A. McCauley	418	.244	1	42	1053	26	30	68	9.9	.973	K. Gleason	60	506	38	17	**2**	2.63
2B	A. Myers	487	.277	2	81	347	352	38	**62**	6.3	.948	T. Vickery	46	382	24	22	0	3.44
SS	B. Allen	456	.226	2	57	**337**	**500**	69	**68**	**6.8**	.924	P. Smith	24	204	8	12	0	4.28
3B	E. Mayer	484	.242	1	70	173	224	55	22	3.9	.878							
RF	S. Thompson	549	.313	4	102	170	29	13	5	1.6	.939							
CF	E. Burke	430	.263	4	50	202	23	24	4	2.6	.904							
LF	B. Hamilton	496	.325	2	49	232	23	34	4	2.3	.882							
C	J. Clements	381	.315	7	74	**503**	92	35	12	**6.9**	.944							
P	K. Gleason	224	.210	0	17	24	95	8	4	2.1	.937							
UT	P. Schriver	223	.274	0	35	272	63	33	12		.910							
P	T. Vickery	159	.208	0	11	17	71	**20**	3	2.3	.815							
UT	B. Grey	128	.242	0	21	69	42	18	4		.860							

Cincinnati

W-77 L-55

Tom Loftus

POS	Player	AB	BA	HR	RBI	PO	A	E	DP	TC/G	FA	Pitcher	G	IP	W	L	SV	ERA
1B	L. Reilly	553	.300	6	86	**1392**	38	**33**	**77**	11.1	.977	B. Rhines	46	401	28	17	0	**1.95**
2B	B. McPhee	528	.256	3	39	**404**	**431**	51	**62**	**6.7**	.942	J. Duryea	33	274	16	12	0	2.92
SS	O. Beard	492	.268	3	72	145	419	65	43	5.6	.897	T. Mullane	25	209	12	10	1	2.24
3B	A. Latham	164	.250	0	15	54	103	27	10	4.5	.853	F. Foreman	25	198	13	10	0	3.95
RF	L. Marr	527	.300	2	73	68	12	6	3	1.3	.930	L. Viau	13	90	7	5	0	4.50
CF	B. Holliday	518	.270	4	75	253	20	15	5	2.2	.948							
LF	J. Knight	481	.312	4	67	224	11	19	0	2.0	.925							
C	J. Harrington	236	.246	1	23	345	73	19	3	6.7	.957							
UT	T. Mullane	286	.276	0	34	114	116	37	7		.861							
C	J. Keenan	202	.139	3	19	244	63	16	5	6.5	.950							
OF	H. Nicol	186	.210	0	19	62	8	6	3	1.7	.921							
P	B. Rhines	154	.188	0	11	23	77	7	3	2.3	.935							

Boston

W-76 L-57

Frank Selee

POS	Player	AB	BA	HR	RBI	PO	A	E	DP	TC/G	FA	Pitcher	G	IP	W	L	SV	ERA
1B	T. Tucker	539	.295	1	62	1341	39	29	53	10.7	**.979**	K. Nichols	48	427	27	19	0	2.21
2B	P. Smith	463	.229	1	53	234	401	**57**	41	5.2	.918	J. Clarkson	44	383	25	18	0	3.27
SS	H. Long	431	.251	8	52	230	352	66	40	6.4	.898	C. Getzien	40	350	23	17	0	3.19
3B	C. McGarr	487	.236	1	51	151	228	27	13	3.5	**.933**							
RF	S. Brodie	514	.296	0	67	225	19	12	6	1.9	.953							
CF	P. Hines	273	.264	2	48	114	4	16	2	1.9	.881							
LF	M. Sullivan	505	.285	6	61	241	13	13	1	2.2	.951							
C	C. Bennett	281	.214	3	40	448	90	23	8	6.6	**.959**							
UT	B. Lowe	207	.280	2	21	103	82	11	2		.944							
UT	L. Hardie	185	.227	3	17	171	49	28	5		.887							
P	K. Nichols	174	.247	0	23	14	85	13	1	2.3	.884							
P	J. Clarkson	173	.249	2	26	21	72	14	3	2.4	.869							
CO	C. Ganzel	163	.270	0	24	144	28	7	4		.961							
P	C. Getzien	147	.231	2	25	14	63	19	2	2.4	.802							
OF	P. Donovan	140	.257	0	9	45	4	6	1	1.7	.891							

New York

W-63 L-68

Jim Mutrie

POS	Player	AB	BA	HR	RBI	PO	A	E	DP	TC/G	FA	Pitcher	G	IP	W	L	SV	ERA
1B	L. Whistler	170	.288	2	29	490	10	9	28	11.3	.982	A. Rusie	67	549	29	**34**	1	2.56
2B	C. Bassett	410	.239	0	54	201	332	27	43	5.6	**.952**	M. Welch	37	292	17	13	0	2.99
SS	J. Glasscock	512	**.336**	1	66	275	421	69	46	6.2	.910	J. Sharrott	25	184	11	10	0	2.89
3B	J. Denny	437	.213	3	42	165	210	47	16	4.0	.889	J. Burkett	21	118	3	10	0	5.57
RF	J. Burkett	401	.309	4	60	108	23	28	4	1.8	.824							
CF	M. Tiernan	553	.304	13	59	210	13	26	5	1.9	.896							
LF	J. Hornung	513	.238	0	65	110	12	9	3	1.7	.931							
C	D. Buckley	266	.256	2	26	365	93	34	4	7.9	.931							
UT	A. Clarke	395	.225	0	49	288	138	55	11		.886							
P	A. Rusie	284	.278	0	28	25	**129**	**20**	5	2.6	.885							
1B	D. Esterbrook	197	.289	0	29	430	13	7	24	10.0	.984							
OF	J. Henry	144	.243	0	16	56	4	9	1	1.9	.870							

Cleveland

W-44 L-88

Gus Schmelz
W-21 L-55

Bob Leadley
W-23 L-33

POS	Player	AB	BA	HR	RBI	PO	A	E	DP	TC/G	FA	Pitcher	G	IP	W	L	SV	ERA
1B	P. Veach	238	.235	0	32	634	40	20	37	10.8	.971	E. Beatin	54	474	22	30	0	3.83
2B	J. Ardner	323	.223	0	35	205	257	40	42	6.0	.920	J. Wadsworth	20	170	2	16	0	5.20
SS	E. McKean	530	.296	7	61	266	433	**75**	46	5.8	.903	C. Young	17	148	9	7	0	3.47
3B	W. Smalley	502	.213	0	42	**221**	**327**	**64**	**27**	4.5	.895	E. Lincoln	15	118	3	11	0	4.42
RF	V. Dailey	246	.289	0	32	103	13	19	2	2.1	.859	L. Viau	13	107	4	9	0	3.36
CF	G. Davis	526	.264	6	73	282	35	18	9	2.5	.946							
LF	B. Gilks	544	.213	0	41	237	20	16	2	2.2	.941							
C	C. Zimmer	444	.214	2	57	480	**188**	**45**	**14**	5.7	.937							
1B	J. Virtue	223	.305	2	25	633	21	12	33	10.7	.982							
P	E. Beatin	191	.141	1	21	30	101	8	**7**	2.6	.942							
O1	T. Dowse	159	.208	0	9	140	10	8	10		.949							
OF	B. West	151	.245	2	29	50	9	12	1	1.9	.831							

NATIONAL LEAGUE 1890, *cont.*

Pittsburgh

W-23 L-113

Guy Hecker

POS	Player	AB	BA	HR	RBI	PO	A	E	DP	TC/G	FA	Pitcher	G	IP	W	L	SV	ERA
1B	G. Hecker	340	.226	0	38	610	31	25	26	9.7	.962	K. Baker	25	178	3	19	0	5.60
2B	S. LaRoque	434	.242	1	40	227	244	38	32	6.5	.925	G. Hecker	14	120	2	9	0	5.11
SS	E. Sales	189	.228	1	23	85	151	35	10	5.3	.871	D. Anderson	13	108	2	11	0	4.67
3B	D. Miller	549	.273	4	66	127	213	60	18	**4.5**	.850	B. Sowders	15	106	3	8	0	4.42
RF	B. Sunday	358	.257	1	33	181	23	27	9	2.7	.883	C. Schmit	11	83	1	9	0	5.83
CF	T. Berger	391	.266	0	40	72	11	8	1	2.2	.912	B. Phillips	10	82	1	9	0	7.57
LF	J. Kelty	207	.237	1	27	100	6	12	1	2.0	.898	B. Gumbert	10	79	4	6	0	5.22
C	H. Decker	354	.274	5	38	267	72	34	5	5.3	.909							
UT	B. Wilson	304	.214	0	21	409	90	60	22		.893							
3B	F. Roat	215	.223	2	17	64	102	30	9	4.5	.847							
OF	F. Osborne	168	.238	1	14	64	8	15	0	2.5	.828							

BATTING AND BASE RUNNING LEADERS

Batting Average
J. Glasscock, NY .336
B. Hamilton, PHI .325
J. Clements, PHI .315
D. O'Brien, BKN .314
S. Thompson, PHI .313

Slugging Average
M. Tiernan, NY .495
J. Clements, PHI .472
L. Reilly, CIN .472
O. Burns, BKN .464
J. Burkett, NY .461

Home Runs
W. Wilmot, CHI 14
O. Burns, BKN 13
M. Tiernan, NY 13
H. Long, BOS 8

Total Bases
M. Tiernan, NY 274
L. Reilly, CIN 261
S. Thompson, PHI 243
W. Wilmot, CHI 240
J. Glasscock, NY 225

Runs Batted In
O. Burns, BKN 128
C. Anson, CHI 107
S. Thompson, PHI 102
W. Wilmot, CHI 99
D. Foutz, BKN 98

Stolen Bases
B. Hamilton, PHI 102
B. Sunday, PIT, PHI 86
H. Collins, BKN 85
W. Wilmot, CHI 76
M. Tiernan, NY 56

Hits
J. Glasscock, NY 172
S. Thompson, PHI 172
M. Tiernan, NY 168
L. Reilly, CIN 166
C. Carroll, CHI 166

Base on Balls
C. Anson, CHI 113
B. Allen, PHI 87
E. McKean, CLE 87
H. Collins, BKN 85

Home Run Percentage
O. Burns, BKN 2.8
W. Wilmot, CHI 2.5
M. Tiernan, NY 2.4
H. Long, BOS 1.9

Runs
H. Collins, BKN 148
C. Carroll, CHI 134
B. Hamilton, PHI 133
M. Tiernan, NY 132

Doubles
S. Thompson, PHI 41
H. Collins, BKN 32
J. Glasscock, NY 32
A. Myers, PHI 29

Triples
L. Reilly, CIN 26
B. McPhee, CIN 22
M. Tiernan, NY 21
O. Beard, CIN 15

PITCHING LEADERS

Winning Percentage
T. Lovett, BKN .732
K. Gleason, PHI .691
P. Luby, CHI .690
B. Caruthers, BKN .676
B. Hutchinson, CHI .627

Earned Run Average
B. Rhines, CIN 1.95
K. Nichols, BOS 2.21
T. Mullane, CIN 2.24
A. Rusie, NY 2.56
K. Gleason, PHI 2.63

Wins
B. Hutchinson, CHI 42
K. Gleason, PHI 38
T. Lovett, BKN 30
A. Rusie, NY 29
B. Rhines, CIN 28

Saves
D. Foutz, BKN 2
K. Gleason, PHI 2
B. Hutchinson, CHI 2

Strikeouts
A. Rusie, NY 341
B. Hutchinson, CHI 289
K. Nichols, BOS 222
K. Gleason, PHI 222
A. Terry, BKN 185

Complete Games
B. Hutchinson, CHI 65
A. Rusie, NY 56
K. Gleason, PHI 54
E. Beatin, CLE 53
K. Nichols, BOS 47

Fewest Hits/9 Innings
A. Rusie, NY 7.15
T. Mullane, CIN 7.54
B. Hutchinson, CHI 7.54
B. Rhines, CIN 7.56

Shutouts
K. Nichols, BOS 7
B. Rhines, CIN 6
K. Gleason, PHI 6
B. Hutchinson, CHI 5

Fewest Walks/9 Innings
C. Young, CLE 1.83
J. Duryea, CIN 1.97
C. Getzien, BOS 2.11
K. Nichols, BOS 2.36

Most Strikeouts/9 Inn.
A. Rusie, NY 5.59
K. Nichols, BOS 4.68
A. Terry, BKN 4.50
B. Hutchinson, CHI 4.31

Innings
B. Hutchinson, CHI 603
A. Rusie, NY 549
K. Gleason, PHI 506
E. Beatin, CLE 474

Games Pitched
B. Hutchinson, CHI 71
A. Rusie, NY 67
K. Gleason, PHI 60
E. Beatin, CLE 54

							Batting						Fielding			Pitching					
	W	L	PCT	GB	R	OR	2B	3B	HR	BA	SA	SB	E	DP	FA	CG	BB	SO	ShO	SV	ERA
Brooklyn	86	43	.667		**884**	620	184	75	43	.264	**.369**	**349**	**320**	92	**.940**	115	401	403	6	2	3.05
Chicago	84	53	.613	6	847	692	146	59	**68**	.260	.356	329	344	89	**.940**	126	481	504	6	**3**	3.24
Philadelphia	78	54	.591	9.5	823	707	**220**	78	23	**.269**	.364	335	398	**122**	.929	122	486	507	8	2	3.32
Cincinnati	77	55	.583		753	633	150	**120**	28	.259	.361	312	382	106	.932	124	407	488	9	1	**2.79**
Boston	76	57	.571		763	**593**	175	62	31	.258	.341	285	359	77	.934	**132**	**354**	506	**13**	1	2.93
New York	63	68	.481	12	713	698	208	89	25	.259	.354	289	449	104	.921	115	607	**612**	6	1	3.06
Cleveland	44	88	.333	31.5	630	832	132	59	21	.232	.299	152	405	108	.929	129	462	306	2	0	4.13
Pittsburgh	23	113	.169	54.5	597	1235	160	43	20	.230	.294	208	607	94	.896	119	573	381	3	0	*5.97*
					6010	6010	1375	585	259	.254	.342	2259	3264	792	.928	982	3771	3707	53	10	*3.56*

AMERICAN ASSOCIATION 1890

Louisville

W-88 L-44

Jack Chapman

POS	Player	AB	BA	HR	RBI	PO	A	E	DP	TC/G	FA	Pitcher	G	IP	W	L	SV	ERA
1B	H. Taylor	553	.306	0		1301	51	25	54	**11.7**	.982	S. Stratton	50	431	34	14	0	**2.36**
2B	T. Shinnick	493	.256	1		288	351	52	42	5.3	.925	R. Ehret	43	359	25	14	2	*2.53*
SS	P. Tomney	386	.277	1		180	406	64	31	**6.0**	.902	G. Meakim	28	192	12	7	1	*2.91*
3B	H. Raymond	521	.259	2		182	241	61	18	4.1	.874	H. Goodall	18	109	8	5	**4**	*3.39*
RF	C. Wolf	543	**.363**	4		199	16	14	5	1.9	.939							
CF	F. Weaver	557	.289	3		227	23	18	4	2.1	.933							
LF	C. Hamburg	485	.272	3		229	16	14	3	1.9	.946							
C	J. Ryan	337	.217	0		415	148	**41**	5	6.8	.932							
P	S. Stratton	189	.323	0		18	111	3	2	2.6	.977							
P	R. Ehret	146	.212	0		9	64	12	2	2.0	.859							

AMERICAN ASSOCIATION 1890, *cont.*

Columbus

W-79 L-55

Al Buckenberger
W-39 L-41

Gus Schmelz
W-38 L-13

Pat Sullivan
W-2 L-1

POS	Player	AB	BA	HR	RBI	PO	A	E	DP	TC/G	FA
1B	M. Lehane	512	.211	0		**1430**	**73**	27	**80**	10.9	**.982**
2B	J. Crooks	485	.221	1		348	345	46	57	5.6	.938
SS	H. Easterday	197	.157	0		82	202	39	20	5.6	.879
3B	C. Reilly	530	.266	4		**205**	**354**	**67**	**26**	**4.6**	.893
RF	J. Sneed	484	.291	2		161	20	24	5	1.6	.883
CF	J. McTamany	466	.258	1		232	17	16	8	2.1	.940
LF	S. Johnson	538	.346	1		164	12	14	1	1.4	.926
C	J. O'Connor	457	.324	2		**539**	146	27	**13**	6.7	**.962**
UT	J. Doyle	298	.268	2		231	153	54	14		.877
SS	B. Wheelock	190	.237	1		92	162	33	12	5.5	.885
P	H. Gastright	169	.213	0		12	55	5	2	1.5	.931

Pitcher	G	IP	W	L	SV	ERA
H. Gastright	48	401	30	14	0	*2.94*
F. Knauss	37	276	17	12	2	*2.81*
J. Easton	37	256	15	14	1	*3.52*
I. Chamberlain	25	175	12	6	0	*2.21*
W. Widner	13	96	4	8	0	*3.28*

St. Louis

W-78 L-58

Tommy McCarthy
W-10 L-8

Chief Roseman
W-17 L-19

Count Campau
W-26 L-14

Tommy McCarthy
W-4 L-1

Joe Gerhardt
W-20 L-16

POS	Player	AB	BA	HR	RBI	PO	A	E	DP	TC/G	FA
1B	E. Cartwright	300	.300	8		706	25	18	37	10.0	.976
2B	B. Higgins	258	.252	0		168	204	19	34	5.8	.951
SS	S. Fuller	526	.278	1		222	389	91	**39**	5.4	.870
3B	J. Davis	71	.254	0		23	53	28	2	5.0	.731
RF	T. McCarthy	548	.350	6		159	19	21	5	2.0	.894
CF	C. Duffee	378	.275	3		120	16	7	8	2.2	.951
LF	C. Campau	314	.322	**10**		113	14	9	1	1.8	.934
C	J. Munyan	342	.266	4		452	115	37	8	7.3	.939
OF	C. Roseman	302	.341	2		61	7	15	2	1.4	.819
OF	T. Gettinger	227	.238	3		62	8	9	1	1.4	.886
P	J. Stivetts	226	.288	7		24	86	13	3	2.3	.894
UT	P. Sweeney	190	.179	0		139	93	37	12		.862
P	T. Ramsey	145	.228	0		12	31	**16**	2	1.3	.729

Pitcher	G	IP	W	L	SV	ERA
J. Stivetts	54	419	27	21	0	*3.52*
T. Ramsey	44	349	24	17	0	*3.69*
B. Hart	26	201	12	8	0	*3.67*
B. Whitrock	16	105	5	6	1	*3.51*

Toledo

W-68 L-64

Charlie Morton

POS	Player	AB	BA	HR	RBI	PO	A	E	DP	TC/G	FA
1B	P. Werden	498	.295	6		1178	59	**35**	57	10.3	.972
2B	P. Nicholson	523	.268	4		294	385	52	45	5.5	.929
SS	F. Scheibeck	485	.241	1		**282**	**412**	**92**	35	5.9	.883
3B	B. Alvord	495	.273	2		203	252	**67**	13	4.5	.872
RF	E. Swartwood	462	.327	3		224	23	20	2	2.1	.925
CF	W. Tebeau	381	.268	1		182	14	10	1	2.2	.951
LF	B. Van Dyke	502	.257	2		172	17	16	0	1.9	.922
C	H. Sage	275	.149	2		336	**153**	27	3	6.4	.948
OP	C. Sprague	199	.236	1		60	18	8	1		.907
P	E. Healy	156	.218	1		24	62	14	2	2.2	.860

Pitcher	G	IP	W	L	SV	ERA
E. Healy	46	389	22	21	0	*2.89*
E. Cushman	40	316	17	21	1	*4.19*
F. Smith	35	286	19	13	0	*3.27*
C. Sprague	19	123	9	5	0	*3.89*

Rochester

W-63 L-63

Pat Powers

POS	Player	AB	BA	HR	RBI	PO	A	E	DP	TC/G	FA
1B	T. O'Brien	273	.190	0		675	20	21	40	10.5	.971
2B	B. Greenwood	437	.222	2		331	343	**59**	59	6.0	.920
SS	M. Phillips	257	.206	0		101	222	29	24	5.5	.918
3B	J. Knowles	491	.281	5		162	303	63	19	4.3	.881
RF	T. Scheffler	445	.245	3		196	29	22	6	2.1	.911
CF	S. Griffin	407	.307	5		159	7	28	1	1.8	.856
LF	H. Lyons	**584**	.260	3		264	25	25	4	2.4	.920
C	D. McGuire	331	.299	4		389	99	32	9	**7.3**	.938
C	D. McKeough	218	.225	0		186	76	20	4	6.0	.929
P	B. Barr	201	.179	2		20	111	10	2	2.5	.929
UT	J. Grim	192	.266	2		151	99	27	15		.903
1B	J. Field	188	.202	4		486	12	18	24	10.1	.965
P	W. Callahan	159	.145	1		14	71	9	6	2.5	.904

Pitcher	G	IP	W	L	SV	ERA
B. Barr	57	493	28	**24**	0	*3.25*
W. Callahan	37	296	18	15	0	*3.28*
C. Titcomb	20	169	10	9	0	*3.74*
B. Miller	13	92	3	7	1	*4.29*
J. Fitzgerald	11	78	3	8	0	4.04

Baltimore

W-15 L-19

Billy Barnie

POS	Player	AB	BA	HR	RBI	PO	A	E	DP	TC/G	FA
1B	T. Power	125	.208	0		259	7	11	8	10.7	.960
2B	R. Mack	95	.284	0		62	76	10	7	5.7	.932
SS	I. Ray	139	.360	1		40	104	17	7	4.2	.894
3B	P. Gilbert	100	.280	1		34	55	10	5	3.4	.899
RF	B. Johnson	95	.295	0		39	6	7	3	2.2	.865
CF	D. Long	77	.156	0		26	5	2	0	1.6	.939
LF	J. Sommer	129	.256	0		69	5	9	3	2.2	.892
C	G. Townsend	67	.239	0		72	34	8	2	6.3	.930
C1	P. Tate	71	.183	0		112	18	7	3		.949
OF	C. Welch	68	.132	0		35	3	1	1*	2.3*	.974
P	L. German	51	.118	0		3	21	4	0	1.6	.857
C	W. Robinson	48	.271	0		83	11	1	3*	8.6	.989
P	S. McMahon	39	.103	0		2*	27*	3	1*	2.7	.906

Pitcher	G	IP	W	L	SV	ERA
L. German	17	132	5	11	0	4.84
S. McMahon	12*	99*	7*	3	0	3.09

Syracuse

W-55 L-72

George Frazer
W-31 L-40

Wally Fessenden
W-4 L-7

George Frazer
W-20 L-25

POS	Player	AB	BA	HR	RBI	PO	A	E	DP	TC/G	FA
1B	M. McQuery	461	.308	2		1146	45	34	63	10.0	.972
2B	C. Childs	493	.345	2		372	367	57	59	6.4	.928
SS	B. McLaughlin	329	.264	2		120	258	41	22	4.9	**.902**
3B	T. O'Rourke	332	.283	1		117	168	44	9	3.8	.866
RF	P. Friel	261	.249	3		77	7	8	2	1.5	.913
CF	R. Wright	348	.305	0		170	15	19	7	2.3	.907
LF	B. Ely	496	.262	0		179	14	18	1	2.7	.915
C	G. Briggs	316	.180	0		200	71	21	6	6.3	.928
P	D. Casey	160	.163	0		22	78	14	4	2.5	.877
P	J. Keefe	157	.191	0		14	71	4	2	2.1	.955
OF	H. Simon	156	.301	2		62	2	4	1	1.8	.941
C	T. O'Rourke	153	.216	0		187	48	24	6	6.5	.907

Pitcher	G	IP	W	L	SV	ERA
D. Casey	45	361	19	22	0	*4.14*
J. Keefe	43	352	17	**24**	0	*4.32*
M. Morrison	17	127	6	9	0	*5.88*
E. Mars	16	121	9	5	0	*4.67*

AMERICAN ASSOCIATION 1890, *cont.*

Philadelphia

W-54 L-78

Bill Sharsig

POS	Player	AB	BA	HR	RBI	PO	A	E	DP	TC/G	FA	Pitcher	G	IP	W	L	SV	ERA
1B	J. O'Brien	433	.261	4		1018	52	26	61	10.1	.976	S. McMahon	48*	410*	29*	18	1	3.34
2B	T. Shaffer	261	.172	0		214	195	35	39	6.4	.921	E. Green	25	191	7	15	1	*5.80*
SS	B. Conroy	404	.171	0		119	257	45	26	5.7	.893	E. Seward	21	154	5	12	0	*4.73*
3B	D. Lyons	339	.354	7		147	203	35	14	4.4	**.909**	D. Esper	18	144	8	9	0	*4.89*
RF	O. Shaffer	390	.282	1		143	17	7	6	1.7	.958	C. Stecher	10	68	0	10	0	*10.32*
CF	C. Welch	396	.268	2		225	23	22	8	2.6	.919							
LF	B. Purcell	463	.276	2		170	17	10	3	1.8	.949							
C	W. Robinson	329	.237	4		412	103	39	10*	6.8	.930							
UT	J. Kappel	208	.240	1		75	92	31	8		.843							
P	S. McMahon	175	.229	2		29*	112*	8	6*	3.1	.946							

Brooklyn

W-26 L-72

Jim Kennedy

POS	Player	AB	BA	HR	RBI	PO	A	E	DP	TC/G	FA	Pitcher	G	IP	W	L	SV	ERA
1B	B. O'Brien	388	.278	4		1015	35	29	66	11.2	.973	E. Daily	27	235	10	15	0	3.95
2B	J. Gerhardt	369	.203	3		359*	348*	47	67*	7.6*	.938*	C. McCullough	26	216	4	21	0	4.59
SS	C. Nelson	223	.251	0		60	198	40	20	5.2	.866	M. Mattimore	19	178	6	13	0	4.44
3B	J. Davis	142	.303	2		49	87	25	9	4.2	.845	C. Murphy	12	95	3	9	0	5.78
RF	E. Daily	394	.239	1		107	17	15	3	2.2	.892							
CF	J. Peltz	384	.227	1		207	18	24	6	2.5	.904							
LF	H. Simon	373	.257	0		176	17	10	4	2.3	.951							
C	J. Toy	160	.181	0		148	86	36	4	6.1	.867							
UT	F. Bowes	232	.220	0		164	67	35	8		.868							
UT	H. Pitz	189	.138	0		156	88	43	6		.850							
SS	F. Fennelly	178	.247	2		70	135	34	8	6.3	.858							

BATTING AND BASE RUNNING LEADERS

Batting Average
- C. Wolf, LOU .363
- D. Lyons, PHI .354
- T. McCarthy, STL .350
- S. Johnson, COL .346
- C. Childs, SYR .345

Slugging Average
- D. Lyons, PHI .531
- C. Childs, SYR .481
- C. Wolf, LOU .479
- T. McCarthy, STL .467
- S. Johnson, COL .461

Home Runs
- C. Campau, STL 10
- E. Cartwright, STL 8
- J. Stivetts, STL 7
- D. Lyons, PHI 7
- P. Werden, TOL 6
- T. McCarthy, STL 6

Total Bases
- C. Wolf, LOU 260
- T. McCarthy, STL 256
- S. Johnson, COL 248
- C. Childs, SYR 237
- P. Werden, TOL 227

Runs Batted In
- (not available)

Stolen Bases
- T. McCarthy, STL 83
- T. Scheffler, ROC 77
- B. Van Dyke, TOL 73
- C. Welch, PHI, BAL 72
- E. Daily, BKN, LOU 62
- T. Shinnick, LOU 62

Hits
- C. Wolf, LOU 197
- T. McCarthy, STL 192
- S. Johnson, COL 186
- C. Childs, SYR 170

Base on Balls
- J. McTamany, COL 112
- J. Crooks, COL 96
- E. Swartwood, TOL 80
- T. Scheffler, ROC 78
- P. Werden, TOL 78

Home Run Percentage
- D. Lyons, PHI 2.1
- S. Griffin, ROC 1.2
- D. McGuire, ROC 1.2
- P. Werden, TOL 1.2

Runs
- J. McTamany, COL 140
- T. McCarthy, STL 137
- S. Fuller, STL 118
- J. Sneed, TOL, COL 117

Doubles
- C. Childs, SYR 33
- D. Lyons, PHI 29
- C. Wolf, LOU 29

Triples
- P. Werden, TOL 20
- S. Johnson, COL 18
- B. Alvord, TOL 16
- J. Sneed, TOL, COL 15

PITCHING LEADERS

Winning Percentage
- S. Stratton, LOU .708
- H. Gastright, COL .682
- I. Chamberlain, STL, COL .682
- R. Ehret, LOU .641
- S. McMahon, PHI, BAL .632
- G. Meakim, LOU .632

Earned Run Average
- S. Stratton, LOU *2.36*
- R. Ehret, LOU *2.53*
- F. Knauss, COL *2.81*
- I. Chamberlain, STL, COL *2.83*
- E. Healy, TOL *2.89*

Wins
- S. McMahon, PHI, BAL 36
- S. Stratton, LOU 34
- H. Gastright, COL 30
- B. Barr, ROC 28
- J. Stivetts, STL 27

Saves
- H. Goodall, LOU 4
- F. Knauss, COL 2
- R. Ehret, LOU 2

Strikeouts
- S. McMahon, PHI, BAL 291
- J. Stivetts, STL 289
- T. Ramsey, STL 257
- E. Healy, TOL 225
- B. Barr, ROC 209

Complete Games
- S. McMahon, PHI, BAL 55
- B. Barr, ROC 52
- E. Healy, TOL 44
- S. Stratton, LOU 44
- H. Gastright, COL 41
- J. Stivetts, STL 41

Fewest Hits/9 Innings
- F. Knauss, COL 6.73
- H. Gastright, COL 7.00
- J. Easton, COL 7.50
- I. Chamberlain, STL, COL 7.50

Shutouts
- I. Chamberlain, STL, COL 6
- R. Ehret, LOU 4
- H. Gastright, COL 4
- S. Stratton, LOU 4

Fewest Walks/9 Innings
- S. Stratton, LOU 1.27
- R. Ehret, LOU 1.98
- T. Ramsey, STL 2.63
- F. Smith, TOL 2.83

Most Strikeouts/9 Inn.
- T. Ramsey, STL 6.63
- J. Stivetts, STL 6.20
- G. Meakim, LOU 5.77
- I. Chamberlain, STL, COL 5.49

Innings
- S. McMahon, PHI, BAL 509
- B. Barr, ROC 493
- S. Stratton, LOU 431
- J. Stivetts, STL 419

Games Pitched
- S. McMahon, PHI, BAL 60
- B. Barr, ROC 57
- J. Stivetts, STL 54
- S. Stratton, LOU 50

							Batting						Fielding			Pitching					
	W	L	PCT	GB	R	OR	2B	3B	HR	BA	SA	SB	E	DP	FA	CG	BB	SO	ShO	SV	ERA
Louisville	88	44	.667		819	588	156	65	15	**.279**	.350	341	380	79	**.933**	114	293	587	13	**7**	***2.58***
Columbus	79	55	.590	10	831	617	159	78	15	.258	.334	353	401	**101**	.931	120	471	624	**14**	3	*2.99*
St. Louis	78	58	.574	12	**870**	736	178	72	**49**	.273	**.370**	307	478	93	.916	118	447	**733**	4	1	*3.67*
Toledo	68	64	.515	20	739	689	152	**108**	24	.252	.348	**421**	419	75	.925	**122**	429	533	4	2	*3.56*
Rochester	63	63	.500	22	709	711	131	64	31	.239	.316	310	416	95	.926	**122**	530	477	5	2	*3.56*
Baltimore	15	19	.441	24	182	**192**	34	16	2	.229	.289	101	**109**	21	.928	36	**123**	134	1	0	*4.03*
Syracuse	55	72	.433	30.5	698	831	151	59	14	.259	.329	292	391	90	.925	115	518	454	5	0	*4.98*
Philadelphia	54	78	.409	34	702	945	**181**	51	24	.235	.314	305	452	93	.918	119	514	461	3	2	*5.22*
Brooklyn	26	72	.265	45	492	733	116	46	14	.221	.293	182	403	92	.909	96	421	230	0	0	*4.78*
					6042	6042	1258	559	188	.249	.327	2612	3449	739	.923	962	3746	4233	49	17	*3.93*

PLAYERS LEAGUE 1890

Boston

W-81 L-48

King Kelly

POS	Player	AB	BA	HR	RBI	PO	A	E	DP	TC/G	FA	Pitcher	G	IP	W	L	SV	ERA
1B	D. Brouthers	460	.330	1	97	1187	73	**49**	78	10.6	.963	O. Radbourn	41	343	27	12	0	3.31
2B	J. Quinn	509	.301	7	82	431	395	51	70	6.7	**.942**	A. Gumbert	39	277	23	12	0	3.96
SS	A. Irwin	354	.260	0	45	137	331	65	44	5.6	.878	B. Daley	34	235	18	7	2	3.60
3B	B. Nash	488	.266	5	90	198	**307**	78	**37**	4.5	.866	M. Kilroy	30	218	9	15	1	4.26
RF	H. Stovey	481	.297	12	83	186	24	18	3	1.7	.921							
CF	T. Brown	543	.276	4	61	276	32	30	8	2.6	.911							
LF	H. Richardson	555	.326	13	**146**	235	13	13	3	2.1	.950							
C	M. Murphy	246	.228	2	32	257	59	34	8	5.2	.903							
UT	K. Kelly	340	.326	4	66	274	145	55	12		.884							
P	O. Radbourn	154	.253	0	16	16	99	8	4	3.0	.935							
P	A. Gumbert	145	.241	3	20	15	83	13	0	2.8	.883							

Brooklyn

W-76 L-56

Monte Ward

POS	Player	AB	BA	HR	RBI	PO	A	E	DP	TC/G	FA	Pitcher	G	IP	W	L	SV	ERA
1B	D. Orr	464	.373	6	124	1009	42	30	67	10.1	.972	G. Weyhing	49	390	30	16	0	3.60
2B	L. Bierbauer	589	.306	7	99	372	**468**	62	**77**	6.8	.931	J. Sowders	39	309	19	16	0	3.82
SS	M. Ward	561	.337	4	60	**303**	**450**	105	59	**6.7**	.878	G. Van Haltren	28	223	15	10	2	4.28
3B	B. Joyce	489	.252	1	78	176	284	**107**	22	4.3	.811	C. Murphy	20	139	4	10	2	4.79
RF	J. McGeachy	443	.244	1	65	206	16	23	1	2.4	.906	G. Hemming	19	123	8	4	3*	3.80
CF	E. Andrews	395	.253	3	38	220	17	23	3	2.8	.912							
LF	E. Seery	394	.223	1	50	216	21	28	3	2.5	.894							
C	T. Kinslow	242	.264	4	46	298	72	37	7	6.4	.909							
OP	G. Van Haltren	376	.335	5	54	138	84	21	6		.914							
C1	P. Cook	218	.252	0	31	319	57	30	20		.926							
C	C. Daily	168	.250	0	35	141	34	24	5	5.0	.879							
P	G. Weyhing	165	.164	1	15	12	55	12	2	1.6	.848							
P	J. Sowders	132	.189	1	20	7	75	7	1	2.3	.921							

New York

W-74 L-57

Buck Ewing

POS	Player	AB	BA	HR	RBI	PO	A	E	DP	TC/G	FA	Pitcher	G	IP	W	L	SV	ERA
1B	R. Connor	484	.349	**14**	103	**1335**	**80**	21	**79**	**11.7**	**.985**	C. Crane	43	330	16	19	1	4.63
2B	D. Shannon	324	.216	3	44	162	262	43	35	6.1	.908	H. O'Day	43	329	22	13	**3**	4.21
SS	D. Richardson	528	.256	4	80	153	263	46	33	6.8	.900	J. Ewing	35	267	18	12	2	4.24
3B	A. Whitney	442	.219	0	45	129	172	47	11	4.0	.865	T. Keefe	30	229	17	11	0	3.38
RF	J. O'Rourke	478	.360	9	115	175	25	15	3	1.9	.930							
CF	G. Gore	399	.318	10	55	146	11	22	3	1.9	.877							
LF	M. Slattery	411	.307	5	67	175	5	19	1	2.1	.905							
C	B. Ewing	352	.338	8	72	372	107	26	7	6.2	**.949**							
OF	D. Johnston	306	.242	1	43	164	18	21	3	2.7	.897							
3S	G. Hatfield	287	.279	1	37	79	156	54	13		.813							
UT	W. Brown	230	.278	4	43	241	49	26	5		.918							
CO	F. Vaughn	166	.265	1	22	112	21	18	3		.881							
P	H. O'Day	150	.227	1	23	11	71	7	0	2.1	.921							
P	C. Crane	146	.315	0	16	17	71	16	0	2.4	.846							

Chicago

W-75 L-62

Charlie Comiskey

POS	Player	AB	BA	HR	RBI	PO	A	E	DP	TC/G	FA	Pitcher	G	IP	W	L	SV	ERA
1B	C. Comiskey	377	.244	0	59	882	41	33	52	10.9	.965	M. Baldwin	**59**	**501**	**34**	24	0	3.31
2B	F. Pfeffer	499	.257	5	80	**441**	387	**76**	73	**7.3**	.916	S. King	56	461	30	22	0	**2.69**
SS	C. Bastian	283	.191	0	29	85	202	39	24	5.1	.880	C. Bartson	25	188	8	10	1	4.26
3B	A. Latham	214	.229	1	20	65	119	25	9	4.0	.880	F. Dwyer	12	69	3	6	1	6.23
RF	H. Duffy	**596**	.320	7	82	255	34	26	5	2.3	.917							
CF	J. Ryan	486	.340	6	89	257	25	25	5	2.6	.919							
LF	T. O'Neill	577	.302	3	75	231	8	19	1	1.9	.926							
C	D. Farrell	451	.290	2	84	428	132	43	12	**6.7**	.929							
UT	J. Boyle	369	.260	1	49	335	154	61	16		.889							
3B	N. Williamson	261	.195	1	26	53	91	34	6	3.4	.809							
UT	D. Darling	221	.258	2	39	296	72	37	24		.909							
P	M. Baldwin	215	.209	1	25	**26**	**146**	15	2	3.2	.920							
P	S. King	185	.168	1	16	22	139	6	**5**	3.0	.964							

Philadelphia

W-68 L-63

Jim Fogarty
W-7 L-9

Charlie Buffinton
W-61 L-54

POS	Player	AB	BA	HR	RBI	PO	A	E	DP	TC/G	FA	Pitcher	G	IP	W	L	SV	ERA
1B	S. Farrar	481	.254	1	69	1238	58	36	**79**	10.5	.973	B. Sanders	43	347	19	18	1	3.76
2B	J. Pickett	407	.280	4	64	236	284	62	46	5.8	.893	P. Knell	35	287	22	11	0	3.83
SS	B. Shindle	584	.322	10	90	266	442	**119**	**67**	6.4	.856	C. Buffinton	36	283	19	15	1	3.81
3B	J. Mulvey	519	.287	6	87	144	227	62	15	3.6	.857	B. Husted	18	129	5	10	0	4.88
RF	J. Fogarty	347	.239	4	58	192	17	8	3	2.4	.963	B. Cunningham	14	109	3	9	0	5.22
CF	M. Griffin	489	.286	6	54	278	33	15	10	2.8	.954							
LF	G. Wood	539	.289	9	102	254	35	34	9	2.4	.895							
C	J. Milligan	234	.295	3	57	260	66	39	**13**	6.2	.893							
UT	B. Hallman	356	.267	1	37	194	103	36	15		.892							
C	L. Cross	245	.298	3	47	191	70	34	7	6.0	.885							
P	B. Sanders	189	.312	0	30	17	93	9	**5**	2.8	.924							
P	C. Buffinton	150	.273	1	24	12	77	14	**5**	2.9	.864							

Pittsburgh

W-60 L-68

Ned Hanlon

POS	Player	AB	BA	HR	RBI	PO	A	E	DP	TC/G	FA	Pitcher	G	IP	W	L	SV	ERA
1B	J. Beckley	516	.324	10	120	1256	58	32	61	11.1	.976	H. Staley	46	388	21	25	0	3.23
2B	Y. Robinson	306	.229	0	38	226	286	65	46	5.9	.887	A. Maul	30	247	16	12	0	3.79
SS	T. Corcoran	503	.233	1	61	210	431	84	36	5.9	.884	P. Galvin	26	217	12	13	0	4.35
3B	W. Kuehne	528	.239	5	73	159	304	82	18	4.3	.850	E. Morris	18	144	8	7	0	4.86
RF	J. Visner	521	.265	3	71	198	18	26	4	1.9	.893	J. Tener	14	117	3	11	0	7.31
CF	N. Hanlon	472	.278	1	44	291	15	30	4	2.8	.911							
LF	J. Fields	526	.283	9	86	153	21	24	3	2.5	.879							
C	F. Carroll	416	.298	2	71	206	50	43	1	5.3	.856							
C	T. Quinn	207	.213	1	15	203	58	33	3	5.3	.888							
P	H. Staley	164	.207	1	25	11	86	6	**5**	2.2	.942							
PO	A. Maul	162	.259	0	21	49	83	15	5		.898							

PLAYERS LEAGUE 1890, *cont.*

Cleveland

W-55 L-75

Henry Larkin
W-34 L-45

Patsy Tebeau
W-21 L-30

POS	Player	AB	BA	HR	RBI	PO	A	E	DP	TC/G	FA	Pitcher	G	IP	W	L	SV	ERA
1B	H. Larkin	506	.332	5	112	1268	40	30	63	10.7	.978	H. Gruber	48	383	22	23	1	4.27
2B	C. Stricker	544	.244	2	65	295	353	68	57	6.6	.905	J. Bakely	43	326	12	25	0	4.47
SS	E. Delahanty	517	.298	3	64	143	244	79	33	6.1	.830	D. O'Brien	25	206	8	16	0	3.40
3B	P. Tebeau	450	.300	5	74	**204**	246	66	25	**4.7**	**.872**	W. McGill	24	184	11	9	0	4.12
RF	P. Radford	466	.292	2	62	137	16	18	5	2.1	.895							
CF	J. McAleer	341	.267	1	42	249	15	17	4	3.3	.940							
LF	P. Browning	493	**.373**	5	93	248	18	32	4	2.5	.893							
C	S. Sutcliffe	386	.329	2	60	264	115	**50**	9	5.1	.883							
C3	J. Brennan	233	.253	0	26	147	73	42	7		.840							
OF	L. Twitchell	233	.223	2	36	61	8	15	1	1.5	.821							
P	H. Gruber	163	.221	0	9	8	109	14	3	2.7	.893							
OF	J. Carney	89	.348	0	21	21	3	4	0	1.5	.857							

Buffalo

W-36 L-96

Jack Rowe
W-22 L-58

Jay Faatz
W-9 L-24

Jack Rowe
W-5 L-14

POS	Player	AB	BA	HR	RBI	PO	A	E	DP	TC/G	FA	Pitcher	G	IP	W	L	SV	ERA
1B	D. White	439	.260	0	47	582	40	19	33	11.2	.970	G. Haddock	35	291	9	**26**	0	5.76
2B	S. Wise	505	.293	6	102	328	375	73	58	6.5	.906	B. Cunningham	25	211	9	15	0	5.84
SS	J. Rowe	504	.250	2	76	228	381	67	56	5.4	**.901**	G. Keefe	25	196	6	16	0	6.52
3B	J. Irwin	308	.234	0	34	79	139	29	13	3.9	.883	L. Twitchell	12	104	5	7	0	4.57
RF	J. Halligan	211	.251	3	33	73	11	18	1	2.4	.824	G. Stafford	12	98	3	9	0	5.14
CF	D. Hoy	493	.298	1	53	289	23	30	9	2.8	.912							
LF	H. Beecher	536	.297	3	90	211	24	55	4	2.3	.810							
C	C. Mack	503	.266	0	53	**449**	**140**	48	**13**	5.7	.925							
UT	S. Clark	260	.265	1	25	168	63	19	14		.924							
OP	L. Twitchell	172	.221	2	17	49	37	7	1		.925							
UT	J. Rainey	166	.235	1	20	72	42	17	8		.870							
P	G. Haddock	146	.247	0	24	20	86	8	2	3.3	.930							

BATTING AND BASE RUNNING LEADERS

Batting Average
P. Browning, CLE .373
D. Orr, BKN .373
J. O'Rourke, NY .360
R. Connor, NY .349
J. Ryan, CHI .340

Slugging Average
R. Connor, NY .548
B. Ewing, NY .545
J. Beckley, PIT .541
D. Orr, BKN .537
P. Browning, CLE .517

Home Runs
R. Connor, NY 14
H. Richardson, BOS 13
H. Stovey, BOS 12
G. Gore, NY 10
J. Beckley, PIT 10
B. Shindle, PHI 10

Total Bases
B. Shindle, PHI 281
H. Duffy, CHI 280
J. Beckley, PIT 279
H. Richardson, BOS 274
R. Connor, NY 265

Runs Batted In
H. Richardson, BOS 146
D. Orr, BKN 124
J. Beckley, PIT 120
J. O'Rourke, NY 115
H. Larkin, CLE 112

Stolen Bases
H. Stovey, BOS 97
T. Brown, BOS 79
H. Duffy, CHI 78
N. Hanlon, PIT 65
M. Ward, BKN 63

Hits
H. Duffy, CHI 191
M. Ward, BKN 189
B. Shindle, PHI 188
P. Browning, CLE 184

Base on Balls
B. Joyce, BKN 123
Y. Robinson, PIT 101
D. Brouthers, BOS 99
D. Hoy, BUF 94

Home Run Percentage
R. Connor, NY 2.9
G. Gore, NY 2.5
H. Stovey, BOS 2.5
H. Richardson, BOS 2.3

Runs
H. Duffy, CHI 161
T. Brown, BOS 146
H. Stovey, BOS 142
M. Ward, BKN 134

Doubles
P. Browning, CLE 40
J. Beckley, PIT 38
J. O'Rourke, NY 37
D. Brouthers, BOS 36
H. Duffy, CHI 36

Triples
J. Beckley, PIT 22
J. Visner, PIT 22
B. Shindle, PHI 21
J. Fields, PIT 20

PITCHING LEADERS

Winning Percentage
B. Daley, BOS .720
O. Radbourn, BOS .692
P. Knell, PHI .667
A. Gumbert, BOS .657
G. Weyhing, BKN .652

Earned Run Average
S. King, CHI 2.69
H. Staley, PIT 3.23
M. Baldwin, CHI 3.31
O. Radbourn, BOS 3.31
T. Keefe, NY 3.38

Wins
M. Baldwin, CHI 34
G. Weyhing, BKN 30
S. King, CHI 30
O. Radbourn, BOS 27
A. Gumbert, BOS 23

Saves
G. Hemming, CLE, BKN 3
H. O'Day, NY 3
G. Van Haltren, BKN 2
J. Ewing, NY 2
C. Murphy, BKN 2
B. Daley, BOS 2

Strikeouts
M. Baldwin, CHI 211
S. King, CHI 185
G. Weyhing, BKN 177
J. Ewing, NY 145
H. Staley, PIT 145

Complete Games
M. Baldwin, CHI 54
S. King, CHI 48
H. Staley, PIT 44
H. Gruber, CLE 39
G. Weyhing, BKN 38

Fewest Hits/9 Innings
S. King, CHI 8.20
C. Crane, NY 8.80
G. Hemming, CLE, BKN 8.88
M. Baldwin, CHI 8.95

Shutouts
S. King, CHI 4
H. Staley, PIT 3
G. Weyhing, BKN 3

Fewest Walks/9 Innings
H. Staley, PIT 1.72
B. Sanders, PHI 1.79
P. Galvin, PIT 2.03
E. Morris, PIT 2.18

Most Strikeouts/9 Inn.
J. Ewing, NY 4.88
B. Daley, BOS 4.21
G. Weyhing, BKN 4.08
W. McGill, CLE 4.02

Innings
M. Baldwin, CHI 501
S. King, CHI 461
G. Weyhing, BKN 390
H. Staley, PIT 388

Games Pitched
M. Baldwin, CHI 59
S. King, CHI 56
G. Weyhing, BKN 49
H. Gruber, CLE 48

							Batting						Fielding			Pitching					
	W	L	PCT	GB	R	OR	2B	3B	HR	BA	SA	SB	E	DP	FA	CG	BB	SO	ShO	SV	ERA
Boston	81	48	.628		992	**767**	**223**	76	53	.282	.398	**412**	460	109	.918	105	467	345	6	2	3.79
Brooklyn	76	56	.576		964	893	186	93	34	.277	.374	272	531	114	.909	111	570	377	4	**7**	3.95
New York	74	57	.565		**1018**	875	204	97	**65**	.284	**.404**	231	**450**	94	**.921**	111	569	449	3	6	4.17
Chicago	75	62	.547		886	770	200	96	30	.264	.361	276	492	107	.918	124	503	**460**	5	2	**3.39**
Philadelphia	68	63	.519	4	941	855	187	**113**	49	.278	.393	203	510	**118**	.910	118	495	361	4	2	4.05
Pittsburgh	60	68	.469	10.5	835	892	168	**113**	36	.260	.370	249	512	80	.907	121	**334**	318	**7**	0	4.22
Cleveland	55	75	.423	16.5	849	1027	213	94	27	**.286**	.386	180	533	103	.907	115	571	325	1	1	4.23
Buffalo	36	96	.273	36.5	793	1199	180	64	20	.260	.337	160	491	116	.914	**125**	673	351	2	0	6.11
					7278	7278	1561	746	314	.274	.378	1983	3979	841	.913	930	4182	2986	32	20	4.24

NATIONAL LEAGUE 1891

Boston

W-87 L-51

Frank Selee

POS	Player	AB	BA	HR	RBI	PO	A	E	DP	TC/G	FA	Pitcher	G	IP	W	L	SV	ERA
1B	T. Tucker	548	.270	2	69	1313	55	34	66	10.0	.976	J. Clarkson	55	461	33	19	**3**	2.79
2B	J. Quinn	508	.240	3	63	275	364	42	44	5.5	.938	K. Nichols	52	426	30	17	**3**	2.39
SS	H. Long	577	.282	7	74	**345**	441	85	**60**	6.3	.902	H. Staley	31	252	20	8	0	2.50
3B	B. Nash	537	.276	5	95	**213**	264	53	20	3.8	.900							
RF	H. Stovey	544	.279	**16**	95	232	22	25	4	2.1	.910							
CF	S. Brodie	523	.260	2	78	268	25	15	9	2.3	.951							
LF	B. Lowe	497	.260	6	74	186	16	16	2	2.0	.927							
C	C. Bennett	256	.215	5	39	383	75	19	**10**	6.4	**.960**							
C	C. Ganzel	263	.259	1	29	288	59	16	3	6.2	.956							
P	J. Clarkson	187	.225	0	26	27	**114**	13	2	2.8	.916							
P	K. Nichols	183	.197	0	27	30	100	7	**5**	2.6	.949							

Chicago

W-82 L-53

Cap Anson

POS	Player	AB	BA	HR	RBI	PO	A	E	DP	TC/G	FA	Pitcher	G	IP	W	L	SV	ERA
1B	C. Anson	540	.291	8	**120**	1407	79	29	**86**	11.1	.981	B. Hutchinson	**66**	**561**	**44**	19	1	2.81
2B	F. Pfeffer	498	.247	7	77	**429**	474	77	**78**	**7.2**	.921	A. Gumbert	32	256	17	11	0	3.58
SS	J. Cooney	465	.245	0	42	145	433	52	39	5.3	**.917**	P. Luby	30	206	8	11	1	4.76
3B	B. Dahlen	549	.260	9	76	120	211	42	13	4.4	.887	E. Stein	14	101	7	6	0	3.74
RF	C. Carroll	515	.256	7	80	168	15	17	5	1.5	.915	T. Vickery	14	80	5	5	0	4.07
CF	J. Ryan	505	.277	9	66	231	25	27	3	2.4	.905							
LF	W. Wilmot	498	.279	11	71	223	15	20	0	2.1	.922							
C	M. Kittridge	296	.209	2	27	384	87	30	5	6.3	.940							
3B	T. Burns	243	.226	1	17	92	107	24	11	4.2	.892							
P	B. Hutchinson	243	.185	2	25	22	103	13	0	2.1	.906							
P	P. Luby	98	.245	2	24	8	42	2	2	1.7	**.962**							
C	P. Schriver	90	.333	1	21	135	27	6	3	6.2	.964							

New York

W-71 L-61

Jim Mutrie

POS	Player	AB	BA	HR	RBI	PO	A	E	DP	TC/G	FA	Pitcher	G	IP	W	L	SV	ERA
1B	R. Connor	479	.290	6	94	1362	56	25	77	11.2	.983	A. Rusie	61	500	33	20	1	2.55
2B	D. Richardson	516	.269	5	51	323	429	38	60	6.9	.952	J. Ewing	33	269	21	8	0	**2.27**
SS	J. Glasscock	369	.241	0	55	164	274	42	39	4.9	.912	M. Welch	22	160	6	9	1	4.28
3B	C. Bassett	524	.260	4	68	143	270	42	18	3.8	**.908**	J. Sharrott	10	69	4	5	1	2.60
RF	M. Tiernan	542	.306	**16**	73	138	16	17	4	1.3	.901							
CF	G. Gore	528	.284	2	48	234	16	25	3	2.1	.909							
LF	J. O'Rourke	555	.295	5	95	195	18	22	1	1.9	.906							
C	D. Buckley	253	.217	4	31	446	83	23	7	**7.5**	.958							
UT	L. Whistler	265	.245	4	38	143	128	49	11		.847							
P	A. Rusie	220	.245	0	15	10	106	**14**	4	2.1	.892							
C	A. Clarke	174	.190	0	21	189	50	22	6	6.2	.916							

Philadelphia

W-68 L-69

Harry Wright

POS	Player	AB	BA	HR	RBI	PO	A	E	DP	TC/G	FA	Pitcher	G	IP	W	L	SV	ERA
1B	W. Brown	441	.243	0	50	997	48	12	60	10.9	**.989**	K. Gleason	53	418	24	22	1	3.51
2B	A. Myers	514	.230	2	69	354	438	53	67	6.3	.937	D. Esper	39	296	20	15	1	3.56
SS	B. Allen	438	.221	1	51	258	426	79	50	**6.5**	.896	J. Thornton	37	269	15	16	2	3.68
3B	B. Shindle	415	.210	0	38	153	248	58	**24**	4.6	.874	T. Keefe	11	78	3	6	1	3.91
RF	S. Thompson	554	.294	8	90	234	32	18	6	2.1	.937							
CF	E. Delahanty	543	.243	4	86	199	22	22	3	2.5	.909							
LF	B. Hamilton	527	**.340**	2	60	287	17	31	7	2.5	.907							
C	J. Clements	423	.310	4	75	415	108	41	**10**	5.3	.927							
UT	E. Mayer	268	.187	0	31	100	105	29	4		.876							
P	K. Gleason	214	.248	0	17	22	73	11	2	2.0	.896							

Cleveland

W-65 L-74

Bob Leadley
W-34 L-34

Patsy Tebeau
W-31 L-40

POS	Player	AB	BA	HR	RBI	PO	A	E	DP	TC/G	FA	Pitcher	G	IP	W	L	SV	ERA
1B	J. Virtue	517	.261	2	72	**1465**	44	**44**	70	11.2	.972	C. Young	55	424	27	22	2	2.85
2B	C. Childs	551	.281	2	83	371	455	**82**	54	6.4	.910	H. Gruber	44	349	17	22	0	4.13
SS	E. McKean	**603**	.282	6	69	248	463	**91**	42	5.7	.887	L. Viau	45	344	18	17	0	3.01
3B	P. Tebeau	249	.261	1	41	102	150	33	13	4.7	.884							
RF	S. Johnson	327	.257	1	46	99	10	16	1	1.6	.872							
CF	G. Davis	570	.289	3	89	257	27	21	1	2.6	.931							
LF	J. McAleer	565	.237	2	61	284	19	25	1	2.4	.924							
C	C. Zimmer	440	.255	3	69	**476**	**181**	45	7	6.1	.936							
UT	J. Doyle	250	.276	0	43	178	73	38	5		.869							
P	C. Young	174	.167	1	18	10	89	9	0	2.0	.917							
OF	J. Burkett	167	.269	0	13	53	5	7	1	1.5	.892							
P	L. Viau	144	.160	0	6	12	79	**14**	2	2.3	.867							
P	H. Gruber	141	.163	1	20	8	90	10	**5**	2.5	.907							
3B	J. Denny	138	.225	0	21	39	60	13	1	3.9	.884							

Brooklyn

W-61 L-76

Monte Ward

POS	Player	AB	BA	HR	RBI	PO	A	E	DP	TC/G	FA	Pitcher	G	IP	W	L	SV	ERA
1B	D. Foutz	521	.257	2	73	1235	47	31	50	10.6	.976	T. Lovett	44	366	23	19	0	3.69
2B	H. Collins	435	.276	3	31	180	222	40	19	6.1	.910	B. Caruthers	38	297	18	14	1	3.12
SS	M. Ward	441	.277	0	39	180	296	66	28	6.2	.878	G. Hemming	27	200	8	15	1	4.96
3B	G. Pinckney	501	.273	2	71	146	261	43	10	3.5	.904	A. Terry	25	194	6	16	1	4.22
RF	O. Burns	470	.285	4	83	173	16	16	5	1.8	.922	B. Inks	13	96	3	10	0	4.02
CF	M. Griffin	521	.267	3	65	353	31	16	7	3.0	.960							
LF	D. O'Brien	395	.253	5	57	203	11	11	1	2.2	.951							
C	T. Kinslow	228	.237	0	33	252	54	26	6	5.4	.922							
C	C. Daily	206	.320	0	30	230	65	24	2	5.8	.925							
UT	T. Daly	200	.250	2	27	289	58	38	8		.901							
PO	B. Caruthers	171	.281	2	23	29	68	10	2		.907							
2B	J. O'Brien	167	.246	0	26	85	102	32	13	5.1	.854							
P	T. Lovett	153	.163	0	17	23	59	6	2	2.0	.932							

NATIONAL LEAGUE 1891, *cont.*

Team	POS	Player	AB	BA	HR	RBI	PO	A	E	DP	TC/G	FA	Pitcher	G	IP	W	L	SV	ERA
Cincinnati	1B	L. Reilly	546	.242	4	64	1104	26	21	60	**11.5**	.982	T. Mullane	51	426	23	26	0	3.23
	2B	B. McPhee	562	.256	6	38	389	**492**	42	72	6.7	**.954**	B. Rhines	48	373	17	24	1	2.87
	SS	G. Smith	512	.201	3	53	240	**507**	75	40	6.0	.909	O. Radbourn	26	218	11	13	0	4.25
W-56 L-81	3B	A. Latham	533	.272	7	53	177	**370**	**75**	**24**	**4.6**	.879	C. Crane	15	117	4	8	0	4.09*
	RF	L. Marr	286	.259	0	32	75	6	16	2	1.3	.835	J. Duryea	10	77	1	9	0	5.38
Tom Loftus	CF	B. Holliday	442	.319	9	84	186	13	13	3	1.9	.939							
	LF	P. Browning	216	.343	0	33	103	6	9	2	2.1	.924							
	C	J. Harrington	333	.228	2	41	388	106	**50**	6	5.9	.908							
	1C	J. Keenan	252	.202	4	33	587	51	30	22		.955							
	OF	J. Halligan	247	.312	3	44	89	6	16	1	1.8	.856							
	P	T. Mullane	209	.148	0	10	22	93	5	2	2.4	.958							
	OF	M. Slattery	158	.209	1	16	91	4	6	1	2.5	.941							
	P	B. Rhines	148	.122	0	5	8	95	7	3	2.3	.936							
Pittsburgh	1B	J. Beckley	554	.292	4	73	1250	**87**	24	63	10.2	.982	M. Baldwin	53	438	22	28	0	2.76
	2B	L. Bierbauer	500	.206	1	47	331	384	55	42	6.4	.929	S. King	48	384	14	**29**	1	3.11
	SS	F. Shugart	320	.275	2	33	172	235	44	34	6.0	.902	P. Galvin	33	247	14	13	0	2.88
W-55 L-80	3B	C. Reilly	415	.219	3	44	128	232	60	8	4.2	.857							
	RF	F. Carroll	353	.218	4	48	160	12	16	2	2.1	.915							
Ned Hanlon	CF	N. Hanlon	455	.266	0	60	219	25	33	1	2.3	.881							
W-31 L-47	LF	P. Browning	203	.291	4	28	115	8	13	0	2.7	.904							
	C	C. Mack	280	.214	0	29	359	79	35	1	6.6	.926							
Bill McGunnigle	UT	D. Miller	548	.285	4	57	339	238	80	13		.878							
W-24 L-33	P	M. Baldwin	177	.153	1	12	**37**	80	13	4	2.5	.900							
	OF	A. Maul	149	.188	0	14	58	7	9	2	1.9	.878							
	P	S. King	148	.169	0	9	19	67	10	**5**	2.0	.896							
	OF	P. Corkhill	145	.228	3	20	77	9	6	3	2.2	.935							
	OF	B. Lally	143	.224	1	17	45	2	9	0	1.4	.839							

BATTING AND BASE RUNNING LEADERS

Batting Average
B. Hamilton, PHI .340
B. Holliday, CIN .319
P. Browning, PIT, CIN .317
J. Clements, PHI .310
M. Tiernan, NY .306

Slugging Average
H. Stovey, BOS .498
M. Tiernan, NY .494
B. Holliday, CIN .473
R. Connor, NY .443
J. Ryan, CHI .434

Home Runs
M. Tiernan, NY 16
H. Stovey, BOS 16
W. Wilmot, CHI 11
B. Holliday, CIN 9
J. Ryan, CHI 9
B. Dahlen, CHI 9

Total Bases
H. Stovey, BOS 271
M. Tiernan, NY 268
G. Davis, CLE 233
J. Beckley, PIT 232
H. Long, BOS 231

Runs Batted In
C. Anson, CHI 120
B. Nash, BOS 95
H. Stovey, BOS 95
J. O'Rourke, NY 95
R. Connor, NY 94

Stolen Bases
B. Hamilton, PHI 111
A. Latham, CIN 87
M. Griffin, BKN 65
H. Long, BOS 60
M. Ward, BKN 57
H. Stovey, BOS 57

Hits
B. Hamilton, PHI 179
E. McKean, CLE 170
M. Tiernan, NY 166
G. Davis, CLE 165

Base on Balls
B. Hamilton, PHI 102
C. Childs, CLE 97
R. Connor, NY 83
H. Long, BOS 80

Home Run Percentage
M. Tiernan, NY 3.0
H. Stovey, BOS 2.9
W. Wilmot, CHI 2.2
B. Holliday, CIN 2.0

Runs
B. Hamilton, PHI 141
H. Long, BOS 129
C. Childs, CLE 120
A. Latham, CIN 119

Doubles
M. Griffin, BKN 36
G. Davis, CLE 35
H. Stovey, BOS 31
M. Tiernan, NY 30

Triples
H. Stovey, BOS 20
J. Beckley, PIT 19
B. McPhee, CIN 16
J. Ryan, CHI 15

PITCHING LEADERS

Winning Percentage
J. Ewing, NY .724
B. Hutchinson, CHI .698
H. Staley, PIT, BOS .649
K. Nichols, BOS .638
J. Clarkson, BOS .635

Earned Run Average
J. Ewing, NY 2.27
K. Nichols, BOS 2.39
A. Rusie, NY 2.55
H. Staley, PIT, BOS 2.58
M. Baldwin, PIT 2.76

Wins
B. Hutchinson, CHI 44
J. Clarkson, BOS 33
A. Rusie, NY 33
K. Nichols, BOS 30
C. Young, CLE 27

Saves
J. Clarkson, BOS 3
K. Nichols, BOS 3
J. Thornton, PHI 2
C. Young, CLE 2

Strikeouts
A. Rusie, NY 337
B. Hutchinson, CHI 261
K. Nichols, BOS 240
M. Baldwin, PIT 197
S. King, PIT 160

Complete Games
B. Hutchinson, CHI 56
A. Rusie, NY 52
M. Baldwin, PIT 48
J. Clarkson, BOS 47
K. Nichols, BOS 45

Fewest Hits/9 Innings
A. Rusie, NY 7.03
M. Baldwin, PIT 7.92
J. Ewing, NY 7.92
B. Hutchinson, CHI 8.15

Shutouts
A. Rusie, NY 6
J. Ewing, NY 5
K. Nichols, BOS 5
B. Hutchinson, CHI 4

Fewest Walks/9 Innings
K. Nichols, BOS 2.18
H. Staley, PIT, BOS 2.22
P. Galvin, PIT 2.26
O. Radbourn, CIN 2.56

Most Strikeouts/9 Inn.
A. Rusie, NY 6.06
K. Nichols, BOS 5.07
J. Ewing, NY 4.61
T. Keefe, NY, PHI 4.32

Innings
B. Hutchinson, CHI 561
A. Rusie, NY 500
J. Clarkson, BOS 461
M. Baldwin, PIT 438

Games Pitched
B. Hutchinson, CHI 66
A. Rusie, NY 61
C. Young, CLE 55
J. Clarkson, BOS 55

							Batting						Fielding			Pitching					
	W	L	PCT	GB	R	OR	2B	3B	HR	BA	SA	SB	E	DP	FA	CG	BB	SO	ShO	SV	ERA
Boston	87	51	.630		**847**	**658**	181	82	51	.255	.356	289	**358**	96	**.938**	**126**	**364**	525	9	**6**	**2.76**
Chicago	82	53	.607	3.5	832	730	159	88	**60**	.253	.359	238	397	**119**	.932	114	475	477	6	3	3.47
New York	71	61	.538		754	711	189	72	47	**.263**	**.361**	224	384	104	.933	117	593	**651**	**11**	3	2.99
Philadelphia	68	69	.496		756	773	180	51	21	.252	.322	232	443	108	.925	105	505	343	3	5	3.73
Cleveland	65	74	.468	4	835	888	183	87	23	.255	.339	242	485	86	.920	118	476	400	1	3	3.50
Brooklyn	61	76	.445	7	765	820	**200**	69	23	.260	.345	**337**	432	73	.924	121	459	407	8	3	3.86
Cincinnati	56	81	.409	12	646	790	148	**90**	40	.242	.335	244	409	101	.931	125	465	393	6	1	3.55
Pittsburgh	55	80	.407	12	679	744	148	71	28	.239	.317	205	475	76	.917	122	465	446	7	2	2.89
					6114	6114	1388	610	293	.252	.342	2011	3383	763	.927	948	3802	3642	51	26	3.34

AMERICAN ASSOCIATION 1891

Team	POS	Player	AB	BA	HR	RBI	PO	A	E	DP	TC/G	FA	Pitcher	G	IP	W	L	SV	ERA
Boston	1B	D. Brouthers	486	**.350**	5	109	1313	34	30	82	10.6	.978	G. Haddock	51	380	34	11	1	2.49
	2B	C. Stricker	514	.216	0	46	**405**	**418**	51	**78**	**6.3**	.942	C. Buffinton	48	364	29	9	1	2.55
	SS	P. Radford	456	.259	0	65	230	453	71	51	5.8	.906	D. O'Brien	40	269	18	13	2	3.65
W-93 L-42	3B	D. Farrell	473	.302	**12**	**110**	87	160	22	8	4.1	.918	B. Daley	19	127	8	6	2	2.98
	RF	H. Duffy	536	.336	8	108	166	23	17	3	1.7	.917							
Arthur Irwin	CF	T. Brown	**589**	.321	5	71	228	23	35	7	2.1	.878							
	LF	H. Richardson	278	.255	7	52	101	5	5	2	1.9	.955							
	C	M. Murphy	402	.216	4	54	**532**	118	31	8	6.5	**.954**							
	3B	B. Joyce	243	.309	3	51	82	149	41	12	4.3	.849							
	P	G. Haddock	185	.243	3	23	21	116	12	2	2.9	.919							
	P	C. Buffinton	181	.188	1	16	10	117	9	3	2.8	.934							
	OF	J. McGeachy	178	.253	1	21	57	4	6	0	1.6	.910							

AMERICAN ASSOCIATION 1891, *cont.*

St. Louis

W-85 L-51

Charlie Comiskey

1B	C. Comiskey	572	.259	2	88	1418	62	31	78	**10.9**	.979	J. Stivetts	**64**	440	33	22	1	2.86
2B	B. Eagan	297	.219	4	43	174	274	34	29	5.9	.929	W. McGill	33	233	18	9	1	2.97
SS	S. Fuller	576	.212	2	61	165	307	79	36	5.4	.857	C. Griffith	27	186	11	8	2	3.33
3B	D. Lyons	451	.315	11	84	151	246	59	16	3.8	.871	J. Neale	15	110	6	4	**3**	4.24
RF	T. McCarthy	570	.309	8	92	161	24	21	5	1.8	.898	G. Rettger	14	93	7	3	1	3.40
CF	D. Hoy	559	.292	5	64	251	26	27	3	2.2	.911							
LF	T. O'Neill	514	.323	10	95	195	5	14	0	1.7	.935							
C	J. Boyle	434	.281	5	79	428	88	35	**11**	6.1	.936							
P	J. Stivetts	302	.305	7	54	22	110	**15**	2	2.3	.898							
UT	J. Munyan	176	.233	0	19	196	53	25	4		.909							

Milwaukee

W-21 L-15

Charlie Cushman

1B	J. Carney	110	.300	3	23	324	20	5*	16	11.3	.986	G. Davies	12	102	7	5	0	2.66
2B	J. Canavan	142	.268	3	21	51	76	20	4	6.1	.864	F. Killen	11	96	7	4	0	1.68
SS	G. Shoch	127	.315	1	16	51	85	10	4	5.8	.932	F. Dwyer	10	86	6	4	0	2.20
3B	G. Alberts	41	.098	0	2	14	21	8	2	3.6	.814							
RF	H. Earl	129	.248	1	17	43	2	1	1	1.5	.978							
CF	E. Burke	144	.236	1	21	70	8	7	3	2.4	.918							
LF	A. Dalrymple	135	.311	1	22	44	6	5	1	1.7	.909							
C	F. Vaughn	99	.333	0	9	103	19	10	5*	6.6	.924							
UT	J. Grim	119	.235	1	14	111	46	15	4		.913							
UT	B. Pettit	80	.175	1	5	22	35	6	1		.905							
P	F. Dwyer	40	.225	0	2	7	20	5	0	3.2	.844							
P	G. Davies	37	.243	0	4	2	18	2	0	1.8	.909							

Baltimore

W-71 L-64

Billy Barnie

1B	P. Werden	552	.290	6	104	**1422**	58	30	79	10.9	.980	S. McMahon	61	**503**	**35**	24	1	2.81
2B	S. Wise	388	.247	1	48	225	299	66	30	6.0	.888	B. Cunningham	30	238	11	14	0	4.01
SS	I. Ray	418	.278	0	58	71	103	28	9	5.1	.861	K. Madden	32	224	13	12	1	4.10
3B	P. Gilbert	513	.230	3	72	**201**	**324**	**84**	**34**	**4.4**	.862	E. Healy	23	170	8	10	0	3.75
RF	B. Johnson	480	.271	2	79	235	28	37	5	2.3	.877							
CF	C. Welch	514	.268	3	55	258	25	16	4	2.6	.946							
LF	G. Van Haltren	566	.318	9	83	143	21	22	7	2.3	.882							
C	W. Robinson	334	.216	2	46	415	80	24	**11**	5.6	.954							
P	S. McMahon	210	.205	1	15	14	**141**	11	4	2.7	.934							
C	G. Townsend	204	.191	0	18	191	68	26	5	4.9	.909							

Philadelphia

W-73 L-66

Bill Sharsig
W-6 L-11

George Wood
W-67 L-55

1B	H. Larkin	526	.279	10	93	987	33	27	56	9.4	.974	G. Weyhing	52	450	31	20	0	3.18
2B	B. Hallman	587	.283	6	69	327	399	55	53	5.5	.930	I. Chamberlain	49	406	22	23	0	4.22
SS	T. Corcoran	511	.254	7	71	**300**	434	72	5	**6.1**	**.911**	B. Sanders	19	145	11	5	0	3.79
3B	J. Mulvey	453	.254	5	66	172	241	49	18	4.1	.894	W. Callahan	13	112	6	6	0	6.43
RF	J. McGeachy	201	.229	2	13	82	10	8	0	2.0	.920							
CF	P. Corkhill	349	.209	0	31	182	14	9	3	2.5	.956							
LF	G. Wood	528	.309	3	61	221	25	16	10	2.1	.939							
C	J. Milligan	455	.303	11	106	470	101	37	9	**7.0**	.939							
UT	L. Cross	402	.301	5	52	297	103	28	12		.935							
OF	J. McTamany	218	.225	3	21	118	10	14	1	2.4	.901							
P	G. Weyhing	198	.111	0	11	27	73	8	2	2.1	.926							
P	I. Chamberlain	176	.188	2	19	20	89	10	2	2.4	.916							
OP	B. Sanders	156	.250	1	19	32	31	8	1		.887							

Columbus

W-61 L-76

Gus Schmelz

1B	M. Lehane	511	.215	1	52	1362	**71**	28	**98**	10.7	**.981**	P. Knell	58	462	28	27	0	2.92
2B	J. Crooks	519	.245	0	46	399	404	36	72	6.1	**.957**	H. Gastright	35	284	12	19	0	3.78
SS	B. Wheelock	498	.229	0	39	248	**474**	81	**65**	5.9	.899	J. Dolan	27	203	12	11	0	4.16
3B	W. Kuehne	261	.215	2	22	85	146	30	15	3.8	.885	J. Easton	20	150	5	12	0	4.43
RF	J. Sneed	366	.257	1	61	142	10	18	4	1.7	.894							
CF	J. McTamany	304	.250	3	35	161	10	13	4	2.3	.929							
LF	C. Duffee	552	.301	10	90	235	33	21	7	2.3	.927							
C	J. Donahue	280	.218	0	35	343	108	28	**11**	6.4	.942							
OC	J. O'Connor	229	.266	0	37	135	37	11	5		.940							
OF	L. Twitchell	224	.277	2	35	67	4	9	0	1.4	.887							
P	P. Knell	215	.158	0	19	**40**	119	10	1	2.9	.941							
C	T. Dowse	201	.224	0	22	254	52	27	6	6.5	.919							

Cincinnati

W-43 L-57

King Kelly

1B	J. Carney	367	.278	3	43	984	45	28*	42	10.7	.974	F. Dwyer	35	289	13	19	0	4.52
2B	Y. Robinson	342	.178	1	37	222	287	78*	33	6.1	.867	C. Crane	32	250	14	14	0	2.45*
SS	J. Canavan	426	.228	7	66	217	304	85*	31	6.0	.860	W. Mains	30	204	12	12	0	2.69
3B	A. Whitney	347	.199	3	33	129	198	35	12	3.9	.903*							
RF	E. Seery	372	.285	4	36	160	17	20	3	2.0	.898							
CF	D. Johnston	376	.221	6	51	193	20	25	4	2.4	.895							
LF	E. Andrews	356	.211	0	26	173	25	8	4	2.5	.961							
C	K. Kelly	283	.297	1	53	217	102	34	11*	5.3	.904							
C	F. Vaughn	175	.257	1	14	170	58	19	6*	5.6	.923							
P	F. Dwyer	141	.284	0	18	15	74	6	1	2.7	.937							

Louisville

W-54 L-83

Jack Chapman

1B	H. Taylor	348	.296	2	35	909	43	21	55	10.8	.978	J. Fitzgerald	31	267	14	17	0	3.44
2B	T. Shinnick	436	.220	1	52	223	325	52	45	5.1	.913	J. Meekin	28	221	9	16	0	4.44
SS	H. Jennings	351	.293	1	58	181	221	49	28	6.6	.891	R. Ehret	26	221	13	13	0	3.47
3B	O. Beard	257	.241	0	24	84	149	32	16	4.3	.879	S. Stratton	20	172	6	13	0	4.08
RF	C. Wolf	528	.256	1	81	185	27	18	5	1.8	.922	J. Doran	15	126	5	10	0	5.43
CF	F. Weaver	556	.282	1	53	290	32	14	7	2.6	.958	E. Daily	15	111	4	8	0	5.74
LF	P. Donovan	439	.321	2	53	214	15	22	0	2.4	.912							
C	J. Ryan	253	.225	2	25	223	83	23	10	5.9	.930							
UT	T. Cahill	430	.253	3	44	385	242	69	31		.901							
C	P. Cook	153	.229	0	23	120	39	16	0	5.0	.909							
3B	W. Kuehne	152	.270	1	17	52	86	16	7	3.9	.896							

AMERICAN ASSOCIATION 1891, *cont.*

Washington

W-44 L-91

Sam Trott
W-4 L-7

Pop Snyder
W-23 L-46

Dan Shannon
W-15 L-34

Sandy Griffin
W-2 L-4

POS	Player	AB	BA	HR	RBI	PO	A	E	DP	TC/G	FA
1B	M. McQuery	261	.241	2	37	701	30	17	39	11.0	.977
2B	T. Dowd	464	.259	1	44	230	287	67	38	5.5	.885
SS	G. Hatfield	500	.256	1	48	211	334	82	40	6.0	.869
3B	B. Alvord	312	.234	0	30	147	210	57	10	5.1	.862
RF	L. Murphy	400	.265	1	35	164	10	25	3	2.0	.874
CF	P. Hines	206	.282	0	31	81	8	15	4	2.2	.856
LF	H. Beecher	235	.243	2	28	109	13	26	4	2.6	.824
C	D. McGuire	413	.303	3	66	442	**130**	**56**	8	6.4	.911
1B	A. McCauley	206	.282	1	31	541	22	18	27	9.8	.969
OC	S. Sutcliffe	201	.353	2	33	115	36	15	4		.910
P	K. Carsey	187	.150	0	15	22	120	12	**5**	2.9	.922
P	F. Foreman	153	.222	4	19	13	66	4	4	1.9	.952

Pitcher	G	IP	W	L	SV	ERA
K. Carsey	54	415	14	**37**	0	4.99
F. Foreman	43	345	18	20	1	3.73
J. Bakely	13	104	2	10	0	5.35

BATTING AND BASE RUNNING LEADERS

Batting Average		Slugging Average		Home Runs	
D. Brouthers, BOS	.350	D. Brouthers, BOS	.512	D. Farrell, BOS	12
H. Duffy, BOS	.336	J. Milligan, PHI	.505	D. Lyons, STL	11
T. O'Neill, STL	.323	D. Farrell, BOS	.474	J. Milligan, PHI	11
T. Brown, BOS	.321	T. Brown, BOS	.469		
G. Van Haltren, BAL	.318	L. Cross, PHI	.458		

Total Bases		Runs Batted In		Stolen Bases	
T. Brown, BOS	276	D. Farrell, BOS	110	T. Brown, BOS	106
G. Van Haltren, BAL	251	D. Brouthers, BOS	109	H. Duffy, BOS	85
D. Brouthers, BOS	249	H. Duffy, BOS	108	G. Van Haltren, BAL	75
H. Duffy, BOS	240	J. Milligan, PHI	106	D. Hoy, STL	59
P. Werden, BAL	234	P. Werden, BAL	104	P. Radford, BOS	55

Hits		Base on Balls		Home Run Percentage	
T. Brown, BOS	189	D. Hoy, STL	117	D. Farrell, BOS	2.5
H. Duffy, BOS	180	J. Crooks, COL	103	D. Lyons, STL	2.4
G. Van Haltren, BAL	180	J. McTamany, COL, PHI	101	J. Milligan, PHI	2.4
T. McCarthy, STL	176	P. Radford, BOS	96	J. Stivetts, STL	2.3

Runs		Doubles		Triples	
T. Brown, BOS	177	J. Milligan, PHI	35	T. Brown, BOS	21
G. Van Haltren, BAL	136	T. Brown, BOS	30	D. Brouthers, BOS	19
H. Duffy, BOS	134	T. O'Neill, STL	28	P. Werden, BAL	18
D. Hoy, STL	134	C. Duffee, COL	28	J. Canavan, CIN, MIL	18

PITCHING LEADERS

Winning Percentage		Earned Run Average		Wins	
C. Buffinton, BOS	.763	C. Crane, CIN	2.45	S. McMahon, BAL	35
G. Haddock, BOS	.756	G. Haddock, BOS	2.49	G. Haddock, BOS	34
C. Griffith, STL, BOS	.609	C. Buffinton, BOS	2.55	J. Stivetts, STL	33
G. Weyhing, PHI	.608	G. Davies, MIL	2.66	G. Weyhing, PHI	31
J. Stivetts, STL	.600	S. McMahon, BAL	2.81	C. Buffinton, BOS	29

Saves		Strikeouts		Complete Games	
J. Neale, STL	3	J. Stivetts, STL	259	S. McMahon, BAL	53
B. Daley, BOS	2	P. Knell, COL	228	G. Weyhing, PHI	51
D. O'Brien, BOS	2	G. Weyhing, PHI	219	P. Knell, COL	47
C. Griffith, STL, BOS	2	S. McMahon, BAL	219	K. Carsey, WAS	46
		I. Chamberlain, PHI	204	I. Chamberlain, PHI	44

Fewest Hits/9 Innings		Shutouts		Fewest Walks/9 Innings	
P. Knell, COL	7.07	G. Haddock, BOS	5	S. Stratton, LOU	1.78
J. Stivetts, STL	7.30	P. Knell, COL	5	B. Sanders, PHI	2.30
C. Buffinton, BOS	7.50	S. McMahon, BAL	5	S. McMahon, BAL	2.67
C. Crane, CIN	7.78			R. Ehret, LOU	2.85

Most Strikeouts/9 Inn.		Innings		Games Pitched	
J. Meekin, LOU	5.74	S. McMahon, BAL	503	J. Stivetts, STL	64
G. Davies, MIL	5.40	P. Knell, COL	462	S. McMahon, BAL	61
J. Stivetts, STL	5.30	G. Weyhing, PHI	450	P. Knell, COL	58
W. McGill, CIN, STL	5.02	J. Stivetts, STL	440	K. Carsey, WAS	54

							Batting						Fielding			Pitching					
	W	L	PCT	GB	R	OR	2B	3B	HR	BA	SA	SB	E	DP	FA	CG	BB	SO	ShO	SV	ERA
Boston	93	42	.689		**1028**	675	163	100	51	**.274**	**.380**	**447**	392	115	.934	108	497	524	**9**	8	3.03
St. Louis	85	51	.625	8.5	959	738	166	51	**57**	.265	.354	279	459	91	.920	101	571	**614**	8	**10**	3.28
Milwaukee	21	15	.583	22.5	227	**156**	58	15	12	.261	.359	47	**116**	20	.922	35	**120**	137	3	0	**2.50**
Baltimore	71	64	.526		850	798	142	99	30	.255	.345	342	503	103	.915	118	472	408	6	2	3.43
Philadelphia	73	66	.525		817	794	**182**	**123**	55	.258	.376	149	389	109	.933	**135**	520	533	3	0	4.01
Columbus	61	76	.445	11	702	777	154	61	20	.237	.308	280	379	**126**	**.935**	118	588	502	6	0	3.75
Cincinnati	43	57	.430	10.5	549	643	105	58	28	.234	.320	164	389	68	.913	86	446	331	2	1	3.44
Louisville	54	83	.394		698	873	127	68	17	.258	.324	227	453	112	.922	125	451	481	**9**	1	4.27
Washington	44	91	.326		691	1067	147	84	19	.251	.330	219	589	95	.900	123	566	486	2	2	4.83
					6521	6521	1244	659	289	.255	.344	2154	3669	839	.922	949	4231	4016	48	24	3.62

NATIONAL LEAGUE 1892

Boston

W-102 L-48

Frank Selee

POS	Player	AB	BA	HR	RBI	PO	A	E	DP	TC/G	FA
1B	T. Tucker	542	.282	1	62	1484	51	**45**	96	10.6	.972
2B	J. Quinn	532	.218	1	59	356	426	40	75	5.7	**.951**
SS	H. Long	646	.280	6	78	297	497	**99**	65	6.3	.889
3B	B. Nash	526	.260	4	95	197	351	62	23	4.5	**.898**
RF	T. McCarthy	603	.242	4	63	219	29	33	4	1.8	.883
CF	H. Duffy	612	.301	5	81	259	17	17	4	2.0	.942
LF	B. Lowe	475	.242	3	57	175	17	15	2	2.3	.928
C	K. Kelly	281	.189	2	41	319	98	40	11	6.3	.912
P	J. Stivetts	240	.296	3	36	17	96	12	5	2.4	.904
C	C. Ganzel	198	.268	0	25	202	50	18	1	5.3	.933
P	K. Nichols	197	.198	2	21	25	88	4	4	2.2	.966

Pitcher	G	IP	W	L	SV	ERA
K. Nichols	53	454	35	16	0	2.83
J. Stivetts	53	415	35	16	1	3.04
H. Staley	37	300	22	10	0	3.03
J. Clarkson	16	146	8	6	0	2.35

NATIONAL LEAGUE 1892, *cont.*

Cleveland

W-93 L-56

Patsy Tebeau

POS	Player	AB	BA	HR	RBI	PO	A	E	DP	TC/G	FA	Pitcher	G	IP	W	L	SV	ERA
1B	J. Virtue	557	.282	2	89	1500	61	26	61	10.8	.984	C. Young	53	453	36	12	0	**1.93**
2B	C. Childs	558	.317	3	53	357	441	53	51	5.9	.938	N. Cuppy	47	376	28	13	1	2.51
SS	E. McKean	531	.262	0	93	207	369	92	29	5.2	.862	J. Clarkson	29	243	17	10	1	2.55
3B	G. Davis	597	.241	5	82	100	166	25	8	3.7	.914	G. Davies	26	216	10	16	0	2.59
RF	J. O'Connor	572	.248	1	58	152	21	12	4	1.7	.935							
CF	J. McAleer	571	.238	4	70	367	25	16	0	2.7	.961							
LF	J. Burkett	608	.275	6	66	271	20	31	7	2.2	.904							
C	C. Zimmer	413	.262	1	64	514	122	42	11	6.1	.938							
3B	P. Tebeau	340	.244	2	49	99	156	25	17	3.8	.911							
P	C. Young	196	.158	1	15	19	122	8	**7**	2.8	.946							
P	N. Cuppy	168	.214	0	24	10	103	6	3	2.5	.950							

Brooklyn

W-95 L-59

Monte Ward

POS	Player	AB	BA	HR	RBI	PO	A	E	DP	TC/G	FA	Pitcher	G	IP	W	L	SV	ERA
1B	D. Brouthers	588	**.335**	5	**124**	1498	105	29	69	10.7	.982	G. Haddock	46	381	29	13	1	3.14
2B	M. Ward	614	.265	1	47	377	472	**74**	48	6.2	.920	E. Stein	48	377	27	16	1	2.84
SS	T. Corcoran	613	.237	1	74	291	495	64	49	5.6	.925	D. Foutz	27	203	13	8	1	3.41
3B	B. Joyce	372	.245	6	45	141	164	49	8	3.8	.862	B. Hart	28	195	9	12	1	3.28
RF	O. Burns	542	.315	4	96	162	16	12	4	1.5	.937	B. Kennedy	26	191	13	8	1	3.86
CF	M. Griffin	452	.277	3	66	267	25	4	7	2.3	.986							
LF	D. O'Brien	490	.243	1	56	222	16	11	3	2.0	.956							
C	C. Daily	278	.234	0	28	342	85	26	9	6.7	.943							
UT	T. Daly	446	.256	4	51	260	170	33	16		.929							
C	T. Kinslow	246	.305	2	40	355	89	32	6	7.2	.933							
OP	D. Foutz	220	.186	1	26	50	60	14	2		.887							
P	G. Haddock	158	.177	0	11	21	80	11	5	2.4	.902							

Philadelphia

W-87 L-66

Harry Wright

POS	Player	AB	BA	HR	RBI	PO	A	E	DP	TC/G	FA	Pitcher	G	IP	W	L	SV	ERA
1B	R. Connor	564	.294	12	73	1483	59	23	99	10.1	**.985**	G. Weyhing	59	470	32	21	**3**	2.66
2B	B. Hallman	586	.292	2	84	335	379	49	60	5.5	.936	K. Carsey	43	318	19	16	1	3.12
SS	B. Allen	563	.227	2	64	331	537	77	**67**	6.2	.919	T. Keefe	39	313	19	16	0	2.36
3B	C. Reilly	331	.196	1	24	106	169	29	13	4.3	.905	D. Esper	21	160	11	6	1	3.42
RF	S. Thompson	609	.305	9	104	223	28	17	7	1.8	.937	P. Knell	11	80	5	5	0	4.05
CF	E. Delahanty	477	.306	6	91	261	25	17	6	2.5	.944							
LF	B. Hamilton	554	.330	3	53	291	26	28	7	2.5	.919							
C	J. Clements	402	.264	8	76	**557**	107	35	12	6.4	.950							
UT	L. Cross	541	.275	4	69	327	236	35	17		.941							
P	G. Weyhing	214	.136	0	13	20	63	20	2	1.7	.806							

Cincinnati

W-82 L-68

Charlie Comiskey

POS	Player	AB	BA	HR	RBI	PO	A	E	DP	TC/G	FA	Pitcher	G	IP	W	L	SV	ERA
1B	C. Comiskey	551	.227	3	71	1469	73	25	**103**	11.1	.984	I. Chamberlain	52	406	19	23	0	3.39
2B	B. McPhee	573	.274	4	60	**451**	471	51	**86**	**6.8**	.948	T. Mullane	37	295	21	13	1	2.59
SS	G. Smith	506	.239	8	63	239	**561**	70	55	6.3	.920	F. Dwyer	33	259	19	10	1	2.33
3B	A. Latham	622	.238	0	44	167	329	66	26	4.0	.883	M. Sullivan	21	166	12	4	0	3.08
RF	B. Holliday	602	.292	**13**	91	271	20	21	6	2.1	.933	B. Rhines	12	84	4	7	0	5.06
CF	P. Browning	307	.303	3	52	152	13	15	0	2.2	.917							
LF	T. O'Neill	419	.251	2	52	188	13	17	3	2.0	.922							
C	M. Murphy	234	.197	2	24	315	67	18	6	5.4	.955							
UT	F. Vaughn	346	.254	2	50	394	80	33	22		.935							
P	I. Chamberlain	160	.225	2	15	16	67	9	0	1.8	.902							

Pittsburgh

W-80 L-73

Al Buckenberger
W-15 L-14

Tom Burns
W-27 L-32

Al Buckenberger
W-38 L-27

POS	Player	AB	BA	HR	RBI	PO	A	E	DP	TC/G	FA	Pitcher	G	IP	W	L	SV	ERA
1B	J. Beckley	614	.236	10	96	**1523**	**132**	38	88	11.2	.978	M. Baldwin	56	440	26	27	0	3.47
2B	L. Bierbauer	649	.236	8	65	385	**555**	49	66	6.5	.950	R. Ehret	39	316	16	20	0	2.65
SS	F. Shugart	554	.267	0	62	303	466	**99**	43	6.5	.886	A. Terry	30	240	18	7	1	2.51
3B	D. Farrell	605	.215	8	77	180	286	64	20	4.0	.879	E. Smith	17	134	6	7	0	3.63
RF	P. Donovan	388	.294	2	26	111	18	19	4	1.6	.872	P. Galvin	12	96	5	6	0	2.63
CF	J. Kelley	205	.239	0	28	101	13	10	4	2.2	.919							
LF	E. Smith	511	.274	4	63	223	15	31	0	2.2	.885							
C	C. Mack	346	.243	1	31	404	**143**	28	11	6.3	**.951**							
UT	D. Miller	623	.254	2	59	413	145	44	22		.927							
OF	P. Corkhill	256	.184	0	25	148	13	8	4	2.5	.953							
P	M. Baldwin	178	.101	1	13	**37**	86	18	2	2.5	.872							

Chicago

W-70 L-76

Cap Anson

POS	Player	AB	BA	HR	RBI	PO	A	E	DP	TC/G	FA	Pitcher	G	IP	W	L	SV	ERA
1B	C. Anson	559	.272	1	74	1491	67	44	62	11.0	.973	B. Hutchinson	**75**	**627**	**37**	36	0	2.74
2B	J. Canavan	439	.166	0	32	282	349	53	40	6.1	.923	A. Gumbert	46	383	22	19	0	3.41
SS	B. Dahlen	581	.291	5	58	178	232	41	29	6.3	.909	P. Luby	31	247	10	16	1	3.13
3B	J. Parrott	333	.201	2	22	115	164	34	7	4.0	.891							
RF	S. Dungan	433	.284	0	53	183	8	20	2	1.9	.905							
CF	J. Ryan	505	.293	10	65	241	26	23	5	2.4	.921							
LF	W. Wilmot	380	.216	2	35	197	8	22	0	2.5	.903							
C	P. Schriver	326	.224	1	34	367	102	36	5	6.2	.929							
OF	G. Decker	291	.227	1	28	73	12	12	3	1.6	.876							
P	B. Hutchinson	263	.217	1	22	21	**156**	13	4	2.5	.932							
SS	J. Cooney	238	.172	0	20	101	211	30	15	5.3	.912							
C	M. Kittridge	229	.179	0	10	359	87	26	5	6.8	.945							
P	A. Gumbert	178	.236	1	8	10	97	9	1	2.5	.922							
PO	P. Luby	163	.190	2	20	28	62	9	3		.909							

NATIONAL LEAGUE 1892, *cont.*

New York

W-71 L-80

Pat Powers

POS	Player	AB	BA	HR	RBI	PO	A	E	DP	TC/G	FA	Pitcher	G	IP	W	L	SV	ERA
1B	B. Ewing	393	.310	7	76	669	49	19	35	10.1	.974	A. Rusie	64	532	31	31	0	2.88
2B	E. Burke	363	.259	6	41	149	181	55	19	6.5	.857	S. King	52	419	23	24	0	3.24
SS	S. Fuller	508	.226	1	48	294	434	92	44	5.8	.888	C. Crane	47	364	16	24	1	3.80
3B	D. Lyons	389	.257	8	51	152	206	53	13	3.8	.871							
RF	M. Tiernan	450	.287	5	66	155	15	19	2	1.6	.899							
CF	H. Lyons	411	.238	0	53	186	16	20	1	2.3	.910							
LF	J. O'Rourke	448	.304	0	56	146	11	15	1	1.5	.913							
C	J. Boyle	436	.183	0	32	418	126	**46**	9	**7.5**	.922							
UT	J. Doyle	366	.298	5	55	231	154	60	13		.865							
P	A. Rusie	252	.210	1	26	27	132	21	5	2.8	.883							
UT	H. Richardson	248	.214	2	34	218	136	24	16		.937							
OF	G. Gore	193	.254	0	11	102	8	8	2	2.2	.932							
P	S. King	167	.210	2	23	22	81	11	4	2.2	.904							
P	C. Crane	163	.245	0	14	27	69	**22**	4	2.5	.814							
1B	J. McMahon	147	.224	1	24	312	13	9	13	9.3	.973							

Louisville

W-63 L-89

Jack Chapman
W-21 L-33

Fred Pfeffer
W-42 L-56

POS	Player	AB	BA	HR	RBI	PO	A	E	DP	TC/G	FA	Pitcher	G	IP	W	L	SV	ERA
1B	L. Whistler	285	.235	5	34	773	32	18	52	11.4*	.978	S. Stratton	42	352	21	19	0	2.92
2B	F. Pfeffer	470	.257	2	76	313	377	50	72	6.4	.932	B. Sanders	31	268	12	19	0	3.22
SS	H. Jennings	594	.222	2	61	**343**	537	90	59	6.4	.907	F. Clausen	24	200	9	13	0	3.06
3B	W. Kuehne	287	.167	0	36	104	160	38	16	4.0	.874	J. Meekin	19	156	7	10	0	4.03
RF	E. Seery	154	.201	0	15	65	10	3	1	1.9	.962	A. Jones	18	147	5	11	0	3.31
CF	T. Brown	**660**	.227	2	45	351	37	34	8	2.8	.919	L. Viau	16	131	4	11	0	3.99
LF	F. Weaver	551	.254	0	57	185	18	22	3	1.8	.902							
C	J. Grim	370	.243	1	36	262	85	22	7	5.3	.940							
UT	H. Taylor	493	.260	0	34	498	74	29	29		.952							
3B	C. Bassett	313	.214	2	35	76	179	41	13	4.1	.861							
PO	S. Stratton	219	.256	0	23	35	91	14	4		.900							
UT	B. Sanders	198	.273	3	18	172	61	12	7		.951							
C	B. Merritt	168	.196	1	13	175	58	15	6	5.4	.940							

Washington

W-58 L-93

Billy Barnie
W-0 L-2

Arthur Irwin
W-46 L-60

Danny Richardson
W-12 L-31

POS	Player	AB	BA	HR	RBI	PO	A	E	DP	TC/G	FA	Pitcher	G	IP	W	L	SV	ERA
1B	H. Larkin	464	.280	8	96	1121	69	38	77	10.5	.969	F. Killen	60	460	29	26	0	3.31
2B	T. Dowd	584	.243	1	50	208	264	58	33	5.4	.891	B. Abbey	27	196	5	18	1	3.45
SS	D. Richardson	551	.240	3	58	225	355	43	45	**6.7**	**.931**	P. Knell	22	170	9	13	0	3.65
3B	Y. Robinson	218	.179	0	19	70	125	34	11	3.9	.852	J. Duryea	18	127	3	10	2	2.41
RF	P. Radford	510	.255	1	37	86	12	7	7	1.7	.933	J. Meekin	14	112	3	10	0	3.46
CF	D. Hoy	593	.280	3	75	275	16	38	3	2.2	.884							
LF	C. Duffee	492	.248	6	51	230	34	25	8	2.3	.913							
C	D. McGuire	315	.232	4	43	381	100	33	8	5.8	.936							
C1	J. Milligan	323	.276	5	43	522	99	24	22		.963							
OF	L. Twitchell	192	.219	0	20	73	5	9	1	1.8	.897							
P	F. Killen	186	.199	4	23	20	121	**22**	2	2.7	.865							
OF	P. Donovan	163	.239	0	12	56	9	12	3	1.9	.844							

St. Louis

W-56 L-94

Jack Glasscock
W-1 L-3

Cub Stricker
W-6 L-17

Jack Crooks
W-27 L-33

George Gore
W-6 L-9

Bob Caruthers
W-16 L-32

POS	Player	AB	BA	HR	RBI	PO	A	E	DP	TC/G	FA	Pitcher	G	IP	W	L	SV	ERA
1B	P. Werden	598	.258	8	84	1467	102	28	81	10.7	.982	K. Gleason	47	400	16	24	0	3.33
2B	J. Crooks	445	.213	7	38	286	300	44	43	6.2	.930	T. Breitenstein	39	282	14	20	0	4.69
SS	J. Glasscock	566	.267	3	72	280	472	69	46	5.9	.916	P. Hawley	20	166	6	14	0	3.19
3B	G. Pinckney	290	.172	0	25	84	161	31	12	3.5	.888	C. Getzien	13	108	5	8	0	5.67
RF	B. Caruthers	513	.277	3	69	159	14	21	2	1.6	.892	B. Caruthers	16	102	2	8	1	5.84
CF	S. Brodie	602	.252	4	60	296	21	19	4	2.5	.943	P. Galvin	12	92	5	7	0	3.23
LF	C. Carroll	407	.273	4	49	181	19	22	1	2.2	.901	F. Dwyer	10	64	2	8	0	5.63
C	D. Buckley	410	.227	5	52	513	123	43	**14**	5.7	.937							
UT	K. Gleason	233	.215	3	25	0	0	0	0									
OF	G. Moriarity	177	.175	3	19	96	9	23	0	2.7	.820							

Baltimore

W-46 L-101

George Van Haltren
W-1 L-10

John Waltz
W-2 L-6

Ned Hanlon
W-43 L-85

POS	Player	AB	BA	HR	RBI	PO	A	E	DP	TC/G	FA	Pitcher	G	IP	W	L	SV	ERA
1B	S. Sutcliffe	276	.279	1	27	678	24	31	39	11.1	.958	S. McMahon	48	397	19	25	1	3.24
2B	C. Stricker	269	.264	3	37	212	224	39	31	6.3	.918	G. Cobb	53	394	10	**37**	0	4.86
SS	T. O'Rourke	239	.310	0	35	104	180	43	17	5.6	.869	T. Vickery	24	176	8	10	0	3.53
3B	B. Shindle	619	.252	3	50	**200**	**382**	**78**	**27**	**4.9**	.882	C. Buffinton	13	97	4	8	0	4.92
RF	G. Van Haltren	556	.302	7	57	217	27	43	5	2.2	.850							
CF	C. Welch	237	.236	1	22	129	4	14	1	2.3	.905							
LF	H. Stovey	283	.272	4	55	109	6	11	2	2.0	.913							
C	W. Robinson	330	.267	2	57	332	86	36	8	5.2	.921							
C	J. Gunson	314	.213	0	32	281	92	32	3	6.0	.921							
SS	G. Shoch	308	.276	1	50	96	197	43	17	5.9	.872							
UT	J. McGraw	286	.269	1	26	165	144	28	16		.917							
1B	L. Whistler	209	.225	2	21	540	26	16	21	11.4*	.973							
OF	P. Ward	186	.290	1	33	53	13	8	4	1.7	.892							
UT	J. Halligan	178	.270	2	43	220	13	19	10		.925							
P	S. McMahon	177	.141	0	18	7	94	12	2	2.4	.894							
P	G. Cobb	172	.209	1	13	12	96	14	0	2.3	.885							

NATIONAL LEAGUE 1892, *cont.*

BATTING AND BASE RUNNING LEADERS

Batting Average
D. Brouthers, BKN .335
B. Hamilton, PHI .330
C. Childs, CLE .317
O. Burns, BKN .315
B. Ewing, NY .310

Slugging Average
E. Delahanty, PHI .495
D. Brouthers, BKN .480
B. Ewing, NY .466
R. Connor, PHI .463
O. Burns, BKN .454

Home Runs
B. Holliday, CIN 13
R. Connor, PHI 12
J. Ryan, CHI 10
J. Beckley, PIT 10
S. Thompson, PHI 9

Total Bases
D. Brouthers, BKN 282
B. Holliday, CIN 270
S. Thompson, PHI 263
R. Connor, PHI 261
H. Duffy, BOS 251

Runs Batted In
D. Brouthers, BKN 124
S. Thompson, PHI 104
H. Larkin, WAS 96
O. Burns, BKN 96
J. Beckley, PIT 96

Stolen Bases
M. Ward, BKN 88
T. Brown, LOU 78
A. Latham, CIN 66
B. Dahlen, CHI 60
D. Hoy, WAS 60

Hits
D. Brouthers, BKN 197
S. Thompson, PHI 186
H. Duffy, BOS 184
B. Hamilton, PHI 183

Base on Balls
J. Crooks, STL 136
C. Childs, CLE 117
R. Connor, PHI 116
T. McCarthy, BOS 93

Home Run Percentage
B. Holliday, CIN 2.2
R. Connor, PHI 2.1
D. Lyons, NY 2.1
J. Clements, PHI 2.0

Runs
C. Childs, CLE 136
B. Hamilton, PHI 132
H. Duffy, BOS 125
R. Connor, PHI 123

Doubles
R. Connor, PHI 37
H. Long, BOS 33
E. Delahanty, PHI 30
D. Brouthers, BKN 30

Triples
E. Delahanty, PHI 21
J. Virtue, CLE 20
D. Brouthers, BKN 20
B. Dahlen, CHI 19
J. Beckley, PIT 19

PITCHING LEADERS

Winning Percentage
C. Young, CLE .750
A. Terry, BAL, PIT .692
G. Haddock, BKN .690
H. Staley, BOS .688
K. Nichols, BOS .686
J. Stivetts, BOS .686

Earned Run Average
C. Young, CLE 1.93
T. Keefe, PHI 2.36
J. Clarkson, BOS, CLE 2.48
N. Cuppy, CLE 2.51
A. Terry, BAL, PIT 2.57

Wins
B. Hutchinson, CHI 37
C. Young, CLE 36
J. Stivetts, BOS 35
K. Nichols, BOS 35
G. Weyhing, PHI 32

Saves
G. Weyhing, PHI 3
J. Duryea, CIN, WAS 2

Strikeouts
B. Hutchinson, CHI 316
A. Rusie, NY 288
G. Weyhing, PHI 202
E. Stein, BKN 190
K. Nichols, BOS 187

Complete Games
B. Hutchinson, CHI 67
A. Rusie, NY 58
K. Nichols, BOS 50
C. Young, CLE 48

Fewest Hits/9 Innings
T. Mullane, CIN 6.77
A. Rusie, NY 6.85
A. Terry, BAL, PIT 6.94
C. Young, CLE 7.21

Shutouts
C. Young, CLE 9
E. Stein, BKN 6
G. Weyhing, PHI 6

Fewest Walks/9 Innings
S. Stratton, LOU 1.79
F. Dwyer, STL, CIN 2.03
B. Sanders, LOU 2.08
C. Young, CLE 2.34

Most Strikeouts/9 Inn.
B. Kennedy, BKN 5.09
A. Rusie, NY 4.87
B. Hutchinson, CHI 4.54
E. Stein, BKN 4.53

Innings
B. Hutchinson, CHI 627
A. Rusie, NY 532
G. Weyhing, PHI 470
F. Killen, WAS 460

Games Pitched
B. Hutchinson, CHI 75
A. Rusie, NY 64
F. Killen, WAS 60
G. Weyhing, PHI 59

							Batting						Fielding			Pitching					
	W	L	PCT	GB	R	OR	2B	3B	HR	BA	SA	SB	E	DP	FA	CG	BB	SO	ShO	SV	ERA
Boston	102	48	.680		862	649	203	51	34	.250	.327	338	454	128	.929	143	460	509	**15**	1	2.86
Cleveland	93	56	.624	8.5	855	**613**	196	96	26	.254	.340	225	407	95	.935	140	**413**	472	11	2	**2.41**
Brooklyn	95	59	.617	9	**935**	733	183	105	30	**.262**	.350	**409**	398	98	**.940**	132	600	597	12	**5**	3.25
Philadelphia	87	66	.569	16.5	860	690	**225**	95	**50**	**.262**	**.367**	216	**393**	128	.939	131	492	502	10	**5**	2.93
Cincinnati	82	68	.547	20	766	731	155	75	44	.241	.322	270	402	**140**	.939	131	535	437	8	2	3.17
Pittsburgh	80	73	.523	23.5	802	796	143	108	38	.236	.322	222	483	113	.927	130	537	455	3	1	3.10
Chicago	70	76	.479	30	635	735	149	92	26	.235	.316	233	424	85	.932	133	424	518	6	1	3.16
New York	71	80	.470	31.5	811	826	173	85	38	.251	.337	301	565	97	.912	139	635	**641**	5	1	3.29
Louisville	63	89	.414	40	649	804	133	61	18	.226	.284	275	471	133	.928	**147**	447	430	9	0	3.34
Washington	58	93	.384	44.5	731	869	148	78	38	.239	.320	276	547	122	.916	129	556	479	5	3	3.46
St. Louis	56	94	.373	46	703	922	138	53	45	.226	.298	209	452	100	.929	139	543	478	4	1	4.20
Baltimore	46	101	.313	54.5	779	1020	160	**111**	30	.254	.343	227	584	100	.910	131	536	437	2	2	4.28
					9388	9388	2006	1010	417	.245	.327	3201	5580	1339	.928	1625	6178	5955	90	24	3.29

First Half

	W	L	PCT	GB
*Boston	52	22	.703	
Brooklyn	51	26	.662	2.5
Philadelphia	46	30	.605	7
Cincinnati	44	31	.587	8.5
Cleveland	40	33	.548	11.5
Pittsburgh	37	39	.487	16
Washington	35	41	.461	18
Chicago	31	39	.443	19
St. Louis	31	42	.425	20.5
New York	31	43	.419	21
Louisville	30	47	.390	23.5
Baltimore	20	55	.267	32.5

Second Half

	W	L	PCT	GB
Cleveland	53	23	.697	
Boston	50	26	.658	3
Brooklyn	44	33	.571	9.5
Pittsburgh	43	34	.558	10.5
Philadelphia	41	36	.532	12.5
New York	40	37	.519	13.5
Chicago	39	37	.513	14
Cincinnati	38	37	.507	14.5
Louisville	33	42	.440	19.5
Baltimore	26	46	.361	25
St. Louis	25	52	.325	28.5
Washington	23	52	.307	29.5

* Defeated Cleveland in playoff 5 games to 0

NATIONAL LEAGUE 1893

Boston

W-86 L-43

Frank Selee

POS	Player	AB	BA	HR	RBI	PO	A	E	DP	TC/G	FA
1B	T. Tucker	486	.284	7	91	1252	39	27	**89**	10.9	.980
2B	B. Lowe	526	.298	14	89	308	409	49	58	6.3	.936
SS	H. Long	552	.288	6	58	271	469	98	**67**	6.8	.883
3B	B. Nash	485	.291	10	123	189	300	41	23	4.1	**.923**
RF	C. Carroll	438	.224	2	54	226	18	22	5	2.2	.917
CF	H. Duffy	560	.362	6	118	313	15	16	6	2.6	.953
LF	T. McCarthy	462	.346	5	111	202	28	25	4	2.4	.902
C	C. Bennett	191	.209	4	27	204	40	12	1	4.3	.953
UT	C. Ganzel	281	.267	1	48	278	49	15	14		.956
P	K. Nichols	177	.220	2	26	21	81	5	5	2.1	.953
P	J. Stivetts	172	.297	3	25	13	50	3	2	1.8	.955
C	B. Merritt	141	.348	3	26	129	25	9	6	4.4	.945
P	H. Staley	113	.265	2	21	3	60	9	2	2.0	.875

Pitcher	G	IP	W	L	SV	ERA
K. Nichols	52	425	34	14	1	3.52
J. Stivetts	38	284	20	12	1	4.41
H. Staley	36	263	18	10	0	5.13
H. Gastright	19	156	12	4	0	5.13

NATIONAL LEAGUE 1893, *cont.*

Pittsburgh

W-81 L-48

Al Buckenberger

1B	J. Beckley	542	.303	5	106	1360	**95**	21	83	11.3	.986
2B	L. Bierbauer	528	.284	4	94	352	441	34	71	6.5	**.959**
SS	J. Glasscock	293	.341	1	74	155	239	28	40	6.4	.934
3B	D. Lyons	490	.306	3	105	**214**	303	46	23	4.3	.918
RF	P. Donovan	499	.317	2	56	178	16	13	5	1.8	.937
CF	G. Van Haltren	529	.338	3	79	227	24	38	3	2.6	.869
LF	E. Smith	518	.346	7	103	271	20	25	7	2.5	.921
C	D. Miller	154	.182	0	17	141	45	17	3	5.1	.916
OF	J. Stenzel	224	.362	4	37	82	4	9	2	2.1	.905
SS	F. Shugart	210	.262	1	32	98	178	37	15	6.1	.882
P	F. Killen	171	.275	4	30	16	103	14	2	2.4	.895
P	R. Ehret	136	.176	1	17	12	80	11	0	2.6	.893
C	C. Mack	133	.286	0	15	128	47	11	5	5.0	.941

F. Killen	55	416	**36**	14	0	3.63
R. Ehret	39	314	18	18	0	3.44
A. Terry	26	170	12	8	0	4.45
A. Gumbert	22	163	11	7	0	5.15

Cleveland

W-73 L-55

Patsy Tebeau

1B	J. Virtue	378	.265	1	60	777	47	21	48	11.6	.975
2B	C. Childs	485	.326	3	65	348	424	62	56	6.8	.926
SS	E. McKean	545	.310	4	133	247	431	74	55	6.0	.902
3B	C. McGarr	249	.309	0	28	93	147	31	7	4.3	.886
RF	B. Ewing	500	.344	6	122	201	14	17	3	2.1	.927
CF	J. McAleer	350	.237	2	41	230	16	19	3	2.9	.928
LF	J. Burkett	511	.348	6	82	239	19	46	5	2.4	.849
C	J. O'Connor	384	.286	3	75	182	62	13	2	4.6	.949
13	P. Tebeau	486	.329	2	102	652	177	41	35		.953
C	C. Zimmer	227	.308	2	41	169	73	8	10	4.5	.968
P	C. Young	187	.235	1	27	27	112	8	1	2.8	.946

C. Young	53	423	34	16	1	3.36
J. Clarkson	36	295	16	17	0	4.45
N. Cuppy	31	244	17	10	0	4.47
C. Hastings	15	92	4	5	1	4.70

Philadelphia

W-72 L-57

Harry Wright

1B	J. Boyle	504	.286	4	81	1066	74	14	71	10.3	.988
2B	B. Hallman	596	.307	4	76	281	370	34	54	5.7	.950
SS	B. Allen	471	.268	8	90	**302**	447	66	65	6.6	.919
3B	C. Reilly	416	.245	4	56	164	235	47	21	4.3	.895
RF	S. Thompson	**600**	.370	11	126	171	17	14	3	1.5	.931
CF	B. Hamilton	355	**.380**	5	44	228	8	16	6	3.1	.937
LF	E. Delahanty	595	.368	**19**	**146**	318	31	19	8	3.1	.948
C	J. Clements	376	.285	17	80	329	75	25	5	4.7	.942
UT	L. Cross	415	.299	4	78	291	182	27	27		.946
OF	T. Turner	155	.323	1	13	79	5	6	2	2.5	.933
OF	J. Sharrott	152	.250	1	22	51	5	12	0	2.1	.824
P	G. Weyhing	147	.150	0	11	31	56	5	3	2.2	.946
P	K. Carsey	145	.186	0	10	17	81	8	1	2.7	.925

G. Weyhing	42	345	23	16	0	4.74
K. Carsey	39	318	20	15	0	4.81
T. Keefe	22	178	10	7	0	4.40
J. Taylor	25	170	10	9	1	4.24

New York

W-68 L-64

Monte Ward

1B	R. Connor	511	.305	11	105	**1423**	83	40	70	**11.5**	.974
2B	M. Ward	588	.328	2	77	348	**464**	**73**	41	6.6	.918
SS	S. Fuller	474	.236	0	51	260	464	71	48	6.1	.911
3B	G. Davis	549	.355	11	119	181	305	**64**	**27**	4.1	.884
RF	M. Tiernan	511	.309	15	102	178	12	15	2	1.6	.927
CF	G. Stafford	281	.281	5	27	129	8	15	4	2.3	.901
LF	E. Burke	537	.279	9	80	278	19	29	2	2.4	.911
C	J. Doyle	318	.321	1	51	186	62	22	7	5.6	.919
P	A. Rusie	212	.269	3	27	23	**114**	15	5	2.7	.901
OF	H. Lyons	187	.273	0	21	113	9	11	3	2.8	.917
C	J. Milligan	147	.231	1	25	188	67	18	5	6.5	.934
P	M. Baldwin	134	.127	0	9	24	52	6	1	1.8	.927
C	P. Wilson	114	.246	2	21	106	20	4	1	4.2	.969

A. Rusie	**56**	**482**	33	21	1	3.23
M. Baldwin	45	331	16	20	2*	4.10
L. German	20	152	8	8	0	4.14

Brooklyn

W-65 L-63

Dave Foutz

1B	D. Brouthers	282	.337	2	59	736	47	11	51	10.3	.986
2B	T. Daly	470	.289	8	70	207	265	44	22	6.3	.915
SS	T. Corcoran	459	.275	2	58	218	444	68	44	6.3	.907
3B	G. Shoch	327	.263	2	54	48	66	9	5	3.3	.927
RF	O. Burns	415	.270	7	60	159	19	13	5	1.8	.932
CF	M. Griffin	362	.285	6	59	232	19	9	8	2.8	.965
LF	D. Foutz	557	.246	7	67	157	10	16	1	2.4	.913
C	T. Kinslow	312	.244	4	45	290	80	27	11	5.2	.932
C	C. Daily	215	.265	1	32	215	46	18	2	5.5	.935
2B	D. Richardson	206	.223	0	27	115	107	12	18	5.1	.949
OF	H. Stovey	175	.251	1	29	115	3	13	0	2.7	.901
P	B. Kennedy	157	.248	0	16	12	109	10	**6**	2.8	.924

B. Kennedy	46	383	25	20	1	3.72
E. Stein	37	298	19	15	0	3.77
G. Haddock	23	151	8	9	0	5.60
D. Daub	12	103	6	6	0	3.84
G. Sharrott	13	95	4	6	1	5.87

Cincinnati

W-65 L-63

Charlie Comiskey

1B	C. Comiskey	259	.220	0	26	675	21	15	57	11.1	.979
2B	B. McPhee	491	.281	3	68	**396**	455	41	**101**	7.0	.954
SS	G. Smith	500	.236	3	56	250	**500**	53	**67**	6.2	**.934**
3B	A. Latham	531	.282	2	49	172	281	55	23	4.0	.892
RF	J. McCarthy	195	.282	0	22	87	7	12	0	2.3	.887
CF	B. Holliday	500	.310	5	89	270	14	17	4	2.4	.944
LF	J. Canavan	461	.226	5	64	243	15	19	0	2.4	.931
C	F. Vaughn	483	.280	1	108	270	77	11	10	4.5	**.969**
C	M. Murphy	200	.235	1	19	162	45	15	6	4.0	.932
1B	F. Motz	156	.256	2	25	426	38	9	27	11.0	.981
OF	P. Ward	150	.280	0	10	54	8	13	4	1.9	.827

F. Dwyer	37	287	18	15	**2**	4.13
I. Chamberlain	34	241	16	12	0	3.73
M. Sullivan	27	184	8	11	1	5.05
T. Parrott	22	154	10	7	0	4.09
T. Mullane	15	122	6	6	1*	4.41
S. King	17	105	5	6	1	4.89

NATIONAL LEAGUE 1893, *cont.*

Baltimore

W-60 L-70

Ned Hanlon

1B	H. Taylor	360	.283	1	54	882	43	23	58	10.8	.976	S. McMahon	43	346	23	18	1	4.37
2B	H. Reitz	490	.286	1	76	315	421	48	62	6.0	.939	T. Mullane	34	245	12	16	1*	4.45
SS	J. McGraw	480	.321	5	64	218	350	67	40	5.4	.894	B. Hawke	29	225	11	16	0	4.76
3B	B. Shindle	521	.261	1	75	176	**308**	63	24	4.4	.885	E. McNabb	21	142	8	7	0	4.12
RF	G. Treadway	458	.260	1	67	192	27	24	4	2.1	.901	K. Baker	15	92	3	8	0	8.44
CF	J. Kelley	502	.305	9	76	307	22	21	4	2.8	.940							
LF	J. Long	226	.212	2	25	109	8	14	1	2.4	.893							
C	W. Robinson	359	.334	3	57	**349**	70	26	8	4.8	.942							
C	B. Clarke	183	.175	1	24	135	45	18	3	5.2	.909							
P	S. McMahon	148	.243	0	22	16	75	**18**	2	2.5	.835							
OF	T. O'Rourke	135	.363	0	19	48	1	1	0	2.0	.980							

Chicago

W-56 L-71

Cap Anson

1B	C. Anson	398	.314	0	91	997	44	20	59	10.5	.981	B. Hutchinson	44	348	16	24	0	4.75
2B	B. Lange	469	.281	8	88	151	181	42	21	6.6	.888	W. McGill	39	303	17	18	0	4.61
SS	B. Dahlen	485	.301	5	64	229	306	65	33	**6.8**	.892	H. Mauck	23	143	8	10	0	4.41
3B	J. Parrott	455	.244	1	65	145	251	42	21	4.4	.904							
RF	S. Dungan	465	.297	2	64	175	20	17	3	2.0	.920							
CF	J. Ryan	341	.299	3	30	162	16	18	2	2.7	.908							
LF	W. Wilmot	392	.301	3	61	198	16	31	1	2.6	.873							
C	M. Kittridge	255	.231	2	30	260	81	22	4	5.2	.939							
UT	G. Decker	328	.271	2	48	333	79	33	25		.926							
C	P. Schriver	229	.284	4	34	215	62	22	8	5.3	.926							
P	B. Hutchinson	162	.253	0	25	13	62	7	3	1.9	.915							
UT	L. Camp	156	.263	2	17	55	66	18	7		.871							

St. Louis

W-57 L-75

Bill Watkins

1B	P. Werden	500	.276	1	94	1194	81	**42**	75	10.6	.968	T. Breitenstein	48	383	19	20	1	**3.18**
2B	J. Quinn	547	.230	0	71	354	366	44	63	5.7	.942	K. Gleason	48	380	21	25	1	4.61
SS	J. Glasscock	195	.287	1	26	85	159	25	19	5.6	.907	P. Hawley	31	227	5	17	1	4.60
3B	J. Crooks	448	.237	1	48	210	286	50	19	**4.4**	.908	D. Clarkson	24	186	12	9	0	3.48
RF	T. Dowd	581	.282	1	54	225	27	15	9	2.0	.944							
CF	S. Brodie	469	.318	2	79	273	21	15	7	2.9	.951							
LF	C. Frank	164	.335	1	17	84	9	7	1	2.5	.930							
C	H. Peitz	362	.254	1	45	296	86	21	7	5.4	.948							
UT	F. Shugart	246	.280	0	28	107	101	34	11		.860							
P	K. Gleason	199	.256	0	20	30	87	12	3	2.7	.907							
SS	B. Ely	178	.253	0	16	98	139	25	16	6.0	.905							
P	T. Breitenstein	160	.181	1	14	**42**	82	8	4	2.8	.939							
C	J. Gunson	151	.272	0	15	130	36	13	4	5.1	.927							
UT	D. Cooley	107	.346	0	21	46	12	4	2		.935							

Louisville

W-50 L-75

Billy Barnie

1B	W. Brown	461	.304	1	85	1082	51	13	76	10.3	.989*	G. Hemming	41	332	18	17	1	5.18
2B	F. Pfeffer	508	.254	3	75	355	398	49	74	6.4	.939	S. Stratton	38	324	12	23	0	5.45
SS	T. O'Rourke	352	.281	0	53	118	176	46	26	5.7	.865	B. Rhodes	20	152	5	12	0	7.60
3B	G. Pinckney	446	.235	1	62	126	279	34	26	3.7	.923	J. Menefee	15	129	8	7	0	4.24
RF	F. Weaver	439	.292	2	49	151	17	16	2	2.2	.913							
CF	T. Brown	529	.240	5	54	339	39	29	13	3.3	.929							
LF	P. Browning	220	.355	1	37	114	5	16	1	2.4	.881							
C	J. Grim	415	.267	3	54	281	112	20	**15**	4.5	.952							
PO	S. Stratton	221	.226	0	16	59	96	8	4		.951							
OF	L. Twitchell	187	.310	1	31	91	6	14	0	2.5	.874							
SS	J. Denny	175	.246	1	22	91	139	20	16	6.0	.920							
P	G. Hemming	158	.203	0	19	19	80	7	2	2.6	.934							

Washington

W-40 L-89

Jim O'Rourke

1B	H. Larkin	319	.317	4	73	781	29	31	48	10.4	.963	D. Esper	42	334	12	**28**	0	4.71
2B	S. Wise	521	.311	5	77	315	302	51	45	**7.3**	.924	A. Maul	37	297	12	21	0	5.30
SS	J. Sullivan	508	.266	2	64	233	396	**102**	34	5.7	.860	J. Meekin	31	245	10	15	0	4.96
3B	J. Mulvey	226	.235	0	19	76	140	31	10	4.5	.874	J. Duryea	17	117	4	10	0	7.54
RF	P. Radford	464	.228	2	34	198	29	25	4	2.0	.901	O. Stocksdale	11	69	2	8	0	8.22
CF	D. Hoy	564	.245	0	45	281	26	37	8	2.6	.892							
LF	J. O'Rourke	547	.287	3	95	174	16	15	2	2.4	.927							
C	D. Farrell	511	.280	4	75	304	**140**	**37**	5	**5.9**	.923							
C	D. McGuire	237	.262	1	26	172	45	27	3	4.9	.889							
UT	C. Stricker	218	.183	0	20	168	146	36	23		.897							
P	D. Esper	143	.287	0	24	14	79	9	0	2.4	.912							
P	A. Maul	134	.254	0	12	11	69	10	1	2.4	.889							
P	J. Meekin	113	.257	3	20	12	53	7	3	2.3	.903							

BATTING AND BASE RUNNING LEADERS

Batting Average

B. Hamilton, PHI	.380
S. Thompson, PHI	.370
E. Delahanty, PHI	.368
H. Duffy, BOS	.362
G. Davis, NY	.355

Slugging Average

E. Delahanty, PHI	.583
G. Davis, NY	.554
S. Thompson, PHI	.530
E. Smith, PIT	.525
B. Hamilton, PHI	.524

Home Runs

E. Delahanty, PHI	19
J. Clements, PHI	17
M. Tiernan, NY	15
B. Lowe, BOS	14

Total Bases

E. Delahanty, PHI	347
S. Thompson, PHI	318
G. Davis, NY	304
E. Smith, PIT	272
E. McKean, CLE	258
H. Duffy, BOS	258

Runs Batted In

E. Delahanty, PHI	146
E. McKean, CLE	133
S. Thompson, PHI	126
B. Nash, BOS	123
B. Ewing, CLE	122

Stolen Bases

T. Brown, LOU	66
T. Dowd, STL	59
A. Latham, CIN	57
E. Burke, NY	54
S. Brodie, STL, BAL	49

PITCHING LEADERS

Winning Percentage

H. Gastright, PIT, BOS	.750
F. Killen, PIT	.720
K. Nichols, BOS	.708
C. Young, CLE	.680
H. Staley, BOS	.643

Earned Run Average

T. Breitenstein, STL	3.18
A. Rusie, NY	3.23
C. Young, CLE	3.36
R. Ehret, PIT	3.44
D. Clarkson, STL	3.48

Wins

F. Killen, PIT	36
C. Young, CLE	34
K. Nichols, BOS	34
A. Rusie, NY	33
B. Kennedy, BKN	25

Saves

T. Colcolough, PIT	2
F. Donnelly, CHI	2
M. Baldwin, PIT, NY	2
F. Dwyer, CIN	2
T. Mullane, CIN, BAL	2

Strikeouts

A. Rusie, NY	208
B. Kennedy, BKN	107
T. Breitenstein, STL	102
C. Young, CLE	102
G. Weyhing, PHI	101

Complete Games

A. Rusie, NY	50
K. Nichols, BOS	44
C. Young, CLE	42
B. Kennedy, BKN	40

NATIONAL LEAGUE 1893, *cont.*

Hits		**Base on Balls**		**Home Run Percentage**		**Fewest Hits/9 Innings**		**Shutouts**		**Fewest Walks/9 Innings**	
S. Thompson, PHI	222	J. Crooks, STL	121	J. Clements, PHI	4.5	A. Rusie, NY	8.42	R. Ehret, PIT	4	C. Young, CLE	2.19
E. Delahanty, PHI	219	C. Childs, CLE	120	E. Delahanty, PHI	3.2	T. Breitenstein, STL	8.44	A. Rusie, NY	4	K. Nichols, BOS	2.50
H. Duffy, BOS	203	P. Radford, WAS	105	M. Tiernan, NY	2.9	F. Killen, PIT	8.68			N. Cuppy, CLE	2.77
G. Davis, NY	195	J. McGraw, BAL	101	B. Lowe, BOS	2.7	B. Kennedy, BKN	8.84			H. Staley, BOS	2.77

Runs		**Doubles**		**Triples**		**Most Strikeouts/9 Inn.**		**Innings**		**Games Pitched**	
H. Long, BOS	149	S. Thompson, PHI	37	P. Werden, STL	29	A. Rusie, NY	3.88	A. Rusie, NY	482	A. Rusie, NY	56
H. Duffy, BOS	147	E. Delahanty, PHI	35	G. Davis, NY	27	J. Meekin, WAS	3.34	K. Nichols, BOS	425	F. Killen, PIT	55
C. Childs, CLE	145	P. Tebeau, CLE	32	E. McKean, CLE	24	P. Hawley, STL	2.89	C. Young, CLE	423	C. Young, CLE	53
J. Burkett, CLE	145	J. Beckley, PIT	32	E. Smith, PIT	23	F. Clausen, LOU, CHI	2.89	F. Killen, PIT	416	K. Nichols, BOS	52
E. Delahanty, PHI	145										

							Batting						Fielding			Pitching					
	W	L	PCT	GB	R	OR	2B	3B	HR	BA	SA	SB	E	DP	FA	CG	BB	SO	ShO	SV	ERA
Boston	86	43	.667		1008	795	178	50	64	.290	.391	243	353	118	.936	**115**	402	253	2	2	4.43
Pittsburgh	81	48	.628		970	**766**	176	**127**	37	.299	.411	210	347	112	.938	104	504	280	**8**	2	4.08
Cleveland	73	55	.570		976	839	222	98	31	.300	.408	252	395	92	.929	110	**356**	242	2	2	4.20
Philadelphia	72	57	.558	1.5	**1011**	841	**246**	90	**79**	**.301**	**.430**	202	**318**	121	**.944**	107	521	283	4	2	4.68
New York	68	64	.515	7	941	845	182	101	62	.293	.410	**299**	432	95	.927	111	581	**395**	6	4	4.29
Brooklyn	65	63	.508	8	775	845	173	83	45	.266	.371	213	385	88	.930	109	547	297	3	3	4.55
Cincinnati	65	63	.508	8	759	814	161	65	28	.259	.340	238	321	**138**	.943	97	549	258	4	**5**	4.59
Baltimore	60	70	.462	14	820	893	164	86	27	.275	.365	233	384	95	.929	104	534	275	1	2	4.97
Chicago	56	71	.441	16.5	829	874	186	93	32	.279	.379	255	421	92	.922	101	553	273	4	**5**	4.81
St. Louis	57	75	.432	18	745	829	152	98	10	.264	.341	250	398	110	.930	114	542	301	3	4	**4.06**
Louisville	50	75	.400	21.5	759	942	178	73	18	.260	.342	203	330	111	.937	113	479	190	4	1	5.90
Washington	40	89	.310	33.5	722	1032	180	83	24	.266	.354	154	497	96	.912	110	574	292	2	0	5.56
					10315	10315	2198	1047	457	.279	.379	2752	4581	1268	.931	1295	6142	3339	43	32	4.68

NATIONAL LEAGUE 1894

Baltimore

W-89 L-39

Ned Hanlon

POS	Player	AB	BA	HR	RBI	PO	A	E	DP	TC/G	FA	Pitcher	G	IP	W	L	SV	ERA
1B	D. Brouthers	525	.347	9	128	1184	65	31	83	10.4	.976	S. McMahon	35	276	25	8	0	4.21
2B	H. Reitz	446	.303	2	105	264	336	20	50	6.4	**.968**	B. Hawke	32	205	16	9	3	5.84
SS	H. Jennings	501	.335	4	109	**307**	499	63	69	**6.8**	.928	K. Gleason	21	172	15	5	0	4.45
3B	J. McGraw	512	.340	1	92	131	247	46	17	3.6	.892	B. Inks	22	133	9	4	1	5.55
RF	W. Keeler	590	.371	5	94	215	25	16	4	2.0	.938	T. Mullane	21	123	6	9	4*	6.31
CF	S. Brodie	573	.366	3	113	310	14	17	4	2.6	.950	D. Esper	16	102	10	2	2	3.88
LF	J. Kelley	507	.393	6	111	276	16	15	3	2.4	.951							
C	W. Robinson	414	.353	1	98	370	84	27	8	4.4	.944							
P	S. McMahon	126	.286	0	25	17	62	5	2	2.4	.940							
2B	F. Bonner	118	.322	0	24	60	62	13	8	5.0	.904							

New York

W-88 L-44

Monte Ward

POS	Player	AB	BA	HR	RBI	PO	A	E	DP	TC/G	FA	Pitcher	G	IP	W	L	SV	ERA
1B	J. Doyle	422	.367	3	100	981	59	**38**	51	**10.9**	.965	A. Rusie	54	444	**36**	13	1	**2.78**
2B	M. Ward	540	.265	0	77	331	446	64	52	6.2	.924	J. Meekin	52	409	33	9	2	3.70
SS	S. Fuller	368	.283	2	46	205	291	65	39	6.3	.884	H. Westervelt	23	141	7	10	0	5.04
3B	G. Davis	477	.352	8	91	150	247	40	18	3.5	.908	L. German	23	134	9	8	1	5.78
RF	M. Tiernan	424	.276	5	77	169	9	15	1	1.7	.922							
CF	G. Van Haltren	519	.331	7	104	299	29	31	5	2.6	.914							
LF	E. Burke	566	.304	5	77	260	17	20	3	2.2	.933							
C	D. Farrell	401	.284	4	66	**460**	**140**	**48**	9	**6.2**	.926							
SO	Y. Murphy	280	.271	0	28	142	149	34	14		.895							
P	A. Rusie	186	.280	3	26	28	**113**	**14**	4	**2.9**	.910							
C1	P. Wilson	175	.331	1	32	246	28	31	9		.898							
P	J. Meekin	170	.282	5	29	15	60	4	3	1.5	.949							

Boston

W-83 L-49

Frank Selee

POS	Player	AB	BA	HR	RBI	PO	A	E	DP	TC/G	FA	Pitcher	G	IP	W	L	SV	ERA
1B	T. Tucker	500	.330	3	100	1108	68	18	82	9.7	.985	K. Nichols	50	407	32	13	0	4.75
2B	B. Lowe	**613**	.346	17	115	345	402	59	62	6.2	.927	J. Stivetts	45	338	26	14	0	4.90
SS	H. Long	475	.324	12	79	217	359	75	52	6.6	.885	H. Staley	27	209	12	10	1	6.81
3B	B. Nash	512	.289	8	87	**204**	**267**	34	**24**	3.8	**.933**	T. Lovett	15	104	8	6	0	5.97
RF	J. Bannon	494	.336	13	114	240	43	41	12	2.5	.873							
CF	H. Duffy	539	**.440**	**18**	**145**	315	27	27	5	3.0	.927							
LF	T. McCarthy	539	.349	13	126	291	28	34	10	2.8	.904							
C	C. Ganzel	266	.278	3	56	184	52	27	6	4.5	.897							
PO	J. Stivetts	244	.328	8	64	49	49	12	2		.891							
C	J. Ryan	201	.269	1	29	168	46	21	7	4.6	.911							
SS	F. Connaughton	171	.345	2	33	62	111	21	11	5.9	.892							
P	K. Nichols	170	.294	0	34	34	67	7	3	2.2	.935							
C	F. Tenney	86	.395	2	21	55	20	9	3	4.2	.893							
P	H. Staley	85	.235	2	25	5	28	6	0	1.4	.846							

NATIONAL LEAGUE 1894, *cont.*

Philadelphia

W-71 L-57

Arthur Irwin

POS	Player	AB	BA	HR	RBI	PO	A	E	DP	TC/G	FA	Pitcher	G	IP	W	L	SV	ERA
1B	J. Boyle	495	.301	4	88	950	61	18	76	9.0	.983	J. Taylor	41	298	23	13	1	4.08
2B	B. Hallman	505	.309	0	66	318	320	48	62	5.8	.930	K. Carsey	35	277	18	12	0	5.56
SS	J. Sullivan	304	.352	3	63	169	224	50	32	5.9	.887	G. Weyhing	38	266	16	14	1	5.81
3B	L. Cross	529	.386	7	125	177	234	36	**24**	**4.5**	.919	G. Harper	12	86	6	6	0	5.32
RF	S. Thompson	437	.407	13	141	159	12	4	2	1.7	.977							
CF	B. Hamilton	544	.404	4	87	361	15	14	4	3.0	.964							
LF	E. Delahanty	489	.407	4	131	212	23	19	4	2.9	.925							
C	J. Clements	159	.346	3	36	178	32	12	4	4.9	.946							
OF	T. Turner	339	.416	1	82	134	7	13	1	2.0	.916							
C	M. Grady	190	.363	0	40	101	29	18	7	3.4	.878							
C	D. Buckley	160	.294	1	26	157	39	7	2	4.8	.966							
SS	B. Allen	149	.255	0	19	87	129	20	15	5.9	.915							
P	J. Taylor	144	.333	0	22	13	68	12	3	2.3	.871							
3B	C. Reilly	135	.296	0	19	34	56	13	3	3.7	.874							

Brooklyn

W-70 L-61

Dave Foutz

POS	Player	AB	BA	HR	RBI	PO	A	E	DP	TC/G	FA	Pitcher	G	IP	W	L	SV	ERA
1B	D. Foutz	293	.307	0	51	658	33	17	37	9.8	.976	B. Kennedy	48	361	24	20	2	4.92
2B	T. Daly	492	.341	8	82	317	354	**68**	52	6.0	.908	E. Stein	45	359	27	14	1	4.54
SS	T. Corcoran	576	.300	5	92	280	439	76	45	6.2	.904	D. Daub	33	215	9	12	0	6.32
3B	B. Shindle	476	.296	4	96	192	226	48	12	4.0	.897	H. Gastright	16	93	2	6	2	6.39
RF	O. Burns	513	.361	5	109	208	15	12	4	1.9	.949							
CF	M. Griffin	405	.365	5	75	297	14	10	5	3.0	.969							
LF	G. Treadway	479	.328	4	102	274	16	35	2	2.7	.892							
C	T. Kinslow	223	.305	2	41	217	47	27	4	4.8	.907							
1B	C. LaChance	257	.323	5	52	508	16	11	26	9.6	.979							
UT	G. Shoch	239	.322	1	37	130	77	17	6		.924							
C	C. Daily	234	.256	0	32	218	61	21	7	5.0	.930							
P	B. Kennedy	161	.304	0	23	7	82	8	4	2.0	.918							
P	E. Stein	146	.260	2	28	20	64	7	1	2.0	.923							

Cleveland

W-68 L-61

Patsy Tebeau

POS	Player	AB	BA	HR	RBI	PO	A	E	DP	TC/G	FA	Pitcher	G	IP	W	L	SV	ERA
1B	P. Tebeau	523	.302	3	89	1077	46	26	66	10.0	.977	C. Young	52	409	26	21	1	3.94
2B	C. Childs	479	.353	2	52	313	374	63	51	6.4	.916	N. Cuppy	43	316	24	15	0	4.56
SS	E. McKean	554	.357	8	128	269	411	71	43	5.8	.905	J. Clarkson	22	151	8	9	0	4.42
3B	C. McGarr	523	.275	2	74	170	242	45	17	3.6	.902	M. Sullivan	13	91	6	5	0	6.35
RF	H. Blake	296	.264	1	51	120	16	10	4	2.0	.932							
CF	J. McAleer	253	.289	2	40	175	9	9	3	3.0	.953							
LF	J. Burkett	523	.358	8	94	242	17	24	5	2.3	.915							
C	C. Zimmer	341	.284	4	65	289	100	15	**16**	4.5	**.963**							
CO	J. O'Connor	330	.315	2	51	249	43	20	4		.936							
OF	B. Ewing	211	.251	2	39	86	7	9	2	2.0	.912							
P	C. Young	186	.215	2	26	16	108	7	4	2.5	.947							
01	W. Tebeau	150	.313	0	25	172	2	13	13		.930							
P	N. Cuppy	135	.259	0	19	17	60	2	**5**	1.8	.975							

Pittsburgh

W-65 L-65

Al Buckenberger
W-53 L-55

Connie Mack
W-12 L-10

POS	Player	AB	BA	HR	RBI	PO	A	E	DP	TC/G	FA	Pitcher	G	IP	W	L	SV	ERA
1B	J. Beckley	533	.343	8	120	**1227**	**84**	30	80	10.2	.978	R. Ehret	46	347	19	21	0	5.14
2B	L. Bierbauer	525	.303	3	107	309	**453**	50	58	6.2	.938	A. Gumbert	37	269	15	14	0	6.02
SS	J. Glasscock	332	.280	1	63	189	295	35	46	6.1	**.933**	F. Killen	28	204	14	11	0	4.50
3B	D. Lyons	254	.323	4	50	119	155	31	11	4.3	.898	T. Colcolough	22	149	8	5	0	7.08
RF	P. Donovan	576	.302	4	76	267	22	21	5	2.3	.932	J. Menefee	13	112	5	8	0	5.40
CF	J. Stenzel	522	.354	13	121	311	23	27	6	2.8	.925							
LF	E. Smith	489	.356	6	72	275	18	21	8	2.5	.933							
C	C. Mack	228	.250	1	21	274	67	19	6	5.2	.947							
3B	F. Hartman	182	.319	2	20	65	97	23	6	3.8	.876							
C	J. Sugden	139	.331	2	23	105	27	13	4	4.7	.910							
P	R. Ehret	135	.170	0	11	12	61	12	2	1.8	.859							
UT	F. Weaver	115	.348	0	24	73	47	15	6		.889							

Chicago

W-57 L-75

Cap Anson

POS	Player	AB	BA	HR	RBI	PO	A	E	DP	TC/G	FA	Pitcher	G	IP	W	L	SV	ERA
1B	C. Anson	347	.395	5	99	739	47	8	52	9.7	**.990**	B. Hutchinson	36	278	14	16	0	6.06
2B	J. Parrott	517	.248	3	64	285	379	49	56	5.8	.931	C. Griffith	36	261	21	14	0	4.92
SS	B. Dahlen	502	.357	15	107	186	253	50	43	7.4	.898	W. McGill	27	208	7	19	0	5.84
3B	C. Irwin	498	.289	8	95	89	123	46	15	3.9	.822	A. Terry	23	163	5	11	0	5.84
RF	J. Ryan	474	.361	3	62	221	22	24	3	2.5	.910	S. Stratton	15	119	8	5	0	6.03
CF	B. Lange	442	.328	6	90	267	25	29	10	2.9	.910							
LF	W. Wilmot	597	.330	5	130	264	16	41	5	2.4	.872							
C	P. Schriver	349	.275	3	47	290	91	32	12	4.7	.923							
UT	G. Decker	384	.313	8	92	497	39	32	32		.944							
C	M. Kittridge	168	.315	0	23	209	36	20	4	5.2	.925							
P	C. Griffith	142	.232	0	15	20	45	4	1	1.9	.942							
P	B. Hutchinson	136	.309	6	16	10	45	5	1	1.7	.917							
PO	S. Stratton	96	.375	3	23	16	21	2	2		.949							

St. Louis

W-56 L-76

Doggie Miller

POS	Player	AB	BA	HR	RBI	PO	A	E	DP	TC/G	FA	Pitcher	G	IP	W	L	SV	ERA
1B	R. Connor	380	.321	7	79	897	68	26	72*	10.0	.974	T. Breitenstein	**56**	**447**	27	25	0	4.79
2B	J. Quinn	405	.286	4	61	341	339	34	**74**	6.7	.952	P. Hawley	53	393	19	**26**	0	4.90
SS	B. Ely	510	.306	12	89	273	442	**79**	51	6.3	.901	D. Clarkson	32	233	8	17	0	6.36
3B	D. Miller	481	.339	8	86	68	96	33	6	3.8	.832							
RF	T. Dowd	524	.271	4	62	199	14	16	4	2.0	.930							
CF	F. Shugart	527	.292	7	72	276	26	29	2	2.7	.912							
LF	C. Frank	319	.279	4	42	161	11	26	4	2.6	.869							
C	H. Peitz	338	.263	3	49	146	51	13	3	5.4	.938							
OF	D. Cooley	206	.296	1	21	74	1	15	1	2.3	.833							
P	T. Breitenstein	182	.220	0	13	**42**	83	9	4	2.4	.933							
P	P. Hawley	163	.264	2	23	29	77	12	2	2.2	.898							

NATIONAL LEAGUE 1894, *cont.*

Cincinnati

W-55 L-75

Charlie Comiskey

POS	Player	AB	BA	HR	RBI	PO	A	E	DP	TC/G	FA
1B	C. Comiskey	220	.264	0	33	536	24	16	36	9.6	.972
2B	B. McPhee	474	.304	5	88	**389**	446	49	72	**7.0**	.945
SS	G. Smith	482	.263	3	76	233	**501**	72	**75**	6.3	.911
3B	A. Latham	524	.313	4	60	158	248	**66**	20	3.7	.860
RF	J. Canavan	356	.272	13	70	188	9	21	6	2.3	.904
CF	D. Hoy	495	.299	5	70	314	29	40	3	3.0	.896
LF	B. Holliday	511	.372	13	119	243	22	25	5	2.4	.914
C	M. Murphy	255	.275	1	37	194	70	29	5	4.0	.901
UT	F. Vaughn	284	.310	7	64	362	64	26	19		.942
UT	T. Parrott	229	.323	4	40	143	87	22	10		.913
P	F. Dwyer	172	.267	2	28	31	62	5	2	2.2	.949
01	J. McCarthy	167	.269	0	21	193	19	13	12		.942
C	B. Merritt	113	.327	1	21	55	26	4	0	3.5	.953

Pitcher	G	IP	W	L	SV	ERA
F. Dwyer	45	348	19	22	1	5.07
T. Parrott	41	309	17	19	1	5.60
I. Chamberlain	23	178	10	9	0	5.77
C. Fisher	11	91	2	8	0	7.32

Washington

W-45 L-87

Gus Schmelz

POS	Player	AB	BA	HR	RBI	PO	A	E	DP	TC/G	FA
1B	E. Cartwright	507	.294	12	106	1219	71	36	63	10.0	.973
2B	P. Ward	347	.303	0	36	167	237	45	21	5.7	.900
SS	F. Scheibeck	196	.230	0	17	108	204	44	15	6.8	.876
3B	B. Joyce	355	.355	17	89	152	183	52	20	3.9	.866
RF	B. Hassamaer	494	.322	4	90	109	11	11	4	1.9	.916
CF	C. Abbey	523	.314	7	101	344	26	37	6	3.2	.909
LF	K. Selbach	372	.306	7	71	153	8	15	2	2.2	.915
C	D. McGuire	425	.306	6	78	288	114	36	8	4.2	.918
UT	P. Radford	325	.240	0	49	219	247	73	23		.865
OF	W. Tebeau	222	.225	0	28	118	8	21	1	2.4	.857
P	W. Mercer	162	.284	2	29	14	68	5	1	1.8	.943
C	D. Dugdale	134	.239	0	16	72	32	15	0	3.6	.874
P	A. Maul	124	.242	2	20	8	49	8	0	2.3	.877

Pitcher	G	IP	W	L	SV	ERA
W. Mercer	49	333	17	23	3	3.76
A. Maul	28	202	11	15	0	5.98
D. Esper	19	122	5	10	0	7.50
M. Sullivan	20	118	2	10	1	6.58
O. Stocksdale	18	117	5	9	0	5.06
C. Petty	16	103	3	8	0	5.59

Louisville

W-36 L-94

Billy Barnie

POS	Player	AB	BA	HR	RBI	PO	A	E	DP	TC/G	FA
1B	L. Lutenberg	250	.192	0	23	593	38	15	54	9.6	.977
2B	F. Pfeffer	409	.308	5	59	255	284	36	58	6.4	.937
SS	D. Richardson	430	.253	1	40	232	360	54	59	6.0	.916
3B	J. Denny	221	.276	0	32	85	124	30	12	4.0	.874
RF	O. Smith	134	.299	3	20	63	5	9	0	2.0	.883
CF	T. Brown	536	.254	9	57	331	21	34	8	3.0	.912
LF	F. Clarke	310	.268	7	48	162	15	23	2	2.6	.885
C	J. Grim	410	.298	7	70	262	100	27	9	5.1	.931
UT	F. Weaver	244	.221	3	24	191	28	11	9		.952
UT	T. O'Rourke	220	.277	0	27	316	41	22	36		.942
OF	L. Twitchell	210	.267	2	32	103	15	12	4	2.5	.908
3B	P. Flaherty	145	.297	0	15	42	70	19	7	3.4	.855

Pitcher	G	IP	W	L	SV	ERA
G. Hemming	35	294	13	19	1	4.37
P. Knell	32	247	7	21	0	5.32
J. Menefee	28	212	8	17	0	4.29
J. Wadsworth	22	173	4	18	0	7.60

BATTING AND BASE RUNNING LEADERS

Batting Average

H. Duffy, BOS	.440
T. Turner, PHI	.416
S. Thompson, PHI	.407
E. Delahanty, PHI	.407
B. Hamilton, PHI	.404

Slugging Average

H. Duffy, BOS	.690
S. Thompson, PHI	.686
B. Joyce, WAS	.648
J. Kelley, BAL	.602
E. Delahanty, PHI	.585

Home Runs

H. Duffy, BOS	18
B. Joyce, WAS	17
B. Lowe, BOS	17
B. Dahlen, CHI	15

Total Bases

H. Duffy, BOS	372
B. Lowe, BOS	319
J. Kelley, BAL	305
W. Keeler, BAL	305
J. Stenzel, PIT	303

Runs Batted In

H. Duffy, BOS	145
S. Thompson, PHI	141
E. Delahanty, PHI	131
W. Wilmot, CHI	130
D. Brouthers, BAL	128
E. McKean, CLE	128

Stolen Bases

B. Hamilton, PHI	98
J. McGraw, BAL	78
W. Wilmot, CHI	74
T. Brown, LOU	66
B. Lange, CHI	65

Hits

H. Duffy, BOS	237
B. Hamilton, PHI	220
W. Keeler, BAL	219
B. Lowe, BOS	212

Base on Balls

B. Hamilton, PHI	126
C. Childs, CLE	107
J. Kelley, BAL	107
J. McGraw, BAL	91
B. Nash, BOS	91

Home Run Percentage

B. Joyce, WAS	4.8
J. Canavan, CIN	3.7
H. Duffy, BOS	3.3
B. Dahlen, CHI	3.0

Runs

B. Hamilton, PHI	192
J. Kelley, BAL	165
W. Keeler, BAL	165
H. Duffy, BOS	160

Doubles

H. Duffy, BOS	51
J. Kelley, BAL	48
W. Wilmot, CHI	45

Triples

H. Reitz, BAL	31
S. Thompson, PHI	27
G. Treadway, BKN	26
R. Connor, NY, STL	25

PITCHING LEADERS

Winning Percentage

J. Meekin, NY	.786
S. McMahon, BAL	.758
A. Rusie, NY	.735
K. Nichols, BOS	.711
E. Stein, BKN	.659

Earned Run Average

A. Rusie, NY	2.78
J. Meekin, NY	3.70
W. Mercer, WAS	3.76
C. Young, CLE	3.94
J. Taylor, PHI	4.08

Wins

A. Rusie, NY	36
J. Meekin, NY	33
K. Nichols, BOS	32
E. Stein, BKN	27
T. Breitenstein, STL	27

Saves

T. Mullane, BAL, CLE	4
B. Hawke, BAL	3
W. Mercer, WAS	3

Strikeouts

A. Rusie, NY	195
T. Breitenstein, STL	140
J. Meekin, NY	133
P. Hawley, STL	120
K. Nichols, BOS	113

Complete Games

T. Breitenstein, STL	46
A. Rusie, NY	45
C. Young, CLE	44
K. Nichols, BOS	40
J. Meekin, NY	40

Fewest Hits/9 Innings

A. Rusie, NY	8.64
J. Meekin, NY	8.89
E. Stein, BKN	9.93
T. Breitenstein, STL	10.00

Shutouts

N. Cuppy, CLE	3
K. Nichols, BOS	3
A. Rusie, NY	3

Fewest Walks/9 Innings

C. Young, CLE	2.33
J. Menefee, LOU, PIT	2.48
K. Gleason, STL, BAL	2.54
H. Staley, BOS	2.63

Most Strikeouts/9 Inn.

A. Rusie, NY	3.95
B. Hawke, BAL	2.99
J. Wadsworth, LOU	2.97
J. Meekin, NY	2.93

Innings

T. Breitenstein, STL	447
A. Rusie, NY	444
C. Young, CLE	409
J. Meekin, NY	409

Games Pitched

T. Breitenstein, STL	56
A. Rusie, NY	54
P. Hawley, STL	53
C. Young, CLE	52
J. Meekin, NY	52

NATIONAL LEAGUE 1894, *cont.*

	W	L	PCT	GB	R	OR	Batting 2B	3B	HR	BA	SA	SB	Fielding E	DP	FA	Pitching CG	BB	SO	ShO	SV	ERA
Baltimore	89	39	.695		1171	820	271	**150**	33	.343	.483	324	**293**	105	**.944**	97	472	275	1	**11**	5.00
New York	88	44	.667	3	940	**789**	197	96	44	.301	.409	319	443	101	.924	111	539	**395**	5	5	**3.83**
Boston	83	49	.629		**1222**	1002	**272**	93	**103**	.331	**.484**	241	415	120	.925	108	**411**	262	3	1	5.41
Philadelphia	71	57	.555		1143	966	252	131	40	**.349**	.476	273	338	111	.935	102	469	262	3	4	5.63
Brooklyn	70	61	.534	2.5	1021	1007	228	130	42	.313	.440	282	390	85	.928	105	555	285	3	5	5.51
Cleveland	68	61	.527	3.5	932	896	241	90	37	.303	.414	220	344	107	.935	107	435	254	**6**	1	4.97
Pittsburgh	65	65	.500	7	955	972	222	123	49	.312	.443	256	354	106	.936	106	457	304	2	0	5.60
Chicago	57	75	.432	16	1041	1066	265	86	65	.314	.441	**327**	452	113	.918	**117**	557	281	0	0	5.68
St. Louis	56	76	.424	17	771	954	171	113	54	.286	.408	190	426	109	.923	114	500	319	2	0	5.29
Cincinnati	55	75	.423	17	910	1085	224	68	60	.294	.410	215	423	119	.925	110	491	219	4	3	5.99
Washington	45	87	.341	28	882	1122	218	118	59	.287	.425	249	499	81	.908	102	446	190	1	4	5.51
Louisville	36	94	.277	36	692	1001	173	88	42	.269	.375	217	428	**130**	.920	113	475	258	2	1	5.45
					11680	11680	2734	1286	628	.308	.434	3113	4805	1287	.927	1292	5807	3304	32	35	5.32

NATIONAL LEAGUE 1895

Baltimore

W-87 L-43

Ned Hanlon

POS	Player	AB	BA	HR	RBI	PO	A	E	DP	TC/G	FA	Pitcher	G	IP	W	L	SV	ERA
1B	S. Carey	490	.261	1	75	1132	43	15	73	9.7	**.987**	B. Hoffer	41	314	31	6	0	3.21
2B	K. Gleason	421	.309	0	74	205	250	51	32	6.0	.899	G. Hemming	34	262	20	13	0	4.05
SS	H. Jennings	529	.386	4	125	**425**	457	56	**71**	**7.2**	**.940**	D. Esper	34	218	10	12	1	3.92
3B	J. McGraw	388	.369	2	48	100	239	47	19	4.1	.878	D. Clarkson	20	142	12	3	0	3.87
RF	W. Keeler	**565**	.377	4	78	244	21	10	5	2.1	.964	S. McMahon	15	122	10	4	0	2.94
CF	S. Brodie	528	.348	2	134	307	23	12	2	2.6	.965							
LF	J. Kelley	518	.365	10	134	260	20	16	5	2.3	.946							
C	W. Robinson	282	.262	0	48	243	78	7	6	4.4	**.979**							
2B	H. Reitz	245	.294	0	29	120	137	17	25	5.7	.938							
C	B. Clarke	241	.290	0	35	176	67	16	8	4.3	.938							

Cleveland

W-84 L-46

Patsy Tebeau

POS	Player	AB	BA	HR	RBI	PO	A	E	DP	TC/G	FA	Pitcher	G	IP	W	L	SV	ERA
1B	P. Tebeau	264	.318	2	52	473	19	4	28	10.1	.992	C. Young	47	370	**35**	10	0	3.24
2B	C. Childs	462	.288	4	90	337	394	**63**	42	**6.7**	.921	N. Cuppy	47	353	26	14	2	3.54
SS	E. McKean	**565**	.342	8	119	246	424	67	42	5.6	.909	B. Wallace	30	229	12	14	1	4.09
3B	C. McGarr	419	.265	2	59	125	217	51	13	3.6	.870	P. Knell	20	117	7	5	0	5.40
RF	H. Blake	315	.276	3	45	119	13	15	3	1.8	.898							
CF	J. McAleer	528	.271	0	68	341	14	25	1	2.9	.934							
LF	J. Burkett	550	**.409**	5	83	273	17	38	4	2.5	.884							
C	C. Zimmer	315	.340	5	56	318	77	10	2	4.8	.975							
C1	J. O'Connor	340	.291	0	58	520	66	16	24		.973							
01	W. Tebeau	337	.326	0	68	480	25	17	12		.967							
P	C. Young	140	.214	0	13	15	**120**	6	2	3.0	.957							
P	N. Cuppy	140	.286	0	25	30	90	4	2	2.6	.968							

Philadelphia

W-78 L-53

Arthur Irwin

POS	Player	AB	BA	HR	RBI	PO	A	E	DP	TC/G	FA	Pitcher	G	IP	W	L	SV	ERA
1B	J. Boyle	**565**	.253	0	67	1245	61	**36**	69	10.1	.973	K. Carsey	44	342	24	16	1	4.92
2B	B. Hallman	539	.314	1	91	299	392	42	57	6.0	.943	J. Taylor	41	335	26	14	1	4.49
SS	J. Sullivan	373	.338	2	50	182	270	62	32	5.8	.879	W. McGill	20	146	10	8	0	5.55
3B	L. Cross	535	.271	2	101	191	**308**	32	23	**4.2**	**.940**	A. Orth	11	88	8	1	1	3.89
RF	S. Thompson	538	.392	**18**	**165**	186	31	13	2	1.9	.943							
CF	B. Hamilton	517	.389	7	74	313	11	31	5	2.9	.913							
LF	E. Delahanty	480	.404	11	106	237	16	15	4	2.6	.944							
C	J. Clements	322	.394	13	75	280	69	11	7	4.1	.969							
OF	T. Turner	210	.386	2	43	89	5	17	0	2.0	.847							
S3	C. Reilly	179	.268	0	25	70	123	23	14		.894							
P	J. Taylor	155	.290	3	35	19	89	5	3	2.8	.956							
P	K. Carsey	141	.291	0	20	9	77	12	2	2.2	.878							
C	M. Grady	123	.325	1	23	103	10	9	2	3.2	.926							

Chicago

W-72 L-58

Cap Anson

POS	Player	AB	BA	HR	RBI	PO	A	E	DP	TC/G	FA	Pitcher	G	IP	W	L	SV	ERA
1B	C. Anson	474	.335	2	91	1176	60	19	**82**	10.3	.985	C. Griffith	42	353	26	14	0	3.93
2B	A. Stewart	365	.241	8	76	252	281	52	53	6.0	.911	A. Terry	38	311	21	14	0	4.80
SS	B. Dahlen	516	.254	7	62	281	**527**	**86**	70	6.9	.904	B. Hutchinson	38	291	13	21	0	4.73
3B	B. Everitt	550	.358	3	88	174	263	75	12	3.9	.854							
RF	J. Ryan	438	.317	6	49	161	18	12	6	1.8	.937							
CF	B. Lange	478	.389	10	98	298	28	27	6	2.9	.924							
LF	W. Wilmot	466	.283	8	72	226	19	23	5	2.5	.914							
C	T. Donahue	219	.269	2	36	234	45	26	8	4.8	.915							
OF	G. Decker	297	.276	2	41	98	3	10	0	1.9	.910							
C	M. Kittridge	212	.226	3	29	197	48	6	4	4.3	.976							
P	C. Griffith	144	.319	1	27	27	81	9	2	2.8	.923							
P	A. Terry	137	.219	1	10	13	81	11	3	2.8	.895							

Boston

W-71 L-60

Frank Selee

POS	Player	AB	BA	HR	RBI	PO	A	E	DP	TC/G	FA	Pitcher	G	IP	W	L	SV	ERA
1B	T. Tucker	462	.249	3	73	1159	82	28	78	10.2	.978	K. Nichols	47	380	26	16	**3**	3.41
2B	B. Lowe	412	.296	7	62	265	336	29	50	6.4	.954	J. Stivetts	38	291	17	17	0	4.64
SS	H. Long	535	.316	9	75	280	409	84	48	6.3	.891	C. Dolan	25	198	11	7	1	4.27
3B	B. Nash	508	.289	10	108	**193**	246	59	**26**	3.8	.882	J. Sullivan	21	179	11	9	0	4.82
RF	J. Bannon	489	.350	6	74	209	30	33	3	2.2	.879							
CF	H. Duffy	531	.352	9	100	322	20	20	7	2.8	.945							
LF	T. McCarthy	452	.290	2	73	199	16	28	2	2.2	.885							
C	C. Ganzel	277	.264	1	52	345	65	16	9	**5.6**	.962							
C	J. Ryan	189	.291	0	18	167	46	11	2	5.2	.951							
OC	F. Tenney	173	.272	1	21	109	24	7	2		.950							
P	J. Stivetts	158	.190	0	24	24	50	3	1	2.0	.961							
P	K. Nichols	157	.236	0	18	29	73	4	2	2.2	.962							

NATIONAL LEAGUE 1895, *cont.*

Team	POS	Player	AB	BA	HR	RBI	PO	A	E	DP	TC/G	FA	Pitcher	G	IP	W	L	SV	ERA
Brooklyn	1B	C. LaChance	536	.312	8	108	1286	53	23	68	10.9	.983	B. Kennedy	39	280	19	12	1	5.12
	2B	T. Daly	455	.281	2	68	318	346	50	42	5.9	.930	E. Stein	32	255	15	13	1	4.72
	SS	T. Corcoran	535	.265	2	69	293	488	64	49	6.7	.924	A. Gumbert	33	234	11	16	1	5.08
W-71 L-60	3B	B. Shindle	477	.279	3	69	142	257	46	16	3.8	.897	D. Daub	25	185	10	10	0	4.29
	RF	G. Treadway	339	.257	7	54	117	7	16	4	1.6	.886	C. Lucid	21	137	10	7	0	5.52
Dave Foutz	CF	M. Griffin	519	.333	4	65	349	23	12	12	2.9	.969							
	LF	J. Anderson	419	.286	9	87	205	11	29	4	2.4	.882							
	C	J. Grim	329	.280	0	44	253	103	20	10	4.1	.947							
	UT	G. Shoch	216	.259	0	29	98	63	14	6		.920							
	C	C. Daily	142	.211	1	11	127	25	7	7	4.1	.956							
	P	B. Kennedy	127	.307	0	21	5	66	5	1	1.9	.934							
	OF	D. Foutz	115	.296	0	21	26	3	4	1	1.6	.879							
Pittsburgh	1B	J. Beckley	530	.328	5	110	**1340**	54	31	76	**11.0**	.978	P. Hawley	**56**	**444**	31	22	1	3.18
	2B	L. Bierbauer	466	.258	0	69	284	**400**	39	52	6.2	.946	B. Hart	36	262	14	17	1	4.75
	SS	M. Cross	393	.257	3	54	254	327	77	42	6.1	.883	B. Foreman	19	140	8	6	2	3.22
W-71 L-61	3B	B. Clingman	382	.259	0	45	137	256	50	16	4.2	.887	F. Killen	13	95	5	5	0	5.49
	RF	P. Donovan	519	.308	1	58	187	11	8	2	1.6	.961	J. Gardner	11	85	8	2	0	2.64
Connie Mack	CF	J. Stenzel	514	.374	7	97	257	23	27	6	2.4	.912							
	LF	E. Smith	480	.302	1	81	250	16	31	2	2.4	.896							
	C	B. Merritt	239	.285	0	27	245	58	21	7	5.1	.935							
	UT	F. Genins	252	.250	2	24	127	99	29	7		.886							
	P	P. Hawley	185	.308	5	42	16	110	13	2	2.5	.906							
	C	J. Sugden	155	.310	1	17	176	57	25	4	5.3	.903							
Cincinnati	1B	B. Ewing	434	.318	5	94	957	79	26	69	10.1	.976	F. Dwyer	37	280	18	15	0	4.24
	2B	B. McPhee	432	.299	1	75	355	366	34	57	6.6	.955	B. Rhines	38	268	19	10	0	4.81
	SS	G. Smith	503	.300	4	74	251	457	59	58	6.0	.923	T. Parrott	41	263	11	18	**3**	5.47
W-66 L-64	3B	A. Latham	460	.311	2	69	126	197	52	13	3.5	.861	F. Foreman	32	219	11	14	1	4.11
	RF	D. Miller	529	.335	8	112	243	25	18	8	2.2	.937	B. Phillips	18	109	6	7	2	6.03
Buck Ewing	CF	G. Hogriever	239	.272	2	34	174	10	13	3	3.0	.934							
	LF	D. Hoy	429	.277	3	55	235	14	33	6	2.6	.883							
	C	F. Vaughn	334	.305	0	48	262	78	24	10	4.7	.934							
	OF	E. Burke	228	.268	1	28	135	8	16	2	2.8	.899							
	UT	T. Parrott	201	.343	3	41	151	70	13	12		.944							
	UT	B. Grey	181	.304	1	29	89	108	24	13		.891							
	OF	B. Holliday	127	.299	0	20	60	3	4	1	2.1	.940							
	P	B. Rhines	113	.221	0	23	17	56	9	3	2.2	.890							
New York	1B	J. Doyle	319	.313	1	66	599	34	21	27	11.3	.968	A. Rusie	49	393	23	23	0	3.73
	2B	G. Stafford	463	.279	3	73	242	329	56	44	5.7	.911	D. Clarke	37	282	18	15	1	3.39
	SS	S. Fuller	458	.225	0	32	270	499	73	59	6.7	.913	J. Meekin	29	226	16	11	0	5.30
	3B	G. Davis	430	.340	5	101	122	175	40	18	4.2	.881	L. German	25	178	7	11	0	5.96
W-66 L-65	RF	M. Tiernan	476	.347	7	70	184	8	11	2	1.7	.946							
	CF	G. Van Haltren	521	.340	8	103	252	26	26	3	2.3	.914							
George Davis	LF	E. Burke	167	.257	1	12	77	8	8	2	2.4	.914							
W-16 L-17	C	D. Farrell	312	.288	1	58	269	67	21	**11**	5.8	.941							
Jack Doyle	C	P. Wilson	238	.235	0	30	214	56	18	8	5.4	.938							
W-32 L-31	UT	Y. Murphy	184	.201	0	16	82	39	18	4		.871							
	P	A. Rusie	179	.246	1	19	19	93	11	4	2.5	.911							
Harvey Watkins	01	T. Bannon	159	.270	0	8	198	18	19	16		.919							
W-18 L-17	OF	O. Burns	114	.307	1	25	42	5	7	0	1.7	.870							
Washington	1B	E. Cartwright	472	.331	3	90	1102	**95**	19	69	10.0	.984	W. Mercer	43	311	13	23	2	4.46
	2B	J. Crooks	409	.279	6	57	327	364	32	43	6.2	**.956**	V. Anderson	29	205	9	16	0	5.89
	SS	F. Scheibeck	167	.186	0	25	95	142	30	17	6.1	.888	O. Stocksdale	20	136	6	11	1	6.09
W-43 L-85	3B	B. Joyce	474	.312	17	95	186	232	**77**	16	3.9	.844	A. Maul	16	136	10	5	0	**2.45**
	RF	B. Hassamaer	358	.279	1	60	104	4	4	1	1.5	.964	J. Malarkey	22	101	0	8	2	5.99
Gus Schmelz	CF	C. Abbey	511	.276	8	84	275	32	33	7	2.6	.903	J. Boyd	14	85	2	11	0	7.07
	LF	K. Selbach	516	.322	6	55	289	21	30	4	2.9	.912							
	C	D. McGuire	533	.336	10	97	**408**	**179**	**40**	**11**	4.8	.936							
	P	W. Mercer	196	.255	1	26	25	58	12	2	2.2	.874							
	UT	J. Boyd	157	.268	1	16	50	55	24	5		.814							
	OF	T. Brown	134	.239	2	16	59	1	6	0	1.9	.909							
St. Louis	1B	R. Connor	398	.329	8	77	953	62	14	60	10.0	.986	T. Breitenstein	54	430	18	**30**	1	4.44
	2B	J. Quinn	543	.311	2	74	**359**	390	43	**63**	5.9	.946	R. Ehret	37	232	6	19	0	6.02
	SS	B. Ely	467	.259	1	46	247	407	53	52	6.0	.925	H. Staley	23	159	6	13	0	5.22
	3B	D. Miller	490	.292	5	74	54	72	26	5	3.3	.829	B. Kissinger	24	141	4	12	0	6.72
W-39 L-92	RF	T. Dowd	505	.323	6	74	218	11	18	3	2.1	.927	J. McDougal	18	115	4	10	0	8.32
	CF	T. Brown	350	.217	1	31	215	15	12	5	2.9	.950							
Al Buckenberger	LF	D. Cooley	563	.339	6	75	320	17	23	1	2.9	.936							
W-16 L-34	C	H. Peitz	334	.284	2	65	260	80	23	10	5.1	.937							
Chris Von Der Ahe	P	T. Breitenstein	218	.193	0	18	**45**	98	**14**	1	2.9	.911							
W-1 L-0	OF	B. Sheehan	180	.317	1	18	56	7	4	1	1.6	.940							
	3B	D. Lyons	129	.295	2	25	61	49	13	2	3.7	.894							
Joe Quinn																			
W-11 L-28																			
Lew Phelan																			
W-11 L-30																			

NATIONAL LEAGUE 1895, *cont.*

Louisville

W-35 L-96

John McCloskey

POS	Player	AB	BA	HR	RBI	PO	A	E	DP	TC/G	FA
1B	H. Spies	276	.268	2	35	439	22	9	30	10.0	.981
2B	J. O'Brien	539	.256	1	50	304	396	46	56	6.0	.938
SS	F. Shugart	473	.264	4	70	178	258	63	39	5.7	.874
3B	J. Collins	373	.279	6	49	131	181	25	12	4.4	.926
RF	T. Gettinger	260	.269	2	32	127	5	13	1	2.3	.910
CF	J. Wright	228	.276	1	30	127	4	5	1	2.3	.963
LF	F. Clarke	550	.347	4	82	344	20	49	4	3.1	.881
C	J. Warner	232	.267	1	20	195	47	18	4	4.1	.931
O3	W. Preston	197	.279	1	24	71	54	33	5		.791
UT	D. Holmes	161	.373	3	20	49	32	21	2		.794
C1	T. Welch	153	.242	1	8	254	41	21	17		.934

Pitcher	G	IP	W	L	SV	ERA
B. Cunningham	31	231	11	16	0	4.75
G. Weyhing	28	213	7	19	0	5.41
M. McDermott	33	207	4	19	0	5.99
B. Inks	28	205	7	20	0	6.40

BATTING AND BASE RUNNING LEADERS

Batting Average

J. Burkett, CLE	.409
E. Delahanty, PHI	.404
J. Clements, PHI	.394
S. Thompson, PHI	.392
B. Lange, CHI	.389

Slugging Average

S. Thompson, PHI	.654
E. Delahanty, PHI	.617
J. Clements, PHI	.612
B. Lange, CHI	.575
J. Kelley, BAL	.546

Home Runs

S. Thompson, PHI	18
B. Joyce, WAS	17
J. Clements, PHI	13
E. Delahanty, PHI	11

Total Bases

S. Thompson, PHI	352
E. Delahanty, PHI	296
J. Burkett, CLE	288
J. Kelley, BAL	283
E. McKean, CLE	283

Runs Batted In

S. Thompson, PHI	165
J. Kelley, BAL	134
S. Brodie, BAL	134
H. Jennings, BAL	125
E. McKean, CLE	119

Stolen Bases

B. Hamilton, PHI	97
B. Lange, CHI	67
J. McGraw, BAL	61
J. Kelley, BAL	54
J. Stenzel, PIT	53
H. Jennings, BAL	53

Hits

J. Burkett, CLE	225
W. Keeler, BAL	213
S. Thompson, PHI	211
H. Jennings, BAL	204

Base on Balls

B. Joyce, WAS	96
B. Hamilton, PHI	96
M. Griffin, BKN	93
E. Delahanty, PHI	86

Home Run Percentage

J. Clements, PHI	4.0
B. Joyce, WAS	3.6
S. Thompson, PHI	3.3
E. Delahanty, PHI	2.3

Runs

B. Hamilton, PHI	166
W. Keeler, BAL	162
H. Jennings, BAL	159
J. Burkett, CLE	153

Doubles

E. Delahanty, PHI	49
S. Thompson, PHI	45
H. Jennings, BAL	41
J. Stenzel, PIT	38
M. Griffin, BKN	38

Triples

K. Selbach, WAS	22
M. Tiernan, NY	21
S. Thompson, PHI	21
D. Cooley, STL	21

PITCHING LEADERS

Winning Percentage

B. Hoffer, BAL	.838
C. Young, CLE	.778
B. Rhines, CIN	.655
N. Cuppy, CLE	.650
C. Griffith, CHI	.650
J. Taylor, PHI	.650

Earned Run Average

A. Maul, WAS	2.45
S. McMahon, BAL	2.94
P. Hawley, PIT	3.18
B. Hoffer, BAL	3.21
B. Foreman, PIT	3.22

Wins

C. Young, CLE	35
B. Hoffer, BAL	31
P. Hawley, PIT	31

Saves

K. Nichols, BOS	3
E. Beam, PHI	3
T. Parrott, CIN	3

Strikeouts

A. Rusie, NY	201
P. Hawley, PIT	142
K. Nichols, BOS	140
T. Breitenstein, STL	127
C. Young, CLE	121

Complete Games

T. Breitenstein, STL	46
P. Hawley, PIT	44
K. Nichols, BOS	42
A. Rusie, NY	42
C. Griffith, CHI	39

Fewest Hits/9 Innings

S. McMahon, BAL	8.09
B. Foreman, PIT	8.44
B. Hoffer, BAL	8.48
A. Rusie, NY	8.79

Shutouts

S. McMahon, BAL	4
B. Hoffer, BAL	4
C. Young, CLE	4
A. Rusie, NY	4
P. Hawley, PIT	4

Fewest Walks/9 Innings

C. Young, CLE	1.83
D. Clarke, NY	1.92
K. Nichols, BOS	2.04
H. Staley, STL	2.21

Most Strikeouts/9 Inn.

A. Rusie, NY	4.60
W. McGill, PHI	4.32
B. Foreman, PIT	3.48
J. Stivetts, BOS	3.43

Innings

P. Hawley, PIT	444
T. Breitenstein, STL	430
A. Rusie, NY	393
K. Nichols, BOS	380

Games Pitched

P. Hawley, PIT	56
T. Breitenstein, STL	54
A. Rusie, NY	49

							Batting						Fielding			Pitching					
	W	L	PCT	GB	R	OR	2B	3B	HR	BA	SA	SB	E	DP	FA	CG	BB	SO	ShO	SV	ERA
Baltimore	87	43	.669		1009	**646**	235	89	25	.324	.427	310	**288**	108	**.946**	104	430	244	**10**	4	**3.80**
Cleveland	84	46	.646	3	917	720	194	67	29	.305	.395	187	348	77	.936	108	**346**	326	6	3	3.90
Philadelphia	78	53	.595	9.5	**1068**	957	**272**	73	**61**	**.330**	**.450**	276	369	93	.933	106	485	330	2	**7**	5.47
Chicago	72	58	.554	15	866	854	171	85	55	.298	.405	260	401	**113**	.928	**119**	432	297	3	1	4.67
Boston	71	60	.542	16.5	907	826	197	57	54	.290	.391	199	364	104	.934	115	363	370	4	4	4.27
Brooklyn	71	60	.542	16.5	867	834	189	77	39	.282	.379	183	325	96	.941	103	395	216	5	6	4.94
Pittsburgh	71	61	.538	17	811	787	190	89	26	.290	.386	257	392	95	.930	106	500	382	4	6	4.05
Cincinnati	66	64	.508	21	903	854	235	**107**	33	.298	.415	**326**	377	112	.931	97	362	245	2	6	4.81
New York	66	65	.504	21.5	852	834	191	90	32	.288	.389	292	438	106	.922	115	415	**409**	6	1	4.51
Washington	43	85	.336	43	837	1048	207	101	55	.287	.412	237	447	96	.917	99	465	258	0	5	5.28
St. Louis	39	92	.298	48.5	747	1032	155	89	36	.281	.373	205	380	94	.930	105	439	280	1	1	5.76
Louisville	35	96	.267	52.5	698	1090	171	73	34	.279	.368	156	477	104	.913	104	469	245	3	1	5.90
					10482	10482	2407	997	479	.296	.399	2888	4606	1198	.930	1281	5101	3602	46	45	4.78

NATIONAL LEAGUE 1896

Baltimore

W-90 L-39

Ned Hanlon

POS	Player	AB	BA	HR	RBI	PO	A	E	DP	TC/G	FA
1B	J. Doyle	487	.339	1	101	1173	42	**32**	85	10.6	.974
2B	H. Reitz	464	.287	4	106	256	335	30	54	5.3	.952
SS	H. Jennings	521	.401	0	121	**377**	476	66	**70**	**7.1**	**.928**
3B	J. Donnelly	396	.328	0	71	140	217	47	15	3.8	.884
RF	W. Keeler	544	.386	4	82	227	20	8	6	2.0	.969
CF	S. Brodie	516	.297	2	87	320	22	10	6	2.7	.972
LF	J. Kelley	519	.364	8	100	280	20	13	3	2.4	.958
C	W. Robinson	245	.347	2	38	260	48	17	5	4.9	.948
C	B. Clarke	300	.297	2	71	203	53	14	5	4.0	.948

Pitcher	G	IP	W	L	SV	ERA
B. Hoffer	35	309	25	7	0	3.38
A. Pond	28	214	16	8	0	3.49
G. Hemming	25	202	15	6	0	4.19
S. McMahon	22	176	11	9	0	3.48
D. Esper	20	156	14	5	0	3.58

NATIONAL LEAGUE 1896, *cont.*

Cleveland

W-80 L-48

Patsy Tebeau

POS	Player	AB	BA	HR	RBI	PO	A	E	DP	TC/G	FA	Pitcher	G	IP	W	L	SV	ERA
1B	P. Tebeau	543	.269	2	94	**1340**	75	21	**88**	**11.8**	.985	C. Young	51	414	28	15	**3**	3.24
2B	C. Childs	498	.355	1	106	**375**	**487**	**53**	**73**	**6.9**	.942	N. Cuppy	46	358	25	14	1	3.12
SS	E. McKean	571	.338	7	112	214	400	57	57	5.0	.915	Z. Wilson	33	240	17	9	1	4.01
3B	C. McGarr	455	.268	1	53	123	228	29	20	3.4	.924	B. Wallace	22	145	10	7	0	3.34
RF	H. Blake	383	.240	1	43	184	17	12	5	2.1	.944							
CF	J. McAleer	455	.288	1	54	278	18	13	5	2.7	.958							
LF	J. Burkett	**586**	**.410**	6	72	269	18	23	4	2.3	.926							
C	C. Zimmer	336	.277	3	46	338	81	12	9	4.7	**.972**							
UT	J. O'Connor	256	.297	1	43	242	40	7	13		.976							
P	C. Young	180	.289	3	28	8	**145**	12	3	3.2	.927							
OP	B. Wallace	149	.235	1	17	42	35	5	4		.939							
P	N. Cuppy	141	.270	1	20	14	106	4	3	2.7	.968							

Cincinnati

W-77 L-50

Buck Ewing

POS	Player	AB	BA	HR	RBI	PO	A	E	DP	TC/G	FA	Pitcher	G	IP	W	L	SV	ERA
1B	B. Ewing	263	.278	1	38	669	49	15	41	10.6	.980	F. Dwyer	36	289	24	11	1	3.15
2B	B. McPhee	433	.305	1	87	297	357	15	56	5.7	**.978**	R. Ehret	34	277	18	14	0	3.42
SS	G. Smith	456	.287	2	71	207	407	49	47	5.5	.926	F. Foreman	27	191	15	6	1	3.68
3B	C. Irwin	476	.296	1	67	**200**	262	34	**28**	3.9	**.931**	C. Fisher	27	160	10	7	2	4.45
RF	D. Miller	504	.321	4	93	199	21	24	7	2.0	.902	B. Rhines	19	143	8	6	0	**2.45**
CF	D. Hoy	443	.298	4	57	303	14	18	3	2.8	.946							
LF	E. Burke	521	.340	1	52	290	13	21	3	2.7	.935							
C	H. Peitz	211	.299	2	34	201	42	8	6	3.7	.968							
1C	F. Vaughn	433	.293	2	66	740	82	21	41		.975							
P	R. Ehret	102	.196	1	20	15	69	7	3	2.7	.923							

Boston

W-74 L-57

Frank Selee

POS	Player	AB	BA	HR	RBI	PO	A	E	DP	TC/G	FA	Pitcher	G	IP	W	L	SV	ERA
1B	T. Tucker	474	.304	2	72	1214	72	20	72	10.7	.985	K. Nichols	49	375	**30**	14	1	2.81
2B	B. Lowe	305	.321	2	48	193	280	17	31	6.7	.965	J. Stivetts	42	329	21	14	0	4.10
SS	H. Long	501	.343	6	100	311	415	83	52	6.7	.897	J. Sullivan	31	225	11	12	1	4.03
3B	J. Collins	304	.296	1	46	134	207	34	16	**4.7**	.909	F. Klobedanz	10	81	6	4	0	3.01
RF	J. Bannon	343	.251	0	50	132	13	16	2	2.1	.901							
CF	B. Hamilton	523	.365	3	52	276	8	20	2	2.3	.934							
LF	H. Duffy	527	.300	5	112	250	15	12	2	2.2	.957							
C	M. Bergen	245	.269	4	37	207	70	24	6	4.8	.920							
OC	F. Tenney	348	.336	2	49	183	40	14	4		.941							
P	J. Stivetts	221	.344	3	49	30	57	5	3	2.2	.946							
3B	J. Harrington	198	.197	1	25	56	102	35	7	3.9	.819							
C	C. Ganzel	179	.263	1	18	139	47	2	4	4.6	.989							
2B	D. McGann	171	.322	2	30	88	111	21	10	5.1	.905							
P	K. Nichols	147	.190	1	24	19	92	0	3	2.3	**1.000**							

Chicago

W-71 L-57

Cap Anson

POS	Player	AB	BA	HR	RBI	PO	A	E	DP	TC/G	FA	Pitcher	G	IP	W	L	SV	ERA
1B	C. Anson	402	.331	2	90	880	54	16	67	9.7	.983	C. Griffith	36	318	23	11	0	3.54
2B	F. Pfeffer	360	.244	2	52	227	307	30	43	6.0	.947	D. Friend	36	291	18	14	0	4.74
SS	B. Dahlen	474	.352	9	74	310	456	71	66	6.7	.915	A. Terry	30	235	15	13	0	4.28
3B	B. Everitt	575	.320	2	46	148	180	44	10	3.8	.882	B. Briggs	26	194	12	8	1	4.31
RF	J. Ryan	489	.305	3	86	207	21	22	4	2.0	.912							
CF	B. Lange	469	.326	4	92	313	18	24	3	2.9	.932							
LF	G. Decker	421	.280	5	61	131	10	11	0	2.1	.928							
C	M. Kittridge	215	.223	1	19	251	56	12	12	5.0	.962							
C	T. Donahue	188	.218	0	20	235	60	20	7	5.5	.937							
3B	B. McCormick	168	.220	1	23	34	72	21	5	3.6	.835							
P	C. Griffith	135	.267	1	16	20	79	9	3	3.0	.917							
2B	H. Truby	109	.257	2	31	76	82	11	17	6.0	.935							

Pittsburgh

W-66 L-63

Connie Mack

POS	Player	AB	BA	HR	RBI	PO	A	E	DP	TC/G	FA	Pitcher	G	IP	W	L	SV	ERA
1B	J. Beckley	217	.253	3	32	558	31	11	42	10.7	.982	F. Killen	**52**	**432**	**30**	18	0	3.41
2B	D. Padden	219	.242	2	24	176	149	24	14	5.7	.931	P. Hawley	49	378	22	21	0	3.57
SS	B. Ely	537	.285	3	77	258	432	62	52	5.9	.918	J. Hughey	25	155	6	8	0	4.99
3B	D. Lyons	436	.307	4	71	165	201	44	15	3.5	.893	C. Hastings	17	104	5	10	1	5.88
RF	P. Donovan	573	.319	3	59	224	24	12	8	2.0	.954							
CF	J. Stenzel	479	.361	2	82	247	13	22	5	2.5	.922							
LF	E. Smith	484	.362	6	94	302	14	18	6	2.7	.946							
C	J. Sugden	301	.296	0	36	284	70	18	12	**5.3**	.952							
C	B. Merritt	282	.291	1	42	242	75	20	5	5.4	.941							
2B	L. Bierbauer	258	.287	0	39	140	206	12	32	6.1	.966							
P	F. Killen	173	.231	2	25	15	115	10	1	2.7	.929							
1B	H. Davis	168	.190	0	23	325	18	12	17	10.1	.966							
P	P. Hawley	163	.239	1	21	12	108	10	2	2.7	.923							

New York

W-64 L-67

Arthur Irwin
W-36 L-53

Bill Joyce
W-28 L-14

POS	Player	AB	BA	HR	RBI	PO	A	E	DP	TC/G	FA	Pitcher	G	IP	W	L	SV	ERA
1B	W. Clark	247	.291	0	33	634	25	17	40	10.4	.975	D. Clarke	48	351	17	24	1	4.26
2B	K. Gleason	541	.299	4	89	329	397	48	38	6.0	.938	J. Meekin	42	334	26	14	0	3.82
SS	F. Connaughton	315	.260	2	43	89	199	35	19	6.0	.892	M. Sullivan	25	185	10	13	0	4.66
3B	G. Davis	494	.320	6	99	117	169	26	11	4.2	.917	E. Doheny	17	108	6	7	0	4.49
RF	M. Tiernan	521	.369	7	89	213	15	7	4	1.8	.970							
CF	G. Van Haltren	562	.351	5	74	272	25	15	4	2.3	.952							
LF	G. Stafford	230	.287	0	40	78	9	10	2	1.8	.897							
C	P. Wilson	253	.237	0	23	256	64	22	4	4.8	.936							
O1	H. Davis	233	.275	2	50	307	13	15	14		.955							
UT	D. Farrell	191	.283	1	37	144	83	26	13		.897							
1B	J. Beckley	182	.302	5	38	418	22	8	18	10.0	.982							
3B	B. Joyce	165	.370	5*	43	71	103	23	4	4.0	.883							
P	D. Clarke	147	.204	0	10	12	72	8	1	1.9	.913							
P	J. Meekin	144	.299	2	16	17	62	8	3	2.1	.908							

NATIONAL LEAGUE 1896, *cont.*

Philadelphia

W-62 L-68

Billy Nash

POS	Player	AB	BA	HR	RBI	PO	A	E	DP	TC/G	FA	Pitcher	G	IP	W	L	SV	ERA
1B	D. Brouthers	218	.344	1	41	566	23	10	44	10.5	.983	J. Taylor	45	359	20	21	1	4.79
2B	B. Hallman	469	.320	2	83	304	368	39	62	5.9	.945	A. Orth	25	196	15	10	0	4.41
SS	B. Hulen	339	.265	0	38	149	205	51	33	5.5	.874	K. Carsey	27	187	11	11	1	5.62
3B	B. Nash	227	.247	3	30	87	148	23	12	4.0	.911	H. Keener	16	113	3	11	0	5.88
RF	S. Thompson	517	.298	12	100	231	28	7	11	2.2	.974							
CF	D. Cooley	287	.307	2	22	130	6	15	2	2.4	.901							
LF	E. Delahanty	499	.397	13	**126**	262	18	14	4	3.0	.952							
C	M. Grady	242	.318	1	44	167	60	14	12	4.0	.942							
3S	L. Cross	406	.256	1	73	165	270	28	26		.940							
OF	J. Sullivan	191	.251	2	24	99	3	4	0	2.4	.962							
C	J. Clements	184	.359	5	45	149	51	7	3	3.9	.966							
1B	N. Lajoie	175	.326	4	42	363	11	2	27	9.6	.995							
P	J. Taylor	157	.185	0	18	19	107	11	3	3.0	.920							
C	J. Boyle	145	.297	1	28	83	21	9	3	4.0	.920							
OF	S. Mertes	143	.238	0	14	85	3	9	0	2.8	.907							

Brooklyn

W-58 L-73

Dave Foutz

POS	Player	AB	BA	HR	RBI	PO	A	E	DP	TC/G	FA	Pitcher	G	IP	W	L	SV	ERA
1B	C. LaChance	348	.284	7	58	956	37	14	62	11.3	.986	B. Kennedy	42	306	17	20	1	4.42
2B	T. Daly	224	.281	3	29	168	190	36	31	6.0	.909	H. Payne	34	242	14	16	0	3.39
SS	T. Corcoran	532	.289	3	73	323	477	64	69	6.5	.926	D. Daub	32	225	12	11	0	3.60
3B	B. Shindle	516	.279	1	61	144	251	38	20	3.3	.912	B. Abbey	25	164	8	8	0	5.15
RF	F. Jones	395	.354	3	46	171	10	14	6	1.9	.928	G. Harper	16	86	4	8	0	5.55
CF	M. Griffin	493	.308	4	51	316	8	13	1	2.8	.961							
LF	T. McCarthy	377	.249	3	47	175	20	17	6	2.1	.920							
C	J. Grim	281	.267	2	35	242	82	21	7	4.5	.939							
01	J. Anderson	430	.314	1	55	538	28	16	30		.973							
2B	G. Shoch	250	.292	1	28	103	184	18	16	4.9	.941							
C	B. Burrell	206	.301	0	23	176	42	17	3	3.9	.928							

Washington

W-58 L-73

Gus Schmelz

POS	Player	AB	BA	HR	RBI	PO	A	E	DP	TC/G	FA	Pitcher	G	IP	W	L	SV	ERA
1B	E. Cartwright	499	.277	1	62	1276	71	30	76	10.4	.978	W. Mercer	46	366	25	18	0	4.13
2B	J. O'Brien	270	.267	4	33	166	228	20	33	5.7	.952	D. McJames	37	280	12	20	1	4.27
SS	G. DeMontreville	533	.343	8	77	305	**479**	**97**	53	6.6	.890	L. German	28	167	2	20	1	6.32
3B	B. Joyce	310	.313	9*	51	50	108	20	6	3.7	.888	S. King	22	145	10	7	1	4.09
RF	B. Lush	352	.247	4	45	142	19	21	4	2.0	.885							
CF	T. Brown	435	.294	2	59	262	7	21	2	2.5	.928							
LF	K. Selbach	487	.304	5	100	303	13	18	3	2.7	.946							
C	D. McGuire	389	.321	2	70	**349**	87	**30**	**14**	4.8	.936							
OF	C. Abbey	301	.262	1	49	105	10	16	0	1.7	.878							
P	W. Mercer	156	.244	1	14	36	89	21	3	3.2	.856							
3B	J. Rogers	154	.279	1	30	27	70	13	2	3.4	.882							
C3	D. Farrell	130	.300	1	30	75	47	5	1		.961							
2B	J. Crooks	84	.286	3	20	49	49	9	5	5.3	.916							

St. Louis

W-40 L-90

Harry Diddlebock
W-7 L-10

Arlie Latham
W-0 L-3

Chris Von Der Ahe
W-0 L-2

Roger Connor
W-8 L-37

Tommy Dowd
W-25 L-38

POS	Player	AB	BA	HR	RBI	PO	A	E	DP	TC/G	FA	Pitcher	G	IP	W	L	SV	ERA
1B	R. Connor	483	.284	11	72	1217	**94**	16	48	10.5	**.988**	T. Breitenstein	44	340	18	26	0	4.48
2B	T. Dowd	521	.265	5	46	182	220	35	22	5.6	.920	B. Hart	42	336	12	**29**	0	5.12
SS	M. Cross	427	.244	6	52	298	394	84	31	6.2	.892	R. Donahue	32	267	7	24	0	5.80
3B	B. Myers	454	.256	0	37	162	242	**62**	16	3.9	.867	B. Kissinger	20	136	2	9	1	6.49
RF	T. Turner	203	.246	1	27	69	4	3	1	1.5	.961							
CF	T. Parrott	474	.291	7	70	276	16	15	7	2.8	.951							
LF	K. Douglass	296	.264	1	28	105	13	14	3	1.8	.894							
C	E. McFarland	290	.241	3	36	276	**117**	16	6	5.1	.961							
OF	J. Sullivan	212	.292	2	21	81	4	4	1	2.0	.955							
2B	J. Quinn	191	.209	1	17	92	167	12	7	5.6	.956							
C	M. Murphy	175	.257	0	11	178	48	18	5	5.1	.926							
OF	D. Cooley	166	.307	0	13	91	2	4	0	2.4	.959							
P	T. Breitenstein	162	.259	0	12	34	89	7	4	3.0	.946							
P	B. Hart	161	.186	0	15	29	106	8	3	3.4	.944							

Louisville

W-38 L-93

John McCloskey
W-2 L-17

Bill McGunnigle
W-36 L-76

POS	Player	AB	BA	HR	RBI	PO	A	E	DP	TC/G	FA	Pitcher	G	IP	W	L	SV	ERA
1B	J. Rogers	290	.259	0	38	591	37	19	42	10.8	.971	C. Fraser	43	349	12	27	1	4.87
2B	J. O'Brien	186	.339	2	24	125	147	24	19	6.0	.919	S. Hill	43	320	9	28	2	4.31
SS	J. Dolan	165	.212	3	18	92	159	16	25	6.1	.940	B. Cunningham	27	189	7	14	1	5.09
3B	B. Clingman	423	.234	2	37	188	**281**	38	21	4.2	.925	A. Herman	14	94	4	6	0	5.63
RF	T. McCreery	441	.351	7	65	177	20	18	4	1.9	.916							
CF	O. Pickering	165	.303	1	22	97	12	12	4	2.7	.901							
LF	F. Clarke	517	.325	9	79	277	18	30	2	2.5	.908							
C	C. Dexter	402	.279	3	37	179	63	26	9	4.9	.903							
UT	D. Miller	324	.275	1	33	202	130	31	14		.915							
1B	P. Cassidy	184	.212	0	12	348	17	10	14	9.9	.973							
P	C. Fraser	146	.151	0	6	**39**	95	**25**	5	**3.7**	.843							
OF	D. Holmes	141	.270	0	18	43	6	13	1	1.9	.790							

BATTING AND BASE RUNNING LEADERS

Batting Average

J. Burkett, CLE	.410
H. Jennings, BAL	.401
E. Delahanty, PHI	.397
W. Keeler, BAL	.386
M. Tiernan, NY	.369

Slugging Average

E. Delahanty, PHI	.631
B. Dahlen, CHI	.553
T. McCreery, LOU	.546
J. Kelley, BAL	.543
J. Burkett, CLE	.541

Home Runs

B. Joyce, WAS, NY	14
E. Delahanty, PHI	13
S. Thompson, PHI	12
R. Connor, STL	11
B. Dahlen, CHI	9
F. Clarke, LOU	9

PITCHING LEADERS

Winning Percentage

B. Hoffer, BAL	.781
G. Hemming, BAL	.714
F. Foreman, CIN	.714
F. Dwyer, CIN	.686
K. Nichols, BOS	.682

Earned Run Average

B. Rhines, CIN	2.45
K. Nichols, BOS	2.81
N. Cuppy, CLE	3.12
F. Dwyer, CIN	3.15
C. Young, CLE	3.24

Wins

K. Nichols, BOS	30
F. Killen, PIT	30
C. Young, CLE	28
J. Meekin, NY	26

NATIONAL LEAGUE 1896, *cont.*

BATTING AND BASE RUNNING LEADERS

Total Bases

J. Burkett, CLE	317
E. Delahanty, PHI	315
J. Kelley, BAL	282
G. Van Haltren, NY	272
W. Keeler, BAL	270

Runs Batted In

E. Delahanty, PHI	126
H. Jennings, BAL	121
H. Duffy, BOS	112
E. McKean, CLE	112
H. Reitz, BAL	106
C. Childs, CLE	106

Stolen Bases

J. Kelley, BAL	87
B. Lange, CHI	84
B. Hamilton, BOS	83
D. Miller, CIN	76
J. Doyle, BAL	73

Hits

J. Burkett, CLE	240
W. Keeler, BAL	210
H. Jennings, BAL	209
E. Delahanty, PHI	198

Base on Balls

B. Hamilton, BOS	110
B. Joyce, WAS, NY	101
C. Childs, CLE	100
J. Kelley, BAL	91

Home Run Percentage

B. Joyce, WAS, NY	2.9
E. Delahanty, PHI	2.6
S. Thompson, PHI	2.3
R. Connor, STL	2.3

Runs

J. Burkett, CLE	160
W. Keeler, BAL	153
B. Hamilton, BOS	152
J. Kelley, BAL	148

Doubles

E. Delahanty, PHI	44
D. Miller, CIN	38
J. Kelley, BAL	31
B. Dahlen, CHI	30

Triples

T. McCreery, LOU	21
G. Van Haltren, NY	21
B. Dahlen, CHI	19
J. Kelley, BAL	19

PITCHING LEADERS

Saves

C. Young, CLE	3
S. Hill, LOU	2
C. Fisher, CIN	2

Strikeouts

C. Young, CLE	140
P. Hawley, PIT	137
F. Killen, PIT	134
T. Breitenstein, STL	114
J. Meekin, NY	110

Complete Games

F. Killen, PIT	44
C. Young, CLE	42
W. Mercer, WAS	38

Fewest Hits/9 Innings

B. Rhines, CIN	8.06
P. Hawley, PIT	9.10
M. Sullivan, NY	9.13
D. Friend, CHI	9.23

Shutouts

C. Young, CLE	5
F. Killen, PIT	5

Fewest Walks/9 Innings

C. Young, CLE	1.35
D. Clarke, NY	1.54
F. Dwyer, CIN	1.87
N. Cuppy, CLE	1.89

Most Strikeouts/9 Inn.

B. Briggs, CHI	3.90
A. Pond, BAL	3.36
D. McJames, WAS	3.31
P. Hawley, PIT	3.26

Innings

F. Killen, PIT	432
C. Young, CLE	414
P. Hawley, PIT	378
K. Nichols, BOS	375

Games Pitched

F. Killen, PIT	52
C. Young, CLE	51
P. Hawley, PIT	49
K. Nichols, BOS	49

							Batting						Fielding			Pitching					
	W	L	PCT	GB	R	OR	2B	3B	HR	BA	SA	SB	E	DP	FA	CG	BB	SO	ShO	SV	ERA
Baltimore	90	39	.698		**995**	662	207	**100**	23	**.328**	**.429**	**441**	296	114	.945	115	339	302	9	1	3.67
Cleveland	80	48	.625	9.5	840	650	207	72	28	.301	.391	175	288	**117**	.949	113	**280**	336	9	**5**	**3.46**
Cincinnati	77	50	.606	12	783	**620**	205	73	19	.294	.388	350	**252**	107	**.951**	105	310	219	**12**	4	3.67
Boston	74	57	.565	17	860	761	175	74	36	.300	.392	241	368	94	.934	110	397	277	6	3	3.78
Chicago	71	57	.555	18.5	815	799	182	97	34	.286	.390	332	366	115	.934	**118**	467	353	2	1	4.41
Pittsburgh	66	63	.512	24	787	741	169	94	27	.292	.385	217	317	103	.941	108	439	**362**	8	1	4.30
New York	64	67	.489	27	829	821	159	87	40	.297	.394	274	365	90	.933	104	403	312	1	2	4.54
Philadelphia	62	68	.477	28.5	890	891	**234**	84	**49**	.295	.413	191	313	112	.941	107	387	243	3	2	5.20
Brooklyn	58	73	.443	33	692	764	174	87	28	.284	.379	198	297	104	.945	97	400	259	3	1	4.25
Washington	58	73	.443	33	818	920	179	79	45	.286	.388	258	398	99	.927	106	435	292	2	3	4.61
St. Louis	40	90	.308	50.5	593	929	134	78	37	.257	.346	185	345	73	.936	115	456	279	1	1	5.33
Louisville	38	93	.290	53	653	997	142	80	37	.261	.351	195	475	110	.916	108	541	288	1	4	5.12
					9555	9555	2167	1005	403	.290	.387	3057	4080	1238	.938	1306	4854	3522	57	28	4.36

NATIONAL LEAGUE 1897

	POS	Player	AB	BA	HR	RBI	PO	A	E	DP	TC/G	FA	Pitcher	G	IP	W	L	SV	ERA
Boston	1B	F. Tenney	**566**	.318	1	85	1248	81	16	69	10.5	.988	K. Nichols	**46**	**368**	**31**	11	**3**	2.64
	2B	B. Lowe	499	.309	5	106	270	404	34	33	5.8	.952	F. Klobedanz	38	309	26	7	0	4.60
W-93 L-39	SS	H. Long	450	.322	3	69	274	353	66	40	6.5	.905	T. Lewis	38	290	21	12	1	3.85
	3B	J. Collins	529	.346	6	132	**214**	**303**	47	**20**	**4.2**	.917	J. Stivetts	18	129	11	4	0	3.41
Frank Selee	RF	C. Stahl	469	.354	4	97	164	17	14	4	1.8	.928	J. Sullivan	13	89	4	5	2	3.94
	CF	B. Hamilton	507	.343	3	61	296	10	12	0	2.5	.962							
	LF	H. Duffy	550	.340	**11**	129	266	12	7	2	2.2	.975							
	C	M. Bergen	327	.248	2	45	351	66	16	4	5.1	.963							
	OP	J. Stivetts	199	.367	2	37	50	39	6	1		.937							
	P	F. Klobedanz	148	.324	1	20	8	47	2	4	1.5	.965							
	P	K. Nichols	147	.265	3	28	29	62	3	1	2.0	.968							
	SS	B. Allen	119	.319	1	24	78	117	16	12	6.6	.924							
Baltimore	1B	J. Doyle	460	.354	1	87	1105	75	25	72	10.6	.979	J. Corbett	37	313	24	8	0	3.11
	2B	H. Reitz	477	.289	2	84	280	**449**	29	**62**	5.9	.962	B. Hoffer	38	303	22	11	0	4.30
W-90 L-40	SS	H. Jennings	439	.355	2	79	335	425	55	54	**7.0**	**.933**	A. Pond	32	248	18	9	0	3.52
	3B	J. McGraw	391	.325	0	48	112	182	38	16	3.2	.886	J. Nops	30	221	20	6	0	2.81
Ned Hanlon	RF	W. Keeler	564	**.424**	1	74	217	12	7	2	1.8	.970							
	CF	J. Stenzel	536	.353	5	116	264	12	20	2	2.3	.932							
	LF	J. Kelley	505	.362	5	118	240	15	11	3	2.0	.959							
	C	B. Clarke	241	.270	1	38	191	38	15	2	4.1	.939							
	UT	J. Quinn	285	.260	1	45	142	176	16	22		.952							
	C	W. Robinson	181	.315	0	23	184	36	8	2	4.8	.965							
	P	J. Corbett	150	.247	0	22	21	76	16	1	3.1	.858							
	10	T. O'Brien	147	.252	0	32	243	15	9	9		.966							
	P	B. Hoffer	139	.237	1	16	22	64	4	4	2.4	.956							
	C	F. Bowerman	130	.315	1	21	155	29	10	1	5.4	.948							
New York	1B	W. Clark	431	.283	1	75	1038	64	18	69	10.5	.984	A. Rusie	38	322	28	10	0	**2.54**
	2B	K. Gleason	540	.319	1	106	309	395	**53**	43	5.9	.930	J. Meekin	37	304	20	11	0	3.76
W-83 L-48	SS	G. Davis	519	.353	10	**134**	**337**	434	62	**67**	6.4	.926	C. Seymour	38	278	18	14	1	3.37
	3B	B. Joyce	388	.304	3	64	165	199	**63**	17	4.0	.852	M. Sullivan	23	149	8	7	2	5.09
Bill Joyce	RF	M. Tiernan	528	.330	5	72	178	11	14	2	1.6	.931							
	CF	G. Van Haltren	564	.330	3	64	267	31	20	4	2.5	.937							
	LF	D. Holmes	306	.268	1	44	113	9	13	2	1.8	.904							
	C	J. Warner	397	.275	2	51	**513**	**127**	**32**	**17**	**6.1**	.952							
	OF	T. McCreery	177	.299	1	28	53	10	7*	1	1.6	.900							
	UT	P. Wilson	154	.299	0	22	222	26	13	9		.950							
	P	A. Rusie	144	.278	0	22	19	77	8	3	2.7	.923							
	P	C. Seymour	137	.241	2	14	15	**98**	**20**	5	3.5	.850							
	P	J. Meekin	137	.299	0	10	14	56	11	2	2.2	.864							

NATIONAL LEAGUE 1897, *cont.*

Team	POS	Player	AB	BA	HR	RBI	PO	A	E	DP	TC/G	FA	Pitcher	G	IP	W	L	SV	ERA
Cincinnati	1B	J. Beckley	365	.345	7	76	830	45	19	56	9.2	.979	T. Breitenstein	40	320	23	12	0	3.62
W-76 L-56	2B	B. McPhee	282	.301	1	39	209	267	17	34	6.1	**.966**	B. Rhines	41	289	21	15	0	4.08
Buck Ewing	SS	C. Ritchey	337	.282	0	41	144	204	40	21	5.5	.897	F. Dwyer	37	247	18	13	0	3.78
	3B	C. Irwin	505	.289	0	74	186	236	27	19	3.4	.940	R. Ehret	34	184	8	10	2	4.78
	RF	D. Miller	440	.316	4	70	203	18	17	2	2.0	.929	B. Dammann	16	95	6	4	0	4.74
	CF	D. Hoy	497	.292	2	42	359	10	26	5	3.1	.934							
	LF	E. Burke	387	.266	1	41	224	11	15	4	2.6	.940							
	C	H. Peitz	266	.293	1	44	260	67	7	8	4.7	**.979**							
	S2	T. Corcoran	445	.288	3	57	286	360	48	51		.931							
	1B	F. Vaughn	199	.291	0	30	342	17	5	19	10.4	.986							
	OF	B. Holliday	195	.313	2	20	76	2	5	0	2.0	.940							
	C	P. Schriver	178	.303	1	30	147	42	8	3	3.7	.959							
	P	T. Breitenstein	124	.266	0	23	16	65	3	3	2.1	.964							

Team	POS	Player	AB	BA	HR	RBI	PO	A	E	DP	TC/G	FA	Pitcher	G	IP	W	L	SV	ERA
Cleveland	1B	P. Tebeau	412	.267	0	59	912	44	6	47	10.5	**.994**	C. Young	**46**	335	21	19	0	3.79
W-69 L-62	2B	C. Childs	444	.338	1	61	319	384	42	42	**6.5**	.944	Z. Wilson	34	264	16	11	0	4.16
Patsy Tebeau	SS	E. McKean	523	.273	2	78	226	385	53	36	5.3	.920	J. Powell	27	225	15	10	0	3.16
	3B	B. Wallace	516	.335	4	112	190	249	34	10	3.6	.928	N. Cuppy	19	139	10	6	0	3.18
	RF	L. Sockalexis	278	.338	3	42	117	10	16	3	2.2	.888							
	CF	O. Pickering	182	.352	1	22	110	5	6	1	2.6	.950							
	LF	J. Burkett	517	.383	2	60	226	18	13	3	2.0	.949							
	C	C. Zimmer	294	.316	0	40	278	81	9	10	4.6	.976							
	UT	J. O'Connor	397	.290	2	69	477	23	16	10		.969							
	P	C. Young	153	.222	0	19	16	88	9	0	2.5	.920							
	C	L. Criger	138	.225	0	22	129	35	11	1	4.7	.937							
	UT	S. McAllister	137	.219	0	11	74	21	9	1		.913							

Team	POS	Player	AB	BA	HR	RBI	PO	A	E	DP	TC/G	FA	Pitcher	G	IP	W	L	SV	ERA
Brooklyn	1B	C. LaChance	520	.308	4	90	1289	64	**30**	**76**	11.0	.978	B. Kennedy	44	343	18	20	1	3.91
W-61 L-71	2B	G. Shoch	284	.278	0	38	188	240	27	25	6.7	.941	H. Payne	40	280	14	17	0	4.63
Billy Barnie	SS	G. Smith	428	.201	0	29	201	399	61	36	5.9	.908	J. Dunn	25	217	14	9	0	4.57
	3B	B. Shindle	542	.284	3	105	185	241	45	13	3.5	.904	C. Fisher	20	149	9	7	1	4.23
	RF	F. Jones	548	.314	0	49	233	22	16	8	2.0	.941	D. Daub	19	138	6	11	0	6.08
	CF	M. Griffin	534	.316	2	56	353	13	17	6	2.9	.956							
	LF	J. Anderson	492	.325	4	85	253	11	18	2	2.5	.936							
	C	J. Grim	290	.248	0	25	241	98	19	8	4.6	.947							
	2B	J. Canavan	240	.217	2	34	157	162	32	18	5.6	.909							
	CO	B. Smith	237	.300	1	39	138	51	19	8		.909							
	P	B. Kennedy	147	.272	1	18	14	87	4	4	2.4	.962							

Team	POS	Player	AB	BA	HR	RBI	PO	A	E	DP	TC/G	FA	Pitcher	G	IP	W	L	SV	ERA
Washington	1B	T. Tucker	352	.338	5	61	856	42	15	58	9.8	.984	W. Mercer	45	332	20	20	2	3.25
W-61 L-71	2B	J. O'Brien	320	.244	3	45	223	260	30	43	6.0	.942	D. McJames	44	324	15	23	2	3.61
Gus Schmelz	SS	G. DeMontreville	**566**	.341	3	93	254	352	**78**	47	6.9	.886	C. Swaim	27	194	10	11	0	4.41
W-9 L-25	3B	C. Reilly	351	.276	2	60	149	224	39	17	4.1	.905	S. King	23	154	6	9	1	4.79
Tom Brown	RF	C. Abbey	300	.260	3	34	126	14	8	1	1.9	.946							
W-52 L-46	CF	T. Brown	469	.292	5	45	252	17	21	5	2.5	.928							
	LF	K. Selbach	486	.313	5	59	305	14	15	2	2.7	.955							
	C	D. McGuire	327	.343	4	53	290	88	21	6	5.5	.947							
	UT	Z. Wrigley	388	.284	3	64	175	209	50	18		.885							
	C	D. Farrell	261	.322	0	53	220	91	18	10	5.2	.945							
	OF	J. Gettman	143	.315	3	29	49	3	1	0	1.5	.981							
	P	W. Mercer	135	.319	0	19	0	0	0	0	—	—							

Team	POS	Player	AB	BA	HR	RBI	PO	A	E	DP	TC/G	FA	Pitcher	G	IP	W	L	SV	ERA
Pittsburgh	1B	H. Davis	429	.305	2	63	570	29	22	26	9.7	.965	F. Killen	42	337	17	23	0	4.46
W-60 L-71	2B	D. Padden	517	.282	2	58	**369**	402	48	36	6.1	.941	P. Hawley	40	311	18	18	0	4.80
Patsy Donovan	SS	B. Ely	516	.283	2	74	308	451	60	41	6.2	.927	J. Hughey	25	149	6	10	1	5.06
	3B	J. Hoffmeister	188	.309	3	36	48	70	31	7	3.1	.792	J. Tannehill	21	142	9	9	1	4.25
	RF	P. Donovan	479	.322	0	57	186	17	11	5	1.8	.949	C. Hastings	16	118	5	4	0	4.58
	CF	S. Brodie	370	.292	2	53	218	11	4	1	2.3	.983	J. Gardner	14	95	5	5	0	5.19
	LF	E. Smith	467	.310	6	54	245	19	28	1	2.4	.904							
	C	J. Sugden	288	.222	0	38	317	82	25	6	5.2	.941							
	C	B. Merritt	209	.263	1	26	202	43	14	6	4.9	.946							
	OP	J. Tannehill	184	.266	0	22	89	53	13	1		.916							
	3B	J. Donnelly	161	.193	0	14	51	87	12	1	3.4	.920							

Team	POS	Player	AB	BA	HR	RBI	PO	A	E	DP	TC/G	FA	Pitcher	G	IP	W	L	SV	ERA
Chicago	1B	C. Anson	424	.285	3	75	933	62	25	67	9.9	.975	C. Griffith	41	344	21	18	1	3.72
W-59 L-73	2B	J. Connor	285	.291	3	38	176	293	32	40	6.6	.936	D. Friend	24	203	12	11	0	4.52
Cap Anson	SS	B. Dahlen	276	.290	6	40	215	291	38	48	7.3	.930	N. Callahan	23	190	12	9	1	4.03
	3B	B. Everitt	379	.314	5	39	119	147	42	9	3.7	.864	B. Briggs	22	187	4	17	0	5.26
	RF	J. Ryan	520	.300	5	85	211	28	14	7	1.9	.945	W. Thornton	16	130	6	7	0	4.70
	CF	B. Lange	479	.340	5	83	264	17	16	4	2.5	.946	R. Denzer	12	95	2	8	0	5.13
	LF	G. Decker	428	.290	5	63	112	12	10	1	1.8	.925							
	C	M. Kittridge	262	.202	1	30	324	75	20	6	5.3	.952							
	3S	B. McCormick	419	.267	2	55	171	268	59	26		.882							
	UT	N. Callahan	360	.292	3	47	147	201	42	25		.892							
	OF	W. Thornton	265	.321	0	55	74	8	23	0	1.8	.781							
	C	T. Donahue	188	.239	0	21	218	64	15	2	5.4	.949							
	P	C. Griffith	162	.235	0	21	23	85	6	3	2.8	.947							

NATIONAL LEAGUE 1897, *cont.*

Philadelphia

W-55 L-77

George Stallings

POS	Player	AB	BA	HR	RBI	PO	A	E	DP	TC/G	FA	Pitcher	G	IP	W	L	SV	ERA
1B	N. Lajoie	545	.361	9	127	1079	37	18	45	10.5	.984	J. Taylor	40	317	16	20	2	4.23
2B	L. Cross	344	.259	3	51	68	120	7	10	5.1	.964	A. Orth	36	282	14	19	0	4.62
SS	S. Gillen	270	.259	0	27	129	197	38	6	5.3	.896	J. Fifield	27	211	5	18	0	5.51
3B	B. Nash	337	.258	0	39	114	146	23	10	3.6	.919	G. Wheeler	26	191	11	10	0	3.96
RF	T. Dowd	391	.292	0	43	116	9	11	3	1.9	.919							
CF	D. Cooley	**566**	.329	4	40	322	16	14	6	2.7	.960							
LF	E. Delahanty	530	.377	5	96	266	23	9	2	2.3	.970							
C	J. Clements	185	.238	6	36	163	40	8	3	4.3	.962							
02	P. Geier	316	.278	1	35	158	129	18	6		.941							
1C	J. Boyle	288	.253	2	36	373	51	12	10		.972							
SS	F. Shugart	163	.252	5	25	104	128	34	15	6.7	.872							
P	A. Orth	152	.329	1	17	9	69	6	1	2.3	.929							
P	J. Taylor	139	.252	1	17	12	89	16	2	2.9	.863							

Louisville

W-52 L-78

Jim Rogers
W-17 L-24

Fred Clarke
W-35 L-54

POS	Player	AB	BA	HR	RBI	PO	A	E	DP	TC/G	FA	Pitcher	G	IP	W	L	SV	ERA
1B	P. Werden	506	.302	5	83	**1318**	**116**	23	70	**11.1**	.984	C. Fraser	35	286	15	19	0	4.09
2B	J. Rogers	150	.147	2	22	86	120	15	12	5.7	.932	B. Cunningham	29	235	14	13	0	4.14
SS	G. Stafford	432	.278	7	53	197	353	70	33	6.0	.887	S. Hill	27	199	7	17	0	3.62
3B	B. Clingman	395	.228	2	47	176	269	25	16	4.2	**.947**	B. Magee	22	155	4	12	0	5.39
RF	T. McCreery	338	.284	4	40	130	13	24	2	1.9	.856							
CF	O. Pickering	246	.252	1	21	134	15	10	2	2.6	.937							
LF	F. Clarke	518	.390	6	67	282	18	24	0	2.6	.926							
C	B. Wilson	381	.213	1	41	338	113	29	7	4.7	.940							
UT	C. Dexter	257	.280	2	46	132	68	27	8		.881							
OF	H. Wagner	237	.338	2	39	101	17	12	5	2.5	.908							
2B	A. Johnson	161	.242	0	23	68	92	22	8	5.5	.879							
2S	J. Dolan	133	.211	0	7	84	113	26	14		.883							

St. Louis

W-29 L-102

Tommy Dowd
W-6 L-22

Hugh Nicol
W-8 L-32

Bill Hallman
W-13 L-36

Chris Von Der Ahe
W-2 L-12

POS	Player	AB	BA	HR	RBI	PO	A	E	DP	TC/G	FA	Pitcher	G	IP	W	L	SV	ERA
1B	M. Grady	322	.280	7	55	797	48	23	54	10.5	.974	R. Donahue	**46**	348	10	**35**	1	6.13
2B	B. Hallman	298	.221	0	26	189	244	28	35	6.0	.939	B. Hart	39	295	9	27	0	6.26
SS	M. Cross	462	.286	4	55	327	**513**	73	47	7.0	.920	K. Carsey	12	99	3	8	0	6.00
3B	F. Hartman	516	.306	2	67	159	253	**63**	14	3.8	.867							
RF	T. Turner	416	.291	2	41	146	10	9	3	1.6	.945							
CF	D. Harley	330	.291	3	35	186	19	23	3	2.6	.899							
LF	B. Lally	355	.279	2	42	192	9	23	2	2.7	.897							
C	K. Douglass	516	.329	6	50	171	64	13	4	4.1	.948							
20	J. Houseman	278	.245	0	21	168	131	24	10		.926							
C	M. Murphy	207	.169	0	12	145	62	11	3	4.1	.950							
P	B. Hart	156	.250	2	14	21	76	8	4	2.7	.924							
P	R. Donahue	155	.213	1	14	24	97	3	1	2.7	.976							
OF	T. Dowd	145	.262	0	9	65	0	6	0	2.4	.915							

BATTING AND BASE RUNNING LEADERS

Batting Average

W. Keeler, BAL	.424
F. Clarke, LOU	.390
J. Burkett, CLE	.383
E. Delahanty, PHI	.377
J. Kelley, BAL	.362

Slugging Average

N. Lajoie, PHI	.569
W. Keeler, BAL	.544
E. Delahanty, PHI	.538
F. Clarke, LOU	.533
G. Davis, NY	.509

Home Runs

H. Duffy, BOS	11
G. Davis, NY	10
N. Lajoie, PHI	9
J. Beckley, NY, CIN	8
M. Grady, PHI, STL	7
G. Stafford, NY, LOU	7

Total Bases

N. Lajoie, PHI	310
W. Keeler, BAL	307
E. Delahanty, PHI	285
F. Clarke, LOU	276
H. Duffy, BOS	265

Runs Batted In

G. Davis, NY	134
J. Collins, BOS	132
H. Duffy, BOS	129
N. Lajoie, PHI	127
J. Kelley, BAL	118

Stolen Bases

B. Lange, CHI	73
J. Stenzel, BAL	69
B. Hamilton, BOS	66
G. Davis, NY	65
W. Keeler, BAL	64

Hits

W. Keeler, BAL	239
F. Clarke, LOU	202
E. Delahanty, PHI	200
J. Burkett, CLE	198

Base on Balls

B. Hamilton, BOS	105
J. McGraw, BAL	99
M. Griffin, BKN	81
K. Selbach, WAS	80

Home Run Percentage

M. Grady, PHI, STL	2.1
H. Duffy, BOS	2.0
G. Davis, NY	1.9
J. Beckley, NY, CIN	1.8

Runs

B. Hamilton, BOS	152
W. Keeler, BAL	145
M. Griffin, BKN	136
F. Jones, BKN	134

Doubles

J. Stenzel, BAL	43
E. Delahanty, PHI	40
N. Lajoie, PHI	40
B. Wallace, CLE	33
J. Ryan, CHI	33

Triples

H. Davis, PIT	28
N. Lajoie, PHI	23
B. Wallace, CLE	21
W. Keeler, BAL	19

PITCHING LEADERS

Winning Percentage

F. Klobedanz, BOS	.788
J. Nops, BAL	.769
J. Corbett, BAL	.750
K. Nichols, BOS	.738
A. Rusie, NY	.737

Earned Run Average

A. Rusie, NY	2.54
K. Nichols, BOS	2.64
J. Nops, BAL	2.81
J. Corbett, BAL	3.11
J. Powell, CLE	3.16

Wins

K. Nichols, BOS	31
A. Rusie, NY	28
F. Klobedanz, BOS	26
J. Corbett, BAL	24
T. Breitenstein, CIN	23

Saves

K. Nichols, BOS	3

Strikeouts

D. McJames, WAS	156
C. Seymour, NY	149
J. Corbett, BAL	149
K. Nichols, BOS	136
A. Rusie, NY	135

Complete Games

C. Griffith, CHI	38
F. Killen, PIT	38
R. Donahue, STL	38
K. Nichols, BOS	37
B. Kennedy, BKN	36

Fewest Hits/9 Innings

C. Seymour, NY	8.23
A. Rusie, NY	8.77
K. Nichols, BOS	8.85
S. Hill, LOU	9.45

Shutouts

D. McJames, WAS	3
W. Mercer, WAS	3

Fewest Walks/9 Innings

C. Young, CLE	1.32
J. Tannehill, PIT	1.52
N. Cuppy, CLE	1.69
K. Nichols, BOS	1.76

Most Strikeouts/9 Inn.

C. Seymour, NY	4.83
D. McJames, WAS	4.34
J. Corbett, BAL	4.28
W. Thornton, CHI	3.80

Innings

K. Nichols, BOS	368
R. Donahue, STL	348
C. Griffith, CHI	344
B. Kennedy, BKN	343

Games Pitched

C. Young, CLE	46
K. Nichols, BOS	46
R. Donahue, STL	46
W. Mercer, WAS	45

NATIONAL LEAGUE 1897, *cont.*

	W	L	PCT	GB	R	OR	2B	3B	HR	BA	SA	SB	E	DP	FA	CG	BB	SO	ShO	SV	ERA
							Batting						Fielding			Pitching					
Boston	93	39	.705		**1025**	**665**	230	83	**45**	.319	**.426**	233	272	80	**.951**	115	393	329	**8**	**7**	3.65
Baltimore	90	40	.692	2	964	674	**243**	66	20	**.325**	.414	**401**	277	110	**.951**	118	382	361	3	0	3.55
New York	83	48	.634	9.5	895	695	188	84	31	.299	.392	328	397	109	.930	118	486	**456**	**8**	3	**3.47**
Cincinnati	76	56	.576	17	763	705	219	69	22	.290	.383	194	273	100	.948	100	329	270	4	2	4.09
Cleveland	69	62	.527	23.5	773	680	192	88	16	.298	.389	181	**261**	74	.950	111	**289**	277	6	0	3.95
Brooklyn	61	71	.462	32	802	845	202	72	22	.279	.365	187	364	99	.936	114	410	256	4	2	4.60
Washington	61	71	.462	32	781	793	194	77	36	.297	.395	208	369	103	.933	103	400	348	7	5	4.01
Pittsburgh	60	71	.458	32.5	676	835	140	**108**	25	.276	.370	170	346	70	.936	112	318	342	2	2	4.67
Chicago	59	73	.447	34	832	894	189	97	38	.282	.386	264	393	**112**	.932	**131**	433	361	2	1	4.53
Philadelphia	55	77	.417	38	752	792	213	83	40	.293	.398	163	296	72	.944	115	364	253	4	2	4.60
Louisville	52	78	.400	40	669	859	160	70	40	.265	.358	195	395	85	.929	114	459	267	2	0	4.42
St. Louis	29	102	.221	63.5	588	1083	149	67	31	.275	.356	172	375	84	.933	109	453	207	1	1	6.21
					9520	9520	2319	964	366	.292	.386	2696	4018	1098	.939	1360	4716	3727	51	25	4.31

NATIONAL LEAGUE 1898

Boston

W-102 L-47

Frank Selee

POS	Player	AB	BA	HR	RBI	PO	A	E	DP	TC/G	FA
1B	F. Tenney	488	.328	0	62	1090	66	23	71	10.1	.980
2B	B. Lowe	559	.272	4	94	397	457	37	63	6.1	.958
SS	H. Long	589	.265	6	99	326	472	67	65	6.1	.923
3B	J. Collins	597	.328	**15**	111	**243**	332	42	20	4.1	.932
RF	C. Stahl	467	.308	3	52	199	14	7	4	1.8	.968
CF	B. Hamilton	417	.369	3	50	189	8	21	2	2.0	.904
LF	H. Duffy	568	.298	8	108	332	18	16	2	2.4	.956
C	M. Bergen	446	.280	3	60	496	109	**24**	4	5.4	.962
UT	G. Yeager	221	.267	3	24	303	40	19	6		.948
P	K. Nichols	158	.241	2	23	21	78	4	1	2.1	.961

Pitcher	G	IP	W	L	SV	ERA
K. Nichols	**50**	388	**31**	12	**4**	2.13
T. Lewis	41	313	26	8	2	2.90
V. Willis	41	311	25	13	0	2.84
F. Klobedanz	35	271	19	10	0	3.89

Baltimore

W-96 L-53

Ned Hanlon

POS	Player	AB	BA	HR	RBI	PO	A	E	DP	TC/G	FA
1B	D. McGann	535	.301	5	106	1416	68	26	78	10.4	.983
2B	G. DeMontreville	567	.328	0	86	303	386	41	35	5.9	.944
SS	H. Jennings	534	.328	1	87	289	368	50	41	6.1	.929
3B	J. McGraw	515	.342	0	53	142	271	46	16	3.4	.900
RF	W. Keeler	561	**.385**	1	44	210	14	9	2	1.8	.961
CF	J. Kelley	464	.321	2	110	235	18	8	4	2.1	.969
LF	D. Holmes	442	.285	1	64	247	13	18	4	2.5	.935
C	W. Robinson	289	.277	0	38	288	72	13	4	4.8	.965
C	B. Clarke	285	.242	0	27	289	69	14	6	5.3	.962
P	J. Hughes	164	.226	2	20	**29**	78	11	1	3.1	.907
OF	J. Stenzel	138	.254	0	22	57	6	5	1	1.9	.926

Pitcher	G	IP	W	L	SV	ERA
D. McJames	45	374	27	15	0	2.36
J. Hughes	38	301	23	12	0	3.20
A. Maul	28	240	20	7	0	2.10
J. Nops	33	235	16	9	0	3.56
F. Kitson	17	119	8	5	0	3.24

Cincinnati

W-92 L-60

Buck Ewing

POS	Player	AB	BA	HR	RBI	PO	A	E	DP	TC/G	FA
1B	J. Beckley	459	.294	4	72	1167	53	21	76	10.5	.983
2B	B. McPhee	486	.249	1	60	299	396	32	74	5.6	.956
SS	T. Corcoran	619	.250	2	87	353	**561**	67	76	6.4	.932
3B	C. Irwin	501	.240	3	55	223	305	34	20	**4.1**	.940
RF	D. Miller	586	.299	3	90	292	23	24	4	2.2	.929
CF	A. McBride	486	.302	2	43	288	18	13	3	2.7	.959
LF	E. Smith	486	.342	1	66	280	15	16	5	2.5	.949
C	H. Peitz	330	.273	1	43	323	90	**24**	12	4.3	.945
UT	H. Steinfeldt	308	.295	0	43	202	158	41	17		.898
1C	F. Vaughn	275	.305	1	46	462	50	17	28		.968

Pitcher	G	IP	W	L	SV	ERA
P. Hawley	43	331	27	11	0	3.37
T. Breitenstein	39	316	20	14	0	3.42
S. Hill	33	262	13	14	0	3.98
F. Dwyer	31	240	16	10	0	3.04
B. Dammann	35	225	16	10	2	3.61

Chicago

W-85 L-65

Tom Burns

POS	Player	AB	BA	HR	RBI	PO	A	E	DP	TC/G	FA
1B	B. Everitt	596	.319	0	69	1519	70	42	**123**	10.9	.974
2B	J. Connor	505	.226	0	67	330	437	44	**75**	5.9	.946
SS	B. Dahlen	521	.290	1	79	369	511	76	**77**	6.7	.921
3B	B. McCormick	530	.247	2	78	152	322	**60**	**31**	3.9	.888
RF	S. Mertes	269	.297	1	47	97	13	15	6	2.1	.880
CF	B. Lange	442	.319	6	69	269	19	9	4	2.7	.970
LF	J. Ryan	572	.323	4	79	267	20	27	2	2.2	.914
C	T. Donahue	396	.220	0	39	450	107	22	**16**	4.7	.962
OP	W. Thornton	210	.295	0	14	74	53	17	5		.882
OF	D. Green	188	.314	4	27	87	10	3	5	2.1	.970
P	N. Callahan	164	.262	0	22	27	63	5	3	3.1	.947
UT	F. Isbell	159	.233	0	8	54	43	19	5		.836
UT	W. Woods	154	.175	0	8	42	87	15	3		.896

Pitcher	G	IP	W	L	SV	ERA
C. Griffith	38	326	24	10	0	**1.88**
N. Callahan	31	274	20	10	0	2.46
W. Thornton	28	215	13	10	0	3.34
W. Woods	27	215	9	13	0	3.14
M. Kilroy	13	100	6	7	0	4.31
F. Isbell	13	81	4	7	0	3.56

Cleveland

W-81 L-68

Patsy Tebeau

POS	Player	AB	BA	HR	RBI	PO	A	E	DP	TC/G	FA
1B	P. Tebeau	477	.258	1	63	956	43	16	43	11.2	.984
2B	C. Childs	413	.288	1	31	273	370	48	37	**6.3**	.931
SS	E. McKean	604	.285	9	94	304	425	53	47	5.2	.932
3B	B. Wallace	593	.270	3	99	201	329	36	19	4.0	.936
RF	H. Blake	474	.245	0	58	234	25	13	3	2.0	.952
CF	J. McAleer	366	.238	0	48	239	10	9	4	2.5	.965
LF	J. Burkett	624	.341	0	42	268	17	19	3	2.0	.938
C	L. Criger	287	.279	1	32	322	105	19	9	5.4	.957
UT	J. O'Connor	478	.249	1	56	761	92	20	36		.977
P	C. Young	154	.253	2	13	12	122	4	2	3.0	.971

Pitcher	G	IP	W	L	SV	ERA
C. Young	46	378	25	13	0	2.53
J. Powell	42	342	23	15	0	3.00
Z. Wilson	33	255	13	18	0	3.60
N. Cuppy	18	128	9	8	0	3.30

NATIONAL LEAGUE 1898, *cont.*

Team	POS	Player	AB	BA	HR	RBI	PO	A	E	DP	TC/G	FA	Pitcher	G	IP	W	L	SV	ERA
Philadelphia	1B	K. Douglass	582	.258	2	48	1236	73	32	74	9.2	.976	W. Piatt	39	306	24	14	0	3.18
W-78 L-71	2B	N. Lajoie	608	.324	6	**127**	**442**	406	46	59	6.1	.949	R. Donahue	35	284	17	17	0	3.55
George Stallings	SS	M. Cross	525	.257	1	50	**404**	506	**93**	65	6.7	.907	A. Orth	32	250	15	13	0	3.02
W-19 L-27	3B	B. Lauder	361	.263	2	67	132	171	47	6	3.6	.866	J. Fifield	21	171	11	9	0	3.31
Bill Shettsline	RF	E. Flick	453	.302	8	81	237	21	19	4	2.1	.931	G. Wheeler	15	112	6	8	0	4.17
W-59 L-44	CF	D. Cooley	629	.312	4	55	352	15	22	2	2.6	.943							
	LF	E. Delahanty	548	.334	4	92	302	20	12	5	2.3	.964							
	C	E. McFarland	429	.282	3	71	420	136	23	7	4.8	.960							
New York	1B	B. Joyce	508	.258	10	91	1252	**87**	**47**	73	10.7	.966	C. Seymour	45	357	25	19	0	3.18
W-77 L-73	2B	K. Gleason	570	.221	0	62	366	**468**	**55**	57	6.2	.938	J. Meekin	38	320	16	18	0	3.77
Bill Joyce	SS	G. Davis	486	.307	2	86	349	421	55	61	**6.8**	.933	A. Rusie	37	300	20	11	1	3.03
W-22 L-21	3B	F. Hartman	475	.272	2	88	146	280	57	16	3.9	.882	E. Doheny	28	213	7	19	0	3.68
Cap Anson	RF	J. Doyle	297	.283	1	43	39	10	8	2	1.5	.860	C. Gettig	17	115	6	3	0	3.83
W-9 L-13	CF	G. Van Haltren	**654**	.312	2	68	299	22	29	5	2.2	.917							
Bill Joyce	LF	M. Tiernan	415	.280	4	49	130	12	4	2	1.4	.973							
W-46 L-39	C	J. Warner	373	.257	0	42	**536**	**139**	22	10	**6.4**	.968							
	PO	C. Seymour	297	.276	4	23	71	119	25	9		.884							
	UT	M. Grady	287	.296	3	49	321	74	34	7		.921							
	UT	C. Gettig	196	.250	0	26	70	103	21	6		.892							
	OF	W. Wilmot	138	.239	2	22	35	4	5	0	1.3	.886							
Pittsburgh	1B	W. Clark	209	.306	1	31	601	27	10	29	11.2	.984	J. Tannehill	43	327	25	13	2	2.95
W-72 L-76	2B	D. Padden	463	.257	2	43	301	407	40	46	5.8	.947	B. Rhines	31	258	12	16	0	3.52
Bill Watkins	SS	B. Ely	519	.212	2	44	311	527	51	58	6.0	**.943**	J. Gardner	25	185	10	13	0	3.21
	3B	B. Grey	528	.229	0	67	172	258	59	16	3.6	.879	F. Killen	23	178	10	11	0	3.75
	RF	P. Donovan	610	.302	0	37	238	21	20	4	1.9	.928	C. Hastings	19	137	4	10	0	3.41
	CF	T. O'Brien	413	.259	1	45	144	15	13	4	2.5	.924	B. Hart	16	125	5	9	1	4.82
	LF	J. McCarthy	537	.289	4	78	296	19	22	4	2.5	.935							
	C	P. Schriver	315	.229	0	32	302	95	18	6	4.5	.957							
	C	F. Bowerman	241	.274	0	29	204	76	16	8	5.0	.946							
	1B	H. Davis	222	.293	1	24	556	22	12	30	11.1	.980							
	OF	T. McCreery	190	.311	2	20	107	6	8	1	2.4	.934							
	OF	S. Brodie	156	.263	0	21	110	4	5	1	2.8	.958							
Louisville	1B	H. Wagner	588	.299	10	105	729	41	22	44	10.6	.972	B. Cunningham	44	362	28	15	0	3.16
W-70 L-81	2B	H. Smith	121	.190	0	13	74	87	16	8	5.4	.910	B. Magee	38	295	16	15	0	3.93
Fred Clarke	SS	C. Ritchey	551	.254	5	51	194	228	37	32	5.7	.919	P. Dowling	36	286	13	20	0	4.16
	3B	B. Clingman	538	.257	0	50	119	191	29	12	4.3	.914	C. Fraser	26	203	7	17	0	5.32
	RF	C. Dexter	421	.314	1	66	148	13	7	2	1.8	.958	R. Ehret	12	89	3	7	0	5.76
	CF	D. Hoy	582	.304	6	66	348	19	21	6	2.6	.946							
	LF	F. Clarke	599	.307	3	47	344	19	23	3	2.6	.940							
	C	M. Kittridge	287	.244	1	31	258	80	20	10	4.2	.944							
	20	G. Stafford	181	.298	1	25	91	82	17	9		.911							
Brooklyn	1B	C. LaChance	526	.247	5	65	807	20	10	53	11.3	.988	B. Kennedy	40	339	16	22	0	3.37
W-54 L-91	2B	B. Hallman	509	.244	2	63	268	419	41	46	5.9	.944	J. Dunn	41	323	16	21	0	3.60
Billy Barnie	SS	G. Magoon	343	.224	1	39	199	357	45	38	6.5	.925	J. Yeager	36	291	12	22	0	3.65
W-15 L-20	3B	B. Shindle	466	.225	1	41	154	278	42	23	4.0	.911	R. Miller	23	152	4	14	0	5.34
Mike Griffin	RF	F. Jones	596	.304	1	69	229	17	14	7	1.8	.946	K. McKenna	14	101	2	6	0	5.63
W-1 L-3	CF	M. Griffin	537	.300	2	40	314	20	9	7	2.6	.974							
Charlie Ebbets	LF	J. Sheckard	408	.277	4	64	213	12	18	2	2.3	.926							
W-38 L-68	C	J. Ryan	301	.189	0	24	289	93	16	13	4.7	.960							
	1B	T. Tucker	283	.279	1	34	797*	49	8	44	11.7*	.991							
	OC	B. Smith	199	.261	0	23	103	24	13	5		.907							
	C	J. Grim	178	.281	0	11	155	56	11	6	4.3	.950							
	P	J. Dunn	167	.246	0	19	22	70	6	2	2.4	.939							
Washington	1B	J. Doyle	177	.305	2	26	344	17	14	23	9.9	.963	G. Weyhing	45	361	15	26	0	4.51
W-51 L-101	2B	H. Reitz	489	.303	2	47	323	401	31	56	5.7	**.959**	W. Mercer	33	234	12	18	0	4.81
Tom Brown	SS	Z. Wrigley	400	.245	2	39	252	326	68	42	6.7	.895	B. Dinneen	29	218	9	16	0	4.00
W-12 L-26	3B	J. Smith	234	.303	3	28	65	74	15	6	3.3	.903	F. Killen	17	128	6	9	0	3.58
Jack Doyle	RF	J. Gettman	567	.277	5	47	234	18	20	4	2.0	.926	C. Swaim	16	101	3	11	1	4.26
W-8 L-9	CF	J. Anderson	430	.305	9	71	200	20	12	3	2.5	.948							
Deacon McGuire	LF	K. Selbach	515	.303	3	60	320	24	19	6	2.8	.948							
W-21 L-47	C	D. McGuire	489	.268	1	57	371	93	16	11	5.2	.967							
Arthur Irwin	C1	D. Farrell	338	.314	1	53	434	96	27	22		.952							
W-10 L-19	UT	W. Mercer	249	.321	2	25	91	116	29	8		.877							
	UT	B. Wagner	223	.224	1	31	82	102	37	8		.833							
	OF	B. Freeman	107	.364	3	21	39	5	1	2	1.6	.978							

NATIONAL LEAGUE 1898, *cont.*

St. Louis

W-39 L-111

Tim Hurst

POS	Player	AB	BA	HR	RBI	PO	A	E	DP	TC/G	FA
1B	G. Decker	286	.259	1	45	772	17	16	31	10.7	.980*
2B	J. Crooks	225	.231	1	20	192	209	17	23	6.3	.959
SS	G. Smith	157	.159	1	9	79	167	26	14	5.3	.904
3B	L. Cross	602	.317	3	79	215	**351**	33	20	4.0	**.945**
RF	T. Dowd	586	.244	0	32	208	11	19	3	1.8	.920
CF	J. Stenzel	404	.282	1	33	257	8	16	2	2.6	.943
LF	D. Harley	549	.246	0	42	311	26	27	3	2.6	.926
C	J. Clements	335	.257	3	41	287	81	11	8	4.4	**.971**
2S	J. Quinn	375	.251	0	36	218	340	31	30		.947
C	J. Sugden	289	.253	0	34	181	88	18	8	4.8	.937
1B	T. Tucker	252	.238	0	20	755*	36	22	40	11.3*	.973
P	J. Taylor	157	.242	1	18	18	**144**	**22**	2	**3.7**	.880

Pitcher	G	IP	W	L	SV	ERA
J. Taylor	**50**	**397**	15	**29**	1	3.90
W. Sudhoff	41	315	11	27	1	4.34
J. Hughey	35	284	7	24	0	3.93
K. Carsey	20	124	2	12	0	6.33

BATTING AND BASE RUNNING LEADERS

Batting Average
- W. Keeler, BAL .385
- B. Hamilton, BOS .369
- J. McGraw, BAL .342
- E. Smith, CIN .342
- J. Burkett, CLE .341

Slugging Average
- J. Anderson, BKN, WAS .494
- J. Collins, BOS .479
- N. Lajoie, PHI .461
- E. Delahanty, PHI .454
- B. Hamilton, BOS .453

Home Runs
- J. Collins, BOS 15
- B. Joyce, NY 10
- H. Wagner, LOU 10
- J. Anderson, BKN, WAS 9
- E. McKean, CLE 9

Total Bases
- J. Collins, BOS 286
- N. Lajoie, PHI 280
- G. Van Haltren, NY 270
- J. Anderson, BKN, WAS 257
- D. Cooley, PHI 256

Runs Batted In
- N. Lajoie, PHI 127
- J. Collins, BOS 111
- J. Kelley, BAL 110
- H. Duffy, BOS 108
- D. McGann, BAL 106

Stolen Bases
- E. Delahanty, PHI 58
- B. Hamilton, BOS 54
- G. DeMontreville, BAL 49
- C. Dexter, LOU 44
- J. McGraw, BAL 43

Hits
- W. Keeler, BAL 216
- J. Burkett, CLE 213
- G. Van Haltren, NY 204
- N. Lajoie, PHI 197

Base on Balls
- J. McGraw, BAL 112
- B. Joyce, NY 88
- B. Hamilton, BOS 87
- E. Flick, PHI 86

Home Run Percentage
- J. Collins, BOS 2.5
- B. Joyce, NY 2.0
- E. Flick, PHI 1.8
- J. Anderson, BKN, WAS 1.7

Runs
- J. McGraw, BAL 143
- H. Jennings, BAL 135
- G. Van Haltren, NY 129
- W. Keeler, BAL 126

Doubles
- N. Lajoie, PHI 43
- E. Delahanty, PHI 36
- B. Dahlen, CHI 35
- J. Collins, BOS 35

Triples
- J. Anderson, BKN, WAS 22
- D. Hoy, LOU 16
- G. Van Haltren, NY 16

PITCHING LEADERS

Winning Percentage
- T. Lewis, BOS .765
- A. Maul, BAL .741
- K. Nichols, BOS .721
- P. Hawley, CIN .711
- C. Griffith, CHI .706

Earned Run Average
- C. Griffith, CHI 1.88
- A. Maul, BAL 2.10
- K. Nichols, BOS 2.13
- D. McJames, BAL 2.36
- N. Callahan, CHI 2.46

Wins
- K. Nichols, BOS 31
- B. Cunningham, LOU 28
- P. Hawley, CIN 27
- D. McJames, BAL 27
- T. Lewis, BOS 26

Saves
- K. Nichols, BOS 4
- P. Hickman, BOS 2
- J. Tannehill, PIT 2
- T. Lewis, BOS 2
- B. Dammann, CIN 2

Strikeouts
- C. Seymour, NY 239
- D. McJames, BAL 178
- V. Willis, BOS 160
- K. Nichols, BOS 138
- W. Piatt, PHI 121

Complete Games
- J. Taylor, STL 42
- B. Cunningham, LOU 41
- C. Young, CLE 40
- D. McJames, BAL 40
- K. Nichols, BOS 40

Fewest Hits/9 Innings
- K. Nichols, BOS 7.33
- V. Willis, BOS 7.64
- T. Lewis, BOS 7.67
- A. Maul, BAL 7.77

Shutouts
- W. Piatt, PHI 6
- J. Powell, CLE 6
- J. Hughes, BAL 5
- J. Tannehill, PIT 5
- K. Nichols, BOS 5

Fewest Walks/9 Innings
- C. Young, CLE 0.98
- F. Dwyer, CIN 1.58
- B. Cunningham, LOU 1.62
- J. Tannehill, PIT 1.74

Most Strikeouts/9 Inn.
- C. Seymour, NY 6.03
- V. Willis, BOS 4.63
- D. McJames, BAL 4.28
- E. Doheny, NY 4.06

Innings
- J. Taylor, STL 397
- K. Nichols, BOS 388
- C. Young, CLE 378
- D. McJames, BAL 374

Games Pitched
- K. Nichols, BOS 50
- J. Taylor, STL 50
- C. Young, CLE 46

							Batting						Fielding			Pitching					
	W	L	PCT	GB	R	OR	2B	3B	HR	BA	SA	SB	E	DP	FA	CG	BB	SO	ShO	SV	ERA
Boston	102	47	.685		872	**614**	190	55	**53**	.290	**.377**	172	310	102	.950	127	470	432	9	**7**	2.98
Baltimore	96	53	.644	6	**933**	623	154	77	12	**.302**	.368	**250**	326	105	.947	138	400	422	12	0	2.90
Cincinnati	92	60	.605	11.5	831	740	207	**101**	19	.271	.359	165	325	128	.950	131	449	294	10	2	3.50
Chicago	85	65	.567	17.5	828	679	175	83	19	.274	.350	220	412	**149**	.936	137	364	323	**13**	0	**2.83**
Cleveland	81	68	.544	21	730	683	162	56	18	.263	.325	93	**301**	95	**.952**	**142**	**309**	339	9	0	3.20
Philadelphia	78	71	.523	24	823	784	**238**	81	33	.280	**.377**	182	379	102	.937	129	399	325	10	0	3.72
New York	77	73	.513	25.5	837	800	190	86	33	.266	.352	214	447	113	.932	141	587	**558**	9	1	3.44
Pittsburgh	72	76	.486	29.5	634	694	140	88	14	.258	.328	107	340	105	.946	131	346	330	10	3	3.41
Louisville	70	81	.464	33	728	833	150	71	32	.267	.342	235	382	114	.939	137	470	271	4	0	4.24
Brooklyn	54	91	.372	46	638	811	156	66	17	.256	.322	130	334	125	.947	134	476	294	1	0	4.01
Washington	51	101	.336	52.5	704	939	177	81	35	.271	.355	197	443	119	.929	129	450	371	0	1	4.52
St. Louis	39	111	.260	63.5	571	929	149	55	13	.247	.305	104	388	97	.939	133	372	288	0	2	4.53
					9129	9129	2088	900	298	.270	.347	2069	4387	1354	.942	1609	5092	4247	87	16	3.61

NATIONAL LEAGUE 1899

Brooklyn

W-101 L-47

Ned Hanlon

POS	Player	AB	BA	HR	RBI	PO	A	E	DP	TC/G	FA
1B	D. McGann	214	.243	2	32	645	31	10	49	11.2	.985*
2B	T. Daly	498	.313	5	88	377	453	**63**	**69**	**6.3**	.929
SS	B. Dahlen	428	.283	4	76	256	377	40	48	6.1	.941
3B	D. Casey	525	.269	1	43	162	258	51	20	3.5	.892
RF	W. Keeler	570	.379	1	61	208	21	5	4	1.7	.979
CF	F. Jones	365	.285	2	38	199	11	12	2	2.3	.946
LF	J. Kelley	538	.325	6	93	307	26	8	7	2.4	.977
C	D. Farrell	254	.299	2	55	251	111	20	9	4.9	.948
01	J. Anderson	439	.269	3	92	537	30	19	27		.968
1B	H. Jennings	216	.296	0	40	446	25	7	24	9.6	.985
C	D. McGuire	157	.318	0	23	144	58*	6	2	4.5	.971

Pitcher	G	IP	W	L	SV	ERA
J. Dunn	41	299	23	13	2	3.70
J. Hughes	35	292	**28**	6	0	2.68
B. Kennedy	40	277	22	9	2	2.79
D. McJames	37	275	19	15	1	3.50

NATIONAL LEAGUE 1899, *cont.*

Team	POS	Player	AB	BA	HR	RBI	PO	A	E	DP	TC/G	FA	Pitcher	G	IP	W	L	SV	ERA
Boston	1B	F. Tenney	603	.347	1	67	1474	**99**	35	**107**	10.7	.978	K. Nichols	42	349	21	19	1	2.94
	2B	B. Lowe	559	.272	4	88	361	461	40	66	5.8	.954	V. Willis	41	343	27	8	2	2.50
W-95 L-57	SS	H. Long	578	.265	6	100	351	435	60	**68**	5.9	.929	T. Lewis	29	235	17	11	0	3.49
	3B	J. Collins	599	.277	5	92	217	**376**	36	23	4.2	.943	J. Meekin	13	108	7	6	0	2.83
Frank Selee	RF	C. Stahl	576	.351	8	53	253	26	9	6	1.9	.969	F. Killen	12	99	7	5	0	4.26
	CF	B. Hamilton	297	.310	1	33	166	11	9	2	2.3	.952	H. Bailey	12	87	6	4	0	3.95
	LF	H. Duffy	588	.279	5	102	344	9	11	1	2.5	.970							
	C	M. Bergen	260	.258	1	34	253	89	16	4	5.0	.955							
	C	B. Clarke	223	.224	2	32	213	69	18	4	5.0	.940							
	OF	G. Stafford	182	.302	3	40	86	0	4	0	2.2	.956							
	OF	C. Frisbee	152	.329	0	20	68	9	11	1	2.2	.875							
Philadelphia	1B	D. Cooley	406	.276	1	31	756	34	24	56	10.3	.971	W. Piatt	39	305	23	15	0	3.45
	2B	N. Lajoie	312	.378	6	70	224	231	22	39	7.1	.954	R. Donahue	35	279	21	8	0	3.39
W-94 L-58	SS	M. Cross	557	.257	3	65	**370**	**529**	**90**	55	6.4	.909	C. Fraser	35	271	21	12	0	3.36
	3B	B. Lauder	583	.268	3	90	210	307	62	22	3.8	.893	A. Orth	21	145	14	3	1	**2.49**
Bill Shettsline	RF	E. Flick	485	.342	2	98	234	24	19	7	2.2	.931	B. Bernhard	21	132	6	6	0	2.65
	CF	R. Thomas	547	.325	0	47	313	22	17	8	2.6	.952	J. Fifield	14	93	3	8	1	4.08
	LF	E. Delahanty	581	**.410**	9	**137**	284	26	10	4	2.2	.969							
	C	E. McFarland	324	.333	1	57	305	125	14	**14**	4.7	.968							
	UT	P. Chiles	338	.320	2	76	330	44	25	18		.937							
	C	K. Douglass	275	.255	0	27	179	76	8	7	4.0	.970							
	2B	J. Dolan	222	.257	1	30	113	190	28	10	5.4	.915							
Baltimore	1B	C. LaChance	472	.307	1	75	1272	40	21	72	10.7	.984	J. McGinnity	48	366	**28**	17	2	2.68
	2B	G. DeMontreville	240	.279	1	36	174	197	15	16	6.4	.961	F. Kitson	40	330	22	16	0	2.76
W-86 L-62	SS	B. Keister	523	.329	3	73	169	283	53	25	5.6	.895	J. Nops	33	259	17	11	0	4.03
	3B	J. McGraw	399	.391	1	33	142	270	24	14	3.7	.945	H. Howell	28	209	13	8	1	3.91
John McGraw	RF	J. Sheckard	536	.295	3	75	298	33	20	14	2.4	.943							
	CF	S. Brodie	531	.309	3	87	310	15	7	5	2.4	.979							
	LF	D. Holmes	553	.320	4	66	321	24	27	5	2.7	.927							
	C	W. Robinson	356	.284	0	47	286	83	20	2	3.7	.949							
	O3	D. Fultz	210	.295	0	18	94	41	16	1		.894							
	SS	G. Magoon	207	.256	0	31	143	215	30	19	6.3	.923							
	1C	P. Crisham	172	.291	0	20	282	23	8	7		.974							
	C	B. Smith	120	.383	0	25	109	26	7	3	3.9	.951							
St. Louis	1B	P. Tebeau	281	.246	1	26	648	22	14	33	10.5	.980	J. Powell	48	373	23	21	0	3.52
	2B	C. Childs	464	.265	1	48	323	355	48	45	5.8	.934	C. Young	44	369	26	16	1	2.58
W-84 L-67	SS	B. Wallace	577	.295	12	108	238	386	55	40	6.8	.919	W. Sudhoff	26	189	13	10	0	3.61
	3B	L. Cross	403	.303	4	64	157	277	18	25*	4.4	.960*	N. Cuppy	21	172	11	8	0	3.15
Patsy Tebeau	RF	E. Heidrick	591	.328	2	82	211	34	20	6	1.8	.925	C. Jones	12	85	6	5	0	3.59
	CF	H. Blake	292	.240	2	41	176	10	4	3	2.2	.979							
	LF	J. Burkett	558	.396	7	71	296	20	21	3	2.4	.938							
	C	L. Criger	258	.256	2	44	228	91	17	6	4.5	.949							
	C1	J. O'Connor	289	.253	0	43	427	76	18	20		.965							
	UT	E. McKean	277	.260	3	40	254	156	34	25		.923							
	1C	O. Schreckengost	277	.278	2	37	516	49	23	35		.961							
	OF	M. Donlin	266	.323	6	27	96	7	15	2	2.3	.873							
Cincinnati	1B	J. Beckley	513	.333	3	99	1291	72	19	74	10.3	.986	N. Hahn	38	309	23	8	0	2.68
	2B	B. McPhee	373	.279	1	65	245	312	26	41	5.5	.955	P. Hawley	34	250	14	17	1	4.24
W-83 L-67	SS	T. Corcoran	537	.277	0	81	281	416	52	52	6.1	.931	B. Phillips	33	228	17	9	1	3.32
	3B	C. Irwin	314	.232	1	52	108	142	25	5	3.5	.909	T. Breitenstein	26	211	13	9	0	3.59
Buck Ewing	RF	D. Miller	323	.251	0	37	148	18	13	4	2.2	.927	J. Taylor	24	168	9	10	2	4.12
	CF	E. Smith	339	.298	1	24	178	12	16	3	2.4	.922							
	LF	K. Selbach	521	.296	3	87	355	27	19	10	2.9	.953							
	C	H. Peitz	290	.272	1	43	**329**	89	10	12	4.7	.977							
	32	H. Steinfeldt	386	.244	0	43	175	239	41	17		.910							
	OF	A. McBride	251	.347	1	23	124	8	7	2	2.2	.950							
	C	B. Wood	194	.314	0	24	160	49	14	3	4.2	.937							
	S3	K. Elberfeld	138	.261	0	22	74	108	25	9		.879							
	OF	S. Crawford	127	.307	1	20	56	9	2	2	2.2	.970							
Pittsburgh	1B	W. Clark	298	.285	0	44	837	36	10	37	11.3	.989	S. Leever	**51**	**379**	21	23	**3**	3.18
	2B	J. O'Brien	279	.226	1	33	211	243	26	32	6.1	.946	J. Tannehill	41	313	24	14	1	2.73
	SS	B. Ely	522	.278	3	72	274	472	58	45	6.1	.928	T. Sparks	28	170	8	6	0	3.86
W-76 L-73	3B	J. Williams	617	.355	9	116	**251**	354	**66**	14	**4.4**	.902	B. Hoffer	23	164	8	10	0	3.63
	RF	P. Donovan	531	.294	1	55	184	9	12	3	1.7	.941	J. Chesbro	19	149	6	9	0	4.11
Bill Watkins	CF	G. Beaumont	437	.352	3	38	235	20	21	6	2.7	.924							
	LF	J. McCarthy	560	.305	3	67	281	18	12	5	2.3	.961							
W-7 L-15	C	F. Bowerman	424	.259	3	53	276	128	**22**	7	5.4	.948							
Patsy Donovan	OF	T. McCreery	455	.323	2	64	198	16	21	2	2.4	.911							
W-69 L-58	C	P. Schriver	301	.282	1	49	275	94	16	6	4.9	.958							
	1B	P. Dillon	121	.256	0	20	301	17	4	16	10.7	.988							

NATIONAL LEAGUE 1899, *cont.*

Chicago

W-75 L-73

Tom Burns

POS	Player	AB	BA	HR	RBI	PO	A	E	DP	TC/G	FA	Pitcher	G	IP	W	L	SV	ERA
1B	B. Everitt	536	.310	1	74	**1491**	95	**47**	103	**12.0**	.971	J. Taylor	41	355	18	21	0	3.76
2B	B. McCormick	376	.258	2	52	200	344	34	47	5.8	.941	C. Griffith	38	320	22	14	0	2.79
SS	G. DeMontreville	310	.281	0	40	192	306	54	38	6.7	.902	N. Callahan	35	294	21	12	0	3.06
3B	H. Wolverton	389	.285	1	49	123	227	57	12	4.2	.860	N. Garvin	24	199	9	13	0	2.85
RF	D. Green	475	.295	6	56	175	22	11	11	1.8	.947	B. Phyle	10	84	1	8	1	4.20
CF	B. Lange	416	.325	1	58	224	22	6	11	2.7	.976							
LF	J. Ryan	525	.301	3	68	266	18	13	6	2.4	.956							
C	T. Donahue	278	.248	0	29	304	100	21	13	4.7	.951							
OF	S. Mertes	426	.298	9	81	197	20	18	4	2.2	.923							
23	J. Connor	234	.205	0	24	101	211	26	25		.923							
C	F. Chance	192	.286	1	22	166	64	12	6	4.2	.950							
SS	G. Magoon	189	.228	0	21	138	216	41	34	6.7	.896							

Louisville

W-75 L-77

Fred Clarke

POS	Player	AB	BA	HR	RBI	PO	A	E	DP	TC/G	FA	Pitcher	G	IP	W	L	SV	ERA
1B	M. Kelley	282	.241	3	33	745	38	21	37	10.6	.974	B. Cunningham	39	324	17	17	0	3.84
2B	C. Ritchey	536	.300	4	71	352	414	51	54	6.0	.938	D. Phillippe	42	321	21	17	1	3.17
SS	B. Clingman	366	.262	2	44	195	381	53	43	5.8	.916	P. Dowling	34	290	13	17	0	3.11
3B	T. Leach	406	.288	5	57	135	200	34	13	4.6	.908	W. Woods	26	186	9	13	0	3.28
RF	C. Dexter	295	.258	1	33	131	16	9	2	2.2	.942	R. Waddell	10	79	7	2	1	3.08
CF	D. Hoy	**633**	.306	5	49	321	21	27	8	2.4	.927	B. Magee	12	71	3	7	0	5.20
LF	F. Clarke	602	.342	5	70	327	20	13	2	2.5	.964							
C	C. Zimmer	262	.298	2	29	184	77	4	6	4.3	.985*							
30	H. Wagner	571	.336	7	113	197	182	24	15		.940							
C	M. Powers	169	.207	0	22	118	27	9	5	4.1	.942							
P	B. Cunningham	154	.260	2	17	**35**	100	8	2	3.7	.944							

New York

W-60 L-90

John Day
W-29 L-35

Fred Hoey
W-31 L-55

POS	Player	AB	BA	HR	RBI	PO	A	E	DP	TC/G	FA	Pitcher	G	IP	W	L	SV	ERA
1B	J. Doyle	448	.299	3	76	1110	69	29	76	10.7	.976	B. Carrick	44	362	16	27	0	4.65
2B	K. Gleason	576	.264	0	59	**403**	**465**	50	60	6.3	.946	C. Seymour	32	268	14	18	0	3.56
SS	G. Davis	416	.337	1	57	311	412	42	57	**7.1**	**.945**	E. Doheny	35	265	14	17	0	4.51
3B	F. Hartman	174	.236	1	16	56	100	20	11	3.5	.886	J. Meekin	18	148	5	11	0	4.37
RF	P. Foster	301	.296	3	57	103	8	6	3	1.4	.949	C. Gettig	18	128	7	8	0	4.43
CF	G. Van Haltren	604	.301	2	58	284	31	23	8	2.2	.932							
LF	T. O'Brien	573	.297	6	77	243	21	19	7	2.2	.933							
C	J. Warner	293	.266	0	19	312	123	**22**	8	**5.6**	.952							
UT	P. Wilson	328	.268	0	42	416	140	49	34		.919							
C3	M. Grady	311	.334	2	54	147	137	26	9		.916							
P	C. Seymour	159	.327	2	27	16	88	**20**	1	**3.9**	.839							

Washington

W-54 L-98

Arthur Irwin

POS	Player	AB	BA	HR	RBI	PO	A	E	DP	TC/G	FA	Pitcher	G	IP	W	L	SV	ERA
1B	D. McGann	280	.343	5	58	667	36	7	37	9.3	.990*	G. Weyhing	43	335	17	21	0	4.54
2B	F. Bonner	347	.274	2	44	192	264	29	34	5.7	.940	B. Dinneen	37	291	14	20	0	3.93
SS	D. Padden	451	.277	2	61	201	281	46	33	6.2	.913	D. McFarlan	32	212	8	18	0	4.76
3B	C. Atherton	242	.248	0	23	91	119	26	7	3.7	.890	W. Mercer	23	186	7	14	0	4.60
RF	B. Freeman	588	.318	**25**	122	220	14	14	3	1.6	.944							
CF	J. Slagle	599	.272	0	41	407	20	21	8	3.1	.953							
LF	J. O'Brien	468	.282	6	51	266	21	23	5	2.6	.926							
C	D. McGuire	199	.271	1	12	178	71*	7	3	4.6	.973							
UT	W. Mercer	375	.299	1	35	109	156	40	8		.869							
UT	S. Barry	247	.287	1	33	254	65	19	13		.944							
1B	P. Cassidy	178	.315	3	32	337	16	11	26	9.8	.970							

Cleveland

W-20 L-134

Lave Cross
W-8 L-30

Joe Quinn
W-12 L-104

POS	Player	AB	BA	HR	RBI	PO	A	E	DP	TC/G	FA	Pitcher	G	IP	W	L	SV	ERA
1B	T. Tucker	456	.241	0	40	1229	58	30	71	10.4	.977	J. Hughey	36	283	4	**30**	0	5.41
2B	J. Quinn	615	.286	0	72	350	440	31	61	5.6	**.962**	C. Knepper	27	220	4	22	0	5.78
SS	H. Lochhead	541	.238	1	43	319	490	81	54	6.1	.909	F. Bates	20	153	1	18	0	7.24
3B	S. Sullivan	473	.245	0	55	110	237	23	21	3.7	.938	C. Schmit	20	138	2	17	0	5.86
RF	S. McAllister	418	.237	1	31	106	10	7	4	1.6	.943	H. Colliflower	14	98	1	11	0	8.17
CF	T. Dowd	605	.278	2	35	341	10	17	2	2.5	.954	W. Sudhoff	11	86	3	8	0	6.98
LF	D. Harley	567	.250	1	50	299	27	27	7	2.5	.924							
C	J. Sugden	250	.276	0	14	196	108	21	11	4.9	.935							
OF	C. Hemphill	202	.277	2	23	61	6	11	1	1.4	.859							
3B	L. Cross	154	.286	1	20	66	81	7	7*	4.1	.955*							

BATTING AND BASE RUNNING LEADERS

Batting Average

E. Delahanty, PHI	.410
J. Burkett, STL	.396
J. McGraw, BAL	.391
W. Keeler, BKN	.379
J. Williams, PIT	.355

Slugging Average

E. Delahanty, PHI	.582
B. Freeman, WAS	.563
J. Williams, PIT	.532
J. Burkett, STL	.500
C. Stahl, BOS	.495

Home Runs

B. Freeman, WAS	25
B. Wallace, STL	12
S. Mertes, CHI	9
E. Delahanty, PHI	9
J. Williams, PIT	9

Total Bases

E. Delahanty, PHI	338
B. Freeman, WAS	331
J. Williams, PIT	328
C. Stahl, BOS	285
H. Wagner, LOU	282

Runs Batted In

E. Delahanty, PHI	137
B. Freeman, WAS	122
J. Williams, PIT	116
H. Wagner, LOU	113
B. Wallace, STL	108

Stolen Bases

J. Sheckard, BAL	77
J. McGraw, BAL	73
E. Heidrick, STL	55
D. Holmes, BAL	50
F. Clarke, LOU	49

Hits

E. Delahanty, PHI	238
J. Burkett, STL	221
J. Williams, PIT	219
W. Keeler, BKN	216

Base on Balls

J. McGraw, BAL	124
R. Thomas, PHI	115
C. Childs, STL	74
G. Van Haltren, NY	74

Home Run Percentage

B. Freeman, WAS	4.3
S. Mertes, CHI	2.1
B. Wallace, STL	2.1
E. Delahanty, PHI	1.5

PITCHING LEADERS

Winning Percentage

J. Hughes, BKN	.824
V. Willis, BOS	.771
N. Hahn, CIN	.742
R. Donahue, PHI	.724
B. Kennedy, BKN	.710

Earned Run Average

A. Orth, PHI	2.49
V. Willis, BOS	2.50
C. Young, STL	2.58
B. Bernhard, PHI	2.65
J. McGinnity, BAL	2.68

Wins

J. Hughes, BKN	28
J. McGinnity, BAL	28
V. Willis, BOS	27
C. Young, STL	26
J. Tannehill, PIT	24

Saves

S. Leever, PIT	3
V. Willis, BOS	2
B. Kennedy, BKN	2
J. Taylor, CIN	2
J. Dunn, BKN	2
J. McGinnity, BAL	2

Strikeouts

N. Hahn, CIN	145
C. Seymour, NY	142
S. Leever, PIT	121
V. Willis, BOS	120
E. Doheny, NY	115

Complete Games

C. Young, STL	40
B. Carrick, NY	40
J. Powell, STL	40
J. Taylor, CHI	39
J. McGinnity, BAL	38

Fewest Hits/9 Innings

V. Willis, BOS	7.28
J. Hughes, BKN	7.71
N. Hahn, CIN	8.16
B. Bernhard, PHI	8.16

Shutouts

V. Willis, BOS	5

Fewest Walks/9 Innings

C. Young, STL	1.07
A. Orth, PHI	1.18
N. Cuppy, STL	1.36
J. Tannehill, PIT	1.47

NATIONAL LEAGUE 1899, *cont.*

BATTING AND BASE RUNNING LEADERS

Runs		Doubles		Triples	
J. McGraw, BAL	140	E. Delahanty, PHI	55	J. Williams, PIT	27
W. Keeler, BKN	140	H. Wagner, LOU	43	B. Freeman, WAS	25
R. Thomas, PHI	137	D. Holmes, BAL	31	C. Stahl, BOS	18
E. Delahanty, PHI	135	H. Long, BOS	30	J. McCarthy, PIT	17
				F. Tenney, BOS	17

PITCHING LEADERS

Most Strikeouts/9 Inn.		Innings		Games Pitched	
C. Seymour, NY	4.76	S. Leever, PIT	379	S. Leever, PIT	51
N. Hahn, CIN	4.22	J. Powell, STL	373	J. McGinnity, BAL	48
E. Doheny, NY	3.90	C. Young, STL	369	J. Powell, STL	48
D. McJames, BKN	3.43	J. McGinnity, BAL	366	C. Young, STL	44
				B. Carrick, NY	44

	W	L	PCT	GB	R	OR	Batting 2B	3B	HR	BA	SA	SB	Fielding E	DP	FA	Pitching CG	BB	SO	ShO	SV	ERA
Brooklyn	101	47	.682		892	658	178	97	26	.291	.382	271	314	125	.948	121	463	331	9	**9**	**3.25**
Boston	95	57	.625	8	858	**645**	178	89	40	.287	.377	185	**303**	124	**.952**	138	432	385	13	4	3.26
Philadelphia	94	58	.618	9	**916**	743	**241**	84	30	**.301**	**.395**	212	379	110	.940	129	370	281	**15**	2	3.47
Baltimore	86	62	.581		827	691	204	71	17	.297	.376	**364**	308	96	.949	133	349	294	9	5	3.31
St. Louis	84	67	.556		819	739	172	89	46	.285	.377	210	397	117	.939	134	**321**	331	7	1	3.36
Cincinnati	83	67	.553	0.5	856	770	194	105	13	.275	.360	228	339	111	.947	130	370	360	8	5	3.70
Pittsburgh	76	73	.510	7	834	765	196	**121**	27	.289	.384	179	361	98	.945	117	437	334	9	4	3.60
Chicago	75	73	.507	7.5	812	763	173	82	27	.277	.359	247	428	**145**	.935	**147**	330	313	8	1	3.37
Louisville	75	77	.493	9.5	827	775	192	68	40	.280	.364	233	394	102	.939	134	323	287	5	2	3.45
New York	60	90	.400	23.5	734	863	161	65	23	.281	.352	234	433	140	.932	138	628	**397**	4	0	4.29
Washington	54	98	.355	30.5	743	983	162	87	**47**	.272	.363	176	403	99	.935	131	422	328	3	0	4.93
Cleveland	20	134	.130	65.5	529	1252	142	50	12	.253	.305	127	388	121	.937	138	527	215	0	0	6.37
					9647	9647	2193	1008	348	.282	.366	2666	4447	1388	.942	1590	4972	3856	90	33	3.86

NATIONAL LEAGUE 1900

Brooklyn

W-82 L-54

Ned Hanlon

POS	Player	AB	BA	HR	RBI	PO	A	E	DP	TC/G	FA	Pitcher	G	IP	W	L	SV	ERA
1B	H. Jennings	441	.272	1	69	1050	76	21	71	10.2	.982	J. McGinnity	44	**347**	**29**	9	0	2.90
2B	T. Daly	343	.312	4	55	233	234	40	39	5.5	.921	B. Kennedy	42	292	20	13	0	3.91
SS	B. Dahlen	483	.259	1	69	321	**517**	55	59	6.7	.938	F. Kitson	40	253	15	13	**4**	4.19
3B	L. Cross	461	.293	4	67	162	282	27	10	4.0	.943*	H. Howell	21	110	6	5	0	3.75
RF	W. Keeler	563	.362	4	68	227	22	16	4	1.9	.940							
CF	F. Jones	552	.310	4	54	315	15	15	3	2.5	.957							
LF	J. Kelley	454	.319	6	91	174	12	8	2	2.5	.959							
C	D. Farrell	273	.275	0	39	252	88	20	8	4.9	.944							
OF	J. Sheckard	273	.300	1	39	171	13	15	3	2.6	.925							
C	D. McGuire	241	.286	0	34	218	77	15	7	4.5	.952							
UT	G. DeMontreville	234	.244	0	28	159	176	25	19		.931							
P	J. McGinnity	145	.193	0	16	15	75	12	4	2.3	.882							

Pittsburgh

W-79 L-60

Fred Clarke

POS	Player	AB	BA	HR	RBI	PO	A	E	DP	TC/G	FA	Pitcher	G	IP	W	L	SV	ERA
1B	D. Cooley	249	.201	0	22	683	20	8	39	10.8	.989	D. Phillippe	38	279	20	13	0	2.84
2B	C. Ritchey	476	.292	1	67	303	357	33	51	5.6	.952	J. Tannehill	29	234	20	6	0	2.88
SS	B. Ely	475	.244	0	51	242	503	52	62	6.1	.935	S. Leever	30	233	15	13	0	2.71
3B	J. Williams	416	.264	5	68	153	254	51	**21**	4.4	.889	J. Chesbro	32	216	15	13	1	3.67
RF	H. Wagner	527	**.381**	4	100	181	11	7	4	1.7	.965	R. Waddell	29	209	8	13	0	**2.37**
CF	G. Beaumont	567	.279	4	50	274	10	17	3	2.2	.944							
LF	F. Clarke	399	.276	3	32	263	8	16	2	2.8	.944							
C	C. Zimmer	271	.295	0	35	**318**	100	17	8	5.6	.961							
10	T. O'Brien	376	.290	3	61	718	27	31	37		.960							
UT	T. Leach	160	.212	1	16	74	117	24	9		.888							
C	J. O'Connor	147	.238	0	19	108	44	9	2	4.0	.944							

Philadelphia

W-75 L-63

Bill Shettsline

POS	Player	AB	BA	HR	RBI	PO	A	E	DP	TC/G	FA	Pitcher	G	IP	W	L	SV	ERA
1B	E. Delahanty	539	.323	2	109	1299	66	27	86	10.7	.981	A. Orth	33	262	12	13	1	3.78
2B	N. Lajoie	451	.337	7	92	287	341	30	**69**	**6.5**	**.954**	R. Donahue	32	240	15	10	0	3.60
SS	M. Cross	466	.202	3	62	**339**	459	**62**	68	6.6	.928	C. Fraser	29	223	16	10	0	3.14
3B	H. Wolverton	383	.282	3	58	122	234	48	16	4.0	.881	B. Bernhard	32	219	15	10	2	4.77
RF	E. Flick	545	.367	11	**110**	232	23	24	6	2.0	.914	W. Piatt	22	161	9	10	0	4.65
CF	R. Thomas	531	.316	0	33	303	19	14	6	2.4	.958	J. Dunn	10	80	5	5	0	4.84
LF	J. Slagle	574	.287	0	45	320	22	29	5	2.6	.922							
C	E. McFarland	344	.305	0	38	278	**137**	16	9	4.6	**.963**							
UT	J. Dolan	257	.198	1	27	136	198	26	17		.928							
C	K. Douglass	160	.300	0	25	138	59	14	4	4.5	.934							
P	A. Orth	129	.310	1	21	15	68	5	3	2.7	.943							
12	P. Chiles	111	.216	1	23	165	42	6	14		.972							

Boston

W-66 L-72

Frank Selee

POS	Player	AB	BA	HR	RBI	PO	A	E	DP	TC/G	FA	Pitcher	G	IP	W	L	SV	ERA
1B	F. Tenney	437	.279	1	56	1021	82	21	50	10.1	.981	B. Dinneen	40	321	20	14	0	3.12
2B	B. Lowe	474	.278	3	71	**323**	335	34	38	5.4	.951	V. Willis	32	236	10	17	0	4.19
SS	H. Long	486	.261	**12**	66	257	454	48	34	6.1	.937	K. Nichols	29	231	13	16	0	3.07
3B	J. Collins	**586**	.304	6	95	**251**	**329**	40	**21**	4.4	.935	T. Lewis	30	209	13	12	0	4.13
RF	B. Freeman	418	.301	6	65	130	3	7	1	1.5	.950	T. Pittinger	18	114	2	9	0	5.13
CF	B. Hamilton	520	.333	1	47	326	14	19	6	2.6	.947	N. Cuppy	17	105	8	4	1	3.08
LF	C. Stahl	553	.295	5	82	277	22	10	4	2.3	.968							
C	B. Clarke	270	.315	1	30	246	104	27	8	5.6	.928							
UT	S. Barry	254	.260	1	37	199	82	23	13		.924							
C	B. Sullivan	238	.273	8	41	227	71	8	10	4.6	.974							
OF	H. Duffy	181	.304	2	31	107	5	5	2	2.4	.957							

NATIONAL LEAGUE 1900, *cont.*

Chicago

W-65 L-75

Tom Loftus

POS	Player	AB	BA	HR	RBI	PO	A	E	DP	TC/G	FA	Pitcher	G	IP	W	L	SV	ERA
1B	J. Ganzel	284	.275	4	32	817	34	17	40	11.1	.980	N. Callahan	32	285	13	16	0	3.82
2B	C. Childs	531	.241	0	44	**323**	**431**	**52**	57	5.9	.935	C. Griffith	30	248	14	13	0	3.05
SS	B. McCormick	379	.219	3	48	161	307	48	32	6.1	.907	N. Garvin	30	246	10	18	0	2.41
3B	B. Bradley	444	.282	5	49	164	291	61	11	**4.9**	.882	J. Taylor	28	222	10	17	1	2.55
RF	J. Ryan	415	.277	5	59	177	12	18	3	2.0	.913	J. Menefee	16	117	9	4	0	3.85
CF	D. Green	389	.298	5	49	218	10	15	2	2.4	.938							
LF	J. McCarthy	503	.294	0	48	233	20	15	4	2.2	.944							
C	T. Donahue	216	.236	0	17	232	63	23	6	4.8	.928							
01	S. Mertes	481	.295	7	60	520	30	26	20		.955							
SS	B. Clingman	159	.208	0	11	81	150	34	19	5.6	.872							
C	F. Chance	149	.295	0	13	155	65	16	2	4.6	.932							
CO	C. Dexter	125	.200	2	20	98	36	6	4		.957							

St. Louis

W-65 L-75

Patsy Tebeau
W-42 L-50

Louie Heilbroner
W-23 L-25

POS	Player	AB	BA	HR	RBI	PO	A	E	DP	TC/G	FA	Pitcher	G	IP	W	L	SV	ERA
1B	D. McGann	444	.297	4	58	1212	58	13	41	10.6	**.990**	C. Young	41	321	19	19	0	3.00
2B	B. Keister	497	.300	1	72	206	315	41	26	4.8	.927	C. Jones	39	293	13	19	0	3.54
SS	B. Wallace	485	.268	4	70	327	447	55	31	6.6	.934	J. Powell	38	288	17	17	0	4.44
3B	J. McGraw	334	.344	2	33	106	213	32	7	3.5	.909	W. Sudhoff	16	127	6	8	0	2.76
RF	P. Donovan	503	.316	0	61	180	13	10	4	1.6	.951	J. Hughey	20	113	5	7	0	5.19
CF	E. Heidrick	339	.301	2	45	215	21	10	4	3.0	.959							
LF	J. Burkett	559	.363	7	68	337	17	25	6	2.7	.934							
C	L. Criger	288	.271	2	38	282	105	19	8	5.4	.953							
01	M. Donlin	276	.326	10	48	308	11	21	14		.938							
C	W. Robinson	210	.248	0	28	189	72	7	3	5.0	.974							
03	P. Dillard	183	.230	0	12	74	47	14	2		.896							

Cincinnati

W-62 L-77

Bob Allen

POS	Player	AB	BA	HR	RBI	PO	A	E	DP	TC/G	FA	Pitcher	G	IP	W	L	SV	ERA
1B	J. Beckley	558	.341	2	94	**1389**	93	30	91	**10.8**	.980	E. Scott	43	323	17	**21**	1	3.82
2B	J. Quinn	266	.274	0	25	154	169	17	24	4.6	.950	N. Hahn	38	303	16	19	0	3.29
SS	T. Corcoran	523	.245	1	54	262	436	60	56	6.1	.921	D. Newton	35	235	9	15	0	4.14
3B	H. Steinfeldt	513	.248	2	66	107	175	24	11	4.6	.922	B. Phillips	29	208	9	11	0	4.28
RF	A. McBride	436	.275	4	59	163	10	16	5	1.7	.915	T. Breitenstein	24	192	10	10	0	3.65
CF	J. Barrett	545	.316	5	42	287	25	24	6	2.5	.929							
LF	S. Crawford	389	.267	7	59	237	18	14	2	2.9	.948							
C	H. Peitz	294	.255	2	34	310	125	19	13	**5.7**	.958							
3B	C. Irwin	333	.273	1	44	74	128	15	11	3.6	.931							
C	M. Kahoe	175	.189	1	9	207	79	11	5	5.8	.963							
C3	B. Wood	139	.266	0	22	68	56	12	5		.912							

New York

W-60 L-78

Buck Ewing
W-21 L-41

George Davis
W-39 L-37

POS	Player	AB	BA	HR	RBI	PO	A	E	DP	TC/G	FA	Pitcher	G	IP	W	L	SV	ERA
1B	J. Doyle	505	.267	1	66	1269	**96**	**41**	**92**	10.6	.971	B. Carrick	**45**	342	19	**21**	0	3.53
2B	K. Gleason	420	.248	1	29	321	326	48	51	6.3	.931	P. Hawley	41	329	18	18	0	3.53
SS	G. Davis	426	.319	3	61	279	450	43	**94**	**6.8**	**.944**	W. Mercer	33	243	13	17	0	3.86
3B	P. Hickman	473	.313	9	91	183	276	**86**	19	4.5	.842	E. Doheny	20	134	4	14	0	5.45
RF	E. Smith	312	.260	2	34	91	10	5	2	1.3	.953							
CF	G. Van Haltren	571	.315	1	51	325	28	23	7	2.7	.939							
LF	K. Selbach	523	.337	4	68	327	25	18	8	2.6	.951							
C	F. Bowerman	270	.241	1	42	232	136	**28**	**15**	5.3	.929							
UT	M. Grady	251	.219	0	27	247	106	37	18		.905							
UT	W. Mercer	248	.294	0	27	75	149	32	11		.875							

BATTING AND BASE RUNNING LEADERS

Batting Average

H. Wagner, PIT	.381
E. Flick, PHI	.367
J. Burkett, STL	.363
W. Keeler, BKN	.362
J. McGraw, STL	.344

Slugging Average

H. Wagner, PIT	.573
E. Flick, PHI	.545
N. Lajoie, PHI	.510
J. Kelley, BKN	.485
P. Hickman, NY	.482

Home Runs

H. Long, BOS	12
E. Flick, PHI	11
M. Donlin, STL	10
P. Hickman, NY	9
B. Sullivan, BOS	8

Total Bases

H. Wagner, PIT	302
E. Flick, PHI	297
J. Burkett, STL	265
W. Keeler, BKN	253
J. Beckley, CIN	242

Runs Batted In

E. Flick, PHI	110
E. Delahanty, PHI	109
H. Wagner, PIT	100
J. Collins, BOS	95
J. Beckley, CIN	94

Stolen Bases

P. Donovan, STL	45
G. Van Haltren, NY	45
J. Barrett, CIN	44
W. Keeler, BKN	41
S. Mertes, CHI	38
H. Wagner, PIT	38

Hits

W. Keeler, BKN	204
J. Burkett, STL	203
H. Wagner, PIT	201
E. Flick, PHI	200

Base on Balls

R. Thomas, PHI	115
B. Hamilton, BOS	107
J. McGraw, STL	85
B. Dahlen, BKN	73

Home Run Percentage

H. Long, BOS	2.5
E. Flick, PHI	2.0
P. Hickman, NY	1.9
S. Crawford, CIN	1.8

Runs

R. Thomas, PHI	131
J. Slagle, PHI	115
J. Barrett, CIN	114
G. Van Haltren, NY	114

Doubles

H. Wagner, PIT	45
N. Lajoie, PHI	33
E. Delahanty, PHI	32
E. Flick, PHI	32

Triples

H. Wagner, PIT	22
J. Kelley, BKN	17
P. Hickman, NY	17
E. Flick, PHI	16
C. Stahl, BOS	16

PITCHING LEADERS

Winning Percentage

J. Tannehill, PIT	.769
J. McGinnity, BKN	.763
C. Fraser, PHI	.615
B. Kennedy, BKN	.606
D. Phillippe, PIT	.606

Earned Run Average

R. Waddell, PIT	2.37
N. Garvin, CHI	2.41
J. Taylor, CHI	2.55
S. Leever, PIT	2.71
W. Sudhoff, STL	2.76

Wins

J. McGinnity, BKN	29
J. Tannehill, PIT	20
D. Phillippe, PIT	20
B. Kennedy, BKN	20
B. Dinneen, BOS	20

Saves

F. Kitson, BKN	4
B. Bernhard, PHI	2

Strikeouts

R. Waddell, PIT	130
N. Hahn, CIN	127
C. Young, STL	115
N. Garvin, CHI	107
B. Dinneen, BOS	107

Complete Games

P. Hawley, NY	34
B. Dinneen, BOS	33

Fewest Hits/9 Innings

R. Waddell, PIT	7.59
N. Garvin, CHI	8.22
K. Nichols, BOS	8.36
B. Dinneen, BOS	8.53

Shutouts

K. Nichols, BOS	4
C. Griffith, CHI	4
C. Young, STL	4
N. Hahn, CIN	4

Fewest Walks/9 Innings

C. Young, STL	1.01
D. Phillippe, PIT	1.35
J. Tannehill, PIT	1.65
E. Scott, CIN	1.84

Most Strikeouts/9 Inn.

R. Waddell, PIT	5.61
N. Garvin, CHI	3.91
N. Hahn, CIN	3.77
D. Newton, CIN	3.38

Innings

J. McGinnity, BKN	347
B. Carrick, NY	342
P. Hawley, NY	329
E. Scott, CIN	323

Games Pitched

B. Carrick, NY	45
J. McGinnity, BKN	44
E. Scott, CIN	43
B. Kennedy, BKN	42

NATIONAL LEAGUE 1900, *cont.*

	W	L	PCT	GB	R	OR	Batting 2B	3B	HR	BA	SA	SB	Fielding E	DP	FA	Pitching CG	BB	SO	ShO	SV	ERA
Brooklyn	82	54	.603		**816**	722	199	81	26	**.293**	**.383**	**274**	303	102	.948	104	405	300	8	**4**	3.89
Pittsburgh	79	60	.568	4.5	733	**612**	185	**100**	25	.272	.368	174	322	106	.945	114	**295**	**415**	11	1	**3.06**
Philadelphia	75	63	.543	8	810	791	187	82	29	.290	.378	205	330	**125**	.945	116	402	284	7	3	4.12
Boston	66	72	.478	17	778	739	163	68	**48**	.283	.373	182	**273**	86	**.953**	116	463	340	8	2	3.72
Chicago	65	75	.464	19	635	751	**202**	51	33	.260	.342	189	418	98	.933	**137**	324	357	9	1	3.23
St. Louis	65	75	.464	19	743	747	141	81	36	.291	.375	243	331	73	.943	117	299	325	**12**	0	3.75
Cincinnati	62	77	.446	21.5	702	745	178	83	33	.266	.354	183	341	120	.945	118	404	399	9	1	3.83
New York	60	78	.435	23	713	823	177	61	23	.279	.357	236	439	124	.928	114	442	277	4	0	3.96
					5930	5930	1432	607	253	.279	.366	1686	2757	834	.942	936	3034	2697	68	12	3.70

NATIONAL LEAGUE 1901

Pittsburgh

W-90 L-49

Fred Clarke

POS	Player	AB	BA	HR	RBI	PO	A	E	DP	TC/G	FA
1B	K. Bransfield	566	.295	0	91	1374	52	28	72	10.5	.981
2B	C. Ritchey	540	.296	1	74	340	**392**	**46**	**53**	5.6	.941
SS	B. Ely	240	.208	0	28	112	215	30	23	5.6	.916
3B	T. Leach	374	.305	1	44	122	196	34	9	3.8	.903
RF	L. Davis	335	.313	2	33	140	18	4	7	1.9	.975
CF	G. Beaumont	558	.332	8	72	289	8	18	2	2.4	.943
LF	F. Clarke	527	.324	6	60	282	13	9	0	2.4	.970
C	C. Zimmer	236	.220	0	21	285	69	9	4	5.3	.975
UT	H. Wagner	556	.353	6	**126**	297	280	48	35		.923
C	J. O'Connor	202	.193	0	22	256	59	7	5	5.5	.978

Pitcher	G	IP	W	L	SV	ERA
D. Phillippe	37	296	22	12	2	2.22
J. Chesbro	36	288	21	10	1	2.38
J. Tannehill	32	252	18	10	1	**2.18**
S. Leever	21	176	14	5	0	2.86

Philadelphia

W-83 L-57

Bill Shettsline

POS	Player	AB	BA	HR	RBI	PO	A	E	DP	TC/G	FA
1B	H. Jennings	302	.275	1	39	745	38	17	20	10.0	.979
2B	B. Hallman	445	.184	0	38	177	261	13	20	5.0	.971*
SS	M. Cross	483	.197	1	44	**343**	445	65	31	6.1	.924
3B	H. Wolverton	379	.309	0	43	114	190	26	9	3.5	**.921**
RF	E. Flick	542	.336	8	88	278	23	12	7	2.3	.962
CF	R. Thomas	479	.309	1	28	283	9	10	2	2.3	.967
LF	E. Delahanty	538	.357	8	108	179	9	10	2	2.4	.949
C	E. McFarland	295	.285	1	32	316	102	13	2	5.8	.970
UT	S. Barry	252	.246	1	22	122	123	31	8		.888
OF	J. Slagle	183	.202	1	20	108	12*	9	3	2.7	.930
C	K. Douglass	173	.324	0	23	201	29	5	2	5.7	.979
C	F. Jacklitsch	120	.250	0	24	126	39	5	3	5.7	.971

Pitcher	G	IP	W	L	SV	ERA
R. Donahue	35	304	21	13	0	2.60
A. Orth	35	282	20	12	0	2.27
B. Duggleby	34	276	19	12	0	2.87
D. White	31	237	14	13	0	3.19
J. Townsend	19	144	9	6	0	3.45

Brooklyn

W-79 L-57

Ned Hanlon

POS	Player	AB	BA	HR	RBI	PO	A	E	DP	TC/G	FA
1B	J. Kelley	492	.309	4	65	984	82	27	63	9.5	.975
2B	T. Daly	520	.315	3	90	**370**	357	43	46	**5.8**	.944
SS	B. Dahlen	513	.261	4	82	301	450	57	49	6.3	.929
3B	C. Irwin	242	.215	0	20	88*	106	9	5	3.1	.956
RF	W. Keeler	589	.355	2	43	181	17	3	4	1.6	.985
CF	T. McCreery	335	.290	3	53	189	9	11	2	2.5	.947
LF	J. Sheckard	558	.353	11	104	287	15	18	5	2.6	.944
C	D. McGuire	301	.296	0	40	415	94	**21**	4	**6.5**	.960
C	D. Farrell	284	.296	1	31	285	90	8	8	6.5	.979
OF	C. Dolan	253	.261	0	29	108	9	4	2	1.9	.967
3B	F. Gatins	197	.228	1	21	56	58	10	5	2.7	.919

Pitcher	G	IP	W	L	SV	ERA
W. Donovan	**45**	351	**25**	15	1	2.77
F. Kitson	38	281	19	11	2	2.98
J. Hughes	31	251	17	12	0	3.27
D. Newton	13	105	6	5	0	2.83
D. McJames	13	91	5	6	0	4.75

St. Louis

W-76 L-64

Patsy Donovan

POS	Player	AB	BA	HR	RBI	PO	A	E	DP	TC/G	FA
1B	D. McGann	426	.289	6	56	1030	50	18	64	10.7	.984
2B	D. Padden	488	.256	2	62	286	336	33	47	5.7	.950
SS	B. Wallace	556	.322	2	91	326	**542**	**66**	**67**	**7.0**	.929
3B	O. Krueger	520	.275	2	79	171	**275**	**60**	11	3.6	.881
RF	P. Donovan	527	.292	1	73	215	19	5	8	1.9	.979
CF	E. Heidrick	502	.339	6	67	258	15	16	2	2.4	.945
LF	J. Burkett	**597**	**.382**	10	75	307	17	27	4	2.5	.923
C	J. Ryan	300	.197	0	31	292	84	7	7	5.9	.982
CO	A. Nichols	308	.244	1	33	256	60	13	9		.960
C1	P. Schriver	166	.271	1	23	273	61	10	13		.971

Pitcher	G	IP	W	L	SV	ERA
J. Powell	**45**	338	19	19	**3**	3.54
J. Harper	39	309	23	13	0	3.62
W. Sudhoff	38	276	17	11	2	3.52
E. Murphy	23	165	10	9	0	4.20

Boston

W-69 L-69

Frank Selee

POS	Player	AB	BA	HR	RBI	PO	A	E	DP	TC/G	FA
1B	F. Tenney	457	.278	1	22	1059	**86**	28	58	10.4	.976
2B	G. DeMontreville	570	.304	5	72	272	344	30	35	5.4	.954
SS	H. Long	518	.228	3	68	304	468	44	55	5.9	**.946**
3B	B. Lowe	491	.255	3	47	149	192	33	12	3.4	.912
RF	J. Slagle	255	.271	0	7	89	11	7	3	1.6	.935
CF	B. Hamilton	349	.292	3	38	232	7	14	4	2.6	.945
LF	D. Cooley	240	.258	0	27	127	5	8	1	2.6	.943
C	M. Kittridge	381	.252	2	40	**581**	**136**	12	7	6.5	**.984**
OF	F. Crolius	200	.240	1	13	65	3	12	1	1.6	.850
UT	P. Moran	180	.211	2	18	299	37	14	8		.960
OF	F. Murphy	176	.261	1	18	97	10	7	1	2.5	.939
P	K. Nichols	163	.282	4	28	27	69	4	1	2.6	.960
P	B. Dinneen	147	.211	1	6	14	72	7	2	2.5	.925

Pitcher	G	IP	W	L	SV	ERA
K. Nichols	38	321	19	16	0	3.22
B. Dinneen	37	309	15	18	0	2.94
V. Willis	38	305	20	17	0	2.36
T. Pittinger	34	281	13	16	0	3.01

NATIONAL LEAGUE 1901, *cont.*

Chicago

W-53 L-86

Tom Loftus

POS	Player	AB	BA	HR	RBI	PO	A	E	DP	TC/G	FA	Pitcher	G	IP	W	L	SV	ERA
1B	J. Doyle	285	.232	0	39	698	60	21	32	10.4	.973	L. Hughes	37	308	11	21	0	3.24
2B	C. Childs	237	.257	0	21	146	192	22	34	5.8	.939	J. Taylor	33	276	13	19	0	3.36
SS	B. McCormick	427	.234	1	32	202	405	59	47	5.9	.911	R. Waddell	29	244	13	15	0	2.81
3B	F. Raymer	463	.233	0	43	79	143	30	5	3.1	.881	M. Eason	27	221	8	17	0	3.59
RF	F. Chance	241	.278	0	36	61	7	5	0	1.5	.932	J. Menefee	21	182	8	13	0	3.80
CF	D. Green	537	.313	6	60	312	17	24	7	2.7	.932							
LF	T. Hartsel	558	.335	7	54	273	16	15	3	2.2	.951							
C	J. Kling	253	.277	0	21	319	75	20	7	6.0	.952							
UT	C. Dexter	460	.267	1	66	618	125	27	32		.965							
C	M. Kahoe	237	.224	1	21	368	74	12	8	7.2	.974							
2B	P. Childs	213	.225	0	14	128	198	14	19	5.6	.959							
OF	C. Dolan	171	.263	0	16	63	9	10	3	2.0	.878							
OP	J. Menefee	152	.257	0	13	52	47	8	1		.925							

New York

W-52 L-85

George Davis

POS	Player	AB	BA	HR	RBI	PO	A	E	DP	TC/G	FA	Pitcher	G	IP	W	L	SV	ERA
1B	J. Ganzel	526	.215	2	66	**1421**	77	21	59	**11.0**	**.986**	D. Taylor	**45**	353	18	**27**	0	3.18
2B	R. Nelson	130	.200	0	7	44	125	22	10	4.9	.885	C. Mathewson	40	336	20	17	0	2.41
SS	G. Davis	495	.309	7	65	296	396	45	42	6.5	.939	B. Phyle	24	169	7	10	1	4.27
3B	S. Strang	493	.282	1	34	127	194	45	**16**	**4.0**	.877							
RF	A. McBride	264	.280	2	29	84	8	5	3	1.5	.948							
CF	G. Van Haltren	544	.342	1	47	263	23	18	5	2.3	.941							
LF	K. Selbach	502	.289	1	56	215	11	14	2	1.9	.942							
C	J. Warner	291	.241	0	20	361	107	16	**11**	5.8	.967							
UT	P. Hickman	401	.282	4	62	154	154	35	10		.898							
C	F. Bowerman	191	.199	0	14	256	67	17	6	7.4	.950							

Cincinnati

W-52 L-87

Bid McPhee

POS	Player	AB	BA	HR	RBI	PO	A	E	DP	TC/G	FA	Pitcher	G	IP	W	L	SV	ERA
1B	J. Beckley	580	.307	3	79	1366	71	**34**	**79**	10.5	.977	N. Hahn	42	**375**	22	19	0	2.71
2B	H. Steinfeldt	382	.249	6	47	138	142	18	23	6.0	.940	B. Phillips	37	281	14	20	0	4.64
SS	G. Magoon	460	.252	1	53	253	345	53	36	5.8	.919	D. Newton	20	168	4	14	0	4.12
3B	C. Irwin	260	.238	0	25	87*	139	27	10	3.8	.893	A. Stimmel	20	153	4	14	0	4.11
RF	S. Crawford	515	.330	**16**	104	209	20	19	6	2.0	.923							
CF	J. Dobbs	435	.274	2	27	189	11	11	4	2.1	.948							
LF	D. Harley	535	.273	4	27	245	20	30	2	2.2	.898							
C	B. Bergen	308	.179	1	17	406	117	16	8	6.2	.970							
UT	H. Peitz	269	.305	1	24	321	127	9	14		.980							
2B	B. Fox	159	.176	0	7	103	134	11	19	5.8	.956							
OF	H. Bay	157	.210	1	3	78	3	4	3	2.1	.953							
P	N. Hahn	141	.170	0	7	14	85	6	4	2.5	.943							

BATTING AND BASE RUNNING LEADERS

Batting Average

J. Burkett, STL	.382
E. Delahanty, PHI	.357
W. Keeler, BKN	.355
J. Sheckard, BKN	.353
H. Wagner, PIT	.353

Slugging Average

J. Sheckard, BKN	.536
E. Delahanty, PHI	.533
S. Crawford, CIN	.528
J. Burkett, STL	.524
E. Flick, PHI	.500

Home Runs

S. Crawford, CIN	16
J. Sheckard, BKN	11
J. Burkett, STL	10
E. Delahanty, PHI	8
E. Flick, PHI	8
G. Beaumont, PIT	8

Total Bases

J. Burkett, STL	313
J. Sheckard, BKN	299
E. Delahanty, PHI	287
H. Wagner, PIT	273
S. Crawford, CIN	272

Runs Batted In

H. Wagner, PIT	126
E. Delahanty, PHI	108
S. Crawford, CIN	104
J. Sheckard, BKN	104
B. Wallace, STL	91
K. Bransfield, PIT	91

Stolen Bases

H. Wagner, PIT	49
T. Hartsel, CHI	41
S. Strang, NY	40
D. Harley, CIN	37
G. Beaumont, PIT	36

Hits

J. Burkett, STL	228
W. Keeler, BKN	209
J. Sheckard, BKN	197
H. Wagner, PIT	196

Base on Balls

R. Thomas, PHI	100
T. Hartsel, CHI	74
L. Davis, BKN, PIT	66
E. Delahanty, PHI	65

Home Run Percentage

S. Crawford, CIN	3.1
J. Sheckard, BKN	2.0
J. Burkett, STL	1.7
H. Steinfeldt, CIN	1.6

Runs

J. Burkett, STL	139
W. Keeler, BKN	123
G. Beaumont, PIT	120
F. Clarke, PIT	118

Doubles

E. Delahanty, PHI	39
J. Beckley, CIN	39
T. Daly, BKN	38
H. Wagner, PIT	37

Triples

J. Sheckard, BKN	19
E. Flick, PHI	17
J. Burkett, STL	17

PITCHING LEADERS

Winning Percentage

J. Chesbro, PIT	.677
D. Phillippe, PIT	.647
J. Tannehill, PIT	.643
J. Harper, STL	.639
F. Kitson, BKN	.633

Earned Run Average

J. Tannehill, PIT	2.18
D. Phillippe, PIT	2.22
A. Orth, PHI	2.27
V. Willis, BOS	2.36
J. Chesbro, PIT	2.38

Wins

W. Donovan, BKN	25
J. Harper, STL	23
D. Phillippe, PIT	22
N. Hahn, CIN	22
J. Chesbro, PIT	21
R. Donahue, PHI	21

Saves

J. Powell, STL	3
W. Sudhoff, STL	2
D. Phillippe, PIT	2
F. Kitson, BKN	2

Strikeouts

N. Hahn, CIN	239
W. Donovan, BKN	226
L. Hughes, CHI	225
C. Mathewson, NY	221
R. Waddell, PIT, CHI	172

Complete Games

N. Hahn, CIN	41
D. Taylor, NY	37
W. Donovan, BKN	36
C. Mathewson, NY	36
R. Donahue, PHI	34

Fewest Hits/9 Innings

J. Townsend, PHI	7.39
C. Mathewson, NY	7.71
V. Willis, BOS	7.72
A. Orth, PHI	7.99

Shutouts

J. Chesbro, PIT	6
A. Orth, PHI	6
V. Willis, BOS	6

Fewest Walks/9 Innings

A. Orth, PHI	1.02
D. Phillippe, PIT	1.16
J. Tannehill, PIT	1.28
B. Duggleby, PHI	1.31

Most Strikeouts/9 Inn.

L. Hughes, CHI	6.57
R. Waddell, PIT, CHI	6.16
C. Mathewson, NY	5.92
W. Donovan, BKN	5.79

Innings

N. Hahn, CIN	375
D. Taylor, NY	353
W. Donovan, BKN	351
J. Powell, STL	338

Games Pitched

J. Powell, STL	45
W. Donovan, BKN	45
D. Taylor, NY	45
N. Hahn, CIN	42

	W	L	PCT	GB	R	OR	Batting 2B	3B	HR	BA	SA	SB	Fielding E	DP	FA	Pitching CG	BB	SO	ShO	SV	ERA
Pittsburgh	90	49	.647		776	**534**	185	92	28	.286	.378	**203**	287	97	.950	119	**244**	505	15	4	**2.58**
Philadelphia	83	57	.593	7.5	668	543	194	58	24	.267	.347	199	**262**	65	**.954**	125	259	480	**16**	0	2.87
Brooklyn	79	57	.581	9.5	744	600	**206**	**97**	32	**.288**	**.390**	178	281	99	.950	111	435	583	7	3	3.14
St. Louis	76	64	.543	14.5	**792**	689	187	**97**	**39**	.285	.383	190	305	**108**	.949	118	332	445	5	**5**	3.68
Boston	69	69	.500	20.5	531	556	135	36	28	.250	.312	157	282	89	.952	128	349	558	11	0	2.90
Chicago	53	86	.381	37	578	699	153	61	18	.258	.326	**203**	336	87	.943	**131**	324	**586**	2	0	3.33
New York	52	85	.380	37	544	755	166	47	19	.255	.321	133	348	81	.941	118	377	542	11	1	3.87
Cincinnati	52	87	.374	38	561	818	179	70	38	.251	.339	137	355	102	.940	126	365	542	4	0	4.17
					5194	5194	1405	558	226	.267	.350	1400	2456	728	.947	976	2685	4241	71	13	3.32

AMERICAN LEAGUE 1901

Team	POS	Player	AB	BA	HR	RBI	PO	A	E	DP	TC/G	FA	Pitcher	G	IP	W	L	SV	ERA
Chicago	1B	F. Isbell	556	.257	3	70	**1387**	**101**	31	79	11.1	.980	R. Patterson	41	312	20	16	0	3.37
W-83 L-53	2B	S. Mertes	545	.277	5	98	337	396	47	54	5.9	.940	C. Griffith	35	267	24	7	1	2.67
Clark Griffith	SS	F. Shugart	415	.251	2	47	223	338	73	32	5.9	.885	N. Callahan	27	215	15	8	0	2.42
	3B	F. Hartman	473	.309	3	89	151	263	49	15	3.9	.894	J. Katoll	27	208	11	10	0	2.81
	RF	F. Jones	521	.311	2	65	216	20	16	5	1.9	.937	E. Harvey	16	92	3	6	1	3.62
	CF	D. Hoy	527	.294	2	60	278	16	13	6	2.3	.958							
	LF	H. McFarland	473	.275	4	59	283	14	17	3	2.4	.946							
	C	B. Sullivan	367	.245	4	56	396	104	17	**13**	5.3	**.967**							
	C	J. Sugden	153	.275	0	19	179	47	7	4	5.5	.970							
	SS	J. Burke	148	.264	0	21	56	94	23	10	5.6	.867							
Boston	1B	B. Freeman	490	.345	12	114	1278	55	**36**	71	10.7	.974	C. Young	43	371	**33**	10	0	**1.62**
W-79 L-57	2B	H. Ferris	523	.250	2	63	359	450	61	**68**	6.3	.930	T. Lewis	39	316	16	17	1	3.53
Jimmy Collins	SS	F. Parent	517	.306	4	59	260	446	63	52	5.6	.918	G. Winter	28	241	16	12	0	2.80
	3B	J. Collins	564	.332	6	94	203	**328**	50	24	**4.2**	.914	F. Mitchell	17	109	6	6	0	3.81
	RF	C. Hemphill	545	.261	3	62	188	22	17	4	1.7	.925	N. Cuppy	13	93	4	6	0	4.15
	CF	C. Stahl	515	.309	6	72	277	12	13	3	2.3	.957							
	LF	T. Dowd	594	.268	3	52	288	11	20	3	2.3	.937							
	C	O. Schreckengost	280	.304	0	38	273	102	**30**	8	5.6	.926							
	C	L. Criger	268	.231	0	24	300	109	14	11	6.2	.967							
	P	C. Young	153	.209	0	17	12	105	3	3	2.8	.975							
Detroit	1B	P. Dillon	281	.288	1	42	777	44	18	57	11.3	.979	R. Miller	38	332	23	13	1	2.95
W-74 L-61	2B	K. Gleason	547	.274	3	75	334	**457**	**64**	67	6.3	.925	E. Siever	38	289	18	15	0	3.24
George Stallings	SS	K. Elberfeld	436	.310	3	76	**332**	411	76	**62**	**6.8**	.907	J. Cronin	30	220	13	15	0	3.89
	3B	D. Casey	540	.283	2	46	133	324	**58**	**25**	4.1	.887	J. Yeager	26	200	12	11	1	2.61
	RF	D. Holmes	537	.294	4	62	217	18	24	5	2.0	.907							
	CF	J. Barrett	542	.293	4	65	300	31	21	7	2.6	.940							
	LF	D. Nance	461	.280	3	66	240	20	19	6	2.1	.932							
	C	F. Buelow	231	.225	2	29	213	84	10	4	4.4	.967							
	UT	S. McAllister	306	.301	3	57	381	66	42	19		.914							
	C	A. Shaw	171	.269	1	23	134	46	12	5	4.6	.938							
Philadelphia	1B	H. Davis	496	.306	8	76	1265	83	33	67	**11.8**	.976	C. Fraser	40	331	22	16	0	3.81
W-74 L-62	2B	N. Lajoie	543	**.422**	**14**	**125**	**395**	381	32	60	**6.8**	**.960**	E. Plank	33	261	17	13	0	3.31
Connie Mack	SS	J. Dolan	338	.216	1	38	88	223	42	30	5.8	.881	B. Bernhard	31	257	17	10	0	4.52
	3B	L. Cross	420	.331	2	73	140	236	33	7	4.1	.919	S. Wiltse	19	166	13	5	0	3.58
	RF	S. Seybold	457	.333	8	90	157	10	8	2	1.8	.954	W. Piatt	18	140	5	12	1	4.63
	CF	D. Fultz	561	.292	0	52	216	13	16	0	2.3	.935							
	LF	M. McIntyre	308	.276	0	46	155	8	14	0	2.2	.921							
	C	M. Powers	431	.251	1	47	**400**	**137**	27	6	5.1	.952							
	OF	J. Hayden	211	.265	0	17	63	11	14	0	1.8	.841							
	OF	P. Geier	211	.232	0	23	80	5	6	1	1.8	.934							
	SS	B. Ely	171	.216	0	16	85	156	23	19	5.9	.913							
Baltimore	1B	B. Hart	206	.311	0	23	561	9	14	28	10.1	.976	J. McGinnity	**48**	**382**	26	20	1	3.56
W-68 L-65	2B	J. Williams	501	.317	7	96	339	412	52	47	6.2	.935	H. Howell	37	295	14	21	0	3.67
John McGraw	SS	B. Keister	442	.328	2	93	231	322	**97**	30	5.8	.851	F. Foreman	24	191	12	6	1	3.67
	3B	J. McGraw	232	.349	0	28	80	107	23	5	3.0	.890	J. Nops	27	177	12	10	1	4.08
	RF	C. Seymour	547	.303	1	77	271	23	17	4	2.3	.945							
	CF	S. Brodie	306	.310	2	41	178	4	7	0	2.3	.963							
	LF	M. Donlin	476	.347	5	67	179	12	17	2	2.8	.918							
	C	R. Bresnahan	295	.268	1	32	199	63	23	3	4.1	.919							
	OF	J. Jackson	364	.250	2	50	234	4	7	1	2.6	**.971**							
	UT	J. Dunn	362	.249	0	36	157	206	53	14		.873							
	C	W. Robinson	239	.301	0	26	235	61	16	4	4.7	.949							
	UT	H. Howell	188	.218	2	26	59	93	16	6		.905							
	P	J. McGinnity	148	.209	0	6	15	104	9	2	2.7	.930							
Washington	1B	M. Grady	347	.285	9	56	575	52	16	34	10.9	.975	B. Carrick	42	324	14	23	0	3.75
W-61 L-73	2B	J. Farrell	555	.272	3	63	176	246	39	43	6.4	.915	W. Lee	36	262	16	16	0	4.40
Jimmy Manning	SS	B. Clingman	480	.242	2	55	290	**462**	55	56	5.9	**.932**	C. Patten	32	254	18	10	0	3.93
	3B	B. Coughlin	508	.278	6	68	**232**	275	43	16	4.0	.922	W. Mercer	24	180	9	13	1	4.56
	RF	S. Dungan	559	.320	1	73	145	15	9	4	1.6	.947	D. Gear	24	163	4	11	0	4.03
	CF	I. Waldron	332*	.322	0	22	140	7	7	0	2.0	.955							
	LF	P. Foster	392	.278	6	53	200	9	17	1	2.2	.925							
	C	B. Clarke	422	.280	3	54	358	122	24	11	4.7	.952							
	2B	J. Quinn	266	.252	3	36	158	177	16	17	5.3	.954							
	OP	D. Gear	199	.236	0	20	56	59	6	3		.950							
	UT	W. Mercer	140	.300	0	16	92	57	15	10		.909							
Cleveland	1B	C. LaChance	548	.303	1	75	1342	58	30	73	10.8	.979	P. Dowling	33	256	11	22*	0	3.86
W-55 L-82	2B	E. Beck	539	.289	6	79	310	404	56	44	5.8	.927	E. Moore	31	251	16	14	0	2.90
Jimmy McAleer	SS	F. Scheibeck	329	.213	0	38	176	268	51	26	5.4	.897	B. Hart	20	158	7	11	0	3.77
	3B	B. Bradley	516	.293	1	55	192	298	37	**25**	4.0	**.930**	E. Scott	17	125	7	6	1	4.40
	RF	J. O'Brien	375	.283	0	39	150	9	10	4	1.8	.941	J. Bracken	12	100	4	8	0	6.21
	CF	O. Pickering	547	.309	0	40	315	22	18	9	2.6	.949	B. Hoffer	16	99	3	8	**3**	4.55
	LF	J. McCarthy	343	.321	0	32	157	9	9	5	2.0	.949	H. McNeal	12	85	5	5	0	4.43
	C	B. Wood	346	.292	1	49	307	106	21	11	5.2	.952							
	OF	E. Harvey	170	.353	1	24	82	7	11	4	2.2	.890							

AMERICAN LEAGUE 1901, *cont.*

Milwaukee

W-48 L-89

Hugh Duffy

POS	Player	AB	BA	HR	RBI	PO	A	E	DP	TC/G	FA
1B	J. Anderson	576	.330	8	99	1310	66	25	**81**	11.2	**.982**
2B	B. Gilbert	492	.270	0	43	319	395	49	66	6.0	.936
SS	W. Conroy	503	.256	5	64	285	408	59	46	6.4	.922
3B	J. Burke	233	.206	0	26	83	132	35	5	3.9	.860
RF	B. Hallman	549	.246	2	47	226	22	26	6	2.0	.905
CF	H. Duffy	286	.308	2	45	141	5	5	0	2.0	.967
LF	G. Hogriever	221	.235	0	16	134	3	15	1	2.8	.901
C	B. Maloney	290	.293	0	22	284	111	20	6	**5.8**	.952
UT	B. Friel	376	.266	4	35	142	183	46	16		.876
OF	I. Waldron	266*	.297	0	29	97	9	14	0	1.9	.883

Pitcher	G	IP	W	L	SV	ERA
B. Reidy	37	301	16	20	0	4.21
N. Garvin	37	257	7	20	2	3.46
B. Husting	34	217	10	15	1	4.27
T. Sparks	29	210	7	16	0	3.51
P. Hawley	26	182	7	14	0	4.59

BATTING AND BASE RUNNING LEADERS

Batting Average
N. Lajoie, PHI .422
M. Donlin, BAL .347
B. Freeman, BOS .345
S. Seybold, PHI .333
J. Collins, BOS .332

Slugging Average
N. Lajoie, PHI .635
B. Freeman, BOS .527
S. Seybold, PHI .499
J. Williams, BAL .495
J. Collins, BOS .495

Home Runs
N. Lajoie, PHI 14
B. Freeman, BOS 12
M. Grady, WAS 9
S. Seybold, PHI 8
H. Davis, PHI 8
J. Anderson, MIL 8

Total Bases
N. Lajoie, PHI 345
J. Collins, BOS 279
J. Anderson, MIL 274
B. Freeman, BOS 258
J. Williams, BAL 248

Runs Batted In
N. Lajoie, PHI 125
B. Freeman, BOS 114
J. Anderson, MIL 99
S. Mertes, CHI 98
J. Williams, BAL 96

Stolen Bases
F. Isbell, CHI 52
S. Mertes, CHI 46
F. Jones, CHI 38
C. Seymour, BAL 38
O. Pickering, CLE 36
D. Fultz, PHI 36

Hits
N. Lajoie, PHI 229
J. Anderson, MIL 190
J. Collins, BOS 187
I. Waldron, MIL, WAS 186

Base on Balls
D. Hoy, CHI 86
F. Jones, CHI 84
J. Barrett, DET 76
H. McFarland, CHI 75

Home Run Percentage
M. Grady, WAS 2.6
N. Lajoie, PHI 2.6
B. Freeman, BOS 2.4
S. Seybold, PHI 1.8

Runs
N. Lajoie, PHI 145
F. Jones, CHI 120
J. Williams, BAL 113
D. Hoy, CHI 112

Doubles
N. Lajoie, PHI 48
J. Anderson, MIL 46
J. Collins, BOS 42
J. Farrell, WAS 32

Triples
B. Keister, BAL 21
J. Williams, BAL 21
S. Mertes, CHI 17
C. Stahl, BOS 16
J. Collins, BOS 16

PITCHING LEADERS

Winning Percentage
C. Griffith, CHI .774
C. Young, BOS .767
N. Callahan, CHI .652
C. Patten, WAS .643
R. Miller, DET .639

Earned Run Average
C. Young, BOS 1.62
N. Callahan, CHI 2.42
J. Yeager, DET 2.61
C. Griffith, CHI 2.67
G. Winter, BOS 2.80

Wins
C. Young, BOS 33
J. McGinnity, BAL 26
C. Griffith, CHI 24
R. Miller, DET 23
C. Fraser, PHI 22

Saves
B. Hoffer, CLE 3
N. Garvin, MIL 2

Strikeouts
C. Young, BOS 158
R. Patterson, CHI 127
P. Dowling, MIL, CLE 124
N. Garvin, MIL 122
C. Fraser, PHI 110

Complete Games
J. McGinnity, BAL 39
C. Young, BOS 38
R. Miller, DET 35
C. Fraser, PHI 35
B. Carrick, WAS 34

Fewest Hits/9 Innings
C. Young, BOS 7.85
N. Callahan, CHI 8.15
E. Moore, CLE 8.38
T. Lewis, BOS 8.51

Shutouts
C. Griffith, CHI 5
C. Young, BOS 5
E. Moore, CLE 4
C. Patten, WAS 4
R. Patterson, CHI 4

Fewest Walks/9 Innings
C. Young, BOS 0.90
D. Gear, WAS 1.21
W. Lee, WAS 1.55
C. Griffith, CHI 1.69

Most Strikeouts/9 Inn.
N. Garvin, MIL 4.27
C. Patten, WAS 3.86
C. Young, BOS 3.83
R. Patterson, CHI 3.66

Innings
J. McGinnity, BAL 382
C. Young, BOS 371
R. Miller, DET 332
C. Fraser, PHI 331

Games Pitched
J. McGinnity, BAL 48
P. Dowling, MIL, CLE 43
C. Young, BOS 43
B. Carrick, WAS 42

							Batting						Fielding			Pitching					
	W	L	PCT	GB	R	OR	2B	3B	HR	BA	SA	SB	E	DP	FA	CG	BB	SO	ShO	SV	ERA
Chicago	83	53	.610		**819**	631	173	89	32	.276	.370	**280**	345	100	.941	110	312	394	**11**	2	**2.98**
Boston	79	57	.581	4	759	**608**	183	104	**37**	.279	.382	157	337	104	**.943**	123	294	**396**	7	1	3.04
Detroit	74	61	.548	8.5	741	694	180	80	29	.279	.370	205	410	**127**	.930	118	313	307	9	2	3.30
Philadelphia	74	62	.544	9	805	761	**239**	86	35	.288	.394	173	337	93	.942	**124**	374	350	6	1	4.00
Baltimore	68	65	.511	13.5	760	750	179	**111**	24	**.294**	**.397**	207	401	76	.926	115	344	271	4	3	3.73
Washington	61	73	.455	21	678	767	191	83	34	.269	.365	127	**323**	97	**.943**	118	**284**	308	8	1	4.09
Cleveland	55	82	.401	28.5	663	827	197	68	12	.271	.348	125	329	99	.942	122	464	334	7	**4**	4.12
Milwaukee	48	89	.350	35.5	641	828	192	66	26	.261	.345	176	393	106	.934	107	395	376	3	**4**	4.06
					5866	5866	1534	687	229	.277	.371	1450	2875	802	.938	937	2780	2736	55	18	3.66

NATIONAL LEAGUE 1902

Pittsburgh

W-103 L-36

Fred Clarke

POS	Player	AB	BA	HR	RBI	PO	A	E	DP	TC/G	FA
1B	K. Bransfield	417	.305	1	69	1064	41	18	40	**11.1**	.984
2B	C. Ritchey	405	.277	2	55	275	341	22	48	5.6	**.966**
SS	W. Conroy	365	.244	1	47	192	327	42	39	5.9	.925
3B	T. Leach	514	.280	**6**	85	170	**316**	39	10	3.9	.926
RF	L. Davis	232	.280	0	20	80	6	5	1	1.5	.945
CF	G. Beaumont	544	**.357**	0	67	260	15	7	8	2.2	.975
LF	F. Clarke	461	.321	2	53	215	13	10	2	2.1	.958
C	H. Smith	185	.189	0	12	265	49	9	3	6.5	.972
UT	H. Wagner	538	.329	3	**91**	532	176	32	33		.957
UT	J. Burke	203	.296	0	26	90	120	23	8		.901
C	J. O'Connor	170	.294	1	28	187	49	5	2	5.7	.979
PO	J. Tannehill	148	.291	1	17	25	57	4	3		.953
C	C. Zimmer	142	.268	0	17	202	48	8	8	6.3	.969

Pitcher	G	IP	W	L	SV	ERA
J. Chesbro	35	286	**28**	6	1	2.17
D. Phillippe	31	272	20	9	0	2.05
J. Tannehill	26	231	20	6	0	1.95
S. Leever	28	222	16	7	2	2.39
E. Doheny	22	188	16	4	0	2.53

NATIONAL LEAGUE 1902, *cont.*

Team	POS	Player	AB	BA	HR	RBI	PO	A	E	DP	TC/G	FA	Pitcher	G	IP	W	L	SV	ERA
Brooklyn	1B	T. McCreery	430	.244	4	57	1032	59	**23**	53	10.3	.979	W. Donovan	35	298	17	15	1	2.78
	2B	T. Flood	476	.218	3	50	297	374	**41**	33	5.4	.942	D. Newton	31	264	15	14	0	2.42
W-75 L-63	SS	B. Dahlen	527	.264	2	74	278	440	66	34	5.7	.916	F. Kitson	31	260	19	12	0	2.84
Ned Hanlon	3B	C. Irwin	458	.273	2	43	173	244	33	21	3.5	.927	J. Hughes	31	254	15	11	0	2.87
	RF	W. Keeler	556	.338	0	38	208	14	5	4	1.7	.978	R. Evans	13	97	5	6	0	2.68
	CF	C. Dolan	**592**	.280	1	54	283	10	20	2	2.2	.936							
	LF	J. Sheckard	486	.270	4	37	284	12	11	6	2.5	.964							
	C	H. Hearne	231	.281	0	28	298	67	13	7	5.8	.966							
	C1	D. Farrell	264	.242	0	24	469	90	12	8		.979							
	P	W. Donovan	161	.168	1	16	20	71	5	2	2.7	.948							
Boston	1B	F. Tenney	489	.315	2	30	1251	**105**	21	75	10.3	**.985**	V. Willis	**51**	**410**	27	**20**	**3**	2.20
	2B	G. DeMontreville	481	.268	0	53	271	294	36	24	5.4	.940	T. Pittinger	46	389	27	16	0	2.52
W-73 L-64	SS	H. Long	429	.228	2	44	279	360	37	46	**6.4**	**.945**	M. Eason	27	206	9	11	0	2.75
Al Buckenberger	3B	E. Gremminger	522	.257	1	66	**222**	282	26	15	3.8	**.951**	J. Malarkey	21	170	8	10	1	2.59
	RF	P. Carney	522	.270	2	65	153	19	13	7	1.4	.930							
	CF	B. Lush	413	.223	2	19	251	24	14	5	2.5	.952							
	LF	D. Cooley	548	.296	0	58	250	7	13	2	2.1	.952							
	C	M. Kittridge	255	.235	2	30	363	99	9	5	6.5	.981							
	C	P. Moran	251	.239	1	24	332	95	8	5	6.1	**.982**							
	UT	C. Dexter	183	.257	1	18	111	113	19	12		.922							
	OF	E. Courtney	165	.218	0	17	71	5	2	0	2.0	.974							
	P	V. Willis	150	.153	0	7	**37**	105	4	**5**	2.9	.973							
	P	T. Pittinger	147	.136	0	10	20	83	6	2	2.4	.945							
Cincinnati	1B	J. Beckley	532	.331	5	69	**1262**	64	**23**	**84**	10.5	.983	N. Hahn	37	321	23	12	0	1.77
	2B	H. Peitz	387	.315	1	60	124	126	22	23	5.7	.919	B. Phillips	34	272	16	16	0	2.48
	SS	T. Corcoran	537	.251	0	54	292	412	56	**49**	5.5	.926	H. Thielman	25	211	8	15	1	3.24
W-70 L-70	3B	H. Steinfeldt	479	.278	1	49	190	315	**49**	**29**	**4.3**	.912	E. Poole	16	138	12	4	0	2.15
Bid McPhee	RF	S. Crawford	555	.333	3	78	208	24	17	5	1.8	.932	B. Ewing	15	118	6	6	0	2.98
W-27 L-37	CF	D. Hoy	279	.290	2	20	149	4	11	1	2.3	.933							
Frank Bancroft	LF	J. Dobbs	256	.297	1	16	146	11	6	2	2.6	.963							
W-9 L-7	C	B. Bergen	322	.180	0	36	406	137	23	13	6.4	.959							
Joe Kelley	OF	C. Seymour	235	.349	2	37	139	10	13	3	2.7	.920							
W-34 L-26	2B	E. Beck	187	.305	1	20	70	92	11	11	5.4	.936							
	2B	G. Magoon	162	.272	0	23	83	144	17	16	6.0	.930							
	UT	J. Kelley	156	.321	1	12	78	59	6	9		.958							
	OF	M. Donlin	143	.294	0	9	59	5	9	1	2.3	.877							
Chicago	1B	F. Chance	236	.284	1	31	391	20	13	21	11.2	.969	J. Taylor	36	325	22	11	1	**1.33**
	2B	B. Lowe	472	.246	0	31	326	406	33	59	**6.5**	.957	P. Williams	31	254	12	16	0	2.51
W-68 L-69	SS	J. Tinker	501	.273	2	54	243	**453**	**72**	47	6.2	.906	J. Menefee	22	197	12	10	0	2.42
Frank Selee	3B	G. Schaefer	291	.196	0	14	103	152	40	11	3.9	.864	C. Lundgren	18	160	9	9	0	1.97
	RF	D. Jones	243	.305	0	14	146	3	7	1	2.4	.955	B. Rhoads	16	118	4	8	1	3.20
	CF	J. Dobbs	235	.302	0	35	122	8	3	5	2.3	.977	J. St. Vrain	12	95	4	6	0	2.08
	LF	J. Slagle	454	.315	0	28	262	15	10	5	2.5	.965							
	C	J. Kling	434	.286	0	57	**471**	**158**	17	**16**	5.8	.974							
	UT	C. Dexter	266	.226	2	26	303	71	27	20		.933							
	UT	J. Menefee	216	.231	0	15	230	57	13	7		.957							
	OF	D. Miller	187	.246	0	13	97	9	5	0	2.2	.955							
	UT	J. Taylor	186	.237	0	17	42	133	9	5		.951							
	OF	B. Congalton	179	.223	1	24	71	6	1	1	1.7	.987							
	01	A. Williams	160	.231	0	14	226	15	11	10		.956							
St. Louis	1B	R. Brashear	388	.276	1	40	751	36	16	49	12.0	.980	M. O'Neill	36	288	18	14	0	2.93
	2B	J. Farrell	565	.250	0	25	297	**422**	40	**72**	6.4	.947	S. Yerkes	39	273	11	**20**	0	3.66
W-56 L-78	SS	O. Krueger	467	.266	0	46	184	390	66	47	6.0	.897	E. Murphy	23	164	9	7	1	3.02
Patsy Donovan	3B	F. Hartman	416	.216	0	52	138	229	37	9	3.8	.908	B. Wicker	22	152	5	13	0	3.19
	RF	P. Donovan	502	.315	0	35	179	30	9	6	1.7	.959	C. Currie	16	127	7	5	0	2.56
	CF	H. Smoot	518	.311	3	48	284	14	22	5	2.5	.931							
	LF	G. Barclay	543	.300	3	53	247	16	28	3	2.1	.904							
	C	J. Ryan	267	.180	0	14	258	86	12	8	5.4	.966							
	1B	A. Nichols	251	.267	1	31	577	24	10	26	10.9	.984							
	C	J. O'Neill	192	.141	0	12	246	79	9	5	5.7	.973							
Philadelphia	1B	H. Jennings	289	.277	1	32	659	46	12	32	10.4	.983	D. White	36	306	16	**20**	1	2.53
	2B	P. Childs	403	.194	0	25	271	349	36	26	5.3	.945	B. Duggleby	33	259	11	17	0	3.38
W-56 L-81	SS	R. Hulswitt	497	.272	0	38	**318**	400	65	37	6.3	.917	H. Iburg	30	236	11	18	0	3.89
Bill Shettsline	3B	B. Hallman	254	.248	0	35	71	147	16	3	3.3	.932	C. Fraser	27	224	12	13	0	3.42
	RF	S. Barry	543	.287	3	57	185	15	13	3	1.6	.939							
	CF	R. Thomas	500	.286	0	24	277	23	8	3	2.2	.974							
	LF	G. Browne	281	.260	0	26	158	14	17	2	2.7	.910							
	C	R. Dooin	333	.231	0	35	433	117	**29**	10	**6.9**	.950							
	1C	K. Douglass	408	.233	0	37	792	63	18	28		.979							
	UT	H. Krug	198	.227	0	14	116	62	12	10		.937							
	PO	D. White	179	.263	1	15	35	84	12	0		.908							

NATIONAL LEAGUE 1902, *cont.*

New York

W-48 L-88

Horace Fogel
W-18 L-23

Heinie Smith
W-5 L-27

John McGraw
W-25 L-38

POS	Player	AB	BA	HR	RBI	PO	A	E	DP	TC/G	FA
1B	D. McGann	227	.300	0	21	634	39	13	38	11.2	.981
2B	H. Smith	511	.252	0	33	**347**	403	37	58	5.7	.953
SS	J. Bean	176	.222	0	5	71	153	28	19	5.3	.889
3B	B. Lauder	482	.237	1	44	189	251	45	17	4.0	.907
RF	J. Dunn	342	.211	0	14	47	4	2	2	1.2	.962
CF	S. Brodie	416	.281	3	42	219	22	12	7	2.3	.953
LF	J. Jones	249	.237	0	19	122	9	15	2	2.2	.897
C	F. Bowerman	367	.253	0	26	428	143	26	10	6.1	.956
OF	G. Browne	216	.319	0	14	104	7	13*	1	2.3*	.895
1B	J. Doyle	186	.301	1	19	490	34	5	28	10.8	.991
UT	R. Bresnahan	178	.292	1	22	164	40	13	8		.940

Pitcher	G	IP	W	L	SV	ERA
C. Mathewson	34	277	14	17	0	2.11
D. Taylor	26	201	7	15	0	2.29
R. Evans	23	176	8	13	0	3.17
J. McGinnity	19	153	8	8	0	2.06
T. Sparks	15	115	4	10	1	3.76
J. Cronin	13	114	5	6	0	2.45

BATTING AND BASE RUNNING LEADERS

Batting Average	
G. Beaumont, PIT	.357
W. Keeler, BKN	.338
S. Crawford, CIN	.333
J. Beckley, CIN	.331
H. Wagner, PIT	.329

Slugging Average	
H. Wagner, PIT	.467
S. Crawford, CIN	.461
F. Clarke, PIT	.453
T. Leach, PIT	.442
J. Beckley, CIN	.429

Home Runs	
T. Leach, PIT	6
J. Beckley, CIN	5
T. McCreery, BKN	4
J. Sheckard, BKN	4

Total Bases	
S. Crawford, CIN	256
H. Wagner, PIT	251
J. Beckley, CIN	228
T. Leach, PIT	227
G. Beaumont, PIT	227

Runs Batted In	
H. Wagner, PIT	91
T. Leach, PIT	85
S. Crawford, CIN	78
B. Dahlen, BKN	74
K. Bransfield, PIT	69
J. Beckley, CIN	69

Stolen Bases	
H. Wagner, PIT	42
J. Slagle, CHI	40
P. Donovan, STL	34
G. Beaumont, PIT	33
H. Smith, NY	32

Hits	
G. Beaumont, PIT	194
W. Keeler, BKN	188
S. Crawford, CIN	185
H. Wagner, PIT	177

Base on Balls	
R. Thomas, PHI	107
B. Lush, BOS	76
F. Tenney, BOS	73
J. Sheckard, BKN	57

Home Run Percentage	
T. Leach, PIT	1.2
J. Beckley, CIN	0.9
T. McCreery, BKN	0.9
J. Sheckard, BKN	0.8

Runs	
H. Wagner, PIT	105
F. Clarke, PIT	104
G. Beaumont, PIT	101
T. Leach, PIT	97

Doubles	
H. Wagner, PIT	33
F. Clarke, PIT	27
B. Dahlen, BKN	26
D. Cooley, BOS	26

Triples	
S. Crawford, CIN	23
T. Leach, PIT	22
H. Wagner, PIT	16
F. Clarke, PIT	14

PITCHING LEADERS

Winning Percentage	
J. Chesbro, PIT	.824
E. Doheny, PIT	.800
J. Tannehill, PIT	.769
S. Leever, PIT	.696
D. Phillippe, PIT	.690

Earned Run Average	
J. Taylor, CHI	1.33
N. Hahn, CIN	1.77
J. Tannehill, PIT	1.95
C. Lundgren, CHI	1.97
D. Phillippe, PIT	2.05

Wins	
J. Chesbro, PIT	28
T. Pittinger, BOS	27
V. Willis, BOS	27
N. Hahn, CIN	23
J. Taylor, CHI	22

Saves	
V. Willis, BOS	3
S. Leever, PIT	2

Strikeouts	
V. Willis, BOS	225
D. White, PHI	185
T. Pittinger, BOS	174
W. Donovan, BKN	170
C. Mathewson, NY	159

Complete Games	
V. Willis, BOS	45
T. Pittinger, BOS	36
N. Hahn, CIN	35
D. White, PHI	34
J. Taylor, CHI	33

Fewest Hits/9 Innings	
D. Newton, BKN	7.08
J. McGinnity, NY	7.18
J. Taylor, CHI	7.51
W. Donovan, BKN	7.56

Shutouts	
C. Mathewson, NY	8
J. Chesbro, PIT	8
J. Taylor, CHI	8
T. Pittinger, BOS	7

Fewest Walks/9 Innings	
D. Phillippe, PIT	0.86
J. Tannehill, PIT	0.97
J. Menefee, CHI	1.19
J. Taylor, CHI	1.19

Most Strikeouts/9 Inn.	
D. White, PHI	5.44
C. Mathewson, NY	5.17
W. Donovan, BKN	5.14
V. Willis, BOS	4.94

Innings	
V. Willis, BOS	410
T. Pittinger, BOS	389
J. Taylor, CHI	325
N. Hahn, CIN	321

Games Pitched	
V. Willis, BOS	51
T. Pittinger, BOS	46
S. Yerkes, STL	39
N. Hahn, CIN	37

							Batting						Fielding			Pitching					
	W	L	PCT	GB	R	OR	2B	3B	HR	BA	SA	SB	E	DP	FA	CG	BB	SO	ShO	SV	ERA
Pittsburgh	103	36	.741		**775**	**440**	**199**	**94**	**19**	**.287**	**.377**	**222**	247	87	.958	131	**250**	**564**	**21**	3	2.30
Brooklyn	75	63	.543	27.5	564	519	147	50	**19**	.257	.320	145	275	79	.952	131	363	536	15	1	2.69
Boston	73	64	.533	29	572	516	142	39	14	.250	.305	189	**240**	90	**.959**	124	372	523	14	**4**	2.61
Cincinnati	70	70	.500	33.5	633	566	188	77	18	.282	.363	131	322	**118**	.945	130	352	430	9	1	2.67
Chicago	68	69	.496	34	530	501	131	40	6	.251	.299	**222**	327	111	.946	**132**	279	437	18	2	**2.21**
St. Louis	56	78	.418	44.5	517	695	116	37	10	.258	.304	158	336	107	.944	112	338	400	7	2	3.47
Philadelphia	56	81	.409	46	484	649	113	42	5	.247	.293	108	305	81	.946	118	334	504	8	2	3.50
New York	48	88	.353	53.5	401	590	149	34	8	.238	.291	187	330	104	.943	118	332	501	11	1	2.82
					4476	4476	1185	413	99	.259	.319	1362	2382	777	.949	996	2620	3895	103	16	2.78

AMERICAN LEAGUE 1902

Philadelphia

W-83 L-53

Connie Mack

POS	Player	AB	BA	HR	RBI	PO	A	E	DP	TC/G	FA
1B	H. Davis	561	.307	6	92	1247	87	22	58	10.6	.984
2B	D. Murphy	291	.313	1	48	167	197	14	22	5.0	.963
SS	M. Cross	497	.231	3	59	**373**	466	66	37	**6.6**	.927
3B	L. Cross	559	.342	0	108	185	306	30	18	3.8	.942
RF	S. Seybold	522	.316	**16**	97	246	11	10	3	2.0	.963
CF	D. Fultz	506	.302	1	49	231	18	10	1	2.3	.961
LF	T. Hartsel	545	.283	5	58	238	18	12	2	2.0	.955
C	O. Schreckengost	284	.324	2	43	367*	108	20*	3	7.0*	.960
C	M. Powers	246	.264	2	39	229	110	18	5	5.3	.950
2B	L. Castro	143	.245	1	15	71	85	14	10	4.7	.918

Pitcher	G	IP	W	L	SV	ERA
E. Plank	36	300	20	15	0	3.30
R. Waddell	33	276	24	7	0	2.05
B. Husting	32	204	14	5	0	3.79
S. Wiltse	19	138	8	8	1	5.15
F. Mitchell	18	108	5	7	1	3.59
H. Wilson	13	96	7	5	0	2.43

AMERICAN LEAGUE 1902, *cont.*

Team	POS	Player	AB	BA	HR	RBI	PO	A	E	DP	TC/G	FA	Pitcher	G	IP	W	L	SV	ERA
St. Louis	1B	J. Anderson	524	.284	4	85	1361	47	22	78	11.3	.985	J. Powell	42	328	22	17	**2**	3.21
W-78 L-58	2B	D. Padden	413	.264	1	40	288	363	22	64	5.8	.967	R. Donahue	35	316	22	11	0	2.76
Jimmy McAleer	SS	B. Wallace	495	.287	1	63	299	474	42	64	6.2	.948	J. Harper	29	222	15	11	0	4.13
	3B	B. McCormick	504	.246	3	51	147	271	44	**26**	3.5	.905	W. Sudhoff	30	220	12	12	0	2.86
	RF	C. Hemphill	416	.317	6	58	164	15	9	6	1.9	.952							
	CF	E. Heidrick	447	.289	3	56	264	16	18	4	2.7	.940							
	LF	J. Burkett	549	.306	5	52	300	17	26	5	2.5	.924							
	C	J. Sugden	203	.246	0	15	192	67	12	**9**	4.4	.956							
	UT	B. Friel	267	.240	2	20	194	94	15	17		.950							
	C	M. Kahoe	197	.244	2	28	214	52	9	4	5.2	.967							
Boston	1B	C. LaChance	541	.279	6	56	**1544**	46	27	80	11.7	.983	C. Young	**45**	**385**	**32**	11	0	2.15
W-77 L-60	2B	H. Ferris	499	.244	8	63	312	**461**	39	59	6.1	.952	B. Dinneen	42	371	21	**21**	0	2.93
Jimmy Collins	SS	F. Parent	**567**	.275	3	62	287	**496**	58	60	6.1	.931	G. Winter	20	168	11	9	0	2.99
	3B	J. Collins	429	.322	6	61	143	255	19	14	3.9	**.954**	T. Sparks	17	143	7	9	0	3.47
	RF	B. Freeman	564	.309	11	**121**	222	15	14	3	1.8	.944							
	CF	C. Stahl	508	.323	2	58	244	15	12	2	2.2	.956							
	LF	P. Dougherty	438	.342	0	34	170	8	20	1	1.9	.899							
	C	L. Criger	266	.256	0	28	330	117	16	6	5.8	.965							
	30	H. Gleason	240	.225	2	25	91	67	11	7		.935							
	C	J. Warner	222	.234	0	12	252	81	7	8	5.3	.979							
	P	C. Young	148	.230	1	12	10	82	7	4	2.2	.929							
	P	B. Dinneen	141	.128	0	9	7	77	4	1	2.1	.955							
Chicago	1B	F. Isbell	515	.252	4	59	1401	**93**	21	**97**	11.4	.986	N. Callahan	35	282	16	14	0	3.60
W-74 L-60	2B	T. Daly	489	.225	1	54	312	370	31	**70**	5.2	.957	R. Patterson	34	268	19	14	0	3.06
Clark Griffith	SS	G. Davis	485	.299	3	93	289	427	37	**72**	5.8	**.951**	W. Piatt	32	246	12	12	0	3.51
	3B	S. Strang	536	.295	3	46	170	334*	62*	21	4.1*	.890	C. Griffith	28	213	15	9	0	4.19
	RF	D. Green	481	.312	0	62	217	11	14	4	1.9	.942	N. Garvin	23	175	10	10	0	2.21
	CF	F. Jones	532	.321	0	54	323	25	10	11	2.7	.972							
	LF	S. Mertes	497	.282	1	79	223	26	21	5	2.3	.922							
	C	B. Sullivan	263	.243	1	26	242	81	11	8	4.8	.967							
	C	E. McFarland	244	.230	1	25	282	71	12	7	5.3	.967							
	PO	N. Callahan	218	.234	0	13	54	107	9	7		.947							
Cleveland	1B	P. Hickman	426	.380	8	94	1079	47	40*	63	11.9*	.966	E. Moore	36	293	17	17	1	2.95
W-69 L-67	2B	N. Lajoie	348	.368	7	64	270	283	15	49	6.6*	.974*	A. Joss	32	269	17	13	0	2.77
Bill Armour	SS	J. Gochnaur	459	.185	0	37	223	447	48	59	5.7	.933	B. Bernhard	27	217	17	5	1	2.20
	3B	B. Bradley	550	.340	11	77	**188**	324	43	21	4.1	.923	C. Wright	21	148	7	11	1	3.95
	RF	E. Flick	424	.297	2	61	156	13	13	2	1.7	.929							
	CF	H. Bay	455	.290	0	23	242	13	7	3	2.4	.973							
	LF	J. McCarthy	359	.284	0	41	178	6	11	0	2.1	.944							
	C	H. Bemis	317	.312	1	29	333	**120**	17	2	5.4	.964							
	OF	O. Pickering	293	.256	3	26	138	5	3	1	2.3	.979							
	C	B. Wood	258	.295	0	40	169	53	14	4	4.5	.941							
Washington	1B	S. Carey	452	.314	0	60	1190	69	14	54	10.6	**.989**	A. Orth	38	324	19	18	0	3.97
W-61 L-75	2B	J. Doyle	312	.247	1	20	145	197	26	17	5.4	.929	C. Patten	36	300	17	16	1	4.05
Tom Loftus	SS	B. Ely	381	.262	1	62	238	350	49	31	6.1	.923	B. Carrick	31	258	11	17	0	4.86
	3B	B. Coughlin	469	.301	6	71	104	157	21	6	4.3	.926	J. Townsend	27	220	9	16	0	4.45
	RF	W. Lee	391	.256	4	45	171	14	17	1	2.1	.916	W. Lee	13	98	5	7	0	5.05
	CF	J. Ryan	484	.320	6	44	280	16	16	0	2.6	.949							
	LF	E. Delahanty	473	**.376**	10	93	236	11	10	0	2.3	.961							
	C	B. Clarke	291	.268	7	42	288	97	11	8	4.6	**.972**							
	UT	B. Keister	483	.300	9	90	229	166	34	14		.921							
	3B	H. Wolverton	249	.249	1	23	86	139	24	8	4.2	.904							
	C	L. Drill	221	.262	1	29	175	51	19	2	4.6	.922							
	P	A. Orth	175	.217	2	10	25	95	10	3	3.4	.923							
Detroit	1B	P. Dillon	243	.206	0	22	709	52	19	45	11.8	.976	W. Mercer	35	282	15	18	1	3.04
W-52 L-83	2B	K. Gleason	441	.247	1	38	**320**	349	**42**	66	6.0	.941	G. Mullin	35	260	13	16	0	3.67
Frank Dwyer	SS	K. Elberfeld	488	.260	1	64	326	459	67	63	6.6	.921	E. Siever	25	188	8	11	1	**1.91**
	3B	D. Casey	520	.273	3	55	174	309	51	17	4.0	.904	R. Miller	20	149	6	12	1	3.69
	RF	D. Holmes	362	.257	2	33	155	16	9	5	2.0	.950	J. Yeager	19	140	6	12	0	4.82
	CF	J. Barrett	509	.303	4	44	326	22	14	6	2.7	.961							
	LF	D. Harley	491	.281	2	44	238	15	19	1	2.2	.930							
	C	D. McGuire	229	.227	2	23	210	65	14	6	4.1	.952							
	UT	S. McAllister	229	.210	1	32	301	67	14	19		.963							
	C	F. Buelow	224	.223	2	29	174	81	**20**	5	4.4	.927							
	1B	E. Beck	162	.296	2	22	343	26	11	24	10.6	.971							
	UT	J. Yeager	161	.242	1	23	59	94	9	3		.944							
Baltimore	1B	D. McGann	250	.316	0	42	658	41	9	52	10.4	.987	H. Howell	26	199	9	15	0	4.12
W-50 L-88	2B	J. Williams	498	.313	8	83	248	332	34	46	5.9	.945	J. McGinnity	25	199	13	10	0	3.44
John McGraw	SS	B. Gilbert	445	.245	2	38	349	410	**78**	**72**	6.5	.907	S. Wiltse	19	164	7	11	0	5.10
W-26 L-31	3B	R. Bresnahan	235	.272	4	34	33	55	12	4	3.3	.880	C. Shields	23	142	4	11	1	4.24
Wilbert Robinson	RF	C. Seymour	280	.268	3	41	121	9	6	2	1.9	.956	J. Katoll	15	123	5	10	0	4.02
W-24 L-57	CF	H. McFarland	242	.322	3	36	152	12	6	1	2.8	.965	I. Butler	16	116	1	10	0	5.34
	LF	K. Selbach	503	.320	3	60	286	17	19	3	2.5	.941	L. Hughes	13	108	7	5	0	3.90
	C	W. Robinson	335	.293	1	57	262	75	18	4	4.1	.949							
	UT	H. Howell	347	.268	2	42	152	208	26	10		.933							
	OF	H. Arndt	248	.254	2	28	106	10	17	1	2.1	.872							
	OF	J. Kelley	222	.311	1	34	101	7	3	2	2.3	.973							
	1B	T. Jones	159	.283	0	14	341	22	17	23	10.3	.955							
	UT	B. Smith	145	.234	0	21	135	34	7	5		.960							
	UT	S. Wiltse	132	.295	2	24	160	44	10	8		.953							

AMERICAN LEAGUE 1902, *cont.*

BATTING AND BASE RUNNING LEADERS

Batting Average
E. Delahanty, WAS .376
N. Lajoie, PHI, CLE .366
P. Hickman, BOS, CLE .363
P. Dougherty, BOS .342
L. Cross, PHI .342

Slugging Average
E. Delahanty, WAS .590
N. Lajoie, PHI, CLE .551
P. Hickman, BOS, CLE .541
B. Bradley, CLE .515
S. Seybold, PHI .506

Home Runs
S. Seybold, PHI 16
P. Hickman, BOS, CLE 11
B. Bradley, CLE 11
B. Freeman, BOS 11
E. Delahanty, WAS 10

Total Bases
P. Hickman, BOS, CLE 289
B. Bradley, CLE 283
B. Freeman, BOS 283
E. Delahanty, WAS 279
S. Seybold, PHI 264

Runs Batted In
B. Freeman, BOS 121
P. Hickman, BOS, CLE 110
L. Cross, PHI 108
S. Seybold, PHI 97
E. Delahanty, WAS 93
G. Davis, CHI 93

Stolen Bases
T. Hartsel, PHI 47
S. Mertes, CHI 46
D. Fultz, PHI 44
B. Gilbert, BAL 38
F. Isbell, CHI 38
S. Strang, CHI 38

Hits
P. Hickman, BOS, CLE 194
L. Cross, PHI 191
B. Bradley, CLE 187
E. Delahanty, WAS 178

Base on Balls
T. Hartsel, PHI 87
S. Strang, CHI 76
J. Barrett, DET 74
J. Burkett, STL 71

Home Run Percentage
S. Seybold, PHI 3.1
B. Clarke, WAS 2.4
E. Delahanty, WAS 2.1
P. Hickman, BOS, CLE 2.1

Runs
D. Fultz, PHI 109
T. Hartsel, PHI 109
S. Strang, CHI 108
B. Bradley, CLE 104

Doubles
E. Delahanty, WAS 43
H. Davis, PHI 43
B. Bradley, CLE 39
L. Cross, PHI 39

Triples
J. Williams, BAL 21
B. Freeman, BOS 19
E. Delahanty, WAS 14
H. Ferris, BOS 14

PITCHING LEADERS

Winning Percentage
B. Bernhard, PHI, CLE .783
R. Waddell, PHI .774
C. Young, BOS .744
R. Donahue, STL .667
C. Griffith, CHI .625

Earned Run Average
E. Siever, DET 1.91
R. Waddell, PHI 2.05
B. Bernhard, PHI, CLE 2.15
C. Young, BOS 2.15
N. Garvin, CHI 2.21

Wins
C. Young, BOS 32
R. Waddell, PHI 24
R. Donahue, STL 22
J. Powell, STL 22
B. Dinneen, BOS 21

Saves
J. Powell, STL 2

Strikeouts
R. Waddell, PHI 210
C. Young, BOS 160
J. Powell, STL 137
B. Dinneen, BOS 136
E. Plank, PHI 107

Complete Games
C. Young, BOS 41
B. Dinneen, BOS 39
A. Orth, WAS 36
J. Powell, STL 36
R. Donahue, STL 33
C. Patten, WAS 33

Fewest Hits/9 Innings
B. Bernhard, PHI, CLE 7.01
R. Waddell, PHI 7.30
A. Joss, CLE 7.52
E. Siever, DET 7.93

Shutouts
A. Joss, CLE 5
E. Siever, DET 4
W. Mercer, DET 4
E. Moore, CLE 4

Fewest Walks/9 Innings
A. Orth, WAS 1.11
C. Young, BOS 1.24
B. Bernhard, PHI, CLE 1.47
E. Siever, DET 1.53

Most Strikeouts/9 Inn.
R. Waddell, PHI 6.84
J. Powell, STL 3.76
C. Young, BOS 3.74
A. Joss, CLE 3.54

Innings
C. Young, BOS 385
B. Dinneen, BOS 371
J. Powell, STL 328
A. Orth, WAS 324

Games Pitched
C. Young, BOS 45
J. Powell, STL 42
B. Dinneen, BOS 42
S. Wiltse, PHI, BAL 38
A. Orth, WAS 38

							Batting						Fielding			Pitching					
	W	L	PCT	GB	R	OR	2B	3B	HR	BA	SA	SB	E	DP	FA	CG	BB	SO	ShO	SV	ERA
Philadelphia	83	53	.610		**775**	636	235	67	38	.287	.389	201	270	75	.953	114	368	**455**	5	2	3.29
St. Louis	78	58	.574	5	619	607	208	61	29	.265	.353	137	274	122	.953	120	343	348	8	2	3.34
Boston	77	60	.562	6.5	664	**600**	195	95	42	.278	.383	132	263	101	**.955**	123	326	431	6	1	**3.02**
Chicago	74	60	.552	8	675	602	170	50	14	.268	.335	**265**	**257**	**125**	**.955**	116	331	346	11	0	3.41
Cleveland	69	67	.507	14	686	667	248	68	33	**.289**	.389	140	287	96	.950	116	411	361	**16**	**3**	3.28
Washington	61	75	.449	22	707	790	**261**	66	**48**	.283	**.396**	121	316	70	.945	**130**	**312**	300	2	1	4.36
Detroit	52	83	.385	30.5	566	657	141	55	22	.251	.320	130	332	111	.943	116	370	245	9	**3**	3.56
Baltimore	50	88	.362	34	715	848	202	**107**	33	.277	.385	189	357	109	.938	119	354	258	3	1	4.33
					5407	5407	1660	569	259	.275	.369	1315	2356	809	.949	954	2815	2744	60	13	3.57

NATIONAL LEAGUE 1903

Pittsburgh

W-91 L-49

Fred Clarke

POS	Player	AB	BA	HR	RBI	PO	A	E	DP	TC/G	FA
1B	K. Bransfield	505	.265	2	57	1347	88	28	**82**	**11.5**	.981
2B	C. Ritchey	506	.287	0	59	281	**460**	30	45	5.6	**.961**
SS	H. Wagner	512	**.355**	5	101	303	397	50	**51**	**6.8**	.933
3B	T. Leach	507	.298	7	87	178	292	**65**	16	**4.2**	.879
RF	J. Sebring	506	.277	4	64	208	20	18	11	2.0	.927
CF	G. Beaumont	**613**	.341	7	68	258	15	15	2	2.0	.948
LF	F. Clarke	427	.351	5	70	168	10	7	3	1.8	.962
C	E. Phelps	273	.282	2	31	315	81	8	7	5.3	.980
UT	O. Krueger	256	.246	1	28	109	113	20	17		.917
C	H. Smith	212	.175	0	19	259	75	9	2	5.7	.974

Pitcher	G	IP	W	L	SV	ERA
D. Phillippe	36	289	24	7	2	2.43
S. Leever	36	284	25	7	1	**2.06**
E. Doheny	27	223	16	8	2	3.19
B. Kennedy	18	125	9	6	0	3.45

New York

W-84 L-55

John McGraw

POS	Player	AB	BA	HR	RBI	PO	A	E	DP	TC/G	FA
1B	D. McGann	482	.270	3	50	1188	64	15	58	9.8	**.988**
2B	B. Gilbert	413	.252	1	40	314	366	47	42	5.7	.935
SS	C. Babb	424	.248	0	46	238	343	56	35	5.6	.912
3B	B. Lauder	395	.281	0	53	140	194	34	10	3.4	.908
RF	G. Browne	591	.313	3	45	212	13	20	4	1.7	.918
CF	R. Bresnahan	406	.350	4	55	150	14	6	6	2.0	.965
LF	S. Mertes	517	.280	7	**104**	265	24	8	5	2.2	.973
C	J. Warner	285	.284	0	34	450	123	8	9	**6.8**	**.986**
OF	G. Van Haltren	280	.257	0	28	136	3	6	1	1.9	.959
UT	J. Dunn	257	.241	0	37	101	173	26	24		.913
C	F. Bowerman	210	.276	1	31	316	66	9	9	7.1	.977
P	J. McGinnity	165	.206	0	11	**31**	94	**16**	3	2.6	.887
P	C. Mathewson	124	.226	1	20	18	93	3	0	2.5	.974

Pitcher	G	IP	W	L	SV	ERA
J. McGinnity	**55**	**434**	**31**	20	2	2.43
C. Mathewson	45	366	30	13	2	2.26
D. Taylor	33	245	13	13	0	4.23
J. Cronin	20	116	6	4	1	3.81
R. Miller	15	85	2	5	**3**	4.13

Chicago

W-82 L-56

Frank Selee

POS	Player	AB	BA	HR	RBI	PO	A	E	DP	TC/G	FA
1B	F. Chance	441	.327	2	81	1204	68	**36**	49	10.8	.972
2B	J. Evers	464	.293	0	52	245	306	37	39	5.3	.937
SS	J. Tinker	460	.291	2	70	229	362	61	37	6.1	.906
3B	D. Casey	435	.290	1	40	143	190	31	5	3.3	.915
RF	D. Harley	386	.231	0	33	162	18	15	2	1.9	.923
CF	D. Jones	497	.282	1	62	249	14	8	3	2.1	.970
LF	J. Slagle	543	.298	0	44	292	16	21	8	2.4	.936
C	J. Kling	491	.297	3	68	**565**	189	24	13	5.9	.969

Pitcher	G	IP	W	L	SV	ERA
J. Taylor	37	312	21	14	1	2.45
J. Weimer	35	282	21	9	0	2.30
B. Wicker	32	247	19	10	1	3.02
C. Lundgren	27	193	10	9	**3**	2.94
J. Menefee	20	147	8	8	0	3.00

NATIONAL LEAGUE 1903, *cont.*

Team	POS	Player	AB	BA	HR	RBI	PO	A	E	DP	TC/G	FA	Pitcher	G	IP	W	L	SV	ERA
Cincinnati	1B	J. Beckley	459	.327	2	81	1127	78	30	56	10.4	.976	N. Hahn	34	296	22	12	0	2.52
W-74 L-65	2B	T. Daly	307	.293	1	38	151	221	25	22	5.0	.937	B. Ewing	29	247	14	13	1	2.77
Joe Kelley	SS	T. Corcoran	459	.246	2	73	263	367	38	42	5.8	.943	J. Sutthoff	30	225	16	10	0	2.80
	3B	H. Steinfeldt	439	.312	6	83	159	212	25	11	3.8	.937	E. Poole	25	184	8	13	0	3.28
	RF	C. Dolan	385	.288	0	58	107	11	8	2	1.4	.937	J. Harper	17	135	6	8	0	4.33
	CF	C. Seymour	558	.342	7	72	318	14	36	2	2.7	.902	B. Phillips	16	118	8	6	0	3.35
	LF	M. Donlin	496	.351	7	67	209	15	25	4	2.1	.900							
	C	H. Peitz	358	.260	0	42	365	93	14	7	6.1	.970							
	UT	J. Kelley	383	.316	3	45	239	86	22	11		.937							
	C	B. Bergen	207	.227	0	19	251	85	7	3	5.9	.980							
Brooklyn	1B	J. Doyle	524	.313	0	91	**1418**	83	29	74	11.0	.981	O. Jones	38	324	20	16	0	2.94
W-70 L-66	2B	T. Flood	309	.249	0	32	195	216	34	37	5.3	.924	H. Schmidt	40	301	21	13	2	3.83
Ned Hanlon	SS	B. Dahlen	474	.262	1	64	296	**477**	42	48	5.9	**.948**	N. Garvin	38	298	15	18	2	3.08
	3B	S. Strang	508	.272	0	38	147	245	37	13	3.5	.914	R. Evans	15	110	4	8	0	3.27
	RF	W. McCreedie	213	.324	0	20	68	6	6	3	1.4	.925	B. Reidy	15	104	7	6	0	3.46
	CF	J. Dobbs	414	.237	2	59	241	11	9	4	2.4	.966							
	LF	J. Sheckard	515	.332	**9**	75	314	36	18	7	2.6	.951							
	C	L. Ritter	259	.236	0	37	309	80	**25**	6	5.6	.940							
	2B	D. Jordan	267	.236	0	21	101	132	18	12	4.6	.928							
	C	F. Jacklitsch	176	.267	1	21	201	71	7	7	5.3	.975							
	OF	D. Gessler	154	.247	0	18	56	4	1	1	1.4	.984							
	OF	T. McCreery	141	.262	0	10	54	4	7	2	1.7	.892							
Boston	1B	F. Tenney	447	.313	3	41	1145	**93**	33	60	10.4	.974	T. Pittinger	44	352	19	**23**	0	3.48
W-58 L-80	2B	E. Abbaticchio	489	.227	1	46	**316**	325	45	35	5.9	.934	V. Willis	33	278	12	18	0	2.98
Al Buckenberger	SS	H. Aubrey	325	.212	0	27	185	301	74	20	6.0	.868	J. Malarkey	32	253	11	16	0	3.09
	3B	E. Gremminger	511	.264	5	56	**217**	**300**	36	**20**	4.0	.935	W. Piatt	25	181	8	13	0	3.18
	RF	P. Carney	392	.240	1	49	112	10	6	4	1.4	.953							
	CF	C. Dexter	457	.223	3	34	177	13	12	6	1.9	.941							
	LF	D. Cooley	553	.289	1	70	246	11	13	4	2.1	.952							
	C	P. Moran	389	.262	7	54	400	**214**	24	**17**	6.0	.962							
	OF	J. Stanley	308	.250	1	47	117	21	15	2	2.0	.902							
	2S	F. Bonner	173	.220	1	10	104	116	15	19		.936							
Philadelphia	1B	K. Douglass	377	.255	1	36	902	51	15	41	10.0	.985	B. Duggleby	36	264	13	18	1	3.75
W-49 L-86	2B	K. Gleason	412	.284	1	49	236	280	22	30	5.3	.959	C. Fraser	31	250	12	17	1	4.50
Chief Zimmer	SS	R. Hulswitt	519	.247	1	58	**354**	430	**81**	43	6.3	.906	T. Sparks	28	248	11	15	0	2.72
	3B	H. Wolverton	494	.308	0	53	182	247	27	8	3.7	**.941**	F. Mitchell	28	227	11	15	0	4.48
	RF	B. Keister	400	.320	3	63	133	22	10	1	1.6	.939	J. McFetridge	14	103	1	11	0	4.91
	CF	R. Thomas	477	.327	1	27	318	19	13	3	2.7	.963							
	LF	S. Barry	550	.276	1	60	211	14	7	2	2.2	.970							
	C	F. Roth	220	.273	0	22	235	82	22	9	5.7	.935							
	OF	J. Titus	280	.286	2	34	126	13	7	2	2.0	.952							
	UT	B. Hallman	198	.212	0	17	148	101	16	6		.940							
	C	R. Dooin	188	.218	0	14	186	82	17	1	5.6	.940							
St. Louis	1B	J. Hackett	351	.228	0	36	947	40	28	63	11.4	.972	C. McFarland	28	229	9	18	0	3.07
W-43 L-94	2B	J. Farrell	519	.272	1	32	281	394	**53**	**52**	**6.2**	.927	T. Brown	26	201	9	13	0	2.60
Patsy Donovan	SS	D. Brain	464	.231	1	60	163	244	41	34	6.2	.908	C. Currie	22	148	4	12	1	4.01
	3B	J. Burke	431	.285	0	42	139	199	33	14	4.0	.911	B. Rhoads	17	129	5	8	0	4.60
	RF	P. Donovan	410	.327	0	39	142	16	8	5	1.6	.952	M. O'Neill	19	115	4	13	0	4.77
	CF	H. Smoot	500	.296	4	49	231	14	15	3	2.0	.942	E. Murphy	15	106	4	8	0	3.31
	LF	G. Barclay	419	.248	0	42	187	13	22	0	2.1	.901	J. Dunleavy	14	102	6	8	0	4.06
	C	J. O'Neill	246	.236	0	27	348	135	14	8	6.7	.972							
	C	J. Ryan	227	.238	1	10	168	65	7	4	5.1	.971							
	OF	J. Dunleavy	193	.249	0	10	58	11	2	5	1.9	.972							
	SS	O. Williams	187	.203	0	9	94	161	33	16	5.5	.885							

BATTING AND BASE RUNNING LEADERS

Batting Average

H. Wagner, PIT	.355
F. Clarke, PIT	.351
M. Donlin, CIN	.351
R. Bresnahan, NY	.350
C. Seymour, CIN	.342

Slugging Average

F. Clarke, PIT	.532
H. Wagner, PIT	.518
M. Donlin, CIN	.516
R. Bresnahan, NY	.493
H. Steinfeldt, CIN	.481

Home Runs

J. Sheckard, BKN	9

Total Bases

G. Beaumont, PIT	272
C. Seymour, CIN	267
H. Wagner, PIT	265
M. Donlin, CIN	256
J. Sheckard, BKN	245

Runs Batted In

S. Mertes, NY	104
H. Wagner, PIT	101
J. Doyle, BKN	91
T. Leach, PIT	87
H. Steinfeldt, CIN	83

Stolen Bases

F. Chance, CHI	67
J. Sheckard, BKN	67
S. Strang, BKN	46
H. Wagner, PIT	46
S. Mertes, NY	45

Hits

G. Beaumont, PIT	209
C. Seymour, CIN	191
G. Browne, NY	185
H. Wagner, PIT	182

Base on Balls

R. Thomas, PHI	107
B. Dahlen, BKN	82
J. Slagle, CHI	81
F. Chance, CHI	78

Home Run Percentage

P. Moran, BOS	1.8
J. Sheckard, BKN	1.7
M. Donlin, CIN	1.4
T. Leach, PIT	1.4

PITCHING LEADERS

Winning Percentage

S. Leever, PIT	.781
D. Phillippe, PIT	.774
J. Weimer, CHI	.700
C. Mathewson, NY	.698
E. Doheny, PIT	.667

Earned Run Average

S. Leever, PIT	2.06
C. Mathewson, NY	2.26
J. Weimer, CHI	2.30
J. McGinnity, NY	2.43
D. Phillippe, PIT	2.43

Wins

J. McGinnity, NY	31
C. Mathewson, NY	30
S. Leever, PIT	25
D. Phillippe, PIT	24
N. Hahn, CIN	22

Saves

R. Miller, NY	3
C. Lundgren, CHI	3

Strikeouts

C. Mathewson, NY	267
J. McGinnity, NY	171
N. Garvin, BKN	154
T. Pittinger, BOS	140
J. Weimer, CHI	128

Complete Games

J. McGinnity, NY	44
C. Mathewson, NY	37
T. Pittinger, BOS	35
N. Hahn, CIN	34
J. Taylor, CHI	33

Fewest Hits/9 Innings

J. Weimer, CHI	7.69
C. Mathewson, NY	7.89
J. Taylor, CHI	7.98
S. Leever, PIT	8.07

Shutouts

S. Leever, PIT	7
N. Hahn, CIN	5
H. Schmidt, BKN	5
D. Phillippe, PIT	4
O. Jones, BKN	4

Fewest Walks/9 Innings

D. Phillippe, PIT	0.90
B. Reidy, BKN	1.21
N. Hahn, CIN	1.43
J. Taylor, CHI	1.64

NATIONAL LEAGUE 1903, *cont.*

BATTING AND BASE RUNNING LEADERS

Runs		Doubles		Triples	
G. Beaumont, PIT	137	F. Clarke, PIT	32	H. Wagner, PIT	19
M. Donlin, CIN	110	H. Steinfeldt, CIN	32	M. Donlin, CIN	18
G. Browne, NY	105	S. Mertes, NY	32	T. Leach, PIT	17
J. Slagle, CHI	104				

PITCHING LEADERS

Most Strikeouts/9 Inn.		Innings		Games Pitched	
C. Mathewson, NY	6.56	J. McGinnity, NY	434	J. McGinnity, NY	55
W. Piatt, BOS	4.97	C. Mathewson, NY	366	C. Mathewson, NY	45
N. Garvin, BKN	4.65	T. Pittinger, BOS	352	T. Pittinger, BOS	44
J. Weimer, CHI	4.09	O. Jones, BKN	324	H. Schmidt, BKN	40

							Batting						Fielding			Pitching					
	W	L	PCT	GB	R	OR	2B	3B	HR	BA	SA	SB	E	DP	FA	CG	BB	SO	ShO	SV	ERA
Pittsburgh	91	49	.650		**793**	613	208	**110**	**34**	.287	**.393**	172	295	100	**.951**	117	384	454	**16**	5	2.91
New York	84	55	.604	6.5	729	**567**	181	49	20	.272	.344	264	287	87	**.951**	115	371	**628**	8	**8**	2.95
Chicago	82	56	.594	8	695	599	191	62	9	.275	.347	259	338	78	.942	117	**354**	451	6	6	**2.77**
Cincinnati	74	65	.532	16.5	765	656	**228**	92	28	**.288**	.390	144	312	84	.946	**126**	378	480	11	1	3.07
Brooklyn	70	66	.515	19	667	682	177	56	15	.265	.339	**273**	**284**	98	**.951**	118	377	438	11	4	3.44
Boston	58	80	.420	32	578	699	176	47	25	.245	.318	159	361	89	.937	125	460	516	5	0	3.34
Philadelphia	49	86	.363	39.5	617	738	186	62	12	.268	.341	120	300	76	.947	**126**	425	381	5	2	3.97
St. Louis	43	94	.314	46.5	505	795	138	65	8	.251	.313	171	354	**111**	.940	111	430	419	4	2	3.76
					5349	5349	1485	543	151	.269	.348	1562	2531	723	.946	955	3179	3767	66	28	3.28

AMERICAN LEAGUE 1903

Boston

W-91 L-47

Jimmy Collins

POS	Player	AB	BA	HR	RBI	PO	A	E	DP	TC/G	FA
1B	C. LaChance	522	.257	1	53	**1471**	57	25	68	11.0	.984
2B	H. Ferris	525	.251	9	66	313	434	**39**	50	5.7	.950
SS	F. Parent	560	.304	4	80	296	456	57	36	5.8	.930
3B	J. Collins	540	.296	5	72	**178**	260	22	**19**	3.5	**.952**
RF	B. Freeman	567	.287	**13**	**104**	195	13	15	2	1.6	.933
CF	C. Stahl	299	.274	2	44	135	11	6	2	2.1	.961
LF	P. Dougherty	**590**	.331	4	59	259	16	14	3	2.1	.952
C	L. Criger	317	.192	3	31	491	**156**	14	**10**	6.9	.979
OF	J. O'Brien	338	.210	3	38	128	9	6	2	2.0	.958

Pitcher	G	IP	W	L	SV	ERA
C. Young	40	**342**	**28**	9	**2**	2.08
B. Dinneen	37	299	21	13	**2**	2.26
L. Hughes	33	245	20	7	0	2.57
N. Gibson	24	183	13	9	0	3.19
G. Winter	24	178	9	8	0	3.08

Philadelphia

W-75 L-60

Connie Mack

POS	Player	AB	BA	HR	RBI	PO	A	E	DP	TC/G	FA
1B	H. Davis	420	.298	5	55	942	63	29	38	9.9	.972
2B	D. Murphy	513	.273	1	60	241	349	32	34	4.7	.949
SS	M. Cross	470	.247	3	45	**305**	396	45	36	5.4	.940
3B	L. Cross	559	.292	2	90	152	228	20	14	2.9	.950
RF	S. Seybold	522	.299	8	84	177	9	7	4	1.6	.964
CF	O. Pickering	512	.281	1	36	272	17	9	5	2.2	.970
LF	T. Hartsel	373	.311	5	26	144	6	5	0	1.6	.968
C	O. Schreckengost	306	.255	3	30	**514**	106	16	4	**8.3**	.975
OF	D. Hoffman	248	.246	2	22	111	4	6	0	2.0	.950
C	M. Powers	247	.227	0	23	349	86	8	3	6.7	.982

Pitcher	G	IP	W	L	SV	ERA
E. Plank	**43**	336	23	16	0	2.38
R. Waddell	39	324	21	16	0	2.44
C. Bender	36	270	17	14	0	3.07
W. Henley	29	186	12	10	0	3.91

Cleveland

W-77 L-63

Bill Armour

POS	Player	AB	BA	HR	RBI	PO	A	E	DP	TC/G	FA
1B	P. Hickman	518	.330	12	97	1310	66	**40**	67	11.3	.972
2B	N. Lajoie	488	**.355**	7	93	**366**	402	36	**61**	**6.5**	.955
SS	J. Gochnaur	438	.185	0	48	236	414	**98**	45	5.6	.869
3B	B. Bradley	543	.315	6	68	151	**299**	**37**	18	3.6	.924
RF	E. Flick	529	.299	2	51	219	15	11	3	1.8	.955
CF	H. Bay	579	.292	1	35	293	13	16	3	2.3	.950
LF	J. McCarthy	415	.265	0	43	178	10	7	5	1.8	.964
C	H. Bemis	314	.261	1	41	315	82	5	6	5.4	**.988**
C	F. Abbott	255	.235	1	25	337	97	**19**	9	6.4	.958

Pitcher	G	IP	W	L	SV	ERA
A. Joss	32	293	18	13	0	2.15
E. Moore	29	239	19	9	1	**1.77**
B. Bernhard	20	166	14	6	0	2.12
R. Donahue	16	137	7	9	0	2.44
C. Wright	15	102	3	9	0	5.75

New York

W-72 L-62

Clark Griffith

POS	Player	AB	BA	HR	RBI	PO	A	E	DP	TC/G	FA
1B	J. Ganzel	476	.277	3	71	1385	94	18	68	**11.6**	**.988**
2B	J. Williams	502	.267	3	82	266	**438**	32	59	5.6	.957
SS	K. Elberfeld	349	.287	0	45	221	291	48	40	6.2*	.914
3B	W. Conroy	503	.272	1	45	164	243	36	11	**3.6**	.919
RF	W. Keeler	515	.318	0	32	177	10	13	4	1.6	.935
CF	H. McFarland	362	.243	5	45	207	9	14	2	2.2	.939
LF	L. Davis	372	.237	0	25	176	7	19	1	2.0	.906
C	M. Beville	258	.194	0	29	296	66	15	4	5.0	.960
OF	D. Fultz	295	.224	0	25	156	11	12	2	2.3	.933
C	J. O'Connor	212	.203	0	12	282	56	4	6	5.4	.988

Pitcher	G	IP	W	L	SV	ERA
J. Chesbro	40	325	21	15	0	2.77
J. Tannehill	32	240	15	15	0	3.27
C. Griffith	25	213	14	11	0	2.70
H. Howell	25	156	9	6	0	3.53
B. Wolfe	20	148	6	9	0	2.97

Detroit

W-65 L-71

Ed Barrow

POS	Player	AB	BA	HR	RBI	PO	A	E	DP	TC/G	FA
1B	C. Carr	548	.281	2	79	1276	**111**	25	60	10.5	.982
2B	H. Smith	336	.223	1	22	200	267	36	30	5.4	.928
SS	S. McAllister	265	.260	0	22	77	129	26	12	5.0	.888
3B	J. Yeager	402	.256	0	43	126	176	26	9	3.1	.921
RF	S. Crawford	550	.335	4	89	225	16	10	3	1.8	.960
CF	J. Barrett	517	.315	2	31	303	19	15	7	2.5	.955
LF	B. Lush	423	.274	1	33	227	17	8	4	2.5	.968
C	D. McGuire	248	.250	0	21	330	73	17	9	6.1	.960
S2	H. Long	239	.222	0	23	161	198	32	18		.918
C	F. Buelow	192	.214	1	13	254	66	13	6	5.6	.961

Pitcher	G	IP	W	L	SV	ERA
G. Mullin	41	321	19	15	**2**	2.25
W. Donovan	35	307	17	16	0	2.29
F. Kitson	31	258	15	16	0	2.58
R. Kisinger	16	119	7	9	0	2.96

AMERICAN LEAGUE 1903, *cont.*

St. Louis

W-65 L-74

Jimmy McAleer

POS	Player	AB	BA	HR	RBI	PO	A	E	DP	TC/G	FA
1B	J. Anderson	550	.284	2	78	1416	91	22	**71**	11.5	.986
2B	B. Friel	351	.228	0	25	108	171	26	15	4.8	.915
SS	B. Wallace	519	.245	1	54	282	**468**	62	53	6.0	.924
3B	H. Hill	317	.243	0	25	110	165	23	10	3.5	.923
RF	C. Hemphill	383	.245	3	29	155	17	7	4	1.7	.961
CF	E. Heidrick	461	.280	1	42	252	17	13	5	2.4	.954
LF	J. Burkett	514	.296	3	40	230	10	15	4	1.9	.941
C	M. Kahoe	244	.189	0	23	333	64	12	8	5.8	.971
C	J. Sugden	241	.216	0	22	321	81	7	6	6.2	.983
23	B. McCormick	207	.217	1	16	79	131	10	14		.955
OF	J. Martin	173	.214	0	7	53	6	1	3	1.6	.983

Pitcher	G	IP	W	L	SV	ERA
J. Powell	38	306	15	19	**2**	2.91
W. Sudhoff	38	294	21	15	0	2.27
E. Siever	31	254	13	14	0	2.48
R. Donahue	16	131	8	7	0	2.75

Chicago

W-60 L-77

Nixey Callahan

POS	Player	AB	BA	HR	RBI	PO	A	E	DP	TC/G	FA
1B	F. Isbell	546	.242	2	59	1180	87	20	57	11.0	.984
2B	G. Magoon	334	.228	0	25	198	253	31	28	5.1	.936
SS	L. Tannehill	503	.225	2	50	291	457	76	**58**	6.0	.908
3B	N. Callahan	439	.292	2	56	113	203	**37**	5	3.5	.895
RF	D. Green	499	.309	6	62	219	16	17	8	1.9	.933
CF	F. Jones	530	.287	0	45	324	11	5	3	2.5	.985
LF	D. Holmes	344	.279	0	18	151	14	6	0	2.1	.965
C	E. McFarland	201	.209	1	19	240	65	10	7	5.6	.968
C	J. Slattery	211	.218	0	20	215	44	7	0	4.8	.974
OF	B. Hallman	207	.208	0	18	114	7	6	0	2.2	.953
2B	T. Daly	150	.207	0	19	96	103	11	12	4.9	.948

Pitcher	G	IP	W	L	SV	ERA
D. White	37	300	17	16	0	2.13
P. Flaherty	40	294	11	**25**	1	3.74
R. Patterson	34	293	15	15	1	2.70
F. Owen	26	167	8	12	1	3.50

Washington

W-43 L-94

Tom Loftus

POS	Player	AB	BA	HR	RBI	PO	A	E	DP	TC/G	FA
1B	B. Clarke	465	.239	2	38	891	44	14	44	10.8	.985
2B	B. McCormick	219	.215	1	24	130	205	14	27	5.5	.960*
SS	C. Moran	373	.225	1	24	216	300	31	37	5.7	**.943**
3B	B. Coughlin	470	.251	1	31	170	224	20	13	3.5	.952
RF	W. Lee	231	.208	0	13	100	6	8	2	2.4	.930
CF	J. Ryan	437	.245	7	46	288	7	9	1	2.7	.970
LF	K. Selbach	536	.250	3	49	251	10	12	2	2.0	.956
C	M. Kittridge	192	.214	0	16	238	76	7	2	5.3	.978
UT	R. Robinson	373	.212	1	20	185	248	43	27		.910
1B	S. Carey	183	.202	0	23	435	23	11	18	10.0	.977
P	A. Orth	162	.302	0	11	17	86	9	0	3.1	.920
OF	E. Delahanty	156	.333	1	21	69	6	3	1	2.0	.962
C	L. Drill	154	.253	0	23	208	47	9	5	5.6	.966

Pitcher	G	IP	W	L	SV	ERA
C. Patten	36	300	11	22	1	3.60
A. Orth	36	280	10	22	**2**	4.34
H. Wilson	30	242	7	18	0	3.31
W. Lee	22	167	8	12	0	3.08
J. Townsend	20	127	2	11	0	4.76
D. Dunkle	14	108	5	9	0	4.24

BATTING AND BASE RUNNING LEADERS

Batting Average

N. Lajoie, CLE	.355
S. Crawford, DET	.335
P. Dougherty, BOS	.331
P. Hickman, CLE	.330
W. Keeler, NY	.318

Slugging Average

N. Lajoie, CLE	.533
P. Hickman, CLE	.502
B. Freeman, BOS	.496
B. Bradley, CLE	.495
S. Crawford, DET	.489

Home Runs

B. Freeman, BOS	13
P. Hickman, CLE	12
H. Ferris, BOS	9
S. Seybold, PHI	8
J. Ryan, WAS	7
N. Lajoie, CLE	7

Total Bases

B. Freeman, BOS	281
B. Bradley, CLE	269
S. Crawford, DET	269
N. Lajoie, CLE	260
P. Hickman, CLE	260

Runs Batted In

B. Freeman, BOS	104
P. Hickman, CLE	97
N. Lajoie, CLE	93
L. Cross, PHI	90
S. Crawford, DET	89

Stolen Bases

H. Bay, CLE	45
O. Pickering, PHI	40
D. Holmes, WAS, CHI	35
P. Dougherty, BOS	35
W. Conroy, NY	33

Hits

P. Dougherty, BOS	195
S. Crawford, DET	184
N. Lajoie, CLE	173
P. Hickman, CLE	171
B. Bradley, CLE	171

Base on Balls

J. Barrett, DET	74
B. Lush, DET	70
O. Pickering, PHI	53
J. Burkett, STL	52

Home Run Percentage

P. Hickman, CLE	2.3
B. Freeman, BOS	2.3
H. Ferris, BOS	1.7
J. Ryan, WAS	1.6

Runs

P. Dougherty, BOS	108
B. Bradley, CLE	103
W. Keeler, NY	95
J. Barrett, DET	95

Doubles

S. Seybold, PHI	45
N. Lajoie, CLE	40
B. Freeman, BOS	39
B. Bradley, CLE	36

Triples

S. Crawford, DET	25
B. Bradley, CLE	22
B. Freeman, BOS	20

PITCHING LEADERS

Winning Percentage

C. Young, BOS	.757
L. Hughes, BOS	.741
E. Moore, CLE	.679
B. Dinneen, BOS	.618
E. Plank, PHI	.590

Earned Run Average

E. Moore, CLE	1.77
C. Young, BOS	2.08
B. Bernhard, CLE	2.12
D. White, CHI	2.13
A. Joss, CLE	2.15

Wins

C. Young, BOS	28
E. Plank, PHI	23
W. Sudhoff, STL	21
B. Dinneen, BOS	21
R. Waddell, PHI	21
J. Chesbro, NY	21

Saves

A. Orth, WAS	2
B. Dinneen, BOS	2
J. Powell, STL	2
G. Mullin, DET	2
C. Young, BOS	2

Strikeouts

R. Waddell, PHI	302
W. Donovan, DET	187
E. Plank, PHI	176
C. Young, BOS	176
G. Mullin, DET	170

Complete Games

W. Donovan, DET	34
C. Young, BOS	34
R. Waddell, PHI	34
J. Powell, STL	33
J. Chesbro, NY	33
E. Plank, PHI	33

Fewest Hits/9 Innings

E. Moore, CLE	7.13
W. Donovan, DET	7.24
A. Joss, CLE	7.35
R. Waddell, PHI	7.61

Shutouts

C. Young, BOS	7
B. Dinneen, BOS	6
G. Mullin, DET	6
L. Hughes, BOS	5
W. Sudhoff, STL	5

Fewest Walks/9 Innings

C. Young, BOS	0.97
B. Bernhard, CLE	1.14
R. Donahue, STL, CLE	1.14
J. Tannehill, NY	1.28

Most Strikeouts/9 Inn.

R. Waddell, PHI	8.39
W. Donovan, DET	5.48
E. Moore, CLE	5.35
J. Powell, STL	4.97

Innings

C. Young, BOS	342
E. Plank, PHI	336
J. Chesbro, NY	325
R. Waddell, PHI	324

Games Pitched

E. Plank, PHI	43
G. Mullin, DET	41
P. Flaherty, CHI	40
C. Young, BOS	40
J. Chesbro, NY	40

							Batting						Fielding			Pitching					
	W	L	PCT	GB	R	OR	2B	3B	HR	BA	SA	SB	E	DP	FA	CG	BB	SO	ShO	SV	ERA
Boston	91	47	.659		**708**	**504**	222	**113**	**48**	**.272**	**.392**	141	239	86	.959	123	269	579	**20**	**4**	**2.57**
Philadelphia	75	60	.556	14.5	597	519	228	68	31	.264	.362	157	**217**	66	**.960**	112	315	**728**	10	1	2.97
Cleveland	77	63	.550	15	639	579	**230**	95	31	.270	.378	176	322	**99**	.946	**125**	271	521	**20**	1	2.66
New York	72	62	.537	17	579	573	193	62	18	.250	.331	160	264	87	.953	111	245	463	8	2	3.08
Detroit	65	71	.478	25	567	539	162	91	12	.268	.351	128	281	82	.950	123	336	554	15	2	2.75
St. Louis	65	74	.468	26.5	500	525	166	78	12	.242	.319	101	268	94	.953	124	**237**	511	12	**4**	2.77
Chicago	60	77	.438	30.5	516	613	176	49	14	.247	.314	**180**	297	85	.949	114	287	391	9	**4**	3.02
Washington	43	94	.314	47.5	437	691	172	72	18	.231	.311	131	260	86	.954	122	306	452	6	3	3.82
					4543	4543	1549	628	184	.255	.345	1174	2148	685	.953	954	2266	4199	100	21	2.95

NATIONAL LEAGUE 1904

New York

W-106 L-47

John McGraw

POS	Player	AB	BA	HR	RBI	PO	A	E	DP	TC/G	FA	Pitcher	G	IP	W	L	SV	ERA
1B	D. McGann	517	.286	6	71	1481	94	15	62	11.3	**.991**	J. McGinnity	**51**	**408**	**35**	8	**5**	**1.61**
2B	B. Gilbert	478	.253	1	54	305	466	44	48	5.6	.946	C. Mathewson	48	368	33	12	0	2.03
SS	B. Dahlen	523	.268	2	**80**	316	**494**	61	**61**	6.0	.930	D. Taylor	37	296	21	15	0	2.34
3B	A. Devlin	474	.281	1	66	126	285	42	10	3.5	.907	H. Wiltse	24	165	13	3	3	2.84
RF	G. Browne	596	.284	4	39	201	20	18	7	1.6	.925	R. Ames	16	115	4	6	3	2.27
CF	R. Bresnahan	402	.284	5	33	151	14	8	9	1.9	.954							
LF	S. Mertes	532	.276	4	78	244	17	12	1	1.9	.956							
C	J. Warner	287	.199	1	15	427	115	10	7	6.4	**.982**							
C	F. Bowerman	289	.232	2	27	413	96	12	11	**6.6**	.977							
OF	M. McCormick	203	.266	1	26	95	3	9	2	1.9	.916							
UT	J. Dunn	181	.309	1	19	61	89	15	7		.909							

Chicago

W-93 L-60

Frank Selee

POS	Player	AB	BA	HR	RBI	PO	A	E	DP	TC/G	FA	Pitcher	G	IP	W	L	SV	ERA
1B	F. Chance	451	.310	6	49	1205	106	13	48	10.8	.990	J. Weimer	37	307	20	14	0	1.91
2B	J. Evers	532	.265	0	47	**381**	**518**	**54**	53	**6.3**	.943	B. Briggs	34	277	19	11	2	2.05
SS	J. Tinker	488	.221	3	41	327	465	64	54	**6.1**	.925	C. Lundgren	31	242	17	10	1	2.60
3B	D. Casey	548	.268	1	43	157	241	39	11	3.3	.911	B. Wicker	30	229	17	8	0	2.67
RF	D. Jones	336	.244	3	39	128	8	10	0	1.5	.932	T. Brown	26	212	15	10	1	1.86
CF	J. McCarthy	432	.264	0	51	213	8	9	0	2.0	.961	F. Corridon	12	100	5	5	0	3.05
LF	J. Slagle	481	.260	1	31	194	15	18	7	1.9	.921							
C	J. Kling	452	.243	2	46	**499**	135	17	6	6.3	.974							
UT	S. Barry	263	.262	1	26	270	73	21	16		.942							
UT	O. Williams	185	.200	0	8	161	67	9	3		.962							
C	J. O'Neill	168	.214	1	19	256	62	6	5	6.6	.981							
PO	B. Wicker	155	.219	0	9	48	34	7	1		.921							

Cincinnati

W-88 L-65

Joe Kelley

POS	Player	AB	BA	HR	RBI	PO	A	E	DP	TC/G	FA	Pitcher	G	IP	W	L	SV	ERA
1B	J. Kelley	449	.281	0	63	1049	76	14	48	9.7	.988	N. Hahn	35	298	16	18	0	2.06
2B	M. Huggins	491	.263	2	30	337	448	46	32	5.9	.945	J. Harper	35	285	23	9	0	2.37
SS	T. Corcoran	578	.230	2	74	353	471	56	54	5.9	**.936**	W. Kellum	31	225	15	10	2	2.60
3B	H. Steinfeldt	349	.244	1	52	153	168	41	13	3.7	.887	T. Walker	24	217	15	8	0	2.24
RF	C. Dolan	465	.284	6	51	157	13	11	0	1.8	.939	B. Ewing	26	212	11	13	0	2.46
CF	C. Seymour	531	.313	5	58	308	20	17	4	2.7	.951	J. Sutthoff	12	90	5	6	0	2.30
LF	F. Odwell	468	.284	1	58	284	18	14	6	2.5	.956							
C	A. Schlei	291	.237	0	32	384	123	12	5	5.9	.977							
3B	O. Woodruff	306	.190	0	20	75	116	14	4	3.4	.932							
C	H. Peitz	272	.243	1	30	255	89	9	10	5.5	.975							
OF	M. Donlin	236	.356	1	38	87	8	14	1	2.1	.872							
OF	J. Sebring	222	.225	0	24	88	11*	0	3	1.8	1.000							

Pittsburgh

W-87 L-66

Fred Clarke

POS	Player	AB	BA	HR	RBI	PO	A	E	DP	TC/G	FA	Pitcher	G	IP	W	L	SV	ERA
1B	K. Bransfield	520	.223	0	60	1454	89	**30**	**70**	11.3	.981	S. Leever	34	253	18	11	0	2.17
2B	C. Ritchey	544	.263	0	51	330	482	36	48	5.4	.958	P. Flaherty	29	242	19	9	0	2.05
SS	H. Wagner	490	**.349**	4	75	274	367	49	46	5.7	.929	M. Lynch	27	223	15	11	0	2.71
3B	T. Leach	579	.257	2	56	**212**	**371**	**60**	18	**4.4**	.907	D. Phillippe	21	167	10	10	1	3.24
RF	J. Sebring	305	.269	0	32	146	16	7	5	2.1	.959	C. Case	18	141	10	5	0	2.94
CF	G. Beaumont	**615**	.301	3	54	287	14	10	6	2.0	.968	R. Miller	19	134	7	8	0	3.35
LF	F. Clarke	278	.306	0	25	135	4	3	2	2.0	.979							
C	E. Phelps	302	.242	0	28	360	97	17	8	5.2	.964							
UT	O. Krueger	268	.194	1	26	115	117	23	10		.910							
OF	M. McCormick	238	.290	2	23	87	7	6	0	1.5	.940							

St. Louis

W-75 L-79

Kid Nichols

POS	Player	AB	BA	HR	RBI	PO	A	E	DP	TC/G	FA	Pitcher	G	IP	W	L	SV	ERA
1B	J. Beckley	551	.325	1	67	**1526**	64	20	65	**11.3**	.988	J. Taylor	41	352	21	19	1	2.22
2B	J. Farrell	509	.255	0	20	297	450	53	**55**	6.2	.934	K. Nichols	36	317	21	13	1	2.02
SS	D. Shay	340	.256	1	18	153	319	46	30	5.3	.911	C. McFarland	32	269	14	17	0	3.21
3B	J. Burke	406	.227	0	37	148	217	42	10	3.4	.897	M. O'Neill	25	220	10	14	0	2.09
RF	S. Shannon	500	.280	1	26	246	18	6	10	2.0	.978	J. Corbett	14	109	5	9	0	4.39
CF	H. Smoot	520	.281	3	66	270	17	10	6	2.2	.966							
LF	G. Barclay	375	.200	1	28	170	7	10	2	1.8	.947							
C	M. Grady	323	.313	5	43	323	77	19	7	5.4	.955							
UT	D. Brain	488	.266	7	72	259	308	45	26		.926							
OF	J. Dunleavy	172	.233	1	14	68	6	1	2	1.7	.987							

Brooklyn

W-56 L-97

Ned Hanlon

POS	Player	AB	BA	HR	RBI	PO	A	E	DP	TC/G	FA	Pitcher	G	IP	W	L	SV	ERA
1B	P. Dillon	511	.258	0	31	1304	99	25	56	10.7	.982	O. Jones	46	377	17	**25**	0	2.75
2B	D. Jordan	252	.179	0	19	142	176	14	17	4.7	.958	J. Cronin	40	307	12	23	0	2.70
SS	C. Babb	521	.265	0	53	**370**	459	65	44	5.9	.927	N. Garvin	23	182	5	15	0	1.68
3B	M. McCormick	347	.184	0	27	138	190	31	**21**	3.5	.914	E. Poole	25	178	8	13	1	3.39
RF	H. Lumley	577	.279	**9**	78	228	26	12	8	1.8	.955	D. Scanlan	13	104	7	6	0	2.16
CF	J. Dobbs	363	.248	0	30	200	6	14	0	2.4	.936							
LF	J. Sheckard	507	.239	1	46	291	16	14	5	2.3	.956							
C	B. Bergen	329	.182	0	12	414	**151**	24	10	6.3	.959							
OF	D. Gessler	341	.290	2	28	170	15	16	2	2.3	.920							
2B	S. Strang	271	.192	1	9	100	164	26	13	4.6	.910							
C	L. Ritter	214	.248	0	19	249	88	12	7	6.1	.966							

Boston

W-55 L-98

Al Buckenberger

POS	Player	AB	BA	HR	RBI	PO	A	E	DP	TC/G	FA	Pitcher	G	IP	W	L	SV	ERA
1B	F. Tenney	533	.270	1	37	1451	**115**	23	66	11.0	.986	V. Willis	43	350	18	**25**	0	2.85
2B	F. Raymer	419	.210	1	27	272	351	27	38	5.7	**.958**	T. Pittinger	38	335	15	21	0	2.66
SS	E. Abbaticchio	579	.256	3	54	367	473	**78**	47	6.0	.915	K. Wilhelm	39	288	14	22	0	3.69
3B	J. Delahanty	499	.285	3	60	158	223	48	12	3.8	.888	T. Fisher	31	214	6	15	0	4.25
RF	R. Cannell	346	.234	0	18	135	5	16	1	1.7	.897	E. McNichol	17	122	2	12	0	4.28
CF	P. Geier	580	.243	1	27	243	20	19	11	2.1	.933							
LF	D. Cooley	467	.272	5	70	201	3	5	4	1.8	.976							
C	T. Needham	269	.260	4	19	326	140	27	8	6.4	.945							
C3	P. Moran	398	.226	4	34	373	197	36	16		.941							
OF	P. Carney	279	.204	0	11	89	12	5	5	1.5	.953							

NATIONAL LEAGUE 1904, *cont.*

Philadelphia

W-52 L-100

Hugh Duffy

POS	Player	AB	BA	HR	RBI	PO	A	E	DP	TC/G	FA
1B	J. Doyle	236	.220	1	22	585	52	15	27	10.0	.977
2B	K. Gleason	587	.274	0	42	379	463	52	44	5.9	.942
SS	R. Hulswitt	406	.244	1	36	273	310	56	42	5.7	.912
3B	H. Wolverton	398	.266	0	49	143	191	27	15	3.5	**.925**
RF	S. Magee	364	.277	3	57	146	19	14	3	1.9	.922
CF	R. Thomas	496	.290	3	29	321	21	9	4	2.5	.974
LF	J. Titus	504	.294	4	55	258	21	14	7	2.1	.952
C	R. Dooin	355	.242	6	36	411	149	**37**	**12**	6.2	.938
10	J. Lush	369	.276	2	42	580	31	34	27		.947
C	F. Roth	229	.258	1	20	241	76	14	8	4.9	.958
S3	S. Donahue	200	.215	0	14	83	106	33	10		.851
UT	B. Hall	163	.160	0	17	149	80	31	13		.881

Pitcher	G	IP	W	L	SV	ERA
C. Fraser	42	302	14	24	1	3.25
B. Duggleby	32	224	12	13	1	3.78
T. Sparks	26	201	7	18	0	2.65
J. Sutthoff	19	164	6	13	0	3.68
J. McPherson	15	128	1	10	0	3.66
F. Mitchell	13	109	4	7	0	3.40
F. Corridon	12	94	6	5	0	2.19

BATTING AND BASE RUNNING LEADERS

Batting Average

H. Wagner, PIT	.349
M. Donlin, CIN, NY	.329
J. Beckley, STL	.325
M. Grady, STL	.313
C. Seymour, CIN	.313

Slugging Average

H. Wagner, PIT	.520
M. Grady, STL	.474
M. Donlin, CIN, NY	.457
C. Seymour, CIN	.439
F. Chance, CHI	.430

Home Runs

H. Lumley, BKN	9
D. Brain, STL	7
R. Dooin, PHI	6
F. Chance, CHI	6
C. Dolan, CIN	6
D. McGann, NY	6

Total Bases

H. Wagner, PIT	255
H. Lumley, BKN	247
C. Seymour, CIN	233
G. Beaumont, PIT	230
J. Beckley, STL	222

Runs Batted In

B. Dahlen, NY	80
S. Mertes, NY	78
H. Lumley, BKN	78
H. Wagner, PIT	75
T. Corcoran, CIN	74

Stolen Bases

H. Wagner, PIT	53
B. Dahlen, NY	47
S. Mertes, NY	47
F. Chance, CHI	42
D. McGann, NY	42

Hits

G. Beaumont, PIT	185
J. Beckley, STL	179
H. Wagner, PIT	171
G. Browne, NY	169

Base on Balls

R. Thomas, PHI	102
M. Huggins, CIN	88
A. Devlin, NY	62
H. Wagner, PIT	59
C. Ritchey, PIT	59

Home Run Percentage

R. Dooin, PHI	1.7
H. Lumley, BKN	1.6
M. Grady, STL	1.5
D. Brain, STL	1.4

Runs

G. Browne, NY	99
H. Wagner, PIT	97
G. Beaumont, PIT	97
M. Huggins, CIN	96

Doubles

H. Wagner, PIT	44
S. Mertes, NY	28
J. Delahanty, BOS	27
B. Dahlen, NY	26
C. Seymour, CIN	26

Triples

H. Lumley, BKN	18
H. Wagner, PIT	14
J. Kelley, CIN	13
J. Tinker, CHI	13
C. Seymour, CIN	13

PITCHING LEADERS

Winning Percentage

J. McGinnity, NY	.814
C. Mathewson, NY	.733
J. Harper, CIN	.719
B. Wicker, CHI	.680
P. Flaherty, PIT	.679

Earned Run Average

J. McGinnity, NY	1.61
N. Garvin, BKN	1.68
T. Brown, CHI	1.86
J. Weimer, CHI	1.91
K. Nichols, STL	2.02

Wins

J. McGinnity, NY	35
C. Mathewson, NY	33
J. Harper, CIN	23
D. Taylor, NY	21
K. Nichols, STL	21
J. Taylor, STL	21

Saves

J. McGinnity, NY	5
R. Ames, NY	3
H. Wiltse, NY	3
B. Milligan, NY	2
B. Briggs, CHI	2
W. Kellum, CIN	2

Strikeouts

C. Mathewson, NY	212
V. Willis, BOS	196
J. Weimer, CHI	177
T. Pittinger, BOS	146
J. McGinnity, NY	144

Complete Games

J. Taylor, STL	39
V. Willis, BOS	39
O. Jones, BKN	38
J. McGinnity, NY	38
K. Nichols, STL	35
T. Pittinger, BOS	35

Fewest Hits/9 Innings

T. Brown, CHI	6.57
J. Weimer, CHI	6.71
J. McGinnity, NY	6.77
N. Garvin, BKN	6.99

Shutouts

J. McGinnity, NY	9
J. Harper, CIN	6

Fewest Walks/9 Innings

N. Hahn, CIN	1.06
D. Phillippe, PIT	1.40
K. Nichols, STL	1.42
W. Kellum, CIN	1.84

Most Strikeouts/9 Inn.

R. Ames, NY	7.28
H. Wiltse, NY	5.74
J. Corbett, STL	5.63
C. Mathewson, NY	5.19

Innings

J. McGinnity, NY	408
O. Jones, BKN	377
C. Mathewson, NY	368
J. Taylor, STL	352

Games Pitched

J. McGinnity, NY	51
C. Mathewson, NY	48
O. Jones, BKN	46
V. Willis, BOS	43

							Batting						Fielding			Pitching					
	W	L	PCT	GB	R	OR	2B	3B	HR	BA	SA	SB	E	DP	FA	CG	BB	SO	ShO	SV	ERA
New York	106	47	.693		**744**	**476**	**202**	65	**31**	**.262**	**.344**	**283**	294	**93**	**.956**	127	349	**707**	**21**	**14**	**2.17**
Chicago	93	60	.608	13	599	517	157	62	22	.248	.315	227	298	89	.954	139	402	618	18	5	2.30
Cincinnati	88	65	.575	18	695	547	189	92	21	.255	.338	179	301	81	.954	142	343	502	12	2	2.35
Pittsburgh	87	66	.569	19	675	592	164	**102**	15	.258	.338	178	**291**	**93**	.955	133	379	455	15	1	2.89
St. Louis	75	79	.487	31.5	602	595	175	66	24	.253	.327	199	307	83	.952	**146**	**319**	529	7	2	2.64
Brooklyn	56	97	.366	50	497	614	159	53	15	.232	.295	205	343	87	.945	135	414	453	12	2	2.70
Boston	55	98	.359	51	491	749	153	50	24	.237	.300	143	348	91	.946	136	500	544	14	0	3.43
Philadelphia	52	100	.342	53.5	571	784	170	54	23	.248	.316	159	403	**93**	.937	131	425	469	10	2	3.39
					4874	4874	1369	544	175	.249	.322	1573	2585	710	.950	1089	3131	4277	109	28	2.73

AMERICAN LEAGUE 1904

Boston

W-95 L-59

Jimmy Collins

POS	Player	AB	BA	HR	RBI	PO	A	E	DP	TC/G	FA
1B	C. LaChance	573	.227	1	47	**1691**	59	14	**65**	11.2	**.992**
2B	H. Ferris	563	.213	3	63	**366**	460	33	42	5.5	.962
SS	F. Parent	591	.291	6	77	327	493	**63**	44	5.7	.929
3B	J. Collins	631	.266	3	67	**191**	320	30	15	3.5	.945
RF	B. Freeman	597	.280	7	84	216	14	11	4	1.5	.954
CF	C. Stahl	587	.295	3	67	293	6	12	0	2.0	.961
LF	K. Selbach	376	.258	0	30	190	8	8	2	2.1	.961
C	L. Criger	299	.211	2	34	502	112	12	7	6.6	.981
C	D. Farrell	198	.212	0	15	234	62	13	6	5.5	.958
OF	P. Dougherty	195*	.272	0	4	95	4	8*	3	2.2	.925

Pitcher	G	IP	W	L	SV	ERA
C. Young	43	380	26	16	1	1.97
B. Dinneen	37	336	23	14	0	2.20
J. Tannehill	33	282	21	11	0	2.04
N. Gibson	33	273	17	14	0	2.21
G. Winter	20	136	8	4	0	2.32

AMERICAN LEAGUE 1904, *cont.*

Team	POS	Player	AB	BA	HR	RBI	PO	A	E	DP	TC/G	FA	Pitcher	G	IP	W	L	SV	ERA
New York	1B	J. Ganzel	465	.260	6	48	1243	63	16	49	11.2	.988	J. Chesbro	**55**	**455**	**41**	12	0	1.82
	2B	J. Williams	559	.263	2	74	315	**465**	40	**52**	5.6	.951	J. Powell	47	390	23	19	0	2.44
W-92 L-59	SS	K. Elberfeld	445	.263	2	46	237	432	48	44	5.9	.933	A. Orth	20	138	11	6	0	2.68
	3B	W. Conroy	489	.243	1	52	137	231	22	8	3.5	.944	L. Hughes	19	136	7	11	0	3.70
Clark Griffith	RF	W. Keeler	543	.343	2	40	186	16	14	7	1.5	.935	C. Griffith	16	100	7	5	0	2.87
	CF	D. Fultz	339	.274	2	32	194	8	5	2	2.3	.976							
	LF	P. Dougherty	452*	.283	6	22	135	14	12	1	1.5	.925							
	C	D. McGuire	322	.208	0	20	530	120	20	**11**	6.9	.970							
	OF	J. Anderson	558	.278	3	82	186	9	9	1	1.8	.956							
	C	R. Kleinow	209	.206	0	16	276	66	12	5	5.7	.966							
	P	J. Chesbro	174	.236	1	17	24	**166**	12	7	3.7	.941							
Chicago	1B	J. Donahue	367	.248	1	48	1067	85	25	49	**11.7**	.979	F. Owen	37	315	21	15	1	1.94
	2B	G. Dundon	373	.228	0	36	186	282	13	25	4.7	**.973**	N. Altrock	38	307	19	14	1	2.96
W-89 L-65	SS	G. Davis	563	.252	1	69	**347**	**514**	58	**62**	**6.0**	.937	D. White	30	228	16	12	0	1.78
	3B	L. Tannehill	547	.229	0	61	180	**369**	31	**22**	**3.8**	.947	F. Smith	26	202	16	9	0	2.09
	RF	D. Green	536	.265	2	62	231	13	9	5	1.7	.964	R. Patterson	22	165	9	9	0	2.29
Nixey Callahan	CF	F. Jones	564	.243	3	43	325	15	8	4	2.3	.977	E. Walsh	18	111	6	3	1	2.60
W-23 L-18	LF	N. Callahan	482	.261	0	54	158	9	4	0	1.6	.977							
	C	B. Sullivan	371	.229	1	44	463	**130**	22	10	5.7	.964							
Fielder Jones	12	F. Isbell	314	.210	1	34	652	128	20	28		.975							
W-66 L-47	OF	D. Holmes	251	.311	1	19	111	8	3	3	1.9	.975							
	C	E. McFarland	160	.275	0	20	195	39	6	2	4.9	.975							
Cleveland	1B	P. Hickman	337	.288	4	45	391	22	14	17	10.7	.967	B. Bernhard	38	321	23	13	0	2.13
	2B	N. Lajoie	554	**.381**	6	**102**	272	255	21	42	**5.8**	.962	R. Donahue	35	277	19	14	0	2.40
	SS	T. Turner	404	.235	1	45	191	376	36	28	5.4	.940	E. Moore	26	228	12	11	0	2.25
W-86 L-65	3B	B. Bradley	607	.300	5	83	178	308	23	18	3.3	**.955**	A. Joss	25	192	14	10	0	**1.59**
	RF	E. Flick	579	.306	6	56	234	19	12	5	1.8	.955	B. Rhoads	22	175	10	9	0	2.87
Bill Armour	CF	H. Bay	506	.261	3	36	281	15	4	6	2.3	.987	O. Hess	21	151	8	7	0	1.67
	LF	B. Lush	477	.258	1	50	269	11	12	4	2.1	.959							
	C	H. Bemis	336	.226	0	25	393	86	21	8	6.3	.958							
	1B	G. Stovall	182	.297	1	31	376	22	9	18	10.7	.978							
Philadelphia	1B	H. Davis	404	.309	**10**	62	1011	57	19	33	10.7	.983	R. Waddell	46	383	25	19	0	1.62
	2B	D. Murphy	557	.287	7	77	280	455	**46**	35	5.2	.941	E. Plank	44	357	26	17	0	2.14
	SS	M. Cross	503	.189	1	38	276	424	47	26	4.9	.937	W. Henley	36	296	15	17	0	2.53
W-81 L-70	3B	L. Cross	607	.290	1	71	164	247	28	15	2.8	.936	C. Bender	29	204	10	11	0	2.87
	RF	S. Seybold	510	.292	3	64	180	12	5	5	1.5	.975							
Connie Mack	CF	O. Pickering	455	.226	0	30	217	13	15	2	2.0	.939							
	LF	T. Hartsel	534	.253	2	25	216	15	10	2	1.6	.959							
	C	O. Schreckengost	311	.186	1	21	**589**	76	14	5	**8.1**	.979							
	OF	D. Hoffman	204	.299	3	24	83	5	6	1	1.8	.936							
	C	M. Powers	184	.190	0	11	338	52	14	6	7.2	.965							
St. Louis	1B	T. Jones	625	.243	2	68	1443	92	19	51	11.6	.988	B. Pelty	39	301	15	18	0	2.84
	2B	D. Padden	453	.238	0	36	288	373	28	31	5.2	.959	H. Howell	34	300	13	21	0	2.19
	SS	B. Wallace	550	.273	2	69	303	482	44	37	6.0	**.947**	F. Glade	35	289	18	15	1	2.27
W-65 L-87	3B	C. Moran	272	.173	0	14	69	169	16	2	3.1	.937	W. Sudhoff	27	222	8	15	0	3.76
	RF	C. Hemphill	438	.256	2	45	177	12	15	5	1.9	.926	E. Siever	29	217	10	15	0	2.65
Jimmy McAleer	CF	E. Heidrick	538	.273	1	36	291	22	12	6	2.5	.963							
	LF	J. Burkett	576	.273	2	27	266	24	18	4	2.1	.942							
	C	J. Sugden	347	.262	0	30	370	94	5	**11**	5.9	**.989**							
	OF	P. Hynes	254	.236	0	15	72	1	8	0	1.3	.901							
	C	M. Kahoe	236	.216	0	12	307	91	13	3	6.0	.968							
	3B	H. Hill	219	.215	0	14	78	79	33*	3	3.4	.826							
	UT	H. Gleason	155	.213	0	6	66	108	15	11		.921							
Detroit	1B	C. Carr	360	.214	0	40	901	99*	17	46	11.1	.983	G. Mullin	45	382	17	23	0	2.40
	2B	B. Lowe	506	.208	0	40	328	402	27	44	5.4	.964	E. Killian	40	332	14	20	1	2.44
	SS	C. O'Leary	456	.213	1	16	308	439	54	48	5.9	.933	W. Donovan	34	293	17	16	0	2.46
W-62 L-90	3B	E. Gremminger	309	.214	1	28	103	123	12	3	2.9	.950	F. Kitson	26	200	8	13	1	3.07
	RF	S. Crawford	571	.250	2	73	230	18	7	8	1.7	.973	J. Stovall	22	147	3	13	0	4.42
Ed Barrow	CF	J. Barrett	624	.268	0	31	339	29	11	6	2.3	.971							
W-32 L-46	LF	M. McIntyre	578	.253	2	46	334	16	15	4	2.4	.959							
	C	L. Drill	160	.244	0	13	195	51	13*	6*	5.3	.950							
Bobby Lowe	UT	R. Robinson	320	.241	0	37	151	216	22	17		.943							
W-30 L-44	3B	B. Coughlin	206	.228	0	17	53	104	12	2	3.0	.929							
	C	B. Wood	175	.246	1	17	232	69	8	5	6.6	.974							
	C1	M. Beville	174	.207	0	13	354	41	16	11		.961							
	1B	P. Hickman	144	.243	2	22	396	23	13	18	11.1	.970							
Washington	1B	J. Stahl	520	.262	3	50	1202	85	**29**	52	11.1	.978	C. Patten	45	358	14	23	**3**	3.07
	2B	B. McCormick	404	.218	0	39	204	355	37	39	5.3	.938	J. Townsend	36	291	5	**26**	0	3.58
	SS	J. Cassidy	581	.241	1	33	249	301	37	38	5.9	.937	B. Jacobson	33	254	6	23	0	3.55
W-38 L-113	3B	H. Hill	290	.197	0	17	86	126	25*	4	3.3	.895	B. Wolfe	17	127	6	9	0	3.27
	RF	P. Donovan	436	.229	0	19	217	15	9	4	2.0	.963	L. Hughes	16	124	2	13	1	3.47
Mal Kittridge	CF	B. O'Neill	365	.244	1	16	141	9	18	1	1.8	.893	D. Dunkle	12	74	2	9	0	4.96
W-1 L-16	LF	F. Huelsman	303	.248	2	30	138	7	6	2	1.8	.960							
	C	M. Kittridge	265	.242	0	24	346	99	8	4	5.7	.982							
Patsy Donovan	C1	B. Clarke	275	.211	0	17	517	86	13	24		.979							
W-37 L-97	3B	B. Coughlin	265	.275	0	17	95	121	14	7	3.6	.939							
	SS	C. Moran	243	.222	0	7	114	171	25	17	5.1	.919							
	OF	K. Selbach	178	.275	0	14	103	5	8	1	2.4	.931							

AMERICAN LEAGUE 1904, *cont.*

BATTING AND BASE RUNNING LEADERS

Batting Average

N. Lajoie, CLE	.381
W. Keeler, NY	.343
H. Davis, PHI	.309
E. Flick, CLE	.306
B. Bradley, CLE	.300

Slugging Average

N. Lajoie, CLE	.554
H. Davis, PHI	.490
E. Flick, CLE	.453
D. Murphy, PHI	.440
P. Hickman, CLE, DET	.437

Home Runs

H. Davis, PHI	10
D. Murphy, PHI	7
B. Freeman, BOS	7

Total Bases

N. Lajoie, CLE	307
E. Flick, CLE	262
C. Stahl, BOS	247
B. Freeman, BOS	246
D. Murphy, PHI	245
P. Dougherty, BOS, NY	245

Runs Batted In

N. Lajoie, CLE	102
B. Freeman, BOS	84
B. Bradley, CLE	83
J. Anderson, NY	82
D. Murphy, PHI	77
F. Parent, BOS	77

Stolen Bases

E. Flick, CLE	42
H. Bay, CLE	38
E. Heidrick, STL	35
G. Davis, CHI	32
N. Lajoie, CLE	31

Hits

N. Lajoie, CLE	211
W. Keeler, NY	186
B. Bradley, CLE	182
P. Dougherty, BOS, NY	181

Base on Balls

J. Barrett, DET	79
J. Burkett, STL	78
T. Hartsel, PHI	75
B. Lush, CLE	72
K. Selbach, WAS, BOS	72

Home Run Percentage

H. Davis, PHI	2.5
J. Ganzel, NY	1.3
D. Murphy, PHI	1.3
P. Hickman, CLE, DET	1.2

Runs

P. Dougherty, BOS, NY	113
E. Flick, CLE	97
B. Bradley, CLE	94
N. Lajoie, CLE	92

Doubles

N. Lajoie, CLE	50
J. Collins, BOS	33

Triples

J. Cassidy, WAS	19
C. Stahl, BOS	19
B. Freeman, BOS	19
E. Flick, CLE	18

PITCHING LEADERS

Winning Percentage

J. Chesbro, NY	.774
J. Tannehill, BOS	.656
F. Smith, CHI	.640
B. Bernhard, CLE	.639
B. Dinneen, BOS	.622

Earned Run Average

A. Joss, CLE	1.59
R. Waddell, PHI	1.62
O. Hess, CLE	1.67
D. White, CHI	1.78
J. Chesbro, NY	1.82

Wins

J. Chesbro, NY	41
E. Plank, PHI	26
C. Young, BOS	26
R. Waddell, PHI	25

Saves

C. Patten, WAS	3

Strikeouts

R. Waddell, PHI	349
J. Chesbro, NY	239
J. Powell, NY	202
E. Plank, PHI	201
C. Young, BOS	200

Complete Games

J. Chesbro, NY	48
G. Mullin, DET	42
C. Young, BOS	40
R. Waddell, PHI	39
J. Powell, NY	38

Fewest Hits/9 Innings

J. Chesbro, NY	6.69
F. Owen, CHI	6.94
F. Smith, CHI	6.98
N. Gibson, BOS	7.12

Shutouts

C. Young, BOS	10
R. Waddell, PHI	8
D. White, CHI	7
G. Mullin, DET	7
E. Plank, PHI	7

Fewest Walks/9 Innings

C. Young, BOS	0.69
J. Tannehill, BOS	1.05
R. Patterson, CHI	1.31
A. Joss, CLE	1.40

Most Strikeouts/9 Inn.

R. Waddell, PHI	8.20
C. Bender, PHI	6.58
E. Moore, CLE	5.49
E. Plank, PHI	5.06

Innings

J. Chesbro, NY	455
J. Powell, NY	390
R. Waddell, PHI	383
G. Mullin, DET	382

Games Pitched

J. Chesbro, NY	55
J. Powell, NY	47
R. Waddell, PHI	46
C. Patten, WAS	45
G. Mullin, DET	45

							Batting						Fielding			Pitching					
	W	L	PCT	GB	R	OR	2B	3B	HR	BA	SA	SB	E	DP	FA	CG	BB	SO	ShO	SV	ERA
Boston	95	59	.617		608	**466**	194	**105**	26	.247	.340	101	242	83	.962	**148**	**233**	612	21	1	**2.12**
New York	92	59	.609	1.5	598	526	195	91	27	.259	.347	163	275	90	.958	123	311	684	15	1	2.57
Chicago	89	65	.578	6	600	482	193	68	14	.242	.316	**216**	**238**	95	**.964**	134	303	550	**26**	3	2.30
Cleveland	86	65	.570	7.5	**647**	482	**225**	90	27	**.262**	**.357**	189	255	86	.959	141	285	627	20	0	2.22
Philadelphia	81	70	.536	12.5	557	503	197	77	**31**	.249	.336	137	250	67	.959	137	366	**887**	**26**	0	2.35
St. Louis	65	87	.428	29	481	604	153	53	10	.239	.293	150	267	78	.960	135	333	577	13	1	2.83
Detroit	62	90	.408	32	505	627	154	70	11	.231	.293	112	273	92	.959	143	433	556	15	2	2.77
Washington	38	113	.252	55.5	437	743	171	57	10	.227	.288	150	314	**97**	.951	137	347	533	8	**4**	3.62
					4433	4433	1482	611	156	.244	.321	1218	2114	688	.959	1098	2611	5026	144	12	2.60

NATIONAL LEAGUE 1905

New York

W-105 L-48

John McGraw

POS	Player	AB	BA	HR	RBI	PO	A	E	DP	TC/G	FA
1B	D. McGann	491	.299	5	75	1350	86	13	59	10.7	**.991**
2B	B. Gilbert	376	.247	0	24	245	367	34	41	5.6	.947
SS	B. Dahlen	520	.242	7	81	313	501	45	58	5.8	.948
3B	A. Devlin	525	.246	2	61	156	**299**	33	14	3.2	.932
RF	G. Browne	536	.293	4	43	175	9	17	1	1.6	.915
CF	M. Donlin	606	.356	7	80	250	17	19	4	1.9	.934
LF	S. Mertes	551	.279	5	108	230	10	10	3	1.7	.960
C	R. Bresnahan	331	.302	0	46	492	114	19	15	**7.2**	.970
C	F. Bowerman	297	.269	3	41	383	66	8	4	6.3	.982
UT	S. Strang	294	.259	3	29	123	144	25	11		.914

Pitcher	G	IP	W	L	SV	ERA
C. Mathewson	43	339	**31**	8	3	**1.27**
J. McGinnity	**46**	320	21	15	3	2.87
R. Ames	34	263	22	8	0	2.74
D. Taylor	32	213	16	9	0	2.66
H. Wiltse	32	197	15	6	3	2.47

Pittsburgh

W-96 L-57

Fred Clarke

POS	Player	AB	BA	HR	RBI	PO	A	E	DP	TC/G	FA
1B	D. Howard	435	.292	2	63	912	48	22	57	10.9	.978
2B	C. Ritchey	533	.255	0	52	279	478	31	**59**	5.2	**.961**
SS	H. Wagner	548	.363	6	101	353	517	60	64	**6.4**	.935
3B	D. Brain	307	.257	3	46	82	170	21	13	3.5	.923
RF	O. Clymer	365	.296	0	23	136	7	2	5	1.6	.986
CF	G. Beaumont	384	.328	3	40	200	12	6	5	2.2	.972
LF	F. Clarke	525	.299	2	51	270	16	7	4	2.1	.976
C	H. Peitz	278	.223	0	27	337	105	16	14	5.3	.965
03	T. Leach	499	.257	2	53	238	134	16	15		.959
1B	B. Clancy	227	.229	2	34	551	27	10	30	11.3	.983

Pitcher	G	IP	W	L	SV	ERA
D. Phillippe	38	279	22	13	0	2.19
S. Leever	33	230	19	6	0	2.70
C. Case	31	217	12	10	1	2.57
M. Lynch	33	206	17	8	2	3.80
P. Flaherty	27	188	9	10	1	3.49
C. Robitaille	17	120	8	5	0	2.92

Chicago

W-92 L-61

Frank Selee
W-37 L-28

Frank Chance
W-55 L-33

POS	Player	AB	BA	HR	RBI	PO	A	E	DP	TC/G	FA
1B	F. Chance	392	.316	2	70	1165	75	13	54	10.9	.990
2B	J. Evers	340	.276	1	37	249	290	36	38	5.8	.937
SS	J. Tinker	547	.247	2	66	345	527	56	**67**	6.2	.940
3B	D. Casey	526	.232	1	56	160	252	22	7	3.1	**.949**
RF	B. Maloney	558	.260	2	56	251	18	13	4	1.9	.954
CF	J. Slagle	568	.269	0	37	306	27	13	6	2.2	.962
LF	W. Schulte	493	.274	1	47	189	14	4	0	1.7	.981
C	J. Kling	380	.218	1	52	**538**	136	24	12	6.6	.966
2B	S. Hofman	287	.237	1	38	138	178	15	13	5.6	.955
C	J. O'Neill	172	.198	0	12	276	63	9	8	7.0	.974
OF	J. McCarthy	170	.276	0	14	63	9	1	4	2.0	.986

Pitcher	G	IP	W	L	SV	ERA
E. Reulbach	34	292	18	14	1	1.42
J. Weimer	33	250	18	12	1	2.27
T. Brown	30	249	18	12	0	2.17
B. Wicker	22	178	13	6	0	2.02
C. Lundgren	23	169	13	5	0	2.24
B. Briggs	20	168	8	8	0	2.14
B. Pfeffer	15	101	4	4	0	2.50

NATIONAL LEAGUE 1905, *cont.*

Philadelphia

W-83 L-69

Hugh Duffy

POS	Player	AB	BA	HR	RBI	PO	A	E	DP	TC/G	FA
1B	K. Bransfield	580	.259	3	76	1398	92	23	**75**	10.0	.985
2B	K. Gleason	608	.247	1	50	**365**	457	46	49	5.6	.947
SS	M. Doolan	492	.254	1	48	299	432	51	45	5.8	.935
3B	E. Courtney	601	.275	2	77	**229**	249	40	13	3.3	.923
RF	J. Titus	548	.308	2	89	255	24	11	4	2.0	.962
CF	R. Thomas	562	.317	0	31	373	27	7	6	2.8	.983
LF	S. Magee	603	.299	5	98	341	19	14	6	2.4	.963
C	R. Dooin	380	.250	0	36	505	152	24	9	6.4	.965

Pitcher	G	IP	W	L	SV	ERA
T. Pittinger	**46**	337	23	14	2	3.10
B. Duggleby	38	289	18	17	0	2.46
T. Sparks	34	260	14	11	1	2.18
F. Corridon	35	212	10	13	1	3.48
K. Nichols	17	139	10	6	0	2.27

Cincinnati

W-79 L-74

Joe Kelley

POS	Player	AB	BA	HR	RBI	PO	A	E	DP	TC/G	FA
1B	S. Barry	494	.324	1	56	1216	61	23	7	10.6	.982
2B	M. Huggins	564	.273	1	38	346	**525**	**51**	55	**6.2**	.945
SS	T. Corcoran	605	.248	2	85	344	**531**	44	**67**	6.1	**.952**
3B	H. Steinfeldt	384	.271	1	39	152	221	33	16	**3.9**	.919
RF	F. Odwell	468	.241	**9**	65	216	18	8	5	1.9	.967
CF	C. Seymour	581	**.377**	8	**121**	347	25	21	12	2.6	.947
LF	J. Kelley	321	.277	1	37	137	11	4	0	1.8	.974
C	A. Schlei	314	.226	1	36	398	**153**	22	**16**	6.4	.962
UT	A. Bridwell	254	.252	0	17	104	118	17	15		.929
OF	J. Sebring	217	.286	2	28	63	6	9	2	1.4	.885
C	E. Phelps	156	.231	0	18	189	55	13	5	5.8	.949

Pitcher	G	IP	W	L	SV	ERA
O. Overall	42	318	17	22	0	2.86
B. Ewing	40	312	20	11	0	2.51
C. Chech	39	268	14	15	0	2.89
J. Harper	26	179	10	13	0	3.87
T. Walker	23	145	9	7	0	3.23

St. Louis

W-58 L-96

Kid Nichols
W-5 L-9

Jimmy Burke
W-34 L-56

Matt Robison
W-19 L-31

POS	Player	AB	BA	HR	RBI	PO	A	E	DP	TC/G	FA
1B	J. Beckley	514	.286	1	57	1442	69	28	56	11.5	.982
2B	H. Arndt	415	.243	2	36	173	254	22	25	5.0	.951
SS	G. McBride	281	.217	2	34	147	273	28	29	5.6	.938
3B	J. Burke	431	.225	1	30	174	238	34	13	3.7	.924
RF	J. Dunleavy	435	.241	1	25	177	25	8	7	1.8	.962
CF	H. Smoot	534	.311	4	58	295	18	8	6	2.3	.975
LF	S. Shannon	544	.268	0	41	299	7	5	3	2.2	.984
C	M. Grady	311	.286	4	41	288	79	17	7	5.4	.956
2S	D. Shay	281	.238	0	28	172	230	35	22		.920
02	J. Clarke	167	.257	3	18	74	49	12	3		.911
SS	D. Brain	158	.228	1	17	58	74	13	4	5.0	.910

Pitcher	G	IP	W	L	SV	ERA
J. Taylor	37	309	15	21	1	3.44
C. McFarland	31	250	8	18	1	3.82
J. Thielman	32	242	15	16	0	3.50
B. Brown	23	179	8	11	0	2.97
W. Egan	23	171	6	15	0	3.58

Boston

W-51 L-103

Fred Tenney

POS	Player	AB	BA	HR	RBI	PO	A	E	DP	TC/G	FA
1B	F. Tenney	549	.288	0	28	**1556**	**152**	32	68	**11.8**	.982
2B	F. Raymer	498	.211	0	31	256	381	34	33	5.0	.949
SS	E. Abbaticchio	**610**	.279	3	41	**386**	468	**75**	53	6.1	.919
3B	H. Wolverton	463	.225	2	55	139	256	28	12	3.5	.934
RF	C. Dolan	433	.275	3	48	175	19	11	2	1.8	.946
CF	R. Cannell	567	.247	0	36	315	14	23	6	2.3	.935
LF	J. Delahanty	461	.258	5	55	186	16	8	1	1.7	.962
C	P. Moran	267	.240	2	22	389	113	7	5	6.5	**.986**
C	T. Needham	271	.218	2	17	292	134	23	6	5.8	.949
32	B. Lauterborn	200	.185	0	9	82	127	27	4		.886
OF	B. Sharpe	170	.182	0	11	55	11	7	3	1.7	.904
P	C. Fraser	156	.224	0	10	36	80	9	1	3.2	.928

Pitcher	G	IP	W	L	SV	ERA
I. Young	43	**378**	20	21	0	2.90
V. Willis	41	342	12	**29**	0	3.21
C. Fraser	39	334	14	22	0	3.29
K. Wilhelm	34	242	3	22	1	4.54

Brooklyn

W-48 L-104

Ned Hanlon

POS	Player	AB	BA	HR	RBI	PO	A	E	DP	TC/G	FA
1B	D. Gessler	431	.290	3	46	1017	79	**33**	54	10.6	.971
2B	C. Malay	349	.252	1	31	138	216	26	17	5.1	.932
SS	P. Lewis	433	.254	3	33	253	371	66	63	5.8	.904
3B	E. Batch	568	.252	5	49	203	246	**57**	**22**	3.5	.887
RF	H. Lumley	505	.293	7	47	177	21	19	4	1.7	.912
CF	J. Dobbs	460	.254	2	36	246	11	17	1	2.2	.938
LF	J. Sheckard	480	.292	3	41	266	24	10	6	2.3	.967
C	L. Ritter	311	.219	1	28	397	106	**26**	4	6.3	.951
C	B. Bergen	247	.190	0	22	371	127	24	8	6.9	.954
S1	C. Babb	235	.187	0	17	388	132	24	32		.956
OF	B. Hall	203	.236	2	15	101	6	7	2	2.7	.939
2B	R. Owens	168	.214	1	20	102	132	18	19	5.9	.929

Pitcher	G	IP	W	L	SV	ERA
H. McIntire	40	309	8	25	1	3.70
D. Scanlan	33	250	14	12	0	2.92
E. Stricklett	33	237	9	18	1	3.34
M. Eason	27	207	5	21	0	4.30
O. Jones	29	174	8	15	1	4.66
F. Mitchell	12	96	3	7	0	4.78

BATTING AND BASE RUNNING LEADERS

Batting Average

C. Seymour, CIN	.377
H. Wagner, PIT	.363
M. Donlin, NY	.356
G. Beaumont, PIT	.328
R. Thomas, PHI	.317

Slugging Average

C. Seymour, CIN	.559
H. Wagner, PIT	.505
M. Donlin, NY	.495
J. Titus, PHI	.436
M. Grady, STL	.434

Home Runs

F. Odwell, CIN	9
C. Seymour, CIN	8
H. Lumley, BKN	7
B. Dahlen, NY	7
M. Donlin, NY	7

Total Bases

C. Seymour, CIN	325
M. Donlin, NY	300
H. Wagner, PIT	277
S. Magee, PHI	253
J. Titus, PHI	239

Runs Batted In

C. Seymour, CIN	121
S. Mertes, NY	108
H. Wagner, PIT	101
S. Magee, PHI	98
J. Titus, PHI	89

Stolen Bases

A. Devlin, NY	59
B. Maloney, CHI	59
H. Wagner, PIT	57
S. Mertes, NY	52
S. Magee, PHI	48

Hits

C. Seymour, CIN	219
M. Donlin, NY	216
H. Wagner, PIT	199
S. Barry, CHI, CIN	182

Base on Balls

M. Huggins, CIN	103
J. Slagle, CHI	97
R. Thomas, PHI	93
F. Chance, CHI	78

Home Run Percentage

F. Odwell, CIN	1.9
H. Lumley, BKN	1.4
C. Seymour, CIN	1.4
B. Dahlen, NY	1.3

PITCHING LEADERS

Winning Percentage

C. Mathewson, NY	.795
S. Leever, PIT	.760
R. Ames, NY	.733
H. Wiltse, NY	.714
M. Lynch, PIT	.680

Earned Run Average

C. Mathewson, NY	1.27
E. Reulbach, CHI	1.42
B. Wicker, CHI	2.02
B. Briggs, CHI	2.14
T. Brown, CHI	2.17

Wins

C. Mathewson, NY	31
T. Pittinger, PHI	23
R. Ames, NY	22
D. Phillippe, PIT	22
J. McGinnity, NY	21

Saves

C. Elliott, NY	6
J. McGinnity, NY	3
H. Wiltse, NY	3
C. Mathewson, NY	3
T. Pittinger, PHI	2
M. Lynch, PIT	2

Strikeouts

C. Mathewson, NY	206
R. Ames, NY	198
O. Overall, CIN	173
B. Ewing, CIN	164
I. Young, BOS	156

Complete Games

I. Young, BOS	41
V. Willis, BOS	36
C. Fraser, BOS	35
J. Taylor, STL	34
C. Mathewson, NY	33

Fewest Hits/9 Innings

E. Reulbach, CHI	6.41
C. Mathewson, NY	6.69
B. Wicker, CHI	7.03
C. Lundgren, CHI	7.03

Shutouts

C. Mathewson, NY	8
I. Young, BOS	7
B. Briggs, CHI	5
E. Reulbach, CHI	5
D. Phillippe, PIT	5

Fewest Walks/9 Innings

D. Phillippe, PIT	1.55
T. Brown, CHI	1.59
I. Young, BOS	1.69
C. Mathewson, NY	1.70

NATIONAL LEAGUE 1905, *cont.*

BATTING AND BASE RUNNING LEADERS

Runs		Doubles		Triples	
M. Donlin, NY	124	C. Seymour, CIN	40	C. Seymour, CIN	21
R. Thomas, PHI	118	J. Titus, PHI	36	S. Mertes, NY	17
M. Huggins, CIN	117	H. Wagner, PIT	32	S. Magee, PHI	17
H. Wagner, PIT	114	M. Donlin, NY	31	H. Smoot, STL	16
				M. Donlin, NY	16

PITCHING LEADERS

Most Strikeouts/9 Inn.		Innings		Games Pitched	
R. Ames, NY	6.78	I. Young, BOS	378	T. Pittinger, PHI	46
H. Wiltse, NY	5.48	V. Willis, BOS	342	J. McGinnity, NY	46
C. Mathewson, NY	5.47	C. Mathewson, NY	339	C. Mathewson, NY	43
O. Overall, CIN	4.90	T. Pittinger, PHI	337	I. Young, BOS	43

							Batting							Fielding			Pitching					
	W	L	PCT	GB	R	OR	2B	3B	HR	BA	SA	SB	E	DP	FA	CG	BB	SO	ShO	SV	ERA
New York	105	48	.686		**778**	505	**191**	88	**39**	**.273**	**.368**	**291**	258	93	.960	118	**364**	**760**	18	**15**	2.39
Pittsburgh	96	57	.627	9	692	570	190	91	22	.266	.350	202	255	112	.961	113	389	512	12	4	2.86
Chicago	92	61	.601	13	667	**442**	157	82	12	.245	.314	267	**248**	99	**.962**	133	385	627	**23**	2	**2.04**
Philadelphia	83	69	.546	21.5	708	602	187	82	16	.260	.336	180	275	99	.957	119	411	516	12	5	2.81
Cincinnati	79	74	.516	26	735	698	160	**101**	27	.269	.354	181	310	**122**	.953	119	439	547	10	1	3.01
St. Louis	58	96	.377	47.5	535	734	140	85	20	.248	.321	162	274	83	.957	135	367	411	10	2	3.59
Boston	51	103	.331	54.5	468	731	148	52	17	.234	.293	132	325	89	.951	**139**	433	533	14	0	3.52
Brooklyn	48	104	.316	56.5	506	807	154	60	29	.246	.317	186	411	101	.936	125	476	556	7	3	3.76
					5089	5089	1327	641	182	.255	.332	1601	2356	798	.955	1001	3264	4462	106	32	3.00

AMERICAN LEAGUE 1905

Philadelphia

W-92 L-56

Connie Mack

POS	Player	AB	BA	HR	RBI	PO	A	E	DP	TC/G	FA	Pitcher	G	IP	W	L	SV	ERA
1B	H. Davis	602	.284	**8**	**83**	1621	91	24	43	11.7	.986	E. Plank	41	347	24	12	0	2.26
2B	D. Murphy	533	.278	6	71	287	387	31	29	4.7	.956	R. Waddell	**46**	329	**27**	10	0	**1.48**
SS	J. Knight	325	.203	3	29	143	188	39	9	4.6	.895	A. Coakley	35	255	18	8	0	1.84
3B	L. Cross	583	.266	0	77	161	249	32	6	3.0	.928	C. Bender	35	229	18	11	0	2.83
RF	S. Seybold	488	.270	6	59	213	13	4	5	1.7	.983	W. Henley	25	184	4	11	0	2.60
CF	D. Hoffman	454	.262	1	35	214	12	14	4	2.0	.942							
LF	T. Hartsel	533	.276	0	28	253	6	17	1	1.9	.938							
C	O. Schreckengost	416	.272	0	45	**790**	114	15	**11**	**8.2**	**.984**							
SS	M. Cross	248	.270	0	24	159	195	27	22	5.0	.929							
OF	B. Lord	238	.239	0	13	94	9	4	3	1.8	.963							

Chicago

W-92 L-60

Fielder Jones

POS	Player	AB	BA	HR	RBI	PO	A	E	DP	TC/G	FA	Pitcher	G	IP	W	L	SV	ERA
1B	J. Donahue	533	.287	1	76	**1645**	**114**	21	**77**	11.9	**.988**	F. Owen	42	334	21	13	0	2.10
2B	G. Dundon	364	.192	0	22	218	321	12	23	5.3	**.978**	N. Altrock	38	316	23	12	0	1.88
SS	G. Davis	550	.278	1	55	330	501	46	**56**	5.6	**.948**	F. Smith	39	292	19	13	0	2.13
3B	L. Tannehill	480	.200	0	39	168	**358**	**39**	**17**	**4.0**	.931	D. White	36	260	17	13	0	1.76
RF	D. Green	379	.243	0	44	119	9	12	3	1.3	.914	E. Walsh	22	137	8	3	0	2.17
CF	F. Jones	568	.245	2	38	337	21	11	5	2.4	.970	R. Patterson	13	89	4	6	0	1.83
LF	D. Holmes	328	.201	0	22	150	11	11	1	1.9	.936							
C	B. Sullivan	323	.201	2	26	389	104	13	8	5.4	.974							
OF	N. Callahan	345	.272	1	43	120	10	6	0	1.5	.956							
UT	F. Isbell	341	.296	2	45	219	136	13	18		.965							
C	E. McFarland	250	.280	0	31	343	88	12	8	6.3	.973							

Detroit

W-79 L-74

Bill Armour

POS	Player	AB	BA	HR	RBI	PO	A	E	DP	TC/G	FA	Pitcher	G	IP	W	L	SV	ERA
1B	P. Lindsay	329	.267	0	31	761	57	18	40	9.5	.978	G. Mullin	44	**348**	21	21	0	2.51
2B	G. Schaefer	554	.244	2	47	**403**	389	37	35	5.5	.955	E. Killian	39	313	23	14	0	2.27
SS	C. O'Leary	512	.213	1	33	358	411	55	40	5.6	.933	W. Donovan	34	281	18	15	0	2.60
3B	B. Coughlin	489	.252	0	44	137	255	37	12	3.1	.914	F. Kitson	33	226	12	14	1	3.47
RF	S. Crawford	575	.297	6	75	152	18	2	3	1.7	.988							
CF	D. Cooley	377	.247	1	32	223	12	10	5	2.5	.959							
LF	M. McIntyre	495	.263	0	30	286	18	10	6	2.4	.968							
C	L. Drill	211	.261	0	24	345	73	13	10	6.2	.970							
OF	P. Hickman	213	.221	2	20	72	7	5	3	1.8	.940							
UT	B. Lowe	181	.193	0	9	93	54	4	1		.974							

Boston

W-78 L-74

Jimmy Collins

POS	Player	AB	BA	HR	RBI	PO	A	E	DP	TC/G	FA	Pitcher	G	IP	W	L	SV	ERA
1B	M. Grimshaw	285	.239	4	35	768	35	16	35	11.1	.980	C. Young	38	321	18	19	0	1.82
2B	H. Ferris	523	.220	6	59	320	**424**	30	38	**5.5**	.961	J. Tannehill	37	272	22	9	0	2.48
SS	F. Parent	602	.234	0	33	294	461	**66**	48	5.4	.920	G. Winter	35	264	16	17	0	2.96
3B	J. Collins	508	.276	4	65	164	268	36	12	3.6	.923	B. Dinneen	31	244	12	14	1	3.73
RF	K. Selbach	418	.246	4	47	186	8	15	1	1.8	.928	N. Gibson	23	134	4	7	0	3.69
CF	C. Stahl	500	.258	0	47	249	11	6	4	2.0	.977							
LF	J. Burkett	573	.257	4	47	276	11	22	0	2.1	.929							
C	L. Criger	313	.198	1	36	539	**147**	20	5	6.5	.972							
10	B. Freeman	455	.240	3	49	647	25	19	20		.973							

Cleveland

W-76 L-78

Nap Lajoie
W-37 L-21

Bill Bradley
W-20 L-21

Nap Lajoie
W-19 L-36

POS	Player	AB	BA	HR	RBI	PO	A	E	DP	TC/G	FA	Pitcher	G	IP	W	L	SV	ERA
1B	C. Carr	306	.235	1	31	940	50	9	33	11.5	.991	A. Joss	33	286	20	12	0	2.01
2B	N. Lajoie	249	.329	2	41	148	177	3	25	5.6	.991	E. Moore	31	269	15	15	0	2.64
SS	T. Turner	582	.263	4	72	285	430	41	49	4.9	.946	B. Rhoads	28	235	16	9	0	2.83
3B	B. Bradley	537	.268	0	51	**187**	312	29	**17**	3.6	**.945**	O. Hess	26	214	10	15	0	3.16
RF	E. Flick	496	**.306**	4	64	177	18	13	3	1.6	.938	B. Bernhard	22	174	7	13	0	3.36
CF	H. Bay	550	.298	0	22	303	14	10	4	2.3	.969	R. Donahue	20	138	6	12	0	3.40
LF	J. Jackson	421	.257	2	31	191	16	11	3	2.1	.950							
C	F. Buelow	236	.174	1	18	262	72	13	4	5.9	.963							
12	G. Stovall	419	.272	1	47	745	160	30	35		.968							
C	H. Bemis	226	.292	0	28	256	52	9	4	5.5	.972							
OP	O. Hess	175	.251	2	13	74	67	9	2		.940							
2B	N. Kahl	131	.221	0	21	60	94	9	3	5.3	.945							

AMERICAN LEAGUE 1905, *cont.*

New York

W-71 L-78

Clark Griffith

POS	Player	AB	BA	HR	RBI	PO	A	E	DP	TC/G	FA	Pitcher	G	IP	W	L	SV	ERA
1B	H. Chase	465	.249	3	49	1171	61	**31**	63	10.4	.975	A. Orth	40	305	18	16	0	2.86
2B	J. Williams	470	.228	6	60	335	332	25	**51**	5.4	.964	J. Chesbro	41	303	19	15	0	2.20
SS	K. Elberfeld	390	.262	0	53	244	317	57	35	5.7	.908	B. Hogg	39	205	9	13	1	3.20
3B	J. Yeager	401	.267	0	42	103	173	23	6	3.3	.923	J. Powell	37	202	8	13	1	3.52
RF	W. Keeler	560	.302	4	38	194	17	7	1	1.6	.968	C. Griffith	25	103	9	6	1	1.67
CF	D. Fultz	422	.232	0	42	252	14	9	2	2.3	.967	A. Puttmann	17	86	2	7	1	4.27
LF	P. Dougherty	418	.263	3	29	173	11	21	2	1.9	.898							
C	R. Kleinow	253	.221	1	24	361	82	10	4	5.5	.978							
UT	W. Conroy	385	.273	2	25	287	142	24	14		.947							
C	D. McGuire	228	.219	0	33	366	69	11	4	6.3	.975							
OF	E. Hahn	160	.319	0	11	83	5	4	1	2.1	.957							

Washington

W-64 L-87

Jake Stahl

POS	Player	AB	BA	HR	RBI	PO	A	E	DP	TC/G	FA	Pitcher	G	IP	W	L	SV	ERA
1B	J. Stahl	501	.244	5	66	1593	94	21	51	**12.2**	.988	C. Patten	42	310	14	22	0	3.14
2B	P. Hickman	360	.311	2	46	170	281	38*	19	5.8	.922	L. Hughes	39	291	17	20	1	2.35
SS	J. Cassidy	576	.215	1	43	308	**520**	**66**	50	5.9	.926	J. Townsend	34	263	7	16	0	2.63
3B	H. Hill	374	.209	1	24	130	206	34	10	3.6	.908	B. Wolfe	28	182	9	13	**2**	2.57
RF	J. Anderson	400	.290	1	38	161	7	7	1	2.0	.960	B. Jacobson	22	144	7	8	0	3.30
CF	C. Jones	544	.208	2	41	240	24	11	6	1.9	.960							
LF	F. Huelsman	421	.271	3	62	189	7	15	2	1.7	.929							
C	M. Heydon	245	.192	1	26	368	125	**23**	7	6.7	.955							
32	R. Nill	319	.182	3	31	138	188	28	15		.921							
OF	P. Knoll	244	.213	0	29	101	8	8	1	1.7	.932							
C	M. Kittridge	238	.164	0	14	323	113	10	8	5.9	.978							
2B	J. Mullin	163	.190	0	13	83	97	14	8	5.0	.928							

St. Louis

W-54 L-99

Jimmy McAleer

POS	Player	AB	BA	HR	RBI	PO	A	E	DP	TC/G	FA	Pitcher	G	IP	W	L	SV	ERA
1B	T. Jones	504	.242	0	48	1502	105	25	52	12.1	.985	H. Howell	38	323	15	22	0	1.98
2B	I. Rockenfield	322	.217	0	16	210	255	37	19	5.3	.926	F. Glade	32	275	6	**25**	0	2.81
SS	B. Wallace	587	.271	1	59	**385**	506	62	40	**6.1**	.935	B. Pelty	31	259	14	14	0	2.75
3B	H. Gleason	535	.217	1	57	118	271	38	8	3.0	.911	W. Sudhoff	32	244	10	20	0	2.99
RF	E. Frisk	429	.261	3	36	117	15	11	2	1.2	.923	J. Buchanan	22	141	5	9	**2**	3.50
CF	B. Koehler	536	.237	2	47	227	24	8	11	2.0	.969							
LF	G. Stone	**632**	.296	7	52	278	15	14	5	2.0	.954							
C	J. Sugden	266	.173	0	23	407	112	9	6	7.4	.983							
OF	J. Van Zandt	322	.233	1	20	69	7	11	0	1.2	.874							

BATTING AND BASE RUNNING LEADERS

Batting Average

E. Flick, CLE	.306
W. Keeler, NY	.302
H. Bay, CLE	.298
S. Crawford, DET	.297
F. Isbell, CHI	.296

Slugging Average

E. Flick, CLE	.466
F. Isbell, CHI	.440
S. Crawford, DET	.433
H. Davis, PHI	.422
G. Stone, STL	.410

Home Runs

H. Davis, PHI	8
G. Stone, STL	7

Total Bases

G. Stone, STL	259
H. Davis, PHI	254
S. Crawford, DET	249
P. Hickman, DET, WAS	232
E. Flick, CLE	231

Runs Batted In

H. Davis, PHI	83
L. Cross, PHI	77
J. Donahue, CHI	76
S. Crawford, DET	75
T. Turner, CLE	72

Stolen Bases

D. Hoffman, PHI	46
D. Fultz, NY	44
J. Stahl, WAS	41
T. Hartsel, PHI	36
H. Bay, CLE	36
H. Davis, PHI	36

Hits

G. Stone, STL	187
S. Crawford, DET	171
H. Davis, PHI	171
W. Keeler, NY	169

Base on Balls

T. Hartsel, PHI	121
F. Jones, CHI	73
K. Selbach, BOS	67
J. Burkett, BOS	67

Home Run Percentage

H. Davis, PHI	1.3
J. Williams, NY	1.3
S. Seybold, PHI	1.2
H. Ferris, BOS	1.1

Runs

H. Davis, PHI	92
F. Jones, CHI	91
H. Bay, CLE	90
T. Hartsel, PHI	88

Doubles

H. Davis, PHI	47
S. Crawford, DET	40
S. Seybold, PHI	37
P. Hickman, DET, WAS	37

Triples

E. Flick, CLE	19
H. Ferris, BOS	16
T. Turner, CLE	14
J. Burkett, BOS	13
G. Stone, STL	13

PITCHING LEADERS

Winning Percentage

R. Waddell, PHI	.730
J. Tannehill, BOS	.710
A. Coakley, PHI	.692
E. Plank, PHI	.667
N. Altrock, CHI	.657

Earned Run Average

R. Waddell, PHI	1.48
D. White, CHI	1.76
C. Young, BOS	1.82
A. Coakley, PHI	1.84
N. Altrock, CHI	1.88

Wins

R. Waddell, PHI	27
E. Plank, PHI	24
E. Killian, DET	23
N. Altrock, CHI	23
J. Tannehill, BOS	22

Saves

J. Buchanan, STL	2
B. Wolfe, WAS	2

Strikeouts

R. Waddell, PHI	287
C. Young, BOS	210
E. Plank, PHI	210
H. Howell, STL	198
F. Smith, CHI	171

Complete Games

E. Plank, PHI	36
H. Howell, STL	35
G. Mullin, DET	35
E. Killian, DET	33
C. Young, BOS	32
F. Owen, CHI	32

Fewest Hits/9 Innings

R. Waddell, PHI	6.33
F. Smith, CHI	6.63
C. Young, BOS	6.96
H. Howell, STL	7.02

Shutouts

E. Killian, DET	8
R. Waddell, PHI	7
J. Tannehill, BOS	6
A. Orth, NY	6

Fewest Walks/9 Innings

C. Young, BOS	0.84
A. Joss, CLE	1.45
F. Owen, CHI	1.51
R. Donahue, CLE	1.63

Most Strikeouts/9 Inn.

R. Waddell, PHI	7.86
C. Young, BOS	5.89
C. Bender, PHI	5.58
H. Howell, STL	5.52

Innings

G. Mullin, DET	348
E. Plank, PHI	347
F. Owen, CHI	334
R. Waddell, PHI	329

Games Pitched

R. Waddell, PHI	46
G. Mullin, DET	44
C. Patten, WAS	42
F. Owen, CHI	42

							Batting						Fielding			Pitching					
	W	L	PCT	GB	R	OR	2B	3B	HR	BA	SA	SB	E	DP	FA	CG	BB	SO	ShO	SV	ERA
Philadelphia	92	56	.622		**623**	492	**256**	51	24	**.255**	**.339**	189	264	64	.958	117	409	**895**	**20**	0	2.19
Chicago	92	60	.605	2	612	**451**	200	55	11	.237	.304	194	**217**	**95**	**.968**	131	329	613	17	0	**1.99**
Detroit	79	74	.516	15.5	512	602	190	54	14	.243	.312	129	265	80	.957	124	474	578	17	1	2.83
Boston	78	74	.513	16	579	564	165	69	**29**	.234	.311	131	294	75	.953	125	**292**	652	15	1	2.84
Cleveland	76	78	.494	19	567	587	211	**72**	18	**.255**	.335	188	229	84	.963	**139**	334	555	16	0	2.85
New York	71	78	.477	21.5	586	622	163	61	23	.248	.319	**200**	293	88	.952	88	396	642	19	**4**	2.93
Washington	64	87	.424	29.5	559	623	193	68	22	.223	.302	169	318	76	.951	118	385	539	11	3	2.87
St. Louis	54	99	.353	40.5	511	608	153	49	16	.232	.289	130	295	78	.955	133	389	633	11	2	2.74
					4549	4549	1531	479	157	.241	.314	1330	2175	640	.957	975	3008	5107	126	11	2.65

NATIONAL LEAGUE 1906

Chicago

W-116 L-36

Frank Chance

POS	Player	AB	BA	HR	RBI	PO	A	E	DP	TC/G	FA
1B	F. Chance	474	.319	3	71	1376	82	16	71	10.8	.989
2B	J. Evers	533	.255	1	51	**344**	441	**44**	51	5.4	.947
SS	J. Tinker	523	.233	1	64	288	472	45	55	5.5	**.944**
3B	H. Steinfeldt	539	.327	3	**83**	160	253	20	13	2.9	**.954**
RF	W. Schulte	563	.281	7	60	218	18	6	7	1.7	.975
CF	J. Slagle	498	.239	0	33	276	9	7	5	2.3	.976
LF	J. Sheckard	549	.262	1	45	264	13	4	1	1.9	.986
C	J. Kling	343	.312	2	46	**520**	126	12	7	**6.9**	**.982**
C	P. Moran	226	.252	0	35	335	78	9	6	6.9	.979
UT	S. Hofman	195	.256	2	20	253	52	7	18		.978

Pitcher	G	IP	W	L	SV	ERA
T. Brown	36	277	26	6	3	**1.04**
J. Pfiester	31	242	20	8	0	1.56
E. Reulbach	33	218	19	4	2	1.65
C. Lundgren	27	208	17	6	2	2.21
J. Taylor	17	147	12	3	0	1.83
O. Overall	18	144	12	3	1	1.88

New York

W-96 L-56

John McGraw

POS	Player	AB	BA	HR	RBI	PO	A	E	DP	TC/G	FA
1B	D. McGann	451	.237	0	37	1391	83	8	61	11.1	**.995**
2B	B. Gilbert	307	.231	1	27	223	324	35	32	**5.9**	.940
SS	B. Dahlen	471	.240	1	49	287	454	49	36	5.5	.938
3B	A. Devlin	498	.299	2	65	171	**355**	31	22	3.8	.944
RF	G. Browne	477	.264	0	38	153	17	12	3	1.5	.934
CF	C. Seymour	269	.320	4	42	129	7	3	3	1.9	.978
LF	S. Shannon	287	.254	0	25	109	4	5	2	1.6	.958
C	R. Bresnahan	405	.281	0	43	407	125	14	6	6.7	.974
20	S. Strang	313	.319	4	49	176	175	21	13		.944
C	F. Bowerman	285	.228	1	42	300	80	6	8	5.8	.984
OF	S. Mertes	253	.237	1	33	119	10	4	0	1.9	.970

Pitcher	G	IP	W	L	SV	ERA
J. McGinnity	**45**	340	**27**	12	2	2.25
C. Mathewson	38	267	22	12	1	2.97
H. Wiltse	38	249	16	11	5	2.27
D. Taylor	31	213	17	9	0	2.20
R. Ames	31	203	12	10	1	2.66

Pittsburgh

W-93 L-60

Fred Clarke

POS	Player	AB	BA	HR	RBI	PO	A	E	DP	TC/G	FA
1B	J. Nealon	556	.255	3	**83**	**1592**	102	23	**90**	11.1	.987
2B	C. Ritchey	484	.269	1	62	326	439	27	59	5.2	**.966**
SS	H. Wagner	516	**.339**	2	71	334	473	51	**57**	6.3	.941
3B	T. Sheehan	315	.241	1	34	104	166	15	11	3.2	.947
RF	B. Ganley	511	.258	0	31	207	16	8	5	1.7	.965
CF	G. Beaumont	310	.265	2	32	148	6	9	2	2.1	.945
LF	F. Clarke	417	.309	1	39	209	15	6	3	2.1	.974
C	G. Gibson	259	.178	0	20	336	97	13	**10**	5.5	.971
30	T. Leach	476	.286	1	39	204	141	20	4		.945
OF	D. Meier	273	.256	0	16	73	5	2	2	1.5	.975
C	H. Peitz	125	.240	0	20	186	45	5	2	6.2	.979

Pitcher	G	IP	W	L	SV	ERA
V. Willis	41	322	22	13	1	1.73
S. Leever	36	260	22	7	0	2.32
L. Leifield	37	256	18	13	1	1.87
D. Phillippe	33	219	15	10	0	2.47
M. Lynch	18	119	6	5	0	2.42

Philadelphia

W-71 L-82

Hugh Duffy

POS	Player	AB	BA	HR	RBI	PO	A	E	DP	TC/G	FA
1B	K. Bransfield	524	.275	1	60	1318	88	29	57	10.3	.980
2B	K. Gleason	494	.227	0	34	215	358	32	39	4.5	.947
SS	M. Doolan	535	.230	1	55	**395**	**480**	**66**	51	6.1	.930
3B	E. Courtney	398	.236	0	42	113	163	23	9	3.1	.923
RF	J. Titus	484	.267	1	57	236	23	7	7	1.9	.974
CF	R. Thomas	493	.254	0	16	340	12	5	5	2.5	.986
LF	S. Magee	563	.282	6	67	316	18	6	2	2.2	.982
C	R. Dooin	351	.245	0	32	475	111	**32**	9	5.8	.948
PO	J. Lush	212	.264	0	15	59	92	12	3		.926
32	P. Sentell	192	.229	1	14	70	105	19	4		.902
C	J. Donovan	166	.199	0	15	222	52	13	4	5.5	.955

Pitcher	G	IP	W	L	SV	ERA
T. Sparks	42	317	19	16	3	2.16
J. Lush	37	281	18	15	0	2.37
B. Duggleby	42	280	13	19	2	2.25
L. Richie	33	206	9	11	0	2.41
T. Pittinger	20	130	8	10	0	3.40

Brooklyn

W-66 L-86

Patsy Donovan

POS	Player	AB	BA	HR	RBI	PO	A	E	DP	TC/G	FA
1B	T. Jordan	450	.262	**12**	78	1240	64	**30**	44	10.6	.978
2B	W. Alperman	441	.252	3	46	245	308	35	25	5.7	.940
SS	P. Lewis	452	.243	0	37	244	393	54	35	5.1	.922
3B	D. Casey	571	.233	0	34	172	272	39	11	3.2	.919
RF	H. Lumley	484	.324	9	61	231	13	13	5	2.0	.949
CF	B. Maloney	566	.221	0	32	355	19	13	6	2.6	.966
LF	J. McCarthy	322	.304	0	35	158	13	14	1	2.2	.924
C	B. Bergen	353	.159	0	19	485	**149**	15	9	6.3	.977
UT	J. Hummel	286	.199	1	21	310	156	18	25		.963
C	L. Ritter	226	.208	0	15	211	61	6	4	5.2	.978
OF	E. Batch	203	.256	0	11	101	5	4	0	2.2	.964

Pitcher	G	IP	W	L	SV	ERA
E. Stricklett	41	292	14	18	5	2.72
D. Scanlan	38	288	18	13	1	3.19
H. McIntire	39	276	13	21	3	2.97
M. Eason	34	227	10	17	0	3.25
J. Pastorius	29	212	10	14	0	3.61

Cincinnati

W-64 L-87

Ned Hanlon

POS	Player	AB	BA	HR	RBI	PO	A	E	DP	TC/G	FA
1B	S. Deal	231	.208	0	21	624	46	10	25	10.5	.985
2B	M. Huggins	545	.292	0	26	341	**458**	**44**	**62**	5.8	.948
SS	T. Corcoran	430	.207	1	33	263	379	40	51	5.8	.941
3B	J. Delahanty	379	.280	1	39	136	170	33	4	3.2	.903
RF	F. Jude	308	.208	1	31	95	14	4	1	1.4	.965
CF	C. Seymour	307	.257	4	38	202	10	7	3	2.8	.968
LF	J. Kelley	465	.228	1	53	184	13	7	5	1.7	.966
C	A. Schlei	388	.245	4	54	455	139	24	8	6.8	.961
10	S. Barry	279	.287	1	33	481	32	8	24		.985
UT	H. Lobert	268	.310	0	19	118	178	20	8		.937
OF	H. Smoot	220	.259	1	17	109	10	7	0	2.1	.944
OF	F. Odwell	202	.223	0	21	94	10	4	0	1.9	.963

Pitcher	G	IP	W	L	SV	ERA
J. Weimer	41	305	20	14	1	2.22
B. Ewing	33	288	13	14	0	2.38
C. Fraser	31	236	10	20	0	2.67
B. Wicker	20	150	6	14	0	2.70
C. Hall	14	95	4	6	1	3.32

St. Louis

W-52 L-98

John McCloskey

POS	Player	AB	BA	HR	RBI	PO	A	E	DP	TC/G	FA
1B	J. Beckley	320	.247	0	44	928	43	13	38	11.6	.987
2B	P. Bennett	**595**	.262	1	34	295	447	41	43	5.1	.948
SS	G. McBride	313	.169	0	13	194	310	30	33	5.9	.944
3B	H. Arndt	256	.270	2	26	108	139	9	15	3.9	.965
RF	A. Burch	335	.266	0	11	155	15	12	6	2.0	.934
CF	H. Smoot	343	.248	0	31	174	8	9	4	2.2	.953
LF	S. Shannon	302	.258	0	25	165	9	5	3	2.2	.972
C	M. Grady	280	.250	3	27	115	67	5	9	3.1	.973
UT	A. Hoelskoetter	317	.224	0	14	109	173	19	10		.937
01	S. Barry	237	.249	0	12	261	16	11	9		.962
OF	S. Mertes	191	.246	0	19	77	4	10	0	1.7	.890
OF	J. Himes	155	.271	0	14	76	10	2	2	2.2	.977

Pitcher	G	IP	W	L	SV	ERA
B. Brown	32	238	8	16	0	2.64
E. Karger	25	192	5	16	1	2.72
F. Beebe	20	161	9	9	0	3.02
J. Taylor	17	155	8	9	0	2.15
C. Druhot	15	130	6	7	0	2.62
G. Thompson	17	103	2	11	0	4.28
W. Egan	16	86	2	9	0	4.59

NATIONAL LEAGUE 1906, *cont.*

Boston

W-49 L-102

Fred Tenney

POS	Player	AB	BA	HR	RBI	PO	A	E	DP	TC/G	FA
1B	F. Tenney	544	.283	1	28	1456	**118**	28	78	**11.2**	.983
2B	A. Strobel	317	.202	1	24	181	259	25	32	5.0	.946
SS	A. Bridwell	459	.227	0	22	322	390	54	43	**6.4**	.930
3B	D. Brain	525	.250	5	45	**208**	321	**48**	**26**	**4.2**	.917
RF	C. Dolan	549	.248	0	39	207	26	18	4	1.7	.928
CF	J. Bates	504	.252	6	54	238	12	11	4	1.9	.958
LF	D. Howard	545	.261	1	54	118	14	13	3	1.7	.910
C	T. Needham	285	.189	1	12	317	114	17	9	5.9	.962
UT	S. Brown	231	.208	0	20	235	88	13	5		.961
C	J. O'Neill	167	.180	0	4	259	72	10	6	7.1	.971
P	B. Pfeffer	158	.196	1	11	13	91	4	0	3.1	.963

Pitcher	G	IP	W	L	SV	ERA
I. Young	43	**358**	16	25	0	2.91
V. Lindaman	39	307	12	23	0	2.43
B. Pfeffer	35	302	13	22	0	2.95
G. Dorner	34	257	8	25*	0	3.88

BATTING AND BASE RUNNING LEADERS

Batting Average
H. Wagner, PIT .339
H. Steinfeldt, CHI .327
H. Lumley, BKN .324
S. Strang, NY .319
F. Chance, CHI .319

Slugging Average
H. Lumley, BKN .477
H. Wagner, PIT .459
S. Strang, NY .435
H. Steinfeldt, CHI .430
F. Chance, CHI .430

Home Runs
T. Jordan, BKN 12
H. Lumley, BKN 9
C. Seymour, CIN, NY 8
W. Schulte, CHI 7
J. Bates, BOS 6
S. Magee, PHI 6

Total Bases
H. Wagner, PIT 237
H. Steinfeldt, CHI 232
H. Lumley, BKN 231
S. Magee, PHI 229
W. Schulte, CHI 223

Runs Batted In
H. Steinfeldt, CHI 83
J. Nealon, PIT 83
C. Seymour, CIN, NY 80
T. Jordan, BKN 78
F. Chance, CHI 71
H. Wagner, PIT 71

Stolen Bases
F. Chance, CHI 57
S. Magee, PHI 55
A. Devlin, NY 54
H. Wagner, PIT 53
J. Evers, CHI 49

Hits
H. Steinfeldt, CHI 176
H. Wagner, PIT 175
C. Seymour, CIN, NY 165
M. Huggins, CIN 159
S. Magee, PHI 159

Base on Balls
R. Thomas, PHI 107
R. Bresnahan, NY 81
J. Titus, PHI 78
B. Dahlen, NY 76

Home Run Percentage
T. Jordan, BKN 2.7
H. Lumley, BKN 1.9
C. Seymour, CIN, NY 1.4
S. Strang, NY 1.3

Runs
F. Chance, CHI 103
H. Wagner, PIT 103
J. Sheckard, CHI 90
J. Nealon, PIT 82

Doubles
H. Wagner, PIT 38
S. Magee, PHI 36
K. Bransfield, PHI 28
H. Steinfeldt, CHI 27
J. Sheckard, CHI 27

Triples
F. Clarke, PIT 13
W. Schulte, CHI 13
H. Lumley, BKN 12
J. Nealon, PIT 12

PITCHING LEADERS

Winning Percentage
E. Reulbach, CHI .826
T. Brown, CHI .813
S. Leever, PIT .759
C. Lundgren, CHI .739
J. Pfiester, CHI .714

Earned Run Average
T. Brown, CHI 1.04
J. Pfiester, CHI 1.56
E. Reulbach, CHI 1.65
V. Willis, PIT 1.73
L. Leifield, PIT 1.87

Wins
J. McGinnity, NY 27
T. Brown, CHI 26
S. Leever, PIT 22
C. Mathewson, NY 22
V. Willis, PIT 22

Saves
G. Ferguson, NY 6
E. Stricklett, BKN 5
H. Wiltse, NY 5

Strikeouts
F. Beebe, CHI, STL 171
B. Pfeffer, BOS 158
R. Ames, NY 156
J. Pfiester, CHI 153
J. Lush, PHI 151
I. Young, BOS 151

Complete Games
I. Young, BOS 37
B. Pfeffer, BOS 33
J. Taylor, STL, CHI 32
V. Willis, PIT 32
V. Lindaman, BOS 32
J. McGinnity, NY 32

Fewest Hits/9 Innings
E. Reulbach, CHI 5.33
T. Brown, CHI 6.43
J. Pfiester, CHI 6.44
F. Beebe, CHI, STL 6.67

Shutouts
T. Brown, CHI 9
L. Leifield, PIT 8

Fewest Walks/9 Innings
D. Phillippe, PIT 1.07
S. Leever, PIT 1.66
T. Sparks, PHI 1.76
B. Ewing, CIN 1.88

Most Strikeouts/9 Inn.
R. Ames, NY 6.90
F. Beebe, CHI, STL 6.67
J. Pfiester, CHI 5.70
O. Overall, CIN, CHI 5.05

Innings
I. Young, BOS 358
J. McGinnity, NY 340
V. Willis, PIT 322
T. Sparks, PHI 317

Games Pitched
J. McGinnity, NY 45
I. Young, BOS 43
B. Duggleby, PHI 42
T. Sparks, PHI 42

							Batting						Fielding			Pitching					
	W	L	PCT	GB	R	OR	2B	3B	HR	BA	SA	SB	E	DP	FA	CG	BB	SO	ShO	SV	ERA
Chicago	116	36	.763		**705**	**381**	181	**71**	20	**.262**	**.339**	283	**194**	100	**.969**	125	446	**702**	**30**	9	**1.76**
New York	96	56	.632	20	625	510	162	53	15	.255	.321	**288**	233	84	.963	105	394	639	19	**16**	2.49
Pittsburgh	93	60	.608	23.5	623	470	164	67	12	.261	.327	162	228	**109**	.964	116	**309**	532	27	2	2.21
Philadelphia	71	82	.464	45.5	528	564	**197**	47	12	.241	.307	180	271	83	.956	108	436	500	21	5	2.58
Brooklyn	66	86	.434	50	496	625	141	68	**25**	.236	.308	175	283	73	.955	119	453	476	22	9	3.13
Cincinnati	64	87	.424	51.5	533	582	140	**71**	16	.238	.304	170	262	97	.959	126	470	567	11	5	2.69
St. Louis	52	98	.347	63	470	607	137	69	10	.235	.296	110	272	92	.957	118	479	559	4	2	3.04
Boston	49	102	.325	66.5	408	649	136	43	16	.226	.281	93	337	102	.947	**137**	436	562	10	0	3.17
					4388	4388	1258	489	126	.244	.310	1461	2080	740	.959	954	3423	4537	144	48	2.63

AMERICAN LEAGUE 1906

Chicago

W-93 L-58

Fielder Jones

POS	Player	AB	BA	HR	RBI	PO	A	E	DP	TC/G	FA
1B	J. Donahue	556	.257	1	57	**1697**	**118**	22	62	**11.9**	**.988**
2B	F. Isbell	549	.279	0	57	292	363	35	36	5.2	.949
SS	G. Davis	484	.277	0	80	263	475	42	44	6.0	.946
3B	L. Tannehill	378	.183	0	33	131	**278**	21	12	**4.3**	.951
RF	B. O'Neill	330	.248	1	21	118	12	7	1	1.5	.949
CF	F. Jones	496	.230	2	34	312	23	4	5	2.4	.988
LF	E. Hahn	484	.227	0	27	164	21	10	3	1.5	.949
C	B. Sullivan	387	.214	2	33	475	134	16	7	5.3	**.974**
OF	P. Dougherty	253	.233	1	27	118	10	2	1	1.8	.985
3B	G. Rohe	225	.258	0	25	66	122	15	6	3.6	.926

Pitcher	G	IP	W	L	SV	ERA
F. Owen	42	293	22	13	2	2.33
N. Altrock	38	288	20	13	0	2.06
E. Walsh	41	278	17	13	1	1.88
D. White	28	219	18	6	0	**1.52**
R. Patterson	21	142	10	7	1	2.09
F. Smith	20	122	5	5	1	3.39

AMERICAN LEAGUE 1906, *cont.*

New York

W-90 L-61

Clark Griffith

POS	Player	AB	BA	HR	RBI	PO	A	E	DP	TC/G	FA	Pitcher	G	IP	W	L	SV	ERA
1B	H. Chase	597	.323	0	76	1504	89	33	54	10.8	.980	A. Orth	45	**339**	**27**	17	0	2.34
2B	J. Williams	501	.277	3	77	336	412	32	34	5.6	.959	J. Chesbro	**49**	325	23	17	1	2.96
SS	K. Elberfeld	346	.306	2	31	200	317	42	18	5.7	.925	B. Hogg	28	206	14	13	0	2.93
3B	F. LaPorte	454	.264	2	54	118	210	35	11	3.2	.904	W. Clarkson	32	151	9	4	0	2.32
RF	W. Keeler	592	.304	2	33	213	16	3	3	1.5	.987	D. Newton	21	125	7	5	0	3.17
CF	D. Hoffman	320	.256	0	23	176	7	12	1	2.0	.938							
LF	F. Delahanty	307	.238	2	41	180	7	9	1	2.1	.954							
C	R. Kleinow	268	.220	0	31	381	102	13	**8**	5.2	.974							
OS	W. Conroy	567	.245	4	54	295	154	21	15		.955							
3O	G. Moriarty	197	.234	0	23	78	79	15	3		.913							

Cleveland

W-89 L-64

Nap Lajoie

POS	Player	AB	BA	HR	RBI	PO	A	E	DP	TC/G	FA	Pitcher	G	IP	W	L	SV	ERA
1B	C. Rossman	396	.308	1	53	1145	45	19	47	11.5	.984	O. Hess	43	334	20	17	**3**	1.83
2B	N. Lajoie	602	.355	0	91	**354**	**415**	21	**76**	6.1	**.973**	B. Rhoads	38	315	22	10	0	1.80
SS	T. Turner	584	.291	2	62	287	**570**	36	**61**	6.1	**.960**	A. Joss	34	282	21	9	1	1.72
3B	B. Bradley	302	.275	2	25	107	177	10	6	3.6	.966	B. Bernhard	31	255	16	15	0	2.54
RF	B. Congalton	419	.320	2	50	174	6	8	0	1.6	.957	J. Townsend	17	93	3	7	0	2.91
CF	E. Flick	**624**	.311	1	62	248	13	5	4	1.8	.981							
LF	J. Jackson	374	.214	0	38	189	5	5	2	1.9	.975							
C	H. Bemis	297	.276	2	30	340	73	16	7	5.3	.963							
UT	G. Stovall	443	.273	0	37	666	153	21	53		.975							
OF	H. Bay	280	.275	0	14	131	8	3	2	2.1	.979							
C	N. Clarke	179	.358	1	21	211	58	5	4	5.1	.982							
P	O. Hess	154	.201	0	11	25	86	6	4	2.7	.949							

Philadelphia

W-78 L-67

Connie Mack

POS	Player	AB	BA	HR	RBI	PO	A	E	DP	TC/G	FA	Pitcher	G	IP	W	L	SV	ERA
1B	H. Davis	551	.292	**12**	**96**	1352	91	**37**	**66**	10.2	.975	R. Waddell	43	273	15	17	0	2.21
2B	D. Murphy	448	.301	2	60	239	308	26	38	4.8	.955	C. Bender	36	238	15	10	**3**	2.53
SS	M. Cross	445	.200	1	40	305	411	47	48	5.7	.938	J. Dygert	35	214	11	13	0	2.70
3B	J. Knight	253	.194	3	20	71	130	17	6	3.3	.922	E. Plank	26	212	19	6	0	2.25
RF	S. Seybold	411	.316	5	59	150	10	13	3	1.5	.925	J. Coombs	23	173	10	10	0	2.50
CF	B. Lord	434	.233	1	44	212	13	14	4	2.1	.941	A. Coakley	22	149	7	8	0	3.14
LF	T. Hartsel	533	.255	1	30	238	15	8	5	1.8	.969							
C	O. Schreckengost	338	.284	1	41	**532**	110	19	7	**7.4**	.971							
OF	H. Armbruster	265	.238	2	24	124	9	4	1	1.9	.971							
C	M. Powers	185	.157	0	7	297	79	10	2	6.8	.974							
3B	R. Oldring	174	.241	0	19	53	87	16	5	3.2	.897							

St. Louis

W-76 L-73

Jimmy McAleer

POS	Player	AB	BA	HR	RBI	PO	A	E	DP	TC/G	FA	Pitcher	G	IP	W	L	SV	ERA
1B	T. Jones	539	.252	0	30	1476	116	25	55	11.3	.985	H. Howell	35	277	15	14	1	2.11
2B	P. O'Brien	524	.233	2	57	254	274	**38**	31	4.7	.933	F. Glade	35	267	15	14	1	2.36
SS	B. Wallace	476	.258	2	67	309	461	41	47	5.9	.949	B. Pelty	34	261	16	11	2	1.59
3B	R. Hartzell	404	.213	0	24	119	209	**41**	11	3.6	.889	J. Powell	28	244	13	14	1	1.77
RF	H. Niles	541	.229	2	31	140	34	6	5	1.7	.967	B. Jacobson	24	155	9	9	0	2.50
CF	C. Hemphill	585	.289	4	62	304	17	13	1	2.2	.961	E. Smith	19	155	8	11	0	3.72
LF	G. Stone	581	**.358**	6	71	295	10	10	3	2.0	.968							
C	J. O'Connor	174	.190	0	11	248	64	3	2	5.8	.990							
C	B. Rickey	201	.284	3	24	233	58	14	2	5.6	.954							
C	T. Spencer	188	.176	0	17	226	60	**20**	3	5.7	.935							
OF	B. Koehler	186	.220	0	15	81	8	4	4	1.8	.957							

Detroit

W-71 L-78

Bill Armour

POS	Player	AB	BA	HR	RBI	PO	A	E	DP	TC/G	FA	Pitcher	G	IP	W	L	SV	ERA
1B	P. Lindsay	499	.224	0	33	1122	66	28	55	10.0	.977	G. Mullin	40	330	21	18	0	2.78
2B	G. Schaefer	446	.238	2	42	348	328	37	42	**6.3**	.948	R. Donahue	28	241	13	14	0	2.73
SS	C. O'Leary	443	.219	2	34	**326**	398	**58**	37	**6.2**	.926	E. Siever	30	223	14	11	0	2.71
3B	B. Coughlin	498	.235	2	60	**188**	265	29	**16**	3.3	.940	W. Donovan	25	212	9	15	0	3.15
RF	S. Crawford	563	.295	2	72	171	19	3	2	1.7	.984	E. Killian	21	150	10	6	2	3.43
CF	T. Cobb	350	.320	1	41	208	14	9	4	2.4	.961	J. Eubank	24	135	4	10	2	3.53
LF	M. McIntyre	493	.260	0	39	254	25	5	8	2.1	.982							
C	B. Schmidt	216	.218	0	10	257	104	16	4	5.6	.958							
OF	D. Jones	323	.260	0	24	193	10	4	3	2.5	.981							
C	F. Payne	222	.270	0	20	177	49	8	3	5.0	.966							

Washington

W-55 L-95

Jake Stahl

POS	Player	AB	BA	HR	RBI	PO	A	E	DP	TC/G	FA	Pitcher	G	IP	W	L	SV	ERA
1B	J. Stahl	482	.222	0	51	1322	78	24	51	10.5	.983	C. Falkenberg	40	299	14	20	1	2.86
2B	H. Schlafly	426	.246	2	30	341	358	28	42	5.9	.961	C. Patten	38	283	19	16	0	2.17
SS	D. Altizer	433	.256	1	27	257	323	43	31	5.5	.931	C. Smith	33	235	9	16	0	2.91
3B	L. Cross	494	.263	1	46	157	242	20	9	3.2	**.952**	L. Hughes	30	204	7	17	0	3.62
RF	P. Hickman	451	.284	9	57	137	12	7	2	1.6	.955	F. Kitson	30	197	6	14	0	3.65
CF	C. Jones	497	.241	3	42	279	20	12	7	2.4	.961							
LF	J. Anderson	583	.271	3	70	286	19	15	2	2.1	.953							
C	H. Wakefield	211	.280	1	21	237	59	17	5	5.2	.946							
UT	R. Nill	315	.235	0	15	148	211	36	21		.909							
OF	J. Stanley	221	.163	0	9	78	7	6	0	1.4	.934							

Boston

W-49 L-105

Jimmy Collins
W-35 L-79

Chick Stahl
W-14 L-26

POS	Player	AB	BA	HR	RBI	PO	A	E	DP	TC/G	FA	Pitcher	G	IP	W	L	SV	ERA
1B	M. Grimshaw	428	.290	0	48	1165	64	16	39	11.3	.987	C. Young	39	288	13	**21**	2	3.19
2B	H. Ferris	495	.244	2	44	316	375	29	41	5.7	.960	J. Harris	30	235	2	**21**	2	3.52
SS	F. Parent	600	.235	1	49	312	472	56	48	5.9	.933	B. Dinneen	28	219	8	19	0	2.92
3B	R. Morgan	307	.215	1	21	126	139	**41**	8	3.5	.866	G. Winter	29	208	6	18	2	4.12
RF	J. Hayden	322	.280	1	13	136	7	4	1	1.7	.973	J. Tannehill	27	196	13	11	0	3.16
CF	C. Stahl	595	.286	4	51	344	24	15	9	2.5	.961	R. Glaze	19	123	4	6	0	3.59
LF	J. Hoey	361	.244	0	24	155	7	15	0	1.9	.915							
C	C. Armbruster	201	.144	0	6	262	99	17	6	5.7	.955							
O1	B. Freeman	392	.250	1	30	467	47	8	22		.985							
OF	K. Selbach	228	.211	0	23	109	6	4	2	2.1	.966							
UT	J. Godwin	193	.187	0	15	79	115	26	11		.882							

AMERICAN LEAGUE 1906, *cont.*

BATTING AND BASE RUNNING LEADERS

Batting Average

G. Stone, STL	.358
N. Lajoie, CLE	.355
H. Chase, NY	.323
T. Cobb, DET	.320
B. Congalton, CLE	.320

Slugging Average

G. Stone, STL	.501
N. Lajoie, CLE	.460
H. Davis, PHI	.459
E. Flick, CLE	.439
P. Hickman, WAS	.421

Home Runs

H. Davis, PHI	12
P. Hickman, WAS	9
G. Stone, STL	6
S. Seybold, PHI	5

Total Bases

G. Stone, STL	291
N. Lajoie, CLE	277
E. Flick, CLE	274
H. Davis, PHI	253
H. Chase, NY	236

Runs Batted In

H. Davis, PHI	96
N. Lajoie, CLE	91
G. Davis, CHI	80
J. Williams, NY	77
H. Chase, NY	76

Stolen Bases

J. Anderson, WAS	39
E. Flick, CLE	39
D. Altizer, WAS	37
F. Isbell, CHI	37
J. Donahue, CHI	36

Hits

N. Lajoie, CLE	214
G. Stone, STL	208
E. Flick, CLE	194
H. Chase, NY	193

Base on Balls

T. Hartsel, PHI	88
F. Jones, CHI	83
E. Hahn, NY, CHI	72
B. Wallace, STL	58

Home Run Percentage

H. Davis, PHI	2.2
P. Hickman, WAS	2.0
S. Seybold, PHI	1.2
G. Stone, STL	1.0

Runs

E. Flick, CLE	98
T. Hartsel, PHI	96
W. Keeler, NY	96
H. Davis, PHI	94

Doubles

N. Lajoie, CLE	49
H. Davis, PHI	42
E. Flick, CLE	33
D. Murphy, PHI	28

Triples

E. Flick, CLE	22
G. Stone, STL	20
S. Crawford, DET	16
H. Ferris, BOS	13

PITCHING LEADERS

Winning Percentage

E. Plank, PHI	.760
D. White, CHI	.750
A. Joss, CLE	.700
B. Rhoads, CLE	.688
F. Owen, CHI	.629

Earned Run Average

D. White, CHI	1.52
B. Pelty, STL	1.59
A. Joss, CLE	1.72
J. Powell, STL	1.77
B. Rhoads, CLE	1.80

Wins

A. Orth, NY	27
J. Chesbro, NY	23
F. Owen, CHI	22
B. Rhoads, CLE	22
A. Joss, CLE	21
G. Mullin, DET	21

Saves

C. Bender, PHI	3
O. Hess, CLE	3

Strikeouts

R. Waddell, PHI	196
C. Falkenberg, WAS	178
E. Walsh, CHI	171
O. Hess, CLE	167
C. Bender, PHI	159

Complete Games

A. Orth, NY	36
G. Mullin, DET	35
O. Hess, CLE	33
B. Rhoads, CLE	31
H. Howell, STL	30
C. Falkenberg, WAS	30

Fewest Hits/9 Innings

B. Pelty, STL	6.53
D. White, CHI	6.57
E. Walsh, CHI	6.95
A. Joss, CLE	7.02

Shutouts

E. Walsh, CHI	10
A. Joss, CLE	9
R. Waddell, PHI	8

Fewest Walks/9 Innings

C. Young, BOS	0.78
R. Patterson, CHI	1.08
N. Altrock, CHI	1.31
A. Joss, CLE	1.37

Most Strikeouts/9 Inn.

R. Waddell, PHI	6.47
C. Bender, PHI	6.00
E. Walsh, CHI	5.53
C. Falkenberg, WAS	5.36

Innings

A. Orth, NY	339
O. Hess, CLE	334
G. Mullin, DET	330
J. Chesbro, NY	325

Games Pitched

J. Chesbro, NY	49
A. Orth, NY	45
R. Waddell, PHI	43
O. Hess, CLE	43

							Batting						Fielding			Pitching					
	W	L	PCT	GB	R	OR	2B	3B	HR	BA	SA	SB	E	DP	FA	CG	BB	SO	ShO	SV	ERA
Chicago	93	58	.616		570	**460**	152	52	7	.230	.286	214	243	80	.963	117	**255**	543	**32**	5	2.13
New York	90	61	.596	3	644	543	166	**77**	17	.266	.339	192	272	69	.957	99	351	605	18	5	2.78
Cleveland	89	64	.582	5	**663**	482	**240**	73	11	**.279**	**.357**	203	**216**	**111**	**.967**	**133**	365	530	27	4	**2.09**
Philadelphia	78	67	.538	12	561	542	213	49	**32**	.247	.330	166	267	86	.956	107	425	**749**	19	4	2.60
St. Louis	76	73	.510	16	558	498	145	60	20	.247	.312	221	290	80	.954	**133**	314	558	17	5	2.23
Detroit	71	78	.477	21	518	599	154	66	10	.242	.306	206	260	86	.959	128	389	469	7	4	3.06
Washington	55	95	.367	37.5	518	664	144	65	26	.238	.309	**233**	279	78	.955	115	451	558	13	1	3.25
Boston	49	105	.318	45.5	462	706	160	75	13	.239	.306	99	335	84	.949	124	285	549	6	**6**	3.41
					4494	4494	1374	517	136	.248	.318	1534	2162	674	.957	956	2835	4561	139	34	2.69

NATIONAL LEAGUE 1907

Chicago

W-107 L-45

Frank Chance

POS	Player	AB	BA	HR	RBI	PO	A	E	DP	TC/G	FA	Pitcher	G	IP	W	L	SV	ERA
1B	F. Chance	382	.293	1	49	1129	80	10	64	11.2	**.992**	O. Overall	35	265	23	8	3	1.70
2B	J. Evers	508	.250	2	51	346	**500**	32	58	5.8	.964	T. Brown	34	233	20	6	3	1.39
SS	J. Tinker	402	.221	1	36	215	390	39	45	5.7	.939	C. Lundgren	28	207	18	7	0	1.17
3B	H. Steinfeldt	542	.266	1	70	161	307	16	18	3.2	**.967**	J. Pfiester	30	195	15	9	0	**1.15**
RF	W. Schulte	342	.287	2	32	130	11	4	1	1.6	.972	E. Reulbach	27	192	17	4	0	1.69
CF	J. Slagle	489	.258	0	32	239	15	10	5	2.0	.962	C. Fraser	22	138	8	5	0	2.28
LF	J. Sheckard	484	.267	1	36	223	13	6	2	1.7	.975	J. Taylor	18	123	6	5	0	3.29
C	J. Kling	334	.284	1	43	**499**	109	8	11	6.3	**.987**							
UT	S. Hofman	470	.268	1	36	433	144	31	36		.949							
C	P. Moran	198	.227	1	19	258	72	9	9	5.7	.973							

Pittsburgh

W-91 L-63

Fred Clarke

POS	Player	AB	BA	HR	RBI	PO	A	E	DP	TC/G	FA	Pitcher	G	IP	W	L	SV	ERA
1B	J. Nealon	381	.257	0	47	998	68	24	35	10.5	.978	V. Willis	39	293	22	11	1	2.34
2B	E. Abbaticchio	496	.262	2	82	320	380	**36**	37	5.0	.951	L. Leifield	40	286	20	16	0	2.33
SS	H. Wagner	515	**.350**	6	82	314	428	49	32	5.7	.938	S. Leever	31	217	14	9	0	1.66
3B	A. Storke	357	.258	1	39	75	123	16	10	3.2	.925	D. Phillippe	35	214	13	11	2	2.61
RF	G. Anderson	413	.206	1	12	207	15	11	4	2.0	.953	H. Camnitz	31	180	13	8	1	2.15
CF	T. Leach	547	.303	4	43	284	15	6	5	2.7	.980							
LF	F. Clarke	501	.289	2	59	298	15	4	2	2.2	.987							
C	G. Gibson	382	.220	3	35	**499**	125	18	12	5.9	.972							
OF	B. Hallman	302	.222	0	15	134	9	5	1	1.8	.966							
3B	T. Sheehan	226	.274	0	25	55	137	12	3	3.6	.941							

Philadelphia

W-83 L-64

Billy Murray

POS	Player	AB	BA	HR	RBI	PO	A	E	DP	TC/G	FA	Pitcher	G	IP	W	L	SV	ERA
1B	K. Bransfield	348	.233	0	38	862	53	21	46	10.2	.978	F. Corridon	37	274	18	14	1	2.46
2B	O. Knabe	444	.255	1	34	293	336	26	53	5.4	.960	T. Sparks	33	265	22	8	1	2.00
SS	M. Doolan	509	.204	1	47	**327**	463	60	**59**	**5.9**	.929	L. Moren	37	255	11	18	1	2.54
3B	E. Courtney	440	.243	2	43	90	143	24	11	3.4	.907	B. Brown	21	130	9	6	0	2.42
RF	J. Titus	523	.275	3	63	198	21	17	3	1.7	.928	L. Richie	25	117	6	6	0	1.77
CF	R. Thomas	419	.243	1	23	274	15	6	4	2.4	.980	T. Pittinger	16	102	9	5	0	3.00
LF	S. Magee	503	.328	4	**85**	297	13	7	7	2.3	.978							
C	R. Dooin	313	.211	0	14	436	123	24	14	6.2	.959							
3B	E. Grant	268	.243	0	19	106	145	23	6	3.7	.916							
C	F. Jacklitsch	202	.213	0	17	270	97	6	**15**	6.4	.984							
OF	F. Osborn	163	.276	0	9	60	2	0	0	1.7	1.000							

NATIONAL LEAGUE 1907, *cont.*

New York

W-82 L-71

John McGraw

POS	Player	AB	BA	HR	RBI	PO	A	E	DP	TC/G	FA
1B	D. McGann	262	.298	2	36	781	55	5	36	10.4	.994
2B	L. Doyle	227	.260	0	16	128	158	26	7	4.5	.917
SS	B. Dahlen	464	.207	0	34	292	426	45	39	5.3	.941
3B	A. Devlin	491	.277	1	54	174	282	29	12	3.5	.940
RF	G. Browne	458	.260	5	37	146	14	10	5	1.4	.941
CF	C. Seymour	473	.294	3	75	300	8	8	4	2.5	.975
LF	S. Shannon	**585**	.265	1	33	282	18	7	3	2.0	.977
C	R. Bresnahan	328	.253	4	38	483	94	8	11	6.2	.986
C1	F. Bowerman	311	.260	0	32	606	79	6	14		.991
OF	S. Strang	306	.252	4	30	112	13	7	5	1.9	.947
2B	T. Corcoran	226	.265	0	24	108	183	19	15	5.0	.939

Pitcher	G	IP	W	L	SV	ERA
C. Mathewson	41	316	**24**	13	2	1.99
J. McGinnity	**47**	310	18	18	**4**	3.16
R. Ames	39	233	10	12	1	2.16
H. Wiltse	33	190	13	12	1	2.18
D. Taylor	28	171	11	7	1	2.42

Brooklyn

W-65 L-83

Patsy Donovan

POS	Player	AB	BA	HR	RBI	PO	A	E	DP	TC/G	FA
1B	T. Jordan	485	.274	4	53	1417	78	**31**	71	10.7	.980
2B	W. Alperman	558	.233	2	39	298	378	33	41	**6.2**	.953
SS	P. Lewis	475	.248	0	30	277	372	43	37	5.1	.938
3B	D. Casey	527	.231	0	19	176	274	21	16	3.4	.955
RF	H. Lumley	454	.267	9	66	171	15	8	7	1.6	.959
CF	B. Maloney	502	.229	0	32	336	18	12	5	2.5	.967
LF	E. Batch	388	.247	0	31	178	14	13	4	2.0	.937
C	L. Ritter	271	.203	0	17	391	103	16	11	5.7	.969
UT	J. Hummel	342	.234	3	31	321	162	16	23		.968

Pitcher	G	IP	W	L	SV	ERA
N. Rucker	37	275	15	13	0	2.06
G. Bell	35	264	8	16	1	2.25
E. Stricklett	29	230	12	14	0	2.27
J. Pastorius	28	222	16	12	0	2.35
H. McIntire	28	200	7	15	0	2.39
D. Scanlan	17	107	6	8	0	3.20

Cincinnati

W-66 L-87

Ned Hanlon

POS	Player	AB	BA	HR	RBI	PO	A	E	DP	TC/G	FA
1B	J. Ganzel	531	.254	2	64	1346	84	14	**89**	10.1	.990
2B	M. Huggins	561	.248	1	31	**353**	443	32	**73**	5.3	.961
SS	H. Lobert	537	.246	1	41	299	382	43	53	5.1	.941
3B	M. Mowrey	448	.252	1	44	167	214	29	14	3.2	.929
RF	M. Mitchell	558	.292	3	47	265	39	12	9	2.2	.962
CF	A. Kruger	317	.233	0	28	199	11	6	3	2.3	.972
LF	F. Odwell	274	.270	0	24	186	9	5	2	2.4	.975
C	L. McLean	374	.289	0	54	365	110	12	12	5.5	.975
OF	L. Davis	266	.229	1	25	160	11	5	3	2.5	.972
UT	J. Kane	262	.248	3	19	120	80	19	2		.913
C	A. Schlei	246	.272	0	27	277	111	8	6	5.9	.980

Pitcher	G	IP	W	L	SV	ERA
B. Ewing	41	333	17	19	0	1.73
A. Coakley	37	265	17	16	1	2.34
J. Weimer	29	209	11	14	0	2.41
R. Hitt	21	153	6	10	0	3.40
D. Mason	25	146	5	12	0	3.14
F. Smith	18	85	2	7	1	2.85

Boston

W-58 L-90

Fred Tenney

POS	Player	AB	BA	HR	RBI	PO	A	E	DP	TC/G	FA
1B	F. Tenney	554	.273	0	26	**1587**	**113**	19	86	**11.5**	.989
2B	C. Ritchey	499	.255	2	51	340	460	24	55	5.7	**.971**
SS	A. Bridwell	509	.218	0	26	325	437	47	57	5.8	**.942**
3B	D. Brain	509	.279	**10**	56	191	323	47	**27**	**4.3**	.916
RF	J. Bates	447	.260	2	49	171	18	4	5	1.6	.979
CF	G. Beaumont	580	.322	4	62	296	30	13	12	2.3	.962
LF	N. Randall	258	.213	0	15	106	9	10	1	1.7	.920
C	T. Needham	260	.196	1	19	281	101	13	9	5.1	.967
C	S. Brown	208	.192	0	14	267	91	11	12	5.9	.970
UT	B. Sweeney	191	.262	0	18	86	106	24	9		.889
OF	D. Howard	187	.273	1	13	54	8	2	2	1.4	.969

Pitcher	G	IP	W	L	SV	ERA
G. Dorner	36	271	12	16	0	3.12
V. Lindaman	34	260	11	15	1	3.63
I. Young	40	245	10	23	1	3.96
P. Flaherty	27	217	12	15	0	2.70
B. Pfeffer	19	144	6	8	0	3.00
J. Boultes	24	140	5	9	0	2.71

St. Louis

W-52 L-101

John McCloskey

POS	Player	AB	BA	HR	RBI	PO	A	E	DP	TC/G	FA
1B	E. Konetchy	330	.252	3	30	922	71	25	46	11.3	.975
2B	P. Bennett	324	.222	0	21	175	208	25	26	4.9	.939
SS	E. Holly	544	.230	1	40	317	**474**	**62**	45	5.8	.927
3B	B. Byrne	558	.256	0	29	**212**	**348**	**49**	24	4.1	.920
RF	S. Barry	292	.247	0	19	94	11	4	0	1.3	.963
CF	J. Burnett	206	.238	0	12	98	8	5	1	1.9	.955
LF	R. Murray	485	.262	7	46	232	25	18	4	2.1	.935
C	D. Marshall	268	.201	2	18	374	**142**	**26**	9	**6.5**	.952
UT	A. Hoelskoetter	396	.247	2	28	450	267	42	40		.945
C	P. Noonan	236	.225	1	16	369	98	24	12	7.0	.951
OF	J. Kelly	197	.188	0	6	85	7	3	4	1.8	.968
OF	T. O'Hara	173	.237	0	5	78	5	5	2	1.9	.943
OF	A. Burch	154	.227	0	5	85	10	8	4	2.1	.922

Pitcher	G	IP	W	L	SV	ERA
S. McGlynn	45	**352**	14	**25**	1	2.91
E. Karger	38	310	15	19	1	2.03
F. Beebe	31	238	7	19	0	2.72
A. Fromme	23	146	5	13	0	2.90
J. Lush	20	144	7	10	0	2.50

BATTING AND BASE RUNNING LEADERS

Batting Average

H. Wagner, PIT	.350
S. Magee, PHI	.328
G. Beaumont, BOS	.322
T. Leach, PIT	.303
C. Seymour, NY	.294

Slugging Average

H. Wagner, PIT	.513
S. Magee, PHI	.455
H. Lumley, BKN	.425
G. Beaumont, BOS	.424
D. Brain, BOS	.420

Home Runs

D. Brain, BOS	10
H. Lumley, BKN	9
R. Murray, STL	7
H. Wagner, PIT	6
G. Browne, NY	5

Total Bases

H. Wagner, PIT	264
G. Beaumont, BOS	246
S. Magee, PHI	229
T. Leach, PIT	221
D. Brain, BOS	214

Runs Batted In

S. Magee, PHI	85
E. Abbaticchio, PIT	82
H. Wagner, PIT	82
C. Seymour, NY	75
H. Steinfeldt, CHI	70

Stolen Bases

H. Wagner, PIT	61
S. Magee, PHI	46
J. Evers, CHI	46
T. Leach, PIT	43
A. Devlin, NY	38

Hits

G. Beaumont, BOS	187
H. Wagner, PIT	180
T. Leach, PIT	166
S. Magee, PHI	165

Base on Balls

R. Thomas, PHI	83
M. Huggins, CIN	83
F. Tenney, BOS	82
S. Shannon, NY	82

Home Run Percentage

H. Lumley, BKN	2.0
D. Brain, BOS	2.0
R. Murray, STL	1.4
S. Strang, NY	1.3

PITCHING LEADERS

Winning Percentage

E. Reulbach, CHI	.810
T. Brown, CHI	.769
O. Overall, CHI	.742
T. Sparks, PHI	.733
C. Lundgren, CHI	.720

Earned Run Average

J. Pfiester, CHI	1.15
C. Lundgren, CHI	1.17
T. Brown, CHI	1.39
S. Leever, PIT	1.66
E. Reulbach, CHI	1.69

Wins

C. Mathewson, NY	24
O. Overall, CHI	23
T. Sparks, PHI	22
V. Willis, PIT	22
T. Brown, CHI	20
L. Leifield, PIT	20

Saves

J. McGinnity, NY	4
T. Brown, CHI	3
O. Overall, CHI	3
C. Mathewson, NY	2
D. Phillippe, PIT	2

Strikeouts

C. Mathewson, NY	178
B. Ewing, CIN	147
R. Ames, NY	146
F. Beebe, STL	141
O. Overall, CHI	139

Complete Games

S. McGlynn, STL	33
B. Ewing, CIN	32
C. Mathewson, NY	31
E. Karger, STL	28
V. Willis, PIT	27

Fewest Hits/9 Innings

C. Lundgren, CHI	5.65
J. Pfiester, CHI	6.60
O. Overall, CHI	6.75
H. Camnitz, PIT	6.75

Shutouts

O. Overall, CHI	8
C. Mathewson, NY	8
C. Lundgren, CHI	7

Fewest Walks/9 Innings

C. Mathewson, NY	1.51
D. Phillippe, PIT	1.51
T. Brown, CHI	1.55
J. McGinnity, NY	1.68

NATIONAL LEAGUE 1907, *cont.*

BATTING AND BASE RUNNING LEADERS / **PITCHING LEADERS**

Runs		Doubles		Triples		Most Strikeouts/9 Inn.		Innings		Games Pitched	
S. Shannon, NY	104	H. Wagner, PIT	38	J. Ganzel, CIN	16	R. Ames, NY	5.63	S. McGlynn, STL	352	J. McGinnity, NY	47
T. Leach, PIT	102	S. Magee, PHI	28	W. Alperman, BKN	16	F. Beebe, STL	5.32	B. Ewing, CIN	333	S. McGlynn, STL	45
H. Wagner, PIT	98	C. Seymour, NY	25	H. Wagner, PIT	14	C. Mathewson, NY	5.07	C. Mathewson, NY	316	C. Mathewson, NY	41
F. Clarke, PIT	97	H. Steinfeldt, CHI	25	G. Beaumont, BOS	14	D. Scanlan, BKN	4.96	E. Karger, STL	310	B. Ewing, CIN	41
								J. McGinnity, NY	310		

							Batting						Fielding			Pitching					
	W	L	PCT	GB	R	OR	2B	3B	HR	BA	SA	SB	E	DP	FA	CG	BB	SO	ShO	SV	ERA
Chicago	107	45	.704		572	**390**	**162**	48	13	.250	.311	235	**211**	110	**.967**	114	402	584	**32**	7	**1.73**
Pittsburgh	91	63	.591	17	**634**	510	133	78	19	**.254**	**.324**	**264**	256	75	.959	111	**368**	497	24	4	2.30
Philadelphia	83	64	.565	21.5	512	476	**162**	65	12	.236	.305	154	256	104	.957	110	422	499	21	3	2.43
New York	82	71	.536	25.5	574	510	160	48	**23**	.251	.317	205	232	75	.963	109	369	**655**	22	**11**	2.45
Brooklyn	65	83	.439	40	446	522	142	63	18	.232	.298	121	262	94	.959	125	463	479	20	1	2.38
Cincinnati	66	87	.431	41.5	526	519	126	**90**	15	.247	.318	158	227	118	.963	118	444	481	10	2	2.41
Boston	58	90	.392	47	502	652	142	61	22	.243	.309	120	249	**128**	.961	121	458	426	9	2	3.33
St. Louis	52	101	.340	55.5	419	606	121	51	19	.232	.288	125	349	105	.947	**126**	499	589	20	2	2.70
					4185	4185	1148	504	141	.243	.309	1382	2042	809	.959	934	3425	4210	158	32	2.47

AMERICAN LEAGUE 1907

Detroit

W-92 L-58

Hughie Jennings

POS	Player	AB	BA	HR	RBI	PO	A	E	DP	TC/G	FA	Pitcher	G	IP	W	L	SV	ERA
1B	C. Rossman	571	.277	0	69	1478	62	30	57	10.3	.981	G. Mullin	46	357	20	20	3	2.59
2B	R. Downs	374	.219	1	42	149	207	27	10	4.8	.930	E. Killian	42	314	25	13	1	1.78
SS	C. O'Leary	465	.241	0	34	**353**	448	44	35	6.1	.948	E. Siever	39	275	18	11	1	2.16
3B	B. Coughlin	519	.243	0	46	163	236	30	9	3.2	.930	W. Donovan	32	271	25	4	1	2.19
RF	T. Cobb	605	**.350**	5	**116**	238	30	11	12	1.9	.961							
CF	S. Crawford	582	.323	4	81	311	22	12	2	2.4	.965							
LF	D. Jones	491	.273	0	27	282	15	9	2	2.4	.971							
C	B. Schmidt	349	.244	0	23	446	132	**34**	**14**	5.9	.944							
UT	G. Schaefer	372	.258	1	32	239	286	23	23		.958							
C	F. Payne	169	.166	0	14	205	55	5	4	5.8	.981							
P	G. Mullin	157	.217	0	13	15	133	6	1	3.3	.961							

Philadelphia

W-88 L-57

Connie Mack

POS	Player	AB	BA	HR	RBI	PO	A	E	DP	TC/G	FA	Pitcher	G	IP	W	L	SV	ERA
1B	H. Davis	582	.266	**8**	87	1475	103	**38**	50	10.8	.976	E. Plank	43	344	24	16	0	2.20
2B	D. Murphy	469	.271	2	57	271	386	24	28	5.6	.965	R. Waddell	44	285	19	13	0	2.15
SS	S. Nicholls	460	.302	0	23	178	258	33	12	5.7	.930	J. Dygert	42	262	21	8	1	2.34
3B	J. Collins	365	.274	0	35	97	185	30	11	3.1	.904	C. Bender	33	219	16	8	3	2.05
RF	S. Seybold	564	.271	5	92	201	19	6	7	1.5	.973	J. Coombs	23	133	6	9	2	3.12
CF	R. Oldring	441	.286	1	40	180	10	5	0	1.7	.974							
LF	T. Hartsel	507	.280	3	29	191	11	7	2	1.5	.967							
C	O. Schreckengost	356	.272	0	38	**640**	**145**	12	4	**8.1**	**.985**							
SS	M. Cross	248	.206	0	18	169	226	19	17	5.6	.954							
OF	B. Lord	170	.182	1	11	91	6	5	0	1.9	.951							
C	M. Powers	159	.182	0	9	313	80	7	8	6.8	.983							

Chicago

W-87 L-64

Fielder Jones

POS	Player	AB	BA	HR	RBI	PO	A	E	DP	TC/G	FA	Pitcher	G	IP	W	L	SV	ERA
1B	J. Donahue	**609**	.259	1	68	**1846**	**140**	12	78	**12.7**	**.994**	E. Walsh	**56**	**422**	24	18	**4**	**1.60**
2B	F. Isbell	486	.243	0	41	276	384	30	41	5.8	.957	F. Smith	41	310	23	10	0	2.47
SS	G. Davis	466	.238	1	52	223	485	38	53	5.7	.949	D. White	46	291	**27**	13	1	2.26
3B	G. Rohe	494	.213	2	51	58	161	25	14	3.2	.898	N. Altrock	30	214	7	13	2	2.57
RF	E. Hahn	592	.255	0	45	182	24	2	6	1.3	.990	R. Patterson	19	96	4	6	0	2.63
CF	F. Jones	559	.261	0	47	307	18	9	6	2.2	.973							
LF	P. Dougherty	533	.270	1	59	209	19	13	4	1.6	.946							
C	B. Sullivan	339	.174	0	36	477	117	10	12	5.6	.983							
P	E. Walsh	154	.162	1	10	35	**227**	4	2	**4.8**	.985							

Cleveland

W-85 L-67

Nap Lajoie

POS	Player	AB	BA	HR	RBI	PO	A	E	DP	TC/G	FA	Pitcher	G	IP	W	L	SV	ERA
1B	G. Stovall	466	.236	1	36	1381	68	25	**90**	12.1	.983	A. Joss	42	339	**27**	11	2	1.83
2B	N. Lajoie	509	.299	2	63	314	**461**	25	**86**	**6.3**	**.969**	G. Liebhardt	38	280	18	14	1	2.05
SS	T. Turner	524	.242	0	46	258	477	39	**67**	5.3	**.950**	B. Rhoads	35	275	15	14	1	2.29
3B	B. Bradley	498	.223	0	34	164	278	29	18	3.4	**.938**	J. Thielman	20	166	11	8	0	2.33
RF	E. Flick	549	.302	3	58	219	22	11	7	1.7	.956	O. Hess	17	93	6	6	1	2.89
CF	J. Birmingham	476	.235	1	33	273	33	17	8	2.4	.947	W. Clarkson	17	91	4	6	0	1.99
LF	B. Hinchman	514	.228	1	50	231	18	11	3	1.7	.958							
C	N. Clarke	390	.269	3	33	470	119	24	9	5.3	.961							
C	H. Bemis	172	.250	0	19	180	42	10	3	4.5	.957							

New York

W-70 L-78

Clark Griffith

POS	Player	AB	BA	HR	RBI	PO	A	E	DP	TC/G	FA	Pitcher	G	IP	W	L	SV	ERA
1B	H. Chase	498	.287	2	68	1144	77	34	50	10.4	.973	A. Orth	36	249	14	**21**	0	2.61
2B	J. Williams	504	.270	2	63	357	393	26	45	5.6	.966	J. Chesbro	30	206	10	10	0	2.53
SS	K. Elberfeld	447	.271	0	51	295	400	52	31	6.3	.930	S. Doyle	29	194	11	11	1	2.65
3B	G. Moriarty	437	.277	0	43	115	160	31	8	3.4	.899	B. Hogg	25	167	10	8	0	3.08
RF	W. Keeler	423	.234	0	17	144	13	5	5	1.5	.969	D. Newton	19	133	7	10	0	3.18
CF	D. Hoffman	517	.253	4	46	286	20	15	4	2.4	.953	B. Keefe	19	58	3	5	3	2.50
LF	W. Conroy	530	.234	3	51	204	10	10	2	2.2	.955							
C	R. Kleinow	269	.264	0	26	318	97	14	5	5.0	.967							
30	F. LaPorte	470	.270	0	48	149	125	30	4		.901							
C	I. Thomas	208	.192	1	24	257	90	17	7	5.5	.953							

AMERICAN LEAGUE 1907, *cont.*

St. Louis

W-69 L-83

Jimmy McAleer

POS	Player	AB	BA	HR	RBI	PO	A	E	DP	TC/G	FA	Pitcher	G	IP	W	L	SV	ERA
1B	T. Jones	549	.250	0	34	1687	103	31	69	11.7	.983	H. Howell	42	316	16	15	3	1.93
2B	H. Niles	492	.289	2	35	280	352	**34**	41	5.7	.949	B. Pelty	36	273	12	**21**	1	2.57
SS	B. Wallace	538	.257	0	70	338	**517**	**54**	54	6.2	.941	J. Powell	32	256	13	16	1	2.68
3B	J. Yeager	436	.239	1	44	108	194	20	12	3.5	.938	F. Glade	24	202	13	9	0	2.67
RF	O. Pickering	576	.276	0	60	210	14	12	5	1.6	.949	B. Dinneen	24	155	7	10	4*	2.43
CF	C. Hemphill	603	.259	0	38	320	12	15	2	2.3	.957							
LF	G. Stone	596	.320	4	59	276	12	9	5	1.9	.970							
C	T. Spencer	230	.265	0	24	250	80	15	6	5.5	.957							
32	R. Hartzell	220	.236	0	13	85	114	14	6		.934							
C	J. Stephens	173	.202	0	11	200	63	9	4	4.9	.967							

Boston

W-59 L-90

Cy Young
W-3 L-3

George Huff
W-2 L-6

Bob Unglaub
W-9 L-20

Deacon McGuire
W-45 L-61

POS	Player	AB	BA	HR	RBI	PO	A	E	DP	TC/G	FA	Pitcher	G	IP	W	L	SV	ERA
1B	B. Unglaub	544	.254	1	62	1504	84	22	71	11.6	.986	C. Young	43	343	21	15	2	1.99
2B	H. Ferris	561	.241	4	60	**424**	459	30	43	6.1	.967	G. Winter	35	257	12	15	1	2.07
SS	H. Wagner	385	.213	2	21	283	387	50	31	**6.6**	.931	R. Glaze	32	182	9	13	0	2.32
3B	J. Knight	364	.212	2	29	129*	211*	28*	15*	3.8*	.924	T. Pruiett	35	174	3	11	3	3.11
RF	B. Congalton	496	.286	2	47	169	18	6	4	1.5	.969	J. Tannehill	18	131	6	7	1	2.47
CF	D. Sullivan	551	.245	1	26	296	16	8	3	2.2	.975	C. Morgan	16	114	6	6	0	1.97
LF	J. Barrett	390	.244	1	28	183	14	7	5	2.1	.966							
C	L. Criger	226	.181	0	14	288	109	9	12	5.4	.978							
UT	F. Parent	409	.276	1	26	195	191	25	20		.939							
C	A. Shaw	198	.192	0	7	294	106	12	10	5.6	.971							
01	M. Grimshaw	181	.204	0	33	163	8	5	10		.972							
3B	J. Collins	158	.291	0	10	46	72	17	2	3.3	.874							

Washington

W-49 L-102

Joe Cantillon

POS	Player	AB	BA	HR	RBI	PO	A	E	DP	TC/G	FA	Pitcher	G	IP	W	L	SV	ERA
1B	J. Anderson	333	.288	0	44	615	32	11	13	10.8	.983	C. Smith	36	259	10	20	0	2.61
2B	J. Delahanty	404	.292	2	54	172	180	22	18	5.5	.941	C. Patten	36	237	12	16	0	3.56
SS	D. Altizer	540	.269	1	42	157	251	32	23	6.2	.927	C. Falkenberg	32	234	6	17	0	2.35
3B	B. Shipke	189	.196	1	9	57	127	11	2	3.1	.944	L. Hughes	34	211	7	14	**4**	3.11
RF	B. Ganley	605	.276	1	35	276	23	19	5	2.1	.940	W. Johnson	14	111	5	9	0	1.87
CF	C. Jones	437	.265	0	37	226	6	8	2	2.2	.967	O. Graham	20	104	4	9	0	3.98
LF	O. Clymer	206	.316	1	16	79	4	8	0	1.8	.912	H. Gehring	15	87	3	7	0	3.31
C	J. Warner	207	.256	0	17	271	64	10	4	5.4	.971							
20	R. Nill	215	.219	0	25	113	106	8	9		.965							
10	P. Hickman	193	.285	1	23	306	20	13	13		.962							
OF	C. Milan	183	.279	0	9	80	12	7	1	2.1	.929							
C	M. Heydon	164	.183	0	9	247	52	12	4	5.5	.961							
3B	L. Cross	161	.199	0	10	38	98	3	2	3.4	.978							

BATTING AND BASE RUNNING LEADERS

Batting Average
T. Cobb, DET .350
S. Crawford, DET .323
G. Stone, STL .320
E. Flick, CLE .302
S. Nicholls, PHI .302

Slugging Average
T. Cobb, DET .473
S. Crawford, DET .460
E. Flick, CLE .412
G. Stone, STL .399
H. Davis, PHI .397

Home Runs
H. Davis, PHI 8
S. Seybold, PHI 5
T. Cobb, DET 5

Total Bases
T. Cobb, DET 286
S. Crawford, DET 268
G. Stone, STL 238
H. Davis, PHI 231
E. Flick, CLE 226

Runs Batted In
T. Cobb, DET 116
S. Seybold, PHI 92
H. Davis, PHI 87
S. Crawford, DET 81
B. Wallace, STL 70

Stolen Bases
T. Cobb, DET 49
W. Conroy, NY 41
E. Flick, CLE 41
B. Ganley, WAS 40
D. Altizer, WAS 38

Hits
T. Cobb, DET 212
G. Stone, STL 191
S. Crawford, DET 188
B. Ganley, WAS 167

Base on Balls
T. Hartsel, PHI 106
E. Hahn, CHI 84
F. Jones, CHI 67
E. Flick, CLE 64

Home Run Percentage
H. Davis, PHI 1.4
S. Seybold, PHI 0.9
T. Cobb, DET 0.8
D. Hoffman, NY 0.8

Runs
S. Crawford, DET 102
D. Jones, DET 101
T. Cobb, DET 97
T. Hartsel, PHI 93

Doubles
H. Davis, PHI 36
S. Crawford, DET 34
N. Lajoie, CLE 30
J. Collins, BOS, PHI 30

Triples
E. Flick, CLE 18
S. Crawford, DET 17
T. Cobb, DET 15
B. Unglaub, BOS 13

PITCHING LEADERS

Winning Percentage
W. Donovan, DET .862
J. Dygert, PHI .724
A. Joss, CLE .711
F. Smith, CHI .697
D. White, CHI .675

Earned Run Average
E. Walsh, CHI 1.60
E. Killian, DET 1.78
A. Joss, CLE 1.83
W. Johnson, WAS 1.87
H. Howell, STL 1.93

Wins
D. White, CHI 27
A. Joss, CLE 27
W. Donovan, DET 25
E. Killian, DET 25
E. Plank, PHI 24
E. Walsh, CHI 24

Saves
L. Hughes, WAS 4
B. Dinneen, BOS, STL 4
E. Walsh, CHI 4

Strikeouts
R. Waddell, PHI 232
E. Walsh, CHI 206
E. Plank, PHI 183
J. Dygert, PHI 151
C. Young, BOS 147

Complete Games
E. Walsh, CHI 37
G. Mullin, DET 35
A. Joss, CLE 34
C. Young, BOS 33
E. Plank, PHI 33

Fewest Hits/9 Innings
J. Dygert, PHI 6.88
G. Winter, BOS 6.94
E. Walsh, CHI 7.27
H. Howell, STL 7.34

Shutouts
E. Plank, PHI 8
R. Waddell, PHI 7
D. White, CHI 7
C. Young, BOS 6
A. Joss, CLE 6

Fewest Walks/9 Innings
D. White, CHI 1.18
N. Altrock, CHI 1.31
C. Young, BOS 1.34
J. Tannehill, BOS 1.37

Most Strikeouts/9 Inn.
R. Waddell, PHI 7.33
W. Johnson, WAS 5.69
J. Dygert, PHI 5.19
J. Coombs, PHI 4.95

Innings
E. Walsh, CHI 422
G. Mullin, DET 357
E. Plank, PHI 344
C. Young, BOS 343

Games Pitched
E. Walsh, CHI 56
D. White, CHI 46
G. Mullin, DET 46
R. Waddell, PHI 44

							Batting						Fielding			Pitching					
	W	L	PCT	GB	R	OR	2B	3B	HR	BA	SA	SB	E	DP	FA	CG	BB	SO	ShO	SV	ERA
Detroit	92	58	.613		**694**	532	179	**76**	11	**.266**	**.336**	192	260	79	.959	120	380	512	15	7	2.33
Philadelphia	88	57	.607	1.5	582	511	**220**	45	**22**	.255	.330	138	263	67	.958	106	378	**789**	**27**	6	2.35
Chicago	87	64	.576	5.5	588	**474**	148	34	6	.237	.283	175	**233**	101	**.966**	112	**305**	604	17	**9**	**2.22**
Cleveland	85	67	.559	8	530	525	182	68	11	.241	.310	193	264	**137**	.960	127	362	513	20	5	2.26
New York	70	78	.473	21	605	665	150	67	14	.249	.314	206	334	79	.947	93	428	511	9	5	3.03
St. Louis	69	83	.454	24	542	555	154	63	9	.253	.312	144	266	97	.959	**129**	352	463	15	**9**	2.61
Boston	59	90	.396	32.5	464	558	155	48	18	.234	.292	124	274	103	.959	100	337	517	17	7	2.45
Washington	49	102	.325	43.5	506	691	137	57	12	.243	.300	**223**	311	69	.952	106	341	569	11	5	3.11
					4511	4511	1325	458	103	.247	.310	1395	2205	732	.958	893	2883	4478	131	53	2.55

NATIONAL LEAGUE 1908

Chicago

W-99 L-55

Frank Chance

POS	Player	AB	BA	HR	RBI	PO	A	E	DP	TC/G	FA	Pitcher	G	IP	W	L	SV	ERA
1B	F. Chance	452	.272	2	55	1291	86	15	56	11.0	.989	T. Brown	44	312	29	9	**5**	1.47
2B	J. Evers	416	.300	0	37	237	361	25	39	5.1	.960	E. Reulbach	46	298	24	7	1	2.03
SS	J. Tinker	548	.266	6	68	314	**570**	39	48	5.9	**.958**	J. Pfiester	33	252	12	10	0	2.00
3B	H. Steinfeldt	539	.241	1	62	166	275	28	15	3.1	.940	O. Overall	37	225	15	11	2	1.92
RF	W. Schulte	386	.236	1	43	148	11	1	3	1.6	.994	C. Fraser	26	163	11	9	2	2.27
CF	J. Slagle	352	.222	0	26	199	6	5	2	2.1	.976	C. Lundgren	23	139	6	9	0	4.22
LF	J. Sheckard	403	.231	2	22	201	13	10	3	1.9	.955							
C	J. Kling	424	.276	4	59	596	149	16	11	**6.5**	.979							
UT	S. Hofman	411	.243	2	42	532	97	23	16		.965							
OF	D. Howard	315	.279	1	26	129	10	5	1	1.8	.965							

New York

W-98 L-56

John McGraw

POS	Player	AB	BA	HR	RBI	PO	A	E	DP	TC/G	FA	Pitcher	G	IP	W	L	SV	ERA
1B	F. Tenney	583	.256	2	49	**1634**	117	18	**68**	11.3	.990	C. Mathewson	**56**	**391**	**37**	11	**5**	**1.43**
2B	L. Doyle	377	.308	0	33	180	291	**33**	28	4.9	.935	H. Wiltse	44	330	23	14	2	2.24
SS	A. Bridwell	467	.285	0	46	277	486	**55**	39	5.6	.933	D. Crandall	32	215	12	12	0	2.93
3B	A. Devlin	534	.253	2	45	**203**	**331**	30	19	3.6	**.947**	J. McGinnity	37	186	11	7	4	2.27
RF	M. Donlin	593	.334	6	106	239	21	6	1	1.7	.977	D. Taylor	27	128	8	5	2	2.33
CF	C. Seymour	587	.267	5	92	340	29	20	9	2.5	.949	R. Ames	18	114	7	4	0	1.81
LF	S. Shannon	268	.224	1	21	114	8	3	3	1.7	.976							
C	R. Bresnahan	449	.283	1	54	**657**	140	12	12	5.8	.985							
OF	M. McCormick	252	.302	0	32	97	3	11	2	1.7	.901							
2B	B. Herzog	160	.300	0	11	61	125	16	19	4.8	.921							

Pittsburgh

W-98 L-56

Fred Clarke

POS	Player	AB	BA	HR	RBI	PO	A	E	DP	TC/G	FA	Pitcher	G	IP	W	L	SV	ERA
1B	H. Swacina	176	.216	0	13	501	19	9	19	10.6	.983	V. Willis	41	305	23	11	0	2.07
2B	E. Abbaticchio	500	.250	1	61	268	423	22	42	5.0	**.969**	N. Maddox	36	261	23	8	1	2.28
SS	H. Wagner	568	**.354**	10	**109**	**354**	469	50	47	5.8	.943	H. Camnitz	38	237	16	9	2	1.56
3B	T. Leach	583	.259	5	41	199	293	33	19	3.5	.937	L. Leifield	34	219	15	14	2	2.10
RF	O. Wilson	529	.227	3	43	258	20	13	3	2.0	.955	S. Leever	38	193	15	7	2	2.10
CF	R. Thomas	386	.256	1	24	269	7	7	4	2.8	.975							
LF	F. Clarke	551	.265	2	53	350	15	10	2	2.5	.973							
C	G. Gibson	486	.228	2	45	607	136	21	10	5.5	.973							
1B	A. Storke	202	.252	1	12	481	17	6	19	10.3	.988							
1B	J. Kane	145	.241	0	22	378	24	14	19	10.4	.966							

Philadelphia

W-83 L-71

Billy Murray

POS	Player	AB	BA	HR	RBI	PO	A	E	DP	TC/G	FA	Pitcher	G	IP	W	L	SV	ERA
1B	K. Bransfield	527	.304	3	71	1472	89	22	67	11.1	.986	G. McQuillan	48	360	23	17	2	1.53
2B	O. Knabe	555	.218	0	27	**344**	**470**	26	42	5.6	.969	T. Sparks	33	263	16	15	2	2.60
SS	M. Doolan	445	.234	2	49	269	419	45	32	5.7	.939	F. Corridon	27	208	14	10	1	2.51
3B	E. Grant	**598**	.244	0	32	197	271	**35**	**22**	3.8	.930	L. Richie	25	158	7	10	1	1.83
RF	J. Titus	539	.286	2	48	215	22	9	3	1.7	.963	L. Moren	28	154	8	9	0	2.92
CF	F. Osborn	555	.267	2	44	359	14	12	3	2.5	.969	B. Foxen	22	147	7	7	0	1.95
LF	S. Magee	508	.283	2	57	279	15	9	5	2.1	.970							
C	R. Dooin	435	.248	0	41	554	**191**	**26**	**17**	5.8	.966							
UT	E. Courtney	160	.181	0	6	157	61	6	7		.973							

Cincinnati

W-73 L-81

John Ganzel

POS	Player	AB	BA	HR	RBI	PO	A	E	DP	TC/G	FA	Pitcher	G	IP	W	L	SV	ERA
1B	J. Ganzel	388	.250	1	53	1116	61	12	52	11.0	**.990**	B. Ewing	37	294	17	15	3	2.21
2B	M. Huggins	498	.239	0	23	302	406	30	45	5.5	.959	B. Spade	35	249	17	12	1	2.74
SS	R. Hulswitt	386	.228	1	28	242	368	42	37	5.5	.936	A. Coakley	32	242	8	18	2	1.86
3B	H. Lobert	570	.293	4	63	121	181	26	11	3.3	.921	B. Campbell	35	221	12	13	1	2.60
RF	M. Mitchell	406	.222	1	37	193	16	9	2	1.8	.959	J. Weimer	15	117	8	7	0	2.39
CF	J. Kane	455	.213	3	23	292	15	6	2	2.5	.981	J. Dubuc	15	85	5	6	0	2.74
LF	D. Paskert	395	.243	1	36	251	15	13	3	2.4	.953							
C	A. Schlei	300	.220	1	22	355	96	18	10	5.3	.962							
C	L. McLean	309	.217	1	28	280	82	14	9	5.4	.963							
3B	M. Mowrey	227	.220	0	23	51	110	11	6	3.1	.936							

Boston

W-63 L-91

Joe Kelley

POS	Player	AB	BA	HR	RBI	PO	A	E	DP	TC/G	FA	Pitcher	G	IP	W	L	SV	ERA
1B	D. McGann	475	.240	2	55	1229	93	16	66	11.1	.988	V. Lindaman	43	271	12	16	1	2.36
2B	C. Ritchey	421	.273	2	36	325	368	24	**46**	**6.0**	.967	P. Flaherty	31	244	12	18	0	3.25
SS	B. Dahlen	524	.239	3	48	291	553	43	**58**	**6.2**	.952	G. Dorner	38	216	8	19	0	3.54
3B	B. Sweeney	418	.244	0	40	174	277	34	14	**3.9**	.930	G. Ferguson	37	208	12	11	0	2.47
RF	G. Browne	536	.228	1	34	248	20	14	8	2.0	.950	I. Young	16	85	4	8	0	2.86
CF	G. Beaumont	476	.267	2	52	259	17	10	3	2.4	.965							
LF	J. Bates	445	.258	1	29	205	15	12	2	2.0	.948							
C	F. Bowerman	254	.228	1	25	228	69	9	12	4.9	.971							
UT	J. Hannifin	257	.206	2	22	152	179	19	15		.946							
OF	J. Kelley	228	.259	2	17	71	5	5	1	2.1	.938							
C	P. Graham	215	.274	0	22	242	75	15	6	5.4	.955							
OF	B. Becker	171	.275	0	7	40	8	3	1	1.2	.941							

Brooklyn

W-53 L-101

Patsy Donovan

POS	Player	AB	BA	HR	RBI	PO	A	E	DP	TC/G	FA	Pitcher	G	IP	W	L	SV	ERA
1B	T. Jordan	515	.247	**12**	60	1462	55	**28**	52	10.6	.982	N. Rucker	42	333	17	19	0	2.08
2B	H. Pattee	264	.216	0	9	158	246	15	15	5.7	.964	K. Wilhelm	42	332	16	22	0	1.87
SS	P. Lewis	415	.219	1	30	227	352	35	33	5.3	.943	H. McIntire	40	288	11	20	2	2.69
3B	T. Sheehan	468	.214	0	29	174	280	34	13	3.4	.930	J. Pastorius	28	214	4	20	0	2.44
RF	H. Lumley	440	.216	4	39	157	13	8	6	1.5	.955	G. Bell	29	155	4	15	1	3.59
CF	B. Maloney	359	.195	3	17	238	11	14	4	2.6	.947							
LF	A. Burch	456	.243	2	18	242	24	8	6	2.4	.971							
C	B. Bergen	302	.175	0	15	470	137	7	9	6.2	**.989**							
UT	J. Hummel	594	.241	4	41	367	182	18	25		.968							
2B	W. Alperman	213	.197	1	15	74	110	13	8	4.7	.934							

NATIONAL LEAGUE 1908, *cont.*

St. Louis

W-49 L-105

John McCloskey

POS	Player	AB	BA	HR	RBI	PO	A	E	DP	TC/G	FA
1B	E. Konetchy	545	.248	5	50	1610	**122**	24	61	**11.4**	.986
2B	B. Gilbert	276	.214	0	10	222	254	24	23	5.6	.952
SS	P. O'Rourke	164	.195	0	16	80	171	41	10	5.5	.860
3B	B. Byrne	439	.191	0	14	183	248	**35**	14	3.8	.925
RF	R. Murray	593	.282	7	62	274	22	28	4	2.1	.914
CF	A. Shaw	367	.264	1	19	179	23	15	7	2.4	.931
LF	J. Delahanty	499	.255	1	44	243	11	6	1	1.9	.977
C	B. Ludwig	187	.182	0	8	227	87	16	2	5.3	.952
UT	C. Charles	454	.205	1	17	215	322	49	25		.916
OF	S. Barry	268	.228	0	11	109	10	4	0	1.8	.967
C	A. Hoelskoetter	155	.232	0	6	182	56	13	6	6.1	.948

Pitcher	G	IP	W	L	SV	ERA
B. Raymond	48	324	15	**25**	2	2.03
J. Lush	38	251	11	18	1	2.12
F. Beebe	29	174	5	13	0	2.63
E. Karger	22	141	4	9	0	3.06
S. Sallee	25	129	3	8	0	3.15
A. Fromme	20	116	5	13	0	2.72
I. Higginbotham	19	107	3	8	0	3.20

BATTING AND BASE RUNNING LEADERS

Batting Average	
H. Wagner, PIT	.354
M. Donlin, NY	.334
L. Doyle, NY	.308
K. Bransfield, PHI	.304
J. Evers, CHI	.300

Slugging Average	
H. Wagner, PIT	.542
M. Donlin, NY	.452
S. Magee, PHI	.417
H. Lobert, CIN	.407
R. Murray, STL	.400

Home Runs	
T. Jordan, BKN	12
H. Wagner, PIT	10
R. Murray, STL	7
J. Tinker, CHI	6
M. Donlin, NY	6

Total Bases	
H. Wagner, PIT	308
M. Donlin, NY	268
R. Murray, STL	237
H. Lobert, CIN	232
T. Leach, PIT	222

Runs Batted In	
H. Wagner, PIT	109
M. Donlin, NY	106
C. Seymour, NY	92
K. Bransfield, PHI	71
J. Tinker, CHI	68

Stolen Bases	
H. Wagner, PIT	53
R. Murray, STL	48
H. Lobert, CIN	47
S. Magee, PHI	40
J. Evers, CHI	36

Hits	
H. Wagner, PIT	201
M. Donlin, NY	198
H. Lobert, CIN	167
R. Murray, STL	167

Base on Balls	
R. Bresnahan, NY	83
F. Tenney, NY	72
J. Evers, CHI	66
F. Clarke, PIT	65

Home Run Percentage	
T. Jordan, BKN	2.3
H. Wagner, PIT	1.8
R. Murray, STL	1.2
J. Tinker, CHI	1.1

Runs	
F. Tenney, NY	101
H. Wagner, PIT	100
T. Leach, PIT	93
J. Evers, CHI	83
F. Clarke, PIT	83

Doubles	
H. Wagner, PIT	39
S. Magee, PHI	30
F. Chance, CHI	27
O. Knabe, PHI	26
M. Donlin, NY	26

Triples	
H. Wagner, PIT	19
H. Lobert, CIN	18
S. Magee, PHI	16
T. Leach, PIT	16

PITCHING LEADERS

Winning Percentage	
E. Reulbach, CHI	.774
C. Mathewson, NY	.771
T. Brown, CHI	.763
N. Maddox, PIT	.742
S. Leever, PIT	.682

Earned Run Average	
C. Mathewson, NY	1.43
T. Brown, CHI	1.47
G. McQuillan, PHI	1.53
H. Camnitz, PIT	1.56
A. Coakley, CIN, CHI	1.78

Wins	
C. Mathewson, NY	37
T. Brown, CHI	29
E. Reulbach, CHI	24

Saves	
C. Mathewson, NY	5
T. Brown, CHI	5
J. McGinnity, NY	4
B. Ewing, CIN	3

Strikeouts	
C. Mathewson, NY	259
N. Rucker, BKN	199
O. Overall, CHI	167
B. Raymond, STL	145
E. Reulbach, CHI	133

Complete Games	
C. Mathewson, NY	34
K. Wilhelm, BKN	33
G. McQuillan, PHI	32
N. Rucker, BKN	30
H. Wiltse, NY	30

Fewest Hits/9 Innings	
T. Brown, CHI	6.17
B. Raymond, STL	6.55
C. Mathewson, NY	6.57
G. McQuillan, PHI	6.58

Shutouts	
C. Mathewson, NY	12
T. Brown, CHI	9

Fewest Walks/9 Innings	
C. Mathewson, NY	0.97
T. Brown, CHI	1.41
T. Sparks, PHI	1.74
B. Ewing, CIN	1.75

Most Strikeouts/9 Inn.	
O. Overall, CHI	6.68
C. Mathewson, NY	5.97
N. Rucker, BKN	5.37
H. Camnitz, PIT	4.49

Innings	
C. Mathewson, NY	391
G. McQuillan, PHI	360
N. Rucker, BKN	333
K. Wilhelm, BKN	332

Games Pitched	
C. Mathewson, NY	56
B. Raymond, STL	48
G. McQuillan, PHI	48
E. Reulbach, CHI	46

							Batting						Fielding			Pitching					
	W	L	PCT	GB	R	OR	2B	3B	HR	BA	SA	SB	E	DP	FA	CG	BB	SO	ShO	SV	ERA
Chicago	99	55	.643		624	461	**197**	56	19	.249	.321	**212**	**206**	76	**.969**	108	437	**668**	**28**	10	2.14
New York	98	56	.636	1	**652**	456	182	43	20	**.267**	**.333**	181	250	79	.962	95	**288**	656	25	**15**	2.14
Pittsburgh	98	56	.636	1	585	469	162	**98**	25	.247	.332	186	226	74	.964	100	406	468	24	8	2.12
Philadelphia	83	71	.539	16	504	**445**	194	68	11	.244	.316	200	238	75	.963	116	379	476	22	6	**2.10**
Cincinnati	73	81	.474	26	489	544	129	77	14	.227	.294	196	255	72	.959	110	415	433	17	7	2.37
Boston	63	91	.409	36	537	622	137	43	17	.239	.293	134	252	**90**	.962	92	423	416	14	1	2.79
Brooklyn	53	101	.344	46	377	516	110	60	**28**	.213	.277	113	247	66	.961	**118**	444	535	20	3	2.47
St. Louis	49	105	.318	50	371	626	134	57	17	.223	.283	150	348	68	.946	97	430	528	13	4	2.64
					4139	4139	1245	502	151	.239	.306	1372	2022	600	.961	836	3222	4180	163	54	2.35

AMERICAN LEAGUE 1908

Detroit

W-90 L-63

Hughie Jennings

POS	Player	AB	BA	HR	RBI	PO	A	E	DP	TC/G	FA
1B	C. Rossman	524	.294	2	71	1429	**102**	29	70	11.3	.981
2B	R. Downs	289	.221	1	35	180	265	36	24	5.9	.925
SS	G. Schaefer	584	.259	3	52	162	254	37	35	6.7	.918
3B	B. Coughlin	405	.215	0	23	129	214	21	12	3.1	.942
RF	T. Cobb	581	**.324**	4	**108**	212	23	14	5	1.7	.944
CF	S. Crawford	**591**	.311	**7**	80	252	9	8	2	2.0	.970
LF	M. McIntyre	569	.295	0	28	329	17	8	4	2.3	.977
C	B. Schmidt	419	.265	1	38	541	**184**	**37**	12	**6.3**	.951
SS	C. O'Leary	211	.251	0	17	130	179	27	15	5.3	.920

Pitcher	G	IP	W	L	SV	ERA
E. Summers	40	301	24	12	1	1.64
G. Mullin	39	291	17	13	0	3.10
W. Donovan	29	243	18	7	0	2.08
E. Willett	30	197	15	8	1	2.28
E. Killian	27	181	12	9	1	2.99

Cleveland

W-90 L-64

Nap Lajoie

POS	Player	AB	BA	HR	RBI	PO	A	E	DP	TC/G	FA
1B	G. Stovall	534	.292	2	45	1509	87	16	**79**	**12.2**	**.990**
2B	N. Lajoie	581	.289	2	74	**450**	**538**	37	**78**	**6.6**	**.964**
SS	G. Perring	310	.216	0	19	74	159	18	15	5.2	.928
3B	B. Bradley	548	.243	1	46	142	209	23	13	3.2	.939
RF	B. Hinchman	464	.231	6	59	106	13	3	1	1.6	.975
CF	J. Birmingham	413	.213	2	38	250	20	12	6	2.3	.957
LF	J. Clarke	492	.242	1	21	220	13	9	1	1.8	.963
C	N. Clarke	290	.241	1	27	327	108	14	6	5.0	.969
C	H. Bemis	277	.224	0	33	326	74	15	5	5.5	.964
OS	T. Turner	201	.239	0	19	65	68	6	4		.957
O1	P. Hickman	197	.234	2	16	248	20	12	7		.957
OF	W. Good	154	.279	1	14	62	0	11	0	1.7	.849

Pitcher	G	IP	W	L	SV	ERA
A. Joss	42	325	24	11	2	**1.16**
B. Rhoads	37	270	18	12	0	1.77
G. Liebhardt	39	262	15	16	0	2.20
H. Berger	29	199	13	8	0	2.12
C. Chech	27	166	11	7	0	1.74

AMERICAN LEAGUE 1908, *cont.*

Chicago

W-88 L-64

Fielder Jones

POS	Player	AB	BA	HR	RBI	PO	A	E	DP	TC/G	FA	Pitcher	G	IP	W	L	SV	ERA
1B	J. Donahue	304	.204	0	22	968	57	6	30	12.4	.994	E. Walsh	**66**	**464**	**40**	15	**6**	1.42
2B	G. Davis	419	.217	0	26	191	314	21	25	5.5	.960	F. Smith	41	298	16	17	1	2.03
SS	F. Parent	391	.207	0	35	212	442	49	33	6.0	.930	D. White	41	296	18	13	0	2.55
3B	L. Tannehill	482	.216	0	35	135	**341**	33	15	3.7	.935	F. Owen	25	140	6	7	0	3.41
RF	E. Hahn	447	.251	0	21	160	4	6	2	1.4	.965	N. Altrock	23	136	5	7	2	2.71
CF	F. Jones	529	.253	1	50	288	17	10	5	2.1	.968							
LF	P. Dougherty	482	.278	0	45	173	7	10	1	1.4	.947							
C	B. Sullivan	430	.191	0	29	553	156	11	11	5.3	**.985**							
OF	J. Anderson	355	.262	0	47	96	9	4	7	1.2	.963							
1B	F. Isbell	320	.247	1	49	824	46	9	30	13.5	.990							
2B	J. Atz	206	.194	0	27	82	137	15	12	5.1	.936							
P	E. Walsh	157	.172	1	10	**41**	**190**	6	**9**	**3.6**	.975							

St. Louis

W-83 L-69

Jimmy McAleer

POS	Player	AB	BA	HR	RBI	PO	A	E	DP	TC/G	FA	Pitcher	G	IP	W	L	SV	ERA
1B	T. Jones	549	.246	1	50	**1616**	90	24	**79**	11.2	.986	H. Howell	41	324	18	18	1	1.89
2B	J. Williams	539	.236	4	53	352	445	31	50	5.6	.963	R. Waddell	43	286	19	14	3	1.89
SS	B. Wallace	487	.253	1	60	286	510	41	45	6.1	**.951**	J. Powell	33	256	16	13	1	2.11
3B	H. Ferris	555	.270	2	74	**222**	316	27	**27**	3.8	**.952**	B. Dinneen	27	167	14	7	0	2.10
RF	R. Hartzell	422	.265	2	32	117	15	8	5	1.7	.943	B. Pelty	20	122	7	4	0	1.99
CF	D. Hoffman	363	.251	1	25	185	19	8	8	2.1	.962	B. Grahame	21	117	6	7	0	2.30
LF	G. Stone	588	.281	5	31	274	11	16	3	2.0	.947	B. Bailey	22	107	3	5	0	3.04
C	T. Spencer	286	.210	0	28	398	109	9	9	5.8	.983							
OF	C. Jones	263	.232	0	17	116	13	5	2	1.9	.963							
OF	A. Schweitzer	182	.291	1	14	86	14	5	3	1.9	.952							

Boston

W-75 L-79

Deacon McGuire
W-53 L-62

Fred Lake
W-22 L-17

POS	Player	AB	BA	HR	RBI	PO	A	E	DP	TC/G	FA	Pitcher	G	IP	W	L	SV	ERA
1B	J. Stahl	258	.248	0	23	830	45	12	34	11.2	.986	C. Young	36	299	21	11	2	1.26
2B	A. McConnell	502	.279	2	43	237	349	**38**	32	5.0	.939	E. Cicotte	39	207	11	12	2	2.43
SS	H. Wagner	526	.247	1	46	**373**	**569**	61	51	**6.6**	.939	C. Morgan	30	205	14	13	1	2.46
3B	H. Lord	558	.260	2	37	181	271	**47**	13	3.5	.906	F. Burchell	31	180	10	8	0	2.96
RF	D. Gessler	435	.308	3	63	162	8	9	4	1.4	.950	G. Winter	22	148	4	14	0	3.05
CF	D. Sullivan	353	.241	0	25	193	18	4	4	2.2	.981	E. Steele	16	118	5	7	0	1.83
LF	J. Thoney	416	.255	2	30	208	12	12	2	2.3	.948	T. Pruiett	13	59	1	7	2	1.99
C	L. Criger	237	.190	0	25	380	120	10	11	6.1	.980							
OF	G. Cravath	277	.256	1	34	128	7	11	3	1.9	.925							
1B	B. Unglaub	266	.263	1	25	744	50	16	22	11.3	.980							
UT	F. LaPorte	156	.237	0	15	67	115	10	7		.948							

Philadelphia

W-68 L-85

Connie Mack

POS	Player	AB	BA	HR	RBI	PO	A	E	DP	TC/G	FA	Pitcher	G	IP	W	L	SV	ERA
1B	H. Davis	513	.248	5	62	1410	86	22	44	10.3	.986	R. Vickers	53	317	18	19	1	2.21
2B	E. Collins	330	.273	1	40	111	127	14	5	5.4	.944	E. Plank	34	245	14	16	1	2.17
SS	S. Nicholls	550	.216	4	31	221	370	56	26	5.4	.913	J. Dygert	41	239	11	15	1	2.87
3B	J. Collins	433	.217	0	30	117	216	26	14	3.1	.928	J. Coombs	26	153	7	5	0	2.00
RF	D. Murphy	525	.265	4	66	145	11	6	4	1.9	.963	C. Bender	18	139	8	9	1	1.75
CF	R. Oldring	434	.221	1	39	246	9	16	3	2.3	.941	B. Schlitzer	24	131	6	8	0	3.16
LF	T. Hartsel	460	.243	4	29	211	6	9	2	1.8	.960							
C	O. Schreckengost	207	.222	0	16	352	91	10	3	6.9	.978							
OP	J. Coombs	220	.255	1	23	102	48	4	4		.974							
C	M. Powers	172	.180	0	7	303	74	13	3	6.5	.967							

Washington

W-67 L-85

Joe Cantillon

POS	Player	AB	BA	HR	RBI	PO	A	E	DP	TC/G	FA	Pitcher	G	IP	W	L	SV	ERA
1B	J. Freeman	531	.252	1	45	1548	66	**41**	69	10.7	.975	L. Hughes	43	276	18	15	4	2.21
2B	J. Delahanty	287	.317	1	30	181	232	16	25	5.4	.963	W. Johnson	36	257	14	14	1	1.64
SS	G. McBride	518	.232	0	34	372	568	52	**58**	6.4	.948	C. Smith	26	184	9	13	1	2.40
3B	B. Shipke	341	.208	0	20	111	190	22	11	2.9	.932	B. Keeley	28	170	6	11	1	2.97
RF	O. Clymer	368	.253	1	35	81	16	7	7	1.3	.933	B. Burns	23	165	6	11	0	1.69
CF	C. Milan	485	.239	1	32	265	18	12	6	2.4	.959	E. Cates	19	115	4	8	0	2.51
LF	B. Ganley	549	.239	1	36	280	13	11	1	2.0	.964							
C	G. Street	394	.206	1	32	**578**	167	21	**14**	6.0	.973							
OF	O. Pickering	373	.225	2	30	135	6	9	1	1.5	.940							
32	B. Unglaub	276	.308	0	29	111	178	15	12		.951							
23	D. Altizer	205	.224	0	18	87	145	13	13		.947							

New York

W-51 L-103

Clark Griffith
W-24 L-32

Kid Elberfeld
W-27 L-71

POS	Player	AB	BA	HR	RBI	PO	A	E	DP	TC/G	FA	Pitcher	G	IP	W	L	SV	ERA
1B	H. Chase	405	.257	1	36	1020	54	22	35	11.4	.980	J. Chesbro	45	289	14	20	1	2.93
2B	H. Niles	361	.249	4	24	166	220	30	15	4.9	.928	J. Lake	38	269	9	**22**	0	3.17
SS	N. Ball	446	.247	0	38	268	438	**80**	28	6.0	.898	R. Manning	41	245	13	16	1	2.94
3B	W. Conroy	531	.237	1	39	179	249	28	12	**3.8**	.939	B. Hogg	24	152	4	16	0	3.01
RF	W. Keeler	323	.263	1	14	123	9	9	2	1.6	.936	A. Orth	21	139	2	13	0	3.42
CF	C. Hemphill	505	.297	0	44	285	13	20	2	2.2	.937	D. Newton	23	88	4	5	1	2.95
LF	J. Stahl	274	.255	2	42	111	14	9	3	2.0	.933							
C	R. Kleinow	279	.168	1	13	281	116	14	5	4.6	.966							
UT	G. Moriarty	348	.236	0	27	609	117	24	30		.968							
C	W. Blair	211	.190	1	13	225	58	12	4	4.9	.959							
OF	I. McIlveen	169	.213	0	8	70	4	4	0	1.8	.949							

BATTING AND BASE RUNNING LEADERS / PITCHING LEADERS

Batting Average		Slugging Average		Home Runs		Winning Percentage		Earned Run Average		Wins	
T. Cobb, DET	.324	T. Cobb, DET	.475	S. Crawford, DET	7	E. Walsh, CHI	.727	A. Joss, CLE	1.16	E. Walsh, CHI	40
S. Crawford, DET	.311	S. Crawford, DET	.457	B. Hinchman, CLE	6	W. Donovan, DET	.720	C. Young, BOS	1.26	E. Summers, DET	24
D. Gessler, BOS	.308	D. Gessler, BOS	.423	H. Niles, NY, BOS	5	A. Joss, CLE	.686	E. Walsh, CHI	1.42	A. Joss, CLE	24
C. Hemphill, NY	.297	C. Rossman, DET	.418	H. Davis, PHI	5	E. Summers, DET	.667	W. Johnson, WAS	1.64	C. Young, BOS	21
M. McIntyre, DET	.295	M. McIntyre, DET	.383	G. Stone, STL	5	C. Young, BOS	.656	E. Summers, DET	1.64	R. Waddell, STL	19

AMERICAN LEAGUE 1908, *cont.*

BATTING AND BASE RUNNING LEADERS

Total Bases

T. Cobb, DET	276
S. Crawford, DET	270
C. Rossman, DET	219
M. McIntyre, DET	218
N. Lajoie, CLE	218

Runs Batted In

T. Cobb, DET	108
S. Crawford, DET	80
H. Ferris, STL	74
N. Lajoie, CLE	74
C. Rossman, DET	71

Stolen Bases

P. Dougherty, CHI	47
C. Hemphill, NY	42
G. Schaefer, DET	40
T. Cobb, DET	39
J. Clarke, CLE	37

Hits

T. Cobb, DET	188
S. Crawford, DET	184
M. McIntyre, DET	168
N. Lajoie, CLE	168

Base on Balls

T. Hartsel, PHI	93
F. Jones, CHI	86
M. McIntyre, DET	83
J. Clarke, CLE	76

Home Run Percentage

B. Hinchman, CLE	1.3
H. Niles, NY, BOS	1.3
S. Crawford, DET	1.2
H. Davis, PHI	1.0

Runs

M. McIntyre, DET	105
S. Crawford, DET	102
G. Schaefer, DET	96
F. Jones, CHI	92

Doubles

T. Cobb, DET	36
C. Rossman, DET	33
S. Crawford, DET	33
N. Lajoie, CLE	32

Triples

T. Cobb, DET	20
J. Stahl, NY, BOS	16
S. Crawford, DET	16
D. Gessler, BOS	14

PITCHING LEADERS

Saves

E. Walsh, CHI	6
L. Hughes, WAS	4
R. Waddell, STL	3

Strikeouts

E. Walsh, CHI	269
R. Waddell, STL	232
L. Hughes, WAS	165
J. Dygert, PHI	164
W. Johnson, WAS	160

Complete Games

E. Walsh, CHI	42
C. Young, BOS	30
A. Joss, CLE	29
H. Howell, STL	27
G. Mullin, DET	26

Fewest Hits/9 Innings

A. Joss, CLE	6.42
F. Smith, CHI	6.44
E. Walsh, CHI	6.65
W. Johnson, WAS	6.78

Shutouts

E. Walsh, CHI	11
A. Joss, CLE	9

Fewest Walks/9 Innings

A. Joss, CLE	0.83
B. Burns, WAS	0.98
E. Walsh, CHI	1.09
C. Young, BOS	1.11

Most Strikeouts/9 Inn.

R. Waddell, STL	7.31
J. Dygert, PHI	6.18
W. Johnson, WAS	5.60
C. Bender, PHI	5.52

Innings

E. Walsh, CHI	464
A. Joss, CLE	325
H. Howell, STL	324
R. Vickers, PHI	317

Games Pitched

E. Walsh, CHI	66
R. Vickers, PHI	53
J. Chesbro, NY	45
L. Hughes, WAS	43
R. Waddell, STL	43

							Batting						Fielding			Pitching					
	W	L	PCT	GB	R	OR	2B	3B	HR	BA	SA	SB	E	DP	FA	CG	BB	SO	ShO	SV	ERA
Detroit	90	63	.588		**647**	547	**199**	86	19	**.264**	**.347**	165	305	95	.953	**120**	318	553	15	5	2.40
Cleveland	90	64	.584	0.5	568	**457**	188	58	18	.239	.309	169	257	95	.962	108	328	548	18	5	**2.02**
Chicago	88	64	.579	1.5	537	470	145	41	3	.224	.271	209	**232**	82	**.966**	107	**284**	623	**23**	**10**	2.22
St. Louis	83	69	.546	6.5	544	483	173	56	**21**	.245	.312	126	237	**97**	.964	107	387	607	16	5	2.15
Boston	75	79	.487	15.5	564	513	116	**88**	14	.246	.312	168	297	71	.955	102	366	624	12	7	2.27
Philadelphia	68	85	.444	22	486	562	183	49	**21**	.223	.291	116	272	68	.957	102	409	**740**	**23**	4	2.57
Washington	67	85	.441	22.5	479	539	131	74	8	.235	.295	170	275	89	.958	105	348	649	14	7	2.34
New York	51	103	.331	39.5	459	713	142	51	12	.236	.291	**230**	337	78	.947	91	457	584	11	3	3.16
					4284	4284	1277	503	116	.239	.303	1353	2212	675	.958	842	2897	4928	132	46	2.39

NATIONAL LEAGUE 1909

Pittsburgh

W-110 L-42

Fred Clarke

POS	Player	AB	BA	HR	RBI	PO	A	E	DP	TC/G	FA	Pitcher	G	IP	W	L	SV	ERA
1B	B. Abstein	512	.260	1	70	1412	65	27	70	11.1	.982	V. Willis	39	290	22	11	0	2.24
2B	D. Miller	560	.279	3	87	260	**426**	34	50	4.8	**.953**	H. Camnitz	41	283	25	6	3	1.62
SS	H. Wagner	495	**.339**	5	**100**	344	430	49	**58**	6.1	.940	N. Maddox	31	203	13	8	0	2.21
3B	J. Barbeau	350	.220	0	25	99	139	29*	8	3.1	.891	L. Leifield	32	202	19	8	0	2.37
RF	O. Wilson	569	.272	4	59	292	19	14	7	2.1	.957	D. Phillippe	22	132	8	3	0	2.32
CF	T. Leach	587	.261	6	43	333	12	11	3	2.6	.969	B. Adams	25	130	12	3	2	1.11
LF	F. Clarke	550	.287	3	68	362	17	5	2	2.5	.987	S. Leever	19	70	8	1	2	2.83
C	G. Gibson	510	.265	2	52	**655**	192	15	9	5.7	**.983**							
3B	B. Byrne	168	.256	0	7	50*	107*	2	3	3.5*	.987							

Chicago

W-104 L-49

Frank Chance

POS	Player	AB	BA	HR	RBI	PO	A	E	DP	TC/G	FA	Pitcher	G	IP	W	L	SV	ERA
1B	F. Chance	324	.272	0	46	901	40	6	43	10.3	.994	T. Brown	**50**	**343**	**27**	9	**7**	1.31
2B	J. Evers	463	.263	1	24	262	354	38	29	5.2	.942	O. Overall	38	285	20	11	2	1.42
SS	J. Tinker	516	.256	4	57	320	470	50	49	5.9	**.940**	E. Reulbach	35	263	19	10	0	1.78
3B	H. Steinfeldt	528	.252	2	59	183	299	31	16	3.4	.940	J. Pfiester	29	197	17	6	0	2.43
RF	W. Schulte	538	.264	4	60	169	14	6	1	1.4	.968	R. Kroh	17	120	9	4	0	1.65
CF	S. Hofman	527	.285	2	58	347	16	13	5	2.5	.965							
LF	J. Sheckard	525	.255	1	43	277	18	10	5	2.1	.967							
C	J. Archer	261	.230	1	30	408	97	21	7	6.6	.960							
C	P. Moran	246	.220	1	23	181	97	8	3	3.9	.972							
1B	D. Howard	203	.197	1	24	593	32	13	29	11.2	.980							
UT	H. Zimmerman	183	.273	0	21	100	93	19	12		.910							

New York

W-92 L-61

John McGraw

POS	Player	AB	BA	HR	RBI	PO	A	E	DP	TC/G	FA	Pitcher	G	IP	W	L	SV	ERA
1B	F. Tenney	375	.235	3	30	1046	72	16	53	**11.6**	.986	C. Mathewson	37	275	25	6	2	**1.14**
2B	L. Doyle	570	.302	6	49	**292**	322	39	**51**	4.6	.940	B. Raymond	39	270	18	12	0	2.47
SS	A. Bridwell	476	.294	0	55	268	439	45	55	5.2	.940	H. Wiltse	37	269	20	11	3	2.00
3B	A. Devlin	491	.265	0	55	191	317	36	**21**	3.8	.934	R. Ames	34	240	15	10	1	2.70
RF	R. Murray	570	.263	**7**	91	222	30	14	1	1.8	.947	R. Marquard	29	173	5	13	0	2.60
CF	B. O'Hara	360	.236	1	30	202	19	5	4	2.0	.978	D. Crandall	30	122	6	4	4	2.88
LF	M. McCormick	413	.291	3	27	144	13	13	6	1.6	.924							
C	A. Schlei	279	.244	0	30	493	127	24	9	**7.2**	.963							
OF	C. Seymour	280	.311	1	30	138	11	5	3	2.1	.968							
1B	F. Merkle	236	.191	0	20	621	27	16	29	9.6	.976							
C	C. Meyers	220	.277	1	30	376	71	17	4	7.3	.963							

Cincinnati

W-77 L-76

Clark Griffith

POS	Player	AB	BA	HR	RBI	PO	A	E	DP	TC/G	FA	Pitcher	G	IP	W	L	SV	ERA
1B	D. Hoblitzell	517	.308	4	67	1444	74	**28**	**80**	10.9	.982	A. Fromme	37	279	19	13	2	1.90
2B	D. Egan	480	.275	2	53	271	376	34	45	**5.9**	.950	H. Gaspar	44	260	18	11	2	2.01
SS	T. Downey	416	.231	1	32	260	363	**62**	54	5.8	.909	J. Rowan	38	226	11	12	0	2.79
3B	H. Lobert	425	.212	4	52	182	204	33	16	3.4	.921	B. Ewing	31	218	11	12	0	2.43
RF	M. Mitchell	523	.310	4	86	262	20	11	3	2.0	.962	B. Campbell	30	148	7	11	2	2.67
CF	R. Oakes	415	.270	3	31	218	15	5	3	2.1	.979	B. Spade	14	98	5	5	0	2.85
LF	B. Bescher	446	.240	1	34	247	14	13	4	2.3	.953	J. Dubuc	19	71	3	5	2	3.66
C	L. McLean	324	.256	2	36	379	119	11	16	5.4	.978							
OF	D. Paskert	322	.252	0	33	172	11	6	3	2.3	.968							
23	M. Huggins	159	.214	0	6	95	125	16	14		.932							

NATIONAL LEAGUE 1909, *cont.*

Team	POS	Player	AB	BA	HR	RBI	PO	A	E	DP	TC/G	FA	Pitcher	G	IP	W	L	SV	ERA
Philadelphia	1B	K. Bransfield	527	.292	1	59	1377	89	16	71	10.7	**.989**	E. Moore	38	300	18	12	0	2.10
	2B	O. Knabe	402	.234	0	33	237	312	36	38	5.4	.938	L. Moren	39	254	16	15	1	2.66
W-74 L-79	SS	M. Doolan	493	.219	1	35	**352**	**484**	54	**58**	**6.1**	.939	G. McQuillan	41	248	13	16	2	2.14
	3B	E. Grant	**631**	.269	1	37	184	310	22	18	3.4	.957	F. Corridon	27	171	11	7	0	2.11
Billy Murray	RF	J. Titus	540	.270	3	46	241	23	8	6	1.8	.971	T. Sparks	24	122	6	11	0	2.96
	CF	J. Bates	266	.293	1	15	130	12	6	3	2.0	.959	H. Coveleski	24	122	6	10	1	2.74
	LF	S. Magee	522	.270	2	66	283	11	9	0	2.1	.970	B. Foxen	18	83	3	7	0	3.35
	C	R. Dooin	468	.224	2	38	517	199	**40**	14	5.4	.947							
	OF	F. Osborn	189	.185	0	19	126	14	3	3	2.6	.979							
	2B	J. Ward	184	.266	0	23	58	77	8	12	3.0	.944							
	OF	P. Deininger	169	.260	0	16	83	5	1	0	2.0	.989							
Brooklyn	1B	T. Jordan	330	.273	3	36	937	29	17	36	10.3	.983	N. Rucker	38	309	13	19	1	2.24
	2B	W. Alperman	420	.248	1	41	266	297	**42**	32	5.6	.931	G. Bell	33	256	16	15	1	2.71
W-55 L-98	SS	T. McMillan	373	.212	0	24	190	310	47	32	5.2	.914	H. McIntire	32	228	7	17	0	3.63
	3B	E. Lennox	435	.262	2	44	167	210	16	18	3.2	**.959**	K. Wilhelm	22	163	3	13	0	3.26
Harry Lumley	RF	H. Lumley	172	.250	0	14	83	9	5	1	1.9	.948	D. Scanlan	19	141	8	7	0	2.93
	CF	A. Burch	601	.271	1	30	320	23	16	4	2.4	.955	G. Hunter	16	113	4	10	0	2.46
	LF	W. Clement	340	.256	0	17	179	14	7	4	2.3	.965	J. Pastorius	12	80	1	9	0	5.76
	C	B. Bergen	346	.139	1	15	536	**202**	18	**18**	6.8	.976							
	UT	J. Hummel	542	.280	4	52	728	207	35	38		.964							
	UT	P. McElveen	258	.198	3	25	147	107	14	11		.948							
	OF	J. Kustus	173	.145	1	11	92	6	5	1	2.1	.951							
St. Louis	1B	E. Konetchy	576	.286	4	80	**1584**	**97**	26	71	11.2	.985	F. Beebe	44	288	15	21	1	2.82
	2B	C. Charles	339	.236	0	29	162	186	31	28	5.3	.918	J. Lush	34	221	11	18	0	3.13
W-54 L-98	SS	R. Hulswitt	289	.280	0	29	147	200	26	16	5.7	.930	S. Sallee	32	219	10	11	0	2.42
	3B	B. Byrne	421	.214	1	33	164*	252*	35	11	4.3*	.922	B. Harmon	21	159	6	11	0	3.68
Roger Bresnahan	RF	S. Evans	498	.259	2	56	212	19	13	10	1.7	.947	L. Backman	21	128	3	11	0	4.14
	CF	A. Shaw	331	.248	2	34	189	14	13	1	2.3	.940	J. Raleigh	15	81	1	10	0	3.79
	LF	R. Ellis	575	.268	3	46	332	28	17	9	2.6	.955							
	C	E. Phelps	306	.248	0	22	330	87	20	11	5.3	.954							
	02	J. Delahanty	411	.214	2	54	203	121	22	11		.936							
	C	R. Bresnahan	234	.244	0	23	211	78	12	3	5.1	.960							
	3B	J. Barbeau	175	.251	0	5	56	72	14*	7	3.1	.901							
	SS	A. Storke	174	.282	0	10	93	135	10	14	5.4	.958							
Boston	1B	F. Stem	245	.208	0	11	656	62	8	31	10.7	.989	A. Mattern	47	316	16	20	3	2.85
	2B	D. Shean	267	.247	1	29	164	209	17	34	5.4	.956	G. Ferguson	36	227	5	**23**	0	3.73
	SS	J. Coffey	257	.187	0	20	133	213	40	18	5.3	.896	K. White	23	148	6	13	0	3.22
W-45 L-108	3B	B. Sweeney	493	.243	1	36	156	243	**43**	14	3.9	.903	L. Richie	22	132	7	7	2	2.32
	RF	B. Becker	562	.246	6	24	222	26	18	8	1.8	.932	B. Brown	18	123	4	10	0	3.14
Harry Smith	CF	G. Beaumont	407	.263	0	60	234	15	8	3	2.3	.969							
W-23 L-54	LF	R. Thomas	281	.263	0	11	155	9	4	1	2.4	.976							
	C	P. Graham	267	.240	0	17	193	111	22	14	4.3	.933							
Frank Bowerman	01	F. Beck	334	.198	3	27	464	26	14	18		.972							
W-22 L-54	OF	J. Bates	236	.288	1	23	123	15	8	0	2.4	.945							
	2B	C. Starr	216	.222	0	6	103	140	18	19	4.8	.931							
	1B	C. Autry	199	.196	0	13	605	38	4	27	10.6	.994							
	SS	B. Dahlen	197	.234	2	16	101	184	29	20	6.4	.908							

BATTING AND BASE RUNNING LEADERS

Batting Average

H. Wagner, PIT	.339
M. Mitchell, CIN	.310
D. Hoblitzell, CIN	.308
L. Doyle, NY	.302
A. Bridwell, NY	.294

Slugging Average

H. Wagner, PIT	.489
M. Mitchell, CIN	.430
L. Doyle, NY	.419
D. Hoblitzell, CIN	.418
M. McCormick, NY	.402

Home Runs

R. Murray, NY	7
B. Becker, BOS	6
L. Doyle, NY	6
T. Leach, PIT	6
H. Wagner, PIT	5

Total Bases

H. Wagner, PIT	242
L. Doyle, NY	239
E. Konetchy, STL	228
M. Mitchell, CIN	225
D. Miller, PIT	222

Runs Batted In

H. Wagner, PIT	100
R. Murray, NY	91
D. Miller, PIT	87
M. Mitchell, CIN	86
E. Konetchy, STL	80

Stolen Bases

B. Bescher, CIN	54
R. Murray, NY	48
D. Egan, CIN	39
S. Magee, PHI	38
A. Burch, BKN	38

Hits

L. Doyle, NY	172
E. Grant, PHI	170
H. Wagner, PIT	168
E. Konetchy, STL	165

Base on Balls

F. Clarke, PIT	80
B. Byrne, STL, PIT	78
J. Evers, CHI	73
J. Sheckard, CHI	72

Home Run Percentage

R. Murray, NY	1.2
B. Becker, BOS	1.1
L. Doyle, NY	1.1
T. Leach, PIT	1.0

Runs

T. Leach, PIT	126
F. Clarke, PIT	97
H. Wagner, PIT	92
B. Byrne, STL, PIT	92

Doubles

H. Wagner, PIT	39
S. Magee, PHI	33
D. Miller, PIT	31
J. Sheckard, CHI	29
T. Leach, PIT	29

Triples

M. Mitchell, CIN	17
S. Magee, PHI	14
E. Konetchy, STL	14
D. Miller, PIT	13

PITCHING LEADERS

Winning Percentage

H. Camnitz, PIT	.806
C. Mathewson, NY	.806
T. Brown, CHI	.750
J. Pfiester, CHI	.739
L. Leifield, PIT	.704

Earned Run Average

C. Mathewson, NY	1.14
T. Brown, CHI	1.31
O. Overall, CHI	1.42
H. Camnitz, PIT	1.62
R. Kroh, CHI	1.65

Wins

T. Brown, CHI	27
C. Mathewson, NY	25
H. Camnitz, PIT	25
V. Willis, PIT	22
H. Wiltse, NY	20
O. Overall, CHI	20

Saves

T. Brown, CHI	7
D. Crandall, NY	4
H. Wiltse, NY	3
L. Richie, PHI, BOS	3
H. Camnitz, PIT	3
A. Mattern, BOS	3

Strikeouts

O. Overall, CHI	205
N. Rucker, BKN	201
E. Moore, PHI	173
T. Brown, CHI	172
R. Ames, NY	156

Complete Games

T. Brown, CHI	32
G. Bell, BKN	29
N. Rucker, BKN	28
C. Mathewson, NY	26

Fewest Hits/9 Innings

C. Mathewson, NY	6.28
A. Fromme, CIN	6.28
O. Overall, CHI	6.44
T. Brown, CHI	6.46

Shutouts

O. Overall, CHI	9
C. Mathewson, NY	8
T. Brown, CHI	8

Fewest Walks/9 Innings

C. Mathewson, NY	1.18
T. Brown, CHI	1.39
H. Wiltse, NY	1.70
N. Maddox, PIT	1.73

Most Strikeouts/9 Inn.

O. Overall, CHI	6.47
R. Ames, NY	5.85
N. Rucker, BKN	5.85
E. Moore, PHI	5.20

Innings

T. Brown, CHI	343
A. Mattern, BOS	316
N. Rucker, BKN	309
E. Moore, PHI	300

Games Pitched

T. Brown, CHI	50
A. Mattern, BOS	47
H. Gaspar, CIN	44
F. Beebe, STL	44

NATIONAL LEAGUE 1909, *cont.*

	W	L	PCT	GB	R	OR	Batting 2B	3B	HR	BA	SA	SB	Fielding E	DP	FA	Pitching CG	BB	SO	ShO	SV	ERA
Pittsburgh	110	42	.724		**699**	447	**218**	**92**	25	**.260**	**.353**	185	**227**	100	**.964**	94	**320**	490	21	9	2.07
Chicago	104	49	.680	6.5	635	**390**	203	60	20	.245	.322	187	244	95	.961	111	364	680	**32**	9	**1.75**
New York	92	61	.601	18.5	623	546	173	68	**26**	.255	.329	230	307	99	.954	105	397	**735**	16	**12**	2.27
Cincinnati	77	76	.503	33.5	606	599	159	72	22	.250	.323	**280**	308	**120**	.952	91	510	477	10	9	2.52
Philadelphia	74	79	.484	36.5	516	518	185	53	12	.244	.309	185	241	97	.961	89	470	610	17	6	2.44
Brooklyn	55	98	.359	55.5	444	627	176	59	16	.229	.296	141	282	86	.954	**126**	528	594	18	2	3.10
St. Louis	54	98	.355	56	583	731	148	56	15	.243	.303	161	322	90	.950	84	483	435	4	2	3.41
Boston	45	108	.294	65.5	435	683	124	43	15	.223	.274	135	340	101	.947	98	543	414	13	6	3.20
					4541	4541	1386	503	151	.244	.314	1504	2271	788	.955	798	3615	4435	131	55	2.60

AMERICAN LEAGUE 1909

Detroit

W-98 L-54

Hughie Jennings

POS	Player	AB	BA	HR	RBI	PO	A	E	DP	TC/G	FA	Pitcher	G	IP	W	L	SV	ERA
1B	C. Rossman	287	.261	0	39	913	36	18	30	12.9	.981	G. Mullin	40	304	**29**	8	1	2.22
2B	G. Schaefer	280	.250	0	22	180	273	16	26	5.5	.966	E. Willett	41	293	21	10	1	2.34
SS	D. Bush	532	.273	0	33	308	**567**	**71**	38	6.0	.925	E. Summers	35	282	19	9	1	2.24
3B	G. Moriarty	473	.273	1	39	117	253	24	11	3.7	**.939**	E. Killian	25	173	11	9	1	1.71
RF	T. Cobb	573	**.377**	**9**	**107**	222	24	14	7	1.7	.946	W. Donovan	21	140	8	7	2	2.31
CF	S. Crawford	589	.314	6	97	297	7	11	2	2.3	.965							
LF	M. McIntyre	476	.244	1	34	217	14	6	1	1.9	.975							
C	B. Schmidt	253	.209	1	28	315	107	**20**	7	5.5	.955							
3B	C. O'Leary	261	.203	0	13	59	118	15	4	3.6	.922							
C	O. Stanage	252	.262	0	21	324	80	15	12	5.4	.964							
OF	D. Jones	204	.279	0	10	103	4	2	1	1.9	.982							
2B	J. Delahanty	150	.253	0	20	88	127	13*	13	5.0	.943							

Philadelphia

W-95 L-58

Connie Mack

POS	Player	AB	BA	HR	RBI	PO	A	E	DP	TC/G	FA	Pitcher	G	IP	W	L	SV	ERA
1B	H. Davis	530	.268	4	75	1432	74	19	65	10.2	.988	E. Plank	34	275	19	10	0	1.70
2B	E. Collins	572	.346	3	56	**373**	**406**	27	**55**	5.3	**.967**	C. Bender	34	250	18	8	1	1.66
SS	J. Barry	409	.215	1	23	196	351	43	40	4.8	.927	C. Morgan	28	229	16	11	0	1.65
3B	F. Baker	541	.305	4	85	**209**	**277**	**42**	16	3.6	.920	H. Krause	32	213	18	8	0	**1.39**
RF	D. Murphy	541	.281	5	69	191	17	5	5	1.4	.977	J. Coombs	31	206	12	11	1	2.32
CF	R. Oldring	326	.230	1	28	174	7	7	1	2.1	.963	J. Dygert	32	137	9	5	0	2.42
LF	B. Ganley	274	.197	0	9	185	9	4	2	2.6	.980							
C	I. Thomas	256	.223	0	31	479	112	9	5	**7.1**	**.985**							
OF	T. Hartsel	267	.270	0	18	140	0	5	0	2.0	.966							
OF	H. Heitmuller	210	.286	0	15	111	4	9	2	2.1	.927							
C	P. Livingston	175	.234	0	15	306	106	13	6	6.6	.969							

Boston

W-88 L-63

Fred Lake

POS	Player	AB	BA	HR	RBI	PO	A	E	DP	TC/G	FA	Pitcher	G	IP	W	L	SV	ERA
1B	J. Stahl	435	.294	6	60	1353	50	20	57	11.3	.986	F. Arellanes	45	231	16	12	**8**	2.18
2B	A. McConnell	453	.238	0	36	251	389	**31**	43	**5.5**	.954	E. Cicotte	27	160	13	5	2	1.97
SS	H. Wagner	430	.256	1	49	282	413	50	40	**6.1**	.933	S. Wood	24	159	11	7	0	2.21
3B	H. Lord	534	.311	0	31	180	268	34	10	3.6	.929	C. Chech	17	107	7	5	0	2.95
RF	D. Gessler	386	.298	0	46	135	18	11	1	1.5	.933	C. Hall	11	60	6	4	0	2.56
CF	T. Speaker	544	.309	7	77	319	35	10	12	2.6	.973							
LF	H. Niles	546	.245	1	38	197	20	11	3	1.9	.952							
C	B. Carrigan	280	.296	1	36	347	110	13	9	6.1	.972							
OF	H. Hooper	255	.282	0	12	124	14	7	3	2.0	.952							
C	P. Donahue	176	.239	2	25	249	71	6	3	5.6	.982							
2S	C. French	167	.251	0	13	86	140	24	14		.904							

Chicago

W-78 L-74

Billy Sullivan

POS	Player	AB	BA	HR	RBI	PO	A	E	DP	TC/G	FA	Pitcher	G	IP	W	L	SV	ERA
1B	F. Isbell	433	.224	0	33	1204	66	8	48	**12.7**	**.994**	F. Smith	**51**	**365**	25	17	1	1.80
2B	J. Atz	381	.236	0	22	202	311	25	40	4.6	.954	J. Scott	36	250	12	12	0	2.30
SS	F. Parent	472	.261	0	30	182	357	41	34	5.9	.929	E. Walsh	31	230	15	11	2	1.41
3B	L. Tannehill	531	.222	0	47	103	168	17	11	3.2	.941	D. White	24	178	11	9	0	1.72
RF	E. Hahn	287	.181	1	16	93	3	1	1	1.3	.990	B. Burns	22	174	7	13	0	1.96
CF	D. Altizer	382	.233	1	20	99	12	6	1	1.9	.949							
LF	P. Dougherty	491	.285	1	55	184	10	12	0	1.5	.942							
C	B. Sullivan	265	.162	0	16	452	119	10	6	6.0	.983							
32	B. Purtell	361	.258	0	40	162	248	24	24		.945							
OP	D. White	192	.234	0	7	71	54	8	1		.940							
C	F. Owens	174	.201	0	17	266	62	14	2	6.0	.959							
OF	W. Cole	165	.236	0	16	83	5	11	1	2.2	.889							
P	F. Smith	127	.173	0	20	**26**	**154**	4	3	3.6	.978							

New York

W-74 L-77

George Stallings

POS	Player	AB	BA	HR	RBI	PO	A	E	DP	TC/G	FA	Pitcher	G	IP	W	L	SV	ERA
1B	H. Chase	474	.283	4	63	1202	71	**28**	53	11.0	.978	J. Warhop	36	243	13	15	2	2.40
2B	F. LaPorte	309	.298	0	31	142	208	23	30	4.5	.938	J. Lake	31	215	14	11	1	1.88
SS	J. Knight	360	.236	0	40	141	204	38	19	4.9	.901	R. Manning	26	173	7	11	1	3.17
3B	J. Austin	437	.231	1	39	176	236	32	**19**	**4.0**	.928	L. Brockett	26	152	10	8	1	2.37
RF	W. Keeler	360	.264	1	32	111	9	4	2	1.3	.968	S. Doyle	17	126	8	6	0	2.58
CF	R. Demmitt	427	.246	4	30	185	22	21	7	2.1	.908	J. Quinn	23	119	9	5	1	1.97
LF	C. Engle	492	.278	3	71	299	17	18	5	2.5	.946	T. Hughes	24	119	7	8	1	2.65
C	R. Kleinow	206	.228	0	15	343	83	15	6	5.7	.966	P. Wilson	14	94	6	5	0	3.17
S3	K. Elberfeld	379	.237	0	26	196	269	26	30		.947							
OF	B. Cree	343	.262	2	27	121	9	7	2	1.8	.949							
OF	C. Hemphill	181	.243	0	10	75	6	2	1	1.8	.976							
C	J. Sweeney	176	.267	0	21	274	83	**20**	7	6.1	.947							

AMERICAN LEAGUE 1909, *cont.*

Cleveland

W-71 L-82

Nap Lajoie
W-57 L-57

Deacon McGuire
W-14 L-25

POS	Player	AB	BA	HR	RBI	PO	A	E	DP	TC/G	FA	Pitcher	G	IP	W	L	SV	ERA
1B	G. Stovall	565	.246	2	49	**1478**	**109**	19	**80**	11.1	.988	C. Young	35	295	19	15	0	2.26
2B	N. Lajoie	469	.324	1	47	193	370	28	**55**	4.9	.953	H. Berger	34	257	13	14	1	2.63
SS	N. Ball	324	.256	1	25	198	289	46	42	5.6	.914	A. Joss	33	243	14	13	0	1.71
3B	B. Bradley	334	.186	0	22	89	157	11	16	3.0	.957	C. Falkenberg	24	165	10	9	0	2.40
RF	W. Good	318	.214	0	17	110	12	6	2	1.6	.953	B. Rhoads	20	133	5	9	0	2.90
CF	J. Birmingham	343	.289	1	38	203	15	12	2	2.3	.948							
LF	B. Hinchman	457	.258	2	53	233	0	20	1	1.9	.921							
C	T. Easterly	287	.261	1	27	335	110	16	9	6.1	.965							
3B	G. Perring	283	.223	0	20	83	151	17	6	3.8	.932							
OF	B. Lord	249	.269	1	25	110	13	1	4	1.8	.992							
OF	E. Flick	235	.255	0	15	87	4	4	1	1.6	.958							
2S	T. Turner	208	.250	0	16	112	176	11	21		.963							
C	N. Clarke	164	.274	0	14	192	65	13	2	6.1	.952							

St. Louis

W-61 L-89

Jimmy McAleer

POS	Player	AB	BA	HR	RBI	PO	A	E	DP	TC/G	FA	Pitcher	G	IP	W	L	SV	ERA
1B	T. Jones	337	.249	0	29	950	70	11	57	10.9	.989	J. Powell	34	239	12	16	3	2.11
2B	J. Williams	374	.195	0	22	221	280	20	42	4.8	.962	R. Waddell	31	220	11	14	0	2.37
SS	B. Wallace	403	.238	1	35	193	279	27	34	5.7	.946	B. Pelty	27	199	11	11	0	2.30
3B	H. Ferris	556	.216	3	58	157	242	27	15	3.7	.937	B. Bailey	32	199	9	10	0	2.44
RF	R. Hartzell	**595**	.271	0	32	120	21	9	5	1.8	.940	B. Grahame	34	187	8	14	1	3.12
CF	D. Hoffman	387	.269	2	26	230	10	8	6	2.3	.968	B. Dinneen	17	112	6	7	0	3.46
LF	G. Stone	310	.287	1	15	147	8	12	4	2.1	.928							
C	L. Criger	212	.170	0	9	387	98	7	16	6.7	.986							
10	A. Griggs	364	.280	0	43	504	38	14	22		.975							
OF	J. McAleese	267	.213	0	12	120	11	13	2	1.8	.910							
C	J. Stephens	223	.220	3	18	335	103	9	9	6.2	.980							

Washington

W-42 L-110

Joe Cantillon

POS	Player	AB	BA	HR	RBI	PO	A	E	DP	TC/G	FA	Pitcher	G	IP	W	L	SV	ERA
1B	J. Donahue	283	.237	0	28	766	36	13	28	10.1	.984	W. Johnson	40	297	13	25	1	2.21
2B	J. Delahanty	302	.222	1	21	177	211	18*	26	4.8	.956	B. Groom	44	261	7	**26**	0	2.87
SS	G. McBride	504	.234	0	34	**341**	499	58	**56**	5.8	**.935**	D. Gray	36	218	5	19	0	3.59
3B	W. Conroy	488	.244	1	20	136	239	25	14	3.3	.938	C. Smith	23	146	3	12	0	3.27
RF	J. Lelivelt	318	.292	0	24	179	14	6	3	2.2	.970	L. Hughes	22	120	4	7	1	2.69
CF	C. Milan	400	.200	1	15	222	19	7	3	2.1	.972							
LF	G. Browne	393	.272	1	16	147	12	11	3	1.7	.935							
C	G. Street	407	.211	0	29	**714**	**210**	18	**18**	6.9	.981							
UT	B. Unglaub	480	.265	3	41	669	121	13	39		.984							

BATTING AND BASE RUNNING LEADERS

Batting Average
T. Cobb, DET .377
E. Collins, PHI .346
N. Lajoie, CLE .324
S. Crawford, DET .314
H. Lord, BOS .311

Slugging Average
T. Cobb, DET .517
S. Crawford, DET .452
E. Collins, PHI .449
F. Baker, PHI .447
T. Speaker, BOS .443

Home Runs
T. Cobb, DET 9
T. Speaker, BOS 7
J. Stahl, BOS 6
S. Crawford, DET 6
D. Murphy, PHI 5

Total Bases
T. Cobb, DET 296
S. Crawford, DET 266
E. Collins, PHI 257
F. Baker, PHI 242
T. Speaker, BOS 241

Runs Batted In
T. Cobb, DET 107
S. Crawford, DET 97
F. Baker, PHI 85
T. Speaker, BOS 77
H. Davis, PHI 75

Stolen Bases
T. Cobb, DET 76
E. Collins, PHI 67
D. Bush, DET 53
P. Dougherty, CHI 36
H. Lord, BOS 36

Hits
T. Cobb, DET 216
E. Collins, PHI 198
S. Crawford, DET 185
T. Speaker, BOS 168

Base on Balls
D. Bush, DET 88
E. Collins, PHI 62
R. Demmitt, NY 55
M. McIntyre, DET 54

Home Run Percentage
T. Cobb, DET 1.6
J. Stahl, BOS 1.4
T. Speaker, BOS 1.3
S. Crawford, DET 1.0

Runs
T. Cobb, DET 116
D. Bush, DET 114
E. Collins, PHI 104
H. Lord, BOS 85

Doubles
S. Crawford, DET 35
N. Lajoie, CLE 33
T. Cobb, DET 33
E. Collins, PHI 30

Triples
F. Baker, PHI 19
D. Murphy, PHI 14
S. Crawford, DET 14

PITCHING LEADERS

Winning Percentage
G. Mullin, DET .784
C. Bender, PHI .692
H. Krause, PHI .692
E. Summers, DET .679
E. Willett, DET .677

Earned Run Average
H. Krause, PHI 1.39
E. Walsh, CHI 1.41
C. Bender, PHI 1.66
E. Plank, PHI 1.70
A. Joss, CLE 1.71

Wins
G. Mullin, DET 29
F. Smith, CHI 25
E. Willett, DET 21
E. Plank, PHI 19
E. Summers, DET 19
C. Young, CLE 19

Saves
F. Arellanes, BOS 8
J. Powell, STL 3

Strikeouts
F. Smith, CHI 177
W. Johnson, WAS 164
H. Berger, CLE 162
C. Bender, PHI 161
R. Waddell, STL 141

Complete Games
F. Smith, CHI 37
C. Young, CLE 30
G. Mullin, DET 29
W. Johnson, WAS 27
C. Morgan, BOS, PHI 26

Fewest Hits/9 Innings
C. Morgan, BOS, PHI 6.26
H. Krause, PHI 6.38
E. Walsh, CHI 6.49
E. Cicotte, BOS 6.59

Shutouts
E. Walsh, CHI 8
H. Krause, PHI 7
F. Smith, CHI 7
J. Coombs, PHI 6

Fewest Walks/9 Innings
A. Joss, CLE 1.15
D. White, CHI 1.57
J. Powell, STL 1.58
C. Bender, PHI 1.62

Most Strikeouts/9 Inn.
H. Krause, PHI 5.87
C. Bender, PHI 5.80
R. Waddell, STL 5.76
H. Berger, CLE 5.67

Innings
F. Smith, CHI 365
G. Mullin, DET 304
W. Johnson, WAS 297
C. Young, CLE 295

Games Pitched
F. Smith, CHI 51
F. Arellanes, BOS 45
B. Groom, WAS 44
E. Willett, DET 41

							Batting						Fielding			Pitching					
	W	L	PCT	GB	R	OR	2B	3B	HR	BA	SA	SB	E	DP	FA	CG	BB	SO	ShO	SV	ERA
Detroit	98	54	.645		**666**	493	**209**	58	19	**.267**	.342	**280**	276	87	.959	**117**	359	528	17	12	2.26
Philadelphia	95	58	.621	3.5	605	**408**	186	**89**	**20**	.257	**.343**	205	**245**	92	.961	111	386	**728**	**27**	3	**1.92**
Boston	88	63	.583	9.5	597	550	151	69	**20**	.263	.333	215	292	95	.955	75	384	555	11	**15**	2.60
Chicago	78	74	.513	20	492	463	145	56	4	.221	.275	211	246	101	**.964**	112	**341**	671	26	4	2.04
New York	74	77	.490	23.5	590	587	143	61	16	.248	.311	187	329	94	.948	94	422	597	18	7	2.68
Cleveland	71	82	.464	27.5	493	532	173	81	10	.241	.313	174	275	**110**	.957	110	349	569	15	3	2.39
St. Louis	61	89	.407	36	441	575	116	45	11	.232	.280	136	267	107	.958	105	383	620	21	4	2.88
Washington	42	110	.276	56	380	656	148	41	9	.223	.275	136	280	100	.957	99	424	653	11	2	3.04
					4264	4264	1271	500	109	.244	.309	1544	2210	786	.957	823	3048	4921	146	50	2.48

NATIONAL LEAGUE 1910

Chicago

W-104 L-50

Frank Chance

POS	Player	AB	BA	HR	RBI	PO	A	E	DP	TC/G	FA	Pitcher	G	IP	W	L	SV	ERA
1B	F. Chance	295	.298	0	36	773	38	3	48	9.4	.996	T. Brown	46	295	25	13	**7**	1.86
2B	J. Evers	433	.263	0	28	282	347	33	55	5.3	.950	K. Cole	33	240	20	4	0	1.80
SS	J. Tinker	473	.288	3	69	277	411	42	54	5.6	.942	H. McIntire	28	176	13	9	0	3.07
3B	H. Steinfeldt	448	.252	2	58	137	246	22	16	3.2	.946	E. Reulbach	24	173	12	8	0	3.12
RF	W. Schulte	559	.301	**10**	68	221	18	8	5	1.6	.968	O. Overall	23	145	12	6	1	2.68
CF	S. Hofman	477	.325	3	86	249	19	7	4	2.5	.975	L. Richie	30	130	11	4	3	2.70
LF	J. Sheckard	507	.256	5	51	308	21	8	3	2.4	.976	J. Pfiester	14	100	6	3	0	1.79
C	J. Kling	297	.269	2	32	407	118	11	10	6.2	.979							
UT	H. Zimmerman	335	.284	3	38	164	181	33	28		.913							
C1	J. Archer	313	.259	2	41	620	97	20	31		.973							
OF	G. Beaumont	172	.267	2	22	107	5	5	0	2.1	.957							

New York

W-91 L-63

John McGraw

POS	Player	AB	BA	HR	RBI	PO	A	E	DP	TC/G	FA	Pitcher	G	IP	W	L	SV	ERA
1B	F. Merkle	506	.292	4	70	1390	84	**29**	**87**	10.4	.981	C. Mathewson	38	318	**27**	9	0	1.90
2B	L. Doyle	575	.285	8	69	313	388	**53**	62	5.0	.930	H. Wiltse	36	235	14	12	1	2.72
SS	A. Bridwell	492	.276	0	48	304	417	41	52	5.4	.946	L. Drucke	34	215	12	10	0	2.47
3B	A. Devlin	493	.260	2	67	179	284	33	20	3.4	.933	D. Crandall	42	208	17	4	4	2.56
RF	R. Murray	553	.277	4	87	246	26	15	3	1.9	.948	R. Ames	33	190	12	11	0	2.22
CF	F. Snodgrass	396	.321	2	44	214	12	7	1	2.3	.970	B. Raymond	19	99	4	11	0	3.81
LF	J. Devore	490	.304	2	27	191	18	16	3	1.7	.929							
C	C. Meyers	365	.285	1	62	**638**	154	25	16	**7.0**	.969							
OF	C. Seymour	287	.265	1	40	137	9	10	1	2.1	.936							
OF	B. Becker	126	.286	3	24	63	7	2	0	1.6	.972							

Pittsburgh

W-86 L-67

Fred Clarke

POS	Player	AB	BA	HR	RBI	PO	A	E	DP	TC/G	FA	Pitcher	G	IP	W	L	SV	ERA
1B	J. Flynn	332	.274	6	52	869	49	22	54	10.1	.977	H. Camnitz	38	260	12	13	2	3.22
2B	D. Miller	444	.227	1	48	263	318	33	45	5.2	.946	B. Adams	34	245	18	9	0	2.24
SS	H. Wagner	556	.320	4	81	**337**	413	51	62	5.8	.936	L. Leifield	40	218	15	12	1	2.64
3B	B. Byrne	602	.296	2	52	167	289	35	11	3.3	.929	K. White	30	153	10	9	2	3.46
RF	O. Wilson	536	.276	4	50	255	23	8	5	2.0	.972	D. Phillippe	31	122	14	2	4	2.29
CF	T. Leach	529	.270	4	52	352	14	13	4	2.9	.966	S. Leever	26	111	6	5	2	2.76
LF	F. Clarke	429	.263	2	63	284	10	10	4	2.6	.967	B. Powell	12	75	4	6	0	2.40
C	G. Gibson	482	.259	3	44	633	**203**	14	8	5.9	**.984**							
OF	V. Campbell	282	.326	4	21	145	8	18	2	2.3	.895							
UT	B. McKechnie	212	.217	0	12	146	166	12	20		.963							
1B	H. Hyatt	175	.263	1	30	323	19	5	19	9.1	.986							

Philadelphia

W-78 L-75

Red Dooin

POS	Player	AB	BA	HR	RBI	PO	A	E	DP	TC/G	FA	Pitcher	G	IP	W	L	SV	ERA
1B	K. Bransfield	427	.239	3	52	1026	51	20	82	10.0	.982	E. Moore	46	283	22	15	0	2.58
2B	O. Knabe	510	.261	1	44	383	381	37	72	5.9	.954	B. Ewing	34	255	16	14	0	3.00
SS	M. Doolan	536	.263	2	57	283	**500**	43	**71**	5.6	**.948**	L. Moren	34	205	13	14	1	3.55
3B	E. Grant	579	.268	1	67	**193**	256	31	22	3.2	.935	G. McQuillan	24	152	9	6	1	**1.60**
RF	J. Titus	535	.241	3	35	226	22	6	4	1.8	.976	E. Stack	20	117	6	7	0	4.00
CF	J. Bates	498	.305	3	61	308	24	16	8	2.7	.954	L. Schettler	27	107	2	6	1	3.20
LF	S. Magee	519	**.331**	6	**123**	285	9	8	2	2.0	.974	B. Foxen	16	78	5	5	0	2.55
C	R. Dooin	331	.242	0	30	472	131	**28**	14	6.9	.956							
UT	J. Walsh	242	.248	3	31	122	101	23	11		.907							
C	P. Moran	199	.236	0	11	278	83	4	5	6.5	.989							

Cincinnati

W-75 L-79

Clark Griffith

POS	Player	AB	BA	HR	RBI	PO	A	E	DP	TC/G	FA	Pitcher	G	IP	W	L	SV	ERA
1B	D. Hoblitzell	**611**	.278	4	70	1454	67	24	64	10.4	.984	H. Gaspar	48	275	15	17	5	2.59
2B	D. Egan	474	.245	0	46	264	381	26	49	5.1	.961	G. Suggs	35	266	19	11	3	2.40
SS	T. McMillan	248	.185	0	13	162	270	34	32	5.7	.927	J. Rowan	42	261	14	13	1	2.93
3B	H. Lobert	314	.309	3	40	123	164	21	11	3.4	.932	F. Beebe	35	214	12	15	0	3.07
RF	M. Mitchell	583	.286	5	88	257	19	12	4	1.9	.958	B. Burns	31	179	8	13	0	3.48
CF	D. Paskert	506	.300	2	46	355	25	17	4	2.9	.957							
LF	B. Bescher	589	.250	4	48	339	16	20	4	2.5	.947							
C	L. McLean	423	.298	2	71	485	158	11	**18**	5.5	.983							
S3	T. Downey	378	.270	2	32	201	281	60	26		.889							
C	T. Clarke	151	.278	1	20	217	52	8	3	4.9	.971							

Brooklyn

W-64 L-90

Bill Dahlen

POS	Player	AB	BA	HR	RBI	PO	A	E	DP	TC/G	FA	Pitcher	G	IP	W	L	SV	ERA
1B	J. Daubert	552	.264	8	50	1418	72	16	81	10.5	.989	N. Rucker	41	**320**	17	18	0	2.58
2B	J. Hummel	578	.244	5	74	344	424	28	67	5.2	**.965**	G. Bell	44	310	10	**27**	1	2.64
SS	T. Smith	321	.181	1	16	254	318	36	57	**6.0**	.941	C. Barger	35	272	15	15	1	2.88
3B	E. Lennox	367	.259	3	32	135	149	15	14	3.0	**.950**	D. Scanlan	34	217	9	11	2	2.61
RF	J. Dalton	273	.227	1	21	129	12	5	3	2.0	.966	E. Knetzer	20	133	7	5	0	3.19
CF	B. Davidson	509	.238	0	34	283	11	12	3	2.3	.961	K. Wilhelm	15	68	3	7	0	4.74
LF	Z. Wheat	606	.284	2	55	354	21	15	6	2.5	.962							
C	B. Bergen	249	.161	0	14	373	151	10	15	6.0	.981							
OF	A. Burch	352	.236	1	20	124	11	6	6	2.0	.957							
3B	P. McElveen	213	.225	1	26	72	78	9	12	2.9	.943							
C	T. Erwin	202	.188	1	10	259	114	20	10	5.8	.949							

St. Louis

W-63 L-90

Roger Bresnahan

POS	Player	AB	BA	HR	RBI	PO	A	E	DP	TC/G	FA	Pitcher	G	IP	W	L	SV	ERA
1B	E. Konetchy	520	.302	3	78	**1499**	**98**	15	81	**11.2**	**.991**	B. Harmon	43	236	13	15	2	4.46
2B	M. Huggins	547	.265	1	36	325	452	30	58	5.3	.963	J. Lush	36	225	14	13	1	3.20
SS	A. Hauser	375	.205	2	36	212	345	41	31	5.1	.931	V. Willis	33	212	9	12	3	3.35
3B	M. Mowrey	489	.282	2	70	171	**301**	**37**	**30**	**3.6**	.927	F. Corridon	30	156	6	14	2	3.81
RF	S. Evans	506	.241	2	73	226	16	8	3	1.8	.968	L. Backman	26	116	6	7	1	3.03
CF	R. Oakes	468	.252	0	43	266	12	18	3	2.3	.939	S. Sallee	18	115	7	8	2	2.97
LF	R. Ellis	550	.258	4	54	268	25	18	4	2.2	.942							
C	E. Phelps	270	.263	0	37	320	84	10	10	5.2	.976							
C	R. Bresnahan	234	.278	0	27	295	100	16	11	5.3	.961							

NATIONAL LEAGUE 1910, *cont.*

Team	POS	Player	AB	BA	HR	RBI	PO	A	E	DP	TC/G	FA	Pitcher	G	IP	W	L	SV	ERA
Boston	1B	B. Sharpe	439	.239	0	29	1122	81	16	72	10.8	.987	A. Mattern	**51**	305	16	19	1	2.98
W-53 L-100	2B	D. Shean	543	.239	3	36	**408**	**493**	44	**92**	**6.4**	.953	B. Brown	46	263	9	23	2	2.67
Fred Lake	SS	B. Sweeney	499	.267	5	46	232	300	**57**	52	5.4	.903	S. Frock	45	255	11	19	2	3.21
	3B	B. Herzog	380	.250	3	32	110	223	31	17	3.5	.915	C. Curtis	43	251	6	24	2	3.55
	RF	D. Miller	482	.286	3	55	203	9	11	3	1.7	.951	G. Ferguson	26	123	8	7	0	3.80
	CF	F. Beck	571	.275	**10**	64	293	19	12	6	2.4	.963							
	LF	B. Collins	584	.241	3	40	355	23	9	2	2.6	.977							
	C	P. Graham	291	.282	0	21	318	132	16	11	5.4	.966							
	SS	E. Abbaticchio	178	.247	0	10	73	149	22	19	5.3	.910							

BATTING AND BASE RUNNING LEADERS

Batting Average		Slugging Average		Home Runs	
S. Magee, PHI	.331	S. Magee, PHI	.507	W. Schulte, CHI	10
V. Campbell, PIT	.326	S. Hofman, CHI	.461	F. Beck, BOS	10
S. Hofman, CHI	.325	W. Schulte, CHI	.460	J. Daubert, BKN	8
F. Snodgrass, NY	.321	F. Merkle, NY	.441	L. Doyle, NY	8
H. Wagner, PIT	.320	V. Campbell, PIT	.436	J. Flynn, PIT	6
				S. Magee, PHI	6

Total Bases		Runs Batted In		Stolen Bases	
S. Magee, PHI	263	S. Magee, PHI	123	B. Bescher, CIN	70
W. Schulte, CHI	257	M. Mitchell, CIN	88	R. Murray, NY	57
B. Byrne, PIT	251	R. Murray, NY	87	D. Paskert, CIN	51
Z. Wheat, BKN	244	S. Hofman, CHI	86	S. Magee, PHI	49
H. Wagner, PIT	240	H. Wagner, PIT	81	J. Devore, NY	43

Hits		Base on Balls		Home Run Percentage	
H. Wagner, PIT	178	M. Huggins, STL	116	J. Flynn, PIT	1.8
B. Byrne, PIT	178	J. Evers, CHI	108	W. Schulte, CHI	1.8
S. Magee, PHI	172	S. Magee, PHI	94	F. Beck, BOS	1.8
Z. Wheat, BKN	172	J. Titus, PHI	93	J. Daubert, BKN	1.4

Runs		Doubles		Triples	
S. Magee, PHI	110	B. Byrne, PIT	43	M. Mitchell, CIN	18
M. Huggins, STL	101	S. Magee, PHI	39	S. Magee, PHI	17
B. Byrne, PIT	101	Z. Wheat, BKN	36	S. Hofman, CHI	16
L. Doyle, NY	97	F. Merkle, NY	35	E. Konetchy, STL	16

PITCHING LEADERS

Winning Percentage		Earned Run Average		Wins	
K. Cole, CHI	.833	G. McQuillan, PHI	1.60	C. Mathewson, NY	27
D. Crandall, NY	.810	K. Cole, CHI	1.80	T. Brown, CHI	25
C. Mathewson, NY	.750	T. Brown, CHI	1.86	E. Moore, PHI	22
B. Adams, PIT	.667	C. Mathewson, NY	1.90	K. Cole, CHI	20
T. Brown, CHI	.658	R. Ames, NY	2.22	G. Suggs, CIN	19

Saves		Strikeouts		Complete Games	
T. Brown, CHI	7	E. Moore, PHI	185	T. Brown, CHI	27
H. Gaspar, CIN	5	C. Mathewson, NY	184	C. Mathewson, NY	27
D. Crandall, NY	4	S. Frock, PIT, BOS	171	N. Rucker, BKN	27
D. Phillippe, PIT	4	L. Drucke, NY	151	C. Barger, BKN	25
		N. Rucker, BKN	147	G. Bell, BKN	25

Fewest Hits/9 Innings		Shutouts		Fewest Walks/9 Innings	
G. McQuillan, PHI	6.44	T. Brown, CHI	7	G. Suggs, CIN	1.62
K. Cole, CHI	6.53	E. Moore, PHI	6	C. Mathewson, NY	1.70
O. Overall, CHI	6.59	A. Mattern, BOS	6	D. Crandall, NY	1.86
D. Scanlan, BKN	7.25	N. Rucker, BKN	6	T. Brown, CHI	1.95

Most Strikeouts/9 Inn.		Innings		Games Pitched	
L. Drucke, NY	6.31	N. Rucker, BKN	320	A. Mattern, BOS	51
S. Frock, PIT, BOS	5.98	C. Mathewson, NY	318	H. Gaspar, CIN	48
E. Moore, PHI	5.88	G. Bell, BKN	310		
O. Overall, CHI	5.72	A. Mattern, BOS	305		

	W	L	PCT	GB	R	OR	Batting 2B	3B	HR	BA	SA	SB	Fielding E	DP	FA	Pitching CG	BB	SO	ShO	SV	ERA
Chicago	104	50	.675		712	**499**	219	**84**	**34**	.268	**.366**	173	**230**	110	.963	99	474	609	**25**	11	**2.51**
New York	91	63	.591	13	**715**	567	204	83	31	**.275**	**.366**	282	291	117	.955	96	397	**717**	9	8	2.68
Pittsburgh	86	67	.562	17.5	655	576	214	83	33	.266	.360	148	245	102	.961	73	**392**	479	13	11	2.83
Philadelphia	78	75	.510	25.5	674	639	**223**	71	22	.255	.338	199	258	132	.960	84	547	657	17	7	3.05
Cincinnati	75	79	.487	29	620	684	150	79	23	.259	.333	**310**	291	103	.955	86	528	497	16	9	3.08
Brooklyn	64	90	.416	40	497	623	166	73	25	.229	.305	151	235	125	**.964**	**103**	545	555	15	4	3.07
St. Louis	63	90	.412	40.5	639	718	167	70	15	.248	.319	179	261	109	.959	83	541	466	4	**12**	3.78
Boston	53	100	.346	50.5	495	701	173	49	31	.246	.317	152	305	**137**	.954	74	599	531	12	7	3.22
					5007	5007	1516	592	214	.256	.338	1594	2116	935	.959	698	4023	4511	111	69	3.03

AMERICAN LEAGUE 1910

Team	POS	Player	AB	BA	HR	RBI	PO	A	E	DP	TC/G	FA	Pitcher	G	IP	W	L	SV	ERA
Philadelphia	1B	H. Davis	492	.248	1	41	1353	64	20	**74**	10.3	.986	J. Coombs	**45**	353	**31**	9	1	1.30
W-102 L-48	2B	E. Collins	583	.322	3	81	**402**	**451**	25	**67**	**5.7**	**.972**	C. Morgan	36	291	18	12	0	1.55
Connie Mack	SS	J. Barry	487	.259	3	60	279	406	**63**	54	5.2	.916	E. Plank	38	250	16	10	2	2.01
	3B	F. Baker	561	.283	2	74	**207**	313	45	**35**	3.9	.920	C. Bender	30	250	23	5	0	1.58
	RF	D. Murphy	560	.300	4	64	209	15	6	5	1.5	.974	H. Krause	16	112	6	6	0	2.88
	CF	R. Oldring	546	.308	4	57	249	14	6	6	2.0	.978							
	LF	T. Hartsel	285	.221	0	22	113	8	7	2	1.5	.945							
	C	J. Lapp	192	.234	0	17	361	88	9	6	7.3	.980							
	OF	B. Lord	288	.278	1	20	142	6	3	2	2.1	.980							
	C	I. Thomas	180	.278	1	19	324	86	14	8	7.1	.967							
New York	1B	H. Chase	524	.290	3	73	1373	65	28	68	11.3	.981	R. Ford	36	300	26	6	1	1.65
W-88 L-63	2B	F. LaPorte	432	.264	2	67	127	220	15	21	4.6	.959	J. Warhop	37	254	14	14	2	2.87
George Stallings	SS	J. Knight	414	.312	3	45	169	247	32	39	5.7	.929	J. Quinn	35	237	18	12	0	2.36
W-78 L-59	3B	J. Austin	432	.218	2	36	204	284	30	10	**3.9**	.942	H. Vaughn	30	222	13	11	1	1.83
Hal Chase	RF	H. Wolter	479	.267	4	42	192	11	13	3	1.7	.940	T. Hughes	23	152	7	9	1	3.50
W-10 L-4	CF	C. Hemphill	351	.239	0	21	159	10	5	2	1.9	.971							
	LF	B. Cree	467	.287	4	73	202	11	10	3	1.7	.955							
	C	J. Sweeney	215	.200	0	13	388	106	13	2	6.5	.974							
	OF	B. Daniels	356	.253	1	17	170	9	8	2	2.2	.957							
	2B	E. Gardner	271	.244	1	24	169	199	25	36	5.6	.936							
	SS	R. Roach	220	.214	0	20	112	173	27	27	5.4	.913							
	C	F. Mitchell	196	.230	0	18	262	69	11	2	5.0	.968							

AMERICAN LEAGUE 1910, *cont.*

Team	POS	Player	AB	BA	HR	RBI	PO	A	E	DP	TC/G	FA	Pitcher	G	IP	W	L	SV	ERA
Detroit	1B	T. Jones	432	.255	0	45	1405	67	23	50	11.1	.985	G. Mullin	38	289	21	12	0	2.87
W-86 L-68	2B	J. Delahanty	378	.294	2	45	246	267	33	36	5.2	.940	E. Summers	30	220	13	12	0	2.53
Hughie Jennings	SS	D. Bush	496	.262	3	34	310	487	51	31	6.0	.940	W. Donovan	26	209	17	7	0	2.42
	3B	G. Moriarty	490	.251	2	60	165	302	37	17	3.8	.927	E. Willett	37	147	16	11	0	3.60
	RF	S. Crawford	588	.289	5	**120**	223	10	9	2	1.6	.963	S. Stroud	28	130	5	9	1	3.25
	CF	T. Cobb	509	**.385**	8	91	305	18	14	4	2.5	.958	R. Works	18	86	3	6	1	3.57
	LF	D. Jones	377	.265	0	24	181	13	9	2	2.0	.956							
	C	O. Stanage	275	.207	2	25	344	148	25	6	6.2	.952							
	OF	M. McIntyre	305	.236	0	25	147	12	9	2	2.2	.946							
	2S	C. O'Leary	211	.242	0	9	116	153	16	12		.944							
	C	B. Schmidt	197	.259	1	23	239	80	9	1	5.0	.973							
Boston	1B	J. Stahl	531	.271	**10**	77	**1488**	60	23	46	11.1	.985	E. Cicotte	36	250	15	11	0	2.74
W-81 L-72	2B	L. Gardner	413	.283	2	36	222	320	32	28	5.1	.944	R. Collins	35	245	13	11	1	1.62
Patsy Donovan	SS	H. Wagner	491	.273	1	52	303	424	57	40	5.6	.927	S. Wood	35	198	12	13	0	1.68
	3B	H. Lord	288	.250	1	32	90	138	18	10	3.5	.927	C. Hall	35	189	12	9	2	1.91
	RF	H. Hooper	584	.267	2	27	241	30	18	7	1.9	.938	E. Karger	27	183	11	7	1	3.19
	CF	T. Speaker	538	.340	7	65	337	20	16	7	2.7	.957	C. Smith	24	156	11	6	1	2.30
	LF	D. Lewis	541	.283	8	68	261	28	17	9	2.1	.944	F. Arellanes	18	100	4	7	0	2.88
	C	B. Carrigan	342	.249	3	53	**495**	134	25	12	5.9	.962							
	UT	C. Engle	363	.264	2	38	129	223	29	17		.924							
	3B	B. Purtell	168	.208	1	15	41	87*	13*	2	3.4	.908							
Cleveland	1B	G. Stovall	521	.261	0	52	1404	**91**	18	60	**11.5**	**.988**	C. Falkenberg	37	257	14	13	1	2.95
W-71 L-81	2B	N. Lajoie	**591**	.384	4	76	387	419	28	60	5.6	.966	W. Mitchell	35	184	12	8	0	2.60
Deacon McGuire	SS	T. Turner	574	.230	0	33	194	320	14	42	5.6	**.973**	C. Young	21	163	7	10	0	2.53
	3B	B. Bradley	214	.196	0	12	89	126	10	8	3.7	.956	E. Koestner	27	145	5	10	2	3.04
	RF	J. Graney	454	.236	1	31	209	14	12	5	2.1	.949	S. Harkness	26	136	10	7	1	3.04
	CF	J. Birmingham	364	.231	0	35	223	24	10	8	2.5	.961	F. Link	22	123	5	6	1	3.30
	LF	A. Kruger	223	.170	0	14	116	10	6	3	2.1	.955	A. Joss	13	107	5	5	0	2.26
	C	T. Easterly	363	.306	0	55	200	104	15	7	4.8	.953	G. Kahler	12	95	6	4	0	1.60
	OF	H. Niles	240	.212	1	18	70	7	2	1	1.4	.975	H. Fanwell	17	92	2	9	0	3.62
	OF	B. Lord	201	.219	0	17	77	14	4	4	1.7	.958							
	C	H. Bemis	167	.216	1	16	186	63	10	4	5.6	.961							
Chicago	1B	C. Gandil	275	.193	2	21	854	57	10	34	12.4	.989	E. Walsh	**45**	370	18	**20**	**5**	**1.27**
W-68 L-85	2B	R. Zeider	498	.217	0	31	205	242	33	31	5.5	.931	D. White	33	246	15	13	1	2.56
Hugh Duffy	SS	L. Blackburne	242	.174	0	10	173	265	43	29	6.5	.911	J. Scott	41	230	8	18	1	2.43
	3B	B. Purtell	368	.234	1	36	117	233*	36*	16	3.8	.907	F. Olmstead	32	184	10	12	0	1.95
	RF	S. Collins	315	.197	1	24	101	11	6	6	1.8	.949	I. Young	27	136	4	8	0	2.72
	CF	P. Meloan	222	.243	0	23	76	16	5	1	1.5	.948	F. Lange	23	131	9	4	0	1.65
	LF	P. Dougherty	443	.248	1	43	158	9	14	2	1.5	.923	F. Smith	19	129	4	9	0	2.03
	C	F. Payne	257	.218	0	19	409	106	14	11	**6.8**	.974							
	OF	F. Parent	258	.178	1	16	92	5	3	1	1.6	.970							
	S1	L. Tannehill	230	.222	1	21	258	144	12	21		.971							
	20	C. French	170	.165	0	4	69	54	10	6		.925							
	3B	H. Lord	165	.297	0	10	44	75	6	4	2.8	.952							
Washington	1B	B. Unglaub	431	.234	0	44	1230	79	20	51	10.7	.985	W. Johnson	**45**	**373**	25	17	1	1.35
W-66 L-85	2B	R. Killefer	345	.229	0	24	173	231	26	27	4.9	.940	B. Groom	34	258	12	17	0	2.76
Jimmy McAleer	SS	G. McBride	514	.230	1	55	**370**	**518**	58	**57**	6.1	.939	D. Gray	34	229	8	19	0	2.63
	3B	K. Elberfeld	455	.251	2	42	139	223	22	15	3.4	**.943**	D. Walker	29	199	11	11	0	3.30
	RF	D. Gessler	487	.259	2	50	161	23	9	3	1.3	.953	D. Reisling	30	191	10	10	1	2.54
	CF	C. Milan	531	.279	0	16	267	30	17	10	2.2	.946							
	LF	J. Lelivelt	347	.265	0	33	149	13	6	5	1.9	.964							
	C	G. Street	257	.202	1	16	417	151	13	8	6.8	**.978**							
	30	W. Conroy	351	.254	1	27	151	91	10	6		.960							
	20	G. Schaefer	229	.275	0	14	89	108	11	16		.947							
St. Louis	1B	P. Newnam	384	.216	2	26	1041	56	**32**	53	11.0	.972	J. Lake	35	261	11	17	2	2.20
W-47 L-107	2B	F. Truesdale	415	.219	1	25	279	313	**56**	41	5.3	.914	B. Bailey	34	192	3	18	0	3.32
Jack O'Connor	SS	B. Wallace	508	.258	0	37	258	344	33	37	**6.5**	.948	B. Pelty	27	165	5	11	0	3.48
	3B	R. Hartzell	542	.218	2	30	123	203	25	19	3.9	.929	F. Ray	21	141	4	10	0	3.58
	RF	A. Schweitzer	379	.230	2	37	149	15	11	3	1.6	.937	J. Powell	21	129	7	11	0	2.30
	CF	D. Hoffman	380	.237	0	27	202	14	9	5	2.1	.960							
	LF	G. Stone	562	.256	0	40	220	20	7	2	1.7	.972							
	C	J. Stephens	299	.241	0	23	418	**156**	17	**18**	6.2	.971							
	UT	A. Griggs	416	.236	2	30	322	120	32	29		.932							
	C	B. Killefer	193	.124	0	7	311	124	**29**	16	6.4	.938							

BATTING AND BASE RUNNING LEADERS

Batting Average		Slugging Average		Home Runs	
T. Cobb, DET	.385	T. Cobb, DET	.554	J. Stahl, BOS	10
N. Lajoie, CLE	.384	N. Lajoie, CLE	.514	T. Cobb, DET	8
T. Speaker, BOS	.340	T. Speaker, BOS	.468	D. Lewis, BOS	8
E. Collins, PHI	.322	D. Murphy, PHI	.436	T. Speaker, BOS	7
J. Knight, NY	.312	R. Oldring, PHI	.430	S. Crawford, DET	5

PITCHING LEADERS

Winning Percentage		Earned Run Average		Wins	
C. Bender, PHI	.821	E. Walsh, CHI	1.27	J. Coombs, PHI	31
R. Ford, NY	.813	J. Coombs, PHI	1.30	R. Ford, NY	26
J. Coombs, PHI	.775	W. Johnson, WAS	1.35	W. Johnson, WAS	25
W. Donovan, DET	.708	C. Morgan, PHI	1.55	C. Bender, PHI	23
G. Mullin, DET	.636	C. Bender, PHI	1.58	G. Mullin, DET	21

AMERICAN LEAGUE 1910, *cont.*

BATTING AND BASE RUNNING LEADERS / PITCHING LEADERS

Total Bases		Runs Batted In		Stolen Bases		Saves		Strikeouts		Complete Games	
N. Lajoie, CLE	304	S. Crawford, DET	120	E. Collins, PHI	81	E. Walsh, CHI	5	W. Johnson, WAS	313	W. Johnson, WAS	38
T. Cobb, DET	282	T. Cobb, DET	91	T. Cobb, DET	65	F. Browning, DET	3	E. Walsh, CHI	258	J. Coombs, PHI	35
T. Speaker, BOS	252	E. Collins, PHI	81	D. Bush, DET	49			J. Coombs, PHI	224	E. Walsh, CHI	33
S. Crawford, DET	249	J. Stahl, BOS	77	R. Zeider, CHI	49			R. Ford, NY	209	R. Ford, NY	29
D. Murphy, PHI	244	N. Lajoie, CLE	76	C. Milan, WAS	44			C. Bender, PHI	155	G. Mullin, DET	27

Hits		Base on Balls		Home Run Percentage		Fewest Hits/9 Innings		Shutouts		Fewest Walks/9 Innings	
N. Lajoie, CLE	227	D. Bush, DET	78	J. Stahl, BOS	1.9	R. Ford, NY	5.83	J. Coombs, PHI	13	E. Walsh, CHI	1.49
T. Cobb, DET	196	C. Milan, WAS	71	T. Cobb, DET	1.6	E. Walsh, CHI	5.89	R. Ford, NY	8	C. Young, CLE	1.49
E. Collins, PHI	188	H. Wolter, NY	66	D. Lewis, BOS	1.5	J. Coombs, PHI	6.32	W. Johnson, WAS	8	R. Collins, BOS	1.51
T. Speaker, BOS	183	T. Cobb, DET	64	T. Speaker, BOS	1.3	W. Johnson, WAS	6.49	E. Walsh, CHI	7	C. Bender, PHI	1.69

Runs		Doubles		Triples		Most Strikeouts/9 Inn.		Innings		Games Pitched	
T. Cobb, DET	106	N. Lajoie, CLE	51	S. Crawford, DET	19	W. Johnson, WAS	7.55	W. Johnson, WAS	373	E. Walsh, CHI	45
T. Speaker, BOS	92	T. Cobb, DET	36	B. Lord, CLE, PHI	18	S. Wood, BOS	6.60	E. Walsh, CHI	370	J. Coombs, PHI	45
N. Lajoie, CLE	92	D. Lewis, BOS	29	D. Murphy, PHI	18	E. Walsh, CHI	6.28	J. Coombs, PHI	353	W. Johnson, WAS	45
D. Bush, DET	90	D. Murphy, PHI	28	B. Cree, NY	16	R. Ford, NY	6.28	R. Ford, NY	300	J. Scott, CHI	41
				J. Stahl, BOS	16						

							Batting						Fielding			Pitching					
	W	L	PCT	GB	R	OR	2B	3B	HR	BA	SA	SB	E	DP	FA	CG	BB	SO	ShO	SV	ERA
Philadelphia	102	48	.680		673	**441**	**194**	**106**	19	**.266**	**.356**	207	**230**	**117**	**.965**	**123**	450	**789**	**24**	5	**1.79**
New York	88	63	.583	14.5	626	557	163	75	20	.248	.322	**288**	284	95	.956	110	**364**	654	14	**8**	2.59
Detroit	86	68	.558	18	**679**	582	192	73	26	.261	.344	249	288	79	.956	108	460	532	17	5	3.00
Boston	81	72	.529	22.5	638	564	175	87	**43**	.259	.351	194	309	80	.954	100	414	670	12	6	2.46
Cleveland	71	81	.467	32	548	657	185	63	9	.244	.308	189	247	112	.964	92	487	614	13	5	2.89
Chicago	68	85	.444	35.5	457	479	115	58	7	.211	.261	183	314	100	.954	103	381	785	23	7	2.01
Washington	66	85	.437	36.5	501	550	145	46	9	.236	.289	192	264	99	.959	119	374	675	19	3	2.46
St. Louis	47	107	.305	57	451	743	131	60	12	.220	.276	169	377	113	.944	100	532	557	9	3	3.09
					4573	4573	1300	568	145	.243	.313	1671	2313	795	.957	855	3462	5276	131	42	2.54

NATIONAL LEAGUE 1911

Team	POS	Player	AB	BA	HR	RBI	PO	A	E	DP	TC/G	FA	Pitcher	G	IP	W	L	SV	ERA
New York	1B	F. Merkle	541	.283	12	84	1375	**117**	**22**	73	10.2	.985	C. Mathewson	45	307	26	13	3	**1.99**
W-99 L-54	2B	L. Doyle	526	.310	13	77	272	340	36	46	4.6	.944	R. Marquard	45	278	24	7	2	2.50
John McGraw	SS	A. Bridwell	263	.270	0	31	129	249	34	26	5.4	.917	R. Ames	34	205	11	10	1	2.68
	3B	A. Devlin	260	.273	0	25	75	144	13	3	2.9	.944	D. Crandall	41	199	15	5	5	2.63
	RF	R. Murray	488	.291	3	78	196	12	10	1	1.7	.954	H. Wiltse	30	187	12	9	0	3.27
	CF	F. Snodgrass	534	.294	1	77	293	31	9	8	2.2	.973	B. Raymond	17	82	6	4	0	3.31
	LF	J. Devore	565	.280	3	50	241	29	19	5	1.9	.934							
	C	C. Meyers	391	.332	1	61	**729**	108	18	11	**6.7**	.979							
	UT	A. Fletcher	326	.319	1	37	153	285	32	27		.932							
	3B	B. Herzog	247	.267	1	26	88	138	18	7	3.8	.926							
	OF	B. Becker	172	.262	1	20	72	7	2	0	1.5	.975							
	P	D. Crandall	113	.239	2	21	9	59	3	2	1.7	.958							
Chicago	1B	V. Saier	259	.259	1	37	715	33	15	44	10.5	.980	T. Brown	**53**	270	21	11	**13**	2.80
W-92 L-62	2B	H. Zimmerman	535	.307	9	85	256	304	32	42	5.5	.946	L. Richie	36	253	15	11	1	2.31
Frank Chance	SS	J. Tinker	536	.278	4	69	**333**	**486**	55	56	**6.1**	**.937**	E. Reulbach	33	222	16	9	0	2.96
	3B	J. Doyle	472	.282	5	62	134	278	**35**	**25**	**3.5**	.922	K. Cole	32	221	18	7	0	3.13
	RF	W. Schulte	577	.300	**21**	**121**	246	19	8	8	1.8	.971	H. McIntire	25	149	11	7	0	4.11
	CF	S. Hofman	512	.252	2	70	230	11	8	5	2.3	.968							
	LF	J. Sheckard	539	.276	4	50	332	32	14	12	2.4	.963							
	C	J. Archer	387	.253	4	41	476	124	14	11	6.0	.977							
	2B	J. Evers	155	.226	0	7	66	90	4	17	4.8	.975							
	OF	W. Good	145	.269	2	21	74	3	6	1	2.1	.928							
Pittsburgh	1B	N. Hunter	209	.254	2	24	504	26	6	44	8.8	.989	L. Leifield	42	318	16	16	1	2.63
W-85 L-69	2B	D. Miller	470	.268	6	78	273	357	38	65	5.2	.943	B. Adams	40	293	22	12	0	2.33
Fred Clarke	SS	H. Wagner	473	**.334**	9	89	221	312	39	55	5.7	.932	H. Camnitz	40	268	20	15	0	3.13
	3B	B. Byrne	598	.259	2	52	181	**282**	**35**	21	3.3	.930	E. Steele	31	166	9	9	2	2.60
	RF	O. Wilson	544	.300	12	107	273	20	7	10	2.1	.977	C. Hendrix	22	119	4	6	1	2.73
	CF	M. Carey	427	.258	5	43	304	11	8	5	2.6	.975	J. Ferry	26	86	6	4	3	3.15
	LF	F. Clarke	392	.324	5	49	216	8	7	3	2.3	.970							
	C	G. Gibson	311	.209	0	19	452	117	12	**16**	5.9	.979							
	OF	T. Leach	386	.238	3	43	208	15	3	3	2.5	.987							
	UT	B. McKechnie	321	.227	2	37	598	109	21	49		.971							
	C	M. Simon	215	.228	0	22	320	75	13	6	6.0	.968							
	SS	A. McCarthy	150	.240	2	31	70	88	3	12	4.9	.981							

NATIONAL LEAGUE 1911, *cont.*

Team	POS	Player	AB	BA	HR	RBI	PO	A	E	DP	TC/G	FA	Pitcher	G	IP	W	L	SV	ERA
Philadelphia	1B	F. Luderus	551	.301	16	99	1373	77	**22**	85	10.1	.985	G. Alexander	48	**367**	**28**	13	3	2.57
	2B	O. Knabe	528	.237	1	42	310	412	38	54	5.4	.950	E. Moore	42	308	15	**19**	1	2.63
W-79 L-73	SS	M. Doolan	512	.238	1	49	295	474	53	**68**	5.7	.936	G. Chalmers	38	209	13	10	4	3.11
	3B	H. Lobert	541	.285	9	72	**202**	213	20	13	3.0	.954	B. Burns	21	121	6	10	0	3.42
Red Dooin	RF	J. Titus	236	.284	8	26	85	10	2	3	1.6	.979	E. Stack	13	78	5	5	0	3.59
	CF	D. Paskert	560	.273	4	47	361	20	8	6	2.5	.979							
	LF	S. Magee	445	.288	15	94	248	14	5	3	2.2	.981							
	C	R. Dooin	247	.328	1	16	436	97	18	5	7.4	.967							
	UT	J. Walsh	289	.270	1	31	148	79	12	14		.950							
	OF	F. Beck	210	.281	3	25	81	7	4	4	1.5	.957							
St. Louis	1B	E. Konetchy	571	.289	6	88	**1652**	71	16	85	**11.0**	**.991**	B. Harmon	51	348	23	16	4	3.13
	2B	M. Huggins	509	.261	1	24	281	439	29	62	5.5	.961	B. Steele	43	287	18	**19**	3	3.73
W-75 L-74	SS	A. Hauser	515	.241	3	46	223	400	**56**	51	5.1	.918	S. Sallee	36	245	15	9	2	2.76
	3B	M. Mowrey	471	.268	0	61	174	267	26	19	3.5	.944	R. Golden	30	149	4	9	0	5.02
Roger Bresnahan	RF	S. Evans	547	.294	5	71	258	17	8	5	1.9	.972	R. Geyer	29	149	9	6	0	3.27
	CF	R. Oakes	551	.263	2	59	364	26	16	8	2.7	.961							
	LF	R. Ellis	555	.250	3	66	297	21	21	3	2.3	.938							
	C	J. Bliss	258	.229	1	27	332	103	22	9	5.4	.952							
	C	R. Bresnahan	227	.278	3	41	323	100	13	9	5.7	.970							
	UT	W. Smith	194	.216	2	19	63	139	14	7		.935							
Cincinnati	1B	D. Hoblitzell	**622**	.289	11	97	1442	91	16	81	9.8	.990	G. Suggs	36	261	15	13	0	3.00
	2B	D. Egan	558	.249	1	56	341	**480**	44	**67**	5.7	.949	H. Gaspar	44	254	10	17	3	3.30
W-70 L-83	SS	T. Downey	360	.261	0	36	198	267	48	26	5.5	.906	B. Keefe	39	234	12	13	3	2.69
	3B	E. Grant	458	.223	1	53	158	208	18	21	3.1	.953	A. Fromme	38	208	10	11	0	3.46
Clark Griffith	RF	M. Mitchell	529	.291	2	84	280	23	9	8	2.2	.971	F. Smith	34	176	10	14	1	3.98
	CF	J. Bates	518	.292	1	61	352	21	13	4	2.6	.966							
	LF	B. Bescher	599	.275	1	45	267	21	14	2	2.0	.954							
	C	L. McLean	328	.287	0	34	414	138	18	**16**	5.8	.968							
	C	T. Clarke	203	.241	1	25	313	74	12	10	4.9	.970							
	SS	J. Esmond	198	.273	1	11	110	104	19	19	5.3	.918							
	OF	F. Beck	87	.184	2	20	25	2	0	0	1.7	1.000							
Brooklyn	1B	J. Daubert	573	.307	5	45	1485	88	18	**91**	10.7	.989	N. Rucker	48	316	22	18	4	2.71
	2B	J. Hummel	477	.270	5	58	296	352	19	58	5.3	**.972**	C. Barger	30	217	11	15	0	3.52
W-64 L-86	SS	B. Tooley	433	.206	1	29	226	340	46	42	5.4	.925	E. Knetzer	35	204	11	12	0	3.49
	3B	E. Zimmerman	417	.185	3	36	167	229	16	24	3.4	**.961**	B. Schardt	39	195	5	15	4	3.59
Bill Dahlen	RF	B. Coulson	521	.234	0	50	253	21	9	5	2.0	.968	D. Scanlan	22	114	3	10	1	3.64
	CF	B. Davidson	292	.233	1	26	168	4	8	1	2.4	.956	G. Bell	19	101	5	6	0	4.28
	LF	Z. Wheat	534	.287	5	76	287	12	14	0	2.3	.955							
	C	B. Bergen	227	.132	0	10	346	121	9	10	5.7	**.981**							
	C	T. Erwin	218	.271	7	34	273	98	11	6	5.2	.971							
	S2	D. Stark	193	.295	0	19	111	134	19	20		.928							
	OF	A. Burch	167	.228	0	7	98	6	3	3	2.5	.972							
Boston	1B	F. Tenney	369	.263	1	36	901	64	15	47	10.5	.985	B. Brown	42	241	8	18	2	4.29
	2B	B. Sweeney	523	.314	3	63	**372**	410	**46**	61	**6.1**	.944	A. Mattern	33	186	4	15	0	4.97
W-44 L-107	SS	B. Herzog	294	.310	5	41	149	248	28	31	5.7	.934	L. Tyler	28	165	7	10	0	5.06
	3B	S. Ingerton	521	.250	5	61	92	119	13	6	3.9	.942	H. Perdue	24	137	6	10	1	4.98
Fred Tenney	RF	D. Miller	577	.333	7	91	243	26	11	4	1.9	.961	O. Weaver	27	121	3	12	0	6.47
	CF	M. Donlin	222	.315	2	34	117	8	12	2	2.4	.912	B. Pfeffer	26	97	7	5	2	4.73
	LF	A. Kaiser	197	.203	2	15	101	6	9	3	2.0	.922	C. Curtis	12	77	1	8	1	4.44
	C	J. Kling	241	.224	2	24	302	106*	21*	6	6.0	.951							
	C	B. Rariden	246	.228	0	21	291	110	20	12	6.5	.952							
	SS	A. Bridwell	182	.291	0	10	78	149	12	19	4.7	.950							
	3B	E. McDonald	175	.206	1	21	63	86	7	10	2.9	.955							
	OF	W. Good	165	.267	0	15	108	13	7	1	3.0	.945							
	UT	H. Spratt	154	.240	2	13	82	75	19	9		.892							
	OF	G. Jackson	147	.347	0	25	74	4	6	1	2.2	.929							
	OF	P. Flaherty	94	.287	2	20	26	2	2	0	1.6	.933							

BATTING AND BASE RUNNING LEADERS

Batting Average
H. Wagner, PIT .334
D. Miller, BOS .333
C. Meyers, NY .332
F. Clarke, PIT .324
A. Fletcher, NY .319

Slugging Average
W. Schulte, CHI .534
L. Doyle, NY .527
H. Wagner, PIT .507
F. Clarke, PIT .492
S. Magee, PHI .483

Home Runs
W. Schulte, CHI 21
F. Luderus, PHI 16
S. Magee, PHI 15
L. Doyle, NY 13
F. Merkle, NY 12
O. Wilson, PIT 12

Total Bases
W. Schulte, CHI 308
L. Doyle, NY 277
F. Luderus, PHI 260
D. Hoblitzell, CIN 258
O. Wilson, PIT 257

Runs Batted In
W. Schulte, CHI 121
O. Wilson, PIT 107
F. Luderus, PHI 99
D. Hoblitzell, CIN 97
S. Magee, PHI 94

Stolen Bases
B. Bescher, CIN 81
J. Devore, NY 61
F. Snodgrass, NY 51
F. Merkle, NY 49
R. Murray, NY 48
B. Herzog, BOS, NY 48

PITCHING LEADERS

Winning Percentage
R. Marquard, NY .774
D. Crandall, NY .750
K. Cole, CHI .720
G. Alexander, PHI .683
C. Mathewson, NY .667

Earned Run Average
C. Mathewson, NY 1.99
L. Richie, CHI 2.31
B. Adams, PIT 2.33
R. Marquard, NY 2.50
G. Alexander, PHI 2.57

Wins
G. Alexander, PHI 28
C. Mathewson, NY 26
R. Marquard, NY 24
B. Harmon, STL 23
B. Adams, PIT 22
N. Rucker, BKN 22

Saves
T. Brown, CHI 13
D. Crandall, NY 5
B. Harmon, STL 4
B. Schardt, BKN 4
G. Chalmers, PHI 4
N. Rucker, BKN 4

Strikeouts
R. Marquard, NY 237
G. Alexander, PHI 227
N. Rucker, BKN 190
E. Moore, PHI 174
B. Harmon, STL 144

Complete Games
G. Alexander, PHI 31
C. Mathewson, NY 29
B. Harmon, STL 28
L. Leifield, PIT 26
B. Adams, PIT 24

NATIONAL LEAGUE 1911, *cont.*

BATTING AND BASE RUNNING LEADERS

Hits

D. Miller, BOS	192
D. Hoblitzell, CIN	180
J. Daubert, BKN	176
W. Schulte, CHI	173

Base on Balls

J. Sheckard, CHI	147
J. Bates, CIN	103
B. Bescher, CIN	102
M. Huggins, STL	96

Home Run Percentage

W. Schulte, CHI	3.6
S. Magee, PHI	3.4
F. Luderus, PHI	2.9
L. Doyle, NY	2.5

Runs

J. Sheckard, CHI	121
M. Huggins, STL	106
B. Bescher, CIN	106
W. Schulte, CHI	105

Doubles

E. Konetchy, STL	38
D. Miller, BOS	36
O. Wilson, PIT	34
B. Sweeney, BOS	33
B. Herzog, BOS, NY	33

Triples

L. Doyle, NY	25
M. Mitchell, CIN	22
W. Schulte, CHI	21
H. Zimmerman, CHI	17
B. Byrne, PIT	17

PITCHING LEADERS

Fewest Hits/9 Innings

G. Alexander, PHI	6.99
R. Marquard, NY	7.16
N. Rucker, BKN	7.27
R. Ames, NY	7.46

Shutouts

B. Adams, PIT	7
G. Alexander, PHI	7

Fewest Walks/9 Innings

C. Mathewson, NY	1.11
B. Adams, PIT	1.29
T. Brown, CHI	1.83
H. Wiltse, NY	1.87

Most Strikeouts/9 Inn.

R. Marquard, NY	7.68
G. Alexander, PHI	5.57
N. Rucker, BKN	5.42
R. Ames, NY	5.18

Innings

G. Alexander, PHI	367
B. Harmon, STL	348
L. Leifield, PIT	318
N. Rucker, BKN	316

Games Pitched

T. Brown, CHI	53
B. Harmon, STL	51
N. Rucker, BKN	48
G. Alexander, PHI	48

	W	L	PCT	GB	R	OR	Batting 2B	3B	HR	BA	SA	SB	Fielding E	DP	FA	Pitching CG	BB	SO	ShO	SV	ERA
New York	99	54	.647		756	**542**	225	105	41	**.279**	**.391**	**347**	255	86	.959	**95**	**369**	**771**	19	11	**2.69**
Chicago	92	62	.597	7.5	**757**	607	218	101	54	.260	.374	214	260	114	.960	85	525	582	12	**16**	2.90
Pittsburgh	85	69	.552	14.5	744	557	206	**106**	48	.262	.371	160	232	**131**	**.963**	91	375	605	14	10	2.84
Philadelphia	79	73	.520	19.5	658	669	214	56	**60**	.259	.359	153	**231**	113	**.963**	90	598	697	**20**	9	3.30
St. Louis	75	74	.503	22	671	745	199	85	27	.252	.340	175	261	106	.960	88	701	561	6	9	3.68
Cincinnati	70	83	.458	29	682	706	180	105	21	.261	.346	290	295	108	.955	77	476	557	4	10	3.26
Brooklyn	64	86	.427	33.5	539	659	151	71	28	.237	.311	184	243	112	.962	81	566	533	14	10	3.39
Boston	44	107	.291	54	699	1021	**249**	54	37	.267	.355	169	347	110	.947	73	672	486	5	6	5.08
					5506	5506	1642	683	316	.260	.356	1692	2124	880	.959	680	4282	4792	94	81	3.39

AMERICAN LEAGUE 1911

Philadelphia

W-101 L-50

Connie Mack

POS	Player	AB	BA	HR	RBI	PO	A	E	DP	TC/G	FA	Pitcher	G	IP	W	L	SV	ERA
1B	S. McInnis	468	.321	3	77	1048	55	17	55	**11.5**	.985	J. Coombs	47	337	**28**	12	2	3.53
2B	E. Collins	493	.365	3	73	**348**	349	24	49	5.5	.967	E. Plank	40	257	23	8	**4**	2.10
SS	J. Barry	442	.265	1	63	268	384	39	49	5.4	.944	C. Morgan	38	250	15	7	1	2.70
3B	F. Baker	592	.334	**11**	115	217	274	30	26	3.5	.942	C. Bender	31	216	17	5	3	2.16
RF	D. Murphy	508	.329	6	66	162	34	8	6	1.5	.961	H. Krause	27	169	11	8	2	3.04
CF	R. Oldring	495	.297	3	59	225	13	5	2	2.0	.979							
LF	B. Lord	574	.310	3	55	271	17	11	5	2.3	.963							
C	I. Thomas	297	.273	0	39	499	150	17	12	**6.5**	.974							
OF	A. Strunk	215	.256	1	21	127	11	3	4	2.3	.979							
1B	H. Davis	183	.197	1	22	427	36	11	21	8.9	.977							
C	J. Lapp	167	.353	1	26	270	47	9	8	5.7	.972							
P	J. Coombs	141	.319	2	23	24	71	**9**	3	2.2	.913							

Detroit

W-89 L-65

Hughie Jennings

POS	Player	AB	BA	HR	RBI	PO	A	E	DP	TC/G	FA	Pitcher	G	IP	W	L	SV	ERA
1B	J. Delahanty	542	.339	3	94	744	21	17	17	10.9	.978	G. Mullin	30	234	18	10	0	3.07
2B	C. O'Leary	256	.266	0	25	169	201	13	19	5.7	.966	E. Willett	38	231	13	14	1	3.66
SS	D. Bush	561	.232	1	36	**372**	**556**	**75**	42	**6.7**	.925	E. Summers	30	179	11	11	0	3.66
3B	G. Moriarty	478	.243	1	60	157	273	33	11	3.6	.929	E. Lafitte	29	172	11	8	1	3.92
RF	S. Crawford	574	.378	7	115	181	16	5	3	1.4	.975	W. Donovan	20	168	10	9	0	3.31
CF	T. Cobb	591	**.420**	8	**144**	376	24	18	10	2.9	.957	R. Works	30	167	11	5	1	3.87
LF	D. Jones	341	.273	0	19	156	15	9	3	2.0	.950	J. Lively	18	114	7	5	0	4.59
C	O. Stanage	503	.264	3	51	**599**	**212**	**41**	13	6.0	.952							
OF	D. Drake	315	.279	1	36	141	4	9	1	1.9	.942							
1B	D. Gainer	248	.302	2	25	671	38	18	36	10.5	.975							

Cleveland

W-80 L-73

Deacon McGuire
W-6 L-11

George Stovall
W-74 L-62

POS	Player	AB	BA	HR	RBI	PO	A	E	DP	TC/G	FA	Pitcher	G	IP	W	L	SV	ERA
1B	G. Stovall	458	.271	0	79	1073	**87**	17	56	10.0	**.986**	V. Gregg	34	244	23	7	0	**1.81**
2B	N. Ball	412	.296	3	45	206	289	29	38	**5.5**	.945	G. Krapp	34	215	13	9	1	3.44
SS	I. Olson	545	.261	1	50	293	428	72	51	5.7	.909	W. Mitchell	30	177	7	14	0	3.76
3B	T. Turner	417	.252	0	28	114	208	10	10	3.5	**.970**	F. Blanding	29	176	7	11	2	3.68
RF	J. Jackson	571	.408	7	83	242	32	12	8	1.9	.958	G. Kahler	30	154	9	8	1	3.27
CF	J. Birmingham	447	.304	2	51	231	19	7	6	2.5	.973	C. Falkenberg	15	107	8	5	1	3.29
LF	J. Graney	527	.269	1	45	258	22	22	5	2.1	.927							
C	G. Fisher	203	.261	0	12	298	96	18	11	7.1	.956							
12	N. Lajoie	315	.365	2	60	479	109	14	33		.977							
OF	T. Easterly	287	.324	1	37	67	7	7	3	1.5	.914							
C	S. Smith	154	.299	1	21	270	62	7	10	7.1	.979							

Boston

W-78 L-75

Patsy Donovan

POS	Player	AB	BA	HR	RBI	PO	A	E	DP	TC/G	FA	Pitcher	G	IP	W	L	SV	ERA
1B	C. Engle	514	.270	2	48	550	43	14	24	9.3	.977	S. Wood	44	277	23	17	3	2.02
2B	H. Wagner	261	.257	1	38	106	104	12	11	5.6	.946	E. Cicotte	35	221	11	15	0	2.81
SS	S. Yerkes	502	.279	1	57	232	337	47	37	5.3	.924	R. Collins	31	204	11	12	1	2.39
3B	L. Gardner	492	.285	4	44	92	161	10	3	3.7	.962	L. Pape	27	176	10	8	0	2.45
RF	H. Hooper	524	.311	4	45	181	27	10	1	1.7	.954	C. Hall	32	147	8	7	**4**	3.73
CF	T. Speaker	500	.334	8	80	297	26	15	5	2.4	.956	E. Karger	25	131	5	8	0	3.37
LF	D. Lewis	469	.307	7	86	203	27	15	4	2.0	.939							
C	B. Carrigan	232	.289	1	30	326	94	12	11	7.0	.972							
1C	B. Williams	284	.239	0	31	727	73	20	28		.976							
C	L. Nunamaker	183	.257	0	19	309	79	11	8	6.8	.972							

AMERICAN LEAGUE 1911, *cont.*

Chicago

W-77 L-74

Hugh Duffy

POS	Player	AB	BA	HR	RBI	PO	A	E	DP	TC/G	FA	Pitcher	G	IP	W	L	SV	ERA
1B	S. Collins	370	.262	4	48	878	67	19	46	9.9	.980	E. Walsh	**56**	**369**	27	18	**4**	2.22
2B	A. McConnell	396	.280	1	34	189	280	13	31	4.7	**.973**	D. White	34	214	10	14	2	2.98
SS	L. Tannehill	516	.254	0	49	262	380	29	37	6.6	**.957**	J. Scott	39	202	14	11	0	2.63
3B	H. Lord	561	.321	3	61	175	226	25	21	3.1	.941	F. Lange	29	162	8	8	0	3.23
RF	M. McIntyre	569	.323	1	52	235	18	14	5	1.8	.948	F. Olmstead	25	118	6	6	2	4.21
CF	P. Bodie	551	.289	4	97	256	24	9	9	2.3	.969	J. Baker	22	94	2	7	1	3.93
LF	N. Callahan	466	.281	3	60	173	10	7	2	1.7	.963	I. Young	24	93	5	6	2	4.37
C	B. Sullivan	256	.215	0	31	447	114	8	13	6.4	**.986**							
UT	R. Zeider	217	.253	2	21	358	92	15	16		.968							
OF	P. Dougherty	211	.289	0	32	78	6	6	1	1.6	.933							
P	E. Walsh	155	.206	0	9	**27**	**159**	8	5	3.5	.959							

New York

W-76 L-76

Hal Chase

POS	Player	AB	BA	HR	RBI	PO	A	E	DP	TC/G	FA	Pitcher	G	IP	W	L	SV	ERA
1B	H. Chase	527	.315	3	62	**1255**	81	**36**	**62**	11.1	.974	R. Ford	37	281	22	11	0	2.27
2B	E. Gardner	357	.263	0	39	181	290	20	44	4.9	.959	R. Caldwell	41	255	14	14	1	3.35
SS	J. Knight	470	.268	3	62	200	247	46	30	6.0	.907	J. Warhop	31	210	12	13	0	4.16
3B	R. Hartzell	527	.296	3	91	158	221	26	18	3.3	.936	J. Quinn	40	175	8	10	2	3.76
RF	H. Wolter	434	.304	4	36	178	18	10	8	1.8	.951	R. Fisher	29	172	10	11	0	3.25
CF	B. Daniels	462	.286	2	31	256	15	17	6	2.4	.941	H. Vaughn	26	146	8	10	0	4.39
LF	B. Cree	520	.348	4	88	245	19	10	2	2.0	.964							
C	W. Blair	222	.194	0	26	379	101	15	12	5.9	.970							
C	J. Sweeney	229	.231	0	18	394	94	18	8	6.1	.964							
SS	O. Johnson	209	.234	3	36	78	126	21	17	4.8	.907							
OF	C. Hemphill	201	.284	1	15	95	4	5	0	1.9	.952							

Washington

W-64 L-90

Jimmy McAleer

POS	Player	AB	BA	HR	RBI	PO	A	E	DP	TC/G	FA	Pitcher	G	IP	W	L	SV	ERA
1B	G. Schaefer	440	.334	0	45	1038	71	23	57	10.5	.980	W. Johnson	40	323	25	13	1	1.89
2B	B. Cunningham	331	.190	3	37	168	244	30	18	4.8	.932	B. Groom	37	255	13	17	2	3.82
SS	G. McBride	557	.235	0	59	353	546	56	**60**	6.2	.941	L. Hughes	34	223	11	17	0	3.47
3B	W. Conroy	346	.231	2	28	87	177	20	11	3.3	.930	D. Walker	32	186	8	13	0	3.39
RF	D. Gessler	450	.282	4	78	130	19	9	2	1.3	.943	D. Gray	28	121	2	13	0	5.06
CF	C. Milan	**616**	.315	3	35	347	33	17	2	2.6	.957							
LF	T. Walker	356	.278	2	39	163	14	16	1	2.1	.917							
C	G. Street	216	.222	0	14	362	102	13	10	6.7	.973							
23	K. Elberfeld	404	.272	0	47	233	297	31	34		.945							
C1	J. Henry	261	.203	0	21	549	123	21	15		.970							
OF	J. Lelivelt	225	.320	0	22	82	11	6	1	2.0	.939							

St. Louis

W-45 L-107

Bobby Wallace

POS	Player	AB	BA	HR	RBI	PO	A	E	DP	TC/G	FA	Pitcher	G	IP	W	L	SV	ERA
1B	J. Black	186	.151	0	7	519	37	16	31	10.6	.972	J. Lake	30	215	10	15	0	3.30
2B	F. LaPorte	507	.314	2	82	287	**398**	**36**	**59**	5.4	.950	J. Powell	31	208	8	**19**	1	3.29
SS	B. Wallace	410	.232	0	31	280	417	42	47	6.0	.943	B. Pelty	28	207	7	15	0	2.83
3B	J. Austin	541	.261	2	45	**228**	**337**	**42**	**27**	**4.1**	.931	E. Hamilton	32	177	5	12	0	3.97
RF	A. Schweitzer	237	.215	0	34	100	13	8	4	1.8	.934	R. Mitchell	28	134	4	8	0	3.84
CF	B. Shotton	572	.255	0	36	356	21	20	2	2.9	.950	L. George	27	116	4	9	0	4.18
LF	H. Hogan	443	.260	2	62	263	26	22	3	2.7	.929	R. Nelson	16	81	3	9	0	5.22
C	N. Clarke	256	.215	0	18	251	111	29	**15**	5.4	.926							
C	J. Stephens	212	.231	0	17	223	94	17	7	5.1	.949							
OF	P. Meloan	206	.262	3	14	69	6	8	1	1.5	.904							
S2	E. Hallinan	169	.207	0	14	118	133	24	24		.913							

BATTING AND BASE RUNNING LEADERS

Batting Average
- T. Cobb, DET .420
- J. Jackson, CLE .408
- S. Crawford, DET .378
- E. Collins, PHI .365
- B. Cree, NY .348

Slugging Average
- T. Cobb, DET .621
- J. Jackson, CLE .590
- S. Crawford, DET .526
- B. Cree, NY .513
- F. Baker, PHI .505

Home Runs
- F. Baker, PHI 11
- T. Speaker, BOS 8
- T. Cobb, DET 8
- D. Lewis, BOS 7
- J. Jackson, CLE 7
- S. Crawford, DET 7

Total Bases
- T. Cobb, DET 367
- J. Jackson, CLE 337
- S. Crawford, DET 302
- F. Baker, PHI 299
- B. Cree, NY 267

Runs Batted In
- T. Cobb, DET 144
- S. Crawford, DET 115
- F. Baker, PHI 115
- P. Bodie, CHI 97
- J. Delahanty, DET 94

Stolen Bases
- T. Cobb, DET 83
- C. Milan, WAS 58
- B. Cree, NY 48
- N. Callahan, CHI 45
- H. Lord, CHI 43

Hits
- T. Cobb, DET 248
- J. Jackson, CLE 233
- S. Crawford, DET 217
- F. Baker, PHI 198

Base on Balls
- D. Bush, DET 98
- D. Gessler, WAS 74
- C. Milan, WAS 74
- H. Hooper, BOS 73

Home Run Percentage
- F. Baker, PHI 1.9
- T. Speaker, BOS 1.6
- D. Lewis, BOS 1.5
- T. Cobb, DET 1.4

Runs
- T. Cobb, DET 147
- D. Bush, DET 126
- J. Jackson, CLE 126
- S. Crawford, DET 109
- C. Milan, WAS 109

Doubles
- T. Cobb, DET 47
- J. Jackson, CLE 45
- F. Baker, PHI 40
- F. LaPorte, STL 37
- B. Lord, PHI 37

Triples
- T. Cobb, DET 24
- B. Cree, NY 22
- J. Jackson, CLE 19
- H. Lord, CHI 18

PITCHING LEADERS

Winning Percentage
- C. Bender, PHI .773
- V. Gregg, CLE .767
- E. Plank, PHI .742
- J. Coombs, PHI .700
- C. Morgan, PHI .682

Earned Run Average
- V. Gregg, CLE 1.81
- W. Johnson, WAS 1.89
- S. Wood, BOS 2.02
- E. Plank, PHI 2.10
- C. Bender, PHI 2.16

Wins
- J. Coombs, PHI 28
- E. Walsh, CHI 27
- W. Johnson, WAS 25
- V. Gregg, CLE 23
- E. Plank, PHI 23
- S. Wood, BOS 23

Saves
- E. Plank, PHI 4
- C. Hall, BOS 4
- E. Walsh, CHI 4
- C. Bender, PHI 3
- S. Wood, BOS 3

Strikeouts
- E. Walsh, CHI 255
- S. Wood, BOS 231
- W. Johnson, WAS 207
- J. Coombs, PHI 185
- R. Ford, NY 158

Complete Games
- W. Johnson, WAS 36
- E. Walsh, CHI 33
- R. Ford, NY 26
- J. Coombs, PHI 26
- G. Mullin, DET 25
- S. Wood, BOS 25

Fewest Hits/9 Innings
- V. Gregg, CLE 6.34
- S. Wood, BOS 7.35
- G. Krapp, CLE 7.63
- C. Morgan, PHI 7.82

Shutouts
- E. Plank, PHI 6
- W. Johnson, WAS 6
- V. Gregg, CLE 5
- S. Wood, BOS 5
- E. Walsh, CHI 5

Fewest Walks/9 Innings
- D. White, CHI 1.47
- J. Lake, STL 1.67
- E. Walsh, CHI 1.76
- J. Warhop, NY 1.89

Most Strikeouts/9 Inn.
- S. Wood, BOS 7.51
- E. Walsh, CHI 6.23
- W. Johnson, WAS 5.76
- J. Scott, CHI 5.70

Innings
- E. Walsh, CHI 369
- J. Coombs, PHI 337
- W. Johnson, WAS 323
- R. Ford, NY 281

Games Pitched
- E. Walsh, CHI 56
- J. Coombs, PHI 47
- S. Wood, BOS 44
- R. Caldwell, NY 41

AMERICAN LEAGUE 1911, *cont.*

	W	L	PCT	GB	R	OR	Batting 2B	3B	HR	BA	SA	SB	Fielding E	DP	FA	Pitching CG	BB	SO	ShO	SV	ERA
Philadelphia	101	50	.669		**861**	**601**	235	93	**35**	**.296**	**.397**	226	**225**	100	**.965**	97	487	739	13	**13**	3.01
Detroit	89	65	.578	13.5	831	776	230	**96**	30	.292	.388	**276**	318	78	.951	**108**	460	538	8	3	3.73
Cleveland	80	73	.523	22	691	712	**238**	81	20	.282	.369	209	302	**108**	.954	93	550	673	6	6	3.37
Boston	78	75	.510	24	680	643	203	66	**35**	.275	.363	190	323	93	.949	87	475	713	10	8	**2.73**
Chicago	77	74	.510	24	719	624	179	92	20	.269	.350	201	252	98	.961	87	**384**	**752**	**16**	11	3.01
New York	76	76	.500	25.5	684	724	190	**96**	26	.272	.363	270	328	99	.949	91	406	667	5	3	3.54
Washington	64	90	.416	38.5	625	766	159	53	16	.258	.320	215	305	90	.953	106	410	628	13	3	3.52
St. Louis	45	107	.296	56.5	567	812	187	63	17	.239	.312	125	358	104	.945	92	463	383	8	1	3.83
					5658	5658	1621	640	199	.273	.358	1712	2411	770	.953	761	3635	5093	79	48	3.34

NATIONAL LEAGUE 1912

	POS	Player	AB	BA	HR	RBI	PO	A	E	DP	TC/G	FA	Pitcher	G	IP	W	L	SV	ERA
New York	1B	F. Merkle	479	.309	11	84	1229	72	**27**	77	10.3	.980	C. Mathewson	43	**310**	23	12	5	2.12
	2B	L. Doyle	558	.330	10	90	313	379	38	68	5.1	.948	R. Marquard	43	295	**26**	11	0	2.57
	SS	A. Fletcher	419	.282	1	57	237	428	**52**	60	5.7	.927	J. Tesreau	36	243	17	7	1	**1.96**
W-103 L-48	3B	B. Herzog	482	.263	2	47	**159**	**308**	29	21	**3.5**	.942	R. Ames	33	179	11	5	1	2.46
	RF	R. Murray	549	.277	3	92	255	20	9	7	2.0	.968	D. Crandall	37	162	13	7	2	3.61
John McGraw	CF	B. Becker	402	.264	6	58	230	20	11	4	2.2	.958	H. Wiltse	28	134	9	6	2	3.16
	LF	F. Snodgrass	535	.269	3	69	229	25	14	4	2.3	.948							
	C	C. Meyers	371	.358	6	54	**576**	111	19	10	5.8	.973							
	OF	J. Devore	327	.275	2	37	155	14	15	3	1.9	.918							
	UT	T. Shafer	163	.288	0	23	80	119	22	10		.900							
Pittsburgh	1B	D. Miller	567	.275	4	87	1385	85	23	**93**	10.2	.985	C. Hendrix	39	289	24	9	1	2.59
	2B	A. McCarthy	401	.277	1	41	237	320	22	52	5.5	.962	H. Camnitz	41	277	22	12	2	2.83
	SS	H. Wagner	558	.324	7	102	341	462	32	**74**	5.8	**.962**	M. O'Toole	37	275	15	17	0	2.71
W-93 L-58	3B	B. Byrne	528	.288	3	35	144	187	18	14	2.7	**.948**	H. Robinson	33	175	12	7	2	2.26
	RF	M. Donlin	244	.316	2	35	102	8	2	1	1.8	.982	B. Adams	28	170	11	8	0	2.91
Fred Clarke	CF	O. Wilson	583	.300	11	95	324	20	14	5	2.4	.961							
	LF	M. Carey	587	.302	5	66	369	19	13	10	2.7	.968							
	C	G. Gibson	300	.240	2	35	484	101	6	11	6.3	**.990**							
	2B	A. Butler	154	.273	1	17	71	99	7	12	4.1	.960							
	OF	H. Hyatt	97	.289	0	22	20	1	1	0	1.5	.955							
Chicago	1B	V. Saier	451	.288	2	61	1165	52	10	67	10.2	.992	L. Cheney	42	303	**26**	10	0	2.85
	2B	J. Evers	478	.341	1	63	319	439	32	71	5.5	.959	J. Lavender	42	252	16	13	3	3.04
	SS	J. Tinker	550	.282	0	75	**354**	470	50	73	**6.2**	.943	L. Richie	39	238	16	8	0	2.95
W-91 L-59	3B	H. Zimmerman	557	**.372**	**14**	**103**	142	242	**35**	16	3.5	.916	E. Reulbach	39	169	10	6	3	3.78
	RF	W. Schulte	553	.264	13	70	219	19	12	6	1.8	.952	C. Smith	21	94	7	4	1	4.21
Frank Chance	CF	T. Leach	265	.242	2	32	181	11	5	4	2.7	.975	T. Brown	15	89	5	6	0	2.64
	LF	J. Sheckard	523	.245	3	47	332	26	14	4	2.5	.962							
	C	J. Archer	385	.283	5	58	504	**149**	**23**	15	5.7	.966							
	OF	W. Miller	241	.307	0	22	109	6	7	2	1.9	.943							
Cincinnati	1B	D. Hoblitzell	558	.294	2	85	1326	87	21	73	9.8	.985	G. Suggs	42	303	19	16	3	2.94
	2B	D. Egan	507	.247	0	52	345	452	22	55	5.5	**.973**	R. Benton	**50**	302	18	21	2	3.10
	SS	J. Esmond	231	.195	1	40	154	180	25	22	4.9	.930	A. Fromme	43	296	16	18	0	2.74
W-75 L-78	3B	A. Phelan	461	.243	3	54	153	250	33	18	3.4	.924	B. Humphries	30	159	9	11	2	3.23
	RF	M. Mitchell	552	.283	4	78	251	18	15	8	2.0	.947							
Hank O'Day	CF	A. Marsans	416	.317	1	38	222	11	6	2	2.4	.975							
	LF	B. Bescher	548	.281	4	38	347	15	14	4	2.6	.963							
	C	L. McLean	333	.243	1	27	425	124	15	16	5.8	.973							
	SS	E. Grant	255	.239	2	20	102	171	15	20	5.1	.948							
	OF	J. Bates	239	.289	1	29	157	15	9	4	2.8	.950							
	C	T. Clarke	146	.281	0	22	239	58	5	7	4.8	.983							
Philadelphia	1B	F. Luderus	572	.257	10	69	**1421**	**104**	15	77	**10.5**	.990	G. Alexander	46	**310**	19	17	2	2.81
	2B	O. Knabe	426	.282	0	46	258	342	30	45	5.1	.952	T. Seaton	44	255	16	12	2	3.28
	SS	M. Doolan	532	.258	1	62	289	**476**	40	49	5.5	.950	E. Moore	31	182	9	14	0	3.31
W-73 L-79	3B	H. Lobert	257	.327	2	33	80	86	4	3	2.7	.976	A. Brennan	27	174	11	9	2	3.57
	RF	G. Cravath	436	.284	11	70	200	26	8	5	2.1	.966	E. Rixey	23	162	10	10	0	2.50
Red Dooin	CF	D. Paskert	540	.315	2	43	336	19	12	4	2.6	.967							
	LF	S. Magee	464	.306	6	72	251	8	10	2	2.2	.963							
	C	B. Killefer	268	.224	1	21	407	134	15	17	**6.5**	.973							
	C	R. Dooin	184	.234	0	22	254	69	14	2	5.8	.958							
	OF	D. Miller	177	.288	0	21	61	9	1	1	1.8	.986							
	3B	T. Downey	171	.292	1	23	57	76	16	3	3.2	.893							
	OF	J. Titus	157	.274	3	22	53	2	5	1	1.4	.917							
St. Louis	1B	E. Konetchy	538	.314	8	82	1392	90	13	77	10.5	.991	S. Sallee	48	294	16	17	**6**	2.60
	2B	M. Huggins	431	.304	0	29	272	337	37	50	5.7	.943	B. Harmon	43	268	18	18	0	3.93
	SS	A. Hauser	479	.259	1	42	262	446	50	54	5.7	.934	B. Steele	40	194	9	13	1	4.69
W-63 L-90	3B	M. Mowrey	408	.255	2	50	131	220	26	**22**	3.5	.931	R. Geyer	41	181	7	14	0	3.28
	RF	S. Evans	491	.283	6	72	219	24	15	2	1.9	.942	J. Willis	31	130	4	9	2	4.44
Roger Bresnahan	CF	R. Oakes	495	.281	3	58	324	15	19	5	2.6	.947							
	LF	L. Magee	458	.290	0	40	198	18	10	2	2.7	.956							
	C	I. Wingo	310	.265	2	44	360	148	**23**	11	5.8	.957							
	OF	R. Ellis	305	.269	4	33	173	10	14	5	2.6	.929							
	3S	W. Smith	219	.256	0	26	81	126	10	10		.954							

NATIONAL LEAGUE 1912, *cont.*

Brooklyn

W-58 L-95

Bill Dahlen

POS	Player	AB	BA	HR	RBI	PO	A	E	DP	TC/G	FA
1B	J. Daubert	559	.308	3	66	1373	76	10	68	10.2	**.993**
2B	G. Cutshaw	357	.280	0	28	192	290	21	31	5.5	.958
SS	B. Tooley	265	.234	2	37	147	214	47	23	5.4	.885
3B	R. Smith	486	.286	4	57	156	251	27	16	3.5	.938
RF	H. Northen	412	.282	2	46	178	11	10	3	2.0	.950
CF	H. Moran	508	.276	1	40	273	24	12	5	2.4	.961
LF	Z. Wheat	453	.305	8	65	285	13	10	2	2.5	.968
C	O. Miller	316	.278	1	31	455	141	15	11	6.5	.975
20	J. Hummel	411	.282	5	54	175	161	11	17		.968
SS	B. Fisher	257	.233	0	26	121	200	29	23	4.7	.917
OF	J. Daley	199	.256	2	13	116	10	7	3	2.4	.947
C	E. Phelps	111	.288	0	23	130	35	4	4	5.3	.976

Pitcher	G	IP	W	L	SV	ERA
N. Rucker	45	298	18	21	4	2.21
P. Ragan	36	208	7	18	1	3.63
E. Yingling	25	163	6	11	0	3.59
E. Stack	28	142	7	5	1	3.36
E. Knetzer	33	140	7	9	0	4.55
F. Allen	20	109	3	9	0	3.63
C. Barger	16	94	1	9	0	5.46
M. Kent	20	93	5	5	0	4.84
C. Curtis	19	80	4	7	0	3.94

Boston

W-52 L-101

Johnny Kling

POS	Player	AB	BA	HR	RBI	PO	A	E	DP	TC/G	FA
1B	B. Houser	332	.286	8	52	759	37	11	48	9.7	.986
2B	B. Sweeney	593	.344	1	100	**459**	**475**	**40**	**76**	**6.4**	.959
SS	F. O'Rourke	196	.122	0	16	92	167	24	16	4.8	.915
3B	E. McDonald	459	.259	2	34	147	216	23	18	3.3	.940
RF	J. Titus	345	.325	2	48	152	12	6	1	1.8	.965
CF	V. Campbell	**624**	.296	3	48	340	20	24	6	2.7	.938
LF	G. Jackson	397	.262	4	48	230	20	15	3	2.5	.943
C	J. Kling	252	.317	2	30	322	108	19	**20**	6.1	.958
UT	A. Devlin	436	.289	0	54	768	140	15	52		.984
03	J. Kirke	359	.320	4	62	99	45	23	4		.862
C	B. Rariden	247	.223	1	14	297	103	15	6	5.7	.964
OF	D. Miller	201	.234	2	24	79	12	5	4	1.9	.948

Pitcher	G	IP	W	L	SV	ERA
L. Tyler	42	256	12	**22**	0	4.18
O. Hess	33	254	12	17	0	3.76
H. Perdue	37	249	13	16	3	3.80
W. Dickson	36	189	3	19	0	3.86
E. Donnelly	37	184	5	10	0	4.35
B. Brown	31	168	4	15	0	4.01

BATTING AND BASE RUNNING LEADERS

Batting Average

H. Zimmerman, CHI	.372
C. Meyers, NY	.358
B. Sweeney, BOS	.344
J. Evers, CHI	.341
L. Doyle, NY	.330

Slugging Average

H. Zimmerman, CHI	.571
O. Wilson, PIT	.513
H. Wagner, PIT	.496
C. Meyers, NY	.477
L. Doyle, NY	.471

Home Runs

H. Zimmerman, CHI	14
W. Schulte, CHI	13
G. Cravath, PHI	11
F. Merkle, NY	11
O. Wilson, PIT	11

Total Bases

H. Zimmerman, CHI	318
O. Wilson, PIT	299
H. Wagner, PIT	277
B. Sweeney, BOS	264
L. Doyle, NY	263

Runs Batted In

H. Zimmerman, CHI	103
H. Wagner, PIT	102
B. Sweeney, BOS	100
O. Wilson, PIT	95
R. Murray, NY	92

Stolen Bases

B. Bescher, CIN	67
M. Carey, PIT	45
F. Snodgrass, NY	43
R. Murray, NY	38
F. Merkle, NY	37
B. Herzog, NY	37

Hits

H. Zimmerman, CHI	207
B. Sweeney, BOS	204
V. Campbell, BOS	185
L. Doyle, NY	184

Base on Balls

J. Sheckard, CHI	122
D. Paskert, PHI	91
M. Huggins, STL	87
B. Bescher, CIN	83

Home Run Percentage

G. Cravath, PHI	2.5
H. Zimmerman, CHI	2.5
W. Schulte, CHI	2.4
F. Merkle, NY	2.3

Runs

B. Bescher, CIN	120
M. Carey, PIT	114
D. Paskert, PHI	102
V. Campbell, BOS	102

Doubles

H. Zimmerman, CHI	41
D. Paskert, PHI	37
H. Wagner, PIT	35
L. Doyle, NY	33
D. Miller, PIT	33

Triples

O. Wilson, PIT	36
R. Murray, NY	20
H. Wagner, PIT	20
J. Daubert, BKN	16

PITCHING LEADERS

Winning Percentage

C. Hendrix, PIT	.727
L. Cheney, CHI	.722
J. Tesreau, NY	.708
R. Marquard, NY	.703
L. Richie, CHI	.667

Earned Run Average

J. Tesreau, NY	1.96
C. Mathewson, NY	2.12
N. Rucker, BKN	2.21
H. Robinson, PIT	2.26
E. Rixey, PHI	2.50

Wins

R. Marquard, NY	26
L. Cheney, CHI	26
C. Hendrix, PIT	24
C. Mathewson, NY	23
H. Camnitz, PIT	22

Saves

S. Sallee, STL	6
C. Mathewson, NY	5
N. Rucker, BKN	4

Strikeouts

G. Alexander, PHI	195
C. Hendrix, PIT	176
R. Marquard, NY	175
R. Benton, CIN	162
N. Rucker, BKN	151

Complete Games

L. Tyler, BOS	29
L. Cheney, CHI	28
C. Mathewson, NY	27
C. Hendrix, PIT	25
G. Alexander, PHI	25
G. Suggs, CIN	25

Fewest Hits/9 Innings

J. Tesreau, NY	6.56
H. Robinson, PIT	7.51
M. O'Toole, PIT	7.75
L. Cheney, CHI	7.77

Shutouts

N. Rucker, BKN	6
M. O'Toole, PIT	6
G. Suggs, CIN	5

Fewest Walks/9 Innings

C. Mathewson, NY	0.99
H. Robinson, PIT	1.54
G. Suggs, CIN	1.66
B. Adams, PIT	1.85

Most Strikeouts/9 Inn.

G. Alexander, PHI	5.66
C. Hendrix, PIT	5.49
R. Marquard, NY	5.35
L. Tyler, BOS	5.06

Innings

G. Alexander, PHI	310
C. Mathewson, NY	310
G. Suggs, CIN	303
L. Cheney, CHI	303

Games Pitched

R. Benton, CIN	50
S. Sallee, STL	48
G. Alexander, PHI	46
N. Rucker, BKN	45

							Batting						Fielding				Pitching				
	W	L	PCT	GB	R	OR	2B	3B	HR	BA	SA	SB	E	DP	FA	CG	BB	SO	ShO	SV	ERA
New York	103	48	.682		**823**	571	231	89	**47**	**.286**	.395	**319**	280	123	.956	93	**338**	652	8	**14**	**2.58**
Pittsburgh	93	58	.616	10	751	**565**	222	**129**	39	.284	**.398**	177	**169**	125	**.972**	**94**	497	**664**	**18**	6	2.85
Chicago	91	59	.607	11.5	756	668	**245**	91	43	.277	.387	164	249	125	.960	80	493	554	14	8	3.42
Cincinnati	75	78	.490	29	656	722	183	89	21	.256	.339	248	247	102	.960	86	452	561	12	10	3.42
Philadelphia	73	79	.480	30.5	670	688	244	68	43	.267	.367	159	231	98	.963	81	515	616	10	8	3.25
St. Louis	63	90	.412	41	659	830	190	77	27	.268	.352	193	274	113	.957	62	560	487	6	11	3.85
Brooklyn	58	95	.379	46	651	754	220	73	32	.268	.358	179	255	96	.959	71	510	553	10	7	3.64
Boston	52	101	.340	52	693	861	227	68	35	.273	.360	137	295	**129**	.954	92	521	542	5	3	4.17
					5659	5659	1762	684	287	.272	.369	1576	2000	911	.960	659	3886	4629	83	67	3.40

AMERICAN LEAGUE 1912

Team	POS	Player	AB	BA	HR	RBI	PO	A	E	DP	TC/G	FA	Pitcher	G	IP	W	L	SV	ERA
Boston	1B	J. Stahl	326	.301	3	60	853	49	18	37	10.0	.980	S. Wood	43	344	**34**	5	1	1.91
	2B	S. Yerkes	523	.252	0	42	244	323	34	39	4.6	.943	B. O'Brien	37	276	20	13	0	2.58
	SS	H. Wagner	504	.274	2	68	332	391	61	43	5.4	.922	H. Bedient	41	231	20	9	2	2.92
W-105 L-47	3B	L. Gardner	517	.315	3	86	167	296	35	16	3.5	.930	R. Collins	27	199	13	8	0	2.53
	RF	H. Hooper	590	.242	2	53	220	22	9	6	1.7	.964	C. Hall	34	191	15	8	2	3.02
Jake Stahl	CF	T. Speaker	580	.383	**10**	98	372	35	18	9	2.8	.958							
	LF	D. Lewis	581	.284	6	109	301	23	18	4	2.2	.947							
	C	B. Carrigan	266	.263	0	24	413	102	16	7	6.1	**.970**							
	UT	C. Engle	171	.234	0	18	248	60	13	15		.960							

Team	POS	Player	AB	BA	HR	RBI	PO	A	E	DP	TC/G	FA	Pitcher	G	IP	W	L	SV	ERA
Washington	1B	C. Gandil	443	.305	2	81	1106	68	12	49	10.1	**.990**	W. Johnson	50	369	33	12	2	**1.39**
	2B	R. Morgan	273	.238	1	30	150	173	21	21	4.6	.939	B. Groom	43	316	24	13	1	2.62
	SS	G. McBride	521	.226	1	52	**349**	498	53	**55**	5.9	**.941**	L. Hughes	31	196	13	10	0	2.94
W-91 L-61	3B	E. Foster	**618**	.285	2	70	168	**348**	45	22	3.6	.920	J. Cashion	26	170	10	6	1	3.17
	RF	D. Moeller	519	.276	6	46	227	25	15	5	2.0	.944							
Clark Griffith	CF	C. Milan	601	.306	1	79	326	31	25	6	2.5	.935							
	LF	H. Shanks	399	.231	1	47	189	14	8	2	1.9	.962							
	C	J. Henry	191	.194	0	9	347	113	11	7	7.5	.977							
	C	E. Ainsmith	186	.226	0	22	415	85	22	5	9.0	.958							
	UT	G. Schaefer	166	.247	0	19	169	30	8	7		.961							
	C	B. Williams	157	.318	0	22	234	74	7	6	7.0	.978							
	P	W. Johnson	144	.264	2	20	15	93	4	4	2.2	.964							

Team	POS	Player	AB	BA	HR	RBI	PO	A	E	DP	TC/G	FA	Pitcher	G	IP	W	L	SV	ERA
Philadelphia	1B	S. McInnis	568	.327	3	101	**1533**	**100**	**27**	**88**	**10.8**	.984	J. Coombs	40	262	21	10	2	3.29
	2B	E. Collins	543	.348	0	64	**387**	426	**38**	**63**	**5.6**	.955	E. Plank	37	260	26	6	2	2.22
	SS	J. Barry	483	.261	0	55	238	438	55	**55**	5.3	.925	B. Brown	34	199	13	11	1	3.66
W-90 L-62	3B	F. Baker	577	.347	**10**	**133**	217	321	34	**25**	**3.8**	.941	B. Houck	30	181	8	8	0	2.94
	RF	B. Lord	378	.238	0	25	148	15	10	5	1.8	.942	C. Bender	27	171	13	8	2	2.74
Connie Mack	CF	R. Oldring	395	.301	1	24	214	8	6	1	2.4	.974	C. Morgan	16	94	3	8	0	3.75
	LF	A. Strunk	412	.289	3	63	278	16	3	3	2.5	.990							
	C	J. Lapp	281	.292	1	35	354	105	20	10	5.8	.958							
	OF	H. Maggert	242	.256	1	13	103	5	7	0	1.9	.939							
	OF	D. Murphy	130	.323	2	20	39	2	5	2	1.3	.891							

Team	POS	Player	AB	BA	HR	RBI	PO	A	E	DP	TC/G	FA	Pitcher	G	IP	W	L	SV	ERA
Chicago	1B	R. Zeider	420	.245	1	42	682	54	16	28	11.4	.979	E. Walsh	**62**	**393**	27	17	**10**	2.15
	2B	M. Rath	591	.272	1	19	353	**463**	31	46	5.4	**.963**	J. Benz	41	238	13	17	0	2.92
	SS	B. Weaver	523	.224	1	43	342	425	**71**	53	5.7	.915	D. White	32	172	8	10	0	3.24
W-78 L-76	3B	H. Lord	570	.267	5	54	127	172	35	11	3.2	.895	F. Lange	31	165	10	10	3	3.27
	RF	S. Collins	575	.292	2	81	177	11	6	0	1.8	.969	E. Cicotte	20	152	9	7	0	2.84
Nixey Callahan	CF	P. Bodie	472	.294	5	72	208	11	7	3	1.7	.969	R. Peters	28	109	5	6	0	4.14
	LF	N. Callahan	408	.272	1	52	166	3	11	0	1.7	.939	G. Mogridge	17	65	3	4	3	4.04
	C	W. Kuhn	178	.202	0	10	318	104	15	8	5.8	.966							
	OF	W. Mattick	285	.260	1	35	154	8	3	1	2.1	.982							
	C	B. Block	136	.257	0	26	222	65	6	4	6.4	.980							

Team	POS	Player	AB	BA	HR	RBI	PO	A	E	DP	TC/G	FA	Pitcher	G	IP	W	L	SV	ERA
Cleveland	1B	A. Griggs	273	.304	0	39	661	43	10	33	10.1	.986	V. Gregg	37	271	20	13	2	2.59
	2B	N. Lajoie	448	.368	0	90	241	249	21	49	5.3	.959	F. Blanding	39	262	18	14	1	2.92
	SS	R. Peckinpaugh	236	.212	1	22	127	188	26	16	5.1	.924	G. Kahler	41	246	12	19	1	3.69
W-75 L-78	3B	T. Turner	370	.308	0	33	129	199	17	21	3.3	**.951**	W. Mitchell	29	164	5	8	1	2.80
	RF	J. Jackson	572	.395	3	90	273	30	16	2	2.1	.950	B. Steen	26	143	9	8	0	3.77
Harry Davis	CF	J. Birmingham	369	.255	0	45	198	18	11	8	2.4	.952	J. Baskette	29	116	8	4	1	3.18
W-54 L-71	LF	B. Ryan	328	.271	1	31	167	11	7	2	2.1	.962							
	C	S. O'Neill	215	.228	0	14	316	108	17	9	6.6	.961							
Joe Birmingham	UT	I. Olson	467	.253	0	33	230	318	44	18		.926							
W-21 L-7	OF	J. Graney	264	.242	0	20	148	11	7	5	2.2	.958							
	C	T. Easterly	186	.296	1	21	226	69	13	11*	6.0	.958							
	1B	D. Johnston	164	.280	1	11	330	17	3	27	8.5	.991							

Team	POS	Player	AB	BA	HR	RBI	PO	A	E	DP	TC/G	FA	Pitcher	G	IP	W	L	SV	ERA
Detroit	1B	G. Moriarty	375	.248	0	54	800	27	11	19	11.8	.987	E. Willett	37	284	17	15	0	3.29
	2B	B. Louden	403	.241	1	36	200	288	25	25	6.0	.951	J. Dubuc	37	250	17	10	3	2.77
	SS	D. Bush	511	.231	2	38	317	**547**	66	45	**6.5**	.929	G. Mullin	30	226	12	17	0	3.54
W-69 L-84	3B	C. Deal	142	.225	0	11	48	113	10	3	4.2	.942	J. Lake	26	163	9	11	1	3.10
	RF	S. Crawford	581	.325	4	109	169	16	3	5	1.3	.984	R. Works	27	157	5	10	1	4.24
Hughie Jennings	CF	T. Cobb	553	**.410**	7	90	324	21	22	5	2.6	.940							
	LF	D. Jones	316	.294	0	24	141	13	6	4	2.0	.963							
	C	O. Stanage	394	.261	0	41	440	**168**	32	**14**	5.4	.950							
	UT	O. Vitt	273	.245	0	19	109	99	11	8		.950							
	20	J. Delahanty	266	.286	0	41	148	120	23	19		.921							
	1B	D. Gainer	179	.240	0	20	547	22	8	25	11.5	.986							

Team	POS	Player	AB	BA	HR	RBI	PO	A	E	DP	TC/G	FA	Pitcher	G	IP	W	L	SV	ERA
St. Louis	1B	G. Stovall	398	.254	0	45	845	68	16	64	9.9	.983	E. Hamilton	41	250	11	14	2	3.24
	2B	D. Pratt	570	.302	5	69	273	326	36	49	5.2	.943	J. Powell	32	235	9	17	0	3.10
	SS	B. Wallace	323	.241	0	31	185	271	28	29	5.6	.942	G. Baumgardner	30	218	11	13	0	3.38
W-53 L-101	3B	J. Austin	536	.252	2	44	**219**	292	**50**	22	3.8	.911	M. Allison	31	169	6	17	1	3.62
	RF	P. Compton	268	.280	2	30	139	9	12	1	2.2	.925	E. Brown	23	120	5	8	0	2.99
Bobby Wallace	CF	B. Shotton	580	.290	2	40	381	20	25	7	2.8	.941							
W-12 L-27	LF	H. Hogan	360	.214	1	36	229	14	7	6	2.5	.972							
	C	J. Stephens	205	.249	0	22	262	110	18	10	5.9	.954							
George Stovall	20	F. LaPorte	266	.312	1	38	123	107	16	24		.935							
W-41 L-74	OF	G. Williams	216	.292	2	32	94	12	8	3	1.8	.930							
	1B	J. Kutina	205	.205	1	18	489	24	8	28	10.2	.985							
	C	P. Krichell	161	.217	0	8	255	72	14	9	6.0	.959							

AMERICAN LEAGUE 1912, *cont.*

Team	POS	Player	AB	BA	HR	RBI	PO	A	E	DP	TC/G	FA	Pitcher	G	IP	W	L	SV	ERA
New York	1B	H. Chase	522	.274	4	58	1162	79	**27**	49	10.5	.979	R. Ford	36	292	13	**21**	0	3.55
	2B	H. Simmons	401	.239	0	41	162	207	21	23	4.4	.946	J. Warhop	39	258	10	19	3	2.86
W-50 L-102	SS	J. Martin	231	.225	0	17	123	201	36	18	5.6	.900	R. Caldwell	30	183	8	16	0	4.47
	3B	D. Paddock	156	.288	1	14	49	69	14	4	3.2	.894	G. McConnell	23	177	8	12	0	2.75
Harry Wolverton	RF	G. Zinn	401	.262	6	55	158	9	20	1	1.8	.893	J. Quinn	18	103	5	7	0	5.79
	CF	R. Hartzell	416	.272	1	38	101	9	7	2	2.1	.940	R. Fisher	17	90	2	8	0	5.88
	LF	B. Daniels	496	.274	2	41	277	13	17	1	2.3	.945	H. Vaughn	15	63	2	8	0	5.14
	C	J. Sweeney	351	.268	0	30	**548**	167	**34**	9	**6.9**	.955							
	UT	D. Sterrett	230	.265	1	32	259	22	5	4		.983							
	OF	B. Cree	190	.332	0	22	123	5	7	1	2.7	.948							
	2B	E. Gardner	160	.281	0	26	93	107	17	11	5.0	.922							
	OF	J. Lelivelt	149	.362	2	23	75	4	3	2	2.3	.963							

BATTING AND BASE RUNNING LEADERS

Batting Average
T. Cobb, DET .410
J. Jackson, CLE .395
T. Speaker, BOS .383
N. Lajoie, CLE .368
E. Collins, PHI .348

Slugging Average
T. Cobb, DET .586
J. Jackson, CLE .579
T. Speaker, BOS .567
F. Baker, PHI .541
S. Crawford, DET .470

Home Runs
F. Baker, PHI 10
T. Speaker, BOS 10
T. Cobb, DET 7
G. Zinn, NY 6
D. Moeller, WAS 6
D. Lewis, BOS 6

Total Bases
J. Jackson, CLE 331
T. Speaker, BOS 329
T. Cobb, DET 324
F. Baker, PHI 312
S. Crawford, DET 273

Runs Batted In
F. Baker, PHI 133
S. Crawford, DET 109
D. Lewis, BOS 109
S. McInnis, PHI 101
T. Speaker, BOS 98

Stolen Bases
C. Milan, WAS 88
E. Collins, PHI 63
T. Cobb, DET 61
T. Speaker, BOS 52
R. Zeider, CHI 47

Hits
T. Cobb, DET 227
J. Jackson, CLE 226
T. Speaker, BOS 222
F. Baker, PHI 200

Base on Balls
D. Bush, DET 117
E. Collins, PHI 101
M. Rath, CHI 95
B. Shotton, STL 86

Home Run Percentage
F. Baker, PHI 1.7
T. Speaker, BOS 1.7
G. Zinn, NY 1.5
T. Cobb, DET 1.3

Runs
E. Collins, PHI 137
T. Speaker, BOS 136
J. Jackson, CLE 121
T. Cobb, DET 119

Doubles
T. Speaker, BOS 53
J. Jackson, CLE 44
F. Baker, PHI 40
D. Lewis, BOS 36

Triples
J. Jackson, CLE 26
T. Cobb, DET 23
F. Baker, PHI 21
S. Crawford, DET 21

PITCHING LEADERS

Winning Percentage
S. Wood, BOS .872
E. Plank, PHI .813
W. Johnson, WAS .733
H. Bedient, BOS .690
J. Coombs, PHI .677

Earned Run Average
W. Johnson, WAS 1.39
S. Wood, BOS 1.91
E. Walsh, CHI 2.15
E. Plank, PHI 2.22
R. Collins, BOS 2.53

Wins
S. Wood, BOS 34
W. Johnson, WAS 33
E. Walsh, CHI 27
E. Plank, PHI 26
B. Groom, WAS 24

Saves
E. Walsh, CHI 10
J. Dubuc, DET 3
G. Mogridge, CHI 3
F. Lange, CHI 3
J. Warhop, NY 3

Strikeouts
W. Johnson, WAS 303
S. Wood, BOS 258
E. Walsh, CHI 254
V. Gregg, CLE 184
B. Groom, WAS 179

Complete Games
S. Wood, BOS 35
W. Johnson, WAS 34
E. Walsh, CHI 32
R. Ford, NY 30
E. Willett, DET 28
B. Groom, WAS 28

Fewest Hits/9 Innings
W. Johnson, WAS 6.32
S. Wood, BOS 6.99
B. Houck, PHI 7.37
E. Walsh, CHI 7.60

Shutouts
S. Wood, BOS 10
W. Johnson, WAS 7
E. Walsh, CHI 6
E. Plank, PHI 5

Fewest Walks/9 Innings
C. Bender, PHI 1.74
W. Johnson, WAS 1.85
R. Collins, BOS 1.90
J. Powell, STL 1.99

Most Strikeouts/9 Inn.
W. Johnson, WAS 7.39
S. Wood, BOS 6.75
V. Gregg, CLE 6.10
E. Walsh, CHI 5.82

Innings
E. Walsh, CHI 393
W. Johnson, WAS 369
S. Wood, BOS 344
B. Groom, WAS 316

Games Pitched
E. Walsh, CHI 62
W. Johnson, WAS 50
S. Wood, BOS 43
B. Groom, WAS 43

							Batting						Fielding			Pitching					
	W	L	PCT	GB	R	OR	2B	3B	HR	BA	SA	SB	E	DP	FA	CG	BB	SO	ShO	SV	ERA
Boston	105	47	.691		**799**	**544**	**269**	84	**29**	.277	**.380**	185	267	88	.957	**108**	**385**	712	**18**	6	2.76
Washington	91	61	.599	14	698	581	202	86	20	.256	.341	**274**	297	92	.954	98	525	**828**	11	6	**2.69**
Philadelphia	90	62	.592	15	779	658	204	**108**	22	**.282**	.377	258	**263**	115	**.959**	100	518	601	11	9	3.32
Chicago	78	76	.506	28	638	646	174	80	17	.255	.329	205	291	102	.956	85	426	697	14	**16**	3.06
Cleveland	75	78	.490	30.5	676	680	218	77	10	.273	.352	194	287	124	.954	94	523	622	7	7	3.30
Detroit	69	84	.451	36.5	720	777	189	86	19	.267	.349	270	338	91	.950	107	517	506	7	5	3.78
St. Louis	53	101	.344	53	552	764	166	71	19	.249	.320	176	341	**127**	.947	85	442	547	8	5	3.71
New York	50	102	.329	55	630	842	168	79	18	.259	.334	247	382	77	.940	105	436	637	4	3	4.13
					5492	5492	1590	671	154	.265	.348	1809	2466	816	.952	782	3772	5150	80	57	3.34

NATIONAL LEAGUE 1913

Team	POS	Player	AB	BA	HR	RBI	PO	A	E	DP	TC/G	FA	Pitcher	G	IP	W	L	SV	ERA
New York	1B	F. Merkle	563	.261	3	69	1463	76	22	86	10.2	.986	C. Mathewson	40	306	25	11	2	**2.06**
	2B	L. Doyle	482	.280	5	73	315	345	31	55	5.3	.955	R. Marquard	42	288	23	10	2	2.50
	SS	A. Fletcher	538	.297	4	71	245	435	50	42	5.4	.932	J. Tesreau	41	282	22	13	0	2.17
	3B	B. Herzog	290	.286	3	31	95	139	13	18	2.9	.947	A. Demaree	31	200	13	4	2	2.21
W-101 L-51	RF	R. Murray	520	.267	2	59	279	24	11	3	2.1	.965	A. Fromme	26	112	11	6	0	4.01
	CF	F. Snodgrass	457	.291	3	49	312	19	11	1	2.6	.968	D. Crandall	35	98	4	4	6	2.86
John McGraw	LF	G. Burns	605	.286	2	54	321	22	13	2	2.4	.963							
	C	C. Meyers	378	.312	3	47	**579**	143	25	12	**6.4**	.967							
	UT	T. Shafer	508	.287	5	52	220	254	43	26		.917							
Philadelphia	1B	F. Luderus	588	.262	18	86	**1533**	**92**	**26**	76	10.7	.984	T. Seaton	52	**322**	**27**	12	1	2.60
	2B	O. Knabe	571	.263	2	53	311	**466**	33	58	5.5	.959	G. Alexander	47	306	22	8	2	2.79
	SS	M. Doolan	518	.218	1	43	**338**	**482**	51	**63**	5.9	.941	A. Brennan	40	207	14	12	1	2.39
W-88 L-63	3B	H. Lobert	573	.300	7	55	**181**	225	11	13	2.9	**.974**	E. Mayer	39	171	9	9	1	3.11
	RF	G. Cravath	525	.341	**19**	**128**	208	20	10	1	1.7	.958	E. Rixey	35	156	9	5	2	3.12
Red Dooin	CF	D. Paskert	454	.262	4	29	330	19	10	8	3.0	.972	G. Chalmers	26	116	3	10	1	4.81
	LF	S. Magee	470	.306	11	70	236	7	8	2	2.0	.968							
	C	B. Killefer	360	.244	0	24	569	**166**	9	**16**	6.3	**.988**							
	OF	B. Becker	306	.324	9	44	172	6	3	1	2.4	.983							

NATIONAL LEAGUE 1913, *cont.*

Chicago

W-88 L-65

Johnny Evers

POS	Player	AB	BA	HR	RBI	PO	A	E	DP	TC/G	FA	Pitcher	G	IP	W	L	SV	ERA
1B	V. Saier	518	.288	14	92	1469	71	**26**	79	10.6	.983	L. Cheney	**54**	305	21	14	**11**	2.57
2B	J. Evers	444	.284	3	49	303	426	30	70	5.6	.960	J. Lavender	40	204	10	14	2	3.66
SS	A. Bridwell	405	.240	1	37	282	399	37	46	5.3	.948	B. Humphries	28	181	16	4	0	2.69
3B	H. Zimmerman	447	.313	9	95	139	232	**36**	18	3.3	.912	G. Pearce	25	163	13	5	0	2.31
RF	W. Schulte	495	.279	9	72	180	13	9	2	1.6	.955	C. Smith	20	138	7	9	0	2.55
CF	T. Leach	454	.289	6	32	270	15	3	5	2.4	.990							
LF	M. Mitchell	278	.259	4	35	176	14	12	0	2.5	.941							
C	J. Archer	367	.267	2	44	454	138	19	6	5.9	.969							
23	A. Phelan	259	.251	2	35	102	147	19	12		.929							
OF	W. Miller	203	.236	1	16	136	9	3	5	2.3	.980							
C	R. Bresnahan	161	.230	1	21	194	67	10	2	4.7	.963							
OF	C. Williams	156	.224	4	32	77	4	2	0	1.9	.976							

Pittsburgh

W-78 L-71

Fred Clarke

POS	Player	AB	BA	HR	RBI	PO	A	E	DP	TC/G	FA	Pitcher	G	IP	W	L	SV	ERA
1B	D. Miller	580	.272	7	90	1400	78	22	67	10.0	.985	B. Adams	43	314	21	10	0	2.15
2B	J. Viox	492	.317	2	65	223	314	23	29	4.5	.959	C. Hendrix	42	241	14	15	3	2.84
SS	H. Wagner	413	.300	3	56	289	323	24	47	**6.1**	.962	H. Robinson	43	196	14	9	0	2.38
3B	B. Byrne	448	.270	1	47	154	176	21	14	3.2	.940	H. Camnitz	36	192	6	17	2	3.74
RF	O. Wilson	580	.266	10	73	301	14	10	3	2.1	.969	M. O'Toole	26	145	6	8	1	3.30
CF	M. Mitchell	199	.271	1	16	150	9	9	0	3.1	.946	G. McQuillan	25	142	8	6	1	3.43
LF	M. Carey	**620**	.277	5	49	363	28	16	6	2.6	.961							
C	M. Simon	255	.247	1	17	393	151	14	6	6.1	.975							
2S	A. Butler	214	.280	0	20	126	144	25	14		.915							
OF	F. Kommers	155	.232	0	22	94	1	2	0	2.4	.979							

Boston

W-69 L-82

George Stallings

POS	Player	AB	BA	HR	RBI	PO	A	E	DP	TC/G	FA	Pitcher	G	IP	W	L	SV	ERA
1B	H. Myers	524	.273	2	50	1344	85	19	57	10.7	.987	L. Tyler	39	290	16	17	2	2.79
2B	B. Sweeney	502	.257	0	47	301	391	**45**	42	5.4	.939	D. Rudolph	33	249	14	13	0	2.92
SS	R. Maranville	571	.247	2	48	317	475	43	49	5.8	.949	O. Hess	29	218	7	17	0	3.83
3B	A. Devlin	210	.229	0	12	83	134	6	4	3.2	.973	H. Perdue	38	212	16	13	1	3.26
RF	J. Titus	269	.297	5	38	94	8	9	1	1.5	.919	B. James	24	136	6	10	0	2.79
CF	L. Mann	407	.253	3	51	250	14	11	2	2.3	.960	W. Dickson	19	128	6	7	0	3.23
LF	J. Connolly	427	.281	5	57	214	16	11	2	1.9	.954							
C	B. Rariden	246	.236	3	30	377	111	12	6	5.7	.976							
UT	F. Smith	285	.228	0	27	104	150	27	11		.904							
OF	B. Lord	235	.251	6	26	81	4	8	0	1.5	.914							
C	B. Whaling	211	.242	0	25	328	84	4	4	5.4	.990							

Brooklyn

W-65 L-84

Bill Dahlen

POS	Player	AB	BA	HR	RBI	PO	A	E	DP	TC/G	FA	Pitcher	G	IP	W	L	SV	ERA
1B	J. Daubert	508	**.350**	2	52	1279	80	13	**91**	9.9	.991	P. Ragan	44	265	15	18	0	3.77
2B	G. Cutshaw	592	.267	7	80	**402**	448	38	**79**	**6.0**	.957	N. Rucker	41	260	14	15	3	2.87
SS	B. Fisher	474	.262	4	54	263	364	**52**	60	5.2	.923	F. Allen	34	175	4	18	2	2.83
3B	R. Smith	540	.296	6	76	175	**295**	34	13	3.3	.933	C. Curtis	30	152	8	9	1	3.26
RF	H. Moran	515	.266	0	26	231	15	13	7	2.0	.950	E. Yingling	26	147	8	8	0	2.58
CF	C. Stengel	438	.272	7	43	270	16	12	1	2.5	.960	E. Reulbach	15	110	7	6	0	2.05
LF	Z. Wheat	535	.301	7	71	338	13	8	7	2.7	.978							
C	O. Miller	320	.272	0	26	448	148	18	13	6.0	.971							
UT	J. Hummel	198	.242	2	24	126	66	8	24		.960							
C	B. Fischer	165	.267	1	12	193	65	7	2	5.2	.974							

Cincinnati

W-64 L-89

Joe Tinker

POS	Player	AB	BA	HR	RBI	PO	A	E	DP	TC/G	FA	Pitcher	G	IP	W	L	SV	ERA
1B	D. Hoblitzell	502	.285	3	68	1373	60	17	76	10.8	.988	C. Johnson	44	269	14	16	0	3.01
2B	H. Groh	397	.282	3	48	249	358	23	43	5.6	.963	G. Suggs	36	199	8	15	2	4.03
SS	J. Tinker	382	.317	1	57	223	320	18	34	5.6	**.968**	G. Packard	39	191	7	11	0	2.97
3B	J. Dodge	323	.241	4	45	96	170	27	10	3.2	.908	R. Ames	31	187	11	13	2	2.88
RF	J. Bates	407	.278	6	51	192	19	12	6	2.0	.946	T. Brown	39	173	11	12	6	2.91
CF	A. Marsans	435	.297	0	38	170	12	7	2	2.0	.963	R. Benton	23	144	11	7	0	3.49
LF	B. Bescher	511	.258	1	37	283	22	10	2	2.3	.968							
C	T. Clarke	330	.264	1	38	378	131	11	5	5.2	.979							
OF	J. Devore	217	.267	3	14	106	9	10	3	2.2	.920							
C	J. Kling	209	.273	0	23	259	94	9	3	5.7	.975							
2S	D. Egan	195	.282	0	22	115	150	12	20		.957							
SS	M. Berghammer	188	.218	1	13	97	143	24	16	5.0	.909							
3B	R. Almeida	130	.262	3	21	42	71	10	6	3.3	.919							

St. Louis

W-51 L-99

Miller Huggins

POS	Player	AB	BA	HR	RBI	PO	A	E	DP	TC/G	FA	Pitcher	G	IP	W	L	SV	ERA
1B	E. Konetchy	502	.273	7	68	1432	91	7	71	**11.0**	**.995**	B. Harmon	42	273	8	21	1	3.92
2B	M. Huggins	381	.286	0	27	266	339	14	44	5.5	**.977**	S. Sallee	49	273	18	15	5	2.70
SS	C. O'Leary	404	.218	0	31	193	297	25	22	5.0	.951	D. Griner	34	225	10	**22**	0	5.08
3B	M. Mowrey	449	.258	0	33	143	284	21	**23**	**3.4**	.953	P. Perritt	36	175	6	14	0	5.25
RF	S. Evans	245	.249	1	31	111	5	2	0	1.6	.983	B. Doak	15	93	2	8	1	3.10
CF	R. Oakes	537	.291	0	49	321	16	11	2	2.4	.968							
LF	L. Magee	529	.265	2	31	250	21	5	5	2.6	.982							
C	I. Wingo	305	.256	2	35	346	132	**28**	12	5.2	.945							
UT	P. Whitted	402	.221	0	38	225	207	27	27		.941							
OF	T. Cather	183	.213	0	12	67	8	7	0	1.4	.915							

BATTING AND BASE RUNNING LEADERS

Batting Average		Slugging Average		Home Runs	
J. Daubert, BKN	.350	G. Cravath, PHI	.568	G. Cravath, PHI	19
G. Cravath, PHI	.341	B. Becker, CIN, PHI	.502	F. Luderus, PHI	18
J. Viox, PIT	.317	H. Zimmerman, CHI	.490	V. Saier, CHI	14
J. Tinker, CIN	.317	S. Magee, PHI	.479	S. Magee, PHI	11
B. Becker, CIN, PHI	.316	V. Saier, CHI	.477	O. Wilson, PIT	10

PITCHING LEADERS

Winning Percentage		Earned Run Average		Wins	
B. Humphries, CHI	.800	C. Mathewson, NY	2.06	T. Seaton, PHI	27
G. Alexander, PHI	.733	B. Adams, PIT	2.15	C. Mathewson, NY	25
R. Marquard, NY	.697	J. Tesreau, NY	2.17	R. Marquard, NY	23
C. Mathewson, NY	.694	A. Demaree, NY	2.21	J. Tesreau, NY	22
T. Seaton, PHI	.692	G. Pearce, CHI	2.31	G. Alexander, PHI	22

NATIONAL LEAGUE 1913, *cont.*

BATTING AND BASE RUNNING LEADERS

Total Bases
- G. Cravath, PHI 298
- F. Luderus, PHI 254
- V. Saier, CHI 247
- H. Lobert, PHI 243
- D. Miller, PIT 243

Runs Batted In
- G. Cravath, PHI 128
- H. Zimmerman, CHI 95
- V. Saier, CHI 92
- D. Miller, PIT 90
- F. Luderus, PHI 86

Stolen Bases
- M. Carey, PIT 61
- H. Myers, BOS 57
- H. Lobert, PHI 41
- G. Burns, NY 40
- G. Cutshaw, BKN 39

Hits
- G. Cravath, PHI 179
- J. Daubert, BKN 178
- G. Burns, NY 173
- H. Lobert, PHI 172
- M. Carey, PIT 172

Base on Balls
- B. Bescher, CIN 94
- M. Huggins, STL 91
- T. Leach, CHI 77
- A. Bridwell, CHI 74

Home Run Percentage
- G. Cravath, PHI 3.6
- F. Luderus, PHI 3.1
- V. Saier, CHI 2.7
- S. Magee, PHI 2.3

Runs
- T. Leach, CHI 99
- M. Carey, PIT 99
- H. Lobert, PHI 98
- V. Saier, CHI 93

Doubles
- R. Smith, BKN 40
- G. Burns, NY 37
- S. Magee, PHI 36
- G. Cravath, PHI 34

Triples
- V. Saier, CHI 21
- D. Miller, PIT 20
- E. Konetchy, STL 17
- G. Cravath, PHI 14
- O. Wilson, PIT 14

PITCHING LEADERS

Saves
- L. Cheney, CHI 11
- D. Crandall, NY 6
- T. Brown, CIN 6
- S. Sallee, STL 5

Strikeouts
- T. Seaton, PHI 168
- J. Tesreau, NY 167
- G. Alexander, PHI 159
- R. Marquard, NY 151
- B. Adams, PIT 144

Complete Games
- L. Tyler, BOS 28
- C. Mathewson, NY 25
- L. Cheney, CHI 25
- B. Adams, PIT 24
- G. Alexander, PHI 23

Fewest Hits/9 Innings
- J. Tesreau, NY 7.09
- T. Seaton, PHI 7.32
- F. Allen, BKN 7.42
- G. Pearce, CHI 7.55

Shutouts
- G. Alexander, PHI 9
- T. Seaton, PHI 6

Fewest Walks/9 Innings
- C. Mathewson, NY 0.62
- B. Humphries, CHI 1.19
- B. Adams, PIT 1.41
- R. Marquard, NY 1.53

Most Strikeouts/9 Inn.
- J. Tesreau, NY 5.33
- C. Hendrix, PIT 5.15
- B. James, BOS 4.84
- R. Marquard, NY 4.72

Innings
- T. Seaton, PHI 322
- B. Adams, PIT 314
- G. Alexander, PHI 306
- C. Mathewson, NY 306

Games Pitched
- L. Cheney, CHI 54
- T. Seaton, PHI 52
- S. Sallee, STL 49
- G. Alexander, PHI 47

	W	L	PCT	GB	R	OR	Batting 2B	3B	HR	BA	SA	SB	Fielding E	DP	FA	Pitching CG	BB	SO	ShO	SV	ERA
New York	101	51	.664		684	**515**	226	70	31	**.273**	.361	**296**	254	107	.961	82	**315**	651	12	**16**	**2.43**
Philadelphia	88	63	.583	12.5	693	636	**257**	78	**73**	.265	**.382**	156	**214**	112	**.968**	77	512	**667**	**20**	11	3.15
Chicago	88	65	.575	13.5	**720**	625	194	**96**	59	.257	.369	181	259	106	.959	89	478	556	12	14	3.13
Pittsburgh	78	71	.523	21.5	673	585	210	86	35	.263	.356	181	226	94	.964	74	434	590	9	7	2.90
Boston	69	82	.457	31.5	641	690	191	60	32	.256	.335	177	273	82	.957	**105**	419	597	12	3	3.19
Brooklyn	65	84	.436	34.5	595	613	193	86	39	.270	.363	188	243	**125**	.961	70	439	548	9	6	3.13
Cincinnati	64	89	.418	37.5	607	717	170	**96**	27	.261	.347	226	251	104	.961	71	456	522	10	10	3.46
St. Louis	51	99	.340	49	523	755	152	72	14	.247	.315	171	219	113	.965	73	476	464	6	10	4.24
					5136	5136	1593	644	310	.262	.354	1576	1939	843	.962	641	3529	4595	90	77	3.20

AMERICAN LEAGUE 1913

Team	POS	Player	AB	BA	HR	RBI	PO	A	E	DP	TC/G	FA	Pitcher	G	IP	W	L	SV	ERA
Philadelphia	1B	S. McInnis	543	.326	4	90	**1504**	80	12	85	10.8	**.992**	E. Plank	41	243	18	10	4	2.60
	2B	E. Collins	534	.345	3	73	314	**449**	28	54	5.3	.965	C. Bender	48	237	21	10	**13**	2.21
	SS	J. Barry	455	.275	3	85	248	403	32	60	5.1	.953	B. Brown	43	235	17	11	1	2.94
W-96 L-57	3B	F. Baker	565	.336	**12**	**126**	**233**	280	**44**	19	3.7	.921	J. Bush	39	200	15	6	3	3.82
	RF	E. Murphy	508	.295	1	30	166	14	11	2	1.4	.942	B. Houck	41	176	14	6	0	4.14
Connie Mack	CF	J. Walsh	303	.254	0	27	184	11	8	4	2.3	.961	B. Shawkey	18	111	6	5	0	2.34
	LF	R. Oldring	538	.283	5	71	236	9	8	3	1.9	.968							
	C	J. Lapp	238	.227	1	20	313	110	14	3	5.7	.968							
	OF	A. Strunk	292	.305	0	46	168	9	7	3	2.3	.962							
	C	W. Schang	207	.266	3	30	317	97	14	9	6.0	.967							
Washington	1B	C. Gandil	550	.318	1	72	1436	**103**	15	**89**	10.7	.990	W. Johnson	47	**346**	**36**	7	2	**1.09**
	2B	R. Morgan	481	.272	0	57	254	359	32	**61**	4.8	.950	B. Groom	37	264	16	16	0	3.23
	SS	G. McBride	499	.214	1	52	316	490	34	62	5.6	**.960**	J. Boehling	38	235	17	7	4	2.14
W-90 L-64	3B	E. Foster	409	.247	1	41	112	217	36	20	3.5	.901	J. Engel	36	165	8	9	0	3.06
	RF	D. Moeller	589	.236	5	42	249	27	22	4	1.9	.926	L. Hughes	36	130	4	12	6	4.30
Clark Griffith	CF	C. Milan	579	.301	3	54	296	20	23	7	2.2	.932							
	LF	H. Shanks	390	.254	1	37	207	13	5	3	2.1	.978							
	C	J. Henry	273	.223	1	26	476	127	11	9	6.4	**.982**							
	UT	F. LaPorte	242	.252	0	18	83	114	9	13		.956							
	C	E. Ainsmith	229	.214	2	20	418	82	17	10	6.5	.967							
Cleveland	1B	D. Johnston	530	.255	2	39	1319	76	15	76	10.6	.989	V. Gregg	44	286	20	13	3	2.24
	2B	N. Lajoie	465	.335	1	68	279	363	20	59	5.3	**.970**	C. Falkenberg	39	276	23	10	0	2.22
	SS	R. Chapman	508	.258	3	39	299	408	48	59	5.5	.936	W. Mitchell	34	217	14	8	0	1.74
W-86 L-66	3B	I. Olson	370	.249	0	32	97	145	12	7	3.5	.953	F. Blanding	41	215	15	10	0	2.55
	RF	J. Jackson	528	.373	7	71	211	28	18	5	1.7	.930	B. Steen	22	128	4	5	2	2.45
Joe Birmingham	CF	N. Leibold	286	.259	0	12	142	12	9	1	2.3	.945	G. Kahler	24	118	5	11	0	3.14
	LF	J. Graney	517	.267	3	68	275	16	9	5	2.0	.970	N. Cullop	23	98	3	7	0	4.42
	C	F. Carisch	222	.216	0	26	391	114	15	10	**6.6**	.971							
	UT	T. Turner	388	.247	0	44	188	279	18	35		.963							
	OF	B. Ryan	243	.296	0	32	138	7	2	2	2.2	.986							
	C	S. O'Neill	234	.295	0	29	353	119	13	9	6.2	.973							
Boston	1B	C. Engle	498	.289	2	50	1239	57	17	55	9.9	.987	D. Leonard	42	259	14	16	1	2.39
	2B	S. Yerkes	487	.267	1	48	220	341	25	31	4.5	.957	H. Bedient	43	259	15	14	5	2.78
	SS	H. Wagner	365	.227	2	34	274	311	39	36	5.9	.938	R. Collins	30	247	19	8	0	2.63
	3B	L. Gardner	473	.281	0	63	126	220	21	13	2.8	.943	S. Wood	23	146	11	5	2	2.29
W-79 L-71	RF	H. Hooper	586	.288	4	40	248	25	9	7	1.9	.968	E. Moseley	24	121	8	5	0	3.13
Jake Stahl	CF	T. Speaker	520	.363	3	81	374	30	25	7	3.1	.942	C. Hall	35	105	5	4	2	3.43
W-39 L-41	LF	D. Lewis	551	.298	0	90	262	29	12	3	2.1	.960	B. O'Brien	15	90	4	9	0	3.69
	C	B. Carrigan	256	.242	0	28	383	127	11	8	6.4	.979							
Bill Carrigan	UT	H. Janvrin	276	.207	3	25	172	177	26	17		.931							
W-40 L-30																			

AMERICAN LEAGUE 1913, *cont.*

Chicago

W-78 L-74

Nixey Callahan

POS	Player	AB	BA	HR	RBI	PO	A	E	DP	TC/G	FA	Pitcher	G	IP	W	L	SV	ERA
1B	H. Chase	384	.286	2	39	1009	71	27*	53	10.9	.976	R. Russell	**51**	316	22	16	4	1.91
2B	M. Rath	295	.200	0	12	159	251	16	32	5.0	.962	J. Scott	48	312	20	**20**	1	1.90
SS	B. Weaver	533	.272	4	52	**392**	**520**	**70**	**73**	**6.5**	.929	E. Cicotte	41	268	18	12	1	1.58
3B	H. Lord	547	.263	1	42	142	221	30	13	2.6	.924	J. Benz	33	151	7	10	1	2.74
RF	S. Collins	535	.239	1	47	244	19	14	3	1.9	.949	D. White	19	103	2	4	0	3.50
CF	P. Bodie	406	.264	8	48	226	14	8	1	2.1	.968	E. Walsh	16	98	8	3	1	2.58
LF	W. Mattick	207	.188	0	11	116	14	3	2	2.1	.977							
C	R. Schalk	401	.244	1	38	**599**	154	15	**18**	6.1	.980							
2B	J. Berger	223	.215	2	20	111	214	14	18	4.9	.959							
OF	L. Chappell	208	.231	0	15	114	5	6	1	2.1	.952							
10	J. Fournier	172	.233	1	23	306	23	5	10		.985							

Detroit

W-66 L-87

Hughie Jennings

POS	Player	AB	BA	HR	RBI	PO	A	E	DP	TC/G	FA	Pitcher	G	IP	W	L	SV	ERA
1B	D. Gainer	363	.267	2	25	1118	50	14	55	**11.6**	.988	J. Dubuc	36	243	15	14	2	2.89
2B	O. Vitt	359	.240	2	33	151	234	16	24	5.1	.960	E. Willett	34	242	13	14	0	3.09
SS	D. Bush	593	.251	1	40	331	510	56	61	5.9	.938	H. Dauss	33	225	13	12	1	2.68
3B	G. Moriarty	347	.239	0	30	122	183	20	9	3.5	.938	M. Hall	30	165	10	12	0	3.27
RF	S. Crawford	**610**	.316	9	83	201	14	8	5	1.6	.964	J. Lake	28	137	8	7	1	3.28
CF	T. Cobb	428	**.390**	4	67	262	22	16	8	2.5	.947							
LF	B. Veach	494	.269	0	64	250	16	24	3	2.1	.917							
C	O. Stanage	241	.224	0	21	277	106	16	6	5.2	.960							
UT	B. Louden	191	.241	0	23	76	146	17	11		.929							
2B	P. Baumann	191	.298	1	22	97	136	14	15	5.0	.943							
C	R. McKee	187	.283	1	20	237	84	17	5	5.5	.950							
OF	H. High	183	.230	0	16	104	8	2	0	2.3	.982							

New York

W-57 L-94

Frank Chance

POS	Player	AB	BA	HR	RBI	PO	A	E	DP	TC/G	FA	Pitcher	G	IP	W	L	SV	ERA
1B	J. Knight	250	.236	0	24	494	45	11	26	11.0	.980	R. Fisher	43	246	12	16	1	3.18
2B	R. Hartzell	490	.259	0	38	203	234	27	29	5.7	.942	R. Ford	33	237	12	18	2	2.66
SS	R. Peckinpaugh	340	.268	1	32	184	303	36	30	5.6	.931	A. Schulz	38	193	7	13	0	3.73
3B	E. Midkiff	284	.197	0	14	102	185	13	12	3.9	.957	G. McConnell	35	180	4	15	3	3.20
RF	B. Daniels	320	.216	0	22	128	15	5	3	1.7	.966	R. Caldwell	27	164	9	8	1	2.41
CF	H. Wolter	425	.254	2	43	228	15	14	1	2.1	.946	R. Keating	28	151	6	12	0	3.21
LF	B. Cree	534	.272	1	63	239	17	3	5	1.8	.988	J. Warhop	15	62	4	6	0	3.75
C	J. Sweeney	351	.265	2	40	511	**180**	26	9	6.4	.964							
3B	F. Maisel	187	.257	0	12	70	83	8	3	3.2	.950							
UT	R. Zeider	159	.233	0	12	138	102	17	13		.934							

St. Louis

W-57 L-96

George Stovall
W-50 L-84

Jimmy Austin
W-2 L-6

Branch Rickey
W-5 L-6

POS	Player	AB	BA	HR	RBI	PO	A	E	DP	TC/G	FA	Pitcher	G	IP	W	L	SV	ERA
1B	G. Stovall	303	.287	1	24	751	65	10	38	10.9	.988	G. Baumgardner	38	253	10	19	1	3.13
2B	D. Pratt	592	.296	2	87	**364**	425	**41**	56	**5.7**	.951	C. Weilman	39	252	10	**20**	0	3.40
SS	M. Balenti	211	.180	0	11	107	169	23	25	5.3	.923	R. Mitchell	33	245	13	16	1	3.01
3B	J. Austin	489	.266	2	42	216	**288**	30	21	**3.8**	**.944**	E. Hamilton	31	217	13	12	1	2.57
RF	G. Williams	538	.273	5	53	225	26	13	7	1.8	.951	W. Leverenz	30	203	6	17	1	2.58
CF	B. Shotton	549	.297	1	28	357	29	20	11	2.8	.951							
LF	J. Johnston	380	.224	2	27	222	23	9	3	2.4	.965							
C	S. Agnew	307	.208	2	24	383	170	**28**	17	5.6	.952							
1B	B. Brief	258	.217	1	26	622	34	9	41	10.7	.986							
SS	B. Wallace	147	.211	0	21	67	96	12	8	4.6	.931							

BATTING AND BASE RUNNING LEADERS

Batting Average
T. Cobb, DET .390
J. Jackson, CLE .373
T. Speaker, BOS .363
E. Collins, PHI .345
F. Baker, PHI .336

Slugging Average
J. Jackson, CLE .551
T. Cobb, DET .535
T. Speaker, BOS .533
F. Baker, PHI .492
S. Crawford, DET .489

Home Runs
F. Baker, PHI 12
S. Crawford, DET 9
P. Bodie, CHI 8
J. Jackson, CLE 7

Total Bases
S. Crawford, DET 298
J. Jackson, CLE 291
F. Baker, PHI 278
T. Speaker, BOS 277
E. Collins, PHI 242

Runs Batted In
F. Baker, PHI 126
S. McInnis, PHI 90
D. Lewis, BOS 90
D. Pratt, STL 87
J. Barry, PHI 85

Stolen Bases
C. Milan, WAS 75
D. Moeller, WAS 62
E. Collins, PHI 55
T. Cobb, DET 52
T. Speaker, BOS 46

Hits
J. Jackson, CLE 197
S. Crawford, DET 193
F. Baker, PHI 190
T. Speaker, BOS 189

Base on Balls
B. Shotton, STL 99
E. Collins, PHI 85
H. Wolter, NY 80
J. Jackson, CLE 80
D. Bush, DET 80

Home Run Percentage
F. Baker, PHI 2.1
P. Bodie, CHI 2.0
S. Crawford, DET 1.5
J. Jackson, CLE 1.3

Runs
E. Collins, PHI 125
F. Baker, PHI 116
J. Jackson, CLE 109
E. Murphy, PHI 105
B. Shotton, STL 105

Doubles
J. Jackson, CLE 39
T. Speaker, BOS 35
F. Baker, PHI 34
S. Crawford, DET 32

Triples
S. Crawford, DET 23
T. Speaker, BOS 22
J. Jackson, CLE 17
T. Cobb, DET 16
G. Williams, STL 16

PITCHING LEADERS

Winning Percentage
W. Johnson, WAS .837
J. Bush, PHI .714
J. Boehling, WAS .708
R. Collins, BOS .704
C. Falkenberg, CLE .697

Earned Run Average
W. Johnson, WAS 1.09
E. Cicotte, CHI 1.58
W. Mitchell, CLE 1.74
J. Scott, CHI 1.90
R. Russell, CHI 1.91

Wins
W. Johnson, WAS 36
C. Falkenberg, CLE 23
R. Russell, CHI 22
C. Bender, PHI 21
V. Gregg, CLE 20
J. Scott, CHI 20

Saves
C. Bender, PHI 13
L. Hughes, WAS 6
H. Bedient, BOS 5
J. Boehling, WAS 4
E. Plank, PHI 4
R. Russell, CHI 4

Strikeouts
W. Johnson, WAS 243
C. Falkenberg, CLE 166
V. Gregg, CLE 166
J. Scott, CHI 158
B. Groom, WAS 156

Complete Games
W. Johnson, WAS 29
R. Russell, CHI 26
J. Scott, CHI 25
G. Baumgardner, STL 23
V. Gregg, CLE 23
C. Falkenberg, CLE 23

Fewest Hits/9 Innings
W. Johnson, WAS 5.98
W. Mitchell, CLE 6.35
W. Leverenz, STL 7.06
R. Russell, CHI 7.09

Shutouts
W. Johnson, WAS 11
R. Russell, CHI 8
E. Plank, PHI 7
C. Falkenberg, CLE 6

Fewest Walks/9 Innings
W. Johnson, WAS 0.99
R. Collins, BOS 1.35
R. Mitchell, STL 1.72
E. Plank, PHI 2.11

Most Strikeouts/9 Inn.
S. Wood, BOS 7.60
W. Johnson, WAS 6.32
W. Mitchell, CLE 5.85
E. Plank, PHI 5.60

Innings
W. Johnson, WAS 346
R. Russell, CHI 316
J. Scott, CHI 312
V. Gregg, CLE 286

Games Pitched
R. Russell, CHI 51
C. Bender, PHI 48
J. Scott, CHI 48
W. Johnson, WAS 47

AMERICAN LEAGUE 1913, *cont.*

	W	L	PCT	GB	R	OR	Batting 2B	3B	HR	BA	SA	SB	Fielding E	DP	FA	Pitching CG	BB	SO	ShO	SV	ERA
Philadelphia	96	57	.627		**794**	592	**223**	80	**33**	**.280**	**.376**	221	**212**	108	**.966**	69	532	630	17	**22**	3.19
Washington	90	64	.584	6.5	596	561	156	80	20	.252	.327	**287**	261	122	.960	78	465	**757**	**23**	20	2.72
Cleveland	86	66	.566	9.5	633	536	205	74	16	.268	.348	191	242	124	.962	95	502	689	18	5	2.52
Boston	79	71	.527	15.5	631	610	221	**101**	17	.269	.364	189	237	84	.961	87	442	710	12	11	2.93
Chicago	78	74	.513	17.5	488	**498**	157	66	23	.236	.310	156	255	104	.960	84	**438**	602	17	8	**2.33**
Detroit	66	87	.431	30	624	716	180	**101**	24	.265	.355	219	300	105	.954	90	504	468	4	7	3.41
New York	57	94	.377	38	529	668	154	45	9	.237	.293	203	293	94	.954	75	455	530	8	7	3.27
St. Louis	57	96	.373	39	528	642	179	73	18	.237	.312	209	301	**125**	.954	**104**	454	476	14	5	3.06
					4823	4823	1475	620	160	.256	.336	1675	2101	866	.959	682	3792	4862	113	85	2.93

NATIONAL LEAGUE 1914

Boston

W-94 L-59

George Stallings

POS	Player	AB	BA	HR	RBI	PO	A	E	DP	TC/G	FA
1B	B. Schmidt	537	.285	1	71	1485	88	16	**109**	10.8	.990
2B	J. Evers	491	.279	1	40	301	397	17	73	5.1	**.976**
SS	R. Maranville	586	.246	4	78	**407**	**574**	**65**	**92**	**6.7**	.938
3B	C. Deal	257	.210	0	23	86	133	12	8	3.1	.948
RF	L. Gilbert	224	.268	5	25	79	14	2	2	1.6	.979
CF	L. Mann	389	.247	4	40	273	24	15	8	2.5	.952
LF	J. Connolly	399	.306	9	65	168	19	5	1	1.6	.974
C	H. Gowdy	366	.243	3	46	475	151	**21**	11	5.6	.968
UT	P. Whitted	218	.261	2	31	161	61	12	9		.949
3B	R. Smith	207	.314	3	37	84*	139*	15	12*	4.0*	.937
C	B. Whaling	172	.209	0	12	272	91	7	7	6.3	.981
OF	H. Moran	154	.266	0	4	59	4	4	0	1.6	.940
OF	T. Cather	145	.297	0	27	57	4	3	1	1.3	.953

Pitcher	G	IP	W	L	SV	ERA
D. Rudolph	42	336	26	10	0	2.35
B. James	46	332	26	7	2	1.90
L. Tyler	38	271	16	13	2	2.69
D. Crutcher	33	159	5	7	0	3.46
O. Hess	14	89	5	6	1	3.03

New York

W-84 L-70

John McGraw

POS	Player	AB	BA	HR	RBI	PO	A	E	DP	TC/G	FA
1B	F. Merkle	512	.258	7	63	1463	88	16	80	10.7	.990
2B	L. Doyle	539	.260	5	63	307	379	29	61	4.9	.959
SS	A. Fletcher	514	.286	2	79	299	446	63	46	6.0	.922
3B	M. Stock	365	.263	3	41	95	261	23	17	3.4	.939
RF	F. Snodgrass	392	.263	0	44	200	11	5	4	2.3	.977
CF	B. Bescher	512	.270	6	35	298	14	13	7	2.6	.960
LF	G. Burns	561	.303	3	60	326	19	18	5	2.4	.950
C	C. Meyers	381	.286	1	55	**487**	150	20	**16**	5.2	.970
UT	E. Grant	282	.277	0	29	97	191	23	16		.926
OF	D. Robertson	256	.266	2	32	101	13	6	2	1.7	.950
C	L. McLean	154	.260	0	14	211	42	7	8	3.5	.973
OF	R. Murray	139	.223	0	23	56	2	0	0	1.2	1.000

Pitcher	G	IP	W	L	SV	ERA
J. Tesreau	42	322	26	10	1	2.37
C. Mathewson	41	312	24	13	2	3.00
R. Marquard	39	268	12	22	2	3.06
A. Demaree	38	224	10	17	0	3.09
A. Fromme	38	138	9	5	2	3.20

St. Louis

W-81 L-72

Miller Huggins

POS	Player	AB	BA	HR	RBI	PO	A	E	DP	TC/G	FA
1B	D. Miller	573	.290	4	88	1019	57	8	46	**11.1**	.993
2B	M. Huggins	509	.263	1	24	328	428	28	58	5.3	.964
SS	A. Butler	274	.201	1	24	155	228	30	24	4.9	.927
3B	Z. Beck	457	.232	3	45	141	264	28	24	3.5	.935
RF	O. Wilson	580	.259	9	73	312	34	6	11	2.3	.983
CF	L. Magee	529	.284	2	40	210	14	7	4	2.3	.970
LF	C. Dolan	421	.240	4	32	182	10	9	2	2.1	.955
C	F. Snyder	326	.230	1	25	419	130	12	12	5.7	**.979**
OF	W. Cruise	256	.227	4	28	158	6	4	1	2.1	.976
C	I. Wingo	237	.300	4	26	276	93	16	7	5.5	.958

Pitcher	G	IP	W	L	SV	ERA
P. Perritt	41	286	16	13	2	2.36
S. Sallee	46	282	18	17	**6**	2.10
B. Doak	36	256	20	6	0	**1.72**
D. Griner	37	179	9	13	2	2.51
H. Perdue	22	153	8	8	1	2.82
H. Robinson	26	126	6	8	0	3.00

Chicago

W-78 L-76

Hank O'Day

POS	Player	AB	BA	HR	RBI	PO	A	E	DP	TC/G	FA
1B	V. Saier	537	.240	18	72	1521	59	22	62	10.5	.986
2B	B. Sweeney	463	.218	1	38	301	426	35	40	5.7	.954
SS	R. Corriden	318	.230	3	29	174	212	46	29	4.5	.894
3B	H. Zimmerman	564	.296	4	87	141	197	**39**	13	3.2	.897
RF	W. Good	580	.272	2	43	242	25	20	10	1.9	.930
CF	T. Leach	577	.263	7	46	321	16	11	5	2.5	.968
LF	W. Schulte	465	.241	5	61	217	9	11	2	1.8	.954
C	R. Bresnahan	248	.278	0	24	365	113	11	6	5.8	.978
C	J. Archer	248	.258	0	19	367	105	13	8	6.4	.973

Pitcher	G	IP	W	L	SV	ERA
L. Cheney	**50**	311	20	18	5	2.54
H. Vaughn	42	294	21	13	1	2.05
J. Lavender	37	214	11	11	0	3.07
B. Humphries	34	171	10	11	0	2.68
G. Pearce	30	141	8	12	1	3.51
Z. Zabel	29	128	4	4	1	2.18

Brooklyn

W-75 L-79

Wilbert Robinson

POS	Player	AB	BA	HR	RBI	PO	A	E	DP	TC/G	FA
1B	J. Daubert	474	**.329**	6	45	1097	48	8	68	9.2	.993
2B	G. Cutshaw	583	.257	2	78	**455**	**444**	38	**74**	**6.1**	.959
SS	D. Egan	337	.226	1	21	150	232	36	21	5.0	.914
3B	R. Smith	330	.245	4	48	136*	193*	22	16*	3.9*	.937
RF	C. Stengel	412	.316	4	60	173	15	7	3	1.6	.964
CF	J. Dalton	442	.319	1	45	240	7	9	2	2.2	.965
LF	Z. Wheat	533	.319	9	89	331	21	14	5	2.5	.962
C	L. McCarty	284	.254	1	30	398	117	16	9	6.3	.970
SS	O. O'Mara	247	.263	1	7	110	183	26	17	5.1	.918
OF	H. Myers	227	.286	0	17	102	4	4	0	1.8	.964
3B	G. Getz	210	.248	0	20	69	134	11	12	3.9	.949
10	J. Hummel	208	.264	0	20	338	21	6	13		.984
C	O. Miller	169	.231	0	9	236	66	11	5	6.3	.965

Pitcher	G	IP	W	L	SV	ERA
J. Pfeffer	43	315	23	12	4	1.97
E. Reulbach	44	256	11	18	3	2.64
P. Ragan	38	208	10	15	3	2.98
R. Aitchison	26	172	12	7	0	2.66
F. Allen	36	171	8	14	0	3.10
N. Rucker	16	104	7	6	0	3.39

NATIONAL LEAGUE 1914, *cont.*

Philadelphia

W-74 L-80

Red Dooin

POS	Player	AB	BA	HR	RBI	PO	A	E	DP	TC/G	FA
1B	F. Luderus	443	.248	12	55	1102	76	**30**	49	10.0	.975
2B	B. Byrne	467	.272	0	26	187	312	35	19	5.3	.934
SS	J. Martin	292	.253	0	21	185	251	33	24	5.7	.930
3B	H. Lobert	505	.275	1	52	188	174	22	10	2.9	**.943**
RF	G. Cravath	499	.299	**19**	100	205	34	18	7	1.8	.930
CF	D. Paskert	451	.264	3	44	303	19	14	4	2.6	.958
LF	B. Becker	514	.325	9	66	270	17	16	3	2.4	.947
C	B. Killefer	299	.234	0	27	464	**154**	14	11	**7.0**	.978
UT	S. Magee	544	.314	15	**103**	549	187	37	20		.952
2B	H. Irelan	165	.236	1	16	98	142	24	12	6.0	.909

Pitcher	G	IP	W	L	SV	ERA
G. Alexander	46	**355**	**27**	15	1	2.38
E. Mayer	48	321	21	19	2	2.58
B. Tincup	28	155	7	10	1	2.61
R. Marshall	27	134	6	7	1	3.75
J. Oeschger	32	124	4	8	1	3.77
E. Rixey	24	103	2	11	0	4.37

Pittsburgh

W-69 L-85

Fred Clarke

POS	Player	AB	BA	HR	RBI	PO	A	E	DP	TC/G	FA
1B	E. Konetchy	563	.249	4	51	**1576**	**93**	8	70	10.9	**.995**
2B	J. Viox	506	.265	1	57	250	400	42	43	5.0	.939
SS	H. Wagner	552	.252	1	50	322	424	39	45	5.9	**.950**
3B	M. Mowrey	284	.254	1	25	83	156	10	8	3.2	.960
RF	M. Mitchell	273	.234	2	23	174	11	3	6	2.5	.984
CF	J. Kelly	508	.222	1	48	319	15	19	3	2.6	.946
LF	M. Carey	**593**	.243	1	31	318	23	12	3	2.3	.966
C	G. Gibson	274	.285	0	30	358	126	13	8	4.9	.974
OF	Z. Collins	182	.242	0	15	92	8	4	2	2.1	.962
UT	A. McCarthy	173	.150	1	14	63	136	11	10		.948

Pitcher	G	IP	W	L	SV	ERA
B. Adams	40	283	13	16	1	2.51
W. Cooper	40	267	16	15	0	2.13
G. McQuillan	45	259	13	17	4	2.98
B. Harmon	37	245	13	17	3	2.53
J. Conzelman	33	101	5	6	1	2.94

Cincinnati

W-60 L-94

Buck Herzog

POS	Player	AB	BA	HR	RBI	PO	A	E	DP	TC/G	FA
1B	D. Hoblitzell	248	.210	0	29	802	31	10	43	11.2	.988
2B	H. Groh	455	.288	2	32	252	394	**44**	56	5.1	.936
SS	B. Herzog	498	.281	1	40	324	474	52	58	6.2	.939
3B	B. Niehoff	484	.242	4	49	154	272	35	15	3.4	.924
RF	H. Moran	395	.235	1	35	175	11	9	4	1.8	.954
CF	B. Daniels	269	.219	0	19	144	7	4	2	2.2	.974
LF	G. Twombly	240	.233	0	19	111	11	4	2	1.9	.968
C	T. Clarke	313	.262	2	25	448	132	16	12	5.5	.973
OF	D. Miller	192	.255	0	33	79	2	2	1	1.8	.976
C	M. Gonzalez	176	.233	0	10	252	101	17	5	4.5	.954
OF	J. Bates	163	.245	2	15	91	4	9	1	1.8	.913
OF	A. Marsans	124	.298	0	22	72	4	7	1	2.3	.916

Pitcher	G	IP	W	L	SV	ERA
R. Ames	47	297	15	**23**	**6**	2.64
R. Benton	41	271	17	18	2	2.96
P. Douglas	45	239	11	18	1	2.56
E. Yingling	34	198	8	13	0	3.45
P. Schneider	29	144	5	13	1	2.81

BATTING AND BASE RUNNING LEADERS

Batting Average	
J. Daubert, BKN	.329
B. Becker, PHI	.325
J. Dalton, BKN	.319
Z. Wheat, BKN	.319
C. Stengel, BKN	.316

Slugging Average	
S. Magee, PHI	.509
G. Cravath, PHI	.499
J. Connolly, BOS	.494
Z. Wheat, BKN	.452
B. Becker, PHI	.446

Home Runs	
G. Cravath, PHI	19
V. Saier, CHI	18
S. Magee, PHI	15
F. Luderus, PHI	12

Total Bases	
S. Magee, PHI	277
G. Cravath, PHI	249
Z. Wheat, BKN	241
H. Zimmerman, CHI	239
G. Burns, NY	234

Runs Batted In	
S. Magee, PHI	103
G. Cravath, PHI	100
Z. Wheat, BKN	89
D. Miller, STL	88
H. Zimmerman, CHI	87

Stolen Bases	
G. Burns, NY	62
B. Herzog, CIN	46
C. Dolan, STL	42
M. Carey, PIT	38
B. Bescher, NY	36
L. Magee, STL	36

Hits	
S. Magee, PHI	171
Z. Wheat, BKN	170
G. Burns, NY	170
B. Becker, PHI	167
H. Zimmerman, CHI	167

Base on Balls	
M. Huggins, STL	105
V. Saier, CHI	94
G. Burns, NY	89
J. Evers, BOS	87

Home Run Percentage	
G. Cravath, PHI	3.8
V. Saier, CHI	3.4
S. Magee, PHI	2.8
F. Luderus, PHI	2.7

Runs	
G. Burns, NY	100
S. Magee, PHI	96
J. Daubert, BKN	89
V. Saier, CHI	87
L. Doyle, NY	87

Doubles	
S. Magee, PHI	39
H. Zimmerman, CHI	36
G. Burns, NY	35
J. Connolly, BOS	28

Triples	
M. Carey, PIT	17
H. Zimmerman, CHI	12
O. Wilson, STL	12
G. Cutshaw, BKN	12

PITCHING LEADERS

Winning Percentage	
B. James, BOS	.788
B. Doak, STL	.769
D. Rudolph, BOS	.722
J. Tesreau, NY	.722
J. Pfeffer, BKN	.657

Earned Run Average	
B. Doak, STL	1.72
B. James, BOS	1.90
J. Pfeffer, BKN	1.97
H. Vaughn, CHI	2.05
S. Sallee, STL	2.10

Wins	
G. Alexander, PHI	27
J. Tesreau, NY	26
B. James, BOS	26
D. Rudolph, BOS	26
C. Mathewson, NY	24

Saves	
R. Ames, CIN	6
S. Sallee, STL	6
L. Cheney, CHI	5
J. Pfeffer, BKN	4
G. McQuillan, PIT	4

Strikeouts	
G. Alexander, PHI	214
J. Tesreau, NY	189
H. Vaughn, CHI	165
L. Cheney, CHI	157
B. James, BOS	156

Complete Games	
G. Alexander, PHI	32
D. Rudolph, BOS	31
B. James, BOS	30
C. Mathewson, NY	29
J. Pfeffer, BKN	27

Fewest Hits/9 Innings	
J. Tesreau, NY	6.65
B. Doak, STL	6.79
L. Cheney, CHI	6.91
P. Douglas, CIN	6.99

Shutouts	
J. Tesreau, NY	8
B. Doak, STL	7
D. Rudolph, BOS	6
G. Alexander, PHI	6
L. Cheney, CHI	6

Fewest Walks/9 Innings	
C. Mathewson, NY	0.66
B. Adams, PIT	1.24
R. Marquard, NY	1.58
D. Rudolph, BOS	1.63

Most Strikeouts/9 Inn.	
G. Alexander, PHI	5.43
J. Tesreau, NY	5.28
H. Vaughn, CHI	5.06
L. Tyler, BOS	4.64

Innings	
G. Alexander, PHI	355
D. Rudolph, BOS	336
B. James, BOS	332
J. Tesreau, NY	322

Games Pitched	
L. Cheney, CHI	50
E. Mayer, PHI	48
R. Ames, CIN	47

							Batting						Fielding			Pitching					
	W	L	PCT	GB	R	OR	2B	3B	HR	BA	SA	SB	E	DP	FA	CG	BB	SO	ShO	SV	ERA
Boston	94	59	.614		657	548	213	60	35	.251	.335	139	246	**143**	.963	**104**	477	606	19	5	2.74
New York	84	70	.545	10.5	**672**	576	**222**	59	30	.265	.348	**239**	254	119	.961	88	**367**	563	**20**	9	2.94
St. Louis	81	72	.529	13	558	**540**	203	65	33	.248	.333	204	239	109	.964	83	422	531	16	11	**2.38**
Chicago	78	76	.506	16.5	605	638	199	74	42	.243	.337	164	310	87	.951	70	528	**651**	14	9	2.71
Brooklyn	75	79	.487	19.5	622	618	172	**90**	31	**.269**	.355	173	248	112	.961	80	466	605	11	10	2.82
Philadelphia	74	80	.481	20.5	651	687	211	52	**62**	.263	**.361**	145	324	81	.950	85	452	650	14	6	3.06
Pittsburgh	69	85	.448	25.5	503	**540**	148	79	18	.233	.303	147	**223**	96	**.966**	86	392	488	10	9	2.70
Cincinnati	60	94	.390	34.5	530	651	142	64	16	.236	.299	224	314	113	.952	74	489	607	15	**14**	2.94
					4798	4798	1510	543	267	.251	.334	1435	2158	860	.959	670	3593	4701	119	73	2.79

AMERICAN LEAGUE 1914

Team	POS	Player	AB	BA	HR	RBI	PO	A	E	DP	TC/G	FA	Pitcher	G	IP	W	L	SV	ERA
Philadelphia	1B	S. McInnis	576	.314	1	95	1423	85	7	**89**	10.2	**.995**	B. Shawkey	38	237	16	8	2	2.73
	2B	E. Collins	526	.344	2	85	354	387	23	55	5.0	**.970**	J. Bush	38	206	16	12	3	3.06
	SS	J. Barry	467	.242	0	42	244	447	39	61	5.2	.947	E. Plank	34	185	15	7	3	2.87
W-99 L-53	3B	F. Baker	570	.319	**9**	97	**221**	292	24	20	3.6	.955	J. Wyckoff	32	185	11	7	2	3.02
	RF	E. Murphy	573	.272	3	43	194	15	13	4	1.5	.941	C. Bender	28	179	17	3	2	2.26
Connie Mack	CF	A. Strunk	404	.275	2	45	280	14	4	3	2.5	.987	H. Pennock	28	152	11	4	3	2.79
	LF	R. Oldring	466	.277	3	49	215	7	8	5	2.0	.965	R. Bressler	29	148	10	4	2	1.77
	C	W. Schang	307	.287	3	45	498	154	**30**	11	6.8	.956							
	OF	J. Walsh	216	.236	3	36	107	7	4	3	2.1	.966							
	C	J. Lapp	199	.231	0	19	330	88	10	4	6.4	.977							
Boston	1B	D. Hoblitzell	229	.319	0	33	627	30	14	22	9.9	.979	R. Collins	39	272	20	13	0	2.51
	2B	S. Yerkes	293	.218	1	23	177	241	12	38	4.7	.972	D. Leonard	36	223	19	5	3	**1.01**
	SS	E. Scott	539	.239	2	37	324	408	39	50	5.4	.949	R. Foster	32	213	14	8	0	1.65
W-91 L-62	3B	L. Gardner	553	.259	3	68	187	**312**	31	18	3.5	.942	H. Bedient	42	177	8	12	2	3.60
	RF	H. Hooper	530	.258	1	41	231	23	7	5	1.9	.973	E. Shore	20	148	10	5	1	1.89
Bill Carrigan	CF	T. Speaker	571	.338	4	90	423	29	15	12	3.0	.968	S. Wood	18	113	9	3	1	2.62
	LF	D. Lewis	510	.278	2	79	254	22	14	2	2.0	.952	A. Johnson	16	99	4	9	0	3.08*
	C	B. Carrigan	178	.253	1	22	350	84	7	8	5.7	**.984**							
	UT	H. Janvrin	492	.238	1	51	669	237	43	50		.955							
	C	H. Cady	159	.258	0	8	217	80	9	1	5.3	.971							
Washington	1B	C. Gandil	526	.259	3	75	1284	**143**	13	84	9.9	.991	W. Johnson	**51**	**372**	**28**	18	1	1.72
	2B	R. Morgan	491	.257	1	49	290	379	37	**58**	4.8	.948	D. Ayers	49	265	12	15	3	2.54
	SS	G. McBride	503	.203	0	24	367	460	36	**72**	5.5	**.958**	J. Shaw	48	257	15	17	**4**	2.70
W-81 L-73	3B	E. Foster	**616**	.282	2	50	200	247	34	**25**	3.1	.929	J. Boehling	27	196	12	8	1	3.03
	RF	D. Moeller	571	.250	1	45	208	19	17	4	1.6	.930	J. Bentley	30	125	5	7	**4**	2.37
Clark Griffith	CF	C. Milan	437	.295	1	39	230	10	13	0	2.2	.949	J. Engel	35	124	7	5	3	2.97
	LF	H. Shanks	500	.224	4	64	276	14	14	3	2.2	.954							
	C	J. Henry	261	.169	0	20	513	124	13	9	**7.1**	.980							
	OF	M. Mitchell	193	.285	1	20	99	11	5	0	2.2	.957							
	C	B. Williams	169	.278	1	22	181	54	6	0	5.5	.975							
Detroit	1B	G. Burns	478	.291	5	57	**1576**	79	**30**	72	**12.3**	.982	H. Coveleski	44	303	22	12	2	2.49
	2B	M. Kavanagh	439	.248	4	35	228	333	43	30	5.3	.929	H. Dauss	45	302	18	15	**4**	2.86
	SS	D. Bush	596	.252	0	32	**425**	**544**	58	64	**6.5**	.944	J. Dubuc	36	224	13	14	1	3.46
W-80 L-73	3B	G. Moriarty	465	.254	1	40	125	**312**	20	16	3.6	.956	P. Cavet	31	151	7	7	2	2.44
	RF	S. Crawford	582	.314	8	**104**	193	18	5	4	1.4	.977	A. Main	32	138	6	6	3	2.67
Hughie Jennings	CF	T. Cobb	345	**.368**	2	57	177	8	10	0	2.0	.949	M. Hall	25	90	4	6	0	2.69
	LF	B. Veach	531	.275	1	72	282	22	11	6	2.2	.965							
	C	O. Stanage	400	.193	0	25	532	**190**	**30**	11	6.2	.960							
	23	O. Vitt	195	.251	0	8	63	154	9	13		.960							
	OF	H. High	184	.266	0	17	92	2	4	1	1.8	.959							
	UT	H. Heilmann	182	.225	2	22	209	31	11	11		.956							
St. Louis	1B	J. Leary	533	.265	0	45	1256	75	17	64	10.4	.987	E. Hamilton	44	302	17	18	2	2.50
	2B	D. Pratt	584	.283	5	65	**358**	423	**46**	48	**5.4**	.944	C. Weilman	44	299	18	13	1	2.08
	SS	D. Lavan	239	.264	1	21	178	193	34	17	5.5	.916	B. James	44	284	15	14	2	2.85
W-71 L-82	3B	J. Austin	466	.238	0	30	183	249	30	18	3.6	.935	G. Baumgardner	45	184	14	13	3	2.79
	RF	G. Williams	499	.253	4	47	200	24	16	2	1.7	.933	W. Leverenz	27	111	1	12	0	3.80
Branch Rickey	CF	B. Shotton	579	.269	0	38	359	15	24	4	2.6	.940	R. Mitchell	28	103	4	5	**4**	4.35
	LF	T. Walker	517	.298	6	78	311	30	10	5	2.4	.972							
	C	S. Agnew	311	.212	0	16	451	163	25	10	5.7	.961							
	SS	B. Wares	215	.209	0	23	128	196	35	23	5.3	.903							
	31	I. Howard	209	.244	0	20	252	63	9	5		.972							
Chicago	1B	J. Fournier	379	.311	6	44	1025	78	25	30	11.6	.978	J. Benz	48	283	14	**19**	2	2.26
	2B	L. Blackburne	474	.222	1	35	239	**433**	26	28	4.9	.963	E. Cicotte	45	269	11	16	3	2.04
	SS	B. Weaver	541	.246	2	28	367	389	**59**	50	6.1	.928	J. Scott	43	253	14	18	1	2.84
W-70 L-84	3B	J. Breton	231	.212	0	24	84	159	24	6	3.4	.910	R. Faber	40	181	10	9	**4**	2.68
	RF	S. Collins	598	.274	3	65	268	21	19	5	2.0	.938	R. Russell	38	167	8	12	1	2.90
Nixey Callahan	CF	P. Bodie	327	.229	3	29	175	14	8	2	2.1	.959	M. Wolfgang	24	119	9	5	0	1.89
	LF	R. Demmitt	515	.258	2	46	217	24	12	3	1.8	.953							
	C	R. Schalk	392	.270	0	36	**613**	183	21	20	6.6	.974							
	1B	H. Chase	206	.267	0	20	632	43	13	27	11.9	.981							
	3B	S. Alcock	156	.173	0	7	57	95	16	10	3.5	.905							
New York	1B	C. Mullen	323	.260	0	44	898	62	6	54	10.4	.994	J. Warhop	37	217	8	15	0	2.37
	2B	L. Boone	370	.222	0	21	238	294	22	32	6.2	.960	R. Caldwell	31	213	17	9	1	1.94
	SS	R. Peckinpaugh	570	.223	3	51	356	500	39	45	5.7	.956	R. Keating	34	210	7	11	1	2.96
	3B	F. Maisel	548	.239	2	47	206	245	**35**	17	3.3	.928	R. Fisher	29	209	10	12	1	2.28
W-70 L-84	RF	D. Cook	470	.283	1	40	171	15	10	2	1.6	.949	M. McHale	31	191	7	16	1	2.97
Frank Chance	CF	B. Cree	275	.309	0	40	190	10	5	4	2.7	.976	K. Cole	33	142	11	9	0	3.30
	LF	R. Hartzell	481	.233	1	32	241	15	7	2	2.1	.973	B. Brown	20	122	5	5	1	3.24
W-60 L-74	C	J. Sweeney	258	.213	1	22	369	120	10	7	6.4	.980							
Roger Peckinpaugh	C	L. Nunamaker	257	.265	2	29	304	126	13	12	6.3	.971							
W-10 L-10	2B	F. Truesdale	217	.212	0	13	121	185	17	19	4.8	.947							
	OF	T. Daley	191	.251	0	9	26	12	6	2	0.8	.864							
	1B	H. Williams	178	.163	1	17	577	25	15	19	10.6	.976							
	OF	B. Holden	165	.182	0	12	98	3	2	0	2.3	.981							

AMERICAN LEAGUE 1914, *cont.*

Cleveland

W-51 L-102

Joe Birmingham

POS	Player	AB	BA	HR	RBI	PO	A	E	DP	TC/G	FA	Pitcher	G	IP	W	L	SV	ERA
1B	D. Johnston	340	.244	0	23	847	36	12	43	10.1	.987	W. Mitchell	39	257	12	17	1	3.19
2B	N. Lajoie	419	.258	0	50	187	215	17	45	5.2	.959	B. Steen	30	201	9	14	0	2.60
SS	R. Chapman	375	.275	2	42	161	187	33	24	5.3	.913	R. Hagerman	37	198	9	15	0	3.09
3B	T. Turner	428	.245	1	33	138	229	14	23	**3.7**	**.963**	G. Morton	25	128	1	13	1	3.02
RF	J. Jackson	453	.338	3	53	195	13	7	4	1.8	.967	F. Blanding	29	116	3	9	1	3.96
CF	N. Leibold	402	.264	0	32	221	22	18	4	2.4	.931	A. Collamore	27	105	3	7	0	3.25
LF	J. Graney	460	.265	1	39	274	15	20	0	2.4	.935	V. Gregg	17	97	9	3	0	3.07
C	S. O'Neill	269	.253	0	20	393	134	24	**22**	6.8	.956							
UT	I. Olson	310	.242	1	20	197	197	17	20		.959							
OF	J. Kirke	242	.273	1	25	73	3	2	1	1.9	.974							
01	R. Wood	220	.236	1	15	209	16	7	13		.970							

BATTING AND BASE RUNNING LEADERS

Batting Average
T. Cobb, DET .368
E. Collins, PHI .344
T. Speaker, BOS .338
J. Jackson, CLE .338
F. Baker, PHI .319

Slugging Average
T. Cobb, DET .513
T. Speaker, BOS .503
S. Crawford, DET .483
J. Jackson, CLE .464
E. Collins, PHI .452

Home Runs
F. Baker, PHI 9
S. Crawford, DET 8
J. Fournier, CHI 6
T. Walker, STL 6
G. Burns, DET 5
D. Pratt, STL 5

Total Bases
T. Speaker, BOS 287
S. Crawford, DET 281
F. Baker, PHI 252
D. Pratt, STL 240
E. Collins, PHI 238

Runs Batted In
S. Crawford, DET 104
F. Baker, PHI 97
S. McInnis, PHI 95
T. Speaker, BOS 90
E. Collins, PHI 85

Stolen Bases
F. Maisel, NY 74
E. Collins, PHI 58
T. Speaker, BOS 42
B. Shotton, STL 40
C. Milan, WAS 38
R. Peckinpaugh, NY 38

Hits
T. Speaker, BOS 193
S. Crawford, DET 183
F. Baker, PHI 182
E. Collins, PHI 181
S. McInnis, PHI 181

Base on Balls
D. Bush, DET 112
E. Collins, PHI 97
E. Murphy, PHI 87
T. Speaker, BOS 77

Home Run Percentage
J. Fournier, CHI 1.6
F. Baker, PHI 1.6
S. Crawford, DET 1.4
T. Walker, STL 1.2

Runs
E. Collins, PHI 122
T. Speaker, BOS 101
E. Murphy, PHI 101
D. Bush, DET 97

Doubles
T. Speaker, BOS 46
D. Lewis, BOS 37
D. Pratt, STL 34
S. Collins, CHI 34

Triples
S. Crawford, DET 26
L. Gardner, BOS 19
T. Speaker, BOS 18
T. Walker, STL 16

PITCHING LEADERS

Winning Percentage
C. Bender, PHI .850
D. Leonard, BOS .792
E. Plank, PHI .682
B. Shawkey, PHI .667
R. Caldwell, NY .654

Earned Run Average
D. Leonard, BOS 1.01
R. Foster, BOS 1.65
W. Johnson, WAS 1.72
E. Shore, BOS 1.89
R. Caldwell, NY 1.94

Wins
W. Johnson, WAS 28
H. Coveleski, DET 22
R. Collins, BOS 20
D. Leonard, BOS 19
C. Weilman, STL 18
H. Dauss, DET 18

Saves
J. Bentley, WAS 4
R. Mitchell, STL 4
H. Dauss, DET 4
R. Faber, CHI 4
J. Shaw, WAS 4

Strikeouts
W. Johnson, WAS 225
W. Mitchell, CLE 179
D. Leonard, BOS 174
J. Shaw, WAS 164
H. Dauss, DET 150

Complete Games
W. Johnson, WAS 33
H. Coveleski, DET 23
R. Caldwell, NY 22
H. Dauss, DET 22

Fewest Hits/9 Innings
D. Leonard, BOS 5.70
R. Caldwell, NY 6.46
E. Shore, BOS 6.77
R. Foster, BOS 6.86

Shutouts
W. Johnson, WAS 9
C. Bender, PHI 7
D. Leonard, BOS 7
R. Collins, BOS 6

Fewest Walks/9 Innings
M. McHale, NY 1.55
W. Johnson, WAS 1.79
J. Warhop, NY 1.83
R. Collins, BOS 1.85

Most Strikeouts/9 Inn.
D. Leonard, BOS 7.03
W. Mitchell, CLE 6.27
J. Shaw, WAS 5.74
W. Johnson, WAS 5.45

Innings
W. Johnson, WAS 372
H. Coveleski, DET 303
H. Dauss, DET 302
E. Hamilton, STL 302

Games Pitched
W. Johnson, WAS 51
D. Ayers, WAS 49
J. Shaw, WAS 48
J. Benz, CHI 48

							Batting						Fielding			Pitching					
	W	L	PCT	GB	R	OR	2B	3B	HR	BA	SA	SB	E	DP	FA	CG	BB	SO	ShO	SV	ERA
Philadelphia	99	53	.651		**749**	529	165	80	**29**	**.272**	**.352**	231	**213**	116	**.966**	89	521	720	24	17	2.78
Boston	91	62	.595	8.5	589	**511**	**226**	**85**	18	.250	.338	177	242	99	.963	88	397	605	24	8	**2.35**
Washington	81	73	.526	19	572	519	176	81	18	.244	.320	220	254	116	.961	75	520	**784**	**25**	**20**	2.54
Detroit	80	73	.523	19.5	615	618	195	84	25	.258	.344	211	286	101	.958	81	498	567	14	12	2.86
St. Louis	71	82	.464	28.5	523	615	185	75	17	.243	.319	233	317	114	.952	81	540	553	15	12	2.85
Chicago	70	84	.455	30	487	560	161	71	19	.239	.311	167	299	90	.955	74	401	660	17	11	2.48
New York	70	84	.455	30	538	550	149	52	12	.229	.287	**251**	238	93	.963	**98**	**390**	563	9	5	2.81
Cleveland	51	102	.333	48.5	538	709	178	70	10	.245	.312	167	300	**119**	.953	69	666	688	10	3	3.21
					4611	4611	1435	598	148	.248	.323	1657	2149	848	.959	655	3933	5140	138	88	2.73

FEDERAL LEAGUE 1914

Indianapolis

W-88 L-65

Bill Phillips

POS	Player	AB	BA	HR	RBI	PO	A	E	DP	TC/G	FA	Pitcher	G	IP	W	L	SV	ERA
1B	C. Carr	441	.293	3	69	1088	59	11	67	10.1	**.991**	C. Falkenberg	**49**	**377**	25	16	3	2.22
2B	F. LaPorte	505	.311	4	**107**	300	373	31	61	5.3	.956	E. Moseley	43	317	19	18	1	3.47
SS	J. Esmond	542	.295	2	49	**317**	448	**67**	54	5.5	.919	G. Kaiserling	37	275	17	10	0	3.11
3B	B. McKechnie	570	.304	2	38	195	**327**	34	**28**	**3.7**	.939	G. Mullin	36	203	14	10	2	2.70
RF	B. Kauff	571	**.370**	8	95	310	31	17	5	2.3	.953	H. Billiard	32	126	8	7	1	3.72
CF	V. Campbell	544	.318	7	44	218	18	19	6	1.9	.925							
LF	A. Scheer	363	.306	3	45	150	13	13	2	1.7	.926							
C	B. Rariden	396	.235	0	47	**714**	**215**	18	14	7.3	.981							
OF	A. Kaiser	187	.230	1	16	98	3	9	0	2.2	.918							
OF	E. Roush	166	.325	1	30	85	5	1	1	2.1	.989							
P	G. Mullin	77	.312	0	21	9	45	5	1	1.6	.915							

Chicago

W-87 L-67

Joe Tinker

POS	Player	AB	BA	HR	RBI	PO	A	E	DP	TC/G	FA	Pitcher	G	IP	W	L	SV	ERA
1B	F. Beck	555	.279	11	77	1614	55	**31**	**86**	10.8	.982	C. Hendrix	**49**	362	**29**	11	5	1.69
2B	J. Farrell	524	.235	0	35	354	**457**	39	54	5.5	.954	M. Fiske	38	198	12	9	0	3.14
SS	J. Tinker	438	.256	2	46	271	408	38	48	**5.7**	.947	E. Lange	36	190	12	10	2	2.23
3B	R. Zeider	452	.274	1	36	151	217	25	27	3.4	.936	D. Watson	26	172	9	11	1	2.04
RF	A. Wickland	536	.276	6	68	252	23	11	3	1.8	.962	M. Prendergast	30	136	5	9	0	2.38
CF	D. Zwilling	592	.313	**15**	95	340	15	14	3	2.4	.962	T. McGuire	24	131	5	7	0	3.70
LF	M. Flack	502	.247	2	39	232	18	7	2	1.9	.973	A. Johnson	16	120	9	5	0	1.58*
C	A. Wilson	440	.291	10	64	674	212	**24**	**19**	6.9	.974							
3B	H. Fritz	174	.213	0	13	34	59	9	7	2.2	.912							

FEDERAL LEAGUE 1914, *cont.*

Team	POS	Player	AB	BA	HR	RBI	PO	A	E	DP	TC/G	FA	Pitcher	G	IP	W	L	SV	ERA
Baltimore	1B	H. Swacina	**617**	.280	0	90	**1616**	**104**	26	74	11.1	.985	J. Quinn	46	343	26	14	1	2.60
W-84 L-70	2B	O. Knabe	469	.226	2	42	287	389	31	49	4.9	.956	G. Suggs	46	319	24	14	3	2.90
Otto Knabe	SS	M. Doolan	486	.245	1	53	305	**476**	42	**55**	5.7	**.949**	K. Wilhelm	47	244	12	17	4	4.03
	3B	J. Walsh	428	.308	10	65	125	217	25	18	3.2	.932	F. Smith	39	175	10	8	2	2.99
	RF	B. Meyer	500	.304	5	40	172	14	17	6	1.5	.916	B. Bailey	19	129	7	9	0	3.08
	CF	V. Duncan	557	.287	2	53	255	20	26	8	2.0	.914	S. Conley	35	125	4	6	0	2.52
	LF	H. Simmons	352	.270	1	38	91	10	12	2	1.5	.894							
	C	F. Jacklitsch	337	.276	2	48	580	167	9	13	6.4	**.988**							
	OF	G. Zinn	225	.280	3	25	82	5	6	1	1.6	.935							
	OF	J. Bates	190	.305	1	29	108	7	6	0	2.1	.950							
	3B	E. Kirkpatrick	174	.253	2	16	28	40	5	1	2.0	.932							
	C	H. Russell	168	.232	0	13	193	44	11	2	5.3	.956							
Buffalo	1B	J. Agler	463	.272	0	20	734	49	12	44	10.5	.985	F. Anderson	37	260	13	16	0	3.08
W-80 L-71	2B	T. Downey	541	.218	2	42	265	388	26	49	5.3	**.962**	G. Krapp	36	253	14	14	0	2.49
Harry Schlafly	SS	B. Louden	431	.313	6	63	299	285	43	34	5.5	.931	R. Ford	35	247	20	6	**6**	1.82
	3B	F. Smith	473	.220	2	45	170	229	30	14	3.4	.930	E. Moore	36	195	10	14	2	4.30
	RF	T. McDonald	250	.296	3	32	94	7	5	2	1.7	.953	A. Schulz	27	171	10	11	1	3.37
	CF	C. Hanford	597	.291	13	90	331	24	10	5	2.4	.973	H. Moran	34	154	11	8	1	4.27
	LF	F. Delahanty	274	.201	2	27	116	8	3	1	1.6	.976							
	C	W. Blair	378	.243	0	33	604	194	13	17	6.3	.984							
	1B	H. Chase	291	.347	3	48	690	38	15	33	10.2	.980							
	OF	E. Booe	241	.224	0	14	86	8	4	2	1.7	.959							
	OF	D. Young	174	.276	4	22	49	2	3	2	1.3	.944							
Brooklyn	1B	H. Myers	305	.220	1	29	784	44	9	47	9.5	.989	T. Seaton	44	303	25	13	2	3.03
W-77 L-77	2B	S. Hofman	515	.287	5	83	232	289	27	39	5.1	.951	E. Lafitte	42	291	16	16	2	2.63
Bill Bradley	SS	E. Gagnier	337	.187	0	25	219	244	33	37	5.6	.933	H. Finneran	27	175	12	11	1	3.18
	3B	T. Wisterzil	534	.257	0	66	**207**	294	23	24	3.5	**.956**	R. Sommers	23	82	4	7	0	4.06
	RF	S. Evans	514	.348	12	96	163	13	11	2	1.7	.941	J. Bluejacket	17	67	4	5	1	3.76
	CF	A. Shaw	376	.324	5	49	198	14	10	4	2.2	.955							
	LF	G. Anderson	364	.316	3	24	176	15	11	2	2.2	.946							
	C	G. Land	335	.275	0	29	490	147	20	11	6.8	.970							
	OF	C. Cooper	399	.241	2	25	188	12	16	4	2.1	.926							
	SS	A. Halt	261	.234	3	25	164	184	43	30	5.5	.890							
	2B	J. Delahanty	214	.290	0	15	104	117	10	15	4.2	.957							
	C	F. Owens	184	.277	2	20	228	67	10	10	5.3	.967							
	OF	D. Murphy	161	.304	4	32	65	8	1	2	1.6	.986							
Kansas City	1B	G. Stovall	450	.284	7	75	1201	70	14	82	**11.1**	.989	G. Packard	42	302	21	13	4	2.89
W-67 L-84	2B	D. Kenworthy	545	.317	**15**	91	**437**	407	**43**	**79**	**6.1**	.952	N. Cullop	44	296	14	17	1	2.34
George Stovall	SS	P. Goodwin	374	.235	1	32	85	208	30	21	4.8	.907	D. Stone	39	187	7	14	0	4.34
	3B	G. Perring	496	.278	2	69	100	223	23	20	3.4	.934	B. Harris	31	154	7	8	1	4.09
	RF	E. Gilmore	530	.287	1	32	196	24	6	7	1.7	.973	P. Henning	28	138	6	12	1	4.83
	CF	A. Kruger	441	.259	4	47	249	14	10	1	2.3	.963	D. Adams	36	136	3	9	3	3.51
	LF	C. Chadbourne	581	.277	1	37	238	34	10	6	1.9	.965	C. Johnson	20	134	9	10	0	3.16
	C	T. Easterly	436	.335	1	67	570	173	**24**	16	6.0	.969							
	OF	C. Coles	194	.253	1	25	52	4	7	0	1.6	.889							
	SS	J. Rawlings	193	.212	0	15	121	222	23	25	6.0	.937							
	UT	C. Daringer	160	.263	0	16	70	142	19	16		.918							
Pittsburgh	1B	H. Bradley	427	.307	0	61	1132	60	12	52	10.2	.990	E. Knetzer	37	272	19	11	1	2.88
W-64 L-86	2B	J. Lewis	394	.234	1	48	304	332	34	33	5.8	.949	H. Camnitz	36	262	14	18	1	3.23
Doc Gessler	SS	E. Holly	350	.246	0	26	238	263	31	30	5.7	.942	W. Dickson	40	257	9	**21**	1	3.16
W-3 L-8	3B	E. Lennox	430	.312	11	84	136	193	16	12	2.8	.954	C. Barger	33	228	10	16	1	4.34
Rebel Oakes	RF	J. Savage	479	.284	1	26	141	15	6	3	1.7	.963	M. Walker	35	169	3	16	0	4.31
W-61 L-78	CF	R. Oakes	571	.312	7	75	313	23	14	2	2.4	.960	G. LaClaire	22	103	5	2	0	4.01
	LF	D. Jones	352	.273	2	24	216	11	7	1	2.5	.970							
	C	C. Berry	411	.238	2	36	550	202	23	18	6.4	.970							
	O2	T. McDonald	223	.318	3	29	77	83	13	10		.925							
	UT	C. Rheam	214	.210	0	20	431	55	16	16		.968							
	OF	F. Delahanty	159	.239	1	7	57	5	1	0	1.8	.984*							
	SS	S. Yerkes	142	.338	1	25	89	139	6	13	6.0	.974							
St. Louis	1B	H. Miller	490	.222	0	46	1256	65	14	48	10.3	.990	B. Groom	42	281	13	20	1	3.24
W-62 L-89	2B	D. Crandall	278	.309	2	41	98	152	20	10	4.3	.926	D. Davenport	33	216	8	13	4	3.46
Three Finger Brown	SS	A. Bridwell	381	.236	1	33	217	291	30	36	5.2	.944	H. Keupper	42	213	8	20	0	4.27
W-50 L-63	3B	A. Boucher	516	.231	2	49	193	263	**42**	18	3.4	.916	D. Crandall	27	196	13	9	0	3.54
Fielder Jones	RF	J. Tobin	529	.270	7	35	185	31	11	3	1.7	.952	E. Willett	27	175	4	16	0	4.22
W-12 L-26	CF	D. Drake	514	.251	3	42	207	16	10	2	2.0	.957	T. Brown	26	175	12	6	0	3.30
	LF	W. Miller	402	.294	4	50	248	15	13	3	2.5	.953							
	C	M. Simon	276	.207	0	21	433	132	9	9	**7.4**	.984							
	2S	J. Misse	306	.196	0	22	229	279	43	29		.922							
	OF	F. Kommers	244	.307	3	41	107	11	12	1	1.9	.908							
	UT	G. Hartley	212	.288	1	25	249	79	11	12		.968							
	OF	L. Kirby	195	.246	2	18	100	7	3	2	2.2	.973							
	C	H. Chapman	181	.210	0	14	247	77	9	8	6.5	.973							

BATTING AND BASE RUNNING LEADERS

Batting Average		Slugging Average		Home Runs	
B. Kauff, IND	.370	S. Evans, BKN	.556	D. Kenworthy, KC	15
S. Evans, BKN	.348	B. Kauff, IND	.534	D. Zwilling, CHI	15
T. Easterly, KC	.335	D. Kenworthy, KC	.525	C. Hanford, BUF	13
A. Shaw, BKN	.324	E. Lennox, PIT	.493	S. Evans, BKN	12
V. Campbell, IND	.318	D. Zwilling, CHI	.480	E. Lennox, PIT	11
				F. Beck, CHI	11

PITCHING LEADERS

Winning Percentage		Earned Run Average		Wins	
R. Ford, BUF	.769	A. Johnson, CHI	1.58	C. Hendrix, CHI	29
C. Hendrix, CHI	.725	C. Hendrix, CHI	1.69	J. Quinn, BAL	26
T. Seaton, BKN	.658	R. Ford, BUF	1.82	T. Seaton, BKN	25
J. Quinn, BAL	.650	D. Watson, CHI, STL	2.01	C. Falkenberg, IND	25
E. Knetzer, PIT	.633	C. Falkenberg, IND	2.22	G. Suggs, BAL	24

FEDERAL LEAGUE 1914, *cont.*

BATTING AND BASE RUNNING LEADERS

Total Bases
- B. Kauff, IND 305
- S. Evans, BKN 286
- D. Kenworthy, KC 286
- D. Zwilling, CHI 284
- C. Hanford, BUF 267

Runs Batted In
- F. LaPorte, IND 107
- S. Evans, BKN 96
- B. Kauff, IND 95
- D. Zwilling, CHI 95
- D. Kenworthy, KC 91

Stolen Bases
- B. Kauff, IND 75
- B. McKechnie, IND 47
- H. Myers, BKN 43
- C. Chadbourne, KC 42

Hits
- B. Kauff, IND 211
- D. Zwilling, CHI 185
- S. Evans, BKN 179
- R. Oakes, PIT 178

Base on Balls
- A. Wickland, CHI 81
- J. Agler, BUF 77
- B. Kauff, IND 72

Home Run Percentage
- D. Kenworthy, KC 2.8
- E. Lennox, PIT 2.6
- D. Zwilling, CHI 2.5
- J. Walsh, BAL 2.3

Runs
- B. Kauff, IND 120
- B. McKechnie, IND 107
- V. Duncan, BAL 99
- S. Evans, BKN 93
- D. Kenworthy, KC 93

Doubles
- B. Kauff, IND 44
- S. Evans, BKN 41
- D. Kenworthy, KC 40
- D. Zwilling, CHI 38

Triples
- S. Evans, BKN 15
- J. Esmond, IND 15
- D. Kenworthy, KC 14

PITCHING LEADERS

Saves
- R. Ford, BUF 6
- C. Hendrix, CHI 5
- D. Davenport, STL 4
- G. Packard, KC 4
- K. Wilhelm, BAL 4

Strikeouts
- C. Falkenberg, IND 236
- E. Moseley, IND 205
- C. Hendrix, CHI 189
- T. Seaton, BKN 172
- B. Groom, STL 167

Complete Games
- C. Hendrix, CHI 34
- C. Falkenberg, IND 33
- E. Moseley, IND 29
- J. Quinn, BAL 27
- T. Seaton, BKN 26
- G. Suggs, BAL 26

Fewest Hits/9 Innings
- C. Hendrix, CHI 6.51
- A. Johnson, CHI 6.60
- R. Ford, BUF 6.91
- G. Krapp, BUF 7.05

Shutouts
- C. Falkenberg, IND 9
- T. Seaton, BKN 7
- C. Hendrix, CHI 6
- G. Suggs, BAL 6

Fewest Walks/9 Innings
- R. Ford, BUF 1.49
- G. Suggs, BAL 1.61
- J. Quinn, BAL 1.71
- C. Hendrix, CHI 1.91

Most Strikeouts/9 Inn.
- B. Bailey, BAL 9.16
- D. Davenport, STL 5.93
- E. Moseley, IND 5.83
- C. Falkenberg, IND 5.63

Innings
- C. Falkenberg, IND 377
- C. Hendrix, CHI 362
- J. Quinn, BAL 343
- G. Suggs, BAL 319

Games Pitched
- C. Hendrix, CHI 49
- C. Falkenberg, IND 49
- K. Wilhelm, BAL 47
- G. Suggs, BAL 46
- J. Quinn, BAL 46

							Batting						Fielding			Pitching					
	W	L	PCT	GB	R	OR	2B	3B	HR	BA	SA	SB	E	DP	FA	CG	BB	SO	ShO	SV	ERA
Indianapolis	88	65	.575		**762**	622	**230**	**90**	33	**.285**	**.383**	**273**	289	113	.956	**104**	476	664	15	8	3.06
Chicago	87	67	.565	1.5	621	**517**	227	50	**51**	.258	.352	171	249	113	**.962**	93	393	650	**17**	8	**2.44**
Baltimore	84	70	.545	4.5	645	628	222	67	32	.268	.357	152	263	105	.960	88	**392**	**732**	15	10	3.13
Buffalo	80	71	.530	7	620	602	177	74	38	.250	.336	228	**242**	109	**.962**	89	505	662	15	**13**	3.16
Brooklyn	77	77	.500	11.5	662	677	225	85	42	.269	.368	220	283	120	.956	91	559	636	11	7	3.33
Kansas City	67	84	.444	20	644	683	226	77	39	.267	.364	171	279	**135**	.957	82	445	600	10	10	3.41
Pittsburgh	64	86	.427	22.5	605	698	180	**90**	34	.262	.352	153	253	92	.960	97	444	510	9	4	3.56
St. Louis	62	89	.411	25	565	697	193	65	26	.247	.326	113	273	94	.957	97	409	661	9	6	3.59
					5124	5124	1680	598	295	.263	.355	1481	2131	881	.959	741	3623	5115	101	66	3.21

NATIONAL LEAGUE 1915

Philadelphia

W-90 L-62

Pat Moran

POS	Player	AB	BA	HR	RBI	PO	A	E	DP	TC/G	FA	Pitcher	G	IP	W	L	SV	ERA
1B	F. Luderus	499	.315	7	62	1409	99	11	76	**10.8**	.993	G. Alexander	49	**376**	**31**	10	3	**1.22**
2B	B. Niehoff	529	.238	2	49	307	411	**41**	55	5.1	.946	E. Mayer	43	275	21	15	2	2.36
SS	D. Bancroft	563	.254	7	30	336	492	64	60	5.8	.928	A. Demaree	32	210	14	11	1	3.05
3B	B. Byrne	387	.209	0	21	98	183	9	9	2.8	**.969**	E. Rixey	29	177	11	12	1	2.39
RF	G. Cravath	522	.285	**24**	**115**	233	28	15	2	1.8	.946	G. Chalmers	26	170	8	9	1	2.48
CF	D. Paskert	328	.244	3	39	181	10	6	2	1.9	.970							
LF	B. Becker	338	.246	11	35	177	5	11	0	2.0	.943							
C	B. Killefer	320	.237	0	24	539	126	19	6	6.5	.972							
OF	P. Whitted	448	.281	1	43	266	7	6	2	2.6	.978							
3B	M. Stock	227	.260	1	15	62	106	5	7	3.1	.971							
C	E. Burns	174	.241	0	16	241	61	6	6	4.6	.981							

Boston

W-83 L-69

George Stallings

POS	Player	AB	BA	HR	RBI	PO	A	E	DP	TC/G	FA	Pitcher	G	IP	W	L	SV	ERA
1B	B. Schmidt	458	.251	2	60	1221	60	17	80	10.2	.987	D. Rudolph	44	341	22	**19**	1	2.37
2B	J. Evers	278	.263	1	22	170	209	16	33	4.8	.959	T. Hughes	**50**	280	16	14	**5**	2.12
SS	R. Maranville	509	.244	2	43	**391**	486	55	63	**6.3**	.941	P. Ragan	33	227	15	12	0	2.46
3B	R. Smith	549	.264	2	65	**170**	**292**	**26**	26	3.1	.947	L. Tyler	32	205	10	9	0	2.86
RF	H. Moran	419	.200	0	21	168	17	7	3	1.6	.964							
CF	S. Magee	571	.280	2	87	346	16	7	4	2.8	.981							
LF	J. Connolly	305	.298	0	23	158	10	5	2	1.9	.971							
C	H. Gowdy	316	.247	2	30	460	148	16	11	5.3	.974							
2B	E. Fitzpatrick	303	.221	0	24	135	160	10	23	4.3	.967							
UT	D. Egan	220	.259	0	21	179	92	16	20		.944							
C	B. Whaling	190	.221	0	13	292	68	5	2	5.1	.986							

Brooklyn

W-80 L-72

Wilbert Robinson

POS	Player	AB	BA	HR	RBI	PO	A	E	DP	TC/G	FA	Pitcher	G	IP	W	L	SV	ERA
1B	J. Daubert	544	.301	2	47	1441	**102**	11	73	10.4	.993	J. Pfeffer	40	292	19	14	3	2.10
2B	G. Cutshaw	566	.246	0	62	**397**	**473**	26	53	**5.8**	**.971**	W. Dell	40	215	11	10	1	2.34
SS	O. O'Mara	577	.244	0	31	319	431	**78**	44	5.6	.906	J. Coombs	29	196	15	10	0	2.58
3B	G. Getz	477	.258	2	46	140	290	22	14	**3.5**	.951	S. Smith	29	174	14	8	2	2.59
RF	C. Stengel	459	.237	3	50	220	13	10	2	1.9	.959	E. Appleton	34	138	4	10	0	3.32
CF	H. Myers	605	.248	2	46	352	23	14	5	2.5	.964	N. Rucker	19	123	9	4	1	2.42
LF	Z. Wheat	528	.258	5	66	345	18	18	4	2.6	.953	P. Douglas	20	117	5	5	0	2.62
C	O. Miller	254	.224	0	25	363	91	9	8	5.5	.981							
C	L. McCarty	276	.239	0	19	310	101	13	5	5.0	.969							

Chicago

W-73 L-80

Roger Bresnahan

POS	Player	AB	BA	HR	RBI	PO	A	E	DP	TC/G	FA	Pitcher	G	IP	W	L	SV	ERA
1B	V. Saier	497	.264	11	64	1348	65	**21**	71	10.3	.985	H. Vaughn	41	270	20	12	1	2.87
2B	H. Zimmerman	520	.265	3	62	211	267	29	30	5.1	.943	J. Lavender	41	220	10	16	3	2.58
SS	B. Fisher	568	.287	5	53	277	434	51	35	5.2	.933	G. Pearce	36	176	13	9	0	3.32
3B	A. Phelan	448	.219	3	35	136	203	22	14	3.3	.939	B. Humphries	31	172	8	13	2	2.31
RF	W. Good	498	.253	2	27	192	13	14	4	1.8	.936	Z. Zabel	36	163	7	10	0	3.20
CF	C. Williams	518	.257	13	64	347	14	12	2	2.5	.968	L. Cheney	25	131	8	9	0	3.56
LF	W. Schulte	550	.249	12	69	280	24	12	3	2.1	.962	P. Standridge	29	112	4	1	0	3.61
C	J. Archer	309	.243	1	27	447	126	13	11	**6.7**	.978	K. Adams	26	107	1	9	0	4.71
C	R. Bresnahan	221	.204	1	19	345	95	8	9	6.6	.982							

NATIONAL LEAGUE 1915, *cont.*

Pittsburgh

W-73 L-81

Fred Clarke

POS	Player	AB	BA	HR	RBI	PO	A	E	DP	TC/G	FA	Pitcher	G	IP	W	L	SV	ERA
1B	D. Johnston	543	.265	5	64	1453	48	13	65	10.3	.991	B. Harmon	37	270	16	17	1	2.50
2B	J. Viox	503	.256	2	45	239	362	29	35	4.7	.954	A. Mamaux	38	252	21	8	0	2.04
SS	H. Wagner	566	.274	6	78	298	395	38	53	5.6	**.948**	B. Adams	40	245	14	14	2	2.87
3B	D. Baird	512	.219	1	53	142	226	24	13	3.0	.939	W. Cooper	38	186	5	16	4	3.30
RF	B. Hinchman	577	.307	5	77	261	17	9	5	1.8	.969	E. Kantlehner	29	163	5	12	2	2.26
CF	Z. Collins	354	.294	1	23	217	11	14	3	2.4	.942	G. McQuillan	30	149	8	10	1	2.84
LF	M. Carey	564	.254	3	27	307	21	6	5	2.4	.982							
C	G. Gibson	351	.251	1	30	551	134	**25**	14	5.9	.965							

St. Louis

W-72 L-81

Miller Huggins

POS	Player	AB	BA	HR	RBI	PO	A	E	DP	TC/G	FA	Pitcher	G	IP	W	L	SV	ERA
1B	D. Miller	553	.264	2	72	1000	50	10	54	12.8	.991	B. Doak	38	276	16	18	1	2.64
2B	M. Huggins	353	.241	2	24	194	315	23	44	5.0	.957	S. Sallee	46	275	13	17	3	2.84
SS	A. Butler	469	.254	1	31	235	351	53	43	4.9	.917	L. Meadows	39	244	13	11	0	2.99
3B	B. Betzel	367	.251	0	27	105	221	22	10	3.3	.937	D. Griner	37	150	5	11	3	2.81
RF	T. Long	507	.294	2	61	236	18	20	1	2.0	.927	H. Robinson	32	143	7	8	0	2.45
CF	O. Wilson	348	.276	3	39	234	20	4	3	2.4	.984	H. Perdue	31	115	6	12	1	4.21
LF	B. Bescher	486	.263	4	34	257	12	8	1	2.1	.971	R. Ames	15	113	9	3	1	2.46
C	F. Snyder	473	.298	2	55	**592**	**204**	14	9	5.6	.983							
OF	C. Dolan	322	.280	2	38	179	4	14	0	2.0	.929							
1B	H. Hyatt	295	.268	2	46	616	21	6	31	7.9	.991							
3B	Z. Beck	223	.233	0	15	59	127	13	10	3.3	.935							

Cincinnati

W-71 L-83

Buck Herzog

POS	Player	AB	BA	HR	RBI	PO	A	E	DP	TC/G	FA	Pitcher	G	IP	W	L	SV	ERA
1B	F. Mollwitz	525	.259	1	51	**1545**	79	7	**107**	10.7	**.996**	G. Dale	49	297	18	17	3	2.46
2B	B. Rodgers	213	.239	0	12	96	170	15	30	5.0	.947	P. Schneider	48	276	13	**19**	2	2.48
SS	B. Herzog	579	.264	1	42	**391**	513	53	**90**	6.3	.945	F. Toney	36	223	15	6	2	1.58
3B	H. Groh	587	.290	3	50	153	280	14	**34**	3.4	.969	R. Benton	35	176	9	13	4*	3.32
RF	T. Griffith	583	.307	4	85	225	11	12	1	1.5	.952	K. Lear	40	168	6	10	0	3.01
CF	R. Killefer	555	.272	1	41	334	17	9	5	2.4	.975	L. McKenry	21	110	5	5	0	2.94
LF	K. Williams	219	.242	0	16	117	11	7	4	2.2	.948							
C	I. Wingo	339	.221	3	29	413	124	19	**15**	5.7	.966							
OF	T. Leach	335	.224	0	17	200	9	9	2	2.3	.959							
C	T. Clarke	226	.288	0	21	294	71	7	7	5.2	.981							
UT	I. Olson	207	.232	0	14	170	166	19	20		.946							
2B	J. Wagner	197	.178	0	13	99	122	9	28	5.0	.961							

New York

W-69 L-83

John McGraw

POS	Player	AB	BA	HR	RBI	PO	A	E	DP	TC/G	FA	Pitcher	G	IP	W	L	SV	ERA
1B	F. Merkle	505	.299	4	62	1123	53	13	62	10.7	.989	J. Tesreau	43	306	19	16	3	2.29
2B	L. Doyle	591	**.320**	4	70	313	396	40	**66**	5.0	.947	P. Perritt	35	220	12	18	0	2.66
SS	A. Fletcher	562	.254	3	74	302	**544**	58	76	6.1	.936	C. Mathewson	27	186	8	14	0	3.58
3B	H. Lobert	386	.251	0	38	109	192	16	9	3.0	.950	S. Stroud	32	184	11	9	1	2.79
RF	D. Robertson	544	.294	3	58	225	13	11	4	1.8	.956	R. Marquard	27	169	9	8	2	3.73
CF	F. Snodgrass	252	.194	0	20	160	12	12	2	1.8	.935	R. Schauer	32	105	2	8	0	3.50
LF	G. Burns	**622**	.272	3	51	278	13	12	4	2.0	.960	R. Benton	10	61	4	5	1*	2.82
C	C. Meyers	289	.232	1	26	464	90	8	**15**	5.1	**.986**							
UT	F. Brainerd	249	.201	1	21	443	94	18	37		.968							
3B	E. Grant	192	.208	0	10	39	57	3	3	1.8	.970							

BATTING AND BASE RUNNING LEADERS

Batting Average

L. Doyle, NY	.320
F. Luderus, PHI	.315
T. Griffith, CIN	.307
B. Hinchman, PIT	.307
J. Daubert, BKN	.301

Slugging Average

G. Cravath, PHI	.510
F. Luderus, PHI	.457
T. Long, STL	.446
V. Saier, CHI	.445
L. Doyle, NY	.442

Home Runs

G. Cravath, PHI	24
C. Williams, CHI	13
W. Schulte, CHI	12
B. Becker, PHI	11
V. Saier, CHI	11

Total Bases

G. Cravath, PHI	266
L. Doyle, NY	261
T. Griffith, CIN	254
B. Hinchman, PIT	253
H. Wagner, PIT	239

Runs Batted In

G. Cravath, PHI	115
S. Magee, BOS	87
T. Griffith, CIN	85
H. Wagner, PIT	78
B. Hinchman, PIT	77

Stolen Bases

M. Carey, PIT	36
B. Herzog, CIN	35
V. Saier, CHI	29
D. Baird, PIT	29
G. Cutshaw, BKN	28

Hits

L. Doyle, NY	189
T. Griffith, CIN	179
B. Hinchman, PIT	177
H. Groh, CIN	170

Base on Balls

G. Cravath, PHI	86
D. Bancroft, PHI	77
J. Viox, PIT	75
M. Huggins, STL	74

Home Run Percentage

G. Cravath, PHI	4.6
B. Becker, PHI	3.3
C. Williams, CHI	2.5
V. Saier, CHI	2.2

Runs

G. Cravath, PHI	89
L. Doyle, NY	86
D. Bancroft, PHI	85
G. Burns, NY	83

Doubles

L. Doyle, NY	40
F. Luderus, PHI	36
V. Saier, CHI	35
R. Smith, BOS	34
S. Magee, BOS	34

Triples

T. Long, STL	25
H. Wagner, PIT	17
T. Griffith, CIN	16
B. Hinchman, PIT	14
G. Burns, NY	14

PITCHING LEADERS

Winning Percentage

G. Alexander, PHI	.756
A. Mamaux, PIT	.724
F. Toney, CIN	.714
H. Vaughn, CHI	.625
J. Coombs, BKN	.600

Earned Run Average

G. Alexander, PHI	1.22
F. Toney, CIN	1.58
A. Mamaux, PIT	2.04
J. Pfeffer, BKN	2.10
T. Hughes, BOS	2.12

Wins

G. Alexander, PHI	31
D. Rudolph, BOS	22
A. Mamaux, PIT	21
E. Mayer, PHI	21
H. Vaughn, CHI	20

Saves

T. Hughes, BOS	5
R. Benton, CIN, NY	5
W. Cooper, PIT	4

Strikeouts

G. Alexander, PHI	241
J. Tesreau, NY	176
T. Hughes, BOS	171
A. Mamaux, PIT	152
H. Vaughn, CHI	148

Complete Games

G. Alexander, PHI	36
D. Rudolph, BOS	30
J. Pfeffer, BKN	26
B. Harmon, PIT	25
J. Tesreau, NY	24

Fewest Hits/9 Innings

G. Alexander, PHI	6.05
F. Toney, CIN	6.47
A. Mamaux, PIT	6.51
T. Hughes, BOS	6.68

Shutouts

G. Alexander, PHI	12
A. Mamaux, PIT	8
J. Tesreau, NY	8
F. Toney, CIN	6
J. Pfeffer, BKN	6

Fewest Walks/9 Innings

C. Mathewson, NY	0.97
B. Humphries, CHI	1.21
B. Adams, PIT	1.25
G. Alexander, PHI	1.53

Most Strikeouts/9 Inn.

G. Alexander, PHI	5.76
T. Hughes, BOS	5.49
A. Mamaux, PIT	5.44
J. Tesreau, NY	5.18

Innings

G. Alexander, PHI	376
D. Rudolph, BOS	341
J. Tesreau, NY	306
G. Dale, CIN	297

Games Pitched

T. Hughes, BOS	50
G. Dale, CIN	49
G. Alexander, PHI	49
P. Schneider, CIN	48

NATIONAL LEAGUE 1915, *cont.*

	W	L	PCT	GB	R	OR	Batting 2B	3B	HR	BA	SA	SB	Fielding E	DP	FA	Pitching CG	BB	SO	ShO	SV	ERA
Philadelphia	90	62	.592		589	**463**	202	39	**58**	.247	.340	121	216	99	**.966**	**98**	342	652	**20**	8	**2.17**
Boston	83	69	.546	7	582	545	**231**	57	17	.240	.319	121	**213**	115	**.966**	95	366	630	15	9	2.57
Brooklyn	80	72	.526	10	536	560	165	75	14	.248	.317	131	238	96	.963	87	473	499	16	7	2.66
Chicago	73	80	.477	17.5	570	620	212	66	53	.244	**.342**	166	268	94	.958	71	480	**657**	18	6	3.11
Pittsburgh	73	81	.474	18	557	520	197	91	24	.246	.334	**182**	214	100	**.966**	91	384	544	18	10	2.60
St. Louis	72	81	.471	18.5	**590**	601	159	**92**	20	**.254**	.333	162	235	109	.964	79	402	538	13	9	2.89
Cincinnati	71	83	.461	20	516	585	194	84	15	.253	.331	156	222	**148**	**.966**	80	497	572	19	**12**	2.84
New York	69	83	.454	21	582	628	195	68	24	.251	.329	155	256	119	.960	78	**325**	637	15	8	3.11
					4522	4522	1555	572	225	.248	.331	1194	1862	880	.964	679	3269	4729	134	69	2.74

AMERICAN LEAGUE 1915

Boston

W-101 L-50

Bill Carrigan

POS	Player	AB	BA	HR	RBI	PO	A	E	DP	TC/G	FA	Pitcher	G	IP	W	L	SV	ERA
1B	D. Hoblitzell	399	.283	2	61	1095	63	15	51	10.0	.987	R. Foster	37	255	19	8	1	2.11
2B	H. Wagner	267	.240	0	29	161	195	28	18	4.9	.927	E. Shore	38	247	19	8	0	1.64
SS	E. Scott	359	.201	0	28	198	298	20	31	5.2	.961	B. Ruth	32	218	18	8	0	2.44
3B	L. Gardner	430	.258	1	55	134	227	26	16	3.0	.933	D. Leonard	32	183	15	7	0	2.36
RF	H. Hooper	566	.235	2	51	255	23	8	7	1.9	.972	S. Wood	25	157	15	5	2	**1.49**
CF	T. Speaker	547	.322	0	69	378	21	10	8	2.7	.976	C. Mays	38	132	6	5	**7**	2.60
LF	D. Lewis	557	.291	2	76	263	15	14	3	1.9	.952	R. Collins	25	105	4	7	2	4.30
C	P. Thomas	203	.236	0	21	325	81	13	7	5.1	.969							
S3	H. Janvrin	316	.269	0	37	122	191	31	16		.910							
2B	J. Barry	248	.262	0	26	143	216	14	19	4.8	.962							
C	H. Cady	205	.278	0	17	313	79	8	12	5.2	.980							
1B	D. Gainer	200	.295	1	29	457	33	6	22	8.9	.988							
P	B. Ruth	92	.315	4	21	17	63	2	3	2.6	.976							

Detroit

W-100 L-54

Hughie Jennings

POS	Player	AB	BA	HR	RBI	PO	A	E	DP	TC/G	FA	Pitcher	G	IP	W	L	SV	ERA
1B	G. Burns	392	.253	5	50	1155	57	17	65	**11.8**	.986	H. Coveleski	**50**	313	22	13	4	2.45
2B	R. Young	378	.243	0	31	233	371	**32**	44	5.3	.950	H. Dauss	46	310	24	13	2	2.50
SS	D. Bush	561	.228	1	44	340	**504**	57	61	5.8	.937	J. Dubuc	39	258	17	12	2	3.21
3B	O. Vitt	560	.250	1	48	**191**	**324**	19	19	**3.5**	**.964**	B. Boland	45	203	13	7	2	3.11
RF	S. Crawford	612	.299	4	**112**	219	8	6	1	1.5	.974	B. Steen	20	79	5	1	4	2.72
CF	T. Cobb	563	**.369**	3	99	328	22	18	7	2.4	.951	B. James	11	67	7	3	0	2.42
LF	B. Veach	569	.313	3	**112**	297	19	8	4	2.1	.975							
C	O. Stanage	300	.223	1	31	395	111	19	0	5.3	.964							
12	M. Kavanagh	332	.295	4	49	559	119	19	23		.973							

Chicago

W-93 L-61

Pants Rowland

POS	Player	AB	BA	HR	RBI	PO	A	E	DP	TC/G	FA	Pitcher	G	IP	W	L	SV	ERA
1B	J. Fournier	422	.322	5	77	674	41	10	31	11.2	.986	R. Faber	**50**	300	24	14	2	2.55
2B	E. Collins	521	.332	4	77	344	**487**	22	54	5.5	**.974**	J. Scott	48	296	24	11	2	2.03
SS	B. Weaver	563	.268	3	49	281	470	49	54	5.4	.939	J. Benz	39	238	15	11	0	2.11
3B	L. Blackburne	283	.216	0	25	88	134	12	13	2.8	.949	R. Russell	41	229	11	10	2	2.59
RF	E. Murphy	273	.315	0	26	113	7	6	0	1.8	.952	E. Cicotte	39	223	13	12	3	3.02
CF	H. Felsch	427	.248	3	53	247	9	11	1	2.3	.959							
LF	S. Collins	576	.257	2	85	197	13	8	2	2.1	.963							
C	R. Schalk	413	.266	1	54	**655**	159	13	8	6.2	**.984**							
30	B. Roth	240	.250	3*	35	79	48	18	1		.876							
OF	J. Jackson	162	.265	2	36	84	6	5	1	2.1	.947							
1B	B. Brief	154	.214	2	17	458	23	7	21	10.6	.986							

Washington

W-85 L-68

Clark Griffith

POS	Player	AB	BA	HR	RBI	PO	A	E	DP	TC/G	FA	Pitcher	G	IP	W	L	SV	ERA
1B	C. Gandil	485	.291	2	64	1237	77	**19**	65	9.9	.986	W. Johnson	47	**337**	**27**	13	4	1.55
2B	R. Morgan	193	.233	0	21	102	175	10	23	5.0	.965	B. Gallia	43	260	17	11	1	2.29
SS	G. McBride	476	.204	1	30	326	422	25	47	5.3	**.968**	J. Boehling	40	229	14	13	0	3.22
3B	E. Foster	**618**	.275	0	52	92	147	21	14	3.3	.919	D. Ayers	40	211	14	9	3	2.21
RF	D. Moeller	438	.226	2	23	167	13	9	6	1.6	.952	J. Shaw	25	133	6	11	1	2.50
CF	C. Milan	573	.288	2	66	352	13	21	3	2.6	.946	H. Harper	19	86	4	4	2	1.77
LF	H. Shanks	492	.250	0	47	151	13	3	1	2.1	.982							
C	J. Henry	277	.220	1	22	478	122	17	4	6.6	.972							
C	B. Williams	197	.244	0	31	213	51	9	4	6.8	.967							
OF	M. Acosta	163	.209	0	18	75	4	3	2	1.5	.963							

New York

W-69 L-83

Wild Bill Donovan

POS	Player	AB	BA	HR	RBI	PO	A	E	DP	TC/G	FA	Pitcher	G	IP	W	L	SV	ERA
1B	W. Pipp	479	.246	4	60	**1396**	**85**	12	**85**	11.1	**.992**	R. Caldwell	36	305	19	16	0	2.89
2B	L. Boone	431	.204	5	43	249	392	23	59	**5.8**	.965	R. Fisher	30	248	18	11	0	2.11
SS	R. Peckinpaugh	540	.220	5	44	291	468	47	60	5.7	.942	J. Warhop	21	143	7	9	0	3.96
3B	F. Maisel	530	.281	4	46	184	223	26	20	3.2	.940	B. Shawkey	16	86	4	7	0	3.26
RF	D. Cook	476	.271	2	33	188	20	9	4	1.7	.959	M. McHale	13	78	3	7	0	4.25
CF	H. High	427	.258	1	43	254	10	5	1	2.3	.981							
LF	R. Hartzell	387	.251	3	60	200	10	8	2	2.0	.963							
C	L. Nunamaker	249	.225	0	17	324	99	16	9	5.7	.964							
23	P. Baumann	219	.292	2	28	129	140	6	20		.978							
OF	B. Cree	196	.214	0	15	97	6	6	1	2.1	.945							
P	R. Caldwell	144	.243	4	20	12	72	1	5	2.4	**.988**							

St. Louis

W-63 L-91

Branch Rickey

POS	Player	AB	BA	HR	RBI	PO	A	E	DP	TC/G	FA	Pitcher	G	IP	W	L	SV	ERA
1B	J. Leary	227	.242	0	15	433	32	7	41	8.9	.985	C. Weilman	47	296	18	19	4	2.34
2B	D. Pratt	602	.291	3	78	**417**	441	31	**82**	5.6	.965	G. Lowdermilk	38	222	9	17	0	3.12
SS	D. Lavan	514	.218	1	48	313	475	**75**	**81**	5.5	.913	E. Hamilton	35	204	9	17	0	2.87
3B	J. Austin	477	.266	1	30	188	264	**41**	**32**	3.5	.917	B. James	34	170	7	10	1	3.59
RF	D. Walsh	150	.220	0	6	66	11	4	0	1.8	.951	E. Koob	28	134	4	5	1	2.36
CF	T. Walker	510	.269	5	49	333	27	23	5	2.8	.940							
LF	B. Shotton	559	.283	1	30	295	15	23	4	2.2	.931							
C	S. Agnew	295	.203	0	19	398	153	**39**	16	5.8	.934							
UT	I. Howard	324	.278	1	43	488	90	12	33		.980							
UT	G. Sisler	274	.285	3	29	413	38	7	21		.985							
C	H. Severeid	203	.222	1	22	247	66	11	2	5.1	.966							

AMERICAN LEAGUE 1915, *cont.*

Team	POS	Player	AB	BA	HR	RBI	PO	A	E	DP	TC/G	FA	Pitcher	G	IP	W	L	SV	ERA
Cleveland	1B	J. Kirke	339	.310	2	40	886	52	13	37	10.9	.986	G. Morton	34	240	16	15	1	2.14
W-57 L-95	2B	B. Wambsganss	375	.195	0	21	138	237	25	24	5.1	.938	W. Mitchell	36	236	11	14	1	2.82
Joe Birmingham	SS	R. Chapman	570	.270	3	67	**378**	469	50	38	**5.8**	.944	R. Hagerman	29	151	6	14	0	3.52
W-12 L-16	3B	W. Barbare	246	.191	0	11	99	141	10	12	3.7	.960	S. Jones	48	146	4	9	4	3.65
Lee Fohl	RF	E. Smith	476	.248	3	67	202	15	18	4	1.9	.923	R. Walker	25	131	4	9	1	3.98
W-45 L-79	CF	N. Leibold	207	.256	0	4	147	10	5	0	3.1	.969	F. Coumbe	30	114	4	7	2	3.47
	LF	J. Graney	404	.260	1	56	227	17	7	1	2.2	.972							
	C	S. O'Neill	386	.236	2	34	556	**175**	24	17	**6.6**	.968							
	01	J. Jackson	299	.331	3	45	352	21	10	12		.974							
	2B	T. Turner	262	.252	0	14	82	136	8	11	4.4	.965							
	OF	B. Southworth	177	.220	0	8	90	7	6	3	2.3	.942							
	OF	B. Roth	144	.299	4*	20	60	5	9	1	1.9	.878							
Philadelphia	1B	S. McInnis	456	.314	0	49	1123	83	13	63	10.2	.989	J. Wyckoff	43	276	10	**22**	0	3.52
W-43 L-109	2B	N. Lajoie	490	.280	1	61	251	332	23	61	5.5	.962	R. Bressler	32	178	4	17	0	5.20
Connie Mack	SS	L. Kopf	386	.225	1	33	152	205	31	24	5.2	.920	J. Bush	25	146	5	15	0	4.14
	3B	W. Schang	359	.248	1	44	64	81	18	9	3.8	.890	T. Sheehan	15	102	4	9	0	4.15
	RF	J. Walsh	417	.206	1	20	231	15	6	1	2.3	.976	T. Knowlson	18	101	4	6	0	3.49
	CF	A. Strunk	485	.297	1	45	225	24	5	4	2.3	.980	B. Shawkey	17	100	6	6	0	4.05
	LF	R. Oldring	408	.248	6	42	212	9	4	3	2.3	.982	H. Pennock	11	44	3	6	1	5.32
	C	J. Lapp	312	.272	2	31	376	115	17	**23**	5.7	.967							
	OF	E. Murphy	260	.231	0	17	55	7	7	0	1.2	.899							
	2B	L. Malone	201	.204	1	17	117	109	20	9	5.7	.919							
	SS	J. Barry	194	.222	0	15	106	150	13	21	5.0	.952							
	C	W. McAvoy	184	.190	0	6	235	130	25	8	6.1	.936							

BATTING AND BASE RUNNING LEADERS

Batting Average

T. Cobb, DET	.369
E. Collins, CHI	.332
J. Fournier, CHI	.322
T. Speaker, BOS	.322
S. McInnis, PHI	.314

Slugging Average

J. Fournier, CHI	.491
T. Cobb, DET	.487
M. Kavanagh, DET	.452
J. Jackson, CLE, CHI	.445
B. Roth, CHI, CLE	.438

Home Runs

B. Roth, CHI, CLE	7
R. Oldring, PHI	6

Total Bases

T. Cobb, DET	274
S. Crawford, DET	264
B. Veach, DET	247
D. Pratt, STL	237
E. Collins, CHI	227

Runs Batted In

B. Veach, DET	112
S. Crawford, DET	112
T. Cobb, DET	99
S. Collins, CHI	85
J. Jackson, CLE, CHI	81

Stolen Bases

T. Cobb, DET	96
F. Maisel, NY	51
E. Collins, CHI	46
B. Shotton, STL	43
C. Milan, WAS	40

Hits

T. Cobb, DET	208
S. Crawford, DET	183
B. Veach, DET	178
T. Speaker, BOS	176

Base on Balls

E. Collins, CHI	119
B. Shotton, STL	118
D. Bush, DET	118
T. Cobb, DET	118

Home Run Percentage

B. Roth, CHI, CLE	1.8
R. Oldring, PHI	1.5
G. Burns, DET	1.3
M. Kavanagh, DET	1.2

Runs

T. Cobb, DET	144
E. Collins, CHI	118
O. Vitt, DET	116
T. Speaker, BOS	108

Doubles

B. Veach, DET	40
D. Lewis, BOS	31
T. Cobb, DET	31
D. Pratt, STL	31
S. Crawford, DET	31

Triples

S. Crawford, DET	19
J. Fournier, CHI	18
B. Roth, CHI, CLE	17
R. Chapman, CLE	17
S. Collins, CHI	17

PITCHING LEADERS

Winning Percentage

S. Wood, BOS	.750
R. Foster, BOS	.704
E. Shore, BOS	.704
B. Ruth, BOS	.692
J. Scott, CHI	.686

Earned Run Average

S. Wood, BOS	1.49
W. Johnson, WAS	1.55
E. Shore, BOS	1.64
J. Scott, CHI	2.03
R. Fisher, NY	2.11

Wins

W. Johnson, WAS	27
J. Scott, CHI	24
R. Faber, CHI	24
H. Dauss, DET	24
H. Coveleski, DET	22

Saves

C. Mays, BOS	7

Strikeouts

W. Johnson, WAS	203
R. Faber, CHI	182
J. Wyckoff, PHI	157
H. Coveleski, DET	150
W. Mitchell, CLE	149

Complete Games

W. Johnson, WAS	35
R. Caldwell, NY	31
H. Dauss, DET	27
J. Scott, CHI	23

Fewest Hits/9 Innings

D. Leonard, BOS	6.38
B. Ruth, BOS	6.86
S. Wood, BOS	6.86
W. Johnson, WAS	6.90

Shutouts

J. Scott, CHI	7
W. Johnson, WAS	7
G. Morton, CLE	6
J. Dubuc, DET	5
R. Foster, BOS	5

Fewest Walks/9 Innings

W. Johnson, WAS	1.50
J. Benz, CHI	1.62
R. Russell, CHI	1.84
E. Cicotte, CHI	1.93

Most Strikeouts/9 Inn.

D. Leonard, BOS	5.69
W. Mitchell, CLE	5.68
R. Faber, CHI	5.47
W. Johnson, WAS	5.43

Innings

W. Johnson, WAS	337
H. Coveleski, DET	313
H. Dauss, DET	310
R. Caldwell, NY	305

Games Pitched

R. Faber, CHI	50
H. Coveleski, DET	50
S. Jones, CLE	48
J. Scott, CHI	48

							Batting						Fielding			Pitching					
	W	L	PCT	GB	R	OR	2B	3B	HR	BA	SA	SB	E	DP	FA	CG	BB	SO	ShO	SV	ERA
Boston	101	50	.669		668	499	202	76	14	.260	.339	118	226	95	.964	82	446	634	19	15	2.39
Detroit	100	54	.649	2.5	**778**	597	**207**	94	23	**.268**	**.358**	**241**	258	107	.961	86	489	550	9	**19**	2.86
Chicago	93	61	.604	9.5	717	509	163	**102**	25	.258	.348	233	222	95	.965	92	**350**	635	17	9	2.43
Washington	85	68	.556	17	569	**491**	152	79	12	.244	.312	186	230	101	.964	87	455	**715**	**21**	13	**2.31**
New York	69	83	.454	32.5	584	588	167	50	**31**	.233	.305	198	**217**	118	**.966**	**101**	517	559	12	2	3.09
St. Louis	63	91	.409	39.5	521	679	166	65	19	.246	.315	202	335	**144**	.949	76	612	566	6	7	3.07
Cleveland	57	95	.375	44.5	539	670	169	79	20	.241	.317	138	280	82	.957	62	518	610	11	10	3.13
Philadelphia	43	109	.283	58.5	545	888	183	72	16	.237	.311	127	338	118	.947	78	827	588	6	2	4.33
					4921	4921	1409	617	160	.248	.326	1443	2106	860	.959	664	4214	4857	101	77	2.95

FEDERAL LEAGUE 1915

Chicago

W-86 L-66

Joe Tinker

POS	Player	AB	BA	HR	RBI	PO	A	E	DP	TC/G	FA	Pitcher	G	IP	W	L	SV	ERA
1B	F. Beck	373	.223	5	38	1073	42	9	57	9.6	.992	G. McConnell	44	303	**25**	10	1	2.20
2B	R. Zeider	494	.227	0	34	208	240	28	39	5.7	.941	C. Hendrix	40	285	16	15	4	3.00
SS	J. Smith	318	.217	4	30	187	246	46*	28	5.2	.904	M. Prendergast	42	254	14	12	0	2.48
3B	H. Fritz	236	.250	3	26	79	106	7	8	2.7	.964	T. Brown	35	236	17	8	3	2.09
RF	M. Flack	523	.314	3	45	226	24	8	5	1.9	.969	D. Black	25	121	6	7	0	2.45
CF	D. Zwilling	548	.286	13	**94**	356	20	8	6	2.6	.979	A. Brennan	19	106	3	9	0	3.74
LF	L. Mann	470	.306	4	58	269	17	9	3	2.3	.969							
C	A. Wilson	269	.305	7	31	391	96	10	6	5.7	.980							
C	B. Fischer	292	.329	4	50	324	100	12	9	5.4	.972							
2B	J. Farrell	222	.216	0	14	138	182	20	26	4.9	.941							
OF	C. Hanford	179	.240	0	22	66	2	2	0	1.6	.971							
3B	T. Wisterzil	164	.244	0	14	65	109	6	6	3.8	.967							

St. Louis

W-87 L-67

Fielder Jones

POS	Player	AB	BA	HR	RBI	PO	A	E	DP	TC/G	FA	Pitcher	G	IP	W	L	SV	ERA
1B	B. Borton	549	.286	3	83	**1571**	58	12	**91**	10.3	.993	D. Davenport	**55**	**393**	22	18	1	2.20
2B	B. Vaughn	521	.280	0	32	249	357	30	43	5.0	.953	D. Crandall	51	313	21	15	0	2.59
SS	E. Johnson	512	.240	7	67	348	477	51	64	5.8	.942	E. Plank	42	268	21	11	3	2.08
3B	C. Deal	223	.323	1	27	76	136	11	9	3.4	.951	B. Groom	37	209	11	11	1	3.27
RF	J. Tobin	**625**	.294	6	51	279	21	11	3	2.0	.965	D. Watson	33	136	9	9	0	3.98
CF	D. Drake	343	.265	1	41	180	10	5	2	2.0	.974							
LF	W. Miller	536	.306	1	63	299	16	12	3	2.1	.963							
C	G. Hartley	394	.274	1	50	565	151	**21**	11	6.5	.972							
3B	A. Kores	201	.234	1	22	80	161	10	12	4.2	.960							
C	H. Chapman	186	.199	1	29	293	79	4	6	7.1	.989							
OF	L. Kirby	178	.213	0	16	87	8	3	2	1.9	.969							
2B	A. Bridwell	175	.229	0	9	60	98	8	9	4.0	.952							

Pittsburgh

W-86 L-67

Rebel Oakes

POS	Player	AB	BA	HR	RBI	PO	A	E	DP	TC/G	FA	Pitcher	G	IP	W	L	SV	ERA
1B	E. Konetchy	576	.314	10	93	1536	81	10	83	10.7	**.994**	F. Allen	41	283	23	12	0	2.51
2B	S. Yerkes	434	.288	1	49	242	322	19	38	5.1	.967	E. Knetzer	41	279	18	15	3	2.58
SS	M. Berghammer	469	.243	0	33	286	359	39	55	5.2	**.943**	C. Rogge	37	254	17	12	0	2.55
3B	M. Mowrey	521	.280	1	49	174	**268**	19	15	3.1	**.959**	B. Hearn	29	176	6	11	0	3.38
RF	B. Kelly	524	.294	4	50	292	27	16	5	2.3	.952	C. Barger	34	153	10	7	5	2.29
CF	R. Oakes	580	.278	0	82	348	12	10	2	2.4	.973	W. Dickson	27	97	6	5	0	4.19
LF	A. Wickland	389	.301	1	30	234	11	8	0	2.3	.968							
C	C. Berry	292	.192	1	26	384	144	11	8	5.4	.980							
UT	J. Lewis	231	.264	0	26	150	152	11	20		.965							
C	P. O'Connor	219	.228	0	16	275	112	5	4	5.9	.987							

Kansas City

W-81 L-72

George Stovall

POS	Player	AB	BA	HR	RBI	PO	A	E	DP	TC/G	FA	Pitcher	G	IP	W	L	SV	ERA
1B	G. Stovall	480	.231	0	44	1417	**87**	20	61	**11.8**	.987	N. Cullop	44	302	22	11	2	2.44
2B	D. Kenworthy	396	.298	3	52	230	283	35	35	5.1	.936	G. Packard	42	282	20	11	2	2.68
SS	J. Rawlings	399	.216	2	24	209	366	46	36	5.2	.926	C. Johnson	46	281	18	17	1	2.75
3B	G. Perring	553	.259	6	67	135	226	16	14	3.7	.958	A. Main	35	230	13	14	3	2.54
RF	E. Gilmore	411	.285	1	47	215	17	5	4	2.0	.979	P. Henning	40	207	8	16	2	3.17
CF	C. Chadbourne	587	.227	1	35	308	24	7	7	2.2	.979							
LF	A. Shaw	448	.281	6	67	184	11	12	0	1.7	.942							
C	T. Easterly	309	.272	3	32	398	132	17	11	6.2	.969							
OF	A. Kruger	240	.237	2	26	116	8	2	2	1.9	.984							
S2	P. Goodwin	229	.236	0	16	106	180	24	17		.923							
C	D. Brown	227	.242	1	26	270	104	15	4	6.0	.961							
3B	B. Bradley	203	.187	0	9	55	95	8	4	2.6	.949							

Newark

W-80 L-72

Bill Phillips
W-26 L-27

Bill McKechnie
W-54 L-45

POS	Player	AB	BA	HR	RBI	PO	A	E	DP	TC/G	FA	Pitcher	G	IP	W	L	SV	ERA
1B	E. Huhn	415	.227	1	41	1001	53	16	68	10.6	.985	E. Reulbach	33	270	20	10	1	2.23
2B	F. LaPorte	550	.253	2	56	**330**	**431**	32	**69**	5.4	.960	E. Moseley	38	268	16	16	0	**1.91**
SS	J. Esmond	569	.258	5	62	**353**	**482**	54	67	5.7	.939	G. Kaiserling	41	261	13	14	2	2.24
3B	B. McKechnie	451	.251	1	43	**184**	226	19	17	3.7	.956	H. Moran	34	206	13	10	0	2.54
RF	V. Campbell	525	.310	1	44	200	15	12	3	1.8	.947	C. Falkenberg	25	172	9	11	1	3.24
CF	E. Roush	551	.298	3	60	331	20	10	3	2.5	.972	T. Seaton	12	75	3	6	1	2.28
LF	A. Scheer	546	.267	2	60	287	16	9	5	2.0	.971							
C	B. Rariden	444	.270	0	40	**709**	**238**	**21**	18	**6.8**	.978							
UT	G. Schaefer	154	.214	0	8	146	31	7	12		.962							

Buffalo

W-74 L-78

Harry Schlafly
W-13 L-28

Walter Blair
W-1 L-1

Harry Lord
W-60 L-49

POS	Player	AB	BA	HR	RBI	PO	A	E	DP	TC/G	FA	Pitcher	G	IP	W	L	SV	ERA
1B	H. Chase	567	.291	**17**	89	1460	83	**26**	84	11.0	.983	A. Schulz	42	310	21	14	0	3.08
2B	B. Louden	469	.281	4	48	191	262	10	36	5.3	.978	H. Bedient	53	269	15	18	**10**	3.17
SS	R. Roach	346	.269	2	31	212	297	22	38	5.8	.959	F. Anderson	36	240	19	13	0	2.51
3B	H. Lord	359	.270	1	21	85	158	14	13	2.8	.946	G. Krapp	38	231	9	19	0	3.51
RF	T. McDonald	251	.271	6	39	93	4	8	1	1.6	.924	R. Ford	21	127	5	9	0	4.52
CF	C. Engle	501	.261	3	71	211	8	7	2	2.3	.969							
LF	B. Meyer	333	.231	1	29	134	9	8	1	1.7	.947							
C	W. Blair	290	.224	2	20	404	150	11	15	5.8	**.981**							
OF	J. Dalton	437	.293	2	46	218	11	8	4	2.0	.966							
OF	S. Hofman	346	.234	0	27	132	16	6	5	1.9	.961							
23	T. Downey	282	.199	1	19	165	193	22	25		.942							
C	N. Allen	215	.205	0	17	347	110	**21**	8	6.0	.956							

Brooklyn

W-70 L-82

Lee Magee
W-53 L-64

John Ganzel
W-17 L-18

POS	Player	AB	BA	HR	RBI	PO	A	E	DP	TC/G	FA	Pitcher	G	IP	W	L	SV	ERA
1B	H. Myers	341	.287	1	36	961	56	10	52	9.6	.990	H. Finneran	37	215	12	13	0	2.80
2B	L. Magee	452	.323	4	49	271	321	**40**	46	**5.5**	.937	D. Marion	35	208	10	9	0	3.20
SS	F. Smith	385	.247	5	58	203	281	42	24	5.6	.920	T. Seaton	32	189	12	11	3	4.56
3B	A. Halt	524	.250	3	64	174	224	**30**	**23**	**3.9**	.930	J. Bluejacket	24	163	9	11	0	3.15
RF	G. Anderson	511	.264	2	39	200	16	10	5	1.7	.956	B. Upham	33	121	7	8	4	3.05
CF	B. Kauff	483	**.342**	12	83	317	32	15	7	2.7	.959	E. Lafitte	17	118	6	9	0	3.98
LF	C. Cooper	527	.294	2	63	274	26	13	3	2.6	.958	F. Wilson	18	102	1	7	0	3.78
C	G. Land	290	.259	0	22	314	114	18	13	5.5	.960	H. Wiltse	18	59	3	5	5	2.28
OF	S. Evans	216	.296	3	30	89	8	4	2	1.7	.960							
3B	T. Wisterzil	106	.311	0	21	45	67	6	7	3.8	.949							

FEDERAL LEAGUE 1915, *cont.*

Team	POS	Player	AB	BA	HR	RBI	PO	A	E	DP	TC/G	FA	Pitcher	G	IP	W	L	SV	ERA
Baltimore	1B	H. Swacina	301	.246	1	38	735	57	11	50	10.7	.986	J. Quinn	44	274	9	**22**	1	3.45
	2B	O. Knabe	320	.253	1	25	203	264	12	52	5.1	**.975**	G. Suggs	35	233	13	17	1	4.14
W-47 L-107	SS	M. Doolan	404	.186	2	21	303	400	40	67*	6.2*	.946	B. Bailey	36	190	5	19	0	4.63
	3B	J. Walsh	401	.302	9	60	131	190	22	15	3.2	.936	C. Bender	26	178	4	16	1	3.99
Otto Knabe	RF	S. Evans	340	.315	1	37	111	12	10	4	1.5	.925	A. Johnson	23	151	7	11	1	3.35
	CF	V. Duncan	531	.267	2	43	257	19	10	6	2.3	.965	G. LaClaire	18	84	2	8	0	2.46
	LF	G. Zinn	312	.269	5	43	139	11	8	4	1.8	.949							
	C	F. Owens	334	.251	3	28	462	146	15	**19**	6.3	.976							
	OF	S. McCandless	406	.214	5	34	209	16	13	**8**	2.3	.945							
	1B	J. Agler	214	.215	0	14	573	44	12	42	10.8	.981							
	UT	E. Kirkpatrick	171	.240	0	19	101	108	20	11		.913							

BATTING AND BASE RUNNING LEADERS

Batting Average

B. Kauff, BKN	.342
B. Fischer, CHI	.329
L. Magee, BKN	.323
E. Konetchy, PIT	.314
M. Flack, CHI	.314

Slugging Average

B. Kauff, BKN	.509
E. Konetchy, PIT	.483
H. Chase, BUF	.471
B. Fischer, CHI	.449
D. Zwilling, CHI	.442

Home Runs

H. Chase, BUF	17
D. Zwilling, CHI	13
B. Kauff, BKN	12
E. Konetchy, PIT	10
J. Walsh, BAL, STL	9

Total Bases

E. Konetchy, PIT	278
H. Chase, BUF	267
J. Tobin, STL	254
B. Kauff, BKN	246
D. Zwilling, CHI	242

Runs Batted In

D. Zwilling, CHI	94
E. Konetchy, PIT	93
H. Chase, BUF	89
B. Kauff, BKN	83
B. Borton, STL	83

Stolen Bases

B. Kauff, BKN	55
M. Mowrey, PIT	40
B. Kelly, PIT	38
M. Flack, CHI	37
L. Magee, BKN	34

Hits

J. Tobin, STL	184
E. Konetchy, PIT	181
S. Evans, BKN, BAL	171
B. Kauff, BKN	165
H. Chase, BUF	165

Base on Balls

B. Borton, STL	92
B. Kauff, BKN	85
M. Berghammer, PIT	83
W. Miller, STL	79

Home Run Percentage

H. Chase, BUF	3.0
A. Wilson, CHI	2.6
B. Kauff, BKN	2.5
D. Zwilling, CHI	2.4

Runs

B. Borton, STL	97
M. Berghammer, PIT	96
S. Evans, BKN, BAL	94
B. Kauff, BKN	92
J. Tobin, STL	92

Doubles

S. Evans, BKN, BAL	34
D. Zwilling, CHI	32
H. Chase, BUF	31
E. Konetchy, PIT	31

Triples

L. Mann, CHI	19
E. Konetchy, PIT	18
B. Kelly, PIT	17
E. Gilmore, KC	15

PITCHING LEADERS

Winning Percentage

G. McConnell, CHI	.714
T. Brown, CHI	.680
N. Cullop, KC	.667
E. Reulbach, NWK	.667
F. Allen, PIT	.657

Earned Run Average

E. Moseley, NWK	1.91
E. Plank, STL	2.08
T. Brown, CHI	2.09
G. McConnell, CHI	2.20
D. Davenport, STL	2.20

Wins

G. McConnell, CHI	25
F. Allen, PIT	23
N. Cullop, KC	22
D. Davenport, STL	22

Saves

H. Bedient, BUF	10
C. Barger, PIT	5
H. Wiltse, BKN	5
C. Hendrix, CHI	4
T. Seaton, BKN, NWK	4
B. Upham, BKN	4

Strikeouts

D. Davenport, STL	229
A. Schulz, BUF	160
G. McConnell, CHI	151
E. Plank, STL	147
F. Anderson, BUF	142
E. Moseley, NWK	142

Complete Games

D. Davenport, STL	30
C. Hendrix, CHI	26
A. Schulz, BUF	25
F. Allen, PIT	24

Fewest Hits/9 Innings

D. Davenport, STL	6.88
A. Main, KC	7.08
E. Plank, STL	7.11
T. Brown, CHI	7.20

Shutouts

D. Davenport, STL	10
E. Plank, STL	6
F. Allen, PIT	6

Fewest Walks/9 Innings

E. Plank, STL	1.81
C. Bender, BAL	1.87
N. Cullop, KC	1.99
J. Quinn, BAL	2.07

Most Strikeouts/9 Inn.

F. Anderson, BUF	5.33
D. Davenport, STL	5.25
E. Plank, STL	4.93
B. Bailey, BAL, CHI	4.91

Innings

D. Davenport, STL	393
D. Crandall, STL	313
A. Schulz, BUF	310
G. McConnell, CHI	303

Games Pitched

D. Davenport, STL	55
H. Bedient, BUF	53
D. Crandall, STL	51
C. Johnson, KC	46

	W	L	PCT	GB	R	OR	Batting						Fielding			Pitching					
							2B	3B	HR	BA	SA	SB	E	DP	FA	CG	BB	SO	ShO	SV	ERA
Chicago	86	66	.566		640	538	185	77	**50**	.257	.352	161	233	102	.964	97	402	576	21	9	2.64
St. Louis	87	67	.565		634	527	199	**81**	23	.261	.345	195	212	111	.967	94	396	**698**	**24**	7	2.73
Pittsburgh	86	67	.562	0.5	592	**524**	180	80	20	.262	.341	224	**182**	98	**.971**	88	441	517	16	11	2.79
Kansas City	81	72	.529	5.5	547	551	200	66	27	.244	.328	144	246	96	.962	95	**390**	526	16	10	2.82
Newark	80	72	.526	6	585	562	**210**	80	17	.252	.334	184	239	124	.963	**100**	453	581	16	5	**2.60**
Buffalo	74	78	.487	12	574	634	193	68	40	.249	.338	184	232	112	.964	79	553	594	14	11	3.38
Brooklyn	70	82	.461	16	**647**	673	205	75	36	**.268**	**.360**	**249**	290	103	.955	78	536	467	10	**13**	3.37
Baltimore	47	107	.305	40	550	760	196	53	36	.244	.325	128	273	**140**	.957	85	466	570	5	4	3.96
					4769	4769	1568	580	249	.255	.340	1469	1907	886	.963	716	3637	4529	122	70	3.04

NATIONAL LEAGUE 1916

Team	POS	Player	AB	BA	HR	RBI	PO	A	E	DP	TC/G	FA	Pitcher	G	IP	W	L	SV	ERA
Brooklyn	1B	J. Daubert	478	.316	3	33	1195	66	9	56	10.1	.993	J. Pfeffer	41	329	25	11	1	1.92
	2B	G. Cutshaw	581	.260	2	63	**361**	**467**	36	51	5.6	.958	L. Cheney	41	253	18	12	0	1.92
W-94 L-60	SS	I. Olson	351	.254	1	38	234	303	47	28	5.7	.920	S. Smith	36	219	14	10	1	2.34
	3B	M. Mowrey	495	.244	0	60	154	291	16	17	3.2	**.965**	R. Marquard	36	205	13	6	5	1.58
Wilbert Robinson	RF	J. Johnston	425	.252	1	26	224	16	9	3	2.3	.964	J. Coombs	27	159	13	8	0	2.66
	CF	H. Myers	412	.262	3	36	242	11	8	5	2.5	.969	W. Dell	32	155	8	9	1	2.26
	LF	Z. Wheat	568	.312	9	73	333	14	9	0	2.4	.975							
	C	C. Meyers	239	.247	0	21	389	95	8	9	6.6	.984							
	OF	C. Stengel	462	.279	8	53	206	14	8	4	1.9	.965							
	C	O. Miller	216	.255	1	17	311	85	13	6	5.9	.968							
	SS	O. O'Mara	193	.202	0	15	117	148	30	13	5.8	.898							
Philadelphia	1B	F. Luderus	508	.281	5	53	1499	71	**28**	83	10.9	.982	G. Alexander	48	**389**	**33**	12	3	**1.55**
	2B	B. Niehoff	548	.243	4	61	285	437	**49**	**65**	5.3	.936	E. Rixey	38	287	22	10	0	1.85
W-91 L-62	SS	D. Bancroft	477	.212	3	33	326	510	**60**	64	**6.3**	.933	A. Demaree	39	285	19	14	1	2.62
	3B	M. Stock	509	.281	1	43	128	213	16	22	3.1	.955	E. Mayer	28	140	7	7	0	3.15
Pat Moran	RF	G. Cravath	448	.283	11	70	182	17	7	2	1.6	.966	C. Bender	27	123	7	7	3	3.74
	CF	D. Paskert	555	.279	8	46	332	14	6	4	2.4	.983	G. McQuillan	21	62	1	7	2	2.76
	LF	P. Whitted	526	.281	6	68	285	13	11	3	2.3	.964							
	C	B. Killefer	286	.217	3	27	443	89	8	15	5.9	**.985**							
	C	E. Burns	219	.233	0	14	283	87	7	5	5.0	.981							

NATIONAL LEAGUE 1916, *cont.*

Team	POS	Player	AB	BA	HR	RBI	PO	A	E	DP	TC/G	FA	Pitcher	G	IP	W	L	SV	ERA
Boston	1B	E. Konetchy	566	.260	3	70	**1626**	**96**	18	**96**	11.0	.990	D. Rudolph	41	312	19	12	3	2.16
	2B	J. Evers	241	.216	0	15	98	175	14	29	4.0	.951	L. Tyler	34	249	17	9	1	2.02
W-89 L-63	SS	R. Maranville	604	.235	4	38	**386**	**515**	50	**79**	6.1	**.947**	P. Ragan	28	182	9	9	0	2.08
	3B	R. Smith	509	.259	3	60	**166**	**299**	**36**	15	3.3	.928	J. Barnes	33	163	6	15	1	2.37
George Stallings	RF	J. Wilhoit	383	.230	2	38	177	12	4	3	1.8	.979	T. Hughes	40	161	16	3	5	2.35
	CF	F. Snodgrass	382	.249	1	32	274	19	5	5	2.7	.983	A. Nehf	22	121	7	5	0	2.01
	LF	S. Magee	419	.241	3	54	220	6	5	0	1.9	.978	F. Allen	19	113	8	2	1	2.07
	C	H. Gowdy	349	.252	1	34	533	158	14	**19**	6.1	.980	E. Reulbach	21	109	7	6	0	2.47
	OF	Z. Collins	268	.209	1	18	114	10	7	3	1.7	.947							
	2B	D. Egan	238	.223	0	16	81	125	11	11	4.1	.949							
	20	E. Fitzpatrick	216	.213	1	18	114	96	9	14		.959							
	P	L. Tyler	93	.204	3	20	9	72	3	3	2.5	.964							
New York	1B	F. Merkle	401	.237	7	44	1183	58	20	61	11.3	.984	J. Tesreau	40	268	18	14	1	2.92
	2B	L. Doyle	441	.268	2	47	270	352	26	53	5.7	.960	P. Perritt	40	251	18	11	2	2.62
W-86 L-66	SS	A. Fletcher	500	.286	3	66	253	497	48	56	6.0	.940	R. Benton	38	239	16	8	2	2.87
	3B	B. McKechnie	260	.246	0	17	70	134	13	8	3.1	.940	F. Anderson	38	188	9	13	2	3.40
John McGraw	RF	D. Robertson	587	.307	**12**	69	248	17	11	5	1.9	.960	F. Schupp	30	140	9	3	1	0.90
	CF	B. Kauff	552	.264	9	74	329	22	14	6	2.4	.962	S. Sallee	15	112	9	4	0	1.37
	LF	G. Burns	**623**	.279	5	41	289	19	12	3	2.1	.963							
	C	B. Rariden	351	.222	1	29	**576**	144	21	10	**6.2**	.972							
	UT	B. Herzog	280	.261	0	25	140	238	17	28		.957							
Chicago	1B	V. Saier	498	.253	7	50	1622	74	27	78	**11.7**	.984	H. Vaughn	44	294	17	15	1	2.20
	2B	O. Knabe	145	.276	0	7	72	128	13	17	5.1	.939	C. Hendrix	36	218	8	16	2	2.68
W-67 L-86	SS	C. Wortman	234	.201	2	16	124	191	32	24	5.0	.908	J. Lavender	36	188	10	14	2	2.82
	3B	H. Zimmerman	398	.291	6	64*	88	198	21	11	4.1*	.932	G. McConnell	28	171	4	12	0	2.57
Joe Tinker	RF	M. Flack	465	.258	3	20	193	22	2	4	1.6	.991	G. Packard	37	155	10	6	5	2.78
	CF	C. Williams	405	.279	**12**	66	260	7	3	0	2.3	.989	M. Prendergast	35	152	6	11	2	2.31
	LF	L. Mann	415	.272	2	29	200	9	6	1	1.9	.972	T. Seaton	31	121	6	6	1	3.27
	C	J. Archer	205	.220	1	30	236	84	7	5	5.0	.979							
	UT	R. Zeider	345	.235	1	22	140	199	21	19		.942							
	OF	W. Schulte	230	.296	5	27	108	8	6	0	1.9	.951							
	SS	E. Mulligan	189	.153	0	9	116	200	40	27	6.1	.888							
	C	B. Fischer	179	.196	1	14	246	73	9	3	5.9	.973							
	OF	J. Kelly	169	.254	2	15	98	4	5	0	2.3	.953							
Pittsburgh	1B	D. Johnston	404	.213	0	39	1042	47	14	44	10.0	.987	A. Mamaux	45	310	21	15	2	2.53
	2B	J. Farmer	166	.271	0	14	53	77	10	6	4.5	.929	W. Cooper	42	246	12	11	2	1.87
W-65 L-89	SS	H. Wagner	432	.287	1	39	226	261	30	32	5.6	.942	F. Miller	30	173	7	10	1	2.29
	3B	D. Baird	430	.216	1	28	90	145	17	12	3.2	.933	B. Harmon	31	173	8	11	0	2.81
Nixey Callahan	RF	B. Hinchman	555	.315	4	76	222	8	9	2	1.9	.962	E. Kantlehner	34	165	5	15	2	3.16
	CF	M. Carey	599	.264	7	42	419	32	8	10	3.0	.983	E. Jacobs	34	153	6	10	0	2.94
	LF	D. Costello	159	.239	0	8	82	0	2	0	2.0	.976	B. Adams	16	72	2	9	0	5.72
	C	W. Schmidt	184	.190	2	15	232	88	8	6	5.8	.976							
	UT	J. Schultz	204	.260	0	22	75	86	22	3		.880							
	OF	W. Schulte	177	.254	0	14	89	2	3	0	2.0	.968							
	3B	H. Warner	168	.238	2	14	60	56	13	5	3.1	.899							
	20	C. Bigbee	164	.250	0	3	81	54	9	7		.938							
Cincinnati	1B	H. Chase	542	**.339**	4	82	932	37	14	66	10.0	.986	F. Toney	41	300	14	17	1	2.28
	2B	B. Louden	439	.219	1	32	238	345	19	48	5.6	**.968**	P. Schneider	44	274	10	19	1	2.69
W-60 L-93	SS	B. Herzog	281	.267	1	24	162	203	27	30	6.0	.931	A. Schulz	44	215	8	19	2	3.14
	3B	H. Groh	553	.269	2	28	123	252	17	**32**	3.6	.957	C. Mitchell	29	195	11	10	0	3.14
Buck Herzog	RF	T. Griffith	595	.266	2	61	238	28	9	5	1.8	.967	E. Knetzer	36	171	5	12	1	2.89
W-34 L-49	CF	E. Roush	272	.287	0	15	192	7	6	1	3.0	.971	E. Moseley	31	150	7	10	1	3.89
	LF	G. Neale	530	.262	0	20	307	20	9	6	2.5	.973							
Ivy Wingo	C	I. Wingo	347	.245	2	40	463	**170**	**28**	15	6.2	.958							
W-1 L-1	OF	R. Killefer	234	.244	1	18	138	6	5	2	2.2	.966							
	1B	F. Mollwitz	183	.224	0	16	482	23	10	29	9.5	.981							
Christy Mathewson	C	T. Clarke	177	.237	0	17	187	58	9	3	5.0	.965							
W-25 L-43																			
St. Louis	1B	D. Miller	505	.238	1	46	948	43	7	60	10.7	**.993**	L. Meadows	**51**	289	12	**23**	2	2.58
	2B	B. Betzel	510	.233	1	37	275	366	27	64	**5.9**	.960	R. Ames	45	228	11	16	**7**	2.64
W-60 L-93	SS	R. Corhan	295	.210	0	18	153	278	39	35	5.6	.917	B. Doak	29	192	12	8	0	2.63
	3B	R. Hornsby	495	.313	6	65	82	174	20	7	3.3	.928	B. Steele	29	148	5	15	0	3.41
Miller Huggins	RF	T. Long	403	.293	1	33	143	13	9	2	1.6	.945	H. Jasper	21	107	5	6	1	3.28
	CF	J. Smith	357	.244	6	34	212	12	12	4	2.0	.949	S. Williams	36	105	6	7	1	4.20
	LF	B. Bescher	561	.235	6	43	284	18	15	2	2.1	.953	M. Watson	18	103	4	6	0	3.06
	C	M. Gonzalez	331	.239	0	29	367	136	10	8	5.5	.981	S. Sallee	16	70	5	5	1	3.47
	C1	F. Snyder	406	.259	0	39	731	138	19	35		.979							
	OF	O. Wilson	355	.239	3	32	181	11	9	3	1.8	.955							
	3B	Z. Beck	184	.223	0	10	45	86	13	7	2.8	.910							

BATTING AND BASE RUNNING LEADERS

Batting Average

H. Chase, CIN	.339
J. Daubert, BKN	.316
B. Hinchman, PIT	.315
R. Hornsby, STL	.313
Z. Wheat, BKN	.312

Slugging Average

Z. Wheat, BKN	.461
H. Chase, CIN	.459
C. Williams, CHI	.459
R. Hornsby, STL	.444
G. Cravath, PHI	.440

Home Runs

C. Williams, CHI	12
D. Robertson, NY	12
G. Cravath, PHI	11
B. Kauff, NY	9
Z. Wheat, BKN	9

PITCHING LEADERS

Winning Percentage

T. Hughes, BOS	.842
G. Alexander, PHI	.733
J. Pfeffer, BKN	.694
E. Rixey, PHI	.688
R. Benton, NY	.667

Earned Run Average

G. Alexander, PHI	1.55
R. Marquard, BKN	1.58
E. Rixey, PHI	1.85
W. Cooper, PIT	1.87
J. Pfeffer, BKN	1.92

Wins

G. Alexander, PHI	33
J. Pfeffer, BKN	25
E. Rixey, PHI	22
A. Mamaux, PIT	21
A. Demaree, PHI	19
D. Rudolph, BOS	19

NATIONAL LEAGUE 1916, *cont.*

BATTING AND BASE RUNNING LEADERS

Total Bases

Z. Wheat, BKN	262
D. Robertson, NY	250
H. Chase, CIN	249
B. Hinchman, PIT	237
G. Burns, NY	229

Runs Batted In

H. Zimmerman, CHI, NY	83
H. Chase, CIN	82
B. Hinchman, PIT	76
B. Kauff, NY	74
Z. Wheat, BKN	73

Stolen Bases

M. Carey, PIT	63
B. Kauff, NY	40
B. Bescher, STL	39
G. Burns, NY	37
B. Herzog, CIN, NY	34

Hits

H. Chase, CIN	184
D. Robertson, NY	180
Z. Wheat, BKN	177
B. Hinchman, PIT	175

Base on Balls

H. Groh, CIN	84
V. Saier, CHI	79
D. Bancroft, PHI	74
B. Kauff, NY	68

Home Run Percentage

C. Williams, CHI	3.0
G. Cravath, PHI	2.5
D. Robertson, NY	2.0
C. Stengel, BKN	1.7

Runs

G. Burns, NY	105
M. Carey, PIT	90
D. Robertson, NY	88
H. Groh, CIN	85

Doubles

B. Niehoff, PHI	42
Z. Wheat, BKN	32
D. Paskert, PHI	30

Triples

B. Hinchman, PIT	16
E. Roush, NY, CIN	15
R. Hornsby, STL	15
B. Kauff, NY	15

PITCHING LEADERS

Saves

R. Ames, STL	7
R. Marquard, BKN	5
G. Packard, CHI	5
T. Hughes, BOS	5

Strikeouts

G. Alexander, PHI	167
L. Cheney, BKN	166
A. Mamaux, PIT	163
F. Toney, CIN	146
H. Vaughn, CHI	144

Complete Games

G. Alexander, PHI	38
J. Pfeffer, BKN	30
D. Rudolph, BOS	27
A. Mamaux, PIT	26
A. Demaree, PHI	25

Fewest Hits/9 Innings

L. Cheney, BKN	6.33
W. Cooper, PIT	6.91
F. Miller, PIT	7.02
P. Ragan, BOS	7.07

Shutouts

G. Alexander, PHI	16
L. Tyler, BOS	6
J. Pfeffer, BKN	6

Fewest Walks/9 Innings

D. Rudolph, BOS	1.10
G. Alexander, PHI	1.16
A. Demaree, PHI	1.52
S. Sallee, STL, NY	1.63

Most Strikeouts/9 Inn.

L. Cheney, BKN	5.91
C. Hendrix, CHI	4.83
A. Mamaux, PIT	4.73
R. Marquard, BKN	4.70

Innings

G. Alexander, PHI	389
J. Pfeffer, BKN	329
D. Rudolph, BOS	312
A. Mamaux, PIT	310

Games Pitched

L. Meadows, STL	51
G. Alexander, PHI	48
R. Ames, STL	45
A. Mamaux, PIT	45

							Batting						Fielding			Pitching					
	W	L	PCT	GB	R	OR	2B	3B	HR	BA	SA	SB	E	DP	FA	CG	BB	SO	ShO	SV	ERA
Brooklyn	94	60	.610		585	471	195	80	28	**.261**	**.345**	187	224	90	.965	96	372	634	22	9	**2.12**
Philadelphia	91	62	.595	2.5	581	489	**223**	53	42	.250	.341	149	234	119	.963	**97**	**295**	601	**26**	9	2.36
Boston	89	63	.586	4	542	**453**	166	73	22	.233	.307	141	**212**	124	**.967**	**97**	325	**644**	21	11	2.19
New York	86	66	.566	7	**597**	504	188	74	42	.253	.343	**206**	217	108	.966	88	310	638	22	11	2.60
Chicago	67	86	.438	26.5	520	541	194	56	**46**	.239	.325	133	286	104	.957	72	365	616	17	13	2.65
Pittsburgh	65	89	.422	29	484	586	147	**91**	20	.240	.316	173	260	97	.959	88	443	596	10	7	2.76
Cincinnati	60	93	.392	33.5	505	617	187	88	14	.254	.331	157	228	**126**	.965	86	458	569	7	6	3.10
St. Louis	60	93	.392	33.5	476	629	155	74	25	.243	.318	182	278	124	.957	58	445	529	11	**14**	3.14
					4290	4290	1455	589	239	.247	.328	1328	1939	892	.962	682	3013	4827	136	80	2.62

AMERICAN LEAGUE 1916

Boston

W-91 L-63

Bill Carrigan

POS	Player	AB	BA	HR	RBI	PO	A	E	DP	TC/G	FA	Pitcher	G	IP	W	L	SV	ERA
1B	D. Hoblitzell	417	.259	0	50	1225	67	15	64	10.4	.989	B. Ruth	44	324	23	12	1	**1.75**
2B	J. Barry	330	.203	0	20	200	282	13	30	5.3	.974	D. Leonard	48	274	18	12	6	2.36
SS	E. Scott	366	.232	0	27	217	339	19	36	4.8	**.967**	C. Mays	44	245	18	13	3	2.39
3B	L. Gardner	493	.308	2	62	149	278	21	24	3.0	.953	E. Shore	38	226	16	10	1	2.63
RF	H. Hooper	575	.271	1	37	266	19	10	5	2.0	.966	R. Foster	33	182	14	7	2	3.06
CF	T. Walker	467	.266	3	46	290	12	13	4	2.5	.959							
LF	D. Lewis	563	.268	1	56	306	16	10	4	2.2	.970							
C	P. Thomas	216	.264	1	21	321	86	8	7	4.6	.981							
S2	H. Janvrin	310	.223	0	26	166	225	27	37		.935							
C	H. Cady	162	.191	0	13	188	49	8	4	3.9	.967							

Chicago

W-89 L-65

Pants Rowland

POS	Player	AB	BA	HR	RBI	PO	A	E	DP	TC/G	FA	Pitcher	G	IP	W	L	SV	ERA
1B	J. Fournier	313	.240	3	44	855	49	20	47	10.9	.978	R. Russell	56	264	18	11	3	2.42
2B	E. Collins	545	.308	0	52	346	415	19	**75**	5.0	**.976**	L. Williams	43	224	13	7	1	2.89
SS	Z. Terry	269	.190	0	17	148	243	27	36	4.5	.935	R. Faber	35	205	17	9	1	2.02
3B	B. Weaver	582	.227	3	38	124	193	20	22	4.0	.941	E. Cicotte	44	187	15	7	5	1.78
RF	S. Collins	527	.243	0	42	238	20	11	6	2.0	.959	J. Scott	32	165	7	14	3	2.72
CF	H. Felsch	546	.300	7	70	340	19	7	5	2.6	.981	J. Benz	28	142	9	5	0	2.03
LF	J. Jackson	592	.341	3	78	290	17	8	5	2.0	.975	M. Wolfgang	27	127	4	6	0	1.98
C	R. Schalk	410	.232	0	41	**653**	**166**	10	25	**6.7**	**.988**	D. Danforth	28	94	6	5	2	3.27
1B	J. Ness	258	.267	1	34	655	31	15	45	10.2	.979							
3B	F. McMullin	187	.257	0	10	74	115	10	11	3.2	.950							

Detroit

W-87 L-67

Hughie Jennings

POS	Player	AB	BA	HR	RBI	PO	A	E	DP	TC/G	FA	Pitcher	G	IP	W	L	SV	ERA
1B	G. Burns	479	.286	4	73	1355	54	22	71	11.5	.985	H. Coveleski	44	324	21	11	2	1.97
2B	R. Young	528	.263	1	45	352	417	27	55	5.5	.966	H. Dauss	39	239	19	12	4	3.21
SS	D. Bush	550	.225	0	34	278	435	34	41	5.2	.954	J. Dubuc	36	170	10	10	1	2.96
3B	O. Vitt	597	.226	0	42	**208**	**385**	22	**32**	**4.1**	**.964**	B. James	30	152	8	12	1	3.68
RF	H. Heilmann	451	.282	2	76	110	10	6	0	1.6	.952	G. Cunningham	35	150	7	10	2	2.75
CF	T. Cobb	542	.371	5	68	325	18	17	9	2.5	.953	B. Boland	46	130	10	3	3	3.94
LF	B. Veach	566	.306	3	91	342	14	12	4	2.5	.967	W. Mitchell	23	128	7	5	0	3.31
C	O. Stanage	291	.237	0	30	387	108	15	11	5.4	.971							
OF	S. Crawford	322	.286	0	42	85	6	2	2	1.2	.978							

New York

W-80 L-74

Wild Bill Donovan

POS	Player	AB	BA	HR	RBI	PO	A	E	DP	TC/G	FA	Pitcher	G	IP	W	L	SV	ERA
1B	W. Pipp	545	.262	**12**	93	1513	99	13	**89**	11.0	.992	B. Shawkey	53	277	24	14	**8**	2.21
2B	J. Gedeon	435	.211	0	27	235	341	27	55	4.9	.955	G. Mogridge	30	195	6	12	0	2.31
SS	R. Peckinpaugh	552	.255	4	58	285	**468**	43	50	5.5	.946	R. Fisher	31	179	11	8	2	3.17
3B	F. Baker	360	.269	10	52	133	210	22	16	3.8	.940	A. Russell	34	171	6	10	6	3.20
RF	F. Gilhooley	223	.278	1	10	93	9	3	3	1.8	.971	N. Cullop	28	167	13	6	1	2.05
CF	L. Magee	510	.257	3	45	301	17	8	3	2.5	.975	R. Caldwell	21	166	5	12	0	2.99
LF	H. High	377	.263	1	28	216	14	12	2	2.2	.950	R. Keating	14	91	5	6	0	3.07
C	L. Nunamaker	260	.296	0	28	353	102	8	13	5.9	.983							
UT	P. Baumann	237	.287	1	25	93	64	8	8		.952							
C	R. Walters	203	.266	0	23	346	102	12	13	7.1	.974							
OF	R. Oldring	158	.234	1	12	66	1	3	3	1.6	.957							
03	F. Maisel	158	.228	0	7	60	26	4	4		.956							

AMERICAN LEAGUE 1916, *cont.*

St. Louis

W-79 L-75

Fielder Jones

POS	Player	AB	BA	HR	RBI	PO	A	E	DP	TC/G	FA	Pitcher	G	IP	W	L	SV	ERA
1B	G. Sisler	580	.305	4	76	1507	83	**24**	85	**11.6**	.985	D. Davenport	**59**	291	12	11	2	2.85
2B	D. Pratt	596	.267	5	**103**	**438**	**491**	**33**	74	**6.1**	.966	C. Weilman	46	276	17	18	2	2.15
SS	D. Lavan	343	.236	0	19	217	386	32	52	**6.0**	.950	E. Plank	37	236	16	15	3	2.33
3B	J. Austin	411	.207	1	28	128	274	26	21	3.5	.939	B. Groom	41	217	13	9	4	2.57
RF	W. Miller	485	.266	1	50	215	12	14	0	1.8	.942	E. Koob	33	167	11	8	2	2.54
CF	A. Marsans	528	.254	1	60	351	25	9	7	2.6	.977	E. Hamilton	23	95	5	7	0	3.30
LF	B. Shotton	**618**	.282	1	36	357	25	20	6	2.6	.950							
C	H. Severeid	293	.273	0	34	313	99	10	6	4.7	.976							
SS	E. Johnson	236	.229	0	19	115	192	21	19	5.5	.936							
C	G. Hartley	222	.225	0	12	263	98	12	10	5.0	.968							

Cleveland

W-77 L-77

Lee Fohl

POS	Player	AB	BA	HR	RBI	PO	A	E	DP	TC/G	FA	Pitcher	G	IP	W	L	SV	ERA
1B	C. Gandil	533	.259	0	72	**1557**	**105**	9	84	11.5	**.995**	J. Bagby	48	279	16	16	5	2.55
2B	I. Howard	246	.187	0	23	108	219	10	17	5.2	.970	S. Coveleski	45	232	15	13	3	3.41
SS	B. Wambsganss	475	.246	0	45	208	325	43	38	5.4	.925	G. Morton	27	150	12	8	0	2.89
3B	T. Turner	428	.262	0	38	87	173	10	10	3.5	.963	E. Klepfer	31	143	6	6	2	2.52
RF	B. Roth	409	.286	4	72	166	20	9	6	1.7	.954	F. Coumbe	29	120	7	5	0	2.02
CF	T. Speaker	546	**.386**	2	83	359	25	10	10	2.6	.975	A. Gould	30	107	5	7	1	2.53
LF	J. Graney	589	.241	5	54	309	22	14	5	2.2	.959	F. Beebe	20	101	5	3	2	2.41
C	S. O'Neill	378	.235	0	29	540	154	**21**	**36**	5.6	.971							
UT	R. Chapman	346	.231	0	27	207	310	32	35		.942							
OF	E. Smith	213	.277	3	40	77	7	3	3	1.5	.966							

Washington

W-76 L-77

Clark Griffith

POS	Player	AB	BA	HR	RBI	PO	A	E	DP	TC/G	FA	Pitcher	G	IP	W	L	SV	ERA
1B	J. Judge	336	.220	0	31	935	69	14	53	9.9	.986	W. Johnson	48	**371**	**25**	20	1	1.89
2B	R. Morgan	315	.267	1	29	133	222	16	34	4.5	.957	B. Gallia	49	284	17	12	2	2.76
SS	G. McBride	466	.227	1	36	282	438	32	53	5.4	.957	H. Harper	36	250	14	10	0	2.45
3B	E. Foster	606	.252	1	44	104	143	19	14	3.2	.929	D. Ayers	43	157	5	9	2	3.78
RF	D. Moeller	240	.246	1	23	94	11	4	3	1.7	.963	J. Boehling	27	140	9	11	0	3.09
CF	C. Milan	565	.273	1	45	372	27	16	8	2.8	.961	J. Shaw	26	106	3	8	1	2.62
LF	H. Shanks	471	.253	1	48	203	19	3	4	2.6	.987							
C	J. Henry	305	.249	0	46	538	124	13	17	5.8	.981							
1C	B. Williams	202	.267	0	20	388	30	6	21		.986							
OF	S. Rice	197	.299	1	17	83	5	4	1	2.0	.957							
3B	J. Leonard	168	.274	0	14	53	65	6	6	3.0	.952							
OF	E. Smith	168	.214	2	27	75	5	1	1	1.8	.988							
OF	H. Rondeau	162	.222	1	28	110	4	5	0	2.5	.958							

Philadelphia

W-36 L-117

Connie Mack

POS	Player	AB	BA	HR	RBI	PO	A	E	DP	TC/G	FA	Pitcher	G	IP	W	L	SV	ERA
1B	S. McInnis	512	.295	1	60	1404	96	12	87	10.8	.992	E. Myers	44	315	14	23	1	3.66
2B	N. Lajoie	426	.246	2	35	254	325	16	61	5.7	.973	J. Bush	40	287	15	**24**	0	2.57
SS	W. Witt	563	.245	2	36	**299**	423	**78**	**59**	5.6	.902	J. Nabors	40	213	1	20	1	3.47
3B	C. Pick	398	.241	0	20	143	230	**42**	25	3.8	.899	T. Sheehan	38	188	1	16	0	3.69
RF	J. Walsh	390	.233	1	27	172	13	12	4	1.7	.939	J. Johnson	12	84	2	8	0	3.74
CF	A. Strunk	544	.316	3	49	291	20	7	5	2.2	.978							
LF	R. Oldring	146	.247	0	14	64	6	8	2	2.0	.897							
C	B. Meyer	138	.232	1	12	217	79	12	5	6.4	.961							
OC	W. Schang	338	.266	7	38	266	77	19	6		.948							
UT	L. McElwee	155	.265	0	10	57	68	14	7		.899							

BATTING AND BASE RUNNING LEADERS

Batting Average
- T. Speaker, CLE .386
- T. Cobb, DET .371
- J. Jackson, CHI .341
- A. Strunk, PHI .316
- L. Gardner, BOS .308

Slugging Average
- T. Speaker, CLE .502
- J. Jackson, CHI .495
- T. Cobb, DET .493
- B. Veach, DET .433
- F. Baker, NY .428

Home Runs
- W. Pipp, NY 12
- F. Baker, NY 10
- W. Schang, PHI 7
- H. Felsch, CHI 7

Total Bases
- J. Jackson, CHI 293
- T. Speaker, CLE 274
- T. Cobb, DET 267
- B. Veach, DET 245
- H. Felsch, CHI 233
- D. Pratt, STL 233

Runs Batted In
- D. Pratt, STL 103
- W. Pipp, NY 93
- B. Veach, DET 91
- T. Speaker, CLE 83
- J. Jackson, CHI 78

Stolen Bases
- T. Cobb, DET 68
- A. Marsans, STL 46
- B. Shotton, STL 41
- E. Collins, CHI 40
- T. Speaker, CLE 35

Hits
- T. Speaker, CLE 211
- J. Jackson, CHI 202
- T. Cobb, DET 201
- G. Sisler, STL 177

Base on Balls
- B. Shotton, STL 111
- J. Graney, CLE 102
- E. Collins, CHI 86
- T. Speaker, CLE 82

Home Run Percentage
- F. Baker, NY 2.8
- W. Pipp, NY 2.2
- W. Schang, PHI 2.1
- E. Smith, CLE, WAS 1.3

Runs
- T. Cobb, DET 113
- J. Graney, CLE 106
- T. Speaker, CLE 102
- B. Shotton, STL 97

Doubles
- T. Speaker, CLE 41
- J. Graney, CLE 41
- J. Jackson, CHI 40
- D. Pratt, STL 35

Triples
- J. Jackson, CHI 21
- E. Collins, CHI 17
- W. Witt, PHI 15
- B. Veach, DET 15

PITCHING LEADERS

Winning Percentage
- E. Cicotte, CHI .682
- B. Ruth, BOS .657
- H. Coveleski, DET .656
- R. Faber, CHI .654
- B. Shawkey, NY .632

Earned Run Average
- B. Ruth, BOS 1.75
- E. Cicotte, CHI 1.78
- W. Johnson, WAS 1.89
- H. Coveleski, DET 1.97
- R. Faber, CHI 2.02

Wins
- W. Johnson, WAS 25
- B. Shawkey, NY 24
- B. Ruth, BOS 23
- H. Coveleski, DET 21
- H. Dauss, DET 19

Saves
- B. Shawkey, NY 8
- A. Russell, NY 6
- D. Leonard, BOS 6
- E. Cicotte, CHI 5
- J. Bagby, CLE 5

Strikeouts
- W. Johnson, WAS 228
- E. Myers, PHI 182
- B. Ruth, BOS 170
- J. Bush, PHI 157
- H. Harper, WAS 149

Complete Games
- W. Johnson, WAS 36
- E. Myers, PHI 31
- J. Bush, PHI 25
- B. Ruth, BOS 23
- H. Coveleski, DET 22

Fewest Hits/9 Innings
- B. Ruth, BOS 6.40
- B. Shawkey, NY 6.64
- E. Cicotte, CHI 6.64
- J. Bush, PHI 6.97

Shutouts
- B. Ruth, BOS 9
- J. Bush, PHI 8
- D. Leonard, BOS 6
- R. Russell, CHI 5

Fewest Walks/9 Innings
- R. Russell, CHI 1.43
- H. Coveleski, DET 1.75
- E. Shore, BOS 1.95
- W. Johnson, WAS 1.99

Most Strikeouts/9 Inn.
- L. Williams, CHI 5.54
- W. Johnson, WAS 5.53
- H. Harper, WAS 5.37
- E. Myers, PHI 5.20

Innings
- W. Johnson, WAS 371
- H. Coveleski, DET 324
- B. Ruth, BOS 324
- E. Myers, PHI 315

Games Pitched
- D. Davenport, STL 59
- R. Russell, CHI 56
- B. Shawkey, NY 53
- B. Gallia, WAS 49

AMERICAN LEAGUE 1916, *cont.*

	W	L	PCT	GB	R	OR	Batting 2B	3B	HR	BA	SA	SB	Fielding E	DP	FA	Pitching CG	BB	SO	ShO	SV	ERA
Boston	91	63	.591		550	**480**	196	56	14	.248	.318	129	**183**	108	**.972**	76	463	584	**24**	16	2.48
Chicago	89	65	.578	2	601	497	194	**100**	17	.251	.339	197	203	**134**	.968	73	**405**	644	20	15	**2.36**
Detroit	87	67	.565	4	**670**	595	202	96	17	**.264**	**.350**	190	211	110	.968	81	578	531	8	13	2.97
New York	80	74	.519	11	577	561	194	59	**35**	.246	.326	179	219	119	.967	84	476	616	12	**17**	2.77
St. Louis	79	75	.513	12	588	545	181	50	14	.245	.307	**234**	248	120	.963	74	478	505	9	13	2.58
Cleveland	77	77	.500	14	630	602	**233**	66	16	.250	.331	160	232	130	.965	65	467	537	9	16	2.89
Washington	76	77	.497	14.5	536	543	170	60	12	.242	.306	185	231	119	.964	84	490	**706**	11	7	2.66
Philadelphia	36	117	.235	54.5	447	776	169	65	19	.242	.313	151	314	126	.951	**94**	715	575	11	3	3.84
					4599	4599	1539	552	144	.249	.324	1425	1841	966	.965	631	4072	4698	104	100	2.82

NATIONAL LEAGUE 1917

New York

W-98 L-56

John McGraw

POS	Player	AB	BA	HR	RBI	PO	A	E	DP	TC/G	FA	Pitcher	G	IP	W	L	SV	ERA
1B	W. Holke	527	.277	2	55	**1635**	70	19	**104**	11.3	.989	F. Schupp	36	272	21	7	0	1.95
2B	B. Herzog	417	.235	2	31	251	327	32	60	5.4	.948	S. Sallee	34	216	18	7	**4**	2.17
SS	A. Fletcher	557	.260	4	56	276	**565**	39	71	5.8	**.956**	R. Benton	35	215	15	9	3	2.72
3B	H. Zimmerman	585	.297	5	**102**	148	**349**	28	22	3.5	.947	P. Perritt	35	215	17	7	1	1.88
RF	D. Robertson	532	.259	**12**	54	266	12	17	1	2.1	.942	J. Tesreau	33	184	13	8	2	3.09
CF	B. Kauff	559	.308	5	68	357	12	9	4	2.5	.976	F. Anderson	38	162	8	8	3	1.44
LF	G. Burns	597	.302	5	45	325	16	9	4	2.3	.974							
C	B. Rariden	266	.271	0	25	354	74	13	7	4.4	.971							
C	L. McCarty	162	.247	2	19	235	43	6	0	5.3	.979							

Philadelphia

W-87 L-65

Pat Moran

POS	Player	AB	BA	HR	RBI	PO	A	E	DP	TC/G	FA	Pitcher	G	IP	W	L	SV	ERA
1B	F. Luderus	522	.261	5	72	1597	**91**	16	91	11.1	.991	G. Alexander	45	**388**	**30**	13	0	**1.86**
2B	B. Niehoff	361	.255	2	42	203	326	31	37	5.8	.945	E. Rixey	39	281	16	**21**	1	2.27
SS	D. Bancroft	478	.243	4	43	274	439	49	56	**6.3**	.936	J. Oeschger	42	262	16	14	0	2.75
3B	M. Stock	564	.264	3	53	132	255	24	16	3.1	.942	E. Mayer	28	160	11	6	0	2.76
RF	G. Cravath	503	.280	**12**	83	209	17	13	3	1.7	.946	J. Lavender	28	129	5	8	1	3.55
CF	D. Paskert	546	.251	4	43	286	19	5	4	2.2	.984	C. Bender	20	113	8	2	2	1.67
LF	P. Whitted	553	.280	3	70	275	19	7	0	2.1	.977							
C	B. Killefer	409	.274	0	31	**617**	138	12	**14**	**6.4**	**.984**							
2B	J. Evers	183	.224	1	12	83	145	4	15	4.7	.983							

St. Louis

W-82 L-70

Miller Huggins

POS	Player	AB	BA	HR	RBI	PO	A	E	DP	TC/G	FA	Pitcher	G	IP	W	L	SV	ERA
1B	G. Paulette	332	.265	0	34	1130	45	8	82	12.7*	.993	B. Doak	44	281	16	20	2	3.10
2B	D. Miller	544	.248	2	45	219	308	22	56	6.0	.960	L. Meadows	43	265	15	9	2	3.09
SS	R. Hornsby	523	.327	8	66	268	527	52	**82**	5.9	.939	R. Ames	43	209	15	10	3	2.71
3B	D. Baird	364	.253	0	24	110	259	23	24	3.8*	.941	M. Watson	41	161	10	13	0	3.51
RF	T. Long	530	.232	3	41	173	9	16	2	1.4	.919	G. Packard	34	153	9	6	2	2.47
CF	J. Smith	462	.297	3	34	233	12	10	6	2.0	.961	O. Horstmann	35	138	9	4	1	3.45
LF	W. Cruise	529	.295	5	59	285	15	11	6	2.0	.965	M. Goodwin	14	85	6	4	0	2.21
C	F. Snyder	313	.236	1	33	341	134	12	10	5.2	.975							
2B	B. Betzel	328	.216	1	17	159	217	15	40	5.2	.962							
C	M. Gonzalez	290	.262	1	28	241	97	8	8	5.1	.977							
3B	F. Smith	165	.182	1	17	62	110	9	5	3.5	.950							

Cincinnati

W-78 L-76

Christy Mathewson

POS	Player	AB	BA	HR	RBI	PO	A	E	DP	TC/G	FA	Pitcher	G	IP	W	L	SV	ERA
1B	H. Chase	**602**	.277	4	86	1499	80	**28**	100	10.6	.983	P. Schneider	46	342	20	19	0	1.98
2B	D. Shean	442	.210	2	35	**332**	**412**	30	**69**	**5.9**	.961	F. Toney	43	340	24	16	1	2.20
SS	L. Kopf	573	.255	2	26	276	470	**68**	59	5.6	.916	M. Regan	32	216	11	10	0	2.71
3B	H. Groh	599	.304	1	53	**178**	331	18	28	3.4	**.966**	C. Mitchell	32	159	9	15	1	3.22
RF	T. Griffith	363	.270	1	45	165	19	5	3	1.9	.974	H. Eller	37	152	10	5	1	2.36
CF	E. Roush	522	**.341**	4	67	335	15	14	0	2.7	.962	J. Ring	24	88	3	7	2	4.40
LF	G. Neale	385	.294	3	33	216	13	5	1	2.0	.979							
C	I. Wingo	399	.266	2	39	459	**151**	**21**	12	5.3	.967							
OF	J. Thorpe	251	.247	4	36	143	7	6	2	2.3	.962							
OF	S. Magee	137	.321	0	23	83	7	1	1	2.2	.989							

Chicago

W-74 L-80

Fred Mitchell

POS	Player	AB	BA	HR	RBI	PO	A	E	DP	TC/G	FA	Pitcher	G	IP	W	L	SV	ERA
1B	F. Merkle	549	.266	3	57	1415	66	26	84	10.8	.983	H. Vaughn	41	296	23	13	0	2.01
2B	L. Doyle	476	.254	6	61	300	348	**33**	54	5.3	.952	P. Douglas	**51**	293	14	20	1	2.55
SS	C. Wortman	190	.174	0	9	85	162	22	26	4.1	.918	C. Hendrix	40	215	10	12	1	2.60
3B	C. Deal	449	.254	0	47	151	254	18	**31**	3.3	.957	A. Demaree	24	141	5	9	1	2.55
RF	M. Flack	447	.248	0	21	199	14	12	3	1.9	.947	P. Carter	23	113	5	8	2	3.26
CF	C. Williams	468	.241	5	42	340	23	15	4	2.8	.960	V. Aldridge	30	107	6	6	2	3.12
LF	L. Mann	444	.273	1	44	203	20	11	2	2.0	.953	M. Prendergast	35	99	3	6	1	3.35
C	A. Wilson	211	.213	2	25	361	92	15	5	6.2	.968	T. Seaton	16	75	5	4	1	2.53
UT	R. Zeider	354	.243	0	27	151	226	28	35		.931							
OF	H. Wolter	353	.249	0	28	131	14	9	5	1.6	.942							
C	R. Elliott	223	.251	0	28	307	93	13	9	5.7	.969							
SS	P. Kilduff	202	.277	0	15	91	128	19	19	4.7	.920							

Boston

W-72 L-81

George Stallings

POS	Player	AB	BA	HR	RBI	PO	A	E	DP	TC/G	FA	Pitcher	G	IP	W	L	SV	ERA
1B	E. Konetchy	474	.272	2	54	1351	70	8	65	11.1	**.994**	J. Barnes	50	295	13	**21**	1	2.68
2B	J. Rawlings	371	.256	2	31	177	290	11	40	5.0	**.977**	D. Rudolph	32	243	13	13	0	3.41
SS	R. Maranville	561	.260	3	43	**341**	474	46	67	6.1	.947	L. Tyler	32	239	14	12	1	2.52
3B	R. Smith	505	.295	2	62	141	264	**33**	27	3.0	.925	A. Nehf	38	233	17	8	0	2.16
RF	W. Rehg	341	.270	1	31	122	9	6	2	1.6	.956	P. Ragan	30	148	6	9	1	2.93
CF	R. Powell	357	.272	4	30	231	14	6	2	2.9	.976	F. Allen	29	112	3	11	0	3.94
LF	J. Kelly	445	.222	3	36	284	16	17	8	2.7	.946							
C	W. Tragesser	297	.222	0	25	433	105	16	11	5.7	.971							
OF	S. Magee	246	.256	1	29	137	7	7	3	2.3	.954							
OF	J. Wilhoit	186	.274	1	10	70	7	6	1	1.6	.928							
UT	E. Fitzpatrick	178	.253	0	17	71	67	15	5		.902							
C	H. Gowdy	154	.214	0	14	204	75	9	3	5.9	.969							

NATIONAL LEAGUE 1917, *cont.*

Brooklyn

W-70 L-81

Wilbert Robinson

POS	Player	AB	BA	HR	RBI	PO	A	E	DP	TC/G	FA	Pitcher	G	IP	W	L	SV	ERA
1B	J. Daubert	468	.261	2	30	1188	82	12	59	10.3	.991	J. Pfeffer	30	266	11	15	0	2.23
2B	G. Cutshaw	487	.259	4	49	319	377	27	43	5.4	.963	L. Cadore	37	264	13	13	3	2.45
SS	I. Olson	580	.269	2	38	283	431	45	53	5.7	.941	R. Marquard	37	233	19	12	0	2.55
3B	M. Mowrey	271	.214	0	25	73	164	12	13	3.1	.952	S. Smith	38	211	12	12	3	3.32
RF	C. Stengel	549	.257	6	73	256	30	9	9	2.0	.969	L. Cheney	35	210	8	12	2	2.35
CF	J. Hickman	370	.219	6	36	222	22	15	6	2.6	.942	J. Coombs	31	141	7	11	0	3.96
LF	Z. Wheat	362	.312	1	41	216	12	5	5	2.1	.979							
C	O. Miller	274	.230	1	17	412	95	11	8	5.7	.979							
UT	H. Myers	471	.268	1	41	410	102	19	15		.964							
OF	J. Johnston	330	.270	0	25	150	8	7	1	1.8	.958							
3B	F. O'Rourke	198	.237	0	15	72	134	10	6	3.7	.954							

Pittsburgh

W-51 L-103

Nixey Callahan
W-20 L-40

Honus Wagner
W-1 L-4

Hugo Bezdek
W-30 L-59

POS	Player	AB	BA	HR	RBI	PO	A	E	DP	TC/G	FA	Pitcher	G	IP	W	L	SV	ERA
1B	H. Wagner	230	.265	0	24	433	22	7	27	9.8	.985	W. Cooper	40	298	17	11	1	2.36
2B	J. Pitler	382	.233	0	23	283	277	20	46	5.5	.966	E. Jacobs	38	227	6	19	2	2.81
SS	C. Ward	423	.236	0	43	206	312	50	49	5.1	.912	F. Miller	38	224	10	19	1	3.13
3B	T. Boeckel	219	.265	0	23	71	116	13	9	3.2	.935	B. Grimes	37	194	3	16	0	3.53
RF	L. King	381	.249	1	35	198	16	7	6	2.2	.968	B. Steele	27	180	5	11	1	2.76
CF	M. Carey	588	.296	1	51	440	28	10	8	3.1	.979	H. Carlson	34	161	7	11	1	2.90
LF	C. Bigbee	469	.239	0	21	235	9	10	2	2.4	.961	A. Mamaux	16	86	2	11	0	5.25
C	B. Fischer	245	.286	3	25	272	77	14	8	5.3	.961							
OF	B. Hinchman	244	.189	2	29	99	5	6	0	2.3	.945							
C	W. Schmidt	183	.246	0	17	229	84	7	9	5.2	.978							

BATTING AND BASE RUNNING LEADERS

Batting Average
E. Roush, CIN .341
R. Hornsby, STL .327
Z. Wheat, BKN .312
B. Kauff, NY .308
H. Groh, CIN .304

Slugging Average
R. Hornsby, STL .484
G. Cravath, PHI .473
E. Roush, CIN .454
Z. Wheat, BKN .423
G. Burns, NY .412

Home Runs
G. Cravath, PHI 12
D. Robertson, NY 12
R. Hornsby, STL 8
J. Hickman, BKN 6
L. Doyle, CHI 6
C. Stengel, BKN 6

Total Bases
R. Hornsby, STL 253
G. Burns, NY 246
H. Groh, CIN 246
G. Cravath, PHI 238
E. Roush, CIN 237
H. Chase, CIN 237

Runs Batted In
H. Zimmerman, NY 102
H. Chase, CIN 86
G. Cravath, PHI 83
C. Stengel, BKN 73
F. Luderus, PHI 72

Stolen Bases
M. Carey, PIT 46
G. Burns, NY 40
B. Kauff, NY 30
R. Maranville, BOS 27
D. Baird, PIT, STL 26

Hits
H. Groh, CIN 182
G. Burns, NY 180
E. Roush, CIN 178
H. Zimmerman, NY 174
M. Carey, PIT 174

Base on Balls
G. Burns, NY 75
H. Groh, CIN 71
G. Cravath, PHI 70
F. Luderus, PHI 65

Home Run Percentage
G. Cravath, PHI 2.4
D. Robertson, NY 2.3
J. Hickman, BKN 1.6
R. Hornsby, STL 1.5

Runs
G. Burns, NY 103
H. Groh, CIN 91
B. Kauff, NY 89
R. Hornsby, STL 86

Doubles
H. Groh, CIN 39
R. Smith, BOS 31
F. Merkle, BKN, CHI 31
G. Cravath, PHI 29

Triples
R. Hornsby, STL 17
G. Cravath, PHI 16
H. Chase, CIN 15
E. Roush, CIN 14
T. Long, STL 14

PITCHING LEADERS

Winning Percentage
F. Schupp, NY .750
S. Sallee, NY .720
P. Perritt, NY .708
G. Alexander, PHI .698
A. Nehf, BOS .680

Earned Run Average
G. Alexander, PHI 1.86
P. Perritt, NY 1.88
F. Schupp, NY 1.95
P. Schneider, CIN 1.98
H. Vaughn, CHI 2.01

Wins
G. Alexander, PHI 30
F. Toney, CIN 24
H. Vaughn, CHI 23
F. Schupp, NY 21
P. Schneider, CIN 20

Saves
S. Sallee, NY 4
L. Cadore, BKN 3
R. Benton, NY 3
F. Anderson, NY 3
S. Smith, BKN 3
R. Ames, STL 3

Strikeouts
G. Alexander, PHI 201
H. Vaughn, CHI 195
P. Douglas, CHI 151
F. Schupp, NY 147
P. Schneider, CIN 142

Complete Games
G. Alexander, PHI 35
F. Toney, CIN 31
J. Barnes, BOS 27
H. Vaughn, CHI 27
F. Schupp, NY 25
P. Schneider, CIN 25

Fewest Hits/9 Innings
F. Schupp, NY 6.68
A. Nehf, BOS 7.60
J. Pfeffer, BKN 7.61
L. Tyler, BOS 7.64

Shutouts
G. Alexander, PHI 8
W. Cooper, PIT 7
F. Toney, CIN 7
F. Schupp, NY 6

Fewest Walks/9 Innings
G. Alexander, PHI 1.35
S. Sallee, NY 1.42
A. Nehf, BOS 1.50
J. Barnes, BOS 1.53

Most Strikeouts/9 Inn.
H. Vaughn, CHI 5.94
F. Schupp, NY 4.86
G. Alexander, PHI 4.67
P. Douglas, CHI 4.63

Innings
G. Alexander, PHI 388
P. Schneider, CIN 342
F. Toney, CIN 340
W. Cooper, PIT 298

Games Pitched
P. Douglas, CHI 51
J. Barnes, BOS 50
P. Schneider, CIN 46
G. Alexander, PHI 45

							Batting						Fielding			Pitching					
	W	L	PCT	GB	R	OR	2B	3B	HR	BA	SA	SB	E	DP	FA	CG	BB	SO	ShO	SV	ERA
New York	98	56	.636		**635**	**457**	170	71	**39**	.261	.343	**162**	**208**	122	**.968**	92	**327**	551	18	**14**	**2.27**
Philadelphia	87	65	.572	10	578	500	**225**	60	38	.248	.339	109	212	112	.967	103	**327**	617	**22**	4	2.46
St. Louis	82	70	.539	15	531	567	159	93	26	.250	.333	159	221	**153**	.967	66	421	502	16	10	3.03
Cincinnati	78	76	.506	20	601	611	196	**100**	26	**.264**	**.354**	153	247	120	.962	95	404	492	12	6	2.66
Chicago	74	80	.481	24	552	567	194	67	17	.239	.313	127	267	121	.959	79	374	**654**	16	9	2.62
Boston	72	81	.471	25.5	536	552	169	75	22	.246	.320	155	224	122	.966	**105**	371	593	21	3	2.77
Brooklyn	70	81	.464	26.5	511	559	159	78	25	.247	.322	130	245	102	.962	99	405	582	7	9	2.78
Pittsburgh	51	103	.331	47	464	595	160	61	9	.238	.298	150	251	119	.961	84	432	509	17	6	3.01
					4408	4408	1432	605	202	.249	.328	1145	1875	971	.964	723	3061	4500	129	61	2.70

AMERICAN LEAGUE 1917

Team	POS	Player	AB	BA	HR	RBI	PO	A	E	DP	TC/G	FA	Pitcher	G	IP	W	L	SV	ERA
Chicago	1B	C. Gandil	553	.273	0	57	1405	77	8	84	10.0	**.995**	E. Cicotte	49	**347**	**28**	12	4	**1.53**
W-100 L-54	2B	E. Collins	564	.289	0	67	**353**	388	24	68	4.9	.969	R. Faber	41	248	16	13	3	1.92
Pants Rowland	SS	S. Risberg	474	.203	1	45	291	352	**61**	57	4.8	.913	L. Williams	45	230	17	8	1	2.97
	3B	B. Weaver	447	.284	3	32	154	218	20	18	3.7	**.949**	R. Russell	35	189	15	5	3	1.95
	RF	N. Leibold	428	.236	0	29	204	18	9	3	1.9	.961	D. Danforth	**50**	173	11	6	**9**	2.65
	CF	H. Felsch	575	.308	6	102	440	24	7	5	3.1	.985	J. Scott	24	125	6	7	1	1.87
	LF	J. Jackson	538	.301	5	75	341	18	6	4	2.5	.984	J. Benz	19	95	7	3	0	2.47
	C	R. Schalk	424	.226	3	51	**624**	148	15	13	5.7	**.981**							
	OF	S. Collins	252	.234	1	14	125	6	1	4	1.8	.992							
	3B	F. McMullin	194	.237	0	12	61	90	11	4	3.1	.932							
Boston	1B	D. Hoblitzell	420	.257	1	47	1274	52	14	58	11.4	.990	B. Ruth	41	326	24	13	2	2.01
W-90 L-62	2B	J. Barry	388	.214	2	30	196	339	14	40	4.7	**.974**	D. Leonard	37	294	16	17	1	2.17
Jack Barry	SS	E. Scott	528	.241	0	50	315	483	39	64	5.3	**.953**	C. Mays	35	289	22	9	0	1.74
	3B	L. Gardner	501	.265	1	61	148	315	**31**	18	3.4	.937	E. Shore	29	227	13	10	1	2.22
	RF	H. Hooper	559	.256	3	45	245	20	8	3	1.8	.971	R. Foster	17	125	8	7	0	2.53
	CF	T. Walker	337	.246	2	37	225	20	7	7	2.6	.972	H. Pennock	24	101	5	5	1	3.31
	LF	D. Lewis	553	.302	1	65	324	20	10	6	2.4	.972							
	C	S. Agnew	260	.208	0	16	297	88	14	5	4.7	.965							
	C	P. Thomas	202	.238	0	24	296	69	5	8	4.8	.986							
	OF	J. Walsh	185	.265	0	12	103	8	2	0	2.4	.982							
	1B	D. Gainer	172	.308	2	19	490	27	6	29	10.5	.989							
	OF	C. Shorten	168	.179	0	16	82	2	2	0	2.0	.977							
Cleveland	1B	J. Harris	369	.304	0	65	1019	86	17	58	**11.8**	.985	J. Bagby	49	321	23	13	7	1.96
W-88 L-66	2B	B. Wambsganss	499	.255	0	43	316	442	**38**	**70**	5.8	.952	S. Coveleski	45	298	19	14	4	1.81
Lee Fohl	SS	R. Chapman	563	.302	3	36	**360**	**528**	59	71	**6.1**	.938	E. Klepfer	41	213	14	4	1	2.37
	3B	J. Evans	385	.190	2	33	138	279	27	20	3.5	.939	G. Morton	35	161	10	10	2	2.74
	RF	B. Roth	495	.285	1	72	228	18	11	6	1.9	.957	F. Coumbe	34	134	8	6	5	2.14
	CF	T. Speaker	523	.352	2	60	365	23	8	5	2.8	.980	O. Lambeth	26	97	7	6	2	3.14
	LF	J. Graney	535	.228	3	35	288	14	13	6	2.2	.959							
	C	S. O'Neill	370	.184	0	29	446	145	12	**19**	4.7	.980							
	1B	L. Guisto	200	.185	0	29	611	33	7	45	11.0	.989							
	32	T. Turner	180	.206	0	15	86	119	4	7		.981							
	OF	E. Smith	161	.261	3	22	64	5	1	2	1.8	.986							
Detroit	1B	G. Burns	407	.226	1	40	1127	57	12	44	11.5	.990	H. Dauss	37	271	17	14	2	2.43
W-78 L-75	2B	R. Young	503	.231	1	35	300	**449**	33	46	5.5	.958	B. Boland	43	238	16	11	6	2.68
Hughie Jennings	SS	D. Bush	581	.281	0	24	281	423	51	41	5.1	.932	H. Ehmke	35	206	10	15	2	2.97
	3B	O. Vitt	512	.254	0	47	164	260	27	18	3.2	.940	B. James	34	198	13	10	1	2.09
	RF	H. Heilmann	556	.281	5	86	200	17	9	4	1.8	.960	W. Mitchell	30	185	12	8	0	2.19
	CF	T. Cobb	**588**	**.383**	7	102	373	27	11	9	2.7	.973	G. Cunningham	44	139	2	7	4	2.91
	LF	B. Veach	571	.319	8	**103**	356	17	17	5	2.5	.956	H. Coveleski	16	69	4	6	0	2.61
	C	O. Stanage	297	.205	0	30	385	88	11	13	5.1	.977							
	C	T. Spencer	192	.240	0	22	250	57	7	10	5.1	.978							
Washington	1B	J. Judge	393	.285	2	30	906	60	12	59	9.8	.988	W. Johnson	47	328	23	16	3	2.30
W-74 L-79	2B	R. Morgan	338	.266	1	33	206	243	18	45	4.9	.961	J. Shaw	47	266	15	14	1	3.21
Clark Griffith	SS	H. Shanks	430	.202	0	28	205	255	35	44	5.5	.929	D. Ayers	40	208	11	10	1	2.17
	3B	E. Foster	554	.235	0	43	95	178	19	15	3.4	.935	B. Gallia	42	208	9	13	1	2.99
	RF	S. Rice	586	.302	0	69	265	26	12	5	2.0	.960	G. Dumont	37	205	5	14	2	2.55
	CF	C. Milan	579	.294	0	48	339	18	14	3	2.4	.962	H. Harper	31	179	11	12	0	3.01
	LF	M. Menosky	322	.258	1	34	208	15	4	3	2.4	.982							
	C	E. Ainsmith	350	.191	0	42	580	154	22	15	**6.4**	.971							
	3B	J. Leonard	297	.192	0	23	78	119	16	15	3.2	.925							
	1B	P. Gharrity	176	.284	0	18	371	29	8	19	8.9	.980							
	C	J. Henry	163	.190	0	18	274	54	4	6	5.6	.988							
New York	1B	W. Pipp	587	.244	**9**	70	1609	**109**	17	**97**	11.2	.990	B. Shawkey	32	236	13	15	0	2.44
W-71 L-82	2B	F. Maisel	404	.198	0	20	219	280	17	37	5.2	.967	R. Caldwell	32	236	13	16	0	2.86
Wild Bill Donovan	SS	R. Peckinpaugh	543	.260	0	41	292	467	54	**84**	5.5	.934	G. Mogridge	29	196	9	11	0	2.98
	3B	F. Baker	553	.282	6	71	**202**	**317**	28	21	3.7	.949	N. Cullop	30	146	5	9	1	3.32
	RF	E. Miller	379	.251	3	35	204	16	9	2	2.0	.961	U. Shocker	26	145	8	5	1	2.61
	CF	T. Hendryx	393	.249	5	44	215	17	11	1	2.3	.955	R. Fisher	23	144	8	9	0	2.19
	LF	H. High	365	.236	1	19	188	16	3	3	2.1	.986	S. Love	33	130	6	5	1	2.35
	C	L. Nunamaker	310	.261	0	33	372	113	12	12	5.5	.976	A. Russell	25	104	7	8	2	2.24
	OF	L. Magee	173	.220	0	8	84	6	6	1	1.9	.938							
	C	R. Walters	171	.263	0	14	263	73	11	6	6.1	.968							
	OF	F. Gilhooley	165	.242	0	8	78	5	6	1	1.9	.933							
St. Louis	1B	G. Sisler	539	.353	2	52	1384	101	**22**	**97**	11.3	.985	D. Davenport	47	281	17	17	2	3.08
W-57 L-97	2B	D. Pratt	450	.247	1	53	324	353	29	64	**5.9**	.959	A. Sothoron	48	277	14	**19**	4	2.83
Fielder Jones	SS	D. Lavan	355	.239	0	30	229	338	47	67	5.6	.923	B. Groom	38	233	8	**19**	3	2.94
	3B	J. Austin	455	.240	0	19	159	248	23	**22**	3.6	.947	E. Koob	39	134	6	14	1	3.91
	RF	B. Jacobson	529	.248	4	55	292	18	8	6	2.4	.975	E. Plank	20	131	5	6	1	1.79
	CF	A. Marsans	257	.230	0	20	155	3	6	1	2.4	.963	T. Rogers	24	109	3	6	0	3.89
	LF	B. Shotton	398	.224	1	20	182	10	16	6	1.9	.923	E. Hamilton	27	83	0	9	1	3.14
	C	H. Severeid	501	.265	1	57	529	**156**	**24**	10	5.1	.966							
	OF	T. Sloan	313	.230	2	25	120	10	5	4	1.8	.963							
	OF	E. Smith	199	.281	0	10	114	12	3	5	2.5	.977							
	UT	E. Johnson	199	.246	2	20	122	197	25	19		.927							

AMERICAN LEAGUE 1917, *cont.*

Philadelphia

W-55 L-98

Connie Mack

POS	Player	AB	BA	HR	RBI	PO	A	E	DP	TC/G	FA	Pitcher	G	IP	W	L	SV	ERA
1B	S. McInnis	567	.303	0	44	**1658**	95	12	81	11.8	.993	J. Bush	37	233	11	17	2	2.47
2B	R. Grover	482	.224	0	34	279	425	29	51	5.3	.960	R. Schauer	33	215	7	16	1	3.14
SS	W. Witt	452	.252	0	28	190	354	38	41	5.2	.935	E. Myers	38	202	9	16	3	4.42
3B	R. Bates	485	.237	2	66	168	267	**31**	17	**3.8**	.933	J. Johnson	34	191	9	12	0	2.78
RF	C. Jamieson	347	.265	0	27	121	12	9	4	1.7	.937	W. Noyes	27	171	10	10	1	2.95
CF	A. Strunk	540	.281	1	45	346	13	5	5	2.5	.986	S. Seibold	33	160	4	16	1	3.94
LF	P. Bodie	557	.291	7	74	258	32	11	7	2.1	.963							
C	W. Schang	316	.285	3	36	260	102	17	11	4.8	.955							
C	B. Meyer	162	.235	0	9	235	66	12	2	5.7	.962							

BATTING AND BASE RUNNING LEADERS

Batting Average
- T. Cobb, DET .383
- G. Sisler, STL .353
- T. Speaker, CLE .352
- B. Veach, DET .319
- H. Felsch, CHI .308

Slugging Average
- T. Cobb, DET .571
- T. Speaker, CLE .486
- B. Veach, DET .457
- G. Sisler, STL .453
- J. Jackson, CHI .429

Home Runs
- W. Pipp, NY 9
- B. Veach, DET 8
- P. Bodie, PHI 7
- T. Cobb, DET 7
- F. Baker, NY 6
- H. Felsch, CHI 6

Total Bases
- T. Cobb, DET 336
- B. Veach, DET 261
- T. Speaker, CLE 254
- G. Sisler, STL 244
- P. Bodie, PHI 233

Runs Batted In
- B. Veach, DET 103
- H. Felsch, CHI 102
- T. Cobb, DET 102
- H. Heilmann, DET 86
- J. Jackson, CHI 75

Stolen Bases
- T. Cobb, DET 55
- E. Collins, CHI 53
- R. Chapman, CLE 52
- B. Roth, CLE 51
- G. Sisler, STL 37

Hits
- T. Cobb, DET 225
- G. Sisler, STL 190
- T. Speaker, CLE 184
- B. Veach, DET 182

Base on Balls
- J. Graney, CLE 94
- E. Collins, CHI 89
- H. Hooper, BOS 80
- D. Bush, DET 80

Home Run Percentage
- W. Pipp, NY 1.5
- B. Veach, DET 1.4
- T. Hendryx, NY 1.3
- P. Bodie, PHI 1.3

Runs
- D. Bush, DET 112
- T. Cobb, DET 107
- R. Chapman, CLE 98
- J. Jackson, CHI 91
- E. Collins, CHI 91

Doubles
- T. Cobb, DET 44
- T. Speaker, CLE 42
- B. Veach, DET 31
- B. Roth, CLE 30
- G. Sisler, STL 30

Triples
- T. Cobb, DET 23
- J. Jackson, CHI 17
- J. Judge, WAS 15

PITCHING LEADERS

Winning Percentage
- R. Russell, CHI .750
- C. Mays, BOS .710
- E. Cicotte, CHI .700
- L. Williams, CHI .680
- B. Ruth, BOS .649

Earned Run Average
- E. Cicotte, CHI 1.53
- C. Mays, BOS 1.74
- S. Coveleski, CLE 1.81
- R. Faber, CHI 1.92
- R. Russell, CHI 1.95

Wins
- E. Cicotte, CHI 28
- B. Ruth, BOS 24
- J. Bagby, CLE 23
- W. Johnson, WAS 23
- C. Mays, BOS 22

Saves
- D. Danforth, CHI 9
- J. Bagby, CLE 7
- B. Boland, DET 6
- F. Coumbe, CLE 5

Strikeouts
- W. Johnson, WAS 188
- E. Cicotte, CHI 150
- D. Leonard, BOS 144
- S. Coveleski, CLE 133
- B. Ruth, BOS 128

Complete Games
- B. Ruth, BOS 35
- W. Johnson, WAS 30
- E. Cicotte, CHI 29
- C. Mays, BOS 27
- D. Leonard, BOS 26
- J. Bagby, CLE 26

Fewest Hits/9 Innings
- S. Coveleski, CLE 6.09
- E. Cicotte, CHI 6.39
- B. Ruth, BOS 6.73
- W. Johnson, WAS 7.11

Shutouts
- S. Coveleski, CLE 9
- W. Johnson, WAS 8
- J. Bagby, CLE 8
- E. Cicotte, CHI 7

Fewest Walks/9 Innings
- R. Russell, CHI 1.52
- G. Mogridge, NY 1.79
- E. Cicotte, CHI 1.82
- W. Johnson, WAS 1.84

Most Strikeouts/9 Inn.
- W. Johnson, WAS 5.16
- H. Harper, WAS 4.97
- J. Bush, PHI 4.67
- D. Leonard, BOS 4.40

Innings
- E. Cicotte, CHI 347
- W. Johnson, WAS 328
- B. Ruth, BOS 326
- J. Bagby, CLE 321

Games Pitched
- D. Danforth, CHI 50
- E. Cicotte, CHI 49
- J. Bagby, CLE 49
- A. Sothoron, STL 48

	W	L	PCT	GB	R	OR	Batting						Fielding			Pitching					
							2B	3B	HR	BA	SA	SB	E	DP	FA	CG	BB	SO	ShO	SV	ERA
Chicago	100	54	.649		**656**	464	152	**80**	19	.253	.326	**219**	204	117	.967	78	**413**	517	**22**	21	**2.16**
Boston	90	62	.592	9	555	**454**	198	64	14	.246	.319	105	**183**	116	**.972**	**115**	**413**	509	15	7	2.20
Cleveland	88	66	.571	12	584	543	**218**	63	14	.245	.322	210	242	136	.964	73	438	451	20	**22**	2.52
Detroit	78	75	.510	21.5	639	577	204	76	26	**.259**	**.344**	163	234	95	.964	78	504	516	20	15	2.56
Washington	74	79	.484	25.5	543	566	173	70	4	.241	.304	166	251	127	.961	84	536	**637**	21	10	2.77
New York	71	82	.464	28.5	524	558	172	52	**27**	.239	.308	136	225	129	.965	87	427	571	10	6	2.66
St. Louis	57	97	.370	43	510	687	183	63	15	.245	.315	157	281	**139**	.957	65	537	429	12	12	3.20
Philadelphia	55	98	.359	44.5	529	691	177	62	17	.254	.322	112	251	106	.961	80	562	516	8	8	3.27
					4540	4540	1477	530	136	.248	.320	1268	1871	965	.964	660	3830	4146	128	101	2.67

NATIONAL LEAGUE 1918

Chicago

W-84 L-45

Fred Mitchell

POS	Player	AB	BA	HR	RBI	PO	A	E	DP	TC/G	FA	Pitcher	G	IP	W	L	SV	ERA
1B	F. Merkle	482	.297	3	65	**1388**	82	15	69	11.5	.990	H. Vaughn	35	**290**	**22**	10	0	**1.74**
2B	R. Zeider	251	.223	0	26	142	207	16	22	4.6	.956	L. Tyler	33	269	19	9	1	2.00
SS	C. Hollocher	**509**	.316	2	38	278	418	53	39	5.7	.929	C. Hendrix	32	233	19	7	0	2.78
3B	C. Deal	414	.239	2	34	144	247	24	21	3.5	.942	P. Douglas	25	157	9	9	2	2.13
RF	M. Flack	478	.257	4	41	199	20	5	5	1.9	.978							
CF	D. Paskert	461	.286	3	59	283	12	6	1	2.5	.980							
LF	L. Mann	489	.288	2	55	229	15	10	3	2.0	.961							
C	B. Killefer	331	.233	0	22	**487**	110	11	12	**5.8**	**.982**							

New York

W-71 L-53

John McGraw

POS	Player	AB	BA	HR	RBI	PO	A	E	DP	TC/G	FA	Pitcher	G	IP	W	L	SV	ERA
1B	W. Holke	326	.252	1	27	938	68	10	50	11.5	.990	P. Perritt	35	233	18	13	0	2.74
2B	L. Doyle	257	.261	3	36	121	221	11	24	4.8	.969	R. Causey	29	158	11	6	2	2.79
SS	A. Fletcher	468	.263	0	47	268	**484**	32	54	6.3	**.959**	A. Demaree	26	142	8	6	1	2.47
3B	H. Zimmerman	463	.272	1	56	128	209	16	8	3.5	.955	S. Sallee	18	132	8	8	2	2.25
RF	R. Youngs	474	.302	1	25	197	22	12	3	1.9	.948							
CF	B. Kauff	270	.315	2	39	147	11	8	4	2.5	.952							
LF	G. Burns	465	.290	4	51	292	10	11	1	2.6	.965							
C	L. McCarty	257	.268	0	24	288	67	9	3	4.9	.975							
C	B. Rariden	183	.224	0	17	195	45	4	3	3.9	.984							

NATIONAL LEAGUE 1918, *cont.*

Cincinnati

W-68 L-60

Christy Mathewson
W-61 L-57

Heinie Groh
W-7 L-3

POS	Player	AB	BA	HR	RBI	PO	A	E	DP	TC/G	FA
1B	H. Chase	259	.301	2	38	607	38	13	59	9.8	.980
2B	L. Magee	459	.290	0	28	275	361	**29**	**73**	5.8	.956
SS	L. Blackburne	435	.228	1	45	319	413	48	**69**	6.2	.938
3B	H. Groh	493	.320	1	37	**180**	253	14	**37**	3.5	**.969**
RF	T. Griffith	427	.265	2	48	201	18	7	3	1.9	.969
CF	E. Roush	435	.333	5	62	320	13	14	2	3.1	.960
LF	G. Neale	371	.270	1	32	249	11	5	2	2.6	.981
C	I. Wingo	323	.254	0	31	315	111	**12**	13	4.7	.973
10	S. Magee	400	.297	2	**76**	685	41	14	40		.981

Pitcher	G	IP	W	L	SV	ERA
H. Eller	37	218	16	12	1	2.36
P. Schneider	33	218	10	15	0	3.51
J. Ring	21	142	9	5	0	2.85
F. Toney	21	137	6	10	2*	2.90
R. Bressler	17	128	8	5	0	2.46
M. Regan	22	80	5	5	2	3.26

Pittsburgh

W-65 L-60

Hugo Bezdek

POS	Player	AB	BA	HR	RBI	PO	A	E	DP	TC/G	FA
1B	F. Mollwitz	432	.269	0	45	1252	73	13	67	11.2	.990
2B	G. Cutshaw	463	.285	5	68	**323**	**366**	26	60	5.7	**.964**
SS	B. Caton	303	.234	0	17	136	276	32	35	5.6	.928
3B	B. McKechnie	435	.255	2	43	162	261	15	26	3.5	.966
RF	B. Southworth	246	.341	2	43	137	12	3	4	2.4	.980
CF	M. Carey	468	.274	3	48	359	25	17	9	3.2	.958
LF	C. Bigbee	310	.255	1	19	168	13	8	1	2.1	.958
C	W. Schmidt	323	.238	0	27	373	**153**	10	**19**	5.2	.981

Pitcher	G	IP	W	L	SV	ERA
W. Cooper	38	273	19	14	**3**	2.11
F. Miller	23	170	11	8	0	2.38
R. Sanders	28	156	7	9	1	2.60
E. Mayer	15	123	9	3	0	2.26
R. Comstock	15	81	5	6	1	3.00

Brooklyn

W-57 L-69

Wilbert Robinson

POS	Player	AB	BA	HR	RBI	PO	A	E	DP	TC/G	FA
1B	J. Daubert	396	.308	2	47	1069	63	10	43	10.9	.991
2B	M. Doolan	308	.179	0	18	230	283	17	37	5.8	.968
SS	I. Olson	506	.239	1	17	265	388	58	42	5.6	.918
3B	O. O'Mara	450	.213	1	24	126	262	20	15	3.4	.951
RF	J. Johnston	484	.281	0	27	178	18	9	4	2.1	.956
CF	H. Myers	407	.256	4	40	294	17	8	7	3.0	.975
LF	Z. Wheat	409	**.335**	0	51	219	11	5	2	2.2	.979
C	O. Miller	228	.193	0	8	276	77	10	6	5.9	.972
OF	J. Hickman	167	.234	1	16	76	9	8	1	2.0	.914
C	M. Wheat	157	.217	1	3	151	50	7	1	5.5	.966

Pitcher	G	IP	W	L	SV	ERA
B. Grimes	**41**	270	19	9	1	2.14
R. Marquard	34	239	9	**18**	0	2.64
L. Cheney	32	201	11	13	1	3.00
J. Coombs	27	189	8	14	0	3.81

Philadelphia

W-55 L-68

Pat Moran

POS	Player	AB	BA	HR	RBI	PO	A	E	DP	TC/G	FA
1B	F. Luderus	468	.288	5	67	1307	**98**	17	**74**	11.4	.988
2B	P. McGaffigan	192	.203	1	8	100	155	14	19	5.1	.948
SS	D. Bancroft	499	.265	0	26	**371**	457	**64**	57	**7.1**	.928
3B	M. Stock	481	.274	1	42	132	273	23	16	3.5	.946
RF	G. Cravath	426	.232	**8**	54	184	19	15	3	1.8	.931
CF	C. Williams	351	.276	6	39	229	10	8	4	2.7	.968
LF	I. Meusel	473	.279	4	62	296	14	9	2	2.7	.972
C	B. Adams	227	.176	0	12	261	69	8	8	4.4	.976
C	E. Burns	184	.207	0	9	184	77	5	3	3.9	.981
2B	H. Pearce	164	.244	0	18	97	157	15	18	5.8	.944

Pitcher	G	IP	W	L	SV	ERA
M. Prendergast	33	252	13	14	1	2.89
B. Hogg	29	228	13	13	1	2.53
J. Oeschger	30	184	6	**18**	**3**	3.03
E. Jacobs	18	123	9	5	1	2.41
M. Watson	23	113	5	7	0	3.43
E. Mayer	13	104	7	4	0	3.12

Boston

W-53 L-71

George Stallings

POS	Player	AB	BA	HR	RBI	PO	A	E	DP	TC/G	FA
1B	E. Konetchy	437	.236	2	56	1226	61	11	69	11.6	**.992**
2B	B. Herzog	473	.228	0	26	240	322	23	43	**5.9**	.961
SS	J. Rawlings	410	.207	0	21	137	256	18	27	5.8	.956
3B	R. Smith	429	.298	2	65	123	**291**	**35**	16	**3.8**	.922
RF	A. Wickland	332	.262	4	32	183	11	5	2	2.1	.975
CF	R. Powell	188	.213	0	20	121	8	7	2	2.6	.949
LF	R. Massey	203	.291	0	18	75	4	3	2	1.8	.963
C	A. Wilson	280	.246	0	19	292	96	9	7	4.7	.977
OF	J. Kelly	155	.232	0	15	93	4	7	0	2.3	.933

Pitcher	G	IP	W	L	SV	ERA
A. Nehf	32	284	15	15	0	2.69
P. Ragan	30	206	8	17	0	3.23
D. Rudolph	21	154	9	10	0	2.57
B. Hearn	17	126	5	6	0	2.49
D. Fillingim	14	113	7	6	0	2.23

St. Louis

W-51 L-78

Jack Hendricks

POS	Player	AB	BA	HR	RBI	PO	A	E	DP	TC/G	FA
1B	G. Paulette	461	.273	0	52	1093	59	**20**	64	**12.1**	.983
2B	B. Fisher	246	.317	2	20	147	232	8	34	6.1	.979
SS	R. Hornsby	416	.281	5	60	208	434	46	55	6.3	.933
3B	D. Baird	316	.247	2	25	99	219	11	12	4.1	.967
RF	W. Cruise	240	.271	6	39	103	4	4	0	1.7	.964
CF	C. Heathcote	348	.259	4	32	222	6	16	0	2.8	.934
LF	A. McHenry	272	.261	1	29	145	14	8	3	2.1	.952
C	M. Gonzalez	349	.252	3	20	362	124	11	17	5.0	.978
UT	B. Betzel	230	.222	0	13	100	103	17	10		.923
OF	J. Smith	166	.211	0	4	87	9	6	6	2.4	.941

Pitcher	G	IP	W	L	SV	ERA
B. Doak	31	211	9	15	1	2.43
R. Ames	27	207	9	14	1	2.31
B. Sherdel	35	182	6	12	0	2.71
G. Packard	30	182	12	12	2	3.50
L. Meadows	30	165	8	14	1	3.59
J. May	29	153	5	6	0	3.83

BATTING AND BASE RUNNING LEADERS

Batting Average		Slugging Average		Home Runs	
Z. Wheat, BKN	.335	E. Roush, CIN	.455	G. Cravath, PHI	8
E. Roush, CIN	.333	J. Daubert, BKN	.429	W. Cruise, STL	6
H. Groh, CIN	.320	R. Hornsby, STL	.416	C. Williams, PHI	6
C. Hollocher, CHI	.316	S. Magee, CIN	.415		
J. Daubert, BKN	.308	A. Wickland, BOS	.398		

Total Bases		Runs Batted In		Stolen Bases	
C. Hollocher, CHI	202	S. Magee, CIN	76	M. Carey, PIT	58
E. Roush, CIN	198	G. Cutshaw, PIT	68	G. Burns, NY	40
H. Groh, CIN	195	F. Luderus, PHI	67	C. Hollocher, CHI	26
L. Mann, CHI	188	R. Smith, BOS	65	D. Baird, STL	25
F. Merkle, CHI	187	F. Merkle, CHI	65	G. Cutshaw, PIT	25

PITCHING LEADERS

Winning Percentage		Earned Run Average		Wins	
C. Hendrix, CHI	.731	H. Vaughn, CHI	1.74	H. Vaughn, CHI	22
E. Mayer, PHI, PIT	.696	L. Tyler, CHI	2.00	C. Hendrix, CHI	19
H. Vaughn, CHI	.688	W. Cooper, PIT	2.11	L. Tyler, CHI	19
B. Grimes, BKN	.679	P. Douglas, CHI	2.13	B. Grimes, BKN	19
L. Tyler, CHI	.679	B. Grimes, BKN	2.14	W. Cooper, PIT	19

Saves		Strikeouts		Complete Games	
F. Toney, CIN, NY	3	H. Vaughn, CHI	148	A. Nehf, BOS	28
F. Anderson, NY	3	W. Cooper, PIT	117	H. Vaughn, CHI	27
J. Oeschger, PHI	3	B. Grimes, BKN	113	W. Cooper, PIT	26
W. Cooper, PIT	3	L. Tyler, CHI	102	L. Tyler, CHI	22
		A. Nehf, BOS	96	C. Hendrix, CHI	21

NATIONAL LEAGUE 1918, *cont.*

BATTING AND BASE RUNNING LEADERS

Hits

C. Hollocher, CHI	161
H. Groh, CIN	158
E. Roush, CIN	145
R. Youngs, NY	143
F. Merkle, CHI	143

Base on Balls

M. Carey, PIT	62
M. Flack, CHI	56
G. Cravath, PHI	54
H. Groh, CIN	54
D. Bancroft, PHI	54

Home Run Percentage

G. Cravath, PHI	1.9
C. Williams, PHI	1.7
A. Wickland, BOS	1.2
R. Hornsby, STL	1.2

Runs

H. Groh, CIN	88
G. Burns, NY	80
M. Flack, CHI	74
C. Hollocher, CHI	72

Doubles

H. Groh, CIN	28
G. Cravath, PHI	27
L. Mann, CHI	27
I. Meusel, PHI	25
F. Merkle, CHI	25

Triples

J. Daubert, BKN	15
A. Wickland, BOS	13
S. Magee, CIN	13
L. Magee, CIN	13

PITCHING LEADERS

Fewest Hits/9 Innings

H. Vaughn, CHI	6.70
B. Grimes, BKN	7.01
W. Cooper, PIT	7.21
L. Tyler, CHI	7.28

Shutouts

L. Tyler, CHI	8
H. Vaughn, CHI	8
B. Grimes, BKN	7
P. Perritt, NY	6

Fewest Walks/9 Innings

S. Sallee, NY	0.82
P. Perritt, NY	1.47
F. Toney, CIN, NY	1.54
G. Packard, STL	1.63

Most Strikeouts/9 Inn.

H. Vaughn, CHI	4.59
W. Cooper, PIT	3.85
B. Grimes, BKN	3.77
L. Cheney, BKN	3.72

Innings

H. Vaughn, CHI	290
A. Nehf, BOS	284
W. Cooper, PIT	273
B. Grimes, BKN	270

Games Pitched

B. Grimes, BKN	41
W. Cooper, PIT	38
H. Eller, CIN	37

							Batting						Fielding			Pitching					
	W	L	PCT	GB	R	OR	2B	3B	HR	BA	SA	SB	E	DP	FA	CG	BB	SO	ShO	SV	ERA
Chicago	84	45	.651		**538**	**393**	164	53	21	.265	.342	159	188	91	.966	92	296	**472**	**25**	6	**2.18**
New York	71	53	.573	10.5	480	415	150	53	13	.260	.330	130	**152**	78	**.970**	74	**228**	330	18	**11**	2.64
Cincinnati	68	60	.531	15.5	530	496	**165**	**84**	15	**.278**	**.366**	128	192	**127**	.964	84	381	321	14	6	3.00
Pittsburgh	65	60	.520	17	466	412	107	72	15	.248	.321	**200**	179	108	.966	85	299	367	12	7	2.48
Brooklyn	57	69	.452	25.5	360	463	121	62	10	.250	.315	113	193	74	.963	85	320	395	17	2	2.81
Philadelphia	55	68	.447	26	430	507	158	28	25	.244	.313	97	211	91	.961	78	369	312	10	6	3.15
Boston	53	71	.427	28.5	424	469	107	59	13	.244	.307	83	184	89	.965	**96**	277	340	13	0	2.90
St. Louis	51	78	.395	33	454	527	147	64	**27**	.244	.325	119	220	116	.962	72	352	361	3	5	2.96
					3682	3682	1119	475	139	.254	.327	1029	1519	774	.965	666	2522	2898	112	43	2.76

AMERICAN LEAGUE 1918

Boston

W-75 L-51

Ed Barrow

POS	Player	AB	BA	HR	RBI	PO	A	E	DP	TC/G	FA	Pitcher	G	IP	W	L	SV	ERA
1B	S. McInnis	423	.272	0	56	1066	71	9	45	**12.2**	**.992**	C. Mays	35	293	21	13	0	2.21
2B	D. Shean	425	.264	0	34	241	341	20	38	5.2	.967	J. Bush	36	273	15	15	2	2.11
SS	E. Scott	443	.221	0	43	270	419	17	38	5.6	**.976**	S. Jones	24	184	16	5	0	2.25
3B	F. Thomas	144	.257	1	11	54	97	5	4	3.8	.968	B. Ruth	20	166	13	7	0	2.22
RF	H. Hooper	474	.289	1	44	221	16	9	8	2.0	.963	D. Leonard	16	126	8	6	0	2.72
CF	A. Strunk	413	.257	0	35	230	13	3	4	2.2	.988							
LF	B. Ruth	317	.300	**11**	66	121	8	7	3	2.3	.949							
C	S. Agnew	199	.166	0	6	254	104	13	10	5.2	.965							
C	W. Schang	225	.244	0	20	188	49	9	4	4.3	.963							
OF	G. Whiteman	214	.266	1	28	95	5	7	1	1.6	.935							

Cleveland

W-73 L-54

Lee Fohl

POS	Player	AB	BA	HR	RBI	PO	A	E	DP	TC/G	FA	Pitcher	G	IP	W	L	SV	ERA
1B	D. Johnston	273	.227	0	25	738	40	9	25	10.8	.989	S. Coveleski	38	311	22	13	1	1.82
2B	B. Wambsganss	315	.295	0	40	204	251	23	35	5.5	.952	J. Bagby	**45**	271	17	16	6	2.69
SS	R. Chapman	446	.267	1	32	**321**	398	49	42	**6.0**	.936	G. Morton	30	215	14	8	0	2.64
3B	J. Evans	243	.263	1	22	91	155	18	17	3.6	.932	F. Coumbe	30	150	13	7	3	3.00
RF	B. Roth	375	.283	1	59	175	16	13	3	1.9	.936	J. Enzmann	30	137	5	7	2	2.37
CF	T. Speaker	471	.318	0	61	352	15	10	6	3.0	.973							
LF	S. Wood	422	.296	5	66	193	10	8	4	2.2	.962							
C	S. O'Neill	359	.242	1	35	409	**154**	10	10	5.1	**.983**							
32	T. Turner	233	.249	0	23	77	170	5	6		.980							
OF	J. Graney	177	.237	0	9	77	2	2	0	1.8	.975							

Washington

W-72 L-56

Clark Griffith

POS	Player	AB	BA	HR	RBI	PO	A	E	DP	TC/G	FA	Pitcher	G	IP	W	L	SV	ERA
1B	J. Judge	502	.261	1	46	1304	92	21	71	10.9	.985	W. Johnson	39	325	**23**	13	3	**1.27**
2B	R. Morgan	300	.233	0	30	172	251	18	29	5.5	.959	H. Harper	35	244	11	10	1	2.18
SS	D. Lavan	464	.278	0	45	275	354	**57**	43	5.9	.917	J. Shaw	41	241	16	12	1	2.42
3B	E. Foster	**519**	.283	0	29	156	281	**30**	31	3.7	.936	D. Ayers	40	220	10	12	3	2.83
RF	W. Schulte	267	.288	0	44	145	10	5	4	2.1	.969							
CF	C. Milan	503	.290	0	56	299	17	9	3	2.6	.972							
LF	B. Shotton	505	.261	0	21	277	15	18	6	2.5	.942							
C	E. Ainsmith	292	.212	0	20	413	131	14	13	**6.3**	.975							
02	H. Shanks	436	.257	1	56	279	143	21	21		.953							

New York

W-60 L-63

Miller Huggins

POS	Player	AB	BA	HR	RBI	PO	A	E	DP	TC/G	FA	Pitcher	G	IP	W	L	SV	ERA
1B	W. Pipp	349	.304	2	44	918	61	12	75	10.9	.988	G. Mogridge	**45**	230	16	13	**7**	2.27
2B	D. Pratt	477	.275	2	55	**340**	386	23	**82**	5.9	.969	S. Love	38	229	13	12	1	3.07
SS	R. Peckinpaugh	446	.231	0	43	260	**439**	28	**75**	6.0	.961	R. Caldwell	24	177	9	8	1	3.06
3B	F. Baker	504	.306	6	68	**175**	282	13	30	**3.7**	**.972**	A. Russell	27	141	7	11	4	3.26
RF	F. Gilhooley	427	.276	1	23	206	15	9	8	2.1	.961	H. Finneran	23	114	3	6	0	3.78
CF	E. Miller	202	.243	1	22	149	13	9	0	2.8	.947	H. Thormahlen	16	113	7	3	0	2.48
LF	P. Bodie	324	.256	3	46	181	17	6	3	2.3	.971							
C	T. Hannah	250	.220	2	21	343	111	12	**16**	5.3	.974							
C	R. Walters	191	.199	0	12	199	47	12	6	5.2	.953							

AMERICAN LEAGUE 1918, *cont.*

Team	POS	Player	AB	BA	HR	RBI	PO	A	E	DP	TC/G	FA	Pitcher	G	IP	W	L	SV	ERA
St. Louis	1B	G. Sisler	452	.341	2	41	1244	95	13	64	11.9	.990	A. Sothoron	29	209	12	12	0	1.94
W-58 L-64	2B	J. Gedeon	441	.213	1	41	309	**409**	17	45	**6.0**	**.977**	D. Davenport	31	180	10	11	1	3.25
Fielder Jones	SS	J. Austin	367	.264	0	20	117	158	18	13	5.1	.939	T. Rogers	29	154	8	10	2	3.27
W-22 L-24	3B	F. Maisel	284	.232	0	16	108	154	14	10	3.5	.949	B. Gallia	19	124	8	6	0	3.48
Jimmy Austin	RF	R. Demmitt	405	.281	1	61	206	25	12	8	2.1	.951	R. Wright	18	111	8	2	0	2.51
W-7 L-9	CF	J. Tobin	480	.277	0	36	244	20	8	8	2.2	.971	U. Shocker	14	95	6	5	2	1.81
Jimmy Burke	LF	E. Smith	286	.269	0	32	164	14	9	4	2.3	.952							
W-29 L-31	C	L. Nunamaker	274	.259	0	22	315	108	9	10	5.3	.979							
	OF	T. Hendryx	219	.279	0	33	108	4	2	2	1.8	.982							
	SS	W. Gerber	171	.240	0	10	109	174	24	20	5.5	.922							
Chicago	1B	C. Gandil	439	.271	0	55	1123	64	10	70	10.5	.992	E. Cicotte	38	266	12	**19**	2	2.64
W-57 L-67	2B	E. Collins	330	.276	2	30	231	285	14	53	5.5	.974	F. Shellenback	28	183	9	12	2	2.66
Pants Rowland	SS	B. Weaver	420	.300	0	29	191	319	32	50	5.5	.941	J. Benz	29	154	8	8	0	2.51
	3B	F. McMullin	235	.277	1	16	74	151	14	9	3.5	.941	D. Danforth	39	139	6	15	2	3.43
	RF	H. Felsch	206	.252	1	20	149	7	7	5	3.1	.957	R. Russell	19	125	7	5	0	2.60
	CF	S. Collins	365	.274	1	56	230	20	7	1	2.8	.973	L. Williams	15	106	6	4	1	2.73
	LF	N. Leibold	440	.250	1	31	259	16	6	5	2.5	.979							
	C	R. Schalk	333	.219	0	22	**422**	114	12	15	5.2	.978							
	OF	E. Murphy	286	.297	0	23	111	3	5	1	1.9	.958							
	UT	S. Risberg	273	.256	1	27	168	160	21	27		.940							
	OF	J. Jackson	65	.354	1	20	36	1	0	0	2.2	1.000							
Detroit	1B	H. Heilmann	286	.276	5	44	367	18	5	11	10.5	.987	H. Dauss	33	250	12	16	3	2.99
W-55 L-71	2B	R. Young	298	.188	0	21	190	271	**30**	28	5.4	.939	B. Boland	29	204	14	10	0	2.65
Hughie Jennings	SS	D. Bush	500	.234	0	22	280	364	48	29	5.4	.931	R. Kallio	30	181	8	14	0	3.62
	3B	O. Vitt	267	.240	0	17	106	137	12	15	3.9	.953	G. Cunningham	27	140	6	7	1	3.15
	RF	G. Harper	227	.242	0	16	125	5	6	2	2.1	.956	B. James	19	122	6	11	0	3.76
	CF	T. Cobb	421	**.382**	3	64	225	12	6	1	2.6	.975	E. Erickson	12	94	4	5	1	2.48
	LF	B. Veach	499	.279	3	**78**	277	14	7	3	2.3	.977							
	C	A. Yelle	144	.174	0	7	172	81	14	5	5.1	.948							
	3B	B. Jones	287	.275	0	21	81	83	11	6	2.8	.937							
	C	O. Stanage	186	.253	1	14	188	54	5	9	5.3	.980							
	OF	F. Walker	167	.198	1	20	102	5	9	1	2.6	.922							
	C	T. Spencer	155	.219	0	8	153	46	7	3	4.3	.966							
Philadelphia	1B	G. Burns	505	.352	6	70	**1384**	**104**	**26**	**109**	11.8	.983	S. Perry	44	**332**	20	**19**	2	1.98
W-52 L-76	2B	J. Dykes	186	.188	0	13	139	189	21	33	6.2	.940	V. Gregg	30	199	9	14	2	3.12
Connie Mack	SS	J. Dugan	406	.195	3	34	211	281	37	46	6.2	.930	W. Adams	32	169	5	12	0	4.42
	3B	L. Gardner	463	.285	1	52	158	**291**	17	**33**	3.7	.964	M. Watson	21	142	7	10	0	3.37
	RF	C. Jamieson	416	.202	0	11	182	15	6	4	2.0	.970	E. Myers	18	95	4	8	1	4.63
	CF	T. Walker	414	.295	**11**	48	242	25	13	4	2.6	.954	B. Geary	16	87	2	5	4	2.69
	LF	M. Kopp	363	.234	0	18	221	20	7	6	2.6	.972							
	C	W. McAvoy	271	.244	0	32	235	123	**15**	15	5.0	.960							
	S2	R. Shannon	225	.240	0	16	155	223	39	40		.906							
	C	C. Perkins	218	.188	1	14	201	103	3	11	5.1	.990							
	OF	M. Acosta	169	.302	0	14	77	7	5	2	2.0	.944							

BATTING AND BASE RUNNING LEADERS

Batting Average		Slugging Average		Home Runs	
T. Cobb, DET	.382	B. Ruth, BOS	.555	B. Ruth, BOS	11
G. Burns, PHI	.352	T. Cobb, DET	.515	T. Walker, PHI	11
G. Sisler, STL	.341	G. Burns, PHI	.467	F. Baker, NY	6
T. Speaker, CLE	.318	G. Sisler, STL	.440	G. Burns, PHI	6
F. Baker, NY	.306	T. Speaker, CLE	.435	H. Heilmann, DET	5
				S. Wood, CLE	5

Total Bases		Runs Batted In		Stolen Bases	
G. Burns, PHI	236	B. Veach, DET	78	G. Sisler, STL	45
T. Cobb, DET	217	G. Burns, PHI	70	B. Roth, CLE	35
F. Baker, NY	206	F. Baker, NY	68	T. Cobb, DET	34
T. Speaker, CLE	205	B. Ruth, BOS	66	R. Chapman, CLE	30
G. Sisler, STL	199	S. Wood, CLE	66	T. Speaker, CLE	27

Hits		Base on Balls		Home Run Percentage	
G. Burns, PHI	178	R. Chapman, CLE	84	B. Ruth, BOS	3.5
T. Cobb, DET	161	D. Bush, DET	79	T. Walker, PHI	2.7
G. Sisler, STL	154	H. Hooper, BOS	75	F. Baker, NY	1.2
F. Baker, NY	154	E. Collins, CHI	73	G. Burns, PHI	1.2

Runs		Doubles		Triples	
R. Chapman, CLE	84	T. Speaker, CLE	33	T. Cobb, DET	14
T. Cobb, DET	83	B. Ruth, BOS	26	H. Hooper, BOS	13
H. Hooper, BOS	81	H. Hooper, BOS	26	B. Veach, DET	13
D. Bush, DET	74	F. Baker, NY	24	B. Roth, CLE	12

PITCHING LEADERS

Winning Percentage		Earned Run Average		Wins	
S. Jones, BOS	.762	W. Johnson, WAS	1.27	W. Johnson, WAS	23
W. Johnson, WAS	.639	S. Coveleski, CLE	1.82	S. Coveleski, CLE	22
S. Coveleski, CLE	.629	A. Sothoron, STL	1.94	C. Mays, BOS	21
C. Mays, BOS	.618	S. Perry, PHI	1.98	S. Perry, PHI	20
J. Shaw, WAS	.571	J. Bush, BOS	2.11	J. Bagby, CLE	17

Saves		Strikeouts		Complete Games	
G. Mogridge, NY	7	W. Johnson, WAS	162	C. Mays, BOS	30
J. Bagby, CLE	6	J. Shaw, WAS	129	S. Perry, PHI	30
B. Geary, PHI	4	J. Bush, BOS	125	W. Johnson, WAS	29
A. Russell, NY	4	G. Morton, CLE	123	J. Bush, BOS	26
		C. Mays, BOS	114	S. Coveleski, CLE	25

Fewest Hits/9 Innings		Shutouts		Fewest Walks/9 Innings	
A. Sothoron, STL	6.55	W. Johnson, WAS	8	E. Cicotte, CHI	1.35
W. Johnson, WAS	6.67	C. Mays, BOS	8	J. Benz, CHI	1.64
H. Harper, WAS	6.71	J. Bush, BOS	7	G. Mogridge, NY	1.68
B. Ruth, BOS	6.76	S. Jones, BOS	5	W. Johnson, WAS	1.94

Most Strikeouts/9 Inn.		Innings		Games Pitched	
G. Morton, CLE	5.16	S. Perry, PHI	332	G. Mogridge, NY	45
J. Shaw, WAS	4.81	W. Johnson, WAS	325	J. Bagby, CLE	45
W. Johnson, WAS	4.49	S. Coveleski, CLE	311	S. Perry, PHI	44
J. Bush, BOS	4.13	C. Mays, BOS	293	J. Shaw, WAS	41

AMERICAN LEAGUE 1918, *cont.*

	W	L	PCT	GB	R	OR	Batting 2B	3B	HR	BA	SA	SB	Fielding E	DP	FA	Pitching CG	BB	SO	ShO	SV	ERA
Boston	75	51	.595		474	**380**	159	54	15	.249	.327	110	**149**	89	**.971**	**105**	380	392	**26**	2	2.31
Cleveland	73	54	.575	2.5	**504**	447	**176**	**67**	9	**.260**	**.341**	**165**	207	82	.962	78	343	364	5	**13**	2.63
Washington	72	56	.563	4	461	412	156	48	5	.256	.316	137	226	95	.960	75	395	**505**	19	8	**2.14**
New York	60	63	.488	13.5	493	475	160	45	20	.257	.330	88	161	**137**	.970	59	463	369	8	**13**	3.03
St. Louis	58	64	.475	15	426	448	152	40	5	.259	.320	138	190	86	.963	67	402	346	8	8	2.75
Chicago	57	67	.460	17	457	446	136	54	9	.256	.321	116	169	98	.967	76	**300**	349	9	8	2.69
Detroit	55	71	.437	20	476	557	141	56	13	.249	.318	123	211	77	.960	74	437	374	8	7	3.40
Philadelphia	52	76	.406	24	412	538	124	44	**22**	.243	.308	83	228	136	.959	80	479	279	13	8	3.22
					3703	3703	1204	408	98	.254	.323	960	1541	800	.964	614	3199	2978	96	67	2.77

NATIONAL LEAGUE 1919

	POS	Player	AB	BA	HR	RBI	PO	A	E	DP	TC/G	FA	Pitcher	G	IP	W	L	SV	ERA
Cincinnati	1B	J. Daubert	537	.276	2	44	1437	80	17	75	11.0	.989	H. Eller	38	248	20	9	2	2.39
W-96 L-44	2B	M. Rath	537	.264	1	29	**345**	**452**	21	**59**	**5.9**	.974	D. Ruether	33	243	19	6	0	1.82
Pat Moran	SS	L. Kopf	503	.270	0	58	273	407	41	39	5.3	.943	S. Sallee	29	228	21	7	0	2.06
	3B	H. Groh	448	.310	5	63	**171**	226	12	**22**	3.4	.971	J. Ring	32	183	10	9	3	2.26
	RF	G. Neale	500	.242	1	54	285	16	13	4	2.3	.959	R. Fisher	26	174	14	5	1	2.17
	CF	E. Roush	504	**.321**	4	71	335	22	4	5	2.7	.989	D. Luque	30	106	9	3	3	2.63
	LF	R. Bressler	165	.206	2	17	105	4	4	1	2.4	.965							
	C	I. Wingo	245	.273	0	27	266	106	12	6	5.1	.969							
	C	B. Rariden	218	.216	1	24	283	67	6	5	5.1	.983							
	OF	S. Magee	163	.215	0	21	98	2	1	0	2.1	.990							
New York	1B	H. Chase	408	.284	5	45	1205	65	21	62	**12.1**	.984	J. Barnes	38	296	**25**	9	1	2.40
W-87 L-53	2B	L. Doyle	381	.289	7	52	214	311	24	48	5.5	.956	R. Benton	35	209	17	11	2	2.63
John McGraw	SS	A. Fletcher	488	.277	3	54	265	**521**	47	49	6.6	.944	F. Toney	24	181	13	6	1	1.84
	3B	H. Zimmerman	444	.255	4	58	122	**268**	**25**	15	3.4	.940	J. Dubuc	36	132	6	4	3	2.66
	RF	R. Youngs	489	.311	2	43	235	23	16	7	2.1	.942	R. Causey	19	105	9	3	0	3.69
	CF	B. Kauff	491	.277	10	67	306	18	17	3	2.5	.950	A. Nehf	13	102	9	2	0	1.50
	LF	G. Burns	534	.303	2	46	290	15	3	4	2.2	.990							
	C	L. McCarty	210	.281	2	21	203	56	8	1	4.5	.970							
	23	F. Frisch	190	.226	2	24	100	130	6	7		.975							
	C	M. Gonzalez	158	.190	0	8	179	49	9	3	4.6	.962							
Chicago	1B	F. Merkle	498	.267	3	62	**1494**	56	**23**	66	11.9	.985	H. Vaughn	38	**307**	21	14	1	1.79
W-75 L-65	2B	C. Pick	269	.242	0	18	135	253	22*	31	5.8	.946	G. Alexander	30	235	16	11	1	**1.72**
Fred Mitchell	SS	C. Hollocher	430	.270	3	26	219	418	40	49	5.9	.941	C. Hendrix	33	206	10	14	0	2.62
	3B	C. Deal	405	.289	2	52	157	233	11	14	3.5	**.973**	S. Martin	35	164	8	8	2	2.47
	RF	M. Flack	469	.294	6	35	194	18	3	1	1.9	.986	P. Douglas	25	162	10	6	0	2.00
	CF	D. Paskert	270	.196	2	29	146	12	5	1	2.0	.969	P. Carter	28	85	5	4	1	2.65
	LF	L. Mann	299	.227	1	22	155	10	3	2	2.2	.982							
	C	B. Killefer	315	.286	0	22	**478**	**124**	8	7	**6.1**	**.987**							
	UT	L. Magee	267	.292	1	17	130	88	13	5		.944							
	OF	T. Barber	230	.313	0	21	123	7	7	1	2.0	.949							
	2B	B. Herzog	193	.275	0	17	81	151	3	14	4.5	.987							
Pittsburgh	1B	F. Mollwitz	168	.173	0	12	478	19	3	21	9.6	.994	W. Cooper	35	287	19	13	1	2.67
W-71 L-68	2B	G. Cutshaw	512	.242	3	51	344	392	15	56	5.4	**.980**	B. Adams	34	263	17	10	1	1.98
Hugo Bezdek	SS	Z. Terry	472	.227	0	27	207	395	25	41	4.9	**.960**	F. Miller	32	202	13	12	0	3.03
	3B	W. Barbare	293	.273	1	34	109	136	10	11	3.2	.961	E. Hamilton	28	160	8	11	1	3.31
	RF	C. Stengel	321	.293	4	43	195	7	9	3	2.4	.957	H. Carlson	22	141	8	10	0	2.23
	CF	C. Bigbee	478	.276	2	27	343	21	11	5	3.0	.971							
	LF	B. Southworth	453	.280	4	61	253	17	9	5	2.3	.968							
	C	W. Schmidt	267	.251	0	29	315	110	8	8	5.1	.982							
	OF	M. Carey	244	.307	0	9	173	5	10	1	3.0	.947							
	1B	V. Saier	166	.223	2	17	493	17	8	18	10.2	.985							
	1B	P. Whitted	131	.389	0	21	311	27	4	21	10.4	.988							
Brooklyn	1B	E. Konetchy	486	.298	1	47	1288	89	9	62	10.5	**.994**	J. Pfeffer	30	267	17	13	0	2.66
W-69 L-71	2B	J. Johnston	405	.281	1	23	157	294	19	31	5.4	.960	L. Cadore	35	251	14	12	0	2.37
Wilbert Robinson	SS	I. Olson	**590**	.278	1	38	349	445	44	57	6.0	.947	A. Mamaux	30	199	10	12	0	2.66
	3B	L. Malone	162	.204	0	11	52	75	9	4	2.9	.934	B. Grimes	25	181	10	11	0	3.47
	RF	T. Griffith	484	.281	6	57	210	20	11	3	1.9	.954	S. Smith	30	173	7	12	1	2.24
	CF	H. Myers	512	.307	5	**73**	358	13	8	5	2.9	.979	C. Mitchell	23	109	7	5	0	3.06
	LF	Z. Wheat	536	.297	5	62	297	9	9	2	2.3	.971							
	C	E. Krueger	226	.248	5	36	305	88	**15**	2	6.2	.963							
	2B	L. Magee	181	.238	0	7	74	124	13	10	5.9	.938							
	C	O. Miller	164	.226	0	5	223	58	10	5	5.7	.966							
Boston	1B	W. Holke	518	.292	0	48	1474	95	11	**86**	11.6	.993	D. Rudolph	37	274	13	18	2	2.17
W-57 L-82	2B	B. Herzog	275	.280	1	25	130	191	16	23	4.8	.953	D. Fillingim	32	186	6	13	2	3.38
George Stallings	SS	R. Maranville	480	.267	5	43	**361**	488	**53**	**74**	**6.9**	.941	A. Nehf	22	169	8	9	0	3.09
	3B	T. Boeckel	365	.249	1	26	98	188	12	11	3.2	.960	R. Keating	22	136	7	11	0	2.98
	RF	R. Powell	470	.236	2	33	213	21	12	7	2.0	.951	A. Demaree	25	128	6	6	3	3.80
	CF	J. Riggert	240	.283	4	17	165	6	9	2	3.0	.950	J. Scott	19	104	6	6	1	3.13
	LF	W. Cruise	241	.216	1	21	124	7	3	1	2.0	.978							
	C	H. Gowdy	219	.279	1	22	230	105	8	11	4.6	.977							
	2B	J. Rawlings	275	.255	1	16	105	169	11	20	4.9	.961							
	03	R. Smith	241	.245	1	25	128	64	9	5		.955							
	C	A. Wilson	191	.257	0	16	213	82	7	4	4.7	.977							
	OF	J. Thorpe	156	.327	1	25	73	2	6	0	2.1	.926							
	OF	L. Mann	145	.283	3	20	82	9	7	1	2.5	.929							

NATIONAL LEAGUE 1919, *cont.*

St. Louis

W-54 L-83

Branch Rickey

POS	Player	AB	BA	HR	RBI	PO	A	E	DP	TC/G	FA
1B	D. Miller	346	.231	1	24	687	40	14	34	10.9	.981
2B	M. Stock	492	.307	0	52	168	254	15	32	5.7	.966
SS	D. Lavan	356	.242	1	25	207	352	43	49	6.1	.929
3B	R. Hornsby	512	.318	8	71	73	151	16	11	3.3	.933
RF	J. Smith	408	.223	0	15	197	19	9	6	2.0	.960
CF	C. Heathcote	401	.279	1	29	225	10	8	3	2.4	.967
LF	A. McHenry	371	.286	1	47	183	20	3	3	2.0	.985
C	V. Clemons	239	.264	2	22	289	89	7	8	5.1	.982
OF	B. Shotton	270	.285	1	20	104	10	9	2	1.8	.927
OF	J. Schultz	229	.253	2	21	75	6	0	1	1.7	1.000
C	F. Snyder	154	.182	0	14	149	80	4	4	4.9	.983

Pitcher	G	IP	W	L	SV	ERA
B. Doak	31	203	13	14	0	3.11
M. Goodwin	33	179	11	9	0	2.51
O. Tuero	**45**	155	5	7	**4**	3.20
B. Sherdel	36	137	5	9	1	3.47
J. May	28	126	3	12	0	3.22
L. Meadows	22	92	4	10*	0	3.03
E. Jacobs	17	85	3	6	1	2.53

Philadelphia

W-47 L-90

Jack Coombs
W-18 L-44

Gavvy Cravath
W-29 L-46

POS	Player	AB	BA	HR	RBI	PO	A	E	DP	TC/G	FA
1B	F. Luderus	509	.293	5	54	1385	**108**	22	82	11.0	.985
2B	G. Paulette	243	.259	1	31	141	173	14	28	6.2	.957
SS	D. Bancroft	335	.272	0	25	242	306	28	43	6.5	.951
3B	L. Blackburne	291	.199	2	19	85	167	18	11	3.8*	.933
RF	L. Callahan	235	.230	1	9	102	13	6	1	2.1	.950
CF	C. Williams	435	.278	9	39	278	13	9	2	2.8	.970
LF	I. Meusel	521	.305	5	59	256	14	9	4	2.2	.968
C	B. Adams	232	.233	1	17	249	90	12	**15**	4.8	.966
02	P. Whitted	289	.249	3	32	169	74	9	8		.964
2S	H. Pearce	244	.180	0	9	129	198	17	30		.951
3B	D. Baird	242	.252	2	30	100	147	13	17	3.9	.950
OF	G. Cravath	214	.341	**12**	45	89	7	9	2	1.9	.914
S2	E. Sicking	185	.216	0	15	117	157	15	37		.948

Pitcher	G	IP	W	L	SV	ERA
G. Smith	31	185	5	11	0	3.22
E. Rixey	23	154	6	12	0	3.97
B. Hogg	22	150	5	12	0	4.43
L. Meadows	18	149	8	10*	0	2.47
G. Packard	21	134	6	8	1	4.15
E. Jacobs	17	129	6	10	0	3.85
F. Woodward	17	101	6	9	0	4.74

BATTING AND BASE RUNNING LEADERS

Batting Average

E. Roush, CIN	.321
R. Hornsby, STL	.318
R. Youngs, NY	.311
H. Groh, CIN	.310
M. Stock, STL	.307

Slugging Average

H. Myers, BKN	.436
L. Doyle, NY	.433
H. Groh, CIN	.431
E. Roush, CIN	.431
R. Hornsby, STL	.430

Home Runs

G. Cravath, PHI	12
B. Kauff, NY	10
C. Williams, PHI	9
R. Hornsby, STL	8
L. Doyle, NY	7

Total Bases

H. Myers, BKN	223
R. Hornsby, STL	220
Z. Wheat, BKN	219
E. Roush, CIN	217
G. Burns, NY	216

Runs Batted In

H. Myers, BKN	73
E. Roush, CIN	71
R. Hornsby, STL	71
B. Kauff, NY	67
H. Groh, CIN	63

Stolen Bases

G. Burns, NY	40
G. Cutshaw, PIT	36
C. Bigbee, PIT	31
J. Smith, STL	30
B. Herzog, BOS, CHI	28
G. Neale, CIN	28

Hits

I. Olson, BKN	164
R. Hornsby, STL	163
E. Roush, CIN	162
G. Burns, NY	162

Base on Balls

G. Burns, NY	82
M. Rath, CIN	64
H. Groh, CIN	56
F. Luderus, PHI	54

Home Run Percentage

C. Williams, PHI	2.1
B. Kauff, NY	2.0
L. Doyle, NY	1.8
R. Hornsby, STL	1.6

Runs

G. Burns, NY	86
H. Groh, CIN	79
J. Daubert, CIN	79
M. Rath, CIN	77

Doubles

R. Youngs, NY	31
F. Luderus, PHI	30
G. Burns, NY	30
B. Kauff, NY	27

Triples

B. Southworth, PIT	14
H. Myers, BKN	14

PITCHING LEADERS

Winning Percentage

D. Ruether, CIN	.760
S. Sallee, CIN	.750
J. Barnes, NY	.735
H. Eller, CIN	.690
B. Adams, PIT	.630

Earned Run Average

G. Alexander, CHI	1.72
H. Vaughn, CHI	1.79
D. Ruether, CIN	1.82
F. Toney, NY	1.84
B. Adams, PIT	1.98

Wins

J. Barnes, NY	25
S. Sallee, CIN	21
H. Vaughn, CHI	21
H. Eller, CIN	20
D. Ruether, CIN	19
W. Cooper, PIT	19

Saves

O. Tuero, STL	4
J. Ring, CIN	3
J. Winters, NY	3
A. Demaree, BOS	3
D. Luque, CIN	3
J. Dubuc, NY	3

Strikeouts

H. Vaughn, CHI	141
H. Eller, CIN	137
G. Alexander, CHI	121
L. Meadows, STL, PHI	116
W. Cooper, PIT	106

Complete Games

W. Cooper, PIT	27
J. Pfeffer, BKN	26
H. Vaughn, CHI	25
D. Rudolph, BOS	24
B. Adams, PIT	23
J. Barnes, NY	23

Fewest Hits/9 Innings

G. Alexander, CHI	6.89
W. Cooper, PIT	7.19
D. Ruether, CIN	7.23
R. Fisher, CIN	7.28

Shutouts

G. Alexander, CHI	9
B. Adams, PIT	7
H. Eller, CIN	7
R. Fisher, CIN	5

Fewest Walks/9 Innings

B. Adams, PIT	0.79
S. Sallee, CIN	0.79
J. Barnes, NY	1.07
L. Cadore, BKN	1.40

Most Strikeouts/9 Inn.

H. Eller, CIN	4.97
G. Alexander, CHI	4.63
L. Meadows, STL, PHI	4.33
H. Vaughn, CHI	4.14

Innings

H. Vaughn, CHI	307
J. Barnes, NY	296
W. Cooper, PIT	287
D. Rudolph, BOS	274

Games Pitched

O. Tuero, STL	45
L. Meadows, STL, PHI	40
H. Eller, CIN	38
J. Barnes, NY	38
H. Vaughn, CHI	38

							Batting						Fielding			Pitching					
	W	L	PCT	GB	R	OR	2B	3B	HR	BA	SA	SB	E	DP	FA	CG	BB	SO	ShO	SV	ERA
Cincinnati	96	44	.686		577	**401**	135	**83**	20	.263	.342	143	**152**	98	**.974**	89	298	407	**23**	9	2.23
New York	87	53	.621	9	**605**	470	204	64	40	**.269**	**.366**	157	216	96	.964	72	305	340	11	**13**	2.70
Chicago	75	65	.536	21	454	407	166	58	21	.256	.332	150	186	87	.969	80	294	**495**	21	5	**2.21**
Pittsburgh	71	68	.511	24.5	472	466	130	82	17	.249	.325	**196**	166	89	.970	92	**263**	391	16	4	2.88
Brooklyn	69	71	.493	27	525	513	167	66	25	.263	.340	112	218	84	.972	**98**	292	476	12	1	2.73
Boston	57	82	.410	38.5	465	563	142	62	24	.253	.324	145	204	111	.966	79	337	374	5	9	3.17
St. Louis	54	83	.394	40.5	463	552	163	52	18	.256	.326	148	217	**112**	.963	55	415	414	6	8	3.23
Philadelphia	47	90	.343	47.5	510	699	**208**	50	**42**	.251	.342	114	219	**112**	.963	93	408	397	6	2	4.17
					4071	4071	1315	517	207	.257	.337	1165	1578	789	.968	658	2612	3294	100	51	2.91

NATIONAL LEAGUE 1919, *cont.*

BATTING AND BASE RUNNING LEADERS

Batting Average

E. Roush, CIN	.321
R. Hornsby, STL	.318
R. Youngs, NY	.311
H. Groh, CIN	.310
M. Stock, STL	.307

Slugging Average

H. Myers, BKN	.436
L. Doyle, NY	.433
H. Groh, CIN	.431
E. Roush, CIN	.431
R. Hornsby, STL	.430

Home Runs

G. Cravath, PHI	12
B. Kauff, NY	10
C. Williams, PHI	9
R. Hornsby, STL	8
L. Doyle, NY	7

Total Bases

H. Myers, BKN	223
R. Hornsby, STL	220
Z. Wheat, BKN	219
E. Roush, CIN	217
G. Burns, NY	216

Runs Batted In

H. Myers, BKN	73
E. Roush, CIN	71
R. Hornsby, STL	71
B. Kauff, NY	67
H. Groh, CIN	63

Stolen Bases

G. Burns, NY	40
G. Cutshaw, PIT	36
C. Bigbee, PIT	31
J. Smith, STL	30
B. Herzog, BOS, CHI	28
G. Neale, CIN	28

Hits

I. Olson, BKN	164
R. Hornsby, STL	163
E. Roush, CIN	162
G. Burns, NY	162

Base on Balls

G. Burns, NY	82
M. Rath, CIN	64
H. Groh, CIN	56
F. Luderus, PHI	54

Home Run Percentage

C. Williams, PHI	2.1
B. Kauff, NY	2.0
L. Doyle, NY	1.8
R. Hornsby, STL	1.6

Runs

G. Burns, NY	86
H. Groh, CIN	79
J. Daubert, CIN	79
M. Rath, CIN	77

Doubles

R. Youngs, NY	31
F. Luderus, PHI	30
G. Burns, NY	30
B. Kauff, NY	27

Triples

B. Southworth, PIT	14
H. Myers, BKN	14

PITCHING LEADERS

Winning Percentage

D. Ruether, CIN	.760
S. Sallee, CIN	.750
J. Barnes, NY	.735
H. Eller, CIN	.690
B. Adams, PIT	.630

Earned Run Average

G. Alexander, CHI	1.72
H. Vaughn, CHI	1.79
D. Ruether, CIN	1.82
F. Toney, NY	1.84
B. Adams, PIT	1.98

Wins

J. Barnes, NY	25
S. Sallee, CIN	21
H. Vaughn, CHI	21
H. Eller, CIN	20
D. Ruether, CIN	19
W. Cooper, PIT	19

Saves

O. Tuero, STL	4
J. Ring, CIN	3
J. Winters, NY	3
A. Demaree, BOS	3
D. Luque, CIN	3
J. Dubuc, NY	3

Strikeouts

H. Vaughn, CHI	141
H. Eller, CIN	137
G. Alexander, CHI	121
L. Meadows, STL, PHI	116
W. Cooper, PIT	106

Complete Games

W. Cooper, PIT	27
J. Pfeffer, BKN	26
H. Vaughn, CHI	25
D. Rudolph, BOS	24
B. Adams, PIT	23
J. Barnes, NY	23

Fewest Hits/9 Innings

G. Alexander, CHI	6.89
W. Cooper, PIT	7.19
D. Ruether, CIN	7.23
R. Fisher, CIN	7.28

Shutouts

G. Alexander, CHI	9
B. Adams, PIT	7
H. Eller, CIN	7
R. Fisher, CIN	5

Fewest Walks/9 Innings

B. Adams, PIT	0.79
S. Sallee, CIN	0.79
J. Barnes, NY	1.07
L. Cadore, BKN	1.40

Most Strikeouts/9 Inn.

H. Eller, CIN	4.97
G. Alexander, CHI	4.63
L. Meadows, STL, PHI	4.33
H. Vaughn, CHI	4.14

Innings

H. Vaughn, CHI	307
J. Barnes, NY	296
W. Cooper, PIT	287
D. Rudolph, BOS	274

Games Pitched

O. Tuero, STL	45
L. Meadows, STL, PHI	40
H. Eller, CIN	38
J. Barnes, NY	38
H. Vaughn, CHI	38

							Batting						Fielding			Pitching					
	W	L	PCT	GB	R	OR	2B	3B	HR	BA	SA	SB	E	DP	FA	CG	BB	SO	ShO	SV	ERA
Cincinnati	96	44	.686		577	**401**	135	**83**	20	.263	.342	143	**152**	98	**.974**	89	298	407	**23**	9	2.23
New York	87	53	.621	9	**605**	470	204	64	40	**.269**	**.366**	157	216	96	.964	72	305	340	11	**13**	2.70
Chicago	75	65	.536	21	454	407	166	58	21	.256	.332	150	186	87	.969	80	294	**495**	21	5	**2.21**
Pittsburgh	71	68	.511	24.5	472	466	130	82	17	.249	.325	**196**	166	89	.970	92	**263**	391	16	4	2.88
Brooklyn	69	71	.493	27	525	513	167	66	25	.263	.340	112	218	84	.972	**98**	292	476	12	1	2.73
Boston	57	82	.410	38.5	465	563	142	62	24	.253	.324	145	204	111	.966	79	337	374	5	9	3.17
St. Louis	54	83	.394	40.5	463	552	163	52	18	.256	.326	148	217	**112**	.963	55	415	414	6	8	3.23
Philadelphia	47	90	.343	47.5	510	699	**208**	50	**42**	.251	.342	114	219	**112**	.963	93	408	397	6	2	4.17
					4071	4071	1315	517	207	.257	.337	1165	1578	789	.968	658	2612	3294	100	51	2.91

AMERICAN LEAGUE 1919

Chicago

W-88 L-52

Kid Gleason

POS	Player	AB	BA	HR	RBI	PO	A	E	DP	TC/G	FA	Pitcher	G	IP	W	L	SV	ERA
1B	C. Gandil	441	.290	1	60	1116	60	3	71	10.3	**.997**	E. Cicotte	40	**307**	**29**	7	1	1.82
2B	E. Collins	518	.319	4	80	**347**	401	20	**66**	5.5	.974	L. Williams	41	297	23	11	1	2.64
SS	S. Risberg	414	.256	2	38	175	278	32	39	5.0	.934	D. Kerr	39	212	13	7	0	2.88
3B	B. Weaver	**571**	.296	3	75	113	200	12	14	3.4	.963	R. Faber	25	162	11	9	0	3.83
RF	N. Leibold	434	.302	0	26	218	26	19	4	2.2	.928	G. Lowdermilk	20	97	5	5	0	2.79
CF	H. Felsch	502	.275	7	86	360	32	13	15	3.0	.968							
LF	J. Jackson	516	.351	7	96	252	15	9	4	2.0	.967							
C	R. Schalk	394	.282	0	34	**551**	130	13	14	5.4	.981							
OF	S. Collins	179	.279	1	16	82	7	4	5	2.0	.957							
3B	F. McMullin	170	.294	0	19	45	90	10	10	3.2	.931							

Cleveland

W-84 L-55

Lee Fohl
W-44 L-34

Tris Speaker
W-40 L-21

POS	Player	AB	BA	HR	RBI	PO	A	E	DP	TC/G	FA	Pitcher	G	IP	W	L	SV	ERA
1B	D. Johnston	331	.305	1	33	957	57	16	57	10.5	.984	S. Coveleski	43	296	24	12	4	2.52
2B	B. Wambsganss	526	.278	2	60	342	436	**30**	60	5.8	.963	J. Bagby	35	241	17	11	3	2.80
SS	R. Chapman	433	.300	3	53	255	347	36	44	5.5	.944	G. Morton	26	147	9	9	0	2.81
3B	L. Gardner	524	.300	2	79	143	**291**	**25**	23	3.3	.946	E. Myers	23	135	8	7	1	3.74
RF	E. Smith	395	.278	9	54	167	12	8	8	1.7	.957	G. Uhle	26	127	10	5	0	2.91
CF	T. Speaker	494	.296	2	63	375	25	7	6	3.0	.983							
LF	J. Graney	461	.234	1	30	281	13	12	2	2.4	.961							
C	S. O'Neill	398	.289	2	47	472	125	14	13	5.0	.977							
OF	S. Wood	192	.255	1	27	90	6	7	1	1.6	.932							
1B	J. Harris	184	.375	1	46	451	38	6	22	10.8	.988							

AMERICAN LEAGUE 1919, *cont.*

New York

W-80 L-59

Miller Huggins

POS	Player	AB	BA	HR	RBI	PO	A	E	DP	TC/G	FA
1B	W. Pipp	523	.275	7	50	**1488**	94	15	77	**11.6**	.991
2B	D. Pratt	527	.292	4	56	315	**491**	26	64	**5.9**	.969
SS	R. Peckinpaugh	453	.305	7	33	271	**434**	43	57	**6.2**	.943
3B	F. Baker	567	.293	10	83	**176**	286	22	**28**	3.4	.955
RF	S. Vick	407	.248	2	27	166	11	9	2	1.9	.952
CF	P. Bodie	475	.278	6	59	293	19	13	6	2.4	.960
LF	D. Lewis	559	.272	7	89	254	13	4	4	1.9	.985
C	M. Ruel	233	.240	0	31	340	90	11	6	5.4	.975
OS	C. Fewster	244	.283	1	15	118	80	17	8		.921
C	T. Hannah	227	.238	1	21	298	66	6	12	5.1	.984

Pitcher	G	IP	W	L	SV	ERA
J. Quinn	38	264	15	14	0	2.63
B. Shawkey	41	261	20	11	4	2.72
H. Thormahlen	30	189	12	10	1	2.62
G. Mogridge	35	187	10	7	0	2.50
C. Mays	13	120	9	3	0	1.65
E. Shore	20	95	5	8	0	4.17
A. Russell	23	91	5	5	1*	3.47

Detroit

W-80 L-60

Hughie Jennings

POS	Player	AB	BA	HR	RBI	PO	A	E	DP	TC/G	FA
1B	H. Heilmann	537	.320	8	95	1402	78	**31**	61	10.8	.979
2B	R. Young	456	.211	1	25	300	389	22	38	5.9	.969
SS	D. Bush	509	.244	0	26	**290**	376	40	38	5.5	.943
3B	B. Jones	439	.260	1	57	134	219	21	14	2.9	.944
RF	I. Flagstead	287	.331	5	41	140	15	8	4	2.0	.951
CF	T. Cobb	497	**.384**	1	70	272	19	8	3	2.4	.973
LF	B. Veach	538	.355	3	101	338	14	12	3	2.6	.967
C	E. Ainsmith	364	.272	3	32	456	107	**22**	7	5.5	.962
OF	C. Shorten	270	.315	0	22	143	2	4	2	2.0	.973

Pitcher	G	IP	W	L	SV	ERA
H. Dauss	34	256	21	9	0	3.55
H. Ehmke	33	249	17	10	0	3.18
B. Boland	35	243	14	16	1	3.04
D. Leonard	29	217	14	13	0	2.77
S. Love	22	90	6	4	1	3.01

Boston

W-66 L-71

Ed Barrow

POS	Player	AB	BA	HR	RBI	PO	A	E	DP	TC/G	FA
1B	S. McInnis	440	.305	1	58	1236	82	7	**84**	11.2	.995
2B	R. Shannon	290	.259	0	17	171	228	11	40	5.2	.973
SS	E. Scott	507	.278	0	38	276	423	17	**63**	5.2	**.976**
3B	O. Vitt	469	.243	0	40	129	254	13	24	3.0	**.967**
RF	H. Hooper	491	.267	3	49	262	19	6	2	2.2	.979
CF	B. Roth	227	.256	0	23	125	7	8	1	2.5	.943
LF	B. Ruth	432	.322	**29**	**114**	230	16	2	6	2.2	.992
C	W. Schang	330	.306	0	55	359	131	14	**15**	4.9	.972
OF	A. Strunk	184	.272	0	17	118	4	4	0	2.6	.968

Pitcher	G	IP	W	L	SV	ERA
S. Jones	35	245	12	20	1	3.75
H. Pennock	32	219	16	8	0	2.71
C. Mays	21	145	5	11	2	2.48
B. Ruth	17	133	9	5	1	2.97
A. Russell	21	120	10	4	4*	2.54
W. Hoyt	13	105	4	6	0	3.25
R. Caldwell	18	86	7	4	0	3.75

St. Louis

W-67 L-72

Jimmy Burke

POS	Player	AB	BA	HR	RBI	PO	A	E	DP	TC/G	FA
1B	G. Sisler	511	.352	10	83	1249	**120**	13	62	10.5	.991
2B	J. Gedeon	437	.254	0	27	290	345	16	44	5.5	**.975**
SS	W. Gerber	462	.227	1	37	287	422	**45**	42	5.4	.940
3B	J. Austin	396	.237	1	21	161	207	24	15	**4.0**	.939
RF	E. Smith	252	.250	1	36	155	13	5	4	2.5	.971
CF	B. Jacobson	455	.323	4	51	270	9	15	2	2.8	.949
LF	J. Tobin	486	.327	6	57	247	16	13	5	2.2	.953
C	H. Severeid	351	.248	0	36	401	106	9	12	5.0	**.983**
OF	K. Williams	227	.300	6	35	168	10	12	3	3.0	.937
OF	R. Demmitt	202	.238	1	19	60	6	10	0	1.6	.868
32	H. Bronkie	196	.255	0	14	75	113	11	13		.945

Pitcher	G	IP	W	L	SV	ERA
A. Sothoron	40	270	20	13	3	2.20
B. Gallia	34	222	12	14	1	3.60
U. Shocker	30	211	13	11	0	2.69
C. Weilman	20	148	10	6	0	2.07
D. Davenport	24	123	2	11	0	3.94
L. Leifield	19	92	6	4	0	2.93

Washington

W-56 L-84

Clark Griffith

POS	Player	AB	BA	HR	RBI	PO	A	E	DP	TC/G	FA
1B	J. Judge	521	.288	2	31	1177	78	15	66	9.5	.988
2B	H. Janvrin	208	.178	1	13	108	120	18	14	4.4	.927
SS	H. Shanks	491	.248	1	54	238	260	42	2	5.7	.922
3B	E. Foster	478	.264	0	26	120	267	22	16	3.6	.946
RF	S. Rice	557	.321	3	71	285	18	12	3	2.2	.962
CF	C. Milan	321	.287	0	37	195	9	10	2	2.5	.953
LF	M. Menosky	342	.287	6	39	222	7	5	1	2.3	.979
C	V. Picinich	212	.274	3	22	303	92	9	5	5.9	.978
CO	P. Gharrity	347	.271	2	43	329	72	15	7		.964
OF	B. Murphy	252	.262	0	28	177	8	8	2	2.6	.959
23	J. Leonard	198	.258	2	20	81	98	8	14		.957

Pitcher	G	IP	W	L	SV	ERA
J. Shaw	**45**	**307**	17	17	**5**	2.73
W. Johnson	39	290	20	14	2	**1.49**
H. Harper	35	208	6	**21**	0	3.72
E. Erickson	20	132	6	11	0	3.95

Philadelphia

W-36 L-104

Connie Mack

POS	Player	AB	BA	HR	RBI	PO	A	E	DP	TC/G	FA
1B	G. Burns	470	.296	8	57	918	71	20	44	11.7	.980
2B	R. Shannon	155	.271	0	14	66	116	10	10	5.2	.948
SS	J. Dugan	387	.271	1	30	228	307	42	39	5.9	.927
3B	F. Thomas	453	.212	2	23	168	242	24	14	3.5	.945
RF	M. Kopp	235	.226	1	12	127	7	11	0	2.2	.924
CF	T. Walker	456	.292	10	64	253	13	19	4	2.5	.933
LF	W. Witt	460	.267	0	33	134	3	4	0	2.4	.972
C	C. Perkins	305	.252	2	29	340	**134**	14	**15**	**5.6**	.971
OF	B. Roth	195	.323	5	29	78	1	2	2	1.7	.975
OF	A. Strunk	194	.211	0	13	98	7	2	0	2.1	.981
1B	D. Burrus	194	.258	0	8	337	21	5	15	9.6	.986
C	W. McAvoy	170	.141	0	11	182	73	7	6	4.6	.973

Pitcher	G	IP	W	L	SV	ERA
R. Naylor	31	205	5	18	0	3.34
W. Kinney	43	203	9	15	2	3.64
J. Johnson	34	202	9	15	0	3.61
S. Perry	25	184	4	17	1	3.58
T. Rogers	23	140	4	12	0	4.31

BATTING AND BASE RUNNING LEADERS

Batting Average		Slugging Average		Home Runs	
T. Cobb, DET	.384	B. Ruth, BOS	.657	B. Ruth, BOS	29
B. Veach, DET	.355	G. Sisler, STL	.530	T. Walker, PHI	10
G. Sisler, STL	.352	B. Veach, DET	.519	G. Sisler, STL	10
J. Jackson, CHI	.351	T. Cobb, DET	.515	F. Baker, NY	10
I. Flagstead, DET	.331	J. Jackson, CHI	.506	E. Smith, CLE	9

PITCHING LEADERS

Winning Percentage		Earned Run Average		Wins	
E. Cicotte, CHI	.806	W. Johnson, WAS	1.49	E. Cicotte, CHI	29
H. Dauss, DET	.700	E. Cicotte, CHI	1.82	S. Coveleski, CLE	24
L. Williams, CHI	.676	C. Weilman, STL	2.07	L. Williams, CHI	23
S. Coveleski, CLE	.667	C. Mays, BOS, NY	2.11	H. Dauss, DET	21
H. Pennock, BOS	.667	A. Sothoron, STL	2.20		

AMERICAN LEAGUE 1919, *cont.*

BATTING AND BASE RUNNING LEADERS

Total Bases
B. Ruth, BOS 284
B. Veach, DET 279
G. Sisler, STL 271
J. Jackson, CHI 261
T. Cobb, DET 256
H. Heilmann, DET 256

Runs Batted In
B. Ruth, BOS 114
B. Veach, DET 101
J. Jackson, CHI 96
H. Heilmann, DET 95
D. Lewis, NY 89

Stolen Bases
E. Collins, CHI 33
T. Cobb, DET 28
G. Sisler, STL 28
S. Rice, WAS 26
H. Hooper, BOS 23
J. Judge, WAS 23

Hits
T. Cobb, DET 191
B. Veach, DET 191
J. Jackson, CHI 181
G. Sisler, STL 180

Base on Balls
J. Graney, CLE 105
B. Ruth, BOS 101
J. Judge, WAS 81
H. Hooper, BOS 79

Home Run Percentage
B. Ruth, BOS 6.7
E. Smith, CLE 2.3
T. Walker, PHI 2.2
G. Sisler, STL 2.0

Runs
B. Ruth, BOS 103
G. Sisler, STL 96
T. Cobb, DET 92
R. Peckinpaugh, NY 89
B. Weaver, CHI 89

Doubles
B. Veach, DET 45
T. Speaker, CLE 38
T. Cobb, DET 36
S. O'Neill, CLE 35

Triples
B. Veach, DET 17
G. Sisler, STL 15
H. Heilmann, DET 15
J. Jackson, CHI 14

PITCHING LEADERS

Saves
J. Shaw, WAS 5
A. Russell, NY, BOS 5
S. Coveleski, CLE 4
B. Shawkey, NY 4
J. Bagby, CLE 3
A. Sothoron, STL 3

Strikeouts
W. Johnson, WAS 147
J. Shaw, WAS 128
L. Williams, CHI 125
B. Shawkey, NY 122
S. Coveleski, CLE 118

Complete Games
E. Cicotte, CHI 30
W. Johnson, WAS 27
L. Williams, CHI 27
C. Mays, BOS, NY 26
S. Coveleski, CLE 24

Fewest Hits/9 Innings
W. Johnson, WAS 7.28
H. Thormahlen, NY 7.39
B. Shawkey, NY 7.51
E. Cicotte, CHI 7.51

Shutouts
W. Johnson, WAS 7

Fewest Walks/9 Innings
E. Cicotte, CHI 1.44
W. Johnson, WAS 1.58
J. Bagby, CLE 1.64
L. Williams, CHI 1.76

Most Strikeouts/9 Inn.
A. Russell, NY, BOS 4.82
W. Johnson, WAS 4.56
W. Kinney, PHI 4.31
D. Leonard, DET 4.22

Innings
E. Cicotte, CHI 307
J. Shaw, WAS 307
L. Williams, CHI 297
S. Coveleski, CLE 296

Games Pitched
J. Shaw, WAS 45
A. Russell, NY, BOS 44
W. Kinney, PHI 43
S. Coveleski, CLE 43

	W	L	PCT	GB	R	OR	Batting 2B	3B	HR	BA	SA	SB	Fielding E	DP	FA	Pitching CG	BB	SO	ShO	SV	ERA
Chicago	88	52	.629		**667**	534	218	70	25	**.287**	.380	**150**	176	116	.969	88	**342**	468	14	3	3.04
Cleveland	84	55	.604	3.5	636	537	**254**	71	25	.278	**.381**	113	201	102	.965	80	362	432	10	**10**	2.92
New York	80	59	.576	7.5	578	**506**	193	49	**45**	.267	.356	101	192	108	.968	85	433	500	14	6	**2.78**
Detroit	80	60	.571	8	618	578	222	**84**	23	.283	**.381**	121	205	81	.964	85	431	428	10	4	3.30
Boston	66	71	.482	20.5	564	552	181	49	33	.261	.344	108	**141**	**118**	**.975**	**89**	420	380	**15**	8	3.30
St. Louis	67	72	.482	20.5	533	567	187	73	31	.264	.355	74	216	98	.963	77	421	415	14	4	3.13
Washington	56	84	.400	32	533	570	177	63	24	.260	.339	142	227	86	.960	69	451	**536**	12	8	3.01
Philadelphia	36	104	.257	52	457	742	175	71	35	.244	.334	103	259	96	.956	72	503	417	1	3	4.26
					4586	4586	1607	530	241	.268	.359	912	1617	805	.965	645	3363	3576	90	46	3.22

NATIONAL LEAGUE 1920

Brooklyn

W-93 L-61

Wilbert Robinson

POS	Player	AB	BA	HR	RBI	PO	A	E	DP	TC/G	FA	Pitcher	G	IP	W	L	SV	ERA
1B	E. Konetchy	497	.308	5	63	1332	79	14	70	11.0	.990	B. Grimes	40	304	23	11	2	2.22
2B	P. Kilduff	478	.272	0	58	316	454	26	69	5.9	.967	L. Cadore	35	254	15	14	0	2.62
SS	I. Olson	637	.254	1	46	275	404	47	48	5.8	.935	J. Pfeffer	30	215	16	9	0	3.01
3B	J. Johnston	635	.291	1	52	159	282	31	21	3.2	.934	A. Mamaux	41	191	12	8	4	2.69
RF	T. Griffith	334	.260	2	30	132	7	4	1	1.6	.972	R. Marquard	28	190	10	7	0	3.23
CF	H. Myers	582	.304	4	80	386	17	9	5	2.7	.978	S. Smith	33	136	11	9	3	1.85
LF	Z. Wheat	583	.328	9	73	287	10	9	5	2.1	.971							
C	O. Miller	301	.289	0	33	**418**	65	7	8	5.5	.986							
OF	B. Neis	249	.253	2	22	145	11	7	4	2.0	.957							

New York

W-86 L-68

John McGraw

POS	Player	AB	BA	HR	RBI	PO	A	E	DP	TC/G	FA	Pitcher	G	IP	W	L	SV	ERA
1B	G. Kelly	590	.266	11	**94**	**1759**	**103**	11	**115**	**12.1**	.994	J. Barnes	43	293	20	15	0	2.64
2B	L. Doyle	471	.285	4	50	278	389	23	61	5.2	.967	A. Nehf	40	281	21	12	0	3.08
SS	D. Bancroft	442	.299	0	31	256*	445*	40	67*	6.9*	.946*	F. Toney	42	278	21	11	1	2.65
3B	F. Frisch	440	.280	4	77	104	251	12	23	3.3	.967	P. Douglas	46	226	14	10	2	2.71
RF	R. Youngs	581	.351	6	78	288	26	22	7	2.2	.935	R. Benton	33	193	9	16	2	3.03
CF	L. King	261	.276	7	42	167	8	9	1	2.2	.951							
LF	G. Burns	631	.287	6	46	336	11	6	5	2.3	.983							
C	F. Snyder	264	.250	3	27	269	92	8	6	4.4	.978							
C	E. Smith	262	.294	1	30	252	73	8	12	4.1	.976							
SS	A. Fletcher	171	.257	0	24	79	154	22	16	6.2	.914							
OF	B. Kauff	157	.274	3	26	111	10	5	0	2.5	.960							

Cincinnati

W-82 L-71

Pat Moran

POS	Player	AB	BA	HR	RBI	PO	A	E	DP	TC/G	FA	Pitcher	G	IP	W	L	SV	ERA
1B	J. Daubert	553	.304	4	48	1358	63	15	90	10.3	.990	J. Ring	42	293	17	16	1	3.23
2B	M. Rath	506	.267	2	28	310	399	17	60	5.8	**.977**	D. Ruether	37	266	16	12	3	2.47
SS	L. Kopf	458	.245	0	59	249	363	47	0	5.4	.929	H. Eller	35	210	13	12	0	2.95
3B	H. Groh	550	.298	0	49	179	252	14	**30**	3.1	.969	D. Luque	37	208	13	9	1	2.51
RF	G. Neale	530	.255	3	46	347	19	5	7	2.5	.987	R. Fisher	33	201	10	11	1	2.73
CF	E. Roush	579	.339	4	90	410	18	11	6	3.2	.975	S. Sallee	21	116	5	6	2	3.34
LF	P. Duncan	576	.295	2	83	334	15	13	4	2.4	.964							
C	I. Wingo	364	.264	2	38	368	115	**21**	**14**	4.7	.958							

Pittsburgh

W-79 L-75

George Gibson

POS	Player	AB	BA	HR	RBI	PO	A	E	DP	TC/G	FA	Pitcher	G	IP	W	L	SV	ERA
1B	C. Grimm	533	.227	2	54	1496	95	8	95	10.8	**.995**	W. Cooper	44	327	24	15	2	2.39
2B	G. Cutshaw	488	.252	0	47	336	423	25	62	**6.1**	.968	B. Adams	35	263	17	13	2	2.16
SS	B. Caton	352	.236	0	27	191	296	37	40	5.5	.929	H. Carlson	39	247	14	13	3	3.36
3B	P. Whitted	494	.261	1	74	166	229	16	16	3.3	.961	E. Hamilton	39	231	10	13	3	3.24
RF	B. Southworth	546	.284	2	53	337	12	3	3	2.5	.991	E. Ponder	33	196	11	15	0	2.62
CF	M. Carey	485	.289	1	35	345	10	12	0	2.8	.967							
LF	C. Bigbee	550	.280	4	32	289	16	9	4	2.4	.971							
C	W. Schmidt	310	.277	0	20	323	109	13	10	4.8	.971							
OF	F. Nicholson	247	.360	4	30	125	9	6	2	2.4	.957							
S2	W. Barbare	186	.274	0	12	75	151	13	20		.946							
C	B. Haeffner	175	.194	0	14	192	48	7	1	4.8	.972							

NATIONAL LEAGUE 1920, *cont.*

Chicago

W-75 L-79

Fred Mitchell

POS	Player	AB	BA	HR	RBI	PO	A	E	DP	TC/G	FA	Pitcher	G	IP	W	L	SV	ERA
1B	F. Merkle	330	.285	3	38	906	54	15	52	11.5	.985	G. Alexander	46	**363**	**27**	14	5	**1.91**
2B	Z. Terry	496	.280	0	52	138	222	9	30	5.9	.976	H. Vaughn	40	301	19	16	0	2.54
SS	C. Hollocher	301	.319	0	22	196	280	23	34	6.2	.954	C. Hendrix	27	204	9	12	0	3.58
3B	C. Deal	450	.240	3	39	129	268	11	22	3.2	**.973**	L. Tyler	27	193	11	12	0	3.31
RF	M. Flack	520	.302	4	49	216	16	8	2	1.8	.967	S. Martin	35	136	4	15	2	4.83
CF	D. Paskert	487	.279	5	71	306	23	15	3	2.5	.956	P. Carter	31	106	3	6	2	4.67
LF	D. Robertson	500	.300	10	75	230	10	8	1	1.9	.968							
C	B. O'Farrell	270	.248	3	19	317	100	19	6	5.1	.956							
1B	T. Barber	340	.265	0	50	739	30	9	40	11.3	.988							
23	B. Herzog	305	.193	0	19	153	241	29	32		.931							
C	B. Killefer	191	.220	0	16	304	80	9	6	6.4	.977							
OF	B. Twombly	183	.235	2	14	91	6	3	0	2.2	.970							

St. Louis

W-75 L-79

Branch Rickey

POS	Player	AB	BA	HR	RBI	PO	A	E	DP	TC/G	FA	Pitcher	G	IP	W	L	SV	ERA
1B	J. Fournier	530	.306	3	61	1373	88	**25**	100	10.8	.983	J. Haines	**47**	302	13	20	2	2.98
2B	R. Hornsby	589	**.370**	9	**94**	**343**	**524**	**34**	**76**	6.0	.962	B. Doak	39	270	20	12	1	2.53
SS	D. Lavan	516	.289	1	63	327	489	**50**	77	6.3	.942	F. Schupp	38	251	16	13	0	3.52
3B	M. Stock	**639**	.319	0	76	158	**300**	30	23	3.1	.939	B. Sherdel	43	170	11	10	**6**	3.28
RF	J. Schultz	320	.263	0	32	147	7	9	3	2.0	.945	M. Goodwin	32	116	3	8	1	4.95
CF	C. Heathcote	489	.284	3	56	296	26	12	3	2.6	.964	E. Jacobs	23	78	4	8	1	5.21
LF	A. McHenry	504	.282	10	65	297	21	16	1	2.5	.952							
C	V. Clemons	338	.281	1	36	408	111	12	11	**5.2**	**.977**							
OF	J. Smith	313	.332	1	28	144	12	6	1	2.0	.963							
UT	H. Janvrin	270	.274	1	28	307	93	13	33		.969							
C	P. Dillhoefer	224	.263	0	13	291	72	18	6	5.2	.953							
OF	B. Shotton	180	.228	1	12	85	9	4	2	1.9	.959							

Boston

W-62 L-90

George Stallings

POS	Player	AB	BA	HR	RBI	PO	A	E	DP	TC/G	FA	Pitcher	G	IP	W	L	SV	ERA
1B	W. Holke	551	.294	3	64	1528	81	14	97	11.3	.991	J. Oeschger	38	299	15	13	0	3.46
2B	C. Pick	383	.274	2	28	219	333	28	45	6.2	.952	J. Scott	44	291	10	21	1	3.53
SS	R. Maranville	493	.266	1	43	354	462	45	62	6.5	.948	D. Fillingim	37	272	12	21	0	3.11
3B	T. Boeckel	582	.268	3	62	**219**	266	**33**	**30**	**3.4**	.936	H. McQuillan	38	226	11	15	5	3.55
RF	W. Cruise	288	.278	1	21	122	10	7	3	1.7	.950	D. Rudolph	18	89	4	8	0	4.04
CF	R. Powell	609	.225	6	29	370	25	18	5	2.8	.956							
LF	L. Mann	424	.276	3	32	228	13	5	1	2.2	.980							
C	M. O'Neil	304	.283	0	28	304	**153**	18	10	4.5	.962							
2B	H. Ford	257	.241	1	30	122	219	10	21	5.9	.972							
OF	J. Sullivan	250	.296	1	28	115	10	3	2	1.9	.977							
OF	E. Eayrs	244	.328	1	24	108	6	6	2	1.9	.950							
C	H. Gowdy	214	.243	0	18	231	104	7	12	4.6	.980							

Philadelphia

W-62 L-91

Gavvy Cravath

POS	Player	AB	BA	HR	RBI	PO	A	E	DP	TC/G	FA	Pitcher	G	IP	W	L	SV	ERA
1B	G. Paulette	562	.288	1	36	1428	99	18	94	11.1	.988	E. Rixey	41	284	11	**22**	2	3.48
2B	J. Rawlings	384	.234	3	30	221	321	17	53	5.8	.970	G. Smith	43	251	13	18	2	3.45
SS	A. Fletcher	379	.296	4	38	223	368	26	47	6.1	.958	L. Meadows	35	247	16	14	0	2.84
3B	R. Miller	338	.219	0	28	89	179	17	15	3.1	.940	R. Causey	35	181	7	14	3	4.32
RF	C. Stengel	445	.292	9	50	212	16	11	1	2.0	.954	B. Hubbell	24	150	9	9	2	3.84
CF	C. Williams	590	.325	**15**	72	388	22	12	4	2.9	.972	B. Gallia	18	72	2	6	2	4.50
LF	I. Meusel	518	.309	14	69	260	16	21	6	2.3	.929							
C	M. Wheat	230	.226	3	20	262	105	15	8	5.2	.961							
UT	D. Miller	343	.254	1	27	254	234	27	48		.948							
OF	B. LeBourveau	261	.257	3	12	133	16	8	1	2.2	.949							
3B	R. Wrightstone	206	.262	3	17	75	109	13	7	3.5	.934							
C	W. Tragesser	176	.210	6	26	157	46	12	4	4.1	.944							
SS	D. Bancroft	171	.298	0	5	106*	153*	5	28*	6.3*	.981*							

BATTING AND BASE RUNNING LEADERS

Batting Average

R. Hornsby, STL	.370
R. Youngs, NY	.351
E. Roush, CIN	.339
Z. Wheat, BKN	.328
C. Williams, PHI	.325

Slugging Average

R. Hornsby, STL	.559
C. Williams, PHI	.497
R. Youngs, NY	.477
I. Meusel, PHI	.473
Z. Wheat, BKN	.463

Home Runs

C. Williams, PHI	15
I. Meusel, PHI	14
G. Kelly, NY	11
D. Robertson, CHI	10
A. McHenry, STL	10

Total Bases

R. Hornsby, STL	329
C. Williams, PHI	293
R. Youngs, NY	277
Z. Wheat, BKN	270
H. Myers, BKN	269

Runs Batted In

R. Hornsby, STL	94
G. Kelly, NY	94
E. Roush, CIN	90
P. Duncan, CIN	83
H. Myers, BKN	80

Stolen Bases

M. Carey, PIT	52
E. Roush, CIN	36
F. Frisch, NY	34
C. Bigbee, PIT	31
G. Neale, CIN	29

Hits

R. Hornsby, STL	218
R. Youngs, NY	204
M. Stock, STL	204
E. Roush, CIN	196

Base on Balls

G. Burns, NY	76
R. Youngs, NY	75
D. Paskert, CHI	64
H. Groh, CIN	60
R. Hornsby, STL	60

Home Run Percentage

I. Meusel, PHI	2.7
C. Williams, PHI	2.5
C. Stengel, PHI	2.0
D. Robertson, CHI	2.0

Runs

G. Burns, NY	115
D. Bancroft, PHI, NY	102
J. Daubert, CIN	97
R. Hornsby, STL	96

Doubles

R. Hornsby, STL	44
H. Myers, BKN	36
C. Williams, PHI	36
D. Bancroft, PHI, NY	36

Triples

H. Myers, BKN	22
R. Hornsby, STL	20
E. Roush, CIN	16
R. Maranville, BOS	15
C. Bigbee, PIT	15

PITCHING LEADERS

Winning Percentage

B. Grimes, BKN	.676
G. Alexander, CHI	.659
F. Toney, NY	.656
J. Pfeffer, BKN	.640
A. Nehf, NY	.636

Earned Run Average

G. Alexander, CHI	1.91
B. Adams, PIT	2.16
B. Grimes, BKN	2.22
W. Cooper, PIT	2.39
D. Ruether, CIN	2.47

Wins

G. Alexander, CHI	27
W. Cooper, PIT	24
B. Grimes, BKN	23
F. Toney, NY	21
A. Nehf, NY	21

Saves

B. Sherdel, STL	6
G. Alexander, CHI	5
H. McQuillan, BOS	5
B. Hubbell, NY, PHI	4
A. Mamaux, BKN	4

Strikeouts

G. Alexander, CHI	173
H. Vaughn, CHI	131
B. Grimes, BKN	131
J. Haines, STL	120
F. Schupp, STL	119

Complete Games

G. Alexander, CHI	33
W. Cooper, PIT	28
B. Grimes, BKN	25
E. Rixey, PHI	25
H. Vaughn, CHI	24

Fewest Hits/9 Innings

D. Luque, CIN	7.28
D. Ruether, CIN	7.96
B. Grimes, BKN	8.03
B. Adams, PIT	8.21

Shutouts

B. Adams, PIT	8
G. Alexander, CHI	7

Fewest Walks/9 Innings

B. Adams, PIT	0.62
W. Cooper, PIT	1.43
A. Nehf, NY	1.44
R. Benton, NY	1.44

Most Strikeouts/9 Inn.

G. Alexander, CHI	4.29
F. Schupp, STL	4.27
R. Marquard, BKN	4.22
H. Vaughn, CHI	3.92

Innings

G. Alexander, CHI	363
W. Cooper, PIT	327
B. Grimes, BKN	304
J. Haines, STL	302

Games Pitched

J. Haines, STL	47
P. Douglas, NY	46
G. Alexander, CHI	46
J. Scott, BOS	44
W. Cooper, PIT	44

NATIONAL LEAGUE 1920, *cont.*

	W	L	PCT	GB	R	OR	Batting 2B	3B	HR	BA	SA	SB	Fielding E	DP	FA	Pitching CG	BB	SO	ShO	SV	ERA
Brooklyn	93	61	.604		660	**528**	205	**99**	28	.277	.367	70	226	118	.966	89	327	**553**	17	10	**2.62**
New York	86	68	.558	7	**682**	543	210	76	46	.269	.363	131	210	**137**	.969	86	297	380	**18**	9	2.80
Cincinnati	82	71	.536	10.5	639	569	169	76	18	.277	.349	158	200	125	.968	90	393	435	12	9	2.84
Pittsburgh	79	75	.513	14	530	552	162	90	16	.257	.332	**181**	**186**	119	**.971**	92	**280**	444	17	10	2.89
Chicago	75	79	.487	18	619	635	223	67	34	.264	.354	115	225	112	.965	**95**	382	508	13	9	3.27
St. Louis	75	79	.487	18	675	682	**238**	96	32	**.289**	**.385**	126	256	136	.961	72	479	529	9	**12**	3.43
Boston	62	90	.408	30	523	670	168	86	23	.260	.339	88	239	125	.964	93	415	368	13	6	3.54
Philadelphia	62	91	.405	30.5	565	714	229	54	**64**	.263	.364	100	232	135	.964	77	444	419	8	11	3.63
					4893	4893	1604	644	261	.270	.357	969	1774	1007	.966	694	3017	3636	107	76	3.13

AMERICAN LEAGUE 1920

	POS	Player	AB	BA	HR	RBI	PO	A	E	DP	TC/G	FA	Pitcher	G	IP	W	L	SV	ERA
Cleveland	1B	D. Johnston	535	.292	2	71	1427	91	12	83	10.4	.992	J. Bagby	**48**	**340**	**31**	12	0	2.89
	2B	B. Wambsganss	565	.244	1	55	414	489	**38**	75	6.2	.960	S. Coveleski	41	315	24	14	2	2.49
W-98 L-56	SS	R. Chapman	435	.303	3	49	243	371	26	43	**5.8**	.959	R. Caldwell	34	238	20	10	0	3.86
	3B	L. Gardner	597	.310	3	118	**156**	**362**	13	**32**	3.4	**.976**	G. Morton	29	137	8	6	1	4.47
Tris Speaker	RF	E. Smith	456	.316	12	103	217	8	7	1	1.8	.970	G. Uhle	27	85	4	5	1	5.21
	CF	T. Speaker	552	.388	8	107	363	24	9	8	2.7	.977							
	LF	C. Jamieson	370	.319	1	40	185	14	7	0	2.1	.966							
	C	S. O'Neill	489	.321	3	55	576	128	17	1	4.9	.976							
	OF	J. Evans	172	.349	0	23	79	6	3	0	2.0	.966							
	OF	S. Wood	137	.270	1	30	71	6	1	0	1.4	.987							
Chicago	1B	S. Collins	495	.303	1	63	1146	63	15	69	10.5	.988	R. Faber	40	319	23	13	1	2.99
	2B	E. Collins	602	.372	3	76	**449**	471	23	76	6.2	**.976**	E. Cicotte	37	303	21	10	2	3.26
W-96 L-58	SS	S. Risberg	458	.266	2	65	238	400	45	59	5.5	.934	L. Williams	39	299	22	14	0	3.91
	3B	B. Weaver	629	.331	2	74	153	276	**31**	15	3.7	.933	D. Kerr	45	254	21	9	**5**	3.37
Kid Gleason	RF	N. Leibold	413	.220	1	28	190	18	5	5	2.0	.977	R. Wilkinson	34	145	7	9	2	4.03
	CF	H. Felsch	556	.338	14	115	385	25	8	10	2.9	.981							
	LF	J. Jackson	570	.382	12	121	314	14	12	2	2.3	.965							
	C	R. Schalk	485	.270	1	61	**581**	138	10	**19**	4.8	**.986**							
	OF	A. Strunk	183	.230	1	14	96	3	2	0	2.1	.980*							
New York	1B	W. Pipp	610	.280	11	76	**1649**	100	15	**101**	**11.5**	.991	C. Mays	45	312	26	11	2	3.06
	2B	D. Pratt	574	.314	4	97	354	**515**	26	**77**	5.8	.971	B. Shawkey	38	268	20	13	2	**2.45**
W-95 L-59	SS	R. Peckinpaugh	534	.270	8	54	263	441	28	56	5.3	.962	J. Quinn	41	253	18	10	3	3.20
	3B	A. Ward	496	.256	11	54	132	303	16	23	**4.0**	.965	R. Collins	36	187	14	8	1	3.17
Miller Huggins	RF	B. Ruth	458	.376	**54**	**137**	259	21	19	3	2.2	.936	H. Thormahlen	29	143	9	6	1	4.14
	CF	P. Bodie	471	.295	7	79	264	12	9	2	2.2	.968	G. Mogridge	26	125	5	9	1	4.31
	LF	D. Lewis	365	.271	4	61	182	14	8	1	2.1	.961							
	C	M. Ruel	261	.268	1	15	317	62	6	2	4.8	.984							
	03	B. Meusel	460	.328	11	83	150	85	20	6		.922							
	C	T. Hannah	259	.247	2	25	308	64	15	1	5.0	.961							
St. Louis	1B	G. Sisler	**631**	**.407**	19	122	1477	**140**	16	87	10.6	.990	D. Davis	38	269	18	12	0	3.17
	2B	J. Gedeon	606	.292	0	61	365	421	29	75	5.3	.964	U. Shocker	38	246	20	10	**5**	2.71
W-76 L-77	SS	W. Gerber	584	.279	2	60	288	**513**	**52**	**65**	5.5	.939	A. Sothoron	36	218	8	15	2	4.70
	3B	J. Austin	280	.271	1	32	108	171	17	14	3.9	.943	C. Weilman	30	183	9	13	2	4.47
Jimmy Burke	RF	J. Tobin	593	.341	4	62	293	18	13	1	2.2	.960	B. Burwell	33	113	6	4	4	3.65
	CF	B. Jacobson	609	.355	9	122	394	18	9	5	2.7	.979	E. Vangilder	24	105	3	8	0	5.50
	LF	K. Williams	521	.307	10	72	331	17	14	6	2.6	.961	B. Bayne	18	100	5	6	0	3.70
	C	H. Severeid	422	.277	2	49	480	111	10	11	**5.1**	.983							
	3B	E. Smith	353	.306	3	55	73	146	20	2	3.4	.916							
	C	J. Billings	155	.277	0	11	138	36	6	1	4.5	.967							
Boston	1B	S. McInnis	559	.297	2	71	1586	91	7	**101**	11.4	**.996**	S. Jones	37	274	13	16	0	3.94
	2B	M. McNally	312	.256	0	23	168	233	30	38	5.7	.930	J. Bush	35	244	15	15	1	4.25
W-72 L-81	SS	E. Scott	569	.269	4	61	**330**	496	23	64	5.5	**.973**	H. Pennock	37	242	16	13	2	3.68
	3B	E. Foster	386	.259	0	41	99	233	15	20	3.9	.957	H. Harper	27	163	5	14	0	3.04
Ed Barrow	RF	M. Menosky	532	.297	3	64	281	17	12	2	2.2	.961	W. Hoyt	22	121	6	6	1	4.38
	CF	T. Hendryx	363	.328	0	73	208	6	8	1	2.3	.964	A. Russell	16	108	5	6	1	3.01
	LF	H. Hooper	536	.312	7	53	263	22	11	2	2.1	.963	E. Myers	12	97	9	1	0	2.13
	C	R. Walters	258	.198	0	28	351	94	9	15	5.3	.980	B. Karr	26	92	3	8	1	4.81
	CO	W. Schang	387	.305	4	51	377	83	18	8		.962							
	3B	O. Vitt	296	.220	1	28	61	148	3	5	3.3	.986							
	2B	C. Brady	180	.228	0	12	111	193	8	21	5.9	.974							
Washington	1B	J. Judge	493	.333	5	51	1194	62	10	67	10.2	.992	T. Zachary	44	263	15	16	2	3.77
	2B	B. Harris	506	.300	1	68	345	401	33	59	5.8	.958	E. Erickson	39	239	12	16	1	3.84
	SS	J. O'Neill	294	.289	1	40	130	251	23	22	5.1	.943	J. Shaw	38	236	11	18	1	4.27
W-68 L-84	3B	F. Ellerbe	336	.292	0	36	101	167	19	8	3.8	.934	H. Courtney	37	188	8	11	0	4.74
	RF	B. Roth	468	.291	9	92	184	15	10	0	1.6	.952	W. Johnson	21	144	8	10	3	3.13
Clark Griffith	CF	S. Rice	624	.338	3	80	454	24	20	5	3.3	.960	A. Schacht	22	99	6	4	1	4.44
	LF	C. Milan	506	.322	3	41	291	15	9	1	2.6	.971	J. Acosta	17	83	5	4	1	4.03
	C	P. Gharrity	428	.245	3	44	409	148	**20**	13	4.8	.965							
	UT	H. Shanks	444	.268	4	37	294	154	17	12		.963							
	UT	R. Shannon	222	.288	0	30	89	148	18	14		.929							

AMERICAN LEAGUE 1920, *cont.*

Detroit

W-61 L-93

Hughie Jennings

POS	Player	AB	BA	HR	RBI	PO	A	E	DP	TC/G	FA
1B	H. Heilmann	543	.309	9	89	1207	80	**19**	52	10.7	.985
2B	R. Young	594	.291	0	33	405	436	27	46	5.8	.969
SS	D. Bush	506	.263	1	33	258	421	45	39	5.2	.938
3B	B. Pinelli	284	.229	0	21	110	183	14	20	4.1	.954
RF	C. Shorten	364	.288	1	40	168	14	2	3	1.9	.989
CF	T. Cobb	428	.334	2	63	246	8	9	2	2.3	.966
LF	B. Veach	612	.307	11	113	357	26	13	4	2.6	.967
C	O. Stanage	238	.231	0	17	248	75	14	4	4.3	.958
OF	I. Flagstead	311	.235	3	35	164	13	6	4	2.2	.967
3B	B. Jones	265	.249	1	18	80	146	14	7	3.6	.942
C	E. Ainsmith	186	.231	1	19	219	55	13	4	4.7	.955
1B	B. Ellison	155	.219	0	21	363	26	1	13	10.3	.997

Pitcher	G	IP	W	L	SV	ERA
H. Dauss	38	270	13	21	0	3.56
H. Ehmke	38	268	15	18	3	3.29
R. Oldham	39	215	8	13	1	3.85
D. Ayers	46	209	7	14	1	3.88
D. Leonard	28	191	10	17	0	4.33

Philadelphia

W-48 L-106

Connie Mack

POS	Player	AB	BA	HR	RBI	PO	A	E	DP	TC/G	FA
1B	I. Griffin	467	.238	0	20	1252	96	13	77	10.8	.990
2B	J. Dykes	546	.256	8	35	305	373	32	38	**6.6**	.955
SS	C. Galloway	298	.201	0	18	184	252	34	22	5.6	.928
3B	F. Thomas	255	.231	1	11	78	140	9	9	3.7	.960
RF	W. Witt	218	.321	1	25	68	2	3	0	1.5	.959
CF	F. Welch	360	.258	4	40	194	14	14	4	2.3	.937
LF	T. Walker	585	.268	17	82	318	26	22	5	2.5	.940
C	C. Perkins	493	.260	5	52	524	**179**	15	15	4.9	.979
UT	J. Dugan	491	.322	3	60	225	328	35	48		.940
OF	A. Strunk	202	.297	0	20	99	2	1	0	1.9	.990*
OC	G. Myatt	196	.250	0	18	83	22	10	3		.913

Pitcher	G	IP	W	L	SV	ERA
S. Perry	42	264	11	**25**	1	3.62
R. Naylor	42	251	10	23	0	3.47
S. Harriss	31	192	9	14	0	4.08
E. Rommel	33	174	7	7	1	2.85
R. Moore	24	133	1	13	0	4.68
D. Keefe	31	130	6	7	0	2.97

BATTING AND BASE RUNNING LEADERS

Batting Average

G. Sisler, STL	.407
T. Speaker, CLE	.388
J. Jackson, CHI	.382
B. Ruth, NY	.376
E. Collins, CHI	.372

Slugging Average

B. Ruth, NY	.847
G. Sisler, STL	.632
J. Jackson, CHI	.589
T. Speaker, CLE	.562
H. Felsch, CHI	.540

Home Runs

B. Ruth, NY	54
G. Sisler, STL	19
T. Walker, PHI	17
H. Felsch, CHI	14
E. Smith, CLE	12
J. Jackson, CHI	12

Total Bases

G. Sisler, STL	399
B. Ruth, NY	388
J. Jackson, CHI	336
T. Speaker, CLE	310
B. Jacobson, STL	305

Runs Batted In

B. Ruth, NY	137
B. Jacobson, STL	122
G. Sisler, STL	122
J. Jackson, CHI	121
L. Gardner, CLE	118

Stolen Bases

S. Rice, WAS	63
G. Sisler, STL	42
B. Roth, WAS	24
M. Menosky, BOS	23
J. Tobin, STL	21

Hits

G. Sisler, STL	257
E. Collins, CHI	224
J. Jackson, CHI	218
B. Jacobson, STL	216

Base on Balls

B. Ruth, NY	148
T. Speaker, CLE	97
H. Hooper, BOS	88
R. Young, DET	85

Home Run Percentage

B. Ruth, NY	11.8
G. Sisler, STL	3.0
T. Walker, PHI	2.9
E. Smith, CLE	2.6

Runs

B. Ruth, NY	158
T. Speaker, CLE	137
G. Sisler, STL	137
E. Collins, CHI	117

Doubles

T. Speaker, CLE	50
G. Sisler, STL	49
J. Jackson, CHI	42

Triples

J. Jackson, CHI	20
G. Sisler, STL	18
H. Hooper, BOS	17

PITCHING LEADERS

Winning Percentage

J. Bagby, CLE	.721
C. Mays, NY	.703
D. Kerr, CHI	.700
E. Cicotte, CHI	.677
U. Shocker, STL	.667
R. Caldwell, CLE	.667

Earned Run Average

B. Shawkey, NY	2.45
S. Coveleski, CLE	2.49
U. Shocker, STL	2.71
J. Bagby, CLE	2.89
R. Faber, CHI	2.99

Wins

J. Bagby, CLE	31
C. Mays, NY	26
S. Coveleski, CLE	24
R. Faber, CHI	23
L. Williams, CHI	22

Saves

U. Shocker, STL	5
D. Kerr, CHI	5
B. Burwell, STL	4
H. Ehmke, DET	3
J. Quinn, NY	3
W. Johnson, WAS	3

Strikeouts

S. Coveleski, CLE	133
L. Williams, CHI	128
B. Shawkey, NY	126
R. Faber, CHI	108
U. Shocker, STL	107

Complete Games

J. Bagby, CLE	30
E. Cicotte, CHI	28
R. Faber, CHI	28
S. Coveleski, CLE	26
C. Mays, NY	26
L. Williams, CHI	26

Fewest Hits/9 Innings

S. Coveleski, CLE	8.11
U. Shocker, STL	8.21
R. Collins, NY	8.22
B. Shawkey, NY	8.27

Shutouts

C. Mays, NY	6
U. Shocker, STL	5
B. Shawkey, NY	5

Fewest Walks/9 Innings

W. Johnson, WAS	1.69
J. Quinn, NY	1.71
S. Coveleski, CLE	1.86
J. Bagby, CLE	2.09

Most Strikeouts/9 Inn.

W. Johnson, WAS	4.89
B. Shawkey, NY	4.24
H. Harper, BOS	3.93
U. Shocker, STL	3.92

Innings

J. Bagby, CLE	340
R. Faber, CHI	319
S. Coveleski, CLE	315
C. Mays, NY	312

Games Pitched

J. Bagby, CLE	48
D. Ayers, DET	46
D. Kerr, CHI	45
C. Mays, NY	45

							Batting						Fielding			Pitching					
	W	L	PCT	GB	R	OR	2B	3B	HR	BA	SA	SB	E	DP	FA	CG	BB	SO	ShO	SV	ERA
Cleveland	98	56	.636		**857**	642	**301**	95	35	.303	.417	73	185	124	.971	93	**401**	466	10	7	3.41
Chicago	96	58	.623	2	794	665	263	**97**	37	.295	.402	108	198	**142**	.968	**112**	405	440	9	10	3.59
New York	95	59	.617	3	838	**629**	268	71	**115**	.280	**.426**	64	193	129	.970	88	420	480	**16**	11	**3.31**
St. Louis	76	77	.497	21.5	797	766	278	84	50	**.308**	.419	121	232	119	.963	84	578	444	9	**14**	4.03
Boston	72	81	.471	25.5	650	698	216	71	22	.269	.351	98	**183**	131	**.972**	91	461	481	11	6	3.82
Washington	68	84	.447	29	723	802	232	81	36	.290	.386	**161**	232	95	.963	80	520	418	10	10	4.17
Detroit	61	93	.396	37	652	833	228	72	30	.270	.358	75	229	95	.965	76	561	**483**	9	7	4.04
Philadelphia	48	106	.312	50	558	834	218	49	44	.252	.337	51	267	126	.959	81	461	423	5	2	3.93
					5869	5869	2004	620	369	.283	.387	751	1719	961	.966	705	3807	3635	79	67	3.79

NATIONAL LEAGUE 1921

Team	POS	Player	AB	BA	HR	RBI	PO	A	E	DP	TC/G	FA	Pitcher	G	IP	W	L	SV	ERA
New York	1B	G. Kelly	587	.308	**23**	122	**1552**	**115**	17	**132**	11.3	.990	A. Nehf	41	261	20	10	1	3.63
W-94 L-59	2B	J. Rawlings	307	.267	1	30	204*	280*	15*	61*	5.8	.970	J. Barnes	42	259	15	9	6	3.10
John McGraw	SS	D. Bancroft	606	.318	6	67	**396**	**546**	39	**105**	6.4	.960	F. Toney	42	249	18	11	3	3.61
	3B	F. Frisch	618	.341	8	100	79	200	19	16	3.2	.936	P. Douglas	40	222	15	10	2	4.22
	RF	R. Youngs	504	.327	3	102	122	11	3	3	1.0	.978	R. Ryan	36	147	7	10	3	3.73
	CF	G. Burns	605	.299	4	61	360	16	11	2	2.6	.972	S. Sallee	37	96	6	4	2	3.64
	LF	I. Meusel	243	.329	2	36	122	10	4	0	2.2	.971							
	C	F. Snyder	309	.320	8	45	299	98	6	7	4.0	.985							
	C	E. Smith	229	.336	10	51	195	56	9	4	3.3	.965							
	OF	C. Walker	192	.286	3	35	247	16	6	5	4.6	.978							
	3B	G. Rapp	181	.215	0	15	55	135	12	12	3.6*	.941							
Pittsburgh	1B	C. Grimm	562	.274	7	71	1517	67	9	93	10.6	.994	W. Cooper	38	**327**	**22**	14	0	3.25
W-90 L-63	2B	G. Cutshaw	350	.340	0	53	196	253	23	36	5.6	.951	W. Glazner	36	234	14	5	1	2.77
George Gibson	SS	R. Maranville	612	.294	1	70	325	529	34	72	5.8	.962	E. Hamilton	35	225	13	15	0	3.36
	3B	C. Barnhart	449	.258	3	62	101	204	14	19	2.7	.956	B. Adams	25	160	14	5	0	2.64
	RF	P. Whitted	403	.283	7	63	247	9	3	6	2.5	.988	J. Morrison	21	144	9	7	0	2.88
	CF	M. Carey	521	.309	7	56	431	15	20	6	3.4	.957	J. Zinn	32	127	7	6	4	3.68
	LF	C. Bigbee	632	.323	3	42	351	27	9	6	2.7	.977	H. Carlson	31	110	4	8	4	4.27
	C	W. Schmidt	393	.282	0	38	**438**	**120**	8	**15**	**5.1**	**.986**							
	23	C. Tierney	442	.299	3	52	191	237	18	37		.960							
	OF	D. Robertson	230	.322	6	48	117	2	5	0	2.1	.960							
St. Louis	1B	J. Fournier	574	.343	16	86	1416	73	19	91	10.1	.987	J. Haines	37	244	18	12	0	3.50
W-87 L-66	2B	R. Hornsby	592	**.397**	21	**126**	305	477	25	59	5.7	.969	B. Doak	32	209	15	6	1	**2.59**
Branch Rickey	SS	D. Lavan	560	.259	2	82	382	540	**49**	88	6.5	.950	B. Pertica	38	208	14	10	2	3.37
	3B	M. Stock	587	.307	3	84	148	243	25	21	2.8	.940	R. Walker	38	171	11	12	3	4.22
	RF	J. Smith	411	.328	7	33	179	11	9	3	1.9	.955	B. Sherdel	38	144	9	8	1	3.18
	CF	L. Mann	256	.328	7	30	174	11	6	2	2.4	.969	J. Pfeffer	18	99	9	3	0	4.29
	LF	A. McHenry	574	.350	17	102	371	13	14	3	2.6	.965	L. North	40	86	4	4	**7**	3.54
	C	V. Clemons	341	.320	2	48	357	101	7	12	4.3	.985							
	OF	J. Schultz	275	.309	6	45	120	7	3	4	1.9	.977							
	OF	H. Mueller	176	.352	1	34	117	5	3	1	2.3	.976							
	C	P. Dillhoefer	162	.241	0	15	170	52	11	0	3.4	.953							
	OF	C. Heathcote	156	.244	0	9	83	5	7	0	1.9	.926							
Boston	1B	W. Holke	579	.261	3	63	1471	86	4	100	10.4	**.997**	J. Oeschger	46	299	20	14	0	3.52
W-79 L-74	2B	H. Ford	555	.279	2	61	297	417	20	48	**6.2**	.973	M. Watson	44	259	14	13	2	3.85
Fred Mitchell	SS	W. Barbare	550	.302	0	49	294	393	31	58	5.9	.957	H. McQuillan	45	250	13	17	5	4.00
	3B	T. Boeckel	592	.313	10	84	**184**	276	**33**	19	3.2	.933	D. Fillingim	44	240	15	10	1	3.45
	RF	B. Southworth	569	.308	7	79	288	25	8	6	2.3	.975	J. Scott	**47**	234	15	13	3	3.70
	CF	R. Powell	624	.306	12	74	377	21	19	3	2.8	.954							
	LF	W. Cruise	344	.346	8	55	232	2	9	3	2.4	.963							
	C	M. O'Neil	277	.249	2	29	276	117	13	8	4.3	.968							
	OF	F. Nicholson	245	.327	5	41	112	4	2	0	2.0	.983							
	C	H. Gowdy	164	.299	2	17	162	50	4	3	4.1	.981							
Brooklyn	1B	R. Schmandt	350	.306	1	43	941	52	11	74	10.9	.989	B. Grimes	37	302	**22**	13	0	2.83
W-77 L-75	2B	P. Kilduff	372	.288	3	45	243	379	24	57	6.2	.963	L. Cadore	35	212	13	14	0	4.17
Wilbert Robinson	SS	I. Olson	**652**	.267	3	35	343	465	**49**	77	6.4	.943	D. Ruether	36	211	10	13	2	4.26
	3B	J. Johnston	624	.325	5	56	162	**312**	**33**	**34**	3.4	.935	C. Mitchell	37	190	11	9	2	2.89
	RF	T. Griffith	455	.312	12	71	215	27	7	5	2.0	.972	S. Smith	35	175	7	11	4	3.90
	CF	H. Myers	549	.288	4	68	278	25	10	5	2.5	.968	J. Miljus	28	94	6	3	1	4.23
	LF	Z. Wheat	568	.320	14	85	283	18	11	3	2.1	.965							
	C	O. Miller	286	.234	1	27	338	107	13	10	5.0	.972							
	OF	B. Neis	230	.257	4	34	126	13	8	1	1.9	.946							
	1B	E. Konetchy	197	.269	3	23	564	28	8*	41	11.1*	.987							
	C	E. Krueger	163	.264	3	20	179	39	7	4	4.3	.969							
Cincinnati	1B	J. Daubert	516	.306	2	64	1290	78	10	98	10.1	.993	D. Luque	41	304	17	19	3	3.38
W-70 L-83	2B	S. Bohne	613	.285	3	44	256	327	16	56	5.9	**.973**	E. Rixey	40	301	19	18	1	2.78
Pat Moran	SS	L. Kopf	367	.218	1	25	195	304	28	39	5.7	.947	R. Marquard	39	266	17	14	0	3.39
	3B	H. Groh	357	.331	0	48	97	188	15	27	3.1	.950	P. Donohue	21	118	7	6	1	3.35
	RF	R. Bressler	323	.307	1	54	155	6	8	2	2.0	.953	L. Brenton	17	60	1	8	1	4.05
	CF	E. Roush	418	.352	4	71	286	9	6	0	2.8	.980							
	LF	P. Duncan	532	.308	2	60	349	19	11	2	2.6	.971							
	C	I. Wingo	295	.268	3	38	318	101	**18**	11	4.8	.959							
	UT	L. Fonseca	297	.276	1	41	307	155	14	30		.971							
	C	B. Hargrave	263	.289	1	38	270	50	9	2	4.5	.973							
	OF	G. Neale	241	.241	0	12	128	7	5	2	2.3	.964							
	SS	S. Crane	215	.233	0	16	129	173	15	32	5.0	.953							
Chicago	1B	R. Grimes	530	.321	6	79	1544	68	12	93	11.0	.993	G. Alexander	31	252	15	13	1	3.39
W-64 L-89	2B	Z. Terry	488	.275	2	45	272	413	20	57	5.7	.972	S. Martin	37	217	11	15	1	4.35
Johnny Evers	SS	C. Hollocher	558	.289	3	37	282	491	30	72	5.9	**.963**	B. Freeman	38	177	9	10	3	4.11
W-41 L-55	3B	C. Deal	422	.289	3	66	122	239	10	19	3.3	**.973**	V. Cheeves	37	163	11	12	0	4.64
Bill Killefer	RF	M. Flack	572	.301	6	37	244	19	3	2	2.0	.989	L. York	40	139	5	9	1	4.73
W-23 L-34	CF	G. Maisel	393	.310	0	43	259	12	6	2	2.6	.978	H. Vaughn	17	109	3	11	0	6.01
	LF	T. Barber	452	.314	1	54	234	23	8	4	2.2	.970							
	C	B. O'Farrell	260	.250	4	32	269	87	12	8	4.1	.967							
	UT	J. Kelleher	301	.309	4	47	192	194	15	31		.963							
	OF	J. Sullivan	240	.329	4	41	122	3	5	0	2.0	.962							
	OF	B. Twombly	175	.377	1	18	81	11	3	0	2.1	.968							
	C	T. Daly	143	.238	0	22	171	48	6	10	4.8	.973							

NATIONAL LEAGUE 1921, *cont.*

Philadelphia

W-51 L-103

Wild Bill Donovan
W-25 L-62

Kaiser Wilhelm
W-26 L-41

POS	Player	AB	BA	HR	RBI	PO	A	E	DP	TC/G	FA
1B	E. Konetchy	268	.321	8	59	771	55	12*	38	11.8*	.986
2B	J. Smith	247	.231	4	22	125	239	11	19	5.7	.971
SS	F. Parkinson	391	.253	5	32	233	404	47	55	**6.5**	.931
3B	R. Wrightstone	372	.296	9	51	58	108	14	6	3.3	.922
RF	B. LeBourveau	281	.295	6	35	126	7	13	2	1.9	.911
CF	C. Williams	562	.320	18	75	382	29	9	5	2.9	.979
LF	I. Meusel	343	.353	12	51	153	18	13	4	2.2	.929
C	F. Bruggy	277	.310	5	28	231	73	15	14	3.7	.953
31	D. Miller	320	.297	0	23	433	96	18	35		.967
10	C. Lee	286	.308	4	29	542	22	10	35		.983
2B	J. Rawlings	254	.291	1	16	138*	215*	17*	32*	6.2	.954
OF	L. King	216	.269	4	32	115	8	12	0	2.4	.911
SS	R. Miller	204	.304	3	26	91	132	22	20	5.3	.910
3B	G. Rapp	202	.277	1	10	62	90	8	7	3.2*	.950
C	J. Peters	155	.290	3	23	116	24	10	0	3.4	.933

Pitcher	G	IP	W	L	SV	ERA
J. Ring	34	246	10	19	1	4.24
G. Smith	39	221	4	**20**	1	4.76
B. Hubbell	36	220	9	16	2	4.33
L. Meadows	28	194	11	16	0	4.31
J. Winters	18	114	5	10	0	3.63
H. Betts	32	101	3	7	4	4.47

BATTING AND BASE RUNNING LEADERS

Batting Average
- R. Hornsby, STL .397
- E. Roush, CIN .352
- A. McHenry, STL .350
- W. Cruise, BOS .346
- J. Fournier, STL .343

Slugging Average
- R. Hornsby, STL .639
- A. McHenry, STL .531
- G. Kelly, NY .528
- I. Meusel, PHI, NY .515
- J. Fournier, STL .505

Home Runs
- G. Kelly, NY 23
- R. Hornsby, STL 21
- C. Williams, PHI 18
- A. McHenry, STL 17
- J. Fournier, STL 16

Total Bases
- R. Hornsby, STL 378
- G. Kelly, NY 310
- A. McHenry, STL 305
- I. Meusel, PHI, NY 302
- F. Frisch, NY 300

Runs Batted In
- R. Hornsby, STL 126
- G. Kelly, NY 122
- R. Youngs, NY 102
- A. McHenry, STL 102
- F. Frisch, NY 100

Stolen Bases
- F. Frisch, NY 49
- M. Carey, PIT 37
- J. Johnston, BKN 28
- S. Bohne, CIN 26
- R. Maranville, PIT 25

Hits
- R. Hornsby, STL 235
- F. Frisch, NY 211
- C. Bigbee, PIT 204
- J. Johnston, BKN 203

Base on Balls
- G. Burns, NY 80
- R. Youngs, NY 71
- M. Carey, PIT 70
- R. Grimes, CHI 70

Home Run Percentage
- G. Kelly, NY 3.9
- R. Hornsby, STL 3.5
- C. Williams, PHI 3.2
- A. McHenry, STL 3.0

Runs
- R. Hornsby, STL 131
- D. Bancroft, NY 121
- F. Frisch, NY 121
- R. Powell, BOS 114

Doubles
- R. Hornsby, STL 44
- G. Kelly, NY 42
- J. Johnston, BKN 41
- R. Grimes, CHI 38

Triples
- R. Hornsby, STL 18
- R. Powell, BOS 18
- C. Grimm, PIT 17
- F. Frisch, NY 17
- C. Bigbee, PIT 17

PITCHING LEADERS

Winning Percentage
- B. Doak, STL .714
- A. Nehf, NY .667
- B. Grimes, BKN .629
- J. Barnes, NY .625
- F. Toney, NY .621

Earned Run Average
- B. Doak, STL 2.59
- B. Adams, PIT 2.64
- W. Glazner, PIT 2.77
- E. Rixey, CIN 2.78
- B. Grimes, BKN 2.83

Wins
- B. Grimes, BKN 22
- W. Cooper, PIT 22
- A. Nehf, NY 20
- J. Oeschger, BOS 20
- E. Rixey, CIN 19

Saves
- L. North, STL 7
- J. Barnes, NY 6
- H. McQuillan, BOS 5

Strikeouts
- B. Grimes, BKN 136
- W. Cooper, PIT 134
- D. Luque, CIN 102
- H. McQuillan, BOS 94

Complete Games
- B. Grimes, BKN 30
- W. Cooper, PIT 29
- D. Luque, CIN 25
- G. Alexander, CHI 21
- J. Ring, PHI 21
- E. Rixey, CIN 21

Fewest Hits/9 Innings
- J. Morrison, PIT 8.19
- W. Glazner, PIT 8.23
- B. Adams, PIT 8.72
- J. Oeschger, BOS 9.12

Shutouts
- 8 tied with 3

Fewest Walks/9 Innings
- B. Adams, PIT 1.01
- G. Alexander, CHI 1.18
- J. Barnes, NY 1.53
- B. Hubbell, PHI 1.55

Most Strikeouts/9 Inn.
- B. Grimes, BKN 4.05
- W. Cooper, PIT 3.69
- B. Doak, STL 3.58
- S. Martin, CHI 3.56

Innings
- W. Cooper, PIT 327
- D. Luque, CIN 304
- B. Grimes, BKN 302
- E. Rixey, CIN 301

Games Pitched
- J. Scott, BOS 47
- J. Oeschger, BOS 46
- H. McQuillan, BOS 45
- D. Fillingim, BOS 44
- M. Watson, BOS 44

							Batting						Fielding			Pitching					
	W	L	PCT	GB	R	OR	2B	3B	HR	BA	SA	SB	E	DP	FA	CG	BB	SO	ShO	SV	ERA
New York	94	59	.614		**840**	637	237	93	75	.298	.421	**137**	187	**155**	.971	71	**295**	357	9	**18**	3.55
Pittsburgh	90	63	.588	4	692	**595**	231	**104**	37	.285	.387	134	172	129	.973	**88**	322	**500**	10	10	**3.17**
St. Louis	87	66	.569	7	809	681	**260**	88	83	**.308**	**.437**	94	219	130	.965	71	399	464	10	16	3.62
Boston	79	74	.516	15	721	697	209	100	61	.290	.400	94	199	122	.969	74	420	382	**11**	12	3.90
Brooklyn	77	75	.507	16.5	667	681	209	85	59	.280	.386	91	232	142	.964	82	361	471	8	12	3.70
Cincinnati	70	83	.458	24	618	649	221	94	20	.278	.370	117	193	139	.969	83	305	408	7	9	3.46
Chicago	64	89	.418	30	668	773	234	56	37	.292	.378	70	**166**	129	**.974**	73	409	441	7	7	4.39
Philadelphia	51	103	.331	43.5	617	919	238	50	**88**	.284	.397	66	295	127	.955	82	371	333	5	8	4.48
					5632	5632	1839	670	460	.289	.397	803	1663	1073	.967	624	2882	3356	67	92	3.78

AMERICAN LEAGUE 1921

New York

W-98 L-55

Miller Huggins

POS	Player	AB	BA	HR	RBI	PO	A	E	DP	TC/G	FA
1B	W. Pipp	588	.296	8	97	1624	89	16	116	11.3	.991
2B	A. Ward	556	.306	5	75	262	409	26	35	5.7	.963
SS	R. Peckinpaugh	577	.288	8	71	318	443	42	75	5.4	.948
3B	F. Baker	330	.294	9	71	84	173	11	16	3.2	.959
RF	B. Meusel	598	.318	24	135	253	28	20	8	2.0	.934
CF	E. Miller	242	.298	4	36	134	10	8	2	2.7	.947
LF	B. Ruth	540	.378	**59**	**171**	348	17	13	6	2.5	.966
C	W. Schang	424	.316	6	55	500	101	19	13	4.7	.969
3B	M. McNally	215	.260	1	24	54	131	5	5	4.0	.974
OF	C. Fewster	207	.280	1	19	71	5	2	1	1.8	.974
P	C. Mays	143	.343	2	22	8	104	2	4	2.3	.982

Pitcher	G	IP	W	L	SV	ERA
C. Mays	**49**	**337**	**27**	9	**7**	3.05
W. Hoyt	43	282	19	13	3	3.09
B. Shawkey	38	245	18	12	2	4.08
R. Collins	28	137	11	5	0	5.44
J. Quinn	33	129	8	7	0	3.48

AMERICAN LEAGUE 1921, *cont.*

Team	POS	Player	AB	BA	HR	RBI	PO	A	E	DP	TC/G	FA	Pitcher	G	IP	W	L	SV	ERA
Cleveland	1B	D. Johnston	384	.297	2	44	960	62	12	72	8.9	.988	S. Coveleski	43	316	23	13	2	3.36
	2B	B. Wambsganss	410	.285	2	46	268	255	20	51	5.3	.963	G. Uhle	41	238	16	13	2	4.01
W-94 L-60	SS	J. Sewell	572	.318	4	91	319	480	47	75	5.5	.944	D. Mails	34	194	14	8	2	3.94
	3B	L. Gardner	586	.319	3	115	179	**335**	**27**	23	3.6	.950	J. Bagby	40	192	14	12	4	4.70
Tris Speaker	RF	E. Smith	431	.290	16	84	183	16	6	1	1.6	.971	R. Caldwell	37	147	6	6	4	4.90
	CF	T. Speaker	506	.362	3	74	345	15	6	2	2.9	.984	A. Sothoron	22	145	12	4	0	3.24
	LF	C. Jamieson	536	.310	1	45	277	17	8	3	2.2	.974	G. Morton	30	108	8	3	0	2.76
	C	S. O'Neill	335	.322	1	50	393	92	9	8	4.7	.982							
	1B	G. Burns	244	.361	0	48	534	41	6	40	8.0	.990							
	2B	R. Stephenson	206	.330	2	34	122	153	17	30	5.4	.942							
	OF	S. Wood	194	.366	4	60	105	3	3	1	1.7	.973							
	OF	J. Evans	153	.333	0	21	90	8	7	2	2.2	.933							
	C	L. Nunamaker	131	.359	0	24	166	31	6	3	4.4	.970							
St. Louis	1B	G. Sisler	582	.371	12	104	1267	108	10	86	10.0	.993	U. Shocker	47	327	**27**	12	4	3.55
	2B	M. McManus	412	.260	3	64	212	269	24	44	5.3	.952	D. Davis	40	265	16	16	0	4.44
W-81 L-73	SS	W. Gerber	436	.278	2	48	269	331	36	60	5.6	.943	E. Vangilder	31	180	11	12	0	3.94
	3B	F. Ellerbe	430	.288	2	48	158	226	19	9	3.8	.953	R. Kolp	37	167	8	7	0	4.97
Lee Fohl	RF	J. Tobin	**671**	.352	8	59	277	28	14	5	2.1	.956	B. Bayne	47	164	11	5	3	4.72
	CF	B. Jacobson	599	.352	5	90	375	7	7	1	2.8	.982	E. Palmero	24	90	4	7	0	5.00
	LF	K. Williams	547	.347	24	117	331	24	26	3	2.6	.932							
	C	H. Severeid	472	.324	2	78	481	117	17	11	4.9	.972							
	S2	D. Lee	180	.167	0	11	138	151	19	30		.938							
Washington	1B	J. Judge	622	.301	7	72	1417	89	6	109	9.9	.996	G. Mogridge	38	288	18	14	0	3.00
	2B	B. Harris	584	.289	0	54	407	481	38	**91**	6.0	.959	W. Johnson	35	264	17	14	1	3.51
W-80 L-73	SS	F. O'Rourke	444	.234	3	54	272	378	**55**	52	5.8	.922	T. Zachary	39	250	18	16	1	3.96
	3B	H. Shanks	562	.302	7	69	**218**	330	23	**35**	3.7	**.960**	E. Erickson	32	179	8	10	0	3.62
George McBride	RF	C. Milan	406	.288	1	40	196	19	16	2	2.4	.931	H. Courtney	30	133	6	9	1	5.63
	CF	S. Rice	561	.330	4	79	380	18	15	3	2.9	.964	J. Acosta	33	116	5	4	3	4.36
	LF	B. Miller	420	.288	9	71	247	13	15	4	2.5	.945	A. Schacht	29	83	6	6	1	4.90
	C	P. Gharrity	387	.310	7	55	408	110	12	14	4.6	.977							
	OF	F. Brower	203	.261	1	35	88	10	9	3	2.3	.916							
	OF	E. Smith	180	.217	2	12	84	10	5	2	2.3	.949							
Boston	1B	S. McInnis	584	.307	0	74	1549	102	1	109	10.9	**.999**	S. Jones	40	299	23	16	1	3.22
	2B	D. Pratt	521	.324	5	100	283	408	28	90	5.4	.961	J. Bush	37	254	16	9	1	3.50
W-75 L-79	SS	E. Scott	576	.262	1	60	**380**	**528**	26	**94**	**6.1**	**.972**	H. Pennock	32	223	12	14	0	4.04
	3B	E. Foster	412	.284	0	30	74	189	16	18	3.0	.943	A. Russell	39	173	7	11	3	4.11
Hugh Duffy	RF	S. Collins	542	.286	4	65	264	22	10	8	2.1	.966	E. Myers	30	172	8	12	0	4.87
	CF	N. Leibold	467	.306	0	30	283	15	16	9	2.7	.949	B. Karr	26	118	8	7	0	3.67
	LF	M. Menosky	477	.300	3	43	278	12	9	3	2.2	.970							
	C	M. Ruel	358	.277	1	43	375	86	11	7	4.3	.977							
	3B	O. Vitt	232	.190	0	12	63	138	8	14	2.9	.962							
	C	R. Walters	169	.201	0	13	232	53	3	11	5.3	.990							
	OF	T. Hendryx	137	.241	0	21	66	2	3	0	1.7	.958							
Detroit	1B	L. Blue	585	.308	5	75	1478	85	16	75	10.4	.990	D. Leonard	36	245	11	13	1	3.75
	2B	R. Young	401	.299	0	29	285	270	31	44	5.5	.947	H. Dauss	32	233	10	15	1	4.33
W-71 L-82	SS	D. Bush	402	.281	0	27	172	260	23	35	5.6	.949	R. Oldham	40	229	11	14	1	4.24
	3B	B. Jones	554	.303	1	72	194	324	**27**	12	**3.9**	.950	H. Ehmke	30	196	13	14	0	4.54
Ty Cobb	RF	H. Heilmann	602	**.394**	19	139	233	10	10	1	1.8	.960	C. Holling	35	136	3	7	4	4.30
	CF	T. Cobb	507	.389	12	101	301	27	10	2	2.8	.970	J. Middleton	38	122	6	11	**7**	5.03
	LF	B. Veach	612	.338	16	128	384	21	11	4	2.8	.974	B. Cole	20	110	7	4	1	4.27
	C	J. Bassler	388	.307	0	56	433	113	14	7	4.9	.975							
	SS	I. Flagstead	259	.305	0	31	111	139	27	8	5.0	.903							
	OF	C. Shorten	217	.272	0	23	101	3	2	2	2.0	.981							
	UT	J. Sargent	178	.253	2	22	112	134	21	21		.921							
Chicago	1B	E. Sheely	563	.304	11	95	**1637**	**119**	**22**	**121**	**11.5**	.988	R. Faber	43	331	25	15	1	**2.48**
	2B	E. Collins	526	.337	2	58	376	458	28	84	6.3	**.968**	D. Kerr	44	309	19	17	1	4.72
W-62 L-92	SS	E. Johnson	613	.295	1	51	291	494	44	80	5.9	.947	R. Wilkinson	36	198	4	20	3	5.13
	3B	E. Mulligan	609	.251	1	45	162	307	22	28	3.2	.955	S. Hodge	36	143	6	8	2	6.56
Kid Gleason	RF	H. Hooper	419	.327	8	58	182	12	5	3	1.8	.975	D. McWeeny	27	98	3	6	2	6.08
	CF	A. Strunk	401	.332	3	69	214	10	7	2	2.1	.970	D. Mulrenan	12	56	2	8	0	7.23
	LF	B. Falk	585	.285	5	82	288	9	13	5	2.1	.958							
	C	R. Schalk	416	.252	0	47	453	129	9	**19**	4.7	**.985**							
	OF	J. Mostil	326	.301	3	42	215	12	13	1	2.6	.946							
	UT	H. McClellan	196	.179	1	14	112	141	8	23		.969							
Philadelphia	1B	J. Walker	423	.258	2	45	1008	49	12	71	10.8	.989	E. Rommel	46	285	16	**23**	3	3.94
	2B	J. Dykes	613	.274	16	77	**434**	**522**	**46**	88	**6.5**	.954	S. Harriss	39	228	11	16	2	4.27
W-53 L-100	SS	C. Galloway	465	.265	3	47	205	305	43	52	5.0	.922	R. Moore	29	192	10	10	0	4.51
	3B	J. Dugan	461	.295	10	58	118	208	16	19	2.9	.953	B. Hasty	35	179	5	16	0	4.87
Connie Mack	RF	W. Witt	629	.315	4	45	288	15	13	3	2.1	.959	D. Keefe	44	173	2	9	1	4.68
	CF	F. Welch	403	.285	7	45	251	16	16	1	2.7	.943	R. Naylor	32	169	3	13	0	4.84
	LF	T. Walker	556	.304	23	101	337	24	17	3	2.7	.955	S. Perry	12	70	3	6	1	4.11
	C	C. Perkins	538	.288	12	73	**540**	**137**	**20**	16	**4.9**	.971							
	1B	F. Brazill	177	.271	0	19	340	22	6	28	10.2	.984							
	SS	E. McCann	157	.223	0	15	56	93	8	13	4.9	.949							

AMERICAN LEAGUE 1921, *cont.*

BATTING AND BASE RUNNING LEADERS

Batting Average		Slugging Average		Home Runs	
H. Heilmann, DET	.394	B. Ruth, NY	.846	B. Ruth, NY	59
T. Cobb, DET	.389	H. Heilmann, DET	.606	K. Williams, STL	24
B. Ruth, NY	.378	T. Cobb, DET	.596	B. Meusel, NY	24
G. Sisler, STL	.371	K. Williams, STL	.561	T. Walker, PHI	23
T. Speaker, CLE	.362	G. Sisler, STL	.560	H. Heilmann, DET	19

Total Bases		Runs Batted In		Stolen Bases	
B. Ruth, NY	457	B. Ruth, NY	171	G. Sisler, STL	35
H. Heilmann, DET	365	H. Heilmann, DET	139	B. Harris, WAS	29
B. Meusel, NY	334	B. Meusel, NY	135	S. Rice, WAS	25
J. Tobin, STL	327	B. Veach, DET	128	T. Cobb, DET	22
G. Sisler, STL	326	K. Williams, STL	117	E. Johnson, CHI	22

Hits		Base on Balls		Home Run Percentage	
H. Heilmann, DET	237	B. Ruth, NY	144	B. Ruth, NY	10.9
J. Tobin, STL	236	L. Blue, DET	103	K. Williams, STL	4.4
G. Sisler, STL	216	R. Peckinpaugh, NY	84	T. Walker, PHI	4.1
B. Jacobson, STL	211	J. Sewell, CLE	80	B. Meusel, NY	4.0

Runs		Doubles		Triples	
B. Ruth, NY	177	T. Speaker, CLE	52	H. Shanks, WAS	19
J. Tobin, STL	132	B. Ruth, NY	44	G. Sisler, STL	18
R. Peckinpaugh, NY	128	H. Heilmann, DET	43	J. Tobin, STL	18
G. Sisler, STL	125	B. Veach, DET	43		

PITCHING LEADERS

Winning Percentage		Earned Run Average		Wins	
C. Mays, NY	.750	R. Faber, CHI	2.48	U. Shocker, STL	27
U. Shocker, STL	.692	G. Mogridge, WAS	3.00	C. Mays, NY	27
J. Bush, BOS	.640	C. Mays, NY	3.05	R. Faber, CHI	25
S. Coveleski, CLE	.639	W. Hoyt, NY	3.09	S. Jones, BOS	23
R. Faber, CHI	.625	S. Jones, BOS	3.22	S. Coveleski, CLE	23

Saves		Strikeouts		Complete Games	
C. Mays, NY	7	W. Johnson, WAS	143	R. Faber, CHI	32
J. Middleton, DET	7	U. Shocker, STL	132	U. Shocker, STL	31
C. Holling, DET	4	B. Shawkey, NY	126	C. Mays, NY	30
U. Shocker, STL	4	R. Faber, CHI	124	S. Coveleski, CLE	29
J. Bagby, CLE	4	D. Leonard, DET	120		
R. Caldwell, CLE	4				

Fewest Hits/9 Innings		Shutouts		Fewest Walks/9 Innings	
R. Faber, CHI	7.97	S. Jones, BOS	5	C. Mays, NY	2.03
J. Bush, BOS	8.63	G. Mogridge, WAS	4	G. Mogridge, WAS	2.06
C. Mays, NY	8.88	R. Faber, CHI	4	J. Bagby, CLE	2.07
B. Shawkey, NY	9.00	U. Shocker, STL	4	T. Zachary, WAS	2.12

Most Strikeouts/9 Inn.		Innings		Games Pitched	
W. Johnson, WAS	4.88	C. Mays, NY	337	C. Mays, NY	49
B. Shawkey, NY	4.63	R. Faber, CHI	331	B. Bayne, STL	47
D. Leonard, DET	4.41	U. Shocker, STL	327	U. Shocker, STL	47
D. Mails, CLE	4.03	S. Coveleski, CLE	316	E. Rommel, PHI	46

							Batting						Fielding			Pitching					
	W	L	PCT	GB	R	OR	2B	3B	HR	BA	SA	SB	E	DP	FA	CG	BB	SO	ShO	SV	ERA
New York	98	55	.641		**948**	708	285	87	**134**	.300	**.464**	89	222	138	.965	**92**	470	**481**	7	15	**3.79**
Cleveland	94	60	.610	4.5	925	712	**355**	90	42	.308	.430	58	204	124	.967	81	**430**	475	**11**	14	3.90
St. Louis	81	73	.526	17.5	835	845	246	**106**	67	.304	.425	92	224	127	.964	79	557	478	9	9	4.62
Washington	80	73	.523	18	704	738	240	96	42	.277	.383	**111**	235	153	.963	80	442	452	8	10	3.97
Boston	75	79	.487	23.5	668	**696**	248	69	17	.277	.361	83	**157**	151	**.975**	88	452	446	9	5	3.98
Detroit	71	82	.464	27	883	852	268	100	58	**.316**	.433	95	232	107	.963	73	495	452	4	**17**	4.40
Chicago	62	92	.403	36.5	683	858	242	82	35	.283	.379	97	200	**155**	.969	86	549	392	7	9	4.94
Philadelphia	53	100	.346	45	657	894	256	64	82	.274	.389	68	274	144	.958	75	548	431	1	7	4.60
					6303	6303	2140	694	477	.292	.408	693	1748	1099	.965	654	3943	3607	56	86	4.27

NATIONAL LEAGUE 1922

New York

W-93 L-61

John McGraw

POS	Player	AB	BA	HR	RBI	PO	A	E	DP	TC/G	FA	Pitcher	G	IP	W	L	SV	ERA
1B	G. Kelly	592	.328	17	107	1642	**103**	13	123	**11.6**	.993	A. Nehf	37	268	19	13	1	3.29
2B	F. Frisch	514	.327	5	51	176	288	12	40	5.6	.975	J. Barnes	37	213	13	8	0	3.51
SS	D. Bancroft	651	.321	4	60	**405**	**579**	**62**	**93**	**6.7**	.941	R. Ryan	46	192	17	12	3	**3.01**
3B	H. Groh	426	.265	3	51	100	207	11	**25**	2.9	**.965**	P. Douglas	24	158	11	4	0	2.63
RF	R. Youngs	559	.331	7	86	280	28	19	6	2.2	.942	C. Jonnard	33	96	6	1	**5**	3.84
CF	C. Stengel	250	.368	7	48	179	7	6	2	2.5	.969	H. McQuillan	15	94	6	5	1	3.82
LF	I. Meusel	617	.331	16	132	279	15	6	1	1.9	.980	F. Toney	13	86	5	6	0	4.17
C	F. Snyder	318	.343	5	51	272	74	7	10	3.6	.980	J. Scott	17	80	8	2	2	4.41
2B	J. Rawlings	308	.282	1	30	166	252	7	44	5.5	.984							
C	E. Smith	234	.278	9	39	214	56	6	3	3.7	.978							
OF	B. Cunningham	229	.328	2	33	155	7	2	3	2.3	.988							

Cincinnati

W-86 L-68

Pat Moran

POS	Player	AB	BA	HR	RBI	PO	A	E	DP	TC/G	FA	Pitcher	G	IP	W	L	SV	ERA
1B	J. Daubert	610	.336	12	66	**1652**	79	11	**127**	11.2	**.994**	E. Rixey	40	**313**	**25**	13	0	3.53
2B	S. Bohne	383	.274	3	51	183	320	22	50	6.2	.958	J. Couch	43	264	16	9	1	3.89
SS	I. Caveney	394	.239	3	54	256	404	47	74	6.0	.934	D. Luque	39	261	13	**23**	0	3.31
3B	B. Pinelli	547	.305	1	72	**204**	**350**	**32**	19	**3.8**	.945	P. Donohue	33	242	18	9	1	3.12
RF	G. Harper	430	.340	2	68	220	15	11	2	2.3	.955	C. Keck	27	131	7	6	1	3.37
CF	G. Burns	631	.285	1	53	386	20	10	3	2.7	.976							
LF	P. Duncan	607	.328	8	94	316	19	10	4	2.3	.971							
C	B. Hargrave	320	.316	7	57	261	60	6	5	3.8	.982							
2B	L. Fonseca	291	.361	4	45	197	251	14	40	6.5	.970							
C	I. Wingo	260	.285	3	45	211	81	11	6	3.9	.964							
OF	E. Roush	165	.352	1	24	96	8	1	0	2.4	.990							

Pittsburgh

W-85 L-69

George Gibson
W-32 L-33

Bill McKechnie
W-53 L-36

POS	Player	AB	BA	HR	RBI	PO	A	E	DP	TC/G	FA	Pitcher	G	IP	W	L	SV	ERA
1B	C. Grimm	593	.292	0	76	1478	68	10	104	10.1	.994	W. Cooper	41	295	23	14	0	3.18
2B	C. Tierney	441	.345	7	86	179	302	18	52	4.8	.964	J. Morrison	45	286	17	11	1	3.43
SS	R. Maranville	**672**	.295	0	63	359	453	33	81	6.1	.961	W. Glazner	34	193	11	12	1	4.38
3B	P. Traynor	571	.282	4	81	147	216	21	19	3.1	.945	B. Adams	27	171	8	11	0	3.57
RF	R. Russell	220	.368	12	75	115	5	4	2	2.1	.968	E. Hamilton	33	160	11	7	2	3.99
CF	M. Carey	629	.329	10	70	449	22	15	4	3.1	.969	H. Carlson	39	145	9	12	2	5.70
LF	C. Bigbee	614	.350	5	99	345	27	17	5	2.6	.956							
C	J. Gooch	353	.329	1	42	382	102	15	10	**4.8**	.970							
30	C. Barnhart	209	.330	1	38	76	34	8	4		.932							
C	W. Schmidt	152	.329	0	22	159	22	1	1	4.6	.995							
OF	R. Rohwer	129	.295	3	22	56	5	4	1	2.2	.938							

NATIONAL LEAGUE 1922, *cont.*

St. Louis

W-85 L-69

Branch Rickey

POS	Player	AB	BA	HR	RBI	PO	A	E	DP	TC/G	FA	Pitcher	G	IP	W	L	SV	ERA
1B	J. Fournier	404	.295	10	61	902	60	18	63	9.0	.982	J. Pfeffer	44	261	19	12	2	3.58
2B	R. Hornsby	623	**.401**	**42**	**152**	**398**	473	30	**81**	5.9	**.967**	B. Sherdel	47	241	17	13	2	3.88
SS	S. Toporcer	352	.324	3	36	168	246	27	31	4.8	.939	J. Haines	29	183	11	9	0	3.84
3B	M. Stock	581	.305	5	79	172	245	22	22	2.9	.950	B. Doak	37	180	11	13	2	5.54
RF	M. Flack	267	.292	2	21	116	5	4	3	1.9	.968	L. North	**53**	150	10	3	4	4.45
CF	J. Smith	510	.310	8	46	282	11	15	3	2.3	.951	C. Barfoot	42	118	4	5	2	4.21
LF	J. Schultz	344	.314	2	64	195	7	5	1	2.3	.976	B. Pertica	34	117	8	8	0	5.91
C	E. Ainsmith	379	.293	13	59	428	99	**20**	14	4.7	.963							
SS	D. Lavan	264	.227	0	27	169	246	28	40	5.4	.937							
OF	A. McHenry	238	.303	5	43	132	13	10	3	2.5	.935							
C	V. Clemons	160	.256	0	15	172	50	1	2	3.5	.996							
OF	H. Mueller	159	.270	3	26	83	6	5	2	2.1	.947							
1B	J. Bottomley	151	.325	5	35	346	12	5	20	10.7	.986							
OF	L. Mann	147	.347	2	20	87	3	2	1	1.6	.978							
OF	R. Blades	130	.300	3	21	61	6	5	0	2.5	.931							
1B	D. Gainer	97	.268	2	23	175	9	4	6	7.2	.979							

Chicago

W-80 L-74

Bill Killefer

POS	Player	AB	BA	HR	RBI	PO	A	E	DP	TC/G	FA	Pitcher	G	IP	W	L	SV	ERA
1B	R. Grimes	509	.354	14	99	1378	68	**19**	106	10.6	.987	V. Aldridge	36	258	16	15	0	3.52
2B	Z. Terry	496	.286	0	67	298	442	28	75	6.1	.964	G. Alexander	33	246	16	13	1	3.63
SS	C. Hollocher	592	.340	3	69	332	502	30	89	5.7	**.965**	T. Osborne	41	184	9	5	3	4.50
3B	M. Krug	450	.276	4	60	129	184	21	19	3.2	.937	V. Cheeves	39	183	12	11	2	4.09
RF	B. Friberg	296	.311	0	23	126	13	4	5	1.9	.972	P. Jones	44	164	8	9	1	4.72
CF	J. Statz	462	.297	1	34	309	16	14	4	3.1	.959	T. Kaufmann	37	153	7	13	3	4.06
LF	H. Miller	466	.352	12	78	219	15	10	3	2.1	.959	G. Stueland	35	111	9	4	0	5.92
C	B. O'Farrell	392	.324	4	60	**446**	**143**	14	**22**	4.8	.977							
OF	C. Heathcote	243	.280	1	34	131	5	2	1	2.3	.986							
OF	T. Barber	226	.310	0	29	78	4	4	2	1.8	.953							
3B	J. Kelleher	193	.259	0	20	44	93	10	9	3.2	.932							
OF	M. Callaghan	175	.257	0	20	85	2	5	0	1.7	.946							

Brooklyn

W-76 L-78

Wilbert Robinson

POS	Player	AB	BA	HR	RBI	PO	A	E	DP	TC/G	FA	Pitcher	G	IP	W	L	SV	ERA
1B	R. Schmandt	396	.268	2	44	1017	65	12	83	9.9	.989	D. Ruether	35	267	21	12	0	3.53
2B	I. Olson	551	.272	1	47	193	283	20	43	5.8	.960	B. Grimes	36	259	17	14	1	4.76
SS	J. Johnston	567	.319	4	49	102	189	16	33	6.1	.948	D. Vance	36	246	18	12	0	3.70
3B	A. High	579	.283	6	65	131	257	17	23	3.1	.958	L. Cadore	29	190	8	15	0	4.35
RF	T. Griffith	329	.316	4	49	167	13	9	4	2.3	.952	S. Smith	28	109	4	8	2	4.56
CF	H. Myers	618	.317	6	89	399	16	11	2	2.8	.974	H. Shriver	25	108	4	6	0	2.99
LF	Z. Wheat	600	.335	16	112	317	14	3	1	2.2	.991							
C	H. DeBerry	259	.301	3	35	309	64	11	5	4.7	.971							
OF	B. Griffith	325	.308	2	35	148	7	3	3	2.1	.981							
C	O. Miller	180	.261	1	23	216	56	9	3	4.9	.968							
1B	C. Mitchell	155	.290	3	28	365	27	3	32	9.4	.992							
P	D. Ruether	125	.208	2	20	9	56	0	**6**	1.9	**1.000**							

Philadelphia

W-57 L-96

Kaiser Wilhelm

POS	Player	AB	BA	HR	RBI	PO	A	E	DP	TC/G	FA	Pitcher	G	IP	W	L	SV	ERA
1B	R. Leslie	513	.271	6	50	1517	63	16	110	11.5	.990	J. Ring	40	249	12	18	1	4.58
2B	F. Parkinson	545	.275	15	70	323	**562**	**34**	78	**6.6**	.963	L. Meadows	33	237	12	18	0	4.03
SS	A. Fletcher	396	.280	7	53	202	379	38	63	5.8	.939	G. Smith	42	194	5	14	0	4.78
3B	G. Rapp	502	.253	0	38	117	249	20	20	3.3	.948	B. Hubbell	35	189	7	15	1	5.00
RF	C. Walker	581	.337	12	89	295	24	15	8	2.3	.955	L. Weinert	34	167	8	11	1	3.40
CF	C. Williams	584	.308	26	92	376	19	11	2	2.7	.973	J. Winters	34	138	6	6	2	5.33
LF	C. Lee	422	.322	17	77	167	10	6	2	2.1	.967	J. Singleton	22	93	1	10	0	5.90
C	B. Henline	430	.316	14	64	400	113	9	13	4.4	**.983**							
3S	R. Wrightstone	331	.305	5	33	109	227	11	25		.968							
OF	B. LeBourveau	167	.269	2	20	77	4	7	1	2.1	.920							
OF	J. Mokan	151	.252	3	27	62	5	7	1	2.4	.905							
C	J. Peters	143	.245	4	24	118	24	7	3	3.8	.953							

Boston

W-53 L-100

Fred Mitchell

POS	Player	AB	BA	HR	RBI	PO	A	E	DP	TC/G	FA	Pitcher	G	IP	W	L	SV	ERA
1B	W. Holke	395	.291	0	46	1017	44	8	65	10.2	.993	M. Watson	41	201	8	14	1	4.70
2B	L. Kopf	466	.266	1	37	175	243	25	35	5.7	.944	F. Miller	31	200	11	13	1	3.51
SS	H. Ford	515	.272	2	60	267	387	32	57	6.0	.953	R. Marquard	39	198	11	15	1	5.09
3B	T. Boeckel	402	.289	6	47	128	168	15	13	2.9	.952	J. Oeschger	46	196	6	21	1	5.06
RF	W. Cruise	352	.278	4	46	212	9	12	3	2.3	.948	H. McQuillan	28	136	5	10	0	4.24
CF	R. Powell	550	.296	6	37	377	18	8	2	3.0	.980	D. Fillingim	25	117	5	9	2	4.54
LF	A. Nixon	318	.264	2	22	189	6	5	0	2.5	.975							
C	M. O'Neil	251	.223	0	26	239	70	7	3	4.0	.978							
UT	W. Barbare	373	.231	0	40	241	238	14	44		.972							
OF	F. Nicholson	222	.252	2	29	125	5	12	0	2.3	.915							
C	H. Gowdy	221	.317	1	27	204	63	8	6	3.8	.971							
C1	F. Gibson	164	.299	3	20	245	28	5	14		.982							
OF	B. Southworth	158	.323	4	18	100	7	5	0	2.7	.955							

BATTING AND BASE RUNNING LEADERS

Batting Average		Slugging Average		Home Runs	
R. Hornsby, STL	.401	R. Hornsby, STL	.722	R. Hornsby, STL	42
R. Grimes, CHI	.354	R. Grimes, CHI	.572	C. Williams, PHI	26
H. Miller, CHI	.352	C. Lee, PHI	.540	C. Lee, PHI	17
C. Bigbee, PIT	.350	C. Tierney, PIT	.515	G. Kelly, NY	17
C. Tierney, PIT	.345	C. Williams, PHI	.514	Z. Wheat, BKN	16
				I. Meusel, NY	16

PITCHING LEADERS

Winning Percentage		Earned Run Average		Wins	
P. Donohue, CIN	.667	R. Ryan, NY	3.01	E. Rixey, CIN	25
E. Rixey, CIN	.658	P. Donohue, CIN	3.12	W. Cooper, PIT	23
J. Couch, CIN	.640	W. Cooper, PIT	3.18	D. Ruether, BKN	21
D. Ruether, BKN	.636	A. Nehf, NY	3.29	J. Pfeffer, STL	19
W. Cooper, PIT	.622	D. Luque, CIN	3.31	A. Nehf, NY	19

NATIONAL LEAGUE 1922, *cont.*

BATTING AND BASE RUNNING LEADERS

Total Bases	
R. Hornsby, STL	450
I. Meusel, NY	314
Z. Wheat, BKN	302
C. Williams, PHI	300
J. Daubert, CIN	300

Runs Batted In	
R. Hornsby, STL	152
I. Meusel, NY	132
Z. Wheat, BKN	112
G. Kelly, NY	107
R. Grimes, CHI	99
C. Bigbee, PIT	99

Stolen Bases	
M. Carey, PIT	51
F. Frisch, NY	31
G. Burns, CIN	30
C. Bigbee, PIT	24
R. Maranville, PIT	24

Hits	
R. Hornsby, STL	250
C. Bigbee, PIT	215
D. Bancroft, NY	209
M. Carey, PIT	207

Base on Balls	
M. Carey, PIT	80
B. O'Farrell, CHI	79
D. Bancroft, NY	79
G. Burns, CIN	78

Home Run Percentage	
R. Hornsby, STL	6.7
C. Williams, PHI	4.5
C. Lee, PHI	4.0
E. Ainsmith, STL	3.4

Runs	
R. Hornsby, STL	141
M. Carey, PIT	140
J. Smith, STL	117
D. Bancroft, NY	117

Doubles	
R. Hornsby, STL	46
R. Grimes, CHI	45
P. Duncan, CIN	44
D. Bancroft, NY	41

Triples	
J. Daubert, CIN	22
I. Meusel, NY	17
C. Bigbee, PIT	15
R. Maranville, PIT	15

PITCHING LEADERS

Saves	
C. Jonnard, NY	5
L. North, STL	4
A. Mamaux, BKN	3
T. Osborne, CHI	3
T. Kaufmann, CHI	3
R. Ryan, NY	3

Strikeouts	
D. Vance, BKN	134
W. Cooper, PIT	129
J. Ring, PHI	116
J. Morrison, PIT	104
B. Grimes, BKN	99

Complete Games	
W. Cooper, PIT	27
D. Ruether, BKN	26
E. Rixey, CIN	26

Fewest Hits/9 Innings	
R. Ryan, NY	9.11
D. Luque, CIN	9.17
D. Vance, BKN	9.49
P. Donohue, CIN	9.56

Shutouts	
D. Vance, BKN	5
J. Morrison, PIT	5
B. Adams, PIT	4
W. Cooper, PIT	4

Fewest Walks/9 Innings	
B. Adams, PIT	0.79
G. Alexander, CHI	1.25
E. Rixey, CIN	1.29
P. Donohue, CIN	1.60

Most Strikeouts/9 Inn.	
D. Vance, BKN	4.91
J. Ring, PHI	4.19
W. Cooper, PIT	3.94
W. Glazner, PIT	3.59

Innings	
E. Rixey, CIN	313
W. Cooper, PIT	295
J. Morrison, PIT	286
A. Nehf, NY	268

Games Pitched	
L. North, STL	53
B. Sherdel, STL	47
R. Ryan, NY	46
J. Oeschger, BOS	46

							Batting						Fielding			Pitching					
	W	L	PCT	GB	R	OR	2B	3B	HR	BA	SA	SB	E	DP	FA	CG	BB	SO	ShO	SV	ERA
New York	93	61	.604		852	**658**	253	90	80	.305	.428	116	194	145	**.970**	73	393	388	7	**15**	**3.45**
Cincinnati	86	68	.558	7	766	677	226	99	45	.296	.401	130	205	147	.968	**88**	**326**	357	8	3	3.53
Pittsburgh	85	69	.552	8	**865**	736	239	**110**	52	**.308**	.419	**145**	**187**	126	**.970**	**88**	358	490	**15**	7	3.98
St. Louis	85	69	.552	8	863	819	**280**	88	107	.301	**.444**	73	239	122	.961	60	447	465	8	12	4.44
Chicago	80	74	.519	13	771	808	248	71	42	.293	.390	97	204	**154**	.968	74	475	402	8	12	4.34
Brooklyn	76	78	.494	17	743	754	235	76	56	.290	.392	79	208	139	.967	82	490	**499**	12	8	4.05
Philadelphia	57	96	.373	35.5	738	920	268	55	**116**	.282	.415	48	225	152	.965	73	460	394	6	5	4.64
Boston	53	100	.346	39.5	596	822	162	73	32	.263	.341	67	215	121	.965	62	489	360	7	6	4.37
					6194	6194	1911	662	530	.292	.404	755	1677	1106	.967	600	3438	3355	71	68	4.10

AMERICAN LEAGUE 1922

New York

W-94 L-60

Miller Huggins

POS	Player	AB	BA	HR	RBI	PO	A	E	DP	TC/G	FA	Pitcher	G	IP	W	L	SV	ERA
1B	W. Pipp	577	.329	9	90	**1667**	88	13	106	**11.6**	.993	B. Shawkey	39	300	20	12	1	2.91
2B	A. Ward	558	.267	7	68	358	**489**	23	73	5.7	.974	W. Hoyt	37	265	19	12	0	3.43
SS	E. Scott	557	.269	3	45	302	**538**	31	74	5.7	**.964**	S. Jones	45	260	13	13	**8**	3.67
3B	F. Baker	234	.278	7	36	68	108	7	7	3.0	.962	J. Bush	39	255	26	7	3	3.31
RF	B. Meusel	473	.319	16	84	202	24	12	0	2.0	.950	C. Mays	34	240	12	14	2	3.60
CF	W. Witt	528	.297	4	40	312	9	8	1	2.4	.976							
LF	B. Ruth	406	.315	35	99	225	14	9	3	2.3	.964							
C	W. Schang	408	.319	1	53	456	102	14	12	4.6	.976							
3B	J. Dugan	252	.286	3	25	59	117	6	10	3.0	.967							
OF	E. Miller	172	.267	3	18	101	7	2	0	2.2	.982							

St. Louis

W-93 L-61

Lee Fohl

POS	Player	AB	BA	HR	RBI	PO	A	E	DP	TC/G	FA	Pitcher	G	IP	W	L	SV	ERA
1B	G. Sisler	586	**.420**	8	105	1293	**125**	17	116	10.2	.988	U. Shocker	48	348	24	17	3	2.97
2B	M. McManus	606	.312	11	109	398	467	**32**	103	5.9	.964	E. Vangilder	43	245	19	13	4	3.42
SS	W. Gerber	604	.267	1	51	**322**	470	47	**93**	5.5	.944	D. Davis	25	174	11	6	0	4.08
3B	F. Ellerbe	342	.246	1	33	137	224	17	20	4.2	.955	R. Kolp	32	170	14	4	0	3.93
RF	J. Tobin	625	.331	13	66	221	15	15	5	1.7	.940	R. Wright	31	154	9	7	5	2.92
CF	B. Jacobson	555	.317	9	102	367	9	12	3	2.8	.969	H. Pruett	39	120	7	7	7	2.33
LF	K. Williams	585	.332	**39**	**155**	372	16	12	4	2.6	.970	B. Bayne	26	93	4	5	2	4.56
C	H. Severeid	517	.321	3	78	552	123	11	10	5.1	.984							
C	P. Collins	127	.307	8	23	129	19	3	4	5.6	.980							

Detroit

W-79 L-75

Ty Cobb

POS	Player	AB	BA	HR	RBI	PO	A	E	DP	TC/G	FA	Pitcher	G	IP	W	L	SV	ERA
1B	L. Blue	584	.300	6	45	1506	75	15	107	11.1	.991	H. Ehmke	45	280	17	17	1	4.22
2B	G. Cutshaw	499	.267	2	61	334	390	21	69	5.6	.972	H. Pillette	40	275	19	12	1	2.85
SS	T. Rigney	536	.300	2	63	262	493	**50**	74	5.2	.938	H. Dauss	39	219	13	13	4	4.20
3B	B. Jones	455	.257	3	44	161	267	17	22	**3.7**	**.962**	R. Oldham	43	212	10	13	3	4.67
RF	H. Heilmann	455	.356	21	92	175	6	10	2	1.7	.948	O. Olsen	37	137	7	6	3	4.53
CF	T. Cobb	526	.401	4	99	330	14	7	3	2.6	.980	S. Johnson	29	97	7	3	1	3.71
LF	B. Veach	618	.327	9	126	375	16	7	3	2.6	.982							
C	J. Bassler	372	.323	0	41	421	113	11	12	4.6	.980							
3B	F. Haney	213	.352	0	25	43	105	10	11	3.8	.937							
2B	D. Clark	185	.292	3	26	72	99	10	16	4.8	.945							
OF	B. Fothergill	152	.322	0	29	50	2	3	1	1.4	.945							

Cleveland

W-78 L-76

Tris Speaker

POS	Player	AB	BA	HR	RBI	PO	A	E	DP	TC/G	FA	Pitcher	G	IP	W	L	SV	ERA
1B	S. McInnis	537	.305	1	78	1376	73	5	96	10.4	**.997**	G. Uhle	50	287	22	16	3	4.07
2B	B. Wambsganss	538	.262	0	47	297	376	27	72	5.6	.961	S. Coveleski	35	277	17	14	2	3.32
SS	J. Sewell	558	.299	2	83	295	462	49	72	**5.8**	.939	G. Morton	38	203	14	9	0	4.00
3B	L. Gardner	470	.285	2	68	133	259	20	**24**	3.2	.951	D. Mails	26	104	4	7	0	5.28
RF	S. Wood	505	.297	8	92	247	18	11	5	2.0	.960	J. Bagby	25	98	4	5	1	6.32
CF	T. Speaker	426	.378	11	71	285	13	5	6	2.8	.983	J. Edwards	25	88	3	8	0	4.70
LF	C. Jamieson	567	.323	3	57	289	18	7	5	2.2	.978	J. Lindsey	29	84	4	5	1	6.02
C	S. O'Neill	392	.311	2	65	450	116	**15**	9	4.5	.974	D. Boone	11	75	4	6	0	4.06
32	R. Stephenson	233	.339	2	32	75	135	12	11		.946							
OF	J. Evans	145	.269	0	22	92	1	3	0	2.0	.969							

AMERICAN LEAGUE 1922, *cont.*

Chicago

W-77 L-77

Kid Gleason

POS	Player	AB	BA	HR	RBI	PO	A	E	DP	TC/G	FA
1B	E. Sheely	526	.317	6	80	1512	103	12	101	10.9	.993
2B	E. Collins	598	.324	1	69	406	451	21	73	5.7	**.976**
SS	E. Johnson	603	.254	0	56	259	468	37	74	5.4	.952
3B	E. Mulligan	372	.234	0	31	94	200	11	14	3.5	.964
RF	H. Hooper	602	.304	11	80	288	19	12	7	2.1	.962
CF	J. Mostil	458	.303	7	70	333	9	12	2	2.7	.966
LF	B. Falk	483	.298	12	79	253	10	10	2	2.1	.963
C	R. Schalk	442	.281	4	60	**591**	**150**	8	16	**5.3**	**.989**
OF	A. Strunk	311	.289	0	33	170	9	2	2	2.4	.989
3B	H. McClellan	301	.226	2	28	77	158	7	15	3.4	.971

Pitcher	G	IP	W	L	SV	ERA
R. Faber	43	**353**	21	17	2	**2.80**
C. Robertson	37	272	14	15	0	3.64
D. Leverett	33	225	13	10	2	3.32
S. Hodge	35	139	7	6	1	4.14
T. Blankenship	24	128	8	10	1	3.81
H. Courtney	18	88	5	6	0	4.93

Washington

W-69 L-85

Clyde Milan

POS	Player	AB	BA	HR	RBI	PO	A	E	DP	TC/G	FA
1B	J. Judge	591	.294	10	81	1413	101	6	**131**	10.3	.996
2B	B. Harris	602	.269	2	40	**479**	483	30	**116**	**6.4**	.970
SS	R. Peckinpaugh	520	.254	2	48	265	524	41	**93**	5.6	.951
3B	B. LaMotte	214	.252	1	23	90	138	11	10	3.9	.954
RF	F. Brower	471	.293	9	71	208	9	5	1	1.8	.977
CF	S. Rice	**633**	.295	6	69	385	23	21	3	2.8	.951
LF	G. Goslin	358	.324	3	53	197	8	15	1	2.4	.932
C	P. Gharrity	273	.256	5	45	282	85	7	9	4.3	.981
30	H. Shanks	272	.283	1	32	125	112	16	16		.937
C	V. Picinich	210	.229	0	19	273	55	8	4	4.4	.976
OF	E. Smith	205	.259	1	23	88	12	9	3	2.2	.917

Pitcher	G	IP	W	L	SV	ERA
W. Johnson	41	280	15	16	4	2.99
G. Mogridge	34	252	18	13	0	3.58
R. Francis	39	225	7	18	2	4.28
T. Zachary	32	185	15	10	1	3.12
E. Erickson	30	142	4	12	2	4.96
J. Brillheart	31	120	4	6	1	3.61
T. Phillips	17	70	3	7	0	4.89

Philadelphia

W-65 L-89

Connie Mack

POS	Player	AB	BA	HR	RBI	PO	A	E	DP	TC/G	FA
1B	J. Hauser	368	.323	9	43	936	55	14	61	10.7	.986
2B	R. Young	470	.223	1	35	302	350	27	53	5.7	.960
SS	C. Galloway	571	.324	6	69	321	493	41	76	5.5	.952
3B	J. Dykes	501	.275	12	68	**186**	**295**	**28**	21	3.6	.945
RF	F. Welch	375	.259	11	49	191	12	11	2	2.1	.949
CF	B. Miller	535	.336	21	90	314	19	8	3	2.5	.977
LF	T. Walker	565	.283	37	99	309	19	15	4	2.3	.956
C	C. Perkins	505	.267	6	69	432	130	9	10	4.0	.984
OF	F. McGowan	300	.230	1	20	210	13	8	2	2.8	.965
1B	D. Johnston	260	.250	1	29	641	31	7	34	10.4	.990

Pitcher	G	IP	W	L	SV	ERA
E. Rommel	**51**	294	**27**	13	2	3.28
S. Harriss	47	230	9	**20**	3	5.02
B. Hasty	28	193	9	14	0	4.25
F. Heimach	37	172	7	11	1	5.03
R. Naylor	35	171	10	15	0	4.73

Boston

W-61 L-93

Hugh Duffy

POS	Player	AB	BA	HR	RBI	PO	A	E	DP	TC/G	FA
1B	G. Burns	558	.306	12	73	1412	94	**20**	103	10.9	.987
2B	D. Pratt	607	.301	6	86	362	484	30	80	5.7	.966
SS	J. Mitchell	203	.251	1	8	98	184	11	31	5.1	.962
3B	J. Dugan	341	.287	3	38	72	143	13	13	3.6	.943
RF	S. Collins	472	.271	1	52	245	6	13	1	2.3	.951
CF	J. Harris	408	.316	6	54	186	15	10	2	2.5	.953
LF	M. Menosky	406	.283	3	32	240	14	6	3	2.5	.977
C	M. Ruel	361	.255	0	28	359	96	10	**17**	4.2	.978
OF	N. Leibold	271	.258	1	18	190	10	7	3	2.9	.966
OF	E. Smith	231	.286	6	32	117	7	7	3	2.2	.947
SS	F. O'Rourke	216	.264	1	17	86	134	22	17	5.0	.909
3S	P. Pittenger	186	.258	0	7	88	148	22	19		.915

Pitcher	G	IP	W	L	SV	ERA
J. Quinn	40	256	13	15	0	3.48
R. Collins	32	211	14	11	0	3.76
H. Pennock	32	202	10	17	1	4.32
A. Ferguson	39	198	9	16	2	4.31
B. Karr	41	183	5	12	1	4.47
A. Russell	34	126	6	7	2	5.01
B. Piercy	29	121	3	9	0	4.67

BATTING AND BASE RUNNING LEADERS

Batting Average
- G. Sisler, STL .420
- T. Cobb, DET .401
- T. Speaker, CLE .378
- H. Heilmann, DET .356
- B. Miller, PHI .336

Slugging Average
- B. Ruth, NY .672
- K. Williams, STL .627
- T. Speaker, CLE .606
- H. Heilmann, DET .598
- G. Sisler, STL .594

Home Runs
- K. Williams, STL 39
- T. Walker, PHI 37
- B. Ruth, NY 35
- H. Heilmann, DET 21
- B. Miller, PHI 21

Total Bases
- K. Williams, STL 367
- G. Sisler, STL 348
- T. Walker, PHI 310
- T. Cobb, DET 297
- B. Miller, PHI 296
- J. Tobin, STL 296

Runs Batted In
- K. Williams, STL 155
- B. Veach, DET 126
- M. McManus, STL 109
- G. Sisler, STL 105
- B. Jacobson, STL 102

Stolen Bases
- G. Sisler, STL 51
- K. Williams, STL 37
- B. Harris, WAS 25
- E. Johnson, CHI 21
- E. Collins, CHI 20
- S. Rice, WAS 20

Hits
- G. Sisler, STL 246
- T. Cobb, DET 211
- J. Tobin, STL 207
- B. Veach, DET 202

Base on Balls
- W. Witt, NY 89
- B. Ruth, NY 84
- L. Blue, DET 82
- T. Speaker, CLE 77

Home Run Percentage
- B. Ruth, NY 8.6
- K. Williams, STL 6.7
- T. Walker, PHI 6.5
- H. Heilmann, DET 4.6

Runs
- G. Sisler, STL 134
- L. Blue, DET 131
- K. Williams, STL 128
- J. Tobin, STL 122

Doubles
- T. Speaker, CLE 48
- D. Pratt, BOS 44
- T. Cobb, DET 42
- G. Sisler, STL 42

Triples
- G. Sisler, STL 18
- T. Cobb, DET 16
- B. Jacobson, STL 16
- J. Judge, WAS 15

PITCHING LEADERS

Winning Percentage
- J. Bush, NY .788
- E. Rommel, PHI .675
- B. Shawkey, NY .625
- H. Pillette, DET .613
- W. Hoyt, NY .613

Earned Run Average
- R. Faber, CHI 2.80
- H. Pillette, DET 2.85
- B. Shawkey, NY 2.91
- U. Shocker, STL 2.97
- W. Johnson, WAS 2.99

Wins
- E. Rommel, PHI 27
- J. Bush, NY 26
- U. Shocker, STL 24
- G. Uhle, CLE 22
- R. Faber, CHI 21

Saves
- S. Jones, NY 8
- H. Pruett, STL 7
- R. Wright, STL 5
- W. Johnson, WAS 4
- H. Dauss, DET 4
- E. Vangilder, STL 4

Strikeouts
- U. Shocker, STL 149
- R. Faber, CHI 148
- B. Shawkey, NY 130
- H. Ehmke, DET 108
- W. Johnson, WAS 105

Complete Games
- R. Faber, CHI 31
- U. Shocker, STL 29
- W. Johnson, WAS 23
- G. Uhle, CLE 23
- E. Rommel, PHI 22

Fewest Hits/9 Innings
- J. Bush, NY 8.46
- R. Faber, CHI 8.52
- B. Shawkey, NY 8.59
- H. Pillette, DET 8.85

Shutouts
- G. Uhle, CLE 5

Fewest Walks/9 Innings
- U. Shocker, STL 1.53
- E. Vangilder, STL 1.76
- C. Mays, NY 1.88
- B. Hasty, PHI 1.92

Most Strikeouts/9 Inn.
- G. Morton, CLE 4.53
- S. Harriss, PHI 4.00
- B. Shawkey, NY 3.90
- U. Shocker, STL 3.85

Innings
- R. Faber, CHI 353
- U. Shocker, STL 348
- B. Shawkey, NY 300
- E. Rommel, PHI 294

Games Pitched
- E. Rommel, PHI 51
- G. Uhle, CLE 50
- U. Shocker, STL 48
- S. Harriss, PHI 47

AMERICAN LEAGUE 1922, *cont.*

	W	L	PCT	GB	R	OR	Batting 2B	3B	HR	BA	SA	SB	Fielding E	DP	FA	Pitching CG	BB	SO	ShO	SV	ERA
New York	94	60	.610		758	**618**	220	75	95	.287	.412	62	157	122	**.975**	**98**	423	458	7	14	3.39
St. Louis	93	61	.604	1	**867**	643	291	**94**	98	**.313**	**.455**	**132**	201	158	.968	79	**421**	**534**	8	**22**	**3.38**
Detroit	79	75	.513	15	828	791	250	87	54	.305	.414	78	191	135	.970	67	473	461	7	15	4.27
Cleveland	78	76	.506	16	768	817	**320**	73	32	.292	.398	89	202	140	.968	76	464	489	**14**	7	4.60
Chicago	77	77	.500	17	691	691	243	62	45	.278	.373	106	**155**	132	**.975**	86	529	484	13	8	3.93
Washington	69	85	.448	25	650	706	229	76	45	.268	.367	94	196	**161**	.969	84	500	422	11	10	3.81
Philadelphia	65	89	.422	29	705	830	229	63	**111**	.269	.400	60	215	119	.966	73	469	373	4	6	4.59
Boston	61	93	.396	33	598	769	250	55	45	.263	.356	60	224	139	.965	71	503	359	10	6	4.30
					5865	5865	2032	585	525	.284	.397	681	1541	1106	.970	634	3782	3580	74	88	4.03

NATIONAL LEAGUE 1923

New York

W-95 L-58

John McGraw

POS	Player	AB	BA	HR	RBI	PO	A	E	DP	TC/G	FA	Pitcher	G	IP	W	L	SV	ERA
1B	G. Kelly	560	.307	16	103	**1568**	60	12	111	**11.3**	.993	H. McQuillan	38	230	15	14	0	3.41
2B	F. Frisch	641	.348	12	111	307	451	21	79	5.8	**.973**	J. Scott	40	220	16	7	1	3.89
SS	D. Bancroft	444	.304	1	31	246	381	43	53	7.0	.936	A. Nehf	34	196	13	10	2	4.50
3B	H. Groh	465	.290	4	48	117	233	9	18	3.0	**.975**	J. Bentley	31	183	13	8	3	4.48
RF	R. Youngs	596	.336	3	87	282	22	13	7	2.1	.959	R. Ryan	**45**	173	16	5	4	3.49
CF	J. O'Connell	252	.250	6	39	145	2	3	1	2.3	.980	M. Watson	17	108	8	5	0	3.43
LF	I. Meusel	595	.297	19	**125**	268	10	15	2	2.0	.949	C. Jonnard	**45**	96	4	3	**5**	3.28
C	F. Snyder	402	.256	5	63	**428**	90	5	**12**	**4.7**	**.990**							
S3	T. Jackson	327	.275	4	37	103	257	23	29		.940							
OF	C. Stengel	218	.339	5	43	115	4	2	1	2.1	.983							
OF	B. Cunningham	203	.271	5	27	123	8	1	2	1.9	.992							

Cincinnati

W-91 L-63

Pat Moran

POS	Player	AB	BA	HR	RBI	PO	A	E	DP	TC/G	FA	Pitcher	G	IP	W	L	SV	ERA
1B	J. Daubert	500	.292	2	54	1224	77	9	95	10.8	.993	D. Luque	41	322	**27**	8	2	**1.93**
2B	S. Bohne	539	.252	3	47	243	333	15	46	6.2	.975	E. Rixey	42	309	20	15	1	2.80
SS	I. Caveney	488	.277	4	63	313	477	**49**	86	6.1	.942	P. Donohue	42	274	21	15	3	3.38
3B	B. Pinelli	423	.277	0	51	131	250	25	17	**3.5**	.938	R. Benton	33	219	14	10	1	3.66
RF	G. Burns	614	.274	3	45	327	11	14	3	2.3	.960	C. Keck	35	87	3	6	2	3.72
CF	E. Roush	527	.351	6	88	337	14	11	3	2.6	.970							
LF	P. Duncan	566	.327	7	83	291	11	2	2	2.1	.993							
C	B. Hargrave	378	.333	10	78	404	90	6	**12**	4.6	.988							
2B	L. Fonseca	237	.278	3	28	123	169	13	27	6.8	.957							
C	I. Wingo	171	.263	1	24	172	44	7	2	3.9	.969							

Pittsburgh

W-87 L-67

Bill McKechnie

POS	Player	AB	BA	HR	RBI	PO	A	E	DP	TC/G	FA	Pitcher	G	IP	W	L	SV	ERA
1B	C. Grimm	563	.345	7	99	1453	81	8	130	10.1	**.995**	J. Morrison	42	302	25	13	2	3.49
2B	J. Rawlings	461	.284	1	45	294	388	30	68	6.0	.958	W. Cooper	39	295	17	**19**	0	3.57
SS	R. Maranville	581	.277	1	41	**332**	**505**	30	**94**	6.1	**.965**	L. Meadows	31	227	16	10	0	3.01
3B	P. Traynor	616	.338	12	101	**191**	**310**	26	30	3.4	.951	B. Adams	26	159	13	7	1	4.42
RF	C. Barnhart	327	.324	9	72	179	14	3	1	2.1	.985	E. Hamilton	28	141	7	9	1	3.77
CF	M. Carey	610	.308	6	63	450	28	19	4	3.2	.962							
LF	C. Bigbee	499	.299	0	54	283	12	3	3	2.4	.990							
C	W. Schmidt	335	.248	0	37	279	88	7	10	3.9	.981							
OF	R. Russell	291	.289	9	58	156	4	5	0	2.2	.970							
C	J. Gooch	202	.277	1	20	217	56	7	7	4.2	.975							
2B	C. Tierney	120	.292	2	23	65	94	10	22*	5.8	.941							
OF	W. Mueller	111	.306	0	20	62	2	4	0	2.6	.941							

Chicago

W-83 L-71

Bill Killefer

POS	Player	AB	BA	HR	RBI	PO	A	E	DP	TC/G	FA	Pitcher	G	IP	W	L	SV	ERA
1B	R. Grimes	216	.329	2	36	629	30	6	46	10.7	.991	G. Alexander	39	305	22	12	2	3.19
2B	G. Grantham	570	.281	8	70	**374**	**518**	**55**	90	**6.3**	.942	V. Aldridge	30	217	16	9	0	3.48
SS	S. Adams	311	.289	4	35	153	248	28	45	5.4	.935	T. Kaufmann	33	206	14	10	3	3.10
3B	B. Friberg	547	.318	12	88	168	294	22	**33**	3.3	.955	T. Osborne	37	180	8	15	1	4.56
RF	C. Heathcote	393	.249	1	27	231	14	5	1	2.2	.980	V. Keen	35	177	12	8	1	3.00
CF	J. Statz	**655**	.319	10	70	438	26	12	7	3.1	.975	F. Fussell	28	76	3	5	3	5.54
LF	H. Miller	485	.301	20	88	256	17	6	4	2.2	.978							
C	B. O'Farrell	452	.319	12	84	418	**118**	13	11	4.4	.976							
SS	C. Hollocher	260	.342	1	28	124	212	13	35	5.4	.963							
C1	G. Hartnett	231	.268	8	39	413	39	5	25		.989							
UT	J. Kelleher	193	.306	6	21	228	84	22	21		.934							
1B	A. Elliott	168	.250	2	29	450	19	4	36	9.1	.992							

St. Louis

W-79 L-74

Branch Rickey

POS	Player	AB	BA	HR	RBI	PO	A	E	DP	TC/G	FA	Pitcher	G	IP	W	L	SV	ERA
1B	J. Bottomley	523	.371	8	94	1264	43	18	95	10.2	.986	J. Haines	37	266	20	13	0	3.11
2B	R. Hornsby	424	**.384**	17	83	192	283	19	47	5.1	.962	B. Sherdel	39	225	15	13	2	4.32
SS	H. Freigau	358	.263	1	35	193	290	37	42	6.0	.929	F. Toney	29	197	11	12	0	3.84
3B	M. Stock	603	.289	2	96	165	261	20	24	3.0	.955	B. Doak	30	185	8	13	0	3.26
RF	M. Flack	505	.291	3	28	242	8	13	4	2.2	.951	J. Pfeffer	26	152	8	9	0	4.02
CF	H. Myers	330	.300	2	48	239	15	6	0	3.0	.977	J. Stuart	37	150	9	5	3	4.27
LF	J. Smith	407	.310	5	41	247	11	7	3	2.5	.974	C. Barfoot	33	101	3	3	1	3.73
C	E. Ainsmith	263	.213	3	34	235	57	6	3	3.7	.980							
OF	R. Blades	317	.246	5	44	194	11	7	1	2.6	.967							
2S	S. Toporcer	303	.254	3	35	192	239	24	57		.947							
OF	H. Mueller	265	.343	5	41	197	9	8	3	2.9	.963							
C	H. McCurdy	185	.265	0	15	157	30	6	4	3.3	.969							

NATIONAL LEAGUE 1923, *cont.*

Brooklyn

W-76 L-78

Wilbert Robinson

POS	Player	AB	BA	HR	RBI	PO	A	E	DP	TC/G	FA	Pitcher	G	IP	W	L	SV	ERA
1B	J. Fournier	515	.351	22	102	1281	82	**21**	90	10.4	.985	B. Grimes	39	**327**	21	18	0	3.58
2B	J. Johnston	625	.325	4	60	221	291	28	25	6.4	.948	D. Vance	37	280	18	15	0	3.50
SS	M. Berg	129	.186	0	6	86	126	22	20	5.0	.906	D. Ruether	34	275	15	14	0	4.22
3B	A. High	426	.270	3	37	98	150	8	15	3.2	.969	L. Dickerman	35	166	8	12	0	3.59
RF	T. Griffith	481	.293	8	66	215	14	18	4	1.9	.927	A. Decatur	36	105	3	3	3	2.67
CF	B. Neis	445	.274	5	37	268	20	18	3	2.8	.941	D. Henry	17	94	4	6	0	3.91
LF	G. Bailey	411	.265	1	42	245	10	11	0	2.7	.959	G. Smith	25	91	3	6	1	3.66
C	Z. Taylor	337	.288	0	46	354	**118**	**16**	6	5.8	.967							
OF	Z. Wheat	349	.375	8	65	135	4	14	1	1.8	.908							
2B	I. Olson	292	.260	1	35	161	244	11	36	5.8	.974							
OF	B. Griffith	248	.294	2	37	111	1	6	0	1.9	.949							
C	H. DeBerry	235	.285	1	48	273	65	10	8	5.8	.971							
3B	B. McCarren	216	.245	3	27	72	106	14	11	2.9	.927							

Boston

W-54 L-100

Fred Mitchell

POS	Player	AB	BA	HR	RBI	PO	A	E	DP	TC/G	FA	Pitcher	G	IP	W	L	SV	ERA
1B	S. McInnis	607	.315	2	95	1500	**89**	14	**136**	10.4	.991	R. Marquard	38	239	11	14	0	3.73
2B	H. Ford	380	.271	2	50	213	300	16	61	5.6	.970	J. Genewich	43	227	13	14	1	3.72
SS	B. Smith	375	.251	0	40	234	360	35	69	**6.2**	.944	J. Barnes	31	195	10	14	2	2.76
3B	T. Boeckel	568	.298	7	79	169	265	**28**	27	3.1	.939	J. Oeschger	44	166	5	15	2	5.68
RF	B. Southworth	611	.319	6	78	326	22	21	6	2.4	.943	T. McNamara	32	139	3	13	0	4.91
CF	R. Powell	338	.302	4	38	214	8	14	0	2.8	.941	L. Benton	35	128	5	9	0	4.99
LF	G. Felix	506	.273	6	44	276	11	15	2	2.5	.950	D. Fillingim	35	100	1	9	0	5.20
C	M. O'Neil	306	.212	0	20	298	104	11	5	4.3	.973							
OF	A. Nixon	321	.274	0	19	214	14	3	4	2.9	.987							
C	E. Smith	191	.288	3	19	141	51	5	7	5.8	.975							

Philadelphia

W-50 L-104

Art Fletcher

POS	Player	AB	BA	HR	RBI	PO	A	E	DP	TC/G	FA	Pitcher	G	IP	W	L	SV	ERA
1B	W. Holke	562	.311	7	70	1425	69	13	**136**	10.3	.991	J. Ring	39	313	18	16	0	3.76
2B	C. Tierney	480	.317	11	65	249	416	17	82*	6.0	.975	W. Glazner	28	161	7	14	1	4.69
SS	H. Sand	470	.228	4	32	277	411	**49**	91	6.1	.934	L. Weinert	38	156	4	17	1	5.42
3B	R. Wrightstone	392	.273	7	57	73	121	12	12	2.9	.942	C. Mitchell	29	139	9	10	0	4.72
RF	C. Walker	527	.281	5	66	284	19	17	5	2.3	.947	R. Head	35	132	2	9	0	6.66
CF	C. Williams	535	.293	**41**	114	350	9	7	3	2.7	.981	P. Behan	31	131	3	12	2	5.50
LF	J. Mokan	400	.313	10	48	235	16	8	0	2.5	.969							
C	B. Henline	330	.324	7	46	288	71	8	8	3.8	.978							
OF	C. Lee	355	.321	11	47	136	4	6	3	1.8	.959							
C	J. Wilson	252	.262	1	25	235	50	12	10	4.3	.960							
UT	F. Parkinson	219	.242	3	28	118	175	18	36		.942							
3B	G. Rapp	179	.263	1	10	58	84	8	9	3.3	.947							

BATTING AND BASE RUNNING LEADERS

Batting Average

R. Hornsby, STL	.384
J. Bottomley, STL	.371
J. Fournier, BKN	.351
E. Roush, CIN	.351
F. Frisch, NY	.348

Slugging Average

R. Hornsby, STL	.627
J. Fournier, BKN	.588
C. Williams, PHI	.576
C. Barnhart, PIT	.563
J. Bottomley, STL	.535

Home Runs

C. Williams, PHI	41
J. Fournier, BKN	22
H. Miller, CHI	20
I. Meusel, NY	19
R. Hornsby, STL	17

Total Bases

F. Frisch, NY	311
C. Williams, PHI	308
J. Fournier, BKN	303
P. Traynor, PIT	301
J. Statz, CHI	288

Runs Batted In

I. Meusel, NY	125
C. Williams, PHI	114
F. Frisch, NY	111
G. Kelly, NY	103
J. Fournier, BKN	102

Stolen Bases

M. Carey, PIT	51
G. Grantham, CHI	43
C. Heathcote, CHI	32
J. Smith, STL	32
F. Frisch, NY	29
J. Statz, CHI	29

Hits

F. Frisch, NY	223
J. Statz, CHI	209
P. Traynor, PIT	208
J. Johnston, BKN	203

Base on Balls

G. Burns, CIN	101
H. Sand, PHI	82
R. Youngs, NY	73
M. Carey, PIT	73

Home Run Percentage

C. Williams, PHI	7.7
J. Fournier, BKN	4.3
H. Miller, CHI	4.1
R. Hornsby, STL	4.0

Runs

R. Youngs, NY	121
M. Carey, PIT	120
F. Frisch, NY	116
J. Johnston, BKN	111

Doubles

E. Roush, CIN	41
G. Grantham, CHI	36
C. Tierney, PIT, PHI	36
J. Bottomley, STL	34

Triples

M. Carey, PIT	19
P. Traynor, PIT	19
E. Roush, CIN	18
B. Southworth, BOS	16

PITCHING LEADERS

Winning Percentage

D. Luque, CIN	.771
R. Ryan, NY	.762
J. Scott, NY	.696
J. Morrison, PIT	.658
G. Alexander, CHI	.647

Earned Run Average

D. Luque, CIN	1.93
E. Rixey, CIN	2.80
V. Keen, CHI	3.00
T. Kaufmann, CHI	3.10
J. Haines, STL	3.11

Wins

D. Luque, CIN	27
J. Morrison, PIT	25
G. Alexander, CHI	22
P. Donohue, CIN	21
B. Grimes, BKN	21

Saves

C. Jonnard, NY	5
R. Ryan, NY	4

Strikeouts

D. Vance, BKN	197
D. Luque, CIN	151
B. Grimes, BKN	119
J. Morrison, PIT	114
J. Ring, PHI	112

Complete Games

B. Grimes, BKN	33
D. Luque, CIN	28
J. Morrison, PIT	27
G. Alexander, CHI	26
W. Cooper, PIT	26

Fewest Hits/9 Innings

D. Luque, CIN	7.80
D. Vance, BKN	8.44
J. Morrison, PIT	8.56
V. Keen, CHI	8.59

Shutouts

D. Luque, CIN	6
J. Barnes, NY, BOS	5
H. McQuillan, NY	5

Fewest Walks/9 Innings

G. Alexander, CHI	0.89
B. Adams, PIT	1.42
J. Genewich, BOS	1.82
E. Rixey, CIN	1.89

Most Strikeouts/9 Inn.

D. Vance, BKN	6.32
D. Luque, CIN	4.22
J. Bentley, NY	3.93
J. Morrison, PIT	3.40

Innings

B. Grimes, BKN	327
D. Luque, CIN	322
J. Ring, PHI	313
E. Rixey, CIN	309

Games Pitched

C. Jonnard, NY	45
R. Ryan, NY	45
J. Oeschger, BOS	44
J. Genewich, BOS	43
J. Barnes, NY, BOS	43

							Batting						Fielding			Pitching					
	W	L	PCT	GB	R	OR	2B	3B	HR	BA	SA	SB	E	DP	FA	CG	BB	SO	ShO	SV	ERA
New York	95	58	.621		**854**	679	248	76	85	**.295**	**.415**	106	**176**	141	**.972**	62	424	453	10	**18**	3.90
Cincinnati	91	63	.591	4.5	708	**629**	237	95	45	.285	.392	96	202	144	.969	88	**359**	450	11	9	**3.21**
Pittsburgh	87	67	.565	8.5	786	696	224	**111**	49	**.295**	.404	154	179	157	.971	92	402	414	5	9	3.87
Chicago	83	71	.539	12.5	756	704	243	52	90	.288	.406	**181**	208	144	.967	80	435	408	8	11	3.82
St. Louis	79	74	.516	16	746	732	**274**	76	63	.286	.398	89	232	141	.963	77	456	398	9	7	3.87
Brooklyn	76	78	.494	19.5	753	741	214	81	62	.285	.387	71	293	137	.955	**94**	477	**549**	8	5	3.73
Boston	54	100	.351	41.5	636	798	213	58	32	.273	.353	57	230	157	.964	55	394	351	**13**	7	4.22
Philadelphia	50	104	.325	45.5	748	1008	259	39	**112**	.278	.401	70	217	**172**	.966	68	549	385	3	8	5.30
					5987	5987	1912	588	538	.286	.394	824	1737	1193	.966	616	3496	3408	67	74	3.99

AMERICAN LEAGUE 1923

Team	POS	Player	AB	BA	HR	RBI	PO	A	E	DP	TC/G	FA	Pitcher	G	IP	W	L	SV	ERA
New York	1B	W. Pipp	569	.304	6	108	1461	81	12	97	10.8	.992	J. Bush	37	276	19	15	0	3.43
	2B	A. Ward	567	.284	10	82	387	**493**	18	86	5.9	**.980**	B. Shawkey	36	259	16	11	1	3.51
W-98 L-54	SS	E. Scott	533	.246	6	60	245	414	27	65	4.5	**.961**	S. Jones	39	243	21	8	4	3.63
	3B	J. Dugan	**644**	.283	7	67	155	300	12	28	3.2	**.974**	W. Hoyt	37	239	17	9	1	3.02
Miller Huggins	RF	B. Ruth	522	.393	**41**	**131**	378	20	11	2	2.8	.973	H. Pennock	35	224	19	6	3	3.33
	CF	W. Witt	596	.314	6	56	357	14	8	4	2.6	.979							
	LF	B. Meusel	460	.313	9	91	206	17	11	2	1.9	.953							
	C	W. Schang	272	.276	2	29	292	60	11	6	4.5	.970							
	C	F. Hofmann	238	.290	3	26	292	34	7	7	4.8	.979							
	OF	E. Smith	183	.306	7	35	86	5	5	2	2.0	.948							

Team	POS	Player	AB	BA	HR	RBI	PO	A	E	DP	TC/G	FA	Pitcher	G	IP	W	L	SV	ERA
Detroit	1B	L. Blue	504	.284	1	46	1347	93	12	74	**11.3**	.992	H. Dauss	50	316	21	13	3	3.62
	2B	F. Haney	503	.282	4	67	162	178	16	29	5.2	.955	H. Pillette	47	250	14	**19**	1	3.85
	SS	T. Rigney	470	.315	1	74	209	383	35	46	4.9	.944	K. Holloway	42	194	11	10	1	4.45
	3B	B. Jones	372	.250	1	40	109	224	16	17	3.6	.954	S. Johnson	37	176	12	7	0	3.98
W-83 L-71	RF	H. Heilmann	524	**.403**	18	115	272	13	12	2	2.3	.960	B. Cole	52	163	13	5	5	4.14
	CF	T. Cobb	556	.340	6	88	362	14	12	2	2.8	.969	R. Collins	17	92	3	7	0	4.87
Ty Cobb	LF	H. Manush	308	.334	4	54	158	6	8	0	2.2	.953	R. Francis	33	79	5	8	1	4.42
	C	J. Bassler	383	.298	0	49	447	133	7	8	4.6	.988							
	UT	D. Pratt	297	.310	0	40	281	179	18	32		.962							
	OF	B. Veach	293	.321	2	39	127	6	8	0	1.7	.943							
	OF	B. Fothergill	241	.315	1	49	121	4	3	0	1.9	.977							

Team	POS	Player	AB	BA	HR	RBI	PO	A	E	DP	TC/G	FA	Pitcher	G	IP	W	L	SV	ERA
Cleveland	1B	F. Brower	397	.285	16	66	1047	66	13	87	10.1	.988	G. Uhle	54	**358**	**26**	16	5	3.77
	2B	B. Wambsganss	345	.290	1	59	252	275	20	46	6.2	.963	S. Coveleski	33	228	13	14	2	**2.76**
	SS	J. Sewell	553	.353	3	109	286	497	**59**	82	5.6	.930	J. Edwards	38	179	10	10	1	3.71
W-82 L-71	3B	R. Lutzke	511	.256	3	65	**186**	**358**	**35**	23	**4.0**	.940	J. Shaute	33	172	10	8	0	3.51
	RF	H. Summa	525	.328	3	69	216	15	11	5	1.8	.955	G. Morton	33	129	6	6	1	4.24
Tris Speaker	CF	T. Speaker	574	.380	17	130	369	26	13	7	2.7	.968	S. Smith	30	124	9	6	1	3.27
	LF	C. Jamieson	**644**	.345	2	51	360	18	10	1	2.6	.974	D. Boone	27	70	4	6	0	6.01
	C	S. O'Neill	330	.248	0	50	354	68	14	3	3.9	.968							
	2B	R. Stephenson	301	.319	5	65	205	214	13	49	6.5	.970							
	C	G. Myatt	220	.286	3	40	188	37	16	3	3.5	.934							
	P	G. Uhle	144	.361	0	22	**18**	89	2	**9**	2.0	.982							
	OF	J. Connolly	109	.303	3	25	42	2	2	0	1.2	.957							

Team	POS	Player	AB	BA	HR	RBI	PO	A	E	DP	TC/G	FA	Pitcher	G	IP	W	L	SV	ERA
Washington	1B	J. Judge	405	.314	2	63	1070	88	8	**113**	10.4	**.993**	W. Johnson	42	261	17	12	4	3.48
	2B	B. Harris	532	.282	2	70	**418**	449	**35**	**120**	**6.3**	.961	G. Mogridge	33	211	13	13	1	3.11
	SS	R. Peckinpaugh	568	.264	2	62	311	**510**	45	**105**	**5.6**	.948	T. Zachary	35	204	10	16	0	4.49
W-75 L-78	3B	O. Bluege	379	.245	2	42	126	247	25	**30**	3.7	.937	A. Russell	52	181	10	8	**9**	3.03
	RF	S. Rice	595	.316-	3	75	307	21	10	8	2.3	.970	P. Zahniser	33	177	9	10	0	3.86
Donie Bush	CF	N. Leibold	315	.305	1	22	186	13	4	2	2.4	.980	C. Warmoth	21	105	7	4	0	4.29
	LF	G. Goslin	600	.300	9	99	310	26	15	5	2.4	.957	B. Hollingsworth	17	73	3	7	0	4.09
	C	M. Ruel	449	.316	0	54	**528**	**146**	14	14	5.2	.980							
	OF	J. Evans	372	.263	0	38	159	5	3	2	2.3	.982							
	C1	P. Gharrity	251	.207	3	33	417	47	8	27		.983							

Team	POS	Player	AB	BA	HR	RBI	PO	A	E	DP	TC/G	FA	Pitcher	G	IP	W	L	SV	ERA
St. Louis	1B	D. Schliebner	444	.275	4	52	1141	79	13	102	9.7	.989	E. Vangilder	41	282	16	17	1	3.06
	2B	M. McManus	582	.309	15	94	386	373	32	86	5.9	.960	U. Shocker	43	277	20	12	5	3.41
	SS	W. Gerber	605	.281	1	62	**334**	461	42	86	5.4	.950	D. Danforth	38	226	16	14	1	3.94
	3B	G. Robertson	251	.247	0	17	86	117	14	6	2.9	.935	R. Kolp	34	171	5	12	1	3.89
W-74 L-78	RF	J. Tobin	637	.317	13	73	269	14	9	3	1.9	.969	D. Davis	19	109	4	6	0	3.62
	CF	B. Jacobson	592	.309	8	81	409	10	11	4	2.9	.974	H. Pruett	32	104	4	7	2	4.31
Lee Fohl	LF	K. Williams	555	.357	29	91	333	23	12	5	2.5	.967	R. Wright	20	83	7	4	0	6.42
W-52 L-49	C	H. Severeid	432	.308	3	51	513	88	4	9	**5.2**	**.993**							
Jimmy Austin	3B	H. Ezzell	279	.244	0	14	88	159	10	13	3.5	.961							
W-22 L-29	C	P. Collins	181	.177	3	30	161	31	4	4	4.2	.980							

Team	POS	Player	AB	BA	HR	RBI	PO	A	E	DP	TC/G	FA	Pitcher	G	IP	W	L	SV	ERA
Philadelphia	1B	J. Hauser	537	.307	16	94	1475	86	15	109	10.8	.990	E. Rommel	**56**	298	18	**19**	5	3.27
	2B	J. Dykes	416	.252	4	43	245	315	21	55	5.7	.964	B. Hasty	44	243	13	15	1	4.44
	SS	C. Galloway	504	.278	2	62	285	408	41	73	5.5	.944	S. Harriss	46	209	10	16	6	4.00
	3B	S. Hale	434	.288	3	51	85	222	28	17	3.1	.916	F. Heimach	40	208	6	12	0	4.32
W-69 L-83	RF	F. Welch	421	.297	4	55	253	13	9	4	2.4	.967	R. Naylor	26	143	12	7	0	3.46
	CF	W. Matthews	485	.274	1	25	316	3	18	0	2.7	.947	R. Walberg	26	115	4	8	0	5.32
Connie Mack	LF	B. Miller	458	.299	12	64	262	10	6	0	2.3	.978							
	C	C. Perkins	500	.270	2	65	475	102	**17**	12	4.3	.971							
	OF	F. McGowan	287	.254	1	19	154	12	5	1	2.2	.971							
	2B	H. Scheer	210	.238	2	21	147	156	9	30	5.1	.971							
	3B	H. Riconda	175	.263	0	12	45	114	15	9	3.7	.914							

Team	POS	Player	AB	BA	HR	RBI	PO	A	E	DP	TC/G	FA	Pitcher	G	IP	W	L	SV	ERA
Chicago	1B	E. Sheely	570	.296	4	88	**1563**	**96**	14	**113**	10.7	.992	C. Robertson	38	255	13	18	0	3.81
	2B	E. Collins	505	.360	5	67	347	430	20	77	5.6	.975	R. Faber	32	232	14	11	0	3.41
	SS	H. McClellan	550	.235	1	41	217	394	27	63	4.6	.958	M. Cvengros	41	215	12	13	3	4.39
W-69 L-85	3B	W. Kamm	544	.292	6	87	173	352	22	29	3.7	.960	T. Blankenship	44	209	9	14	0	4.27
	RF	H. Hooper	576	.288	10	65	272	15	12	3	2.1	.960	D. Leverett	38	193	10	13	3	4.06
Kid Gleason	CF	J. Mostil	546	.291	3	64	422	21	12	5	3.2	.974	S. Thurston	44	192	7	8	4	3.05
	LF	B. Falk	274	.307	5	38	148	6	8	3	2.0	.951							
	C	R. Schalk	382	.228	1	44	481	93	10	**20**	4.8	.983							
	OF	R. Elsh	209	.249	0	24	127	7	6	1	2.5	.957							
	OF	B. Barrett	162	.272	2	23	89	5	6	1	2.5	.940							

AMERICAN LEAGUE 1923, *cont.*

Boston

W-61 L-91

Frank Chance

POS	Player	AB	BA	HR	RBI	PO	A	E	DP	TC/G	FA
1B	G. Burns	551	.328	7	82	1485	92	**16**	103	10.9	.990
2B	C. Fewster	284	.236	0	15	103	140	16	21	5.4	.938
SS	J. Mitchell	347	.225	0	19	184	264	18	40	5.4	.961
3B	H. Shanks	464	.254	3	57	89	169	17	16	3.2	.938
RF	I. Flagstead	382	.312	8	53	218	33	10	8	2.6	.962
CF	D. Reichle	361	.258	1	39	190	10	5	2	2.2	.976
LF	J. Harris	483	.335	13	76	289	13	10	2	2.4	.968
C	V. Picinich	268	.276	2	31	247	89	15	7	4.3	.957
UT	N. McMillan	459	.253	0	42	261	327	35	48		.944
OF	S. Collins	342	.231	0	18	164	17	9	2	2.1	.953
C	A. DeVormer	209	.258	0	18	181	48	5	3	4.3	.979
OF	M. Menosky	188	.229	0	25	103	12	10	1	2.6	.920
2B	P. Pittenger	177	.215	0	15	77	86	7	12	4.0	.959

Pitcher	G	IP	W	L	SV	ERA
H. Ehmke	43	317	20	17	3	3.78
J. Quinn	42	243	13	17	7	3.89
A. Ferguson	34	198	9	13	0	4.04
B. Piercy	30	187	8	17	0	3.41
G. Murray	39	178	7	11	0	4.91
C. Fullerton	37	143	2	15	1	5.09

BATTING AND BASE RUNNING LEADERS

Batting Average

H. Heilmann, DET	.403
B. Ruth, NY	.393
T. Speaker, CLE	.380
E. Collins, CHI	.360
K. Williams, STL	.357

Slugging Average

B. Ruth, NY	.764
H. Heilmann, DET	.632
K. Williams, STL	.623
T. Speaker, CLE	.610
J. Harris, BOS	.520

Home Runs

B. Ruth, NY	41
K. Williams, STL	29
H. Heilmann, DET	18
T. Speaker, CLE	17
F. Brower, CLE	16
J. Hauser, PHI	16

Winning Percentage

H. Pennock, NY	.760
S. Jones, NY	.724
W. Hoyt, NY	.654
U. Shocker, STL	.625
G. Uhle, CLE	.619

Total Bases

B. Ruth, NY	399
T. Speaker, CLE	350
K. Williams, STL	346
H. Heilmann, DET	331
J. Tobin, STL	303

Runs Batted In

B. Ruth, NY	131
T. Speaker, CLE	130
H. Heilmann, DET	115
J. Sewell, CLE	109
W. Pipp, NY	108

Stolen Bases

E. Collins, CHI	47
J. Mostil, CHI	41
B. Harris, WAS	23
S. Rice, WAS	20
C. Jamieson, CLE	19

Saves

A. Russell, WAS	9
J. Quinn, BOS	7
S. Harriss, PHI	6

Hits

C. Jamieson, CLE	222
T. Speaker, CLE	218
H. Heilmann, DET	211
B. Ruth, NY	205

Base on Balls

B. Ruth, NY	170
J. Sewell, CLE	98
L. Blue, DET	96
T. Speaker, CLE	93

Home Run Percentage

B. Ruth, NY	7.9
K. Williams, STL	5.2
F. Brower, CLE	4.0
H. Heilmann, DET	3.4

Fewest Hits/9 Innings

B. Shawkey, NY	8.07
W. Hoyt, NY	8.56
J. Bush, NY	8.59
D. Danforth, STL	8.79

Runs

B. Ruth, NY	151
T. Speaker, CLE	133
C. Jamieson, CLE	130
H. Heilmann, DET	121

Doubles

T. Speaker, CLE	59
G. Burns, BOS	47
B. Ruth, NY	45
H. Heilmann, DET	44

Triples

S. Rice, WAS	18
G. Goslin, WAS	18
J. Mostil, CHI	15
J. Tobin, STL	15

Most Strikeouts/9 Inn.

W. Johnson, WAS	4.48
B. Shawkey, NY	4.35
J. Bush, NY	4.08
D. Danforth, STL	3.82

PITCHING LEADERS

Earned Run Average

S. Coveleski, CLE	2.76
W. Hoyt, NY	3.02
E. Vangilder, STL	3.06
G. Mogridge, WAS	3.11
E. Rommel, PHI	3.27

Wins

G. Uhle, CLE	26
S. Jones, NY	21
H. Dauss, DET	21
U. Shocker, STL	20
H. Ehmke, BOS	20

Strikeouts

W. Johnson, WAS	130
B. Shawkey, NY	125
J. Bush, NY	125
H. Ehmke, BOS	121
U. Shocker, STL	109
G. Uhle, CLE	109

Complete Games

G. Uhle, CLE	29
H. Ehmke, BOS	28
U. Shocker, STL	24
J. Bush, NY	23
H. Dauss, DET	22

Shutouts

S. Coveleski, CLE	5
E. Vangilder, STL	4
H. Dauss, DET	4

Fewest Walks/9 Innings

U. Shocker, STL	1.59
S. Coveleski, CLE	1.66
J. Quinn, BOS	1.96
H. Dauss, DET	2.22

Innings

G. Uhle, CLE	358
H. Ehmke, BOS	317
H. Dauss, DET	316
E. Rommel, PHI	298

Games Pitched

E. Rommel, PHI	56
G. Uhle, CLE	54
A. Russell, WAS	52
B. Cole, DET	52

							Batting						Fielding			Pitching					
	W	L	PCT	GB	R	OR	2B	3B	HR	BA	SA	SB	E	DP	FA	CG	BB	SO	ShO	SV	ERA
New York	98	54	.645		823	**622**	231	79	**105**	.291	**.422**	69	**144**	131	**.977**	**102**	491	**506**	9	10	**3.66**
Detroit	83	71	.539	16	831	741	270	69	41	.300	.401	87	200	103	.968	61	**459**	447	9	12	4.09
Cleveland	82	71	.536	16.5	**888**	746	**301**	75	59	**.301**	.420	79	226	143	.964	76	466	407	**10**	11	3.91
Washington	75	78	.490	23.5	720	747	224	**93**	26	.274	.367	102	216	**182**	.966	70	559	474	8	**16**	3.99
St. Louis	74	78	.487	24	688	720	248	62	82	.281	.398	64	177	145	.971	83	528	488	**10**	10	3.93
Philadelphia	69	83	.454	29	661	761	229	65	52	.271	.370	72	221	127	.965	65	550	400	6	12	4.08
Chicago	69	85	.448	30	692	741	254	57	42	.279	.373	**191**	184	138	.971	74	534	467	5	11	4.03
Boston	61	91	.401	37	584	809	253	54	34	.261	.351	77	232	126	.963	78	520	412	3	11	4.20
					5887	5887	2010	554	441	.282	.388	741	1600	1095	.968	609	4107	3601	60	93	3.99

NATIONAL LEAGUE 1924

New York

W-93 L-60

John McGraw
W-16 L-13

Hughie Jennings
W-32 L-12

John McGraw
W-45 L-35

POS	Player	AB	BA	HR	RBI	PO	A	E	DP	TC/G	FA
1B	G. Kelly	571	.324	21	**136**	1309	60	10	105	11.0	.993
2B	F. Frisch	603	.328	7	69	**391**	537	27	100	**6.7**	.972
SS	T. Jackson	596	.302	11	76	332	534	**58**	101	6.1	.937
3B	H. Groh	559	.281	2	46	121	286	7	13	2.9	**.983**
RF	R. Youngs	526	.356	10	74	236	17	12	3	2.0	.955
CF	H. Wilson	383	.295	10	57	230	8	8	2	2.4	.967
LF	I. Meusel	549	.310	6	102	287	4	10	0	2.2	.967
C	F. Snyder	354	.302	5	53	308	79	5	8	3.6	.987
OF	B. Southworth	281	.256	3	36	167	5	12	2	2.5	.935
C	H. Gowdy	191	.325	4	37	223	51	5	8	3.6	.982
1B	B. Terry	163	.239	5	24	325	14	4	30	8.2	.988

Pitcher	G	IP	W	L	SV	ERA
V. Barnes	35	229	16	10	3	3.06
J. Bentley	28	188	16	5	1	3.78
H. McQuillan	27	184	14	8	3	2.69
A. Nehf	30	172	14	4	2	3.62
W. Dean	26	126	6	12	0	5.01
R. Ryan	37	125	8	6	5	4.26
M. Watson	22	100	7	4	0	3.79
C. Jonnard	34	90	4	5	5	2.41

NATIONAL LEAGUE 1924, *cont.*

Team	POS	Player	AB	BA	HR	RBI	PO	A	E	DP	TC/G	FA	Pitcher	G	IP	W	L	SV	ERA
Brooklyn	1B	J. Fournier	563	.334	**27**	116	1388	**99**	22	102	9.9	.985	B. Grimes	38	**311**	22	13	1	3.82
W-92 L-62	2B	A. High	582	.328	6	61	295	437	27	52	5.7	.964	D. Vance	35	309	**28**	6	0	**2.16**
Wilbert Robinson	SS	J. Mitchell	243	.263	1	16	131	216	18	30	5.7	.951	D. Ruether	30	167	8	13	3	3.94
	3B	M. Stock	561	.242	2	52	139	200	**25**	14	2.6	.931	B. Doak	21	149	11	5	0	3.07
	RF	T. Griffith	482	.251	3	67	210	9	8	3	1.6	.965	A. Decatur	31	128	10	9	1	4.07
	CF	E. Brown	455	.308	5	78	311	3	8	0	2.8	.975	T. Osborne	21	104	6	5	0	5.09
	LF	Z. Wheat	566	.375	14	97	288	13	11	4	2.2	.965							
	C	Z. Taylor	345	.290	1	39	388	96	6	13	**5.3**	**.988**							
	SS	J. Johnston	315	.298	2	29	136	203	22	32	5.7	.939							
	C	H. DeBerry	218	.243	3	26	394	57	3	8	7.2	.993							
	OF	B. Neis	211	.303	4	26	114	5	8	1	2.0	.937							
Pittsburgh	1B	C. Grimm	542	.288	2	63	**1596**	72	8	**139**	11.1	**.995**	W. Cooper	38	269	20	14	1	3.28
W-90 L-63	2B	R. Maranville	594	.266	2	71	365	**568**	26	**109**	6.3	**.973**	R. Kremer	**41**	259	18	10	1	3.19
Bill McKechnie	SS	G. Wright	**616**	.287	7	111	310	**601**	52	**102**	**6.3**	.946	J. Morrison	**41**	238	11	16	2	3.75
	3B	P. Traynor	545	.294	5	82	179	268	15	**31**	3.3	.968	L. Meadows	36	229	13	12	0	3.26
	RF	C. Barnhart	344	.276	3	51	186	8	6	3	2.3	.970	E. Yde	33	194	16	3	0	2.83
	CF	M. Carey	599	.297	7	55	428	16	16	3	3.1	.965							
	LF	K. Cuyler	466	.354	9	85	246	19	16	4	2.5	.943							
	C	J. Gooch	224	.290	0	25	198	47	3	12	3.6	.988							
	OF	C. Bigbee	282	.262	0	15	155	9	10	2	2.3	.943							
	03	E. Moore	209	.359	2	13	92	30	1	2		.992							
	C	W. Schmidt	177	.243	1	20	166	51	3	6	3.9	.986							
	C	E. Smith	111	.369	4	21	127	23	4	3	4.4	.974							
Cincinnati	1B	J. Daubert	405	.281	1	31	1128	74	12	84	**11.9**	.990	E. Rixey	35	238	15	14	1	2.76
W-83 L-70	2B	H. Critz	413	.322	3	35	229	357	27	58	6.4	.956	C. Mays	37	226	20	9	0	3.15
Jack Hendricks	SS	I. Caveney	337	.273	4	32	200	310	42	59	6.1	.924	P. Donohue	35	222	16	9	0	3.60
	3B	B. Pinelli	510	.306	0	70	**182**	**318**	23	21	**3.7**	.956	D. Luque	31	219	10	15	0	3.16
	RF	C. Walker	397	.300	4	46	213	14	5	4	2.1	.978	T. Sheehan	39	167	9	11	1	3.24
	CF	E. Roush	483	.348	3	72	270	10	12	4	2.5	.959	R. Benton	32	163	7	9	1	2.77
	LF	P. Duncan	319	.270	2	37	124	3	10	0	1.7	.927	J. May	38	99	3	3	**6**	3.00
	C	B. Hargrave	312	.301	3	33	322	80	7	7	4.5	.983							
	10	R. Bressler	383	.347	4	49	561	35	9	36		.985							
	UT	S. Bohne	349	.255	4	46	194	294	23	40		.955							
	OF	G. Burns	336	.256	2	33	168	13	7	4	2.1	.963							
	C	I. Wingo	192	.286	1	23	215	50	3	7	4.1	.989							
Chicago	1B	H. Cotter	310	.261	4	33	873	59	10	72	10.5	.989	V. Aldridge	32	244	15	12	0	3.50
W-81 L-72	2B	G. Grantham	469	.316	12	60	273	426	**44**	78	6.3	.941	V. Keen	40	235	15	14	3	3.80
Bill Killefer	SS	S. Adams	418	.280	1	27	169	277	28	62	5.4	.941	T. Kaufmann	34	208	16	11	0	4.02
	3B	B. Friberg	495	.279	5	82	163	268	21	21	3.2	.954	E. Jacobs	38	190	11	12	1	3.74
	RF	C. Heathcote	392	.309	0	30	228	7	5	3	2.2	.979	G. Alexander	21	169	12	5	0	3.03
	CF	J. Statz	549	.277	3	49	373	22	16	5	3.1	.961	S. Blake	29	106	6	6	1	4.57
	LF	D. Grigsby	411	.299	3	48	244	16	7	4	2.2	.974	R. Wheeler	29	101	3	6	0	3.91
	C	G. Hartnett	354	.299	16	67	369	97	**18**	12	4.6	.963							
	SS	C. Hollocher	286	.245	2	21	156	248	13	42	5.9	.969							
	C	B. O'Farrell	183	.240	3	28	204	40	4	5	4.4	.984							
	1B	R. Grimes	177	.299	5	34	530	12	10	40	11.0	.982							
	OF	O. Vogel	172	.267	1	24	101	7	5	2	2.1	.956							
	OF	B. Weis	133	.278	0	23	81	8	2	2	2.5	.978							
	UT	B. Barrett	133	.241	5	21	123	80	13	20		.940							
	OF	H. Miller	131	.336	4	25	54	1	3	0	1.8	.948							
St. Louis	1B	J. Bottomley	528	.316	14	111	1297	48	**24**	110	10.3	.982	J. Haines	35	223	8	19	0	4.41
W-65 L-89	2B	R. Hornsby	536	**.424**	25	94	301	517	30	102	5.9	.965	A. Sothoron	29	197	10	16	0	3.57
Branch Rickey	SS	J. Cooney	383	.295	1	57	242	322	18	68	5.9	.969	B. Sherdel	35	169	8	9	1	3.42
	3B	H. Freigau	376	.269	2	39	127	171	13	24	3.2	.958	J. Stuart	28	159	9	11	0	4.75
	RF	J. Smith	459	.283	2	33	251	18	9	8	2.4	.968	E. Dyer	29	137	8	11	0	4.61
	CF	W. Holm	293	.294	0	23	162	9	2	1	2.7	.988	L. Dickerman	18	120	7	4	0	2.41
	LF	R. Blades	456	.311	11	68	256	6	12	1	2.5	.956	H. Bell	28	113	3	8	1	4.92
	C	M. Gonzalez	402	.296	3	53	**413**	96	7	**15**	4.3	.986							
	01	H. Mueller	296	.264	2	37	335	15	9	17		.975							
	OF	M. Flack	209	.263	2	21	90	9	3	0	2.0	.971							
	3S	S. Toporcer	198	.313	1	24	54	103	7	8		.957							
	OF	T. Douthit	173	.277	0	13	118	5	3	2	2.5	.976							
	OF	C. Hafey	91	.253	2	22	48	3	4	1	2.3	.927							
Philadelphia	1B	W. Holke	563	.300	6	64	1516	90	12	134	10.9	.993	J. Ring	32	215	10	12	0	3.97
W-55 L-96	2B	H. Ford	530	.272	3	53	337	543	27	96	6.3	.970	H. Carlson	38	204	8	17	2	4.86
Art Fletcher	SS	H. Sand	539	.245	6	40	**333**	460	34	95	6.0	**.959**	B. Hubbell	36	179	10	9	2	4.83
	3B	R. Wrightstone	388	.307	7	58	114	154	16	19	2.9	.944	C. Mitchell	30	165	6	13	1	5.62
	RF	G. Harper	411	.294	16	55	219	13	2	4	2.1	.991	W. Glazner	35	157	7	16	0	5.92
	CF	C. Williams	558	.328	24	93	368	13	15	0	2.7	.962	H. Betts	37	144	7	10	2	4.30
	LF	J. Mokan	366	.260	7	44	195	9	3	1	2.2	.986	J. Couch	37	137	4	8	3	4.73
	C	B. Henline	289	.284	5	35	248	76	9	12	4.0	.973							
	OF	J. Schultz	284	.282	5	29	137	7	6	0	2.0	.960							
	C	J. Wilson	280	.279	6	39	240	93	11	14	4.2	.968							
	UT	F. Parkinson	156	.212	1	19	63	127	7	23		.964							

NATIONAL LEAGUE 1924, *cont.*

Boston

W-53 L-100

Dave Bancroft
W-27 L-38

Dick Rudolph
W-11 L-27

Dave Bancroft
W-15 L-35

POS	Player	AB	BA	HR	RBI	PO	A	E	DP	TC/G	FA
1B	S. McInnis	581	.291	1	59	1435	95	10	129	10.5	.994
2B	C. Tierney	505	.259	6	58	235	399	24	83	5.7	.964
SS	B. Smith	347	.228	2	38	180	273	20	54	5.9	.958
3B	E. Padgett	502	.255	1	46	95	194	10	23	2.6	.967
RF	C. Stengel	461	.280	5	39	211	12	5	4	1.8	.978
CF	F. Wilson	215	.237	1	15	140	5	4	1	2.7	.973
LF	B. Cunningham	437	.272	1	40	243	16	8	3	2.4	.970
C	M. O'Neil	362	.246	0	22	362	**108**	7	8	4.5	.985
SS	D. Bancroft	319	.279	2	21	186	259	18	57	5.9	.961
C	F. Gibson	229	.310	1	30	159	52	6	4	4.7	.972
OF	G. Felix	204	.211	1	10	147	6	8	1	3.2	.950
OF	R. Powell	188	.261	1	15	117	9	7	3	2.9	.947

Pitcher	G	IP	W	L	SV	ERA
J. Barnes	37	268	15	**20**	0	3.23
J. Genewich	34	200	10	19	1	5.21
J. Cooney	34	181	8	9	2	3.18
T. McNamara	35	179	8	12	0	5.18
J. Yeargin	32	141	1	11	0	5.09
L. Benton	30	128	5	7	1	4.15
D. Stryker	20	73	3	8	0	6.01

BATTING AND BASE RUNNING LEADERS

Batting Average
R. Hornsby, STL .424
Z. Wheat, BKN .375
R. Youngs, NY .356
K. Cuyler, PIT .354
E. Roush, CIN .348

Slugging Average
R. Hornsby, STL .696
C. Williams, PHI .552
Z. Wheat, BKN .549
K. Cuyler, PIT .539
J. Fournier, BKN .536

Home Runs
J. Fournier, BKN 27
R. Hornsby, STL 25
C. Williams, PHI 24
G. Kelly, NY 21
G. Hartnett, CHI 16
G. Harper, CIN, PHI 16

Total Bases
R. Hornsby, STL 373
Z. Wheat, BKN 311
C. Williams, PHI 308
G. Kelly, NY 303
J. Fournier, BKN 302

Runs Batted In
G. Kelly, NY 136
J. Fournier, BKN 116
J. Bottomley, STL 111
G. Wright, PIT 111
I. Meusel, NY 102

Stolen Bases
M. Carey, PIT 49
K. Cuyler, PIT 32
C. Heathcote, CHI 26
J. Smith, STL 24
P. Traynor, PIT 24

Hits
R. Hornsby, STL 227
Z. Wheat, BKN 212
F. Frisch, NY 198
A. High, BKN 191

Base on Balls
R. Hornsby, STL 89
J. Fournier, BKN 83
R. Youngs, NY 77
C. Williams, PHI 67

Home Run Percentage
J. Fournier, BKN 4.8
R. Hornsby, STL 4.7
G. Hartnett, CHI 4.5
C. Williams, PHI 4.3

Runs
R. Hornsby, STL 121
F. Frisch, NY 121
M. Carey, PIT 113
R. Youngs, NY 112

Doubles
R. Hornsby, STL 43
Z. Wheat, BKN 41
G. Kelly, NY 37

Triples
E. Roush, CIN 21
R. Maranville, PIT 20
G. Wright, PIT 18
K. Cuyler, PIT 16

PITCHING LEADERS

Winning Percentage
E. Yde, PIT .842
D. Vance, BKN .824
J. Bentley, NY .762
C. Mays, CIN .690
R. Kremer, PIT .643

Earned Run Average
D. Vance, BKN 2.16
H. McQuillan, NY 2.69
E. Rixey, CIN 2.76
E. Yde, PIT 2.83
G. Alexander, CHI 3.03

Wins
D. Vance, BKN 28
B. Grimes, BKN 22
C. Mays, CIN 20
W. Cooper, PIT 20
R. Kremer, PIT 18

Saves
J. May, CIN 6
C. Jonnard, NY 5
R. Ryan, NY 5

Strikeouts
D. Vance, BKN 262
B. Grimes, BKN 135
D. Luque, CIN 86
J. Morrison, PIT 85
T. Kaufmann, CHI 79

Complete Games
D. Vance, BKN 30
B. Grimes, BKN 30
W. Cooper, PIT 25
J. Barnes, BOS 21
V. Aldridge, CHI 20

Fewest Hits/9 Innings
D. Vance, BKN 6.94
E. Yde, PIT 7.93
J. Morrison, PIT 8.07
E. Rixey, CIN 8.27

Shutouts
6 tied with 4

Fewest Walks/9 Innings
G. Alexander, CHI 1.33
W. Cooper, PIT 1.34
C. Mays, CIN 1.43
P. Donohue, CIN 1.46

Most Strikeouts/9 Inn.
D. Vance, BKN 7.64
B. Grimes, BKN 3.91
A. Nehf, NY 3.77
D. Luque, CIN 3.53

Innings
B. Grimes, BKN 311
D. Vance, BKN 309
W. Cooper, PIT 269
J. Barnes, BOS 268

Games Pitched
J. Morrison, PIT 41
R. Kremer, PIT 41
V. Keen, CHI 40
T. Sheehan, CIN 39

							Batting						Fielding			Pitching					
	W	L	PCT	GB	R	OR	2B	3B	HR	BA	SA	SB	E	DP	FA	CG	BB	SO	ShO	SV	ERA
New York	93	60	.608		**857**	641	269	81	**95**	**.300**	**.432**	82	186	160	.971	71	392	406	4	**21**	3.62
Brooklyn	92	62	.597	1.5	717	675	227	54	72	.287	.391	34	196	121	.968	**98**	403	**640**	10	5	3.64
Pittsburgh	90	63	.588	3	724	588	222	**122**	43	.287	.399	**181**	183	161	.971	85	323	364	**15**	5	3.27
Cincinnati	83	70	.542	10	649	**579**	236	111	36	.290	.397	103	217	142	.966	77	**293**	451	14	9	**3.12**
Chicago	81	72	.529	12	698	699	207	59	66	.276	.378	137	218	153	.966	85	438	416	4	6	3.83
St. Louis	65	89	.422	28.5	740	750	**270**	87	67	.290	.411	86	191	162	.969	79	486	393	7	6	4.15
Philadelphia	55	96	.364	37	676	849	256	56	94	.275	.397	57	175	**168**	.972	59	469	349	7	10	4.87
Boston	53	100	.346	40	520	800	194	52	25	.256	.327	74	**168**	154	**.973**	66	402	364	10	4	4.46
					5581	5581	1881	622	498	.283	.391	754	1534	1221	.970	620	3206	3383	71	66	3.87

AMERICAN LEAGUE 1924

Washington

W-92 L-62

Bucky Harris

POS	Player	AB	BA	HR	RBI	PO	A	E	DP	TC/G	FA
1B	J. Judge	516	.324	3	79	1276	86	8	108	9.8	.994
2B	B. Harris	544	.268	1	58	393	386	26	**100**	5.6	.968
SS	R. Peckinpaugh	523	.272	2	73	278	487	29	**81**	5.1	.963
3B	O. Bluege	402	.281	2	49	88	195	16	11	2.9	.946
RF	S. Rice	**646**	.334	1	76	331	18	12	4	2.3	.967
CF	N. Leibold	246	.293	0	20	148	7	1	0	2.2	.994
LF	G. Goslin	579	.344	12	**129**	369	12	16	4	2.6	.960
C	M. Ruel	501	.283	0	57	**612**	**112**	15	**23**	**5.0**	.980
OF	E. McNeely	179	.330	0	15	105	3	3	1	2.6	.973
OF	W. Matthews	169	.302	0	13	121	7	2	2	3.0	.985
3B	D. Prothro	159	.333	0	24	40	68	10	6	2.6	.915

Pitcher	G	IP	W	L	SV	ERA
W. Johnson	38	278	**23**	7	0	**2.72**
G. Mogridge	30	213	16	11	0	3.76
T. Zachary	33	203	15	9	2	2.75
F. Marberry	**50**	195	11	12	**15**	3.09
J. Martina	24	125	6	8	0	4.67
C. Ogden	16	108	9	5	0	2.59
P. Zahniser	24	92	5	7	0	4.40
A. Russell	37	82	5	1	8	4.37

AMERICAN LEAGUE 1924, *cont.*

New York

W-89 L-63

Miller Huggins

POS	Player	AB	BA	HR	RBI	PO	A	E	DP	TC/G	FA	Pitcher	G	IP	W	L	SV	ERA
1B	W. Pipp	589	.295	9	113	1447	106	9	106	10.2	**.994**	H. Pennock	40	286	21	9	3	2.83
2B	A. Ward	400	.253	8	66	303	385	19	60	5.9	.973	J. Bush	39	252	17	16	1	3.57
SS	E. Scott	548	.250	4	64	322	455	27	80	5.3	.966	W. Hoyt	46	247	18	13	4	3.79
3B	J. Dugan	610	.302	3	56	177	250	17	22	3.0	.962	B. Shawkey	38	208	16	11	0	4.12
RF	B. Ruth	529	**.378**	**46**	121	340	18	14	4	2.4	.962	S. Jones	36	179	9	6	3	3.63
CF	W. Witt	600	.297	1	36	362	11	9	1	2.7	.976							
LF	B. Meusel	579	.325	12	120	252	17	14	4	2.0	.951							
C	W. Schang	356	.292	5	52	423	89	15	9	4.8	.972							
C	F. Hofmann	166	.175	1	11	179	45	2	2	4.2	.991							

Detroit

W-86 L-68

Ty Cobb

POS	Player	AB	BA	HR	RBI	PO	A	E	DP	TC/G	FA	Pitcher	G	IP	W	L	SV	ERA
1B	L. Blue	395	.311	2	50	1099	85	17	72	**11.1**	.986	E. Whitehill	35	233	17	9	0	3.86
2B	D. Pratt	429	.303	1	77	133	192	18	38	5.4	.948	R. Collins	34	216	14	7	0	3.21
SS	T. Rigney	499	.289	4	93	273	463	25	72	5.2	**.967**	L. Stoner	36	216	11	11	0	4.72
3B	B. Jones	393	.272	0	47	108	196	14	12	3.0	.956	K. Holloway	49	181	14	6	3	4.07
RF	H. Heilmann	570	.346	10	113	263	31	9	6	2.1	.970	H. Dauss	40	131	12	11	6	4.59
CF	T. Cobb	625	.338	4	74	417	12	6	8	2.8	.986	B. Cole	28	109	3	9	2	4.69
LF	H. Manush	422	.289	9	68	224	4	5	1	2.2	.979	S. Johnson	29	104	5	4	3	4.93
C	J. Bassler	379	.346	1	68	402	103	11	11	4.2	.979	E. Wells	29	102	6	8	4	4.06
3B	F. Haney	256	.309	1	30	48	146	14	9	3.5	.933							
2B	L. Burke	241	.253	0	17	125	167	13	30	5.3	.957							
2B	F. O'Rourke	181	.276	0	19	115	140	8	27	6.6	.970							
OF	B. Fothergill	166	.301	0	15	89	2	3	1	2.1	.968							
C	L. Woodall	165	.309	0	24	174	41	3	5	3.5	.986							
OF	A. Wingo	150	.287	1	26	59	3	5	2	1.6	.925							

St. Louis

W-74 L-78

George Sisler

POS	Player	AB	BA	HR	RBI	PO	A	E	DP	TC/G	FA	Pitcher	G	IP	W	L	SV	ERA
1B	G. Sisler	636	.305	9	74	1319	**111**	**23**	114	9.6	.984	U. Shocker	39	239	16	13	1	4.17
2B	M. McManus	442	.333	5	80	324	365	20	67	6.0	.972	D. Danforth	41	220	15	12	4	4.51
SS	W. Gerber	496	.272	0	55	317	422	**42**	77	5.3	.946	E. Wingard	36	218	13	12	1	3.51
3B	G. Robertson	439	.319	4	52	112	203	14	22	3.0	.957	D. Davis	29	160	11	13	0	4.10
RF	J. Tobin	569	.299	2	48	248	19	12	5	2.1	.957	E. Vangilder	43	145	5	10	1	5.76
CF	B. Jacobson	579	.318	19	97	484	7	7	4	3.3	.986	R. Kolp	25	97	5	7	0	5.68
LF	K. Williams	398	.324	18	84	257	13	9	2	2.6	.968							
C	H. Severeid	432	.308	4	48	436	104	6	12	4.2	**.989**							
OF	J. Evans	209	.254	0	18	118	3	4	1	2.6	.968							
UT	N. McMillan	201	.279	0	27	132	122	11	19		.958							

Philadelphia

W-71 L-81

Connie Mack

POS	Player	AB	BA	HR	RBI	PO	A	E	DP	TC/G	FA	Pitcher	G	IP	W	L	SV	ERA
1B	J. Hauser	562	.288	27	115	**1513**	94	12	**131**	11.1	.993	E. Rommel	43	278	18	15	1	3.95
2B	M. Bishop	294	.255	2	21	189	273	15	50	6.0	.969	F. Heimach	40	198	14	12	0	4.73
SS	C. Galloway	464	.276	2	48	285	389	34	71	5.5	.952	S. Baumgartner	36	181	13	6	4	2.88
3B	H. Riconda	281	.253	1	21	95	147	19	14	3.6	.927	D. Burns	37	154	6	8	1	5.08
RF	B. Miller	398	.342	6	62	172	11	5	4	2.0	.973	S. Gray	34	152	8	7	2	3.98
CF	A. Simmons	594	.308	8	102	390	17	10	4	2.7	.976	R. Meeker	30	146	5	12	0	4.68
LF	B. Lamar	367	.330	7	48	184	13	6	4	2.3	.970	S. Harriss	36	123	6	10	2	4.68
C	C. Perkins	392	.242	0	32	415	102	9	9	4.1	.983							
2B	J. Dykes	410	.312	3	50	213	253	19	46	6.2	.961							
OF	F. Welch	293	.290	5	31	120	15	2	2	1.9	.985							
3B	S. Hale	261	.318	2	17	39	108	8	10	2.8	.948							
OF	P. Strand	167	.228	0	13	80	3	1	0	1.9	.988							

Cleveland

W-67 L-86

Tris Speaker

POS	Player	AB	BA	HR	RBI	PO	A	E	DP	TC/G	FA	Pitcher	G	IP	W	L	SV	ERA
1B	G. Burns	462	.310	4	66	1227	110	18	85	10.7	.987	J. Shaute	46	283	20	**17**	2	3.75
2B	C. Fewster	322	.267	0	36	194	229	17	36	4.7	.961	S. Smith	39	248	12	14	1	3.02
SS	J. Sewell	594	.316	4	104	**349**	**514**	36	76	**5.9**	.960	S. Coveleski	37	240	15	16	0	4.04
3B	R. Lutzke	341	.243	0	42	154	238	**22**	25	**4.0**	.947	G. Uhle	28	196	9	15	1	4.77
RF	H. Summa	390	.290	2	38	167	10	11	2	2.0	.941							
CF	T. Speaker	486	.344	9	65	323	20	13	3	2.8	.963							
LF	C. Jamieson	594	.359	3	53	330	11	9	6	2.5	.974							
C	G. Myatt	342	.342	8	73	248	63	7	7	3.3	.978							
OF	P. McNulty	291	.268	0	26	137	9	6	2	2.0	.961							
2B	R. Stephenson	240	.371	4	44	114	179	12	20	5.3	.961							
C	L. Sewell	165	.291	0	17	171	42	9	5	4.0	.959							
1B	F. Brower	107	.280	3	20	187	17	2	11	7.9	.990							

Boston

W-67 L-87

Lee Fohl

POS	Player	AB	BA	HR	RBI	PO	A	E	DP	TC/G	FA	Pitcher	G	IP	W	L	SV	ERA
1B	J. Harris	491	.301	3	77	1266	101	10	100	10.8	.993	H. Ehmke	45	**315**	19	**17**	4	3.46
2B	B. Wambsganss	636	.274	0	49	**459**	**490**	**37**	98	**6.4**	.962	A. Ferguson	40	235	14	**17**	2	3.79
SS	D. Lee	288	.253	0	29	198	246	30	43	5.3	.937	J. Quinn	43	228	12	13	7	3.20
3B	D. Clark	325	.277	2	54	88	173	15	8	3.0	.946	C. Fullerton	33	152	7	12	2	4.32
RF	I. Boone	486	.333	13	96	189	17	5	3	1.7	.976	B. Piercy	22	115	5	7	0	6.20
CF	I. Flagstead	560	.305	5	43	370	9	10	2	2.7	.974	G. Murray	28	80	2	9	0	6.72
LF	B. Veach	519	.295	5	99	268	15	13	2	2.3	.956							
C	S. O'Neill	307	.238	0	38	342	75	13	2	4.7	.970							
3B	H. Ezzell	273	.275	0	32	59	127	2	6	3.0	.989							
OF	S. Collins	240	.292	0	28	85	4	4	0	1.7	.957							
UT	H. Shanks	193	.259	0	25	118	129	9	23		.965							
C	V. Picinich	158	.266	1	24	155	36	10	2	3.9	.950							

AMERICAN LEAGUE 1924, *cont.*

Chicago

W-66 L-87

Johnny Evers
W-10 L-11

Ed Walsh
W-1 L-2

Eddie Collins
W-14 L-13

Johnny Evers
W-41 L-61

POS	Player	AB	BA	HR	RBI	PO	A	E	DP	TC/G	FA	Pitcher	G	IP	W	L	SV	ERA
1B	E. Sheely	535	.320	3	103	1423	79	14	97	10.4	.991	S. Thurston	38	291	20	14	1	3.80
2B	E. Collins	556	.349	6	86	396	446	20	83	5.7	**.977**	T. Lyons	41	216	12	11	3	4.87
SS	B. Barrett	406	.271	2	56	167	199	39	36	5.3	.904	R. Faber	21	161	9	11	0	3.85
3B	W. Kamm	528	.254	6	93	**190**	**312**	15	**31**	3.6	**.971**	S. Connally	44	160	7	13	6	4.05
RF	H. Hooper	476	.328	10	62	251	22	4	8	2.3	.986	T. Blankenship	25	125	7	6	1	5.17
CF	J. Mostil	385	.325	4	49	281	13	8	2	3.0	.974	M. Cvengros	26	106	3	12	0	5.88
LF	B. Falk	526	.352	6	99	292	26	10	4	2.4	.970	C. Robertson	17	97	4	10	0	4.99
C	B. Crouse	305	.259	1	44	298	97	**23**	9	4.6	.945							
OF	M. Archdeacon	288	.319	0	25	173	8	8	2	2.5	.958							

BATTING AND BASE RUNNING LEADERS

Batting Average

B. Ruth, NY	.378
C. Jamieson, CLE	.359
B. Falk, CHI	.352
E. Collins, CHI	.349
J. Bassler, DET	.346

Slugging Average

B. Ruth, NY	.739
H. Heilmann, DET	.533
K. Williams, STL	.533
B. Jacobson, STL	.528
G. Myatt, CLE	.518

Home Runs

B. Ruth, NY	46
J. Hauser, PHI	27
B. Jacobson, STL	19
K. Williams, STL	18
I. Boone, BOS	13

Total Bases

B. Ruth, NY	391
B. Jacobson, STL	306
H. Heilmann, DET	304
G. Goslin, WAS	299
J. Hauser, PHI	290

Runs Batted In

G. Goslin, WAS	129
B. Ruth, NY	121
B. Meusel, NY	120
J. Hauser, PHI	115
H. Heilmann, DET	113
W. Pipp, NY	113

Stolen Bases

E. Collins, CHI	42
B. Meusel, NY	26
S. Rice, WAS	24
T. Cobb, DET	23
C. Jamieson, CLE	21

Hits

S. Rice, WAS	216
C. Jamieson, CLE	213
T. Cobb, DET	211
B. Ruth, NY	200

Base on Balls

B. Ruth, NY	142
J. Hauser, PHI	102
E. Sheely, CHI	95
E. Collins, CHI	89

Home Run Percentage

B. Ruth, NY	8.7
J. Hauser, PHI	4.8
K. Williams, STL	4.5
B. Jacobson, STL	3.3

Runs

B. Ruth, NY	143
T. Cobb, DET	115
E. Collins, CHI	108
H. Hooper, CHI	107
H. Heilmann, DET	107

Doubles

H. Heilmann, DET	45
J. Sewell, CLE	45
B. Jacobson, STL	41
B. Wambsganss, BOS	41

Triples

W. Pipp, NY	19
G. Goslin, WAS	17
H. Heilmann, DET	16
S. Rice, WAS	14

PITCHING LEADERS

Winning Percentage

W. Johnson, WAS	.767
H. Pennock, NY	.700
E. Whitehill, DET	.654
T. Zachary, WAS	.625
G. Mogridge, WAS	.593
B. Shawkey, NY	.593

Earned Run Average

W. Johnson, WAS	2.72
T. Zachary, WAS	2.75
H. Pennock, NY	2.83
S. Baumgartner, PHI	2.88
S. Smith, CLE	3.02

Wins

W. Johnson, WAS	23
H. Pennock, NY	21
J. Shaute, CLE	20
S. Thurston, CHI	20
H. Ehmke, BOS	19

Saves

F. Marberry, WAS	15
A. Russell, WAS	8
J. Quinn, BOS	7
S. Connally, CHI	6
H. Dauss, DET	6

Strikeouts

W. Johnson, WAS	158
H. Ehmke, BOS	119
B. Shawkey, NY	114
H. Pennock, NY	101
U. Shocker, STL	84

Complete Games

S. Thurston, CHI	28
H. Ehmke, BOS	26
H. Pennock, NY	25
E. Rommel, PHI	21
J. Shaute, CLE	21

Fewest Hits/9 Innings

W. Johnson, WAS	7.55
R. Collins, DET	8.29
T. Zachary, WAS	8.79
E. Wingard, STL	8.88

Shutouts

W. Johnson, WAS	6
D. Davis, STL	5
U. Shocker, STL	4
H. Pennock, NY	4
H. Ehmke, BOS	4

Fewest Walks/9 Innings

S. Smith, CLE	1.53
U. Shocker, STL	1.84
S. Thurston, CHI	1.86
H. Pennock, NY	2.01

Most Strikeouts/9 Inn.

W. Johnson, WAS	5.12
B. Shawkey, NY	4.94
H. Ehmke, BOS	3.40
H. Pennock, NY	3.17

Innings

H. Ehmke, BOS	315
S. Thurston, CHI	291
H. Pennock, NY	286
J. Shaute, CLE	283

Games Pitched

F. Marberry, WAS	50
K. Holloway, DET	49
W. Hoyt, NY	46
J. Shaute, CLE	46

							Batting						Fielding			Pitching					
	W	L	PCT	GB	R	OR	2B	3B	HR	BA	SA	SB	E	DP	FA	CG	BB	SO	ShO	SV	ERA
Washington	92	62	.597		755	**613**	255	**88**	22	.294	.387	115	171	149	.972	74	505	469	**13**	**25**	**3.35**
New York	89	63	.586	2	798	667	248	86	**98**	.289	**.426**	69	**156**	131	**.974**	76	522	**487**	**13**	13	3.86
Detroit	86	68	.558	6	**849**	796	**315**	76	35	**.298**	.404	100	187	142	.971	60	**466**	441	5	20	4.19
St. Louis	74	78	.487	17	764	797	265	62	67	.294	.408	85	183	141	.969	66	512	382	11	7	4.55
Philadelphia	71	81	.467	20	685	778	251	59	63	.281	.389	79	180	**157**	.971	68	597	371	8	10	4.39
Cleveland	67	86	.438	24.5	755	814	306	59	41	.296	.399	84	205	130	.967	**87**	503	315	7	7	4.40
Boston	67	87	.435	25	725	801	300	61	30	.277	.374	79	210	124	.967	73	519	414	8	16	4.36
Chicago	66	87	.431	25.5	793	858	254	58	41	.288	.382	**138**	229	136	.963	76	512	360	1	11	4.75
					6124	6124	2194	549	397	.290	.396	749	1521	1110	.969	580	4136	3239	66	109	4.23

NATIONAL LEAGUE 1925

Pittsburgh

W-95 L-58

Bill McKechnie

POS	Player	AB	BA	HR	RBI	PO	A	E	DP	TC/G	FA	Pitcher	G	IP	W	L	SV	ERA
1B	G. Grantham	359	.326	8	52	925	44	11	96	9.6	.989	L. Meadows	35	255	19	10	1	3.67
2B	E. Moore	547	.298	6	77	307	401	**36**	82	6.1	.952	R. Kremer	40	215	17	8	2	3.69
SS	G. Wright	614	.308	18	121	338	**530**	56	**109**	6.0	.939	V. Aldridge	30	213	15	7	0	3.63
3B	P. Traynor	591	.320	6	106	**226**	**303**	24	**41**	**3.7**	**.957**	J. Morrison	**44**	211	17	14	**4**	3.88
RF	K. Cuyler	617	.357	17	102	362	21	13	4	2.6	.967	E. Yde	33	207	17	9	0	4.13
CF	M. Carey	542	.343	5	44	363	20	20	2	3.1	.950	B. Adams	33	101	6	5	3	5.42
LF	C. Barnhart	539	.325	4	114	295	11	12	2	2.3	.962							
C	E. Smith	329	.313	8	64	317	77	13	**15**	4.2	.968							
C	J. Gooch	215	.298	0	30	172	39	7	8	2.9	.968							
1B	S. McInnis	155	.368	0	24	377	24	3	40	8.8	.993							

NATIONAL LEAGUE 1925, *cont.*

Team	POS	Player	AB	BA	HR	RBI	PO	A	E	DP	TC/G	FA	Pitcher	G	IP	W	L	SV	ERA
New York	1B	B. Terry	489	.319	11	70	1270	77	14	83	**10.8**	.990	J. Scott	36	240	14	15	3	3.15
	2B	G. Kelly	586	.309	20	99	273	394	13	68	6.3	.981	V. Barnes	32	222	15	11	2	3.53
	SS	T. Jackson	411	.285	9	59	277	366	40	64	6.2	.941	K. Greenfield	29	172	12	8	0	3.88
W-86 L-66	3B	F. Lindstrom	356	.287	4	33	123	147	12	9	2.9	.957	J. Bentley	28	157	11	9	0	5.04
	RF	R. Youngs	500	.264	6	53	214	24	12	2	2.0	.952	A. Nehf	29	155	11	9	1	3.77
John McGraw	CF	B. Southworth	473	.292	6	44	289	7	11	1	2.6	.964	W. Dean	33	151	10	7	1	4.64
	LF	I. Meusel	516	.328	21	111	244	16	11	2	2.2	.959							
W-10 L-4	C	F. Snyder	325	.240	11	51	336	71	6	7	4.3	**.985**							
Hughie Jennings	UT	F. Frisch	502	.331	11	48	215	393	37	45		.943							
W-21 L-11	OF	H. Wilson	180	.239	6	30	75	3	2	2	1.6	.975							
John McGraw																			
W-55 L-51																			
Cincinnati	1B	W. Holke	232	.280	1	20	642	35	2	60	10.4	.997	P. Donohue	42	**301**	21	14	2	3.08
	2B	H. Critz	541	.277	2	51	340	542	27	**96**	6.3	.970	D. Luque	36	291	16	18	0	**2.63**
	SS	I. Caveney	358	.249	2	47	209	349	35	72	5.3	.941	E. Rixey	39	287	21	11	1	2.88
W-80 L-73	3B	B. Pinelli	492	.283	2	49	113	265	22	21	3.7	.945	R. Benton	33	147	9	10	1	4.05
	RF	C. Walker	509	.318	6	71	332	12	6	4	2.5	.983	J. May	36	137	8	9	2	3.87
Jack Hendricks	CF	E. Roush	540	.339	8	83	343	15	8	3	2.7	.978	C. Mays	12	52	3	5	2	3.31
	LF	B. Zitzmann	301	.252	0	21	135	5	6	0	1.6	.959							
	C	B. Hargrave	273	.300	2	33	283	42	7	1	4.0	.979							
	10	R. Bressler	319	.348	4	61	602	23	12	46		.981							
	OF	E. Smith	284	.271	8	46	139	8	5	5	1.9	.967							
	3B	C. Dressen	215	.274	3	19	40	95	7	8	3.0	.951							
	SS	S. Bohne	214	.257	2	24	84	138	16	24	4.9	.933							
St. Louis	1B	J. Bottomley	619	.367	21	128	**1466**	74	**21**	**133**	10.2	.987	J. Haines	29	207	13	14	0	4.57
	2B	R. Hornsby	504	**.403**	**39**	**143**	287	416	34	95	5.4	.954	B. Sherdel	32	200	15	6	1	3.11
	SS	S. Toporcer	268	.284	2	26	141	215	15	40	5.6	.960	F. Rhem	30	170	8	13	1	4.92
W-77 L-76	3B	L. Bell	586	.285	11	88	151	284	**36**	39	3.1	.924	A. Sothoron	28	156	10	10	0	4.05
	RF	C. Hafey	358	.302	5	57	180	9	9	2	2.3	.955	A. Reinhart	20	145	11	5	0	3.05
Branch Rickey	CF	H. Mueller	243	.313	1	26	165	6	8	3	2.5	.955	D. Mails	21	131	7	7	0	4.60
W-13 L-25	LF	R. Blades	462	.342	12	57	266	13	6	4	2.5	.979	L. Dickerman	29	131	4	11	1	5.58
	C	B. O'Farrell	317	.278	3	32	324	67	10	5	4.4	.975	E. Dyer	27	82	4	3	3	4.15
Rogers Hornsby	OF	R. Shinners	251	.295	7	36	161	2	3	1	2.5	.982							
W-64 L-51	OF	J. Smith	243	.251	4	31	152	7	7	2	2.6	.958							
	OF	M. Flack	241	.249	0	28	103	8	1	1	1.9	.991							
	S2	J. Cooney	187	.273	0	18	97	137	6	31		.975							
	SS	T. Thevenow	175	.269	0	17	98	169	14	18	5.6	.950							
Boston	1B	D. Burrus	588	.340	5	87	1416	**85**	15	110	10.0	**.990**	J. Cooney	31	246	14	14	0	3.48
	2B	D. Gautreau	279	.262	0	23	171	231	10	39	6.1	.976	J. Barnes	32	216	11	16	0	4.53
	SS	D. Bancroft	479	.319	2	49	300	459	44	81	**6.4**	**.945**	L. Benton	31	183	14	7	1	3.09
W-70 L-83	3B	B. Marriott	370	.268	1	40	96	187	22	13	3.4	.928	J. Genewich	34	169	12	10	0	3.99
	RF	J. Welsh	484	.312	7	63	237	27	11	7	2.4	.960	K. Graham	34	157	7	12	1	4.41
Dave Bancroft	CF	G. Felix	459	.307	2	66	328	15	10	3	3.1	.972	R. Ryan	37	123	2	8	2	6.31
	LF	B. Neis	355	.285	5	45	282	8	9	1	3.4	.970	R. Marquard	26	72	2	8	0	5.75
	C	F. Gibson	316	.278	2	50	271	60	11	7	3.9	.968							
	OF	D. Harris	340	.265	5	36	217	12	9	3	2.6	.962							
	2S	E. Padgett	256	.305	0	29	118	152	11	29		.961							
	C	M. O'Neil	222	.257	2	30	208	31	7	3	3.6	.972							
	3B	A. High	219	.288	4	28	47	93	3	7	2.4	.979							
	OF	L. Mann	184	.342	2	20	116	7	1	1	2.2	.992							
	UT	B. Smith	174	.282	0	23	78	145	17	20		.929							
Brooklyn	1B	J. Fournier	545	.350	22	130	1317	82	15	105	9.8	.989	D. Vance	31	265	**22**	9	0	3.53
	2B	M. Stock	615	.328	1	62	305	477	18	74	5.7	.978	B. Grimes	33	247	12	**19**	0	5.04
	SS	J. Mitchell	336	.250	0	18	184	266	25	49	5.3	.947	R. Ehrhardt	36	208	10	14	1	5.03
W-68 L-85	3B	J. Johnston	431	.297	2	43	76	110	24	10	2.6	.886	T. Osborne	41	175	8	15	1	4.94
	RF	D. Cox	434	.329	7	64	197	14	7	4	2.0	.968	J. Petty	28	153	9	9	0	4.88
Wilbert Robinson	CF	E. Brown	618	.306	5	99	449	7	13	3	3.1	.972	B. Hubbell	33	87	3	6	1	5.30
	LF	Z. Wheat	616	.359	14	103	320	7	13	2	2.3	.962							
	C	Z. Taylor	352	.310	3	44	294	102	17	12	4.3	.959							
	3B	C. Tierney	265	.257	2	39	54	102	6	6	2.7	.963							
	SS	H. Ford	216	.273	1	15	126	185	11	33	4.9	.966							
	C	H. DeBerry	193	.259	2	24	309	50	7	4	6.7	.981							
Philadelphia	1B	C. Hawks	320	.322	5	45	775	45	12	64	9.2	.986	J. Ring	38	270	14	16	0	4.37
	2B	B. Friberg	304	.270	5	22	181	257	16	37	5.9	.965	H. Carlson	35	234	13	14	0	4.23
	SS	H. Sand	496	.278	3	55	**352**	420	**60**	91	5.8	.928	C. Mitchell	32	199	10	17	1	5.28
	3B	C. Huber	436	.284	5	54	107	199	17	16	2.7	.947	A. Decatur	25	128	4	13	2	5.27
W-68 L-85	RF	C. Williams	314	.331	13	60	173	12	2	3	1.9	.989	J. Knight	33	105	7	6	3	6.84
	CF	G. Harper	495	.349	18	97	319	16	10	5	2.7	.971	H. Betts	35	97	4	5	1	5.55
Art Fletcher	LF	G. Burns	349	.292	1	22	189	9	2	2	2.3	.990	J. Couch	34	94	5	6	2	5.44
	C	J. Wilson	335	.328	3	54	275	50	6	9	3.7	.982							
	21	L. Fonseca	467	.319	7	60	648	245	20	68		.978							
	OF	F. Leach	292	.312	5	28	178	2	9	1	2.9	.952							
	UT	R. Wrightstone	286	.346	14	61	152	62	16	11		.930							
	C	B. Henline	263	.304	8	48	209	53	12	9	4.0	.956							
	OF	J. Mokan	209	.330	6	42	120	1	2	0	1.8	.984							

NATIONAL LEAGUE 1925, *cont.*

Chicago

W-68 L-86

Bill Killefer
W-33 L-42

Rabbit Maranville
W-23 L-30

George Gibson
W-12 L-14

POS	Player	AB	BA	HR	RBI	PO	A	E	DP	TC/G	FA
1B	C. Grimm	519	.306	10	76	1317	73	15	125	10.1	.989
2B	S. Adams	**627**	.287	2	48	**354**	**551**	16	90	**6.4**	**.983**
SS	R. Maranville	266	.233	0	23	162	261	20	51	6.0	.955
3B	H. Freigau	476	.307	8	71	98	185	27	20	3.2	.913
RF	C. Heathcote	380	.263	5	39	241	21	8	8	2.7	.970
CF	M. Brooks	349	.281	13	72	249	9	6	2	3.0	.977
LF	A. John	226	.301	0	37	124	5	2	3	2.3	.985
C	G. Hartnett	398	.289	24	67	**409**	**114**	**23**	**15**	**5.0**	.958
OF	T. Griffith	235	.285	7	27	109	9	8	1	2.1	.937
C	M. Gonzalez	197	.264	3	18	155	31	2	7	3.8	.989
OF	B. Weis	180	.267	2	25	78	3	3	0	1.8	.964
3S	P. Pittenger	173	.312	0	15	71	127	11	13		.947
OF	D. Grigsby	137	.255	0	20	81	4	3	2	2.3	.966

Pitcher	G	IP	W	L	SV	ERA
G. Alexander	32	236	15	11	0	3.39
S. Blake	36	231	10	18	2	4.86
W. Cooper	32	212	12	14	0	4.28
T. Kaufmann	31	196	13	13	2	4.50
G. Bush	42	182	6	13	**4**	4.30
P. Jones	28	124	6	6	0	4.65

BATTING AND BASE RUNNING LEADERS

Batting Average		Slugging Average		Home Runs	
R. Hornsby, STL	.403	R. Hornsby, STL	.756	R. Hornsby, STL	39
J. Bottomley, STL	.367	K. Cuyler, PIT	.593	G. Hartnett, CHI	24
Z. Wheat, BKN	.359	J. Bottomley, STL	.578	J. Fournier, BKN	22
K. Cuyler, PIT	.357	J. Fournier, BKN	.569	I. Meusel, NY	21
J. Fournier, BKN	.350	G. Harper, PHI	.558	J. Bottomley, STL	21

Total Bases		Runs Batted In		Stolen Bases	
R. Hornsby, STL	381	R. Hornsby, STL	143	M. Carey, PIT	46
K. Cuyler, PIT	366	J. Fournier, BKN	130	K. Cuyler, PIT	41
J. Bottomley, STL	358	J. Bottomley, STL	128	S. Adams, CHI	26
Z. Wheat, BKN	333	G. Wright, PIT	121	E. Roush, CIN	22
J. Fournier, BKN	310	C. Barnhart, PIT	114	F. Frisch, NY	21

Hits		Base on Balls		Home Run Percentage	
J. Bottomley, STL	227	J. Fournier, BKN	86	R. Hornsby, STL	7.7
Z. Wheat, BKN	221	R. Hornsby, STL	83	G. Hartnett, CHI	6.0
K. Cuyler, PIT	220	E. Moore, PIT	73	C. Williams, PHI	4.1
R. Hornsby, STL	203	R. Youngs, NY	66	I. Meusel, NY	4.1
		M. Carey, PIT	66		

Runs		Doubles		Triples	
K. Cuyler, PIT	144	J. Bottomley, STL	44	K. Cuyler, PIT	26
R. Hornsby, STL	133	K. Cuyler, PIT	43	C. Walker, CIN	16
Z. Wheat, BKN	125	Z. Wheat, BKN	42	E. Roush, CIN	16
P. Traynor, PIT	114	R. Hornsby, STL	41	J. Fournier, BKN	16
		D. Burrus, BOS	41		

PITCHING LEADERS

Winning Percentage		Earned Run Average		Wins	
B. Sherdel, STL	.714	D. Luque, CIN	2.63	D. Vance, BKN	22
D. Vance, BKN	.710	E. Rixey, CIN	2.88	E. Rixey, CIN	21
V. Aldridge, PIT	.682	A. Reinhart, STL	3.05	P. Donohue, CIN	21
R. Kremer, PIT	.680	P. Donohue, CIN	3.08	L. Meadows, PIT	19
E. Rixey, CIN	.656	L. Benton, BOS	3.09		

Saves		Strikeouts		Complete Games	
G. Bush, CHI	4	D. Vance, BKN	221	P. Donohue, CIN	27
J. Morrison, PIT	4	D. Luque, CIN	140	D. Vance, BKN	26
		S. Blake, CHI	93	D. Luque, CIN	22
		J. Ring, PHI	93	E. Rixey, CIN	22
		V. Aldridge, PIT	88	J. Ring, PHI	21

Fewest Hits/9 Innings		Shutouts		Fewest Walks/9 Innings	
D. Luque, CIN	8.13	D. Vance, BKN	4	G. Alexander, CHI	1.11
L. Benton, BOS	8.35	H. Carlson, PHI	4	P. Donohue, CIN	1.47
D. Vance, BKN	8.38	D. Luque, CIN	4	E. Rixey, CIN	1.47
V. Aldridge, PIT	9.20	P. Donohue, CIN	3	J. Cooney, BOS	1.83

Most Strikeouts/9 Inn.		Innings		Games Pitched	
D. Vance, BKN	7.50	P. Donohue, CIN	301	J. Morrison, PIT	44
D. Luque, CIN	4.33	D. Luque, CIN	291	G. Bush, CHI	42
V. Aldridge, PIT	3.71	E. Rixey, CIN	287	P. Donohue, CIN	42
S. Blake, CHI	3.62	J. Ring, PHI	270	T. Osborne, BKN	41

							Batting						Fielding			Pitching					
	W	L	PCT	GB	R	OR	2B	3B	HR	BA	SA	SB	E	DP	FA	CG	BB	SO	ShO	SV	ERA
Pittsburgh	95	58	.621		**912**	715	**316**	**105**	77	**.307**	**.448**	**159**	224	**171**	.964	77	387	386	2	**13**	3.87
New York	86	66	.566	8.5	736	702	239	61	**114**	.283	.415	79	199	129	.968	80	408	446	6	8	3.94
Cincinnati	80	73	.523	15	690	**643**	221	90	44	.285	.387	108	203	161	.968	**92**	**324**	437	**11**	12	**3.38**
St. Louis	77	76	.503	18	828	764	292	80	109	.299	.445	70	204	156	.966	82	470	428	8	7	4.36
Boston	70	83	.458	25	708	802	260	70	41	.292	.390	77	221	145	.964	77	458	351	5	4	4.39
Brooklyn	68	85	.444	27	786	866	250	80	64	.296	.406	37	210	130	.966	82	477	**518**	4	4	4.77
Philadelphia	68	85	.444	27	812	930	288	58	100	.295	.425	48	211	147	.966	69	444	371	8	9	5.02
Chicago	68	86	.442	27.5	723	773	254	70	85	.275	.396	94	**198**	161	**.969**	75	485	435	5	10	4.41
					6195	6195	2120	614	634	.292	.414	672	1670	1200	.966	634	3453	3372	49	67	4.27

AMERICAN LEAGUE 1925

Washington

W-96 L-55

Bucky Harris

POS	Player	AB	BA	HR	RBI	PO	A	E	DP	TC/G	FA
1B	J. Judge	376	.314	8	66	901	71	7	92	9.0	**.993**
2B	B. Harris	551	.287	1	66	402	429	26	**107**	6.0	.970
SS	R. Peckinpaugh	422	.294	4	64	215	345	28	71	4.7	.952
3B	O. Bluege	522	.287	4	79	158	285	22	29	3.2	.953
RF	S. Rice	649	.350	1	87	339	20	12	7	2.4	.968
CF	E. McNeely	385	.286	3	37	259	13	7	3	2.5	.975
LF	G. Goslin	601	.334	18	113	385	24	12	1	2.8	.971
C	M. Ruel	393	.310	0	54	**491**	**103**	**11**	**18**	**4.8**	.982
10	J. Harris	300	.323	12	59	461	41	6	40		.988
P	W. Johnson	97	.433	2	20	5	37	0	2	1.4	**1.000**

Pitcher	G	IP	W	L	SV	ERA
S. Coveleski	32	241	20	5	0	**2.84**
W. Johnson	30	229	20	7	0	3.07
D. Ruether	30	223	18	7	0	3.87
T. Zachary	38	218	12	15	2	3.85
F. Marberry	**55**	93	8	6	**15**	3.47

AMERICAN LEAGUE 1925, *cont.*

Philadelphia

W-88 L-64

Connie Mack

POS	Player	AB	BA	HR	RBI	PO	A	E	DP	TC/G	FA
1B	J. Poole	480	.298	5	67	1166	65	23	102	10.2	.982
2B	M. Bishop	368	.280	4	27	233	352	26	53	5.9	.957
SS	C. Galloway	481	.241	3	71	296	431	35	89	5.1	.954
3B	S. Hale	391	.345	8	63	98	173	24	19	3.1	.919
RF	B. Miller	474	.319	10	81	158	7	5	1	1.5	.971
CF	A. Simmons	**658**	.384	24	129	447	8	16	2	3.1	.966
LF	B. Lamar	568	.356	3	77	283	18	15	4	2.4	.953
C	M. Cochrane	420	.331	6	55	419	79	8	9	3.8	.984
32	J. Dykes	465	.323	5	55	225	302	21	45		.962
OF	F. Welch	202	.277	4	41	85	6	3	3	1.6	.968

Pitcher	G	IP	W	L	SV	ERA
E. Rommel	52	261	**21**	10	3	3.69
S. Harriss	46	252	19	12	1	3.50
L. Grove	45	197	10	12	1	4.75
S. Gray	32	196	16	8	3	3.40
R. Walberg	53	192	8	14	7	3.99
S. Baumgartner	37	113	6	3	3	3.57
J. Quinn	18	100	6	3	0	3.88

St. Louis

W-82 L-71

George Sisler

POS	Player	AB	BA	HR	RBI	PO	A	E	DP	TC/G	FA
1B	G. Sisler	649	.345	12	105	1330	**131**	**26**	120	9.9	.983
2B	M. McManus	587	.288	13	90	**430**	**479**	**31**	93	**6.1**	.967
SS	B. LaMotte	356	.272	2	51	220	270	39	57	5.7	.926
3B	G. Robertson	582	.271	14	76	**201**	287	**32**	**41**	3.4	.938
RF	H. Rice	354	.359	11	47	175	13	3	1	2.2	.984
CF	B. Jacobson	540	.341	15	76	383	18	13	9	3.0	.969
LF	K. Williams	411	.331	25	105	242	11	12	4	2.6	.955
C	L. Dixon	205	.224	1	19	233	70	6	8	4.1	.981
OF	H. Bennett	298	.279	2	37	140	12	14	1	2.3	.916
SS	W. Gerber	246	.272	0	19	144	206	19	39	5.2	.949
C	P. Hargrave	225	.284	8	43	211	44	5	4	4.2	.981
OF	J. Tobin	193	.301	2	27	61	1	0	0	1.6	1.000
OF	J. Evans	159	.314	0	20	96	3	0	2	2.1	1.000
C	H. Severeid	109	.367	1	21	114	24	1	3	4.5	.993

Pitcher	G	IP	W	L	SV	ERA
M. Gaston	42	239	15	14	1	4.41
J. Bush	33	214	14	14	0	4.97
E. Vangilder	52	193	14	8	6	4.70
D. Davis	35	180	12	7	1	4.59
J. Giard	30	161	10	5	0	5.04
D. Danforth	38	159	7	9	2	4.36
E. Wingard	32	153	9	10	0	5.06

Detroit

W-81 L-73

Ty Cobb

POS	Player	AB	BA	HR	RBI	PO	A	E	DP	TC/G	FA
1B	L. Blue	532	.306	3	94	1480	101	19	115	10.8	.988
2B	F. O'Rourke	482	.293	5	57	309	382	21	67	6.0	**.971**
SS	J. Tavener	453	.245	0	47	229	398	24	73	4.9	.963
3B	F. Haney	398	.279	0	40	115	207	16	22	3.2	.953
RF	H. Heilmann	573	**.393**	13	133	278	9	9	1	2.0	.970
CF	T. Cobb	415	.378	12	102	267	9	15	1	2.8	.948
LF	A. Wingo	440	.370	5	68	282	16	9	6	2.5	.971
C	J. Bassler	344	.279	0	52	375	87	8	14	4.0	.983
OF	H. Manush	277	.303	5	47	153	7	3	0	2.2	.982
OF	B. Fothergill	204	.353	2	28	120	6	3	2	2.2	.977
2B	L. Burke	180	.289	0	24	100	130	9	27	4.6	.962
C	L. Woodall	171	.205	0	13	165	38	7	4	2.8	.967

Pitcher	G	IP	W	L	SV	ERA
E. Whitehill	35	239	11	11	2	4.66
H. Dauss	35	228	16	11	1	3.16
K. Holloway	38	158	13	4	2	4.62
L. Stoner	34	152	10	9	1	4.26
R. Collins	26	140	6	11	0	4.56
E. Wells	35	134	6	9	2	6.23
D. Leonard	18	126	11	4	0	4.51
J. Doyle	45	118	4	7	8	5.93

Chicago

W-79 L-75

Eddie Collins

POS	Player	AB	BA	HR	RBI	PO	A	E	DP	TC/G	FA
1B	E. Sheely	600	.315	9	111	**1565**	95	20	**136**	**11.0**	.988
2B	E. Collins	425	.346	3	80	290	346	20	74	5.7	.970
SS	I. Davis	562	.240	0	61	313	472	**53**	**97**	**5.8**	.937
3B	W. Kamm	509	.279	6	83	182	**310**	22	32	**3.4**	**.957**
RF	H. Hooper	442	.265	6	55	231	16	6	4	2.0	.976
CF	J. Mostil	605	.299	2	50	446	11	7	5	3.0	.985
LF	B. Falk	602	.301	4	99	306	18	14	4	2.2	.959
C	R. Schalk	343	.274	0	52	368	99	8	15	3.8	.983
UT	B. Barrett	245	.363	3	40	132	131	19	24		.933
C	B. Crouse	131	.351	2	25	104	36	7	5	3.1	.952

Pitcher	G	IP	W	L	SV	ERA
T. Lyons	43	263	**21**	11	3	3.26
R. Faber	34	238	12	11	0	3.78
T. Blankenship	40	222	17	8	1	3.16
S. Thurston	36	175	10	14	1	6.17
C. Robertson	24	137	8	12	0	5.26
M. Cvengros	22	105	3	9	0	4.30
S. Connally	40	105	6	7	8	4.64

Cleveland

W-70 L-84

Tris Speaker

POS	Player	AB	BA	HR	RBI	PO	A	E	DP	TC/G	FA
1B	G. Burns	488	.336	6	79	1195	82	14	94	10.2	.989
2B	C. Fewster	294	.248	1	38	222	237	30	41	5.7	.939
SS	J. Sewell	608	.336	1	98	**314**	**529**	29	80	5.7	**.967**
3B	R. Lutzke	238	.218	1	16	61	129	13	9	2.9	.936
RF	P. McNulty	373	.314	6	43	206	16	8	2	2.1	.965
CF	T. Speaker	429	.389	12	87	311	16	11	9	3.1	.967
LF	C. Jamieson	557	.296	4	42	324	16	16	4	2.6	.955
C	G. Myatt	358	.271	11	54	273	53	9	2	3.4	.973
32	F. Spurgeon	376	.287	0	32	155	250	21	30		.951
OF	C. Lee	230	.322	4	42	129	7	7	2	2.0	.951
OF	H. Summa	224	.330	0	25	83	2	3	0	1.6	.966
C	L. Sewell	220	.232	0	18	216	54	8	13	4.2	.971

Pitcher	G	IP	W	L	SV	ERA
S. Smith	31	237	11	14	1	4.86
G. Uhle	29	211	13	11	0	4.10
B. Karr	32	198	11	12	0	4.78
J. Miller	32	190	10	13	2	3.31
G. Buckeye	30	153	13	8	0	3.65
J. Shaute	26	131	4	12	4	5.43

New York

W-69 L-85

Miller Huggins

POS	Player	AB	BA	HR	RBI	PO	A	E	DP	TC/G	FA
1B	L. Gehrig	437	.295	20	68	1126	53	13	72	10.5	.989
2B	A. Ward	439	.246	4	38	246	317	20	57	5.2	.966
SS	P. Wanninger	403	.236	1	22	214	296	30	59	4.9	.944
3B	J. Dugan	404	.292	0	31	118	202	10	19	3.4	.970
RF	B. Ruth	359	.290	25	66	207	15	6	3	2.3	.974
CF	E. Combs	593	.342	3	61	401	12	9	2	2.8	.979
LF	B. Meusel	624	.290	**33**	**138**	249	9	4	6	2.0	.985
C	B. Bengough	283	.258	0	23	325	83	3	12	4.4	**.993**
OF	B. Paschal	247	.360	12	56	117	6	6	0	2.0	.953
1B	W. Pipp	178	.230	3	24	399	38	4	40	9.4	.991
2S	E. Johnson	170	.282	5	17	87	107	9	21		.956
C	W. Schang	167	.240	2	24	172	55	6	8	4.0	.974
32	H. Shanks	155	.258	1	18	64	87	6	13		.962

Pitcher	G	IP	W	L	SV	ERA
H. Pennock	47	**277**	16	17	2	2.96
S. Jones	43	247	15	**21**	2	4.63
U. Shocker	41	244	12	12	2	3.65
W. Hoyt	46	243	11	14	6	4.00
B. Shawkey	33	186	6	14	0	4.11

AMERICAN LEAGUE 1925, *cont.*

Boston

W-47 L-105

Lee Fohl

POS	Player	AB	BA	HR	RBI	PO	A	E	DP	TC/G	FA
1B	P. Todt	544	.278	11	75	1408	100	13	126	10.9	.991
2B	B. Wambsganss	360	.231	1	41	254	326	26	60	5.9	.957
SS	D. Lee	255	.224	0	19	188	260	37	64	5.8	.924
3B	D. Prothro	415	.313	0	51	115	211	19	16	3.2	.945
RF	I. Boone	476	.330	9	68	198	9	13	1	1.9	.941
CF	I. Flagstead	572	.280	6	61	429	24	11	6	3.2	.976
LF	R. Carlyle	276	.326	7	49	122	5	13	0	2.1	.907
C	V. Picinich	251	.255	1	25	222	53	9	3	3.8	.968
OF	T. Vache	252	.313	3	48	87	2	9	0	1.8	.908
OF	D. Williams	218	.229	0	13	117	4	6	1	2.4	.953
3B	H. Ezzell	186	.285	0	15	53	89	13	5	3.3	.916
2B	B. Rogell	169	.195	0	17	98	145	17	29	5.3	.935
SS	B. Connolly	107	.262	0	21	60	72	7	13	4.1	.950

Pitcher	G	IP	W	L	SV	ERA
H. Ehmke	34	261	9	20	1	3.73
T. Wingfield	41	254	12	19	2	3.96
R. Ruffing	37	217	9	18	1	5.01
P. Zahniser	37	177	5	12	1	5.15
J. Quinn	19	105	7	8	0	4.37
B. Ross	33	94	3	8	0	6.20

BATTING AND BASE RUNNING LEADERS

Batting Average

H. Heilmann, DET	.393
T. Speaker, CLE	.389
A. Simmons, PHI	.384
T. Cobb, DET	.378
A. Wingo, DET	.370

Slugging Average

K. Williams, STL	.613
T. Cobb, DET	.598
A. Simmons, PHI	.596
T. Speaker, CLE	.578
H. Heilmann, DET	.569

Home Runs

B. Meusel, NY	33
B. Ruth, NY	25
K. Williams, STL	25
A. Simmons, PHI	24
L. Gehrig, NY	20

Total Bases

A. Simmons, PHI	392
B. Meusel, NY	338
G. Goslin, WAS	329
H. Heilmann, DET	326
G. Sisler, STL	311

Runs Batted In

B. Meusel, NY	138
H. Heilmann, DET	133
A. Simmons, PHI	129
G. Goslin, WAS	113
E. Sheely, CHI	111

Stolen Bases

J. Mostil, CHI	43
G. Goslin, WAS	26
S. Rice, WAS	26
E. Collins, CHI	19
L. Blue, DET	19
I. Davis, CHI	19

Hits

A. Simmons, PHI	253
S. Rice, WAS	227
H. Heilmann, DET	225
G. Sisler, STL	224

Base on Balls

W. Kamm, CHI	90
J. Mostil, CHI	90
M. Bishop, PHI	87
E. Collins, CHI	87

Home Run Percentage

K. Williams, STL	6.1
B. Meusel, NY	5.3
L. Gehrig, NY	4.6
J. Harris, BOS, WAS	4.1

Runs

J. Mostil, CHI	135
A. Simmons, PHI	122
E. Combs, NY	117
G. Goslin, WAS	116

Doubles

M. McManus, STL	44
E. Sheely, CHI	43
A. Simmons, PHI	43
G. Burns, CLE	41

Triples

G. Goslin, WAS	20
J. Mostil, CHI	16
G. Sisler, STL	15

PITCHING LEADERS

Winning Percentage

S. Coveleski, WAS	.800
W. Johnson, WAS	.741
D. Ruether, WAS	.720
T. Blankenship, CHI	.680
E. Rommel, PHI	.677

Earned Run Average

S. Coveleski, WAS	2.84
H. Pennock, NY	2.96
W. Johnson, WAS	3.07
H. Dauss, DET	3.16
T. Blankenship, CHI	3.16

Wins

E. Rommel, PHI	21
T. Lyons, CHI	21
W. Johnson, WAS	20
S. Coveleski, WAS	20
S. Harriss, PHI	19

Saves

F. Marberry, WAS	15
J. Doyle, DET	8
S. Connally, CHI	8
R. Walberg, PHI	7
W. Hoyt, NY	6
E. Vangilder, STL	6

Strikeouts

L. Grove, PHI	116
W. Johnson, WAS	108
S. Harriss, PHI	95
H. Ehmke, BOS	95
S. Jones, NY	92

Complete Games

S. Smith, CLE	22
H. Ehmke, BOS	22
H. Pennock, NY	21
T. Lyons, CHI	19
T. Wingfield, BOS	18

Fewest Hits/9 Innings

W. Johnson, WAS	8.29
S. Coveleski, WAS	8.59
H. Pennock, NY	8.68
T. Blankenship, CHI	8.84

Shutouts

T. Lyons, CHI	5
J. Giard, STL	4
S. Gray, PHI	4

Fewest Walks/9 Innings

S. Smith, CLE	1.82
J. Quinn, BOS, PHI	1.85
U. Shocker, NY	2.14
R. Faber, CHI	2.23

Most Strikeouts/9 Inn.

W. Johnson, WAS	4.24
S. Gray, PHI	3.68
S. Harriss, PHI	3.39
S. Jones, NY	3.36

Innings

H. Pennock, NY	277
T. Lyons, CHI	263
E. Rommel, PHI	261
H. Ehmke, BOS	261

Games Pitched

F. Marberry, WAS	55
R. Walberg, PHI	53
E. Vangilder, STL	52
E. Rommel, PHI	52

							Batting						Fielding			Pitching					
	W	L	PCT	GB	R	OR	2B	3B	HR	BA	SA	SB	E	DP	FA	CG	BB	SO	ShO	SV	ERA
Washington	96	55	.636		829	**669**	251	71	56	.303	.411	**134**	170	**166**	.972	69	543	464	10	**21**	**3.67**
Philadelphia	88	64	.579	8.5	830	714	298	79	76	**.307**	.434	67	211	148	.966	61	544	**495**	8	18	3.89
St. Louis	82	71	.536	15	897	909	**304**	68	**110**	.298	**.439**	85	226	164	.964	67	675	419	7	10	4.85
Detroit	81	73	.526	16.5	**903**	829	277	**84**	50	.302	.413	97	173	143	.972	66	556	419	2	18	4.61
Chicago	79	75	.513	18.5	811	771	299	59	38	.284	.385	129	200	162	.968	71	**489**	374	**12**	13	4.34
Cleveland	70	84	.455	27.5	782	810	285	58	52	.297	.399	90	210	146	.967	**93**	493	345	6	9	4.49
New York	69	85	.448	28.5	706	774	247	74	**110**	.275	.410	67	**160**	150	**.974**	80	505	492	8	13	4.33
Boston	47	105	.309	49.5	639	921	257	64	41	.266	.364	42	271	150	.957	68	510	310	6	6	4.97
					6397	6397	2218	557	533	.292	.407	711	1621	1229	.967	575	4315	3318	59	108	4.39

NATIONAL LEAGUE 1926

St. Louis

W-89 L-65

Rogers Hornsby

POS	Player	AB	BA	HR	RBI	PO	A	E	DP	TC/G	FA
1B	J. Bottomley	603	.299	19	**120**	1607	54	**19**	118	10.9	.989
2B	R. Hornsby	527	.317	11	93	245	433	27	73	5.3	.962
SS	T. Thevenow	563	.256	2	63	**371**	**597**	45	98	**6.5**	.956
3B	L. Bell	581	.325	17	100	165	254	22	25	2.8	.950
RF	B. Southworth	391	.317	11	69	228	5	7	0	2.4	.971
CF	T. Douthit	530	.308	3	52	440	14	20	2	3.4	.958
LF	R. Blades	416	.305	8	43	229	10	5	1	2.3	.980
C	B. O'Farrell	492	.293	7	68	**466**	117	10	12	4.1	.983
OF	C. Hafey	225	.271	4	38	106	6	3	1	2.1	.974
OF	H. Mueller	191	.267	3	28	106	7	6	3	2.3	.950
OF	W. Holm	144	.285	0	21	75	1	3	1	2.0	.962

Pitcher	G	IP	W	L	SV	ERA
F. Rhem	34	258	**20**	7	0	3.21
B. Sherdel	34	235	16	12	0	3.49
J. Haines	33	183	13	4	1	3.25
V. Keen	26	152	10	9	0	4.56
G. Alexander	23	148	9	7	2	2.91
A. Reinhart	27	143	10	5	0	4.22
H. Bell	27	85	6	6	2	3.18

NATIONAL LEAGUE 1926, *cont.*

Team	POS	Player	AB	BA	HR	RBI	PO	A	E	DP	TC/G	FA	Pitcher	G	IP	W	L	SV	ERA
Cincinnati	1B	W. Pipp	574	.291	6	99	**1710**	92	15	**140**	**11.7**	.992	P. Donohue	47	**286**	**20**	14	2	3.37
W-87 L-67	2B	H. Critz	607	.270	3	79	357	**588**	18	**107**	6.2	**.981**	C. Mays	39	281	19	12	1	3.14
Jack Hendricks	SS	F. Emmer	224	.196	0	18	141	242	34	40	5.3	.918	D. Luque	34	234	13	16	0	3.43
	3B	C. Dressen	474	.266	4	48	108	**284**	14	19	**3.3**	.966	E. Rixey	37	233	14	8	0	3.40
	RF	C. Walker	571	.306	6	78	325	21	14	8	2.4	.961	J. May	45	168	13	9	3	3.22
	CF	E. Roush	563	.323	7	79	304	12	15	2	2.3	.955	R. Lucas	39	154	8	5	2	3.68
	LF	C. Christensen	329	.350	0	41	170	6	4	2	1.9	.978							
	C	B. Hargrave	326	**.353**	6	62	276	50	4	7	3.5	**.988**							
	OF	R. Bressler	297	.357	1	51	155	4	5	1	2.0	.970							
	C	V. Picinich	240	.263	2	31	240	52	10	6	3.5	.967							
	3S	B. Pinelli	207	.222	0	24	52	141	11	9		.946							
	SS	H. Ford	197	.279	0	18	152	190	13	57	6.2	.963							
Pittsburgh	1B	G. Grantham	449	.318	8	70	1203	66	13	106	9.7	.990	R. Kremer	37	231	**20**	6	5	**2.61**
W-84 L-69	2B	H. Rhyne	366	.251	2	39	167	220	13	46	6.1	.967	L. Meadows	36	227	**20**	9	0	3.97
Bill McKechnie	SS	G. Wright	458	.308	8	77	242	382	49	82	5.8	.927	V. Aldridge	30	190	10	13	1	4.07
	3B	P. Traynor	574	.317	3	92	**182**	279	**23**	**39**	3.3	.952	E. Yde	37	187	8	7	0	3.65
	RF	P. Waner	536	.336	8	79	307	21	8	3	2.4	.976	D. Songer	35	126	7	8	2	3.13
	CF	M. Carey	324	.222	0	28	225	8	14	3	3.0	.943	J. Morrison	26	122	6	8	2	3.38
	LF	K. Cuyler	614	.321	8	92	405	19	14	4	2.8	.968	J. Bush	19	111	6	6	3	3.01
	C	E. Smith	292	.346	2	46	307	63	14	10	3.9	.964							
	C	J. Gooch	218	.271	1	42	202	38	5	6	3.1	.980							
	OF	C. Barnhart	203	.192	0	10	101	5	1	1	1.8	.991							
	2B	J. Rawlings	181	.232	0	20	126	164	9	25	5.1	.970							
Chicago	1B	C. Grimm	524	.277	8	82	1416	68	18	139	10.2	.988	C. Root	42	271	18	**17**	2	2.82
W-82 L-72	2B	S. Adams	**624**	.309	0	39	324	485	**29**	93	6.2	.965	S. Blake	39	198	11	12	1	3.60
Joe McCarthy	SS	J. Cooney	513	.251	1	47	344	492	24	**107**	6.1	**.972**	T. Kaufmann	26	170	9	7	2	3.02
	3B	H. Freigau	508	.270	3	51	133	242	13	22	2.9	**.966**	P. Jones	30	160	12	7	2	3.09
	RF	C. Heathcote	510	.276	10	53	306	22	5	8	2.5	.985	G. Bush	35	157	13	9	2	2.86
	CF	H. Wilson	529	.321	**21**	109	348	11	10	5	2.6	.973	B. Osborn	31	136	6	5	1	3.63
	LF	R. Stephenson	281	.338	3	44	126	7	7	0	1.9	.950	B. Piercy	19	90	6	5	0	4.48
	C	G. Hartnett	284	.275	8	41	307	86	9	6	4.6	.978							
	C	M. Gonzalez	253	.249	1	23	306	53	4	5	4.7	.989							
	OF	P. Scott	189	.286	3	34	114	7	4	2	2.1	.968							
	OF	J. Kelly	176	.335	0	32	58	3	3	0	1.6	.953							
New York	1B	G. Kelly	499	.303	13	80	1196	79	9	89	11.3	**.993**	J. Scott	**50**	226	13	15	5	4.34
W-74 L-77	2B	F. Frisch	545	.314	5	44	261	471	19	69	5.9	.975	K. Greenfield	39	223	13	12	1	3.96
John McGraw	SS	T. Jackson	385	.327	8	51	256	351	24	71	5.8	.962	F. Fitzsimmons	37	219	14	10	0	2.88
	3B	F. Lindstrom	543	.302	9	76	151	251	16	23	3.0	.962	V. Barnes	31	185	8	13	1	2.87
	RF	R. Youngs	372	.306	4	43	170	18	5	5	2.1	.974	J. Ring	39	183	11	10	2	4.57
	CF	T. Tyson	335	.293	3	35	232	9	5	5	2.7	.980	H. McQuillan	33	167	11	10	0	3.72
	LF	I. Meusel	449	.292	6	65	197	10	9	1	1.9	.958	C. Davies	38	89	2	4	**6**	3.94
	C	P. Florence	188	.229	2	14	212	41	**17**	7	3.6	.937							
	OF	H. Mueller	305	.249	4	29	194	13	11	2	2.7	.950							
	1B	B. Terry	225	.289	5	43	391	31	9	36	11.3	.979							
	SS	D. Farrell	171	.287	2	23	106	124	12	22	4.6	.950							
	OF	B. Southworth	116	.328	5	30	62	2	2	1	2.4	.970							
Brooklyn	1B	B. Herman	496	.319	11	81	918	60	14	55	9.8	.986	J. Petty	38	276	17	**17**	1	2.84
W-71 L-82	2B	C. Fewster	337	.243	2	24	225	297	26	38	5.3	.953	B. Grimes	30	225	12	13	0	3.71
Wilbert Robinson	SS	J. Butler	501	.269	1	68	243	317	30	43	5.8	.949	D. McWeeny	42	216	11	13	1	3.04
	3B	B. Marriott	360	.267	3	42	80	173	20	6	2.6	.927	B. McGraw	33	174	9	13	1	4.59
	RF	D. Cox	398	.296	1	45	201	12	8	2	1.9	.964	D. Vance	24	169	9	10	1	3.89
	CF	G. Felix	432	.280	3	53	270	11	13	2	2.4	.956	J. Barnes	31	158	10	11	1	5.24
	LF	Z. Wheat	411	.290	5	35	202	9	10	3	2.2	.955	R. Ehrhardt	44	97	2	5	4	3.90
	C	M. O'Neil	201	.209	0	20	247	53	11	5	4.2	.965							
	OF	M. Jacobson	288	.247	0	23	191	5	5	2	2.3	.975							
	1B	J. Fournier	243	.284	11	48	548	28	8	19	9.1	.986							
	SS	R. Maranville	234	.235	0	24	138	192	18	28	5.8	.948							
	C	C. Hargreaves	208	.250	2	23	224	65	4	6	4.2	.986							
Boston	1B	D. Burrus	486	.270	3	61	1153	**103**	12	97	9.8	.991	L. Benton	43	232	14	14	1	3.85
W-66 L-86	2B	D. Gautreau	266	.267	0	8	170	205	23	42	5.4	.942	J. Genewich	37	216	8	16	2	3.88
Dave Bancroft	SS	D. Bancroft	453	.311	1	44	317	398	33	75	6.1	.956	B. Smith	33	193	10	13	1	3.91
	3B	A. High	476	.296	2	66	99	155	10	15	3.3	.962	J. Wertz	32	189	11	9	0	3.28
	RF	J. Welsh	490	.278	3	57	283	23	11	8	2.5	.965	G. Mogridge	39	142	6	10	3	4.50
	CF	J. Smith	322	.311	2	25	206	8	6	0	2.7	.973	B. Hearn	34	117	4	9	2	4.22
	LF	E. Brown	612	.328	2	84	401	10	15	2	2.8	.965	H. Goldsmith	19	101	5	7	0	4.37
	C	Z. Taylor	432	.255	0	42	394	**123**	8	**17**	**4.3**	.985							
	3S	E. Taylor	272	.268	0	33	117	174	13	28		.957							
	OF	F. Wilson	236	.237	0	23	121	6	9	1	2.4	.934							
	2B	E. Moore	184	.266	0	15	90	123	6	27	5.8	.973							
	OF	L. Mann	129	.302	1	20	79	5	3	0	1.9	.966							

NATIONAL LEAGUE 1926, *cont.*

Philadelphia

W-58 L-93

Art Fletcher

POS	Player	AB	BA	HR	RBI	PO	A	E	DP	TC/G	FA	Pitcher	G	IP	W	L	SV	ERA
1B	J. Bentley	240	.258	2	27	516	28	4	41	9.8	.993	H. Carlson	35	267	17	12	0	3.23
2B	B. Friberg	478	.268	1	51	**381**	512	22	89	**6.4**	.976	C. Mitchell	28	179	9	14	1	4.58
SS	H. Sand	567	.272	4	37	358	495	**55**	88	6.1	.939	C. Willoughby	47	168	8	12	1	5.95
3B	C. Huber	376	.245	1	34	110	214	15	22	2.9	.956	W. Dean	33	164	8	16	0	6.10
RF	C. Williams	336	.345	18	53	143	14	6	3	1.8	.963	D. Ulrich	45	148	8	13	1	4.08
CF	F. Leach	492	.329	11	71	313	15	7	2	2.7	.979	J. Knight	35	143	3	12	2	6.62
LF	J. Mokan	456	.303	6	62	221	16	8	4	2.0	.967							
C	J. Wilson	279	.305	4	32	228	78	16	5	4.1	.950							
UT	R. Wrightstone	368	.307	7	57	549	125	19	64		.973							
OF	A. Nixon	311	.293	4	41	206	7	5	3	2.5	.977							
C	B. Henline	283	.283	2	30	217	46	8	9	3.5	.970							
OF	G. Harper	194	.314	7	38	111	2	7	1	2.2	.942							

BATTING AND BASE RUNNING LEADERS

Batting Average

B. Hargrave, CIN	.353
C. Christensen, CIN	.350
E. Smith, PIT	.346
C. Williams, PHI	.345
P. Waner, PIT	.336

Slugging Average

C. Williams, PHI	.568
H. Wilson, CHI	.539
P. Waner, PIT	.528
B. Hargrave, CIN	.525
L. Bell, STL	.518

Home Runs

H. Wilson, CHI	21
J. Bottomley, STL	19
C. Williams, PHI	18
L. Bell, STL	17
B. Southworth, NY, STL	16

Total Bases

J. Bottomley, STL	305
L. Bell, STL	301
H. Wilson, CHI	285
P. Waner, PIT	283
K. Cuyler, PIT	282

Runs Batted In

J. Bottomley, STL	120
H. Wilson, CHI	109
L. Bell, STL	100
B. Southworth, NY, STL	99
W. Pipp, CIN	99

Stolen Bases

K. Cuyler, PIT	35
S. Adams, CHI	27
T. Douthit, STL	23
F. Frisch, NY	23
R. Youngs, NY	21

Hits

E. Brown, BOS	201
K. Cuyler, PIT	197
S. Adams, CHI	193
L. Bell, STL	189

Base on Balls

H. Wilson, CHI	69
P. Waner, PIT	66
H. Sand, PHI	66
D. Bancroft, BOS	64

Home Run Percentage

C. Williams, PHI	5.4
H. Wilson, CHI	4.0
B. Southworth, NY, STL	3.2
J. Bottomley, STL	3.2

Runs

K. Cuyler, PIT	113
P. Waner, PIT	101
B. Southworth, NY, STL	99
H. Sand, PHI	99

Doubles

J. Bottomley, STL	40
E. Roush, CIN	37
H. Wilson, CHI	36

Triples

P. Waner, PIT	22
C. Walker, CIN	20
P. Traynor, PIT	17

PITCHING LEADERS

Winning Percentage

R. Kremer, PIT	.769
F. Rhem, STL	.741
L. Meadows, PIT	.690
C. Mays, CIN	.613
P. Donohue, CIN	.588

Earned Run Average

R. Kremer, PIT	2.61
C. Root, CHI	2.82
J. Petty, BKN	2.84
F. Fitzsimmons, NY	2.88
T. Kaufmann, CHI	3.02

Wins

L. Meadows, PIT	20
R. Kremer, PIT	20
F. Rhem, STL	20
P. Donohue, CIN	20
C. Mays, CIN	19

Saves

C. Davies, NY	6
R. Kremer, PIT	5
J. Scott, NY	5
R. Ehrhardt, BKN	4

Strikeouts

D. Vance, BKN	140
C. Root, CHI	127
J. May, CIN	103
L. Benton, BOS	103
J. Petty, BKN	101

Complete Games

C. Mays, CIN	24
J. Petty, BKN	23
C. Root, CHI	21
H. Carlson, PHI	20
F. Rhem, STL	20

Fewest Hits/9 Innings

J. Petty, BKN	8.03
F. Rhem, STL	8.41
P. Jones, CHI	8.48
G. Alexander, CHI, STL	8.58

Shutouts

P. Donohue, CIN	5
B. Smith, BOS	4
S. Blake, CHI	4

Fewest Walks/9 Innings

P. Donohue, CIN	1.23
G. Alexander, CHI, STL	1.39
H. Carlson, PHI	1.58
C. Mays, CIN	1.70

Most Strikeouts/9 Inn.

D. Vance, BKN	7.46
P. Jones, CHI	4.49
S. Blake, CHI	4.33
C. Root, CHI	4.21

Innings

P. Donohue, CIN	286
C. Mays, CIN	281
J. Petty, BKN	276
C. Root, CHI	271

Games Pitched

J. Scott, NY	50
C. Willoughby, PHI	47
P. Donohue, CIN	47
J. May, CIN	45
D. Ulrich, PHI	45

							Batting						Fielding			Pitching					
	W	L	PCT	GB	R	OR	2B	3B	HR	BA	SA	SB	E	DP	FA	CG	BB	SO	ShO	SV	ERA
St. Louis	89	65	.578		**817**	678	259	82	**90**	.286	**.415**	83	198	141	.969	**90**	397	365	10	6	3.67
Cincinnati	87	67	.565	2	747	651	242	**120**	35	**.290**	.400	51	183	160	.972	88	**324**	424	**14**	8	3.42
Pittsburgh	84	69	.549	4.5	769	689	243	106	44	.285	.396	91	220	161	.965	83	455	387	12	**18**	3.67
Chicago	82	72	.532	7	682	**602**	**291**	49	66	.278	.390	85	**162**	**174**	**.974**	77	486	508	13	14	**3.26**
New York	74	77	.490	13.5	663	668	214	58	73	.278	.384	**94**	186	150	.970	61	427	419	4	15	3.77
Brooklyn	71	82	.464	17.5	623	705	246	62	40	.263	.358	76	229	95	.963	83	472	**517**	5	9	3.82
Boston	66	86	.434	22	624	719	209	62	16	.277	.350	81	208	150	.967	60	455	408	9	9	4.03
Philadelphia	58	93	.384	29.5	687	900	244	50	75	.281	.390	47	224	153	.964	68	454	331	5	5	5.19
					5612	5612	1948	589	439	.280	.385	608	1610	1184	.968	610	3470	3359	72	84	3.85

AMERICAN LEAGUE 1926

New York

W-91 L-63

Miller Huggins

POS	Player	AB	BA	HR	RBI	PO	A	E	DP	TC/G	FA	Pitcher	G	IP	W	L	SV	ERA
1B	L. Gehrig	572	.313	16	107	1566	73	15	87	10.7	.991	H. Pennock	40	266	23	11	2	3.62
2B	T. Lazzeri	589	.275	18	114	298	461	31	72	5.3	.961	U. Shocker	41	258	19	11	2	3.38
SS	M. Koenig	617	.271	5	62	281	422	**52**	66	5.4	.931	W. Hoyt	40	218	16	12	4	3.85
3B	J. Dugan	434	.288	1	64	122	221	16	10	2.9	.955	S. Jones	39	161	9	8	5	4.98
RF	B. Ruth	495	.372	**47**	**145**	308	11	7	5	2.2	.979	M. Thomas	33	140	6	6	0	4.23
CF	E. Combs	606	.299	8	56	375	8	12	2	2.7	.970	B. Shawkey	29	104	8	7	3	3.62
LF	B. Meusel	413	.315	12	81	211	4	9	1	2.1	.960							
C	P. Collins	290	.286	7	35	394	76	14	**14**	4.8	.971							
OF	B. Paschal	258	.287	7	33	134	10	10	0	2.1	.935							
3B	M. Gazella	168	.232	0	21	37	78	11	5	2.8	.913							

Cleveland

W-88 L-66

Tris Speaker

POS	Player	AB	BA	HR	RBI	PO	A	E	DP	TC/G	FA	Pitcher	G	IP	W	L	SV	ERA
1B	G. Burns	603	.358	4	114	1499	99	19	122	10.7	.988	G. Uhle	39	**318**	**27**	11	1	2.83
2B	F. Spurgeon	614	.295	0	49	341	**479**	**32**	**93**	5.7	.962	D. Levsen	33	237	16	13	0	3.41
SS	J. Sewell	578	.324	4	85	**326**	463	37	86	5.4	.955	J. Shaute	34	207	14	10	1	3.53
3B	R. Lutzke	475	.261	0	59	160	302	19	27	3.4	.960	S. Smith	27	188	11	10	0	3.73
RF	H. Summa	581	.308	4	76	328	18	9	5	2.3	.975	G. Buckeye	32	166	6	9	0	3.10
CF	T. Speaker	539	.304	7	86	394	20	8	7	2.8	.981	B. Karr	30	113	5	6	1	5.00
LF	C. Jamieson	555	.299	2	45	293	15	13	5	2.2	.960	J. Miller	18	83	7	4	1	3.27
C	L. Sewell	433	.238	0	46	437	**91**	9	3	4.3	.983							

AMERICAN LEAGUE 1926, *cont.*

Philadelphia

W-83 L-67

Connie Mack

POS	Player	AB	BA	HR	RBI	PO	A	E	DP	TC/G	FA
1B	J. Poole	361	.294	8	63	887	55	8	71	9.4	.992
2B	M. Bishop	400	.265	0	33	235	365	8	55	5.1	**.987**
SS	C. Galloway	408	.240	0	49	274	315	41	49	4.7	.935
3B	J. Dykes	429	.287	1	44	95	188	15	16	3.9	.950
RF	W. French	397	.305	1	36	186	12	6	7	2.1	.971
CF	A. Simmons	581	.343	19	109	333	11	9	5	2.4	.975
LF	B. Lamar	419	.284	5	50	199	10	10	2	2.1	.954
C	M. Cochrane	370	.273	8	47	**502**	90	**15**	9	**5.3**	.975
3B	S. Hale	327	.281	4	43	82	152	13	16	3.2	.947
1B	J. Hauser	229	.192	8	36	630	35	3	39	10.3	.996
OF	F. Welch	174	.282	4	23	75	4	2	1	1.7	.975

Pitcher	G	IP	W	L	SV	ERA
L. Grove	45	258	13	13	6	**2.51**
E. Rommel	37	219	11	11	0	3.08
J. Quinn	31	164	10	11	1	3.41
R. Walberg	40	151	12	10	2	2.80
S. Gray	38	151	11	12	0	3.64
H. Ehmke	20	147	12	4	0	2.81
J. Pate	47	113	9	0	6	2.71

Washington

W-81 L-69

Bucky Harris

POS	Player	AB	BA	HR	RBI	PO	A	E	DP	TC/G	FA
1B	J. Judge	453	.291	7	92	1145	95	8	90	9.8	.994
2B	B. Harris	537	.283	1	63	**356**	427	30	74	5.8	.963
SS	B. Myer	434	.304	1	62	215	297	40	47	4.7	.928
3B	O. Bluege	487	.271	3	65	139	256	20	15	3.1	.952
RF	S. Rice	**641**	.337	3	76	342	25	15	5	2.5	.961
CF	E. McNeely	442	.303	0	48	274	9	9	3	2.4	.969
LF	G. Goslin	567	.354	17	108	373	25	15	8	2.8	.964
C	M. Ruel	368	.299	1	53	452	81	6	13	4.6	**.989**
10	J. Harris	257	.307	5	55	354	20	3	20		.992

Pitcher	G	IP	W	L	SV	ERA
W. Johnson	33	262	15	16	0	3.61
S. Coveleski	36	245	14	11	1	3.12
D. Ruether	23	169	12	6	0	4.84
F. Marberry	**64**	138	12	7	**22**	3.00
G. Crowder	19	100	7	4	1	3.96

Chicago

W-81 L-72

Eddie Collins

POS	Player	AB	BA	HR	RBI	PO	A	E	DP	TC/G	FA
1B	E. Sheely	525	.299	6	89	1380	84	8	87	10.2	**.995**
2B	E. Collins	375	.344	1	62	228	307	15	53	5.4	.973
SS	B. Hunnefield	470	.274	3	48	185	259	32	44	4.9	.933
3B	W. Kamm	480	.294	0	62	**177**	**323**	11	16	**3.6**	**.978**
RF	B. Barrett	368	.307	6	61	179	8	6	2	1.9	.969
CF	J. Mostil	600	.328	4	42	440	15	15	4	3.2	.968
LF	B. Falk	566	.345	8	108	338	16	3	4	2.3	.992
C	R. Schalk	226	.265	0	32	251	45	7	6	3.8	.977
OF	S. Harris	222	.252	2	27	106	6	6	2	1.9	.949
2B	R. Morehart	192	.318	0	21	71	136	11	13	4.5	.950

Pitcher	G	IP	W	L	SV	ERA
T. Lyons	39	284	18	16	2	3.01
T. Thomas	44	249	15	12	2	3.80
T. Blankenship	29	209	13	10	1	3.61
R. Faber	27	185	15	9	0	3.56
J. Edwards	32	142	6	9	1	4.18
S. Thurston	31	134	6	8	3	5.02
S. Connally	31	108	6	5	3	3.16

Detroit

W-79 L-75

Ty Cobb

POS	Player	AB	BA	HR	RBI	PO	A	E	DP	TC/G	FA
1B	L. Blue	429	.287	1	52	1153	56	17	95	11.2	.986
2B	C. Gehringer	459	.277	1	48	255	323	16	56	5.3	.973
SS	J. Tavener	532	.265	1	58	300	470	39	**92**	5.2	.952
3B	J. Warner	311	.251	0	34	105	175	13	9	3.1	.956
RF	H. Heilmann	502	.367	9	103	228	18	7	4	1.9	.972
CF	H. Manush	498	**.378**	14	86	283	7	10	3	2.5	.967
LF	B. Fothergill	387	.367	3	73	245	3	10	0	2.5	.961
C	C. Manion	176	.199	0	14	227	48	8	2	3.8	.972
32	F. O'Rourke	363	.242	1	41	181	256	23	42		.950
OF	A. Wingo	298	.282	1	45	155	13	14	2	2.5	.923
1B	J. Neun	242	.298	0	15	433	22	3	34	9.3	.993
OF	T. Cobb	233	.339	4	62	109	4	6	2	2.2	.950
C	J. Bassler	174	.305	0	22	223	61	0	6	4.5	1.000

Pitcher	G	IP	W	L	SV	ERA
E. Whitehill	36	252	16	13	0	3.99
S. Gibson	35	196	12	9	2	3.48
E. Wells	36	178	12	10	0	4.15
L. Stoner	32	160	7	10	0	5.47
K. Holloway	36	139	4	6	2	5.12
H. Dauss	35	124	12	6	9	4.20
R. Collins	30	122	8	8	1	2.73
A. Johns	35	113	6	4	1	5.35

St. Louis

W-62 L-92

George Sisler

POS	Player	AB	BA	HR	RBI	PO	A	E	DP	TC/G	FA
1B	G. Sisler	613	.290	7	71	1467	87	21	**141**	10.6	.987
2B	O. Melillo	385	.255	1	30	225	297	19	65	6.1	.965
SS	W. Gerber	411	.270	0	42	261	358	37	**92**	5.1	.944
3B	M. McManus	549	.284	9	68	119	197	14	17	3.9	.958
RF	B. Miller	353	.331	4	50	219	12	15	2	2.6	.939
CF	H. Rice	578	.313	9	59	300	22	10	4	2.5	.970
LF	K. Williams	347	.280	17	74	189	12	11	2	2.3	.948
C	W. Schang	285	.330	8	50	224	75	10	7	3.8	.968
3B	G. Robertson	247	.251	1	19	58	112	14	9	3.3	.924
C	P. Hargrave	235	.281	7	37	165	50	5	7	3.7	.977
OF	H. Bennett	225	.267	1	26	106	9	6	3	2.4	.950
OF	C. Durst	219	.237	3	16	143	5	3	0	2.6	.980
OF	B. Jacobson	182	.286	2	21	105	2	4	0	2.2	.964

Pitcher	G	IP	W	L	SV	ERA
T. Zachary	34	247	14	15	0	3.60
M. Gaston	32	214	10	**18**	0	4.33
E. Vangilder	42	181	9	11	1	5.17
E. Wingard	39	169	5	8	3	3.57
W. Ballou	43	154	11	10	2	4.79
J. Giard	22	90	3	10	0	7.00
D. Davis	27	83	3	8	1	4.66

Boston

W-46 L-107

Lee Fohl

POS	Player	AB	BA	HR	RBI	PO	A	E	DP	TC/G	FA
1B	P. Todt	599	.255	7	69	**1755**	**126**	**22**	114	**12.4**	.988
2B	B. Regan	403	.263	4	34	264	392	24	66	**6.4**	.965
SS	T. Rigney	525	.270	4	53	286	**492**	25	80	**5.5**	**.969**
3B	F. Haney	462	.221	0	52	149	322	**21**	**30**	3.6	.957
RF	B. Jacobson	394	.305	6	69	193	7	4	1	2.1	.980
CF	I. Flagstead	415	.299	3	31	264	14	5	4	2.9	.982
LF	S. Rosenthal	285	.267	4	34	100	0	4	0	1.6	.962
C	A. Gaston	301	.223	0	21	284	69	7	5	3.7	.981
2B	M. Herrera	237	.257	0	19	112	168	11	23	6.1	.962
OF	J. Tobin	209	.273	1	14	79	7	3	1	1.7	.966
OF	W. Shaner	191	.283	0	21	106	3	4	2	2.4	.965
OF	F. Bratschi	167	.275	0	19	55	1	3	0	1.6	.949
OF	R. Carlyle	164	.287	2	16	62	4	7	0	2.0	.904

Pitcher	G	IP	W	L	SV	ERA
H. Wiltse	37	196	8	15	0	4.22
T. Wingfield	43	191	11	16	3	4.44
P. Zahniser	30	172	6	**18**	0	4.97
R. Ruffing	37	166	6	15	2	4.39
T. Welzer	40	141	4	3	0	4.79
S. Harriss	21	113	6	10	0	4.46
F. Heimach	20	102	2	9	0	5.65
H. Ehmke	14	97	3	10	0	5.46

BATTING AND BASE RUNNING LEADERS

Batting Average		Slugging Average		Home Runs	
H. Manush, DET	.378	B. Ruth, NY	.737	B. Ruth, NY	47
B. Ruth, NY	.372	A. Simmons, PHI	.566	A. Simmons, PHI	19
B. Fothergill, DET	.367	H. Manush, DET	.564	T. Lazzeri, NY	18
H. Heilmann, DET	.367	L. Gehrig, NY	.549	K. Williams, STL	17
G. Burns, CLE	.358	G. Goslin, WAS	.543	G. Goslin, WAS	17

PITCHING LEADERS

Winning Percentage		Earned Run Average		Wins	
G. Uhle, CLE	.711	L. Grove, PHI	2.51	G. Uhle, CLE	27
H. Pennock, NY	.676	G. Uhle, CLE	2.83	H. Pennock, NY	23
U. Shocker, NY	.633	T. Lyons, CHI	3.01	U. Shocker, NY	19
R. Faber, CHI	.625	E. Rommel, PHI	3.08	T. Lyons, CHI	18
W. Hoyt, NY	.571	S. Coveleski, WAS	3.12		

AMERICAN LEAGUE 1926, *cont.*

BATTING AND BASE RUNNING LEADERS

Total Bases
B. Ruth, NY 365
A. Simmons, PHI 329
L. Gehrig, NY 314
G. Goslin, WAS 308
G. Burns, CLE 298

Runs Batted In
B. Ruth, NY 145
T. Lazzeri, NY 114
G. Burns, CLE 114
A. Simmons, PHI 109
B. Falk, CHI 108
G. Goslin, WAS 108

Stolen Bases
J. Mostil, CHI 35
S. Rice, WAS 25
B. Hunnefield, CHI 24
E. McNeely, WAS 18
J. Sewell, CLE 17

Hits
G. Burns, CLE 216
S. Rice, WAS 216
G. Goslin, WAS 201
A. Simmons, PHI 199

Base on Balls
B. Ruth, NY 144
M. Bishop, PHI 116
T. Rigney, BOS 108
L. Gehrig, NY 105

Home Run Percentage
B. Ruth, NY 9.5
K. Williams, STL 4.9
A. Simmons, PHI 3.3
T. Lazzeri, NY 3.1

Runs
B. Ruth, NY 139
L. Gehrig, NY 135
J. Mostil, CHI 120
E. Combs, NY 113

Doubles
G. Burns, CLE 64
A. Simmons, PHI 53
T. Speaker, CLE 52
B. Jacobson, STL, BOS 51

Triples
L. Gehrig, NY 20
C. Gehringer, DET 17
G. Goslin, WAS 15
J. Mostil, CHI 15

PITCHING LEADERS

Saves
F. Marberry, WAS 22
H. Dauss, DET 9
L. Grove, PHI 6
J. Pate, PHI 6
S. Jones, NY 5

Strikeouts
L. Grove, PHI 194
G. Uhle, CLE 159
T. Thomas, CHI 127
W. Johnson, WAS 125
E. Whitehill, DET 109

Complete Games
G. Uhle, CLE 32
T. Lyons, CHI 24
W. Johnson, WAS 22
L. Grove, PHI 20
H. Pennock, NY 19
U. Shocker, NY 19

Fewest Hits/9 Innings
L. Grove, PHI 7.92
T. Thomas, CHI 8.13
G. Uhle, CLE 8.48
T. Lyons, CHI 8.50

Shutouts
E. Wells, DET 4

Fewest Walks/9 Innings
H. Pennock, NY 1.45
S. Smith, CLE 1.48
E. Rommel, PHI 2.22
U. Shocker, NY 2.47

Most Strikeouts/9 Inn.
L. Grove, PHI 6.77
T. Thomas, CHI 4.59
G. Uhle, CLE 4.50
W. Johnson, WAS 4.30

Innings
G. Uhle, CLE 318
T. Lyons, CHI 284
H. Pennock, NY 266
W. Johnson, WAS 262

Games Pitched
F. Marberry, WAS 64
J. Pate, PHI 47
L. Grove, PHI 45
T. Thomas, CHI 44

							Batting						Fielding			Pitching					
	W	L	PCT	GB	R	OR	2B	3B	HR	BA	SA	SB	E	DP	FA	CG	BB	SO	ShO	SV	ERA
New York	91	63	.591		**847**	713	262	75	**121**	.289	**.437**	79	210	117	.966	64	478	486	4	20	3.86
Cleveland	88	66	.571	3	738	612	**333**	49	27	.289	.386	88	173	153	.972	**96**	**450**	381	**11**	4	3.40
Philadelphia	83	67	.553	6	677	**570**	259	65	61	.269	.383	56	171	131	.972	62	451	**571**	10	16	**3.00**
Washington	81	69	.540	8	802	761	244	**97**	43	**.292**	.401	**122**	184	129	.969	65	566	418	5	**26**	4.34
Chicago	81	72	.529	9.5	730	665	314	60	32	.289	.390	121	**165**	122	**.973**	85	506	458	**11**	12	3.74
Detroit	79	75	.513	12	793	830	281	90	36	.291	.398	88	193	151	.969	57	555	469	10	18	4.41
St. Louis	62	92	.403	29	682	845	253	78	72	.276	.394	62	235	**167**	.963	64	654	337	5	9	4.66
Boston	46	107	.301	44.5	562	835	249	54	32	.256	.343	48	193	143	.970	53	546	336	6	5	4.72
					5831	5831	2195	568	424	.281	.391	664	1524	1113	.969	546	4206	3456	62	110	4.02

NATIONAL LEAGUE 1927

	POS	Player	AB	BA	HR	RBI	PO	A	E	DP	TC/G	FA	Pitcher	G	IP	W	L	SV	ERA
Pittsburgh	1B	J. Harris	411	.326	5	73	1056	78	11	84	9.9	.990	L. Meadows	40	299	19	10	0	3.40
	2B	G. Grantham	531	.305	8	66	279	363	32	65	5.4	.953	C. Hill	43	278	22	11	3	3.24
W-94 L-60	SS	G. Wright	570	.281	9	105	**296**	430	**45**	82	5.4	.942	V. Aldridge	35	239	15	10	1	4.25
	3B	P. Traynor	573	.342	5	106	**212**	265	19	**23**	3.5	.962	R. Kremer	35	226	19	8	2	**2.47**
Donie Bush	RF	P. Waner	623	**.380**	9	**131**	326	20	7	4	2.5	.980	J. Dawson	20	81	3	7	0	4.46
	CF	L. Waner	629	.355	2	27	396	9	10	0	2.8	.976	J. Miljus	19	76	8	3	0	1.90
	LF	C. Barnhart	360	.319	3	54	222	5	5	2	2.5	.978							
	C	J. Gooch	291	.258	2	48	285	57	9	7	3.9	.974							
	OF	K. Cuyler	285	.309	3	31	195	6	4	0	2.8	.980							
	C	E. Smith	189	.270	5	25	187	32	3	2	3.6	.986							
	2B	H. Rhyne	168	.274	0	17	105	101	8	19	4.8	.963							
St. Louis	1B	J. Bottomley	574	.303	19	124	**1656**	70	20	**149**	11.5	.989	J. Haines	38	301	24	10	1	2.72
	2B	F. Frisch	617	.337	10	78	396	**641**	22	**104**	**6.9**	**.979**	G. Alexander	37	268	21	10	3	2.52
	SS	H. Schuble	218	.257	4	28	120	192	29	36	5.2	.915	B. Sherdel	39	232	17	12	**6**	3.53
W-92 L-61	3B	L. Bell	390	.259	9	65	85	142	**24**	13	2.5	.904	F. Rhem	27	169	10	12	0	4.41
	RF	W. Holm	419	.286	3	66	201	3	7	0	2.2	.967							
Bob O'Farrell	CF	T. Douthit	488	.262	5	50	396	8	15	4	3.4	.964							
	LF	C. Hafey	346	.329	18	63	179	19	4	7	2.1	.980							
	C	F. Snyder	194	.258	1	30	174	37	4	5	3.5	.981							
	OF	B. Southworth	306	.301	2	39	153	6	5	2	2.0	.970							
	3S	S. Toporcer	290	.248	0	19	86	157	12	21		.953							
	SS	T. Thevenow	191	.194	0	4	111	199	18	38	5.6	.945							
	OF	R. Blades	180	.317	2	29	64	0	6	0	1.4	.914							
	C	B. O'Farrell	178	.264	0	18	141	45	4	5	3.6	.979							
	C	J. Schulte	156	.288	9	32	172	45	10	6	3.8	.956							
New York	1B	B. Terry	580	.326	20	121	1621	**105**	12	135	**11.6**	.993	B. Grimes	39	260	19	8	2	3.54
	2B	R. Hornsby	568	.361	26	125	299	582	25	98	5.8	.972	F. Fitzsimmons	42	245	17	10	3	3.72
	SS	T. Jackson	469	.318	14	98	287	**444**	37	**85**	**6.2**	.952	V. Barnes	35	229	14	11	2	3.98
W-92 L-62	3B	F. Lindstrom	562	.306	7	58	93	178	9	12	3.2	.968	L. Benton	29	173	13	5	2	3.95
	RF	G. Harper	483	.331	16	87	299	13	8	5	2.3	.975	D. Henry	45	164	11	6	4	4.23
John McGraw	CF	E. Roush	570	.304	7	58	327	19	9	4	2.6	.975	B. Clarkson	26	87	3	9	2	4.36
W-70 L-52	LF	H. Mueller	190	.289	3	19	100	1	6	0	1.9	.944							
	C	Z. Taylor	258	.233	0	21	267	51	9	8	4.0	.972							
Rogers Hornsby	3B	A. Reese	355	.265	4	21	50	126	17	14	3.0	.912							
W-22 L-10	OF	M. Ott	163	.282	1	19	52	2	1	1	1.7	.982							
	OF	T. Tyson	159	.264	1	17	73	5	6	1	2.0	.929							
	SS	D. Farrell	142	.387	3	34	77	116	17	19	5.8	.919							
	C	A. DeVormer	141	.248	2	21	115	27	7	0	2.8	.953							

NATIONAL LEAGUE 1927, *cont.*

Team	POS	Player	AB	BA	HR	RBI	PO	A	E	DP	TC/G	FA	Pitcher	G	IP	W	L	SV	ERA
Chicago	1B	C. Grimm	543	.311	2	74	1437	99	15	117	10.6	.990	C. Root	**48**	**309**	**26**	15	2	3.76
	2B	C. Beck	391	.258	2	44	238	358	19	62	6.2	.969	S. Blake	32	224	13	14	0	3.29
	SS	W. English	334	.290	1	28	177	281	29	47	5.8	.940	G. Bush	36	193	10	10	2	3.03
W-85 L-68	3B	S. Adams	**647**	.292	0	49	45	107	6	12	3.0	.962	H. Carlson	27	184	12	8	0	3.17
	RF	E. Webb	332	.301	14	52	171	14	8	5	2.2	.959	J. Brillheart	32	129	4	2	0	4.13
Joe McCarthy	CF	H. Wilson	551	.318	**30**	129	400	13	14	3	2.9	.967	P. Jones	30	113	7	8	0	4.07
	LF	R. Stephenson	579	.344	7	82	297	18	8	5	2.2	.975	B. Osborn	24	108	5	5	0	4.18
	C	G. Hartnett	449	.294	10	80	**479**	**99**	**16**	**21**	**4.8**	.973							
	OF	C. Heathcote	228	.294	2	25	136	13	2	7	2.6	.987							
	3B	E. Pick	181	.171	2	15	60	71	13	9	2.9	.910							
	OF	P. Scott	156	.314	0	21	70	3	1	1	2.1	.986							
Cincinnati	1B	W. Pipp	443	.260	2	41	1145	66	5	86	10.7	**.996**	R. Lucas	37	240	18	11	2	3.38
	2B	H. Critz	396	.278	4	49	239	388	20	69	5.7	.969	J. May	44	236	15	12	1	3.51
	SS	H. Ford	409	.274	1	46	218	323	27	75	5.5	.952	D. Luque	29	231	13	12	0	3.20
W-75 L-78	3B	C. Dressen	548	.292	2	55	131	**315**	15	20	3.2	**.967**	E. Rixey	34	220	12	10	1	3.48
	RF	C. Walker	527	.292	6	80	316	15	15	8	2.5	.957	P. Donohue	33	191	6	16	1	4.11
Jack Hendricks	CF	E. Allen	359	.295	2	20	250	6	3	3	2.6	.988	C. Mays	14	82	3	7	0	3.51
	LF	R. Bressler	467	.291	3	77	261	15	8	5	2.4	.972	A. Nehf	21	45	3	5	4	5.56
	C	B. Hargrave	305	.308	0	35	261	57	4	10	3.5	**.988**							
	OF	B. Zitzmann	232	.284	0	24	135	2	6	0	2.4	.958							
	1B	G. Kelly	222	.270	5	21	456	32	4	46	10.0	.992							
	OF	C. Christensen	185	.254	0	16	106	6	5	3	2.3	.957							
	C	V. Picinich	173	.254	0	12	218	31	5	8	4.2	.980							
	P	R. Lucas	150	.313	0	28	7	51	1	2	1.6	.983							
Brooklyn	1B	B. Herman	412	.272	14	73	968	68	**21**	64	10.1	.980	D. Vance	34	273	16	15	1	2.70
	2B	J. Partridge	572	.260	7	40	330	454	**52**	63	6.0	.938	J. Petty	42	272	13	18	1	2.98
	SS	J. Butler	521	.238	2	57	214	251	20	49	5.4	.959	J. Elliott	30	188	6	13	3	3.30
W-65 L-88	3B	B. Barrett	355	.259	5	38	76	167	21	12	2.8	.920	D. McWeeny	34	164	4	8	1	3.56
	RF	M. Carey	538	.266	1	54	331	19	11	6	2.6	.970	B. Doak	27	145	11	8	0	3.48
Wilbert Robinson	CF	J. Statz	507	.274	1	21	371	14	4	5	3.2	.990	R. Ehrhardt	46	96	3	7	2	3.57
	LF	G. Felix	445	.265	0	57	221	13	13	1	2.1	.947	J. Barnes	18	79	2	10	0	5.72
	C	H. DeBerry	201	.234	1	21	339	59	5	8	6.0	.988	W. Clark	27	74	7	2	2	2.32
	01	H. Hendrick	458	.310	4	50	556	37	10	37		.983							
	SS	J. Flowers	231	.234	2	20	137	184	19	29	5.2	.944							
	C	B. Henline	177	.266	1	18	216	50	15	6	4.7	.947							
Boston	1B	J. Fournier	374	.283	10	53	901	63	11	63	9.6	.989	B. Smith	41	261	10	18	3	3.76
	2B	D. Gautreau	236	.246	0	20	136	196	12	22	6.0	.965	K. Greenfield	27	190	11	14	0	3.84
	SS	D. Bancroft	375	.243	1	31	275	329	39	66	6.2	.939	J. Genewich	40	181	11	8	1	3.83
W-60 L-94	3B	A. High	384	.302	4	46	93	122	20	9	2.6	.915	J. Wertz	42	164	4	10	1	4.55
	RF	L. Richbourg	450	.309	2	34	233	10	12	0	2.3	.953	C. Robertson	28	154	7	17	0	4.72
Dave Bancroft	CF	J. Welsh	497	.288	9	54	377	24	13	6	3.2	.969	F. Edwards	29	92	2	8	0	4.99
	LF	E. Brown	558	.306	2	75	335	10	7	1	2.3	.980	G. Mogridge	20	49	6	4	5	3.70
	C	S. Hogan	229	.288	3	32	215	54	4	3	4.5	.985							
	UT	D. Farrell	424	.292	1	58	252	335	37	47		.941							
	UT	E. Moore	411	.302	1	32	200	223	16	36		.964							
	1B	D. Burrus	220	.318	0	32	505	44	16	51	9.3	.972							
	OF	J. Smith	183	.317	1	24	106	7	6	1	2.5	.950							
	C	F. Gibson	167	.222	0	19	130	35	6	3	3.6	.965							
Philadelphia	1B	R. Wrightstone	533	.306	6	75	1268	90	15	114	10.1	.989	J. Scott	**48**	233	9	**21**	1	5.09
	2B	F. Thompson	597	.303	1	70	**424**	485	35	97	6.2	.963	A. Ferguson	31	227	8	16	0	4.84
	SS	H. Sand	535	.299	1	49	201	247	24	36	5.5	.949	D. Ulrich	32	193	8	11	1	3.17
W-51 L-103	3B	B. Friberg	335	.233	1	28	124	226	15	**23**	**3.5**	.959	H. Pruett	31	186	7	17	1	6.05
	RF	C. Williams	492	.274	**30**	98	241	22	8	8	2.1	.970	L. Sweetland	21	104	2	10	0	6.16
Stuffy McInnis	CF	F. Leach	536	.306	12	83	385	26	8	10	3.0	.981	C. Willoughby	35	98	3	7	2	6.54
	LF	D. Spalding	442	.296	0	25	250	7	2	1	2.3	.992	H. Carlson	11	64	4	5	1	5.23
	C	J. Wilson	443	.275	2	45	377	82	12	12	3.8	.975							
	SS	J. Cooney	259	.270	0	15	155	238	8	51	5.4	.980*							
	OF	J. Mokan	213	.286	0	33	97	5	4	0	1.7	.962							
	OF	A. Nixon	154	.312	0	18	121	3	4	0	2.9	.969							

BATTING AND BASE RUNNING LEADERS

Batting Average
P. Waner, PIT .380
R. Hornsby, NY .361
L. Waner, PIT .355
R. Stephenson, CHI .344
P. Traynor, PIT .342

Slugging Average
C. Hafey, STL .590
R. Hornsby, NY .586
H. Wilson, CHI .579
P. Waner, PIT .543
B. Terry, NY .529

Home Runs
C. Williams, PHI 30
H. Wilson, CHI 30
R. Hornsby, NY 26
B. Terry, NY 20
J. Bottomley, STL 19

Total Bases
P. Waner, PIT 338
R. Hornsby, NY 333
H. Wilson, CHI 319
B. Terry, NY 307
J. Bottomley, STL 292

Runs Batted In
P. Waner, PIT 131
H. Wilson, CHI 129
R. Hornsby, NY 125
J. Bottomley, STL 124
B. Terry, NY 121

Stolen Bases
F. Frisch, STL 48
M. Carey, BKN 32
H. Hendrick, BKN 29
S. Adams, CHI 26
L. Richbourg, BOS 24

Hits
P. Waner, PIT 237
L. Waner, PIT 223
F. Frisch, STL 208
R. Hornsby, NY 205

Base on Balls
R. Hornsby, NY 86
G. Harper, NY 84
G. Grantham, PIT 74
J. Bottomley, STL 74

Home Run Percentage
C. Williams, PHI 6.1
H. Wilson, CHI 5.4
C. Hafey, STL 5.2
R. Hornsby, NY 4.6

PITCHING LEADERS

Winning Percentage
L. Benton, BOS, NY .708
J. Haines, STL .706
B. Grimes, NY .704
R. Kremer, PIT .704
G. Alexander, STL .677

Earned Run Average
R. Kremer, PIT 2.47
G. Alexander, STL 2.52
D. Vance, BKN 2.70
J. Haines, STL 2.72
J. Petty, BKN 2.98

Wins
C. Root, CHI 26
J. Haines, STL 24
C. Hill, PIT 22
G. Alexander, STL 21

Saves
B. Sherdel, STL 6
A. Nehf, CIN, CHI 5
G. Mogridge, BOS 5
D. Henry, NY 4

Strikeouts
D. Vance, BKN 184
C. Root, CHI 145
J. May, CIN 121
B. Grimes, NY 102
J. Petty, BKN 101

Complete Games
D. Vance, BKN 25
J. Haines, STL 25
L. Meadows, PIT 25
G. Alexander, STL 22
C. Hill, PIT 22

Fewest Hits/9 Innings
D. Vance, BKN 7.97
R. Kremer, PIT 8.16
J. Haines, STL 8.17
C. Hill, PIT 8.43

Shutouts
J. Haines, STL 6
R. Lucas, CIN 4
C. Root, CHI 4
R. Kremer, PIT 3

Fewest Walks/9 Innings
G. Alexander, STL 1.28
R. Lucas, CIN 1.46
P. Donohue, CIN 1.51
H. Carlson, PHI, CHI 1.63

NATIONAL LEAGUE 1927, *cont.*

BATTING AND BASE RUNNING LEADERS						PITCHING LEADERS					
Runs		**Doubles**		**Triples**		**Most Strikeouts/9 Inn.**		**Innings**		**Games Pitched**	
R. Hornsby, NY	133	R. Stephenson, CHI	46	P. Waner, PIT	17	D. Vance, BKN	6.06	C. Root, CHI	309	J. Scott, PHI	48
L. Waner, PIT	133	P. Waner, PIT	40	J. Bottomley, STL	15	J. Elliott, BKN	4.73	J. Haines, STL	301	C. Root, CHI	48
H. Wilson, CHI	119	C. Dressen, CIN	36	F. Thompson, PHI	14	J. May, CIN	4.62	L. Meadows, PIT	299	R. Ehrhardt, BKN	46
P. Waner, PIT	113	F. Lindstrom, NY	36	B. Terry, NY	13	H. Pruett, PHI	4.35	C. Hill, PIT	278	D. Henry, NY	45

							Batting						Fielding			Pitching					
	W	L	PCT	GB	R	OR	2B	3B	HR	BA	SA	SB	E	DP	FA	CG	BB	SO	ShO	SV	ERA
Pittsburgh	94	60	.610		**817**	659	258	78	54	**.305**	.412	65	187	130	.969	**90**	418	435	10	10	3.66
St. Louis	92	61	.601	1.5	754	665	264	**79**	84	.278	.408	**110**	213	**170**	.966	89	363	394	**14**	11	3.57
New York	92	62	.597	2	**817**	720	251	62	**109**	.297	**.427**	73	195	160	.969	65	453	442	7	**16**	3.97
Chicago	85	68	.556	8.5	750	661	**266**	63	74	.284	.400	65	181	152	.971	75	514	465	11	5	3.65
Cincinnati	75	78	.490	18.5	643	653	222	77	29	.278	.367	62	**165**	160	**.973**	87	**316**	407	12	12	3.54
Brooklyn	65	88	.425	28.5	541	**619**	195	74	39	.253	.342	106	229	117	.963	74	418	**574**	7	10	**3.36**
Boston	60	94	.390	34	651	771	216	61	37	.279	.363	100	231	130	.963	52	468	402	3	11	4.22
Philadelphia	51	103	.331	43	678	903	216	46	57	.280	.370	68	169	152	.972	81	462	377	5	6	5.35
					5651	5651	1888	540	483	.282	.386	649	1570	1171	.968	613	3412	3496	69	81	3.91

AMERICAN LEAGUE 1927

New York

W-110 L-44

Miller Huggins

POS	Player	AB	BA	HR	RBI	PO	A	E	DP	TC/G	FA	Pitcher	G	IP	W	L	SV	ERA
1B	L. Gehrig	584	.373	47	**175**	**1662**	88	15	108	**11.4**	.992	W. Hoyt	36	256	**22**	7	1	2.63
2B	T. Lazzeri	570	.309	18	102	213	398	18	60	5.6	.971	W. Moore	50	213	19	7	**13**	**2.28**
SS	M. Koenig	526	.285	3	62	262	423	**47**	76	**6.0**	.936	H. Pennock	34	210	19	8	2	3.00
3B	J. Dugan	387	.269	2	43	93	196	19	15	2.8	.938	U. Shocker	31	200	18	6	0	2.84
RF	B. Ruth	540	.356	**60**	164	328	14	13	4	2.4	.963	D. Ruether	27	184	13	6	0	3.38
CF	E. Combs	**648**	.356	6	64	411	6	14	0	2.8	.968	G. Pipgras	29	166	10	3	0	4.11
LF	B. Meusel	516	.337	8	103	249	15	14	1	2.1	.950	M. Thomas	21	89	7	4	0	4.87
C	P. Collins	251	.275	7	36	267	56	8	1	3.7	.976							
2B	R. Morehart	195	.256	1	20	101	175	16	27	5.5	.945							
C	J. Grabowski	195	.277	0	25	197	47	4	3	3.6	.984							
OF	C. Durst	129	.248	0	25	47	1	1	0	1.4	.980							

Philadelphia

W-91 L-63

Connie Mack

POS	Player	AB	BA	HR	RBI	PO	A	E	DP	TC/G	FA	Pitcher	G	IP	W	L	SV	ERA
1B	J. Dykes	417	.324	3	60	816	49	10	59	10.7	.989	L. Grove	51	262	20	13	9	3.19
2B	M. Bishop	372	.277	0	22	211	342	19	48	5.4	.967	R. Walberg	46	249	16	12	4	3.97
SS	J. Boley	370	.311	1	52	182	318	26	49	4.6	.951	J. Quinn	34	207	15	10	1	3.17
3B	S. Hale	501	.313	5	81	152	247	16	**46**	3.2	.961	H. Ehmke	30	190	12	10	0	4.22
RF	T. Cobb	490	.357	5	93	243	9	8	2	2.1	.969	E. Rommel	30	147	11	3	1	4.36
CF	A. Simmons	406	.392	15	108	247	10	4	2	2.5	.985	S. Gray	37	141	9	6	3	4.60
LF	W. French	326	.304	0	41	190	6	9	2	2.2	.956							
C	M. Cochrane	432	.338	12	80	**559**	85	9	11	**5.3**	.986							
OF	B. Lamar	324	.299	4	47	148	9	8	1	2.1	.952							
OF	Z. Wheat	247	.324	1	38	105	8	2	1	1.9	.983							
2B	E. Collins	225	.338	1	15	124	150	10	31	5.1	.965							
SS	C. Galloway	181	.265	0	22	115	150	15	20	4.6	.946							
1B	J. Foxx	130	.323	3	20	258	15	7	10	8.8	.975							

Washington

W-85 L-69

Bucky Harris

POS	Player	AB	BA	HR	RBI	PO	A	E	DP	TC/G	FA	Pitcher	G	IP	W	L	SV	ERA
1B	J. Judge	522	.308	2	71	1309	71	6	79	10.2	**.996**	H. Lisenbee	39	242	18	9	0	3.57
2B	B. Harris	475	.267	1	55	**316**	413	21	68	5.9	**.972**	S. Thurston	29	205	13	13	0	4.47
SS	B. Reeves	380	.255	1	39	194	296	41	36	5.5	.923	B. Hadley	30	199	14	6	0	2.85
3B	O. Bluege	503	.274	1	66	185	**337**	21	20	3.7	.961	F. Marberry	56	155	10	7	9	4.64
RF	S. Rice	603	.297	2	65	258	12	7	2	2.0	.975	G. Braxton	**58**	155	10	9	**13**	2.95
CF	T. Speaker	523	.327	2	73	278	12	10	5	2.5	.967	T. Zachary	15	110	4	7	0	3.67
LF	G. Goslin	581	.334	13	120	356	8	17	3	2.6	.955	W. Johnson	18	108	5	6	0	5.10
C	M. Ruel	428	.308	1	52	495	100	7	8	4.7	**.988**	B. Burke	36	100	3	2	0	3.96
OF	E. McNeely	185	.276	0	16	81	3	2	1	1.8	.977	G. Crowder	15	67	4	7	0	4.54
C	B. Tate	131	.313	1	24	148	24	4	4	4.5	.977							

Detroit

W-82 L-71

George Moriarty

POS	Player	AB	BA	HR	RBI	PO	A	E	DP	TC/G	FA	Pitcher	G	IP	W	L	SV	ERA
1B	L. Blue	365	.260	1	42	1019	68	18	99	10.6	.984	E. Whitehill	41	236	16	14	3	3.36
2B	C. Gehringer	508	.317	4	61	304	**438**	27	**84**	**6.4**	.965	L. Stoner	38	215	10	13	5	3.98
SS	J. Tavener	419	.274	5	59	246	356	33	79	5.6	.948	S. Gibson	33	190	11	12	0	3.69
3B	J. Warner	559	.267	1	45	156	277	**24**	34	3.3	.947	K. Holloway	36	183	11	12	6	4.07
RF	H. Heilmann	505	**.398**	14	120	218	11	8	5	1.8	.966	R. Collins	30	173	13	7	0	4.69
CF	H. Manush	593	.298	6	80	361	9	11	3	2.5	.971	O. Carroll	31	172	10	6	0	3.98
LF	B. Fothergill	527	.359	9	114	315	3	13	1	2.4	.961							
C	L. Woodall	246	.280	0	39	265	72	1	6	3.9	.997							
UT	M. McManus	369	.268	9	69	245	263	17	54		.968							
1B	J. Neun	204	.324	0	27	548	30	12	45	11.1	.980							
C	J. Bassler	200	.285	0	24	206	56	7	8	4.0	.974							
OF	A. Wingo	137	.234	0	20	43	6	6	2	1.6	.891							

Chicago

W-70 L-83

Ray Schalk

POS	Player	AB	BA	HR	RBI	PO	A	E	DP	TC/G	FA	Pitcher	G	IP	W	L	SV	ERA
1B	B. Clancy	464	.300	3	53	1184	81	11	76	10.4	.991	T. Lyons	39	**308**	**22**	14	2	2.84
2B	A. Ward	463	.270	5	56	275	437	27	66	5.4	.963	T. Thomas	40	**308**	19	16	1	2.98
SS	B. Hunnefield	365	.285	2	36	150	210	26	38	4.9	.933	T. Blankenship	37	237	12	17	0	5.06
3B	W. Kamm	540	.270	0	59	**236**	279	15	21	3.6	**.972**	S. Connally	43	198	10	15	5	4.08
RF	B. Barrett	556	.286	4	83	289	22	12	6	2.2	.963	R. Faber	18	111	4	7	0	4.55
CF	A. Metzler	543	.319	3	61	397	16	15	6	3.2	.965							
LF	B. Falk	535	.327	9	83	372	22	9	9	2.8	.978							
C	H. McCurdy	262	.286	1	27	261	55	9	8	4.0	.972							
C	B. Crouse	222	.239	0	20	202	79	8	10	3.6	.972							
SS	R. Peckinpaugh	217	.295	0	23	101	170	10	30	4.7	.964							

AMERICAN LEAGUE 1927, *cont.*

Team	POS	Player	AB	BA	HR	RBI	PO	A	E	DP	TC/G	FA	Pitcher	G	IP	W	L	SV	ERA
Cleveland	1B	G. Burns	549	.319	3	78	1362	102	15	111	10.6	.990	W. Hudlin	43	265	18	12	0	4.01
W-66 L-87	2B	L. Fonseca	428	.311	2	40	229	304	15	51	5.7	.973	J. Shaute	45	230	9	16	2	4.22
Jack McCallister	SS	J. Sewell	569	.316	1	92	**361**	**480**	33	80	5.7	**.962**	G. Buckeye	35	205	10	17	1	3.96
	3B	R. Lutzke	311	.251	0	41	120	199	21	24	3.5	.938	J. Miller	34	185	10	8	0	3.21
	RF	H. Summa	574	.286	4	74	242	12	12	3	1.8	.955	G. Uhle	25	153	8	9	1	4.34
	CF	F. Eichrodt	267	.221	0	25	170	13	4	6	2.3	.979	D. Levsen	25	80	3	7	0	5.49
	LF	C. Jamieson	489	.309	0	36	300	13	10	2	2.5	.969	G. Grant	25	75	4	6	1	4.46
	C	L. Sewell	470	.294	0	53	402	**119**	**20**	**14**	4.3	.963							
	3B	J. Hodapp	240	.304	5	40	69	132	14	15	3.2	.935							
	2B	F. Spurgeon	179	.251	1	19	124	150	18	28	5.6	.938							
St. Louis	1B	G. Sisler	614	.327	5	97	1374	**131**	**24**	**138**	10.3	.984	M. Gaston	37	254	13	17	1	5.00
W-59 L-94	2B	O. Melillo	356	.225	0	26	229	293	**36**	72	5.5	.935	E. Vangilder	44	203	10	12	1	4.79
Dan Howley	SS	W. Gerber	438	.224	0	45	290	427	41	**91**	5.4	.946	S. Jones	30	190	8	14	0	4.32
	3B	F. O'Rourke	538	.268	1	39	183	244	20	27	**3.7**	.955	E. Wingard	38	156	2	13	0	6.56
	RF	H. Rice	520	.287	7	68	277	26	20	7	2.5	.938	L. Stewart	27	156	8	11	1	4.28
	CF	B. Miller	492	.325	5	75	309	9	10	3	2.6	.970	E. Nevers	27	95	3	8	2	4.94
	LF	K. Williams	421	.323	17	74	260	15	10	4	2.5	.965	W. Ballou	21	90	5	6	0	4.78
	C	W. Schang	263	.319	5	42	213	73	7	10	3.9	.976	T. Zachary	13	78	4	6	0	4.37
	23	S. Adams	259	.266	0	29	159	190	21	35		.943	G. Crowder	21	74	3	5	3	5.01
	OF	H. Bennett	256	.266	3	30	118	5	7	1	2.4	.946							
	C	S. O'Neill	191	.230	1	22	180	57	4	8	4.0	.983							
	OF	F. Schulte	189	.317	3	34	117	3	11	0	2.7	.916							
Boston	1B	P. Todt	516	.236	6	52	1401	112	13	121	11.0	.991	H. Wiltse	36	219	10	18	1	5.10
W-51 L-103	2B	B. Regan	468	.274	2	66	283	397	28	76	5.9	.960	S. Harriss	44	218	14	**21**	1	4.18
Bill Carrigan	SS	B. Myer	469	.288	2	47	239	311	35	64	5.8	.940	T. Welzer	37	182	6	11	1	4.46
	3B	B. Rogell	207	.266	2	28	49	123	6	8	3.4	.966	D. MacFayden	34	160	5	8	2	4.27
	RF	J. Tobin	374	.310	2	40	152	10	9	4	1.8	.947	R. Ruffing	26	158	5	13	2	4.66
	CF	I. Flagstead	466	.285	4	69	326	19	5	4	2.7	.986	J. Russell	34	147	4	9	0	4.10
	LF	W. Shaner	406	.273	3	49	220	13	11	1	2.3	.955	D. Lundgren	30	136	5	12	0	6.27
	C	G. Hartley	244	.275	1	31	214	51	9	5	3.2	.967							
	UT	J. Rothrock	428	.259	1	36	323	284	26	63		.959							
	OF	C. Carlyle	278	.234	1	28	127	10	5	0	1.7	.965							
	C	F. Hofmann	217	.272	0	24	241	59	18	4	3.9	.943							
	3B	R. Rollings	184	.266	0	9	39	66	7	2	2.5	.938							
	OF	B. Jacobson	155	.245	0	24	90	4	2	0	2.5	.979							

BATTING AND BASE RUNNING LEADERS

Batting Average
- H. Heilmann, DET .398
- A. Simmons, PHI .392
- L. Gehrig, NY .373
- B. Fothergill, DET .359
- T. Cobb, PHI .357

Slugging Average
- B. Ruth, NY .772
- L. Gehrig, NY .765
- A. Simmons, PHI .645
- H. Heilmann, DET .616
- K. Williams, STL .527

Home Runs
- B. Ruth, NY 60
- L. Gehrig, NY 47
- T. Lazzeri, NY 18
- K. Williams, STL 17
- A. Simmons, PHI 15

Total Bases
- L. Gehrig, NY 447
- B. Ruth, NY 417
- E. Combs, NY 331
- H. Heilmann, DET 311
- G. Goslin, WAS 300

Runs Batted In
- L. Gehrig, NY 175
- B. Ruth, NY 164
- H. Heilmann, DET 120
- G. Goslin, WAS 120
- B. Fothergill, DET 114

Stolen Bases
- G. Sisler, STL 27
- B. Meusel, NY 24
- J. Neun, DET 22
- T. Cobb, PHI 22
- T. Lazzeri, NY 22

Hits
- E. Combs, NY 231
- L. Gehrig, NY 218
- H. Heilmann, DET 201
- G. Sisler, STL 201

Base on Balls
- B. Ruth, NY 138
- L. Gehrig, NY 109
- M. Bishop, PHI 105
- H. Heilmann, DET 72

Home Run Percentage
- B. Ruth, NY 11.1
- L. Gehrig, NY 8.0
- K. Williams, STL 4.0
- A. Simmons, PHI 3.7

Runs
- B. Ruth, NY 158
- L. Gehrig, NY 149
- E. Combs, NY 137
- C. Gehringer, DET 110

Doubles
- L. Gehrig, NY 52
- G. Burns, CLE 51
- H. Heilmann, DET 50
- J. Sewell, CLE 48

Triples
- E. Combs, NY 23
- L. Gehrig, NY 18
- H. Manush, DET 18
- G. Goslin, WAS 15

PITCHING LEADERS

Winning Percentage
- W. Hoyt, NY .759
- U. Shocker, NY .750
- W. Moore, NY .731
- H. Pennock, NY .704
- H. Lisenbee, WAS .667

Earned Run Average
- W. Moore, NY 2.28
- W. Hoyt, NY 2.63
- U. Shocker, NY 2.84
- T. Lyons, CHI 2.84
- B. Hadley, WAS 2.85

Wins
- W. Hoyt, NY 22
- T. Lyons, CHI 22
- L. Grove, PHI 20
- H. Pennock, NY 19
- W. Moore, NY 19
- T. Thomas, CHI 19

Saves
- W. Moore, NY 13
- G. Braxton, WAS 13
- L. Grove, PHI 9
- F. Marberry, WAS 9
- K. Holloway, DET 6
- J. Pate, PHI 6

Strikeouts
- L. Grove, PHI 174
- R. Walberg, PHI 136
- T. Thomas, CHI 107
- H. Lisenbee, WAS 105
- G. Braxton, WAS 95
- E. Whitehill, DET 95

Complete Games
- T. Lyons, CHI 30
- T. Thomas, CHI 24
- W. Hoyt, NY 23
- M. Gaston, STL 21
- H. Pennock, NY 18
- W. Hudlin, CLE 18

Fewest Hits/9 Innings
- W. Moore, NY 7.82
- T. Thomas, CHI 7.93
- B. Hadley, WAS 8.02
- H. Lisenbee, WAS 8.22

Shutouts
- H. Lisenbee, WAS 4

Fewest Walks/9 Innings
- J. Quinn, PHI 1.61
- U. Shocker, NY 1.85
- W. Hoyt, NY 1.90
- T. Lyons, CHI 1.96

Most Strikeouts/9 Inn.
- L. Grove, PHI 5.97
- R. Walberg, PHI 4.91
- R. Ruffing, BOS 4.38
- G. Uhle, CLE 4.05

Innings
- T. Lyons, CHI 308
- T. Thomas, CHI 308
- W. Hudlin, CLE 265
- L. Grove, PHI 262

Games Pitched
- G. Braxton, WAS 58
- F. Marberry, WAS 56
- L. Grove, PHI 51
- W. Moore, NY 50

							Batting						Fielding			Pitching					
	W	L	PCT	GB	R	OR	2B	3B	HR	BA	SA	SB	E	DP	FA	CG	BB	SO	ShO	SV	ERA
New York	110	44	.714		**975**	**599**	291	**103**	**158**	**.307**	**.489**	90	195	123	.969	82	**409**	431	**11**	20	**3.20**
Philadelphia	91	63	.591	19	841	726	281	70	56	.303	.414	98	190	124	.970	66	442	**553**	8	**24**	3.95
Washington	85	69	.552	25	782	730	268	87	29	.287	.386	133	195	125	.969	62	491	497	10	23	3.95
Detroit	82	71	.536	27.5	845	805	282	100	51	.289	.409	**141**	206	**173**	.968	75	577	421	5	17	4.12
Chicago	70	83	.458	39.5	662	708	285	61	36	.278	.378	90	**178**	131	**.971**	**85**	440	365	10	8	3.91
Cleveland	66	87	.431	43.5	668	766	**321**	52	26	.283	.379	63	201	146	.968	72	508	366	5	8	4.27
St. Louis	59	94	.386	50.5	724	904	262	59	55	.276	.380	91	248	166	.960	80	604	385	4	8	4.95
Boston	51	103	.331	59	597	856	271	78	28	.259	.357	82	228	162	.964	63	558	381	6	7	4.68
					6094	6094	2261	610	439	.285	.399	788	1641	1150	.967	585	4029	3399	59	115	4.13

NATIONAL LEAGUE 1928

Team	POS	Player	AB	BA	HR	RBI	PO	A	E	DP	TC/G	FA	Pitcher	G	IP	W	L	SV	ERA
St. Louis	1B	J. Bottomley	576	.325	**31**	**136**	1454	52	**20**	113	10.3	.987	B. Sherdel	38	249	21	10	**5**	2.86
	2B	F. Frisch	547	.300	10	86	383	474	21	80	6.3	**.976**	G. Alexander	34	244	16	9	2	3.36
W-95 L-59	SS	R. Maranville	366	.240	1	34	236	362	19	57	5.5	.969	J. Haines	33	240	20	8	0	3.18
	3B	W. Holm	386	.277	3	47	100	145	22	9	3.2	.918	F. Rhem	28	170	11	8	3	4.14
Bill McKechnie	RF	G. Harper	272	.305	17	58	156	13	2	2	2.0	.988	C. Mitchell	19	150	8	9	0	3.30
	CF	T. Douthit	648	.295	3	43	547	10	9	4	3.7	.984	S. Johnson	34	120	8	4	3	3.90
	LF	C. Hafey	520	.337	27	111	287	13	11	3	2.3	.965	A. Reinhart	23	75	4	6	2	2.87
	C	J. Wilson	411	.258	2	50	394*	82*	8	13*	4.0	.983							
	3B	A. High	368	.285	6	37	56	117	12	10	2.5	.935							
	OF	W. Roettger	261	.341	6	44	152	2	3	1	2.4	.981							
	SS	T. Thevenow	171	.205	0	13	100	158	19	29	4.3	.931							
New York	1B	B. Terry	568	.326	17	101	**1584**	78	12	**148**	**11.2**	.993	L. Benton	42	310	**25**	9	4	2.73
	2B	A. Cohen	504	.274	9	59	304	434	24	90	6.0	.969	F. Fitzsimmons	40	261	20	9	1	3.68
W-93 L-61	SS	T. Jackson	537	.270	14	77	354	**547**	45	112	**6.3**	.952	J. Genewich	26	158	11	4	3	3.18
	3B	F. Lindstrom	646	.358	14	107	145	**340**	21	34	3.3	**.958**	C. Hubbell	20	124	10	6	1	2.83
John McGraw	RF	M. Ott	435	.322	18	77	214	14	7	4	2.0	.970	V. Aldridge	22	119	4	7	2	4.83
	CF	J. Welsh	476	.307	9	54	310	8	6	3	2.8	.981	J. Faulkner	38	117	9	8	2	3.53
	LF	L. O'Doul	354	.319	8	46	149	4	6	0	1.7	.962	D. Henry	17	64	3	6	1	3.80
	C	S. Hogan	411	.333	10	71	389	57	10	11	3.7	.978							
	UT	A. Reese	406	.308	6	44	232	136	16	21		.958							
	OF	L. Mann	193	.264	2	25	97	3	5	1	1.5	.952							
	OF	E. Roush	163	.252	2	13	100	7	5	0	2.9	.955							
	C	B. O'Farrell	133	.195	2	20	138	27	2	1	2.7	.988							
Chicago	1B	C. Grimm	547	.294	5	62	1458	70	10	147	10.5	**.993**	P. Malone	42	251	18	13	2	2.84
	2B	F. Maguire	574	.279	1	41	**410**	**524**	23	**126**	**6.9**	.976	S. Blake	34	241	17	11	1	2.47
W-91 L-63	SS	W. English	475	.299	2	34	245	382	36	85	5.8	.946	C. Root	40	237	14	18	2	3.57
	3B	C. Beck	483	.257	3	52	74	156	10	24	2.8	.958	G. Bush	42	204	15	6	2	3.83
Joe McCarthy	RF	K. Cuyler	499	.285	17	79	257	18	5	3	2.2	.982	A. Nehf	31	177	13	7	0	2.65
	CF	H. Wilson	520	.313	**31**	120	321	11	14	2	2.4	.960	P. Jones	39	154	10	6	3	4.03
	LF	R. Stephenson	512	.324	8	90	268	10	5	1	2.1	.982							
	C	G. Hartnett	388	.302	14	57	455	**103**	6	14	**4.8**	**.989**							
	3B	J. Butler	174	.270	0	16	51	120	9	9	3.1	.950							
	C	M. Gonzalez	158	.272	1	21	198	35	4	8	5.3	.983							
	OF	E. Webb	140	.250	3	23	65	4	1	0	2.3	.986							
Pittsburgh	1B	G. Grantham	440	.323	10	85	1117	71	17	83	10.1	.986	B. Grimes	**48**	**331**	**25**	14	3	2.99
	2B	S. Adams	539	.276	0	38	265	343	18	54	5.9	.971	C. Hill	36	237	16	10	2	3.53
W-85 L-67	SS	G. Wright	407	.310	8	66	194	301	39	59	5.3	.927	R. Kremer	34	219	15	13	0	4.64
	3B	P. Traynor	569	.337	3	124	175	296	**27**	15	**3.5**	.946	F. Fussell	28	160	8	9	1	3.61
Donie Bush	RF	P. Waner	602	.370	6	86	299	14	8	0	2.5	.975	J. Dawson	31	129	7	7	3	3.29
	CF	L. Waner	**659**	.335	5	61	418	15	9	4	2.9	.980	E. Brame	24	96	7	4	0	5.08
	LF	F. Brickell	202	.322	3	41	107	6	5	1	2.4	.958	J. Miljus	21	70	5	7	1	5.30
	C	C. Hargreaves	260	.285	1	32	230	47	11*	7	3.7	.962							
	2S	D. Bartell	233	.305	1	36	158	199	16	40		.957							
	OF	C. Barnhart	196	.296	4	30	96	3	3	0	2.1	.971							
	OF	P. Scott	177	.311	5	33	90	5	2	5	2.3	.979							
	OF	A. Comorosky	176	.295	2	34	118	2	4	1	2.5	.968							
Cincinnati	1B	G. Kelly	402	.296	3	58	894	69	9	99	9.8	.991	E. Rixey	43	291	19	18	2	3.43
	2B	H. Critz	641	.296	5	52	333	497	25	124	5.6	.971	D. Luque	33	234	11	10	1	3.57
	SS	H. Ford	506	.241	0	54	**355**	508	25	**128**	6.0	**.972**	R. Kolp	44	209	13	10	3	3.19
W-78 L-74	3B	C. Dressen	498	.291	1	59	122	283	**27**	27	3.2	.938	R. Lucas	27	167	13	9	1	3.39
	RF	C. Walker	427	.279	6	73	289	9	14	3	2.6	.955	P. Donohue	23	150	7	11	0	4.74
Jack Hendricks	CF	E. Allen	485	.305	1	62	348	12	7	4	2.8	.981							
	LF	B. Zitzmann	266	.297	3	33	155	4	7	2	2.1	.958							
	C	V. Picinich	324	.302	7	35	279	65	6	6	3.8	.983							
	1B	W. Pipp	272	.283	2	26	673	40	8	69	10.0	.989							
	OF	M. Callaghan	238	.290	0	24	140	5	3	2	2.1	.980							
	OF	P. Purdy	223	.309	0	25	137	3	5	1	2.4	.966							
	C	B. Hargrave	190	.295	0	23	181	37	2	2	3.9	.991							
Brooklyn	1B	D. Bissonette	587	.320	25	106	1482	77	**20**	95	10.2	.987	D. Vance	38	280	22	10	2	**2.09**
	2B	J. Flowers	339	.274	2	44	260	270	16	46	5.8	.971	D. McWeeny	42	244	14	14	1	3.17
	SS	D. Bancroft	515	.247	0	51	350	484	46	66	5.9	.948	J. Petty	40	234	15	15	1	4.04
W-77 L-76	3B	H. Hendrick	425	.318	11	59	74	200	26	19	3.3	.913	W. Clark	40	195	12	9	3	2.68
	RF	B. Herman	486	.340	12	91	225	12	16	2	2.0	.937	J. Elliott	41	192	9	14	1	3.89
Wilbert Robinson	CF	M. Carey	296	.247	2	19	202	8	3	1	2.2	.986	B. Doak	28	99	3	8	3	3.26
	LF	R. Bressler	501	.295	4	70	254	7	4	0	1.9	.985							
	C	H. DeBerry	258	.252	0	23	377	56	10	5	5.5	.977							
	UT	H. Riconda	281	.224	3	35	181	222	20	25		.953							
	OF	T. Tyson	210	.271	1	21	130	6	5	3	2.6	.965							
	OF	J. Statz	171	.234	0	16	107	3	4	2	1.5	.965							
Boston	1B	G. Sisler	491	.340	4	68	1188	86*	15	100	10.9	.988	B. Smith	38	244	13	17	2	3.87
	2B	R. Hornsby	486	**.387**	21	94	295	450	21	85	5.5	.973	E. Brandt	38	225	9	**21**	0	5.07
	SS	D. Farrell	483	.215	3	43	289	418	**51**	73	5.7	.933	A. Delaney	39	192	9	17	2	3.79
W-50 L-103	3B	L. Bell	591	.277	10	91	**177**	314	**27**	**37**	3.4	.948	K. Greenfield	32	144	3	11	0	5.32
	RF	L. Richbourg	612	.337	2	52	367	8	11	1	2.6	.972	J. Cooney	24	90	3	7	1	4.32
Jack Slattery	CF	J. Smith	254	.280	1	32	165	4	2	0	2.6	.988	J. Genewich	13	81	3	7	0	4.13
W-11 L-20	LF	E. Brown	523	.268	2	59	302	6	13	3	2.5	.960							
	C	Z. Taylor	399	.251	2	30	367	83	7	8	3.7	.985							
Rogers Hornsby	OF	E. Moore	215	.237	2	18	131	7	6	3	2.7	.958							
W-39 L-83																			

NATIONAL LEAGUE 1928, *cont.*

Philadelphia

W-43 L-109

Burt Shotton

POS	Player	AB	BA	HR	RBI	PO	A	E	DP	TC/G	FA
1B	D. Hurst	396	.285	19	64	964	68	12	92	10.0	.989
2B	F. Thompson	634	.287	3	50	409	509	**32**	109	6.3	.966
SS	H. Sand	426	.211	0	38	290	410	36	94	5.4	.951
3B	P. Whitney	585	.301	10	103	171	293	22	27	3.3	.955
RF	C. Klein	253	.360	11	34	128	7	3	0	2.2	.978
CF	D. Sothern	579	.285	5	38	358	19	14	7	2.9	.964
LF	F. Leach	588	.304	13	96	296	11	7	5	2.6	.978
C	W. Lerian	239	.272	2	25	239	61	7	12	4.1	.977
OF	C. Williams	238	.256	12	37	118	9	0	0	1.8	1.000
C	S. Davis	163	.282	3	18	149	46	4	7	4.1	.980

Pitcher	G	IP	W	L	SV	ERA
R. Benge	40	202	8	18	1	4.55
J. Ring	35	173	4	17	1	6.40
L. Sweetland	37	135	3	15	2	6.58
A. Ferguson	34	135	5	10	2	5.88
B. McGraw	39	132	7	8	1	4.64
C. Willoughby	35	131	6	5	1	5.30
A. Walsh	38	122	4	9	2	6.18
R. Miller	33	108	0	12	1	5.42

BATTING AND BASE RUNNING LEADERS

Batting Average
R. Hornsby, BOS .387
P. Waner, PIT .370
F. Lindstrom, NY .358
G. Sisler, BOS .340
B. Herman, BKN .340

Slugging Average
R. Hornsby, BOS .632
J. Bottomley, STL .628
C. Hafey, STL .604
H. Wilson, CHI .588
P. Waner, PIT .547

Home Runs
H. Wilson, CHI 31
J. Bottomley, STL 31
C. Hafey, STL 27
D. Bissonette, BKN 25
R. Hornsby, BOS 21

Total Bases
J. Bottomley, STL 362
F. Lindstrom, NY 330
P. Waner, PIT 329
D. Bissonette, BKN 319
C. Hafey, STL 314

Runs Batted In
J. Bottomley, STL 136
P. Traynor, PIT 124
H. Wilson, CHI 120
C. Hafey, STL 111
F. Lindstrom, NY 107

Stolen Bases
K. Cuyler, CHI 37
F. Frisch, STL 29
C. Walker, CIN 19
F. Thompson, PHI 19
M. Carey, BKN 18
H. Critz, CIN 18

Hits
F. Lindstrom, NY 231
P. Waner, PIT 223
L. Waner, PIT 221
L. Richbourg, BOS 206

Base on Balls
R. Hornsby, BOS 107
T. Douthit, STL 84
R. Bressler, BKN 80
H. Wilson, CHI 77
P. Waner, PIT 77

Home Run Percentage
H. Wilson, CHI 6.0
G. Harper, NY, STL 5.8
J. Bottomley, STL 5.4
C. Hafey, STL 5.2

Runs
P. Waner, PIT 142
J. Bottomley, STL 123
L. Waner, PIT 121
T. Douthit, STL 111

Doubles
P. Waner, PIT 50
C. Hafey, STL 46
R. Hornsby, BOS 42
J. Bottomley, STL 42

Triples
J. Bottomley, STL 20
P. Waner, PIT 19
L. Waner, PIT 14
R. Bressler, BKN 13
D. Bissonette, BKN 13

PITCHING LEADERS

Winning Percentage
L. Benton, NY .735
J. Haines, STL .714
G. Bush, CHI .714
F. Fitzsimmons, NY .690
D. Vance, BKN .688

Earned Run Average
D. Vance, BKN 2.09
S. Blake, CHI 2.47
A. Nehf, CHI 2.65
W. Clark, BKN 2.68
L. Benton, NY 2.73

Wins
L. Benton, NY 25
B. Grimes, PIT 25
D. Vance, BKN 22
B. Sherdel, STL 21
J. Haines, STL 20
F. Fitzsimmons, NY 20

Saves
H. Haid, STL 5
B. Sherdel, STL 5
L. Benton, NY 4
H. Carlson, CHI 4

Strikeouts
D. Vance, BKN 200
P. Malone, CHI 155
C. Root, CHI 122
B. Grimes, PIT 97
L. Benton, NY 90

Complete Games
L. Benton, NY 28
B. Grimes, PIT 28
D. Vance, BKN 24
B. Sherdel, STL 20
J. Haines, STL 20

Fewest Hits/9 Innings
D. Vance, BKN 7.26
S. Blake, CHI 7.82
P. Malone, CHI 7.83
D. McWeeny, BKN 8.04

Shutouts
R. Lucas, CIN 4
S. Blake, CHI 4
D. McWeeny, BKN 4
D. Vance, BKN 4
B. Grimes, PIT 4

Fewest Walks/9 Innings
G. Alexander, STL 1.37
B. Sherdel, STL 2.03
L. Benton, NY 2.06
E. Rixey, CIN 2.07

Most Strikeouts/9 Inn.
D. Vance, BKN 6.42
P. Malone, CHI 5.57
C. Root, CHI 4.63
W. Clark, BKN 3.93

Innings
B. Grimes, PIT 331
L. Benton, NY 310
E. Rixey, CIN 291
D. Vance, BKN 280

Games Pitched
B. Grimes, PIT 48
R. Kolp, CIN 44
E. Rixey, CIN 43

							Batting						Fielding			Pitching					
	W	L	PCT	GB	R	OR	2B	3B	HR	BA	SA	SB	E	DP	FA	CG	BB	SO	ShO	SV	ERA
St. Louis	95	59	.617		807	636	**292**	70	113	.281	.425	82	160	134	.974	**83**	**399**	422	4	**21**	3.38
New York	93	61	.604	2	807	653	276	59	**118**	.293	**.430**	62	178	175	.972	79	405	399	7	16	3.67
Chicago	91	63	.591	4	714	**615**	251	64	92	.278	.402	**83**	**156**	176	**.975**	75	508	531	12	14	3.40
Pittsburgh	85	67	.559	9	**837**	704	246	**100**	52	**.309**	.421	64	201	123	.967	82	446	385	8	11	3.95
Cincinnati	78	74	.513	16	648	686	229	67	32	.280	.368	**83**	162	**194**	.974	68	410	355	11	11	3.94
Brooklyn	77	76	.503	17.5	665	640	229	70	66	.266	.374	81	217	113	.965	75	468	**551**	**16**	15	**3.25**
Boston	50	103	.327	44.5	631	878	241	41	52	.275	.367	60	193	141	.969	54	524	343	1	6	4.83
Philadelphia	43	109	.283	51	660	957	257	47	85	.267	.382	53	181	171	.971	42	671	403	4	11	5.52
					5769	5769	2021	518	610	.281	.396	568	1448	1227	.971	558	3831	3389	63	105	3.99

AMERICAN LEAGUE 1928

New York

W-101 L-53

Miller Huggins

POS	Player	AB	BA	HR	RBI	PO	A	E	DP	TC/G	FA
1B	L. Gehrig	562	.374	27	**142**	**1488**	79	**18**	112	10.3	.989
2B	T. Lazzeri	404	.332	10	82	236	331	26	56	5.1	.956
SS	M. Koenig	533	.319	4	63	260	328	49	69	5.1	.923
3B	J. Dugan	312	.276	6	34	87	129	11	13	2.5	.952
RF	B. Ruth	536	.323	**54**	**142**	304	9	8	0	2.1	.975
CF	E. Combs	626	.310	7	56	424	11	9	7	3.0	.980
LF	B. Meusel	518	.297	11	113	259	16	7	6	2.2	.975
C	J. Grabowski	202	.238	1	21	265	32	4	8	4.0	.987
2S	L. Durocher	296	.270	0	31	158	274	18	42		.960
3B	G. Robertson	251	.291	1	36	75	112	15	5	2.9	.926
C	B. Bengough	161	.267	0	9	206	37	2	7	4.2	.992

Pitcher	G	IP	W	L	SV	ERA
G. Pipgras	46	**301**	**24**	13	3	3.38
W. Hoyt	42	273	23	7	**8**	3.36
H. Pennock	28	211	17	6	3	2.56
H. Johnson	31	199	14	9	0	4.30
A. Shealy	23	96	8	6	2	5.06
W. Moore	35	60	4	4	2	4.18

AMERICAN LEAGUE 1928, *cont.*

Team	POS	Player	AB	BA	HR	RBI	PO	A	E	DP	TC/G	FA	Pitcher	G	IP	W	L	SV	ERA
Philadelphia	1B	J. Hauser	300	.260	16	59	811	41	12	51	9.8	.986	L. Grove	39	262	**24**	8	4	2.58
W-98 L-55	2B	M. Bishop	472	.316	6	50	284	371	15	62	5.4	**.978**	R. Walberg	38	236	17	12	1	3.55
Connie Mack	SS	J. Boley	425	.264	0	49	244	320	30	51	4.5	.949	J. Quinn	31	211	18	7	1	2.90
	3B	S. Hale	314	.309	4	58	86	189	**20**	17	3.7	.932	E. Rommel	43	174	13	5	4	3.06
	RF	T. Cobb	353	.323	1	40	154	7	6	0	2.0	.964	G. Earnshaw	26	158	7	7	1	3.81
	CF	B. Miller	510	.329	8	85	298	8	10	2	2.4	.968	H. Ehmke	23	139	9	8	0	3.62
	LF	A. Simmons	464	.351	15	107	231	10	3	2	2.1	.988	O. Orwoll	27	106	6	5	2	4.58
	C	M. Cochrane	468	.293	10	57	**645**	71	**25**	8	**5.7**	.966							
	UT	J. Foxx	400	.328	13	79	412	154	17	32		.971							
	OF	M. Haas	332	.280	6	39	175	9	5	1	2.3	.974							
	UT	J. Dykes	242	.277	5	30	166	164	9	21		.973							
	OF	T. Speaker	191	.267	3	29	111	8	3	1	2.4	.975							
	1P	O. Orwoll	170	.306	0	22	328	41	7	32		.981							
St. Louis	1B	L. Blue	549	.281	14	80	1472	**107**	17	**121**	10.4	.989	S. Gray	35	263	20	12	3	3.19
W-82 L-72	2B	O. Brannan	483	.244	10	66	272	434	26	74	5.4	.964	G. Crowder	41	244	21	5	2	3.69
Dan Howley	SS	R. Kress	560	.273	3	81	**318**	400	**55**	99	5.2	.929	J. Ogden	38	243	15	16	2	4.15
	3B	F. O'Rourke	391	.263	1	62	149	160	15	13	3.4	.954	G. Blaeholder	38	214	10	15	3	4.37
	RF	E. McNeely	496	.236	0	44	229	19	4	2	2.1	.984	L. Stewart	29	143	7	9	3	4.67
	CF	F. Schulte	556	.286	7	85	419	21	12	6	3.2	.973	D. Coffman	29	86	4	5	1	6.09
	LF	H. Manush	638	.378	13	108	355	6	3	2	2.4	.992							
	C	W. Schang	245	.286	3	39	263	46	5	5	3.8	.984							
	C	C. Manion	243	.226	2	31	302	49	7	10	5.0	.980							
	OF	F. McGowan	168	.363	2	18	99	3	4	1	2.3	.962							
	3B	L. Bettencourt	159	.283	4	24	38	68	6	4	2.7	.946							
Washington	1B	J. Judge	542	.306	3	93	1412	92	6	118	10.1	.996	B. Hadley	33	232	12	13	0	3.54
W-75 L-79	2B	B. Harris	358	.204	0	28	251	326	18	61	6.2	.970	S. Jones	30	225	17	7	0	2.84
Bucky Harris	SS	B. Reeves	353	.303	3	42	159	190	35	32	5.8	.909	G. Braxton	38	218	13	11	6	**2.51**
	3B	O. Bluege	518	.297	2	75	150	**330**	**20**	34	**3.5**	.960	F. Marberry	**48**	161	13	13	3	3.85
	RF	S. Rice	616	.328	2	55	240	11	7	5	1.8	.973	M. Gaston	28	149	6	12	0	5.51
	CF	R. Barnes	417	.302	6	51	255	16	6	2	2.7	.978	L. Brown	27	107	4	4	1	4.04
	LF	G. Goslin	456	**.379**	17	102	266	14	11	4	2.3	.962	T. Zachary	20	103	6	9	0	5.44
	C	M. Ruel	350	.257	0	55	397	73	5	5	4.7	**.989**							
	OF	S. West	378	.302	3	40	210	13	1	0	1.9	**.996**							
	SS	J. Cronin	227	.242	0	25	133	190	16	42	5.4	.953							
	2B	J. Hayes	210	.257	0	22	101	123	6	26	5.6	.974							
	C	E. Kenna	118	.297	1	20	104	26	8	3	4.1	.942							
Chicago	1B	B. Clancy	487	.271	2	37	1175	93	12	104	10.0	.991	T. Thomas	36	283	17	16	2	3.08
W-72 L-82	2B	B. Hunnefield	333	.294	2	24	160	239	14	47	5.0	.966	T. Lyons	39	240	15	14	6	3.98
Ray Schalk	SS	B. Cissell	443	.260	1	60	255	360	41	77	5.3	.938	G. Adkins	36	225	10	16	1	3.73
W-32 L-42	3B	W. Kamm	552	.308	1	84	**243**	278	12	33	3.4	**.977**	R. Faber	27	201	13	9	0	3.75
Lena Blackburne	RF	A. Metzler	464	.304	3	55	288	11	10	3	2.3	.968	T. Blankenship	27	158	9	11	0	4.61
W-40 L-40	CF	J. Mostil	503	.270	0	51	394	18	10	3	3.2	.976	E. Walsh	14	78	4	7	0	4.96
	LF	B. Falk	286	.290	1	37	164	9	5	0	2.3	.972							
	C	B. Crouse	218	.252	2	20	196	61	11	3	3.5	.959							
	OF	C. Reynolds	291	.323	2	36	135	6	3	2	1.9	.979							
	2S	B. Redfern	261	.234	0	35	166	223	24	39		.942							
	O2	B. Barrett	235	.277	3	26	122	62	5	7		.974							
	C	M. Berg	224	.246	0	29	256	52	3	8	4.3	.990							
Detroit	1B	B. Sweeney	309	.252	0	19	675	55	5	51	9.8	.993	O. Carroll	34	231	16	12	2	3.27
W-68 L-86	2B	C. Gehringer	603	.320	6	74	377	**507**	35	101	6.0	.962	E. Whitehill	31	196	11	16	0	4.31
George Moriarty	SS	J. Tavener	473	.260	5	52	302	405	42	81	**5.7**	.944	V. Sorrell	29	171	8	11	0	4.79
	3B	M. McManus	500	.288	8	73	114	183	14	12	3.4	.955	E. Vangilder	38	156	11	10	5	3.91
	RF	H. Heilmann	558	.328	14	107	215	17	7	2	1.9	.971	L. Stoner	36	126	5	8	4	4.35
	CF	H. Rice	510	.302	6	81	346	9	14	0	2.9	.962	K. Holloway	30	120	4	8	2	4.34
	LF	B. Fothergill	347	.317	3	63	179	6	8	0	2.1	.959	S. Gibson	20	120	5	8	0	5.42
	C	P. Hargrave	321	.274	10	63	301	35	8	5	3.9	.977	H. Billings	21	111	5	10	0	5.12
	OF	A. Wingo	242	.285	2	30	144	5	5	1	2.2	.968	G. Smith	39	106	1	1	3	4.42
	3B	J. Warner	206	.214	0	13	62	107	10	6	3.4	.944							
	C	L. Woodall	186	.210	0	13	218	44	2	3	4.3	.992							
	OF	J. Stone	113	.354	2	21	49	2	2	0	2.0	.962							
Cleveland	1B	L. Fonseca	263	.327	3	36	541	41	0	65	10.4	1.000	J. Shaute	36	254	13	17	2	4.04
W-62 L-92	2B	C. Lind	**650**	.294	1	54	**390**	505	**37**	**116**	**6.1**	.960	W. Hudlin	42	220	14	14	7	4.04
Roger Peckinpaugh	SS	J. Sewell	588	.323	4	70	297	**438**	28	**103**	5.6	**.963**	G. Uhle	31	214	12	17	1	4.07
	3B	J. Hodapp	449	.323	2	73	103	220	19	20	3.4	.944	J. Miller	25	158	8	9	0	4.44
	RF	H. Summa	504	.284	3	57	223	12	7	5	1.8	.971	G. Grant	28	155	10	8	0	5.04
	CF	S. Langford	427	.276	4	50	239	5	7	2	2.3	.972	B. Bayne	37	109	2	5	3	5.13
	LF	C. Jamieson	433	.307	1	37	282	22	5	1	2.8	.984							
	C	L. Sewell	411	.270	3	52	430	**117**	16	**13**	4.8	.972							
	UT	E. Morgan	265	.313	4	54	387	69	18	41		.962							
	1B	G. Burns	209	.249	5	30	470	38	8	44	9.7	.984							

AMERICAN LEAGUE 1928, *cont.*

Boston

W-57 L-96

Bill Carrigan

POS	Player	AB	BA	HR	RBI	PO	A	E	DP	TC/G	FA	Pitcher	G	IP	W	L	SV	ERA
1B	P. Todt	539	.252	12	73	1486	94	5	96	**11.0**	**.997**	R. Ruffing	42	289	10	**25**	2	3.89
2B	B. Regan	511	.264	7	75	294	467	29	87	5.8	.963	E. Morris	47	258	19	15	5	3.53
SS	W. Gerber	300	.213	0	28	201	328	25	50	5.4	.955	J. Russell	32	201	11	14	0	3.84
3B	B. Myer	536	.313	1	44	137	306	14	**35**	3.2	.969	D. MacFayden	33	195	9	15	0	4.75
RF	D. Taitt	482	.299	3	61	251	19	7	8	2.0	.975	S. Harriss	27	128	8	11	1	4.63
CF	I. Flagstead	510	.290	1	39	346	18	10	4	2.8	.973							
LF	K. Williams	462	.303	8	67	253	10	8	0	2.1	.970							
C	F. Hofmann	199	.226	0	16	223	44	5	7	3.8	.982							
UT	J. Rothrock	344	.267	3	22	242	61	12	14		.962							
S2	B. Rogell	296	.233	0	29	150	232	23	34		.943							
C	C. Berry	177	.260	1	19	153	34	8	2	3.1	.959							
C	J. Heving	158	.259	0	11	153	25	6	2	3.0	.967							

BATTING AND BASE RUNNING LEADERS

Batting Average
- G. Goslin, WAS .379
- H. Manush, STL .378
- L. Gehrig, NY .374
- A. Simmons, PHI .351
- T. Lazzeri, NY .332

Slugging Average
- B. Ruth, NY .709
- L. Gehrig, NY .648
- G. Goslin, WAS .614
- H. Manush, STL .575
- A. Simmons, PHI .558

Home Runs
- B. Ruth, NY 54
- L. Gehrig, NY 27
- G. Goslin, WAS 17
- J. Hauser, PHI 16
- A. Simmons, PHI 15

Total Bases
- B. Ruth, NY 380
- H. Manush, STL 367
- L. Gehrig, NY 364
- E. Combs, NY 290
- H. Heilmann, DET 283

Runs Batted In
- B. Ruth, NY 142
- L. Gehrig, NY 142
- B. Meusel, NY 113
- H. Manush, STL 108
- A. Simmons, PHI 107
- H. Heilmann, DET 107

Stolen Bases
- B. Myer, BOS 30
- J. Mostil, CHI 23
- H. Rice, DET 20
- B. Cissell, CHI 18
- O. Bluege, WAS 18

Hits
- H. Manush, STL 241
- L. Gehrig, NY 210
- S. Rice, WAS 202
- E. Combs, NY 194

Base on Balls
- B. Ruth, NY 135
- L. Blue, STL 105
- M. Bishop, PHI 97
- L. Gehrig, NY 95

Home Run Percentage
- B. Ruth, NY 10.1
- L. Gehrig, NY 4.8
- G. Goslin, WAS 3.7
- J. Foxx, PHI 3.3

Runs
- B. Ruth, NY 163
- L. Gehrig, NY 139
- E. Combs, NY 118
- L. Blue, STL 116

Doubles
- L. Gehrig, NY 47
- H. Manush, STL 47
- B. Meusel, NY 45
- F. Schulte, STL 44

Triples
- E. Combs, NY 21
- H. Manush, STL 20
- C. Gehringer, DET 16

PITCHING LEADERS

Winning Percentage
- G. Crowder, STL .808
- W. Hoyt, NY .767
- L. Grove, PHI .750
- H. Pennock, NY .739
- J. Quinn, PHI .720

Earned Run Average
- G. Braxton, WAS 2.51
- H. Pennock, NY 2.56
- L. Grove, PHI 2.58
- S. Jones, WAS 2.84
- J. Quinn, PHI 2.90

Wins
- L. Grove, PHI 24
- G. Pipgras, NY 24
- W. Hoyt, NY 23
- G. Crowder, STL 21
- S. Gray, STL 20

Saves
- W. Hoyt, NY 8
- W. Hudlin, CLE 7
- G. Braxton, WAS 6
- T. Lyons, CHI 6
- E. Morris, BOS 5
- E. Vangilder, DET 5

Strikeouts
- L. Grove, PHI 183
- G. Pipgras, NY 139
- T. Thomas, CHI 129
- R. Ruffing, BOS 118
- G. Earnshaw, PHI 117

Complete Games
- R. Ruffing, BOS 25
- L. Grove, PHI 24
- T. Thomas, CHI 24
- G. Pipgras, NY 22

Fewest Hits/9 Innings
- G. Braxton, WAS 7.30
- L. Grove, PHI 7.84
- S. Jones, WAS 8.37
- H. Johnson, NY 8.50

Shutouts
- H. Pennock, NY 5
- S. Jones, WAS 4
- J. Quinn, PHI 4
- L. Grove, PHI 4
- G. Pipgras, NY 4

Fewest Walks/9 Innings
- J. Quinn, PHI 1.45
- H. Pennock, NY 1.71
- G. Braxton, WAS 1.81
- J. Russell, BOS 1.83

Most Strikeouts/9 Inn.
- L. Grove, PHI 6.29
- H. Johnson, NY 4.97
- R. Walberg, PHI 4.28
- E. Whitehill, DET 4.26

Innings
- G. Pipgras, NY 301
- R. Ruffing, BOS 289
- T. Thomas, CHI 283
- W. Hoyt, NY 273

Games Pitched
- F. Marberry, WAS 48
- E. Morris, BOS 47
- G. Pipgras, NY 46
- E. Rommel, PHI 43

							Batting						Fielding			Pitching					
	W	L	PCT	GB	R	OR	2B	3B	HR	BA	SA	SB	E	DP	FA	CG	BB	SO	ShO	SV	ERA
New York	101	53	.656		**894**	685	269	79	**133**	**.296**	**.450**	51	194	136	.968	83	452	487	13	**21**	3.74
Philadelphia	98	55	.641	2.5	829	**615**	**323**	75	89	.295	.436	59	181	124	.970	81	**424**	**607**	**15**	16	**3.36**
St. Louis	82	72	.532	19	772	742	276	76	63	.274	.393	76	189	146	.969	80	454	456	6	15	4.17
Washington	75	79	.487	26	718	705	277	93	40	.284	.393	110	**178**	146	**.972**	77	466	462	**15**	10	3.88
Chicago	72	82	.468	29	656	725	231	77	24	.270	.358	**139**	186	149	.970	**88**	501	418	6	11	3.98
Detroit	68	86	.442	33	744	804	265	**97**	62	.279	.401	113	218	140	.965	65	567	451	5	16	4.32
Cleveland	62	92	.403	39	674	830	299	61	34	.285	.382	50	221	**187**	.965	71	511	416	4	15	4.47
Boston	57	96	.373	43.5	589	770	260	62	38	.264	.361	99	**178**	139	.971	70	452	407	5	9	4.39
					5876	5876	2200	620	483	.281	.397	697	1545	1167	.969	615	3827	3704	69	113	4.04

NATIONAL LEAGUE 1929

Chicago

W-98 L-54

Joe McCarthy

POS	Player	AB	BA	HR	RBI	PO	A	E	DP	TC/G	FA	Pitcher	G	IP	W	L	SV	ERA
1B	C. Grimm	463	.298	10	91	1228	74	10	114	10.9	.992	C. Root	43	272	19	6	5	3.47
2B	R. Hornsby	602	.380	39	149	286	**547**	23	**106**	5.5	.973	G. Bush	**50**	271	18	7	**8**	3.66
SS	W. English	608	.276	1	52	332	497	39	107	6.0	.955	P. Malone	40	267	**22**	10	2	3.57
3B	N. McMillan	495	.271	5	55	131	226	**21**	21	3.2	.944	S. Blake	35	218	14	13	1	4.29
RF	K. Cuyler	509	.360	15	102	288	15	8	6	2.4	.974	A. Nehf	32	121	8	5	1	5.59
CF	H. Wilson	574	.345	39	**159**	380	14	12	4	2.7	.970	H. Carlson	31	112	11	5	2	5.16
LF	R. Stephenson	495	.362	17	110	245	9	4	4	2.0	.984	M. Cvengros	32	64	5	4	2	4.64
C	Z. Taylor	215	.274	1	31	247	36	6	4	4.5*	.979							
OF	C. Heathcote	224	.313	2	31	131	4	2	2	2.6	.985							
3B	C. Beck	190	.211	0	9	18	70	2	5	2.7	.978							
C	M. Gonzalez	167	.240	0	18	212	34	2	7	4.1	.992							

NATIONAL LEAGUE 1929, *cont.*

Team	POS	Player	AB	BA	HR	RBI	PO	A	E	DP	TC/G	FA	Pitcher	G	IP	W	L	SV	ERA
Pittsburgh	1B	E. Sheely	485	.293	6	88	1292	83	5	102	9.9	**.996**	B. Grimes	33	233	17	7	2	3.13
	2B	G. Grantham	349	.307	12	90	205	239	15	54	6.0	.967	E. Brame	37	230	16	11	0	4.55
W-88 L-65	SS	D. Bartell	610	.302	2	57	179	246	21	21	4.6	.953	R. Kremer	34	222	18	10	0	4.26
	3B	P. Traynor	540	.356	4	108	148	238	20	23	3.1	.951	J. Petty	36	184	11	10	0	3.71
Donie Bush	RF	P. Waner	596	.336	15	100	328	15	5	5	2.4	.986	S. Swetonic	41	144	8	10	5	4.82
W-67 L-51	CF	L. Waner	**662**	.353	5	74	450	22	6	6	3.2	.987	L. French	30	123	7	5	1	4.90
	LF	A. Comorosky	473	.321	6	97	256	6	10	3	2.2	.963	H. Meine	22	108	7	6	1	4.50
	C	C. Hargreaves	328	.268	1	44	308	56	7	7	3.6	.981							
Jewel Ens	C	R. Hemsley	235	.289	0	37	240	48	14	7	3.8	.954							
W-21 L-14	UT	S. Adams	196	.260	0	11	75	130	17	14		.923							
	SS	S. Clarke	178	.264	2	21	73	132	18	19	5.4	.919							
	P	E. Brame	116	.310	4	25	7	36	3	0	1.2	.935							
New York	1B	B. Terry	607	.372	14	117	**1575**	111	11	**146**	**11.4**	.994	C. Hubbell	39	268	18	11	1	3.69
	2B	A. Cohen	347	.294	5	47	227	315	20	52	6.0	.964	L. Benton	39	237	11	17	3	4.14
W-84 L-67	SS	T. Jackson	551	.294	21	94	329	**552**	28	**110**	**6.1**	**.969**	F. Fitzsimmons	37	222	15	11	1	4.10
	3B	F. Lindstrom	549	.319	15	91	134	258	14	24	3.2	.966	B. Walker	29	178	14	7	0	**3.09**
John McGraw	RF	M. Ott	545	.328	42	152	335	26	10	12	2.5	.973	C. Mays	37	123	7	2	4	4.32
	CF	E. Roush	450	.324	8	52	248	18	5	5	2.5	.982	D. Henry	27	101	5	6	1	3.82
	LF	F. Leach	411	.290	8	47	149	2	4	0	1.6	.974	J. Scott	30	92	7	6	1	3.53
	C	S. Hogan	317	.300	5	45	286	47	7	5	3.7	.979	J. Genewich	21	85	3	7	1	6.78
	OF	C. Fullis	274	.288	7	29	151	3	6	0	2.1	.963							
	C	B. O'Farrell	248	.306	4	42	254	22	6	2	3.4	.979							
	2B	A. Reese	209	.263	0	21	104	163	11	24	6.3	.960							
	32	D. Farrell	178	.213	0	16	87	114	13	18		.939							
	PH	P. Crawford	57	.298	3	24													
St. Louis	1B	J. Bottomley	560	.314	29	137	1347	75	13	122	9.9	.991	B. Sherdel	33	196	10	15	0	5.93
	2B	F. Frisch	527	.334	5	74	295	374	21	66	5.7	.970	S. Johnson	42	182	13	7	3	3.60
W-78 L-74	SS	C. Gelbert	512	.262	3	65	**338**	499	**46**	95	6.0	.948	J. Haines	28	180	13	10	0	5.71
	3B	A. High	603	.295	10	63	91	204	10	17	2.5	**.967**	C. Mitchell	25	173	8	11	0	4.27
Billy Southworth	RF	E. Orsatti	346	.332	3	39	176	12	5	5	2.5	.974	H. Haid	38	155	9	9	4	4.07
W-43 L-45	CF	T. Douthit	613	.336	9	62	442	8	12	1	3.1	.974	F. Frankhouse	30	133	7	2	1	4.12
	LF	C. Hafey	517	.338	29	125	278	8	10	1	2.3	.966	G. Alexander	22	132	9	8	0	3.89
	C	J. Wilson	394	.325	4	71	**410**	**80**	14	**16**	4.2	.972							
Gabby Street	OF	W. Roettger	269	.253	3	42	137	4	1	0	2.1	.993							
W-1 L-0	OF	W. Holm	176	.233	0	14	115	4	7	2	2.9	.944							
	C	E. Smith	145	.345	1	22	131	21	6	1	3.2	.962							
Bill McKechnie																			
W-34 L-29																			
Philadelphia	1B	D. Hurst	589	.304	31	125	1509	**112**	24	125	10.7	.985	C. Willoughby	49	243	15	14	4	4.99
	2B	F. Thompson	623	.324	4	53	**395**	512	**33**	103	**6.4**	.965	L. Sweetland	43	204	13	11	2	5.11
	SS	T. Thevenow	317	.227	0	35	188	296	24	56	5.6	.953	R. Benge	38	199	11	15	4	6.29
W-71 L-82	3B	P. Whitney	612	.327	8	115	**168**	**333**	17	**29**	**3.4**	.967	P. Collins	43	153	9	7	5	5.75
	RF	C. Klein	616	.356	**43**	145	321	18	12	3	2.4	.966	H. Elliott	40	114	3	7	2	6.06
Burt Shotton	CF	D. Sothern	294	.306	5	27	193	9	7	2	2.9	.967	L. Koupal	15	87	5	5	2	4.78
	LF	L. O'Doul	638	**.398**	32	122	320	14	10	5	2.2	.971	B. McGraw	41	86	5	5	4	5.73
	C	W. Lerian	273	.223	7	25	271	69	5	13	3.3	**.986**	H. Smythe	19	69	4	6	1	5.24
	SO	B. Friberg	455	.301	7	55	234	195	28	33		.939							
	C	S. Davis	263	.342	7	48	198	47	10	7	2.6	.961							
	OF	H. Peel	156	.269	0	19	94	2	1	1	2.5	.990							
	PH	C. Williams	65	.292	5	21	27	1	1	0	2.6	.966							
Brooklyn	1B	D. Bissonette	431	.281	12	75	1093	47	15	70	10.2	.987	W. Clark	41	**279**	16	**19**	1	3.74
	2B	E. Moore	402	.296	0	48	135	228	17	31	5.1	.955	D. Vance	31	231	14	13	0	3.89
	SS	D. Bancroft	358	.277	1	44	224	309	25	45	5.5	.955	R. Moss	39	182	11	6	0	5.04
W-70 L-83	3B	W. Gilbert	569	.304	3	58	137	271	19	16	3.0	.956	C. Dudley	35	157	6	14	0	5.69
	RF	B. Herman	569	.381	21	113	244	10	16	2	1.9	.941	D. McWeeny	36	146	4	10	1	6.10
Wilbert Robinson	CF	J. Frederick	628	.328	24	75	410	13	11	1	3.0	.975	J. Morrison	39	137	13	7	**8**	4.48
	LF	R. Bressler	456	.318	9	77	263	7	13	0	2.3	.954							
	C	V. Picinich	273	.260	4	31	311	62	8	8	4.5	.979							
	UT	H. Hendrick	384	.354	14	82	467	62	16	29		.971							
	C	H. DeBerry	210	.262	1	25	304	36	3	3	5.0	.991							
	2B	B. Rhiel	205	.278	4	25	94	137	5	16	5.0	.979							
Cincinnati	1B	G. Kelly	577	.293	5	103	1537	103	11	127	11.2	.993	R. Lucas	32	270	19	12	0	3.60
	2B	H. Critz	425	.247	1	50	210	395	16	72	5.9	**.974**	E. Rixey	35	201	10	13	1	4.16
	SS	H. Ford	529	.276	3	50	239	368	30	86	5.9	.953	J. May	41	199	10	14	3	4.61
W-66 L-88	3B	C. Dressen	401	.244	1	36	77	157	17	9	2.6	.932	P. Donohue	32	178	10	13	0	5.42
	RF	C. Walker	492	.313	7	83	298	11	10	2	2.3	.969	D. Luque	32	176	5	16	0	4.50
Jack Hendricks	CF	E. Allen	538	.292	6	64	393	12	5	2	3.0	.988	R. Kolp	30	145	8	10	0	4.03
	LF	E. Swanson	574	.300	4	43	317	9	10	2	2.4	.970							
	C	J. Gooch	287	.300	0	34	251	61	8	7	3.7	.975							
	C	C. Sukeforth	237	.354	1	33	171	40	4	4	2.8	.981							
	SS	P. Pittenger	210	.295	0	27	107	153	12	37	5.4	.956							
	3B	J. Stripp	187	.214	3	20	49	120	7	4	3.2	.960							
	OF	P. Purdy	181	.271	1	16	84	3	2	0	2.1	.978							

NATIONAL LEAGUE 1929, *cont.*

Team	POS	Player	AB	BA	HR	RBI	PO	A	E	DP	TC/G	FA	Pitcher	G	IP	W	L	SV	ERA
Boston	1B	G. Sisler	629	.326	2	79	1398	111	**28**	131	10.0	.982	B. Smith	34	231	11	17	3	4.68
	2B	F. Maguire	496	.252	0	41	334	437	23	94	5.8	.971	S. Seibold	33	206	12	17	1	4.73
W-56 L-98	SS	R. Maranville	560	.284	0	55	319	536	35	104	6.1	.961	P. Jones	35	188	7	15	0	4.64
	3B	L. Bell	483	.298	9	72	107	198	15	15	2.5	.953	E. Brandt	26	168	8	13	0	5.53
Judge Fuchs	RF	L. Richbourg	557	.305	3	56	323	14	10	2	2.6	.971	B. Cantwell	27	157	4	13	2	4.47
	CF	E. Clark	279	.315	1	30	216	7	5	3	3.1	.978	D. Leverett	24	98	3	7	1	6.36
	LF	G. Harper	457	.291	10	68	266	7	8	2	2.2	.972	B. Cunningham	17	92	4	6	1	4.52
	C	A. Spohrer	342	.272	2	48	314	57	**18**	5	3.6	.954							
	OF	J. Welsh	186	.290	2	16	177	6	4	1	3.7	.979							

BATTING AND BASE RUNNING LEADERS

Batting Average
- L. O'Doul, PHI .398
- B. Herman, BKN .381
- R. Hornsby, CHI .380
- B. Terry, NY .372
- R. Stephenson, CHI .362

Slugging Average
- R. Hornsby, CHI .679
- C. Klein, PHI .657
- M. Ott, NY .635
- C. Hafey, STL .632
- L. O'Doul, PHI .622

Home Runs
- C. Klein, PHI 43
- M. Ott, NY 42
- H. Wilson, CHI 39
- R. Hornsby, CHI 39
- L. O'Doul, PHI 32

Total Bases
- R. Hornsby, CHI 409
- C. Klein, PHI 405
- L. O'Doul, PHI 397
- H. Wilson, CHI 355
- B. Herman, BKN 348

Runs Batted In
- H. Wilson, CHI 159
- M. Ott, NY 152
- R. Hornsby, CHI 149
- C. Klein, PHI 145
- J. Bottomley, STL 137

Stolen Bases
- K. Cuyler, CHI 43
- E. Swanson, CIN 33
- F. Frisch, STL 24
- E. Allen, CIN 21
- B. Herman, BKN 21

Hits
- L. O'Doul, PHI 254
- L. Waner, PIT 234
- R. Hornsby, CHI 229
- B. Terry, NY 226

Base on Balls
- M. Ott, NY 113
- G. Grantham, PIT 93
- P. Waner, PIT 89
- R. Hornsby, CHI 87

Home Run Percentage
- M. Ott, NY 7.7
- C. Klein, PHI 7.0
- H. Wilson, CHI 6.8
- R. Hornsby, CHI 6.5

Runs
- R. Hornsby, CHI 156
- L. O'Doul, PHI 152
- M. Ott, NY 138
- H. Wilson, CHI 135

Doubles
- J. Frederick, BKN 52
- C. Hafey, STL 47
- R. Hornsby, CHI 47
- G. Kelly, CIN 45
- C. Klein, PHI 45

Triples
- L. Waner, PIT 20
- C. Walker, CIN 15
- P. Waner, PIT 15
- P. Whitney, PHI 14

PITCHING LEADERS

Winning Percentage
- C. Root, CHI .760
- G. Bush, CHI .720
- B. Grimes, PIT .708
- P. Malone, CHI .688
- R. Kremer, PIT .643

Earned Run Average
- B. Walker, NY 3.09
- B. Grimes, PIT 3.13
- C. Root, CHI 3.47
- P. Malone, CHI 3.57
- R. Lucas, CIN 3.60

Wins
- P. Malone, CHI 22
- R. Lucas, CIN 19
- C. Root, CHI 19
- R. Kremer, PIT 18
- C. Hubbell, NY 18
- G. Bush, CHI 18

Saves
- G. Bush, CHI 8
- J. Morrison, BKN 8
- L. Koupal, BKN, PHI 6
- C. Root, CHI 5
- P. Collins, PHI 5
- S. Swetonic, PIT 5

Strikeouts
- P. Malone, CHI 166
- W. Clark, BKN 140
- D. Vance, BKN 126
- C. Root, CHI 124
- C. Hubbell, NY 106

Complete Games
- R. Lucas, CIN 28

Fewest Hits/9 Innings
- R. Lucas, CIN 8.90
- C. Hubbell, NY 9.17
- R. Kremer, PIT 9.18
- S. Johnson, STL 9.18

Shutouts
- P. Malone, CHI 5
- F. Fitzsimmons, NY 4
- C. Root, CHI 4

Fewest Walks/9 Innings
- D. Vance, BKN 1.83
- R. Lucas, CIN 1.93
- J. Petty, PIT 2.05
- C. Hubbell, NY 2.25

Most Strikeouts/9 Inn.
- P. Malone, CHI 5.60
- D. Vance, BKN 4.90
- W. Clark, BKN 4.52
- J. May, CIN 4.16

Innings
- W. Clark, BKN 279
- C. Root, CHI 272
- G. Bush, CHI 271
- R. Lucas, CIN 270

Games Pitched
- G. Bush, CHI 50
- C. Willoughby, PHI 49
- P. Collins, PHI 43
- L. Sweetland, PHI 43
- C. Root, CHI 43

							Batting						Fielding			Pitching					
	W	L	PCT	GB	R	OR	2B	3B	HR	BA	SA	SB	E	DP	FA	CG	BB	SO	ShO	SV	ERA
Chicago	98	54	.645		**982**	758	**310**	45	140	.303	.452	103	**154**	**169**	**.975**	79	537	548	**14**	21	4.16
Pittsburgh	88	65	.575	10.5	904	780	285	**116**	60	.303	.430	94	181	136	.970	79	439	409	5	13	4.36
New York	84	67	.556	13.5	897	**709**	251	47	136	.296	.436	85	158	163	**.975**	68	**387**	431	9	13	**3.97**
St. Louis	78	74	.513	20	831	806	**310**	84	100	.293	.438	72	174	149	.971	**83**	474	453	6	8	4.66
Philadelphia	71	82	.464	27.5	897	1032	305	51	**153**	**.309**	**.467**	59	191	153	.969	45	616	369	5	**24**	6.13
Brooklyn	70	83	.458	28.5	755	888	282	69	99	.291	.427	80	192	113	.968	59	549	**549**	7	16	4.92
Cincinnati	66	88	.429	33	686	760	258	79	34	.281	.379	**134**	162	148	.974	75	413	347	5	8	4.41
Boston	56	98	.364	43	657	876	252	78	32	.280	.375	65	204	146	.967	78	530	366	4	12	5.12
					6609	6609	2253	569	754	.294	.426	692	1416	1177	.971	566	3945	3472	55	115	4.72

AMERICAN LEAGUE 1929

Team	POS	Player	AB	BA	HR	RBI	PO	A	E	DP	TC/G	FA	Pitcher	G	IP	W	L	SV	ERA
Philadelphia	1B	J. Foxx	517	.354	33	117	1226	74	6	98	9.2	.995	L. Grove	42	275	20	6	4	**2.81**
	2B	M. Bishop	475	.232	3	36	301	371	21	58	5.4	.970	R. Walberg	40	268	18	11	4	3.60
	SS	J. Boley	303	.251	2	47	161	229	15	50	4.6	.963	G. Earnshaw	44	255	**24**	8	1	3.29
W-104 L-46	3B	S. Hale	379	.277	1	40	90	171	12	13	2.8	.956	J. Quinn	35	161	11	9	2	3.97
	RF	B. Miller	556	.335	8	93	311	10	10	4	2.3	.970	B. Shores	39	153	11	6	7	3.60
Connie Mack	CF	M. Haas	578	.313	16	82	373	10	7	2	2.8	.982	E. Rommel	32	114	12	2	4	2.85
	LF	A. Simmons	581	.365	34	**157**	349	19	4	2	2.6	.989							
	C	M. Cochrane	514	.331	7	95	**659**	77	13	9	**5.5**	**.983**							
	UT	J. Dykes	401	.327	13	79	203	273	33	41		.935							
New York	1B	L. Gehrig	553	.300	35	126	1458	82	9	134	10.1	.994	G. Pipgras	39	225	18	12	0	4.23
	2B	T. Lazzeri	545	.354	18	106	368	467	**27**	**101**	5.9	.969	W. Hoyt	30	202	10	9	1	4.24
	SS	L. Durocher	341	.246	0	32	197	299	22	59	5.6	.958	E. Wells	31	193	13	9	0	4.33
W-88 L-66	3B	G. Robertson	309	.298	0	35	80	116	7	6	2.6	.966	R. Sherid	33	160	6	6	1	3.49
	RF	B. Ruth	499	.345	**46**	154	240	5	4	2	1.9	.984	H. Pennock	27	158	9	11	2	4.90
Miller Huggins	CF	E. Combs	586	.345	3	65	358	10	13	5	2.7	.966	F. Heimach	35	135	11	6	4	4.01
W-82 L-61	LF	B. Meusel	391	.261	10	57	206	9	7	2	2.3	.968	T. Zachary	26	120	12	0	2	2.48
	C	B. Dickey	447	.324	10	65	476	**95**	12	**13**	4.6	.979	W. Moore	41	62	6	4	8	4.06
Art Fletcher	S3	M. Koenig	373	.292	3	41	137	216	32	34		.917							
W-6 L-5	3B	L. Lary	236	.309	5	26	38	95	8	10	2.6	.943							
	OF	C. Durst	202	.257	4	31	151	5	2	1	2.2	.987							
	OF	S. Byrd	170	.312	5	28	108	6	6	2	2.2	.950							

AMERICAN LEAGUE 1929, *cont.*

Team	POS	Player	AB	BA	HR	RBI	PO	A	E	DP	TC/G	FA	Pitcher	G	IP	W	L	SV	ERA
Cleveland	1B	L. Fonseca	566	**.369**	6	103	1486	**107**	8	**141**	**10.9**	.995	W. Hudlin	40	280	17	15	1	3.34
W-81 L-71	2B	J. Hodapp	294	.327	4	51	162	271	10	32	6.2	.977	W. Ferrell	43	243	21	10	5	3.60
Roger Peckinpaugh	SS	J. Tavener	250	.212	2	27	158	275	25	59	5.1	.945	J. Miller	29	206	14	12	0	3.58
	3B	J. Sewell	578	.315	7	73	163	**336**	13	28	3.4	.975	J. Shaute	26	162	8	8	0	4.28
	RF	B. Falk	430	.309	13	94	219	15	14	4	2.0	.944	J. Miljus	34	128	8	8	2	5.19
	CF	E. Averill	602	.331	18	97	388	14	14	3	2.7	.966	K. Holloway	25	119	6	5	0	3.03
	LF	C. Jamieson	364	.291	0	26	192	8	4	1	2.2	.980	J. Zinn	18	105	4	6	2	5.04
	C	L. Sewell	406	.236	1	39	433	81	**18**	11	4.3	.966							
	OF	E. Morgan	318	.318	3	37	100	8	11	1	1.5	.908							
	SS	R. Gardner	256	.262	1	24	175	240	21	50	5.3	.952							
	2B	C. Lind	224	.241	0	13	190	209	18	60	6.5	.957							
	02	D. Porter	192	.328	1	24	95	63	8	8		.952							
St. Louis	1B	L. Blue	573	.293	6	61	**1491**	88	10	127	10.5	.994	S. Gray	43	**305**	18	15	1	3.72
W-79 L-73	2B	O. Melillo	494	.296	5	67	342	**519**	24	98	6.3	.973	G. Crowder	40	267	17	15	4	3.92
Dan Howley	SS	R. Kress	557	.305	9	107	312	441	43	**94**	5.5	**.946**	G. Blaeholder	42	222	14	15	2	4.18
	3B	F. O'Rourke	585	.251	2	62	171	242	25	**30**	2.9	.943	R. Collins	26	155	11	6	1	4.00
	RF	F. McGowan	441	.254	2	51	257	16	7	5	2.4	.975	L. Stewart	23	149	9	6	0	3.25
	CF	F. Schulte	446	.307	3	71	361	12	4	2	3.3	.989	J. Ogden	34	131	4	8	0	4.93
	LF	H. Manush	574	.355	6	81	293	11	4	3	2.2	.987	C. Kimsey	24	64	3	6	1	5.04
	C	W. Schang	249	.237	5	36	268	56	4	6	3.9	.988							
	OF	E. McNeely	230	.243	1	18	96	4	2	0	1.6	.980							
	C	R. Ferrell	144	.229	0	20	140	35	7	3	4.0	.962							
Washington	1B	J. Judge	543	.315	6	71	1323	88	6	116	10.0	**.996**	F. Marberry	**49**	250	19	12	**11**	3.06
W-71 L-81	2B	B. Myer	563	.300	3	82	205	271	21	51	5.6	.958	B. Hadley	37	194	6	16	0	5.65
Walter Johnson	SS	J. Cronin	494	.281	8	61	285	**459**	**62**	92	5.6	.923	G. Braxton	37	182	12	10	4	4.85
	3B	J. Hayes	424	.276	2	57	56	132	11	15	3.2	.945	L. Brown	40	168	8	7	0	4.18
	RF	S. Rice	616	.323	1	62	272	20	9	5	2.0	.970	S. Jones	24	154	9	9	0	3.92
	CF	S. West	510	.267	3	75	376	25	9	8	2.9	.978	B. Burke	37	141	6	8	0	4.79
	LF	G. Goslin	553	.288	18	91	299	7	10	1	2.2	.968	M. Thomas	22	125	7	8	2	3.52
	C	B. Tate	265	.294	0	30	291	49	10	10	4.7	.971	A. Liska	24	94	3	9	0	4.77
	UT	O. Bluege	220	.295	5	31	74	145	6	24		.973							
	C	M. Ruel	188	.245	0	20	247	52	3	6	4.8	.990							
Detroit	1B	D. Alexander	626	.343	25	137	1443	90	**18**	129	10.0	.988	G. Uhle	32	249	15	11	0	4.08
W-70 L-84	2B	C. Gehringer	634	.339	13	106	**404**	501	23	93	6.0	**.975**	E. Whitehill	38	245	14	15	1	4.62
Bucky Harris	SS	H. Schuble	258	.233	2	28	141	216	46	43	4.7	.886	V. Sorrell	36	226	14	15	1	5.18
	3B	M. McManus	599	.280	18	90	206	289	14	29	3.4	.972	O. Carroll	34	202	9	17	1	4.63
	RF	H. Heilmann	453	.344	15	120	193	8	7	3	1.8	.966	E. Yde	29	87	7	3	0	5.30
	CF	H. Rice	536	.304	6	69	345	16	15	6	3.0	.960	L. Stoner	24	53	3	3	4	5.26
	LF	R. Johnson	**640**	.314	10	69	377	25	31	5	3.0	.928							
	C	E. Phillips	221	.235	2	21	255	34	10	4	4.7	.967							
	OF	B. Fothergill	277	.354	6	62	116	2	4	1	2.1	.967							
	C	P. Hargrave	185	.330	3	26	175	38	6	7	4.6	.973							
	C	M. Shea	162	.290	3	24	157	32	7	4	3.9	.964							
Chicago	1B	A. Shires	353	.312	3	41	815	58	8	78	10.0	.991	T. Thomas	36	260	14	18	1	3.19
W-59 L-93	2B	J. Kerr	419	.258	1	39	307	459	23	84	**6.5**	.971	T. Lyons	37	259	14	20	2	4.10
Lena Blackburne	SS	B. Cissell	618	.280	5	62	**357**	**459**	55	90	**5.7**	.937	R. Faber	31	234	13	13	0	3.88
	3B	W. Kamm	523	.268	3	63	**221**	270	11	27	**3.5**	**.978**	H. McKain	34	158	6	9	1	3.65
	RF	C. Reynolds	517	.317	11	67	268	13	15	5	2.3	.949	G. Adkins	31	138	2	11	0	5.33
	CF	D. Hoffman	337	.258	3	37	237	4	4	2	2.8	.984	E. Walsh	24	129	6	11	0	5.65
	LF	A. Metzler	568	.275	2	49	316	16	14	3	2.5	.960							
	C	M. Berg	351	.288	0	47	290	86	7	12	3.6	.982							
	1B	B. Clancy	290	.283	3	45	647	49	6	47	9.5	.991							
	OF	C. Watwood	278	.302	2	18	188	7	12	2	2.7	.942							
Boston	1B	P. Todt	534	.262	4	64	1467	102	14	128	10.3	.991	R. Ruffing	35	244	9	**22**	1	4.86
W-58 L-96	2B	B. Regan	371	.288	1	54	193	282	19	66	5.4	.962	M. Gaston	39	244	12	19	2	3.73
Bill Carrigan	SS	H. Rhyne	346	.251	0	38	220	297	36	71	4.9	.935	J. Russell	35	226	6	18	0	3.94
	3B	B. Reeves	460	.248	2	28	152	242	**38**	27	3.3	.912	D. MacFayden	32	221	10	18	0	3.62
	RF	B. Barrett	370	.270	3	35	204	16	6	4	2.1	.973	E. Morris	33	208	14	14	1	4.45
	CF	J. Rothrock	473	.300	6	59	342	12	11	3	2.9	.970	B. Bayne	27	84	5	5	0	6.72
	LF	R. Scarritt	540	.294	1	71	302	16	19	6	2.3	.944							
	C	C. Berry	207	.242	1	21	236	51	5	8	4.1	.983							
	UT	B. Narleski	260	.277	0	25	146	200	15	41		.958							
	OF	E. Bigelow	211	.284	1	26	63	5	4	1	1.2	.944							
	C	J. Heving	188	.319	0	23	207	40	3	4	4.5	.988							
	OF	K. Williams	139	.345	3	21	75	3	3	2	2.3	.963							

BATTING AND BASE RUNNING LEADERS

Batting Average		Slugging Average		Home Runs	
L. Fonseca, CLE	.369	B. Ruth, NY	.697	B. Ruth, NY	46
A. Simmons, PHI	.365	A. Simmons, PHI	.642	L. Gehrig, NY	35
H. Manush, STL	.355	J. Foxx, PHI	.625	A. Simmons, PHI	34
T. Lazzeri, NY	.354	L. Gehrig, NY	.582	J. Foxx, PHI	33
J. Foxx, PHI	.354	D. Alexander, DET	.580	D. Alexander, DET	25

PITCHING LEADERS

Winning Percentage		Earned Run Average		Wins	
L. Grove, PHI	.769	L. Grove, PHI	2.81	G. Earnshaw, PHI	24
G. Earnshaw, PHI	.750	F. Marberry, WAS	3.06	W. Ferrell, CLE	21
W. Ferrell, CLE	.677	T. Thomas, CHI	3.19	L. Grove, PHI	20
R. Walberg, PHI	.621	G. Earnshaw, PHI	3.29	F. Marberry, WAS	19
F. Marberry, WAS	.613	W. Hudlin, CLE	3.34		

AMERICAN LEAGUE 1929, *cont.*

BATTING AND BASE RUNNING LEADERS

Total Bases	
A. Simmons, PHI	373
D. Alexander, DET	363
B. Ruth, NY	348
C. Gehringer, DET	337
J. Foxx, PHI	323

Runs Batted In	
A. Simmons, PHI	157
B. Ruth, NY	154
D. Alexander, DET	137
L. Gehrig, NY	126
H. Heilmann, DET	120

Stolen Bases	
C. Gehringer, DET	28
B. Cissell, CHI	26
B. Miller, PHI	24
J. Rothrock, BOS	23
R. Johnson, DET	20

Hits	
D. Alexander, DET	215
C. Gehringer, DET	215
A. Simmons, PHI	212
L. Fonseca, CLE	209

Base on Balls	
M. Bishop, PHI	128
L. Blue, STL	126
L. Gehrig, NY	122
J. Foxx, PHI	103

Home Run Percentage	
B. Ruth, NY	9.2
J. Foxx, PHI	6.4
L. Gehrig, NY	6.3
A. Simmons, PHI	5.9

Runs	
C. Gehringer, DET	131
R. Johnson, DET	128
L. Gehrig, NY	127
J. Foxx, PHI	123

Doubles	
H. Manush, STL	45
C. Gehringer, DET	45
R. Johnson, DET	45
L. Fonseca, CLE	44

Triples	
C. Gehringer, DET	19
R. Scarritt, BOS	17
B. Miller, PHI	16

PITCHING LEADERS

Saves	
F. Marberry, WAS	11
W. Moore, NY	8
B. Shores, PHI	7
W. Ferrell, CLE	5

Strikeouts	
L. Grove, PHI	170
G. Earnshaw, PHI	149
G. Pipgras, NY	125
F. Marberry, WAS	121
R. Ruffing, BOS	109
S. Gray, STL	109

Complete Games	
T. Thomas, CHI	24
G. Uhle, DET	23
S. Gray, STL	23
W. Hudlin, CLE	22
T. Lyons, CHI	21
L. Grove, PHI	21

Fewest Hits/9 Innings	
G. Earnshaw, PHI	8.23
E. Wells, NY	8.33
F. Marberry, WAS	8.38
R. Walberg, PHI	8.61

Shutouts	
G. Blaeholder, STL	4
D. MacFayden, BOS	4
G. Crowder, STL	4
S. Gray, STL	4

Fewest Walks/9 Innings	
J. Russell, BOS	1.59
T. Thomas, CHI	2.08
G. Uhle, DET	2.10
W. Hudlin, CLE	2.34

Most Strikeouts/9 Inn.	
L. Grove, PHI	5.56
G. Earnshaw, PHI	5.27
G. Pipgras, NY	4.99
F. Marberry, WAS	4.35

Innings	
S. Gray, STL	305
W. Hudlin, CLE	280
L. Grove, PHI	275
R. Walberg, PHI	268

Games Pitched	
F. Marberry, WAS	49
G. Earnshaw, PHI	44
W. Ferrell, CLE	43
S. Gray, STL	43

							Batting						Fielding			Pitching					
	W	L	PCT	GB	R	OR	2B	3B	HR	BA	SA	SB	E	DP	FA	CG	BB	SO	ShO	SV	ERA
Philadelphia	104	46	.693		901	**615**	288	76	122	.296	.451	61	**146**	117	**.975**	72	487	**573**	8	**24**	**3.44**
New York	88	66	.571	18	899	775	262	74	**142**	.295	.450	51	178	152	.971	64	485	484	12	18	4.17
Cleveland	81	71	.533	24	717	736	294	79	62	.294	.417	75	198	**162**	.968	80	488	389	8	10	4.05
St. Louis	79	73	.520	26	733	713	276	63	46	.276	.380	72	156	148	**.975**	83	**462**	415	**15**	10	4.08
Washington	71	81	.467	34	730	776	244	66	48	.276	.375	86	195	156	.968	61	496	494	3	17	4.34
Detroit	70	84	.455	36	**926**	928	**339**	**97**	110	**.299**	**.453**	95	242	149	.961	82	646	467	5	9	4.96
Chicago	59	93	.388	46	627	792	240	74	37	.268	.363	**106**	188	153	.970	78	505	328	5	7	4.41
Boston	58	96	.377	48	605	803	285	69	28	.267	.365	85	218	159	.965	**84**	496	416	9	5	4.43
					6138	6138	2228	598	595	.284	.407	631	1521	1196	.969	604	4065	3566	65	100	4.24

NATIONAL LEAGUE 1930

	POS	Player	AB	BA	HR	RBI	PO	A	E	DP	TC/G	FA	Pitcher	G	IP	W	L	SV	ERA
St. Louis	1B	J. Bottomley	487	.304	15	97	1164	41	12	127	9.8	.990	B. Hallahan	35	237	15	9	2	4.66
	2B	F. Frisch	540	.346	10	114	307	473	25	93	**6.5**	.969	S. Johnson	32	188	12	10	2	4.65
	SS	C. Gelbert	513	.304	3	72	322	472	44	104	6.0	.947	J. Haines	29	182	13	8	1	4.30
W-92 L-62	3B	S. Adams	570	.314	0	55	66	159	8	18	2.2	**.966**	B. Grimes	22	152	13	6	0	3.01
	RF	G. Watkins	391	.373	17	87	163	10	8	4	2.0	.956	F. Rhem	26	140	12	8	0	4.45
Gabby Street	CF	T. Douthit	**664**	.303	7	93	425	8	16	3	2.9	.964	H. Bell	39	115	4	3	**8**	3.90
	LF	C. Hafey	446	.336	26	107	189	11	5	0	1.8	.976	A. Grabowski	33	106	6	4	1	4.84
	C	J. Wilson	362	.318	1	58	456	67	7	**11**	5.0	.987	J. Lindsey	39	106	7	5	5	4.43
	OF	S. Fisher	254	.374	8	61	122	6	5	0	2.0	.962							
	C	G. Mancuso	227	.366	7	59	277	33	10	2	5.2	.969							
	3B	A. High	215	.279	2	29	34	68	1	5	2.1	.990							
	OF	R. Blades	101	.396	4	25	66	1	3	0	2.2	.957							
Chicago	1B	C. Grimm	429	.289	6	66	1040	68	6	103	9.9	**.995**	P. Malone	45	272	**20**	9	4	3.94
	2B	F. Blair	578	.273	6	59	257	429	30	83	6.2	.958	G. Bush	46	225	15	10	3	6.20
	SS	W. English	638	.335	14	59	173	251	16	57	5.6	.964	C. Root	37	220	16	14	3	4.33
W-90 L-64	3B	L. Bell	248	.278	5	47	63	102	9	14	2.5	.948	S. Blake	34	187	10	14	0	4.82
	RF	K. Cuyler	642	.355	13	134	377	21	8	7	2.6	.980	B. Teachout	40	153	11	4	0	4.06
Joe McCarthy	CF	H. Wilson	585	.356	**56**	**190**	357	9	19	2	2.5	.951	B. Osborn	35	127	10	6	1	4.97
W-86 L-64	LF	R. Stephenson	341	.367	5	68	132	5	6	1	1.8	.958							
	C	G. Hartnett	508	.339	37	122	**646**	**68**	8	**11**	**5.3**	**.989**							
Rogers Hornsby	S2	C. Beck	244	.213	6	34	149	233	20	53		.950							
W-4 L-0	OF	D. Taylor	219	.283	2	37	97	3	3	0	2.0	.971							
	1B	G. Kelly	166	.331	3	19	414	32	1	31	11.5	.998							
New York	1B	B. Terry	633	**.401**	23	129	**1538**	**128**	17	128	**10.9**	.990	B. Walker	39	245	17	15	1	3.93
	2B	H. Critz	558	.265	4	50	346*	413*	22	88*	6.3	.972*	C. Hubbell	37	242	17	12	2	3.87
	SS	T. Jackson	431	.339	13	82	218	441	30	72	6.0	.956	F. Fitzsimmons	41	224	19	7	1	4.25
W-87 L-67	3B	F. Lindstrom	609	.379	22	106	132	291	21	24	3.0	.953	H. Pruett	45	136	5	4	3	4.78
	RF	M. Ott	521	.349	25	119	320	23	11	6	2.4	.969	C. Mitchell	24	129	10	3	0	3.98
John McGraw	CF	W. Roettger	420	.283	5	51	233	9	2	1	2.1	.992	J. Heving	41	90	7	5	6	5.22
	LF	F. Leach	544	.327	13	71	208	11	5	4	1.8	.978	P. Donohue	18	87	7	6	1	6.13
	C	S. Hogan	389	.339	13	75	386	46	8	5	4.6	.982	J. Genewich	18	61	2	5	3	5.61
	C	B. O'Farrell	249	.301	4	54	259	34	8	0	4.4	.973							
	OF	E. Allen	238	.307	7	31	122	6	2	0	2.1	.985							
	S2	D. Marshall	223	.309	0	21	106	175	12	28		.959							
	OF	A. Reese	172	.273	4	25	66	1	3	0	2.2	.957							

NATIONAL LEAGUE 1930, *cont.*

Brooklyn

W-86 L-68

Wilbert Robinson

POS	Player	AB	BA	HR	RBI	PO	A	E	DP	TC/G	FA	Pitcher	G	IP	W	L	SV	ERA
1B	D. Bissonette	572	.336	16	113	1427	72	**20**	**142**	10.4	.987	D. Vance	35	259	17	15	0	**2.61**
2B	M. Finn	273	.278	3	30	182	235	23	63	5.4	.948	W. Clark	44	200	13	13	6	4.18
SS	G. Wright	532	.321	22	126	297	462	28	97	5.9	.964	D. Luque	31	199	14	8	2	4.30
3B	W. Gilbert	623	.294	3	67	130	312	**26**	27	3.1	.944	J. Elliott	35	198	10	7	1	3.95
RF	B. Herman	614	.393	35	130	260	10	6	1	1.8	.978	R. Phelps	36	180	14	7	0	4.11
CF	J. Frederick	616	.334	17	76	394	12	4	3	2.9	.990	R. Moss	36	118	9	6	1	5.10
LF	R. Bressler	335	.299	3	52	200	5	1	1	2.3	.995	S. Thurston	24	106	6	4	1	3.40
C	A. Lopez	421	.309	6	57	465	66	9	9	4.3	.983							
2B	J. Flowers	253	.320	2	50	153	200	19	42	5.7	.949							
UT	E. Moore	196	.281	1	20	117	115	10	23		.959							
OF	H. Hendrick	167	.257	5	28	68	4	4	2	1.8	.947							

Pittsburgh

W-80 L-74

Jewel Ens

POS	Player	AB	BA	HR	RBI	PO	A	E	DP	TC/G	FA	Pitcher	G	IP	W	L	SV	ERA
1B	G. Suhr	542	.286	17	107	1445	79	13	**142**	10.2	.992	R. Kremer	39	**276**	**20**	12	0	5.02
2B	G. Grantham	552	.324	18	99	324	488	**36**	84	6.0	.958	L. French	42	275	17	**18**	1	4.36
SS	D. Bartell	475	.320	4	75	304	458	48	111	**6.4**	.941	E. Brame	32	236	17	8	1	4.70
3B	P. Traynor	497	.366	9	119	130	268	25	18	3.3	.941	G. Spencer	41	157	8	9	4	5.40
RF	P. Waner	589	.368	8	77	344	9	15	4	2.6	.959	H. Meine	20	117	6	8	1	6.14
CF	L. Waner	260	.362	1	36	165	6	3	1	2.7	.983	S. Swetonic	23	97	6	6	5	4.47
LF	A. Comorosky	597	.313	12	119	337	12	11	2	2.4	.969							
C	R. Hemsley	324	.253	2	45	325	50	8	**11**	3.9	.979							
OF	F. Brickell	219	.297	1	14	134	3	7	1	2.4	.951							
C	A. Bool	216	.259	7	46	190	42	8	4	3.7	.967							
UT	C. Engle	216	.264	0	15	113	161	15	18		.948							
OF	I. Flagstead	156	.250	2	21	70	4	3	1	1.9	.961							
P	E. Brame	116	.353	3	22	1	39	2	0	1.3	.952							

Boston

W-70 L-84

Bill McKechnie

POS	Player	AB	BA	HR	RBI	PO	A	E	DP	TC/G	FA	Pitcher	G	IP	W	L	SV	ERA
1B	G. Sisler	431	.309	3	67	915	81	13	103	9.4	.987	S. Seibold	36	251	15	16	2	4.12
2B	F. Maguire	516	.267	0	52	387	476	28	104	6.1	.969	B. Smith	38	220	10	14	5	4.26
SS	R. Maranville	558	.281	2	43	343	445	29	98	5.9	**.965**	B. Cantwell	31	173	9	15	2	4.88
3B	B. Chatham	404	.267	5	56	89	152	21	26	2.8	.920	T. Zachary	24	151	11	5	0	4.58
RF	L. Richbourg	529	.304	3	54	294	9	9	4	2.4	.971	E. Brandt	41	147	4	11	1	5.01
CF	J. Welsh	422	.275	3	36	329	8	7	2	3.1	.980	B. Sherdel	21	119	6	5	1	4.75
LF	W. Berger	555	.310	38	119	307	10	11	3	2.3	.966	F. Frankhouse	27	111	7	6	0	5.61
C	A. Spohrer	356	.317	2	37	322	36	**16**	4	3.5	.957	B. Cunningham	36	107	5	6	0	5.48
OF	E. Clark	233	.296	3	28	165	3	4	0	2.7	.977							
1B	J. Neun	212	.325	2	23	431	31	4	46	8.5	.991							
OF	R. Moore	191	.288	2	34	70	3	1	0	2.2	.986							
C	B. Cronin	178	.253	0	17	203	31	4	5	3.7	.983							

Cincinnati

W-59 L-95

Dan Howley

POS	Player	AB	BA	HR	RBI	PO	A	E	DP	TC/G	FA	Pitcher	G	IP	W	L	SV	ERA
1B	J. Stripp	464	.306	3	64	722	38	3	76	10.2	.996	B. Frey	44	245	11	**18**	1	4.70
2B	H. Ford	424	.231	1	34	152	217	6	45	5.7	.984	R. Lucas	33	211	14	16	1	5.38
SS	L. Durocher	354	.243	3	32	216	350	24	77	5.7	.959	L. Benton	35	178	7	12	1	5.12
3B	T. Cuccinello	443	.312	10	78	85	181	23	15	2.7	.920	R. Kolp	37	168	7	12	3	4.22
RF	H. Heilmann	459	.333	19	91	279	16	14	5	2.9	.955	E. Rixey	32	164	9	13	0	5.10
CF	B. Meusel	443	.289	10	62	223	8	9	3	2.1	.963	J. May	26	112	3	11	0	5.77
LF	C. Walker	472	.307	8	51	241	5	9	2	2.1	.965	A. Campbell	23	58	2	4	4	5.43
C	C. Sukeforth	296	.284	1	19	234	46	7	8	3.5	.976							
OF	E. Swanson	301	.309	2	22	178	5	7	1	2.7	.963							
C	J. Gooch	276	.243	2	30	233	42	13	4	3.6	.955							
OF	M. Callaghan	225	.276	0	16	142	3	2	1	2.7	.986							
2B	P. Crawford	224	.290	3	26	94	153	8	23	4.7	.969							
1B	G. Kelly	188	.287	5	35	503	35	4	44	10.8	.993							

Philadelphia

W-52 L-102

Burt Shotton

POS	Player	AB	BA	HR	RBI	PO	A	E	DP	TC/G	FA	Pitcher	G	IP	W	L	SV	ERA
1B	D. Hurst	391	.327	17	78	845	59	15	92	9.6	.984	P. Collins	47	239	16	11	3	4.78
2B	F. Thompson	478	.282	4	46	287	386	32	95	6.3	.955	R. Benge	38	226	11	15	1	5.70
SS	T. Thevenow	573	.286	0	78	**344**	**554**	**56**	**113**	6.1	.941	L. Sweetland	34	167	7	15	0	7.71
3B	P. Whitney	606	.342	8	117	**186**	**313**	18	**29**	**3.5**	.965	C. Willoughby	41	153	4	17	1	7.59
RF	C. Klein	648	.386	40	170	362	44	17	10	2.7	.960	H. Collard	30	127	6	12	0	6.80
CF	D. Sothern	347	.280	5	36	217	15	8	3	2.9	.967	H. Elliott	**48**	117	6	11	0	7.67
LF	L. O'Doul	528	.383	22	97	262	3	13	1	2.1	.953							
C	S. Davis	329	.313	14	65	307	50	5	5	3.8	.986							
UT	B. Friberg	331	.341	4	42	185	175	21	29		.945							
1B	M. Sherlock	299	.324	0	38	623	51	7	57	9.7	.990							
OF	F. Brickell	240	.246	0	17	151	6	6	0	3.1	.963							
C	T. Rensa	172	.285	3	31	131	20	11	5	3.3	.932							
C	H. McCurdy	148	.331	1	25	97	16	4	1	2.9	.966							

BATTING AND BASE RUNNING LEADERS

Batting Average

B. Terry, NY	.401
B. Herman, BKN	.393
C. Klein, PHI	.386
L. O'Doul, PHI	.383
F. Lindstrom, NY	.379

Slugging Average

H. Wilson, CHI	.723
C. Klein, PHI	.687
B. Herman, BKN	.678
C. Hafey, STL	.652
G. Hartnett, CHI	.630

Home Runs

H. Wilson, CHI	56
C. Klein, PHI	40
W. Berger, BOS	38
G. Hartnett, CHI	37
B. Herman, BKN	35

Total Bases

C. Klein, PHI	445
H. Wilson, CHI	423
B. Herman, BKN	416
B. Terry, NY	392
K. Cuyler, CHI	351

Runs Batted In

H. Wilson, CHI	190
C. Klein, PHI	170
K. Cuyler, CHI	134
B. Herman, BKN	130
B. Terry, NY	129

Stolen Bases

K. Cuyler, CHI	37
P. Waner, PIT	18
B. Herman, BKN	18
J. Stripp, CIN	15
F. Frisch, STL	15
F. Lindstrom, NY	15

PITCHING LEADERS

Winning Percentage

F. Fitzsimmons, NY	.731
P. Malone, CHI	.690
E. Brame, PIT	.680
R. Kremer, PIT	.625
B. Hallahan, STL	.625

Earned Run Average

D. Vance, BKN	2.61
C. Hubbell, NY	3.87
B. Walker, NY	3.93
P. Malone, CHI	3.94
B. Grimes, BOS, STL	4.07

Wins

P. Malone, CHI	20
R. Kremer, PIT	20
F. Fitzsimmons, NY	19

Saves

H. Bell, STL	8
W. Clark, BKN	6
J. Heving, NY	6
B. Smith, BOS	5
J. Lindsey, STL	5
S. Swetonic, PIT	5

Strikeouts

B. Hallahan, STL	177
D. Vance, BKN	173
P. Malone, CHI	142
C. Root, CHI	124
C. Hubbell, NY	117

Complete Games

E. Brame, PIT	22
P. Malone, CHI	22
L. French, PIT	21
D. Vance, BKN	20
S. Seibold, BOS	20

NATIONAL LEAGUE 1930, *cont.*

BATTING AND BASE RUNNING LEADERS

Hits		Base on Balls		Home Run Percentage		Fewest Hits/9 Innings	
B. Terry, NY	254	H. Wilson, CHI	105	H. Wilson, CHI	9.6	D. Vance, BKN	8.39
C. Klein, PHI	250	M. Ott, NY	103	G. Hartnett, CHI	7.3	B. Hallahan, STL	8.84
B. Herman, BKN	241	W. English, CHI	100	W. Berger, BOS	6.8	F. Fitzsimmons, NY	9.23
F. Lindstrom, NY	231	G. Grantham, PIT	81	C. Klein, PHI	6.2	B. Walker, NY	9.46
Runs		**Doubles**		**Triples**		**Most Strikeouts/9 Inn.**	
C. Klein, PHI	158	C. Klein, PHI	59	A. Comorosky, PIT	23	B. Hallahan, STL	6.71
K. Cuyler, CHI	155	K. Cuyler, CHI	50	P. Waner, PIT	18	D. Vance, BKN	6.02
W. English, CHI	152	B. Herman, BKN	48	W. English, CHI	17	C. Root, CHI	5.07
H. Wilson, CHI	146	A. Comorosky, PIT	47	K. Cuyler, CHI	17	P. Malone, CHI	4.70

PITCHING LEADERS

Shutouts		Fewest Walks/9 Innings	
C. Root, CHI	4	R. Lucas, CIN	1.88
D. Vance, BKN	4	D. Vance, BKN	1.91
C. Hubbell, NY	3	R. Kremer, PIT	2.05
L. French, PIT	3	E. Brame, PIT	2.14
Innings		**Games Pitched**	
R. Kremer, PIT	276	H. Elliott, PHI	48
L. French, PIT	275	P. Collins, PHI	47
P. Malone, CHI	272	G. Bush, CHI	46
D. Vance, BKN	259	H. Pruett, NY	45
		P. Malone, CHI	45

	W	L	PCT	GB	R	OR	Batting 2B	3B	HR	BA	SA	SB	Fielding E	DP	FA	Pitching CG	BB	SO	ShO	SV	ERA
St. Louis	92	62	.597		**1004**	784	**373**	89	104	.314	.471	72	183	**176**	.970	63	477	**641**	5	**21**	4.40
Chicago	90	64	.584	2	998	870	305	72	**171**	.309	**.481**	70	170	167	.973	67	528	601	6	12	4.80
New York	87	67	.565	5	959	814	264	83	143	**.319**	.473	59	164	164	**.974**	64	439	522	6	19	4.59
Brooklyn	86	68	.558	6	871	**738**	303	73	122	.304	.454	53	174	167	.972	74	**394**	526	**13**	15	**4.03**
Pittsburgh	80	74	.519	12	891	928	285	**119**	86	.303	.449	**76**	216	164	.965	**80**	438	393	7	13	5.24
Boston	70	84	.455	22	693	835	246	78	66	.281	.393	69	178	167	.971	71	475	424	6	11	4.91
Cincinnati	59	95	.383	33	665	857	265	67	74	.281	.400	48	**161**	164	.973	61	**394**	361	6	11	5.08
Philadelphia	52	102	.338	40	944	1199	345	44	126	.315	.458	34	239	169	.962	54	543	384	3	7	6.71
					7025	7025	2386	625	892	.303	.447	481	1485	1338	.970	534	3688	3852	52	109	4.97

AMERICAN LEAGUE 1930

Philadelphia

W-102 L-52

Connie Mack

POS	Player	AB	BA	HR	RBI	PO	A	E	DP	TC/G	FA
1B	J. Foxx	562	.335	37	156	**1362**	79	14	101	9.5	.990
2B	M. Bishop	441	.252	10	38	267	418	17	61	5.5	.976
SS	J. Boley	420	.276	4	55	221	296	16	62	4.4	**.970**
3B	J. Dykes	435	.301	6	73	124	191	13	18	2.7	.960
RF	B. Miller	585	.303	9	100	309	10	8	3	2.1	.976
CF	M. Haas	532	.299	2	68	360	11	9	5	2.9	.976
LF	A. Simmons	554	**.381**	36	165	275	10	3	1	2.1	.990
C	M. Cochrane	487	.357	10	85	**654**	**69**	5	**11**	**5.6**	**.993**
S3	E. McNair	237	.266	0	34	93	104	17	12		.921
2S	D. Williams	191	.262	3	22	108	149	12	23		.955

Pitcher	G	IP	W	L	SV	ERA
G. Earnshaw	49	296	22	13	2	4.44
L. Grove	**50**	291	**28**	5	**9**	**2.54**
R. Walberg	38	205	13	12	1	4.69
B. Shores	31	159	12	4	0	4.19
R. Mahaffey	33	153	9	5	0	5.01
E. Rommel	35	130	9	4	3	4.28
J. Quinn	35	90	9	7	6	4.42

Washington

W-94 L-60

Walter Johnson

POS	Player	AB	BA	HR	RBI	PO	A	E	DP	TC/G	FA
1B	J. Judge	442	.326	10	80	1050	67	2	95	9.6	**.998**
2B	B. Myer	541	.303	2	61	330	405	27	89	5.7	.965
SS	J. Cronin	587	.346	13	126	**336**	**509**	35	**95**	**5.7**	.960
3B	O. Bluege	476	.290	3	69	138	**258**	15	20	3.1	.964
RF	S. Rice	593	.349	1	73	297	13	12	4	2.2	.963
CF	S. West	411	.328	6	67	310	8	9	1	2.8	.972
LF	H. Manush	356	.362	7	65	159	5	2	0	1.9	.988
C	R. Spencer	321	.255	0	36	395	44	5	3	4.8	.989
OF	D. Harris	205	.317	4	44	106	8	2	3	2.0	.983
C	M. Ruel	198	.253	0	26	243	32	4	5	4.7	.986
OF	G. Goslin	188	.271	7	38	72	2	5	1	1.7	.937
UT	J. Hayes	166	.283	1	20	149	110	5	33		.981

Pitcher	G	IP	W	L	SV	ERA
B. Hadley	42	260	15	11	2	3.73
G. Crowder	27	202	15	9	1	3.60
L. Brown	38	197	16	12	0	4.25
F. Marberry	33	185	15	5	1	4.09
S. Jones	25	183	15	7	0	4.07
A. Liska	32	151	9	7	1	3.29
B. Burke	24	74	3	4	3	3.63
G. Braxton	15	27	3	2	5	3.29

New York

W-86 L-68

Bob Shawkey

POS	Player	AB	BA	HR	RBI	PO	A	E	DP	TC/G	FA
1B	L. Gehrig	581	.379	41	**174**	1298	**89**	15	109	9.2	.989
2B	T. Lazzeri	571	.303	9	121	184	245	13	39	5.7	.971
SS	L. Lary	464	.289	3	52	224	324	35	58	5.2	.940
3B	B. Chapman	513	.316	10	81	100	149	**24**	11	3.0	.912
RF	B. Ruth	518	.359	**49**	153	266	10	10	0	2.0	.965
CF	H. Rice	346	.298	7	74	244	7	8	2	3.0	.969
LF	E. Combs	532	.344	7	82	275	5	9	1	2.1	.969
C	B. Dickey	366	.339	5	65	418	51	**11**	5	4.8	.977
OF	S. Byrd	218	.284	6	31	119	2	1	0	1.4	.992
OF	D. Cooke	216	.255	6	29	133	2	3	1	1.9	.978
2B	J. Reese	188	.346	3	18	86	99	5	26	4.0	.974
P	R. Ruffing	99	.374	4	21	3	27	2	0	0.9	.938

Pitcher	G	IP	W	L	SV	ERA
G. Pipgras	44	221	15	15	4	4.11
R. Ruffing	34	198	15	5	1	4.14
R. Sherid	37	184	12	13	4	5.23
H. Johnson	44	175	14	11	2	4.67
H. Pennock	25	156	11	7	0	4.32
E. Wells	27	151	12	3	0	5.20

Cleveland

W-81 L-73

Roger Peckinpaugh

POS	Player	AB	BA	HR	RBI	PO	A	E	DP	TC/G	FA
1B	E. Morgan	584	.349	26	136	1275	80	18	116	9.2	.987
2B	J. Hodapp	635	.354	9	121	**403**	557	30	103	6.4	.970
SS	J. Goldman	306	.242	1	44	203	246	26	54	5.1	.945
3B	J. Sewell	353	.289	0	48	83	184	14	16	2.9	.950
RF	D. Porter	480	.350	4	57	189	12	8	4	1.8	.962
CF	E. Averill	534	.339	19	119	345	11	19	5	2.8	.949
LF	C. Jamieson	366	.301	1	52	162	7	8	0	1.9	.955
C	L. Sewell	292	.257	1	43	283	49	9	5	4.5	.974
OF	B. Seeds	277	.285	3	32	156	6	8	0	2.4	.953
C	G. Myatt	265	.294	2	37	214	43	6	8	3.7	.977
OF	B. Falk	191	.325	4	36	84	4	3	3	2.2	.967
SS	E. Montague	179	.263	1	16	84	104	17	19	4.5	.917
3S	J. Burnett	170	.312	0	20	44	105	11	14		.931

Pitcher	G	IP	W	L	SV	ERA
W. Ferrell	43	297	25	13	3	3.31
W. Hudlin	37	217	13	16	1	4.57
C. Brown	35	214	11	12	1	4.97
M. Harder	36	175	11	10	2	4.21
P. Appleton	39	119	8	7	1	4.02

AMERICAN LEAGUE 1930, *cont.*

Detroit

W-75 L-79

Bucky Harris

POS	Player	AB	BA	HR	RBI	PO	A	E	DP	TC/G	FA
1B	D. Alexander	602	.326	20	135	1338	71	**22**	**132**	9.3	.985
2B	C. Gehringer	610	.330	16	98	399	501	19	97	6.0	**.979**
SS	M. Koenig	267	.240	1	16	115	181	25	40	4.6	.922
3B	M. McManus	484	.320	9	89	**152**	241	14	**23**	3.1	**.966**
RF	R. Johnson	462	.275	2	35	218	15	16	4	2.1	.936
CF	L. Funk	527	.275	4	65	354	8	13	4	2.9	.965
LF	J. Stone	422	.313	3	56	222	5	8	1	2.2	.966
C	R. Hayworth	227	.278	0	22	277	27	7	4	4.1	.977
S3	B. Akers	233	.279	9	40	119	184	20	43		.938
OF	H. Rice	128	.305	2	24	66	2	4	0	2.1	.944
P	G. Uhle	117	.308	2	21	10	29	1	2	1.2	.975

Pitcher	G	IP	W	L	SV	ERA
G. Uhle	33	239	12	12	3	3.65
V. Sorrell	35	233	16	11	1	3.86
E. Whitehill	34	221	17	13	1	4.24
C. Hogsett	33	146	9	8	1	5.42
W. Hoyt	26	136	9	8	4	4.78
C. Sullivan	40	94	1	5	5	6.53
W. Wyatt	21	86	4	5	2	3.57

St. Louis

W-64 L-90

Bill Killefer

POS	Player	AB	BA	HR	RBI	PO	A	E	DP	TC/G	FA
1B	L. Blue	425	.235	4	42	1110	68	16	91	**10.8**	.987
2B	O. Melillo	574	.256	5	59	384	**572**	21	**107**	**6.6**	.979
SS	R. Kress	614	.313	16	112	271	349	**41**	83	5.4	.938
3B	F. O'Rourke	400	.268	1	41	116	150	14	16	3.3	.950
RF	T. Gullic	308	.250	4	44	136	12	5	3	1.9	.967
CF	F. Schulte	392	.278	5	62	250	5	9	2	2.7	.966
LF	G. Goslin	396	.326	30	100	237	13	7	0	2.5	.973
C	R. Ferrell	314	.268	1	41	336	66	7	5	4.0	.983
O1	E. McNeely	235	.272	0	20	302	18	8	30		.976
OF	R. Badgro	234	.239	1	27	112	8	6	3	2.1	.952
OF	A. Metzler	209	.258	1	23	114	2	6	0	2.2	.951
OF	H. Manush	198	.328	2	29	96	5	1	0	2.1	.990
3B	S. Hale	190	.274	2	25	46	80	7	5	2.8	.947

Pitcher	G	IP	W	L	SV	ERA
L. Stewart	35	271	20	12	0	3.45
D. Coffman	38	196	8	18	1	5.14
G. Blaeholder	37	191	11	13	4	4.61
R. Collins	35	172	9	7	2	4.35
S. Gray	27	168	4	15	0	6.28
C. Kimsey	42	113	6	10	1	6.35
R. Stiles	20	102	3	6	0	5.89
G. Crowder	13	77	3	7	1	4.66

Chicago

W-62 L-92

Donie Bush

POS	Player	AB	BA	HR	RBI	PO	A	E	DP	TC/G	FA
1B	B. Clancy	234	.244	3	27	583	24	3	38	9.7	.995
2B	B. Cissell	562	.270	2	48	251	336	**32**	60	5.8	.948
SS	G. Mulleavy	289	.263	0	28	137	219	32	41	5.3	.918
3B	W. Kamm	331	.269	3	47	142	209	23	17	**3.6**	.939
RF	S. Jolley	616	.313	16	114	249	17	14	4	1.9	.950
CF	R. Barnes	266	.248	1	31	179	6	12	3	2.7	.939
LF	C. Reynolds	563	.359	22	100	336	11	9	1	2.7	.975
C	B. Tate	230	.317	0	27	219	40	5	5	3.8	.981
1O	C. Watwood	427	.302	2	51	707	46	11	59		.986
2B	J. Kerr	266	.289	3	27	130	166	6	33	5.9	.980
OF	B. Fothergill	135	.296	0	24	49	2	7	0	1.9	.879

Pitcher	G	IP	W	L	SV	ERA
T. Lyons	42	**298**	22	15	1	3.78
P. Caraway	38	193	10	10	1	3.86
R. Faber	29	169	8	13	1	4.21
T. Thomas	34	169	5	13	0	5.22
D. Henry	35	155	2	17	0	4.88
E. Walsh	37	104	1	4	0	5.38
G. Braxton	19	91	4	10	1	6.45
H. McKain	32	89	6	4	5	5.56

Boston

W-52 L-102

Heinie Wagner

POS	Player	AB	BA	HR	RBI	PO	A	E	DP	TC/G	FA
1B	P. Todt	383	.269	11	62	1001	65	8	84	10.3	.993
2B	B. Regan	507	.266	3	53	308	439	29	92	6.1	.963
SS	H. Rhyne	296	.203	0	23	188	284	28	63	4.7	.944
3B	O. Miller	370	.286	0	40	78	160	13	13	3.0	.948
RF	E. Webb	449	.323	16	66	200	8	9	4	1.9	.959
CF	T. Oliver	**646**	.293	0	46	477	9	9	3	3.2	.982
LF	R. Scarritt	447	.289	2	48	256	5	9	0	2.5	.967
C	C. Berry	256	.289	6	35	279	56	4	4	4.0	.988
OF	C. Durst	302	.245	1	24	145	4	5	1	2.1	.968
3B	B. Reeves	272	.217	2	18	63	125	22	21	3.4	.895
1B	B. Sweeney	243	.309	4	30	541	30	2	49	10.2	.997
C	J. Heving	220	.277	0	17	195	37	3	7	3.3	.987
SS	R. Warstler	162	.185	1	13	100	149	14	30	4.9	.947

Pitcher	G	IP	W	L	SV	ERA
M. Gaston	38	273	13	**20**	2	3.92
D. MacFayden	36	269	11	14	2	4.21
H. Lisenbee	37	237	10	17	0	4.40
J. Russell	35	230	9	**20**	0	5.45
E. Durham	33	140	4	15	1	4.69
E. Morris	18	65	4	9	0	4.13

BATTING AND BASE RUNNING LEADERS

Batting Average
- A. Simmons, PHI .381
- L. Gehrig, NY .379
- B. Ruth, NY .359
- C. Reynolds, CHI .359
- M. Cochrane, PHI .357

Slugging Average
- B. Ruth, NY .732
- L. Gehrig, NY .721
- A. Simmons, PHI .708
- J. Foxx, PHI .637
- G. Goslin, WAS, STL .601
- E. Morgan, CLE .601

Home Runs
- B. Ruth, NY 49
- L. Gehrig, NY 41
- J. Foxx, PHI 37
- G. Goslin, WAS, STL 37
- A. Simmons, PHI 36

Total Bases
- L. Gehrig, NY 419
- A. Simmons, PHI 392
- B. Ruth, NY 379
- J. Foxx, PHI 358
- G. Goslin, WAS, STL 351
- E. Morgan, CLE 351

Runs Batted In
- L. Gehrig, NY 174
- A. Simmons, PHI 165
- J. Foxx, PHI 156
- B. Ruth, NY 153
- G. Goslin, WAS, STL 138

Stolen Bases
- M. McManus, DET 23
- C. Gehringer, DET 19
- R. Johnson, DET 17
- G. Goslin, WAS, STL 17
- J. Cronin, WAS 17

Hits
- J. Hodapp, CLE 225
- L. Gehrig, NY 220
- A. Simmons, PHI 211
- S. Rice, WAS 207

Base on Balls
- B. Ruth, NY 136
- M. Bishop, PHI 128
- L. Gehrig, NY 101
- J. Foxx, PHI 93

Home Run Percentage
- B. Ruth, NY 9.5
- L. Gehrig, NY 7.1
- J. Foxx, PHI 6.6
- A. Simmons, PHI 6.5

Runs
- A. Simmons, PHI 152
- B. Ruth, NY 150
- C. Gehringer, DET 144
- L. Gehrig, NY 143

Doubles
- J. Hodapp, CLE 51
- H. Manush, STL, WAS 49
- E. Morgan, CLE 47
- C. Gehringer, DET 47

Triples
- E. Combs, NY 22
- C. Reynolds, CHI 18
- L. Gehrig, NY 17
- A. Simmons, PHI 16

PITCHING LEADERS

Winning Percentage
- L. Grove, PHI .848
- F. Marberry, WAS .750
- S. Jones, WAS .682
- W. Ferrell, CLE .658
- R. Ruffing, BOS, NY .652

Earned Run Average
- L. Grove, PHI 2.54
- W. Ferrell, CLE 3.31
- L. Stewart, STL 3.45
- G. Uhle, DET 3.65
- B. Hadley, WAS 3.73

Wins
- L. Grove, PHI 28
- W. Ferrell, CLE 25
- G. Earnshaw, PHI 22
- T. Lyons, CHI 22
- L. Stewart, STL 20

Saves
- L. Grove, PHI 9
- G. Braxton, WAS, CHI 6
- J. Quinn, PHI 6
- C. Sullivan, DET 5
- H. McKain, CHI 5

Strikeouts
- L. Grove, PHI 209
- G. Earnshaw, PHI 193
- B. Hadley, WAS 162
- W. Ferrell, CLE 143
- R. Ruffing, BOS, NY 131

Complete Games
- T. Lyons, CHI 29
- G. Crowder, STL, WAS 25
- W. Ferrell, CLE 25
- L. Stewart, STL 23
- L. Grove, PHI 22

Fewest Hits/9 Innings
- B. Hadley, WAS 8.37
- L. Grove, PHI 8.44
- G. Crowder, STL, WAS 8.88
- M. Gaston, BOS 8.97

Shutouts
- G. Pipgras, NY 3
- G. Earnshaw, PHI 3

Fewest Walks/9 Innings
- H. Pennock, NY 1.15
- T. Lyons, CHI 1.72
- L. Grove, PHI 1.86
- J. Russell, BOS 2.08

Most Strikeouts/9 Inn.
- L. Grove, PHI 6.46
- G. Earnshaw, PHI 5.87
- B. Hadley, WAS 5.60
- R. Ruffing, BOS, NY 5.32

Innings
- T. Lyons, CHI 298
- W. Ferrell, CLE 297
- G. Earnshaw, PHI 296
- L. Grove, PHI 291

Games Pitched
- L. Grove, PHI 50
- G. Earnshaw, PHI 49
- H. Johnson, NY 44
- G. Pipgras, NY 44

AMERICAN LEAGUE 1930, *cont.*

	W	L	PCT	GB	R	OR	Batting 2B	3B	HR	BA	SA	SB	Fielding E	DP	FA	Pitching CG	BB	SO	ShO	SV	ERA
Philadelphia	102	52	.662		951	751	319	74	125	.294	.452	48	**145**	121	**.975**	72	488	**672**	**8**	**21**	4.28
Washington	94	60	.610	8	892	**689**	300	98	57	.302	.426	**101**	159	150	.974	**78**	504	524	4	14	**3.96**
New York	86	68	.558	16	**1062**	898	298	**110**	**152**	**.309**	**.488**	91	207	132	.965	65	524	572	6	15	4.88
Cleveland	81	73	.526	21	890	915	**358**	59	72	.304	.431	51	237	156	.962	69	528	441	4	14	4.88
Detroit	75	79	.487	27	783	833	298	90	82	.284	.421	98	192	156	.967	68	570	574	3	17	4.70
St. Louis	64	90	.416	38	751	886	289	67	75	.268	.391	93	188	152	.970	68	449	470	5	10	5.07
Chicago	62	92	.403	40	729	884	255	90	63	.276	.391	74	235	136	.962	67	**407**	471	2	10	4.71
Boston	52	102	.338	50	612	814	257	67	47	.264	.364	42	196	**161**	.968	**78**	488	356	4	5	4.70
					6670	6670	2374	655	673	.288	.421	598	1559	1164	.968	565	3958	4080	36	106	4.65

NATIONAL LEAGUE 1931

St. Louis

W-101 L-53

Gabby Street

POS	Player	AB	BA	HR	RBI	PO	A	E	DP	TC/G	FA	Pitcher	G	IP	W	L	SV	ERA
1B	J. Bottomley	382	.348	9	75	897	43	12	95	10.2	.987	B. Hallahan	37	249	**19**	9	4	3.29
2B	F. Frisch	518	.311	4	82	290	424	19	93	5.7	.974	B. Grimes	29	212	17	9	0	3.65
SS	C. Gelbert	447	.289	1	62	281	435	31	91	5.7	.959	P. Derringer	35	212	18	8	2	3.36
3B	S. Adams	608	.293	1	40	118	223	13	**29**	2.6	**.963**	F. Rhem	33	207	11	10	1	3.56
RF	G. Watkins	503	.288	13	51	263	12	12	4	2.2	.958	S. Johnson	32	186	11	9	2	3.00
CF	P. Martin	413	.300	7	75	282	10	10	2	2.7	.967	J. Haines	19	122	12	3	0	3.02
LF	C. Hafey	450	**.349**	16	95	226	4	4	1	2.0	.983	J. Lindsey	35	75	6	4	7	2.77
C	J. Wilson	383	.274	0	51	**498**	75	9	15	**5.3**	.985							
1B	R. Collins	279	.301	4	59	563	42	3	54	8.9	.995							
C	G. Mancuso	187	.262	1	23	239	40	8	6	5.1	.972							
OF	E. Orsatti	158	.291	0	19	83	0	1	0	1.9	.988							
OF	T. Douthit	133	.331	1	21	105	0	3	0	3.0	.972							

New York

W-87 L-65

John McGraw

POS	Player	AB	BA	HR	RBI	PO	A	E	DP	TC/G	FA	Pitcher	G	IP	W	L	SV	ERA
1B	B. Terry	611	.349	9	112	1411	**105**	16	108	10.0	.990	F. Fitzsimmons	35	254	18	11	0	3.05
2B	B. Hunnefield	196	.270	1	17	112	140	13	27	4.7	.951	C. Hubbell	36	247	14	12	3	2.66
SS	T. Jackson	555	.310	5	71	303	**496**	25	79	5.7	**.970**	B. Walker	37	239	17	9	3	**2.26**
3B	J. Vergez	565	.278	13	81	146	268	30	23	2.9	.932	C. Mitchell	27	190	13	11	0	4.07
RF	F. Lindstrom	303	.300	5	36	150	4	4	1	2.2	.975	J. Berly	27	111	7	8	0	3.88
CF	M. Ott	497	.292	29	115	332	20	7	4	2.6	.981	J. Heving	22	42	1	6	3	4.89
LF	F. Leach	515	.309	6	61	239	6	6	1	2.0	.976							
C	S. Hogan	396	.301	12	65	469	54	2	10	4.6	**.996**							
OF	C. Fullis	302	.328	3	28	154	5	2	4	2.4	.988							
OF	E. Allen	298	.329	5	43	151	2	4	1	2.0	.975							
2B	H. Critz	238	.290	4	17	139	164	5	27	5.7	.984							
2B	D. Marshall	194	.201	0	10	102	135	11	26	5.3	.956							
C	B. O'Farrell	174	.224	1	19	223	27	5	1	3.2	.980							

Chicago

W-84 L-70

Rogers Hornsby

POS	Player	AB	BA	HR	RBI	PO	A	E	DP	TC/G	FA	Pitcher	G	IP	W	L	SV	ERA
1B	C. Grimm	531	.331	4	66	1357	79	10	107	10.0	**.993**	C. Root	39	251	17	14	2	3.48
2B	R. Hornsby	357	.331	16	90	107	205	16	24	4.8	.951	B. Smith	36	240	15	12	2	3.22
SS	W. English	634	.319	2	53	**322**	441	28	75	5.7	.965	P. Malone	36	228	16	9	0	3.90
3B	L. Bell	252	.282	4	32	66	118	11	18	2.8	.944	G. Bush	39	180	16	8	2	4.49
RF	K. Cuyler	613	.330	9	88	347	11	11	4	2.4	.970	L. Sweetland	26	130	8	7	0	5.04
CF	H. Wilson	395	.261	13	61	210	9	5	1	2.2	.978	J. May	31	79	5	5	2	3.87
LF	R. Stephenson	263	.319	1	52	134	1	2	1	1.7	.985							
C	G. Hartnett	380	.282	8	70	444	68	10	**16**	5.0	.981							
32	B. Jurges	293	.201	0	23	108	198	11	32		.965							
OF	D. Taylor	270	.300	5	41	170	3	2	0	2.6	.989							
21	F. Blair	240	.258	2	29	245	120	12	28		.968							
OF	V. Barton	239	.238	13	50	133	2	5	0	2.3	.964							
C	R. Hemsley	204	.309	3	31	236	40	7	5	4.3	.975							

Brooklyn

W-79 L-73

Wilbert Robinson

POS	Player	AB	BA	HR	RBI	PO	A	E	DP	TC/G	FA	Pitcher	G	IP	W	L	SV	ERA
1B	D. Bissonette	587	.290	12	87	**1460**	66	16	136	10.1	.990	W. Clark	34	233	14	10	1	3.20
2B	M. Finn	413	.274	0	45	260	331	15	65	5.4	.975	D. Vance	30	219	11	13	0	3.38
SS	G. Slade	272	.239	1	29	173	274	25	54	5.8	.947	R. Phelps	28	149	7	9	0	5.00
3B	W. Gilbert	552	.266	0	46	125	**295**	23	14	3.1	.948	S. Thurston	24	143	9	9	0	3.97
RF	B. Herman	610	.313	18	97	287	24	13	7	2.2	.960	F. Heimach	31	135	9	7	1	3.46
CF	J. Frederick	611	.270	17	71	398	10	15	2	2.9	.965	J. Shaute	25	129	11	8	0	4.83
LF	L. O'Doul	512	.336	7	75	285	4	14	0	2.3	.954	D. Luque	19	103	7	6	0	4.56
C	A. Lopez	360	.269	0	40	390	69	11	6	4.5	.977	J. Quinn	39	64	5	4	**15**	2.66
SS	G. Wright	268	.284	9	32	151	255	25	52	5.7	.942							
C	E. Lombardi	182	.297	4	23	218	23	4	5	4.9	.984							
2B	F. Thompson	181	.265	1	21	89	120	12	36	3.5	.946							
OF	R. Bressler	153	.281	0	26	54	1	1	0	1.6	.982							

Pittsburgh

W-75 L-79

Jewel Ens

POS	Player	AB	BA	HR	RBI	PO	A	E	DP	TC/G	FA	Pitcher	G	IP	W	L	SV	ERA
1B	G. Suhr	270	.211	4	32	684	39	5	72	9.6	.993	H. Meine	36	**284**	**19**	13	0	2.98
2B	G. Grantham	465	.305	10	46	114	142	23	34	5.5	.918	L. French	39	276	15	13	1	3.26
SS	T. Thevenow	404	.213	0	38	245	432	25	92	5.8	.964	R. Kremer	30	230	11	15	0	3.33
3B	P. Traynor	615	.298	2	103	**172**	284	**37**	21	**3.2**	.925	G. Spencer	38	187	11	12	3	3.42
RF	P. Waner	559	.322	6	70	342	28	9	8	2.7	.976	E. Brame	26	180	9	13	0	4.21
CF	L. Waner	**681**	.314	4	57	484	20	11	5	3.4	.979							
LF	A. Comorosky	350	.243	1	48	214	4	5	2	2.5	.978							
C	E. Phillips	353	.232	7	44	293	49	5	12	3.4	.986							
OF	W. Jensen	267	.243	3	17	182	2	5	1	2.8	.974							
2B	T. Piet	167	.299	0	24	103	133	3	17	5.4	.987							
2B	H. Grossklos	161	.280	0	20	92	115	4	35	5.4	.981							
C	E. Grace	150	.280	1	20	128	23	4	5	3.4	.974							

NATIONAL LEAGUE 1931, *cont.*

Philadelphia

W-66 L-88

Burt Shotton

POS	Player	AB	BA	HR	RBI	PO	A	E	DP	TC/G	FA	Pitcher	G	IP	W	L	SV	ERA
1B	D. Hurst	489	.305	11	91	1206	104	**18**	117	9.8	.986	J. Elliott	**52**	249	**19**	14	5	4.27
2B	L. Mallon	375	.309	1	45	231	290	24	57	5.6	.956	R. Benge	38	247	14	18	2	3.17
SS	D. Bartell	554	.289	0	34	315	432	**41**	**96**	**5.9**	.948	P. Collins	42	240	12	16	4	3.86
3B	P. Whitney	501	.287	9	74	131	217	19	1	2.9	.948	C. Dudley	30	179	8	14	0	3.52
RF	B. Arlett	418	.313	18	72	196	14	10	6	2.3	.955	F. Watt	38	123	5	5	2	4.84
CF	F. Brickell	514	.253	1	31	341	8	8	2	2.9	.978	S. Bolen	28	99	3	12	0	6.39
LF	C. Klein	594	.337	**31**	**121**	292	13	9	0	2.1	.971	S. Blake	14	71	4	5	1	5.58
C	S. Davis	393	.326	4	51	420	**78**	3	10	4.4	.994							
23	B. Friberg	353	.261	1	26	180	252	20	43		.956							
C	H. McCurdy	150	.287	1	25	157	27	6	1	4.2	.968							

Boston

W-64 L-90

Bill McKechnie

POS	Player	AB	BA	HR	RBI	PO	A	E	DP	TC/G	FA	Pitcher	G	IP	W	L	SV	ERA
1B	E. Sheely	538	.273	1	77	1374	70	12	108	10.2	.992	E. Brandt	33	250	18	11	2	2.92
2B	F. Maguire	492	.228	0	26	372	478	21	94	**5.9**	**.976**	T. Zachary	33	229	11	15	2	3.10
SS	R. Maranville	562	.260	0	33	271	432	38	93	5.4	.949	S. Seibold	33	206	10	18	0	4.67
3B	B. Urbanski	303	.238	0	17	76	145	9	15	3.4	.961	B. Cantwell	33	156	7	9	2	3.63
RF	W. Schulmerich	327	.309	2	43	190	6	7	0	2.3	.966	B. Sherdel	27	138	6	10	0	4.25
CF	W. Berger	617	.323	19	84	457	16	11	5	3.1	.977	B. Cunningham	33	137	3	12	1	4.48
LF	R. Worthington	491	.291	4	44	242	8	3	1	2.0	.988	F. Frankhouse	26	127	8	8	1	4.03
C	A. Spohrer	350	.240	0	27	392	54	8	5	4.1	.982							
OF	L. Richbourg	286	.287	2	29	154	3	3	2	2.3	.981							
03	R. Moore	192	.260	3	34	71	39	6	3		.948							
3B	B. Dreesen	180	.222	1	10	28	83	11	1	2.6	.910							

Cincinnati

W-58 L-96

Dan Howley

POS	Player	AB	BA	HR	RBI	PO	A	E	DP	TC/G	FA	Pitcher	G	IP	W	L	SV	ERA
1B	H. Hendrick	530	.315	1	75	1348	67	18*	147*	10.5*	.987	S. Johnson	42	262	11	**19**	0	3.77
2B	T. Cuccinello	575	.315	2	93	**376**	**499**	**28**	**128**	5.9	.969	R. Lucas	29	238	14	13	0	3.59
SS	L. Durocher	361	.227	1	29	212	344	20	86	4.8	.965	L. Benton	38	204	10	15	2	3.35
3B	J. Stripp	426	.324	3	42	101	191	13	22	3.2	.957	B. Frey	34	134	8	12	2	4.92
RF	E. Crabtree	443	.269	4	37	240	19	7	6	2.6	.974	E. Rixey	22	127	4	7	0	3.91
CF	T. Douthit	374	.262	0	24	286	6	5	3	3.1	.983	O. Carroll	29	107	3	9	0	5.53
LF	E. Roush	376	.271	1	41	197	5	4	1	2.3	.981	R. Kolp	30	107	4	9	1	4.96
C	C. Sukeforth	351	.256	0	25	300	59	**13**	9	3.5	.965	J. Ogden	22	89	4	8	1	2.93
OF	N. Cullop	334	.263	8	48	177	5	6	3	2.3	.968							
OF	C. Heathcote	252	.258	0	28	164	13	2	4	3.0	.989							
OF	W. Roettger	185	.351	1	20	95	3	1	1	2.3	.990							
SS	H. Ford	175	.229	0	13	107	162	13	41	3.9	.954							
C	A. Asbjornson	118	.305	0	22	82	24	2	2	3.5	.981							

BATTING AND BASE RUNNING LEADERS

Batting Average

C. Hafey, STL	.349
B. Terry, NY	.349
J. Bottomley, STL	.348
C. Klein, PHI	.337
L. O'Doul, BKN	.336

Slugging Average

C. Klein, PHI	.584
R. Hornsby, CHI	.574
C. Hafey, STL	.569
M. Ott, NY	.545
B. Arlett, PHI	.538

Home Runs

C. Klein, PHI	31
M. Ott, NY	29
W. Berger, BOS	19
B. Arlett, PHI	18
B. Herman, BKN	18

Total Bases

C. Klein, PHI	347
B. Terry, NY	323
B. Herman, BKN	320
W. Berger, BOS	316
K. Cuyler, CHI	290

Runs Batted In

C. Klein, PHI	121
M. Ott, NY	115
B. Terry, NY	112
P. Traynor, PIT	103
B. Herman, BKN	97

Stolen Bases

F. Frisch, STL	28
B. Herman, BKN	17
P. Martin, STL	16
S. Adams, STL	16
G. Watkins, STL	15

Hits

L. Waner, PIT	214
B. Terry, NY	213
K. Cuyler, CHI	202
W. English, CHI	202

Base on Balls

M. Ott, NY	80
P. Waner, PIT	73
K. Cuyler, CHI	72
G. Grantham, PIT	71

Home Run Percentage

M. Ott, NY	5.8
C. Klein, PHI	5.2
R. Hornsby, CHI	4.5
B. Arlett, PHI	4.3

Runs

C. Klein, PHI	121
B. Terry, NY	121
W. English, CHI	117
K. Cuyler, CHI	110

Doubles

S. Adams, STL	46
W. Berger, BOS	44
D. Bartell, PHI	43
B. Herman, BKN	43
B. Terry, NY	43

Triples

B. Terry, NY	20
B. Herman, BKN	16
P. Traynor, PIT	15
D. Bissonette, BKN	14

PITCHING LEADERS

Winning Percentage

P. Derringer, STL	.692
B. Hallahan, STL	.679
G. Bush, CHI	.667
B. Walker, NY	.654
B. Grimes, STL	.654

Earned Run Average

B. Walker, NY	2.26
C. Hubbell, NY	2.66
E. Brandt, BOS	2.92
H. Meine, PIT	2.98
S. Johnson, STL	3.00

Wins

B. Hallahan, STL	19
J. Elliott, PHI	19
H. Meine, PIT	19
P. Derringer, STL	18
E. Brandt, BOS	18
F. Fitzsimmons, NY	18

Saves

J. Quinn, BKN	15
J. Lindsey, STL	7
J. Elliott, PHI	5
P. Collins, PHI	4
B. Hallahan, STL	4

Strikeouts

B. Hallahan, STL	159
C. Hubbell, NY	156
D. Vance, BKN	150
P. Derringer, STL	134
C. Root, CHI	131

Complete Games

R. Lucas, CIN	24
E. Brandt, BOS	23
H. Meine, PIT	22
C. Hubbell, NY	21
L. French, PIT	20

Fewest Hits/9 Innings

C. Hubbell, NY	7.76
B. Walker, NY	7.97
E. Brandt, BOS	8.21
F. Fitzsimmons, NY	8.59

Shutouts

B. Walker, NY	6
P. Derringer, STL	4
C. Hubbell, NY	4
F. Fitzsimmons, NY	4

Fewest Walks/9 Innings

S. Johnson, STL	1.40
R. Lucas, CIN	1.47
W. Clark, BKN	2.01
T. Zachary, BOS	2.08

Most Strikeouts/9 Inn.

D. Vance, BKN	6.17
B. Hallahan, STL	5.75
P. Derringer, STL	5.70
C. Hubbell, NY	5.68

Innings

H. Meine, PIT	284
L. French, PIT	276
S. Johnson, CIN	262
F. Fitzsimmons, NY	254

Games Pitched

J. Elliott, PHI	52
P. Collins, PHI	42
S. Johnson, CIN	42

							Batting						Fielding			Pitching					
	W	L	PCT	GB	R	OR	2B	3B	HR	BA	SA	SB	E	DP	FA	CG	BB	SO	ShO	SV	ERA
St. Louis	101	53	.656		815	614	**353**	74	60	.286	.411	**114**	160	169	**.974**	80	449	**626**	**17**	**20**	3.45
New York	87	65	.572	13	768	**599**	251	64	**101**	**.289**	.416	83	**159**	126	**.974**	**90**	421	571	**17**	12	**3.30**
Chicago	84	70	.545	17	**828**	710	340	67	83	**.289**	**.422**	49	169	141	.973	80	524	541	8	8	3.97
Brooklyn	79	73	.520	21	681	673	240	**77**	71	.276	.390	45	187	154	.969	64	**351**	546	9	18	3.84
Pittsburgh	75	79	.487	26	636	691	243	70	41	.266	.360	59	194	167	.968	89	442	345	9	5	3.66
Philadelphia	66	88	.429	35	684	828	299	52	81	.279	.400	42	210	149	.966	60	511	499	4	16	4.58
Boston	64	90	.416	37	533	680	221	59	34	.258	.341	46	170	141	.973	78	406	419	12	9	3.90
Cincinnati	58	96	.377	43	592	742	241	70	21	.269	.352	24	165	**194**	.973	70	399	317	4	6	4.22
					5537	5537	2188	533	492	.277	.387	462	1414	1241	.971	611	3503	3864	80	94	3.87

AMERICAN LEAGUE 1931

Philadelphia

W-107 L-45

Connie Mack

POS	Player	AB	BA	HR	RBI	PO	A	E	DP	TC/G	FA	Pitcher	G	IP	W	L	SV	ERA
1B	J. Foxx	515	.291	30	120	964	49	7	89	9.1	.993	R. Walberg	44	**291**	20	12	3	3.74
2B	M. Bishop	497	.294	5	37	314	414	12	84	5.7	.984	L. Grove	41	289	**31**	4	5	**2.06**
SS	D. Williams	294	.269	6	40	152	214	27	59	5.5	.931	G. Earnshaw	43	282	21	7	6	3.67
3B	J. Dykes	355	.273	3	46	105	153	7	19	3.0	.974	R. Mahaffey	30	162	15	4	2	4.21
RF	B. Miller	534	.281	8	77	305	7	4	1	2.3	.987	E. Rommel	25	118	7	5	0	2.97
CF	M. Haas	440	.323	8	56	272	6	3	4	2.8	.989	W. Hoyt	16	111	10	5	0	4.22
LF	A. Simmons	513	**.390**	22	128	287	10	4	0	2.4	.987							
C	M. Cochrane	459	.349	17	89	560	63	9	9	5.4	.986							
UT	E. McNair	280	.271	5	33	97	155	19	36		.930							
SS	J. Boley	224	.228	0	20	102	149	12	31	4.2	.954							
OF	D. Cramer	223	.260	2	20	133	5	3	1	2.6	.979							
1B	P. Todt	197	.244	5	44	403	13	2	36	8.0	.995							
OF	J. Moore	143	.224	2	21	70	3	2	2	2.1	.973							

New York

W-94 L-59

Joe McCarthy

POS	Player	AB	BA	HR	RBI	PO	A	E	DP	TC/G	FA	Pitcher	G	IP	W	L	SV	ERA
1B	L. Gehrig	619	.341	**46**	**184**	1352	58	13	120	9.2	.991	L. Gomez	40	243	21	9	3	2.63
2B	T. Lazzeri	484	.267	8	83	216	288	22	52	5.8	.958	R. Ruffing	37	237	16	14	2	4.41
SS	L. Lary	610	.280	10	107	321	484	46	85	5.5	.946	H. Johnson	40	196	13	8	4	4.72
3B	J. Sewell	484	.302	6	64	131	227	18	14	3.1	.952	H. Pennock	25	189	11	6	0	4.28
RF	B. Ruth	534	.373	**46**	163	237	5	7	2	1.8	.972	G. Pipgras	36	138	7	6	3	3.79
CF	E. Combs	563	.318	5	58	335	5	9	2	2.7	.974	E. Wells	27	117	9	5	2	4.32
LF	B. Chapman	600	.315	17	122	300	14	12	1	2.4	.963	R. Sherid	17	74	5	5	2	5.69
C	B. Dickey	477	.327	6	78	**670**	78	3	6	**6.0**	**.996**							
OF	S. Byrd	248	.270	3	32	148	3	4	1	1.8	.974							
2B	J. Reese	245	.241	3	26	173	168	10	44	5.8	.972							

Washington

W-92 L-62

Walter Johnson

POS	Player	AB	BA	HR	RBI	PO	A	E	DP	TC/G	FA	Pitcher	G	IP	W	L	SV	ERA
1B	J. Kuhel	524	.269	8	85	1255	57	12	119	9.5	.991	L. Brown	42	259	15	14	0	3.20
2B	B. Myer	591	.293	4	56	333	398	12	87	5.4	**.984**	G. Crowder	44	234	18	11	2	3.88
SS	J. Cronin	611	.306	12	126	**323**	488	43	**94**	5.5	.950	F. Marberry	45	219	16	4	7	3.45
3B	O. Bluege	570	.272	8	98	151	**286**	18	24	3.0	**.960**	C. Fischer	46	191	13	9	3	4.38
RF	S. Rice	413	.310	0	42	221	7	7	2	2.2	.970	B. Hadley	**55**	180	11	10	8	3.06
CF	S. West	526	.333	3	91	402	13	4	3	3.3	.990	S. Jones	25	148	9	10	1	4.32
LF	H. Manush	616	.307	6	70	245	5	6	1	1.8	.977	B. Burke	30	129	8	3	2	4.27
C	R. Spencer	483	.275	1	60	642	69	11	9	5.0	.985							
OF	D. Harris	231	.312	5	50	111	4	6	1	2.0	.950							
OF	H. Rice	162	.265	0	15	89	3	3	0	2.3	.968							

Cleveland

W-78 L-76

Roger Peckinpaugh

POS	Player	AB	BA	HR	RBI	PO	A	E	DP	TC/G	FA	Pitcher	G	IP	W	L	SV	ERA
1B	E. Morgan	462	.351	11	86	1114	72	**19**	102	10.3	.984	W. Ferrell	40	276	22	12	3	3.75
2B	J. Hodapp	468	.295	2	56	274	413	22	73	5.9	.969	W. Hudlin	44	254	15	14	4	4.60
SS	E. Montague	193	.285	1	26	127	202	27	30	5.6	.924	C. Brown	39	233	11	15	0	4.71
3B	W. Kamm	410	.295	0	66	129*	208	19	29*	3.1*	.947	M. Harder	40	194	13	14	1	4.36
RF	D. Porter	414	.312	1	38	184	7	6	0	1.8	.970	S. Connally	17	86	5	5	1	4.20
CF	E. Averill	**627**	.333	32	143	398	9	10	3	2.7	.976							
LF	J. Vosmik	591	.320	7	117	315	12	10	2	2.3	.970							
C	L. Sewell	375	.275	1	53	384	61	9	5	4.3	.980							
UT	J. Burnett	427	.300	1	52	194	296	34	52		.935							
C	G. Myatt	195	.246	1	29	176	34	2	2	3.7	.991							
OF	B. Falk	161	.304	2	28	55	1	3	0	1.8	.949							
P	W. Ferrell	116	.319	9	30	19	**74**	3	3	2.4	.969							

St. Louis

W-63 L-91

Bill Killefer

POS	Player	AB	BA	HR	RBI	PO	A	E	DP	TC/G	FA	Pitcher	G	IP	W	L	SV	ERA
1B	J. Burns	570	.260	4	70	1346	**125**	11	**131**	10.4	.993	S. Gray	43	258	11	**24**	2	5.09
2B	O. Melillo	617	.306	2	75	**428**	**543**	**32**	**118**	**6.6**	.968	L. Stewart	36	258	14	17	0	4.40
SS	J. Levey	498	.209	5	38	269	398	**58**	92	5.2	.920	G. Blaeholder	35	226	11	15	0	4.53
3B	R. Kress	605	.311	16	114	92	141	16	12	3.0	.936	D. Coffman	32	169	9	13	1	3.88
RF	T. Jenkins	230	.265	3	25	93	6	5	1	1.8	.952	R. Collins	17	107	5	5	0	3.79
CF	F. Schulte	553	.304	9	65	361	13	11	4	2.9	.971	W. Hebert	23	103	6	7	0	5.07
LF	G. Goslin	591	.328	24	105	319	14	14	1	2.3	.960	C. Kimsey	42	94	4	6	7	4.39
C	R. Ferrell	386	.306	3	57	412	**86**	**14**	**11**	4.7	.973							
3B	L. Storti	273	.220	3	26	78	134	17	20	3.4	.926							
OF	L. Bettencourt	206	.257	3	26	99	6	4	1	1.9	.963							

Boston

W-62 L-90

Shano Collins

POS	Player	AB	BA	HR	RBI	PO	A	E	DP	TC/G	FA	Pitcher	G	IP	W	L	SV	ERA
1B	B. Sweeney	498	.295	1	58	1283	92	9	89	**11.2**	**.993**	J. Russell	36	232	10	18	0	5.16
2B	R. Warstler	181	.243	0	10	74	135	15	20	5.3	.933	D. MacFayden	35	231	16	12	0	4.02
SS	H. Rhyne	565	.273	0	51	295	**502**	31	74	**5.6**	**.963**	W. Moore	53	185	11	13	**10**	3.88
3B	O. Miller	389	.272	0	43	75	147	11	12	3.1	.953	E. Durham	38	165	8	10	0	4.25
RF	E. Webb	589	.333	14	103	270	21	16	5	2.0	.948	H. Lisenbee	41	165	5	12	0	5.19
CF	T. Oliver	586	.276	0	70	433	15	3	4	3.0	.993	E. Morris	37	131	5	7	0	4.75
LF	J. Rothrock	475	.278	4	42	153	9	3	1	2.1	.982	M. Gaston	23	119	2	13	0	4.46
C	C. Berry	357	.283	6	49	312	78	6	8	3.9	.985	B. Kline	28	98	5	5	0	4.41
3B	U. Pickering	341	.252	9	52	90	143	8	8	3.3	.967							
OF	A. Van Camp	324	.275	0	33	107	3	3	0	1.9	.973							

Detroit

W-61 L-93

Bucky Harris

POS	Player	AB	BA	HR	RBI	PO	A	E	DP	TC/G	FA	Pitcher	G	IP	W	L	SV	ERA
1B	D. Alexander	517	.325	3	87	1197	53	16	91	10.0	.987	E. Whitehill	34	272	13	16	0	4.06
2B	C. Gehringer	383	.311	4	53	224	236	10	54	6.0	.979	V. Sorrell	35	247	13	14	1	4.12
SS	B. Rogell	185	.303	2	24	91	182	12	26	5.9	.958	G. Uhle	29	193	11	12	2	3.50
3B	M. McManus	362	.271	3	53	92	172	14	18	3.5	.950	T. Bridges	35	173	8	16	0	4.99
RF	R. Johnson	621	.279	8	55	332	25	15	8	2.5	.960	A. Herring	35	165	7	13	1	4.31
CF	H. Walker	252	.286	0	16	170	4	7	1	2.7	.961	C. Hogsett	22	112	3	9	2	5.93
LF	J. Stone	584	.327	10	76	319	11	14	6	2.3	.959	W. Hoyt	16	92	3	8	0	5.87
C	R. Hayworth	273	.256	0	25	334	61	11	5	4.6	.973							
UT	M. Owen	377	.223	3	39	308	220	24	46		.957							
2S	M. Koenig	364	.253	1	39	191	236	28	41		.938							
OF	G. Walker	189	.296	1	28	99	2	5	1	2.4	.953							
OF	F. Doljack	187	.278	4	20	140	8	12	1	3.0	.925							

AMERICAN LEAGUE 1931, *cont.*

Chicago

W-56 L-97

Donie Bush

POS	Player	AB	BA	HR	RBI	PO	A	E	DP	TC/G	FA
1B	L. Blue	589	.304	1	62	**1452**	81	16	105	10.0	.990
2B	J. Kerr	444	.268	2	50	297	366	22	78	5.9	.968
SS	B. Cissell	409	.220	1	46	168	233	24	47	5.1	.944
3B	B. Sullivan	363	.275	2	33	96	152	**24**	9	3.3	.912
RF	C. Reynolds	462	.290	6	77	233	10	13	3	2.3	.949
CF	C. Watwood	367	.283	1	47	259	13	16	2	2.8	.944
LF	L. Fonseca	465	.299	2	71	183	4	5	1	2.0	.974
C	B. Tate	273	.267	0	22	310	69	5	**11**	4.5	.987
OF	B. Fothergill	312	.282	3	56	169	2	5	0	2.4	.972
SS	L. Appling	297	.232	1	28	147	232	42	37	5.5	.900
C	F. Grube	265	.219	1	24	248	50	7	3	3.8	.977
3B	I. Jeffries	223	.224	2	16	69	100	9	4	2.9	.949
OF	M. Simons	189	.275	0	12	112	3	6	0	2.1	.950
OF	S. Jolley	110	.300	3	28	29	1	5	1	1.5	.857

Pitcher	G	IP	W	L	SV	ERA
V. Frasier	46	254	13	15	4	4.46
T. Thomas	42	242	10	14	2	4.80
P. Caraway	51	220	10	**24**	2	6.22
R. Faber	44	184	10	14	1	3.82
H. McKain	27	112	6	9	0	5.71
T. Lyons	22	101	4	6	0	4.01

BATTING AND BASE RUNNING LEADERS

Batting Average

A. Simmons, PHI	.390
B. Ruth, NY	.373
E. Morgan, CLE	.351
M. Cochrane, PHI	.349
L. Gehrig, NY	.341

Slugging Average

B. Ruth, NY	.700
L. Gehrig, NY	.662
A. Simmons, PHI	.641
E. Averill, CLE	.576
J. Foxx, PHI	.567

Home Runs

B. Ruth, NY	46
L. Gehrig, NY	46
E. Averill, CLE	32
J. Foxx, PHI	30
G. Goslin, STL	24

Total Bases

L. Gehrig, NY	410
B. Ruth, NY	374
E. Averill, CLE	361
A. Simmons, PHI	329
G. Goslin, STL	328

Runs Batted In

L. Gehrig, NY	184
B. Ruth, NY	163
E. Averill, CLE	143
A. Simmons, PHI	128
J. Cronin, WAS	126

Stolen Bases

B. Chapman, NY	61
R. Johnson, DET	33
J. Burns, STL	19
B. Cissell, CHI	18
T. Lazzeri, NY	18

Hits

L. Gehrig, NY	211
E. Averill, CLE	209
A. Simmons, PHI	200
B. Ruth, NY	199

Base on Balls

B. Ruth, NY	128
L. Blue, CHI	127
L. Gehrig, NY	117
M. Bishop, PHI	112

Home Run Percentage

B. Ruth, NY	8.6
L. Gehrig, NY	7.4
J. Foxx, PHI	5.8
E. Averill, CLE	5.1

Runs

L. Gehrig, NY	163
B. Ruth, NY	149
E. Averill, CLE	140
E. Combs, NY	120
B. Chapman, NY	120

Doubles

E. Webb, BOS	67
D. Alexander, DET	47
R. Kress, STL	46
J. Cronin, WAS	44

Triples

R. Johnson, DET	19
L. Blue, CHI	15
L. Gehrig, NY	15
C. Reynolds, CHI	14
J. Vosmik, CLE	14

PITCHING LEADERS

Winning Percentage

L. Grove, PHI	.886
F. Marberry, WAS	.800
R. Mahaffey, PHI	.789
G. Earnshaw, PHI	.750
L. Gomez, NY	.700

Earned Run Average

L. Grove, PHI	2.06
L. Gomez, NY	2.63
L. Brown, WAS	3.20
F. Marberry, WAS	3.45
G. Uhle, DET	3.50

Wins

L. Grove, PHI	31
W. Ferrell, CLE	22
L. Gomez, NY	21
G. Earnshaw, PHI	21
R. Walberg, PHI	20

Saves

W. Moore, BOS	10
B. Hadley, WAS	8
F. Marberry, WAS	7
C. Kimsey, STL	7
G. Earnshaw, PHI	6

Strikeouts

L. Grove, PHI	175
G. Earnshaw, PHI	152
L. Gomez, NY	150
R. Ruffing, NY	132
B. Hadley, WAS	124

Complete Games

L. Grove, PHI	27
W. Ferrell, CLE	27
G. Earnshaw, PHI	23
E. Whitehill, DET	22
L. Stewart, STL	20

Fewest Hits/9 Innings

L. Gomez, NY	7.63
L. Grove, PHI	7.76
G. Earnshaw, PHI	8.15
D. Coffman, STL	8.45

Shutouts

L. Grove, PHI	4
G. Earnshaw, PHI	3

Fewest Walks/9 Innings

H. Pennock, NY	1.43
S. Gray, STL	1.88
L. Grove, PHI	1.93
C. Brown, CLE	2.12

Most Strikeouts/9 Inn.

L. Gomez, NY	5.56
T. Bridges, DET	5.46
L. Grove, PHI	5.46
R. Ruffing, NY	5.01

Innings

R. Walberg, PHI	291
L. Grove, PHI	289
G. Earnshaw, PHI	282
W. Ferrell, CLE	276

Games Pitched

B. Hadley, WAS	55
W. Moore, BOS	53
P. Caraway, CHI	51
C. Fischer, WAS	46
V. Frasier, CHI	46

							Batting						Fielding			Pitching					
	W	L	PCT	GB	R	OR	2B	3B	HR	BA	SA	SB	E	DP	FA	CG	BB	SO	ShO	SV	ERA
Philadelphia	107	45	.704		858	**626**	311	64	118	.287	.435	27	**141**	151	**.976**	**97**	457	574	**12**	16	**3.47**
New York	94	59	.614	13.5	**1067**	760	277	78	**155**	**.297**	**.457**	**138**	169	131	.972	78	543	**686**	4	17	4.20
Washington	92	62	.597	16	843	691	308	**93**	49	.285	.400	72	142	148	**.976**	60	498	582	6	**24**	3.76
Cleveland	78	76	.506	30	885	833	**321**	69	71	.296	.419	63	232	143	.963	76	561	470	6	9	4.63
St. Louis	63	91	.409	45	722	870	287	62	76	.271	.390	73	232	**160**	.963	65	**448**	436	4	10	4.76
Boston	62	90	.408	45	625	800	289	34	37	.262	.349	43	188	127	.970	61	473	365	5	10	4.60
Detroit	61	93	.396	47	651	836	292	69	43	.268	.371	117	220	139	.964	93	597	511	5	6	4.56
Chicago	56	97	.366	51.5	704	939	238	69	27	.260	.343	94	245	131	.961	54	588	420	6	10	5.05
					6355	6355	2323	538	576	.278	.395	627	1569	1130	.968	584	4165	4044	48	102	4.38

NATIONAL LEAGUE 1932

Chicago

W-90 L-64

Rogers Hornsby
W-53 L-46

Charlie Grimm
W-37 L-18

POS	Player	AB	BA	HR	RBI	PO	A	E	DP	TC/G	FA
1B	C. Grimm	570	.307	7	80	1429	123	11	**127**	10.5	.993
2B	B. Herman	656	.314	1	51	401	**527**	**38**	102	**6.3**	.961
SS	B. Jurges	396	.253	2	52	223	394	23	69	**6.2**	**.964**
3B	W. English	522	.272	3	47	96	173	12	13	3.0	.957
RF	K. Cuyler	446	.291	10	77	239	7	8	1	2.3	.969
CF	J. Moore	443	.305	13	64	272	12	5	2	2.7	.983
LF	R. Stephenson	583	.324	4	85	298	7	5	2	2.1	.984
C	G. Hartnett	406	.271	12	52	484	75	10	8	**4.9**	.982
3B	S. Hack	178	.236	2	19	36	90	12	5	2.7	.913
C	R. Hemsley	151	.238	4	20	173	17	5	3	4.1	.974
OF	L. Richbourg	148	.257	1	21	70	2	1	1	2.2	.986

Pitcher	G	IP	W	L	SV	ERA
L. Warneke	35	277	**22**	6	0	**2.37**
G. Bush	40	239	19	11	0	3.21
P. Malone	37	237	15	17	0	3.38
C. Root	39	216	15	10	3	3.58
B. Grimes	30	141	6	11	1	4.78
B. Smith	34	119	4	3	2	4.61

NATIONAL LEAGUE 1932, *cont.*

Team	POS	Player	AB	BA	HR	RBI	PO	A	E	DP	TC/G	FA	Pitcher	G	IP	W	L	SV	ERA
Pittsburgh	1B	G. Suhr	581	.263	5	81	1388	84	**18**	111	9.7	.988	L. French	**47**	274	18	16	4	3.02
W-86 L-68	2B	T. Piet	574	.282	7	85	378	454	26	80	5.6	.970	B. Swift	39	214	14	10	4	3.61
George Gibson	SS	A. Vaughan	497	.318	4	61	247	403	**46**	74	5.4	.934	H. Meine	28	172	12	9	1	3.86
	3B	P. Traynor	513	.329	2	68	173	222	**27**	14	**3.3**	.936	B. Harris	37	168	10	9	2	3.64
	RF	P. Waner	630	.341	7	82	367	13	10	3	2.5	.974	S. Swetonic	24	163	11	6	0	2.82
	CF	L. Waner	565	.333	3	38	426	9	6	0	3.4	.986	G. Spencer	39	138	4	8	1	4.97
	LF	A. Comorosky	370	.286	4	46	255	4	5	2	2.9	.981	L. Chagnon	30	128	9	6	0	3.94
	C	E. Grace	390	.274	7	55	364	48	1	10	3.6	**.998**							
	OF	D. Barbee	327	.257	5	55	190	5	5	2	2.6	.975							
	S3	T. Thevenow	194	.237	0	26	82	126	14	24		.937							

Team	POS	Player	AB	BA	HR	RBI	PO	A	E	DP	TC/G	FA	Pitcher	G	IP	W	L	SV	ERA
Brooklyn	1B	G. Kelly	202	.243	4	22	575	36	10	48	10.0	.984	W. Clark	40	273	20	12	0	3.49
W-81 L-73	2B	T. Cuccinello	597	.281	12	77	385	525	25	**113**	6.1	.973	V. Mungo	39	223	13	11	2	4.43
Max Carey	SS	G. Wright	446	.274	10	60	231	386	40	83	5.4	.939	D. Vance	27	176	12	11	1	4.20
	3B	J. Stripp	534	.303	6	64	92	201	14	22	3.3	.954	F. Heimach	36	168	9	4	0	3.97
	RF	H. Wilson	481	.297	23	123	220	14	11	4	2.0	.955	S. Thurston	28	153	12	8	0	4.06
	CF	D. Taylor	395	.324	11	48	271	8	3	1	2.9	.989	J. Shaute	34	117	7	7	4	4.62
	LF	L. O'Doul	595	**.368**	21	90	317	4	7	0	2.2	.979	J. Quinn	42	87	3	7	**8**	3.30
	C	A. Lopez	404	.275	1	43	456	**82**	13	10	4.4	.976							
	OF	J. Frederick	384	.299	16	56	201	6	5	2	2.4	.976							
	SS	G. Slade	250	.240	1	23	101	148	15	30	4.8	.943							
	1B	B. Clancy	196	.306	0	16	524	40	2	55	10.7	.996							
	3B	M. Finn	189	.238	0	14	34	92	9	7	2.7	.933							

Team	POS	Player	AB	BA	HR	RBI	PO	A	E	DP	TC/G	FA	Pitcher	G	IP	W	L	SV	ERA
Philadelphia	1B	D. Hurst	579	.339	24	**143**	1341	94	10	105	9.6	**.993**	E. Holley	34	228	11	14	0	3.95
W-78 L-76	2B	L. Mallon	347	.259	5	31	199	228	20	42	5.1	.955	R. Benge	41	222	13	12	6	4.05
Burt Shotton	SS	D. Bartell	614	.308	1	53	**359**	**529**	34	83	6.0	.963	S. Hansen	39	191	10	10	2	3.72
	3B	P. Whitney	624	.298	13	124	**177**	**276**	19	**31**	3.1	**.960**	P. Collins	43	184	14	12	3	5.27
	RF	C. Klein	650	.348	**38**	137	331	29	15	3	2.4	.960	F. Rhem	26	169	11	7	1	3.74
	CF	K. Davis	576	.309	5	57	411	15	11	6	3.3	.975	J. Elliott	39	166	11	10	0	5.42
	LF	H. Lee	595	.303	18	85	380	11	14	3	2.7	.965							
	C	S. Davis	402	.336	14	70	408	54	6	**15**	3.9	.987							
	2B	B. Friberg	154	.240	0	14	107	137	11	22	4.6	.957							

Team	POS	Player	AB	BA	HR	RBI	PO	A	E	DP	TC/G	FA	Pitcher	G	IP	W	L	SV	ERA
Boston	1B	A. Shires	298	.238	5	30	715	48	9	61	9.4	.988	E. Brandt	35	254	16	16	1	3.97
W-77 L-77	2B	R. Maranville	571	.235	0	37	**402**	473	22	91	6.0	**.975**	H. Betts	31	222	13	11	1	2.80
Bill McKechnie	SS	B. Urbanski	563	.272	8	46	316	461	44	**91**	6.0	.946	B. Brown	35	213	14	7	1	3.30
	3B	F. Knothe	344	.238	1	36	81	168	14	7	3.0	.947	T. Zachary	32	212	12	11	0	3.10
	RF	W. Schulmerich	404	.260	11	57	232	11	8	5	2.5	.968	B. Cantwell	37	146	13	11	5	2.96
	CF	W. Berger	602	.307	17	73	396	10	3	3	3.1	.993	S. Seibold	28	137	3	10	0	4.68
	LF	R. Worthington	435	.303	8	61	216	8	3	2	2.2	.987	F. Frankhouse	37	109	4	6	0	3.56
	C	A. Spohrer	335	.269	0	33	374	62	4	2	4.4	.991							
	UT	R. Moore	351	.293	3	43	258	67	5	34		.985							
	OF	F. Leach	223	.247	1	29	126	2	3	0	2.6	.977							
	C	P. Hargrave	217	.263	4	33	206	39	8	4	3.5	.968							
	1B	B. Jordan	212	.321	2	29	514	31	5	48	11.2	.991							
	OF	D. Holland	156	.295	1	18	94	3	1	0	2.5	.990							

Team	POS	Player	AB	BA	HR	RBI	PO	A	E	DP	TC/G	FA	Pitcher	G	IP	W	L	SV	ERA
New York	1B	B. Terry	643	.350	28	117	**1493**	**137**	14	125	**10.7**	.991	C. Hubbell	40	284	18	11	2	2.50
W-72 L-82	2B	H. Critz	**659**	.276	2	50	392	471	23	94	5.9	.974	F. Fitzsimmons	35	238	11	11	0	4.43
John McGraw	SS	D. Marshall	226	.248	0	28	119	199	27	37	5.5	.922	B. Walker	31	163	8	12	2	4.14
W-17 L-23	3B	J. Vergez	376	.261	6	43	94	208	21	22	2.9	.935	J. Mooney	29	125	6	10	0	5.05
Bill Terry	RF	M. Ott	566	.318	**38**	123	347	11	6	5	2.4	.984	H. Bell	35	120	8	4	2	3.67
W-55 L-59	CF	F. Lindstrom	595	.271	15	92	315	18	6	2	2.6	.982	D. Luque	38	110	6	7	5	4.01
	LF	J. Moore	361	.305	2	27	160	6	3	10	2.0	.982	H. Schumacher	27	101	5	6	0	3.55
	C	S. Hogan	502	.287	8	77	**522**	71	10	11	4.4	.983	W. Hoyt	18	97	5	7	0	3.42
	OF	C. Fullis	235	.298	1	21	97	1	1	0	1.8	.990	S. Gibson	41	82	4	8	3	4.85
	3S	G. English	204	.225	2	19	77	133	14	18		.938							
	SS	T. Jackson	195	.256	4	38	106	166	22	31	5.7	.925							

Team	POS	Player	AB	BA	HR	RBI	PO	A	E	DP	TC/G	FA	Pitcher	G	IP	W	L	SV	ERA
St. Louis	1B	R. Collins	549	.279	21	91	701	46	1	72	9.2	.999	D. Dean	**46**	**286**	18	15	2	3.30
W-72 L-82	2B	J. Reese	309	.265	2	26	209	220	9	48	5.7	.979	P. Derringer	39	233	11	14	0	4.05
Gabby Street	SS	C. Gelbert	455	.268	1	45	246	389	37	69	5.5	.945	T. Carleton	44	196	10	13	0	4.08
	3B	J. Flowers	247	.255	2	18	59	91	3	10	2.8	.980	B. Hallahan	25	176	12	7	1	3.11
	RF	G. Watkins	458	.312	9	63	267	11	15	1	2.4	.949	S. Johnson	32	165	5	14	2	4.92
	CF	P. Martin	323	.238	4	34	151	10	4	3	2.4	.976	A. Stout	36	74	4	5	1	4.40
	LF	E. Orsatti	375	.336	2	44	197	3	5	0	2.1	.976							
	C	G. Mancuso	310	.284	5	43	454	53	12	7	6.3	.977							
	23	F. Frisch	486	.292	3	60	252	309	14	58		.976							
	1B	J. Bottomley	311	.296	11	48	662	41	10	67	9.6	.986							
	C	J. Wilson	274	.248	2	28	326	55	7	9	5.2	.982							
	OF	R. Blades	201	.229	3	29	117	2	3	0	2.0	.975							

Team	POS	Player	AB	BA	HR	RBI	PO	A	E	DP	TC/G	FA	Pitcher	G	IP	W	L	SV	ERA
Cincinnati	1B	H. Hendrick	398	.302	4	40	922	60	14	72	10.6	.986	R. Lucas	31	269	13	17	0	2.94
W-60 L-94	2B	G. Grantham	493	.292	6	39	258	347	26	45	5.5	.959	S. Johnson	42	245	13	15	2	3.27
Dan Howley	SS	L. Durocher	457	.217	1	33	283	429	30	76	5.2	.960	O. Carroll	32	210	10	**19**	1	4.50
	3B	W. Gilbert	420	.214	1	40	90	198	22	16	2.8	.929	L. Benton	35	180	6	13	2	4.31
	RF	B. Herman	577	.326	16	87	392	18	13	6	2.9	.969	R. Kolp	32	160	6	10	1	3.89
	CF	E. Crabtree	402	.274	2	35	288	9	3	3	3.2	.990	B. Frey	28	131	4	10	0	4.32
	LF	W. Roettger	347	.277	3	43	214	3	2	2	2.3	.991	E. Rixey	25	112	5	5	0	2.66
	C	E. Lombardi	413	.303	11	68	288	76	**14**	6	3.5	.963							
	OF	T. Douthit	333	.243	0	25	251	6	4	2	3.0	.985							
	UT	J. Morrissey	269	.242	0	13	144	240	8	38		.980							
	OF	C. Hafey	253	.344	2	36	131	5	5	0	1.7	.965							
	3B	A. High	191	.188	0	12	34	62	5	2	2.2	.950							

NATIONAL LEAGUE 1932, *cont.*

BATTING AND BASE RUNNING LEADERS

Batting Average

L. O'Doul, BKN	.368
B. Terry, NY	.350
C. Klein, PHI	.348
P. Waner, PIT	.341
D. Hurst, PHI	.339

Slugging Average

C. Klein, PHI	.646
M. Ott, NY	.601
B. Terry, NY	.580
L. O'Doul, BKN	.555
D. Hurst, PHI	.547

Home Runs

M. Ott, NY	38
C. Klein, PHI	38
B. Terry, NY	28
D. Hurst, PHI	24
H. Wilson, BKN	23

Total Bases

C. Klein, PHI	420
B. Terry, NY	373
M. Ott, NY	340
L. O'Doul, BKN	330
P. Waner, PIT	318

Runs Batted In

D. Hurst, PHI	143
C. Klein, PHI	137
P. Whitney, PHI	124
H. Wilson, BKN	123
M. Ott, NY	123

Stolen Bases

C. Klein, PHI	20
T. Piet, PIT	19
G. Watkins, STL	18
F. Frisch, STL	18
K. Davis, PHI	16

Hits

C. Klein, PHI	226
B. Terry, NY	225
L. O'Doul, BKN	219
P. Waner, PIT	215

Base on Balls

M. Ott, NY	100
D. Hurst, PHI	65
D. Bartell, PHI	64
G. Suhr, PIT	63

Home Run Percentage

M. Ott, NY	6.7
C. Klein, PHI	5.8
H. Wilson, BKN	4.8
B. Terry, NY	4.4

Runs

C. Klein, PHI	152
B. Terry, NY	124
L. O'Doul, BKN	120
M. Ott, NY	119

Doubles

P. Waner, PIT	62
C. Klein, PHI	50
R. Stephenson, CHI	49
D. Bartell, PHI	48

Triples

B. Herman, CIN	19
G. Suhr, PIT	16
C. Klein, PHI	15

PITCHING LEADERS

Winning Percentage

L. Warneke, CHI	.786
G. Bush, CHI	.633
W. Clark, BKN	.625
F. Rhem, STL, PHI	.625
C. Hubbell, NY	.621

Earned Run Average

L. Warneke, CHI	2.37
C. Hubbell, NY	2.50
H. Betts, BOS	2.80
S. Swetonic, PIT	2.82
R. Lucas, CIN	2.94

Wins

L. Warneke, CHI	22
W. Clark, BKN	20
G. Bush, CHI	19
L. French, PIT	18
C. Hubbell, NY	18
D. Dean, STL	18

Saves

J. Quinn, BKN	8
R. Benge, PHI	6
D. Luque, NY	5
B. Cantwell, BOS	5

Strikeouts

D. Dean, STL	191
C. Hubbell, NY	137
P. Malone, CHI	120
T. Carleton, STL	113
B. Brown, BOS	110

Complete Games

R. Lucas, CIN	28
L. Warneke, CHI	25
C. Hubbell, NY	22
L. French, PIT	20
E. Brandt, BOS	19
W. Clark, BKN	19

Fewest Hits/9 Innings

S. Swetonic, PIT	7.41
L. Warneke, CHI	8.03
C. Hubbell, NY	8.24
P. Malone, CHI	8.43

Shutouts

S. Swetonic, PIT	4
L. Warneke, CHI	4
D. Dean, STL	4

Fewest Walks/9 Innings

B. Swift, PIT	1.09
R. Lucas, CIN	1.17
C. Hubbell, NY	1.27
H. Betts, BOS	1.42

Most Strikeouts/9 Inn.

D. Dean, STL	6.01
B. Hallahan, STL	5.51
P. Malone, CHI	4.56
C. Hubbell, NY	4.34

Innings

D. Dean, STL	286
C. Hubbell, NY	284
L. Warneke, CHI	277
L. French, PIT	274

Games Pitched

L. French, PIT	47
D. Dean, STL	46
T. Carleton, STL	44
P. Collins, PHI	43

	W	L	PCT	GB	R	OR	Batting 2B	3B	HR	BA	SA	SB	Fielding E	DP	FA	Pitching CG	BB	SO	ShO	SV	ERA
Chicago	90	64	.584		720	**633**	296	60	69	.278	.392	48	173	146	.973	79	409	527	9	7	**3.44**
Pittsburgh	86	68	.558	4	701	711	274	**90**	47	.285	.394	71	185	124	.969	72	338	377	12	12	3.75
Brooklyn	81	73	.526	9	752	747	296	59	109	.283	.419	61	183	**169**	.971	61	403	499	7	16	4.28
Philadelphia	78	76	.506	12	**844**	796	**330**	67	**122**	**.292**	**.442**	71	194	133	.968	59	450	459	4	**17**	4.47
Boston	77	77	.500	13	649	655	262	53	63	.265	.366	36	**152**	145	**.976**	72	420	440	8	8	3.53
New York	72	82	.468	18	755	706	263	54	116	.276	.406	31	191	143	.969	57	387	506	3	16	3.83
St. Louis	72	82	.468	18	684	717	307	51	76	.269	.385	**92**	175	155	.971	70	455	**681**	**13**	9	3.97
Cincinnati	60	94	.390	30	575	715	265	68	47	.263	.362	35	178	129	.971	**83**	**276**	359	6	6	3.79
					5680	5680	2293	502	649	.276	.396	445	1431	1144	.971	553	3138	3848	62	91	3.88

AMERICAN LEAGUE 1932

New York

W-107 L-47

Joe McCarthy

POS	Player	AB	BA	HR	RBI	PO	A	E	DP	TC/G	FA	Pitcher	G	IP	W	L	SV	ERA
1B	L. Gehrig	596	.349	34	151	1293	75	18	101	8.9	.987	L. Gomez	37	265	24	7	1	4.21
2B	T. Lazzeri	510	.300	15	113	362	405	17	70	5.9	.978	R. Ruffing	35	259	18	7	2	3.09
SS	F. Crosetti	398	.241	5	57	155	216	25	49	4.8	.937	G. Pipgras	32	219	16	9	0	4.19
3B	J. Sewell	503	.272	11	68	122	221	9	15	2.9	.974	J. Allen	33	192	17	4	4	3.70
RF	B. Ruth	457	.341	41	137	209	10	9	1	1.8	.961	H. Pennock	22	147	9	5	0	4.60
CF	E. Combs	591	.321	9	65	343	6	12	3	2.6	.967	D. MacFayden	17	121	7	5	1	3.93
LF	B. Chapman	581	.299	10	107	303	13	17	2	2.2	.949							
C	B. Dickey	423	.310	15	84	639	53	9	6	**6.5**	.987							
SS	L. Lary	280	.232	3	39	152	218	23	39	4.9	.941							
OF	S. Byrd	209	.297	8	30	129	4	5	1	1.5	.964							

Philadelphia

W-94 L-60

Connie Mack

POS	Player	AB	BA	HR	RBI	PO	A	E	DP	TC/G	FA	Pitcher	G	IP	W	L	SV	ERA
1B	J. Foxx	585	.364	**58**	**169**	1328	79	9	115	10.0	**.994**	L. Grove	44	292	25	10	7	**2.84**
2B	M. Bishop	409	.254	5	37	232	340	7	68	5.5	**.988**	R. Walberg	41	272	17	10	1	4.73
SS	E. McNair	554	.285	18	95	242	391	31	89	5.0	.953	G. Earnshaw	36	245	19	13	0	4.77
3B	J. Dykes	558	.265	7	90	142	251	8	20	2.8	**.980**	R. Mahaffey	37	223	13	13	0	5.09
RF	D. Cramer	384	.336	3	46	233	7	6	2	2.9	.976	T. Freitas	23	150	12	5	0	3.83
CF	M. Haas	558	.305	6	65	372	6	5	2	2.8	.987							
LF	A. Simmons	**670**	.322	35	151	290	9	6	4	2.0	.980							
C	M. Cochrane	518	.293	23	112	**652**	**94**	5	**15**	5.5	**.993**							
OF	B. Miller	305	.295	8	58	180	3	4	0	2.2	.979							
2B	D. Williams	215	.251	4	24	122	175	15	30	5.9	.952							

Washington

W-93 L-61

Walter Johnson

POS	Player	AB	BA	HR	RBI	PO	A	E	DP	TC/G	FA	Pitcher	G	IP	W	L	SV	ERA
1B	J. Kuhel	347	.291	4	52	761	45	5	64	9.5	.994	G. Crowder	50	**327**	**26**	13	1	3.33
2B	B. Myer	577	.279	5	52	352	426	20	97	5.7	.975	M. Weaver	43	234	22	10	2	4.08
SS	J. Cronin	557	.318	6	116	**306**	**448**	32	**95**	5.6	**.959**	L. Brown	46	203	15	12	5	4.44
3B	O. Bluege	507	.258	5	64	158	295	14	**28**	3.1	.970	F. Marberry	**54**	198	8	4	**13**	4.01
RF	C. Reynolds	406	.305	9	63	229	3	4	0	2.5	.983	T. Thomas	18	117	8	7	0	3.54
CF	S. West	554	.287	6	83	450	15	10	7	3.3	.979							
LF	H. Manush	625	.342	14	116	318	6	4	3	2.2	.988							
C	R. Spencer	317	.246	1	41	313	44	8	9	3.7	.978							
1B	J. Judge	291	.258	3	29	668	46	2	71	9.2	.997							
OF	S. Rice	288	.323	1	34	132	7	4	2	2.1	.972							
C	M. Berg	195	.236	1	26	229	35	0	9	3.5	1.000							
OF	D. Harris	156	.327	6	29	66	3	5	0	2.2	.932							

AMERICAN LEAGUE 1932, *cont.*

Team	POS	Player	AB	BA	HR	RBI	PO	A	E	DP	TC/G	FA	Pitcher	G	IP	W	L	SV	ERA
Cleveland	1B	E. Morgan	532	.293	4	68	**1430**	74	**23**	100	10.8	.985	W. Ferrell	38	288	23	13	1	3.66
	2B	B. Cissell	541	.320	6	93	329	475	30*	82	6.5*	.964	C. Brown	37	263	15	12	1	4.08
	SS	J. Burnett	512	.297	4	53	184	304	28	52	5.0	.946	M. Harder	39	255	15	13	0	3.75
W-87 L-65	3B	W. Kamm	524	.286	3	83	**164**	**299**	16	20	**3.2**	.967	W. Hudlin	33	182	12	8	2	4.71
	RF	D. Porter	621	.308	4	62	269	2	5	0	1.9	.982	O. Hildebrand	27	129	8	6	0	3.69
Roger Peckinpaugh	CF	E. Averill	631	.314	32	124	412	12	16	3	2.9	.964	J. Russell	18	113	5	7	1	4.70
	LF	J. Vosmik	621	.312	10	97	432	12	5	4	2.9	.989	S. Connally	35	112	8	6	3	4.33
	C	L. Sewell	300	.253	2	52	306	50	8	8	4.3	.978							
	C	G. Myatt	252	.246	8	46	211	32	3	3	3.8	.988							
	SS	E. Montague	192	.245	0	24	91	129	27	22	4.3	.891							
Detroit	1B	H. Davis	590	.269	4	74	1327	75	16	123	10.1	.989	E. Whitehill	33	244	16	12	0	4.54
	2B	C. Gehringer	618	.298	19	107	**396**	495	**30**	**110**	6.1	.967	V. Sorrell	32	234	14	14	0	4.03
	SS	B. Rogell	554	.271	9	61	275	433	42	88	5.4	.944	W. Wyatt	43	206	9	13	1	5.03
W-76 L-75	3B	H. Schuble	340	.271	5	52	70	152	14	10	3.1	.941	T. Bridges	34	201	14	12	1	3.36
	RF	E. Webb	338	.287	3	51	163	8	6	0	2.1	.955	C. Hogsett	47	178	11	9	7	3.54
Bucky Harris	CF	G. Walker	480	.323	8	78	309	9	17	1	2.9	.949	G. Uhle	33	147	6	6	5	4.48
	LF	J. Stone	582	.297	17	108	334	11	14	2	2.5	.961							
	C	R. Hayworth	338	.293	2	44	399	59	4	8	4.4	.991							
	UT	B. Rhiel	250	.280	3	38	150	65	5	21		.977							
	OF	J. White	208	.260	2	21	96	6	4	2	2.3	.962							
	OF	R. Johnson	195	.251	3	22	102	3	8	0	2.4	.929							
	3B	N. Richardson	155	.219	0	12	51	92	2	8	2.2	.986							
St. Louis	1B	J. Burns	617	.305	11	70	1399	**101**	12	**130**	10.1	.992	L. Stewart	41	260	14	19	1	4.61
	2B	O. Melillo	612	.242	3	66	393	**526**	18	**110**	6.1	.981	G. Blaeholder	42	258	14	14	0	4.70
	SS	J. Levey	568	.280	4	63	284	439	**47**	83	5.1	.939	B. Hadley	40	230	13	20*	1	5.53
W-63 L-91	3B	A. Scharein	303	.304	0	42	100	172	10	22	3.7	.965	S. Gray	52	207	8	12	4	4.53
	RF	B. Campbell	593	.285	14	85	297	12	20	4	2.4	.939	W. Hebert	35	108	1	12	1	6.48
Bill Killefer	CF	F. Schulte	565	.294	9	73	331	9	5	1	2.7	.986	C. Fischer	24	97	3	7	0	5.57
	LF	G. Goslin	572	.299	17	104	330	16	18	5	2.4	.951							
	C	R. Ferrell	438	.315	2	65	486	78	8	9	4.8	.986							
	3B	L. Storti	193	.259	3	26	50	81	6	8	2.7	.956							
Chicago	1B	L. Blue	373	.249	0	43	1014	88	16	106	10.6	.986	T. Lyons	33	231	10	15	2	3.28
	2B	J. Hayes	475	.257	2	54	241	346	20	78	6.3	.967	S. Jones	30	200	10	15	0	4.22
	SS	L. Appling	489	.274	3	63	195	287	37	66	6.1	.929	M. Gaston	28	167	7	17	1	4.00
W-49 L-102	3B	C. Selph	396	.283	0	51	83	120	20	14	3.1	.910	V. Frasier	29	146	3	13	0	6.23
	RF	B. Seeds	434	.290	2	45	234	7	9	1	2.2	.964	P. Gregory	33	118	5	3	0	4.51
Lew Fonseca	CF	L. Funk	440	.259	2	40	318	15	7	4	2.8	.979	R. Faber	42	106	2	11	6	3.74
	LF	B. Fothergill	346	.295	7	50	136	4	7	0	1.7	.952							
	C	F. Grube	277	.282	0	31	303	55	**16**	5	4.1	.957							
	UT	R. Kress	515	.285	9	57	281	201	32	41		.938							
	1B	B. Sullivan	307	.316	1	45	485	35	5	42	10.1	.990							
	C	C. Berry	226	.305	4	31	212	52	5	5	3.8	.981							
	OF	J. Hodapp	176	.227	3	20	58	0	2	0	1.9	.967							
Boston	1B	D. Alexander	376	.372*	8	56	1051	67	9	93	11.2*	.992	B. Weiland	43	196	6	16	1	4.51
	2B	M. Olson	403	.248	0	25	266	324	28	68	5.8	.955	E. Durham	34	175	6	13	0	3.80
	SS	R. Warstler	388	.211	0	34	254	373	41	84	**6.2**	.939	B. Kline	47	172	11	13	2	5.28
W-43 L-111	3B	U. Pickering	457	.260	2	40	110	222	**21**	22	2.8	.941	I. Andrews	25	142	8	6	0	3.81
	RF	R. Johnson	348	.299	11	47	167	6	13	0	2.2	.930	W. Moore	37	84	4	10	4	5.23
Shano Collins	CF	T. Oliver	455	.264	0	37	328	12	6	4	3.0	.983	D. MacFayden	12	78	1	10	0	5.10
W-11 L-44	LF	S. Jolley	531	.309	18	99	234	12	15	3	2.1	.943	J. Welch	20	72	4	6	0	5.23
	C	B. Tate	273	.245	2	26	244	50	8	7	4.0	.974							
Marty McManus	23	M. McManus	302	.235	5	24	147	227	17	28		.957							
W-32 L-67	OF	C. Watwood	266	.248	0	30	101	3	6	0	2.4	.945							
	C	E. Connolly	222	.225	0	21	233	55	13	0	4.0	.957							
	SS	H. Rhyne	207	.227	0	14	92	161	9	31	4.8	.966							
	OF	E. Webb	192	.281	5	27	74	7	3	2	1.7	.964							
	OF	G. Stumpf	169	.201	1	18	78	2	4	0	1.6	.952							

BATTING AND BASE RUNNING LEADERS

Batting Average

D. Alexander, DET, BOS	.367
J. Foxx, PHI	.364
L. Gehrig, NY	.349
H. Manush, WAS	.342
B. Ruth, NY	.341

Slugging Average

J. Foxx, PHI	.749
B. Ruth, NY	.661
L. Gehrig, NY	.621
E. Averill, CLE	.569
A. Simmons, PHI	.548

Home Runs

J. Foxx, PHI	58
B. Ruth, NY	41
A. Simmons, PHI	35
L. Gehrig, NY	34
E. Averill, CLE	32

Total Bases

J. Foxx, PHI	438
L. Gehrig, NY	370
A. Simmons, PHI	367
E. Averill, CLE	359
H. Manush, WAS	325

Runs Batted In

J. Foxx, PHI	169
L. Gehrig, NY	151
A. Simmons, PHI	151
B. Ruth, NY	137
E. Averill, CLE	124

Stolen Bases

B. Chapman, NY	38
G. Walker, DET	30
R. Johnson, DET, BOS	20
B. Cissell, CHI, CLE	18

Hits

A. Simmons, PHI	216
H. Manush, WAS	214
J. Foxx, PHI	213
L. Gehrig, NY	208

Base on Balls

B. Ruth, NY	130
J. Foxx, PHI	116
M. Bishop, PHI	110
L. Gehrig, NY	108

Home Run Percentage

J. Foxx, PHI	9.9
B. Ruth, NY	9.0
L. Gehrig, NY	5.7
A. Simmons, PHI	5.2

PITCHING LEADERS

Winning Percentage

J. Allen, NY	.810
L. Gomez, NY	.774
R. Ruffing, NY	.720
L. Grove, PHI	.714
M. Weaver, WAS	.688

Earned Run Average

L. Grove, PHI	2.84
R. Ruffing, NY	3.09
T. Lyons, CHI	3.28
G. Crowder, WAS	3.33
T. Bridges, DET	3.36

Wins

G. Crowder, WAS	26
L. Grove, PHI	25
L. Gomez, NY	24
W. Ferrell, CLE	23
M. Weaver, WAS	22

Saves

F. Marberry, WAS	13
W. Moore, BOS, NY	8
L. Grove, PHI	7
C. Hogsett, DET	7
R. Faber, CHI	6

Strikeouts

R. Ruffing, NY	190
L. Grove, PHI	188
L. Gomez, NY	176
B. Hadley, CHI, STL	145
G. Pipgras, NY	111

Complete Games

L. Grove, PHI	27
W. Ferrell, CLE	26
R. Ruffing, NY	22

Fewest Hits/9 Innings

J. Allen, NY	7.59
R. Ruffing, NY	7.61
T. Bridges, DET	7.79
L. Grove, PHI	8.30

Shutouts

T. Bridges, DET	4
L. Grove, PHI	4

Fewest Walks/9 Innings

C. Brown, CLE	1.71
G. Crowder, WAS	2.12
M. Harder, CLE	2.40
L. Grove, PHI	2.44

AMERICAN LEAGUE 1932, *cont.*

BATTING AND BASE RUNNING LEADERS / **PITCHING LEADERS**

Runs		Doubles		Triples		Most Strikeouts/9 Inn.		Innings		Games Pitched	
J. Foxx, PHI	151	E. McNair, PHI	47	J. Cronin, WAS	18	R. Ruffing, NY	6.60	G. Crowder, WAS	327	F. Marberry, WAS	54
A. Simmons, PHI	144	C. Gehringer, DET	44	T. Lazzeri, NY	16	L. Gomez, NY	5.97	L. Grove, PHI	292	S. Gray, STL	52
E. Combs, NY	143	J. Cronin, WAS	43	B. Myer, WAS	16	L. Grove, PHI	5.80	W. Ferrell, CLE	288	G. Crowder, WAS	50
L. Gehrig, NY	138			B. Chapman, NY	15	B. Hadley, CHI, STL	5.26	R. Walberg, PHI	272		

							Batting						Fielding			Pitching					
	W	L	PCT	GB	R	OR	2B	3B	HR	BA	SA	SB	E	DP	FA	CG	BB	SO	ShO	SV	ERA
New York	107	47	.695		**1002**	724	279	82	160	.286	.454	77	188	124	.969	**95**	561	**770**	**11**	15	**3.98**
Philadelphia	94	60	.610	13	981	752	303	51	**173**	**.290**	**.457**	38	**124**	142	**.979**	**95**	511	595	10	10	4.45
Washington	93	61	.604	14	840	**716**	303	**100**	61	.284	.408	70	125	157	**.979**	66	526	437	10	**22**	4.16
Cleveland	87	65	.572	19	845	747	**310**	74	78	.285	.413	52	191	129	.969	94	**446**	439	6	8	4.12
Detroit	76	75	.503	29.5	799	787	291	80	80	.273	.401	**103**	187	154	.969	67	592	521	9	17	4.30
St. Louis	63	91	.409	44	736	898	274	69	67	.276	.388	69	188	156	.969	63	574	496	8	11	5.01
Chicago	49	102	.325	56.5	667	897	274	56	36	.267	.360	89	264	**170**	.958	50	580	379	2	12	4.82
Boston	43	111	.279	64	566	915	253	57	53	.251	.351	46	233	165	.963	42	612	365	2	7	5.02
					6436	6436	2287	569	708	.276	.404	544	1500	1197	.969	572	4402	4002	58	102	4.48

NATIONAL LEAGUE 1933

New York

W-91 L-61

Bill Terry

POS	Player	AB	BA	HR	RBI	PO	A	E	DP	TC/G	FA	Pitcher	G	IP	W	L	SV	ERA
1B	B. Terry	475	.322	6	58	1246	76	11	103	**11.4**	.992	C. Hubbell	45	**309**	**23**	12	5	**1.66**
2B	H. Critz	558	.246	2	33	316	**541**	16	87	6.6	**.982**	H. Schumacher	35	259	19	12	1	2.16
SS	B. Ryan	525	.238	3	48	296	**494**	42	95	5.7	.950	F. Fitzsimmons	36	252	16	11	0	2.90
3B	J. Vergez	458	.271	16	72	101	222	25	17	2.8	.928	R. Parmelee	32	218	13	8	0	3.17
RF	M. Ott	580	.283	23	103	283	12	5	3	2.0	.983	H. Bell	38	105	6	5	5	2.05
CF	K. Davis	434	.258	7	37	248	7	3	3	2.2	.988	D. Luque	35	80	8	2	4	2.69
LF	J. Moore	524	.292	0	42	266	19	10	6	2.2	.966							
C	G. Mancuso	481	.264	6	56	**580**	83	**19**	15	4.8	.972							
OF	L. O'Doul	229	.306	9	35	109	4	3	0	1.8	.974							
1B	S. Leslie	137	.321	3	27	371	21	4	28	11.3	.990							

Pittsburgh

W-87 L-67

George Gibson

POS	Player	AB	BA	HR	RBI	PO	A	E	DP	TC/G	FA	Pitcher	G	IP	W	L	SV	ERA
1B	G. Suhr	566	.267	10	75	1451	90	14	**151**	10.1	.991	L. French	47	291	18	13	1	2.72
2B	T. Piet	362	.323	1	42	241	305	26	61	5.9	.955	B. Swift	37	218	14	10	0	3.13
SS	A. Vaughan	573	.314	9	97	310	487	**46**	95	5.5	.945	H. Meine	32	207	15	8	0	3.65
3B	P. Traynor	624	.304	1	82	**176**	**300**	**27**	16	**3.3**	.946	S. Swetonic	31	165	12	12	0	3.50
RF	P. Waner	618	.309	7	70	346	16	7	2	2.4	.981	H. Smith	28	145	8	7	1	2.86
CF	F. Lindstrom	538	.310	5	55	388	7	5	2	3.1	.988	W. Hoyt	36	117	5	7	4	2.92
LF	L. Waner	500	.276	0	26	267	9	5	2	2.5	.982	L. Chagnon	39	100	6	4	1	3.69
C	E. Grace	291	.289	3	44	305	37	7	7	4.0	.980	B. Harris	31	59	4	4	5	3.22
2B	T. Thevenow	253	.312	0	34	137	172	8	31	5.2	.975							
OF	W. Jensen	196	.296	0	15	95	1	2	0	2.5	.980							
OF	A. Comorosky	162	.284	1	15	66	1	0	0	2.2	1.000							

Chicago

W-86 L-68

Charlie Grimm

POS	Player	AB	BA	HR	RBI	PO	A	E	DP	TC/G	FA	Pitcher	G	IP	W	L	SV	ERA
1B	C. Grimm	384	.247	3	37	979	84	4	94	10.3	**.996**	L. Warneke	36	287	18	13	1	2.00
2B	B. Herman	619	.279	0	44	**466**	512	**45**	**114**	**6.7**	.956	G. Bush	41	259	20	12	2	2.75
SS	B. Jurges	487	.269	5	50	298	476	34	95	5.7	.958	C. Root	35	242	15	10	0	2.60
3B	W. English	398	.261	3	41	80	173	7	9	2.5	**.973**	P. Malone	31	186	10	14	0	3.91
RF	B. Herman	508	.289	16	93	252	12	12	1	2.1	.957	B. Tinning	32	175	13	6	1	3.18
CF	F. Demaree	515	.272	6	51	321	12	12	1	2.6	.965	L. Nelson	24	76	5	5	1	3.21
LF	R. Stephenson	346	.329	4	51	187	5	3	2	2.1	.985	B. Grimes	17	70	3	6	3	3.49
C	G. Hartnett	490	.276	16	88	550	77	7	**17**	4.5	.989							
OF	K. Cuyler	262	.317	5	35	130	2	3	0	2.0	.978							
3S	M. Koenig	218	.284	3	25	65	132	14	24		.934							
1B	H. Hendrick	189	.291	4	23	328	23	6	31	9.4	.983							

Boston

W-83 L-71

Bill McKechnie

POS	Player	AB	BA	HR	RBI	PO	A	E	DP	TC/G	FA	Pitcher	G	IP	W	L	SV	ERA
1B	B. Jordan	588	.286	4	46	**1513**	88	14	117	10.8	.991	E. Brandt	41	288	18	14	4	2.60
2B	R. Maranville	478	.218	0	38	362	384	22	82	5.4	.971	B. Cantwell	40	255	20	10	2	2.62
SS	B. Urbanski	566	.251	0	35	299	473	38	91	5.7	.953	F. Frankhouse	43	245	16	15	2	3.16
3B	P. Whitney	382	.246	8	49	77	187	8	23*	3.2	.971	H. Betts	35	242	11	11	4	2.79
RF	R. Moore	497	.302	8	70	275	11	6	1	2.4	.979	T. Zachary	26	125	7	9	2	3.53
CF	W. Berger	528	.313	27	106	382	6	9	4	2.9	.977							
LF	H. Lee	312	.221	1	28	207	6	5	2	2.5	.977							
C	S. Hogan	328	.253	3	30	280	56	1	11	3.5	**.997**							
OF	J. Mowry	249	.221	0	20	155	2	1	0	2.5	.994							
C	A. Spohrer	184	.250	1	12	150	26	5	4	2.8	.972							
3B	F. Knothe	158	.228	1	6	34	56	2	6	2.8	.978							
3B	D. Gyselman	155	.239	0	12	45	93	11	4	3.5	.926							

St. Louis

W-82 L-71

Gabby Street
W-46 L-45

Frankie Frisch
W-36 L-26

POS	Player	AB	BA	HR	RBI	PO	A	E	DP	TC/G	FA	Pitcher	G	IP	W	L	SV	ERA
1B	R. Collins	493	.310	10	68	1054	79	7	82	9.3	.994	D. Dean	**48**	293	20	18	4	3.04
2B	F. Frisch	585	.303	4	66	371	378	14	71	5.8	.982	T. Carleton	44	277	17	11	3	3.38
SS	L. Durocher	395	.258	2	41	238	358	24	64	5.0	.961*	B. Hallahan	36	244	16	13	0	3.50
3B	P. Martin	599	.316	8	57	139	273	25	14	3.0	.943	B. Walker	29	158	9	10	0	3.42
RF	G. Watkins	525	.278	5	62	295	9	15	3	2.4	.953	J. Haines	32	115	9	6	1	2.50
CF	E. Orsatti	436	.298	0	38	274	5	4	1	2.8	.986	D. Vance	28	99	6	2	3	3.55
LF	J. Medwick	595	.306	18	98	318	17	7	2	2.3	.980							
C	J. Wilson	369	.255	1	45	498	58	10	13	**5.3**	.982							
OF	E. Allen	261	.241	0	36	179	8	3	1	2.8	.984							
UT	P. Crawford	224	.268	0	21	287	62	6	25		.983							
C	B. O'Farrell	163	.239	2	20	211	19	7	1	4.7	.970							
2B	R. Hornsby	83	.325	2	21	24	35	2	7	3.6	.967							

NATIONAL LEAGUE 1933, *cont.*

Brooklyn

W-65 L-88

Max Carey

POS	Player	AB	BA	HR	RBI	PO	A	E	DP	TC/G	FA
1B	S. Leslie	364	.286	5	46	855	49	17	44	9.7	.982
2B	T. Cuccinello	485	.252	9	65	311	334	15	64	5.5	.977
SS	J. Jordan	211	.256	0	17	104	182	9	25	5.8	.969
3B	J. Stripp	537	.277	1	51	170	264	15	17	3.2	.967
RF	J. Frederick	556	.308	7	64	289	8	9	1	2.2	.971
CF	D. Taylor	358	.285	9	40	247	4	6	1	2.8	.977
LF	H. Wilson	360	.267	9	54	181	3	7	0	2.1	.963
C	A. Lopez	372	.301	3	41	449	**84**	5	14	4.3	.991
OF	B. Boyle	338	.299	0	31	195	2	5	0	2.2	.975
UT	J. Flowers	210	.233	2	22	130	158	11	21		.963
SS	G. Wright	192	.255	1	18	95	124	15	29	4.6	.936
OF	J. Hutcheson	184	.234	6	21	84	8	1	2	2.1	.989
OF	L. O'Doul	159	.252	5	21	88	1	5	0	2.3	.947

Pitcher	G	IP	W	L	SV	ERA
B. Beck	43	257	12	20	1	3.54
V. Mungo	41	248	16	15	0	2.72
R. Benge	37	229	10	17	1	3.42
O. Carroll	33	226	13	15	0	3.78
S. Thurston	32	131	6	8	3	4.52
J. Shaute	41	108	3	4	2	3.49

Philadelphia

W-60 L-92

Burt Shotton

POS	Player	AB	BA	HR	RBI	PO	A	E	DP	TC/G	FA
1B	D. Hurst	550	.267	8	76	1355	**114**	**23**	132	10.5	.985
2B	J. Warner	340	.224	0	22	177	224	11	45	5.8	.973
SS	D. Bartell	587	.271	1	37	**381**	493	45	**100**	**6.0**	.951
3B	J. McLeod	232	.194	0	15	60	120	17	8	2.9	.914
RF	C. Klein	606	**.368**	**28**	**120**	339	21	5	5	2.4	.986
CF	C. Fullis	**647**	.309	1	45	410	15	10	3	2.9	.977
LF	W. Schulmerich	365	.334	8	59	210	6	5	0	2.3	.977
C	S. Davis	495	.349	9	65	395	69	8	9	3.6	.983
2B	M. Finn	169	.237	0	13	107	164	10	34	5.5	.964
OF	H. Lee	167	.287	0	12	97	5	2	0	2.3	.981

Pitcher	G	IP	W	L	SV	ERA
E. Holley	30	207	13	15	0	3.53
S. Hansen	32	168	6	14	1	4.44
J. Elliott	35	162	6	10	2	3.84
C. Moore	36	161	8	9	1	3.74
P. Collins	42	151	8	13	**6**	4.11
F. Rhem	28	126	5	14	2	6.57

Cincinnati

W-58 L-94

Donie Bush

POS	Player	AB	BA	HR	RBI	PO	A	E	DP	TC/G	FA
1B	J. Bottomley	549	.250	13	83	1511	72	15	112	11.0	.991
2B	J. Morrissey	534	.230	0	26	187	295	18	46	5.7	.964
SS	O. Bluege	291	.213	0	18	162	256	28	48	4.7	.937
3B	S. Adams	538	.262	1	22	121	272	15	15	3.1	.963
RF	H. Rice	510	.261	0	54	315	14	3	3	2.4	.991
CF	C. Hafey	568	.303	7	62	364	16	5	5	2.7	.987
LF	J. Moore	514	.263	1	44	329	12	9	4	2.7	.974
C	E. Lombardi	350	.283	4	47	223	52	8	3	3.0	.972
2B	G. Grantham	260	.204	4	28	160	189	19	33	5.1	.948
OF	W. Roettger	209	.239	1	17	124	4	3	2	2.4	.977

Pitcher	G	IP	W	L	SV	ERA
P. Derringer	33	231	7	25*	1	3.23
R. Lucas	29	220	10	16	0	3.40
S. Johnson	34	211	7	18	1	3.49
L. Benton	34	153	10	11	2	3.71
R. Kolp	30	150	6	9	3	3.53
B. Frey	37	132	6	4	0	3.82

BATTING AND BASE RUNNING LEADERS

Batting Average

C. Klein, PHI	.368
S. Davis, PHI	.349
T. Piet, PIT	.323
B. Terry, NY	.322
W. Schulmerich, BOS, PHI	.318

Slugging Average

C. Klein, PHI	.602
W. Berger, BOS	.566
B. Herman, CHI	.502
J. Medwick, STL	.497
A. Vaughan, PIT	.478

Home Runs

C. Klein, PHI	28
W. Berger, BOS	27
M. Ott, NY	23
J. Medwick, STL	18

Total Bases

C. Klein, PHI	365
W. Berger, BOS	299
J. Medwick, STL	296
P. Waner, PIT	282
A. Vaughan, PIT	274

Runs Batted In

C. Klein, PHI	120
W. Berger, BOS	106
M. Ott, NY	103
J. Medwick, STL	98
A. Vaughan, PIT	97

Stolen Bases

P. Martin, STL	26
F. Frisch, STL	18
C. Fullis, PHI	18
C. Klein, PHI	15
E. Orsatti, STL	14

Hits

C. Klein, PHI	223
C. Fullis, PHI	200
P. Waner, PIT	191
P. Traynor, PIT	190

Base on Balls

M. Ott, NY	75
G. Suhr, PIT	72
P. Martin, STL	67
A. Vaughan, PIT	64

Home Run Percentage

W. Berger, BOS	5.1
C. Klein, PHI	4.6
M. Ott, NY	4.0
L. O'Doul, BKN, NY	3.6

Runs

P. Martin, STL	122
C. Klein, PHI	101
P. Waner, PIT	101
M. Ott, NY	98

Doubles

C. Klein, PHI	44
J. Medwick, STL	40
F. Lindstrom, PIT	39
P. Waner, PIT	38

Triples

A. Vaughan, PIT	19
P. Waner, PIT	16
B. Herman, CHI	12
P. Martin, STL	12

PITCHING LEADERS

Winning Percentage

B. Cantwell, BOS	.667
C. Hubbell, NY	.657
H. Meine, PIT	.652
G. Bush, CHI	.625
H. Schumacher, NY	.613

Earned Run Average

C. Hubbell, NY	1.66
L. Warneke, CHI	2.00
H. Schumacher, NY	2.16
E. Brandt, BOS	2.60
C. Root, CHI	2.60

Wins

C. Hubbell, NY	23
B. Cantwell, BOS	20
G. Bush, CHI	20
D. Dean, STL	20
H. Schumacher, NY	19

Saves

P. Collins, PHI	6
C. Hubbell, NY	5
H. Bell, NY	5
B. Harris, PIT	5

Strikeouts

D. Dean, STL	199
C. Hubbell, NY	156
T. Carleton, STL	147
L. Warneke, CHI	133
R. Parmelee, NY	132

Complete Games

D. Dean, STL	26
L. Warneke, CHI	26
E. Brandt, BOS	23
C. Hubbell, NY	22

Fewest Hits/9 Innings

H. Schumacher, NY	6.92
C. Hubbell, NY	7.46
R. Parmelee, NY	7.87
E. Brandt, BOS	8.01

Shutouts

C. Hubbell, NY	10
H. Schumacher, NY	7
L. French, PIT	5

Fewest Walks/9 Innings

R. Lucas, CIN	0.74
C. Hubbell, NY	1.37
B. Swift, PIT	1.48
L. French, PIT	1.70

Most Strikeouts/9 Inn.

D. Dean, STL	6.11
R. Parmelee, NY	5.44
T. Carleton, STL	4.78
C. Hubbell, NY	4.55

Innings

C. Hubbell, NY	309
D. Dean, STL	293
L. French, PIT	291
E. Brandt, BOS	288

Games Pitched

D. Dean, STL	48
L. French, PIT	47
A. Liska, PHI	45
C. Hubbell, NY	45

							Batting						Fielding			Pitching					
	W	L	PCT	GB	R	OR	2B	3B	HR	BA	SA	SB	E	DP	FA	CG	BB	SO	ShO	SV	ERA
New York	91	61	.599		636	**515**	204	41	**82**	.263	.361	31	178	156	.973	75	400	555	**22**	15	**2.71**
Pittsburgh	87	67	.565	5	667	619	249	**84**	39	**.285**	**.383**	34	166	133	.972	70	313	401	16	12	3.27
Chicago	86	68	.558	6	646	536	**256**	51	72	.271	.380	52	168	**163**	.973	**95**	413	488	16	9	2.93
Boston	83	71	.539	9	552	531	217	56	54	.252	.345	25	**138**	148	**.978**	85	355	383	14	**16**	2.96
St. Louis	82	71	.536	9.5	**687**	609	**256**	61	57	.276	.378	**99**	162	119	.973	73	452	**635**	10	**16**	3.37
Brooklyn	65	88	.425	26.5	617	695	224	51	62	.263	.359	82	177	120	.971	71	374	415	9	10	3.73
Philadelphia	60	92	.395	31	607	760	240	41	60	.274	.369	55	183	156	.970	52	410	341	10	13	4.34
Cincinnati	58	94	.382	33	496	643	208	37	34	.246	.320	30	177	139	.971	74	**257**	310	13	8	3.42
					4908	4908	1854	422	460	.266	.362	408	1349	1134	.973	595	2974	3528	110	99	3.34

AMERICAN LEAGUE 1933

Washington

W-99 L-53

Joe Cronin

POS	Player	AB	BA	HR	RBI	PO	A	E	DP	TC/G	FA
1B	J. Kuhel	602	.322	11	107	**1498**	61	7	126	10.2	**.996**
2B	B. Myer	530	.302	4	61	356	417	17	92	6.1	.978
SS	J. Cronin	602	.309	5	118	297	528	34	95	5.7	**.960**
3B	O. Bluege	501	.261	6	71	116	247	13	25	2.7	.965
RF	G. Goslin	549	.297	10	64	261	17	10	7	2.3	.965
CF	F. Schulte	550	.295	5	87	433	10	9	4	3.2	.980
LF	H. Manush	658	.336	5	95	325	10	6	1	2.3	.982
C	L. Sewell	474	.264	2	61	516	61	6	12	4.1	.990
OF	D. Harris	177	.260	5	38	79	1	3	0	1.8	.964
UT	B. Boken	133	.278	3	26	72	91	7	13		.959

Pitcher	G	IP	W	L	SV	ERA
G. Crowder	**52**	299	**24**	15	4	3.97
E. Whitehill	39	270	22	8	1	3.33
L. Stewart	34	231	15	6	0	3.82
M. Weaver	23	152	10	5	0	3.25
T. Thomas	35	135	7	7	3	4.80
J. Russell	50	124	12	6	**13**	2.69
B. McAfee	27	53	3	2	5	6.62

New York

W-91 L-59

Joe McCarthy

POS	Player	AB	BA	HR	RBI	PO	A	E	DP	TC/G	FA
1B	L. Gehrig	593	.334	32	139	1290	64	9	102	9.0	.993
2B	T. Lazzeri	523	.294	18	104	338	407	**25**	71	5.6	.968
SS	F. Crosetti	451	.253	9	60	245	384	43	58	5.1	.936
3B	J. Sewell	524	.273	2	54	123	224	13	27	2.7	.964
RF	B. Ruth	459	.301	34	103	215	9	7	4	1.8	.970
CF	E. Combs	419	.298	5	60	227	3	6	1	2.3	.975
LF	B. Chapman	565	.312	9	98	288	24	8	4	2.2	.975
C	B. Dickey	478	.318	14	97	**721**	82	6	15	**6.4**	.993
OF	D. Walker	328	.274	15	51	194	7	8	1	2.7	.962

Pitcher	G	IP	W	L	SV	ERA
R. Ruffing	35	235	9	14	3	3.91
L. Gomez	35	235	16	10	2	3.18
J. Allen	25	185	15	7	1	4.39
R. Van Atta	26	157	12	4	1	4.18
J. Brown	21	74	7	5	0	5.23
H. Pennock	23	65	7	4	4	5.54
W. Moore	35	62	5	6	8	5.52

Philadelphia

W-79 L-72

Connie Mack

POS	Player	AB	BA	HR	RBI	PO	A	E	DP	TC/G	FA
1B	J. Foxx	573	**.356**	**48**	**163**	1402	**93**	15	98	10.1	.990
2B	M. Bishop	391	.294	4	42	254	359	16	52	5.6	.975
SS	D. Williams	408	.289	11	73	199	243	38	34	5.7	.921
3B	P. Higgins	567	.314	14	99	**159**	270	**24**	23	**3.0**	.947
RF	E. Coleman	388	.281	6	68	178	5	10	2	2.2	.948
CF	D. Cramer	**661**	.295	8	75	387	13	12	2	2.7	.971
LF	B. Johnson	535	.290	21	93	298	16	16	3	2.3	.952
C	M. Cochrane	429	.322	15	60	476	67	6	8	4.3	.989
S2	E. McNair	310	.261	7	48	169	216	17	39		.958
OF	L. Finney	240	.267	3	32	136	6	8	1	2.4	.947

Pitcher	G	IP	W	L	SV	ERA
L. Grove	45	275	**24**	8	6	3.20
S. Cain	38	218	13	12	1	4.25
R. Walberg	40	201	9	13	4	4.88
R. Mahaffey	33	179	13	10	0	5.17
G. Earnshaw	21	118	5	10	0	5.97

Cleveland

W-75 L-76

Roger Peckinpaugh
W-26 L-25

Bibb Falk
W-1 L-0

Walter Johnson
W-48 L-51

POS	Player	AB	BA	HR	RBI	PO	A	E	DP	TC/G	FA
1B	H. Boss	438	.269	1	53	1062	71	7	89	10.4	.994
2B	O. Hale	351	.276	10	64	213	259	23	45	6.8	.954
SS	B. Knickerbocker	279	.226	2	32	151	233	25	37	5.1	.939
3B	W. Kamm	447	.282	1	47	153	221	6	16	2.9	**.984**
RF	D. Porter	499	.267	0	41	236	9	1	3	2.0	.996
CF	E. Averill	599	.301	11	92	390	8	12	3	2.8	.971
LF	J. Vosmik	438	.263	4	56	242	15	4	3	2.3	.985
C	R. Spencer	227	.203	0	23	258	42	3	4	4.2	.990
2S	B. Cissell	409	.230	6	33	238	351	28	47		.955
UT	J. Burnett	261	.272	1	29	124	198	23	31		.933
C	F. Pytlak	248	.310	2	33	246	57	0	11	4.4	1.000
OF	M. Galatzer	160	.237	1	17	74	4	2	0	2.0	.975
PO	W. Ferrell	140	.271	7	26	43	49	0	5		1.000

Pitcher	G	IP	W	L	SV	ERA
M. Harder	43	253	15	17	4	2.95
O. Hildebrand	36	220	16	11	0	3.76
W. Ferrell	28	201	11	12	0	4.21
C. Brown	33	185	11	12	1	3.41
W. Hudlin	34	147	5	13	1	3.97
M. Pearson	19	135	10	5	0	**2.33**
S. Connally	41	103	5	3	1	4.89

Detroit

W-75 L-79

Bucky Harris
W-73 L-79

Del Baker
W-2 L-0

POS	Player	AB	BA	HR	RBI	PO	A	E	DP	TC/G	FA
1B	H. Greenberg	449	.301	12	87	1133	63	14	111	10.3	.988
2B	C. Gehringer	628	.325	12	105	358	**542**	17	**111**	5.9	.981
SS	B. Rogell	587	.295	0	57	**326**	526	51	**116**	5.8	.944
3B	M. Owen	550	.262	2	65	143	226	22	19	2.9	.944
RF	J. Stone	574	.280	11	80	280	11	9	1	2.1	.970
CF	P. Fox	535	.288	7	57	313	5	7	0	2.6	.978
LF	G. Walker	483	.280	9	64	234	10	15	3	2.3	.942
C	R. Hayworth	425	.245	1	45	546	79	4	14	4.7	.994
OF	J. White	234	.252	2	34	122	4	3	1	2.4	.977
1B	H. Davis	173	.214	0	14	433	13	10	33	10.4	.978
OF	F. Doljack	147	.286	0	22	74	6	5	3	2.3	.941

Pitcher	G	IP	W	L	SV	ERA
F. Marberry	37	238	16	11	2	3.29
T. Bridges	33	233	14	12	2	3.09
V. Sorrell	36	233	11	15	1	3.79
C. Fischer	35	183	11	15	3	3.55
S. Rowe	19	123	7	4	0	3.58
C. Hogsett	45	116	6	10	9	4.50
V. Frasier	20	104	5	5	0	6.64

Chicago

W-67 L-83

Lew Fonseca

POS	Player	AB	BA	HR	RBI	PO	A	E	DP	TC/G	FA
1B	R. Kress	467	.248	10	78	1169	60	**28**	83	**11.3**	.978
2B	J. Hayes	535	.258	2	47	344	497	16	89	6.2	.981
SS	L. Appling	612	.322	6	85	314	**534**	**55**	107	**6.0**	.939
3B	J. Dykes	554	.260	1	68	132	**296**	21	22	3.0	.953
RF	E. Swanson	539	.306	1	63	281	7	8	0	2.1	.973
CF	M. Haas	585	.287	1	51	347	9	6	2	2.5	.983
LF	A. Simmons	605	.331	14	119	372	15	4	1	2.7	.990
C	F. Grube	256	.230	0	23	266	44	5	5	3.8	.984
C	C. Berry	271	.255	2	28	260	39	4	1	3.7	.987

Pitcher	G	IP	W	L	SV	ERA
T. Lyons	36	228	10	**21**	1	4.38
S. Jones	27	177	10	12	0	3.36
M. Gaston	30	167	8	12	0	4.85
E. Durham	24	139	10	6	0	4.48
J. Heving	40	118	7	5	6	2.67
J. Miller	26	106	5	6	0	5.62
P. Gregory	23	104	4	11	0	4.95
R. Faber	36	86	3	4	5	3.44

Boston

W-63 L-86

Marty McManus

POS	Player	AB	BA	HR	RBI	PO	A	E	DP	TC/G	FA
1B	D. Alexander	313	.281	5	40	728	47	6	51	9.9	.992
2B	J. Hodapp	413	.312	3	54	273	334	**25**	65	6.3	.960
SS	R. Warstler	322	.217	1	17	150	275	22	40	5.1	.951
3B	M. McManus	366	.284	3	36	79	123	9	9	2.8	.957
RF	R. Johnson	483	.313	10	95	280	14	25	3	2.6	.922
CF	D. Cooke	454	.291	5	54	257	6	12	5	2.3	.956
LF	S. Jolley	411	.282	9	65	178	12	9	3	2.0	.955
C	R. Ferrell	421	.297	3	72	500	76*	6*	9	5.0	.990
S3	B. Werber	425	.259	3	39	167	257	39	43		.916
OF	T. Oliver	244	.258	0	23	187	9	3	3	2.3	.985
10	B. Seeds	230	.243	0	23	422	22	8	33		.982
3B	B. Walters	195	.256	4	28	42	84	8	11	3.1	.940
1B	J. Judge	108	.296	0	22	259	12	0	21	9.7	1.000

Pitcher	G	IP	W	L	SV	ERA
G. Rhodes	34	232	12	15	0	4.03
B. Weiland	39	216	8	14	3	3.87
L. Brown	33	163	8	11	1	4.02
H. Johnson	25	155	8	6	1	4.06
I. Andrews	34	140	7	13	1	4.95
J. Welch	47	129	4	9	3	4.60
G. Pipgras	22	128	9	8	1	4.07
B. Kline	46	127	7	8	4	4.54

AMERICAN LEAGUE 1933, *cont.*

St. Louis

W-55 L-96

Bill Killefer
W-34 L-57

Allen Sothoron
W-2 L-6

Rogers Hornsby
W-19 L-33

POS	Player	AB	BA	HR	RBI	PO	A	E	DP	TC/G	FA
1B	J. Burns	556	.288	7	71	1336	81	12	**129**	10.0	.992
2B	O. Melillo	496	.292	3	79	**362**	451	7	110	**6.3**	**.991**
SS	J. Levey	529	.195	2	36	298	428	42	73	5.6	.945
3B	A. Scharein	471	.204	0	26	113	208	17	**31**	3.6	.950
RF	B. Campbell	567	.277	16	106	250	18	14	4	2.0	.950
CF	S. West	517	.300	11	48	329	14	4	3	2.7	.988
LF	C. Reynolds	475	.286	8	71	269	8	10	3	2.3	.965
C	M. Shea	279	.262	1	27	328	60	2	15*	4.6	.995*
UT	T. Gullic	304	.243	5	35	229	74	5	8		.984
32	L. Storti	210	.195	3	21	105	113	8	26		.965
OF	D. Garms	189	.317	4	24	91	5	4	1	2.1	.960

Pitcher	G	IP	W	L	SV	ERA
B. Hadley	45	**317**	15	20	3	3.92
G. Blaeholder	38	256	15	19	0	4.72
E. Wells	36	204	6	14	1	4.20
R. Stiles	31	115	3	7	1	5.01
S. Gray	38	112	7	4	4	4.10
W. Hebert	33	88	4	6	0	5.30
D. Coffman	21	81	3	7	1	5.89

BATTING AND BASE RUNNING LEADERS

Batting Average
- J. Foxx, PHI .356
- H. Manush, WAS .336
- L. Gehrig, NY .334
- A. Simmons, CHI .331
- C. Gehringer, DET .325

Slugging Average
- J. Foxx, PHI .703
- L. Gehrig, NY .605
- B. Ruth, NY .582
- M. Cochrane, PHI .515
- B. Johnson, PHI .505

Home Runs
- J. Foxx, PHI 48
- B. Ruth, NY 34
- L. Gehrig, NY 32
- B. Johnson, PHI 21
- T. Lazzeri, NY 18

Total Bases
- J. Foxx, PHI 403
- L. Gehrig, NY 359
- H. Manush, WAS 302
- C. Gehringer, DET 294
- A. Simmons, CHI 291

Runs Batted In
- J. Foxx, PHI 163
- L. Gehrig, NY 139
- A. Simmons, CHI 119
- J. Cronin, WAS 118
- J. Kuhel, WAS 107

Stolen Bases
- B. Chapman, NY 27
- G. Walker, DET 26
- E. Swanson, CHI 19
- J. Kuhel, WAS 17
- B. Werber, NY, BOS 15
- T. Lazzeri, NY 15

Hits
- H. Manush, WAS 221
- J. Foxx, PHI 204
- C. Gehringer, DET 204
- A. Simmons, CHI 200

Base on Balls
- B. Ruth, NY 114
- M. Bishop, PHI 106
- M. Cochrane, PHI 106
- J. Foxx, PHI 96

Home Run Percentage
- J. Foxx, PHI 8.4
- B. Ruth, NY 7.4
- L. Gehrig, NY 5.4
- B. Johnson, PHI 3.9

Runs
- L. Gehrig, NY 138
- J. Foxx, PHI 125
- H. Manush, WAS 115
- B. Chapman, NY 112

Doubles
- J. Cronin, WAS 45
- B. Johnson, PHI 44
- J. Burns, STL 43
- B. Rogell, DET 42
- C. Gehringer, DET 42

Triples
- H. Manush, WAS 17
- E. Combs, NY 16
- E. Averill, CLE 16
- B. Myer, WAS 15

PITCHING LEADERS

Winning Percentage
- L. Grove, PHI .750
- E. Whitehill, WAS .733
- L. Stewart, WAS .714
- J. Allen, NY .682
- G. Crowder, WAS .615
- L. Gomez, NY .615

Earned Run Average
- M. Pearson, CLE 2.33
- M. Harder, CLE 2.95
- T. Bridges, DET 3.09
- L. Gomez, NY 3.18
- L. Grove, PHI 3.20

Wins
- L. Grove, PHI 24
- G. Crowder, WAS 24
- E. Whitehill, WAS 22
- O. Hildebrand, CLE 16
- L. Gomez, NY 16
- F. Marberry, DET 16

Saves
- J. Russell, WAS 13
- C. Hogsett, DET 9
- W. Moore, NY 8
- J. Hevina, CHI 6
- L. Grove, PHI 6

Strikeouts
- L. Gomez, NY 163
- B. Hadley, STL 149
- R. Ruffing, NY 122
- T. Bridges, DET 120
- J. Allen, NY 119

Complete Games
- L. Grove, PHI 21
- B. Hadley, STL 19
- E. Whitehill, WAS 19
- R. Ruffing, NY 18
- T. Bridges, DET 17
- G. Crowder, WAS 17

Fewest Hits/9 Innings
- M. Pearson, CLE 7.38
- T. Bridges, DET 7.42
- B. Weiland, BOS 8.20
- J. Allen, NY 8.33

Shutouts
- O. Hildebrand, CLE 6
- L. Gomez, NY 4
- G. Blaeholder, STL 3

Fewest Walks/9 Innings
- C. Brown, CLE 1.65
- F. Marberry, DET 2.30
- L. Stewart, WAS 2.34
- M. Harder, CLE 2.38

Most Strikeouts/9 Inn.
- L. Gomez, NY 6.25
- J. Allen, NY 5.80
- R. Ruffing, NY 4.67
- T. Bridges, DET 4.64

Innings
- B. Hadley, STL 317
- G. Crowder, WAS 299
- L. Grove, PHI 275
- E. Whitehill, WAS 270

Games Pitched
- G. Crowder, WAS 52
- J. Russell, WAS 50
- J. Welch, BOS 47
- B. Kline, BOS 46

	W	L	PCT	GB	R	OR	Batting 2B	3B	HR	BA	SA	SB	Fielding E	DP	FA	Pitching CG	BB	SO	ShO	SV	ERA
Washington	99	53	.651		850	**665**	281	**86**	60	**.287**	.402	65	**131**	149	**.979**	68	**452**	447	5	**26**	3.82
New York	91	59	.607	7	**927**	768	241	75	**144**	.283	.440	**74**	165	122	.972	70	612	**711**	8	22	4.36
Philadelphia	79	72	.523	19.5	875	853	**297**	56	140	.285	**.441**	33	203	121	.966	69	644	423	6	14	4.81
Cleveland	75	76	.497	23.5	654	669	218	77	50	.261	.360	36	156	127	.974	**74**	465	437	**12**	7	**3.71**
Detroit	75	79	.487	25	722	733	283	78	57	.269	.380	68	178	**167**	.971	69	561	575	6	17	3.96
Chicago	67	83	.447	31	683	814	231	53	43	.272	.360	43	186	143	.970	53	519	423	8	13	4.45
Boston	63	86	.423	34.5	700	758	294	56	50	.271	.377	62	204	133	.966	60	591	473	4	14	4.35
St. Louis	55	96	.364	43.5	669	820	244	64	64	.253	.360	70	149	162	.976	55	531	426	7	10	4.82
					6080	6080	2089	545	608	.273	.390	451	1372	1124	.972	518	4375	3915	56	123	4.29

NATIONAL LEAGUE 1934

St. Louis

W-95 L-58

Frankie Frisch

POS	Player	AB	BA	HR	RBI	PO	A	E	DP	TC/G	FA
1B	R. Collins	600	.333	**35**	128	1289	**110**	13	115	9.2	.991
2B	F. Frisch	550	.305	3	75	294	351	15	74	5.7	.977
SS	L. Durocher	500	.260	3	70	320	407	33	86	5.2	.957
3B	P. Martin	454	.289	5	49	85	195	**19**	7	2.8	.936
RF	J. Rothrock	**647**	.284	11	72	343	10	9	4	2.4	.975
CF	E. Orsatti	337	.300	0	31	207	5	3	0	2.4	.986
LF	J. Medwick	620	.319	18	106	322	10	14	1	2.3	.960
C	S. Davis	347	.300	9	65	459	42	6	7	**5.4**	.988
UT	B. Whitehead	332	.277	1	24	158	220	16	38		.959
C	B. DeLancey	253	.316	13	40	363	35	8	5	5.3	.980
OF	C. Fullis	199	.261	0	26	124	2	4	1	2.3	.969

Pitcher	G	IP	W	L	SV	ERA
D. Dean	50	312	**30**	7	7	2.66
T. Carleton	40	241	16	11	2	4.26
P. Dean	39	233	19	11	2	3.43
B. Hallahan	32	163	8	12	0	4.26
B. Walker	24	153	12	4	0	3.12

NATIONAL LEAGUE 1934, *cont.*

Team	POS	Player	AB	BA	HR	RBI	PO	A	E	DP	TC/G	FA	Pitcher	G	IP	W	L	SV	ERA
New York	1B	B. Terry	602	.354	8	83	**1592**	105	10	**131**	**11.2**	**.994**	C. Hubbell	49	313	21	12	**8**	**2.30**
	2B	H. Critz	571	.242	6	40	**353**	**510**	19	**90**	**6.4**	**.978**	H. Schumacher	41	297	23	10	0	3.18
W-93 L-60	SS	T. Jackson	523	.268	16	101	283	458	**43**	60	**6.0**	.945	F. Fitzsimmons	38	263	18	14	1	3.04
	3B	J. Vergez	320	.200	7	27	86	195	17	11	2.9	.943	R. Parmelee	22	153	10	6	0	3.42
Bill Terry	RF	M. Ott	582	.326	**35**	**135**	286	12	8	1	2.0	.974	J. Bowman	30	107	5	4	3	3.61
	CF	G. Watkins	296	.247	6	33	165	3	10	1	2.2	.944	A. Smith	30	67	3	5	5	4.32
	LF	J. Moore	580	.331	15	61	242	8	12	1	2.0	.954	H. Bell	22	54	4	3	6	3.67
	C	G. Mancuso	383	.245	7	46	448	67	**12**	7	4.3	.977	D. Luque	26	42	4	3	7	3.83
	UT	B. Ryan	385	.242	2	41	159	283	26	33		.944							
	OF	H. Leiber	187	.241	2	25	99	3	3	1	2.1	.971							
	OF	L. O'Doul	177	.316	9	46	60	1	2	0	1.7	.968							
Chicago	1B	C. Grimm	267	.296	5	47	683	43	4	39	9.9	.995	L. Warneke	43	291	22	10	3	3.21
	2B	B. Herman	456	.303	3	42	278	385	17	64	6.1	.975	B. Lee	35	214	13	14	1	3.40
W-86 L-65	SS	B. Jurges	358	.246	8	33	205	334	19	63	5.7	.966	G. Bush	40	209	18	10	2	3.83
	3B	S. Hack	402	.289	1	21	102	198	16	10	2.9	.949	P. Malone	34	191	14	7	0	3.53
Charlie Grimm	RF	B. Herman	467	.304	14	84	192	7	6	2	1.8	.971	J. Weaver	27	159	11	9	0	3.91
	CF	K. Cuyler	559	.338	6	69	319	15	10	1	2.4	.971	B. Tinning	39	129	4	6	3	3.34
	LF	C. Klein	435	.301	20	80	222	6	9	2	2.2	.962	C. Root	34	118	4	7	0	4.28
	C	G. Hartnett	438	.299	22	90	**605**	**86**	3	**11**	5.4	**.996**							
	S3	W. English	421	.278	3	31	72	126	8	27		.961							
	OF	T. Stainback	359	.306	2	46	185	4	9	1	2.1	.955							
	2B	A. Galan	192	.260	5	22	90	106	8	16	4.7	.961							
Boston	1B	B. Jordan	489	.311	2	58	1165	66	14	85	10.6	.989	E. Brandt	40	255	16	14	5	3.53
	2B	M. McManus	435	.276	8	47	156	247	15	39	5.7	.964	F. Frankhouse	37	234	17	9	1	3.20
W-78 L-73	SS	B. Urbanski	605	.293	7	53	298	457	31	84	5.4	**.961**	H. Betts	40	213	17	10	3	4.06
	3B	P. Whitney	563	.259	12	79	105	**227**	11	11	**3.1**	**.968**	F. Rhem	25	153	8	8	0	3.60
Bill McKechnie	RF	T. Thompson	343	.265	0	37	205	12	8	3	2.7	.964	B. Cantwell	27	143	5	11	5	4.33
	CF	W. Berger	615	.298	34	121	385	9	9	2	2.7	.978	B. Smith	39	122	6	9	5	4.66
	LF	H. Lee	521	.292	8	79	317	5	5	1	2.6	.985							
	C	A. Spohrer	265	.223	0	17	296	45	8	5	3.6	.977							
	01	R. Moore	422	.284	7	64	496	23	12	24		.977							
	C	S. Hogan	279	.262	4	34	291	53	5	8	3.9	.986							
	2B	L. Mallon	166	.295	0	18	92	145	8	17	5.8	.967							
Pittsburgh	1B	G. Suhr	573	.283	13	103	1326	75	9	108	9.3	.994	L. French	49	264	12	18	1	3.58
	2B	C. Lavagetto	304	.220	3	46	214	234	18	39	5.6	.961	B. Swift	37	213	11	13	0	3.98
W-74 L-76	SS	A. Vaughan	558	.333	12	94	329	480	41	77	5.7	.952	R. Birkofer	41	204	11	12	1	4.10
	3B	P. Traynor	444	.309	1	61	**116**	176	14	16	2.8	.954	W. Hoyt	48	191	15	6	5	2.93
George Gibson	RF	P. Waner	599	**.362**	14	90	323	15	5	1	2.4	.985	R. Lucas	29	173	10	9	0	4.38
W-27 L-24	CF	L. Waner	611	.283	1	48	405	8	9	1	3.0	.979	H. Meine	26	106	7	6	0	4.32
	LF	F. Lindstrom	383	.290	4	49	181	8	2	1	2.1	.990							
Pie Traynor	C	E. Grace	289	.270	4	24	304	26	6	4	4.0	.982							
W-47 L-52	23	T. Thevenow	446	.271	0	54	214	280	19	37		.963							
	OF	W. Jensen	283	.290	0	27	143	1	1	0	2.2	.993							
	C	T. Padden	237	.321	0	22	297	20	7	3	4.3	.978							
Brooklyn	1B	S. Leslie	546	.332	9	102	1262	93	9	104	9.9	.993	V. Mungo	45	**315**	18	16	3	3.37
	2B	T. Cuccinello	528	.261	14	94	246	347	16	54	6.0	.974	R. Benge	36	227	14	12	0	4.32
W-71 L-81	SS	L. Frey	490	.284	8	57	232	375	35	81	5.9	.945	D. Leonard	44	184	14	11	5	3.28
	3B	J. Stripp	384	.315	1	40	93	147	15	**20**	2.7	.941	J. Babich	25	135	7	11	1	4.20
Casey Stengel	RF	B. Boyle	472	.305	7	48	275	20	9	1	2.5	.970	T. Zachary	22	102	5	6	2	4.43
	CF	L. Koenecke	460	.320	14	73	310	6	2	0	2.6	.994	L. Munns	33	99	3	7	0	4.71
	LF	D. Taylor	405	.299	7	57	188	8	5	1	1.9	.975							
	C	A. Lopez	439	.273	7	54	542	62	11	4	4.5	.982							
	S2	J. Jordan	369	.266	0	43	157	246	19	40		.955							
	OF	J. Frederick	307	.296	4	35	121	11	6	3	1.8	.957							
	OF	H. Wilson	172	.262	6	27	71	3	2	3*	1.8	.974							
Philadelphia	1B	D. Camilli	378	.265	12	68	882	55	14*	102	9.3	.985	C. Davis	**51**	274	19	17	5	2.95
	2B	L. Chiozza	484	.304	0	44	215	257	**31**	37	5.9	.938	P. Collins	45	254	13	18	1	4.18
W-56 L-93	SS	D. Bartell	604	.310	0	37	**350**	**483**	40	**93**	6.0	.954	S. Hansen	50	151	6	12	3	5.42
	3B	B. Walters	300	.260	4	38	74	136	11	12	2.8	.950	S. Johnson	42	134	5	9	3	3.50
Jimmie Wilson	RF	J. Moore	458	.343	11	93	244	18	5	2	2.3	.981	C. Moore	35	127	4	9	0	6.47
	CF	K. Davis	393	.293	3	48	304	13	3	3	3.2	.991	E. Moore	20	122	5	7	1	4.05
	LF	E. Allen	581	.330	10	85	337	19	8	3	2.5	.978							
	C	A. Todd	302	.318	4	41	291	32	8	7	4.0	.976							
	C	J. Wilson	277	.292	3	35	265	42	4	7	4.0	.987							
	2B	I. Jeffries	175	.246	4	19	122	157	11	42	5.6	.962							
	32	M. Haslin	166	.265	1	11	61	89	8	9		.949							
	1B	D. Hurst	130	.262	2	21	317	17	2	30	8.4	.994							
Cincinnati	1B	J. Bottomley	556	.284	11	78	1303	77	15	106	10.0	.989	P. Derringer	47	261	15	21	4	3.59
	2B	T. Piet	421	.259	1	38	126	149	15	27	5.9	.948	B. Frey	39	245	11	16	2	3.52
W-52 L-99	SS	G. Slade	555	.285	4	52	200	315	26	60	5.6	.952	S. Johnson	46	216	7	**22**	3	5.22
	3B	M. Koenig	633	.272	1	67	57	130	14	1	3.1	.930	T. Freitas	30	153	6	12	1	4.01
Bob O'Farrell	RF	A. Comorosky	446	.258	0	40	285	5	9	1	2.5	.970	A. Stout	41	141	6	8	1	4.86
W-30 L-60	CF	C. Hafey	535	.293	18	67	380	7	13	1	2.9	.968							
	LF	H. Pool	358	.327	2	50	196	8	10	1	2.3	.953							
	C	E. Lombardi	417	.305	9	62	383	61	5	8	4.0	.989							
Burt Shotton	32	S. Adams	278	.252	0	14	92	156	8	21		.969							
W-1 L-0	OF	W. Schulmerich	209	.263	5	19	121	1	3	1	2.2	.976							
Chuck Dressen																			
W-21 L-39																			

NATIONAL LEAGUE 1934, *cont.*

BATTING AND BASE RUNNING LEADERS

Batting Average
- P. Waner, PIT .362
- B. Terry, NY .354
- K. Cuyler, CHI .338
- R. Collins, STL .333
- A. Vaughan, PIT .333

Slugging Average
- R. Collins, STL .615
- M. Ott, NY .591
- W. Berger, BOS .546
- P. Waner, PIT .539
- J. Medwick, STL .529

Home Runs
- M. Ott, NY 35
- R. Collins, STL 35
- W. Berger, BOS 34
- G. Hartnett, CHI 22
- C. Klein, CHI 20

Total Bases
- R. Collins, STL 369
- M. Ott, NY 344
- W. Berger, BOS 336
- J. Medwick, STL 328
- P. Waner, PIT 323

Runs Batted In
- M. Ott, NY 135
- R. Collins, STL 128
- W. Berger, BOS 121
- J. Medwick, STL 106
- G. Suhr, PIT 103

Stolen Bases
- P. Martin, STL 23
- K. Cuyler, CHI 15
- D. Bartell, PHI 13
- D. Taylor, BKN 12

Hits
- P. Waner, PIT 217
- B. Terry, NY 213
- R. Collins, STL 200
- J. Medwick, STL 198

Base on Balls
- A. Vaughan, PIT 94
- M. Ott, NY 85
- L. Koenecke, BKN 70
- S. Leslie, BKN 69

Home Run Percentage
- M. Ott, NY 6.0
- R. Collins, STL 5.8
- W. Berger, BOS 5.5
- G. Hartnett, CHI 5.0

Runs
- P. Waner, PIT 122
- M. Ott, NY 119
- R. Collins, STL 116
- A. Vaughan, PIT 115

Doubles
- K. Cuyler, CHI 42
- E. Allen, PHI 42
- A. Vaughan, PIT 41
- R. Collins, STL 40
- J. Medwick, STL 40

Triples
- J. Medwick, STL 18
- P. Waner, PIT 16
- G. Suhr, PIT 13
- R. Collins, STL 12

PITCHING LEADERS

Winning Percentage
- D. Dean, STL .811
- W. Hoyt, PIT .714
- H. Schumacher, NY .697
- L. Warneke, CHI .688
- F. Frankhouse, BOS .654

Earned Run Average
- C. Hubbell, NY 2.30
- D. Dean, STL 2.66
- C. Davis, PHI 2.95
- F. Fitzsimmons, NY 3.04
- B. Walker, STL 3.12

Wins
- D. Dean, STL 30
- H. Schumacher, NY 23
- L. Warneke, CHI 22
- C. Hubbell, NY 21
- P. Dean, STL 19
- C. Davis, PHI 19

Saves
- C. Hubbell, NY 8
- D. Dean, STL 7
- D. Luque, NY 7
- H. Bell, NY 6

Strikeouts
- D. Dean, STL 195
- V. Mungo, BKN 184
- P. Dean, STL 150
- L. Warneke, CHI 143
- P. Derringer, CIN 122

Complete Games
- D. Dean, STL 24
- C. Hubbell, NY 23
- L. Warneke, CHI 23
- V. Mungo, BKN 22
- E. Brandt, BOS 20

Fewest Hits/9 Innings
- C. Hubbell, NY 8.22
- D. Dean, STL 8.32
- L. Warneke, CHI 8.43
- V. Mungo, BKN 8.56

Shutouts
- D. Dean, STL 7
- P. Dean, STL 5
- C. Hubbell, NY 5
- B. Lee, CHI 4

Fewest Walks/9 Innings
- C. Hubbell, NY 1.06
- B. Frey, CIN 1.54
- D. Leonard, BKN 1.67
- F. Fitzsimmons, NY 1.74

Most Strikeouts/9 Inn.
- P. Dean, STL 5.79
- D. Dean, STL 5.63
- V. Mungo, BKN 5.25
- B. Walker, STL 4.47

Innings
- V. Mungo, BKN 315
- C. Hubbell, NY 313
- D. Dean, STL 312
- H. Schumacher, NY 297

Games Pitched
- C. Davis, PHI 51
- S. Hansen, PHI 50
- D. Dean, STL 50
- C. Hubbell, NY 49
- L. French, PIT 49

							Batting						Fielding			Pitching					
	W	L	PCT	GB	R	OR	2B	3B	HR	BA	SA	SB	E	DP	FA	CG	BB	SO	ShO	SV	ERA
St. Louis	95	58	.621		**799**	656	**294**	75	104	**.288**	**.425**	**69**	166	**141**	.972	**78**	411	**689**	**15**	16	3.69
New York	93	60	.608	2	760	**583**	240	41	**126**	.275	.405	19	179	**141**	.972	66	**351**	499	12	**30**	**3.19**
Chicago	86	65	.570	8	705	639	263	44	101	.279	.402	59	**137**	135	**.977**	73	417	633	11	9	3.76
Boston	78	73	.517	16	683	714	233	44	83	.272	.378	30	169	120	.972	62	405	462	11	20	4.11
Pittsburgh	74	76	.493	19.5	735	713	281	**77**	52	.287	.398	44	145	118	.975	61	354	487	8	8	4.20
Brooklyn	71	81	.467	23.5	748	795	284	52	79	.281	.396	55	180	**141**	.970	66	476	520	6	12	4.48
Philadelphia	56	93	.376	37	675	794	286	35	56	.284	.384	52	197	140	.966	52	437	416	8	15	4.76
Cincinnati	52	99	.344	42	590	801	227	65	55	.266	.364	34	181	136	.970	51	389	438	3	19	4.37
					5695	5695	2108	433	656	.279	.394	362	1354	1072	.972	509	3240	4144	74	129	4.07

AMERICAN LEAGUE 1934

Detroit

W-101 L-53

Mickey Cochrane

POS	Player	AB	BA	HR	RBI	PO	A	E	DP	TC/G	FA	Pitcher	G	IP	W	L	SV	ERA
1B	H. Greenberg	593	.339	26	139	1454	84	16	124	10.2	.990	T. Bridges	36	275	22	11	1	3.67
2B	C. Gehringer	601	.356	11	127	355	**516**	17	100	5.8	.981	S. Rowe	45	266	24	8	1	3.45
SS	B. Rogell	592	.296	3	100	259	**518**	31	99	5.2	.962	E. Auker	43	205	15	7	1	3.42
3B	M. Owen	565	.317	8	96	**202**	253	21	33	3.1	.956	F. Marberry	38	156	15	5	3	4.57
RF	P. Fox	516	.285	2	45	245	13	7	4	2.2	.974	V. Sorrell	28	130	6	9	2	4.79
CF	J. White	384	.313	0	44	225	9	10	2	2.4	.959	C. Fischer	20	95	6	4	1	4.37
LF	G. Goslin	614	.305	13	100	290	15	15	2	2.1	.953							
C	M. Cochrane	437	.320	2	76	517	69	7	7	4.8	.988							
OF	G. Walker	347	.300	6	39	191	5	11	2	2.6	.947							
C	R. Hayworth	167	.293	0	27	226	23	4	3	4.7	.984							
P	S. Rowe	109	.303	2	22	9	46	0	3	1.2	**1.000**							

New York

W-94 L-60

Joe McCarthy

POS	Player	AB	BA	HR	RBI	PO	A	E	DP	TC/G	FA	Pitcher	G	IP	W	L	SV	ERA
1B	L. Gehrig	579	**.363**	**49**	**165**	1284	80	8	126	9.0	.994	L. Gomez	38	**282**	**26**	5	1	**2.33**
2B	T. Lazzeri	438	.267	14	67	218	265	12	52	5.4	.976	R. Ruffing	36	256	19	11	0	3.93
SS	F. Crosetti	554	.265	11	67	242	356	35	77	5.3	.945	J. Murphy	40	208	14	10	4	3.12
3B	J. Saltzgaver	350	.271	6	36	71	130	10	10	2.5	.953	J. Broaca	26	177	12	9	0	4.16
RF	B. Ruth	365	.288	22	84	197	3	8	0	1.9	.962	J. DeShong	31	134	6	7	3	4.11
CF	B. Chapman	588	.308	5	86	368	12	13	2	2.6	.967							
LF	S. Byrd	191	.246	3	23	156	2	2	1	1.5	.988							
C	B. Dickey	395	.322	12	72	527	49	8	13	**5.6**	.986							
S3	R. Rolfe	279	.287	0	18	121	159	19	31		.936							
OF	M. Hoag	251	.267	3	34	142	7	4	2	1.8	.974							
OF	E. Combs	251	.319	2	25	145	1	1	0	2.4	.993							
2B	D. Heffner	241	.261	0	25	158	179	10	46	5.1	.971							
C	A. Jorgens	183	.208	0	20	288	20	5	7	5.6	.984							
OF	G. Selkirk	176	.313	5	38	90	3	1	1	2.0	.989							

Cleveland

W-85 L-69

Walter Johnson

POS	Player	AB	BA	HR	RBI	PO	A	E	DP	TC/G	FA	Pitcher	G	IP	W	L	SV	ERA
1B	H. Trosky	625	.330	35	142	**1487**	**86**	**22**	**145**	10.4	.986	M. Harder	44	255	20	12	4	2.61
2B	O. Hale	563	.302	13	101	408	480	**41**	107	**6.8**	.956	M. Pearson	39	255	18	13	2	4.52
SS	B. Knickerbocker	593	.317	4	67	262	451	28	106	5.1	.962	O. Hildebrand	33	198	11	9	1	4.50
3B	W. Kamm	386	.269	0	42	109	248	8	24	3.1	**.978**	W. Hudlin	36	195	15	10	4	4.75
RF	S. Rice	335	.293	1	33	129	2	5	0	1.7	.963	L. Brown	38	117	5	10	6	3.85
CF	E. Averill	598	.313	31	113	410	12	13	3	2.8	.970							
LF	J. Vosmik	405	.341	6	78	199	7	5	2	2.0	.976							
C	F. Pytlak	289	.260	0	35	325	38	4	4	4.2	.989							
3B	J. Burnett	208	.293	3	30	43	59	2	6	2.5	.981							
OF	M. Galatzer	196	.270	0	15	91	7	2	0	2.0	.980							
OF	B. Seeds	186	.247	0	18	83	2	2	0	1.8	.977							

AMERICAN LEAGUE 1934, *cont.*

Team	POS	Player	AB	BA	HR	RBI	PO	A	E	DP	TC/G	FA	Pitcher	G	IP	W	L	SV	ERA
Boston	1B	E. Morgan	528	.267	3	79	1283	56	16	111	9.9	.988	G. Rhodes	44	219	12	12	2	4.56
W-76 L-76	2B	B. Cissell	416	.267	4	44	280	281	24	62	6.1	.959	J. Welch	41	206	13	15	0	4.49
Bucky Harris	SS	L. Lary	419	.241	2	54	260	396	24	66	5.3	.965*	F. Ostermueller	33	199	10	13	3	3.49
	3B	B. Werber	623	.321	11	67	136	**323**	29	25	**3.8**	.941	W. Ferrell	26	181	14	5	1	3.63
	RF	M. Solters	365	.299	7	58	197	11	15	1	2.5	.933	H. Johnson	31	124	6	8	1	5.36
	CF	C. Reynolds	413	.303	4	86	244	6	6	3	2.6	.977	L. Grove	22	109	8	8	0	6.50
	LF	R. Johnson	569	.320	7	119	260	12	15	1	2.1	.948	R. Walberg	30	105	6	7	1	4.04
	C	R. Ferrell	437	.297	1	48	**531**	72	6	7	4.8	**.990**							
	OF	D. Porter	265	.302	0	56	109	1	7	1	1.6	.940							
	2B	M. Bishop	253	.261	1	22	147	155	3	37	5.4	.990							
	OF	D. Cooke	168	.244	1	26	79	1	2	0	1.9	.976							
Philadelphia	1B	J. Foxx	539	.334	44	130	1378	85	10	133	**10.5**	.993	J. Marcum	37	232	14	11	0	4.50
W-68 L-82	2B	R. Warstler	419	.236	1	36	228	392	20	87	6.0	.969	S. Cain	36	231	9	17	0	4.41
Connie Mack	SS	E. McNair	599	.280	17	82	**305**	489	**41**	**109**	5.5	.951	B. Dietrich	39	208	11	12	3	4.68
	3B	P. Higgins	543	.330	16	90	147	247	**37**	**34**	3.0	.914	J. Cascarella	42	194	12	15	1	4.68
	RF	E. Coleman	329	.280	14	60	140	8	3	2	1.8	.980	A. Benton	32	155	7	9	1	4.88
	CF	D. Cramer	**649**	.311	6	46	385	12	6	0	2.7	.985	R. Mahaffey	37	129	6	7	2	5.37
	LF	B. Johnson	547	.307	34	92	304	17	11	3	2.4	.967							
	C	C. Berry	269	.268	0	34	339	48	5	9	4.0	.987							
	OF	L. Finney	272	.279	1	28	112	3	7	1	2.3	.943							
	C	F. Hayes	248	.226	6	30	279	36	15	4	3.7	.955							
	2B	D. Williams	205	.273	2	17	110	171	13	31	5.5	.956							
	OF	B. Miller	177	.243	1	22	72	2	0	1	1.6	1.000							
St. Louis	1B	J. Burns	612	.257	13	73	1365	81	12	132	9.5	.992	B. Newsom	47	262	16	**20**	5	4.01
W-67 L-85	2B	O. Melillo	552	.241	2	55	**412**	462	17	**110**	6.3	**.981**	G. Blaeholder	39	234	14	18	3	4.22
Rogers Hornsby	SS	A. Strange	430	.233	1	45	260	392	31	84	5.5	.955	B. Hadley	39	213	10	16	1	4.35
	3B	H. Clift	572	.260	14	56	150	245	30	28	3.0	.929	D. Coffman	40	173	9	10	3	4.53
	RF	B. Campbell	481	.279	9	74	230	14	17	3	2.1	.935	I. Andrews	43	139	4	11	3	4.66
	CF	S. West	482	.326	9	55	303	14	9	3	2.7	.972	J. Knott	45	138	10	3	4	4.96
	LF	R. Pepper	564	.298	7	101	299	15	12	4	2.4	.963							
	C	R. Hemsley	431	.309	2	52	487	**92**	**16**	**15**	5.2	.973							
	UT	O. Bejma	262	.271	2	29	129	145	11	27		.961							
	OF	D. Garms	232	.293	0	31	111	2	7	0	2.1	.942							
	C	F. Grube	170	.288	0	11	186	21	8	4	3.9	.963							
Washington	1B	J. Kuhel	263	.289	3	25	618	23	4	62	10.2	.994	E. Whitehill	32	235	14	11	0	4.52
W-66 L-86	2B	B. Myer	524	.305	3	57	367	420	20	101	6.0	.975	M. Weaver	31	205	11	15	0	4.79
Joe Cronin	SS	J. Cronin	504	.284	7	101	246	486	38	86	**6.1**	.951	B. Burke	37	168	8	8	0	3.21
	3B	C. Travis	392	.319	1	53	88	210	20	23	3.2	.937	J. Russell	**54**	158	5	10	**7**	4.17
	RF	J. Stone	419	.315	7	67	245	13	9	3	2.4	.966	L. Stewart	24	152	7	11	0	4.03
	CF	F. Schulte	524	.298	3	73	351	5	5	0	2.7	.986	T. Thomas	33	133	8	9	1	5.47
	LF	H. Manush	556	.349	11	89	293	5	6	2	2.3	.980	A. McColl	42	112	3	4	1	3.86
	C	E. Phillips	169	.195	2	16	162	21	3	4	3.5	.984	G. Crowder	29	101	4	10	3	6.79
	UT	O. Bluege	285	.246	0	11	114	202	10	28		.969							
	OF	D. Harris	235	.251	2	37	103	7	3	1	1.8	.973							
	1B	P. Susko	224	.286	2	25	608	40	8	58	11.3	.988							
	C	L. Sewell	207	.237	2	21	143	23	1	6	3.3	.994							
	UT	R. Kress	171	.228	4	24	327	32	2	21		.994							
Chicago	1B	Z. Bonura	510	.302	27	110	1239	77	5	94	10.4	**.996**	G. Earnshaw	33	227	14	11	0	4.52
W-53 L-99	2B	J. Hayes	226	.257	1	31	147	188	7	35	5.6	.980	T. Lyons	30	205	11	13	1	4.87
Lew Fonseca	SS	L. Appling	452	.303	2	61	243	341	34	55	5.6	.945	M. Gaston	29	194	6	19	0	5.85
W-4 L-11	3B	J. Dykes	456	.268	7	82	74	160	14	9	3.4	.944	S. Jones	27	183	8	12	0	5.11
Jimmy Dykes	RF	E. Swanson	426	.298	0	34	193	4	4	1	1.9	.980	L. Tietje	34	176	5	14	0	4.81
W-49 L-88	CF	M. Haas	351	.268	2	22	204	5	2	1	2.4	.991	P. Gallivan	35	127	4	7	1	5.61
	LF	A. Simmons	558	.344	18	104	286	14	4	3	2.2	.987	J. Heving	33	88	1	7	4	7.26
	C	E. Madjeski	281	.221	5	32	348	49	11	11	5.2	.973	W. Wyatt	23	68	4	11	2	7.18
	2B	B. Boken	297	.236	3	40	121	165	22	28	5.4	.929							
	OF	J. Conlan	225	.249	0	16	122	5	6	1	2.5	.955							
	3B	M. Hopkins	210	.214	2	28	63	136	9	4	3.3	.957							
	C	M. Shea	176	.159	0	5	240	35	8	4	4.7	.972							
	OF	F. Uhalt	165	.242	0	16	85	2	6	1	2.3	.935							

BATTING AND BASE RUNNING LEADERS

Batting Average

L. Gehrig, NY	.363
C. Gehringer, DET	.356
H. Manush, WAS	.349
A. Simmons, CHI	.344
J. Vosmik, CLE	.341

Slugging Average

L. Gehrig, NY	.706
J. Foxx, PHI	.653
H. Greenberg, DET	.600
H. Trosky, CLE	.598
E. Averill, CLE	.569

Home Runs

L. Gehrig, NY	49
J. Foxx, PHI	44
H. Trosky, CLE	35
B. Johnson, PHI	34
E. Averill, CLE	31

Total Bases

L. Gehrig, NY	409
H. Trosky, CLE	374
H. Greenberg, DET	356
J. Foxx, PHI	352
E. Averill, CLE	340

Runs Batted In

L. Gehrig, NY	165
H. Trosky, CLE	142
H. Greenberg, DET	139
J. Foxx, PHI	130
C. Gehringer, DET	127

Stolen Bases

B. Werber, BOS	40
J. White, DET	28
B. Chapman, NY	26
P. Fox, DET	25
G. Walker, DET	20

PITCHING LEADERS

Winning Percentage

L. Gomez, NY	.839
S. Rowe, DET	.750
F. Marberry, DET	.750
E. Auker, DET	.682
T. Bridges, DET	.667

Earned Run Average

L. Gomez, NY	2.33
M. Harder, CLE	2.61
J. Murphy, NY	3.12
E. Auker, DET	3.42
S. Rowe, DET	3.45

Wins

L. Gomez, NY	26
S. Rowe, DET	24
T. Bridges, DET	22
M. Harder, CLE	20
R. Ruffing, NY	19

Saves

J. Russell, WAS	7
L. Brown, CLE	6
B. Newsom, STL	5

Strikeouts

L. Gomez, NY	158
T. Bridges, DET	151
R. Ruffing, NY	149
S. Rowe, DET	149
M. Pearson, CLE	140

Complete Games

L. Gomez, NY	25
T. Bridges, DET	23
T. Lyons, CHI	21
S. Rowe, DET	20
R. Ruffing, NY	19
M. Pearson, CLE	19

AMERICAN LEAGUE 1934, *cont.*

BATTING AND BASE RUNNING LEADERS

Hits		Base on Balls		Home Run Percentage	
C. Gehringer, DET	214	J. Foxx, PHI	111	L. Gehrig, NY	8.5
L. Gehrig, NY	210	L. Gehrig, NY	109	J. Foxx, PHI	8.2
H. Trosky, CLE	206	B. Ruth, NY	103	B. Johnson, PHI	6.2
D. Cramer, PHI	202	B. Myer, WAS	102	B. Ruth, NY	6.0

Runs		Doubles		Triples	
C. Gehringer, DET	134	H. Greenberg, DET	63	B. Chapman, NY	13
B. Werber, BOS	129	C. Gehringer, DET	50	H. Manush, WAS	11
L. Gehrig, NY	128	E. Averill, CLE	48		
E. Averill, CLE	128	H. Trosky, CLE	45		

PITCHING LEADERS

Fewest Hits/9 Innings		Shutouts		Fewest Walks/9 Innings	
L. Gomez, NY	7.13	M. Harder, CLE	6	W. Ferrell, BOS	2.44
R. Ruffing, NY	8.15	L. Gomez, NY	6	E. Auker, DET	2.46
T. Bridges, DET	8.15	R. Ruffing, NY	5	G. Blaeholder, STL	2.61
J. Murphy, NY	8.36	B. Dietrich, PHI	4	S. Rowe, DET	2.74
		S. Rowe, DET	4		

Most Strikeouts/9 Inn.		Innings		Games Pitched	
R. Ruffing, NY	5.23	L. Gomez, NY	282	J. Russell, WAS	54
L. Gomez, NY	5.05	T. Bridges, DET	275	B. Newsom, STL	47
S. Rowe, DET	5.04	S. Rowe, DET	266	J. Knott, STL	45
M. Pearson, CLE	4.95	B. Newsom, STL	262	S. Rowe, DET	45

							Batting						Fielding			Pitching					
	W	L	PCT	GB	R	OR	2B	3B	HR	BA	SA	SB	E	DP	FA	CG	BB	SO	ShO	SV	ERA
Detroit	101	53	.656		**958**	708	**349**	53	74	**.300**	.424	**124**	159	150	**.974**	74	**488**	640	10	14	4.06
New York	94	60	.610	7	842	**669**	226	61	135	.278	.419	71	**157**	151	.973	**83**	542	**656**	**13**	10	**3.76**
Cleveland	85	69	.552	16	814	763	340	46	100	.287	.423	52	172	164	.972	72	582	554	8	19	4.28
Boston	76	76	.500	24	820	775	287	**70**	51	.274	.383	116	188	141	.969	68	543	538	8	9	4.32
Philadelphia	68	82	.453	31	764	838	236	50	**144**	.280	**.425**	57	196	166	.967	68	693	480	8	8	5.01
St. Louis	67	85	.441	33	674	800	252	59	62	.268	.373	42	187	160	.969	50	632	499	6	**20**	4.49
Washington	66	86	.434	34	729	806	278	**70**	51	.278	.382	49	162	**167**	**.974**	61	503	412	3	12	4.68
Chicago	53	99	.349	47	704	946	237	40	71	.263	.363	36	207	126	.966	72	628	506	4	8	5.41
					6305	6305	2205	449	688	.278	.399	547	1428	1225	.970	548	4611	4285	60	100	4.50

NATIONAL LEAGUE 1935

Team	POS	Player	AB	BA	HR	RBI	PO	A	E	DP	TC/G	FA	Pitcher	G	IP	W	L	SV	ERA
Chicago	1B	P. Cavarretta	589	.275	8	82	1347	98	**20**	**129**	10.1	.986	L. Warneke	42	262	20	13	4	3.06
W-100 L-54	2B	B. Herman	666	.341	7	83	**416**	**520**	35	**109**	**6.3**	**.964**	B. Lee	39	252	20	6	1	2.96
Charlie Grimm	SS	B. Jurges	519	.241	1	59	**348**	**484**	31	**99**	**5.9**	**.964**	L. French	42	246	17	10	2	2.96
	3B	S. Hack	427	.311	4	64	87	237	20	21	3.1	.942	C. Root	38	201	15	8	2	3.08
	RF	C. Klein	434	.293	21	73	215	11	10	7	2.1	.958	T. Carleton	31	171	11	8	1	3.89
	CF	F. Demaree	385	.325	2	66	204	13	6	3	2.3	.973	R. Henshaw	31	143	13	5	1	3.28
	LF	A. Galan	646	.314	12	79	351	12	8	4	2.4	.978							
	C	G. Hartnett	413	.344	13	91	477	**77**	9	**11**	5.1	**.984**							
	03	F. Lindstrom	342	.275	3	62	167	40	7	7		.967							
	C	K. O'Dea	202	.257	6	38	213	27	9	3	4.0	.964							
	OF	K. Cuyler	157	.268	4	18	98	5	2	1	2.5	.981							
St. Louis	1B	R. Collins	578	.313	23	122	1269	95	18	107	9.2	.987	D. Dean	50	**325**	**28**	12	5	3.04
W-96 L-58	2B	F. Frisch	354	.294	1	55	193	252	8	48	5.1	.982	P. Dean	46	270	19	12	5	3.37
Frankie Frisch	SS	L. Durocher	513	.265	8	78	313	420	28	81	5.4	.963	B. Walker	37	193	13	8	1	3.82
	3B	P. Martin	539	.299	9	54	113	171	30	17	2.8	.904	B. Hallahan	40	181	15	8	1	3.42
	RF	J. Rothrock	502	.273	3	56	283	5	6	1	2.3	.980	E. Heusser	33	123	5	5	2	2.92
	CF	T. Moore	456	.287	6	53	354	11	6	3	3.2	.984	J. Haines	30	115	6	5	2	3.59
	LF	J. Medwick	634	.353	23	126	352	8	13	0	2.4	.965	P. Collins	26	83	7	6	2	4.57
	C	B. DeLancey	301	.279	6	41	372	29	12	6	5.0	.971							
	2B	B. Whitehead	338	.263	0	33	172	218	8	43	5.0	.980							
	C	S. Davis	315	.317	1	60	335	34	3	2	4.6	.992							
	OF	E. Orsatti	221	.240	1	24	115	3	3	2	2.0	.975							
	3S	C. Gelbert	168	.292	2	21	62	95	5	16		.969							
	P	D. Dean	128	.234	2	21	13	42	2	0	1.1	.965							
New York	1B	B. Terry	596	.341	6	64	1379	**99**	6	105	**10.4**	**.996**	C. Hubbell	42	303	23	12	0	3.27
W-91 L-62	2B	M. Koenig	396	.283	3	37	123	206	11	20	5.3	.968	H. Schumacher	33	262	19	9	0	2.89
Bill Terry	SS	D. Bartell	539	.262	14	53	339	424	37	71	5.8	.954	R. Parmelee	34	226	14	10	0	4.22
	3B	T. Jackson	511	.301	9	80	139	220	20	13	3.0	.947	S. Castleman	29	174	15	6	0	4.09
	RF	M. Ott	593	.322	31	114	285	17	3	7	2.2	.990	A. Smith	40	124	10	8	5	3.41
	CF	H. Leiber	613	.331	22	107	357	5	13	2	2.4	.965	F. Fitzsimmons	18	94	4	8	0	4.02
	LF	J. Moore	**681**	.295	15	71	342	11	10	2	2.3	.972	A. Stout	40	88	1	4	5	4.91
	C	G. Mancuso	447	.298	5	56	**484**	71	16	4	4.5	.972							
	2B	H. Critz	219	.187	2	14	140	175	11	31	5.5	.966							
	2B	A. Cuccinello	165	.248	4	20	113	140	13	26	5.5	.951							
	C	H. Danning	152	.243	2	20	153	22	4	6	4.1	.978							
	P	H. Schumacher	107	.196	2	21	14	**89**	0	4	**3.1**	**1.000**							
Pittsburgh	1B	G. Suhr	529	.272	10	81	1315	73	15	83	9.4	.989	C. Blanton	35	254	18	13	1	**2.58**
W-86 L-67	2B	P. Young	494	.265	7	82	282	315	30	47	5.9	.952	G. Bush	41	204	11	11	2	4.32
Pie Traynor	SS	A. Vaughan	499	**.385**	19	99	249	422	35	55	5.2	.950	B. Swift	39	204	15	8	1	2.70
	3B	T. Thevenow	408	.238	0	47	94	161	13	11	3.3	.951	J. Weaver	33	176	14	8	0	3.42
	RF	P. Waner	549	.321	11	78	283	13	5	2	2.2	.983	W. Hoyt	39	164	7	11	6	3.40
	CF	L. Waner	537	.309	0	46	350	5	4	1	3.0	.989	R. Birkofer	37	150	9	7	1	4.07
	LF	W. Jensen	627	.324	8	62	290	6	7	1	2.1	.977	R. Lucas	20	126	8	6	0	3.44
	C	T. Padden	302	.272	1	30	425	64	**17**	2	**5.4**	.966							
	2B	C. Lavagetto	231	.290	0	19	92	120	11	10	5.3	.951							
	C	E. Grace	224	.263	3	29	269	35	3	9	4.4	.990							
	3B	P. Traynor	204	.279	1	36	59	84	18	2	3.3	.888							
	OF	B. Hafey	184	.228	6	16	125	5	4	3	2.9	.970							

NATIONAL LEAGUE 1935, *cont.*

Brooklyn

W-70 L-83

Casey Stengel

POS	Player	AB	BA	HR	RBI	PO	A	E	DP	TC/G	FA	Pitcher	G	IP	W	L	SV	ERA
1B	S. Leslie	520	.308	5	93	1233	81	14	106	9.6	.989	V. Mungo	37	214	16	10	2	3.65
2B	T. Cuccinello	360	.292	8	53	158	186	8	48	5.5	.977	W. Clark	33	207	13	8	0	3.30
SS	L. Frey	515	.262	11	77	264	388	**44**	72	5.5	.937	G. Earnshaw	25	166	8	12	0	4.12
3B	J. Stripp	373	.306	3	43	63	162	9	17	2.7	.962	T. Zachary	25	158	7	12	4	3.59
RF	B. Boyle	475	.272	4	44	244	18	10	5	2.2	.963	J. Babich	37	143	7	14	0	6.66
CF	F. Bordagaray	422	.282	1	39	227	14	5	2	2.3	.980	D. Leonard	43	138	2	9	**8**	3.92
LF	D. Taylor	352	.290	7	59	193	4	6	0	2.1	.970	R. Benge	23	125	9	9	1	4.48
C	A. Lopez	379	.251	3	39	472	65	11	8	4.3	.980							
UT	J. Bucher	473	.302	7	58	194	188	18	29		.955							
OF	L. Koenecke	325	.283	4	27	222	3	8	0	2.6	.966							
2S	J. Jordan	295	.278	0	30	174	273	12	39		.974							
C	B. Phelps	121	.364	5	22	118	16	6	4	4.1	.957							

Cincinnati

W-68 L-85

Chuck Dressen

POS	Player	AB	BA	HR	RBI	PO	A	E	DP	TC/G	FA	Pitcher	G	IP	W	L	SV	ERA
1B	J. Bottomley	399	.258	1	49	934	53	8	74	10.3	.992	P. Derringer	45	277	22	13	2	3.51
2B	A. Kampouris	499	.246	7	62	367	411	35	88	5.8	.957	A. Hollingsworth	38	173	6	13	0	3.89
SS	B. Myers	445	.267	5	36	230	335	37	77	5.4	.939	G. Schott	33	159	8	11	0	3.91
3B	L. Riggs	532	.278	5	46	132	**269**	**31**	21	**3.2**	.928	T. Freitas	31	144	5	10	2	4.57
RF	I. Goodman	592	.269	12	72	322	17	14	4	2.4	.960	S. Johnson	30	130	5	11	0	6.23
CF	S. Byrd	416	.262	9	52	284	10	9	1	2.6	.970	B. Frey	38	114	6	10	2	6.85
LF	B. Herman	349	.335	10	58	156	5	4	0	2.2	.976	D. Brennan	38	114	5	5	5	3.15
C	E. Lombardi	332	.343	12	64	298	49	6	4	4.3	.983	L. Herrmann	29	108	3	5	0	3.58
13	B. Sullivan	241	.266	2	36	368	61	4	40		.991							
OF	K. Cuyler	223	.251	2	22	123	5	2	2	2.3	.985							
C	G. Campbell	218	.257	3	30	238	36	4	1	4.2	.986							
UT	G. Slade	196	.281	1	14	91	115	11	20		.949							

Philadelphia

W-64 L-89

Jimmie Wilson

POS	Player	AB	BA	HR	RBI	PO	A	E	DP	TC/G	FA	Pitcher	G	IP	W	L	SV	ERA
1B	D. Camilli	602	.261	25	83	**1442**	96	**20**	118	10.0	.987	C. Davis	44	231	16	14	2	3.66
2B	L. Chiozza	472	.284	3	47	296	405	**39**	54	6.2	.947	O. Jorgens	**53**	188	10	15	2	4.83
SS	M. Haslin	407	.265	3	52	212	249	34	52	5.7	.931	S. Johnson	37	175	10	8	6	3.56
3B	J. Vergez	546	.249	9	63	**188**	222	20	**25**	2.9	**.953**	J. Bivin	47	162	2	9	1	5.79
RF	J. Moore	600	.323	19	93	233	18	7	6	1.7	.973	B. Walters	24	151	9	9	0	4.17
CF	E. Allen	645	.307	8	63	412	26	9	6	2.9	.980	J. Bowman	33	148	7	10	1	4.25
LF	G. Watkins	600	.270	17	76	325	18	15	4	2.4	.958							
C	A. Todd	328	.290	3	42	292	37	11	5	3.9	.968							
C	J. Wilson	290	.279	1	37	329	44	7	9	4.9	.982							
S2	C. Gomez	222	.230	0	16	150	216	19	36		.951							

Boston

W-38 L-115

Bill McKechnie

POS	Player	AB	BA	HR	RBI	PO	A	E	DP	TC/G	FA	Pitcher	G	IP	W	L	SV	ERA
1B	B. Jordan	470	.279	5	35	857	66	16	59	9.9	.983	F. Frankhouse	40	231	11	15	0	4.76
2B	L. Mallon	412	.274	2	25	166	219	10	31	5.4	.975	B. Cantwell	39	211	4	**25**	0	4.61
SS	B. Urbanski	514	.230	4	30	258	356	40	52	5.1	.939	B. Smith	46	203	8	18	5	3.94
3B	P. Whitney	458	.273	4	60	83	144	10	8	3.2	.958	E. Brandt	29	175	5	19	0	5.00
RF	R. Moore	407	.275	4	42	161	10	9	3	2.3	.950	H. Betts	44	160	2	9	0	5.47
CF	W. Berger	589	.295	**34**	**130**	458	8	17	1	3.2	.965	D. MacFayden	28	152	5	13	0	5.10
LF	H. Lee	422	.303	0	39	273	7	11	0	2.6	.962							
C	A. Spohrer	260	.242	1	16	230	45	12	4	3.2	.958							
OF	T. Thompson	297	.273	4	30	184	9	7	3	2.4	.965							
UT	J. Coscarart	284	.236	1	29	115	177	14	20		.954							
C	S. Hogan	163	.301	2	25	175	25	2	2	3.6	.990							

BATTING AND BASE RUNNING LEADERS

Batting Average

A. Vaughan, PIT	.385
J. Medwick, STL	.353
G. Hartnett, CHI	.344
E. Lombardi, CIN	.343
B. Herman, CHI	.341

Slugging Average

A. Vaughan, PIT	.607
J. Medwick, STL	.576
M. Ott, NY	.555
W. Berger, BOS	.548
G. Hartnett, CHI	.545

Home Runs

W. Berger, BOS	34
M. Ott, NY	31
D. Camilli, PHI	25
R. Collins, STL	23
J. Medwick, STL	23

Total Bases

J. Medwick, STL	365
M. Ott, NY	329
W. Berger, BOS	323
B. Herman, CHI	317
H. Leiber, NY	314

Runs Batted In

W. Berger, BOS	130
J. Medwick, STL	126
R. Collins, STL	122
M. Ott, NY	114
H. Leiber, NY	107

Stolen Bases

A. Galan, CHI	22
P. Martin, STL	20
F. Bordagaray, BKN	18
S. Hack, CHI	14
I. Goodman, CIN	14

Hits

B. Herman, CHI	227
J. Medwick, STL	224

Base on Balls

A. Vaughan, PIT	97
A. Galan, CHI	87
M. Ott, NY	82
G. Suhr, PIT	70

Home Run Percentage

W. Berger, BOS	5.8
M. Ott, NY	5.2
C. Klein, CHI	4.8
D. Camilli, PHI	4.2

Runs

A. Galan, CHI	133
J. Medwick, STL	132
P. Martin, STL	121
M. Ott, NY	113
B. Herman, CHI	113

Doubles

B. Herman, CHI	57
J. Medwick, STL	46
E. Allen, PHI	46
P. Martin, STL	41
A. Galan, CHI	41

Triples

I. Goodman, CIN	18
L. Waner, PIT	14
J. Medwick, STL	13

PITCHING LEADERS

Winning Percentage

B. Lee, CHI	.769
S. Castleman, NY	.714
D. Dean, STL	.700
H. Schumacher, NY	.679
C. Hubbell, NY	.657

Earned Run Average

C. Blanton, PIT	2.58
B. Swift, PIT	2.70
H. Schumacher, NY	2.89
L. French, CHI	2.96
B. Lee, CHI	2.96

Wins

D. Dean, STL	28
C. Hubbell, NY	23
P. Derringer, CIN	22
B. Lee, CHI	20
L. Warneke, CHI	20

Saves

D. Leonard, BKN	8
S. Johnson, PHI	6
W. Hoyt, PIT	6

Strikeouts

D. Dean, STL	190
C. Hubbell, NY	150
V. Mungo, BKN	143
P. Dean, STL	143
C. Blanton, PIT	142

Complete Games

D. Dean, STL	29
C. Hubbell, NY	24
C. Blanton, PIT	23
L. Warneke, CHI	20
P. Derringer, CIN	20

Fewest Hits/9 Innings

C. Blanton, PIT	7.79
H. Schumacher, NY	8.08
R. Parmelee, NY	8.52
B. Swift, PIT	8.53

Shutouts

F. Fitzsimmons, NY	4
J. Weaver, PIT	4
V. Mungo, BKN	4
L. French, CHI	4
C. Blanton, PIT	4

Fewest Walks/9 Innings

W. Clark, BKN	1.22
C. Hubbell, NY	1.46
P. Derringer, CIN	1.59
L. French, CHI	1.61

Most Strikeouts/9 Inn.

V. Mungo, BKN	6.00
D. Dean, STL	5.26
C. Blanton, PIT	5.02
P. Dean, STL	4.77

Innings

D. Dean, STL	325
C. Hubbell, NY	303
P. Derringer, CIN	277
P. Dean, STL	270

Games Pitched

O. Jorgens, PHI	53
D. Dean, STL	50
J. Bivin, PHI	47
B. Smith, BOS	46
P. Dean, STL	46

NATIONAL LEAGUE 1935, *cont.*

	W	L	PCT	GB	R	OR	Batting 2B	3B	HR	BA	SA	SB	Fielding E	DP	FA	Pitching CG	BB	SO	ShO	SV	ERA
Chicago	100	54	.649		**847**	**597**	**303**	62	88	**.288**	.414	66	186	**163**	.970	**81**	400	589	12	14	**3.26**
St. Louis	96	58	.623	4	829	625	286	59	86	.284	.405	71	**164**	133	**.972**	73	382	**594**	9	18	3.54
New York	91	62	.595	8.5	770	675	248	56	**123**	.286	**.416**	32	174	129	**.972**	76	411	524	10	11	3.78
Pittsburgh	86	67	.562	13.5	743	647	255	**90**	66	.285	.402	30	190	94	.968	76	**312**	549	**15**	11	3.42
Brooklyn	70	83	.458	29.5	711	767	235	62	59	.277	.376	60	188	146	.969	62	436	480	11	**20**	4.22
Cincinnati	68	85	.444	31.5	646	772	244	68	73	.265	.378	**72**	204	139	.966	59	438	500	9	12	4.30
Philadelphia	64	89	.418	35.5	685	871	249	32	92	.269	.378	52	228	145	.963	53	505	475	8	15	4.76
Boston	38	115	.248	61.5	575	852	233	33	75	.263	.362	20	197	101	.967	54	404	355	6	5	4.93
					5806	5806	2053	462	662	.277	.391	403	1531	1050	.968	534	3288	4066	80	106	4.03

AMERICAN LEAGUE 1935

Detroit

W-93 L-58

Mickey Cochrane

POS	Player	AB	BA	HR	RBI	PO	A	E	DP	TC/G	FA	Pitcher	G	IP	W	L	SV	ERA
1B	H. Greenberg	619	.328	**36**	**170**	1437	**99**	13	142	10.2	.992	S. Rowe	42	276	19	13	3	3.69
2B	C. Gehringer	610	.330	19	108	349	**489**	13	99	5.7	**.985**	T. Bridges	36	274	21	10	1	3.51
SS	B. Rogell	560	.275	6	71	280	512	24	**104**	5.4	**.971**	G. Crowder	33	241	16	10	0	4.26
3B	M. Owen	483	.263	2	71	148	215	16	19	2.9	.958	E. Auker	36	195	18	7	0	3.83
RF	P. Fox	517	.321	15	73	244	9	3	1	2.0	.988	J. Sullivan	25	126	6	6	0	3.51
CF	J. White	412	.240	2	32	247	7	10	1	2.7	.962	C. Hogsett	40	97	6	6	5	3.54
LF	G. Goslin	590	.292	9	109	326	6	12	2	2.4	.965							
C	M. Cochrane	411	.319	5	47	504	50	6	6	5.1	.989							
OF	G. Walker	362	.301	7	53	204	2	10	1	2.5	.954							
C	R. Hayworth	175	.309	0	22	211	35	1	4	5.1	.996							
P	S. Rowe	109	.312	3	28	11	42	1	1	1.3	.981							

New York

W-89 L-60

Joe McCarthy

POS	Player	AB	BA	HR	RBI	PO	A	E	DP	TC/G	FA	Pitcher	G	IP	W	L	SV	ERA
1B	L. Gehrig	535	.329	30	119	1337	82	15	96	9.6	.990	L. Gomez	34	246	12	15	1	3.18
2B	T. Lazzeri	477	.273	13	83	285	329	19	72	5.4	.970	R. Ruffing	30	222	16	11	0	3.12
SS	F. Crosetti	305	.256	8	50	153	261	16	42	4.9	.963	J. Broaca	29	201	15	7	0	3.58
3B	R. Rolfe	639	.300	5	67	166	239	15	16	3.1	**.964**	J. Allen	23	167	13	6	0	3.61
RF	G. Selkirk	491	.312	11	94	269	9	7	1	2.2	.975	V. Tamulis	30	161	10	5	1	4.09
CF	B. Chapman	553	.289	8	74	372	25	15	7	3.0	.964	J. Murphy	40	117	10	5	5	4.08
LF	J. Hill	392	.293	4	33	203	9	11	1	2.4	.951	J. Brown	20	87	6	5	0	3.61
C	B. Dickey	448	.279	14	81	**536**	62	3	7	**5.1**	**.995**	P. Malone	29	56	3	5	3	5.43
OF	E. Combs	298	.282	3	35	143	2	1	0	2.1	.993							

Cleveland

W-82 L-71

Walter Johnson
W-46 L-48

Steve O'Neill
W-36 L-23

POS	Player	AB	BA	HR	RBI	PO	A	E	DP	TC/G	FA	Pitcher	G	IP	W	L	SV	ERA
1B	H. Trosky	632	.271	26	113	**1567**	88	11	129	10.9	.993	M. Harder	42	287	22	11	2	3.29
2B	B. Berger	461	.258	5	43	309	419	27	91	6.3	.964	W. Hudlin	36	232	15	11	5	3.69
SS	B. Knickerbocker	540	.298	0	55	247	453	32	82	5.7	.956	M. Pearson	30	182	8	13	0	4.90
3B	O. Hale	589	.304	16	101	160	**312**	**31**	17	3.4	.938	T. Lee	32	181	7	10	1	4.04
RF	B. Campbell	308	.325	7	54	129	2	1	1	1.8	.992	O. Hildebrand	34	171	9	8	5	3.94
CF	E. Averill	563	.288	19	79	371	6	7	2	2.8	.982	L. Brown	42	122	8	7	4	3.61
LF	J. Vosmik	620	.348	10	110	347	5	5	3	2.4	.986	L. Stewart	24	91	6	6	2	5.44
C	E. Phillips	220	.273	1	41	233	18	5	3	3.7	.980							
2S	R. Hughes	266	.293	0	14	151	215	13	44		.966							
OF	M. Galatzer	259	.301	0	19	134	7	10	0	1.9	.934							
OF	A. Wright	160	.237	2	18	56	4	1	0	1.3	.984							

Boston

W-78 L-75

Joe Cronin

POS	Player	AB	BA	HR	RBI	PO	A	E	DP	TC/G	FA	Pitcher	G	IP	W	L	SV	ERA
1B	B. Dahlgren	525	.263	9	63	1433	69	**18**	109	10.2	.988	W. Ferrell	41	**322**	**25**	14	0	3.52
2B	O. Melillo	399	.261	1	39	286	372	18	85	6.4*	.973	L. Grove	35	273	20	12	1	**2.70**
SS	J. Cronin	556	.295	9	95	264	431	37	86	5.3	.949	G. Rhodes	34	146	2	10	2	5.41
3B	B. Werber	462	.255	14	61	**174**	264	27	20	**3.8**	.942	J. Welch	31	143	10	9	2	4.47
RF	D. Cooke	294	.306	3	34	172	4	5	1	2.2	.972	R. Walberg	44	143	5	9	3	3.91
CF	M. Almada	607	.290	3	59	337	22	12	3	2.5	.968	F. Ostermueller	22	138	7	8	1	3.92
LF	R. Johnson	553	.315	3	66	267	21	17	1	2.1	.944							
C	R. Ferrell	458	.301	3	61	520	79	**13**	**12**	4.7	.979							
UT	D. Williams	251	.251	3	25	122	154	12	21		.958							
OF	C. Reynolds	244	.270	6	35	146	7	4	0	2.5	.975							
P	W. Ferrell	150	.347	7	32	9	76	2	1	2.1	.977							
OF	B. Miller	138	.304	3	26	48	2	2	0	1.8	.962							

Chicago

W-74 L-78

Jimmy Dykes

POS	Player	AB	BA	HR	RBI	PO	A	E	DP	TC/G	FA	Pitcher	G	IP	W	L	SV	ERA
1B	Z. Bonura	550	.295	21	92	1421	83	9	109	**11.0**	.994	J. Whitehead	28	222	13	13	0	3.72
2B	J. Hayes	329	.267	4	45	202	275	17	48	5.8	.966	V. Kennedy	31	212	11	11	1	3.91
SS	L. Appling	525	.307	1	71	**335**	**556**	**39**	93	**6.1**	.958	T. Lyons	23	191	15	8	0	3.02
3B	J. Dykes	403	.288	4	61	100	166	13	12	2.8	.953	L. Tietje	30	170	9	15	0	4.30
RF	M. Haas	327	.291	2	40	183	4	2	1	2.3	.989	S. Jones	21	140	8	7	0	4.05
CF	A. Simmons	525	.267	16	79	349	5	7	1	2.9	.981	R. Phelps	27	125	4	8	1	4.82
LF	R. Radcliff	623	.286	10	68	231	8	8	1	1.7	.968	C. Fischer	24	89	5	5	0	6.19
C	L. Sewell	421	.285	2	67	399	83	6	10	4.4	.988	W. Wyatt	30	52	4	3	5	6.75
OF	G. Washington	339	.283	8	47	137	10	4	2	1.9	.974							
2B	T. Piet	292	.298	3	27	129	216	9	32	6.0	.975							

Washington

W-67 L-86

Bucky Harris

POS	Player	AB	BA	HR	RBI	PO	A	E	DP	TC/G	FA	Pitcher	G	IP	W	L	SV	ERA
1B	J. Kuhel	633	.261	2	74	1425	87	14	**150**	10.1	.991	E. Whitehill	34	279	14	13	0	4.29
2B	B. Myer	616	**.349**	5	100	**460**	473	20	**138**	6.3	.979	B. Hadley	35	230	10	15	0	4.92
SS	O. Bluege	320	.263	0	34	117	177	10	32	5.2	.967	B. Newsom	28	198	11	12*	2	4.45
3B	C. Travis	534	.318	0	61	136	254	15	**29**	3.6	.963	E. Linke	40	178	11	7	3	5.01
RF	J. Stone	454	.315	1	78	224	12	11	4	2.2	.955	J. Russell	43	126	4	9	3	5.71
CF	J. Powell	551	.312	6	98	361	10	9	4	2.8	.976	L. Pettit	41	109	8	5	3	4.95
LF	H. Manush	479	.273	4	56	251	8	4	5	2.4	.985							
C	C. Bolton	375	.304	2	55	356	52	12	8	4.0	.971							
SS	R. Kress	252	.298	2	42	118	204	12	53	6.3	.964							
OF	F. Schulte	224	.268	2	23	96	2	2	0	1.8	.980							
OF	D. Miles	216	.264	0	29	92	5	3	1	2.2	.970							
C	S. Holbrook	135	.259	2	25	145	12	8	0	3.5	.952							

AMERICAN LEAGUE 1935, *cont.*

St. Louis

W-65 L-87

Rogers Hornsby

POS	Player	AB	BA	HR	RBI	PO	A	E	DP	TC/G	FA
1B	J. Burns	549	.286	5	67	1239	57	11	115	9.3	.992
2B	T. Carey	296	.291	0	42	189	253	18	52	6.1	.961
SS	L. Lary	371	.288	2	35	258	306	22	66	6.3	.962
3B	H. Clift	475	.295	11	69	130	240	26	12	3.1	.934
RF	E. Coleman	397	.287	17	71	173	11	5	1	1.9	.974
CF	S. West	527	.300	10	70	449	7	5	2	3.4	.989
LF	M. Solters	552	.330	18	104	328	18	4	1	2.8	.989
C	R. Hemsley	504	.290	0	48	510	**105**	**13**	10	4.5	.979
OF	R. Pepper	261	.253	4	37	103	5	2	1	1.9	.982
O1	B. Bell	220	.250	3	17	187	8	9	11		.956
UT	J. Burnett	206	.223	0	26	71	136	13	18		.941
2B	O. Bejma	198	.192	2	26	105	153	13	32	5.8	.952

Pitcher	G	IP	W	L	SV	ERA
I. Andrews	50	213	13	7	1	3.54
J. Knott	48	188	11	8	**7**	4.60
J. Walkup	55	181	6	9	0	6.25
R. Van Atta	53*	170	9	16	3	5.34
S. Cain	31	168	9	8	0	5.26
F. Thomas	49	147	7	15	1	4.78
D. Coffman	41	144	5	11	2	6.14

Philadelphia

W-58 L-91

Connie Mack

POS	Player	AB	BA	HR	RBI	PO	A	E	DP	TC/G	FA
1B	J. Foxx	535	.346	**36**	115	1109	77	3	107	9.8	**.997**
2B	R. Warstler	496	.250	3	59	308	482	**34**	94	6.1	.959
SS	E. McNair	526	.270	4	57	232	346	27	78	5.0	.955
3B	P. Higgins	524	.296	23	94	162	214	21	15	3.0	.947
RF	W. Moses	345	.325	5	35	157	7	10	1	2.2	.943
CF	D. Cramer	**644**	.332	3	70	429	6	11	1	3.0	.975
LF	B. Johnson	582	.299	28	109	337	13	20	4	2.5	.946
C	P. Richards	257	.245	4	29	293	40	8	5	4.3	.977
OF	L. Finney	410	.273	0	31	145	5	9	1	2.1	.943
C	C. Berry	190	.253	3	29	189	37	3	7	4.1	.987

Pitcher	G	IP	W	L	SV	ERA
J. Marcum	39	243	17	12	3	4.08
B. Dietrich	43	185	7	13	3	5.39
G. Blaeholder	23	149	6	10	0	3.99
W. Wilshere	27	142	9	9	1	4.05
R. Mahaffey	27	136	8	4	0	3.90

BATTING AND BASE RUNNING LEADERS

Batting Average
B. Myer, WAS .349
J. Vosmik, CLE .348
J. Foxx, PHI .346
D. Cramer, PHI .332
C. Gehringer, DET .330

Slugging Average
J. Foxx, PHI .636
H. Greenberg, DET .628
L. Gehrig, NY .583
J. Vosmik, CLE .537
P. Fox, DET .513

Home Runs
J. Foxx, PHI 36
H. Greenberg, DET 36
L. Gehrig, NY 30
B. Johnson, PHI 28
H. Trosky, CLE 26

Total Bases
H. Greenberg, DET 389
J. Foxx, PHI 340
J. Vosmik, CLE 333
M. Solters, BOS, STL 314
L. Gehrig, NY 312

Runs Batted In
H. Greenberg, DET 170
L. Gehrig, NY 119
J. Foxx, PHI 115
H. Trosky, CLE 113
M. Solters, BOS, STL 112

Stolen Bases
B. Werber, BOS 29
L. Lary, WAS, STL 28
M. Almada, BOS 20
J. White, DET 19
B. Chapman, NY 17

Hits
J. Vosmik, CLE 216
B. Myer, WAS 215
D. Cramer, PHI 214
H. Greenberg, DET 203

Base on Balls
L. Gehrig, NY 132
L. Appling, CHI 122
J. Foxx, PHI 114
M. Cochrane, DET 96
B. Myer, WAS 96

Home Run Percentage
J. Foxx, PHI 6.7
H. Greenberg, DET 5.8
L. Gehrig, NY 5.6
B. Johnson, PHI 4.8

Runs
L. Gehrig, NY 125
C. Gehringer, DET 123
H. Greenberg, DET 121
J. Foxx, PHI 118
B. Chapman, NY 118

Doubles
J. Vosmik, CLE 47
H. Greenberg, DET 46
M. Solters, BOS, STL 45
P. Fox, DET 38
B. Chapman, NY 38

Triples
J. Vosmik, CLE 20
J. Stone, WAS 18
H. Greenberg, DET 16
J. Cronin, BOS 14

PITCHING LEADERS

Winning Percentage
E. Auker, DET .720
J. Broaca, NY .682
T. Bridges, DET .677
M. Harder, CLE .667
T. Lyons, CHI .652

Earned Run Average
L. Grove, BOS 2.70
T. Lyons, CHI 3.02
R. Ruffing, NY 3.12
L. Gomez, NY 3.18
M. Harder, CLE 3.29

Wins
W. Ferrell, BOS 25
M. Harder, CLE 22
T. Bridges, DET 21
L. Grove, BOS 20
S. Rowe, DET 19

Saves
J. Knott, STL 7
W. Hudlin, CLE 5
O. Hildebrand, CLE 5
W. Wyatt, CHI 5
J. Murphy, NY 5
C. Hogsett, DET 5

Strikeouts
T. Bridges, DET 163
S. Rowe, DET 140
L. Gomez, NY 138
L. Grove, BOS 121
J. Allen, NY 113

Complete Games
W. Ferrell, BOS 31
L. Grove, BOS 23
T. Bridges, DET 23
S. Rowe, DET 21

Fewest Hits/9 Innings
J. Allen, NY 8.03
R. Ruffing, NY 8.15
L. Gomez, NY 8.16
J. Whitehead, CHI 8.46

Shutouts
S. Rowe, DET 6
T. Bridges, DET 4
M. Harder, CLE 4

Fewest Walks/9 Innings
M. Harder, CLE 1.66
L. Grove, BOS 2.14
S. Rowe, DET 2.22
I. Andrews, STL 2.24

Most Strikeouts/9 Inn.
J. Allen, NY 6.09
T. Bridges, DET 5.35
L. Gomez, NY 5.05
S. Rowe, DET 4.57

Innings
W. Ferrell, BOS 322
M. Harder, CLE 287
E. Whitehill, WAS 279
S. Rowe, DET 276

Games Pitched
R. Van Atta, NY, STL 58
J. Walkup, STL 55
I. Andrews, STL 50
F. Thomas, STL 49

							Batting						Fielding			Pitching					
	W	L	PCT	GB	R	OR	2B	3B	HR	BA	SA	SB	E	DP	FA	CG	BB	SO	ShO	SV	ERA
Detroit	93	58	.616		**919**	665	301	83	106	**.290**	**.435**	70	**128**	154	**.978**	**87**	522	584	**16**	11	3.82
New York	89	60	.597	3	818	**632**	255	70	104	.280	.416	68	151	114	.974	76	516	**594**	12	13	**3.60**
Cleveland	82	71	.536	12	776	739	**324**	77	93	.284	.421	63	177	147	.972	67	**457**	498	11	**21**	4.15
Boston	78	75	.510	16	718	732	281	63	69	.276	.392	**89**	194	136	.969	82	520	470	6	11	4.05
Chicago	74	78	.487	19.5	738	750	262	42	74	.275	.382	46	146	133	.976	80	574	436	8	8	4.38
Washington	67	86	.438	27	823	903	255	**95**	32	.285	.381	54	171	**186**	.972	67	613	456	5	12	5.25
St. Louis	65	87	.428	28.5	718	930	291	51	73	.270	.384	45	187	138	.970	42	640	435	4	15	5.26
Philadelphia	58	91	.389	34	710	869	243	44	**112**	.279	.406	42	190	150	.968	58	704	469	7	10	5.12
					6220	6220	2212	525	663	.280	.402	477	1344	1158	.972	559	4546	3942	69	101	4.45

NATIONAL LEAGUE 1936

New York

W-92 L-62

Bill Terry

POS	Player	AB	BA	HR	RBI	PO	A	E	DP	TC/G	FA	Pitcher	G	IP	W	L	SV	ERA
1B	S. Leslie	417	.295	6	54	1030	68	10	81	11.2	.991	C. Hubbell	42	304	**26**	6	3	**2.31**
2B	B. Whitehead	632	.278	4	47	442	552	**32**	107	**6.7**	.969	H. Schumacher	35	214	11	13	1	3.49
SS	D. Bartell	510	.298	8	42	317	**559**	40	**106**	**6.4**	.956	A. Smith	43	209	14	13	2	3.78
3B	T. Jackson	465	.230	7	53	99	196	15	8	2.7	.952	F. Gabler	43	162	9	8	6	3.12
RF	M. Ott	534	.328	**33**	135	250	20	4	3	1.9	.985	F. Fitzsimmons	28	141	10	7	2	3.32
CF	H. Leiber	337	.279	9	67	165	9	7	3	2.1	.961	H. Gumbert	39	141	11	3	0	3.90
LF	J. Moore	649	.316	7	63	291	25	6	3	2.2	.981	S. Castleman	29	112	4	7	1	5.64
C	G. Mancuso	519	.301	9	63	**524**	104	**15**	**15**	4.7	.977	D. Coffman	42	102	7	5	7	3.90
OF	J. Ripple	311	.305	7	47	190	5	4	**10**	2.6	.980							
1B	B. Terry	229	.310	2	39	525	41	2	55	10.1	.996							

Chicago

W-87 L-67

Charlie Grimm

POS	Player	AB	BA	HR	RBI	PO	A	E	DP	TC/G	FA	Pitcher	G	IP	W	L	SV	ERA
1B	P. Cavarretta	458	.273	9	56	980	71	14	93	9.3	.987	B. Lee	43	259	18	11	1	3.31
2B	B. Herman	632	.334	5	93	**457**	492	24	110	6.4	**.975**	L. French	43	252	18	9	3	3.39
SS	B. Jurges	429	.280	1	42	249	379	26	80	5.6	.960	L. Warneke	40	241	16	13	1	3.44
3B	S. Hack	561	.298	6	78	121	202	17	13	2.4	.950	T. Carleton	35	197	14	10	1	3.65
RF	F. Demaree	605	.350	16	96	285	16	10	1	2.0	.968	C. Davis	24	153	11	9	1	3.00
CF	A. Galan	575	.264	8	81	381	9	5	3	2.7	.987	R. Henshaw	39	129	6	5	1	3.97
LF	E. Allen	373	.295	3	39	191	2	4	2	2.2	.980	C. Root	33	74	3	6	1	4.15
C	G. Hartnett	424	.307	7	64	504	75	5	8	**5.1**	**.991**							
C	K. O'Dea	189	.307	2	38	211	27	5	1	4.4	.979							
SS	W. English	182	.247	0	20	75	127	5	27	4.9	.976							
OF	J. Gill	174	.253	7	28	72	3	5	1	2.0	.938							

St. Louis

W-87 L-67

Frankie Frisch

POS	Player	AB	BA	HR	RBI	PO	A	E	DP	TC/G	FA	Pitcher	G	IP	W	L	SV	ERA
1B	J. Mize	414	.329	19	93	897	66	6	63	10.0	.994	D. Dean	**51**	**315**	24	13	**11**	3.17
2B	S. Martin	332	.298	6	41	169	242	22	50	5.2	.949	R. Parmelee	37	221	11	11	2	4.56
SS	L. Durocher	510	.286	1	58	300	392	21	80	5.2	**.971**	J. Winford	39	192	11	10	3	3.80
3B	C. Gelbert	280	.229	3	27	60	104	6	11	2.8	.965	E. Heusser	42	104	7	3	3	5.43
RF	P. Martin	572	.309	11	76	226	13	6	5	1.9	.976	J. Haines	25	99	7	5	1	3.90
CF	T. Moore	590	.264	5	47	418	14	10	7	3.3	.977	P. Dean	17	92	5	5	1	4.60
LF	J. Medwick	636	.351	18	**138**	367	16	6	4	2.5	.985	B. Walker	21	80	5	6	1	5.87
C	S. Davis	363	.273	4	59	390	59	7	7	4.4	.985							
2B	F. Frisch	303	.274	1	26	124	176	11	27	5.1	.965							
1B	R. Collins	277	.292	13	48	475	37	5	48	8.5	.990							
C	B. Ogrodowski	237	.228	1	20	314	32	4	6	4.1	.989							
32	A. Garibaldi	232	.276	1	20	97	119	11	7		.952							

Pittsburgh

W-84 L-70

Pie Traynor

POS	Player	AB	BA	HR	RBI	PO	A	E	DP	TC/G	FA	Pitcher	G	IP	W	L	SV	ERA
1B	G. Suhr	583	.312	11	118	1432	93	10	100	9.8	**.993**	B. Swift	45	262	16	16	2	4.01
2B	P. Young	475	.248	6	77	318	361	24	39	5.7	.966	C. Blanton	44	236	13	15	3	3.51
SS	A. Vaughan	568	.335	9	78	**327**	477	47	86	5.5	.945	J. Weaver	38	226	14	8	0	4.31
3B	B. Brubaker	554	.289	6	102	**134**	209	**22**	8	2.5	.940	R. Lucas	27	176	15	4	0	3.18
RF	P. Waner	585	**.373**	5	94	323	15	14	7	2.4	.960	M. Brown	47	165	10	11	3	3.87
CF	L. Waner	414	.321	1	31	245	2	4	2	2.7	.984	W. Hoyt	22	117	7	5	1	2.70
LF	W. Jensen	**696**	.283	10	58	338	6	9	1	2.3	.975	R. Birkofer	34	109	7	5	0	4.69
C	T. Padden	281	.249	1	31	342	62	10	6	4.8	.976							
C	A. Todd	267	.273	2	28	332	39	9	2	5.4	.976							
OF	F. Schulte	238	.261	1	17	129	1	3	1	2.4	.977							
2B	C. Lavagetto	197	.244	2	26	85	110	10	24	5.5	.951							

Cincinnati

W-74 L-80

Chuck Dressen

POS	Player	AB	BA	HR	RBI	PO	A	E	DP	TC/G	FA	Pitcher	G	IP	W	L	SV	ERA
1B	L. Scarsella	485	.313	3	65	1109	84	13	90	**10.5**	.989	P. Derringer	**51**	282	19	19	5	4.02
2B	A. Kampouris	355	.239	5	46	270	376	21	71	5.6	.969	A. Hollingsworth	29	184	9	10	0	4.16
SS	B. Myers	323	.269	6	27	225	304	35	73	5.8	.938	G. Schott	31	180	11	11	1	3.80
3B	L. Riggs	538	.257	6	57	122	**267**	13	**19**	2.9	.968	B. Hallahan	23	135	5	9	0	4.33
RF	I. Goodman	489	.284	17	71	274	6	8	2	2.4	.972	B. Frey	31	131	10	8	0	4.25
CF	K. Cuyler	567	.326	7	74	322	9	9	3	2.4	.974	P. Davis	26	126	8	8	5	3.58
LF	B. Herman	380	.279	13	71	175	3	6	0	2.0	.967	L. Stine	40	122	3	8	2	5.03
C	E. Lombardi	387	.333	12	68	330	54	**15**	10	3.8	.962	D. Brennan	41	94	5	2	9	4.39
UT	T. Thevenow	321	.234	0	36	178	248	23	49		.949							
OF	H. Walker	258	.275	4	23	158	4	5	2	2.3	.970							
C	G. Campbell	235	.268	1	40	257	49	5	9	4.4	.984							
02	C. Chapman	219	.247	1	22	85	49	4	6		.971							

Boston

W-71 L-83

Bill McKechnie

POS	Player	AB	BA	HR	RBI	PO	A	E	DP	TC/G	FA	Pitcher	G	IP	W	L	SV	ERA
1B	B. Jordan	555	.323	3	66	1307	96	10	**137**	10.4	.993	D. MacFayden	37	267	17	13	0	2.87
2B	T. Cuccinello	565	.308	7	86	383	**559**	28	**128**	6.5	.971	T. Chaplin	40	231	10	15	2	4.12
SS	B. Urbanski	494	.261	0	26	188	211	27	56	5.3	.937	J. Lanning	28	153	7	11	0	3.65
3B	J. Coscarart	367	.245	2	44	91	168	18	16	2.9	.935	B. Reis	35	139	6	5	0	4.48
RF	G. Moore	637	.290	13	67	314	32	8	0	2.3	.977	B. Smith	35	136	6	7	8	3.77
CF	W. Berger	534	.288	25	91	384	10	14	1	3.1	.966	B. Cantwell	34	133	9	9	2	3.04
LF	H. Lee	565	.253	3	64	319	5	9	1	2.2	.973	R. Benge	21	115	7	9	0	5.79
C	A. Lopez	426	.242	8	50	447	**107**	14	9	4.5	.975							
SS	R. Warstler	304	.211	0	17	157	278	24	59	6.2	.948							
01	T. Thompson	266	.286	4	36	359	20	5	19		.987							

Brooklyn

W-67 L-87

Casey Stengel

POS	Player	AB	BA	HR	RBI	PO	A	E	DP	TC/G	FA	Pitcher	G	IP	W	L	SV	ERA
1B	B. Hassett	635	.310	3	82	1401	**121**	**26**	89	9.9	.983	V. Mungo	45	312	18	19	3	3.35
2B	J. Jordan	398	.234	2	28	209	247	14	41	4.8	.970	F. Frankhouse	41	234	13	10	2	3.65
SS	L. Frey	524	.279	4	60	238	331	**51**	52	5.3	.918	E. Brandt	38	234	11	13	2	3.50
3B	J. Stripp	439	.317	1	60	132	174	10	13	3.0	**.968**	M. Butcher	38	148	6	6	2	3.96
RF	F. Bordagaray	372	.315	4	31	207	8	2	0	2.4	.991	W. Clark	33	120	7	11	2	4.42
CF	J. Cooney	507	.282	0	30	336	11	2	3	2.7	.994	G. Jeffcoat	40	96	5	6	3	4.52
LF	G. Watkins	364	.255	4	43	183	5	6	1	2.0	.969	G. Earnshaw	19	93	4	9	1	5.32
C	R. Berres	267	.240	1	13	436	59	6	7	4.8	.988	T. Baker	35	88	1	8	2	4.72
UT	J. Bucher	370	.251	2	41	145	138	19	15		.937							
C	B. Phelps	319	.367	5	57	334	49	9	6	4.0	.977							
OF	E. Wilson	173	.347	3	25	72	3	6	0	1.7	.926							

NATIONAL LEAGUE 1936, *cont.*

Philadelphia

W-54 L-100

Jimmie Wilson

POS	Player	AB	BA	HR	RBI	PO	A	E	DP	TC/G	FA
1B	D. Camilli	530	.315	28	102	**1446**	79	18	122	10.3	.988
2B	C. Gomez	332	.232	0	28	137	229	20	33	5.4	.948
SS	L. Norris	581	.265	11	76	317	345	45	70	5.8	.936
3B	P. Whitney	411	.294	6	59	106	212	15	15	3.0*	.955
RF	C. Klein	492	.309	20	87	213	13	17	2	2.1	.930
CF	L. Chiozza	572	.297	1	48	235	7	7	10	2.8	.972
LF	J. Moore	472	.328	16	68	214	5	12	1	2.1	.948
C	E. Grace	221	.249	4	32	217	29	6	3	3.9	.976
OF	E. Sulik	404	.287	6	36	227	6	7	1	2.3	.971
C	J. Wilson	230	.278	1	27	187	31	9	5	3.6	.960
C	B. Atwood	192	.302	2	29	184	27	6	3	4.1	.972

Pitcher	G	IP	W	L	SV	ERA
B. Walters	40	258	11	**21**	0	4.26
C. Passeau	49	217	11	15	3	3.48
J. Bowman	40	204	9	20	1	5.04
O. Jorgens	39	167	8	8	0	4.79
S. Johnson	39	111	5	7	7	4.30

BATTING AND BASE RUNNING LEADERS

Batting Average
- P. Waner, PIT .373
- B. Phelps, BKN .367
- J. Medwick, STL .351
- F. Demaree, CHI .350
- A. Vaughan, PIT .335

Slugging Average
- M. Ott, NY .588
- D. Camilli, PHI .577
- J. Mize, STL .577
- J. Medwick, STL .577
- P. Waner, PIT .520

Home Runs
- M. Ott, NY 33
- D. Camilli, PHI 28
- W. Berger, BOS 25
- C. Klein, CHI, PHI 25
- J. Mize, STL 19

Total Bases
- J. Medwick, STL 367
- M. Ott, NY 314
- C. Klein, CHI, PHI 308
- D. Camilli, PHI 306
- P. Waner, PIT 304

Runs Batted In
- J. Medwick, STL 138
- M. Ott, NY 135
- G. Suhr, PIT 118
- C. Klein, CHI, PHI 105
- D. Camilli, PHI 102
- B. Brubaker, PIT 102

Stolen Bases
- P. Martin, STL 23
- S. Martin, STL 17
- S. Hack, CHI 17
- L. Chiozza, PHI 17

Hits
- J. Medwick, STL 223
- P. Waner, PIT 218
- F. Demaree, CHI 212
- B. Herman, CHI 211

Base on Balls
- A. Vaughan, PIT 118
- D. Camilli, PHI 116
- M. Ott, NY 111
- G. Suhr, PIT 95

Home Run Percentage
- M. Ott, NY 6.2
- D. Camilli, PHI 5.3
- R. Collins, STL 4.7
- W. Berger, BOS 4.7

Runs
- A. Vaughan, PIT 122
- P. Martin, STL 121
- M. Ott, NY 120
- J. Medwick, STL 115

Doubles
- J. Medwick, STL 64
- B. Herman, CHI 57
- P. Waner, PIT 53
- T. Moore, STL 39

Triples
- I. Goodman, CIN 14
- D. Camilli, PHI 13
- J. Medwick, STL 13

PITCHING LEADERS

Winning Percentage
- C. Hubbell, NY .813
- R. Lucas, PIT .789
- L. French, CHI .667
- D. Dean, STL .649
- B. Lee, CHI .621

Earned Run Average
- C. Hubbell, NY 2.31
- D. MacFayden, BOS 2.87
- D. Dean, STL 3.17
- R. Lucas, PIT 3.18
- B. Lee, CHI 3.31

Wins
- C. Hubbell, NY 26
- D. Dean, STL 24
- P. Derringer, CIN 19
- L. French, CHI 18
- B. Lee, CHI 18
- V. Mungo, BKN 18

Saves
- D. Dean, STL 11
- D. Brennan, CIN 9
- B. Smith, BOS 8
- S. Johnson, PHI 7
- D. Coffman, NY 7

Strikeouts
- V. Mungo, BKN 238
- D. Dean, STL 195
- C. Blanton, PIT 127
- C. Hubbell, NY 123
- P. Derringer, CIN 121

Complete Games
- D. Dean, STL 28
- C. Hubbell, NY 25
- V. Mungo, BKN 22
- D. MacFayden, BOS 21
- B. Lee, CHI 20

Fewest Hits/9 Innings
- C. Hubbell, NY 7.85
- V. Mungo, BKN 7.94
- B. Lee, CHI 8.28
- D. Dean, STL 8.86

Shutouts
- 7 tied with 4

Fewest Walks/9 Innings
- R. Lucas, PIT 1.33
- P. Derringer, CIN 1.34
- D. Dean, STL 1.51
- C. Hubbell, NY 1.69

Most Strikeouts/9 Inn.
- V. Mungo, BKN 6.87
- D. Dean, STL 5.57
- C. Blanton, PIT 4.85
- J. Weaver, PIT 4.31

Innings
- D. Dean, STL 315
- V. Mungo, BKN 312
- C. Hubbell, NY 304
- P. Derringer, CIN 282

Games Pitched
- D. Dean, STL 51
- P. Derringer, CIN 51
- C. Passeau, PHI 49
- M. Brown, PIT 47

							Batting						Fielding			Pitching					
	W	L	PCT	GB	R	OR	2B	3B	HR	BA	SA	SB	E	DP	FA	CG	BB	SO	ShO	SV	ERA
New York	92	62	.597		742	621	237	48	97	.281	.395	31	168	164	.974	58	401	500	12	22	**3.46**
Chicago	87	67	.565	5	755	**603**	275	36	76	**.286**	.392	68	**146**	156	**.976**	**77**	434	597	**18**	10	3.53
St. Louis	87	67	.565	5	795	794	**332**	60	88	.281	**.410**	**69**	156	134	.974	65	477	561	5	**24**	4.48
Pittsburgh	84	70	.545	8	**804**	718	283	**80**	60	**.286**	.397	37	199	113	.967	67	**379**	559	5	12	3.89
Cincinnati	74	80	.481	18	722	760	224	73	82	.274	.388	68	191	150	.969	50	418	459	6	23	4.22
Boston	71	83	.461	21	631	715	207	44	68	.265	.356	23	189	**175**	.971	60	451	421	7	13	3.94
Brooklyn	67	87	.435	25	662	752	263	43	33	.272	.353	55	208	107	.966	59	528	**654**	7	18	3.98
Philadelphia	54	100	.351	38	726	874	250	46	**103**	.281	.401	50	252	144	.959	51	515	454	7	14	4.64
					5837	5837	2071	430	607	.278	.387	401	1509	1143	.970	487	3603	4205	67	136	4.02

AMERICAN LEAGUE 1936

New York

W-102 L-51

Joe McCarthy

POS	Player	AB	BA	HR	RBI	PO	A	E	DP	TC/G	FA
1B	L. Gehrig	579	.354	**49**	152	1377	82	9	128	9.5	.994
2B	T. Lazzeri	537	.287	14	109	346	414	**25**	88	5.3	.968
SS	F. Crosetti	632	.288	15	78	320	463	**43**	95	5.5	.948
3B	R. Rolfe	568	.319	10	70	162	265	19	20	3.4	**.957**
RF	G. Selkirk	493	.308	18	107	290	10	8	3	2.3	.974
CF	J. Powell	324	.306	7	48	196	6	5	2	2.5	.976
LF	J. DiMaggio	637	.323	29	125	339	22	8	2	2.7	.978
C	B. Dickey	423	.362	22	107	499	61	14	10	**5.4**	.976
OF	M. Hoag	156	.301	3	34	82	2	4	1	2.3	.955
OF	B. Chapman	139	.266	1	21	106	3	4	0	3.1	.965
C	J. Glenn	129	.271	1	20	167	24	6	2	4.5	.970
P	R. Ruffing	127	.291	5	22	13	56	1	6	2.1	.986
P	M. Pearson	91	.253	1	20	12	39	1	3	1.6	.981

Pitcher	G	IP	W	L	SV	ERA
R. Ruffing	33	271	20	12	0	3.85
M. Pearson	33	223	19	7	1	3.71
J. Broaca	37	206	12	7	3	4.24
L. Gomez	31	189	13	7	0	4.39
B. Hadley	31	174	14	4	1	4.35
P. Malone	35	135	12	4	**9**	3.81
J. Murphy	27	88	9	3	5	3.38

AMERICAN LEAGUE 1936, *cont.*

Team	POS	Player	AB	BA	HR	RBI	PO	A	E	DP	TC/G	FA	Pitcher	G	IP	W	L	SV	ERA
Detroit	1B	J. Burns	558	.283	4	63	1280	73	8	126	9.9	.994	T. Bridges	39	295	**23**	11	0	3.60
W-83 L-71	2B	C. Gehringer	641	.354	15	116	397	**524**	**25**	**116**	**6.1**	**.974**	S. Rowe	41	245	19	10	3	4.51
Mickey Cochrane W-29 L-24	SS	B. Rogell	585	.274	6	68	286	462	27	98	5.3	**.965**	E. Auker	35	215	13	16	0	4.89
Del Baker W-18 L-16	3B	M. Owen	583	.295	9	105	**190**	281	24	**28**	3.2	.952	V. Sorrell	30	131	6	7	3	5.28
Mickey Cochrane W-36 L-31	RF	G. Walker	550	.353	12	93	280	14	16	5	2.5	.948	R. Lawson	41	128	8	6	3	5.48
	CF	A. Simmons	568	.327	13	112	352	8	5	1	2.6	.986							
	LF	G. Goslin	572	.315	24	125	266	11	13	1	2.0	.955							
	C	R. Hayworth	250	.240	1	30	305	28	4	5	4.2	.988							
	OF	P. Fox	220	.305	4	26	118	3	4	0	2.3	.968							
Chicago	1B	Z. Bonura	587	.330	12	137	**1500**	**107**	7	**150**	**11.1**	**.996**	V. Kennedy	35	274	21	9	0	4.63
W-81 L-70	2B	J. Hayes	417	.312	5	84	216	334	12	70	6.3	.979	J. Whitehead	34	231	13	13	1	4.64
Jimmy Dykes	SS	L. Appling	526	**.388**	6	128	320	471	41	**119**	**6.1**	.951	S. Cain	30	195	14	10	0	4.75
	3B	J. Dykes	435	.267	7	60	108	240	18	14	2.9	.951	T. Lyons	26	182	10	13	0	5.14
	RF	M. Haas	408	.284	0	46	176	7	2	2	1.9	.989	M. Stratton	16	95	5	7	0	5.21
	CF	M. Kreevich	550	.307	5	69	300	17	12	5	2.5	.964	C. Brown	38	83	6	2	5	4.99
	LF	R. Radcliff	618	.335	8	82	213	6	15	2	1.8	.936	R. Phelps	15	69	4	6	0	6.03
	C	L. Sewell	451	.251	5	73	461	**87**	9	12	4.4	.984							
	23	T. Piet	352	.273	7	42	167	317	18	49		.964							
	OF	L. Rosenthal	317	.281	3	47	243	7	6	3	3.2	.977							
Washington	1B	J. Kuhel	588	.321	16	118	1452	73	10	138	10.3	.993	B. Newsom	43	286	17	15	2	4.32
W-82 L-71	2B	O. Bluege	319	.288	1	55	128	158	2	35	5.5	.993	J. DeShong	34	224	18	10	2	4.63
Bucky Harris	SS	C. Travis	517	.317	2	92	135	213	23	53	5.2	.938	E. Whitehill	28	212	14	11	0	4.87
	3B	B. Lewis	601	.291	6	67	152	297	**32**	24	3.5	.933	P. Appleton	38	202	14	9	3	3.53
	RF	C. Reynolds	293	.276	4	41	142	8	5	0	2.2	.968	J. Cascarella	22	139	9	8	1	4.07
	CF	B. Chapman	401	.332	4	60	271	10	12	4	3.0	.959	M. Weaver	26	91	6	4	1	4.35
	LF	J. Stone	437	.341	15	90	249	12	9	5	2.4	.967							
	C	C. Bolton	289	.291	2	51	287	44	7	4	4.1	.979							
	S2	R. Kress	391	.284	8	51	229	312	29	73		.949							
	OF	J. Hill	233	.305	0	34	83	5	3	1	1.5	.967							
	C	W. Millies	215	.312	0	25	205	40	8	3	3.5	.968							
	OF	J. Powell	214	.290	1	30	115	2	6	1	2.3	.951							
	2B	B. Myer	156	.269	0	15	120	143	4	31	6.2	.985							
	OF	F. Sington	94	.319	1	28	52	1	3	0	2.2	.946							
Cleveland	1B	H. Trosky	629	.343	42	**162**	1367	85	**22**	126	9.8	.985	J. Allen	36	243	20	10	1	3.44
W-80 L-74	2B	R. Hughes	638	.295	0	63	**421**	466	**25**	98	6.0	.973	M. Harder	36	225	15	15	1	5.17
Steve O'Neill	SS	B. Knickerbocker	618	.294	8	73	313	486	40	97	5.4	.952	O. Hildebrand	36	175	10	11	4	4.90
	3B	O. Hale	620	.316	14	87	169	**323**	28	26	**3.5**	.946	D. Galehouse	36	148	8	7	1	4.85
	RF	R. Weatherly	349	.335	8	53	164	15	5	2	2.2	.973	L. Brown	24	140	8	10	1	4.17
	CF	E. Averill	614	.378	28	126	369	11	12	2	2.6	.969	G. Blaeholder	35	134	8	4	0	5.09
	LF	J. Vosmik	506	.287	7	94	258	11	6	1	2.0	.978	T. Lee	43	127	3	5	3	4.89
	C	B. Sullivan	319	.351	2	48	324	40	12	8	5.2	.968							
	C	F. Pytlak	224	.321	0	31	224	35	1	6	4.5	.996							
	OF	B. Campbell	172	.372	6	30	68	4	3	2	1.6	.960							
Boston	1B	J. Foxx	585	.338	41	143	1226	76	12	108	9.5	.991	W. Ferrell	39	**301**	20	15	0	4.19
W-74 L-80	2B	O. Melillo	327	.226	0	32	239	242	10	59	5.3	.980	L. Grove	35	253	17	12	2	**2.81**
Joe Cronin	SS	E. McNair	494	.285	4	74	171	230	14	47	4.9	.966	F. Ostermueller	43	181	10	16	2	4.87
	3B	B. Werber	535	.275	10	67	112	161	19	16	2.9	.935	J. Marcum	31	174	8	13	1	4.81
	RF	M. Almada	320	.253	1	21	144	9	2	2	1.9	.987	J. Wilson	43	136	6	8	3	4.42
	CF	D. Cramer	643	.292	0	41	443	20	12	6	3.1	.975	R. Walberg	24	100	5	4	0	4.40
	LF	D. Cooke	341	.273	6	47	207	3	6	2	2.4	.972							
	C	R. Ferrell	410	.312	8	55	**556**	55	8	5	5.1	**.987**							
	OF	H. Manush	313	.291	0	45	110	3	4	1	1.6	.966							
	UT	J. Kroner	298	.292	4	62	146	211	18	36		.952							
	SS	J. Cronin	295	.281	2	43	115	191	23	34	5.5	.930							
	P	W. Ferrell	135	.267	5	24	9	42	2	2	1.4	.962							
St. Louis	1B	J. Bottomley	544	.298	12	95	1250	47	10	103	9.3	.992	C. Hogsett	39	215	13	15	1	5.52
W-57 L-95	2B	T. Carey	488	.273	1	57	308	434	**25**	82	6.0	.967	J. Knott	47	193	9	17	6	7.29
Rogers Hornsby	SS	L. Lary	620	.289	2	52	**339**	**495**	38	88	5.6	.956	I. Andrews	36	191	7	12	1	4.84
	3B	H. Clift	576	.302	20	73	158	310	24	27	3.2	.951	E. Caldwell	41	189	7	16	2	6.00
	RF	B. Bell	616	.344	11	123	291	11	8	6	2.2	.974	T. Thomas	36	180	11	9	0	5.26
	CF	S. West	533	.278	7	70	442	10	8	2	3.1	.983	R. Van Atta	**52**	123	4	7	2	6.60
	LF	M. Solters	628	.291	17	134	356	16	17	5	2.6	.956							
	C	R. Hemsley	377	.263	2	39	340	68	13	**16**	3.7	.969							
	C	T. Giuliani	198	.217	0	13	226	29	9	7	4.0	.966							
	OF	E. Coleman	137	.292	2	34	31	0	2	0	1.8	.939							
	OF	R. Pepper	124	.282	2	23	31	1	2	0	1.9	.941							
Philadelphia	1B	L. Finney	**653**	.302	1	41	782	34	8	70	10.6	.990	H. Kelley	35	235	15	12	3	3.86
W-53 L-100	2B	R. Warstler	236	.250	1	24	139	265	11	45	6.3	.973	G. Rhodes	35	216	9	**20**	1	5.74
Connie Mack	SS	S. Newsome	471	.225	0	46	273	417	31	87	5.9	.957	B. Ross	30	201	9	14	0	5.83
	3B	P. Higgins	550	.289	12	80	151	266	26	24	3.1	.941	H. Fink	34	189	8	16	3	5.39
	RF	G. Puccinelli	457	.278	11	78	245	11	14	1	2.3	.948	B. Dietrich	21	72	4	6	3	6.53
	CF	W. Moses	585	.345	7	66	396	12	11	3	2.9	.974							
	LF	B. Johnson	566	.292	25	121	289	13	12	3	2.4	.962							
	C	F. Hayes	505	.271	10	67	489	69	**16**	8	4.0	.972							
	1B	C. Dean	342	.287	1	48	680	37	8	62	9.4	.989							
	2B	A. Niemiec	203	.197	1	20	134	180	9	32	6.2	.972							

AMERICAN LEAGUE 1936, *cont.*

BATTING AND BASE RUNNING LEADERS

Batting Average
- L. Appling, CHI .388
- E. Averill, CLE .378
- B. Dickey, NY .362
- C. Gehringer, DET .354
- L. Gehrig, NY .354

Slugging Average
- L. Gehrig, NY .696
- H. Trosky, CLE .644
- J. Foxx, BOS .631
- E. Averill, CLE .627
- B. Dickey, NY .617

Home Runs
- L. Gehrig, NY 49
- H. Trosky, CLE 42
- J. Foxx, BOS 41
- J. DiMaggio, NY 29
- E. Averill, CLE 28

Total Bases
- H. Trosky, CLE 405
- L. Gehrig, NY 403
- E. Averill, CLE 385
- J. Foxx, BOS 369
- J. DiMaggio, NY 367

Runs Batted In
- H. Trosky, CLE 162
- L. Gehrig, NY 152
- J. Foxx, BOS 143
- Z. Bonura, CHI 137
- M. Solters, STL 134

Stolen Bases
- L. Lary, STL 37
- J. Powell, WAS, NY 26
- B. Werber, BOS 23
- B. Chapman, NY, WAS 20
- R. Hughes, CLE 20

Hits
- E. Averill, CLE 232
- C. Gehringer, DET 227
- H. Trosky, CLE 216
- B. Bell, STL 212

Base on Balls
- L. Gehrig, NY 130
- L. Lary, STL 117
- H. Clift, STL 115
- J. Foxx, BOS 105

Home Run Percentage
- L. Gehrig, NY 8.5
- J. Foxx, BOS 7.0
- H. Trosky, CLE 6.7
- B. Dickey, NY 5.2

Runs
- L. Gehrig, NY 167
- H. Clift, STL 145
- C. Gehringer, DET 144
- F. Crosetti, NY 137

Doubles
- C. Gehringer, DET 60
- G. Walker, DET 55
- B. Chapman, NY, WAS 50
- O. Hale, CLE 50

Triples
- R. Rolfe, NY 15
- E. Averill, CLE 15
- J. DiMaggio, NY 15
- B. Johnson, PHI 14

PITCHING LEADERS

Winning Percentage
- M. Pearson, NY .731
- V. Kennedy, CHI .700
- T. Bridges, DET .676
- J. Allen, CLE .667
- S. Rowe, DET .655

Earned Run Average
- L. Grove, BOS 2.81
- J. Allen, CLE 3.44
- P. Appleton, WAS 3.53
- T. Bridges, DET 3.60
- M. Pearson, NY 3.71

Wins
- T. Bridges, DET 23
- V. Kennedy, CHI 21
- J. Allen, CLE 20
- R. Ruffing, NY 20
- W. Ferrell, BOS 20

Saves
- P. Malone, NY 9
- J. Knott, STL 6
- C. Brown, CHI 5
- J. Murphy, NY 5
- O. Hildebrand, CLE 4

Strikeouts
- T. Bridges, DET 175
- J. Allen, CLE 165
- B. Newsom, WAS 156
- L. Grove, BOS 130
- M. Pearson, NY 118

Complete Games
- W. Ferrell, BOS 28
- T. Bridges, DET 26
- R. Ruffing, NY 25
- B. Newsom, WAS 24
- L. Grove, BOS 22

Fewest Hits/9 Innings
- M. Pearson, NY 7.71
- L. Grove, BOS 8.42
- J. Allen, CLE 8.67
- L. Gomez, NY 8.78

Shutouts
- L. Grove, BOS 6
- T. Bridges, DET 5
- J. Allen, CLE 4
- S. Rowe, DET 4
- B. Newsom, WAS 4

Fewest Walks/9 Innings
- T. Lyons, CHI 2.23
- L. Grove, BOS 2.31
- S. Rowe, DET 2.35
- I. Andrews, STL 2.35

Most Strikeouts/9 Inn.
- J. Allen, CLE 6.11
- T. Bridges, DET 5.35
- L. Gomez, NY 5.01
- B. Newsom, WAS 4.91

Innings
- W. Ferrell, BOS 301
- T. Bridges, DET 295
- B. Newsom, WAS 286
- V. Kennedy, CHI 274

Games Pitched
- R. Van Atta, STL 52
- J. Knott, STL 47

							Batting						Fielding			Pitching					
	W	L	PCT	GB	R	OR	2B	3B	HR	BA	SA	SB	E	DP	FA	CG	BB	SO	ShO	SV	ERA
New York	102	51	.667		**1065**	**731**	315	83	**182**	.300	**.483**	76	163	148	.973	77	663	**624**	6	**21**	**4.17**
Detroit	83	71	.539	19.5	921	871	326	55	94	.300	.431	72	**153**	159	**.975**	76	562	526	**13**	13	5.00
Chicago	81	70	.536	20	920	873	282	56	60	.292	.397	66	168	**174**	.973	**80**	578	414	5	8	5.06
Washington	82	71	.536	20	889	799	293	**84**	62	.295	.414	**103**	182	163	.970	78	588	462	8	14	4.58
Cleveland	80	74	.519	22.5	921	862	**357**	82	123	**.304**	.461	66	178	154	.971	**80**	607	619	6	12	4.83
Boston	74	80	.481	28.5	775	764	288	62	86	.276	.400	54	165	139	.972	78	**552**	584	11	9	4.39
St. Louis	57	95	.375	44.5	804	1064	299	66	79	.279	.403	62	188	143	.969	54	609	399	3	13	6.24
Philadelphia	53	100	.346	49	714	1045	240	60	72	.269	.376	59	209	152	.965	68	696	405	3	12	6.08
					7009	7009	2400	548	758	.289	.421	558	1406	1232	.971	591	4855	4033	55	102	5.04

NATIONAL LEAGUE 1937

New York

W-95 L-57

Bill Terry

POS	Player	AB	BA	HR	RBI	PO	A	E	DP	TC/G	FA	Pitcher	G	IP	W	L	SV	ERA
1B	J. McCarthy	420	.279	10	65	1123	82	16	89	11.1	.987	C. Hubbell	39	262	**22**	8	4	3.20
2B	B. Whitehead	574	.286	5	52	**394**	514	24	**106**	6.1	**.974**	C. Melton	46	248	20	9	**7**	2.61
SS	D. Bartell	516	.306	14	62	281	476	33	96	**6.2**	.958	H. Schumacher	38	218	13	12	1	3.60
3B	L. Chiozza	439	.232	4	29	90	171	17	9	3.0	.939	H. Gumbert	34	200	10	11	1	3.68
RF	M. Ott	545	.294	**31**	95	156	13	0	1	1.9	1.000	S. Castleman	23	160	11	6	0	3.31
CF	J. Ripple	426	.317	5	66	193	6	4	1	1.8	.980	D. Coffman	42	80	8	3	3	3.04
LF	J. Moore	580	.310	6	57	226	12	6	0	1.7	.975							
C	H. Danning	292	.288	8	51	332	57	7	7	4.6	.982							
C	G. Mancuso	287	.279	4	39	410	69	9	4	6.0	.982							
OF	W. Berger	199	.291	12	43	107	4	4	0	2.2	.965							
1B	S. Leslie	191	.309	3	30	444	38	5	45	11.1	.990							
OF	H. Leiber	184	.293	4	32	78	1	1	0	1.7	.988							

Chicago

W-93 L-61

Charlie Grimm

POS	Player	AB	BA	HR	RBI	PO	A	E	DP	TC/G	FA	Pitcher	G	IP	W	L	SV	ERA
1B	R. Collins	456	.274	16	71	1068	80	11	94	10.4	.991	B. Lee	42	272	14	15	3	3.54
2B	B. Herman	564	.335	8	65	384	468	**41**	97	**6.5**	.954	T. Carleton	32	208	16	8	0	3.15
SS	B. Jurges	450	.298	1	65	258	370	16	74	5.0	**.975**	L. French	42	208	16	10	0	3.98
3B	S. Hack	582	.297	2	63	**151**	**247**	13	**25**	2.7	.968	C. Root	43	179	13	5	5	3.38
RF	F. Demaree	615	.324	17	115	283	17	6	6	2.0	.980	R. Parmelee	33	146	7	8	0	5.13
CF	J. Marty	290	.290	5	44	196	4	5	0	2.4	.976	C. Bryant	38	135	9	3	3	4.26
LF	A. Galan	611	.252	18	78	328	9	7	3	2.5	.980	C. Davis	28	124	10	5	1	4.08
C	G. Hartnett	356	.354	12	82	436	65	2	7	5.0	**.996**	C. Shoun	37	93	7	7	0	5.61
01	P. Cavarretta	329	.286	5	56	454	40	10	28		.980							
C	K. O'Dea	219	.301	4	32	234	29	4	4	4.2	.985							
UT	L. Frey	198	.278	1	22	90	101	10	18		.950							
OF	T. Stainback	160	.231	0	14	99	4	2	1	2.1	.981							

Pittsburgh

W-86 L-68

Pie Traynor

POS	Player	AB	BA	HR	RBI	PO	A	E	DP	TC/G	FA	Pitcher	G	IP	W	L	SV	ERA
1B	G. Suhr	575	.278	5	97	1452	91	11	108	10.3	.993	C. Blanton	36	243	14	12	0	3.30
2B	L. Handley	480	.250	3	37	296	375	35	67	5.6	.950	R. Bauers	34	188	13	6	1	2.88
SS	A. Vaughan	469	.322	5	72	231	335	26	58	5.5	.956	E. Brandt	33	176	11	10	2	3.11
3B	B. Brubaker	413	.254	6	48	98	216	16	16	2.9	.952	B. Swift	36	164	9	10	3	3.95
RF	P. Waner	619	.354	2	74	271	16	9	3	2.0	.970	J. Bowman	30	128	8	8	1	4.57
CF	L. Waner	537	.330	1	45	312	8	4	0	2.6	.988	R. Lucas	20	126	8	10	0	4.27
LF	W. Jensen	509	.279	5	45	256	5	10	1	2.3	.963	J. Weaver	32	110	8	5	0	3.20
C	A. Todd	514	.307	8	86	**603**	**89**	**20**	**15**	**5.6**	.972	M. Brown	50	108	7	2	**7**	4.18
UT	P. Young	408	.260	9	54	195	328	24	52		.956	J. Tobin	20	87	6	3	1	3.00
OF	J. Dickshot	264	.254	3	33	109	5	6	2	1.9	.950							

NATIONAL LEAGUE 1937, *cont.*

St. Louis

W-81 L-73

Frankie Frisch

POS	Player	AB	BA	HR	RBI	PO	A	E	DP	TC/G	FA	Pitcher	G	IP	W	L	SV	ERA
1B	J. Mize	560	.364	25	113	1308	67	17	104	9.7	.988	B. Weiland	41	264	15	14	0	3.54
2B	J. Brown	525	.276	2	53	235	360	22	57	5.5	.964	L. Warneke	36	239	18	11	0	4.53
SS	L. Durocher	477	.203	1	47	279	381	28	72	5.1	.959	D. Dean	27	197	13	10	1	2.69
3B	D. Gutteridge	447	.271	7	61	133	176	7	18	3.0	.978	S. Johnson	38	192	12	12	1	3.32
RF	D. Padgett	446	.314	10	74	225	9	11	5	2.2	.955	M. Ryba	38	135	9	6	0	4.13
CF	T. Moore	461	.267	5	43	307	9	4	2	3.0	.988	R. Harrell	35	97	3	7	1	5.87
LF	J. Medwick	**633**	**.374**	**31**	**154**	329	9	4	1	2.2	.988							
C	B. Ogrodowski	279	.233	3	31	387	50	7	2	5.1	.984							
OF	P. Martin	339	.304	5	38	204	12	6	3	2.7	.973							
30	F. Bordagaray	300	.293	1	37	105	72	9	2		.952							
C	M. Owen	234	.231	0	20	287	49	9	6	4.4	.974							
2B	S. Martin	223	.260	1	17	93	134	13	27	5.0	.946							

Boston

W-79 L-73

Bill McKechnie

POS	Player	AB	BA	HR	RBI	PO	A	E	DP	TC/G	FA	Pitcher	G	IP	W	L	SV	ERA
1B	E. Fletcher	539	.247	1	38	**1587**	108	12	**117**	**11.5**	.993	L. Fette	35	259	20	10	0	2.88
2B	T. Cuccinello	575	.271	11	80	330	**524**	29	92	5.8	.967	J. Turner	33	257	20	11	1	**2.38**
SS	R. Warstler	555	.223	3	36	298	**493**	**49**	85	5.6	.942	D. MacFayden	32	246	14	14	0	2.93
3B	G. English	269	.290	2	37	61	121	8	9	2.7	.958	G. Bush	32	181	8	15	1	3.54
RF	G. Moore	561	.283	16	70	340	21	8	1	2.5	.978	J. Lanning	32	117	5	7	2	3.93
CF	V. DiMaggio	493	.256	13	69	351	21	7	2	2.9	.982	I. Hutchinson	31	92	4	6	0	3.73
LF	D. Garms	478	.259	2	37	168	1	4	0	2.1	.977	F. Gabler	19	76	4	7	2	5.09
C	A. Lopez	334	.204	3	38	342	83	7	5	4.2	.984							
OF	R. Johnson	260	.277	3	22	131	5	5	0	2.2	.965							
C	R. Mueller	187	.251	2	26	169	44	1	6	3.8	.995							
3B	E. Mayo	172	.227	1	18	57	73	6	2	2.7	.956							
OF	W. Berger	113	.274	5	22	51	1	0	0	1.9	1.000							

Brooklyn

W-62 L-91

Burleigh Grimes

POS	Player	AB	BA	HR	RBI	PO	A	E	DP	TC/G	FA	Pitcher	G	IP	W	L	SV	ERA
1B	B. Hassett	556	.304	1	53	1125	**116**	**20**	96	9.6	.984	M. Butcher	39	192	11	15	0	4.27
2B	C. Lavagetto	503	.282	8	70	229	294	28	56	5.5	.949	L. Hamlin	39	186	11	13	1	3.59
SS	W. English	378	.238	1	42	220	303	24	51	4.7	.956	F. Frankhouse	33	179	10	13	0	4.27
3B	J. Stripp	300	.243	1	26	75	91	5	4	2.6	.971	W. Hoyt	27	167	7	7	0	3.23
RF	H. Manush	466	.333	4	73	187	7	6	1	1.6	.970	V. Mungo	25	161	9	11	3	2.91
CF	J. Cooney	430	.293	0	37	279	9	7	2	2.7	.976	R. Henshaw	42	156	5	12	2	5.07
LF	T. Winsett	350	.237	5	42	209	6	9	1	2.2	.960	F. Fitzsimmons	13	91	4	8	0	4.27
C	B. Phelps	409	.313	7	58	465	76	16	10	5.0	.971							
23	J. Bucher	380	.253	4	37	165	192	23	35		.939							
OF	G. Brack	372	.274	5	38	208	10	7	0	2.2	.969							

Philadelphia

W-61 L-92

Jimmie Wilson

POS	Player	AB	BA	HR	RBI	PO	A	E	DP	TC/G	FA	Pitcher	G	IP	W	L	SV	ERA
1B	D. Camilli	475	.339	27	80	1256	99	8	104	10.4	**.994**	C. Passeau	50	**292**	14	18	2	4.34
2B	D. Young	360	.194	0	24	200	333	28	63	5.2	.950	B. Walters	37	246	14	15	0	4.75
SS	G. Scharein	511	.241	0	57	**335**	456	44	**98**	5.7	.947	W. LaMaster	50	220	15	**19**	4	5.31
3B	P. Whitney	487	.341	8	79	136	238	7	17	2.9	**.982**	H. Mulcahy	**56**	216	8	18	3	5.13
RF	C. Klein	406	.325	15	57	175	11	10	3	1.9	.949	O. Jorgens	52	141	3	4	3	4.41
CF	H. Martin	579	.283	8	49	353	9	8	1	2.7	.978	S. Johnson	32	138	4	10	3	5.02
LF	M. Arnovich	410	.290	10	60	237	10	7	5	2.4	.972							
C	B. Atwood	279	.244	2	32	290	48	11	5	4.4	.968							
UT	L. Norris	381	.257	9	36	212	264	22	43		.956							
OF	E. Browne	332	.292	6	52	92	7	2	1	1.9	.980							
OF	J. Moore	307	.319	9	59	124	9	8	1	2.0	.943							
C	E. Grace	223	.211	6	29	275	30	3	10	4.8	.990							

Cincinnati

W-56 L-98

Chuck Dressen
W-51 L-78

Bobby Wallace
W-5 L-20

POS	Player	AB	BA	HR	RBI	PO	A	E	DP	TC/G	FA	Pitcher	G	IP	W	L	SV	ERA
1B	B. Jordan	316	.282	1	28	669	46	8	55	9.5	.989	L. Grissom	50	224	12	17	6	3.26
2B	A. Kampouris	458	.249	17	71	367	439	33	87	5.7	.961	P. Derringer	43	223	10	14	1	4.04
SS	B. Myers	335	.251	7	43	190	360	30	67	4.8	.948	P. Davis	42	218	11	13	3	3.59
3B	L. Riggs	384	.242	6	45	112	223	**21**	16	**3.6**	.941	A. Hollingsworth	43	202	9	15	5	3.91
RF	I. Goodman	549	.273	12	55	291	13	8	0	2.2	.974	G. Schott	37	154	4	13	1	2.97
CF	C. Hafey	257	.261	9	41	128	5	4	0	2.1	.971	B. Hallahan	21	63	3	9	0	6.14
LF	K. Cuyler	406	.271	0	32	174	8	5	1	1.8	.973							
C	E. Lombardi	368	.334	9	59	333	58	11	3	4.5	.973							
1B	L. Scarsella	329	.246	3	34	589	37	10	55	9.8	.984							
OF	H. Walker	221	.249	1	19	135	5	1	3	2.4	.993							
C	S. Davis	209	.268	3	33	300	40	7	3	5.9	.980							
OF	P. Weintraub	177	.271	3	20	78	3	2	1	1.8	.976							
3B	J. Outlaw	165	.273	0	11	41	87	12	4	3.4	.914							

BATTING AND BASE RUNNING LEADERS

Batting Average		Slugging Average		Home Runs	
J. Medwick, STL	.374	J. Medwick, STL	.641	M. Ott, NY	31
J. Mize, STL	.364	J. Mize, STL	.595	J. Medwick, STL	31
G. Hartnett, CHI	.354	D. Camilli, PHI	.587	D. Camilli, PHI	27
P. Waner, PIT	.354	G. Hartnett, CHI	.548	J. Mize, STL	25
P. Whitney, PHI	.341	M. Ott, NY	.523	A. Galan, CHI	18

Total Bases		Runs Batted In		Stolen Bases	
J. Medwick, STL	406	J. Medwick, STL	154	A. Galan, CHI	23
J. Mize, STL	333	F. Demaree, CHI	115	S. Hack, CHI	16
F. Demaree, CHI	298	J. Mize, STL	113	T. Moore, STL	13
M. Ott, NY	285	G. Suhr, PIT	97	C. Lavagetto, BKN	13
D. Camilli, PHI	279	M. Ott, NY	95	G. Scharein, PHI	13
				B. Hassett, BKN	13

PITCHING LEADERS

Winning Percentage		Earned Run Average		Wins	
C. Hubbell, NY	.733	J. Turner, BOS	2.38	C. Hubbell, NY	22
C. Melton, NY	.690	C. Melton, NY	2.61	C. Melton, NY	20
L. Fette, BOS	.667	D. Dean, STL	2.69	J. Turner, BOS	20
T. Carleton, CHI	.667	R. Bauers, PIT	2.88	L. Fette, BOS	20
J. Turner, BOS	.645	L. Fette, BOS	2.88	L. Warneke, STL	18

Saves		Strikeouts		Complete Games	
C. Melton, NY	7	C. Hubbell, NY	159	J. Turner, BOS	24
M. Brown, PIT	7	L. Grissom, CIN	149	L. Fette, BOS	23
L. Grissom, CIN	6	C. Blanton, PIT	143	B. Weiland, STL	21
A. Hollingsworth, CIN	5	C. Melton, NY	142		
C. Root, CHI	5	W. LaMaster, PHI	135		
		C. Passeau, PHI	135		

NATIONAL LEAGUE 1937, *cont.*

BATTING AND BASE RUNNING LEADERS

Hits
- J. Medwick, STL 237
- P. Waner, PIT 219
- J. Mize, STL 204
- F. Demaree, CHI 199

Base on Balls
- M. Ott, NY 102
- D. Camilli, PHI 90
- G. Suhr, PIT 83
- S. Hack, CHI 83

Home Run Percentage
- M. Ott, NY 5.7
- D. Camilli, PHI 5.7
- J. Medwick, STL 4.9
- J. Mize, STL 4.5

Runs
- J. Medwick, STL 111
- B. Herman, CHI 106
- S. Hack, CHI 106
- A. Galan, CHI 104
- F. Demaree, CHI 104

Doubles
- J. Medwick, STL 56
- J. Mize, STL 40
- D. Bartell, NY 38
- B. Phelps, BKN 37
- J. Moore, NY 37

Triples
- A. Vaughan, PIT 17
- G. Suhr, PIT 14
- L. Handley, PIT 12
- I. Goodman, CIN 12

PITCHING LEADERS

Fewest Hits/9 Innings
- V. Mungo, BKN 7.60
- L. Grissom, CIN 7.77
- C. Melton, NY 7.84
- T. Carleton, CHI 7.91

Shutouts
- L. Grissom, CIN 5
- J. Turner, BOS 5
- L. Fette, BOS 5

Fewest Walks/9 Innings
- D. Dean, STL 1.51
- W. Hoyt, PIT, BKN 1.66
- J. Turner, BOS 1.82
- S. Castleman, NY 1.85

Most Strikeouts/9 Inn.
- V. Mungo, BKN 6.82
- L. Grissom, CIN 6.00
- R. Bauers, PIT 5.66
- W. LaMaster, PHI 5.51

Innings
- C. Passeau, PHI 292
- B. Lee, CHI 272
- B. Weiland, STL 264
- C. Hubbell, NY 262

Games Pitched
- H. Mulcahy, PHI 56
- O. Jorgens, PHI 52

							Batting						Fielding			Pitching					
	W	L	PCT	GB	R	OR	2B	3B	HR	BA	SA	SB	E	DP	FA	CG	BB	SO	ShO	SV	ERA
New York	95	57	.625		732	602	251	41	**111**	.278	.403	45	159	143	.974	67	404	**653**	11	17	3.43
Chicago	93	61	.604	3	**811**	682	253	74	96	**.287**	**.416**	71	**151**	141	**.975**	73	502	596	11	13	3.97
Pittsburgh	86	68	.558	10	704	646	223	**86**	47	.285	.384	32	181	135	.970	67	428	643	12	17	3.56
St. Louis	81	73	.526	15	789	733	**264**	67	94	.282	.406	**78**	164	127	.973	81	448	573	10	4	3.95
Boston	79	73	.520	16	579	**556**	200	41	63	.247	.339	45	157	128	**.975**	**85**	**372**	387	**16**	10	**3.22**
Brooklyn	62	91	.405	33.5	616	772	258	53	37	.265	.354	69	217	127	.964	63	476	592	5	8	4.13
Philadelphia	61	92	.399	34.5	724	869	258	37	103	.273	.391	66	184	**157**	.970	59	501	529	6	15	5.06
Cincinnati	56	98	.364	40	612	707	215	59	73	.254	.360	53	208	139	.966	64	533	581	10	**18**	3.94
					5567	5567	1922	458	624	.271	.382	459	1421	1097	.971	559	3664	4554	81	102	3.91

AMERICAN LEAGUE 1937

New York

W-102 L-52

Joe McCarthy

POS	Player	AB	BA	HR	RBI	PO	A	E	DP	TC/G	FA
1B	L. Gehrig	569	.351	37	159	1370	74	**16**	113	9.3	.989
2B	T. Lazzeri	446	.244	14	70	251	382	22	64	5.2	.966
SS	F. Crosetti	611	.234	11	49	313	467	43	86	5.6	.948
3B	R. Rolfe	648	.276	4	62	195	309	20	27	3.4	.962
RF	M. Hoag	362	.301	3	46	181	8	9	2	2.0	.955
CF	J. DiMaggio	621	.346	**46**	167	413	21	17	4	3.0	.962
LF	J. Powell	365	.263	3	45	201	5	4	2	2.2	.981
C	B. Dickey	530	.332	29	133	**692**	**80**	7	11	5.7	.991
OF	G. Selkirk	256	.328	18	68	140	9	2	1	2.2	.987
OF	T. Henrich	206	.320	8	42	90	6	3	1	1.7	.970
2S	D. Heffner	201	.249	0	21	123	126	6	30		.976

Pitcher	G	IP	W	L	SV	ERA
L. Gomez	34	278	**21**	11	0	**2.33**
R. Ruffing	31	256	20	7	0	2.98
B. Hadley	29	178	11	8	0	5.30
M. Pearson	22	145	9	3	1	3.17
J. Murphy	39	110	13	4	10	4.17
P. Malone	28	92	4	4	6	5.48
K. Wicker	16	88	7	3	0	4.40
S. Chandler	12	82	7	4	0	2.84
F. Makosky	26	58	5	2	3	4.97

Detroit

W-89 L-65

Mickey Cochrane
W-16 L-13

Del Baker
W-34 L-20

Mickey Cochrane
W-39 L-32

POS	Player	AB	BA	HR	RBI	PO	A	E	DP	TC/G	FA
1B	H. Greenberg	594	.337	40	**183**	**1477**	102	13	133	10.3	.992
2B	C. Gehringer	564	**.371**	14	96	331	485	12	102	5.8	**.986**
SS	B. Rogell	536	.276	8	64	323	451	26	103	5.5	**.968**
3B	M. Owen	396	.288	1	45	108	219	10	17	3.2	**.970**
RF	P. Fox	628	.331	12	82	321	6	8	0	2.3	.976
CF	J. White	305	.246	0	21	216	4	6	0	2.8	.973
LF	G. Walker	635	.335	18	113	316	9	15	2	2.3	.956
C	R. York	375	.307	35	103	190	27	9	6	4.2	.960
OF	C. Laabs	242	.240	8	37	133	2	4	0	2.2	.971
OF	G. Goslin	181	.238	4	35	81	2	4	1	2.2	.954
C	B. Tebbetts	162	.191	2	16	155	25	7	1	3.9	.963

Pitcher	G	IP	W	L	SV	ERA
E. Auker	39	253	17	9	1	3.88
T. Bridges	34	245	15	12	0	4.07
R. Lawson	37	217	18	7	1	5.26
J. Wade	33	165	7	10	0	5.39
B. Poffenberger	29	137	10	5	3	4.65
G. Gill	31	128	11	4	1	4.51
S. Coffman	28	101	7	5	0	4.37
J. Russell	25	40	2	5	4	7.59

Chicago

W-86 L-68

Jimmy Dykes

POS	Player	AB	BA	HR	RBI	PO	A	E	DP	TC/G	FA
1B	Z. Bonura	447	.345	19	100	1114	63	13	123	**10.3**	.989
2B	J. Hayes	573	.229	2	79	**353**	**490**	14	**115**	**6.0**	.984
SS	L. Appling	574	.317	4	77	280	**541**	**49**	**111**	5.6	.944
3B	T. Piet	332	.235	4	38	83	163	16	12	3.0	.939
RF	D. Walker	593	.302	9	95	270	10	14	1	1.9	.952
CF	M. Kreevich	583	.302	12	73	401	13	5	4	3.0	.988
LF	R. Radcliff	584	.325	4	79	273	9	10	5	2.1	.966
C	L. Sewell	412	.269	1	61	502	72	9	11	4.9	.985
13	J. Dykes	85	.306	1	23	152	27	1	15		.994

Pitcher	G	IP	W	L	SV	ERA
V. Kennedy	32	221	14	13	0	5.09
T. Lee	30	205	12	10	0	3.52
T. Lyons	22	169	12	7	0	4.15
J. Whitehead	26	166	11	8	0	4.07
M. Stratton	22	165	15	5	0	2.40
B. Dietrich	29	143	8	10	1	4.90
C. Brown	**53**	100	7	7	**18**	3.42

Cleveland

W-83 L-71

Steve O'Neill

POS	Player	AB	BA	HR	RBI	PO	A	E	DP	TC/G	FA
1B	H. Trosky	601	.298	32	128	1403	76	10	131	9.8	.993
2B	J. Kroner	283	.237	2	26	155	189	11	45	5.5	.969
SS	L. Lary	644	.290	8	77	**325**	489	31	95	5.4	.963
3B	O. Hale	561	.267	6	82	96	199	11	24	3.4	.964
RF	B. Campbell	448	.301	4	61	204	14	5	5	1.8	.978
CF	E. Averill	609	.299	21	92	362	11	9	3	2.4	.976
LF	M. Solters	589	.323	20	109	283	19	15	3	2.1	.953
C	F. Pytlak	397	.315	1	44	559	**80**	9	**13**	5.6	.986
32	R. Hughes	346	.277	1	40	157	233	13	32		.968
C	B. Sullivan	168	.286	3	22	146	20	9	1	4.6	.949

Pitcher	G	IP	W	L	SV	ERA
M. Harder	38	234	15	12	2	4.28
D. Galehouse	36	201	9	14	3	4.57
W. Hudlin	35	176	12	11	2	4.10
J. Allen	24	173	15	1	0	2.55
B. Feller	26	149	9	7	1	3.39
E. Whitehill	33	147	8	8	2	6.49
J. Heving	40	73	8	4	5	4.83

AMERICAN LEAGUE 1937, *cont.*

Team	POS	Player	AB	BA	HR	RBI	PO	A	E	DP	TC/G	FA	Pitcher	G	IP	W	L	SV	ERA
Boston	1B	J. Foxx	569	.285	36	127	1287	**106**	8	122	9.3	**.994**	L. Grove	32	262	17	9	0	3.02
	2B	E. McNair	455	.292	12	76	242	316	18	67	5.4	.969	J. Wilson	51	221	16	10	7	3.70
W-80 L-72	SS	J. Cronin	570	.307	18	110	300	414	31	89	5.0	.958	B. Newsom	30	208	13	10	0	4.38
	3B	P. Higgins	570	.302	9	106	161	258	29	29	2.9	.935	J. Marcum	37	184	13	11	3	4.85
Joe Cronin	RF	B. Chapman	423	.307	7	57	262	9	4	1	2.5	.985	A. McKain	36	137	8	8	2	4.66
	CF	D. Cramer	560	.305	0	51	365	12	12	4	2.9	.969	R. Walberg	32	105	5	7	1	5.59
	LF	B. Mills	505	.295	7	58	239	8	14	0	2.2	.946	F. Ostermueller	25	87	3	7	1	4.98
	C	G. Desautels	305	.243	0	27	491	44	4	4	**5.7**	**.993**							
	OF	F. Gaffke	184	.288	6	34	80	3	3	0	1.7	.965							
	C	M. Berg	141	.255	0	20	208	24	5	2	5.0	.979							

Team	POS	Player	AB	BA	HR	RBI	PO	A	E	DP	TC/G	FA	Pitcher	G	IP	W	L	SV	ERA
Washington	1B	J. Kuhel	547	.283	6	61	1242	85	9	**141**	9.8	.993	J. DeShong	37	264	14	15	1	4.90
	2B	B. Myer	430	.293	1	65	308	338	**23**	90	5.6	.966	W. Ferrell	25	208*	11	13	0	3.94
W-73 L-80	SS	C. Travis	526	.344	3	66	229	396	23	99	5.0	.965	M. Weaver	30	189	12	9	0	4.20
	3B	B. Lewis	**668**	.314	10	79	146	293	29	32	3.0	.938	P. Appleton	35	168	8	15	2	4.39
Bucky Harris	RF	J. Stone	542	.330	6	88	300	15	5	3	2.3	.984	E. Linke	36	129	6	1	3	5.60
	CF	M. Almada	433	.309	4	33	308	16	12	3	3.4	.964	C. Fischer	17	72	4	5	2	4.38
	LF	A. Simmons	419	.279	8	84	240	7	4	5	2.5	.984	S. Cohen	33	55	2	4	4	3.11
	C	R. Ferrell	279	.229	1	32	341	42	5	5	4.6	.987							
	OF	F. Sington	228	.237	3	36	120	4	5	0	2.0	.961							
	C	W. Millies	179	.223	0	28	199	33	7	7	4.3	.971							

Team	POS	Player	AB	BA	HR	RBI	PO	A	E	DP	TC/G	FA	Pitcher	G	IP	W	L	SV	ERA
Philadelphia	1B	C. Dean	309	.262	2	31	705	38	7	55	9.6	.991	G. Caster	34	232	12	19	0	4.43
	2B	R. Peters	339	.260	3	43	138	170	11	34	4.6	.966	H. Kelley	41	205	13	**21**	0	5.36
W-54 L-97	SS	S. Newsome	438	.253	1	30	256	408	32	76	**5.7**	.954	E. Smith	38	197	4	17	5	3.94
	3B	B. Werber	493	.292	7	70	132	260	17	25	3.3	.958	B. Thomas	35	170	8	15	0	4.99
Connie Mack	RF	W. Moses	649	.320	25	86	323	16	15	4	2.3	.958	B. Ross	28	147	5	10	0	4.89
W-39 L-80	CF	J. Hill	242	.293	1	37	163	4	8	0	2.6	.954	L. Nelson	30	116	4	9	2	5.90
	LF	B. Johnson	477	.306	25	108	313	14	8	3	2.5	.976							
	C	E. Brucker	317	.259	6	37	323	48	11	**13**	4.2	.971							
Earle Mack	10	L. Finney	379	.251	1	20	519	30	12	39		.979							
W-15 L-17	OF	J. Rothrock	232	.267	0	21	130	2	1	0	2.3	.992							
	C	F. Hayes	188	.261	10	38	208	23	7	4	4.3	.971							
	2B	W. Ambler	162	.216	0	11	107	149	12	34	4.8	.955							
	P	L. Nelson	113	.354	4	29	3	14	0	0	0.6	1.000							

Team	POS	Player	AB	BA	HR	RBI	PO	A	E	DP	TC/G	FA	Pitcher	G	IP	W	L	SV	ERA
St. Louis	1B	H. Davis	450	.276	3	35	1065	54	10	108	10.1	.991	O. Hildebrand	30	201	8	17	1	5.14
	2B	T. Carey	487	.275	1	40	202	253	8	58	5.3	.983	J. Knott	38	191	8	18	2	4.89
W-46 L-108	SS	B. Knickerbocker	491	.261	4	61	205	368	25	59	5.2	.958	C. Hogsett	37	177	6	19	2	6.29
	3B	H. Clift	571	.306	29	118	**198**	**405**	**34**	**50**	**4.1**	.947	J. Walkup	27	150	9	12	0	7.36
Rogers Hornsby	RF	B. Bell	642	.340	14	117	222	22	4	6	1.9	.984	J. Bonetti	28	143	4	11	1	5.84
W-25 L-52	CF	S. West	457	.328	7	58	298	17	4	6	3.0	.987	B. Trotter	34	122	2	9	1	5.81
	LF	J. Vosmik	594	.325	4	93	333	12	10	4	2.5	.972	L. Koupal	26	106	4	9	0	6.56
	C	R. Hemsley	334	.222	3	28	332	70	**13**	**13**	4.4	.969							
Jim Bottomley	OF	E. Allen	320	.316	0	31	186	8	4	1	2.5	.980							
W-21 L-56	C	B. Huffman	176	.273	1	24	140	20	5	4	3.9	.970							

BATTING AND BASE RUNNING LEADERS

Batting Average
C. Gehringer, DET .371
L. Gehrig, NY .351
J. DiMaggio, NY .346
Z. Bonura, CHI .345
C. Travis, WAS .344

Slugging Average
J. DiMaggio, NY .673
H. Greenberg, DET .668
R. York, DET .651
L. Gehrig, NY .643
Z. Bonura, CHI .573

Home Runs
J. DiMaggio, NY 46
H. Greenberg, DET 40
L. Gehrig, NY 37
J. Foxx, BOS 36
R. York, DET 35

Total Bases
J. DiMaggio, NY 418
H. Greenberg, DET 397
L. Gehrig, NY 366
W. Moses, PHI 357
H. Trosky, CLE 329

Runs Batted In
H. Greenberg, DET 183
J. DiMaggio, NY 167
L. Gehrig, NY 159
B. Dickey, NY 133
H. Trosky, CLE 128

Stolen Bases
B. Werber, PHI 35
B. Chapman, WAS, BOS 35
G. Walker, DET 23
J. Hill, WAS, PHI 18
L. Appling, CHI 18
L. Lary, CLE 18

Hits
B. Bell, STL 218
J. DiMaggio, NY 215
G. Walker, DET 213
B. Lewis, WAS 210

Base on Balls
L. Gehrig, NY 127
H. Greenberg, DET 102
J. Foxx, BOS 99
B. Johnson, PHI 98
H. Clift, STL 98

Home Run Percentage
R. York, DET 9.3
J. DiMaggio, NY 7.4
H. Greenberg, DET 6.7
L. Gehrig, NY 6.5

Runs
J. DiMaggio, NY 151
R. Rolfe, NY 143
L. Gehrig, NY 138
H. Greenberg, DET 137

Doubles
B. Bell, STL 51
H. Greenberg, DET 49
W. Moses, PHI 48
J. Vosmik, STL 47

Triples
M. Kreevich, CHI 16
D. Walker, CHI 16
J. Stone, WAS 15
J. DiMaggio, NY 15

PITCHING LEADERS

Winning Percentage
J. Allen, CLE .938
M. Stratton, CHI .750
R. Ruffing, NY .741
R. Lawson, DET .720
L. Gomez, NY .656

Earned Run Average
L. Gomez, NY 2.33
M. Stratton, CHI 2.40
J. Allen, CLE 2.55
R. Ruffing, NY 2.98
L. Grove, BOS 3.02

Wins
L. Gomez, NY 21
R. Ruffing, NY 20
R. Lawson, DET 18
E. Auker, DET 17
L. Grove, BOS 17

Saves
C. Brown, CHI 18
J. Murphy, NY 10
J. Wilson, BOS 7
P. Malone, NY 6
E. Smith, PHI 5
J. Heving, CLE 5

Strikeouts
L. Gomez, NY 194
B. Newsom, WAS, BOS 166
L. Grove, BOS 153
B. Feller, CLE 150
T. Bridges, DET 138

Complete Games
W. Ferrell, BOS, WAS 26
L. Gomez, NY 25
R. Ruffing, NY 22
L. Grove, BOS 21
J. DeShong, WAS 20

Fewest Hits/9 Innings
L. Gomez, NY 7.53
M. Stratton, CHI 7.76
E. Smith, PHI 8.15
J. Allen, CLE 8.17

Shutouts
L. Gomez, NY 6
M. Stratton, CHI 5
R. Ruffing, NY 5
P. Appleton, WAS 4
J. Whitehead, CHI 4

Fewest Walks/9 Innings
M. Stratton, CHI 2.02
W. Hudlin, CLE 2.05
R. Ruffing, NY 2.39
T. Lyons, CHI 2.39

Most Strikeouts/9 Inn.
L. Gomez, NY 6.27
J. Wilson, BOS 5.57
B. Newsom, WAS, BOS 5.43
L. Grove, BOS 5.26

Innings
W. Ferrell, BOS, WAS 281
L. Gomez, NY 278
B. Newsom, WAS, BOS 275
J. DeShong, WAS 264

Games Pitched
C. Brown, CHI 53
J. Wilson, BOS 51
H. Kelley, PHI 41
B. Newsom, WAS, BOS 41

AMERICAN LEAGUE 1937, *cont.*

	W	L	PCT	GB	R	OR	Batting 2B	3B	HR	BA	SA	SB	Fielding E	DP	FA	Pitching CG	BB	SO	ShO	SV	ERA
New York	102	52	.662		**979**	**671**	282	73	**174**	.283	**.456**	60	170	134	.972	**82**	**506**	652	**15**	**21**	**3.65**
Detroit	89	65	.578	13	935	841	309	62	150	**.292**	.452	89	**147**	149	**.976**	70	635	485	6	11	4.87
Chicago	86	68	.558	16	780	730	280	76	67	.280	.400	70	174	173	.971	70	532	533	**15**	**21**	4.17
Cleveland	83	71	.539	19	817	768	304	76	103	.280	.423	76	159	153	.974	64	563	630	4	15	4.39
Boston	80	72	.526	21	821	775	269	64	100	.281	.411	79	177	139	.970	74	597	**682**	6	14	4.48
Washington	73	80	.477	28.5	757	841	245	**84**	47	.279	.379	61	170	**181**	.972	75	676	535	5	14	4.58
Philadelphia	54	97	.358	46.5	699	854	278	60	94	.267	.397	**95**	198	150	.967	65	613	469	6	9	4.85
St. Louis	46	108	.299	56	715	1023	**327**	44	71	.285	.399	30	173	166	.972	55	653	468	2	8	6.00
					6503	6503	2294	539	806	.281	.415	560	1368	1245	.972	555	4775	4454	59	113	4.62

NATIONAL LEAGUE 1938

Team	POS	Player	AB	BA	HR	RBI	PO	A	E	DP	TC/G	FA	Pitcher	G	IP	W	L	SV	ERA
Chicago	1B	R. Collins	490	.267	13	61	1264	111	6	118	10.2	**.996**	B. Lee	44	291	**22**	9	2	**2.66**
W-89 L-63	2B	B. Herman	624	.277	1	56	**404**	517	18	111	6.2	**.981**	C. Bryant	44	270	19	11	2	3.10
Charlie Grimm	SS	B. Jurges	465	.245	1	47	277	417	34	82	5.4	.953	L. French	43	201	10	19	0	3.80
W-45 L-36	3B	S. Hack	609	.320	4	67	**178**	300	23	**26**	**3.3**	.954	T. Carleton	33	168	10	9	0	5.42
Gabby Hartnett	RF	F. Demaree	476	.273	8	62	199	12	6	1	1.7	.972	C. Root	44	161	8	7	8	2.86
W-44 L-27	CF	C. Reynolds	497	.302	3	67	328	10	6	4	2.8	.983	J. Russell	42	102	6	1	3	3.34
	LF	A. Galan	395	.286	6	69	211	10	3	3	2.2	.987	V. Page	13	68	5	4	1	3.84
	C	G. Hartnett	299	.274	10	59	358	40	2	8	4.8	.995							
	01	P. Cavarretta	268	.239	1	28	277	21	4	14		.987							
	C	K. O'Dea	247	.263	3	33	294	32	10	3	4.7	.970							
	OF	J. Marty	235	.243	7	35	143	6	2	1	2.2	.987							
	UT	T. Lazzeri	120	.267	5	23	49	75	7	12		.947							
Pittsburgh	1B	G. Suhr	530	.294	3	64	**1512**	81	12	**150**	11.1	.993	R. Bauers	40	243	13	14	3	3.07
W-86 L-64	2B	P. Young	562	.278	4	79	370	**554**	26	**120**	**6.4**	.973	J. Tobin	40	241	14	12	0	3.47
Pie Traynor	SS	A. Vaughan	541	.322	7	68	**306**	**507**	33	**107**	5.8	.961	C. Blanton	29	173	11	7	0	3.70
	3B	L. Handley	570	.268	6	51	119	**304**	23	**26**	3.3	.948	B. Klinger	28	159	12	5	1	2.99
	RF	P. Waner	625	.280	6	69	284	11	7	0	2.1	.977	B. Swift	36	150	7	5	4	3.24
	CF	L. Waner	619	.313	5	57	341	15	5	5	2.5	.986	M. Brown	**51**	133	15	9	5	3.80
	LF	J. Rizzo	555	.301	23	111	284	5	15	1	2.2	.951							
	C	A. Todd	491	.265	7	75	**574**	**89**	10	7	**5.1**	**.985**							
New York	1B	J. McCarthy	470	.272	8	59	1315	77	10	111	**11.2**	.993	C. Melton	36	243	14	14	0	3.89
W-83 L-67	2B	A. Kampouris	268	.246	5	37	198	255	13	52	5.9	.972	H. Gumbert	38	236	15	13	0	4.01
Bill Terry	SS	D. Bartell	481	.262	9	49	288	447	37	85	**6.1**	.952	H. Schumacher	28	185	13	8	0	3.50
	3B	M. Ott	527	.311	**36**	116	98	238	15	14	3.1	.957	C. Hubbell	24	179	13	10	1	3.07
	RF	J. Ripple	501	.261	10	60	236	13	6	2	1.9	.976	B. Lohrman	31	152	9	6	0	3.32
	CF	H. Leiber	360	.269	12	65	181	6	5	3	2.2	.974	D. Coffman	**51**	111	8	4	**12**	3.48
	LF	J. Moore	506	.302	11	56	214	8	5	1	2.0	.978	J. Brown	43	90	5	3	5	1.80
	C	H. Danning	448	.306	9	60	449	50	8	7	4.4	.984							
	OF	B. Seeds	296	.291	9	52	147	6	2	2	2.0	.987							
	20	L. Chiozza	179	.235	3	17	80	111	11	9		.946							
	S3	G. Myatt	170	.306	3	10	77	128	17	24		.923							
	C	G. Mancuso	158	.348	2	15	184	24	5	5	4.8	.977							
	1B	S. Leslie	154	.253	1	16	304	15	4	21	10.1	.988							
Cincinnati	1B	F. McCormick	**640**	.327	5	106	1441	95	7	127	10.2	.995	P. Derringer	41	**307**	21	14	3	2.93
W-82 L-68	2B	L. Frey	501	.265	4	36	278	390	25	80	5.7	.964	J. Vander Meer	32	225	15	10	0	3.12
Bill McKechnie	SS	B. Myers	442	.253	12	47	255	380	41	74	5.5	.939	B. Walters	27	168	11	6	1	3.69
	3B	L. Riggs	531	.252	2	55	146	280	24	18	3.2	.947	P. Davis	29	168	7	12	1	3.97
	RF	I. Goodman	568	.292	30	92	306	10	4	1	2.3	.988	J. Weaver	30	129	6	4	3	3.13
	CF	H. Craft	612	.270	15	83	436	15	8	3	3.0	.983	W. Moore	19	90	6	4	0	3.49
	LF	W. Berger	407	.307	16	56	192	7	7	2	2.1	.966	G. Schott	31	83	5	5	2	4.45
	C	E. Lombardi	489	**.342**	19	95	512	73	9	8	4.8	.985	J. Cascarella	33	61	4	7	4	4.57
	OF	D. Cooke	233	.275	2	33	126	4	5	1	2.6	.963							
Boston	1B	E. Fletcher	529	.272	6	48	1424	**126**	**15**	108	10.7	.990	J. Turner	35	268	14	18	0	3.46
W-77 L-75	2B	T. Cuccinello	555	.265	9	76	323	458	21	84	5.5	.974	L. Fette	33	240	11	13	1	3.15
Casey Stengel	SS	R. Warstler	467	.231	0	40	285	428	**48**	76	5.6	.937	D. MacFayden	29	220	14	9	0	2.95
	3B	J. Stripp	229	.275	1	19	61	111	6	12	3.1	.966*	I. Hutchinson	36	151	9	8	4	2.74
	RF	J. Cooney	432	.271	0	17	209	6	4	2	2.0	.982	M. Shoffner	26	140	8	7	1	3.54
	CF	V. DiMaggio	540	.228	14	61	415	19	12	10	3.0	.973	J. Lanning	32	138	8	7	0	3.72
	LF	M. West	418	.234	10	63	205	6	3	2	2.0	.986	D. Errickson	34	123	9	7	6	3.15
	C	R. Mueller	274	.237	4	35	239	47	2	4	3.8	.993							
	03	D. Garms	428	.315	0	47	174	104	11	8		.962							
	C	A. Lopez	236	.267	1	14	240	42	3	4	4.0	.989							
	OF	G. Moore	180	.272	3	19	97	4	2	0	2.2	.981							
	3B	G. English	165	.248	2	21	33	75	5	3	2.6	.956							

NATIONAL LEAGUE 1938, *cont.*

St. Louis

W-71 L-80

Frankie Frisch
W-63 L-72

Mike Gonzalez
W-8 L-8

POS	Player	AB	BA	HR	RBI	PO	A	E	DP	TC/G	FA	Pitcher	G	IP	W	L	SV	ERA
1B	J. Mize	531	.337	27	102	1297	93	**15**	117	10.0	.989	B. Weiland	35	228	16	11	1	3.59
2B	S. Martin	417	.278	1	27	225	301	18	59	5.5	.967	B. McGee	47	216	7	12	5	3.21
SS	L. Myers	227	.242	1	19	110	195	18	36	4.7	.944	L. Warneke	31	197	13	8	0	3.97
3B	D. Gutteridge	552	.255	9	64	94	148	14	17	3.5	.945	C. Davis	40	173	12	8	3	3.63
RF	E. Slaughter	395	.276	8	58	189	7	6	0	2.2	.970	R. Henshaw	27	130	5	11	0	4.02
CF	T. Moore	312	.272	4	21	219	5	3	1	3.0	.987	M. Macon	38	129	4	11	2	4.11
LF	J. Medwick	590	.322	21	**122**	330	12	9	6	2.4	.974	C. Shoun	40	117	6	6	1	4.14
C	M. Owen	397	.267	4	36	463	67	11	8	4.7	.980							
OF	D. Padgett	388	.271	8	65	140	14	6	3	2.3	.962							
UT	J. Brown	382	.301	0	38	195	264	21	55		.956							
OF	P. Martin	269	.294	2	38	138	1	2	1	2.3	.986							
3B	J. Stripp	199	.286	0	18	53	76	3	9	2.6	.977*							
OF	F. Bordagaray	156	.282	0	21	67	3	3	0	2.5	.959							

Brooklyn

W-69 L-80

Burleigh Grimes

POS	Player	AB	BA	HR	RBI	PO	A	E	DP	TC/G	FA	Pitcher	G	IP	W	L	SV	ERA
1B	D. Camilli	509	.251	24	100	1356	95	8	129	10.1	.995	L. Hamlin	44	237	12	15	6	3.68
2B	J. Hudson	498	.261	2	37	304	395	**27**	79	5.5	.963	F. Fitzsimmons	27	203	11	8	0	3.02
SS	L. Durocher	479	.219	1	56	287	399	24	90	5.0	**.966**	T. Pressnell	43	192	11	14	3	3.56
3B	C. Lavagetto	487	.273	6	79	136	229	**28**	**26**	3.0	.929	V. Tamulis	38	160	12	6	2	3.83
RF	G. Rosen	473	.281	4	51	263	19	3	4	2.5	.989	B. Posedel	33	140	8	9	1	5.66
CF	E. Koy	521	.299	11	76	306	7	5	4	2.4	.984	V. Mungo	24	133	4	11	0	3.92
LF	B. Hassett	335	.293	0	40	154	0	9	0	2.3	.945	M. Butcher	24	73	5	4	2	6.56
C	B. Phelps	208	.308	5	46	218	25	5	5	4.5	.980							
OF	K. Cuyler	253	.273	2	23	125	9	1	1	2.0	.993							
OF	T. Stainback	104	.327	0	20	52	1	1	0	2.3	.981							

Philadelphia

W-45 L-105

Jimmie Wilson
W-45 L-103

Hans Lobert
W-0 L-2

POS	Player	AB	BA	HR	RBI	PO	A	E	DP	TC/G	FA	Pitcher	G	IP	W	L	SV	ERA
1B	P. Weintraub	351	.311	4	45	913	75	12	70	10.2	.988	H. Mulcahy	46	267	10	**20**	1	4.61
2B	E. Mueller	444	.250	4	34	229	266	17	44	4.6	.967	C. Passeau	44	239	11	18	1	4.52
SS	D. Young	340	.229	0	31	156	263	30	44	5.2	.933	A. Hollingsworth	24	174	5	16	0	3.82
3B	P. Whitney	300	.277	3	38	68	131	14	8	2.8	.934	P. Sivess	39	116	3	6	3	5.51
RF	C. Klein	458	.247	8	61	229	8	10	1	2.1	.960	M. Butcher	12	98	4	8	0	2.93
CF	H. Martin	466	.298	3	39	298	7	11	2	2.7	.965	B. Walters	12	83	4	8	0	5.23
LF	M. Arnovich	502	.275	4	72	327	18	6	0	2.6	.983	W. LaMaster	18	64	4	7	0	7.77
C	B. Atwood	281	.196	3	28	350	53	**13**	**12**	4.4	.969							
S2	G. Scharein	390	.238	1	29	246	327	37	57		.939							
3B	B. Jordan	310	.300	0	18	42	103	4	13	2.6	.973							
OF	G. Brack	282	.287	4	28	156	5	6	2	2.5	.964							
C	S. Davis	215	.247	2	23	217	27	5	5	4.0	.980							

BATTING AND BASE RUNNING LEADERS

Batting Average
E. Lombardi, CIN .342
J. Mize, STL .337
F. McCormick, CIN .327
J. Medwick, STL .322
A. Vaughan, PIT .322

Slugging Average
J. Mize, STL .614
M. Ott, NY .583
J. Medwick, STL .536
I. Goodman, CIN .533
E. Lombardi, CIN .524

Home Runs
M. Ott, NY 36
I. Goodman, CIN 30
J. Mize, STL 27
D. Camilli, BKN 24
J. Rizzo, PIT 23

Total Bases
J. Mize, STL 326
J. Medwick, STL 316
M. Ott, NY 307
I. Goodman, CIN 303
J. Rizzo, PIT 285

Runs Batted In
J. Medwick, STL 122
M. Ott, NY 116
J. Rizzo, PIT 111
F. McCormick, CIN 106
J. Mize, STL 102

Stolen Bases
S. Hack, CHI 16
C. Lavagetto, BKN 15
E. Koy, BKN 15
A. Vaughan, PIT 14
D. Gutteridge, STL 14

Hits
F. McCormick, CIN 209
S. Hack, CHI 195
L. Waner, PIT 194
J. Medwick, STL 190

Base on Balls
D. Camilli, BKN 119
M. Ott, NY 118
A. Vaughan, PIT 104
S. Hack, CHI 94

Home Run Percentage
M. Ott, NY 6.8
I. Goodman, CIN 5.3
J. Mize, STL 5.1
D. Camilli, BKN 4.7

Runs
M. Ott, NY 116
S. Hack, CHI 109
D. Camilli, BKN 106
I. Goodman, CIN 103

Doubles
J. Medwick, STL 47
F. McCormick, CIN 40
H. Martin, PHI 36
P. Young, PIT 36

Triples
J. Mize, STL 16
D. Gutteridge, STL 15
G. Suhr, PIT 14
E. Koy, BKN 13
L. Riggs, CIN 13

PITCHING LEADERS

Winning Percentage
B. Lee, CHI .710
C. Bryant, CHI .633
M. Brown, PIT .625
P. Derringer, CIN .600
J. Vander Meer, CIN .600

Earned Run Average
B. Lee, CHI 2.66
P. Derringer, CIN 2.93
D. MacFayden, BOS 2.95
B. Klinger, PIT 2.99
F. Fitzsimmons, BKN 3.02

Wins
B. Lee, CHI 22
P. Derringer, CIN 21
C. Bryant, CHI 19
B. Weiland, STL 16

Saves
D. Coffman, NY 12
C. Root, CHI 8
L. Hamlin, BKN 6
D. Errickson, BOS 6

Strikeouts
C. Bryant, CHI 135
P. Derringer, CIN 132
J. Vander Meer, CIN 125
B. Lee, CHI 121
B. Weiland, STL 117
R. Bauers, PIT 117

Complete Games
P. Derringer, CIN 26
J. Turner, BOS 22
B. Walters, PHI, CIN 20
D. MacFayden, BOS 19
B. Lee, CHI 19

Fewest Hits/9 Innings
J. Vander Meer, CIN 7.07
R. Bauers, PIT 7.67
C. Bryant, CHI 7.82
B. Klinger, PIT 8.59

Shutouts
B. Lee, CHI 9
D. MacFayden, BOS 5
L. Warneke, STL 4
H. Schumacher, NY 4
P. Derringer, CIN 4

Fewest Walks/9 Innings
P. Derringer, CIN 1.44
C. Hubbell, NY 1.66
J. Turner, BOS 1.81
F. Fitzsimmons, BKN 1.91

Most Strikeouts/9 Inn.
C. Hubbell, NY 5.23
J. Vander Meer, CIN 4.99
B. Weiland, STL 4.61
C. Bryant, CHI 4.49

Innings
P. Derringer, CIN 307
B. Lee, CHI 291
C. Bryant, CHI 270
J. Turner, BOS 268

Games Pitched
M. Brown, PIT 51
D. Coffman, NY 51
B. McGee, STL 47
H. Mulcahy, PHI 46

							Batting						Fielding			Pitching					
	W	L	PCT	GB	R	OR	2B	3B	HR	BA	SA	SB	E	DP	FA	CG	BB	SO	ShO	SV	ERA
Chicago	89	63	.586		713	**598**	242	70	65	.269	.377	49	**135**	151	**.978**	67	454	**583**	**16**	**18**	**3.37**
Pittsburgh	86	64	.573	2	707	630	265	66	65	**.279**	.388	47	163	**168**	.974	57	432	557	8	15	3.46
New York	83	67	.553	5	705	637	210	36	**125**	.271	.396	31	168	147	.973	59	**389**	497	8	**18**	3.62
Cincinnati	82	68	.547	6	723	634	251	57	110	.277	.406	19	172	133	.971	72	463	542	11	16	3.62
Boston	77	75	.507	12	561	618	199	39	54	.250	.333	49	173	136	.972	**83**	465	413	15	12	3.40
St. Louis	71	80	.470	17.5	**725**	721	**288**	74	91	**.279**	**.407**	55	199	145	.967	58	474	534	10	16	3.84
Brooklyn	69	80	.463	18.5	704	710	225	**79**	61	.257	.367	**66**	157	148	.973	56	446	469	12	14	4.07
Philadelphia	45	105	.300	43	550	840	233	29	40	.254	.333	38	201	135	.966	68	582	492	3	6	4.93
					5388	5388	1913	450	611	.267	.376	354	1368	1163	.972	520	3705	4087	83	115	3.79

AMERICAN LEAGUE 1938

Team	POS	Player	AB	BA	HR	RBI	PO	A	E	DP	TC/G	FA	Pitcher	G	IP	W	L	SV	ERA
New York	1B	L. Gehrig	576	.295	29	114	1483	100	14	**157**	10.2	.991	R. Ruffing	31	247	**21**	7	0	3.31
	2B	J. Gordon	458	.255	25	97	290	450	**31**	98	**6.1**	.960	L. Gomez	32	239	18	12	0	3.35
	SS	F. Crosetti	631	.263	9	55	**352**	**506**	**47**	**120**	**5.8**	.948	M. Pearson	28	202	16	7	0	3.97
W-99 L-53	3B	R. Rolfe	631	.311	10	80	151	294	19	26	3.1	.959	S. Chandler	23	172	14	5	0	4.03
	RF	T. Henrich	471	.270	22	91	239	14	4	1	2.0	.984	B. Hadley	29	167	9	8	1	3.60
Joe McCarthy	CF	J. DiMaggio	599	.324	32	140	366	20	15	4	2.8	.963	S. Sundra	25	94	6	4	0	4.80
	LF	G. Selkirk	335	.254	10	62	176	7	5	3	2.0	.973	J. Murphy	32	91	8	2	**11**	4.24
	C	B. Dickey	454	.313	27	115	**518**	**94**	8	7	4.9	.987							
	OF	M. Hoag	267	.277	0	48	132	5	5	3	2.0	.965							
	OF	J. Powell	164	.256	2	20	86	1	2	0	2.1	.978							
	2B	B. Knickerbocker	128	.250	1	21	78	86	3	23	4.9	.982							
	C	J. Glenn	123	.260	0	25	134	15	4	3	3.8	.974							
Boston	1B	J. Foxx	565	**.349**	50	**175**	1282	116	**19**	153	9.5	.987	J. Bagby	43	199	15	11	2	4.21
	2B	B. Doerr	509	.289	5	80	372	420	26	**118**	5.6	.968	J. Wilson	37	195	15	15	1	4.30
	SS	J. Cronin	530	.325	17	94	304	449	36	110	5.6	.954	F. Ostermueller	31	177	13	5	2	4.58
W-88 L-61	3B	P. Higgins	524	.303	5	106	140	272	39	28	3.3	.914	L. Grove	24	164	14	4	1	**3.08**
	RF	B. Chapman	480	.340	6	80	267	15	10	5	2.3	.966	E. Dickman	32	104	5	5	0	5.28
Joe Cronin	CF	D. Cramer	**658**	.301	0	71	417	15	6	3	3.0	.986	A. McKain	37	100	5	4	6	4.52
	LF	J. Vosmik	621	.324	9	86	302	14	7	4	2.2	.978	J. Marcum	15	92	5	6	0	4.09
	C	G. Desautels	333	.291	2	48	423	52	7	7	4.5	.985	J. Heving	16	82	8	1	2	3.73
	C	J. Peacock	195	.303	1	39	177	12	3	2	3.4	.984	B. Harris	13	80	5	5	1	4.03
	OF	R. Nonnenkamp	180	.283	0	18	85	5	3	1	2.4	.968							
Cleveland	1B	H. Trosky	554	.334	19	110	1232	102	10	124	9.1	.993	B. Feller	39	278	17	11	1	4.08
	2B	O. Hale	496	.278	8	69	304	343	25	72	5.3	.963	M. Harder	38	240	17	10	4	3.83
	SS	L. Lary	568	.268	3	51	296	399	26	88	5.1	.964	J. Allen	30	200	14	8	0	4.18
W-86 L-66	3B	K. Keltner	576	.276	26	113	141	271	19	19	2.9	.956	E. Whitehill	26	160	9	8	0	5.56
	RF	B. Campbell	511	.290	12	72	220	13	8	3	2.0	.967	W. Hudlin	29	127	8	8	1	4.89
Ossie Vitt	CF	E. Averill	482	.330	14	93	331	14	9	2	2.7	.975	D. Galehouse	36	114	7	8	3	4.34
	LF	J. Heath	502	.343	21	112	254	5	7	2	2.2	.974	J. Humphries	**45**	103	9	8	6	5.23
	C	F. Pytlak	364	.308	1	43	475	56	7	11	**5.4**	.987							
	OF	R. Weatherly	210	.262	2	18	110	7	3	3	2.2	.975							
	C	R. Hemsley	203	.296	2	28	358	38	8	5	7.0	.980							
	OF	M. Solters	199	.201	2	22	91	4	3	3	2.1	.969							
Detroit	1B	H. Greenberg	556	.315	**58**	146	**1484**	**120**	14	146	10.4	.991	V. Kennedy	33	190	12	9	2	5.06
	2B	C. Gehringer	568	.306	20	107	**393**	**455**	21	115	5.7	.976	G. Gill	24	164	12	9	0	4.12
	SS	B. Rogell	501	.259	3	55	291	431	31	101	5.6	.959	E. Auker	27	161	11	10	0	5.27
W-84 L-70	3B	D. Ross	265	.260	1	30	90	157	14	15	3.5	.946	T. Bridges	25	151	13	9	1	4.59
	RF	P. Fox	634	.293	7	96	301	13	2	2	2.1	.994	R. Lawson	27	127	8	9	1	5.46
Mickey Cochrane	CF	C. Morgan	306	.284	0	27	192	6	4	2	2.7	.980	H. Eisenstat	32	125	9	6	4	3.73
W-47 L-51	LF	D. Walker	454	.308	6	43	224	8	5	1	2.1	.979	B. Poffenberger	25	125	6	7	1	4.82
	C	R. York	463	.298	33	127	406	70	5	10	4.1	.990	S. Coffman	39	96	4	4	2	6.02
Del Baker	3B	M. Christman	318	.248	1	44	86	146	4	14	3.4	.983							
W-37 L-19	OF	C. Laabs	211	.237	7	37	128	4	4	1	2.6	.971							
	OF	J. White	206	.262	0	15	141	4	5	0	2.7	.967							
	C	B. Tebbetts	143	.294	1	25	108	20	2	4	2.5	.985							
Washington	1B	Z. Bonura	540	.289	22	114	1209	93	9	132	10.2	**.993**	D. Leonard	33	223	12	15	0	3.43
	2B	B. Myer	437	.336	6	71	308	355	12	91	5.6	**.982**	P. Appleton	43	164	7	9	5	4.60
	SS	C. Travis	567	.335	5	67	304	457	40	113	5.6	.950	K. Chase	32	150	9	10	1	5.58
W-75 L-76	3B	B. Lewis	656	.296	12	91	161	**329**	**47**	**32**	**3.6**	.912	W. Ferrell	23	149	13	8	0	5.92
	RF	G. Case	433	.305	2	40	207	7	8	2	2.2	.964	H. Kelley	38	148	9	8	1	4.49
Bucky Harris	CF	S. West	344	.302	5	47	221	4	4	3	2.7	.983	M. Weaver	31	139	7	6	0	5.24
	LF	A. Simmons	470	.302	21	95	232	4	4	1	2.1	.983	J. DeShong	31	131	5	8	0	6.58
	C	R. Ferrell	411	.292	1	58	512	69	**11**	**15**	4.5	.981	J. Krakauskas	29	121	7	5	0	3.12
	OF	T. Wright	263	.350	2	36	107	3	2	3	1.9	.982	C. Hogsett	31	91	5	6	3	6.03
	OF	J. Stone	213	.244	3	28	107	5	3	0	2.2	.974							
	OF	M. Almada	197	.244	1	15	147	7	5	1	3.4	.969							
	2B	O. Bluege	184	.261	0	21	85	110	2	26	5.2	.990							
Chicago	1B	J. Kuhel	412	.267	8	51	1136	59	14	97	**10.9**	.988	T. Lee	33	245	13	12	1	3.49
	2B	J. Hayes	238	.328	1	20	146	183	8	51	5.5	.976	T. Lyons	23	195	9	11	0	3.70
	SS	L. Appling	294	.303	0	44	149	258	20	37	5.5	.953	M. Stratton	26	186	15	9	2	4.01
W-65 L-83	3B	M. Owen	577	.281	6	55	136	305	24	29	3.3	.948	J. Whitehead	32	183	10	11	2	4.76
	RF	H. Steinbacher	399	.331	4	61	202	7	8	2	2.1	.963	J. Rigney	38	167	9	9	1	3.56
Jimmy Dykes	CF	M. Kreevich	489	.297	6	73	379	7	10	2	3.1	.975	J. Knott	20	131	5	10	0	4.05
	LF	G. Walker	442	.305	16	87	197	9	9	2	2.0	.958							
	C	L. Sewell	211	.213	0	27	205	55	4	7	4.1	.985							
	OF	R. Radcliff	503	.330	5	81	230	5	5	0	2.4	.979							
	S2	B. Berger	470	.217	3	36	230	341	36	78		.941							
	C	T. Rensa	165	.248	3	19	185	36	4	4	3.9	.982							
St. Louis	1B	G. McQuinn	602	.324	12	82	1207	90	10	134	8.8	.992	B. Newsom	44	**330**	20	16	1	5.08
	2B	D. Heffner	473	.245	2	69	365	363	22	103	5.3	.971	L. Mills	30	210	10	12	0	5.31
	SS	R. Kress	566	.302	7	79	321	388	26	100	4.9	**.965**	O. Hildebrand	23	163	8	10	0	5.69
W-55 L-97	3B	H. Clift	534	.290	34	118	**176**	306	19	31	3.4	**.962**	R. Van Atta	25	104	4	7	0	6.06
	RF	B. Bell	526	.262	13	84	266	12	6	3	2.2	.979	J. Walkup	18	94	1	12	0	6.80
Gabby Street	CF	M. Almada	436	.342	3	37	247	9	9	1	2.6	.966	F. Johnson	17	69	3	7	3	5.61
W-53 L-90	LF	B. Mills	466	.285	3	46	235	9	9	2	2.2	.964							
	C	B. Sullivan	375	.277	7	49	441	65	5	10	5.2	**.990**							
Oscar Melillo	OF	M. Mazzera	204	.279	6	29	74	7	2	1	1.8	.976							
W-2 L-7	C	T. Heath	194	.227	2	22	315	42	5	5	5.6	.986							
	OF	S. West	165	.309	1	27	101	0	3	0	2.5	.971							

AMERICAN LEAGUE 1938, *cont.*

Philadelphia

W-53 L-99

Connie Mack

POS	Player	AB	BA	HR	RBI	PO	A	E	DP	TC/G	FA
1B	L. Finney	454	.275	10	48	574	24	6	35	9.4	.990
2B	D. Lodigiani	325	.280	6	44	193	233	21	45	5.6	.953
SS	W. Ambler	393	.234	0	38	209	310	32	54	4.8	.942
3B	B. Werber	499	.259	11	69	168	266	30	21	3.5	.935
RF	W. Moses	589	.307	8	49	304	11	11	3	2.3	.966
CF	B. Johnson	563	.313	30	113	400	21	16	3	2.9	.963
LF	S. Chapman	406	.259	17	63	229	8	12	0	2.2	.952
C	F. Hayes	316	.291	11	55	319	38	9	2	4.1	.975
2B	S. Sperry	253	.273	0	27	121	185	13	26	5.3	.959
1B	D. Siebert	194	.284	0	28	403	41	0	35	9.7	1.000
C	E. Brucker	171	.374	3	35	188	20	3	1	4.8	.986

Pitcher	G	IP	W	L	SV	ERA
G. Caster	42	280	16	**20**	1	4.37
B. Thomas	42	212	9	14	0	4.92
L. Nelson	32	191	10	11	2	5.65
B. Ross	29	184	9	16	0	5.32
E. Smith	43	131	3	10	4	5.92
N. Potter	35	111	2	12	5	6.47

BATTING AND BASE RUNNING LEADERS

Batting Average

J. Foxx, BOS	.349
J. Heath, CLE	.343
B. Chapman, BOS	.340
B. Myer, WAS	.336
C. Travis, WAS	.335

Slugging Average

J. Foxx, BOS	.704
H. Greenberg, DET	.683
J. Heath, CLE	.602
J. DiMaggio, NY	.581
R. York, DET	.579

Home Runs

H. Greenberg, DET	58
J. Foxx, BOS	50
H. Clift, STL	34
R. York, DET	33
J. DiMaggio, NY	32

Total Bases

J. Foxx, BOS	398
H. Greenberg, DET	380
J. DiMaggio, NY	348
B. Johnson, PHI	311
J. Heath, CLE	302

Runs Batted In

J. Foxx, BOS	175
H. Greenberg, DET	146
J. DiMaggio, NY	140
R. York, DET	127
H. Clift, STL	118

Stolen Bases

F. Crosetti, NY	27
L. Lary, CLE	23
B. Werber, PHI	19
B. Lewis, WAS	17
P. Fox, DET	16

Hits

J. Vosmik, BOS	201
D. Cramer, BOS	198
J. Foxx, BOS	197
M. Almada, WAS, STL	197

Base on Balls

H. Greenberg, DET	119
J. Foxx, BOS	119
H. Clift, STL	118
C. Gehringer, DET	112

Home Run Percentage

H. Greenberg, DET	10.4
J. Foxx, BOS	8.8
R. York, DET	7.1
H. Clift, STL	6.4

Runs

H. Greenberg, DET	144
J. Foxx, BOS	139
C. Gehringer, DET	133
R. Rolfe, NY	132

Doubles

J. Cronin, BOS	51
G. McQuinn, STL	42
B. Chapman, BOS	40
H. Trosky, CLE	40

Triples

J. Heath, CLE	18
E. Averill, CLE	15
J. DiMaggio, NY	13

PITCHING LEADERS

Winning Percentage

R. Ruffing, NY	.750
M. Pearson, NY	.696
M. Harder, CLE	.630
M. Stratton, CHI	.625
B. Feller, CLE	.607

Earned Run Average

L. Grove, BOS	3.08
R. Ruffing, NY	3.31
L. Gomez, NY	3.35
D. Leonard, WAS	3.43
T. Lee, CHI	3.49

Wins

R. Ruffing, NY	21
B. Newsom, STL	20
L. Gomez, NY	18
M. Harder, CLE	17
B. Feller, CLE	17

Saves

J. Murphy, NY	11
A. McKain, BOS	6
J. Humphries, CLE	6
N. Potter, PHI	5
P. Appleton, WAS	5

Strikeouts

B. Feller, CLE	240
B. Newsom, STL	226
L. Mills, STL	134
L. Gomez, NY	129
R. Ruffing, NY	127

Complete Games

B. Newsom, STL	31
R. Ruffing, NY	22
L. Gomez, NY	20
B. Feller, CLE	20
G. Caster, PHI	20

Fewest Hits/9 Innings

B. Feller, CLE	7.29
J. Allen, CLE	8.51
M. Pearson, NY	8.82
D. Leonard, WAS	8.91

Shutouts

R. Ruffing, NY	4
L. Gomez, NY	4
J. Wilson, BOS	3
D. Leonard, WAS	3

Fewest Walks/9 Innings

D. Leonard, WAS	2.14
M. Harder, CLE	2.33
T. Lyons, CHI	2.40
S. Chandler, NY	2.46

Most Strikeouts/9 Inn.

B. Feller, CLE	7.78
B. Newsom, STL	6.17
T. Bridges, DET	6.02
L. Mills, STL	5.73

Innings

B. Newsom, STL	330
G. Caster, PHI	280
B. Feller, CLE	278
R. Ruffing, NY	247

Games Pitched

J. Humphries, CLE	45
B. Newsom, STL	44
E. Smith, PHI	43
P. Appleton, WAS	43
J. Bagby, BOS	43

							Batting						Fielding			Pitching					
	W	L	PCT	GB	R	OR	2B	3B	HR	BA	SA	SB	E	DP	FA	CG	BB	SO	ShO	SV	ERA
New York	99	53	.651		**966**	**710**	283	63	**174**	.274	**.446**	**91**	169	169	.973	**91**	566	567	**10**	13	**3.91**
Boston	88	61	.591	9.5	902	751	298	56	98	**.299**	.434	55	190	172	.968	67	**528**	484	**10**	15	4.46
Cleveland	86	66	.566	13	847	782	**300**	**89**	113	.281	.434	83	151	145	.974	68	681	**717**	5	**17**	4.60
Detroit	84	70	.545	16	862	795	219	52	137	.272	.411	76	147	172	**.976**	75	608	435	2	11	4.79
Washington	75	76	.497	23.5	814	873	278	72	85	.293	.416	65	180	**179**	.970	59	655	515	6	11	4.94
Chicago	65	83	.439	32	709	752	239	55	67	.277	.383	56	196	155	.967	83	550	432	5	9	4.36
St. Louis	55	97	.362	44	755	962	273	36	92	.281	.397	51	**145**	163	.975	71	737	632	3	7	5.80
Philadelphia	53	99	.349	46	726	956	243	62	98	.270	.396	65	206	119	.965	56	599	473	4	12	5.48
					6581	6581	2133	485	864	.281	.415	542	1384	1274	.971	570	4924	4255	45	95	4.79

NATIONAL LEAGUE 1939

Cincinnati

W-97 L-57

Bill McKechnie

POS	Player	AB	BA	HR	RBI	PO	A	E	DP	TC/G	FA
1B	F. McCormick	630	.332	18	**128**	**1518**	100	7	**153**	10.4	**.996**
2B	L. Frey	484	.291	11	55	324	412	18	83	**6.1**	.976
SS	B. Myers	509	.281	9	56	309	512	**42**	**110**	5.7	.951
3B	B. Werber	599	.289	5	57	165	**308**	**34**	**32**	**3.4**	.933
RF	I. Goodman	470	.323	7	84	246	16	5	4	2.2	.981
CF	H. Craft	502	.257	13	67	300	13	6	4	2.4	.981
LF	W. Berger	329	.258	14	44	158	6	5	0	1.8	.970
C	E. Lombardi	450	.287	20	85	536	63	**10**	7	**5.1**	.984
OF	L. Gamble	221	.267	0	14	87	5	1	0	1.7	.989
C	W. Hershberger	174	.345	0	32	204	21	3	2	3.8	.987
OF	N. Bongiovanni	159	.258	0	16	89	1	1	1	2.3	.989

Pitcher	G	IP	W	L	SV	ERA
B. Walters	39	**319**	**27**	11	0	**2.29**
P. Derringer	38	301	25	7	0	2.93
W. Moore	42	188	13	12	3	3.45
L. Grissom	33	154	9	7	0	4.10
J. Thompson	42	152	13	5	2	2.54
J. Vander Meer	30	129	5	9	0	4.67

St. Louis

W-92 L-61

Ray Blades

POS	Player	AB	BA	HR	RBI	PO	A	E	DP	TC/G	FA
1B	J. Mize	564	**.349**	**28**	108	1348	90	**19**	123	9.6	.987
2B	S. Martin	425	.268	3	30	242	304	13	62	5.2	**.977**
SS	J. Brown	**645**	.298	3	51	208	349	25	67	5.6	.957
3B	D. Gutteridge	524	.269	7	54	136	203	24	24	2.5	.934
RF	E. Slaughter	604	.320	12	86	348	18	12	5	2.5	.968
CF	T. Moore	417	.295	17	77	291	16	2	1	2.6	.994
LF	J. Medwick	606	.332	14	117	313	10	8	1	2.2	.976
C	M. Owen	344	.259	3	35	452	52	9	7	4.1	.982
03	P. Martin	281	.306	3	37	128	34	7	2		.959
C	D. Padgett	233	.399	5	53	249	18	6	5	4.5	.978

Pitcher	G	IP	W	L	SV	ERA
C. Davis	49	248	22	16	7	3.63
M. Cooper	45	211	12	6	4	3.25
B. Bowman	51	169	13	5	**9**	2.60
L. Warneke	34	162	13	7	2	3.78
B. McGee	43	156	12	5	0	3.81
B. Weiland	32	146	10	12	1	3.57
C. Shoun	**53**	103	3	1	**9**	3.76

NATIONAL LEAGUE 1939, *cont.*

Team	POS	Player	AB	BA	HR	RBI	PO	A	E	DP	TC/G	FA	Pitcher	G	IP	W	L	SV	ERA
Brooklyn	1B	D. Camilli	565	.290	26	104	1515	**129**	17	138	10.6	.990	L. Hamlin	40	270	20	13	0	3.64
W-84 L-69	2B	P. Coscarart	419	.277	4	43	256	338	25	69	5.8	.960	H. Casey	40	227	15	10	1	2.93
Leo Durocher	SS	L. Durocher	390	.277	1	34	228	322	25	73	5.1	.957	V. Tamulis	39	159	9	8	4	4.37
	3B	C. Lavagetto	587	.300	10	87	163	278	24	28	3.1	.948	T. Pressnell	31	157	9	7	2	4.02
	RF	A. Parks	239	.272	1	19	125	2	3	0	2.0	.977	F. Fitzsimmons	27	151	7	9	3	3.87
	CF	G. Moore	306	.225	3	39	140	8	6	3	1.8	.961	W. Wyatt	16	109	8	3	0	2.31
	LF	E. Koy	425	.278	8	67	252	4	10	1	2.3	.962	I. Hutchinson	41	106	5	2	1	4.34
	C	B. Phelps	323	.285	6	42	361	40	8	6	4.4	.980	R. Evans	24	64	1	8	1	5.18
	S2	J. Hudson	343	.254	2	32	175	259	18	56		.960							
	C	A. Todd	245	.278	5	32	284	35	5	5	4.4	.985							
	OF	D. Walker	225	.280	2	38	144	5	5	3	2.6	.968							
	OF	T. Stainback	201	.269	3	19	121	0	8	0	2.3	.938							
	OF	G. Rosen	183	.251	1	12	106	0	0	0	2.3	1.000							
	OF	J. Ripple	106	.330	0	28	55	0	0	0	2.0	1.000							
Chicago	1B	R. Russell	542	.273	9	79	1383	83	18	109	10.4	.988	B. Lee	37	282	19	15	0	3.44
W-84 L-70	2B	B. Herman	623	.307	7	70	**377**	**485**	**29**	**95**	5.7	.967	C. Passeau	34	221	13	9	3	3.05
Gabby Hartnett	SS	D. Bartell	336	.238	3	34	241	307	33	62	5.8	.943	L. French	36	194	15	8	1	3.29
	3B	S. Hack	641	.298	8	56	**177**	278	21	15	3.1	.956	C. Root	35	167	8	8	4	4.03
	RF	J. Gleeson	332	.223	4	45	175	5	8	1	2.1	.957	V. Page	27	139	7	7	1	3.88
	CF	H. Leiber	365	.310	24	88	249	5	6	0	2.7	.977	D. Dean	19	96	6	4	0	3.36
	LF	A. Galan	549	.304	6	71	290	6	9	0	2.1	.970	E. Whitehill	24	89	4	7	1	5.14
	C	G. Hartnett	306	.278	12	59	336	47	3	3	4.5	.992	J. Russell	39	69	4	3	3	3.67
	OF	C. Reynolds	281	.246	4	44	168	5	5	1	2.5	.972							
	C	G. Mancuso	251	.231	2	17	333	36	7	6	4.9	.981							
	OF	B. Nicholson	220	.295	5	38	123	5	6	0	2.3	.955							
	SS	B. Mattick	178	.287	0	23	102	179	22	28	6.3	.927							
New York	1B	Z. Bonura	455	.321	11	85	1205	90	11	110	10.7	.992	H. Gumbert	36	244	18	11	0	4.32
W-77 L-74	2B	B. Whitehead	335	.239	2	24	232	320	17	60	6.3	.970	C. Melton	41	207	12	15	5	3.56
Bill Terry	SS	B. Jurges	543	.285	6	63	295	482	28	95	5.9	**.965**	B. Lohrman	38	186	12	13	1	4.07
	3B	T. Hafey	256	.242	6	26	61	130	8	10	2.8	.960	H. Schumacher	29	182	13	10	0	4.81
	RF	M. Ott	396	.308	27	80	175	6	5	2	1.9	.973	C. Hubbell	29	154	11	9	2	2.75
	CF	F. Demaree	560	.304	11	79	329	11	5	2	2.3	.986	M. Salvo	32	136	4	10	1	4.63
	LF	J. Moore	562	.269	10	47	260	13	4	2	2.0	.986	J. Brown	31	56	4	0	7	4.15
	C	H. Danning	520	.313	16	74	**550**	**80**	6	**13**	4.8	**.991**							
	2B	A. Kampouris	201	.249	5	29	146	179	9	34	5.4	.973							
	OF	B. Seeds	173	.266	5	26	77	2	2	0	1.6	.975							
Pittsburgh	1B	E. Fletcher	370	.303	12	71	1010	56	8	97	10.6*	.993	B. Klinger	37	225	14	**17**	0	4.36
W-68 L-85	2B	P. Young	293	.276	3	29	202	270	16	61	5.8	.967	M. Brown	47	200	9	13	7	3.37
Pie Traynor	SS	A. Vaughan	595	.306	6	62	**330**	**531**	34	103	**5.9**	.962	J. Bowman	37	185	10	14	1	4.48
	3B	L. Handley	376	.285	1	42	83	180	18	14	2.8	.936	R. Sewell	52	176	10	9	2	4.08
	RF	P. Waner	461	.328	3	45	206	12	5	4	2.1	.978	J. Tobin	25	145	9	9	0	4.52
	CF	L. Waner	379	.285	0	24	225	9	2	1	2.6	.992	B. Swift	36	130	5	7	4	3.89
	LF	J. Rizzo	330	.261	6	55	186	2	5	0	2.2	.974							
	C	R. Mueller	180	.233	2	18	203	32	7	5	3.0	.971							
	23	B. Brubaker	345	.232	7	43	183	286	26	47		.947							
	OF	C. Klein	270	.300	11	47	133	4	7	0	2.2	.951							
	OF	F. Bell	262	.286	2	34	152	6	4	0	2.4	.975							
	C	R. Berres	231	.229	0	16	269	36	2	4	3.8	.993							
	1B	G. Suhr	204	.289	1	31	521	23	4	42	10.5	.993							
Boston	1B	B. Hassett	590	.308	2	60	1143	112	**19**	127	10.0	.985	B. Posedel	33	221	15	13	0	3.92
W-63 L-88	2B	T. Cuccinello	310	.306	2	40	208	246	14	66	5.8	.970	D. MacFayden	33	192	8	14	2	3.90
Casey Stengel	SS	E. Miller	296	.267	4	31	183	275	14	76	6.1	.970	J. Turner	25	158	4	11	0	4.28
	3B	H. Majeski	367	.272	7	54	111	196	18	19	3.3	.945	L. Fette	27	146	10	10	0	2.96
	RF	D. Garms	513	.298	2	37	183	6	7	2	2.0	.964	M. Shoffner	25	132	4	6	1	3.13
	CF	J. Cooney	368	.274	2	27	236	10	2	2	2.1	.992	J. Lanning	37	129	5	6	4	3.42
	LF	M. West	449	.285	19	82	287	8	8	2	2.4	.974	D. Errickson	28	128	6	9	1	4.00
	C	A. Lopez	412	.252	8	49	424	72	7	11	3.9	.986	J. Sullivan	31	114	6	9	2	3.64
	UT	R. Warstler	342	.243	0	24	194	301	20	75		.961							
	OF	A. Simmons	330	.282	7	43	158	7	3	2	2.0	.982							
	UT	S. Sisti	215	.228	1	11	136	152	8	8		.973							
Philadelphia	1B	G. Suhr	198	.318	3	24	520	37	3	50	9.3	.995	H. Mulcahy	38	226	9	16	4	4.99
W-45 L-106	2B	R. Hughes	237	.228	1	16	183	184	6	30	5.7	.984	K. Higbe	34	187	10	14	2	4.85
Doc Prothro	SS	G. Scharein	399	.238	1	33	258	331	26	69	5.3	.958	B. Beck	34	183	7	14	3	4.73
	3B	P. May	464	.287	2	62	153	263	19	28	3.3	**.956**	I. Pearson	26	125	2	13	0	5.76
	RF	J. Marty	299	.254	9	44	176	9	5	3	2.4	.974	S. Johnson	22	111	8	8	2	3.81
	CF	H. Martin	393	.282	1	22	276	5	7	1	3.0	.976	M. Butcher	19	104	2	13*	0	5.61
	LF	M. Arnovich	491	.324	5	67	335	10	6	0	2.7	.983	R. Harrell	22	95	3	7	0	5.42
	C	S. Davis	202	.307	0	23	260	40	0	1	3.5	1.000	A. Hollingsworth	15	60	1	9	0	5.85
	UT	E. Mueller	341	.279	9	43	163	166	11	38		.968							
	OF	G. Brack	270	.289	6	41	89	4	4	1	2.0	.959							
	OF	L. Scott	232	.280	1	26	109	7	5	1	2.2	.959							
	SS	D. Young	217	.263	3	20	70	104	10	16	3.3	.946							
	1B	J. Bolling	211	.289	3	13	392	38	8	35	9.1	.982							
	C	W. Millies	205	.234	0	12	229	37	**10**	3	3.3	.964							

BATTING AND BASE RUNNING LEADERS

Batting Average		Slugging Average		Home Runs	
J. Mize, STL	.349	J. Mize, STL	.626	J. Mize, STL	28
F. McCormick, CIN	.332	M. Ott, NY	.581	M. Ott, NY	27
J. Medwick, STL	.332	H. Leiber, CHI	.556	D. Camilli, BKN	26
P. Waner, PIT	.328	D. Camilli, BKN	.524	H. Leiber, CHI	24
M. Arnovich, PHI	.324	I. Goodman, CIN	.515	E. Lombardi, CIN	20

PITCHING LEADERS

Winning Percentage		Earned Run Average		Wins	
P. Derringer, CIN	.781	B. Walters, CIN	2.29	B. Walters, CIN	27
B. Walters, CIN	.711	C. Hubbell, NY	2.75	P. Derringer, CIN	25
L. French, CHI	.652	H. Casey, BKN	2.93	C. Davis, STL	22
H. Gumbert, NY	.621	P. Derringer, CIN	2.93	L. Hamlin, BKN	20
L. Hamlin, BKN	.606	L. Fette, BOS	2.96	B. Lee, CHI	19

NATIONAL LEAGUE 1939, *cont.*

BATTING AND BASE RUNNING LEADERS / PITCHING LEADERS

Total Bases		Runs Batted In		Stolen Bases		Saves		Strikeouts		Complete Games	
J. Mize, STL	353	F. McCormick, CIN	128	L. Handley, PIT	17	C. Shoun, STL	9	C. Passeau, PHI, CHI	137	B. Walters, CIN	31
F. McCormick, CIN	312	J. Medwick, STL	117	S. Hack, CHI	17	B. Bowman, STL	9	B. Walters, CIN	137	P. Derringer, CIN	28
J. Medwick, STL	307	J. Mize, STL	108	B. Werber, CIN	15	J. Brown, NY	7	M. Cooper, STL	130	B. Lee, CHI	20
D. Camilli, BKN	296	D. Camilli, BKN	104	C. Lavagetto, BKN	14	M. Brown, PIT	7	P. Derringer, CIN	128	L. Hamlin, BKN	19
E. Slaughter, STL	291	H. Leiber, CHI	88	B. Hassett, BOS	13	C. Davis, STL	7	B. Lee, CHI	105	B. Posedel, BOS	18

Hits		Base on Balls		Home Run Percentage		Fewest Hits/9 Innings		Shutouts		Fewest Walks/9 Innings	
F. McCormick, CIN	209	D. Camilli, BKN	110	M. Ott, NY	6.8	B. Walters, CIN	7.05	L. Fette, BOS	6	P. Derringer, CIN	1.05
J. Medwick, STL	201	M. Ott, NY	100	H. Leiber, CHI	6.6	L. Fette, BOS	7.58	B. Posedel, BOS	5	C. Hubbell, NY	1.40
J. Mize, STL	197	J. Mize, STL	92	J. Mize, STL	5.0	L. Hamlin, BKN	8.51	P. Derringer, CIN	5	C. Davis, STL	1.74
E. Slaughter, STL	193	B. Werber, CIN	91	D. Camilli, BKN	4.6	C. Hubbell, NY	8.77	B. McGee, STL	4	L. Hamlin, BKN	1.80

Runs		Doubles		Triples		Most Strikeouts/9 Inn.		Innings		Games Pitched	
B. Werber, CIN	115	E. Slaughter, STL	52	B. Herman, CHI	18	L. French, CHI	4.55	B. Walters, CIN	319	C. Shoun, STL	53
S. Hack, CHI	112	J. Medwick, STL	48	I. Goodman, CIN	16	C. Passeau, PHI, CHI	4.49	P. Derringer, CIN	301	R. Sewell, PIT	52
B. Herman, CHI	111	J. Mize, STL	44	J. Mize, STL	14	K. Higbe, CHI, PHI	4.07	B. Lee, CHI	282	B. Bowman, STL	51
D. Camilli, BKN	105	F. McCormick, CIN	41	D. Camilli, BKN	12	B. Walters, CIN	3.87	C. Passeau, PHI, CHI	274	C. Davis, STL	49

	W	L	PCT	GB	R	OR	Batting 2B	3B	HR	BA	SA	SB	Fielding E	DP	FA	Pitching CG	BB	SO	ShO	SV	ERA
Cincinnati	97	57	.630		767	**595**	269	60	98	.278	.405	46	162	170	.974	**86**	499	**637**	13	9	**3.27**
St. Louis	92	61	.601	4.5	**779**	633	**332**	**62**	98	**.294**	**.432**	44	177	140	.971	45	498	603	**18**	**32**	3.59
Brooklyn	84	69	.549	12.5	708	645	265	57	78	.265	.380	59	176	157	.972	69	**399**	528	9	13	3.64
Chicago	84	70	.545	13	724	678	263	**62**	91	.266	.391	**61**	186	126	.970	72	430	584	8	13	3.80
New York	77	74	.510	18.5	703	685	211	38	**116**	.272	.396	26	**153**	152	**.975**	55	478	505	6	20	4.07
Pittsburgh	68	85	.444	28.5	666	721	261	60	63	.276	.384	44	168	153	.972	53	423	524	10	15	4.15
Boston	63	88	.417	32.5	572	659	199	39	56	.264	.348	41	181	**178**	.971	68	513	430	11	15	3.71
Philadelphia	45	106	.298	50.5	553	856	232	40	49	.261	.351	47	171	133	.970	67	579	447	3	12	5.17
					5472	5472	2032	418	649	.272	.386	368	1374	1209	.972	515	3819	4258	78	129	3.92

AMERICAN LEAGUE 1939

	POS	Player	AB	BA	HR	RBI	PO	A	E	DP	TC/G	FA	Pitcher	G	IP	W	L	SV	ERA
New York	1B	B. Dahlgren	531	.235	15	89	1303	68	**13**	**140**	9.6	.991	R. Ruffing	28	233	21	7	0	2.93
	2B	J. Gordon	567	.284	28	111	**370**	**461**	28	**116**	5.7	.967	L. Gomez	26	198	12	8	0	3.41
W-106 L-45	SS	F. Crosetti	**656**	.233	10	56	**323**	460	26	**118**	5.3	**.968**	B. Hadley	26	154	12	6	2	2.98
	3B	R. Rolfe	648	.329	14	80	151	282	19	22	3.0	.958	A. Donald	24	153	13	3	1	3.71
Joe McCarthy	RF	C. Keller	398	.334	11	83	213	5	7	1	2.1	.969	M. Pearson	22	146	12	5	0	4.49
	CF	J. DiMaggio	462	**.381**	30	126	328	13	5	2	3.0	.986	O. Hildebrand	21	127	10	4	2	3.06
	LF	G. Selkirk	418	.306	21	101	254	4	3	1	2.1	.989	S. Sundra	24	121	11	1	0	2.76
	C	B. Dickey	480	.302	24	105	**571**	57	7	8	5.0	**.989**	M. Russo	21	116	8	3	2	2.41
	OF	T. Henrich	347	.277	9	57	205	7	2	1	2.4	.991	J. Murphy	38	61	3	6	**19**	4.40
	P	R. Ruffing	114	.307	1	20	8	32	2	2	1.5	.952							
Boston	1B	J. Foxx	467	.360	**35**	105	1101	91	10	104	9.8	.992	L. Grove	23	191	15	4	0	**2.54**
	2B	B. Doerr	525	.318	12	73	336	431	19	95	**6.2**	.976	J. Wilson	36	177	11	11	2	4.67
W-89 L-62	SS	J. Cronin	520	.308	19	107	306	437	32	93	**5.5**	.959	F. Ostermueller	34	159	11	7	4	4.24
	3B	J. Tabor	577	.289	14	95	144	**338**	**40**	32	3.5	.923	E. Auker	31	151	9	10	0	5.36
Joe Cronin	RF	T. Williams	565	.327	31	**145**	318	11	19	3	2.3	.945	D. Galehouse	30	147	9	10	0	4.54
	CF	D. Cramer	589	.311	0	56	356	12	6	0	2.8	.984	E. Dickman	48	114	8	3	5	4.43
	LF	J. Vosmik	554	.276	7	84	296	9	8	0	2.2	.974	J. Heving	46	107	11	3	7	3.70
	C	J. Peacock	274	.277	0	36	314	33	10	6	4.3	.972	J. Bagby	21	80	5	5	0	7.09
	10	L. Finney	249	.325	1	46	328	12	6	28		.983							
	C	G. Desautels	226	.243	0	21	310	48	2	5	4.9	.994							
	2B	T. Carey	161	.242	0	20	75	87	0	19	4.6	1.000							
Cleveland	1B	H. Trosky	448	.335	25	104	1004	97	9	97	9.4	.992	B. Feller	39	**297**	**24**	9	1	2.85
	2B	O. Hale	253	.312	4	48	141	146	10	31	4.1	.966	A. Milnar	37	209	14	12	3	3.79
W-87 L-67	SS	S. Webb	269	.264	2	26	165	203	27	40	4.9	.932	M. Harder	29	208	15	9	1	3.50
	3B	K. Keltner	587	.325	13	97	**187**	297	13	**40**	3.2	**.974**	J. Allen	28	175	9	7	0	4.58
Ossie Vitt	RF	B. Campbell	450	.287	8	72	200	12	13	3	2.0	.942	W. Hudlin	27	143	9	10	3	4.91
	CF	B. Chapman	545	.290	6	82	356	12	11	0	2.6	.971	H. Eisenstat	26	104	6	7	2	3.30
	LF	J. Heath	431	.292	14	69	263	7	10	2	2.6	.964							
	C	R. Hemsley	395	.263	2	36	499	58	9	7	**5.3**	.984							
	UT	O. Grimes	364	.269	4	56	501	192	22	75		.969							
	OF	R. Weatherly	323	.310	1	32	146	3	6	1	2.0	.961							
	SS	L. Boudreau	225	.258	0	19	103	184	14	31	5.7	.953							
	C	F. Pytlak	183	.268	0	14	227	24	0	5	4.9	1.000							
Chicago	1B	J. Kuhel	546	.300	15	56	1256	72	11	113	**9.8**	.992	T. Lee	33	235	15	11	3	4.21
	2B	O. Bejma	307	.251	8	44	170	199	7	36	4.6	.981	J. Rigney	35	219	15	8	0	3.70
W-85 L-69	SS	L. Appling	516	.314	0	56	289	**461**	**39**	78	5.3	.951	E. Smith	29	177	9	11	0	3.67
	3B	E. McNair	479	.324	7	82	90	194	19	23	2.9	.937	T. Lyons	21	173	14	6	0	2.76
Jimmy Dykes	RF	L. Rosenthal	324	.265	10	51	193	5	2	1	2.2	.990	J. Knott	25	150	11	6	0	4.15
	CF	M. Kreevich	541	.323	5	77	419	18	11	4	3.2	.975	B. Dietrich	25	128	7	8	0	5.22
	LF	G. Walker	598	.291	13	111	365	11	13	3	2.6	.967	C. Brown	**61**	118	11	10	18	3.88
	C	M. Tresh	352	.259	0	38	480	59	8	7	4.6	.985							
	OF	R. Radcliff	397	.264	2	53	130	1	4	0	1.7	.970							
	2B	J. Hayes	269	.249	0	23	172	201	10	51	5.6	.974							
	3B	M. Owen	194	.237	0	15	63	99	8	11	3.1	.953							

AMERICAN LEAGUE 1939, *cont.*

Detroit

W-81 L-73

Del Baker

POS	Player	AB	BA	HR	RBI	PO	A	E	DP	TC/G	FA	Pitcher	G	IP	W	L	SV	ERA
1B	H. Greenberg	500	.312	33	112	1205	75	9	108	9.5	**.993**	B. Newsom	35	246	17	10	2	3.37
2B	C. Gehringer	406	.325	16	86	245	312	13	67	5.3	**.977**	T. Bridges	29	198	17	7	2	3.50
SS	F. Croucher	324	.269	5	40	139	256	28	47	4.5	.934	S. Rowe	28	164	10	12	0	4.99
3B	P. Higgins	489	.276	8	76	140	241	36	22	3.2	.914	D. Trout	33	162	9	10	2	3.61
RF	P. Fox	519	.295	7	66	275	12	9	3	2.3	.970	A. Benton	37	150	6	8	5	4.56
CF	B. McCosky	611	.311	4	58	428	7	6	2	3.0	.986	A. McKain	32	130	5	6	4	3.68
LF	E. Averill	309	.262	10	58	157	3	4	0	2.0	.976							
C	B. Tebbetts	341	.261	4	53	449	**64**	**16**	10	5.3	.970							
C	R. York	329	.307	20	68	283	38	5	5	4.9	.985							
2S	B. McCoy	192	.302	1	33	108	150	11	25		.959							
OF	R. Cullenbine	179	.240	6	23	81	2	9	1	2.0	.902							
S3	B. Rogell	174	.230	2	23	76	130	15	24		.932							
S2	R. Kress	157	.242	1	22	77	116	11	28		.946							
OF	D. Walker	154	.305	4	19	93	4	3	1	2.7	.970							
OF	B. Bell	134	.239	0	24	73	4	0	1	2.1	1.000							

Washington

W-65 L-87

Bucky Harris

POS	Player	AB	BA	HR	RBI	PO	A	E	DP	TC/G	FA	Pitcher	G	IP	W	L	SV	ERA
1B	M. Vernon	276	.257	1	30	690	40	11	75	9.9	.985	D. Leonard	34	269	20	8	0	3.54
2B	J. Bloodworth	318	.289	4	40	226	219	13	66	6.3	.972	K. Chase	32	232	10	19	0	3.80
SS	C. Travis	476	.292	5	63	194	359	24	74	4.9	.958	J. Krakauskas	39	217	11	17	1	4.60
3B	B. Lewis	536	.319	10	75	122	326	32	31	**3.6**	.933	J. Haynes	27	173	8	12	0	5.36
RF	G. Case	530	.302	2	35	332	7	16	2	2.9	.955	A. Carrasquel	40	159	5	9	2	4.69
CF	S. West	390	.282	3	52	232	7	2	3	2.7	.992	P. Appleton	40	103	5	10	6	4.56
LF	T. Wright	499	.309	4	93	236	10	13	4	2.1	.950							
C	R. Ferrell	274	.281	0	31	327	46	9	9	4.6	.976							
OF	B. Estalella	280	.275	8	41	157	3	6	1	2.2	.964							
2B	B. Myer	258	.302	1	32	175	188	12	48	5.8	.968							
OF	J. Welaj	201	.274	1	33	113	2	3	1	2.1	.975							
S3	C. Gelbert	188	.255	3	29	60	122	7	20		.963							
C	T. Giuliani	172	.250	0	18	201	28	5	3	4.7	.979							

Philadelphia

W-55 L-97

Connie Mack
W-25 L-37

Earle Mack
W-30 L-60

POS	Player	AB	BA	HR	RBI	PO	A	E	DP	TC/G	FA	Pitcher	G	IP	W	L	SV	ERA
1B	D. Siebert	402	.294	6	47	874	74	9	73	9.7	.991	L. Nelson	35	198	10	13	1	4.78
2B	J. Gantenbein	348	.290	4	36	165	179	19	26	4.8	.948	N. Potter	41	196	8	12	2	6.60
SS	S. Newsome	248	.222	0	17	176	221	21	44	4.5	.950	B. Ross	29	174	6	14	0	6.00
3B	D. Lodigiani	393	.260	6	44	103	181	17	8	3.4	.944	B. Beckmann	27	155	7	11	0	5.39
RF	W. Moses	437	.307	3	33	209	10	8	2	2.2	.965	G. Caster	28	136	9	9	0	4.90
CF	S. Chapman	498	.269	15	64	350	11	17	2	3.2	.955	C. Pippen	25	119	4	11	1	5.99
LF	B. Johnson	544	.338	23	114	369	15	13	3	2.6	.967	C. Dean	54	117	5	8	7	5.25
C	F. Hayes	431	.283	20	83	380	60	10	**12**	3.9	.978	B. Joyce	30	108	3	5	0	6.69
23	B. Nagel	341	.252	12	39	134	218	21	32		.944							
OF	D. Miles	320	.300	1	37	146	4	5	1	2.0	.968							
SS	W. Ambler	227	.211	0	24	126	184	15	31	4.2	.954							
C	E. Brucker	172	.291	3	31	150	18	0	5	3.6	1.000							
1B	N. Etten	155	.252	3	29	376	19	4	29	9.7	.990							

St. Louis

W-43 L-111

Fred Haney

POS	Player	AB	BA	HR	RBI	PO	A	E	DP	TC/G	FA	Pitcher	G	IP	W	L	SV	ERA
1B	G. McQuinn	617	.316	20	94	**1377**	**116**	11	122	9.8	.993	J. Kramer	40	212	9	16	0	5.83
2B	J. Berardino	468	.256	5	58	315	339	**29**	67	6.0	.958	V. Kennedy	33	192	9	17*	0	5.73
SS	D. Heffner	375	.267	1	35	138	218	21	33	5.2	.944	B. Trotter	41	157	6	13	0	5.34
3B	H. Clift	526	.270	15	84	184	324	25	34	3.6	.953	R. Lawson	36	151	3	7	0	5.32
RF	M. Hoag	482	.295	10	75	218	13	7	2	2.0	.971	L. Mills	34	144	4	11	2	6.55
CF	C. Laabs	317	.300	10	62	199	7	6	0	2.7	.972	B. Harris	28	126	3	12	0	5.71
LF	J. Gallagher	266	.282	9	40	143	8	9	1	2.4	.944	G. Gill	27	95	1	12	0	7.11
C	J. Glenn	286	.273	4	29	280	48	11	4	4.1	.968							
OF	B. Sullivan	332	.289	5	50	139	7	7	3	2.6	.954							
SS	M. Christman	222	.216	0	20	151	209	15	45	5.9	.960							
OF	J. Grace	207	.304	3	22	83	9	3	0	1.8	.968							
OF	M. Mazzera	111	.297	3	22	56	1	1	0	2.3	.983							

BATTING AND BASE RUNNING LEADERS

Batting Average
- J. DiMaggio, NY .381
- J. Foxx, BOS .360
- B. Johnson, PHI .338
- H. Trosky, CLE .335
- C. Keller, NY .334

Slugging Average
- J. Foxx, BOS .694
- J. DiMaggio, NY .671
- H. Greenberg, DET .622
- T. Williams, BOS .609
- H. Trosky, CLE .589

Home Runs
- J. Foxx, BOS 35
- H. Greenberg, DET 33
- T. Williams, BOS 31
- J. DiMaggio, NY 30
- J. Gordon, NY 28

Total Bases
- T. Williams, BOS 344
- J. Foxx, BOS 324
- R. Rolfe, NY 321
- G. McQuinn, STL 318
- H. Greenberg, DET 311

Runs Batted In
- T. Williams, BOS 145
- J. DiMaggio, NY 126
- B. Johnson, PHI 114
- H. Greenberg, DET 112
- J. Gordon, NY 111
- G. Walker, CHI 111

Stolen Bases
- G. Case, WAS 51
- P. Fox, DET 23
- M. Kreevich, CHI 23
- B. McCosky, DET 20
- B. Chapman, CLE 18
- J. Kuhel, CHI 18

Hits
- R. Rolfe, NY 213
- G. McQuinn, STL 195
- K. Keltner, CLE 191
- B. McCosky, DET 190

Base on Balls
- H. Clift, STL 111
- T. Williams, BOS 107
- L. Appling, CHI 105
- G. Selkirk, NY 103

Home Run Percentage
- J. Foxx, BOS 7.5
- H. Greenberg, DET 6.6
- J. DiMaggio, NY 6.5
- R. York, DET 6.1

Runs
- R. Rolfe, NY 139
- T. Williams, BOS 131
- J. Foxx, BOS 130
- B. McCosky, DET 120

Doubles
- R. Rolfe, NY 46
- T. Williams, BOS 44
- H. Greenberg, DET 42
- G. McQuinn, STL 37

Triples
- B. Lewis, WAS 16
- B. McCosky, DET 14
- B. Campbell, CLE 13
- G. McQuinn, STL 13

PITCHING LEADERS

Winning Percentage
- L. Grove, BOS .789
- R. Ruffing, NY .750
- B. Feller, CLE .727
- D. Leonard, WAS .714
- T. Bridges, DET .708

Earned Run Average
- L. Grove, BOS 2.54
- T. Lyons, CHI 2.76
- B. Feller, CLE 2.85
- R. Ruffing, NY 2.93
- L. Gomez, NY 3.41

Wins
- B. Feller, CLE 24
- R. Ruffing, NY 21
- D. Leonard, WAS 20
- B. Newsom, STL, DET 20
- T. Bridges, DET 17

Saves
- J. Murphy, NY 19
- C. Brown, CHI 18
- C. Dean, PHI 7
- J. Heving, BOS 7
- P. Appleton, WAS 6

Strikeouts
- B. Feller, CLE 246
- B. Newsom, STL, DET 192
- T. Bridges, DET 129
- J. Rigney, CHI 119
- K. Chase, WAS 118

Complete Games
- B. Feller, CLE 24
- B. Newsom, STL, DET 24
- R. Ruffing, NY 22
- D. Leonard, WAS 21
- L. Grove, BOS 17

Fewest Hits/9 Innings
- B. Feller, CLE 6.89
- L. Gomez, NY 7.86
- R. Ruffing, NY 8.14
- K. Chase, WAS 8.34

Shutouts
- R. Ruffing, NY 5
- B. Feller, CLE 4
- B. Newsom, STL, DET 3

Fewest Walks/9 Innings
- T. Lyons, CHI 1.36
- D. Leonard, WAS 1.97
- T. Lee, CHI 2.68
- L. Grove, BOS 2.73

Most Strikeouts/9 Inn.
- B. Feller, CLE 7.46
- B. Newsom, STL, DET 5.92
- T. Bridges, DET 5.86
- J. Rigney, CHI 4.90

Innings
- B. Feller, CLE 297
- B. Newsom, STL, DET 292
- D. Leonard, WAS 269
- T. Lee, CHI 235

Games Pitched
- C. Brown, CHI 61
- C. Dean, PHI 54
- E. Dickman, BOS 48
- J. Heving, BOS 46

AMERICAN LEAGUE 1939, *cont.*

	W	L	PCT	GB	R	OR	Batting 2B	3B	HR	BA	SA	SB	Fielding E	DP	FA	Pitching CG	BB	SO	ShO	SV	ERA
New York	106	45	.702		**967**	**556**	259	55	**166**	.287	**.451**	72	**126**	159	**.978**	**87**	567	565	**15**	**26**	**3.31**
Boston	89	62	.589	17	890	795	287	57	124	**.291**	.436	42	180	147	.970	52	543	539	4	20	4.56
Cleveland	87	67	.565	20.5	797	700	**291**	**79**	85	.280	.413	72	180	148	.970	69	602	614	10	13	4.08
Chicago	85	69	.552	22.5	755	737	220	56	64	.275	.374	**113**	167	140	.972	62	**454**	535	5	21	4.31
Detroit	81	73	.526	26.5	849	762	277	67	124	.279	.426	88	198	147	.967	64	574	**633**	8	16	4.29
Washington	65	87	.428	41.5	702	797	249	**79**	44	.278	.379	94	205	**167**	.966	72	602	521	4	10	4.60
Philadelphia	55	97	.362	51.5	711	1022	282	55	98	.271	.400	60	210	131	.964	50	579	397	6	12	5.79
St. Louis	43	111	.279	64.5	733	1035	242	50	91	.268	.381	48	199	144	.968	56	739	516	3	3	6.01
					6404	6404	2107	498	796	.279	.407	589	1465	1183	.969	512	4660	4320	55	121	4.62

NATIONAL LEAGUE 1940

Team	POS	Player	AB	BA	HR	RBI	PO	A	E	DP	TC/G	FA	Pitcher	G	IP	W	L	SV	ERA
Cincinnati	1B	F. McCormick	**618**	.309	19	127	**1587**	98	8	**146**	10.9	**.995**	B. Walters	36	**305**	**22**	10	0	**2.48**
W-100 L-53	2B	L. Frey	563	.266	8	54	**366**	**512**	21	**111**	6.0	.977	P. Derringer	37	297	20	12	0	3.06
Bill McKechnie	SS	B. Myers	282	.202	5	30	155	269	17	62	5.0	.961	J. Thompson	33	225	16	9	0	3.32
	3B	B. Werber	584	.277	12	48	139	287	17	24	3.1	**.962**	J. Turner	24	187	14	7	0	2.89
	RF	I. Goodman	519	.258	12	63	252	6	8	0	2.0	.970	W. Moore	25	117	8	8	1	3.63
	CF	H. Craft	422	.244	6	48	284	7	1	2	2.7	.997	J. Beggs	37	77	12	3	**7**	2.00
	LF	M. McCormick	417	.300	1	30	266	9	4	2	2.6	.986							
	C	E. Lombardi	376	.319	14	74	397	46	5	5	4.4	.989							
	SS	E. Joost	278	.216	1	24	145	240	16	48	5.1	.960							
	OF	M. Arnovich	211	.284	0	21	129	5	0	0	2.2	1.000							
	C	W. Hershberger	123	.309	0	26	121	11	2	0	3.6	.985							
	OF	J. Ripple	101	.307	4	20	45	0	0	0	1.5	1.000							
Brooklyn	1B	D. Camilli	512	.287	23	96	1299	79	11	85	9.9	.992	W. Wyatt	37	239	15	14	0	3.46
W-88 L-65	2B	P. Coscarart	506	.237	9	58	326	379	31	58	5.3	.958	L. Hamlin	33	182	9	8	0	3.06
Leo Durocher	SS	P. Reese	312	.272	5	28	190	238	18	41	5.4	.960	V. Tamulis	41	154	8	5	2	3.09
	3B	C. Lavagetto	448	.257	4	43	137	191	**24**	12	3.0	.932	H. Casey	44	154	11	8	2	3.62
	RF	J. Vosmik	404	.282	1	42	193	9	5	1	2.1	.976	T. Carleton	34	149	6	6	2	3.81
	CF	D. Walker	556	.308	6	66	360	6	10	3	2.8	.973	C. Davis	22	137	8	7	2	3.81
	LF	J. Medwick	423	.300	14	66	240	7	5	0	2.4	.980	F. Fitzsimmons	20	134	16	2	1	2.81
	C	B. Phelps	370	.295	13	61	428	35	11	3	4.8	.977	T. Pressnell	24	68	6	5	2	3.69
	OF	J. Wasdell	230	.278	3	37	70	1	4	0	1.8	.947							
	30	P. Reiser	225	.293	3	20	59	58	5	7		.959							
	S2	J. Hudson	179	.218	0	19	94	145	15	20		.941							
	SS	L. Durocher	160	.231	1	14	102	131	10	22	4.6	.959							
St. Louis	1B	J. Mize	579	.314	**43**	**137**	1376	80	14	105	9.6	.990	L. Warneke	33	232	16	10	0	3.14
W-84 L-69	2B	J. Orengo	415	.287	7	56	204	216	21	45	5.7	.952	M. Cooper	38	231	11	12	3	3.63
Ray Blades	SS	M. Marion	435	.278	3	46	245	366	33	76	5.2	.949	B. McGee	38	218	16	10	0	3.80
W-14 L-24	3B	S. Martin	369	.238	4	32	52	89	4	2	2.0	.972	C. Shoun	**54**	197	13	11	5	3.92
Mike Gonzalez	RF	E. Slaughter	516	.306	17	73	267	8	3	5	2.1	.989	B. Bowman	28	114	7	5	0	4.33
W-1 L-5	CF	T. Moore	537	.304	17	64	383	11	5	4	3.0	.987	M. Lanier	35	105	9	6	3	3.34
Billy Southworth	LF	E. Koy	348	.310	8	52	192	2	6	0	2.2	.970							
W-69 L-40	C	M. Owen	307	.264	0	27	378	56	9	8	3.9	.980							
	UT	J. Brown	454	.280	0	30	198	243	22	42		.952							
	C	D. Padgett	240	.242	6	41	243	34	11	5	4.0	.962							
	OF	P. Martin	228	.316	3	39	103	8	3	0	1.8	.974							
	OF	J. Medwick	158	.304	3	20	81	1	1	0	2.2	.988							
Pittsburgh	1B	E. Fletcher	510	.273	16	104	1512	**104**	11	128	**11.1**	.993	R. Sewell	33	190	16	5	1	2.80
W-78 L-76	2B	F. Gustine	524	.281	1	55	288	402	**43**	92	5.6	.941	J. Bowman	32	188	9	10	2	4.46
Frankie Frisch	SS	A. Vaughan	594	.300	7	95	308	**542**	**52**	94	5.8	.942	M. Brown	48	173	10	9	**7**	3.49
	3B	L. Handley	302	.281	1	19	84	139	18	12	3.0	.925	K. Heintzelman	39	165	8	8	3	4.47
	RF	B. Elliott	551	.292	5	64	302	12	7	0	2.2	.978	B. Klinger	39	142	8	13	3	5.39
	CF	V. DiMaggio	356	.289	19	54	220	13	5	3	2.2	.979	M. Butcher	35	136	8	9	2	6.01
	LF	M. Van Robays	572	.273	11	116	276	10	11	3	2.1	.963	J. Lanning	38	116	8	4	2	4.05
	C	S. Davis	285	.326	5	39	288	61	12	11	4.1	.967	D. Lanahan	40	108	6	8	2	4.25
	3B	D. Garms	358	**.355**	5	57	65	123	7	15	3.0	.964	D. MacFayden	35	91	5	4	2	3.55
	OF	P. Waner	238	.290	1	32	62	3	1	0	1.5	.985							
	C	A. Lopez	174	.259	1	24	224	29	2	7	4.3	.992*							
	OF	L. Waner	166	.259	0	3	90	3	1	1	2.2	.989							
	2B	P. Young	136	.250	2	20	51	79	13	9	4.3	.909							
Chicago	1B	P. Cavarretta	193	.280	2	22	524	30	5	57	10.8	.991	C. Passeau	46	281	20	13	5	2.50
W-75 L-79	2B	B. Herman	558	.292	5	57	**366**	448	22	94	**6.2**	.974	L. French	40	246	14	14	2	3.29
Gabby Hartnett	SS	B. Mattick	441	.218	0	33	233	431	38	76	5.6	.946	B. Lee	37	211	9	17	0	5.03
	3B	S. Hack	603	.317	8	40	**175**	**302**	23	**27**	3.4	.954	V. Olsen	34	173	13	9	0	2.97
	RF	B. Nicholson	491	.297	25	98	235	10	13	2	2.1	.950	K. Raffensberger	43	115	7	9	3	3.38
	CF	H. Leiber	440	.302	17	86	187	8	3	0	1.9	.985	J. Mooty	20	114	6	6	1	2.92
	LF	J. Gleeson	485	.313	5	61	273	14	5	3	2.4	.983	C. Root	36	113	2	4	1	3.82
	C	A. Todd	381	.255	6	42	418	59	8	11	4.7	.984							
	OF	D. Dallessandro	287	.268	1	36	156	1	5	0	2.2	.969							
	1B	R. Russell	215	.247	5	33	518	18	10	22	10.7	.982							
	OF	A. Galan	209	.230	3	22	114	6	2	2	2.3	.984							
	1B	Z. Bonura	182	.264	4	20	408	40	4	34	10.3	.991							
	S2	R. Warstler	159	.226	1	18	90	141	14	20		.943							

NATIONAL LEAGUE 1940, *cont.*

New York

W-72 L-80

Bill Terry

POS	Player	AB	BA	HR	RBI	PO	A	E	DP	TC/G	FA	Pitcher	G	IP	W	L	SV	ERA
1B	B. Young	556	.286	17	101	1505	86	13	112	10.9	.992	H. Gumbert	35	237	12	14	2	3.76
2B	T. Cuccinello	307	.208	5	36	106	130	3	17	5.1	.987	H. Schumacher	34	227	13	13	1	3.25
SS	M. Witek	433	.256	3	31	192	307	22	46	5.9	.958	C. Hubbell	31	214	11	12	0	3.65
3B	B. Whitehead	568	.282	4	36	68	130	11	5	2.8	.947	B. Lohrman	31	195	10	15	1	3.78
RF	M. Ott	536	.289	19	79	210	9	4	2	2.0	.982	C. Melton	37	167	10	11	2	4.91
CF	F. Demaree	460	.302	7	61	233	6	5	5	2.1	.980	J. Brown	41	55	2	4	**7**	3.42
LF	J. Moore	543	.276	6	46	259	9	5	1	2.1	.982	R. Lynn	33	42	4	3	3	3.83
C	H. Danning	524	.300	13	91	**634**	**91**	**15**	**13**	**5.6**	.980							
OF	J. Rucker	277	.296	4	23	121	3	6	0	2.3	.954							
SS	B. Jurges	214	.252	2	36	123	196	11	36	5.2	.967							
OF	B. Seeds	155	.290	4	16	64	3	1	0	1.7	.985							

Boston

W-65 L-87

Casey Stengel

POS	Player	AB	BA	HR	RBI	PO	A	E	DP	TC/G	FA	Pitcher	G	IP	W	L	SV	ERA
1B	B. Hassett	458	.234	0	27	877	91	**21**	102	10.1	.979	D. Errickson	34	236	12	13	4	3.16
2B	B. Rowell	486	.305	3	58	251	360	30	81	5.6	.953	B. Posedel	35	233	12	17	1	4.13
SS	E. Miller	569	.276	14	79	**405**	487	28	**122**	**6.1**	**.970**	J. Sullivan	36	177	10	14	1	3.55
3B	S. Sisti	459	.251	6	34	117	192	21	21	3.2	.936	M. Salvo	21	161	10	9	0	3.08
RF	M. West	524	.261	7	72	220	16	6	1	2.4	.975	N. Strincevich	32	129	4	8	1	5.53
CF	J. Cooney	365	.318	0	21	238	5	2	0	2.5	.992	J. Tobin	15	96	7	3	0	3.83
LF	C. Ross	569	.281	17	89	347	12	14	2	2.5	.962							
C	R. Berres	229	.192	0	14	254	56	6	6	3.7	.981							
OF	G. Moore	363	.292	5	39	198	11	3	3	2.3	.986							

Philadelphia

W-50 L-103

Doc Prothro

POS	Player	AB	BA	HR	RBI	PO	A	E	DP	TC/G	FA	Pitcher	G	IP	W	L	SV	ERA
1B	A. Mahan	544	.244	2	39	1380	102	12	120	10.3	.992	K. Higbe	41	283	14	19	1	3.72
2B	H. Schulte	436	.236	1	21	282	317	12	70	5.1	**.980**	H. Mulcahy	36	280	13	**22**	0	3.60
SS	B. Bragan	474	.222	7	44	268	443	49	83	5.8	.936	I. Pearson	29	145	3	14	1	5.45
3B	P. May	501	.293	1	48	139	297	21	12	**3.4**	.954	S. Johnson	37	138	5	14	1	4.88
RF	C. Klein	354	.218	7	37	180	4	3	2	1.6	.984	B. Beck	29	129	4	9	0	4.31
CF	J. Marty	455	.270	13	50	296	7	8	0	2.6	.974	L. Smoll	33	109	2	8	0	5.37
LF	J. Rizzo	367	.292	20	53	207	6	7	2	2.4	.968							
C	B. Warren	289	.246	12	34	326	63	10	9	4.1	.975							
UT	E. Mueller	263	.247	3	28	146	96	5	13		.980							
C	B. Atwood	203	.192	0	22	238	43	3	3	4.1	.989							
OF	M. Mazzera	156	.237	0	13	62	5	1	2	1.6	.985							

BATTING AND BASE RUNNING LEADERS

Batting Average

D. Garms, PIT	.355
E. Lombardi, CIN	.319
J. Cooney, BOS	.318
S. Hack, CHI	.317
J. Mize, STL	.314

Slugging Average

J. Mize, STL	.636
B. Nicholson, CHI	.534
D. Camilli, BKN	.529
V. DiMaggio, CIN, PIT	.519
E. Slaughter, STL	.504

Home Runs

J. Mize, STL	43
B. Nicholson, CHI	25
J. Rizzo, PIT, CIN, PHI	24
D. Camilli, BKN	23

Total Bases

J. Mize, STL	368
F. McCormick, CIN	298
J. Medwick, STL, BKN	280
D. Camilli, BKN	271
A. Vaughan, PIT	269

Runs Batted In

J. Mize, STL	137
F. McCormick, CIN	127
M. Van Robays, PIT	116
E. Fletcher, PIT	104
B. Young, NY	101

Stolen Bases

L. Frey, CIN	22
S. Hack, CHI	21
T. Moore, STL	18
B. Werber, CIN	16
P. Reese, BKN	15

Hits

S. Hack, CHI	191
F. McCormick, CIN	191
J. Mize, STL	182
A. Vaughan, PIT	178

Base on Balls

E. Fletcher, PIT	119
M. Ott, NY	100
D. Camilli, BKN	89
A. Vaughan, PIT	88

Home Run Percentage

J. Mize, STL	7.4
V. DiMaggio, CIN, PIT	5.3
B. Nicholson, CHI	5.1
J. Rizzo, PIT, CIN, PHI	4.8

Runs

A. Vaughan, PIT	113
J. Mize, STL	111
B. Werber, CIN	105
L. Frey, CIN	102

Doubles

F. McCormick, CIN	44
A. Vaughan, PIT	40
J. Gleeson, CHI	39
S. Hack, CHI	38

Triples

A. Vaughan, PIT	15
C. Ross, BOS	14
D. Camilli, BKN	13
E. Slaughter, STL	13
J. Mize, STL	13

PITCHING LEADERS

Winning Percentage

F. Fitzsimmons, BKN	.889
R. Sewell, PIT	.762
B. Walters, CIN	.688
J. Thompson, CIN	.640
P. Derringer, CIN	.625

Earned Run Average

B. Walters, CIN	2.48
C. Passeau, CHI	2.50
R. Sewell, PIT	2.80
F. Fitzsimmons, BKN	2.81
J. Turner, CIN	2.89

Wins

B. Walters, CIN	22
C. Passeau, CHI	20
P. Derringer, CIN	20

Saves

J. Brown, NY	7
M. Brown, PIT	7
J. Beggs, CIN	7
C. Passeau, CHI	5
C. Shoun, STL	5

Strikeouts

K. Higbe, PHI	137
W. Wyatt, BKN	124
C. Passeau, CHI	124
H. Schumacher, NY	123
P. Derringer, CIN	115
B. Walters, CIN	115

Complete Games

B. Walters, CIN	29
P. Derringer, CIN	26
H. Mulcahy, PHI	21
C. Passeau, CHI	20
K. Higbe, PHI	20

Fewest Hits/9 Innings

B. Walters, CIN	7.11
K. Higbe, PHI	7.70
J. Thompson, CIN	7.87
R. Sewell, PIT	8.02

Shutouts

M. Salvo, BOS	5
B. Lohrman, NY	5
W. Wyatt, BKN	5

Fewest Walks/9 Innings

P. Derringer, CIN	1.46
J. Turner, CIN	1.54
F. Fitzsimmons, BKN	1.67
L. Warneke, STL	1.82

Most Strikeouts/9 Inn.

H. Schumacher, NY	4.88
W. Wyatt, BKN	4.66
K. Higbe, PHI	4.36
J. Thompson, CIN	4.11

Innings

B. Walters, CIN	305
P. Derringer, CIN	297
K. Higbe, PHI	283
C. Passeau, CHI	281

Games Pitched

C. Shoun, STL	54
M. Brown, PIT	48
C. Passeau, CHI	46
H. Casey, BKN	44

							Batting						Fielding			Pitching					
	W	L	PCT	GB	R	OR	2B	3B	HR	BA	SA	SB	E	DP	FA	CG	BB	SO	ShO	SV	ERA
Cincinnati	100	53	.654		707	**528**	264	38	89	.266	.379	72	**117**	158	**.981**	**91**	445	557	10	11	**3.05**
Brooklyn	88	65	.575	12	697	621	256	**70**	93	.260	.383	56	183	110	.970	65	**393**	**634**	**17**	14	3.50
St. Louis	84	69	.549	16	747	699	266	61	**119**	.275	**.411**	**97**	174	134	.971	71	488	550	10	14	3.83
Pittsburgh	78	76	.506	22.5	**809**	783	**276**	68	76	**.276**	.394	69	217	160	.966	49	492	491	8	**24**	4.36
Chicago	75	79	.487	25.5	681	636	272	48	86	.267	.384	63	199	143	.968	69	430	564	12	14	3.54
New York	72	80	.474	27.5	663	659	201	46	91	.267	.374	45	139	132	.977	57	473	606	11	18	3.79
Boston	65	87	.428	34.5	623	745	219	50	59	.256	.349	48	184	**169**	.970	76	573	435	9	12	4.36
Philadelphia	50	103	.327	50	494	750	180	35	75	.238	.331	25	181	136	.970	66	475	485	5	8	4.40
					5421	5421	1934	416	688	.263	.376	475	1394	1142	.972	544	3769	4322	82	115	3.85

AMERICAN LEAGUE 1940

Team	POS	Player	AB	BA	HR	RBI	PO	A	E	DP	TC/G	FA	Pitcher	G	IP	W	L	SV	ERA
Detroit	1B	R. York	588	.316	33	134	1390	107	15	101	9.8	.990	B. Newsom	36	264	21	5	0	2.83
	2B	C. Gehringer	515	.313	10	81	276	374	19	72	4.8	.972	T. Bridges	29	198	12	9	0	3.37
	SS	D. Bartell	528	.233	7	53	295	394	34	74	5.2	.953	S. Rowe	27	169	16	3	0	3.46
W-90 L-64	3B	P. Higgins	480	.271	13	76	133	239	29	16	3.1	.928	J. Gorsica	29	160	7	7	0	4.33
	RF	P. Fox	350	.289	5	48	169	6	6	0	2.1	.967	H. Newhouser	28	133	9	9	0	4.86
Del Baker	CF	B. McCosky	589	.340	4	57	349	7	6	2	2.6	.983	D. Trout	33	101	3	7	2	4.47
	LF	H. Greenberg	573	.340	**41**	**150**	298	14	15	1	2.2	.954	A. Benton	42	79	6	10	**17**	4.42
	C	B. Tebbetts	379	.296	4	46	572	**89**	**17**	**10**	**6.3**	.975	F. Hutchinson	17	76	3	7	0	5.68
	OF	B. Campbell	297	.283	8	44	133	6	6	0	2.0	.959							
	C	B. Sullivan	220	.309	3	41	292	29	8	4	5.8	.976							
	OF	E. Averill	118	.280	2	20	23	2	1	0	1.2	.962							
Cleveland	1B	H. Trosky	522	.295	25	93	1207	70	11	129	9.3	.991	B. Feller	**43**	**320**	**27**	11	4	**2.61**
	2B	R. Mack	530	.283	12	69	323	417	27	109	5.3	.965	A. Milnar	37	242	18	10	3	3.27
	SS	L. Boudreau	627	.295	9	101	277	**454**	24	**116**	4.9	**.968**	M. Harder	31	186	12	11	0	4.06
W-89 L-65	3B	K. Keltner	543	.254	15	77	170	277	22	27	3.2	.953	A. Smith	31	183	15	7	2	3.44
	RF	B. Bell	444	.279	4	58	193	5	6	1	2.1	.971	J. Allen	32	139	9	8	5	3.44
Ossie Vitt	CF	R. Weatherly	578	.303	12	59	370	10	12	3	2.9	.969	J. Dobson	40	100	3	7	3	4.95
	LF	B. Chapman	548	.286	4	50	307	10	12	3	2.3	.964							
	C	R. Hemsley	416	.267	4	42	591	65	4	8	5.6	**.994**							
	OF	J. Heath	356	.219	14	50	197	6	6	1	2.3	.971							
New York	1B	B. Dahlgren	568	.264	12	73	**1488**	75	15	143	10.2	.990	R. Ruffing	30	226	15	12	0	3.38
	2B	J. Gordon	616	.281	30	103	374	**505**	23	116	5.8	.975	M. Russo	30	189	14	8	1	3.28
	SS	F. Crosetti	546	.194	4	31	246	396	31	73	4.6	.954	S. Chandler	27	172	8	7	0	4.60
W-88 L-66	3B	R. Rolfe	588	.250	10	53	161	288	24	24	3.4	.949	M. Breuer	27	164	8	9	0	4.55
	RF	C. Keller	500	.286	21	93	317	5	11	2	2.4	.967	A. Donald	24	119	8	3	0	3.03
Joe McCarthy	CF	J. DiMaggio	508	**.352**	31	133	359	5	8	2	2.9	.978	M. Pearson	16	110	7	5	0	3.69
	LF	G. Selkirk	379	.269	19	71	220	9	9	6	2.1	.962	E. Bonham	12	99	9	3	0	1.90
	C	B. Dickey	372	.247	9	54	425	55	3	9	4.7	.994	S. Sundra	27	99	4	6	2	5.53
	OF	T. Henrich	293	.307	10	53	147	10	5	2	2.1	.969	B. Hadley	25	80	3	5	2	5.74
	C	B. Rosar	228	.298	4	37	258	30	5	8	4.7	.983	J. Murphy	35	63	8	4	9	3.69
Boston	1B	J. Foxx	515	.297	36	119	844	79	9	87	9.8	.990	J. Bagby	36	183	10	16	2	4.73
	2B	B. Doerr	595	.291	22	105	**401**	480	21	**118**	6.0	.977	J. Wilson	41	158	12	6	5	5.08
	SS	J. Cronin	548	.285	24	111	252	443	**38**	89	5.0	.948	L. Grove	22	153	7	6	0	3.99
W-82 L-72	3B	J. Tabor	459	.285	21	81	143	267	**33**	25	**3.7**	.926	F. Ostermueller	31	144	5	9	0	4.95
	RF	D. DiMaggio	418	.301	8	46	239	16	6	5	2.8	.977	H. Hash	34	120	7	7	3	4.95
Joe Cronin	CF	D. Cramer	**661**	.303	1	51	333	11	11	2	2.4	.969	D. Galehouse	25	120	6	6	0	5.17
	LF	T. Williams	561	.344	23	113	302	13	13	2	2.3	.960	J. Heving	39	119	12	7	3	4.01
	C	G. Desautels	222	.225	0	17	325	27	3	8	5.1	.992	E. Dickman	35	100	8	6	3	6.03
	01	L. Finney	534	.320	5	73	652	33	7	41		.990							
Chicago	1B	J. Kuhel	603	.280	27	94	1395	91	18	112	9.7	.988	J. Rigney	39	281	14	18	3	3.11
	2B	S. Webb	334	.237	1	29	143	229	12	44	5.2	.969	T. Lee	28	228	12	13	0	3.47
	SS	L. Appling	566	.348	0	79	**307**	436	37	83	5.2	.953	E. Smith	32	207	14	9	0	3.21
W-82 L-72	3B	B. Kennedy	606	.252	3	52	**178**	322	**33**	25	3.5	.938	T. Lyons	22	186	12	8	0	3.24
	RF	T. Wright	581	.337	5	88	278	11	11	2	2.1	.963	J. Knott	25	158	11	9	0	4.56
Jimmy Dykes	CF	M. Kreevich	582	.265	8	55	428	12	8	3	3.1	.982	B. Dietrich	23	150	10	6	0	4.03
	LF	M. Solters	428	.308	12	80	266	6	8	2	2.6	.971	C. Brown	37	66	4	6	10	3.68
	C	M. Tresh	480	.281	1	64	**619**	69	12	7	5.2	.983							
	OF	L. Rosenthal	276	.301	6	42	208	4	5	0	2.4	.977							
	2B	E. McNair	251	.227	7	31	128	170	13	27	4.8	.958							
St. Louis	1B	G. McQuinn	594	.279	16	84	1436	**124**	13	**157**	**10.5**	**.992**	E. Auker	38	264	16	11	0	3.96
	2B	D. Heffner	487	.236	3	53	311	426	17	102	**6.0**	**.977**	V. Kennedy	34	222	12	17	0	5.59
	SS	J. Berardino	523	.258	16	85	250	336	**38**	83	**5.6**	.939	B. Harris	35	194	11	15	1	4.93
W-67 L-87	3B	H. Clift	523	.273	20	87	161	**329**	21	**32**	3.5	**.959**	J. Niggeling	28	154	7	11	0	4.45
	RF	C. Laabs	218	.271	10	40	124	3	4	1	2.1	.969	B. Trotter	36	98	7	6	2	3.77
Fred Haney	CF	W. Judnich	519	.303	24	89	356	7	4	4	2.8	.989	R. Lawson	30	72	5	3	4	5.13
	LF	R. Radcliff	584	.342	7	81	282	8	8	2	2.1	.973	J. Kramer	16	65	3	7	0	6.26
	C	B. Swift	398	.244	0	39	389	55	9	8	3.5	.980							
	OF	R. Cullenbine	257	.230	7	31	114	5	3	2	2.1	.975							
	OF	J. Grace	229	.258	5	25	86	6	4	0	1.9	.958							
	OF	M. Hoag	191	.262	3	26	64	4	2	0	1.5	.971							
	SS	A. Strange	167	.186	0	6	65	112	7	24	5.3	.962							
Washington	1B	Z. Bonura	311	.273	3	45	712	42	14	70	9.7	.982	D. Leonard	35	289	14	**19**	0	3.49
	2B	J. Bloodworth	469	.245	11	70	260	274	12	74	5.7	.978	K. Chase	35	262	15	17	0	3.23
	SS	J. Pofahl	406	.234	2	36	191	302	25	69	4.6	.952	S. Hudson	38	252	17	16	1	4.57
W-64 L-90	3B	C. Travis	528	.322	2	76	116	265	27	30	3.6	.934	W. Masterson	31	130	3	13	2	4.90
	RF	B. Lewis	600	.317	6	63	206	11	9	1	2.0	.960	J. Krakauskas	32	109	1	6	2	6.44
Bucky Harris	CF	G. Case	656	.293	5	56	384	10	12	0	2.6	.970	R. Monteagudo	27	101	2	6	2	6.08
	LF	G. Walker	595	.294	13	96	285	10	10	2	2.2	.967							
	C	R. Ferrell	326	.273	0	28	427	67	10	5	5.1	.980							
	OF	J. Welaj	215	.256	3	21	132	1	3	0	2.6	.978							
	2B	B. Myer	210	.290	0	29	119	176	10	34	5.6	.967							
	C	J. Early	206	.257	5	14	276	41	10	5	5.8	.969							

AMERICAN LEAGUE 1940, *cont.*

Team	POS	Player	AB	BA	HR	RBI	PO	A	E	DP	TC/G	FA	Pitcher	G	IP	W	L	SV	ERA
Philadelphia	1B	D. Siebert	595	.286	5	77	1322	119	**22**	112	9.5	.985	J. Babich	31	229	14	13	0	3.73
W-54 L-100	2B	B. McCoy	490	.257	7	62	261	392	**34**	82	5.3	.951	N. Potter	31	201	9	14	0	4.44
Connie Mack	SS	A. Brancato	298	.191	1	23	136	180	17	35	4.2	.949	G. Caster	36	178	4	**19**	2	6.56
	3B	A. Rubeling	376	.245	4	38	96	184	20	13	3.1	.933	C. Dean	30	159	6	13	1	6.61
	RF	W. Moses	537	.309	9	50	295	10	8	1	2.4	.974	B. Ross	24	156	5	10	1	4.38
	CF	S. Chapman	508	.276	23	75	348	13	14	2	2.9	.963	B. Beckmann	34	127	8	4	1	4.17
	LF	B. Johnson	512	.268	31	103	310	15	13	4	2.5	.962	E. Heusser	41	110	6	13	5	4.99
	C	F. Hayes	465	.308	16	70	515	63	**17**	9	4.4	.971	P. Vaughan	18	99	2	9	2	5.35
	OF	D. Miles	236	.301	1	23	117	3	7	0	2.5	.945							
	SS	B. Lillard	206	.238	1	21	112	157	23	28	4.2	.921							
	3B	J. Gantenbein	197	.239	4	23	31	75	8	11	2.5	.930							

BATTING AND BASE RUNNING LEADERS

Batting Average
J. DiMaggio, NY .352
L. Appling, CHI .348
T. Williams, BOS .344
R. Radcliff, STL .342
H. Greenberg, DET .340

Slugging Average
H. Greenberg, DET .670
J. DiMaggio, NY .626
T. Williams, BOS .594
R. York, DET .583
J. Foxx, BOS .581

Home Runs
H. Greenberg, DET 41
J. Foxx, BOS 36
R. York, DET 33
J. DiMaggio, NY 31
B. Johnson, PHI 31

Total Bases
H. Greenberg, DET 384
R. York, DET 343
T. Williams, BOS 333
J. DiMaggio, NY 318
J. Gordon, NY 315

Runs Batted In
H. Greenberg, DET 150
R. York, DET 134
J. DiMaggio, NY 133
J. Foxx, BOS 119
T. Williams, BOS 113

Stolen Bases
G. Case, WAS 35
G. Walker, WAS 21
J. Gordon, NY 18
M. Kreevich, CHI 15
B. Lewis, WAS 15

Hits
R. Radcliff, STL 200
B. McCosky, DET 200
D. Cramer, BOS 200
L. Appling, CHI 197

Base on Balls
C. Keller, NY 106
H. Clift, STL 104
J. Foxx, BOS 101
C. Gehringer, DET 101

Home Run Percentage
H. Greenberg, DET 7.2
J. Foxx, BOS 7.0
J. DiMaggio, NY 6.1
B. Johnson, PHI 6.1

Runs
T. Williams, BOS 134
H. Greenberg, DET 129
B. McCosky, DET 123
J. Gordon, NY 112

Doubles
H. Greenberg, DET 50
R. York, DET 46
L. Boudreau, CLE 46
T. Williams, BOS 43

Triples
B. McCosky, DET 19
C. Keller, NY 15
L. Finney, BOS 15
T. Williams, BOS 14

PITCHING LEADERS

Winning Percentage
S. Rowe, DET .842
B. Newsom, DET .808
B. Feller, CLE .711
A. Smith, CLE .682
A. Milnar, CLE .643

Earned Run Average
B. Feller, CLE 2.61
B. Newsom, DET 2.83
J. Rigney, CHI 3.11
E. Smith, CHI 3.21
K. Chase, WAS 3.23

Wins
B. Feller, CLE 27
B. Newsom, DET 21
A. Milnar, CLE 18
S. Hudson, WAS 17
S. Rowe, DET 16
E. Auker, STL 16

Saves
A. Benton, DET 17
C. Brown, CHI 10
J. Murphy, NY 9

Strikeouts
B. Feller, CLE 261
B. Newsom, DET 164
J. Rigney, CHI 141
T. Bridges, DET 133
K. Chase, WAS 129

Complete Games
B. Feller, CLE 31
T. Lee, CHI 24
D. Leonard, WAS 23

Fewest Hits/9 Innings
B. Feller, CLE 6.88
J. Rigney, CHI 7.70
E. Smith, CHI 7.77
T. Bridges, DET 7.79

Shutouts
T. Lyons, CHI 4
A. Milnar, CLE 4
B. Feller, CLE 4

Fewest Walks/9 Innings
T. Lyons, CHI 1.79
T. Lee, CHI 2.21
S. Rowe, DET 2.29
D. Leonard, WAS 2.43

Most Strikeouts/9 Inn.
B. Feller, CLE 7.33
T. Bridges, DET 6.06
B. Newsom, DET 5.59
E. Smith, CHI 5.17

Innings
B. Feller, CLE 320
D. Leonard, WAS 289
J. Rigney, CHI 281
B. Newsom, DET 264
E. Auker, STL 264

Games Pitched
B. Feller, CLE 43
A. Benton, DET 42
E. Heusser, PHI 41
J. Wilson, BOS 41

							Batting						Fielding			Pitching					
	W	L	PCT	GB	R	OR	2B	3B	HR	BA	SA	SB	E	DP	FA	CG	BB	SO	ShO	SV	ERA
Detroit	90	64	.584		**888**	717	**312**	65	134	**.286**	.442	66	194	116	.968	59	570	**752**	10	**23**	4.01
Cleveland	89	65	.578	1	710	**637**	287	61	101	.265	.398	53	**149**	164	**.975**	72	512	686	**13**	22	**3.63**
New York	88	66	.571	2	817	671	243	66	**155**	.259	.418	59	152	158	**.975**	76	511	559	10	14	3.89
Boston	82	72	.532	8	872	825	301	**80**	145	**.286**	**.449**	55	173	156	.972	51	625	613	4	16	4.89
Chicago	82	72	.532	8	735	672	238	63	73	.278	.387	52	185	125	.969	**83**	**480**	574	10	18	3.74
St. Louis	67	87	.435	23	757	882	278	58	118	.263	.401	51	158	**179**	.974	64	646	439	4	9	5.12
Washington	64	90	.416	26	665	811	266	67	52	.271	.374	**94**	194	166	.968	74	618	618	6	7	4.59
Philadelphia	54	100	.351	36	703	932	242	53	105	.262	.387	48	238	131	.960	72	534	488	4	12	5.22
					6147	6147	2167	513	883	.271	.407	478	1443	1195	.970	551	4496	4729	61	121	4.39

NATIONAL LEAGUE 1941

Team	POS	Player	AB	BA	HR	RBI	PO	A	E	DP	TC/G	FA	Pitcher	G	IP	W	L	SV	ERA
Brooklyn	1B	D. Camilli	529	.285	**34**	**120**	1379	98	16	107	10.1	.989	K. Higbe	**48**	298	**22**	9	3	3.14
W-100 L-54	2B	B. Herman	536	.291	3	41	297	354	20	64	5.0	.970	W. Wyatt	38	288	**22**	10	1	2.34
Leo Durocher	SS	P. Reese	595	.229	2	46	**346**	473	**47**	76	**5.7**	.946	H. Casey	45	162	14	11	7	3.89
	3B	C. Lavagetto	441	.277	1	78	117	215	22	17	3.0	.938	C. Davis	28	154	13	7	2	2.97
	RF	D. Walker	531	.311	9	71	309	19	8	8	2.3	.976	L. Hamlin	30	136	8	8	1	4.24
	CF	P. Reiser	536	**.343**	14	76	356	14	7	0	2.8	.981							
	LF	J. Medwick	538	.318	18	88	270	11	5	2	2.2	.983							
	C	M. Owen	386	.231	1	44	**530**	64	3	7	4.7	.995							
	OF	J. Wasdell	265	.298	4	48	84	2	4	0	1.7	.956							
	3B	L. Riggs	197	.305	5	36	48	75	9	4	3.1	.932							
	P	W. Wyatt	109	.239	3	22	11	47	2	5	1.6	.967							

NATIONAL LEAGUE 1941, *cont.*

St. Louis

W-97 L-56

Billy Southworth

POS	Player	AB	BA	HR	RBI	PO	A	E	DP	TC/G	FA	Pitcher	G	IP	W	L	SV	ERA
1B	J. Mize	473	.317	16	100	1157	82	8	104	10.2	.994	L. Warneke	37	246	17	9	0	3.15
2B	C. Crespi	560	.279	4	46	**382**	421	32	**94**	5.8	.962	E. White	32	210	17	7	2	2.40
SS	M. Marion	547	.252	3	58	299	**489**	38	85	5.3	.954	M. Cooper	29	187	13	9	0	3.91
3B	J. Brown	549	.306	3	56	135	276	15	22	3.5	.965	M. Lanier	35	153	10	8	3	2.82
RF	E. Slaughter	425	.311	13	76	173	5	10	1	1.7	.947	H. Gumbert	33	144	11	5	1	2.74
CF	T. Moore	493	.294	6	68	293	14	5	3	2.6	.984	H. Krist	37	114	10	0	2	4.03
LF	J. Hopp	445	.303	4	50	213	4	4	1	2.4	.982	I. Hutchinson	29	47	1	5	5	3.86
C	G. Mancuso	328	.229	2	37	482	58	6	6	5.2	.989							
OF	D. Padgett	324	.247	5	44	115	1	5	0	2.0	.959							
C	W. Cooper	200	.245	1	20	247	39	10	11	4.7	.966							
OF	C. Triplett	185	.286	3	21	78	4	3	0	1.8	.965							
OF	E. Crabtree	167	.341	5	28	71	2	0	0	1.5	1.000							

Cincinnati

W-88 L-66

Bill McKechnie

POS	Player	AB	BA	HR	RBI	PO	A	E	DP	TC/G	FA	Pitcher	G	IP	W	L	SV	ERA
1B	F. McCormick	603	.269	17	97	**1464**	92	8	**130**	10.2	**.995**	B. Walters	37	**302**	19	15	2	2.83
2B	L. Frey	543	.254	6	59	340	432	24	93	5.5	**.970**	P. Derringer	29	228	12	14	1	3.31
SS	E. Joost	537	.253	4	40	310	415	45	85	5.2	.942	J. Vander Meer	33	226	16	13	0	2.82
3B	B. Werber	418	.239	4	46	120	256	16	30	3.7	.959	E. Riddle	33	217	19	4	1	**2.24**
RF	J. Gleeson	301	.233	3	34	153	1	3	0	1.9	.981	J. Turner	23	113	6	4	0	3.11
CF	H. Craft	413	.249	10	59	280	6	5	1	2.5	.983	J. Thompson	27	109	6	6	1	4.87
LF	M. McCormick	369	.287	4	31	240	9	6	2	2.5	.976	J. Beggs	37	57	4	3	5	3.79
C	E. Lombardi	398	.264	10	60	496	70	10	9	5.0	.983							
OF	E. Koy	204	.250	2	27	92	3	1	1	2.0	.990							
C	D. West	172	.215	1	17	209	21	7	3	3.7	.970							
3B	C. Aleno	169	.243	1	18	41	77	3	6	3.0	.975							
OF	L. Waner	164	.256	0	6	68	3	1	1	1.6	.986							

Pittsburgh

W-81 L-73

Frankie Frisch

POS	Player	AB	BA	HR	RBI	PO	A	E	DP	TC/G	FA	Pitcher	G	IP	W	L	SV	ERA
1B	E. Fletcher	521	.288	11	74	1444	**118**	14	113	**10.4**	.991	R. Sewell	39	249	14	**17**	2	3.72
2B	F. Gustine	463	.270	1	46	269	317	28	45	5.9	.954	M. Butcher	33	236	17	12	0	3.05
SS	A. Vaughan	374	.316	6	38	172	289	20	42	5.0	.958	K. Heintzelman	35	196	11	11	0	3.44
3B	L. Handley	459	.288	0	33	125	247	21	19	3.4	.947	J. Lanning	34	176	11	11	1	3.13
RF	B. Elliott	527	.273	3	76	281	9	9	2	2.2	.970	B. Klinger	35	117	9	4	4	3.93
CF	V. DiMaggio	528	.267	21	100	391	11	10	3	2.7	.976	D. Dietz	33	100	7	2	1	2.33
LF	M. Van Robays	457	.282	4	78	292	9	8	3	2.6	.974							
C	A. Lopez	317	.265	5	43	345	54	8	5	3.6	.980							
2B	S. Martin	233	.305	0	19	127	154	8	26	5.5	.972							
SS	A. Anderson	223	.215	1	10	97	161	19	29	4.8	.931							
30	D. Garms	220	.264	3	42	73	44	9	1		.929							
OF	B. Stewart	172	.267	0	10	71	5	3	2	1.9	.962							

New York

W-74 L-79

Bill Terry

POS	Player	AB	BA	HR	RBI	PO	A	E	DP	TC/G	FA	Pitcher	G	IP	W	L	SV	ERA
1B	B. Young	574	.265	25	104	1395	87	21	124	10.0	.986	H. Schumacher	30	206	12	10	1	3.36
2B	B. Whitehead	403	.228	1	23	288	285	18	60	5.7	.970	C. Melton	42	194	8	11	1	3.01
SS	B. Jurges	471	.293	5	61	230	432	30	82	5.2	.957	C. Hubbell	26	164	11	9	1	3.57
3B	D. Bartell	373	.303	5	35	91	169	11	16	3.2	.959	B. Lohrman	33	159	9	10	3	4.02
RF	M. Ott	525	.286	27	90	256	19	9	3	2.0	.968	B. Carpenter	29	132	11	6	2	3.83
CF	J. Rucker	**622**	.288	1	42	344	13	12	5	2.6	.967	B. McGee	22	106	2	9	0	4.91
LF	J. Moore	428	.273	7	40	237	5	7	0	2.1	.972	B. Bowman	29	80	6	7	1	5.71
C	H. Danning	459	.244	7	56	**530**	77	4	8	**5.3**	.993	J. Brown	31	57	1	5	**8**	3.32
3B	J. Orengo	252	.214	4	25	74	132	9	12	3.6	.958							
OF	M. Arnovich	207	.280	2	22	103	5	2	0	1.8	.982							
C	G. Hartnett	150	.300	5	26	138	15	1	1	4.5	.994							

Chicago

W-70 L-84

Jimmie Wilson

POS	Player	AB	BA	HR	RBI	PO	A	E	DP	TC/G	FA	Pitcher	G	IP	W	L	SV	ERA
1B	B. Dahlgren	359	.281	16	59	957	38	9	84	10.2	.991	C. Passeau	34	231	14	14	0	3.35
2B	L. Stringer	512	.246	5	53	356	**455**	34	84	**6.2**	.960	V. Olsen	37	186	10	8	1	3.15
SS	B. Sturgeon	433	.245	0	25	215	366	27	68	4.8	.956	B. Lee	28	167	8	14	1	3.76
3B	S. Hack	586	.317	7	45	138	295	21	22	3.0	.954	J. Mooty	33	153	8	9	4	3.35
RF	B. Nicholson	532	.254	26	98	293	10	9	2	2.2	.971	P. Erickson	32	141	5	7	1	3.70
CF	P. Cavarretta	346	.286	6	40	128	3	1	2	2.0	.992	L. French	26	138	5	14	0	4.63
LF	D. Dallessandro	486	.272	6	85	292	4	4	0	2.3	.987	C. Root	19	107	8	7	0	5.40
C	C. McCullough	418	.227	9	53	481	64	10	6	4.7	.982							
OF	L. Novikoff	203	.241	5	24	92	3	0	0	1.8	1.000							
01	H. Leiber	162	.216	7	25	192	8	5	13		.976							
C	B. Scheffing	132	.242	1	20	126	17	5	1	4.4	.966							

Boston

W-62 L-92

Casey Stengel

POS	Player	AB	BA	HR	RBI	PO	A	E	DP	TC/G	FA	Pitcher	G	IP	W	L	SV	ERA
1B	B. Hassett	405	.296	1	33	895	78	9	92	9.9	.991	J. Tobin	33	238	12	12	0	3.10
2B	B. Rowell	483	.267	7	60	265	312	**40**	81	5.5	.935	M. Salvo	35	195	7	16	0	4.06
SS	E. Miller	585	.239	6	68	336	485	29	**112**	5.5	**.966**	A. Johnson	43	183	7	15	1	3.53
3B	S. Sisti	541	.259	1	45	162	287	**41**	28	3.6	.916	D. Errickson	38	166	6	12	1	4.78
RF	G. Moore	397	.272	5	43	229	13	8	2	2.3	.968	A. Javery	34	161	10	11	1	4.31
CF	J. Cooney	442	.319	0	29	274	9	1	3	2.6	.996	T. Earley	33	139	6	8	3	2.53
LF	M. West	484	.277	12	68	302	13	6	5	2.4	.981	F. LaManna	35	73	5	4	1	5.33
C	R. Berres	279	.201	1	19	356	64	2	3	3.5	**.995**							
OF	P. Waner	294	.279	2	46	129	7	5	3	1.8	.965							
C	P. Masi	180	.222	3	18	194	31	5	3	2.8	.978							
2B	S. Roberge	167	.216	0	15	95	132	5	31	5.0	.978							
1B	B. Dahlgren	166	.235	7	30	379	28	3	45	10.5	.993							

NATIONAL LEAGUE 1941, *cont.*

Philadelphia

W-43 L-111

Doc Prothro

POS	Player	AB	BA	HR	RBI	PO	A	E	DP	TC/G	FA	Pitcher	G	IP	W	L	SV	ERA
1B	N. Etten	540	.311	14	79	1286	89	**23**	124	9.3	.984	J. Podgajny	34	181	9	12	0	4.62
2B	D. Murtaugh	347	.219	0	11	233	247	11	49	5.8	.978	T. Hughes	34	170	9	14	0	4.45
SS	B. Bragan	557	.251	4	69	322	437	45	86	5.2	.944	C. Blanton	28	164	6	13	0	4.51
3B	P. May	490	.267	0	39	**194**	**324**	15	**31**	**3.8**	**.972**	S. Johnson	39	163	5	12	2	4.52
RF	S. Benjamin	480	.235	3	27	185	11	4	3	1.8	.980	I. Pearson	46	136	4	14	6	3.57
CF	J. Marty	477	.268	8	39	286	7	11	0	2.3	.964	L. Grissom	29	131	2	13	0	3.97
LF	D. Litwhiler	590	.305	18	66	393	12	15	3	2.8	.964	F. Hoerst	37	106	3	10	0	5.20
C	B. Warren	345	.214	9	35	412	**84**	**14**	**16**	4.6	.973	B. Beck	34	95	1	9	0	4.63
OF	J. Rizzo	235	.217	4	24	114	8	4	2	2.0	.968							
UT	E. Mueller	233	.227	1	22	114	107	6	21		.974							
C	M. Livingston	207	.203	0	18	263	34	8	5	4.3	.974							
2S	H. Marnie	158	.241	0	11	129	103	2	24		.991							

BATTING AND BASE RUNNING LEADERS

Batting Average
- P. Reiser, BKN .343
- J. Cooney, BOS .319
- J. Medwick, BKN .318
- S. Hack, CHI .317
- J. Mize, STL .317

Slugging Average
- P. Reiser, BKN .558
- D. Camilli, BKN .556
- J. Mize, STL .535
- J. Medwick, BKN .517
- E. Slaughter, STL .496

Home Runs
- D. Camilli, BKN 34
- M. Ott, NY 27
- B. Nicholson, CHI 26
- B. Young, NY 25
- B. Dahlgren, BOS, CHI 23

Total Bases
- P. Reiser, BKN 299
- D. Camilli, BKN 294
- J. Medwick, BKN 278
- D. Litwhiler, PHI 275
- B. Young, NY 265

Runs Batted In
- D. Camilli, BKN 120
- B. Young, NY 104
- J. Mize, STL 100
- V. DiMaggio, PIT 100
- B. Nicholson, CHI 98

Stolen Bases
- D. Murtaugh, PHI 18
- S. Benjamin, PHI 17
- L. Handley, PIT 16
- L. Frey, CIN 16
- J. Hopp, STL 15

Hits
- S. Hack, CHI 186
- P. Reiser, BKN 184
- D. Litwhiler, PHI 180
- J. Rucker, NY 179

Base on Balls
- E. Fletcher, PIT 118
- D. Camilli, BKN 104
- M. Ott, NY 100
- S. Hack, CHI 99

Home Run Percentage
- D. Camilli, BKN 6.4
- M. Ott, NY 5.1
- B. Nicholson, CHI 4.9
- B. Dahlgren, BOS, CHI 4.4

Runs
- P. Reiser, BKN 117
- S. Hack, CHI 111
- J. Medwick, BKN 100
- E. Fletcher, PIT 95
- J. Rucker, NY 95

Doubles
- J. Mize, STL 39
- P. Reiser, BKN 39
- J. Rucker, NY 38
- D. Dallessandro, CHI 36

Triples
- P. Reiser, BKN 17
- E. Fletcher, PIT 13
- J. Hopp, STL 11
- B. Elliott, PIT 10
- J. Medwick, BKN 10

PITCHING LEADERS

Winning Percentage
- E. Riddle, CIN .826
- K. Higbe, BKN .710
- E. White, STL .708
- W. Wyatt, BKN .688
- L. Warneke, STL .654

Earned Run Average
- E. Riddle, CIN 2.24
- W. Wyatt, BKN 2.34
- E. White, STL 2.40
- J. Vander Meer, CIN 2.82
- B. Walters, CIN 2.83

Wins
- W. Wyatt, BKN 22
- K. Higbe, BKN 22
- E. Riddle, CIN 19
- B. Walters, CIN 19

Saves
- J. Brown, NY 8
- B. Crouch, PHI, STL 7
- H. Casey, BKN 7
- I. Pearson, PHI 6
- I. Hutchinson, STL 5
- J. Beggs, CIN 5

Strikeouts
- J. Vander Meer, CIN 202
- W. Wyatt, BKN 176
- B. Walters, CIN 129
- K. Higbe, BKN 121
- M. Cooper, STL 118

Complete Games
- B. Walters, CIN 27
- W. Wyatt, BKN 23
- J. Tobin, BOS 20
- C. Passeau, CHI 20
- M. Butcher, PIT 19
- K. Higbe, BKN 19

Fewest Hits/9 Innings
- J. Vander Meer, CIN 6.84
- W. Wyatt, BKN 6.96
- E. White, STL 7.24
- K. Higbe, BKN 7.37

Shutouts
- W. Wyatt, BKN 7
- J. Vander Meer, CIN 6
- C. Davis, BKN 5
- B. Walters, CIN 5

Fewest Walks/9 Innings
- C. Davis, BKN 1.57
- C. Passeau, CHI 2.03
- P. Derringer, CIN 2.13
- J. Tobin, BOS 2.27

Most Strikeouts/9 Inn.
- J. Vander Meer, CIN 8.03
- M. Cooper, STL 5.69
- W. Wyatt, BKN 5.49
- E. White, STL 5.01

Innings
- B. Walters, CIN 302
- K. Higbe, BKN 298
- W. Wyatt, BKN 288
- R. Sewell, PIT 249

Games Pitched
- K. Higbe, BKN 48
- I. Pearson, PHI 46
- H. Casey, BKN 45
- J. Hutchings, CIN, BOS 44

							Batting						Fielding			Pitching					
	W	L	PCT	GB	R	OR	2B	3B	HR	BA	SA	SB	E	DP	FA	CG	BB	SO	ShO	SV	ERA
Brooklyn	100	54	.649		**800**	581	**286**	**69**	**101**	**.272**	**.405**	36	162	125	.974	66	495	603	17	**22**	**3.14**
St. Louis	97	56	.634	2.5	734	589	254	56	70	**.272**	.377	47	172	146	.973	64	502	**659**	15	20	3.19
Cincinnati	88	66	.571	12	616	**564**	213	33	64	.247	.337	**68**	**152**	147	**.975**	**89**	510	627	**19**	10	3.17
Pittsburgh	81	73	.526	19	690	643	233	65	56	.268	.368	59	196	130	.968	71	492	410	8	12	3.48
New York	74	79	.484	25.5	667	706	248	35	95	.260	.371	36	160	144	.974	55	539	566	12	18	3.94
Chicago	70	84	.455	30	666	670	239	25	99	.253	.365	39	180	139	.970	74	**449**	548	8	9	3.72
Boston	62	92	.403	38	592	720	231	38	48	.251	.334	61	191	**174**	.969	62	554	446	10	9	3.95
Philadelphia	43	111	.279	57	501	793	188	38	64	.244	.331	65	187	147	.969	35	606	552	4	9	4.50
					5266	5266	1892	359	597	.258	.361	411	1400	1152	.971	516	4147	4411	93	109	3.64

AMERICAN LEAGUE 1941

New York

W-101 L-53

Joe McCarthy

POS	Player	AB	BA	HR	RBI	PO	A	E	DP	TC/G	FA	Pitcher	G	IP	W	L	SV	ERA
1B	J. Sturm	524	.239	3	36	1099	85	12	117	9.6	.990	M. Russo	28	210	14	10	1	3.09
2B	J. Gordon	588	.276	24	87	332	397	**32**	**109**	5.8	.958	R. Ruffing	23	186	15	6	0	3.54
SS	P. Rizzuto	515	.307	3	46	252	399	29	**109**	**5.3**	.957	S. Chandler	28	164	10	4	4	3.19
3B	R. Rolfe	561	.264	8	42	140	263	23	28	3.2	.946	A. Donald	22	159	9	5	0	3.57
RF	T. Henrich	538	.277	31	85	280	13	6	4	2.2	.980	L. Gomez	23	156	15	5	0	3.74
CF	J. DiMaggio	541	.357	30	**125**	385	16	9	5	2.9	.978	M. Breuer	26	141	9	7	2	4.09
LF	C. Keller	507	.298	33	122	328	7	7	2	2.5	.980	E. Bonham	23	127	9	6	2	2.98
C	B. Dickey	348	.284	7	71	422	45	3	11	4.5	**.994**	J. Murphy	35	77	8	3	**15**	1.98
C	B. Rosar	209	.287	1	36	246	24	1	6	4.5	.996							
UT	G. Priddy	174	.213	1	26	167	119	8	46		.973							
OF	G. Selkirk	164	.220	6	25	84	4	3	2	1.9	.967							
SS	F. Crosetti	148	.223	1	22	80	89	10	20	5.6	.944							
P	R. Ruffing	89	.303	2	22	7	21	0	3	1.2	**1.000**							

AMERICAN LEAGUE 1941, *cont.*

Team	POS	Player	AB	BA	HR	RBI	PO	A	E	DP	TC/G	FA	Pitcher	G	IP	W	L	SV	ERA
Boston	1B	J. Foxx	487	.300	19	105	1155	**112**	10	105	10.3	.992	D. Newsome	36	214	19	10	0	4.13
W-84 L-70	2B	B. Doerr	500	.282	16	93	290	389	20	85	5.3	.971	M. Harris	35	194	8	14	1	3.25
Joe Cronin	SS	J. Cronin	518	.311	16	95	225	324	24	64	4.8	.958	C. Wagner	29	187	12	8	0	3.07
	3B	J. Tabor	498	.279	16	101	123	277	**30**	24	3.4	.930	J. Dobson	27	134	12	5	0	4.49
	RF	L. Finney	497	.288	4	53	181	7	11	2	2.2	.945	L. Grove	21	134	7	7	0	4.37
	CF	D. DiMaggio	584	.283	8	58	386	16	15	2	2.9	.964	M. Ryba	40	121	7	3	6	4.46
	LF	T. Williams	456	**.406**	**37**	120	262	11	11	2	2.1	.961	J. Wilson	27	116	4	13	1	5.03
	C	F. Pytlak	336	.271	2	39	416	41	4	7	5.1	.991							
	OF	P. Fox	268	.302	0	31	123	5	3	2	2.1	.977							
	C	J. Peacock	261	.284	0	27	298	33	4	7	4.8	.988							
	SS	S. Newsome	227	.225	2	17	95	133	10	28	3.4	.958							
	OF	S. Spence	203	.232	2	28	97	6	0	2	2.0	1.000							
Chicago	1B	J. Kuhel	600	.250	12	63	**1444**	108	10	113	**10.3**	.994	T. Lee	35	300	22	11	1	**2.37**
W-77 L-77	2B	B. Knickerbocker	343	.245	7	29	204	221	13	58	5.0	.970	E. Smith	34	263	13	17	1	3.18
Jimmy Dykes	SS	L. Appling	592	.314	1	57	294	**473**	42	95	5.3	.948	J. Rigney	30	237	13	13	0	3.84
	3B	D. Lodigiani	322	.239	4	40	120	187	12	22	3.7	.962	T. Lyons	22	187	12	10	0	3.70
	RF	T. Wright	513	.322	10	97	279	8	8	3	2.2	.973	B. Dietrich	19	109	5	8	0	5.35
	CF	M. Kreevich	436	.232	0	37	302	7	2	2	2.8	.994	B. Ross	20	108	3	8	0	3.16
	LF	M. Hoag	380	.255	1	44	215	6	10	1	2.3	.957	J. Hallett	22	75	5	5	0	6.03
	C	M. Tresh	390	.251	0	33	**488**	81	11	12	5.0	.981							
	2B	D. Kolloway	280	.271	3	24	118	181	14	23	5.0	.955							
	3B	B. Kennedy	257	.206	1	29	88	153	17	12	3.6	.934							
	OF	M. Solters	251	.259	4	43	135	7	5	1	2.3	.966							
	OF	B. Chapman	190	.226	2	19	122	4	1	1	2.6	.992							
Cleveland	1B	H. Trosky	310	.294	11	51	727	54	9	77	9.3	.989	B. Feller	**44**	**343**	**25**	13	2	3.15
W-75 L-79	2B	R. Mack	501	.228	9	44	363	386	23	**109**	5.3	.970	A. Milnar	35	229	12	19	0	4.36
Roger Peckinpaugh	SS	L. Boudreau	579	.257	10	56	**296**	444	26	97	5.2	**.966**	A. Smith	29	207	12	13	0	3.83
	3B	K. Keltner	581	.269	23	84	181	**346**	16	**36**	**3.6**	**.971**	J. Bagby	33	201	9	15	2	4.04
	RF	J. Heath	585	.340	24	123	259	20	15	1	1.9	.949	C. Brown	41	74	3	3	5	3.27
	CF	R. Weatherly	363	.289	3	37	208	1	7	1	2.5	.968	J. Heving	27	71	5	2	5	2.29
	LF	G. Walker	445	.283	6	48	257	9	5	0	2.6	.982	M. Harder	15	69	5	4	1	5.24
	C	R. Hemsley	288	.240	2	24	401	42	9	8	4.7	.980							
	OF	S. Campbell	328	.250	3	35	202	6	4	0	2.7	.981							
	1B	O. Grimes	244	.238	4	24	544	31	3	53	9.3	.995							
	C	G. Desautels	189	.201	1	17	300	32	1	5	5.0	.997							
Detroit	1B	R. York	590	.259	27	111	1393	110	**21**	111	9.8	.986	B. Newsom	43	250	12	**20**	2	4.60
W-75 L-79	2B	C. Gehringer	436	.220	3	46	279	324	11	59	5.3	**.982**	H. Newhouser	33	173	9	11	0	4.79
Del Baker	SS	F. Croucher	489	.254	2	39	270	361	44	85	5.0	.935	J. Gorsica	33	171	9	11	2	4.47
	3B	P. Higgins	540	.298	11	73	153	304	26	14	3.3	.946	A. Benton	38	158	15	6	7	2.97
	RF	B. Campbell	512	.275	15	93	241	5	6	1	1.9	.976	D. Trout	37	152	9	9	2	3.74
	CF	B. McCosky	494	.324	3	55	328	6	5	2	2.8	.985	T. Bridges	25	148	9	12	0	3.41
	LF	R. Radcliff	379	.317	3	39	155	6	5	1	1.9	.970	S. Rowe	27	139	8	6	1	4.14
	C	B. Tebbetts	359	.284	2	47	461	**83**	13	11	**5.7**	.977							
	C	B. Sullivan	234	.282	3	29	339	33	9	7	6.0	.976							
	OF	P. Mullin	220	.345	5	23	117	2	7	0	2.5	.944							
	OF	T. Stainback	200	.245	2	10	107	3	6	0	1.5	.948							
St. Louis	1B	G. McQuinn	495	.297	18	80	1138	109	6	109	10.0	**.995**	E. Auker	34	216	14	15	0	5.50
W-70 L-84	2B	D. Heffner	399	.233	0	17	224	307	14	52	5.2	.974	B. Muncrief	36	214	13	9	1	3.65
Fred Haney W-15 L-29	SS	J. Berardino	469	.271	5	89	261	305	27	81	4.8	.954	D. Galehouse	30	190	9	10	0	3.64
Luke Sewell W-55 L-55	3B	H. Clift	584	.255	17	84	**195**	316	22	27	3.5	.959	B. Harris	34	187	12	14	1	5.21
	RF	C. Laabs	392	.278	15	59	217	6	4	2	2.3	.982	J. Niggeling	24	168	7	9	0	3.80
	CF	W. Judnich	546	.284	14	83	383	11	8	3	2.9	.980	G. Caster	32	104	3	7	3	5.00
	LF	R. Cullenbine	501	.317	9	98	258	12	10	3	2.3	.964							
	C	R. Ferrell	321	.252	2	23	340	51	2	11	4.0	.995							
	OF	J. Grace	362	.309	6	60	164	13	3	1	2.0	.983							
	2B	J. Lucadello	351	.279	2	31	147	185	13	36	4.9	.962							
	C	B. Swift	170	.259	0	21	180	22	3	3	3.5	.985							
Washington	1B	M. Vernon	531	.299	9	93	1186	80	10	**122**	9.7	.992	D. Leonard	34	256	18	13	0	3.45
W-70 L-84	2B	J. Bloodworth	506	.245	7	66	**380**	**436**	24	107	**6.4**	.971	S. Hudson	33	250	13	14	0	3.46
Bucky Harris	SS	C. Travis	608	.359	7	101	279	388	25	99	5.1	.964	K. Chase	33	206	6	18	0	5.08
	3B	G. Archie	379	.269	3	48	71	150	15	12	3.2	.936	S. Sundra	28	168	9	13	0	5.29
	RF	B. Lewis	569	.297	9	72	229	16	7	3	2.6	.972	R. Anderson	32	112	4	6	0	4.18
	CF	D. Cramer	**660**	.273	2	66	369	9	6	1	2.5	.984	A. Carrasquel	35	97	6	2	2	3.44
	LF	G. Case	649	.271	2	53	362	21	10	3	2.6	.975	B. Zuber	36	96	6	4	2	5.42
	C	J. Early	355	.287	10	54	385	52	**16**	**13**	4.5	.965	W. Masterson	34	78	4	3	3	5.97
	C	A. Evans	159	.277	1	19	195	24	7	6	4.4	.969							
Philadelphia	1B	D. Siebert	467	.334	5	79	1102	106	12	95	9.9	.990	P. Marchildon	30	204	10	15	0	3.57
W-64 L-90	2B	B. McCoy	517	.271	8	61	285	423	27	87	5.4	.963	J. Knott	27	194	13	11	0	4.40
Connie Mack	SS	A. Brancato	530	.234	2	49	263	395	**61**	80	5.2	.915	L. McCrabb	26	157	9	13	2	5.49
	3B	P. Suder	531	.245	4	52	175	271	20	25	3.4	.957	L. Harris	33	132	4	4	2	4.78
	RF	W. Moses	438	.301	4	35	263	12	7	5	2.6	.975	B. Beckmann	22	130	5	9	1	4.57
	CF	S. Chapman	552	.322	25	106	416	21	15	5	3.2	.967	T. Ferrick	36	119	8	10	7	3.77
	LF	B. Johnson	552	.275	22	107	287	17	3	0	2.5	.990	B. Hadley	25	102	4	6	3	5.01
	C	F. Hayes	439	.280	12	63	403	65	8	11	3.9	.983							
	OF	E. Collins	219	.242	0	12	119	3	4	1	2.5	.968							
	OF	D. Miles	170	.312	0	15	79	2	0	1	2.3	1.000							

AMERICAN LEAGUE 1941, *cont.*

BATTING AND BASE RUNNING LEADERS

Batting Average

T. Williams, BOS	.406
C. Travis, WAS	.359
J. DiMaggio, NY	.357
J. Heath, CLE	.340
D. Siebert, PHI	.334

Slugging Average

T. Williams, BOS	.735
J. DiMaggio, NY	.643
J. Heath, CLE	.586
C. Keller, NY	.580
S. Chapman, PHI	.543

Home Runs

T. Williams, BOS	37
C. Keller, NY	33
T. Henrich, NY	31
J. DiMaggio, NY	30
R. York, DET	27

Total Bases

J. DiMaggio, NY	348
J. Heath, CLE	343
T. Williams, BOS	335
C. Travis, WAS	316
S. Chapman, PHI	300

Runs Batted In

J. DiMaggio, NY	125
J. Heath, CLE	123
C. Keller, NY	122
T. Williams, BOS	120
R. York, DET	111

Stolen Bases

G. Case, WAS	33
J. Kuhel, CHI	20
J. Heath, CLE	18
M. Kreevich, CHI	17
J. Tabor, BOS	17

Hits

C. Travis, WAS	218
J. Heath, CLE	199
J. DiMaggio, NY	193
L. Appling, CHI	186

Base on Balls

T. Williams, BOS	145
R. Cullenbine, STL	121
H. Clift, STL	113
C. Keller, NY	102

Home Run Percentage

T. Williams, BOS	8.1
C. Keller, NY	6.5
T. Henrich, NY	5.8
J. DiMaggio, NY	5.5

Runs

T. Williams, BOS	135
J. DiMaggio, NY	122
D. DiMaggio, BOS	117
H. Clift, STL	108

Doubles

L. Boudreau, CLE	45
J. DiMaggio, NY	43
W. Judnich, STL	40
J. Kuhel, CHI	39
C. Travis, WAS	39

Triples

J. Heath, CLE	20
C. Travis, WAS	19
K. Keltner, CLE	13

PITCHING LEADERS

Winning Percentage

L. Gomez, NY	.750
R. Ruffing, NY	.714
A. Benton, DET	.714
T. Lee, CHI	.667
B. Feller, CLE	.658

Earned Run Average

T. Lee, CHI	2.37
C. Wagner, BOS	3.07
M. Russo, NY	3.09
B. Feller, CLE	3.15
E. Smith, CHI	3.18

Wins

B. Feller, CLE	25
T. Lee, CHI	22
D. Newsome, BOS	19
D. Leonard, WAS	18

Saves

J. Murphy, NY	15
A. Benton, DET	7
T. Ferrick, PHI	7
M. Ryba, BOS	6
J. Heving, CLE	5
C. Brown, CLE	5

Strikeouts

B. Feller, CLE	260
B. Newsom, DET	175
T. Lee, CHI	130
J. Rigney, CHI	119
M. Harris, BOS	111
E. Smith, CHI	111

Complete Games

T. Lee, CHI	30
B. Feller, CLE	28
E. Smith, CHI	21
T. Lyons, CHI	19
D. Leonard, WAS	19

Fewest Hits/9 Innings

B. Feller, CLE	7.45
T. Lee, CHI	7.73
T. Bridges, DET	7.80
A. Donald, NY	7.98

Shutouts

B. Feller, CLE	6
J. Humphries, CHI	4
S. Chandler, NY	4
D. Leonard, WAS	4

Fewest Walks/9 Innings

T. Lyons, CHI	1.78
D. Leonard, WAS	1.90
B. Muncrief, STL	2.23
R. Ruffing, NY	2.62

Most Strikeouts/9 Inn.

B. Feller, CLE	6.82
B. Newsom, DET	6.29
T. Bridges, DET	5.49
M. Harris, BOS	5.15

Innings

B. Feller, CLE	343
T. Lee, CHI	300
E. Smith, CHI	263
D. Leonard, WAS	256

Games Pitched

B. Feller, CLE	44
B. Newsom, DET	43
C. Brown, CLE	41
M. Ryba, BOS	40

							Batting						Fielding			Pitching					
	W	L	PCT	GB	R	OR	2B	3B	HR	BA	SA	SB	E	DP	FA	CG	BB	SO	ShO	SV	ERA
New York	101	53	.656		830	**631**	243	60	**151**	.269	.419	51	165	**196**	.973	75	598	589	13	**26**	3.53
Boston	84	70	.545	17	**865**	750	**304**	55	124	**.283**	**.430**	67	172	139	.972	70	611	574	8	11	4.19
Chicago	77	77	.500	24	638	649	245	47	47	.255	.343	**91**	180	145	.971	**106**	**521**	564	**14**	4	**3.52**
Cleveland	75	79	.487	26	677	668	249	**84**	103	.256	.393	63	**142**	158	**.976**	68	660	617	10	19	3.90
Detroit	75	79	.487	26	686	743	247	55	81	.263	.375	43	186	129	.969	52	645	**697**	8	16	4.18
St. Louis	70	84	.455	31	765	823	281	58	91	.266	.390	50	151	156	.975	65	549	454	7	10	4.72
Washington	70	84	.455	31	728	798	257	80	52	.272	.376	79	187	169	.969	69	603	544	8	7	4.35
Philadelphia	64	90	.416	37	713	840	240	69	85	.268	.387	27	200	150	.967	64	557	386	3	18	4.83
					5902	5902	2066	508	734	.266	.389	471	1383	1242	.971	569	4744	4425	71	111	4.15

NATIONAL LEAGUE 1942

	POS	Player	AB	BA	HR	RBI	PO	A	E	DP	TC/G	FA	Pitcher	G	IP	W	L	SV	ERA
St. Louis	1B	J. Hopp	314	.258	3	37	746	44	14	68	9.1	.983	M. Cooper	37	279	**22**	7	0	**1.78**
W-106 L-48	2B	C. Crespi	292	.243	0	35	219	190	14	42	5.1	.967	J. Beazley	43	215	21	6	3	2.13
Billy Southworth	SS	M. Marion	485	.276	0	54	296	448	31	87	5.3	.960	H. Gumbert	38	163	9	5	5	3.26
	3B	W. Kurowski	366	.254	9	42	124	194	19	19	3.2	.944	M. Lanier	34	160	13	8	2	2.98
	RF	E. Slaughter	591	.318	13	98	287	15	4	2	2.0	.987	E. White	26	128	7	5	2	2.52
	CF	T. Moore	489	.288	6	49	271	9	4	0	2.3	.986	M. Dickson	36	121	6	3	2	2.91
	LF	S. Musial	467	.315	10	72	296	6	5	0	2.3	.984	H. Krist	34	118	13	3	1	2.51
	C	W. Cooper	438	.281	7	65	519	62	**17**	6	**5.2**	.972	H. Pollet	27	109	7	5	0	2.88
	23	J. Brown	**606**	.256	1	71	296	326	24	65		.963	L. Warneke	12	82	6	4	0	3.29
	1B	R. Sanders	282	.252	5	39	626	35	6	54	8.7	.991							
	C	K. O'Dea	192	.234	5	32	247	37	6	6	5.9	.979							
	OF	H. Walker	191	.314	0	16	115	6	4	0	2.2	.968							
	OF	C. Triplett	154	.273	1	23	82	2	3	0	1.9	.966							
Brooklyn	1B	D. Camilli	524	.252	26	109	1334	85	12	123	9.5	.992	K. Higbe	38	222	16	11	0	3.25
W-104 L-50	2B	B. Herman	571	.256	2	65	**383**	402	22	**97**	5.3	.973	W. Wyatt	31	217	19	7	0	2.73
Leo Durocher	SS	P. Reese	564	.255	3	53	**337**	**482**	35	**99**	**5.7**	.959	C. Davis	32	206	15	6	2	2.36
	3B	A. Vaughan	495	.277	2	49	118	208	14	18	2.9	.959	L. French	38	148	15	4	0	1.83
	RF	D. Walker	393	.290	6	54	207	8	3	2	2.0	.986	E. Head	36	137	10	6	4	3.56
	CF	P. Reiser	480	.310	10	64	277	9	9	2	2.4	.969	J. Allen	27	118	10	6	3	3.20
	LF	J. Medwick	553	.300	4	96	287	5	3	1	2.1	.990	H. Casey	50	112	6	3	**13**	2.25
	C	M. Owen	421	.259	0	44	**595**	**66**	9	12	5.0	.987							
	OF	J. Rizzo	217	.230	4	27	124	6	3	1	1.9	.977							
	OF	A. Galan	209	.263	0	22	101	2	1	0	1.9	.990							
	3B	L. Riggs	180	.278	3	22	36	65	6	7	2.3	.944							
New York	1B	J. Mize	541	.305	26	**110**	1393	74	8	98	**10.7**	**.995**	H. Schumacher	29	216	12	13	0	3.04
W-85 L-67	2B	M. Witek	553	.260	5	48	371	**441**	18	72	5.6	**.978**	B. Carpenter	28	186	11	10	0	3.15
Mel Ott	SS	B. Jurges	464	.256	2	30	251	401	15	67	5.4	.978	B. Lohrman	26	158	13	4	0	2.56
	3B	B. Werber	370	.205	1	13	79	227	24	14	3.5	.927	C. Hubbell	24	157	11	8	0	3.95
	RF	M. Ott	549	.295	**30**	93	269	15	3	3	1.9	.990	C. Melton	23	144	11	5	1	2.63
	CF	W. Marshall	401	.257	11	59	222	13	6	4	2.3	.975	H. Feldman	31	114	7	1	0	3.16
	LF	B. Barna	331	.257	6	58	169	4	3	0	2.0	.983	B. McGee	31	104	6	3	1	2.93
	C	H. Danning	408	.279	1	34	459	55	11	7	4.5	.979	A. Adams	**61**	88	7	4	11	1.84
	3S	D. Bartell	316	.244	5	24	135	191	14	27		.959							
	OF	B. Young	287	.279	11	59	101	4	3	2	2.0	.972							
	OF	B. Maynard	190	.247	4	32	103	6	2	2	1.9	.982							
	OF	H. Leiber	147	.218	4	23	93	2	1	1	2.3	.990							

NATIONAL LEAGUE 1942, *cont.*

Team	POS	Player	AB	BA	HR	RBI	PO	A	E	DP	TC/G	FA	Pitcher	G	IP	W	L	SV	ERA
Cincinnati	1B	F. McCormick	564	.277	13	89	**1403**	101	10	**132**	10.5	.993	R. Starr	37	277	15	13	0	2.67
W-76 L-76	2B	L. Frey	523	.266	2	39	340	424	18	95	5.6	.977	B. Walters	34	254	15	14	0	2.66
Bill McKechnie	SS	E. Joost	562	.224	6	41	248	380	**45**	79	5.2	.933	J. Vander Meer	33	244	18	12	0	2.43
	3B	B. Haas	585	.239	6	54	160	273	35	**33**	3.2	.925	P. Derringer	29	209	10	11	0	3.06
	RF	M. Marshall	530	.255	7	43	245	3	6	2	2.0	.976	E. Riddle	29	158	7	11	0	3.69
	CF	G. Walker	422	.230	5	50	277	7	8	2	2.7	.973	J. Thompson	29	102	4	7	0	3.36
	LF	E. Tipton	207	.222	4	18	126	3	3	0	2.3	.977	J. Beggs	38	89	6	5	8	2.13
	C	R. Lamanno	371	.264	12	43	421	59	11	7	4.7	.978							
	OF	I. Goodman	226	.243	0	15	101	7	1	2	1.9	.991							

Team	POS	Player	AB	BA	HR	RBI	PO	A	E	DP	TC/G	FA	Pitcher	G	IP	W	L	SV	ERA
Pittsburgh	1B	E. Fletcher	506	.289	7	57	1379	**118**	12	104	10.5	.992	R. Sewell	40	248	17	15	2	3.41
W-66 L-81	2B	F. Gustine	388	.229	2	35	227	312	26	53	5.2	.954	B. Klinger	37	153	8	11	1	3.24
Frankie Frisch	SS	P. Coscarart	487	.228	3	29	203	315	26	50	5.0	.952	M. Butcher	24	151	5	8	1	2.93
	3B	B. Elliott	560	.296	9	89	**173**	**285**	**36**	22	**3.5**	.927	D. Dietz	40	134	6	9	3	3.95
	RF	J. Barrett	332	.247	0	26	202	11	6	4	2.3	.973	K. Heintzelman	27	130	8	11	0	4.57
	CF	V. DiMaggio	496	.238	15	75	383	20	9	5	3.0	.978	J. Lanning	34	119	6	8	1	3.32
	LF	J. Wasdell	409	.259	3	38	191	8	9	1	2.1	.957	L. Hamlin	23	112	4	4	0	3.94
	C	A. Lopez	289	.256	1	26	327	53	2	**14**	3.9	**.995**	H. Gornicki	25	112	5	6	2	2.57
	OF	M. Van Robays	328	.232	1	46	199	6	3	3	2.5	.986	L. Wilkie	35	107	6	7	1	4.19
	C	B. Phelps	257	.284	9	41	244	40	12	5	4.1	.959							
	UT	B. Stewart	183	.219	0	20	87	23	3	0		.973							
	SS	A. Anderson	166	.271	0	7	77	103	11	17	4.0	.942							

Team	POS	Player	AB	BA	HR	RBI	PO	A	E	DP	TC/G	FA	Pitcher	G	IP	W	L	SV	ERA
Chicago	1B	P. Cavarretta	482	.270	3	54	567	44	5	48	10.1	.992	C. Passeau	35	278	19	14	0	2.68
W-68 L-86	2B	L. Stringer	406	.236	9	41	268	343	**29**	59	5.7	.955	B. Lee	32	220	13	13	0	3.85
Jimmie Wilson	SS	L. Merullo	515	.256	2	37	299	438	42	80	5.4	.946	H. Bithorn	38	171	9	14	2	3.68
	3B	S. Hack	553	.300	6	39	154	261	15	21	3.1	**.965**	V. Olsen	32	140	6	9	1	4.49
	RF	B. Nicholson	588	.294	21	78	327	18	5	2	2.3	.986	B. Fleming	33	134	5	6	2	3.01
	CF	D. Dallessandro	264	.261	4	43	134	6	2	1	2.2	.986	L. Warneke	15	99	5	7	2	2.27
	LF	L. Novikoff	483	.300	7	64	232	11	9	2	2.1	.964	J. Schmitz	23	87	3	7	2	3.43
	C	C. McCullough	337	.282	5	31	386	61	9	10	4.7	.980							
	UT	R. Russell	302	.242	8	41	392	90	14	40		.972							
	1B	J. Foxx	205	.205	3	19	489	24	9	32	10.0	.983							
	OF	C. Gilbert	179	.184	0	7	99	6	2	2	2.3	.981							
	2S	B. Sturgeon	162	.247	0	7	112	163	4	33		.986							

Team	POS	Player	AB	BA	HR	RBI	PO	A	E	DP	TC/G	FA	Pitcher	G	IP	W	L	SV	ERA
Boston	1B	M. West	452	.254	16	56	807	47	8	66	10.1	.991	J. Tobin	37	**288**	12	**21**	0	3.97
W-59 L-89	2B	S. Sisti	407	.211	4	35	304	351	20	66	5.4	.970	A. Javery	42	261	12	16	0	3.03
Casey Stengel	SS	E. Miller	534	.243	6	47	285	450	13	78	5.2	**.983**	L. Tost	35	148	10	10	0	3.53
	3B	N. Fernandez	577	.255	6	55	123	206	31	16	3.7	.914	M. Salvo	25	131	7	8	0	3.03
	RF	P. Waner	333	.258	1	39	150	6	5	3	1.7	.969	T. Earley	27	113	6	11	1	4.71
	CF	T. Holmes	558	.278	4	41	373	16	4	4	2.8	.990	J. Sain	40	97	4	7	6	3.90
	LF	C. Ross	220	.195	5	19	123	2	1	0	2.2	.992							
	C	E. Lombardi	309	**.330**	11	46	251	41	6	3	3.5	.980							
	C	C. Kluttz	210	.267	1	31	200	29	5	5	4.1	.979							
	1B	B. Gremp	207	.217	3	19	504	33	5	45	8.7	.991							
	OF	J. Cooney	198	.207	0	7	59	2	1	0	1.1	.984							
	OF	F. Demaree	187	.225	3	24	114	4	0	1	2.4	1.000							
	23	S. Roberge	172	.215	1	12	87	127	6	19		.973							

Team	POS	Player	AB	BA	HR	RBI	PO	A	E	DP	TC/G	FA	Pitcher	G	IP	W	L	SV	ERA
Philadelphia	1B	N. Etten	459	.264	8	41	1152	83	**19**	99	9.3	.985	T. Hughes	40	253	12	18	1	3.06
W-42 L-109	2B	A. Glossop	454	.225	4	40	322	351	27	79	**5.9**	.961	R. Melton	42	209	9	20	4	3.70
Hans Lobert	SS	B. Bragan	335	.218	2	15	161	238	26	49	5.4	.939	S. Johnson	39	195	8	19	0	3.69
	3B	P. May	345	.238	0	18	109	227	13	23	3.3	.963	J. Podgajny	43	187	6	14	0	3.91
	RF	R. Northey	402	.251	5	31	206	12	11	2	2.1	.952	F. Hoerst	33	151	4	16	1	5.20
	CF	L. Waner	287	.261	0	10	170	6	6	0	2.4	.967							
	LF	D. Litwhiler	591	.271	9	56	308	9	0	0	2.1	1.000							
	C	B. Warren	225	.209	7	20	264	50	9	4	4.1	.972							
	UT	D. Murtaugh	506	.241	0	27	302	377	43	61		.940							
	OF	E. Koy	258	.244	4	26	149	4	3	1	2.0	.981							
	C	M. Livingston	239	.205	2	22	275	36	4	8	4.0	.987							
	OF	S. Benjamin	210	.224	2	8	75	7	2	1	1.9	.976							
	OP	E. Naylor	168	.196	0	14	66	11	1	0		.987							

BATTING AND BASE RUNNING LEADERS

Batting Average		**Slugging Average**		**Home Runs**	
E. Lombardi, BOS	.330	J. Mize, NY	.521	M. Ott, NY	30
E. Slaughter, STL	.318	M. Ott, NY	.497	D. Camilli, BKN	26
S. Musial, STL	.315	E. Slaughter, STL	.494	J. Mize, NY	26
P. Reiser, BKN	.310	S. Musial, STL	.490	B. Nicholson, CHI	21
J. Mize, NY	.305	E. Lombardi, BOS	.482	M. West, BOS	16

Total Bases		**Runs Batted In**		**Stolen Bases**	
E. Slaughter, STL	292	J. Mize, NY	110	P. Reiser, BKN	20
J. Mize, NY	282	D. Camilli, BKN	109	P. Reese, BKN	15
B. Nicholson, CHI	280	E. Slaughter, STL	98	N. Fernandez, BOS	15
M. Ott, NY	273	J. Medwick, BKN	96	J. Hopp, STL	14
D. Camilli, BKN	247	M. Ott, NY	93	L. Merullo, CHI	14

PITCHING LEADERS

Winning Percentage		**Earned Run Average**		**Wins**	
L. French, BKN	.789	M. Cooper, STL	1.78	M. Cooper, STL	22
J. Beazley, STL	.778	J. Beazley, STL	2.13	J. Beazley, STL	21
M. Cooper, STL	.759	C. Davis, BKN	2.36	W. Wyatt, BKN	19
W. Wyatt, BKN	.731	J. Vander Meer, CIN	2.43	C. Passeau, CHI	19
C. Davis, BKN	.714	B. Lohrman, STL, NY	2.48	J. Vander Meer, CIN	18

Saves		**Strikeouts**		**Complete Games**	
H. Casey, BKN	13	J. Vander Meer, CIN	186	J. Tobin, BOS	28
A. Adams, NY	11	M. Cooper, STL	152	C. Passeau, CHI	24
J. Beggs, CIN	8	K. Higbe, BKN	115	M. Cooper, STL	22
J. Sain, BOS	6	B. Walters, CIN	109	B. Walters, CIN	21
H. Gumbert, STL	5	R. Melton, PHI	107	J. Vander Meer, CIN	21

NATIONAL LEAGUE 1942, *cont.*

BATTING AND BASE RUNNING LEADERS

Hits
- E. Slaughter, STL 188
- B. Nicholson, CHI 173
- S. Hack, CHI 166
- J. Medwick, BKN 166
- B. Elliott, PIT 166

Base on Balls
- M. Ott, NY 109
- E. Fletcher, PIT 105
- D. Camilli, BKN 97
- S. Hack, CHI 94

Home Run Percentage
- M. Ott, NY 5.5
- D. Camilli, BKN 5.0
- J. Mize, NY 4.8
- B. Young, NY 3.8

Runs
- M. Ott, NY 118
- E. Slaughter, STL 100
- J. Mize, NY 97
- S. Hack, CHI 91

Doubles
- M. Marion, STL 38
- J. Medwick, BKN 37
- S. Hack, CHI 36
- B. Herman, BKN 34

Triples
- E. Slaughter, STL 17
- B. Nicholson, CHI 11
- S. Musial, STL 10
- D. Litwhiler, PHI 9

PITCHING LEADERS

Fewest Hits/9 Innings
- M. Cooper, STL 6.69
- J. Vander Meer, CIN 6.93
- K. Higbe, BKN 7.31
- R. Starr, CIN 7.42

Shutouts
- M. Cooper, STL 10
- C. Davis, BKN 5
- R. Sewell, PIT 5
- A. Javery, BOS 5

Fewest Walks/9 Innings
- L. Warneke, STL, CHI 1.79
- B. Lohrman, STL, NY 1.85
- C. Hubbell, NY 1.94
- C. Melton, NY 2.07

Most Strikeouts/9 Inn.
- J. Vander Meer, CIN 6.86
- M. Cooper, STL 4.91
- K. Higbe, BKN 4.67
- R. Melton, PHI 4.60

Innings
- J. Tobin, BOS 288
- M. Cooper, STL 279
- C. Passeau, CHI 278
- R. Starr, CIN 277

Games Pitched
- A. Adams, NY 61
- H. Casey, BKN 50
- J. Beazley, STL 43
- J. Podgajny, PHI 43

							Batting						Fielding			Pitching					
	W	L	PCT	GB	R	OR	2B	3B	HR	BA	SA	SB	E	DP	FA	CG	BB	SO	ShO	SV	ERA
St. Louis	106	48	.688		**755**	**482**	**282**	**69**	60	**.268**	**.379**	71	169	137	.972	70	473	**651**	**18**	15	**2.55**
Brooklyn	104	50	.675	2	742	510	263	34	62	.265	.362	**79**	**138**	150	**.977**	67	493	612	16	**24**	2.84
New York	85	67	.559	20	675	600	162	35	**109**	.254	.361	39	**138**	128	**.977**	70	493	497	12	13	3.31
Cincinnati	76	76	.500	29	527	545	198	39	66	.231	.321	42	177	158	.971	**80**	526	616	12	8	2.82
Pittsburgh	66	81	.449	36.5	585	631	173	49	54	.245	.330	41	184	129	.969	64	**435**	426	13	11	3.58
Chicago	68	86	.442	38	591	665	224	41	75	.254	.353	61	170	**169**	.973	71	525	507	10	14	3.60
Boston	59	89	.399	44	515	645	210	19	68	.240	.329	49	142	138	.976	68	518	414	9	8	3.76
Philadelphia	42	109	.278	62.5	394	706	168	37	44	.232	.306	37	194	147	.968	51	605	472	2	6	4.12
					4784	4784	1680	323	538	.249	.343	419	1312	1156	.973	541	4068	4195	92	99	3.32

AMERICAN LEAGUE 1942

New York

W-103 L-51

Joe McCarthy

POS	Player	AB	BA	HR	RBI	PO	A	E	DP	TC/G	FA	Pitcher	G	IP	W	L	SV	ERA
1B	B. Hassett	538	.284	5	48	1128	118	11	130	9.5	.991	E. Bonham	28	226	21	5	0	2.27
2B	J. Gordon	538	.322	18	103	354	442	**28**	**121**	5.6	.966	S. Chandler	24	201	16	5	0	2.38
SS	P. Rizzuto	553	.284	4	68	**324**	445	30	**114**	5.5	.962	R. Ruffing	24	194	14	7	0	3.21
3B	F. Crosetti	285	.242	4	23	70	105	9	14	3.0	.951	H. Borowy	25	178	15	4	1	2.52
RF	T. Henrich	483	.267	13	67	219	10	3	5	1.9	.987	M. Breuer	27	164	8	9	1	3.07
CF	J. DiMaggio	610	.305	21	114	409	10	8	3	2.8	.981	A. Donald	20	148	11	3	0	3.11
LF	C. Keller	544	.292	26	108	321	10	5	1	2.2	.985	L. Gomez	13	80	6	4	0	4.28
C	B. Dickey	268	.295	2	37	322	44	9	7	4.7	.976	J. Murphy	31	58	4	10	**11**	3.41
3B	R. Rolfe	265	.219	8	25	57	132	8	16	3.3	.959							
C	B. Rosar	209	.230	2	34	249	26	1	7	4.8	.996							
UT	G. Priddy	189	.280	2	28	146	114	9	26		.967							

Boston

W-93 L-59

Joe Cronin

POS	Player	AB	BA	HR	RBI	PO	A	E	DP	TC/G	FA	Pitcher	G	IP	W	L	SV	ERA
1B	T. Lupien	463	.281	3	70	1091	68	9	99	9.7	.992	T. Hughson	38	**281**	**22**	6	4	2.59
2B	B. Doerr	545	.290	15	102	376	453	21	105	**6.0**	**.975**	C. Wagner	29	205	14	11	0	3.29
SS	J. Pesky	620	.331	2	51	320	**465**	37	94	**5.6**	.955	J. Dobson	30	183	11	9	0	3.30
3B	J. Tabor	508	.252	12	75	**168**	236	**33**	24	3.2	.924	D. Newsome	24	158	8	10	0	5.01
RF	L. Finney	397	.285	3	61	199	8	5	1	2.2	.976	O. Judd	31	150	8	10	2	3.89
CF	D. DiMaggio	622	.286	14	48	439	19	6	7	3.1	.987	B. Butland	23	111	7	1	1	2.51
LF	T. Williams	522	**.356**	**36**	**137**	313	15	4	4	2.2	.988	Y. Terry	20	85	6	5	1	3.92
C	B. Conroy	250	.200	4	20	324	40	11	6	4.5	.971	M. Brown	34	60	9	3	6	3.43
C	J. Peacock	286	.266	0	25	280	44	4	8	4.0	.988							
OF	P. Fox	256	.262	3	42	111	2	4	0	1.6	.966							
31	J. Cronin	79	.304	4	24	46	26	6	7		.923							

St. Louis

W-82 L-69

Luke Sewell

POS	Player	AB	BA	HR	RBI	PO	A	E	DP	TC/G	FA	Pitcher	G	IP	W	L	SV	ERA
1B	G. McQuinn	554	.262	12	78	1384	105	13	116	**10.4**	.991	E. Auker	35	249	14	13	0	4.08
2B	D. Gutteridge	616	.255	1	50	**377**	**454**	23	94	5.9	.973	J. Niggeling	28	206	15	11	0	2.66
SS	V. Stephens	575	.294	14	92	290	415	**42**	82	5.2	.944	D. Galehouse	32	191	12	12	1	3.62
3B	H. Clift	541	.274	7	55	160	287	28	28	3.4	.941	A. Hollingsworth	33	161	10	6	4	2.96
RF	C. Laabs	520	.275	27	99	276	13	9	3	2.1	.970	B. Muncrief	24	134	6	8	0	3.89
CF	W. Judnich	457	.313	17	82	330	4	3	0	2.8	.991	S. Sundra	20	111	8	3	0	3.82
LF	G. McQuillen	339	.283	3	47	156	2	5	0	2.1	.969	G. Caster	39	80	8	2	5	2.81
C	R. Ferrell	273	.223	0	26	356	57	6	7	4.4	.986							
OF	M. Chartak	237	.249	9	43	142	10	4	3	2.4	.974							
C	F. Hayes	159	.252	2	17	175	25	6	2	4.0	.971							
OF	T. Criscola	158	.297	1	13	0	0	0	0	—	—							

Cleveland

W-75 L-79

Lou Boudreau

POS	Player	AB	BA	HR	RBI	PO	A	E	DP	TC/G	FA	Pitcher	G	IP	W	L	SV	ERA
1B	L. Fleming	548	.292	14	82	**1503**	90	12	**152**	10.3	**.993**	J. Bagby	38	271	17	9	1	2.96
2B	R. Mack	481	.225	2	45	340	434	25	105	5.6	.969	M. Harder	29	199	13	14	0	3.44
SS	L. Boudreau	506	.283	2	58	281	426	26	107	5.0	**.965**	C. Dean	27	173	8	11	1	3.81
3B	K. Keltner	624	.287	6	78	166	**353**	30	**38**	**3.6**	**.945**	A. Smith	30	168	10	15	0	3.96
RF	O. Hockett	601	.250	7	48	284	12	6	3	2.1	.980	A. Milnar	28	157	6	8	0	4.13
CF	R. Weatherly	473	.258	5	39	324	7	3	4	2.9	.991	V. Kennedy	28	108	4	8	1	4.08
LF	J. Heath	568	.278	10	76	326	12	7	3	2.4	.980	J. Heving	27	46	5	3	3	4.86
C	O. Denning	214	.210	1	19	213	36	2	6	3.2	.992							
OF	B. Mills	195	.277	1	26	142	4	4	2	2.8	.973							
C	J. Hegan	170	.194	0	11	227	32	6	7	4.0	.977							
C	G. Desautels	162	.247	0	9	180	16	5	0	3.3	.975							

AMERICAN LEAGUE 1942, *cont.*

Team	POS	Player	AB	BA	HR	RBI	PO	A	E	DP	TC/G	FA	Pitcher	G	IP	W	L	SV	ERA
Detroit	1B	R. York	577	.260	21	90	1413	**146**	19	117	10.4	.988	A. Benton	35	227	7	13	2	2.90
W-73 L-81	2B	J. Bloodworth	533	.242	13	57	334	431	22	66	5.9	.972	D. Trout	35	223	12	18	0	3.43
Del Baker	SS	B. Hitchcock	280	.211	0	29	157	199	21	39	4.7	.944	H. White	34	217	12	12	1	2.91
	3B	P. Higgins	499	.267	11	79	134	243	30	24	3.0	.926	H. Newhouser	38	184	8	14	5	2.45
	RF	B. Harris	398	.271	9	45	164	5	10	2	1.7	.944	T. Bridges	23	174	9	7	1	2.74
	CF	D. Cramer	**630**	.263	0	43	352	15	7	6	2.5	.981	V. Trucks	28	168	14	8	0	2.74
	LF	B. McCosky	600	.293	7	50	351	7	7	2	2.4	.981							
	C	B. Tebbetts	308	.247	1	27	**446**	69	**12**	10	**5.4**	.977							
	03	D. Ross	226	.274	3	30	94	30	7	4		.947							
	C	D. Parsons	188	.197	2	11	274	44	6	6	5.2	.981							
	SS	M. Franklin	154	.260	2	16	67	79	5	14	4.7	.967							
	OF	R. Radcliff	144	.250	1	20	43	1	1	1	1.9	.978							

Team	POS	Player	AB	BA	HR	RBI	PO	A	E	DP	TC/G	FA	Pitcher	G	IP	W	L	SV	ERA
Chicago	1B	J. Kuhel	413	.249	4	52	1085	70	11	94	10.4	.991	J. Humphries	28	228	12	12	0	2.68
W-66 L-82	2B	D. Kolloway	601	.273	3	60	308	345	23	80	5.8	.966	E. Smith	29	215	7	**20**	1	3.98
Jimmy Dykes	SS	L. Appling	543	.262	3	53	269	418	38	77	5.1	.948	T. Lyons	20	180	14	6	0	**2.10**
	3B	B. Kennedy	412	.231	0	38	99	207	14	17	3.3	.956	B. Dietrich	26	160	6	11	0	4.89
	RF	W. Moses	577	.270	7	49	323	14	7	3	2.4	.980	B. Ross	22	113	5	7	1	5.00
	CF	M. Hoag	412	.240	2	37	266	12	8	4	2.6	.972	J. Haynes	**40**	103	8	5	6	2.62
	LF	T. Wright	300	.333	0	47	176	6	6	1	2.3	.968	J. Wade	15	86	5	5	0	4.10
	C	M. Tresh	233	.232	0	15	258	37	7	2	4.2	.977	O. Grove	12	66	4	6	0	5.16
	C	T. Turner	182	.242	3	21	199	35	7	5	4.5	.971							
	3B	D. Lodigiani	168	.280	0	15	40	96	8	4	3.3	.944							
	OF	S. West	151	.232	0	25	112	1	2	1	2.6	.983							

Team	POS	Player	AB	BA	HR	RBI	PO	A	E	DP	TC/G	FA	Pitcher	G	IP	W	L	SV	ERA
Washington	1B	M. Vernon	621	.271	9	86	1360	95	**26**	109	9.8	.982	S. Hudson	35	239	10	17	2	4.36
W-62 L-89	2B	E. Clary	240	.275	0	16	162	181	11	37	5.1	.969	B. Newsom	30	214	11	17	0	4.93
Bucky Harris	SS	J. Sullivan	357	.235	0	42	217	235	31	51	5.3	.936	E. Wynn	30	190	10	16	0	5.12
	3B	B. Estalella	429	.277	8	65	89	134	14	4	3.0	.941	A. Carrasquel	35	152	7	7	4	3.43
	RF	B. Campbell	378	.278	5	63	188	4	9	1	2.3	.955	W. Masterson	25	143	5	9	2	3.34
	CF	S. Spence	629	.323	4	79	395	7	11	0	2.8	.973	B. Zuber	37	127	9	9	1	3.84
	LF	G. Case	513	.320	5	43	270	4	14	1	2.4	.951							
	C	J. Early	353	.204	3	46	392	**71**	9	**11**	4.8	.981							
	UT	J. Pofahl	283	.208	0	28	166	204	18	45		.954							
	UT	B. Repass	259	.239	2	23	142	178	12	21		.964							
	03	R. Cullenbine	241	.286	2	35	125	69	11	5		.946							
	C	A. Evans	223	.229	0	10	254	42	**12**	5	4.6	.961							

Team	POS	Player	AB	BA	HR	RBI	PO	A	E	DP	TC/G	FA	Pitcher	G	IP	W	L	SV	ERA
Philadelphia	1B	D. Siebert	612	.260	2	74	1345	104	16	109	9.6	.989	P. Marchildon	38	244	17	14	1	4.20
W-55 L-99	2B	B. Knickerbocker	289	.253	1	19	178	220	15	45	5.1	.964	R. Wolff	32	214	12	15	3	3.32
Connie Mack	SS	P. Suder	476	.256	4	54	141	193	16	31	5.1	.954	L. Harris	26	166	11	15	0	3.74
	3B	B. Blair	484	.279	5	66	143	234	28	21	3.2	.931	R. Christopher	30	165	4	13	1	3.82
	RF	E. Valo	459	.251	2	40	264	5	10	0	2.3	.964	D. Fowler	31	140	6	11	1	4.95
	CF	M. Kreevich	444	.255	1	30	314	4	6	0	3.0	.981	H. Besse	30	133	2	9	1	6.50
	LF	B. Johnson	550	.291	13	80	318	18	13	1	2.3	.963	J. Knott	20	95	2	10	0	5.57
	C	H. Wagner	288	.236	1	30	371	47	6	7	4.5	**.986**							
	OF	D. Miles	346	.272	0	22	177	6	3	0	2.3	.984							
	2S	C. Davis	272	.224	2	26	175	210	19	30		.953							
	C	B. Swift	192	.229	0	15	253	39	9	3	5.0	.970							

BATTING AND BASE RUNNING LEADERS

Batting Average

T. Williams, BOS	.356
J. Pesky, BOS	.331
S. Spence, WAS	.323
J. Gordon, NY	.322
G. Case, WAS	.320

Slugging Average

T. Williams, BOS	.648
C. Keller, NY	.513
W. Judnich, STL	.499
J. DiMaggio, NY	.498
C. Laabs, STL	.498

Home Runs

T. Williams, BOS	36
C. Laabs, STL	27
C. Keller, NY	26
R. York, DET	21
J. DiMaggio, NY	21

Total Bases

T. Williams, BOS	338
J. DiMaggio, NY	304
C. Keller, NY	279
D. DiMaggio, BOS	272
S. Spence, WAS	272

Runs Batted In

T. Williams, BOS	137
J. DiMaggio, NY	114
C. Keller, NY	108
J. Gordon, NY	103
B. Doerr, BOS	102

Stolen Bases

G. Case, WAS	44
M. Vernon, WAS	25
J. Kuhel, CHI	22
P. Rizzuto, NY	22
M. Hoag, CHI	17
L. Appling, CHI	17

Hits

J. Pesky, BOS	205
S. Spence, WAS	203
T. Williams, BOS	186
J. DiMaggio, NY	186

Base on Balls

T. Williams, BOS	145
C. Keller, NY	114
H. Clift, STL	106
L. Fleming, CLE	106

Home Run Percentage

T. Williams, BOS	6.9
C. Laabs, STL	5.2
C. Keller, NY	4.8
W. Judnich, STL	3.7

Runs

T. Williams, BOS	141
J. DiMaggio, NY	123
D. DiMaggio, BOS	110
H. Clift, STL	108

Doubles

D. Kolloway, CHI	40
H. Clift, STL	39
J. Heath, CLE	37
D. DiMaggio, BOS	36

Triples

S. Spence, WAS	15
J. Heath, CLE	13
J. DiMaggio, NY	13
G. McQuillen, STL	12

PITCHING LEADERS

Winning Percentage

E. Bonham, NY	.808
H. Borowy, NY	.789
T. Hughson, BOS	.786
S. Chandler, NY	.762
J. Bagby, CLE	.654

Earned Run Average

T. Lyons, CHI	2.10
E. Bonham, NY	2.27
S. Chandler, NY	2.38
H. Newhouser, DET	2.45
H. Borowy, NY	2.52

Wins

T. Hughson, BOS	22
E. Bonham, NY	21
P. Marchildon, PHI	17
J. Bagby, CLE	17
S. Chandler, NY	16

Saves

J. Murphy, NY	11
M. Brown, BOS	6
J. Haynes, CHI	6
H. Newhouser, DET	5
G. Caster, STL	5

Strikeouts

B. Newsom, WAS	113
T. Hughson, BOS	113
A. Benton, DET	110
P. Marchildon, PHI	110
J. Niggeling, STL	107

Complete Games

E. Bonham, NY	22
T. Hughson, BOS	22
T. Lyons, CHI	20
S. Hudson, WAS	19
E. Smith, CHI	18
P. Marchildon, PHI	18

Fewest Hits/9 Innings

H. Newhouser, DET	6.71
J. Niggeling, STL	7.55
J. Dobson, BOS	7.64
S. Chandler, NY	7.89

Shutouts

E. Bonham, NY	6

Fewest Walks/9 Innings

E. Bonham, NY	0.96
T. Lyons, CHI	1.30
R. Ruffing, NY	1.91
J. Bagby, CLE	2.13

Most Strikeouts/9 Inn.

H. Newhouser, DET	5.05
T. Bridges, DET	5.02
B. Newsom, WAS	4.76
J. Niggeling, STL	4.67

Innings

T. Hughson, BOS	281
J. Bagby, CLE	271
E. Auker, STL	249
P. Marchildon, PHI	244

Games Pitched

J. Haynes, CHI	40
G. Caster, STL	39

AMERICAN LEAGUE 1942, *cont.*

	W	L	PCT	GB	R	OR	Batting 2B	3B	HR	BA	SA	SB	Fielding E	DP	FA	Pitching CG	BB	SO	ShO	SV	ERA
New York	103	51	.669		**801**	**507**	223	57	**108**	.269	.394	69	**142**	**190**	**.976**	**88**	**431**	558	**18**	**17**	**2.91**
Boston	93	59	.612	9	761	594	**244**	55	103	**.276**	**.403**	68	157	156	.974	84	553	500	11	**17**	3.44
St. Louis	82	69	.543	19.5	730	637	239	**62**	98	.259	.385	37	167	143	.972	68	505	488	12	13	3.59
Cleveland	75	79	.487	28	590	659	223	58	50	.253	.345	69	163	175	.974	61	560	448	12	11	3.59
Detroit	73	81	.474	30	589	587	217	37	76	.246	.344	39	194	142	.969	65	598	**671**	12	14	3.13
Chicago	66	82	.446	34	538	609	214	36	25	.246	.318	**114**	173	144	.970	86	473	432	8	8	3.58
Washington	62	89	.411	39.5	653	817	224	49	40	.258	.341	98	222	133	.962	68	558	496	12	11	4.58
Philadelphia	55	99	.357	48	549	801	213	46	33	.249	.325	44	188	124	.969	67	639	546	5	9	4.48
					5211	5211	1797	400	533	.257	.357	538	1406	1207	.971	587	4317	4139	90	100	3.66

NATIONAL LEAGUE 1943

St. Louis

W-105 L-49

Billy Southworth

POS	Player	AB	BA	HR	RBI	PO	A	E	DP	TC/G	FA	Pitcher	G	IP	W	L	SV	ERA
1B	R. Sanders	478	.280	11	73	1302	71	7	**142**	9.8	.995	M. Cooper	37	274	**21**	8	3	2.30
2B	L. Klein	627	.287	7	62	301	356	18	99	5.4	.973	M. Lanier	32	213	15	7	3	1.90
SS	M. Marion	418	.280	1	52	232	424	20	93	5.3	.970	H. Krist	34	164	11	5	3	2.90
3B	W. Kurowski	522	.287	13	70	**166**	255	21	29	3.2	.952	H. Brecheen	29	135	9	6	4	2.26
RF	S. Musial	617	**.357**	13	81	376	15	7	4	2.6	.982	H. Gumbert	21	133	10	5	0	2.84
CF	H. Walker	564	.294	2	53	321	14	12	4	2.4	.965	H. Pollet	16	118	8	4	0	**1.75**
LF	D. Litwhiler	258	.279	7	31	139	7	0	1	2.1	1.000	M. Dickson	31	116	8	2	0	3.58
C	W. Cooper	449	.318	9	81	504	49	**14**	5	**5.1**	.975	G. Munger	32	93	9	5	2	3.95
03	D. Garms	249	.257	0	22	111	25	9	5		.938	A. Brazle	13	88	8	2	0	1.53
01	J. Hopp	241	.224	2	25	286	17	12	23		.962	E. White	14	79	5	5	0	3.78
C	K. O'Dea	203	.281	3	25	237	32	3	6	4.9	.989							

Cincinnati

W-87 L-67

Bill McKechnie

POS	Player	AB	BA	HR	RBI	PO	A	E	DP	TC/G	FA	Pitcher	G	IP	W	L	SV	ERA
1B	F. McCormick	472	.303	8	59	1156	85	6	116	10.4	.995	J. Vander Meer	36	289	15	16	0	2.87
2B	L. Frey	586	.263	2	43	399	461	13	**112**	6.1	**.985**	E. Riddle	36	260	**21**	11	3	2.63
SS	E. Miller	576	.224	2	71	**335**	543	19	**123**	5.8	**.979**	B. Walters	34	246	15	15	0	3.54
3B	S. Mesner	504	.272	0	52	132	274	**24**	29	3.3	.944	R. Starr	36	217	11	10	1	3.64
RF	M. Marshall	508	.236	4	39	240	12	5	4	2.0	.981	C. Shoun	45	147	14	5	7	3.06
CF	G. Walker	429	.245	3	54	231	8	5	3	2.3	.980	J. Beggs	39	115	7	6	6	2.34
LF	E. Tipton	493	.288	9	49	298	8	5	2	2.2	.984							
C	R. Mueller	427	.260	8	52	**579**	**100**	8	**17**	4.9	.988							
UT	B. Haas	332	.262	4	44	432	97	9	52		.983							
OF	E. Crabtree	254	.276	2	26	135	4	9	2	2.3	.939							

Brooklyn

W-81 L-72

Leo Durocher

POS	Player	AB	BA	HR	RBI	PO	A	E	DP	TC/G	FA	Pitcher	G	IP	W	L	SV	ERA
1B	D. Camilli	353	.246	6	43	853	60	7	78	9.7	.992	K. Higbe	35	185	13	10	0	3.70
2B	B. Herman	585	.330	2	100	291	322	18	69	5.4	.971	W. Wyatt	26	181	14	5	0	2.49
SS	A. Vaughan	610	.305	5	66	175	291	17	55	4.9	.965	E. Head	47	170	9	10	6	3.66
3B	F. Bordagaray	268	.302	0	19	28	26	7	0	2.4	.885	C. Davis	31	164	10	13	3	3.78
RF	D. Walker	540	.302	5	71	262	20	9	2	2.1	.969	B. Newsom	22	125	9	4	1	3.02
CF	A. Galan	495	.287	9	67	347	12	7	1	3.0	.981	R. Melton	30	119	5	8	0	3.92
LF	L. Olmo	238	.303	4	37	128	6	6	0	2.5	.957	L. Webber	54	116	2	2	**10**	3.81
C	M. Owen	365	.260	0	54	414	47	6	11	4.7	.987	M. Macon	25	77	7	5	0	5.96
OF	P. Waner	225	.311	1	26	116	4	5	1	2.2	.960							
C	B. Bragan	220	.264	2	24	253	34	8	6	5.2	.973							
UT	A. Glossop	217	.171	3	21	102	161	24	24		.916							
1B	H. Schultz	182	.269	1	34	386	33	6	27	9.4	.986							
OF	J. Medwick	173	.272	0	25	65	2	2	0	1.6	.971							

Pittsburgh

W-80 L-74

Frankie Frisch

POS	Player	AB	BA	HR	RBI	PO	A	E	DP	TC/G	FA	Pitcher	G	IP	W	L	SV	ERA
1B	E. Fletcher	544	.283	9	70	**1541**	**108**	6	141	**10.7**	**.996**	R. Sewell	35	265	**21**	9	3	2.54
2B	P. Coscarart	491	.242	0	48	186	263	18	54	5.5	.961	B. Klinger	33	195	11	8	0	2.72
SS	F. Gustine	414	.290	0	43	135	230	24	41	5.7	.938	M. Butcher	33	194	10	8	1	2.60
3B	B. Elliott	581	.315	7	101	149	**294**	**24**	**34**	3.1	.949	W. Hebert	34	184	10	11	0	2.98
RF	J. Barrett	290	.231	1	32	165	6	2	0	1.7	.988	H. Gornicki	42	147	9	13	4	3.98
CF	V. DiMaggio	580	.248	15	88	457	16	7	3	3.1	.985	X. Rescigno	37	133	6	9	2	3.05
LF	J. Russell	533	.259	4	44	285	16	3	3	2.3	.990							
C	A. Lopez	372	.263	1	39	378	66	4	9	3.9	**.991**							
OF	M. Van Robays	236	.288	1	35	120	5	8	1	2.2	.940							
OF	T. O'Brien	232	.310	2	26	76	4	3	0	1.7	.964							
C	B. Baker	172	.273	1	26	157	29	4	3	3.4	.979							
2B	A. Rubeling	168	.262	0	9	87	138	6	27	5.3	.974							
SS	H. Geary	166	.151	1	13	92	127	10	25	5.0	.956							

Chicago

W-74 L-79

Jimmie Wilson

POS	Player	AB	BA	HR	RBI	PO	A	E	DP	TC/G	FA	Pitcher	G	IP	W	L	SV	ERA
1B	P. Cavarretta	530	.291	8	73	1290	67	**18**	103	10.3	.987	C. Passeau	35	257	15	12	1	2.91
2B	E. Stanky	510	.245	0	47	362	416	27	78	**6.1**	.966	H. Bithorn	39	250	18	12	2	2.60
SS	L. Merullo	453	.254	1	25	218	396	39	68	5.2	.940	P. Derringer	32	174	10	14	3	3.57
3B	S. Hack	533	.289	3	35	149	264	17	11	3.2	.960	H. Wyse	38	156	9	7	5	2.94
RF	B. Nicholson	608	.309	**29**	**128**	340	16	8	2	2.4	.978	E. Hanyzewski	33	130	8	7	0	2.56
CF	P. Lowrey	480	.292	1	63	315	13	6	4	3.0	.982	B. Lee	13	78	3	7	0	3.56
LF	I. Goodman	225	.320	3	45	120	2	4	1	2.1	.968							
C	C. McCullough	266	.237	2	23	271	25	7	2	3.7	.977							
OF	L. Novikoff	233	.279	0	28	96	2	2	1	1.6	.980							
OF	D. Dallessandro	176	.222	1	31	87	2	3	0	2.0	.967							

NATIONAL LEAGUE 1943, *cont.*

Team	POS	Player	AB	BA	HR	RBI	PO	A	E	DP	TC/G	FA	Pitcher	G	IP	W	L	SV	ERA
Boston	1B	J. McCarthy	313	.304	2	33	839	53	4	51	11.5	.996	A. Javery	41	**303**	17	16	0	3.21
	2B	C. Ryan	457	.212	1	24	224	306	21	41	5.5	.962	N. Andrews	36	284	14	**20**	0	2.57
W-68 L-85	SS	W. Wietelmann	534	.215	0	39	307	**581**	**40**	91	**6.1**	.957	R. Barrett	38	255	12	18	0	3.18
	3B	E. Joost	421	.185	2	20	104	171	16	15	4.3	.945	J. Tobin	33	250	14	14	0	2.66
Bob Coleman	RF	C. Workman	615	.249	10	67	310	22	4	7	2.3	.988	M. Salvo	21	99	5	7	0	3.47
W-21 L-25	CF	T. Holmes	**629**	.270	5	41	408	18	3	3	2.8	.993							
	LF	B. Nieman	335	.251	7	46	195	12	8	1	2.3	.963							
Casey Stengel	C	P. Masi	238	.273	2	28	192	40	2	1	3.2	.991							
W-47 L-60	OF	C. Ross	285	.218	7	32	165	8	4	1	2.3	.977							
	1B	K. Farrell	280	.268	0	21	740	50	3	61	11.5	.996							
	C	C. Kluttz	207	.246	0	20	176	43	6	5	4.1	.973							
Philadelphia	1B	J. Wasdell	522	.261	4	67	749	56	10	62	9.9	.988	A. Gerheauser	38	215	10	19	0	3.60
	2B	D. Murtaugh	451	.273	1	35	321	345	18	76	6.1	.974	T. Kraus	34	200	9	15	2	3.16
W-64 L-90	SS	G. Stewart	336	.211	2	24	128	232	20	41	4.9	.947	S. Rowe	27	199	14	8	1	2.94
	3B	P. May	415	.282	1	48	142	280	16	20	**3.3**	**.963**	D. Barrett	23	169	10	9	1	2.39
Bucky Harris	RF	R. Northey	586	.278	16	68	292	19	7	6	2.2	.978	S. Johnson	21	113	8	3	2	3.27
W-38 L-52	CF	B. Adams	418	.256	4	38	298	6	5	8	2.9	.984	C. Fuchs	17	78	2	7	1	4.29
	LF	C. Triplett	360	.272	14	52	184	11	6	0	2.2	.970							
Freddie Fitzsimmons	C	M. Livingston	265	.249	3	18	268	49	4	5	3.8	.988*							
W-26 L-38	UT	B. Dahlgren	508	.287	5	56	800	151	24	81		.975							
	2B	R. Hamrick	160	.200	0	9	67	78	6	9	4.9	.960							
	SS	C. Brewster	159	.220	0	12	73	110	20	18	4.4	.901							
New York	1B	J. Orengo	266	.218	6	29	730	61	6	49	9.7	.992	C. Melton	34	186	9	13	0	3.19
	2B	M. Witek	622	.314	6	55	**401**	**505**	**31**	90	6.1	.967	J. Wittig	40	164	5	15	4	4.23
W-55 L-98	SS	B. Jurges	481	.229	4	29	209	303	24	44	5.4	.955	V. Mungo	45	154	3	7	2	3.91
	3B	D. Bartell	337	.270	5	28	62	131	4	9	3.6	.980	A. Adams	**70**	140	11	7	9	2.82
Mel Ott	RF	M. Ott	380	.234	18	47	219	12	6	1	2.1	.975	R. Fischer	22	131	5	10	1	4.61
	CF	J. Rucker	505	.273	2	46	300	9	10	3	2.7	.969	K. Chase	21	129	4	12	0	4.11
	LF	J. Medwick	324	.281	5	45	130	9	5	2	1.9	.965	H. Feldman	31	105	4	5	0	4.30
	C	G. Mancuso	252	.198	2	20	336	40	10	1	5.0	.974	B. Lohrman	17	80	5	6	1	5.15
	UT	S. Gordon	474	.251	9	63	551	148	17	59		.976							
	OF	B. Maynard	393	.206	9	32	157	10	2	0	2.3	.988							
	C	E. Lombardi	295	.305	10	51	296	36	10	8	4.7	.971							

BATTING AND BASE RUNNING LEADERS

Batting Average

S. Musial, STL	.357
B. Herman, BKN	.330
W. Cooper, STL	.318
B. Elliott, PIT	.315
M. Witek, NY	.314

Slugging Average

S. Musial, STL	.562
B. Nicholson, CHI	.531
W. Cooper, STL	.463
B. Elliott, PIT	.444
C. Triplett, STL, PHI	.439

Home Runs

B. Nicholson, CHI	29
M. Ott, NY	18
R. Northey, PHI	16
C. Triplett, STL, PHI	15
V. DiMaggio, PIT	15

Total Bases

S. Musial, STL	347
B. Nicholson, CHI	323
B. Elliott, PIT	258
L. Klein, STL	257
R. Northey, PHI	252
A. Vaughan, BKN	252

Runs Batted In

B. Nicholson, CHI	128
B. Elliott, PIT	101
B. Herman, BKN	100
V. DiMaggio, PIT	88
W. Cooper, STL	81
S. Musial, STL	81

Stolen Bases

A. Vaughan, BKN	20
P. Lowrey, CHI	13
F. Gustine, PIT	12
J. Russell, PIT	12
C. Workman, BOS	12

Hits

S. Musial, STL	220
M. Witek, NY	195
B. Herman, BKN	193
B. Nicholson, CHI	188

Base on Balls

A. Galan, BKN	103
M. Ott, NY	95
E. Fletcher, PIT	95
E. Stanky, CHI	92

Home Run Percentage

B. Nicholson, CHI	4.8
M. Ott, NY	4.7
C. Triplett, STL, PHI	3.9
E. Lombardi, NY	3.4

Runs

A. Vaughan, BKN	112
S. Musial, STL	108
B. Nicholson, CHI	95
P. Cavarretta, CHI	93

Doubles

S. Musial, STL	48
V. DiMaggio, PIT	41
B. Herman, BKN	41
A. Vaughan, BKN	39

Triples

S. Musial, STL	20
L. Klein, STL	14
P. Lowrey, CHI	12
B. Elliott, PIT	12

PITCHING LEADERS

Winning Percentage

M. Cooper, STL	.724
R. Sewell, PIT	.700
M. Lanier, STL	.682
E. Riddle, CIN	.656
H. Bithorn, CHI	.600

Earned Run Average

H. Pollet, STL	1.75
M. Lanier, STL	1.90
M. Cooper, STL	2.30
W. Wyatt, BKN	2.49
R. Sewell, PIT	2.54

Wins

E. Riddle, CIN	21
R. Sewell, PIT	21
M. Cooper, STL	21
H. Bithorn, CHI	18
A. Javery, BOS	17

Saves

L. Webber, BKN	10
A. Adams, NY	9
C. Shoun, CIN	7
E. Head, BKN	6
J. Beggs, CIN	6

Strikeouts

J. Vander Meer, CIN	174
M. Cooper, STL	141
A. Javery, BOS	134
M. Lanier, STL	123
K. Higbe, BKN	108

Complete Games

R. Sewell, PIT	25
J. Tobin, BOS	24
M. Cooper, STL	24
N. Andrews, BOS	23
B. Walters, CIN	21
J. Vander Meer, CIN	21

Fewest Hits/9 Innings

H. Pollet, STL	6.31
W. Wyatt, BKN	6.92
J. Vander Meer, CIN	7.10
M. Cooper, STL	7.49

Shutouts

H. Bithorn, CHI	7
M. Cooper, STL	6

Fewest Walks/9 Innings

S. Rowe, PHI	1.31
P. Derringer, CHI	2.02
W. Wyatt, BKN	2.14
W. Hebert, PIT	2.20

Most Strikeouts/9 Inn.

J. Vander Meer, CIN	5.42
M. Lanier, STL	5.19
H. Pollet, STL	4.64
M. Cooper, STL	4.63

Innings

A. Javery, BOS	303
J. Vander Meer, CIN	289
N. Andrews, BOS	284
M. Cooper, STL	274

Games Pitched

A. Adams, NY	70
L. Webber, BKN	54
E. Head, BKN	47
C. Shoun, CIN	45
V. Mungo, NY	45

							Batting						Fielding			Pitching					
	W	L	PCT	GB	R	OR	2B	3B	HR	BA	SA	SB	E	DP	FA	CG	BB	SO	ShO	SV	ERA
St. Louis	105	49	.682		679	**475**	259	72	70	**.279**	**.391**	40	151	183	.976	**94**	477	**639**	**21**	15	**2.57**
Cincinnati	87	67	.565	18	608	543	229	47	43	.256	.340	49	**125**	**193**	**.980**	78	581	498	18	17	3.13
Brooklyn	81	72	.529	23.5	**716**	674	**263**	35	39	.272	.357	58	168	137	.972	50	637	588	12	**22**	3.88
Pittsburgh	80	74	.519	25	669	605	240	**73**	42	.262	.357	**64**	170	159	.973	74	421	396	11	12	3.06
Chicago	74	79	.484	30.5	632	600	207	56	52	.261	.351	53	168	138	.973	67	**394**	513	12	14	3.24
Boston	68	85	.444	36.5	465	612	202	36	39	.233	.309	56	176	139	.972	87	440	409	13	4	3.25
Philadelphia	64	90	.416	41	571	676	186	36	66	.249	.335	29	189	143	.969	66	456	431	11	14	3.79
New York	55	98	.359	49.5	558	713	153	33	**81**	.247	.335	35	166	140	.973	35	626	588	6	19	4.08
					4898	4898	1739	388	432	.257	.347	384	1313	1232	.974	551	4032	4062	104	117	3.37

AMERICAN LEAGUE 1943

New York

W-98 L-56

Joe McCarthy

POS	Player	AB	BA	HR	RBI	PO	A	E	DP	TC/G	FA	Pitcher	G	IP	W	L	SV	ERA
1B	N. Etten	583	.271	14	107	1410	79	**17**	148	9.8	.989	S. Chandler	30	253	**20**	4	0	**1.64**
2B	J. Gordon	543	.249	17	69	407	**490**	**29**	114	**6.1**	.969	E. Bonham	28	226	15	8	1	2.27
SS	F. Crosetti	348	.233	2	20	194	260	26	58	5.3	.946	B. Wensloff	29	223	13	11	1	2.54
3B	B. Johnson	592	.280	5	94	**183**	**326**	18	**32**	3.4	.966	H. Borowy	29	217	14	9	0	2.82
RF	B. Metheny	360	.261	9	36	156	1	6	0	1.8	.963	A. Donald	22	119	6	4	0	4.60
CF	J. Lindell	441	.245	4	51	269	11	10	1	2.4	.966	B. Zuber	20	118	8	4	1	3.89
LF	C. Keller	512	.271	31	86	338	8	2	0	2.5	.994	M. Russo	24	102	5	10	1	3.72
C	B. Dickey	242	.351	4	33	322	37	2	5	5.1	.994	J. Murphy	37	68	12	4	8	2.51
OF	R. Weatherly	280	.264	7	28	174	2	3	0	2.6	.983							
SS	S. Stirnweiss	274	.219	1	25	110	192	20	50	4.7	.938							
OF	T. Stainback	231	.260	0	10	141	3	1	2	2.4	.993							
C	K. Sears	187	.278	2	22	233	31	7	5	5.4	.974							
C	R. Hemsley	180	.239	2	24	234	31	5	3	5.2	.981							

Washington

W-84 L-69

Ossie Bluege

POS	Player	AB	BA	HR	RBI	PO	A	E	DP	TC/G	FA	Pitcher	G	IP	W	L	SV	ERA
1B	M. Vernon	553	.268	7	70	1351	75	14	125	10.1	.990	E. Wynn	37	257	18	12	0	2.91
2B	G. Priddy	560	.271	4	62	364	411	23	105	6.0	.971	D. Leonard	31	220	11	13	1	3.28
SS	J. Sullivan	456	.208	1	55	276	445	**41**	89	**5.7**	.946	M. Candini	28	166	11	7	1	2.49
3B	E. Clary	254	.256	0	19	86	119	12	6	3.2	.945	M. Haefner	36	165	11	5	6	2.29
RF	G. Case	613	.294	1	52	318	8	5	2	2.4	.985	A. Carrasquel	39	144	11	7	5	3.68
CF	S. Spence	570	.267	12	88	396	12	7	1	2.8	.983	J. Mertz	33	117	5	7	3	4.63
LF	B. Johnson	438	.265	7	63	212	11	1	1	2.5	.996	R. Scarborough	24	86	4	4	3	2.83
C	J. Early	423	.258	5	60	443	83	**11**	10	4.4	.980	E. Pyle	18	73	4	8	1	4.09
OF	G. Moore	254	.268	2	39	125	5	2	0	2.3	.985							
C	T. Giuliani	133	.226	0	20	154	24	7	1	3.8	.962							
OF	J. Powell	132	.265	0	20	83	4	2	0	2.7	.978							

Cleveland

W-82 L-71

Lou Boudreau

POS	Player	AB	BA	HR	RBI	PO	A	E	DP	TC/G	FA	Pitcher	G	IP	W	L	SV	ERA
1B	M. Rocco	405	.240	5	46	1012	61	5	111	10.0	**.995**	J. Bagby	36	**273**	17	14	1	3.10
2B	R. Mack	545	.220	7	62	381	444	28	123	5.6	.967	A. Smith	29	208	17	7	1	2.55
SS	L. Boudreau	539	.286	3	67	**328**	488	25	**122**	5.5	**.970**	A. Reynolds	34	199	11	12	3	2.99
3B	K. Keltner	427	.260	4	39	113	228	11	24	3.3	.969	V. Kennedy	28	147	10	7	0	2.45
RF	R. Cullenbine	488	.289	8	56	245	14	5	6	2.2	.981	M. Harder	19	135	8	7	0	3.06
CF	O. Hockett	601	.276	2	51	347	13	15	3	2.7	.960	J. Salveson	23	86	5	3	3	3.35
LF	J. Heath	424	.274	18	79	264	4	9	1	2.5	.968	C. Dean	17	76	5	5	0	4.50
C	B. Rosar	382	.283	1	41	480	**91**	10	11	5.1	.983	J. Heving	30	72	1	1	9	2.75
OF	H. Edwards	297	.276	3	28	173	4	3	0	2.4	.983	M. Naymick	29	63	4	4	2	2.30
UT	R. Peters	215	.219	1	19	66	98	11	17		.937							
C	G. Desautels	185	.205	0	19	251	28	5	4	4.3	.982							

Chicago

W-82 L-72

Jimmy Dykes

POS	Player	AB	BA	HR	RBI	PO	A	E	DP	TC/G	FA	Pitcher	G	IP	W	L	SV	ERA
1B	J. Kuhel	531	.213	5	46	1471	106	8	143	10.4	.995	O. Grove	32	216	15	9	2	2.75
2B	D. Kolloway	348	.216	1	33	246	240	16	71	5.9	.968	J. Humphries	28	188	11	11	0	3.30
SS	L. Appling	585	**.328**	3	80	300	**500**	36	115	5.4	.957	E. Smith	25	188	11	11	0	3.69
3B	R. Hodgin	407	.314	1	50	34	120	9	7	2.9	.945	B. Dietrich	26	187	12	10	0	2.80
RF	W. Moses	599	.245	3	48	370	12	8	2	2.6	.979	B. Ross	21	149	11	7	0	3.19
CF	T. Tucker	528	.235	3	39	399	14	5	1	3.2	.988	T. Lee	19	127	5	9	0	4.18
LF	G. Curtright	488	.291	3	48	301	7	9	1	2.5	.972	J. Haynes	35	109	7	2	3	2.96
C	M. Tresh	279	.215	0	20	321	62	7	4	4.6	.982	G. Maltzberger	37	99	7	4	**14**	2.46
2B	S. Webb	213	.235	0	22	118	169	14	35	5.6	.953	J. Wade	21	84	3	7	0	3.01
3B	J. Grant	197	.259	4	22	43	115	19	11	3.5	.893							
C	T. Turner	154	.240	2	11	186	34	5	5	4.6	.978							

Detroit

W-78 L-76

Steve O'Neill

POS	Player	AB	BA	HR	RBI	PO	A	E	DP	TC/G	FA	Pitcher	G	IP	W	L	SV	ERA
1B	R. York	571	.271	**34**	**118**	1349	**149**	15	105	9.8	.990	D. Trout	44	247	**20**	12	6	2.48
2B	J. Bloodworth	474	.241	6	52	349	393	21	74	5.9	.972	V. Trucks	33	203	16	10	2	2.84
SS	J. Hoover	575	.243	4	38	301	393	**41**	84	5.1	.944	H. Newhouser	37	196	8	17	1	3.04
3B	P. Higgins	523	.277	10	84	156	253	**26**	22	3.2	.940	T. Bridges	25	192	12	7	0	2.39
RF	B. Harris	354	.254	6	32	192	6	8	2	2.1	.961	H. White	32	178	7	12	2	3.39
CF	D. Cramer	606	.300	1	43	346	9	4	3	2.6	.989	S. Overmire	29	147	7	6	1	3.18
LF	D. Wakefield	**633**	.316	7	79	314	11	14	1	2.2	.959	J. Gorsica	35	96	4	5	5	3.36
C	P. Richards	313	.220	5	33	**537**	86	9	**12**	**6.3**	**.986**							
UT	D. Ross	247	.267	0	18	106	65	9	10		.950							
23	J. Wood	164	.323	1	17	70	64	12	6		.918							

St. Louis

W-72 L-80

Luke Sewell

POS	Player	AB	BA	HR	RBI	PO	A	E	DP	TC/G	FA	Pitcher	G	IP	W	L	SV	ERA
1B	G. McQuinn	449	.243	12	74	1072	86	9	88	9.6	.992	D. Galehouse	31	224	11	11	1	2.77
2B	D. Gutteridge	538	.273	1	36	328	331	**29**	64	5.2	.958	S. Sundra	32	208	15	11	0	3.25
SS	V. Stephens	512	.289	22	91	220	339	34	51	4.8	.943	B. Muncrief	35	205	13	12	1	2.81
3B	H. Clift	379	.232	3	25	126	252	20	20	3.8*	.950	N. Potter	33	168	10	5	1	2.78
RF	M. Chartak	344	.256	10	37	160	4	5	2	2.2	.970	A. Hollingsworth	35	154	6	13	3	4.21
CF	M. Byrnes	429	.280	4	50	289	13	1	3	2.7	.997	J. Niggeling	20	150	6	8	0	3.17
LF	C. Laabs	580	.250	17	85	346	16	9	4	2.5	.976	G. Caster	35	76	6	8	8	2.12
C	F. Hayes	250	.188	5	30	301	40	6	8	4.6	.983							
UT	M. Christman	336	.271	2	35	279	172	3	41		.993							
OF	A. Zarilla	228	.254	2	17	123	5	5	2	2.2	.962							
C	R. Ferrell	209	.239	0	20	327	52	5	7	5.5	.987							
OF	M. Kreevich	161	.255	0	10	146	5	1	1	3.0	.993							

Boston

W-68 L-84

Joe Cronin

POS	Player	AB	BA	HR	RBI	PO	A	E	DP	TC/G	FA	Pitcher	G	IP	W	L	SV	ERA
1B	T. Lupien	608	.255	4	47	**1487**	118	12	**149**	**10.6**	.993	T. Hughson	35	266	12	15	2	2.64
2B	B. Doerr	604	.270	16	75	**415**	**490**	9	**132**	5.9	**.990**	J. Dobson	25	164	7	11	0	3.12
SS	S. Newsome	449	.265	1	22	222	310	21	69	5.6	.962	Y. Terry	30	164	7	9	1	3.52
3B	J. Tabor	537	.242	13	85	135	261	**26**	**32**	3.2	.938	O. Judd	23	155	11	6	0	2.90
RF	P. Fox	489	.288	2	44	261	10	11	2	2.3	.961	D. Newsome	25	154	8	13	0	4.49
CF	C. Metkovich	321	.246	5	27	183	6	9	3	2.6	.955	M. Ryba	40	144	7	5	2	3.26
LF	L. Culberson	312	.272	3	34	211	10	5	2	2.9	.978	P. Woods	23	101	5	6	1	4.92
C	R. Partee	299	.281	0	31	349	57	7	11	4.5	.983	M. Brown	**49**	93	6	6	9	2.12
SS	E. Lake	216	.199	3	16	128	195	13	43	5.3	.961							
OF	J. Lazor	208	.226	0	13	135	7	3	0	2.3	.979							
PH	J. Cronin	77	.312	5	29	12	18	1	1	3.1	.968							

AMERICAN LEAGUE 1943, *cont.*

Philadelphia

W-49 L-105

Connie Mack

POS	Player	AB	BA	HR	RBI	PO	A	E	DP	TC/G	FA
1B	D. Siebert	558	.251	1	72	1332	111	15	117	10.1	.990
2B	P. Suder	475	.221	3	41	231	269	15	58	5.4	.971
SS	I. Hall	544	.256	0	54	298	435	40	91	5.2	.948
3B	E. Mayo	471	.219	0	28	176	223	10	18	3.3	**.976**
RF	J. Welaj	281	.242	0	15	187	3	8	0	2.8	.960
CF	J. White	500	.248	1	30	335	8	12	2	2.7	.966
LF	B. Estalella	367	.259	11	63	225	5	6	1	2.4	.975
C	H. Wagner	289	.239	1	26	340	56	8	3	4.1	.980
OF	E. Valo	249	.221	3	18	134	4	2	0	2.2	.986
C	B. Swift	224	.192	1	11	278	53	8	9	4.4	.976
2B	D. Heffner	178	.208	0	8	98	127	5	27	4.9	.978
OF	J. Tyack	155	.258	0	23	82	4	2	0	2.3	.977

Pitcher	G	IP	W	L	SV	ERA
J. Flores	31	231	12	14	0	3.11
R. Wolff	41	221	10	15	6	3.54
L. Harris	32	216	7	**21**	1	4.20
D. Black	33	208	6	16	1	4.20
O. Arntzen	32	164	4	13	0	4.22
R. Christopher	24	133	5	8	2	3.45
E. Fagan	18	37	2	6	3	6.27

BATTING AND BASE RUNNING LEADERS

Batting Average
L. Appling, CHI .328
D. Wakefield, DET .316
R. Hodgin, CHI .314
D. Cramer, DET .300
G. Case, WAS .294

Slugging Average
R. York, DET .527
C. Keller, NY .525
V. Stephens, STL .482
J. Heath, CLE .481
D. Wakefield, DET .434

Home Runs
R. York, DET 34
C. Keller, NY 31
V. Stephens, STL 22
J. Heath, CLE 18
J. Gordon, NY 17
C. Laabs, STL 17

Total Bases
R. York, DET 301
D. Wakefield, DET 275
C. Keller, NY 269
B. Doerr, BOS 249
V. Stephens, STL 247

Runs Batted In
R. York, DET 118
N. Etten, NY 107
B. Johnson, NY 94
V. Stephens, STL 91
S. Spence, WAS 88

Stolen Bases
G. Case, WAS 61
W. Moses, CHI 56
T. Tucker, CHI 29
L. Appling, CHI 27
M. Vernon, WAS 24

Hits
D. Wakefield, DET 200
L. Appling, CHI 192
D. Cramer, DET 182
G. Case, WAS 180

Base on Balls
C. Keller, NY 106
J. Gordon, NY 98
R. Cullenbine, CLE 96
L. Boudreau, CLE 90
L. Appling, CHI 90

Home Run Percentage
C. Keller, NY 6.1
R. York, DET 6.0
V. Stephens, STL 4.3
J. Heath, CLE 4.2

Runs
G. Case, WAS 102
C. Keller, NY 97
D. Wakefield, DET 91
R. York, DET 90

Doubles
D. Wakefield, DET 38
G. Case, WAS 36
D. Gutteridge, STL 35
N. Etten, NY 35

Triples
J. Lindell, NY 12
W. Moses, CHI 12
C. Keller, NY 11
R. York, DET 11

PITCHING LEADERS

Winning Percentage
S. Chandler, NY .833
A. Smith, CLE .708
E. Bonham, NY .652
D. Trout, DET .625
O. Grove, CHI .625

Earned Run Average
S. Chandler, NY 1.64
E. Bonham, NY 2.27
T. Bridges, DET 2.39
D. Trout, DET 2.48
B. Wensloff, NY 2.54

Wins
D. Trout, DET 20
S. Chandler, NY 20
E. Wynn, WAS 18
A. Smith, CLE 17
J. Bagby, CLE 17

Saves
G. Maltzberger, CHI 14
J. Heving, CLE 9
M. Brown, BOS 9
G. Caster, STL 8
J. Murphy, NY 8

Strikeouts
A. Reynolds, CLE 151
H. Newhouser, DET 144
S. Chandler, NY 134
T. Bridges, DET 124
V. Trucks, DET 118

Complete Games
S. Chandler, NY 20
T. Hughson, BOS 20
O. Grove, CHI 18
B. Wensloff, NY 18
D. Trout, DET 18

Fewest Hits/9 Innings
A. Reynolds, CLE 6.34
J. Niggeling, STL, WAS 6.66
S. Chandler, NY 7.01
B. Wensloff, NY 7.21

Shutouts
S. Chandler, NY 5
D. Trout, DET 5
E. Bonham, NY 4
T. Hughson, BOS 4

Fewest Walks/9 Innings
D. Leonard, WAS 1.88
S. Chandler, NY 1.92
E. Bonham, NY 2.07
B. Muncrief, STL 2.11

Most Strikeouts/9 Inn.
A. Reynolds, CLE 6.84
H. Newhouser, DET 6.62
T. Bridges, DET 5.82
V. Trucks, DET 5.24

Innings
J. Bagby, CLE 273
T. Hughson, BOS 266
E. Wynn, WAS 257
S. Chandler, NY 253

Games Pitched
M. Brown, BOS 49
D. Trout, DET 44
R. Wolff, PHI 41
M. Ryba, BOS 40

							Batting						Fielding			Pitching					
	W	L	PCT	GB	R	OR	2B	3B	HR	BA	SA	SB	E	DP	FA	CG	BB	SO	ShO	SV	ERA
New York	98	56	.636		**669**	**542**	218	**59**	**100**	.256	**.376**	46	160	166	.974	**83**	489	653	14	13	**2.93**
Washington	84	69	.549	13.5	666	595	245	50	47	.254	.347	142	179	145	.971	61	540	495	16	**21**	3.18
Cleveland	82	71	.536	15.5	600	577	**246**	45	55	.255	.350	47	157	**183**	.975	64	606	585	14	20	3.15
Chicago	82	72	.532	16	573	594	193	46	33	.247	.320	**173**	166	167	.973	70	501	476	12	19	3.20
Detroit	78	76	.506	20	632	560	200	47	77	**.261**	.359	40	177	130	.971	67	549	**706**	**18**	20	3.00
St. Louis	72	80	.474	25	596	604	229	36	78	.245	.349	37	**152**	127	.975	64	**488**	572	10	14	3.41
Boston	68	84	.447	29	563	607	223	42	57	.244	.332	86	153	179	**.976**	62	615	513	13	16	3.45
Philadelphia	49	105	.318	49	497	717	174	44	26	.232	.297	55	162	148	.973	73	536	503	5	13	4.05
					4796	4796	1728	369	473	.249	.341	626	1306	1245	.974	544	4324	4503	102	136	3.30

NATIONAL LEAGUE 1944

St. Louis

W-105 L-49

Billy Southworth

POS	Player	AB	BA	HR	RBI	PO	A	E	DP	TC/G	FA
1B	R. Sanders	601	.295	12	102	1370	64	8	**142**	9.5	**.994**
2B	E. Verban	498	.257	0	43	319	380	23	**105**	4.9	.968
SS	M. Marion	506	.267	6	63	268	461	21	90	5.2	**.972**
3B	W. Kurowski	555	.270	20	87	**188**	281	17	20	3.3	**.965**
RF	S. Musial	568	.347	12	94	353	16	5	2	2.6	.987
CF	J. Hopp	527	.336	11	72	316	2	1	1	2.4	.997
LF	D. Litwhiler	492	.264	15	82	294	6	8	1	2.3	.974
C	W. Cooper	397	.317	13	72	442	40	10	7	**5.1**	.980
C	K. O'Dea	265	.249	6	37	326	34	2	4	5.2	.994
OF	A. Bergamo	192	.286	2	19	83	0	1	0	1.7	.988

Pitcher	G	IP	W	L	SV	ERA
M. Cooper	34	252	22	7	1	2.46
M. Lanier	33	224	17	12	0	2.65
T. Wilks	36	207	17	4	0	2.65
H. Brecheen	30	189	16	5	0	2.85
A. Jurisich	30	130	7	9	1	3.39
G. Munger	21	121	11	3	2	1.34
F. Schmidt	37	114	7	3	5	3.15

NATIONAL LEAGUE 1944, *cont.*

Team	POS	Player	AB	BA	HR	RBI	PO	A	E	DP	TC/G	FA	Pitcher	G	IP	W	L	SV	ERA
Pittsburgh	1B	B. Dahlgren	599	.289	12	101	1440	128	**20**	105	10.1	.987	R. Sewell	38	286	21	12	2	3.18
	2B	P. Coscarart	554	.264	4	42	371	389	26	71	5.8	.967	F. Ostermueller	28	205	11	7	1	2.73
W-90 L-63	SS	F. Gustine	405	.230	2	42	183	330	34	52	4.7	.938	M. Butcher	35	199	13	11	1	3.12
Frankie Frisch	3B	B. Elliott	538	.297	10	108	169	**285**	**27**	**22**	**3.4**	.944	N. Strincevich	40	190	14	7	2	3.08
	RF	J. Barrett	568	.269	7	83	373	12	11	4	2.7	.972	P. Roe	39	185	13	11	1	3.11
	CF	V. DiMaggio	342	.240	9	50	234	8	4	4	2.4	.984	X. Rescigno	48	124	10	8	5	4.35
	LF	J. Russell	580	.312	8	66	345	20	5	7	2.5	.986	C. Cuccurullo	32	106	2	1	4	4.06
	C	A. Lopez	331	.230	1	34	372	52	7	6	3.7	**.984**	R. Starr	27	90	6	5	3	5.02
	OF	F. Colman	226	.270	6	53	102	4	4	0	2.1	.964							
	UT	A. Rubeling	184	.245	4	30	70	56	2	7		.984							
	SS	F. Zak	160	.300	0	11	93	162	14	24	4.0	.948							
	OF	T. O'Brien	156	.250	3	20	50	5	2	1	1.2	.965							
Cincinnati	1B	F. McCormick	581	.305	20	102	**1508**	**135**	13	130	**10.8**	.992	B. Walters	34	285	**23**	8	1	2.40
	2B	W. Williams	**653**	.240	1	35	377	**542**	27	97	**6.1**	**.971**	C. Shoun	38	203	13	10	2	3.02
W-89 L-65	SS	E. Miller	536	.209	4	55	**357**	**544**	27	**100**	**6.0**	.971	E. Heusser	30	193	13	11	2	**2.38**
Bill McKechnie	3B	S. Mesner	414	.242	1	47	120	246	19	21	3.2	.951	T. de la Cruz	34	191	9	9	1	3.25
	RF	G. Walker	478	.278	5	62	293	3	10	0	2.6	.967	H. Gumbert	24	155	10	8	2	3.30
	CF	D. Clay	356	.250	0	17	272	4	2	0	2.8	.993	A. Carter	33	148	11	7	3	2.61
	LF	E. Tipton	479	.301	3	36	329	8	6	1	2.5	.983	J. Konstanty	20	113	6	4	0	2.80
	C	R. Mueller	555	.286	10	73	471	**65**	9	5	3.5	.983							
	OF	M. Marshall	229	.245	4	23	131	6	5	3	2.4	.965							
	OF	T. Criscola	157	.229	0	14	80	4	2	0	2.5	.977							
Chicago	1B	P. Cavarretta	614	.321	5	82	1337	77	11	121	10.3	.992	H. Wyse	41	257	16	15	1	3.15
	2B	D. Johnson	608	.278	2	71	**385**	462	**47**	85	5.8	.947	C. Passeau	34	227	15	9	3	2.89
W-75 L-79	SS	L. Merullo	193	.212	1	16	115	167	19	26	5.4	.937	P. Derringer	42	180	7	13	3	4.15
Jimmie Wilson	3B	S. Hack	383	.282	3	32	96	164	17	7	3.7	.939	B. Fleming	39	158	9	10	0	3.13
W-1 L-9	RF	B. Nicholson	582	.287	**33**	**122**	305	18	7	4	2.1	.979	B. Chipman	26	129	9	9	2	3.49
Roy Johnson	CF	A. Pafko	469	.269	6	62	333	24	6	4	3.0	.983	H. Vandenburg	35	126	7	4	2	3.63
W-0 L-1	LF	D. Dallessandro	381	.304	8	74	212	9	4	2	2.1	.982	P. Erickson	33	124	5	9	1	3.55
Charlie Grimm	C	D. Williams	262	.240	0	27	317	50	7	7	4.9	.981	R. Lynn	22	84	5	4	1	4.06
W-74 L-69	3S	R. Hughes	478	.287	1	28	220	303	20	54		.963							
	SS	B. Schuster	154	.221	1	14	57	100	9	18	4.4	.946							
New York	1B	P. Weintraub	361	.316	13	77	928	72	8	72	10.2	.992	B. Voiselle	43	**313**	21	16	0	3.02
	2B	G. Hausmann	466	.266	1	30	301	350	27	66	5.6	.960	H. Feldman	40	205	11	13	2	4.16
W-67 L-87	SS	B. Kerr	548	.266	9	63	328	507	**40**	81	5.9	.954	E. Pyle	31	164	7	10	0	4.34
Mel Ott	3B	H. Luby	323	.254	2	35	83	134	13	14	3.5	.943	A. Adams	**65**	138	8	11	**13**	4.25
	RF	M. Ott	399	.288	26	82	199	6	3	0	2.0	.986	R. Fischer	38	129	6	14	2	5.18
	CF	J. Rucker	587	.244	6	39	310	14	5	0	2.4	.985	J. Allen	18	84	4	7	0	4.07
	LF	J. Medwick	490	.337	7	85	290	8	2	2	2.5	.993							
	C	E. Lombardi	373	.255	10	58	350	47	**13**	**11**	4.1	.968							
	13	N. Reyes	374	.289	8	53	580	120	12	49		.983							
	3B	B. Jurges	246	.211	1	23	48	124	7	7	2.9	.961							
	C	G. Mancuso	195	.251	1	25	249	37	7	4	4.1	.976							
	OF	R. Treadway	170	.300	0	5	87	3	4	0	2.5	.957							
Boston	1B	B. Etchison	308	.214	8	33	757	48	6	64	9.5	.993	J. Tobin	43	299	18	19	3	3.01
	2B	C. Ryan	332	.295	4	25	210	272	13	57	6.2	.974	N. Andrews	37	257	16	15	2	3.22
W-65 L-89	SS	W. Wietelmann	417	.240	2	32	215	287	24	60	5.1	.954	A. Javery	40	254	10	19	3	3.54
Bob Coleman	3B	D. Phillips	489	.258	1	53	84	177	19	**22**	3.1	.932	R. Barrett	42	230	9	16	2	4.06
	RF	C. Workman	418	.208	11	53	161	16	3	3	1.7	.983	I. Hutchinson	40	120	9	7	1	4.21
	CF	T. Holmes	631	.309	13	73	426	14	4	7	2.9	.991							
	LF	B. Nieman	468	.265	16	65	261	13	7	2	2.2	.975							
	C	P. Masi	251	.275	3	23	180	34	5	3	3.5	.977							
	1B	M. Macon	366	.273	3	36	625	49	16	62	9.6	.977							
	C	C. Kluttz	229	.279	2	19	199	40	5	5	4.2	.980							
	OF	A. Wright	195	.256	7	35	88	2	3	1	2.0	.968							
	C	S. Hofferth	180	.200	1	26	158	22	3	3	3.9	.984							
	OF	C. Ross	154	.227	5	26	75	8	0	2	2.2	1.000							
Brooklyn	1B	H. Schultz	526	.255	11	83	1091	85	14	90	8.8	.988	H. Gregg	39	198	9	16	2	5.46
	2B	E. Stanky	261	.276	0	16	132	138	11	28	4.8	.961	C. Davis	31	194	10	11	4	3.34
W-63 L-91	SS	B. Bragan	266	.267	0	17	77	109	9	16	3.8	.954	R. Melton	37	187	9	13	0	3.46
Leo Durocher	3B	F. Bordagaray	501	.281	6	51	107	150	15	14	2.8	.945	L. Webber	48	140	7	8	3	4.94
	RF	D. Walker	535	**.357**	13	91	260	17	11	4	2.1	.962	C. McLish	23	84	3	10	0	7.82
	CF	G. Rosen	264	.261	0	23	199	12	2	0	3.3	.991							
	LF	A. Galan	547	.318	12	93	323	10	4	3	2.3	.988							
	C	M. Owen	461	.273	1	42	**506**	57	12	8	4.6	.979							
	UT	L. Olmo	520	.258	9	85	316	138	27	18		.944							
	1B	J. Bolling	131	.351	1	25	206	20	2	7	8.4	.991							

NATIONAL LEAGUE 1944, *cont.*

Philadelphia

W-61 L-92

Freddie Fitzsimmons

POS	Player	AB	BA	HR	RBI	PO	A	E	DP	TC/G	FA
1B	T. Lupien	597	.283	5	52	1453	103	13	114	10.4	.992
2B	M. Mullen	464	.267	0	31	291	316	23	52	5.5	.963
SS	R. Hamrick	292	.205	1	23	160	293	25	55	6.5	.948
3B	G. Stewart	377	.220	0	29	77	181	10	12	3.2	.963
RF	R. Northey	570	.288	22	104	286	24	6	7	2.1	.981
CF	B. Adams	584	.283	17	64	449	14	10	1	3.1	.979
LF	J. Wasdell	451	.277	3	40	243	6	5	0	2.1	.980
C	B. Finley	281	.249	1	21	289	34	11	7	4.5	.967
UT	C. Letchas	396	.237	0	33	219	300	16	54		.970
C	J. Peacock	253	.225	0	21	274	38	3	4	4.3	.990
3B	T. Cieslak	220	.245	2	11	35	72	15	1	2.5	.877
OF	C. Triplett	184	.234	1	25	90	3	1	1	2.1	.989

Pitcher	G	IP	W	L	SV	ERA
K. Raffensberger	37	259	13	**20**	0	3.06
C. Schanz	40	241	13	16	3	3.32
D. Barrett	37	221	12	18	0	3.86
B. Lee	31	208	10	11	1	3.15
A. Gerheauser	30	183	8	16	0	4.58

BATTING AND BASE RUNNING LEADERS

Batting Average
- D. Walker, BKN .357
- S. Musial, STL .347
- J. Medwick, NY .337
- J. Hopp, STL .336
- P. Cavarretta, CHI .321

Slugging Average
- S. Musial, STL .549
- B. Nicholson, CHI .545
- M. Ott, NY .544
- D. Walker, BKN .529
- P. Weintraub, NY .524

Home Runs
- B. Nicholson, CHI 33
- M. Ott, NY 26
- R. Northey, PHI 22
- W. Kurowski, STL 20
- F. McCormick, CIN 20

Total Bases
- B. Nicholson, CHI 317
- S. Musial, STL 312
- T. Holmes, BOS 288
- D. Walker, BKN 283
- R. Northey, PHI 283

Runs Batted In
- B. Nicholson, CHI 122
- B. Elliott, PIT 108
- R. Northey, PHI 104
- F. McCormick, CIN 102
- R. Sanders, STL 102

Stolen Bases
- J. Barrett, PIT 28
- T. Lupien, PHI 18
- R. Hughes, CHI 16
- J. Hopp, STL 15
- B. Kerr, NY 14

Hits
- S. Musial, STL 197
- P. Cavarretta, CHI 197
- T. Holmes, BOS 195
- D. Walker, BKN 191

Base on Balls
- A. Galan, BKN 101
- B. Nicholson, CHI 93
- M. Ott, NY 90
- S. Musial, STL 90

Home Run Percentage
- M. Ott, NY 6.5
- B. Nicholson, CHI 5.7
- R. Northey, PHI 3.9
- W. Kurowski, STL 3.6

Runs
- B. Nicholson, CHI 116
- S. Musial, STL 112
- J. Russell, PIT 109
- J. Hopp, STL 106
- P. Cavarretta, CHI 106

Doubles
- S. Musial, STL 51
- A. Galan, BKN 43
- T. Holmes, BOS 42

Triples
- J. Barrett, PIT 19
- B. Elliott, PIT 16
- P. Cavarretta, CHI 15
- S. Musial, STL 14
- J. Russell, PIT 14

PITCHING LEADERS

Winning Percentage
- T. Wilks, STL .810
- H. Brecheen, STL .762
- M. Cooper, STL .759
- B. Walters, CIN .742
- R. Sewell, PIT .636

Earned Run Average
- E. Heusser, CIN 2.38
- B. Walters, CIN 2.40
- M. Cooper, STL 2.46
- M. Lanier, STL 2.65
- T. Wilks, STL 2.65

Wins
- B. Walters, CIN 23
- M. Cooper, STL 22
- R. Sewell, PIT 21
- B. Voiselle, NY 21
- J. Tobin, BOS 18

Saves
- A. Adams, NY 13
- F. Schmidt, STL 5
- X. Rescigno, PIT 5
- C. Davis, BKN 4
- C. Cuccurullo, PIT 4

Strikeouts
- B. Voiselle, NY 161
- M. Lanier, STL 141
- A. Javery, BOS 137
- K. Raffensberger, PHI 136
- F. Ostermueller, BKN, PIT 97
- M. Cooper, STL 97

Complete Games
- J. Tobin, BOS 28
- B. Walters, CIN 27
- B. Voiselle, NY 25
- R. Sewell, PIT 24
- M. Cooper, STL 22

Fewest Hits/9 Innings
- B. Walters, CIN 7.36
- T. Wilks, STL 7.51
- M. Lanier, STL 7.70
- E. Heusser, CIN 7.71

Shutouts
- M. Cooper, STL 7
- B. Walters, CIN 6
- M. Butcher, PIT 5
- M. Lanier, STL 5
- J. Tobin, BOS 5

Fewest Walks/9 Innings
- K. Raffensberger, PHI 1.57
- N. Strincevich, PIT 1.75
- C. Davis, BKN 1.81
- C. Shoun, CIN 1.87

Most Strikeouts/9 Inn.
- M. Lanier, STL 5.66
- A. Javery, BOS 4.85
- K. Raffensberger, PHI 4.73
- B. Voiselle, NY 4.63

Innings
- B. Voiselle, NY 313
- J. Tobin, BOS 299
- R. Sewell, PIT 286
- B. Walters, CIN 285

Games Pitched
- A. Adams, NY 65
- X. Rescigno, PIT 48
- L. Webber, BKN 48
- J. Tobin, BOS 43
- B. Voiselle, NY 43

							Batting						Fielding			Pitching					
	W	L	PCT	GB	R	OR	2B	3B	HR	BA	SA	SB	E	DP	FA	CG	BB	SO	ShO	SV	ERA
St. Louis	105	49	.682		**772**	**490**	**274**	59	**100**	**.275**	**.402**	37	**112**	**162**	**.982**	89	468	**637**	**26**	12	**2.67**
Pittsburgh	90	63	.588	14.5	744	662	248	**80**	70	.265	.379	**87**	191	122	.970	77	435	452	10	19	3.44
Cincinnati	89	65	.578	16	573	537	229	31	51	.254	.338	51	137	153	.978	**93**	**384**	359	17	12	2.97
Chicago	75	79	.487	30	702	669	236	46	71	.261	.360	53	186	151	.970	70	452	535	11	13	3.59
New York	67	87	.435	38	682	773	191	47	93	.263	.370	38	179	128	.971	47	587	499	4	**21**	4.29
Boston	65	89	.422	40	593	674	250	39	79	.246	.353	37	182	160	.971	70	527	454	13	12	3.67
Brooklyn	63	91	.409	42	690	832	255	51	56	.269	.366	43	197	112	.966	50	660	487	4	13	4.68
Philadelphia	61	92	.399	43.5	539	658	199	42	55	.251	.336	32	177	138	.972	66	459	496	11	6	3.64
					5295	5295	1882	395	575	.260	.363	378	1361	1126	.973	562	3972	3919	96	108	3.62

AMERICAN LEAGUE 1944

St. Louis

W-89 L-65

Luke Sewell

POS	Player	AB	BA	HR	RBI	PO	A	E	DP	TC/G	FA
1B	G. McQuinn	516	.250	11	72	1332	72	9	116	9.7	**.994**
2B	D. Gutteridge	603	.245	3	36	368	407	**35**	95	5.5	.957
SS	V. Stephens	559	.293	20	**109**	239	480	35	71	5.3	.954
3B	M. Christman	547	.271	6	83	**172**	316	14	34	3.5	**.972**
RF	G. Moore	390	.238	6	58	208	5	7	2	2.2	.968
CF	M. Byrnes	407	.295	4	45	282	7	7	1	2.4	.976
LF	M. Kreevich	402	.301	5	44	282	4	4	0	2.9	.986
C	F. Mancuso	244	.205	1	24	311	35	**17**	9	4.2	.953
OF	A. Zarilla	288	.299	6	45	167	4	4	1	2.2	.977
C	R. Hayworth	269	.223	1	25	336	39	13	4	4.5	.966
OF	C. Laabs	201	.234	5	23	108	3	0	2	2.0	1.000

Pitcher	G	IP	W	L	SV	ERA
J. Kramer	33	257	17	13	0	2.49
N. Potter	32	232	19	7	0	2.83
B. Muncrief	33	219	13	8	1	3.08
S. Jakucki	35	198	13	9	3	3.55
D. Galehouse	24	153	9	10	0	3.12
A. Hollingsworth	26	93	5	7	1	4.47
G. Caster	42	81	6	6	**12**	2.44

AMERICAN LEAGUE 1944, *cont.*

Team	POS	Player	AB	BA	HR	RBI	PO	A	E	DP	TC/G	FA	Pitcher	G	IP	W	L	SV	ERA
Detroit	1B	R. York	583	.276	18	98	1453	107	**17**	**163**	10.4	.989	D. Trout	49	**352**	27	14	0	**2.12**
W-88 L-66	2B	E. Mayo	607	.249	5	63	384	458	19	**120**	6.0	.978	H. Newhouser	47	312	**29**	9	2	2.22
Steve O'Neill	SS	J. Hoover	441	.236	0	29	256	405	48	102	**6.0**	.932	R. Gentry	37	204	12	14	0	4.24
	3B	P. Higgins	543	.297	7	76	146	311	**22**	21	3.3	.954	S. Overmire	32	200	11	11	1	3.07
	RF	J. Outlaw	535	.273	3	57	254	14	10	2	2.0	.964	J. Gorsica	34	162	6	14	4	4.11
	CF	D. Cramer	578	.292	2	42	337	13	7	2	2.5	.980							
	LF	D. Wakefield	276	.355	12	53	155	3	6	1	2.1	.963							
	C	P. Richards	300	.237	3	37	413	60	10	**13**	**5.4**	.979							
	OF	C. Hostetler	265	.298	0	20	129	5	2	1	2.1	.985							
	C	B. Swift	247	.255	1	19	288	48	6	4	4.5	.982							
	OF	D. Ross	167	.210	2	15	67	2	3	1	1.9	.958							
	UT	J. Orengo	154	.201	0	10	124	124	20	24		.925							
	P	D. Trout	133	.271	5	24	21	**94**	**4**	**8**	2.4	.966							
New York	1B	N. Etten	573	.293	**22**	91	1382	106	16	144	9.8	.989	H. Borowy	35	253	17	12	2	2.64
W-83 L-71	2B	S. Stirnweiss	643	.319	8	43	**433**	**481**	17	113	**6.0**	**.982**	M. Dubiel	30	232	13	13	0	3.38
Joe McCarthy	SS	M. Milosevich	312	.247	0	32	176	281	22	68	5.3	.954	E. Bonham	26	214	12	9	0	2.99
	3B	O. Grimes	387	.279	5	46	105	189	17	14	3.2	.945	A. Donald	30	159	13	10	0	3.34
	RF	B. Metheny	518	.239	14	67	232	8	11	2	1.9	.956	B. Zuber	22	107	5	7	0	4.21
	CF	J. Lindell	594	.300	18	103	468	9	7	3	3.2	.986	J. Page	19	103	5	7	0	4.56
	LF	H. Martin	328	.302	9	47	177	8	7	4	2.4	.964	J. Turner	35	42	4	4	7	3.46
	C	M. Garbark	299	.261	1	33	372	47	5	9	5.0	.988							
	C	R. Hemsley	284	.268	2	26	298	41	6	7	4.5	.983							
	3B	D. Savage	239	.264	4	24	66	109	10	11	3.1	.946							
	SS	F. Crosetti	197	.239	5	30	115	150	11	33	5.0	.960							
	OF	E. Levy	153	.242	4	29	75	2	3	0	2.2	.963							
Boston	1B	L. Finney	251	.287	0	32	521	23	7	53	9.3	.987	T. Hughson	28	203	18	5	5	2.26
W-77 L-77	2B	B. Doerr	468	.325	15	81	341	363	17	96	5.8	.976	P. Woods	38	171	4	8	0	3.27
Joe Cronin	SS	S. Newsome	472	.242	0	41	249	421	26	79	5.5	.963	J. Bowman	26	168	12	8	0	4.81
	3B	J. Tabor	438	.285	13	72	125	258	20	14	3.5	.950	E. O'Neill	28	152	6	11	0	4.63
	RF	P. Fox	496	.315	1	64	228	7	3	1	2.0	.987	M. Ryba	42	138	12	7	2	3.33
	CF	C. Metkovich	549	.277	9	59	242	8	10	2	3.2	.962	C. Hausmann	32	137	4	7	2	3.42
	LF	B. Johnson	525	.324	17	106	270	23	7	3	2.1	.977	Y. Terry	27	133	6	10	0	4.21
	C	R. Partee	280	.243	2	41	326	40	4	5	4.4	.989	F. Barrett	38	90	8	7	8	3.69
	OF	L. Culberson	282	.238	2	21	182	6	4	2	2.7	.979							
	32	J. Bucher	277	.274	4	31	99	138	11	25		.956							
	C	H. Wagner	223	.332	1	38	299	29	10	4	5.3	.970							
	OF	T. McBride	216	.245	0	24	113	8	1	1	2.1	.992							
	1B	J. Cronin	191	.241	5	28	428	27	9	39	9.5	.981							
Cleveland	1B	M. Rocco	**653**	.266	13	70	**1467**	**138**	11	158	10.4	.993	S. Gromek	35	204	10	9	1	2.56
W-72 L-82	2B	R. Mack	284	.232	0	29	226	243	24	73	5.9	.951	M. Harder	30	196	12	10	0	3.71
Lou Boudreau	SS	L. Boudreau	584	**.327**	3	67	**339**	**516**	19	**134**	5.9	**.978**	A. Smith	28	182	7	13	0	3.42
	3B	K. Keltner	573	.295	13	91	168	**369**	18	**37**	**3.7**	.968	E. Klieman	47	178	11	13	5	3.38
	RF	R. Cullenbine	571	.284	16	80	275	15	10	6	2.0	.967	A. Reynolds	28	158	11	8	1	3.30
	CF	O. Hockett	457	.289	1	50	275	6	5	1	2.6	.983	J. Heving	**63**	119	8	3	10	1.96
	LF	P. Seerey	342	.234	15	39	196	8	3	1	2.4	.986	R. Poat	36	81	4	8	1	5.13
	C	B. Rosar	331	.263	0	30	409	59	5	**13**	4.8	**.989**							
	2B	R. Peters	282	.223	1	24	151	181	8	45	5.4	.976							
	OF	M. Hoag	277	.285	1	27	171	9	10*	3	2.9	.947							
	OF	P. O'Dea	173	.318	0	13	72	2	4	1	1.9	.949							
	OF	J. Heath	151	.331	5	33	76	4	4	2	2.3	.952							
Philadelphia	1B	B. McGhee	287	.289	1	19	701	46	8	51	10.1	.989	B. Newsom	37	265	13	15	1	2.82
W-72 L-82	2B	I. Hall	559	.268	0	45	248	286	11	40	5.6	.980	R. Christopher	35	215	14	14	1	2.97
Connie Mack	SS	E. Busch	484	.271	0	40	204	330	34	50	5.1	.940	L. Hamlin	29	190	6	12	0	3.74
	3B	G. Kell	514	.268	0	44	167	289	20	25	3.4	.958	J. Flores	27	186	9	11	0	3.39
	RF	J. White	267	.221	1	21	162	5	9	2	2.4	.949	D. Black	29	177	10	12	0	4.06
	CF	B. Estalella	506	.298	7	60	318	12	4	4	2.6	.988	L. Harris	23	174	10	9	0	3.30
	LF	F. Garrison	449	.269	4	37	289	6	4	0	2.5	.987	J. Berry	53	111	10	8	**12**	1.94
	C	F. Hayes	581	.248	13	78	**636**	**89**	13	10	4.8	.982							
	10	D. Siebert	468	.306	6	52	759	53	10	60		.988							
	OF	H. Epps	229	.262	0	13	141	4	4	1	2.5	.973							
Chicago	1B	H. Trosky	497	.241	10	70	1310	57	9	122	**10.6**	.993	B. Dietrich	36	246	16	**17**	0	3.62
W-71 L-83	2B	R. Schalk	587	.220	1	44	360	391	28	109	5.5	.964	O. Grove	34	235	14	15	0	3.72
Jimmy Dykes	SS	S. Webb	513	.211	0	30	202	461	39	81	5.2	.944	E. Lopat	27	210	11	10	0	3.26
	3B	R. Hodgin	465	.295	1	51	77	215	18	22	3.8	.942	J. Humphries	30	169	8	10	1	3.67
	RF	W. Moses	535	.280	3	34	267	7	7	2	2.1	.975	J. Haynes	33	154	5	6	2	2.57
	CF	T. Tucker	446	.287	2	46	414	12	4	2	3.6	.991	T. Lee	15	113	3	9	0	3.02
	LF	E. Carnett	457	.276	1	60	199	7	11	0	2.5	.949	G. Maltzberger	46	91	10	5	**12**	2.96
	C	M. Tresh	312	.260	0	25	370	47	8	5	4.6	.981							
	OF	G. Curtright	198	.253	2	23	101	8	6	3	2.3	.948							
	3B	G. Clarke	169	.260	0	27	36	107	9	6	3.4	.941							
	OF	J. Dickshot	162	.253	0	15	72	3	2	1	1.9	.974							

AMERICAN LEAGUE 1944, *cont.*

Washington

W-64 L-90

Ossie Bluege

POS	Player	AB	BA	HR	RBI	PO	A	E	DP	TC/G	FA
1B	J. Kuhel	518	.278	4	51	1251	83	**17**	119	9.8	.987
2B	G. Myatt	538	.284	0	40	341	299	29	81	5.5	.957
SS	J. Sullivan	471	.251	0	30	276	426	**50**	89	5.4	.934
3B	G. Torres	524	.267	0	58	120	297	21	25	3.6	.952
RF	J. Powell	367	.240	1	37	196	5	4	0	2.3	.980
CF	S. Spence	592	.316	18	100	434	29	5	9	3.1	.989
LF	G. Case	465	.249	2	32	288	7	9	2	2.7	.970
C	R. Ferrell	339	.277	0	25	403	71	9	8	5.0	.981
OF	R. Ortiz	316	.253	5	35	165	2	9	1	2.2	.949
C	M. Guerra	210	.281	1	29	211	32	10	8	4.4	.960
2B	F. Vaughn	109	.257	1	21	61	70	8	16	5.3	.942

Pitcher	G	IP	W	L	SV	ERA
D. Leonard	32	229	14	14	0	3.06
M. Haefner	31	228	12	15	1	3.04
E. Wynn	33	208	8	**17**	2	3.38
J. Niggeling	24	206	10	8	0	2.32
R. Wolff	33	155	4	15	2	4.99
A. Carrasquel	43	134	8	7	2	3.43
M. Candini	28	103	6	7	1	4.11

BATTING AND BASE RUNNING LEADERS

Batting Average

L. Boudreau, CLE	.327
B. Doerr, BOS	.325
B. Johnson, BOS	.324
S. Stirnweiss, NY	.319
S. Spence, WAS	.316

Slugging Average

B. Doerr, BOS	.528
B. Johnson, BOS	.528
J. Lindell, NY	.500
S. Spence, WAS	.486
N. Etten, NY	.466
K. Keltner, CLE	.466

Home Runs

N. Etten, NY	22
V. Stephens, STL	20
R. York, DET	18
S. Spence, WAS	18
J. Lindell, NY	18

Total Bases

J. Lindell, NY	297
S. Stirnweiss, NY	296
S. Spence, WAS	288
B. Johnson, BOS	277
N. Etten, NY	267
K. Keltner, CLE	267

Runs Batted In

V. Stephens, STL	109
B. Johnson, BOS	106
J. Lindell, NY	103
S. Spence, WAS	100
R. York, DET	98

Stolen Bases

S. Stirnweiss, NY	55
G. Case, WAS	49
G. Myatt, WAS	26
W. Moses, CHI	21
D. Gutteridge, STL	20

Hits

S. Stirnweiss, NY	205
L. Boudreau, CLE	191
S. Spence, WAS	187
J. Lindell, NY	178

Base on Balls

N. Etten, NY	97
B. Johnson, BOS	95
R. Cullenbine, CLE	87
G. McQuinn, STL	85

Home Run Percentage

P. Seerey, CLE	4.4
N. Etten, NY	3.8
V. Stephens, STL	3.6
B. Johnson, BOS	3.2

Runs

S. Stirnweiss, NY	125
B. Johnson, BOS	106
R. Cullenbine, CLE	98
B. Doerr, BOS	95

Doubles

L. Boudreau, CLE	45
K. Keltner, CLE	41
B. Johnson, BOS	40
P. Fox, BOS	38

Triples

J. Lindell, NY	16
S. Stirnweiss, NY	16
D. Gutteridge, STL	11
B. Doerr, BOS	10

PITCHING LEADERS

Winning Percentage

T. Hughson, BOS	.783
H. Newhouser, DET	.763
N. Potter, STL	.731
D. Trout, DET	.659
H. Borowy, NY	.586

Earned Run Average

D. Trout, DET	2.12
H. Newhouser, DET	2.22
T. Hughson, BOS	2.26
J. Niggeling, WAS	2.32
J. Kramer, STL	2.49

Wins

H. Newhouser, DET	29
D. Trout, DET	27
N. Potter, STL	19
T. Hughson, BOS	18
H. Borowy, NY	17
J. Kramer, STL	17

Saves

G. Caster, STL	12
G. Maltzberger, CHI	12
J. Berry, PHI	12
J. Heving, CLE	10
F. Barrett, BOS	8

Strikeouts

H. Newhouser, DET	187
D. Trout, DET	144
B. Newsom, PHI	142
J. Kramer, STL	124
J. Niggeling, WAS	121

Complete Games

D. Trout, DET	33
H. Newhouser, DET	25
T. Hughson, BOS	19
E. Wynn, WAS	19
M. Dubiel, NY	19
H. Borowy, NY	19

Fewest Hits/9 Innings

S. Gromek, CLE	7.07
J. Niggeling, WAS	7.17
H. Newhouser, DET	7.61
T. Hughson, BOS	7.61

Shutouts

D. Trout, DET	7
H. Newhouser, DET	6
S. Jakucki, STL	4
R. Gentry, DET	4

Fewest Walks/9 Innings

L. Harris, PHI	1.34
D. Leonard, WAS	1.45
E. Bonham, NY	1.73
T. Hughson, BOS	1.81

Most Strikeouts/9 Inn.

H. Newhouser, DET	5.39
J. Niggeling, WAS	5.29
S. Gromek, CLE	5.08
T. Hughson, BOS	4.96

Innings

D. Trout, DET	352
H. Newhouser, DET	312
B. Newsom, PHI	265
J. Kramer, STL	257

Games Pitched

J. Heving, CLE	63
J. Berry, PHI	53
D. Trout, DET	49
E. Klieman, CLE	47
H. Newhouser, DET	47

	W	L	PCT	GB	R	OR	Batting 2B	3B	HR	BA	SA	SB	Fielding E	DP	FA	Pitching CG	BB	SO	ShO	SV	ERA
St. Louis	89	65	.578		684	587	223	45	72	.252	.352	44	171	142	.972	71	469	**581**	16	17	3.17
Detroit	88	66	.571	1	658	**581**	220	44	60	.263	.354	61	190	184	.970	**87**	452	568	**20**	8	**3.09**
New York	83	71	.539	6	674	617	216	**74**	**96**	.264	**.387**	91	**156**	170	**.974**	78	532	529	9	13	3.39
Boston	77	77	.500	12	**739**	676	**277**	56	69	**.270**	.380	60	171	154	.972	58	592	524	5	17	3.82
Cleveland	72	82	.468	17	643	677	270	50	70	.266	.372	48	165	**192**	**.974**	48	621	524	7	**18**	3.65
Philadelphia	72	82	.468	17	525	594	169	47	36	.257	.327	42	176	127	.971	72	**390**	534	9	14	3.26
Chicago	71	83	.461	18	543	662	210	55	23	.247	.320	66	183	154	.970	64	420	481	5	17	3.58
Washington	64	90	.416	25	592	664	186	42	33	.261	.330	**127**	218	156	.964	83	475	503	12	11	3.49
					5058	5058	1771	413	459	.260	.353	539	1430	1279	.971	561	3951	4244	83	115	3.43

NATIONAL LEAGUE 1945

Chicago

W-98 L-56

Charlie Grimm

POS	Player	AB	BA	HR	RBI	PO	A	E	DP	TC/G	FA
1B	P. Cavarretta	498	**.355**	6	97	1149	77	9	83	10.3	.993
2B	D. Johnson	557	.302	2	58	309	440	19	74	5.6	.975
SS	L. Merullo	394	.239	2	37	209	336	30	49	4.9	.948
3B	S. Hack	597	.323	2	43	**195**	312	13	27	**3.6**	**.975**
RF	B. Nicholson	559	.243	13	88	300	12	3	4	2.1	.990
CF	A. Pafko	534	.298	12	110	371	11	2	0	2.7	.995
LF	P. Lowrey	523	.283	7	89	280	17	4	1	2.2	.987
C	M. Livingston	224	.254	2	23	263	27	3	2	4.3	.990
UT	R. Hughes	222	.261	0	8	120	157	13	28		.955
C	P. Gillespie	163	.288	3	25	161	20	2	1	4.1	.989
1B	H. Becker	133	.286	2	27	222	12	0	21	8.4	1.000

Pitcher	G	IP	W	L	SV	ERA
H. Wyse	38	278	22	10	0	2.68
C. Passeau	34	227	17	9	1	2.46
P. Derringer	35	214	16	11	4	3.45
R. Prim	34	165	13	8	2	2.40
H. Borowy	15	122	11	2	1	2.13*
P. Erickson	28	108	7	4	3	3.32
H. Vandenburg	30	95	6	3	2	3.49

NATIONAL LEAGUE 1945, *cont.*

Team	POS	Player	AB	BA	HR	RBI	PO	A	E	DP	TC/G	FA	Pitcher	G	IP	W	L	SV	ERA
St. Louis	1B	R. Sanders	537	.276	8	78	1259	90	**19**	113	9.6	.986	R. Barrett	36	247*	21*	9	0	2.74
W-95 L-59	2B	E. Verban	597	.278	0	72	398	406	18	95	5.3	**.978**	K. Burkhart	42	217	18	8	2	2.90
Billy Southworth	SS	M. Marion	430	.277	1	59	237	372	21	70	5.2	.967	B. Donnelly	31	166	8	10	2	3.52
	3B	W. Kurowski	511	.323	21	102	172	235	15	28	3.2	.964	H. Brecheen	24	157	15	4	2	2.52
	RF	J. Hopp	446	.289	3	44	244	5	5	2	2.4	.980	G. Dockins	31	126	8	6	0	3.21
	CF	B. Adams	578	.292	20	101	382	9	9	3	2.9	.978	T. Wilks	18	98	4	7	0	2.93
	LF	R. Schoendienst	565	.278	1	47	286	10	5	1	2.6	.983	J. Creel	26	87	5	4	2	4.14
	C	K. O'Dea	307	.254	4	43	321	50	2	**14**	4.1	**.995**							
	OF	A. Bergamo	304	.316	3	44	146	9	5	3	2.1	.969							
	C	D. Rice	253	.261	1	28	284	39	2	6	4.2	.994							
Brooklyn	1B	A. Galan	576	.307	9	92	558	34	7	53	9.1	.988	H. Gregg	42	254	18	13	2	3.47
W-87 L-67	2B	E. Stanky	555	.258	1	39	**429**	441	**34**	**101**	**5.9**	.962	V. Lombardi	38	204	10	11	4	3.31
Leo Durocher	SS	E. Basinski	336	.262	0	33	166	262	34	59	4.6	.926	C. Davis	24	150	10	10	0	3.25
	3B	F. Bordagaray	273	.256	2	49	54	93	19	7	2.9	.886	A. Herring	22	124	7	4	2	3.48
	RF	D. Walker	607	.300	8	**124**	346	18	3	4	2.4	.992	T. Seats	31	122	10	7	0	4.36
	CF	G. Rosen	606	.325	12	75	392	7	3	1	2.9	.993	C. King	42	112	5	5	3	4.09
	LF	L. Olmo	556	.313	10	110	225	8	7	2	2.3	.971	R. Branca	16	110	5	6	1	3.04
	C	M. Sandlock	195	.282	2	17	196	20	2	3	4.6	.991	C. Buker	42	87	7	2	5	3.30
	1B	E. Stevens	201	.274	4	29	478	38	7	40	9.5	.987	L. Webber	17	75	7	3	0	3.58
	SS	T. Brown	196	.245	2	19	93	164	23	27	5.1	.918							
	3B	B. Hart	161	.230	3	27	54	62	11	8	3.3	.913							
Pittsburgh	1B	B. Dahlgren	531	.250	5	75	1373	93	6	**115**	10.4	**.996**	P. Roe	33	235	14	13	1	2.87
W-82 L-72	2B	P. Coscarart	392	.242	8	38	257	361	14	74	5.2	.978	N. Strincevich	36	228	16	10	2	3.31
Frankie Frisch	SS	F. Gustine	478	.280	2	66	177	291	**35**	52	4.8	.930	R. Sewell	33	188	11	9	1	4.07
	3B	B. Elliott	541	.290	8	108	94	178	21	18	3.6	.928	M. Butcher	28	169	10	8	0	3.03
	RF	J. Barrett	507	.256	15	67	318	8	8	0	2.5	.976	A. Gerheauser	32	140	5	10	1	3.91
	CF	A. Gionfriddo	409	.284	2	42	235	6	9	2	2.4	.964	K. Gables	29	139	11	7	1	4.15
	LF	J. Russell	510	.284	12	77	313	9	9	1	2.4	.973	X. Rescigno	44	79	3	5	9	5.72
	C	A. Lopez	243	.218	0	18	326	38	3	7	4.0	.992							
	3B	L. Handley	312	.298	1	32	85	183	15	13	3.6	.947							
	C	B. Salkeld	267	.311	15	52	279	40	9	8	3.8	.973							
	SS	V. Barnhart	201	.269	0	19	104	166	21	31	4.8	.928							
	OF	T. O'Brien	161	.335	0	18	72	2	3	0	1.7	.961							
	10	F. Colman	153	.209	4	30	143	14	1	10		.994							
New York	1B	P. Weintraub	283	.272	10	42	774	60	6	49	10.9	.993	B. Voiselle	41	232	14	14	0	4.49
W-78 L-74	2B	G. Hausmann	623	.279	2	45	376	**489**	29	65	5.8	.968	H. Feldman	35	218	12	13	1	3.27
Mel Ott	SS	B. Kerr	546	.249	4	40	**333**	**515**	32	**81**	**5.9**	.964	V. Mungo	26	183	14	7	0	3.20
	3B	N. Reyes	431	.288	5	44	111	232	14	12	3.1	.961	J. Brewer	28	160	8	6	0	3.83
	RF	M. Ott	451	.308	21	79	217	11	4	1	2.0	.983	A. Adams	65	113	11	9	**15**	3.42
	CF	J. Rucker	429	.273	7	51	256	6	6	2	2.7	.978	S. Emmerich	31	100	4	4	0	4.86
	LF	D. Gardella	430	.272	18	71	182	6	9	1	2.1	.954	A. Hansen	23	93	4	3	3	4.66
	C	E. Lombardi	368	.307	19	70	**425**	49	8	8	**5.0**	.983	R. Fischer	31	77	3	8	1	5.63
	OF	R. Treadway	224	.241	4	23	107	3	7	0	2.0	.940							
	C	C. Kluttz	222	.279	4	21	195	32	5	5	4.1	.978							
	3B	B. Jurges	176	.324	3	24	40	94	9	3	3.3	.937							
Boston	1B	V. Shupe	283	.269	0	15	650	53	8	81	9.2	.989	J. Tobin	27	197	9	14	0	3.84
W-67 L-85	2B	W. Wietelmann	428	.271	4	33	222	232	13	58	5.4	.972	B. Logan	34	187	7	11	1	3.18
Bob Coleman	SS	D. Culler	527	.262	2	30	252	386	31	71	5.3	.954	J. Hutchings	57	185	7	6	3	3.75
W-42 L-51	3B	C. Workman	514	.274	25	87	97	205	**30**	18	3.1	.910	N. Andrews	21	138	7	12	0	4.58
Del Bissonette	RF	T. Holmes	636	.352	**28**	117	334	13	6	4	2.3	.983	E. Wright	15	111	8	3	0	2.51
W-25 L-34	CF	C. Gillenwater	517	.288	7	72	451	24	10	5	3.5	.979	B. Lee	16	106	6	3	0	2.79
	LF	B. Nieman	247	.247	14	56	132	4	10	1	2.6	.932	M. Cooper	20	78	7	4	1	3.35
	C	P. Masi	371	.272	7	46	335	**52**	8	7	4.2	.980	D. Hendrickson	37	73	4	8	5	4.91
	1B	J. Mack	260	.231	3	44	635	48	6	48	10.6	.991							
	OF	J. Medwick	218	.284	0	26	78	7	0	2	2.2	1.000							
	C	S. Hofferth	170	.235	3	15	168	31	4	7	4.5	.980							
Cincinnati	1B	F. McCormick	580	.276	10	81	**1469**	**118**	9	104	**10.6**	.994	E. Heusser	31	223	11	16	1	3.71
W-61 L-93	2B	W. Williams	482	.237	0	27	295	393	22	61	5.3	.969	J. Bowman	25	186	11	13	0	3.59
Bill McKechnie	SS	E. Miller	421	.238	13	49	245	382	16	61	5.6	**.975**	B. Walters	22	168	10	10	0	2.68
	3B	S. Mesner	540	.254	1	52	170	**326**	15	**35**	3.5	.971	H. Fox	45	164	8	13	0	4.93
	RF	A. Libke	449	.283	4	53	223	13	9	6	2.3	.963	V. Kennedy	24	158	5	12	1	4.00
	CF	D. Clay	**656**	.280	1	50	446	10	5	3	3.0	.989							
	LF	E. Tipton	331	.242	5	34	192	2	6	1	2.4	.970							
	C	A. Lakeman	258	.256	8	31	226	31	10	4	3.6	.963							
	OF	G. Walker	316	.253	2	21	123	4	5	1	2.0	.962							
	C	A. Unser	204	.265	3	21	207	30	11	5	4.1	.956							
	2S	K. Wahl	194	.201	0	10	135	170	15	22		.953							
	OF	D. Sipek	156	.244	0	13	68	2	2	0	2.3	.972							
	OF	H. Sauer	116	.293	5	20	69	0	2	0	2.5	.972							

NATIONAL LEAGUE 1945, *cont.*

Philadelphia

W-46 L-108

Freddie Fitzsimmons
W-18 L-51

Ben Chapman
W-28 L-57

POS	Player	AB	BA	HR	RBI	PO	A	E	DP	TC/G	FA
1B	J. Wasdell	500	.300	7	60	597	43	7	51	10.3	.989
2B	F. Daniels	230	.200	0	10	171	215	18	41	5.4	.955
SS	B. Mott	289	.221	0	22	134	189	19	41	5.4	.944
3B	J. Antonelli	504	.256	1	28	129	201	14	24	3.2	.959
RF	V. Dinges	397	.287	1	36	132	10	2	5	2.2	.986
CF	V. DiMaggio	452	.257	19	84	337	16	2	4	2.9	.994
LF	C. Triplett	363	.240	7	46	202	3	12	1	2.4	.945
C	G. Mancuso	176	.199	0	16	215	34	3	4	3.6	.988
UT	G. Crawford	302	.295	2	24	152	148	17	18		.946
UT	J. Foxx	224	.268	7	38	304	54	8	19		.978
OF	R. Monteagudo	193	.301	0	15	61	6	6	2	2.1	.918
C	A. Seminick	188	.239	6	26	198	30	5	3	3.3	.979
OF	J. Powell	173	.231	1	14	67	5	1	2	1.7	.986
SS	W. Flager	168	.250	2	15	98	145	14	25	5.4	.946

Pitcher	G	IP	W	L	SV	ERA
D. Barrett	36	191	7	**20**	1	5.43
A. Karl	**67**	181	9	8	**15**	2.99
C. Schanz	35	145	4	15	5	4.35
C. Sproull	34	130	4	10	1	5.94
D. Mauney	20	123	6	10	1	3.08
O. Judd	23	83	5	4	2	3.81
T. Kraus	19	82	4	9	0	5.40

BATTING AND BASE RUNNING LEADERS

Batting Average	
P. Cavarretta, CHI	.355
T. Holmes, BOS	.352
G. Rosen, BKN	.325
S. Hack, CHI	.323
W. Kurowski, STL	.323

Slugging Average	
T. Holmes, BOS	.577
W. Kurowski, STL	.511
P. Cavarretta, CHI	.500
M. Ott, NY	.499
L. Olmo, BKN	.462

Home Runs	
T. Holmes, BOS	28
C. Workman, BOS	25
B. Adams, PHI, STL	22
M. Ott, NY	21
W. Kurowski, STL	21

Total Bases	
T. Holmes, BOS	367
G. Rosen, BKN	279
B. Adams, PHI, STL	279
D. Walker, BKN	266
W. Kurowski, STL	261

Runs Batted In	
D. Walker, BKN	124
T. Holmes, BOS	117
A. Pafko, CHI	110
L. Olmo, BKN	110
B. Adams, PHI, STL	109

Stolen Bases	
R. Schoendienst, STL	26
J. Barrett, PIT	25
D. Clay, CIN	19
J. Russell, PIT	15
L. Olmo, BKN	15
T. Holmes, BOS	15

Hits	
T. Holmes, BOS	224
G. Rosen, BKN	197
S. Hack, CHI	193
D. Clay, CIN	184

Base on Balls	
E. Stanky, BKN	148
A. Galan, BKN	114
S. Hack, CHI	99
B. Nicholson, CHI	92

Home Run Percentage	
C. Workman, BOS	4.9
M. Ott, NY	4.7
T. Holmes, BOS	4.4
V. DiMaggio, PHI	4.2

Runs	
E. Stanky, BKN	128
G. Rosen, BKN	126
T. Holmes, BOS	125
A. Galan, BKN	114

Doubles	
T. Holmes, BOS	47
D. Walker, BKN	42
B. Elliott, PIT	36
A. Galan, BKN	36

Triples	
L. Olmo, BKN	13
A. Pafko, CHI	12
J. Rucker, NY	11
G. Rosen, BKN	11

PITCHING LEADERS

Winning Percentage	
H. Brecheen, STL	.789
K. Burkhart, STL	.692
H. Wyse, CHI	.688
R. Barrett, BOS, STL	.657
C. Passeau, CHI	.654

Earned Run Average	
H. Borowy, CHI	2.13
C. Passeau, CHI	2.46
H. Brecheen, STL	2.52
B. Walters, CIN	2.68
H. Wyse, CHI	2.68

Wins	
R. Barrett, BOS, STL	23
H. Wyse, CHI	22
K. Burkhart, STL	18
H. Gregg, BKN	18
C. Passeau, CHI	17

Saves	
A. Karl, PHI	15
A. Adams, NY	15
X. Rescigno, PIT	9
C. Schanz, PHI	5
C. Buker, BKN	5
D. Hendrickson, BOS	5

Strikeouts	
P. Roe, PIT	148
H. Gregg, BKN	139
B. Voiselle, NY	115
V. Mungo, NY	101
J. Hutchings, BOS	99

Complete Games	
R. Barrett, BOS, STL	24
H. Wyse, CHI	23
C. Passeau, CHI	19
N. Strincevich, PIT	18
E. Heusser, CIN	18

Fewest Hits/9 Innings	
H. Borowy, CHI	7.72
H. Brecheen, STL	7.78
H. Gregg, BKN	7.82
C. Passeau, CHI	8.13

Shutouts	
C. Passeau, CHI	5
K. Burkhart, STL	4
B. Donnelly, STL	4
E. Heusser, CIN	4
B. Voiselle, NY	4

Fewest Walks/9 Innings	
C. Davis, BKN	1.26
R. Barrett, BOS, STL	1.71
P. Roe, PIT	1.76
H. Wyse, CHI	1.78

Most Strikeouts/9 Inn.	
P. Roe, PIT	5.67
H. Gregg, BKN	4.92
B. Voiselle, NY	4.45
C. Passeau, CHI	3.89

Innings	
R. Barrett, BOS, STL	285
H. Wyse, CHI	278
H. Gregg, BKN	254
P. Roe, PIT	235

Games Pitched	
A. Karl, PHI	67
A. Adams, NY	65
J. Hutchings, BOS	57
H. Fox, CIN	45
R. Barrett, BOS, STL	45

	W	L	PCT	GB	R	OR	Batting						Fielding			Pitching					
							2B	3B	HR	BA	SA	SB	E	DP	FA	CG	BB	SO	ShO	SV	ERA
Chicago	98	56	.636		735	**532**	229	52	57	**.277**	.372	69	**121**	124	**.980**	**86**	**385**	541	15	14	**2.98**
St. Louis	95	59	.617	3	756	583	256	44	64	.273	.371	55	137	150	.977	77	497	510	**18**	9	3.24
Brooklyn	87	67	.565	11	**795**	724	257	**71**	57	.271	.376	75	230	144	.962	61	586	**557**	7	18	3.70
Pittsburgh	82	72	.532	16	753	686	**259**	56	72	.267	.377	81	178	141	.971	73	455	518	8	16	3.76
New York	78	74	.513	19	668	700	175	35	**114**	.269	**.379**	38	166	112	.973	53	529	530	13	21	4.06
Boston	67	85	.441	30	721	728	229	25	101	.267	.374	**82**	193	**160**	.969	57	557	404	7	13	4.04
Cincinnati	61	93	.396	37	536	694	221	26	56	.249	.333	71	146	138	.976	77	534	372	11	6	4.00
Philadelphia	46	108	.299	52	548	865	197	27	56	.246	.326	54	234	150	.962	31	608	433	4	**26**	4.64
					5512	5512	1823	336	577	.265	.363	525	1405	1119	.971	515	4151	3865	83	123	3.80

AMERICAN LEAGUE 1945

Detroit

W-88 L-65

Steve O'Neill

POS	Player	AB	BA	HR	RBI	PO	A	E	DP	TC/G	FA
1B	R. York	595	.264	18	87	**1464**	113	**19**	142	10.3	.988
2B	E. Mayo	501	.285	10	54	326	393	15	91	5.9	**.980**
SS	S. Webb	407	.199	0	21	215	343	25	71	5.6	.957
3B	B. Maier	486	.263	1	34	142	226	25	19	3.2	.936
RF	R. Cullenbine	523	.277	18	93	321	23	7	3	2.4	.980
CF	D. Cramer	541	.275	6	58	314	7	3	4	2.3	.991
LF	J. Outlaw	446	.271	0	34	192	13	7	6	2.0	.967
C	B. Swift	279	.233	0	24	358	60	5	12	4.5	.988
OF	H. Greenberg	270	.311	13	60	129	3	0	0	1.8	1.000
C	P. Richards	234	.256	3	32	361	44	2	7	4.9	.995
SS	J. Hoover	222	.257	1	17	126	163	17	35	4.5	.944

Pitcher	G	IP	W	L	SV	ERA
H. Newhouser	40	**313**	**25**	9	2	**1.81**
D. Trout	41	246	18	15	2	3.14
A. Benton	31	192	13	8	3	2.02
S. Overmire	31	162	9	9	4	3.88
L. Mueller	26	135	6	8	1	3.68
J. Tobin	14	58	4	5	1	3.55

AMERICAN LEAGUE 1945, *cont.*

Team	POS	Player	AB	BA	HR	RBI	PO	A	E	DP	TC/G	FA	Pitcher	G	IP	W	L	SV	ERA
Washington	1B	J. Kuhel	533	.285	2	75	1323	94	16	101	10.2	.989	R. Wolff	33	250	20	10	2	2.12
W-87 L-67	2B	G. Myatt	490	.296	1	39	228	231	13	48	5.0	.972	M. Haefner	37	238	16	14	3	3.47
Ossie Bluege	SS	G. Torres	562	.237	0	48	**272**	437	35	65	5.1	.953	M. Pieretti	44	233	14	13	2	3.32
	3B	H. Clift	375	.211	8	53	111	214	23	18	3.1	.934	D. Leonard	31	216	17	7	1	2.13
	RF	B. Lewis	258	.333	2	37	151	8	3	3	2.3	.981	J. Niggeling	26	177	7	12	0	3.16
	CF	G. Binks	550	.278	6	81	321	13	8	4	2.7	.977	A. Carrasquel	35	123	7	5	1	2.71
	LF	G. Case	504	.294	1	31	316	17	7	3	2.8	.979							
	C	R. Ferrell	286	.266	1	38	331	64	4	3	4.8	.990							
	2B	F. Vaughn	268	.235	1	25	177	189	21	35	5.1	.946							
	OF	M. Kreevich	158	.278	1	23	98	2	3	0	2.6*	.971							
St. Louis	1B	G. McQuinn	483	.277	7	61	1143	105	11	87	9.3	.991	N. Potter	32	255	15	11	0	2.47
W-81 L-70	2B	D. Gutteridge	543	.238	2	49	334	334	21	66	5.4	.970	J. Kramer	29	193	10	15	2	3.36
Luke Sewell	SS	V. Stephens	571	.289	**24**	89	256	439	28	69	5.0	**.961**	S. Jakucki	30	192	12	10	2	3.51
	3B	M. Christman	289	.277	4	34	79	137	6	12	2.9	.973	T. Shirley	32	184	8	12	0	3.63
	RF	G. Moore	354	.260	5	50	184	10	6	0	2.0	.970	A. Hollingsworth	26	173	12	9	1	2.70
	CF	M. Kreevich	295	.237	2	21	230	4	2	0	3.0	.992	B. Muncrief	27	146	13	4	1	2.72
	LF	M. Byrnes	442	.249	8	59	319	12	4	0	2.7	.988							
	C	F. Mancuso	365	.268	1	38	467	55	6	10	4.6	.989							
	UT	L. Schulte	430	.247	0	36	167	245	23	24		.947							
	OF	P. Gray	234	.218	0	13	162	3	7	1	2.8	.959							
	O1	L. Finney	213	.277	2	22	233	18	2	14		.992							
	OF	B. Martin	185	.200	2	16	116	7	1	2	2.6	.992							
	C	R. Hayworth	160	.194	0	17	216	23	2	5	4.4	.992							
New York	1B	N. Etten	565	.285	18	**111**	1401	94	17	**149**	9.9	.989	B. Bevens	29	184	13	9	0	3.67
W-81 L-71	2B	S. Stirnweiss	**632**	**.309**	10	64	**432**	492	**29**	**119**	**6.3**	.970	E. Bonham	23	181	8	11	0	3.29
Joe McCarthy	SS	F. Crosetti	441	.238	4	48	264	380	37	86	5.4	.946	A. Gettel	27	155	9	8	3	3.90
	3B	O. Grimes	480	.265	4	45	162	296	**31**	**35**	3.5	.937	M. Dubiel	26	151	10	9	0	4.64
	RF	B. Metheny	509	.248	8	53	227	12	4	2	1.9	.984	H. Borowy	18	132	10	5	0	3.13*
	CF	T. Stainback	327	.257	5	32	233	10	8	6	3.0	.968	B. Zuber	21	127	5	11	1	3.19
	LF	H. Martin	408	.267	7	53	233	8	4	1	2.4	.984	J. Page	20	102	6	3	0	2.82
	C	M. Garbark	176	.216	1	26	202	41	7	10	4.2	.972	R. Ruffing	11	87	7	3	0	2.89
	OF	R. Derry	253	.225	13	45	170	4	4	2	2.6	.978	J. Turner	30	54	3	4	**10**	3.64
	OF	C. Keller	163	.301	10	34	110	4	0	0	2.6	1.000							
	C	A. Robinson	160	.281	8	24	186	16	0	3	4.5	1.000							
	OF	J. Lindell	159	.283	1	20	108	2	2	0	2.7	.982							
Cleveland	1B	M. Rocco	565	.264	10	56	1203	115	10	112	9.4	**.992**	S. Gromek	33	251	19	9	1	2.55
W-73 L-72	2B	D. Meyer	524	.292	7	48	317	313	14	66	5.0	.978	A. Reynolds	44	247	18	12	4	3.20
Lou Boudreau	SS	L. Boudreau	346	.306	3	48	217	289	9	73	5.3	.983	J. Bagby	25	159	8	11	1	3.73
	3B	D. Ross	363	.262	2	43	119	175	13	14	2.9	.958	A. Smith	21	134	5	12	1	3.84
	RF	P. Seerey	414	.237	14	56	227	7	6	3	2.1	.975	E. Klieman	38	126	5	8	4	3.85
	CF	F. Mackiewicz	359	.273	2	37	288	11	4	4	2.7	.987	P. Center	31	86	6	3	1	3.99
	LF	J. Heath	370	.305	15	61	214	3	6	1	2.2	.973	M. Harder	11	76	3	7	0	3.67
	C	F. Hayes	385	.236	6	43	508*	63	7	23*	4.9*	.988*							
	UT	A. Cihocki	283	.212	0	24	154	208	15	42		.960							
	OF	P. O'Dea	221	.235	1	21	118	4	1	2	2.3	.992							
	OF	L. Fleming	140	.329	3	22	59	2	4	2	2.0	.938							
Chicago	1B	K. Farrell	396	.258	0	34	913	74	11	76	10.3	.989	T. Lee	29	228	15	12	0	2.44
W-71 L-78	2B	R. Schalk	513	.248	1	65	380	389	18	90	5.9	.977	O. Grove	33	217	14	12	1	3.44
Jimmy Dykes	SS	C. Michaels	445	.245	2	54	259	426	**47**	74	5.8	.936	E. Lopat	26	199	10	13	1	4.11
	3B	T. Cuccinello	402	.308	2	49	73	221	20	22	2.8	.936	J. Humphries	22	153	6	14	1	4.24
	RF	W. Moses	569	.295	2	50	329	12	8	1	2.5	.977	B. Dietrich	18	122	7	10	0	4.19
	CF	O. Hockett	417	.293	2	55	273	7	5	3	2.7	.982	E. Caldwell	27	105	6	7	4	3.59
	LF	J. Dickshot	486	.302	4	58	253	13	8	3	2.2	.971	J. Haynes	14	104	5	5	1	3.55
	C	M. Tresh	458	.249	0	47	575	**102**	**11**	7	4.6	.984							
	OF	G. Curtright	324	.281	4	32	196	8	3	0	2.5	.986							
	1B	B. Nagel	220	.209	3	27	503	34	9	42	9.6	.984							
	3B	F. Baker	208	.250	0	19	36	99	4	6	2.4	.971							
Boston	1B	C. Metkovich	539	.260	5	62	935	76	15	96	10.6	.985	B. Ferriss	35	265	21	10	2	2.96
W-71 L-83	2B	S. Newsome	438	.290	1	48	206	231	17	54	5.5	.963	J. Wilson	23	144	6	8	0	3.30
Joe Cronin	SS	E. Lake	473	.279	11	51	265	**459**	40	**112**	**5.9**	.948	E. O'Neill	24	142	8	11	0	5.15
	3B	J. Tobin	278	.252	0	21	82	151	12	17	3.4	.951	C. Hausmann	31	125	5	7	2	5.04
	RF	J. Lazor	335	.310	5	45	141	6	6	0	1.9	.961	M. Ryba	34	123	7	6	2	2.49
	CF	L. Culberson	331	.275	6	45	219	14	8	6	2.6	.967	P. Woods	24	107	4	7	2	4.19
	LF	B. Johnson	529	.280	12	74	296	15	8	4	2.3	.975	R. Heflin	20	102	4	10	0	4.06
	C	B. Garbark	199	.261	0	17	249	31	2	9	4.2	.993	F. Barrett	37	86	4	3	3	2.62
	OF	T. McBride	344	.305	1	47	180	10	3	4	2.4	.984	V. Johnson	26	85	6	4	2	4.01
	2B	B. Steiner	304	.257	3	20	202	213	14	63	5.6	.967							
	OF	P. Fox	208	.245	0	20	84	5	1	1	1.6	.989							
	3B	T. LaForest	204	.250	2	16	45	97	5	11	3.3	.966							
	1B	D. Camilli	198	.212	2	19	505	44	5	62	10.3	.991							
Philadelphia	1B	D. Siebert	573	.267	7	51	1427	**135**	14	129	**10.7**	.991	B. Newsom	36	257	8	**20**	0	3.29
W-52 L-98	2B	I. Hall	616	.261	0	50	422	**498**	21	108	6.2	.978	R. Christopher	33	227	13	13	2	3.17
Connie Mack	SS	E. Busch	416	.250	0	35	209	370	29	67	5.2	.952	J. Flores	29	191	7	10	1	3.43
	3B	G. Kell	567	.272	4	56	**186**	**345**	20	32	**3.7**	**.964**	J. Berry	**52**	130	8	7	5	2.35
	RF	H. Peck	449	.276	5	39	190	9	12	3	1.9	.943	L. Knerr	27	130	5	11	0	4.22
	CF	B. Estalella	451	.299	8	52	314	10	4	3	2.6	.988	D. Black	26	125	5	11	0	5.17
	LF	C. Metro	200	.210	3	15	100	5	3	0	1.9	.972	C. Gassaway	24	118	4	7	0	3.74
	C	B. Rosar	300	.210	1	25	338	54	5	6	4.7	.987	S. Gerkin	21	102	0	12	0	3.62
	OF	B. McGhee	250	.252	0	19	84	2	1	0	1.8	.989							
	OF	M. Smith	203	.212	0	11	120	4	3	0	2.0	.976							
	SS	B. Wilkins	154	.260	0	4	74	118	16	23	5.2	.923							

AMERICAN LEAGUE 1945, *cont.*

BATTING AND BASE RUNNING LEADERS

Batting Average
S. Stirnweiss, NY .309
T. Cuccinello, CHI .308
J. Dickshot, CHI .302
B. Estalella, PHI .299
G. Myatt, WAS .296

Slugging Average
S. Stirnweiss, NY .476
V. Stephens, STL .473
R. Cullenbine, CLE, DET .444
N. Etten, NY .437
B. Estalella, PHI .435

Home Runs
V. Stephens, STL 24
R. Cullenbine, CLE, DET 18
N. Etten, NY 18
R. York, DET 18
J. Heath, CLE 15

Total Bases
S. Stirnweiss, NY 301
V. Stephens, STL 270
N. Etten, NY 247
R. York, DET 246
W. Moses, CHI 239

Runs Batted In
N. Etten, NY 111
R. Cullenbine, CLE, DET 93
V. Stephens, STL 89
R. York, DET 87
G. Binks, WAS 81

Stolen Bases
S. Stirnweiss, NY 33
G. Myatt, WAS 30
G. Case, WAS 30
C. Metkovich, BOS 19
J. Dickshot, CHI 18

Hits
S. Stirnweiss, NY 195
W. Moses, CHI 168
V. Stephens, STL 165
N. Etten, NY 161
I. Hall, PHI 161

Base on Balls
R. Cullenbine, CLE, DET 112
E. Lake, BOS 106
O. Grimes, NY 97
N. Etten, NY 90

Home Run Percentage
V. Stephens, STL 4.2
P. Seerey, CLE 3.4
R. Cullenbine, CLE, DET 3.4
N. Etten, NY 3.2

Runs
S. Stirnweiss, NY 107
V. Stephens, STL 90
R. Cullenbine, CLE, DET 83

Doubles
W. Moses, CHI 35
G. Binks, WAS 32
S. Stirnweiss, NY 32
G. McQuinn, STL 31

Triples
S. Stirnweiss, NY 22
W. Moses, CHI 15
J. Kuhel, WAS 13
J. Dickshot, CHI 10

PITCHING LEADERS

Winning Percentage
H. Newhouser, DET .735
D. Leonard, WAS .708
S. Gromek, CLE .679
B. Ferriss, BOS .677
R. Wolff, WAS .667

Earned Run Average
H. Newhouser, DET 1.81
A. Benton, DET 2.02
R. Wolff, WAS 2.12
D. Leonard, WAS 2.13
T. Lee, CHI 2.44

Wins
H. Newhouser, DET 25
B. Ferriss, BOS 21
R. Wolff, WAS 20
S. Gromek, CLE 19
D. Trout, DET 18
A. Reynolds, CLE 18

Saves
J. Turner, NY 10
J. Berry, PHI 5

Strikeouts
H. Newhouser, DET 212
N. Potter, STL 129
B. Newsom, PHI 127
A. Reynolds, CLE 112
T. Lee, CHI 108
R. Wolff, WAS 108

Complete Games
H. Newhouser, DET 29
B. Ferriss, BOS 26
R. Wolff, WAS 21
S. Gromek, CLE 21
N. Potter, STL 21

Fewest Hits/9 Innings
H. Newhouser, DET 6.86
R. Wolff, WAS 7.20
N. Potter, STL 7.47
B. Muncrief, STL 8.16

Shutouts
H. Newhouser, DET 8
A. Benton, DET 5
B. Ferriss, BOS 5

Fewest Walks/9 Innings
E. Bonham, NY 1.10
D. Leonard, WAS 1.46
R. Wolff, WAS 1.91
S. Gromek, CLE 2.37

Most Strikeouts/9 Inn.
H. Newhouser, DET 6.09
J. Kramer, STL 4.62
N. Potter, STL 4.55
B. Newsom, PHI 4.44

Innings
H. Newhouser, DET 313
B. Ferriss, BOS 265
B. Newsom, PHI 257
N. Potter, STL 255

Games Pitched
J. Berry, PHI 52
M. Pieretti, WAS 44
A. Reynolds, CLE 44
D. Trout, DET 41

							Batting						Fielding			Pitching					
	W	L	PCT	GB	R	OR	2B	3B	HR	BA	SA	SB	E	DP	FA	CG	BB	SO	ShO	SV	ERA
Detroit	88	65	.575		633	565	**227**	47	77	.256	.361	60	158	173	.975	78	538	**588**	**19**	**16**	2.99
Washington	87	67	.565	1.5	622	562	197	**63**	27	.258	.334	**110**	183	124	.970	82	**440**	550	**19**	11	**2.92**
St. Louis	81	70	.536	6	597	**548**	215	37	63	.249	.341	25	143	123	.976	**91**	506	570	10	8	3.14
New York	81	71	.533	6.5	**676**	606	189	61	**93**	.259	**.373**	64	175	170	.971	78	485	474	9	14	3.45
Cleveland	73	72	.503	11	557	**548**	216	48	65	.255	.359	19	**126**	149	**.977**	76	501	497	14	12	3.31
Chicago	71	78	.477	15	596	633	204	55	22	**.262**	.337	78	180	139	.970	84	448	486	13	13	3.69
Boston	71	83	.461	17.5	599	674	225	44	50	.260	.346	72	169	**198**	.973	71	656	490	15	13	3.80
Philadelphia	52	98	.347	34.5	494	638	201	37	33	.245	.316	25	168	160	.973	65	571	531	11	8	3.62
					4774	4774	1674	392	430	.256	.346	453	1302	1236	.973	625	4145	4186	110	95	3.36

NATIONAL LEAGUE 1946

St. Louis

W-98 L-58

Eddie Dyer

POS	Player	AB	BA	HR	RBI	PO	A	E	DP	TC/G	FA
1B	S. Musial	**624**	**.365**	16	103	1056	65	**13**	119	9.9	.989
2B	R. Schoendienst	606	.281	0	34	340	354	11	87	5.5	**.984**
SS	M. Marion	498	.233	3	46	**290**	**480**	21	**105**	**5.5**	.973
3B	W. Kurowski	519	.301	14	89	**175**	**249**	15	**17**	3.2	**.966**
RF	E. Slaughter	609	.300	18	**130**	284	23	6	6	2.0	.981
CF	H. Walker	346	.237	3	27	215	11	6	2	2.5	.974
LF	E. Dusak	275	.240	9	42	139	12	1	1	2.0	.993
C	J. Garagiola	211	.237	3	22	260	25	3	6	4.1	.990
OF	T. Moore	278	.263	3	28	158	5	3	0	2.5	.982
10	D. Sisler	235	.260	3	42	334	31	6	31		.984
OF	B. Adams	173	.185	5	22	95	1	1	1	1.7	.990

Pitcher	G	IP	W	L	SV	ERA
H. Pollet	40	**266**	**21**	10	5	**2.10**
H. Brecheen	36	231	15	15	3	2.49
M. Dickson	47	184	15	6	1	2.88
A. Brazle	37	153	11	10	0	3.29
J. Beazley	19	103	7	5	0	4.46
K. Burkhart	25	100	6	3	2	2.88

Brooklyn

W-96 L-60

Leo Durocher

POS	Player	AB	BA	HR	RBI	PO	A	E	DP	TC/G	FA
1B	E. Stevens	310	.242	10	60	716	48	11	59	7.8	.986
2B	E. Stanky	483	.273	0	36	**356**	359	17	**88**	5.2	.977
SS	P. Reese	542	.284	5	60	285	463	26	104	5.1	.966
3B	C. Lavagetto	242	.236	3	27	70	108	14	11	2.9	.927
RF	D. Walker	576	.319	9	116	237	15	8	3	1.7	.969
CF	C. Furillo	335	.284	3	35	292	9	5	4	2.7	.984
LF	P. Reiser	423	.277	11	73	205	14	5	2	2.3	.978
C	B. Edwards	292	.267	1	25	431	53	9	9	**5.4**	.982
UT	A. Galan	274	.310	3	38	211	44	16	3		.941
OF	D. Whitman	265	.260	2	31	178	5	0	0	2.2	1.000
1B	H. Schultz	249	.253	3	27	576	58	7	65	7.4	.989
C	F. Anderson	199	.256	2	14	258	35	11	5	4.3	.964
32	B. Herman	184	.288	0	28	73	91	5	13		.970

Pitcher	G	IP	W	L	SV	ERA
J. Hatten	42	222	14	11	2	2.84
K. Higbe	42	211	17	8	1	3.03
V. Lombardi	41	193	13	10	3	2.89
H. Behrman	47	151	11	5	4	2.93
H. Gregg	26	117	6	4	2	2.99
H. Casey	46	100	11	5	5	1.99
R. Melton	24	100	6	3	1	1.99
A. Herring	35	86	7	2	5	3.35

NATIONAL LEAGUE 1946, *cont.*

Chicago

W-82 L-71

Charlie Grimm

POS	Player	AB	BA	HR	RBI	PO	A	E	DP	TC/G	FA
1B	E. Waitkus	441	.304	4	55	992	81	4	76	10.2	.996
2B	D. Johnson	314	.242	1	19	192	228	8	34	5.2	.981
SS	B. Jurges	221	.222	0	17	119	204	8	26	4.5	.976
3B	S. Hack	323	.285	0	26	102	168	9	6	3.1	.968
RF	P. Cavarretta	510	.294	8	78	196	7	7	2	2.4	.967
CF	P. Lowrey	540	.257	4	54	308	15	7	3	2.6	.979
LF	M. Rickert	392	.263	7	47	200	5	6	1	2.0	.972
C	C. McCullough	307	.287	4	34	390	40	4	4	4.9	.991
OF	B. Nicholson	296	.220	8	41	179	4	5	1	2.3	.973
SS	B. Sturgeon	294	.296	1	21	109	158	19	31	4.0	.934
OF	A. Pafko	234	.282	3	39	165	13	4	4	2.8	.978
2B	L. Stringer	209	.244	3	19	135	150	13	17	4.8	.956
C	M. Livingston	176	.256	2	20	239	25	5	3	4.8	.981
3B	J. Ostrowski	160	.212	3	12	33	80	8	5	2.4	.934

Pitcher	G	IP	W	L	SV	ERA
J. Schmitz	41	224	11	11	2	2.61
H. Wyse	40	201	14	12	1	2.68
H. Borowy	32	201	12	10	0	3.76
P. Erickson	32	137	9	7	0	2.43
E. Kush	40	130	9	2	2	3.05
C. Passeau	21	129	9	8	0	3.13
B. Chipman	34	109	6	5	2	3.13
H. Bithorn	26	87	6	5	1	3.84

Boston

W-81 L-72

Billy Southworth

POS	Player	AB	BA	HR	RBI	PO	A	E	DP	TC/G	FA
1B	R. Sanders	259	.243	6	35	659	61	9	57	9.5	.988
2B	C. Ryan	502	.241	1	48	285	317	20	53	5.2	.968
SS	D. Culler	482	.255	0	33	279	380	36	68	5.3	.948
3B	N. Fernandez	372	.255	2	42	83	150	15	10	3.1	.940
RF	T. Holmes	568	.310	6	79	294	17	4	7	2.2	.987
CF	C. Gillenwater	224	.228	1	14	180	6	4	2	2.4	.979
LF	B. Rowell	293	.280	3	31	168	8	4	2	2.1	.978
C	P. Masi	397	.267	3	62	**470**	56	10	5	4.3	.981
10	J. Hopp	445	.333	3	48	670	45	11	45		.985
UT	B. Herman	252	.306	3	22	279	116	11	48		.973
OF	D. Litwhiler	247	.291	8	38	128	2	2	0	2.0	.985
3B	S. Roberge	169	.231	2	20	63	80	4	11	3.1	.973
OF	M. McCormick	164	.262	1	16	109	1	3	0	2.4	.973
C	D. Padgett	98	.255	2	21	65	12	5	1	3.2	.939

Pitcher	G	IP	W	L	SV	ERA
J. Sain	37	265	20	14	2	2.21
M. Cooper	28	199	13	11	1	3.12
E. Wright	36	176	12	9	0	3.52
B. Lee	25	140	10	9	0	4.18
S. Johnson	28	127	6	5	1	2.76
W. Spahn	24	126	8	5	1	2.94

Philadelphia

W-69 L-85

Ben Chapman

POS	Player	AB	BA	HR	RBI	PO	A	E	DP	TC/G	FA
1B	F. McCormick	504	.284	11	66	1185	98	1	92	9.6	**.999**
2B	E. Verban	473	.275	0	34	353	381*	28*	83	5.5	.963
SS	S. Newsome	375	.232	1	23	179	310	23	53	4.8	.955
3B	J. Tabor	463	.268	10	50	156	221	18	**17**	3.2	.954
RF	R. Northey	438	.249	16	62	194	7	6	3	1.9	.971
CF	J. Wyrostek	545	.281	6	45	388	18	8	4	2.9	.981
LF	D. Ennis	540	.313	17	73	332	16	9	4	2.6	.975
C	A. Seminick	406	.264	12	52	461	61	**14**	**12**	4.5	.974
UT	R. Hughes	276	.236	0	22	123	144	11	27		.960
OF	C. Gilbert	260	.242	1	17	154	9	0	4	2.4	1.000

Pitcher	G	IP	W	L	SV	ERA
K. Raffensberger	39	196	8	15	**6**	3.63
O. Judd	30	173	11	12	2	3.53
S. Rowe	17	136	11	4	0	2.12
C. Schanz	32	116	6	6	4	5.80
T. Hughes	29	111	6	9	1	4.38
D. Mauney	24	90	6	4	2	2.70
A. Karl	39	65	3	7	5	4.96

Cincinnati

W-67 L-87

Bill McKechnie
W-64 L-86

Hank Gowdy
W-3 L-1

POS	Player	AB	BA	HR	RBI	PO	A	E	DP	TC/G	FA
1B	B. Haas	535	.264	3	50	1346	91	9	**140**	**11.0**	.994
2B	B. Adams	311	.244	4	24	190	251	15	67	6.2	.967
SS	E. Miller	299	.194	6	36	184	297	15	79	5.6	.970
3B	G. Hatton	436	.271	14	69	108	194	**19**	14	2.8	.941
RF	A. Libke	431	.253	5	42	191	14	6	4	1.8	.972
CF	D. Clay	435	.228	2	22	312	10	4	3	2.7	.988
LF	E. Lukon	312	.250	12	34	190	5	3	1	2.4	.985
C	R. Mueller	378	.254	8	48	405	**65**	3	**12**	4.7	**.994**
20	L. Frey	333	.246	3	24	210	176	15	33		.963
23	B. Zientara	280	.289	0	16	114	219	11	38		.968
SS	C. Corbitt	274	.248	1	16	126	229	20	45	4.9	.947
C	R. Lamanno	239	.243	1	30	222	37	7	6	4.4	.974
OF	M. West	202	.213	5	18	112	6	6	3	2.1	.952

Pitcher	G	IP	W	L	SV	ERA
J. Vander Meer	29	204	10	12	0	3.17
E. Blackwell	33	194	9	13	0	2.45
J. Beggs	28	190	12	10	1	2.32
E. Heusser	29	168	7	14	2	3.22
B. Walters	22	151	10	7	0	2.56
J. Hetki	32	126	6	6	1	2.99
H. Gumbert	36	119	6	8	4	3.24

Pittsburgh

W-63 L-91

Frankie Frisch
W-62 L-89

Spud Davis
W-1 L-2

POS	Player	AB	BA	HR	RBI	PO	A	E	DP	TC/G	FA
1B	E. Fletcher	532	.256	4	66	**1356**	**106**	8	97	10.0	.995
2B	F. Gustine	495	.259	8	52	290	328	21	61	**5.7**	.967
SS	B. Cox	411	.290	2	36	235	323	**39**	59	5.2	.935
3B	L. Handley	416	.238	1	28	107	237	15	13	**3.5**	.958
RF	B. Elliott	486	.263	5	68	188	8	1	5	2.1	.995
CF	J. Russell	516	.277	8	50	308	7	11	1	2.4	.966
LF	R. Kiner	502	.247	**23**	81	339	6	11	0	2.5	.969
C	A. Lopez	150	.307	1	12	173	30	3	4	3.7	.985
UT	J. Brown	241	.241	0	12	127	168	16	28		.949
C	B. Salkeld	160	.294	3	19	176	31	6	3	4.2	.972

Pitcher	G	IP	W	L	SV	ERA
F. Ostermueller	27	193	13	10	0	2.84
N. Strincevich	32	176	10	15	1	3.58
K. Heintzelman	32	158	8	12	1	3.77
R. Sewell	25	149	8	12	0	3.68
E. Bahr	27	137	8	6	0	2.63
J. Hallett	35	115	5	7	0	3.29
K. Gables	32	101	2	4	1	5.27
J. Lanning	27	91	4	5	1	3.07
P. Roe	21	70	3	8	2	5.14

New York

W-61 L-93

Mel Ott

POS	Player	AB	BA	HR	RBI	PO	A	E	DP	TC/G	FA
1B	J. Mize	377	.337	22	70	928	83	11	80	10.1	.989
2B	B. Blattner	420	.255	11	49	285	315	15	62	5.4	.976
SS	B. Kerr	497	.249	6	40	240	400	12	66	5.2	**.982**
3B	B. Rigney	360	.236	3	31	77	143	8	8	3.1	.965
RF	G. Rosen	310	.281	5	30	200	3	5	0	2.5	.976
CF	W. Marshall	510	.282	13	48	253	14	6	2	2.2	.978
LF	S. Gordon	450	.293	5	45	197	8	1	0	2.0	.995
C	W. Cooper	280	.268	8	46	277	38	9	3	4.4	.972
10	B. Young	291	.278	7	33	492	24	7	25		.987
23	M. Witek	284	.264	4	29	138	150	20	23		.935
OF	J. Graham	270	.219	14	47	105	7	6	0	1.9	.949
C	E. Lombardi	238	.290	12	39	272	36	7	7	5.0	.978
OF	J. Rucker	197	.264	1	13	91	1	5	0	1.8	.948

Pitcher	G	IP	W	L	SV	ERA
D. Koslo	40	265	14	**19**	1	3.63
M. Kennedy	38	187	9	10	1	3.42
B. Voiselle	36	178	9	15	0	3.74
K. Trinkle	**48**	151	7	14	2	3.87
J. Thompson	39	63	4	6	4	1.29

NATIONAL LEAGUE 1946, *cont.*

BATTING AND BASE RUNNING LEADERS

Batting Average
S. Musial, STL .365
J. Hopp, BOS .333
D. Walker, BKN .319
D. Ennis, PHI .313
T. Holmes, BOS .310

Slugging Average
S. Musial, STL .587
D. Ennis, PHI .485
E. Slaughter, STL .465
W. Kurowski, STL .462
D. Walker, BKN .448

Home Runs
R. Kiner, PIT 23
J. Mize, NY 22
E. Slaughter, STL 18
D. Ennis, PHI 17
R. Northey, PHI 16
S. Musial, STL 16

Total Bases
S. Musial, STL 366
E. Slaughter, STL 283
D. Ennis, PHI 262
D. Walker, BKN 258
T. Holmes, BOS 241

Runs Batted In
E. Slaughter, STL 130
D. Walker, BKN 116
S. Musial, STL 103
W. Kurowski, STL 89
R. Kiner, PIT 81

Stolen Bases
P. Reiser, BKN 34
B. Haas, CIN 22
J. Hopp, BOS 21
B. Adams, CIN 16
D. Walker, BKN 14

Hits
S. Musial, STL 228
D. Walker, BKN 184
E. Slaughter, STL 183
T. Holmes, BOS 176

Base on Balls
E. Stanky, BKN 137
E. Fletcher, PIT 111
P. Cavarretta, CHI 88
P. Reese, BKN 87

Home Run Percentage
R. Kiner, PIT 4.6
R. Northey, PHI 3.7
G. Hatton, CIN 3.2
D. Ennis, PHI 3.1

Runs
S. Musial, STL 124
E. Slaughter, STL 100
E. Stanky, BKN 98
R. Schoendienst, STL 94

Doubles
S. Musial, STL 50
T. Holmes, BOS 35
W. Kurowski, STL 32
B. Herman, BKN, BOS 31

Triples
S. Musial, STL 20
P. Cavarretta, CHI 10
P. Reese, BKN 10
D. Walker, BKN 9

PITCHING LEADERS

Winning Percentage
M. Dickson, STL .714
K. Higbe, BKN .680
H. Pollet, STL .677
J. Sain, BOS .588
H. Brecheen, STL .500

Earned Run Average
H. Pollet, STL 2.10
J. Sain, BOS 2.21
J. Beggs, CIN 2.32
E. Blackwell, CIN 2.45
H. Brecheen, STL 2.49

Wins
H. Pollet, STL 21
J. Sain, BOS 20
K. Higbe, BKN 17
M. Dickson, STL 15
H. Brecheen, STL 15

Saves
K. Raffensberger, PHI 6
H. Pollet, STL 5
A. Herring, BKN 5
A. Karl, PHI 5
H. Casey, BKN 5

Strikeouts
J. Schmitz, CHI 135
K. Higbe, BKN 134
J. Sain, BOS 129
D. Koslo, NY 121
H. Brecheen, STL 117

Complete Games
J. Sain, BOS 24
H. Pollet, STL 22
D. Koslo, NY 17
F. Ostermueller, PIT 16
M. Cooper, BOS 15

Fewest Hits/9 Innings
M. Kennedy, NY 7.38
J. Schmitz, CHI 7.38
E. Blackwell, CIN 7.41
K. Higbe, BKN 7.60

Shutouts
E. Blackwell, CIN 6
J. Vander Meer, CIN 5
H. Brecheen, STL 5
M. Cooper, BOS 4
H. Pollet, STL 4

Fewest Walks/9 Innings
M. Cooper, BOS 1.76
K. Raffensberger, PHI 1.79
J. Beggs, CIN 1.85
N. Strincevich, PIT 2.25

Most Strikeouts/9 Inn.
K. Higbe, BKN 5.72
J. Schmitz, CHI 5.42
E. Blackwell, CIN 4.63
H. Brecheen, STL 4.55

Innings
H. Pollet, STL 266
J. Sain, BOS 265
D. Koslo, NY 265
H. Brecheen, STL 231

Games Pitched
K. Trinkle, NY 48
H. Behrman, BKN 47
M. Dickson, STL 47
H. Casey, BKN 46

	W	L	PCT	GB	R	OR	Batting 2B	3B	HR	BA	SA	SB	Fielding E	DP	FA	Pitching CG	BB	SO	ShO	SV	ERA
*St. Louis	98	58	.628		**712**	**545**	**265**	56	81	**.265**	**.381**	58	**124**	167	**.980**	**75**	493	607	**18**	15	**3.01**
Brooklyn	96	60	.615	2	701	570	233	**66**	55	.260	.361	**100**	174	154	.972	52	671	**647**	14	**28**	3.05
Chicago	82	71	.536	14.5	626	581	223	50	56	.254	.346	43	146	119	.976	59	527	609	14	11	3.24
Boston	81	72	.529	15.5	630	592	238	48	44	.264	.353	60	169	129	.972	74	478	531	10	12	3.37
Philadelphia	69	85	.448	28	560	705	209	40	80	.258	.359	41	148	144	.975	55	542	490	11	23	3.99
Cincinnati	67	87	.435	30	523	570	206	33	65	.239	.327	82	155	**192**	.975	69	**467**	506	16	11	3.07
Pittsburgh	63	91	.409	34	552	668	202	52	60	.250	.344	48	184	127	.970	61	541	458	10	6	3.72
New York	61	93	.396	36	612	685	176	37	**121**	.255	.374	46	159	121	.973	48	660	581	8	13	3.92
					4916	4916	1752	382	562	.256	.356	478	1259	1153	.974	493	4379	4429	101	119	3.42

* Defeated Brooklyn in playoff 2 games to 0

AMERICAN LEAGUE 1946

Boston

W-104 L-50

Joe Cronin

POS	Player	AB	BA	HR	RBI	PO	A	E	DP	TC/G	FA	Pitcher	G	IP	W	L	SV	ERA
1B	R. York	579	.276	17	119	**1327**	**116**	8	**154**	9.4	.994	T. Hughson	39	278	20	11	3	2.75
2B	B. Doerr	583	.271	18	116	**420**	**483**	13	**129**	6.1	**.986**	B. Ferriss	40	274	25	6	3	3.25
SS	J. Pesky	**621**	.335	2	55	296	479	25	96	5.2	.969	M. Harris	34	223	17	9	0	3.64
3B	R. Russell	274	.208	6	35	59	137	12	24	3.0	.942	J. Dobson	32	167	13	7	0	3.24
RF	C. Metkovich	281	.246	4	25	125	3	7	0	1.7	.948	J. Bagby	21	107	7	6	0	3.71
CF	D. DiMaggio	534	.316	7	73	390	9	6	2	2.9	.985	E. Johnson	29	80	5	4	3	3.71
LF	T. Williams	514	.342	38	123	325	7	10	2	2.3	.971	B. Klinger	28	57	3	2	**9**	2.37
C	H. Wagner	370	.230	6	52	**553**	39	10	3	5.2	.983							
3B	P. Higgins	200	.275	2	28	52	109	9	14	2.9	.947							
OF	L. Culberson	179	.313	3	18	87	1	3	0	1.9	.967							
OF	W. Moses	175	.206	2	17	92	3	2	1	2.2	.979							

Detroit

W-92 L-62

Steve O'Neill

POS	Player	AB	BA	HR	RBI	PO	A	E	DP	TC/G	FA	Pitcher	G	IP	W	L	SV	ERA
1B	H. Greenberg	523	.277	**44**	**127**	1272	93	**15**	110	**9.9**	.989	H. Newhouser	37	292	**26**	9	1	**1.94**
2B	J. Bloodworth	249	.245	5	36	157	184	9	46	4.9	.974	D. Trout	38	276	17	13	3	2.34
SS	E. Lake	587	.254	8	31	232	391	35	85	4.2	.947	V. Trucks	32	237	14	9	0	3.23
3B	G. Kell	434	.327	4	41	105*	210*	5	22*	3.0*	.984*	F. Hutchinson	28	207	14	11	2	3.09
RF	R. Cullenbine	328	.335	15	56	125	12	5	1	1.8	.965	A. Benton	28	141	11	7	1	3.65
CF	H. Evers	304	.266	4	33	196	2	5	0	2.7	.975	S. Overmire	24	97	5	7	1	4.62
LF	D. Wakefield	396	.268	12	59	210	6	8	1	2.2	.964							
C	B. Tebbetts	280	.243	1	34	486	53	10	4	6.3	.982							
03	J. Outlaw	299	.261	2	31	101	64	7	4		.959							
OF	P. Mullin	276	.246	3	35	121	8	7	1	1.8	.949							
OF	D. Cramer	204	.294	1	26	89	2	0	0	1.8	1.000							
2B	E. Mayo	202	.252	0	22	96	125	8	28	4.7	.965							
2B	S. Webb	169	.219	0	17	97	143	7	28	4.9	.972							

AMERICAN LEAGUE 1946, *cont.*

New York

W-87 L-67

Joe McCarthy
W-22 L-13

Bill Dickey
W-57 L-48

Johnny Neun
W-8 L-6

POS	Player	AB	BA	HR	RBI	PO	A	E	DP	TC/G	FA	Pitcher	G	IP	W	L	SV	ERA
1B	N. Etten	323	.232	9	49	717	55	7	80	9.3	.991	S. Chandler	34	257	20	8	2	2.10
2B	J. Gordon	376	.210	11	47	281	346	17	87	6.0	.974	B. Bevens	31	250	16	13	0	2.23
SS	P. Rizzuto	471	.257	2	38	267	378	26	97	**5.4**	.961	J. Page	31	136	9	8	3	3.57
3B	S. Stirnweiss	487	.251	0	37	66	152	2	18	2.8	.991	R. Gumpert	33	133	11	3	1	2.31
RF	T. Henrich	565	.251	19	83	224	10	2	5	2.1	.992	E. Bonham	18	105	5	8	3	3.70
CF	J. DiMaggio	503	.290	25	95	314	15	6	3	2.6	.982	A. Gettel	26	103	6	7	0	2.97
LF	C. Keller	538	.275	30	101	324	4	7	0	2.2	.979	J. Murphy	27	45	4	2	7	3.40
C	A. Robinson	330	.297	16	64	410	50	8	5	4.9	.983							
OF	J. Lindell	332	.259	10	40	159	8	3	3	2.3	.982							
3B	B. Johnson	296	.260	4	35	71	163	11	15	3.3	.955							

Washington

W-76 L-78

Ossie Bluege

POS	Player	AB	BA	HR	RBI	PO	A	E	DP	TC/G	FA	Pitcher	G	IP	W	L	SV	ERA
1B	M. Vernon	587	**.353**	8	85	1320	101	**15**	133	9.8	.990	M. Haefner	33	228	14	11	1	2.85
2B	G. Priddy	511	.254	6	58	378	428	**32**	105	**6.1**	.962	B. Newsom	24	178	11	8	1	2.78
SS	C. Travis	465	.252	1	56	133	196	14	45	4.6	.959	D. Leonard	26	162	10	10	0	3.56
3B	B. Hitchcock	354	.212	0	25	53	87	12	7	3.3	.921	R. Scarborough	32	156	7	11	1	4.05
RF	B. Lewis	582	.292	7	45	304	16	10	5	2.3	.970	S. Hudson	31	142	8	11	1	3.60
CF	S. Spence	578	.292	16	87	412	15	8	3	2.9	.982	R. Wolff	21	122	5	8	0	2.58
LF	J. Grace	321	.302	2	31	185	4	8	2	2.7	.959	E. Wynn	17	107	8	5	0	3.11
C	A. Evans	272	.254	2	30	336	30	**13**	5	4.7	.966	W. Masterson	29	91	5	6	1	6.01
UT	S. Robertson	230	.200	6	19	88	132	19	22		.921							
C	J. Early	189	.201	4	18	246	45	12	7	4.7	.960							
UT	G. Torres	185	.254	0	13	82	137	11	20		.952							
OF	J. Heath	166	.283	4	27	92	3	3	0	2.1	.969							

Chicago

W-74 L-80

Jimmy Dykes
W-10 L-20

Ted Lyons
W-64 L-60

POS	Player	AB	BA	HR	RBI	PO	A	E	DP	TC/G	FA	Pitcher	G	IP	W	L	SV	ERA
1B	H. Trosky	299	.254	2	31	729	33	7	63	9.6	.991	E. Lopat	29	231	13	13	0	2.73
2B	D. Kolloway	482	.280	3	53	235	281	15	74	5.9	.972	O. Grove	33	205	8	13	0	3.02
SS	L. Appling	582	.309	1	55	252	**505**	**39**	**99**	5.3	.951	J. Haynes	32	177	7	9	2	3.76
3B	D. Lodigiani	155	.245	0	13	41	88	9	4	3.1	.935	E. Smith	24	145	8	11	1	2.85
RF	T. Wright	422	.275	7	52	217	5	2	0	2.1	.991	F. Papish	31	138	7	5	0	2.74
CF	T. Tucker	438	.288	1	36	276	11	3	1	2.6	.990	E. Caldwell	39	91	13	4	8	2.08
LF	B. Kennedy	411	.258	5	34	157	10	6	1	2.3	.965	J. Rigney	15	83	5	5	0	4.03
C	M. Tresh	217	.217	0	21	330	48	2	**13**	4.8	.995	R. Hamner	25	71	2	7	1	4.42
2B	C. Michaels	291	.258	1	22	185	195	17	51	6.0	.957							
OF	R. Hodgin	258	.252	0	25	114	3	2	0	2.1	.983							
OF	W. Platt	247	.251	3	32	130	4	4	1	2.3	.971							
1B	J. Kuhel	238	.273	4	20	596	38	4	65	10.3	.994							
C	F. Hayes	179	.212	2	16	199	32	5	4	4.7*	.979							
OF	W. Moses	168	.274	4	16	84	2	0	0	2.4	1.000							

Cleveland

W-68 L-86

Lou Boudreau

POS	Player	AB	BA	HR	RBI	PO	A	E	DP	TC/G	FA	Pitcher	G	IP	W	L	SV	ERA
1B	L. Fleming	306	.278	8	42	607	62	11	60	8.5	.984	B. Feller	**48**	**371**	**26**	15	4	2.18
2B	D. Meyer	207	.232	0	16	110	150	6	26	4.2	.977	R. Embree	28	200	8	12	0	3.46
SS	L. Boudreau	515	.293	6	62	**315**	405	22	94	5.3	**.970**	A. Reynolds	31	183	11	15	0	3.88
3B	K. Keltner	398	.241	13	45	112	195	11	18	2.8	.965	S. Gromek	29	154	5	15	4	4.33
RF	H. Edwards	458	.301	10	54	226	13	8	1	2.0	.968	B. Lemon	32	94	4	5	1	2.49
CF	P. Seerey	404	.225	26	62	248	4	5	1	2.2	.981	J. Berry	21	37	3	6	1	3.38
LF	G. Case	484	.225	1	22	226	5	4	0	2.0	.983							
C	J. Hegan	271	.236	0	17	486	47	5	11	6.2	.991							
2B	J. Conway	258	.225	0	18	125	131	12	27	5.4	.955							
OF	F. Mackiewicz	258	.260	0	16	172	2	3	1	2.5	.983							
2B	R. Mack	171	.205	1	9	118	142	8	37	4.4	.970							
C	F. Hayes	156	.256	3	18	302	16	6	2	6.5*	.981							

St. Louis

W-66 L-88

Luke Sewell
W-53 L-71

Zack Taylor
W-13 L-17

POS	Player	AB	BA	HR	RBI	PO	A	E	DP	TC/G	FA	Pitcher	G	IP	W	L	SV	ERA
1B	C. Stevens	432	.248	3	27	1020	86	6	98	9.3	**.995**	J. Kramer	31	195	13	11	0	3.19
2B	J. Berardino	582	.265	5	68	374	414	23	96	5.7	.972	D. Galehouse	30	180	8	12	0	3.65
SS	V. Stephens	450	.307	14	64	224	343	30	71	5.3	.950	S. Zoldak	35	170	9	11	2	3.43
3B	M. Christman	458	.258	1	41	61	171	6	21	3.1	.975	N. Potter	23	145	8	9	0	3.72
RF	A. Zarilla	371	.259	4	43	236	13	7	6	2.4	.973	T. Shirley	27	140	6	12	0	4.96
CF	W. Judnich	511	.262	15	72	409	6	2	2	3.0	.995	B. Muncrief	29	115	3	12	0	4.99
LF	J. Heath	316	.275	12	57	147	5	6	1	1.9	.962	S. Ferens	34	88	2	9	0	4.50
C	F. Mancuso	262	.240	3	23	298	31	9	3	4.0	.973	T. Ferrick	25	32	4	1	5	2.78
OF	C. Laabs	264	.261	16	52	151	5	2	2	2.2	.987							
3B	B. Dillinger	225	.280	0	11	56	98	13	11	3.1	.922							
32	J. Lucadello	210	.248	1	15	84	102	7	14		.964							
C	H. Helf	182	.192	6	21	251	51	11	7	4.5	.965							
OF	G. McQuillen	166	.241	1	12	77	8	2	0	1.8	.977							
OF	J. Grace	161	.230	1	13	82	6	3	1	2.1	.967							

Philadelphia

W-49 L-105

Connie Mack

POS	Player	AB	BA	HR	RBI	PO	A	E	DP	TC/G	FA	Pitcher	G	IP	W	L	SV	ERA
1B	G. McQuinn	484	.225	3	35	1098	99	**15**	107	9.0	.988	P. Marchildon	36	227	13	**16**	1	3.49
2B	G. Handley	251	.251	0	21	159	146	17	32	4.7	.947	D. Fowler	32	206	9	**16**	0	3.28
SS	P. Suder	455	.281	2	50	151	204	15	39	5.5	.959	B. Savage	40	164	3	15	2	4.06
3B	H. Majeski	264	.250	1	25	78	159	8	22	3.4	.967	J. Flores	29	155	9	7	1	2.32
RF	E. Valo	348	.307	1	31	182	7	5	0	2.2	.974	L. Knerr	30	148	3	**16**	0	5.40
CF	B. McCosky	308	.354	1	34	207	2	4	0	2.5	.981	L. Harris	34	125	3	14	0	5.24
LF	S. Chapman	545	.261	20	67	369	13	12	4	2.7	.970	R. Christopher	30	119	5	7	0	4.30
C	B. Rosar	424	.283	2	47	532	**73**	0	9	5.2	**1.000**							
OF	T. Stainback	291	.244	0	20	153	5	6	1	2.5	.963							
SS	J. Wallaesa	194	.196	5	11	111	130	22	31	4.5	.916							
2B	O. Grimes	191	.262	1	20	98	105	9	30	4.9	.958							
2B	I. Hall	185	.249	0	19	105	113	6	20	5.6	.973							
OF	R. Derry	184	.207	0	14	127	3	2	2	2.6	.985							

AMERICAN LEAGUE 1946, *cont.*

BATTING AND BASE RUNNING LEADERS

Batting Average

M. Vernon, WAS	.353
T. Williams, BOS	.342
J. Pesky, BOS	.335
G. Kell, PHI, DET	.322
D. DiMaggio, BOS	.316

Slugging Average

T. Williams, BOS	.667
H. Greenberg, DET	.604
C. Keller, NY	.533
J. DiMaggio, NY	.511
H. Edwards, CLE	.509

Home Runs

H. Greenberg, DET	44
T. Williams, BOS	38
C. Keller, NY	30
P. Seerey, CLE	26
J. DiMaggio, NY	25

Total Bases

T. Williams, BOS	343
H. Greenberg, DET	316
M. Vernon, WAS	298
C. Keller, NY	287
S. Spence, WAS	287

Runs Batted In

H. Greenberg, DET	127
T. Williams, BOS	123
R. York, BOS	119
B. Doerr, BOS	116
C. Keller, NY	101

Stolen Bases

G. Case, CLE	28
S. Stirnweiss, NY	18
E. Lake, DET	15
P. Rizzuto, NY	14
D. Kolloway, CHI	14
M. Vernon, WAS	14

Hits

J. Pesky, BOS	208
M. Vernon, WAS	207
L. Appling, CHI	180
T. Williams, BOS	176

Base on Balls

T. Williams, BOS	156
C. Keller, NY	113
E. Lake, DET	103
R. Cullenbine, DET	88

Home Run Percentage

H. Greenberg, DET	8.4
T. Williams, BOS	7.4
P. Seerey, CLE	6.4
C. Keller, NY	5.6

Runs

T. Williams, BOS	142
J. Pesky, BOS	115
E. Lake, DET	105
C. Keller, NY	98

Doubles

M. Vernon, WAS	51
S. Spence, WAS	50
J. Pesky, BOS	43
T. Williams, BOS	37

Triples

H. Edwards, CLE	16
B. Lewis, WAS	13
G. Kell, PHI, DET	10
C. Keller, NY	10
S. Spence, WAS	10

PITCHING LEADERS

Winning Percentage

B. Ferriss, BOS	.806
H. Newhouser, DET	.743
S. Chandler, NY	.714
M. Harris, BOS	.654
T. Hughson, BOS	.645

Earned Run Average

H. Newhouser, DET	1.94
S. Chandler, NY	2.10
B. Feller, CLE	2.18
B. Bevens, NY	2.23
D. Trout, DET	2.34

Wins

H. Newhouser, DET	26
B. Feller, CLE	26
B. Ferriss, BOS	25
S. Chandler, NY	20
T. Hughson, BOS	20

Saves

B. Klinger, BOS	9
E. Caldwell, CHI	8
J. Murphy, NY	7
T. Ferrick, CLE, STL	6

Strikeouts

B. Feller, CLE	348
H. Newhouser, DET	275
T. Hughson, BOS	172
V. Trucks, DET	161
D. Trout, DET	151

Complete Games

B. Feller, CLE	36
H. Newhouser, DET	29
B. Ferriss, BOS	26
D. Trout, DET	23
T. Hughson, BOS	21

Fewest Hits/9 Innings

H. Newhouser, DET	6.62
B. Feller, CLE	6.71
S. Chandler, NY	6.99
B. Bevens, NY	7.68

Shutouts

B. Feller, CLE	10
S. Chandler, NY	6
H. Newhouser, DET	6
B. Ferriss, BOS	6
T. Hughson, BOS	6

Fewest Walks/9 Innings

T. Hughson, BOS	1.65
E. Lopat, CHI	1.87
B. Ferriss, BOS	2.33
D. Galehouse, STL	2.60

Most Strikeouts/9 Inn.

H. Newhouser, DET	8.47
B. Feller, CLE	8.43
V. Trucks, DET	6.12
F. Hutchinson, DET	6.00

Innings

B. Feller, CLE	371
H. Newhouser, DET	292
T. Hughson, BOS	278
D. Trout, DET	276

Games Pitched

B. Feller, CLE	48
B. Savage, PHI	40
B. Ferriss, BOS	40
E. Caldwell, CHI	39
T. Hughson, BOS	39

							Batting						Fielding			Pitching					
	W	L	PCT	GB	R	OR	2B	3B	HR	BA	SA	SB	E	DP	FA	CG	BB	SO	ShO	SV	ERA
Boston	104	50	.675		**792**	594	**268**	50	109	**.271**	**.402**	45	**139**	165	**.977**	79	501	667	15	**20**	3.38
Detroit	92	62	.597	12	704	567	212	41	108	.258	.374	65	155	138	.974	**94**	**497**	**896**	**18**	15	3.22
New York	87	67	.565	17	684	**547**	208	50	**136**	.248	.387	48	150	**174**	.975	68	552	653	17	17	3.13
Washington	76	78	.494	28	608	706	260	**63**	60	.260	.366	51	211	162	.966	71	547	537	8	10	3.74
Chicago	74	80	.481	30	562	595	206	44	37	.257	.333	**78**	175	170	.972	62	508	550	9	16	**3.10**
Cleveland	68	86	.442	36	537	637	233	56	79	.245	.356	57	147	147	.975	63	649	789	16	13	3.62
St. Louis	66	88	.429	38	621	711	220	46	84	.251	.356	23	159	157	.974	63	573	574	13	12	3.95
Philadelphia	49	105	.318	55	529	680	220	51	40	.253	.338	39	167	141	.971	61	577	562	10	5	3.90
					5037	5037	1827	401	653	.255	.364	406	1303	1254	.973	561	4404	5228	106	108	3.50

NATIONAL LEAGUE 1947

Brooklyn

W-94 L-60

Clyde Sukeforth
W-2 L-0

Burt Shotton
W-92 L-60

POS	Player	AB	BA	HR	RBI	PO	A	E	DP	TC/G	FA	Pitcher	G	IP	W	L	SV	ERA
1B	J. Robinson	590	.297	12	48	1323	92	16	**144**	9.5	.989	R. Branca	43	280	21	12	1	2.67
2B	E. Stanky	559	.252	3	53	402	406	12	**123**	5.6	**.985**	J. Hatten	42	225	17	8	0	3.63
SS	P. Reese	476	.284	12	73	266	441	25	99	5.2	.966	V. Lombardi	33	175	12	11	3	2.99
3B	S. Jorgensen	441	.274	5	67	116	235	19	26	2.9	.949	H. Taylor	33	162	10	5	1	3.11
RF	D. Walker	529	.306	9	94	261	9	10	0	1.9	.964	H. Gregg	37	104	4	5	1	5.87
CF	C. Furillo	437	.295	8	88	287	9	7	3	2.5	.977	H. Behrman	40	92	5	3	8	5.48
LF	P. Reiser	388	.309	5	46	240	3	3	0	2.3	.988	C. King	29	88	6	5	0	2.77
C	B. Edwards	471	.295	9	80	**592**	58	11	**11**	5.2	.983	H. Casey	46	77	10	4	**18**	3.99
OF	G. Hermanski	189	.275	7	39	105	5	2	0	1.7	.982							
03	A. Vaughan	126	.325	2	25	56	20	0	3		1.000							

St. Louis

W-89 L-65

Eddie Dyer

POS	Player	AB	BA	HR	RBI	PO	A	E	DP	TC/G	FA	Pitcher	G	IP	W	L	SV	ERA
1B	S. Musial	587	.312	19	95	1360	77	8	138	9.7	.994	M. Dickson	47	232	13	16	3	3.07
2B	R. Schoendienst	**659**	.253	3	48	357	404	19	109	5.5	.976	G. Munger	40	224	16	5	3	3.37
SS	M. Marion	540	.272	4	74	**329**	452	15	**104**	5.3	**.981**	H. Brecheen	29	223	16	11	1	3.30
3B	W. Kurowski	513	.310	27	104	140	250	19	17	2.9	.954	H. Pollet	37	176	9	11	2	4.34
RF	E. Dusak	328	.284	6	28	178	13	6	2	2.2	.970	A. Brazle	44	168	14	8	4	2.84
CF	T. Moore	460	.283	7	45	292	6	5	2	2.5	.983	J. Hearn	37	162	12	7	1	3.22
LF	E. Slaughter	551	.294	10	86	306	15	6	5	2.3	.982	K. Burkhart	34	95	3	6	1	5.21
C	D. Rice	261	.218	12	44	380	33	8	7	4.5	.981							
OF	R. Northey	311	.293	15	63	122	8	7	1	1.5	.949							
C	J. Garagiola	183	.257	5	25	281	23	4	2	4.2	.987							
OF	J. Medwick	150	.307	4	28	56	3	0	2	1.4	1.000							

Boston

W-86 L-68

Billy Southworth

POS	Player	AB	BA	HR	RBI	PO	A	E	DP	TC/G	FA	Pitcher	G	IP	W	L	SV	ERA
1B	E. Torgeson	399	.281	16	78	1033	76	**18**	83	9.6	.984	W. Spahn	40	**290**	21	10	3	**2.33**
2B	C. Ryan	544	.265	5	69	393	432	**23**	88	5.7	.973	J. Sain	38	266	21	12	1	3.52
SS	D. Culler	214	.248	0	19	106	212	11	31	4.4	.967	R. Barrett	36	211	11	12	1	3.55
3B	B. Elliott	555	.317	22	113	129	302	20	25	3.0	**.956**	B. Voiselle	22	131	8	7	0	4.32
RF	T. Holmes	618	.309	9	53	336	12	4	4	2.4	.989	S. Johnson	36	113	6	8	2	4.23
CF	J. Hopp	430	.288	2	32	296	2	6	0	2.4	.980							
LF	B. Rowell	384	.276	5	40	202	4	12	0	2.2	.945							
C	P. Masi	411	.304	9	50	411	58	5	1	3.9	**.989**							
OF	M. McCormick	284	.285	3	36	155	4	3	0	2.1	.981							
OF	D. Litwhiler	226	.261	7	31	119	2	3	0	1.9	.976							
1B	F. McCormick	212	.354	2	43	428	26	2	31	9.5	.996							
SS	N. Fernandez	209	.206	2	21	89	146	17	22	4.1	.933							

NATIONAL LEAGUE 1947, *cont.*

New York

W-81 L-73

Mel Ott

POS	Player	AB	BA	HR	RBI	PO	A	E	DP	TC/G	FA	Pitcher	G	IP	W	L	SV	ERA
1B	J. Mize	586	.302	**51**	**138**	**1380**	**117**	6	120	9.8	**.996**	L. Jansen	42	248	21	5	1	3.16
2B	B. Rigney	531	.267	17	59	184	229	11	41	5.9	.974	D. Koslo	39	217	15	10	0	4.39
SS	B. Kerr	547	.287	7	49	270	**460**	17	77	**5.4**	.977	M. Kennedy	34	148	9	12	0	4.85
3B	L. Lohrke	329	.240	11	35	118	187	20	20	2.9	.938	C. Hartung	23	138	9	7	0	4.57
RF	W. Marshall	587	.291	36	107	334	19	10	6	2.3	.972	K. Trinkle	**62**	94	8	4	10	3.75
CF	B. Thomson	545	.283	29	85	330	12	7	2	2.7	.980	H. Iott	20	71	3	8	0	5.93
LF	S. Gordon	437	.272	13	57	254	12	8	0	2.2	.971							
C	W. Cooper	515	.305	35	122	560	51	**13**	8	4.7	.979							
OF	L. Gearhart	179	.246	6	17	94	4	4	1	2.3	.961							
2B	M. Witek	160	.219	3	17	102	125	4	27	5.8	.983							
C	E. Lombardi	110	.282	4	21	86	11	2	2	4.1	.980							

Cincinnati

W-73 L-81

Johnny Neun

POS	Player	AB	BA	HR	RBI	PO	A	E	DP	TC/G	FA	Pitcher	G	IP	W	L	SV	ERA
1B	B. Young	364	.283	14	79	730	56	8	66	8.5	.990	E. Blackwell	33	273	**22**	8	0	2.47
2B	B. Zientara	418	.258	2	24	243	247	12	53	5.0	.976	J. Vander Meer	30	186	9	14	0	4.40
SS	E. Miller	545	.268	19	87	295	445	21	88	5.0	.972	K. Peterson	37	152	6	13	2	4.25
3B	G. Hatton	524	.281	16	77	143	248	26	18	3.1	.938	B. Lively	38	123	4	7	0	4.68
RF	F. Baumholtz	643	.283	5	45	282	18	7	2	2.0	.977	B. Walters	20	122	8	8	0	5.75
CF	B. Haas	482	.286	3	67	170	2	8	0	2.6	.956	E. Erautt	36	119	4	9	0	5.07
LF	A. Galan	392	.314	6	61	246	2	3	0	2.1	.988	K. Raffensberger	19	107	6	5	1	4.13
C	R. Lamanno	413	.257	5	50	556	**62**	9	6	**5.8**	.986	H. Gumbert	46	90	10	10	10	3.89
2B	B. Adams	217	.272	4	20	172	177	12	46	5.2	.967							
OF	E. Lukon	200	.205	11	33	103	4	0	2	1.9	1.000							
C	R. Mueller	192	.250	6	33	221	28	4	2	4.6	.984							
OF	T. Tatum	176	.273	1	16	117	6	0	3	2.5	1.000							
OF	C. Vollmer	155	.219	1	13	125	2	2	0	2.0	.984							

Chicago

W-69 L-85

Charlie Grimm

POS	Player	AB	BA	HR	RBI	PO	A	E	DP	TC/G	FA	Pitcher	G	IP	W	L	SV	ERA
1B	E. Waitkus	514	.292	2	35	1161	101	8	109	**10.1**	.994	J. Schmitz	38	207	13	**18**	4	3.22
2B	D. Johnson	402	.259	3	26	255	291	17	65	5.2	.970	D. Lade	34	187	11	10	0	3.94
SS	L. Merullo	373	.241	0	29	219	322	**29**	77	5.3	.949	H. Borowy	40	183	8	12	2	4.38
3B	P. Lowrey	448	.281	5	37	83	194	16	21	3.2	.945	P. Erickson	40	174	7	12	1	4.34
RF	B. Nicholson	487	.244	26	75	281	7	3	1	2.1	.990	H. Wyse	37	142	6	9	1	4.31
CF	A. Pafko	513	.302	13	66	327	9	5	3	2.7	.985	B. Chipman	32	135	7	6	0	3.68
LF	P. Cavarretta	459	.314	2	63	203	11	5	3	2.2	.977	E. Kush	47	91	8	3	5	3.36
C	B. Scheffing	363	.264	5	50	379	52	7	4	4.5	.984	C. Passeau	19	63	2	6	2	6.25
3B	S. Hack	240	.271	0	12	64	136	8	11	3.2	.962							
C	C. McCullough	234	.252	3	30	280	35	5	3	5.0	.984							
S2	B. Sturgeon	232	.254	0	21	135	192	6	42		.982							
OF	C. Aberson	140	.279	4	20	62	7	6	1	1.9	.920							

Philadelphia

W-62 L-92

Ben Chapman

POS	Player	AB	BA	HR	RBI	PO	A	E	DP	TC/G	FA	Pitcher	G	IP	W	L	SV	ERA
1B	H. Schultz	403	.223	6	35	986	67	7	92	9.3	.993	D. Leonard	32	235	17	12	0	2.68
2B	E. Verban	540	.285	0	42	**450**	**453**	17	111	**5.9**	.982	S. Rowe	31	196	14	10	1	4.32
SS	S. Newsome	310	.229	2	22	131	247	12	60	4.6	.969	O. Judd	32	147	4	15	0	4.60
3B	L. Handley	277	.253	0	42	87	144	6	8	2.9	.975	K. Heintzelman	24	136	7	10	1	4.04
RF	J. Wyrostek	454	.273	5	51	261	11	8	2	2.2	.971	T. Hughes	29	127	4	11	1	3.47
CF	H. Walker	488	.371*	1	41	350	15	13	2	3.0	.966	B. Donnelly	38	121	4	6	5	2.98
LF	D. Ennis	541	.275	12	81	320	12	7	2	2.5	.979	A. Jurisich	34	118	1	7	3	4.94
C	A. Seminick	337	.252	13	50	438	53	11	6	4.7	.978	C. Schanz	34	102	2	4	2	4.16
3B	J. Tabor	251	.235	4	31	68	96	15	8	2.7	.916	F. Schmidt	29	77	5	8	0	4.70
SS	R. LaPointe	211	.308	1	15	82	158	11	25	4.6	.956							
1C	A. Lakeman	182	.159	6	19	286	18	4	16		.987							
OF	B. Adams	182	.247	2	15	78	5	4	2	1.7	.954							
C	D. Padgett	158	.316	0	24	111	16	5	1	3.4	.962							

Pittsburgh

W-62 L-92

Billy Herman

W-61 L-92

Bill Burwell

W-1 L-0

POS	Player	AB	BA	HR	RBI	PO	A	E	DP	TC/G	FA	Pitcher	G	IP	W	L	SV	ERA
1B	H. Greenberg	402	.249	25	74	983	79	9	85	9.0	.992	K. Higbe	46	225	11	17	5	3.72
2B	J. Bloodworth	316	.250	7	48	222	206	9	56	5.0	.979	F. Ostermueller	26	183	12	10	0	3.84
SS	B. Cox	529	.274	15	54	220	388	20	63	4.9	.968	E. Bonham	33	150	11	8	3	3.85
3B	F. Gustine	616	.297	9	67	**198**	**330**	**31**	**35**	**3.6**	.945	P. Roe	38	144	4	15	2	5.25
RF	W. Westlake	407	.273	17	69	239	8	3	0	2.3	.988	R. Sewell	24	121	6	4	0	3.57
CF	J. Russell	478	.253	8	51	343	6	7	3	3.0	.980	J. Bagby	37	116	5	4	0	4.67
LF	R. Kiner	565	.313	**51**	127	390	8	7	1	2.7	.983	M. Queen	14	74	3	7	0	4.01
C	D. Howell	214	.276	4	25	272	30	8	2	4.2	.974							
OF	C. Rikard	324	.287	4	32	177	2	4	0	2.3	.978							
C	C. Kluttz	232	.302	6	42	247	55	4	7	4.4	.987							
2B	E. Basinski	161	.199	4	17	116	130	7	34	4.5	.972							
1B	E. Fletcher	157	.242	1	22	324	25	5	28	7.1	.986							

BATTING AND BASE RUNNING LEADERS

Batting Average

H. Walker, STL, PHI	.363
B. Elliott, BOS	.317
P. Cavarretta, CHI	.314
R. Kiner, PIT	.313
S. Musial, STL	.312

Slugging Average

R. Kiner, PIT	.639
J. Mize, NY	.614
W. Cooper, NY	.586
W. Kurowski, STL	.544
W. Marshall, NY	.528

Home Runs

R. Kiner, PIT	51
J. Mize, NY	51
W. Marshall, NY	36
W. Cooper, NY	35
B. Thomson, NY	29

Total Bases

R. Kiner, PIT	361
J. Mize, NY	360
W. Marshall, NY	310
W. Cooper, NY	302
S. Musial, STL	296

Runs Batted In

J. Mize, NY	138
R. Kiner, PIT	127
W. Cooper, NY	122
B. Elliott, BOS	113
W. Marshall, NY	107

Stolen Bases

J. Robinson, BKN	29
P. Reiser, BKN	14
J. Hopp, BOS	13
H. Walker, STL, PHI	13
E. Torgeson, BOS	11

PITCHING LEADERS

Winning Percentage

L. Jansen, NY	.808
G. Munger, STL	.762
E. Blackwell, CIN	.733
J. Hatten, BKN	.680
W. Spahn, BOS	.677

Earned Run Average

W. Spahn, BOS	2.33
E. Blackwell, CIN	2.47
R. Branca, BKN	2.67
D. Leonard, PHI	2.68
M. Dickson, STL	3.07

Wins

E. Blackwell, CIN	22
L. Jansen, NY	21
J. Sain, BOS	21
R. Branca, BKN	21
W. Spahn, BOS	21

Saves

H. Casey, BKN	18
K. Trinkle, NY	10
H. Gumbert, CIN	10
H. Behrman, PIT, BKN	8

Strikeouts

E. Blackwell, CIN	193
R. Branca, BKN	148
J. Sain, BOS	132
G. Munger, STL	123
W. Spahn, BOS	123

Complete Games

E. Blackwell, CIN	23
J. Sain, BOS	22
W. Spahn, BOS	22
L. Jansen, NY	20
D. Leonard, PHI	19

NATIONAL LEAGUE 1947, *cont.*

BATTING AND BASE RUNNING LEADERS

Hits		Base on Balls		Home Run Percentage	
T. Holmes, BOS	191	H. Greenberg, PIT	104	R. Kiner, PIT	9.0
H. Walker, STL, PHI	186	P. Reese, BKN	104	J. Mize, NY	8.7
S. Musial, STL	183	E. Stanky, BKN	103	W. Cooper, NY	6.8
F. Gustine, PIT	183	R. Kiner, PIT	98	H. Greenberg, PIT	6.2

Runs		Doubles		Triples	
J. Mize, NY	137	E. Miller, CIN	38	H. Walker, STL, PHI	16
J. Robinson, BKN	125	B. Elliott, BOS	35	E. Slaughter, STL	13
R. Kiner, PIT	118	C. Ryan, BOS	33	S. Musial, STL	13
S. Musial, STL	113	T. Holmes, BOS	33	F. Baumholtz, CIN	9
				R. Schoendienst, STL	9

PITCHING LEADERS

Fewest Hits/9 Innings		Shutouts		Fewest Walks/9 Innings	
H. Taylor, BKN	7.22	W. Spahn, BOS	7	L. Jansen, NY	2.07
E. Blackwell, CIN	7.48	G. Munger, STL	6	S. Rowe, PHI	2.07
W. Spahn, BOS	7.61	E. Blackwell, CIN	6	D. Leonard, PHI	2.18
R. Branca, BKN	8.07	M. Dickson, STL	4	K. Raffensberger, PHI, CIN	2.26
		R. Branca, BKN	4		

Most Strikeouts/9 Inn.		Innings		Games Pitched	
E. Blackwell, CIN	6.36	W. Spahn, BOS	290	K. Trinkle, NY	62
G. Munger, STL	4.93	R. Branca, BKN	280	H. Behrman, PIT, BKN	50
R. Branca, BKN	4.76	E. Blackwell, CIN	273	K. Higbe, BKN, PIT	50
J. Sain, BOS	4.47	J. Sain, BOS	266	E. Kush, CHI	47
				M. Dickson, STL	47

	W	L	PCT	GB	R	OR	Batting 2B	3B	HR	BA	SA	SB	Fielding E	DP	FA	Pitching CG	BB	SO	ShO	SV	ERA
Brooklyn	94	60	.610		774	668	241	50	83	.272	.384	**88**	129	164	.978	47	626	592	**14**	**34**	3.82
St. Louis	89	65	.578	5	780	634	235	**65**	115	.270	.401	28	**128**	**169**	**.979**	65	495	**642**	13	20	**3.53**
Boston	86	68	.558	8	701	**622**	**265**	42	85	**.275**	.390	58	153	124	.974	**74**	**453**	486	**14**	13	3.62
New York	81	73	.526	13	**830**	761	220	48	**221**	.271	**.454**	29	155	136	.974	58	590	553	6	14	4.44
Cincinnati	73	81	.474	21	681	755	242	43	95	.259	.375	46	138	134	.977	54	589	633	13	13	4.41
Chicago	69	85	.448	25	567	722	231	48	71	.259	.361	22	150	159	.975	46	618	571	8	15	4.10
Philadelphia	62	92	.403	32	589	687	210	52	60	.258	.352	60	152	140	.974	70	501	514	8	14	3.96
Pittsburgh	62	92	.403	32	744	817	216	44	156	.261	.406	30	149	131	.975	44	592	501	9	13	4.68
					5666	5666	1860	392	886	.266	.390	361	1154	1157	.976	458	4464	4492	85	136	4.07

AMERICAN LEAGUE 1947

New York

W-97 L-57

Bucky Harris

POS	Player	AB	BA	HR	RBI	PO	A	E	DP	TC/G	FA	Pitcher	G	IP	W	L	SV	ERA
1B	G. McQuinn	517	.304	13	80	1198	93	8	120	9.1	.994	A. Reynolds	34	242	19	8	2	3.20
2B	S. Stirnweiss	571	.256	5	41	337	402	13	107	5.1	.983	S. Shea	27	179	14	5	1	3.07
SS	P. Rizzuto	549	.273	2	60	340	450	25	111	5.4	.969	B. Bevens	28	165	7	13	0	3.82
3B	B. Johnson	494	.285	10	95	136	204	17	12	2.7	.952	J. Page	56	141	14	8	**17**	2.48
RF	T. Henrich	550	.287	16	98	278	13	5	2	2.2	.983	S. Chandler	17	128	9	5	0	**2.46**
CF	J. DiMaggio	534	.315	20	97	316	2	1	0	2.3	.997	B. Newsom	17	116	7	5	0	2.80
LF	J. Lindell	476	.275	11	67	308	6	7	1	2.7	.978	V. Raschi	15	105	7	2	0	3.87
C	A. Robinson	252	.270	5	36	346	38	1	3	5.2	.997	K. Drews	30	92	6	6	1	4.91
CO	Y. Berra	293	.280	11	54	307	18	9	5		.973							
OF	C. Keller	151	.238	13	36	85	2	3	0	2.1	.967							

Detroit

W-85 L-69

Steve O'Neill

POS	Player	AB	BA	HR	RBI	PO	A	E	DP	TC/G	FA	Pitcher	G	IP	W	L	SV	ERA
1B	R. Cullenbine	464	.224	24	78	1184	**139**	15	111	9.7	.989	H. Newhouser	40	285	17	**17**	2	2.87
2B	E. Mayo	535	.279	6	48	326	365	12	80	5.0	.983	F. Hutchinson	33	220	18	10	2	3.03
SS	E. Lake	602	.211	12	46	268	441	**43**	94	4.8	.943	D. Trout	32	186	10	11	2	3.48
3B	G. Kell	588	.320	5	93	167	**333**	**20**	25	**3.4**	.962	V. Trucks	36	181	10	12	2	4.53
RF	P. Mullin	398	.256	15	62	229	10	3	2	2.3	.988	S. Overmire	28	141	11	5	0	3.77
CF	H. Evers	460	.296	10	67	354	10	8	2	3.0	.978	A. Benton	36	133	6	7	7	4.40
LF	D. Wakefield	368	.283	8	51	197	10	11	2	2.2	.950	A. Houtteman	23	111	7	2	0	3.42
C	B. Swift	279	.251	1	21	401	45	5	6	4.6	.989	H. White	35	85	4	5	2	3.61
OF	V. Wertz	333	.288	6	44	160	6	6	0	2.1	.965							
C	H. Wagner	191	.288	5	33	275	25	3	3	4.3	.990							
OF	D. Cramer	157	.268	2	30	79	3	3	0	2.4	.965							

Boston

W-83 L-71

Joe Cronin

POS	Player	AB	BA	HR	RBI	PO	A	E	DP	TC/G	FA	Pitcher	G	IP	W	L	SV	ERA
1B	J. Jones	404	.235	16	76	1018*	73	10	11	10.1*	.991	J. Dobson	33	229	18	8	1	2.95
2B	B. Doerr	561	.258	17	95	376	**466**	16	**118**	**5.9**	.981	B. Ferriss	33	218	12	11	0	4.04
SS	J. Pesky	**638**	.324	0	39	251	391	16	90	4.9	.976	T. Hughson	29	189	12	11	0	3.33
3B	S. Dente	168	.232	0	11	40	83	8	11	2.8	.939	D. Galehouse	21	149	11	7	0	3.32
RF	S. Mele	453	.302	12	73	233	10	2	1	2.1	.992	E. Johnson	45	142	12	11	8	2.97
CF	D. DiMaggio	513	.283	8	71	413	19	10	4	3.3	.977	H. Dorish	41	136	7	8	2	4.70
LF	T. Williams	528	**.343**	**32**	**114**	347	10	9	2	2.3	.975							
C	B. Tebbetts	291	.299	1	28	332	50	10*	6	4.4	.974							
OF	W. Moses	255	.275	2	27	109	2	3	0	2.0	.974							
3S	E. Pellagrini	231	.203	4	19	73	142	14	17		.939							
1B	R. York	184	.212	6	27	395	36	2	45*	9.0	.995*							
C	R. Partee	169	.231	0	16	207	26	6	4	4.4	.975							

Cleveland

W-80 L-74

Lou Boudreau

POS	Player	AB	BA	HR	RBI	PO	A	E	DP	TC/G	FA	Pitcher	G	IP	W	L	SV	ERA
1B	E. Robinson	318	.245	14	52	800	55	5	79	9.9	.994	B. Feller	42	**299**	**20**	11	3	2.68
2B	J. Gordon	562	.272	29	93	341	**466**	18	110	5.3	.978	D. Black	30	191	10	12	0	3.92
SS	L. Boudreau	538	.307	4	67	305	475	14	**120**	5.4	**.982**	B. Lemon	37	167	11	5	3	3.44
3B	K. Keltner	541	.257	11	76	156	266	12	**29**	2.9	.972	R. Embree	27	163	8	10	0	3.15
RF	H. Edwards	393	.260	15	59	199	3	2	0	2.0	.990	A. Gettel	31	149	11	10	0	3.20
CF	C. Metkovich	473	.254	5	40	349	2	4	2	3.0	.989	E. Klieman	**58**	92	5	4	**17**	3.03
LF	D. Mitchell	493	.316	1	34	252	8	6	1	2.3	.977	B. Stephens	31	92	5	10	1	4.01
C	J. Hegan	378	.249	4	42	**566**	54	7	**14**	**4.7**	.989	S. Gromek	29	84	3	5	4	3.74
OF	H. Peck	392	.293	8	44	166	5	3	3	1.8	.983	M. Harder	15	80	6	4	0	4.50
1B	L. Fleming	281	.242	4	43	662	63	8	78	9.5	.989							
OF	P. Seerey	216	.171	11	29	105	7	5	1	1.7	.957							

AMERICAN LEAGUE 1947, *cont.*

Philadelphia

W-78 L-76

Connie Mack

POS	Player	AB	BA	HR	RBI	PO	A	E	DP	TC/G	FA	Pitcher	G	IP	W	L	SV	ERA
1B	F. Fain	461	.291	7	71	1141	101	**19**	118	9.6	.985	P. Marchildon	35	277	19	9	0	3.22
2B	P. Suder	528	.241	5	60	304	413	10	94	5.2	**.986**	D. Fowler	36	227	12	11	0	2.81
SS	E. Joost	540	.206	13	64	**370**	452	38	100	**5.7**	.956	B. McCahan	29	165	10	5	0	3.32
3B	H. Majeski	479	.280	8	72	160	263	5	28	3.2	**.988**	J. Coleman	32	160	6	12	1	4.32
RF	E. Valo	370	.300	5	36	205	9	6	0	2.1	.973	J. Flores	28	151	4	13	0	3.39
CF	S. Chapman	551	.252	14	83	428	16	6	2	3.1	.987	B. Savage	44	146	8	10	2	3.76
LF	B. McCosky	546	.328	1	52	346	8	6	2	2.6	.983	C. Scheib	21	116	4	6	0	5.04
C	B. Rosar	359	.259	1	33	406	**70**	2	12	4.7	**.996**	R. Christopher	44	81	10	7	12	2.90
OF	G. Binks	333	.258	2	34	157	8	6	1	2.3	.965							
C	M. Guerra	209	.215	0	18	203	36	9	5	4.0	.964							

Chicago

W-70 L-84

Ted Lyons

POS	Player	AB	BA	HR	RBI	PO	A	E	DP	TC/G	FA	Pitcher	G	IP	W	L	SV	ERA
1B	R. York	400	.243	15	64	932	71	5	104*	9.9	.995*	E. Lopat	31	253	16	13	0	2.81
2B	D. Kolloway	485	.278	2	35	274	306	**23**	76	6.1	.962	F. Papish	38	199	12	12	3	3.26
SS	L. Appling	503	.306	8	49	232	422	35	86	5.3	.949	J. Haynes	29	182	14	6	0	2.42
3B	F. Baker	371	.264	0	22	84	253	7	28	3.4	.980	O. Grove	25	136	6	8	0	4.44
RF	B. Kennedy	428	.262	6	48	204	8	7	3	2.1	.968	B. Gillespie	25	118	5	8	0	4.73
CF	D. Philley	551	.258	2	45	355	9	5	2	2.8	.986	E. Harrist	33	94	3	8	5	3.56
LF	T. Wright	401	.324	4	54	198	6	6	1	2.1	.971	T. Lee	21	87	3	7	1	4.47
C	M. Tresh	274	.241	0	20	313	38	9	10	4.0	.975	P. Gebrian	27	66	2	3	5	4.48
23	C. Michaels	355	.273	3	34	208	264	15	61		.969	G. Maltzberger	33	64	1	4	5	3.39
OF	T. Tucker	254	.236	1	17	171	5	4	2	2.8	.978	E. Caldwell	40	54	1	4	8	3.64
C	G. Dickey	211	.223	1	27	285	35	5	5	4.1	.985							
SO	J. Wallaesa	205	.195	7	32	129	95	5	22		.978							
OF	R. Hodgin	180	.294	1	24	99	2	1	0	2.5	.990							
1B	J. Jones	171	.240	3	20	444*	31	6	49	11.2*	.988							

Washington

W-64 L-90

Ossie Bluege

POS	Player	AB	BA	HR	RBI	PO	A	E	DP	TC/G	FA	Pitcher	G	IP	W	L	SV	ERA
1B	M. Vernon	600	.265	7	85	1299	105	**19**	123	9.2	.987	W. Masterson	35	253	12	16	1	3.13
2B	G. Priddy	505	.214	3	49	**382**	405	16	89	5.5	.980	E. Wynn	33	247	17	15	0	3.64
SS	M. Christman	374	.222	1	33	203	291	11	75	4.8	.978	M. Haefner	31	193	10	14	1	3.64
3B	E. Yost	428	.238	0	14	125	198	14	11	3.0	.958	R. Scarborough	33	161	6	13	0	3.41
RF	B. Lewis	506	.261	6	48	259	11	9	2	2.1	.968	S. Hudson	20	106	6	9	0	5.60
CF	S. Spence	506	.279	16	73	408	12	7	3	3.0	.984	B. Newsom	14	84	4	6	0	4.09
LF	J. Grace	234	.248	3	17	162	4	4	0	2.5	.976	T. Ferrick	31	60	1	7	9	3.15
C	A. Evans	319	.241	2	23	389	48	5	**14**	4.7	.989							
OF	S. Robertson	266	.233	1	23	126	5	7	1	2.5	.949							
3B	C. Travis	204	.216	1	10	28	68	7	6	2.6	.932							
OF	T. McBride	166	.271	0	15	103	2	3	0	2.1	.972							

St. Louis

W-59 L-95

Muddy Ruel

POS	Player	AB	BA	HR	RBI	PO	A	E	DP	TC/G	FA	Pitcher	G	IP	W	L	SV	ERA
1B	W. Judnich	500	.258	18	64	1067	76	13	118	9.0	.989	J. Kramer	33	199	11	16	1	4.97
2B	J. Berardino	306	.261	1	20	242	221	11	61	5.5	.977	E. Kinder	34	194	8	15	1	4.49
SS	V. Stephens	562	.279	15	83	283	**494**	24	113	5.4	.970	F. Sanford	34	187	7	16	4	3.71
3B	B. Dillinger	571	.294	3	37	**169**	265	19	21	3.3	.958	B. Muncrief	31	176	8	14	0	4.90
RF	A. Zarilla	380	.224	3	38	209	6	3	0	2.0	.986	S. Zoldak	35	171	9	10	1	3.47
CF	P. Lehner	483	.248	7	48	344	1	7	0	2.8	.980	C. Fannin	26	146	6	8	1	3.58
LF	J. Heath	491	.251	27	85	297	7	4	4	2.2	.987	N. Potter	32	123	4	10	2	4.04
C	L. Moss	274	.157	6	27	362	43	7	6	4.3	.983							
OF	R. Coleman	343	.259	2	30	174	7	3	**4**	2.0	.984							
UT	B. Hitchcock	275	.222	1	28	209	190	14	45		.966							
C	J. Early	214	.224	3	19	301	43	4	5	4.1	.989							

BATTING AND BASE RUNNING LEADERS

Batting Average
T. Williams, BOS .343
B. McCosky, PHI .328
J. Pesky, BOS .324
T. Wright, CHI .324
G. Kell, DET .320

Slugging Average
T. Williams, BOS .634
J. DiMaggio, NY .522
J. Gordon, CLE .496
T. Henrich, NY .485
J. Heath, STL .485

Home Runs
T. Williams, BOS 32
J. Gordon, CLE 29
J. Heath, STL 27
R. Cullenbine, DET 24
R. York, BOS, CHI 21

Total Bases
T. Williams, BOS 335
J. DiMaggio, NY 279
J. Gordon, CLE 279
T. Henrich, NY 267
J. Pesky, BOS 250

Runs Batted In
T. Williams, BOS 114
T. Henrich, NY 98
J. DiMaggio, NY 97
J. Jones, CHI, BOS 96
B. Johnson, NY 95
B. Doerr, BOS 95

Stolen Bases
B. Dillinger, STL 34
D. Philley, CHI 21
M. Vernon, WAS 12
J. Pesky, BOS 12

Hits
J. Pesky, BOS 207
G. Kell, DET 188
T. Williams, BOS 181
B. McCosky, PHI 179

Base on Balls
T. Williams, BOS 162
R. Cullenbine, DET 137
E. Lake, DET 120
E. Joost, PHI 114

Home Run Percentage
T. Williams, BOS 6.1
J. Heath, STL 5.5
R. Cullenbine, DET 5.2
J. Gordon, CLE 5.2

Runs
T. Williams, BOS 125
T. Henrich, NY 109
J. Pesky, BOS 106
S. Stirnweiss, NY 102

Doubles
L. Boudreau, CLE 45
T. Williams, BOS 40
T. Henrich, NY 35
J. DiMaggio, NY 31

Triples
T. Henrich, NY 13
M. Vernon, WAS 12
D. Philley, CHI 11

PITCHING LEADERS

Winning Percentage
A. Reynolds, NY .704
J. Dobson, BOS .692
P. Marchildon, PHI .679
B. Feller, CLE .645
F. Hutchinson, DET .643

Earned Run Average
S. Chandler, NY 2.46
B. Feller, CLE 2.68
D. Fowler, PHI 2.81
E. Lopat, CHI 2.81
H. Newhouser, DET 2.87

Wins
B. Feller, CLE 20
A. Reynolds, NY 19
P. Marchildon, PHI 19
F. Hutchinson, DET 18
J. Dobson, BOS 18

Saves
E. Klieman, CLE 17
J. Page, NY 17
R. Christopher, PHI 12
T. Ferrick, WAS 9
E. Caldwell, CHI 8
E. Johnson, BOS 8

Strikeouts
B. Feller, CLE 196
H. Newhouser, DET 176
W. Masterson, WAS 135
A. Reynolds, NY 129
P. Marchildon, PHI 128

Complete Games
H. Newhouser, DET 24
E. Lopat, CHI 22
E. Wynn, WAS 22
P. Marchildon, PHI 21
B. Feller, CLE 20

Fewest Hits/9 Innings
S. Shea, NY 6.40
B. Feller, CLE 6.92
S. Chandler, NY 7.03
P. Marchildon, PHI 7.42

Shutouts
B. Feller, CLE 5
M. Haefner, WAS 4
A. Reynolds, NY 4
W. Masterson, WAS 4

Fewest Walks/9 Innings
D. Galehouse, STL, BOS 2.48
F. Hutchinson, DET 2.50
E. Lopat, CHI 2.60
J. Dobson, BOS 2.87

Most Strikeouts/9 Inn.
B. Feller, CLE 5.90
T. Hughson, BOS 5.66
H. Newhouser, DET 5.56
E. Kinder, STL 5.09

Innings
B. Feller, CLE 299
H. Newhouser, DET 285
P. Marchildon, PHI 277
E. Lopat, CHI 253
W. Masterson, WAS 253

Games Pitched
E. Klieman, CLE 58
J. Page, NY 56
E. Johnson, BOS 45
R. Christopher, PHI 44
B. Savage, PHI 44

AMERICAN LEAGUE 1947, *cont.*

	W	L	PCT	GB	R	OR	Batting 2B	3B	HR	BA	SA	SB	Fielding E	DP	FA	Pitching CG	BB	SO	ShO	SV	ERA
New York	97	57	.630		**794**	**568**	230	**72**	**115**	**.271**	**.407**	27	109	151	.981	73	628	**691**	14	21	**3.39**
Detroit	85	69	.552	12	714	642	**234**	42	103	.258	.377	52	155	142	.975	**77**	**531**	648	**15**	18	3.57
Boston	83	71	.539	14	720	669	206	54	103	.265	.382	41	137	172	.977	64	575	586	13	19	3.81
Cleveland	80	74	.519	17	687	588	**234**	51	112	.259	.385	29	**104**	178	**.983**	55	628	590	13	**29**	3.44
Philadelphia	78	76	.506	19	633	614	218	52	61	.252	.349	37	143	161	.976	70	597	493	12	15	3.51
Chicago	70	84	.455	27	553	661	211	41	53	.256	.342	**91**	155	**180**	.975	47	603	522	11	27	3.64
Washington	64	90	.416	33	496	675	186	48	42	.241	.321	53	143	151	.976	67	579	551	**15**	12	3.97
St. Louis	59	95	.383	38	564	744	189	52	90	.241	.350	69	134	169	.977	50	604	552	7	13	4.33
					5161	5161	1708	412	679	.255	.364	399	1080	1304	.977	503	4745	4633	100	154	3.71

NATIONAL LEAGUE 1948

Boston

W-91 L-62

Billy Southworth

POS	Player	AB	BA	HR	RBI	PO	A	E	DP	TC/G	FA	Pitcher	G	IP	W	L	SV	ERA
1B	E. Torgeson	438	.253	10	67	1069	81	8	85	9.0	.993	J. Sain	42	**315**	**24**	15	1	2.60
2B	E. Stanky	247	.320	2	29	168	202	7	45	5.7	.981	W. Spahn	36	257	15	12	1	3.71
SS	A. Dark	543	.322	3	48	253	393	25	66	5.0	.963	B. Voiselle	37	216	13	13	2	3.63
3B	B. Elliott	540	.283	23	100	**146**	298	26	18	3.1	.945	V. Bickford	33	146	11	5	1	3.27
RF	T. Holmes	585	.325	6	61	283	8	5	4	2.2	.983	R. Barrett	34	128	7	8	0	3.65
CF	M. McCormick	343	.303	1	39	187	7	5	3	2.0	.975	B. Hogue	40	86	8	2	2	3.23
LF	J. Heath	364	.319	20	76	223	6	2	2	2.2	.991	C. Shoun	36	74	5	1	4	4.01
C	P. Masi	376	.253	5	44	458	39	6	5	4.6	.988							
OF	J. Russell	322	.264	9	54	246	3	2	0	3.0	.992							
OF	C. Conatser	224	.277	3	23	146	3	4	1	2.0	.974							
2S	S. Sisti	221	.244	0	21	140	173	14	32		.957							
C	B. Salkeld	198	.242	8	28	254	32	3	5	4.9	.990							
1B	F. McCormick	180	.250	4	34	343	33	5	30	7.6	.987							

St. Louis

W-85 L-69

Eddie Dyer

POS	Player	AB	BA	HR	RBI	PO	A	E	DP	TC/G	FA	Pitcher	G	IP	W	L	SV	ERA
1B	N. Jones	481	.254	10	81	1148	63	17	98	9.6	.986	M. Dickson	42	252	12	16	1	4.14
2B	R. Schoendienst	408	.272	4	36	230	269	10	57	5.3	.980	H. Brecheen	33	233	20	7	1	**2.24**
SS	M. Marion	567	.252	4	43	263	445	19	80	5.1	**.974**	H. Pollet	36	186	13	8	0	4.54
3B	D. Lang	323	.269	4	31	81	188	10	13	2.9	.964	G. Munger	39	166	10	11	0	4.50
RF	E. Slaughter	549	.321	11	90	330	9	10	1	2.4	.971	A. Brazle	42	156	10	6	1	3.80
CF	T. Moore	207	.232	4	18	131	2	1	0	1.9	.993	T. Wilks	57	131	6	6	13	2.62
LF	S. Musial	611	**.376**	39	**131**	347	10	7	3	2.3	.981	J. Hearn	34	90	8	6	1	4.22
C	D. Rice	290	.197	4	34	447	46	2	5	5.0	**.996**							
UT	E. Dusak	311	.209	6	19	191	80	5	14		.982							
OF	R. Northey	246	.321	13	64	85	2	1	0	1.3	.989							
2S	R. LaPointe	222	.225	0	15	142	158	12	36		.962							
3B	W. Kurowski	220	.214	2	33	55	100	10	7	2.5	.939							

Brooklyn

W-84 L-70

Leo Durocher
W-35 L-37

Ray Blades
W-1 L-0

Burt Shotton
W-48 L-33

POS	Player	AB	BA	HR	RBI	PO	A	E	DP	TC/G	FA	Pitcher	G	IP	W	L	SV	ERA
1B	G. Hodges	481	.249	11	70	830	60	13	85	9.4	.986	R. Barney	44	247	15	13	0	3.10
2B	J. Robinson	574	.296	12	85	308	315	13	80	5.5	**.980**	R. Branca	36	216	14	9	1	3.51
SS	P. Reese	566	.274	9	75	**335**	453	31	**93**	**5.5**	.962	J. Hatten	42	209	13	10	0	3.58
3B	B. Cox	237	.249	3	15	51	107	7	7	2.4	.958	P. Roe	34	178	12	8	2	2.63
RF	G. Hermanski	400	.290	15	60	225	13	7	1	2.1	.971	E. Palica	41	125	6	6	3	4.45
CF	C. Furillo	364	.297	4	44	274	13	5	2	2.8	.983	H. Behrman	34	91	5	4	7	4.05
LF	M. Rackley	281	.327	0	15	143	7	8	1	2.1	.949	W. Ramsdell	27	50	4	4	4	5.19
C	R. Campanella	279	.258	9	45	413	45	9	**12**	6.0	.981							
UT	B. Edwards	286	.276	8	54	264	43	12	2		.962							
23	E. Miksis	221	.213	2	16	122	143	9	19		.967							
OF	D. Whitman	165	.291	0	20	93	3	1	0	2.0	.990							
OF	G. Shuba	161	.267	4	32	87	1	6	1	1.7	.936							
OF	D. Snider	160	.244	5	21	87	5	1	0	2.0	.989							
1B	P. Ward	146	.260	1	21	268	20	3	21	7.7	.990							
3B	T. Brown	145	.241	2	20	43	60	7	7	2.6	.936							
OF	A. Vaughan	123	.244	3	22	47	4	0	0	2.0	1.000							

Pittsburgh

W-83 L-71

Billy Meyer

POS	Player	AB	BA	HR	RBI	PO	A	E	DP	TC/G	FA	Pitcher	G	IP	W	L	SV	ERA
1B	E. Stevens	429	.254	10	69	1021	83	4	94	9.5	**.996**	B. Chesnes	25	194	14	6	0	3.57
2B	D. Murtaugh	514	.290	1	71	**375**	**412**	17	**95**	**5.5**	.979	E. Riddle	28	191	12	10	1	3.49
SS	S. Rojek	**641**	.290	4	51	262	**475**	29	91	4.9	.962	V. Lombardi	38	163	10	9	4	3.70
3B	F. Gustine	449	.267	9	42	119	256	21	21	3.3	.947	K. Higbe	56	158	8	7	10	3.36
RF	D. Walker	408	.316	2	54	168	4	4	0	1.6	.977	E. Bonham	22	136	6	10	0	4.31
CF	W. Westlake	428	.285	17	65	274	8	7	2	2.3	.976	F. Ostermueller	23	134	8	11	0	4.42
LF	R. Kiner	555	.265	**40**	123	382	6	10	1	2.6	.975	R. Sewell	21	122	13	3	0	3.48
C	E. Fitz Gerald	262	.267	1	35	338	36	15	4	4.1	.961	E. Singleton	38	92	4	6	2	4.97
OF	J. Hopp	392	.278	1	31	192	3	0	1	2.4	1.000							
C	C. Kluttz	271	.221	4	20	298	54	8	8	4.0	.978							
3B	E. Bockman	176	.239	4	23	50	100	6	9	3.1	.962							
10	M. West	146	.178	8	21	209	20	2	14		.991							

New York

W-78 L-76

Mel Ott
W-37 L-38

Leo Durocher
W-41 L-38

POS	Player	AB	BA	HR	RBI	PO	A	E	DP	TC/G	FA	Pitcher	G	IP	W	L	SV	ERA
1B	J. Mize	560	.289	**40**	125	**1359**	**111**	13	**114**	9.8	.991	L. Jansen	42	277	18	12	2	3.61
2B	B. Rigney	424	.264	10	43	258	275	**18**	48	5.2	.967	S. Jones	55	201	16	8	5	3.35
SS	B. Kerr	496	.240	0	46	269	456	25	72	5.2	.967	R. Poat	39	158	11	10	0	4.34
3B	S. Gordon	521	.299	30	107	126	220	19	19	3.2	**.948**	C. Hartung	36	153	8	8	1	4.75
RF	W. Marshall	537	.272	14	86	266	16	5	2	2.0	.983	D. Koslo	35	149	8	10	3	3.87
CF	W. Lockman	584	.286	18	59	388	6	5	0	2.8	.987	M. Kennedy	25	114	3	9	0	4.01
LF	B. Thomson	471	.248	16	63	313	10	10	2	2.7	.970	A. Hansen	36	100	5	3	1	2.97
C	W. Cooper	290	.266	16	54	307	21	7	3	4.2	.979	K. Trinkle	53	71	4	5	7	3.18
32	L. Lohrke	280	.250	5	31	125	170	22	21		.931							

NATIONAL LEAGUE 1948, *cont.*

Team	POS	Player	AB	BA	HR	RBI	PO	A	E	DP	TC/G	FA	Pitcher	G	IP	W	L	SV	ERA
Philadelphia	1B	D. Sisler	446	.274	11	56	986	73	**18**	88	9.0	.983	D. Leonard	34	226	11	**18**	0	2.51
W-66 L-88	2B	G. Hamner	446	.260	3	48	210	224	15	46	5.2	.967	C. Simmons	31	170	7	12	0	4.87
Ben Chapman	SS	E. Miller	468	.246	14	61	229	341	20	63	4.8	.966	M. Dubiel	37	150	9	10	4	3.89
W-37 L-42	3B	P. Caballero	351	.245	0	19	105	147	10	14	3.3	.962	S. Rowe	30	148	10	10	2	4.07
Dusty Cooke	RF	D. Ennis	589	.290	30	95	297	15	14	4	2.2	.957	R. Roberts	20	147	7	9	0	3.19
W-6 L-6	CF	R. Ashburn	463	.333	2	40	344	14	7	2	3.1	.981	B. Donnelly	26	132	5	7	2	3.69
Eddie Sawyer	LF	J. Blatnik	415	.260	6	45	220	9	13	1	2.3	.946	K. Heintzelman	27	130	6	11	2	4.29
W-23 L-40	C	A. Seminick	391	.225	13	44	**541**	**74**	**22**	8	**5.1**	.965							
	31	B. Haas	333	.282	4	34	366	107	24	26		.952							
	OF	H. Walker	332	.292	2	23	198	6	4	1	2.6	.981							
	UT	B. Rowell	196	.240	1	22	76	42	12	7		.908							
	2B	E. Verban	169	.231	0	11	104	126	6	25	4.4	.975							
Cincinnati	1B	T. Kluszewski	379	.274	12	57	833	65	9	60	9.3	.990	J. Vander Meer	33	232	17	14	0	3.41
W-64 L-89	2B	B. Adams	262	.298	1	21	160	143	11	33	4.9	.965	K. Raffensberger	40	180	11	12	0	3.84
Johnny Neun	SS	V. Stallcup	539	.228	3	65	264	433	32	84	4.9	.956	H. Fox	34	171	6	9	1	4.53
W-44 L-56	3B	G. Hatton	458	.240	9	44	141	243	28	21	3.3	.932	H. Wehmeier	33	147	11	8	0	5.86
Bucky Walters	RF	F. Baumholtz	415	.296	4	30	216	11	3	2	2.1	.987	E. Blackwell	22	139	7	9	1	4.54
W-20 L-33	CF	J. Wyrostek	512	.273	17	76	331	8	8	1	2.7	.977	K. Peterson	43	137	2	15	1	4.60
	LF	H. Sauer	530	.260	35	97	270	14	8	6	2.2	.973	H. Gumbert	**61**	106	10	8	**17**	3.47
	C	R. Lamanno	385	.242	0	27	537	49	13	11	4.8	.978							
	OF	D. Litwhiler	338	.275	14	44	165	3	2	2	2.0	.988							
	UT	C. Corbitt	258	.256	0	18	138	160	7	24		.977							
	2B	B. Zientara	187	.187	0	7	143	140	3	32	4.8	.990							
Chicago	1B	E. Waitkus	562	.295	7	44	1064	92	9	77	**10.0**	.992	J. Schmitz	34	242	18	13	1	2.64
W-64 L-90	2B	H. Schenz	337	.261	1	14	184	190	10	45	4.9	.974	R. Meyer	29	165	10	10	0	3.66
Charlie Grimm	SS	R. Smalley	361	.216	4	36	189	351	**34**	70	4.6	.941	D. McCall	30	151	4	13	0	4.82
	3B	A. Pafko	548	.312	26	101	125	**314**	**29**	**29**	**3.4**	.938	B. Rush	36	133	5	11	0	3.92
	RF	B. Nicholson	494	.261	19	67	244	7	5	1	1.9	.980	H. Borowy	39	127	5	10	1	4.89
	CF	H. Jeffcoat	473	.279	4	42	307	12	8	3	2.7	.976	R. Hamner	27	111	5	9	0	4.69
	LF	P. Lowrey	435	.294	2	54	225	9	4	2	2.3	.983	C. Chambers	29	104	2	9	0	4.43
	C	B. Scheffing	293	.300	5	45	332	36	4	5	4.8	.989	D. Lade	19	87	5	6	0	4.02
	10	P. Cavarretta	334	.278	3	40	446	32	3	46		.994	J. Dobernic	54	86	7	2	1	3.15
	2B	E. Verban	248	.294	1	16	134	164	11	47	5.5	.964							
	OF	C. Maddern	214	.252	4	27	98	6	2	0	1.9	.981							
	C	C. McCullough	172	.209	1	7	225	25	7	5	5.0	.973							
	C	R. Walker	171	.275	5	26	178	22	4	3	4.6	.980							

BATTING AND BASE RUNNING LEADERS

Batting Average
S. Musial, STL .376
R. Ashburn, PHI .333
T. Holmes, BOS .325
A. Dark, BOS .322
E. Slaughter, STL .321

Slugging Average
S. Musial, STL .702
J. Mize, NY .564
S. Gordon, NY .537
R. Kiner, PIT .533
D. Ennis, PHI .525

Home Runs
R. Kiner, PIT 40
J. Mize, NY 40
S. Musial, STL 39
H. Sauer, CIN 35
S. Gordon, NY 30
D. Ennis, PHI 30

Total Bases
S. Musial, STL 429
J. Mize, NY 316
D. Ennis, PHI 309
R. Kiner, PIT 296
A. Pafko, CHI 283

Runs Batted In
S. Musial, STL 131
J. Mize, NY 125
R. Kiner, PIT 123
S. Gordon, NY 107
A. Pafko, CHI 101

Stolen Bases
R. Ashburn, PHI 32
P. Reese, BKN 25
S. Rojek, PIT 24
J. Robinson, BKN 22
E. Torgeson, BOS 19

Hits
S. Musial, STL 230
T. Holmes, BOS 190
S. Rojek, PIT 186
E. Slaughter, STL 176

Base on Balls
B. Elliott, BOS 131
R. Kiner, PIT 112
J. Mize, NY 94

Home Run Percentage
R. Kiner, PIT 7.2
J. Mize, NY 7.1
H. Sauer, CIN 6.6
S. Musial, STL 6.4

Runs
S. Musial, STL 135
W. Lockman, NY 117
J. Mize, NY 110
J. Robinson, BKN 108

Doubles
S. Musial, STL 46
D. Ennis, PHI 40
A. Dark, BOS 39
J. Robinson, BKN 38

Triples
S. Musial, STL 18
J. Hopp, PIT 12
E. Slaughter, STL 11
E. Waitkus, CHI 10
W. Lockman, NY 10

PITCHING LEADERS

Winning Percentage
H. Brecheen, STL .741
S. Jones, NY .667
J. Sain, BOS .615
L. Jansen, NY .600
J. Schmitz, CHI .581

Earned Run Average
H. Brecheen, STL 2.24
D. Leonard, PHI 2.51
J. Sain, BOS 2.60
J. Schmitz, CHI 2.64
R. Barney, BKN 3.10

Wins
J. Sain, BOS 24
H. Brecheen, STL 20
J. Schmitz, CHI 18
L. Jansen, NY 18
J. Vander Meer, CIN 17

Saves
H. Gumbert, CIN 17
T. Wilks, STL 13
K. Higbe, PIT 10
H. Behrman, BKN 7
K. Trinkle, NY 7

Strikeouts
H. Brecheen, STL 149
R. Barney, BKN 138
J. Sain, BOS 137
L. Jansen, NY 126
R. Branca, BKN 122

Complete Games
J. Sain, BOS 28
H. Brecheen, STL 21
J. Schmitz, CHI 18
D. Leonard, PHI 16
W. Spahn, BOS 16

Fewest Hits/9 Innings
J. Schmitz, CHI 6.92
R. Barney, BKN 7.04
H. Brecheen, STL 7.44
V. Bickford, BOS 7.71

Shutouts
H. Brecheen, STL 7
K. Raffensberger, CIN 4
R. Barney, BKN 4
L. Jansen, NY 4
J. Sain, BOS 4

Fewest Walks/9 Innings
L. Jansen, NY 1.75
H. Brecheen, STL 1.89
D. Leonard, PHI 2.15
J. Sain, BOS 2.37

Most Strikeouts/9 Inn.
H. Brecheen, STL 5.75
R. Branca, BKN 5.09
R. Barney, BKN 5.04
J. Vander Meer, CIN 4.66

Innings
J. Sain, BOS 315
L. Jansen, NY 277
W. Spahn, BOS 257
M. Dickson, STL 252

Games Pitched
H. Gumbert, CIN 61
T. Wilks, STL 57
K. Higbe, PIT 56
S. Jones, NY 55

							Batting						Fielding			Pitching					
	W	L	PCT	GB	R	OR	2B	3B	HR	BA	SA	SB	E	DP	FA	CG	BB	SO	ShO	SV	ERA
Boston	91	62	.595		739	**584**	**272**	49	95	**.275**	.399	43	143	132	.976	**70**	**430**	579	10	17	**3.38**
St. Louis	85	69	.552	6.5	742	646	238	**58**	105	.263	.389	24	**119**	138	**.980**	60	476	635	13	18	3.91
Brooklyn	84	70	.545	7.5	744	667	256	54	91	.261	.381	**114**	161	151	.973	52	633	**670**	9	**22**	3.75
Pittsburgh	83	71	.539	8.5	706	699	191	54	108	.263	.380	68	137	150	.977	65	564	519	5	19	4.15
New York	78	76	.506	13.5	**780**	704	210	49	**164**	.256	**.408**	51	156	134	.974	54	551	527	**15**	21	3.93
Philadelphia	66	88	.429	25.5	591	729	227	39	91	.259	.368	68	210	126	.964	61	561	552	6	15	4.08
Cincinnati	64	89	.418	27	588	752	221	37	104	.247	.365	42	158	135	.973	40	572	599	9	20	4.47
Chicago	64	90	.416	27.5	597	706	225	44	87	.262	.369	39	172	**152**	.972	51	609	636	7	10	4.00
					5487	5487	1840	384	845	.261	.382	449	1256	1118	.974	453	4396	4717	74	142	3.96

AMERICAN LEAGUE 1948

Team	POS	Player	AB	BA	HR	RBI	PO	A	E	DP	TC/G	FA	Pitcher	G	IP	W	L	SV	ERA
Cleveland	1B	E. Robinson	493	.254	16	83	1213	79	7	123	9.9	**.995**	B. Lemon	43	**294**	20	14	2	2.82
W-97 L-58	2B	J. Gordon	550	.280	32	124	330	436	23	97	5.5	.971	B. Feller	44	280	19	15	3	3.56
Lou Boudreau	SS	L. Boudreau	560	.355	18	106	297	483	20	**119**	5.3	**.975**	G. Bearden	37	230	20	7	1	**2.43**
	3B	K. Keltner	558	.297	31	119	123	**312**	14	27	2.9	.969	S. Gromek	38	130	9	3	2	2.84
	RF	L. Doby	439	.301	14	66	287	12	14	3	2.7	.955	S. Zoldak	23	106	9	6	0	2.81
	CF	T. Tucker	242	.260	1	19	172	5	0	2	2.7	1.000	R. Christopher	45	59	3	2	**17**	2.90
	LF	D. Mitchell	608	.336	4	56	307	12	3	3	2.3	.991							
	C	J. Hegan	472	.248	14	61	**637**	**76**	7	**17**	**5.1**	.990							
	OF	A. Clark	271	.310	9	38	108	4	2	1	1.8	.982							
	OF	W. Judnich	218	.257	2	29	93	4	3	0	2.0	.970							
	OF	H. Edwards	160	.269	3	18	76	1	1	0	1.9	.987							
	P	B. Lemon	119	.286	5	21	**23**	**86**	4	8	**2.6**	.965							
Boston	1B	B. Goodman	445	.310	1	66	1101	69	8	118	**10.1**	.993	J. Dobson	38	245	16	10	2	3.56
W-96 L-59	2B	B. Doerr	527	.285	27	111	366	430	6	119	5.8	.993	M. Parnell	35	212	15	8	0	3.14
Joe McCarthy	SS	V. Stephens	635	.269	29	137	269	**540**	**24**	113	5.4	.971	J. Kramer	29	205	18	5	0	4.35
	3B	J. Pesky	565	.281	3	55	121	303	**22**	**35**	3.2	.951	E. Kinder	28	178	10	7	0	3.74
	RF	S. Spence	391	.235	12	61	206	4	5	1	2.3	.977	D. Galehouse	27	137	8	8	3	4.00
	CF	D. DiMaggio	**648**	.285	9	87	503	13	10	4	3.4	.981	B. Ferriss	31	115	7	3	3	5.23
	LF	T. Williams	509	**.369**	25	127	289	9	5	2	2.3	.983	M. Harris	20	114	7	10	0	5.30
	C	B. Tebbetts	446	.280	5	68	470	56	**10**	8	4.3	.981	E. Johnson	35	91	10	4	5	4.53
	OF	W. Moses	189	.259	2	29	101	2	2	1	2.3	.981							
	OF	S. Mele	180	.233	2	25	99	2	3	0	1.9	.971							
	23	B. Hitchcock	124	.298	1	20	54	82	4	15		.971							
	C	M. Batts	118	.314	1	24	118	18	2	3	3.4	.986							
New York	1B	G. McQuinn	302	.248	11	41	693	48	5	79	8.3	.993	A. Reynolds	39	236	16	7	3	3.77
W-94 L-60	2B	S. Stirnweiss	515	.252	3	32	346	364	5	103	5.1	**.993**	E. Lopat	33	227	17	11	0	3.65
Bucky Harris	SS	P. Rizzuto	464	.252	6	50	259	348	17	85	4.9	.973	V. Raschi	36	223	19	8	1	3.84
	3B	B. Johnson	446	.294	12	64	147	213	20	25	**3.2**	.947	S. Shea	28	156	9	10	1	3.41
	RF	T. Henrich	588	.308	25	100	216	8	5	4	2.2	.978	T. Byrne	31	134	8	5	2	3.30
	CF	J. DiMaggio	594	.320	**39**	**155**	441	8	13	1	3.0	.972	J. Page	**55**	108	7	8	16	4.26
	LF	J. Lindell	309	.317	13	55	165	7	1	1	2.2	.994							
	C	G. Niarhos	228	.268	0	19	376	33	4	7	5.0	.990							
	CO	Y. Berra	469	.305	14	98	390	40	9	7		.979							
	UT	B. Brown	363	.300	3	48	130	173	18	33		.944							
	OF	C. Keller	247	.267	6	44	126	1	3	0	2.0	.977							
Philadelphia	1B	F. Fain	520	.281	7	88	1284	**120**	**16**	148	9.8	.989	P. Marchildon	33	226	9	15	0	4.53
W-84 L-70	2B	P. Suder	519	.241	7	60	342	461	10	114	5.5	.988	J. Coleman	33	216	14	13	0	4.09
Connie Mack	SS	E. Joost	509	.250	16	55	**325**	409	20	115	**5.6**	.973	D. Fowler	29	205	15	8	2	3.78
	3B	H. Majeski	590	.310	12	120	163	268	11	19	3.1	**.975**	C. Scheib	32	199	14	8	0	3.94
	RF	E. Valo	383	.305	3	46	231	4	4	1	2.2	.983	L. Brissie	39	194	14	10	5	4.13
	CF	S. Chapman	445	.258	13	70	368	8	7	2	3.2	.982	C. Harris	45	94	5	2	5	4.13
	LF	B. McCosky	515	.326	0	46	277	9	3	1	2.2	.990	B. McCahan	17	87	4	7	0	5.71
	C	B. Rosar	302	.255	4	41	335	39	1	10	4.2	**.997**	B. Savage	33	75	5	1	5	6.21
	OF	D. White	253	.245	1	28	108	3	5	1	2.1	.957							
	OF	R. Coleman	210	.243	0	21	126	7	3	3	2.6	.978							
	C	M. Guerra	142	.211	1	23	163	20	5	1	4.0	.973							
	P	C. Scheib	104	.298	2	21	14	36	1	5	1.6	.980							
Detroit	1B	G. Vico	521	.267	8	58	1169	85	15	112	8.9	.988	H. Newhouser	39	272	**21**	12	1	3.01
W-78 L-76	2B	E. Mayo	370	.249	2	42	202	223	11	48	5.1	.975	F. Hutchinson	33	221	13	11	0	4.32
Steve O'Neill	SS	J. Lipon	458	.290	5	52	211	346	17	63	4.9	.970	V. Trucks	43	212	14	13	2	3.78
	3B	G. Kell	368	.304	2	44	108	146	8	15	2.8	.969	D. Trout	32	184	10	14	2	3.43
	RF	P. Mullin	496	.288	23	80	274	7	8	0	2.2	.972	A. Houtteman	43	164	2	16	10	4.66
	CF	H. Evers	538	.314	10	103	392	8	11	0	3.0	.973	S. Overmire	37	66	3	4	3	5.97
	LF	V. Wertz	391	.248	7	67	196	11	10	3	2.2	.954							
	C	B. Swift	292	.223	4	33	476	55	5	13	4.8	.991							
	OF	D. Wakefield	322	.276	11	53	198	3	11	1	2.5	.948							
	S2	N. Berry	256	.266	0	16	138	199	17	46		.952							
	2B	E. Lake	198	.263	2	18	110	132	7	31	5.5	.972							
	3B	J. Outlaw	198	.283	0	25	39	87	11	8	2.9	.920							
St. Louis	1B	C. Stevens	287	.261	1	26	737	56	7	89	9.4	.991	F. Sanford	42	227	12	**21**	2	4.64
W-59 L-94	2B	G. Priddy	560	.296	8	79	**407**	**471**	**29**	**132**	**6.2**	.968	C. Fannin	34	214	10	14	1	4.17
Zack Taylor	SS	E. Pellagrini	290	.238	2	27	194	292	18	85	5.1	.964	N. Garver	38	198	7	11	5	3.41
	3B	B. Dillinger	644	.321	2	44	187	242	20	30	2.9	.955	B. Kennedy	26	132	7	8	0	4.70
	RF	A. Zarilla	529	.329	12	74	322	5	13	0	2.5	.962	B. Stephens	43	123	3	6	3	6.02
	CF	P. Lehner	333	.276	2	46	223	4	6	2	2.6	.974	F. Biscan	47	99	6	7	2	6.11
	LF	W. Platt	454	.271	7	82	230	5	13	2	2.2	.948	J. Ostrowski	26	78	4	6	3	5.97
	C	L. Moss	335	.257	14	46	357	52	5	8	4.0	.988							
	SS	S. Dente	267	.270	0	22	138	207	15	46	4.7	.958							
	OF	D. Kokos	258	.298	4	40	126	8	5	2	2.0	.964							
	1B	H. Arft	248	.238	5	38	598	43	3	81	9.3	.995							
	C	R. Partee	231	.203	0	17	297	22	6	7	4.3	.982							
	OF	D. Lund	161	.248	3	25	72	3	0	0	1.7	1.000							

AMERICAN LEAGUE 1948, *cont.*

Team	POS	Player	AB	BA	HR	RBI	PO	A	E	DP	TC/G	FA	Pitcher	G	IP	W	L	SV	ERA
Washington	1B	M. Vernon	558	.242	3	48	1297	113	15	128	9.5	.989	E. Wynn	33	198	8	19	0	5.82
W-56 L-97	2B	A. Kozar	577	.250	1	58	348	444	27	89	5.5	.967	W. Masterson	33	188	8	15	2	3.83
Joe Kuhel	SS	M. Christman	409	.259	1	40	207	259	15	59	4.7	.969	R. Scarborough	31	185	15	8	1	2.82
	3B	E. Yost	555	.249	2	50	**189**	240	15	21	3.1	.966	S. Hudson	39	182	4	16	1	5.88
	RF	B. Stewart	401	.279	7	69	265	5	7	1	2.4	.975	M. Haefner	28	148	5	13	0	4.02
	CF	C. Gillenwater	221	.244	3	21	186	4	5	0	2.9	.974	D. Thompson	46	131	6	10	4	3.84
	LF	G. Coan	513	.232	7	60	341	11	11	3	2.8	.970	T. Ferrick	37	74	2	5	10	4.15
	C	J. Early	246	.220	1	28	268	51	3	7	3.5	.991							
	OF	E. Wooten	258	.256	1	23	178	9	4	2	2.6	.979							
	C	A. Evans	228	.259	2	28	245	38	5	6	3.4	.983							
	OF	T. McBride	206	.257	1	29	108	7	2	3	2.1	.983							
	OF	S. Robertson	187	.246	2	22	105	3	7	0	2.3	.939							
	SS	J. Sullivan	173	.208	0	12	94	138	12	33	4.3	.951							

Team	POS	Player	AB	BA	HR	RBI	PO	A	E	DP	TC/G	FA	Pitcher	G	IP	W	L	SV	ERA
Chicago	1B	T. Lupien	617	.246	6	54	**1436**	92	11	**155**	10.0	.993	B. Wight	34	223	9	20	1	4.80
W-51 L-101	2B	D. Kolloway	417	.273	6	38	241	276	18	62	6.4	.966	J. Haynes	27	150	9	10	0	3.97
Ted Lyons	SS	C. Michaels	484	.248	5	56	164	285	20	65	5.5	.957	A. Gettel	22	148	8	10	1	4.01
	3B	L. Appling	497	.314	0	47	84	163	15	13	3.6	.943	M. Pieretti	21	120	8	10	1	4.95
	RF	T. Wright	455	.279	4	61	227	9	3	3	2.1	.987	H. Judson	40	107	4	5	8	4.78
	CF	D. Philley	488	.287	5	42	381	22	9	6	3.2	.978	F. Papish	32	95	2	8	4	5.00
	LF	P. Seerey	340	.229	18	64	198	9	4	5	2.3	.981	O. Grove	32	88	2	10	1	6.16
	C	A. Robinson	326	.252	8	39	303	50	4	4	3.9	.989	G. Moulder	33	86	3	6	2	6.41
	3B	F. Baker	335	.215	0	18	78	170	10	17	3.6	.961							
	OF	R. Hodgin	331	.266	1	34	184	9	6	0	2.5	.970							
	C	R. Weigel	163	.233	0	26	108	19	4	4	3.4	.969							

BATTING AND BASE RUNNING LEADERS

Batting Average
T. Williams, BOS .369
L. Boudreau, CLE .355
D. Mitchell, CLE .336
A. Zarilla, STL .329
B. McCosky, PHI .326

Slugging Average
T. Williams, BOS .615
J. DiMaggio, NY .598
T. Henrich, NY .554
L. Boudreau, CLE .534
K. Keltner, CLE .522

Home Runs
J. DiMaggio, NY 39
J. Gordon, CLE 32
K. Keltner, CLE 31
V. Stephens, BOS 29
B. Doerr, BOS 27

Total Bases
J. DiMaggio, NY 355
T. Henrich, NY 326
T. Williams, BOS 313
L. Boudreau, CLE 299
V. Stephens, BOS 299

Runs Batted In
J. DiMaggio, NY 155
V. Stephens, BOS 137
T. Williams, BOS 127
J. Gordon, CLE 124
H. Majeski, PHI 120

Stolen Bases
B. Dillinger, STL 28
G. Coan, WAS 23
M. Vernon, WAS 15
D. Mitchell, CLE 13

Hits
B. Dillinger, STL 207
D. Mitchell, CLE 204
L. Boudreau, CLE 199
J. DiMaggio, NY 190

Base on Balls
T. Williams, BOS 126
E. Joost, PHI 119
F. Fain, PHI 113
D. DiMaggio, BOS 101

Home Run Percentage
J. DiMaggio, NY 6.6
J. Gordon, CLE 5.8
K. Keltner, CLE 5.6
B. Doerr, BOS 5.1

Runs
T. Henrich, NY 138
D. DiMaggio, BOS 127
T. Williams, BOS 124
J. Pesky, BOS 124

Doubles
T. Williams, BOS 44
T. Henrich, NY 42
H. Majeski, PHI 41
G. Priddy, STL 40
D. DiMaggio, BOS 40

Triples
T. Henrich, NY 14
B. Stewart, NY, WAS 13
P. Mullin, DET 11
E. Yost, WAS 11
J. DiMaggio, NY 11

PITCHING LEADERS

Winning Percentage
J. Kramer, BOS .783
G. Bearden, CLE .741
V. Raschi, NY .704
A. Reynolds, NY .696
M. Parnell, BOS .652
D. Fowler, PHI .652
R. Scarborough, WAS .652

Earned Run Average
G. Bearden, CLE 2.43
B. Lemon, CLE 2.82
H. Newhouser, DET 3.01
M. Parnell, BOS 3.14
D. Trout, DET 3.43

Wins
H. Newhouser, DET 21
G. Bearden, CLE 20
B. Lemon, CLE 20
V. Raschi, NY 19
B. Feller, CLE 19

Saves
R. Christopher, CLE 17
J. Page, NY 16
A. Houtteman, DET 10
T. Ferrick, WAS 10
H. Judson, CHI 8

Strikeouts
B. Feller, CLE 164
B. Lemon, CLE 147
H. Newhouser, DET 143
L. Brissie, PHI 127
V. Raschi, NY 124

Complete Games
B. Lemon, CLE 20
H. Newhouser, DET 19
V. Raschi, NY 18
B. Feller, CLE 18

Fewest Hits/9 Innings
B. Lemon, CLE 7.08
G. Bearden, CLE 7.33
B. Feller, CLE 8.19
H. Newhouser, DET 8.23

Shutouts
B. Lemon, CLE 10
G. Bearden, CLE 6
V. Raschi, NY 6
J. Dobson, BOS 5

Fewest Walks/9 Innings
F. Hutchinson, DET 1.95
E. Lopat, NY 2.62
J. Kramer, BOS 2.81
V. Raschi, NY 2.99

Most Strikeouts/9 Inn.
L. Brissie, PHI 5.89
B. Feller, CLE 5.27
V. Raschi, NY 5.01
H. Newhouser, DET 4.73

Innings
B. Lemon, CLE 294
B. Feller, CLE 280
H. Newhouser, DET 272
J. Dobson, BOS 245

Games Pitched
J. Page, NY 55
A. Widmar, STL 49
F. Biscan, STL 47
D. Thompson, WAS 46

							Batting						Fielding			Pitching					
	W	L	PCT	GB	R	OR	2B	3B	HR	BA	SA	SB	E	DP	FA	CG	BB	SO	ShO	SV	ERA
*Cleveland	97	58	.626		840	**568**	242	54	**155**	**.282**	.431	54	114	183	**.982**	66	628	595	**26**	**30**	**3.22**
Boston	96	59	.619	1	**907**	720	**277**	40	121	.274	.409	38	116	174	.981	70	592	513	11	13	4.20
New York	94	60	.610	2.5	857	633	251	**75**	139	.278	**.432**	24	120	161	.979	62	641	654	16	24	3.75
Philadelphia	84	70	.545	12.5	729	735	231	47	68	.260	.362	39	**113**	180	.981	**74**	638	486	7	18	4.43
Detroit	78	76	.506	18.5	700	726	219	58	78	.267	.375	22	155	143	.974	60	**589**	**678**	5	22	4.15
St. Louis	59	94	.386	37	671	849	251	62	63	.271	.378	63	168	**190**	.972	35	737	531	4	20	5.01
Washington	56	97	.366	40	578	796	203	**75**	31	.244	.331	**76**	154	144	.974	42	734	446	4	22	4.65
Chicago	51	101	.336	44.5	559	814	172	39	55	.251	.331	46	160	176	.974	35	673	403	2	23	4.89
					5841	5841	1846	450	710	.266	.381	362	1100	1351	.977	444	5232	4306	75	172	4.29

* Defeated Boston in a 1 game playoff

AMERICAN LEAGUE 1948, *cont.*

BATTING AND BASE RUNNING LEADERS

Batting Average
T. Williams, BOS .369
L. Boudreau, CLE .355
D. Mitchell, CLE .336
A. Zarilla, STL .329
B. McCosky, PHI .326

Slugging Average
T. Williams, BOS .615
J. DiMaggio, NY .598
T. Henrich, NY .554
L. Boudreau, CLE .534
K. Keltner, CLE .522

Home Runs
J. DiMaggio, NY 39
J. Gordon, CLE 32
K. Keltner, CLE 31
V. Stephens, BOS 29
B. Doerr, BOS 27

Total Bases
J. DiMaggio, NY 355
T. Henrich, NY 326
T. Williams, BOS 313
L. Boudreau, CLE 299
V. Stephens, BOS 299

Runs Batted In
J. DiMaggio, NY 155
V. Stephens, BOS 137
T. Williams, BOS 127
J. Gordon, CLE 124
H. Majeski, PHI 120

Stolen Bases
B. Dillinger, STL 28
G. Coan, WAS 23
M. Vernon, WAS 15
D. Mitchell, CLE 13

Hits
B. Dillinger, STL 207
D. Mitchell, CLE 204
L. Boudreau, CLE 199
J. DiMaggio, NY 190

Base on Balls
T. Williams, BOS 126
E. Joost, PHI 119
F. Fain, PHI 113
D. DiMaggio, BOS 101

Home Run Percentage
J. DiMaggio, NY 6.6
J. Gordon, CLE 5.8
K. Keltner, CLE 5.6
B. Doerr, BOS 5.1

Runs
T. Henrich, NY 138
D. DiMaggio, BOS 127
T. Williams, BOS 124
J. Pesky, BOS 124

Doubles
T. Williams, BOS 44
T. Henrich, NY 42
H. Majeski, PHI 41
G. Priddy, STL 40
D. DiMaggio, BOS 40

Triples
T. Henrich, NY 14
B. Stewart, NY, WAS 13
P. Mullin, DET 11
E. Yost, WAS 11
J. DiMaggio, NY 11

PITCHING LEADERS

Winning Percentage
J. Kramer, BOS .783
G. Bearden, CLE .741
V. Raschi, NY .704
A. Reynolds, NY .696
M. Parnell, BOS .652
D. Fowler, PHI .652
R. Scarborough, WAS .652

Earned Run Average
G. Bearden, CLE 2.43
B. Lemon, CLE 2.82
H. Newhouser, DET 3.01
M. Parnell, BOS 3.14
D. Trout, DET 3.43

Wins
H. Newhouser, DET 21
G. Bearden, CLE 20
B. Lemon, CLE 20
V. Raschi, NY 19
B. Feller, CLE 19

Saves
R. Christopher, CLE 17
J. Page, NY 16
A. Houtteman, DET 10
T. Ferrick, WAS 10
H. Judson, CHI 8

Strikeouts
B. Feller, CLE 164
B. Lemon, CLE 147
H. Newhouser, DET 143
L. Brissie, PHI 127
V. Raschi, NY 124

Complete Games
B. Lemon, CLE 20
H. Newhouser, DET 19
V. Raschi, NY 18
B. Feller, CLE 18

Fewest Hits/9 Innings
B. Lemon, CLE 7.08
G. Bearden, CLE 7.33
B. Feller, CLE 8.19
H. Newhouser, DET 8.23

Shutouts
B. Lemon, CLE 10
G. Bearden, CLE 6
V. Raschi, NY 6
J. Dobson, BOS 5

Fewest Walks/9 Innings
F. Hutchinson, DET 1.95
E. Lopat, NY 2.62
J. Kramer, BOS 2.81
V. Raschi, NY 2.99

Most Strikeouts/9 Inn.
L. Brissie, PHI 5.89
B. Feller, CLE 5.27
V. Raschi, NY 5.01
H. Newhouser, DET 4.73

Innings
B. Lemon, CLE 294
B. Feller, CLE 280
H. Newhouser, DET 272
J. Dobson, BOS 245

Games Pitched
J. Page, NY 55
A. Widmar, STL 49
F. Biscan, STL 47
D. Thompson, WAS 46

	W	L	PCT	GB	R	OR	Batting 2B	3B	HR	BA	SA	SB	Fielding E	DP	FA	Pitching CG	BB	SO	ShO	SV	ERA
*Cleveland	97	58	.626		840	**568**	242	54	**155**	**.282**	.431	54	114	183	**.982**	66	628	595	**26**	**30**	**3.22**
Boston	96	59	.619	1	**907**	720	**277**	40	121	.274	.409	38	116	174	.981	70	592	513	11	13	4.20
New York	94	60	.610	2.5	857	633	251	**75**	139	.278	**.432**	24	120	161	.979	62	641	654	16	24	3.75
Philadelphia	84	70	.545	12.5	729	735	231	47	68	.260	.362	39	**113**	180	.981	**74**	638	486	7	18	4.43
Detroit	78	76	.506	18.5	700	726	219	58	78	.267	.375	22	155	143	.974	60	**589**	**678**	5	22	4.15
St. Louis	59	94	.386	37	671	849	251	62	63	.271	.378	63	168	**190**	.972	35	737	531	4	20	5.01
Washington	56	97	.366	40	578	796	203	**75**	31	.244	.331	**76**	154	144	.974	42	734	446	4	22	4.65
Chicago	51	101	.336	44.5	559	814	172	39	55	.251	.331	46	160	176	.974	35	673	403	2	23	4.89
					5841	5841	1846	450	710	.266	.381	362	1100	1351	.977	444	5232	4306	75	172	4.29

* Defeated Boston in a 1 game playoff

NATIONAL LEAGUE 1949

Team	POS	Player	AB	BA	HR	RBI	PO	A	E	DP	TC/G	FA	Pitcher	G	IP	W	L	SV	ERA
Brooklyn	1B	G. Hodges	596	.285	23	115	**1336**	80	7	**142**	9.1	**.995**	D. Newcombe	38	244	17	8	1	3.17
W-97 L-57	2B	J. Robinson	593	**.342**	16	124	395	421	16	**119**	5.3	.981	P. Roe	30	213	15	6	1	2.79
Burt Shotton	SS	P. Reese	617	.279	16	73	**316**	454	18	93	5.1	**.977**	J. Hatten	37	187	12	8	2	4.18
	3B	B. Cox	390	.233	8	40	104	213	12	28	3.3	.964	R. Branca	34	187	13	5	1	4.39
	RF	C. Furillo	549	.322	18	106	286	13	11	2	2.2	.965	J. Banta	48	152	10	6	3	3.37
	CF	D. Snider	552	.292	23	92	355	12	6	2	2.6	.984	R. Barney	38	141	9	8	1	4.41
	LF	G. Hermanski	224	.299	8	42	140	7	3	1	1.9	.980	E. Palica	49	97	8	9	6	3.62
	C	R. Campanella	436	.287	22	82	**684**	55	11	5	**5.9**	.985							
	C	B. Edwards	148	.209	8	25	184	13	2	0	4.9	.990							
St. Louis	1B	N. Jones	380	.300	8	62	876	40	**15**	85	9.5	.984	H. Pollet	39	231	20	9	1	2.77
W-96 L-58	2B	R. Schoendienst	640	.297	3	54	**399**	**424**	11	105	**6.0**	**.987**	H. Brecheen	32	215	14	11	1	3.35
Eddie Dyer	SS	M. Marion	515	.272	5	70	242	441	17	74	5.2	.976	A. Brazle	39	206	14	8	0	3.18
	3B	E. Kazak	326	.304	6	42	64	175	19	20	3.2	.926	G. Munger	35	188	15	8	2	3.87
	RF	S. Musial	612	.338	36	123	326	10	3	5	2.2	.991	G. Staley	45	171	10	10	6	2.73
	CF	C. Diering	369	.263	3	38	300	7	4	1	2.5	.987	T. Wilks	**59**	118	10	3	**9**	3.73
	LF	E. Slaughter	568	.336	13	96	330	10	6	1	2.3	.983							
	C	D. Rice	284	.236	4	29	355	29	3	4	4.2	**.992**							
	OF	R. Northey	265	.260	7	50	93	4	2	2	1.4	.980							
	3B	T. Glaviano	258	.267	6	36	67	181	19	15	3.7	.929							
	1B	R. Nelson	244	.221	4	32	564	24	0	48	8.4	1.000							
	C	J. Garagiola	241	.261	3	26	332	35	6	1	4.7	.984							

NATIONAL LEAGUE 1949, *cont.*

Team	POS	Player	AB	BA	HR	RBI	PO	A	E	DP	TC/G	FA	Pitcher	G	IP	W	L	SV	ERA
Philadelphia	1B	D. Sisler	412	.289	7	50	815	40	11	93	9.0	.987	K. Heintzelman	33	250	17	10	0	3.02
W-81 L-73	2B	E. Miller	266	.207	6	29	240	189	6	54	5.3	.986	R. Roberts	43	227	15	15	4	3.69
Eddie Sawyer	SS	G. Hamner	**662**	.263	6	53	280	**506**	32	**101**	5.3	.961	R. Meyer	37	213	17	8	1	3.08
	3B	W. Jones	532	.244	19	77	**181**	**308**	**27**	19	**3.6**	.948	H. Borowy	28	193	12	12	0	4.19
	RF	B. Nicholson	299	.234	11	40	185	10	1	1	2.2	.995	C. Simmons	38	131	4	10	1	4.59
	CF	R. Ashburn	**662**	.284	1	37	514	13	11	3	3.5	.980	J. Konstanty	53	97	9	5	7	3.25
	LF	D. Ennis	610	.302	25	110	359	16	13	1	2.5	.966	S. Rowe	23	65	3	7	0	4.82
	C	A. Seminick	334	.243	24	68	411	54	**12**	6	4.9	.975							
	OF	S. Hollmig	251	.255	2	26	108	5	5	1	1.8	.958							
	C	S. Lopata	240	.271	8	27	236	19	7	2	4.5	.973							
	1B	E. Waitkus	209	.306	1	28	452	36	3	51	9.1	.994							
	2B	M. Goliat	189	.212	3	19	140	143	9	31	5.8	.969							
	3B	B. Blattner	97	.247	5	21	11	11	1	2	0.4	.957							
Boston	1B	E. Fletcher	413	.262	11	51	965	71	9	96	8.6	.991	W. Spahn	38	**302**	**21**	14	0	3.07
W-75 L-79	2B	E. Stanky	506	.285	1	42	357	354	15	92	5.4	.979	J. Sain	37	243	10	17	0	4.81
Billy Southworth	SS	A. Dark	529	.276	3	53	232	387	25	76	5.2	.961	V. Bickford	37	231	16	11	0	4.25
W-55 L-54	3B	B. Elliott	482	.280	17	76	141	300	17	27	3.5	.963	B. Voiselle	30	169	7	8	1	4.04
Johnny Cooney	RF	T. Holmes	380	.266	8	59	210	10	3	4	2.2	.987	N. Potter	41	97	6	11	7	4.19
W-20 L-25	CF	J. Russell	415	.231	8	54	269	3	7	3	2.3	.975	J. Antonelli	22	96	3	7	0	3.56
	LF	M. Rickert	277	.292	6	49	149	9	3	2	2.1	.981	B. Hall	31	74	6	4	0	4.36
	C	D. Crandall	228	.263	4	34	287	39	6	5	5.3	.982							
	UT	S. Sisti	268	.257	5	22	156	80	7	11		.971							
	OF	P. Reiser	221	.271	8	40	139	5	3	2	2.3	.980							
	OF	E. Sauer	214	.266	3	31	134	3	4	1	2.0	.972							
	UT	C. Ryan	208	.250	6	20	118	131	8	24		.969							
	C	B. Salkeld	161	.255	5	25	230	21	5	3	4.1	.980							
	OF	J. Heath	111	.306	9	23	56	2	1	1	1.9	.983							
New York	1B	J. Mize	388	.263	18	62	906	65	6	77	9.7*	.994	L. Jansen	37	260	15	16	0	3.85
W-73 L-81	2B	H. Thompson	275	.280	9	34	197	175	15	44	5.6	.961	M. Kennedy	38	223	12	14	1	3.43
Leo Durocher	SS	B. Kerr	220	.209	0	19	125	224	15	33	4.1	.959	D. Koslo	38	212	11	14	4	**2.50**
	3B	S. Gordon	489	.284	26	90	112	206	14	18	2.7	.958	S. Jones	42	207	15	12	0	3.34
	RF	W. Marshall	499	.307	12	70	292	13	8	3	2.3	.974	C. Hartung	33	155	9	11	0	5.00
	CF	B. Thomson	641	.309	27	109	488	10	9	4	3.3	.982							
	LF	W. Lockman	617	.301	11	65	353	10	10	1	2.5	.973							
	C	W. Westrum	169	.243	7	28	224	18	5	4	4.0	.980							
	UT	B. Rigney	389	.278	6	47	185	317	32	46		.940							
	UT	L. Lohrke	180	.267	5	22	86	143	9	13		.962							
	C	R. Mueller	170	.224	5	23	197	21	4	2	4.0	.982							
	C	W. Cooper	147	.211	4	21	148	18*	3	2	4.2	.982							
Pittsburgh	1B	J. Hopp	371	.318	5	39	642	44	7	69	9.0	.990	M. Dickson	44	224	12	14	0	3.29
W-71 L-83	2B	M. Basgall	308	.218	2	26	224	224	13	58	4.7	.972	B. Werle	35	221	12	13	0	4.24
Billy Meyer	SS	S. Rojek	557	.244	0	31	240	461	25	92	5.0	.966	C. Chambers	34	177	13	7	0	3.96
	3B	P. Castiglione	448	.268	6	43	100	213	14	26	3.3	.957	B. Chesnes	27	145	7	13	1	5.88
	RF	W. Westlake	525	.282	23	104	319	12	6	4	2.4	.982	V. Lombardi	34	134	5	5	1	4.57
	CF	D. Restelli	232	.250	12	40	167	4	7	2	2.9	.961	E. Bonham	18	89	7	4	0	4.25
	LF	R. Kiner	549	.310	**54**	**127**	311	12	7	3	2.2	.979	E. Riddle	16	74	1	8	1	5.33
	C	C. McCullough	241	.237	4	21	363	39	6	**8**	4.5	.985	H. Casey	33	39	4	1	5	4.66
	2B	D. Murtaugh	236	.203	2	24	202	182	10	58	5.3	.975							
	1B	E. Stevens	221	.262	4	32	533	58	3	65	10.2	.995							
	3B	E. Bockman	220	.223	6	19	59	127	8	14	2.9	.959							
	OF	T. Saffell	205	.322	2	25	122	2	1	1	2.4	.992							
	OF	D. Walker	181	.282	1	18	58	2	1	0	1.6	.984							
	C	E. Fitz Gerald	160	.263	2	18	163	22	5	5	3.4	.974							
Cincinnati	1B	T. Kluszewski	531	.309	8	68	1140	65	14	109	9.1	.989	K. Raffensberger	41	284	18	17	0	3.39
W-62 L-92	2B	J. Bloodworth	452	.261	9	59	229	234	9	56	5.1	.981	H. Fox	38	215	6	**19**	0	3.98
Bucky Walters	SS	V. Stallcup	575	.254	3	45	256	437	27	87	5.1	.963	H. Wehmeier	33	213	11	12	0	4.68
W-61 L-90	3B	G. Hatton	537	.263	11	69	143	290	11	**29**	3.3	**.975**	J. Vander Meer	28	160	5	10	0	4.90
Luke Sewell	RF	J. Wyrostek	474	.249	9	46	293	10	9	1	2.4	.971	E. Erautt	39	113	4	11	1	3.36
W-1 L-2	CF	L. Merriman	287	.230	4	26	214	7	7	1	2.7	.969	B. Lively	31	103	4	6	1	3.92
	LF	P. Lowrey	309	.275	2	25	202	7	1	2	2.7	.995	E. Blackwell	30	77	5	5	1	4.23
	C	W. Cooper	307	.280	16	62	316	43*	8	3	4.8	.978							
	OF	H. Walker	314	.318	1	23	177	7	7	1	2.5	.963							
	OF	D. Litwhiler	292	.291	11	48	143	6	2	1	1.8	.987							
	2B	B. Adams	277	.253	0	25	162	138	5	29	4.8	.984							
	C	D. Howell	172	.244	2	18	191	35	3	2	4.1	.987							
Chicago	1B	H. Reich	386	.280	3	34	759	83*	9	57	10.0	.989	J. Schmitz	36	207	11	13	3	4.35
W-61 L-93	2B	E. Verban	343	.289	0	22	218	249	**17**	60	5.5	.965	B. Rush	35	201	10	18	4	4.07
Charlie Grimm	SS	R. Smalley	477	.245	8	35	265	438	**39**	91	**5.6**	.947	D. Leonard	33	180	7	16	0	4.15
W-19 L-31	3B	F. Gustine	261	.226	4	27	52	110	12	13	3.2	.931	M. Dubiel	32	148	6	9	4	4.14
Frankie Frisch	RF	H. Jeffcoat	363	.245	2	26	250	12	10	2	2.7	.963	D. Lade	36	130	4	5	1	5.00
W-42 L-62	CF	A. Pafko	519	.281	18	69	217	8	3	2	2.3	.987	W. Hacker	30	126	5	8	0	4.23
	LF	H. Sauer	357	.291	27	83	199	10	4	2	2.2	.981	B. Chipman	38	113	7	8	1	3.97
	C	M. Owen	198	.273	2	18	219	35	8	5	4.4	.969	B. Muncrief	34	75	5	6	2	4.56
	1B	P. Cavarretta	360	.294	8	49	673	63	5	58	10.6	.993							
	3S	B. Ramazzotti	190	.179	0	6	48	112	3	15		.982							
	OF	H. Edwards	176	.290	7	21	80	4	1	2	1.7	.988							
	C	R. Walker	172	.244	3	22	166	23	7	2	4.6	.964							
	OF	F. Baumholtz	164	.226	1	15	67	3	1	3	1.7	.986							
	OF	H. Walker	159	.264	1	14	69	3	4	0	1.9	.947							

NATIONAL LEAGUE 1949, *cont.*

BATTING AND BASE RUNNING LEADERS

Batting Average

J. Robinson, BKN	.342
S. Musial, STL	.338
E. Slaughter, STL	.336
C. Furillo, BKN	.322
R. Kiner, PIT	.310

Slugging Average

R. Kiner, PIT	.658
S. Musial, STL	.624
J. Robinson, BKN	.528
D. Ennis, PHI	.525
B. Thomson, NY	.518

Home Runs

R. Kiner, PIT	54
S. Musial, STL	36
H. Sauer, CIN, CHI	31
B. Thomson, NY	27
S. Gordon, NY	26

Total Bases

S. Musial, STL	382
R. Kiner, PIT	361
B. Thomson, NY	332
D. Ennis, PHI	320
J. Robinson, BKN	313

Runs Batted In

R. Kiner, PIT	127
J. Robinson, BKN	124
S. Musial, STL	123
G. Hodges, BKN	115
D. Ennis, PHI	110

Stolen Bases

J. Robinson, BKN	37
P. Reese, BKN	26
G. Hermanski, BKN	12
H. Jeffcoat, CHI	12
D. Snider, BKN	12
W. Lockman, NY	12

Hits

S. Musial, STL	207
J. Robinson, BKN	203
B. Thomson, NY	198
E. Slaughter, STL	191

Base on Balls

R. Kiner, PIT	117
P. Reese, BKN	116
E. Stanky, BOS	113
S. Musial, STL	107

Home Run Percentage

R. Kiner, PIT	9.8
H. Sauer, CIN, CHI	6.1
S. Musial, STL	5.9
S. Gordon, NY	5.3

Runs

P. Reese, BKN	132
S. Musial, STL	128
J. Robinson, BKN	122
R. Kiner, PIT	116

Doubles

S. Musial, STL	41
D. Ennis, PHI	39
G. Hatton, CIN	38
J. Robinson, BKN	38

Triples

E. Slaughter, STL	13
S. Musial, STL	13
J. Robinson, BKN	12
D. Ennis, PHI	11
R. Ashburn, PHI	11

PITCHING LEADERS

Winning Percentage

P. Roe, BKN	.714
H. Pollet, STL	.690
D. Newcombe, BKN	.680
R. Meyer, PHI	.680
G. Munger, STL	.652

Earned Run Average

D. Koslo, NY	2.50
H. Pollet, STL	2.77
P. Roe, BKN	2.79
K. Heintzelman, PHI	3.02
W. Spahn, BOS	3.07

Wins

W. Spahn, BOS	21
H. Pollet, STL	20
K. Raffensberger, CIN	18
R. Meyer, PHI	17
D. Newcombe, BKN	17
K. Heintzelman, PHI	17

Saves

T. Wilks, STL	9
J. Konstanty, PHI	7
N. Potter, BOS	7
G. Staley, STL	6
E. Palica, BKN	6

Strikeouts

W. Spahn, BOS	151
D. Newcombe, BKN	149
L. Jansen, NY	113
R. Branca, BKN	109
P. Roe, BKN	109

Complete Games

W. Spahn, BOS	25
K. Raffensberger, CIN	20
D. Newcombe, BKN	19
H. Pollet, STL	17
L. Jansen, NY	17

Fewest Hits/9 Innings

D. Koslo, NY	8.19
D. Newcombe, BKN	8.21
M. Kennedy, NY	8.38
R. Meyer, PHI	8.41

Shutouts

H. Pollet, STL	5
D. Newcombe, BKN	5
K. Heintzelman, PHI	5
K. Raffensberger, CIN	5

Fewest Walks/9 Innings

D. Koslo, NY	1.83
P. Roe, BKN	1.86
B. Werle, PIT	2.08
L. Jansen, NY	2.15

Most Strikeouts/9 Inn.

D. Newcombe, BKN	5.49
C. Chambers, PIT	4.72
P. Roe, BKN	4.61
W. Spahn, BOS	4.50

Innings

W. Spahn, BOS	302
K. Raffensberger, CIN	284
L. Jansen, NY	260
K. Heintzelman, PHI	250

Games Pitched

T. Wilks, STL	59
J. Konstanty, PHI	53
E. Palica, BKN	49
J. Banta, BKN	48

	W	L	PCT	GB	R	OR	Batting 2B	3B	HR	BA	SA	SB	Fielding E	DP	FA	Pitching CG	BB	SO	ShO	SV	ERA
Brooklyn	97	57	.630		**879**	651	236	47	**152**	.274	**.419**	**117**	**122**	162	**.980**	62	582	**743**	**15**	17	3.80
St. Louis	96	58	.623	1	766	**616**	**281**	54	102	**.277**	.404	17	146	149	.976	64	506	606	13	**19**	**3.45**
Philadelphia	81	73	.526	16	662	668	232	**55**	122	.254	.388	27	156	141	.974	58	**502**	495	12	15	3.89
Boston	75	79	.487	22	706	719	246	33	103	.258	.374	28	148	144	.976	**68**	520	591	12	11	3.99
New York	73	81	.474	24	736	693	203	52	147	.261	.401	43	161	134	.973	**68**	544	516	10	9	3.82
Pittsburgh	71	83	.461	26	681	760	191	41	126	.259	.384	48	132	**173**	.978	53	535	556	9	15	4.57
Cincinnati	62	92	.403	35	627	770	264	35	86	.260	.368	31	138	150	.977	55	640	538	10	6	4.33
Chicago	61	93	.396	36	593	773	212	53	97	.256	.373	53	186	160	.970	44	564	532	8	17	4.50
					5650	5650	1865	370	935	.262	.389	364	1189	1213	.976	472	4393	4577	89	109	4.04

AMERICAN LEAGUE 1949

New York

W-97 L-57

Casey Stengel

POS	Player	AB	BA	HR	RBI	PO	A	E	DP	TC/G	FA	Pitcher	G	IP	W	L	SV	ERA
1B	T. Henrich	411	.287	24	85	445	28	2	64	9.1	.996	V. Raschi	38	275	21	10	0	3.34
2B	J. Coleman	447	.275	2	42	298	315	12	102	5.1	**.981**	E. Lopat	31	215	15	10	1	3.26
SS	P. Rizzuto	614	.275	5	64	329	440	23	118	5.2	**.971**	A. Reynolds	35	214	17	6	1	4.00
3B	B. Brown	343	.283	6	61	84	158	13	17	3.0	.949	T. Byrne	32	196	15	7	0	3.72
RF	H. Bauer	301	.272	10	45	156	11	4	3	1.8	.977	J. Page	**60**	135	13	8	**27**	2.59
CF	C. Mapes	304	.247	7	38	228	14	6	4	2.3	.976	F. Sanford	29	95	7	3	0	3.87
LF	G. Woodling	296	.270	5	44	163	5	3	1	1.7	.982							
C	Y. Berra	415	.277	20	91	544	60	7	**18**	**5.6**	.989							
3B	B. Johnson	329	.249	8	56	77	136	11	16	2.8	.951							
OF	J. DiMaggio	272	.346	14	67	195	1	3	0	2.6	.985							
OF	J. Lindell	211	.242	6	27	114	4	2	1	1.8	.983							
1B	D. Kryhoski	177	.294	1	27	363	31	7	39	7.9	.983							
2B	S. Stirnweiss	157	.261	0	11	121	106	6	34	4.6	.974							

Boston

W-96 L-58

Joe McCarthy

POS	Player	AB	BA	HR	RBI	PO	A	E	DP	TC/G	FA	Pitcher	G	IP	W	L	SV	ERA
1B	B. Goodman	443	.298	0	56	1069	79	9	148	9.9	**.992**	M. Parnell	39	**295**	**25**	7	2	**2.77**
2B	B. Doerr	541	.309	18	109	395	439	17	134	**6.1**	.980	E. Kinder	43	252	23	6	4	3.36
SS	V. Stephens	610	.290	39	**159**	257	**508**	27	**128**	5.1	.966	J. Dobson	33	213	14	12	2	3.85
3B	J. Pesky	604	.306	2	69	**184**	**333**	16	**48**	**3.6**	.970	C. Stobbs	26	152	11	6	0	4.03
RF	A. Zarilla	474	.281	9	71	241	6	4	4	2.1	.984	J. Kramer	21	112	6	8	1	5.16
CF	D. DiMaggio	605	.307	8	60	420	13	10	1	3.1	.977	W. Masterson	18	55	3	4	4	4.25
LF	T. Williams	566	.343	**43**	**159**	337	12	6	3	2.3	.983							
C	B. Tebbetts	404	.270	5	48	481	51	**11**	13	4.6	.980							
C	M. Batts	157	.242	3	31	193	23	5	2	4.4	.977							

Cleveland

W-89 L-65

Lou Boudreau

POS	Player	AB	BA	HR	RBI	PO	A	E	DP	TC/G	FA	Pitcher	G	IP	W	L	SV	ERA
1B	M. Vernon	584	.291	18	83	**1438**	**155**	14	168	**10.5**	.991	B. Lemon	37	280	22	10	1	2.99
2B	J. Gordon	541	.251	20	84	297	430	15	123	5.1	.980	B. Feller	36	211	15	14	0	3.75
SS	L. Boudreau	475	.284	4	60	176	272	8	78	5.2	.982	M. Garcia	41	176	14	5	2	2.36
3B	K. Keltner	246	.232	8	30	51	145	4	11	2.9	.980	E. Wynn	26	165	11	7	0	4.15
RF	B. Kennedy	424	.276	9	57	190	12	2	4	2.1	.990	A. Benton	40	136	9	6	10	2.12
CF	L. Doby	547	.280	24	85	355	7	9	2	2.5	.976	G. Bearden	32	127	8	8	0	5.10
LF	D. Mitchell	**640**	.317	3	56	337	10	2	2	2.3	.994	S. Gromek	27	92	4	6	0	3.33
C	J. Hegan	468	.224	8	55	**651**	**73**	7	16	4.8	.990	S. Paige	31	83	4	7	5	3.04
SS	R. Boone	258	.252	4	26	162	210	21	58	5.2	.947							
OF	T. Tucker	197	.244	0	14	119	2	2	0	2.4	.984							

AMERICAN LEAGUE 1949, *cont.*

Detroit

W-87 L-67

Red Rolfe

POS	Player	AB	BA	HR	RBI	PO	A	E	DP	TC/G	FA	Pitcher	G	IP	W	L	SV	ERA
1B	P. Campbell	255	.278	3	30	461	38	7	67	6.8	.986	H. Newhouser	38	292	18	11	1	3.36
2B	N. Berry	329	.237	0	18	225	234	14	56	5.0	.970	V. Trucks	41	275	19	11	4	2.81
SS	J. Lipon	439	.251	3	59	240	364	22	92	5.2	.965	A. Houtteman	34	204	15	10	0	3.71
3B	G. Kell	522	**.343**	3	59	154	271	11	23	3.3	.975	T. Gray	34	195	10	10	1	3.51
RF	V. Wertz	608	.304	20	133	302	14	6	4	2.1	.981	F. Hutchinson	33	189	15	7	1	2.96
CF	J. Groth	348	.293	11	73	247	8	9	3	2.7	.966	D. Trout	33	59	3	6	3	4.40
LF	H. Evers	432	.303	7	72	319	12	2	2	2.7	.994							
C	A. Robinson	331	.269	13	56	458	44	7	9	4.7	.986							
21	D. Kolloway	483	.294	2	47	607	184	18	93		.978							
OF	P. Mullin	310	.268	12	59	169	4	2	0	2.2	.989							
UT	E. Lake	240	.196	1	15	113	167	10	37		.966							
C	B. Swift	189	.238	2	18	232	26	3	6	3.8	.989							

Philadelphia

W-81 L-73

Connie Mack

POS	Player	AB	BA	HR	RBI	PO	A	E	DP	TC/G	FA	Pitcher	G	IP	W	L	SV	ERA
1B	F. Fain	525	.263	3	78	1275	122	**22**	**194**	9.5	.984	A. Kellner	38	245	20	12	1	3.75
2B	P. Suder	445	.267	10	75	203	259	12	85	5.3	.975	J. Coleman	33	240	13	14	1	3.86
SS	E. Joost	525	.263	23	81	**352**	442	25	126	**5.7**	.969	L. Brissie	34	229	16	11	3	4.28
3B	H. Majeski	448	.277	9	67	117	219	15	37	3.1	.957	D. Fowler	31	214	15	11	1	3.75
RF	W. Moses	308	.276	1	25	169	7	3	3	1.9	.983	C. Scheib	38	183	9	12	0	5.12
CF	S. Chapman	589	.278	24	108	450	11	10	3	3.1	.979	B. Shantz	33	127	6	8	2	3.40
LF	E. Valo	547	.283	5	85	395	8	8	0	2.7	.981							
C	M. Guerra	298	.265	3	31	328	48	7	3	4.0	.982							
2B	N. Fox	247	.255	0	21	191	196	7	68	5.1	.982							
OF	D. White	169	.213	0	10	89	4	1	0	2.0	.989							
OF	T. Wright	149	.235	2	25	60	5	2	0	1.9	.970							

Chicago

W-63 L-91

Jack Onslow

POS	Player	AB	BA	HR	RBI	PO	A	E	DP	TC/G	FA	Pitcher	G	IP	W	L	SV	ERA
1B	C. Kress	353	.278	1	44	907	66	6	103	10.3	.994	B. Wight	35	245	15	13	1	3.31
2B	C. Michaels	561	.308	6	83	392	**484**	22	**135**	5.8	.976	R. Gumpert	34	234	13	16	1	3.81
SS	L. Appling	492	.301	5	58	253	450	26	95	5.2	.964	B. Pierce	32	172	7	15	0	3.88
3B	F. Baker	388	.260	1	40	106	269	9	31	3.1	**.977**	B. Kuzava	29	157	10	6	0	4.02
RF	D. Philley	598	.286	0	44	282	16	7	3	2.1	.977	M. Pieretti	39	116	4	6	4	5.51
CF	C. Metkovich	338	.237	5	45	212	1	7	0	2.5	.968	H. Judson	26	108	1	14	1	4.58
LF	H. Adams	208	.293	0	16	112	4	3	1	2.5	.975	M. Surkont	44	96	3	5	4	4.78
C	D. Wheeler	192	.240	1	22	210	36	6	4	4.3	.976	M. Haefner	14	80	4	6	1	4.37
01	S. Souchock	252	.234	7	37	346	21	6	30		.984							
OF	G. Zernial	198	.318	5	38	73	4	0	0	1.7	1.000							
C	J. Tipton	191	.204	3	19	203	32	2	4	4.5	.992							
C	E. Malone	170	.271	1	16	186	22	2	2	4.1	.990							
OF	J. Ostrowski	158	.266	5	31	81	3	5	0	2.2	.944							

St. Louis

W-53 L-101

Zack Taylor

POS	Player	AB	BA	HR	RBI	PO	A	E	DP	TC/G	FA	Pitcher	G	IP	W	L	SV	ERA
1B	J. Graham	500	.238	24	79	1118	87	19	120	9.0	.984	N. Garver	41	224	12	**17**	3	3.98
2B	G. Priddy	544	.290	11	63	**407**	415	**27**	96	5.9	.968	B. Kennedy	48	154	4	11	1	4.69
SS	E. Pellagrini	235	.238	2	15	164	227	16	52	5.4	.961	C. Fannin	30	143	8	14	1	6.17
3B	B. Dillinger	544	.324	1	51	166	209	**25**	22	3.0	.938	A. Papai	42	142	4	11	2	5.06
RF	D. Kokos	501	.261	23	77	290	16	6	5	2.3	.981	J. Ostrowski	40	141	8	8	2	4.79
CF	S. Spence	314	.245	13	45	205	10	1	2	2.5	.995	K. Drews	31	140	4	12	0	6.64
LF	R. Sievers	471	.306	16	91	314	14	9	1	2.7	.973	R. Embree	35	127	3	13	1	5.37
C	S. Lollar	284	.261	8	49	279	39	4	3	3.5	.988	T. Ferrick	50	104	6	4	6	3.88
OF	P. Lehner	297	.229	3	37	153	1	2	0	2.8	.987							
C	L. Moss	278	.291	10	39	283	41	10	9	4.0	.970							
OF	W. Platt	244	.258	3	29	135	3	2	0	2.4	.986							
SS	J. Sullivan	243	.226	0	18	117	144	16	35	3.9	.942							

Washington

W-50 L-104

Joe Kuhel

POS	Player	AB	BA	HR	RBI	PO	A	E	DP	TC/G	FA	Pitcher	G	IP	W	L	SV	ERA
1B	E. Robinson	527	.294	18	78	1299	100	18	133	9.9	.987	S. Hudson	40	209	8	**17**	1	4.22
2B	A. Kozar	350	.269	4	31	232	235	11	57	4.7	.977	R. Scarborough	34	200	13	11	0	4.60
SS	S. Dente	590	.273	1	53	314	462	**35**	106	5.3	.957	P. Calvert	34	161	6	**17**	1	5.43
3B	E. Yost	435	.253	9	45	158	232	19	23	3.4	.954	M. Harris	23	129	2	12	0	5.16
RF	B. Stewart	388	.284	8	43	207	8	4	3	2.1	.982	L. Hittle	36	109	5	7	0	4.21
CF	C. Vollmer	443	.253	14	59	324	3	6	1	2.9	.982	J. Haynes	37	96	2	9	2	6.26
LF	G. Coan	358	.218	3	25	225	8	6	3	2.5	.975	D. Weik	27	95	3	12	1	5.38
C	A. Evans	321	.271	2	42	322	47	3	2	3.5	**.992**	M. Haefner	19	92	5	5	0	4.42
UT	S. Robertson	374	.251	11	42	185	253	25	43		.946							
OF	S. Mele	264	.242	3	25	108	5	4	3	1.9	.966							
OF	B. Lewis	257	.245	3	28	136	4	3	1	2.1	.979							

BATTING AND BASE RUNNING LEADERS

Batting Average

G. Kell, DET	.343
T. Williams, BOS	.343
B. Dillinger, STL	.324
D. Mitchell, CLE	.317
B. Doerr, BOS	.309

Slugging Average

T. Williams, BOS	.650
V. Stephens, BOS	.539
T. Henrich, NY	.526
B. Doerr, BOS	.497
Y. Berra, NY	.480

Home Runs

T. Williams, BOS	43
V. Stephens, BOS	39
T. Henrich, NY	24
J. Graham, STL	24
L. Doby, CLE	24
S. Chapman, PHI	24

Total Bases

T. Williams, BOS	368
V. Stephens, BOS	329
V. Wertz, DET	283
D. Mitchell, CLE	274
B. Doerr, BOS	269

Runs Batted In

T. Williams, BOS	159
V. Stephens, BOS	159
V. Wertz, DET	133
B. Doerr, BOS	109
S. Chapman, PHI	108

Stolen Bases

B. Dillinger, STL	20
P. Rizzuto, NY	18
E. Valo, PHI	14
D. Philley, CHI	13

PITCHING LEADERS

Winning Percentage

E. Kinder, BOS	.793
M. Parnell, BOS	.781
A. Reynolds, NY	.739
B. Lemon, CLE	.688
T. Byrne, NY	.682
F. Hutchinson, DET	.682

Earned Run Average

M. Parnell, BOS	2.77
V. Trucks, DET	2.81
B. Lemon, CLE	2.99
E. Lopat, NY	3.26
B. Wight, CHI	3.31

Wins

M. Parnell, BOS	25
E. Kinder, BOS	23
B. Lemon, CLE	22
V. Raschi, NY	21
A. Kellner, PHI	20

Saves

J. Page, NY	27
A. Benton, CLE	10
T. Ferrick, STL	6
S. Paige, CLE	5

Strikeouts

V. Trucks, DET	153
H. Newhouser, DET	144
E. Kinder, BOS	138
B. Lemon, CLE	138
T. Byrne, NY	129

Complete Games

M. Parnell, BOS	27
B. Lemon, CLE	22
H. Newhouser, DET	22
V. Raschi, NY	21
A. Kellner, PHI	19
E. Kinder, BOS	19

AMERICAN LEAGUE 1949, *cont.*

BATTING AND BASE RUNNING LEADERS

Hits
D. Mitchell, CLE	203
T. Williams, BOS	194
D. DiMaggio, BOS	186
J. Pesky, BOS	185
V. Wertz, DET	185

Base on Balls
T. Williams, BOS	162
E. Joost, PHI	149
F. Fain, PHI	136
L. Appling, CHI	121

Home Run Percentage
T. Williams, BOS	7.6
V. Stephens, BOS	6.4
T. Henrich, NY	5.8
Y. Berra, NY	4.8

Runs
T. Williams, BOS	150
E. Joost, PHI	128
D. DiMaggio, BOS	126
V. Stephens, BOS	113

Doubles
T. Williams, BOS	39
G. Kell, DET	38
D. DiMaggio, BOS	34
A. Zarilla, STL, BOS	33

Triples
D. Mitchell, CLE	23
B. Dillinger, STL	13
E. Valo, PHI	12

PITCHING LEADERS

Fewest Hits/9 Innings
T. Byrne, NY	5.74
B. Lemon, CLE	6.79
V. Trucks, DET	6.84
M. Parnell, BOS	7.86

Shutouts
E. Kinder, BOS	6
V. Trucks, DET	6
M. Garcia, CLE	5

Fewest Walks/9 Innings
A. Houtteman, DET	2.61
E. Lopat, NY	2.88
R. Gumpert, CHI	3.19
H. Newhouser, DET	3.42

Most Strikeouts/9 Inn.
T. Byrne, NY	5.92
V. Trucks, DET	5.01
E. Kinder, BOS	4.93
L. Brissie, PHI	4.63

Innings
M. Parnell, BOS	295
H. Newhouser, DET	292
B. Lemon, CLE	280
V. Trucks, DET	275
V. Raschi, NY	275

Games Pitched
J. Page, NY	60
D. Welteroth, WAS	52
T. Ferrick, STL	50
B. Kennedy, STL	48

	W	L	PCT	GB	R	OR	Batting 2B	3B	HR	BA	SA	SB	Fielding E	DP	FA	Pitching CG	BB	SO	ShO	SV	ERA
New York	97	57	.630		829	637	215	60	115	.269	.400	58	138	195	.977	59	812	**671**	12	**36**	3.69
Boston	96	58	.623	1	**896**	667	**272**	36	**131**	**.282**	**.420**	43	120	207	.980	84	661	598	16	16	3.97
Cleveland	89	65	.578	8	675	**574**	194	58	112	.260	.384	44	**103**	192	**.983**	65	**611**	594	10	19	**3.36**
Detroit	87	67	.565	10	751	655	215	51	88	.267	.378	39	131	174	.978	70	628	631	**19**	12	3.77
Philadelphia	81	73	.526	16	726	725	214	49	82	.260	.369	36	140	**217**	.976	**85**	758	490	9	11	4.23
Chicago	63	91	.409	34	648	737	207	**66**	43	.257	.347	**62**	141	180	.977	57	693	502	10	17	4.30
St. Louis	53	101	.344	44	667	913	213	30	117	.254	.377	38	166	154	.971	43	685	432	3	16	5.21
Washington	50	104	.325	47	584	868	207	41	81	.254	.356	46	161	168	.973	44	779	451	9	9	5.10
					5776	5776	1737	391	769	.263	.379	366	1100	1487	.977	507	5627	4369	88	136	4.20

NATIONAL LEAGUE 1950

Philadelphia

W-91 L-63

Eddie Sawyer

POS	Player	AB	BA	HR	RBI	PO	A	E	DP	TC/G	FA	Pitcher	G	IP	W	L	SV	ERA
1B	E. Waitkus	641	.284	2	44	**1387**	99	10	142	**9.7**	.993	R. Roberts	40	304	20	11	1	3.02
2B	M. Goliat	483	.234	13	64	345	393	21	89	5.5	.972	C. Simmons	31	215	17	8	1	3.40
SS	G. Hamner	637	.270	11	82	293	513	48	100	5.4	.944	B. Miller	35	174	11	6	1	3.57
3B	W. Jones	610	.267	25	88	**190**	**323**	25	30	3.4	.954	R. Meyer	32	160	9	11	1	5.30
RF	D. Ennis	595	.311	31	**126**	279	10	9	3	2.0	.970	J. Konstanty	**74**	152	16	7	**22**	2.66
CF	R. Ashburn	594	.303	2	41	405	8	5	2	2.8	.988	B. Church	31	142	8	6	1	2.73
LF	D. Sisler	523	.296	13	83	293	9	4	0	2.2	.987	K. Heintzelman	23	125	3	9	0	4.09
C	A. Seminick	393	.288	24	68	551	54	**15**	9	5.0	.976							

Brooklyn

W-89 L-65

Burt Shotton

POS	Player	AB	BA	HR	RBI	PO	A	E	DP	TC/G	FA	Pitcher	G	IP	W	L	SV	ERA
1B	G. Hodges	561	.283	32	113	1273	100	8	**159**	9.0	**.994**	D. Newcombe	40	267	19	11	3	3.70
2B	J. Robinson	518	.328	14	81	359	390	11	**133**	5.3	**.986**	P. Roe	36	251	19	11	1	3.30
SS	P. Reese	531	.260	11	52	282	398	26	94	5.3	.963	E. Palica	43	201	13	8	1	3.58
3B	B. Cox	451	.257	8	44	102	233	15	35	3.3	**.957**	R. Branca	43	142	7	9	7	4.69
RF	C. Furillo	620	.305	18	106	246	18	8	2	1.8	.971	D. Bankhead	41	129	9	4	3	5.50
CF	D. Snider	620	.321	31	107	378	15	7	1	2.6	.983	C. Erskine	22	103	7	6	1	4.72
LF	G. Hermanski	289	.298	7	34	172	5	2	0	2.3	.989	B. Podbielan	20	73	5	4	1	5.33
C	R. Campanella	437	.281	31	89	**683**	54	11	14	**6.1**	.985	J. Banta	16	41	4	4	2	4.35
OF	J. Russell	214	.229	10	32	131	3	1	0	2.5	.993							
3B	B. Morgan	199	.226	7	21	33	121	5	15	3.1	.969							
OF	T. Brown	86	.291	8	20	31	2	3	0	2.3	.917							

New York

W-86 L-68

Leo Durocher

POS	Player	AB	BA	HR	RBI	PO	A	E	DP	TC/G	FA	Pitcher	G	IP	W	L	SV	ERA
1B	T. Gilbert	322	.220	4	32	784	65	10	80	7.7	.988	L. Jansen	40	275	19	13	3	3.01
2B	E. Stanky	527	.300	8	52	**407**	**418**	20	128	5.6	.976	S. Maglie	47	206	18	4	1	2.71
SS	A. Dark	587	.279	16	67	288	465	30	101	5.1	.962	S. Jones	40	199	13	16	2	4.61
3B	H. Thompson	512	.289	20	91	136	303	**26**	**43**	3.4	.944	D. Koslo	40	187	13	15	3	3.91
RF	D. Mueller	525	.291	7	84	205	7	3	2	1.7	.986	J. Hearn	16	125	11	3	0	1.94*
CF	B. Thomson	563	.252	25	85	394	15	9	5	2.8	.978	M. Kennedy	36	114	5	4	2	4.72
LF	W. Lockman	532	.295	6	52	305	11	7	3	2.5	.978	J. Kramer	35	87	3	6	1	3.53
C	W. Westrum	437	.236	23	71	608	**71**	1	**21**	4.9	**.999**							
10	M. Irvin	374	.299	15	66	568	50	12	62		.981							

Boston

W-83 L-71

Billy Southworth

POS	Player	AB	BA	HR	RBI	PO	A	E	DP	TC/G	FA	Pitcher	G	IP	W	L	SV	ERA
1B	E. Torgeson	576	.290	23	87	1365	**110**	**21**	126	9.6	.986	V. Bickford	40	**312**	19	14	0	3.47
2B	R. Hartsfield	419	.277	7	24	236	247	**26**	53	5.3	.949	W. Spahn	41	293	**21**	17	1	3.16
SS	B. Kerr	507	.227	2	46	310	471	28	97	5.2	.965	J. Sain	37	278	20	13	0	3.94
3B	B. Elliott	531	.305	24	107	141	256	20	26	3.0	.952	B. Chipman	27	124	7	7	1	4.43
RF	T. Holmes	322	.298	9	51	151	6	0	0	1.8	1.000	B. Hogue	36	63	3	5	7	5.03
CF	S. Jethroe	582	.273	18	58	355	17	12	6	2.7	.969							
LF	S. Gordon	481	.304	27	103	278	8	3	1	2.3	.990							
C	W. Cooper	337	.329	14	60	386	47	12	9	5.1	.973							
OF	W. Marshall	298	.235	5	40	150	11	7	2	2.0	.958							
C	D. Crandall	255	.220	4	37	311	41	12	7	4.9	.967							
OF	L. Olmo	154	.227	5	22	74	1	2	0	1.4	.974							

NATIONAL LEAGUE 1950, *cont.*

St. Louis

W-78 L-75

Eddie Dyer

POS	Player	AB	BA	HR	RBI	PO	A	E	DP	TC/G	FA	Pitcher	G	IP	W	L	SV	ERA
1B	R. Nelson	235	.247	1	20	596	51	5	66	9.3	.992	H. Pollet	37	232	14	13	2	3.29
2B	R. Schoendienst	**642**	.276	7	63	393	403	12	124	5.7	.985	M. Lanier	27	181	11	9	0	3.13
SS	M. Marion	372	.247	4	40	180	313	11	73	5.0	**.978**	G. Staley	42	170	13	13	3	4.99
3B	T. Glaviano	410	.285	11	44	103	255	25	16	**3.6**	.935	A. Brazle	46	165	11	9	6	4.10
RF	E. Slaughter	556	.290	10	101	260	9	6	1	1.9	.978	H. Brecheen	27	163	8	11	1	3.80
CF	C. Diering	204	.250	3	18	178	8	2	2	2.3	.989	G. Munger	32	155	7	8	0	3.90
LF	B. Howerton	313	.281	10	59	183	2	6	0	2.0	.969	C. Boyer	36	120	7	7	1	3.52
C	D. Rice	414	.244	9	54	572	63	10	12	5.0	.984							
01	S. Musial	555	**.346**	28	109	760	39	8	67		.990							
3B	E. Kazak	207	.256	5	23	36	95	9	7	2.9	.936							
SS	E. Miller	172	.227	3	22	72	173	5	29	4.9	.980							
OF	H. Walker	150	.207	0	7	92	3	3	0	2.1	.969							
C	J. Garagiola	88	.318	2	20	99	8	0	2	3.6	1.000							

Cincinnati

W-66 L-87

Luke Sewell

POS	Player	AB	BA	HR	RBI	PO	A	E	DP	TC/G	FA	Pitcher	G	IP	W	L	SV	ERA
1B	T. Kluszewski	538	.307	25	111	1123	61	15	101	9.2	.987	E. Blackwell	40	261	17	15	4	2.97
2B	C. Ryan	367	.259	3	43	304	283	16	13	5.9*	.973	K. Raffensberger	38	239	14	19	0	4.26
SS	V. Stallcup	483	.251	8	54	253	389	18	79	4.9	.973	H. Wehmeier	41	230	10	18	4	5.67
3B	G. Hatton	438	.260	11	54	145	230	18	19	3.1	.954	H. Fox	34	187	11	8	1	4.33
RF	J. Wyrostek	509	.285	8	76	238	8	5	0	1.9	.980	W. Ramsdell	27	157	7	12	0	3.72
CF	L. Merriman	298	.258	2	31	181	4	2	1	2.2	.989	F. Smith	38	91	2	7	3	3.87
LF	B. Usher	321	.259	6	35	190	7	3	1	2.1	.985							
C	D. Howell	224	.223	2	22	338	26	5	4	4.6	.986							
OF	J. Adcock	372	.293	8	55	177	6	6	3	2.5	.968							
23	B. Adams	348	.282	3	25	170	200	14	34		.964							
OF	P. Lowrey	264	.227	1	11	153	4	2	1	2.2	.987							
C	J. Pramesa	228	.307	5	30	328	37	7	2	5.1	.981							

Chicago

W-64 L-89

Frankie Frisch

POS	Player	AB	BA	HR	RBI	PO	A	E	DP	TC/G	FA	Pitcher	G	IP	W	L	SV	ERA
1B	P. Ward	285	.253	6	33	734	73	4	78	10.7	.995	B. Rush	39	255	13	**20**	1	3.71
2B	W. Terwilliger	480	.242	10	32	314	380	24	80	5.7	.967	J. Schmitz	39	193	10	16	0	4.99
SS	R. Smalley	557	.230	21	85	**332**	**541**	**51**	**115**	**6.0**	.945	P. Minner	39	190	8	13	4	4.11
3B	B. Serena	435	.239	17	61	122	274	23	24	3.4	.945	F. Hiller	38	153	12	5	1	3.53
RF	B. Borkowski	256	.273	4	29	150	3	4	1	2.4	.975	M. Dubiel	39	143	6	10	2	4.16
CF	A. Pafko	514	.304	36	92	342	12	8	1	2.5	.978	D. Lade	34	118	5	6	2	4.74
LF	H. Sauer	540	.274	32	103	236	12	9	1	2.1	.965	J. Klippstein	33	105	2	9	1	5.25
C	M. Owen	259	.243	2	21	318	39	8	8	4.2	.978	D. Leonard	35	74	5	1	6	3.77
1B	P. Cavarretta	256	.273	10	31	606	47	9	55	9.9	.986							
C	R. Walker	213	.230	6	16	240	34	7	6	4.5	.975							
OF	C. Mauro	185	.227	1	10	86	2	5	0	1.9	.946							
OF	H. Jeffcoat	179	.235	2	18	83	6	3	0	1.7	.967							
OF	R. Northey	114	.281	4	20	38	3	1	2	1.6	.976							
OF	H. Edwards	110	.364	2	21	38	2	1	0	1.4	.976							

Pittsburgh

W-57 L-96

Billy Meyer

POS	Player	AB	BA	HR	RBI	PO	A	E	DP	TC/G	FA	Pitcher	G	IP	W	L	SV	ERA
1B	J. Hopp	318	.340	8	47	534	32	6	61	8.2	.990	C. Chambers	37	249	12	15	0	4.30
2B	D. Murtaugh	367	.294	2	37	273	292	14	84	5.4	.976	M. Dickson	51	225	10	15	3	3.80
SS	S. Rojek	230	.257	0	17	102	160	9	39	4.0	.967	B. Werle	48	215	8	16	8	4.60
3B	N. Fernandez	198	.258	6	27	48	101	12	6	3.1	.925	B. MacDonald	32	153	8	10	1	4.29
RF	G. Bell	422	.282	8	53	203	10	5	3	2.1	.977	V. Law	27	128	7	9	0	4.92
CF	W. Westlake	477	.285	24	95	329	4	3	3	2.7	.991	M. Queen	33	120	5	14	0	5.98
LF	R. Kiner	547	.272	**47**	118	287	13	11	2	2.1	.965							
C	C. McCullough	279	.254	6	34	362	45	6	3	4.1	.985							
SS	D. O'Connell	315	.292	8	32	147	228	9	47	5.9	.977							
UT	P. Castiglione	263	.255	3	22	116	125	10	23		.960							
3B	B. Dillinger	222	.288	1	9	60	116	8	13	3.6	.957							
1B	J. Phillips	208	.293	5	34	450	39	7	46	9.2	.986							
OF	T. Saffell	182	.203	2	6	128	5	1	0	3.1	.993							
OF	T. Beard	177	.232	4	12	112	4	2	0	2.4	.983							
C	R. Mueller	156	.269	6	24	204	30	1	3	3.7	.996							

BATTING AND BASE RUNNING LEADERS

Batting Average

S. Musial, STL	.346
J. Robinson, BKN	.328
D. Snider, BKN	.321
D. Ennis, PHI	.311
T. Kluszewski, CIN	.307

Slugging Average

S. Musial, STL	.596
A. Pafko, CHI	.591
R. Kiner, PIT	.590
S. Gordon, BOS	.557
D. Snider, BKN	.553

Home Runs

R. Kiner, PIT	47
A. Pafko, CHI	36
H. Sauer, CHI	32
G. Hodges, BKN	32

Total Bases

D. Snider, BKN	343
S. Musial, STL	331
D. Ennis, PHI	328
R. Kiner, PIT	323
A. Pafko, CHI	304

Runs Batted In

D. Ennis, PHI	126
R. Kiner, PIT	118
G. Hodges, BKN	113
T. Kluszewski, CIN	111
S. Musial, STL	109

Stolen Bases

S. Jethroe, BOS	35
P. Reese, BKN	17
D. Snider, BKN	16
E. Torgeson, BOS	15
R. Ashburn, PHI	14

Hits

D. Snider, BKN	199
S. Musial, STL	192
C. Furillo, BKN	189
D. Ennis, PHI	185

Base on Balls

E. Stanky, NY	144
R. Kiner, PIT	122
E. Torgeson, BOS	119
W. Westrum, NY	92

Home Run Percentage

R. Kiner, PIT	8.6
R. Campanella, BKN	7.1
A. Pafko, CHI	7.0
H. Sauer, CHI	5.9

PITCHING LEADERS

Winning Percentage

S. Maglie, NY	.818
J. Konstanty, PHI	.696
C. Simmons, PHI	.680
R. Roberts, PHI	.645
D. Newcombe, BKN	.633
P. Roe, BKN	.633

Earned Run Average

J. Hearn, STL, NY	2.49
S. Maglie, NY	2.71
E. Blackwell, CIN	2.97
L. Jansen, NY	3.01
R. Roberts, PHI	3.02

Wins

W. Spahn, BOS	21
J. Sain, BOS	20
R. Roberts, PHI	20

Saves

J. Konstanty, PHI	22
B. Werle, PIT	8
R. Branca, BKN	7
B. Hogue, BOS	7
D. Leonard, CHI	6
A. Brazle, STL	6

Strikeouts

W. Spahn, BOS	191
E. Blackwell, CIN	188
L. Jansen, NY	161
C. Simmons, PHI	146
R. Roberts, PHI	146

Complete Games

V. Bickford, BOS	27
J. Sain, BOS	25
W. Spahn, BOS	25
L. Jansen, NY	21
R. Roberts, PHI	21

Fewest Hits/9 Innings

J. Hearn, STL, NY	5.64
E. Blackwell, CIN	7.00
S. Maglie, NY	7.38
C. Simmons, PHI	7.46

Shutouts

J. Hearn, STL, NY	5
S. Maglie, NY	5
L. Jansen, NY	5
R. Roberts, PHI	5

Fewest Walks/9 Innings

K. Raffensberger, CIN	1.51
L. Jansen, NY	1.80
J. Sain, BOS	2.26
R. Roberts, PHI	2.28

NATIONAL LEAGUE 1950, *cont.*

BATTING AND BASE RUNNING LEADERS

Runns

E. Torgeson, BOS	120
E. Stanky, NY	115
R. Kiner, PIT	112
D. Snider, BKN	109

Doubles

R. Schoendienst, STL	43
S. Musial, STL	41
J. Robinson, BKN	39
T. Kluszewski, CIN	37

Triples

R. Ashburn, PHI	14
G. Bell, PIT	11
D. Snider, BKN	10
R. Smalley, CHI	9
R. Schoendienst, STL	9

PITCHING LEADERS

Most Strikeouts/9 Inn.

E. Blackwell, CIN	6.48
C. Simmons, PHI	6.12
W. Spahn, BOS	5.87
E. Palica, BKN	5.86

Innings

V. Bickford, BOS	312
R. Roberts, PHI	304
W. Spahn, BOS	293
J. Sain, BOS	278

Games Pitched

J. Konstanty, PHI	74
M. Dickson, PIT	51
B. Werle, PIT	48
S. Maglie, NY	47

	W	L	PCT	GB	R	OR	Batting 2B	3B	HR	BA	SA	SB	Fielding E	DP	FA	Pitching CG	BB	SO	ShO	SV	ERA
Philadelphia	91	63	.591		722	**624**	225	55	125	.265	.396	33	151	155	.975	57	**530**	620	13	**27**	**3.50**
Brooklyn	89	65	.578	2	**847**	724	247	46	**194**	**.272**	**.444**	**77**	**127**	**183**	**.979**	62	591	**772**	10	21	4.28
New York	86	68	.558	5	735	643	204	50	133	.258	.392	42	137	181	.977	70	536	596	**19**	15	3.71
Boston	83	71	.539	8	785	736	246	36	148	.263	.405	71	182	146	.970	**88**	554	615	7	10	4.14
St. Louis	78	75	.510	12.5	693	670	255	50	102	.259	.386	23	130	172	.978	57	535	603	10	14	3.97
Cincinnati	66	87	.431	24.5	654	734	**257**	27	99	.260	.376	37	140	132	.976	67	582	686	7	13	4.32
Chicago	64	89	.418	26.5	643	772	224	47	161	.248	.401	46	201	169	.968	55	593	559	9	19	4.28
Pittsburgh	57	96	.373	33.5	681	857	227	**59**	138	.264	.406	43	136	165	.977	42	616	556	6	16	4.96
					5760	5760	1885	370	1100	.261	.401	372	1204	1303	.975	498	4537	5007	81	135	4.14

AMERICAN LEAGUE 1950

New York

W-98 L-56

Casey Stengel

POS	Player	AB	BA	HR	RBI	PO	A	E	DP	TC/G	FA
1B	J. Collins	205	.234	8	28	480	36	7	62	5.3	.987
2B	J. Coleman	522	.287	6	69	384	384	18	137	5.2	.977
SS	P. Rizzuto	617	.324	7	66	**301**	452	14	123	4.9	**.982**
3B	B. Johnson	327	.260	6	40	82	169	11	20	2.6	.958
RF	H. Bauer	415	.320	13	70	228	8	3	3	2.2	.987
CF	J. DiMaggio	525	.301	32	122	363	9	9	1	2.8	.976
LF	G. Woodling	449	.283	6	60	263	16	2	3	2.4	.993
C	Y. Berra	597	.322	28	124	**777**	**64**	13	**16**	**5.8**	.985
OF	C. Mapes	356	.247	12	61	183	8	10	4	2.0	.950
3B	B. Brown	277	.267	4	37	63	140	9	13	2.6	.958
1B	J. Mize	274	.277	25	72	490	31	2	73	7.3	.996
1B	T. Henrich	151	.272	6	34	224	7	3	23	6.9	.987

Pitcher	G	IP	W	L	SV	ERA
V. Raschi	33	257	21	8	1	4.00
A. Reynolds	35	241	16	12	2	3.74
E. Lopat	35	236	18	8	1	3.47
T. Byrne	31	203	15	9	0	4.74
F. Sanford	26	113	5	4	0	4.55
W. Ford	20	112	9	1	1	2.81
T. Ferrick	30	57	8	4	9	3.65
J. Page	37	55	3	7	13	5.04

Detroit

W-95 L-59

Red Rolfe

POS	Player	AB	BA	HR	RBI	PO	A	E	DP	TC/G	FA
1B	D. Kolloway	467	.289	6	62	1087	85	13	133	**10.0**	.989
2B	G. Priddy	618	.277	13	75	440	**542**	19	**150**	**6.4**	.981
SS	J. Lipon	601	.293	2	63	273	**483**	**33**	**126**	**5.4**	.958
3B	G. Kell	**641**	.340	8	101	186	315	9	30	3.2	**.982**
RF	V. Wertz	559	.308	27	123	286	5	10	3	2.1	.967
CF	J. Groth	566	.306	12	85	374	9	6	0	2.5	.985
LF	H. Evers	526	.323	21	103	325	15	1	3	2.5	.997
C	A. Robinson	283	.226	9	37	355	42	3	4	3.9	.993
1B	D. Kryhoski	169	.219	4	19	409	27	4	44	9.4	.991
OF	P. Mullin	142	.218	6	23	62	4	0	1	2.1	1.000
P	F. Hutchinson	95	.326	0	20	17	50	4	6	1.8	.944

Pitcher	G	IP	W	L	SV	ERA
A. Houtteman	41	275	19	12	4	3.54
F. Hutchinson	39	232	17	8	0	3.96
H. Newhouser	35	214	15	13	3	4.34
D. Trout	34	185	13	5	4	3.75
T. Gray	27	149	10	7	1	4.40
H. White	42	111	9	6	1	4.54

Boston

W-94 L-60

Joe McCarthy
W-31 L-28

Steve O'Neill
W-63 L-32

POS	Player	AB	BA	HR	RBI	PO	A	E	DP	TC/G	FA
1B	W. Dropo	559	.322	34	**144**	1142	77	15	147	9.2	.988
2B	B. Doerr	586	.294	27	120	**443**	431	11	130	5.9	**.988**
SS	V. Stephens	628	.295	30	**144**	258	431	13	115	4.8	.981
3B	J. Pesky	490	.312	1	49	160	257	11	29	**3.7**	.974
RF	A. Zarilla	471	.325	9	74	230	12	6	1	1.9	.976
CF	D. DiMaggio	588	.328	7	70	390	15	7	2	2.9	.983
LF	T. Williams	334	.317	28	97	165	7	8	0	2.1	.956
C	B. Tebbetts	268	.310	8	45	285	44	4	5	4.5	.988
UT	B. Goodman	424	**.354**	4	68	344	89	9	28		.980
C	M. Batts	238	.273	4	34	306	29	2	3	4.6	.994
OF	C. Vollmer	169	.284	7	37	80	3	4	0	2.2	.954
OF	T. Wright	107	.318	0	20	40	1	2	1	1.8	.953

Pitcher	G	IP	W	L	SV	ERA
M. Parnell	40	249	18	10	3	3.61
E. Kinder	48	207	14	12	9	4.26
J. Dobson	39	207	15	10	4	4.18
C. Stobbs	32	169	12	7	1	5.10
M. McDermott	38	130	7	3	5	5.19
W. Masterson	33	129	8	6	1	5.64
W. Nixon	22	101	8	6	2	6.04

Cleveland

W-92 L-62

Lou Boudreau

POS	Player	AB	BA	HR	RBI	PO	A	E	DP	TC/G	FA
1B	L. Easter	540	.280	28	107	1100	82	11	114	9.3	.991
2B	J. Gordon	368	.236	19	57	224	283	16	69	5.0	.969
SS	R. Boone	365	.301	7	58	178	267	26	64	4.6	.945
3B	A. Rosen	554	.287	**37**	116	151	**322**	15	24	3.2	.969
RF	B. Kennedy	540	.291	9	54	294	13	4	3	2.2	.987
CF	L. Doby	503	.326	25	102	367	2	5	1	2.7	.987
LF	D. Mitchell	506	.308	3	49	236	3	7	1	1.9	.972
C	J. Hegan	415	.219	14	58	656	**64**	5	14	5.6	.993
SS	L. Boudreau	260	.269	1	29	118	170	4	44	4.8	.986
2B	B. Avila	201	.299	1	21	153	135	5	46	4.7	.983
OF	A. Clark	163	.215	6	21	75	2	1	0	1.9	.987
P	B. Lemon	136	.272	6	26	22	66	4	6	2.1	.957

Pitcher	G	IP	W	L	SV	ERA
B. Lemon	44	**288**	**23**	11	3	3.84
B. Feller	35	247	16	11	0	3.43
E. Wynn	32	214	18	8	0	**3.20**
M. Garcia	33	184	11	11	0	3.86
S. Gromek	31	113	10	7	0	3.65
S. Zoldak	33	64	4	2	4	3.96
A. Benton	36	63	4	2	4	3.57
J. Flores	28	53	3	3	4	3.74

AMERICAN LEAGUE 1950, *cont.*

	POS	Player	AB	BA	HR	RBI	PO	A	E	DP	TC/G	FA	Pitcher	G	IP	W	L	SV	ERA
Washington	1B	M. Vernon	327	.306	9	65	743	61	8	93	9.6	.990*	S. Hudson	30	238	14	14	0	4.09
	2B	C. Michaels	388	.250	4	47	298	323	16*	91	6.1	.975	B. Kuzava	22	155	8	7	0	3.95
	SS	S. Dente	603	.239	2	59	225	406	32	88	5.2	.952	C. Marrero	27	152	6	10	1	4.50
W-67 L-87	3B	E. Yost	573	.295	11	58	**205**	307	**30**	**45**	3.5	.945	S. Consuegra	21	125	7	8	2	4.40
	RF	B. Stewart	378	.267	4	35	202	10	2	3	2.1	.991	J. Haynes	27	102	7	5	0	5.84
Bucky Harris	CF	I. Noren	542	.295	14	98	357	20	6	5	3.2	.984	M. Harris	**53**	98	5	9	**15**	4.78
	LF	G. Coan	366	.303	7	50	220	4	7	1	2.4	.970							
	C	A. Evans	289	.235	2	30	289	23	4	8	3.6	.987							
	OF	S. Mele	435	.274	12	86	192	8	2	0	2.0	.990							
	C	M. Grasso	195	.287	1	22	238	38	**17**	6	4.2	.942							
	OF	J. Ostrowski	141	.227	4	23	105	3	6	1	2.5	.947							
Chicago	1B	E. Robinson	424	.314	20	73	982*	60	14	105	8.9	.987	B. Pierce	33	219	12	16	1	3.98
	2B	N. Fox	457	.247	0	30	340	344	18	100	5.8	.974	B. Wight	30	206	10	16	0	3.58
	SS	C. Carrasquel	524	.282	4	46	234	458	28	113	5.1	.961	B. Cain	34	172	9	12	2	3.93
	3B	H. Majeski	414	.309	6	46	115	246	11	31	3.3	.970	R. Gumpert	40	155	5	12	0	4.75
W-60 L-94	RF	M. Rickert	278	.237	4	27	150	3	5	1	2.0	.968	R. Scarborough	27	149	10	13	1	5.30
	CF	D. Philley	619	.242	14	80	367	19	8	8	2.6	.980	H. Judson	46	112	2	3	0	3.94
Jack Onslow	LF	G. Zernial	543	.280	29	93	306	9	10	2	2.4	.969	K. Holcombe	24	96	3	10	1	4.59
W-8 L-22	C	P. Masi	377	.279	7	55	440	52	2	9	4.3	**.996**	L. Aloma	42	88	7	2	4	3.80
Red Corriden	3B	F. Baker	186	.317	0	11	50	102	2	7	2.9	.987							
W-52 L-72	1B	G. Goldsberry	127	.268	2	25	235	29	3	37	6.7	.989							
St. Louis	1B	D. Lenhardt	480	.273	22	81	618	39	8	77	7.7	.988	N. Garver	37	260	13	18	0	3.39
	2B	O. Friend	372	.237	8	50	244	302	22	62	6.1	.961	A. Widmar	36	195	7	15	4	4.76
	SS	T. Upton	389	.237	2	30	198	328	30	65	4.8	.946	S. Overmire	31	161	9	12	0	4.19
	3B	B. Sommers	137	.255	0	14	25	52	7	5	2.3	.917	D. Starr	32	124	7	5	2	5.02
W-58 L-96	RF	K. Wood	369	.225	13	62	162	16	9	2	2.0	.952	H. Dorish	29	109	4	9	0	6.44
	CF	R. Coleman	384	.271	8	55	253	7	4	1	2.7	.985	C. Fannin	25	102	5	9	1	6.53
Zack Taylor	LF	D. Kokos	490	.261	18	67	342	8	11	2	2.8	.970	D. Johnson	25	96	5	6	1	6.09
	C	S. Lollar	396	.280	13	65	367	48	8	9	3.9	.981	D. Pillette	24	74	3	5	2	7.09
	OF	R. Sievers	370	.238	10	57	222	12	4	3	3.1	.983							
	23	S. Stirnweiss	326	.218	1	24	191	206	12	51		.971							
	1B	H. Arft	280	.268	1	32	701	51	4	59	9.0	.995							
	C	L. Moss	222	.266	8	34	204	20	10	4	3.9	.957							
	OF	J. Delsing	209	.263	0	15	150	4	1	3	2.9	.994							
	SS	B. DeMars	178	.247	0	13	113	123	17	32	4.7	.933							
Philadelphia	1B	F. Fain	522	.282	10	83	1286	**124**	**19**	**192**	9.5	.987	L. Brissie	46	246	7	19	8	4.02
	2B	B. Hitchcock	399	.273	1	54	297	319	21	105	6.0	.967	A. Kellner	36	225	8	**20**	2	5.47
	SS	E. Joost	476	.233	18	58	241	389	29	117	5.0	.956	B. Shantz	36	215	8	14	0	4.61
W-52 L-102	3B	B. Dillinger	356	.309	3	41	92	173	12	18	3.3	.957	H. Wyse	41	171	9	14	0	5.85
	RF	E. Valo	446	.280	10	46	264	9	5	3	2.4	.982	B. Hooper	45	170	15	10	5	5.02
Connie Mack	CF	S. Chapman	553	.251	23	95	428	11	10	4	3.2	.978	C. Scheib	43	106	3	10	3	7.22
	LF	P. Lehner	427	.309	9	52	247	10	5	1	2.6	.981							
	C	M. Guerra	252	.282	2	26	253	33	3	8	3.7	.990							
	3B	K. Wahl	280	.257	2	27	70	141	12	11	3.7	.946							
	OF	W. Moses	265	.264	2	21	147	7	2	2	2.5	.987							
	UT	P. Suder	248	.246	8	35	167	181	9	55		.975							
	C	J. Tipton	184	.266	6	20	201	24	3	3	3.9	.987							
	OF	B. McCosky	179	.240	0	11	73	1	1	1	1.8	.987							

BATTING AND BASE RUNNING LEADERS

Batting Average
B. Goodman, BOS .354
G. Kell, DET .340
D. DiMaggio, BOS .328
L. Doby, CLE .326
A. Zarilla, BOS .325

Slugging Average
J. DiMaggio, NY .585
W. Dropo, BOS .583
H. Evers, DET .551
L. Doby, CLE .545
A. Rosen, CLE .543

Home Runs
A. Rosen, CLE 37
W. Dropo, BOS 34
J. DiMaggio, NY 32
V. Stephens, BOS 30
G. Zernial, CHI 29

Total Bases
W. Dropo, BOS 326
V. Stephens, BOS 321
Y. Berra, NY 318
G. Kell, DET 310
J. DiMaggio, NY 307

Runs Batted In
W. Dropo, BOS 144
V. Stephens, BOS 144
Y. Berra, NY 124
V. Wertz, DET 123
J. DiMaggio, NY 122

Stolen Bases
D. DiMaggio, BOS 15
E. Valo, PHI 12
P. Rizzuto, NY 12
G. Coan, WAS 10
J. Lipon, DET 9

Hits
G. Kell, DET 218
P. Rizzuto, NY 200
D. DiMaggio, BOS 193
Y. Berra, NY 192

Base on Balls
E. Yost, WAS 141
F. Fain, PHI 133
J. Pesky, BOS 104
B. Hitchcock, PHI 103

Home Run Percentage
A. Rosen, CLE 6.7
J. DiMaggio, NY 6.1
W. Dropo, BOS 6.1
G. Zernial, CHI 5.3

Runs
D. DiMaggio, BOS 131
P. Rizzuto, NY 125
V. Stephens, BOS 125
Y. Berra, NY 116

Doubles
G. Kell, DET 56
V. Wertz, DET 37
P. Rizzuto, NY 36
H. Evers, DET 35

Triples
H. Evers, DET 11
B. Doerr, BOS 11
D. DiMaggio, BOS 11

PITCHING LEADERS

Winning Percentage
V. Raschi, NY .724
E. Lopat, NY .692
E. Wynn, CLE .692
F. Hutchinson, DET .680
B. Lemon, CLE .676

Earned Run Average
E. Wynn, CLE 3.20
N. Garver, STL 3.39
B. Feller, CLE 3.43
E. Lopat, NY 3.47
A. Houtteman, DET 3.54

Wins
B. Lemon, CLE 23
V. Raschi, NY 21
A. Houtteman, DET 19
E. Wynn, CLE 18
E. Lopat, NY 18
M. Parnell, BOS 18

Saves
M. Harris, WAS 15
J. Page, NY 13
T. Ferrick, STL, NY 11
E. Kinder, BOS 9
L. Brissie, PHI 8

Strikeouts
B. Lemon, CLE 170
A. Reynolds, NY 160
V. Raschi, NY 155
E. Wynn, CLE 143
B. Feller, CLE 119

Complete Games
N. Garver, STL 22
B. Lemon, CLE 22
M. Parnell, BOS 21
A. Houtteman, DET 21
S. Hudson, WAS 17
V. Raschi, NY 17

Fewest Hits/9 Innings
E. Wynn, CLE 6.99
B. Pierce, CHI 7.76
B. Cain, CHI 8.02
A. Reynolds, NY 8.04

Shutouts
A. Houtteman, DET 4

Fewest Walks/9 Innings
F. Hutchinson, DET 1.86
E. Lopat, NY 2.48
D. Trout, DET 3.12
A. Houtteman, DET 3.24

Most Strikeouts/9 Inn.
E. Wynn, CLE 6.02
A. Reynolds, NY 5.98
V. Raschi, NY 5.44
B. Lemon, CLE 5.31

Innings
B. Lemon, CLE 288
A. Houtteman, DET 275
N. Garver, STL 260
V. Raschi, NY 257

Games Pitched
M. Harris, WAS 53
E. Kinder, BOS 48
T. Ferrick, STL, NY 46
H. Judson, CHI 46
L. Brissie, PHI 46

AMERICAN LEAGUE 1950, *cont.*

	W	L	PCT	GB	R	OR	Batting 2B	3B	HR	BA	SA	SB	Fielding E	DP	FA	Pitching CG	BB	SO	ShO	SV	ERA
New York	98	56	.636		914	691	234	**70**	159	.282	.441	41	119	188	.980	66	708	**712**	**12**	**31**	4.15
Detroit	95	59	.617	3	837	713	285	50	114	.282	.417	23	120	194	**.981**	**72**	**553**	576	9	20	4.12
Boston	94	60	.610	4	**1027**	804	**287**	61	161	**.302**	**.464**	32	**111**	181	**.981**	66	748	630	6	28	4.88
Cleveland	92	62	.597	6	806	**654**	222	46	**164**	.269	.422	40	129	160	.978	69	647	674	11	16	**3.74**
Washington	67	87	.435	31	690	813	190	53	76	.260	.360	**42**	167	181	.972	59	648	486	7	18	4.66
Chicago	60	94	.390	38	625	749	172	47	93	.260	.364	19	140	181	.977	62	734	566	7	9	4.41
St. Louis	58	96	.377	40	684	916	235	43	106	.246	.370	39	196	155	.967	56	651	448	7	14	5.20
Philadelphia	52	102	.338	46	670	913	204	53	100	.261	.378	**42**	155	**208**	.974	50	729	466	3	18	5.49
					6253	6253	1829	423	973	.270	.402	278	1137	1448	.976	500	5418	4558	62	154	4.58

NATIONAL LEAGUE 1951

New York

W-98 L-59

Leo Durocher

POS	Player	AB	BA	HR	RBI	PO	A	E	DP	TC/G	FA
1B	W. Lockman	614	.282	12	73	1045	89	16	113	**9.7**	.986
2B	E. Stanky	515	.247	14	43	356	412	18	117	5.6	.977
SS	A. Dark	646	.303	14	69	**295**	**465**	**45**	**114**	5.2	.944
3B	H. Thompson	264	.235	8	33	64	120	15	16	2.8	.925
RF	D. Mueller	469	.277	16	69	233	5	4	1	2.1	.983
CF	W. Mays	464	.274	20	68	353	12	9	2	3.1	.976
LF	M. Irvin	558	.312	24	**121**	237	10	1	1	2.2	.996
C	W. Westrum	361	.219	20	70	554	62	8	9	5.1	**.987**
03	B. Thomson	518	.293	32	101	258	139	20	14		.952
C	R. Noble	141	.234	5	26	144	8	4	3	3.8	.974

Pitcher	G	IP	W	L	SV	ERA
S. Maglie	42	298	**23**	6	4	2.93
L. Jansen	39	278	**23**	11	0	3.04
J. Hearn	34	211	17	9	0	3.62
D. Koslo	39	150	10	9	3	3.31
G. Spencer	57	132	10	4	6	3.75
S. Jones	41	120	6	11	4	4.26

Brooklyn

W-97 L-60

Chuck Dressen

POS	Player	AB	BA	HR	RBI	PO	A	E	DP	TC/G	FA
1B	G. Hodges	582	.268	40	103	1365	**126**	12	**171**	9.5	.992
2B	J. Robinson	548	.338	19	88	**390**	**435**	7	**137**	5.4	**.992**
SS	P. Reese	616	.286	10	84	292	422	35	106	4.9	.953
3B	B. Cox	455	.279	9	51	140	264	14	26	3.0	.967
RF	C. Furillo	**667**	.295	16	91	330	24	5	6	2.3	.986
CF	D. Snider	606	.277	29	101	382	12	5	1	2.7	.987
LF	A. Pafko	277	.249	18	58	144	8	1	0	2.0	.993
C	R. Campanella	505	.325	33	108	**722**	**72**	**11**	**12**	**5.8**	.986

Pitcher	G	IP	W	L	SV	ERA
D. Newcombe	40	272	20	9	0	3.28
P. Roe	34	258	22	3	0	3.04
R. Branca	42	204	13	12	3	3.26
C. Erskine	46	190	16	12	4	4.46
C. King	48	121	14	7	6	4.15

St. Louis

W-81 L-73

Marty Marion

POS	Player	AB	BA	HR	RBI	PO	A	E	DP	TC/G	FA
1B	N. Jones	300	.263	3	41	698	48	7	7	10.6	.991
2B	R. Schoendienst	553	.289	6	54	339	386	7	113	5.9	.990
SS	S. Hemus	420	.281	2	32	181	344	19	72	**5.2**	.965
3B	B. Johnson	442	.262	14	64	99	316	10	32	3.4	.976*
RF	E. Slaughter	409	.281	4	64	198	10	1	3	2.0	.995
CF	P. Lowrey	370	.303	5	40	220	6	4	3	2.7	.983
LF	S. Musial	578	**.355**	32	108	216	13	6	4	2.6	.974
C	D. Rice	374	.251	9	47	447	66	8	**12**	4.3	.985
OF	W. Westlake	267	.255	6	39	154	7	3	1	2.4	.982
OF	H. Rice	236	.254	4	38	116	6	6	0	2.0	.953
SS	S. Rojek	186	.274	0	14	95	131	6	36	4.5	.974

Pitcher	G	IP	W	L	SV	ERA
G. Staley	42	227	19	13	3	3.81
T. Poholsky	38	195	7	13	1	4.43
M. Lanier	31	160	11	9	1	3.26
A. Brazle	56	154	6	5	7	3.09
H. Brecheen	24	139	8	4	2	3.25
C. Chambers	21	129	11	6	0	3.83
G. Munger	23	95	4	6	0	5.32
J. Presko	15	89	7	4	2	3.45

Boston

W-76 L-78

Billy Southworth
W-28 L-31

Tommy Holmes
W-48 L-47

POS	Player	AB	BA	HR	RBI	PO	A	E	DP	TC/G	FA
1B	E. Torgeson	581	.263	24	92	1330	107	**17**	137	9.4	.988
2B	R. Hartsfield	450	.271	6	31	336	293	20	87	5.7	.969
SS	B. Kerr	172	.186	1	18	110	173	9	34	4.6	.969
3B	B. Elliott	480	.285	15	70	138	242	**24**	31	3.2	.941
RF	W. Marshall	469	.281	11	62	220	11	0	3	1.8	1.000
CF	S. Jethroe	572	.280	18	65	356	18	10	5	2.7	.974
LF	S. Gordon	550	.287	29	109	249	4	4	1	2.1	.984
C	W. Cooper	342	.313	18	59	367	57	8	9	4.8	.981
2S	S. Sisti	362	.279	2	38	220	227	18	47		.961
C	E. St. Claire	220	.282	1	25	267	29	7	5	4.9	.977
OF	B. Addis	199	.276	1	24	107	1	2	1	2.4	.982
SS	J. Logan	169	.219	0	16	98	155	11	31	4.6	.958

Pitcher	G	IP	W	L	SV	ERA
W. Spahn	39	311	22	14	0	2.98
M. Surkont	37	237	12	16	1	3.99
V. Bickford	25	165	11	9	0	3.12
J. Sain	26	160	5	13	1	4.21
C. Nichols	33	156	11	8	2	**2.88**
J. Wilson	20	110	7	7	1	5.40
B. Chipman	33	52	4	3	4	4.85

Philadelphia

W-73 L-81

Eddie Sawyer

POS	Player	AB	BA	HR	RBI	PO	A	E	DP	TC/G	FA
1B	E. Waitkus	610	.257	1	46	1214	94	10	121	9.2	.992
2B	P. Caballero	161	.186	1	11	133	124	4	37	4.6	.985
SS	G. Hamner	589	.255	9	72	255	458	31	93	5.0	.958
3B	W. Jones	564	.285	22	81	190	286	17	**33**	3.4	.966
RF	D. Ennis	532	.267	15	73	268	14	9	3	2.0	.969
CF	R. Ashburn	643	.344	4	63	538	15	7	6	3.6	.988
LF	D. Sisler	428	.287	8	52	233	8	8	3	2.2	.968
C	A. Seminick	291	.227	11	37	378	47	9	6	4.8	.979
C	D. Wilber	245	.278	8	34	326	26	8	5	4.9	.978
2B	E. Pellagrini	197	.234	5	30	80	110	2	19	3.6	.990
UT	T. Brown	196	.219	10	32	174	36	8	14		.963
OF	B. Nicholson	170	.241	8	30	75	1	1	0	1.9	.987

Pitcher	G	IP	W	L	SV	ERA
R. Roberts	44	**315**	21	15	2	3.03
B. Church	38	247	15	11	1	3.53
R. Meyer	28	168	8	9	0	3.48
J. Thompson	29	119	4	8	1	3.85
K. Heintzelman	35	118	6	12	2	4.18
J. Konstanty	58	116	4	11	9	4.05
K. Johnson	20	106	5	8	0	4.57

NATIONAL LEAGUE 1951, *cont.*

Team	POS	Player	AB	BA	HR	RBI	PO	A	E	DP	TC/G	FA	Pitcher	G	IP	W	L	SV	ERA
Cincinnati	1B	T. Kluszewski	607	.259	13	77	**1381**	88	5	115	9.6	**.997**	K. Raffensberger	42	249	16	**17**	5	3.44
W-68 L-86	2B	C. Ryan	473	.237	16	53	332	344	**21**	73	5.8	.970	E. Blackwell	38	232	16	15	2	3.45
Luke Sewell	SS	V. Stallcup	428	.241	8	49	190	333	17	61	4.6	**.969**	H. Fox	40	228	9	14	2	3.83
	3B	G. Hatton	331	.254	4	37	103	178	8	24	3.3	.972	W. Ramsdell	31	196	9	**17**	0	4.04
	RF	J. Wyrostek	537	.311	2	61	255	8	8	2	1.9	.970	H. Wehmeier	39	185	7	10	2	3.70
	CF	L. Merriman	359	.242	5	36	309	5	1	2	3.1	.997	H. Perkowski	35	102	3	6	1	2.82
	LF	J. Adcock	395	.243	10	47	221	8	4	2	2.2	.983	F. Smith	50	76	5	5	11	3.20
	C	D. Howell	207	.251	2	18	275	24	4	5	4.2	.987							
	32	B. Adams	403	.266	5	24	184	215	18	33		.957							
	OF	B. Usher	303	.208	5	25	218	9	6	4	2.4	.974							
	C	J. Pramesa	227	.229	6	22	241	27	9	4	4.4	.968							
	SS	R. McMillan	199	.211	1	8	78	132	8	23	4.0	.963							
	OF	H. Edwards	127	.315	3	20	64	0	1	0	1.9	.985							
Pittsburgh	1B	J. Phillips	156	.237	0	12	322	21	3	37	6.5	.991	M. Dickson	45	289	20	16	2	4.02
W-64 L-90	2B	D. Murtaugh	151	.199	1	11	110	113	7	35	3.5	.970	M. Queen	39	168	7	9	0	4.44
Billy Meyer	SS	G. Strickland	454	.216	9	47	222	386	37	89	5.2	.943	B. Werle	59	150	8	6	6	5.65
	3B	P. Castiglione	482	.261	7	42	103	228	15	25	3.5	.957	B. Friend	34	150	6	10	0	4.27
	RF	G. Bell	600	.278	16	89	267	18	4	4	2.0	.986	H. Pollet	21	129	6	10	0	5.04
	CF	C. Metkovich	423	.293	3	40	171	4	1	0	2.6	.994	V. Law	28	114	6	9	2	4.50
	LF	R. Kiner	531	.309	**42**	109	195	7	7	1	2.2	.967	T. Wilks	48*	83	3	5	12*	2.83
	C	C. McCullough	259	.297	8	39	364	52	5	10	4.9	.988							
	OF	B. Howerton	219	.274	11	37	93	3	5	1	1.9	.950							
	C	J. Garagiola	212	.255	9	35	255	30	4	4	4.7	.986							
	1B	R. Nelson	195	.267	1	14	275	24	3	32	9.4	.990							
	3B	W. Westlake	181	.282	16	45	32	87	12	12	3.9	.908							
Chicago	1B	C. Connors	201	.239	2	18	452	33	8	41	8.6	.984	B. Rush	37	211	11	12	2	3.83
W-62 L-92	2B	E. Miksis	421	.266	4	35	279	317	19	71	6.0*	.969	P. Minner	33	202	6	**17**	1	3.79
Frankie Frisch	SS	R. Smalley	238	.231	8	31	117	190	15	42	4.4	.953	C. McLish	30	146	4	10	0	4.45
W-35 L-45	3B	R. Jackson	557	.275	16	76	**198**	**323**	**24**	32	**3.8**	.956	F. Hiller	24	141	6	12	1	4.84
Phil Cavarretta	RF	H. Jeffcoat	278	.273	4	27	166	11	2	5	2.1	.989	T. Lown	31	127	4	9	0	5.46
W-27 L-47	CF	F. Baumholtz	560	.284	2	50	307	6	8	2	2.3	.975	B. Kelly	35	124	7	4	0	4.66
	LF	H. Sauer	525	.263	30	89	286	19	6	2	2.4	.981	J. Klippstein	35	124	6	6	2	4.29
	C	S. Burgess	219	.251	2	20	210	35	5	6	3.9	.980	D. Leonard	41	82	10	6	3	2.64
	OF	G. Hermanski	231	.281	3	20	134	9	5	1	2.0	.966							
	1B	P. Cavarretta	206	.311	6	28	444	42	3	51	9.2	.994							
	2B	W. Terwilliger	192	.214	0	10	136	142	9	37	5.9	.969							
	OF	A. Pafko	178	.264	12	35	119	6	1	3	2.6	.992							
	1B	D. Fondy	170	.271	3	20	387	27	10	40	9.6	.976							
	SS	J. Cusick	164	.177	2	16	78	147	11	25	4.2	.953							
	SS	B. Ramazzotti	158	.247	1	15	73	137	11	32	4.3	.950							

BATTING AND BASE RUNNING LEADERS

Batting Average

S. Musial, STL	.355
R. Ashburn, PHI	.344
J. Robinson, BKN	.338
R. Campanella, BKN	.325
M. Irvin, NY	.312

Slugging Average

R. Kiner, PIT	.627
S. Musial, STL	.614
R. Campanella, BKN	.590
B. Thomson, NY	.562
G. Hodges, BKN	.527

Home Runs

R. Kiner, PIT	42
G. Hodges, BKN	40
R. Campanella, BKN	33
B. Thomson, NY	32
S. Musial, STL	32

Total Bases

S. Musial, STL	355
R. Kiner, PIT	333
G. Hodges, BKN	307
R. Campanella, BKN	298
D. Snider, BKN	293
A. Dark, NY	293

Runs Batted In

M. Irvin, NY	121
R. Kiner, PIT	109
S. Gordon, BOS	109
R. Campanella, BKN	108
S. Musial, STL	108

Stolen Bases

S. Jethroe, BOS	35
R. Ashburn, PHI	29
J. Robinson, BKN	25
E. Torgeson, BOS	20
P. Reese, BKN	20

Hits

R. Ashburn, PHI	221
S. Musial, STL	205
C. Furillo, BKN	197
A. Dark, NY	196

Base on Balls

R. Kiner, PIT	137
E. Stanky, NY	127
W. Westrum, NY	104
E. Torgeson, BOS	102

Home Run Percentage

R. Kiner, PIT	7.9
G. Hodges, BKN	6.9
A. Pafko, CHI, BKN	6.6
R. Campanella, BKN	6.5

Runs

R. Kiner, PIT	124
S. Musial, STL	124
G. Hodges, BKN	118
A. Dark, NY	114

Doubles

A. Dark, NY	41
T. Kluszewski, CIN	35
R. Campanella, BKN	33
J. Robinson, BKN	33

Triples

S. Musial, STL	12
G. Bell, PIT	12
M. Irvin, NY	11
F. Baumholtz, CHI	10
S. Jethroe, BOS	10

PITCHING LEADERS

Winning Percentage

P. Roe, BKN	.880
S. Maglie, NY	.793
D. Newcombe, BKN	.690
L. Jansen, NY	.676
J. Hearn, NY	.654

Earned Run Average

C. Nichols, BOS	2.88
S. Maglie, NY	2.93
W. Spahn, BOS	2.98
R. Roberts, PHI	3.03
P. Roe, BKN	3.04

Wins

L. Jansen, NY	23
S. Maglie, NY	23
P. Roe, BKN	22
W. Spahn, BOS	22
R. Roberts, PHI	21

Saves

T. Wilks, STL, PIT	13
F. Smith, CIN	11
J. Konstanty, PHI	9
A. Brazle, STL	7

Strikeouts

D. Newcombe, BKN	164
W. Spahn, BOS	164
S. Maglie, NY	146
L. Jansen, NY	145
B. Rush, CHI	129

Complete Games

W. Spahn, BOS	26
S. Maglie, NY	22
R. Roberts, PHI	22
P. Roe, BKN	19
M. Dickson, PIT	19

Fewest Hits/9 Innings

S. Maglie, NY	7.67
D. Newcombe, BKN	7.78
E. Blackwell, CIN	7.90
R. Branca, BKN	7.94

Shutouts

W. Spahn, BOS	7
R. Roberts, PHI	6
K. Raffensberger, CIN	5

Fewest Walks/9 Innings

K. Raffensberger, CIN	1.38
L. Jansen, NY	1.81
R. Roberts, PHI	1.83
P. Roe, BKN	2.24

Most Strikeouts/9 Inn.

M. Queen, PIT	6.58
B. Rush, CHI	5.49
D. Newcombe, BKN	5.43
R. Branca, BKN	5.21

Innings

R. Roberts, PHI	315
W. Spahn, BOS	311
S. Maglie, NY	298
M. Dickson, PIT	289

Games Pitched

T. Wilks, STL, PIT	65
B. Werle, PIT	59
J. Konstanty, PHI	58
G. Spencer, NY	57

NATIONAL LEAGUE 1951, *cont.*

	W	L	PCT	GB	R	OR	Batting 2B	Batting 3B	Batting HR	Batting BA	Batting SA	SB	Fielding E	Fielding DP	Fielding FA	Pitching CG	Pitching BB	Pitching SO	Pitching ShO	Pitching SV	ERA
*New York	98	59	.624		781	**641**	201	53	179	.260	.418	55	171	175	.972	64	**482**	625	9	18	**3.48**
Brooklyn	97	60	.618	1	**855**	672	**249**	37	**184**	**.275**	**.434**	**89**	129	**192**	.979	64	549	**693**	10	13	3.88
St. Louis	81	73	.526	15.5	683	671	230	**57**	95	.264	.382	30	**125**	187	**.980**	58	558	546	9	**23**	3.95
Boston	76	78	.494	20.5	723	662	234	37	130	.262	.394	78	145	157	.976	**73**	595	604	10	12	3.75
Philadelphia	73	81	.474	23.5	648	644	199	47	108	.260	.375	64	138	146	.977	57	496	570	**19**	15	3.81
Cincinnati	68	86	.442	28.5	559	667	215	33	88	.248	.351	44	140	141	.977	55	490	584	14	**23**	3.70
Pittsburgh	64	90	.416	32.5	689	845	218	56	137	.258	.397	26	170	178	.972	40	627	582	9	22	4.78
Chicago	62	92	.403	34.5	614	750	200	47	103	.250	.364	63	181	161	.971	48	572	544	10	10	4.34
					5552	5552	1746	367	1024	.260	.389	449	1199	1337	.976	459	4369	4748	90	136	3.96

* Defeated Brooklyn in playoff 2 games to 1

AMERICAN LEAGUE 1951

Team	POS	Player	AB	BA	HR	RBI	PO	A	E	DP	TC/G	FA	Pitcher	G	IP	W	L	SV	ERA
New York	1B	J. Collins	262	.286	9	48	556	56	8	65	5.4	.987	V. Raschi	35	258	21	10	0	3.27
W-98 L-56	2B	J. Coleman	362	.249	3	43	245	268	17	84	5.2	.968	E. Lopat	31	235	21	9	0	2.91
Casey Stengel	SS	P. Rizzuto	540	.274	2	43	317	407	24	113	5.2	.968	A. Reynolds	40	221	17	8	7	3.05
	3B	B. Brown	313	.268	6	51	80	151	11	14	2.7	.955	T. Morgan	27	125	9	3	2	3.68
	RF	H. Bauer	348	.296	10	54	188	7	2	1	1.8	.990	S. Shea	25	96	5	5	0	4.33
	CF	J. DiMaggio	415	.263	12	71	288	11	3	3	2.7	.990	J. Ostrowski	34	95	6	4	5	3.49
	LF	G. Woodling	420	.281	15	71	265	5	2	0	2.3	.993	B. Kuzava	23	82	8	4	5	2.40
	C	Y. Berra	547	.294	27	88	**693**	**82**	**13**	**25**	**5.6**	.984							
	32	G. McDougald	402	.306	14	63	174	249	14	46		.968							
	OF	M. Mantle	341	.267	13	65	135	4	6	1	1.7	.959							
	1B	J. Mize	332	.259	10	49	632	44	4	86	7.3	.994							
	OF	J. Jensen	168	.298	8	25	106	6	3	1	2.4	.974							
Cleveland	1B	L. Easter	486	.270	27	103	1043	68	14	108	9.0	.988	E. Wynn	37	**274**	20	13	1	3.02
W-93 L-61	2B	B. Avila	542	.304	10	58	349	417	14	87	5.7	.982	B. Lemon	42	263	17	**14**	2	3.52
Al Lopez	SS	R. Boone	544	.233	12	51	311	425	**33**	108	5.1	.957	M. Garcia	47	254	20	13	6	3.15
	3B	A. Rosen	573	.265	24	102	157	277	19	20	2.9	.958	B. Feller	33	250	**22**	8	0	3.50
	RF	B. Kennedy	321	.246	7	29	174	9	6	2	1.8	.968	L. Brissie	54	112	4	3	9	3.20
	CF	L. Doby	447	.295	20	69	321	12	8	3	2.6	.977	S. Gromek	27	107	7	4	1	2.77
	LF	D. Mitchell	510	.290	11	62	253	3	2	0	2.1	.992							
	C	J. Hegan	416	.238	6	43	597	66	6	8	5.2	**.991**							
	01	H. Simpson	332	.229	7	24	458	20	8	29		.984							
	OF	S. Chapman	246	.228	6	36	132	2	2	1	1.6	.985							
Boston	1B	W. Dropo	360	.239	11	57	878	63	12	91	10.2	.987	M. Parnell	36	221	18	11	2	3.26
W-87 L-67	2B	B. Doerr	402	.289	13	73	303	311	12	99	5.9	.981	R. Scarborough	37	184	12	9	0	5.09
Steve O'Neill	SS	J. Pesky	480	.313	3	41	204	340	22	74	5.3	.961	M. McDermott	34	172	8	8	3	3.35
	3B	V. Stephens	377	.300	17	78	105	207	7	19	3.6	.978	C. Stobbs	34	170	10	9	0	4.76
	RF	C. Vollmer	386	.251	22	85	206	5	3	0	2.0	.986	E. Kinder	**63**	127	11	2	**14**	2.55
	CF	D. DiMaggio	**639**	.296	12	72	376	15	11	1	2.8	.973	W. Nixon	33	125	7	4	1	4.90
	LF	T. Williams	531	.318	30	126	315	12	4	6	2.3	.988	B. Wight	34	118	7	7	0	5.10
	C	L. Moss	202	.198	3	26	284	28	5	4	4.6	.984	L. Kiely	17	113	7	7	0	3.34
	UT	B. Goodman	546	.297	0	50	742	170	14	96		.985	H. Taylor	31	81	4	9	2	5.75
	SS	L. Boudreau	273	.267	5	47	80	153	12	45	4.7	.951							
	C	B. Rosar	170	.229	1	13	235	20	1	6	4.6	.996							
	3B	F. Hatfield	163	.172	2	14	40	124	7	15	3.5	.959							
Chicago	1B	E. Robinson	564	.282	29	117	**1296**	91	**17**	**143**	9.6	.988	B. Pierce	37	240	15	**14**	2	3.03
W-81 L-73	2B	N. Fox	604	.313	4	55	413	449	17	112	**6.0**	.981	S. Rogovin	22	193	11	7	0	2.48*
Paul Richards	SS	C. Carrasquel	538	.264	2	58	306	**477**	20	107	5.5	**.975**	K. Holcombe	28	159	11	12	0	3.78
	3B	B. Dillinger	299	.301	0	20	70	116	14	10	2.9	.930	J. Dobson	28	147	7	6	3	3.62
	RF	A. Zarilla	382	.257	10	60	164	7	3	2	1.5	.983	R. Gumpert	33	142	9	8	2	4.32
	CF	J. Busby	477	.283	5	68	360	16	7	4	2.8	.982	L. Kretlow	26	137	6	9	0	4.20
	LF	M. Minoso	516	.324	10	74	145	4	6	0	1.9	.961	H. Judson	27	122	5	6	1	3.77
	C	P. Masi	225	.271	4	28	299	24	7	7	4.2	.979	H. Dorish	32	97	5	6	0	3.54
	OF	B. Stewart	217	.276	6	40	111	4	2	0	1.9	.983							
	OF	D. Lenhardt	199	.266	10	45	116	2	2	0	2.3	.983							
	OF	R. Coleman	181	.276	3	21	141	3	3	1	2.9	.980							
	C	G. Niarhos	168	.256	1	10	240	31	4	5	4.7	.985							
Detroit	1B	D. Kryhoski	421	.287	12	57	964	81	9	95	9.4	.991	T. Gray	34	197	7	**14**	1	4.06
W-73 L-81	2B	G. Priddy	584	.260	8	57	**437**	**463**	18	**118**	6.0	.980	D. Trout	42	192	9	**14**	5	4.04
Red Rolfe	SS	J. Lipon	487	.265	0	38	244	364	**33**	80	5.1	.949	F. Hutchinson	31	188	10	10	2	3.68
	3B	G. Kell	598	.319	2	59	175	**310**	20	**34**	**3.4**	**.960**	V. Trucks	37	154	13	8	1	4.33
	RF	V. Wertz	501	.285	27	94	254	7	3	1	2.0	.989	B. Cain	35	149	11	10	2	4.70
	CF	J. Groth	428	.299	3	49	266	12	2	3	2.5	.993	M. Stuart	29	124	4	6	1	3.77
	LF	H. Evers	393	.224	11	46	234	9	6	1	2.3	.976	G. Bearden	37	106	3	4	0	4.33
	C	J. Ginsberg	304	.260	8	37	388	56	10	7	4.8	.978	H. Newhouser	15	96	6	6	0	3.92
	OF	P. Mullin	295	.281	12	51	151	4	10	1	2.0	.939	H. White	38	76	3	4	4	4.74
	1B	D. Kolloway	212	.255	1	17	452	49	4	53	8.6	.992							
	OF	S. Souchock	188	.245	11	28	92	3	6	1	1.7	.941							
	UT	N. Berry	157	.229	0	9	78	127	12	22		.945							
	PH	C. Keller	62	.258	3	21	22	0	0	0	2.8	1.000							

AMERICAN LEAGUE 1951, *cont.*

Team	POS	Player	AB	BA	HR	RBI	PO	A	E	DP	TC/G	FA	Pitcher	G	IP	W	L	SV	ERA
Philadelphia	1B	F. Fain	425	**.344**	6	57	931	**113**	11	124	**9.8**	.990	A. Kellner	33	210	11	**14**	2	4.46
W-70 L-84	2B	P. Suder	440	.245	1	42	274	313	8	93	5.8	**.987**	B. Shantz	32	205	18	10	0	3.94
Jimmy Dykes	SS	E. Joost	553	.289	19	78	**325**	422	20	**115**	**5.5**	.974	B. Hooper	38	189	12	10	5	4.38
	3B	H. Majeski	323	.285	5	42	82	217	8	17	3.5	.974	C. Scheib	46	143	1	12	10	4.47
	RF	E. Valo	444	.302	7	55	247	5	5	0	2.2	.981	M. Martin	35	138	11	4	0	3.78
	CF	D. Philley	468	.263	7	59	299	15	7	4	2.7	.978	S. Zoldak	26	128	6	10	0	3.16
	LF	G. Zernial	552	.274	33*	125*	321	17	9	3	2.5	.974	D. Fowler	22	125	5	11	0	5.62
	C	J. Tipton	213	.239	3	20	230	52	9	12	4.0	.969	J. Kucab	30	75	4	3	4	4.22
	32	B. Hitchcock	222	.306	1	36	92	150	14	30		.945							
	1B	L. Limmer	214	.159	5	30	450	40	6	54	8.6	.988							
	C	J. Astroth	187	.246	2	19	228	18	2	2	4.4	.992							
	OF	A. Clark	161	.248	4	22	60	2	1	1	2.0	.984							
Washington	1B	M. Vernon	546	.293	9	87	1157	87	8	121	9.1	**.994**	C. Marrero	25	187	11	9	0	3.90
W-62 L-92	2B	C. Michaels	485	.258	4	45	258	391	**24**	86	5.3	.964	S. Consuegra	40	146	7	8	3	4.01
Bucky Harris	SS	P. Runnels	273	.278	0	25	159	176	18	41	4.8	.949	D. Johnson	21	144	7	11	0	3.95
	3B	E. Yost	568	.283	12	65	**203**	234	21	22	3.0	.954	S. Hudson	23	139	5	12	0	5.13
	RF	S. Mele	558	.274	5	94	263	8	2	1	2.2	.993	B. Porterfield	19	133	9	8	0	3.24
	CF	I. Noren	509	.279	8	86	420	15	10	1	3.5	.978	J. Moreno	31	133	5	11	2	4.88
	LF	G. Coan	538	.303	9	62	374	17	14	2	3.1	.965	M. Harris	41	87	6	8	4	3.81
	C	M. Guerra	214	.201	1	20	192	25	5	0	3.4	.977	A. Sima	18	77	3	7	0	4.79
	SS	S. Dente	273	.238	0	29	128	173	12	43	4.8	.962							
	OF	M. McCormick	243	.288	1	23	134	7	5	0	2.4	.966							
	S2	G. Verble	177	.203	0	15	101	123	5	28		.978							
	C	M. Grasso	175	.206	1	14	182	26	7	6	4.4	.967							
	C	C. Kluttz	159	.308	1	22	162	15	6	2	4.2	.967							
St. Louis	1B	H. Arft	345	.261	7	42	820	86	10	100	9.4	.989	N. Garver	33	246	20	12	0	3.73
W-52 L-102	2B	B. Young	611	.260	1	31	361	462	17	**118**	5.7	.980	D. Pillette	35	191	6	**14**	0	4.99
Zack Taylor	SS	B. Jennings	195	.179	0	13	141	165	15	39	5.0	.953	T. Byrne	19	123	4	10	0	3.82
	3B	F. Marsh	445	.243	4	43	137	225	**28**	31	3.3	.928	A. Widmar	26	108	4	9	0	6.52
	RF	K. Wood	333	.237	15	44	179	7	8	0	1.9	.959	J. McDonald	16	84	4	7	1	4.07
	CF	J. Delsing	449	.249	8	45	340	15	6	5	2.9	.983	L. Sleater	20	81	1	9	1	5.11
	LF	R. Coleman	341	.282	5	55	185	9	5	1	2.3	.975	S. Paige	23	62	3	4	5	4.79
	C	S. Lollar	310	.252	8	44	361	48	2	8	4.8	.995							
	C	M. Batts	248	.302	5	31	259	30	12*	4	4.7	.960							
	OF	C. Mapes	201	.274	7	30	111	4	2	1	2.2	.983							
	SS	J. Bero	160	.212	5	17	91	137	11	30	4.3	.954							

BATTING AND BASE RUNNING LEADERS

Batting Average
- F. Fain, PHI .344
- M. Minoso, CLE, CHI .326
- G. Kell, DET .319
- T. Williams, BOS .318
- N. Fox, CHI .313

Slugging Average
- T. Williams, BOS .556
- L. Doby, CLE .512
- G. Zernial, CHI, PHI .511
- V. Wertz, DET .511
- M. Minoso, CLE, CHI .500

Home Runs
- G. Zernial, CHI, PHI 33
- T. Williams, BOS 30
- E. Robinson, CHI 29
- L. Easter, CLE 27
- V. Wertz, DET 27
- Y. Berra, NY 27

Total Bases
- T. Williams, BOS 295
- G. Zernial, CHI, PHI 292
- E. Robinson, CHI 279
- Y. Berra, NY 269
- D. DiMaggio, BOS 267

Runs Batted In
- G. Zernial, CHI, PHI 129
- T. Williams, BOS 126
- E. Robinson, CHI 117
- L. Easter, CLE 103
- A. Rosen, CLE 102

Stolen Bases
- M. Minoso, CLE, CHI 31
- J. Busby, CHI 26
- P. Rizzuto, NY 18
- G. McDougald, NY 14
- C. Carrasquel, CHI 14
- B. Avila, CLE 14

Hits
- G. Kell, DET 191
- N. Fox, CHI 189
- D. DiMaggio, BOS 189
- M. Minoso, CLE, CHI 173

Base on Balls
- T. Williams, BOS 144
- E. Yost, WAS 126
- E. Joost, PHI 106
- L. Doby, CLE 101

Home Run Percentage
- G. Zernial, CHI, PHI 5.8
- T. Williams, BOS 5.6
- L. Easter, CLE 5.6
- V. Wertz, DET 5.4

Runs
- D. DiMaggio, BOS 113
- M. Minoso, CLE, CHI 112
- T. Williams, BOS 109
- E. Yost, WAS 109

Doubles
- S. Mele, WAS 36
- E. Yost, WAS 36
- G. Kell, DET 36

Triples
- M. Minoso, CLE, CHI 14
- R. Coleman, STL, CHI 12
- N. Fox, CHI 12
- B. Young, STL 9

PITCHING LEADERS

Winning Percentage
- B. Feller, CLE .733
- E. Lopat, NY .700
- A. Reynolds, NY .680
- V. Raschi, NY .677
- B. Shantz, PHI .643

Earned Run Average
- S. Rogovin, DET, CHI 2.78
- E. Lopat, NY 2.91
- E. Wynn, CLE 3.02
- B. Pierce, CHI 3.03
- A. Reynolds, NY 3.05

Wins
- B. Feller, CLE 22
- E. Lopat, NY 21
- V. Raschi, NY 21
- N. Garver, STL 20
- M. Garcia, CLE 20
- E. Wynn, CLE 20

Saves
- E. Kinder, BOS 14
- C. Scheib, PHI 10
- L. Brissie, PHI, CLE 9
- A. Reynolds, NY 7
- M. Garcia, CLE 6

Strikeouts
- V. Raschi, NY 164
- E. Wynn, CLE 133
- B. Lemon, CLE 132
- T. Gray, DET 131
- M. McDermott, BOS 127

Complete Games
- N. Garver, STL 24
- E. Wynn, CLE 21
- E. Lopat, NY 20
- B. Pierce, CHI 18
- S. Rogovin, DET, CHI 17
- B. Lemon, CLE 17

Fewest Hits/9 Innings
- A. Reynolds, NY 6.96
- M. McDermott, BOS 7.38
- E. Wynn, CLE 7.45
- S. Rogovin, DET, CHI 7.85

Shutouts
- A. Reynolds, NY 7
- E. Lopat, NY 5
- B. Shantz, PHI 4
- B. Feller, CLE 4
- V. Raschi, NY 4

Fewest Walks/9 Innings
- F. Hutchinson, DET 1.29
- E. Lopat, NY 2.72
- B. Pierce, CHI 2.73
- B. Hooper, PHI 2.90

Most Strikeouts/9 Inn.
- M. McDermott, BOS 6.65
- T. Gray, DET 5.97
- V. Raschi, NY 5.71
- V. Trucks, DET 5.21

Innings
- E. Wynn, CLE 274
- B. Lemon, CLE 263
- V. Raschi, NY 258
- M. Garcia, CLE 254

Games Pitched
- E. Kinder, BOS 63
- L. Brissie, PHI, CLE 56
- M. Garcia, CLE 47
- C. Scheib, PHI 46

							Batting						Fielding			Pitching					
	W	L	PCT	GB	R	OR	2B	3B	HR	BA	SA	SB	E	DP	FA	CG	BB	SO	ShO	SV	ERA
New York	98	56	.636		798	621	208	48	**140**	.269	**.408**	78	144	190	.975	66	562	**664**	**24**	22	3.56
Cleveland	93	61	.604	5	696	**594**	208	35	**140**	.256	.389	52	**134**	151	**.978**	**76**	577	642	10	19	**3.38**
Boston	87	67	.565	11	**804**	725	233	32	127	.266	.392	20	141	184	.977	46	599	658	7	**24**	4.14
Chicago	81	73	.526	17	714	644	229	**64**	86	**.270**	.385	**99**	151	176	.975	74	**549**	572	11	14	3.50
Detroit	73	81	.474	25	685	741	231	35	104	.265	.380	37	163	166	.973	51	602	597	8	17	4.29
Philadelphia	70	84	.455	28	736	745	**262**	43	102	.262	.386	48	136	**204**	**.978**	52	569	437	7	22	4.47
Washington	62	92	.403	36	672	764	242	45	54	.263	.355	45	160	148	.973	58	630	475	6	13	4.49
St. Louis	52	102	.338	46	611	882	223	47	86	.247	.357	35	172	179	.971	56	801	550	5	9	5.17
					5716	5716	1836	349	839	.262	.382	414	1201	1398	.975	479	4889	4595	78	140	4.13

NATIONAL LEAGUE 1952

Team	POS	Player	AB	BA	HR	RBI	PO	A	E	DP	TC/G	FA	Pitcher	G	IP	W	L	SV	ERA
Brooklyn	1B	G. Hodges	508	.254	32	102	1322	**116**	11	152	9.5	.992	C. Erskine	33	207	14	6	2	2.70
W-96 L-57	2B	J. Robinson	510	.308	19	75	353	400	20	**113**	5.3	.974	B. Loes	39	187	13	8	1	2.69
Chuck Dressen	SS	P. Reese	559	.272	6	58	282	376	21	89	4.7	.969	B. Wade	37	180	11	9	3	3.60
	3B	B. Cox	455	.259	6	34	100	157	8	26	2.7	**.970**	P. Roe	27	159	11	2	0	3.12
	RF	C. Furillo	425	.247	8	59	225	12	3	2	1.8	.988	J. Black	56	142	15	4	15	2.15
	CF	D. Snider	534	.303	21	92	341	13	3	3	2.5	.992	C. Van Cuyk	23	98	5	6	1	5.16
	LF	A. Pafko	551	.287	19	85	229	18	3	2	1.8	.988	J. Rutherford	22	97	7	7	2	4.25
	C	R. Campanella	468	.269	22	97	662	55	4	7	**5.9**	**.994**	C. Labine	25	77	8	4	0	5.14
	OF	G. Shuba	256	.305	9	40	116	2	1	0	1.8	.992							
	3B	B. Morgan	191	.236	7	16	45	107	5	10	2.6	.968							
New York	1B	W. Lockman	606	.290	13	58	**1435**	111	13	**155**	**10.1**	.992	J. Hearn	37	224	14	7	1	3.78
W-92 L-62	2B	D. Williams	540	.254	13	55	279	375	18	102	4.9	.973	S. Maglie	35	216	18	8	1	2.92
Leo Durocher	SS	A. Dark	589	.301	14	73	**324**	423	27	**116**	5.2	.965	L. Jansen	34	167	11	11	2	4.09
	3B	B. Thomson	608	.270	24	108	82	184	17	13	3.1	.940	D. Koslo	41	166	10	7	5	3.19
	RF	D. Mueller	456	.281	12	49	221	8	3	4	1.9	.987	H. Wilhelm	**71**	159	15	3	11	**2.43**
	CF	H. Thompson	423	.260	17	67	182	5	4	1	2.7	.979	M. Lanier	37	137	7	12	5	3.94
	LF	B. Elliott	272	.228	10	35	83	6	2	0	1.4	.978	G. Spencer	35	60	3	5	3	5.55
	C	W. Westrum	322	.220	14	43	481	64	12	**11**	5.0	.978							
	OF	D. Rhodes	176	.250	10	36	97	3	9	0	1.9	.917							
	OF	W. Mays	127	.236	4	23	109	6	1	2	3.4	.991							
	OF	M. Irvin	126	.310	4	21	44	3	0	1	1.5	1.000							
St. Louis	1B	D. Sisler	418	.261	13	60	1022	84	17*	116	9.9	.985	G. Staley	35	240	17	14	0	3.27
W-88 L-66	2B	R. Schoendienst	620	.303	7	67	**399**	424	19	108	**5.9**	.977	V. Mizell	30	190	10	8	0	3.65
Eddie Stanky	SS	S. Hemus	570	.268	15	52	253	452	29	104	5.0	.960	J. Presko	28	147	7	10	0	4.05
	3B	B. Johnson	282	.252	2	34	56	177	12	10	2.8	.951	C. Boyer	23	110	6	6	0	4.24
	RF	E. Slaughter	510	.300	11	101	250	11	3	3	1.9	.989	A. Brazle	46	109	12	5	**16**	2.72
	CF	S. Musial	578	**.336**	21	91	298	6	4	2	2.3	.987	H. Brecheen	25	100	7	5	2	3.32
	LF	P. Lowrey	374	.286	1	48	174	3	4	1	1.7	.978	E. Yuhas	54	99	12	2	6	2.72
	C	D. Rice	495	.259	11	65	**677**	**81**	6	8	5.2	.992							
	OF	H. Rice	295	.288	7	45	132	5	4	0	1.7	.972							
	3B	T. Glaviano	162	.241	3	19	46	95	10	5	2.9	.934							
Philadelphia	1B	E. Waitkus	499	.289	2	49	1281	95	12	119	9.7	.991	R. Roberts	39	**330**	**28**	7	2	2.59
W-87 L-67	2B	C. Ryan	577	.241	12	49	348	**462**	**23**	95	5.4	.972	R. Meyer	37	232	13	14	1	3.14
Eddie Sawyer	SS	G. Hamner	596	.275	17	87	267	470	**38**	102	5.1	.951	K. Drews	33	229	14	15	0	2.72
W-28 L-35	3B	W. Jones	541	.250	18	72	**216**	281	16	**31**	**3.5**	.969	C. Simmons	28	201	14	8	0	2.82
Steve O'Neill	RF	J. Wyrostek	321	.274	1	37	202	10	6	1	2.5	.972	J. Konstanty	42	80	5	3	6	3.94
W-59 L-32	CF	R. Ashburn	613	.282	1	42	428	23	9	5	3.0	.980	A. Hansen	43	77	5	6	4	3.26
	LF	D. Ennis	592	.289	20	107	277	11	9	1	2.0	.970							
	C	S. Burgess	371	.296	6	56	439	47	11	6	4.8	.978							
	C	S. Lopata	179	.274	4	27	274	21	4	6	5.4	.987							
	OF	M. Clark	155	.335	1	15	81	5	0	1	2.3	1.000							
Chicago	1B	D. Fondy	554	.300	10	67	1257	103	14	92	9.6	.990	B. Rush	34	250	17	13	0	2.70
W-77 L-77	2B	E. Miksis	383	.232	2	19	126	140	14	22	5.2	.950	J. Klippstein	41	203	9	14	3	4.44
Phil Cavarretta	SS	R. Smalley	261	.222	5	30	139	200	17	33	4.3	.952	W. Hacker	33	185	15	9	1	2.58
	3B	R. Jackson	379	.232	9	34	91	203	13	13	3.0	.958	P. Minner	28	181	14	9	0	3.74
	RF	F. Baumholtz	409	.325	4	35	248	10	7	3	2.6	.974	T. Lown	33	157	4	11	0	4.37
	CF	H. Jeffcoat	297	.219	4	30	218	16	1	2	2.5	.996	B. Kelly	31	125	4	9	0	3.59
	LF	H. Sauer	567	.270	**37**	**121**	327	17	6	3	2.3	.983	D. Leonard	45	67	2	2	11	2.16
	C	T. Atwell	362	.290	2	31	451	50	12	2	5.1	.977							
	32	B. Serena	390	.274	15	61	198	234	8	30		.982							
	OF	B. Addis	292	.295	1	20	160	8	2	2	2.2	.988							
	OF	G. Hermanski	275	.255	4	34	146	7	3	3	2.1	.981							
	SS	T. Brown	200	.320	3	24	58	85	14	17	4.0	.911							
	2B	B. Ramazzotti	183	.284	1	12	90	143	5	28	4.8	.979							
Cincinnati	1B	T. Kluszewski	497	.320	16	86	1121	66	8	116	9.0	**.993**	K. Raffensberger	38	247	17	13	1	2.81
W-69 L-85	2B	G. Hatton	433	.212	9	57	316	289	6	68	5.1	**.990**	H. Perkowski	33	194	12	10	0	3.80
Luke Sewell	SS	R. McMillan	540	.244	7	57	297	**495**	24	101	5.3	.971	H. Wehmeier	33	190	9	11	0	5.15
W-39 L-59	3B	B. Adams	**637**	.283	6	48	176	**328**	**20**	28	3.4	.962	B. Church	29	153	5	9	0	4.34
Earle Brucker	RF	W. Marshall	397	.267	8	46	188	13	3	2	1.9	.985	F. Hiller	28	124	5	8	1	4.63
W-3 L-2	CF	B. Borkowski	377	.252	4	24	219	5	2	1	2.2	.991	F. Smith	53	122	12	11	7	3.75
Rogers Hornsby	LF	J. Adcock	378	.278	13	52	189	5	3	1	2.3	.985	E. Blackwell	23	102	3	12	0	5.38
W-27 L-24	C	A. Seminick	336	.256	14	50	416	47	**13**	7	4.8	.973	B. Podbielan	24	87	4	5	1	2.80
	OF	H. Edwards	184	.283	6	28	80	2	1	0	1.6	.988							
	OF	W. Westlake	183	.202	3	14	127	5	1	0	2.4	.992							
	OF	C. Abrams	158	.278	2	13	87	1	0	1	2.0	1.000							
	OF	J. Greengrass	68	.309	5	24	55	0	2	0	3.4	.965							
Boston	1B	E. Torgeson	382	.230	5	34	931	73	11	86	9.7	.989	W. Spahn	40	290	14	19	3	2.98
W-64 L-89	2B	J. Dittmer	326	.193	7	41	228	267	9	60	5.6	.982	J. Wilson	33	234	12	14	0	4.23
Tommy Holmes	SS	J. Logan	456	.283	4	42	247	385	18	81	**5.6**	**.972**	M. Surkont	31	215	12	13	0	3.77
W-13 L-22	3B	E. Mathews	528	.242	25	58	160	259	19	21	3.1	.957	V. Bickford	26	161	7	12	0	3.74
Charlie Grimm	RF	B. Thorpe	292	.260	3	26	132	9	4	3	2.0	.972	L. Burdette	45	137	6	11	7	3.61
W-51 L-67	CF	S. Jethroe	608	.232	13	58	413	10	13	3	2.9	.970	E. Johnson	29	92	6	3	1	4.11
	LF	S. Gordon	522	.289	25	75	263	9	1	0	1.9	.996							
	C	W. Cooper	349	.235	10	55	417	55	8	8	5.4	.983							
	UT	S. Sisti	245	.212	4	24	142	129	16	22		.944							
	OF	J. Daniels	219	.187	2	14	119	6	3	2	1.5	.977							
	1B	G. Crowe	217	.258	4	20	476	42	8	40	9.6	.985							
	C	P. Burris	168	.220	2	21	208	16	0	3	4.5	1.000							

NATIONAL LEAGUE 1952, *cont.*

Pittsburgh

W-42 L-112

Billy Meyer

POS	Player	AB	BA	HR	RBI	PO	A	E	DP	TC/G	FA
1B	T. Bartirome	355	.220	0	16	909	72	11	91	8.4	.989
2B	J. Merson	398	.246	5	38	190	214	9	59	5.1	.978
SS	D. Groat	384	.284	1	29	229	272	25	61	5.6	.952
3B	P. Castiglione	214	.266	4	18	67	129	10	7	3.6	.951
RF	G. Bell	468	.250	16	59	202	8	6	2	1.8	.972
CF	B. Del Greco	341	.217	1	20	246	11	6	3	2.8	.977
LF	R. Kiner	516	.244	**37**	87	250	9	8	0	1.8	.970
C	J. Garagiola	344	.273	8	54	418	63	11	9	4.7	.978
10	C. Metkovich	373	.271	7	41	602	34	7	59		.989
UT	C. Koshorek	322	.261	0	15	149	232	18	47		.955
2S	G. Strickland	232	.177	5	22	142	217	19	54		.950
C	C. McCullough	172	.233	1	15	227	38	5	4	4.4	.981

Pitcher	G	IP	W	L	SV	ERA
M. Dickson	43	278	14	**21**	2	3.57
H. Pollet	31	214	7	16	0	4.12
B. Friend	35	185	7	17	0	4.18
W. Main	48	153	2	12	2	4.46
T. Wilks	44	72	5	5	4	3.61

BATTING AND BASE RUNNING LEADERS

Batting Average	
S. Musial, STL	.336
F. Baumholtz, CHI	.325
T. Kluszewski, CIN	.320
J. Robinson, BKN	.308
D. Snider, BKN	.303

Slugging Average	
S. Musial, STL	.538
H. Sauer, CHI	.531
T. Kluszewski, CIN	.509
R. Kiner, PIT	.500
G. Hodges, BKN	.500

Home Runs	
R. Kiner, PIT	37
H. Sauer, CHI	37
G. Hodges, BKN	32
S. Gordon, BOS	25
E. Mathews, BOS	25

Total Bases	
S. Musial, STL	311
H. Sauer, CHI	301
B. Thomson, NY	293
D. Ennis, PHI	281
D. Snider, BKN	264

Runs Batted In	
H. Sauer, CHI	121
B. Thomson, NY	108
D. Ennis, PHI	107
G. Hodges, BKN	102
E. Slaughter, STL	101

Stolen Bases	
P. Reese, BKN	30
S. Jethroe, BOS	28
J. Robinson, BKN	24
R. Ashburn, PHI	16
D. Fondy, CHI	13
C. Ryan, PHI	13

Hits	
S. Musial, STL	194
R. Schoendienst, STL	188
B. Adams, CIN	180
A. Dark, NY	177

Base on Balls	
R. Kiner, PIT	110
G. Hodges, BKN	107
J. Robinson, BKN	106
S. Hemus, STL	96
S. Musial, STL	96

Home Run Percentage	
R. Kiner, PIT	7.2
H. Sauer, CHI	6.5
G. Hodges, BKN	6.3
S. Gordon, BOS	4.8

Runs	
S. Hemus, STL	105
S. Musial, STL	105
J. Robinson, BKN	104
W. Lockman, NY	99

Doubles	
S. Musial, STL	42
R. Schoendienst, STL	40
R. McMillan, CIN	32
H. Sauer, CHI	31
R. Ashburn, PHI	31

Triples	
B. Thomson, NY	14
E. Slaughter, STL	12
T. Kluszewski, CIN	11
D. Ennis, PHI	10

PITCHING LEADERS

Winning Percentage	
H. Wilhelm, NY	.833
R. Roberts, PHI	.800
J. Black, BKN	.789
S. Maglie, NY	.692
W. Hacker, CHI	.625

Earned Run Average	
H. Wilhelm, NY	2.43
W. Hacker, CHI	2.58
R. Roberts, PHI	2.59
B. Loes, BKN	2.69
B. Rush, CHI	2.70

Wins	
R. Roberts, PHI	28
S. Maglie, NY	18
G. Staley, STL	17
K. Raffensberger, CIN	17
B. Rush, CHI	17

Saves	
A. Brazle, STL	16
J. Black, BKN	15
D. Leonard, CHI	11
H. Wilhelm, NY	11
L. Burdette, BOS	7
F. Smith, CIN	7

Strikeouts	
W. Spahn, BOS	183
B. Rush, CHI	157
R. Roberts, PHI	148
V. Mizell, STL	146
C. Simmons, PHI	141

Complete Games	
R. Roberts, PHI	30
M. Dickson, PIT	21
W. Spahn, BOS	19
K. Raffensberger, CIN	18
B. Rush, CHI	17

Fewest Hits/9 Innings	
W. Hacker, CHI	7.01
H. Wilhelm, NY	7.17
C. Erskine, BKN	7.27
B. Rush, CHI	7.37

Shutouts	
C. Simmons, PHI	6
K. Raffensberger, CIN	6

Fewest Walks/9 Innings	
R. Roberts, PHI	1.23
W. Hacker, CHI	1.51
K. Raffensberger, CIN	1.64
G. Staley, STL	1.95

Most Strikeouts/9 Inn.	
V. Mizell, STL	6.92
C. Simmons, PHI	6.30
H. Wilhelm, NY	6.10
B. Wade, BKN	5.90

Innings	
R. Roberts, PHI	330
W. Spahn, BOS	290
M. Dickson, PIT	278
B. Rush, CHI	250

Games Pitched	
H. Wilhelm, NY	71
J. Black, BKN	56
E. Yuhas, STL	54
F. Smith, CIN	53

							Batting						Fielding			Pitching					
	W	L	PCT	GB	R	OR	2B	3B	HR	BA	SA	SB	E	DP	FA	CG	BB	SO	ShO	SV	ERA
Brooklyn	96	57	.627		**775**	603	199	32	**153**	.262	**.399**	**90**	**106**	169	**.982**	45	544	**773**	11	24	3.53
New York	92	62	.597	4.5	722	639	186	**56**	151	.256	**.399**	30	158	**175**	.974	49	538	655	11	**31**	3.59
St. Louis	88	66	.571	8.5	677	630	**247**	54	97	**.267**	.391	33	141	159	.977	49	501	712	11	27	3.66
Philadelphia	87	67	.565	9.5	657	**552**	237	45	93	.260	.376	60	150	145	.975	**80**	**373**	609	**16**	16	**3.07**
Chicago	77	77	.500	19.5	628	631	223	45	107	.264	.383	50	146	123	.976	59	534	661	15	15	3.58
Cincinnati	69	85	.448	27.5	615	659	212	45	104	.249	.366	32	107	145	**.982**	56	517	579	11	12	4.01
Boston	64	89	.418	32	569	651	187	31	110	.233	.343	58	154	143	.975	63	525	687	11	13	3.78
Pittsburgh	42	112	.273	54.5	515	793	181	30	92	.231	.331	43	182	167	.970	43	615	564	4	8	4.65
					5158	5158	1672	338	907	.253	.374	396	1144	1226	.976	444	4147	5240	90	146	3.73

AMERICAN LEAGUE 1952

New York

W-95 L-59

Casey Stengel

POS	Player	AB	BA	HR	RBI	PO	A	E	DP	TC/G	FA
1B	J. Collins	428	.280	18	59	1047	73	11	123	9.5	.990
2B	B. Martin	363	.267	3	33	244	323	9	92	5.4	.984
SS	P. Rizzuto	578	.254	2	43	308	**458**	19	**116**	**5.2**	.976
3B	G. McDougald	555	.263	11	78	124	273	13	**38**	**3.5**	.968
RF	H. Bauer	553	.293	17	74	233	16	4	2	1.8	.984
CF	M. Mantle	549	.311	23	87	347	15	12	5	2.7	.968
LF	G. Woodling	408	.309	12	63	241	12	1	4	2.2	.996
C	Y. Berra	534	.273	30	98	**700**	**73**	6	**10**	**5.6**	.992
OF	I. Noren	272	.235	5	21	95	3	0	1	1.6	1.000
1B	J. Mize	137	.263	4	29	218	18	3	32	8.9	.987

Pitcher	G	IP	W	L	SV	ERA
A. Reynolds	35	244	20	8	6	**2.06**
V. Raschi	31	223	16	6	0	2.78
E. Lopat	20	149	10	5	0	2.53
J. Sain	35	148	11	6	7	3.46
B. Kuzava	28	133	8	8	3	3.45
T. Morgan	16	94	5	4	2	3.07
B. Miller	21	88	4	6	0	3.48
B. Hogue	27	47	3	5	4	5.32

AMERICAN LEAGUE 1952, *cont.*

Cleveland

W-93 L-61

Al Lopez

POS	Player	AB	BA	HR	RBI	PO	A	E	DP	TC/G	FA	Pitcher	G	IP	W	L	SV	ERA
1B	L. Easter	437	.263	31	97	940	90	18	87	8.9	.983	B. Lemon	42	**310**	22	11	4	2.50
2B	B. Avila	597	.300	7	45	355	431	**28**	81	5.5	.966	M. Garcia	46	292	22	11	4	2.37
SS	R. Boone	316	.263	7	45	177	251	27	55	4.7	.941	E. Wynn	42	286	23	12	3	2.90
3B	A. Rosen	567	.302	28	**105**	159	256	18	25	2.9	.958	B. Feller	30	192	9	13	0	4.74
RF	H. Simpson	545	.266	10	65	226	11	3	4	1.9	.988	S. Gromek	29	123	7	7	1	3.67
CF	L. Doby	519	.276	**32**	104	398	11	6	3	3.1	.986							
LF	D. Mitchell	511	.323	5	58	258	2	2	0	2.0	.992							
C	J. Hegan	333	.225	4	41	498	53	7	7	5.2	.987							
OF	J. Fridley	175	.251	4	16	87	3	2	0	1.7	.978							
C	J. Tipton	105	.248	6	22	118	18	4	1	4.0	.971							

Chicago

W-81 L-73

Paul Richards

POS	Player	AB	BA	HR	RBI	PO	A	E	DP	TC/G	FA	Pitcher	G	IP	W	L	SV	ERA
1B	E. Robinson	594	.296	22	104	**1329**	89	14	**145**	9.2	.990	B. Pierce	33	255	15	12	1	2.57
2B	N. Fox	**648**	.296	0	39	**406**	**433**	13	111	5.6	**.985**	S. Rogovin	33	232	14	9	1	3.85
SS	C. Carrasquel	359	.248	1	42	176	248	16	50	4.4	.964	J. Dobson	29	201	14	10	1	2.51
3B	H. Rodriguez	407	.265	1	40	145	232	16	26	3.5	.959	M. Grissom	28	166	12	10	0	3.74
RF	S. Mele	423	.248	14	59	157	8	0	1	1.5	1.000	C. Stobbs	38	135	7	12	1	3.13
CF	R. Coleman	195	.215	2	14	130	5	3	0	1.9	.978	H. Dorish	39	91	8	4	**11**	2.47
LF	M. Minoso	569	.281	13	61	322	11	7	3	2.4	.979	L. Aloma	25	40	3	1	6	4.28
C	S. Lollar	375	.240	13	50	590	53	7	4	5.4	.989							
OF	B. Stewart	225	.267	5	30	108	1	2	0	1.9	.982							
OF	J. Rivera	201	.249	3	18	157	2	2	1	3.0	.988							
OF	T. Wright	132	.258	1	21	60	2	2	0	1.9	.969							

Philadelphia

W-79 L-75

Jimmy Dykes

POS	Player	AB	BA	HR	RBI	PO	A	E	DP	TC/G	FA	Pitcher	G	IP	W	L	SV	ERA
1B	F. Fain	538	**.327**	2	59	1245	**150**	**22**	124	**9.8**	.984	B. Shantz	33	280	**24**	7	0	2.48
2B	S. Kell	213	.221	0	17	143	169	12	35	4.8	.963	A. Kellner	34	231	12	14	0	4.36
SS	E. Joost	540	.244	20	75	278	431	**28**	81	5.0	.962	H. Byrd	37	228	15	15	2	3.31
3B	B. Hitchcock	407	.246	1	56	105	222	**20**	26	3.3	.942	C. Scheib	30	158	11	7	2	4.39
RF	E. Valo	388	.281	5	47	223	7	9	1	2.0	.962	B. Hooper	43	144	8	15	6	5.18
CF	D. Philley	586	.263	7	71	442	13	4	3	3.1	.991							
LF	G. Zernial	549	.262	29	100	302	6	9	0	2.2	.972							
C	J. Astroth	337	.249	1	36	436	36	4	9	4.7	.992							
UT	P. Suder	228	.241	1	20	136	179	8	40		.975							
2B	C. Michaels	200	.250	1	18	151	133	2	30	5.2	.993							
OF	A. Clark	186	.274	7	29	78	2	1	0	1.7	.988							
3B	H. Majeski	117	.256	2	20	33	87	3	9	3.6	.976							

Washington

W-78 L-76

Bucky Harris

POS	Player	AB	BA	HR	RBI	PO	A	E	DP	TC/G	FA	Pitcher	G	IP	W	L	SV	ERA
1B	M. Vernon	569	.251	10	80	1291	115	10	139	9.3	**.993**	B. Porterfield	31	231	13	14	0	2.72
2B	F. Baker	263	.262	0	33	151	176	2	36	4.8	.994	C. Marrero	22	184	11	8	0	2.88
SS	P. Runnels	555	.285	1	64	**314**	406	25	97	5.1	.966	S. Shea	22	169	11	7	0	2.93
3B	E. Yost	587	.233	12	49	**212**	249	18	26	3.1	.962	W. Masterson	24	161	9	8	2	3.70
RF	J. Jensen	570	.286	10	80	283	17	7	1	2.1	.977	J. Moreno	26	147	9	9	0	3.97
CF	J. Busby	512	.244	2	47	430	4	3	0	3.4	.993	R. Gumpert	20	104	4	9	0	4.24
LF	G. Coan	332	.205	5	20	185	4	3	1	2.2	.984	S. Consuegra	30	74	6	0	5	3.05
C	M. Grasso	361	.216	0	27	485	64	**17**	4	5.0	.970							
OF	K. Wood	210	.238	6	32	161	6	8	1	3.1	.954							
2B	M. Hoderlein	208	.269	0	17	138	168	7	43	5.4	.978							

Boston

W-76 L-78

Lou Boudreau

POS	Player	AB	BA	HR	RBI	PO	A	E	DP	TC/G	FA	Pitcher	G	IP	W	L	SV	ERA
1B	D. Gernert	367	.243	19	67	877	67	12	104	9.7	.987	M. Parnell	33	214	12	12	2	3.62
2B	B. Goodman	513	.306	4	56	284	340	16	95	**6.2**	.975	M. McDermott	30	162	10	9	0	3.72
SS	J. Lipon	234	.205	0	18	118	218	6	53	5.0	.982*	S. Hudson	21	134	7	9	0	3.62
3B	G. Kell	276	.319	6	40	75	138	9	14	3.0	.959	D. Trout	26	134	9	8	1	3.64
RF	F. Throneberry	310	.258	5	23	141	9	7	5	1.8	.955	D. Brodowski	20	115	5	5	0	4.40
CF	D. DiMaggio	486	.294	6	33	303	12	8	4	2.6	.975	W. Nixon	23	104	5	4	0	4.86
LF	H. Evers	401	.262	14	59	219	8	6	3	2.2	.974	E. Kinder	23	98	5	6	4	2.58
C	S. White	381	.281	10	49	464	59	9	7	4.8	.983	I. Delock	39	95	4	9	5	4.26
S3	V. Stephens	295	.254	7	44	110	227	16	48		.955	R. Scarborough	28	77	1	5	4	4.81
23	T. Lepcio	274	.263	5	26	164	212	14	46		.964	A. Benton	24	38	4	3	6	2.39
OF	C. Vollmer	250	.264	11	50	143	3	0	1	2.1	1.000							
SO	J. Piersall	161	.267	1	16	79	78	9	13		.946							
C	D. Wilber	135	.267	3	23	160	22	1	5	4.7	.995							
1B	W. Dropo	132	.265	6	27	319	21	2	31	9.8	.994							
OF	D. Lenhardt	105	.295	7	24	52	0	1	0	2.0	.981							

St. Louis

W-64 L-90

Rogers Hornsby
W-22 L-29

Marty Marion
W-42 L-61

POS	Player	AB	BA	HR	RBI	PO	A	E	DP	TC/G	FA	Pitcher	G	IP	W	L	SV	ERA
1B	D. Kryhoski	342	.243	11	42	680	49	8	80	8.6	.989	D. Pillette	30	205	10	13	0	3.59
2B	B. Young	575	.247	4	39	380	407	13	**127**	5.4	.984	T. Byrne	29	196	7	14	0	4.68
SS	J. De Maestri	186	.226	1	18	105	156	17	29	3.6	.939	B. Cain	29	170	12	10	2	4.13
3B	J. Dyck	402	.269	15	64	79	152	9	14	3.2	.962	G. Bearden	34	151	7	8	0	4.30
RF	B. Nieman	478	.289	18	74	230	10	6	5	2.0	.976	N. Garver	21	149	7	10	0	3.69
CF	J. Rivera	336	.256	4	30	273	7	7	1	3.3	.976	S. Paige	46	138	12	10	10	3.07
LF	J. Delsing	298	.255	1	34	206	4	3	2	2.5	.986	E. Harrist	36	117	2	8	5	4.01
C	C. Courtney	413	.286	5	50	487	60	2	7	4.9	**.996**							
S3	F. Marsh	247	.279	2	27	87	162	17	39		.936							
1B	G. Goldsberry	227	.229	3	17	524	40	10	56	8.0	.983							
SS	M. Marion	186	.247	2	19	105	138	5	41	3.9	.980							
3B	C. Michaels	166	.265	3	25	43	88	12	12	3.4	.916							

AMERICAN LEAGUE 1952, *cont.*

Detroit

W-50 L-104

Red Rolfe
W-23 L-49

Fred Hutchinson
W-27 L-55

POS	Player	AB	BA	HR	RBI	PO	A	E	DP	TC/G	FA
1B	W. Dropo	459	.279	23	70	1005	78	12	104	9.5	.989
2B	G. Priddy	279	.283	4	20	211	209	14	48	5.8	.968
SS	N. Berry	189	.228	0	13	90	158	9	26	3.9	.965
3B	F. Hatfield	441	.236	2	25	114	253*	12	32	3.5	.968*
RF	V. Wertz	285	.246	17	51	134	8	2	3	1.8	.986
CF	J. Groth	524	.284	4	51	329	14	5	3	2.5	.986
LF	P. Mullin	255	.251	7	35	131	6	3	2	2.2	.979
C	J. Ginsberg	307	.221	6	36	442	41	8	7	4.9	.984
OF	S. Souchock	265	.249	13	45	103	4	4	2	2.0	.964
2B	A. Federoff	231	.242	0	14	136	184	8	42	4.7	.976
OF	C. Mapes	193	.197	9	23	86	3	3	1	1.5	.967
S2	J. Pesky	177	.254	1	9	105	137	11	37		.957
C	M. Batts	173	.237	3	13	262	36	5	4	5.5	.983
1B	D. Kolloway	173	.243	2	21	252	28	6	15	8.9	.979

Pitcher	G	IP	W	L	SV	ERA
T. Gray	35	224	12	17	0	4.14
A. Houtteman	35	221	8	**20**	1	4.36
V. Trucks	35	197	5	19	1	3.97
H. Newhouser	25	154	9	9	0	3.74
B. Wight	23	144	5	9	0	3.88
B. Hoeft	34	125	2	7	4	4.32
H. White	41	63	1	8	5	3.69

BATTING AND BASE RUNNING LEADERS

Batting Average
F. Fain, PHI .327
D. Mitchell, CLE .323
M. Mantle, NY .311
G. Kell, DET, BOS .311
G. Woodling, NY .309

Slugging Average
L. Doby, CLE .541
M. Mantle, NY .530
A. Rosen, CLE .524
L. Easter, CLE .513
V. Wertz, DET, STL .506

Home Runs
L. Doby, CLE 32
L. Easter, CLE 31
Y. Berra, NY 30
G. Zernial, PHI 29
W. Dropo, BOS, DET 29

Total Bases
A. Rosen, CLE 297
M. Mantle, NY 291
W. Dropo, BOS, DET 282
L. Doby, CLE 281
E. Robinson, CHI 277

Runs Batted In
A. Rosen, CLE 105
L. Doby, CLE 104
E. Robinson, CHI 104
G. Zernial, PHI 100
Y. Berra, NY 98

Stolen Bases
M. Minoso, CHI 22
J. Rivera, STL, CHI 21
J. Jensen, NY, WAS 18
P. Rizzuto, NY 17
F. Throneberry, BOS 16

Hits
N. Fox, CHI 192
B. Avila, CLE 179
F. Fain, PHI 176
E. Robinson, CHI 176

Base on Balls
E. Yost, WAS 129
E. Joost, PHI 122
F. Fain, PHI 105
E. Valo, PHI 101

Home Run Percentage
L. Easter, CLE 7.1
L. Doby, CLE 6.2
Y. Berra, NY 5.6
V. Wertz, DET, STL 5.5

Runs
L. Doby, CLE 104
B. Avila, CLE 102
A. Rosen, CLE 101
Y. Berra, NY 97

Doubles
F. Fain, PHI 43
M. Mantle, NY 37
M. Vernon, WAS 33
E. Robinson, CHI 33

Triples
B. Avila, CLE 11
H. Simpson, CLE 10
P. Rizzuto, NY 10
N. Fox, CHI 10

PITCHING LEADERS

Winning Percentage
B. Shantz, PHI .774
V. Raschi, NY .727
A. Reynolds, NY .714
B. Lemon, CLE .667
M. Garcia, CLE .667

Earned Run Average
A. Reynolds, NY 2.06
M. Garcia, CLE 2.37
B. Shantz, PHI 2.48
B. Lemon, CLE 2.50
J. Dobson, CHI 2.51

Wins
B. Shantz, PHI 24
E. Wynn, CLE 23
M. Garcia, CLE 22
B. Lemon, CLE 22
A. Reynolds, NY 20

Saves
H. Dorish, CHI 11
S. Paige, STL 10
J. Sain, NY 7

Strikeouts
A. Reynolds, NY 160
E. Wynn, CLE 153
B. Shantz, PHI 152
B. Pierce, CHI 144
M. Garcia, CLE 143

Complete Games
B. Lemon, CLE 28
B. Shantz, PHI 27
A. Reynolds, NY 24
E. Wynn, CLE 19
M. Garcia, CLE 19

Fewest Hits/9 Innings
B. Lemon, CLE 6.86
V. Raschi, NY 7.02
A. Reynolds, NY 7.15
J. Dobson, CHI 7.36

Shutouts
A. Reynolds, NY 6
M. Garcia, CLE 6
B. Shantz, PHI 5
B. Lemon, CLE 5

Fewest Walks/9 Innings
B. Shantz, PHI 2.03
D. Pillette, STL 2.41
C. Marrero, WAS 2.59
A. Houtteman, DET 2.65

Most Strikeouts/9 Inn.
M. McDermott, BOS 6.50
A. Reynolds, NY 5.89
V. Trucks, DET 5.89
T. Gray, DET 5.54

Innings
B. Lemon, CLE 310
M. Garcia, CLE 292
E. Wynn, CLE 286
B. Shantz, PHI 280

Games Pitched
B. Kennedy, CHI 47
S. Paige, STL 46
M. Garcia, CLE 46
B. Hooper, PHI 43

							Batting						Fielding			Pitching				
	W	L	PCT	GB	R	OR	2B	3B	HR	BA	SA	SB	E	DP	FA	CG	BB	SO	ShO	SV	ERA
New York	95	59	.617		727	**557**	221	**56**	129	**.267**	.403	52	127	**199**	.979	72	581	666	**17**	27	**3.14**
Cleveland	93	61	.604	2	**763**	606	211	49	**148**	.262	**.404**	46	155	141	.975	**80**	556	671	16	18	3.32
Chicago	81	73	.526	14	610	568	199	38	80	.252	.348	**61**	**123**	158	**.980**	53	578	**774**	13	**28**	3.25
Philadelphia	79	75	.513	16	664	723	212	35	89	.253	.359	52	140	148	.977	73	**526**	562	11	16	4.15
Washington	78	76	.506	17	598	608	225	44	50	.239	.326	48	132	152	.978	75	577	574	10	15	3.37
Boston	76	78	.494	19	668	658	**233**	34	113	.255	.377	59	145	181	.976	53	623	624	7	24	3.80
St. Louis	64	90	.416	31	604	733	225	46	82	.250	.356	30	155	176	.974	48	598	581	6	18	4.12
Detroit	50	104	.325	45	557	738	190	37	103	.243	.352	27	152	145	.975	51	591	702	10	14	4.25
					5191	5191	1716	339	794	.253	.366	375	1129	1300	.977	505	4630	5154	90	160	3.67

NATIONAL LEAGUE 1953

Brooklyn

W-105 L-49

Chuck Dressen

POS	Player	AB	BA	HR	RBI	PO	A	E	DP	TC/G	FA
1B	G. Hodges	520	.302	31	122	1025	99	8	105	8.9	.993
2B	J. Gilliam	605	.278	6	63	332	426	19	102	5.2	.976
SS	P. Reese	524	.271	13	61	265	380	23	83	4.9	.966
3B	B. Cox	327	.291	10	44	86	142	6	20	2.6	.974
RF	C. Furillo	479	**.344**	21	92	232	11	3	3	1.9	.988
CF	D. Snider	590	.336	42	126	370	7	5	3	2.5	.987
LF	J. Robinson	484	.329	12	95	145	9	3	0	2.1	.981
C	R. Campanella	519	.312	41	**142**	**807**	57	10	9	**6.2**	.989
3S	B. Morgan	196	.260	7	33	71	105	10	19		.946
OF	G. Shuba	169	.254	5	23	59	1	1	1	1.4	.984
1B	W. Belardi	163	.239	11	34	283	23	5	34	8.2	.984

Pitcher	G	IP	W	L	SV	ERA
C. Erskine	39	247	20	6	3	3.54
R. Meyer	34	191	15	5	0	4.56
B. Loes	32	163	14	8	0	4.54
P. Roe	25	157	11	3	0	4.36
B. Milliken	37	118	8	4	2	3.37
J. Podres	33	115	9	4	0	4.23
C. Labine	37	110	11	6	7	2.77
B. Wade	32	90	7	5	3	3.79
J. Hughes	48	86	4	3	9	3.47
J. Black	34	73	6	3	5	5.33

Milwaukee

W-92 L-62

Charlie Grimm

POS	Player	AB	BA	HR	RBI	PO	A	E	DP	TC/G	FA
1B	J. Adcock	590	.285	18	80	1389	96	13	146	9.5	.991
2B	J. Dittmer	504	.266	9	63	290	343	**23**	95	4.8	.965
SS	J. Logan	611	.273	11	73	**295**	481	20	104	5.3	**.975**
3B	E. Mathews	579	.302	**47**	135	154	311	**30**	33	3.2	.939
RF	A. Pafko	516	.297	17	72	241	5	6	1	1.8	.976
CF	B. Bruton	613	.250	1	41	397	15	9	5	2.8	.979
LF	S. Gordon	464	.274	19	75	245	10	6	2	1.9	.977
C	D. Crandall	382	.272	15	51	566	**62**	9	**13**	5.9	.986
OF	J. Pendleton	251	.299	7	27	141	7	6	1	1.5	.961

Pitcher	G	IP	W	L	SV	ERA
W. Spahn	35	266	**23**	7	3	**2.10**
J. Antonelli	31	175	12	12	1	3.18
L. Burdette	46	175	15	5	8	3.24
M. Surkont	28	170	11	5	0	4.18
B. Buhl	30	154	13	8	0	2.97
D. Liddle	31	129	7	6	2	3.08
J. Wilson	20	114	4	9	0	4.34

NATIONAL LEAGUE 1953, *cont.*

Team	POS	Player	AB	BA	HR	RBI	PO	A	E	DP	TC/G	FA	Pitcher	G	IP	W	L	SV	ERA
Philadelphia	1B	E. Torgeson	379	.274	11	64	916	65	13	83	9.5	.987	R. Roberts	44	**347**	**23**	16	2	2.75
W-83 L-71	2B	G. Hamner	609	.276	21	92	194	290	15	65	5.4	.970	C. Simmons	32	238	16	13	0	3.21
Steve O'Neill	SS	T. Kazanski	360	.217	2	27	185	239	23	53	4.7	.949	K. Drews	47	185	9	10	3	4.52
	3B	W. Jones	481	.225	19	70	**176**	253	11	36	3.0	**.975**	J. Konstanty	48	171	14	10	5	4.43
	RF	J. Wyrostek	409	.271	6	47	192	11	8	2	1.9	.962	B. Miller	35	157	8	9	2	4.00
	CF	R. Ashburn	622	.330	2	57	496	18	5	4	3.3	.990	S. Ridzik	42	124	9	6	0	3.77
	LF	D. Ennis	578	.285	29	125	284	14	6	4	2.0	.980							
	C	S. Burgess	312	.292	4	36	395	23	3	8	4.4	**.993**							
	2B	C. Ryan	247	.296	5	26	134	166	13	39	4.8	.958							
	1B	E. Waitkus	247	.291	1	16	480	37	6	65	8.9	.989							
	C	S. Lopata	234	.239	8	31	344	27	5	2	4.7	.987							
	OF	M. Clark	198	.298	0	19	104	2	1	0	2.1	.991							
St. Louis	1B	S. Bilko	570	.251	21	84	**1446**	**124**	15	145	**10.3**	.991	H. Haddix	36	253	20	9	1	3.06
W-83 L-71	2B	R. Schoendienst	564	.342	15	79	**365**	**430**	14	**109**	5.8	**.983**	G. Staley	40	230	18	9	4	3.99
Eddie Stanky	SS	S. Hemus	585	.279	14	61	257	476	**27**	90	5.1	.964	V. Mizell	33	224	13	11	0	3.49
	3B	R. Jablonski	604	.268	21	112	94	278	27	27	2.5	.932	J. Presko	34	162	6	13	1	5.01
	RF	E. Slaughter	492	.291	6	89	235	2	1	0	1.7	.996	S. Miller	40	138	7	8	4	5.56
	CF	R. Repulski	567	.275	15	66	361	7	5	1	2.4	.987	A. Brazle	60	92	6	7	**18**	4.21
	LF	S. Musial	593	.337	30	113	294	9	5	1	2.0	.984	H. White	49	85	6	5	7	2.98
	C	D. Rice	419	.236	6	37	627	60	8	6	5.1	.988							
	OF	P. Lowrey	182	.269	5	27	42	1	0	0	1.1	1.000							
New York	1B	W. Lockman	607	.295	9	61	1042	100	13	96	9.6	.989	R. Gomez	29	204	13	11	0	3.40
W-70 L-84	2B	D. Williams	340	.297	3	34	191	254	8	54	4.8	.982	J. Hearn	36	197	9	12	0	4.53
Leo Durocher	SS	A. Dark	**647**	.300	23	88	219	343	19	79	5.3	.967	L. Jansen	36	185	11	16	1	4.14
	3B	H. Thompson	388	.302	24	74	90	194	13	18	2.9	.956	S. Maglie	27	145	8	9	0	4.15
	RF	D. Mueller	480	.333	6	60	203	7	6	0	1.8	.972	H. Wilhelm	**68**	145	7	8	15	3.04
	CF	B. Thomson	608	.288	26	106	391	16	7	0	2.7	.983	D. Koslo	37	112	6	12	2	4.76
	LF	M. Irvin	444	.329	21	97	244	10	7	4	2.3	.973	A. Corwin	48	107	6	4	2	4.98
	C	W. Westrum	290	.224	12	30	441	53	9	9	4.7	.982	A. Worthington	20	102	4	8	0	3.44
	UT	D. Spencer	408	.208	20	56	179	269	32	52		.933							
	32	B. Hofman	169	.266	12	34	55	83	7	18		.952							
	OF	D. Rhodes	163	.233	11	30	76	6	3	4	1.8	.965							
	1B	T. Gilbert	160	.169	3	16	381	26	2	34	9.3	.995							
Cincinnati	1B	T. Kluszewski	570	.316	40	108	1285	58	7	**149**	9.2	**.995**	H. Perkowski	33	193	12	11	2	4.52
W-68 L-86	2B	R. Bridges	432	.227	1	21	329	320	16	94	**5.8**	.976	B. Podbielan	36	186	6	16	1	4.73
Rogers Hornsby	SS	R. McMillan	557	.233	5	43	288	**519**	23	**114**	**5.4**	.972	K. Raffensberger	26	174	7	14	0	3.93
W-64 L-82	3B	B. Adams	607	.275	8	49	159	**324**	25	**39**	3.4	.951	J. Nuxhall	30	142	9	11	2	4.32
Buster Mills	RF	W. Marshall	357	.266	17	62	187	11	1	1	2.1	.995	F. Baczewski	24	138	11	4	1	3.45
W-4 L-4	CF	G. Bell	610	.300	30	105	447	16	11	5	3.1	.977	J. Collum	30	125	7	11	3	3.75
	LF	J. Greengrass	606	.285	20	100	341	11	6	0	2.3	.983	F. Smith	50	84	8	1	2	5.49
	C	A. Seminick	387	.235	19	64	436	44	9	2	4.4	.982	C. King	35	76	3	6	2	5.21
	OF	B. Borkowski	249	.269	7	29	104	3	2	0	1.6	.982							
	2B	G. Hatton	159	.233	7	22	56	49	1	15	3.0	.991							
	C	H. Landrith	154	.240	3	16	179	13	3	4	4.1	.985							
Chicago	1B	D. Fondy	595	.309	18	78	1274	115	**18**	105	9.4	.987	W. Hacker	39	222	12	**19**	2	4.38
W-65 L-89	2B	E. Miksis	577	.251	8	39	210	262	**23**	65	5.4	.954	P. Minner	31	201	12	15	1	4.21
Phil Cavarretta	SS	R. Smalley	253	.249	6	25	153	191	25	39	4.8	.932	J. Klippstein	48	168	10	11	6	4.83
	3B	R. Jackson	498	.285	19	66	141	265	22	24	3.2	.949	B. Rush	29	167	9	14	0	4.54
	RF	H. Sauer	395	.263	19	60	221	5	7	1	2.2	.970	T. Lown	49	148	8	7	3	5.16
	CF	F. Baumholtz	520	.306	3	25	290	6	6	0	2.3	.980	H. Pollet	25	111	5	6	1	4.12
	LF	R. Kiner	414	.283	28	87	211	6	8	2	1.9	.964	B. Church	27	104	4	5	1	5.00
	C	C. McCullough	229	.258	6	23	273	31	4	7	4.2	.987	D. Leonard	45	63	2	3	8	4.60
	23	B. Serena	275	.251	10	52	135	160	7	31		.977							
	C	J. Garagiola	228	.272	1	21	296	34	4	2	4.9	.988							
	OF	H. Jeffcoat	183	.235	4	22	175	6	5	2	1.9	.973							
Pittsburgh	1B	P. Ward	281	.210	8	27	693	64	7	65	9.8	.991	M. Dickson	45	201	10	**19**	4	4.53
W-50 L-104	2B	J. O'Brien	279	.247	2	22	172	210	7	48	5.1	.982	P. LaPalme	35	176	8	16	2	4.59
Fred Haney	SS	E. O'Brien	261	.238	0	14	122	207	23	39	4.3	.935	J. Lindell	27	176	5	16	0	4.71
	3B	D. O'Connell	588	.294	7	55	119	221	15	16	**3.4**	.958	B. Friend	32	171	8	11	0	4.90
	RF	C. Abrams	448	.286	15	43	205	13	6	3	2.0	.973	B. Hall	37	152	3	12	1	5.39
	CF	C. Bernier	310	.213	3	31	220	8	7	1	2.7	.970	R. Face	41	119	6	8	0	6.58
	LF	F. Thomas	455	.255	30	102	306	17	8	1	2.8	.976	J. Hetki	54	118	3	6	3	3.95
	C	M. Sandlock	186	.231	0	12	290	49	3	4	5.3	.991							
	1B	P. Smith	389	.283	4	44	622	52	10	53	9.2	.985							
	OF	H. Rice	286	.311	4	42	167	14	5	2	2.7	.973							
	SS	D. Cole	235	.272	0	23	139	192	12	40	4.5	.965							
	23	E. Pellagrini	174	.253	4	19	75	95	6	13		.966							
	3B	P. Castiglione	159	.208	4	21	44	88	3	6	3.1	.978							
	OF	R. Kiner	148	.270	7	29	71	5	0	1	1.9	1.000							

BATTING AND BASE RUNNING LEADERS

Batting Average		Slugging Average		Home Runs	
C. Furillo, BKN	.344	D. Snider, BKN	.627	E. Mathews, MIL	47
R. Schoendienst, STL	.342	E. Mathews, MIL	.627	D. Snider, BKN	42
S. Musial, STL	.337	R. Campanella, BKN	.611	R. Campanella, BKN	41
D. Snider, BKN	.336	S. Musial, STL	.609	T. Kluszewski, CIN	40
D. Mueller, NY	.333	C. Furillo, BKN	.580	R. Kiner, PIT, CHI	35

PITCHING LEADERS

Winning Percentage		Earned Run Average		Wins	
C. Erskine, BKN	.769	W. Spahn, MIL	2.10	W. Spahn, MIL	23
W. Spahn, MIL	.767	R. Roberts, PHI	2.75	R. Roberts, PHI	23
R. Meyer, BKN	.750	B. Buhl, MIL	2.97	C. Erskine, BKN	20
L. Burdette, MIL	.750	H. Haddix, STL	3.06	H. Haddix, STL	20
H. Haddix, STL	.690	J. Antonelli, MIL	3.18	G. Staley, STL	18

NATIONAL LEAGUE 1953, *cont.*

BATTING AND BASE RUNNING LEADERS

Total Bases	
D. Snider, BKN	370
E. Mathews, MIL	363
S. Musial, STL	361
T. Kluszewski, CIN	325
G. Bell, CIN	320

Runs Batted In	
R. Campanella, BKN	142
E. Mathews, MIL	135
D. Snider, BKN	126
D. Ennis, PHI	125
G. Hodges, BKN	122

Stolen Bases	
B. Bruton, MIL	26
P. Reese, BKN	22
J. Gilliam, BKN	21
J. Robinson, BKN	17
D. Snider, BKN	16

Hits	
R. Ashburn, PHI	205
S. Musial, STL	200
D. Snider, BKN	198
A. Dark, NY	194

Base on Balls	
S. Musial, STL	105
R. Kiner, PIT, CHI	100
J. Gilliam, BKN	100
E. Mathews, MIL	99

Home Run Percentage	
E. Mathews, MIL	8.1
R. Campanella, BKN	7.9
D. Snider, BKN	7.1
T. Kluszewski, CIN	7.0

Runs	
D. Snider, BKN	132
S. Musial, STL	127
A. Dark, NY	126
J. Gilliam, BKN	125

Doubles	
S. Musial, STL	53
A. Dark, NY	41
C. Furillo, BKN	38
D. Snider, BKN	38

Triples	
J. Gilliam, BKN	17
B. Bruton, MIL	14
S. Hemus, STL	11
D. Fondy, CHI	11

PITCHING LEADERS

Saves	
A. Brazle, STL	18
H. Wilhelm, NY	15
J. Hughes, BKN	9
D. Leonard, CHI	8
L. Burdette, MIL	8

Strikeouts	
R. Roberts, PHI	198
C. Erskine, BKN	187
V. Mizell, STL	173
H. Haddix, STL	163
W. Spahn, MIL	148

Complete Games	
R. Roberts, PHI	33
W. Spahn, MIL	24
C. Simmons, PHI	19
H. Haddix, STL	19
C. Erskine, BKN	16

Fewest Hits/9 Innings	
W. Spahn, MIL	7.15
R. Gomez, NY	7.32
V. Mizell, STL	7.74
B. Buhl, MIL	7.76

Shutouts	
H. Haddix, STL	6
W. Spahn, MIL	5
R. Roberts, PHI	5
C. Simmons, PHI	4
C. Erskine, BKN	4

Fewest Walks/9 Innings	
R. Roberts, PHI	1.58
K. Raffensberger, CIN	1.71
P. Minner, CHI	1.79
G. Staley, STL	2.11

Most Strikeouts/9 Inn.	
V. Mizell, STL	6.94
C. Erskine, BKN	6.82
J. Antonelli, MIL	6.72
J. Klippstein, CHI	6.07

Innings	
R. Roberts, PHI	347
W. Spahn, MIL	266
H. Haddix, STL	253
C. Erskine, BKN	247

Games Pitched	
H. Wilhelm, NY	68
A. Brazle, STL	60
J. Hetki, PIT	54
F. Smith, CIN	50

							Batting						Fielding			Pitching					
	W	L	PCT	GB	R	OR	2B	3B	HR	BA	SA	SB	E	DP	FA	CG	BB	SO	ShO	SV	ERA
Brooklyn	105	49	.682		**955**	689	274	59	**208**	**.285**	**.474**	**90**	**118**	161	**.980**	51	509	**819**	11	29	4.10
Milwaukee	92	62	.597	13	738	**589**	227	52	156	.266	.415	46	143	169	.976	72	539	738	**14**	15	**3.30**
Philadelphia	83	71	.539	22	716	666	228	**62**	115	.265	.396	42	147	161	.975	**76**	**410**	637	13	15	3.80
St. Louis	83	71	.539	22	768	713	**281**	56	140	.273	.424	18	138	161	.977	51	533	732	11	**36**	4.23
New York	70	84	.455	35	768	747	195	45	176	.271	.422	31	151	151	.975	46	610	647	10	20	4.25
Cincinnati	68	86	.442	37	714	788	190	34	166	.261	.403	25	129	**176**	.978	47	488	506	7	15	4.64
Chicago	65	89	.422	40	633	835	204	57	137	.260	.399	49	193	141	.967	38	554	623	3	22	4.79
Pittsburgh	50	104	.325	55	622	887	178	49	99	.247	.356	41	163	139	.973	49	577	607	4	10	5.22
					5914	5914	1777	414	1197	.266	.411	342	1182	1259	.975	430	4220	5309	73	162	4.29

AMERICAN LEAGUE 1953

New York

W-99 L-52

Casey Stengel

POS	Player	AB	BA	HR	RBI	PO	A	E	DP	TC/G	FA
1B	J. Collins	387	.269	17	44	826	65	10	100	8.0	.989
2B	B. Martin	587	.257	15	75	376	390	12	**121**	5.3	.985
SS	P. Rizzuto	413	.271	2	54	214	409	24	100	4.9	.963
3B	G. McDougald	541	.285	10	83	147	299	**22**	36	3.4	.953
RF	H. Bauer	437	.304	10	57	230	13	2	3	1.9	.992
CF	M. Mantle	461	.295	21	92	322	10	6	2	2.8	.982
LF	G. Woodling	395	.306	10	58	240	6	1	2	2.1	.996
C	Y. Berra	503	.296	27	108	566	64	9	9	4.8	.986
OF	I. Noren	345	.267	6	46	208	11	2	1	2.3	.991
1B	D. Bollweg	155	.297	6	24	323	15	6	37	8.0	.983
1B	J. Mize	104	.250	4	27	113	7	0	19	8.0	1.000

Pitcher	G	IP	W	L	SV	ERA
W. Ford	32	207	18	6	0	3.00
J. Sain	40	189	14	7	9	3.00
V. Raschi	28	181	13	6	1	3.33
E. Lopat	25	178	16	4	0	**2.42**
A. Reynolds	41	145	13	7	13	3.41
J. McDonald	27	130	9	7	0	3.82
B. Kuzava	33	92	6	5	4	3.31
T. Gorman	40	77	4	5	6	3.39

Cleveland

W-92 L-62

Al Lopez

POS	Player	AB	BA	HR	RBI	PO	A	E	DP	TC/G	FA
1B	B. Glynn	411	.243	3	30	1036	81	8	133	8.3	**.993**
2B	B. Avila	559	.286	8	55	346	**445**	11	114	5.7	**.986**
SS	G. Strickland	419	.284	5	47	238	400	17	**103**	5.4	.974
3B	A. Rosen	599	.336	**43**	**145**	174	**338**	19	**38**	**3.4**	.964
RF	W. Westlake	218	.330	9	46	128	3	5	2	1.9	.963
CF	L. Doby	513	.263	29	102	354	10	6	3	2.5	.984
LF	D. Mitchell	500	.300	13	60	224	2	7	1	1.9	.970
C	J. Hegan	299	.217	9	37	399	42	**11**	3	4.3	.976
OF	H. Simpson	242	.227	7	22	118	4	4	0	1.8	.968
1B	L. Easter	211	.303	7	31	442	30	9	54	8.6	.981
OF	B. Kennedy	161	.236	3	22	91	2	0	0	1.0	1.000
SS	R. Boone	112	.241	4	21	64	94	8	24	5.4	.952

Pitcher	G	IP	W	L	SV	ERA
B. Lemon	41	**287**	21	15	1	3.36
M. Garcia	38	272	18	9	0	3.25
E. Wynn	36	252	17	12	0	3.93
B. Feller	25	176	10	7	0	3.59
D. Hoskins	26	113	9	3	1	3.99
A. Houtteman	22	109	7	7	3	3.80
B. Hooper	43	69	5	4	7	4.02

Chicago

W-89 L-65

Paul Richards

POS	Player	AB	BA	HR	RBI	PO	A	E	DP	TC/G	FA
1B	F. Fain	446	.256	6	52	1108	106	13	98	9.7	.989
2B	N. Fox	624	.285	3	72	**451**	426	15	101	**5.8**	.983
SS	C. Carrasquel	552	.279	2	47	278	462	18	87	5.1	**.976**
3B	B. Elliott	208	.260	4	32	54	104	6	9	2.8	.963
RF	S. Mele	481	.274	12	82	213	14	1	1	1.7	.996
CF	J. Rivera	567	.259	11	78	385	15	10	5	2.6	.976
LF	M. Minoso	556	.313	15	104	279	15	10	3	2.1	.967
C	S. Lollar	334	.287	8	54	470	51	3	2	4.9	**.994**
10	B. Boyd	165	.297	3	23	301	16	1	25		.997
C	R. Wilson	164	.250	0	10	282	24	6	1	5.0	.981
OF	T. Wright	132	.250	2	25	44	1	1	0	1.4	.978

Pitcher	G	IP	W	L	SV	ERA
B. Pierce	40	271	18	12	3	2.72
V. Trucks	24	176	15	6	1	2.86
M. Fornieles	39	153	8	7	3	3.59
H. Dorish	55	146	10	6	18	3.40
S. Rogovin	22	131	7	12	1	5.22
S. Consuegra	29	124	7	5	3	2.54
J. Dobson	23	101	5	5	1	3.67
B. Keegan	22	99	7	5	1	2.74

AMERICAN LEAGUE 1953, *cont.*

Team	POS	Player	AB	BA	HR	RBI	PO	A	E	DP	TC/G	FA	Pitcher	G	IP	W	L	SV	ERA
Boston	1B	D. Gernert	494	.253	21	71	1223	84	**19**	139	**9.8**	.986	M. Parnell	38	241	21	8	0	3.06
W-84 L-69	2B	B. Goodman	514	.313	2	41	267	306	15	88	5.3	.974	M. McDermott	32	206	18	10	0	3.01
Lou Boudreau	SS	M. Bolling	323	.263	5	28	174	321	23	71	4.8	.956	H. Brown	30	166	11	6	0	4.65
	3B	G. Kell	460	.307	12	73	114	231	10	23	2.9	**.972**	S. Hudson	30	156	6	9	2	3.52
	RF	J. Piersall	585	.272	3	52	352	15	5	7	2.5	.987	W. Nixon	23	117	4	8	0	3.93
	CF	T. Umphlett	495	.283	3	59	382	12	7	1	2.9	.983	E. Kinder	**69**	107	10	6	**27**	1.85
	LF	H. Evers	300	.240	11	31	161	3	2	0	1.8	.988	B. Henry	21	86	5	5	1	3.26
	C	S. White	476	.273	13	64	**588**	**68**	9	9	**5.1**	.986							
	OF	G. Stephens	221	.204	3	18	113	2	4	0	1.7	.966							
	32	F. Baker	172	.273	0	24	67	93	4	18		.976							
	UT	T. Lepcio	161	.236	4	11	96	155	6	37		.977							
	C	D. Wilber	112	.241	7	29	90	7	2	0	3.5	.980							
	OF	T. Williams	91	.407	13	34	31	1	1	1	1.3	.970							
Washington	1B	M. Vernon	608	**.337**	15	115	**1376**	94	12	**158**	**9.8**	.992	B. Porterfield	34	255	**22**	10	0	3.35
W-76 L-76	2B	W. Terwilliger	464	.252	4	46	333	395	13	108	5.6	.982	W. Masterson	29	166	10	12	0	3.63
Bucky Harris	SS	P. Runnels	486	.257	2	50	195	324	23	87	4.5	.958	S. Shea	23	165	12	7	0	3.94
	3B	E. Yost	577	.272	9	45	**190**	300	18	31	3.3	.965	C. Stobbs	27	153	11	8	0	3.29
	RF	J. Jensen	552	.266	10	84	274	9	5	0	2.0	.983	C. Marrero	22	146	8	7	2	3.03
	CF	J. Busby	586	.312	6	82	482	15	6	4	3.4	.988	S. Dixon	43	120	5	8	3	3.75
	LF	C. Vollmer	408	.260	11	74	227	8	5	1	2.3	.979	J. Schmitz	24	108	2	7	4	3.68
	C	E. Fitz Gerald	288	.250	3	39	319	33	4	3	4.2	.989							
	C	M. Grasso	196	.209	2	22	219	24	4	4	4.2	.984							
	OF	G. Coan	168	.196	2	17	105	2	0	1	2.3	1.000							
Detroit	1B	W. Dropo	606	.248	13	96	1260	**127**	14	121	9.3	.990	N. Garver	30	198	11	11	1	4.45
W-60 L-94	2B	J. Pesky	308	.292	2	24	166	183	3	49	4.8	.991	B. Hoeft	29	198	9	14	2	4.83
Fred Hutchinson	SS	H. Kuenn	**679**	.308	2	48	**308**	441	21	78	5.0	.973	T. Gray	30	176	10	15	0	4.60
	3B	R. Boone	385	.312	22	93	111	211	14	32	3.5	.958	S. Gromek	19	126	6	8	1	4.51
	RF	D. Lund	421	.257	9	47	275	12	6	0	2.4	.980	D. Marlowe	42	120	6	7	0	5.26
	CF	J. Delsing	479	.288	11	62	354	7	3	2	2.7	.992	R. Branca	17	102	4	7	1	4.15
	LF	B. Nieman	508	.281	15	69	271	10	6	1	2.1	.979	R. Herbert	43	88	4	6	6	5.24
	C	M. Batts	374	.278	6	42	463	44	7	7	5.0	.986							
	32	F. Hatfield	311	.254	3	19	120	208	9	34		.973							
	OF	S. Souchock	278	.302	11	46	144	7	6	3	2.0	.962							
	2B	G. Priddy	196	.235	1	24	111	106	5	28	4.9	.977							
	C	J. Bucha	158	.222	1	14	218	22	4	4	4.4	.984							
Philadelphia	1B	E. Robinson	615	.247	22	102	1366	71	17	135	9.4	.988	H. Byrd	40	237	11	**20**	0	5.51
W-59 L-95	2B	C. Michaels	411	.251	12	42	304	302	**19**	81	5.7	.970	M. Fricano	39	211	9	12	0	3.88
Jimmy Dykes	SS	J. De Maestri	420	.255	6	35	191	297	18	53	4.7	.964	A. Kellner	25	202	11	12	0	3.93
	3B	L. Babe	343	.224	0	20	114	192	16	24	3.5	.950	C. Bishop	39	161	3	14	2	5.66
	RF	D. Philley	620	.303	9	59	296	18	6	0	2.0	.981	M. Martin	58	156	10	12	7	4.43
	CF	E. McGhee	358	.263	1	29	319	4	6	0	3.3	.982	B. Shantz	16	106	5	9	0	4.09
	LF	G. Zernial	556	.284	42	108	300	17	9	2	2.3	.972	C. Scheib	28	96	3	7	2	4.88
	C	J. Astroth	260	.296	3	24	341	47	5	**13**	5.0	.987							
	32	P. Suder	454	.286	4	35	178	279	10	42		.979							
	C	R. Murray	268	.284	6	41	330	45	4	8	4.9	.989							
	SS	E. Joost	177	.249	6	15	102	147	11	33	5.1	.958							
	OF	C. Mauro	165	.267	0	17	119	5	4	0	2.6	.969							
St. Louis	1B	D. Kryhoski	338	.278	16	50	685	66	6	7	8.6	.992	D. Larsen	38	193	7	12	2	4.16
W-54 L-100	2B	B. Young	537	.255	4	25	397	363	18	120	5.3	.977	D. Pillette	31	167	7	13	0	4.48
Marty Marion	SS	B. Hunter	567	.219	1	37	284	**512**	**25**	99	**5.4**	.970	D. Littlefield	36	152	7	12	0	5.08
	3B	J. Dyck	334	.213	9	27	62	101	13	12	3.5	.926	S. Paige	57	117	3	9	11	3.53
	RF	V. Wertz	440	.268	19	70	243	15	7	4	2.2	.974	H. Brecheen	26	117	5	13	1	3.07
	CF	J. Groth	557	.253	10	57	425	18	4	5	3.2	.991	M. Stuart	60	114	8	2	7	3.94
	LF	D. Kokos	299	.241	13	38	152	5	6	1	2.0	.963	B. Cain	32	100	4	10	1	6.23
	C	C. Courtney	355	.251	4	19	436	47	10	7	4.8	.980	V. Trucks	16	88	5	4	2	3.07
	OF	D. Lenhardt	303	.317	10	35	148	8	5	1	2.1	.969	B. Holloman	22	65	3	7	0	5.23
	1B	R. Sievers	285	.270	8	35	604	31	5	64	8.4	.992							
	C	L. Moss	239	.276	2	28	296	21	7	4	4.6	.978							
	3B	V. Stephens	165	.321	4	17	54	91	7	9	3.3	.954							
	3B	B. Elliott	160	.250	5	29	51	93	7	12	3.4	.954							

BATTING AND BASE RUNNING LEADERS

Batting Average

M. Vernon, WAS	.337
A. Rosen, CLE	.336
B. Goodman, BOS	.313
M. Minoso, CHI	.313
J. Busby, WAS	.312

Slugging Average

A. Rosen, CLE	.613
G. Zernial, PHI	.559
Y. Berra, NY	.523
R. Boone, CLE, DET	.519
M. Vernon, WAS	.518

Home Runs

A. Rosen, CLE	43
G. Zernial, PHI	42
L. Doby, CLE	29
Y. Berra, NY	27
R. Boone, CLE, DET	26

Total Bases

A. Rosen, CLE	367
M. Vernon, WAS	315
G. Zernial, PHI	311
Y. Berra, NY	263
D. Philley, PHI	263

Runs Batted In

A. Rosen, CLE	145
M. Vernon, WAS	115
R. Boone, CLE, DET	114
Y. Berra, NY	108
G. Zernial, PHI	108

Stolen Bases

M. Minoso, CHI	25
J. Rivera, CHI	22
J. Jensen, WAS	18
J. Busby, WAS	13
D. Philley, PHI	13

PITCHING LEADERS

Winning Percentage

E. Lopat, NY	.800
W. Ford, NY	.750
M. Parnell, BOS	.724
B. Porterfield, WAS	.688
M. Garcia, CLE	.667
V. Trucks, STL, CHI	.667

Earned Run Average

E. Lopat, NY	2.42
B. Pierce, CHI	2.72
V. Trucks, STL, CHI	2.93
W. Ford, NY	3.00
J. Sain, NY	3.00

Wins

B. Porterfield, WAS	22
M. Parnell, BOS	21
B. Lemon, CLE	21
V. Trucks, STL, CHI	20

Saves

E. Kinder, BOS	27
H. Dorish, CHI	18
A. Reynolds, NY	13
S. Paige, STL	11
J. Sain, NY	9

Strikeouts

B. Pierce, CHI	186
V. Trucks, STL, CHI	149
E. Wynn, CLE	138
M. Parnell, BOS	136
M. Garcia, CLE	134

Complete Games

B. Porterfield, WAS	24
B. Lemon, CLE	23
M. Garcia, CLE	21
B. Pierce, CHI	19
V. Trucks, STL, CHI	17

AMERICAN LEAGUE 1953, *cont.*

BATTING AND BASE RUNNING LEADERS

Hits

H. Kuenn, DET	209
M. Vernon, WAS	205
A. Rosen, CLE	201
D. Philley, PHI	188

Base on Balls

E. Yost, WAS	123
F. Fain, CHI	108
L. Doby, CLE	96
D. Gernert, BOS	88

Home Run Percentage

G. Zernial, PHI	7.6
A. Rosen, CLE	7.2
L. Doby, CLE	5.7
Y. Berra, NY	5.4

Runs

A. Rosen, CLE	115
E. Yost, WAS	107
M. Mantle, NY	105
M. Minoso, CHI	104

Doubles

M. Vernon, WAS	43
G. Kell, BOS	41
S. White, BOS	34
B. Goodman, BOS	33
H. Kuenn, DET	33

Triples

J. Rivera, CHI	16
M. Vernon, WAS	11
J. Piersall, BOS	9
D. Philley, PHI	9

PITCHING LEADERS

Fewest Hits/9 Innings

B. Pierce, CHI	7.16
M. McDermott, BOS	7.37
V. Raschi, NY	7.46
W. Masterson, WAS	7.85

Shutouts

B. Porterfield, WAS	9
B. Pierce, CHI	7
V. Trucks, STL, CHI	5
M. Parnell, BOS	5
B. Lemon, CLE	5

Fewest Walks/9 Innings

E. Lopat, NY	1.61
J. Sain, NY	2.14
A. Kellner, PHI	2.28
B. Porterfield, WAS	2.58

Most Strikeouts/9 Inn.

B. Pierce, CHI	6.17
T. Gray, DET	5.88
W. Masterson, WAS	5.14
M. Parnell, BOS	5.08

Innings

B. Lemon, CLE	287
M. Garcia, CLE	272
B. Pierce, CHI	271
V. Trucks, STL, CHI	264

Games Pitched

E. Kinder, BOS	69
M. Stuart, STL	60
M. Martin, PHI	58
S. Paige, STL	57

	W	L	PCT	GB	R	OR	Batting 2B	3B	HR	BA	SA	SB	Fielding E	DP	FA	Pitching CG	BB	SO	ShO	SV	ERA
New York	99	52	.656		**801**	**547**	226	52	139	**.273**	**.417**	34	126	182	.979	50	500	604	**16**	**39**	**3.20**
Cleveland	92	62	.597	8.5	770	627	201	29	**160**	.270	.410	33	127	**197**	.979	**81**	519	586	11	15	3.64
Chicago	89	65	.578	11.5	716	592	226	**53**	74	.258	.364	**73**	125	144	**.980**	57	583	**714**	**16**	33	3.41
Boston	84	69	.549	16	656	632	255	37	101	.264	.384	33	148	173	.975	41	584	642	14	37	3.59
Washington	76	76	.500	23.5	687	614	230	**53**	69	.263	.368	65	**120**	173	.979	76	**478**	515	**16**	10	3.66
Detroit	60	94	.390	40.5	695	923	**259**	44	108	.266	.387	30	135	149	.978	50	585	645	2	16	5.25
Philadelphia	59	95	.383	41.5	632	799	205	38	116	.256	.372	41	137	161	.977	51	594	566	6	11	4.67
St. Louis	54	100	.351	46.5	555	778	214	25	112	.249	.363	17	152	165	.974	28	626	639	7	24	4.48
					5512	5512	1816	331	879	.262	.383	326	1070	1344	.978	434	4469	4911	88	185	3.99

NATIONAL LEAGUE 1954

New York

W-97 L-57

Leo Durocher

POS	Player	AB	BA	HR	RBI	PO	A	E	DP	TC/G	FA	Pitcher	G	IP	W	L	SV	ERA
1B	W. Lockman	570	.251	16	60	1261	88	**18**	122	9.4	.987	J. Antonelli	39	259	21	7	2	**2.30**
2B	D. Williams	544	.222	9	46	353	396	14	112	5.4	**.982**	R. Gomez	37	222	17	9	0	2.88
SS	A. Dark	**644**	.293	20	70	289	487	**36**	105	5.3	.956	S. Maglie	34	218	14	6	2	3.26
3B	H. Thompson	448	.263	26	86	125	267	23	27	3.2	.945	J. Hearn	29	130	8	8	1	4.15
RF	D. Mueller	619	.342	4	71	263	14	6	5	1.8	.979	D. Liddle	28	127	9	4	0	3.06
CF	W. Mays	565	**.345**	41	110	448	13	7	9	3.1	.985	M. Grissom	56	122	10	7	19	2.35
LF	M. Irvin	432	.262	19	64	274	7	7	0	2.3	.976	H. Wilhelm	57	111	12	4	7	2.10
C	W. Westrum	246	.187	8	27	419	45	7	8	4.8	.985							
C	R. Katt	200	.255	9	33	265	23	8	4	3.6	.973							
OF	D. Rhodes	164	.341	15	50	62	1	1	0	1.7	.984							
UT	B. Hofman	125	.224	8	30	192	32	4	25		.982							

Brooklyn

W-92 L-62

Walter Alston

POS	Player	AB	BA	HR	RBI	PO	A	E	DP	TC/G	FA	Pitcher	G	IP	W	L	SV	ERA
1B	G. Hodges	579	.304	42	130	**1381**	**132**	7	129	**9.9**	.995	C. Erskine	38	260	18	15	1	4.15
2B	J. Gilliam	607	.282	13	52	340	388	17	99	5.2	.977	R. Meyer	36	180	11	6	0	3.99
SS	P. Reese	554	.309	10	69	270	426	25	74	5.2	.965	J. Podres	29	152	11	7	0	4.27
3B	D. Hoak	261	.245	7	26	71	139	11	12	2.9	.950	B. Loes	28	148	13	5	0	4.14
RF	C. Furillo	547	.294	19	96	306	10	9	3	2.2	.972	D. Newcombe	29	144	9	8	0	4.55
CF	D. Snider	584	.341	40	130	360	8	7	1	2.5	.981	C. Labine	47	108	7	6	5	4.15
LF	S. Amoros	263	.274	9	34	149	6	2	1	2.2	.987	J. Hughes	**60**	87	8	4	**24**	3.22
C	R. Campanella	397	.207	19	51	600	58	7	7	**6.0**	.989							
O3	J. Robinson	386	.311	15	59	153	99	7	6		.973							
3B	B. Cox	226	.235	2	17	57	90	6	7	2.6	.961							
C	R. Walker	155	.181	5	23	259	19	1	4	5.9	.996							

Milwaukee

W-89 L-65

Charlie Grimm

POS	Player	AB	BA	HR	RBI	PO	A	E	DP	TC/G	FA	Pitcher	G	IP	W	L	SV	ERA
1B	J. Adcock	500	.308	23	87	1229	67	6	125	9.8	.995	W. Spahn	39	283	21	12	3	3.14
2B	D. O'Connell	541	.279	2	37	244	314	12	83	5.5	.979	L. Burdette	38	238	15	14	0	2.76
SS	J. Logan	560	.275	8	66	324	**489**	26	104	**5.4**	**.969**	G. Conley	28	194	14	9	0	2.96
3B	E. Mathews	476	.290	40	103	112	254	13	**28**	3.0	.966	J. Wilson	27	128	8	2	0	3.52
RF	A. Pafko	510	.286	14	69	245	9	8	3	1.9	.969	C. Nichols	35	122	9	11	1	4.41
CF	B. Bruton	567	.284	4	30	350	14	7	3	2.6	.981	D. Jolly	47	111	11	6	10	2.43
LF	H. Aaron	468	.280	13	69	223	5	7	0	2.0	.970	B. Buhl	31	110	2	7	3	4.00
C	D. Crandall	463	.242	21	64	**665**	**79**	8	11	5.5	.989							
2B	J. Dittmer	192	.245	6	20	119	141	6	31	4.8	.977							
OF	J. Pendleton	173	.220	1	16	90	5	5	0	2.0	.950							

Philadelphia

W-75 L-79

Steve O'Neill
W-40 L-37

Terry Moore
W-35 L-42

POS	Player	AB	BA	HR	RBI	PO	A	E	DP	TC/G	FA	Pitcher	G	IP	W	L	SV	ERA
1B	E. Torgeson	490	.271	5	54	1146	74	12	103	9.3	.990	R. Roberts	45	**337**	**23**	15	4	2.97
2B	G. Hamner	596	.299	13	89	361	412	17	97	5.2	.978	C. Simmons	34	253	14	15	1	2.81
SS	B. Morgan	455	.262	14	50	237	361	29	71	4.9	.954	M. Dickson	40	226	10	**20**	3	3.78
3B	W. Jones	535	.271	12	56	**184**	277	15	23	**3.4**	**.968**	B. Miller	30	150	7	9	0	4.56
RF	M. Clark	233	.240	1	24	114	9	5	2	2.0	.961	H. Wehmeier	25	138	10	8	0	3.85
CF	R. Ashburn	559	.313	1	41	483	12	8	2	3.3	.984							
LF	D. Ennis	556	.261	25	119	303	9	14	1	2.3	.957							
C	S. Burgess	345	.368	4	46	356	30	**10**	4	4.4	.975							
OF	D. Schell	272	.283	7	33	143	4	4	0	2.2	.974							
C	S. Lopata	259	.290	14	42	336	26	4	1	4.9	.989							
OF	J. Wyrostek	259	.239	3	28	90	5	1	1	1.7	.990							

NATIONAL LEAGUE 1954, *cont.*

Team	POS	Player	AB	BA	HR	RBI	PO	A	E	DP	TC/G	FA	Pitcher	G	IP	W	L	SV	ERA
Cincinnati	1B	T. Kluszewski	573	.326	**49**	**141**	1237	101	5	**166**	9.0	**.996**	A. Fowler	40	228	12	10	0	3.83
W-74 L-80	2B	J. Temple	505	.307	0	44	**428**	374	22	117	5.7	.973	C. Valentine	36	194	12	11	1	4.45
Birdie Tebbetts	SS	R. McMillan	588	.250	4	42	**341**	464	34	**129**	**5.4**	.959	J. Nuxhall	35	167	12	5	0	3.89
	3B	B. Adams	390	.269	3	23	127	186	16	24	3.5	.951	B. Podbielan	27	131	7	10	0	5.36
	RF	W. Post	451	.255	18	83	231	13	11	2	2.2	.957	F. Baczewski	29	130	6	6	0	5.26
	CF	G. Bell	619	.299	17	101	406	12	6	2	2.8	.986	H. Perkowski	28	96	2	8	0	6.11
	LF	J. Greengrass	542	.280	27	95	298	9	10	0	2.3	.968	H. Judson	37	93	5	7	3	3.95
	C	A. Seminick	247	.235	7	30	327	44	4	11	4.6	.989	F. Smith	50	81	5	8	20	2.67
	3B	C. Harmon	286	.238	2	25	70	129	8	19	3.1	.961	J. Collum	36	79	7	3	0	3.74
	C	E. Bailey	183	.197	9	20	194	20	6	2	3.6	.973							
	OF	B. Borkowski	162	.265	1	19	69	3	0	0	2.0	1.000							

Team	POS	Player	AB	BA	HR	RBI	PO	A	E	DP	TC/G	FA	Pitcher	G	IP	W	L	SV	ERA
St. Louis	1B	J. Cunningham	310	.284	11	50	814	68	10	96	10.5	.989	H. Haddix	43	260	18	13	4	3.57
W-72 L-82	2B	R. Schoendienst	610	.315	5	79	394	**477**	18	**137**	**6.2**	.980	V. Raschi	30	179	8	9	0	4.73
Eddie Stanky	SS	A. Grammas	401	.264	2	29	252	432	24	100	5.0	.966	B. Lawrence	35	159	15	6	1	3.74
	3B	R. Jablonski	611	.296	12	104	122	**298**	**34**	25	3.0	.925	G. Staley	48	156	7	13	2	5.26
	RF	S. Musial	591	.330	35	126	271	13	3	4	1.9	.990	T. Poholsky	25	106	5	7	0	3.06
	CF	W. Moon	635	.304	12	76	387	11	9	2	2.8	.978	A. Brazle	58	84	5	4	8	4.16
	LF	R. Repulski	619	.283	19	79	302	4	8	0	2.1	.975	J. Presko	37	72	4	9	0	6.91
	C	B. Sarni	380	.300	9	70	486	41	2	**12**	4.5	**.996**							
	1B	T. Alston	244	.246	4	34	552	72	7	57	9.7	.989							
	UT	S. Hemus	214	.304	2	27	85	151	10	29		.959							

Team	POS	Player	AB	BA	HR	RBI	PO	A	E	DP	TC/G	FA	Pitcher	G	IP	W	L	SV	ERA
Chicago	1B	D. Fondy	568	.285	9	49	1228	119	9	129	9.8	.993	B. Rush	33	236	13	15	0	3.77
W-64 L-90	2B	G. Baker	541	.275	13	61	355	385	**25**	102	5.7	.967	P. Minner	32	218	11	11	1	3.96
Stan Hack	SS	E. Banks	593	.275	19	79	312	475	34	105	5.3	.959	W. Hacker	39	159	6	13	2	4.25
	3B	R. Jackson	484	.273	19	67	118	266	18	21	3.2	.955	J. Klippstein	36	148	4	11	1	5.29
	RF	H. Sauer	520	.288	41	103	282	8	11	2	2.1	.963	H. Pollet	20	128	8	10	0	3.58
	CF	D. Talbot	403	.241	1	19	245	10	4	1	2.4	.985	J. Davis	46	128	11	7	4	3.52
	LF	R. Kiner	557	.285	22	73	298	6	9	1	2.1	.971	H. Jeffcoat	43	104	5	6	7	5.19
	C	J. Garagiola	153	.281	5	21	191	23	4	0	4.0	.982	D. Cole	18	84	3	8	0	5.36
	OF	F. Baumholtz	303	.297	4	28	168	2	2	0	2.4	.988							
	C	W. Cooper	158	.310	7	32	190	31	5	4	4.7	.978							

Team	POS	Player	AB	BA	HR	RBI	PO	A	E	DP	TC/G	FA	Pitcher	G	IP	W	L	SV	ERA
Pittsburgh	1B	B. Skinner	470	.249	8	46	1026	84	16	87	9.5	.986	M. Surkont	33	208	9	18	0	4.41
W-53 L-101	2B	C. Roberts	496	.232	1	36	357	394	24	82	5.9	.969	B. Friend	35	170	7	12	2	5.07
Fred Haney	SS	G. Allie	418	.199	3	30	192	260	23	59	5.0	.952	V. Law	39	162	9	13	3	5.51
	3B	D. Cole	486	.270	1	40	48	112	10	7	3.1	.941	D. Littlefield	23	155	10	11	0	3.60
	RF	S. Gordon	363	.306	12	49	121	9	3	1	1.8	.977	B. Purkey	36	131	3	8	0	5.07
	CF	F. Thomas	577	.298	23	94	418	14	5	2	2.9	.989	J. Thies	33	130	3	9	0	3.87
	LF	J. Lynch	284	.239	8	36	127	10	5	2	1.7	.965	P. LaPalme	33	121	4	10	0	5.52
	C	T. Atwell	287	.289	3	26	360	39	4	4	4.6	.990	G. O'Donnell	21	87	3	9	1	4.53
	UT	P. Ward	360	.269	7	48	419	69	15	34		.970	J. Hetki	58	83	4	4	9	4.99
	OF	D. Hall	310	.239	2	27	235	5	11	1	2.5	.956							
	C	J. Shepard	227	.304	3	22	257	46	7	5	4.6	.977							

BATTING AND BASE RUNNING LEADERS

Batting Average

W. Mays, NY	.345
D. Mueller, NY	.342
D. Snider, BKN	.341
S. Musial, STL	.330
T. Kluszewski, CIN	.326

Slugging Average

W. Mays, NY	.667
D. Snider, BKN	.647
T. Kluszewski, CIN	.642
S. Musial, STL	.607
E. Mathews, MIL	.603

Home Runs

T. Kluszewski, CIN	49
G. Hodges, BKN	42
H. Sauer, CHI	41
W. Mays, NY	41
E. Mathews, MIL	40
D. Snider, BKN	40

Total Bases

D. Snider, BKN	378
W. Mays, NY	377
T. Kluszewski, CIN	368
S. Musial, STL	359
G. Hodges, BKN	335

Runs Batted In

T. Kluszewski, CIN	141
G. Hodges, BKN	130
D. Snider, BKN	130
S. Musial, STL	126
D. Ennis, PHI	119

Stolen Bases

B. Bruton, MIL	34
J. Temple, CIN	21
D. Fondy, CHI	20
W. Moon, STL	18
R. Ashburn, PHI	11

Hits

D. Mueller, NY	212
D. Snider, BKN	199
W. Mays, NY	195
S. Musial, STL	195

Base on Balls

R. Ashburn, PHI	125
E. Mathews, MIL	113
S. Musial, STL	103
H. Thompson, NY	90
P. Reese, BKN	90

Home Run Percentage

T. Kluszewski, CIN	8.6
E. Mathews, MIL	8.4
H. Sauer, CHI	7.9
W. Mays, NY	7.3

Runs

D. Snider, BKN	120
S. Musial, STL	120
W. Mays, NY	119
R. Ashburn, PHI	111

Doubles

S. Musial, STL	41
D. Snider, BKN	39
G. Hamner, PHI	39
R. Repulski, STL	39

Triples

W. Mays, NY	13
G. Hamner, PHI	11
D. Snider, BKN	10

PITCHING LEADERS

Winning Percentage

J. Antonelli, NY	.750
B. Lawrence, STL	.714
R. Gomez, NY	.654
W. Spahn, MIL	.636
R. Roberts, PHI	.605

Earned Run Average

J. Antonelli, NY	2.30
L. Burdette, MIL	2.76
C. Simmons, PHI	2.81
R. Gomez, NY	2.88
G. Conley, MIL	2.96

Wins

R. Roberts, PHI	23
J. Antonelli, NY	21
W. Spahn, MIL	21
H. Haddix, STL	18
C. Erskine, BKN	18

Saves

J. Hughes, BKN	24
F. Smith, CIN	20
M. Grissom, NY	19
D. Jolly, MIL	10
J. Hetki, PIT	9

Strikeouts

R. Roberts, PHI	185
H. Haddix, STL	184
C. Erskine, BKN	166
J. Antonelli, NY	152
W. Spahn, MIL	136

Complete Games

R. Roberts, PHI	29
W. Spahn, MIL	23
C. Simmons, PHI	21
J. Antonelli, NY	18
L. Burdette, MIL	13
H. Haddix, STL	13

Fewest Hits/9 Innings

J. Antonelli, NY	7.27
R. Roberts, PHI	7.73
G. Conley, MIL	7.92
B. Lawrence, STL	8.00

Shutouts

J. Antonelli, NY	6

Fewest Walks/9 Innings

R. Roberts, PHI	1.50
P. Minner, CHI	2.06
W. Hacker, CHI	2.10
L. Burdette, MIL	2.34

Most Strikeouts/9 Inn.

H. Haddix, STL	6.38
C. Erskine, BKN	5.74
D. Littlefield, PIT	5.34
J. Antonelli, NY	5.29

Innings

R. Roberts, PHI	337
W. Spahn, MIL	283
H. Haddix, STL	260
C. Erskine, BKN	260

Games Pitched

J. Hughes, BKN	60
A. Brazle, STL	58
J. Hetki, PIT	58
H. Wilhelm, NY	57

NATIONAL LEAGUE 1954, *cont.*

	W	L	PCT	GB	R	OR	Batting 2B	3B	HR	BA	SA	SB	Fielding E	DP	FA	Pitching CG	BB	SO	ShO	SV	ERA
New York	97	57	.630		732	**550**	194	42	**186**	.264	.424	30	154	172	.975	45	613	692	**19**	33	**3.09**
Brooklyn	92	62	.597	5	778	740	246	56	**186**	.270	**.444**	46	129	138	.978	39	533	**762**	8	**36**	4.31
Milwaukee	89	65	.578	8	670	556	217	41	139	.265	.401	54	**116**	171	**.981**	63	553	698	13	21	3.19
Philadelphia	75	79	.487	22	659	614	243	**58**	102	.267	.395	30	145	133	.975	**78**	**450**	570	14	12	3.59
Cincinnati	74	80	.481	23	729	763	221	46	147	.262	.406	47	137	**194**	.977	34	547	537	8	27	4.50
St. Louis	72	82	.468	25	**799**	790	**285**	**58**	119	**.281**	.421	**63**	146	178	.976	40	535	680	11	18	4.50
Chicago	64	90	.416	33	700	766	229	45	159	.263	.412	46	154	164	.974	41	619	622	6	19	4.51
Pittsburgh	53	101	.344	44	557	845	181	57	76	.248	.350	21	173	136	.971	37	564	525	4	15	4.92
					5624	5624	1816	403	1114	.265	.407	337	1154	1286	.976	377	4414	5086	83	181	4.08

AMERICAN LEAGUE 1954

Cleveland

W-111 L-43

Al Lopez

POS	Player	AB	BA	HR	RBI	PO	A	E	DP	TC/G	FA	Pitcher	G	IP	W	L	SV	ERA
1B	B. Glynn	171	.251	5	18	424	35	6	38	4.8	.987	E. Wynn	40	**271**	**23**	11	2	2.73
2B	B. Avila	555	**.341**	15	67	356	**406**	**19**	100	**5.5**	.976	M. Garcia	45	259	19	8	5	**2.64**
SS	G. Strickland	361	.213	6	37	193	321	21	61	4.8	.961	B. Lemon	36	258	**23**	7	0	2.72
3B	A. Rosen	466	.300	24	102	110	149	11	14	3.1	.959	A. Houtteman	32	188	15	7	0	3.35
RF	D. Philley	452	.226	12	60	237	6	4	0	1.9	.984	B. Feller	19	140	13	3	0	3.09
CF	L. Doby	577	.272	**32**	**126**	411	14	2	6	2.8	.995	D. Mossi	40	93	6	1	7	1.94
LF	A. Smith	481	.281	11	50	241	8	4	1	2.3	.984	R. Narleski	42	89	3	3	13	2.22
C	J. Hegan	423	.234	11	40	661	49	4	9	5.2	**.994**	H. Newhouser	26	47	7	2	7	2.51
1B	V. Wertz	295	.275	14	48	557	52	7	57	7.4	.989							
OF	W. Westlake	240	.263	11	42	131	1	5	0	2.0	.964							
3B	R. Regalado	180	.250	2	24	62	84	5	7	3.0	.967							
SS	S. Dente	169	.266	1	19	66	133	6	33	3.4	.971							

New York

W-103 L-51

Casey Stengel

POS	Player	AB	BA	HR	RBI	PO	A	E	DP	TC/G	FA	Pitcher	G	IP	W	L	SV	ERA
1B	J. Collins	343	.271	12	46	759	60	7	105	7.1	.992	W. Ford	34	211	16	8	1	2.82
2B	G. McDougald	394	.259	12	48	224	233	5	84	5.0	.989	B. Grim	37	199	20	6	0	3.26
SS	P. Rizzuto	307	.195	2	15	184	294	16	84	3.9	.968	E. Lopat	26	170	12	4	0	3.55
3B	A. Carey	411	.302	8	65	154	283	15	32	**3.8**	.967	A. Reynolds	36	157	13	4	7	3.32
RF	H. Bauer	377	.294	12	54	179	6	2	1	1.7	.989	T. Morgan	32	143	11	5	1	3.34
CF	M. Mantle	543	.300	27	102	327	20	9	5	2.5	.975	H. Byrd	25	132	9	7	0	2.99
LF	I. Noren	426	.319	12	66	242	9	5	2	2.2	.980	J. Sain	45	77	6	6	**22**	3.16
C	Y. Berra	584	.307	22	125	**717**	63	8	**14**	5.3	.990							
OF	G. Woodling	304	.250	3	40	164	5	3	1	1.9	.983							
2B	J. Coleman	300	.217	3	21	183	198	9	62	4.9	.977							
1B	B. Skowron	215	.340	7	41	395	28	6	48	7.0	.986							
1B	E. Robinson	142	.261	3	27	227	19	5	21	8.7	.980							

Chicago

W-94 L-60

Paul Richards
W-91 L-54

Marty Marion
W-3 L-6

POS	Player	AB	BA	HR	RBI	PO	A	E	DP	TC/G	FA	Pitcher	G	IP	W	L	SV	ERA
1B	F. Fain	235	.302	5	51	565	31	8	54	9.4	.987	V. Trucks	40	265	19	12	3	2.79
2B	N. Fox	631	.319	2	47	**400**	392	9	**103**	5.2	**.989**	B. Keegan	31	210	16	9	2	3.09
SS	C. Carrasquel	620	.255	12	62	280	492	20	**102**	5.1	**.975**	B. Pierce	36	189	9	10	3	3.48
3B	C. Michaels	282	.262	7	44	95	180	12	10	3.2	.958	J. Harshman	35	177	14	8	1	2.95
RF	J. Rivera	490	.286	13	61	255	5	11	0	1.9	.959	S. Consuegra	39	154	16	3	3	2.69
CF	J. Groth	422	.275	7	60	314	7	4	3	2.6	.988	D. Johnson	46	144	8	7	7	3.13
LF	M. Minoso	568	.320	19	116	340	14	8	3	2.5	.978	H. Dorish	37	109	6	4	6	2.72
C	S. Lollar	316	.244	7	34	395	38	3	8	4.7	.993	M. Martin	35	70	5	4	5	2.06
13	G. Kell	233	.283	5	48	272	56	4	31		.988							
C	M. Batts	158	.228	3	19	225	19	2	3	5.9	.992							
1B	P. Cavarretta	158	.316	3	24	261	17	2	29	6.4	.993							

Boston

W-69 L-85

Lou Boudreau

POS	Player	AB	BA	HR	RBI	PO	A	E	DP	TC/G	FA	Pitcher	G	IP	W	L	SV	ERA
1B	H. Agganis	434	.251	11	57	1064	**89**	12	101	9.8	.990	F. Sullivan	36	206	15	12	1	3.14
2B	T. Lepcio	398	.256	8	45	233	230	14	58	6.0	.971	W. Nixon	31	200	11	12	0	4.06
SS	M. Bolling	370	.249	6	36	186	370	**32**	73	**5.5**	.946	T. Brewer	33	163	10	9	0	4.65
3B	G. Hatton	302	.281	5	33	77	204	10	20	3.1	.966*	L. Kiely	28	131	5	8	0	3.50
RF	J. Piersall	474	.285	8	38	249	10	4	2	2.1	.985	H. Brown	40	118	1	8	0	4.12
CF	J. Jensen	580	.276	25	117	331	12	5	0	2.3	.986	E. Kinder	48	107	8	8	15	3.62
LF	T. Williams	386	.345	29	89	213	5	4	0	1.9	.982	B. Henry	24	96	3	7	0	4.52
C	S. White	493	.282	14	75	677	**80**	**16**	11	**5.8**	.979	M. Parnell	19	92	3	7	0	3.70
UT	B. Goodman	489	.303	1	36	393	248	14	90		.979	S. Hudson	33	71	3	4	5	4.42
UT	B. Consolo	242	.227	1	11	113	184	15	30		.952							
OF	K. Olson	227	.260	1	20	122	10	6	1	1.8	.957							
10	S. Mele	132	.318	7	23	188	9	2	18		.990							

Detroit

W-68 L-86

Fred Hutchinson

POS	Player	AB	BA	HR	RBI	PO	A	E	DP	TC/G	FA	Pitcher	G	IP	W	L	SV	ERA
1B	W. Dropo	320	.281	4	44	681	54	3	60	7.8	.996	S. Gromek	36	253	18	16	1	2.74
2B	F. Bolling	368	.236	6	38	248	232	13	54	4.4	.974	N. Garver	35	246	14	11	1	2.81
SS	H. Kuenn	**656**	.306	5	48	**294**	**496**	28	85	5.3	.966	G. Zuverink	35	203	9	13	4	3.59
3B	R. Boone	543	.295	20	85	**170**	332	19	22	3.5	.964	B. Hoeft	34	175	7	15	1	4.58
RF	A. Kaline	504	.276	4	43	283	16	9	0	2.3	.971	A. Aber	32	125	5	11	3	3.97
CF	B. Tuttle	530	.266	7	58	364	18	6	3	2.7	.985	D. Marlowe	38	84	5	4	2	4.18
LF	J. Delsing	371	.248	6	38	221	5	1	0	2.1	.996							
C	F. House	352	.250	9	38	434	56	4	7	4.6	.992							
OF	B. Nieman	251	.263	8	35	119	2	2	0	2.0	.984							
1B	W. Belardi	250	.232	11	24	636	51	8	54	8.8	.988							
2B	F. Hatfield	218	.294	2	25	114	126	7	29	4.6	.972							
C	R. Wilson	170	.282	2	22	245	25	1	7	5.1	.996							

AMERICAN LEAGUE 1954, *cont.*

Washington

W-66 L-88

Bucky Harris

POS	Player	AB	BA	HR	RBI	PO	A	E	DP	TC/G	FA	Pitcher	G	IP	W	L	SV	ERA
1B	M. Vernon	597	.290	20	97	**1365**	76	11	**144**	**9.8**	**.992**	B. Porterfield	32	244	13	15	0	3.32
2B	W. Terwilliger	337	.208	3	24	213	243	13	72	5.2	.972	M. McDermott	30	196	7	15	1	3.44
SS	P. Runnels	488	.268	3	56	174	313	24	69	4.8	.953	J. Schmitz	29	185	11	8	1	2.91
3B	E. Yost	539	.256	11	47	**170**	**347**	17	29	3.4	.968	C. Stobbs	31	182	11	11	0	4.10
RF	T. Umphlett	342	.219	1	33	169	13	2	4	1.8	.989	D. Stone	31	179	12	10	0	3.22
CF	J. Busby	628	.298	7	80	491	6	6	1	3.2	.988	C. Pascual	48	119	4	7	3	4.22
LF	R. Sievers	514	.232	24	102	296	10	9	1	2.4	.971	S. Shea	23	71	2	9	0	6.18
C	E. Fitz Gerald	360	.289	4	40	396	38	12	5	4.2	.973							
OF	T. Wright	171	.246	1	17	84	0	0	0	2.0	1.000							
2B	J. Pesky	158	.253	0	9	92	91	4	22	5.1	.979							
C	J. Tipton	157	.223	1	10	220	30	2	6	4.8	.992							
SS	J. Snyder	154	.234	0	17	81	145	5	31	4.8	.978							

Baltimore

W-54 L-100

Jimmy Dykes

POS	Player	AB	BA	HR	RBI	PO	A	E	DP	TC/G	FA	Pitcher	G	IP	W	L	SV	ERA
1B	E. Waitkus	311	.283	2	33	618	48	0	72	8.5	1.000	B. Turley	35	247	14	15	0	3.46
2B	B. Young	432	.245	4	24	299	310	15	76	4.9	.976	J. Coleman	33	221	13	17	0	3.50
SS	B. Hunter	411	.243	2	27	249	333	**32**	76	5.0	.948	D. Larsen	29	202	3	**21**	0	4.37
3B	V. Stephens	365	.285	8	46	102	186	10	19	3.1	.966	D. Pillette	25	179	10	14	0	3.12
RF	C. Abrams	423	.293	6	25	248	6	6	1	2.3	.977	L. Kretlow	32	167	6	11	0	4.37
CF	C. Diering	418	.258	2	29	330	17	6	6	3.0	.983	B. Chakales	38	89	3	7	3	3.73
LF	J. Fridley	240	.246	4	36	132	1	2	0	2.0	.985							
C	C. Courtney	397	.270	4	37	539	53	6	8	5.4	.990							
3B	B. Kennedy	323	.251	6	45	81	131	14	10	3.2	.938							
1B	D. Kryhoski	300	.260	1	34	591	52	5	52	9.4	.992							
OF	G. Coan	265	.279	2	20	148	1	5	0	2.3	.968							
OF	S. Mele	230	.239	5	32	97	5	4	1	1.7	.962							
SS	J. Brideweser	204	.265	0	12	67	103	10	22	3.8	.944							

Philadelphia

W-51 L-103

Eddie Joost

POS	Player	AB	BA	HR	RBI	PO	A	E	DP	TC/G	FA	Pitcher	G	IP	W	L	SV	ERA
1B	L. Limmer	316	.231	14	32	597	56	8	63	8.4	.988	A. Portocarrero	34	248	9	18	0	4.06
2B	S. Jacobs	508	.258	0	26	347	300	17	98	5.1	.974	A. Kellner	27	174	6	17	0	5.39
SS	J. De Maestri	539	.230	8	40	285	406	25	90	5.0	.965	M. Fricano	37	152	5	11	1	5.16
3B	J. Finigan	487	.302	7	51	151	305	**25**	**34**	3.5	.948	B. Trice	19	119	7	8	0	5.60
RF	B. Renna	422	.232	13	53	226	13	7	5	2.1	.972	S. Dixon	38*	107	5	7	4	4.86
CF	B. Wilson	323	.238	15	33	270	7	3	4	3.1	.989	J. Gray	18	105	3	12	0	6.51
LF	V. Power	462	.255	8	38	256	13	4	3	2.7	.985	C. Bishop	20	96	4	6	1	4.41
C	J. Astroth	226	.221	1	23	300	39	4	5	4.8	.988	M. Burtschy	46	95	5	4	4	3.80
OF	G. Zernial	336	.250	14	62	180	4	9	1	2.1	.953							
1B	D. Bollweg	268	.224	5	24	530	51	**13**	55	8.4	.978							
OF	E. Valo	224	.214	1	33	135	3	5	1	2.3	.965							
23	P. Suder	205	.200	0	16	97	134	8	25		.967							
C	B. Shantz	164	.256	1	17	170	28	5	1	4.0	.975							

BATTING AND BASE RUNNING LEADERS

Batting Average
- B. Avila, CLE .341
- M. Minoso, CHI .320
- I. Noren, NY .319
- N. Fox, CHI .319
- Y. Berra, NY .307

Slugging Average
- T. Williams, BOS .635
- M. Minoso, CHI .535
- M. Mantle, NY .525
- A. Rosen, CLE .506
- M. Vernon, WAS .492

Home Runs
- L. Doby, CLE 32
- T. Williams, BOS 29
- M. Mantle, NY 27
- J. Jensen, BOS 25
- A. Rosen, CLE 24
- R. Sievers, WAS 24

Total Bases
- M. Minoso, CHI 304
- M. Vernon, WAS 294
- M. Mantle, NY 285
- Y. Berra, NY 285
- L. Doby, CLE 279

Runs Batted In
- L. Doby, CLE 126
- Y. Berra, NY 125
- J. Jensen, BOS 117
- M. Minoso, CHI 116

Stolen Bases
- J. Jensen, BOS 22
- J. Rivera, CHI 18
- M. Minoso, CHI 18
- S. Jacobs, PHI 17
- J. Busby, WAS 17

Hits
- N. Fox, CHI 201
- H. Kuenn, DET 201
- B. Avila, CLE 189
- J. Busby, WAS 187

Base on Balls
- T. Williams, BOS 136
- E. Yost, WAS 131
- M. Mantle, NY 102
- A. Smith, CLE 88

Home Run Percentage
- T. Williams, BOS 7.5
- L. Doby, CLE 5.5
- A. Rosen, CLE 5.2
- M. Mantle, NY 5.0

Runs
- M. Mantle, NY 129
- M. Minoso, CHI 119
- B. Avila, CLE 112
- N. Fox, CHI 111

Doubles
- M. Vernon, WAS 33
- A. Smith, CLE 29
- M. Minoso, CHI 29

Triples
- M. Minoso, CHI 18
- P. Runnels, WAS 15
- M. Vernon, WAS 14
- M. Mantle, NY 12

PITCHING LEADERS

Winning Percentage
- S. Consuegra, CHI .842
- B. Grim, NY .769
- B. Lemon, CLE .767
- M. Garcia, CLE .704
- A. Houtteman, CLE .682

Earned Run Average
- M. Garcia, CLE 2.64
- S. Consuegra, CHI 2.69
- B. Lemon, CLE 2.72
- E. Wynn, CLE 2.73
- S. Gromek, DET 2.74

Wins
- B. Lemon, CLE 23
- E. Wynn, CLE 23
- B. Grim, NY 20
- M. Garcia, CLE 19
- V. Trucks, CHI 19

Saves
- J. Sain, NY 22
- E. Kinder, BOS 15
- R. Narleski, CLE 13

Strikeouts
- B. Turley, BAL 185
- E. Wynn, CLE 155
- V. Trucks, CHI 152
- B. Pierce, CHI 148
- J. Harshman, CHI 134

Complete Games
- B. Porterfield, WAS 21
- B. Lemon, CLE 21
- E. Wynn, CLE 20
- S. Gromek, DET 17

Fewest Hits/9 Innings
- B. Turley, BAL 6.48
- W. Ford, NY 7.26
- E. Wynn, CLE 7.48
- J. Coleman, BAL 7.48

Shutouts
- V. Trucks, CHI 5
- M. Garcia, CLE 5

Fewest Walks/9 Innings
- E. Lopat, NY 1.75
- S. Gromek, DET 2.03
- S. Consuegra, CHI 2.05
- N. Garver, DET 2.27

Most Strikeouts/9 Inn.
- B. Pierce, CHI 7.06
- J. Harshman, CHI 6.81
- B. Turley, BAL 6.73
- B. Hoeft, DET 5.86

Innings
- E. Wynn, CLE 271
- V. Trucks, CHI 265
- M. Garcia, CLE 259
- B. Lemon, CLE 258

Games Pitched
- S. Dixon, WAS, PHI 54
- E. Kinder, BOS 48
- C. Pascual, WAS 48
- M. Martin, PHI, CHI 48

							Batting						Fielding			Pitching					
	W	L	PCT	GB	R	OR	2B	3B	HR	BA	SA	SB	E	DP	FA	CG	BB	SO	ShO	SV	ERA
Cleveland	111	43	.721		746	**504**	188	39	**156**	.262	.403	30	128	148	.979	**77**	**486**	678	12	36	**2.78**
New York	103	51	.669	8	**805**	563	215	59	133	**.268**	**.408**	34	126	**198**	.979	51	552	655	15	**37**	3.26
Chicago	94	60	.610	17	711	521	203	47	94	.267	.379	**98**	**108**	149	**.982**	60	517	701	**21**	33	3.05
Boston	69	85	.448	42	700	728	**244**	41	123	.266	.395	51	176	163	.972	41	612	**707**	9	22	4.01
Detroit	68	86	.442	43	584	664	215	41	90	.258	.367	48	129	131	.978	58	506	603	13	13	3.81
Washington	66	88	.429	45	632	680	188	**69**	81	.246	.355	37	137	172	.977	69	573	562	10	7	3.84
Baltimore	54	100	.351	57	483	668	195	49	52	.251	.338	30	147	152	.975	58	688	668	6	8	3.88
Philadelphia	51	103	.331	60	542	875	191	41	94	.236	.342	30	169	163	.972	49	685	555	3	13	5.18
					5203	5203	1639	386	823	.257	.373	358	1120	1276	.977	463	4619	5129	89	169	3.73

NATIONAL LEAGUE 1955

Team	POS	Player	AB	BA	HR	RBI	PO	A	E	DP	TC/G	FA	Pitcher	G	IP	W	L	SV	ERA
Brooklyn	1B	G. Hodges	546	.289	27	102	1274	105	12	126	**10.0**	.991	D. Newcombe	34	234	20	5	0	3.20
W-98 L-55	2B	J. Gilliam	538	.249	7	40	213	269	16	64	5.0	.968	C. Erskine	31	195	11	8	1	3.79
Walter Alston	SS	P. Reese	553	.282	10	61	239	404	23	86	4.7	.965	J. Podres	27	159	9	10	0	3.95
	3B	J. Robinson	317	.256	8	36	74	180	9	18	3.1	.966	C. Labine	**60**	144	13	5	11	3.24
	RF	C. Furillo	523	.314	26	95	249	10	5	4	1.9	.981	B. Loes	22	128	10	4	0	3.59
	CF	D. Snider	538	.309	42	**136**	348	9	4	0	2.5	.989	K. Spooner	29	99	8	6	2	3.65
	LF	S. Amoros	388	.247	10	51	201	10	6	1	2.0	.972	R. Craig	21	91	5	3	2	2.78
	C	R. Campanella	446	.318	32	107	**672**	54	6	8	**6.0**	.992	E. Roebuck	47	84	5	6	12	4.71
	2S	D. Zimmer	280	.239	15	50	182	199	12	63		.969	D. Bessent	24	63	8	1	3	2.70
	3B	D. Hoak	279	.240	5	19	82	183	11	15	3.5	.960							
	P	D. Newcombe	117	.359	7	23	15	24	4	5	1.3	.907							
Milwaukee	1B	G. Crowe	303	.281	15	55	677	61	8	62	9.4	.989	W. Spahn	39	246	17	14	1	3.26
W-85 L-69	2B	D. O'Connell	453	.225	6	40	309	357	13	76	**6.0**	.981	L. Burdette	42	230	13	8	0	4.03
Charlie Grimm	SS	J. Logan	595	.297	13	83	268	**511**	30	100	5.3	.963	B. Buhl	38	202	13	11	1	3.21
	3B	E. Mathews	499	.289	41	101	140	**280**	21	23	**3.2**	.952	G. Conley	22	158	11	7	0	4.16
	RF	H. Aaron	602	.314	27	106	254	9	9	2	2.2	.967	C. Nichols	34	144	9	8	1	4.00
	CF	B. Bruton	**636**	.275	9	47	412	17	14	6	3.0	.968	R. Crone	33	140	10	9	0	3.46
	LF	B. Thomson	343	.257	12	56	182	5	6	0	2.1	.969	E. Johnson	40	92	5	7	4	3.42
	C	D. Crandall	440	.236	26	62	611	67	**10**	8	5.3	.985							
	1B	J. Adcock	288	.264	15	45	725	44	8	68	10.0	.990							
	OF	A. Pafko	252	.266	5	34	96	1	2	0	1.7	.980							
	OF	C. Tanner	243	.247	6	27	101	4	2	0	1.7	.981							
New York	1B	G. Harris	263	.232	12	36	617	50	12	65	9.1	.982	J. Antonelli	38	235	14	16	1	3.33
W-80 L-74	2B	W. Terwilliger	257	.257	1	18	212	240	7	70	5.9	.985	J. Hearn	39	227	14	16	0	3.73
Leo Durocher	SS	A. Dark	475	.282	9	45	213	324	21	70	4.9	.962	R. Gomez	33	185	9	10	1	4.56
	3B	H. Thompson	432	.245	17	63	104	262	**22**	23	3.1	.943	S. Maglie	23	130	9	5	0	3.75
	RF	D. Mueller	605	.306	8	83	239	5	6	1	1.7	.976	D. Liddle	33	106	10	4	1	4.23
	CF	W. Mays	580	.319	**51**	127	407	23	8	8	2.9	.982	H. Wilhelm	59	103	4	1	0	3.93
	LF	W. Lockman	576	.273	15	49	167	4	3	1	2.1	.983	W. McCall	42	95	6	5	3	3.69
	C	R. Katt	326	.215	7	28	482	45	7	7	4.4	.987	R. Monzant	28	95	4	8	0	3.99
	2B	D. Williams	247	.251	4	15	139	162	10	39	4.4	.968	M. Grissom	55	89	5	4	8	2.92
	UT	B. Hofman	207	.266	10	28	259	59	1	30		.997							
	OF	D. Rhodes	187	.305	6	32	68	2	1	0	1.6	.986							
	SS	B. Gardner	187	.203	3	17	65	122	12	28	5.2	.940							
	30	S. Gordon	144	.243	7	25	57	61	0	6		1.000							
Philadelphia	1B	M. Blaylock	259	.208	3	24	528	44	5	35	7.5	.991	R. Roberts	41	**305**	**23**	14	3	3.28
W-77 L-77	2B	B. Morgan	483	.232	10	49	192	204	8	46	4.6	.980	M. Dickson	36	216	12	11	0	3.50
Mayo Smith	SS	R. Smalley	260	.196	7	39	136	205	9	32	4.0	.974	H. Wehmeier	31	194	10	12	0	4.41
	3B	W. Jones	516	.258	16	81	**202**	235	18	22	3.1	**.960**	C. Simmons	25	130	8	8	0	4.92
	RF	J. Greengrass	323	.272	12	37	159	10	2	0	2.1	.988	J. Meyer	50	110	6	11	**16**	3.43
	CF	R. Ashburn	533	**.338**	3	42	387	10	7	3	2.9	.983	B. Miller	40	90	8	4	1	2.41
	LF	D. Ennis	564	.296	29	120	298	9	4	2	2.1	.987							
	C	A. Seminick	289	.246	11	34	435	45	3	6	5.5	.994*							
	2B	G. Hamner	405	.257	5	43	152	183	14	39	4.3	.960							
	C	S. Lopata	303	.271	22	58	332	37	2	9	5.6	.995							
	OF	G. Gorbous	224	.237	4	23	113	10	2	2	2.2	.984							
Cincinnati	1B	T. Kluszewski	612	.314	47	113	**1388**	86	8	**153**	9.7	**.995**	J. Nuxhall	50	257	17	12	3	3.47
W-75 L-79	2B	J. Temple	588	.281	0	50	408	410	24	**119**	5.7	.971	A. Fowler	46	208	11	10	2	3.90
Birdie Tebbetts	SS	R. McMillan	470	.268	1	37	290	495	25	**111**	5.4	.969	J. Klippstein	39	138	9	10	0	3.39
	3B	R. Bridges	168	.286	1	18	48	88	5	7	2.4	.965	J. Collum	32	134	9	8	1	3.63
	RF	W. Post	601	.309	40	109	298	13	7	2	2.1	.978	G. Staley	30	120	5	8	0	4.66
	CF	G. Bell	610	.308	27	104	364	4	5	0	2.4	.987	R. Minarcin	41	116	5	9	1	4.90
	LF	S. Palys	222	.230	7	30	116	3	1	0	2.2	.992	J. Black	32	102	5	2	3	4.22
	C	S. Burgess	421	.306	20	77	457	35	7	6	4.7	.986	H. Freeman	52	92	7	4	11	2.16
	03	R. Jablonski	221	.240	9	28	69	46	11	3		.913							
	30	C. Harmon	198	.253	5	28	114	50	6	4		.965							
	OF	B. Thurman	152	.217	7	22	54	2	3	0	1.6	.949							
	3B	B. Adams	150	.273	2	20	35	88	4	11	3.0	.969							
Chicago	1B	D. Fondy	574	.265	17	65	1304	**107**	**13**	135	9.7	.991	S. Jones	36	242	14	**20**	0	4.10
W-72 L-81	2B	G. Baker	609	.268	11	52	**432**	**444**	**30**	114	5.9	.967	B. Rush	33	234	13	11	0	3.50
Stan Hack	SS	E. Banks	596	.295	44	117	290	482	22	102	5.2	**.972**	W. Hacker	35	213	11	15	3	4.27
	3B	R. Jackson	499	.265	21	70	125	247	20	**26**	2.9	.949	P. Minner	22	158	9	9	0	3.48
	RF	J. King	301	.256	11	45	184	10	2	2	2.1	.990	J. Davis	42	134	7	11	3	4.44
	CF	E. Miksis	481	.235	9	41	267	6	3	1	2.5	.989	H. Jeffcoat	50	101	8	6	6	2.95
	LF	H. Sauer	261	.211	12	28	122	4	2	1	1.9	.984	H. Pollet	24	61	4	3	5	5.61
	C	H. Chiti	338	.231	11	41	495	**69**	9	**10**	5.1	.984							
	OF	F. Baumholtz	280	.289	1	27	131	3	1	1	2.1	.993							
	OF	B. Speake	261	.218	12	43	90	4	4	1	1.8	.959							
	OF	J. Bolger	160	.206	0	7	125	1	6	0	2.6	.955							
St. Louis	1B	S. Musial	562	.319	33	108	925	92	8	93	9.3	.992	H. Haddix	37	208	12	16	1	4.46
W-68 L-86	2B	R. Schoendienst	553	.268	11	51	296	381	10	96	4.8	**.985**	L. Jackson	37	177	9	14	2	4.31
Eddie Stanky	SS	A. Grammas	366	.240	3	25	235	340	19	76	4.7	.968	L. Arroyo	35	159	11	8	0	4.19
W-17 L-19	3B	K. Boyer	530	.264	18	62	124	253	19	24	2.8	.952	T. Poholsky	30	151	9	11	0	3.81
Harry Walker	RF	W. Moon	593	.295	19	76	188	5	5	1	2.0	.975	W. Schmidt	20	130	7	6	0	2.78
W-51 L-67	CF	B. Virdon	534	.281	17	68	339	7	12	1	2.5	.966	B. Lawrence	46	96	3	8	1	6.56
	LF	R. Repulski	512	.270	23	73	260	5	7	1	1.9	.974	P. LaPalme	56	92	4	3	3	2.75
	C	B. Sarni	325	.255	3	34	482	39	7	8	5.3	.987							
	32	S. Hemus	206	.243	5	21	56	90	5	10		.967							
	C	N. Burbrink	170	.276	0	15	261	24	6	4	5.3	.979							

NATIONAL LEAGUE 1955, *cont.*

Pittsburgh

W-60 L-94

Fred Haney

POS	Player	AB	BA	HR	RBI	PO	A	E	DP	TC/G	FA
1B	D. Long	419	.291	16	79	968	97	**13**	114	9.1	.988
2B	J. O'Brien	278	.299	1	25	185	220	13	53	5.4	.969
SS	D. Groat	521	.267	4	51	**330**	450	**32**	107	**5.4**	.961
3B	G. Freese	455	.253	14	44	55	127	11	16	3.0	.943
RF	R. Clemente	474	.255	5	47	253	18	6	5	2.3	.978
CF	E. O'Brien	236	.233	0	8	132	8	1	1	2.5	.993
LF	F. Thomas	510	.245	25	72	307	8	5	3	2.3	.984
C	J. Shepard	264	.239	2	23	288	34	6	6	4.3	.982
OF	J. Lynch	282	.284	5	28	104	11	6	3	1.7	.950
UT	D. Cole	239	.226	0	21	103	158	10	25		.963
C	T. Atwell	207	.213	1	18	334	24	3	3	5.4	.992
1B	P. Ward	179	.212	5	25	384	35	1	41	8.8	.998
3B	G. Freese	179	.257	3	22	50	82	9	3	2.8	.936
OF	R. Mejias	167	.216	3	21	67	8	6	2	1.9	.926

Pitcher	G	IP	W	L	SV	ERA
V. Law	43	201	10	10	1	3.81
B. Friend	44	200	14	9	2	**2.83**
M. Surkont	35	166	7	14	2	5.57
R. Kline	36	137	6	13	2	4.15
D. Littlefield	35	130	5	12	0	5.12
R. Face	42	126	5	7	5	3.58
L. Donoso	25	95	4	6	1	5.31
D. Hall	15	94	6	6	1	3.91
B. Purkey	14	68	2	7	1	5.32

BATTING AND BASE RUNNING LEADERS

Batting Average

R. Ashburn, PHI	.338
W. Mays, NY	.319
S. Musial, STL	.319
R. Campanella, BKN	.318
H. Aaron, MIL	.314

Slugging Average

W. Mays, NY	.659
D. Snider, BKN	.628
E. Mathews, MIL	.601
E. Banks, CHI	.596
T. Kluszewski, CIN	.585

Home Runs

W. Mays, NY	51
T. Kluszewski, CIN	47
E. Banks, CHI	44
D. Snider, BKN	42
E. Mathews, MIL	41

Total Bases

W. Mays, NY	382
T. Kluszewski, CIN	358
E. Banks, CHI	355
W. Post, CIN	345
D. Snider, BKN	338

Runs Batted In

D. Snider, BKN	136
W. Mays, NY	127
D. Ennis, PHI	120
E. Banks, CHI	117
T. Kluszewski, CIN	113

Stolen Bases

B. Bruton, MIL	25
W. Mays, NY	24
K. Boyer, STL	22
J. Temple, CIN	19
J. Gilliam, BKN	15

Hits

T. Kluszewski, CIN	192
H. Aaron, MIL	189
G. Bell, CIN	188
W. Post, CIN	186

Base on Balls

E. Mathews, MIL	109
R. Ashburn, PHI	105
D. Snider, BKN	104
H. Thompson, NY	84

Home Run Percentage

W. Mays, NY	8.8
E. Mathews, MIL	8.2
D. Snider, BKN	7.8
T. Kluszewski, CIN	7.7

Runs

D. Snider, BKN	126
W. Mays, NY	123
W. Post, CIN	116
T. Kluszewski, CIN	116

Doubles

J. Logan, MIL	37
H. Aaron, MIL	37
D. Snider, BKN	34
W. Post, CIN	33

Triples

D. Long, PIT	13
W. Mays, NY	13
B. Bruton, MIL	12
R. Clemente, PIT	11

PITCHING LEADERS

Winning Percentage

D. Newcombe, BKN	.800
R. Roberts, PHI	.622
J. Nuxhall, CIN	.586
W. Spahn, MIL	.548

Earned Run Average

B. Friend, PIT	2.83
D. Newcombe, BKN	3.20
B. Buhl, MIL	3.21
W. Spahn, MIL	3.26
R. Roberts, PHI	3.28

Wins

R. Roberts, PHI	23
D. Newcombe, BKN	20
W. Spahn, MIL	17
J. Nuxhall, CIN	17

Saves

J. Meyer, PHI	16
E. Roebuck, BKN	12
H. Freeman, CIN	11
C. Labine, BKN	11
M. Grissom, NY	8

Strikeouts

S. Jones, CHI	198
R. Roberts, PHI	160
H. Haddix, STL	150
D. Newcombe, BKN	143
J. Antonelli, NY	143

Complete Games

R. Roberts, PHI	26
D. Newcombe, BKN	17
W. Spahn, MIL	16
J. Nuxhall, CIN	14
B. Rush, CHI	14
J. Antonelli, NY	14

Fewest Hits/9 Innings

S. Jones, CHI	6.52
B. Buhl, MIL	7.50
B. Rush, CHI	7.85
J. Antonelli, NY	7.88

Shutouts

J. Nuxhall, CIN	5
M. Dickson, PHI	4
S. Jones, CHI	4

Fewest Walks/9 Innings

D. Newcombe, BKN	1.46
R. Roberts, PHI	1.56
W. Hacker, CHI	1.82
B. Friend, PIT	2.34

Most Strikeouts/9 Inn.

S. Jones, CHI	7.37
H. Haddix, STL	6.49
J. Podres, BKN	6.44
G. Conley, MIL	6.09

Innings

R. Roberts, PHI	305
J. Nuxhall, CIN	257
W. Spahn, MIL	246
S. Jones, CHI	242

Games Pitched

C. Labine, BKN	60
H. Wilhelm, NY	59
P. LaPalme, STL	56
M. Grissom, NY	55

							Batting						Fielding			Pitching					
	W	L	PCT	GB	R	OR	2B	3B	HR	BA	SA	SB	E	DP	FA	CG	BB	SO	ShO	SV	ERA
Brooklyn	98	55	.641		**857**	**650**	**230**	44	**201**	**.271**	**.448**	**79**	133	156	.978	46	483	**773**	11	**37**	**3.68**
Milwaukee	85	69	.552	13.5	743	668	219	55	182	.261	.427	42	152	155	.975	**61**	591	654	5	12	3.85
New York	80	74	.519	18.5	702	673	173	34	169	.260	.402	38	142	165	.976	52	560	721	6	14	3.77
Philadelphia	77	77	.500	21.5	675	666	214	50	132	.255	.395	44	**110**	117	**.981**	58	477	657	11	21	3.93
Cincinnati	75	79	.487	23.5	761	684	216	28	181	.270	.425	51	139	169	.977	38	**443**	576	**12**	22	3.95
Chicago	72	81	.471	26	626	713	187	55	164	.247	.398	37	147	147	.975	47	601	686	10	23	4.17
St. Louis	68	86	.442	30.5	654	757	228	36	143	.261	.400	64	146	152	.975	42	549	730	10	15	4.56
Pittsburgh	60	94	.390	38.5	560	767	210	**60**	91	.244	.361	22	166	**175**	.972	41	536	622	5	16	4.39
					5578	5578	1677	362	1263	.259	.407	377	1135	1236	.976	385	4240	5419	70	160	4.04

AMERICAN LEAGUE 1955

New York

W-96 L-58

Casey Stengel

POS	Player	AB	BA	HR	RBI	PO	A	E	DP	TC/G	FA
1B	B. Skowron	288	.319	12	61	517	37	6	63	7.6	.989
2B	G. McDougald	533	.285	13	53	352	348	11	**119**	5.6	**.985**
SS	B. Hunter	255	.227	3	20	115	249	16	60	3.9	.958
3B	A. Carey	510	.257	7	47	**154**	**301**	22	**37**	**3.5**	.954
RF	H. Bauer	492	.278	20	53	248	13	5	3	2.0	.981
CF	M. Mantle	517	.306	**37**	99	372	11	2	2	2.7	.995
LF	I. Noren	371	.253	8	59	238	9	5	0	2.0	.980
C	Y. Berra	541	.272	27	108	**721**	54	**13**	10	5.4	.984
OF	E. Howard	279	.290	10	43	124	10	3	3	1.8	.978
1B	J. Collins	278	.234	13	45	395	42	1	63	6.0	.998
1B	E. Robinson	173	.208	16	42	390	20	2	35	9.0	.995
OF	B. Cerv	85	.341	3	22	25	1	0	0	1.3	1.000

Pitcher	G	IP	W	L	SV	ERA
W. Ford	39	254	**18**	7	2	2.63
B. Turley	36	247	17	13	1	3.06
T. Byrne	27	160	16	5	2	3.15
J. Kucks	29	127	8	7	0	3.41
D. Larsen	19	97	9	2	2	3.06
B. Grim	26	92	7	5	4	4.19
E. Lopat	16	87	4	8	0	3.74
J. Konstanty	45	74	7	2	11	2.32
T. Morgan	40	72	7	3	10	3.25

AMERICAN LEAGUE 1955, *cont.*

Team	POS	Player	AB	BA	HR	RBI	PO	A	E	DP	TC/G	FA	Pitcher	G	IP	W	L	SV	ERA
Cleveland	1B	V. Wertz	257	.253	14	55	449	33	8	49	7.8	.984	E. Wynn	32	230	17	11	0	2.82
W-93 L-61	2B	B. Avila	537	.272	13	61	348	342	13	108	5.0	.982	H. Score	33	227	16	10	0	2.85
Al Lopez	SS	G. Strickland	388	.209	2	34	221	360	14	84	4.6	**.976**	B. Lemon	35	211	**18**	10	2	3.88
	3B	A. Rosen	492	.244	21	81	119	195	12	17	3.1	.963	M. Garcia	38	211	11	13	3	4.02
	RF	A. Smith	607	.306	22	77	206	5	5	1	1.8	.977	A. Houtteman	35	124	10	6	0	3.98
	CF	L. Doby	491	.291	26	75	313	6	2	1	2.5	.994	R. Narleski	**60**	112	9	1	**19**	3.71
	LF	R. Kiner	321	.243	18	54	141	2	2	0	1.7	.986	D. Mossi	57	82	4	3	9	2.42
	C	J. Hegan	304	.220	9	40	583	34	2	**12**	**5.6**	**.997**							
	OF	G. Woodling	259	.278	5	35	129	4	1	0	1.9	.993*							
	OF	D. Pope	104	.298	6	22	62	0	3	0	2.1	.954							
Chicago	1B	W. Dropo	453	.280	19	79	1101	62	6	104	8.4	.995	B. Pierce	33	206	15	10	1	**1.97**
W-91 L-63	2B	N. Fox	**636**	.311	6	59	**399**	**483**	**24**	110	**5.9**	.974	D. Donovan	29	187	15	9	0	3.32
Marty Marion	SS	C. Carrasquel	523	.256	11	52	222	424	18	81	4.6	.973	J. Harshman	32	179	11	7	0	3.36
	3B	G. Kell	429	.312	8	81	83	165	6	8	2.4	**.976**	V. Trucks	32	175	13	8	0	3.96
	RF	J. Rivera	454	.264	10	52	288	22	6	7	2.2	.981	S. Consuegra	44	126	6	5	7	2.64
	CF	J. Busby	337	.243	1	27	243	6	4	3	2.6	.984	C. Johnson	17	99	7	4	0	3.45
	LF	M. Minoso	517	.288	10	70	287	19	9	3	2.3	.971	H. Byrd	25	91	4	6	1	4.65
	C	S. Lollar	426	.261	16	61	664	62	4	**12**	5.4	.995	M. Fornieles	26	86	6	3	2	3.86
	OF	B. Nieman	272	.283	11	53	118	4	3	2	1.6	.976	D. Howell	35	74	8	3	9	2.93
	3B	B. Kennedy	214	.304	9	43	32	73	7	10	2.0	.938							
Boston	1B	N. Zauchin	477	.239	27	93	1137	84	6	106	9.7	**.995**	F. Sullivan	35	**260**	**18**	13	0	2.91
W-84 L-70	2B	B. Goodman	599	.294	0	52	348	373	23	93	5.2	.969	W. Nixon	31	208	12	10	0	4.07
Pinky Higgins	SS	B. Klaus	541	.283	7	60	207	391	28	55	5.0	.955	T. Brewer	31	193	11	10	0	4.20
	3B	G. Hatton	380	.245	4	49	97	225	8	22	3.0	.976	G. Susce	29	144	9	7	1	3.06
	RF	J. Jensen	574	.275	26	**116**	281	11	7	3	2.0	.977	I. Delock	29	144	9	7	3	3.76
	CF	J. Piersall	515	.283	13	62	425	7	3	2	3.0	.993	L. Kiely	33	90	3	3	6	2.80
	LF	T. Williams	320	.356	28	83	170	5	2	0	1.9	.989	T. Hurd	43	81	8	6	5	3.01
	C	S. White	544	.261	11	64	671	**71**	12	8	5.3	.984	E. Kinder	43	67	5	5	18	2.84
	OF	G. Stephens	157	.293	3	18	82	7	5	1	1.3	.947							
	OF	F. Throneberry	144	.257	6	27	69	3	3	0	2.2	.960							
Detroit	1B	E. Torgeson	300	.283	9	50	695	53	6	79	9.1	.992	F. Lary	36	235	14	15	1	3.10
W-79 L-75	2B	F. Hatfield	413	.232	8	33	216	251	12	74	5.2	.975	N. Garver	33	231	12	16	0	3.98
Bucky Harris	SS	H. Kuenn	620	.306	8	62	253	378	29	83	4.7	.956	B. Hoeft	32	220	16	7	0	2.99
	3B	R. Boone	500	.284	20	**116**	135	252	19	33	3.2	.953	S. Gromek	28	181	13	10	0	3.98
	RF	A. Kaline	588	**.340**	27	102	306	14	7	4	2.2	.979	D. Maas	18	87	5	6	0	4.88
	CF	B. Tuttle	603	.279	14	78	442	12	7	2	3.0	.985	B. Birrer	36	80	4	3	3	4.15
	LF	J. Delsing	356	.239	10	60	178	3	1	1	1.8	.995	A. Aber	39	80	6	3	3	3.38
	C	F. House	328	.259	15	53	423	35	6	5	5.0	.987							
	C	R. Wilson	241	.220	2	17	292	25	5	5	4.5	.984							
	2B	H. Malmberg	208	.216	0	19	155	181	5	42	5.2	.985							
	OF	B. Phillips	184	.234	3	23	128	2	1	0	2.0	.992							
	1B	F. Fain	140	.264	2	23	370	29	5	42	9.2	.988							
	1B	J. Phillips	117	.316	1	20	236	13	2	16	7.2	.992							
Kansas City	1B	V. Power	596	.319	19	76	**1281**	**130**	**10**	**140**	**9.9**	.993	A. Ditmar	35	175	12	12	1	5.03
W-63 L-91	2B	J. Finigan	545	.255	9	68	236	228	12	72	5.3	.975	A. Kellner	30	163	11	8	0	4.20
Lou Boudreau	SS	J. De Maestri	457	.249	6	37	206	358	21	78	4.8	.964	B. Shantz	23	125	5	10	0	4.54
	3B	H. Lopez	483	.290	15	68	104	233	**23**	26	3.9	.936	A. Ceccarelli	31	124	4	7	0	5.31
	RF	E. Slaughter	267	.322	5	34	126	5	2	2	1.7	.985	A. Portocarrero	24	111	5	9	0	4.77
	CF	H. Simpson	396	.301	5	52	262	5	6	2	2.7	.978	T. Gorman	57	109	7	6	18	3.55
	LF	G. Zernial	413	.254	30	84	231	9	9	4	2.4	.964	V. Raschi	20	101	4	6	0	5.42
	C	J. Astroth	274	.252	5	23	420	50	5	9	4.8	.989	C. Boyer	30	98	5	5	0	6.22
	OF	E. Valo	283	.364	3	37	147	5	2	2	2.1	.987							
	OF	B. Wilson	273	.223	15	38	186	4	6	0	2.4	.969							
	OF	B. Renna	249	.213	7	28	118	5	1	2	1.6	.992							
	C	B. Shantz	217	.258	1	12	261	27	3	8	3.7	.990							
Baltimore	1B	G. Triandos	481	.277	12	65	839	69	**10**	92	8.9	.989	J. Wilson	34	235	12	**18**	0	3.44
W-57 L-97	2B	F. Marsh	303	.218	2	19	197	158	6	51	4.8	.983	E. Palica	33	170	5	11	2	4.14
Paul Richards	SS	W. Miranda	487	.255	1	38	**300**	**481**	**34**	**101**	**5.3**	.958	R. Moore	46	152	10	10	6	3.92
	3B	W. Causey	175	.194	1	9	25	79	10	10	2.1	.912	B. Wight	19	117	6	8	2	2.45
	RF	C. Abrams	309	.243	6	32	191	7	3	1	2.1	.985	G. Zuverink	28	86	4	3	4	2.19
	CF	C. Diering	371	.256	3	31	242	6	6	2	2.4	.976	H. Dorish	35	66	3	3	6	3.15
	LF	D. Philley	311	.299	6	41	154	6	5	2	2.0	.970							
	C	H. Smith	424	.271	4	52	497	58	8	9	4.5	.986							
	OF	D. Pope	222	.248	1	30	152	3	0	1	2.1	1.000							
	OF	J. Dyck	197	.279	2	22	86	4	1	1	2.0	.989							
	32	B. Cox	194	.211	3	14	53	95	3	9		.980							
	2B	B. Young	186	.199	1	8	121	146	4	42	4.7	.985							
	OF	H. Evers	185	.238	6	30	106	1	1	0	2.0	.991							
	1B	B. Hale	182	.357	0	29	300	33	9	25	7.8	.974							
Washington	1B	M. Vernon	538	.301	14	85	1258	69	8	137	9.3	.994	D. Stone	43	180	6	13	1	4.15
W-53 L-101	2B	P. Runnels	503	.284	2	49	349	338	17	107	5.3	.976	B. Porterfield	30	178	10	17	0	4.45
Chuck Dressen	SS	J. Valdivielso	294	.221	2	28	160	317	22	69	5.3	.956	J. Schmitz	32	165	7	10	1	3.71
	3B	E. Yost	375	.243	7	48	100	217	19	22	3.1	.943	M. McDermott	31	156	10	10	1	3.75
	RF	C. Paula	351	.299	6	45	154	5	10	3	2.0	.941	C. Stobbs	41	140	4	14	3	5.00
	CF	T. Umphlett	323	.217	2	19	237	8	3	1	2.4	.988	P. Ramos	45	130	5	11	5	3.88
	LF	R. Sievers	509	.271	25	106	247	5	3	0	2.0	.988	C. Pascual	43	129	2	12	3	6.14
	C	E. Fitz Gerald	236	.237	4	19	304	30	6	5	4.7	.982	T. Abernathy	40	119	5	9	0	5.96
	OF	E. Oravetz	263	.270	0	25	117	1	4	0	2.1	.967							
	C	C. Courtney	238	.298	2	30	252	27	5	4	4.2	.982							
	OF	J. Busby	191	.230	6	14	132	1	1	0	2.9	.993							
	OF	J. Groth	183	.219	2	17	121	2	2	1	2.6	.984							

AMERICAN LEAGUE 1955, *cont.*

BATTING AND BASE RUNNING LEADERS

Batting Average

A. Kaline, DET	.340
V. Power, KC	.319
G. Kell, CHI	.312
N. Fox, CHI	.311
H. Kuenn, DET	.306

Slugging Average

M. Mantle, NY	.611
A. Kaline, DET	.546
G. Zernial, KC	.508
L. Doby, CLE	.505
V. Power, KC	.505

Home Runs

M. Mantle, NY	37
G. Zernial, KC	30
T. Williams, BOS	28
N. Zauchin, BOS	27
Y. Berra, NY	27
A. Kaline, DET	27

Total Bases

A. Kaline, DET	321
M. Mantle, NY	316
V. Power, KC	301
A. Smith, CLE	287
J. Jensen, BOS	275

Runs Batted In

R. Boone, DET	116
J. Jensen, BOS	116
Y. Berra, NY	108
R. Sievers, WAS	106
A. Kaline, DET	102

Stolen Bases

J. Rivera, CHI	25
M. Minoso, CHI	19
J. Jensen, BOS	16
J. Busby, WAS, CHI	12
A. Smith, CLE	11

Hits

A. Kaline, DET	200
N. Fox, CHI	198
V. Power, KC	190
H. Kuenn, DET	190

Base on Balls

M. Mantle, NY	113
B. Goodman, BOS	99
E. Yost, WAS	95
F. Fain, DET, CLE	94

Home Run Percentage

G. Zernial, KC	7.3
M. Mantle, NY	7.2
N. Zauchin, BOS	5.7
L. Doby, CLE	5.3

Runs

A. Smith, CLE	123
M. Mantle, NY	121
A. Kaline, DET	121
B. Tuttle, DET	102

Doubles

H. Kuenn, DET	38
V. Power, KC	34
B. Goodman, BOS	31
S. White, BOS	30
J. Finigan, KC	30

Triples

A. Carey, NY	11
M. Mantle, NY	11
V. Power, KC	10

PITCHING LEADERS

Winning Percentage

T. Byrne, NY	.762
W. Ford, NY	.720
B. Hoeft, DET	.696
B. Lemon, CLE	.643
D. Donovan, CHI	.625

Earned Run Average

B. Pierce, CHI	1.97
W. Ford, NY	2.63
E. Wynn, CLE	2.82
H. Score, CLE	2.85
F. Sullivan, BOS	2.91

Wins

B. Lemon, CLE	18
W. Ford, NY	18
F. Sullivan, BOS	18
E. Wynn, CLE	17
B. Turley, NY	17

Saves

R. Narleski, CLE	19
E. Kinder, BOS	18
T. Gorman, KC	18
J. Konstanty, NY	11
T. Morgan, NY	10

Strikeouts

H. Score, CLE	245
B. Turley, NY	210
B. Pierce, CHI	157
W. Ford, NY	137
B. Hoeft, DET	133

Complete Games

W. Ford, NY	18
B. Hoeft, DET	17

Fewest Hits/9 Innings

B. Turley, NY	6.13
H. Score, CLE	6.26
W. Ford, NY	6.67
B. Pierce, CHI	7.09

Shutouts

B. Hoeft, DET	7
B. Pierce, CHI	6
E. Wynn, CLE	6
B. Turley, NY	6

Fewest Walks/9 Innings

S. Gromek, DET	1.84
D. Donovan, CHI	2.31
M. Garcia, CLE	2.39
N. Garver, DET	2.61

Most Strikeouts/9 Inn.

H. Score, CLE	9.70
B. Turley, NY	7.66
B. Pierce, CHI	6.87
J. Harshman, CHI	5.82

Innings

F. Sullivan, BOS	260
W. Ford, NY	254
B. Turley, NY	247
F. Lary, DET	235
J. Wilson, BAL	235

Games Pitched

R. Narleski, CLE	60
T. Gorman, KC	57
D. Mossi, CLE	57
H. Dorish, CHI, BAL	48

							Batting						Fielding			Pitching					
	W	L	PCT	GB	R	OR	2B	3B	HR	BA	SA	SB	E	DP	FA	CG	BB	SO	ShO	SV	ERA
New York	96	58	.623		762	569	179	**55**	**175**	.260	**.418**	55	128	**180**	.978	52	689	731	**18**	33	**3.23**
Cleveland	93	61	.604	3	698	601	195	31	148	.257	.394	28	**108**	152	**.981**	45	558	**877**	13	**36**	3.39
Chicago	91	63	.591	5	725	**557**	204	36	116	**.268**	.388	**69**	111	147	**.981**	55	**499**	720	17	23	3.37
Boston	84	70	.545	12	755	652	**241**	39	137	.264	.402	43	136	140	.977	44	582	674	9	34	3.72
Detroit	79	75	.513	17	**775**	658	211	38	130	.266	.394	41	139	159	.976	**66**	517	629	15	12	3.79
Kansas City	63	91	.409	33	638	911	189	46	121	.261	.382	22	146	174	.976	29	707	572	7	23	5.35
Baltimore	57	97	.370	39	540	754	177	39	54	.240	.320	34	167	159	.972	35	625	595	9	22	4.21
Washington	53	101	.344	43	598	789	178	54	80	.248	.351	25	154	170	.974	37	637	607	9	16	4.62
					5491	5491	1574	338	961	.258	.381	317	1089	1281	.977	363	4814	5405	97	199	3.96

NATIONAL LEAGUE 1956

	POS	Player	AB	BA	HR	RBI	PO	A	E	DP	TC/G	FA	Pitcher	G	IP	W	L	SV	ERA
Brooklyn	1B	G. Hodges	550	.265	32	87	1190	103	10	105	9.4	.992	D. Newcombe	38	268	**27**	7	0	3.06
	2B	J. Gilliam	594	.300	6	43	233	326	11	64	5.6	.981	R. Craig	35	199	12	11	1	3.71
	SS	P. Reese	572	.257	9	46	263	367	23	79	4.8	.965	S. Maglie	28	191	13	5	0	2.87
W-93 L-61	3B	R. Jackson	307	.274	8	53	84	184	2	19	3.4	.993	C. Erskine	31	186	13	11	0	4.25
	RF	C. Furillo	523	.289	21	83	230	10	4	2	1.7	.984	C. Labine	62	116	10	6	**19**	3.35
Walter Alston	CF	D. Snider	542	.292	**43**	101	358	11	6	1	2.5	.984	D. Drysdale	25	99	5	5	0	2.64
	LF	S. Amoros	292	.260	16	58	123	3	6	0	1.5	.955	E. Roebuck	43	89	5	4	1	3.93
	C	R. Campanella	388	.219	20	73	**659**	49	11	3	5.9	.985	D. Bessent	38	79	4	3	9	2.50
	UT	J. Robinson	357	.275	10	43	169	230	9	37		.978							
	C	R. Walker	146	.212	3	20	184	20	3	4	4.8	.986							
Milwaukee	1B	J. Adcock	454	.291	38	103	1086	75	6	109	9.0	**.995**	W. Spahn	39	281	20	11	3	2.78
	2B	D. O'Connell	498	.239	2	42	295	381	10	98	5.0	.985	L. Burdette	39	256	19	10	1	**2.70**
	SS	J. Logan	545	.281	15	46	266	467	24	94	5.1	.968	B. Buhl	38	217	18	8	0	3.32
W-92 L-62	3B	E. Mathews	552	.272	37	95	133	287	**25**	22	3.0	.944	R. Crone	35	170	11	10	2	3.87
	RF	H. Aaron	609	**.328**	26	92	316	17	13	4	2.3	.962	G. Conley	31	158	8	9	3	3.13
Charlie Grimm	CF	B. Bruton	525	.272	8	56	391	10	13	1	2.9	.969	T. Phillips	23	88	5	3	2	2.26
W-24 L-22	LF	B. Thomson	451	.235	20	74	257	7	7	0	2.0	.974	E. Johnson	36	51	4	3	6	3.71
	C	D. Crandall	311	.238	16	48	448	44	2	9	4.5	**.996**	D. Jolly	29	46	2	3	7	3.74
Fred Haney	C	D. Rice	188	.213	3	17	271	21	5	2	4.6	.983							
W-68 L-40	1B	F. Torre	159	.258	0	16	390	42	3	34	4.9	.993							
Cincinnati	1B	T. Kluszewski	517	.302	35	102	1166	89	13	**110**	9.7	.990	B. Lawrence	49	219	19	10	0	3.99
	2B	J. Temple	**632**	.285	2	41	**389**	**432**	16	89	5.4	.981	J. Klippstein	37	211	12	11	1	4.09
	SS	R. McMillan	479	.263	3	62	**319**	**511**	21	**105**	**5.7**	**.975**	J. Nuxhall	44	201	13	11	3	3.72
W-91 L-63	3B	R. Jablonski	407	.256	15	66	117	172	9	11	2.3	.970	A. Fowler	45	178	11	11	1	4.05
	RF	W. Post	539	.249	36	83	292	16	10	1	2.3	.969	H. Jeffcoat	38	171	8	2	2	3.84
Birdie Tebbetts	CF	G. Bell	603	.292	29	84	330	12	5	4	2.3	.986	H. Freeman	64	109	14	5	18	3.40
	LF	F. Robinson	572	.290	38	83	323	5	8	1	2.2	.976							
	C	E. Bailey	383	.300	28	75	511	52	9	**10**	5.4	.984							
	C	S. Burgess	229	.275	12	39	257	18	0	2	5.0	1.000							
	1B	G. Crowe	144	.250	10	23	225	25	3	15	7.9	.988							
	OF	B. Thurman	139	.295	8	22	39	2	2	1	1.5	.953							

NATIONAL LEAGUE 1956, *cont.*

St. Louis

W-76 L-78

Fred Hutchinson

POS	Player	AB	BA	HR	RBI	PO	A	E	DP	TC/G	FA	Pitcher	G	IP	W	L	SV	ERA
1B	S. Musial	594	.310	27	**109**	870	90	7	96	9.4	.993	V. Mizell	33	209	14	14	0	3.62
2B	D. Blasingame	587	.261	0	27	280	303	8	89	6.0	.986	T. Poholsky	33	203	9	14	0	3.59
SS	A. Dark	413	.286	4	37	178	292	20	66	4.9	.959	M. Dickson	28	196	13	8	0	3.07
3B	K. Boyer	595	.306	26	98	130	**309**	18	**37**	3.1	.961	H. Wehmeier	34	171	12	9	1	3.69
RF	W. Moon	540	.298	16	68	159	8	2	2	1.7	.988	W. Schmidt	33	148	6	8	1	3.84
CF	B. Del Greco	270	.215	5	18	217	3	3	0	2.3	.987	L. McDaniel	39	116	7	6	0	3.40
LF	R. Repulski	376	.277	11	55	187	3	5	0	2.0	.974	L. Jackson	51	85	2	2	9	4.11
C	H. Smith	227	.282	5	23	300	34	6	3	5.2	.982	J. Collum	38	60	6	2	7	4.20
OF	W. Lockman	193	.249	0	10	103	2	5	0	1.9	.955							
C	R. Katt	158	.259	6	20	231	16	4	0	5.3	.984							
OF	H. Sauer	151	.298	5	24	55	2	0	1	1.5	1.000							
C	B. Sarni	148	.291	5	22	219	25*	2	1*	6.0	.992							
UT	B. Morgan	113	.195	3	20	42	56	6	6		.942							

Philadelphia

W-71 L-83

Mayo Smith

POS	Player	AB	BA	HR	RBI	PO	A	E	DP	TC/G	FA	Pitcher	G	IP	W	L	SV	ERA
1B	M. Blaylock	460	.254	10	50	949	72	8	86	8.3	.992	R. Roberts	43	297	19	**18**	3	4.45
2B	T. Kazanski	379	.211	4	34	246	261	11	68	4.5	.979	H. Haddix	31	207	12	8	2	3.48
SS	G. Hamner	401	.224	4	42	177	302	32	69	4.6	.937	C. Simmons	33	198	15	10	0	3.36
3B	W. Jones	520	.277	17	78	**202**	264	13	23	**3.2**	**.973**	B. Miller	49	122	3	6	5	3.24
RF	E. Valo	291	.289	5	37	167	4	6	0	2.0	.966	S. Miller	24	107	5	8	0	4.47
CF	R. Ashburn	628	.303	3	50	503	11	9	3	3.4	.983	S. Rogovin	22	107	7	6	0	4.98
LF	D. Ennis	630	.260	26	95	269	8	11	0	1.9	.962	J. Meyer	41	96	7	11	2	4.41
C	S. Lopata	535	.267	32	95	573	24	11	**10**	**6.0**	.982							
OF	J. Greengrass	215	.205	5	25	104	3	1	1	1.7	.991							
2B	S. Hemus	187	.289	5	24	94	93	5	18	3.9	.974							
SS	R. Smalley	168	.226	0	16	81	142	12	32	3.9	.949							
C	A. Seminick	161	.199	7	23	266	23	7	2	5.5	.976							

New York

W-67 L-87

Bill Rigney

POS	Player	AB	BA	HR	RBI	PO	A	E	DP	TC/G	FA	Pitcher	G	IP	W	L	SV	ERA
1B	B. White	508	.256	22	59	**1256**	**111**	15	106	**10.0**	.989	J. Antonelli	41	258	20	13	1	2.86
2B	R. Schoendienst	334	.296	2	14	199	215	3	52	4.9	.993*	R. Gomez	40	196	7	17	0	4.58
SS	D. Spencer	489	.221	14	42	113	169	6	33	4.4	.979	A. Worthington	28	166	7	14	0	3.97
3B	F. Castleman	385	.226	14	45	90	213	17	10	3.0	.947	J. Hearn	30	129	5	11	1	3.97
RF	D. Mueller	453	.269	5	41	180	4	2	2	1.6	.989	D. Littlefield	31	97	4	4	2	4.08
CF	W. Mays	578	.296	36	84	415	14	9	6	2.9	.979	J. Margoneri	23	92	6	6	0	3.93
LF	J. Brandt	351	.299	11	47	165	8	2	0	1.8	.989	H. Wilhelm	64	89	4	9	8	3.83
C	B. Sarni	238	.231	5	23	367	36*	3	9*	5.4	.993	W. McCall	46	77	3	4	7	3.61
OF	D. Rhodes	244	.217	8	33	85	6	4	1	1.4	.958							
SS	A. Dark	206	.252	2	17	89	132	9	27	4.8	.961							
3B	H. Thompson	183	.235	8	29	25	94	12	7	3.0	.908							
OF	W. Lockman	169	.272	1	10	69	3	3	1	1.9	.960							
SS	E. Bressoud	163	.227	0	9	67	125	10	26	4.2	.950							

Pittsburgh

W-66 L-88

Bobby Bragan

POS	Player	AB	BA	HR	RBI	PO	A	E	DP	TC/G	FA	Pitcher	G	IP	W	L	SV	ERA
1B	D. Long	517	.263	27	91	1201	99	**24**	92	9.6	.982	B. Friend	49	**314**	17	17	3	3.46
2B	B. Mazeroski	255	.243	3	14	163	242	8	56	5.1	.981	R. Kline	44	264	14	**18**	2	3.38
SS	D. Groat	520	.273	0	37	287	420	**34**	74	5.3	.954	V. Law	39	196	8	16	2	4.32
3B	F. Thomas	588	.282	25	80	118	176	18	21	2.8	.942	R. Face	**68**	135	12	13	6	3.52
RF	R. Clemente	543	.311	7	60	274	17	13	2	2.2	.957	G. Munger	35	107	3	4	2	4.04
CF	B. Virdon	509	.334	8	37	334	10	4	2	2.7	.989	N. King	38	60	4	1	5	3.15
LF	L. Walls	474	.274	11	54	284	10	10	1	2.3	.967							
C	J. Shepard	256	.242	7	30	356	36	4	4	4.6	.990							
01	B. Skinner	233	.202	5	29	216	8	2	21		.991							
C	H. Foiles	222	.212	7	25	291	30	4	8	4.5	.988							
32	G. Freese	207	.208	3	14	69	115	4	9		.979							

Chicago

W-60 L-94

Stan Hack

POS	Player	AB	BA	HR	RBI	PO	A	E	DP	TC/G	FA	Pitcher	G	IP	W	L	SV	ERA
1B	D. Fondy	543	.269	9	46	1048	94	17	101	8.7	.985	B. Rush	32	240	13	10	0	3.19
2B	G. Baker	546	.258	12	57	362	426	**25**	**99**	**5.8**	.969	S. Jones	33	189	9	14	0	3.91
SS	E. Banks	538	.297	28	85	279	357	25	92	4.8	.962	W. Hacker	34	168	3	13	0	4.66
3B	D. Hoak	424	.215	5	37	122	158	15	16	2.7	.949	D. Kaiser	27	150	4	9	0	3.59
RF	W. Moryn	529	.285	23	67	268	18	5	2	2.1	.983	J. Davis	46	120	5	7	2	3.66
CF	P. Whisenant	314	.239	11	46	242	6	2	0	2.7	.992	T. Lown	61	111	9	8	13	3.58
LF	M. Irvin	339	.271	15	50	216	6	2	0	2.3	.991	V. Valentinetti	42	95	6	4	1	3.78
C	H. Landrith	312	.221	4	32	483	55	**14**	9	5.6	.975	J. Brosnan	30	95	5	9	1	3.79
UT	E. Miksis	356	.239	9	27	144	151	7	14		.977							
OF	J. King	317	.249	15	54	187	10	2	2	2.4	.990							
OF	S. Drake	215	.256	2	15	142	3	1	1	2.8	.993							
C	H. Chiti	203	.212	4	18	327	35	7	2	5.5	.981							

BATTING AND BASE RUNNING LEADERS

Batting Average

H. Aaron, MIL	.328
B. Virdon, STL, PIT	.319
R. Clemente, PIT	.311
S. Musial, STL	.310
K. Boyer, STL	.306

Slugging Average

D. Snider, BKN	.598
J. Adcock, MIL	.597
H. Aaron, MIL	.558
F. Robinson, CIN	.558
W. Mays, NY	.557

Home Runs

D. Snider, BKN	43
J. Adcock, MIL	38
F. Robinson, CIN	38
E. Mathews, MIL	37
W. Post, CIN	36
W. Mays, NY	36

Total Bases

H. Aaron, MIL	340
D. Snider, BKN	324
W. Mays, NY	322
F. Robinson, CIN	319
S. Musial, STL	310

Runs Batted In

S. Musial, STL	109
J. Adcock, MIL	103
T. Kluszewski, CIN	102
D. Snider, BKN	101
K. Boyer, STL	98

Stolen Bases

W. Mays, NY	40
J. Gilliam, BKN	21
B. White, NY	15
J. Temple, CIN	14
P. Reese, BKN	13

PITCHING LEADERS

Winning Percentage

D. Newcombe, BKN	.794
B. Buhl, MIL	.692
L. Burdette, MIL	.655
B. Lawrence, CIN	.655
W. Spahn, MIL	.645

Earned Run Average

L. Burdette, MIL	2.70
W. Spahn, MIL	2.78
J. Antonelli, NY	2.86
S. Maglie, BKN	2.87
D. Newcombe, BKN	3.06

Wins

D. Newcombe, BKN	27
J. Antonelli, NY	20
W. Spahn, MIL	20
B. Lawrence, CIN	19
L. Burdette, MIL	19
R. Roberts, PHI	19

Saves

C. Labine, BKN	19
H. Freeman, CIN	18
T. Lown, CHI	13
L. Jackson, STL	9
D. Bessent, BKN	9

Strikeouts

S. Jones, CHI	176
H. Haddix, STL, PHI	170
B. Friend, PIT	166
R. Roberts, PHI	157
V. Mizell, STL	153

Complete Games

R. Roberts, PHI	22
W. Spahn, MIL	20
B. Friend, PIT	19
D. Newcombe, BKN	18
L. Burdette, MIL	16

NATIONAL LEAGUE 1956, *cont.*

BATTING AND BASE RUNNING LEADERS

Hits
H. Aaron, MIL 200
R. Ashburn, PHI 190
B. Virdon, STL, PIT 185
S. Musial, STL 184

Base on Balls
D. Snider, BKN 99
J. Gilliam, BKN 95
W. Jones, PHI 92
E. Mathews, MIL 91

Home Run Percentage
J. Adcock, MIL 8.4
D. Snider, BKN 7.9
T. Kluszewski, CIN 6.8
E. Mathews, MIL 6.7

Runs
F. Robinson, CIN 122
D. Snider, BKN 112
H. Aaron, MIL 106
E. Mathews, MIL 103

Doubles
H. Aaron, MIL 34
S. Lopata, PHI 33
D. Snider, BKN 33
S. Musial, STL 33

Triples
B. Bruton, MIL 15
H. Aaron, MIL 14
L. Walls, PIT 11
W. Moon, STL 11

PITCHING LEADERS

Fewest Hits/9 Innings
S. Maglie, BKN 7.26
D. Newcombe, BKN 7.35
S. Jones, CHI 7.39
V. Mizell, STL 7.42

Shutouts
L. Burdette, MIL 6
J. Antonelli, NY 6
D. Newcombe, BKN 5
B. Friend, PIT 4

Fewest Walks/9 Innings
R. Roberts, PHI 1.21
D. Newcombe, BKN 1.54
W. Spahn, MIL 1.66
A. Fowler, CIN 1.77

Most Strikeouts/9 Inn.
S. Jones, CHI 8.40
H. Haddix, STL, PHI 6.64
V. Mizell, STL 6.60
J. Nuxhall, CIN 5.38

Innings
B. Friend, PIT 314
R. Roberts, PHI 297
W. Spahn, MIL 281
D. Newcombe, BKN 268

Games Pitched
R. Face, PIT 68
H. Freeman, CIN 64
H. Wilhelm, NY 64
C. Labine, BKN 62

							Batting						Fielding			Pitching					
	W	L	PCT	GB	R	OR	2B	3B	HR	BA	SA	SB	E	DP	FA	CG	BB	SO	ShO	SV	ERA
Brooklyn	93	61	.604		720	601	212	36	179	.258	.419	65	**111**	149	**.981**	46	441	**772**	**12**	**30**	3.57
Milwaukee	92	62	.597	1	709	**569**	212	54	177	.259	.423	29	130	159	.979	**64**	467	639	**12**	27	**3.11**
Cincinnati	91	63	.591	2	**775**	658	201	32	**221**	.266	**.441**	45	113	147	**.981**	47	458	653	4	29	3.85
St. Louis	76	78	.494	17	678	698	**234**	49	124	**.268**	.399	41	134	**172**	.978	41	546	709	**12**	**30**	3.97
Philadelphia	71	83	.461	22	668	738	207	49	121	.252	.381	45	144	140	.975	57	**437**	750	4	15	4.20
New York	67	87	.435	26	540	650	192	45	145	.244	.382	**67**	144	143	.976	31	551	765	9	28	3.78
Pittsburgh	66	88	.429	27	588	653	199	**57**	110	.257	.380	24	162	140	.973	37	469	662	8	24	3.74
Chicago	60	94	.390	33	597	708	202	50	142	.244	.382	55	144	141	.976	37	613	744	6	17	3.96
					5275	5275	1659	372	1219	.256	.401	371	1082	1191	.977	360	3982	5694	67	200	3.77

AMERICAN LEAGUE 1956

New York

W-97 L-57

Casey Stengel

POS	Player	AB	BA	HR	RBI	PO	A	E	DP	TC/G	FA	Pitcher	G	IP	W	L	SV	ERA
1B	B. Skowron	464	.308	23	90	968	**80**	7	**138**	8.8	.993	W. Ford	31	226	19	6	1	**2.47**
2B	B. Martin	458	.264	9	49	241	260	10	84	4.9	.980	J. Kucks	34	224	18	9	0	3.85
SS	G. McDougald	438	.311	13	56	177	273	14	77	5.0	.970	D. Larsen	38	180	11	5	1	3.26
3B	A. Carey	422	.237	7	50	114	265	21	26	3.1	.948	T. Sturdivant	32	158	16	8	5	3.30
RF	H. Bauer	539	.241	26	84	242	10	8	2	1.8	.969	B. Turley	27	132	8	4	1	5.05
CF	M. Mantle	533	**.353**	**52**	**130**	370	10	4	3	2.7	.990	T. Byrne	37	110	7	3	6	3.36
LF	E. Howard	290	.262	5	34	97	2	1	0	1.5	.990	R. Coleman	29	88	3	5	2	3.67
C	Y. Berra	521	.298	30	105	**732**	55	**11**	**15**	**5.9**	.986	B. Grim	26	75	6	1	5	2.77
O1	J. Collins	262	.225	7	43	346	32	1	37		.997	T. Morgan	41	71	6	7	11	4.16
UT	J. Coleman	183	.257	0	18	138	152	9	46		.970							
OF	N. Siebern	162	.204	4	21	100	1	3	0	2.0	.971							
OF	B. Cerv	115	.304	3	25	59	4	1	2	1.5	.984							

Cleveland

W-88 L-66

Al Lopez

POS	Player	AB	BA	HR	RBI	PO	A	E	DP	TC/G	FA	Pitcher	G	IP	W	L	SV	ERA
1B	V. Wertz	481	.264	32	106	**971**	77	9	99	7.9	.991	E. Wynn	38	278	20	9	2	2.72
2B	B. Avila	513	.224	10	54	322	351	16	83	5.1	.977	B. Lemon	39	255	20	14	3	3.03
SS	C. Carrasquel	474	.243	7	48	240	352	20	70	4.3	.967	H. Score	35	249	20	9	0	2.53
3B	A. Rosen	416	.267	15	61	89	219	18	20	2.8	.945	M. Garcia	35	198	11	12	0	3.78
RF	R. Colavito	322	.276	21	65	177	6	6	0	1.9	.968	D. Mossi	48	88	6	5	11	3.59
CF	J. Busby	494	.235	12	50	344	3	4	0	2.6	.989							
LF	A. Smith	526	.274	16	71	248	6	5	1	2.1	.981							
C	J. Hegan	315	.222	6	34	648	28	10	2	5.8	.985							
OF	G. Woodling	317	.262	8	38	154	3	3	0	1.9	.981							
UT	G. Strickland	171	.211	3	17	118	145	5	34		.981							
1B	P. Ward	150	.253	6	21	226	21	3	20	4.2	.988							
OF	S. Mele	114	.254	4	20	29	2	1	0	1.6	.969							

Chicago

W-85 L-69

Marty Marion

POS	Player	AB	BA	HR	RBI	PO	A	E	DP	TC/G	FA	Pitcher	G	IP	W	L	SV	ERA
1B	W. Dropo	361	.266	8	52	855	50	6	95	7.8	**.993**	B. Pierce	35	276	20	9	1	3.32
2B	N. Fox	**649**	.296	4	52	**478**	**396**	12	**124**	**5.8**	**.986**	D. Donovan	34	235	12	10	0	3.64
SS	L. Aparicio	533	.266	3	56	**250**	**474**	**35**	91	5.0	.954	J. Harshman	34	227	15	11	0	3.10
3B	F. Hatfield	321	.262	7	33	83	189	11	21	2.8	.961	J. Wilson	28	160	9	12	0	4.06
RF	J. Rivera	491	.255	12	66	271	9	7	4	2.1	.976	B. Keegan	20	105	5	7	0	3.93
CF	L. Doby	504	.268	24	102	371	4	5	2	2.8	.987	G. Staley	26	102	8	3	0	2.92
LF	M. Minoso	545	.316	21	88	284	10	8	1	2.0	.974	D. Howell	34	64	5	6	4	4.62
C	S. Lollar	450	.293	11	75	679	40	5	6	5.5	**.993**							
1O	D. Philley	279	.265	4	47	349	19	7	31		.981							
3B	S. Esposito	184	.228	3	25	41	109	6	17	2.6	.962							
C	L. Moss	127	.244	10	22	149	10	1	1	3.3	.994							
PH	R. Northey	48	.354	3	23	4	1	0	0	1.3	1.000							

Boston

W-84 L-70

Pinky Higgins

POS	Player	AB	BA	HR	RBI	PO	A	E	DP	TC/G	FA	Pitcher	G	IP	W	L	SV	ERA
1B	M. Vernon	403	.310	15	84	930	58	**11**	96	**9.3**	.989	T. Brewer	32	244	19	9	0	3.50
2B	B. Goodman	399	.293	2	38	215	266	**17**	69	5.2	.966	F. Sullivan	34	242	14	7	0	3.42
SS	D. Buddin	377	.239	5	37	213	370	29	**98**	**5.4**	.953	W. Nixon	23	145	9	8	0	4.21
3B	B. Klaus	520	.271	7	59	120	242	21	18	**3.6**	.945	D. Sisler	39	142	9	8	3	4.62
RF	J. Jensen	578	.315	20	97	291	13	12	2	2.1	.962	M. Parnell	21	131	7	6	0	3.77
CF	J. Piersall	601	.293	14	87	455	10	4	1	3.0	.991	I. Delock	48	128	13	7	9	4.21
LF	T. Williams	400	.345	24	82	174	7	5	2	1.7	.973	B. Porterfield	25	126	3	12	0	5.14
C	S. White	392	.245	5	44	547	**60**	10	13	5.4	.984	T. Hurd	40	76	3	4	5	5.33
O1	D. Gernert	306	.291	16	68	367	41	4	38		.990							
2B	T. Lepcio	284	.261	15	51	143	166	11	47	5.6	.966							
C	P. Daley	187	.267	5	29	228	14	2	1	4.3	.992							

AMERICAN LEAGUE 1956, *cont.*

Team	POS	Player	AB	BA	HR	RBI	PO	A	E	DP	TC/G	FA	Pitcher	G	IP	W	L	SV	ERA
Detroit	1B	E. Torgeson	318	.264	12	42	623	32	5	62	8.0	.992	F. Lary	41	**294**	**21**	13	1	3.15
W-82 L-72	2B	F. Bolling	366	.281	7	45	223	260	11	72	4.8	.978	P. Foytack	43	256	15	13	1	3.59
Bucky Harris	SS	H. Kuenn	591	.332	12	88	219	388	20	86	4.4	**.968**	B. Hoeft	38	248	20	14	0	4.06
	3B	R. Boone	481	.308	25	81	151	243	17	23	3.2	.959	S. Gromek	40	141	8	6	4	4.28
	RF	A. Kaline	617	.314	27	128	343	18	6	4	2.4	.984	V. Trucks	22	120	6	5	1	3.83
	CF	B. Tuttle	546	.253	9	65	348	13	9	2	2.7	.976	A. Aber	42	63	4	4	7	3.43
	LF	C. Maxwell	500	.326	28	87	281	12	4	1	2.2	.987							
	C	F. House	321	.240	10	44	450	33	7	8	5.6	.986							
	C	R. Wilson	228	.289	7	38	393	34	4	7	5.5	.991							
	1B	J. Phillips	224	.295	1	20	422	32	9	49	8.3	.981							
	03	B. Kennedy	177	.232	4	22	87	40	12	3		.914							
	S2	J. Brideweser	156	.218	0	10	111	134	5	32		.980							
	1B	W. Belardi	154	.279	6	15	240	17	3	21	8.4	.988							
Baltimore	1B	B. Boyd	225	.311	2	11	469	24	5	46	8.3	.990	R. Moore	32	185	12	7	0	4.18
W-69 L-85	2B	B. Gardner	515	.231	11	50	274	331	16	76	4.7	.974	C. Johnson	26	184	9	10	0	3.43
Paul Richards	SS	W. Miranda	461	.217	2	34	229	436	26	91	4.7	.962	B. Wight	35	175	9	12	0	4.02
	3B	G. Kell	345	.261	8	37	97	165	7	19	2.8	.974*	H. Brown	35	152	9	7	2	4.04
	RF	T. Francona	445	.258	9	57	240	10	6	1	2.1	.977	E. Palica	29	116	4	11	0	4.49
	CF	D. Williams	353	.286	11	37	205	2	2	0	2.6	.990	M. Fornieles	30	111	4	7	1	3.97
	LF	B. Nieman	388	.322	12	64	243	4	5	1	2.2	.980	D. Ferrarese	36	102	4	10	2	5.03
	C	G. Triandos	452	.279	21	88	417	50	5	12	5.3	.989	G. Zuverink	**62**	97	7	6	**16**	4.16
	C	H. Smith	229	.262	3	18	313	33	2	11	4.9	.994	B. Loes	21	57	2	7	3	4.76
	1B	B. Hale	207	.237	1	24	366	29	10	33	7.9	.975							
	OF	J. Pyburn	156	.173	2	11	114	5	3	3	1.6	.975							
Washington	1B	P. Runnels	578	.310	8	76	693	49	4	73	9.2	.995	C. Stobbs	37	240	15	15	1	3.60
W-59 L-95	2B	H. Plews	256	.270	1	25	137	166	**17**	38	4.8	.947	C. Pascual	39	189	6	18	2	5.87
Chuck Dressen	SS	J. Valdivielso	246	.236	4	29	144	266	23	58	4.8	.947	P. Ramos	37	152	12	10	0	5.27
	3B	E. Yost	515	.231	11	53	**164**	**303**	18	**31**	3.6	.963	D. Stone	41	132	5	7	3	6.27
	RF	J. Lemon	538	.271	27	96	301	11	12	6	2.3	.963	B. Wiesler	37	123	3	12	0	6.44
	CF	K. Olson	313	.246	4	22	192	4	2	0	2.0	.990	B. Stewart	33	105	5	7	2	5.57
	LF	W. Herzog	421	.245	4	35	240	9	5	0	2.5	.980	B. Chakales	43	96	4	4	4	4.03
	C	C. Courtney	283	.300	5	44	290	35	7	7	4.4	.979	C. Grob	37	79	4	5	1	7.83
	01	R. Sievers	550	.253	29	95	784	54	9	76		.989	B. Byerly	25	52	2	4	4	2.96
	C	L. Berberet	207	.261	4	27	266	28	1	6	5.0	.997							
Kansas City	1B	V. Power	530	.309	14	63	671	62	5	73	9.7	.993	A. Ditmar	44	254	12	**22**	1	4.42
W-52 L-102	2B	J. Finigan	250	.216	2	21	114	105	7	35	4.3	.969	T. Gorman	52	171	9	10	3	3.83
Lou Boudreau	SS	J. De Maestri	434	.233	6	39	210	407	23	95	4.8	.964	J. Crimian	54	129	4	8	3	5.51
	3B	H. Lopez	561	.273	18	69	152	254	**26**	23	3.6	.940	W. Burnette	18	121	6	8	0	2.89
	RF	H. Simpson	543	.293	21	105	188	3	7	2	1.8	.965	L. Kretlow	25	119	4	9	0	5.31
	CF	J. Groth	244	.258	5	37	140	8	0	3	1.8	1.000	T. Herriage	31	103	1	13	0	6.64
	LF	L. Skizas	297	.316	11	39	148	9	4	0	2.2	.975	B. Shantz	45	101	2	7	9	4.35
	C	T. Thompson	268	.272	1	27	328	38	7	7	5.5	.981	A. Kellner	20	92	7	4	0	4.32
	OF	G. Zernial	272	.224	16	44	111	9	2	1	1.8	.984							
	OF	A. Pilarcik	239	.251	4	22	154	9	4	1	2.5	.976							
	OF	E. Slaughter	223	.278	2	23	105	1	2	0	1.9	.981							
	C	J. Ginsberg	195	.246	1	12	238	28	3	3	4.7	.989							
	1B	E. Robinson	172	.198	2	12	360	19	9	43	8.3	.977							
	C	H. Smith	142	.275	2	24	183	22	3	3	5.8	.986							

BATTING AND BASE RUNNING LEADERS

Batting Average
M. Mantle, NY .353
T. Williams, BOS .345
H. Kuenn, DET .332
C. Maxwell, DET .326
B. Nieman, CHI, BAL .320

Slugging Average
M. Mantle, NY .705
T. Williams, BOS .605
C. Maxwell, DET .534
Y. Berra, NY .534
A. Kaline, DET .530

Home Runs
M. Mantle, NY 52
V. Wertz, CLE 32
Y. Berra, NY 30
R. Sievers, WAS 29
C. Maxwell, DET 28

Total Bases
M. Mantle, NY 376
A. Kaline, DET 327
J. Jensen, BOS 287
M. Minoso, CHI 286
Y. Berra, NY 278
H. Kuenn, DET 278

Runs Batted In
M. Mantle, NY 130
A. Kaline, DET 128
V. Wertz, CLE 106
Y. Berra, NY 105
H. Simpson, KC 105

Stolen Bases
L. Aparicio, CHI 21
J. Rivera, CHI 20
B. Avila, CLE 17
M. Minoso, CHI 12
T. Francona, BAL 11
J. Jensen, BOS 11

Hits
H. Kuenn, DET 196
A. Kaline, DET 194
N. Fox, CHI 192
M. Mantle, NY 188

Base on Balls
E. Yost, WAS 151
M. Mantle, NY 112
T. Williams, BOS 102
L. Doby, CHI 102

Home Run Percentage
M. Mantle, NY 9.8
V. Wertz, CLE 6.7
T. Williams, BOS 6.0
Y. Berra, NY 5.8

Runs
M. Mantle, NY 132
N. Fox, CHI 109
M. Minoso, CHI 106

Doubles
J. Piersall, BOS 40
H. Kuenn, DET 32
A. Kaline, DET 32

Triples
J. Lemon, WAS 11
H. Simpson, KC 11
M. Minoso, CHI 11
J. Jensen, BOS 11

PITCHING LEADERS

Winning Percentage
W. Ford, NY .760
E. Wynn, CLE .690
B. Pierce, CHI .690
H. Score, CLE .690
T. Brewer, BOS .679

Earned Run Average
W. Ford, NY 2.47
H. Score, CLE 2.53
E. Wynn, CLE 2.72
B. Lemon, CLE 3.03
J. Harshman, CHI 3.10

Wins
F. Lary, DET 21
B. Hoeft, DET 20
H. Score, CLE 20
B. Lemon, CLE 20
B. Pierce, CHI 20
E. Wynn, CLE 20

Saves
G. Zuverink, BAL 16
D. Mossi, CLE 11
T. Morgan, NY 11
B. Shantz, KC 9
I. Delock, BOS 9

Strikeouts
H. Score, CLE 263
B. Pierce, CHI 192
P. Foytack, DET 184
B. Hoeft, DET 172
F. Lary, DET 165

Complete Games
B. Pierce, CHI 21
B. Lemon, CLE 21
F. Lary, DET 20
W. Ford, NY 18
B. Hoeft, DET 18
E. Wynn, CLE 18

Fewest Hits/9 Innings
H. Score, CLE 5.85
D. Larsen, NY 6.66
J. Harshman, CHI 7.27
T. Brewer, BOS 7.37

Shutouts
H. Score, CLE 5

Fewest Walks/9 Innings
C. Stobbs, WAS 2.02
D. Donovan, CHI 2.26
J. Kucks, NY 2.89
E. Wynn, CLE 2.95

Most Strikeouts/9 Inn.
H. Score, CLE 9.49
C. Pascual, WAS 7.73
P. Foytack, DET 6.47
B. Pierce, CHI 6.25

Innings
F. Lary, DET 294
E. Wynn, CLE 278
B. Pierce, CHI 276
P. Foytack, DET 256

Games Pitched
G. Zuverink, BAL 62
J. Crimian, KC 54
T. Gorman, KC 52
D. Mossi, CLE 48
I. Delock, BOS 48

AMERICAN LEAGUE 1956, *cont.*

	W	L	PCT	GB	R	OR	Batting 2B	3B	HR	BA	SA	SB	Fielding E	DP	FA	Pitching CG	BB	SO	ShO	SV	ERA
New York	97	57	.630		**857**	631	193	55	**190**	.270	**.434**	51	136	**214**	.977	50	652	732	9	**35**	3.63
Cleveland	88	66	.571	9	712	**581**	199	23	153	.244	.381	40	129	130	.978	**67**	564	**845**	**17**	24	**3.32**
Chicago	85	69	.552	12	776	634	218	43	128	.267	.397	**70**	**122**	160	**.979**	65	**524**	722	11	13	3.73
Boston	84	70	.545	13	780	751	**261**	45	139	.275	.419	28	169	168	.972	50	668	712	8	20	4.17
Detroit	82	72	.532	15	789	699	209	50	150	**.279**	.420	43	140	151	.976	62	655	788	10	15	4.06
Baltimore	69	85	.448	28	571	705	198	34	91	.244	.350	39	137	142	.977	38	547	715	10	24	4.20
Washington	59	95	.383	38	652	924	198	**62**	112	.250	.377	37	171	173	.972	36	730	663	1	18	5.33
Kansas City	52	102	.338	45	619	831	204	41	112	.252	.370	40	166	187	.973	30	679	636	3	18	4.86
					5756	5756	1680	353	1075	.260	.394	348	1170	1325	.976	398	5019	5813	69	167	4.16

NATIONAL LEAGUE 1957

Milwaukee

W-95 L-59

Fred Haney

POS	Player	AB	BA	HR	RBI	PO	A	E	DP	TC/G	FA	Pitcher	G	IP	W	L	SV	ERA
1B	F. Torre	364	.272	5	40	859	71	4	89	8.0	**.996**	W. Spahn	39	271	**21**	11	3	2.69
2B	R. Schoendienst	394	.310	6	32	238	282	7	72	5.7	.987	L. Burdette	37	257	17	9	0	3.72
SS	J. Logan	494	.273	10	49	263	**440**	**29**	94	**5.7**	.960	B. Buhl	34	217	18	7	0	2.74
3B	E. Mathews	572	.292	32	94	131	**299**	**16**	27	3.0	.964	G. Conley	35	148	9	9	1	3.16
RF	H. Aaron	615	.322	**44**	**132**	346	9	6	0	2.4	.983	B. Trowbridge	32	126	7	5	1	3.64
CF	B. Bruton	306	.278	5	30	206	5	4	2	2.7	.981	J. Pizarro	24	99	5	6	0	4.62
LF	W. Covington	328	.284	21	65	150	9	3	1	1.8	.981	E. Johnson	30	65	7	3	4	3.88
C	D. Crandall	383	.253	15	46	414	**59**	6	11	4.7	.987	D. McMahon	32	47	2	3	9	1.54
OF	A. Pafko	220	.277	8	27	108	1	2	1	1.6	.982							
1B	J. Adcock	209	.287	12	38	477	30	2	60	9.1	.996							
2B	D. O'Connell	183	.235	1	8	128	145	5	43	5.8	.982							
UT	F. Mantilla	182	.236	4	21	87	136	12	28		.949							
OF	B. Thomson	148	.236	4	23	78	2	1	0	2.1	.988							
C	D. Rice	144	.229	9	20	235	14	2	3	5.2	.992							
OF	B. Hazle	134	.403	7	27	57	1	6	0	1.6	.906							

St. Louis

W-87 L-67

Fred Hutchinson

POS	Player	AB	BA	HR	RBI	PO	A	E	DP	TC/G	FA	Pitcher	G	IP	W	L	SV	ERA
1B	S. Musial	502	**.351**	29	102	1167	99	10	**131**	**9.8**	.992	L. Jackson	41	210	15	9	1	3.47
2B	D. Blasingame	**650**	.271	8	58	372	**512**	14	**128**	**5.8**	.984	L. McDaniel	30	191	15	9	0	3.49
SS	A. Dark	583	.290	4	64	**276**	419	25	**105**	5.2	.965	S. Jones	28	183	12	9	0	3.60
3B	E. Kasko	479	.273	1	35	100	224	13	21	2.8	.961	H. Wehmeier	36	165	10	7	0	4.31
RF	D. Ennis	490	.286	24	105	180	3	11	0	1.5	.943	V. Mizell	33	149	8	10	0	3.74
CF	K. Boyer	544	.265	19	62	275	2	1	1	2.6	.996	W. Schmidt	40	117	10	3	0	4.78
LF	W. Moon	516	.295	24	73	245	8	9	1	2.0	.966	V. McDaniel	17	87	7	5	0	3.22
C	H. Smith	333	.279	2	37	468	42	5	8	5.3	.990	L. Merritt	44	65	1	2	7	3.31
10	J. Cunningham	261	.318	9	52	360	18	3	17		.992	H. Wilhelm	40	55	1	4	11	4.25
C	H. Landrith	214	.243	3	26	339	29	5	3	5.6	.987	B. Muffett	23	44	3	2	8	2.25
OF	B. Smith	185	.211	3	18	138	6	4	4	1.9	.973							

Brooklyn

W-84 L-70

Walter Alston

POS	Player	AB	BA	HR	RBI	PO	A	E	DP	TC/G	FA	Pitcher	G	IP	W	L	SV	ERA
1B	G. Hodges	579	.299	27	98	**1317**	115	14	115	9.6	.990	D. Drysdale	34	221	17	9	0	2.69
2B	J. Gilliam	617	.250	2	37	**407**	390	11	90	5.5	**.986**	D. Newcombe	28	199	11	12	0	3.49
SS	C. Neal	448	.270	12	62	151	298	24	60	4.7	.949	J. Podres	31	196	12	9	3	**2.66**
3B	P. Reese	330	.224	1	29	51	166	13	5	3.1	.943	D. McDevitt	22	119	7	4	0	3.25
RF	C. Furillo	395	.306	12	66	153	7	2	1	1.5	.988	R. Craig	32	111	6	9	0	4.61
CF	D. Snider	508	.274	40	92	304	6	3	1	2.3	.990	C. Labine	58	105	5	7	**17**	3.44
LF	G. Cimoli	532	.293	10	57	265	11	6	2	2.0	.979	S. Koufax	34	104	5	4	0	3.88
C	R. Campanella	330	.242	13	62	618	51	5	5	**6.7**	**.993**	S. Maglie	19	101	6	6	1	2.93
3S	D. Zimmer	269	.219	6	19	99	170	13	20		.954	E. Roebuck	44	96	8	2	8	2.71
OF	S. Amoros	238	.277	7	26	122	2	2	0	1.9	.984							
C	R. Walker	166	.181	2	23	230	20	2	3	5.0	.992							
OF	E. Valo	161	.273	4	26	57	0	0	0	1.6	1.000							

Cincinnati

W-80 L-74

Birdie Tebbetts

POS	Player	AB	BA	HR	RBI	PO	A	E	DP	TC/G	FA	Pitcher	G	IP	W	L	SV	ERA
1B	G. Crowe	494	.271	31	92	932	86	11	86	8.6	.989	B. Lawrence	49	250	16	13	4	3.52
2B	J. Temple	557	.284	0	37	391	372	20	81	5.4	.974	H. Jeffcoat	37	207	12	13	0	4.52
SS	R. McMillan	448	.272	1	55	253	418	16	86	4.5	**.977**	J. Nuxhall	39	174	10	10	1	4.75
3B	D. Hoak	529	.293	19	89	**193**	269	14	**29**	**3.2**	**.971**	D. Gross	43	148	7	9	1	4.31
RF	W. Post	467	.244	20	74	252	12	4	4	2.2	.985	J. Klippstein	46	146	8	11	3	5.05
CF	G. Bell	510	.292	13	61	311	7	4	1	2.7	.988	T. Acker	49	109	10	5	4	4.97
LF	F. Robinson	611	.322	29	75	336	11	4	3	2.6	.989	H. Freeman	52	84	7	2	8	4.52
C	E. Bailey	391	.261	20	48	542	41	5	5	5.1	.991	R. Sanchez	38	62	3	2	5	4.76
C	S. Burgess	205	.283	14	39	223	15	3	0	5.4	.988							
OF	B. Thurman	190	.247	16	40	75	3	1	1	1.8	.987							
1B	T. Kluszewski	127	.268	6	21	161	15	2	11	7.7	.989							

Philadelphia

W-77 L-77

Mayo Smith

POS	Player	AB	BA	HR	RBI	PO	A	E	DP	TC/G	FA	Pitcher	G	IP	W	L	SV	ERA
1B	E. Bouchee	574	.293	17	76	1182	**125**	**16**	93	8.6	.988	R. Roberts	39	250	10	**22**	2	4.07
2B	G. Hamner	502	.227	10	62	260	282	**21**	54	4.5	.963	J. Sanford	33	237	19	8	0	3.08
SS	C. Fernandez	500	.262	5	51	241	377	26	69	4.3	.960	C. Simmons	32	212	12	11	0	3.44
3B	W. Jones	440	.218	9	47	140	197	12	18	2.8	.966	H. Haddix	27	171	10	13	0	4.06
RF	R. Repulski	516	.260	20	68	264	6	9	2	2.1	.968	D. Cardwell	30	128	4	8	1	4.91
CF	R. Ashburn	626	.297	0	33	502	18	7	7	3.4	.987	D. Farrell	52	83	10	2	10	2.38
LF	H. Anderson	400	.268	17	61	213	5	3	1	2.0	.986	B. Miller	32	60	2	5	6	2.69
C	S. Lopata	388	.237	18	67	634	36	8	9	6.3	.988							
OF	B. Bowman	237	.266	6	23	123	8	10	2	1.7	.929							
32	T. Kazanski	185	.265	3	11	63	95	5	21		.969							
C	J. Lonnett	160	.169	5	15	305	16	1	3	5.0	.997							

NATIONAL LEAGUE 1957, *cont.*

New York

W-69 L-85

Bill Rigney

POS	Player	AB	BA	HR	RBI	PO	A	E	DP	TC/G	FA	Pitcher	G	IP	W	L	SV	ERA
1B	W. Lockman	456	.248	7	30	981	71	10	94	10.4	.991	R. Gomez	38	238	15	13	0	3.78
2B	D. O'Connell	364	.266	7	28	156	194	7	50	5.3	.980	J. Antonelli	40	212	12	18	0	3.77
SS	D. Spencer	534	.249	11	50	213	342	**29**	95	5.3	.950	C. Barclay	37	183	9	9	0	3.44
3B	R. Jablonski	305	.289	9	57	44	130	11	15	2.6	.941	A. Worthington	55	158	8	11	4	4.22
RF	D. Mueller	450	.258	6	37	174	13	2	4	1.6	.989	S. Miller	38	124	7	9	1	3.63
CF	W. Mays	585	.333	35	97	422	14	9	5	3.0	.980	R. Crone	25	121	4	8	1	4.33
LF	H. Sauer	378	.259	26	76	125	4	1	0	1.3	.992	M. Grissom	55	83	4	4	14	2.61
C	V. Thomas	241	.249	6	31	396	31	4	8	4.9	.991							
2B	R. Schoendienst	254	.307	9	33	141	166	5	41	5.5	.984							
3B	O. Virgil	226	.235	4	24	27	111	11	10	2.4	.926							
1B	G. Harris	225	.240	9	31	502	37	8	53	9.0	.985							
OF	B. Thomson	215	.242	8	38	124	2	1	0	1.8	.992							
OF	D. Rhodes	190	.205	4	19	63	0	0	0	1.4	1.000							
C	R. Katt	165	.230	2	17	238	25	5	4	3.9	.981							

Chicago

W-62 L-92

Bob Scheffing

POS	Player	AB	BA	HR	RBI	PO	A	E	DP	TC/G	FA	Pitcher	G	IP	W	L	SV	ERA
1B	D. Long	397	.305	21	62	908	72	5	81	9.5	.995	M. Drabowsky	36	240	13	15	0	3.53
2B	B. Morgan	425	.207	5	27	220	343	14	58	5.0	.976	D. Drott	38	229	15	11	0	3.58
SS	E. Banks	594	.285	43	102	168	261	11	59	4.4	.975	B. Rush	31	205	6	16	0	4.38
3B	B. Adams	187	.251	1	10	43	68	6	5	2.5	.949	D. Elston	39	144	6	7	8	3.56
RF	W. Moryn	568	.289	19	88	276	13	12	3	2.0	.960	D. Hillman	32	103	6	11	1	4.35
CF	C. Tanner	318	.286	7	42	156	5	2	2	2.0	.988	J. Brosnan	41	99	5	5	0	3.38
LF	L. Walls	366	.240	6	33	174	6	3	0	1.9	.984	T. Lown	**67**	93	5	7	12	3.77
C	C. Neeman	415	.258	10	39	**703**	56	8	**13**	6.5	.990							
01	B. Speake	418	.232	16	50	480	41	7	21		.987							
OF	J. Bolger	273	.275	5	29	152	4	2	1	2.5	.987							
UT	J. Kindall	181	.160	6	12	73	109	15	10		.924							

Pittsburgh

W-62 L-92

Bobby Bragan
W-36 L-67

Danny Murtaugh
W-26 L-25

POS	Player	AB	BA	HR	RBI	PO	A	E	DP	TC/G	FA	Pitcher	G	IP	W	L	SV	ERA
1B	D. Fondy	323	.313	2	35	698	54	14	63	10.5	.982	B. Friend	40	**277**	14	18	0	3.38
2B	B. Mazeroski	526	.283	8	54	308	443	17	96	5.3	.978	R. Kline	40	205	9	16	0	4.04
SS	D. Groat	501	.315	7	54	226	380	20	74	5.1	.968	B. Purkey	48	180	11	14	2	3.86
3B	G. Freese	346	.283	6	31	62	132	**16**	16	2.8	.924	V. Law	31	173	10	8	1	2.87
RF	R. Clemente	451	.253	4	30	272	9	6	1	2.6	.979	L. Arroyo	54	131	3	11	1	4.68
CF	B. Virdon	561	.251	8	50	403	13	6	2	3.0	.986	R. Face	59	94	4	6	10	3.07
LF	B. Skinner	387	.305	13	45	172	9	7	2	2.0	.963							
C	H. Foiles	281	.270	9	36	436	32	**9**	2	4.4	.981							
UT	F. Thomas	594	.290	23	89	729	119	25	60		.971							
UT	G. Baker	365	.266	2	36	129	219	20	35		.946							

BATTING AND BASE RUNNING LEADERS

Batting Average

S. Musial, STL	.351
W. Mays, NY	.333
F. Robinson, CIN	.322
H. Aaron, MIL	.322
D. Groat, PIT	.315

Slugging Average

W. Mays, NY	.626
S. Musial, STL	.612
H. Aaron, MIL	.600
D. Snider, BKN	.587
E. Banks, CHI	.579

Home Runs

H. Aaron, MIL	44
E. Banks, CHI	43
D. Snider, BKN	40
W. Mays, NY	35
E. Mathews, MIL	32

Total Bases

H. Aaron, MIL	369
W. Mays, NY	366
E. Banks, CHI	344
F. Robinson, CIN	323
E. Mathews, MIL	309

Runs Batted In

H. Aaron, MIL	132
D. Ennis, STL	105
S. Musial, STL	102
E. Banks, CHI	102
G. Hodges, BKN	98

Stolen Bases

W. Mays, NY	38
J. Gilliam, BKN	26
D. Blasingame, STL	21
J. Temple, CIN	19
C. Fernandez, PHI	18

Hits

R. Schoendienst, NY, MIL	200
H. Aaron, MIL	198
F. Robinson, CIN	197
W. Mays, NY	195

Base on Balls

J. Temple, CIN	94
R. Ashburn, PHI	94
E. Mathews, MIL	90
E. Bouchee, PHI	84

Home Run Percentage

D. Snider, BKN	7.9
E. Banks, CHI	7.2
H. Aaron, MIL	7.2
G. Crowe, CIN	6.3

Runs

H. Aaron, MIL	118
E. Banks, CHI	113
W. Mays, NY	112
E. Mathews, MIL	109

Doubles

D. Hoak, CIN	39
S. Musial, STL	38
E. Bouchee, PHI	35
E. Banks, CHI	34

Triples

W. Mays, NY	20
B. Virdon, PIT	11
B. Bruton, MIL	9
E. Mathews, MIL	9

PITCHING LEADERS

Winning Percentage

B. Buhl, MIL	.720
J. Sanford, PHI	.704
W. Spahn, MIL	.656
L. Burdette, MIL	.654
D. Drysdale, BKN	.654

Earned Run Average

J. Podres, BKN	2.66
D. Drysdale, BKN	2.69
W. Spahn, MIL	2.69
B. Buhl, MIL	2.74
V. Law, PIT	2.87

Wins

W. Spahn, MIL	21
J. Sanford, PHI	19
B. Buhl, MIL	18
D. Drysdale, BKN	17
L. Burdette, MIL	17

Saves

C. Labine, BKN	17
M. Grissom, NY	14
T. Lown, CHI	12
H. Wilhelm, STL	11
R. Face, PIT	10
D. Farrell, PHI	10

Strikeouts

J. Sanford, PHI	188
D. Drott, CHI	170
M. Drabowsky, CHI	170
S. Jones, STL	154
D. Drysdale, BKN	148

Complete Games

W. Spahn, MIL	18
B. Friend, PIT	17
R. Gomez, NY	16
J. Sanford, PHI	15

Fewest Hits/9 Innings

J. Sanford, PHI	7.38
J. Podres, BKN	7.71
D. Drott, CHI	7.86
B. Buhl, MIL	7.93

Shutouts

J. Podres, BKN	6
D. Newcombe, BKN	4
D. Drysdale, BKN	4
W. Spahn, MIL	4

Fewest Walks/9 Innings

D. Newcombe, BKN	1.49
R. Roberts, PHI	1.55
V. Law, PIT	1.67
B. Purkey, PIT	1.90

Most Strikeouts/9 Inn.

S. Jones, STL	7.59
H. Haddix, PHI	7.17
J. Sanford, PHI	7.15
D. Drott, CHI	6.68

Innings

B. Friend, PIT	277
W. Spahn, MIL	271
L. Burdette, MIL	257
B. Lawrence, CIN	250
R. Roberts, PHI	250

Games Pitched

T. Lown, CHI	67
R. Face, PIT	59
C. Labine, BKN	58
M. Grissom, NY	55
A. Worthington, NY	55

							Batting						Fielding			Pitching					
	W	L	PCT	GB	R	OR	2B	3B	HR	BA	SA	SB	E	DP	FA	CG	BB	SO	ShO	SV	ERA
Milwaukee	95	59	.617		**772**	613	221	**62**	**199**	.269	**.442**	35	120	173	.981	**60**	570	693	9	24	3.47
St. Louis	87	67	.565	8	737	666	235	43	132	**.274**	.405	58	131	168	.979	46	506	778	11	**29**	3.78
Brooklyn	84	70	.545	11	690	**591**	188	38	147	.253	.387	60	127	136	.979	44	456	**891**	**18**	**29**	**3.35**
Cincinnati	80	74	.519	15	747	781	**251**	33	187	.269	.432	51	**107**	139	**.982**	40	429	707	5	**29**	4.62
Philadelphia	77	77	.500	18	623	656	213	44	117	.250	.375	57	136	117	.976	54	**412**	858	9	23	3.80
New York	69	85	.448	26	643	701	171	54	157	.252	.393	**64**	161	**180**	.974	35	471	701	9	20	4.01
Chicago	62	92	.403	33	628	722	223	31	147	.244	.380	28	149	140	.975	30	601	859	5	26	4.13
Pittsburgh	62	92	.403	33	586	696	231	60	92	.268	.384	46	170	143	.972	47	421	663	9	15	3.88
					5426	5426	1733	365	1178	.260	.400	399	1101	1196	.977	356	3866	6150	75	195	3.88

AMERICAN LEAGUE 1957

New York

W-98 L-56

Casey Stengel

POS	Player	AB	BA	HR	RBI	PO	A	E	DP	TC/G	FA	Pitcher	G	IP	W	L	SV	ERA
1B	B. Skowron	457	.304	17	88	1026	86	9	116	**9.7**	.992	T. Sturdivant	28	202	16	6	0	2.54
2B	B. Richardson	305	.256	0	19	206	223	9	60	4.7	.979	J. Kucks	37	179	8	10	2	3.56
SS	G. McDougald	539	.289	13	62	247	391	16	**104**	5.4	.976	B. Turley	32	176	13	6	3	2.71
3B	A. Carey	247	.255	6	33	66	147	5	9	2.7	.977	B. Shantz	30	173	11	5	5	**2.45**
RF	H. Bauer	479	.259	18	65	200	7	3	1	1.6	.986	D. Larsen	27	140	10	4	0	3.74
CF	M. Mantle	474	.365	34	94	324	6	7	1	2.4	.979	W. Ford	24	129	11	5	0	2.57
LF	E. Slaughter	209	.254	5	34	97	2	0	0	1.5	1.000	A. Ditmar	46	127	8	3	6	3.25
C	Y. Berra	482	.251	24	82	**704**	61	4	12	**6.4**	.995	T. Byrne	30	85	4	6	2	4.36
UT	T. Kubek	431	.297	3	39	189	183	20	33		.949	B. Grim	46	72	12	8	**19**	2.63
OC	E. Howard	356	.253	8	44	246	16	6	4		.978							
01	H. Simpson	224	.250	7	39	198	13	3	19		.986							
23	J. Coleman	157	.268	2	12	89	115	7	33		.967							

Chicago

W-90 L-64

Al Lopez

POS	Player	AB	BA	HR	RBI	PO	A	E	DP	TC/G	FA	Pitcher	G	IP	W	L	SV	ERA
1B	E. Torgeson	251	.295	7	46	612	29	1	72	9.2	.998	B. Pierce	37	257	**20**	12	2	3.26
2B	N. Fox	619	.317	6	61	**453**	**453**	13	**141**	**5.9**	.986	D. Donovan	28	221	16	6	0	2.77
SS	L. Aparicio	575	.257	3	41	246	**449**	20	85	5.0	.972	J. Wilson	30	202	15	8	0	3.48
3B	B. Phillips	393	.270	7	42	91	227	14	17	3.4	.958	J. Harshman	30	151	8	8	1	4.10
RF	J. Landis	274	.212	2	16	192	8	3	4	2.3	.985	B. Keegan	30	143	10	8	2	3.53
CF	L. Doby	416	.288	14	79	255	3	4	0	2.4	.985	B. Fischer	33	124	7	8	1	3.48
LF	M. Minoso	568	.310	12	103	293	9	5	2	2.0	.984	G. Staley	47	105	5	1	7	2.06
C	S. Lollar	351	.256	11	70	454	45	1	5	5.2	.998	D. Howell	37	68	6	5	6	3.29
OF	J. Rivera	402	.256	14	52	141	6	4	0	1.8	.974	P. LaPalme	35	40	1	4	7	3.35
1B	W. Dropo	223	.256	13	49	483	39	7	49	7.7	.987							
3S	S. Esposito	176	.205	2	15	80	165	9	22		.965							

Boston

W-82 L-72

Pinky Higgins

POS	Player	AB	BA	HR	RBI	PO	A	E	DP	TC/G	FA	Pitcher	G	IP	W	L	SV	ERA
1B	D. Gernert	316	.237	14	58	681	50	8	82	10.4	.989	F. Sullivan	31	241	14	11	0	2.73
2B	T. Lepcio	232	.241	9	37	136	194	8	58	5.0	.976	T. Brewer	32	238	16	13	0	3.85
SS	B. Klaus	477	.252	10	42	204	417	25	93	5.5	.961	W. Nixon	29	191	12	13	0	3.68
3B	F. Malzone	634	.292	15	103	**151**	**370**	**25**	**31**	**3.6**	**.954**	M. Fornieles	25	125	8	7	2	3.52
RF	J. Jensen	544	.281	23	103	251	16	11	4	1.9	.960	D. Sisler	22	122	7	8	1	4.71
CF	J. Piersall	609	.261	19	63	397	12	4	0	2.7	.990	B. Porterfield	28	102	4	4	1	4.05
LF	T. Williams	420	**.388**	38	87	215	2	1	0	1.7	.995	I. Delock	49	94	9	8	11	3.83
C	S. White	340	.215	3	31	489	49	8	**13**	4.9	.985	G. Susce	29	88	7	3	1	4.28
1B	M. Vernon	270	.241	7	38	662	51	6	47	10.3	.992							
2B	G. Mauch	222	.270	2	28	127	153	11	41	5.0	.962							
SS	B. Consolo	196	.270	4	19	61	149	15	30	5.4	.933							
C	P. Daley	191	.225	3	25	289	20	0	5	4.0	**1.000**							
OF	G. Stephens	173	.266	3	26	70	4	1	2	0.8	.987							

Detroit

W-78 L-76

Jack Tighe

POS	Player	AB	BA	HR	RBI	PO	A	E	DP	TC/G	FA	Pitcher	G	IP	W	L	SV	ERA
1B	R. Boone	462	.273	12	65	972	45	10	103	8.8	.990	J. Bunning	45	**267**	**20**	8	1	2.69
2B	F. Bolling	576	.259	15	40	394	401	**16**	112	5.6	.980	F. Lary	40	238	11	16	3	3.98
SS	H. Kuenn	624	.277	9	44	225	354	**27**	86	4.5	.955	D. Maas	45	219	10	14	6	3.28
3B	R. Bertoia	295	.275	4	28	76	125	10	8	2.5	.953	P. Foytack	38	212	14	11	1	3.14
RF	A. Kaline	577	.295	23	90	319	13	5	2	2.3	.985	B. Hoeft	34	207	9	11	1	3.48
CF	B. Tuttle	451	.251	5	47	331	5	6	1	2.7	.982	H. Byrd	37	59	4	3	5	3.36
LF	C. Maxwell	492	.276	24	82	317	6	1	1	2.4	.997							
C	F. House	348	.259	7	36	535	54	2	5	6.1	.997							
C	R. Wilson	178	.242	3	13	277	29	0	5	5.2	1.000							
3B	J. Finigan	174	.270	0	17	58	108	8	9	2.9	.954							
10	D. Philley	173	.283	2	16	219	25	2	19		.992							

Baltimore

W-76 L-76

Paul Richards

POS	Player	AB	BA	HR	RBI	PO	A	E	DP	TC/G	FA	Pitcher	G	IP	W	L	SV	ERA
1B	B. Boyd	485	.318	4	34	**1073**	70	10	107	8.7	.991	C. Johnson	35	242	14	11	0	3.20
2B	B. Gardner	**644**	.262	6	55	393	424	11	96	5.6	**.987**	R. Moore	34	227	11	13	0	3.72
SS	W. Miranda	314	.194	0	20	166	324	17	59	4.4	.966	B. Loes	31	155	12	7	4	3.24
3B	G. Kell	310	.297	9	44	66	122	4	15	2.4	.979	H. Brown	25	150	7	8	1	3.90
RF	A. Pilarcik	407	.278	9	49	234	15	1	2	2.0	.996	B. O'Dell	35	140	4	10	4	2.69
CF	J. Busby	288	.250	3	19	233	8	4	1	2.9	.984	B. Wight	27	121	6	6	0	3.64
LF	B. Nieman	445	.276	13	70	237	6	5	0	2.1	.980	G. Zuverink	**56**	113	10	6	9	2.48
C	G. Triandos	418	.254	19	72	580	**64**	5	**13**	5.4	.992	K. Lehman	30	68	8	3	6	2.78
OF	T. Francona	279	.233	7	38	119	0	1	0	1.6	.992							
UT	B. Goodman	263	.308	3	33	134	110	11	20		.957							
C	J. Ginsberg	175	.274	1	18	252	20	4	6	4.2	.986							
UT	D. Williams	167	.234	1	17	150	41	2	15		.990							
OF	J. Durham	157	.185	4	17	70	1	0	0	1.2	1.000							

Cleveland

W-76 L-77

Kerby Farrell

POS	Player	AB	BA	HR	RBI	PO	A	E	DP	TC/G	FA	Pitcher	G	IP	W	L	SV	ERA
1B	V. Wertz	515	.282	28	105	1025	83	**14**	**122**	8.1	.988	E. Wynn	40	263	14	17	1	4.31
2B	B. Avila	463	.268	5	48	280	254	9	72	5.1	.983	M. Garcia	38	211	12	8	0	3.75
SS	C. Carrasquel	392	.276	8	57	212	357	24	75	4.9	.960	D. Mossi	36	159	11	10	2	4.13
3B	A. Smith	507	.247	11	49	95	156	24	16	3.3	.913	R. Narleski	46	154	11	5	16	3.09
RF	R. Colavito	461	.252	25	84	268	12	11	2	2.2	.962	C. McLish	42	144	9	7	1	2.74
CF	R. Maris	358	.235	14	51	266	10	7	2	2.5	.975	B. Lemon	21	117	6	11	0	4.60
LF	G. Woodling	430	.321	19	78	225	10	2	0	2.1	.992	B. Daley	34	87	2	8	2	4.43
C	J. Hegan	148	.216	4	15	287	14	0	4	5.2	1.000							
UT	L. Raines	244	.262	2	16	84	109	13	15		.937							
03	D. Williams	205	.283	6	17	94	31	6	5		.954							
UT	G. Strickland	201	.234	1	19	146	164	6	38		.981							
C	R. Nixon	185	.281	2	18	268	31	5	5	5.3	.984							
C	D. Brown	114	.263	4	22	190	18	3	4	6.4	.986							

AMERICAN LEAGUE 1957, *cont.*

Kansas City

W-59 L-94

Lou Boudreau
W-36 L-67

Harry Craft
W-23 L-27

POS	Player	AB	BA	HR	RBI	PO	A	E	DP	TC/G	FA	Pitcher	G	IP	W	L	SV	ERA
1B	V. Power	467	.259	14	42	968	**99**	2	95	9.5	**.998**	N. Garver	24	145	6	13	0	3.84
2B	B. Hunter	319	.191	8	29	111	152	7	40	4.2	.974	T. Morgan	46	144	9	7	7	4.64
SS	J. De Maestri	461	.245	9	33	**248**	387	13	87	4.8	**.980**	A. Kellner	28	133	6	5	0	4.27
3B	H. Lopez	391	.294	11	35	117	227	23	20	3.3	.937	R. Terry	21	131	4	11	0	3.38
RF	B. Cerv	345	.272	11	44	157	6	6	1	1.9	.964	J. Urban	31	129	7	4	0	3.34
CF	W. Held	326	.239	20	50	266	12	1	2	3.0	.996	T. Gorman	38	125	5	9	3	3.83
LF	G. Zernial	437	.236	27	69	213	4	11	1	2.0	.952	V. Trucks	48	116	9	7	7	3.03
C	H. Smith	360	.303	13	41	463	55	**9**	8	5.1	.983	A. Portocarrero	33	115	4	9	0	3.92
OF	L. Skizas	376	.245	18	44	119	5	3	2	1.7	.976	W. Burnette	38	113	7	12	1	4.30
23	B. Martin	265	.257	9	27	150	135	5	32		.983							
C	T. Thompson	230	.204	7	19	272	29	2	7	4.9	.993							
10	H. Simpson	179	.296	6	24	272	24	2	21		.993							
1B	I. Noren	160	.212	2	16	191	12	2	24	8.2	.990							
2B	M. Graff	155	.181	0	10	110	127	3	36	4.5	.988							

Washington

W-55 L-99

Chuck Dressen
W-4 L-16

Cookie Lavagetto
W-51 L-83

POS	Player	AB	BA	HR	RBI	PO	A	E	DP	TC/G	FA	Pitcher	G	IP	W	L	SV	ERA
1B	P. Runnels	473	.230	2	35	616	44	3	59	9.2	.995	P. Ramos	43	231	12	16	0	4.79
2B	H. Plews	329	.271	1	26	199	175	8	42	4.8	.979	C. Stobbs	42	212	8	**20**	1	5.36
SS	R. Bridges	391	.228	3	47	226	382	18	77	5.8*	.971	C. Pascual	29	176	8	17	0	4.10
3B	E. Yost	414	.251	9	38	109	207	16	18	3.1	.952	R. Kemmerer	39	172	7	11	0	4.96
RF	J. Lemon	518	.284	17	64	227	4	7	2	1.8	.971	T. Clevenger	52	140	7	6	8	4.19
CF	B. Usher	295	.261	5	27	228	7	5	2	2.5	.979	D. Hyde	52	109	4	3	1	4.12
LF	R. Sievers	572	.301	**42**	**114**	254	6	4	2	2.0	.985	B. Byerly	47	95	6	6	6	3.13
C	L. Berberet	264	.261	7	36	349	48	0	8	5.2	**1.000**	T. Abernathy	26	85	2	10	0	6.78
2S	M. Bolling	277	.227	4	19	168	232	11	53		.973							
10	A. Schult	247	.263	4	35	366	15	6	35		.984							
C	C. Courtney	232	.267	6	27	288	35	2	6	5.5	.994							
OF	F. Throneberry	195	.185	2	12	116	2	2	0	2.1	.983							
1B	J. Becquer	186	.226	2	22	300	19	0	29	7.4	1.000							

BATTING AND BASE RUNNING LEADERS

Batting Average
T. Williams, BOS .388
M. Mantle, NY .365
G. Woodling, CLE .321
B. Boyd, BAL .318
N. Fox, CHI .317

Slugging Average
T. Williams, BOS .731
M. Mantle, NY .665
R. Sievers, WAS .579
G. Woodling, CLE .521
V. Wertz, CLE .485

Home Runs
R. Sievers, WAS 42
T. Williams, BOS 38
M. Mantle, NY 34
V. Wertz, CLE 28
G. Zernial, KC 27

Total Bases
R. Sievers, WAS 331
M. Mantle, NY 315
T. Williams, BOS 307
A. Kaline, DET 276
F. Malzone, BOS 271

Runs Batted In
R. Sievers, WAS 114
V. Wertz, CLE 105
J. Jensen, BOS 103
M. Minoso, CHI 103
F. Malzone, BOS 103

Stolen Bases
L. Aparicio, CHI 28
J. Rivera, CHI 18
M. Minoso, CHI 18
M. Mantle, NY 16

Hits
N. Fox, CHI 196
F. Malzone, BOS 185
M. Minoso, CHI 176
M. Mantle, NY 173
H. Kuenn, DET 173

Base on Balls
M. Mantle, NY 146
T. Williams, BOS 119
A. Smith, CLE 79
M. Minoso, CHI 79

Home Run Percentage
T. Williams, BOS 9.0
R. Sievers, WAS 7.3
M. Mantle, NY 7.2
V. Wertz, CLE 5.4

Runs
M. Mantle, NY 121
N. Fox, CHI 110
J. Piersall, BOS 103
R. Sievers, WAS 99

Doubles
M. Minoso, CHI 36
B. Gardner, BAL 36
F. Malzone, BOS 31
H. Kuenn, DET 30

Triples
H. Simpson, KC, NY 9
H. Bauer, NY 9
G. McDougald, NY 9
B. Boyd, BAL 8
N. Fox, CHI 8

PITCHING LEADERS

Winning Percentage
D. Donovan, CHI .727
T. Sturdivant, NY .727
J. Bunning, DET .714
J. Wilson, CHI .652
B. Pierce, CHI .625

Earned Run Average
B. Shantz, NY 2.45
T. Sturdivant, NY 2.54
J. Bunning, DET 2.69
B. Turley, NY 2.71
F. Sullivan, BOS 2.73

Wins
B. Pierce, CHI 20
J. Bunning, DET 20
T. Sturdivant, NY 16
D. Donovan, CHI 16
T. Brewer, BOS 16

Saves
B. Grim, NY 19
R. Narleski, CLE 16
I. Delock, BOS 11
G. Zuverink, BAL 9
T. Clevenger, WAS 8

Strikeouts
E. Wynn, CLE 184
J. Bunning, DET 182
C. Johnson, BAL 177
B. Pierce, CHI 171
B. Turley, NY 152

Complete Games
D. Donovan, CHI 16
B. Pierce, CHI 16
T. Brewer, BOS 15
J. Bunning, DET 14
C. Johnson, BAL 14
F. Sullivan, BOS 14

Fewest Hits/9 Innings
B. Turley, NY 6.12
J. Bunning, DET 7.20
P. Foytack, DET 7.43
T. Sturdivant, NY 7.59

Shutouts
J. Wilson, CHI 5
B. Turley, NY 4
B. Pierce, CHI 4

Fewest Walks/9 Innings
F. Sullivan, BOS 1.80
D. Donovan, CHI 1.84
B. Shantz, NY 2.08
B. Loes, BAL 2.14

Most Strikeouts/9 Inn.
B. Turley, NY 7.76
C. Johnson, BAL 6.58
E. Wynn, CLE 6.30
J. Bunning, DET 6.13

Innings
J. Bunning, DET 267
E. Wynn, CLE 263
B. Pierce, CHI 257
C. Johnson, BAL 242

Games Pitched
G. Zuverink, BAL 56
D. Hyde, WAS 52
T. Clevenger, WAS 52
I. Delock, BOS 49

							Batting						Fielding			Pitching					
	W	L	PCT	GB	R	OR	2B	3B	HR	BA	SA	SB	E	DP	FA	CG	BB	SO	ShO	SV	ERA
New York	98	56	.636		**723**	**534**	200	**54**	145	**.268**	**.409**	49	123	**183**	.980	41	580	**810**	13	**42**	**3.00**
Chicago	90	64	.584	8	707	566	208	41	106	.260	.375	**109**	**107**	169	**.982**	**59**	**470**	665	**16**	27	3.35
Boston	82	72	.532	16	721	668	**231**	32	153	.262	.405	29	149	179	.976	55	498	692	9	23	3.88
Detroit	78	76	.506	20	614	614	224	37	116	.257	.378	36	121	151	.980	52	505	756	9	21	3.56
Baltimore	76	76	.500	21	597	588	191	39	87	.252	.353	57	112	159	.981	44	493	767	13	25	3.46
Cleveland	76	77	.497	21.5	682	722	199	26	140	.252	.382	40	153	154	.974	46	618	807	7	23	4.05
Kansas City	59	94	.386	38.5	563	710	195	40	**166**	.244	.394	35	125	162	.979	26	565	626	6	19	4.19
Washington	55	99	.357	43	603	808	215	38	111	.244	.363	13	128	159	.979	31	580	691	5	16	4.85
					5210	5210	1663	307	1024	.255	.382	368	1018	1316	.979	354	4309	5814	78	196	3.79

NATIONAL LEAGUE 1958

Team	POS	Player	AB	BA	HR	RBI	PO	A	E	DP	TC/G	FA	Pitcher	G	IP	W	L	SV	ERA
Milwaukee	1B	F. Torre	372	.309	6	55	960	80	6	85	8.6	**.994**	W. Spahn	38	**290**	**22**	11	1	3.07
	2B	R. Schoendienst	427	.262	1	24	233	301	7	77	5.2	**.987**	L. Burdette	40	275	20	10	0	2.91
W-92 L-62	SS	J. Logan	530	.226	11	53	273	**481**	**32**	99	5.5	.959	B. Rush	28	147	10	6	0	3.42
	3B	E. Mathews	546	.251	31	77	116	**351**	22	24	3.3	.955	C. Willey	23	140	9	7	0	2.70
Fred Haney	RF	H. Aaron	601	.326	30	95	305	12	5	0	2.1	.984	J. Jay	18	97	7	5	0	2.14
	CF	B. Bruton	325	.280	3	28	203	6	5	0	2.2	.977	J. Pizarro	16	97	6	4	1	2.70
	LF	W. Covington	294	.330	24	74	118	3	6	2	1.5	.953	D. McMahon	38	59	7	2	8	3.68
	C	D. Crandall	427	.272	18	63	**659**	**64**	7	6	5.9	**.990**							
	1B	J. Adcock	320	.275	19	54	525	36	6	55	8.0	.989							
	02	F. Mantilla	226	.221	7	19	114	49	4	12		.976							
	OF	A. Pafko	164	.238	3	23	107	2	0	0	1.2	1.000							
Pittsburgh	1B	T. Kluszewski	301	.292	4	37	591	36	4	62	8.8	.994	B. Friend	38	274	**22**	14	0	3.68
	2B	B. Mazeroski	567	.275	19	68	344	**496**	17	118	**5.6**	.980	R. Kline	32	237	13	**16**	0	3.53
W-84 L-70	SS	D. Groat	584	.300	3	66	**307**	461	20	**127**	5.3	.975	V. Law	35	202	14	12	3	3.96
	3B	F. Thomas	562	.281	35	109	122	240	**29**	21	2.8	.926	C. Raydon	31	134	8	4	1	3.62
Danny Murtaugh	RF	R. Clemente	519	.289	6	50	312	22	6	3	2.5	.982	G. Witt	18	106	9	2	0	1.61
	CF	B. Virdon	604	.267	9	46	401	11	3	0	2.9	.993	B. Porterfield	37	88	4	6	5	3.29
	LF	B. Skinner	529	.321	13	70	232	19	6	2	1.8	.977	R. Face	57	84	5	2	**20**	2.89
	C	H. Foiles	264	.205	8	30	456	41	5	5	4.9	.990	D. Gross	40	75	5	7	7	3.98
	1B	D. Stuart	254	.268	16	48	529	49	**16**	69	9.3	.973							
	OF	R. Mejias	157	.268	5	19	104	3	3	0	1.9	.973							
San Francisco	1B	O. Cepeda	603	.312	25	96	**1322**	97	**16**	131	**9.8**	.989	J. Antonelli	41	242	16	13	3	3.28
	2B	D. O'Connell	306	.232	3	23	222	278	7	70	4.9	.986	R. Gomez	42	208	10	12	1	4.38
W-80 L-74	SS	D. Spencer	539	.256	17	74	238	438	**32**	95	5.3	.955	S. Miller	41	182	6	9	0	**2.47**
	3B	J. Davenport	434	.256	12	41	92	221	13	19	2.5	.960	M. McCormick	42	178	11	8	1	4.59
Bill Rigney	RF	W. Kirkland	418	.258	14	56	187	12	8	4	1.8	.961	A. Worthington	54	151	11	7	6	3.63
	CF	W. Mays	600	.347	29	96	429	17	9	2	3.0	.980	R. Monzant	43	151	8	11	1	4.72
	LF	F. Alou	182	.253	4	16	126	2	2	1	1.9	.985	M. Grissom	51	65	7	5	10	3.99
	C	B. Schmidt	393	.244	14	54	616	54	**12**	**10**	5.5	.982							
	OF	H. Sauer	236	.250	12	46	93	3	5	1	1.5	.950							
	3B	R. Jablonski	230	.230	12	46	49	91	8	2	2.6	.946							
	OF	L. Wagner	221	.317	13	35	89	5	5	0	1.7	.949							
Cincinnati	1B	G. Crowe	345	.275	7	61	713	53	6	65	8.3	.992	B. Purkey	37	250	17	11	0	3.60
	2B	J. Temple	542	.306	3	47	**395**	353	16	90	5.4	.979	H. Haddix	29	184	8	7	0	3.52
W-76 L-78	SS	R. McMillan	393	.229	1	25	278	394	14	81	4.7	**.980**	B. Lawrence	46	181	8	13	5	4.13
	3B	D. Hoak	417	.261	6	50	132	244	14	29	3.5	.964	J. Nuxhall	36	176	12	11	0	3.79
Birdie Tebbetts	RF	J. Lynch	420	.312	16	68	154	5	5	2	1.6	.970	D. Newcombe	20	133	7	7	1	3.85
W-52 L-61	CF	G. Bell	385	.252	10	46	235	7	1	2	2.3	.996	T. Acker	38	125	4	3	1	4.55
	LF	F. Robinson	554	.269	31	83	310	12	3	1	2.4	.991	A. Kellner	18	82	7	3	0	2.30
Jimmy Dykes	C	E. Bailey	360	.250	11	59	438	44	6	6	4.9	.988	H. Jeffcoat	49	75	6	8	9	3.72
W-24 L-17	C	S. Burgess	251	.283	6	31	297	21	4	2	5.6	.988							
	UT	A. Grammas	216	.218	0	12	126	174	6	32		.980							
	OF	P. Whisenant	203	.236	11	40	122	3	0	1	1.9	1.000							
	OF	B. Thurman	178	.230	4	20	80	2	2	1	2.0	.976							
	1B	W. Dropo	162	.290	7	31	300	27	0	31	7.6	1.000							
Chicago	1B	D. Long	480	.271	20	75	1173	84	10	130	9.2	.992	T. Phillips	39	170	7	10	1	4.76
	2B	T. Taylor	497	.235	6	27	311	374	23	103	5.2	.968	G. Hobbie	55	168	10	6	2	3.74
W-72 L-82	SS	E. Banks	**617**	.313	**47**	**129**	292	468	**32**	100	5.1	.960	D. Drott	39	167	7	11	0	5.43
	3B	A. Dark	464	.295	3	43	107	225	18	24	3.2	.949	D. Hillman	31	126	4	8	1	3.15
Bob Scheffing	RF	L. Walls	513	.304	24	72	241	10	2	1	1.9	.992	M. Drabowsky	22	126	9	11	0	4.51
	CF	B. Thomson	547	.283	21	82	353	13	4	3	2.5	.989	D. Elston	**69**	97	9	8	10	2.88
	LF	W. Moryn	512	.264	26	77	265	4	6	1	2.0	.978	J. Briggs	20	96	5	5	0	4.52
	C	S. Taylor	301	.259	6	36	460	23	6	4	5.6	.988	B. Henry	44	81	5	4	6	2.88
	32	J. Goryl	219	.242	4	14	91	153	16	26		.938							
	C	C. Neeman	201	.259	12	29	340	25	3	6	5.2	.992							
St. Louis	1B	S. Musial	472	.337	17	62	1019	**100**	13	127	9.1	.989	S. Jones	35	250	14	13	0	2.88
	2B	D. Blasingame	547	.274	2	36	312	380	**26**	97	5.2	.964	L. Jackson	49	198	13	13	8	3.68
	SS	E. Kasko	259	.220	2	22	111	186	12	47	4.0	.961	V. Mizell	30	190	10	14	0	3.42
W-72 L-82	3B	K. Boyer	570	.307	23	90	**156**	350	20	**41**	**3.7**	.962	J. Brosnan	33	115	8	4	7	3.44
	RF	W. Moon	290	.238	7	38	122	5	2	0	1.6	.984	B. Mabe	31	112	3	9	0	4.51
Fred Hutchinson	CF	C. Flood	422	.261	10	41	346	18	8	3	3.1	.978	L. McDaniel	26	109	5	7	0	5.80
W-69 L-75	LF	D. Ennis	329	.261	3	47	122	11	1	2	1.6	.993	B. Muffett	35	84	4	6	5	4.93
	C	H. Smith	220	.227	1	24	346	22	4	4	5.2	.989							
Stan Hack	OC	G. Green	442	.281	13	55	428	35	9	5		.981							
W-3 L-7	10	J. Cunningham	337	.312	12	57	418	26	3	21		.993							
	S2	G. Freese	191	.257	6	16	77	77	12	14		.928							
	OF	I. Noren	178	.264	4	22	75	1	2	0	1.0	.974							
Los Angeles	1B	G. Hodges	475	.259	22	64	907	69	8	**134**	8.1	.992	D. Drysdale	44	212	12	13	0	4.17
	2B	C. Neal	473	.254	22	65	334	343	17	**121**	5.3	.976	J. Podres	39	210	13	15	1	3.72
W-71 L-83	SS	D. Zimmer	455	.262	17	60	265	372	23	100	**5.8**	.965	S. Koufax	40	159	11	11	1	4.48
	3B	D. Gray	197	.249	9	30	56	139	15	18	3.8	.929	S. Williams	27	119	9	7	0	4.01
Walter Alston	RF	C. Furillo	411	.290	18	83	187	5	5	0	1.7	.975	C. Labine	52	104	6	6	14	4.15
	CF	D. Snider	327	.312	15	58	151	4	2	0	1.7	.987	F. Kipp	40	102	6	6	0	5.01
	LF	G. Cimoli	325	.246	9	27	180	10	5	2	1.9	.974	J. Klippstein	45	90	3	5	9	3.80
	C	J. Roseboro	384	.271	14	43	594	36	8	5	**6.1**	.987							
	UT	J. Gilliam	555	.261	2	43	245	176	12	37		.972							
	01	N. Larker	253	.277	4	29	239	17	5	18		.981							

NATIONAL LEAGUE 1958, *cont.*

Philadelphia

W-69 L-85

Mayo Smith
W-39 L-45

Eddie Sawyer
W-30 L-40

POS	Player	AB	BA	HR	RBI	PO	A	E	DP	TC/G	FA	Pitcher	G	IP	W	L	SV	ERA
1B	E. Bouchee	334	.257	9	39	690	58	5	59	8.5	.993	R. Roberts	35	270	17	14	0	3.24
2B	S. Hemus	334	.284	8	36	188	220	13	52	5.0	.969	R. Semproch	36	204	13	11	0	3.92
SS	C. Fernandez	522	.230	6	51	296	415	18	88	4.9	.975	J. Sanford	38	186	10	13	0	4.44
3B	W. Jones	398	.271	14	60	137	186	11	13	3.0	**.967**	C. Simmons	29	168	7	14	1	4.38
RF	W. Post	379	.282	12	62	185	12	10	0	2.3	.952	D. Cardwell	16	108	3	6	0	4.51
CF	R. Ashburn	615	**.350**	2	33	495	8	8	2	3.4	.984	D. Farrell	54	94	8	9	11	3.35
LF	H. Anderson	515	.301	23	97	155	4	4	1	1.9	.975	J. Meyer	37	90	3	6	2	3.59
C	S. Lopata	258	.248	9	33	418	28	6	6	5.7	.987							
UT	T. Kazanski	289	.228	3	35	140	175	8	41		.975							
OF	R. Repulski	238	.244	13	40	90	3	5	0	1.8	.949							
01	D. Philley	207	.309	3	31	183	12	1	12		.995							
OF	B. Bowman	184	.288	8	24	82	1	1	0	1.5	.988							
C	C. Sawatski	183	.230	5	12	271	17	4	2	5.5	.986							

BATTING AND BASE RUNNING LEADERS

Batting Average

R. Ashburn, PHI	.350
W. Mays, SF	.347
S. Musial, STL	.337
H. Aaron, MIL	.326
B. Skinner, PIT	.321

Slugging Average

E. Banks, CHI	.614
W. Mays, SF	.583
H. Aaron, MIL	.546
F. Thomas, PIT	.528
S. Musial, STL	.528

Home Runs

E. Banks, CHI	47
F. Thomas, PIT	35
E. Mathews, MIL	31
F. Robinson, CIN	31
H. Aaron, MIL	30

Total Bases

E. Banks, CHI	379
W. Mays, SF	350
H. Aaron, MIL	328
O. Cepeda, SF	309
F. Thomas, PIT	297

Runs Batted In

E. Banks, CHI	129
F. Thomas, PIT	109
H. Anderson, PHI	97
W. Mays, SF	96
O. Cepeda, SF	96

Stolen Bases

W. Mays, SF	31
R. Ashburn, PHI	30
T. Taylor, CHI	21
D. Blasingame, STL	20
J. Gilliam, LA	18

Hits

R. Ashburn, PHI	215
W. Mays, SF	208
H. Aaron, MIL	196
E. Banks, CHI	193

Base on Balls

R. Ashburn, PHI	97
J. Temple, CIN	91
E. Mathews, MIL	85
J. Cunningham, STL	82

Home Run Percentage

E. Banks, CHI	7.6
F. Thomas, PIT	6.2
E. Mathews, MIL	5.7
F. Robinson, CIN	5.6

Runs

W. Mays, SF	121
E. Banks, CHI	119
H. Aaron, MIL	109
K. Boyer, STL	101

Doubles

O. Cepeda, SF	38
D. Groat, PIT	36
S. Musial, STL	35
H. Anderson, PHI	34
H. Aaron, MIL	34

Triples

R. Ashburn, PHI	13
W. Mays, SF	11
B. Virdon, PIT	11
E. Banks, CHI	11

PITCHING LEADERS

Winning Percentage

W. Spahn, MIL	.667
L. Burdette, MIL	.667
B. Friend, PIT	.611
B. Purkey, CIN	.607
J. Antonelli, SF	.552

Earned Run Average

S. Miller, SF	2.47
S. Jones, STL	2.88
L. Burdette, MIL	2.91
W. Spahn, MIL	3.07
R. Roberts, PHI	3.24

Wins

B. Friend, PIT	22
W. Spahn, MIL	22
L. Burdette, MIL	20
B. Purkey, CIN	17
R. Roberts, PHI	17

Saves

R. Face, PIT	20
C. Labine, LA	14
D. Farrell, PHI	11
J. Klippstein, CIN, LA	10
M. Grissom, SF	10
D. Elston, CHI	10

Strikeouts

S. Jones, STL	225
W. Spahn, MIL	150
J. Podres, LA	143
J. Antonelli, SF	143
B. Friend, PIT	135

Complete Games

W. Spahn, MIL	23
R. Roberts, PHI	21
L. Burdette, MIL	19
B. Purkey, CIN	17
B. Friend, PIT	16

Fewest Hits/9 Innings

S. Jones, STL	7.34
S. Koufax, LA	7.49
S. Miller, SF	7.91
W. Spahn, MIL	7.98

Shutouts

C. Willey, MIL	4
J. Jay, MIL	3
G. Witt, PIT	3
B. Purkey, CIN	3
L. Burdette, MIL	3

Fewest Walks/9 Innings

L. Burdette, MIL	1.63
R. Roberts, PHI	1.70
V. Law, PIT	1.73
B. Purkey, CIN	1.76

Most Strikeouts/9 Inn.

S. Jones, STL	8.10
S. Koufax, LA	7.43
D. Drott, CHI	6.83
J. Podres, LA	6.12

Innings

W. Spahn, MIL	290
L. Burdette, MIL	275
B. Friend, PIT	274
R. Roberts, PHI	270

Games Pitched

D. Elston, CHI	69
R. Face, PIT	57
J. Klippstein, CIN, LA	57
G. Hobbie, CHI	55

							Batting						Fielding			Pitching					
	W	L	PCT	GB	R	OR	2B	3B	HR	BA	SA	SB	E	DP	FA	CG	BB	SO	ShO	SV	ERA
Milwaukee	92	62	.597		675	**541**	221	21	167	**.266**	.412	26	120	152	.980	**72**	426	773	**16**	17	**3.21**
Pittsburgh	84	70	.545	8	662	607	229	**68**	134	.264	.410	30	133	173	.978	43	470	679	10	**41**	3.56
San Francisco	80	74	.519	12	**727**	698	**250**	42	170	.263	.422	64	152	156	.975	38	512	775	7	25	3.98
Cincinnati	76	78	.494	16	695	621	242	40	123	.258	.389	61	**100**	148	**.983**	50	**419**	705	7	20	3.73
Chicago	72	82	.468	20	709	725	207	49	**182**	.265	**.426**	39	150	161	.975	27	619	805	5	24	4.22
St. Louis	72	82	.468	20	619	704	216	39	111	.261	.380	44	153	163	.974	45	567	822	6	25	4.12
Los Angeles	71	83	.461	21	668	761	166	50	172	.251	.402	**73**	146	**198**	.975	30	606	**855**	7	31	4.47
Philadelphia	69	85	.448	23	664	762	238	56	124	**.266**	.400	51	129	136	.978	51	446	778	6	15	4.32
					5419	5419	1769	365	1183	.262	.405	388	1083	1287	.977	356	4065	6192	64	198	3.95

AMERICAN LEAGUE 1958

New York

W-92 L-62

Casey Stengel

POS	Player	AB	BA	HR	RBI	PO	A	E	DP	TC/G	FA	Pitcher	G	IP	W	L	SV	ERA
1B	B. Skowron	465	.273	14	73	1040	71	8	112	9.5	**.993**	B. Turley	33	245	**21**	7	1	2.97
2B	G. McDougald	503	.250	14	65	265	298	13	97	5.0	.977	W. Ford	30	219	14	7	1	**2.01**
SS	T. Kubek	559	.265	2	48	242	453	28	98	5.4	.961	A. Ditmar	38	140	9	8	4	3.42
3B	A. Carey	315	.286	12	45	99	195	12	22	3.1	.961	B. Shantz	33	126	7	6	0	3.36
RF	H. Bauer	452	.268	12	50	186	7	4	0	1.6	.980	J. Kucks	34	126	8	8	4	3.93
CF	M. Mantle	519	.304	**42**	97	331	5	8	2	2.3	.977	D. Larsen	19	114	9	6	0	3.07
LF	N. Siebern	460	.300	14	55	259	8	5	2	2.0	.982	D. Maas	22	101	7	3	0	3.82
C	Y. Berra	433	.266	22	90	509	41	0	8	**6.5**	**1.000**	R. Duren	44	76	6	4	**20**	2.02
CO	E. Howard	376	.314	11	66	409	27	2	8		.995							
3B	J. Lumpe	232	.254	3	32	57	126	11	13	3.0	.943							
2B	B. Richardson	182	.247	0	14	104	110	6	35	4.3	.973							

AMERICAN LEAGUE 1958, *cont.*

Chicago

W-82 L-72

Al Lopez

POS	Player	AB	BA	HR	RBI	PO	A	E	DP	TC/G	FA	Pitcher	G	IP	W	L	SV	ERA
1B	E. Torgeson	188	.266	10	30	470	30	11	54	7.0	.978	D. Donovan	34	248	15	14	0	3.01
2B	N. Fox	623	.300	0	49	**444**	399	13	**117**	5.5	.985	B. Pierce	35	245	17	11	2	2.68
SS	L. Aparicio	557	.266	2	40	**289**	**463**	21	90	5.3	.973	E. Wynn	40	240	14	16	2	4.13
3B	B. Goodman	425	.299	0	40	67	204	14	16	2.6	.951	J. Wilson	28	156	9	9	1	4.10
RF	J. Rivera	276	.225	9	35	153	7	1	3	1.6	.994	R. Moore	32	137	9	7	2	3.82
CF	J. Landis	523	.277	15	64	331	9	5	1	2.4	.986	G. Staley	50	85	4	5	8	3.16
LF	A. Smith	480	.252	12	58	249	9	8	2	1.9	.970	T. Lown	27	41	3	3	8	3.98
C	S. Lollar	421	.273	20	84	597	63	9	8	5.8	.987							
30	B. Phillips	260	.273	5	30	122	87	8	13		.963							
1B	R. Boone	246	.244	7	41	511	34	8	45	8.8	.986							
C	E. Battey	168	.226	8	26	220	27	3	6	5.1	.988							
OF	D. Mueller	166	.253	0	16	57	3	2	1	1.4	.968							
1B	R. Jackson	146	.233	7	21	289	16	1	29	8.1	.997							

Boston

W-79 L-75

Pinky Higgins

POS	Player	AB	BA	HR	RBI	PO	A	E	DP	TC/G	FA	Pitcher	G	IP	W	L	SV	ERA
1B	D. Gernert	431	.237	20	69	**1101**	**93**	11	**118**	**10.6**	.991	T. Brewer	33	227	12	12	0	3.72
2B	P. Runnels	568	.322	8	59	267	320	9	88	**5.6**	.985	F. Sullivan	32	199	13	9	3	3.57
SS	D. Buddin	497	.237	12	43	269	445	**31**	**102**	**5.5**	.958	I. Delock	31	160	14	8	2	3.38
3B	F. Malzone	**627**	.295	15	87	139	**378**	**27**	**36**	**3.5**	.950	D. Sisler	30	149	8	9	0	4.94
RF	J. Jensen	548	.286	35	**122**	293	14	6	3	2.0	.981	M. Wall	52	114	8	9	10	3.62
CF	J. Piersall	417	.237	8	48	314	8	5	2	2.6	.985	M. Fornieles	37	111	4	6	1	4.96
LF	T. Williams	411	**.328**	26	85	154	3	7	0	1.4	.957	L. Kiely	47	81	5	2	12	3.00
C	S. White	328	.259	6	35	450	38	6	8	4.8	.988							
OF	G. Stephens	270	.219	9	25	149	5	4	2	1.4	.975							
C	L. Berberet	167	.210	2	18	234	18	4	2	5.2	.984							

Cleveland

W-77 L-76

Bobby Bragan
W-31 L-36

Joe Gordon
W-46 L-40

POS	Player	AB	BA	HR	RBI	PO	A	E	DP	TC/G	FA	Pitcher	G	IP	W	L	SV	ERA
1B	M. Vernon	355	.293	8	55	774	50	11	90	8.7	.987	C. McLish	39	226	16	8	1	2.99
2B	B. Avila	375	.253	5	30	175	177	5	62	4.4	.986	M. Grant	44	204	10	11	4	3.84
SS	B. Hunter	190	.195	0	9	124	165	16	46	4.1	.948	R. Narleski	44	183	13	10	1	4.07
3B	B. Harrell	229	.218	7	19	21	50	1	7	1.6	.986	G. Bell	33	182	12	10	1	3.31
RF	R. Colavito	489	.303	41	113	243	14	5	6	2.0	.981	D. Mossi	43	102	7	8	3	3.90
CF	L. Doby	247	.283	13	45	141	5	0	0	2.1	1.000	H. Wilhelm	30	90	2	7	5	2.49
LF	M. Minoso	556	.302	24	80	301	13	8	1	2.2	.975	H. Woodeshick	14	72	6	6	0	3.64
C	R. Nixon	376	.301	9	46	499	31	5	4	5.3	.991							
UT	V. Power	385	.317	12	53	365	172	8	68		.985							
2S	B. Moran	257	.226	1	18	174	210	15	56		.962							
OF	G. Geiger	195	.231	1	6	133	3	2	2	2.6	.986							
OF	R. Maris	182	.225	9	27	109	6	4*	1	2.5	.966							
C	D. Brown	173	.237	7	20	278	23	4	6	4.9	.987							
S3	C. Carrasquel	156	.256	2	21	54	84	8	17		.945							
31	P. Ward	148	.338	4	21	162	40	2	12		.990							

Detroit

W-77 L-77

Jack Tighe
W-21 L-28

Bill Norman
W-56 L-49

POS	Player	AB	BA	HR	RBI	PO	A	E	DP	TC/G	FA	Pitcher	G	IP	W	L	SV	ERA
1B	G. Harris	451	.273	20	83	942	79	**15**	90	8.5	.986	F. Lary	39	**260**	16	15	1	2.90
2B	F. Bolling	610	.269	14	75	342	**445**	12	109	5.2	**.985**	P. Foytack	39	230	15	13	1	3.44
SS	B. Martin	498	.255	7	42	159	229	17	58	4.6	.958	J. Bunning	35	220	14	12	0	3.52
3B	R. Bertoia	240	.233	6	27	70	139	11	13	3.2	.950	B. Hoeft	36	143	10	9	3	4.15
RF	A. Kaline	543	.313	16	85	316	23	2	4	2.4	.994	H. Moford	25	110	4	9	1	3.61
CF	H. Kuenn	561	.319	8	54	358	9	6	1	2.7	.984	H. Aguirre	44	70	3	4	5	3.75
LF	C. Maxwell	397	.272	13	65	201	4	3	0	1.8	.986							
C	R. Wilson	298	.299	3	29	565	34	5	6	6.0	.992							
SS	C. Veal	207	.256	0	16	95	160	5	30	4.5	.981							
3B	O. Virgil	193	.244	3	19	55	101	3	7	3.2	.981							
OF	G. Zernial	124	.323	5	23	30	1	2	0	1.4	.939							
1B	R. Boone	114	.237	6	20	236	15	3	26	7.9	.988							

Baltimore

W-74 L-79

Paul Richards

POS	Player	AB	BA	HR	RBI	PO	A	E	DP	TC/G	FA	Pitcher	G	IP	W	L	SV	ERA
1B	B. Boyd	401	.309	7	36	757	53	5	85	8.2	.994	J. Harshman	34	236	12	15	4	2.89
2B	B. Gardner	560	.225	3	33	349	350	11	113	4.7	.985	B. O'Dell	41	221	14	11	8	2.97
SS	W. Miranda	214	.201	1	8	137	216	14	53	3.6	.962	A. Portocarrero	32	205	15	11	2	3.25
3B	B. Robinson	463	.238	3	32	**151**	275	21	30	3.2	.953	M. Pappas	31	135	10	10	0	4.06
RF	A. Pilarcik	379	.243	1	24	213	5	3	0	1.9	.986	C. Johnson	26	118	6	9	1	3.88
CF	J. Busby	215	.237	3	19	196	1	1	0	1.9	.995	B. Loes	32	114	3	9	5	3.63
LF	G. Woodling	413	.276	15	65	181	7	5	1	1.7	.974	H. Brown	19	97	7	5	1	3.07
C	G. Triandos	474	.245	30	79	**698**	61	**10**	11	5.8	.987	G. Zuverink	45	69	2	2	7	3.39
UT	D. Williams	409	.276	4	32	359	61	8	27		.981							
OF	B. Nieman	366	.325	16	60	145	3	6	0	1.5	.961							
SS	F. Castleman	200	.170	3	14	102	165	10	37	3.0	.964							
1B	J. Marshall	191	.215	5	19	382	19	0	37	7.7	1.000							

Kansas City

W-73 L-81

Harry Craft

POS	Player	AB	BA	HR	RBI	PO	A	E	DP	TC/G	FA	Pitcher	G	IP	W	L	SV	ERA
1B	V. Power	205	.302	4	27	439	48	4	54	9.6	.992	R. Terry	40	217	11	13	2	4.24
2B	H. Lopez	564	.261	17	73	251	282	**14**	78	5.7	.974	N. Garver	31	201	12	11	1	4.03
SS	J. De Maestri	442	.219	6	38	226	417	13	95	4.8	**.980**	R. Herbert	42	175	8	8	3	3.50
3B	H. Smith	315	.273	5	46	44	87	7	9	3.2	.949	J. Urban	30	132	8	11	1	5.93
RF	R. Maris	401	.247	19	53	194	9	5	3	2.1	.976	B. Grim	26	114	7	6	0	3.56
CF	B. Tuttle	511	.231	11	51	311	12	4	2	2.3	.988	M. Dickson	27	99	9	5	1	3.27
LF	B. Cerv	515	.305	38	104	311	13	5	3	2.4	.985	T. Gorman	50	90	4	4	8	3.51
C	H. Chiti	295	.268	9	44	425	41	6	9	5.7	.987	D. Tomanek	36	72	5	5	5	3.61
13	P. Ward	268	.254	6	24	358	76	12	34		.973	D. Maas	10	55	4	5	1	3.90
2B	M. Baxes	231	.212	0	8	134	151	9	40	4.8	.969							
OF	B. Martyn	226	.261	2	23	112	4	4	2	1.9	.967							
1B	H. Simpson	212	.264	7	27	384	18	4	44	9.4	.990							
C	F. House	202	.252	4	24	236	22	2	4	4.7	.992							
3S	C. Carrasquel	160	.213	2	13	53	97	4	16		.974							

AMERICAN LEAGUE 1958, *cont.*

Washington

W-61 L-93

Cookie Lavagetto

POS	Player	AB	BA	HR	RBI	PO	A	E	DP	TC/G	FA
1B	N. Zauchin	303	.228	15	37	749	56	4	74	8.9	.995
2B	K. Aspromonte	253	.225	5	27	139	184	12	49	4.7	.964
SS	R. Bridges	377	.263	5	28	191	331	13	73	4.8	.976
3B	E. Yost	406	.224	8	37	109	186	11	20	2.7	**.964**
RF	J. Lemon	501	.246	26	75	255	8	6	2	2.0	.978
CF	A. Pearson	530	.275	3	33	338	6	7	1	2.5	.980
LF	R. Sievers	550	.295	39	108	216	5	2	0	2.0	.991
C	C. Courtney	450	.251	8	62	682	**64**	7	**17**	5.9	.991
23	H. Plews	380	.258	2	29	156	208	16	45		.958
OF	N. Chrisley	233	.215	5	26	117	6	1	2	1.8	.992
SS	O. Alvarez	196	.209	0	5	113	158	9	33	4.4	.968
1B	J. Becquer	164	.238	0	12	319	34	2	26	8.5	.994

Pitcher	G	IP	W	L	SV	ERA
P. Ramos	43	259	14	**18**	3	4.23
R. Kemmerer	40	224	6	15	0	4.61
C. Pascual	31	177	8	12	0	3.15
H. Griggs	32	137	3	11	0	5.52
T. Clevenger	**55**	124	9	9	6	4.35
D. Hyde	53	103	10	3	18	1.75
V. Valentinetti	23	96	4	6	0	5.08

BATTING AND BASE RUNNING LEADERS

Batting Average
T. Williams, BOS .328
P. Runnels, BOS .322
H. Kuenn, DET .319
A. Kaline, DET .313
V. Power, KC, CLE .312

Slugging Average
R. Colavito, CLE .620
B. Cerv, KC .592
M. Mantle, NY .592
T. Williams, BOS .584
R. Sievers, WAS .544

Home Runs
M. Mantle, NY 42
R. Colavito, CLE 41
R. Sievers, WAS 39
B. Cerv, KC 38
J. Jensen, BOS 35

Total Bases
M. Mantle, NY 307
B. Cerv, KC 305
R. Colavito, CLE 303
R. Sievers, WAS 299
J. Jensen, BOS 293

Runs Batted In
J. Jensen, BOS 122
R. Colavito, CLE 113
R. Sievers, WAS 108
B. Cerv, KC 104
M. Mantle, NY 97

Stolen Bases
L. Aparicio, CHI 29
J. Rivera, CHI 21
J. Landis, CHI 19
M. Mantle, NY 18
M. Minoso, CLE 14

Hits
N. Fox, CHI 187
F. Malzone, BOS 185
V. Power, KC, CLE 184
P. Runnels, BOS 183

Base on Balls
M. Mantle, NY 129
J. Jensen, BOS 99
T. Williams, BOS 98
P. Runnels, BOS 87

Home Run Percentage
R. Colavito, CLE 8.4
M. Mantle, NY 8.1
B. Cerv, KC 7.4
R. Sievers, WAS 7.1

Runs
M. Mantle, NY 127
P. Runnels, BOS 103
V. Power, KC, CLE 98
M. Minoso, CLE 94

Doubles
H. Kuenn, DET 39
V. Power, KC, CLE 37
A. Kaline, DET 34
P. Runnels, BOS 32

Triples
V. Power, KC, CLE 10
J. Lemon, WAS 9
B. Tuttle, KC 9
L. Aparicio, CHI 9

PITCHING LEADERS

Winning Percentage
B. Turley, NY .750
C. McLish, CLE .667
B. Pierce, CHI .607
A. Portocarrero, BAL .577
P. Foytack, DET .536

Earned Run Average
W. Ford, NY 2.01
B. Pierce, CHI 2.68
J. Harshman, BAL 2.89
F. Lary, DET 2.90
B. O'Dell, BAL 2.97

Wins
B. Turley, NY 21
B. Pierce, CHI 17
C. McLish, CLE 16
F. Lary, DET 16

Saves
R. Duren, NY 20
D. Hyde, WAS 18
L. Kiely, BOS 12
M. Wall, BOS 10

Strikeouts
E. Wynn, CHI 179
J. Bunning, DET 177
B. Turley, NY 168
J. Harshman, BAL 161
C. Pascual, WAS 146

Complete Games
B. Turley, NY 19
B. Pierce, CHI 19
F. Lary, DET 19
J. Harshman, BAL 17
P. Foytack, DET 16
D. Donovan, CHI 16

Fewest Hits/9 Innings
B. Turley, NY 6.53
G. Bell, CLE 6.97
W. Ford, NY 7.14
B. Pierce, CHI 7.49

Shutouts
W. Ford, NY 7
B. Turley, NY 6
D. Donovan, CHI 4
E. Wynn, CHI 4
P. Ramos, WAS 4

Fewest Walks/9 Innings
D. Donovan, CHI 1.92
B. O'Dell, BAL 2.07
F. Sullivan, BOS 2.21
F. Lary, DET 2.35

Most Strikeouts/9 Inn.
C. Pascual, WAS 7.41
J. Bunning, DET 7.25
E. Wynn, CHI 6.72
B. Turley, NY 6.16

Innings
F. Lary, DET 260
P. Ramos, WAS 259
D. Donovan, CHI 248
B. Turley, NY 245
B. Pierce, CHI 245

Games Pitched
T. Clevenger, WAS 55
D. Tomanek, CLE, KC 54
D. Hyde, WAS 53
M. Wall, BOS 52

	W	L	PCT	GB	R	OR	Batting 2B	3B	HR	BA	SA	SB	Fielding E	DP	FA	Pitching CG	BB	SO	ShO	SV	ERA
New York	92	62	.597		**759**	577	212	39	**164**	**.268**	**.416**	48	128	**182**	.978	53	557	796	**21**	**33**	**3.22**
Chicago	82	72	.532	10	634	615	191	42	101	.257	.367	**101**	114	160	.981	55	515	751	15	25	3.61
Boston	79	75	.513	13	697	691	**229**	30	155	.256	.400	29	145	172	.976	44	521	695	5	28	3.92
Cleveland	77	76	.503	14.5	694	635	210	31	161	.258	.403	50	152	171	.974	51	604	766	2	20	3.73
Detroit	77	77	.500	15	659	606	**229**	41	109	.266	.389	48	**106**	140	**.982**	**59**	437	**797**	8	19	3.59
Baltimore	74	79	.484	17.5	521	**575**	195	19	108	.241	.350	33	114	159	.980	55	**403**	749	15	28	3.40
Kansas City	73	81	.474	19	642	713	196	**50**	138	.247	.381	22	125	166	.979	42	467	720	9	25	4.15
Washington	61	93	.396	31	553	747	161	38	121	.240	.357	22	118	163	.980	28	558	762	6	28	4.53
					5159	5159	1623	290	1057	.254	.383	353	1002	1313	.979	387	4062	6036	81	206	3.77

NATIONAL LEAGUE 1959

Los Angeles

W-88 L-68

Walter Alston

POS	Player	AB	BA	HR	RBI	PO	A	E	DP	TC/G	FA
1B	G. Hodges	413	.276	25	80	891	66	8	77	8.5	**.992**
2B	C. Neal	616	.287	19	83	**386**	413	9	**110**	5.4	**.989**
SS	D. Zimmer	249	.165	4	28	115	226	10	43	4.0	.972
3B	J. Gilliam	553	.282	3	34	121	245	16	18	2.9	.958
RF	D. Snider	370	.308	23	88	157	2	4	1	1.5	.975
CF	D. Demeter	371	.256	18	70	223	5	4	1	1.9	.983
LF	W. Moon	543	.302	19	74	224	13	4	2	1.7	.983
C	J. Roseboro	397	.232	10	38	**848**	54	8	10	**7.8**	.991
10	N. Larker	311	.289	8	49	491	48	5	53		.991
OF	R. Fairly	244	.238	4	23	97	8	4	1	1.2	.963
SS	M. Wills	242	.260	0	7	121	220	12	39	4.3	.966

Pitcher	G	IP	W	L	SV	ERA
D. Drysdale	44	271	17	13	2	3.46
J. Podres	34	195	14	9	0	4.11
S. Koufax	35	153	8	6	2	4.05
R. Craig	29	153	11	5	0	2.06
D. McDevitt	39	145	10	8	4	3.97
S. Williams	35	125	5	5	0	3.97
L. Sherry	23	94	7	2	3	2.19
C. Labine	56	85	5	10	9	3.93

NATIONAL LEAGUE 1959, *cont.*

Milwaukee

W-86 L-70

Fred Haney

POS	Player	AB	BA	HR	RBI	PO	A	E	DP	TC/G	FA	Pitcher	G	IP	W	L	SV	ERA
1B	J. Adcock	404	.292	25	76	761	80	2	67	9.5	.998	W. Spahn	40	**292**	**21**	15	0	2.96
2B	F. Mantilla	251	.215	3	19	97	126	7	26	3.8	.970	L. Burdette	41	290	**21**	15	1	4.07
SS	J. Logan	470	.291	13	50	260	431	18	78	5.1	.975	B. Buhl	31	198	15	9	0	2.86
3B	E. Mathews	594	.306	**46**	114	144	305	18	21	3.2	.961	J. Jay	34	136	6	11	0	4.09
RF	H. Aaron	629	**.355**	39	123	261	12	5	3	1.8	.982	J. Pizarro	29	134	6	2	0	3.77
CF	B. Bruton	478	.289	6	41	309	6	3	2	2.4	.991	C. Willey	26	117	5	9	0	4.15
LF	W. Covington	373	.279	7	45	148	6	6	2	1.7	.963	B. Rush	31	101	5	6	0	2.40
C	D. Crandall	518	.257	21	72	783	**71**	5	**15**	5.9	**.994**	D. McMahon	60	81	5	3	**15**	2.57
1B	F. Torre	263	.228	1	33	622	46	4	43	7.7	.994							
2B	B. Avila	172	.238	3	19	103	131	8	21	4.7	.967							

San Francisco

W-83 L-71

Bill Rigney

POS	Player	AB	BA	HR	RBI	PO	A	E	DP	TC/G	FA	Pitcher	G	IP	W	L	SV	ERA
1B	O. Cepeda	605	.317	27	105	929	70	16	74	8.3	.984	J. Antonelli	40	282	19	10	1	3.10
2B	D. Spencer	555	.265	12	62	350	413	24	82	5.2	.970	S. Jones	50	271	**21**	15	4	**2.83**
SS	E. Bressoud	315	.251	9	26	151	267	11	37	4.7	.974	M. McCormick	47	226	12	16	4	3.99
3B	J. Davenport	469	.258	6	38	91	221	7	15	2.6	**.978**	J. Sanford	36	222	15	12	1	3.16
RF	W. Kirkland	463	.272	22	68	212	8	7	0	1.9	.969	S. Miller	59	168	8	7	8	2.84
CF	W. Mays	575	.313	34	104	353	6	6	2	2.5	.984							
LF	J. Brandt	429	.270	12	57	176	10	3	2	1.6	.984							
C	H. Landrith	283	.251	3	29	576	45	5	5	5.7	.992							
OF	F. Alou	247	.275	10	33	111	2	3	0	1.7	.974							
SS	A. Rodgers	228	.250	6	24	110	197	22	35	5.0	.933							
1B	W. McCovey	192	.354	13	38	424	29	5	29	9.0	.989							
C	B. Schmidt	181	.243	5	20	307	30	0	1	4.8	1.000							
OF	L. Wagner	129	.225	5	22	48	0	3	0	1.8	.941							

Pittsburgh

W-78 L-76

Danny Murtaugh

POS	Player	AB	BA	HR	RBI	PO	A	E	DP	TC/G	FA	Pitcher	G	IP	W	L	SV	ERA
1B	D. Stuart	397	.297	27	78	831	81	**22**	87	8.9	.976	V. Law	34	266	18	9	1	2.98
2B	B. Mazeroski	493	.241	7	59	303	373	13	100	5.2	.981	B. Friend	35	235	8	**19**	0	4.03
SS	D. Groat	593	.275	5	51	**301**	473	**29**	**97**	**5.5**	.964	H. Haddix	31	224	12	12	0	3.13
3B	D. Hoak	564	.294	8	65	**169**	**322**	20	31	**3.3**	.961	R. Kline	33	186	11	13	0	4.26
RF	R. Clemente	432	.296	4	50	229	10	13	1	2.4	.948	B. Daniels	34	101	7	9	1	5.45
CF	B. Virdon	519	.254	8	41	404	16	9	5	3.0	.979	R. Face	57	93	18	1	10	2.70
LF	B. Skinner	547	.280	13	61	285	9	11	1	2.1	.964							
C	S. Burgess	377	.297	11	59	441	39	8	4	4.8	.984							
OF	R. Mejias	276	.236	7	28	155	8	5	2	2.0	.970							
1B	R. Nelson	175	.291	6	32	337	18	2	45	6.4	.994							
C	D. Kravitz	162	.253	3	21	198	19	3	3	4.9	.986							

Chicago

W-74 L-80

Bob Scheffing

POS	Player	AB	BA	HR	RBI	PO	A	E	DP	TC/G	FA	Pitcher	G	IP	W	L	SV	ERA
1B	D. Long	296	.236	14	37	731	49	12	63	9.3	.985	B. Anderson	37	235	12	13	0	4.13
2B	T. Taylor	624	.280	8	38	352	**456**	**25**	105	**5.6**	.970	G. Hobbie	46	234	16	13	0	3.69
SS	E. Banks	589	.304	45	**143**	271	**519**	12	95	5.2	**.985**	D. Hillman	39	191	8	11	0	3.53
3B	A. Dark	477	.264	6	45	111	255	20	20	2.9	.948	M. Drabowsky	31	142	5	10	0	4.13
RF	L. Walls	354	.257	8	33	203	1	7	0	1.8	.967	B. Henry	**65**	134	9	8	12	2.68
CF	G. Altman	420	.245	12	47	278	7	3	2	2.4	.990	A. Ceccarelli	18	102	5	5	0	4.76
LF	B. Thomson	374	.259	11	52	223	9	3	4	2.0	.987	J. Buzhardt	31	101	4	5	0	4.97
C	S. Taylor	353	.269	13	43	497	37	**10**	1	5.0	.982	D. Elston	**65**	98	10	8	13	3.32
OF	W. Moryn	381	.234	14	48	175	9	2	1	1.8	.989							
1B	J. Marshall	294	.252	11	40	558	51	2	52	8.5	.997							
UT	E. Averill	186	.237	10	34	197	49	13	4		.950							
OF	I. Noren	156	.321	4	19	81	4	0	1	2.1	1.000							

Cincinnati

W-74 L-80

Mayo Smith
W-35 L-45

Fred Hutchinson
W-39 L-35

POS	Player	AB	BA	HR	RBI	PO	A	E	DP	TC/G	FA	Pitcher	G	IP	W	L	SV	ERA
1B	F. Robinson	540	.311	36	125	998	75	17	**111**	8.7	.984	D. Newcombe	30	222	13	8	1	3.16
2B	J. Temple	598	.311	8	67	322	390	19	96	4.9	.974	B. Purkey	38	218	13	18	1	4.25
SS	E. Kasko	329	.283	2	31	182	271	11	61	5.5	.976	O. Pena	46	136	5	9	5	4.76
3B	W. Jones	233	.249	7	31	92	105	7	9	3.0	.966	J. Nuxhall	28	132	9	9	1	4.24
RF	G. Bell	580	.293	19	115	269	15	1	1	2.0	.996	J. O'Toole	28	129	5	8	0	5.15
CF	V. Pinson	**648**	.316	20	84	423	11	7	4	2.9	.984	B. Lawrence	43	128	7	12	10	4.77
LF	J. Lynch	379	.269	17	58	180	5	4	3	1.9	.979	J. Brosnan	26	83	8	3	2	3.35
C	E. Bailey	379	.264	12	40	549	64	6	6	5.3	.990	J. Hook	17	79	5	5	0	5.13
UT	F. Thomas	374	.225	12	47	206	126	19	19		.946							
SS	R. McMillan	246	.264	9	24	163	205	10	50	5.2	.974							
C	D. Dotterer	161	.267	2	17	230	20	2	3	4.9	.992							
P	D. Newcombe	105	.305	3	21	14	31	1	4	1.5	.978							

St. Louis

W-71 L-83

Solly Hemus

POS	Player	AB	BA	HR	RBI	PO	A	E	DP	TC/G	FA	Pitcher	G	IP	W	L	SV	ERA
1B	S. Musial	341	.255	14	44	623	63	7	72	7.7	.990	L. Jackson	40	256	14	13	0	3.30
2B	D. Blasingame	615	.289	1	24	362	439	17	104	5.5	.979	V. Mizell	31	201	13	10	0	4.20
SS	A. Grammas	368	.269	3	30	216	373	22	80	4.7	.964	E. Broglio	35	181	7	12	0	4.72
3B	K. Boyer	563	.309	28	94	134	300	20	**32**	3.2	.956	L. McDaniel	62	132	14	12	**15**	3.82
RF	J. Cunningham	458	.345	7	60	201	5	6	1	1.8	.972	G. Blaylock	26	100	4	5	0	5.13
CF	G. Cimoli	519	.279	8	72	267	12	6	2	2.0	.979	M. Bridges	27	76	6	3	1	4.26
LF	B. White	517	.302	12	72	175	2	7	1	2.0	.962							
C	H. Smith	452	.270	13	50	758	60	9	13	5.9	.989							
OF	C. Flood	208	.255	7	26	147	1	5	1	1.4	.967							
OF	G. Oliver	172	.244	6	28	62	1	3	0	1.6	.955							
PH	G. Crowe	103	.301	8	29	82	12	0	9	6.7	1.000							

Philadelphia

W-64 L-90

Eddie Sawyer

POS	Player	AB	BA	HR	RBI	PO	A	E	DP	TC/G	FA	Pitcher	G	IP	W	L	SV	ERA
1B	E. Bouchee	499	.285	15	74	**1127**	**95**	17	96	**9.2**	.986	R. Roberts	35	257	15	17	0	4.27
2B	S. Anderson	477	.218	0	34	343	403	12	70	5.0	.984	J. Owens	31	221	12	12	1	3.21
SS	J. Koppe	422	.261	7	28	218	347	27	67	5.2	.954	G. Conley	25	180	12	7	1	3.00
3B	G. Freese	400	.268	23	70	83	156	**22**	15	2.4	.916	D. Cardwell	25	153	9	10	0	4.06
RF	W. Post	468	.254	22	94	226	12	2	3	2.0	.992	R. Semproch	30	112	3	10	3	5.40
CF	R. Ashburn	564	.266	1	20	359	4	11	1	2.5	.971	R. Gomez	20	72	3	8	1	6.10
LF	H. Anderson	508	.240	14	63	283	17	6	4	2.2	.980	D. Farrell	38	57	1	6	6	4.74
C	C. Sawatski	198	.293	9	43	306	23	7	4	4.9	.979							
01	D. Philley	254	.291	7	37	238	15	4	18		.984							
3B	W. Jones	160	.269	7	24	40	76	3	5	2.6	.975							

NATIONAL LEAGUE 1959, *cont.*

BATTING AND BASE RUNNING LEADERS

Batting Average
- H. Aaron, MIL .355
- J. Cunningham, STL .345
- O. Cepeda, SF .317
- V. Pinson, CIN .316
- W. Mays, SF .313

Slugging Average
- H. Aaron, MIL .636
- E. Banks, CHI .596
- E. Mathews, MIL .593
- F. Robinson, CIN .583
- W. Mays, SF .583

Home Runs
- E. Mathews, MIL 46
- E. Banks, CHI 45
- H. Aaron, MIL 39
- F. Robinson, CIN 36
- W. Mays, SF 34

Total Bases
- H. Aaron, MIL 400
- E. Mathews, MIL 352
- E. Banks, CHI 351
- W. Mays, SF 335
- V. Pinson, CIN 330

Runs Batted In
- E. Banks, CHI 143
- F. Robinson, CIN 125
- H. Aaron, MIL 123
- G. Bell, CIN 115
- E. Mathews, MIL 114

Stolen Bases
- W. Mays, SF 27
- J. Gilliam, LA 23
- O. Cepeda, SF 23
- T. Taylor, CHI 23
- V. Pinson, CIN 21

Hits
- H. Aaron, MIL 223
- V. Pinson, CIN 205
- O. Cepeda, SF 192
- J. Temple, CIN 186

Base on Balls
- J. Gilliam, LA 96
- J. Cunningham, STL 88
- W. Moon, LA 81
- E. Mathews, MIL 80

Home Run Percentage
- E. Mathews, MIL 7.7
- E. Banks, CHI 7.6
- F. Robinson, CIN 6.7
- H. Aaron, MIL 6.2

Runs
- V. Pinson, CIN 131
- W. Mays, SF 125
- E. Mathews, MIL 118
- H. Aaron, MIL 116

Doubles
- V. Pinson, CIN 47
- H. Aaron, MIL 46
- W. Mays, SF 43
- G. Cimoli, STL 40

Triples
- W. Moon, LA 11
- C. Neal, LA 11
- A. Dark, CHI 9
- B. White, STL 9
- V. Pinson, CIN 9

PITCHING LEADERS

Winning Percentage
- R. Face, PIT .947
- V. Law, PIT .667
- J. Antonelli, SF .655
- B. Buhl, MIL .625

Earned Run Average
- S. Jones, SF 2.83
- S. Miller, SF 2.84
- B. Buhl, MIL 2.86
- W. Spahn, MIL 2.96
- V. Law, PIT 2.98

Wins
- S. Jones, SF 21
- L. Burdette, MIL 21
- W. Spahn, MIL 21
- J. Antonelli, SF 19
- R. Face, PIT 18
- V. Law, PIT 18

Saves
- D. McMahon, MIL 15
- L. McDaniel, STL 15
- D. Elston, CHI 13
- B. Henry, CHI 12
- B. Lawrence, CIN 10
- R. Face, PIT 10

Strikeouts
- D. Drysdale, LA 242
- S. Jones, SF 209
- S. Koufax, LA 173
- J. Antonelli, SF 165
- M. McCormick, SF 151

Complete Games
- W. Spahn, MIL 21
- V. Law, PIT 20
- L. Burdette, MIL 20
- R. Roberts, PHI 19
- D. Newcombe, CIN 17
- J. Antonelli, SF 17

Fewest Hits/9 Innings
- H. Haddix, PIT 7.58
- S. Jones, SF 7.71
- G. Hobbie, CHI 7.85
- D. Drysdale, LA 7.88

Shutouts
- 7 tied with 4

Fewest Walks/9 Innings
- D. Newcombe, CIN 1.09
- L. Burdette, MIL 1.18
- R. Roberts, PHI 1.22
- B. Purkey, CIN 1.78

Most Strikeouts/9 Inn.
- D. Drysdale, LA 8.05
- S. Jones, SF 6.95
- J. Podres, LA 6.69
- E. Broglio, STL 6.60

Innings
- W. Spahn, MIL 292
- L. Burdette, MIL 290
- J. Antonelli, SF 282
- S. Jones, SF 271
- D. Drysdale, LA 271

Games Pitched
- D. Elston, CHI 65
- B. Henry, CHI 65
- L. McDaniel, STL 62
- D. McMahon, MIL 60

							Batting						Fielding			Pitching					
	W	L	PCT	GB	R	OR	2B	3B	HR	BA	SA	SB	E	DP	FA	CG	BB	SO	ShO	SV	ERA
*Los Angeles	88	68	.564		705	670	196	46	148	.257	.396	**84**	**114**	154	**.981**	43	614	**1077**	14	**26**	3.79
Milwaukee	86	70	.551	2	724	623	216	36	**177**	.265	.417	41	127	138	.979	**69**	429	775	**18**	18	3.51
San Francisco	83	71	.539	4	705	**613**	239	35	167	.261	.414	81	152	118	.974	52	500	873	12	23	**3.47**
Pittsburgh	78	76	.506	9	651	680	230	42	112	.263	.384	32	154	**165**	.975	48	**418**	730	7	17	3.90
Chicago	74	80	.481	13	673	688	209	44	163	.249	.398	32	140	142	.977	30	519	765	11	25	4.01
Cincinnati	74	80	.481	13	**764**	738	**258**	34	161	**.274**	**.427**	65	126	157	.978	44	456	690	7	**26**	4.31
St. Louis	71	83	.461	16	641	725	244	**49**	118	.269	.400	65	146	158	.975	36	564	846	8	25	4.34
Philadelphia	64	90	.416	23	599	725	196	38	113	.242	.362	39	154	132	.973	54	474	769	8	15	4.27
					5462	5462	1788	324	1159	.260	.400	439	1113	1164	.976	376	3974	6525	85	175	3.95

* Defeated Milwaukee in playoff 2 games to 0

AMERICAN LEAGUE 1959

	POS	Player	AB	BA	HR	RBI	PO	A	E	DP	TC/G	FA	Pitcher	G	IP	W	L	SV	ERA
Chicago	1B	E. Torgeson	277	.220	9	45	717	37	13	58	7.4	.983	E. Wynn	37	**256**	**22**	10	0	3.17
	2B	N. Fox	**624**	.306	2	70	**364**	**453**	10	93	5.3	**.988**	B. Shaw	47	231	18	6	3	2.69
W-94 L-60	SS	L. Aparicio	612	.257	6	51	**282**	**460**	23	87	**5.0**	**.970**	B. Pierce	34	224	14	15	0	3.62
	3B	B. Phillips	379	.264	5	40	90	202	15	13	3.1	.951	D. Donovan	31	180	9	10	0	3.66
Al Lopez	RF	J. McAnany	210	.276	0	27	106	6	4	4	1.7	.966	B. Latman	37	156	8	5	0	3.75
	CF	J. Landis	515	.272	5	60	420	10	3	2	2.9	.993	G. Staley	**67**	116	8	5	14	2.24
	LF	A. Smith	472	.237	17	55	303	8	6	2	2.5	.981	T. Lown	60	93	9	2	**15**	2.89
	C	S. Lollar	505	.265	22	84	623	51	5	**14**	5.6	.993							
	3B	B. Goodman	268	.250	1	28	57	135	10	10	2.7	.950							
	OF	J. Rivera	177	.220	4	19	75	5	2	3	1.2	.976							
	C	J. Romano	126	.294	5	25	169	16	4	5	5.0	.979							
Cleveland	1B	V. Power	595	.289	10	60	**1039**	**110**	6	**98**	**9.5**	**.995**	C. McLish	35	235	19	8	1	3.63
	2B	B. Martin	242	.260	9	24	147	149	1	37	4.4	.997	G. Bell	44	234	16	11	5	4.04
	SS	W. Held	525	.251	29	71	177	277	18	43	4.6	.962	M. Grant	38	165	10	7	3	4.14
	3B	G. Strickland	441	.238	3	48	69	131	6	11	2.6	.971	H. Score	30	161	9	11	0	4.71
W-89 L-65	RF	R. Colavito	588	.257	**42**	111	319	7	5	1	2.1	.985	J. Perry	44	153	12	10	4	2.65
	CF	J. Piersall	317	.246	4	30	216	3	4	2	2.5	.982	M. Garcia	29	72	3	6	1	4.00
Joe Gordon	LF	M. Minoso	570	.302	21	92	314	14	5	1	2.3	.985							
	C	R. Nixon	258	.240	1	29	374	31	6	8	5.6	.985							
	01	T. Francona	399	.363	20	79	432	21	5	21		.989							
	23	J. Baxes	247	.239	15	34	123	148	15	31		.948							
New York	1B	B. Skowron	282	.298	15	59	626	43	6	68	9.4	.991	W. Ford	35	204	16	10	1	3.04
	2B	B. Richardson	469	.301	2	33	256	292	17	85	5.2	.970	A. Ditmar	38	202	13	9	1	2.90
	SS	T. Kubek	512	.279	6	51	121	217	11	42	5.2	.968	B. Turley	33	154	8	11	0	4.32
W-79 L-75	3B	H. Lopez	406	.283	16	69	66	147	17	15	3.0	.926	D. Maas	38	138	14	8	4	4.43
	RF	H. Bauer	341	.238	9	39	139	2	4	0	1.3	.972	R. Terry	24	127	3	7	0	3.39
Casey Stengel	CF	M. Mantle	541	.285	31	75	366	7	2	3	2.6	.995	D. Larsen	25	125	6	7	0	4.33
	LF	N. Siebern	380	.271	11	53	175	1	2	0	1.9	.989	J. Coates	37	100	6	1	3	2.87
	C	Y. Berra	472	.284	19	69	**698**	61	2	9	**6.6**	**.997**	B. Shantz	33	95	7	3	3	2.38
	UT	E. Howard	443	.273	18	73	712	49	10	41		.987	R. Duren	41	77	3	6	14	1.88
	UT	G. McDougald	434	.251	4	34	190	345	10	70		.982							
	1B	M. Throneberry	192	.240	8	22	337	27	4	40	6.8	.989							
	OF	E. Slaughter	99	.172	6	21	27	0	1	0	1.1	.964							

AMERICAN LEAGUE 1959, *cont.*

Detroit

W-76 L-78

Bill Norman
W-2 L-15

Jimmy Dykes
W-74 L-63

POS	Player	AB	BA	HR	RBI	PO	A	E	DP	TC/G	FA	Pitcher	G	IP	W	L	SV	ERA
1B	G. Harris	349	.221	9	39	728	57	6	59	8.5	.992	J. Bunning	40	250	17	13	1	3.89
2B	F. Bolling	459	.266	13	55	281	340	8	81	5.0	.987	P. Foytack	39	240	14	14	1	4.64
SS	R. Bridges	381	.268	3	35	179	293	24	66	4.5	.952	D. Mossi	34	228	17	9	0	3.36
3B	E. Yost	521	.278	21	61	**168**	259	17	21	3.0	**.962**	F. Lary	32	223	17	10	0	3.55
RF	H. Kuenn	561	**.353**	9	71	247	6	3	0	1.9	.988	R. Narleski	42	104	4	12	5	5.78
CF	A. Kaline	511	.327	27	94	364	4	4	0	2.7	.989	T. Morgan	46	93	1	4	9	3.98
LF	C. Maxwell	518	.251	31	95	285	6	4	1	2.2	.986	D. Sisler	32	52	1	3	7	4.01
C	L. Berberet	338	.216	13	44	511	39	6	4	5.9	.989							
C	R. Wilson	228	.263	4	35	374	25	5	8	6.3	.988							
UT	T. Lepcio	215	.279	7	24	96	143	11	30		.956							
1B	B. Osborne	209	.191	3	21	377	27	7	36	7.3	.983							
1B	G. Zernial	132	.227	7	26	197	10	6	20	6.7	.972							

Boston

W-75 L-79

Pinky Higgins
W-31 L-42

Rudy York
W-0 L-1

Bill Jurges
W-44 L-36

POS	Player	AB	BA	HR	RBI	PO	A	E	DP	TC/G	FA	Pitcher	G	IP	W	L	SV	ERA
1B	D. Gernert	298	.262	11	42	552	49	3	54	8.1	.995	T. Brewer	36	215	10	12	2	3.76
2B	P. Runnels	560	.314	6	57	273	272	10	82	5.5	.982	J. Casale	31	180	13	8	0	4.31
SS	D. Buddin	485	.241	10	53	235	412	**35**	**89**	4.5	.949	F. Sullivan	30	178	9	11	1	3.95
3B	F. Malzone	604	.280	19	92	134	**357**	24	**40**	**3.3**	.953	B. Monbouquette	34	152	7	7	0	4.15
RF	J. Jensen	535	.277	28	**112**	311	12	6	4	2.3	.982	I. Delock	28	134	11	6	0	2.95
CF	G. Geiger	335	.245	11	48	173	5	2	1	1.9	.989	F. Baumann	26	96	6	4	1	4.05
LF	T. Williams	272	.254	10	43	94	4	3	0	1.3	.970	M. Fornieles	46	82	5	3	11	3.07
C	S. White	377	.284	1	42	557	56	6	8	5.2	.990	L. Kiely	41	56	3	3	7	4.20
OF	G. Stephens	270	.278	3	39	141	11	3	0	1.8	.981	M. Wall	26	49	2	5	3	5.51
OF	M. Keough	251	.243	7	27	147	5	1	1	2.2	.993							
1B	V. Wertz	247	.275	7	49	440	38	4	44	7.5	.992							
2B	P. Green	172	.233	1	10	109	132	7	38	5.5	.972							
C	P. Daley	169	.225	1	11	245	28	1	5	4.7	.996							

Baltimore

W-74 L-80

Paul Richards

POS	Player	AB	BA	HR	RBI	PO	A	E	DP	TC/G	FA	Pitcher	G	IP	W	L	SV	ERA
1B	B. Boyd	415	.265	3	41	927	46	**15**	88	9.1	.985	H. Wilhelm	32	226	15	11	0	**2.19**
2B	B. Gardner	401	.217	6	27	333	392	**18**	**104**	**5.3**	.976	M. Pappas	33	209	15	9	3	3.27
SS	C. Carrasquel	346	.223	4	28	124	237	11	63	4.2	.970	B. O'Dell	38	199	10	12	1	2.93
3B	B. Robinson	313	.284	4	24	92	187	13	25	3.4	.955	J. Walker	30	182	11	10	4	2.92
RF	G. Woodling	440	.300	14	77	210	2	4	0	1.7	.981	H. Brown	31	164	11	9	3	3.79
CF	W. Tasby	505	.250	13	48	320	13	11	4	2.5	.968	B. Loes	37	64	4	7	14	4.06
LF	B. Nieman	360	.292	21	60	171	6	5	0	1.9	.973							
C	G. Triandos	393	.216	25	73	597	**63**	**13**	5	5.4	.981							
S3	B. Klaus	321	.249	3	25	120	231	13	28		.964							
OF	A. Pilarcik	273	.282	3	16	133	3	3	1	1.3	.978							
C	J. Ginsberg	166	.181	1	14	241	29	2	4	4.4	.993							
1B	W. Dropo	151	.278	6	21	386	18	4	42	7.6	.990							

Kansas City

W-66 L-88

Harry Craft

POS	Player	AB	BA	HR	RBI	PO	A	E	DP	TC/G	FA	Pitcher	G	IP	W	L	SV	ERA
1B	K. Hadley	288	.253	10	39	656	42	8	66	7.4	.989	B. Daley	39	216	16	13	1	3.16
2B	W. Terwilliger	180	.267	2	18	144	166	9	42	5.1	.972	N. Garver	32	201	10	13	1	3.71
SS	J. De Maestri	352	.244	6	34	167	320	22	63	4.4	.957	R. Herbert	37	184	11	11	1	4.85
3B	D. Williams	488	.266	16	75	83	164	11	10	3.2	.957	J. Kucks	33	151	8	11	1	3.87
RF	R. Maris	433	.273	16	72	231	7	6	4	2.1	.975	B. Grim	40	125	6	10	4	4.09
CF	B. Tuttle	463	.300	7	43	294	17	5	3	2.6	.984	R. Coleman	29	81	2	10	2	4.56
LF	B. Cerv	463	.285	20	87	231	8	5	2	2.1	.980	T. Sturdivant	36	72	2	6	5	4.65
C	F. House	347	.236	1	30	447	43	9	7	5.3	.982							
2S	J. Lumpe	403	.243	3	28	218	306	12	80		.978							
3B	H. Smith	292	.288	5	31	85	119	10	10	2.8	.953							
OF	R. Snyder	243	.313	3	21	127	9	2	2	2.2	.986							
C	H. Chiti	162	.272	5	25	228	25	3	5	5.4	.988							
2B	H. Lopez	135	.281	6	24	81	71	11	15	4.9	.933							

Washington

W-63 L-91

Cookie Lavagetto

POS	Player	AB	BA	HR	RBI	PO	A	E	DP	TC/G	FA	Pitcher	G	IP	W	L	SV	ERA
1B	R. Sievers	385	.242	21	49	846	72	10	72	10.0	.989	C. Pascual	32	239	17	10	0	2.64
2B	R. Bertoia	308	.237	8	29	139	198	10	40	4.9	.971	P. Ramos	37	234	13	**19**	0	4.16
SS	B. Consolo	202	.213	0	10	111	229	17	44	4.8	.952	R. Kemmerer	37	206	8	17	0	4.50
3B	H. Killebrew	546	.242	**42**	105	129	325	**30**	18	3.2	.938	B. Fischer	34	187	9	11	0	4.28
RF	F. Throneberry	327	.251	10	42	136	7	7	2	1.7	.953	T. Clevenger	50	117	8	5	8	3.91
CF	B. Allison	570	.261	30	85	333	8	9	1	2.3	.974	H. Griggs	37	98	2	8	2	5.25
LF	J. Lemon	531	.279	33	100	281	4	9	0	2.1	.969	C. Stobbs	41	91	1	8	7	2.98
C	H. Naragon	195	.241	0	11	262	13	2	0	5.1	.993	D. Hyde	37	54	2	5	4	4.97
SS	R. Samford	237	.224	5	22	92	177	15	33	4.4	.947							
2B	K. Aspromonte	225	.244	2	14	101	137	10	25	4.8	.960							
1B	J. Becquer	220	.268	1	26	454	32	5	38	9.3	.990							
OF	L. Green	190	.242	2	15	89	4	2	0	1.6	.979							
C	C. Courtney	189	.233	2	18	213	11	3	2	4.3	.987							

BATTING AND BASE RUNNING LEADERS

Batting Average

H. Kuenn, DET	.353
A. Kaline, DET	.327
P. Runnels, BOS	.314
N. Fox, CHI	.306
M. Minoso, CLE	.302

Slugging Average

A. Kaline, DET	.530
H. Killebrew, WAS	.516
M. Mantle, NY	.514
R. Colavito, CLE	.512
J. Lemon, WAS	.510

Home Runs

H. Killebrew, WAS	42
R. Colavito, CLE	42
J. Lemon, WAS	33
C. Maxwell, DET	31
M. Mantle, NY	31

Total Bases

R. Colavito, CLE	301
H. Killebrew, WAS	282
H. Kuenn, DET	281
M. Mantle, NY	278
B. Allison, WAS	275

Runs Batted In

J. Jensen, BOS	112
R. Colavito, CLE	111
H. Killebrew, WAS	105
J. Lemon, WAS	100
C. Maxwell, DET	95

Stolen Bases

L. Aparicio, CHI	56
M. Mantle, NY	21
J. Landis, CHI	20
J. Jensen, BOS	20
B. Allison, WAS	13

PITCHING LEADERS

Winning Percentage

B. Shaw, CHI	.750
C. McLish, CLE	.704
E. Wynn, CHI	.688
D. Mossi, DET	.654
C. Pascual, WAS	.630
F. Lary, DET	.630

Earned Run Average

H. Wilhelm, BAL	2.19
C. Pascual, WAS	2.64
B. Shaw, CHI	2.69
A. Ditmar, NY	2.90
J. Walker, BAL	2.92

Wins

E. Wynn, CHI	22
C. McLish, CLE	19
B. Shaw, CHI	18

Saves

T. Lown, CHI	15
R. Duren, NY	14
B. Loes, BAL	14
G. Staley, CHI	14
M. Fornieles, BOS	11

Strikeouts

J. Bunning, DET	201
C. Pascual, WAS	185
E. Wynn, CHI	179
H. Score, CLE	147
H. Wilhelm, BAL	139

Complete Games

C. Pascual, WAS	17
M. Pappas, BAL	15
D. Mossi, DET	15
J. Bunning, DET	14
E. Wynn, CHI	14

AMERICAN LEAGUE 1959, *cont.*

BATTING AND BASE RUNNING LEADERS

Hits		Base on Balls		Home Run Percentage	
H. Kuenn, DET	198	E. Yost, DET	135	H. Killebrew, WAS	7.7
N. Fox, CHI	191	P. Runnels, BOS	95	R. Colavito, CLE	7.1
P. Runnels, BOS	176	M. Mantle, NY	94	J. Lemon, WAS	6.2
M. Minoso, CLE	172	D. Buddin, BOS	92	C. Maxwell, DET	6.0
V. Power, CLE	172				

Runs		Doubles		Triples	
E. Yost, DET	115	H. Kuenn, DET	42	B. Allison, WAS	9
M. Mantle, NY	104	F. Malzone, BOS	34	G. McDougald, NY	8
V. Power, CLE	102	N. Fox, CHI	34		
J. Jensen, BOS	101	D. Williams, KC	33		
		P. Runnels, BOS	33		

PITCHING LEADERS

Fewest Hits/9 Innings		Shutouts		Fewest Walks/9 Innings	
H. Score, CLE	6.89	C. Pascual, WAS	6	H. Brown, BAL	1.76
A. Ditmar, NY	6.95	E. Wynn, CHI	5	F. Lary, DET	1.86
H. Wilhelm, BAL	7.09	M. Pappas, BAL	4	N. Garver, KC	1.88
E. Wynn, CHI	7.11			D. Mossi, DET	1.93

Most Strikeouts/9 Inn.		Innings		Games Pitched	
H. Score, CLE	8.23	E. Wynn, CHI	256	G. Staley, CHI	67
J. Bunning, DET	7.25	J. Bunning, DET	250	T. Lown, CHI	60
C. Pascual, WAS	6.98	P. Foytack, DET	240	T. Clevenger, WAS	50
B. Turley, NY	6.47	C. Pascual, WAS	239	B. Shaw, CHI	47

	W	L	PCT	GB	R	OR	Batting 2B	3B	HR	BA	SA	SB	Fielding E	DP	FA	Pitching CG	BB	SO	ShO	SV	ERA
Chicago	94	60	.610		669	**588**	220	**46**	97	.250	.364	**113**	130	141	**.979**	44	525	761	13	**36**	**3.29**
Cleveland	89	65	.578	5	**745**	646	216	25	**167**	**.263**	**.408**	33	126	138	.978	**58**	635	799	7	23	3.75
New York	79	75	.513	15	687	647	224	40	153	.260	.402	45	131	160	.978	38	594	**836**	**15**	28	3.60
Detroit	76	78	.494	18	713	732	196	30	160	.258	.400	34	**124**	131	.978	53	**432**	829	9	24	4.20
Boston	75	79	.487	19	726	696	**248**	28	125	.256	.385	68	131	**167**	.978	38	589	724	9	25	4.17
Baltimore	74	80	.481	20	551	621	182	23	109	.238	.345	36	147	163	.976	45	476	735	**15**	30	3.56
Kansas City	66	88	.429	28	681	760	231	43	117	**.263**	.390	34	159	156	.973	44	492	703	8	21	4.35
Washington	63	91	.409	31	619	701	173	32	163	.237	.379	51	162	140	.973	46	467	694	10	21	4.01
					5391	5391	1690	267	1091	.253	.384	414	1110	1196	.977	366	4210	6081	86	208	3.87

NATIONAL LEAGUE 1960

Pittsburgh

W-95 L-59

Danny Murtaugh

POS	Player	AB	BA	HR	RBI	PO	A	E	DP	TC/G	FA	Pitcher	G	IP	W	L	SV	ERA
1B	D. Stuart	438	.260	23	83	920	77	**14**	90	9.4	.986	B. Friend	38	276	18	12	1	3.00
2B	B. Mazeroski	538	.273	11	64	**413**	**449**	10	**127**	**5.8**	**.989**	V. Law	35	272	20	9	0	3.08
SS	D. Groat	573	**.325**	2	50	237	443	24	92	**5.2**	.966	H. Haddix	29	172	11	10	1	3.97
3B	D. Hoak	553	.282	16	79	132	**324**	**25**	34	3.1	.948	V. Mizell	23	156	13	5	0	3.12
RF	R. Clemente	570	.314	16	94	246	19	8	2	1.9	.971	R. Face	**68**	115	10	8	24	2.90
CF	B. Virdon	409	.264	8	40	272	10	5	0	2.6	.983	F. Green	45	70	8	4	3	3.21
LF	B. Skinner	571	.273	15	86	250	13	5	2	1.9	.981							
C	S. Burgess	337	.294	7	39	485	38	3	7	5.9	**.994**							
OF	G. Cimoli	307	.267	0	28	181	5	7	1	2.1	.964							
C	H. Smith	258	.295	11	45	356	30	6	5	5.5	.985							
1B	R. Nelson	200	.300	7	35	463	37	2	48	6.9	.996							

Milwaukee

W-88 L-66

Chuck Dressen

POS	Player	AB	BA	HR	RBI	PO	A	E	DP	TC/G	FA	Pitcher	G	IP	W	L	SV	ERA
1B	J. Adcock	514	.298	25	91	**1229**	104	9	105	**9.9**	**.993**	L. Burdette	45	276	19	13	4	3.36
2B	C. Cottier	229	.227	3	19	180	214	13	40	4.4	.968	W. Spahn	40	268	**21**	10	2	3.50
SS	J. Logan	482	.245	7	42	235	417	30	77	5.0	.956	B. Buhl	36	239	16	9	0	3.09
3B	E. Mathews	548	.277	39	124	**141**	280	22	23	2.9	.950	C. Willey	28	145	6	7	0	4.35
RF	H. Aaron	590	.292	40	**126**	320	13	6	6	2.2	.982	J. Jay	32	133	9	8	1	3.24
CF	B. Bruton	629	.286	12	54	351	10	5	3	2.5	.986	J. Pizarro	21	115	6	7	0	4.55
LF	W. Covington	281	.249	10	35	106	2	4	1	1.6	.964	D. McMahon	48	64	3	6	10	5.94
C	D. Crandall	537	.294	19	77	**764**	**70**	10	9	6.0	.988	R. Piche	37	48	3	5	9	3.56
2B	R. Schoendienst	226	.257	1	19	120	148	10	34	4.5	.964							

St. Louis

W-86 L-68

Solly Hemus

POS	Player	AB	BA	HR	RBI	PO	A	E	DP	TC/G	FA	Pitcher	G	IP	W	L	SV	ERA
1B	B. White	554	.283	16	79	994	65	11	**109**	8.7	.990	L. Jackson	43	**282**	18	13	0	3.48
2B	J. Javier	451	.237	4	21	272	338	**24**	71	5.3	.962	E. Broglio	52	226	**21**	9	0	2.74
SS	D. Spencer	507	.258	16	58	215	323	31	66	4.1	.946	R. Sadecki	26	157	9	9	0	3.78
3B	K. Boyer	552	.304	32	97	140	300	19	**37**	**3.1**	.959	C. Simmons	23	152	7	4	0	2.66
RF	J. Cunningham	492	.280	6	39	184	6	10	1	1.7	.950	R. Kline	34	118	4	9	1	6.04
CF	C. Flood	396	.237	8	38	290	7	2	0	2.2	.993	L. McDaniel	65	116	12	4	**26**	2.09
LF	S. Musial	331	.275	17	63	97	2	1	0	1.7	.990							
C	H. Smith	337	.228	2	28	664	61	7	9	5.9	.990							
OF	W. Moryn	200	.245	11	35	100	4	1	0	1.7	.990							
UT	A. Grammas	196	.245	4	17	102	171	9	33		.968							
OF	B. Nieman	188	.287	4	31	63	0	4	0	1.2	.940							
C	C. Sawatski	179	.229	6	27	279	25	2	5	4.6	.993							

Los Angeles

W-82 L-72

Walter Alston

POS	Player	AB	BA	HR	RBI	PO	A	E	DP	TC/G	FA	Pitcher	G	IP	W	L	SV	ERA
1B	N. Larker	440	.323	5	78	914	80	7	81	8.4	.993	D. Drysdale	41	269	15	14	2	2.84
2B	C. Neal	477	.256	8	40	250	291	13	78	4.1	.977	J. Podres	34	228	14	12	0	3.08
SS	M. Wills	516	.295	0	27	260	431	**40**	78	5.0	.945	S. Williams	38	207	14	10	1	3.00
3B	J. Gilliam	557	.248	5	40	101	262	15	21	2.9	.960	S. Koufax	37	175	8	13	1	3.91
RF	F. Howard	448	.268	23	77	177	8	3	1	1.6	.984	L. Sherry	57	142	14	10	7	3.79
CF	T. Davis	352	.276	11	44	151	7	4	2	1.9	.975	E. Roebuck	58	117	8	3	8	2.78
LF	W. Moon	469	.299	13	69	194	15	3	3	1.7	.986	R. Craig	21	116	8	3	0	3.27
C	J. Roseboro	287	.213	8	42	640	48	5	**10**	**8.0**	.993							
OF	D. Snider	235	.243	14	36	108	3	4	1	1.5	.965							
1B	G. Hodges	197	.198	8	30	403	33	2	40	4.8	.995							
OF	D. Demeter	168	.274	9	29	92	2	1	1	1.5	.989							

NATIONAL LEAGUE 1960, *cont.*

San Francisco

W-79 L-75

Bill Rigney
W-33 L-25

Tom Sheehan
W-46 L-50

POS	Player	AB	BA	HR	RBI	PO	A	E	DP	TC/G	FA	Pitcher	G	IP	W	L	SV	ERA
1B	W. McCovey	260	.238	13	51	557	39	9	42	8.5	.985	M. McCormick	40	253	15	12	3	**2.70**
2B	D. Blasingame	523	.235	2	31	318	329	14	66	5.0	.979	S. Jones	39	234	18	14	0	3.19
SS	E. Bressoud	386	.225	9	43	191	339	22	53	4.8	.960	J. Sanford	37	219	12	14	0	3.82
3B	J. Davenport	363	.251	6	38	77	171	10	12	2.5	**.961**	B. O'Dell	43	203	8	13	2	3.20
RF	W. Kirkland	515	.252	21	65	252	16	6	5	1.9	.978	J. Antonelli	41	112	6	7	11	3.77
CF	W. Mays	595	.319	29	103	392	12	8	2	2.7	.981	S. Miller	47	102	7	6	2	3.90
LF	O. Cepeda	569	.297	24	96	163	10	3	3	1.9	.983	B. Loes	37	46	3	2	5	4.93
C	B. Schmidt	344	.267	8	37	631	31	**13**	6	6.3	.981							
32	J. Amalfitano	328	.277	1	27	99	184	14	24		.953							
OF	F. Alou	322	.264	8	44	156	5	7	0	1.8	.958							
UT	A. Rodgers	217	.244	2	22	112	129	12	26		.953							
C	H. Landrith	190	.242	1	20	346	23	**13**	5	5.5	.966							

Cincinnati

W-67 L-87

Fred Hutchinson

POS	Player	AB	BA	HR	RBI	PO	A	E	DP	TC/G	FA	Pitcher	G	IP	W	L	SV	ERA
1B	F. Robinson	464	.297	31	83	663	54	5	60	9.3	.993	B. Purkey	41	253	17	11	0	3.60
2B	B. Martin	317	.246	3	16	228	207	11	52	4.6	.975	J. Hook	36	222	11	18	0	4.50
SS	R. McMillan	399	.236	10	42	171	315	18	68	4.3	.964	J. O'Toole	34	196	12	12	1	3.80
3B	E. Kasko	479	.292	6	51	98	186	10	20	3.4	.966	C. McLish	37	151	4	14	0	4.16
RF	G. Bell	515	.262	12	62	239	13	3	1	1.9	.988	J. Nuxhall	38	112	1	8	0	4.42
CF	V. Pinson	**652**	.287	20	61	401	11	8	1	2.7	.981	J. Brosnan	57	99	7	2	12	2.36
LF	W. Post	249	.281	17	38	125	8	2	0	2.0	.985	D. Newcombe	16	83	4	6	0	4.57
C	E. Bailey	441	.261	13	67	621	52	7	8	5.3	.990	B. Henry	51	68	1	5	17	3.19
1B	G. Coleman	251	.271	6	32	559	63	1	69	9.4	.998							
OF	J. Lynch	159	.289	6	27	41	1	4	1	1.4	.913							
3B	W. Jones	149	.268	3	27	43	59	4	5	2.3	.962							

Chicago

W-60 L-94

Charlie Grimm
W-6 L-11

Lou Boudreau
W-54 L-83

POS	Player	AB	BA	HR	RBI	PO	A	E	DP	TC/G	FA	Pitcher	G	IP	W	L	SV	ERA
1B	E. Bouchee	299	.237	5	44	709	56	7	56	9.6	.991	G. Hobbie	46	259	16	**20**	1	3.97
2B	J. Kindall	246	.240	2	23	147	218	13	44	4.6	.966	B. Anderson	38	204	9	11	1	4.11
SS	E. Banks	597	.271	**41**	117	**283**	**488**	18	**94**	5.1	**.977**	D. Cardwell	31	177	8	14	0	4.37
3B	R. Santo	347	.251	9	44	78	144	13	6	2.5	.945	D. Ellsworth	31	177	7	13	0	3.72
RF	B. Will	475	.255	6	53	224	10	2	2	2.0	.992	D. Elston	60	127	8	9	11	3.40
CF	R. Ashburn	547	.291	0	40	317	11	8	2	2.3	.976	S. Morehead	45	123	2	9	4	3.94
LF	G. Altman	334	.266	13	51	144	2	1	0	1.9	.993							
C	M. Thacker	90	.156	0	6	170	23	4	2	3.9	.980							
UT	F. Thomas	479	.238	21	64	528	92	17	40		.973							
23	D. Zimmer	368	.258	6	35	208	266	16	30		.967							

Philadelphia

W-59 L-95

Eddie Sawyer
W-0 L-1

Andy Cohen
W-1 L-0

Gene Mauch
W-58 L-94

POS	Player	AB	BA	HR	RBI	PO	A	E	DP	TC/G	FA	Pitcher	G	IP	W	L	SV	ERA
1B	P. Herrera	512	.281	17	71	1017	**109**	**14**	88	8.5	.988	R. Roberts	35	237	12	16	1	4.02
2B	T. Taylor	505	.287	4	35	283	356	21	67	5.4	.968	J. Buzhardt	30	200	5	16	0	3.86
SS	R. Amaro	264	.231	0	16	153	230	14	47	4.3	.965	G. Conley	29	183	8	14	0	3.68
3B	A. Dark	198	.242	3	14	57	84	7	7	2.8	.953	J. Owens	31	150	4	14	0	5.04
RF	K. Walters	426	.239	8	37	220	17	3	4	2.0	.988	D. Green	23	109	3	6	0	4.06
CF	B. Del Greco	300	.237	10	26	247	10	8	1	3.0	.970	C. Short	42	107	6	9	3	3.94
LF	J. Callison	288	.260	9	30	176	7	2	4	2.2	.989	D. Farrell	59	103	10	6	11	2.70
C	J. Coker	252	.214	6	34	394	43	8	5	5.9	.982	A. Mahaffey	14	93	7	3	0	2.31
OF	T. Curry	245	.261	6	34	96	2	8	0	1.7	.925							
OF	T. Gonzalez	241	.299	6	33	146	6	3	0	2.3	.981							
OF	B. Smith	217	.286	4	27	125	4	0	1	1.8	1.000							
UT	L. Walls	181	.199	3	19	75	49	6	8		.954							
SS	J. Koppe	170	.171	1	13	107	133	11	23	4.6	.956							
C	C. Neeman	160	.181	4	13	252	31	6	2	5.6	.979							
C	C. Dalrymple	158	.272	4	21	172	25	7	3	4.3	.966							

BATTING AND BASE RUNNING LEADERS

Batting Average

D. Groat, PIT	.325
N. Larker, LA	.323
W. Mays, SF	.319
R. Clemente, PIT	.314
K. Boyer, STL	.304

Slugging Average

F. Robinson, CIN	.595
H. Aaron, MIL	.566
K. Boyer, STL	.562
W. Mays, SF	.555
E. Banks, CHI	.554

Home Runs

E. Banks, CHI	41
H. Aaron, MIL	40
E. Mathews, MIL	39
K. Boyer, STL	32
F. Robinson, CIN	31

Total Bases

H. Aaron, MIL	334
E. Banks, CHI	331
W. Mays, SF	330
K. Boyer, STL	310
V. Pinson, CIN	308

Runs Batted In

H. Aaron, MIL	126
E. Mathews, MIL	124
E. Banks, CHI	117
W. Mays, SF	103
K. Boyer, STL	97

Stolen Bases

M. Wills, LA	50
V. Pinson, CIN	32
T. Taylor, CHI, PHI	26
W. Mays, SF	25
B. Bruton, MIL	22

Hits

W. Mays, SF	190
V. Pinson, CIN	187
D. Groat, PIT	186
B. Bruton, MIL	180

Base on Balls

R. Ashburn, CHI	116
E. Mathews, MIL	111
J. Gilliam, LA	96
F. Robinson, CIN	82

Home Run Percentage

E. Mathews, MIL	7.1
E. Banks, CHI	6.9
H. Aaron, MIL	6.8
F. Robinson, CIN	6.7

Runs

B. Bruton, MIL	112
E. Mathews, MIL	108
W. Mays, SF	107
V. Pinson, CIN	107

Doubles

V. Pinson, CIN	37
O. Cepeda, SF	36
F. Robinson, CIN	33
B. Skinner, PIT	33

Triples

B. Bruton, MIL	13
W. Mays, SF	12
V. Pinson, CIN	12
H. Aaron, MIL	11

PITCHING LEADERS

Winning Percentage

E. Broglio, STL	.700
V. Law, PIT	.690
W. Spahn, MIL	.677
B. Buhl, MIL	.640
B. Purkey, CIN	.607

Earned Run Average

M. McCormick, SF	2.70
E. Broglio, STL	2.74
D. Drysdale, LA	2.84
S. Williams, LA	3.00
B. Friend, PIT	3.00

Wins

E. Broglio, STL	21
W. Spahn, MIL	21
V. Law, PIT	20
L. Burdette, MIL	19

Saves

L. McDaniel, STL	26
R. Face, PIT	24
B. Henry, CIN	17
J. Brosnan, CIN	12

Strikeouts

D. Drysdale, LA	246
S. Koufax, LA	197
S. Jones, SF	190
E. Broglio, STL	188
B. Friend, PIT	183

Complete Games

L. Burdette, MIL	18
W. Spahn, MIL	18
V. Law, PIT	18
G. Hobbie, CHI	16
B. Friend, PIT	16

Fewest Hits/9 Innings

E. Broglio, STL	6.84
S. Koufax, LA	6.84
S. Williams, LA	7.03
D. Drysdale, LA	7.16

Shutouts

J. Sanford, SF	6
D. Drysdale, LA	5

Fewest Walks/9 Innings

L. Burdette, MIL	1.14
R. Roberts, PHI	1.29
V. Law, PIT	1.33
B. Friend, PIT	1.47

Most Strikeouts/9 Inn.

S. Koufax, LA	10.13
D. Drysdale, LA	8.23
S. Williams, LA	7.60
E. Broglio, STL	7.48

Innings

L. Jackson, STL	282
L. Burdette, MIL	276
B. Friend, PIT	276
V. Law, PIT	272

Games Pitched

R. Face, PIT	68
L. McDaniel, STL	65
D. Elston, CHI	60
D. Farrell, PHI	59

NATIONAL LEAGUE 1960, *cont.*

	W	L	PCT	GB	R	OR	Batting 2B	3B	HR	BA	SA	SB	Fielding E	DP	FA	Pitching CG	BB	SO	ShO	SV	ERA
Pittsburgh	95	59	.617		**734**	**593**	**236**	56	120	**.276**	.407	34	128	**163**	**.979**	47	**386**	811	11	33	3.49
Milwaukee	88	66	.571	7	724	658	198	48	**170**	.265	**.417**	69	141	137	.976	**55**	518	807	13	28	3.76
St. Louis	86	68	.558	9	639	616	213	48	138	.254	.393	48	141	152	.976	37	511	906	11	30	3.64
Los Angeles	82	72	.532	13	662	**593**	216	38	126	.255	.383	**95**	**125**	142	**.979**	46	564	**1122**	13	20	**3.40**
San Francisco	79	75	.513	16	671	631	220	**62**	130	.255	.393	86	166	117	.972	**55**	512	897	**16**	26	3.44
Cincinnati	67	87	.435	28	640	692	230	40	140	.250	.388	73	**125**	155	**.979**	33	442	740	8	**35**	4.00
Chicago	60	94	.390	35	634	776	213	48	119	.243	.369	51	143	133	.977	36	565	805	6	25	4.35
Philadelphia	59	95	.383	36	546	691	196	44	99	.239	.351	45	155	129	.974	45	439	736	6	16	4.01
					5250	5250	1722	384	1042	.255	.388	501	1124	1128	.977	354	3937	6824	84	213	3.76

AMERICAN LEAGUE 1960

New York

W-97 L-57

Casey Stengel

POS	Player	AB	BA	HR	RBI	PO	A	E	DP	TC/G	FA	Pitcher	G	IP	W	L	SV	ERA
1B	B. Skowron	538	.309	26	91	**1202**	115	**12**	130	9.4	.991	A. Ditmar	34	200	15	9	0	3.06
2B	B. Richardson	460	.252	1	26	312	337	18	103	4.7	.973	W. Ford	33	193	12	9	0	3.08
SS	T. Kubek	568	.273	14	62	228	443	22	84	5.1	.968	B. Turley	34	173	9	3	5	3.27
3B	C. Boyer	393	.242	14	46	102	219	11	24	3.4	.967	R. Terry	35	167	10	8	1	3.40
RF	R. Maris	499	.283	39	**112**	263	6	4	1	2.1	.985	J. Coates	35	149	13	3	1	4.28
CF	M. Mantle	527	.275	**40**	94	326	9	3	1	2.3	.991	E. Grba	24	81	6	4	1	3.68
LF	H. Lopez	408	.284	9	42	199	8	5	2	2.0	.976	D. Maas	35	70	5	1	4	4.09
C	E. Howard	323	.245	6	39	410	40	6	9	5.0	.987	B. Shantz	42	68	5	4	11	2.79
CO	Y. Berra	359	.276	15	62	312	24	5	6		.985	R. Duren	42	49	3	4	9	4.96
32	G. McDougald	337	.258	8	34	127	236	13	31		.965	L. Arroyo	29	41	5	1	7	2.88
OF	B. Cerv	216	.250	8	28	101	6	2	0	2.1	.982							

Baltimore

W-89 L-65

Paul Richards

POS	Player	AB	BA	HR	RBI	PO	A	E	DP	TC/G	FA	Pitcher	G	IP	W	L	SV	ERA
1B	J. Gentile	384	.292	21	98	885	52	7	98	7.6	.993	C. Estrada	36	209	**18**	11	2	3.58
2B	M. Breeding	551	.267	3	43	359	422	18	116	5.3	.977	M. Pappas	30	206	15	11	0	3.37
SS	R. Hansen	530	.255	22	86	**325**	456	29	110	5.3	.964	J. Fisher	40	198	12	11	2	3.41
3B	B. Robinson	595	.294	14	88	**171**	**328**	12	34	**3.4**	**.977**	S. Barber	36	182	10	7	2	3.22
RF	G. Stephens	193	.238	5	11	124	5	1	0	1.7	.992	H. Brown	30	159	12	5	0	3.06
CF	J. Brandt	511	.254	15	65	284	10	5	2	2.1	.983	H. Wilhelm	41	147	11	8	7	3.31
LF	G. Woodling	435	.283	11	62	202	7	1	0	1.7	.995	J. Walker	29	118	3	4	5	3.74
C	G. Triandos	364	.269	12	54	516	45	6	5	5.4	.989							
OF	A. Pilarcik	194	.247	4	17	75	4	0	0	1.1	1.000							
1B	W. Dropo	179	.268	4	21	397	27	3	50	6.4	.993							
OF	J. Busby	159	.258	0	12	133	2	2	1	1.9	.985							
C	C. Courtney	154	.227	1	12	246	23	7	2	4.8	.975							

Chicago

W-87 L-67

Al Lopez

POS	Player	AB	BA	HR	RBI	PO	A	E	DP	TC/G	FA	Pitcher	G	IP	W	L	SV	ERA
1B	R. Sievers	444	.295	28	93	1079	63	8	117	**10.1**	.993	E. Wynn	36	237	13	12	1	3.49
2B	N. Fox	**605**	.289	2	59	**412**	**447**	13	**126**	**5.9**	.985	B. Pierce	32	196	14	7	0	3.62
SS	L. Aparicio	600	.277	2	61	305	**551**	18	**117**	**5.7**	**.979**	B. Shaw	36	193	13	13	0	4.06
3B	G. Freese	455	.273	17	79	88	263	20	29	3.0	.946	F. Baumann	44	185	13	6	3	**2.67**
RF	A. Smith	536	.315	12	72	252	5	9	2	1.9	.966	R. Kemmerer	36	121	6	3	2	2.98
CF	J. Landis	494	.253	10	49	372	10	6	3	2.6	.985	G. Staley	64	115	13	8	10	2.42
LF	M. Minoso	591	.311	20	105	282	14	6	3	2.0	.980	H. Score	23	114	5	10	0	3.72
C	S. Lollar	421	.252	7	46	555	54	3	**12**	5.0	**.995**	D. Donovan	33	79	6	1	3	5.38
1B	T. Kluszewski	181	.293	5	39	325	19	1	38	8.8	.997	T. Lown	45	67	2	3	5	3.88

Cleveland

W-76 L-78

Joe Gordon
W-49 L-46

Jo-Jo White
W-1 L-0

Jimmy Dykes
W-26 L-32

POS	Player	AB	BA	HR	RBI	PO	A	E	DP	TC/G	FA	Pitcher	G	IP	W	L	SV	ERA
1B	V. Power	580	.288	10	84	1177	**145**	5	**145**	9.0	**.996**	J. Perry	41	261	**18**	10	1	3.62
2B	K. Aspromonte	459	.290	10	48	192	215	10	63	5.2	.976	M. Grant	33	160	9	8	0	4.40
SS	W. Held	376	.258	21	67	208	345	19	87	5.2	.967	G. Bell	28	155	9	10	1	4.13
3B	B. Phillips	304	.207	4	33	87	135	11	18	2.7	.953	B. Latman	31	147	7	7	0	4.03
RF	H. Kuenn	474	.308	9	54	222	7	8	3	2.0	.966	D. Stigman	41	134	5	11	9	4.51
CF	J. Piersall	486	.282	18	66	355	5	3	0	2.7	.992	B. Locke	32	123	3	5	2	3.37
LF	T. Francona	544	.292	17	79	278	4	3	0	2.1	.989	J. Klippstein	49	74	5	5	**14**	2.91
C	J. Romano	316	.272	16	52	470	30	6	6	5.1	.988							
2B	J. Temple	381	.268	2	19	169	164	9	55	4.4	.974							
SS	M. de la Hoz	160	.256	6	23	58	94	8	13	4.2	.950							

Washington

W-73 L-81

Cookie Lavagetto

POS	Player	AB	BA	HR	RBI	PO	A	E	DP	TC/G	FA	Pitcher	G	IP	W	L	SV	ERA
1B	J. Becquer	298	.252	4	35	611	38	7	59	8.5	.989	P. Ramos	43	**274**	11	**18**	2	3.45
2B	B. Gardner	592	.257	9	56	355	407	**21**	101	5.4	.973	D. Lee	44	165	8	7	3	3.44
SS	J. Valdivielso	268	.213	2	19	178	294	23	68	4.3	.954	C. Pascual	26	152	12	8	2	3.03
3B	R. Bertoia	460	.265	4	45	94	227	13	19	3.0	.961	J. Kralick	35	151	8	6	1	3.04
RF	B. Allison	501	.251	15	69	290	10	11	3	2.2	.965	T. Clevenger	53	129	5	11	7	4.20
CF	L. Green	330	.294	5	33	219	4	2	0	2.3	.991	C. Stobbs	40	119	12	7	2	3.32
LF	J. Lemon	528	.269	38	100	251	11	11	1	1.9	.960	H. Woodeshick	41	115	4	5	4	4.70
C	E. Battey	466	.270	15	60	**749**	**65**	**15**	10	**6.1**	.982	R. Moore	37	66	3	2	13	2.88
13	H. Killebrew	442	.276	31	80	629	135	17	76		.978							
OF	D. Dobbek	248	.218	10	30	141	5	4	1	1.9	.973							
SS	B. Consolo	174	.207	3	15	83	158	16	36	3.1	.938							
OF	F. Throneberry	157	.248	1	23	52	2	3	0	1.7	.947							

AMERICAN LEAGUE 1960, *cont.*

Detroit

W-71 L-83

Jimmy Dykes W-44 L-52

Billy Hitchcock W-1 L-0

Joe Gordon W-26 L-31

POS	Player	AB	BA	HR	RBI	PO	A	E	DP	TC/G	FA	Pitcher	G	IP	W	L	SV	ERA
1B	N. Cash	353	.286	18	63	739	59	7	68	8.1	.991	F. Lary	38	**274**	15	15	1	3.51
2B	F. Bolling	536	.254	9	59	375	377	17	93	5.6	.978	J. Bunning	36	252	11	14	0	2.79
SS	C. Fernandez	435	.241	4	35	226	381	**34**	67	4.9	.947	D. Mossi	23	158	9	8	0	3.47
3B	E. Yost	497	.260	14	47	155	208	**26**	18	2.7	.933	B. Bruce	34	130	4	7	0	3.74
RF	R. Colavito	555	.249	35	87	271	11	7	5	2.0	.976	P. Burnside	31	114	7	7	2	4.28
CF	A. Kaline	551	.278	15	68	367	5	5	1	2.7	.987	P. Foytack	28	97	2	11	2	6.14
LF	C. Maxwell	482	.237	24	81	254	5	1	0	2.2	.996	H. Aguirre	37	95	5	3	10	2.85
C	L. Berberet	232	.194	5	23	396	36	3	4	5.4	.993	D. Sisler	41	80	7	5	6	2.48
1B	S. Bilko	222	.207	9	25	501	36	5	47	8.7	.991							
OF	N. Chrisley	220	.255	5	24	101	2	2	0	2.2	.981							

Boston

W-65 L-89

Bill Jurges W-15 L-27

Del Baker W-2 L-5

Pinky Higgins W-48 L-57

POS	Player	AB	BA	HR	RBI	PO	A	E	DP	TC/G	FA	Pitcher	G	IP	W	L	SV	ERA
1B	V. Wertz	443	.282	19	103	841	78	**12**	89	8.0	.987	B. Monbouquette	35	215	14	11	0	3.64
2B	P. Runnels	528	**.320**	2	35	274	360	9	99	5.0	**.986**	T. Brewer	34	187	10	15	1	4.82
SS	D. Buddin	428	.245	6	36	230	356	30	79	5.0	.951	F. Sullivan	40	154	6	16	1	5.10
3B	F. Malzone	595	.271	14	79	159	318	**26**	**36**	3.3	.948	I. Delock	24	129	9	10	0	4.73
RF	L. Clinton	298	.228	6	37	165	4	6	2	2.0	.966	B. Muffett	23	125	6	4	0	3.24
CF	W. Tasby	385	.281	7	37	232	6	5	1	2.4	.979	M. Fornieles	**70**	109	10	5	**14**	2.64
LF	T. Williams	310	.316	29	72	131	6	1	1	1.6	.993	T. Sturdivant	40	101	3	3	1	4.97
C	R. Nixon	272	.298	5	33	354	26	5	3	5.2	.987	J. Casale	29	96	2	9	0	6.17
2S	P. Green	260	.242	3	21	151	169	11	33		.967							
OF	G. Geiger	245	.302	9	33	121	9	0	1	2.0	1.000							
OF	R. Repulski	136	.243	3	20	56	0	0	0	1.7	1.000							
OF	B. Thomson	114	.263	5	20	65	1	2	1	2.5	.971							

Kansas City

W-58 L-96

Bob Elliott

POS	Player	AB	BA	HR	RBI	PO	A	E	DP	TC/G	FA	Pitcher	G	IP	W	L	SV	ERA
1B	M. Throneberry	236	.250	11	41	508	40	5	56	7.8	.991	R. Herbert	37	253	14	15	1	3.28
2B	J. Lumpe	574	.272	8	53	355	364	13	99	5.5	.982	B. Daley	37	231	16	16	0	4.56
SS	K. Hamlin	428	.224	2	24	195	341	25	61	4.0	.955	D. Hall	29	182	8	13	0	4.05
3B	A. Carey	343	.233	12	53	95	180	7	26	3.1	.975	N. Garver	28	122	4	9	0	3.83
RF	R. Snyder	304	.260	4	26	135	4	2	2	1.5	.986	K. Johnson	42	120	5	10	3	4.26
CF	B. Tuttle	559	.256	8	40	381	16	5	3	2.7	.988	J. Kucks	31	114	4	10	0	6.00
LF	N. Siebern	520	.279	19	69	151	4	2	0	2.1	.987	D. Larsen	22	84	1	10	0	5.38
C	P. Daley	228	.263	5	25	263	33	3	3	4.9	.990							
UT	D. Williams	420	.288	12	65	376	131	11	28		.979							
OF	H. Bauer	255	.275	3	31	85	4	2	1	1.4	.978							
OF	W. Herzog	252	.266	8	38	128	4	2	1	1.9	.985							
C	H. Chiti	190	.221	5	28	263	24	5	1	5.6	.983							
C	D. Kravitz	175	.234	4	14	216	16	7	3	5.1	.971							

BATTING AND BASE RUNNING LEADERS

Batting Average

P. Runnels, BOS	.320
A. Smith, CHI	.315
M. Minoso, CHI	.311
B. Skowron, NY	.309
H. Kuenn, CLE	.308

Slugging Average

R. Maris, NY	.581
M. Mantle, NY	.558
H. Killebrew, WAS	.534
R. Sievers, CHI	.534
B. Skowron, NY	.528

Home Runs

M. Mantle, NY	40
R. Maris, NY	39
J. Lemon, WAS	38
R. Colavito, DET	35
H. Killebrew, WAS	31

Total Bases

M. Mantle, NY	294
R. Maris, NY	290
B. Skowron, NY	284
M. Minoso, CHI	284
J. Lemon, WAS	268

Runs Batted In

R. Maris, NY	112
M. Minoso, CHI	105
V. Wertz, BOS	103
J. Lemon, WAS	100
J. Gentile, BAL	98

Stolen Bases

L. Aparicio, CHI	51
J. Landis, CHI	23
L. Green, WAS	21
A. Kaline, DET	19
J. Piersall, CLE	18

Hits

M. Minoso, CHI	184
B. Robinson, BAL	175
N. Fox, CHI	175
P. Runnels, BOS	169
A. Smith, CHI	169

Base on Balls

E. Yost, DET	125
M. Mantle, NY	111
B. Allison, WAS	92
G. Woodling, BAL	84

Home Run Percentage

R. Maris, NY	7.8
M. Mantle, NY	7.6
J. Lemon, WAS	7.2
H. Killebrew, WAS	7.0

Runs

M. Mantle, NY	119
R. Maris, NY	98
J. Landis, CHI	89
M. Minoso, CHI	89

Doubles

T. Francona, CLE	36
B. Skowron, NY	34
G. Freese, CHI	32
M. Minoso, CHI	32

Triples

N. Fox, CHI	10
B. Robinson, BAL	9

PITCHING LEADERS

Winning Percentage

J. Perry, CLE	.643
A. Ditmar, NY	.625
C. Estrada, BAL	.621
M. Pappas, BAL	.577
F. Lary, DET	.500
B. Daley, KC	.500

Earned Run Average

F. Baumann, CHI	2.67
J. Bunning, DET	2.79
H. Brown, BAL	3.06
A. Ditmar, NY	3.06
W. Ford, NY	3.08

Wins

C. Estrada, BAL	18
J. Perry, CLE	18
B. Daley, KC	16
A. Ditmar, NY	15
M. Pappas, BAL	15
F. Lary, DET	15

Saves

J. Klippstein, CLE	14
M. Fornieles, BOS	14
R. Moore, CHI, WAS	13
B. Shantz, NY	11
H. Aguirre, DET	10
G. Staley, CHI	10

Strikeouts

J. Bunning, DET	201
P. Ramos, WAS	160
E. Wynn, CHI	158
F. Lary, DET	149
C. Estrada, BAL	144

Complete Games

F. Lary, DET	15
R. Herbert, KC	14
P. Ramos, WAS	14
B. Daley, KC	13
E. Wynn, CHI	13

Fewest Hits/9 Innings

C. Estrada, BAL	6.99
B. Turley, NY	7.17
S. Barber, BAL	7.33
J. Bunning, DET	7.75

Shutouts

W. Ford, NY	4
E. Wynn, CHI	4
J. Perry, CLE	4

Fewest Walks/9 Innings

H. Brown, BAL	1.25
D. Mossi, DET	1.82
D. Hall, KC	1.88
F. Lary, DET	2.03

Most Strikeouts/9 Inn.

J. Bunning, DET	7.18
G. Bell, CLE	6.34
C. Estrada, BAL	6.21
E. Wynn, CHI	5.99

Innings

F. Lary, DET	274
P. Ramos, WAS	274
J. Perry, CLE	261
R. Herbert, KC	253

Games Pitched

M. Fornieles, BOS	70
G. Staley, CHI	64
T. Clevenger, WAS	53
M. Kutyna, KC	51
R. Moore, CHI, WAS	51

AMERICAN LEAGUE 1960, *cont.*

							Batting						Fielding			Pitching					
	W	L	PCT	GB	R	OR	2B	3B	HR	BA	SA	SB	E	DP	FA	CG	BB	SO	ShO	SV	ERA
New York	97	57	.630		**746**	627	215	40	**193**	.260	**.426**	37	129	162	.979	38	609	712	**16**	**42**	**3.52**
Baltimore	89	65	.578	8	682	**606**	206	33	123	.253	.377	37	**108**	172	**.982**	**48**	552	785	11	22	**3.52**
Chicago	87	67	.565	10	741	617	**242**	38	112	**.270**	.396	**122**	109	**175**	**.982**	42	533	695	11	26	3.60
Cleveland	76	78	.494	21	667	693	218	20	127	.267	.388	58	128	165	.978	32	636	771	10	30	3.95
Washington	73	81	.474	24	672	696	205	**43**	147	.244	.384	52	165	159	.973	34	538	775	10	35	3.77
Detroit	71	83	.461	26	633	644	188	34	150	.239	.375	66	138	138	.977	40	**474**	**824**	7	25	3.64
Boston	65	89	.422	32	658	775	234	32	124	.261	.389	34	141	156	.976	34	580	767	6	23	4.62
Kansas City	58	96	.377	39	615	756	212	34	110	.249	.366	16	127	149	.979	44	525	664	4	14	4.38
					5414	5414	1720	274	1086	.255	.388	422	1045	1276	.978	312	4447	5993	75	217	3.88

NATIONAL LEAGUE 1961

Cincinnati

W-93 L-61

Fred Hutchinson

POS	Player	AB	BA	HR	RBI	PO	A	E	DP	TC/G	FA
1B	G. Coleman	520	.287	26	87	1162	**121**	11	93	8.6	.991
2B	D. Blasingame	450	.222	1	21	277	304	17	53	5.2	.972
SS	E. Kasko	469	.271	2	27	201	286	18	59	4.5	.964
3B	G. Freese	575	.277	26	87	123	254	20	23	2.6	.950
RF	F. Robinson	545	.323	37	124	284	15	3	3	2.0	.990
CF	V. Pinson	607	.343	16	87	391	19	10	4	2.7	.976
LF	W. Post	282	.294	20	57	133	7	6	3	1.8	.959
C	J. Zimmerman	204	.206	0	10	374	22	10	8	5.3	.975
OF	G. Bell	235	.255	3	33	112	1	1	0	1.5	.991
SS	L. Cardenas	198	.308	5	24	83	133	6	21	3.5	.973
OF	J. Lynch	181	.315	13	50	53	2	3	0	1.3	.948

Pitcher	G	IP	W	L	SV	ERA
J. O'Toole	39	253	19	9	2	3.10
J. Jay	34	247	**21**	10	0	3.53
B. Purkey	36	246	16	12	1	3.73
K. Hunt	29	136	9	10	0	3.96
J. Maloney	27	95	6	7	2	4.37
J. Brosnan	53	80	10	4	16	3.04
B. Henry	47	53	2	1	16	2.19

Los Angeles

W-89 L-65

Walter Alston

POS	Player	AB	BA	HR	RBI	PO	A	E	DP	TC/G	FA
1B	G. Hodges	215	.242	8	31	454	37	1	44	4.9	.998
2B	C. Neal	341	.235	10	48	211	246	11	63	4.5	.976
SS	M. Wills	**613**	.282	1	31	253	428	29	104	4.8	.959
3B	J. Gilliam	439	.244	4	32	48	104	7	9	2.1	.956
RF	T. Davis	460	.278	15	58	143	3	4	2	1.7	.973
CF	W. Davis	339	.254	12	45	224	4	4	1	2.0	.983
LF	W. Moon	463	.328	17	88	186	5	6	1	1.5	.970
C	J. Roseboro	394	.251	18	59	**877**	56	13	**16**	**7.6**	.986
1B	N. Larker	282	.270	5	38	589	52	3	68	7.5	.995
OF	F. Howard	267	.296	15	45	79	6	6	0	1.4	.934
OF	R. Fairly	245	.322	10	48	85	7	1	1	1.3	.989
OF	D. Snider	233	.296	16	56	113	6	3	3	1.8	.975
3B	D. Spencer	189	.243	8	27	42	92	5	14	2.4	.964
C	N. Sherry	121	.256	5	21	253	16	2	3	6.0	.993

Pitcher	G	IP	W	L	SV	ERA
S. Koufax	42	256	18	13	1	3.52
D. Drysdale	40	244	13	10	0	3.69
S. Williams	41	235	15	12	0	3.90
J. Podres	32	183	18	5	0	3.74
R. Craig	40	113	5	6	2	6.15
L. Sherry	53	95	4	4	15	3.90
R. Perranoski	53	92	7	5	6	2.65
D. Farrell	50	89	6	6	10	5.06

San Francisco

W-85 L-69

Alvin Dark

POS	Player	AB	BA	HR	RBI	PO	A	E	DP	TC/G	FA
1B	W. McCovey	328	.271	18	50	669	55	11	55	8.8	.985
2B	J. Amalfitano	384	.255	2	23	201	223	13	48	4.6	.970
SS	J. Pagan	434	.253	5	46	227	334	21	55	4.4	.964
3B	J. Davenport	436	.278	12	65	119	235	13	25	2.8	**.965**
RF	F. Alou	415	.289	18	52	196	10	2	1	1.7	.990
CF	W. Mays	572	.308	40	123	385	7	8	3	2.6	.980
LF	H. Kuenn	471	.265	5	46	157	9	2	0	1.8	.988
C	E. Bailey	340	.238	13	51	629	40	10	4	6.6	.985
10	O. Cepeda	585	.311	**46**	**142**	774	51	5	50		.994
2B	C. Hiller	240	.237	2	12	133	158	8	34	4.5	.973
OF	M. Alou	200	.310	6	24	85	2	2	0	1.5	.978

Pitcher	G	IP	W	L	SV	ERA
M. McCormick	40	250	13	16	0	3.20
J. Sanford	38	217	13	9	0	4.22
J. Marichal	29	185	13	10	0	3.89
B. O'Dell	46	130	7	5	2	3.59
S. Jones	37	128	8	8	1	4.49
S. Miller	63	122	14	5	**17**	2.66
B. Loes	26	115	6	5	0	4.24
D. LeMay	27	83	3	6	3	3.56

Milwaukee

W-83 L-71

Chuck Dressen
W-71 L-58

Birdie Tebbetts
W-12 L-13

POS	Player	AB	BA	HR	RBI	PO	A	E	DP	TC/G	FA
1B	J. Adcock	562	.285	35	108	**1471**	102	11	133	**10.7**	**.993**
2B	F. Bolling	585	.262	15	56	326	489	10	112	5.6	**.988**
SS	R. McMillan	505	.220	7	48	**257**	**496**	19	110	5.0	**.975**
3B	E. Mathews	572	.306	32	91	**168**	281	18	30	3.1	.961
RF	L. Maye	373	.271	14	41	169	6	5	0	1.9	.972
CF	H. Aaron	603	.327	34	120	377	13	7	3	2.6	.982
LF	F. Thomas	423	.284	25	67	202	4	10	0	2.0	.954
C	J. Torre	406	.278	10	42	494	50	10	4	4.9	.982

Pitcher	G	IP	W	L	SV	ERA
L. Burdette	40	**272**	18	11	0	4.00
W. Spahn	38	263	**21**	13	0	**3.02**
B. Buhl	32	188	9	10	0	4.11
C. Willey	35	160	6	12	0	3.83
D. Nottebart	38	126	6	7	3	4.06
B. Hendley	19	97	5	7	0	3.90
D. McMahon	53	92	6	4	8	2.84

St. Louis

W-80 L-74

Solly Hemus
W-33 L-41

Johnny Keane
W-47 L-33

POS	Player	AB	BA	HR	RBI	PO	A	E	DP	TC/G	FA
1B	B. White	591	.286	20	90	1373	104	17	125	9.9	.989
2B	J. Javier	445	.279	2	41	239	332	20	82	5.2	.966
SS	A. Grammas	170	.212	0	21	81	136	9	29	3.5	.960
3B	K. Boyer	589	.329	24	95	117	**346**	24	23	3.2	.951
RF	C. James	349	.255	4	44	151	3	6	1	1.8	.963
CF	C. Flood	335	.322	2	21	241	13	4	4	2.2	.984
LF	S. Musial	372	.288	15	70	149	9	1	0	1.5	.994
C	J. Schaffer	153	.255	1	16	244	23	1	6	3.9	.996
OF	J. Cunningham	322	.286	7	40	131	2	5	1	1.6	.964
SS	B. Lillis	230	.217	0	21	73	134	16	19	4.0	.928
OF	D. Taussig	188	.287	2	25	123	6	1	2	1.5	.992
C	C. Sawatski	174	.299	10	33	218	19	1	3	4.0	.996
SS	D. Spencer	130	.254	4	21	66	109	8	26	4.9	.956

Pitcher	G	IP	W	L	SV	ERA
R. Sadecki	31	223	14	10	0	3.72
B. Gibson	35	211	13	12	1	3.24
L. Jackson	33	211	14	11	0	3.75
C. Simmons	30	196	9	10	0	3.13
E. Broglio	29	175	9	12	0	4.12
L. McDaniel	55	94	10	6	9	4.87

NATIONAL LEAGUE 1961, *cont.*

Pittsburgh

W-75 L-79

Danny Murtaugh

POS	Player	AB	BA	HR	RBI	PO	A	E	DP	TC/G	FA	Pitcher	G	IP	W	L	SV	ERA
1B	D. Stuart	532	.301	35	117	1152	99	**21**	**141**	9.6	.983	B. Friend	41	236	14	**19**	1	3.85
2B	B. Mazeroski	558	.265	13	59	**410**	**505**	**23**	**144**	**6.2**	.975	J. Gibbon	30	195	13	10	0	3.32
SS	D. Groat	596	.275	6	55	235	473	**32**	**117**	5.1	.957	H. Haddix	29	156	10	6	0	4.10
3B	D. Hoak	503	.298	12	61	137	267	20	29	3.0	.953	E. Francis	23	103	2	8	0	4.21
RF	R. Clemente	572	**.351**	23	89	256	27	9	5	2.0	.969	V. Mizell	25	100	7	10	0	5.04
CF	B. Virdon	599	.260	9	58	384	6	6	4	2.7	.985	C. Labine	56	93	4	1	8	3.69
LF	B. Skinner	381	.268	3	42	175	5	5	1	1.9	.973	R. Face	62	92	6	12	**17**	3.82
C	S. Burgess	323	.303	12	52	426	27	4	4	5.0	**.991**	B. Shantz	43	89	6	3	2	3.32
C	H. Smith	193	.223	3	26	290	18	3	1	4.8	.990							
OF	J. Christopher	186	.263	0	14	86	2	2	1	1.6	.978							

Chicago

W-64 L-90

Vedie Himsl W-5 L-6
Harry Craft W-4 L-8
Vedie Himsl W-5 L-12
El Tappe W-2 L-0
Harry Craft

Vedie Himsl W-0 L-3
El Tappe W-35 L-43
Lou Klein W-5 L-6
El Tappe W-5 L-11

POS	Player	AB	BA	HR	RBI	PO	A	E	DP	TC/G	FA	Pitcher	G	IP	W	L	SV	ERA
1B	E. Bouchee	319	.248	12	38	852	76	16	97	8.8	.983	D. Cardwell	39	259	15	14	0	3.82
2B	D. Zimmer	477	.252	13	40	282	323	17	99	5.4	.973	G. Hobbie	36	199	7	13	2	4.26
SS	E. Banks	511	.278	29	80	173	358	19	68	**5.3**	.965	D. Ellsworth	37	187	10	11	0	3.86
3B	R. Santo	578	.284	23	83	157	307	**31**	**41**	**3.2**	.937	J. Curtis	31	180	10	13	0	4.89
RF	G. Altman	518	.303	27	96	258	11	6	2	2.1	.978	B. Anderson	57	152	7	10	8	4.26
CF	A. Heist	321	.255	7	37	211	9	5	0	2.3	.978	D. Elston	58	93	6	7	8	5.59
LF	B. Williams	529	.278	25	86	220	9	11	3	1.8	.954	B. Schultz	41	67	7	6	7	2.70
C	D. Bertell	267	.273	2	33	396	49	8	10	5.0	.982							
2S	J. Kindall	310	.242	9	44	206	233	26	61		.944							
OF	R. Ashburn	307	.257	0	19	131	4	3	0	1.8	.978							
C	S. Taylor	235	.238	8	23	319	25	4	5	4.6	.989							
1S	A. Rodgers	214	.266	6	23	404	83	9	44		.982							

Philadelphia

W-47 L-107

Gene Mauch

POS	Player	AB	BA	HR	RBI	PO	A	E	DP	TC/G	FA	Pitcher	G	IP	W	L	SV	ERA
1B	P. Herrera	400	.258	13	51	1003	96	8	104	9.6	.993	A. Mahaffey	36	219	11	**19**	0	4.10
2B	T. Taylor	400	.250	2	26	231	270	10	74	5.6	.980	J. Buzhardt	41	202	6	18	0	4.49
SS	R. Amaro	381	.257	1	32	243	379	19	91	4.9	.970	F. Sullivan	49	159	3	16	6	4.29
3B	C. Smith	411	.248	9	47	75	194	22	19	3.1	.924	D. Ferrarese	42	139	5	12	1	3.76
RF	D. Demeter	382	.257	20	68	173	9	1	2	2.3	.995	D. Green	42	128	2	4	1	4.85
CF	T. Gonzalez	426	.277	12	58	246	7	4	4	2.2	.984	C. Short	39	127	6	12	1	5.94
LF	J. Callison	455	.266	9	47	227	10	8	2	2.0	.967	R. Roberts	26	117	1	10	0	5.85
C	C. Dalrymple	378	.220	5	42	551	**86**	**14**	10	5.3	.978	J. Owens	20	107	5	10	0	4.47
UT	B. Malkmus	342	.231	7	31	210	299	12	67		.977	J. Baldschun	**65**	100	5	3	3	3.88
UT	L. Walls	261	.280	8	30	247	59	8	33		.975							
OF	K. Walters	180	.228	2	14	73	4	2	0	1.4	.975							
OF	B. Smith	174	.253	2	18	91	8	3	1	2.2	.971							
OF	W. Covington	165	.303	7	26	53	4	3	1	1.3	.950							

BATTING AND BASE RUNNING LEADERS

Batting Average
R. Clemente, PIT .351
V. Pinson, CIN .343
K. Boyer, STL .329
W. Moon, LA .328
H. Aaron, MIL .327

Slugging Average
F. Robinson, CIN .611
O. Cepeda, SF .609
H. Aaron, MIL .594
W. Mays, SF .584
D. Stuart, PIT .581

Home Runs
O. Cepeda, SF 46
W. Mays, SF 40
F. Robinson, CIN 37
D. Stuart, PIT 35
J. Adcock, MIL 35

Total Bases
H. Aaron, MIL 358
O. Cepeda, SF 356
W. Mays, SF 334
F. Robinson, CIN 333
R. Clemente, PIT 320

Runs Batted In
O. Cepeda, SF 142
F. Robinson, CIN 124
W. Mays, SF 123
H. Aaron, MIL 120
D. Stuart, PIT 117

Stolen Bases
M. Wills, LA 35
V. Pinson, CIN 23
F. Robinson, CIN 22
H. Aaron, MIL 21
W. Mays, SF 18

Hits
V. Pinson, CIN 208
R. Clemente, PIT 201
H. Aaron, MIL 197
K. Boyer, STL 194

Base on Balls
E. Mathews, MIL 93
W. Moon, LA 89
W. Mays, SF 81
J. Gilliam, LA 79

Home Run Percentage
O. Cepeda, SF 7.9
W. Mays, SF 7.0
F. Robinson, CIN 6.8
D. Stuart, PIT 6.6

Runs
W. Mays, SF 129
F. Robinson, CIN 117
H. Aaron, MIL 115
K. Boyer, STL 109

Doubles
H. Aaron, MIL 39
V. Pinson, CIN 34
F. Robinson, CIN 32
W. Mays, SF 32
R. Santo, CHI 32

Triples
G. Altman, CHI 12
J. Callison, PHI 11
K. Boyer, STL 11
B. White, STL 11

PITCHING LEADERS

Winning Percentage
J. Podres, LA .783
J. O'Toole, CIN .679
J. Jay, CIN .677
L. Burdette, MIL .621
W. Spahn, MIL .618

Earned Run Average
W. Spahn, MIL 3.02
J. O'Toole, CIN 3.10
C. Simmons, STL 3.13
M. McCormick, SF 3.20
B. Gibson, STL 3.24

Wins
J. Jay, CIN 21
W. Spahn, MIL 21
J. O'Toole, CIN 19
J. Podres, LA 18
S. Koufax, LA 18
L. Burdette, MIL 18

Saves
R. Face, PIT 17
S. Miller, SF 17
B. Henry, CIN 16
J. Brosnan, CIN 16
L. Sherry, LA 15

Strikeouts
S. Koufax, LA 269
S. Williams, LA 205
D. Drysdale, LA 182
J. O'Toole, CIN 178
B. Gibson, STL 166

Complete Games
W. Spahn, MIL 21
S. Koufax, LA 15
J. Jay, CIN 14
L. Burdette, MIL 14

Fewest Hits/9 Innings
S. Koufax, LA 7.46
J. Jay, CIN 7.90
B. Gibson, STL 7.92
R. Sadecki, STL 7.92

Shutouts
J. Jay, CIN 4
W. Spahn, MIL 4

Fewest Walks/9 Innings
L. Burdette, MIL 1.09
B. Friend, PIT 1.72
B. Purkey, CIN 1.86
W. Spahn, MIL 2.19

Most Strikeouts/9 Inn.
S. Koufax, LA 9.47
S. Williams, LA 7.84
B. Gibson, STL 7.07
D. Drysdale, LA 6.71

Innings
L. Burdette, MIL 272
W. Spahn, MIL 263
D. Cardwell, CHI 259
S. Koufax, LA 256

Games Pitched
J. Baldschun, PHI 65
S. Miller, SF 63
R. Face, PIT 62
D. Elston, CHI 58

							Batting						Fielding			Pitching					
	W	L	PCT	GB	R	OR	2B	3B	HR	BA	SA	SB	E	DP	FA	CG	BB	SO	ShO	SV	ERA
Cincinnati	93	61	.604		710	**653**	**247**	35	158	.270	.421	70	134	124	.977	46	500	829	**12**	**40**	3.78
Los Angeles	89	65	.578	4	735	697	193	40	157	.262	.405	**86**	144	162	.975	40	544	**1105**	10	35	4.04
San Francisco	85	69	.552	8	**773**	655	219	32	183	.264	**.423**	79	133	126	.977	39	502	924	9	30	3.77
Milwaukee	83	71	.539	10	712	656	199	34	**188**	.258	.415	70	**111**	152	**.982**	**57**	493	652	8	16	3.89
St. Louis	80	74	.519	13	703	668	236	51	103	.271	.393	46	166	165	.972	49	570	823	10	24	**3.74**
Pittsburgh	75	79	.487	18	694	675	232	**57**	128	**.273**	.410	26	150	**187**	.975	34	**400**	759	9	29	3.92
Chicago	64	90	.416	29	689	800	238	51	176	.255	.418	35	183	175	.970	34	465	755	6	25	4.48
Philadelphia	47	107	.305	46	584	796	185	50	103	.243	.357	56	146	179	.976	29	521	775	9	13	4.61
					5600	5600	1749	350	1196	.262	.405	468	1167	1270	.975	328	3995	6622	73	212	4.03

AMERICAN LEAGUE 1961

New York

W-109 L-53

Ralph Houk

POS	Player	AB	BA	HR	RBI	PO	A	E	DP	TC/G	FA
1B	B. Skowron	561	.267	28	89	1228	102	10	**146**	9.0	.993
2B	B. Richardson	662	.261	3	49	**413**	376	18	**136**	5.0	.978
SS	T. Kubek	617	.276	8	46	261	449	30	107	**5.1**	.959
3B	C. Boyer	504	.224	11	55	151	**353**	17	36	**3.7**	.967
RF	R. Maris	590	.269	**61**	**141**	266	9	9	1	1.8	.968
CF	M. Mantle	514	.317	54	128	351	6	6	0	2.4	.983
LF	Y. Berra	395	.271	22	61	161	7	2	2	2.0	.988
C	E. Howard	446	.348	21	77	635	43	5	4	6.2	.993
OF	H. Lopez	243	.222	3	22	123	7	3	0	1.8	.977
C	J. Blanchard	243	.305	21	54	268	18	3	2	6.0	.990
OF	B. Cerv	118	.271	6	20	55	2	1	0	1.9	.983

Pitcher	G	IP	W	L	SV	ERA
W. Ford	39	**283**	**25**	4	0	3.21
B. Stafford	36	195	14	9	2	2.68
R. Terry	31	188	16	3	0	3.15
R. Sheldon	35	163	11	5	0	3.60
J. Coates	43	141	11	5	5	3.44
B. Daley	23	130	8	9	0	3.96
L. Arroyo	**65**	119	15	5	**29**	2.19

Detroit

W-101 L-61

Bob Scheffing

POS	Player	AB	BA	HR	RBI	PO	A	E	DP	TC/G	FA
1B	N. Cash	535	**.361**	41	132	**1231**	127	11	121	8.7	.992
2B	J. Wood	663	.258	11	69	380	396	**25**	83	4.9	.969
SS	C. Fernandez	435	.248	3	40	207	312	23	59	4.5	.958
3B	S. Boros	396	.270	5	62	115	192	15	15	2.8	.953
RF	A. Kaline	586	.324	19	82	378	9	4	3	2.7	.990
CF	B. Bruton	596	.257	17	63	410	4	5	2	2.7	.988
LF	R. Colavito	583	.290	45	140	329	16	9	4	2.2	.975
C	D. Brown	308	.266	16	45	460	38	5	7	5.5	.990
SS	D. McAuliffe	285	.256	6	33	79	115	14	29	3.8	.933
C	M. Roarke	229	.223	2	22	383	22	5	5	4.8	.988

Pitcher	G	IP	W	L	SV	ERA
F. Lary	36	275	23	9	0	3.24
J. Bunning	38	268	17	11	1	3.19
D. Mossi	35	240	15	7	1	2.96
P. Foytack	32	170	11	10	0	3.93
P. Regan	32	120	10	7	2	5.25
T. Fox	39	57	5	2	12	1.41
H. Aguirre	45	55	4	4	8	3.25

Baltimore

W-95 L-67

Paul Richards
W-78 L-57

Lum Harris
W-17 L-10

POS	Player	AB	BA	HR	RBI	PO	A	E	DP	TC/G	FA
1B	J. Gentile	486	.302	46	**141**	1209	100	14	129	9.2	.989
2B	J. Adair	386	.264	9	37	233	237	6	57	4.4	.987
SS	R. Hansen	533	.248	12	51	256	437	30	**110**	4.9	.959
3B	B. Robinson	**668**	.287	7	61	151	331	14	34	3.0	**.972**
RF	W. Herzog	323	.291	5	35	143	2	0	0	1.5	1.000
CF	J. Brandt	516	.297	16	72	293	6	8	2	2.3	.974
LF	R. Snyder	312	.292	1	13	168	3	6	0	1.6	.966
C	G. Triandos	397	.244	17	63	642	55	8	**9**	6.2	.989
OF	D. Williams	310	.206	8	24	86	4	3	1	1.2	.968
2B	M. Breeding	244	.209	1	16	179	179	11	53	4.6	.970
OF	E. Robinson	222	.266	8	30	136	6	4	3	1.8	.973
OF	D. Philley	144	.250	1	23	21	0	0	0	0.8	1.000

Pitcher	G	IP	W	L	SV	ERA
S. Barber	37	248	18	12	1	3.33
C. Estrada	33	212	15	9	0	3.69
J. Fisher	36	196	10	13	1	3.90
M. Pappas	26	178	13	9	1	3.04
H. Brown	27	167	10	6	1	3.19
B. Hoeft	35	138	7	4	3	2.02
D. Hall	29	122	7	5	4	3.09
H. Wilhelm	51	110	9	7	18	2.30

Chicago

W-86 L-76

Al Lopez

POS	Player	AB	BA	HR	RBI	PO	A	E	DP	TC/G	FA
1B	R. Sievers	492	.295	27	92	1096	94	8	93	9.1	.993
2B	N. Fox	606	.251	2	51	**413**	407	15	97	5.3	.982
SS	L. Aparicio	625	.272	6	45	264	**487**	30	86	5.0	**.962**
3B	A. Smith	532	.278	28	93	58	161	12	12	2.9	.948
RF	F. Robinson	432	.310	11	59	218	7	2	0	2.1	.991
CF	J. Landis	534	.283	22	85	389	9	5	3	2.9	.988
LF	M. Minoso	540	.280	14	82	273	10	13	2	2.0	.956
C	S. Lollar	337	.282	7	41	464	48	1	6	4.8	**.998**
13	J. Martin	274	.230	5	32	353	118	10	38		.979
C	C. Carreon	229	.271	4	27	395	25	2	6	5.9	.995

Pitcher	G	IP	W	L	SV	ERA
J. Pizarro	39	195	14	7	2	3.05
F. Baumann	53	188	10	13	3	5.61
B. Pierce	39	180	10	9	3	3.80
C. McLish	31	162	10	13	1	4.38
R. Herbert	21	138	9	6	0	4.05
E. Wynn	17	110	8	2	0	3.51
T. Lown	59	101	7	5	11	2.76
D. Larsen	25	74	7	2	2	4.12
W. Hacker	42	57	3	3	8	3.77

Cleveland

W-78 L-83

Jimmy Dykes
W-77 L-83

Mel Harder
W-1 L-0

POS	Player	AB	BA	HR	RBI	PO	A	E	DP	TC/G	FA
1B	V. Power	563	.268	5	63	1154	**142**	8	101	**9.2**	.994
2B	J. Temple	518	.276	3	30	239	317	18	79	4.4	.969
SS	W. Held	509	.267	23	78	258	393	27	90	4.7	.960
3B	B. Phillips	546	.264	18	72	**188**	246	19	23	3.2	.958
RF	W. Kirkland	525	.259	27	95	290	12	8	5	2.2	.974
CF	J. Piersall	484	.322	6	40	328	9	3	3	2.8	.991
LF	T. Francona	592	.301	16	85	289	5	4	1	2.2	.987
C	J. Romano	509	.299	21	80	752	58	9	8	5.8	.989
UT	M. de la Hoz	173	.260	3	23	77	116	9	10		.955
OF	C. Essegian	166	.289	12	35	85	5	3	1	1.9	.968

Pitcher	G	IP	W	L	SV	ERA
M. Grant	35	245	15	9	0	3.86
G. Bell	34	228	12	16	0	4.10
J. Perry	35	224	10	17	0	4.71
B. Latman	45	177	13	5	5	4.02
W. Hawkins	30	133	7	9	1	4.06
B. Locke	37	95	4	4	2	4.53
F. Funk	56	92	11	11	11	3.31

Boston

W-76 L-86

Pinky Higgins

POS	Player	AB	BA	HR	RBI	PO	A	E	DP	TC/G	FA
1B	P. Runnels	360	.317	3	38	701	50	4	92	6.7	**.995**
2B	C. Schilling	646	.259	5	62	397	**449**	8	121	5.4	**.991**
SS	D. Buddin	339	.263	6	42	204	294	23	70	4.8	.956
3B	F. Malzone	590	.266	14	87	136	304	**23**	**45**	3.1	.950
RF	J. Jensen	498	.263	13	66	274	14	4	2	2.2	.986
CF	G. Geiger	499	.232	18	64	324	12	4	1	2.5	.988
LF	C. Yastrzemski	583	.266	11	80	248	12	10	1	1.8	.963
C	J. Pagliaroni	376	.242	16	58	586	39	**10**	5	5.9	.984
1B	V. Wertz	317	.262	11	60	664	67	7	65	8.6	.991
OF	C. Hardy	281	.263	3	36	142	7	6	3	2.0	.961
C	R. Nixon	242	.289	1	19	330	24	9	2	5.5	.975
SS	P. Green	219	.260	6	27	84	166	16	35	4.7	.940

Pitcher	G	IP	W	L	SV	ERA
B. Monbouquette	32	236	14	14	0	3.39
G. Conley	33	200	11	14	1	4.91
D. Schwall	25	179	15	7	0	3.22
I. Delock	28	156	6	9	0	4.90
T. Stallard	43	133	2	7	2	4.88
M. Fornieles	57	119	9	8	15	4.68
B. Muffett	38	113	3	11	2	5.67
A. Earley	33	50	2	4	7	3.99

Minnesota

W-70 L-90

Cookie Lavagetto
W-19 L-30

Sam Mele
W-2 L-5

Cookie Lavagetto
W-4 L-6

Sam Mele
W-45 L-49

POS	Player	AB	BA	HR	RBI	PO	A	E	DP	TC/G	FA
1B	H. Killebrew	541	.288	46	122	972	67	14	91	8.8	.987
2B	B. Martin	374	.246	6	36	217	224	17	61	4.4	.963
SS	Z. Versalles	510	.280	7	53	229	371	30	74	4.9	.952
3B	B. Tuttle	370	.246	5	38	66	165	14	15	2.9	.943
RF	B. Allison	556	.245	29	105	300	14	8	3	2.1	.975
CF	L. Green	600	.285	9	50	356	3	8	0	2.4	.978
LF	J. Lemon	423	.258	14	52	182	7	12	0	1.7	.940
C	E. Battey	460	.302	17	55	**812**	**60**	6	**9**	**6.7**	.993

Pitcher	G	IP	W	L	SV	ERA
P. Ramos	42	264	11	**20**	2	3.95
C. Pascual	35	252	15	16	0	3.46
J. Kralick	33	242	13	11	0	3.61
J. Kaat	36	201	9	17	0	3.90
D. Lee	37	115	3	6	3	3.52
R. Moore	46	56	4	4	14	3.67

AMERICAN LEAGUE 1961, *cont.*

Los Angeles

W-70 L-91

Bill Rigney

POS	Player	AB	BA	HR	RBI	PO	A	E	DP	TC/G	FA	Pitcher	G	IP	W	L	SV	ERA
1B	S. Bilko	294	.279	20	59	577	61	7	56	7.5	.989	K. McBride	38	242	12	15	1	3.65
2B	K. Aspromonte	238	.223	2	14	156	196	11	55	5.9	.970	E. Grba	40	212	11	13	2	4.25
SS	J. Koppe	338	.251	5	40	127	250	21	51	4.5	.947	T. Bowsfield	41	157	11	8	0	3.73
3B	E. Yost	213	.202	3	15	57	103	6	4	2.5	.964	R. Moeller	33	113	4	8	0	5.83
RF	A. Pearson	427	.288	7	41	233	7	11	2	2.2	.956	R. Kline	26	105	3	6	1	4.90
CF	K. Hunt	479	.255	25	84	261	6	14	1	2.1	.950	J. Donohue	38	100	4	6	5	4.31
LF	L. Wagner	453	.280	28	79	187	12	6	2	1.8	.971	R. Duren	40	99	6	12	2	5.18
C	E. Averill	323	.266	21	59	542	38	5	6	6.6	.991	T. Morgan	59	92	8	2	10	2.36
OF	L. Thomas	450	.284	24	70	159	9	6	1	2.0	.966	A. Fowler	53	89	5	8	11	3.64
03	G. Thomas	282	.280	13	59	96	63	13	5		.924							
1B	T. Kluszewski	263	.243	15	39	520	28	6	51	8.4	.989							
2S	R. Bridges	229	.240	2	15	145	196	6	35		.983							
3B	G. Leek	199	.226	5	20	54	127	8	11	3.9	.958							
2B	B. Moran	173	.260	2	22	108	116	8	31	4.5	.966							
C	E. Sadowski	164	.232	4	12	295	17	4	4	5.6	.987							

Kansas City

W-61 L-100

Joe Gordon
W-26 L-33

Hank Bauer
W-35 L-67

POS	Player	AB	BA	HR	RBI	PO	A	E	DP	TC/G	FA	Pitcher	G	IP	W	L	SV	ERA
1B	N. Siebern	560	.296	18	98	907	76	11	88	9.1	.989	J. Archer	39	205	9	15	5	3.20
2B	J. Lumpe	569	.293	3	54	403	426	18	105	**5.8**	.979	N. Bass	40	171	11	11	0	4.69
SS	D. Howser	611	.280	3	45	**299**	427	**38**	85	4.9	.950	J. Walker	36	168	8	14	2	4.82
3B	W. Causey	312	.276	8	49	102	193	14	20	3.5	.955	B. Shaw	26	150	9	10	0	4.31
RF	D. Johnson	283	.216	8	42	104	6	6	0	2.0	.948	J. Nuxhall	37	128	5	8	1	5.34
CF	B. Del Greco	239	.230	5	21	168	8	3	2	2.5	.983	E. Rakow	45	125	2	8	1	4.76
LF	L. Posada	344	.253	7	53	205	8	6	0	2.1	.973	B. Kunkel	58	89	3	4	4	5.18
C	H. Sullivan	331	.242	6	40	387	32	7	7	4.8	.984	B. Daley	16	64	4	8	1	4.95
C	J. Pignatano	243	.243	4	22	379	35	9	7	5.1	.979							
OF	G. Stephens	183	.208	4	26	114	6	4	4*	2.3	.968							
OF	J. Hankins	173	.185	3	6	97	1	3	0	1.6	.970							
1B	M. Throneberry	130	.238	6	24	241	25	1	31	8.9	.996							

Washington

W-61 L-100

Mickey Vernon

POS	Player	AB	BA	HR	RBI	PO	A	E	DP	TC/G	FA	Pitcher	G	IP	W	L	SV	ERA
1B	D. Long	377	.249	17	49	827	62	**15**	87	9.5	.983	J. McClain	33	212	8	18	1	3.86
2B	C. Cottier	337	.234	2	34	233	316	10	73	5.6	.982	B. Daniels	32	212	12	11	0	3.44
SS	C. Veal	218	.202	0	8	130	172	8	43	4.9	.974	D. Donovan	23	169	10	10	0	**2.40**
3B	D. O'Connell	493	.260	1	37	75	173	16	14	3.6	.939	M. Kutyna	50	143	6	8	3	3.97
RF	M. Keough	390	.249	9	34	213	7	5	2	2.3	.978	E. Hobaugh	26	126	7	9	0	4.42
CF	W. Tasby	494	.251	17	63	332	5	5	0	2.5	.985	P. Burnside	33	113	4	9	2	4.53
LF	C. Hinton	339	.260	6	34	175	6	7	4	2.0	.963	J. Gabler	29	93	3	8	4	4.86
C	G. Green	364	.280	18	62	326	22	5	3	4.5	.986	D. Sisler	45	60	2	8	11	4.18
OF	G. Woodling	342	.313	10	57	154	8	2	0	1.8	.988							
OF	J. King	263	.270	11	46	138	7	3	2	1.6	.980							
3B	B. Klaus	251	.227	7	30	40	107	6	3	3.0	.961							
SS	B. Johnson	224	.295	6	28	110	172	13	31	5.2	.956							
C	P. Daley	203	.192	2	17	285	35	4	6	4.5	.988							
3B	H. Bright	183	.240	4	21	47	95	11	14	3.8	.928							
1B	B. Zipfel	170	.200	4	18	429	25	8	40	10.5	.983							

BATTING AND BASE RUNNING LEADERS

Batting Average

N. Cash, DET	.361
A. Kaline, DET	.324
J. Piersall, CLE	.322
M. Mantle, NY	.317
J. Gentile, BAL	.302

Slugging Average

M. Mantle, NY	.687
N. Cash, DET	.662
J. Gentile, BAL	.646
R. Maris, NY	.620
H. Killebrew, MIN	.606

Home Runs

R. Maris, NY	61
M. Mantle, NY	54
J. Gentile, BAL	46
H. Killebrew, MIN	46
R. Colavito, DET	45

Total Bases

R. Maris, NY	366
N. Cash, DET	354
M. Mantle, NY	353
R. Colavito, DET	338
H. Killebrew, MIN	328

Runs Batted In

J. Gentile, BAL	141
R. Maris, NY	141
R. Colavito, DET	140
N. Cash, DET	132
M. Mantle, NY	128

Stolen Bases

L. Aparicio, CHI	53
D. Howser, KC	37
J. Wood, DET	30
C. Hinton, WAS	22
B. Bruton, DET	22

Hits

N. Cash, DET	193
B. Robinson, BAL	192
A. Kaline, DET	190
T. Francona, CLE	178

Base on Balls

M. Mantle, NY	126
N. Cash, DET	124
R. Colavito, DET	113
H. Killebrew, MIN	107

Home Run Percentage

M. Mantle, NY	10.5
R. Maris, NY	10.3
J. Gentile, BAL	9.5
H. Killebrew, MIN	8.5

Runs

M. Mantle, NY	132
R. Maris, NY	132
R. Colavito, DET	129
N. Cash, DET	119

Doubles

A. Kaline, DET	41
T. Kubek, NY	38
B. Robinson, BAL	38
N. Siebern, KC	36

Triples

J. Wood, DET	14
M. Keough, WAS	9
J. Lumpe, KC	9

PITCHING LEADERS

Winning Percentage

W. Ford, NY	.862
R. Terry, NY	.842
L. Arroyo, NY	.750
F. Lary, DET	.719
D. Mossi, DET	.682
D. Schwall, BOS	.682

Earned Run Average

D. Donovan, WAS	2.40
B. Stafford, NY	2.68
D. Mossi, DET	2.96
M. Pappas, BAL	3.04
J. Pizarro, CHI	3.05

Wins

W. Ford, NY	25
F. Lary, DET	23
S. Barber, BAL	18
J. Bunning, DET	17
R. Terry, NY	16

Saves

L. Arroyo, NY	29
H. Wilhelm, BAL	18
M. Fornieles, BOS	15
R. Moore, MIN	14
T. Fox, DET	12

Strikeouts

C. Pascual, MIN	221
W. Ford, NY	209
J. Bunning, DET	194
J. Pizarro, CHI	188
K. McBride, LA	180

Complete Games

F. Lary, DET	22
C. Pascual, MIN	15
S. Barber, BAL	14

Fewest Hits/9 Innings

C. Estrada, BAL	6.75
M. Pappas, BAL	6.79
S. Barber, BAL	7.03
C. Pascual, MIN	7.31

Shutouts

C. Pascual, MIN	8
S. Barber, BAL	8
M. Pappas, BAL	4
F. Lary, DET	4
J. Bunning, DET	4

Fewest Walks/9 Innings

D. Mossi, DET	1.76
H. Brown, BAL	1.78
D. Donovan, WAS	1.87
R. Terry, NY	2.01

Most Strikeouts/9 Inn.

J. Pizarro, CHI	8.69
C. Pascual, MIN	7.88
C. Estrada, BAL	6.79
K. McBride, LA	6.70

Innings

W. Ford, NY	283
F. Lary, DET	275
J. Bunning, DET	268
P. Ramos, MIN	264

Games Pitched

L. Arroyo, NY	65
T. Lown, CHI	59
T. Morgan, LA	59
B. Kunkel, KC	58

AMERICAN LEAGUE 1961, *cont.*

							Batting						Fielding			Pitching					
	W	L	PCT	GB	R	OR	2B	3B	HR	BA	SA	SB	E	DP	FA	CG	BB	SO	ShO	SV	ERA
New York	109	53	.673		827	612	194	40	**240**	.263	**.442**	28	**124**	**180**	**.980**	47	542	866	14	**39**	3.46
Detroit	101	61	.623	8	**841**	671	215	**53**	180	**.266**	.421	98	146	147	.976	**62**	**469**	836	12	30	3.55
Baltimore	95	67	.586	14	691	**588**	227	36	149	.254	.390	39	128	173	**.980**	54	617	926	**21**	33	**3.22**
Chicago	86	76	.531	23	765	726	216	46	138	.265	.395	**100**	128	138	**.980**	39	498	814	3	33	4.06
Cleveland	78	83	.484	30.5	737	752	**257**	39	150	**.266**	.406	34	139	142	.977	35	599	801	12	23	4.15
Boston	76	86	.469	33	729	792	251	37	112	.254	.374	56	144	170	.977	35	679	831	6	30	4.29
Minnesota	70	90	.438	38	707	778	215	40	167	.250	.397	47	174	150	.971	49	570	914	14	23	4.28
Los Angeles	70	91	.435	38.5	744	784	218	22	189	.245	.398	37	192	154	.969	25	713	**973**	5	34	4.31
Kansas City	61	100	.379	47.5	683	863	216	47	90	.247	.354	58	175	160	.972	32	629	703	5	23	4.74
Washington	61	100	.379	47.5	618	776	217	44	119	.244	.367	81	156	171	.975	39	586	666	8	21	4.23
					7342	7342	2226	404	1534	.255	.394	578	1506	1585	.976	417	5902	8330	100	289	4.03

NATIONAL LEAGUE 1962

San Francisco

W-103 L-62

Alvin Dark

POS	Player	AB	BA	HR	RBI	PO	A	E	DP	TC/G	FA	Pitcher	G	IP	W	L	SV	ERA
1B	O. Cepeda	625	.306	35	114	1353	88	13	125	9.1	.991	B. O'Dell	43	281	19	14	0	3.53
2B	C. Hiller	602	.276	3	48	367	417	**29**	105	5.0	.964	J. Sanford	39	265	24	7	0	3.43
SS	J. Pagan	580	.259	7	57	286	461	21	84	4.7	**.973**	J. Marichal	37	263	18	11	1	3.36
3B	J. Davenport	485	.297	14	58	125	256	19	28	2.8	.953	B. Pierce	30	162	16	6	1	3.49
RF	F. Alou	561	.316	25	98	262	7	8	3	1.8	.971	S. Miller	59	107	5	8	19	4.12
CF	W. Mays	621	.304	**49**	141	429	6	4	1	2.7	.991	M. McCormick	28	99	5	5	0	5.38
LF	H. Kuenn	487	.304	10	68	160	3	5	1	1.6	.970	B. Bolin	41	92	7	3	5	3.62
C	T. Haller	272	.261	18	55	472	38	4	6	5.6	.992	D. Larsen	49	86	5	4	11	4.38
C	E. Bailey	254	.232	17	45	419	25	6	3	6.0	.987							
OF	W. McCovey	229	.293	20	54	81	2	2	1	1.5	.976							
OF	M. Alou	195	.292	3	14	80	3	2	0	1.5	.976							

Los Angeles

W-102 L-63

Walter Alston

POS	Player	AB	BA	HR	RBI	PO	A	E	DP	TC/G	FA	Pitcher	G	IP	W	L	SV	ERA
1B	R. Fairly	460	.278	14	71	968	43	11	76	8.5	.989	D. Drysdale	43	**314**	**25**	9	1	2.83
2B	L. Burright	249	.205	4	30	176	206	15	35	3.6	.962	J. Podres	40	255	15	13	0	3.81
SS	M. Wills	**695**	.299	6	48	295	493	36	86	5.0	.956	S. Williams	40	186	14	12	1	4.46
3B	J. Gilliam	588	.270	4	43	51	126	11	12	2.1	.941	S. Koufax	28	184	14	7	1	**2.54**
RF	F. Howard	493	.296	31	119	187	19	6	4	1.6	.972	E. Roebuck	64	119	10	2	9	3.09
CF	W. Davis	600	.285	21	85	379	13	15	0	2.6	.963	R. Perranoski	**70**	107	6	6	20	2.85
LF	T. Davis	665	**.346**	27	**153**	240	9	10	0	1.8	.961	L. Sherry	58	90	7	3	11	3.20
C	J. Roseboro	389	.249	7	55	**842**	57	**14**	10	**7.1**	.985	J. Moeller	19	86	6	5	1	5.25
01	W. Moon	244	.242	4	31	300	20	7	29		.979							
OF	D. Snider	158	.278	5	30	56	3	2	0	1.6	.967							
C	D. Camilli	88	.284	4	22	162	8	3	1	4.4	.983							

Cincinnati

W-98 L-64

Fred Hutchinson

POS	Player	AB	BA	HR	RBI	PO	A	E	DP	TC/G	FA	Pitcher	G	IP	W	L	SV	ERA
1B	G. Coleman	476	.277	28	86	1021	83	12	100	8.7	.989	B. Purkey	37	288	23	5	0	2.81
2B	D. Blasingame	494	.281	2	35	334	352	17	66	5.1	.976	J. Jay	39	273	21	14	0	3.76
SS	L. Cardenas	589	.294	10	60	273	443	21	84	4.9	.972	J. O'Toole	36	252	16	13	0	3.50
3B	E. Kasko	533	.278	4	41	101	204	19	18	2.8	.941	J. Maloney	22	115	9	7	1	3.51
RF	F. Robinson	609	.342	39	136	315	10	2	2	2.0	.994	J. Klippstein	40	109	7	6	4	4.47
CF	V. Pinson	619	.292	23	100	344	13	4	1	2.4	.989	J. Brosnan	48	65	4	4	13	3.34
LF	W. Post	285	.263	17	62	110	5	8	0	1.4	.935	B. Henry	40	37	4	2	11	4.58
C	J. Edwards	452	.254	8	50	807	**92**	12	**11**	7.0	.987							
OF	J. Lynch	288	.281	12	57	89	7	3	1	1.4	.970							
OF	M. Keough	230	.278	7	27	88	2	3	1	1.3	.968							
3B	D. Zimmer	192	.250	2	16	45	66	6	6	2.7	.949							
C	H. Foiles	131	.275	7	25	249	14	5	1	6.5	.981							

Pittsburgh

W-93 L-68

Danny Murtaugh

POS	Player	AB	BA	HR	RBI	PO	A	E	DP	TC/G	FA	Pitcher	G	IP	W	L	SV	ERA
1B	D. Stuart	394	.228	16	64	868	78	**17**	98	9.5	.982	B. Friend	39	262	18	14	1	3.06
2B	B. Mazeroski	572	.271	14	81	**425**	**509**	14	**138**	**6.0**	.985	A. McBean	33	190	15	10	0	3.70
SS	D. Groat	678	.294	2	61	**314**	**521**	**38**	**126**	**5.4**	.956	E. Francis	36	176	9	8	0	3.07
3B	D. Hoak	411	.241	5	48	93	220	10	19	2.8	**.969**	H. Haddix	28	141	9	6	0	4.20
RF	R. Clemente	538	.312	10	74	269	19	8	1	2.1	.973	V. Law	23	139	10	7	0	3.94
CF	B. Virdon	663	.247	6	47	360	11	9	0	2.4	.976	T. Sturdivant	49	125	9	5	2	3.73
LF	B. Skinner	510	.302	20	75	210	6	9	0	1.6	.960	R. Face	63	91	8	7	**28**	1.88
C	S. Burgess	360	.328	13	61	550	45	7	5	6.0	.988	D. Olivo	62	84	5	1	7	2.77
1B	D. Clendenon	222	.302	7	28	382	24	4	44	7.9	.990							

Milwaukee

W-86 L-76

Birdie Tebbetts

POS	Player	AB	BA	HR	RBI	PO	A	E	DP	TC/G	FA	Pitcher	G	IP	W	L	SV	ERA
1B	J. Adcock	391	.248	29	78	907	57	3	72	8.6	**.997**	W. Spahn	34	269	18	14	0	3.04
2B	F. Bolling	406	.271	9	43	252	298	6	70	4.7	**.989**	B. Shaw	38	225	15	9	2	2.80
SS	R. McMillan	468	.246	12	41	243	424	19	85	5.1	.972	B. Hendley	35	200	11	13	1	3.60
3B	E. Mathews	536	.265	29	90	141	283	16	22	3.1	.964	L. Burdette	37	144	10	9	2	4.89
RF	M. Jones	333	.255	10	36	142	3	4	0	1.6	.973	T. Cloninger	24	111	8	3	0	4.30
CF	H. Aaron	592	.323	45	128	340	11	7	1	2.3	.980	C. Raymond	26	43	5	5	10	2.74
LF	L. Maye	349	.244	10	41	209	2	5	1	2.3	.977							
C	D. Crandall	350	.297	8	45	460	54	3	7	5.7	**.994**							
1B	T. Aaron	334	.231	8	38	507	45	6	55	5.1	.989							
C	J. Torre	220	.282	5	26	325	39	5	4	5.9	.986							
OF	G. Bell	214	.285	5	24	75	3	1	0	1.4	.987							
S2	A. Samuel	209	.206	3	20	81	155	10	29		.959							

NATIONAL LEAGUE 1962, *cont.*

Team	POS	Player	AB	BA	HR	RBI	PO	A	E	DP	TC/G	FA	Pitcher	G	IP	W	L	SV	ERA
St. Louis	1B	B. White	614	.324	20	102	1221	94	9	114	9.1	.993	L. Jackson	36	252	16	11	0	3.75
	2B	J. Javier	598	.263	7	39	344	414	18	96	5.1	.977	B. Gibson	32	234	15	13	1	2.85
W-84 L-78	SS	J. Gotay	369	.255	2	27	179	339	24	65	4.5	.956	E. Broglio	34	222	12	9	0	3.00
	3B	K. Boyer	611	.291	24	98	158	318	22	**34**	3.1	.956	R. Washburn	34	176	12	9	0	4.10
Johnny Keane	RF	C. James	388	.276	8	59	156	7	2	1	1.4	.988	C. Simmons	31	154	10	10	0	3.51
	CF	C. Flood	635	.296	12	70	387	12	4	5	2.7	.990	L. McDaniel	55	107	3	10	14	4.12
	LF	S. Musial	433	.330	19	82	164	6	4	1	1.5	.977	R. Sadecki	22	102	6	8	1	5.54
	C	G. Oliver	345	.258	14	45	494	46	5	7	5.6	.991	B. Shantz	28	58	5	3	4	2.18
	C	C. Sawatski	222	.252	13	42	354	24	1	4	5.4	.997							
	SS	D. Maxvill	189	.222	1	18	111	169	11	41	3.8	.962							
	1B	F. Whitfield	158	.266	8	34	282	25	4	32	8.2	.987							
Philadelphia	1B	R. Sievers	477	.262	21	80	975	93	10	102	8.3	.991	A. Mahaffey	41	274	19	14	0	3.94
	2B	T. Taylor	625	.259	7	43	372	385	22	101	5.2	.972	J. Hamilton	41	182	9	12	2	5.09
W-81 L-80	SS	B. Wine	311	.244	4	25	140	237	8	51	4.3	.979	D. Bennett	31	175	9	9	3	3.81
	3B	D. Demeter	550	.307	29	107	91	177	18	18	2.7	.937	C. McLish	32	155	11	5	1	4.25
Gene Mauch	RF	J. Callison	603	.300	23	83	327	24	7	7	2.4	.980	C. Short	47	142	11	9	3	3.42
	CF	T. Gonzalez	437	.302	20	63	268	8	0	2	2.4	1.000	D. Green	37	129	6	6	1	3.83
	LF	T. Savage	335	.266	7	39	185	4	5	1	1.8	.974	J. Baldschun	67	113	12	7	13	2.96
	C	C. Dalrymple	370	.276	11	54	635	61	9	**11**	5.9	.987							
	OF	W. Covington	304	.283	9	44	98	3	6	2	1.2	.944							
	UT	B. Klaus	248	.206	4	20	93	142	9	21		.963							
	SS	R. Amaro	226	.243	0	19	143	224	12	50	4.9	.968							
	1B	F. Torre	168	.310	0	20	347	37	8	40	5.2	.980							
Houston	1B	N. Larker	506	.263	9	63	1148	103	11	103	9.3	.991	D. Farrell	43	242	10	20	4	3.02
	2B	J. Amalfitano	380	.237	1	27	230	268	17	72	4.7	.967	K. Johnson	33	197	7	16	0	3.84
W-64 L-96	SS	B. Lillis	457	.249	1	30	169	290	13	54	4.8	.972	B. Bruce	32	175	10	9	0	4.06
	3B	B. Aspromonte	534	.266	11	59	150	233	13	21	2.8	.967	J. Golden	37	153	7	11	1	4.07
Harry Craft	RF	R. Mejias	566	.286	24	76	217	10	13	2	1.7	.946	H. Woodeshick	31	139	5	16	0	4.39
	CF	C. Warwick	477	.260	16	60	262	12	4	1	2.2	.986	D. McMahon	51	77	5	5	8	1.53
	LF	A. Spangler	418	.285	5	35	183	7	8	2	1.6	.960	R. Kemmerer	36	68	5	3	3	4.10
	C	H. Smith	345	.235	12	35	570	65	9	9	7.0	.986							
	OF	J. Pendleton	321	.246	8	36	126	4	5	0	1.5	.963							
	C	M. Ranew	218	.234	4	24	357	35	8	1	6.9	.980							
Chicago	1B	E. Banks	610	.269	37	104	**1458**	**106**	11	**134**	**10.6**	.993	B. Buhl	34	212	12	13	0	3.69
	2B	K. Hubbs	661	.260	5	49	363	489	15	103	5.5	.983	D. Ellsworth	37	209	9	20	1	5.09
	SS	A. Rodgers	461	.278	5	44	239	433	28	91	5.3	.960	D. Cardwell	41	196	7	16	4	4.92
W-59 L-103	3B	R. Santo	604	.227	17	83	**161**	**332**	**23**	33	**3.3**	.955	C. Koonce	35	191	10	10	0	3.97
	RF	G. Altman	534	.318	22	74	234	8	7	3	1.9	.972	G. Hobbie	42	162	5	14	0	5.22
El Tappe	CF	L. Brock	434	.263	9	35	243	7	9	2	2.4	.965	B. Anderson	57	108	2	7	4	5.02
W-4 L-16	LF	B. Williams	618	.298	22	91	273	18	10	4	1.9	.967	B. Schultz	51	78	5	5	5	3.82
	C	D. Bertell	215	.302	2	18	306	36	5	0	4.6	.986	D. Elston	57	66	4	8	8	2.44
Lou Klein	OF	D. Landrum	238	.282	1	15	122	3	4	3	2.2	.969							
W-12 L-18																			
Charlie Metro																			
W-43 L-69																			
New York	1B	M. Throneberry	357	.244	16	49	785	77	17*	87	9.1	.981	R. Craig	42	233	10	**24**	3	4.51
	2B	C. Neal	508	.260	11	58	187	240	13	54	5.2	.970	A. Jackson	36	231	8	20	0	4.40
W-40 L-120	SS	E. Chacon	368	.236	2	27	204	332	22	64	5.1	.961	J. Hook	37	214	8	19	0	4.84
	3B	F. Mantilla	466	.275	11	59	76	179	14	22	2.8	.948	B. Miller	33	144	1	12	1	4.89
Casey Stengel	RF	R. Ashburn	389	.306	7	28	187	9	5	1	2.1	.975	C. Anderson	50	131	3	17	4	5.35
	CF	J. Hickman	392	.245	13	46	265	7	8	0	2.3	.971	B. Moorhead	38	105	0	2	0	4.53
	LF	F. Thomas	571	.266	34	94	216	14	9	0	1.9	.962	K. MacKenzie	42	80	5	4	1	4.95
	C	C. Cannizzaro	133	.241	0	9	218	34	7	3	4.6	.973							
	UT	R. Kanehl	351	.248	4	27	235	230	32	57		.936							
	OF	J. Christopher	271	.244	6	32	133	5	4	4	1.5	.972							
	OF	G. Woodling	190	.274	5	24	68	0	1	0	1.4	.986							
	C	S. Taylor	158	.222	3	20	202	25	2	3	4.6	.991							

BATTING AND BASE RUNNING LEADERS

Batting Average		Slugging Average		Home Runs	
T. Davis, LA	.346	F. Robinson, CIN	.624	W. Mays, SF	49
F. Robinson, CIN	.342	H. Aaron, MIL	.618	H. Aaron, MIL	45
S. Musial, STL	.330	W. Mays, SF	.615	F. Robinson, CIN	39
B. White, STL	.324	F. Howard, LA	.560	E. Banks, CHI	37
H. Aaron, MIL	.323	T. Davis, LA	.535	O. Cepeda, SF	35

Total Bases		Runs Batted In		Stolen Bases	
W. Mays, SF	382	T. Davis, LA	153	M. Wills, LA	104
F. Robinson, CIN	380	W. Mays, SF	141	W. Davis, LA	32
H. Aaron, MIL	366	F. Robinson, CIN	136	J. Javier, STL	26
T. Davis, LA	356	H. Aaron, MIL	128	V. Pinson, CIN	26
O. Cepeda, SF	324	F. Howard, LA	119	T. Taylor, PHI	20

PITCHING LEADERS

Winning Percentage		Earned Run Average		Wins	
B. Purkey, CIN	.821	S. Koufax, LA	2.54	D. Drysdale, LA	25
J. Sanford, SF	.774	B. Shaw, MIL	2.80	J. Sanford, SF	24
D. Drysdale, LA	.735	B. Purkey, CIN	2.81	B. Purkey, CIN	23
B. Pierce, SF	.727	D. Drysdale, LA	2.83	J. Jay, CIN	21
B. Shaw, MIL	.625	B. Gibson, STL	2.85	A. Mahaffey, PHI	19
				B. O'Dell, SF	19

Saves		Strikeouts		Complete Games	
R. Face, PIT	28	D. Drysdale, LA	232	W. Spahn, MIL	22
R. Perranoski, LA	20	S. Koufax, LA	216	A. Mahaffey, PHI	20
S. Miller, SF	19	B. Gibson, STL	208	B. O'Dell, SF	20
L. McDaniel, STL	14	D. Farrell, HOU	203	D. Drysdale, LA	19
J. Brosnan, CIN	13	B. O'Dell, SF	195	J. Marichal, SF	18
J. Baldschun, PHI	13			B. Purkey, CIN	18

NATIONAL LEAGUE 1962, *cont.*

BATTING AND BASE RUNNING LEADERS

Hits

T. Davis, LA	230
F. Robinson, CIN	208
M. Wills, LA	208
B. White, STL	199
D. Groat, PIT	199

Base on Balls

E. Mathews, MIL	101
J. Gilliam, LA	93
R. Ashburn, NY	81
W. Mays, SF	78

Home Run Percentage

W. Mays, SF	7.9
H. Aaron, MIL	7.6
F. Robinson, CIN	6.4
F. Howard, LA	6.3

Runs

F. Robinson, CIN	134
W. Mays, SF	130
M. Wills, LA	130
H. Aaron, MIL	127

Doubles

F. Robinson, CIN	51
W. Mays, SF	36
D. Groat, PIT	34

Triples

W. Davis, LA	10
J. Callison, PHI	10
B. Virdon, PIT	10
M. Wills, LA	10

PITCHING LEADERS

Fewest Hits/9 Innings

S. Koufax, LA	6.54
B. Gibson, STL	6.70
D. Bennett, PHI	7.42
D. Drysdale, LA	7.79

Shutouts

B. Gibson, STL	5
B. Friend, PIT	5

Fewest Walks/9 Innings

B. Shaw, MIL	1.76
B. Friend, PIT	1.82
W. Spahn, MIL	1.84
B. Pierce, SF	1.94

Most Strikeouts/9 Inn.

S. Koufax, LA	10.55
K. Johnson, HOU	8.13
B. Gibson, STL	8.01
D. Bennett, PHI	7.68

Innings

D. Drysdale, LA	314
B. Purkey, CIN	288
B. O'Dell, SF	281
A. Mahaffey, PHI	274

Games Pitched

R. Perranoski, LA	70
J. Baldschun, PHI	67
E. Roebuck, LA	64
R. Face, PIT	63

							Batting						Fielding			Pitching					
	W	L	PCT	GB	R	OR	2B	3B	HR	BA	SA	SB	E	DP	FA	CG	BB	SO	ShO	SV	ERA
*San Francisco	103	62	.624		**878**	690	235	32	**204**	**.278**	**.441**	73	142	153	.977	**62**	503	886	10	39	3.79
Los Angeles	102	63	.618	1	842	697	192	**65**	140	.268	.400	**198**	193	144	.970	44	588	**1104**	8	**46**	3.62
Cincinnati	98	64	.605	3.5	802	685	**252**	40	167	.270	.417	66	145	144	.977	51	567	964	13	35	3.75
Pittsburgh	93	68	.578	8	706	**626**	240	**65**	108	.268	.394	50	152	**177**	.976	40	466	897	13	41	**3.37**
Milwaukee	86	76	.531	15.5	730	665	204	38	181	.252	.403	57	**124**	154	**.980**	59	**407**	802	10	24	3.68
St. Louis	84	78	.519	17.5	774	664	221	31	137	.271	.394	86	132	170	.979	53	517	914	**17**	25	3.55
Philadelphia	81	80	.503	20	705	759	199	39	142	.260	.390	79	138	167	.977	43	574	863	7	24	4.28
Houston	64	96	.400	36.5	592	717	170	47	105	.246	.351	42	173	149	.973	34	471	1047	9	19	3.83
Chicago	59	103	.364	42.5	632	827	196	56	126	.253	.377	78	146	171	.977	29	601	783	4	26	4.54
New York	40	120	.250	60.5	617	948	166	40	139	.240	.361	59	210	167	.967	43	571	772	4	10	5.04
					7278	7278	2075	453	1449	.261	.393	788	1555	1596	.975	458	5265	9032	95	289	3.95

* Defeated Los Angeles in playoff 2 games to 1

AMERICAN LEAGUE 1962

New York

W-96 L-66

Ralph Houk

POS	Player	AB	BA	HR	RBI	PO	A	E	DP	TC/G	FA	Pitcher	G	IP	W	L	SV	ERA
1B	B. Skowron	478	.270	23	80	1054	77	10	101	8.5	.991	R. Terry	43	**299**	**23**	12	2	3.19
2B	B. Richardson	**692**	.302	8	59	378	452	15	**116**	5.2	.982	W. Ford	38	258	17	8	0	2.90
SS	T. Tresh	622	.286	20	93	201	312	16	51	4.8	.970	B. Stafford	35	213	14	9	0	3.67
3B	C. Boyer	566	.272	18	68	**187**	**396**	22	**41**	**3.9**	.964	J. Bouton	36	133	7	7	2	3.99
RF	R. Maris	590	.256	33	100	316	4	3	0	2.1	.991	R. Sheldon	34	118	7	8	1	5.49
CF	M. Mantle	377	.321	30	89	214	4	5	1	1.9	.978	J. Coates	50	118	7	6	6	4.44
LF	H. Lopez	335	.275	6	48	176	3	3	0	2.2	.984	B. Daley	43	105	7	5	4	3.59
C	E. Howard	494	.279	21	91	713	44	4	12	5.9	.995	M. Bridges	52	72	8	4	18	3.14
OF	J. Blanchard	246	.232	13	39	76	2	1	0	1.7	.987	L. Arroyo	27	34	1	3	7	4.81
CO	Y. Berra	232	.224	10	35	238	17	6	6		.977							
SS	T. Kubek	169	.314	4	17	71	117	9	27	5.6	.954							

Minnesota

W-91 L-71

Sam Mele

POS	Player	AB	BA	HR	RBI	PO	A	E	DP	TC/G	FA	Pitcher	G	IP	W	L	SV	ERA
1B	V. Power	611	.290	16	63	1193	**134**	10	**133**	9.4	.993	J. Kaat	39	269	18	14	1	3.14
2B	B. Allen	573	.269	12	64	357	394	13	109	4.8	.983	C. Pascual	34	258	20	11	0	3.32
SS	Z. Versalles	568	.241	17	67	**335**	**501**	26	**127**	**5.4**	.970	J. Kralick	39	243	12	11	0	3.86
3B	R. Rollins	624	.298	16	96	137	324	**28**	33	3.1	.943	D. Stigman	40	143	12	5	3	3.66
RF	B. Allison	519	.266	29	102	287	10	7	1	2.1	.977	J. Bonikowski	30	100	5	7	2	3.88
CF	L. Green	619	.271	14	63	361	8	2	2	2.4	.995	L. Stange	44	95	4	3	3	4.45
LF	H. Killebrew	552	.243	**48**	**126**	227	5	8	0	1.6	.967	R. Moore	49	65	8	3	9	4.73
C	E. Battey	522	.280	11	57	**872**	**82**	9	9	**6.6**	.991	B. Pleis	21	45	2	5	3	4.40
1B	D. Mincher	121	.240	9	29	211	13	5	17	9.2	.978	F. Sullivan	21	33	4	1	5	3.24

Los Angeles

W-86 L-76

Bill Rigney

POS	Player	AB	BA	HR	RBI	PO	A	E	DP	TC/G	FA	Pitcher	G	IP	W	L	SV	ERA
1B	L. Thomas	583	.290	26	104	735	42	14	66	8.8	.982	D. Chance	50	207	14	10	8	2.96
2B	B. Moran	659	.282	17	74	**422**	477	13	103	**5.7**	.986	B. Belinsky	33	187	10	11	1	3.56
SS	J. Koppe	375	.227	4	40	197	356	25	63	4.9	.957	E. Grba	40	176	8	9	1	4.54
3B	F. Torres	451	.259	11	74	110	250	24	20	3.1	.938	D. Lee	27	153	8	8	2	3.11
RF	G. Thomas	181	.238	4	12	107	4	5	1	2.3	.957	K. McBride	24	149	11	5	0	3.50
CF	A. Pearson	614	.261	5	42	366	8	4	0	2.4	.989	T. Bowsfield	34	139	9	8	1	4.40
LF	L. Wagner	612	.268	37	107	269	7	8	1	1.8	.972	A. Fowler	48	77	4	3	5	2.81
C	B. Rodgers	565	.258	6	61	826	73	**10**	**14**	6.1	.989	R. Duren	42	71	2	9	8	4.42
OF	E. Averill	187	.219	4	22	70	2	0	0	1.5	1.000	J. Spring	57	65	4	2	6	4.02
SS	J. Fregosi	175	.291	3	23	96	150	15	35	5.0	.943	T. Morgan	48	59	5	2	9	2.91
1B	S. Bilko	164	.287	8	38	371	28	2	36	8.0	.995	D. Osinski	33	54	6	4	4	2.82

Detroit

W-85 L-76

Bob Scheffing

POS	Player	AB	BA	HR	RBI	PO	A	E	DP	TC/G	FA	Pitcher	G	IP	W	L	SV	ERA
1B	N. Cash	507	.243	39	89	1081	116	10	94	8.3	.992	J. Bunning	41	258	19	10	6	3.59
2B	J. Wood	367	.226	8	30	185	197	**20**	33	4.5	.950	H. Aguirre	42	216	16	8	3	**2.21**
SS	C. Fernandez	503	.249	20	59	235	336	24	53	4.3	.960	D. Mossi	35	180	11	13	1	4.19
3B	S. Boros	356	.228	16	47	105	151	19	15	2.6	.931	P. Regan	35	171	11	9	0	4.04
RF	A. Kaline	398	.304	29	94	225	8	4	1	2.4	.983	P. Foytack	29	144	10	7	0	4.39
CF	B. Bruton	561	.278	16	74	394	5	7	2	2.8	.983	R. Kline	36	77	3	6	2	4.31
LF	R. Colavito	601	.273	37	112	359	10	3	1	2.3	.992	R. Nischwitz	48	65	4	5	4	3.90
C	D. Brown	431	.241	12	40	742	42	5	8	6.0	.994	T. Fox	44	58	3	1	16	1.71
UT	D. McAuliffe	471	.263	12	63	260	257	30	45		.945							
OF	B. Morton	195	.262	4	17	110	4	1	1	1.9	.991							

AMERICAN LEAGUE 1962, *cont.*

Chicago

W-85 L-77

Al Lopez

POS	Player	AB	BA	HR	RBI	PO	A	E	DP	TC/G	FA
1B	J. Cunningham	526	.295	8	70	1282	90	8	118	9.7	**.994**
2B	N. Fox	621	.267	2	54	376	428	8	93	5.3	**.990**
SS	L. Aparicio	581	.241	7	40	280	452	20	102	4.9	**.973**
3B	A. Smith	511	.292	16	82	76	185	18	8	2.7	.935
RF	M. Hershberger	427	.262	4	46	236	7	4	0	1.8	.984
CF	J. Landis	534	.228	15	61	360	2	2	1	2.5	.995
LF	F. Robinson	600	.312	11	109	278	13	8	2	1.9	.973
C	C. Carreon	313	.256	4	37	519	30	3	5	5.9	.995
C	S. Lollar	220	.268	2	26	298	23	3	0	4.9	.991
OF	C. Maxwell	206	.296	9	43	100	2	1	1	1.8	.990
32	B. Sadowski	130	.231	6	24	33	62	2	9		.979

Pitcher	G	IP	W	L	SV	ERA
R. Herbert	35	237	20	9	0	3.27
J. Pizarro	36	203	12	14	1	3.81
E. Fisher	57	183	9	5	5	3.10
E. Wynn	27	168	7	15	0	4.46
J. Buzhardt	28	152	8	12	0	4.19
F. Baumann	40	120	7	6	4	3.38
J. Horlen	20	109	7	6	0	4.89
D. Zanni	44	86	6	5	5	3.75
T. Lown	42	56	4	2	6	3.04

Cleveland

W-80 L-82

Mel McGaha
W-78 L-82

Mel Harder
W-2 L-0

POS	Player	AB	BA	HR	RBI	PO	A	E	DP	TC/G	FA
1B	T. Francona	621	.272	14	70	1402	127	**22**	5	**9.8**	.986
2B	J. Kindall	530	.232	13	55	358	**494**	19	114	5.7	.978
SS	W. Held	466	.249	19	58	221	371	27	101	4.7	.956
3B	B. Phillips	562	.258	10	54	175	243	10	16	3.0	.977
RF	W. Kirkland	419	.200	21	72	233	11	7	0	2.0	.972
CF	T. Cline	375	.248	2	28	238	3	2	1	2.3	.992
LF	C. Essegian	336	.274	21	50	154	1	1	0	1.7	.994
C	J. Romano	459	.261	25	81	657	63	7	6	5.6	.990
OF	A. Luplow •	318	.277	14	45	162	4	7	0	2.0	.960
OF	W. Tasby	199	.241	4	17	105	1	0	0	1.6	1.000
OF	D. Dillard	174	.230	5	14	54	1	2	0	1.1	.965
OF	G. Green	143	.280	11	28	51	2	2	1	1.7	.964

Pitcher	G	IP	W	L	SV	ERA
D. Donovan	34	251	20	10	0	3.59
P. Ramos	37	201	10	12	1	3.71
J. Perry	35	194	12	12	0	4.14
B. Latman	45	179	8	13	5	4.17
M. Grant	26	150	7	10	0	4.27
G. Bell	57	108	10	9	12	4.26
S. McDowell	25	88	3	7	1	6.06

Baltimore

W-77 L-85

Billy Hitchcock

POS	Player	AB	BA	HR	RBI	PO	A	E	DP	TC/G	FA
1B	J. Gentile	545	.251	33	87	1214	121	16	121	9.0	.988
2B	M. Breeding	240	.246	2	18	146	196	8	47	4.8	.977
SS	J. Adair	538	.284	11	48	216	285	16	72	4.6	.969
3B	B. Robinson	634	.303	23	86	163	339	11	32	3.2	**.979**
RF	R. Snyder	416	.305	9	40	218	8	6	2	1.9	.974
CF	J. Brandt	505	.255	19	75	310	9	8	2	2.4	.976
LF	B. Powell	400	.242	15	53	184	1	6	0	1.7	.969
C	G. Triandos	207	.159	6	23	355	28	6	2	6.2	.985
2B	J. Temple	270	.263	1	17	141	169	6	41	4.5	.981
OF	W. Herzog	263	.266	7	35	132	4	3	0	2.0	.978
C	C. Lau	197	.294	6	37	269	15	1	1	5.1	.996
SS	R. Hansen	196	.173	3	17	114	159	10	37	4.4	.965
O1	D. Williams	178	.247	1	18	180	13	0	13		1.000
OF	D. Nicholson	173	.173	9	15	111	4	2	0	1.5	.983
C	H. Landrith	167	.222	4	17	289	34	6	5	5.5	.982

Pitcher	G	IP	W	L	SV	ERA
C. Estrada	34	223	9	**17**	0	3.83
M. Pappas	35	205	12	10	0	4.03
R. Roberts	27	191	10	9	0	2.78
J. Fisher	32	152	7	9	1	5.09
S. Barber	28	140	9	6	0	3.46
D. Hall	43	118	6	6	6	2.28
B. Hoeft	57	114	4	8	7	4.59
H. Wilhelm	52	93	7	10	15	1.94
H. Brown	22	86	6	4	1	4.10

Boston

W-76 L-84

Pinky Higgins

POS	Player	AB	BA	HR	RBI	PO	A	E	DP	TC/G	FA
1B	P. Runnels	562	**.326**	10	60	1309	104	10	125	9.4	.993
2B	C. Schilling	413	.230	7	35	267	331	9	85	5.1	.985
SS	E. Bressoud	599	.277	14	68	291	482	**28**	107	5.2	.965
3B	F. Malzone	619	.283	21	95	154	313	16	32	3.1	.967
RF	L. Clinton	398	.294	18	75	185	6	4	1	1.9	.979
CF	G. Geiger	466	.249	16	54	287	8	4	1	2.3	.987
LF	C. Yastrzemski	646	.296	19	94	329	15	11	3	2.2	.969
C	J. Pagliaroni	260	.258	11	37	411	33	6	4	6.2	.987
OF	C. Hardy	362	.215	8	36	205	7	2	1	2.0	.991
C	B. Tillman	249	.229	14	38	389	19	7	1	6.3	.983
2B	B. Gardner	199	.271	0	12	67	91	6	21	4.3	.963

Pitcher	G	IP	W	L	SV	ERA
G. Conley	34	242	15	14	1	3.95
B. Monbouquette	35	235	15	13	0	3.33
E. Wilson	31	191	12	8	0	3.90
D. Schwall	33	182	9	15	0	4.94
D. Radatz	**62**	125	9	6	**24**	2.24
G. Cisco	23	83	4	7	0	6.72
M. Fornieles	42	82	3	6	5	5.36
A. Earley	38	68	4	5	5	5.80

Kansas City

W-72 L-90

Hank Bauer

POS	Player	AB	BA	HR	RBI	PO	A	E	DP	TC/G	FA
1B	N. Siebern	600	.308	25	117	**1405**	127	10	122	9.5	.994
2B	J. Lumpe	641	.301	10	83	343	435	11	97	5.1	.986
SS	D. Howser	286	.238	6	34	138	191	13	37	4.8	.962
3B	E. Charles	535	.288	17	74	145	285	16	27	3.2	.964
RF	G. Cimoli	550	.275	10	71	231	8	8	2	1.7	.968
CF	B. Del Greco	338	.254	9	38	245	9	4	0	2.1	.984
LF	M. Jimenez	479	.301	11	69	185	7	3	0	1.6	.985
C	H. Sullivan	274	.248	4	29	447	31	**10**	2	5.2	.980
OF	J. Tartabull	310	.277	0	22	185	6	5	0	2.3	.974
UT	W. Causey	305	.252	4	38	143	200	14	25		.961
C	J. Azcue	223	.229	2	25	363	42	6	5	5.9	.985
OF	G. Alusik	209	.273	11	35	87	3	3	0	1.9	.968

Pitcher	G	IP	W	L	SV	ERA
E. Rakow	42	235	14	**17**	1	4.25
D. Pfister	41	196	4	14	1	4.54
J. Walker	31	143	8	9	0	5.90
B. Fischer	34	128	4	12	2	3.95
J. Wyatt	59	125	10	7	11	4.46
D. Segui	37	117	8	5	6	3.86
D. Wickersham	30	110	11	4	1	4.17
O. Pena	13	90	6	4	0	3.01
G. Jones	21	33	3	2	6	6.34

Washington

W-60 L-101

Mickey Vernon

POS	Player	AB	BA	HR	RBI	PO	A	E	DP	TC/G	FA
1B	H. Bright	392	.273	17	67	800	70	10	83	8.9	.989
2B	C. Cottier	443	.242	6	40	368	354	14	100	5.5	.981
SS	K. Hamlin	292	.253	3	22	126	210	13	47	4.0	.963
3B	B. Johnson	466	.288	12	43	79	142	13	12	3.3	.944
RF	J. King	333	.243	11	35	178	9	4	4	1.9	.979
CF	J. Piersall	471	.244	4	31	308	5	1	0	2.4	.997
LF	C. Hinton	542	.310	17	75	233	7	3	1	1.8	.988
C	K. Retzer	340	.285	8	37	488	44	8	5	5.5	.985
C	B. Schmidt	256	.242	10	31	342	40	1	3	4.4	**.997**
32	D. O'Connell	236	.263	2	18	70	141	10	21		.955
OF	D. Lock	225	.253	12	37	144	2	4	0	2.2	.973
3B	J. Schaive	225	.253	6	29	42	105	5	7	3.1	.967
1B	D. Long	191	.241	4	24	459	32	2	67	9.7	.996
1O	B. Zipfel	184	.239	6	21	228	17	8	13		.968
OF	J. Hicks	174	.224	6	14	74	1	3	1	1.9	.962

Pitcher	G	IP	W	L	SV	ERA
D. Stenhouse	34	197	11	12	0	3.65
D. Rudolph	37	176	8	10	0	3.62
T. Cheney	37	173	7	9	1	3.17
B. Daniels	44	161	7	16	2	4.85
C. Osteen	28	150	8	13	1	3.65
P. Burnside	40	150	5	11	2	4.45
S. Hamilton	41	107	3	8	2	3.77
M. Kutyna	54	78	5	6	0	4.04
J. Hannan	42	68	2	4	4	3.31

AMERICAN LEAGUE 1962, *cont.*

BATTING AND BASE RUNNING LEADERS

Batting Average

P. Runnels, BOS	.326
M. Mantle, NY	.321
F. Robinson, CHI	.312
C. Hinton, WAS	.310
N. Siebern, KC	.308

Slugging Average

M. Mantle, NY	.605
H. Killebrew, MIN	.545
R. Colavito, DET	.514
N. Cash, DET	.513
B. Allison, MIN	.511

Home Runs

H. Killebrew, MIN	48
N. Cash, DET	39
R. Colavito, DET	37
L. Wagner, LA	37
J. Gentile, BAL	33
R. Maris, NY	33

Total Bases

R. Colavito, DET	309
B. Robinson, BAL	308
L. Wagner, LA	306
C. Yastrzemski, BOS	303
H. Killebrew, MIN	301

Runs Batted In

H. Killebrew, MIN	126
N. Siebern, KC	117
R. Colavito, DET	112
F. Robinson, CHI	109
L. Wagner, LA	107

Stolen Bases

L. Aparicio, CHI	31
C. Hinton, WAS	28
J. Wood, DET	24
E. Charles, KC	20

Hits

B. Richardson, NY	209
J. Lumpe, KC	193
B. Robinson, BAL	192
C. Yastrzemski, BOS	191

Base on Balls

M. Mantle, NY	122
N. Siebern, KC	110
H. Killebrew, MIN	106
N. Cash, DET	104

Home Run Percentage

H. Killebrew, MIN	8.7
M. Mantle, NY	8.0
N. Cash, DET	7.7
R. Colavito, DET	6.2

Runs

A. Pearson, LA	115
N. Siebern, KC	114
B. Allison, MIN	102
C. Yastrzemski, BOS	99
B. Richardson, NY	99

Doubles

F. Robinson, CHI	45
C. Yastrzemski, BOS	43
E. Bressoud, BOS	40
B. Richardson, NY	38

Triples

G. Cimoli, KC	15
L. Clinton, BOS	10
F. Robinson, CHI	10
J. Lumpe, KC	10

PITCHING LEADERS

Winning Percentage

R. Herbert, CHI	.690
W. Ford, NY	.680
D. Donovan, CLE	.667
H. Aguirre, DET	.667
R. Terry, NY	.657

Earned Run Average

H. Aguirre, DET	2.21
R. Roberts, BAL	2.78
W. Ford, NY	2.90
D. Chance, LA	2.96
E. Fisher, CHI	3.10

Wins

R. Terry, NY	23
R. Herbert, CHI	20
D. Donovan, CLE	20
C. Pascual, MIN	20
J. Bunning, DET	19

Saves

D. Radatz, BOS	24
M. Bridges, NY	18
T. Fox, DET	16
H. Wilhelm, BAL	15
G. Bell, CLE	12

Strikeouts

C. Pascual, MIN	206
J. Bunning, DET	184
R. Terry, NY	176
J. Pizarro, CHI	173
J. Kaat, MIN	173

Complete Games

C. Pascual, MIN	18
D. Donovan, CLE	16
J. Kaat, MIN	16
R. Terry, NY	14
J. Bunning, DET	12
R. Herbert, CHI	12

Fewest Hits/9 Innings

H. Aguirre, DET	6.75
T. Cheney, WAS	6.96
B. Belinsky, LA	7.16
E. Wilson, BOS	7.67

Shutouts

C. Pascual, MIN	5
D. Donovan, CLE	5
J. Kaat, MIN	5
K. McBride, LA	4
B. Monbouquette, BOS	4

Fewest Walks/9 Innings

D. Donovan, CLE	1.69
R. Terry, NY	1.72
D. Mossi, DET	1.80
R. Roberts, BAL	1.93

Most Strikeouts/9 Inn.

J. Pizarro, CHI	7.66
T. Cheney, WAS	7.63
C. Pascual, MIN	7.20
B. Belinsky, LA	6.97

Innings

R. Terry, NY	299
J. Kaat, MIN	269
C. Pascual, MIN	258
J. Bunning, DET	258
W. Ford, NY	258

Games Pitched

D. Radatz, BOS	62
J. Wyatt, KC	59

	W	L	PCT	GB	R	OR	Batting 2B	3B	HR	BA	SA	SB	Fielding E	DP	FA	Pitching CG	BB	SO	ShO	SV	ERA
New York	96	66	.593		**817**	680	240	29	199	**.267**	**.426**	42	131	151	.979	33	499	838	10	42	3.70
Minnesota	91	71	.562	5	798	713	215	39	185	.260	.412	33	129	**173**	.979	**53**	**493**	**948**	11	27	3.89
Los Angeles	86	76	.531	10	718	706	232	35	137	.250	.380	46	175	153	.972	23	616	858	**15**	**47**	3.70
Detroit	85	76	.528	10.5	758	692	191	36	**209**	.248	.411	69	156	114	.974	46	503	873	8	35	3.81
Chicago	85	77	.525	11	707	**658**	250	56	92	.257	.372	76	**110**	153	**.982**	50	537	821	13	28	3.73
Cleveland	80	82	.494	16	682	745	202	22	180	.245	.388	35	139	168	.977	45	594	780	12	31	4.14
Baltimore	77	85	.475	19	652	680	225	34	156	.248	.387	45	122	152	.980	32	549	898	8	33	**3.69**
Boston	76	84	.475	19	707	756	**257**	53	146	.258	.403	39	131	152	.979	34	632	923	10	40	4.22
Kansas City	72	90	.444	24	745	837	220	**58**	116	.263	.386	76	132	131	.979	32	655	825	4	33	4.79
Washington	60	101	.373	35.5	599	716	206	38	132	.250	.373	**99**	139	160	.978	38	593	771	11	13	4.04
					7183	7183	2238	400	1552	.255	.394	560	1364	1507	.978	386	5671	8535	102	329	3.97

NATIONAL LEAGUE 1963

Los Angeles

W-99 L-63

Walter Alston

POS	Player	AB	BA	HR	RBI	PO	A	E	DP	TC/G	FA	Pitcher	G	IP	W	L	SV	ERA
1B	R. Fairly	490	.271	12	77	884	45	5	74	7.8	**.995**	D. Drysdale	42	315	19	17	0	2.63
2B	J. Gilliam	525	.282	6	49	242	277	8	61	4.4	.985	S. Koufax	40	311	**25**	5	0	**1.88**
SS	M. Wills	527	.302	0	34	171	322	21	47	4.7	.959	J. Podres	37	198	14	12	1	3.54
3B	K. McMullen	233	.236	5	28	47	133	13	8	2.7	.933	B. Miller	42	187	10	8	1	2.89
RF	F. Howard	417	.273	28	64	190	4	8	0	1.8	.960	R. Perranoski	**69**	129	16	3	21	1.67
CF	W. Davis	515	.245	9	60	337	16	8	3	2.4	.978	L. Sherry	36	80	2	6	3	3.73
LF	T. Davis	556	**.326**	16	88	181	7	6	3	1.5	.969							
C	J. Roseboro	470	.236	9	49	908	66	8	6	7.3	.992							
OF	W. Moon	343	.262	8	48	125	2	5	0	1.4	.962							
1B	B. Skowron	237	.203	4	19	518	34	5	44	8.4	.991							
SS	D. Tracewski	217	.226	1	10	92	196	13	32	3.7	.957							
2B	N. Oliver	163	.239	1	9	109	112	9	26	4.0	.961							

St. Louis

W-93 L-69

Johnny Keane

POS	Player	AB	BA	HR	RBI	PO	A	E	DP	TC/G	FA	Pitcher	G	IP	W	L	SV	ERA
1B	B. White	658	.304	27	109	1389	105	13	126	9.3	.991	B. Gibson	36	255	18	9	0	3.39
2B	J. Javier	609	.263	9	46	**377**	415	25	93	5.1	.969	E. Broglio	39	250	18	8	0	2.99
SS	D. Groat	631	.319	6	73	257	448	26	91	4.6	.964	C. Simmons	32	233	15	9	0	2.48
3B	K. Boyer	617	.285	24	111	129	293	**34**	23	2.9	.925	R. Sadecki	36	193	10	10	1	4.10
RF	G. Altman	464	.274	9	47	220	8	5	1	1.9	.979	R. Taylor	54	133	9	7	11	2.84
CF	C. Flood	**662**	.302	5	63	401	12	5	2	2.6	.988	L. Burdette	21	98	3	8	2	3.75
LF	C. James	347	.268	10	45	169	4	1	1	1.7	.994	B. Shantz	55	79	6	4	11	2.61
C	T. McCarver	405	.289	4	51	722	55	5	7	6.2	.994	E. Bauta	38	53	3	4	3	3.93
OF	S. Musial	337	.255	12	58	121	1	4	0	1.3	.968							
P	B. Gibson	87	.207	3	20	27	28	5	0	1.7	.917							

San Francisco

W-88 L-74

Alvin Dark

POS	Player	AB	BA	HR	RBI	PO	A	E	DP	TC/G	FA	Pitcher	G	IP	W	L	SV	ERA
1B	O. Cepeda	579	.316	34	97	1262	83	**21**	91	9.1	.985	J. Marichal	41	**321**	**25**	8	0	2.41
2B	C. Hiller	417	.223	6	33	224	277	19	48	4.8	.963	J. Sanford	42	284	16	13	0	3.51
SS	J. Pagan	483	.234	6	39	262	375	20	69	4.6	.970	B. O'Dell	36	222	14	10	1	3.16
3B	J. Davenport	460	.252	4	36	122	183	12	9	2.5	.962	B. Bolin	47	137	10	6	7	3.28
RF	F. Alou	565	.281	20	82	279	9	4	2	1.9	.986	J. Fisher	36	116	6	10	1	4.58
CF	W. Mays	596	.314	38	103	397	7	8	1	2.6	.981	B. Pierce	38	99	3	11	8	4.27
LF	W. McCovey	564	.280	**44**	102	220	7	14	0	1.8	.942	D. Larsen	46	62	7	7	3	3.05
C	E. Bailey	308	.263	21	68	560	44	8	3	7.0	.987							
03	H. Kuenn	417	.290	6	31	115	60	13	3		.931							
C	T. Haller	298	.255	14	44	499	38	3	7	6.4	.994							

NATIONAL LEAGUE 1963, *cont.*

Team	POS	Player	AB	BA	HR	RBI	PO	A	E	DP	TC/G	FA	Pitcher	G	IP	W	L	SV	ERA
Philadelphia	1B	R. Sievers	450	.240	19	82	981	77	12	93	8.5	.989	C. McLish	32	210	13	11	0	3.26
W-87 L-75	2B	T. Taylor	640	.281	5	49	319	396	10	86	4.9	**.986**	R. Culp	34	203	14	11	0	2.97
Gene Mauch	SS	B. Wine	418	.215	6	44	220	359	17	73	4.5	.971	C. Short	38	198	9	12	0	2.95
	3B	D. Hoak	377	.231	6	24	88	205	13	13	2.9	.958	A. Mahaffey	26	149	7	10	0	3.99
	RF	J. Callison	626	.284	26	78	298	26	2	4	2.1	.994	D. Green	40	120	7	5	2	3.23
	CF	T. Gonzalez	555	.306	4	66	263	11	4	2	1.8	.986	D. Bennett	23	119	9	5	1	2.64
	LF	W. Covington	353	.303	17	64	114	4	8	0	1.2	.937	J. Baldschun	65	114	11	7	16	2.30
	C	C. Dalrymple	452	.252	10	40	881	**90**	19	**16**	7.0	.981	J. Klippstein	49	112	5	6	8	1.93
	UT	D. Demeter	515	.258	22	83	375	86	14	15		.971	R. Duren	33	87	6	2	2	3.30
	S3	R. Amaro	217	.217	2	19	105	169	13	28		.955							
Cincinnati	1B	G. Coleman	365	.247	14	59	752	65	11	66	7.7	.987	J. Maloney	33	250	23	7	0	2.77
W-86 L-76	2B	P. Rose	623	.273	6	41	360	366	22	78	4.8	.971	J. O'Toole	33	234	17	14	0	2.88
Fred Hutchinson	SS	L. Cardenas	565	.235	7	48	270	420	20	84	4.5	**.972**	J. Nuxhall	35	217	15	8	2	2.61
	3B	G. Freese	217	.244	6	26	44	103	11	8	2.5	.930	J. Tsitouris	30	191	12	8	0	3.16
	RF	T. Harper	408	.260	10	37	224	7	4	1	2.0	.983	J. Jay	30	170	7	18	1	4.29
	CF	V. Pinson	652	.313	22	106	357	9	8	0	2.3	.979	B. Purkey	21	137	6	10	0	3.55
	LF	F. Robinson	482	.259	21	91	237	13	4	1	1.8	.984	A. Worthington	50	81	4	4	10	2.99
	C	J. Edwards	495	.259	11	67	**1008**	87	6	**16**	**7.4**	**.995**	B. Henry	47	52	1	3	14	4.15
	3B	E. Kasko	199	.241	3	10	41	75	5	5	2.5	.959							
	OF	B. Skinner	194	.253	3	17	74	3	0	1	1.5	1.000							
	1B	D. Pavletich	183	.208	5	18	317	16	3	20	5.9	.991							
	10	M. Keough	172	.227	6	21	250	24	2	25		.993							
	3B	D. Spencer	155	.239	1	23	45	92	3	9	2.9	.979							
Milwaukee	1B	G. Oliver	296	.250	11	47	440	19	7	39	8.5	.985	W. Spahn	33	260	23	7	0	2.60
W-84 L-78	2B	F. Bolling	542	.244	5	43	326	379	14	107	5.1	.981	D. Lemaster	46	237	11	14	1	3.04
Bobby Bragan	SS	R. McMillan	320	.250	4	29	143	283	9	60	4.6	.979	B. Hendley	41	169	9	9	3	3.93
	3B	E. Mathews	547	.263	23	84	113	276	13	23	**3.3**	**.968**	B. Shaw	48	159	7	11	13	2.66
	RF	H. Aaron	631	.319	**44**	**130**	267	10	6	1	1.8	.979	T. Cloninger	41	145	9	11	1	3.78
	CF	M. Jones	228	.219	3	22	135	1	3	0	1.7	.978	B. Sadowski	19	117	5	7	0	2.62
	LF	L. Maye	442	.271	11	34	231	4	4	1	2.2	.983	L. Burdette	15	84	6	5	0	3.63
	C	J. Torre	501	.293	14	71	584	46	4	9	6.0	.994	C. Raymond	45	53	4	6	5	5.40
	UT	D. Menke	518	.234	11	50	234	398	24	67		.963							
	C	D. Crandall	259	.201	3	28	413	38	4	2	6.1	.991							
	OF	T. Cline	174	.236	0	10	116	5	1	3	2.0	.992							
Chicago	1B	E. Banks	432	.227	18	64	1178	78	9	97	10.1	.993	D. Ellsworth	37	291	22	10	0	2.11
W-82 L-80	2B	K. Hubbs	566	.235	8	47	338	493	22	96	5.6	.974	L. Jackson	37	275	14	18	0	2.55
Bob Kennedy	SS	A. Rodgers	516	.229	5	33	**271**	**454**	**35**	**100**	5.1	.954	B. Buhl	37	226	11	14	0	3.38
	3B	R. Santo	630	.297	25	99	**136**	**374**	26	25	3.3	.951	G. Hobbie	36	165	7	10	0	3.92
	RF	L. Brock	547	.258	9	37	269	17	8	7	2.1	.973	P. Toth	27	131	5	9	0	3.10
	CF	E. Burton	322	.230	12	41	151	6	4	1	1.8	.975	L. McDaniel	57	88	13	7	**22**	2.86
	LF	B. Williams	612	.286	25	95	298	13	4	2	2.0	.987							
	C	D. Bertell	322	.233	2	14	549	84	8	15	6.5	.988							
	OF	D. Landrum	227	.242	1	10	100	3	3	0	1.9	.972							
Pittsburgh	1B	D. Clendenon	563	.275	15	57	**1450**	**118**	15	**154**	**10.5**	.991	B. Friend	39	269	17	16	0	2.34
W-74 L-88	2B	B. Mazeroski	534	.245	8	52	340	**506**	14	**131**	**6.2**	.984	D. Cardwell	33	214	13	15	0	3.07
Danny Murtaugh	SS	D. Schofield	541	.246	3	32	232	366	21	95	**5.3**	.966	D. Schwall	33	168	6	12	0	3.33
	3B	B. Bailey	570	.228	12	45	113	332	32	**38**	3.1	.933	J. Gibbon	37	147	5	12	1	3.30
	RF	R. Clemente	600	.320	17	76	239	11	11	2	1.7	.958	A. McBean	55	122	13	3	11	2.57
	CF	B. Virdon	554	.269	8	53	323	6	4	2	2.3	.988	T. Sisk	57	108	1	3	1	2.92
	LF	W. Stargell	304	.243	11	47	78	3	4	0	1.3	.953	E. Francis	33	97	4	6	0	4.53
	C	J. Pagliaroni	252	.230	11	26	435	56	6	4	5.8	.988	B. Veale	34	78	5	2	3	1.04
	C	S. Burgess	264	.280	6	37	364	40	4	4	5.7	.990	R. Face	56	70	3	9	16	3.23
	OF	J. Lynch	237	.266	10	36	70	2	3	0	1.2	.960							
	SS	J. Logan	181	.232	0	9	74	122	17	28	4.8	.920							
Houston	1B	R. Staub	513	.224	6	45	881	58	10	52	8.7	.989	K. Johnson	37	224	11	17	1	2.65
W-66 L-96	2B	E. Fazio	228	.184	2	5	132	145	8	18	3.4	.972	D. Farrell	34	202	14	13	1	3.02
Harry Craft	SS	B. Lillis	469	.198	1	19	223	336	25	52	4.7	.957	D. Nottebart	31	193	11	8	0	3.17
	3B	B. Aspromonte	468	.214	8	49	134	213	23	4	2.8	.938	B. Bruce	30	170	5	9	0	3.59
	RF	C. Warwick	528	.254	7	47	240	7	3	2	1.8	.988	H. Brown	26	141	5	11	0	3.31
	CF	H. Goss	411	.209	9	44	276	7	2	2	2.3	.993	H. Woodeshick	55	114	11	9	10	1.97
	LF	A. Spangler	430	.281	4	27	215	5	3	1	2.0	.987	D. Drott	27	98	2	12	0	4.98
	C	J. Bateman	404	.210	10	59	690	81	**23**	7	6.9	.971	D. McMahon	49	80	1	5	5	4.05
	12	P. Runnels	388	.253	2	23	590	104	6	49		.991							
	23	J. Temple	322	.264	1	17	146	188	16	19		.954							
	OS	J. Wynn	250	.244	4	27	121	33	8	3		.951							
New York	1B	T. Harkness	375	.211	10	41	898	112	14	73	9.7	.986	R. Craig	46	236	5	**22**	2	3.78
W-51 L-111	2B	R. Hunt	533	.272	10	42	350	416	**26**	85	5.6	.967	A. Jackson	37	227	13	17	1	3.96
Casey Stengel	SS	A. Moran	331	.193	1	23	189	332	27	57	4.7	.951	C. Willey	30	183	9	14	0	3.10
	3B	C. Neal	253	.225	3	18	61	135	8	10	3.1	.961	G. Cisco	51	156	7	15	0	4.34
	RF	D. Snider	354	.243	14	45	139	5	2	0	1.4	.986	T. Stallard	39	155	6	17	1	4.71
	CF	J. Hickman	494	.229	17	51	149	6	6	2	2.0	.963	J. Hook	41	153	4	14	1	5.48
	LF	F. Thomas	420	.260	15	60	158	8	2	1	1.8	.988	L. Bearnarth	58	126	3	8	4	3.42
	C	C. Coleman	247	.178	3	9	418	54	15	9	5.4	.969							
	OF	E. Kranepool	273	.209	2	14	78	5	4	1	1.6	.954							
	UT	R. Kanehl	191	.241	1	9	128	35	12	7		.931							
	OF	J. Hicks	159	.226	5	22	83	1	3	0	2.1	.966							

NATIONAL LEAGUE 1963, *cont.*

BATTING AND BASE RUNNING LEADERS

Batting Average

T. Davis, LA	.326
R. Clemente, PIT	.320
H. Aaron, MIL	.319
D. Groat, STL	.319
O. Cepeda, SF	.316

Slugging Average

H. Aaron, MIL	.586
W. Mays, SF	.582
W. McCovey, SF	.566
O. Cepeda, SF	.563
V. Pinson, CIN	.514

Home Runs

W. McCovey, SF	44
H. Aaron, MIL	44
W. Mays, SF	38
O. Cepeda, SF	34
F. Howard, LA	28

Total Bases

H. Aaron, MIL	370
W. Mays, SF	347
V. Pinson, CIN	335
O. Cepeda, SF	326
B. White, STL	323

Runs Batted In

H. Aaron, MIL	130
K. Boyer, STL	111
B. White, STL	109
V. Pinson, CIN	106
W. Mays, SF	103

Stolen Bases

M. Wills, LA	40
H. Aaron, MIL	31
V. Pinson, CIN	27
F. Robinson, CIN	26
W. Davis, LA	25

Hits

V. Pinson, CIN	204
H. Aaron, MIL	201
D. Groat, STL	201
B. White, STL	200
C. Flood, STL	200

Base on Balls

E. Mathews, MIL	124
F. Robinson, CIN	81
H. Aaron, MIL	78
K. Boyer, STL	70

Home Run Percentage

W. McCovey, SF	7.8
H. Aaron, MIL	7.0
W. Mays, SF	6.4
O. Cepeda, SF	5.9

Runs

H. Aaron, MIL	121
W. Mays, SF	115
C. Flood, STL	112
B. White, STL	106

Doubles

D. Groat, STL	43
V. Pinson, CIN	37
T. Gonzalez, PHI	36
B. Williams, CHI	36
J. Callison, PHI	36

Triples

V. Pinson, CIN	14
T. Gonzalez, PHI	12
L. Brock, CHI	11
J. Callison, PHI	11
D. Groat, STL	11

PITCHING LEADERS

Winning Percentage

R. Perranoski, LA	.842
S. Koufax, LA	.833
W. Spahn, MIL	.767
J. Maloney, CIN	.767
J. Marichal, SF	.758

Earned Run Average

S. Koufax, LA	1.88
D. Ellsworth, CHI	2.11
B. Friend, PIT	2.34
J. Marichal, SF	2.41
C. Simmons, STL	2.48

Wins

S. Koufax, LA	25
J. Marichal, SF	25
J. Maloney, CIN	23
W. Spahn, MIL	23
D. Ellsworth, CHI	22

Saves

L. McDaniel, CHI	22
R. Perranoski, LA	21
R. Face, PIT	16
J. Baldschun, PHI	16
B. Henry, CIN	14

Strikeouts

S. Koufax, LA	306
J. Maloney, CIN	265
D. Drysdale, LA	251
J. Marichal, SF	248
B. Gibson, STL	204

Complete Games

W. Spahn, MIL	22
S. Koufax, LA	20
D. Ellsworth, CHI	19
J. Marichal, SF	18
D. Drysdale, LA	17

Fewest Hits/9 Innings

S. Koufax, LA	6.19
R. Culp, PHI	6.55
J. Maloney, CIN	6.58
D. Ellsworth, CHI	6.90

Shutouts

S. Koufax, LA	11
W. Spahn, MIL	7
C. Simmons, STL	6
J. Maloney, CIN	6

Fewest Walks/9 Innings

B. Friend, PIT	1.47
D. Farrell, HOU	1.56
J. Nuxhall, CIN	1.62
D. Drysdale, LA	1.63

Most Strikeouts/9 Inn.

J. Maloney, CIN	9.53
S. Koufax, LA	8.86
R. Culp, PHI	7.79
C. Short, PHI	7.27

Innings

J. Marichal, SF	321
D. Drysdale, LA	315
S. Koufax, LA	311
D. Ellsworth, CHI	291

Games Pitched

R. Perranoski, LA	69
J. Baldschun, PHI	65
L. Bearnarth, NY	58
L. McDaniel, CHI	57
T. Sisk, PIT	57

							Batting						Fielding			Pitching					
	W	L	PCT	GB	R	OR	2B	3B	HR	BA	SA	SB	E	DP	FA	CG	BB	SO	ShO	SV	ERA
Los Angeles	99	63	.611		640	**550**	178	34	110	.251	.357	**124**	159	129	.975	51	402	**1095**	**24**	29	**2.85**
St. Louis	93	69	.574	6	**747**	628	**231**	**66**	128	**.271**	.403	77	147	136	.976	49	463	978	17	32	3.32
San Francisco	88	74	.543	11	725	641	206	35	**197**	.258	**.414**	55	156	113	.975	46	464	954	9	30	3.35
Philadelphia	87	75	.537	12	642	578	228	54	126	.252	.381	56	142	147	.978	45	553	1052	12	31	3.09
Cincinnati	86	76	.531	13	648	594	225	44	122	.246	.371	92	135	127	.978	55	425	1048	22	**36**	3.29
Milwaukee	84	78	.519	15	677	603	204	39	139	.244	.370	75	**129**	161	**.980**	**56**	489	924	18	25	3.26
Chicago	82	80	.506	17	570	578	205	44	127	.238	.363	68	155	172	.976	45	400	851	15	28	3.08
Pittsburgh	74	88	.457	25	567	595	181	49	108	.250	.359	57	182	**195**	.972	34	457	900	16	33	3.10
Houston	66	96	.407	33	464	640	170	39	62	.220	.301	39	162	100	.974	36	**378**	937	16	20	3.44
New York	51	111	.315	48	501	774	156	35	96	.219	.315	41	210	151	.967	42	529	806	5	12	4.12
					6181	6181	1984	439	1215	.245	.363	684	1577	1431	.975	459	4560	9545	154	276	3.29

AMERICAN LEAGUE 1963

New York

W-104 L-57

Ralph Houk

POS	Player	AB	BA	HR	RBI	PO	A	E	DP	TC/G	FA
1B	J. Pepitone	580	.271	27	89	1140	103	6	111	8.7	.995
2B	B. Richardson	**630**	.265	3	48	335	424	12	**105**	5.1	.984
SS	T. Kubek	557	.257	7	44	227	403	13	80	4.9	.980
3B	C. Boyer	557	.251	12	54	165	309	23	32	**3.5**	.954
RF	R. Maris	312	.269	23	53	162	6	2	1	2.0	.988
CF	T. Tresh	520	.269	25	71	305	6	6	1	2.2	.981
LF	H. Lopez	433	.249	14	52	187	11	9	2	1.7	.957
C	E. Howard	487	.287	28	85	786	51	5	8	6.4	.994
OF	J. Blanchard	218	.225	16	45	76	2	1	0	1.2	.987
UT	P. Linz	186	.269	2	12	69	103	4	17		.977
OF	M. Mantle	172	.314	15	35	99	2	1	0	2.0	.990
1B	H. Bright	157	.236	7	23	263	8	4	32	•7.9	.985
C	Y. Berra	147	.293	8	28	244	13	3	5	7.4	.988

Pitcher	G	IP	W	L	SV	ERA
W. Ford	38	**269**	**24**	7	1	2.74
R. Terry	40	268	17	15	1	3.22
J. Bouton	40	249	21	7	1	2.53
A. Downing	24	176	13	5	0	2.56
S. Williams	29	146	9	8	0	3.20
B. Stafford	28	90	4	8	3	6.02
H. Reniff	48	89	4	3	18	2.62
S. Hamilton	34	62	5	1	5	2.60

Chicago

W-94 L-68

Al Lopez

POS	Player	AB	BA	HR	RBI	PO	A	E	DP	TC/G	FA
1B	T. McCraw	280	.254	6	33	673	47	5	65	7.5	.993
2B	N. Fox	539	.260	2	42	305	342	8	71	4.9	**.988**
SS	R. Hansen	482	.226	13	67	247	**483**	13	95	5.2	.983
3B	P. Ward	600	.295	22	84	156	302	**38**	27	3.2	.923
RF	F. Robinson	527	.283	13	71	245	8	4	4	1.9	.984
CF	J. Landis	396	.225	13	45	264	6	2	0	2.2	.993
LF	D. Nicholson	449	.229	22	70	213	10	7	1	1.9	.970
C	J. Martin	259	.205	5	28	468	48	9	9	5.4	.983
OF	M. Hershberger	476	.279	3	45	230	13	6	3	2.1	.976
C	C. Carreon	270	.274	2	35	429	36	6	7	5.1	.987
2S	A. Weis	210	.271	0	18	123	168	10	41		.967
1B	J. Cunningham	210	.286	1	31	535	24	6	39	9.7	.989

Pitcher	G	IP	W	L	SV	ERA
G. Peters	41	243	19	8	1	**2.33**
R. Herbert	33	225	13	10	0	3.24
J. Pizarro	32	215	16	8	1	2.39
H. Wilhelm	55	136	5	8	21	2.64
J. Buzhardt	19	126	9	4	0	2.42
J. Horlen	33	124	11	7	0	3.27
E. Fisher	33	121	9	8	0	3.95
J. Brosnan	45	73	3	8	14	2.84

AMERICAN LEAGUE 1963, *cont.*

Team	POS	Player	AB	BA	HR	RBI	PO	A	E	DP	TC/G	FA	Pitcher	G	IP	W	L	SV	ERA
Minnesota	1B	V. Power	541	.270	10	52	896	76	8	86	7.9	.992	C. Pascual	31	248	21	9	0	2.46
W-91 L-70	2B	B. Allen	421	.240	9	43	236	256	12	65	3.9	.976	D. Stigman	33	241	15	15	0	3.25
Sam Mele	SS	Z. Versalles	621	.261	10	54	**301**	448	30	87	4.9	.961	J. Kaat	31	178	10	10	1	4.19
	3B	R. Rollins	531	.307	16	61	121	225	26	22	2.8	.930	J. Perry	35	168	9	9	1	3.74
	RF	B. Allison	527	.271	35	91	326	11	10	4	2.4	.971	L. Stange	32	165	12	5	0	2.62
	CF	J. Hall	497	.260	33	80	306	13	6	5	2.3	.982	B. Dailey	66	109	6	3	21	1.99
	LF	H. Killebrew	515	.258	**45**	96	219	7	3	0	1.7	.987	G. Roggenburk	36	50	2	4	4	2.16
	C	E. Battey	508	.285	26	84	**861**	**66**	6	11	6.4	.994							
	OF	L. Green	280	.239	4	27	165	1	2	0	1.4	.988							
	1B	D. Mincher	225	.258	17	42	446	27	8	34	8.0	.983							
	UT	J. Goryl	150	.287	9	24	75	92	7	18		.960							
Baltimore	1B	J. Gentile	496	.248	24	72	1185	110	6	**122**	9.1	**.995**	S. Barber	39	259	20	13	0	2.75
W-86 L-76	2B	J. Adair	382	.228	6	30	242	268	8	67	5.0	.985	R. Roberts	35	251	14	13	0	3.33
Billy Hitchcock	SS	L. Aparicio	601	.250	5	45	275	403	12	76	4.8	**.983**	M. Pappas	34	217	16	9	0	3.03
	3B	B. Robinson	589	.251	11	67	153	**330**	12	**43**	3.1	**.976**	M. McCormick	25	136	6	8	0	4.30
	RF	R. Snyder	429	.256	7	36	238	5	3	1	1.9	.988	D. McNally	29	126	7	8	1	4.58
	CF	J. Brandt	451	.248	15	61	272	9	4	1	2.1	.986	S. Miller	**71**	112	5	8	**27**	2.24
	LF	B. Powell	491	.265	25	82	181	6	6	1	1.6	.969	D. Hall	47	112	5	5	12	2.98
	C	J. Orsino	379	.272	19	56	636	37	7	8	6.2	.990							
	OF	A. Smith	368	.272	10	39	160	6	5	0	1.8	.971							
	2B	B. Johnson	254	.295	8	32	97	131	3	34	4.6	.987							
	C	D. Brown	171	.246	2	13	317	23	5	7	5.9	.986							
	UT	B. Saverine	167	.234	1	12	99	89	2	19		.989							
	OF	J. Gaines	126	.286	6	20	52	0	3	0	1.4	.945							
Cleveland	1B	F. Whitfield	346	.251	21	54	690	51	10	64	8.2	.987	M. Grant	38	229	13	14	1	3.69
W-79 L-83	2B	W. Held	416	.248	17	61	188	251	8	50	4.7	.982	D. Donovan	30	206	11	13	0	4.24
Birdie Tebbetts	SS	L. Brown	247	.255	5	18	71	126	13	17	4.6	.938	J. Kralick	28	197	13	9	0	2.92
	3B	M. Alvis	602	.274	22	67	**170**	285	28	32	3.1	.942	P. Ramos	36	185	9	8	0	3.12
	RF	W. Kirkland	427	.230	15	47	234	11	4	2	2.2	.984	B. Latman	38	149	7	12	2	4.94
	CF	V. Davalillo	370	.292	7	36	247	10	3	0	2.9	.988	G. Bell	58	119	8	5	5	2.95
	LF	T. Francona	500	.228	10	41	215	2	3	0	1.8	.986	J. Walker	39	88	6	6	1	4.91
	C	J. Azcue	320	.284	14	46	564	42	5	13*	6.7	.992	T. Abernathy	43	59	7	2	12	2.88
	OF	A. Luplow	295	.234	7	27	157	7	1	1	1.9	.994							
	1B	J. Adcock	283	.251	13	49	608	36	3	46	8.3	.995							
	C	J. Romano	255	.216	10	34	408	28	3	5	6.2	.993							
	S2	J. Kindall	234	.205	5	20	131	183	9	31		.972							
	SS	D. Howser	162	.247	1	10	80	90	9	15	4.1	.950							
	2B	M. de la Hoz	150	.267	5	25	63	89	6	20	4.6	.962							
Detroit	1B	N. Cash	493	.270	26	79	1161	99	7	93	8.9	.994	J. Bunning	39	248	12	13	1	3.88
W-79 L-83	2B	J. Wood	351	.271	11	27	188	202	17	47	5.0	.958	H. Aguirre	38	226	14	15	0	3.67
Bob Scheffing	SS	D. McAuliffe	568	.262	13	61	220	356	22	68	4.5	.963	P. Regan	38	189	15	9	1	3.86
W-24 L-36	3B	B. Phillips	464	.246	5	45	116	226	14	26	3.0	.961	M. Lolich	33	144	5	9	0	3.55
Chuck Dressen	RF	A. Kaline	551	.312	27	101	257	5	2	0	1.9	.992	D. Mossi	24	123	7	7	2	3.74
W-55 L-47	CF	B. Bruton	524	.256	8	48	339	6	3	3	2.5	.991	F. Lary	16	107	4	9	0	3.27
	LF	R. Colavito	597	.271	22	91	319	10	4	0	2.1	.988	B. Faul	28	97	5	6	1	4.64
	C	G. Triandos	327	.239	14	41	535	29	1	4	6.3	**.998**	T. Fox	46	80	8	6	11	3.59
	C	B. Freehan	300	.243	9	36	407	22	2	5	5.9	.995							
	UT	D. Wert	251	.259	7	25	85	173	10	20		.963							
	2B	G. Smith	171	.216	0	17	120	157	5	28	5.4	.982							
Boston	1B	D. Stuart	612	.261	42	**118**	**1207**	**134**	**29**	100	8.8	.979	B. Monbouquette	37	267	20	10	0	3.81
W-76 L-85	2B	C. Schilling	576	.234	8	33	276	369	10	74	4.6	.985	E. Wilson	37	211	11	16	0	3.76
Johnny Pesky	SS	E. Bressoud	497	.260	20	60	260	351	24	76	4.6	.962	D. Morehead	29	175	10	13	0	3.81
	3B	F. Malzone	580	.291	15	71	151	283	16	18	3.0	.964	J. Lamabe	65	151	7	4	6	3.15
	RF	L. Clinton	560	.232	22	77	319	7	6	0	2.3	.982	D. Radatz	66	132	15	6	25	1.97
	CF	G. Geiger	399	.263	16	44	234	11	4	1	2.6	.984	B. Heffner	20	125	4	9	0	4.26
	LF	C. Yastrzemski	570	**.321**	14	68	283	18	6	3	2.0	.980	A. Earley	53	116	3	7	1	4.75
	C	B. Tillman	307	.225	8	32	621	26	5	5	**6.9**	.992							
	OF	R. Mejias	357	.227	11	39	177	6	5	1	2.2	.973							
	C	R. Nixon	287	.268	5	30	483	22	4	1	6.7	.992							
	UT	F. Mantilla	178	.315	6	15	83	74	4	19		.975							
Kansas City	1B	N. Siebern	556	.272	16	83	1193	102	12	95	**10.0**	.991	D. Wickersham	38	238	12	15	1	4.09
W-73 L-89	2B	J. Lumpe	595	.271	5	59	341	452	10	92	5.2	.988	O. Pena	35	217	12	**20**	0	3.69
Ed Lopat	SS	W. Causey	554	.280	8	44	266	402	15	81	5.1	.978	E. Rakow	34	174	9	10	0	3.92
	3B	E. Charles	603	.267	15	79	153	310	25	19	3.1	.949	M. Drabowsky	26	174	7	13	0	3.05
	RF	G. Cimoli	529	.263	4	48	256	14	4	3	2.0	.985	D. Segui	38	167	9	6	0	3.77
	CF	B. Del Greco	306	.212	8	29	207	5	4	0	2.0	.981	T. Bowsfield	41	111	5	7	3	4.45
	LF	J. Tartabull	242	.240	1	19	135	3	2	1	2.0	.986	B. Fischer	45	96	9	6	3	3.57
	C	D. Edwards	240	.250	6	35	341	30	5	4	6.0	.987	J. Wyatt	63	92	6	4	21	3.13
	OF	C. Essegian	231	.225	5	27	95	2	1	0	1.8	.990							
	10	K. Harrelson	226	.230	6	23	326	17	7	24		.980							
	OF	G. Alusik	221	.267	9	37	98	5	0	1	1.6	1.000							
	C	C. Lau	187	.294	3	26	258	15	5	2	5.6	.982							

AMERICAN LEAGUE 1963, *cont.*

Los Angeles

W-70 L-91

Bill Rigney

POS	Player	AB	BA	HR	RBI	PO	A	E	DP	TC/G	FA	Pitcher	G	IP	W	L	SV	ERA
1B	L. Thomas	528	.220	9	55	961	84	4	88	10.1	.996	K. McBride	36	251	13	12	0	3.26
2B	B. Moran	597	.275	7	65	**352**	**455**	**22**	98	**5.5**	.973	D. Chance	45	248	13	18	3	3.19
SS	J. Fregosi	592	.287	9	50	271	446	27	90	4.9	.964	D. Osinski	47	159	8	8	0	3.28
3B	F. Torres	463	.261	4	51	101	237	22	29	3.0	.939	D. Lee	40	154	8	11	1	3.68
RF	B. Perry	166	.253	3	14	86	1	5	0	1.7	.946	J. Navarro	57	90	4	5	12	2.89
CF	A. Pearson	578	.304	6	47	340	10	6	5	2.4	.983	A. Fowler	57	89	5	3	10	2.42
LF	L. Wagner	550	.291	26	90	254	7	11	1	1.9	.960	B. Belinsky	13	77	2	9	0	5.75
C	B. Rodgers	300	.233	4	23	416	48	**10**	5	5.6	.979	P. Foytack	25	70	5	5	0	3.71
1B	C. Dees	202	.307	3	27	474	32	7	41	9.2	.986							
C	E. Sadowski	174	.172	4	15	340	38	1	7	5.6	.997							
OF	G. Thomas	167	.210	4	15	63	1	4	0	1.7	.941							
OF	B. Sadowski	144	.250	1	22	41	0	0	0	1.6	1.000							

Washington

W-56 L-106

Mickey Vernon
W-14 L-26

Eddie Yost
W-0 L-1

Gil Hodges
W-42 L-79

POS	Player	AB	BA	HR	RBI	PO	A	E	DP	TC/G	FA	Pitcher	G	IP	W	L	SV	ERA
1B	B. Osborne	358	.212	12	44	713	55	9	68	9.6	.988	C. Osteen	40	212	9	14	0	3.35
2B	C. Cottier	337	.205	5	21	200	221	16	49	5.1	.963	D. Rudolph	37	174	7	19	1	4.55
SS	E. Brinkman	514	.228	7	45	241	462	**37**	**97**	**5.2**	.950	B. Daniels	35	169	5	10	1	4.38
3B	D. Zimmer	298	.248	13	44	88	173	18	17	3.6	.935	T. Cheney	23	136	8	9	0	2.71
RF	J. King	459	.231	24	62	213	13	3	2	1.9	.987	J. Duckworth	37	121	4	12	0	6.04
CF	D. Lock	531	.252	27	82	377	14	8	6	2.7	.980	R. Kline	62	94	3	8	17	2.79
LF	C. Hinton	566	.269	15	55	274	8	3	1	2.3	.989	S. Ridzik	20	90	5	6	1	4.82
C	K. Retzer	265	.242	5	31	320	35	7	5	4.5	.981	D. Stenhouse	16	87	3	9	0	4.55
1B	D. Phillips	321	.237	10	32	655	59	4	73	10.6	.994							
OF	M. Minoso	315	.229	4	30	103	4	5	0	1.5	.955							
2B	D. Blasingame	254	.256	2	12	162	177	3	52	5.3	.991							
C	D. Leppert	211	.237	6	24	281	20	5	4	5.1	.984							
32	M. Breeding	197	.274	1	14	76	110	11	15		.944							

BATTING AND BASE RUNNING LEADERS

Batting Average

C. Yastrzemski, BOS	.321
A. Kaline, DET	.312
R. Rollins, MIN	.307
A. Pearson, LA	.304
P. Ward, CHI	.295

Slugging Average

H. Killebrew, MIN	.555
B. Allison, MIN	.533
E. Howard, NY	.528
D. Stuart, BOS	.521
J. Hall, MIN	.521

Home Runs

H. Killebrew, MIN	45
D. Stuart, BOS	42
B. Allison, MIN	35
J. Hall, MIN	33
E. Howard, NY	28

Total Bases

D. Stuart, BOS	319
P. Ward, CHI	289
H. Killebrew, MIN	286
A. Kaline, DET	283
B. Allison, MIN	281

Runs Batted In

D. Stuart, BOS	118
A. Kaline, DET	101
H. Killebrew, MIN	96
B. Allison, MIN	91
R. Colavito, DET	91

Stolen Bases

L. Aparicio, BAL	40
C. Hinton, WAS	25
J. Wood, DET	18
R. Snyder, BAL	18
A. Pearson, LA	17

Hits

C. Yastrzemski, BOS	183
P. Ward, CHI	177
A. Pearson, LA	176
A. Kaline, DET	172

Base on Balls

C. Yastrzemski, BOS	95
A. Pearson, LA	92
B. Allison, MIN	90
N. Cash, DET	89

Home Run Percentage

H. Killebrew, MIN	8.7
D. Stuart, BOS	6.9
B. Allison, MIN	6.6
J. Hall, MIN	6.6

Runs

B. Allison, MIN	99
A. Pearson, LA	92
T. Tresh, NY	91
C. Yastrzemski, BOS	91
R. Colavito, DET	91

Doubles

C. Yastrzemski, BOS	40
P. Ward, CHI	34
F. Torres, LA	32
W. Causey, KC	32
M. Alvis, CLE	32

Triples

Z. Versalles, MIN	13
C. Hinton, WAS	12
J. Fregosi, LA	12
G. Cimoli, KC	11

PITCHING LEADERS

Winning Percentage

W. Ford, NY	.774
J. Bouton, NY	.750
D. Radatz, BOS	.714
G. Peters, CHI	.704
C. Pascual, MIN	.700

Earned Run Average

G. Peters, CHI	2.33
J. Pizarro, CHI	2.39
C. Pascual, MIN	2.46
J. Bouton, NY	2.53
A. Downing, NY	2.56

Wins

W. Ford, NY	24
C. Pascual, MIN	21
J. Bouton, NY	21
S. Barber, BAL	20
B. Monbouquette, BOS	20

Saves

S. Miller, BAL	27
D. Radatz, BOS	25
B. Dailey, MIN	21
J. Wyatt, KC	21
H. Wilhelm, CHI	21

Strikeouts

C. Pascual, MIN	202
J. Bunning, DET	196
D. Stigman, MIN	193
G. Peters, CHI	189
W. Ford, NY	189

Complete Games

C. Pascual, MIN	18
R. Terry, NY	18
D. Stigman, MIN	15
H. Aguirre, DET	14
R. Herbert, CHI	14

Fewest Hits/9 Innings

A. Downing, NY	5.84
J. Bouton, NY	6.89
M. Drabowsky, KC	6.97
D. Morehead, BOS	7.06

Shutouts

R. Herbert, CHI	7
J. Bouton, NY	6

Fewest Walks/9 Innings

D. Donovan, CLE	1.22
R. Terry, NY	1.31
R. Herbert, CHI	1.40
B. Monbouquette, BOS	1.42

Most Strikeouts/9 Inn.

A. Downing, NY	8.76
P. Ramos, CLE	8.24
C. Pascual, MIN	7.32
D. Stigman, MIN	7.21

Innings

W. Ford, NY	269
R. Terry, NY	268
B. Monbouquette, BOS	267
S. Barber, BAL	259

Games Pitched

S. Miller, BAL	71
B. Dailey, MIN	66
D. Radatz, BOS	66
J. Lamabe, BOS	65

							Batting						Fielding			Pitching					
	W	L	PCT	GB	R	OR	2B	3B	HR	BA	SA	SB	E	DP	FA	CG	BB	SO	ShO	SV	ERA
New York	104	57	.646		714	547	197	35	188	.252	.403	42	110	162	.982	**59**	476	965	17	31	3.07
Chicago	94	68	.580	10.5	683	**544**	208	**40**	114	.250	.365	64	131	163	.979	49	**440**	932	**19**	39	**2.97**
Minnesota	91	70	.565	13	**767**	602	223	35	**225**	**.255**	**.430**	32	144	140	.976	58	459	941	12	30	3.28
Baltimore	86	76	.531	18.5	644	621	207	32	146	.249	.380	**97**	**99**	157	**.984**	35	507	913	8	**43**	3.45
Cleveland	79	83	.488	25.5	635	702	214	29	169	.239	.381	59	143	129	.977	40	478	**1018**	11	25	3.79
Detroit	79	83	.488	25.5	700	703	195	36	148	.252	.382	73	113	124	.981	42	477	930	6	28	3.90
Boston	76	85	.472	28	666	704	**247**	34	171	.252	.400	27	135	119	.978	29	539	1009	6	32	3.97
Kansas City	73	89	.451	31.5	615	704	225	38	95	.247	.353	47	127	131	.980	35	540	887	9	29	3.92
Los Angeles	70	91	.435	34	597	660	208	38	95	.250	.354	43	163	155	.974	30	578	889	9	31	3.52
Washington	56	106	.346	48.5	578	812	190	35	138	.227	.351	68	182	**165**	.971	29	537	744	8	25	4.42
					6599	6599	2114	352	1489	.247	.380	552	1347	1445	.978	406	5031	9228	105	313	3.63

NATIONAL LEAGUE 1964

Team	POS	Player	AB	BA	HR	RBI	PO	A	E	DP	TC/G	FA	Pitcher	G	IP	W	L	SV	ERA
St. Louis	1B	B. White	631	.303	21	102	1513	101	6	**125**	10.1	**.996**	B. Gibson	40	287	19	12	1	3.01
	2B	J. Javier	535	.241	12	65	**360**	401	**27**	97	5.1	.966	C. Simmons	34	244	18	9	0	3.43
W-93 L-69	SS	D. Groat	636	.292	1	70	249	**499**	**40**	**91**	4.9	.949	R. Sadecki	37	220	20	11	1	3.68
	3B	K. Boyer	628	.295	24	**119**	131	337	24	30	3.0	.951	R. Craig	39	166	7	9	5	3.25
Johnny Keane	RF	M. Shannon	253	.261	9	43	110	7	2	2	1.4	.983	R. Taylor	63	101	8	4	7	4.62
	CF	C. Flood	**679**	.311	5	46	391	10	5	2	2.5	.988	M. Cuellar	32	72	5	5	4	4.50
	LF	L. Brock	419	.348	12	44	180	7	10	0	1.9	.949	B. Schultz	30	49	1	3	14	1.64
	C	T. McCarver	465	.288	9	52	762	43	**11**	9	6.0	.987							
	OF	C. James	233	.223	5	17	76	3	3	0	1.4	.963							
Cincinnati	1B	D. Johnson	477	.273	21	79	940	81	10	82	7.9	.990	J. O'Toole	30	220	17	7	0	2.66
	2B	P. Rose	516	.269	4	34	263	301	12	63	4.5	.979	J. Maloney	31	216	15	10	0	2.71
	SS	L. Cardenas	597	.251	9	69	**336**	436	32	87	4.9	.960	B. Purkey	34	196	11	9	1	3.04
W-92 L-70	3B	S. Boros	370	.257	2	31	95	204	12	18	2.7	.961	J. Jay	34	183	11	11	2	3.39
	RF	F. Robinson	568	.306	29	96	279	7	4	3	1.9	.986	J. Tsitouris	37	175	9	13	2	3.80
Fred Hutchinson	CF	V. Pinson	625	.266	23	84	299	14	9	1	2.1	.972	J. Nuxhall	32	155	9	8	2	4.07
W-54 L-45	LF	T. Harper	317	.243	4	22	149	4	1	2	1.7	.994	S. Ellis	52	122	10	3	14	2.57
	C	J. Edwards	423	.281	7	55	**890**	**73**	8	**17**	**8.1**	.992	B. McCool	40	89	6	5	7	2.42
Dick Sisler	32	C. Ruiz	311	.244	2	16	95	149	11	28		.957	B. Henry	37	52	2	2	6	0.87
W-3 L-3	OF	M. Keough	276	.257	9	28	105	4	1	1	1.4	.991							
	1B	G. Coleman	198	.242	5	27	352	35	4	28	8.0	.990							
Fred Hutchinson																			
W-6 L-4																			
Dick Sisler																			
W-29 L-18																			
Philadelphia	1B	J. Herrnstein	303	.234	6	25	488	22	5	33	7.6	.990	J. Bunning	41	284	19	8	2	2.63
	2B	T. Taylor	570	.251	4	46	325	358	16	94	4.7	.977	C. Short	42	221	17	9	2	2.20
	SS	B. Wine	283	.212	4	34	153	257	15	55	3.9	.965	D. Bennett	41	208	12	14	1	3.68
W-92 L-70	3B	D. Allen	632	.318	29	91	154	325	**41**	30	3.2	.921	A. Mahaffey	34	157	12	9	0	4.52
	RF	J. Callison	654	.274	31	104	319	19	4	3	2.1	.988	R. Culp	30	135	8	7	0	4.13
Gene Mauch	CF	T. Gonzalez	421	.278	4	40	243	5	1	2	2.1	.996	J. Baldschun	71	118	6	9	21	3.12
	LF	W. Covington	339	.280	13	58	99	4	3	0	1.0	.972	E. Roebuck	60	77	5	3	12	2.21
	C	C. Dalrymple	382	.238	6	46	737	61	7	11	6.5	.991							
	UT	C. Rojas	340	.291	2	31	164	76	7	11		.972							
	S1	R. Amaro	299	.264	4	34	295	200	10	55		.980							
	C	G. Triandos	188	.250	8	33	371	24	6	4	6.3	.985							
	1B	F. Thomas	143	.294	7	26	297	28	8	37	8.5	.976							
San Francisco	1B	O. Cepeda	529	.304	31	97	1211	80	**18**	89	9.4	.986	J. Marichal	33	269	21	8	0	2.48
	2B	H. Lanier	383	.274	2	28	224	294	11	48	5.4	.979	G. Perry	44	206	12	11	5	2.75
	SS	J. Pagan	367	.223	1	28	204	302	22	52	4.0	.958	B. Bolin	38	175	6	9	1	3.25
W-90 L-72	3B	J. Hart	566	.286	31	81	139	277	28	24	3.0	.937	B. Hendley	30	163	10	11	0	3.64
	RF	J. Alou	376	.274	3	28	172	8	5	2	1.7	.973	R. Herbel	40	161	9	9	1	3.07
Alvin Dark	CF	W. Mays	578	.296	**47**	111	370	10	6	4	2.5	.984	J. Sanford	18	106	5	7	1	3.30
	LF	W. McCovey	364	.220	18	54	96	5	7	1	1.3	.935	B. Shaw	61	93	7	6	11	3.76
	C	T. Haller	388	.253	16	48	739	50	9	12	7.1	.989	B. O'Dell	36	85	8	7	2	5.40
	OF	H. Kuenn	351	.262	4	22	97	2	5	0	1.2	.952							
	UT	J. Davenport	297	.236	2	26	138	237	11	29		.972							
	OF	M. Alou	250	.264	1	14	120	2	3	1	1.6	.976							
	2B	C. Hiller	205	.180	1	17	111	143	6	29	4.3	.977							
	C	D. Crandall	195	.231	3	11	402	30	3	7	6.7	.993							
	OF	D. Snider	167	.210	4	17	44	2	1	0	1.1	.979							
Milwaukee	1B	G. Oliver	279	.276	13	49	622	34	12	50	8.8	.982	T. Cloninger	38	243	19	14	2	3.56
	2B	F. Bolling	352	.199	5	34	212	255	7	68	4.1	**.985**	D. Lemaster	39	221	17	11	1	4.15
	SS	D. Menke	505	.283	20	65	253	422	25	76	5.0	.964	W. Spahn	38	174	6	13	4	5.29
W-88 L-74	3B	E. Mathews	502	.233	23	74	130	247	15	19	3.1	.962	H. Fischer	37	168	11	10	2	4.01
	RF	H. Aaron	570	.328	24	95	270	13	5	5	2.1	.983	B. Sadowski	51	167	9	10	5	4.10
Bobby Bragan	CF	L. Maye	588	.304	10	74	264	7	11	1	2.1	.961	W. Blasingame	28	117	9	5	2	4.24
	LF	R. Carty	455	.330	22	88	176	5	4	1	1.5	.978	B. Tiefenauer	46	73	4	6	13	3.21
	C	J. Torre	601	.321	20	109	518	46	3	4	5.9	**.995**							
	OF	F. Alou	415	.253	9	51	191	2	5	0	2.2	.975							
	C	E. Bailey	271	.262	5	34	416	28	8	3	5.7	.982							
	UT	M. de la Hoz	189	.291	4	12	65	109	10	17		.946							
Los Angeles	1B	R. Fairly	454	.256	10	74	1081	82	15	89	8.4	.987	D. Drysdale	40	**321**	18	16	0	2.18
	2B	N. Oliver	321	.243	0	21	194	247	15	44	4.7	.967	S. Koufax	29	223	19	5	1	**1.74**
	SS	M. Wills	630	.275	2	34	273	422	27	77	4.8	.963	P. Ortega	34	157	7	9	1	4.00
W-80 L-82	3B	J. Gilliam	334	.228	2	27	54	121	12	7	2.2	.936	J. Moeller	27	145	7	13	0	4.21
	RF	F. Howard	433	.226	24	69	183	2	4	0	1.5	.979	B. Miller	**74**	138	7	7	9	2.62
Walter Alston	CF	W. Davis	613	.294	12	77	400	16	7	2	2.7	.983	R. Perranoski	72	125	5	7	14	3.09
	LF	T. Davis	592	.275	14	86	264	9	5	1	1.9	.982	L. Miller	16	80	4	8	0	4.18
	C	J. Roseboro	414	.287	3	45	809	64	6	8	6.9	.993							
	UT	D. Tracewski	304	.247	1	26	152	218	15	35		.961							
	30	D. Griffith	238	.290	4	23	57	56	23	3		.831							
	01	W. Parker	214	.257	3	10	326	26	6	18		.983							

NATIONAL LEAGUE 1964, *cont.*

Team	POS	Player	AB	BA	HR	RBI	PO	A	E	DP	TC/G	FA	Pitcher	G	IP	W	L	SV	ERA
Pittsburgh	1B	D. Clendenon	457	.282	12	64	1153	75	14	116	10.4	.989	B. Veale	40	280	18	12	0	2.74
W-80 L-82	2B	B. Mazeroski	601	.268	10	64	346	**543**	23	**122**	**5.6**	.975	B. Friend	35	240	13	18	0	3.33
Danny Murtaugh	SS	D. Schofield	398	.246	3	36	184	349	28	78	5.1	.950	V. Law	35	192	12	13	0	3.61
	3B	B. Bailey	530	.281	11	51	81	218	18	19	3.0	.943	J. Gibbon	28	147	10	7	0	3.68
	RF	R. Clemente	622	**.339**	12	87	289	13	10	2	2.0	.968	S. Blass	24	105	5	8	0	4.04
	CF	B. Virdon	473	.243	3	27	243	5	6	1	1.9	.976	A. McBean	58	90	8	3	22	1.91
	LF	M. Mota	271	.277	5	32	120	4	5	1	1.4	.961	R. Face	55	80	3	3	4	5.20
	C	J. Pagliaroni	302	.295	10	36	584	42	5	5	6.6	.992							
	01	W. Stargell	421	.273	21	78	565	24	10	50		.983							
	OF	J. Lynch	297	.273	16	66	59	0	1	0	0.8	.983							
	3B	G. Freese	289	.225	9	40	48	112	14	12	2.4	.920							
	SS	G. Alley	209	.211	6	13	100	211	11	43	5.3	.966							
	C	S. Burgess	171	.246	2	17	237	18	2	3	5.8	.992							
Chicago	1B	E. Banks	591	.264	23	95	**1565**	**132**	10	122	**10.9**	.994	L. Jackson	40	298	**24**	11	0	3.14
W-76 L-86	2B	J. Amalfitano	324	.241	4	27	201	254	17	47	5.5	.964	D. Ellsworth	37	257	14	18	0	3.75
Bob Kennedy	SS	A. Rodgers	448	.239	12	46	232	428	24	68	**5.4**	.965	B. Buhl	36	228	15	14	0	3.83
	3B	R. Santo	592	.313	30	114	**156**	**367**	20	**31**	**3.4**	.963	L. Burdette	28	131	9	9	0	4.88
	RF	L. Gabrielson	272	.246	5	23	116	5	2	0	1.8	.984	E. Broglio	18	100	4	7	1	4.04
	CF	B. Cowan	497	.241	19	50	297	2	10	0	2.3	.968	L. McDaniel	63	95	1	7	15	3.88
	LF	B. Williams	645	.312	33	98	233	14	13	0	1.6	.950							
	C	D. Bertell	353	.238	4	35	531	52	**11**	3	5.4	.981							
	2S	J. Stewart	415	.253	3	33	214	307	12	64		.977							
	OF	L. Brock	215	.251	2	14	86	8	4*	1	1.9	.959							
Houston	1B	W. Bond	543	.254	20	85	685	40	8	46	9.6	.989	K. Johnson	35	218	11	16	0	3.63
	2B	N. Fox	442	.265	0	28	231	317	13	51	4.9	.977	B. Bruce	35	202	15	9	0	2.76
	SS	E. Kasko	448	.243	0	22	228	388	14	72	4.9	**.978**	D. Farrell	32	198	11	10	0	3.27
W-66 L-96	3B	B. Aspromonte	553	.280	12	69	133	261	11	10	2.6	**.973**	D. Nottebart	28	157	6	11	0	3.90
	RF	J. Gaines	307	.254	7	34	130	4	6	1	1.7	.957	H. Brown	27	132	3	15	1	3.95
Harry Craft	CF	M. White	280	.271	0	27	127	4	3	1	1.9	.978	J. Owens	48	118	8	7	6	3.28
W-61 L-88	LF	A. Spangler	449	.245	4	38	185	3	7	1	1.5	.964	D. Larsen	30	103	4	8	1	2.26
	C	J. Grote	298	.181	3	24	522	52	9	5	5.9	.985	C. Raymond	38	80	5	5	0	2.82
Lum Harris	UT	B. Lillis	332	.268	0	17	169	236	10	40		.976	H. Woodeshick	61	78	2	9	**23**	2.76
W-5 L-8	10	R. Staub	292	.216	8	35	512	30	9	34		.984							
	C	J. Bateman	221	.190	5	19	400	43	6	4	6.2	.987							
	OF	J. Wynn	219	.224	5	18	129	8	6	3	2.2	.958							
New York	1B	E. Kranepool	420	.257	10	45	975	80	10	78	10.2	.991	J. Fisher	40	228	10	17	0	4.23
	2B	R. Hunt	475	.303	6	42	244	317	12	73	5.3	.979	T. Stallard	36	226	10	**20**	0	3.79
W-53 L-109	SS	R. McMillan	379	.211	1	25	217	353	14	64	5.3	.976	A. Jackson	40	213	11	16	1	4.26
	3B	C. Smith	443	.239	20	58	89	166	23	9	3.3	.917	G. Cisco	36	192	6	19	0	3.62
Casey Stengel	RF	J. Christopher	543	.300	16	76	251	10	7	2	1.8	.974	B. Wakefield	62	120	3	5	2	3.61
	CF	J. Hickman	409	.257	11	57	237	8	6	1	2.2	.976	L. Bearnarth	44	78	5	5	3	4.15
	LF	G. Altman	422	.230	9	47	202	12	7	3	2.0	.968	W. Hunter	41	49	3	3	5	4.41
	C	J. Gonder	341	.270	7	35	397	70	10	7	4.9	.979							
	UT	R. Kanehl	254	.232	1	11	161	125	6	26		.979							
	C	H. Taylor	225	.240	4	23	182	28	4	5	4.8	.981							
	OF	L. Elliot	224	.228	9	22	130	2	2	1	2.1	.985							
	32	B. Klaus	209	.244	2	11	81	128	6	14		.972							
	01	F. Thomas	197	.254	3	19	200	16	1	12		.995							
	C	C. Cannizzaro	164	.311	0	10	225	28	3	6	4.8	.988							

BATTING AND BASE RUNNING LEADERS

Batting Average
R. Clemente, PIT .339
R. Carty, MIL .330
H. Aaron, MIL .328
J. Torre, MIL .321
D. Allen, PHI .318

Slugging Average
W. Mays, SF .607
R. Santo, CHI .564
D. Allen, PHI .557
R. Carty, MIL .554
F. Robinson, CIN .548

Home Runs
W. Mays, SF 47
B. Williams, CHI 33
O. Cepeda, SF 31
J. Hart, SF 31
J. Callison, PHI 31

Total Bases
D. Allen, PHI 352
W. Mays, SF 351
B. Williams, CHI 343
R. Santo, CHI 334
J. Callison, PHI 322

Runs Batted In
K. Boyer, STL 119
R. Santo, CHI 114
W. Mays, SF 111
J. Torre, MIL 109
J. Callison, PHI 104

Stolen Bases
M. Wills, LA 53
L. Brock, CHI, STL 43
W. Davis, LA 42
T. Harper, CIN 24
F. Robinson, CIN 23

Hits
R. Clemente, PIT 211
C. Flood, STL 211
D. Allen, PHI 201
B. Williams, CHI 201

Base on Balls
R. Santo, CHI 86
E. Mathews, MIL 85
W. Mays, SF 82
F. Robinson, CIN 79

Home Run Percentage
W. Mays, SF 8.1
O. Cepeda, SF 5.9
J. Hart, SF 5.5
B. Williams, CHI 5.1

Runs
D. Allen, PHI 125
W. Mays, SF 121
L. Brock, CHI, STL 111
F. Robinson, CIN 103
H. Aaron, MIL 103

Doubles
L. Maye, MIL 44
R. Clemente, PIT 40
B. Williams, CHI 39
F. Robinson, CIN 38
D. Allen, PHI 38

Triples
R. Santo, CHI 13
D. Allen, PHI 13
V. Pinson, CIN 11
L. Brock, CHI, STL 11

PITCHING LEADERS

Winning Percentage
S. Koufax, LA .792
J. Marichal, SF .724
J. O'Toole, CIN .708
J. Bunning, PHI .704
L. Jackson, CHI .686

Earned Run Average
S. Koufax, LA 1.74
D. Drysdale, LA 2.18
C. Short, PHI 2.20
J. Marichal, SF 2.48
J. Bunning, PHI 2.63

Wins
L. Jackson, CHI 24
J. Marichal, SF 21
R. Sadecki, STL 20

Saves
H. Woodeshick, HOU 23
A. McBean, PIT 22
J. Baldschun, PHI 21
L. McDaniel, CHI 15

Strikeouts
B. Veale, PIT 250
B. Gibson, STL 245
D. Drysdale, LA 237
S. Koufax, LA 223
J. Bunning, PHI 219

Complete Games
J. Marichal, SF 22
D. Drysdale, LA 21
L. Jackson, CHI 19
B. Gibson, STL 17
D. Ellsworth, CHI 16

Fewest Hits/9 Innings
S. Koufax, LA 6.22
D. Drysdale, LA 6.78
C. Short, PHI 7.10
B. Veale, PIT 7.14

Shutouts
S. Koufax, LA 7
H. Fischer, MIL 5
V. Law, PIT 5
J. Bunning, PHI 5
D. Drysdale, LA 5

Fewest Walks/9 Innings
J. Bunning, PHI 1.46
B. Bruce, HOU 1.47
V. Law, PIT 1.50
J. Marichal, SF 1.74

Most Strikeouts/9 Inn.
S. Koufax, LA 9.00
J. Maloney, CIN 8.92
B. Veale, PIT 8.05
B. Gibson, STL 7.67

Innings
D. Drysdale, LA 321
L. Jackson, CHI 298
B. Gibson, STL 287
J. Bunning, PHI 284

Games Pitched
B. Miller, LA 74
R. Perranoski, LA 72
J. Baldschun, PHI 71
L. McDaniel, CHI 63
R. Taylor, STL 63

NATIONAL LEAGUE 1964, *cont.*

	W	L	PCT	GB	R	OR	Batting 2B	3B	HR	BA	SA	SB	Fielding E	DP	FA	Pitching CG	BB	SO	ShO	SV	ERA
St. Louis	93	69	.574		715	652	240	53	109	**.272**	.392	73	172	147	.973	47	410	877	10	38	3.43
Cincinnati	92	70	.568	1	660	**566**	220	38	130	.249	.372	90	**130**	137	**.979**	54	436	**1122**	14	35	3.07
Philadelphia	92	70	.568	1	693	632	241	51	130	.258	.391	30	157	150	.975	37	440	1009	17	**41**	3.36
San Francisco	90	72	.556	3	656	587	185	38	**165**	.246	.382	64	159	136	.975	48	480	1023	17	30	3.19
Milwaukee	88	74	.543	5	**803**	744	**274**	32	159	**.272**	**.418**	53	143	139	.977	45	452	906	14	39	4.12
Los Angeles	80	82	.494	13	614	572	180	39	79	.250	.340	**141**	170	126	.973	47	458	1062	**19**	27	**2.95**
Pittsburgh	80	82	.494	13	663	636	225	**54**	121	.264	.389	39	177	**179**	.972	42	476	951	14	29	3.52
Chicago	76	86	.469	17	649	724	239	50	145	.251	.390	70	162	147	.975	**58**	423	737	11	19	4.08
Houston	66	96	.407	27	495	628	162	41	70	.229	.315	40	149	124	.976	30	**353**	852	9	31	3.41
New York	53	109	.327	40	569	776	195	31	103	.246	.348	36	167	154	.974	40	466	717	10	15	4.25
					6517	6517	2161	427	1211	.254	.374	636	1586	1439	.975	448	4394	9256	135	304	3.54

AMERICAN LEAGUE 1964

	POS	Player	AB	BA	HR	RBI	PO	A	E	DP	TC/G	FA	Pitcher	G	IP	W	L	SV	ERA
New York	1B	J. Pepitone	613	.251	28	100	**1333**	**121**	18	**128**	9.5	.988	J. Bouton	38	271	18	13	0	3.02
W-99 L-63	2B	B. Richardson	**679**	.267	4	50	**400**	410	15	108	5.3	.982	W. Ford	39	245	17	6	1	2.13
Yogi Berra	SS	T. Kubek	415	.229	8	31	186	307	11	52	5.1	.978	A. Downing	37	244	13	8	2	3.47
	3B	C. Boyer	510	.218	8	52	118	278	13	28	**3.3**	.968	R. Terry	27	115	7	11	4	4.54
	RF	R. Maris	513	.281	26	71	250	6	1	0	1.9	.996	R. Sheldon	19	102	5	2	1	3.61
	CF	M. Mantle	465	.303	35	111	217	3	5	1	1.7	.978	M. Stottlemyre	13	96	9	3	0	2.06
	LF	T. Tresh	533	.246	16	73	259	7	1	0	1.8	.996	P. Mikkelsen	50	86	7	4	12	3.56
	C	E. Howard	550	.313	15	84	**939**	67	2	9	6.9	**.998**	H. Reniff	41	69	6	4	9	3.12
	S3	P. Linz	368	.250	5	25	121	275	20	42		.952	S. Hamilton	30	60	7	2	3	3.28
	OF	H. Lopez	285	.260	10	34	130	2	4	1	1.3	.971							
	CO	J. Blanchard	161	.255	7	28	139	8	2	1		.987							
Chicago	1B	T. McCraw	368	.261	6	36	601	37	5	57	7.7	.992	G. Peters	37	274	**20**	8	0	2.50
W-98 L-64	2B	A. Weis	328	.247	2	23	199	255	16	64	4.1	.966	J. Pizarro	33	239	19	9	0	2.56
Al Lopez	SS	R. Hansen	575	.261	20	68	**292**	**514**	21	**105**	**5.2**	.975	J. Horlen	32	211	13	9	0	1.88
	3B	P. Ward	539	.282	23	94	126	309	19	24	3.3	.958	J. Buzhardt	31	160	10	8	0	2.98
	RF	M. Hershberger	452	.230	2	31	231	10	4	2	1.8	.984	H. Wilhelm	73	131	12	9	27	1.99
	CF	J. Landis	298	.208	1	18	183	7	1	2	1.9	.995	E. Fisher	59	125	6	3	9	3.02
	LF	F. Robinson	525	.301	11	59	225	5	3	0	1.7	.987	R. Herbert	20	112	6	7	0	3.47
	C	J. Martin	294	.197	4	22	530	43	8	6	4.8	.986	D. Mossi	34	40	3	1	7	2.92
	2B	D. Buford	442	.262	4	30	196	198	13	60	4.4	.968							
	OF	D. Nicholson	294	.204	13	39	136	4	4	0	1.6	.972							
	1B	B. Skowron	273	.293	4	38	621	40	1	53	9.5*	.998							
	C	J. McNertney	186	.215	3	23	360	30	5	5	5.7	.987							
Baltimore	1B	N. Siebern	478	.245	12	56	1171	101	6	121	8.6	.995	M. Pappas	37	252	16	7	0	2.97
W-97 L-65	2B	J. Adair	569	.248	9	47	395	422	5	107	5.4	**.994**	W. Bunker	29	214	19	5	0	2.69
Hank Bauer	SS	L. Aparicio	578	.266	10	37	260	437	15	98	4.9	**.979**	R. Roberts	31	204	13	7	0	2.91
	3B	B. Robinson	612	.317	28	**118**	**153**	**327**	14	**40**	3.0	**.972**	D. McNally	30	159	9	11	0	3.67
	RF	S. Bowens	501	.263	22	71	249	8	5	1	1.9	.981	S. Barber	36	157	9	13	1	3.84
	CF	J. Brandt	523	.243	13	47	345	14	7	2	2.7	.981	S. Miller	66	97	7	7	23	3.06
	LF	B. Powell	424	.290	39	99	178	13	5	1	1.6	.974	H. Haddix	49	90	5	5	10	2.31
	C	D. Brown	230	.257	8	32	380	29	5	4	4.9	.988	D. Hall	45	88	9	1	7	1.85
	C	J. Orsino	248	.222	8	23	384	31	10	3	6.4	.976							
	UT	B. Johnson	210	.248	3	29	164	77	5	27		.980							
	OF	W. Kirkland	150	.200	3	22	86	7	1	3	1.6	.989							
Detroit	1B	N. Cash	479	.257	23	83	1105	92	4	97	8.8	**.997**	D. Wickersham	40	254	19	12	1	3.44
W-85 L-77	2B	J. Lumpe	624	.256	6	46	339	394	13	95	4.7	.983	M. Lolich	44	232	18	9	2	3.26
Chuck Dressen	SS	D. McAuliffe	557	.241	24	66	262	467	**32**	84	4.8	.958	H. Aguirre	32	162	5	10	1	3.79
	3B	D. Wert	525	.257	9	55	126	283	15	30	3.0	.965	E. Rakow	42	152	8	9	3	3.72
	RF	A. Kaline	525	.293	17	68	278	6	3	2	2.1	.990	P. Regan	32	147	5	10	1	5.03
	CF	G. Thomas	308	.286	12	44	164	4	2	1	1.9	.988	D. McLain	19	100	4	5	0	4.05
	LF	G. Brown	426	.272	15	54	205	4	4	0	2.0	.981	J. Sparma	21	84	5	6	0	3.00
	C	B. Freehan	520	.300	18	80	923	61	7	7	7.0	.993	F. Gladding	42	67	7	4	7	3.07
	OF	D. Demeter	441	.256	22	80	164	3	0	1	1.9	1.000	L. Sherry	38	66	7	5	11	3.66
	OF	B. Bruton	296	.277	5	33	143	7	2	3	1.9	.987	T. Fox	32	61	4	3	5	3.39
Los Angeles	1B	J. Adcock	366	.268	21	64	959	54	7	94	9.7	.993	D. Chance	46	**278**	**20**	9	4	**1.65**
W-82 L-80	2B	B. Knoop	486	.216	7	38	357	**522**	**20**	**123**	**5.6**	.978	F. Newman	32	190	13	10	0	2.75
Bill Rigney	SS	J. Fregosi	505	.277	18	72	225	421	23	89	4.9	.966	B. Latman	40	138	6	10	2	3.85
	3B	F. Torres	277	.231	12	28	73	122	6	10	2.8	.970	B. Lee	64	137	6	5	19	1.51
	RF	L. Clinton	306	.248	9	38	123	12	2	3	1.6	.985	B. Belinsky	23	135	9	8	0	2.86
	CF	A. Pearson	265	.223	2	16	132	1	3	1	2.1	.978	K. McBride	29	116	4	13	1	5.26
	LF	W. Smith	359	.301	11	51	128	2	3	0	1.5	.977	D. Lee	33	89	5	4	2	2.72
	C	B. Rodgers	514	.243	4	54	884	**87**	**13**	**14**	6.7	.987	B. Duliba	58	73	6	4	9	3.59
	UT	T. Satriano	255	.200	1	17	383	72	8	32		.983							
	OF	J. Piersall	255	.314	2	13	115	2	0	2	1.6	1.000							
	OF	B. Perry	221	.276	3	16	115	2	3	0	1.9	.975							
	13	V. Power	221	.249	3	13	302	79	3	26		.992							
	OF	E. Kirkpatrick	219	.242	2	22	90	3	3	0	1.5	.969							
	3B	B. Moran	198	.268	0	11	47	86	10	5	3.0	.930							
	OF	L. Thomas	172	.273	2	24	71	4	4	1	1.7	.949							

AMERICAN LEAGUE 1964, *cont.*

Cleveland

W-79 L-83

George Strickland
W-33 L-39

Birdie Tebbetts
W-46 L-44

POS	Player	AB	BA	HR	RBI	PO	A	E	DP	TC/G	FA	Pitcher	G	IP	W	L	SV	ERA
1B	B. Chance	390	.279	14	75	567	24	7	47	7.4	.988	J. Kralick	30	191	12	7	0	3.21
2B	L. Brown	335	.230	12	40	185	270	9	56	4.5	.981	S. McDowell	31	173	11	6	1	2.70
SS	D. Howser	637	.256	3	52	291	463	20	100	4.8	.974	D. Donovan	30	158	7	9	1	4.55
3B	M. Alvis	381	.252	18	53	83	191	13	18	2.7	.955	S. Siebert	41	156	7	9	3	3.23
RF	T. Francona	270	.248	8	24	65	2	1	0	1.0	.985	P. Ramos	36	133	7	10	0	5.14
CF	V. Davalillo	577	.270	6	51	346	11	5	5	2.5	.986	L. Tiant	19	127	10	4	1	2.83
LF	L. Wagner	641	.253	31	100	254	5	11	0	1.7	.959	G. Bell	56	106	8	6	4	4.33
C	J. Romano	352	.241	19	47	714	38	7	3	**7.9**	.991	D. McMahon	70	101	6	4	16	2.41
UT	W. Held	364	.236	18	49	183	182	14	40		.963	T. John	25	94	2	9	0	3.91
1B	F. Whitfield	293	.270	10	29	596	36	5	63	8.1	.992	L. Stange	23	92	4	8	0	4.12
UT	C. Salmon	283	.307	4	25	191	67	2	14		.992	T. Abernathy	53	73	2	6	11	4.33
C	J. Azcue	271	.273	4	34	510	36	4	2	7.2	.993							

Minnesota

W-79 L-83

Sam Mele

POS	Player	AB	BA	HR	RBI	PO	A	E	DP	TC/G	FA	Pitcher	G	IP	W	L	SV	ERA
1B	B. Allison	492	.287	32	86	715	55	11	63	8.4	.986	C. Pascual	36	267	15	12	0	3.30
2B	B. Allen	243	.214	6	20	161	173	7	40	4.8	.979	J. Kaat	36	243	17	11	1	3.22
SS	Z. Versalles	659	.259	20	64	271	427	31	89	4.6	.957	D. Stigman	32	190	6	15	0	4.03
3B	R. Rollins	596	.270	12	68	134	297	**24**	17	3.1	.947	M. Grant	26	166	11	9	1	2.82
RF	T. Oliva	672	**.323**	32	94	313	5	6	0	2.0	.981	J. Arrigo	41	105	7	4	1	3.84
CF	J. Hall	510	.282	25	75	323	13	5	0	2.5	.985	J. Roland	30	94	2	6	3	4.10
LF	H. Killebrew	577	.270	**49**	111	232	1	7	0	1.5	.971	A. Worthington	41	72	5	6	14	1.37
C	E. Battey	405	.272	12	52	813	52	9	4	7.0	.990	J. Perry	42	65	6	3	2	3.44
1B	D. Mincher	287	.237	23	56	549	43	5	50	7.9	.992							

Boston

W-72 L-90

Johnny Pesky
W-70 L-90

Billy Herman
W-2 L-0

POS	Player	AB	BA	HR	RBI	PO	A	E	DP	TC/G	FA	Pitcher	G	IP	W	L	SV	ERA
1B	D. Stuart	603	.279	33	114	1159	104	**24**	105	8.3	.981	B. Monbouquette	36	234	13	14	1	4.04
2B	D. Jones	374	.230	6	39	181	193	16	41	4.6	.959	E. Wilson	33	202	11	12	0	4.49
SS	E. Bressoud	566	.293	15	55	248	411	19	78	4.3	.972	J. Lamabe	39	177	9	13	1	5.89
3B	F. Malzone	537	.264	13	56	141	259	17	24	2.9	.959	D. Morehead	32	167	8	15	0	4.97
RF	L. Thomas	401	.257	13	42	176	6	1	1	1.7	.995	B. Heffner	55	159	7	9	6	4.08
CF	C. Yastrzemski	567	.289	15	67	372	19	11	3	2.7	.973	D. Radatz	79	157	16	9	**29**	2.29
LF	T. Conigliaro	404	.290	24	52	176	7	5	0	1.8	.973	E. Connolly	27	81	4	11	0	4.91
C	B. Tillman	425	.278	17	61	897	49	11	5	7.3	.989							
UT	F. Mantilla	425	.289	30	64	173	146	5	29		.985							
C	R. Nixon	163	.233	1	20	273	11	3	3	6.4	.990							
2B	C. Schilling	163	.196	0	7	89	101	5	20	4.6	.974							

Washington

W-62 L-100

Gil Hodges

POS	Player	AB	BA	HR	RBI	PO	A	E	DP	TC/G	FA	Pitcher	G	IP	W	L	SV	ERA
1B	B. Skowron	262	.271	13	41	591	40	4	41	9.6*	.994	C. Osteen	37	257	15	13	0	3.33
2B	D. Blasingame	506	.267	1	34	259	336	14	70	4.5	.977	B. Narum	38	199	9	15	0	4.30
SS	E. Brinkman	447	.224	8	34	234	364	19	75	4.9	.969	B. Daniels	33	163	8	10	0	3.70
3B	J. Kennedy	482	.230	7	35	97	190	16	14	2.9	.947	A. Koch	32	114	3	10	0	4.89
RF	J. King	415	.241	18	56	240	10	7	0	2.1	.973	S. Ridzik	49	112	5	5	2	2.89
CF	D. Lock	512	.248	28	80	354	19	5	3	2.5	.987	J. Hannan	49	106	4	7	3	4.16
LF	C. Hinton	514	.274	11	53	258	7	4	3	2.1	.985	D. Stenhouse	26	88	2	7	1	4.81
C	M. Brumley	426	.244	2	35	628	44	6	4	5.1	.991	R. Kline	61	81	10	7	14	2.32
3B	D. Zimmer	341	.246	12	38	68	143	10	6	2.5	.955	J. Duckworth	30	56	1	6	3	4.34
1B	D. Phillips	234	.231	2	23	473	39	3	50	8.4	.994							
OF	F. Valentine	212	.226	4	20	86	2	2	1	1.6	.978							

Kansas City

W-57 L-105

Ed Lopat
W-17 L-35

Mel McGaha
W-40 L-70

POS	Player	AB	BA	HR	RBI	PO	A	E	DP	TC/G	FA	Pitcher	G	IP	W	L	SV	ERA
1B	J. Gentile	439	.251	28	71	1018	84	13	92	8.7	.988	O. Pena	40	219	12	14	0	4.43
2B	D. Green	435	.264	11	37	262	361	6	69	5.2	.990	D. Segui	40	217	8	**17**	0	4.56
SS	W. Causey	604	.281	8	49	266	352	21	75	4.9	.967	J. O'Donoghue	39	174	10	14	0	4.92
3B	E. Charles	557	.241	16	63	138	259	19	25	2.8	.954	M. Drabowsky	53	168	5	13	1	5.29
RF	R. Colavito	588	.274	34	102	275	10	8	1	1.8	.973	J. Wyatt	**81**	128	9	8	20	3.59
CF	N. Mathews	573	.239	14	60	384	5	13	2	2.6	.968	T. Bowsfield	50	119	4	7	0	4.10
LF	M. Jimenez	204	.225	12	38	59	3	4	1	1.3	.939	W. Stock	50	93	6	3	5	1.94
C	D. Edwards	294	.224	5	28	469	31	7	5	6.4	.986							
SO	B. Campaneris	269	.257	4	22	97	96	5	14		.975							
C	B. Bryan	220	.241	13	36	317	22	3	5	5.3	.991							
OF	G. Alusik	204	.240	3	19	61	1	1	1	1.4	.984							

BATTING AND BASE RUNNING LEADERS

Batting Average		Slugging Average		Home Runs	
T. Oliva, MIN	.323	B. Powell, BAL	.606	H. Killebrew, MIN	49
B. Robinson, BAL	.317	M. Mantle, NY	.591	B. Powell, BAL	39
E. Howard, NY	.313	T. Oliva, MIN	.557	M. Mantle, NY	35
M. Mantle, NY	.303	B. Allison, MIN	.553	R. Colavito, KC	34
F. Robinson, CHI	.301	H. Killebrew, MIN	.548	D. Stuart, BOS	33

Total Bases		Runs Batted In		Stolen Bases	
T. Oliva, MIN	374	B. Robinson, BAL	118	L. Aparicio, BAL	57
B. Robinson, BAL	319	D. Stuart, BOS	114	A. Weis, CHI	22
H. Killebrew, MIN	316	M. Mantle, NY	111	V. Davalillo, CLE	21
R. Colavito, KC	298	H. Killebrew, MIN	111	D. Howser, CLE	20
D. Stuart, BOS	296	R. Colavito, KC	102	C. Hinton, WAS	17

Hits		Base on Balls		Home Run Percentage	
T. Oliva, MIN	217	N. Siebern, BAL	106	B. Powell, BAL	9.2
B. Robinson, BAL	194	M. Mantle, NY	99	H. Killebrew, MIN	8.5
B. Richardson, NY	181	H. Killebrew, MIN	93	M. Mantle, NY	7.5
E. Howard, NY	172	B. Allison, MIN	92	B. Allison, MIN	6.5

PITCHING LEADERS

Winning Percentage		Earned Run Average		Wins	
W. Bunker, BAL	.792	D. Chance, LA	1.65	G. Peters, CHI	20
W. Ford, NY	.739	J. Horlen, CHI	1.88	D. Chance, LA	20
G. Peters, CHI	.714	W. Ford, NY	2.13	W. Bunker, BAL	19
M. Pappas, BAL	.696	G. Peters, CHI	2.50	J. Pizarro, CHI	19
D. Chance, LA	.690	J. Pizarro, CHI	2.56	D. Wickersham, DET	19

Saves		Strikeouts		Complete Games	
D. Radatz, BOS	29	A. Downing, NY	217	D. Chance, LA	15
H. Wilhelm, CHI	27	C. Pascual, MIN	213	C. Pascual, MIN	14
S. Miller, BAL	23	D. Chance, LA	207	J. Kaat, MIN	13
J. Wyatt, KC	20	G. Peters, CHI	205	C. Osteen, WAS	13
B. Lee, LA	19	M. Lolich, DET	192	M. Pappas, BAL	13

Fewest Hits/9 Innings		Shutouts		Fewest Walks/9 Innings	
J. Horlen, CHI	6.07	D. Chance, LA	11	B. Monbouquette, BOS	1.54
D. Chance, LA	6.27	W. Ford, NY	8	M. Pappas, BAL	1.72
W. Bunker, BAL	6.77	M. Pappas, BAL	7	F. Newman, LA	1.85
G. Peters, CHI	7.14	M. Lolich, DET	6	J. Bouton, NY	1.99

AMERICAN LEAGUE 1964, *cont.*

BATTING AND BASE RUNNING LEADERS

Runs		Doubles		Triples	
T. Oliva, MIN	109	T. Oliva, MIN	43	R. Rollins, MIN	10
D. Howser, CLE	101	E. Bressoud, BOS	41	Z. Versalles, MIN	10
H. Killebrew, MIN	95	B. Robinson, BAL	35	J. Fregosi, LA	9
L. Wagner, CLE	94	Z. Versalles, MIN	33	C. Yastrzemski, BOS	9
Z. Versalles, MIN	94			T. Oliva, MIN	9

PITCHING LEADERS

Most Strikeouts/9 Inn.		Innings		Games Pitched	
S. McDowell, CLE	9.19	D. Chance, LA	278	J. Wyatt, KC	81
A. Downing, NY	8.00	G. Peters, CHI	274	D. Radatz, BOS	79
O. Pena, KC	7.55	J. Bouton, NY	271	H. Wilhelm, CHI	73
D. Stigman, MIN	7.53	C. Pascual, MIN	267	D. McMahon, CLE	70

	W	L	PCT	GB	R	OR	Batting 2B	3B	HR	BA	SA	SB	Fielding E	DP	FA	Pitching CG	BB	SO	ShO	SV	ERA
New York	99	63	.611		730	577	208	35	162	.253	.387	54	109	158	.983	46	504	989	18	**45**	3.15
Chicago	98	64	.605	1	642	**501**	184	40	106	.247	.353	75	122	164	.981	44	**401**	955	20	**45**	**2.72**
Baltimore	97	65	.599	2	679	567	229	20	162	.248	.387	78	**95**	159	**.985**	44	456	939	17	41	3.16
Detroit	85	77	.525	14	699	678	199	**57**	157	.253	.395	60	111	137	.982	35	536	993	11	35	3.84
Los Angeles	82	80	.506	17	544	551	186	27	102	.242	.344	49	138	**168**	.978	30	530	965	**28**	41	2.91
Cleveland	79	83	.488	20	689	693	208	22	164	.247	.380	**79**	118	149	.981	37	565	**1162**	16	37	3.75
Minnesota	79	83	.488	20	**737**	678	227	46	**221**	.252	**.427**	46	145	131	.977	**47**	545	1099	4	29	3.57
Boston	72	90	.444	27	688	793	**253**	29	186	**.258**	.416	18	138	123	.977	21	571	1094	9	38	4.50
Washington	62	100	.383	37	578	733	199	28	125	.231	.348	47	127	145	.979	27	505	794	5	26	3.98
Kansas City	57	105	.352	42	621	836	216	29	166	.239	.379	34	158	152	.974	18	614	966	6	27	4.71
					6607	6607	2109	333	1551	.247	.382	540	1261	1486	.980	349	5227	9956	134	364	3.63

NATIONAL LEAGUE 1965

Los Angeles

W-97 L-65

Walter Alston

POS	Player	AB	BA	HR	RBI	PO	A	E	DP	TC/G	FA	Pitcher	G	IP	W	L	SV	ERA
1B	W. Parker	542	.238	8	51	1434	95	5	112	10.0	**.997**	S. Koufax	43	**336**	**26**	8	2	**2.04**
2B	J. Lefebvre	544	.250	12	69	349	429	24	91	5.1	.970	D. Drysdale	44	308	23	12	1	2.77
SS	M. Wills	650	.286	0	33	267	**535**	25	89	**5.3**	.970	C. Osteen	40	287	15	15	0	2.79
3B	J. Kennedy	105	.171	1	5	35	64	3	5	1.1	.971	J. Podres	27	134	7	6	1	3.43
RF	R. Fairly	555	.274	9	70	262	7	5	1	1.9	.982	R. Perranoski	59	105	6	6	17	2.24
CF	W. Davis	558	.238	10	57	318	6	11	1	2.4	.967	B. Miller	61	103	6	7	9	2.97
LF	L. Johnson	468	.259	12	58	199	3	3	2	1.6	.985	H. Reed	38	78	7	5	1	3.12
C	J. Roseboro	437	.233	8	57	824	55	5	7	6.7	.994							
3B	J. Gilliam	372	.280	4	39	55	135	8	13	2.5	.960							
3B	D. Tracewski	186	.215	1	20	30	103	7	6	2.6	.950							

San Francisco

W-95 L-67

Herman Franks

POS	Player	AB	BA	HR	RBI	PO	A	E	DP	TC/G	FA	Pitcher	G	IP	W	L	SV	ERA
1B	W. McCovey	540	.276	39	92	1310	87	13	93	9.0	.991	J. Marichal	39	295	22	13	1	2.13
2B	H. Lanier	522	.226	0	39	294	445	18	75	4.8	.976	B. Shaw	42	235	16	9	2	2.64
SS	D. Schofield	379	.203	2	19	145	274	7	52	4.6	.984*	G. Perry	47	196	8	12	1	4.19
3B	J. Hart	591	.299	23	96	134	231	**32**	16	2.8	.919	R. Herbel	47	171	12	9	1	3.85
RF	J. Alou	543	.298	9	52	238	7	5	0	1.8	.980	B. Bolin	45	163	14	6	2	2.76
CF	W. Mays	558	.317	**52**	112	337	13	6	4	2.4	.983	J. Sanford	23	91	4	5	2	3.96
LF	M. Alou	324	.231	2	18	139	6	2	1	1.4	.986	F. Linzy	57	82	9	3	21	1.43
C	T. Haller	422	.251	16	49	**864**	50	**12**	9	7.0	.987	M. Murakami	45	74	4	1	8	3.75
UT	J. Davenport	271	.251	4	31	97	147	14	21		.946							
OF	L. Gabrielson	269	.301	4	26	112	3	3	1	1.5	.975							

Pittsburgh

W-90 L-72

Harry Walker

POS	Player	AB	BA	HR	RBI	PO	A	E	DP	TC/G	FA	Pitcher	G	IP	W	L	SV	ERA
1B	D. Clendenon	612	.301	14	96	1572	**119**	**28**	**161**	10.9	.984	B. Veale	39	266	17	12	0	2.84
2B	B. Mazeroski	494	.271	6	54	290	439	9	**113**	**5.8**	**.988**	D. Cardwell	37	240	13	10	0	3.18
SS	G. Alley	500	.252	5	47	163	376	18	79	5.1	.968	B. Friend	34	222	8	12	0	3.24
3B	B. Bailey	626	.256	11	49	96	243	22	25	2.5	.939	V. Law	29	217	17	9	0	2.15
RF	R. Clemente	589	**.329**	10	65	288	16	10	1	2.2	.968	A. McBean	62	114	6	6	18	2.29
CF	B. Virdon	481	.279	4	24	260	3	8	1	2.1	.970	T. Sisk	38	111	7	3	0	3.40
LF	W. Stargell	533	.272	27	107	208	12	8	3	1.7	.965	J. Gibbon	31	106	4	9	1	4.51
C	J. Pagliaroni	403	.268	17	65	669	42	4	**14**	5.5	.994	D. Schwall	43	77	9	6	4	2.92
OF	M. Mota	294	.279	4	29	127	5	2	1	1.4	.985							
UT	A. Rodgers	178	.287	2	25	88	110	8	27		.961							

Cincinnati

W-89 L-73

Dick Sisler

POS	Player	AB	BA	HR	RBI	PO	A	E	DP	TC/G	FA	Pitcher	G	IP	W	L	SV	ERA
1B	T. Perez	281	.260	12	47	525	40	6	55	6.1	.989	S. Ellis	44	264	22	10	2	3.79
2B	P. Rose	**670**	.312	11	81	**382**	403	20	93	5.0	.975	J. Maloney	33	255	20	9	0	2.54
SS	L. Cardenas	557	.287	11	57	**292**	440	19	**92**	4.8	.975	J. Jay	37	156	9	8	1	4.22
3B	D. Johnson	616	.287	32	**130**	132	266	22	26	2.6	.948	J. Nuxhall	32	149	11	4	2	3.45
RF	F. Robinson	582	.296	33	113	282	5	3	1	1.9	.990	J. Tsitouris	31	131	6	9	1	4.95
CF	V. Pinson	669	.305	22	94	354	9	3	1	2.3	.992	J. O'Toole	29	128	3	10	1	5.92
LF	T. Harper	646	.257	18	64	277	6	5	0	1.8	.983	B. McCool	62	105	9	10	21	4.27
C	J. Edwards	371	.267	17	51	761	61	8	9	**7.5**	.990							
1B	G. Coleman	325	.302	14	57	621	48	6	52	7.6	.991							
C	D. Pavletich	191	.319	8	32	335	16	5	5	6.6	.986							

Milwaukee

W-86 L-76

Bobby Bragan

POS	Player	AB	BA	HR	RBI	PO	A	E	DP	TC/G	FA	Pitcher	G	IP	W	L	SV	ERA
1B	G. Oliver	392	.270	21	58	374	37	7	30	8.0	.983	T. Cloninger	40	279	24	11	1	3.29
2B	F. Bolling	535	.264	7	50	310	393	17	90	4.9	.976	W. Blasingame	38	225	16	10	1	3.77
SS	W. Woodward	265	.208	0	11	146	243	9	61	3.7	.977	K. Johnson	29	180	13	8	2	3.21
3B	E. Mathews	546	.251	32	95	113	301	19	19	2.8	.956	D. Lemaster	32	146	7	13	0	4.43
RF	H. Aaron	570	.318	32	89	298	9	4	2	2.1	.987	B. Sadowski	34	123	5	9	3	4.32
CF	M. Jones	504	.262	31	75	239	2	5	2	1.8	.980	H. Fischer	31	123	8	9	0	3.89
LF	F. Alou	555	.297	23	78	148	2	3	0	1.7	.980	B. O'Dell	62	111	10	6	18	2.18
C	J. Torre	523	.291	27	80	589	43	6	4	6.4	.991	P. Niekro	41	75	2	3	6	2.89
OF	R. Carty	271	.310	10	35	112	3	5	1	1.6	.958							
OF	T. Cline	220	.191	0	10	119	5	4	1	1.5	.969							
SS	D. Menke	181	.243	4	18	65	140	7	22	3.9	.967							
UT	M. de la Hoz	176	.256	2	11	61	99	8	20		.952							

NATIONAL LEAGUE 1965, *cont.*

Philadelphia

W-85 L-76

Gene Mauch

POS	Player	AB	BA	HR	RBI	PO	A	E	DP	TC/G	FA
1B	D. Stuart	538	.234	28	95	1119	98	17	100	8.6	.986
2B	T. Taylor	323	.229	3	27	169	220	17	51	4.7	.958
SS	B. Wine	394	.228	5	33	221	387	21	84	4.7	.967
3B	D. Allen	619	.302	20	85	129	305	26	**29**	2.9	.943
RF	J. Callison	619	.262	32	101	313	21	6	2	2.1	.982
CF	T. Gonzalez	370	.295	13	41	167	3	3	1	1.7	.983
LF	A. Johnson	262	.294	8	28	109	3	4	0	1.4	.966
C	C. Dalrymple	301	.213	4	23	657	**70**	5	10	7.2˙	.993
20	C. Rojas	521	.303	3	42	264	236	7	57		.986
OF	W. Covington	235	.247	15	45	88	2	3	0	1.5	.968
OF	J. Briggs	229	.236	4	23	110	2	2	0	1.7	.982
1S	R. Amaro	184	.212	0	15	172	126	10	32		.968
C	P. Corrales	174	.224	2	15	358	24	7	2	6.3	.982

Pitcher	G	IP	W	L	SV	ERA
C. Short	47	297	18	11	2	2.82
J. Bunning	39	291	19	9	0	2.60
R. Culp	33	204	14	10	0	3.22
R. Herbert	25	131	5	8	1	3.86
B. Belinsky	30	110	4	9	1	4.84
G. Wagner	59	105	7	7	7	3.00
J. Baldschun	65	99	5	8	6	3.82
E. Roebuck	44	50	5	3	3	3.40

St. Louis

W-80 L-81

Red Schoendienst

POS	Player	AB	BA	HR	RBI	PO	A	E	DP	TC/G	FA
1B	B. White	543	.289	24	73	1308	109	11	114	9.9	.992
2B	J. Javier	229	.227	2	23	128	179	8	40	4.6	.975
SS	D. Groat	587	.254	0	52	242	450	27	86	4.9	.962
3B	K. Boyer	535	.260	13	75	113	250	12	18	2.6	**.968**
RF	M. Shannon	244	.221	3	25	170	5	1	1	1.7	.994
CF	C. Flood	617	.310	11	83	349	7	5	3	2.4	.986
LF	L. Brock	631	.288	16	69	272	11	12	1	1.9	.959
C	T. McCarver	409	.276	11	48	687	43	4	4	6.6	**.995**
UT	P. Gagliano	363	.240	8	53	201	169	16	34		.959
OF	T. Francona	174	.259	5	19	35	0	1	0	1.1	.972
2S	J. Buchek	166	.247	3	21	92	154	5	38		.980
OF	B. Skinner	152	.309	5	26	43	0	3	0	1.4	.935

Pitcher	G	IP	W	L	SV	ERA
B. Gibson	38	299	20	12	1	3.07
C. Simmons	34	203	9	15	0	4.08
T. Stallard	40	194	11	8	0	3.38
R. Sadecki	36	173	6	15	1	5.21
B. Purkey	32	124	10	9	2	5.79
R. Washburn	28	119	9	11	2	3.62
N. Briles	37	82	3	3	4	3.50
H. Woodeshick	51	60	3	2	15	1.81
D. Dennis	41	55	2	3	6	2.29

Chicago

W-72 L-90

Bob Kennedy
W-24 L-32

Lou Klein
W-48 L-58

POS	Player	AB	BA	HR	RBI	PO	A	E	DP	TC/G	FA
1B	E. Banks	612	.265	28	106	**1682**	93	15	143	**11.0**	.992
2B	G. Beckert	614	.239	3	30	326	**494**	23	101	5.5	.973
SS	D. Kessinger	309	.201	0	14	176	338	**28**	69	5.2	.948
3B	R. Santo	608	.285	33	101	**155**	**373**	24	27	**3.4**	.957
RF	B. Williams	645	.315	34	108	296	10	10	2	1.9	.968
CF	D. Landrum	425	.226	6	34	241	3	3	0	2.1	.988
LF	D. Clemens	340	.221	4	26	145	7	3	0	1.5	.981
C	V. Roznovsky	172	.221	3	15	270	30	5	6	4.8	.984
OS	J. Stewart	282	.223	0	19	117	58	8	11		.956
OF	G. Altman	196	.235	4	23	66	0	4	0	1.6	.943
SS	R. Pena	170	.218	2	12	74	151	17	29	4.8	.930
C	C. Krug	169	.201	5	24	273	27	6	5	5.3	.980
C	E. Bailey	150	.253	5	23	237	23	5	3	4.9	.981

Pitcher	G	IP	W	L	SV	ERA
L. Jackson	39	257	14	21	0	3.85
D. Ellsworth	36	222	14	15	1	3.81
B. Buhl	32	184	13	11	0	4.39
C. Koonce	38	173	7	9	0	3.69
T. Abernathy	**84**	136	4	6	**31**	2.57
L. McDaniel	71	129	5	6	2	2.59
B. Faul	17	97	6	6	0	3.54

Houston

W-65 L-97

Lum Harris

POS	Player	AB	BA	HR	RBI	PO	A	E	DP	TC/G	FA
1B	W. Bond	407	.263	7	47	650	49	12	52	9.6	.983
2B	J. Morgan	601	.271	14	40	348	492	**27**	82	5.5	.969
SS	B. Lillis	408	.221	0	20	188	273	15	49	4.6	.968
3B	B. Aspromonte	578	.263	5	52	123	281	16	25	2.9	.962
RF	R. Staub	410	.256	14	63	202	12	11	1	2.0	.951
CF	J. Wynn	564	.275	22	73	382	13	9	1	2.6	.978
LF	L. Maye	415	.251	3	36	177	6	9	1	1.9	.953
C	R. Brand	391	.235	2	37	585	54	8	8	6.3	.988
OF	J. Gaines	229	.227	6	31	83	1	8	0	1.4	.913
1B	J. Gentile	227	.242	7	31	544	43	4	41	8.7	.993
SS	E. Kasko	215	.247	1	10	96	152	6	27	4.3	.976

Pitcher	G	IP	W	L	SV	ERA
B. Bruce	35	230	9	18	0	3.72
D. Farrell	33	208	11	11	1	3.50
D. Nottebart	29	158	4	15	0	4.67
L. Dierker	26	147	7	8	0	3.50
D. Giusti	38	131	8	7	3	4.32
C. Raymond	33	96	7	4	5	2.90
J. Owens	50	71	6	5	8	3.28
R. Taylor	32	58	1	5	4	6.40
H. Woodeshick	27	32	3	4	3	3.06

New York

W-50 L-112

Casey Stengel
W-31 L-64

Wes Westrum
W-19 L-48

POS	Player	AB	BA	HR	RBI	PO	A	E	DP	TC/G	FA
1B	E. Kranepool	525	.253	10	53	1375	93	12	116	10.1	.992
2B	C. Hiller	286	.238	5	21	145	182	14	39	4.3	.959
SS	R. McMillan	528	.242	1	42	248	477	27	80	4.9	.964
3B	C. Smith	499	.244	16	62	119	281	18	27	3.2	.957
RF	J. Lewis	477	.245	15	45	257	14	7	3	2.0	.975
CF	J. Hickman	369	.236	15	40	136	3	5	0	1.6	.965
LF	R. Swoboda	399	.228	19	50	188	9	11	2	1.9	.947
C	C. Cannizzaro	251	.183	0	7	435	69	**12**	8	4.6	.977
OF	J. Christopher	437	.249	5	40	180	3	2	0	1.7	.989
UT	B. Klaus	288	.191	2	12	179	254	11	54		.975
2B	R. Hunt	196	.240	1	10	106	128	5	17	5.2	.979

Pitcher	G	IP	W	L	SV	ERA
J. Fisher	43	254	8	**24**	1	3.94
A. Jackson	37	205	8	20	1	4.34
W. Spahn	20	126	4	12	0	4.36
G. Cisco	35	112	4	8	0	4.49
T. McGraw	37	98	2	7	1	3.32
T. Parsons	35	91	1	10	1	4.67
G. Kroll	32	87	6	6	1	4.45

BATTING AND BASE RUNNING LEADERS

Batting Average

R. Clemente, PIT	.329
H. Aaron, MIL	.318
W. Mays, SF	.317
B. Williams, CHI	.315
P. Rose, CIN	.312

Slugging Average

W. Mays, SF	.645
H. Aaron, MIL	.560
B. Williams, CHI	.552
F. Robinson, CIN	.540
W. McCovey, SF	.539

Home Runs

W. Mays, SF	52
W. McCovey, SF	39
B. Williams, CHI	34
F. Robinson, CIN	33
R. Santo, CHI	33

Total Bases

W. Mays, SF	360
B. Williams, CHI	356
V. Pinson, CIN	324
H. Aaron, MIL	319
D. Johnson, CIN	317

Runs Batted In

D. Johnson, CIN	130
F. Robinson, CIN	113
W. Mays, SF	112
B. Williams, CHI	108
W. Stargell, PIT	107

Stolen Bases

M. Wills, LA	94
L. Brock, STL	63
J. Wynn, HOU	43
T. Harper, CIN	35
W. Davis, LA	25

PITCHING LEADERS

Winning Percentage

S. Koufax, LA	.765
J. Maloney, CIN	.690
S. Ellis, CIN	.688
T. Cloninger, MIL	.686
J. Bunning, PHI	.679

Earned Run Average

S. Koufax, LA	2.04
J. Marichal, SF	2.13
V. Law, PIT	2.15
J. Maloney, CIN	2.54
J. Bunning, PHI	2.60

Wins

S. Koufax, LA	26
T. Cloninger, MIL	24
D. Drysdale, LA	23
S. Ellis, CIN	22
J. Marichal, SF	22

Saves

T. Abernathy, CHI	31
F. Linzy, SF	21
B. McCool, CIN	21
A. McBean, PIT	18
H. Woodeshick, HOU, STL	18
B. O'Dell, MIL	18

Strikeouts

S. Koufax, LA	382
B. Veale, PIT	276
B. Gibson, STL	270
J. Bunning, PHI	268
J. Maloney, CIN	244

Complete Games

S. Koufax, LA	27
J. Marichal, SF	24
B. Gibson, STL	20
D. Drysdale, LA	20
T. Cloninger, MIL	16

NATIONAL LEAGUE 1965, *cont.*

BATTING AND BASE RUNNING LEADERS

Hits

P. Rose, CIN	209
V. Pinson, CIN	204
B. Williams, CHI	203
R. Clemente, PIT	194

Base on Balls

J. Morgan, HOU	97
W. McCovey, SF	88
R. Santo, CHI	88
J. Wynn, HOU	84

Home Run Percentage

W. Mays, SF	9.3
W. McCovey, SF	7.2
M. Jones, MIL	6.2
E. Mathews, MIL	5.9

Runs

T. Harper, CIN	126
W. Mays, SF	118
P. Rose, CIN	117
B. Williams, CHI	115

Doubles

H. Aaron, MIL	40
B. Williams, CHI	39
L. Brock, STL	35
P. Rose, CIN	35

Triples

J. Callison, PHI	16
R. Clemente, PIT	14
D. Clendenon, PIT	14
D. Allen, PHI	14

PITCHING LEADERS

Fewest Hits/9 Innings

S. Koufax, LA	5.79
J. Maloney, CIN	6.66
J. Marichal, SF	6.83
B. Bolin, SF	6.90

Shutouts

J. Marichal, SF	10
S. Koufax, LA	8
B. Veale, PIT	7
J. Bunning, PHI	7
D. Drysdale, LA	7

Fewest Walks/9 Innings

J. Marichal, SF	1.40
V. Law, PIT	1.45
B. Bruce, HOU	1.49
D. Farrell, HOU	1.51

Most Strikeouts/9 Inn.

S. Koufax, LA	10.24
B. Veale, PIT	9.34
J. Maloney, CIN	8.60
J. Bunning, PHI	8.29

Innings

S. Koufax, LA	336
D. Drysdale, LA	308
B. Gibson, STL	299
C. Short, PHI	297

Games Pitched

T. Abernathy, CHI	84
H. Woodeshick, HOU, STL	78
L. McDaniel, CHI	71
J. Baldschun, PHI	65

							Batting							Fielding			Pitching					
	W	L	PCT	GB	R	OR	2B	3B	HR	BA	SA	SB	E	DP	FA	CG	BB	SO	ShO	SV	ERA
Los Angeles	97	65	.599		608	**521**	193	32	78	.245	.335	**172**	134	135	.979	**58**	425	1079	**23**	34	**2.81**
San Francisco	95	67	.586	2	682	593	169	43	159	.252	.385	47	148	124	.976	42	408	1060	17	**42**	3.20
Pittsburgh	90	72	.556	7	675	580	217	57	111	.265	.382	51	152	**189**	.977	49	469	882	17	27	3.01
Cincinnati	89	73	.549	8	**825**	704	**268**	**61**	183	**.273**	**.439**	82	**117**	142	**.981**	43	587	**1113**	9	34	3.88
Milwaukee	86	76	.531	11	708	633	243	28	**196**	.256	.416	64	140	145	.978	43	541	966	4	38	3.52
Philadelphia	85	76	.528	11.5	654	667	205	53	144	.250	.384	46	157	153	.975	50	466	1071	18	21	3.53
St. Louis	80	81	.497	16.5	707	674	234	46	109	.254	.371	100	130	152	.979	40	467	916	11	35	3.77
Chicago	72	90	.444	25	635	723	202	33	134	.238	.358	65	171	166	.974	33	481	855	9	35	3.78
Houston	65	97	.401	32	569	711	188	42	97	.237	.340	90	166	130	.974	29	**388**	931	7	26	3.84
New York	50	112	.309	47	495	752	203	27	107	.221	.327	28	171	153	.974	29	498	776	11	14	4.06
					6558	6558	2122	422	1318	.249	.374	745	1486	1489	.977	416	4730	9649	126	306	3.54

AMERICAN LEAGUE 1965

Minnesota

W-102 L-60

Sam Mele

POS	Player	AB	BA	HR	RBI	PO	A	E	DP	TC/G	FA	Pitcher	G	IP	W	L	SV	ERA
1B	D. Mincher	346	.251	22	65	818	45	7	64	8.8	.992	M. Grant	41	270	**21**	7	0	3.30
2B	J. Kindall	342	.196	6	36	242	252	19	62	4.8	.963	J. Kaat	45	264	18	11	2	2.83
SS	Z. Versalles	**666**	.273	19	77	248	487	**39**	**105**	4.8	.950	J. Perry	36	168	12	7	0	2.63
3B	R. Rollins	469	.249	5	32	112	229	15	21	3.2	.958	C. Pascual	27	156	9	3	0	3.35
RF	T. Oliva	576	**.321**	16	98	284	10	11	3	2.1	.964	D. Boswell	27	106	6	5	0	3.40
CF	J. Hall	522	.285	20	86	282	7	7	2	2.1	.976	A. Worthington	62	80	10	7	21	2.13
LF	B. Allison	438	.233	23	78	231	11	7	4	2.0	.972	J. Merritt	16	77	5	4	2	3.17
C	E. Battey	394	.297	6	60	652	56	**10**	**10**	5.6	.986	J. Klippstein	56	76	9	3	5	2.24
13	H. Killebrew	401	.269	25	75	743	113	12	67		.986	D. Stigman	33	70	4	2	4	4.37
OF	S. Valdespino	245	.261	1	22	94	4	1	1	1.7	.990	B. Pleis	41	51	4	4	4	2.98
OF	J. Nossek	170	.218	2	16	64	1	2	1	1.4	.970							

Chicago

W-95 L-67

Al Lopez

POS	Player	AB	BA	HR	RBI	PO	A	E	DP	TC/G	FA	Pitcher	G	IP	W	L	SV	ERA
1B	B. Skowron	559	.274	18	78	**1297**	74	8	**116**	9.5	.994	J. Horlen	34	219	13	13	0	2.88
2B	D. Buford	586	.283	10	47	326	357	13	93	5.0	.981	J. Buzhardt	32	189	13	8	1	3.01
SS	R. Hansen	587	.235	11	66	287	**527**	26	97	**5.2**	.969	T. John	39	184	14	7	3	3.09
3B	P. Ward	507	.247	10	57	97	319	21	22	3.3	.952	G. Peters	33	176	10	12	0	3.62
RF	F. Robinson	577	.265	14	66	254	6	4	0	1.7	.985	E. Fisher	**82**	165	15	7	24	2.40
CF	K. Berry	472	.218	12	42	331	6	7	1	2.2	.980	B. Howard	30	148	9	8	0	3.47
LF	D. Cater	514	.270	14	55	174	6	4	2	1.4	.978	H. Wilhelm	66	144	7	7	20	1.81
C	J. Martin	230	.261	2	21	348	41	7	4	3.5	.982							
C	J. Romano	356	.242	18	48	569	**61**	5	**10**	5.7	.992							
10	T. McCraw	273	.238	5	21	336	24	4	18		.989							
PH	S. Burgess	77	.286	2	24	17	3	0	0	4.0	1.000							

Baltimore

W-94 L-68

Hank Bauer

POS	Player	AB	BA	HR	RBI	PO	A	E	DP	TC/G	FA	Pitcher	G	IP	W	L	SV	ERA
1B	B. Powell	472	.248	17	72	538	52	5	50	7.6	.992	M. Pappas	34	221	13	9	0	2.60
2B	J. Adair	582	.259	7	66	**395**	**446**	12	99	**5.4**	**.986**	S. Barber	37	221	15	10	0	2.69
SS	L. Aparicio	564	.225	8	40	238	439	20	87	4.9	**.971**	D. McNally	35	199	11	6	0	2.85
3B	B. Robinson	559	.297	18	80	144	296	15	36	3.2	.967	W. Bunker	34	189	10	8	2	3.38
RF	R. Snyder	345	.270	1	29	188	4	0	0	1.8	1.000	S. Miller	67	119	14	7	24	1.89
CF	P. Blair	364	.234	5	25	241	5	2	0	2.1	.992	R. Roberts	20	115	5	7	0	3.38
LF	C. Blefary	462	.260	22	70	227	10	5	3	1.8	.979	D. Hall	48	94	11	8	12	3.07
C	D. Brown	255	.231	5	30	466	40	9	6	5.6	.983	J. Miller	16	93	6	4	0	3.18
1B	N. Siebern	297	.256	8	32	631	48	6	64	9.0	.991	J. Palmer	27	92	5	4	1	3.72
UT	B. Johnson	273	.242	5	27	310	106	9	29		.979							
OF	J. Brandt	243	.243	8	24	143	6	6	0	1.8	.961							
C	J. Orsino	232	.233	9	28	342	25	5	3	6.0	.987							
OF	S. Bowens	203	.163	7	20	108	3	2	1	1.7	.982							

Detroit

W-89 L-73

Bob Swift
W-24 L-18

Chuck Dressen
W-65 L-55

POS	Player	AB	BA	HR	RBI	PO	A	E	DP	TC/G	FA	Pitcher	G	IP	W	L	SV	ERA
1B	N. Cash	467	.266	30	82	1091	**97**	9	96	8.6	.992	M. Lolich	43	244	15	9	3	3.44
2B	J. Lumpe	502	.257	4	39	281	308	9	69	4.3	.985	D. McLain	33	220	16	6	1	2.61
SS	D. McAuliffe	404	.260	15	54	190	286	22	58	4.4	.956	H. Aguirre	32	208	14	10	0	3.59
3B	D. Wert	609	.261	12	54	163	331	12	33	3.1	**.976**	D. Wickersham	34	195	9	14	0	3.78
RF	A. Kaline	399	.281	18	72	193	2	3	0	1.8	.985	J. Sparma	30	167	13	8	0	3.18
CF	D. Demeter	389	.278	16	58	158	1	2	1	2.0	.988	L. Sherry	39	78	3	6	5	3.10
LF	W. Horton	512	.273	29	104	249	7	3	1	1.8	.988	T. Fox	42	78	6	4	10	2.78
C	B. Freehan	431	.234	10	43	**865**	57	4	4	**7.2**	.996	F. Gladding	46	70	6	2	5	2.83
OF	G. Brown	227	.256	10	43	108	1	3	0	2.0	.973	O. Pena	30	57	4	6	4	2.51
OF	J. Northrup	219	.205	2	16	82	0	2	0	1.6	.976							
SS	R. Oyler	194	.186	5	13	79	156	11	17	4.3	.955							
OF	G. Thomas	169	.213	3	10	87	4	5	0	1.6	.948							

AMERICAN LEAGUE 1965, *cont.*

Team	POS	Player	AB	BA	HR	RBI	PO	A	E	DP	TC/G	FA	Pitcher	G	IP	W	L	SV	ERA
Cleveland	1B	F. Whitfield	468	.293	26	90	932	80	7	79	8.4	.993	S. McDowell	42	273	17	11	4	**2.18**
W-87 L-75	2B	P. Gonzalez	400	.253	5	39	265	287	11	59	5.0	.980	L. Tiant	41	196	11	11	1	3.53
Birdie Tebbetts	SS	L. Brown	438	.253	8	40	167	262	10	55	4.6	.977	S. Siebert	39	189	16	8	1	2.43
	3B	M. Alvis	604	.247	21	61	**169**	264	19	17	2.9	.958	R. Terry	30	166	11	6	0	3.69
	RF	R. Colavito	592	.287	26	**108**	265	9	0	1	1.7	1.000	L. Stange	41	132	8	4	0	3.34
	CF	V. Davalillo	505	.301	5	40	320	5	4	0	2.5	.988	G. Bell	60	104	6	5	17	3.04
	LF	L. Wagner	517	.294	28	79	175	3	8	0	1.4	.957	J. Kralick	30	86	5	11	0	4.92
	C	J. Azcue	335	.230	2	35	714	53	5	2	7.1	.994	D. McMahon	58	85	3	3	11	3.28
	UT	C. Hinton	431	.255	18	54	408	71	13	30		.974							
	SS	D. Howser	307	.235	1	6	119	173	7	33	4.1	.977							
New York	1B	J. Pepitone	531	.247	18	62	1036	71	3	104	**9.7**	**.997**	M. Stottlemyre	37	**291**	20	9	0	2.63
W-77 L-85	2B	B. Richardson	664	.247	6	47	372	403	15	**121**	5.0	.981	W. Ford	37	244	16	13	1	3.24
Johnny Keane	SS	T. Kubek	339	.218	5	35	134	237	14	53	4.1	.964	A. Downing	35	212	12	14	0	3.40
	3B	C. Boyer	514	.251	18	58	134	**354**	16	**46**	**3.4**	.968	J. Bouton	30	151	4	15	0	4.82
	RF	H. Lopez	283	.261	7	39	94	3	6	0	1.4	.942	B. Stafford	22	111	3	8	0	3.56
	CF	T. Tresh	602	.279	26	74	283	11	9	1	2.0	.970	P. Ramos	65	92	5	5	19	2.92
	LF	M. Mantle	361	.255	19	46	165	3	6	0	1.6	.966	H. Reniff	51	85	3	4	3	3.80
	C	E. Howard	391	.233	9	45	614	43	6	6	7.0	.991	P. Mikkelsen	41	82	4	9	1	3.28
	SS	P. Linz	285	.207	2	16	126	205	16	29	4.9	.954							
	OF	R. Repoz	218	.220	12	28	133	1	1	0	2.0	.993							
	1B	R. Barker	205	.254	7	31	398	45	4	41	7.3	.991							
	OF	R. Maris	155	.239	8	27	66	1	2	0	1.6	.971							
California	1B	V. Power	197	.259	1	20	419	41	2	35	4.3	.996	F. Newman	36	261	14	16	0	2.93
W-75 L-87	2B	B. Knoop	465	.269	7	43	331	402	**22**	89	5.3	.971	D. Chance	36	226	15	10	0	3.15
Bill Rigney	SS	J. Fregosi	602	.277	15	64	**312**	481	26	93	5.1	.968	M. Lopez	35	215	14	13	1	2.93
	3B	P. Schaal	483	.224	9	45	101	321	13	20	2.8	.970	G. Brunet	41	197	9	11	2	2.56
	RF	A. Pearson	360	.278	4	21	166	5	2	1	1.7	.988	B. Lee	69	131	9	7	23	1.92
	CF	J. Cardenal	512	.250	11	57	286	12	11	2	2.4	.964	R. May	30	124	4	9	0	3.92
	LF	W. Smith	459	.261	14	57	187	10	4	1	1.6	.980							
	C	B. Rodgers	411	.209	1	32	682	52	7	7	5.8	.991							
	1B	J. Adcock	349	.241	14	47	789	45	3	68	8.6	.996							
	OF	L. Clinton	222	.243	1	8	107	6	2	1	1.6	.983							
Washington	1B	D. Nen	246	.260	6	31	519	61	4	48	9.0	.993	P. Richert	34	194	15	12	0	2.60
W-70 L-92	2B	D. Blasingame	403	.223	1	18	235	248	8	68	4.5	.984	P. Ortega	35	180	12	15	0	5.11
Gil Hodges	SS	E. Brinkman	444	.185	5	35	292	369	25	76	4.6	.964	B. Narum	46	174	4	12	0	4.46
	3B	K. McMullen	555	.263	18	54	155	299	**22**	29	3.4	.954	M. McCormick	44	158	8	8	1	3.36
	RF	W. Held	332	.247	16	54	175	5	7	2	1.8	.963	B. Daniels	33	116	5	13	1	4.72
	CF	D. Lock	418	.215	16	39	278	6	9	3	2.2	.969	S. Ridzik	63	110	6	4	8	4.02
	LF	F. Howard	516	.289	21	84	204	5	4	0	1.5	.981	H. Koplitz	33	107	4	7	1	4.05
	C	M. Brumley	216	.208	3	15	376	25	4	2	6.1	.990	R. Kline	74	99	7	6	**29**	2.63
	2S	K. Hamlin	362	.273	4	22	185	210	12	45		.971							
	OF	W. Kirkland	312	.231	14	54	151	3	2	0	1.7	.987							
	OF	J. King	258	.213	14	49	127	7	1	1	1.5	.993							
	UT	D. Zimmer	226	.199	2	17	181	81	12	7		.956							
	1B	J. Cunningham	201	.229	3	20	393	24	6	44	7.2	.986							
	1B	B. Chance	199	.256	4	14	391	25	5	39	8.8	.988							
	C	D. Camilli	193	.192	3	18	319	23	7	2	5.9	.980							
Boston	1B	L. Thomas	521	.271	22	75	1035	**97**	**18**	86	9.1	.984	E. Wilson	36	231	13	14	0	3.98
W-62 L-100	2B	F. Mantilla	534	.275	18	92	251	286	13	64	4.5	.976	B. Monbouquette	35	229	10	**18**	0	3.70
Billy Herman	SS	R. Petrocelli	323	.232	13	33	151	278	19	45	4.8	.958	D. Morehead	34	193	10	**18**	0	4.06
	3B	F. Malzone	364	.239	3	34	79	170	8	19	2.7	.969	J. Lonborg	32	185	9	17	0	4.47
	RF	T. Conigliaro	521	.269	**32**	82	277	11	7	1	2.2	.976	D. Bennett	34	142	5	7	0	4.38
	CF	L. Green	373	.276	7	24	198	2	4	1	2.1	.980	D. Radatz	63	124	9	11	22	3.91
	LF	C. Yastrzemski	494	.312	20	72	222	11	3	2	1.8	.987							
	C	B. Tillman	368	.215	6	35	676	45	9	6	6.9	.988							
	3B	D. Jones	367	.270	5	37	63	163	17	14	3.0	.930							
	OF	J. Gosger	324	.256	9	35	195	4	5	2	2.5	.975							
	SS	E. Bressoud	296	.226	8	25	147	195	13	45	4.1	.963							
	2B	C. Schilling	171	.240	3	9	90	116	5	22	5.1	.976							
	1B	T. Horton	163	.294	7	23	311	24	7	30	7.8	.980							
Kansas City	1B	K. Harrelson	483	.238	23	66	1044	70	9	93	9.0	.992	F. Talbot	39	198	10	12	0	4.14
W-59 L-103	2B	D. Green	474	.232	15	55	252	341	12	73	4.8	.980	R. Sheldon	32	187	10	8	0	3.95
Mel McGaha	SS	B. Campaneris	578	.270	6	42	187	269	30	50	4.5	.938	J. O'Donoghue	34	178	9	**18**	0	3.95
W-5 L-21	3B	E. Charles	480	.269	8	56	150	251	12	28	3.2	.971	D. Segui	40	163	5	15	0	4.64
Haywood Sullivan	RF	M. Hershberger	494	.231	5	48	238	14	3	7	1.8	.988	C. Hunter	32	133	8	8	0	4.26
W-54 L-82	CF	J. Landis	364	.239	3	36	258	0	4	0	2.4	.985	W. Stock	62	100	0	4	4	5.24
	LF	T. Reynolds	270	.237	1	22	154	8	3	2	2.0	.982	J. Wyatt	65	89	2	6	18	3.25
	C	B. Bryan	325	.252	14	51	527	44	9	6	6.1	.984	D. Mossi	51	55	5	8	7	3.74
	UT	W. Causey	513	.261	3	34	221	313	15	60		.973	J. Aker	34	51	4	3	3	3.16
	OF	J. Tartabull	218	.312	1	19	133	5	2	0	2.6	.986							
	C	R. Lachemann	216	.227	9	29	361	27	8	3	5.3	.980							
	OF	N. Mathews	184	.212	2	15	103	1	2	0	1.9	.981							
	1B	J. Gentile	118	.246	10	22	239	17	5	24	7.5	.981							

BATTING AND BASE RUNNING LEADERS

Batting Average

T. Oliva, MIN	.321
C. Yastrzemski, BOS	.312
V. Davalillo, CLE	.301
B. Robinson, BAL	.297
L. Wagner, CLE	.294

Slugging Average

C. Yastrzemski, BOS	.536
T. Conigliaro, BOS	.512
N. Cash, DET	.512
L. Wagner, CLE	.495
T. Oliva, MIN	.491

Home Runs

T. Conigliaro, BOS	32
N. Cash, DET	30
W. Horton, DET	29
L. Wagner, CLE	28

PITCHING LEADERS

Winning Percentage

M. Grant, MIN	.750
D. McLain, DET	.727
M. Stottlemyre, NY	.690
E. Fisher, CHI	.682
S. Siebert, CLE	.667

Earned Run Average

S. McDowell, CLE	2.18
E. Fisher, CHI	2.40
S. Siebert, CLE	2.43
G. Brunet, CAL	2.56
P. Richert, WAS	2.60

Wins

M. Grant, MIN	21
M. Stottlemyre, NY	20
J. Kaat, MIN	18
S. McDowell, CLE	17

AMERICAN LEAGUE 1965, *cont.*

BATTING AND BASE RUNNING LEADERS

Total Bases		Runs Batted In		Stolen Bases		Saves	
Z. Versalles, MIN	308	R. Colavito, CLE	108	B. Campaneris, KC	51	R. Kline, WAS	29
T. Tresh, NY	287	W. Horton, DET	104	J. Cardenal, CAL	37	S. Miller, BAL	24
T. Oliva, MIN	283	T. Oliva, MIN	98	Z. Versalles, MIN	27	E. Fisher, CHI	24
R. Colavito, CLE	277	F. Mantilla, BOS	92	V. Davalillo, CLE	26	B. Lee, CAL	23
T. Conigliaro, BOS	267	F. Whitfield, CLE	90	L. Aparicio, BAL	26	D. Radatz, BOS	22

Hits		Base on Balls		Home Run Percentage		Fewest Hits/9 Innings	
T. Oliva, MIN	185	R. Colavito, CLE	93	N. Cash, DET	6.4	S. McDowell, CLE	5.87
Z. Versalles, MIN	182	C. Blefary, BAL	88	T. Conigliaro, BOS	6.1	E. Fisher, CHI	6.42
R. Colavito, CLE	170	F. Mantilla, BOS	79	W. Horton, DET	5.7	S. Siebert, CLE	6.63
T. Tresh, NY	168	N. Cash, DET	77	L. Wagner, CLE	5.4	P. Richert, WAS	6.77

Runs		Doubles		Triples		Most Strikeouts/9 Inn.	
Z. Versalles, MIN	126	C. Yastrzemski, BOS	45	B. Campaneris, KC	12	S. McDowell, CLE	10.71
T. Oliva, MIN	107	Z. Versalles, MIN	45	Z. Versalles, MIN	12	S. Siebert, CLE	9.11
T. Tresh, NY	94	T. Oliva, MIN	40	L. Aparicio, BAL	10	M. Lolich, DET	8.35
D. Buford, CHI	93	T. Tresh, NY	29	W. Smith, CAL	9	D. McLain, DET	7.84

PITCHING LEADERS

Strikeouts		Complete Games	
S. McDowell, CLE	325	M. Stottlemyre, NY	18
M. Lolich, DET	226	S. McDowell, CLE	14
D. McLain, DET	192	M. Grant, MIN	14
S. Siebert, CLE	191	D. McLain, DET	13
A. Downing, NY	179		

Shutouts		Fewest Walks/9 Innings	
M. Grant, MIN	6	R. Terry, CLE	1.25
D. McLain, DET	4	B. Monbouquette, BOS	1.57
D. Chance, CAL	4	J. Horlen, CHI	1.60
J. Horlen, CHI	4	W. Ford, NY	1.84
M. Stottlemyre, NY	4		

Innings		Games Pitched	
M. Stottlemyre, NY	291	E. Fisher, CHI	82
S. McDowell, CLE	273	R. Kline, WAS	74
M. Grant, MIN	270	B. Lee, CAL	69
J. Kaat, MIN	264	J. Dickson, KC	68

	W	L	PCT	GB	R	OR	Batting 2B	3B	HR	BA	SA	SB	Fielding E	DP	FA	Pitching CG	BB	SO	ShO	SV	ERA
Minnesota	102	60	.630		**774**	600	**257**	42	150	**.254**	.399	92	172	158	.973	32	503	934	12	45	3.14
Chicago	95	67	.586	7	647	**555**	200	38	125	.246	.364	50	127	156	.980	21	**460**	946	14	**53**	2.99
Baltimore	94	68	.580	8	641	578	227	38	125	.238	.363	67	126	152	.980	32	510	939	**15**	41	**2.98**
Detroit	89	73	.549	13	680	602	190	27	162	.238	.374	57	116	126	**.981**	**45**	509	1069	14	31	3.35
Cleveland	87	75	.537	15	663	613	198	21	156	.250	.379	109	**114**	127	**.981**	41	500	**1156**	13	41	3.30
New York	77	85	.475	25	611	604	196	31	149	.235	.364	35	137	**166**	.978	41	511	1001	11	31	3.28
California	75	87	.463	27	527	569	200	36	92	.239	.341	107	123	149	**.981**	39	563	847	14	33	3.17
Washington	70	92	.432	32	591	721	179	33	136	.228	.350	30	143	148	.976	21	633	867	8	40	3.93
Boston	62	100	.383	40	669	791	244	40	**165**	.251	**.400**	47	162	129	.974	33	543	993	9	25	4.24
Kansas City	59	103	.364	43	585	755	186	**59**	110	.240	.358	**110**	139	142	.977	18	574	882	7	32	4.24
					6388	6388	2077	365	1370	.242	.369	704	1359	1453	.978	323	5306	9634	117	372	3.46

NATIONAL LEAGUE 1966

	POS	Player	AB	BA	HR	RBI	PO	A	E	DP	TC/G	FA	Pitcher	G	IP	W	L	SV	ERA
Los Angeles	1B	W. Parker	475	.253	12	51	1118	70	9	74	8.6	.992	S. Koufax	41	**323**	**27**	9	0	**1.73**
W-95 L-67	2B	J. Lefebvre	544	.274	24	74	246	332	12	59	5.0	.980	D. Drysdale	40	274	13	16	0	3.42
Walter Alston	SS	M. Wills	594	.273	1	39	227	453	23	79	5.1	.967	C. Osteen	39	240	17	14	0	2.85
	3B	J. Kennedy	274	.201	3	24	39	127	6	10	2.0	.965	D. Sutton	37	226	12	12	0	2.99
	RF	R. Fairly	351	.288	14	61	110	2	3	0	1.2	.974	P. Regan	65	117	14	1	**21**	1.62
	CF	W. Davis	624	.284	11	61	347	9	11	0	2.4	.970	B. Miller	46	84	4	2	5	2.77
	LF	L. Johnson	526	.272	17	73	249	8	4	2	1.8	.985	R. Perranoski	55	82	6	7	7	3.18
	C	J. Roseboro	445	.276	9	53	**904**	65	7	11	**7.1**	.993							
	OF	T. Davis	313	.313	3	27	98	5	3	1	1.3	.972							
	3B	J. Gilliam	235	.217	1	16	40	103	7	8	2.1	.953							
	OF	A. Ferrara	115	.270	5	23	43	0	2	0	1.4	.956							

	POS	Player	AB	BA	HR	RBI	PO	A	E	DP	TC/G	FA	Pitcher	G	IP	W	L	SV	ERA
San Francisco	1B	W. McCovey	502	.295	36	96	1287	81	22	91	9.6	.984	J. Marichal	37	307	25	6	0	2.23
W-93 L-68	2B	H. Lanier	459	.231	3	37	254	313	5	66	5.1	.991	G. Perry	36	256	21	8	0	2.99
Herman Franks	SS	T. Fuentes	541	.261	9	40	145	233	17	44	5.2	.957	B. Bolin	36	224	11	10	1	2.89
	3B	J. Hart	578	.285	33	93	100	282	24	24	2.9	.941	R. Herbel	32	130	4	5	1	4.16
	RF	O. Brown	348	.233	7	33	163	12	4	1	1.6	.978	L. McDaniel	64	122	10	5	6	2.66
	CF	W. Mays	552	.288	37	103	370	8	7	2	2.6	.982	R. Sadecki	26	105	3	7	0	5.40
	LF	J. Alou	370	.259	1	20	141	4	5	1	1.5	.967	F. Linzy	51	100	7	11	16	2.96
	C	T. Haller	471	.240	27	67	797	57	8	5	6.3	.991	B. Priddy	38	91	6	3	1	3.96
	UT	J. Davenport	305	.249	9	30	107	201	14	27		.957	J. Gibbon	37	81	4	6	1	3.67
	OF	L. Gabrielson	240	.217	4	16	72	1	4	0	1.1	.948							
	OF	C. Peterson	190	.237	2	19	62	2	0	1	1.3	1.000							

	POS	Player	AB	BA	HR	RBI	PO	A	E	DP	TC/G	FA	Pitcher	G	IP	W	L	SV	ERA
Pittsburgh	1B	D. Clendenon	571	.299	28	98	**1452**	96	**24**	**182**	**10.3**	.985	B. Veale	38	268	16	12	0	3.02
W-92 L-70	2B	B. Mazeroski	621	.262	16	82	**411**	**538**	8	**161**	**5.9**	**.992**	W. Fryman	36	182	12	9	1	3.81
Harry Walker	SS	G. Alley	579	.299	7	43	235	472	15	**128**	5.0	.979	V. Law	31	178	12	8	0	4.05
	3B	B. Bailey	380	.279	13	46	57	201	12	20	2.8	.956	S. Blass	34	156	11	7	0	3.87
	RF	R. Clemente	638	.317	29	119	318	17	12	3	2.3	.965	T. Sisk	34	150	10	5	1	4.14
	CF	M. Alou	535	**.342**	2	27	264	11	8	3	2.1	.972	P. Mikkelsen	71	126	9	8	14	3.07
	LF	W. Stargell	485	.315	33	102	180	9	11	0	1.6	.945	D. Cardwell	32	102	6	6	1	4.60
	C	J. Pagliaroni	374	.235	11	49	613	37	2	6	5.5	**.997**	A. McBean	47	87	4	3	3	3.22
	3B	J. Pagan	368	.264	4	54	57	166	12	18	2.8	.949	R. Face	54	70	6	6	18	2.70
	OF	M. Mota	322	.332	5	46	150	3	1	0	1.6	.994							

NATIONAL LEAGUE 1966, *cont.*

Team	POS	Player	AB	BA	HR	RBI	PO	A	E	DP	TC/G	FA	Pitcher	G	IP	W	L	SV	ERA
Philadelphia	1B	B. White	577	.276	22	103	1422	**109**	9	118	9.7	**.994**	J. Bunning	43	314	19	14	1	2.41
	2B	C. Rojas	626	.268	6	55	218	288	9	68	4.9	.983	C. Short	42	272	20	10	0	3.54
	SS	D. Groat	584	.260	2	53	260	454	19	79	**5.3**	.974	L. Jackson	35	247	15	13	0	2.99
W-87 L-75	3B	D. Allen	524	.317	40	110	81	180	9	15	3.0	.967	B. Buhl	32	132	6	8	1	4.77
	RF	J. Callison	612	.276	11	55	275	12	3	2	1.9	.990	R. Culp	34	111	7	4	1	5.04
	CF	J. Briggs	255	.282	10	23	126	3	3	0	1.9	.977	D. Knowles	69	100	6	5	13	3.05
Gene Mauch	LF	T. Gonzalez	384	.286	6	40	206	7	3	1	1.8	.986	R. Wise	22	99	5	6	0	3.71
	C	C. Dalrymple	331	.245	4	39	615	48	5	5	6.1	.993							
	23	T. Taylor	434	.242	5	40	187	281	9	45		.981							
	C	B. Uecker	207	.208	7	30	368	33	6	7	5.4	.985							
	OF	J. Brandt	164	.250	1	15	78	3	1	0	1.2	.988							
	1B	F. Alou	**666**	.327	31	74	769	53	10	63	9.2	.988	T. Cloninger	39	258	14	11	1	4.12
Atlanta	2B	W. Woodward	455	.264	0	43	154	208	10	46	4.7	.973	K. Johnson	32	216	14	8	0	3.30
	SS	D. Menke	454	.251	15	60	165	282	21	50	4.4	.955	D. Lemaster	27	171	11	8	0	3.74
	3B	E. Mathews	452	.250	16	53	114	237	20	31	2.9	.946	C. Carroll	**73**	144	8	7	11	2.37
W-85 L-77	RF	H. Aaron	603	.279	**44**	**127**	315	12	4	5	2.1	.988	D. Kelley	20	81	7	5	0	3.22
	CF	M. Jones	417	.264	23	66	251	1	5	0	2.3	.981	W. Blasingame	16	68	3	7	0	5.32
Bobby Bragan	LF	R. Carty	521	.326	15	76	226	8	7	0	1.9	.971	C. Olivo	47	66	5	4	7	4.23
W-52 L-59	C	J. Torre	546	.315	36	101	607	67	11	9	6.0	.984	T. Abernathy	38	65	4	4	4	3.86
Billy Hitchcock	2B	F. Bolling	227	.211	1	18	134	150	5	35	4.3	.983	B. O'Dell	24	41	2	3	6	2.40
W-33 L-18	C	G. Oliver	191	.194	8	24	286	22	3	3	6.5	.990							
	P	T. Cloninger	111	.234	5	23	14	43	**8**	1	1.7	.877							
	1B	O. Cepeda	452	.303	17	58	1109	62	13	111	9.9	.989	B. Gibson	35	280	21	12	0	2.44
St. Louis	2B	J. Javier	460	.228	7	31	306	364	13	89	4.7	.981	A. Jackson	36	233	13	15	0	2.51
	SS	D. Maxvill	394	.244	0	24	219	428	22	88	5.2	.967	R. Washburn	27	170	11	9	0	3.76
	3B	C. Smith	391	.266	10	43	84	213	11	26	2.9	.964	N. Briles	49	154	4	15	6	3.21
W-83 L-79	RF	M. Shannon	459	.288	16	64	247	10	4	4	2.0	.985	L. Jaster	26	152	11	5	0	3.26
	CF	C. Flood	626	.267	10	78	391	5	0	1	2.5	1.000	J. Hoerner	57	76	5	1	13	1.54
Red Schoendienst	LF	L. Brock	643	.285	15	46	269	9	19	1	1.9	.936							
	C	T. McCarver	543	.274	12	68	841	62	7	7	6.1	.992							
	2S	J. Buchek	284	.236	4	25	148	220	18	52		.953							
	3B	P. Gagliano	213	.254	2	15	30	77	2	7	2.7	.982							
	1B	T. Perez	257	.265	4	39	530	23	6	46	7.5	.989	J. Maloney	32	225	16	8	0	2.80
Cincinnati	2B	P. Rose	654	.313	16	70	385	344	14	79	5.3	.981	S. Ellis	41	221	12	19	0	5.29
	SS	L. Cardenas	568	.255	20	81	**279**	446	15	87	4.6	**.980**	M. Pappas	33	210	12	11	0	4.29
	3B	T. Helms	542	.284	9	49	110	208	13	16	2.9	.961	J. O'Toole	25	142	5	7	0	3.55
W-76 L-84	RF	T. Harper	553	.278	5	31	257	5	1	2	1.8	.996	J. Nuxhall	35	130	6	8	0	4.50
	CF	V. Pinson	618	.288	16	76	344	9	13	1	2.4	.964	D. Nottebart	59	111	5	4	11	3.07
Don Heffner	LF	D. Johnson	505	.257	24	81	141	4	3	1	1.4	.980	B. McCool	57	105	8	8	18	2.48
W-37 L-46	C	J. Edwards	282	.191	6	39	617	40	5	3	6.8	.992	T. Davidson	54	85	5	4	4	3.90
Dave Bristol	C	D. Pavletich	235	.294	12	38	323	30	9	2	6.6	.975							
W-39 L-38	OF	A. Shamsky	234	.231	21	47	104	3	3	1	1.5	.973							
	1B	G. Coleman	227	.251	5	37	399	29	6	33	6.7	.986							
	1B	C. Harrison	434	.256	9	52	974	78	8	68	9.3	.992	M. Cuellar	38	227	12	10	2	2.22
Houston	2B	J. Morgan	425	.285	5	42	256	316	21	61	5.1	.965	D. Giusti	34	210	15	14	0	4.20
	SS	S. Jackson	596	.292	3	25	270	449	**37**	73	5.0	.951	L. Dierker	29	187	10	8	0	3.18
	3B	B. Aspromonte	560	.252	8	52	149	261	16	18	2.9	**.962**	D. Farrell	32	153	6	10	2	4.60
W-72 L-90	RF	R. Staub	554	.280	13	81	289	13	12	2	2.1	.962	B. Bruce	25	130	3	13	0	5.34
	CF	J. Wynn	418	.256	18	62	259	6	6	4	2.6	.978	B. Latman	31	103	2	7	1	2.71
Grady Hatton	LF	L. Maye	358	.288	9	36	145	4	8	0	1.6	.949	C. Raymond	62	92	7	5	16	3.13
	C	J. Bateman	433	.279	17	70	731	63	**15**	**14**	6.7	.981	J. Owens	40	50	4	7	2	4.68
	OF	D. Nicholson	280	.246	10	31	139	11	5	0	1.7	.968							
	OF	R. Davis	194	.247	2	19	98	9	2	1	2.3	.982							
	UT	B. Lillis	164	.232	0	11	99	109	10	24		.954							
	UT	F. Mantilla	151	.219	6	22	124	46	4	11		.977							
	1B	E. Kranepool	464	.254	16	57	1161	85	10	100	9.5	.992	J. Fisher	38	230	11	14	0	3.68
New York	2B	R. Hunt	479	.288	3	33	295	384	21	81	5.7	.970	D. Ribant	39	188	11	9	3	3.20
	SS	E. Bressoud	405	.225	10	49	135	252	16	52	4.3	.960	B. Shaw	26	168	11	10	0	3.92
	3B	K. Boyer	496	.266	14	61	113	292	21	33	3.3	.951	J. Hamilton	57	149	6	13	13	3.93
W-66 L-95	RF	A. Luplow	334	.251	7	31	147	4	2	1	1.5	.987	R. Gardner	41	134	4	8	1	5.12
	CF	C. Jones	495	.275	8	57	275	10	6	2	2.3	.979	B. Friend	22	86	5	8	1	4.40
Wes Westrum	LF	R. Swoboda	342	.222	8	50	145	7	2	0	1.6	.987	D. Selma	30	81	4	6	1	4.24
	C	J. Grote	317	.237	3	31	516	55	11	7	5.1	.981	T. McGraw	15	62	2	9	0	5.34
	UT	C. Hiller	254	.280	2	14	110	153	5	32		.981							
	SS	R. McMillan	220	.214	1	12	112	203	8	35	4.5	.975							
	OF	L. Elliot	199	.246	5	32	73	10	8	0	1.7	.912							
	OF	J. Lewis	166	.193	5	20	77	2	1	1	1.6	.988							
	1B	E. Banks	511	.272	15	75	1178	81	10	88	9.8	.992	D. Ellsworth	38	269	8	**22**	0	3.98
Chicago	2B	G. Beckert	656	.287	1	59	373	402	**24**	89	5.3	.970	K. Holtzman	34	221	11	16	0	3.79
	SS	D. Kessinger	533	.274	1	43	202	**474**	35	68	4.8	.951	F. Jenkins	60	182	6	8	5	3.31
	3B	R. Santo	561	.312	30	94	**150**	**391**	**25**	**36**	**3.7**	.956	B. Hands	41	159	8	13	2	4.58
W-59 L-103	RF	B. Williams	648	.276	29	91	319	9	8	3	2.1	.976	C. Koonce	45	109	5	5	2	3.81
	CF	A. Phillips	416	.262	16	36	258	14	6	2	2.5	.978	B. Hendley	43	90	4	5	7	3.91
Leo Durocher	LF	B. Browne	419	.243	16	51	200	3	7	0	1.8	.967	C. Simmons	19	77	4	7	0	4.07
	C	R. Hundley	526	.236	19	63	871	**85**	14	8	6.5	.986							
	01	J. Boccabella	206	.228	6	25	230	18	1	13		.996							
	OF	G. Altman	185	.222	5	17	42	4	2	0	1.1	.958							

NATIONAL LEAGUE 1966, *cont.*

BATTING AND BASE RUNNING LEADERS

Batting Average
- M. Alou, PIT .342
- F. Alou, ATL .327
- R. Carty, ATL .326
- D. Allen, PHI .317
- R. Clemente, PIT .317

Slugging Average
- D. Allen, PHI .632
- W. McCovey, SF .586
- W. Stargell, PIT .581
- J. Torre, ATL .560
- W. Mays, SF .556

Home Runs
- H. Aaron, ATL 44
- D. Allen, PHI 40
- W. Mays, SF 37
- W. McCovey, SF 36
- J. Torre, ATL 36

Total Bases
- F. Alou, ATL 355
- R. Clemente, PIT 342
- D. Allen, PHI 331
- H. Aaron, ATL 325
- W. Mays, SF 307

Runs Batted In
- H. Aaron, ATL 127
- R. Clemente, PIT 119
- D. Allen, PHI 110
- W. Mays, SF 103
- B. White, PHI 103

Stolen Bases
- L. Brock, STL 74
- S. Jackson, HOU 49
- M. Wills, LA 38
- A. Phillips, PHI, CHI 32
- T. Harper, CIN 29

Hits
- F. Alou, ATL 218
- P. Rose, CIN 205
- R. Clemente, PIT 202
- G. Beckert, CHI 188

Base on Balls
- R. Santo, CHI 95
- J. Morgan, HOU 89
- W. McCovey, SF 76
- H. Aaron, ATL 76

Home Run Percentage
- D. Allen, PHI 7.6
- H. Aaron, ATL 7.3
- W. McCovey, SF 7.2
- W. Stargell, PIT 6.8

Runs
- F. Alou, ATL 122
- H. Aaron, ATL 117
- D. Allen, PHI 112
- R. Clemente, PIT 105

Doubles
- J. Callison, PHI 40
- P. Rose, CIN 38
- V. Pinson, CIN 35
- F. Alou, ATL 32

Triples
- T. McCarver, STL 13
- L. Brock, STL 12
- R. Clemente, PIT 11

PITCHING LEADERS

Winning Percentage
- J. Marichal, SF .806
- S. Koufax, LA .750
- G. Perry, SF .724
- C. Short, PHI .667
- J. Maloney, CIN .667

Earned Run Average
- S. Koufax, LA 1.73
- M. Cuellar, HOU 2.22
- J. Marichal, SF 2.23
- J. Bunning, PHI 2.41
- B. Gibson, STL 2.44

Wins
- S. Koufax, LA 27
- J. Marichal, SF 25
- G. Perry, SF 21
- B. Gibson, STL 21
- C. Short, PHI 20

Saves
- P. Regan, LA 21
- R. Face, PIT 18
- B. McCool, CIN 18
- C. Raymond, HOU 16
- F. Linzy, SF 16

Strikeouts
- S. Koufax, LA 317
- J. Bunning, PHI 252
- B. Veale, PIT 229
- B. Gibson, STL 225
- J. Marichal, SF 222

Complete Games
- S. Koufax, LA 27
- J. Marichal, SF 25
- B. Gibson, STL 20
- C. Short, PHI 19
- J. Bunning, PHI 16

Fewest Hits/9 Innings
- J. Marichal, SF 6.68
- S. Koufax, LA 6.72
- B. Gibson, STL 6.74
- J. Maloney, CIN 6.97

Shutouts
- 6 tied with 5

Fewest Walks/9 Innings
- J. Marichal, SF 1.05
- V. Law, PIT 1.22
- G. Perry, SF 1.41
- D. Drysdale, LA 1.48

Most Strikeouts/9 Inn.
- S. Koufax, LA 8.83
- J. Maloney, CIN 8.65
- D. Sutton, LA 8.34
- B. Veale, PIT 7.68

Innings
- S. Koufax, LA 323
- J. Bunning, PHI 314
- J. Marichal, SF 307
- B. Gibson, STL 280

Games Pitched
- C. Carroll, ATL 73
- P. Mikkelsen, PIT 71
- D. Knowles, PHI 69
- P. Regan, LA 65

							Batting						Fielding			Pitching					
	W	L	PCT	GB	R	OR	2B	3B	HR	BA	SA	SB	E	DP	FA	CG	BB	SO	ShO	SV	ERA
Los Angeles	95	67	.586		606	**490**	201	27	108	.256	.362	94	133	128	.979	**52**	**356**	**1084**	**20**	35	**2.62**
San Francisco	93	68	.578	1.5	675	626	195	31	181	.248	.392	29	168	131	.974	**52**	359	973	14	27	3.24
Pittsburgh	92	70	.568	3	759	641	**238**	**66**	158	**.279**	**.428**	64	141	**215**	.978	35	463	898	12	**43**	3.52
Philadelphia	87	75	.537	8	696	640	224	49	117	.258	.378	56	**113**	147	**.982**	**52**	412	928	15	23	3.57
Atlanta	85	77	.525	10	**782**	683	220	32	**207**	.263	.424	59	154	139	.976	37	485	884	10	36	3.68
St. Louis	83	79	.512	12	571	577	196	61	108	.251	.368	**144**	145	166	.977	47	448	892	19	32	3.11
Cincinnati	76	84	.475	18	692	702	232	33	149	.260	.395	70	122	133	.980	28	490	1043	10	35	4.08
Houston	72	90	.444	23	612	695	203	35	112	.255	.365	90	174	126	.972	34	391	929	13	26	3.76
New York	66	95	.410	28.5	587	761	187	35	98	.239	.342	55	159	171	.975	37	521	773	9	22	4.17
Chicago	59	103	.364	36	644	809	203	43	140	.254	.380	76	166	132	.974	28	479	908	6	24	4.33
					6624	6624	2099	412	1378	.256	.383	737	1475	1488	.977	402	4404	9312	128	303	3.61

AMERICAN LEAGUE 1966

	POS	Player	AB	BA	HR	RBI	PO	A	E	DP	TC/G	FA	Pitcher	G	IP	W	L	SV	ERA
Baltimore	1B	B. Powell	491	.287	34	109	1094	68	13	96	8.6	.989	D. McNally	34	213	13	6	0	3.17
	2B	D. Johnson	501	.257	7	56	288	347	**19**	75	5.2	.971	J. Palmer	30	208	15	10	0	3.46
W-97 L-63	SS	L. Aparicio	**659**	.276	6	41	**303**	441	17	104	5.0	**.978**	E. Watt	43	146	9	7	4	3.83
	3B	B. Robinson	620	.269	23	100	174	**313**	12	26	3.2	**.976**	W. Bunker	29	143	10	6	0	4.29
Hank Bauer	RF	F. Robinson	576	**.316**	**49**	**122**	254	4	4	0	1.7	.985	S. Barber	25	133	10	5	0	2.29
	CF	P. Blair	303	.277	6	33	204	4	2	2	1.7	.990	J. Miller	23	101	4	8	0	4.74
	LF	R. Snyder	373	.306	3	41	209	6	3	2	2.1	.986	M. Drabowsky	44	96	6	0	7	2.81
	C	A. Etchebarren	412	.221	11	50	799	65	10	7	7.2	.989	S. Miller	51	92	9	4	18	2.25
	OF	C. Blefary	419	.255	23	64	159	5	4	0	1.5	.976	E. Fisher	44*	72	5	3	13	2.64
	OF	S. Bowens	243	.210	6	20	114	7	5	2	1.9	.960	D. Hall	32	66	6	2	7	3.95

	POS	Player	AB	BA	HR	RBI	PO	A	E	DP	TC/G	FA	Pitcher	G	IP	W	L	SV	ERA
Minnesota	1B	D. Mincher	431	.251	14	62	995	85	9	62	8.4	.992	J. Kaat	41	**305**	**25**	13	0	2.75
	2B	B. Allen	319	.238	5	30	191	214	11	46	4.7	.974	M. Grant	35	249	13	13	0	3.25
W-89 L-73	SS	Z. Versalles	543	.249	7	36	195	377	**35**	69	4.5	.942	J. Perry	33	184	11	7	0	2.54
	3B	H. Killebrew	569	.281	39	110	83	190	14	11	2.7	.951	D. Boswell	28	169	12	5	0	3.14
Sam Mele	RF	T. Oliva	622	.307	25	87	335	9	10	3	2.2	.972	J. Merritt	31	144	7	14	3	3.38
	CF	T. Uhlaender	367	.226	2	22	258	4	4	2	2.7	.985	C. Pascual	21	103	8	6	0	4.89
	LF	J. Hall	356	.239	20	47	175	6	4	1	1.8	.978	A. Worthington	65	91	6	3	16	2.46
	C	E. Battey	364	.255	4	34	705	45	4	9	6.7	.995	P. Cimino	35	65	2	5	4	2.92
	UT	C. Tovar	465	.260	2	41	254	274	14	44		.974							
	3B	R. Rollins	269	.245	10	40	54	107	8	13	2.6	.953							
	OF	B. Allison	168	.220	8	19	86	3	3	0	1.6	.967							

	POS	Player	AB	BA	HR	RBI	PO	A	E	DP	TC/G	FA	Pitcher	G	IP	W	L	SV	ERA
Detroit	1B	N. Cash	603	.279	32	93	1271	**114**	**17**	118	8.9	.988	D. McLain	38	264	20	14	0	3.92
	2B	J. Lumpe	385	.231	1	26	202	223	4	51	4.5	.991	M. Lolich	40	204	14	14	3	4.77
W-88 L-74	SS	D. McAuliffe	430	.274	23	56	160	292	17	49	4.5	.964	E. Wilson	23	163	13	6	0	2.59
	3B	D. Wert	559	.268	11	70	128	253	11	20	2.6	.972	D. Wickersham	38	141	8	3	1	3.20
Chuck Dressen	RF	J. Northrup	419	.265	16	58	241	8	5	1	2.2	.980	O. Pena	54	108	4	2	7	3.08
W-16 L-10	CF	A. Kaline	479	.288	29	88	279	7	2	1	2.1	.993	J. Podres	36	108	4	5	4	3.43
Bob Swift	LF	W. Horton	526	.262	27	100	233	4	5	1	1.8	.979	H. Aguirre	30	104	3	9	0	3.82
W-32 L-25	C	B. Freehan	492	.234	12	46	**898**	56	4	11	**7.3**	**.996**	B. Monbouquette	30	103	7	8	0	4.73
Frank Skaff	OF	M. Stanley	235	.289	3	19	163	6	0	1	2.1	1.000	L. Sherry	55	78	8	5	20	3.82
W-40 L-39	2B	J. Wood	230	.252	2	27	109	100	7	25	4.2	.968							
	SS	R. Oyler	210	.171	1	9	107	194	11	42	4.5	.965							
	OF	G. Brown	169	.266	7	27	46	4	1	1	1.2	.980							

AMERICAN LEAGUE 1966, *cont.*

Chicago

W-83 L-79

Eddie Stanky

POS	Player	AB	BA	HR	RBI	PO	A	E	DP	TC/G	FA	Pitcher	G	IP	W	L	SV	ERA
1B	T. McCraw	389	.229	5	48	843	67	9	56	7.6	.990	T. John	34	223	14	11	0	2.62
2B	A. Weis	187	.155	0	9	130	173	4	44	3.2	.987	J. Horlen	37	211	10	13	1	2.43
SS	J. Adair	370	.243	4	36	109	236	9	35	4.7	.975	G. Peters	30	205	12	10	0	**1.98**
3B	D. Buford	607	.244	8	52	98	301	**26**	24	3.2	.939	J. Buzhardt	33	150	6	11	1	3.83
RF	F. Robinson	342	.237	5	35	148	2	6	0	1.4	.962	B. Howard	27	149	9	5	0	2.30
CF	T. Agee	629	.273	22	86	376	12	7	7	2.5	.982	J. Lamabe	34	121	7	9	0	3.93
LF	K. Berry	443	.271	8	34	208	10	2	1	1.6	.991	B. Locker	56	95	9	8	12	2.46
C	J. Romano	329	.231	15	47	622	46	4	7	6.6	.994	J. Pizarro	34	89	8	6	3	3.76
1B	B. Skowron	337	.249	6	29	722	60	7	75	8.1	.991	H. Wilhelm	46	81	5	2	6	1.66
OF	P. Ward	251	.219	3	28	83	3	1	1	1.5	.989	E. Fisher	23*	35	1	3	6	2.29
SS	L. Elia	195	.205	3	22	103	186	14	39	4.0	.954							
2B	W. Causey	164	.244	0	13	86	110	4	15	3.3	.980							
C	J. Martin	157	.255	2	20	243	23	5	3	4.3	.982							

Cleveland

W-81 L-81

Birdie Tebbetts
W-66 L-57

George Strickland
W-15 L-24

POS	Player	AB	BA	HR	RBI	PO	A	E	DP	TC/G	FA	Pitcher	G	IP	W	L	SV	ERA
1B	F. Whitfield	502	.241	27	78	1104	76	11	96	9.0	.991	G. Bell	40	254	14	15	0	3.22
2B	P. Gonzalez	352	.233	2	17	237	257	8	62	4.8	.984	S. Siebert	34	241	16	8	1	2.80
SS	L. Brown	340	.229	3	17	131	238	15	45	4.3	.961	S. McDowell	35	194	9	8	3	2.87
3B	M. Alvis	596	.245	17	55	**180**	280	20	24	3.1	.958	S. Hargan	38	192	13	10	0	2.48
RF	R. Colavito	533	.238	30	72	261	10	5	0	1.9	.982	L. Tiant	46	155	12	11	8	2.79
CF	V. Davalillo	344	.250	3	19	208	6	3	1	2.0	.986	J. O'Donoghue	32	108	6	8	0	3.83
LF	L. Wagner	549	.279	23	66	185	4	2	0	1.4	.990	T. Kelley	31	95	4	8	0	4.34
C	J. Azcue	302	.275	9	37	588	40	7	3	6.5	.989	D. Radatz	39	57	0	3	10	4.61
UT	C. Salmon	422	.256	7	40	315	225	19	53		.966							
OF	C. Hinton	348	.256	12	50	176	6	5	1	1.8	.973							

California

W-80 L-82

Bill Rigney

POS	Player	AB	BA	HR	RBI	PO	A	E	DP	TC/G	FA	Pitcher	G	IP	W	L	SV	ERA
1B	N. Siebern	336	.247	5	41	1014	65	7	96	11.0	.994	D. Chance	41	260	12	17	1	3.08
2B	B. Knoop	590	.232	17	72	**381**	**488**	17	**135**	**5.5**	**.981**	G. Brunet	41	212	13	13	0	3.31
SS	J. Fregosi	611	.252	13	67	297	**531**	**35**	**125**	**5.3**	.959	M. Lopez	37	199	7	14	1	3.93
3B	P. Schaal	386	.244	6	24	97	249	19	21	2.8	.948	J. Sanford	50	108	13	7	5	3.83
RF	E. Kirkpatrick	312	.192	9	44	151	4	1	1	1.5	.994	F. Newman	21	103	4	7	0	4.73
CF	J. Cardenal	561	.276	16	48	351	10	3	4	2.5	.992	B. Lee	61	102	5	4	16	2.74
LF	R. Reichardt	319	.288	16	44	153	8	4	1	1.9	.976	C. Wright	20	91	4	7	0	3.74
C	B. Rodgers	454	.236	7	48	662	**69**	6	7	5.5	.992	M. Rojas	47	84	7	4	10	2.88
OF	J. Johnstone	254	.264	3	17	114	2	3	1	2.0	.975	L. Burdette	54	80	7	2	5	3.39
1B	J. Adcock	231	.273	18	48	565	39	2	60	8.5	.997							
UT	T. Satriano	226	.239	0	24	283	58	6	13		.983							
OF	W. Smith	195	.185	1	20	71	4	2	1	1.5	.974							

Kansas City

W-74 L-86

Alvin Dark

POS	Player	AB	BA	HR	RBI	PO	A	E	DP	TC/G	FA	Pitcher	G	IP	W	L	SV	ERA
1B	K. Harrelson	210	.224	5	22	485	48	8	42	9.3	.985	L. Krausse	36	178	14	9	3	2.99
2B	D. Green	507	.250	9	62	300	389	15	86	5.1	.979	C. Hunter	30	177	9	11	0	4.02
SS	B. Campaneris	573	.267	5	42	283	350	19	80	4.7	.971	J. Nash	18	127	12	1	1	2.06
3B	E. Charles	385	.286	9	42	85	201	11	21	2.9	.963	P. Lindblad	38	121	5	10	1	4.17
RF	M. Hershberger	538	.253	2	57	285	14	7	3	2.1	.977	J. Aker	66	113	8	4	**32**	1.99
CF	J. Gosger	272	.224	5	27	158	3	1	0	2.1	.994	B. Odom	14	90	5	5	0	2.49
LF	L. Stahl	312	.250	5	34	142	6	3	1	1.6	.980	C. Dobson	14	84	4	6	0	4.09
C	P. Roof	369	.209	7	44	680	52	11	7	6.0	.985	R. Sheldon	14	69	4	7	0	3.13
UT	D. Cater	425	.292	7	52	545	104	9	55		.986							
O1	R. Repoz	319	.216	11	34	445	22	5	27		.989							
OF	J. Nossek	230	.261	1	27	161	8	3	1	2.2	.983							
UT	O. Chavarria	191	.241	2	10	105	86	7	23		.965							

Washington

W-71 L-88

Gil Hodges

POS	Player	AB	BA	HR	RBI	PO	A	E	DP	TC/G	FA	Pitcher	G	IP	W	L	SV	ERA
1B	D. Nen	235	.213	6	30	566	38	6	44	8.0	.990	P. Richert	36	246	14	14	0	3.37
2B	B. Saverine	406	.251	5	24	149	169	9	35	4.7	.972	M. McCormick	41	216	11	14	0	3.46
SS	E. Brinkman	582	.229	7	48	263	501	28	83	5.0	.965	P. Ortega	33	197	12	12	0	3.92
3B	K. McMullen	524	.233	13	54	125	280	21	26	3.0	.951	J. Hannan	30	114	3	9	0	4.26
RF	F. Valentine	508	.276	16	59	290	6	6	2	2.2	.980	C. Cox	66	113	4	5	7	3.50
CF	D. Lock	386	.233	16	48	295	8	7	1	2.4	.977	B. Humphreys	58	112	7	3	3	2.82
LF	F. Howard	493	.278	18	71	216	5	4	1	1.7	.982	R. Kline	63	90	6	4	23	2.39
C	P. Casanova	429	.254	13	44	674	53	**14**	**12**	6.2	.981	D. Segui	21	72	3	7	0	5.00
OF	J. King	310	.248	10	30	147	4	2	0	1.8	.987							
1B	K. Harrelson	250	.248	7	28	641	38	6	53	9.8	.991							
2B	D. Blasingame	200	.215	1	11	119	132	4	32	4.4	.984							
OF	W. Kirkland	163	.190	6	17	56	3	1	0	0.9	.983							

Boston

W-72 L-90

Billy Herman
W-64 L-82

Pete Runnels
W-8 L-8

POS	Player	AB	BA	HR	RBI	PO	A	E	DP	TC/G	FA	Pitcher	G	IP	W	L	SV	ERA
1B	G. Scott	601	.245	27	90	**1362**	112	14	**130**	9.4	.991	J. Lonborg	45	182	10	10	2	3.86
2B	G. Smith	403	.213	8	37	239	287	17	76	5.0	.969	J. Santiago	35	172	12	13	2	3.66
SS	R. Petrocelli	522	.238	18	59	206	381	28	69	4.8	.954	D. Brandon	40	158	8	8	2	3.31
3B	J. Foy	554	.262	15	63	150	279	21	**28**	**3.2**	.953	L. Stange	28	153	7	9	0	3.35
RF	T. Conigliaro	558	.265	28	93	244	8	7	1	1.8	.973	E. Wilson	15	101	5	5	0	3.84
CF	D. Demeter	226	.292	9	29	109	3	2	0	2.0	.982	D. McMahon	49	78	8	7	9	2.65
LF	C. Yastrzemski	594	.278	16	80	310	15	5	2	2.1	.985	J. Wyatt	42	72	3	4	8	3.14
C	M. Ryan	369	.214	2	32	685	50	6	7	6.5	.992	K. Sanders	24	47	3	6	2	3.80
2B	D. Jones	252	.234	4	23	129	121	10	26	3.7	.962							
C	B. Tillman	204	.230	3	24	372	24	4	5	5.6	.990							
OF	J. Tartabull	195	.277	0	11	90	1	1	0	2.0	.989							
OF	G. Thomas	173	.237	5	20	84	4	0	0	1.8	1.000							

AMERICAN LEAGUE 1966, *cont.*

New York

W-70 L-89

Johnny Keane
W-4 L-16

Ralph Houk
W-66 L-73

POS	Player	AB	BA	HR	RBI	PO	A	E	DP	TC/G	FA	Pitcher	G	IP	W	L	SV	ERA
1B	J. Pepitone	585	.255	31	83	1044	92	6	92	**9.6**	**.995**	M. Stottlemyre	37	251	12	**20**	1	3.80
2B	B. Richardson	610	.251	7	42	322	408	15	91	5.1	.980	F. Peterson	34	215	12	11	0	3.31
SS	H. Clarke	312	.266	6	28	102	154	8	37	4.2	.970	A. Downing	30	200	10	11	0	3.56
3B	C. Boyer	500	.240	14	57	87	226	11	12	3.8	.966	F. Talbot	23	124	7	7	0	4.15
RF	R. Maris	348	.233	13	43	133	3	1	0	1.4	.993	J. Bouton	24	120	3	8	1	2.69
CF	M. Mantle	333	.288	23	56	172	2	0	0	1.8	1.000	H. Reniff	56	95	3	7	9	3.21
LF	T. Tresh	537	.233	27	68	181	12	3	3	2.3	.985	S. Hamilton	44	90	8	3	3	3.00
C	E. Howard	410	.256	6	35	553	44	9	6	6.1	.985	P. Ramos	52	90	3	9	13	3.61
OF	R. White	316	.225	7	20	153	3	7	0	2.0	.957	D. Womack	42	75	7	3	4	2.64
C	J. Gibbs	182	.258	3	20	295	27	4	4	6.0	.988							
OF	L. Clinton	159	.220	5	21	80	2	2	0	1.3	.976							

BATTING AND BASE RUNNING LEADERS

Batting Average
F. Robinson, BAL .316
T. Oliva, MIN .307
A. Kaline, DET .288
B. Powell, BAL .287
H. Killebrew, MIN .281

Slugging Average
F. Robinson, BAL .637
H. Killebrew, MIN .538
A. Kaline, DET .534
B. Powell, BAL .532
D. McAuliffe, DET .509

Home Runs
F. Robinson, BAL 49
H. Killebrew, MIN 39
B. Powell, BAL 34
N. Cash, DET 32
J. Pepitone, NY 31

Total Bases
F. Robinson, BAL 367
T. Oliva, MIN 312
H. Killebrew, MIN 306
N. Cash, DET 288
T. Agee, CHI 281

Runs Batted In
F. Robinson, BAL 122
H. Killebrew, MIN 110
B. Powell, BAL 109
W. Horton, DET 100
B. Robinson, BAL 100

Stolen Bases
B. Campaneris, KC 52
D. Buford, CHI 51
T. Agee, CHI 44
L. Aparicio, BAL 25
J. Cardenal, CAL 24

Hits
T. Oliva, MIN 191
F. Robinson, BAL 182
L. Aparicio, BAL 182
T. Agee, CHI 172

Base on Balls
H. Killebrew, MIN 103
J. Foy, BOS 91
F. Robinson, BAL 87
T. Tresh, NY 86

Home Run Percentage
F. Robinson, BAL 8.5
B. Powell, BAL 6.9
H. Killebrew, MIN 6.9
A. Kaline, DET 6.1

Runs
F. Robinson, BAL 122
T. Oliva, MIN 99
N. Cash, DET 98
T. Agee, CHI 98

Doubles
C. Yastrzemski, BOS 39
B. Robinson, BAL 35
F. Robinson, BAL 34
J. Fregosi, CAL 32
T. Oliva, MIN 32

Triples
B. Knoop, CAL 11
B. Campaneris, KC 10
E. Brinkman, WAS 9

PITCHING LEADERS

Winning Percentage
S. Siebert, CLE .667
J. Kaat, MIN .658
E. Wilson, BOS, DET .621
J. Palmer, BAL .600
D. McLain, DET .588

Earned Run Average
G. Peters, CHI 1.98
J. Horlen, CHI 2.43
S. Hargan, CLE 2.48
J. Perry, MIN 2.54
T. John, CHI 2.62

Wins
J. Kaat, MIN 25
D. McLain, DET 20
E. Wilson, BOS, DET 18
S. Siebert, CLE 16
J. Palmer, BAL 15

Saves
J. Aker, KC 32
R. Kline, WAS 23
L. Sherry, DET 20
E. Fisher, CHI, BAL 19
S. Miller, BAL 18

Strikeouts
S. McDowell, CLE 225
J. Kaat, MIN 205
E. Wilson, BOS, DET 200
P. Richert, WAS 195
G. Bell, CLE 194

Complete Games
J. Kaat, MIN 19
D. McLain, DET 14
E. Wilson, BOS, DET 13
G. Bell, CLE 12

Fewest Hits/9 Innings
S. McDowell, CLE 6.02
D. Boswell, MIN 6.38
G. Peters, CHI 6.86
D. McLain, DET 6.98

Shutouts
L. Tiant, CLE 5
S. McDowell, CLE 5
T. John, CHI 5

Fewest Walks/9 Innings
J. Kaat, MIN 1.62
F. Peterson, NY 1.67
M. Grant, MIN 1.77
G. Peters, CHI 1.98

Most Strikeouts/9 Inn.
S. McDowell, CLE 10.42
D. Boswell, MIN 9.19
M. Lolich, DET 7.64
P. Richert, WAS 7.14

Innings
J. Kaat, MIN 305
E. Wilson, BOS, DET 264
D. McLain, DET 264
D. Chance, CAL 260

Games Pitched
E. Fisher, CHI, BAL 67
J. Aker, KC 66
C. Cox, WAS 66
A. Worthington, MIN 65

							Batting						Fielding			Pitching					
	W	L	PCT	GB	R	OR	2B	3B	HR	BA	SA	SB	E	DP	FA	CG	BB	SO	ShO	SV	ERA
Baltimore	97	63	.606		**755**	601	**243**	35	175	**.258**	**.409**	55	**115**	142	**.981**	23	514	1070	13	**51**	3.32
Minnesota	89	73	.549	9	663	581	219	33	144	.249	.382	67	139	118	.977	**52**	**392**	1015	11	28	3.13
Detroit	88	74	.543	10	719	698	224	45	**179**	.251	.406	41	120	142	.980	36	520	1026	11	38	3.85
Chicago	83	79	.512	15	574	**517**	193	40	87	.231	.331	**153**	159	149	.976	38	403	896	**22**	34	**2.68**
Cleveland	81	81	.500	17	574	586	156	25	155	.237	.360	53	138	132	.977	49	489	**1111**	15	28	3.23
California	80	82	.494	18	604	643	179	54	122	.232	.354	80	136	**186**	.979	31	511	836	12	40	3.56
Kansas City	74	86	.463	23	564	648	212	**56**	70	.236	.337	132	138	154	.977	19	630	854	11	47	3.55
Washington	71	88	.447	25.5	557	659	185	40	126	.234	.355	53	142	139	.977	25	448	866	6	35	3.70
Boston	72	90	.444	26	655	731	228	44	145	.240	.376	35	155	153	.975	32	577	977	10	31	3.92
New York	70	89	.440	26.5	611	612	182	36	162	.235	.374	49	142	142	.977	29	443	842	7	32	3.42
					6276	6276	2021	408	1365	.240	.368	718	1384	1457	.978	334	4927	9493	118	364	3.44

NATIONAL LEAGUE 1967

St. Louis

W-101 L-60

Red Schoendienst

POS	Player	AB	BA	HR	RBI	PO	A	E	DP	TC/G	FA	Pitcher	G	IP	W	L	SV	ERA
1B	O. Cepeda	563	.325	25	**111**	1304	90	10	103	9.3	.993	D. Hughes	37	222	16	6	3	2.67
2B	J. Javier	520	.281	14	64	311	352	24	72	5.0	.965	S. Carlton	30	193	14	9	1	2.98
SS	D. Maxvill	476	.227	1	41	236	470	19	74	4.9	.974	R. Washburn	27	186	10	7	0	3.53
3B	M. Shannon	482	.245	12	77	88	239	29	18	2.9	.919	B. Gibson	24	175	13	7	0	2.98
RF	R. Maris	410	.261	9	55	224	5	2	1	2.0	.991	N. Briles	49	155	14	5	6	2.43
CF	C. Flood	514	.335	5	50	314	4	4	1	2.6	.988	L. Jaster	34	152	9	7	3	3.01
LF	L. Brock	**689**	.299	21	76	272	12	13	2	1.9	.956	A. Jackson	38	107	9	4	1	3.95
C	T. McCarver	471	.295	14	69	819	**67**	3	10	**6.8**	**.997**	R. Willis	65	81	6	5	10	2.67
OF	B. Tolan	265	.253	6	32	118	4	1	1	1.5	.992	J. Hoerner	57	66	4	4	15	2.59
UT	P. Gagliano	217	.221	2	21	115	99	8	16		.964	J. Lamabe	23	48	3	4	4	2.83
OF	A. Johnson	175	.223	1	12	91	7	3	2	1.8	.970							

NATIONAL LEAGUE 1967, *cont.*

Team	POS	Player	AB	BA	HR	RBI	PO	A	E	DP	TC/G	FA	Pitcher	G	IP	W	L	SV	ERA
San Francisco	1B	W. McCovey	456	.276	31	91	1221	81	**15**	102	10.4	.989	G. Perry	39	293	15	17	1	2.61
	2B	T. Fuentes	344	.209	5	29	274	313	12	79	4.6	.980	M. McCormick	40	262	**22**	10	0	2.85
	SS	H. Lanier	525	.213	0	42	197	440	17	73	4.8	.974	J. Marichal	26	202	14	10	0	2.76
	3B	J. Hart	578	.289	29	99	60	177	16	10	2.8	.937	R. Sadecki	35	188	12	6	0	2.78
W-91 L-71	RF	O. Brown	412	.267	13	53	190	5	3	0	1.7	.985	R. Herbel	42	126	4	5	1	3.08
	CF	W. Mays	486	.263	22	70	277	3	7	0	2.1	.976	B. Bolin	37	120	6	8	0	4.88
Herman Franks	LF	J. Alou	510	.292	5	30	195	5	11	2	1.7	.948	F. Linzy	57	96	7	7	17	1.51
	C	T. Haller	455	.251	14	49	797	64	3	5	6.4	.997	L. McDaniel	41	73	2	6	3	3.72
	UT	J. Davenport	295	.275	5	30	83	192	4	24		.986							
	OF	K. Henderson	179	.190	4	14	86	3	5	1	1.8	.947							
	1B	J. Hiatt	153	.275	6	26	288	17	3	25	8.6	.990							
	1B	E. Banks	573	.276	23	95	**1383**	**91**	10	111	10.1	.993	F. Jenkins	38	289	20	13	0	2.80
Chicago	2B	G. Beckert	597	.280	5	40	327	422	**25**	89	5.4	.968	R. Nye	35	205	13	10	0	3.20
	SS	D. Kessinger	580	.231	0	42	215	457	19	77	4.8	.973	J. Niekro	36	170	10	7	0	3.34
	3B	R. Santo	586	.300	31	98	**187**	**393**	26	**33**	**3.8**	.957	R. Culp	30	153	8	11	0	3.89
W-87 L-74	RF	T. Savage	225	.218	5	33	133	5	3	1	1.6	.979	B. Hands	49	150	7	8	6	2.46
	CF	A. Phillips	448	.268	17	70	340	13	7	0	2.6	.981	C. Simmons	17	82	3	7	0	4.94
Leo Durocher	LF	B. Williams	634	.278	28	84	271	3	3	1	1.7	.989	C. Hartenstein	45	73	9	5	10	3.08
	C	R. Hundley	539	.267	14	60	**865**	59	4	7	6.1	.996	B. Stoneman	28	63	2	4	4	3.29
	OF	L. Thomas	191	.220	2	23	60	2	2	0	1.5	.969							
	1B	L. May	438	.265	12	57	621	43	4	49	8.2	.994	G. Nolan	33	227	14	8	0	2.58
Cincinnati	2B	T. Helms	497	.274	2	35	185	224	9	50	4.8	.978	M. Pappas	34	218	16	13	0	3.35
	SS	L. Cardenas	379	.256	2	21	190	316	15	57	4.8	.971	J. Maloney	30	196	15	11	0	3.25
	3B	T. Perez	600	.290	26	102	113	221	13	13	2.5	.963	M. Queen	31	196	14	8	0	2.76
W-87 L-75	RF	T. Harper	365	.225	7	22	208	6	1	0	2.2	.995	S. Ellis	32	176	8	11	0	3.84
	CF	V. Pinson	650	.288	18	66	341	4	5	1	2.2	.986	T. Abernathy	**70**	106	6	3	**28**	1.27
Dave Bristol	LF	P. Rose	585	.301	12	76	211	5	4	0	1.8	.982	B. McCool	31	97	3	7	2	3.42
	C	J. Edwards	209	.206	2	20	454	30	5	4	6.7	.990	J. Arrigo	32	74	6	6	1	3.16
	1B	D. Johnson	361	.224	13	53	587	41	2	47	7.8	.997							
	UT	C. Ruiz	250	.220	0	13	131	168	10	33		.968							
	C	D. Pavletich	231	.238	6	34	383	31	6	5	6.4	.986							
	1B	B. White	308	.250	8	33	775	52	6	85	8.8	.993	J. Bunning	40	**302**	17	15	0	2.29
Philadelphia	2B	C. Rojas	528	.259	4	45	282	360	15	92	4.8	.977	L. Jackson	40	262	13	15	0	3.10
	SS	B. Wine	363	.190	2	28	201	390	12	90	4.5	**.980**	C. Short	29	199	9	11	1	2.39
	3B	D. Allen	463	.307	23	77	95	249	**35**	23	3.1	.908	R. Wise	36	181	11	11	0	3.28
W-82 L-80	RF	J. Callison	556	.261	14	64	286	12	7	1	2.1	.977	D. Ellsworth	32	125	6	7	0	4.38
	CF	J. Briggs	332	.232	9	30	182	2	4	0	2.0	.979	D. Farrell	50	92	9	6	12	2.05
Gene Mauch	LF	T. Gonzalez	508	.339	9	59	260	10	2	1	1.9	.993	D. Hall	48	86	10	8	8	2.20
	C	C. Dalrymple	268	.172	3	21	558	59	4	7	6.4	.994	J. Boozer	28	75	5	4	1	4.10
	UT	T. Taylor	462	.238	2	34	524	182	9	73		.987							
	OF	D. Lock	313	.252	14	51	172	8	5	2	1.9	.973							
	C	G. Oliver	263	.224	7	34	425	30	6	3	5.8	.987							
	SS	G. Sutherland	231	.247	1	19	77	115	15	33	3.1	.928							
	1B	D. Clendenon	478	.249	13	56	1199	89	**15**	**122**	**10.6**	.988	T. Sisk	37	208	13	13	1	3.34
Pittsburgh	2B	B. Mazeroski	639	.261	9	77	**417**	**498**	18	**131**	**5.7**	.981	B. Veale	33	203	16	8	0	3.64
	SS	G. Alley	550	.287	6	55	**257**	**500**	26	**105**	**5.4**	.967	D. Ribant	38	172	9	8	0	4.08
	3B	M. Wills	616	.302	3	45	98	343	24	31	3.2	.948	A. McBean	51	131	7	4	4	2.54
W-81 L-81	RF	R. Clemente	585	**.357**	23	110	273	17	9	4	2.1	.970	S. Blass	32	127	6	8	0	3.55
	CF	M. Alou	550	.338	2	28	249	9	3	3	1.9	.989	W. Fryman	28	113	3	8	1	4.05
Harry Walker	LF	W. Stargell	462	.271	20	73	140	12	10	1	1.7	.938	J. Pizarro	50	107	8	10	9	3.95
W-42 L-42	C	J. May	325	.271	3	22	550	52	4	9	5.5	.993	B. O'Dell	27	87	5	6	0	5.82
Danny Murtaugh	OF	M. Mota	349	.321	4	56	153	9	2	2	1.7	.988	R. Face	61	74	7	5	17	2.42
W-39 L-39	UT	J. Pagan	211	.289	1	19	73	109	7	14		.963							
	1B	F. Alou	574	.274	15	43	774	28	6	67	9.5	.993	D. Lemaster	31	215	9	9	0	3.34
Atlanta	2B	W. Woodward	429	.226	0	25	270	339	11	81	5.2	**.982**	K. Johnson	29	210	13	9	0	2.74
	SS	D. Menke	418	.227	7	39	181	349	19	65	4.4	.965	P. Niekro	46	207	11	9	9	**1.87**
	3B	C. Boyer	572	.245	26	96	166	291	14	30	3.1	**.970**	P. Jarvis	32	194	15	10	0	3.66
W-77 L-85	RF	H. Aaron	600	.307	**39**	109	321	12	7	3	2.2	.979	D. Kelley	39	98	2	9	2	3.77
	CF	M. Jones	454	.253	17	50	252	7	4	1	2.1	.985	C. Carroll	42	93	6	12	0	5.52
Billy Hitchcock	LF	R. Carty	444	.255	15	64	203	7	9	3	2.0	.959	J. Ritchie	52	82	4	6	2	3.17
W-77 L-82	C	J. Torre	477	.277	20	68	580	63	6	**12**	5.7	.991	T. Cloninger	16	77	4	7	0	5.17
Ken Silvestri	1B	T. Francona	254	.248	6	25	503	32	5	36	9.6	.991	C. Upshaw	30	45	2	3	8	2.58
W-0 L-3													C. Raymond	28	34	4	1	5	2.62
	1B	W. Parker	413	.247	5	31	913	68	4	72	8.8	**.996**	C. Osteen	39	288	17	17	0	3.22
Los Angeles	2B	R. Hunt	388	.263	3	33	211	224	9	50	4.9	.980	D. Drysdale	38	282	13	16	0	2.74
	SS	G. Michael	223	.202	0	7	117	204	17	30	4.1	.950	D. Sutton	37	233	11	15	1	3.95
	3B	J. Lefebvre	494	.261	8	50	49	205	12	12	2.9	.955	B. Singer	32	204	12	8	0	2.64
W-73 L-89	RF	R. Fairly	486	.220	10	55	129	8	2	1	1.4	.986	R. Perranoski	**70**	110	6	7	16	2.45
	CF	W. Davis	569	.257	6	41	300	6	9	2	2.3	.971	J. Brewer	30	101	5	4	1	2.68
Walter Alston	LF	L. Johnson	330	.270	11	41	153	7	4	0	1.8	.976	P. Regan	55	96	6	9	6	2.99
	C	J. Roseboro	334	.272	4	24	550	60	10	6	5.8	.984	B. Miller	52	86	2	9	0	4.31
	OF	A. Ferrara	347	.277	16	50	135	1	3	0	1.5	.978							
	30	B. Bailey	322	.227	4	28	77	152	14	11		.942							
	OF	L. Gabrielson	238	.261	7	29	92	7	2	0	1.5	.980							
	2S	N. Oliver	232	.237	0	7	124	157	12	35		.959							
	SS	D. Schofield	232	.216	2	15	107	213	8	37	4.8	.976							
	C	J. Torborg	196	.214	2	12	413	30	5	3	6.0	.989							

NATIONAL LEAGUE 1967, *cont.*

Houston

W-69 L-93

Grady Hatton

POS	Player	AB	BA	HR	RBI	PO	A	E	DP	TC/G	FA
1B	E. Mathews	328	.238	10	38	572	40	8	50	7.8	.987
2B	J. Morgan	494	.275	6	42	297	344	14	67	5.0	.979
SS	S. Jackson	520	.237	0	25	204	379	**35**	63	4.8	.943
3B	B. Aspromonte	486	.294	6	58	130	237	14	17	2.9	.963
RF	R. Staub	546	.333	10	74	269	10	11	2	2.0	.962
CF	J. Wynn	594	.249	37	107	364	4	12	1	2.4	.968
LF	R. Davis	285	.256	7	38	114	7	3	2	1.5	.976
C	J. Bateman	252	.190	2	17	483	46	6	5	7.5	.989
2S	J. Gotay	234	.282	2	15	91	137	8	27		.966
C	R. Brand	215	.242	0	18	397	36	1	3	6.5	.998
OF	N. Miller	190	.205	1	14	84	3	3	1	1.7	.967
1B	C. Harrison	177	.243	2	26	438	27	6	24	8.0	.987
1B	D. Rader	162	.333	2	26	263	18	8	26	8.0	.972

Pitcher	G	IP	W	L	SV	ERA
M. Cuellar	36	246	16	11	1	3.03
D. Giusti	37	222	11	15	1	4.18
D. Wilson	31	184	10	9	0	2.79
B. Belinsky	27	115	3	9	0	4.68
L. Dierker	15	99	6	5	0	3.36
W. Blasingame	15	77	4	7	0	5.96
C. Sembera	45	60	2	6	3	4.83
D. Eilers	35	59	6	4	1	3.94

New York

W-61 L-101

Wes Westrum
W-57 L-94

Salty Parker
W-4 L-7

POS	Player	AB	BA	HR	RBI	PO	A	E	DP	TC/G	FA
1B	E. Kranepool	469	.269	10	54	1137	87	10	103	8.9	.992
2B	J. Buchek	411	.236	14	41	203	255	11	54	4.9	.977
SS	B. Harrelson	540	.254	1	28	254	467	32	88	5.1	.958
3B	E. Charles	323	.238	3	31	85	201	17	16	3.4	.944
RF	R. Swoboda	449	.281	13	53	190	8	9	0	1.9	.957
CF	C. Jones	411	.246	5	30	210	5	5	3	1.9	.977
LF	T. Davis	577	.302	16	73	231	5	6	0	1.6	.975
C	J. Grote	344	.195	4	23	609	62	7	8	5.7	.990
UT	B. Johnson	230	.348	5	27	222	105	7	37		.979
3B	K. Boyer	166	.235	3	13	27	84	6	7	2.7	.949

Pitcher	G	IP	W	L	SV	ERA
T. Seaver	35	251	16	13	0	2.76
J. Fisher	39	220	9	**18**	0	4.70
D. Cardwell	26	118	5	9	0	3.57
B. Shaw	23	99	3	9	0	4.29
R. Taylor	50	73	4	6	8	2.34
D. Shaw	40	51	4	5	3	2.98
H. Reniff	29	43	3	3	4	3.35

BATTING AND BASE RUNNING LEADERS

Batting Average
- R. Clemente, PIT .357
- T. Gonzalez, PHI .339
- M. Alou, PIT .338
- C. Flood, STL .335
- R. Staub, HOU .333

Slugging Average
- H. Aaron, ATL .573
- D. Allen, PHI .566
- R. Clemente, PIT .554
- W. McCovey, SF .535
- O. Cepeda, STL .524

Home Runs
- H. Aaron, ATL 39
- J. Wynn, HOU 37
- W. McCovey, SF 31
- R. Santo, CHI 31
- J. Hart, SF 29

Total Bases
- H. Aaron, ATL 344
- L. Brock, STL 325
- R. Clemente, PIT 324
- B. Williams, CHI 305
- R. Santo, CHI 300

Runs Batted In
- O. Cepeda, STL 111
- R. Clemente, PIT 110
- H. Aaron, ATL 109
- J. Wynn, HOU 107
- T. Perez, CIN 102

Stolen Bases
- L. Brock, STL 52
- J. Morgan, HOU 29
- M. Wills, PIT 29
- V. Pinson, CIN 26
- A. Phillips, CHI 24

Hits
- R. Clemente, PIT 209
- L. Brock, STL 206
- V. Pinson, CIN 187
- M. Alou, PIT 186
- M. Wills, PIT 186

Base on Balls
- R. Santo, CHI 96
- J. Morgan, HOU 81
- A. Phillips, CHI 80
- J. Hart, SF 77

Home Run Percentage
- W. McCovey, SF 6.8
- H. Aaron, ATL 6.5
- J. Wynn, HOU 6.2
- R. Santo, CHI 5.3

Runs
- H. Aaron, ATL 113
- L. Brock, STL 113
- R. Santo, CHI 107
- R. Clemente, PIT 103

Doubles
- R. Staub, HOU 44
- O. Cepeda, STL 37
- H. Aaron, ATL 37

Triples
- V. Pinson, CIN 13
- B. Williams, CHI 12
- L. Brock, STL 12
- J. Morgan, HOU 11

PITCHING LEADERS

Winning Percentage
- D. Hughes, STL .727
- M. McCormick, SF .688
- B. Veale, PIT .667
- F. Jenkins, CHI .606
- P. Jarvis, ATL .600

Earned Run Average
- P. Niekro, ATL 1.87
- J. Bunning, PHI 2.29
- C. Short, PHI 2.39
- G. Nolan, CIN 2.58
- G. Perry, SF 2.61

Wins
- M. McCormick, SF 22
- F. Jenkins, CHI 20
- C. Osteen, LA 17
- J. Bunning, PHI 17

Saves
- T. Abernathy, CIN 28
- R. Face, PIT 17
- F. Linzy, SF 17
- R. Perranoski, LA 16
- J. Hoerner, STL 15

Strikeouts
- J. Bunning, PHI 253
- F. Jenkins, CHI 236
- G. Perry, SF 230
- G. Nolan, CIN 206
- M. Cuellar, HOU 203

Complete Games
- F. Jenkins, CHI 20
- J. Marichal, SF 18
- T. Seaver, NY 18
- G. Perry, SF 18
- M. Cuellar, HOU 16
- J. Bunning, PHI 16

Fewest Hits/9 Innings
- D. Hughes, STL 6.64
- D. Wilson, HOU 6.90
- G. Perry, SF 7.10
- M. Queen, CIN 7.13

Shutouts
- J. Bunning, PHI 6
- G. Nolan, CIN 5
- M. McCormick, SF 5
- C. Osteen, LA 5

Fewest Walks/9 Innings
- M. Pappas, CIN 1.57
- C. Osteen, LA 1.62
- K. Johnson, ATL 1.63
- J. Niekro, CHI 1.70

Most Strikeouts/9 Inn.
- G. Nolan, CIN 8.18
- B. Veale, PIT 7.94
- S. Carlton, STL 7.83
- D. Wilson, HOU 7.78

Innings
- J. Bunning, PHI 302
- G. Perry, SF 293
- F. Jenkins, CHI 289
- C. Osteen, LA 288

Games Pitched
- T. Abernathy, CIN 70
- R. Perranoski, LA 70
- R. Willis, STL 65
- R. Face, PIT 61

							Batting						Fielding			Pitching					
	W	L	PCT	GB	R	OR	2B	3B	HR	BA	SA	SB	E	DP	FA	CG	BB	SO	ShO	SV	ERA
St. Louis	101	60	.627		695	557	225	40	115	.263	.379	**102**	140	127	.978	44	431	956	17	**45**	3.05
San Francisco	91	71	.562	10.5	652	**551**	201	39	140	.245	.372	22	134	149	.979	**64**	453	990	17	25	**2.92**
Chicago	87	74	.540	14	**702**	624	211	49	128	.251	.378	63	**121**	143	**.981**	47	463	888	7	28	3.48
Cincinnati	87	75	.537	14.5	604	563	251	54	109	.248	.372	92	**121**	124	.980	34	498	**1065**	**18**	39	3.05
Philadelphia	82	80	.506	19.5	612	581	221	47	103	.242	.357	79	137	174	.978	46	403	967	17	23	3.10
Pittsburgh	81	81	.500	20.5	679	693	193	**62**	91	**.277**	**.380**	79	141	**186**	.978	35	561	820	5	35	3.74
Atlanta	77	85	.475	24.5	631	640	191	29	**158**	.240	.372	55	138	148	.978	35	449	862	5	32	3.47
Los Angeles	73	89	.451	28.5	519	595	203	38	82	.236	.332	56	160	144	.975	41	**393**	967	17	24	3.21
Houston	69	93	.426	32.5	626	742	**259**	46	93	.249	.364	88	159	120	.974	35	485	1060	8	21	4.03
New York	61	101	.377	40.5	498	672	178	23	83	.238	.325	58	157	147	.975	36	536	893	10	19	3.73
					6218	6218	2133	427	1102	.249	.363	694	1408	1462	.978	417	4672	9468	121	291	3.38

AMERICAN LEAGUE 1967

Team	POS	Player	AB	BA	HR	RBI	PO	A	E	DP	TC/G	FA	Pitcher	G	IP	W	L	SV	ERA
Boston	1B	G. Scott	565	.303	19	82	**1321**	94	**19**	**115**	9.4	.987	J. Lonborg	39	273	**22**	9	0	3.16
W-92 L-70	2B	M. Andrews	494	.263	8	40	303	345	16	63	4.8	.976	L. Stange	35	182	8	10	1	2.77
Dick Williams	SS	R. Petrocelli	491	.259	17	66	223	432	19	73	4.8	.972	G. Bell	29	165	12	8	3	3.16
	3B	J. Foy	446	.251	16	49	109	204	**27**	13	2.9	.921	D. Brandon	39	158	5	11	3	4.17
	RF	T. Conigliaro	349	.287	20	67	172	5	3	1	1.9	.983	J. Santiago	50	145	12	4	5	3.59
	CF	R. Smith	565	.246	15	61	335	10	6	3	2.4	.983	J. Wyatt	60	93	10	7	20	2.60
	LF	C. Yastrzemski	579	**.326**	**44**	**121**	297	13	7	1	2.0	.978							
	C	M. Ryan	226	.199	2	27	473	34	6	11	6.5	.988							
	UT	J. Adair	316	.291	3	26	105	175	8	30		.972							
	OF	J. Tartabull	247	.223	0	10	90	3	1	1	1.1	.989							
	32	D. Jones	159	.289	3	25	23	60	6	6		.933							
Detroit	1B	N. Cash	488	.242	22	72	1135	**112**	6	89	8.6	**.995**	E. Wilson	39	264	**22**	11	0	3.27
W-91 L-71	2B	D. McAuliffe	557	.239	22	65	270	307	**21**	74	4.1	.965	D. McLain	37	235	17	16	0	3.79
Mayo Smith	SS	R. Oyler	367	.207	1	29	185	374	21	61	4.0	.964	J. Sparma	37	218	16	9	0	3.76
	3B	D. Wert	534	.257	6	40	112	280	9	21	2.9	.978	M. Lolich	31	204	14	13	0	3.04
	RF	A. Kaline	458	.308	25	78	217	14	4	2	1.8	.983	D. Wickersham	36	85	4	5	4	2.74
	CF	J. Northrup	495	.271	10	61	271	3	8	1	2.0	.972	F. Gladding	42	77	6	4	12	1.99
	LF	W. Horton	401	.274	19	67	165	5	5	2	1.6	.971	J. Hiller	23	65	4	3	3	2.63
	C	B. Freehan	517	.282	20	74	**950**	63	8	9	6.9	.992	M. Marshall	37	59	1	3	10	1.98
	OF	M. Stanley	333	.210	7	24	216	3	4	2	1.7	.982	F. Lasher	17	30	2	1	9	3.90
	2B	J. Lumpe	177	.232	4	17	70	85	6	12	3.0	.963							
Minnesota	1B	H. Killebrew	547	.269	**44**	113	1283	86	11	100	8.6	.992	D. Chance	41	**284**	20	14	1	2.73
W-91 L-71	2B	R. Carew	514	.292	8	51	289	314	15	60	4.6	.976	J. Kaat	42	263	16	13	0	3.04
Sam Mele	SS	Z. Versalles	581	.200	6	50	229	454	**30**	81	4.5	.958	J. Merritt	37	228	13	7	0	2.53
W-25 L-25	3B	R. Rollins	339	.245	6	39	83	153	9	13	2.5	.963	D. Boswell	37	223	14	12	0	3.27
Cal Ermer	RF	T. Oliva	557	.289	17	83	286	8	4	2	2.0	.987	J. Perry	37	131	8	7	0	3.03
W-66 L-46	CF	T. Uhlaender	415	.258	6	49	255	6	1	3	2.2	.996	M. Grant	27	95	5	6	0	4.72
	LF	B. Allison	496	.258	24	75	220	6	5	0	1.6	.978	A. Worthington	59	92	8	9	16	2.84
	C	J. Zimmerman	234	.167	1	12	572	44	5	7	6.0	.992	R. Kline	54	72	7	1	5	3.77
	UT	C. Tovar	**649**	.267	6	47	307	184	17	23		.967							
	C	R. Nixon	170	.235	1	22	308	26	2	1	4.9	.994							
	1B	R. Reese	101	.248	4	20	93	3	1	5	2.7	.990							
Chicago	1B	T. McCraw	453	.236	11	45	1167	110	11	92	**10.5**	.991	G. Peters	38	260	16	11	0	2.28
W-89 L-73	2B	W. Causey	292	.226	1	28	153	199	8	36	3.8	.978	J. Horlen	35	258	19	7	0	**2.06**
Eddie Stanky	SS	R. Hansen	498	.233	8	51	243	**482**	27	**91**	4.8	.964	T. John	31	178	10	13	0	2.47
	3B	D. Buford	535	.241	4	32	95	250	19	16	3.0	.948	B. Locker	**77**	125	7	5	20	2.09
	RF	K. Berry	485	.241	7	41	233	9	2	1	1.7	.992	B. Howard	30	113	3	10	0	3.43
	CF	T. Agee	529	.234	14	52	337	6	11	2	2.3	.969	W. Wood	51	95	4	2	4	2.45
	LF	P. Ward	467	.233	18	62	107	3	1	0	1.2	.991	H. Wilhelm	49	89	8	3	12	1.31
	C	J. Martin	252	.234	4	22	478	39	7	3	5.5	.987	J. Buzhardt	28	89	3	9	0	3.96
	OF	W. Williams	275	.240	3	15	112	6	2	2	1.6	.983							
	OF	R. Colavito	190	.221	3	29	83	2	2	3	1.5	.977							
	C	D. Josephson	189	.238	1	9	292	24	0	3	5.4	1.000							
	31	K. Boyer	180	.261	4	21	154	79	5	16		.979							
California	1B	D. Mincher	487	.273	25	76	1177	88	8	92	9.0	.994	G. Brunet	40	250	11	**19**	1	3.31
W-84 L-77	2B	B. Knoop	511	.245	9	38	**376**	392	11	**91**	4.9	.986	J. McGlothlin	32	197	12	8	0	2.96
Bill Rigney	SS	J. Fregosi	590	.290	9	56	258	435	25	73	4.8	.965	R. Clark	32	174	12	11	0	2.59
	3B	P. Schaal	272	.188	6	20	73	156	7	9	2.7	.970	M. Rojas	72	122	12	9	**27**	2.52
	RF	J. Hall	401	.249	16	55	197	6	2	1	1.7	.990	J. Hamilton	26	119	9	6	0	3.24
	CF	J. Cardenal	381	.236	6	27	195	10	3	0	2.1	.986	B. Kelso	69	112	5	3	11	2.97
	LF	R. Reichardt	498	.265	17	69	254	10	7	4	2.0	.974	C. Wright	20	77	5	5	0	3.26
	C	B. Rodgers	429	.219	6	41	728	**73**	7	11	6.0	.991							
	OF	J. Johnstone	230	.209	2	10	141	3	4	0	2.3	.973							
	UT	T. Satriano	201	.224	4	21	150	85	7	10		.971							
	OF	B. Morton	201	.313	0	32	83	1	0	0	1.4	1.000							
	OF	R. Repoz	176	.250	5	20	135	3	5	0	2.3	.965							
Baltimore	1B	B. Powell	415	.234	13	55	903	64	14	82	8.6	.986	T. Phoebus	33	208	14	9	0	3.33
W-76 L-85	2B	D. Johnson	510	.247	10	64	340	348	13	75	4.9	.981	P. Richert	26	132	7	10	2	2.99
Hank Bauer	SS	L. Aparicio	546	.233	4	31	221	333	25	67	4.4	.957	B. Dillman	32	124	5	9	3	4.35
	3B	B. Robinson	610	.269	22	77	147	**405**	11	37	3.6	**.980**	D. McNally	24	119	7	7	0	4.54
	RF	F. Robinson	479	.311	30	94	191	7	2	2	1.6	.990	J. Hardin	19	111	8	3	0	2.27
	CF	P. Blair	552	.293	11	64	369	13	6	3	2.7	.985	E. Watt	49	104	3	5	8	2.26
	LF	C. Blefary	554	.242	22	81	170	13	6	5	1.8	.968	M. Drabowsky	43	95	7	5	12	1.60
	C	A. Etchebarren	330	.215	7	35	673	57	8	10	6.7	.989	G. Brabender	14	94	6	4	0	3.35
	OF	R. Snyder	275	.236	4	23	127	3	2	0	1.9	.985	W. Bunker	29	88	3	7	1	4.09
	S2	M. Belanger	184	.174	1	10	98	134	9	23		.963	S. Miller	42	81	3	10	8	2.55
	C	L. Haney	164	.268	3	20	311	31	3	3	6.1	.991	S. Barber	15	75	4	9	0	4.10
Washington	1B	M. Epstein	284	.229	9	29	718	54	10	72	9.8	.987	P. Ortega	34	220	10	10	0	3.03
W-76 L-85	2B	B. Allen	254	.193	3	18	177	200	4	57	5.1	.990	C. Pascual	28	165	12	10	0	3.28
Gil Hodges	SS	E. Brinkman	320	.188	1	18	160	309	10	54	4.4	**.979**	B. Moore	27	144	7	11	0	3.76
	3B	K. McMullen	563	.245	16	67	153	348	18	**38**	**3.6**	.965	J. Coleman	28	134	8	9	0	4.63
	RF	C. Peterson	405	.240	8	46	190	5	6	1	2.0	.970	D. Knowles	61	113	6	8	14	2.70
	CF	F. Valentine	457	.234	11	44	258	7	3	0	2.0	.989	B. Priddy	46	110	3	7	4	3.44
	LF	F. Howard	519	.256	36	89	210	5	3	1	1.5	.986	B. Humphreys	48	106	6	2	4	4.17
	C	P. Casanova	528	.248	9	53	827	70	15	**19**	6.7	.984	F. Bertaina	18	96	6	5	0	2.92
	UT	T. Cullen	402	.236	2	31	219	361	27	67		.956	D. Lines	54	86	2	5	4	3.36
	OF	H. Allen	292	.233	3	17	148	1	3	1	1.5	.980	C. Cox	54	73	7	4	1	2.96
	1B	D. Nen	238	.218	6	29	516	42	3	49	8.6	.995	D. Baldwin	58	69	2	4	12	1.70
	2B	B. Saverine	233	.236	0	8	80	98	8	22	3.9	.957							
	OF	E. Stroud	204	.201	1	10	117	1	2	0	1.5	.983							

AMERICAN LEAGUE 1967, *cont.*

Team	POS	Player	AB	BA	HR	RBI	PO	A	E	DP	TC/G	FA	Pitcher	G	IP	W	L	SV	ERA
Cleveland	1B	T. Horton	363	.281	10	44	763	46	7	62	8.7	.991	S. McDowell	37	236	13	15	0	3.85
W-75 L-87	2B	V. Fuller	206	.223	7	21	133	144	4	39	4.4	.986	S. Hargan	30	223	14	13	0	2.62
Joe Adcock	SS	L. Brown	485	.227	7	37	233	414	22	90	4.5	.967	L. Tiant	33	214	12	9	2	2.74
	3B	M. Alvis	637	.256	21	70	**169**	304	17	20	3.0	.965	S. Siebert	34	185	10	12	4	2.38
	RF	C. Hinton	498	.245	10	37	239	5	6	0	1.8	.976	J. O'Donoghue	33	131	8	9	2	3.24
	CF	V. Davalillo	359	.287	2	22	202	5	3	1	1.7	.986	O. Pena	48	88	0	3	8	3.36
	LF	L. Wagner	433	.242	15	54	142	4	3	1	1.3	.980	S. Williams	16	79	6	4	1	2.62
	C	J. Azcue	295	.251	11	34	636	57	1	4	**8.1**	**.999**	G. Culver	53	75	7	3	3	3.96
	OF	L. Maye	297	.259	9	27	102	2	2	0	1.4	.981	B. Allen	47	54	0	5	5	2.98
	C	D. Sims	272	.202	12	37	561	56	7	7	7.3	.989							
	1B	F. Whitfield	257	.218	9	31	494	40	4	51	8.2	.993							
	UT	C. Salmon	203	.227	2	19	199	103	5	26		.984							
	OF	R. Colavito	191	.241	5	21	75	2	3	0	1.6	.962							
	2B	P. Gonzalez	189	.228	1	8	114	120	7	29	3.8	.971							
New York	1B	M. Mantle	440	.245	22	55	1089	91	8	82	9.1	.993	M. Stottlemyre	36	255	15	15	0	2.96
W-72 L-90	2B	H. Clarke	588	.272	3	29	348	**410**	8	79	**5.5**	**.990**	A. Downing	31	202	14	10	0	2.63
Ralph Houk	SS	R. Amaro	417	.223	1	17	212	374	16	73	**4.9**	.973	F. Peterson	36	181	8	14	0	3.47
	3B	C. Smith	425	.224	9	38	92	283	21	22	3.4	.947	F. Talbot	29	139	6	8	0	4.22
	RF	S. Whitaker	441	.243	11	50	202	12	4	6	1.9	.982	B. Monbouquette	33	133	6	5	1	2.36
	CF	J. Pepitone	501	.251	13	64	277	7	7	1	2.4	.976	T. Tillotson	43	98	3	9	2	4.03
	LF	T. Tresh	448	.219	14	53	198	9	6	1	1.8	.972	S. Barber	17	98	6	9	0	4.05
	C	J. Gibbs	374	.233	4	25	582	55	**16**	7	6.6	.975	D. Womack	65	97	5	6	18	2.41
	OF	B. Robinson	342	.196	7	29	169	10	6	1	1.8	.968	S. Hamilton	44	62	2	4	4	3.48
	O3	R. White	214	.224	2	18	79	29	10	1		.915							
	C	E. Howard	199	.196	3	17	289	26	5	5	6.7	.984							
	S3	J. Kennedy	179	.196	1	17	74	151	16	21		.934							
Kansas City	1B	R. Webster	360	.256	11	51	615	41	7	42	8.0	.989	C. Hunter	35	260	13	17	0	2.81
	2B	J. Donaldson	377	.276	0	28	210	230	8	40	4.4	.982	J. Nash	37	222	12	17	0	3.76
W-62 L-99	SS	B. Campaneris	601	.248	3	32	**259**	365	**30**	75	4.5	.954	C. Dobson	32	198	10	10	0	3.69
	3B	D. Green	349	.198	5	37	54	86	8	5	2.5	.946	L. Krausse	48	160	7	17	6	4.28
Alvin Dark	RF	M. Hershberger	480	.254	1	49	206	17	4	2	1.7	.982	P. Lindblad	46	116	5	8	6	3.58
W-52 L-69	CF	R. Monday	406	.251	14	58	260	14	8	6	2.5	.972	B. Odom	29	104	3	8	0	5.04
	LF	J. Gosger	356	.242	5	36	201	6	4	1	1.9	.981	T. Pierce	49	98	3	4	7	3.04
	C	P. Roof	327	.205	6	24	677	55	7	6	6.5	.991	J. Aker	57	88	3	8	12	4.30
Luke Appling	UT	D. Cater	529	.270	4	46	424	109	13	35		.976							
W-10 L-30	1B	K. Harrelson	174	.305	6	30	333	25	3	21	8.0	.992							
	OF	J. Nossek	166	.205	0	10	105	2	2	0	1.7	.982							

BATTING AND BASE RUNNING LEADERS

Batting Average
C. Yastrzemski, BOS .326
F. Robinson, BAL .311
A. Kaline, DET .308
G. Scott, BOS .303
P. Blair, BAL .293

Slugging Average
C. Yastrzemski, BOS .622
F. Robinson, BAL .576
H. Killebrew, MIN .558
A. Kaline, DET .541
F. Howard, WAS .511

Home Runs
H. Killebrew, MIN 44
C. Yastrzemski, BOS 44
F. Howard, WAS 36
F. Robinson, BAL 30
A. Kaline, DET 25
D. Mincher, CAL 25

Total Bases
C. Yastrzemski, BOS 360
H. Killebrew, MIN 305
F. Robinson, BAL 276
F. Howard, WAS 265
B. Robinson, BAL 265

Runs Batted In
C. Yastrzemski, BOS 121
H. Killebrew, MIN 113
F. Robinson, BAL 94
F. Howard, WAS 89
T. Oliva, MIN 83

Stolen Bases
B. Campaneris, KC 55
D. Buford, CHI 34
T. Agee, CHI 28
T. McCraw, CHI 24
H. Clarke, NY 21

Hits
C. Yastrzemski, BOS 189
C. Tovar, MIN 173
G. Scott, BOS 171
J. Fregosi, CAL 171

Base on Balls
H. Killebrew, MIN 131
M. Mantle, NY 107
D. McAuliffe, DET 105
C. Yastrzemski, BOS 91

Home Run Percentage
H. Killebrew, MIN 8.0
C. Yastrzemski, BOS 7.6
F. Howard, WAS 6.9
F. Robinson, BAL 6.3

Runs
C. Yastrzemski, BOS 112
H. Killebrew, MIN 105
C. Tovar, MIN 98
A. Kaline, DET 94

Doubles
T. Oliva, MIN 34
C. Tovar, MIN 32
C. Yastrzemski, BOS 31
D. Johnson, BAL 30

Triples
P. Blair, BAL 12
D. Buford, CHI 9

PITCHING LEADERS

Winning Percentage
J. Horlen, CHI .731
J. Lonborg, BOS .710
E. Wilson, DET .667
J. Sparma, DET .640
G. Peters, CHI .593

Earned Run Average
J. Horlen, CHI 2.06
G. Peters, CHI 2.28
S. Siebert, CLE 2.38
T. John, CHI 2.47
J. Merritt, MIN 2.53

Wins
E. Wilson, DET 22
J. Lonborg, BOS 22
D. Chance, MIN 20
J. Horlen, CHI 19
D. McLain, DET 17

Saves
M. Rojas, CAL 27
B. Locker, CHI 20
J. Wyatt, BOS 20
D. Womack, NY 18
A. Worthington, MIN 16

Strikeouts
J. Lonborg, BOS 246
S. McDowell, CLE 236
D. Chance, MIN 220
L. Tiant, CLE 219
G. Peters, CHI 215

Complete Games
D. Chance, MIN 18
S. Hargan, CLE 15
J. Lonborg, BOS 15
J. Horlen, CHI 13
C. Hunter, KC 13
J. Kaat, MIN 13

Fewest Hits/9 Innings
G. Peters, CHI 6.47
D. Boswell, MIN 6.55
J. Horlen, CHI 6.56
S. Siebert, CLE 6.60

Shutouts
S. Hargan, CLE 6
T. John, CHI 6
J. McGlothlin, CAL 6
M. Lolich, DET 6
J. Horlen, CHI 6

Fewest Walks/9 Innings
J. Merritt, MIN 1.19
J. Kaat, MIN 1.44
L. Stange, BOS 1.59
J. Horlen, CHI 2.02

Most Strikeouts/9 Inn.
L. Tiant, CLE 9.22
S. McDowell, CLE 8.99
D. Boswell, MIN 8.25
J. Lonborg, BOS 8.10

Innings
D. Chance, MIN 284
J. Lonborg, BOS 273
E. Wilson, DFT 264
J. Kaat, MIN 263

Games Pitched
B. Locker, CHI 77
M. Rojas, CAL 72
B. Kelso, CAL 69
D. Womack, NY 65

							Batting						Fielding			Pitching					
	W	L	PCT	GB	R	OR	2B	3B	HR	BA	SA	SB	E	DP	FA	CG	BB	SO	ShO	SV	ERA
Boston	92	70	.568		**722**	614	**216**	39	**158**	**.255**	**.395**	68	142	142	.977	41	477	1010	9	44	3.36
Detroit	91	71	.562	1	683	587	192	36	152	.243	.376	37	131	126	.979	46	472	1038	17	40	3.32
Minnesota	91	71	.562	1	671	590	**216**	48	131	.240	.369	55	132	123	.978	**58**	**396**	1089	18	24	3.14
Chicago	89	73	.549	3	531	**491**	181	34	89	.225	.320	124	138	149	.979	36	465	927	**24**	39	**2.45**
California	84	77	.522	7.5	567	587	170	37	114	.238	.349	40	**111**	135	**.982**	19	525	892	14	**46**	3.19
Baltimore	76	85	.472	15.5	654	592	215	44	138	.240	.372	54	124	144	.980	29	566	1034	17	36	3.32
Washington	76	85	.472	15.5	550	637	168	25	115	.223	.326	53	144	**167**	.978	24	495	878	14	39	3.38
Cleveland	75	87	.463	17	559	613	213	35	131	.235	.359	53	117	138	.981	49	559	**1189**	14	27	3.25
New York	72	90	.444	20	522	621	166	17	100	.225	.317	63	154	144	.976	37	480	898	16	27	3.24
Kansas City	62	99	.385	29.5	533	660	212	**50**	69	.233	.330	**132**	132	120	.978	26	558	990	10	34	3.68
					5992	5992	1949	365	1197	.236	.351	679	1325	1388	.979	365	4993	9945	153	356	3.23

NATIONAL LEAGUE 1968

Team	POS	Player	AB	BA	HR	RBI	PO	A	E	DP	TC/G	FA	Pitcher	G	IP	W	L	SV	ERA
St. Louis	1B	O. Cepeda	600	.248	16	73	1362	90	17	109	9.5	.988	B. Gibson	34	305	22	9	0	**1.12**
	2B	J. Javier	519	.260	4	52	304	339	16	68	4.7	.976	N. Briles	33	244	19	11	0	2.81
	SS	D. Maxvill	459	.253	1	24	232	458	22	81	4.7	.969	S. Carlton	34	232	13	11	0	2.99
	3B	M. Shannon	576	.266	15	79	110	310	21	25	2.8	.952	R. Washburn	31	215	14	8	0	2.26
W-97 L-65	RF	R. Maris	310	.255	5	45	169	4	3	1	2.1	.983	L. Jaster	31	154	9	13	0	3.51
	CF	C. Flood	618	.301	5	60	386	11	7	4	2.7	.983	J. Hoerner	47	49	8	2	17	1.47
Red Schoendienst	LF	L. Brock	660	.279	6	51	269	9	14	1	1.9	.952	W. Granger	34	44	4	2	4	2.25
	C	T. McCarver	434	.253	5	48	708	54	11	6	7.1	.986							
	OF	B. Tolan	278	.230	5	17	116	3	4	1	1.8	.967							
	C	J. Edwards	230	.239	3	29	350	25	3	2	7.0	.992							
San Francisco	1B	W. McCovey	523	.293	**36**	**105**	1305	103	**21**	91	9.8	.985	J. Marichal	38	**326**	**26**	9	0	2.43
	2B	R. Hunt	529	.250	2	28	289	410	**20**	66	4.9	.972	G. Perry	39	291	16	15	1	2.45
	SS	H. Lanier	486	.206	0	27	**282**	496	17	72	5.3	**.979**	R. Sadecki	38	254	12	**18**	0	2.91
	3B	J. Davenport	272	.224	1	17	49	120	7	12	2.1	.960	M. McCormick	38	198	12	14	1	3.58
W-88 L-74	RF	B. Bonds	307	.254	9	35	169	6	4	1	2.2	.978	B. Bolin	34	177	10	5	0	1.99
	CF	W. Mays	498	.289	23	79	301	7	7	2	2.2	.978	F. Linzy	57	95	9	8	12	2.08
Herman Franks	LF	J. Alou	419	.263	0	39	175	10	2	2	1.8	.989							
	C	D. Dietz	301	.272	6	38	497	37	**13**	10	6.1	.976							
	30	J. Hart	480	.258	23	78	165	112	19	12		.936							
	OF	T. Cline	291	.223	1	28	93	6	3	1	1.5	.971							
	C	J. Hiatt	224	.232	4	34	328	31	2	4	6.2	.994							
	UT	F. Johnson	174	.190	1	7	61	83	9	6		.941							
	OF	D. Marshall	174	.264	1	16	58	3	5	3	1.3	.924							
Chicago	1B	E. Banks	552	.246	32	83	1379	88	6	118	10.0	.996	F. Jenkins	40	308	20	15	0	2.63
	2B	G. Beckert	643	.294	4	37	356	461	19	107	5.4	.977	B. Hands	38	259	16	10	0	2.89
	SS	D. Kessinger	655	.240	1	32	263	**573**	**33**	**97**	**5.5**	.962	K. Holtzman	34	215	11	14	1	3.35
	3B	R. Santo	577	.246	26	98	130	**378**	15	**33**	3.2	**.971**	J. Niekro	34	177	14	10	2	4.31
W-84 L-78	RF	J. Hickman	188	.223	5	23	115	4	3	0	1.8	.975	R. Nye	27	133	7	12	1	3.80
	CF	A. Phillips	439	.241	13	33	311	11	7	3	2.3	.979	P. Regan	68	127	10	5	25*	2.20
Leo Durocher	LF	B. Williams	642	.288	30	98	261	4	9	0	1.7	.967							
	C	R. Hundley	553	.226	7	65	885	81	5	11	6.1	.995							
	OF	L. Johnson	205	.244	1	14	97	0	3	0	1.8	.970							
	OF	A. Spangler	177	.271	2	18	71	2	2	1	1.6	.973							
	OF	W. Smith	142	.275	5	25	42	1	0	0	1.1	1.000							
Cincinnati	1B	L. May	559	.290	22	80	1040	70	5	86	9.1	.996	G. Culver	42	226	11	16	2	3.23
	2B	T. Helms	507	.288	2	47	322	370	15	82	5.6	.979	J. Maloney	33	207	16	10	0	3.61
	SS	L. Cardenas	452	.235	7	41	221	388	29	66	4.7	.955	J. Arrigo	36	205	12	10	0	3.33
	3B	T. Perez	625	.282	18	92	**151**	343	**25**	**33**	**3.2**	.952	G. Nolan	23	150	9	4	0	2.40
W-83 L-79	RF	P. Rose	626	**.335**	10	49	268	20	3	4	2.0	.990	T. Abernathy	**78**	135	10	7	13	2.46
	CF	V. Pinson	499	.271	5	48	258	7	6	0	2.2	.978	C. Carroll	58	122	7	7	17	2.29
Dave Bristol	LF	A. Johnson	603	.312	2	58	243	8	14	2	1.9	.947							
	C	J. Bench	564	.275	15	82	**942**	**102**	9	10	6.8	.991							
	OF	M. Jones	234	.252	10	34	82	1	1	0	1.4	.988							
	1B	F. Whitfield	171	.257	6	32	285	21	6	28	7.6	.981							
Atlanta	1B	D. Johnson	342	.208	8	33	738	46	3	66	8.1	.996	P. Niekro	37	257	14	12	2	2.59
	2B	F. Millan	570	.289	1	33	330	438	16	91	5.4	.980	P. Jarvis	34	256	16	12	0	2.60
	SS	S. Jackson	358	.226	1	19	132	307	22	35	4.7	.952	R. Reed	35	202	11	10	0	3.35
	3B	C. Boyer	273	.227	4	17	74	135	4	17	3.1	.981	K. Johnson	31	135	5	8	0	3.47
W-81 L-81	RF	H. Aaron	606	.287	29	86	330	13	3	2	2.3	.991	M. Pappas	22	121	10	8	0	2.37
	CF	F. Alou	**662**	.317	11	57	379	8	8	2	2.5	.980	C. Upshaw	52	117	8	7	13	2.47
Lum Harris	LF	M. Lum	232	.224	3	21	115	7	3	0	1.3	.976	J. Britton	34	90	4	6	3	3.09
	C	J. Torre	424	.271	10	55	492	37	2	7	5.8	**.996**	G. Stone	17	75	7	4	0	2.76
	UT	M. Martinez	356	.230	0	12	169	264	18	44		.960	C. Raymond	36	60	3	5	10	2.83
	01	T. Francona	346	.286	2	47	382	12	4	18		.990							
	01	T. Aaron	283	.244	1	25	287	20	5	13		.984							
	C	B. Tillman	236	.220	5	20	359	29	4	7	5.2	.990							
	3B	B. Johnson	187	.262	0	11	45	101	8	9	3.2	.948							
Pittsburgh	1B	D. Clendenon	584	.257	17	87	**1587**	**128**	17	**134**	**11.2**	.990	B. Veale	36	245	13	14	0	2.05
	2B	B. Mazeroski	506	.251	3	42	319	**467**	15	107	**5.6**	.981	S. Blass	33	220	18	6	0	2.12
	SS	G. Alley	474	.245	4	39	162	394	15	86	5.2	.974	A. McBean	36	198	9	12	0	3.58
	3B	M. Wills	627	.278	0	31	105	276	17	27	2.8	.957	B. Moose	38	171	8	12	3	2.74
W-80 L-82	RF	R. Clemente	502	.291	18	57	297	9	5	1	2.4	.984	J. Bunning	27	160	4	14	0	3.88
	CF	M. Alou	558	.332	0	52	298	8	5	0	2.2	.984	R. Kline	56	113	12	5	7	1.68
Larry Shepard	LF	W. Stargell	435	.237	24	67	144	12	9	0	1.5	.945	D. Ellis	26	104	6	5	0	2.50
	C	J. May	416	.219	1	33	752	70	10	10	6.2	.988	T. Sisk	33	96	5	5	1	3.28
	OF	M. Mota	331	.281	1	33	149	5	3	1	1.7	.981	R. Face	43	52	2	4	13	2.60
	SS	F. Patek	208	.255	2	18	80	164	6	23	4.8	.976							
	UT	J. Pagan	163	.221	4	21	40	65	7	7		.938							
Los Angeles	1B	W. Parker	468	.239	3	27	939	69	1	74	8.9	**.999**	B. Singer	37	256	13	17	0	2.88
	2B	P. Popovich	418	.232	2	25	172	229	7	48	4.6	.983	C. Osteen	39	254	12	**18**	0	3.08
	SS	Z. Versalles	403	.196	2	24	204	380	28	62	5.1	.954	D. Drysdale	31	239	14	12	0	2.15
	3B	B. Bailey	322	.227	8	39	81	164	12	14	2.9	.953	D. Sutton	35	208	11	15	1	2.60
W-76 L-86	RF	R. Fairly	441	.234	4	43	159	13	2	7	1.7	.989	M. Kekich	25	115	2	10	0	3.91
	CF	W. Davis	643	.250	7	31	345	9	10	2	2.3	.973	M. Grant	37	95	6	4	3	2.08
Walter Alston	LF	L. Gabrielson	304	.270	10	35	114	6	3	1	1.4	.976	J. Brewer	54	76	8	3	14	2.49
	C	T. Haller	474	.285	4	53	863	81	6	**23**	6.8	.994	J. Billingham	50	71	3	0	8	2.14
	2B	J. Lefebvre	286	.241	5	31	126	137	6	29	4.3	.978							
	31	K. Boyer	221	.271	6	41	275	64	10	29		.971							
	OF	W. Crawford	175	.251	4	14	78	6	3	1	1.8	.966							

NATIONAL LEAGUE 1968, *cont.*

Philadelphia

W-76 L-86

Gene Mauch
W-27 L-27

George Myatt
W-1 L-0

Bob Skinner
W-48 L-59

POS	Player	AB	BA	HR	RBI	PO	A	E	DP	TC/G	FA
1B	B. White	385	.239	9	40	982	77	6	94	9.6	.994
2B	C. Rojas	621	.232	9	48	**365**	424	10	**110**	5.3	**.987**
SS	R. Pena	500	.260	1	38	230	434	32	93	5.2	.954
3B	T. Taylor	547	.250	3	38	112	315	15	25	3.2	.966
RF	J. Callison	398	.244	14	40	187	10	0	1	1.8	1.000
CF	T. Gonzalez	416	.264	3	38	227	4	5	1	2.0	.979
LF	D. Allen	521	.263	33	90	208	5	6	0	1.6	.973
C	M. Ryan	296	.179	1	15	501	62	5	7	5.9	.991
01	J. Briggs	338	.254	7	31	423	23	7	33		.985
OF	D. Lock	248	.210	8	34	145	2	7	1	2.0	.955
C	C. Dalrymple	241	.207	3	26	463	34	5	3	6.3	.990

Pitcher	G	IP	W	L	SV	ERA
C. Short	42	270	19	13	1	2.94
L. Jackson	34	244	13	17	0	2.77
W. Fryman	34	214	12	14	0	2.78
R. Wise	30	182	9	15	0	4.54
J. James	29	116	4	4	0	4.28
D. Farrell	54	83	4	6	12	3.48
G. Wagner	44	78	4	4	8	3.00

New York

W-73 L-89

Gil Hodges

POS	Player	AB	BA	HR	RBI	PO	A	E	DP	TC/G	FA
1B	E. Kranepool	373	.231	3	20	921	75	6	76	8.9	.994
2B	P. Linz	258	.209	0	17	136	162	10	36	4.3	.968
SS	B. Harrelson	402	.219	0	14	199	317	15	58	5.0	.972
3B	E. Charles	369	.276	15	53	69	200	13	19	2.7	.954
RF	R. Swoboda	450	.242	11	59	217	14	6	4	1.9	.975
CF	T. Agee	368	.217	5	17	216	6	5	2	1.8	.978
LF	C. Jones	509	.297	14	55	226	7	9	0	1.7	.963
C	J. Grote	404	.282	3	31	754	60	5	8	**7.1**	.994
OF	A. Shamsky	345	.238	12	48	128	6	1	2	1.6	.993
2B	K. Boswell	284	.261	4	11	154	203	13	37	5.4	.965
S2	A. Weis	274	.172	1	14	138	242	14	43		.964
C	J. Martin	244	.225	3	31	334	24	2	4	6.8	.994
UT	J. Buchek	192	.182	1	11	57	91	7	11		.955
OF	L. Stahl	183	.235	3	10	110	5	2	1	2.5	.983

Pitcher	G	IP	W	L	SV	ERA
T. Seaver	36	278	16	12	1	2.20
J. Koosman	35	264	19	12	0	2.08
D. Cardwell	29	180	7	13	1	2.95
D. Selma	33	170	9	10	0	2.75
N. Ryan	21	134	6	9	0	3.09
C. Koonce	55	97	6	4	11	2.42
A. Jackson	25	93	3	7	3	3.69
J. McAndrew	12	79	4	7	0	2.28
R. Taylor	58	77	1	5	13	2.70

Houston

W-72 L-90

Grady Hatton
W-23 L-38

Harry Walker
W-49 L-52

POS	Player	AB	BA	HR	RBI	PO	A	E	DP	TC/G	FA
1B	R. Staub	591	.291	6	72	1313	93	11	100	9.6	.992
2B	D. Menke	542	.249	6	56	269	285	10	47	4.7	.982
SS	H. Torres	466	.223	1	24	159	391	24	55	4.5	.958
3B	D. Rader	333	.267	6	43	83	168	19	14	3.1	.930
RF	N. Miller	257	.237	6	28	131	1	4	1	1.8	.971
CF	R. Davis	217	.212	1	12	131	4	4	0	2.7	.971
LF	J. Wynn	542	.269	26	67	298	20	4	8	2.1	.988
C	J. Bateman	350	.249	4	33	690	49	11	6	6.9	.985
30	B. Aspromonte	409	.225	1	46	110	153	10	9		.963
OF	L. Thomas	201	.194	1	11	67	5	2	0	1.5	.973
OF	D. Simpson	177	.186	3	11	63	2	2	1	1.4	.970
2B	J. Gotay	165	.248	1	11	116	103	4	28	4.6	.982

Pitcher	G	IP	W	L	SV	ERA
D. Giusti	37	251	11	14	1	3.19
L. Dierker	32	234	12	15	0	3.31
D. Lemaster	33	224	10	15	0	2.81
D. Wilson	33	209	13	16	0	3.28
M. Cuellar	28	171	8	11	1	2.74
J. Buzhardt	39	84	4	4	5	3.12
S. Shea	30	35	4	4	6	3.38

BATTING AND BASE RUNNING LEADERS

Batting Average

P. Rose, CIN	.335
M. Alou, PIT	.332
F. Alou, ATL	.317
A. Johnson, CIN	.312
C. Flood, STL	.301

Slugging Average

W. McCovey, SF	.545
D. Allen, PHI	.520
B. Williams, CHI	.500
H. Aaron, ATL	.498
W. Mays, SF	.488

Home Runs

W. McCovey, SF	36
D. Allen, PHI	33
E. Banks, CHI	32
B. Williams, CHI	30
H. Aaron, ATL	29

Total Bases

B. Williams, CHI	321
H. Aaron, ATL	302
P. Rose, CIN	294
F. Alou, ATL	290
W. McCovey, SF	285

Runs Batted In

W. McCovey, SF	105
R. Santo, CHI	98
B. Williams, CHI	98
T. Perez, CIN	92
D. Allen, PHI	90

Stolen Bases

L. Brock, STL	62
M. Wills, PIT	52
W. Davis, LA	36
H. Aaron, ATL	28
C. Jones, NY	23

Hits

P. Rose, CIN	210
F. Alou, ATL	210
G. Beckert, CHI	189
A. Johnson, CIN	188

Base on Balls

R. Santo, CHI	96
J. Wynn, HOU	90
R. Hunt, SF	78
D. Allen, PHI	74

Home Run Percentage

W. McCovey, SF	6.9
D. Allen, PHI	6.3
E. Banks, CHI	5.8
J. Wynn, HOU	4.8

Runs

G. Beckert, CHI	98
P. Rose, CIN	94
T. Perez, CIN	93
L. Brock, STL	92

Doubles

L. Brock, STL	46
P. Rose, CIN	42
J. Bench, CIN	40
R. Staub, HOU	37
F. Alou, ATL	37

Triples

L. Brock, STL	14
R. Clemente, PIT	12
W. Davis, LA	10
D. Allen, PHI	9

PITCHING LEADERS

Winning Percentage

S. Blass, PIT	.750
J. Marichal, SF	.743
B. Gibson, STL	.710
N. Briles, STL	.633
B. Hands, CHI	.615
J. Maloney, CIN	.615

Earned Run Average

B. Gibson, STL	1.12
B. Bolin, SF	1.99
B. Veale, PIT	2.05
J. Koosman, NY	2.08
S. Blass, PIT	2.12

Wins

J. Marichal, SF	26
B. Gibson, STL	22
F. Jenkins, CHI	20
N. Briles, STL	19
J. Koosman, NY	19
C. Short, PHI	19

Saves

P. Regan, LA, CHI	25
J. Hoerner, STL	17
C. Carroll, ATL, CIN	17
J. Brewer, LA	14

Strikeouts

B. Gibson, STL	268
F. Jenkins, CHI	260
B. Singer, LA	227
J. Marichal, SF	218
R. Sadecki, SF	206

Complete Games

J. Marichal, SF	30
B. Gibson, STL	28
F. Jenkins, CHI	20
G. Perry, SF	19
J. Koosman, NY	17

Fewest Hits/9 Innings

B. Gibson, STL	5.85
B. Bolin, SF	6.52
B. Veale, PIT	6.86
P. Jarvis, ATL	7.10

Shutouts

B. Gibson, STL	13
D. Drysdale, LA	8
S. Blass, PIT	7
J. Koosman, NY	7

Fewest Walks/9 Innings

B. Hands, CHI	1.25
J. Marichal, SF	1.27
T. Seaver, NY	1.55
M. Pappas, CIN, ATL	1.57

Most Strikeouts/9 Inn.

B. Singer, LA	7.97
B. Gibson, STL	7.92
J. Maloney, CIN	7.87
F. Jenkins, CHI	7.60

Innings

J. Marichal, SF	326
F. Jenkins, CHI	308
B. Gibson, STL	305
G. Perry, SF	291

Games Pitched

T. Abernathy, CIN	78
P. Regan, LA, CHI	73
C. Carroll, ATL, CIN	68
R. Taylor, NY	58

NATIONAL LEAGUE 1968, *cont.*

	W	L	PCT	GB	R	OR	Batting 2B	3B	HR	BA	SA	SB	Fielding E	DP	FA	Pitching CG	BB	SO	ShO	SV	ERA
St. Louis	97	65	.599		583	**472**	227	**48**	73	.249	.346	110	140	135	.978	63	375	971	**30**	32	**2.49**
San Francisco	88	74	.543	9	599	529	162	33	108	.239	.341	50	162	125	.975	**77**	**344**	942	20	16	2.71
Chicago	84	78	.519	13	612	611	203	43	**130**	.242	.366	41	**119**	149	**.981**	46	392	894	12	32	3.41
Cincinnati	83	79	.512	14	**690**	673	**281**	36	106	**.273**	**.389**	59	144	144	.978	24	573	963	16	**38**	3.56
Atlanta	81	81	.500	16	514	549	179	31	80	.252	.339	83	125	139	.980	44	362	871	16	29	2.92
Pittsburgh	80	82	.494	17	583	532	180	44	80	.252	.343	**130**	139	162	.979	42	485	897	19	30	2.74
Los Angeles	76	86	.469	21	470	509	202	36	67	.230	.319	57	144	144	.977	38	414	994	23	31	2.69
Philadelphia	76	86	.469	21	543	615	178	30	100	.233	.333	58	127	**163**	.980	42	421	935	12	27	3.36
New York	73	89	.451	24	473	499	178	30	81	.228	.315	72	133	142	.979	45	430	1014	25	32	2.72
Houston	72	90	.444	25	510	588	205	28	66	.231	.317	44	156	129	.975	50	479	**1021**	12	23	3.26
					5577	5577	1995	359	891	.243	.341	704	1389	1432	.978	471	4275	9502	185	290	2.99

AMERICAN LEAGUE 1968

Detroit

W-103 L-59

Mayo Smith

POS	Player	AB	BA	HR	RBI	PO	A	E	DP	TC/G	FA	Pitcher	G	IP	W	L	SV	ERA
1B	N. Cash	411	.263	25	63	924	88	8	66	8.7	.992	D. McLain	41	**336**	**31**	6	0	1.96
2B	D. McAuliffe	570	.249	16	56	288	348	9	79	4.4	.986	E. Wilson	34	224	13	12	0	2.85
SS	R. Oyler	215	.135	1	12	139	207	8	31	3.2	.977	M. Lolich	39	220	17	9	1	3.19
3B	D. Wert	536	.200	12	37	142	284	15	22	2.9	.966	J. Sparma	34	182	10	10	0	3.70
RF	J. Northrup	580	.264	21	90	321	7	7	1	2.2	.979	J. Hiller	39	128	9	6	2	2.39
CF	M. Stanley	583	.259	11	60	297	7	0	2	2.3	1.000	P. Dobson	47	125	5	8	7	2.66
LF	W. Horton	512	.285	36	85	212	6	6	2	1.6	.973	D. Patterson	38	68	2	3	7	2.12
C	B. Freehan	540	.263	25	84	**971**	73	6	**15**	7.6	.994	F. Lasher	34	49	5	1	5	3.33
OF	A. Kaline	327	.287	10	53	131	1	3	0	1.8	.978							
SS	T. Matchick	227	.203	3	14	53	118	9	20	3.1	.950							
UT	D. Tracewski	212	.156	4	15	82	157	5	27		.980							

Baltimore

W-91 L-71

Hank Bauer
W-43 L-37

Earl Weaver
W-48 L-34

POS	Player	AB	BA	HR	RBI	PO	A	E	DP	TC/G	FA	Pitcher	G	IP	W	L	SV	ERA
1B	B. Powell	550	.249	22	85	**1293**	79	14	102	9.3	.990	D. McNally	35	273	22	10	0	1.95
2B	D. Johnson	504	.242	9	56	260	330	13	67	4.7	.978	J. Hardin	35	244	18	13	0	2.51
SS	M. Belanger	472	.208	2	21	248	444	22	73	4.9	.969	T. Phoebus	36	241	15	15	0	2.62
3B	B. Robinson	608	.253	17	75	168	**353**	16	31	3.3	**.970**	D. Leonhard	28	126	7	7	1	3.13
RF	F. Robinson	421	.268	15	52	173	5	7	0	1.6	.962	G. Brabender	37	125	6	7	3	3.32
CF	P. Blair	421	.211	7	38	271	10	2	2	2.1	.993	E. Watt	59	83	5	5	11	2.27
LF	C. Blefary	451	.200	15	39	144	9	6	1	1.7	.962	P. Richert	36	62	6	3	6	3.47
C	A. Etchebarren	189	.233	5	20	414	29	1	3	6.3	.998	M. Drabowsky	45	61	4	4	7	1.91
O2	D. Buford	426	.282	15	46	239	111	8	22		.978							
OF	C. Motton	217	.198	8	25	91	2	1	0	1.7	.989							
C	E. Hendricks	183	.202	7	23	303	21	3	3	6.2	.991							

Cleveland

W-86 L-75

Alvin Dark

POS	Player	AB	BA	HR	RBI	PO	A	E	DP	TC/G	FA	Pitcher	G	IP	W	L	SV	ERA
1B	T. Horton	477	.249	14	59	972	63	8	80	8.1	.992	S. McDowell	38	269	15	14	0	1.81
2B	V. Fuller	244	.242	0	18	112	129	3	24	3.3	.988	L. Tiant	34	258	21	9	0	**1.60**
SS	L. Brown	495	.234	6	35	255	371	22	70	4.2	.966	S. Siebert	31	206	12	10	0	2.97
3B	M. Alvis	452	.223	8	37	114	202	13	18	2.6	.960	S. Williams	44	194	13	11	9	2.50
RF	T. Harper	235	.217	6	26	121	0	2	0	1.1	.984	S. Hargan	32	158	8	15	0	4.15
CF	J. Cardenal	583	.257	7	44	367	12	10	7	2.5	.974	E. Fisher	54	95	4	2	4	2.85
LF	L. Maye	299	.281	4	26	123	4	2	0	1.6	.984	M. Paul	36	92	5	8	3	3.93
C	J. Azcue	357	.280	4	42	699	50	3	11	**7.8**	**.996**	V. Romo	40	83	5	3	12	1.62
C	D. Sims	361	.249	11	44	523	41	**10**	7	6.8	.983							
UT	C. Salmon	276	.214	3	12	152	145	8	29		.974							
OF	R. Snyder	217	.281	2	23	106	4	1	3	2.1	.991							
OF	L. Johnson	202	.257	5	23	87	5	1	1	1.6	.989							
2B	D. Nelson	189	.233	0	19	115	114	3	26	3.9	.987							
OF	V. Davalillo	180	.239	2	13	84	4	3	1	1.9	.967							

Boston

W-86 L-76

Dick Williams

POS	Player	AB	BA	HR	RBI	PO	A	E	DP	TC/G	FA	Pitcher	G	IP	W	L	SV	ERA
1B	G. Scott	350	.171	3	25	807	55	11	68	7.8	.987	R. Culp	35	216	16	6	0	2.91
2B	M. Andrews	536	.271	7	45	330	375	17	93	5.2	.976	G. Bell	35	199	11	11	1	3.12
SS	R. Petrocelli	406	.234	12	46	169	360	12	66	4.6	**.978**	D. Ellsworth	31	196	16	7	0	3.03
3B	J. Foy	515	.225	10	60	116	313	**30**	**36**	3.1	.935	J. Santiago	18	124	9	4	0	2.25
RF	K. Harrelson	535	.275	35	**109**	241	8	0	1	1.9	1.000	J. Lonborg	23	113	6	10	0	4.29
CF	R. Smith	558	.265	15	69	390	8	6	1	2.6	.985	J. Pizarro	19	108	6	8	2	3.59
LF	C. Yastrzemski	539	**.301**	23	74	301	12	3	3	2.0	.991	G. Waslewski	34	105	4	7	2	3.67
C	R. Gibson	231	.225	3	20	428	36	8	7	6.4	.983	L. Stange	50	103	5	5	12	3.93
12	D. Jones	354	.234	5	29	481	65	3	55		.995	J. Stephenson	23	69	2	8	0	5.64
UT	J. Adair	208	.216	2	12	90	139	8	22		.966	S. Lyle	49	66	6	1	11	2.74
C	E. Howard	203	.241	5	18	377	30	2	3	6.0	.995							

New York

W-83 L-79

Ralph Houk

POS	Player	AB	BA	HR	RBI	PO	A	E	DP	TC/G	FA	Pitcher	G	IP	W	L	SV	ERA
1B	M. Mantle	435	.237	18	54	1195	76	15	91	9.8	.988	M. Stottlemyre	36	279	21	12	0	2.45
2B	H. Clarke	579	.230	2	26	**357**	**444**	13	80	**5.9**	.984	S. Bahnsen	37	267	17	12	0	2.05
SS	T. Tresh	507	.195	11	52	199	409	31	70	**5.4**	.951	F. Peterson	36	212	12	11	0	2.63
3B	B. Cox	437	.229	7	41	98	279	17	22	3.0	.957	S. Barber	20	128	6	5	0	3.23
RF	B. Robinson	342	.240	6	40	195	3	3	1	2.1	.985	F. Talbot	29	99	1	9	0	3.36
CF	J. Pepitone	380	.245	15	56	190	4	4	1	2.2	.980	J. Verbanic	40	97	6	7	4	3.15
LF	R. White	577	.267	17	62	283	14	1	4	1.9	.997	B. Monbouquette	17	89	5	7	0	4.43
C	J. Gibbs	423	.213	3	29	642	55	6	7	5.8	.991	D. Womack	45	62	3	7	2	3.21
OF	A. Kosco	466	.240	15	59	160	9	7	0	1.9	.960	L. McDaniel	24	51	4	1	10	1.75
C	F. Fernandez	135	.170	7	30	240	27	3	2	6.0	.989	S. Hamilton	40	51	2	2	11	2.13

AMERICAN LEAGUE 1968, *cont.*

Oakland

W-82 L-80

Bob Kennedy

POS	Player	AB	BA	HR	RBI	PO	A	E	DP	TC/G	FA
1B	D. Cater	504	.290	6	62	985	68	5	89	8.7	**.995**
2B	J. Donaldson	363	.220	2	27	169	263	13	48	4.5	.971
SS	B. Campaneris	**642**	.276	4	38	**279**	458	**34**	86	5.0	.956
3B	S. Bando	605	.251	9	67	**188**	272	17	27	2.9	.964
RF	R. Jackson	553	.250	29	74	269	14	12	5	2.0	.959
CF	R. Monday	482	.274	8	49	299	11	7	3	2.2	.978
LF	M. Hershberger	246	.272	5	32	128	5	3	0	1.5	.978
C	D. Duncan	246	.191	7	28	474	41	7	5	6.6	.987
2B	D. Green	202	.233	6	18	124	170	8	35	5.0	.974
C	J. Pagliaroni	199	.246	6	20	375	16	1	3	6.2	.997
1B	R. Webster	196	.214	3	23	454	27	6	33	8.9	.988
OF	J. Rudi	181	.177	1	12	77	1	1	0	1.4	.987

Pitcher	G	IP	W	L	SV	ERA
C. Hunter	36	234	13	13	1	3.35
B. Odom	32	231	16	10	0	2.45
J. Nash	34	229	13	13	0	2.28
C. Dobson	35	225	12	14	0	3.00
L. Krausse	36	185	10	11	4	3.11
D. Segui	52	83	6	5	6	2.39
J. Aker	54	75	4	4	11	4.10
E. Sprague	47	69	3	4	4	3.28

Minnesota

W-79 L-83

Cal Ermer

POS	Player	AB	BA	HR	RBI	PO	A	E	DP	TC/G	FA
1B	R. Reese	332	.259	4	28	620	38	6	36	7.6	.991
2B	R. Carew	461	.273	1	42	262	280	**18**	48	4.8	.968
SS	J. Hernandez	199	.176	2	17	119	197	25	43	4.3	.927
3B	C. Tovar	613	.272	6	47	48	147	14	8	2.8	.933
RF	T. Oliva	470	.289	18	68	227	7	4	1	1.9	.983
CF	T. Uhlaender	488	.283	7	52	283	3	4	1	2.2	.986
LF	B. Allison	469	.247	22	52	166	4	6	0	1.5	.966
C	J. Roseboro	380	.216	8	39	689	52	7	5	6.4	.991
1B	H. Killebrew	295	.210	17	40	594	56	4	50	8.5	.994
23	F. Quilici	229	.245	1	22	121	165	3	30		.990
3S	R. Clark	227	.185	1	13	73	157	16	18		.935
3B	R. Rollins	203	.241	6	30	28	93	9	4	2.3	.931

Pitcher	G	IP	W	L	SV	ERA
D. Chance	43	292	16	16	1	2.53
J. Merritt	38	238	12	16	1	3.25
J. Kaat	30	208	14	12	0	2.94
D. Boswell	34	190	10	13	0	3.32
J. Perry	32	139	8	6	1	2.27
R. Perranoski	66	87	8	7	6	3.10
A. Worthington	54	76	4	5	**18**	2.71

California

W-67 L-95

Bill Rigney

POS	Player	AB	BA	HR	RBI	PO	A	E	DP	TC/G	FA
1B	D. Mincher	399	.236	13	48	949	59	9	90	9.0	.991
2B	B. Knoop	494	.249	3	39	350	425	15	**94**	5.2	.981
SS	J. Fregosi	614	.244	9	49	273	454	29	**92**	4.8	.962
3B	A. Rodriguez	223	.242	1	16	61	113	15	18	2.7	.921
RF	R. Repoz	375	.240	13	54	226	4	3	1	2.0	.987
CF	V. Davalillo	339	.298	1	18	212	4	1	2	2.5	.995
LF	R. Reichardt	534	.255	21	73	267	9	3	2	1.9	.989
C	B. Rodgers	258	.190	1	14	407	50	7	11	5.3	.985
C	T. Satriano	297	.253	8	35	404	40	5	6	5.3	.989
UT	C. Hinton	267	.195	7	23	390	60	7	32		.985
3B	P. Schaal	219	.210	2	16	61	142	9	13	3.7	.958
OF	B. Morton	163	.270	1	18	64	1	1	1	1.3	.985

Pitcher	G	IP	W	L	SV	ERA
G. Brunet	39	245	13	**17**	0	2.86
J. McGlothlin	40	208	10	15	3	3.54
S. Ellis	42	164	9	10	2	3.95
C. Wright	41	126	10	6	3	3.94
T. Murphy	15	99	5	6	0	2.17
R. Clark	21	94	1	11	0	3.53
M. Pattin	52	84	4	4	3	2.79
A. Messersmith	28	81	4	2	4	2.21
T. Burgmeier	56	73	1	4	5	4.33
M. Rojas	38	55	4	3	6	4.25

Chicago

W-67 L-95

Eddie Stanky
W-34 L-45

Les Moss
W-0 L-2

Al Lopez
W-6 L-5

Les Moss
W-12 L-22

Al Lopez
W-15 L-21

POS	Player	AB	BA	HR	RBI	PO	A	E	DP	TC/G	FA
1B	T. McCraw	477	.235	9	44	1285	**93**	**20**	**103**	**10.4**	.986
2B	S. Alomar	363	.253	0	12	188	221	**18**	48	4.3	.958
SS	L. Aparicio	622	.264	4	36	269	**535**	19	**92**	5.3	.977
3B	P. Ward	399	.216	15	50	59	151	12	7	2.9	.946
RF	B. Bradford	281	.217	5	24	162	4	6	0	1.7	.965
CF	K. Berry	504	.252	7	32	352	11	7	2	2.5	.981
LF	T. Davis	456	.268	8	50	171	8	7	2	1.6	.962
C	D. Josephson	434	.247	6	45	641	**86**	7	**15**	6.0	.990
C	J. McNertney	169	.219	3	18	299	39	5	8	5.4	.985
OF	B. Voss	167	.156	2	15	73	5	3	3	1.5	.963
OF	L. Wagner	162	.284	1	18	48	0	3	0	1.1	.941

Pitcher	G	IP	W	L	SV	ERA
J. Horlen	35	224	12	14	0	2.37
J. Fisher	35	181	8	13	0	2.99
T. John	25	177	10	5	0	1.98
G. Peters	31	163	4	13	1	3.76
W. Wood	**88**	159	13	12	16	1.87
C. Carlos	29	122	4	14	0	3.90
B. Priddy	35	114	3	11	0	3.63
H. Wilhelm	72	94	4	4	12	1.73
B. Locker	70	90	5	4	10	2.29

Washington

W-65 L-96

Jim Lemon

POS	Player	AB	BA	HR	RBI	PO	A	E	DP	TC/G	FA
1B	M. Epstein	385	.234	13	33	947	70	13	83	9.4	.987
2B	B. Allen	373	.241	6	40	263	271	5	63	4.9	**.991**
SS	R. Hansen	275	.185	8	28	137	256	15	45	5.0	.963
3B	K. McMullen	557	.248	20	62	185	296	19	26	**3.4**	.962
RF	E. Stroud	306	.239	4	23	139	2	3	1	1.7	.979
CF	D. Unser	635	.230	1	30	388	22	5	10	2.7	.988
LF	F. Howard	598	.274	**44**	106	160	11	8	1	1.7	.955
C	P. Casanova	322	.196	4	25	472	46	6	3	5.7	.989
OF	C. Peterson	226	.204	3	18	82	2	0	0	1.6	1.000
SS	E. Brinkman	193	.187	0	6	97	197	10	28	4.1	.967
2B	F. Coggins	171	.175	0	7	122	122	12	33	4.9	.953
C	J. French	165	.194	1	10	268	42	5	2	5.9	.984
OF	B. Alyea	150	.267	6	23	76	0	0	0	1.9	1.000

Pitcher	G	IP	W	L	SV	ERA
J. Coleman	33	223	12	16	0	3.27
C. Pascual	31	201	13	12	0	2.69
J. Hannan	25	140	10	6	0	3.01
D. Bosman	46	139	2	9	1	3.69
F. Bertaina	27	127	7	13	0	4.66
B. Moore	32	118	4	6	3	3.37
P. Ortega	31	116	5	12	0	4.98
D. Higgins	59	100	4	4	13	3.25
B. Humphreys	56	93	5	7	2	3.69

BATTING AND BASE RUNNING LEADERS

Batting Average

C. Yastrzemski, BOS	.301
D. Cater, OAK	.290
T. Oliva, MIN	.289
W. Horton, DET	.285
T. Uhlaender, MIN	.283

Slugging Average

F. Howard, WAS	.552
W. Horton, DET	.543
K. Harrelson, BOS	.518
C. Yastrzemski, BOS	.495
T. Oliva, MIN	.477

Home Runs

F. Howard, WAS	44
W. Horton, DET	36
K. Harrelson, BOS	35
R. Jackson, OAK	29
N. Cash, DET	25
B. Freehan, DET	25

PITCHING LEADERS

Winning Percentage

D. McLain, DET	.838
R. Culp, BOS	.727
L. Tiant, CLE	.700
D. Ellsworth, BOS	.696
D. McNally, BAL	.688

Earned Run Average

L. Tiant, CLE	1.60
S. McDowell, CLE	1.81
D. McNally, BAL	1.95
D. McLain, DET	1.96
T. John, CHI	1.98

Wins

D. McLain, DET	31
D. McNally, BAL	22
L. Tiant, CLE	21
M. Stottlemyre, NY	21
J. Hardin, BAL	18

AMERICAN LEAGUE 1968, *cont.*

BATTING AND BASE RUNNING LEADERS

Total Bases		Runs Batted In		Stolen Bases	
F. Howard, WAS	330	K. Harrelson, BOS	109	B. Campaneris, OAK	62
W. Horton, DET	278	F. Howard, WAS	106	J. Cardenal, CLE	40
K. Harrelson, BOS	277	J. Northrup, DET	90	C. Tovar, MIN	35
C. Yastrzemski, BOS	267	W. Horton, DET	85	D. Buford, BAL	27
J. Northrup, DET	259	B. Powell, BAL	85	J. Foy, BOS	26

Hits		Base on Balls		Home Run Percentage	
B. Campaneris, OAK	177	C. Yastrzemski, BOS	119	F. Howard, WAS	7.4
C. Tovar, MIN	167	M. Mantle, NY	106	W. Horton, DET	7.0
F. Howard, WAS	164	J. Foy, BOS	84	K. Harrelson, BOS	6.5
L. Aparicio, CHI	164	D. McAuliffe, DET	82	R. Jackson, OAK	5.2

Runs		Doubles		Triples	
D. McAuliffe, DET	95	R. Smith, BOS	37	J. Fregosi, CAL	13
C. Yastrzemski, BOS	90	B. Robinson, BAL	36	T. McCraw, CHI	12
R. White, NY	89	C. Yastrzemski, BOS	32	E. Stroud, WAS	10
C. Tovar, MIN	89	C. Tovar, MIN	31	D. McAuliffe, DET	10

PITCHING LEADERS

Saves		Strikeouts		Complete Games	
A. Worthington, MIN	18	S. McDowell, CLE	283	D. McLain, DET	28
W. Wood, CHI	16	D. McLain, DET	280	L. Tiant, CLE	19
D. Higgins, WAS	13	L. Tiant, CLE	264	M. Stottlemyre, NY	19
V. Romo, CLE	12	D. Chance, MIN	234	D. McNally, BAL	18
L. Stange, BOS	12	D. McNally, BAL	202	J. Hardin, BAL	16
H. Wilhelm, CHI	12				

Fewest Hits/9 Innings		Shutouts		Fewest Walks/9 Innings	
L. Tiant, CLE	5.30	L. Tiant, CLE	9	F. Peterson, NY	1.23
D. McNally, BAL	5.77			D. McLain, DET	1.69
S. McDowell, CLE	6.06			D. Ellsworth, BOS	1.70
S. Siebert, CLE	6.33			J. Kaat, MIN	1.73

Most Strikeouts/9 Inn.		Innings		Games Pitched	
S. McDowell, CLE	9.47	D. McLain, DET	336	W. Wood, CHI	88
L. Tiant, CLE	9.20	D. Chance, MIN	292	H. Wilhelm, CHI	72
M. Lolich, DET	8.06	M. Stottlemyre, NY	279	B. Locker, CHI	70
R. Culp, BOS	7.90	D. McNally, BAL	273	R. Perranoski, MIN	66

							Batting						Fielding			Pitching					
	W	L	PCT	GB	R	OR	2B	3B	HR	BA	SA	SB	E	DP	FA	CG	BB	SO	ShO	SV	ERA
Detroit	103	59	.636		**671**	**492**	190	39	**185**	.235	**.385**	26	**105**	133	**.983**	**59**	486	1115	19	29	2.71
Baltimore	91	71	.562	12	579	497	**215**	28	133	.225	.352	78	120	131	.981	53	502	1044	16	31	**2.66**
Cleveland	86	75	.534	16.5	516	504	210	36	75	.234	.327	115	127	130	.979	48	540	**1157**	**23**	32	**2.66**
Boston	86	76	.531	17	614	611	207	17	125	.236	.352	76	128	147	.979	55	523	972	17	31	3.33
New York	83	79	.512	20	536	531	154	34	109	.214	.318	90	139	142	.979	45	424	831	14	27	2.79
Oakland	82	80	.506	21	569	544	192	40	94	**.240**	.343	**147**	145	136	.976	45	505	997	18	29	2.94
Minnesota	79	83	.488	24	562	546	207	**41**	105	.237	.350	98	170	117	.973	46	**414**	996	14	29	2.89
California	67	95	.414	36	498	615	170	33	83	.227	.318	62	140	**156**	.977	29	519	869	11	31	3.43
Chicago	67	95	.414	36	463	527	169	33	71	.228	.311	90	151	152	.977	20	451	834	11	**40**	2.75
Washington	65	96	.404	37.5	524	665	160	37	124	.224	.336	29	148	144	.976	26	517	826	11	28	3.64
					5532	5532	1874	338	1104	.230	.339	811	1373	1388	.978	426	4881	9641	154	307	2.98

NATIONAL LEAGUE 1969

		POS	Player	AB	BA	HR	RBI	PO	A	E	DP	TC/G	FA	Pitcher	G	IP	W	L	SV	ERA
East	New York	1B	E. Kranepool	353	.238	11	49	809	64	6	76	8.3	.993	T. Seaver	36	273	**25**	7	0	2.21
		2B	K. Boswell	362	.279	3	32	190	229	18	51	4.6	.959	J. Koosman	32	241	17	9	0	2.28
	W-100 L-62	SS	B. Harrelson	395	.248	0	24	243	347	19	70	5.1	.969	G. Gentry	35	234	13	12	0	3.43
		3B	W. Garrett	400	.218	1	39	40	115	8	10	2.3	.951	D. Cardwell	30	152	8	10	0	3.01
	Gil Hodges	RF	R. Swoboda	327	.235	9	52	163	5	2	0	1.8	.988	J. McAndrew	27	135	6	7	0	3.47
		CF	T. Agee	565	.271	26	76	334	7	5	0	2.4	.986	T. McGraw	42	100	9	3	12	2.24
		LF	C. Jones	483	.340	12	75	223	4	2	0	1.9	.991	N. Ryan	25	89	6	3	1	3.53
		C	J. Grote	365	.252	6	40	718	63	7	11	7.0	.991	C. Koonce	40	83	6	3	7	4.99
		OF	A. Shamsky	303	.300	14	47	117	2	1	2	1.5	.992	R. Taylor	59	76	9	4	13	2.72
		S2	A. Weis	247	.215	2	23	138	218	13	50		.965							
		OF	R. Gaspar	215	.228	1	14	104	12	2	**6**	1.3	.983							
		3B	B. Pfeil	211	.232	0	10	32	88	3	8	2.5	.976							
		1B	D. Clendenon	202	.252	12	37	418	25	7	46	7.8	.984							
		C	J. Martin	177	.209	4	21	275	9	1	2	5.9	.996							
		3B	E. Charles	169	.207	3	18	37	86	7	9	2.5	.946							
	Chicago	1B	E. Banks	565	.253	23	106	**1419**	87	4	116	9.9	**.997**	F. Jenkins	43	311	21	15	1	3.21
		2B	G. Beckert	543	.291	1	37	262	401	**24**	71	5.3	.965	B. Hands	41	300	20	14	0	2.49
		SS	D. Kessinger	664	.273	4	53	**266**	**542**	20	**101**	5.3	**.976**	K. Holtzman	39	261	17	13	0	3.59
	W-92 L-70	3B	R. Santo	575	.289	29	123	**144**	334	27	23	3.2	.947	D. Selma	36	169	10	8	1	3.63
		RF	J. Hickman	338	.237	21	54	153	6	3	0	1.3	.981	P. Regan	71	112	12	6	17	3.70
	Leo Durocher	CF	D. Young	272	.239	6	27	191	4	5	0	2.0	.975	T. Abernathy	56	85	4	3	3	3.18
		LF	B. Williams	642	.293	21	95	250	15	12	2	1.7	.957	R. Nye	34	69	3	5	3	5.09
		C	R. Hundley	522	.255	18	64	978	**79**	8	**17**	7.1	.992							
		OF	A. Spangler	213	.211	4	23	75	1	4	0	1.4	.950							
		O1	W. Smith	195	.246	9	25	185	9	3	14		.985							
	Pittsburgh	1B	A. Oliver	463	.285	17	70	869	49	8	87	8.7	.991	B. Veale	34	226	13	14	0	3.23
		2B	B. Mazeroski	227	.229	3	25	134	192	4	46	5.1	.988	D. Ellis	35	219	11	17	0	3.58
		SS	F. Patek	460	.239	5	32	227	399	30	81	4.5	.954	S. Blass	38	210	16	10	2	4.46
	W-88 L-74	3B	R. Hebner	459	.301	8	47	79	240	19	31	2.7	.944	B. Moose	44	170	14	3	4	2.91
		RF	R. Clemente	507	.345	19	91	226	14	5	1	1.8	.980	J. Bunning	25	156	10	9	0	3.81
	Larry Shepard	CF	M. Alou	**698**	.331	1	48	327	10	8	4	2.1	.977	L. Walker	31	119	4	6	0	3.63
	W-84 L-73	LF	W. Stargell	522	.307	29	92	159	4	5	1	1.4	.970	C. Hartenstein	56	96	5	4	10	3.94
		C	M. Sanguillen	459	.303	5	57	825	71	**17**	11	8.1	.981	B. Dal Canton	57	86	8	2	5	3.35
	Alex Grammas	2S	G. Alley	285	.246	8	32	145	213	11	56		.970	J. Gibbon	35	51	5	1	9	1.93
	W-4 L-1	3O	J. Pagan	274	.285	9	42	56	76	5	7		.964							
		O1	C. Taylor	221	.348	4	33	267	16	8	26		.973							
		C	J. May	190	.232	7	23	325	22	2	3	6.7	.994							
		UT	J. Martinez	168	.268	1	16	86	132	6	31		.973							

NATIONAL LEAGUE 1969, *cont.*

	Team	POS	Player	AB	BA	HR	RBI	PO	A	E	DP	TC/G	FA	Pitcher	G	IP	W	L	SV	ERA
	St. Louis	1B	J. Torre	602	.289	18	101	1270	83	6	117	9.4	.996	B. Gibson	35	314	20	13	0	2.18
	W-87 L-75	2B	J. Javier	493	.282	10	42	244	374	21	70	4.5	.967	S. Carlton	31	236	17	11	0	2.17
	Red Schoendienst	SS	D. Maxvill	372	.175	2	32	216	408	20	78	4.9	.969	N. Briles	36	228	15	13	0	3.51
		3B	M. Shannon	551	.254	12	55	123	258	22	22	2.7	.945	R. Washburn	28	132	3	8	1	3.07
		RF	V. Pinson	495	.255	10	70	218	6	1	2	1.8	.996	C. Taylor	27	127	7	5	0	2.55
		CF	C. Flood	606	.285	4	57	362	14	4	2	2.5	.989	M. Torrez	24	108	10	4	0	3.58
		LF	L. Brock	655	.298	12	47	255	7	14	2	1.8	.949	D. Giusti	22	100	3	7	0	3.60
		C	T. McCarver	515	.260	7	51	925	66	14	10	7.4	.986	M. Grant	30	63	7	5	7	4.12
														J. Hoerner	45	53.	2	3	15	2.89
	Philadelphia	1B	D. Allen	438	.288	32	89	1024	54	16	100	9.4	.985	G. Jackson	38	253	14	18	1	3.34
	W-63 L-99	2B	C. Rojas	391	.228	4	30	259	229	10	68	5.2	.980	W. Fryman	36	228	12	15	0	4.42
	Bob Skinner	SS	D. Money	450	.229	6	42	212	443	21	82	5.4	.969	R. Wise	33	220	15	13	0	3.23
	W-44 L-64	3B	T. Taylor	557	.262	3	30	57	150	7	8	3.0	.967	J. Johnson	33	147	6	13	1	4.29
	George Myatt	RF	J. Callison	495	.265	16	64	273	12	3	3	2.2	.990	B. Champion	23	117	5	10	1	5.00
	W-19 L-35	CF	L. Hisle	482	.266	20	56	324	11	8	2	2.5	.977	L. Palmer	26	90	2	8	0	5.20
		LF	J. Briggs	361	.238	12	46	197	6	6	0	1.9	.971	D. Farrell	46	74	3	4	3	4.01
		C	M. Ryan	446	.204	12	44	769	**79**	8	13	6.5	.991	B. Wilson	37	62	2	5	6	3.34
		UT	D. Johnson	475	.255	17	80	250	99	11	12		.969							
		3B	R. Joseph	264	.273	6	37	49	103	7	11	2.7	.956							
		OF	R. Stone	222	.239	1	24	85	6	2	0	1.3	.978							
		S2	T. Harmon	201	.239	0	16	94	168	7	42		.974							
	Montreal	1B	B. Bailey	358	.265	9	53	704	67	6	77	9.1	.992	B. Stoneman	42	236	11	19	0	4.39
	W-52 L-110	2B	G. Sutherland	544	.239	3	35	318	381	21	**110**	5.2	.971	J. Robertson	38	180	5	16	1	3.96
	Gene Mauch	SS	B. Wine	370	.200	3	25	208	367	**31**	96	5.1	.949	M. Wegener	32	166	5	14	0	4.40
		3B	C. Laboy	562	.258	18	83	115	307	25	28	2.9	.944	D. McGinn	74	132	7	10	6	3.94
		RF	R. Staub	549	.302	29	79	265	16	10	2	1.9	.966	G. Waslewski	30	109	3	7	1	3.29
		CF	A. Phillips	199	.216	4	7	99	3	2	0	2.0	.981	H. Reed	31	106	6	7	1	4.84
		LF	M. Jones	455	.270	22	79	226	6	10	0	1.9	.959	S. Renko	18	103	6	7	0	4.02
		C	R. Brand	287	.258	0	20	492	44	8	7	6.5	.985	R. Face	44	59	4	2	5	3.94
		1B	R. Fairly	253	.289	12	39	409	36	4	53	8.6	.991							
		C	J. Bateman	235	.209	8	19	433	26	7	5	7.1	.985							
		OF	T. Cline	209	.239	2	12	77	2	1	1	2.0	.988							
		SS	M. Wills	189	.222	0	8	72	139	11	31	4.8	.950							
West	**Atlanta**	1B	O. Cepeda	573	.257	22	88	1318	101	9	91	9.3	.994	P. Niekro	40	284	23	13	1	2.57
	W-93 L-69	2B	F. Millan	652	.267	6	57	**373**	**444**	17	72	5.1	**.980**	R. Reed	36	241	18	10	0	3.47
	Lum Harris	SS	S. Jackson	318	.239	1	27	161	254	17	48	4.5	.961	P. Jarvis	37	217	13	11	0	4.44
		3B	C. Boyer	496	.250	14	57	139	275	15	18	3.0	**.965**	G. Stone	36	165	13	10	3	3.65
		RF	H. Aaron	547	.300	44	97	267	11	5	3	2.0	.982	M. Pappas	26	144	6	10	0	3.63
		CF	F. Alou	476	.282	5	32	260	4	3	1	2.3	.989	C. Upshaw	62	105	6	4	27	2.91
		LF	T. Gonzalez	320	.294	10	50	173	1	2	0	2.1	.989	J. Britton	24	88	7	5	1	3.78
		C	B. Didier	352	.256	0	32	633	52	4	3	6.0	.994							
		OF	R. Carty	304	.342	16	58	118	0	6	0	1.6	.952							
		SS	G. Garrido	227	.220	0	10	99	192	8	32	3.7	.973							
		UT	B. Aspromonte	198	.253	3	24	74	46	8	2		.938							
		C	B. Tillman	190	.195	12	29	309	15	4	5	4.8	.988							
		OF	M. Lum	168	.268	1	22	119	2	1	1	1.4	.992							
		01	T. Francona	88	.295	2	22	64	4	2	4		.971							
	San Francisco	1B	W. McCovey	491	.320	**45**	**126**	1392	79	12	116	**10.0**	.992	G. Perry	40	**325**	19	14	0	2.49
	W-90 L-72	2B	R. Hunt	478	.262	3	41	254	356	13	67	5.0	.979	J. Marichal	37	300	21	11	0	**2.10**
	Clyde King	SS	H. Lanier	495	.228	0	35	252	530	25	98	**5.4**	.969	M. McCormick	32	197	11	9	0	3.34
		3B	J. Davenport	303	.241	2	42	77	158	8	15	2.3	.967	B. Bolin	30	146	7	7	0	4.44
		RF	B. Bonds	622	.259	32	90	339	9	8	2	2.3	.978	R. Sadecki	29	138	5	8	0	4.24
		CF	W. Mays	403	.283	13	58	199	4	5	0	1.9	.976	F. Linzy	58	116	14	9	11	3.65
		LF	K. Henderson	374	.225	6	44	175	10	6	2	1.7	.969							
		C	D. Dietz	244	.230	11	35	432	31	13	5	6.5	.973							
		OF	D. Marshall	267	.232	2	33	106	3	5	0	1.3	.956							
		23	D. Mason	250	.228	0	13	132	174	18	36		.944							
		OF	J. Hart	236	.254	3	26	80	2	5	1	1.3	.943							
		C	J. Hiatt	194	.196	7	34	335	30	3	6	6.1	.992							
		3S	T. Fuentes	183	.295	1	14	50	117	13	18		.928							
		1B	B. Burda	161	.230	6	27	206	12	1	15	4.9	.995							
	Cincinnati	1B	L. May	607	.278	38	110	1387	102	11	**128**	9.6	.993	J. Merritt	42	251	17	9	0	4.37
	W-89 L-73	2B	T. Helms	480	.269	1	40	320	344	17	87	**5.4**	.975	T. Cloninger	35	190	11	17	0	5.02
	Dave Bristol	SS	W. Woodward	241	.261	0	15	147	248	14	36	4.4	.966	J. Maloney	30	179	12	5	0	2.77
		3B	T. Perez	629	.294	37	122	136	**342**	**32**	**35**	3.2	.937	C. Carroll	71	151	12	6	7	3.52
		RF	P. Rose	627	**.348**	16	82	316	10	4	3	2.1	.988	W. Granger	**90**	145	9	6	27	2.79
		CF	B. Tolan	637	.305	21	93	362	6	10	3	2.5	.974	J. Fisher	34	113	4	4	1	5.50
		LF	A. Johnson	523	.315	17	88	222	5	18	1	1.9	.927	G. Nolan	16	109	8	8	0	3.55
		C	J. Bench	532	.293	26	90	793	76	7	10	6.0	.992	G. Culver	32	101	5	7	4	4.28
		OF	J. Stewart	221	.253	4	24	68	4	2	0	1.1	.973	J. Arrigo	20	91	4	7	0	4.14
		SS	D. Chaney	209	.191	0	15	115	191	17	44	3.5	.947							
		UT	C. Ruiz	196	.245	0	13	120	147	12	36		.957							

NATIONAL LEAGUE 1969, *cont.*

Los Angeles

W-85 L-77

Walter Alston

POS	Player	AB	BA	HR	RBI	PO	A	E	DP	TC/G	FA	Pitcher	G	IP	W	L	SV	ERA
1B	W. Parker	471	.278	13	68	1189	79	6	87	10.0	.995	C. Osteen	41	321	20	15	0	2.66
2B	T. Sizemore	590	.271	4	46	283	331	13	76	5.3	.979	B. Singer	41	316	20	12	1	2.34
SS	M. Wills	434	.297	4	39	168	357	17	61	5.2	.969	D. Sutton	41	293	17	18	0	3.47
3B	B. Sudakis	462	.234	14	53	98	272	21	26	**3.2**	.946	A. Foster	24	103	3	9	0	4.37
RF	A. Kosco	424	.248	19	74	153	6	3	2	1.5	.981	J. Brewer	59	88	7	6	20	2.56
CF	W. Davis	498	.311	11	59	271	8	6	1	2.3	.979	P. Mikkelsen	48	81	7	5	4	2.78
LF	W. Crawford	389	.247	11	41	177	5	5	0	1.7	.973	A. McBean	31	48	2	6	4	3.91
C	T. Haller	445	.263	6	39	800	48	7	4	6.5	.992							
OF	M. Mota	294	.323	3	30	118	8	4	2	1.6	.969							
32	J. Lefebvre	275	.236	4	44	96	181	6	23		.979							
OF	B. Russell	212	.226	5	15	132	4	3	1	1.6	.978							
OF	L. Gabrielson	178	.270	1	18	50	1	1	0	1.1	.981							

Houston

W-81 L-81

Harry Walker

POS	Player	AB	BA	HR	RBI	PO	A	E	DP	TC/G	FA	Pitcher	G	IP	W	L	SV	ERA
1B	C. Blefary	542	.253	12	67	1235	**103**	**17**	117	8.9	.987	L. Dierker	39	305	20	13	0	2.33
2B	J. Morgan	535	.236	15	43	303	328	18	79	4.9	.972	D. Lemaster	38	245	13	17	1	3.16
SS	D. Menke	553	.269	10	90	161	356	24	63	4.1	.956	D. Wilson	34	225	16	12	0	4.00
3B	D. Rader	569	.246	11	83	126	307	25	34	3.0	.945	T. Griffin	31	188	11	10	0	3.54
RF	N. Miller	409	.264	4	50	172	7	3	3	1.6	.984	J. Ray	40	115	8	2	0	3.91
CF	J. Wynn	495	.269	33	87	318	9	5	3	2.2	.985	J. Billingham	52	83	6	7	2	4.23
LF	J. Alou	452	.248	5	34	173	8	14	1	1.7	.928	F. Gladding	57	73	4	8	**29**	4.19
C	J. Edwards	496	.232	6	50	**1135**	**79**	7	9	**8.1**	**.994**							
UT	M. Martinez	198	.308	0	15	77	66	11	8		.929							

San Diego

W-52 L-110

Preston Gomez

POS	Player	AB	BA	HR	RBI	PO	A	E	DP	TC/G	FA	Pitcher	G	IP	W	L	SV	ERA
1B	N. Colbert	483	.255	24	66	1217	87	13	96	9.8	.990	C. Kirby	35	216	7	**20**	0	3.79
2B	J. Arcia	302	.215	0	10	162	176	8	33	5.1	.977	J. Niekro	37	202	8	17	0	3.70
SS	T. Dean	273	.176	2	9	139	255	9	41	4.2	.978	A. Santorini	32	185	8	14	0	3.94
3B	E. Spiezio	355	.234	13	43	93	198	19	10	3.2	.939	T. Sisk	53	143	2	13	6	4.78
RF	O. Brown	568	.264	20	61	269	14	7	4	2.0	.976	D. Kelley	27	136	4	8	0	3.57
CF	C. Gaston	391	.230	2	28	243	12	11	4	2.4	.959	G. Ross	46	110	3	12	3	4.19
LF	A. Ferrara	366	.260	14	56	131	5	6	2	1.5	.958	J. Baldschun	61	77	7	2	1	4.79
C	C. Cannizzaro	418	.220	4	33	644	69	9	8	5.5	.988	J. Podres	17	65	5	6	0	4.29
UT	R. Pena	472	.250	4	30	289	285	13	54		.978	B. McCool	54	59	3	5	7	4.27
OF	I. Murrell	247	.255	3	25	137	3	6	0	2.0	.959							
2B	J. Sipin	229	.223	2	9	106	173	7	41	4.8	.976							
3B	V. Kelly	209	.244	3	15	42	91	4	10	2.8	.971							
OF	T. Gonzalez	182	.225	2	8	114	2	3	0	2.4	.975							
OF	L. Stahl	162	.198	3	10	48	3	1	0	1.4	.981							

BATTING AND BASE RUNNING LEADERS

Batting Average
P. Rose, CIN .348
R. Clemente, PIT .345
C. Jones, NY .340
M. Alou, PIT .331
W. McCovey, SF .320

Slugging Average
W. McCovey, SF .656
H. Aaron, ATL .607
D. Allen, PHI .573
W. Stargell, PIT .556
R. Clemente, PIT .544

Home Runs
W. McCovey, SF 45
H. Aaron, ATL 44
L. May, CIN 38
T. Perez, CIN 37
J. Wynn, HOU 33

Total Bases
H. Aaron, ATL 332
T. Perez, CIN 331
W. McCovey, SF 322
L. May, CIN 321
P. Rose, CIN 321

Runs Batted In
W. McCovey, SF 126
R. Santo, CHI 123
T. Perez, CIN 122
L. May, CIN 110
E. Banks, CHI 106

Stolen Bases
L. Brock, STL 53
J. Morgan, HOU 49
B. Bonds, SF 45
M. Wills, MON, LA 40
B. Tolan, CIN 26

Hits
M. Alou, PIT 231
P. Rose, CIN 218
L. Brock, STL 195
B. Tolan, CIN 194

Base on Balls
J. Wynn, HOU 148
W. McCovey, SF 121
J. Morgan, HOU 110
R. Staub, MON 110

Home Run Percentage
W. McCovey, SF 9.2
H. Aaron, ATL 8.0
D. Allen, PHI 7.3
J. Wynn, HOU 6.7

Runs
B. Bonds, SF 120
P. Rose, CIN 120
J. Wynn, HOU 113
D. Kessinger, CHI 109

Doubles
M. Alou, PIT 41
D. Kessinger, CHI 38
P. Rose, CIN 33
B. Williams, CHI 33
L. Brock, STL 33

Triples
R. Clemente, PIT 12
P. Rose, CIN 11
B. Tolan, CIN 10
B. Williams, CHI 10
L. Brock, STL 10

PITCHING LEADERS

Winning Percentage
T. Seaver, NY .781
J. Marichal, SF .656
J. Merritt, CIN .654
J. Koosman, NY .654
R. Reed, ATL .643

Earned Run Average
J. Marichal, SF 2.10
S. Carlton, STL 2.17
B. Gibson, STL 2.18
T. Seaver, NY 2.21
J. Koosman, NY 2.28

Wins
T. Seaver, NY 25
P. Niekro, ATL 23
J. Marichal, SF 21
F. Jenkins, CHI 21

Saves
F. Gladding, HOU 29
C. Upshaw, ATL 27
W. Granger, CIN 27
J. Brewer, LA 20
P. Regan, CHI 17

Strikeouts
F. Jenkins, CHI 273
B. Gibson, STL 269
B. Singer, LA 247
D. Wilson, HOU 235
G. Perry, SF 233

Complete Games
B. Gibson, STL 28
J. Marichal, SF 27
G. Perry, SF 26
F. Jenkins, CHI 23
P. Niekro, ATL 21

Fewest Hits/9 Innings
T. Seaver, NY 6.65
J. Maloney, CIN 6.79
B. Singer, LA 6.95
J. Koosman, NY 6.98

Shutouts
J. Marichal, SF 8
C. Osteen, LA 7
F. Jenkins, CHI 7
J. Koosman, NY 6
K. Holtzman, CHI 6

Fewest Walks/9 Innings
J. Marichal, SF 1.62
P. Niekro, ATL 1.81
F. Jenkins, CHI 2.05
J. Niekro, CHI, SD 2.07

Most Strikeouts/9 Inn.
T. Griffin, HOU 9.57
D. Wilson, HOU 9.40
B. Moose, PIT 8.74
D. Selma, SD, CHI 8.54

Innings
G. Perry, SF 325
C. Osteen, LA 321
B. Singer, LA 316
B. Gibson, STL 314

Games Pitched
W. Granger, CIN 90
D. McGinn, MON 74
P. Regan, CHI 71
C. Carroll, CIN 71

NATIONAL LEAGUE 1969, *cont.*

		W	L	PCT	GB	R	OR	Batting 2B	3B	HR	BA	SA	SB	Fielding E	DP	FA	Pitching CG	BB	SO	ShO	SV	ERA
East	New York	100	62	.617		632	541	184	41	109	.242	.351	66	122	146	.980	51	517	1012	**28**	35	2.99
	Chicago	92	70	.568	8	720	611	215	40	142	.253	.384	30	136	149	.979	58	475	1017	22	27	3.34
	Pittsburgh	88	74	.543	12	725	652	220	**52**	119	**.277**	.398	74	155	169	.975	39	553	1124	9	33	3.61
	St. Louis	87	75	.537	13	595	**540**	**228**	44	90	.253	.359	87	138	144	.978	63	511	1004	12	26	**2.94**
	Philadelphia	63	99	.389	37	645	745	227	35	137	.241	.372	73	136	157	.978	47	570	921	14	21	4.17
	Montreal	52	110	.321	48	582	791	202	33	125	.240	.359	52	184	**179**	.971	26	702	973	8	21	4.33
West	Atlanta	93	69	.574		691	631	195	22	141	.258	.380	59	**115**	114	**.981**	38	438	893	7	42	3.53
	San Francisco	90	72	.556	3	713	636	187	28	136	.242	.361	71	169	155	.974	**71**	461	906	15	17	3.25
	Cincinnati	89	73	.549	4	**798**	768	224	42	**171**	**.277**	**.422**	79	168	158	.973	23	611	818	11	**44**	4.13
	Los Angeles	85	77	.525	8	645	561	185	**52**	97	.254	.359	80	126	130	.980	47	**420**	975	20	31	3.09
	Houston	81	81	.500	12	676	668	208	40	104	.240	.352	**101**	153	136	.975	52	547	**1221**	11	34	3.60
	San Diego	52	110	.321	41	468	746	180	42	99	.225	.329	45	156	140	.975	16	592	764	9	25	4.24
						7890	7890	2455	471	1470	.250	.369	817	1758	1777	.977	531	6397	11628	166	356	3.60

AMERICAN LEAGUE 1969

		POS	Player	AB	BA	HR	RBI	PO	A	E	DP	TC/G	FA	Pitcher	G	IP	W	L	SV	ERA
East	Baltimore	1B	B. Powell	533	.304	37	121	1192	84	7	105	8.9	.995	M. Cuellar	39	291	23	11	0	2.38
	W-109 L-53	2B	D. Johnson	511	.280	7	57	355	369	12	93	5.2	.984	D. McNally	41	269	20	7	0	3.22
	Earl Weaver	SS	M. Belanger	530	.287	2	50	251	449	23	79	4.9	.968	T. Phoebus	35	202	14	7	0	3.52
		3B	B. Robinson	598	.234	23	84	163	**370**	13	37	3.5	**.976**	J. Palmer	26	181	16	4	0	2.34
		RF	F. Robinson	539	.308	32	100	226	9	3	2	1.8	.987	J. Hardin	30	138	6	7	1	3.60
		CF	P. Blair	625	.285	26	76	407	14	5	5	2.8	.988	D. Leonhard	37	94	7	4	1	2.49
		LF	D. Buford	554	.291	11	64	228	7	4	1	1.9	.983	E. Watt	56	71	5	2	16	1.65
		C	E. Hendricks	295	.244	12	38	479	40	1	2	6.0	**.998**	D. Hall	39	66	5	2	6	1.92
		C	A. Etchebarren	217	.249	3	26	380	27	4	1	5.7	.990	P. Richert	44	57	7	4	12	2.20
		OF	M. Rettenmund	190	.247	4	25	107	3	1	0	1.4	.991							
		OF	C. Motton	89	.303	6	21	26	0	0	0	1.3	1.000							
	Detroit	1B	N. Cash	483	.280	22	74	1016	96	7	99	8.4	.994	D. McLain	42	**325**	**24**	9	0	2.80
	W-90 L-72	2B	D. McAuliffe	271	.262	11	33	167	196	9	40	5.2	.976	M. Lolich	37	281	19	11	1	3.14
	Mayo Smith	SS	T. Tresh	331	.224	13	37	118	187	11	38	4.1	.965	E. Wilson	35	215	12	10	0	3.31
		3B	D. Wert	423	.225	14	50	114	259	13	20	3.0	.966	M. Kilkenny	39	128	8	6	2	3.37
		RF	A. Kaline	456	.272	21	69	192	9	7	4	1.8	.966	P. Dobson	49	105	5	10	9	3.60
		CF	J. Northrup	543	.295	25	66	323	8	5	2	2.3	.985	J. Hiller	40	99	4	4	4	3.99
		LF	W. Horton	508	.262	28	91	272	8	8	0	2.1	.972	J. Sparma	23	93	6	8	0	4.76
		C	B. Freehan	489	.262	16	49	**821**	49	7	7	**7.3**	.992	D. McMahon	34	37	3	5	11	3.89
		OS	M. Stanley	592	.235	16	70	300	137	10	22		.978							
		23	T. Matchick	298	.242	0	32	104	167	7	34		.975							
		C	J. Price	192	.234	9	28	337	18	4	4	7.0	.989							
		2B	I. Brown	170	.229	5	12	75	100	7	18	4.0	.962							
	Boston	1B	D. Jones	336	.220	3	33	692	54	6	61	9.3	.992	R. Culp	32	227	17	8	0	3.81
	W-87 L-75	2B	M. Andrews	464	.293	15	59	297	334	18	82	5.4	.972	M. Nagy	33	197	12	2	0	3.11
	Dick Williams	SS	R. Petrocelli	535	.297	40	97	269	466	14	103	4.9	**.981**	S. Siebert	43	163	14	10	5	3.80
	W-82 L-71	3B	G. Scott	549	.253	16	52	106	203	15	29	3.0	.954	J. Lonborg	29	144	7	11	0	4.51
	Eddie Popowski	RF	T. Conigliaro	506	.255	20	82	207	4	4	2	1.6	.981	L. Stange	41	137	6	9	3	3.68
	W-5 L-4	CF	R. Smith	543	.309	25	93	321	8	14	1	2.5	.959	V. Romo	52	127	7	9	11	3.18
		LF	C. Yastrzemski	603	.255	40	111	246	17	4	2	1.9	.985	S. Lyle	71	103	8	3	17	2.54
		C	R. Gibson	287	.251	3	27	466	41	11	2	6.2	.979	R. Jarvis	29	100	5	6	1	4.75
		UT	S. O'Brien	263	.243	9	29	65	143	15	30		.933	B. Landis	45	82	5	5	1	5.25
		UT	D. Schofield	226	.257	2	20	97	150	7	30		.972							
		OF	J. Lahoud	218	.188	9	21	91	3	2	0	1.5	.979							
	Washington	1B	M. Epstein	403	.278	30	85	1035	69	11	99	9.4	.990	J. Coleman	40	248	12	13	1	3.27
	W-86 L-76	2B	B. Allen	365	.247	9	45	239	281	14	70	4.9	.974	D. Bosman	31	193	14	5	1	**2.19**
	Ted Williams	SS	E. Brinkman	576	.266	2	43	248	511	19	92	5.2	.976	C. Cox	52	172	12	7	0	2.78
		3B	K. McMullen	562	.272	19	87	**185**	347	13	35	**3.5**	.976	J. Hannan	35	158	7	6	0	3.64
		RF	H. Allen	271	.277	1	17	120	6	9	2	1.5	.933	B. Moore	31	134	9	8	0	4.30
		CF	D. Unser	581	.286	7	57	339	8	10	3	2.4	.972	D. Higgins	55	85	10	9	16	3.48
		LF	F. Howard	592	.296	48	111	147	3	4	0	1.4	.974	J. Shellenback	30	85	4	7	1	4.04
		C	P. Casanova	379	.216	4	37	583	59	5	5	5.3	.992	D. Knowles	53	84	9	2	13	2.24
		2B	T. Cullen	249	.209	1	15	166	188	7	44	3.4	.981	B. Humphreys	47	80	3	3	5	3.05
		OF	L. Maye	238	.290	9	26	100	1	6	1	1.6	.944	D. Baldwin	43	67	2	4	4	4.05
		OF	B. Alyea	237	.249	11	40	84	6	6	0	1.4	.938							
		OF	E. Stroud	206	.252	4	29	109	1	2	0	1.3	.982							
	New York	1B	J. Pepitone	513	.242	27	70	**1254**	74	7	118	**10.1**	**.995**	M. Stottlemyre	39	303	20	14	0	2.82
	W-80 L-81	2B	H. Clarke	**641**	.285	4	48	**373**	**429**	15	**112**	5.2	.982	F. Peterson	37	272	17	16	0	2.55
	Ralph Houk	SS	G. Michael	412	.272	2	31	205	365	19	64	5.0	.968	S. Bahnsen	40	221	9	16	1	3.83
		3B	J. Kenney	447	.257	2	34	63	207	7	20	3.3	.975	B. Burbach	31	141	6	8	0	3.65
		RF	B. Murcer	564	.259	26	82	212	4	8	0	1.9	.964	A. Downing	30	131	7	5	0	3.38
		CF	R. Woods	171	.175	1	7	129	2	0	0	2.0	1.000	M. Kekich	28	105	4	6	1	4.54
		LF	R. White	448	.290	7	74	267	9	3	1	2.2	.989	L. McDaniel	51	84	5	6	5	3.55
		C	J. Gibbs	219	.224	0	18	364	31	4	6	6.0	.990	J. Aker	38	66	8	4	11	2.06
		C	F. Fernandez	229	.223	12	29	321	29	2	2	5.4	.994							
		OF	B. Robinson	222	.171	3	21	99	5	4	0	1.7	.963							
		OF	J. Hall	212	.236	3	26	78	1	3	0	1.6	.963							
		3B	B. Cox	191	.215	2	17	37	122	11	14	3.0	.935							

AMERICAN LEAGUE 1969, *cont.*

Cleveland

W-62 L-99

Alvin Dark

POS	Player	AB	BA	HR	RBI	PO	A	E	DP	TC/G	FA
1B	T. Horton	625	.278	27	93	1179	**100**	**14**	**130**	8.2	.989
2B	V. Fuller	254	.236	4	22	217	192	9	53	4.1	.978
SS	L. Brown	469	.239	4	24	172	276	19	59	4.6	.959
3B	M. Alvis	191	.225	1	15	49	96	4	10	2.6	.973
RF	K. Harrelson	519	.222	27	84	257	7	4	2	1.9	.985
CF	J. Cardenal	557	.257	11	45	327	9	6	2	2.4	.982
LF	R. Snyder	266	.248	2	24	144	2	6	1	1.8	.961
C	D. Sims	326	.236	18	45	634	51	6	8	6.8	.991
3B	L. Klimchock	258	.287	6	26	46	82	9	7	2.4	.934
23	Z. Versalles	217	.226	1	13	100	125	6	24		.974
SS	E. Leon	213	.239	3	19	114	185	15	43	4.9	.952
OF	R. Scheinblum	199	.186	1	13	71	4	2	1	1.5	.974
OF	F. Baker	172	.256	3	15	71	5	4	0	1.7	.950

Pitcher	G	IP	W	L	SV	ERA
S. McDowell	39	285	18	14	1	2.94
L. Tiant	38	250	9	**20**	0	3.71
S. Williams	61	178	6	14	12	3.94
S. Hargan	32	144	5	14	0	5.70
D. Ellsworth	34	135	6	9	0	4.13
M. Paul	47	117	5	10	2	3.61
J. Pizarro	48	83	3	3	4	3.16

West

Minnesota

W-97 L-65

Billy Martin

POS	Player	AB	BA	HR	RBI	PO	A	E	DP	TC/G	FA
1B	R. Reese	419	.322	16	69	924	56	7	97	8.4	.993
2B	R. Carew	458	**.332**	8	56	244	302	17	80	4.8	.970
SS	L. Cardenas	578	.280	10	70	**310**	**570**	32	**126**	**5.7**	.965
3B	H. Killebrew	555	.276	**49**	**140**	75	185	20	12	2.7	.929
RF	T. Oliva	637	.309	24	101	311	14	6	3	2.2	.982
CF	C. Tovar	535	.288	11	52	225	9	4	3	2.1	.983
LF	T. Uhlaender	554	.273	8	62	278	8	1	1	1.9	.997
C	J. Roseboro	361	.263	3	32	585	52	**13**	**16**	5.9	.980
OF	G. Nettles	225	.222	7	26	76	2	1	0	1.5	.987
OF	B. Allison	189	.228	8	27	91	2	0	1	1.6	1.000
C	G. Mitterwald	187	.257	5	13	340	33	5	6	6.0	.987
OF	C. Manuel	164	.207	2	24	57	2	2	0	1.3	.967

Pitcher	G	IP	W	L	SV	ERA
J. Perry	46	262	20	6	0	2.82
D. Boswell	39	256	20	12	0	3.23
J. Kaat	40	242	14	13	1	3.49
T. Hall	31	141	8	7	0	3.33
R. Perranoski	75	120	9	10	**31**	2.11
B. Miller	48	119	5	5	3	3.02
D. Woodson	44	110	7	5	1	3.67

Oakland

W-88 L-74

Hank Bauer
W-80 L-69

John McNamara
W-8 L-5

POS	Player	AB	BA	HR	RBI	PO	A	E	DP	TC/G	FA
1B	D. Cater	584	.262	10	76	1087	97	9	112	9.0	.992
2B	D. Green	483	.275	12	64	302	379	10	93	5.3	**.986**
SS	B. Campaneris	547	.260	2	25	220	391	21	72	5.1	.967
3B	S. Bando	609	.281	31	113	178	321	**24**	36	3.2	.954
RF	R. Jackson	549	.275	47	118	278	14	11	2	2.0	.964
CF	R. Monday	399	.271	12	54	262	3	10	0	2.3	.964
LF	T. Reynolds	315	.257	2	20	184	5	4	2	2.2	.979
C	P. Roof	247	.235	2	19	493	40	9	4	5.1	.983
S2	T. Kubiak	305	.249	2	27	153	215	10	41		.974
OF	J. Tartabull	266	.267	0	11	134	2	1	0	2.2	.993
C	D. Duncan	127	.126	3	22	209	15	4	1	4.1	.982
1B	T. Francona	85	.341	3	20	158	6	2	11	8.7	.988

Pitcher	G	IP	W	L	SV	ERA
C. Hunter	38	247	12	15	0	3.35
C. Dobson	35	235	15	13	0	3.86
B. Odom	32	231	15	6	0	2.92
L. Krausse	43	140	7	7	7	4.44
R. Fingers	60	119	6	7	12	3.71
J. Nash	26	115	8	8	0	3.67
P. Lindblad	60	78	9	6	9	4.14

California

W-71 L-91

Bill Rigney
W-11 L-28

Lefty Phillips
W-60 L-63

POS	Player	AB	BA	HR	RBI	PO	A	E	DP	TC/G	FA
1B	J. Spencer	386	.254	10	31	926	66	9	81	9.4	.991
2B	S. Alomar	559	.250	1	30	294	354	21*	94	5.0	.969
SS	J. Fregosi	580	.260	12	47	255	465	21	88	4.6	.972
3B	A. Rodriguez	561	.232	7	49	145	352	**24**	**42**	3.3	.954
RF	B. Voss	349	.261	2	40	175	11	1	3	1.7	.995
CF	J. Johnstone	540	.270	10	59	331	12	6	4	2.4	.983
LF	R. Reichardt	493	.254	13	68	244	13	5	4	1.9	.981
C	J. Azcue	248	.218	1	19	437	52*	4	10	6.2	.992
01	R. Repoz	219	.164	8	19	296	22	2	26		.994
OF	B. Morton	172	.244	7	32	70	5	0	1	1.5	1.000

Pitcher	G	IP	W	L	SV	ERA
A. Messersmith	40	250	16	11	2	2.52
T. Murphy	36	216	10	16	0	4.21
J. McGlothlin	37	201	8	16	0	3.18
R. May	43	180	10	13	2	3.44
G. Brunet	23	101	6	7	0	3.84
K. Tatum	45	86	7	2	22	1.36
H. Wilhelm	44	66	5	7	10	2.47

Kansas City

W-69 L-93

Joe Gordon

POS	Player	AB	BA	HR	RBI	PO	A	E	DP	TC/G	FA
1B	M. Fiore	339	.274	12	35	696	94	10	54	8.8	.988
2B	J. Adair	432	.250	5	48	223	261	8	41	4.5	.984
SS	J. Hernandez	504	.222	4	40	306	375	**33**	60	5.0	.954
3B	J. Foy	519	.262	11	71	117	209	12	20	3.0	.964
RF	P. Kelly	417	.264	8	32	237	12	5	3	2.4	.980
CF	B. Oliver	394	.254	13	43	199	11	5	4	2.2	.977
LF	L. Piniella	493	.282	11	68	278	13	7	1	2.3	.977
C	E. Rodriguez	267	.236	2	20	433	39	5	2	5.3	.990
OF	E. Kirkpatrick	315	.257	14	49	180	8	1	1	2.3	.995
1B	C. Harrison	213	.221	3	18	415	36	3	27	8.3	.993
C	B. Martinez	205	.229	4	23	290	25	9	7	5.9	.972
3B	P. Schaal	205	.263	1	13	27	77	12	3	2.4	.897
2S	J. Rios	196	.224	1	5	101	105	9	23		.958
OF	J. Keough	166	.187	0	7	82	2	0	1	1.7	1.000
OF	H. Taylor	89	.270	3	21	19	1	2	1	1.2	.909

Pitcher	G	IP	W	L	SV	ERA
W. Bunker	35	223	12	11	2	3.23
D. Drago	41	201	11	13	1	3.77
B. Butler	34	194	9	10	0	3.90
R. Nelson	29	193	7	13	0	3.31
J. Rooker	28	158	4	16	0	3.75
M. Hedlund	34	125	3	6	2	3.24
M. Drabowsky	52	98	11	9	11	2.94
D. Wickersham	34	50	2	3	5	3.96

Chicago

W-68 L-94

Al Lopez
W-8 L-9

Don Gutteridge
W-60 L-85

POS	Player	AB	BA	HR	RBI	PO	A	E	DP	TC/G	FA
1B	G. Hopkins	373	.265	8	46	903	51	6	81	9.5	.994
2B	B. Knoop	345	.229	6	41	271	320	9	76	5.8*	.985
SS	L. Aparicio	599	.280	5	51	248	563	20	94	5.4	.976
3B	B. Melton	556	.255	23	87	112	322	22	36	3.1	.952
RF	W. Williams	471	.304	3	32	183	13	3	4	1.8	.985
CF	K. Berry	297	.232	4	18	215	7	0	1	1.9	1.000
LF	C. May	367	.281	18	62	154	10	3	0	1.7	.982
C	E. Herrmann	290	.231	8	31	420	41	8	7	5.1	.983
OF	B. Bradford	273	.256	11	27	141	5	6	1	1.7	.961
10	T. McCraw	240	.258	2	25	302	15	3	21		.991
UT	P. Ward	199	.246	6	32	193	48	3	13		.988
C	D. Pavletich	188	.245	6	33	195	26	6	3	4.5	.974
UT	R. Hansen	185	.259	2	22	216	83	8	28		.974
C	D. Josephson	162	.241	1	20	227	27	4	1	5.5	.984

Pitcher	G	IP	W	L	SV	ERA
J. Horlen	36	236	13	16	0	3.78
T. John	33	232	9	11	0	3.25
G. Peters	36	219	10	15	0	4.53
B. Wynne	20	129	7	7	0	4.06
W. Wood	**76**	120	10	11	15	3.01
D. Osinski	51	61	5	5	2	3.56

AMERICAN LEAGUE 1969, *cont.*

Seattle

W-64 L-98

Joe Schultz

POS	Player	AB	BA	HR	RBI	PO	A	E	DP	TC/G	FA
1B	D. Mincher	427	.246	25	78	1033	93	6	98	9.3	.995
2B	J. Donaldson	338	.234	1	19	209	242	12	56	5.1	.974
SS	R. Oyler	255	.165	7	22	143	266	15	47	4.0	.965
3B	T. Harper	537	.235	9	41	70	123	10	9	3.4	.951
RF	S. Hovley	329	.277	3	20	175	8	2	3	2.2	.989
CF	W. Comer	481	.245	15	54	287	14	6	6	2.2	.980
LF	T. Davis	454	.271	6	80	174	3	6	0	1.6	.967
C	J. McNertney	410	.241	8	55	697	67	9	13	6.3	.988
OF	M. Hegan	267	.292	8	37	100	7	5	1	1.8	.955
UT	G. Gil	221	.222	0	17	65	130	9	16		.956
3B	R. Rollins	187	.225	4	21	42	103	8	6	3.3	.948
UT	R. Clark	163	.196	0	12	79	116	9	17		.956
1B	G. Goossen	139	.309	10	24	265	23	2	15	9.4	.993

Pitcher	G	IP	W	L	SV	ERA
G. Brabender	40	202	13	14	0	4.36
M. Pattin	34	159	7	12	0	5.62
D. Segui	66	142	12	6	12	3.35
F. Talbot	25	115	5	8	0	4.16
J. Gelnar	39	109	3	10	3	3.31
M. Marshall	20	88	3	10	0	5.13
S. Barber	25	86	4	7	0	4.80
B. Locker	51	78	3	3	6	2.18
J. O'Donoghue	55	70	2	2	6	2.96
G. Bell	13	61	2	6	2	4.70

BATTING AND BASE RUNNING LEADERS

Batting Average
R. Carew, MIN	.332
R. Smith, BOS	.309
T. Oliva, MIN	.309
F. Robinson, BAL	.308
B. Powell, BAL	.304

Slugging Average
R. Jackson, OAK	.608
R. Petrocelli, BOS	.589
H. Killebrew, MIN	.584
F. Howard, WAS	.574
B. Powell, BAL	.559

Home Runs
H. Killebrew, MIN	49
F. Howard, WAS	48
R. Jackson, OAK	47
R. Petrocelli, BOS	40
C. Yastrzemski, BOS	40

Total Bases
F. Howard, WAS	340
R. Jackson, OAK	334
H. Killebrew, MIN	324
T. Oliva, MIN	316
R. Petrocelli, BOS	315

Runs Batted In
H. Killebrew, MIN	140
B. Powell, BAL	121
R. Jackson, OAK	118
S. Bando, OAK	113
F. Howard, WAS	111
C. Yastrzemski, BOS	111

Stolen Bases
T. Harper, SEA	73
B. Campaneris, OAK	62
C. Tovar, MIN	45
P. Kelly, KC	40
J. Foy, KC	37

Hits
T. Oliva, MIN	197
H. Clarke, NY	183
P. Blair, BAL	178
F. Howard, WAS	175

Base on Balls
H. Killebrew, MIN	145
R. Jackson, OAK	114
S. Bando, OAK	111
F. Howard, WAS	102

Home Run Percentage
H. Killebrew, MIN	8.8
R. Jackson, OAK	8.6
F. Howard, WAS	8.1
R. Petrocelli, BOS	7.5

Runs
R. Jackson, OAK	123
F. Robinson, BAL	111
F. Howard, WAS	111
H. Killebrew, MIN	106
S. Bando, OAK	106

Doubles
T. Oliva, MIN	39
R. Jackson, OAK	36
D. Johnson, BAL	34
R. Petrocelli, BOS	32
P. Blair, BAL	32

Triples
D. Unser, WAS	8
R. Smith, BOS	7
H. Clarke, NY	7

PITCHING LEADERS

Winning Percentage
J. Palmer, BAL	.800
J. Perry, MIN	.769
D. McNally, BAL	.741
D. McLain, DET	.727
B. Odom, OAK	.714

Earned Run Average
D. Bosman, WAS	2.19
J. Palmer, BAL	2.34
M. Cuellar, BAL	2.38
A. Messersmith, CAL	2.52
F. Peterson, NY	2.55

Wins
D. McLain, DET	24
M. Cuellar, BAL	23
D. Boswell, MIN	20
J. Perry, MIN	20
D. McNally, BAL	20
M. Stottlemyre, NY	20

Saves
R. Perranoski, MIN	31
K. Tatum, CAL	22
S. Lyle, BOS	17
E. Watt, BAL	16
D. Higgins, WAS	16

Strikeouts
S. McDowell, CLE	279
M. Lolich, DET	271
A. Messersmith, CAL	211
D. Boswell, MIN	190
J. Coleman, WAS	182
M. Cuellar, BAL	182

Complete Games
M. Stottlemyre, NY	24
D. McLain, DET	23
S. McDowell, CLE	18
M. Cuellar, BAL	18
F. Peterson, NY	16

Fewest Hits/9 Innings
A. Messersmith, CAL	6.08
J. Palmer, BAL	6.51
M. Cuellar, BAL	6.60
M. Lolich, DET	6.86

Shutouts
D. McLain, DET	9
J. Palmer, BAL	6
M. Cuellar, BAL	5

Fewest Walks/9 Innings
F. Peterson, NY	1.42
D. Bosman, WAS	1.82
D. McLain, DET	1.86
J. Perry, MIN	2.27

Most Strikeouts/9 Inn.
S. McDowell, CLE	8.81
M. Lolich, DET	8.69
A. Messersmith, CAL	7.60
B. Butler, KC	7.25

Innings
D. McLain, DET	325
M. Stottlemyre, NY	303
M. Cuellar, BAL	291
S. McDowell, CLE	285

Games Pitched
W. Wood, CHI	76
R. Perranoski, MIN	75
S. Lyle, BOS	71
B. Locker, CHI, SEA	68

		W	L	PCT	GB	R	OR	Batting 2B	3B	HR	BA	SA	SB	Fielding E	DP	FA	Pitching CG	BB	SO	ShO	SV	ERA
East	Baltimore	109	53	.673		779	**517**	234	29	175	.265	.414	82	**101**	145	**.984**	50	**498**	897	**20**	36	**2.83**
	Detroit	90	72	.556	19	701	601	188	29	182	.242	.387	35	130	130	.979	**55**	586	**1032**	**20**	28	3.32
	Boston	87	75	.537	22	743	736	234	37	**197**	.251	**.415**	41	157	**178**	.975	30	685	935	7	41	3.93
	Washington	86	76	.531	23	694	644	171	40	148	.251	.378	52	140	159	.978	28	656	835	10	41	3.49
	New York	80	81	.497	28.5	562	587	210	**44**	94	.235	.344	119	131	158	.979	53	522	801	13	20	3.23
	Cleveland	62	99	.385	46.5	573	717	173	24	119	.237	.345	85	145	153	.976	35	681	1000	7	22	3.94
West	Minnesota	97	65	.599		**790**	618	**246**	32	163	**.268**	.408	115	150	177	.977	41	524	906	8	**43**	3.25
	Oakland	88	74	.543	9	740	678	210	28	148	.249	.376	100	137	162	.978	42	586	887	14	36	3.71
	California	71	91	.438	26	528	652	151	29	88	.230	.319	54	136	164	.978	25	517	885	9	39	3.55
	Kansas City	69	93	.426	28	586	688	179	32	98	.240	.338	129	157	114	.975	42	560	894	10	25	3.72
	Chicago	68	94	.420	29	625	723	210	27	112	.247	.357	54	122	163	.981	29	564	810	10	25	4.21
	Seattle	64	98	.395	33	639	799	179	27	125	.234	.346	**167**	167	149	.974	21	653	963	6	33	4.35
						7960	7960	2385	378	1649	.246	.369	1033	1673	1852	.978	451	7032	10845	134	389	3.63

NATIONAL LEAGUE 1970

East

Pittsburgh

W-89 L-73

Danny Murtaugh

POS	Player	AB	BA	HR	RBI	PO	A	E	DP	TC/G	FA
1B	B. Robertson	390	.287	27	82	907	78	5	107	10.0	.995
2B	B. Mazeroski	367	.229	7	39	227	325	7	87	5.5	.987
SS	G. Alley	426	.244	8	41	202	381	15	84	**5.5**	.975
3B	R. Hebner	420	.290	11	46	64	235	19	24	2.7	.940
RF	R. Clemente	412	.352	14	60	189	12	7	2	2.0	.966
CF	M. Alou	**677**	.297	1	47	297	15	8	1	2.1	.975
LF	W. Stargell	474	.264	31	85	184	16	5	1	1.6	.976
C	M. Sanguillen	486	.325	7	61	775	66	10	12	6.8	.988
01	A. Oliver	551	.270	12	83	718	52	9	69		.988
SS	F. Patek	237	.245	1	19	122	212	10	42	5.3	.971
3B	J. Pagan	230	.265	7	29	43	91	6	14	2.6	.957
2B	D. Cash	210	.314	1	28	147	156	8	46	5.7	.974

Pitcher	G	IP	W	L	SV	ERA
B. Veale	34	202	10	15	0	3.92
D. Ellis	30	202	13	10	0	3.21
S. Blass	31	197	10	12	0	3.52
B. Moose	28	190	11	10	0	3.98
L. Walker	42	163	15	6	3	3.04
D. Giusti	66	103	9	3	26	3.06
B. Dal Canton	41	85	9	4	1	4.55

NATIONAL LEAGUE 1970, *cont.*

Chicago

W-84 L-78

Leo Durocher

POS	Player	AB	BA	HR	RBI	PO	A	E	DP	TC/G	FA	Pitcher	G	IP	W	L	SV	ERA
1B	J. Hickman	514	.315	32	115	563	60	6	46	8.5	.990	F. Jenkins	40	313	22	16	0	3.39
2B	G. Beckert	591	.288	3	36	302	412	**22**	88	5.3	.970	K. Holtzman	39	288	17	11	0	3.38
SS	D. Kessinger	631	.266	1	39	257	**501**	22	86	5.1	.972	B. Hands	39	265	18	15	1	3.70
3B	R. Santo	555	.267	26	114	143	320	27	36	3.2	.945	M. Pappas	21	145	10	8	0	2.68
RF	J. Callison	477	.264	19	68	244	8	7	3	1.8	.973	J. Decker	24	109	2	7	0	4.62
CF	C. James	176	.210	3	14	115	5	0	1	1.3	1.000	P. Regan	54	76	5	9	12	4.74
LF	B. Williams	636	.322	42	129	259	13	3	1	1.7	.989							
C	R. Hundley	250	.244	7	36	455	26	5	2	6.7	.990							
1B	E. Banks	222	.252	12	44	528	35	4	53	9.1	.993							
OF	J. Pepitone	213	.268	12	44	121	1	1	0	2.2	.992							
UT	P. Popovich	186	.253	4	20	75	97	4	26		.977							
C	J. Hiatt	178	.242	2	22	380	22	4	1	6.4	.990							
1B	W. Smith	167	.216	5	24	318	11	2	32	7.7	.994							

New York

W-83 L-79

Gil Hodges

POS	Player	AB	BA	HR	RBI	PO	A	E	DP	TC/G	FA	Pitcher	G	IP	W	L	SV	ERA
1B	D. Clendenon	396	.288	22	97	722	62	7	72	7.9	.991	T. Seaver	37	291	18	12	0	**2.81**
2B	K. Boswell	351	.254	5	44	204	244	2	49	4.5	.996	J. Koosman	30	212	12	7	0	3.14
SS	B. Harrelson	564	.243	1	42	**305**	401	21	84	4.7	.971	G. Gentry	32	188	9	9	1	3.69
3B	J. Foy	322	.236	6	37	90	179	18	20	3.0	.937	J. McAndrew	32	184	10	14	2	3.57
RF	R. Swoboda	245	.233	9	40	117	3	2	1	1.2	.984	R. Sadecki	28	139	8	4	0	3.88
CF	T. Agee	636	.286	24	75	374	4	13	3	2.6	.967	N. Ryan	27	132	7	11	1	3.41
LF	C. Jones	506	.277	10	63	243	10	5	3	2.0	.981	T. McGraw	57	91	4	6	10	3.26
C	J. Grote	415	.255	2	34	**855**	46	8	12	**7.3**	.991	R. Taylor	57	66	5	4	13	3.95
01	A. Shamsky	403	.293	11	49	482	37	2	30		.996	D. Frisella	30	66	8	3	1	3.00
32	W. Garrett	366	.254	12	45	151	205	12	34		.967							
OF	K. Singleton	198	.263	5	26	90	1	3	0	1.8	.968							
OF	D. Marshall	189	.243	6	29	71	2	2	0	1.7	.973							

St. Louis

W-76 L-86

Red Schoendienst

POS	Player	AB	BA	HR	RBI	PO	A	E	DP	TC/G	FA	Pitcher	G	IP	W	L	SV	ERA
1B	J. Hague	451	.271	14	68	672	48	4	65	8.8	.994	B. Gibson	34	294	**23**	7	0	3.12
2B	J. Javier	513	.251	2	42	329	413	15	84	5.5	.980	S. Carlton	34	254	10	**19**	0	3.72
SS	D. Maxvill	399	.201	0	28	216	426	12	80	4.8	**.982**	M. Torrez	30	179	8	10	0	4.22
3B	J. Torre	624	.325	21	100	68	133	11	12	2.9	.948	J. Reuss	20	127	7	8	0	4.11
RF	L. Lee	264	.227	6	23	120	3	4	0	1.6	.969	C. Taylor	56	124	6	7	8	3.12
CF	J. Cardenal	552	.293	10	74	276	6	9	0	2.2	.969	N. Briles	30	107	6	7	0	6.22
LF	L. Brock	664	.304	13	57	247	9	10	2	1.8	.962	F. Linzy	47	61	3	5	2	3.67
C	T. Simmons	284	.243	3	24	466	37	5	2	6.4	.990							
13	D. Allen	459	.279	34	101	703	108	16	70		.981							
OF	C. Taylor	245	.249	6	45	66	3	1	1	1.5	.986							
OF	V. Davalillo	183	.311	1	33	67	3	2	1	1.3	.972							
3B	M. Shannon	174	.213	0	22	32	59	8	4	1.9	.919							

Philadelphia

W-73 L-88

Frank Lucchesi

POS	Player	AB	BA	HR	RBI	PO	A	E	DP	TC/G	FA	Pitcher	G	IP	W	L	SV	ERA
1B	D. Johnson	574	.256	27	93	1178	73	6	104	8.2	.995	R. Wise	35	220	13	14	0	4.17
2B	D. Doyle	413	.208	2	16	251	228	11	55	4.8	.978	J. Bunning	34	219	10	15	0	4.11
SS	L. Bowa	547	.250	0	34	202	418	13	69	4.4	.979	C. Short	36	199	9	16	1	4.30
3B	D. Money	447	.295	14	66	131	236	15	27	3.2	.961	G. Jackson	32	150	5	15	0	5.28
RF	R. Stone	321	.262	3	39	148	5	5	0	1.6	.968	B. Lersch	42	138	6	3	3	3.26
CF	L. Hisle	405	.205	10	44	262	5	6	0	2.3	.978	D. Selma	73	134	8	9	22	2.75
LF	J. Briggs	341	.270	9	47	188	7	4	1	2.1	.980	W. Fryman	27	128	8	6	0	4.08
C	M. Ryan	134	.179	2	11	238	15	2	1	5.5	.992	L. Palmer	38	102	1	2	0	5.47
UT	T. Taylor	439	.301	9	55	220	215	5	48		.989	J. Hoerner	44	58	9	5	9	2.64
OF	O. Gamble	275	.262	1	19	148	4	7	0	2.1	.956							
OF	B. Browne	270	.248	10	36	150	4	4	1	1.8	.975							
C	T. McCarver	164	.287	4	14	314	18	3	2	7.6	.991							

Montreal

W-73 L-89

Gene Mauch

POS	Player	AB	BA	HR	RBI	PO	A	E	DP	TC/G	FA	Pitcher	G	IP	W	L	SV	ERA
1B	R. Fairly	385	.288	15	61	944	90	5	112	8.8	.995	C. Morton	43	285	18	11	0	3.60
2B	G. Sutherland	359	.206	3	26	178	254	11	72	4.6	.975	S. Renko	41	223	13	11	1	4.32
SS	B. Wine	501	.232	3	51	284	481	19	**137**	4.9	.976	B. Stoneman	40	208	7	15	0	4.59
3B	C. Laboy	432	.199	5	53	105	194	17	19	2.4	.946	D. McGinn	52	131	7	10	0	5.43
RF	R. Staub	569	.274	30	94	308	14	5	4	2.0	.985	M. Wegener	25	104	3	6	0	5.28
CF	A. Phillips	214	.238	6	21	130	1	2	0	1.8	.985	H. Reed	57	89	6	5	5	3.13
LF	M. Jones	271	.240	14	32	118	3	4	1	1.4	.968	C. Raymond	59	83	6	7	23	4.45
C	J. Bateman	520	.237	15	68	824	62	**15**	**19**	6.6	.983	M. Marshall	24	65	3	7	3	3.48
UT	B. Bailey	352	.287	28	84	179	86	8	18		.971							
2B	M. Staehle	321	.218	0	26	152	208	14	53	4.1	.963							
OF	J. Gosger	274	.263	5	37	124	5	0	1	1.8	1.000							
OF	J. Fairey	211	.242	3	25	86	1	2	0	1.5	.978							

West

Cincinnati

W-102 L-60

Sparky Anderson

POS	Player	AB	BA	HR	RBI	PO	A	E	DP	TC/G	FA	Pitcher	G	IP	W	L	SV	ERA
1B	L. May	605	.253	34	94	1362	109	10	**143**	9.7	.993	G. Nolan	37	251	18	7	0	3.26
2B	T. Helms	575	.237	1	45	350	410	13	**107**	5.2	**.983**	J. Merritt	35	234	20	12	0	4.08
SS	D. Concepcion	265	.260	1	19	137	244	22	51	4.3	.945	J. McGlothlin	35	211	14	10	0	3.58
3B	T. Perez	587	.317	40	129	131	286	**35**	34	3.0	.923	W. Simpson	26	176	14	3	0	3.02
RF	P. Rose	649	.316	15	52	309	8	1	2	2.0	.997	T. Cloninger	30	148	9	7	1	3.83
CF	B. Tolan	589	.316	16	80	349	7	8	0	2.4	.978	C. Carroll	65	104	9	4	16	2.60
LF	B. Carbo	365	.310	21	63	177	8	4	2	1.6	.979	W. Granger	67	85	6	5	**35**	2.65
C	J. Bench	605	.293	**45**	**148**	755	73	12	12	6.0	.986	D. Gullett	44	78	5	2	6	2.42
SS	W. Woodward	264	.223	1	14	101	226	9	48	4.4	.973							
OF	H. McRae	165	.248	8	23	52	1	1	0	1.2	.981							

NATIONAL LEAGUE 1970, *cont.*

Los Angeles

W-87 L-74

Walter Alston

POS	Player	AB	BA	HR	RBI	PO	A	E	DP	TC/G	FA	Pitcher	G	IP	W	L	SV	ERA
1B	W. Parker	614	.319	10	111	**1498**	125	7	116	**10.1**	**.996**	D. Sutton	38	260	15	13	0	4.08
2B	T. Sizemore	340	.306	1	34	194	232	7	47	5.0	.984	C. Osteen	37	259	16	14	0	3.82
SS	M. Wills	522	.270	0	34	171	396	24	58	4.7	.959	A. Foster	33	199	10	13	0	4.25
3B	B. Grabarkewitz	529	.289	17	84	88	190	12	19	3.0	.959	J. Moeller	31	135	7	9	4	3.93
RF	M. Mota	417	.305	3	37	172	8	5	3	1.7	.973	S. Vance	20	115	7	7	0	3.13
CF	W. Davis	593	.305	8	93	342	12	3	4	2.5	.992	B. Singer	16	106	8	5	0	3.14
LF	W. Crawford	299	.234	8	40	160	9	7	1	1.9	.960	J. Brewer	58	89	7	6	24	3.13
C	T. Haller	325	.286	10	47	524	26	4	7	5.2	.993	P. Mikkelsen	33	62	4	2	6	2.76
2B	J. Lefebvre	314	.252	4	44	142	177	4	34	4.6	.988	J. Pena	29	57	4	3	4	4.42
OF	B. Russell	278	.259	0	28	167	8	3	1	2.3	.983							
C3	B. Sudakis	269	.264	14	44	188	99	14	9		.953							
OF	A. Kosco	224	.228	8	27	101	2	2	0	1.8	.981							

San Francisco

W-86 L-76

Clyde King
W-19 L-23

Charlie Fox
W-67 L-53

POS	Player	AB	BA	HR	RBI	PO	A	E	DP	TC/G	FA	Pitcher	G	IP	W	L	SV	ERA
1B	W. McCovey	495	.289	39	126	1217	**134**	**15**	117	9.4	.989	G. Perry	41	**329**	**23**	13	0	3.20
2B	R. Hunt	367	.281	6	41	162	173	11	38	4.1	.968	J. Marichal	34	243	12	10	0	4.11
SS	H. Lanier	438	.231	2	41	256	397	22	83	5.2	.967	R. Robertson	41	184	8	9	1	4.84
3B	A. Gallagher	282	.266	4	28	70	128	6	12	2.2	.971	F. Reberger	45	152	7	8	2	5.57
RF	B. Bonds	663	.302	26	78	326	14	11	7	2.2	.969	R. Bryant	34	96	5	8	0	4.78
CF	W. Mays	478	.291	28	83	269	6	7	3	2.2	.975	D. McMahon	61	94	9	5	19	2.97
LF	K. Henderson	554	.294	17	88	272	15	10	2	2.1	.966	S. Pitlock	18	87	5	5	0	4.66
C	D. Dietz	493	.300	22	107	820	58	14	9	6.4	.984	J. Johnson	33	65	3	4	3	4.27
UT	T. Fuentes	435	.267	2	32	202	324	19	57		.965							
3B	J. Hart	255	.282	8	37	39	69	11	2	2.1	.908							
01	F. Johnson	161	.273	3	31	199	14	5	16		.977							
S2	B. Heise	154	.234	1	22	78	124	13	24		.940							

Houston

W-79 L-83

Harry Walker

POS	Player	AB	BA	HR	RBI	PO	A	E	DP	TC/G	FA	Pitcher	G	IP	W	L	SV	ERA
1B	B. Watson	327	.272	11	61	695	39	6	54	8.9	.992	L. Dierker	37	270	16	12	1	3.87
2B	J. Morgan	548	.268	8	52	349	430	17	98	**5.6**	.979	J. Billingham	46	188	13	9	0	3.97
SS	D. Menke	562	.304	13	92	192	394	**28**	66	4.6	.954	D. Wilson	29	184	11	6	0	3.91
3B	D. Rader	576	.252	25	87	**147**	**357**	18	**39**	**3.4**	**.966**	D. Lemaster	39	162	7	12	3	4.56
RF	J. Alou	458	.306	1	44	169	6	7	2	1.7	.962	T. Griffin	23	111	3	13	0	5.76
CF	C. Cedeno	355	.310	7	42	211	1	7	0	2.4	.968	J. Ray	52	105	6	3	5	3.26
LF	J. Wynn	554	.282	27	88	293	14	4	4	2.1	.987	R. Cook	41	82	4	4	2	3.73
C	J. Edwards	458	.221	7	49	854	**74**	5	11	6.7	**.995**	J. Bouton	29	73	4	6	0	5.42
10	J. Pepitone	279	.251	14	35	428	30	3	45		.993	F. Gladding	63	71	7	4	18	4.06
OF	N. Miller	226	.239	4	29	101	6	6	1	1.6	.947							
OF	T. Davis	213	.282	3	30	71	4	4	1	1.5	.949							

Atlanta

W-76 L-86

Lum Harris

POS	Player	AB	BA	HR	RBI	PO	A	E	DP	TC/G	FA	Pitcher	G	IP	W	L	SV	ERA
1B	O. Cepeda	567	.305	34	111	1288	112	12	100	9.5	.992	P. Jarvis	36	254	16	16	0	3.61
2B	F. Millan	590	.310	2	37	337	359	15	83	5.0	.979	P. Niekro	34	230	12	18	0	4.27
SS	S. Jackson	328	.259	0	20	123	240	26	40	4.5	.933	J. Nash	34	212	13	9	0	4.08
3B	C. Boyer	475	.246	16	62	107	268	18	21	3.1	.954	G. Stone	35	207	11	11	0	3.87
RF	H. Aaron	516	.298	38	118	246	6	6	1	2.1	.977	R. Reed	21	135	7	10	0	4.40
CF	T. Gonzalez	430	.265	7	55	235	1	3	0	2.0	.987	H. Wilhelm	50	78	6	4	13	3.10
LF	R. Carty	478	**.366**	25	101	219	5	6	0	1.7	.974	B. Priddy	41	73	5	5	8	5.42
C	B. Tillman	223	.238	11	30	404	22	5	0	6.2	.988							
SS	G. Garrido	367	.264	1	19	119	233	9	36	4.5	.975							
OF	M. Lum	291	.254	7	28	168	3	2	0	1.8	.988							
C	H. King	204	.260	11	30	316	14	5	1	5.4	.985							
C	B. Didier	168	.149	0	7	297	25	4	3	5.7	.988							

San Diego

W-63 L-99

Preston Gomez

POS	Player	AB	BA	HR	RBI	PO	A	E	DP	TC/G	FA	Pitcher	G	IP	W	L	SV	ERA
1B	N. Colbert	572	.259	38	86	1406	90	14	126	9.9	.991	P. Dobson	40	251	14	15	1	3.76
2B	D. Campbell	581	.219	12	40	**359**	**455**	**22**	96	5.5	.974	C. Kirby	36	215	10	16	0	4.52
SS	J. Arcia	229	.223	0	17	89	146	11	32	3.7	.955	D. Coombs	35	188	10	14	0	3.30
3B	E. Spiezio	316	.285	12	42	66	178	12	10	2.8	.953	D. Roberts	43	182	8	14	1	3.81
RF	O. Brown	534	.292	23	89	258	12	10	3	2.0	.964	R. Herbel	64*	111	7	5	9	4.95
CF	C. Gaston	584	.318	29	93	310	7	8	0	2.3	.975	M. Corkins	24	111	5	6	0	4.62
LF	I. Murrell	347	.245	12	35	183	8	6	2	2.0	.970	A. Santorini	21	76	1	8	1	6.04
C	C. Cannizzaro	341	.279	5	42	559	44	12	5	5.6	.980	T. Dukes	53	69	1	6	10	4.04
OF	A. Ferrara	372	.277	13	51	119	2	4	0	1.3	.968							
S3	S. Huntz	352	.219	11	37	118	257	20	39		.949							
C	B. Barton	188	.218	4	16	347	28	2	5	6.4	.995							

BATTING AND BASE RUNNING LEADERS

Batting Average

R. Carty, ATL	.366
J. Torre, STL	.325
M. Sanguillen, PIT	.325
B. Williams, CHI	.322
W. Parker, LA	.319

Slugging Average

W. McCovey, SF	.612
T. Perez, CIN	.589
J. Bench, CIN	.587
B. Williams, CHI	.586
R. Carty, ATL	.584

Home Runs

J. Bench, CIN	45
B. Williams, CHI	42
T. Perez, CIN	40
W. McCovey, SF	39
H. Aaron, ATL	38
N. Colbert, SD	38

Total Bases

B. Williams, CHI	373
J. Bench, CIN	355
T. Perez, CIN	346
B. Bonds, SF	334
C. Gaston, SD	317

Runs Batted In

J. Bench, CIN	148
T. Perez, CIN	129
B. Williams, CHI	129
W. McCovey, SF	126
H. Aaron, ATL	118

Stolen Bases

B. Tolan, CIN	57
L. Brock, STL	51
B. Bonds, SF	48
J. Morgan, HOU	42
W. Davis, LA	38

PITCHING LEADERS

Winning Percentage

B. Gibson, STL	.767
G. Nolan, CIN	.720
L. Walker, PIT	.714
G. Perry, SF	.639
J. Merritt, CIN	.625

Earned Run Average

T. Seaver, NY	2.81
W. Simpson, CIN	3.02
L. Walker, PIT	3.04
B. Gibson, STL	3.12
J. Koosman, NY	3.14

Wins

B. Gibson, STL	23
G. Perry, SF	23
F. Jenkins, CHI	22
J. Merritt, CIN	20

Saves

W. Granger, CIN	35
D. Giusti, PIT	26
J. Brewer, LA	24
C. Raymond, MON	23
D. Selma, PHI	22

Strikeouts

T. Seaver, NY	283
B. Gibson, STL	274
F. Jenkins, CHI	274
G. Perry, SF	214
K. Holtzman, CHI	202

Complete Games

F. Jenkins, CHI	24
B. Gibson, STL	23
G. Perry, SF	23
T. Seaver, NY	19
L. Dierker, HOU	17

NATIONAL LEAGUE 1970, *cont.*

BATTING AND BASE RUNNING LEADERS

Hits

B. Williams, CHI	205
P. Rose, CIN	205
J. Torre, STL	203
L. Brock, STL	202

Base on Balls

W. McCovey, SF	137
R. Staub, MON	112
D. Dietz, SF	109
J. Wynn, HOU	106

Home Run Percentage

W. McCovey, SF	7.9
J. Bench, CIN	7.4
D. Allen, STL	7.4
H. Aaron, ATL	7.4

Runs

B. Williams, CHI	137
B. Bonds, SF	134
P. Rose, CIN	120
L. Brock, STL	114

Doubles

W. Parker, LA	47
W. McCovey, SF	39
P. Rose, CIN	37
D. Dietz, SF	36
B. Bonds, SF	36

Triples

W. Davis, LA	16
D. Kessinger, CHI	14
R. Clemente, PIT	10
B. Bonds, SF	10

PITCHING LEADERS

Fewest Hits/9 Innings

W. Simpson, CIN	6.39
T. Seaver, NY	7.11
L. Walker, PIT	7.12
G. Gentry, NY	7.42

Shutouts

G. Perry, SF	5
D. Ellis, PIT	4
C. Osteen, LA	4
C. Morton, MON	4
D. Sutton, LA	4

Fewest Walks/9 Innings

F. Jenkins, CHI	1.73
J. Marichal, SF	1.78
C. Osteen, LA	1.81
J. McAndrew, NY	1.86

Most Strikeouts/9 Inn.

T. Seaver, NY	8.75
B. Gibson, STL	8.39
B. Veale, PIT	7.93
F. Jenkins, CHI	7.88

Innings

G. Perry, SF	329
F. Jenkins, CHI	313
B. Gibson, STL	294
T. Seaver, NY	291

Games Pitched

R. Herbel, SD, NY	76
D. Selma, PHI	73
F. Linzy, SF, STL	67
W. Granger, CIN	67

		W	L	PCT	GB	R	OR	Batting 2B	3B	HR	BA	SA	SB	Fielding E	DP	FA	Pitching CG	BB	SO	ShO	SV	ERA
East	Pittsburgh	89	73	.549		729	664	235	**70**	130	**.270**	.406	66	137	**195**	.979	36	625	990	13	43	3.70
	Chicago	84	78	.519	5	806	679	228	44	179	.259	.415	39	137	146	.978	**59**	**475**	1000	9	25	3.76
	New York	83	79	.512	6	695	**630**	211	42	120	.249	.370	118	124	136	.979	47	575	**1064**	10	32	**3.46**
	St. Louis	76	86	.469	13	744	747	218	51	113	.263	.379	117	150	159	.977	51	632	960	11	20	4.05
	Philadelphia	73	88	.453	15.5	594	730	224	58	101	.238	.356	72	**114**	134	**.981**	24	538	1047	8	36	4.17
	Montreal	73	89	.451	16	687	807	211	35	136	.237	.365	65	141	193	.977	29	716	914	10	32	4.50
West	Cincinnati	102	60	.630		775	681	253	45	**191**	**.270**	**.436**	115	151	173	.976	32	592	843	15	**60**	3.71
	Los Angeles	87	74	.540	14.5	749	684	233	67	87	**.270**	.382	**138**	135	135	.978	37	496	880	**17**	42	3.82
	San Francisco	86	76	.531	16	**831**	826	**257**	35	165	.262	.409	83	170	153	.973	50	604	931	7	30	4.50
	Houston	79	83	.488	23	744	763	250	47	129	.259	.391	114	140	144	.978	36	577	942	6	35	4.23
	Atlanta	76	86	.469	26	736	772	215	24	160	**.270**	.404	58	141	118	.977	45	478	960	9	24	4.35
	San Diego	63	99	.389	39	681	788	208	36	172	.246	.391	60	158	159	.975	24	611	886	9	32	4.38
						8771	8771	2743	554	1683	.258	.392	1045	1698	1845	.977	470	6919	11417	124	411	4.05

AMERICAN LEAGUE 1970

East

Baltimore

W-108 L-54

Earl Weaver

POS	Player	AB	BA	HR	RBI	PO	A	E	DP	TC/G	FA	Pitcher	G	IP	W	L	SV	ERA
1B	B. Powell	526	.297	35	114	1209	89	10	107	9.0	.992	J. Palmer	39	**305**	20	10	0	2.71
2B	D. Johnson	530	.281	10	53	**379**	390	8	101	5.2	.990	M. Cuellar	40	298	**24**	8	0	3.47
SS	M. Belanger	459	.218	1	36	212	412	19	78	4.5	.970	D. McNally	40	296	**24**	9	0	3.22
3B	B. Robinson	608	.276	18	94	157	321	17	30	3.2	.966	J. Hardin	36	145	6	5	1	3.54
RF	F. Robinson	471	.306	25	78	221	9	3	3	1.9	.987	T. Phoebus	27	135	5	5	0	3.07
CF	P. Blair	480	.267	18	65	368	10	4	3	3.0	.990	D. Hall	32	61	10	5	3	3.10
LF	D. Buford	504	.272	17	66	221	13	3	3	1.8	.987	E. Watt	53	55	7	7	12	3.27
C	E. Hendricks	322	.242	12	41	509	35	8	6	5.8	.986	P. Richert	50	55	7	2	13	1.96
OF	M. Rettenmund	338	.322	18	58	201	6	5	1	2.3	.976							
C	A. Etchebarren	230	.243	4	28	392	29	7	3	5.6	.984							
UT	C. Salmon	172	.250	7	22	61	87	9	12		.943							
01	T. Crowley	152	.257	5	20	138	6	2	9		.986							

New York

W-93 L-69

Ralph Houk

POS	Player	AB	BA	HR	RBI	PO	A	E	DP	TC/G	FA	Pitcher	G	IP	W	L	SV	ERA
1B	D. Cater	582	.301	6	76	981	70	8	79	8.1	.992	M. Stottlemyre	37	271	15	13	0	3.09
2B	H. Clarke	**686**	.251	4	46	**379**	**478**	18	95	5.6	.979	F. Peterson	39	260	20	11	0	2.91
SS	G. Michael	435	.214	2	38	248	379	**28**	78	5.3	.957	S. Bahnsen	36	233	14	11	0	3.32
3B	J. Kenney	404	.193	4	35	111	300	17	18	3.2	.960	L. McDaniel	62	112	9	5	29	2.01
RF	C. Blefary	269	.212	9	37	103	1	3	0	1.4	.972	S. Kline	16	100	6	6	0	3.42
CF	B. Murcer	581	.251	23	78	375	15	3	3	2.5	.992	R. Klimkowski	45	98	6	7	1	2.66
LF	R. White	609	.296	22	94	315	6	2	0	2.0	.994	J. Aker	41	70	4	2	16	2.06
C	T. Munson	453	.302	6	53	631	**80**	8	11	5.8	.989	S. Hamilton	35	45	4	3	3	2.78
1B	J. Ellis	226	.248	7	29	449	37	4	35	9.2	.992							
OF	R. Woods	225	.227	8	27	108	6	3	1	1.5	.974							
C	J. Gibbs	153	.301	8	26	208	19	3	1	5.2	.987							

Boston

W-87 L-75

Eddie Kasko

POS	Player	AB	BA	HR	RBI	PO	A	E	DP	TC/G	FA	Pitcher	G	IP	W	L	SV	ERA
1B	C. Yastrzemski	566	.329	40	102	696	61	8	62	8.1	.990	R. Culp	33	251	17	14	0	3.05
2B	M. Andrews	589	.253	17	65	342	350	**19**	74	4.8	.973	S. Siebert	33	223	15	8	0	3.43
SS	R. Petrocelli	583	.261	29	103	262	393	20	77	4.8	.970	G. Peters	34	222	16	11	0	4.05
3B	G. Scott	480	.296	16	63	71	113	13	13	2.9	.934	K. Brett	41	139	8	9	2	4.08
RF	T. Conigliaro	560	.266	36	116	252	7	6	1	1.8	.977	M. Nagy	23	129	6	5	0	4.47
CF	R. Smith	580	.303	22	74	361	15	9	1	2.7	.977	V. Romo	48	108	7	3	6	4.08
LF	B. Conigliaro	398	.271	18	58	201	8	7	0	2.0	.968	S. Lyle	63	67	1	7	20	3.90
C	G. Moses	315	.263	6	35	578	45	6	3	7.1	.990	G. Wagner	38	40	3	1	7	3.38
3S	L. Alvarado	183	.224	1	10	45	134	8	17		.957							
C	T. Satriano	165	.236	3	13	318	19	5	5	6.7	.985							

AMERICAN LEAGUE 1970, *cont.*

Team	POS	Player	AB	BA	HR	RBI	PO	A	E	DP	TC/G	FA	Pitcher	G	IP	W	L	SV	ERA
Detroit	1B	N. Cash	370	.259	15	53	868	70	10	76	8.3	.989	M. Lolich	40	273	14	**19**	0	3.79
W-79 L-83	2B	D. McAuliffe	530	.234	12	50	280	333	16	75	5.0	.975	J. Niekro	38	213	12	13	0	4.06
Mayo Smith	SS	C. Gutierrez	415	.243	0	22	183	326	23	60	3.9	.957	L. Cain	29	181	12	7	0	3.83
	3B	D. Wert	363	.218	6	33	94	191	14	20	2.6	.953	M. Kilkenny	36	129	7	6	0	5.16
	RF	A. Kaline	467	.278	16	71	156	3	2	1	1.8	.988	J. Hiller	47	104	6	6	3	3.03
	CF	M. Stanley	568	.252	13	47	317	3	0	0	2.4	1.000	E. Wilson	18	96	4	6	0	4.41
	LF	W. Horton	371	.305	17	69	154	10	3	1	1.7	.982	T. Timmerman	61	85	6	7	27	4.13
	C	B. Freehan	395	.241	16	52	742	42	2	6	6.9	**.997**	D. Patterson	43	78	7	1	2	4.85
	OF	J. Northrup	504	.262	24	80	284	4	2	1	2.1	.993							
	UT	E. Maddox	258	.248	3	24	104	100	14	10		.936							
	UT	D. Jones	191	.220	6	21	111	99	4	26		.981							
	OF	G. Brown	124	.226	3	24	37	1	2	0	1.5	.950							
Cleveland	1B	T. Horton	413	.269	17	59	898	73	6	106	8.7	.994	S. McDowell	39	**305**	20	12	0	2.92
W-76 L-86	2B	E. Leon	549	.248	10	56	342	378	13	102	5.2	.982	R. Hand	35	160	6	13	3	3.83
Alvin Dark	SS	J. Heidemann	445	.211	6	37	216	354	23	79	4.5	.961	D. Chance	45	155	9	8	4	4.24
	3B	G. Nettles	549	.235	26	62	134	358	17	40	3.3	**.967**	S. Hargan	23	143	11	3	0	2.90
	RF	V. Pinson	574	.286	24	82	265	8	5	3	2.0	.982	S. Dunning	19	94	4	9	0	4.98
	CF	T. Uhlaender	473	.268	11	46	225	5	2	1	1.7	.991	D. Higgins	58	90	4	6	11	4.00
	LF	R. Foster	477	.268	23	60	188	6	7	0	1.5	.965	M. Paul	30	88	2	8	0	4.81
	C	R. Fosse	450	.307	18	61	**854**	70	10	7	**7.8**	.989	P. Hennigan	42	72	6	3	3	4.00
	UT	D. Sims	345	.264	23	56	505	34	8	18		.985	R. Austin	31	68	2	5	3	4.76
	UT	C. Hinton	195	.318	9	29	229	15	2	14		.992	F. Lasher	43	58	1	7	5	4.06
	OF	B. Bradford	163	.196	7	23	117	1	2	0	1.9	.983							
Washington	1B	M. Epstein	430	.256	20	56	1100	70	10	104	**9.7**	.992	D. Bosman	36	231	16	12	0	3.00
W-70 L-92	2B	T. Cullen	262	.214	1	18	211	262	3	65	4.3	**.994**	J. Coleman	39	219	8	12	0	3.58
Ted Williams	SS	E. Brinkman	625	.262	1	40	**301**	**569**	23	**103**	**5.7**	.974	C. Cox	37	192	8	12	1	4.45
	3B	A. Rodriguez	547	.247	19	76	97	343*	18	36*	3.4	.961	J. Hannan	42	128	9	11	0	4.01
	RF	D. Unser	322	.258	5	30	173	8	3	2	1.8	.984	D. Knowles	71	119	2	14	27	2.04
	CF	E. Stroud	433	.266	5	32	271	8	2	3	2.4	.993	G. Brunet	24	118	8	6	0	4.42
	LF	F. Howard	566	.283	**44**	**126**	172	6	5	4	1.5	.973	J. Shellenback	39	117	6	7	0	3.69
	C	P. Casanova	328	.229	6	30	461	48	6	**12**	5.2	.988	J. Grzenda	49	85	3	6	6	4.98
	OF	R. Reichardt	277	.253	15	46	134	0	2	0	1.7	.985	H. Pina	61	71	5	3	6	2.79
	2B	B. Allen	261	.234	8	29	169	175	11	47	4.4	.969							
	OF	L. Maye	255	.263	7	30	75	4	0	1	1.2	1.000							
	C	J. French	166	.211	1	13	267	23	8	4	4.8	.973							
West **Minnesota**	1B	R. Reese	501	.261	10	56	1118	82	10	94	8.3	.992	J. Perry	40	279	**24**	12	0	3.03
W-98 L-64	2B	D. Thompson	302	.219	0	22	144	204	5	35	4.4	.986	J. Kaat	45	230	14	10	0	3.56
Bill Rigney	SS	L. Cardenas	588	.247	11	65	280	487	17	91	4.9	.978	B. Blyleven	27	164	10	9	0	3.18
	3B	H. Killebrew	527	.271	41	113	108	203	17	14	2.4	.948	T. Hall	52	155	11	6	4	2.55
	RF	T. Oliva	628	.325	23	107	351	12	12	4	2.4	.968	B. Zepp	43	151	9	4	2	3.22
	CF	C. Tovar	650	.300	10	54	370	12	9	1	2.6	.977	S. Williams	68	113	10	1	15	1.99
	LF	J. Holt	319	.266	3	40	201	2	1	0	1.6	.995	R. Perranoski	67	111	7	8	**34**	2.43
	C	G. Mitterwald	369	.222	15	46	740	62	3	8	6.9	.996	L. Tiant	18	93	7	3	0	3.39
	OF	B. Alyea	258	.291	16	61	93	4	2	0	1.3	.980	D. Boswell	18	69	3	7	0	6.39
	2B	R. Carew	191	.366	4	28	73	122	8	26	4.5	.961							
	30	R. Renick	179	.229	7	25	52	54	2	5		.981							
	C	P. Ratliff	149	.268	5	22	183	11	4	4	3.7	.980							
Oakland	1B	D. Mincher	463	.246	27	74	1109	91	**12**	107	8.8	.990	C. Dobson	41	267	16	15	0	3.74
W-89 L-73	2B	D. Green	384	.190	4	29	259	332	13	66	4.8	.978	C. Hunter	40	262	18	14	0	3.81
John McNamara	SS	B. Campaneris	603	.279	22	64	267	414	19	92	4.9	.973	D. Segui	47	162	10	10	2	**2.56**
	3B	S. Bando	502	.263	20	75	**158**	258	20	22	2.9	.954	B. Odom	29	156	9	8	0	3.81
	RF	R. Jackson	426	.237	23	66	251	8	12	0	1.9	.956	R. Fingers	45	148	7	9	2	3.65
	CF	R. Monday	376	.290	10	37	257	3	5	2	2.4	.981	M. Grant	72	123	6	2	24	1.83
	LF	F. Alou	575	.271	8	55	287	11	7	3	2.1	.977	P. Lindblad	62	63	8	2	3	2.71
	C	F. Fernandez	252	.214	15	44	405	25	3	6	5.7	.993	B. Locker	38	56	3	3	4	2.88
	01	J. Rudi	350	.309	11	42	302	18	4	17		.988							
	C	D. Duncan	232	.259	10	29	373	28	9	9	5.6	.978							
	OF	T. Davis	200	.290	1	27	51	1	2	0	1.2	.963							
	C	G. Tenace	105	.305	7	20	180	18	2	7	6.7	.990							
California	1B	J. Spencer	511	.274	12	68	**1212**	85	7	**131**	9.2	**.995**	C. Wright	39	261	22	12	0	2.83
W-86 L-76	2B	S. Alomar	672	.251	2	36	375	460	18	**119**	**5.6**	.979	T. Murphy	39	227	16	13	0	4.24
Lefty Phillips	SS	J. Fregosi	601	.278	22	82	264	468	20	99	5.0	.973	R. May	38	209	7	13	0	4.00
	3B	K. McMullen	422	.232	14	61	128	266	17	32	3.4*	.959	A. Messersmith	37	195	11	10	5	3.00
	RF	R. Repoz	407	.238	18	47	203	6	1	2	1.9	.995	E. Fisher	67	130	4	4	8	3.05
	CF	J. Johnstone	320	.237	11	39	200	7	4	3	2.1	.981	K. Tatum	62	89	7	4	17	2.93
	LF	A. Johnson	614	**.329**	14	86	269	11	12	0	1.9	.959	G. Garrett	32	75	5	6	0	2.64
	C	J. Azcue	351	.242	2	25	587	51	6	10	5.8	.991	M. Queen	34	60	3	6	9	4.20
	C	T. Egan	210	.238	4	20	367	31	5	4	5.1	.988							
	OF	B. Voss	181	.243	3	30	86	7	2	1	1.7	.979							
	OF	J. Tatum	181	.238	0	6	108	2	2	0	1.9	.982							
	01	B. Cowan	134	.276	5	25	95	6	2	7		.981							

AMERICAN LEAGUE 1970, *cont.*

Kansas City

W-65 L-97

Charlie Metro
W-19 L-33

Bob Lemon
W-46 L-64

POS	Player	AB	BA	HR	RBI	PO	A	E	DP	TC/G	FA
1B	B. Oliver	612	.260	27	99	1020	65	8	100	9.5	.993
2B	C. Rojas	384	.260	2	28	217	283	9	69	5.2	.982
SS	J. Hernandez	238	.231	2	10	142	187	17	38	4.5	.951
3B	P. Schaal	380	.268	5	35	69	159	15	12	2.5	.938
RF	P. Kelly	452	.235	6	38	254	8	10	2	2.3	.963
CF	A. Otis	620	.284	11	58	388	15	4	6	2.6	.990
LF	L. Piniella	542	.301	11	88	247	6	4	2	1.8	.984
C	E. Kirkpatrick	424	.229	18	62	463	61	**12**	**12**	6.0	.978
S2	R. Severson	240	.250	1	22	127	202	12	45		.965
C	E. Rodriguez	231	.225	1	15	451	32	6	5	6.5	.988
01	J. Keough	183	.322	4	21	176	13	4	13		.979

Pitcher	G	IP	W	L	SV	ERA
D. Drago	35	240	9	15	0	3.75
B. Johnson	40	214	8	13	4	3.07
J. Rooker	38	204	10	15	1	3.53
B. Butler	25	141	4	12	0	3.77
W. Bunker	24	122	2	11	0	4.20
D. Morehead	28	122	3	5	1	3.61
A. Fitzmorris	43	118	8	5	1	4.42
T. Burgmeier	41	68	6	6	1	3.18
T. Abernathy	36	56	9	3	12	2.57

Milwaukee

W-65 L-97

Dave Bristol

POS	Player	AB	BA	HR	RBI	PO	A	E	DP	TC/G	FA
1B	M. Hegan	476	.244	11	52	1097	**113**	7	104	8.8	.994
2B	T. Kubiak	540	.252	4	41	233	238	5	63	5.2	.989
SS	R. Pena	416	.238	3	42	149	272	8	58	4.3	.981*
3B	T. Harper	604	.296	31	82	123	275	**24**	23	3.3	.943
RF	R. Snyder	276	.232	4	31	140	1	5	0	1.4	.966
CF	D. May	342	.240	7	31	255	6	3	0	2.7	.989
LF	D. Walton	397	.257	17	66	162	4	6	0	1.5	.965
C	P. Roof	321	.227	13	37	596	47	8	6	6.1	.988
C	J. McNertney	296	.243	6	22	387	46	7	3	4.7	.984
OF	T. Savage	276	.279	12	50	119	3	6	0	1.6	.953
OF	B. Burda	222	.248	4	20	71	3	1	1	1.2	.987

Pitcher	G	IP	W	L	SV	ERA
M. Pattin	37	233	14	12	0	3.40
L. Krausse	37	216	13	18	0	4.75
S. Lockwood	27	174	5	12	0	4.29
B. Bolin	32	132	5	11	1	4.91
G. Brabender	29	129	6	15	1	6.00
A. Downing	17	94	2	10	0	3.34
J. Gelnar	53	92	4	3	4	4.21
K. Sanders	50	92	5	2	13	1.76

Chicago

W-56 L-106

Don Gutteridge
W-49 L-87

Bill Adair
W-4 L-6

Chuck Tanner
W-3 L-13

POS	Player	AB	BA	HR	RBI	PO	A	E	DP	TC/G	FA
1B	G. Hopkins	287	.286	6	29	629	42	9	67	8.8	.987
2B	B. Knoop	402	.229	5	36	276	403	11	102	5.5	.984
SS	L. Aparicio	552	.313	5	43	251	483	18	99	5.2	.976
3B	B. Melton	514	.263	33	96	47	179	18	19	3.5	.926
RF	W. Williams	315	.251	3	15	119	12	7	1	1.7	.949
CF	K. Berry	463	.276	7	50	331	9	4	2	2.5	.988
LF	C. May	555	.285	12	68	203	12	2	2	1.5	.991
C	E. Herrmann	297	.283	19	52	433	51	6	10	5.6	.988
32	S. O'Brien	441	.247	8	44	155	264	23	49		.948
10	T. McCraw	332	.220	6	31	427	35	9	34		.981
C	D. Josephson	285	.316	4	41	353	38	6	7	4.7	.985

Pitcher	G	IP	W	L	SV	ERA
T. John	37	269	12	17	0	3.28
G. Janeski	35	206	10	17	0	4.76
J. Horlen	28	172	6	16	0	4.87
W. Wood	**77**	122	9	13	21	2.80
J. Crider	32	91	4	7	4	4.45
B. Johnson	18	90	4	7	0	4.80
D. Murphy	51	81	2	3	5	5.67
B. Miller	15	70	4	6	0	5.01

BATTING AND BASE RUNNING LEADERS

Batting Average
A. Johnson, CAL .329
C. Yastrzemski, BOS .329
T. Oliva, MIN .325
L. Aparicio, CHI .313
F. Robinson, BAL .306

Slugging Average
C. Yastrzemski, BOS .592
B. Powell, BAL .549
H. Killebrew, MIN .546
F. Howard, WAS .546
T. Harper, MIL .522

Home Runs
F. Howard, WAS 44
H. Killebrew, MIN 41
C. Yastrzemski, BOS 40
T. Conigliaro, BOS 36
B. Powell, BAL 35

Total Bases
C. Yastrzemski, BOS 335
T. Oliva, MIN 323
T. Harper, MIL 315
F. Howard, WAS 309
B. Powell, BAL 289

Runs Batted In
F. Howard, WAS 126
T. Conigliaro, BOS 116
B. Powell, BAL 114
H. Killebrew, MIN 113
T. Oliva, MIN 107

Stolen Bases
B. Campaneris, OAK 42
T. Harper, MIL 38
S. Alomar, CAL 35
P. Kelly, KC 34
A. Otis, KC 33

Hits
T. Oliva, MIN 204
A. Johnson, CAL 202
C. Tovar, MIN 195
C. Yastrzemski, BOS 186

Base on Balls
F. Howard, WAS 132
H. Killebrew, MIN 128
C. Yastrzemski, BOS 128
S. Bando, OAK 118

Home Run Percentage
H. Killebrew, MIN 7.8
F. Howard, WAS 7.8
C. Yastrzemski, BOS 7.1
B. Powell, BAL 6.7

Runs
C. Yastrzemski, BOS 125
C. Tovar, MIN 120
R. Smith, BOS 109
R. White, NY 109

Doubles
A. Otis, KC 36
T. Oliva, MIN 36
C. Tovar, MIN 36
T. Harper, MIL 35

Triples
C. Tovar, MIN 13
M. Stanley, DET 11
A. Otis, KC 9

PITCHING LEADERS

Winning Percentage
M. Cuellar, BAL .750
D. McNally, BAL .727
J. Palmer, BAL .667
J. Perry, MIN .667
S. Siebert, BOS .652

Earned Run Average
D. Segui, OAK 2.56
J. Palmer, BAL 2.71
C. Wright, CAL 2.83
F. Peterson, NY 2.91
S. McDowell, CLE 2.92

Wins
J. Perry, MIN 24
D. McNally, BAL 24
M. Cuellar, BAL 24
C. Wright, CAL 22

Saves
R. Perranoski, MIN 34
L. McDaniel, NY 29
T. Timmerman, DET 27
D. Knowles, WAS 27
M. Grant, OAK 24

Strikeouts
S. McDowell, CLE 304
M. Lolich, DET 230
B. Johnson, KC 206
J. Palmer, BAL 199
R. Culp, BOS 197

Complete Games
M. Cuellar, BAL 21
S. McDowell, CLE 19
J. Palmer, BAL 17
D. McNally, BAL 16
R. Culp, BOS 15

Fewest Hits/9 Innings
A. Messersmith, CAL 6.65
S. McDowell, CLE 6.96
D. Segui, OAK 7.22
B. Johnson, KC 7.49

Shutouts
J. Palmer, BAL 5
C. Dobson, OAK 5
G. Peters, BOS 4
M. Cuellar, BAL 4
J. Perry, MIN 4

Fewest Walks/9 Innings
F. Peterson, NY 1.38
J. Perry, MIN 1.84
C. Cox, WAS 2.06
M. Cuellar, BAL 2.08

Most Strikeouts/9 Inn.
S. McDowell, CLE 8.97
B. Johnson, KC 8.66
L. Cain, DET 7.76
M. Lolich, DET 7.58

Innings
S. McDowell, CLE 305
J. Palmer, BAL 305
M. Cuellar, BAL 298
D. McNally, BAL 296

Games Pitched
W. Wood, CHI 77
M. Grant, OAK 72
D. Knowles, WAS 71
S. Williams, MIN 68

		W	L	PCT	GB	R	OR	Batting					SB	Fielding			Pitching					ERA
								2B	3B	HR	BA	SA		E	DP	FA	CG	BB	SO	ShO	SV	
East	Baltimore	108	54	.667		**792**	**574**	213	25	179	.257	.401	84	117	148	.981	**60**	469	941	12	31	**3.15**
	New York	93	69	.574	15	680	612	208	**41**	111	.251	.365	105	130	146	.980	36	**451**	777	6	49	3.25
	Boston	87	75	.537	21	786	722	**252**	28	**203**	**.262**	**.428**	50	156	131	.974	38	594	1003	8	44	3.90
	Detroit	79	83	.488	29	666	731	207	38	148	.238	.374	29	133	142	.978	33	623	1045	9	39	4.09
	Cleveland	76	86	.469	32	649	675	197	23	183	.249	.394	25	133	168	.979	34	689	**1076**	8	35	3.91
	Washington	70	92	.432	38	626	689	184	28	138	.238	.358	72	**116**	173	**.982**	20	611	823	11	40	3.80
West	Minnesota	98	64	.605		744	605	230	**41**	153	**.262**	.403	57	123	130	.980	26	486	940	12	**58**	3.23
	Oakland	89	73	.549	9	678	593	208	24	171	.249	.392	**131**	141	152	.977	33	542	858	**15**	40	3.30
	California	86	76	.531	12	631	630	197	40	114	.251	.363	69	127	169	.980	21	559	922	10	49	3.48
	Kansas City	65	97	.401	33	611	705	202	**41**	97	.244	.348	97	152	162	.976	30	641	915	11	25	3.78
	Milwaukee	65	97	.401	33	613	751	202	24	126	.242	.358	91	136	142	.978	31	587	895	2	27	4.20
	Chicago	56	106	.346	42	633	822	192	20	123	.253	.362	54	165	**187**	.975	20	556	762	6	30	4.54
						8109	8109	2492	373	1746	.250	.379	864	1629	1850	.978	382	6808	10957	110	467	3.72

NATIONAL LEAGUE 1971

		POS	Player	AB	BA	HR	RBI	PO	A	E	DP	TC/G	FA	Pitcher	G	IP	W	L	SV	ERA
East	Pittsburgh	1B	B. Robertson	469	.271	26	72	1089	**128**	9	107	**9.7**	.993	S. Blass	33	240	15	8	0	2.85
	W-97 L-65	2B	D. Cash	478	.289	2	34	228	304	7	80	5.1	.987	D. Ellis	31	227	19	9	0	3.05
	Danny Murtaugh	SS	G. Alley	348	.227	6	28	187	316	22	55	4.9	.958	B. Johnson	31	175	9	10	0	3.45
		3B	R. Hebner	388	.271	17	67	89	172	14	21	2.5	.949	L. Walker	28	160	10	8	0	3.54
		RF	R. Clemente	522	.341	13	86	267	11	2	4	2.3	.993	B. Moose	30	140	11	7	1	4.11
		CF	A. Oliver	529	.282	14	64	305	4	6	2	2.7	.981	N. Briles	37	136	8	4	1	3.04
		LF	W. Stargell	511	.295	**48**	125	237	8	4	4	1.8	.984	B. Kison	18	95	6	5	0	3.41
		C	M. Sanguillen	533	.319	7	81	712	**72**	5	**12**	5.8	.994	D. Giusti	58	86	5	6	**30**	2.93
		OF	V. Davalillo	295	.285	1	33	112	5	2	0	2.0	.983	M. Grant	42	75	5	3	7	3.60
		OF	G. Clines	273	.308	1	24	146	8	3	2	2.1	.981							
		SS	J. Hernandez	233	.206	3	26	105	235	18	42	4.8	.950							
		2B	B. Mazeroski	193	.254	1	16	95	121	3	22	4.8	.986							
		C	M. May	126	.278	6	25	168	12	0	3	5.8	1.000							
	St. Louis	1B	J. Hague	380	.226	16	54	618	50	3	63	7.4	.996	S. Carlton	37	273	20	9	0	3.56
	W-90 L-72	2B	T. Sizemore	478	.264	3	42	206	237	11	55	4.9	.976	B. Gibson	31	246	16	13	0	3.04
	Red Schoendienst	SS	D. Maxvill	356	.225	0	24	188	413	13	71	4.4	.979	R. Cleveland	34	222	12	12	0	4.01
		3B	J. Torre	634	**.363**	24	**137**	**136**	271	**21**	22	2.7	.951	J. Reuss	36	211	14	14	0	4.78
		RF	M. Alou	609	.315	7	74	203	8	4	0	2.3	.981	C. Zachary	23	90	3	10	0	5.30
		CF	J. Cruz	292	.274	9	27	197	2	5	1	2.5	.975	M. Drabowsky	51	60	6	1	8	3.45
		LF	L. Brock	640	.313	7	61	262	7	14	3	1.8	.951	F. Linzy	50	59	4	3	6	2.14
		C	T. Simmons	510	.304	7	77	747	52	9	11	6.2	.989	D. Shaw	45	51	7	2	2	2.65
		OF	J. Cardenal	301	.243	7	48	181	9	6	1	2.4	.969							
		2B	J. Javier	259	.259	3	28	163	186	8	45	4.5	.978							
		OF	L. Melendez	173	.225	0	11	90	3	4	0	1.5	.959							
		1B	J. Beauchamp	162	.235	2	16	311	19	6	27	7.6	.982							
		C	J. McNertney	128	.289	4	22	192	7	3	1	5.6	.985							
	Chicago	1B	J. Pepitone	427	.307	16	61	872	64	9	75	9.9	.990	F. Jenkins	39	**325**	**24**	13	0	2.77
	W-83 L-79	2B	G. Beckert	530	.342	2	42	275	382	9	76	5.2	.986	M. Pappas	35	261	17	14	0	3.52
	Leo Durocher	SS	D. Kessinger	617	.258	2	38	263	512	27	**97**	5.2	.966	B. Hands	36	242	12	18	0	3.42
		3B	R. Santo	555	.267	21	88	118	274	17	**29**	2.7	.958	K. Holtzman	30	195	9	15	0	4.48
		RF	J. Callison	290	.210	8	38	158	3	3	0	1.8	.982	J. Pizarro	16	101	7	6	0	3.48
		CF	B. Davis	301	.256	0	28	213	5	4	1	2.4	.982	P. Regan	48	73	5	5	6	3.95
		LF	B. Williams	594	.301	28	93	284	8	7	3	1.9	.977							
		C	C. Cannizzaro	197	.213	5	23	311	26	6	2	4.9	.983							
		01	J. Hickman	383	.256	19	60	470	34	3	28		.994							
		2B	P. Popovich	226	.217	4	28	74	119	3	26	4.9	.985							
		P	F. Jenkins	115	.243	6	20	**31**	48	**7**	1	2.2	.919							
	New York	1B	E. Kranepool	421	.280	14	58	786	61	2	67	7.9	**.998**	T. Seaver	36	286	20	10	0	**1.76**
	W-83 L-79	2B	K. Boswell	392	.273	5	40	191	234	12	56	4.0	.973	G. Gentry	32	203	12	11	0	3.24
	Gil Hodges	SS	B. Harrelson	547	.252	0	32	257	441	16	86	5.1	.978	J. Koosman	26	166	6	11	0	3.04
		3B	B. Aspromonte	342	.225	5	33	76	145	8	10	2.4	.965	R. Sadecki	34	163	7	7	0	2.93
		RF	K. Singleton	298	.245	13	46	143	5	4	0	1.6	.974	N. Ryan	30	152	10	14	0	3.97
		CF	T. Agee	425	.285	14	50	265	7	6	0	2.6	.978	T. McGraw	51	111	11	4	8	1.70
		LF	C. Jones	505	.319	14	69	248	4	5	1	1.9	.981	D. Frisella	53	91	8	5	12	1.98
		C	J. Grote	403	.270	2	35	**892**	41	9	4	**7.7**	.990	C. Williams	31	90	5	6	0	4.80
		UT	T. Foli	288	.226	0	24	150	199	12	43		.967							
		1B	D. Clendenon	263	.247	11	37	505	37	8	49	7.6	.985							
		OF	D. Marshall	214	.238	3	21	92	2	1	0	1.5	.989							
		3B	W. Garrett	202	.213	1	11	30	89	4	7	2.3	.967							
		OF	D. Hahn	178	.236	1	11	140	2	4	1	1.8	.973							
		C	D. Dyer	169	.231	2	18	336	21	3	3	6.8	.992							
	Montreal	1B	R. Fairly	447	.257	13	71	1108	104	10	110	9.1	.992	B. Stoneman	39	295	17	16	0	3.14
	W-71 L-90	2B	R. Hunt	520	.279	5	38	270	370	14	72	4.9	.979	S. Renko	40	276	15	14	0	3.75
	Gene Mauch	SS	B. Wine	340	.200	1	16	221	321	10	76	4.6	.982	C. Morton	36	214	10	18	1	4.79
		3B	B. Bailey	545	.251	14	83	69	194	11	14	2.3	**.960**	E. McAnally	31	178	11	12	0	3.89
		RF	R. Staub	599	.311	19	97	290	20	18	5	2.0	.945	J. Strohmayer	27	114	7	5	1	4.34
		CF	B. Day	371	.283	4	33	262	10	5	1	2.3	.982	M. Marshall	66	111	5	8	23	4.30
		LF	J. Fairey	200	.245	1	19	85	7	3	1	1.6	.968							
		C	J. Bateman	492	.242	10	56	726	56	12	**12**	5.8	.985							
		2S	G. Sutherland	304	.257	4	26	154	249	21	59		.950							
		1C	J. Boccabella	177	.220	3	15	334	33	4	30		.989							
	Philadelphia	1B	D. Johnson	582	.265	34	95	1219	88	7	124	9.7	.995	R. Wise	38	272	17	14	0	2.88
	W-67 L-95	2B	D. Doyle	342	.231	3	24	241	264	17	62	5.7	.967	B. Lersch	38	214	5	14	0	3.79
	Frank Lucchesi	SS	L. Bowa	**650**	.249	0	25	272	**560**	11	**97**	**5.4**	**.987**	C. Short	31	173	7	14	1	3.85
		3B	J. Vukovich	217	.166	0	14	58	137	9	8	2.8	.956	K. Reynolds	35	162	5	9	0	4.50
		RF	R. Freed	348	.221	6	37	184	4	2	1	1.8	.989	W. Fryman	37	149	10	7	2	3.38
		CF	W. Montanez	599	.255	30	99	364	11	11	3	2.4	.972	J. Bunning	29	110	5	12	1	5.48
		LF	O. Gamble	280	.221	6	23	125	4	4	1	1.7	.970	B. Champion	37	109	3	5	0	4.38
		C	T. McCarver	474	.278	8	46	673	51	11	8	5.9	.985	D. Brandon	52	83	6	6	4	3.90
		UT	D. Money	439	.223	7	38	167	197	11	21		.971	J. Hoerner	49	73	4	5	9	1.97
		2B	T. Harmon	221	.204	0	12	122	166	4	39	5.0	.986	B. Wilson	38	59	4	6	7	3.05
		OF	R. Stone	185	.227	2	23	76	5	3	0	1.6	.964							

NATIONAL LEAGUE 1971, *cont.*

		POS	Player	AB	BA	HR	RBI	PO	A	E	DP	TC/G	FA	Pitcher	G	IP	W	L	SV	ERA
West	**San Francisco**	1B	W. McCovey	329	.277	18	70	828	63	**15**	80	9.5	.983	G. Perry	37	280	16	12	0	2.76
	W-90 L-72	2B	T. Fuentes	630	.273	4	52	373	465	**23**	109	5.7	.973	J. Marichal	37	279	18	11	0	2.94
	Charlie Fox	SS	C. Speier	601	.235	8	46	239	517	**33**	95	5.1	.958	J. Cumberland	45	185	9	6	2	2.92
		3B	A. Gallagher	429	.277	5	57	88	204	15	18	2.4	.951	R. Bryant	27	140	7	10	0	3.79
		RF	B. Bonds	619	.288	33	102	329	10	2	1	2.2	.994	S. Stone	24	111	5	9	0	4.14
		CF	W. Mays	417	.271	18	61	192	2	6	1	2.4	.970	J. Johnson	67	109	12	9	18	2.97
		LF	K. Henderson	504	.264	15	65	277	3	10	1	2.1	.966	D. McMahon	61	82	10	6	4	4.06
		C	D. Dietz	453	.252	19	72	712	37	14	4	5.7	.982							
		3B	H. Lanier	206	.233	1	13	33	79	5	6	1.4	.957							
		OF	J. Rosario	192	.224	0	13	151	1	0	0	2.3	1.000							
		10	D. Kingman	115	.278	6	24	168	9	4	9		.978							
	Los Angeles	1B	W. Parker	533	.274	6	62	1215	97	5	113	8.9	.996	D. Sutton	38	265	17	12	1	2.55
	W-89 L-73	2B	J. Lefebvre	388	.245	12	68	244	260	6	69	5.0	.988	A. Downing	37	262	20	9	0	2.68
	Walter Alston	SS	M. Wills	601	.281	3	44	220	484	16	86	5.0	.978	C. Osteen	38	259	14	11	0	3.51
		3B	S. Garvey	225	.227	7	26	53	161	14	11	2.9	.939	B. Singer	31	203	10	17	0	4.17
		RF	B. Buckner	358	.277	5	41	165	5	1	0	2.0	.994	D. Alexander	17	92	6	6	0	3.82
		CF	W. Davis	641	.309	10	74	404	7	8	0	2.7	.981	J. Brewer	55	81	6	5	22	1.89
		LF	W. Crawford	342	.281	9	40	146	5	3	1	1.6	.981	P. Mikkelsen	41	74	8	5	5	3.65
		C	D. Sims	230	.274	6	25	345	33	3	5	5.1	.992							
		UT	D. Allen	549	.295	23	90	382	151	21	38		.962							
		UT	B. Valentine	281	.249	1	25	123	176	16	31		.949							
		OF	M. Mota	269	.312	0	34	108	3	4	1	1.4	.965							
		20	B. Russell	211	.227	2	15	130	109	7	21		.972							
		C	T. Haller	202	.267	5	32	320	34	8	3	5.4	.978							
	Atlanta	1B	H. Aaron	495	.327	47	118	629	38	3	56	9.4	.996	P. Niekro	42	269	15	14	2	2.98
	W-82 L-80	2B	F. Millan	577	.289	2	45	373	437	15	120	5.9	.982	R. Reed	32	222	13	14	0	3.73
	Lum Harris	SS	M. Perez	410	.227	4	32	195	382	27	91	4.8	.955	G. Stone	27	173	6	8	0	3.59
		3B	D. Evans	260	.242	12	38	71	138	14	13	3.1	.937	P. Jarvis	35	162	6	14	1	4.11
		RF	M. Lum	454	.269	13	55	286	10	3	2	2.4	.990	T. Kelley	28	143	9	5	0	2.96
		CF	S. Jackson	547	.258	2	25	336	8	7	0	2.4	.980	J. Nash	32	133	9	7	2	4.94
		LF	R. Garr	639	.343	9	44	315	15	11	3	2.2	.968	C. Upshaw	49	82	11	6	17	3.51
		C	E. Williams	497	.260	33	87	375	35	8	4	5.8	.981	B. Priddy	40	64	4	9	4	4.22
		1B	O. Cepeda	250	.276	14	44	586	49	5	60	10.2	.992							
		C	H. King	198	.207	5	19	274	23	5	0	5.0	.983							
		3S	Z. Versalles	194	.191	5	22	61	105	13	13		.927							
	Cincinnati	1B	L. May	553	.278	39	98	1261	78	8	118	9.4	.994	G. Nolan	35	245	12	15	0	3.16
	W-79 L-83	2B	T. Helms	547	.258	3	52	**395**	468	9	**130**	**5.9**	**.990**	D. Gullett	35	218	16	6	0	2.64
	Sparky Anderson	SS	D. Concepcion	327	.205	1	20	160	294	12	62	4.2	.974	J. McGlothlin	30	171	8	12	0	3.21
		3B	T. Perez	609	.269	25	91	113	**304**	18	26	**2.9**	.959	R. Grimsley	26	161	10	7	0	3.58
		RF	P. Rose	632	.304	13	44	306	13	2	1	2.0	.994	W. Simpson	22	117	4	7	0	4.77
		CF	G. Foster	368	.234	10	50	267	8	4	3	2.7	.986	J. Merritt	28	107	1	11	0	4.37
		LF	H. McRae	337	.264	9	34	167	6	6	1	2.0	.966	W. Granger	**70**	100	7	6	11	3.33
		C	J. Bench	562	.238	27	61	687	59	9	9	5.4	.988	C. Carroll	61	94	10	4	15	2.49
		OF	B. Carbo	310	.219	5	20	154	7	3	0	1.8	.982	J. Gibbon	50	64	5	6	11	2.95
		S3	W. Woodward	273	.242	0	18	114	236	7	44		.980							
	Houston	1B	D. Menke	475	.246	1	43	845	59	3	77	9.0	.997	D. Wilson	35	268	16	10	0	2.45
	W-79 L-83	2B	J. Morgan	583	.256	13	56	336	**482**	12	93	5.3	.986	J. Billingham	33	228	10	16	0	3.39
	Harry Walker	SS	R. Metzger	562	.235	0	26	**275**	459	17	91	5.1	.977	K. Forsch	33	188	8	8	0	2.54
		3B	D. Rader	484	.244	12	56	93	275	**21**	28	2.9	.946	L. Dierker	24	159	12	6	0	2.72
		RF	J. Wynn	404	.203	7	45	232	9	3	5	2.1	.988	W. Blasingame	30	158	9	11	0	4.61
		CF	C. Cedeno	611	.264	10	81	345	6	4	0	2.3	.989	J. Ray	47	98	10	4	3	2.11
		LF	B. Watson	468	.288	9	67	131	2	2	0	1.6	.985	G. Culver	59	95	5	8	7	2.65
		C	J. Edwards	317	.233	1	23	555	48	3	7	5.8	**.995**	F. Gladding	48	51	4	5	12	2.12
		OF	J. Alou	433	.279	2	40	229	7	4	3	2.2	.983							
		C	J. Hiatt	174	.276	1	16	329	20	3	6	5.4	.991							
	San Diego	1B	N. Colbert	565	.264	27	84	**1372**	106	10	**125**	9.7	.993	D. Roberts	37	270	14	17	0	2.10
	W-61 L-100	2B	D. Mason	344	.212	2	11	188	231	15	47	4.8	.965	C. Kirby	38	267	15	13	0	2.83
	Preston Gomez	SS	E. Hernandez	549	.222	0	12	260	445	**33**	82	5.2	.955	S. Arlin	36	228	9	**19**	0	3.47
		3B	E. Spiezio	308	.231	7	36	57	168	9	12	2.6	.962	T. Phoebus	29	133	3	11	0	4.47
		RF	O. Brown	484	.273	9	55	263	9	5	2	2.1	.982	F. Norman	20	127	3	12	0	3.32
		CF	C. Gaston	518	.228	17	61	271	8	5	1	2.1	.982	A. Severinsen	59	70	2	5	8	3.47
		LF	L. Stahl	308	.253	8	36	141	11	2	4	2.1	.987	B. Miller	38	64	7	3	7	1.41
		C	B. Barton	376	.250	5	23	698	67	**15**	10	6.6	.981							
		23	D. Campbell	365	.227	7	29	169	254	17	48		.961							
		OF	L. Lee	256	.273	4	21	86	6	8	1	1.5	.920							
		OF	I. Murrell	255	.235	7	24	133	2	3	0	1.9	.978							
		32	G. Jestadt	189	.291	0	13	63	141	12	11		.944							

BATTING AND BASE RUNNING LEADERS

Batting Average		Slugging Average		Home Runs	
J. Torre, STL	.363	H. Aaron, ATL	.669	W. Stargell, PIT	48
R. Garr, ATL	.343	W. Stargell, PIT	.628	H. Aaron, ATL	47
G. Beckert, CHI	.342	J. Torre, STL	.555	L. May, CIN	39
R. Clemente, PIT	.341	L. May, CIN	.532	D. Johnson, PHI	34
H. Aaron, ATL	.327	B. Bonds, SF	.512	E. Williams, ATL	33
				B. Bonds, SF	33

PITCHING LEADERS

Winning Percentage		Earned Run Average		Wins	
D. Gullett, CIN	.727	T. Seaver, NY	1.76	F. Jenkins, CHI	24
S. Carlton, STL	.690	D. Roberts, SD	2.10	A. Downing, LA	20
A. Downing, LA	.690	D. Wilson, HOU	2.45	S. Carlton, STL	20
D. Ellis, PIT	.679	K. Forsch, HOU	2.54	T. Seaver, NY	20
T. Seaver, NY	.667	D. Sutton, LA	2.55	D. Ellis, PIT	19

NATIONAL LEAGUE 1971, *cont.*

BATTING AND BASE RUNNING LEADERS

Total Bases
J. Torre, STL 352
H. Aaron, ATL 331
W. Stargell, PIT 321
B. Bonds, SF 317
B. Williams, CHI 300

Runs Batted In
J. Torre, STL 137
W. Stargell, PIT 125
H. Aaron, ATL 118
B. Bonds, SF 102
W. Montanez, PHI 99

Stolen Bases
L. Brock, STL 64
J. Morgan, HOU 40
R. Garr, ATL 30
T. Agee, NY 28
B. Harrelson, NY 28
L. Bowa, PHI 28

Hits
J. Torre, STL 230
R. Garr, ATL 219
L. Brock, STL 200
W. Davis, LA 198

Base on Balls
W. Mays, SF 112
D. Dietz, SF 97
B. Bailey, MON 97
D. Allen, LA 93

Home Run Percentage
H. Aaron, ATL 9.5
W. Stargell, PIT 9.4
L. May, CIN 7.1
E. Williams, ATL 6.6

Runs
L. Brock, STL 126
B. Bonds, SF 110
W. Stargell, PIT 104
R. Garr, ATL 101

Doubles
C. Cedeno, HOU 40
L. Brock, STL 37
R. Staub, MON 34
J. Torre, STL 34

Triples
R. Metzger, HOU 11
J. Morgan, HOU 11
W. Davis, LA 10
C. Gaston, SD 9

PITCHING LEADERS

Saves
D. Giusti, PIT 30
M. Marshall, MON 23
J. Brewer, LA 22
J. Johnson, SF 18
C. Upshaw, ATL 17

Strikeouts
T. Seaver, NY 289
F. Jenkins, CHI 263
B. Stoneman, MON 251
C. Kirby, SD 231
D. Sutton, LA 194

Complete Games
F. Jenkins, CHI 30
T. Seaver, NY 21
B. Gibson, STL 20
B. Stoneman, MON 20

Fewest Hits/9 Innings
D. Wilson, HOU 6.55
T. Seaver, NY 6.61
C. Kirby, SD 7.18
G. Gentry, NY 7.40

Shutouts
B. Gibson, STL 5
S. Blass, PIT 5
M. Pappas, CHI 5
A. Downing, LA 5

Fewest Walks/9 Innings
F. Jenkins, CHI 1.02
J. Marichal, SF 1.81
G. Stone, ATL 1.82
B. Hands, CHI 1.86

Most Strikeouts/9 Inn.
T. Seaver, NY 9.09
C. Kirby, SD 7.79
B. Stoneman, MON 7.66
F. Jenkins, CHI 7.28

Innings
F. Jenkins, CHI 325
B. Stoneman, MON 295
T. Seaver, NY 286
G. Perry, SF 280

Games Pitched
W. Granger, CIN 70
J. Johnson, SF 67
M. Marshall, MON 66
C. Carroll, CIN 61
D. McMahon, SF 61

		W	L	PCT	GB	R	OR	Batting 2B	3B	HR	BA	SA	SB	Fielding E	DP	FA	Pitching CG	BB	SO	ShO	SV	ERA
East	Pittsburgh	97	65	.599		**788**	599	223	**61**	**154**	.274	**.416**	65	133	164	.979	43	470	813	15	**48**	3.31
	St. Louis	90	72	.556	7	739	699	225	54	95	**.275**	.385	**124**	142	155	.978	56	576	911	14	22	3.87
	Chicago	83	79	.512	14	637	648	202	34	128	.258	.378	44	126	150	.980	**75**	411	900	17	13	3.61
	New York	83	79	.512	14	588	**550**	203	29	98	.249	.351	89	114	135	.981	42	529	**1157**	13	22	**3.00**
	Montreal	71	90	.441	25.5	622	729	197	29	88	.246	.343	51	150	164	.976	49	658	829	8	25	4.12
	Philadelphia	67	95	.414	30	558	688	209	35	123	.233	.350	63	122	158	.981	31	525	838	10	25	3.71
West	San Francisco	90	72	.556		706	644	224	36	140	.247	.378	101	179	153	.972	45	471	831	14	30	3.33
	Los Angeles	89	73	.549	1	663	587	213	38	95	.266	.370	76	131	159	.979	48	**399**	853	**18**	33	3.23
	Atlanta	82	80	.506	8	643	699	192	30	153	.257	.385	57	146	**180**	.977	40	485	823	11	31	3.75
	Cincinnati	79	83	.488	11	586	581	203	28	138	.241	.366	59	**103**	174	**.984**	27	501	750	11	38	3.35
	Houston	79	83	.488	11	585	567	**230**	52	71	.240	.340	101	106	152	.983	43	475	914	10	25	3.13
	San Diego	61	100	.379	28.5	486	610	184	31	96	.233	.332	70	161	144	.974	47	559	923	10	17	3.23
						7601	7601	2505	457	1379	.252	.366	900	1613	1888	.979	546	6059	10542	151	329	3.47

AMERICAN LEAGUE 1971

East

Baltimore

W-101 L-57

Earl Weaver

POS	Player	AB	BA	HR	RBI	PO	A	E	DP	TC/G	FA	Pitcher	G	IP	W	L	SV	ERA
1B	B. Powell	418	.256	22	92	1031	67	5	97	8.9	.995	M. Cuellar	38	292	20	9	0	3.08
2B	D. Johnson	510	.282	18	72	361	367	12	**103**	5.3	.984	J. Palmer	37	282	20	9	0	2.68
SS	M. Belanger	500	.266	0	35	280	443	16	77	5.0	.978	P. Dobson	38	282	20	8	1	2.90
3B	B. Robinson	589	.272	20	92	131	354	16	35	3.2	.968	D. McNally	30	224	21	5	0	2.89
RF	M. Rettenmund	491	.318	11	75	292	7	7	4	2.3	.977	D. Hall	27	43	6	6	1	5.02
CF	P. Blair	516	.262	10	44	331	4	3	1	2.4	.991	E. Watt	35	40	3	1	11	1.80
LF	D. Buford	449	.290	19	54	217	6	3	0	2.0	.987	T. Dukes	28	38	1	5	4	3.55
C	E. Hendricks	316	.250	9	42	429	33	7	5	5.2	.985	P. Richert	35	36	3	5	4	3.50
OF	F. Robinson	455	.281	28	99	177	3	5	0	2.0	.973							
C	A. Etchebarren	222	.270	9	29	337	24	5	2	5.2	.986							

Detroit

W-91 L-71

Billy Martin

POS	Player	AB	BA	HR	RBI	PO	A	E	DP	TC/G	FA	Pitcher	G	IP	W	L	SV	ERA
1B	N. Cash	452	.283	32	91	1020	75	9	105	8.4	.992	M. Lolich	45	**376**	**25**	14	0	2.92
2B	D. McAuliffe	477	.208	18	57	322	308	8	86	5.2	.987	J. Coleman	39	286	20	9	0	3.15
SS	E. Brinkman	527	.228	1	37	235	**513**	15	91	4.8	.980	L. Cain	26	145	10	9	0	4.34
3B	A. Rodriguez	604	.253	15	39	127	341	23	33	3.2	.953	J. Niekro	31	122	6	7	1	4.50
RF	A. Kaline	405	.294	15	54	207	6	0	0	1.7	1.000	F. Scherman	69	113	11	6	20	2.71
CF	M. Stanley	401	.292	7	41	315	10	4	3	2.4	.988	D. Chance	31	90	4	6	0	3.50
LF	W. Horton	450	.289	22	72	176	8	7	1	1.6	.963	M. Kilkenny	30	86	4	5	1	5.02
C	B. Freehan	516	.277	21	71	**912**	50	4	6	6.7	.996	T. Timmerman	52	84	7	6	4	3.86
OF	J. Northrup	459	.270	16	71	205	4	4	0	2.0	.981							
OF	G. Brown	195	.338	11	29	68	2	1	0	1.3	.986							
2B	T. Taylor	181	.287	3	19	114	107	1	29	4.4	.995							

Boston

W-85 L-77

Eddie Kasko

POS	Player	AB	BA	HR	RBI	PO	A	E	DP	TC/G	FA	Pitcher	G	IP	W	L	SV	ERA
1B	G. Scott	537	.263	24	78	1256	75	11	122	9.4	.992	R. Culp	35	242	14	16	0	3.61
2B	D. Griffin	483	.244	3	27	311	344	9	90	5.4	.986	S. Siebert	32	235	16	10	0	2.91
SS	L. Aparicio	491	.232	4	45	194	338	16	56	4.5	.971	G. Peters	34	214	14	11	1	4.37
3B	R. Petrocelli	553	.251	28	89	118	334	11	37	3.0	**.976**	J. Lonborg	27	168	10	7	0	4.13
RF	R. Smith	618	.283	30	96	386	15	14	2	2.6	.966	B. Lee	47	102	9	2	2	2.74
CF	B. Conigliaro	351	.262	11	33	232	5	4	2	2.4	.983	B. Bolin	52	70	5	3	6	4.24
LF	C. Yastrzemski	508	.254	15	70	281	16	2	4	2.0	.993	K. Tatum	36	54	2	4	9	4.17
C	D. Josephson	306	.245	10	39	491	32	6	5	6.1	.989	S. Lyle	50	52	6	4	16	2.77
2S	J. Kennedy	272	.276	5	22	112	150	13	34		.953							
OF	J. Lahoud	256	.215	14	32	139	4	1	3	2.1	.993							
C	B. Montgomery	205	.239	2	24	361	15	4	3	5.8	.989							

AMERICAN LEAGUE 1971, *cont.*

New York

W-82 L-80

Ralph Houk

POS	Player	AB	BA	HR	RBI	PO	A	E	DP	TC/G	FA	Pitcher	G	IP	W	L	SV	ERA
1B	D. Cater	428	.276	4	50	564	62	3	54	8.1	.995	F. Peterson	37	274	15	13	1	3.05
2B	H. Clarke	625	.250	2	41	**386**	**455**	16	97	5.5	.981	M. Stottlemyre	35	270	16	12	0	2.87
SS	G. Michael	456	.224	3	35	243	474	20	88	**5.4**	.973	S. Bahnsen	36	242	14	12	0	3.35
3B	J. Kenney	325	.262	0	20	69	237	15	20	2.9	.953	S. Kline	31	222	12	13	0	2.96
RF	F. Alou	461	.289	8	69	129	3	2	0	1.7	.985	M. Kekich	37	170	10	9	0	4.08
CF	B. Murcer	529	.331	25	94	317	10	5	1	2.3	.985	L. McDaniel	44	70	5	10	4	5.01
LF	R. White	524	.292	19	84	306	8	0	1	2.2	1.000	J. Aker	41	56	4	4	4	2.57
C	T. Munson	451	.251	10	42	547	67	1	4	5.3	**.998**							
1B	J. Ellis	238	.244	3	34	625	35	7	66	10.3	.990							
C	J. Gibbs	206	.218	5	21	229	12	3	1	4.8	.988							
OF	R. Blomberg	199	.322	7	31	96	1	3	1	1.8	.970							
3B	R. Hansen	145	.207	2	20	16	51	6	9	2.4	.918							
OF	R. Swoboda	138	.261	2	20	80	2	3	0	1.8	.965							

Washington

W-63 L-96

Ted Williams

POS	Player	AB	BA	HR	RBI	PO	A	E	DP	TC/G	FA	Pitcher	G	IP	W	L	SV	ERA
1B	D. Mincher	323	.291	10	45	705	59	8	80	8.8	.990	D. Bosman	35	237	12	16	0	3.72
2B	T. Cullen	403	.191	2	26	165	213	1	47	4.9	.997	D. McLain	33	217	10	**22**	0	4.27
SS	T. Harrah	383	.230	2	22	181	307	23	69	4.4	.955	P. Broberg	18	125	5	9	0	3.46
3B	D. Nelson	329	.280	5	33	63	149	14	15	2.7	.938	C. Cox	54	124	5	7	7	3.99
RF	D. Unser	581	.255	9	41	394	10	8	2	2.7	.981	B. Gogolewski	27	124	6	5	0	2.76
CF	E. Maddox	258	.217	1	18	197	7	2	1	2.0	.990	J. Shellenback	40	120	3	11	0	3.52
LF	F. Howard	549	.279	26	83	141	7	1	0	1.5	.993	P. Lindblad	43	84	6	4	8	2.58
C	P. Casanova	311	.203	5	26	416	40	7	4	5.6	.985	J. Grzenda	46	70	5	2	5	1.93
CO	D. Billings	349	.246	6	48	378	37	4	5		.990							
23	B. Allen	229	.266	4	22	85	126	10	16		.955							
2B	L. Randle	215	.219	2	13	178	178	12	50	5.6	.967							
01	T. McCraw	207	.213	7	25	134	2	5	3		.965							
OF	J. Burroughs	181	.232	5	25	82	3	3	0	1.8	.966							
OF	L. Biittner	171	.257	0	16	72	6	5	0	2.0	.940							

Cleveland

W-60 L-102

Alvin Dark
W-42 L-61

Johnny Lipon
W-18 L-41

POS	Player	AB	BA	HR	RBI	PO	A	E	DP	TC/G	FA	Pitcher	G	IP	W	L	SV	ERA
1B	C. Chambliss	415	.275	9	48	943	55	8	85	9.3	.992	S. McDowell	35	215	13	17	1	3.39
2B	E. Leon	429	.261	4	35	235	271	9	71	4.8	.983	S. Dunning	31	184	8	14	1	4.50
SS	J. Heidemann	240	.208	0	9	113	188	7	34	3.8	.977	A. Foster	36	182	8	12	0	4.15
3B	G. Nettles	598	.261	28	86	**159**	**412**	16	**54**	**3.7**	.973	R. Lamb	43	158	6	12	1	3.36
RF	R. Foster	396	.245	18	45	174	9	6	2	1.8	.968	V. Colbert	50	143	7	6	2	3.97
CF	V. Pinson	566	.263	11	35	305	11	7	2	2.3	.978	S. Hargan	37	113	1	13	1	6.21
LF	T. Uhlaender	500	.288	2	47	245	6	2	0	1.9	.992	P. Hennigan	57	82	4	3	14	4.94
C	R. Fosse	486	.276	12	62	748	**73**	10	**16**	6.6	.988	E. Farmer	43	79	5	4	4	4.33
OF	T. Ford	196	.194	2	14	107	4	0	0	2.0	1.000							
OF	F. Baker	181	.210	1	23	65	2	1	1	1.3	.985							

West

Oakland

W-101 L-60

Dick Williams

POS	Player	AB	BA	HR	RBI	PO	A	E	DP	TC/G	FA	Pitcher	G	IP	W	L	SV	ERA
1B	M. Epstein	329	.234	18	51	714	52	4	93*	8.0	.995	V. Blue	39	312	24	8	0	**1.82**
2B	D. Green	475	.244	12	49	366	384	11	98	5.3	.986	C. Hunter	37	274	21	11	0	2.96
SS	B. Campaneris	569	.251	5	47	231	303	**26**	85	4.2	.954	C. Dobson	30	189	15	5	0	3.81
3B	S. Bando	538	.271	24	94	141	267	12	22	2.7	.971	D. Segui	26	146	10	8	0	3.14
RF	R. Jackson	567	.277	32	80	285	15	7	3	2.1	.977	B. Odom	25	141	10	12	0	4.28
CF	R. Monday	355	.245	18	56	238	6	4	1	2.2	.984	R. Fingers	48	129	4	6	17	3.00
LF	J. Rudi	513	.267	10	52	249	5	1	1	2.1	.996	B. Locker	47	72	7	2	6	2.88
C	D. Duncan	363	.253	15	40	678	41	**12**	3	**7.2**	.984	D. Knowles	43	53	5	2	7	3.59
OF	A. Mangual	287	.286	4	30	163	3	2	1	2.1	.988							
10	T. Davis	219	.324	3	42	274	30	5	24		.984							
UT	L. Brown	189	.196	1	9	82	141	6	31		.974							
C	G. Tenace	179	.274	7	25	300	20	2	3	6.2	.994							

Kansas City

W-85 L-76

Bob Lemon

POS	Player	AB	BA	HR	RBI	PO	A	E	DP	TC/G	FA	Pitcher	G	IP	W	L	SV	ERA
1B	G. Hopkins	295	.278	9	47	669	57	7	76	8.8	.990	D. Drago	35	241	17	11	0	2.99
2B	C. Rojas	414	.300	6	59	252	293	5	76	5.0	**.991**	M. Hedlund	32	206	15	8	0	2.71
SS	F. Patek	591	.267	6	36	**301**	459	25	**107**	5.3	.968	P. Splittorff	22	144	8	9	0	2.69
3B	P. Schaal	548	.274	11	63	107	335	**28**	31	2.9	.940	B. Dal Canton	25	141	8	6	0	3.45
RF	J. Keough	351	.248	3	30	164	4	3	1	1.7	.982	A. Fitzmorris	36	127	7	5	0	4.18
CF	A. Otis	555	.301	15	79	404	10	4	4	2.9	.990	J. York	53	93	5	5	3	2.90
LF	L. Piniella	448	.279	3	51	201	6	3	2	1.8	.986	T. Burgmeier	67	88	9	7	17	1.74
C	J. May	218	.252	1	24	314	38	1	6	5.0	.997	T. Abernathy	63	81	4	6	23	2.56
10	B. Oliver	373	.244	8	52	564	34	8	52		.987	K. Wright	21	78	3	6	1	3.69
OC	E. Kirkpatrick	365	.219	9	46	412	30	8	6		.982							
1B	C. Harrison	143	.217	2	21	335	24	3	31	9.3	.992							

Chicago

W-79 L-83

Chuck Tanner

POS	Player	AB	BA	HR	RBI	PO	A	E	DP	TC/G	FA	Pitcher	G	IP	W	L	SV	ERA
1B	C. May	500	.294	7	70	1189	71	**18**	90	**9.8**	.986	W. Wood	44	334	22	13	1	1.91
2B	M. Andrews	330	.282	12	47	177	191	**17**	51	5.1	.956	T. Bradley	45	286	15	15	2	2.96
SS	L. Alvarado	264	.216	0	8	89	189	12	34	4.1	.959	T. John	38	229	13	16	0	3.62
3B	B. Melton	543	.269	**33**	86	116	371	16	26	3.4	.968	B. Johnson	53	178	12	10	14	2.93
RF	W. Williams	361	.294	8	35	157	4	0	2	1.8	1.000	J. Horlen	34	137	8	9	2	4.27
CF	J. Johnstone	388	.260	16	40	232	9	8	1	2.1	.968	S. Kealey	54	77	2	2	6	3.86
LF	R. Reichardt	496	.278	19	62	283	4	4	0	2.3	.986	V. Romo	45	72	1	7	5	3.38
C	E. Herrmann	294	.214	11	35	556	56	3	5	6.3	.995							
20	R. McKinney	369	.271	8	46	192	160	10	34		.972							
SS	L. Richard	260	.231	2	17	87	210	**26**	30	4.8	.920							
C	T. Egan	251	.239	10	34	443	41	7	2	6.4	.986							
OF	P. Kelly	213	.291	3	22	100	7	1	0	1.8	.991							
SS	R. Morales	185	.243	2	14	66	138	5	14	3.7	.976							
OF	M. Hershberger	177	.260	2	15	96	1	4	0	1.7	.960							

AMERICAN LEAGUE 1971, *cont.*

California

W-76 L-86

Lefty Phillips

POS	Player	AB	BA	HR	RBI	PO	A	E	DP	TC/G	FA
1B	J. Spencer	510	.237	18	59	**1296**	**93**	5	117	9.6	**.996**
2B	S. Alomar	**689**	.260	4	42	350	432	9	100	**5.8**	.989
SS	J. Fregosi	347	.233	5	33	93	237	22	31	4.8	.938
3B	K. McMullen	593	.250	21	68	137	344	17	27	3.2	.966
RF	R. Repoz	297	.199	13	42	172	6	0	2	1.8	1.000
CF	K. Berry	298	.221	3	22	237	5	3	0	2.4	.988
LF	T. Gonzalez	314	.245	3	38	146	4	2	1	1.7	.987
C	J. Stephenson	279	.219	3	25	434	33	4	3	5.4	.992
OF	M. Rivers	268	.265	1	12	159	5	4	2	2.2	.976
OF	T. Conigliaro	266	.222	4	15	155	6	1	1	2.3	.994
SS	S. O'Brien	251	.199	5	21	87	136	9	30	4.5	.961
OF	A. Johnson	242	.260	2	21	84	3	7	0	1.5	.926
C	G. Moses	181	.227	4	15	299	38	8	3	5.5	.977
OF	B. Cowan	174	.276	4	20	69	1	0	0	1.8	1.000

Pitcher	G	IP	W	L	SV	ERA
C. Wright	37	277	16	17	0	2.99
A. Messersmith	38	277	20	13	0	2.99
T. Murphy	37	243	6	17	0	3.78
R. May	32	208	11	12	0	3.03
E. Fisher	57	119	10	8	3	2.72
L. Allen	54	94	4	6	15	2.49
D. LaRoche	56	72	5	1	9	2.50

Minnesota

W-74 L-86

Bill Rigney

POS	Player	AB	BA	HR	RBI	PO	A	E	DP	TC/G	FA
1B	R. Reese	329	.219	10	39	673	43	4	71	7.6	.994
2B	R. Carew	577	.307	2	48	321	329	16	76	4.7	.976
SS	L. Cardenas	554	.264	18	75	266	445	11	89	4.7	**.985**
3B	S. Braun	343	.254	5	35	48	106	11	7	2.3	.933
RF	T. Oliva	487	**.337**	22	81	216	6	7	3	1.9	.969
CF	J. Holt	340	.259	1	29	209	4	3	2	2.0	.986
LF	C. Tovar	657	.311	1	45	348	14	5	3	2.4	.986
C	G. Mitterwald	388	.250	13	44	656	53	10	7	6.0	.986
13	H. Killebrew	500	.254	28	**119**	700	149	13	55		.985
OF	J. Nettles	168	.250	6	24	139	3	2	1	2.3	.986

Pitcher	G	IP	W	L	SV	ERA
B. Blyleven	38	278	16	15	0	2.82
J. Perry	40	270	17	17	1	4.23
J. Kaat	39	260	13	14	0	3.32
R. Corbin	52	140	8	11	3	4.11
T. Hall	48	130	4	7	9	3.32
S. Williams	46	78	4	5	4	4.15
R. Perranoski	36	43	1	4	5	6.75

Milwaukee

W-69 L-92

Dave Bristol

POS	Player	AB	BA	HR	RBI	PO	A	E	DP	TC/G	FA
1B	J. Briggs	375	.264	21	59	458	40	5	53	8.4	.990
2B	R. Theobald	388	.276	1	23	233	311	15	81	5.0	.973
SS	R. Auerbach	236	.203	1	9	120	193	12	31	4.2	.963
3B	T. Harper	585	.258	14	52	71	115	13	10	2.8	.935
RF	B. Voss	275	.251	10	30	151	1	2	1	1.9	.987
CF	D. May	501	.277	16	65	342	10	9	3	2.5	.975
LF	J. Cardenal	198	.258	3	32	133	6	3	0	2.7	.979
C	E. Rodriguez	319	.210	1	30	520	67	5	8	5.2	.992
UT	R. Pena	274	.237	3	28	290	112	4	38		.990
UT	A. Kosco	264	.227	10	39	264	25	3	23		.990
2S	T. Kubiak	260	.227	3	17	171	222	14	44		.966
SS	B. Heise	189	.254	0	7	85	138	9	36	4.5	.961

Pitcher	G	IP	W	L	SV	ERA
M. Pattin	36	265	14	14	0	3.12
B. Parsons	36	245	13	17	0	3.20
S. Lockwood	33	208	10	15	0	3.33
L. Krausse	43	180	8	12	0	2.95
J. Slaton	26	148	10	8	0	3.77
K. Sanders	**83**	136	7	12	**31**	1.92

BATTING AND BASE RUNNING LEADERS

Batting Average
T. Oliva, MIN	.337
B. Murcer, NY	.331
M. Rettenmund, BAL	.318
C. Tovar, MIN	.311
R. Carew, MIN	.307

Slugging Average
T. Oliva, MIN	.546
B. Murcer, NY	.543
N. Cash, DET	.531
F. Robinson, BAL	.510
R. Jackson, OAK	.508

Home Runs
B. Melton, CHI	33
N. Cash, DET	32
R. Jackson, OAK	32
R. Smith, BOS	30

Total Bases
R. Smith, BOS	302
R. Jackson, OAK	288
B. Murcer, NY	287
B. Melton, CHI	267
T. Oliva, MIN	266

Runs Batted In
H. Killebrew, MIN	119
F. Robinson, BAL	99
R. Smith, BOS	96
B. Murcer, NY	94
S. Bando, OAK	94

Stolen Bases
A. Otis, KC	52
F. Patek, KC	49
S. Alomar, CAL	39
B. Campaneris, OAK	34
V. Pinson, CLE	25
T. Harper, MIL	25

Hits
C. Tovar, MIN	204
S. Alomar, CAL	179
R. Carew, MIN	177
B. Murcer, NY	175
R. Smith, BOS	175

Base on Balls
H. Killebrew, MIN	114
C. Yastrzemski, BOS	106
P. Schaal, KC	103
B. Murcer, NY	91
R. Petrocelli, BOS	91

Home Run Percentage
N. Cash, DET	7.1
F. Robinson, BAL	6.2
B. Melton, CHI	6.1
R. Jackson, OAK	5.6

Runs
D. Buford, BAL	99
B. Murcer, NY	94
C. Tovar, MIN	94
R. Carew, MIN	88

Doubles
R. Smith, BOS	33
P. Schaal, KC	31
T. Oliva, MIN	30
A. Rodriguez, DET	30

Triples
F. Patek, KC	11
R. Carew, MIN	10
P. Blair, BAL	8

PITCHING LEADERS

Winning Percentage
D. McNally, BAL	.808
V. Blue, OAK	.750
C. Dobson, OAK	.750
P. Dobson, BAL	.714

Earned Run Average
V. Blue, OAK	1.82
W. Wood, CHI	1.91
J. Palmer, BAL	2.68
M. Hedlund, KC	2.71
B. Blyleven, MIN	2.82

Wins
M. Lolich, DET	25
V. Blue, OAK	24
W. Wood, CHI	22
D. McNally, BAL	21
C. Hunter, OAK	21

Saves
K. Sanders, MIL	31
T. Abernathy, KC	23
F. Scherman, DET	20
R. Fingers, OAK	17
T. Burgmeier, KC	17

Strikeouts
M. Lolich, DET	308
V. Blue, OAK	301
J. Coleman, DET	236
B. Blyleven, MIN	224
W. Wood, CHI	210

Complete Games
M. Lolich, DET	29
V. Blue, OAK	24
W. Wood, CHI	22
M. Cuellar, BAL	21
J. Palmer, BAL	20

Fewest Hits/9 Innings
V. Blue, OAK	6.03
S. McDowell, CLE	6.70
R. May, CAL	6.92
A. Messersmith, CAL	7.28

Shutouts
V. Blue, OAK	8
M. Stottlemyre, NY	7
W. Wood, CHI	7
T. Bradley, CHI	6

Fewest Walks/9 Innings
F. Peterson, NY	1.38
S. Kline, NY	1.50
J. Kaat, MIN	1.63
W. Wood, CHI	1.67

Most Strikeouts/9 Inn.
V. Blue, OAK	8.68
S. McDowell, CLE	8.04
B. Johnson, CHI	7.74
J. Coleman, DET	7.43

Innings
M. Lolich, DET	376
W. Wood, CHI	334
V. Blue, OAK	312
M. Cuellar, BAL	292

Games Pitched
K. Sanders, MIL	83
F. Scherman, DET	69
T. Burgmeier, KC	67
T. Abernathy, KC	63

AMERICAN LEAGUE 1971, *cont.*

								Batting						Fielding			Pitching					
		W	L	PCT	GB	R	OR	2B	3B	HR	BA	SA	SB	E	DP	FA	CG	BB	SO	ShO	SV	ERA
East	Baltimore	101	57	.639		**742**	**530**	207	25	158	**.261**	.398	66	112	148	.981	**71**	**416**	793	15	22	**3.00**
	Detroit	91	71	.562	12	701	645	214	38	**179**	.254	**.405**	35	**106**	156	**.983**	53	609	**1000**	11	32	3.64
	Boston	85	77	.525	18	691	667	**246**	28	161	.252	.397	51	116	149	.981	44	535	871	11	35	3.83
	New York	82	80	.506	21	648	641	195	**43**	97	.254	.360	75	125	159	.981	67	423	707	15	12	3.45
	Washington	63	96	.396	38.5	537	660	189	30	86	.230	.326	68	141	170	.977	30	554	762	10	26	3.70
	Cleveland	60	102	.370	43	543	747	200	20	109	.238	.342	57	116	159	.981	21	770	937	7	32	4.28
West	Oakland	101	60	.627		691	564	195	25	160	.252	.384	80	117	157	.981	57	501	999	18	36	3.06
	Kansas City	85	76	.528	16	603	566	225	40	80	.250	.353	**130**	134	**178**	.978	34	496	775	15	**44**	3.25
	Chicago	79	83	.488	22.5	617	597	185	30	138	.250	.373	83	160	128	.975	46	468	976	19	32	3.13
	California	76	86	.469	25.5	511	576	213	18	96	.231	.329	72	131	159	.980	39	607	904	11	32	3.10
	Minnesota	74	86	.463	26.5	654	670	197	31	116	.260	.372	66	118	134	.980	43	529	895	9	25	3.82
	Milwaukee	69	92	.429	32	534	609	160	23	104	.229	.329	82	138	152	.977	32	569	795	**23**	32	3.38
						7472	7472	2426	351	1484	.247	.364	865	1514	1849	.980	537	6477	10414	164	360	3.47

NATIONAL LEAGUE 1972

East

Pittsburgh

W-96 L-59

Bill Virdon

POS	Player	AB	BA	HR	RBI	PO	A	E	DP	TC/G	FA	Pitcher	G	IP	W	L	SV	ERA
1B	W. Stargell	495	.293	33	112	881	40	**15**	96	9.3	.984	S. Blass	33	250	19	8	0	2.49
2B	D. Cash	425	.282	3	30	260	342	5	81	6.3	.992	B. Moose	31	226	13	10	1	2.91
SS	G. Alley	347	.248	3	36	181	339	16	88	4.7	.970	N. Briles	28	196	14	11	0	3.08
3B	R. Hebner	427	.300	19	72	76	210	9	17	2.4	.969	D. Ellis	25	163	15	7	0	2.70
RF	R. Clemente	378	.312	10	60	199	5	0	2	2.2	1.000	B. Kison	32	152	9	7	3	3.26
CF	A. Oliver	565	.312	12	89	332	4	5	1	2.5	.985	B. Johnson	31	116	4	4	3	2.96
LF	V. Davalillo	368	.318	4	28	181	4	4	0	1.9	.979	L. Walker	26	93	4	6	2	3.40
C	M. Sanguillen	520	.298	7	71	721	50	9	4	6.1	.988	D. Giusti	54	75	7	4	22	1.93
20	R. Stennett	370	.286	3	30	192	164	9	43		.975	R. Hernandez	53	70	5	0	14	1.67
OF	G. Clines	311	.334	0	17	131	7	6	0	1.7	.958	B. Miller	36	54	5	2	3	2.65
1B	B. Robertson	306	.193	12	41	502	60	4	57	6.4	.993							
SS	J. Hernandez	176	.188	1	14	110	180	22	34	4.6	.929							

Chicago

W-85 L-70

Leo Durocher
W-46 L-44

Whitey Lockman
W-39 L-26

POS	Player	AB	BA	HR	RBI	PO	A	E	DP	TC/G	FA	Pitcher	G	IP	W	L	SV	ERA
1B	J. Hickman	368	.272	17	64	670	70	6	61	9.7	.992	F. Jenkins	36	289	20	12	0	3.21
2B	G. Beckert	474	.270	3	43	256	396	16	71	5.7	.976	B. Hooton	33	218	11	14	0	2.80
SS	D. Kessinger	577	.274	1	39	259	504	28	90	5.4	.965	M. Pappas	29	195	17	7	0	2.77
3B	R. Santo	464	.302	17	74	108	274	21	19	3.1	.948	B. Hands	32	189	11	8	0	2.99
RF	J. Cardenal	533	.291	17	70	223	11	7	1	1.8	.971	R. Reuschel	21	129	10	8	0	2.93
CF	R. Monday	434	.249	11	42	268	6	1	2	2.1	.996	T. Phoebus	37	83	3	3	6	3.78
LF	B. Williams	574	**.333**	37	122	233	9	4	0	1.7	.984	J. Aker	48	67	6	6	17	2.96
C	R. Hundley	357	.218	5	30	569	53	3	7	5.5	**.995**	J. Pizarro	16	59	4	5	1	3.97
UT	C. Fanzone	222	.225	8	42	243	115	9	21		.975							
1B	J. Pepitone	214	.262	8	21	552	31	2	51	8.9	.997							

New York

W-83 L-73

Yogi Berra

POS	Player	AB	BA	HR	RBI	PO	A	E	DP	TC/G	FA	Pitcher	G	IP	W	L	SV	ERA
1B	E. Kranepool	327	.269	8	34	705	48	3	65	7.0	.996	T. Seaver	35	262	21	12	0	2.92
2B	K. Boswell	355	.211	9	33	208	183	4	53	4.2	.990	J. Matlack	34	244	15	10	0	2.32
SS	B. Harrelson	418	.215	1	24	191	334	16	51	4.7	.970	G. Gentry	32	164	7	10	0	4.01
3B	J. Fregosi	340	.232	5	32	71	144	15	9	2.7	.935	J. Koosman	34	163	11	12	1	4.14
RF	R. Staub	239	.293	9	38	108	4	2	2	1.8	.982	J. McAndrew	28	161	11	8	1	2.80
CF	T. Agee	422	.227	13	47	273	6	11	1	2.7	.962	T. McGraw	54	106	8	6	27	1.70
LF	C. Jones	375	.245	5	52	136	8	2	1	1.7	.986	D. Frisella	39	67	5	8	9	3.34
C	D. Dyer	325	.231	8	36	690	61	5	**12**	**8.3**	.993							
OF	J. Milner	362	.238	17	38	160	7	6	0	1.9	.965							
UT	T. Martinez	330	.224	1	19	175	194	5	30		.987							
3B	W. Garrett	298	.232	2	29	66	150	9	13	2.7	.960							
C	J. Grote	205	.210	3	21	405	42	1	5	7.6	.998							
OF	W. Mays	195	.267	8	19	109	3	3	1	2.3	.974							
OF	D. Marshall	156	.250	4	11	70	0	2	0	1.7	.972							

St. Louis

W-75 L-81

Red Schoendienst

POS	Player	AB	BA	HR	RBI	PO	A	E	DP	TC/G	FA	Pitcher	G	IP	W	L	SV	ERA
1B	M. Alou	404	.314	3	31	535	40	7	53	8.8	.988	B. Gibson	34	278	19	11	0	2.46
2B	T. Sizemore	439	.264	2	38	222	342	14	68	5.2	.976	R. Wise	35	269	16	16	0	3.11
SS	D. Maxvill	276	.221	1	23	145	243	8	56	4.2	.980	R. Cleveland	33	231	14	15	0	3.94
3B	J. Torre	544	.289	11	81	102	182	11	17	2.5	.963	A. Santorini	30	134	8	11	0	4.11
RF	L. Melendez	332	.238	5	28	206	5	9	0	2.1	.959	S. Spinks	16	118	5	5	0	2.67
CF	J. Cruz	332	.235	2	23	220	9	5	5	2.3	.979	D. Segui	33	56	3	1	9	3.07
LF	L. Brock	621	.311	3	42	253	6	13	1	1.8	.952							
C	T. Simmons	594	.303	16	96	**842**	**78**	8	6	6.9	.991							
OF	B. Carbo	302	.258	7	34	162	15*	6	3	2.0	.967							
UT	E. Crosby	276	.217	0	19	130	197	10	42		.970							

Montreal

W-70 L-86

Gene Mauch

POS	Player	AB	BA	HR	RBI	PO	A	E	DP	TC/G	FA	Pitcher	G	IP	W	L	SV	ERA
1B	M. Jorgensen	372	.231	13	47	757	56	4	66	10.8	.995	B. Stoneman	36	251	12	14	0	2.98
2B	R. Hunt	443	.253	0	18	257	353	11	61	5.1	.982	M. Torrez	34	243	16	12	0	3.33
SS	T. Foli	540	.241	2	35	**281**	487	27	94	5.4	.966	C. Morton	27	172	7	13	0	3.92
3B	B. Bailey	489	.233	16	57	83	250	22	21	2.6	.938	E. McAnally	29	170	6	15	0	3.81
RF	K. Singleton	507	.274	14	50	236	9	7	3	1.8	.972	B. Moore	22	148	9	9	0	3.47
CF	B. Day	386	.233	0	30	225	7	5	3	2.0	.979	M. Marshall	**65**	116	14	8	18	1.78
LF	R. Fairly	446	.278	17	68	125	8	2	2	1.9	.985	S. Renko	30	97	1	10	0	5.20
C	J. Boccabella	207	.227	1	10	316	33	6	6	4.9	.983							
CO	T. McCarver	239	.251	5	20	312	24	4	2		.988							
OF	R. Woods	221	.258	10	31	110	2	1	0	1.5	.991							
C	T. Humphrey	215	.186	1	9	322	37	5	4	5.6	.986							
2B	H. Torres	181	.155	2	7	86	132	8	28	3.8	.965							
OF	C. Mashore	176	.227	3	23	80	3	1	0	1.1	.988							

NATIONAL LEAGUE 1972, *cont.*

	POS	Player	AB	BA	HR	RBI	PO	A	E	DP	TC/G	FA	Pitcher	G	IP	W	L	SV	ERA
Philadelphia	1B	T. Hutton	381	.260	4	38	555	36	5	46	6.9	.992	S. Carlton	41	**346**	**27**	10	0	**1.97**
	2B	D. Doyle	442	.249	1	26	265	288	10	66	4.7	.982	K. Reynolds	33	154	2	15	0	4.26
W-59 L-97	SS	L. Bowa	579	.250	1	31	212	494	9	88	4.8	**.987**	W. Twitchell	49	140	5	9	1	4.06
	3B	D. Money	536	.222	15	52	**139**	316	10	**31**	3.1	**.978**	B. Champion	30	133	4	14	0	5.09
	RF	B. Robinson	188	.239	8	21	109	2	2	1	1.6	.982	W. Fryman	23	120	4	10	1	4.36
Frank Lucchesi	CF	W. Montanez	531	.247	13	64	318	15	5	2	2.6	.985	D. Brandon	42	104	7	7	2	3.45
W-26 L-50	LF	G. Luzinski	563	.281	18	68	255	9	11	2	1.9	.960	B. Lersch	36	101	4	6	0	3.04
	C	J. Bateman	252	.222	3	17	447	38	14*	6	6.2	.972	D. Selma	46	99	2	9	3	5.56
Paul Owens	1B	D. Johnson	230	.213	9	31	479	24	9	43	8.3	.982							
W-33 L-47	2B	T. Harmon	218	.284	2	13	106	136	1	31	4.9	.996							
West																			
Cincinnati	1B	T. Perez	515	.283	21	90	1207	68	9	111	9.4	.993	J. Billingham	36	218	12	12	1	3.18
	2B	J. Morgan	552	.292	16	73	**370**	436	8	92	5.5	**.990**	R. Grimsley	30	198	14	8	1	3.05
	SS	D. Concepcion	378	.209	2	29	194	365	18	75	5.1	.969	G. Nolan	25	176	15	5	0	1.99
W-95 L-59	3B	D. Menke	447	.233	9	50	85	258	16	20	2.8	.955	J. McGlothlin	31	145	9	8	0	3.91
	RF	C. Geronimo	255	.275	4	29	150	10	3	1	1.5	.982	D. Gullett	31	135	9	10	2	3.94
Sparky Anderson	CF	B. Tolan	604	.283	8	82	401	9	4	3	2.8	.990	W. Simpson	24	130	8	5	0	4.14
	LF	P. Rose	**645**	.307	6	57	330	15	2	2	2.3	.994	T. Hall	47	124	10	1	8	2.61
	C	J. Bench	538	.270	**40**	**125**	735	56	6	9	6.2	.992	P. Borbon	62	122	8	3	11	3.17
	SS	D. Chaney	196	.250	2	19	83	149	9	24	3.8	.963	C. Carroll	**65**	96	6	4	**37**	2.25
	10	J. Hague	138	.246	4	20	196	9	0	13		1.000							
	03	H. McRae	97	.278	5	26	16	14	6	1		.833							
Houston	1B	L. May	592	.284	29	98	**1318**	76	6	**133**	9.6	.996	D. Wilson	33	228	15	10	0	2.68
	2B	T. Helms	518	.259	5	60	353	**441**	17	**115**	**5.8**	.979	L. Dierker	31	215	15	8	0	3.40
	SS	R. Metzger	641	.222	2	38	238	504	22	**101**	5.0	.971	J. Reuss	33	192	9	13	1	4.17
W-84 L-69	3B	D. Rader	553	.237	22	90	119	**340**	20	**31**	3.2	.958	D. Roberts	35	192	12	7	2	4.50
	RF	J. Wynn	542	.273	24	90	284	8	5	2	2.1	.983	K. Forsch	30	156	6	8	0	3.91
Harry Walker	CF	C. Cedeno	559	.320	22	82	345	9	7	1	2.6	.981	G. Culver	45	97	6	2	2	3.05
W-67 L-54	LF	B. Watson	548	.312	16	86	218	6	5	0	1.6	.978	T. Griffin	39	94	5	4	3	3.24
	C	J. Edwards	332	.268	5	40	645	41	8	8	6.6	.988	J. Ray	54	90	10	9	8	4.30
Salty Parker	C	L. Howard	157	.223	2	13	323	15	7	2	6.5	.980	F. Gladding	42	49	5	6	14	2.77
W-1 L-0																			
Leo Durocher																			
W-16 L-15																			
Los Angeles	1B	W. Parker	427	.279	4	59	1074	68	4	91	9.6	**.997**	D. Sutton	33	273	19	9	0	2.08
	2B	L. Lacy	243	.259	0	12	125	161	8	38	5.1	.973	C. Osteen	33	252	20	11	0	2.64
	SS	B. Russell	434	.272	4	34	197	439	**34**	69	**5.5**	.949	A. Downing	31	203	9	9	0	2.98
W-85 L-70	3B	S. Garvey	294	.269	9	30	71	187	**28**	18	3.4	.902	T. John	29	187	11	5	0	2.89
	RF	F. Robinson	342	.251	19	59	168	6	6	2	1.9	.967	B. Singer	26	169	6	16	0	3.67
Walter Alston	CF	W. Davis	615	.289	19	79	373	10	5	1	2.7	.987	J. Brewer	51	78	8	7	17	1.26
	LF	M. Mota	371	.323	5	48	141	3	1	1	1.5	.993	P. Mikkelsen	33	58	5	5	5	4.06
	C	C. Cannizzaro	200	.240	2	18	312	26	6	4	4.8	.983	P. Richert	37	52	2	3	6	2.25
	UT	B. Valentine	391	.274	3	32	178	245	23	38		.948							
	01	B. Buckner	383	.319	5	37	434	22	4	28		.991							
	OF	W. Crawford	243	.251	8	27	111	2	2	0	1.6	.983							
	2B	J. Lefebvre	169	.201	5	24	66	82	2	21	4.5	.987							
Atlanta	1B	H. Aaron	449	.265	34	77	968	66	14	75	**9.6**	.987	P. Niekro	38	282	16	12	0	3.06
	2B	F. Millan	498	.257	1	38	273	339	8	67	5.2	.987	R. Reed	31	213	11	15	0	3.93
	SS	M. Perez	479	.228	1	28	220	378	27	73	4.4	.957	R. Schueler	37	145	5	8	2	3.66
W-70 L-84	3B	D. Evans	418	.254	19	71	126	273	25	20	**3.4**	.941	T. Kelley	27	116	5	7	0	4.58
	RF	M. Lum	369	.228	9	38	241	4	6	1	2.3	.976	G. Stone	31	111	6	11	1	5.51
Lum Harris	CF	D. Baker	446	.321	17	76	344	8	4	1	2.9	.989	P. Jarvis	37	99	11	7	2	4.09
W-47 L-57	LF	R. Garr	554	.325	12	53	246	8	10	1	2.0	.962	C. Upshaw	42	54	3	5	13	3.67
	C	E. Williams	565	.258	28	87	584	49	13	7	5.6	.980							
Eddie Mathews	OF	R. Carty	271	.277	6	29	139	3	3	1	1.9	.979							
W-23 L-27	OF	O. Brown	164	.226	3	16	82	7	10	2	1.7	.899							
San Francisco	1B	W. McCovey	263	.213	14	35	617	32	9	52	8.9	.986	R. Bryant	35	214	14	7	0	2.90
	2B	T. Fuentes	572	.264	7	53	361	417	**29**	89	5.3	.964	J. Barr	44	179	8	10	2	2.87
	SS	C. Speier	562	.269	15	71	243	**517**	20	69	5.2	.974	J. Marichal	25	165	6	16	0	3.71
W-69 L-86	3B	A. Gallagher	233	.223	2	18	64	120	5	7	2.7	.974	S. McDowell	28	164	10	8	0	4.34
	RF	B. Bonds	626	.259	26	80	345	8	8	3	2.4	.978	S. Stone	27	124	6	8	0	2.98
Charlie Fox	CF	G. Maddox	458	.266	12	58	279	7	6	3	2.4	.979	D. Carrithers	25	90	4	8	1	5.80
	LF	K. Henderson	439	.257	18	51	247	14	7	3	2.2	.974	J. Willoughby	11	88	6	4	0	2.35
	C	D. Rader	459	.259	6	41	661	45	11	7	5.6	.985	J. Johnson	48	73	8	6	8	4.44
	UT	D. Kingman	472	.225	29	83	496	159	22	49		.968	R. Moffitt	40	71	1	5	4	3.68
	1B	E. Goodson	150	.280	6	30	299	27	3	28	7.8	.991	D. McMahon	44	63	3	3	5	3.71
San Diego	1B	N. Colbert	563	.250	38	111	1290	**103**	6	119	9.3	.996	S. Arlin	38	250	10	**21**	0	3.60
	2B	D. Thomas	500	.230	5	36	197	239	15	52	5.4	.967	C. Kirby	34	239	12	14	0	3.13
	SS	E. Hernandez	329	.195	1	15	169	319	19	59	4.7	.963	F. Norman	42	212	9	11	2	3.44
W-58 L-95	3B	D. Roberts	418	.244	5	33	62	166	17	20	2.9	.931	M. Caldwell	42	164	7	11	2	4.01
	RF	C. Gaston	379	.269	7	44	158	10	4	3	1.8	.977	M. Corkins	47	140	6	9	6	3.54
Preston Gomez	CF	J. Morales	347	.239	4	18	214	8	3	2	2.3	.987	B. Greif	34	125	5	16	2	5.60
W-4 L-7	LF	L. Lee	370	.300	12	47	186	6	5	2	2.1	.975	G. Ross	60	92	4	3	3	2.45
	C	F. Kendall	273	.216	6	18	504	41	3	11	6.7	.995							
Don Zimmer	OF	J. Jeter	326	.221	7	21	222	1	3	0	2.5	.987							
W-54 L-88	OF	L. Stahl	297	.226	7	20	139	4	2	1	1.9	.986							
	23	G. Jestadt	256	.246	6	22	104	131	13	27		.948							

NATIONAL LEAGUE 1972, *cont.*

BATTING AND BASE RUNNING LEADERS

Batting Average

B. Williams, CHI	.333
R. Garr, ATL	.325
D. Baker, ATL	.321
C. Cedeno, HOU	.320
B. Watson, HOU	.312

Slugging Average

B. Williams, CHI	.606
W. Stargell, PIT	.558
J. Bench, CIN	.541
C. Cedeno, HOU	.537
H. Aaron, ATL	.514

Home Runs

J. Bench, CIN	40
N. Colbert, SD	38
B. Williams, CHI	37
H. Aaron, ATL	34
W. Stargell, PIT	33

Total Bases

B. Williams, CHI	348
C. Cedeno, HOU	300
J. Bench, CIN	291
L. May, HOU	290
N. Colbert, SD	286

Runs Batted In

J. Bench, CIN	125
B. Williams, CHI	122
W. Stargell, PIT	112
N. Colbert, SD	111
L. May, HOU	98

Stolen Bases

L. Brock, STL	63
J. Morgan, CIN	58
C. Cedeno, HOU	55
B. Bonds, SF	44
B. Tolan, CIN	42

Hits

P. Rose, CIN	198
L. Brock, STL	193
B. Williams, CHI	191
R. Garr, ATL	180
T. Simmons, STL	180

Base on Balls

J. Morgan, CIN	115
J. Wynn, HOU	103
J. Bench, CIN	100
H. Aaron, ATL	92

Home Run Percentage

H. Aaron, ATL	7.6
J. Bench, CIN	7.4
N. Colbert, SD	6.7
W. Stargell, PIT	6.7

Runs

J. Morgan, CIN	122
B. Bonds, SF	118
J. Wynn, HOU	117
P. Rose, CIN	107

Doubles

W. Montanez, PHI	39
C. Cedeno, HOU	39
T. Simmons, STL	36
B. Williams, CHI	34

Triples

L. Bowa, PHI	13
P. Rose, CIN	11
M. Sanguillen, PIT	8
C. Cedeno, HOU	8
L. Brock, STL	8

PITCHING LEADERS

Winning Percentage

G. Nolan, CIN	.750
S. Carlton, PHI	.730
M. Pappas, CHI	.708
S. Blass, PIT	.704
D. Ellis, PIT	.682

Earned Run Average

S. Carlton, PHI	1.97
G. Nolan, CIN	1.99
D. Sutton, LA	2.08
J. Matlack, NY	2.32
B. Gibson, STL	2.46

Wins

S. Carlton, PHI	27
T. Seaver, NY	21
C. Osteen, LA	20
F. Jenkins, CHI	20

Saves

C. Carroll, CIN	37
T. McGraw, NY	27
D. Giusti, PIT	22
M. Marshall, MON	18
J. Aker, CHI	17
J. Brewer, LA	17

Strikeouts

S. Carlton, PHI	310
T. Seaver, NY	249
B. Gibson, STL	208
D. Sutton, LA	207
F. Jenkins, CHI	184

Complete Games

S. Carlton, PHI	30
B. Gibson, STL	23
F. Jenkins, CHI	23
R. Wise, STL	20
D. Sutton, LA	18

Fewest Hits/9 Innings

D. Sutton, LA	6.14
S. Carlton, PHI	6.68
B. Gibson, STL	7.32
T. Seaver, NY	7.39

Shutouts

D. Sutton, LA	9
S. Carlton, PHI	8
F. Norman, SD	6
L. Dierker, HOU	5
F. Jenkins, CHI	5

Fewest Walks/9 Innings

M. Pappas, CHI	1.34
G. Nolan, CIN	1.53
P. Niekro, ATL	1.69
D. Ellis, PIT	1.82

Most Strikeouts/9 Inn.

T. Seaver, NY	8.55
J. Reuss, HOU	8.16
J. Koosman, NY	8.12
S. Carlton, PHI	8.06

Innings

S. Carlton, PHI	346
F. Jenkins, CHI	289
P. Niekro, ATL	282
B. Gibson, STL	278

Games Pitched

C. Carroll, CIN	65
M. Marshall, MON	65
P. Borbon, CIN	62
G. Ross, SD	60

		W	L	PCT	GB	R	OR	Batting 2B	3B	HR	BA	SA	SB	Fielding E	DP	FA	Pitching CG	BB	SO	ShO	SV	ERA
East	Pittsburgh	96	59	.619		691	**512**	**251**	**47**	110	**.274**	**.397**	49	136	**171**	.978	39	433	838	15	48	2.81
	Chicago	85	70	.548	11	685	567	206	40	133	.257	.387	69	132	148	.979	54	**421**	824	19	32	3.22
	New York	83	73	.532	13.5	528	578	175	31	105	.225	.332	41	116	122	.980	32	486	**1059**	12	41	3.27
	St. Louis	75	81	.481	21.5	568	600	214	42	70	.260	.355	104	141	146	.977	**64**	531	912	13	13	3.42
	Montreal	70	86	.449	26.5	513	609	156	22	91	.234	.325	68	134	141	.978	39	579	888	11	23	3.60
	Philadelphia	59	97	.378	37.5	503	635	200	36	98	.236	.344	42	116	142	.981	43	536	927	13	15	3.67
West	Cincinnati	95	59	.617		707	557	214	44	124	.251	.380	**140**	**110**	143	**.982**	25	435	806	15	**60**	3.21
	Houston	84	69	.549	10.5	**708**	636	233	38	134	.258	.393	111	116	151	.980	38	498	971	14	31	3.77
	Los Angeles	85	70	.548	10.5	584	527	178	39	98	.256	.360	82	162	145	.974	50	429	856	**23**	29	**2.78**
	Atlanta	70	84	.455	25	628	730	186	17	144	.258	.382	47	156	130	.974	40	512	732	4	27	4.27
	San Francisco	69	86	.445	26.5	662	649	211	36	**150**	.244	.384	123	156	121	.974	44	507	771	8	23	3.70
	San Diego	58	95	.379	36.5	488	665	168	38	102	.227	.332	78	144	146	.976	39	618	960	17	19	3.78
						7265	7265	2392	430	1359	.248	.364	954	1619	1706	.978	507	5985	10544	164	361	3.46

AMERICAN LEAGUE 1972

East

Detroit

W-86 L-70

Billy Martin

POS	Player	AB	BA	HR	RBI	PO	A	E	DP	TC/G	FA	Pitcher	G	IP	W	L	SV	ERA
1B	N. Cash	440	.259	22	61	1060	70	8	102	8.5	.993	M. Lolich	41	327	22	14	0	2.50
2B	D. McAuliffe	408	.240	8	30	266	249	13	63	4.6	.975	J. Coleman	40	280	19	14	0	2.80
SS	E. Brinkman	516	.203	6	49	233	495	7	81	4.7	**.990**	T. Timmerman	34	150	8	10	0	2.89
3B	A. Rodriguez	601	.236	13	56	**150**	348	16	33	**3.4**	.969	W. Fryman	16	114	10	3	0	2.05
RF	J. Northrup	426	.261	8	42	215	8	5	2	1.8	.978	C. Seelbach	61	112	9	8	14	2.89
CF	M. Stanley	435	.234	14	55	309	9	2	1	2.3	.994	F. Scherman	57	94	7	3	12	3.64
LF	W. Horton	333	.231	11	36	131	6	0	0	1.4	1.000	B. Slayback	23	82	5	6	0	3.18
C	B. Freehan	374	.262	10	56	648	57	8	9	6.8	.989							
OF	A. Kaline	278	.313	10	32	111	5	1	0	1.4	.991							
OF	G. Brown	252	.230	10	31	122	5	3	1	1.8	.977							
2B	T. Taylor	228	.303	1	20	121	108	8	25	3.5	.966							

Boston

W-85 L-70

Eddie Kasko

POS	Player	AB	BA	HR	RBI	PO	A	E	DP	TC/G	FA	Pitcher	G	IP	W	L	SV	ERA
1B	D. Cater	317	.237	8	39	656	61	5	65	8.0	.993	M. Pattin	38	253	17	13	0	3.23
2B	D. Griffin	470	.260	2	35	321	331	15	81	5.2	.978	S. Siebert	32	196	12	12	0	3.80
SS	L. Aparicio	436	.257	3	39	183	304	16	54	4.6	.968	L. Tiant	43	179	15	6	3	**1.91**
3B	R. Petrocelli	521	.240	15	75	146	278	13	**38**	3.0	.970	J. Curtis	26	154	11	8	0	3.73
RF	R. Smith	467	.270	21	74	247	8	5	2	2.0	.981	L. McGlothen	22	145	8	7	0	3.41
CF	T. Harper	556	.254	14	49	321	4	5	4	2.3	.985	R. Culp	16	105	5	8	0	4.46
LF	C. Yastrzemski	455	.264	12	68	141	10	4	1	1.9	.974	B. Lee	47	84	7	4	5	3.20
C	C. Fisk	457	.293	22	61	**846**	**72**	**15**	10	**7.1**	.984	D. Newhauser	31	37	4	2	4	2.43
OF	B. Oglivie	253	.241	8	30	98	5	2	2	1.6	.981							
UT	J. Kennedy	212	.245	2	22	110	141	13	34		.951							

AMERICAN LEAGUE 1972, *cont.*

Baltimore

W-80 L-74

Earl Weaver

POS	Player	AB	BA	HR	RBI	PO	A	E	DP	TC/G	FA	Pitcher	G	IP	W	L	SV	ERA
1B	B. Powell	465	.252	21	81	1116	70	**15**	111	9.0	.988	J. Palmer	36	274	21	10	0	2.07
2B	D. Johnson	376	.221	5	32	286	307	6	81	5.2	**.990**	P. Dobson	38	268	16	**18**	0	2.65
SS	M. Belanger	285	.186	2	16	180	285	12	53	4.5	.975	M. Cuellar	35	248	18	12	0	2.57
3B	B. Robinson	556	.250	8	64	129	333	11	27	3.1	**.977**	D. McNally	36	241	13	17	0	2.95
RF	M. Rettenmund	301	.233	6	21	174	6	2	2	1.9	.989	D. Alexander	35	106	6	8	2	2.45
CF	P. Blair	477	.233	8	49	337	10	3	1	2.5	.991	R. Harrison	39	94	3	4	4	2.30
LF	D. Buford	408	.206	5	22	173	6	2	1	1.7	.989	E. Watt	38	46	2	3	7	2.15
C	J. Oates	253	.261	4	21	391	31	2	4	5.2	**.995**	G. Jackson	32	41	1	1	8	2.63
UT	B. Grich	460	.278	12	50	299	338	20	81		.970							
OF	D. Baylor	320	.253	11	38	152	2	4	0	1.9	.975							
OF	T. Crowley	247	.231	11	29	95	2	1	1	1.4	.990							
C	A. Etchebarren	188	.202	2	21	334	22	3	2	5.1	.992							

New York

W-79 L-76

Ralph Houk

POS	Player	AB	BA	HR	RBI	PO	A	E	DP	TC/G	FA	Pitcher	G	IP	W	L	SV	ERA
1B	R. Blomberg	299	.268	14	49	813	32	13	88	9.0	.985	M. Stottlemyre	36	260	14	**18**	0	3.22
2B	H. Clarke	547	.241	3	37	347	**399**	11	**104**	**5.3**	.985	F. Peterson	35	250	17	15	0	3.24
SS	G. Michael	391	.233	1	32	218	437	21	89	5.6	.969	S. Kline	32	236	16	9	0	2.40
3B	C. Sanchez	250	.248	0	22	47	167	14	13	3.4	.939	M. Kekich	29	175	10	13	0	3.70
RF	J. Callison	275	.258	9	34	127	4	1	1	1.8	.992	S. Lyle	59	108	9	5	**35**	1.91
CF	B. Murcer	585	.292	33	96	382	11	3	1	2.6	.992	R. Gardner	20	97	8	5	0	3.06
LF	R. White	556	.270	10	54	323	8	2	1	2.1	.994							
C	T. Munson	511	.280	7	46	575	71	**15**	11	5.0	.977							
1B	F. Alou	324	.278	6	37	648	54	7	69	7.5	.990							
32	B. Allen	220	.227	9	21	75	132	9	26		.958							
OF	R. Torres	199	.211	3	13	86	4	2	0	1.5	.978							
C	J. Ellis	136	.294	5	25	127	11	5	1	5.7	.965							

Cleveland

W-72 L-84

Ken Aspromonte

POS	Player	AB	BA	HR	RBI	PO	A	E	DP	TC/G	FA	Pitcher	G	IP	W	L	SV	ERA
1B	C. Chambliss	466	.292	6	44	1109	56	8	109	**9.9**	.993	G. Perry	41	343	**24**	16	1	1.92
2B	J. Brohamer	527	.233	5	35	285	393	16	87	5.3	.977	D. Tidrow	39	237	14	15	0	2.77
SS	F. Duffy	385	.239	3	27	197	360	13	75	4.5	.977	M. Wilcox	32	156	7	14	0	3.40
3B	G. Nettles	557	.253	17	70	114	**358**	**21**	27	3.3	.957	R. Lamb	34	108	5	6	0	3.08
RF	B. Bell	466	.255	9	36	274	10	3	4	2.3	.990	S. Dunning	16	105	6	4	0	3.26
CF	D. Unser	383	.238	1	17	248	10	3	1	2.2	.989	P. Hennigan	38	67	5	3	6	2.69
LF	A. Johnson	356	.239	8	37	145	4	7	1	1.6	.955	E. Farmer	46	61	2	5	7	4.43
C	R. Fosse	457	.241	10	41	713	70	12	9	6.4	.985	S. Mingori	41	57	0	6	10	3.95
01	T. McCraw	391	.258	7	33	504	28	3	29		.994							
2S	E. Leon	225	.200	4	16	103	179	6	39		.979							
OF	J. Lowenstein	151	.212	6	21	77	7	0	3	1.4	1.000							

Milwaukee

W-65 L-91

Dave Bristol
W-10 L-20

Roy McMillan
W-1 L-1

Del Crandall
W-54 L-70

POS	Player	AB	BA	HR	RBI	PO	A	E	DP	TC/G	FA	Pitcher	G	IP	W	L	SV	ERA
1B	G. Scott	578	.266	20	88	1210	73	10	106	9.3	.992	J. Lonborg	33	223	14	12	1	2.83
2B	R. Theobald	391	.220	1	19	193	299	6	68	4.4	.988	B. Parsons	33	214	13	13	0	3.91
SS	R. Auerbach	554	.218	2	30	256	452	30	90	4.8	.959	S. Lockwood	29	170	8	15	0	3.60
3B	M. Ferraro	381	.255	2	29	93	174	14	16	2.4	.950	J. Colborn	39	148	7	7	0	3.10
RF	J. Lahoud	316	.237	12	34	189	2	5	0	2.0	.974	K. Brett	26	133	7	12	0	4.53
CF	D. May	500	.238	9	45	376	9	6	3	2.8	.985	G. Ryerson	20	102	3	8	0	3.62
LF	J. Briggs	418	.266	21	65	194	6	4	1	1.9	.980	K. Sanders	62	92	2	9	17	3.13
C	E. Rodriguez	355	.285	2	35	542	54	10	6	5.3	.983	F. Linzy	47	77	2	2	12	3.04
UT	B. Heise	271	.266	0	12	125	170	6	31		.980							
OF	B. Conigliaro	191	.230	7	16	120	5	1	2	2.5	.992							
OF	O. Brown	179	.279	3	25	116	8	1	3	2.2	.992							

West

Oakland

W-93 L-62

Dick Williams

POS	Player	AB	BA	HR	RBI	PO	A	E	DP	TC/G	FA	Pitcher	G	IP	W	L	SV	ERA
1B	M. Epstein	455	.270	26	70	1111	73	12	101	8.7	.990	C. Hunter	38	295	21	7	0	2.04
2B	T. Cullen	142	.261	0	15	103	117	11	24	3.6	.952	K. Holtzman	39	265	19	11	0	2.51
SS	B. Campaneris	**625**	.240	8	32	**283**	494	18	93	5.4	.977	B. Odom	31	194	15	6	0	2.50
3B	S. Bando	535	.236	15	77	123	337	19	29	3.2	.960	V. Blue	25	151	6	10	0	2.80
RF	A. Mangual	272	.246	5	32	166	4	5	2	2.4	.971	R. Fingers	65	111	11	9	21	2.51
CF	R. Jackson	499	.265	25	75	301	5	9	5	2.3	.971	D. Hamilton	25	101	6	6	0	2.93
LF	J. Rudi	593	.305	19	75	247	9	2	1	1.8	.992	B. Locker	56	78	6	1	10	2.65
C	D. Duncan	403	.218	19	59	661	43	5	9	6.3	.993	D. Knowles	54	66	5	1	11	1.36
C	G. Tenace	227	.225	5	32	266	18	6	1	5.9	.979							

Chicago

W-87 L-67

Chuck Tanner

POS	Player	AB	BA	HR	RBI	PO	A	E	DP	TC/G	FA	Pitcher	G	IP	W	L	SV	ERA
1B	D. Allen	506	.308	**37**	**113**	1234	67	7	94	9.1	.995	W. Wood	49	**377**	**24**	17	0	2.51
2B	M. Andrews	505	.220	7	50	**354**	325	**19**	69	4.8	.973	T. Bradley	40	260	15	14	0	2.98
SS	R. Morales	287	.206	2	20	120	213	11	32	4.0	.968	S. Bahnsen	43	252	21	16	0	3.60
3B	E. Spiezio	277	.238	2	22	67	172	12	11	3.4	.952	T. Forster	62	100	6	5	29	2.25
RF	P. Kelly	402	.261	5	24	173	8	6	3	1.7	.968	D. Lemonds	31	95	4	7	0	2.95
CF	R. Reichardt	291	.251	8	43	157	2	3	1	1.8	.981	G. Gossage	36	80	7	1	2	4.28
LF	C. May	523	.308	12	68	215	13	4	2	1.6	.983							
C	E. Herrmann	354	.249	10	40	641	69	8	10	6.4	.989							
OF	J. Johnstone	261	.188	4	17	154	5	2	1	1.7	.988							
SS	L. Alvarado	254	.213	4	29	98	213	14	28	4.0	.957							
OF	W. Williams	221	.249	2	11	93	6	1	2	1.8	.990							
3B	B. Melton	208	.245	7	30	47	125	12	12	3.3	.935							

Minnesota

W-77 L-77

Bill Rigney
W-36 L-34

Frank Quilici
W-41 L-43

POS	Player	AB	BA	HR	RBI	PO	A	E	DP	TC/G	FA	Pitcher	G	IP	W	L	SV	ERA
1B	H. Killebrew	433	.231	26	74	995	**99**	9	82	8.5	.992	B. Blyleven	39	287	17	17	0	2.73
2B	R. Carew	535	**.318**	0	51	331	378	16	85	5.2	.978	D. Woodson	36	252	14	14	0	2.71
SS	D. Thompson	573	.276	4	48	247	468	**32**	76	5.2	.957	J. Perry	35	218	13	16	0	3.34
3B	E. Soderholm	287	.188	13	39	66	163	14	17	3.1	.942	R. Corbin	31	162	8	9	0	2.61
RF	C. Tovar	548	.265	2	31	287	10	5	2	2.2	.983	J. Kaat	15	113	10	2	0	2.07
CF	B. Darwin	513	.267	22	80	289	8	6	1	2.1	.980	D. LaRoche	62	95	5	7	10	2.84
LF	S. Brye	253	.241	0	12	170	9	1	1	1.9	.994	W. Granger	63	90	4	6	19	3.00
C	G. Mitterwald	163	.184	1	8	272	33	5	4	5.1	.984							
UT	S. Braun	402	.289	2	50	110	207	13	26		.961							
OF	J. Nettles	235	.204	4	15	156	5	3	1	2.1	.982							
1B	R. Reese	197	.218	5	26	392	30	5	55	4.4	.988							
C	G. Borgmann	175	.234	3	14	304	31	12	4	6.2	.965							

AMERICAN LEAGUE 1972, *cont.*

Kansas City

W-76 L-78

Bob Lemon

POS	Player	AB	BA	HR	RBI	PO	A	E	DP	TC/G	FA	Pitcher	G	IP	W	L	SV	ERA
1B	J. Mayberry	503	.298	25	100	**1338**	82	7	**141**	9.8	**.995**	D. Drago	34	239	12	17	0	3.01
2B	C. Rojas	487	.261	3	53	265	360	9	82	4.8	.986	P. Splittorff	35	216	12	12	0	3.12
SS	F. Patek	518	.212	0	32	230	**510**	22	**113**	**5.6**	.971	R. Nelson	34	173	11	6	2	2.08
3B	P. Schaal	435	.228	6	41	77	245	18	16	2.8	.947	B. Dal Canton	35	132	6	6	2	3.40
RF	R. Scheinblum	450	.300	8	66	215	6	8	2	1.9	.965	M. Hedlund	29	113	5	7	0	4.78
CF	A. Otis	540	.293	11	54	351	6	3	3	2.6	.992	A. Fitzmorris	38	101	2	5	3	3.74
LF	L. Piniella	574	.312	11	72	275	8	7	2	1.9	.976	J. Rooker	18	72	5	6	0	4.38
C	E. Kirkpatrick	364	.275	9	43	590	49	6	5	6.0	.991	T. Abernathy	45	58	3	4	5	1.71
OF	S. Hovley	196	.270	3	24	103	6	2	0	1.6	.982	T. Burgmeier	51	55	6	2	9	4.25

California

W-75 L-80

Del Rice

POS	Player	AB	BA	HR	RBI	PO	A	E	DP	TC/G	FA	Pitcher	G	IP	W	L	SV	ERA
1B	B. Oliver	509	.269	19	70	1079	54	7	93	9.0	.994	N. Ryan	39	284	19	16	0	2.28
2B	S. Alomar	610	.239	1	25	350	388	17	92	4.9	.977	C. Wright	35	251	18	11	0	2.98
SS	L. Cardenas	551	.223	6	42	241	471	22	82	4.9	.970	R. May	35	205	12	11	1	2.94
3B	K. McMullen	472	.269	9	34	89	267	11	26	2.7	.970	A. Messersmith	25	170	8	11	2	2.81
RF	L. Stanton	402	.251	12	39	225	6	4	2	1.9	.983	R. Clark	26	110	4	9	1	4.50
CF	K. Berry	409	.289	5	39	272	13	0	5	2.5	1.000	L. Allen	42	85	3	7	5	3.49
LF	V. Pinson	484	.275	7	49	205	11	2	3	1.6	.991	E. Fisher	43	81	4	5	4	3.76
C	A. Kusnyer	179	.207	2	13	362	33	10	3	6.4	.975	S. Barber	34	58	4	4	2	2.02
1O	J. Spencer	212	.222	1	14	289	23	3	25		.990							
OF	M. Rivers	159	.214	0	7	105	0	2	0	2.2	.981							

Texas

W-54 L-100

Ted Williams

POS	Player	AB	BA	HR	RBI	PO	A	E	DP	TC/G	FA	Pitcher	G	IP	W	L	SV	ERA
1B	F. Howard	287	.244	9	31	441	27	9	39	7.2	.981	P. Broberg	39	176	5	12	1	4.30
2B	L. Randle	249	.193	2	21	151	166	16	38	5.1	.952	D. Bosman	29	173	8	10	0	3.64
SS	T. Harrah	374	.259	1	31	166	308	20	64	4.7	.960	R. Hand	30	171	10	14	0	3.32
3B	D. Nelson	499	.226	2	28	107	222	19	25	2.9	.945	M. Paul	49	162	8	9	1	2.17
RF	T. Ford	429	.235	14	50	242	11	6	2	2.2	.977	B. Gogolewski	36	151	4	11	2	4.23
CF	J. Lovitto	330	.224	1	19	233	7	6	2	2.4	.976	D. Stanhouse	24	105	2	9	0	3.77
LF	T. Grieve	142	.204	3	11	60	6	1	0	1.4	.985	P. Lindblad	**66**	100	5	8	9	2.61
C	D. Billings	469	.254	5	58	478	45	10	**13**	5.8	.981	J. Panther	58	94	5	9	0	4.12
O1	L. Biittner	382	.259	3	31	503	41	8	37		.986	H. Pina	60	76	2	7	15	3.20
OF	E. Maddox	294	.252	0	10	199	7	2	4	2.2	.990	C. Cox	35	65	3	5	4	4.41
1B	D. Mincher	191	.236	6	39	467	44	3	45	8.7	.994							
2B	V. Harris	186	.140	0	10	110	132	10	29	4.3	.960							

BATTING AND BASE RUNNING LEADERS

Batting Average
R. Carew, MIN .318
L. Piniella, KC .312
D. Allen, CHI .308
C. May, CHI .308
J. Rudi, OAK .305

Slugging Average
D. Allen, CHI .603
C. Fisk, BOS .538
B. Murcer, NY .537
J. Mayberry, KC .507
M. Epstein, OAK .490

Home Runs
D. Allen, CHI 37
B. Murcer, NY 33
H. Killebrew, MIN 26
M. Epstein, OAK 26
R. Jackson, OAK 25
J. Mayberry, KC 25

Total Bases
B. Murcer, NY 314
D. Allen, CHI 305
J. Rudi, OAK 288
J. Mayberry, KC 255
L. Piniella, KC 253

Runs Batted In
D. Allen, CHI 113
J. Mayberry, KC 100
B. Murcer, NY 96
G. Scott, MIL 88
B. Powell, BAL 81

Stolen Bases
B. Campaneris, OAK 52
D. Nelson, TEX 51
F. Patek, KC 33
P. Kelly, CHI 32
A. Otis, KC 28

Hits
J. Rudi, OAK 181
L. Piniella, KC 179
B. Murcer, NY 171
R. Carew, MIN 170

Base on Balls
D. Allen, CHI 99
R. White, NY 99
H. Killebrew, MIN 94
C. May, CHI 79

Home Run Percentage
D. Allen, CHI 7.3
H. Killebrew, MIN 6.0
M. Epstein, OAK 5.7
B. Murcer, NY 5.6

Runs
B. Murcer, NY 102
J. Rudi, OAK 94
T. Harper, BOS 92
D. Allen, CHI 90

Doubles
L. Piniella, KC 33
J. Rudi, OAK 32
B. Murcer, NY 30
T. Harper, BOS 29
R. White, NY 29

Triples
C. Fisk, BOS 9
J. Rudi, OAK 9
P. Blair, BAL 8
P. Kelly, CHI 7
B. Murcer, NY 7

PITCHING LEADERS

Winning Percentage
C. Hunter, OAK .750
B. Odom, OAK .714
L. Tiant, BOS .714
J. Palmer, BAL .677
S. Kline, NY .640

Earned Run Average
L. Tiant, BOS 1.91
G. Perry, CLE 1.92
C. Hunter, OAK 2.04
J. Palmer, BAL 2.07
R. Nelson, KC 2.08

Wins
G. Perry, CLE 24
W. Wood, CHI 24
M. Lolich, DET 22
S. Bahnsen, CHI 21
J. Palmer, BAL 21
C. Hunter, OAK 21

Saves
S. Lyle, NY 35
T. Forster, CHI 29
R. Fingers, OAK 21
W. Granger, MIN 19
K. Sanders, MIL 17

Strikeouts
N. Ryan, CAL 329
M. Lolich, DET 250
G. Perry, CLE 234
B. Blyleven, MIN 228
J. Coleman, DET 222

Complete Games
G. Perry, CLE 29
M. Lolich, DET 23
N. Ryan, CAL 20
W. Wood, CHI 20
J. Palmer, BAL 18

Fewest Hits/9 Innings
N. Ryan, CAL 5.26
C. Hunter, OAK 6.10
R. Nelson, KC 6.23
L. Tiant, BOS 6.44

Shutouts
N. Ryan, CAL 9
W. Wood, CHI 8
M. Stottlemyre, NY 7

Fewest Walks/9 Innings
F. Peterson, NY 1.58
R. Nelson, KC 1.61
S. Kline, NY 1.68
K. Holtzman, OAK 1.77

Most Strikeouts/9 Inn.
N. Ryan, CAL 10.43
A. Messersmith, CAL 7.52
R. May, CAL 7.42
T. Bradley, CHI 7.23

Innings
W. Wood, CHI 377
G. Perry, CLE 343
M. Lolich, DET 327
C. Hunter, OAK 295

Games Pitched
P. Lindblad, TEX 66
R. Fingers, OAK 65
W. Granger, MIN 63

		W	L	PCT	GB	R	OR	Batting 2B	3B	HR	BA	SA	SB	Fielding E	DP	FA	Pitching CG	BB	SO	ShO	SV	ERA
East	Detroit	86	70	.551		558	514	179	32	122	.237	.356	17	**96**	137	**.984**	46	465	952	11	33	2.96
	Boston	85	70	.548	0.5	**640**	620	**229**	**34**	124	.248	**.376**	66	130	141	.978	48	512	918	20	25	3.47
	Baltimore	80	74	.519	5	519	**430**	193	29	100	.229	.339	78	100	150	.983	**62**	**395**	788	20	21	**2.54**
	New York	79	76	.510	6.5	557	527	201	24	103	.249	.357	71	134	**179**	.978	35	419	625	19	39	3.05
	Cleveland	72	84	.462	14	472	519	187	18	91	.234	.330	49	116	157	.981	47	534	846	13	25	2.97
	Milwaukee	65	91	.417	21	493	595	167	22	88	.235	.328	64	139	145	.977	37	486	740	14	32	3.45
West	Oakland	93	62	.600		604	457	195	29	**134**	.240	.366	87	130	146	.979	42	418	862	**23**	**43**	2.58
	Chicago	87	67	.565	5.5	566	538	170	28	108	.238	.346	100	135	136	.977	36	431	936	14	42	3.12
	Minnesota	77	77	.500	15.5	537	535	182	31	93	.244	.344	53	159	133	.974	37	444	838	17	34	2.86
	Kansas City	76	78	.494	16.5	580	545	220	26	78	**.255**	.353	85	120	164	.980	44	405	801	16	28	3.24
	California	75	80	.484	18	454	533	171	26	78	.242	.330	57	114	135	.981	57	620	**1000**	18	16	3.06
	Texas	54	100	.351	38.5	461	628	166	17	56	.217	.290	**126**	166	147	.972	11	613	868	8	34	3.53
						6441	6441	2260	316	1175	.239	.343	853	1539	1770	.979	502	5742	10174	193	372	3.07

NATIONAL LEAGUE 1973

East

New York

W-82 L-79

Yogi Berra

POS	Player	AB	BA	HR	RBI	PO	A	E	DP	TC/G	FA	Pitcher	G	IP	W	L	SV	ERA
1B	J. Milner	451	.239	23	72	771	47	9	66	8.7	.989	T. Seaver	36	290	19	10	0	**2.08**
2B	F. Millan	638	.290	3	37	410	411	9	99	5.4	.989	J. Koosman	35	263	14	15	0	2.84
SS	B. Harrelson	356	.258	0	20	153	315	10	49	4.6	.979	J. Matlack	34	242	14	16	0	3.20
3B	W. Garrett	504	.256	16	58	80	280	22	36	2.9	.942	G. Stone	27	148	12	3	1	2.80
RF	R. Staub	585	.279	15	76	297	17	7	5	2.1	.978	T. McGraw	60	119	5	6	25	3.87
CF	D. Hahn	262	.229	2	21	176	2	2	0	2.1	.989	R. Sadecki	31	117	5	4	1	3.39
LF	C. Jones	339	.260	11	48	168	6	6	0	2.0	.967	H. Parker	38	97	8	4	5	3.35
C	J. Grote	285	.256	1	32	545	34	3	0	**7.2**	.995	J. McAndrew	23	80	3	8	1	5.38
10	E. Kranepool	284	.239	1	35	448	28	2	39		.996	B. Capra	24	42	2	7	4	3.86
UT	T. Martinez	263	.255	1	14	119	139	12	15		.956							
OF	W. Mays	209	.211	6	25	103	2	1	0	2.4	.991							
C	D. Dyer	189	.185	1	9	308	26	2	7	5.6	.994							

St. Louis

W-81 L-81

Red Schoendienst

POS	Player	AB	BA	HR	RBI	PO	A	E	DP	TC/G	FA	Pitcher	G	IP	W	L	SV	ERA
1B	J. Torre	519	.287	13	69	833	60	6	80	7.9	.993	R. Wise	35	259	16	12	0	3.37
2B	T. Sizemore	521	.282	1	54	312	463	15	83	**5.7**	.981	R. Cleveland	32	224	14	10	0	3.01
SS	M. Tyson	469	.243	1	33	202	352	**33**	68	4.6	.944	A. Foster	35	204	13	9	0	3.14
3B	K. Reitz	426	.235	6	42	85	211	8	19	2.3	**.974**	B. Gibson	25	195	12	10	0	2.77
RF	L. Melendez	341	.267	2	35	196	8	2	4	2.2	.990	D. Segui	65	100	7	6	17	2.78
CF	J. Cruz	406	.227	10	57	276	2	6	1	2.4	.979	T. Murphy	19	89	3	7	0	3.76
LF	L. Brock	650	.297	7	63	310	3	12	1	2.0	.963	R. Folkers	34	82	4	4	3	3.61
C	T. Simmons	619	.310	13	91	**888**	74	13	13	6.4	.987	O. Pena	42	62	4	4	6	2.18
1B	T. McCarver	331	.266	3	49	545	30	8	47	7.6	.986	A. Hrabosky	44	56	2	4	5	2.09
OF	B. Carbo	308	.286	8	40	171	11	4	3	2.0	.978	W. Granger	33	47	2	4	5	4.24

Pittsburgh

W-80 L-82

Bill Virdon
W-67 L-69

Danny Murtaugh
W-13 L-13

POS	Player	AB	BA	HR	RBI	PO	A	E	DP	TC/G	FA	Pitcher	G	IP	W	L	SV	ERA
1B	B. Robertson	397	.239	14	40	957	79	5	91	9.7	.995	N. Briles	33	219	14	13	0	2.84
2B	D. Cash	436	.271	2	31	227	276	11	46	5.6	.979	B. Moose	33	201	12	13	0	3.53
SS	D. Maxvill	217	.189	0	17	105	234	10	46	4.7	.971	D. Ellis	28	192	12	14	0	3.05
3B	R. Hebner	509	.271	25	74	92	260	23	19	2.7	.939	J. Rooker	41	170	10	6	5	2.85
RF	R. Zisk	333	.324	10	54	139	12	2	4	1.8	.987	L. Walker	37	122	7	12	1	4.65
CF	A. Oliver	654	.292	20	99	238	5	9	0	2.3	.964	D. Giusti	67	99	9	2	20	2.37
LF	W. Stargell	522	.299	**44**	**119**	261	14	7	1	2.0	.975	B. Johnson	50	92	4	2	4	3.62
C	M. Sanguillen	589	.282	12	65	493	35	9	9	6.0	.983	R. Hernandez	59	90	4	5	11	2.41
2S	R. Stennett	466	.242	10	55	277	348	14	84		.978	S. Blass	23	89	3	9	0	9.85
OF	G. Clines	304	.263	1	23	145	6	5	0	2.0	.968							
C	M. May	283	.269	7	31	402	36	12	4	5.7	.973							

Montreal

W-79 L-83

Gene Mauch

POS	Player	AB	BA	HR	RBI	PO	A	E	DP	TC/G	FA	Pitcher	G	IP	W	L	SV	ERA
1B	M. Jorgensen	413	.230	9	47	990	80	5	88	8.7	**.995**	S. Renko	36	250	15	11	1	2.81
2B	R. Hunt	401	.309	0	18	219	280	9	54	5.0	.982	M. Torrez	35	208	9	12	0	4.46
SS	T. Foli	458	.240	2	36	245	396	27	84	**5.4**	.960	M. Marshall	**92**	179	14	11	**31**	2.66
3B	B. Bailey	513	.273	26	86	93	275	17	25	2.6	.956	B. Moore	35	176	7	16	0	4.49
RF	K. Singleton	560	.302	23	103	278	20	5	3	1.9	.983	E. McAnally	27	147	7	9	0	4.04
CF	R. Woods	318	.230	3	31	208	7	5	1	1.9	.977	S. Rogers	17	134	10	5	0	1.54
LF	R. Fairly	413	.298	17	49	182	4	5	0	1.6	.974	B. Stoneman	29	97	4	8	1	6.80
C	J. Boccabella	403	.233	7	46	610	65	**14**	10	5.9	.980	T. Walker	54	92	7	5	4	3.63
1B	H. Breeden	258	.275	15	43	515	45	5	50	8.6	.991							
S2	P. Frias	225	.231	0	22	120	211	15	46		.957							
OF	B. Day	207	.275	4	28	86	2	0	0	1.7	1.000							

Chicago

W-77 L-84

Whitey Lockman

POS	Player	AB	BA	HR	RBI	PO	A	E	DP	TC/G	FA	Pitcher	G	IP	W	L	SV	ERA
1B	J. Hickman	201	.244	3	20	398	31	5	37	8.5	.988	F. Jenkins	38	271	14	16	0	3.89
2B	G. Beckert	372	.255	0	29	163	262	7	50	4.9	.984	B. Hooton	42	240	14	17	0	3.67
SS	D. Kessinger	577	.262	0	43	**274**	526	30	**109**	5.3	.964	R. Reuschel	36	237	14	15	0	3.00
3B	R. Santo	536	.267	20	77	107	271	20	17	2.7	.950	M. Pappas	30	162	7	12	0	4.28
RF	J. Cardenal	522	.303	11	68	234	13	5	2	1.8	.980	B. Bonham	44	152	7	5	6	3.02
CF	R. Monday	554	.267	26	56	317	9	9	2	2.3	.973	B. Locker	63	106	10	6	18	2.55
LF	B. Williams	576	.288	20	86	253	14	4	1	2.0	.985	J. Aker	47	64	4	5	12	4.08
C	R. Hundley	368	.226	10	43	648	59	5	7	5.8	.993							
2B	P. Popovich	280	.236	2	24	171	247	8	53	5.1	.981							
C	K. Rudolph	170	.206	2	17	259	28	9	4	4.6	.970							
UT	C. Fanzone	150	.273	6	22	193	41	8	13		.967							
1B	P. Bourque	139	.209	7	20	327	35	5	32	9.7	.986							

Philadelphia

W-71 L-91

Danny Ozark

POS	Player	AB	BA	HR	RBI	PO	A	E	DP	TC/G	FA	Pitcher	G	IP	W	L	SV	ERA
1B	W. Montanez	552	.263	11	65	785	52	5	87	8.5	.994	S. Carlton	40	**293**	13	**20**	0	3.90
2B	D. Doyle	370	.273	3	26	231	296	14	71	4.7	.974	W. Twitchell	34	223	13	9	0	2.50
SS	L. Bowa	446	.211	0	23	191	361	12	87	4.6	.979	K. Brett	31	212	13	9	0	3.44
3B	M. Schmidt	367	.196	18	52	101	251	17	30	3.0	.954	J. Lonborg	38	199	13	16	0	4.88
RF	B. Robinson	452	.288	25	65	227	8	5	1	2.1	.979	D. Ruthven	25	128	6	9	1	4.21
CF	D. Unser	440	.289	11	52	329	14	4	4	2.6	.988	B. Lersch	42	98	3	6	1	4.39
LF	G. Luzinski	610	.285	29	97	262	7	2	1	1.7	.993	M. Scarce	52	71	1	8	12	2.42
C	B. Boone	521	.261	10	61	868	**89**	10	16	6.7	.990							
UT	C. Tovar	328	.268	1	21	113	113	12	32		.950							
1B	T. Hutton	247	.263	5	29	527	43	1	61	8.0	.998							
OF	M. Anderson	193	.254	9	28	99	4	2	1	1.6	.981							

West

Cincinnati

W-99 L-63

Sparky Anderson

POS	Player	AB	BA	HR	RBI	PO	A	E	DP	TC/G	FA	Pitcher	G	IP	W	L	SV	ERA
1B	T. Perez	564	.314	27	101	**1318**	85	**13**	**131**	9.4	.991	J. Billingham	40	**293**	19	10	0	3.04
2B	J. Morgan	576	.290	26	82	**417**	440	9	**106**	5.6	.990	R. Grimsley	38	242	13	10	1	3.23
SS	D. Concepcion	328	.287	8	46	165	292	12	56	5.3	.974	D. Gullett	45	228	18	8	2	3.51
3B	D. Menke	241	.191	3	26	68	189	9	19	2.2	.966	F. Norman	24	166	12	6	0	3.30
RF	C. Geronimo	324	.210	4	33	243	9	2	2	2.0	.992	P. Borbon	80	121	11	4	14	2.15
CF	B. Tolan	457	.206	9	51	279	9	10	1	2.5	.966	T. Hall	54	104	8	5	8	3.47
LF	P. Rose	**680**	**.338**	5	64	343	15	3	0	2.3	.992	C. Carroll	53	93	8	8	14	3.69
C	J. Bench	557	.253	25	104	693	61	4	7	5.7	.995							
3B	D. Driessen	366	.301	4	47	62	150	12	19	2.6	.946							
SS	D. Chaney	227	.181	0	14	103	216	12	44	4.4	.964							
OF	A. Kosco	118	.280	9	21	50	1	0	0	1.4	1.000							

NATIONAL LEAGUE 1973, *cont.*

Team	POS	Player	AB	BA	HR	RBI	PO	A	E	DP	TC/G	FA	Pitcher	G	IP	W	L	SV	ERA
Los Angeles	1B	B. Buckner	575	.275	8	46	888	50	2	93	10.1	.998	D. Sutton	33	256	18	10	0	2.42
W-95 L-66	2B	D. Lopes	535	.275	6	37	319	379	11	90	5.3	.984	A. Messersmith	33	250	14	10	0	2.70
Walter Alston	SS	B. Russell	615	.265	4	56	243	**560**	31	106	5.1	.963	C. Osteen	33	237	16	11	0	3.31
	3B	R. Cey	507	.245	15	80	111	**328**	18	**39**	3.1	.961	T. John	36	218	16	7	0	3.10
	RF	W. Crawford	457	.295	14	66	250	13	6	4	1.9	.978	A. Downing	30	193	9	9	0	3.31
	CF	W. Davis	599	.285	16	77	344	6	7	0	2.4	.980	J. Brewer	56	72	6	8	20	3.01
	LF	M. Mota	293	.314	0	23	96	4	0	0	1.4	1.000	C. Hough	37	72	4	2	5	2.76
	C	J. Ferguson	487	.263	25	88	757	57	3	**17**	6.7	**.996**	P. Richert	39	51	3	3	7	3.18
	1B	S. Garvey	349	.304	8	50	718	26	5	58	9.9	.993	G. Culver	28	42	4	4	2	3.00
	OF	T. Paciorek	195	.262	5	18	92	2	2	0	1.2	.979							
San Francisco	1B	W. McCovey	383	.266	29	75	930	76	12	89	8.7	.988	R. Bryant	41	270	**24**	12	0	3.54
W-88 L-74	2B	T. Fuentes	656	.277	6	63	386	**478**	6	102	5.4	**.993**	J. Barr	41	231	11	17	2	3.82
Charlie Fox	SS	C. Speier	542	.249	11	71	255	470	**33**	92	5.1	.956	T. Bradley	35	224	13	12	0	3.90
	3B	E. Goodson	384	.302	12	53	64	171	23	13	2.8	.911	J. Marichal	34	209	11	15	0	3.79
	RF	B. Bonds	643	.283	39	96	346	12	11	5	2.3	.970	J. Willoughby	39	123	4	5	1	4.70
	CF	G. Maddox	587	.319	11	76	370	4	12	0	2.8	.969	E. Sosa	71	107	10	4	18	3.28
	LF	G. Matthews	540	.300	12	58	277	11	5	0	2.0	.983	R. Moffitt	60	100	4	4	14	2.43
	C	D. Rader	462	.229	9	41	701	48	7	5	5.1	.991	D. McMahon	22	30	4	0	6	1.50
	31	D. Kingman	305	.203	24	55	313	146	22	30		.954							
	10	G. Thomasson	235	.285	4	30	312	15	6	15		.982							
Houston	1B	L. May	545	.270	28	105	1220	78	9	112	9.1	.993	J. Reuss	41	279	16	13	0	3.74
W-82 L-80	2B	T. Helms	543	.287	4	61	325	438	9	104	5.3	.988	D. Roberts	39	249	17	11	0	2.85
Leo Durocher	SS	R. Metzger	580	.250	1	35	231	429	12	83	4.5	**.982**	D. Wilson	37	239	11	16	2	3.20
	3B	D. Rader	574	.254	21	89	**134**	296	**25**	24	3.0	.945	K. Forsch	46	201	9	12	4	4.20
	RF	J. Wynn	481	.220	20	55	270	9	4	1	2.1	.986	T. Griffin	25	100	4	6	0	4.15
	CF	C. Cedeno	525	.320	25	70	357	10	7	2	2.8	.981	J. Crawford	48	70	2	4	6	4.50
	LF	B. Watson	573	.312	16	94	271	8	9	0	2.0	.969	J. Ray	42	69	6	4	6	4.43
	C	S. Jutze	278	.223	0	18	450	31	8	4	5.7	.984	J. York	41	53	3	4	6	4.42
	C	J. Edwards	250	.244	5	27	435	22	5	3	6.1	.989							
	OF	T. Agee	204	.235	8	15	114	2	2	2	1.8	.983							
Atlanta	1B	M. Lum	513	.294	16	82	707	42	7	64	9.0	.991	C. Morton	38	256	15	10	0	3.41
W-76 L-85	2B	D. Johnson	559	.270	43	99	383	464	**30**	**106**	5.7	.966	P. Niekro	42	245	13	10	4	3.31
Eddie Mathews	SS	M. Perez	501	.250	8	57	215	416	25	78	4.7	.962	R. Schueler	39	186	8	7	2	3.86
	3B	D. Evans	595	.281	41	104	124	325	22	33	**3.2**	.953	R. Harrison	38	177	11	8	5	4.16
	RF	H. Aaron	392	.301	40	96	206	5	5	0	2.1	.977	R. Reed	20	116	4	11	1	4.42
	CF	D. Baker	604	.288	21	99	390	10	7	1	2.6	.983	G. Gentry	16	87	4	6	1	3.41
	LF	R. Garr	668	.299	11	55	293	9	10	2	2.1	.968	T. House	52	67	4	2	4	4.70
	C	J. Oates	322	.248	4	27	409	57	9	6	5.5	.981	P. Dobson	12	58	3	7	0	4.97
	C	P. Casanova	236	.216	7	18	330	48	9	3	5.0	.977	D. Frisella	42	45	1	2	8	4.20
	OS	S. Jackson	206	.209	0	12	93	89	6	10		.968							
	1B	F. Tepedino	148	.304	4	29	331	28	3	30	6.2	.992							
	1C	D. Dietz	139	.295	3	24	325	29	6	19		.983							
San Diego	1B	N. Colbert	529	.270	22	80	1300	**98**	11	124	**9.8**	.992	B. Greif	36	199	10	17	1	3.21
W-60 L-102	2B	R. Morales	244	.164	0	16	176	239	5	45	5.3	.988	C. Kirby	34	192	8	18	0	4.79
Don Zimmer	SS	D. Thomas	404	.238	0	22	115	227	32	39	5.1	.914	S. Arlin	34	180	11	14	0	5.10
	3B	D. Roberts	479	.286	21	64	77	245	20	25	3.1	.942	R. Troedson	50	152	7	9	1	4.25
	RF	C. Gaston	476	.250	16	57	198	16	12	4	1.9	.947	M. Caldwell	55	149	5	14	10	3.74
	CF	J. Grubb	389	.311	8	37	229	11	3	1	2.4	.988	R. Jones	20	140	7	6	0	3.16
	LF	J. Morales	388	.281	9	34	214	5	2	1	2.2	.991	M. Corkins	47	122	5	8	3	4.50
	C	F. Kendall	507	.282	10	59	749	64	13	7	6.0	.984	V. Romo	49	88	2	3	7	3.70
	OF	L. Lee	333	.237	3	30	154	7	5	0	2.0	.970							
	SS	E. Hernandez	247	.223	0	9	106	190	7	42	4.5	.977							
	32	D. Hilton	234	.197	5	16	79	141	6	19		.973							
	O1	I. Murrell	210	.229	9	21	249	16	5	14		.981							
	OF	G. Locklear	154	.240	3	25	77	2	4	0	2.2	.952							

BATTING AND BASE RUNNING LEADERS

Batting Average

P. Rose, CIN	.338
C. Cedeno, HOU	.320
G. Maddox, SF	.319
T. Perez, CIN	.314
B. Watson, HOU	.312

Slugging Average

W. Stargell, PIT	.646
D. Evans, ATL	.556
D. Johnson, ATL	.546
C. Cedeno, HOU	.537
B. Bonds, SF	.530

Home Runs

W. Stargell, PIT	44
D. Johnson, ATL	43
D. Evans, ATL	41
H. Aaron, ATL	40
B. Bonds, SF	39

Total Bases

B. Bonds, SF	341
W. Stargell, PIT	337
D. Evans, ATL	331
D. Johnson, ATL	305
A. Oliver, PIT	303

Runs Batted In

W. Stargell, PIT	119
L. May, HOU	105
J. Bench, CIN	104
D. Evans, ATL	104
K. Singleton, MON	103

Stolen Bases

L. Brock, STL	70
J. Morgan, CIN	67
C. Cedeno, HOU	56
B. Bonds, SF	43
D. Lopes, LA	36

Hits

P. Rose, CIN	230
R. Garr, ATL	200
L. Brock, STL	193
T. Simmons, STL	192

Base on Balls

D. Evans, ATL	124
K. Singleton, MON	123
J. Morgan, CIN	111
W. McCovey, SF	105

Home Run Percentage

H. Aaron, ATL	10.2
W. Stargell, PIT	8.4
D. Johnson, ATL	7.7
D. Evans, ATL	6.9

PITCHING LEADERS

Winning Percentage

T. John, LA	.696
D. Gullett, CIN	.692
R. Bryant, SF	.667
J. Billingham, CIN	.655
T. Seaver, NY	.655

Earned Run Average

T. Seaver, NY	2.08
D. Sutton, LA	2.42
W. Twitchell, PHI	2.50
M. Marshall, MON	2.66
A. Messersmith, LA	2.70

Wins

R. Bryant, SF	24
T. Seaver, NY	19
J. Billingham, CIN	19
D. Gullett, CIN	18
D. Sutton, LA	18

Saves

M. Marshall, MON	31
T. McGraw, NY	25
D. Giusti, PIT	20
J. Brewer, LA	20
E. Sosa, SF	18
B. Locker, CHI	18

Strikeouts

T. Seaver, NY	251
S. Carlton, PHI	223
J. Matlack, NY	205
D. Sutton, LA	200
A. Messersmith, LA	177
J. Reuss, HOU	177

Complete Games

T. Seaver, NY	18
S. Carlton, PHI	18
J. Billingham, CIN	16
D. Sutton, LA	14
R. Wise, STL	14
J. Matlack, NY	14

Fewest Hits/9 Innings

T. Seaver, NY	6.80
D. Sutton, LA	6.88
W. Twitchell, PHI	6.93
D. Wilson, HOU	7.03

Shutouts

J. Billingham, CIN	7
D. Roberts, HOU	6
W. Twitchell, PHI	5
R. Wise, STL	5

Fewest Walks/9 Innings

J. Marichal, SF	1.59
F. Jenkins, CHI	1.89
J. Barr, SF	1.91
D. Sutton, LA	1.97

NATIONAL LEAGUE 1973, *cont.*

BATTING AND BASE RUNNING LEADERS

Runs		Doubles		Triples	
B. Bonds, SF	131	W. Stargell, PIT	43	R. Metzger, HOU	14
J. Morgan, CIN	116	A. Oliver, PIT	38	G. Matthews, SF	10
P. Rose, CIN	115	R. Staub, NY	36	G. Maddox, SF	10
D. Evans, ATL	114	T. Simmons, STL	36	W. Davis, LA	9
		P. Rose, CIN	36		

PITCHING LEADERS

Most Strikeouts/9 Inn.		Innings		Games Pitched	
T. Seaver, NY	7.79	S. Carlton, PHI	293	M. Marshall, MON	92
B. Moore, MON	7.71	J. Billingham, CIN	293	P. Borbon, CIN	80
J. Matlack, NY	7.62	T. Seaver, NY	290	E. Sosa, SF	71
D. Sutton, LA	7.02	J. Reuss, HOU	279	D. Giusti, PIT	67

		W	L	PCT	GB	R	OR	Batting 2B	3B	HR	BA	SA	SB	Fielding E	DP	FA	Pitching CG	BB	SO	ShO	SV	ERA
East	New York	82	79	.509		608	588	198	24	85	.246	.338	27	126	140	.980	47	490	**1027**	15	40	3.27
	St. Louis	81	81	.500	1.5	643	603	240	35	75	.259	.357	100	159	149	.975	42	486	867	14	36	3.25
	Pittsburgh	80	82	.494	2.5	704	693	**257**	44	154	.261	.405	23	151	156	.976	26	564	839	11	**44**	3.74
	Montreal	79	83	.488	3.5	668	702	190	23	125	.251	.364	77	163	156	.974	26	681	866	6	38	3.73
	Chicago	77	84	.478	5	614	655	201	21	117	.247	.357	65	157	155	.975	27	**438**	885	13	40	3.66
	Philadelphia	71	91	.438	11.5	642	717	218	29	134	.249	.371	51	134	**179**	.979	**49**	632	919	11	22	4.00
West	Cincinnati	99	63	.611		741	621	232	34	137	.254	.383	**148**	**115**	162	**.982**	39	518	801	**17**	43	3.43
	Los Angeles	95	66	.590	3.5	675	**565**	219	29	110	.263	.371	109	125	166	.981	45	461	961	15	38	**3.00**
	San Francisco	88	74	.543	11	739	702	212	**52**	161	.262	.407	112	163	138	.974	33	485	787	8	**44**	3.79
	Houston	82	80	.506	17	681	672	216	35	134	.251	.376	92	116	140	.981	45	575	907	14	26	3.78
	Atlanta	76	85	.472	22.5	**799**	774	219	34	**206**	**.266**	**.427**	84	166	142	.974	34	575	803	9	35	4.25
	San Diego	60	102	.370	39	548	770	198	26	112	.244	.351	88	170	152	.973	34	548	845	10	23	4.16
						8062	8062	2600	386	1550	.254	.376	976	1745	1835	.977	447	6453	10507	143	429	3.67

AMERICAN LEAGUE 1973

East

Baltimore

W-97 L-65

Earl Weaver

POS	Player	AB	BA	HR	RBI	PO	A	E	DP	TC/G	FA	Pitcher	G	IP	W	L	SV	ERA
1B	B. Powell	370	.265	11	54	988	77	12	95	9.7	.989	J. Palmer	38	296	22	9	1	**2.40**
2B	B. Grich	581	.251	12	50	**431**	**509**	5	**130**	**5.8**	**.995**	M. Cuellar	38	267	18	13	0	3.27
SS	M. Belanger	470	.226	0	27	241	**530**	23	100	5.2	.971	D. McNally	38	266	17	17	0	3.21
3B	B. Robinson	549	.257	9	72	129	354	15	25	3.2	.970	D. Alexander	29	175	12	8	0	3.86
RF	R. Coggins	389	.319	7	41	220	6	3	3	2.3	.987	B. Reynolds	42	111	7	5	9	1.95
CF	P. Blair	500	.280	10	64	369	14	4	4	2.7	.990	J. Jefferson	18	101	6	5	0	4.10
LF	D. Baylor	405	.286	11	51	204	5	4	0	1.9	.981	G. Jackson	45	80	8	0	9	1.91
C	E. Williams	459	.237	22	83	407	33	6	5	4.7	.987	E. Watt	30	71	3	4	5	3.30
DH	T. Davis	552	.306	7	89													
OF	A. Bumbry	356	.337	7	34	134	2	3	0	1.6	.978							
OF	M. Rettenmund	321	.262	9	44	196	4	3	1	2.3	.985							
C	A. Etchebarren	152	.257	2	23	201	14	2	5	4.3	.991							

Boston

W-89 L-73

Eddie Kasko
W-88 L-73

Eddie Popowski
W-1 L-0

POS	Player	AB	BA	HR	RBI	PO	A	E	DP	TC/G	FA	Pitcher	G	IP	W	L	SV	ERA
1B	C. Yastrzemski	540	.296	19	95	912	56	6	85	9.1	.994	B. Lee	38	285	17	11	1	2.74
2B	D. Griffin	396	.255	1	33	294	284	6	77	5.2	.990	L. Tiant	35	272	20	13	0	3.34
SS	L. Aparicio	499	.271	0	49	190	404	21	68	4.7	.966	J. Curtis	35	221	13	13	0	3.58
3B	R. Petrocelli	356	.244	13	45	73	224	6	22	3.1	.980	M. Pattin	34	219	15	15	1	4.31
RF	R. Miller	441	.261	6	43	301	4	7	1	2.3	.978	R. Moret	30	156	13	2	3	3.17
CF	R. Smith	423	.303	21	69	275	8	5	1	2.8	.983	B. Bolin	39	53	3	4	15	2.72
LF	T. Harper	566	.281	17	71	251	13	4	2	1.9	.985	B. Veale	32	36	2	3	11	3.50
C	C. Fisk	508	.246	26	71	**739**	50	**14**	8	6.1	.983							
DH	O. Cepeda	550	.289	20	86													
OF	D. Evans	282	.223	10	32	178	4	1	0	1.6	.995							
S2	M. Guerrero	219	.233	0	11	106	183	8	49		.973							
13	D. Cater	195	.313	1	24	303	56	6	45		.984							
C	B. Montgomery	128	.320	7	25	168	19	5	2	5.8	.974							

Detroit

W-85 L-77

Billy Martin
W-71 L-63

Joe Schultz
W-14 L-14

POS	Player	AB	BA	HR	RBI	PO	A	E	DP	TC/G	FA	Pitcher	G	IP	W	L	SV	ERA
1B	N. Cash	363	.262	19	40	856	64	8	72	8.1	.991	M. Lolich	42	309	16	15	0	3.82
2B	D. McAuliffe	343	.274	12	47	217	265	7	62	4.8	.986	J. Coleman	40	288	23	15	0	3.53
SS	E. Brinkman	515	.237	7	40	249	480	24	89	4.6	.968	J. Perry	35	203	14	13	0	4.03
3B	A. Rodriguez	555	.222	9	58	135	335	14	30	3.0	.971	W. Fryman	34	170	6	13	0	5.35
RF	J. Northrup	404	.307	12	44	207	6	4	2	1.9	.982	J. Hiller	**65**	125	10	5	**38**	1.44
CF	M. Stanley	602	.244	17	57	420	10	3	3	2.8	.993							
LF	W. Horton	411	.316	17	53	160	2	10	0	1.6	.942							
C	B. Freehan	380	.234	6	29	584	50	3	3	6.5	**.995**							
DH	G. Brown	377	.236	12	50													
O1	A. Kaline	310	.255	10	45	347	13	1	32		.997							
2B	T. Taylor	275	.229	5	24	134	165	4	37	4.2	.987							
C	D. Sims	252	.242	8	30	375	39	9	7	6.2	.979							
DH	F. Howard	227	.256	12	29													
OF	D. Sharon	178	.242	7	16	124	5	4	1	1.5	.970							

New York

W-80 L-82

Ralph Houk

POS	Player	AB	BA	HR	RBI	PO	A	E	DP	TC/G	FA	Pitcher	G	IP	W	L	SV	ERA
1B	F. Alou	280	.236	4	27	467	30	6	43	7.5	.988	M. Stottlemyre	38	273	16	16	0	3.07
2B	H. Clarke	590	.263	2	35	378	442	18	107	5.7	.979	D. Medich	34	235	14	9	0	2.95
SS	G. Michael	418	.225	3	47	208	433	23	84	5.1	.965	F. Peterson	31	184	8	15	0	3.95
3B	G. Nettles	552	.234	22	81	117	**410**	26	39	**3.5**	.953	L. McDaniel	47	160	12	6	10	2.86
RF	M. Alou	497	.296	2	28	146	6	4	2	1.8	.974	P. Dobson	22	142	9	8	0	4.17
CF	B. Murcer	616	.304	22	95	380	14	6	2	2.5	.985	S. McDowell	16	96	5	8	0	3.95
LF	R. White	**639**	.246	18	60	339	4	8	0	2.2	.977	S. Lyle	51	82	5	9	27	2.51
C	T. Munson	519	.301	20	74	673	**80**	12	**11**	5.4	.984	S. Kline	14	74	4	7	0	4.01
DH	J. Hart	339	.254	13	52													
D1	R. Blomberg	301	.329	12	57	359	28	8	38		.980							

AMERICAN LEAGUE 1973, *cont.*

	POS	Player	AB	BA	HR	RBI	PO	A	E	DP	TC/G	FA	Pitcher	G	IP	W	L	SV	ERA
Milwaukee	1B	G. Scott	604	.306	24	107	1388	**118**	9	144	9.6	.994	J. Colborn	43	314	20	12	1	3.18
W-74 L-88	2B	P. Garcia	580	.245	15	54	405	470	**27**	111	5.6	.970	J. Slaton	38	276	13	15	0	3.71
Del Crandall	SS	T. Johnson	465	.213	0	32	**253**	381	25	88	4.9	.962	J. Bell	31	184	9	9	1	3.97
	3B	D. Money	556	.284	11	61	112	224	10	24	2.8	**.971**	S. Lockwood	37	155	5	12	0	3.90
	RF	B. Coluccio	438	.224	15	58	236	12	2	3	2.3	.992	B. Champion	37	136	5	8	1	3.70
	CF	D. May	624	.303	25	93	401	9	9	3	2.8	.979	E. Rodriguez	30	76	9	7	5	3.30
	LF	J. Briggs	488	.246	18	57	294	9	10	1	2.3	.968	C. Short	42	72	3	5	2	5.13
	C	D. Porter	350	.254	16	67	372	47	10	9	4.8	.977	F. Linzy	42	63	2	6	13	3.57
	DH	O. Brown	296	.280	7	32													
	C	E. Rodriguez	290	.269	0	30	324	40	5	5	4.9	.986							
	DO	J. Lahoud	225	.204	5	26	85	2	0	1		1.000							
	OD	B. Mitchell	130	.223	5	20	24	0	1	0		.960							
Cleveland	1B	C. Chambliss	572	.273	11	53	1437	114	**14**	153	10.2	.991	G. Perry	41	344	19	19	0	3.38
W-71 L-91	2B	J. Brohamer	300	.220	4	29	215	279	15	67	5.2	.971	D. Tidrow	42	275	14	16	0	4.42
Ken Aspromonte	SS	F. Duffy	361	.263	8	50	198	377	8	82	5.1	**.986**	M. Wilcox	26	134	8	10	0	5.83
	3B	B. Bell	631	.268	14	59	**144**	363	22	**44**	3.4	.958	T. Timmerman	29	124	8	7	2	4.92
	RF	R. Torres	312	.205	7	28	191	9	5	1	1.8	.976	B. Strom	27	123	2	10	0	4.61
	CF	G. Hendrick	440	.268	21	61	242	7	3	1	2.3	.988	T. Hilgendorf	48	95	5	3	6	3.14
	LF	C. Spikes	506	.237	23	73	202	13	8	0	2.0	.964	J. Johnson	39	60	5	6	5	6.18
	C	D. Duncan	344	.233	17	43	533	41	7	8	**6.8**	.988	K. Sanders	15	27	5	1	5	1.65
	DH	O. Gamble	390	.267	20	44													
	CD	J. Ellis	437	.270	14	68	370	27	8	5		.980							
	OF	W. Williams	350	.289	8	38	123	7	4	0	2.2	.970							
	UT	J. Lowenstein	305	.292	6	40	124	85	7	22		.968							
	SS	L. Cardenas	195	.215	0	12	87	154	9	33	3.7	.964							
	2B	T. Ragland	183	.257	0	12	136	166	5	43	4.7	.984							
West																			
Oakland	1B	G. Tenace	510	.259	24	84	1095	61	13	104	8.7	.989	K. Holtzman	40	297	21	13	0	2.97
W-94 L-68	2B	D. Green	332	.262	3	42	264	297	7	86	4.3	.988	V. Blue	37	264	20	9	0	3.28
Dick Williams	SS	B. Campaneris	601	.250	4	46	228	496	23	87	5.0	.969	C. Hunter	36	256	21	5	0	3.34
	3B	S. Bando	592	.287	29	98	126	281	22	24	2.7	.949	B. Odom	30	150	5	12	0	4.49
	RF	R. Jackson	539	.293	**32**	**117**	302	4	9	0	2.2	.971	R. Fingers	62	127	7	8	22	1.92
	CF	B. North	554	.285	5	34	429	14	9	5	3.3	.980	D. Knowles	52	99	6	8	9	3.09
	LF	J. Rudi	437	.270	12	66	231	6	2	2	2.0	.992	H. Pina	47	88	6	3	8	2.76
	C	R. Fosse	492	.256	7	52	712	63	10	5	5.6	.987	D. Hamilton	16	70	6	4	0	4.39
	DH	D. Johnson	464	.246	19	81													
	OF	A. Mangual	192	.224	3	13	88	2	5	0	1.9	.947							
	2B	T. Kubiak	182	.220	3	17	89	129	6	28	2.7	.973							
Kansas City	1B	J. Mayberry	510	.278	26	100	**1457**	81	9	**156**	**10.4**	.994	P. Splittorff	38	262	20	11	0	3.99
W-88 L-74	2B	C. Rojas	551	.276	6	69	302	424	13	114	5.4	.982	S. Busby	37	238	16	15	0	4.24
Jack McKeon	SS	F. Patek	501	.234	5	45	242	503	26	**115**	**5.7**	.966	D. Drago	37	213	12	14	0	4.23
	3B	P. Schaal	396	.288	8	42	77	237	**30**	14	2.8	.913	G. Garber	48	153	9	9	11	4.24
	RF	E. Kirkpatrick	429	.263	6	45	198	3	2	0	1.9	.990	D. Bird	54	102	4	4	20	3.00
	CF	A. Otis	583	.300	26	93	330	10	5	4	2.6	.986	B. Dal Canton	32	97	4	3	3	4.82
	LF	L. Piniella	513	.250	9	69	196	9	3	3	1.6	.986	A. Fitzmorris	15	89	8	3	0	2.83
	C	F. Healy	279	.276	6	34	429	43	10	4	5.2	.979	K. Wright	25	81	6	5	0	4.89
	DH	H. McRae	338	.234	9	50													
	UT	K. Bevacqua	276	.257	2	40	120	90	9	20		.959							
	OF	S. Hovley	232	.254	2	24	114	4	3	1	1.5	.975							
Minnesota	1B	J. Lis	253	.245	9	25	626	48	9	59	7.1	.987	B. Blyleven	40	325	20	17	0	2.52
W-81 L-81	2B	R. Carew	580	**.350**	6	62	383	413	13	96	5.5	.984	J. Kaat	29	182	11	12	0	4.41
Frank Quilici	SS	D. Thompson	347	.225	1	36	131	326	24	50	5.1	.950	J. Decker	29	170	10	10	0	4.17
	3B	S. Braun	361	.283	6	42	79	175	16	21	2.6	.941	R. Corbin	51	148	8	5	14	3.03
	RF	B. Darwin	560	.252	18	90	233	13	5	1	1.8	.980	B. Hands	39	142	7	10	2	3.49
	CF	L. Hisle	545	.272	15	64	337	11	9	0	2.5	.975	D. Woodson	23	141	10	8	0	3.95
	LF	J. Holt	441	.297	11	58	193	6	2	2	2.0	.990	D. Goltz	32	106	6	4	1	5.25
	C	G. Mitterwald	432	.259	16	64	676	59	6	6	6.1	.992	B. Campbell	28	52	3	3	7	3.14
	DH	T. Oliva	571	.291	16	92							K. Sanders	27	44	2	4	8	6.09
	UT	J. Terrell	438	.265	1	32	170	298	18	55		.963							
	OF	S. Brye	278	.263	6	33	209	4	3	1	2.5	.986							
	1B	H. Killebrew	248	.242	5	32	431	45	1	42	8.4	.998							
California	1B	M. Epstein	312	.215	8	32	710	50	5	61	8.9	.993	N. Ryan	41	326	21	16	1	2.87
W-79 L-83	2B	S. Alomar	470	.238	0	28	243	267	11	70	4.7	.979	B. Singer	40	316	20	14	0	3.22
Bobby Winkles	SS	R. Meoli	305	.223	2	23	122	252	**27**	52	4.2	.933	C. Wright	37	257	11	19	0	3.68
	3B	A. Gallagher	311	.273	0	26	59	185	10	13	2.6	.961	R. May	34	185	7	17	0	4.38
	RF	L. Stanton	306	.235	8	34	160	5	6	2	1.6	.965	D. Sells	51	68	7	2	10	3.71
	CF	K. Berry	415	.284	3	36	309	5	1	0	2.4	.997							
	LF	V. Pinson	466	.260	8	57	210	11	8	2	1.9	.965							
	C	J. Torborg	255	.220	1	18	611	37	6	2	6.4	.991							
	DH	F. Robinson	534	.266	30	97													
	UT	B. Oliver	544	.265	18	89	396	121	11	26		.979							
	UT	T. McCraw	264	.265	3	24	268	25	1	28		.997							
	OF	R. Scheinblum	229	.328	3	21	92	3	3	0	1.8	.969							
	UT	W. Llenas	130	.269	1	25	42	37	1	3		.988							

AMERICAN LEAGUE 1973, *cont.*

Chicago

W-77 L-85

Chuck Tanner

POS	Player	AB	BA	HR	RBI	PO	A	E	DP	TC/G	FA	Pitcher	G	IP	W	L	SV	ERA
1B	T. Muser	309	.285	4	30	680	38	6	70	8.1	.992	W. Wood	49	**359**	**24**	20	0	3.46
2B	J. Orta	425	.266	6	40	254	300	18	75	4.7	.969	S. Bahnsen	42	282	18	**21**	0	3.57
SS	E. Leon	399	.228	3	30	198	382	17	78	4.9	.972	S. Stone	36	176	6	11	1	4.24
3B	B. Melton	560	.277	20	87	115	347	23	31	3.2	.953	T. Forster	51	173	6	11	16	3.23
RF	P. Kelly	550	.280	1	44	254	9	6	2	1.9	.978	E. Fisher	26	111	6	7	0	4.88
CF	B. Sharp	196	.276	4	22	146	10	3	2	2.3	.981	C. Acosta	48	97	10	6	18	2.23
LF	C. May	553	.268	20	96	118	7	1	0	1.8	.992							
C	E. Herrmann	379	.224	10	39	617	70	11	**11**	6.1	.984							
DH	M. Andrews	159	.201	0	10													
OF	J. Jeter	300	.240	7	26	144	3	7	0	2.1	.955							
OD	K. Henderson	262	.260	6	32	102	1	3	0		.972							
1B	D. Allen	250	.316	16	41	597	43	4	55	9.6	.994							
UT	J. Hairston	210	.271	0	23	194	13	5	11		.976							
UT	L. Alvarado	203	.232	0	20	120	158	9	31		.969							
OF	B. Bradford	168	.238	8	15	114	9	1	2	2.4	.992							

Texas

W-57 L-105

Whitey Herzog W-47 L-91

Del Wilber W-1 L-0

Billy Martin W-9 L-14

POS	Player	AB	BA	HR	RBI	PO	A	E	DP	TC/G	FA	Pitcher	G	IP	W	L	SV	ERA
1B	J. Spencer	352	.267	4	43	790	67	1	110	8.7	.999*	J. Bibby	26	180	9	10	1	3.25
2B	D. Nelson	576	.286	7	48	327	364	11	98	5.0	.984	J. Merritt	35	160	5	13	1	4.05
SS	J. Mason	238	.206	3	19	113	206	18	43	4.6	.947	B. Gogolewski	49	124	3	6	6	4.21
3B	T. Harrah	461	.260	10	50	39	79	8	4	2.4	.937	S. Siebert	25	120	7	11	2	3.99
RF	J. Burroughs	526	.279	30	85	304	13	8	2	2.2	.975	P. Broberg	22	119	5	9	0	5.60
CF	V. Harris	555	.249	8	44	297	5	7	1	2.7	.977	D. Clyde	18	93	4	8	0	5.03
LF	L. Biittner	258	.252	1	12	91	6	2	1	1.7	.980	M. Paul	36	87	5	4	2	4.97
C	K. Suarez	278	.248	1	27	501	44	6	4	6.1	.989	J. Brown	25	67	5	5	2	3.90
DH	A. Johnson	624	.287	8	68							S. Foucault	32	56	2	4	8	3.86
OD	R. Carty	306	.232	3	33	87	2	0	0		1.000							
C	D. Billings	280	.179	3	32	356	32	10	3	5.5	.975							
UT	B. Sudakis	235	.255	15	43	216	62	5	21		.982							
OF	E. Maddox	172	.238	1	17	144	7	3	1	1.7	.981							
OF	T. Grieve	123	.309	7	21	68	0	0	0	1.2	1.000							

BATTING AND BASE RUNNING LEADERS

Batting Average

R. Carew, MIN	.350
G. Scott, MIL	.306
T. Davis, BAL	.306
B. Murcer, NY	.304
D. May, MIL	.303

Slugging Average

R. Jackson, OAK	.531
S. Bando, OAK	.498
F. Robinson, CAL	.489
G. Scott, MIL	.488
T. Munson, NY	.487

Home Runs

R. Jackson, OAK	32
J. Burroughs, TEX	30
F. Robinson, CAL	30
S. Bando, OAK	29

Total Bases

S. Bando, OAK	295
G. Scott, MIL	295
D. May, MIL	295
R. Jackson, OAK	286
B. Murcer, NY	286

Runs Batted In

R. Jackson, OAK	117
G. Scott, MIL	107
J. Mayberry, KC	100
S. Bando, OAK	98
F. Robinson, CAL	97

Stolen Bases

T. Harper, BOS	54
B. North, OAK	53
D. Nelson, TEX	43
R. Carew, MIN	41
F. Patek, KC	36

Hits

R. Carew, MIN	203
D. May, MIL	189
B. Murcer, NY	187
G. Scott, MIL	185

Base on Balls

J. Mayberry, KC	122
B. Grich, BAL	107
C. Yastrzemski, BOS	105
G. Tenace, OAK	101

Home Run Percentage

R. Jackson, OAK	5.9
J. Burroughs, TEX	5.7
F. Robinson, CAL	5.6
C. Fisk, BOS	5.1

Runs

R. Jackson, OAK	99
B. North, OAK	98
R. Carew, MIN	98
G. Scott, MIL	98

Doubles

P. Garcia, MIL	32
S. Bando, OAK	32
C. Chambliss, CLE	30
R. Carew, MIN	30
G. Scott, MIL	30

Triples

A. Bumbry, BAL	11
R. Carew, MIN	11
J. Orta, CHI	10
R. Coggins, BAL	9

PITCHING LEADERS

Winning Percentage

C. Hunter, OAK	.808
J. Palmer, BAL	.710
V. Blue, OAK	.690
P. Splittorff, KC	.645
J. Colborn, MIL	.625

Earned Run Average

J. Palmer, BAL	2.40
B. Blyleven, MIN	2.52
B. Lee, BOS	2.74
N. Ryan, CAL	2.87
D. Medich, NY	2.95

Wins

W. Wood, CHI	24
J. Coleman, DET	23
J. Palmer, BAL	22
C. Hunter, OAK	21
K. Holtzman, OAK	21
N. Ryan, CAL	21

Saves

J. Hiller, DET	38
S. Lyle, NY	27
R. Fingers, OAK	22
D. Bird, KC	20
C. Acosta, CHI	18

Strikeouts

N. Ryan, CAL	383
B. Blyleven, MIN	258
B. Singer, CAL	241
G. Perry, CLE	238
M. Lolich, DET	214

Complete Games

G. Perry, CLE	29
N. Ryan, CAL	26
B. Blyleven, MIN	25
L. Tiant, BOS	23
J. Colborn, MIL	22

Fewest Hits/9 Innings

J. Bibby, TEX	6.05
N. Ryan, CAL	6.57
J. Palmer, BAL	6.84
L. Tiant, BOS	7.18

Shutouts

B. Blyleven, MIN	9
G. Perry, CLE	7
J. Palmer, BAL	6

Fewest Walks/9 Innings

J. Kaat, MIN, CHI	1.73
B. Blyleven, MIN	1.86
K. Holtzman, OAK	2.00
W. Wood, CHI	2.28

Most Strikeouts/9 Inn.

N. Ryan, CAL	10.57
J. Bibby, TEX	7.75
B. Blyleven, MIN	7.14
S. Stone, CHI	7.04

Innings

W. Wood, CHI	359
G. Perry, CLE	344
N. Ryan, CAL	326
B. Blyleven, MIN	325

Games Pitched

J. Hiller, DET	65
R. Fingers, OAK	62
D. Bird, KC	54
D. Knowles, OAK	52

		W	L	PCT	GB	R	OR	Batting 2B	3B	HR	BA	SA	SB	Fielding E	DP	FA	Pitching CG	BB	SO	ShO	SV	ERA
East	Baltimore	97	65	.599		754	**561**	229	**48**	119	.266	.389	**146**	119	184	.981	67	475	715	14	26	**3.07**
	Boston	89	73	.549	8	738	647	235	30	147	.267	**.401**	114	127	162	.979	67	499	808	10	33	3.65
	Detroit	85	77	.525	12	642	674	213	32	157	.254	.390	28	**112**	144	**.982**	39	493	911	11	**46**	3.90
	New York	80	82	.494	17	641	610	212	17	131	.261	.378	47	156	172	.976	47	**457**	708	16	39	3.34
	Milwaukee	74	88	.457	23	708	731	229	40	145	.253	.388	110	145	167	.977	50	623	671	11	28	3.98
	Cleveland	71	91	.438	26	680	826	205	29	**158**	.256	.387	60	139	174	.978	55	602	883	9	21	4.58
West	Oakland	94	68	.580		**758**	615	216	28	147	.260	.389	128	137	170	.978	46	494	797	16	41	3.29
	Kansas City	88	74	.543	6	755	752	239	40	114	.261	.381	105	167	**192**	.974	40	617	790	7	41	4.21
	Minnesota	81	81	.500	13	738	692	**240**	44	120	**.270**	.393	87	139	147	.978	48	519	880	**18**	34	3.77
	California	79	83	.488	15	629	657	183	29	93	.253	.348	59	156	153	.975	**72**	614	**1010**	13	19	3.57
	Chicago	77	85	.475	17	652	705	228	38	111	.256	.372	83	144	165	.977	48	574	848	15	35	3.86
	Texas	57	105	.352	37	619	844	195	29	110	.255	.361	91	161	164	.974	35	680	831	10	27	4.64
						8314	8314	2624	404	1552	.259	.381	1058	1702	1994	.977	614	6647	9852	150	390	3.82

NATIONAL LEAGUE 1974

East

Pittsburgh

W-88 L-74

Danny Murtaugh

POS	Player	AB	BA	HR	RBI	PO	A	E	DP	TC/G	FA
1B	B. Robertson	236	.229	16	48	494	37	5	44	8.5	.991
2B	R. Stennett	673	.291	7	56	**441**	475	19	115	**6.1**	.980
SS	F. Taveras	333	.246	0	26	170	321	31	60	4.2	.941
3B	R. Hebner	550	.291	18	68	115	304	**28**	34	3.2	.937
RF	R. Zisk	536	.313	17	100	312	9	5	3	2.3	.985
CF	A. Oliver	617	.321	11	85	284	3	4	1	3.0	.986
LF	W. Stargell	508	.301	25	96	253	8	9	1	2.0	.967
C	M. Sanguillen	596	.287	7	68	713	76	12	8	5.3	.985
OF	G. Clines	276	.225	0	14	177	6	2	1	2.4	.989
1B	E. Kirkpatrick	271	.247	6	38	512	31	4	55	9.3	.993
OF	D. Parker	220	.282	4	29	101	5	4	1	2.2	.964
SS	M. Mendoza	163	.221	0	15	77	187	10	21	3.1	.964

Pitcher	G	IP	W	L	SV	ERA
J. Rooker	33	263	15	11	0	2.77
J. Reuss	35	260	16	11	0	3.50
K. Brett	27	191	13	9	0	3.30
D. Ellis	26	177	12	9	0	3.15
B. Kison	40	129	9	8	2	3.49
D. Giusti	64	106	7	5	12	3.31
L. Demery	19	95	6	6	0	4.26

St. Louis

W-86 L-75

Red Schoendienst

POS	Player	AB	BA	HR	RBI	PO	A	E	DP	TC/G	FA
1B	J. Torre	529	.282	11	70	1165	**102**	10	**144**	9.2	.992
2B	T. Sizemore	504	.250	2	47	335	412	15	109	6.0	.980
SS	M. Tyson	422	.223	1	37	231	410	30	**108**	4.7	.955
3B	K. Reitz	579	.271	7	54	131	278	11	29	2.8	**.974**
RF	R. Smith	517	.309	23	100	275	9	7	3	2.2	.976
CF	B. McBride	559	.309	6	56	395	9	4	1	2.8	.990
LF	L. Brock	635	.306	3	48	283	8	10	2	2.0	.967
C	T. Simmons	599	.272	20	103	717	82	11	13	5.7	.986
OF	J. Cruz	161	.261	5	20	76	2	2	1	1.5	.975

Pitcher	G	IP	W	L	SV	ERA
B. Gibson	33	240	11	13	0	3.83
L. McGlothen	31	237	16	12	0	2.70
J. Curtis	33	195	10	14	1	3.78
A. Foster	31	162	7	10	0	3.89
S. Siebert	28	134	8	8	0	3.83
B. Forsch	19	100	7	4	0	2.97
R. Folkers	55	90	6	2	2	3.00
A. Hrabosky	65	88	8	1	9	2.97
M. Garman	64	82	7	2	6	2.63

Philadelphia

W-80 L-82

Danny Ozark

POS	Player	AB	BA	HR	RBI	PO	A	E	DP	TC/G	FA
1B	W. Montanez	527	.304	7	79	1216	79	10	126	9.5	.992
2B	D. Cash	**687**	.300	2	58	396	**519**	22	**141**	5.8	.977
SS	L. Bowa	669	.275	1	36	256	462	12	104	4.5	**.984**
3B	M. Schmidt	568	.282	**36**	116	134	**404**	26	40	3.5	.954
RF	M. Anderson	395	.251	5	34	238	12	5	3	1.9	.980
CF	D. Unser	454	.264	11	61	300	13	6	0	2.4	.981
LF	G. Luzinski	302	.272	7	48	146	10	3	0	1.9	.981
C	B. Boone	488	.242	3	52	**825**	77	**22**	7	6.3	.976
OF	B. Robinson	280	.236	5	29	162	8	5	0	2.0	.971
10	T. Hutton	208	.240	4	33	285	15	2	25		.993
OF	J. Johnstone	200	.295	6	30	88	4	3	1	1.6	.968

Pitcher	G	IP	W	L	SV	ERA
S. Carlton	39	291	16	13	0	3.22
J. Lonborg	39	283	17	13	0	3.21
D. Ruthven	35	213	9	13	0	4.01
R. Schueler	44	203	11	16	1	3.72
W. Twitchell	25	112	6	9	0	5.22
M. Scarce	58	70	3	8	5	5.01

Montreal

W-79 L-82

Gene Mauch

POS	Player	AB	BA	HR	RBI	PO	A	E	DP	TC/G	FA
1B	M. Jorgensen	287	.310	11	59	606	51	1	47	7.2	.998
2B	J. Cox	236	.220	2	26	148	220	12	45	5.3	.968
SS	T. Foli	441	.254	0	39	220	412	19	85	**5.4**	.971
3B	R. Hunt	403	.268	0	26	37	140	11	14	2.5	.941
RF	K. Singleton	511	.276	9	74	224	7	11	0	1.7	.955
CF	W. Davis	611	.295	12	89	369	8	12	1	2.6	.969
LF	B. Bailey	507	.280	20	73	105	8	3	3	1.5	.974
C	B. Foote	420	.262	11	60	640	**83**	12	12	6.0	.984
2S	L. Lintz	319	.238	0	20	168	250	18	48		.959
1B	R. Fairly	282	.245	12	43	572	42	7	41	9.3	.989
1B	H. Breeden	190	.247	2	20	422	31	6	43	8.2	.987

Pitcher	G	IP	W	L	SV	ERA
S. Rogers	38	254	15	**22**	0	4.46
S. Renko	37	228	12	16	0	4.03
M. Torrez	32	186	15	8	0	3.58
D. Blair	22	146	11	7	0	3.27
E. McAnally	25	129	6	13	0	4.47
C. Taylor	61	108	6	2	11	2.17
T. Walker	33	92	4	5	2	3.82
J. Montague	46	83	3	4	3	3.14
D. Murray	32	70	1	1	10	1.03

New York

W-71 L-91

Yogi Berra

POS	Player	AB	BA	HR	RBI	PO	A	E	DP	TC/G	FA
1B	J. Milner	507	.252	20	63	1147	77	7	103	9.3	.994
2B	F. Millan	518	.268	1	33	374	315	15	81	5.3	.979
SS	B. Harrelson	331	.227	1	13	196	325	17	65	5.5	.968
3B	W. Garrett	522	.224	13	53	111	318	20	31	3.1	.955
RF	R. Staub	561	.258	19	78	262	19	5	5	1.9	.983
CF	D. Hahn	323	.251	4	28	217	8	3	0	2.2	.987
LF	C. Jones	461	.282	13	60	220	8	7	0	2.0	.970
C	J. Grote	319	.257	5	36	549	36	7	1	6.3	.988
UT	T. Martinez	334	.219	2	43	164	257	20	38		.955
OF	D. Schneck	254	.205	5	25	179	7	5	2	2.3	.974
UT	K. Boswell	222	.216	2	15	94	113	6	18		.972
01	E. Kranepool	217	.300	4	24	207	9	5	18		.977

Pitcher	G	IP	W	L	SV	ERA
J. Matlack	34	265	13	15	0	2.41
J. Koosman	35	265	15	11	0	3.36
T. Seaver	32	236	11	11	0	3.20
H. Parker	40	131	4	12	4	3.92
B. Apodaca	35	103	6	6	3	3.50
R. Sadecki	34	101	8	8	0	3.48
T. McGraw	41	89	6	11	3	4.15

Chicago

W-66 L-96

Whitey Lockman
W-41 L-52

Jim Marshall
W-25 L-44

POS	Player	AB	BA	HR	RBI	PO	A	E	DP	TC/G	FA
1B	A. Thornton	303	.261	10	46	760	70	7	61	9.3	.992
2B	V. Harris	200	.195	0	11	122	144	16	20	5.0	.943
SS	D. Kessinger	599	.259	1	42	**259**	476	32	87	5.1	.958
3B	B. Madlock	453	.313	9	54	84	229	18	14	2.7	.946
RF	J. Cardenal	542	.293	13	72	262	15	10	4	2.1	.965
CF	R. Monday	538	.294	20	58	302	10	5	5	2.3	.984
LF	J. Morales	534	.273	15	82	266	5	7	2	1.9	.975
C	S. Swisher	280	.214	5	27	493	50	7	8	6.1	.987
10	B. Williams	404	.280	16	68	635	53	11	50		.984
C	G. Mitterwald	215	.251	7	28	335	40	10	4	5.7	.974
UT	C. Fanzone	158	.190	4	22	87	82	15	14		.918

Pitcher	G	IP	W	L	SV	ERA
B. Bonham	44	243	11	**22**	1	3.85
R. Reuschel	41	241	13	12	0	4.29
B. Hooton	48	176	7	11	1	4.81
S. Stone	38	170	8	6	0	4.13
K. Frailing	55	125	6	9	1	3.89
D. LaRoche	49	92	5	6	5	4.79
O. Zamora	56	84	3	9	10	3.11
H. Pina	34	47	3	4	4	4.02

West

Los Angeles

W-102 L-60

Walter Alston

POS	Player	AB	BA	HR	RBI	PO	A	E	DP	TC/G	FA
1B	S. Garvey	642	.312	21	111	**1536**	62	8	108	**10.3**	.995
2B	D. Lopes	530	.266	10	35	309	360	**24**	71	4.8	.965
SS	B. Russell	553	.269	5	65	194	491	**39**	68	4.5	.946
3B	R. Cey	577	.262	18	97	155	365	22	25	3.4	.959
RF	W. Crawford	468	.295	11	61	225	3	8	1	1.8	.966
CF	J. Wynn	535	.271	32	108	365	10	3	3	2.6	.992
LF	B. Buckner	580	.314	7	58	235	4	6	0	1.8	.976
C	S. Yeager	316	.266	12	41	552	58	5	4	**6.6**	.992
C	J. Ferguson	349	.252	16	57	436	40	6	2	5.9	.988
OF	T. Paciorek	175	.240	1	24	83	1	5	1	1.2	.944

Pitcher	G	IP	W	L	SV	ERA
A. Messersmith	39	292	**20**	6	0	2.59
D. Sutton	40	276	19	9	0	3.23
M. Marshall	**106**	208	15	12	**21**	2.42
D. Rau	36	198	13	11	0	3.73
T. John	22	153	13	3	0	2.59
A. Downing	21	98	5	6	0	3.67
C. Hough	49	96	9	4	1	3.75

NATIONAL LEAGUE 1974, *cont.*

Team	POS	Player	AB	BA	HR	RBI	PO	A	E	DP	TC/G	FA	Pitcher	G	IP	W	L	SV	ERA
Cincinnati	1B	T. Perez	596	.265	28	101	1292	75	6	111	8.7	**.996**	D. Gullett	36	243	17	11	0	3.04
	2B	J. Morgan	512	.293	22	67	344	385	13	92	5.2	.982	C. Kirby	36	231	12	9	0	3.27
W-98 L-64	SS	D. Concepcion	594	.281	14	82	239	**536**	30	99	5.0	.963	J. Billingham	36	212	19	11	0	3.95
	3B	D. Driessen	470	.281	7	56	67	192	24	19	2.2	.915	F. Norman	35	186	13	12	0	3.15
Sparky Anderson	RF	C. Geronimo	474	.281	7	54	355	13	5	2	2.6	.987	P. Borbon	73	139	10	7	14	3.24
	CF	G. Foster	276	.264	7	41	172	2	2	1	1.8	.989	C. Carroll	57	101	12	5	6	2.14
	LF	P. Rose	652	.284	3	51	346	11	1	3	2.2	.997							
	C	J. Bench	621	.280	33	**129**	757	68	6	**16**	6.1	.993							
	OF	K. Griffey	227	.251	2	19	115	5	0	1	1.7	1.000							
	OF	M. Rettenmund	208	.216	6	28	103	3	0	0	1.5	1.000							
	OF	T. Crowley	125	.240	1	20	29	1	0	0	1.4	1.000							
Atlanta	1B	D. Johnson	454	.251	15	62	641	54	5	57	9.6	.993	P. Niekro	41	**302**	**20**	13	1	2.38
	2B	M. Perez	447	.260	2	34	225	311	8	64	5.3	.985	C. Morton	38	275	16	12	0	3.14
	SS	C. Robinson	452	.230	0	29	238	395	29	73	4.7	.956	B. Capra	39	217	16	8	1	**2.28**
W-88 L-74	3B	D. Evans	571	.240	25	79	**185**	367	26	**45**	**3.6**	.955	R. Reed	28	186	10	11	0	3.39
	RF	D. Baker	574	.256	20	69	359	10	7	2	2.5	.981	R. Harrison	20	126	6	11	0	4.71
Eddie Mathews	CF	R. Office	248	.246	3	31	171	0	1	0	1.4	.994	T. House	56	103	6	2	11	1.92
W-50 L-49	LF	R. Garr	606	**.353**	11	54	255	8	9	2	2.0	.967	M. Leon	34	75	4	7	3	2.64
	C	J. Oates	291	.223	1	21	434	55	4	4	5.4	.992	D. Frisella	36	42	3	4	6	5.14
Clyde King	10	M. Lum	361	.233	11	50	554	26	4	44		.993							
W-38 L-25	OF	H. Aaron	340	.268	20	69	142	3	2	0	1.7	.986							
	C	V. Correll	202	.238	4	29	282	40	4	4	5.5	.988							
	1B	F. Tepedino	169	.231	0	16	307	26	4	35	7.3	.988							
Houston	1B	L. May	556	.268	24	85	1253	88	8	116	9.3	.994	L. Dierker	33	224	11	10	0	2.89
	2B	T. Helms	452	.279	5	50	308	360	10	99	5.1	**.985**	T. Griffin	34	211	14	10	0	3.54
W-81 L-81	SS	R. Metzger	572	.253	0	30	238	451	17	85	4.9	.976	D. Wilson	33	205	11	13	0	3.07
	3B	D. Rader	533	.257	17	78	128	347	17	28	3.2	.965	D. Roberts	34	204	10	12	1	3.40
Preston Gomez	RF	G. Gross	589	.314	0	36	296	15	2	4	2.1	.994	C. Osteen	23	138	9	9	0	3.71
	CF	C. Cedeno	610	.269	26	102	446	11	3	4	2.9	.993	K. Forsch	70	103	8	7	10	2.80
	LF	B. Watson	524	.298	11	67	202	7	4	2	1.5	.981	M. Cosgrove	45	90	7	3	2	3.49
	C	M. May	405	.289	7	54	525	63	4	10	5.1	**.993**	F. Scherman	53	61	2	5	4	4.13
	C1	C. Johnson	171	.228	10	29	270	18	4	17		.986							
San Francisco	1B	D. Kingman	350	.223	18	55	680	60	**13**	66	8.3	.983	J. Barr	44	240	13	9	2	2.74
	2B	T. Fuentes	390	.249	0	22	238	287	11	70	5.2	.979	J. D'Acquisto	38	215	12	14	0	3.77
	SS	C. Speier	501	.250	9	53	210	445	21	82	5.0	.969	M. Caldwell	31	189	14	5	0	2.95
W-72 L-90	3B	S. Ontiveros	343	.265	4	33	64	144	16	16	3.0	.929	T. Bradley	30	134	8	11	0	5.17
	RF	B. Bonds	567	.256	21	71	305	11	11	3	2.2	.966	R. Bryant	41	127	3	15	0	5.60
Charlie Fox	CF	G. Maddox	538	.284	8	50	345	3	5	0	2.7	.986	R. Moffitt	61	102	5	7	15	4.50
W-34 L-42	LF	G. Matthews	561	.287	16	82	281	9	9	2	2.0	.970	E. Sosa	68	101	9	7	6	3.48
	C	D. Rader	323	.291	1	26	461	38	8	4	4.7	.984	C. Williams	39	100	1	3	0	2.79
Wes Westrum	OF	G. Thomasson	315	.244	2	29	149	4	3	1	2.1	.981							
W-38 L-48	1B	E. Goodson	298	.272	6	48	593	30	2	52	8.6	.997							
	UT	M. Phillips	283	.219	2	20	125	195	19	33		.944							
	UT	B. Miller	198	.278	0	16	55	161	12	11		.947							
	2B	C. Arnold	174	.241	1	26	64	86	4	16	5.0	.974							
San Diego	1B	W. McCovey	344	.253	22	63	815	47	11	59	8.4	.987	B. Greif	43	226	9	19	1	4.66
	2B	D. Thomas	523	.247	3	41	232	294	13	45	5.2	.976	D. Freisleben	33	212	9	14	0	3.65
W-60 L-102	SS	E. Hernandez	512	.232	0	34	229	449	24	64	4.8	.966	R. Jones	40	208	8	**22**	2	4.46
	3B	D. Roberts	318	.167	5	18	83	170	12	15	2.6	.955	D. Spillner	30	148	9	11	0	4.01
John McNamara	RF	D. Winfield	498	.265	20	75	276	11	12	2	2.3	.960	L. Hardy	76	102	9	4	2	4.68
	CF	J. Grubb	444	.286	8	42	321	8	8	1	2.8	.976	V. Romo	54	71	5	5	9	4.56
	LF	B. Tolan	357	.266	8	40	161	5	5	0	1.9	.971							
	C	F. Kendall	424	.231	8	45	631	64	12	12	5.3	.983							
	10	N. Colbert	368	.207	14	54	605	52	9	43		.986							
	OF	C. Gaston	267	.213	6	33	119	7	1	1	2.0	.992							
	3B	D. Hilton	217	.240	1	12	51	94	8	13	2.8	.948							
	2B	G. Beckert	172	.256	0	7	70	80	10	16	4.4	.938							

BATTING AND BASE RUNNING LEADERS

Batting Average		Slugging Average		Home Runs	
R. Garr, ATL	.353	M. Schmidt, PHI	.546	M. Schmidt, PHI	36
A. Oliver, PIT	.321	W. Stargell, PIT	.537	J. Bench, CIN	33
G. Gross, HOU	.314	R. Smith, STL	.528	J. Wynn, LA	32
B. Buckner, LA	.314	J. Bench, CIN	.507	T. Perez, CIN	28
B. Madlock, CHI	.313	R. Garr, ATL	.503	C. Cedeno, HOU	26

Total Bases		Runs Batted In		Stolen Bases	
J. Bench, CIN	315	J. Bench, CIN	129	L. Brock, STL	118
M. Schmidt, PHI	310	M. Schmidt, PHI	116	D. Lopes, LA	59
R. Garr, ATL	305	S. Garvey, LA	111	J. Morgan, CIN	58
S. Garvey, LA	301	J. Wynn, LA	108	C. Cedeno, HOU	57
A. Oliver, PIT	293	T. Simmons, STL	103	L. Lintz, MON	50

PITCHING LEADERS

Winning Percentage		Earned Run Average		Wins	
A. Messersmith, LA	.769	B. Capra, ATL	2.28	A. Messersmith, LA	20
D. Sutton, LA	.679	P. Niekro, ATL	2.38	P. Niekro, ATL	20
B. Capra, ATL	.667	J. Matlack, NY	2.41	J. Billingham, CIN	19
M. Torrez, MON	.652	M. Marshall, LA	2.42	D. Sutton, LA	19
J. Billingham, CIN	.633	A. Messersmith, LA	2.59	D. Gullett, CIN	17
				J. Lonborg, PHI	17

Saves		Strikeouts		Complete Games	
M. Marshall, LA	21	S. Carlton, PHI	240	P. Niekro, ATL	18
R. Moffitt, SF	15	A. Messersmith, LA	221	S. Carlton, PHI	17
P. Borbon, CIN	14	T. Seaver, NY	201	J. Lonborg, PHI	16
D. Giusti, PIT	12	J. Matlack, NY	195	J. Rooker, PIT	15
C. Taylor, MON	11	P. Niekro, ATL	195	J. Matlack, NY	14
T. House, ATL	11			J. Reuss, PIT	14

NATIONAL LEAGUE 1974, *cont.*

BATTING AND BASE RUNNING LEADERS

Hits

R. Garr, ATL	214
D. Cash, PHI	206
S. Garvey, LA	200
A. Oliver, PIT	198

Base on Balls

D. Evans, ATL	126
J. Morgan, CIN	120
J. Wynn, LA	108
M. Schmidt, PHI	106
P. Rose, CIN	106

Home Run Percentage

M. Schmidt, PHI	6.3
J. Wynn, LA	6.0
J. Bench, CIN	5.3
W. Stargell, PIT	4.9

Runs

P. Rose, CIN	110
M. Schmidt, PHI	108
J. Bench, CIN	108
J. Morgan, CIN	107

Doubles

P. Rose, CIN	45
A. Oliver, PIT	38
J. Bench, CIN	38
W. Stargell, PIT	37

Triples

R. Garr, ATL	17
A. Oliver, PIT	12
D. Cash, PHI	11
R. Metzger, HOU	10
L. Bowa, PHI	10

PITCHING LEADERS

Fewest Hits/9 Innings

B. Capra, ATL	6.76
A. Messersmith, LA	7.00
P. Niekro, ATL	7.42
D. Gullett, CIN	7.44

Shutouts

J. Matlack, NY	7
P. Niekro, ATL	6

Fewest Walks/9 Innings

J. Barr, SF	1.76
R. Reed, ATL	1.98
D. Ellis, PIT	2.08
J. Lonborg, PHI	2.23

Most Strikeouts/9 Inn.

T. Seaver, NY	7.67
S. Carlton, PHI	7.42
B. Bonham, CHI	7.07
J. D'Acquisto, SF	6.99

Innings

P. Niekro, ATL	302
A. Messersmith, LA	292
S. Carlton, PHI	291
J. Lonborg, PHI	283

Games Pitched

M. Marshall, LA	106
L. Hardy, SD	76
P. Borbon, CIN	73
K. Forsch, HOU	70

		W	L	PCT	GB	R	OR	Batting 2B	3B	HR	BA	SA	SB	Fielding E	DP	FA	Pitching CG	BB	SO	ShO	SV	ERA
East	Pittsburgh	88	74	.543		751	657	238	46	114	**.274**	.391	55	162	154	.975	**51**	543	721	9	17	3.49
	St. Louis	86	75	.534	1.5	677	643	216	46	83	.265	.365	**172**	147	**192**	.977	37	616	794	13	20	3.48
	Philadelphia	80	82	.494	8	676	701	233	**50**	95	.261	.373	115	148	168	.976	46	682	892	4	19	3.92
	Montreal	79	82	.491	8.5	662	657	201	29	86	.254	.350	124	153	157	.976	35	544	822	8	**27**	3.60
	New York	71	91	.438	17	572	646	183	22	96	.235	.329	43	158	150	.975	46	504	908	15	14	3.42
	Chicago	66	96	.407	22	669	826	221	42	110	.251	.365	78	199	141	.969	23	576	895	6	26	4.28
West	Los Angeles	102	60	.630		**798**	**561**	231	34	**139**	.272	**.401**	149	157	122	.975	33	**464**	**943**	19	23	**2.97**
	Cincinnati	98	64	.605	4	776	631	**271**	35	135	.260	.394	146	134	151	.979	34	536	875	11	**27**	3.42
	Atlanta	88	74	.543	14	661	563	202	37	120	.249	.363	72	132	161	.979	46	488	772	**21**	22	3.05
	Houston	81	81	.500	21	653	632	222	41	110	.263	.378	108	**113**	161	**.982**	36	601	738	18	18	3.48
	San Francisco	72	90	.444	30	634	723	228	38	93	.252	.358	107	175	153	.972	27	559	756	11	25	3.80
	San Diego	60	102	.370	42	541	830	196	27	99	.229	.330	85	170	126	.973	25	715	855	7	19	4.61
						8070	8070	2642	447	1280	.255	.366	1254	1848	1836	.976	439	6828	9971	142	257	3.63

AMERICAN LEAGUE 1974

East

Baltimore

W-91 L-71

Earl Weaver

POS	Player	AB	BA	HR	RBI	PO	A	E	DP	TC/G	FA	Pitcher	G	IP	W	L	SV	ERA
1B	B. Powell	344	.265	12	45	866	61	4	102	9.1	.996	R. Grimsley	40	296	18	13	1	3.07
2B	B. Grich	582	.263	19	82	**484**	**453**	20	**132**	**6.0**	.979	M. Cuellar	38	269	22	10	0	3.11
SS	M. Belanger	493	.225	5	36	243	**552**	13	100	**5.2**	**.984**	D. McNally	39	259	16	10	1	3.58
3B	B. Robinson	553	.288	7	59	115	**410**	18	**44**	**3.5**	.967	J. Palmer	26	179	7	12	0	3.27
RF	R. Coggins	411	.243	4	32	238	3	4	1	2.3	.984	D. Alexander	30	114	6	9	0	4.03
CF	P. Blair	552	.261	17	62	447	7	7	2	3.1	.985	W. Garland	20	91	5	5	1	2.97
LF	D. Baylor	489	.272	10	59	218	1	5	0	1.7	.978	B. Reynolds	54	69	7	5	7	2.74
C	E. Williams	413	.254	14	52	308	33	6	5	4.6	.983	G. Jackson	49	67	6	4	12	2.55
DH	T. Davis	626	.289	11	84													
OF	A. Bumbry	270	.233	1	19	115	7	6	0	1.9	.953							
OF	J. Fuller	189	.222	7	28	116	3	5	1	2.1	.960							
C	A. Etchebarren	180	.222	2	15	269	19	7	3	4.9	.976							
UT	E. Cabell	174	.241	3	17	223	45	4	18		.985							

New York

W-89 L-73

Bill Virdon

POS	Player	AB	BA	HR	RBI	PO	A	E	DP	TC/G	FA	Pitcher	G	IP	W	L	SV	ERA
1B	C. Chambliss	400	.242	6	43	873	78	8	93	9.0	.992	P. Dobson	39	281	19	15	0	3.07
2B	S. Alomar	279	.269	1	27	140	136	9	37	3.8	.968	D. Medich	38	280	19	15	0	3.60
SS	J. Mason	440	.250	5	37	241	430	25	87	4.6	.964	D. Tidrow	33	191	11	9	1	3.86
3B	G. Nettles	566	.246	22	75	**147**	377	21	29	3.5	.961	R. May	17	114	8	4	0	2.29
RF	B. Murcer	606	.274	10	88	297	21	7	2	2.1	.978	S. Lyle	66	114	9	3	15	1.66
CF	E. Maddox	466	.303	3	45	334	18	5	4	2.6	.986	M. Stottlemyre	16	113	6	7	0	3.58
LF	L. Piniella	518	.305	9	70	265	16	3	0	2.2	.989	C. Upshaw	36	60	1	5	6	3.00
C	T. Munson	517	.261	13	60	743	**75**	**22**	10	6.1	.974							
DH	R. Blomberg	264	.311	10	48													
OD	R. White	473	.275	7	43	141	2	1	1		.993							
D1	B. Sudakis	259	.232	7	39	277	23	3	31		.990							
2S	G. Michael	177	.260	0	13	121	169	9	40		.970							

Boston

W-84 L-78

Darrell Johnson

POS	Player	AB	BA	HR	RBI	PO	A	E	DP	TC/G	FA	Pitcher	G	IP	W	L	SV	ERA
1B	C. Cooper	414	.275	8	43	637	40	12	66	9.3	.983	L. Tiant	38	311	22	13	0	2.92
2B	D. Griffin	312	.266	0	33	178	242	9	53	4.7	.979	B. Lee	38	282	17	15	0	3.51
SS	M. Guerrero	284	.246	0	23	136	266	13	50	4.5	.969	R. Cleveland	41	221	12	14	0	4.32
3B	R. Petrocelli	454	.267	15	76	83	219	12	23	2.7	.962	D. Drago	33	176	7	10	3	3.48
RF	D. Evans	463	.281	10	70	294	8	3	2	2.5	.990	R. Moret	31	173	9	10	2	3.75
CF	J. Beniquez	389	.267	5	33	264	4	6	2	2.8	.978	D. Segui	58	108	6	8	10	4.00
LF	C. Yastrzemski	515	.301	15	79	99	2	4	1	1.7	.962							
C	B. Montgomery	254	.252	4	38	318	28	8	3	4.5	.977							
DH	T. Harper	443	.237	5	24													
SS	R. Burleson	384	.284	4	44	142	249	18	41	4.6	.956							
OF	B. Carbo	338	.249	12	61	164	5	1	1	2.0	.994							
OF	R. Miller	280	.261	5	22	253	7	3	3	2.5	.989							
23	D. McAuliffe	272	.210	5	24	150	177	11	37		.967							
C	C. Fisk	187	.299	11	26	267	26	6	2	6.0	.980							
1D	D. Cater	126	.246	5	20	126	10	0	9		1.000							

AMERICAN LEAGUE 1974, *cont.*

Cleveland

W-77 L-85

Ken Aspromonte

POS	Player	AB	BA	HR	RBI	PO	A	E	DP	TC/G	FA	Pitcher	G	IP	W	L	SV	ERA
1B	J. Ellis	477	.285	10	64	667	37	6	57	10.3	.992	G. Perry	37	322	21	13	0	2.52
2B	J. Brohamer	315	.270	2	30	203	269	6	67	4.8	.987	J. Perry	36	252	17	12	0	2.96
SS	F. Duffy	549	.233	8	48	242	491	15	83	4.7	.980	F. Peterson	29	153	9	14	0	4.35
3B	B. Bell	423	.262	7	46	112	274	15	31	3.5	.963	D. Bosman	25	127	7	5	0	4.11
RF	C. Spikes	568	.271	22	80	284	16	10	3	2.0	.968	T. Buskey	51	93	2	6	17	3.19
CF	G. Hendrick	495	.279	19	67	355	9	4	2	2.8	.989	F. Beene	32	73	4	4	2	4.93
LF	J. Lowenstein	508	.242	8	48	200	6	3	1	2.1	.986	S. Kline	16	71	3	8	0	5.07
C	D. Duncan	425	.200	16	46	557	47	15	7	4.6	.976	T. Hilgendorf	35	48	4	3	3	4.88
DH	O. Gamble	454	.291	19	59													
OF	L. Lee	232	.233	5	25	131	5	6	1	2.3	.958							

Milwaukee

W-76 L-86

Del Crandall

POS	Player	AB	BA	HR	RBI	PO	A	E	DP	TC/G	FA	Pitcher	G	IP	W	L	SV	ERA
1B	G. Scott	604	.281	17	82	**1345**	**114**	12	**137**	**9.9**	**.992**	J. Slaton	40	250	13	16	0	3.92
2B	P. Garcia	452	.199	12	54	382	365	23	102	5.5	.970	C. Wright	38	232	9	20	0	4.42
SS	R. Yount	344	.250	3	26	148	327	19	55	4.6	.962	J. Colborn	33	224	10	13	0	4.06
3B	D. Money	**629**	.283	15	65	131	336	5	42	3.0	**.989**	K. Kobel	34	169	6	14	0	3.99
RF	D. May	477	.226	10	42	249	10	3	2	2.2	.989	B. Champion	31	162	11	4	0	3.61
CF	B. Coluccio	394	.223	6	31	346	10	4	2	2.7	.989	T. Murphy	70	123	10	10	20	1.90
LF	J. Briggs	554	.253	17	73	309	10	9	2	2.2	.973	E. Rodriguez	43	112	7	4	4	3.62
C	D. Porter	432	.241	12	56	484	60	12	8	4.8	.978							
DH	B. Mitchell	173	.243	5	20													
OF	K. Berry	267	.240	1	24	187	8	1	1	2.4	.995							
S2	T. Johnson	245	.245	0	25	138	230	9	51		.976							
C	C. Moore	204	.245	0	19	229	28	4	5	4.3	.985							
UT	M. Hegan	190	.237	7	32	136	5	1	12		.993							

Detroit

W-72 L-90

Ralph Houk

POS	Player	AB	BA	HR	RBI	PO	A	E	DP	TC/G	FA	Pitcher	G	IP	W	L	SV	ERA
1B	B. Freehan	445	.297	18	60	590	36	4	49	9.7	.994	M. Lolich	41	308	16	**21**	0	4.15
2B	G. Sutherland	619	.254	5	49	337	360	17	101	4.9	.976	J. Coleman	41	286	14	12	0	4.31
SS	E. Brinkman	502	.221	14	54	237	493	21	88	5.0	.972	J. LaGrow	37	216	8	19	0	4.67
3B	A. Rodriguez	571	.222	5	49	132	389	21	40	3.4	.961	J. Hiller	59	150	17	14	13	2.64
RF	J. Northrup	376	.237	11	42	209	5	6	0	2.3	.973	W. Fryman	27	142	6	9	0	4.31
CF	M. Stanley	394	.221	8	34	252	4	2	2	2.8	.992	L. Walker	28	92	5	5	0	4.99
LF	W. Horton	238	.298	15	47	106	2	6	0	1.8	.947							
C	G. Moses	198	.237	4	19	377	26	6	6	5.5	.985							
DH	A. Kaline	558	.262	13	64													
OF	R. LeFlore	254	.260	2	13	151	8	**11**	3	2.9	.935							
OF	B. Oglivie	252	.270	4	29	87	3	5	0	1.5	.947							

West

Oakland

W-90 L-72

Alvin Dark

POS	Player	AB	BA	HR	RBI	PO	A	E	DP	TC/G	FA	Pitcher	G	IP	W	L	SV	ERA
1B	G. Tenace	484	.211	26	73	816	41	4	80	8.1	.995	C. Hunter	41	318	**25**	12	0	**2.49**
2B	D. Green	287	.213	2	22	233	243	8	67	4.8	.983	V. Blue	40	282	17	15	0	3.26
SS	B. Campaneris	527	.290	2	41	207	423	22	76	4.9	.966	K. Holtzman	39	255	19	17	0	3.07
3B	S. Bando	498	.243	22	103	113	287	23	28	3.0	.946	R. Fingers	**76**	119	9	5	18	2.65
RF	R. Jackson	506	.289	29	93	296	8	10	2	2.5	.968	D. Hamilton	29	117	7	4	0	3.15
CF	B. North	543	.260	4	33	437	9	4	2	3.3	.991	P. Lindblad	45	101	4	4	6	2.05
LF	J. Rudi	593	.293	22	99	234	7	4	0	1.8	.984	G. Abbott	19	96	5	7	0	3.00
C	L. Haney	121	.165	2	3	218	18	2	1	3.3	.992							
DH	J. Alou	220	.268	2	15													
OD	A. Mangual	365	.233	9	43	142	5	6	0		.961							
DO	C. Washington	221	.285	0	19	63	2	1	0		.985							
UT	T. Kubiak	220	.209	0	18	129	175	6	38		.981							
C	R. Fosse	204	.196	4	23	299	28	9	6	4.9	.973							
1D	D. Johnson	174	.195	7	23	211	9	2	15		.991							

Texas

W-84 L-76

Billy Martin

POS	Player	AB	BA	HR	RBI	PO	A	E	DP	TC/G	FA	Pitcher	G	IP	W	L	SV	ERA
1B	M. Hargrove	415	.323	4	66	631	72	9	57	7.8	.987	F. Jenkins	41	328	**25**	12	0	2.83
2B	D. Nelson	474	.236	3	42	295	337	20	74	5.4	.969	J. Bibby	41	264	19	19	0	4.74
SS	T. Harrah	573	.260	21	74	**281**	466	**29**	98	4.9	.963	J. Brown	35	217	13	12	0	3.57
3B	L. Randle	520	.302	1	49	92	167	18	23	3.1	.935	S. Hargan	37	187	12	9	0	3.95
RF	J. Burroughs	554	.301	25	**118**	231	10	7	5	1.7	.972	S. Foucault	69	144	8	9	12	2.25
CF	J. Lovitto	283	.223	2	26	201	7	6	1	2.0	.972	D. Clyde	28	117	3	9	0	4.38
LF	C. Tovar	562	.292	4	58	331	13	7	3	2.6	.980							
C	J. Sundberg	368	.247	3	36	722	69	8	**15**	6.1	.990							
DH	J. Spencer	352	.278	7	44													
OF	A. Johnson	453	.291	4	41	168	6	8	2	2.2	.956							
DO	T. Grieve	259	.255	9	32	62	5	0	1		1.000							
13	J. Fregosi	230	.261	12	34	331	73	5	35		.988							

Minnesota

W-82 L-80

Frank Quilici

POS	Player	AB	BA	HR	RBI	PO	A	E	DP	TC/G	FA	Pitcher	G	IP	W	L	SV	ERA
1B	C. Kusick	201	.239	8	26	479	42	2	45	7.0	.996	B. Blyleven	37	281	17	17	0	2.66
2B	R. Carew	599	**.364**	3	55	375	416	**33**	114	5.6	.960	J. Decker	37	249	16	14	0	3.29
SS	D. Thompson	264	.250	4	25	127	183	12	39	3.7	.963	D. Goltz	28	174	10	10	1	3.26
3B	E. Soderholm	464	.276	10	51	100	273	17	19	3.0	.956	V. Albury	32	164	8	9	0	4.12
RF	B. Darwin	575	.264	25	94	254	8	8	1	1.9	.970	B. Campbell	63	120	8	7	19	2.63
CF	S. Brye	488	.283	2	41	301	10	1	2	2.4	.997	B. Hands	35	115	4	5	3	4.46
LF	L. Hisle	510	.286	19	79	279	4	6	1	2.1	.979	R. Corbin	29	112	7	6	0	5.30
C	G. Borgmann	345	.252	3	45	652	52	2	4	5.5	**.997**	B. Butler	26	99	4	6	1	4.09
DH	T. Oliva	459	.285	13	57							T. Burgmeier	50	92	5	3	4	4.52
OF	S. Braun	453	.280	8	40	180	10	7	2	1.8	.964							
D1	H. Killebrew	333	.222	13	54	218	21	2	21		.992							
UT	J. Terrell	229	.245	0	19	114	179	9	35		.970							
1B	J. Holt	197	.254	0	16	449	43	2	57	7.4	.996							
SS	L. Gomez	168	.208	0	3	97	190	12	37	4.0	.960							

AMERICAN LEAGUE 1974, *cont.*

Chicago

W-80 L-80

Chuck Tanner

POS	Player	AB	BA	HR	RBI	PO	A	E	DP	TC/G	FA	Pitcher	G	IP	W	L	SV	ERA
1B	D. Allen	462	.301	**32**	88	998	49	**15**	112	8.5	.986	W. Wood	42	320	20	19	0	3.60
2B	J. Orta	525	.316	10	67	297	313	18	93	5.1	.971	J. Kaat	42	277	21	13	0	2.92
SS	B. Dent	496	.274	5	45	251	499	22	**108**	5.0	.972	S. Bahnsen	38	216	12	15	0	4.71
3B	B. Melton	495	.242	21	63	100	272	**24**	29	3.2	.939	T. Forster	59	134	7	8	**24**	3.63
RF	B. Sharp	320	.253	4	24	210	3	3	0	2.2	.986	B. Johnson	18	122	10	4	0	2.73
CF	K. Henderson	602	.292	20	95	462	7	6	3	2.9	.987	S. Pitlock	40	106	3	3	1	4.42
LF	C. May	551	.249	8	58	245	11	3	1	2.0	.988	G. Gossage	39	89	4	6	1	4.15
C	E. Herrmann	367	.259	10	39	561	55	8	8	5.8	.987							
DH	P. Kelly	424	.281	4	21													
UT	R. Santo	375	.221	5	41	135	148	8	49		.973							
CO	B. Downing	293	.225	10	39	337	30	2	5		.995							
1B	T. Muser	206	.291	1	18	419	13	1	46	5.4	.998							

Kansas City

W-77 L-85

Jack McKeon

POS	Player	AB	BA	HR	RBI	PO	A	E	DP	TC/G	FA	Pitcher	G	IP	W	L	SV	ERA
1B	J. Mayberry	427	.234	22	69	963	61	10	101	9.8	.990	S. Busby	38	292	22	14	0	3.39
2B	C. Rojas	542	.271	6	60	292	368	9	94	4.7	**.987**	P. Splittorff	36	226	13	19	0	4.10
SS	F. Patek	537	.225	3	38	250	493	25	**108**	5.2	.967	A. Fitzmorris	34	190	13	6	1	2.79
3B	G. Brett	457	.282	2	47	102	279	21	16	3.0	.948	B. Dal Canton	31	175	8	10	0	3.14
RF	V. Pinson	406	.276	6	41	188	9	4	2	1.8	.980	M. Pattin	25	117	3	7	0	4.00
CF	A. Otis	552	.284	12	73	425	8	6	3	3.1	.986	L. McDaniel	38	107	1	4	1	3.45
LF	J. Wohlford	501	.271	2	44	273	7	5	4	2.1	.982	N. Briles	18	103	5	7	0	4.02
C	F. Healy	445	.252	9	53	620	64	16	4	5.1	.977	D. Bird	55	92	7	6	10	2.74
DH	H. McRae	539	.310	15	88													
OF	A. Cowens	269	.242	1	25	151	13	2	2	1.6	.988							
1B	T. Solaita	239	.268	7	30	508	40	5	36	8.5	.991							
UT	F. White	204	.221	1	18	119	189	12	40		.962							

California

W-68 L-94

Bobby Winkles
W-30 L-44

Whitey Herzog
W-2 L-2

Dick Williams
W-36 L-48

POS	Player	AB	BA	HR	RBI	PO	A	E	DP	TC/G	FA	Pitcher	G	IP	W	L	SV	ERA
1B	J. Doherty	223	.256	3	15	538	30	5	55	8.2	.991	N. Ryan	42	**333**	22	16	0	2.89
2B	D. Doyle	511	.260	1	34	311	404	12	99	5.0	.983	F. Tanana	39	269	14	19	0	3.11
SS	D. Chalk	465	.252	5	31	168	269	**29**	55	4.7	.938	A. Hassler	23	162	7	11	1	2.61
3B	P. Schaal	165	.248	2	20	24	78	11	9	2.2	.903	D. Lange	21	114	3	8	0	3.79
RF	L. Stanton	415	.267	11	62	226	11	6	0	2.1	.975	B. Singer	14	109	7	4	0	2.97
CF	M. Rivers	466	.285	3	31	309	9	2	3	2.8	.994	E. Figueroa	25	105	2	8	0	3.69
LF	J. Lahoud	325	.271	13	44	156	6	4	2	1.6	.976							
C	E. Rodriguez	395	.253	7	36	**782**	**75**	7	7	**6.3**	.992							
DH	F. Robinson	427	.251	20	63													
UT	B. Valentine	371	.261	3	39	160	116	17	10		.942							
13	B. Oliver	359	.248	8	55	400	83	12	46		.976							
01	B. Bochte	196	.270	5	26	248	9	5	16		.981							
OF	M. Nettles	175	.274	0	8	99	0	1	0	1.9	.990							

BATTING AND BASE RUNNING LEADERS

Batting Average

R. Carew, MIN	.364
J. Orta, CHI	.316
H. McRae, KC	.310
L. Piniella, NY	.305
E. Maddox, NY	.303

Slugging Average

D. Allen, CHI	.563
R. Jackson, OAK	.514
J. Burroughs, TEX	.504
J. Rudi, OAK	.484
B. Freehan, DET	.479

Home Runs

D. Allen, CHI	32
R. Jackson, OAK	29
G. Tenace, OAK	26
J. Burroughs, TEX	25
B. Darwin, MIN	25

Total Bases

J. Rudi, OAK	287
K. Henderson, CHI	281
J. Burroughs, TEX	279
R. Carew, MIN	267
G. Scott, MIL	261
D. Money, MIL	261

Runs Batted In

J. Burroughs, TEX	118
S. Bando, OAK	103
J. Rudi, OAK	99
K. Henderson, CHI	95
B. Darwin, MIN	94

Stolen Bases

B. North, OAK	54
R. Carew, MIN	38
J. Lowenstein, CLE	36
B. Campaneris, OAK	34
F. Patek, KC	33

Hits

R. Carew, MIN	218
T. Davis, BAL	181
D. Money, MIL	178
K. Henderson, CHI	176

Base on Balls

G. Tenace, OAK	110
C. Yastrzemski, BOS	104
J. Burroughs, TEX	91
B. Grich, BAL	90

Home Run Percentage

D. Allen, CHI	6.9
R. Jackson, OAK	5.7
G. Tenace, OAK	5.4
J. Mayberry, KC	5.2

Runs

C. Yastrzemski, BOS	93
B. Grich, BAL	92
R. Jackson, OAK	90
A. Otis, KC	87

Doubles

J. Rudi, OAK	39
H. McRae, KC	36
G. Scott, MIL	36
K. Henderson, CHI	35

Triples

M. Rivers, CAL	11
A. Otis, KC	9

PITCHING LEADERS

Winning Percentage

M. Cuellar, BAL	.688
F. Jenkins, TEX	.676
C. Hunter, OAK	.676
L. Tiant, BOS	.629
G. Perry, CLE	.618
J. Kaat, CHI	.618

Earned Run Average

C. Hunter, OAK	2.49
G. Perry, CLE	2.52
A. Hassler, CAL	2.61
B. Blyleven, MIN	2.66
A. Fitzmorris, KC	2.79

Wins

C. Hunter, OAK	25
F. Jenkins, TEX	25
M. Cuellar, BAL	22
S. Busby, KC	22
L. Tiant, BOS	22
N. Ryan, CAL	22

Saves

T. Forster, CHI	24
T. Murphy, MIL	20
B. Campbell, MIN	19
T. Buskey, NY, CLE	18
R. Fingers, OAK	18

Strikeouts

N. Ryan, CAL	367
B. Blyleven, MIN	249
F. Jenkins, TEX	225
G. Perry, CLE	216
M. Lolich, DET	202

Complete Games

F. Jenkins, TEX	29
G. Perry, CLE	28
M. Lolich, DET	27
N. Ryan, CAL	26
L. Tiant, BOS	25

Fewest Hits/9 Innings

N. Ryan, CAL	5.97
G. Perry, CLE	6.43
B. Dal Canton, KC	6.94
A. Hassler, CAL	7.33

Shutouts

L. Tiant, BOS	7
C. Hunter, OAK	6
F. Jenkins, TEX	6
M. Cuellar, BAL	5
J. Bibby, TEX	5

Fewest Walks/9 Innings

F. Jenkins, TEX	1.23
C. Hunter, OAK	1.30
K. Holtzman, OAK	1.80
J. Kaat, CHI	2.05

Most Strikeouts/9 Inn.

N. Ryan, CAL	9.92
B. Blyleven, MIN	7.98
F. Jenkins, TEX	6.17
S. Busby, KC	6.10

Innings

N. Ryan, CAL	333
F. Jenkins, TEX	328
G. Perry, CLE	322
W. Wood, CHI	320

Games Pitched

R. Fingers, OAK	76
T. Murphy, MIL	70
S. Foucault, TEX	69
S. Lyle, NY	66

AMERICAN LEAGUE 1974, *cont.*

		W	L	PCT	GB	R	OR	Batting 2B	3B	HR	BA	SA	SB	Fielding E	DP	FA	Pitching CG	BB	SO	ShO	SV	ERA
East	Baltimore	91	71	.562		659	612	226	27	116	.256	.370	145	128	174	**.980**	57	480	701	**16**	25	3.27
	New York	89	73	.549	2	671	623	220	30	101	.263	.368	53	142	158	.977	53	528	829	13	24	3.32
	Boston	84	78	.519	7	**696**	661	**236**	31	109	.264	.377	104	145	156	.977	**71**	463	751	12	18	3.72
	Cleveland	77	85	.475	14	662	694	201	19	131	.255	.370	79	146	157	.977	45	479	650	8	27	3.80
	Milwaukee	76	86	.469	15	647	660	228	**49**	120	.244	.369	106	**127**	168	**.980**	43	493	621	11	24	3.77
	Detroit	72	90	.444	19	620	768	200	35	131	.247	.366	67	158	155	.975	54	621	869	7	15	4.17
West	Oakland	90	72	.556		689	**551**	205	37	132	.247	.373	**164**	141	154	.977	49	**430**	755	12	28	**2.95**
	Texas	84	76	.525	5	690	698	198	39	99	**.272**	.377	113	163	164	.974	62	449	871	**16**	12	3.82
	Minnesota	82	80	.506	8	673	669	190	37	111	**.272**	.378	74	151	164	.976	43	513	934	11	**29**	3.64
	Chicago	80	80	.500	9	684	721	225	23	**135**	.268	**.389**	64	147	**188**	.977	55	548	826	11	**29**	3.94
	Kansas City	77	85	.475	13	667	662	232	42	89	.259	.364	146	152	166	.976	54	482	731	14	17	3.51
	California	68	94	.420	22	618	657	203	31	95	.254	.356	119	147	150	.977	64	649	**986**	13	12	3.52
						7976	7976	2564	400	1369	.258	.371	1234	1747	1954	.977	650	6135	9524	144	260	3.62

NATIONAL LEAGUE 1975

		POS	Player	AB	BA	HR	RBI	PO	A	E	DP	TC/G	FA	Pitcher	G	IP	W	L	SV	ERA
East	Pittsburgh	1B	W. Stargell	461	.295	22	90	1121	54	10	112	9.7	.992	J. Reuss	32	237	18	11	0	2.54
		2B	R. Stennett	616	.286	7	62	379	463	18	98	6.0	.979	J. Rooker	28	197	13	11	0	2.97
		SS	F. Taveras	378	.212	0	23	200	369	28	74	4.5	.953	B. Kison	33	192	12	11	0	3.23
	W-92 L-69	3B	R. Hebner	472	.246	15	57	86	244	19	17	2.8	.946	D. Ellis	27	140	8	9	0	3.79
		RF	D. Parker	558	.308	25	101	311	7	9	2	2.3	.972	J. Candelaria	18	121	8	6	0	2.75
	Danny Murtaugh	CF	A. Oliver	628	.280	18	84	380	5	5	3	2.5	.987	K. Brett	23	118	9	5	0	3.36
		LF	R. Zisk	504	.290	20	75	264	7	7	1	2.0	.975	L. Demery	45	115	7	5	4	2.90
		C	M. Sanguillen	481	.328	9	58	650	53	9	4	5.4	.987	D. Giusti	61	92	5	4	17	2.93
		OF	B. Robinson	200	.280	6	33	107	3	1	1	1.9	.991	R. Hernandez	46	64	7	2	5	2.95
	Philadelphia	1B	D. Allen	416	.233	12	62	900	70	**18**	79	8.7	.982	S. Carlton	37	255	15	14	0	3.56
		2B	D. Cash	**699**	.305	4	57	**400**	481	17	**126**	5.5	.981	T. Underwood	35	219	14	13	0	4.15
		SS	L. Bowa	583	.305	2	38	227	403	25	82	4.9	.962	L. Christenson	29	172	11	6	1	3.66
	W-86 L-76	3B	M. Schmidt	562	.249	**38**	95	132	368	24	30	3.5	.954	J. Lonborg	27	159	8	6	0	4.13
		RF	M. Anderson	247	.259	4	28	161	6	4	0	1.6	.977	W. Twitchell	36	134	5	10	0	4.43
	Danny Ozark	CF	G. Maddox	374	.291	4	46	288	10	5	4	3.1	.983	G. Garber	**71**	110	10	12	14	3.60
		LF	G. Luzinski	596	.300	34	**120**	248	10	9	0	1.7	.966	T. McGraw	56	103	9	6	14	2.97
		C	B. Boone	289	.246	2	20	456	44	5	7	5.5	.990	T. Hilgendorf	53	97	7	3	0	2.13
		OF	J. Johnstone	350	.329	7	54	152	10	4	3	1.6	.976							
		C	J. Oates	269	.286	1	25	429	44	5	10*	5.8	.990							
		1B	T. Hutton	165	.248	3	24	307	32	2	37	4.8	.994							
		OF	O. Brown	145	.303	6	26	67	0	0	0	1.8	1.000							
	New York	1B	E. Kranepool	325	.323	4	43	666	46	2	51	8.7	.997	T. Seaver	36	280	**22**	9	0	2.38
		2B	F. Millan	676	.283	1	56	379	420	23	95	5.1	.972	J. Koosman	36	240	14	13	2	3.41
		SS	M. Phillips	383	.256	1	28	185	334	31*	52	4.8	.944	J. Matlack	33	229	16	12	0	3.38
	W-82 L-80	3B	W. Garrett	274	.266	6	34	64	160	8	24	2.5	.966	R. Tate	26	138	5	13	0	4.43
		RF	R. Staub	574	.282	19	105	267	15	4	3	1.9	.986	H. Webb	29	115	7	6	0	4.07
	Yogi Berra	CF	D. Unser	531	.294	10	53	362	13	5	2	2.6	.987	R. Baldwin	54	97	3	5	6	3.34
	W-56 L-53	LF	D. Kingman	502	.231	36	88	134	3	6	0	2.0	.958	B. Apodaca	46	85	3	4	13	1.48
		C	J. Grote	386	.295	2	39	706	55	4	8	**6.9**	**.995**							
	Roy McMillan	3B	J. Torre	361	.247	6	35	61	148	11	14	2.7	.950							
	W-26 L-27	01	J. Milner	220	.191	7	29	267	27	3	21		.990							
		OF	G. Clines	203	.227	0	10	98	9	2	2	1.8	.982							
		C	J. Stearns	169	.189	3	10	297	40	2	9	6.3	.994							
		OF	M. Vail	162	.302	3	17	92	9	3	1	2.9	.971							
	St. Louis	1B	R. Smith	477	.302	19	76	524	33	10	51	8.6	.982	L. McGlothen	35	239	15	13	0	3.92
		2B	T. Sizemore	562	.240	3	49	329	405	21	82	4.9	.972	B. Forsch	34	230	15	10	0	2.86
		SS	M. Tyson	368	.266	2	37	154	246	12	44	4.3	.971	R. Reed	24	176	9	8	0	3.23
	W-82 L-80	3B	K. Reitz	592	.269	5	63	124	279	23	21	2.7	.946	J. Curtis	39	147	8	9	1	3.43
		RF	B. McBride	413	.300	5	36	289	4	3	1	2.8	.990	J. Denny	25	136	10	7	0	3.97
	Red Schoendienst	CF	W. Davis	350	.291	6	50	187	5	6	2	2.2	.970	B. Gibson	22	109	3	10	2	5.04
		LF	L. Brock	528	.309	3	47	247	5	9	0	2.0	.966	A. Hrabosky	65	97	13	3	**22**	1.67
		C	T. Simmons	581	.332	18	100	803	62	**15**	5	5.7	.983	E. Rasmussen	14	81	5	5	0	3.78
		OF	L. Melendez	291	.265	2	27	169	3	3	1	2.0	.983	M. Garman	66	79	3	8	10	2.39
		1B	R. Fairly	229	.301	7	37	351	33	8	33	7.0	.980							
		1B	K. Hernandez	188	.250	3	20	469	36	2	34	9.1	.996							
		SS	M. Guerrero	184	.239	0	11	76	198	13	29	4.5	.955							
	Chicago	1B	A. Thornton	372	.293	18	60	982	77	13	88	9.5	.988	R. Burris	36	238	15	10	0	4.12
		2B	M. Trillo	545	.248	7	70	350	**509**	**29**	103	5.8	.967	R. Reuschel	38	234	11	**17**	1	3.73
		SS	D. Kessinger	601	.243	0	46	205	436	22	100	4.7	.967	B. Bonham	38	229	13	15	0	4.72
	W-75 L-87	3B	B. Madlock	514	**.354**	7	64	79	250	20	14	2.7	.943	S. Stone	33	214	12	8	0	3.95
		RF	J. Cardenal	574	.317	9	68	313	14	8	3	2.2	.976	D. Knowles	58	88	6	9	15	5.83
	Jim Marshall	CF	R. Monday	491	.267	17	60	315	6	9	0	2.5	.973	O. Zamora	52	71	5	2	10	5.07
		LF	J. Morales	578	.270	12	91	273	11	6	1	1.9	.979	G. Zahn	16	63	2	7	1	4.45
		C	S. Swisher	254	.213	1	22	426	36	10	5	5.1	.979							
		10	P. LaCock	249	.229	6	30	479	45	6	39		.989							
		C	G. Mitterwald	200	.220	5	26	247	32	7	4	4.8	.976							
		C	T. Hosley	141	.255	6	20	254	16	9	3	5.3	.968							

NATIONAL LEAGUE 1975, *cont.*

Montreal

W-75 L-87

Gene Mauch

POS	Player	AB	BA	HR	RBI	PO	A	E	DP	TC/G	FA	Pitcher	G	IP	W	L	SV	ERA
1B	M. Jorgensen	445	.261	18	67	1150	91	7	123	9.4	.994	S. Rogers	35	252	11	12	0	3.29
2B	P. Mackanin	448	.225	12	44	300	410	25	100	5.8	.966	S. Renko	31	170	6	12	1	4.08
SS	T. Foli	572	.238	1	29	**260**	**497**	21	**104**	5.2	.973	D. Warthen	40	168	8	6	3	3.11
3B	L. Parrish	532	.274	10	65	105	291	35	33	3.0	.919	D. Blair	30	163	8	15	0	3.81
RF	L. Biittner	346	.315	3	28	166	8	5	0	1.9	.972	W. Fryman	38	157	9	12	3	3.32
CF	P. Mangual	514	.245	9	45	308	8	9	2	2.4	.972	D. Murray	63	111	15	8	9	3.97
LF	G. Carter	503	.270	17	68	150	1	4	1	1.7	.974	D. Carrithers	19	101	5	3	0	3.30
C	B. Foote	387	.194	7	30	590	50	10	**10**	5.7	.985	D. DeMola	60	98	4	7	1	4.13
OF	B. Bailey	227	.273	5	30	88	4	2	1	1.5	.979	C. Taylor	54	74	2	2	6	3.53
OF	J. Dwyer	175	.286	3	20	86	8	4	1	1.9	.959							
1B	J. Morales	163	.301	2	24	201	26	4	19	8.6	.983							

West

Cincinnati

W-108 L-54

Sparky Anderson

POS	Player	AB	BA	HR	RBI	PO	A	E	DP	TC/G	FA	Pitcher	G	IP	W	L	SV	ERA
1B	T. Perez	511	.282	20	109	1192	72	9	113	9.6	.993	G. Nolan	32	211	15	9	0	3.16
2B	J. Morgan	498	.327	17	94	356	425	11	96	5.6	**.986**	J. Billingham	33	208	15	10	0	4.11
SS	D. Concepcion	507	.274	5	49	238	445	16	102	**5.4**	.977	F. Norman	34	188	12	4	0	3.73
3B	P. Rose	662	.317	7	74	106	230	13	21	2.5	.963	D. Gullett	22	160	15	4	0	2.42
RF	K. Griffey	463	.305	4	46	202	6	7	0	1.8	.967	P. Darcy	27	131	11	5	1	3.57
CF	C. Geronimo	501	.257	6	53	408	12	3	5	2.9	.993	P. Borbon	67	125	9	5	5	2.95
LF	G. Foster	463	.300	23	78	299	11	3	3	2.5	.990	C. Kirby	26	111	10	6	0	4.70
C	J. Bench	530	.283	28	110	568	51	7	9	5.2	.989	C. Carroll	56	96	7	5	7	2.63
10	D. Driessen	210	.281	7	38	309	20	5	34		.985	W. McEnaney	70	91	5	2	15	2.47
OF	M. Rettenmund	188	.239	2	19	99	1	0	1	1.6	1.000	R. Eastwick	58	90	5	3	**22**	2.60
UT	D. Chaney	160	.219	2	26	77	164	7	27		.972							
UT	D. Flynn	127	.268	1	20	57	118	2	20		.989							

Los Angeles

W-88 L-74

Walter Alston

POS	Player	AB	BA	HR	RBI	PO	A	E	DP	TC/G	FA	Pitcher	G	IP	W	L	SV	ERA
1B	S. Garvey	659	.319	18	95	**1500**	77	8	96	**9.9**	**.995**	A. Messersmith	42	**322**	19	14	1	2.29
2B	D. Lopes	618	.262	8	41	307	377	15	58	5.1	.979	D. Rau	38	258	15	9	0	3.10
SS	B. Russell	252	.206	0	14	94	230	11	27	4.0	.967	D. Sutton	35	254	16	13	0	2.87
3B	R. Cey	566	.283	25	101	144	309	19	23	3.0	.960	B. Hooton	31	224	18	7	0	2.82
RF	W. Crawford	373	.263	9	46	201	2	2	0	1.8	.990	M. Marshall	57	109	9	14	13	3.30
CF	J. Wynn	412	.248	18	58	282	6	5	2	2.4	.983	C. Hough	38	61	3	7	4	2.95
LF	B. Buckner	288	.243	6	31	138	4	2	0	2.0	.986							
C	S. Yeager	452	.228	12	54	**806**	62	7	4	6.5	.992							
O2	L. Lacy	306	.314	7	40	151	75	13	11		.946							
OF	J. Hale	204	.211	6	22	128	2	3	0	2.0	.977							
CO	J. Ferguson	202	.208	5	23	215	20	2	4		.992							
SS	R. Auerbach	170	.224	0	12	77	137	9	17	2.8	.960							

San Francisco

W-80 L-81

Wes Westrum

POS	Player	AB	BA	HR	RBI	PO	A	E	DP	TC/G	FA	Pitcher	G	IP	W	L	SV	ERA
1B	W. Montanez	518	.305	8	85	1150	81*	8	114*	9.2	.994	J. Barr	35	244	13	14	0	3.06
2B	D. Thomas	540	.276	6	48	348	372	19	100	5.2	.974	J. Montefusco	35	244	15	9	0	2.88
SS	C. Speier	487	.271	10	69	247	420	12	81	5.0	**.982**	P. Falcone	34	190	12	11	0	4.17
3B	S. Ontiveros	325	.289	3	31	64	188	21	14	3.1	.923	M. Caldwell	38	163	7	13	1	4.80
RF	B. Murcer	526	.298	11	91	201	10	4	3	1.5	.981	E. Halicki	24	160	9	13	0	3.49
CF	V. Joshua	507	.318	7	43	279	10	2	3	2.5	.993	C. Williams	55	98	5	3	3	3.49
LF	G. Matthews	425	.280	12	58	225	11	8	2	2.2	.967	G. Lavelle	65	82	6	3	8	2.96
C	D. Rader	292	.291	5	31	457	37	8	7	5.3	.984	R. Moffitt	55	74	4	5	11	3.89
OF	G. Thomasson	326	.227	7	32	172	9	4	2	2.5	.978							
3B	B. Miller	309	.239	1	31	66	120	10	11	2.9	.949							
C	M. Hill	182	.214	5	23	282	27	2	7	5.2	.994							

San Diego

W-71 L-91

John McNamara

POS	Player	AB	BA	HR	RBI	PO	A	E	DP	TC/G	FA	Pitcher	G	IP	W	L	SV	ERA
1B	W. McCovey	413	.252	23	68	979	73	15	94	9.3	.986	R. Jones	37	285	20	12	0	**2.24**
2B	T. Fuentes	565	.280	4	43	389	448	26	105	**6.1**	.970	J. McIntosh	37	183	8	15	0	3.69
SS	E. Hernandez	344	.218	0	19	168	327	18	70	4.6	.965	D. Freisleben	36	181	5	14	0	4.28
3B	T. Kubiak	196	.224	0	14	36	110	7	9	2.4	.954	D. Spillner	37	167	5	13	1	4.26
RF	D. Winfield	509	.267	15	76	302	9	9	1	2.3	.972	R. Folkers	45	142	6	11	0	4.18
CF	J. Grubb	553	.269	4	38	334	3	3	0	2.4	.991	B. Strom	18	120	8	8	0	2.55
LF	B. Tolan	506	.255	5	43	230	5	7	1	2.0	.971	D. Frisella	65	98	1	6	9	3.12
C	F. Kendall	286	.199	0	24	337	38	9	6	4.5	.977	B. Greif	59	72	4	6	9	3.88
13	M. Ivie	377	.249	8	46	539	138	23	54		.967							
UT	H. Torres	352	.259	5	26	128	338	13	55		.973							
OF	G. Locklear	237	.321	5	27	92	4	3	1	1.9	.970							
C	R. Hundley	180	.206	2	14	237	20	8	3	5.2	.970							
OF	D. Sharon	160	.194	4	20	91	1	5	0	1.7	.948							

Atlanta

W-67 L-94

Clyde King
W-58 L-76

Connie Ryan
W-9 L-18

POS	Player	AB	BA	HR	RBI	PO	A	E	DP	TC/G	FA	Pitcher	G	IP	W	L	SV	ERA
1B	E. Williams	383	.240	11	50	844	50	10	77	10.0	.989	C. Morton	39	278	17	16	0	3.50
2B	M. Perez	461	.275	2	34	259	341	9	74	5.3	.985	P. Niekro	39	276	15	15	1	3.20
SS	L. Blanks	471	.234	3	38	183	414	25	68	4.8	.960	T. House	58	79	7	7	11	3.19
3B	D. Evans	567	.243	22	73	**161**	**381**	**36**	**41**	**3.7**	.938	B. Capra	12	78	4	7	0	4.27
RF	D. Baker	494	.261	19	72	287	10	3	0	2.2	.990	J. Easterly	21	69	2	9	0	4.96
CF	R. Office	355	.290	3	30	229	6	8	0	2.3	.967	B. Dal Canton	26	67	2	7	3	3.36
LF	R. Garr	625	.278	6	31	298	12	11	2	2.2	.966							
C	V. Correll	325	.215	11	39	413	63	13	2	5.0	.973							
10	M. Lum	364	.228	8	36	657	34	5	41		.993							
OF	D. May	203	.276	12	40	103	3	4	2	2.1	.964							
2B	R. Gilbreath	202	.243	2	16	121	125	5	29	4.8	.980							
C	B. Pocoroba	188	.255	1	22	237	25	8	2	4.4	.970							

NATIONAL LEAGUE 1975, *cont.*

Team	POS	Player	AB	BA	HR	RBI	PO	A	E	DP	TC/G	FA	Pitcher	G	IP	W	L	SV	ERA
Houston	1B	B. Watson	485	.324	18	85	1077	69	8	106	9.8	.993	L. Dierker	34	232	14	16	0	4.00
	2B	R. Andrews	277	.238	0	19	191	237	8	65	4.6	.982	J. Richard	33	203	12	10	0	4.39
W-64 L-97	SS	R. Metzger	450	.227	2	26	186	441	15	83	5.1	.977	D. Roberts	32	198	8	14	1	4.27
	3B	D. Rader	448	.223	12	48	111	257	11	24	3.1	**.971**	D. Konieczny	32	171	6	13	0	4.47
Preston Gomez	RF	J. Cruz	315	.257	9	49	187	6	4	0	2.1	.980	K. Forsch	34	109	4	8	2	3.22
W-47 L-80	CF	C. Cedeno	500	.288	13	63	322	8	6	2	2.6	.982	J. Niekro	40	88	6	4	4	3.07
	LF	G. Gross	483	.294	0	41	216	14	10	2	2.0	.958	J. Crawford	44	87	3	5	4	3.62
Bill Virdon	C	M. May	386	.241	4	52	568	**70**	9	8	6.3	.986	T. Griffin	17	79	3	8	0	5.35
W-17 L-17	OF	W. Howard	392	.283	0	21	194	7	1	0	2.1	.995	W. Granger	55	74	2	5	5	3.65
	UT	E. Cabell	348	.264	2	43	197	58	6	17		.977							
	1C	C. Johnson	340	.276	20	65	602	37	12	37		.982							
	23	K. Boswell	178	.242	0	21	54	103	6	13		.963							

BATTING AND BASE RUNNING LEADERS

Batting Average
B. Madlock, CHI .354
T. Simmons, STL .332
M. Sanguillen, PIT .328
J. Morgan, CIN .327
B. Watson, HOU .324

Slugging Average
D. Parker, PIT .541
G. Luzinski, PHI .540
M. Schmidt, PHI .523
J. Bench, CIN .519
G. Foster, CIN .518

Home Runs
M. Schmidt, PHI 38
D. Kingman, NY 36
G. Luzinski, PHI 34
J. Bench, CIN 28
D. Parker, PIT 25
R. Cey, LA 25

Total Bases
G. Luzinski, PHI 322
S. Garvey, LA 314
D. Parker, PIT 302
M. Schmidt, PHI 294
P. Rose, CIN 286

Runs Batted In
G. Luzinski, PHI 120
J. Bench, CIN 110
T. Perez, CIN 109
R. Staub, NY 105

Stolen Bases
D. Lopes, LA 77
J. Morgan, CIN 67
L. Brock, STL 56
C. Cedeno, HOU 50
J. Cardenal, CHI 34

Hits
D. Cash, PHI 213
S. Garvey, LA 210
P. Rose, CIN 210
T. Simmons, STL 193

Base on Balls
J. Morgan, CIN 132
J. Wynn, LA 110
D. Evans, ATL 105
M. Schmidt, PHI 101

Home Run Percentage
D. Kingman, NY 7.2
M. Schmidt, PHI 6.8
G. Luzinski, PHI 5.7
J. Bench, CIN 5.3

Runs
P. Rose, CIN 112
D. Cash, PHI 111
D. Lopes, LA 108
J. Morgan, CIN 107

Doubles
P. Rose, CIN 47
D. Cash, PHI 40
J. Bench, CIN 39
A. Oliver, PIT 39

Triples
R. Garr, ATL 11
G. Gross, HOU 10
V. Joshua, SF 10
D. Parker, PIT 10
D. Kessinger, CHI 10

PITCHING LEADERS

Winning Percentage
D. Gullett, CIN .789
T. Seaver, NY .710
B. Hooton, CHI, LA .667
D. Murray, MON .652

Earned Run Average
R. Jones, SD 2.24
A. Messersmith, LA 2.29
T. Seaver, NY 2.38
J. Reuss, PIT 2.54
B. Forsch, STL 2.86

Wins
T. Seaver, NY 22
R. Jones, SD 20
A. Messersmith, LA 19
B. Hooton, CHI, LA 18
J. Reuss, PIT 18

Saves
R. Eastwick, CIN 22
A. Hrabosky, STL 22
D. Giusti, PIT 17
W. McEnaney, CIN 15
D. Knowles, CHI 15

Strikeouts
T. Seaver, NY 243
J. Montefusco, SF 215
A. Messersmith, LA 213
S. Carlton, PHI 192
J. Richard, HOU 176

Complete Games
A. Messersmith, LA 19
R. Jones, SD 18
J. Reuss, PIT 15
T. Seaver, NY 15
L. Dierker, HOU 14
S. Carlton, PHI 14

Fewest Hits/9 Innings
A. Messersmith, LA 6.82
D. Warthen, MON 6.96
T. Seaver, NY 6.98
D. Sutton, LA 7.16

Shutouts
A. Messersmith, LA 7
J. Reuss, PIT 6
R. Jones, SD 6
T. Seaver, NY 5

Fewest Walks/9 Innings
G. Nolan, CIN 1.24
R. Jones, SD 1.77
R. Reed, ATL, STL 1.91
D. Rau, LA 2.13

Most Strikeouts/9 Inn.
J. Montefusco, SF 7.93
T. Seaver, NY 7.81
J. Richard, HOU 7.80
D. Warthen, MON 6.86

Innings
A. Messersmith, LA 322
R. Jones, SD 285
T. Seaver, NY 280
C. Morton, ATL 278

Games Pitched
G. Garber, PHI 71
W. McEnaney, CIN 70
P. Borbon, CIN 67
D. Tomlin, SD 67

								Batting						Fielding			Pitching					
		W	L	PCT	GB	R	OR	2B	3B	HR	BA	SA	SB	E	DP	FA	CG	BB	SO	ShO	SV	ERA
East	Pittsburgh	92	69	.571		712	565	255	47	**138**	.263	**.402**	49	151	147	.976	43	551	768	14	31	3.02
	Philadelphia	86	76	.531	6.5	735	694	**283**	42	125	.269	**.402**	126	152	156	.976	33	546	897	11	30	3.82
	New York	82	80	.506	10.5	646	625	217	34	101	.256	.361	32	151	144	.976	40	580	**989**	14	31	3.39
	St. Louis	82	80	.506	10.5	662	689	239	46	81	**.273**	.375	116	171	140	.973	33	571	824	13	36	3.58
	Chicago	75	87	.463	17.5	712	827	229	41	95	.259	.368	67	179	152	.972	27	551	850	8	33	4.57
	Montreal	75	87	.463	17.5	601	690	216	31	98	.244	.348	108	180	**179**	.973	30	665	831	12	25	3.73
West	Cincinnati	108	54	.667		**840**	586	278	37	124	.271	.401	**168**	**102**	173	**.984**	22	487	663	8	**50**	3.37
	Los Angeles	88	74	.543	20	648	**534**	217	31	118	.248	.365	138	127	106	.979	**51**	**448**	894	**18**	21	**2.92**
	San Francisco	80	81	.497	27.5	659	671	235	45	84	.259	.365	99	146	164	.976	37	612	856	9	24	3.74
	San Diego	71	91	.438	37	552	683	215	22	78	.244	.335	85	188	163	.971	40	521	713	12	20	3.51
	Atlanta	67	94	.416	40.5	583	739	179	28	107	.244	.346	55	175	147	.972	32	519	669	4	25	3.93
	Houston	64	97	.398	43.5	664	711	218	**54**	84	.254	.359	133	137	166	.979	39	679	839	6	25	4.05
						8014	8014	2781	458	1233	.257	.369	1176	1859	1837	.976	427	6730	9793	129	351	3.64

AMERICAN LEAGUE 1975

		POS	Player	AB	BA	HR	RBI	PO	A	E	DP	TC/G	FA	Pitcher	G	IP	W	L	SV	ERA
East	**Boston**	1B	C. Yastrzemski	543	.269	14	60	1202	87	5	103	9.2	.996	B. Lee	41	260	17	9	0	3.95
		2B	D. Griffin	287	.240	1	29	195	215	14	45	4.3	.967	L. Tiant	35	260	18	14	0	4.02
	W-95 L-65	SS	R. Burleson	580	.252	6	62	267	498	29	102	5.0	.963	R. Wise	35	255	19	12	0	3.95
		3B	R. Petrocelli	402	.239	7	59	85	229	13	13	2.9	.960	R. Cleveland	31	171	13	9	0	4.43
	Darrell Johnson	RF	D. Evans	412	.274	13	56	281	15	4	8	2.6	.987	R. Moret	36	145	14	3	1	3.60
		CF	F. Lynn	528	.331	21	105	404	11	7	1	2.9	.983	D. Pole	18	90	4	6	0	4.42
		LF	J. Rice	564	.309	22	102	162	6	0	0	1.9	1.000	D. Drago	40	73	2	2	15	3.84
		C	C. Fisk	263	.331	10	52	347	30	8	2	5.4	.979	D. Segui	33	71	2	5	6	4.82
		DH	C. Cooper	305	.311	14	44							J. Willoughby	24	48	5	2	8	3.54
		OF	B. Carbo	319	.257	15	50	157	7	4	1	2.0	.976							
		2B	D. Doyle	310	.310	4	36	141	193	9	35	4.1	.974							
		UT	J. Beniquez	254	.291	2	17	110	17	1	2		.992							
		C	B. Montgomery	195	.226	2	26	210	23	3	6	4.5	.987							
		3B	B. Heise	126	.214	0	21	36	90	8	7	3.0	.940							

AMERICAN LEAGUE 1975, *cont.*

Team	POS	Player	AB	BA	HR	RBI	PO	A	E	DP	TC/G	FA	Pitcher	G	IP	W	L	SV	ERA
Baltimore	1B	L. May	580	.262	20	99	**1312**	106	10	**138**	9.9	.993	J. Palmer	39	323	**23**	11	1	**2.09**
W-90 L-69	2B	B. Grich	524	.260	13	57	**423**	**484**	21	**122**	**6.2**	.977	M. Torrez	36	271	20	9	0	3.06
Earl Weaver	SS	M. Belanger	442	.226	3	27	259	508	17	**105**	5.2	.978	M. Cuellar	36	256	14	12	0	3.66
	3B	B. Robinson	482	.201	6	53	96	326	9	30	3.0	**.979**	R. Grimsley	35	197	10	13	0	4.07
	RF	K. Singleton	586	.300	15	55	283	9	3	2	1.9	.990	D. Alexander	32	133	8	8	1	3.04
	CF	P. Blair	440	.218	5	31	327	8	3	1	2.4	.991	W. Garland	29	87	2	5	4	3.71
	LF	D. Baylor	524	.282	25	76	268	8	5	0	2.1	.982	G. Jackson	41	48	4	3	7	3.35
	C	D. Duncan	307	.205	12	41	397	41	8	5	4.7	.982	D. Miller	30	46	6	3	8	2.72
	DH	T. Davis	460	.283	6	57													
	DO	A. Bumbry	349	.269	2	32	70	2	0	1		1.000							
	C	E. Hendricks	223	.215	8	38	332	36	2	3	4.5	**.995**							
	OF	J. Northrup	194	.273	5	29	91	2	2	0	1.6	.979							
	UT	D. DeCinces	167	.251	4	23	92	115	7	20		.967							
New York	1B	C. Chambliss	562	.304	9	72	1222	106	12	113	9.1	.991	C. Hunter	39	**328**	**23**	14	0	2.58
W-83 L-77	2B	S. Alomar	489	.239	2	39	340	368	11	93	4.8	**.985**	D. Medich	38	272	16	16	0	3.50
Bill Virdon	SS	J. Mason	223	.152	2	16	134	209	16	45	3.9	.955	R. May	32	212	14	12	0	3.06
W-53 L-51	3B	G. Nettles	581	.267	21	91	135	**379**	19	31	3.4	.964	P. Dobson	33	208	11	14	0	4.07
Billy Martin	RF	B. Bonds	529	.270	32	85	287	12	4	6	2.3	.987	L. Gura	26	151	7	8	0	3.51
W-30 L-26	CF	E. Maddox	218	.307	1	23	157	5	0	3	2.9	1.000	S. Lyle	49	89	5	7	6	3.12
	LF	R. White	556	.290	12	59	303	11	5	0	2.4	.984	D. Tidrow	37	69	6	3	5	3.13
	C	T. Munson	597	.318	12	102	700	95	**23**	**14**	**6.3**	.972	T. Martinez	23	37	1	2	8	2.68
	DH	E. Herrmann	200	.255	6	30													
	SS	F. Stanley	252	.222	0	15	105	189	7	36	3.6	.977							
	OF	L. Piniella	199	.196	0	22	65	5	1	0	1.5	.986							
	UT	W. Williams	185	.281	5	16	57	4	1	0		.984							
Cleveland	1B	B. Powell	435	.297	27	86	997	69	3	92	8.8	**.997**	D. Eckersley	34	187	13	7	2	2.60
W-79 L-80	2B	D. Kuiper	346	.292	0	25	192	230	12	65	5.0	.972	F. Peterson	25	146	14	8	0	3.94
Frank Robinson	SS	F. Duffy	482	.243	1	47	225	464	16	85	4.9	.977	D. Hood	29	135	6	10	0	4.39
	3B	B. Bell	553	.271	10	59	**146**	330	25	29	3.3	.950	R. Harrison	19	126	7	7	0	4.79
	RF	C. Spikes	345	.229	11	33	176	13	5	5	1.9	.974	G. Perry	15	122	6	9	0	3.55
	CF	G. Hendrick	561	.258	24	86	338	4	6	1	2.4	.983	J. Bibby	24	113	5	9	1	3.20
	LF	O. Gamble	348	.261	15	45	146	8	2	2	1.9	.987	E. Raich	18	93	7	8	0	5.54
	C	A. Ashby	254	.224	5	32	441	43	5	6	5.6	.990	D. LaRoche	61	82	5	3	17	2.19
	DH	R. Carty	383	.308	18	64							T. Buskey	50	77	5	3	7	2.57
	OF	R. Manning	480	.285	3	35	331	12	9	2	3.0	.974							
	C	J. Ellis	296	.230	7	32	396	44	11	3	5.4	.976							
	UT	J. Lowenstein	265	.242	12	33	61	16	2	1		.975							
	2B	J. Brohamer	217	.244	6	16	166	162	8	52	5.1	.976							
	DH	F. Robinson	118	.237	9	24													
Milwaukee	1B	G. Scott	617	.285	**36**	**109**	1202	**109**	14	118	9.2	.989	P. Broberg	38	220	14	16	0	4.13
W-68 L-94	2B	P. Garcia	302	.225	6	38	230	293	8	67	5.6	.985	J. Slaton	37	217	11	18	0	4.52
Del Crandall	SS	R. Yount	558	.267	8	52	273	402	**44**	80	5.0	.939	J. Colborn	36	206	11	13	2	4.27
W-67 L-94	3B	D. Money	405	.277	15	43	95	179	14	22	2.9	.951	B. Travers	28	136	6	11	1	4.29
Harvey Kuenn	RF	S. Lezcano	429	.247	11	43	240	10	6	1	2.0	.977	T. Hausman	29	112	3	6	0	4.10
W-1 L-0	CF	G. Thomas	240	.179	10	28	215	5	9	1	2.0	.961	B. Champion	27	110	6	6	0	5.89
	LF	B. Mitchell	229	.249	9	41	128	2	1	1	1.8	.992	E. Rodriguez	43	88	7	0	7	3.49
	C	D. Porter	409	.232	18	60	532	82	13	10	5.1	.979	T. Murphy	52	72	1	9	20	4.60
	DH	H. Aaron	465	.234	12	60													
	OF	B. Sharp	373	.255	1	34	294	12	2	4	2.5	.994							
	32	K. Bevacqua	258	.229	2	24	145	159	12	32		.962							
	CO	C. Moore	241	.290	1	29	234	23	10	2		.963							
	01	M. Hegan	203	.251	5	22	241	21	2	19		.992							
	OF	B. Darwin	186	.247	8	23	82	5	2	1	2.1	.978							
	2B	B. Sheldon	181	.287	0	14	87	122	5	33	4.9	.977							
Detroit	1B	J. Pierce	170	.235	8	22	407	26	13	38	9.1	.971	M. Lolich	32	241	12	18	0	3.78
W-57 L-102	2B	G. Sutherland	503	.258	6	39	278	365	21	83	5.2	.968	J. Coleman	31	201	10	18	0	5.55
Ralph Houk	SS	T. Veryzer	404	.252	5	48	215	358	24	62	4.7	.960	V. Ruhle	32	190	11	12	0	4.03
	3B	A. Rodriguez	507	.245	13	60	136	375	25	33	**3.5**	.953	L. LaGrow	32	164	7	14	0	4.38
	RF	L. Roberts	447	.257	10	38	268	10	5	2	2.2	.982	R. Bare	29	151	8	13	0	4.48
	CF	R. LeFlore	550	.258	8	37	317	13	9	3	2.5	.973	T. Walker	36	115	3	8	0	4.45
	LF	B. Oglivie	332	.286	9	36	192	4	5	1	2.3	.975	D. Lemanczyk	26	109	2	7	0	4.46
	C	B. Freehan	427	.246	14	47	582	64	6	8	5.8	.991	J. Hiller	36	71	2	3	14	2.17
	DH	W. Horton	615	.275	25	92													
	01	D. Meyer	470	.236	8	47	571	41	12	39		.981							
	UT	M. Stanley	164	.256	3	19	183	22	2	9		.990							
West																			
Oakland	1B	J. Rudi	468	.278	21	75	732	36	7	64	8.5	.991	V. Blue	39	278	22	11	1	3.01
W-98 L-64	2B	P. Garner	488	.246	6	54	354	426	**26**	93	5.0	.968	K. Holtzman	39	266	18	14	0	3.14
Alvin Dark	SS	B. Campaneris	509	.265	4	46	199	378	23	58	4.4	.962	R. Fingers	**75**	127	10	6	24	2.98
	3B	S. Bando	562	.230	15	78	122	314	15	**36**	2.8	.967	D. Bosman	22	123	11	4	0	3.52
	RF	R. Jackson	593	.253	**36**	104	315	13	12	5	2.3	.965	P. Lindblad	68	122	9	1	7	2.72
	CF	B. North	524	.273	1	43	420	10	11	1	3.2	.975	J. Todd	58	122	8	3	12	2.29
	LF	C. Washington	590	.308	10	77	305	8	7	1	2.2	.978	G. Abbott	30	114	5	5	0	4.25
	C	G. Tenace	498	.255	29	87	541	63	10	10	4.9	.984	S. Bahnsen	21	100	6	7	0	3.24
	DH	B. Williams	520	.244	23	81													

AMERICAN LEAGUE 1975, *cont.*

Team	POS	Player	AB	BA	HR	RBI	PO	A	E	DP	TC/G	FA	Pitcher	G	IP	W	L	SV	ERA
Kansas City	1B	J. Mayberry	554	.291	34	106	1199	100	**16**	105	**10.0**	.988	S. Busby	34	260	18	12	0	3.08
	2B	C. Rojas	406	.254	2	37	233	303	11	65	4.7	.980	A. Fitzmorris	35	242	16	12	0	3.57
W-91 L-71	SS	F. Patek	483	.228	5	45	231	405	27	78	4.9	.959	D. Leonard	32	212	15	7	0	3.77
	3B	G. Brett	**634**	.308	11	89	131	355	**26**	27	3.2	.949	M. Pattin	44	177	10	10	5	3.25
Jack McKeon	RF	A. Cowens	328	.277	4	42	214	4	5	2	2.0	.978	P. Splittorff	35	159	9	10	1	3.17
W-50 L-46	CF	A. Otis	470	.247	9	46	310	9	4	3	2.5	.988	N. Briles	24	112	6	6	2	4.26
	LF	H. McRae	480	.306	5	71	207	7	3	2	1.9	.986	D. Bird	51	105	9	6	11	3.25
Whitey Herzog	C	B. Martinez	226	.226	3	23	361	39	8	4	5.2	.980							
W-41 L-25	DH	H. Killebrew	312	.199	14	44													
	OF	J. Wohlford	353	.255	0	30	175	9	9	1	1.9	.953							
	OF	V. Pinson	319	.223	4	22	144	6	1	0	1.8	.993							
	2S	F. White	304	.250	7	36	179	265	11	55		.976							
	D1	T. Solaita	231	.260	16	44	282	28	2	24		.994							
	C	F. Healy	188	.255	2	18	258	17	5	2	5.5	.982							

Team	POS	Player	AB	BA	HR	RBI	PO	A	E	DP	TC/G	FA	Pitcher	G	IP	W	L	SV	ERA
Texas	1B	J. Spencer	403	.266	11	47	844	70	5	92	9.3	.995	F. Jenkins	37	270	17	18	0	3.93
	2B	L. Randle	601	.276	4	57	205	232	12	61	5.7	.973	S. Hargan	33	189	9	10	0	3.80
W-79 L-83	SS	T. Harrah	522	.293	20	93	198	375	22	68	5.0	.963	G. Perry	22	184	12	8	0	3.03
	3B	R. Howell	383	.251	10	51	80	214	21	32	2.7	.933	J. Umbarger	56	131	8	7	2	4.12
Billy Martin	RF	J. Burroughs	585	.226	29	94	249	10	9	2	1.8	.966	B. Hands	18	110	6	7	0	4.02
W-44 L-51	CF	D. Moates	175	.274	3	14	114	6	2	1	2.4	.984	S. Foucault	59	107	8	4	10	4.12
	LF	M. Hargrove	519	.303	11	62	187	2	7	0	2.0	.964	C. Wright	25	93	4	6	0	4.44
Frank Lucchesi	C	J. Sundberg	472	.199	6	36	**791**	**101**	17	11	5.9	.981	S. Thomas	46	81	4	4	3	3.10
W-35 L-32	DH	C. Tovar	427	.258	3	28							J. Brown	17	70	5	5	0	4.22
	OD	T. Grieve	369	.276	14	61	93	3	1	0		.990							
	SS	R. Smalley	250	.228	3	33	80	175	16	30	4.6	.941							
	1B	J. Fregosi	191	.262	7	33	355	34	6	31	7.3	.985							
	OF	W. Davis	169	.249	5	17	100	1	1	1	2.4	.990							
	2B	M. Cubbage	143	.224	4	21	67	111	7	24	5.0	.962							

Team	POS	Player	AB	BA	HR	RBI	PO	A	E	DP	TC/G	FA	Pitcher	G	IP	W	L	SV	ERA
Minnesota	1B	C. Kusick	156	.237	6	27	372	31	4	45	8.0	.990	B. Blyleven	35	276	15	10	0	3.00
	2B	R. Carew	535	**.359**	14	80	285	369	18	79	5.5	.973	J. Hughes	37	250	16	14	0	3.82
W-76 L-83	SS	D. Thompson	355	.270	5	37	138	245	24	40	4.1	.941	D. Goltz	32	243	14	14	0	3.67
	3B	E. Soderholm	419	.286	11	58	94	277	12	14	3.4	.969	V. Albury	32	135	6	7	1	4.53
Frank Quilici	RF	L. Bostock	369	.282	0	29	188	3	3	0	2.1	.985	B. Campbell	47	121	4	6	5	3.79
	CF	D. Ford	440	.280	15	59	246	3	3	2	2.1	.988	R. Corbin	18	90	5	7	0	5.12
	LF	S. Braun	453	.302	11	45	195	6	6	1	2.0	.971	T. Burgmeier	46	76	5	8	11	3.09
	C	G. Borgmann	352	.207	2	33	618	81	8	6	5.7	.989							
	DH	T. Oliva	455	.270	13	58													
	UT	J. Terrell	385	.286	1	36	267	232	14	60		.973							
	1O	J. Briggs	264	.231	7	39	483	55	8	38		.985							
	OF	L. Hisle	255	.314	11	51	118	2	3	0	2.1	.976							
	OF	S. Brye	246	.252	9	34	112	7	2	0	1.7	.983							
	OD	B. Darwin	169	.219	5	18	28	3	1	0		.969							
	C	P. Roof	126	.302	7	21	245	30	3	4	4.4	.989							

Team	POS	Player	AB	BA	HR	RBI	PO	A	E	DP	TC/G	FA	Pitcher	G	IP	W	L	SV	ERA
Chicago	1B	C. May	454	.271	8	53	508	46	6	54	8.9	.989	J. Kaat	43	304	20	14	0	3.11
	2B	J. Orta	542	.304	11	83	354	354	16	95	5.4	.978	W. Wood	43	291	16	**20**	0	4.11
W-75 L-86	SS	B. Dent	602	.264	3	58	**279**	**543**	16	**105**	**5.3**	**.981**	C. Osteen	37	204	7	16	0	4.36
	3B	B. Melton	512	.240	15	70	131	313	**26**	23	3.4	.945	G. Gossage	62	142	9	8	**26**	1.84
Chuck Tanner	RF	P. Kelly	471	.274	9	45	222	4	2	1	2.0	.991	J. Jefferson	22	108	5	9	0	5.10
	CF	K. Henderson	513	.251	9	53	394	7	4	0	3.0	.990	D. Hamilton	30	70	6	5	6	2.84
	LF	N. Nyman	327	.226	2	28	177	6	8	0	2.0	.958	S. Bahnsen	12	67	4	6	0	6.01
	C	B. Downing	420	.240	7	41	730	84	8	5	6.0	.990	T. Forster	17	37	3	3	4	2.19
	DH	D. Johnson	555	.232	18	72													
	UT	B. Stein	226	.270	3	21	87	118	9	21		.958							
	OF	J. Hairston	219	.283	0	23	111	6	6	1	2.1	.951							

Team	POS	Player	AB	BA	HR	RBI	PO	A	E	DP	TC/G	FA	Pitcher	G	IP	W	L	SV	ERA
California	1B	B. Bochte	375	.285	3	48	850	51	12	90	8.7	.987	F. Tanana	34	257	16	9	0	2.62
	2B	J. Remy	569	.258	1	46	336	427	14	111	5.3	.982	E. Figueroa	33	245	16	13	0	2.91
W-72 L-89	SS	M. Miley	224	.174	4	26	107	186	19	53	4.5	.939	N. Ryan	28	198	14	12	0	3.45
	3B	D. Chalk	513	.273	3	56	108	333	11	30	3.0	.976	B. Singer	29	179	7	15	1	4.98
Dick Williams	RF	L. Stanton	440	.261	14	82	230	16	10	2	2.0	.961	A. Hassler	30	133	3	12	0	5.94
	CF	M. Rivers	616	.284	1	53	371	13	9	3	2.6	.977	D. Lange	30	102	4	6	1	5.21
	LF	M. Nettles	294	.231	0	23	186	4	5	0	2.2	.974	D. Kirkwood	44	84	6	5	7	3.11
	C	E. Rodriguez	226	.235	3	27	492	33	5	2	5.9	.991							
	DH	T. Harper	285	.239	3	31													
	OF	D. Collins	319	.266	3	29	159	3	2	2	2.2	.988							
	DO	J. Lahoud	192	.214	6	33	41	1	0	0		1.000							

BATTING AND BASE RUNNING LEADERS

Batting Average		Slugging Average		Home Runs	
R. Carew, MIN	.359	F. Lynn, BOS	.566	R. Jackson, OAK	36
F. Lynn, BOS	.331	J. Mayberry, KC	.547	G. Scott, MIL	36
T. Munson, NY	.318	B. Powell, CLE	.524	J. Mayberry, KC	34
J. Rice, BOS	.309	G. Scott, MIL	.515	B. Bonds, NY	32
C. Washington, OAK	.308	B. Bonds, NY	.512	G. Tenace, OAK	29
				J. Burroughs, TEX	29

PITCHING LEADERS

Winning Percentage		Earned Run Average		Wins	
M. Torrez, BAL	.690	J. Palmer, BAL	2.09	J. Palmer, BAL	23
D. Leonard, KC	.682	C. Hunter, NY	2.58	C. Hunter, NY	23
J. Palmer, BAL	.676	D. Eckersley, CLE	2.60	V. Blue, OAK	22
V. Blue, OAK	.667	F. Tanana, CAL	2.62	M. Torrez, BAL	20
B. Lee, BOS	.654	E. Figueroa, CAL	2.91	J. Kaat, CHI	20

AMERICAN LEAGUE 1975, *cont.*

BATTING AND BASE RUNNING LEADERS

Total Bases

G. Scott, MIL	318
J. Mayberry, KC	303
R. Jackson, OAK	303
F. Lynn, BOS	299
G. Brett, KC	289

Runs Batted In

G. Scott, MIL	109
J. Mayberry, KC	106
F. Lynn, BOS	105
R. Jackson, OAK	104
J. Rice, BOS	102
T. Munson, NY	102

Stolen Bases

M. Rivers, CAL	70
C. Washington, OAK	40
A. Otis, KC	39
R. Carew, MIN	35
J. Remy, CAL	34

Hits

G. Brett, KC	195
R. Carew, MIN	192
T. Munson, NY	190
C. Washington, OAK	182

Base on Balls

J. Mayberry, KC	119
K. Singleton, BAL	118
B. Grich, BAL	107
G. Tenace, OAK	106

Home Run Percentage

B. Powell, CLE	6.2
J. Mayberry, KC	6.1
R. Jackson, OAK	6.1
B. Bonds, NY	6.0

Runs

F. Lynn, BOS	103
J. Mayberry, KC	95
B. Bonds, NY	93
J. Rice, BOS	92

Doubles

F. Lynn, BOS	47
R. Jackson, OAK	39
H. McRae, KC	38
J. Mayberry, KC	38
C. Chambliss, NY	38

Triples

M. Rivers, CAL	13
G. Brett, KC	13
J. Orta, CHI	10
A. Cowens, KC	8

PITCHING LEADERS

Saves

G. Gossage, CHI	26
R. Fingers, OAK	24
T. Murphy, MIL	20
D. LaRoche, CLE	17
D. Drago, BOS	15

Strikeouts

F. Tanana, CAL	269
B. Blyleven, MIN	233
G. Perry, CLE, TEX	233
J. Palmer, BAL	193
V. Blue, OAK	189

Complete Games

C. Hunter, NY	30
G. Perry, CLE, TEX	25
J. Palmer, BAL	25
F. Jenkins, TEX	22
B. Blyleven, MIN	20

Fewest Hits/9 Innings

C. Hunter, NY	6.80
N. Ryan, CAL	6.91
J. Palmer, BAL	7.05
D. Eckersley, CLE	7.09

Shutouts

J. Palmer, BAL	10
C. Hunter, NY	7

Fewest Walks/9 Innings

F. Jenkins, TEX	1.87
G. Perry, CLE, TEX	2.06
R. Grimsley, BAL	2.15
J. Palmer, BAL	2.23

Most Strikeouts/9 Inn.

F. Tanana, CAL	9.41
N. Ryan, CAL	8.45
B. Blyleven, MIN	7.61
D. Eckersley, CLE	7.33

Innings

C. Hunter, NY	328
J. Palmer, BAL	323
G. Perry, CLE, TEX	306
J. Kaat, CHI	304

Games Pitched

R. Fingers, OAK	75
P. Lindblad, OAK	68
G. Gossage, CHI	62
D. LaRoche, CLE	61

									Batting						Fielding			Pitching					
		W	L	PCT	GB	R	OR	2B	3B	HR	BA	SA	SB	E	DP	FA	CG	BB	SO	ShO	SV	ERA
East	Boston	95	65	.594		**796**	709	**284**	44	134	**.275**	**.417**	66	139	142	.977	62	**490**	720	11	31	3.99
	Baltimore	90	69	.566	4.5	682	**553**	224	33	124	.252	.373	104	**107**	**175**	**.983**	**70**	500	717	**19**	21	**3.17**
	New York	83	77	.519	12	681	588	230	39	110	.264	.382	102	135	148	.978	**70**	502	809	11	20	3.29
	Cleveland	79	80	.497	15.5	688	703	201	25	**153**	.261	.392	106	134	156	.978	37	599	800	6	32	3.84
	Milwaukee	68	94	.420	28	675	792	242	34	146	.250	.389	65	180	162	.971	36	624	643	10	34	4.34
	Detroit	57	102	.358	37.5	570	786	171	39	125	.249	.366	63	173	141	.972	52	533	787	10	17	4.29
West	Oakland	98	64	.605		758	606	220	33	151	.254	.391	183	143	140	.977	36	523	784	10	**44**	3.29
	Kansas City	91	71	.562	7	710	649	263	**58**	118	.261	.394	155	154	151	.976	52	498	815	11	25	3.49
	Texas	79	83	.488	19	714	733	208	17	134	.256	.371	102	191	173	.971	60	518	792	16	17	3.90
	Minnesota	76	83	.478	20.5	724	736	215	28	121	.271	.386	81	170	147	.973	57	617	846	7	22	4.05
	Chicago	75	86	.466	22.5	655	703	209	38	94	.255	.358	101	140	155	.978	34	655	799	7	39	3.93
	California	72	89	.447	25.5	628	723	195	41	55	.246	.328	**220**	184	164	.971	59	613	**975**	**19**	16	3.89
						8281	8281	2662	429	1465	.258	.379	1348	1850	1854	.975	625	6672	9487	137	318	3.79

NATIONAL LEAGUE 1976

		POS	Player	AB	BA	HR	RBI	PO	A	E	DP	TC/G	FA	Pitcher	G	IP	W	L	SV	ERA
East	Philadelphia	1B	D. Allen	298	.268	15	49	671	44	8	71	8.5	.989	S. Carlton	35	253	20	7	0	3.13
	W-101 L-61	2B	D. Cash	**666**	.284	1	56	407	424	10	**118**	5.3	**.988**	J. Kaat	38	228	12	14	0	3.48
	Danny Ozark	SS	L. Bowa	624	.248	0	49	180	492	17	90	4.4	.975	J. Lonborg	33	222	18	10	1	3.08
		3B	M. Schmidt	584	.262	**38**	107	139	**377**	21	29	**3.4**	.961	L. Christenson	32	169	13	8	0	3.68
		RF	J. Johnstone	440	.318	5	53	266	8	5	1	2.3	.982	T. Underwood	33	156	10	5	2	3.53
		CF	G. Maddox	531	.330	6	68	441	10	5	0	3.2	.989	R. Reed	59	128	8	7	14	2.46
		LF	G. Luzinski	533	.304	21	95	204	8	8	0	1.5	.964	T. McGraw	58	97	7	6	11	2.50
		C	B. Boone	361	.271	4	54	557	36	4	5	5.5	.993	G. Garber	59	93	9	3	11	2.82
		10	B. Tolan	272	.261	5	35	395	14	5	36		.988							
		OF	O. Brown	209	.254	5	30	105	7	6	2	1.6	.949							
		C	T. McCarver	155	.277	3	29	254	9	0	1	6.4	1.000							
	Pittsburgh	1B	W. Stargell	428	.257	20	65	1037	53	13	76	9.9	.988	J. Candelaria	32	220	16	7	1	3.15
	W-92 L-70	2B	R. Stennett	654	.257	2	60	**430**	502	18	111	**6.1**	.981	J. Reuss	31	209	14	9	2	3.53
	Danny Murtaugh	SS	F. Taveras	519	.258	0	24	210	481	35	74	5.1	.952	J. Rooker	30	199	15	8	1	3.35
		3B	R. Hebner	434	.249	8	51	87	236	16	16	2.7	.953	B. Kison	31	193	14	9	1	3.08
		RF	D. Parker	537	.313	13	90	294	12	14	0	2.4	.956	D. Medich	29	179	8	11	0	3.51
		CF	A. Oliver	443	.323	12	61	301	4	5	0	2.9	.984	L. Demery	36	145	10	7	2	3.17
		LF	R. Zisk	581	.289	21	89	300	11	4	2	2.1	.987	K. Tekulve	64	103	5	3	9	2.45
		C	M. Sanguillen	389	.290	2	36	518	52	**13**	7	5.3	.978	B. Moose	53	88	3	9	10	3.70
		03	B. Robinson	393	.303	21	64	164	53	8	7		.964	D. Giusti	40	58	5	4	6	4.32
		C	D. Dyer	184	.223	3	9	279	37	2	4	5.5	.994							
		1B	B. Robertson	129	.217	2	25	257	17	1	28	9.5	.996							
	New York	1B	E. Kranepool	415	.292	10	49	675	33	3	48	8.3	.996	T. Seaver	35	271	14	11	0	2.59
	W-86 L-76	2B	F. Millan	531	.282	1	35	311	315	15	68	4.7	.977	J. Matlack	35	262	17	10	0	2.95
	Joe Frazier	SS	B. Harrelson	359	.234	1	26	183	330	20	44	4.6	.962	J. Koosman	34	247	21	10	0	2.70
		3B	R. Staiger	304	.220	2	26	55	209	9	18	2.9	.967	M. Lolich	31	193	8	13	0	3.22
		RF	J. Milner	443	.271	15	78	195	7	3	2	1.8	.985	C. Swan	23	132	6	9	0	3.55
		CF	D. Unser	276	.228	5	25	180	5	1	0	2.4	.995	S. Lockwood	56	94	10	7	19	2.67
		LF	D. Kingman	474	.238	37	86	202	10	9	0	2.0	.959	B. Apodaca	43	90	3	7	5	2.80
		C	J. Grote	323	.272	4	28	617	49	5	6	**7.1**	.993							
		1B	J. Torre	310	.306	5	31	590	49	7	40	8.3	.989							
		OF	B. Boisclair	286	.287	2	13	156	3	3	1	1.9	.981							
		UT	M. Phillips	262	.256	4	29	115	191	11	26		.965							
		3B	W. Garrett	251	.223	4	26	47	137	10	12	3.0	.948							
		C	R. Hodges	155	.226	4	24	262	18	7	0	5.5	.976							

NATIONAL LEAGUE 1976, *cont.*

Chicago

W-75 L-87

Jim Marshall

POS	Player	AB	BA	HR	RBI	PO	A	E	DP	TC/G	FA	Pitcher	G	IP	W	L	SV	ERA
1B	P. LaCock	244	.221	8	28	435	30	12	47	8.8	.975	R. Reuschel	38	260	14	12	1	3.46
2B	M. Trillo	582	.239	4	59	349	**527**	17	103	5.7	.981	R. Burris	37	249	15	13	0	3.11
SS	M. Kelleher	337	.228	0	22	147	289	9	52	4.4	.980	B. Bonham	32	196	9	13	0	4.27
3B	B. Madlock	514	**.339**	15	84	107	234	14	21	2.6	.961	S. Renko	28	163	8	11	0	3.86
RF	J. Morales	537	.274	16	67	273	12	5	6	2.1	.983	B. Sutter	52	83	6	3	10	2.71
CF	R. Monday	534	.272	32	77	278	4	2	0	2.8	.993	J. Coleman	39	79	2	8	4	4.10
LF	J. Cardenal	521	.299	8	47	246	10	5	1	2.0	.981	D. Knowles	58	72	5	7	9	2.88
C	S. Swisher	377	.236	5	42	574	49	11	6	5.9	.983	O. Zamora	40	55	5	3	3	5.24
OF	J. Wallis	338	.254	5	21	193	11	5	3	2.3	.976							
C	G. Mitterwald	303	.215	5	28	320	40	7	2	5.7	.981							
SS	D. Rosello	227	.242	1	11	128	217	12	45	4.2	.966							
10	L. Biittner	192	.245	0	17	266	34	4	20		.987							

St. Louis

W-72 L-90

Red Schoendienst

POS	Player	AB	BA	HR	RBI	PO	A	E	DP	TC/G	FA	Pitcher	G	IP	W	L	SV	ERA
1B	K. Hernandez	374	.289	7	46	862	**107**	10	87	8.9	.990	P. Falcone	32	212	12	16	0	3.23
2B	M. Tyson	245	.286	3	28	158	237	12	54	5.5	.971	J. Denny	30	207	11	9	0	**2.52**
SS	D. Kessinger	502	.239	1	40	212	350	18	84	5.1	.969	L. McGlothen	33	205	13	15	0	3.91
3B	H. Cruz	526	.228	13	71	100	270	**26**	19	2.7	.934	B. Forsch	33	194	8	10	0	3.94
RF	W. Crawford	392	.304	9	50	209	6	4	1	2.0	.982	E. Rasmussen	43	150	6	12	0	3.53
CF	J. Mumphrey	384	.258	1	26	261	6	2	1	2.9	.993	J. Curtis	37	134	6	11	1	4.50
LF	L. Brock	498	.301	4	67	221	6	4	0	1.9	.983	A. Hrabosky	68	95	8	6	13	3.30
C	T. Simmons	546	.291	5	75	493	66	4	4	5.0	.993	B. Greif	47	55	1	5	6	4.12
OF	B. McBride	272	.335	3	24	201	5	4	0	3.2	.981							
UT	V. Harris	259	.228	1	19	173	103	14	21		.952							
SS	G. Templeton	213	.291	1	17	111	172	24	41	5.8	.922							
OF	M. Anderson	199	.291	1	12	106	5	2	1	1.9	.982							
C	J. Ferguson	189	.201	4	21	238	32	6	6	5.8	.978							
UT	R. Smith	170	.218	8	23	184	44	2	18		.991							
1B	R. Fairly	110	.264	0	21	174	21	1	19	7.3	.995							

Montreal

W-55 L-107

Karl Kuehl
W-43 L-85

Charlie Fox
W-12 L-22

POS	Player	AB	BA	HR	RBI	PO	A	E	DP	TC/G	FA	Pitcher	G	IP	W	L	SV	ERA
1B	M. Jorgensen	343	.254	6	23	599	57	7	59	8.2	.989	S. Rogers	33	230	7	**17**	1	3.21
2B	P. Mackanin	380	.224	8	33	201	289	18	60	5.1	.965	W. Fryman	34	216	13	13	2	3.37
SS	T. Foli	546	.264	6	54	247	469	18	**102**	5.0	.975	D. Stanhouse	34	184	9	12	1	3.77
3B	L. Parrish	543	.232	11	61	122	310	25	**35**	3.0	.945	D. Carrithers	34	140	6	12	0	4.43
RF	E. Valentine	305	.279	7	39	162	12	5	4	2.0	.972	D. Murray	**81**	113	4	9	13	3.26
CF	P. Mangual	215	.260	3	16	146	3	5	1	2.5	.968	D. Warthen	23	90	2	10	0	5.30
LF	J. White	278	.245	2	21	157	4	3	0	1.8	.982							
C	B. Foote	350	.234	7	27	476	59	6	**13**	5.6	.989							
CO	G. Carter	311	.219	6	38	364	42	2	8		.995							
OF	D. Unser	220	.227	7	15	108	5	2	2	1.8	.983							
1B	E. Williams	190	.237	8	29	377	41	8	37	9.1	.981							
OF	B. Rivera	185	.276	2	19	89	7	5	3	1.8	.950							
1B	A. Thornton	183	.191	9	24	326	26	2	43	8.2	.994							
2B	W. Garrett	177	.243	2	11	121	157	5	32	5.2	.982							
1C	J. Morales	158	.316	4	37	137	21	3	9		.981							

West

Cincinnati

W-102 L-60

Sparky Anderson

POS	Player	AB	BA	HR	RBI	PO	A	E	DP	TC/G	FA	Pitcher	G	IP	W	L	SV	ERA
1B	T. Perez	527	.260	19	91	1158	73	5	110	9.1	.996	G. Nolan	34	239	15	9	0	3.46
2B	J. Morgan	472	.320	27	111	342	335	13	85	5.2	.981	P. Zachry	38	204	14	7	0	2.74
SS	D. Concepcion	576	.281	9	69	**304**	**506**	27	93	**5.6**	.968	F. Norman	33	180	12	7	0	3.10
3B	P. Rose	665	.323	10	63	115	293	13	25	2.6	**.969**	J. Billingham	34	177	12	10	1	4.32
RF	K. Griffey	562	.336	6	74	270	10	6	2	2.0	.979	S. Alcala	30	132	11	4	0	4.70
CF	C. Geronimo	486	.307	2	49	386	4	6	2	2.7	.985	D. Gullett	23	126	11	3	1	3.00
LF	G. Foster	562	.306	29	**121**	322	9	2	3	2.3	.994	P. Borbon	69	121	4	3	8	3.35
C	J. Bench	465	.234	16	74	**651**	60	2	11	5.6	**.997**	R. Eastwick	71	108	11	5	**26**	2.08
UT	D. Flynn	219	.283	1	20	107	152	4	33		.985	W. McEnaney	55	72	2	6	7	4.88
10	D. Driessen	219	.247	7	44	314	23	2	33		.994							
OF	M. Lum	136	.228	3	20	48	0	0	0	1.3	1.000							
OF	B. Bailey	124	.298	6	23	35	2	1	1	1.2	.974							

Los Angeles

W-92 L-70

Walter Alston
W-90 L-68

Tom Lasorda
W-2 L-2

POS	Player	AB	BA	HR	RBI	PO	A	E	DP	TC/G	FA	Pitcher	G	IP	W	L	SV	ERA
1B	S. Garvey	631	.317	13	80	**1583**	67	3	138	10.2	**.998**	D. Sutton	35	268	21	10	0	3.06
2B	D. Lopes	427	.241	4	20	218	266	18	56	5.0	.964	D. Rau	34	231	16	12	0	2.57
SS	B. Russell	554	.274	5	65	251	476	28	90	5.1	.963	B. Hooton	33	227	11	15	0	3.26
3B	R. Cey	502	.277	23	80	111	334	16	22	3.2	.965	T. John	31	207	10	10	0	3.09
RF	R. Smith	225	.280	10	26	130	3	2	2	2.3	.985	R. Rhoden	27	181	12	3	0	2.98
CF	D. Baker	384	.242	4	39	254	3	1	1	2.4	.996	C. Hough	77	143	12	8	18	2.21
LF	B. Buckner	642	.301	7	60	315	7	5	0	2.1	.985	M. Marshall	30	63	4	3	8	4.45
C	S. Yeager	359	.214	11	35	522	**77**	9	9	5.3	.985							
2B	T. Sizemore	266	.241	0	18	168	191	5	51	5.1	.986							
OC	J. Ferguson	185	.222	6	18	156	12	6	2		.966							

Houston

W-80 L-82

Bill Virdon

POS	Player	AB	BA	HR	RBI	PO	A	E	DP	TC/G	FA	Pitcher	G	IP	W	L	SV	ERA
1B	B. Watson	585	.313	16	102	1395	96	15	126	9.7	.990	J. Richard	39	291	20	15	0	2.75
2B	R. Andrews	410	.256	0	23	228	354	14	66	5.6	.977	L. Dierker	28	188	13	14	0	3.69
SS	R. Metzger	481	.210	0	29	253	462	10	93	4.8	**.986**	J. Andujar	28	172	9	10	0	3.61
3B	E. Cabell	586	.273	2	43	128	263	17	24	2.9	.958	J. Niekro	36	118	4	8	0	3.36
RF	J. Cruz	439	.303	4	61	265	10	8	4	2.3	.972	D. Larson	13	92	5	8	0	3.03
CF	C. Cedeno	575	.297	18	83	377	11	8	5	2.7	.980	K. Forsch	52	92	4	3	19	2.15
LF	G. Gross	426	.286	0	27	208	13	5	4	2.0	.978	B. McLaughlin	17	79	4	5	1	2.85
C	E. Herrmann	265	.204	3	25	412	37	6	5	5.8	.987	G. Pentz	40	64	3	3	5	2.95
UT	C. Johnson	318	.226	10	49	468	35	9	10		.982							
OF	L. Roberts	235	.289	7	33	99	1	2	0	1.7	.980							
OF	W. Howard	191	.220	1	18	96	2	4	1	1.6	.961							
UT	J. DaVanon	107	.290	1	20	53	94	7	16		.955							

NATIONAL LEAGUE 1976, *cont.*

San Francisco

W-74 L-88

Bill Rigney

POS	Player	AB	BA	HR	RBI	PO	A	E	DP	TC/G	FA	Pitcher	G	IP	W	L	SV	ERA
1B	D. Evans	257	.222	10	36	681	68	7	53	9.1	.991	J. Montefusco	37	253	16	14	0	2.84
2B	M. Perez	332	.259	2	26	189	273	10	51	5.3	.979	J. Barr	37	252	15	12	0	2.89
SS	C. Speier	495	.226	3	40	225	441	18	81	5.1	.974	E. Halicki	32	186	12	14	0	3.62
3B	K. Reitz	577	.267	5	66	140	303	19	32	3.0	.959	G. Lavelle	65	110	10	6	12	2.69
RF	B. Murcer	533	.259	23	90	282	11	12	2	2.1	.961	R. Dressler	25	108	3	10	0	4.43
CF	L. Herndon	337	.288	2	23	226	8	8	4	2.2	.967	M. Caldwell	50	107	1	7	2	4.86
LF	G. Matthews	587	.279	20	84	265	8	7	0	1.8	.975	J. D'Acquisto	28	106	3	8	0	5.35
C	D. Rader	255	.263	1	22	349	32	6	4	4.8	.984	R. Moffitt	58	103	6	6	14	2.27
01	G. Thomasson	328	.259	8	38	436	20	12	28		.974							
2B	D. Thomas	272	.232	2	19	160	212	14	52	5.6	.964							
1B	W. Montanez	230	.309	2	20	583	51*	7*	54*	11.1*	.989							

San Diego

W-73 L-89

John McNamara

POS	Player	AB	BA	HR	RBI	PO	A	E	DP	TC/G	FA	Pitcher	G	IP	W	L	SV	ERA
1B	M. Ivie	405	.291	7	70	1020	70	5	89	8.1	.995	R. Jones	40	**315**	**22**	14	0	2.74
2B	T. Fuentes	520	.263	2	36	339	387	**22**	91	5.9	.971	B. Strom	36	211	12	16	0	3.29
SS	E. Hernandez	340	.256	1	24	132	344	18	64	4.9	.964	D. Freisleben	34	172	10	13	1	3.51
3B	D. Rader	471	.257	9	55	109	318	20	22	3.3	.955	B. Metzger	77	123	11	4	16	2.92
RF	J. Grubb	384	.284	5	27	183	3	5	0	1.9	.974	D. Spillner	32	107	2	11	0	5.06
CF	W. Davis	493	.268	5	46	349	6	3	2	2.8	.992							
LF	D. Winfield	492	.283	13	69	304	15	6	4	2.4	.982							
C	F. Kendall	456	.246	2	39	582	54	4	6	4.4	.994							
OF	J. Turner	281	.267	5	37	115	6	5	0	1.7	.960							
SS	H. Torres	215	.195	4	15	64	160	12	29	3.7	.949							
UT	T. Kubiak	212	.236	0	26	77	110	4	21		.979							
1B	W. McCovey	202	.203	7	36	420	44	4	39	9.2	.991							

Atlanta

W-70 L-92

Dave Bristol

POS	Player	AB	BA	HR	RBI	PO	A	E	DP	TC/G	FA	Pitcher	G	IP	W	L	SV	ERA
1B	W. Montanez	420	.321	9	64	986	56*	15*	87*	10.3*	.986	P. Niekro	38	271	17	11	0	3.29
2B	R. Gilbreath	383	.251	1	32	239	311	14	76	5.4	.975	D. Ruthven	36	240	14	**17**	0	4.20
SS	D. Chaney	496	.252	1	50	243	466	**37**	88	4.9	.950	A. Messersmith	29	207	11	11	1	3.04
3B	J. Royster	533	.248	5	45	**156**	306	18	**35**	3.2	.962	C. Morton	26	140	4	9	0	4.18
RF	K. Henderson	435	.262	13	61	219	3	3	0	1.8	.987	F. LaCorte	19	105	3	12	0	4.71
CF	R. Office	359	.281	4	34	204	3	3	2	2.3	.986	A. Devine	48	73	5	6	9	3.21
LF	J. Wynn	449	.207	17	66	287	17	9	2	2.3	.971	E. Sosa	21	35	4	4	3	5.35
C	V. Correll	200	.225	5	16	319	36	7	1	5.6	.981							
OF	T. Paciorek	324	.290	4	36	115	3	2	0	1.4	.983							
OF	D. May	214	.215	3	23	98	5	3	1	1.8	.972							
C1	E. Williams	184	.212	9	26	298	18	1	9		.997							
2B	L. Lacy	180	.272	3	20	88	101	6	25	4.4	.969							
C	B. Pocoroba	174	.241	0	14	273	39	7	5	5.9	.978							
OF	C. Gaston	134	.291	4	25	42	1	1	0	1.6	.977							

BATTING AND BASE RUNNING LEADERS

Batting Average

B. Madlock, CHI	.339
K. Griffey, CIN	.336
G. Maddox, PHI	.330
P. Rose, CIN	.323
J. Morgan, CIN	.320

Slugging Average

J. Morgan, CIN	.576
G. Foster, CIN	.530
M. Schmidt, PHI	.524
R. Monday, CHI	.507
D. Kingman, NY	.506

Home Runs

M. Schmidt, PHI	38
D. Kingman, NY	37
R. Monday, CHI	32
G. Foster, CIN	29
J. Morgan, CIN	27

Total Bases

M. Schmidt, PHI	306
P. Rose, CIN	299
G. Foster, CIN	298
S. Garvey, LA	284
J. Morgan, CIN	272
W. Montanez, SF, ATL	272

Runs Batted In

G. Foster, CIN	121
J. Morgan, CIN	111
M. Schmidt, PHI	107
B. Watson, HOU	102
G. Luzinski, PHI	95

Stolen Bases

D. Lopes, LA	63
J. Morgan, CIN	60
F. Taveras, PIT	58
C. Cedeno, HOU	58
L. Brock, STL	56

Hits

P. Rose, CIN	215
W. Montanez, SF, ATL	206
S. Garvey, LA	200
B. Buckner, LA	193

Base on Balls

J. Wynn, ATL	127
J. Morgan, CIN	114
M. Schmidt, PHI	100
R. Cey, LA	89

Home Run Percentage

D. Kingman, NY	7.8
M. Schmidt, PHI	6.5
R. Monday, CHI	6.0
J. Morgan, CIN	5.7

Runs

P. Rose, CIN	130
J. Morgan, CIN	113
M. Schmidt, PHI	112
K. Griffey, CIN	111

Doubles

P. Rose, CIN	42
J. Johnstone, PHI	38
G. Maddox, PHI	37
S. Garvey, LA	37

Triples

D. Cash, PHI	12
C. Geronimo, CIN	11
W. Davis, SD	10
D. Parker, PIT	10

PITCHING LEADERS

Winning Percentage

S. Carlton, PHI	.741
J. Candelaria, PIT	.696
D. Sutton, LA	.677
J. Koosman, NY	.677
J. Rooker, PIT	.652

Earned Run Average

J. Denny, STL	2.52
D. Rau, LA	2.57
T. Seaver, NY	2.59
J. Koosman, NY	2.70
P. Zachry, CIN	2.74

Wins

R. Jones, SD	22
J. Koosman, NY	21
D. Sutton, LA	21
S. Carlton, PHI	20
J. Richard, HOU	20

Saves

R. Eastwick, CIN	26
K. Forsch, HOU	19
S. Lockwood, NY	19
C. Hough, LA	18
B. Metzger, SD	16

Strikeouts

T. Seaver, NY	235
J. Richard, HOU	214
J. Koosman, NY	200
S. Carlton, PHI	195
P. Niekro, ATL	173

Complete Games

R. Jones, SD	25
J. Koosman, NY	17
J. Matlack, NY	16
D. Sutton, LA	15
J. Richard, HOU	14

Fewest Hits/9 Innings

J. Richard, HOU	6.84
T. Seaver, NY	7.01
J. Candelaria, PIT	7.08
A. Messersmith, ATL	7.22

Shutouts

J. Matlack, NY	6
J. Montefusco, SF	6
T. Seaver, NY	5
R. Jones, SD	5

Fewest Walks/9 Innings

G. Nolan, CIN	1.02
J. Kaat, PHI	1.27
R. Jones, SD	1.43
J. Matlack, NY	1.96

Most Strikeouts/9 Inn.

T. Seaver, NY	7.80
J. Koosman, NY	7.29
S. Carlton, PHI	6.95
J. Richard, HOU	6.62

Innings

R. Jones, SD	315
J. Richard, HOU	291
T. Seaver, NY	271
P. Niekro, ATL	271

Games Pitched

D. Murray, MON	81
B. Metzger, SD	77
C. Hough, LA	77
R. Eastwick, CIN	71

NATIONAL LEAGUE 1976, *cont.*

		W	L	PCT	GB	R	OR	Batting 2B	3B	HR	BA	SA	SB	Fielding E	DP	FA	Pitching CG	BB	SO	ShO	SV	ERA
East	Philadelphia	101	61	.623		770	557	259	45	110	.272	.395	127	115	148	.981	34	**397**	918	9	44	3.10
	Pittsburgh	92	70	.568	9	708	630	249	56	110	.267	.391	130	163	142	.975	45	460	762	12	35	3.37
	New York	86	76	.531	15	615	**538**	198	34	102	.246	.352	66	131	116	.979	**53**	419	**1025**	**18**	25	**2.94**
	Chicago	75	87	.463	26	611	728	216	24	105	.251	.356	74	140	145	.978	27	490	850	12	33	3.93
	St. Louis	72	90	.444	29	629	671	243	57	63	.260	.359	123	174	163	.973	35	581	731	15	26	3.61
	Montreal	55	107	.340	46	531	734	224	32	94	.235	.340	86	155	**179**	.976	26	659	783	10	21	3.99
West	Cincinnati	102	60	.630		**857**	633	**271**	**63**	**141**	**.280**	**.424**	**210**	**102**	157	**.984**	33	491	790	12	**45**	3.51
	Los Angeles	92	70	.568	10	608	543	200	34	91	.251	.349	144	128	154	.980	47	479	747	17	28	3.02
	Houston	80	82	.494	22	625	657	195	50	66	.256	.347	150	140	155	.978	42	662	780	17	29	3.55
	San Francisco	74	88	.457	28	595	686	211	37	85	.246	.345	88	186	153	.971	27	518	746	**18**	31	3.53
	San Diego	73	89	.451	29	570	662	216	37	64	.247	.337	92	141	148	.978	47	543	652	11	18	3.65
	Atlanta	70	92	.432	32	620	700	170	30	82	.245	.334	74	167	151	.973	33	564	818	13	27	3.87
						7739	7739	2652	499	1113	.255	.361	1364	1742	1811	.977	449	6263	9602	164	362	3.51

AMERICAN LEAGUE 1976

East

New York
W-97 L-62

Billy Martin

POS	Player	AB	BA	HR	RBI	PO	A	E	DP	TC/G	FA	Pitcher	G	IP	W	L	SV	ERA
1B	C. Chambliss	641	.293	17	96	1440	109	9	123	10.1	.994	C. Hunter	36	299	17	15	0	3.53
2B	W. Randolph	430	.267	1	40	307	415	19	87	**6.0**	.974	E. Figueroa	34	257	19	10	0	3.02
SS	F. Stanley	260	.238	1	20	145	251	7	36	3.7	.983	D. Ellis	32	212	17	8	0	3.19
3B	G. Nettles	583	.254	**32**	93	137	**383**	19	**30**	**3.4**	.965	K. Holtzman	21	149	9	7	0	4.17
RF	O. Gamble	340	.232	17	57	199	10	4	3	2.0	.981	D. Alexander	19	137	10	5	0	3.29
CF	M. Rivers	590	.312	8	67	407	6	6	0	3.1	.986	S. Lyle	64	104	7	8	**23**	2.26
LF	R. White	626	.286	14	65	380	9	5	1	2.5	.987	D. Tidrow	47	92	4	5	10	2.63
C	T. Munson	616	.302	17	105	537	78	12	8	5.2	.981							
DH	C. May	288	.278	3	40													
OD	L. Piniella	327	.281	3	38	106	4	2	0		.982							
SS	J. Mason	217	.180	1	14	128	245	13	47	4.2	.966							
UT	S. Alomar	163	.239	1	10	95	114	7	18		.968							

Baltimore
W-88 L-74

Earl Weaver

POS	Player	AB	BA	HR	RBI	PO	A	E	DP	TC/G	FA	Pitcher	G	IP	W	L	SV	ERA
1B	T. Muser	326	.227	1	30	683	62	7	65	6.9	.991	J. Palmer	40	**315**	**22**	13	0	2.51
2B	B. Grich	518	.266	13	54	**389**	400	12	91	5.7	.985	W. Garland	38	232	20	7	1	2.68
SS	M. Belanger	522	.270	1	40	239	**545**	14	97	5.2	.982	R. May	24	152	11	7	0	3.78
3B	D. DeCinces	440	.234	11	42	96	208	19	9	3.0	.941	R. Grimsley	28	137	8	7	0	3.94
RF	R. Jackson	498	.277	27	91	284	8	11	3	2.5	.964	M. Cuellar	26	107	4	13	1	4.96
CF	P. Blair	375	.197	3	16	327	6	7	1	2.4	.979	D. Miller	49	89	2	4	7	2.93
LF	K. Singleton	544	.278	13	70	278	9	5	2	2.2	.983	T. Martinez	28	42	3	1	8	2.59
C	D. Duncan	284	.204	4	17	371	35	6	9	4.4	.985							
DH	L. May	530	.258	25	**109**													
OF	A. Bumbry	450	.251	9	36	251	9	3	2	2.3	.989							
DO	A. Mora	220	.218	6	25	55	3	3	0		.951							
3B	B. Robinson	218	.211	3	11	59	126	6	11	2.7	.969							
C	R. Dempsey	174	.213	0	10	263	34	4	8	5.2	.987							

Boston
W-83 L-79

Darrell Johnson
W-41 L-45

Don Zimmer
W-42 L-34

POS	Player	AB	BA	HR	RBI	PO	A	E	DP	TC/G	FA	Pitcher	G	IP	W	L	SV	ERA
1B	C. Yastrzemski	546	.267	21	102	829	52	2	78	9.4	.998	L. Tiant	38	279	21	12	0	3.06
2B	D. Doyle	432	.250	0	26	209	311	12	67	4.7	.977	R. Wise	34	224	14	11	0	3.54
SS	R. Burleson	540	.291	7	42	274	478	34	88	5.2	.957	F. Jenkins	30	209	12	11	0	3.27
3B	B. Hobson	269	.234	8	34	60	146	14	11	2.9	.936	R. Cleveland	41	170	10	9	2	3.07
RF	D. Evans	501	.242	17	62	324	15	2	4	2.4	.994	D. Pole	31	121	6	5	0	4.31
CF	F. Lynn	507	.314	10	65	367	13	6	4	3.0	.984	R. Jones	24	104	5	3	0	3.38
LF	J. Rice	581	.282	25	85	199	8	7	0	2.2	.967	J. Willoughby	54	99	3	12	10	2.82
C	C. Fisk	487	.255	17	58	649	73	12	9	5.5	.984	B. Lee	24	96	5	7	3	5.63
DH	C. Cooper	451	.282	15	78							T. Murphy	37	81	4	5	8	3.44
OF	R. Miller	269	.283	0	27	220	4	2	1	2.8	.991							
3B	R. Petrocelli	240	.212	3	24	57	120	6	11	2.5	.967							
UT	S. Dillard	167	.275	1	15	58	102	11	21		.936							

Cleveland
W-81 L-78

Frank Robinson

POS	Player	AB	BA	HR	RBI	PO	A	E	DP	TC/G	FA	Pitcher	G	IP	W	L	SV	ERA
1B	B. Powell	293	.215	9	33	698	61	10	76	8.6	.987	P. Dobson	35	217	16	12	0	3.48
2B	D. Kuiper	506	.263	0	37	300	365	9	92	5.3	**.987**	D. Eckersley	36	199	13	12	1	3.44
SS	F. Duffy	392	.212	2	30	222	344	10	83	4.4	**.983**	J. Brown	32	180	9	11	0	4.25
3B	B. Bell	604	.281	7	60	104	330	20	23	2.9	.956	J. Bibby	34	163	13	7	1	3.20
RF	C. Spikes	334	.237	3	31	185	7	3	0	2.0	.985	R. Waits	26	124	7	9	0	3.99
CF	R. Manning	552	.292	6	43	359	8	5	1	2.7	.987	J. Kern	50	118	10	7	15	2.36
LF	G. Hendrick	551	.265	25	81	288	13	4	6	2.1	.987	S. Thomas	37	106	4	4	6	2.29
C	A. Ashby	247	.239	4	32	475	51	7	7	6.2	.987	D. LaRoche	61	96	1	4	21	2.25
DH	R. Carty	552	.310	13	83							T. Buskey	39	94	5	4	1	3.64
S2	L. Blanks	328	.280	5	41	152	213	11	53		.971							
C	R. Fosse	276	.301	2	30	483	42	7	9	**6.3**	.987							
OF	J. Lowenstein	229	.205	2	14	97	7	3	1	1.8	.972							
OF	T. Smith	164	.256	2	12	90	4	2	0	1.9	.979							

Detroit
W-74 L-87

Ralph Houk

POS	Player	AB	BA	HR	RBI	PO	A	E	DP	TC/G	FA	Pitcher	G	IP	W	L	SV	ERA
1B	J. Thompson	412	.218	17	54	1157	88	8	104	**10.7**	.994	D. Roberts	36	252	16	17	0	4.00
2B	P. Garcia	227	.198	3	20	168	219	17	53	5.2	.958	M. Fidrych	31	250	19	9	0	**2.34**
SS	T. Veryzer	354	.234	1	25	164	313	17	53	5.1	.966	V. Ruhle	32	200	9	12	0	3.92
3B	A. Rodriguez	480	.240	8	50	120	280	9	21	3.2	**.978**	R. Bare	30	134	7	8	0	4.63
RF	R. Staub	589	.299	15	96	218	8	7	3	1.8	.970	J. Hiller	56	121	12	8	13	2.38
CF	R. LeFlore	544	.316	4	39	381	14	11	1	3.1	.973	J. Crawford	32	109	1	8	2	4.53
LF	A. Johnson	429	.268	6	45	159	7	8	1	1.9	.954	D. Lemanczyk	20	81	4	6	0	5.11
C	B. Freehan	237	.270	5	27	312	28	6	2	5.7	.983							
DH	W. Horton	401	.262	14	56													
OF	B. Oglivie	305	.285	15	47	136	7	2	0	2.3	.986							
OF	D. Meyer	294	.252	2	16	76	4	1	1	1.7	.988							
2S	C. Scrivener	222	.221	2	16	134	221	11	46		.970							
UT	M. Stanley	214	.257	4	29	187	47	5	14		.979							

AMERICAN LEAGUE 1976, *cont.*

Milwaukee

W-66 L-95

Alex Grammas

POS	Player	AB	BA	HR	RBI	PO	A	E	DP	TC/G	FA	Pitcher	G	IP	W	L	SV	ERA
1B	G. Scott	606	.274	18	77	1393	107	13	133	9.8	.991	J. Slaton	38	293	14	15	0	3.44
2B	T. Johnson	273	.275	0	14	161	222	8	42	3.9	.980	B. Travers	34	240	15	16	0	2.81
SS	R. Yount	638	.252	2	54	**290**	510	31	**104**	5.2	.963	J. Colborn	32	226	9	15	0	3.71
3B	D. Money	439	.267	12	62	96	202	13	21	3.0	.958	J. Augustine	39	172	9	12	0	3.30
RF	G. Thomas	227	.198	8	36	210	4	3	0	2.3	.986	E. Rodriguez	45	136	5	13	8	3.64
CF	V. Joshua	423	.267	5	28	268	10	5	4	2.7	.982	B. Castro	39	70	4	6	8	3.45
LF	S. Lezcano	513	.285	7	56	345	10	10	3	2.6	.973	D. Frisella	32	49	5	2	9	2.74
C	D. Porter	389	.208	5	32	491	52	14	7	5.0	.975							
DH	H. Aaron	271	.229	10	35													
CO	C. Moore	241	.191	3	16	249	44	9	1		.970							
UT	M. Hegan	218	.248	5	31	88	6	2	8		.979							
OD	B. Carbo	183	.235	3	15	71	5	0	1		1.000							
OF	B. Sharp	180	.244	0	11	108	7	3	2	2.1	.975							

West

Kansas City

W-90 L-72

Whitey Herzog

POS	Player	AB	BA	HR	RBI	PO	A	E	DP	TC/G	FA	Pitcher	G	IP	W	L	SV	ERA
1B	J. Mayberry	594	.232	13	95	**1484**	105	7	132	10.0	.996	D. Leonard	35	259	17	10	0	3.51
2B	F. White	446	.229	2	46	255	387	18	75	5.1	.973	A. Fitzmorris	35	220	15	11	0	3.07
SS	F. Patek	432	.241	1	43	233	426	26	87	4.8	.962	D. Bird	39	198	12	10	2	3.36
3B	G. Brett	**645**	**.333**	7	67	**140**	335	26	22	3.2	.948	P. Splittorff	26	159	11	8	0	3.96
RF	A. Cowens	581	.265	3	59	329	13	5	3	2.3	.986	M. Pattin	44	141	8	14	5	2.49
CF	A. Otis	592	.279	18	86	373	5	3	1	2.5	.992	M. Littell	60	104	8	4	16	2.08
LF	T. Poquette	344	.302	2	34	188	1	4	0	2.0	.979	A. Hassler	19	100	5	6	0	2.89
C	B. Martinez	267	.228	5	34	420	40	4	4	4.9	.991	S. Mingori	55	85	5	5	10	2.33
DH	H. McRae	527	.332	8	73													
OF	J. Wohlford	293	.249	1	24	189	6	5	0	2.2	.975							
C	B. Stinson	209	.263	2	25	304	30	7	4	4.3	.979							

Oakland

W-87 L-74

Chuck Tanner

POS	Player	AB	BA	HR	RBI	PO	A	E	DP	TC/G	FA	Pitcher	G	IP	W	L	SV	ERA
1B	G. Tenace	417	.249	22	66	577	31	3	47	8.7	.995	V. Blue	37	298	18	13	0	2.36
2B	P. Garner	555	.261	8	74	378	**465**	22	91	5.4	.975	M. Torrez	39	266	16	12	0	2.50
SS	B. Campaneris	536	.256	1	52	231	490	23	66	5.0	.969	S. Bahnsen	35	143	8	7	0	3.34
3B	S. Bando	550	.240	27	84	125	304	17	26	2.9	.962	P. Mitchell	26	142	9	7	0	4.25
RF	C. Washington	490	.257	5	53	276	10	11	2	2.4	.963	R. Fingers	70	135	13	11	20	2.47
CF	B. North	590	.276	2	31	397	8	9	1	2.9	.978	P. Lindblad	65	115	6	5	5	3.05
LF	J. Rudi	500	.270	13	94	258	6	3	2	2.1	.989	D. Bosman	27	112	4	2	0	4.10
C	L. Haney	177	.226	0	10	290	45	9	2	4.0	.974	J. Todd	49	83	7	8	4	3.80
DH	B. Williams	351	.211	11	41													
UT	D. Baylor	595	.247	15	68	781	45	12	40		.986							
UT	K. McMullen	186	.220	5	23	222	39	2	20		.992							

Minnesota

W-85 L-77

Gene Mauch

POS	Player	AB	BA	HR	RBI	PO	A	E	DP	TC/G	FA	Pitcher	G	IP	W	L	SV	ERA
1B	R. Carew	605	.331	9	90	1394	108	16	**149**	10.0	.989	D. Goltz	36	249	14	14	0	3.36
2B	B. Randall	475	.267	1	34	327	423	**24**	**124**	5.1	.969	J. Hughes	37	177	9	14	0	4.98
SS	R. Smalley	384	.271	2	36	189	338	18	70	5.3	.967	B. Singer	26	172	9	9	0	3.77
3B	M. Cubbage	342	.260	3	49	71	209	18	22	3.0	.940	B. Campbell	**78**	168	17	5	20	3.01
RF	D. Ford	514	.267	20	86	267	6	9	1	2.0	.968	S. Luebber	38	119	4	5	2	4.00
CF	L. Bostock	474	.323	4	60	320	10	4	2	2.7	.988	P. Redfern	23	118	8	8	0	3.51
LF	L. Hisle	581	.272	14	96	361	16	6	1	2.5	.984	T. Burgmeier	57	115	8	1	1	2.50
C	B. Wynegar	534	.260	10	69	650	78	**16**	6	5.4	.978	E. Bane	17	79	4	7	0	5.11
DH	C. Kusick	266	.259	11	36													
UT	S. Braun	417	.288	3	61	71	32	6	3		.945							
OF	S. Brye	258	.264	2	23	147	1	2	0	1.9	.987							
UT	J. Terrell	171	.246	0	8	82	122	8	27		.962							

California

W-76 L-86

Dick Williams
W-39 L-57

Norm Sherry
W-37 L-29

POS	Player	AB	BA	HR	RBI	PO	A	E	DP	TC/G	FA	Pitcher	G	IP	W	L	SV	ERA
1B	B. Bochte	466	.258	2	49	489	39	5	37	9.0	.991	F. Tanana	34	288	19	10	0	2.44
2B	J. Remy	502	.263	0	28	279	406	16	77	5.3	.977	N. Ryan	39	284	17	**18**	0	3.36
SS	D. Chalk	438	.217	0	33	141	293	13	45	4.4	.971	G. Ross	34	225	8	16	0	3.00
3B	R. Jackson	410	.227	8	40	85	222	16	19	2.8	.950	P. Hartzell	37	166	7	4	2	2.77
RF	B. Bonds	378	.265	10	54	199	9	5	3	2.2	.977	D. Kirkwood	28	158	6	12	0	4.61
CF	R. Torres	264	.205	6	27	195	5	2	0	1.9	.990	S. Monge	32	118	6	7	0	3.36
LF	D. Collins	365	.263	4	28	160	3	1	0	2.3	.994	D. Drago	43	79	7	8	6	4.42
C	A. Etchebarren	247	.227	0	21	539	46	12	7	5.9	.980							
DH	T. Davis	219	.265	3	26													
UT	B. Melton	341	.208	6	42	227	36	3	22		.989							
2S	M. Guerrero	268	.284	1	18	129	172	14	32		.956							
1O	D. Briggs	248	.214	1	14	358	26	5	33		.987							
OF	L. Stanton	231	.190	2	25	128	1	2	0	1.7	.985							
1B	T. Solaita	215	.270	9	33	451	54	1	32	9.4	.998							
C	T. Humphrey	196	.245	1	19	397	42	9	4	6.3	.980							
OF	B. Jones	166	.211	6	17	98	6	1	0	1.7	.990							

Texas

W-76 L-86

Frank Lucchesi

POS	Player	AB	BA	HR	RBI	PO	A	E	DP	TC/G	FA	Pitcher	G	IP	W	L	SV	ERA
1B	M. Hargrove	541	.287	7	58	1222	110	**21**	103	9.6	.984	G. Perry	32	250	15	14	0	3.24
2B	L. Randle	539	.224	1	51	291	319	18	63	5.6	.971	N. Briles	32	210	11	9	1	3.26
SS	T. Harrah	584	.260	15	67	**290**	473	**36**	81	**5.5**	.955	B. Blyleven	24	202	9	11	0	2.76
3B	R. Howell	491	.253	8	53	103	245	**28**	20	2.9	.926	J. Umbarger	30	197	10	12	0	3.15
RF	J. Burroughs	604	.237	18	86	289	12	4	3	2.0	.987	S. Hargan	35	124	8	8	1	3.63
CF	J. Beniquez	478	.255	0	33	410	18	6	3	3.1	.986	S. Foucault	46	76	8	8	5	3.32
LF	G. Clines	446	.276	0	38	215	9	3	1	2.2	.987	J. Hoerner	41	35	0	4	8	5.14
C	J. Sundberg	448	.228	3	34	**719**	**96**	7	**11**	5.9	**.991**							
DH	T. Grieve	546	.255	20	81													
UT	D. Thompson	196	.214	1	13	60	117	4	12		.978							

AMERICAN LEAGUE 1976, *cont.*

	POS	Player	AB	BA	HR	RBI	PO	A	E	DP	TC/G	FA	Pitcher	G	IP	W	L	SV	ERA
Chicago	1B	J. Spencer	518	.253	14	70	1206	**112**	2	116	9.2	**.998**	G. Gossage	31	224	9	17	1	3.94
W-64 L-97	2B	J. Brohamer	354	.251	7	40	263	334	10	74	5.2	.984	B. Johnson	32	211	9	16	0	4.73
Paul Richards	SS	B. Dent	562	.246	2	52	279	468	18	96	4.8	.976	K. Brett	27	201	10	12	1	3.32
	3B	K. Bell	230	.248	5	20	70	124	6	10	3.0	.970	F. Barrios	35	142	5	9	3	4.31
	RF	R. Garr	527	.300	4	36	254	7	6	2	2.1	.978	T. Forster	29	111	2	12	1	4.38
	CF	C. Lemon	451	.246	4	38	353	12	3	1	2.8	.992	P. Vuckovich	33	110	7	4	0	4.66
	LF	J. Orta	636	.274	14	72	156	9	5	1	2.2	.971	D. Hamilton	45	90	6	6	10	3.60
	C	B. Downing	317	.256	3	30	450	38	6	4	5.3	.988	C. Carroll	29	77	4	4	6	2.57
	DH	P. Kelly	311	.254	5	34													
	23	B. Stein	392	.268	4	36	153	241	19	39		.954							
	D1	L. Johnson	222	.320	4	33	210	18	4	20		.983							
	C	J. Essian	199	.246	0	21	319	53	10	10	5.0	.974							

BATTING AND BASE RUNNING LEADERS

Batting Average
G. Brett, KC .333
H. McRae, KC .332
R. Carew, MIN .331
L. Bostock, MIN .323
R. LeFlore, DET .316

Slugging Average
R. Jackson, BAL .502
J. Rice, BOS .482
G. Nettles, NY .475
F. Lynn, BOS .467
R. Carew, MIN .463

Home Runs
G. Nettles, NY 32
R. Jackson, BAL 27
S. Bando, OAK 27
L. May, BAL 25
G. Hendrick, CLE 25
J. Rice, BOS 25

Total Bases
G. Brett, KC 298
C. Chambliss, NY 283
J. Rice, BOS 280
R. Carew, MIN 280
G. Nettles, NY 277

Runs Batted In
L. May, BAL 109
T. Munson, NY 105
C. Yastrzemski, BOS 102
L. Hisle, MIN 96
R. Staub, DET 96
C. Chambliss, NY 96

Stolen Bases
B. North, OAK 75
R. LeFlore, DET 58
B. Campaneris, OAK 54
D. Baylor, OAK 52
F. Patek, KC 51

Hits
G. Brett, KC 215
R. Carew, MIN 200
C. Chambliss, NY 188
T. Munson, NY 186

Base on Balls
M. Hargrove, TEX 97
T. Harrah, TEX 91
B. Grich, BAL 86
R. Staub, DET 83
R. White, NY 83

Home Run Percentage
G. Nettles, NY 5.5
R. Jackson, BAL 5.4
S. Bando, OAK 4.9
L. May, BAL 4.7

Runs
R. White, NY 104
R. Carew, MIN 97
M. Rivers, NY 95
G. Brett, KC 94

Doubles
A. Otis, KC 40
D. Evans, BOS 34
H. McRae, KC 34
R. Carty, CLE 34
G. Brett, KC 34

Triples
G. Brett, KC 14
P. Garner, OAK 12
R. Carew, MIN 12
T. Poquette, KC 10

PITCHING LEADERS

Winning Percentage
B. Campbell, MIN .773
W. Garland, BAL .741
D. Ellis, NY .680
M. Fidrych, DET .679
F. Tanana, CAL .655
E. Figueroa, NY .655

Earned Run Average
M. Fidrych, DET 2.34
V. Blue, OAK 2.36
F. Tanana, CAL 2.44
M. Torrez, OAK 2.50
J. Palmer, BAL 2.51

Wins
J. Palmer, BAL 22
L. Tiant, BOS 21
W. Garland, BAL 20
M. Fidrych, DET 19
E. Figueroa, NY 19
F. Tanana, CAL 19

Saves
S. Lyle, NY 23
D. LaRoche, CLE 21
B. Campbell, MIN 20
R. Fingers, OAK 20
M. Littell, KC 16

Strikeouts
N. Ryan, CAL 327
F. Tanana, CAL 261
B. Blyleven, MIN, TEX 219
D. Eckersley, CLE 200
C. Hunter, NY 173

Complete Games
M. Fidrych, DET 24
F. Tanana, CAL 23
J. Palmer, BAL 23
G. Perry, TEX 21
C. Hunter, NY 21
N. Ryan, CAL 21

Fewest Hits/9 Innings
N. Ryan, CAL 6.12
F. Tanana, CAL 6.63
D. Eckersley, CLE 7.01
J. Palmer, BAL 7.29

Shutouts
N. Ryan, CAL 7
B. Blyleven, MIN, TEX 6
V. Blue, OAK 6
J. Palmer, BAL 6

Fewest Walks/9 Innings
D. Bird, KC 1.41
F. Jenkins, BOS 1.85
G. Perry, TEX 1.87
V. Blue, OAK 1.90

Most Strikeouts/9 Inn.
N. Ryan, CAL 10.36
D. Eckersley, CLE 9.05
F. Tanana, CAL 8.16
B. Blyleven, MIN, TEX 6.62

Innings
J. Palmer, BAL 315
C. Hunter, NY 299
B. Blyleven, MIN, TEX 298
V. Blue, OAK 298

Games Pitched
B. Campbell, MIN 78
R. Fingers, OAK 70
P. Lindblad, OAK 65
S. Lyle, NY 64

		W	L	PCT	GB	R	OR	Batting 2B	3B	HR	BA	SA	SB	Fielding E	DP	FA	Pitching CG	BB	SO	ShO	SV	ERA
East	New York	97	62	.610		730	**575**	231	36	120	.269	.389	163	126	141	.980	62	448	674	15	37	**3.19**
	Baltimore	88	74	.543	10.5	619	598	213	28	119	.243	.358	150	**118**	157	**.982**	59	489	678	16	23	3.31
	Boston	83	79	.512	15.5	716	660	257	53	**134**	.263	**.402**	95	141	148	.978	49	**409**	673	13	27	3.52
	Cleveland	81	78	.509	16	615	615	189	38	85	.263	.359	75	121	159	.980	30	533	928	**17**	**46**	3.48
	Detroit	74	87	.460	24	609	709	207	38	101	.257	.365	107	168	161	.974	55	550	738	12	20	3.87
	Milwaukee	66	95	.410	32	570	655	170	38	88	.246	.340	62	152	160	.975	45	567	677	10	27	3.64
West	Kansas City	90	72	.556		713	611	**259**	**57**	65	.269	.371	218	139	147	.978	41	493	735	12	35	3.21
	Oakland	87	74	.540	2.5	686	598	208	33	113	.246	.361	**341**	144	130	.977	39	415	711	15	29	3.26
	Minnesota	85	77	.525	5	**743**	704	222	51	81	**.274**	.375	146	172	**182**	.973	29	610	762	11	23	3.72
	California	76	86	.469	14	550	631	210	23	63	.235	.318	126	150	139	.977	**64**	553	**992**	15	17	3.36
	Texas	76	86	.469	14	616	652	213	26	80	.250	.341	87	156	142	.976	63	461	773	15	15	3.47
	Chicago	64	97	.398	25.5	586	745	209	46	73	.255	.349	120	130	155	.979	54	600	802	10	22	4.25
						7753	7753	2588	467	1122	.256	.361	1690	1717	1821	.977	590	6128	9143	161	321	3.52

NATIONAL LEAGUE 1977

		POS	Player	AB	BA	HR	RBI	PO	A	E	DP	TC/G	FA	Pitcher	G	IP	W	L	SV	ERA
East	**Philadelphia**	1B	R. Hebner	397	.285	18	62	927	65	9	91	9.7	.991	S. Carlton	36	283	**23**	10	0	2.64
	W-101 L-61	2B	T. Sizemore	519	.281	4	47	348	427	11	**104**	5.2	.986	L. Christenson	34	219	19	6	0	4.07
	Danny Ozark	SS	L. Bowa	624	.280	4	41	222	518	13	94	4.9	.983	R. Lerch	32	169	10	6	0	5.06
		3B	M. Schmidt	544	.274	38	101	106	**396**	19	33	**3.5**	.964	J. Kaat	35	160	6	11	0	5.40
		RF	B. McBride	280	.339	11	41	140	6	2	1	2.0	.986	J. Lonborg	25	158	11	4	0	4.10
		CF	G. Maddox	571	.292	14	74	383	7	9	2	2.9	.977	R. Reed	60	124	7	5	15	2.76
		LF	G. Luzinski	554	.309	39	130	205	11	8	2	1.5	.964	G. Garber	64	103	8	6	19	2.36
		C	B. Boone	440	.284	11	66	653	80	8	9	5.7	.989	T. McGraw	45	79	7	3	9	2.62
		OF	J. Johnstone	363	.284	15	59	163	9	0	1	1.9	1.000	W. Brusstar	46	71	7	2	3	2.66
		OF	J. Martin	215	.260	6	28	117	4	2	1	1.2	.984							
		C	T. McCarver	169	.320	6	30	233	14	3	3	6.0	.988							
		1B	D. Johnson	156	.321	8	36	291	14	0	26	7.1	1.000							

NATIONAL LEAGUE 1977, *cont.*

	POS	Player	AB	BA	HR	RBI	PO	A	E	DP	TC/G	FA	Pitcher	G	IP	W	L	SV	ERA
Pittsburgh	1B	B. Robinson	507	.304	26	104	695	34	6	62	8.5	.992	J. Candelaria	33	231	20	5	0	**2.34**
W-96 L-66	2B	R. Stennett	453	.336	5	51	269	315	11	70	5.3	.982	J. Reuss	33	208	10	13	0	4.11
Chuck Tanner	SS	F. Taveras	544	.252	1	29	178	449	25	62	4.5	.962	J. Rooker	30	204	14	9	0	3.09
	3B	P. Garner	585	.260	17	77	98	240	10	28	3.3	.971	B. Kison	33	193	9	10	0	4.90
	RF	D. Parker	637	**.338**	21	88	389	26	15	0	2.7	.965	G. Gossage	72	133	11	9	26	1.62
	CF	O. Moreno	492	.240	7	34	366	10	9	4	2.6	.977	O. Jones	34	108	3	7	0	5.08
	LF	A. Oliver	568	.308	19	82	305	6	6	1	2.1	.981	K. Tekulve	72	103	10	1	7	3.06
	C	D. Dyer	270	.241	3	19	502	41	2	10	5.9	**.996**	G. Jackson	49	91	5	3	4	3.86
	C	E. Ott	311	.264	7	38	455	49	9	6	5.7	.982	L. Demery	39	90	6	5	1	5.10
	1B	W. Stargell	186	.274	13	35	449	27	7	26	8.8	.986	T. Forster	33	87	6	4	1	4.45
	UT	F. Gonzalez	181	.276	4	27	43	66	2	6		.982							
St. Louis	1B	K. Hernandez	560	.291	15	91	1453	106	12	**146**	9.9	.992	E. Rasmussen	34	233	11	17	0	3.48
W-83 L-79	2B	M. Tyson	418	.246	7	57	267	423	15	99	5.2	.979	B. Forsch	35	217	20	7	0	3.48
Vern Rapp	SS	G. Templeton	621	.322	8	79	285	453	32	98	5.1	.958	J. Denny	26	150	8	8	0	4.50
	3B	K. Reitz	587	.261	17	79	121	320	9	**35**	2.9	**.980**	J. Urrea	41	140	7	6	4	3.15
	RF	H. Cruz	339	.236	6	42	154	9	6	1	1.6	.964	P. Falcone	27	124	4	8	1	5.44
	CF	J. Mumphrey	463	.287	2	38	291	8	9	1	2.3	.971	T. Underwood	19	100	6	9	0	4.95
	LF	L. Brock	489	.272	2	46	184	2	9	1	1.5	.954	B. Metzger	58	93	4	2	7	3.11
	C	T. Simmons	516	.318	21	95	683	75	10	5	5.4	.987	C. Carroll	51	90	4	2	4	2.50
	OF	T. Scott	292	.291	3	41	223	5	1	0	2.6	.996	A. Hrabosky	65	86	6	5	10	4.40
	OF	B. McBride	122	.262	4	20	48	2	0	0	1.5	1.000	R. Eastwick	41	54	3	7	4	4.70
	1B	R. Freed	83	.398	5	21	102	7	0	13	6.1	1.000							
Chicago	1B	B. Buckner	426	.284	11	60	966	58	10	75	10.4	.990	R. Reuschel	39	252	20	10	1	2.79
W-81 L-81	2B	M. Trillo	504	.280	7	57	330	**467**	**25**	81	**5.5**	.970	R. Burris	39	221	14	16	0	4.72
Herman Franks	SS	I. DeJesus	624	.266	3	40	234	**595**	33	94	5.6	.962	B. Bonham	34	215	10	13	0	4.35
	3B	S. Ontiveros	546	.299	10	68	100	324	20	24	2.9	.955	M. Krukow	34	172	8	14	0	4.40
	RF	B. Murcer	554	.265	27	89	237	11	5	5	1.7	.980	G. Hernandez	67	110	8	7	4	3.03
	CF	J. Morales	490	.290	11	69	247	8	4	3	2.0	.985	B. Sutter	62	107	7	3	31	1.35
	LF	G. Gross	239	.322	5	32	109	3	1	0	1.6	.991	P. Reuschel	69	107	5	6	4	4.37
	C	G. Mitterwald	349	.238	9	43	621	78	8	13	6.5	.989							
	10	L. Biittner	493	.298	12	62	792	65	11	51		.987							
	OF	G. Clines	239	.293	3	41	68	3	1	0	1.1	.986							
	OF	J. Cardenal	226	.239	3	18	85	1	1	0	1.4	.989							
	C	S. Swisher	205	.190	5	15	327	38	9	3	5.2	.976							
Montreal	1B	T. Perez	559	.283	19	91	1312	110	11	88	9.7	.992	S. Rogers	40	302	17	16	0	3.10
W-75 L-87	2B	D. Cash	650	.289	0	43	343	443	11	73	5.2	.986	J. Brown	42	186	9	12	0	4.50
Dick Williams	SS	C. Speier	531	.235	5	38	236	435	21	75	5.0	.970	D. Stanhouse	47	158	10	10	10	3.42
	3B	L. Parrish	402	.246	11	46	81	225	21	11	2.8	.936	W. Twitchell	22	139	6	5	0	4.21
	RF	E. Valentine	508	.293	25	76	232	9	7	1	2.0	.972	S. Bahnsen	23	127	8	9	0	4.82
	CF	A. Dawson	525	.282	19	65	352	9	4	1	2.7	.989	S. Alcala	31	102	2	6	2	4.69
	LF	W. Cromartie	620	.282	5	50	319	10	8	1	2.2	.976	J. Kerrigan	66	89	3	5	11	3.24
	C	G. Carter	522	.284	31	84	**811**	**101**	9	**14**	6.3	.990	W. McEnaney	69	87	3	5	3	3.93
	OF	D. Unser	289	.273	12	40	120	2	3	0	1.7	.976	B. Atkinson	55	83	7	2	7	3.36
	3B	W. Garrett	159	.270	2	22	34	101	0	2	2.8	1.000							
New York	1B	J. Milner	388	.255	12	57	672	48	4	64	8.3	.994	J. Koosman	32	227	8	**20**	0	3.49
W-64 L-98	2B	F. Millan	314	.248	2	21	197	188	9	43	4.4	.977	N. Espinosa	32	200	10	13	0	3.42
Joe Frazier	SS	B. Harrelson	269	.178	1	12	141	239	6	41	3.9	.984	J. Matlack	26	169	7	15	0	4.21
W-15 L-30	3B	L. Randle	513	.304	5	27	98	221	13	25	3.0	.961	C. Swan	26	147	9	10	0	4.22
Joe Torre	RF	M. Vail	279	.262	8	35	159	5	6	2	2.0	.965	P. Zachry	19	120	7	6	0	3.76
W-49 L-68	CF	L. Mazzilli	537	.250	6	46	386	9	3	1	2.6	.992	S. Lockwood	63	104	4	8	20	3.38
	LF	S. Henderson	350	.297	12	65	189	4	4	1	2.0	.980	T. Seaver	13	96	7	3	0	3.00
	C	J. Stearns	431	.251	12	55	742	76	15	12	**6.6**	.982	B. Apodaca	59	84	4	8	5	3.43
	OF	B. Boisclair	307	.293	4	44	140	1	6	0	1.6	.959							
	S2	D. Flynn	282	.191	0	14	155	203	13	38		.965							
	O1	E. Kranepool	281	.281	10	40	347	30	4	21		.990							
	OF	D. Kingman	211	.209	9	28	76	0	2	0	1.7	.974							
	UT	J. Youngblood	182	.253	0	11	99	88	7	21		.964							
West																			
Los Angeles	1B	S. Garvey	646	.297	33	115	**1606**	55	8	137	**10.4**	**.995**	D. Sutton	33	240	14	8	0	3.19
W-98 L-64	2B	D. Lopes	502	.283	11	53	287	380	14	74	5.2	.979	B. Hooton	32	223	12	7	1	2.62
Tom Lasorda	SS	B. Russell	634	.278	4	51	234	523	29	**102**	5.1	.963	T. John	31	220	20	7	0	2.78
	3B	R. Cey	564	.241	30	110	138	346	18	29	3.3	.964	R. Rhoden	31	216	16	10	0	3.75
	RF	R. Smith	488	.307	32	87	240	7	5	0	1.8	.980	D. Rau	32	212	14	8	0	3.44
	CF	R. Monday	392	.230	15	48	208	3	2	0	1.9	.991	C. Hough	70	127	6	12	22	3.33
	LF	D. Baker	533	.291	30	86	227	8	3	2	1.6	.987	M. Garman	49	63	4	4	12	2.71
	C	S. Yeager	387	.256	16	55	690	89	**18**	12	6.5	.977							
	UT	L. Lacy	169	.266	6	21	56	69	4	11		.969							
	OF	G. Burke	169	.254	1	13	98	1	3	0	1.4	.971							
Cincinnati	1B	D. Driessen	536	.300	17	91	1182	75	7	116	8.5	.994	F. Norman	35	221	14	13	0	3.38
W-88 L-74	2B	J. Morgan	521	.288	22	78	**351**	359	5	100	4.7	**.993**	T. Seaver	20	165	14	3	0	2.34
Sparky Anderson	SS	D. Concepcion	572	.271	8	64	280	490	11	101	5.0	**.986**	J. Billingham	36	162	10	10	0	5.22
	3B	P. Rose	**655**	.311	9	64	98	268	16	18	2.4	.958	P. Borbon	73	127	10	5	18	3.19
	RF	K. Griffey	585	.318	12	57	298	10	3	3	2.1	.990	P. Moskau	20	108	6	6	0	4.00
	CF	C. Geronimo	492	.266	10	52	375	9	3	2	2.6	.992	D. Capilla	22	106	7	8	0	4.23
	LF	G. Foster	615	.320	**52**	**149**	352	12	3	1	2.3	.992	D. Murray	61	102	7	2	4	4.94
	C	J. Bench	494	.275	31	109	705	66	10	10	5.8	.987	P. Zachry	12	75	3	7	0	5.04
													W. Fryman	17	75	5	5	1	5.40
													R. Eastwick	23	43	2	2	7	2.91

NATIONAL LEAGUE 1977, *cont.*

Team	POS	Player	AB	BA	HR	RBI	PO	A	E	DP	TC/G	FA	Pitcher	G	IP	W	L	SV	ERA
Houston	1B	B. Watson	554	.289	22	110	1331	**118**	9	100	10.0	.994	J. Richard	36	267	18	12	0	2.97
W-81 L-81	2B	A. Howe	413	.264	8	58	192	279	7	49	5.0	.985	M. Lemongello	34	215	9	14	0	3.47
Bill Virdon	SS	R. Metzger	269	.186	0	16	130	260	11	45	4.2	.973	J. Niekro	44	181	13	8	5	3.03
	3B	E. Cabell	625	.282	16	68	**140**	280	**23**	17	3.1	.948	J. Andujar	26	159	11	8	0	3.68
	RF	J. Cruz	579	.299	17	87	311	11	9	1	2.1	.973	F. Bannister	24	143	8	9	0	4.03
	CF	C. Cedeno	530	.279	14	71	335	14	1	2	2.6	.997	J. Sambito	54	89	5	5	7	2.33
	LF	T. Puhl	229	.301	0	10	119	3	1	0	2.1	.992	K. Forsch	42	86	5	8	8	2.72
	C	J. Ferguson	421	.257	16	61	634	80	11	10	5.9	.985	B. McLaughlin	46	85	4	7	5	4.24
	S2	J. Gonzalez	383	.245	1	27	154	293	27	56		.943							
	OF	W. Howard	187	.257	2	13	100	2	1	1	1.7	.990							
	OF	C. Johnson	144	.299	10	23	49	4	3	0	1.6	.946							
San Francisco	1B	W. McCovey	478	.280	28	86	1072	60	**13**	93	8.4	.989	E. Halicki	37	258	16	12	0	3.31
W-75 L-87	2B	R. Andrews	436	.264	0	25	225	314	20	66	4.9	.964	J. Barr	38	234	12	16	0	4.77
Joe Altobelli	SS	T. Foli	368	.228	4	27	184	302	13	72	4.9	.974	B. Knepper	27	166	11	9	0	3.36
	3B	B. Madlock	533	.302	12	46	96	220	17	16	2.6	.949	J. Montefusco	26	157	7	12	0	3.50
	RF	J. Clark	413	.252	13	51	226	11	6	2	2.1	.975	C. Williams	55	119	6	5	0	4.01
	CF	T. Whitfield	326	.285	7	36	167	4	5	0	2.1	.972	G. Lavelle	73	118	7	7	20	2.06
	LF	G. Thomasson	446	.256	17	71	255	2	11	1	2.4	.959	R. Moffitt	64	88	4	9	11	3.58
	C	M. Hill	320	.250	9	50	505	57	6	4	5.6	.989	L. McGlothen	21	80	2	9	0	5.63
	UT	D. Thomas	506	.267	8	44	307	158	14	24		.971							
	UT	D. Evans	461	.254	17	72	324	83	13	15		.969							
	OF	R. Elliott	167	.240	7	26	68	5	2	1	1.6	.973							
	UT	V. Harris	165	.261	2	14	69	96	8	21		.954							
	C	G. Alexander	119	.303	5	20	174	8	6	0	5.7	.968							
San Diego	1B	M. Ivie	489	.272	9	66	863	56	7	76	8.8	.992	B. Shirley	39	214	12	18	0	3.70
W-69 L-93	2B	M. Champion	507	.229	1	43	301	348	17	82	4.5	.974	B. Owchinko	30	170	9	12	0	4.45
John McNamara	SS	B. Almon	613	.261	2	43	**303**	538	**41**	87	**5.7**	.954	T. Griffin	38	151	6	9	0	4.47
W-20 L-28	3B	T. Ashford	249	.217	3	24	32	145	12	14	2.6	.937	R. Jones	27	147	6	12	0	4.59
Bob Skinner	RF	G. Richards	525	.290	5	32	193	13	8	0	2.0	.963	D. Freisleben	33	139	7	9	0	4.60
W-1 L-0	CF	G. Hendrick	541	.311	23	81	386	11	7	2	2.8	.983	R. Fingers	**78**	132	8	9	**35**	3.00
Alvin Dark	LF	D. Winfield	615	.275	25	92	368	15	11	3	2.5	.972	D. Spillner	76	123	7	6	6	3.73
W-48 L-65	C	G. Tenace	437	.233	15	61	523	61	12	9	6.0	.980	R. Sawyer	56	111	7	6	0	5.84
	OF	J. Turner	289	.246	10	48	114	10	7	2	1.9	.947	D. Tomlin	76	102	4	4	3	3.00
	C	D. Roberts	186	.220	1	23	254	24	5	2	4.5	.982							
	3B	D. Rader	170	.271	5	27	43	104	6	9	3.0	.961							
	01	D. Kingman	168	.238	11	39	142	14	3	5		.981							
Atlanta	1B	W. Montanez	544	.287	20	68	1129	70	10	88	9.0	.992	P. Niekro	44	**330**	16	**20**	0	4.04
W-61 L-101	2B	R. Gilbreath	407	.243	8	43	277	305	13	61	4.9	.978	D. Ruthven	25	151	7	13	0	4.23
Dave Bristol	SS	P. Rockett	264	.254	1	24	152	209	23	38	4.6	.940	B. Capra	45	139	6	11	0	5.37
W-8 L-21	3B	J. Moore	361	.260	5	34	86	189	17	10	2.8	.942	A. Messersmith	16	102	5	4	0	4.41
Ted Turner	RF	G. Matthews	555	.283	17	64	262	11	10	1	2.0	.965	E. Solomon	18	89	6	6	0	4.55
W-0 L-1	CF	R. Office	428	.241	5	39	249	8	3	3	2.5	.988	D. Campbell	65	89	0	6	13	3.03
Vern Benson	LF	J. Burroughs	579	.271	41	114	249	9	7	3	1.7	.974	R. Camp	54	79	6	3	10	3.99
W-1 L-0	C	B. Pocoroba	321	.290	8	44	542	78	7	8	6.3	.989	D. Collins	40	71	3	9	2	5.07
Dave Bristol	UT	J. Royster	445	.216	6	28	182	267	28	40		.941							
W-52 L-79	OF	B. Bonnell	360	.300	1	45	181	3	2	1	2.5	.989							
	S2	D. Chaney	209	.201	3	15	113	182	8	30		.974							
	PH	C. Gaston	85	.271	3	21													

BATTING AND BASE RUNNING LEADERS

Batting Average
D. Parker, PIT .338
G. Templeton, STL .322
G. Foster, CIN .320
K. Griffey, CIN .318
T. Simmons, STL .318

Slugging Average
G. Foster, CIN .631
G. Luzinski, PHI .594
R. Smith, LA .576
M. Schmidt, PHI .574
J. Bench, CIN .540

Home Runs
G. Foster, CIN 52
J. Burroughs, ATL 41
G. Luzinski, PHI 39
M. Schmidt, PHI 38
S. Garvey, LA 33

Total Bases
G. Foster, CIN 388
D. Parker, PIT 338
G. Luzinski, PHI 329
S. Garvey, LA 322
M. Schmidt, PHI 312

Runs Batted In
G. Foster, CIN 149
G. Luzinski, PHI 130
S. Garvey, LA 115
J. Burroughs, ATL 114
B. Watson, HOU 110
R. Cey, LA 110

Stolen Bases
F. Taveras, PIT 70
C. Cedeno, HOU 61
G. Richards, SD 56
O. Moreno, PIT 53
J. Morgan, CIN 49

Hits
D. Parker, PIT 215
P. Rose, CIN 204
G. Templeton, STL 200
G. Foster, CIN 197

Base on Balls
G. Tenace, SD 125
J. Morgan, CIN 117
R. Smith, LA 104
M. Schmidt, PHI 104

Home Run Percentage
G. Foster, CIN 8.5
J. Burroughs, ATL 7.1
G. Luzinski, PHI 7.0
M. Schmidt, PHI 7.0

PITCHING LEADERS

Winning Percentage
J. Candelaria, PIT .800
T. Seaver, NY, CIN .778
L. Christenson, PHI .760
T. John, LA .741
B. Forsch, STL .741

Earned Run Average
J. Candelaria, PIT 2.34
T. Seaver, NY, CIN 2.58
B. Hooton, LA 2.62
S. Carlton, PHI 2.64
T. John, LA 2.78

Wins
S. Carlton, PHI 23
T. Seaver, NY, CIN 21
B. Forsch, STL 20
T. John, LA 20
J. Candelaria, PIT 20
R. Reuschel, CHI 20

Saves
R. Fingers, SD 35
B. Sutter, CHI 31
G. Gossage, PIT 26
C. Hough, LA 22
S. Lockwood, NY 20
G. Lavelle, SF 20

Strikeouts
P. Niekro, ATL 262
J. Richard, HOU 214
S. Rogers, MON 206
S. Carlton, PHI 198
T. Seaver, NY, CIN 196

Complete Games
P. Niekro, ATL 20
T. Seaver, NY, CIN 19
S. Carlton, PHI 17
S. Rogers, MON 17
J. Richard, HOU 13

Fewest Hits/9 Innings
T. Seaver, NY, CIN 6.85
J. Richard, HOU 7.15
S. Carlton, PHI 7.28
B. Hooton, LA 7.43

Shutouts
T. Seaver, NY, CIN 7
R. Reuschel, CHI 4
S. Rogers, MON 4

Fewest Walks/9 Innings
J. Candelaria, PIT 1.95
T. John, LA 2.05
D. Rau, LA 2.08
J. Barr, SF 2.15

NATIONAL LEAGUE 1977, *cont.*

BATTING AND BASE RUNNING LEADERS

Runs		Doubles		Triples	
G. Foster, CIN	124	D. Parker, PIT	44	G. Templeton, STL	18
K. Griffey, CIN	117	D. Cash, MON	42	G. Richards, SD	11
M. Schmidt, PHI	114	K. Hernandez, STL	41	M. Schmidt, PHI	11
J. Morgan, CIN	113	W. Cromartie, MON	41	B. Almon, SD	11

PITCHING LEADERS

Most Strikeouts/9 Inn.		Innings		Games Pitched	
J. Koosman, NY	7.61	P. Niekro, ATL	330	R. Fingers, SD	78
J. Richard, HOU	7.21	S. Rogers, MON	302	D. Spillner, SD	76
P. Niekro, ATL	7.15	S. Carlton, PHI	283	D. Tomlin, SD	76
T. Seaver, NY, CIN	6.75	J. Richard, HOU	267	B. Metzger, SD, STL	75

								Batting						Fielding			Pitching					
		W	L	PCT	GB	R	OR	2B	3B	HR	BA	SA	SB	E	DP	FA	CG	BB	SO	ShO	SV	ERA
East	Philadelphia	101	61	.623		**847**	668	266	56	186	**.279**	**.448**	135	120	168	.981	31	482	856	4	**47**	3.71
	Pittsburgh	96	66	.593	5	734	665	278	57	133	.274	.413	**260**	145	137	.977	25	485	890	**15**	39	3.61
	St. Louis	83	79	.512	18	737	688	252	56	96	.270	.388	134	139	**174**	.978	26	532	768	10	31	3.81
	Chicago	81	81	.500	20	692	739	271	37	111	.266	.387	64	153	147	.977	16	489	**942**	10	44	4.01
	Montreal	75	87	.463	26	665	736	**294**	50	138	.260	.402	88	129	128	.980	31	579	856	11	33	4.01
	New York	64	98	.395	37	587	663	227	30	88	.244	.346	98	134	132	.978	27	490	911	12	28	3.77
West	Los Angeles	98	64	.605		769	**582**	223	28	**191**	.266	.418	114	124	160	.981	34	**438**	930	13	39	**3.22**
	Cincinnati	88	74	.543	10	802	725	269	42	181	.274	.436	170	**95**	154	**.984**	33	544	868	12	32	4.22
	Houston	81	81	.500	17	680	650	263	**60**	114	.254	.385	187	142	136	.978	**37**	545	871	11	28	3.54
	San Francisco	75	87	.463	23	673	711	227	41	134	.253	.383	90	179	136	.972	27	529	854	10	33	3.75
	San Diego	69	93	.426	29	692	834	245	49	120	.249	.375	133	189	142	.971	6	673	827	5	44	4.43
	Atlanta	61	101	.377	37	678	895	218	20	139	.254	.376	82	175	127	.972	28	701	915	5	31	4.85
						8556	8556	3033	526	1631	.262	.396	1555	1724	1741	.977	321	6487	10488	118	429	3.91

AMERICAN LEAGUE 1977

East

	POS	Player	AB	BA	HR	RBI	PO	A	E	DP	TC/G	FA	Pitcher	G	IP	W	L	SV	ERA
New York	1B	C. Chambliss	600	.287	17	90	1368	98	16	129	9.4	.989	E. Figueroa	32	239	16	11	0	3.58
W-100 L-62	2B	W. Randolph	551	.274	4	40	350	454	16	108	5.6	.980	M. Torrez	31	217	14	12	0	3.86
Billy Martin	SS	B. Dent	477	.247	8	49	250	434	18	90	4.5	.974	R. Guidry	31	211	16	7	1	2.82
	3B	G. Nettles	589	.255	37	107	132	321	12	31	3.0	.974	D. Gullett	22	158	14	4	0	3.59
	RF	R. Jackson	525	.286	32	110	236	7	13	0	2.0	.949	D. Tidrow	49	151	11	4	5	3.16
	CF	M. Rivers	565	.326	12	69	380	11	7	1	2.9	.982	C. Hunter	22	143	9	9	0	4.72
	LF	R. White	519	.268	14	52	301	7	6	4	2.3	.981	S. Lyle	**72**	137	13	5	26	2.17
	C	T. Munson	595	.308	18	100	657	73	12	4	5.5	.984							
	DH	C. May	181	.227	2	16													
	OD	L. Piniella	339	.330	12	45	77	2	2	0		.975							
	OF	P. Blair	164	.262	4	25	125	1	4	0	1.6	.969							
	UT	C. Johnson	142	.296	12	31	145	14	1	13		.994							
Baltimore	1B	L. May	585	.253	27	99	907	56	5	101	8.8	.995	J. Palmer	39	**319**	**20**	11	0	2.91
W-97 L-64	2B	B. Smith	367	.215	5	29	260	272	5	78	5.2	.991	R. May	37	252	18	14	0	3.61
Earl Weaver	SS	M. Belanger	402	.206	2	30	244	417	10	82	4.7	**.985**	M. Flanagan	36	235	15	10	1	3.64
	3B	D. DeCinces	522	.259	19	69	124	**330**	20	**34**	3.2	.958	R. Grimsley	34	218	14	10	0	3.96
	RF	K. Singleton	536	.328	24	99	278	8	4	2	1.9	.986	D. Martinez	42	167	14	7	4	4.10
	CF	A. Bumbry	518	.317	4	41	329	7	3	0	2.6	.991	S. McGregor	29	114	3	5	4	4.42
	LF	P. Kelly	360	.256	10	49	181	2	3	1	1.7	.984	T. Martinez	41	50	5	1	9	2.70
	C	R. Dempsey	270	.226	3	34	416	52	11	10	5.3	.977	D. Drago	36	40	6	3	3	3.63
	DH	E. Murray	611	.283	27	88													
	2B	R. Dauer	304	.243	5	25	179	213	7	55	4.8	.982							
	OF	A. Mora	233	.245	13	44	66	2	0	0	1.2	1.000							
	C	D. Skaggs	216	.287	1	24	344	34	2	4	4.8	.995							
Boston	1B	G. Scott	584	.269	33	95	1446	115	**24**	150	10.1	.985	F. Jenkins	28	193	10	10	0	3.68
W-97 L-64	2B	D. Doyle	455	.240	2	49	230	412	14	90	4.8	.979	R. Cleveland	36	190	11	8	2	4.26
Don Zimmer	SS	R. Burleson	**663**	.293	3	52	**285**	482	24	111	5.1	.970	L. Tiant	32	189	12	8	0	4.53
	3B	B. Hobson	593	.265	30	112	128	272	23	27	2.7	.946	B. Stanley	41	151	8	7	3	3.99
	RF	B. Carbo	228	.289	15	34	131	5	7	1	2.1	.951	B. Campbell	69	140	13	9	**31**	2.96
	CF	F. Lynn	497	.260	18	76	333	7	2	1	2.7	.994	B. Lee	27	128	9	5	1	4.42
	LF	C. Yastrzemski	558	.296	28	102	287	16	0	1	2.2	1.000	R. Wise	26	128	11	5	0	4.78
	C	C. Fisk	536	.315	26	102	779	69	11	7	5.7	.987	M. Paxton	29	108	10	5	0	3.83
	DH	J. Rice	644	.320	**39**	114							J. Willoughby	31	55	6	2	2	4.94
	OF	D. Evans	230	.287	14	36	126	2	1	0	2.0	.992							
	OF	R. Miller	189	.254	0	24	118	5	1	3	1.6	.992							
Detroit	1B	J. Thompson	585	.270	31	105	**1599**	97	16	135	**10.8**	.991	D. Rozema	28	218	15	7	0	3.10
W-74 L-88	2B	T. Fuentes	615	.309	5	51	**379**	459	**26**	**115**	**5.7**	.970	F. Arroyo	38	209	8	18	0	4.18
Ralph Houk	SS	T. Veryzer	350	.197	2	28	185	377	18	62	4.7	.969	B. Sykes	32	133	5	7	0	4.40
	3B	A. Rodriguez	306	.219	10	32	60	222	8	19	3.1	.972	D. Roberts	22	129	4	10	0	5.16
	RF	B. Oglivie	450	.262	21	61	236	10	6	3	2.1	.976	J. Crawford	37	126	7	8	1	4.79
	CF	R. LeFlore	652	.325	16	57	365	12	11	0	2.5	.972	J. Hiller	45	124	8	14	7	3.56
	LF	S. Kemp	552	.257	18	88	252	10	5	1	1.8	.981	M. Wilcox	20	106	6	2	0	3.65
	C	M. May	397	.249	12	46	551	78	9	**12**	5.7	.986	M. Fidrych	11	81	6	4	0	2.89
	DH	R. Staub	623	.278	22	101							S. Foucault	44	74	7	7	13	3.16
	3B	P. Mankowski	286	.276	3	27	73	196	10	15	3.3	.964							
	OF	M. Stanley	222	.230	8	23	101	2	3	0	1.9	.972							
	C	J. Wockenfuss	164	.274	9	25	175	20	3	2	5.4	.985							

AMERICAN LEAGUE 1977, *cont.*

Cleveland

W-71 L-90

Frank Robinson
W-26 L-31

Jeff Torborg
W-45 L-59

POS	Player	AB	BA	HR	RBI	PO	A	E	DP	TC/G	FA	Pitcher	G	IP	W	L	SV	ERA
1B	A. Thornton	433	.263	28	70	1026	71	6	97	9.4	.995	W. Garland	38	283	13	**19**	0	3.59
2B	D. Kuiper	610	.277	1	50	334	449	12	104	5.4	.985	D. Eckersley	33	247	14	13	0	3.53
SS	F. Duffy	334	.201	4	31	145	301	15	62	3.8	.967	J. Bibby	37	207	12	13	2	3.57
3B	B. Bell	479	.292	11	64	111	253	15	23	3.2	.960	R. Waits	37	135	9	7	2	4.00
RF	J. Norris	440	.270	2	37	320	9	6	1	2.7	.982	P. Dobson	33	133	3	12	1	6.16
CF	R. Manning	252	.226	5	18	191	2	2	0	2.9	.990	A. Fitzmorris	29	133	6	10	0	5.41
LF	B. Bochte	392	.304	5	43	161	7	6	1	2.3	.966	D. Hood	41	105	2	1	0	3.00
C	F. Kendall	317	.249	3	39	506	35	5	5	5.4	.991	J. Kern	60	92	8	10	18	3.42
DH	R. Carty	461	.280	15	80													
OF	P. Dade	461	.291	3	45	167	10	2	2	1.8	.989							
UT	L. Blanks	322	.286	6	38	100	181	11	27		.962							
C	R. Fosse	238	.265	6	27	427	48	8	4	6.3	.983							
OF	R. Pruitt	219	.288	2	32	104	2	3	0	1.6	.972							

Milwaukee

W-67 L-95

Alex Grammas

POS	Player	AB	BA	HR	RBI	PO	A	E	DP	TC/G	FA	Pitcher	G	IP	W	L	SV	ERA
1B	C. Cooper	643	.300	20	78	1386	118	12	134	10.2	.992	J. Slaton	32	221	10	14	0	3.58
2B	D. Money	570	.279	25	83	256	357	12	82	5.4	.981	J. Augustine	33	209	12	18	0	4.48
SS	R. Yount	605	.288	4	49	256	449	26	94	4.8	.964	M. Haas	32	198	10	12	0	4.32
3B	S. Bando	580	.250	17	82	96	277	13	31	2.9	.966	E. Rodriguez	42	143	5	6	4	4.34
RF	S. Lezcano	400	.273	21	49	238	11	3	2	2.3	.988	L. Sorensen	23	142	7	10	0	4.37
CF	V. Joshua	536	.261	9	49	311	8	10	0	2.3	.970	B. Travers	19	122	4	12	0	5.24
LF	J. Wohlford	391	.248	2	36	246	6	5	1	2.1	.981	M. Caldwell	21	94	5	8	0	4.60
C	C. Moore	375	.248	5	45	566	78	**13**	10	4.8	.980	B. Castro	51	69	8	6	13	4.17
DH	J. Quirk	221	.217	3	13													
OF	S. Brye	241	.249	7	28	166	8	0	1	2.1	1.000							

Toronto

W-54 L-107

Roy Hartsfield

POS	Player	AB	BA	HR	RBI	PO	A	E	DP	TC/G	FA	Pitcher	G	IP	W	L	SV	ERA
1B	D. Ault	445	.245	11	64	1113	103	16	91	10.1	.987	D. Lemanczyk	34	252	13	16	0	4.25
2B	S. Staggs	291	.258	2	28	169	194	13	35	5.2	.965	J. Garvin	34	245	10	18	0	4.19
SS	H. Torres	266	.241	5	26	82	165	5	29	3.7	.980	J. Jefferson	33	217	9	17	0	4.31
3B	R. Howell	364	.316	10	44	81	165	12	12	3.0	.953	P. Vuckovich	53	148	7	7	8	3.47
RF	O. Velez	360	.256	16	62	140	5	4	1	1.9	.973	M. Willis	43	107	2	6	5	3.95
CF	G. Woods	227	.216	0	17	154	4	1	0	2.7	.994	J. Byrd	17	87	2	13	0	6.21
LF	A. Woods	440	.284	6	35	215	6	7	1	2.0	.969	J. Johnson	43	86	2	4	5	4.60
C	A. Ashby	396	.210	2	29	619	71	11	11	5.7	.984	J. Clancy	13	77	4	9	0	5.03
DH	R. Fairly	458	.279	19	64							B. Singer	13	60	2	8	0	6.75
OS	B. Bailor	496	.310	5	32	235	165	12	27		.971							
3D	D. Rader	313	.240	13	40	38	103	5	2		.966							
UT	D. McKay	274	.197	3	22	141	205	14	36		.961							
OD	S. Ewing	244	.287	4	34	65	1	3	0		.957							
OF	J. Scott	233	.240	2	15	127	3	5	2	2.0	.963							
OF	S. Bowling	194	.206	1	13	139	14	2	0	1.8	.987							

West

Kansas City

W-102 L-60

Whitey Herzog

POS	Player	AB	BA	HR	RBI	PO	A	E	DP	TC/G	FA	Pitcher	G	IP	W	L	SV	ERA
1B	J. Mayberry	543	.230	23	82	1296	81	7	118	9.5	**.995**	D. Leonard	38	293	**20**	12	1	3.04
2B	F. White	474	.245	5	50	310	434	8	86	4.9	**.989**	J. Colborn	36	239	18	14	0	3.62
SS	F. Patek	497	.262	5	60	252	413	29	70	4.5	.958	P. Splittorff	37	229	16	6	0	3.69
3B	G. Brett	564	.312	22	88	115	325	20	33	**3.4**	.957	A. Hassler	29	156	9	6	0	4.21
RF	A. Cowens	606	.312	23	112	307	14	6	1	2.1	.982	M. Pattin	31	128	10	3	0	3.59
CF	A. Otis	478	.251	17	78	326	10	3	0	2.4	.991	D. Bird	53	118	11	4	14	3.89
LF	T. Poquette	342	.292	2	33	177	4	0	1	1.9	1.000	L. Gura	52	106	8	5	10	3.14
C	D. Porter	425	.275	16	60	663	61	**13**	4	5.9	.982	M. Littell	48	105	8	4	12	3.60
DH	H. McRae	641	.298	21	92							S. Mingori	43	64	2	4	4	3.09
UT	P. LaCock	218	.303	3	29	203	19	2	16		.991							
OF	J. Zdeb	195	.297	2	23	93	4	3	0	1.1	.970							
C	J. Wathan	119	.328	2	21	130	9	1	0	4.0	.993							

Texas

W-94 L-68

Frank Lucchesi
W-31 L-31

Eddie Stanky
W-1 L-0

Connie Ryan
W-2 L-4

Billy Hunter
W-60 L-33

POS	Player	AB	BA	HR	RBI	PO	A	E	DP	TC/G	FA	Pitcher	G	IP	W	L	SV	ERA
1B	M. Hargrove	525	.305	18	69	1393	100	11	134	9.9	.993	G. Perry	34	238	15	12	0	3.37
2B	B. Wills	541	.287	9	62	321	**492**	15	89	5.5	.982	D. Alexander	34	237	17	11	0	3.65
SS	B. Campaneris	552	.254	5	46	269	483	25	91	5.2	.968	B. Blyleven	30	235	14	12	0	2.72
3B	T. Harrah	539	.263	27	87	108	278	15	20	2.5	.963	D. Ellis	23	167	10	6	1	2.91
RF	D. May	340	.241	7	42	181	8	6	2	1.8	.969	N. Briles	30	108	6	4	1	4.07
CF	J. Beniquez	424	.269	10	50	311	10	4	1	2.6	.988	A. Devine	56	106	11	6	15	3.57
LF	C. Washington	521	.284	12	68	255	11	6	3	2.1	.978	P. Lindblad	42	99	4	5	4	4.18
C	J. Sundberg	453	.291	6	65	**801**	**103**	5	**12**	**6.1**	**.994**	R. Moret	18	72	3	3	4	3.75
DH	W. Horton	519	.289	15	75							D. Knowles	42	50	5	2	4	3.24
OF	K. Henderson	244	.258	5	23	113	0	2	0	1.8	.983							
OF	T. Grieve	236	.225	7	30	77	5	2	1	1.4	.976							
UT	K. Bevacqua	96	.333	5	28	42	31	1	4		.986							

Chicago

W-90 L-72

Bob Lemon

POS	Player	AB	BA	HR	RBI	PO	A	E	DP	TC/G	FA	Pitcher	G	IP	W	L	SV	ERA
1B	J. Spencer	470	.247	18	69	977	90	10	76	8.6	.991	F. Barrios	33	231	14	7	0	4.13
2B	J. Orta	564	.282	11	84	287	335	19	64	4.6	.970	S. Stone	31	207	15	12	0	4.52
SS	A. Bannister	560	.275	3	57	259	325	**40**	51	4.7	.936	K. Kravec	26	167	11	8	0	4.10
3B	E. Soderholm	460	.280	25	67	99	249	8	18	2.8	**.978**	C. Knapp	27	146	12	7	0	4.81
RF	R. Zisk	531	.290	30	101	210	9	4	3	2.0	.982	W. Wood	24	123	7	8	0	4.98
CF	C. Lemon	553	.273	19	67	512	12	12	2	3.6	.978	L. LaGrow	66	99	7	3	25	2.45
LF	R. Garr	543	.300	10	54	225	10	3	2	1.9	.987	B. Johnson	29	92	4	5	2	4.01
C	J. Essian	322	.273	10	44	592	62	9	8	6.0	.986	K. Brett	13	83	6	4	0	4.99
DH	O. Gamble	408	.297	31	83							D. Hamilton	55	67	4	5	9	3.63
D1	L. Johnson	374	.302	18	65	346	32	4	31		.990							
C	B. Downing	169	.284	4	25	320	28	6	5	5.8	.983							
32	J. Brohamer	152	.257	2	20	54	100	8	15		.951							
OF	W. Nordhagen	124	.315	4	22	50	1	3	0	1.2	.944							

AMERICAN LEAGUE 1977, *cont.*

Minnesota

W-84 L-77

Gene Mauch

POS	Player	AB	BA	HR	RBI	PO	A	E	DP	TC/G	FA	Pitcher	G	IP	W	L	SV	ERA
1B	R. Carew	616	**.388**	14	100	1459	**121**	10	**161**	10.5	.994	D. Goltz	39	303	**20**	11	0	3.36
2B	B. Randall	306	.239	0	22	222	297	8	74	5.2	.985	P. Thormodsgard	37	218	11	15	0	4.62
SS	R. Smalley	584	.231	6	56	255	**504**	33	**116**	**5.3**	.958	G. Zahn	34	198	12	14	0	4.68
3B	M. Cubbage	417	.264	9	55	90	266	18	29	3.0	.952	T. Johnson	71	147	16	7	15	3.12
RF	D. Ford	453	.267	11	60	205	9	8	2	1.6	.964	P. Redfern	30	137	6	9	0	5.19
CF	L. Bostock	593	.336	14	90	349	10	4	0	2.4	.989	R. Schueler	52	135	8	7	3	4.40
LF	L. Hisle	546	.302	28	**119**	287	11	8	2	2.3	.974	T. Burgmeier	61	97	6	4	7	5.10
C	B. Wynegar	532	.261	10	79	676	84	5	8	5.4	.993							
DH	C. Kusick	268	.254	12	45													
DO	G. Adams	269	.338	6	49	60	3	2	1		.969							
DH	R. Chiles	261	.264	3	36													
UT	J. Terrell	214	.224	1	20	58	129	6	20		.969							
2B	R. Wilfong	171	.246	1	13	114	164	12	40	4.4	.959							
OF	B. Gorinski	118	.195	3	22	44	0	3	0	1.3	.936							

California

W-74 L-88

Norm Sherry
W-39 L-42

Dave Garcia
W-35 L-46

POS	Player	AB	BA	HR	RBI	PO	A	E	DP	TC/G	FA	Pitcher	G	IP	W	L	SV	ERA
1B	T. Solaita	324	.241	14	53	641	57	7	50	7.7	.990	N. Ryan	37	299	19	16	0	2.77
2B	J. Remy	575	.252	4	44	307	420	19	90	4.9	.975	F. Tanana	31	241	15	9	0	**2.54**
SS	R. Mulliniks	271	.269	3	21	112	229	13	37	4.6	.963	P. Hartzell	41	189	8	12	4	3.57
3B	D. Chalk	519	.277	3	45	114	266	21	21	2.8	.948	K. Brett	21	142	7	10	0	4.25
RF	B. Bonds	592	.264	37	115	272	5	4	0	2.0	.986	W. Simpson	27	122	6	12	0	5.83
CF	G. Flores	342	.278	1	26	177	5	4	2	2.2	.978	D. Miller	41	92	4	4	4	3.02
LF	J. Rudi	242	.264	13	53	131	3	0	0	2.2	1.000	D. LaRoche	46	81	6	5	13	3.10
C	T. Humphrey	304	.227	2	34	661	63	8	10	6.0	.989							
DH	D. Baylor	561	.251	25	75													
UT	R. Jackson	292	.243	8	28	314	75	6	33		.985							
UT	M. Guerrero	244	.283	1	28	61	105	2	18		.988							
OF	T. Bosley	212	.297	0	19	130	1	5	0	2.5	.963							
SS	B. Grich	181	.243	7	23	88	141	4	23	4.5	.983							

Seattle

W-64 L-98

Darrell Johnson

POS	Player	AB	BA	HR	RBI	PO	A	E	DP	TC/G	FA	Pitcher	G	IP	W	L	SV	ERA
1B	D. Meyer	582	.273	22	90	1407	109	12	134	9.6	.992	G. Abbott	36	204	12	13	0	4.46
2B	J. Baez	305	.259	1	17	151	250	11	54	5.4	.973	J. Montague	47	182	8	12	4	4.30
SS	C. Reynolds	420	.248	4	28	197	397	28	86	4.6	.955	D. Pole	25	122	7	12	0	5.16
3B	B. Stein	556	.259	13	67	**146**	255	15	20	2.8	.964	E. Romo	58	114	8	10	16	2.84
RF	L. Stanton	454	.275	27	90	175	9	9	2	2.1	.953	D. Segui	40	111	0	7	2	5.68
CF	R. Jones	597	.263	24	76	465	11	9	3	3.1	.981	M. Kekich	41	90	5	4	3	5.60
LF	S. Braun	451	.235	5	31	186	11	5	3	2.0	.975	T. House	26	89	4	5	1	3.93
C	B. Stinson	297	.269	8	32	494	43	9	11	5.5	.984	G. Wheelock	17	88	6	9	0	4.91
DH	J. Bernhardt	305	.243	7	30													
OD	D. Collins	402	.239	5	28	124	6	2	2		.985							
OF	C. Lopez	297	.283	8	34	160	11	5	3	2.0	.972							
2S	L. Milbourne	242	.219	2	21	120	209	11	46		.968							
2B	J. Cruz	199	.256	1	7	114	171	5	29	5.4	.983							

Oakland

W-63 L-98

Jack McKeon
W-26 L-27

Bobby Winkles
W-37 L-71

POS	Player	AB	BA	HR	RBI	PO	A	E	DP	TC/G	FA	Pitcher	G	IP	W	L	SV	ERA
1B	D. Allen	171	.240	5	31	389	37	7	36	8.7	.984	V. Blue	38	280	14	**19**	0	3.83
2B	M. Perez	373	.231	2	23	192	287	13	48	4.7	.974	R. Langford	37	208	8	**19**	0	4.02
SS	R. Picciolo	419	.200	2	22	213	381	21	70	4.2	.966	D. Medich	26	148	10	6	0	4.69
3B	W. Gross	485	.233	22	63	126	242	**27**	26	2.7	.932	J. Coleman	43	128	4	4	2	2.95
RF	J. Tyrone	294	.245	5	26	167	5	9	0	2.2	.950	B. Lacey	64	122	6	8	7	3.02
CF	T. Armas	363	.240	13	53	294	9	6	4	2.8	.981	P. Torrealba	41	117	4	6	2	2.62
LF	M. Page	501	.307	21	75	279	11	14	0	2.3	.954	D. Bair	45	83	4	6	8	3.47
C	J. Newman	162	.222	4	15	251	36	9	5	3.1	.970	D. Giusti	40	60	3	3	6	3.00
DH	M. Sanguillen	571	.275	6	58													
2S	R. Scott	364	.261	0	20	198	270	21	49		.957							
UT	E. Williams	348	.241	13	38	305	26	3	14		.991							
10	M. Jorgensen	203	.246	8	32	365	32	4	26		.990							
UT	R. McKinney	198	.177	6	21	213	27	9	22		.964							
OF	B. North	184	.261	1	9	112	1	2	0	2.2	.983							
OF	L. Murray	162	.179	1	9	114	3	1	3	1.5	.992							

BATTING AND BASE RUNNING LEADERS

Batting Average

R. Carew, MIN	.388
L. Bostock, MIN	.336
K. Singleton, BAL	.328
M. Rivers, NY	.326
R. LeFlore, DET	.325

Slugging Average

J. Rice, BOS	.593
R. Carew, MIN	.570
R. Jackson, NY	.550
L. Hisle, MIN	.533
G. Brett, KC	.532

Home Runs

J. Rice, BOS	39
G. Nettles, NY	37
B. Bonds, CAL	37
G. Scott, BOS	33
R. Jackson, NY	32

Total Bases

J. Rice, BOS	382
R. Carew, MIN	351
H. McRae, KC	330
A. Cowens, KC	318
R. LeFlore, DET	310

Runs Batted In

L. Hisle, MIN	119
B. Bonds, CAL	115
J. Rice, BOS	114
B. Hobson, BOS	112
A. Cowens, KC	112

Stolen Bases

F. Patek, KC	53
M. Page, OAK	42
J. Remy, CAL	41
B. Bonds, CAL	41
R. LeFlore, DET	39

Hits

R. Carew, MIN	239
R. LeFlore, DET	212
J. Rice, BOS	206
L. Bostock, MIN	199

Base on Balls

T. Harrah, TEX	109
K. Singleton, BAL	107
M. Hargrove, TEX	103
W. Gross, OAK	86

Home Run Percentage

O. Gamble, CHI	7.6
A. Thornton, CLE	6.5
G. Nettles, NY	6.3
B. Bonds, CAL	6.3

PITCHING LEADERS

Winning Percentage

P. Splittorff, KC	.727
R. Guidry, NY	.696
T. Johnson, MIN	.696
D. Rozema, DET	.682
J. Palmer, BAL	.645
D. Goltz, MIN	.645

Earned Run Average

F. Tanana, CAL	2.54
B. Blyleven, TEX	2.72
N. Ryan, CAL	2.77
R. Guidry, NY	2.82
J. Palmer, BAL	2.91

Wins

D. Leonard, KC	20
D. Goltz, MIN	20
J. Palmer, BAL	20
N. Ryan, CAL	19
J. Colborn, KC	18
R. May, BAL	18

Saves

B. Campbell, BOS	31
S. Lyle, NY	26
L. LaGrow, CHI	25
J. Kern, CLE	18
D. LaRoche, CLE, CAL	17

Strikeouts

N. Ryan, CAL	341
D. Leonard, KC	244
F. Tanana, CAL	205
J. Palmer, BAL	193
D. Eckersley, CLE	191

Complete Games

N. Ryan, CAL	22
J. Palmer, BAL	22
D. Leonard, KC	21
W. Garland, CLE	21
F. Tanana, CAL	20

Fewest Hits/9 Innings

N. Ryan, CAL	5.96
B. Blyleven, TEX	6.93
J. Palmer, BAL	7.42
R. Guidry, NY	7.42

Shutouts

F. Tanana, CAL	7
R. Guidry, NY	5
B. Blyleven, TEX	5
D. Leonard, KC	5

Fewest Walks/9 Innings

D. Rozema, DET	1.40
F. Jenkins, BOS	1.68
P. Hartzell, CAL	1.81
D. Eckersley, CLE	1.97

AMERICAN LEAGUE 1977, *cont.*

BATTING AND BASE RUNNING LEADERS

Runs		Doubles		Triples	
R. Carew, MIN	128	H. McRae, KC	54	R. Carew, MIN	16
C. Fisk, BOS	106	R. Jackson, NY	39	J. Rice, BOS	15
G. Brett, KC	105	C. Lemon, CHI	38	A. Cowens, KC	14
		R. Carew, MIN	38	G. Brett, KC	13

PITCHING LEADERS

Most Strikeouts/9 Inn.		Innings		Games Pitched	
N. Ryan, CAL	10.26	J. Palmer, BAL	319	S. Lyle, NY	72
F. Tanana, CAL	7.65	D. Goltz, MIN	303	T. Johnson, MIN	71
R. Guidry, NY	7.51	N. Ryan, CAL	299	B. Campbell, BOS	69
D. Leonard, KC	7.49	D. Leonard, KC	293	B. McClure, MIL	68

								Batting						Fielding			Pitching					
		W	L	PCT	GB	R	OR	2B	3B	HR	BA	SA	SB	E	DP	FA	CG	BB	SO	ShO	SV	ERA
East	New York	100	62	.617		831	**651**	267	47	184	.281	.444	93	132	151	.979	52	486	758	16	34	3.61
	Baltimore	97	64	.602	2.5	719	653	231	25	148	.261	.393	90	**106**	**189**	**.983**	**65**	494	737	11	23	3.74
	Boston	97	64	.602	2.5	859	712	258	56	**213**	.281	**.465**	66	133	162	.978	40	**378**	758	13	40	4.16
	Detroit	74	88	.457	26	714	751	228	45	166	.264	.410	60	142	153	.978	44	470	784	3	23	4.13
	Cleveland	71	90	.441	28.5	676	739	221	46	100	.269	.380	87	130	145	.979	45	550	876	8	30	4.10
	Milwaukee	67	95	.414	33	639	765	255	46	125	.258	.389	85	139	165	.978	38	566	719	6	25	4.32
	Toronto	54	107	.335	45.5	605	822	230	41	100	.252	.365	65	164	133	.974	40	623	771	3	20	4.57
West	Kansas City	102	60	.630		822	**651**	**299**	**77**	146	.277	.436	170	137	145	.978	41	499	850	15	**42**	**3.52**
	Texas	94	68	.580	8	767	657	265	39	135	.270	.405	154	117	156	.982	49	471	864	**17**	31	3.56
	Chicago	90	72	.556	12	844	771	254	52	192	.278	.444	42	159	125	.974	34	516	842	3	40	4.25
	Minnesota	84	77	.522	17.5	**867**	776	273	60	123	**.282**	.417	105	143	184	.978	35	507	737	4	25	4.38
	California	74	88	.457	28	675	695	233	40	131	.255	.386	159	147	137	.976	53	572	**965**	13	26	3.76
	Seattle	64	98	.395	38	624	855	218	33	133	.256	.381	110	147	162	.976	18	578	785	1	31	4.83
	Oakland	63	98	.391	38.5	605	749	176	37	117	.240	.352	**176**	190	136	.970	32	560	788	4	26	4.05
						10247	10247	3408	644	2013	.266	.405	1462	1986	2143	.977	586	7270	11234	117	416	4.07

NATIONAL LEAGUE 1978

East

Philadelphia

W-90 L-72

Danny Ozark

POS	Player	AB	BA	HR	RBI	PO	A	E	DP	TC/G	FA	Pitcher	G	IP	W	L	SV	ERA
1B	R. Hebner	435	.283	17	71	987	49	6	86	8.9	.994	S. Carlton	34	247	16	13	0	2.84
2B	T. Sizemore	351	.219	0	25	232	302	12	61	5.1	.978	L. Christenson	33	228	13	14	0	3.24
SS	L. Bowa	654	.294	3	43	224	502	10	87	4.7	**.986**	R. Lerch	33	184	11	8	0	3.96
3B	M. Schmidt	513	.251	21	78	98	324	16	**34**	3.2	.963	D. Ruthven	20	151	13	5	0	2.99
RF	B. McBride	472	.269	10	49	234	8	1	3	2.0	.996	J. Kaat	26	140	8	5	0	4.11
CF	G. Maddox	598	.288	11	68	444	7	8	1	3.0	.983	J. Lonborg	22	114	8	10	0	5.21
LF	G. Luzinski	540	.265	35	101	232	7	4	2	1.6	.984	R. Reed	66	109	3	4	17	2.23
C	B. Boone	435	.283	12	62	619	55	6	6	5.3	**.991**	T. McGraw	55	90	8	7	9	3.20
OF	J. Martin	266	.271	9	36	148	8	2	1	1.4	.987							
1B	J. Cardenal	201	.249	4	33	360	17	4	39	7.6	.990							

Pittsburgh

W-88 L-73

Chuck Tanner

POS	Player	AB	BA	HR	RBI	PO	A	E	DP	TC/G	FA	Pitcher	G	IP	W	L	SV	ERA
1B	W. Stargell	390	.295	28	97	875	57	6	76	8.4	.994	B. Blyleven	34	244	14	10	0	3.02
2B	R. Stennett	333	.243	3	35	164	208	11	40	4.8	.971	D. Robinson	35	228	14	6	1	3.47
SS	F. Taveras	654	.278	0	38	216	448	38	80	4.5	.946	J. Candelaria	30	189	12	11	1	3.24
3B	P. Garner	528	.261	10	66	67	172	18	12	3.2	.930	J. Rooker	28	163	9	11	0	4.25
RF	D. Parker	581	**.334**	30	117	302	12	13	3	2.2	.960	K. Tekulve	**91**	135	8	7	31	2.33
CF	O. Moreno	515	.235	2	33	409	9	7	2	2.8	.984	J. Bibby	34	107	8	7	1	3.53
LF	B. Robinson	499	.246	14	80	235	8	3	2	1.9	.988	B. Kison	28	96	6	6	0	3.19
C	E. Ott	379	.269	9	38	537	42	**15**	7	6.1	.975	G. Jackson	60	77	7	5	5	3.27
OF	J. Milner	295	.271	6	38	118	1	0	0	1.7	1.000	E. Whitson	43	74	5	6	4	3.28
1C	M. Sanguillen	220	.264	3	16	438	20	0	26		1.000							
C	D. Dyer	175	.211	0	13	326	22	3	2	6.4	.991							

Chicago

W-79 L-83

Herman Franks

POS	Player	AB	BA	HR	RBI	PO	A	E	DP	TC/G	FA	Pitcher	G	IP	W	L	SV	ERA
1B	B. Buckner	446	.323	5	74	1075	83	6	85	11.1	.995	R. Reuschel	35	243	14	15	0	3.41
2B	M. Trillo	552	.261	4	55	354	**505**	19	**99**	**5.9**	.978	D. Lamp	37	224	7	15	0	3.29
SS	I. DeJesus	619	.278	3	35	232	**558**	27	96	5.1	.967	R. Burris	40	199	7	13	1	4.75
3B	S. Ontiveros	276	.243	1	22	57	194	9	16	3.4	.965	D. Roberts	35	142	6	8	1	5.26
RF	B. Murcer	499	.281	9	64	225	8	5	0	1.7	.979	M. Krukow	27	138	9	3	0	3.91
CF	G. Gross	347	.265	1	39	182	6	4	1	1.7	.979	D. Moore	71	103	9	7	4	4.11
LF	D. Kingman	395	.266	28	79	170	8	4	2	1.8	.978	B. Sutter	64	99	8	10	27	3.18
C	D. Rader	305	.203	3	36	412	51	11	7	4.2	.977	G. Hernandez	54	60	8	2	3	3.75
10	L. Biittner	343	.257	4	50	601	53	9	53		.986							
OF	G. Clines	229	.258	0	17	84	6	2	0	1.4	.978							
3B	R. Scott	227	.282	0	15	43	101	11	15	2.6	.929							
OF	M. Vail	180	.333	4	33	50	1	1	0	1.2	.981							

Montreal

W-76 L-86

Dick Williams

POS	Player	AB	BA	HR	RBI	PO	A	E	DP	TC/G	FA	Pitcher	G	IP	W	L	SV	ERA
1B	T. Perez	544	.290	14	78	1181	82	11	116	8.8	.991	R. Grimsley	36	263	20	11	0	3.05
2B	D. Cash	658	.252	3	43	**362**	400	11	91	4.9	**.986**	S. Rogers	30	219	13	10	1	2.47
SS	C. Speier	501	.251	5	51	245	467	18	93	4.9	.975	R. May	27	144	8	10	0	3.88
3B	L. Parrish	520	.277	15	70	122	288	23	20	3.1	.947	D. Schatzeder	29	144	7	7	0	3.06
RF	E. Valentine	570	.289	25	76	296	24	10	3	2.3	.970	W. Twitchell	33	112	4	12	0	5.38
CF	A. Dawson	609	.253	25	72	411	17	5	2	2.8	.988	H. Dues	25	99	5	6	1	2.36
LF	W. Cromartie	607	.297	10	56	340	24	8	5	2.4	.978	W. Fryman	19	95	5	7	1	3.61
C	G. Carter	533	.255	20	72	**781**	83	10	**9**	5.8	.989	S. Bahnsen	44	75	1	5	7	3.84
10	D. Unser	179	.196	2	15	232	12	2	16		.992	D. Knowles	60	72	3	3	6	2.38
												M. Garman	47	61	4	6	13	4.40

NATIONAL LEAGUE 1978, *cont.*

St. Louis

W-69 L-93

Vern Rapp
W-6 L-11

Jack Krol
W-1 L-1

Ken Boyer
W-62 L-81

POS	Player	AB	BA	HR	RBI	PO	A	E	DP	TC/G	FA	Pitcher	G	IP	W	L	SV	ERA
1B	K. Hernandez	542	.255	11	64	1436	96	10	124	9.8	.994	J. Denny	33	234	14	11	0	2.96
2B	M. Tyson	377	.233	3	26	246	306	13	78	4.6	.977	B. Forsch	34	234	11	17	0	3.69
SS	G. Templeton	647	.280	2	47	**285**	523	**40**	**108**	**5.5**	.953	P. Vuckovich	45	198	12	12	1	2.55
3B	K. Reitz	540	.246	10	75	111	314	12	18	2.9	**.973**	S. Martinez	22	138	9	8	0	3.65
RF	J. Morales	457	.239	4	46	254	5	6	0	2.1	.977	M. Littell	72	106	4	8	11	2.80
CF	G. Hendrick	382	.288	17	67	241	5	1	0	2.4	.996	J. Urrea	27	99	4	9	0	5.36
LF	J. Mumphrey	367	.262	2	37	178	10	1	1	1.6	.995	B. Schultz	62	83	2	4	6	3.80
C	T. Simmons	516	.287	22	80	670	**88**	9	6	5.7	.988							
OF	L. Brock	298	.221	0	12	114	2	3	0	1.5	.975							
OF	T. Scott	219	.228	1	14	100	6	6	0	1.5	.946							
2B	M. Phillips	164	.268	1	28	93	110	6	24	3.8	.971							
1B	R. Freed	92	.239	2	20	110	10	1	13	8.1	.992							

New York

W-66 L-96

Joe Torre

POS	Player	AB	BA	HR	RBI	PO	A	E	DP	TC/G	FA	Pitcher	G	IP	W	L	SV	ERA
1B	W. Montanez	609	.256	17	96	1350	**104**	8	**138**	9.3	.995	J. Koosman	38	235	3	15	2	3.75
2B	D. Flynn	532	.237	0	36	249	299	8	70	4.3	.986	C. Swan	29	207	9	6	0	**2.43**
SS	T. Foli	413	.257	1	27	190	314	18	78	4.7	.966	N. Espinosa	32	204	11	15	0	4.72
3B	L. Randle	437	.233	2	35	108	215	11	21	2.7	.967	P. Zachry	21	138	10	6	0	3.33
RF	E. Maddox	389	.257	2	39	155	8	2	3	2.1	.988	M. Bruhert	27	134	4	11	0	4.77
CF	L. Mazzilli	542	.273	16	61	386	8	5	3	2.8	.987	K. Kobel	32	108	5	6	0	2.92
LF	S. Henderson	587	.266	10	65	315	18	11	3	2.2	.968	S. Lockwood	57	91	7	13	15	3.56
C	J. Stearns	477	.264	15	73	711	84	12	7	5.7	.985	D. Murray	53	86	8	5	5	3.65
UT	J. Youngblood	266	.252	7	30	160	96	6	21		.977							
OF	B. Boisclair	214	.224	4	15	114	3	2	0	1.7	.983							

West

Los Angeles

W-95 L-67

Tom Lasorda

POS	Player	AB	BA	HR	RBI	PO	A	E	DP	TC/G	FA	Pitcher	G	IP	W	L	SV	ERA
1B	S. Garvey	639	.316	21	113	**1546**	74	9	121	**10.1**	.994	D. Sutton	34	238	15	11	0	3.55
2B	D. Lopes	587	.278	17	58	337	424	**20**	88	5.3	.974	B. Hooton	32	236	19	10	0	2.71
SS	B. Russell	625	.286	3	46	245	533	31	91	5.2	.962	T. John	33	213	17	10	1	3.30
3B	R. Cey	555	.270	23	84	116	336	16	26	3.0	.966	D. Rau	30	199	15	9	0	3.26
RF	R. Smith	447	.295	29	93	220	8	12	4	1.9	.950	R. Rhoden	30	165	10	8	0	3.65
CF	R. Monday	342	.254	19	57	209	3	1	0	2.1	.995	B. Welch	23	111	7	4	3	2.03
LF	D. Baker	522	.262	11	66	250	13	4	1	1.8	.985	C. Hough	55	93	5	5	7	3.29
C	S. Yeager	228	.193	4	23	373	55	5	3	4.8	.988	T. Forster	47	65	5	4	22	1.94
OF	B. North	304	.234	0	10	232	2	6	1	2.3	.975							
UT	L. Lacy	245	.261	13	40	114	64	9	7		.952							
C	J. Ferguson	198	.237	7	28	284	23	5	2	5.0	.984							

Cincinnati

W-92 L-69

Sparky Anderson

POS	Player	AB	BA	HR	RBI	PO	A	E	DP	TC/G	FA	Pitcher	G	IP	W	L	SV	ERA
1B	D. Driessen	524	.250	16	70	1264	93	6	92	9.0	**.996**	T. Seaver	36	260	16	14	0	2.87
2B	J. Morgan	441	.236	13	75	252	290	11	49	4.5	.980	F. Norman	36	177	11	9	1	3.71
SS	D. Concepcion	565	.301	6	67	255	459	23	72	4.8	.969	T. Hume	42	174	8	11	1	4.14
3B	P. Rose	655	.302	7	52	117	256	15	23	2.5	.961	P. Moskau	26	145	6	4	1	3.97
RF	K. Griffey	614	.288	10	63	296	13	10	2	2.1	.969	B. Bonham	23	140	11	5	0	3.54
CF	C. Geronimo	296	.226	5	27	259	4	5	1	2.3	.981	M. Sarmiento	63	127	9	7	5	4.39
LF	G. Foster	604	.281	**40**	**120**	319	10	10	1	2.2	.971	D. Bair	70	100	7	6	28	1.98
C	J. Bench	393	.260	23	73	605	48	7	6	**6.2**	.989	P. Borbon	62	99	8	2	4	5.00
OF	M. Lum	146	.267	6	23	69	6	1	2	1.8	.987	M. LaCoss	16	96	4	8	0	4.50
												D. Tomlin	57	62	9	1	4	5.81

San Francisco

W-89 L-73

Joe Altobelli

POS	Player	AB	BA	HR	RBI	PO	A	E	DP	TC/G	FA	Pitcher	G	IP	W	L	SV	ERA
1B	W. McCovey	351	.228	12	64	721	44	10	49	8.0	.987	B. Knepper	36	260	17	11	0	2.63
2B	B. Madlock	447	.309	15	44	223	299	14	48	4.7	.974	V. Blue	35	258	18	10	0	2.79
SS	J. LeMaster	272	.235	1	14	135	260	14	40	4.3	.966	J. Montefusco	36	239	11	9	0	3.80
3B	D. Evans	547	.243	20	78	**147**	**348**	**25**	25	**3.4**	.952	E. Halicki	29	199	9	10	1	2.85
RF	J. Clark	592	.306	25	98	320	16	6	5	2.3	.982	J. Barr	32	163	8	11	1	3.53
CF	L. Herndon	471	.259	1	32	369	3	10	0	2.6	.974	G. Lavelle	67	98	13	10	14	3.31
LF	T. Whitfield	488	.289	10	32	249	7	3	2	1.8	.988	R. Moffitt	70	82	8	4	12	3.29
C	M. Hill	358	.243	3	36	586	56	9	3	5.6	.986							
1B	M. Ivie	318	.308	11	55	550	18	3	33	7.5	.995							
SS	R. Metzger	235	.260	0	17	112	184	8	30	4.1	.974							
OF	H. Cruz	197	.223	6	24	82	5	2	3	1.7	.978							
2B	R. Andrews	177	.220	1	11	120	131	6	23	4.1	.977							
01	J. Dwyer	173	.225	5	22	197	14	2	14		.991							

San Diego

W-84 L-78

Roger Craig

POS	Player	AB	BA	HR	RBI	PO	A	E	DP	TC/G	FA	Pitcher	G	IP	W	L	SV	ERA
1B	G. Tenace	401	.224	16	61	668	37	5	61	8.9	.993	G. Perry	37	261	**21**	6	0	2.72
2B	F. Gonzalez	320	.250	2	29	190	256	8	68	4.8	.982	R. Jones	37	253	13	14	0	2.88
SS	O. Smith	590	.258	1	46	264	548	25	98	5.3	.970	B. Owchinko	36	202	10	13	0	3.56
3B	B. Almon	405	.252	0	21	72	221	21	20	2.8	.933	B. Shirley	50	166	8	11	5	3.69
RF	O. Gamble	375	.275	7	47	172	12	4	3	1.8	.979	E. Rasmussen	27	146	12	10	0	4.06
CF	G. Richards	555	.308	4	45	210	8	8	0	1.8	.965	R. Fingers	67	107	6	13	**37**	2.52
LF	D. Winfield	587	.308	24	97	321	7	7	1	2.2	.979	J. D'Acquisto	45	93	4	3	10	2.13
C	R. Sweet	226	.221	1	11	337	33	6	3	4.9	.984							
UT	D. Thomas	352	.227	3	26	328	168	12	39		.976							
OF	J. Turner	225	.280	8	37	91	5	3	0	1.7	.970							
1B	B. Perkins	217	.240	2	33	538	41	4	56	9.9	.993							
UT	T. Ashford	155	.245	3	26	108	53	6	22		.964							

NATIONAL LEAGUE 1978, *cont.*

Houston

W-74 L-88

Bill Virdon

POS	Player	AB	BA	HR	RBI	PO	A	E	DP	TC/G	FA	Pitcher	G	IP	W	L	SV	ERA
1B	B. Watson	461	.289	14	79	974	95	9	63	8.4	.992	J. Richard	36	275	18	11	0	3.11
2B	A. Howe	420	.293	7	55	224	289	12	51	4.9	.977	M. Lemongello	33	210	9	14	1	3.94
SS	J. Sexton	141	.206	2	6	59	95	3	18	2.7	.981	J. Niekro	35	203	14	14	0	3.86
3B	E. Cabell	**660**	.295	7	71	136	274	18	15	2.8	.958	T. Dixon	30	140	7	11	1	3.99
RF	J. Cruz	565	.315	10	83	311	4	8	0	2.1	.975	K. Forsch	52	133	10	6	7	2.71
CF	C. Cedeno	192	.281	7	23	149	2	2	1	3.1	.987	J. Andujar	35	111	5	7	1	3.41
LF	T. Puhl	585	.289	3	35	386	6	3	2	2.7	.992	F. Bannister	28	110	3	9	0	4.83
C	L. Pujols	153	.131	1	11	271	33	6	2	5.6	.981	J. Sambito	62	88	4	9	11	3.07
OF	D. Walling	247	.251	3	36	140	4	3	2	1.9	.980							
2B	J. Gonzalez	223	.233	1	16	62	112	3	21	3.3	.983							
SS	R. Landestoy	218	.266	0	9	65	132	4	18	4.0	.980							
10	D. Bergman	186	.231	0	12	328	16	4	26		.989							
C	J. Ferguson	150	.207	7	22	288	29	2	0	6.3	.994							

Atlanta

W-69 L-93

Bobby Cox

POS	Player	AB	BA	HR	RBI	PO	A	E	DP	TC/G	FA	Pitcher	G	IP	W	L	SV	ERA
1B	D. Murphy	530	.226	23	79	1137	92	**20**	84	9.7	.984	P. Niekro	44	**334**	19	**18**	1	2.88
2B	J. Royster	529	.259	2	35	186	193	10	39	5.2	.974	P. Hanna	29	140	7	13	0	5.14
SS	D. Chaney	245	.224	3	20	97	189	7	30	3.8	.976	M. Mahler	34	135	4	11	0	4.67
3B	B. Horner	323	.266	23	63	81	199	13	17	3.3	.956	E. Solomon	37	106	4	6	2	4.08
RF	G. Matthews	474	.285	18	62	238	10	8	0	2.0	.969	L. McWilliams	15	99	9	3	0	2.82
CF	R. Office	404	.250	9	40	291	4	3	2	2.2	.990	G. Garber	43	78	4	4	22	2.53
LF	J. Burroughs	488	.301	23	77	224	13	6	2	1.7	.975	J. Easterly	37	78	3	6	1	5.65
C	B. Pocoroba	289	.242	6	34	454	43	5	1	6.4	.990	A. Devine	31	65	5	4	3	5.95
32	R. Gilbreath	326	.245	3	31	108	204	9	22		.972	T. Boggs	16	59	2	8	0	6.71
OF	B. Bonnell	304	.240	1	16	172	7	3	1	1.7	.984							
C	J. Nolan	213	.230	4	22	295	24	7	3	5.3	.979							
1B	B. Beall	185	.243	1	16	275	24	4	23	7.6	.987							
2B	G. Hubbard	163	.258	2	13	102	130	5	30	5.4	.979							

BATTING AND BASE RUNNING LEADERS

Batting Average

D. Parker, PIT	.334
S. Garvey, LA	.316
J. Cruz, HOU	.315
B. Madlock, SF	.309
D. Winfield, SD	.308

Slugging Average

D. Parker, PIT	.585
R. Smith, LA	.559
G. Foster, CIN	.546
J. Clark, SF	.537
J. Burroughs, ATL	.529

Home Runs

G. Foster, CIN	40
G. Luzinski, PHI	35
D. Parker, PIT	30
R. Smith, LA	29
W. Stargell, PIT	28
D. Kingman, CHI	28

Total Bases

D. Parker, PIT	340
G. Foster, CIN	330
S. Garvey, LA	319
J. Clark, SF	318
D. Winfield, SD	293

Runs Batted In

G. Foster, CIN	120
D. Parker, PIT	117
S. Garvey, LA	113
G. Luzinski, PHI	101
J. Clark, SF	98

Stolen Bases

O. Moreno, PIT	71
F. Taveras, PIT	46
D. Lopes, LA	45
I. DeJesus, CHI	41
O. Smith, SD	40

Hits

S. Garvey, LA	202
P. Rose, CIN	198
E. Cabell, HOU	195
D. Parker, PIT	194

Base on Balls

J. Burroughs, ATL	117
D. Evans, SF	105
G. Tenace, SD	101
G. Luzinski, PHI	100

Home Run Percentage

G. Foster, CIN	6.6
R. Smith, LA	6.5
G. Luzinski, PHI	6.5
D. Parker, PIT	5.2

Runs

I. DeJesus, CHI	104
P. Rose, CIN	103
D. Parker, PIT	102
G. Foster, CIN	97

Doubles

P. Rose, CIN	51
J. Clark, SF	46
T. Simmons, STL	40
L. Parrish, MON	39

Triples

G. Templeton, STL	13
G. Richards, SD	12
D. Parker, PIT	12

PITCHING LEADERS

Winning Percentage

G. Perry, SD	.778
B. Hooton, LA	.655
R. Grimsley, MON	.645
V. Blue, SF	.643
T. John, LA	.630

Earned Run Average

C. Swan, NY	2.43
S. Rogers, MON	2.47
P. Vuckovich, STL	2.55
B. Knepper, SF	2.63
B. Hooton, LA	2.71

Wins

G. Perry, SD	21
R. Grimsley, MON	20
B. Hooton, LA	19
P. Niekro, ATL	19
V. Blue, SF	18
J. Richard, HOU	18

Saves

R. Fingers, SD	37
K. Tekulve, PIT	31
D. Bair, CIN	28
B. Sutter, CHI	27
G. Garber, PHI, ATL	25

Strikeouts

J. Richard, HOU	303
P. Niekro, ATL	248
T. Seaver, CIN	226
B. Blyleven, PIT	182
J. Montefusco, SF	177

Complete Games

P. Niekro, ATL	22
R. Grimsley, MON	19
B. Knepper, SF	16
J. Richard, HOU	16
S. Carlton, PHI	12
D. Sutton, LA	12

Fewest Hits/9 Innings

J. Richard, HOU	6.28
C. Swan, NY	7.13
B. Hooton, LA	7.47
E. Halicki, SF	7.51

Shutouts

B. Knepper, SF	6
E. Halicki, SF	4
B. Blyleven, PIT	4
V. Blue, SF	4
P. Niekro, ATL	4

Fewest Walks/9 Innings

L. Christenson, PHI	1.86
J. Barr, SF	1.93
R. Reuschel, CHI	2.00
E. Halicki, SF	2.04

Most Strikeouts/9 Inn.

J. Richard, HOU	9.92
T. Seaver, CIN	7.82
P. Vuckovich, STL	6.77
B. Blyleven, PIT	6.71

Innings

P. Niekro, ATL	334
J. Richard, HOU	275
R. Grimsley, MON	263
G. Perry, SD	261

Games Pitched

K. Tekulve, PIT	91
M. Littell, STL	72
D. Moore, CHI	71
D. Bair, CIN	70
R. Moffitt, SF	70

		W	L	PCT	GB	R	OR	Batting 2B	3B	HR	BA	SA	SB	Fielding E	DP	FA	Pitching CG	BB	SO	ShO	SV	ERA
East	Philadelphia	90	72	.556		708	586	248	32	133	.258	.388	152	**104**	155	**.983**	38	**393**	813	9	29	3.33
	Pittsburgh	88	73	.547	1.5	684	637	239	**54**	115	.257	.385	**213**	167	133	.973	30	499	880	13	44	3.41
	Chicago	79	83	.488	11	664	724	224	48	72	**.264**	.361	110	144	154	.978	24	539	768	7	38	4.05
	Montreal	76	86	.469	14	633	611	269	31	121	.254	.379	80	134	150	.979	42	572	740	13	32	3.42
	St. Louis	69	93	.426	21	600	657	263	44	79	.249	.358	97	136	155	.978	32	600	859	13	22	3.58
	New York	66	96	.407	24	607	690	227	47	86	.245	.352	100	132	159	.979	21	531	775	7	26	3.87
West	Los Angeles	95	67	.586		**727**	**573**	251	27	**149**	**.264**	**.402**	137	140	138	.978	46	440	800	16	38	**3.12**
	Cincinnati	92	69	.571	2.5	710	688	**270**	32	136	.256	.393	137	134	120	.978	16	567	908	10	46	3.81
	San Francisco	89	73	.549	6	613	594	240	41	117	.248	.374	87	146	118	.977	42	453	840	**17**	29	3.30
	San Diego	84	78	.519	11	591	598	208	42	75	.252	.348	152	160	**171**	.975	21	483	744	10	**55**	3.28
	Houston	74	88	.457	21	605	634	231	45	70	.258	.355	178	133	109	.978	**48**	578	**930**	**17**	23	3.63
	Atlanta	69	93	.426	26	600	750	191	39	123	.244	.363	90	153	126	.975	29	624	848	12	32	4.08
						7742	7742	2861	482	1276	.254	.372	1533	1683	1688	.978	389	6279	9905	144	414	3.57

AMERICAN LEAGUE 1978

	POS	Player	AB	BA	HR	RBI	PO	A	E	DP	TC/G	FA	Pitcher	G	IP	W	L	SV	ERA
East																			
New York	1B	C. Chambliss	625	.274	12	90	1366	111	4	119	9.6	**.997**	R. Guidry	35	274	**25**	3	0	**1.74**
W-100 L-63	2B	W. Randolph	499	.279	3	42	296	400	16	80	5.3	.978	E. Figueroa	35	253	20	9	0	2.99
Billy Martin	SS	B. Dent	379	.243	5	40	178	341	10	56	4.3	.981	D. Tidrow	31	185	7	11	0	3.84
W-52 L-42	3B	G. Nettles	587	.276	27	93	109	326	11	**30**	2.8	.975	G. Gossage	63	134	10	11	**27**	2.01
Dick Howser	RF	R. Jackson	511	.274	27	97	212	6	3	1	2.1	.986	J. Beattie	25	128	6	9	0	3.73
W-0 L-1	CF	M. Rivers	559	.265	11	48	384	8	8	2	2.9	.980	C. Hunter	21	118	12	6	0	3.58
Bob Lemon	LF	L. Piniella	472	.314	6	69	213	4	7	0	2.2	.969	S. Lyle	59	112	9	3	9	3.47
W-48 L-20	C	T. Munson	617	.297	6	71	666	61	10	4	5.9	.986							
	DH	C. Johnson	174	.184	6	19													
	OF	R. White	346	.269	8	43	128	1	1	0	1.8	.992							
	DH	J. Spencer	150	.227	7	24													
	OF	G. Thomasson	116	.276	3	20	101	4	3	1	2.2	.972							
Boston	1B	G. Scott	412	.233	12	54	1052	55	10	99	9.9	.991	D. Eckersley	35	268	20	8	0	2.99
W-99 L-64	2B	J. Remy	583	.278	2	44	327	444	13	**114**	5.6	.983	M. Torrez	36	250	16	13	0	3.96
Don Zimmer	SS	R. Burleson	626	.248	5	49	285	482	15	100	5.4	.981	L. Tiant	32	212	13	8	0	3.31
	3B	B. Hobson	512	.250	17	80	122	261	**43**	25	3.2	.899	B. Lee	28	177	10	10	0	3.46
	RF	D. Evans	497	.247	24	63	305	14	6	2	2.3	.982	B. Stanley	52	142	15	2	10	2.60
	CF	F. Lynn	541	.298	22	82	408	11	7	2	2.9	.984	J. Wright	24	116	8	4	0	3.57
	LF	J. Rice	**677**	.315	**46**	**139**	245	13	3	1	2.3	.989	D. Drago	37	77	4	4	7	3.03
	C	C. Fisk	571	.284	20	88	733	90	**17**	13	5.5	.980	B. Campbell	29	51	7	5	4	3.91
	DH	B. Bailey	94	.191	4	9													
	UT	C. Yastrzemski	523	.277	17	81	523	49	5	49		.991							
	UT	J. Brohamer	244	.234	1	25	64	103	5	18		.971							
Milwaukee	1B	C. Cooper	407	.312	13	54	842	66	11	71	10.9	.988	M. Caldwell	37	293	22	9	1	2.36
W-93 L-69	2B	P. Molitor	521	.273	6	45	197	283	12	57	5.4	.976	L. Sorensen	37	281	18	12	1	3.21
George Bamberger	SS	R. Yount	502	.293	9	71	246	453	30	78	**5.8**	.959	J. Augustine	35	188	13	12	0	4.54
	3B	S. Bando	540	.285	17	78	89	329	14	25	3.2	.968	B. Travers	28	176	12	11	0	4.41
	RF	S. Lezcano	442	.292	15	61	262	18	6	5	2.3	.979	A. Replogle	32	149	9	5	0	3.92
	CF	G. Thomas	452	.246	32	86	345	5	6	0	2.6	.983	E. Rodriguez	32	105	5	5	2	3.93
	LF	B. Oglivie	469	.303	18	72	187	5	4	0	2.2	.980	B. McClure	44	65	2	6	9	3.74
	C	C. Moore	268	.269	5	31	314	41	6	3	3.8	.983	B. Castro	42	50	5	4	8	1.81
	DH	L. Hisle	520	.290	34	115													
	UT	D. Money	518	.293	14	54	705	216	9	88		.990							
	C	B. Martinez	256	.219	1	20	327	32	8	7	4.1	.978							
	DO	D. Davis	218	.248	5	26	54	2	0	0		1.000							
Baltimore	1B	E. Murray	610	.285	27	95	**1504**	106	5	143	10.3	.997	J. Palmer	38	**296**	21	12	0	2.46
W-90 L-71	2B	R. Dauer	459	.264	6	46	193	239	1	60	5.0	.998	M. Flanagan	40	281	19	15	0	4.03
Earl Weaver	SS	M. Belanger	348	.213	0	16	184	409	9	76	4.5	**.985**	D. Martinez	40	276	16	11	0	3.52
	3B	D. DeCinces	511	.286	28	80	111	280	10	27	3.1	.975	S. McGregor	35	233	15	13	1	3.32
	RF	K. Singleton	502	.293	20	81	244	1	6	0	1.8	.976	D. Stanhouse	56	75	6	9	24	2.89
	CF	L. Harlow	460	.243	8	26	313	7	7	2	2.4	.979	T. Martinez	42	69	3	3	5	4.83
	LF	P. Kelly	274	.274	11	40	123	3	4	1	1.6	.969							
	C	R. Dempsey	441	.259	6	32	636	79	11	**14**	5.4	.985							
	DH	L. May	556	.246	25	80													
	2B	B. Smith	250	.260	5	30	146	208	5	43	4.3	.986							
	OF	A. Mora	229	.214	8	14	129	4	3	0	2.0	.978							
	OF	C. Lopez	193	.238	4	20	151	7	2	2	1.4	.988							
	SS	K. Garcia	186	.263	0	13	86	173	15	35	3.7	.945							
Detroit	1B	J. Thompson	589	.287	26	96	1503	92	11	**153**	**10.6**	.993	J. Slaton	35	234	17	11	0	4.12
W-86 L-76	2B	L. Whitaker	484	.285	3	58	301	458	17	95	5.7	.978	M. Wilcox	29	215	13	12	0	3.76
Ralph Houk	SS	A. Trammell	448	.268	2	34	239	421	14	95	4.8	.979	D. Rozema	28	209	9	12	0	3.14
	3B	A. Rodriguez	385	.265	7	43	79	228	4	20	2.4	**.987**	J. Billingham	30	202	15	8	0	3.88
	RF	T. Corcoran	324	.265	1	27	186	6	3	4	1.8	.985	J. Morris	28	106	3	5	0	4.33
	CF	R. LeFlore	666	.297	12	62	440	9	11	4	3.0	.976	K. Young	14	106	6	7	0	2.81
	LF	S. Kemp	582	.277	15	79	325	11	8	2	2.2	.977	B. Sykes	22	94	6	6	2	3.94
	C	M. May	352	.250	10	37	406	58	10	5	5.0	.979	J. Hiller	51	92	9	4	15	2.34
	DH	R. Staub	642	.273	24	121							S. Foucault	24	37	2	4	4	3.16
	C	L. Parrish	288	.219	14	41	353	39	5	5	5.0	.987							
	3B	P. Mankowski	222	.275	4	20	42	129	5	17	2.2	.972							
	OF	J. Wockenfuss	187	.283	7	22	89	2	2	0	1.5	.978							
Cleveland	1B	A. Thornton	508	.262	33	105	1327	106	7	106	9.9	.995	R. Waits	34	230	13	15	0	3.20
W-69 L-90	2B	D. Kuiper	547	.283	0	43	341	408	16	91	5.1	.979	R. Wise	33	213	9	**19**	0	4.32
Jeff Torborg	SS	T. Veryzer	421	.271	1	32	177	375	21	58	4.4	.963	M. Paxton	33	191	12	11	1	3.86
	3B	B. Bell	556	.282	6	62	125	**355**	15	**30**	**3.6**	.970	D. Hood	36	155	5	6	0	4.47
	RF	P. Dade	307	.254	3	20	171	6	7	2	2.3	.962	D. Clyde	28	153	8	11	0	4.28
	CF	R. Manning	566	.263	3	50	377	7	2	1	2.7	.995	J. Kern	58	99	10	10	13	3.08
	LF	J. Grubb	378	.265	14	61	199	14	6	4	2.0	.973	S. Monge	48	85	4	3	6	2.76
	C	G. Alexander	324	.235	17	62	305	34	6	3	5.2	.983							
	DH	B. Carbo	174	.287	4	16													
	OF	J. Norris	315	.283	2	27	153	6	2	2	2.1	.988							
	UT	T. Cox	227	.233	1	19	100	42	4	6		.973							
	S2	L. Blanks	193	.254	2	20	81	138	13	25		.944							
	CO	R. Pruitt	187	.235	6	17	199	15	4	4		.982							
	DH	W. Horton	169	.249	5	22													

AMERICAN LEAGUE 1978, *cont.*

	POS	Player	AB	BA	HR	RBI	PO	A	E	DP	TC/G	FA	Pitcher	G	IP	W	L	SV	ERA
Toronto	1B	J. Mayberry	515	.250	22	70	1143	52	8	120	8.7	.993	J. Jefferson	31	212	7	16	0	4.38
	2B	D. McKay	504	.238	7	45	310	408	12	96	5.2	.984	T. Underwood	31	198	6	14	0	4.10
	SS	L. Gomez	413	.223	0	32	247	400	16	97	4.3	.976	J. Clancy	31	194	10	12	0	4.09
W-59 L-102	3B	R. Howell	551	.270	8	61	109	306	22	27	3.3	.950	J. Garvin	26	145	4	12	0	5.54
	RF	B. Bailor	621	.264	1	52	303	15	12	7	2.6	.964	B. Moore	37	144	6	9	0	4.86
Roy Hartsfield	CF	R. Bosetti	568	.259	5	42	417	17	6	1	3.3	.986	D. Lemanczyk	29	137	4	14	0	6.26
	LF	A. Woods	220	.241	3	25	131	2	3	0	2.3	.978	M. Willis	44	101	3	7	7	4.56
	C	R. Cerone	282	.223	3	20	426	44	4	7	5.6	.992	T. Murphy	50	94	6	9	7	3.93
	DH	R. Carty	387	.284	20	68							V. Cruz	32	47	7	3	9	1.71
	C	A. Ashby	264	.261	9	29	399	38	6	6	5.5	.986							
	OF	O. Velez	248	.266	9	38	150	10	3	4	2.2	.982							
	UT	W. Upshaw	224	.237	1	17	131	4	7	5		.951							
	OF	T. Hutton	173	.254	2	9	85	2	0	0	1.6	1.000							
West — **Kansas City**	1B	P. LaCock	322	.295	5	48	700	39	5	67	7.0	.993	D. Leonard	40	295	21	17	0	3.33
	2B	F. White	461	.275	7	50	325	385	16	96	5.2	.978	P. Splittorff	39	262	19	13	0	3.40
	SS	F. Patek	440	.248	2	46	240	350	**32**	84	4.5	.949	L. Gura	35	222	16	4	0	2.72
W-92 L-70	3B	G. Brett	510	.294	9	62	104	289	16	25	3.2	.961	R. Gale	31	192	14	8	0	3.09
	RF	A. Cowens	485	.274	5	63	275	10	3	5	2.3	.990	D. Bird	40	99	6	6	1	5.29
Whitey Herzog	CF	A. Otis	486	.298	22	96	382	9	2	1	2.9	.995	M. Pattin	32	79	3	3	4	3.32
	LF	W. Wilson	198	.217	0	16	171	6	4	2	1.6	.978	A. Hrabosky	58	75	8	7	20	2.88
	C	D. Porter	520	.265	18	78	608	62	8	10	4.7	.988	S. Mingori	45	69	1	4	7	2.74
	DH	H. McRae	623	.273	16	72													
	01	C. Hurdle	417	.264	7	56	544	30	12	48		.980							
	OF	T. Poquette	204	.216	4	30	144	5	7	0	2.5	.955							
	1C	J. Wathan	190	.300	2	28	385	28	2	20		.995							
California	1B	R. Fairly	235	.217	10	40	482	31	1	47	6.6	.998	F. Tanana	33	239	18	12	0	3.65
	2B	B. Grich	487	.251	6	42	325	419	13	77	5.3	.983	N. Ryan	31	235	10	13	0	3.71
	SS	D. Chalk	470	.253	1	34	168	237	19	46	4.4	.955	C. Knapp	30	188	14	8	0	4.21
W-87 L-75	3B	C. Lansford	453	.294	8	52	93	182	17	18	2.5	.942	D. Aase	29	179	11	8	0	4.03
	RF	L. Bostock	568	.296	5	71	366	7	4	2	2.6	.989	P. Hartzell	54	157	6	10	6	3.44
Dave Garcia	CF	R. Miller	475	.263	1	37	353	9	4	5	2.8	.989	K. Brett	31	100	3	5	1	4.95
W-25 L-20	LF	J. Rudi	497	.256	17	79	231	4	2	1	2.1	.992	D. LaRoche	59	96	10	9	25	2.81
	C	B. Downing	412	.255	7	46	681	82	5	6	**6.0**	.993							
Jim Fregosi	DH	D. Baylor	591	.255	34	99													
W-62 L-55	13	R. Jackson	387	.297	6	57	605	88	7	56		.990							
	OF	K. Landreaux	260	.223	5	23	138	6	2	0	1.8	.986							
Texas	1B	M. Hargrove	494	.251	7	40	1221	**116**	**17**	90	9.7	.987	J. Matlack	35	270	15	13	1	2.27
	2B	B. Wills	539	.250	9	57	**350**	**526**	17	84	**5.7**	.981	F. Jenkins	34	249	18	8	0	3.04
	SS	B. Campaneris	269	.186	1	17	151	263	20	44	4.9	.954	D. Alexander	31	191	9	10	0	3.86
W-87 L-75	3B	T. Harrah	450	.229	12	59	54	167	8	15	2.5	.965	D. Medich	28	171	9	8	2	3.74
	RF	B. Bonds	475	.265	29	82	213	13	7	5	2.1	.970	D. Ellis	22	141	9	7	0	4.20
Billy Hunter	CF	J. Beniquez	473	.260	11	50	309	8	9	1	2.6	.972	S. Comer	30	117	11	5	1	2.30
W-86 L-75	LF	A. Oliver	525	.324	14	89	219	8	3	1	2.1	.987	J. Umbarger	32	98	5	8	1	4.88
	C	J. Sundberg	518	.278	6	58	**769**	**91**	3	**14**	5.8	**.997**	R. Cleveland	53	76	5	7	12	3.09
Pat Corrales	DH	R. Zisk	511	.262	22	85							L. Barker	29	52	1	5	4	4.82
W-1 L-0	UT	K. Bevacqua	248	.222	6	30	62	116	18	12		.908							
	UT	J. Lowenstein	176	.222	5	21	34	42	6	2		.927							
Minnesota	1B	R. Carew	564	**.333**	5	70	1362	105	16	134	10.0	.989	R. Erickson	37	266	14	13	0	3.96
	2B	B. Randall	330	.270	0	21	231	345	10	81	5.1	.983	G. Zahn	35	252	14	14	0	3.03
	SS	R. Smalley	586	.273	19	77	**287**	**527**	25	**121**	5.3	.970	D. Goltz	29	220	15	10	0	2.49
W-73 L-89	3B	M. Cubbage	394	.282	7	57	65	233	9	24	2.7	.971	G. Serum	34	184	9	9	1	4.10
	RF	H. Powell	381	.247	3	31	219	9	4	2	2.0	.983	M. Marshall	54	99	10	12	21	2.36
Gene Mauch	CF	D. Ford	592	.274	11	82	376	6	9	2	2.6	.977	D. Jackson	19	92	4	6	0	4.48
	LF	W. Norwood	428	.255	8	46	227	7	14	1	2.2	.944	S. Perzanowski	13	57	2	7	1	5.24
	C	B. Wynegar	454	.229	4	45	582	70	8	12	5.0	.988							
	DH	G. Adams	310	.258	7	35													
	OF	B. Rivera	251	.271	3	23	162	5	3	0	1.8	.982							
	DH	J. Morales	242	.314	2	38													
	3B	L. Wolfe	235	.234	3	25	60	143	10	9	2.6	.953							
	2B	R. Wilfong	199	.266	1	11	152	196	5	37	4.4	.986							
	OF	R. Chiles	198	.268	1	22	108	3	4	0	1.9	.965							
	UT	C. Kusick	191	.173	4	20	228	22	4	14		.984							
Chicago	1B	L. Johnson	498	.273	8	72	887	71	8	74	8.9	.992	S. Stone	30	212	12	12	0	4.37
	2B	J. Orta	420	.274	13	53	275	290	9	62	5.0	.984	K. Kravec	30	203	11	16	0	4.08
	SS	D. Kessinger	431	.255	1	31	171	321	13	60	4.1	.974	F. Barrios	33	196	9	15	0	4.05
W-71 L-90	3B	E. Soderholm	457	.258	20	67	**128**	245	14	17	3.0	.964	W. Wood	28	168	10	10	0	5.20
	RF	C. Washington	314	.264	6	31	159	6	7	0	2.1	.959	J. Willoughby	59	93	1	6	13	3.86
Bob Lemon	CF	C. Lemon	357	.300	13	55	284	8	5	2	3.1	.983	L. LaGrow	52	88	6	5	16	4.40
W-34 L-40	LF	R. Garr	443	.275	3	29	205	5	9	2	2.0	.959							
	C	B. Nahorodny	347	.236	8	35	486	53	11	6	5.3	.980							
Larry Doby	DH	R. Blomberg	156	.231	5	22													
W-37 L-50	OD	B. Molinaro	286	.262	6	27	88	2	0	0		1.000							
	UT	G. Pryor	222	.261	2	15	100	202	11	31		.965							
	OF	T. Bosley	219	.269	2	13	155	3	4	0	2.5	.975							
	UT	W. Nordhagen	206	.301	5	35	87	12	6	2		.943							
	C	M. Colbern	141	.270	2	20	203	19	7	1	4.9	.969							

AMERICAN LEAGUE 1978, *cont.*

Oakland

W-69 L-93

Bobby Winkles
W-24 L-15

Jack McKeon
W-45 L-78

POS	Player	AB	BA	HR	RBI	PO	A	E	DP	TC/G	FA
1B	D. Revering	521	.271	16	46	1013	110	13	98	8.2	.989
2B	M. Edwards	414	.273	1	23	228	309	**20**	71	4.2	.964
SS	M. Guerrero	505	.275	3	38	258	330	26	67	4.3	.958
3B	W. Gross	285	.200	7	23	72	150	20	22	2.3	.917
RF	T. Armas	239	.213	2	13	214	3	2	0	2.6	.991
CF	J. Wallis	279	.237	6	26	187	7	4	5	2.5	.980
LF	M. Page	516	.285	17	70	211	4	6	0	1.9	.973
C	J. Essian	278	.223	3	26	431	78	10	12	4.4	.981
DH	G. Alexander	174	.207	10	22						
3B	T. Duncan	319	.257	2	37	63	119	9	4	2.3	.953
C1	J. Newman	268	.239	9	32	399	41	12	20		.973
OF	M. Dilone	258	.229	1	14	195	3	3	1	2.0	.985
OF	G. Burke	200	.235	1	14	152	1	2	0	2.3	.987
OF	D. Alston	173	.208	1	10	86	0	4	0	1.8	.956
DH	R. Carty	141	.277	11	31						

Pitcher	G	IP	W	L	SV	ERA
M. Keough	32	197	8	15	0	3.24
J. Johnson	33	186	11	10	0	3.39
R. Langford	37	176	7	13	0	3.43
P. Broberg	35	166	10	12	0	4.62
S. Renko	27	151	6	12	0	4.29
D. Heaverlo	69	130	3	6	10	3.25
B. Lacey	**74**	120	8	9	5	3.01
E. Sosa	68	109	8	2	14	2.64
A. Wirth	16	81	5	6	0	3.43

Seattle

W-56 L-104

Darrell Johnson

POS	Player	AB	BA	HR	RBI	PO	A	E	DP	TC/G	FA
1B	D. Meyer	444	.227	8	56	1104	79	13	119	9.9	.989
2B	J. Cruz	550	.235	1	25	286	472	10	101	5.4	**.987**
SS	C. Reynolds	548	.292	5	44	243	461	29	102	5.0	.960
3B	B. Stein	403	.261	4	37	72	244	24	21	3.1	.929
RF	L. Roberts	472	.301	22	92	296	10	8	4	2.5	.975
CF	R. Jones	472	.235	6	46	393	10	6	2	3.2	.985
LF	B. Bochte	486	.263	11	51	172	7	3	2	2.0	.984
C	B. Stinson	364	.258	11	55	472	60	7	7	4.4	.987
DH	L. Stanton	302	.182	3	24						
OF	T. Paciorek	251	.299	4	30	95	3	2	0	1.9	.980
UT	L. Milbourne	234	.226	2	20	92	169	9	27		.967
OF	J. Hale	211	.171	4	22	160	1	2	0	1.7	.988
D1	B. Robertson	174	.230	8	28	141	8	0	16		1.000
13	J. Bernhardt	165	.230	2	12	263	63	6	21		.982

Pitcher	G	IP	W	L	SV	ERA
P. Mitchell	29	168	8	14	0	4.18
G. Abbott	29	155	7	15	0	5.27
R. Honeycutt	26	134	5	11	0	4.89
T. House	34	116	5	4	0	4.66
J. Colborn	20	114	3	10	0	5.37
S. Rawley	52	111	4	9	4	4.12
E. Romo	56	107	11	7	10	3.69
B. McLaughlin	20	107	4	8	0	4.37
J. Todd	49	107	3	4	3	3.88
D. Pole	21	99	4	11	0	6.48

BATTING AND BASE RUNNING LEADERS

Batting Average
R. Carew, MIN .333
A. Oliver, TEX .324
J. Rice, BOS .315
L. Piniella, NY .314
B. Oglivie, MIL .303

Slugging Average
J. Rice, BOS .600
L. Hisle, MIL .533
D. DeCinces, BAL .526
A. Otis, KC .525
A. Thornton, CLE .516

Home Runs
J. Rice, BOS 46
L. Hisle, MIL 34
D. Baylor, CAL 34
A. Thornton, CLE 33
G. Thomas, MIL 32

Total Bases
J. Rice, BOS 406
E. Murray, BAL 293
D. Baylor, CAL 279
R. Staub, DET 279
J. Thompson, DET 278

Runs Batted In
J. Rice, BOS 139
R. Staub, DET 121
L. Hisle, MIL 115
A. Thornton, CLE 105
R. Carty, TOR, OAK 99
D. Baylor, CAL 99

Stolen Bases
R. LeFlore, DET 68
J. Cruz, SEA 59
B. Wills, TEX 52
M. Dilone, OAK 50
W. Wilson, KC 46

Hits
J. Rice, BOS 213
R. LeFlore, DET 198
R. Carew, MIN 188
T. Munson, NY 183

Base on Balls
M. Hargrove, TEX 107
K. Singleton, BAL 98
S. Kemp, DET 97
A. Thornton, CLE 93

Home Run Percentage
G. Thomas, MIL 7.1
J. Rice, BOS 6.8
L. Hisle, MIL 6.5
A. Thornton, CLE 6.5

Runs
R. LeFlore, DET 126
J. Rice, BOS 121
D. Baylor, CAL 103
A. Thornton, CLE 97

Doubles
G. Brett, KC 45
C. Fisk, BOS 39
H. McRae, KC 39
D. DeCinces, BAL 37

Triples
J. Rice, BOS 15
R. Carew, MIN 10
D. Ford, MIN 10
R. Garr, CHI 9
R. Yount, MIL 9

PITCHING LEADERS

Winning Percentage
R. Guidry, NY .893
B. Stanley, BOS .882
L. Gura, KC .800
D. Eckersley, BOS .714
M. Caldwell, MIL .710

Earned Run Average
R. Guidry, NY 1.74
J. Matlack, TEX 2.27
M. Caldwell, MIL 2.36
J. Palmer, BAL 2.46
D. Goltz, MIN 2.49

Wins
R. Guidry, NY 25
M. Caldwell, MIL 22
D. Leonard, KC 21
J. Palmer, BAL 21
E. Figueroa, NY 20
D. Eckersley, BOS 20

Saves
G. Gossage, NY 27
D. LaRoche, CAL 25
D. Stanhouse, BAL 24
M. Marshall, MIN 21
A. Hrabosky, KC 20

Strikeouts
N. Ryan, CAL 260
R. Guidry, NY 248
D. Leonard, KC 183
M. Flanagan, BAL 167
D. Eckersley, BOS 162

Complete Games
M. Caldwell, MIL 23
D. Leonard, KC 20
J. Palmer, BAL 19
J. Matlack, TEX 18
L. Sorensen, MIL 17
M. Flanagan, BAL 17

Fewest Hits/9 Innings
R. Guidry, NY 6.15
N. Ryan, CAL 7.01
L. Gura, KC 7.43
J. Palmer, BAL 7.48

Shutouts
R. Guidry, NY 9
M. Caldwell, MIL 6
J. Palmer, BAL 6
L. Tiant, BOS 5

Fewest Walks/9 Innings
F. Jenkins, TEX 1.48
L. Sorensen, MIL 1.60
M. Caldwell, MIL 1.66
J. Matlack, TEX 1.70

Most Strikeouts/9 Inn.
N. Ryan, CAL 9.96
R. Guidry, NY 8.16
K. Kravec, CHI 6.83
T. Underwood, TOR 6.33

Innings
J. Palmer, BAL 296
D. Leonard, KC 295
M. Caldwell, MIL 293
L. Sorensen, MIL 281
M. Flanagan, BAL 281

Games Pitched
B. Lacey, OAK 74
D. Heaverlo, OAK 69
E. Sosa, OAK 68
G. Gossage, NY 63

		W	L	PCT	GB	R	OR	Batting 2B	3B	HR	BA	SA	SB	Fielding E	DP	FA	Pitching CG	BB	SO	ShO	SV	ERA
East	*New York	100	63	.613		735	**582**	228	38	125	.267	.388	98	113	136	**.982**	39	478	817	16	**36**	**3.18**
	Boston	99	64	.607	1	796	657	270	46	172	.267	.424	74	146	172	.977	57	464	706	15	26	3.54
	Milwaukee	93	69	.574	6.5	**804**	650	265	38	**173**	**.276**	**.432**	95	150	144	.977	62	**398**	577	**19**	24	3.65
	Baltimore	90	71	.559	9	659	633	248	19	154	.258	.396	75	**110**	166	**.982**	**65**	509	754	16	33	3.56
	Detroit	86	76	.531	13.5	714	653	218	34	129	.271	.392	90	118	**177**	.981	60	503	684	12	21	3.64
	Cleveland	69	90	.434	29	639	694	223	45	106	.261	.379	64	123	142	.980	36	568	739	6	28	3.97
	Toronto	59	102	.366	40	590	775	217	39	98	.250	.359	28	131	163	.979	35	614	758	5	23	4.55
West	Kansas City	92	70	.568		743	634	**305**	**59**	98	.268	.399	**216**	150	152	.976	53	478	657	14	33	3.44
	California	87	75	.537	5	691	666	226	28	108	.259	.370	86	136	136	.978	44	599	**892**	13	33	3.65
	Texas	87	75	.537	5	692	632	216	36	132	.253	.381	196	153	140	.976	54	421	776	12	25	3.42
	Minnesota	73	89	.451	19	666	678	259	47	82	.267	.375	99	146	171	.977	48	520	703	9	26	3.69
	Chicago	71	90	.441	20.5	634	731	221	41	106	.264	.379	83	139	130	.977	38	586	710	9	33	4.22
	Oakland	69	93	.426	23	532	690	200	31	100	.245	.351	144	179	142	.971	26	582	750	11	29	3.62
	Seattle	56	104	.350	35	614	834	229	37	97	.248	.359	123	141	172	.978	28	567	630	4	20	4.72
						9509	9509	3325	538	1680	.261	.385	1471	1935	2143	.978	645	7287	10153	161	390	3.77

* Defeated Boston in a 1 game playoff

NATIONAL LEAGUE 1979

		POS	Player	AB	BA	HR	RBI	PO	A	E	DP	TC/G	FA	Pitcher	G	IP	W	L	SV	ERA
East	Pittsburgh	1B	W. Stargell	424	.281	32	82	949	47	3	102	8.8	**.997**	B. Blyleven	37	237	12	5	0	3.61
		2B	R. Stennett	319	.238	0	24	172	282	12	63	4.6	.974	J. Candelaria	33	207	14	9	0	3.22
		SS	T. Foli	525	.291	1	65	255	404	15	97	5.1	.978	B. Kison	33	172	13	7	0	3.19
	W-98 L-64	3B	B. Madlock	311	.328	7	44	63	153	7	12	2.6	.969	D. Robinson	29	161	8	8	0	3.86
		RF	D. Parker	622	.310	25	94	341	15	15	1	2.3	.960	J. Bibby	34	138	12	4	0	2.80
	Chuck Tanner	CF	O. Moreno	**695**	.282	8	69	490	11	13	3	3.2	.975	K. Tekulve	**94**	134	10	8	31	2.75
		LF	B. Robinson	421	.264	24	75	161	6	3	0	1.4	.982	E. Romo	84	129	10	5	5	3.00
		C	E. Ott	403	.273	7	51	612	53	4	6	5.8	.994	J. Rooker	19	104	4	7	0	4.59
		23	P. Garner	549	.293	11	59	222	378	21	74		.966	G. Jackson	72	82	8	5	14	2.96
		01	J. Milner	326	.276	16	60	367	20	8	28		.980							
		C	S. Nicosia	191	.288	4	13	320	25	3	4	5.4	.991							
		OF	L. Lacy	182	.247	5	15	70	3	2	0	1.8	.973							
	Montreal	1B	T. Perez	489	.270	13	73	1114	65	11	81	9.2	.991	S. Rogers	37	249	13	12	0	3.00
		2B	R. Scott	562	.238	3	42	301	324	13	71	**5.6**	.980	B. Lee	33	222	16	10	0	3.04
		SS	C. Speier	344	.227	7	26	194	355	17	52	5.1	.970	S. Sanderson	34	168	9	8	1	3.43
		3B	L. Parrish	544	.307	30	82	119	290	23	25	2.8	.947	D. Schatzeder	32	162	10	5	1	2.83
	W-95 L-65	RF	E. Valentine	548	.276	21	82	281	10	5	2	2.1	.983	R. Grimsley	32	151	10	9	0	5.36
		CF	A. Dawson	639	.275	25	92	394	7	5	1	2.7	.988	D. Palmer	36	123	10	2	2	2.63
	Dick Williams	LF	W. Cromartie	659	.275	8	46	343	16	9	4	2.3	.976	E. Sosa	62	97	8	7	18	1.95
		C	G. Carter	505	.283	22	75	**751**	**88**	9	**12**	6.1	.989	R. May	33	94	10	3	0	2.30
		2B	D. Cash	187	.321	2	19	88	110	6	18	4.3	.971	W. Fryman	44	58	3	6	10	2.79
	St. Louis	1B	K. Hernandez	610	**.344**	11	105	**1489**	**146**	8	**145**	**10.3**	.995	P. Vuckovich	34	233	15	10	0	3.59
		2B	K. Oberkfell	369	.301	1	35	213	323	8	65	4.6	**.985**	B. Forsch	33	219	11	11	0	3.82
		SS	G. Templeton	672	.314	9	62	**292**	525	**34**	**102**	**5.7**	.960	S. Martinez	32	207	15	8	0	3.26
		3B	K. Reitz	605	.268	8	73	124	290	12	26	2.7	.972	J. Denny	31	206	8	11	0	4.85
	W-86 L-76	RF	G. Hendrick	493	.300	16	75	254	20	2	7	2.0	.993	J. Fulgham	20	146	10	6	0	2.53
		CF	T. Scott	587	.259	6	68	427	14	7	5	3.0	.984	M. Littell	63	82	9	4	13	2.20
	Ken Boyer	LF	L. Brock	405	.304	5	38	152	7	7	2	1.7	.958	D. Knowles	48	49	2	5	6	4.04
		C	T. Simmons	448	.283	26	87	606	69	10	10	5.6	.985	B. Schultz	31	42	4	3	3	4.50
		OF	J. Mumphrey	339	.295	3	32	180	3	3	0	1.6	.984							
		2B	M. Tyson	190	.221	5	20	125	184	8	42	4.5	.975							
		OF	D. Iorg	179	.291	1	21	51	2	2	0	1.4	.964							
	Philadelphia	1B	P. Rose	628	.331	4	59	1424	87	8	124	9.6	.995	S. Carlton	35	251	18	11	0	3.62
		2B	M. Trillo	431	.260	6	42	270	368	10	84	5.5	.985	R. Lerch	37	214	10	13	0	3.74
		SS	L. Bowa	539	.241	0	31	229	448	6	80	4.7	**.991**	N. Espinosa	33	212	14	12	0	3.65
	W-84 L-78	3B	M. Schmidt	541	.253	45	114	114	361	23	**36**	3.2	.954	D. Ruthven	20	122	7	5	0	4.28
		RF	B. McBride	582	.280	12	60	341	12	4	3	2.4	.989	L. Christenson	19	106	5	10	0	4.50
	Danny Ozark	CF	G. Maddox	548	.281	13	61	433	13	2	2	3.2	.996	R. Reed	61	102	13	8	5	4.15
	W-65 L-67	LF	G. Luzinski	452	.252	18	81	156	3	9	1	1.3	.946	T. McGraw	65	84	4	3	16	5.14
		C	B. Boone	398	.286	9	58	527	65	7	8	5.1	.988	R. Eastwick	51	83	3	6	6	4.88
	Dallas Green	OF	G. Gross	174	.333	0	15	82	5	2	2	1.2	.978							
	W-19 L-11	01	D. Unser	141	.298	6	29	118	5	3	6		.976							
	Chicago	1B	B. Buckner	591	.284	14	66	1258	124	7	118	9.9	.995	R. Reuschel	36	239	18	12	0	3.62
		2B	T. Sizemore	330	.248	2	24	230	312	15*	68	5.8	.973	L. McGlothen	42	212	13	14	2	4.12
		SS	I. DeJesus	636	.283	5	52	235	507	32	97	4.8	.959	D. Lamp	38	200	11	10	0	3.51
		3B	S. Ontiveros	519	.285	4	57	98	268	23	27	2.7	.941	M. Krukow	28	165	9	9	0	4.20
	W-80 L-82	RF	S. Thompson	346	.289	2	29	161	7	5	3	1.7	.971	K. Holtzman	23	118	6	9	0	4.58
		CF	J. Martin	534	.272	19	73	297	11	6	4	2.2	.981	D. Tidrow	63	103	11	5	4	2.71
	Herman Franks	LF	D. Kingman	532	.288	**48**	115	240	11	12	3	1.9	.954	B. Sutter	62	101	6	6	**37**	2.23
	W-78 L-77	C	B. Foote	429	.254	16	56	713	63	**17**	9	**6.1**	.979							
	Joey Amalfitano	01	L. Biittner	272	.290	3	50	282	23	6	24		.981							
	W-2 L-5	OF	B. Murcer	190	.258	7	22	110	4	0	0	2.1	1.000							
		OF	M. Vail	179	.335	7	35	51	3	2	0	1.4	.964							
		2B	S. Dillard	166	.283	5	24	111	132	3	31	4.1	.988							
	New York	1B	W. Montanez	410	.234	5	47	905	76	11	95	9.2	.989	C. Swan	35	251	14	13	0	3.30
		2B	D. Flynn	555	.243	4	61	**369**	380	13	**98**	5.1	.983	P. Falcone	33	184	6	14	0	4.16
		SS	F. Taveras	635	.263	1	33	270	438	25	88	4.8	.966	K. Kobel	30	162	6	8	0	3.50
		3B	R. Hebner	473	.268	10	79	99	246	22	26	2.7	.940	N. Allen	50	99	6	10	8	3.55
	W-63 L-99	RF	J. Youngblood	590	.275	16	60	308	18	5	3	2.3	.985	D. Murray	58	97	4	8	4	4.82
		CF	L. Mazzilli	597	.303	15	79	358	12	4	1	2.6	.989	D. Ellis	17	85	3	7	0	6.04
	Joe Torre	LF	S. Henderson	350	.306	5	39	201	6	2	3	2.2	.990	A. Hassler	29	80	4	5	4	3.71
		C	J. Stearns	538	.243	9	66	628	85	12	11	6.0	.983	T. Hausman	19	79	2	6	2	2.73
		OF	E. Maddox	224	.268	1	12	129	5	2	1	2.1	.985	E. Glynn	46	60	1	4	7	3.00
		UT	A. Trevino	207	.271	0	20	229	71	9	14		.971	S. Lockwood	27	42	2	5	9	1.50
West	Cincinnati	1B	D. Driessen	515	.250	18	75	1289	79	9	112	9.6	.993	T. Seaver	32	215	16	6	0	3.14
		2B	J. Morgan	436	.250	9	32	259	329	12	74	5.0	.980	M. LaCoss	35	206	14	8	0	3.50
		SS	D. Concepcion	590	.281	16	84	284	495	27	**102**	5.4	.967	F. Norman	34	195	11	13	0	3.65
		3B	R. Knight	551	.318	10	79	120	262	15	26	2.7	.962	B. Bonham	29	176	9	7	0	3.78
	W-90 L-71	RF	K. Griffey	380	.316	8	32	175	8	3	1	2.0	.984	T. Hume	57	163	10	9	17	2.76
		CF	C. Geronimo	356	.239	4	38	291	11	2	2	2.6	.993	P. Moskau	21	106	5	4	0	3.91
	John McNamara	LF	G. Foster	440	.302	30	98	214	7	4	1	1.9	.982	F. Pastore	30	95	6	7	4	4.26
		C	J. Bench	464	.276	22	80	619	68	10	11	5.5	.986	D. Bair	65	94	11	7	16	4.31
		OF	D. Collins	396	.318	3	35	159	2	4	2	1.8	.976							
		2B	J. Kennedy	220	.273	1	17	95	144	5	28	4.1	.980							
		OF	H. Cruz	182	.242	4	27	119	8	2	4	1.9	.984							

NATIONAL LEAGUE 1979, *cont.*

Houston

W-89 L-73

Bill Virdon

POS	Player	AB	BA	HR	RBI	PO	A	E	DP	TC/G	FA	Pitcher	G	IP	W	L	SV	ERA
1B	C. Cedeno	470	.262	6	54	832	33	**17**	79	9.7	.981	J. Richard	38	292	18	13	0	**2.71**
2B	R. Landestoy	282	.270	0	30	166	234	12	53	3.6	.971	J. Niekro	38	264	**21**	11	0	3.00
SS	C. Reynolds	555	.265	0	39	208	428	23	88	4.6	.965	J. Andujar	46	194	12	12	4	3.43
3B	E. Cabell	603	.272	6	67	109	178	13	11	2.3	.957	K. Forsch	26	178	11	6	0	3.03
RF	J. Leonard	411	.290	0	47	227	6	10	1	2.0	.959	R. Williams	31	121	4	7	0	3.27
CF	T. Puhl	600	.287	8	49	352	7	0	3	2.4	1.000	J. Sambito	63	91	8	7	22	1.78
LF	J. Cruz	558	.289	9	72	320	7	14	0	2.2	.959							
C	A. Ashby	336	.202	2	35	548	57	8	5	5.8	.987							
23	A. Howe	355	.248	6	33	173	258	7	39		.984							
UT	J. Gonzalez	181	.249	0	10	92	146	5	27		.979							
1B	B. Watson	163	.239	3	18	371	33	3	23	9.3	.993							
OF	D. Walling	147	.327	3	31	65	2	1	0	1.6	.985							

Los Angeles

W-79 L-83

Tom Lasorda

POS	Player	AB	BA	HR	RBI	PO	A	E	DP	TC/G	FA	Pitcher	G	IP	W	L	SV	ERA
1B	S. Garvey	648	.315	28	110	1402	93	7	101	9.3	.995	R. Sutcliffe	39	242	17	10	0	3.46
2B	D. Lopes	582	.265	28	73	341	**384**	14	82	4.9	.981	D. Sutton	33	226	12	15	1	3.82
SS	B. Russell	627	.271	7	56	218	452	30	70	4.7	.957	B. Hooton	29	212	11	10	0	2.97
3B	R. Cey	487	.281	28	81	123	265	9	25	2.6	**.977**	J. Reuss	39	160	7	14	3	3.54
RF	G. Thomasson	315	.248	14	45	194	4	4	1	2.0	.980	C. Hough	42	151	7	5	0	4.77
CF	D. Thomas	406	.256	5	44	269	10	1	4	2.4	.996	B. Welch	25	81	5	6	5	4.00
LF	D. Baker	554	.274	23	88	289	14	3	4	2.0	.990	D. Patterson	36	53	4	1	6	5.26
C	S. Yeager	310	.216	13	41	513	56	9	7	5.6	.984	L. LaGrow	31	37	5	1	4	3.41
CO	J. Ferguson	363	.262	20	69	414	37	9	8		.980							
OF	R. Smith	234	.274	10	32	159	5	2	0	2.7	.988							

San Francisco

W-71 L-91

Joe Altobelli
W-61 L-79

Dave Bristol
W-10 L-12

POS	Player	AB	BA	HR	RBI	PO	A	E	DP	TC/G	FA	Pitcher	G	IP	W	L	SV	ERA
1B	M. Ivie	402	.286	27	89	724	40	4	51	7.8	.995	V. Blue	34	237	14	14	0	5.01
2B	J. Strain	257	.241	1	12	147	188	6	32	5.1	.982	B. Knepper	34	207	9	12	0	4.65
SS	J. LeMaster	343	.254	3	29	160	303	20	32	4.6	.959	J. Montefusco	22	137	3	8	0	3.94
3B	D. Evans	562	.253	17	70	**129**	**369**	**30**	28	**3.3**	.943	E. Halicki	33	126	5	8	0	4.57
RF	J. Clark	527	.273	26	86	261	13	5	7	2.0	.982	J. Curtis	27	121	10	9	0	4.17
CF	B. North	460	.259	5	30	300	8	4	2	2.4	.987	E. Whitson	18	100	5	8	0	3.95
LF	L. Herndon	354	.257	7	36	196	10	8	2	1.8	.963	P. Nastu	25	100	3	4	0	4.32
C	D. Littlejohn	193	.197	1	13	366	43	6	7	6.6	.986	G. Lavelle	70	97	7	9	20	2.51
OF	T. Whitfield	394	.287	5	44	167	10	8	3	1.7	.957	T. Griffin	59	94	5	6	2	3.93
1B	W. McCovey	353	.249	15	57	740	48	10	60	9.0	.987	G. Minton	46	80	4	3	4	1.80
SS	R. Metzger	259	.251	0	31	108	219	15	34	4.4	.956	P. Borbon	30	46	4	3	3	4.89
2B	B. Madlock	249	.261	7	41	137	144	7	32	4.6	.976							
C	M. Hill	169	.207	3	15	283	31	3	4	5.5	.991							

San Diego

W-68 L-93

Roger Craig

POS	Player	AB	BA	HR	RBI	PO	A	E	DP	TC/G	FA	Pitcher	G	IP	W	L	SV	ERA
1B	D. Briggs	227	.207	8	30	326	28	5	20	7.2	.986	R. Jones	39	263	11	12	0	3.63
2B	F. Gonzalez	323	.217	9	34	217	225	11	52	4.4	.976	G. Perry	32	233	12	11	0	3.05
SS	O. Smith	587	.211	0	27	256	**555**	20	86	5.4	.976	B. Shirley	49	205	8	16	0	3.38
3B	P. Dade	283	.276	1	19	44	162	11	12	3.1	.949	E. Rasmussen	45	157	6	9	3	3.27
RF	J. Turner	448	.248	9	61	197	7	9	2	1.9	.958	B. Owchinko	42	149	6	12	0	3.74
CF	G. Richards	545	.279	4	41	320	7	9	2	2.5	.973	J. D'Acquisto	51	134	9	13	2	4.90
LF	D. Winfield	597	.308	34	**118**	344	14	5	3	2.3	.986	R. Fingers	54	84	9	9	13	4.50
C	G. Tenace	463	.263	20	67	413	51	1	10	4.9	**.998**	S. Mura	38	73	4	4	2	3.08
UT	K. Bevacqua	297	.253	1	34	115	156	11	21		.961	M. Lee	46	65	2	4	5	4.29
C	B. Fahey	209	.287	3	19	277	33	2	5	4.6	.994							
01	J. Johnstone	201	.294	0	32	185	18	4	10		.981							
2B	B. Almon	198	.227	1	8	116	150	4	37	4.4	.985							
3B	B. Evans	162	.216	1	14	30	108	7	12	2.7	.952							

Atlanta

W-66 L-94

Bobby Cox

POS	Player	AB	BA	HR	RBI	PO	A	E	DP	TC/G	FA	Pitcher	G	IP	W	L	SV	ERA
1B	D. Murphy	384	.276	21	57	685	42	15	61	9.8	.980	P. Niekro	44	**342**	**21**	**20**	0	3.39
2B	G. Hubbard	325	.231	3	29	193	268	**15**	57	5.2	.968	E. Solomon	31	186	7	14	0	4.21
SS	P. Frias	475	.259	1	44	229	432	32	79	5.1	.954	R. Matula	28	171	8	10	0	4.16
3B	B. Horner	487	.314	33	98	56	143	15	11	2.6	.930	T. Brizzolara	20	107	6	9	0	5.30
RF	J. Burroughs	397	.224	11	47	175	8	7	1	1.7	.963	G. Garber	68	106	6	16	25	4.33
CF	B. Bonnell	375	.259	12	45	220	8	4	2	1.9	.983	M. Mahler	26	100	5	11	0	5.85
LF	G. Matthews	631	.304	27	90	292	12	8	4	2.0	.974	J. McLaughlin	37	69	5	3	5	2.48
C	B. Benedict	204	.225	0	15	344	35	6	3	5.1	.984							
32	J. Royster	601	.273	3	51	261	405	22	62		.968							
OF	R. Office	277	.249	2	37	164	4	2	0	1.8	.988							
C	J. Nolan	230	.248	4	21	328	27	6	2	4.9	.983							
1B	M. Lum	217	.249	6	27	414	30	1	36	8.7	.998							
OF	C. Spikes	93	.280	3	21	16	0	3	0	1.3	.842							

BATTING AND BASE RUNNING LEADERS

Batting Average

K. Hernandez, STL	.344
P. Rose, PHI	.331
R. Knight, CIN	.318
S. Garvey, LA	.315
B. Horner, ATL	.314

Slugging Average

D. Kingman, CHI	.613
M. Schmidt, PHI	.564
G. Foster, CIN	.561
D. Winfield, SD	.558
B. Horner, ATL	.552

Home Runs

D. Kingman, CHI	48
M. Schmidt, PHI	45
D. Winfield, SD	34
B. Horner, ATL	33
W. Stargell, PIT	32

Total Bases

D. Winfield, SD	333
D. Parker, PIT	327
D. Kingman, CHI	326
S. Garvey, LA	322
G. Matthews, ATL	317

Runs Batted In

D. Winfield, SD	118
D. Kingman, CHI	115
M. Schmidt, PHI	114
S. Garvey, LA	110
K. Hernandez, STL	105

Stolen Bases

O. Moreno, PIT	77
B. North, SF	58
D. Lopes, LA	44
F. Taveras, PIT, NY	44
R. Scott, MON	39

PITCHING LEADERS

Winning Percentage

T. Seaver, CIN	.727
J. Niekro, HOU	.656
S. Martinez, STL	.652
R. Sutcliffe, LA	.630
S. Carlton, PHI	.621

Earned Run Average

J. Richard, HOU	2.71
T. Hume, CIN	2.76
D. Schatzeder, MON	2.83
B. Hooton, LA	2.97
J. Niekro, HOU	3.00
S. Rogers, MON	3.00

Wins

J. Niekro, HOU	21
P. Niekro, ATL	21
R. Reuschel, CHI	18
S. Carlton, PHI	18
J. Richard, HOU	18

Saves

B. Sutter, CHI	37
K. Tekulve, PIT	31
G. Garber, ATL	25
J. Sambito, HOU	22
G. Lavelle, SF	20

Strikeouts

J. Richard, HOU	313
S. Carlton, PHI	213
P. Niekro, ATL	208
B. Blyleven, PIT	172
L. McGlothen, CHI	147

Complete Games

P. Niekro, ATL	23
J. Richard, HOU	19
S. Carlton, PHI	13
S. Rogers, MON	13
B. Hooton, LA	12

NATIONAL LEAGUE 1979, *cont.*

BATTING AND BASE RUNNING LEADERS

Hits

G. Templeton, STL	211
K. Hernandez, STL	210
P. Rose, PHI	208
S. Garvey, LA	204

Base on Balls

M. Schmidt, PHI	120
G. Tenace, SD	105
D. Lopes, LA	97
B. North, SF	96

Home Run Percentage

D. Kingman, CHI	9.0
M. Schmidt, PHI	8.3
G. Foster, CIN	6.8
B. Horner, ATL	6.8

Runs

K. Hernandez, STL	116
O. Moreno, PIT	110
M. Schmidt, PHI	109
D. Lopes, LA	109
D. Parker, PIT	109

Doubles

K. Hernandez, STL	48
W. Cromartie, MON	46
D. Parker, PIT	45
K. Reitz, STL	41

Triples

G. Templeton, STL	19
B. McBride, PHI	12
A. Dawson, MON	12
O. Moreno, PIT	12

PITCHING LEADERS

Fewest Hits/9 Innings

J. Richard, HOU	6.78
S. Carlton, PHI	7.24
J. Niekro, HOU	7.53
D. Schatzeder, MON	7.56

Shutouts

T. Seaver, CIN	5
S. Rogers, MON	5
J. Niekro, HOU	5
S. Carlton, PHI	4
J. Richard, HOU	4

Fewest Walks/9 Innings

K. Forsch, HOU	1.77
J. Candelaria, PIT	1.78
T. Hume, CIN	1.82
B. Lee, MON	1.86

Most Strikeouts/9 Inn.

J. Richard, HOU	9.65
S. Carlton, PHI	7.64
S. Sanderson, MON	7.39
B. Blyleven, PIT	6.53

Innings

P. Niekro, ATL	342
J. Richard, HOU	292
J. Niekro, HOU	264
R. Jones, SD	263

Games Pitched

K. Tekulve, PIT	94
E. Romo, PIT	84
G. Jackson, PIT	72
G. Lavelle, SF	70

		W	L	PCT	GB	R	OR	Batting 2B	3B	HR	BA	SA	SB	Fielding E	DP	FA	Pitching CG	BB	SO	ShO	SV	ERA
East	Pittsburgh	98	64	.605		**775**	643	264	52	148	.272	**.416**	180	134	163	.979	24	504	904	7	**52**	3.41
	Montreal	95	65	.594	2	701	**581**	273	42	143	.264	.408	121	131	123	.979	33	**450**	813	18	39	**3.14**
	St. Louis	86	76	.531	12	731	693	**279**	**63**	100	**.278**	.401	116	132	166	.980	38	501	788	10	25	3.72
	Philadelphia	84	78	.519	14	683	718	250	53	119	.266	.396	128	**106**	148	**.983**	33	477	787	14	29	4.16
	Chicago	80	82	.494	18	706	707	250	43	135	.269	.403	73	159	163	.975	20	521	**933**	11	44	3.88
	New York	63	99	.389	35	593	706	255	41	74	.250	.350	135	140	**168**	.978	16	607	819	10	36	3.84
West	Cincinnati	90	71	.559		731	644	266	31	132	.264	.396	99	124	152	.980	27	485	773	10	40	3.58
	Houston	89	73	.549	1.5	583	582	224	52	49	.256	.344	**190**	138	146	.978	**55**	504	854	**19**	31	3.19
	Los Angeles	79	83	.488	11.5	739	717	220	24	**183**	.263	.412	106	118	123	.981	30	555	811	6	34	3.83
	San Francisco	71	91	.438	19.5	672	751	192	36	125	.246	.365	140	163	138	.974	25	577	880	6	34	4.16
	San Diego	68	93	.422	22	603	681	193	53	93	.242	.348	100	141	154	.978	29	513	779	7	25	3.69
	Atlanta	66	94	.412	23.5	669	763	220	28	126	.256	.377	98	183	139	.970	32	494	779	3	34	4.18
						8186	8186	2886	518	1427	.261	.385	1486	1669	1783	.978	362	6188	9920	121	423	3.73

AMERICAN LEAGUE 1979

East

Baltimore

W-102 L-57

Earl Weaver

POS	Player	AB	BA	HR	RBI	PO	A	E	DP	TC/G	FA	Pitcher	G	IP	W	L	SV	ERA
1B	E. Murray	606	.295	25	99	**1456**	107	10	135	10.0	.994	D. Martinez	40	**292**	15	16	0	3.67
2B	R. Dauer	479	.257	9	61	213	260	10	68	4.7	.979	M. Flanagan	39	266	**23**	9	0	3.08
SS	K. Garcia	417	.247	5	24	173	271	21	66	4.1	.955	S. Stone	32	186	11	7	0	3.77
3B	D. DeCinces	422	.230	16	61	99	247	13	21	3.0	.964	S. McGregor	27	175	13	6	0	3.34
RF	K. Singleton	570	.295	35	111	247	8	5	2	1.8	.981	J. Palmer	23	156	10	6	0	3.29
CF	A. Bumbry	569	.285	7	49	367	7	7	1	2.6	.982	S. Stewart	31	118	8	5	1	3.51
LF	G. Roenicke	376	.261	25	64	246	10	5	1	2.0	.981	T. Martinez	39	78	10	3	3	2.88
C	R. Dempsey	368	.239	6	41	615	**81**	7	13	**5.7**	.990	D. Stanhouse	52	73	7	3	21	2.84
DH	L. May	456	.254	19	69													
SS	M. Belanger	198	.167	0	9	110	195	3	38	3.1	.990							
OF	J. Lowenstein	197	.254	11	34	120	4	1	2	1.7	.992							
2B	B. Smith	189	.249	6	33	107	142	5	33	4.0	.980							
OD	P. Kelly	153	.288	9	25	36	0	0	0		1.000							

Milwaukee

W-95 L-66

George Bamberger

POS	Player	AB	BA	HR	RBI	PO	A	E	DP	TC/G	FA	Pitcher	G	IP	W	L	SV	ERA
1B	C. Cooper	590	.308	24	106	1323	78	10	119	10.5	.993	M. Caldwell	30	235	16	6	0	3.29
2B	P. Molitor	584	.322	9	62	289	413	15	81	**5.9**	.979	L. Sorensen	34	235	15	14	0	3.98
SS	R. Yount	577	.267	8	51	267	517	25	97	5.4	.969	J. Slaton	32	213	15	9	0	3.63
3B	S. Bando	476	.246	9	43	87	222	12	16	2.9	.963	B. Travers	30	187	14	8	0	3.90
RF	S. Lezcano	473	.321	28	101	281	10	4	2	2.2	.986	M. Haas	29	185	11	11	0	4.77
CF	G. Thomas	557	.244	**45**	123	435	4	4	0	2.9	.991	J. Augustine	43	86	9	6	5	3.45
LF	B. Oglivie	514	.282	29	81	252	7	4	0	2.2	.985	R. Cleveland	29	55	1	5	4	6.71
C	C. Moore	337	.300	5	38	414	58	10	7	4.5	.979	B. McClure	36	51	5	2	5	3.88
DH	D. Davis	335	.266	12	41							B. Castro	39	44	3	1	6	2.05
UT	D. Money	350	.237	6	38	240	117	2	33		.994							
32	J. Gantner	208	.284	2	22	78	147	7	24		.970							
C	B. Martinez	196	.270	4	26	198	39	8	2	3.6	.967							
OF	J. Wohlford	175	.263	1	17	126	0	4	0	2.4	.969							

Boston

W-91 L-69

Don Zimmer

POS	Player	AB	BA	HR	RBI	PO	A	E	DP	TC/G	FA	Pitcher	G	IP	W	L	SV	ERA
1B	B. Watson	312	.337	13	53	525	47	7	58	10.0	.988	M. Torrez	36	252	16	13	0	4.50
2B	J. Remy	306	.297	0	29	147	205	11	43	4.8	.970	D. Eckersley	33	247	17	10	0	2.99
SS	R. Burleson	627	.278	5	60	272	523	16	109	5.3	**.980**	B. Stanley	40	217	16	12	1	3.98
3B	B. Hobson	528	.261	28	93	110	251	25	17	2.7	.935	S. Renko	27	171	11	9	0	4.11
RF	D. Evans	489	.274	21	58	307	15	4	5	2.2	.988	C. Rainey	20	104	8	5	1	3.81
CF	F. Lynn	531	**.333**	39	122	381	10	5	4	2.8	.987	D. Drago	53	89	10	6	13	3.03
LF	J. Rice	619	.325	39	130	241	8	4	1	2.0	.984	B. Campbell	41	55	3	4	9	4.25
C	G. Allenson	241	.203	3	22	407	40	9	3	4.4	.980							
DH	C. Yastrzemski	518	.270	21	87													
DC	C. Fisk	320	.272	10	42	155	8	3	1		.982							
23	J. Brohamer	192	.266	1	11	74	140	5	27		.977							
1B	G. Scott	156	.224	4	23	400	25	6	40	10.5	.986							
OF	T. Poquette	154	.331	2	23	73	2	4	1	1.8	.949							

AMERICAN LEAGUE 1979, *cont.*

New York

W-89 L-71

Bob Lemon
W-34 L-31

Billy Martin
W-55 L-40

POS	Player	AB	BA	HR	RBI	PO	A	E	DP	TC/G	FA	Pitcher	G	IP	W	L	SV	ERA
1B	C. Chambliss	554	.280	18	63	1299	95	7	135	**10.5**	.995	T. John	37	276	21	9	0	2.97
2B	W. Randolph	574	.270	5	61	**355**	**478**	13	**128**	5.5	.985	R. Guidry	33	236	18	8	2	**2.78**
SS	B. Dent	431	.230	2	32	219	512	17	107	5.3	.977	L. Tiant	30	196	13	8	0	3.90
3B	G. Nettles	521	.253	20	73	110	339	16	30	3.2	.966	E. Figueroa	16	105	4	6	0	4.11
RF	R. Jackson	465	.297	29	89	274	7	4	2	2.3	.986	C. Hunter	19	105	2	9	0	5.31
CF	M. Rivers	286	.287	3	25	147	4	4	0	2.2	.974	R. Davis	44	85	14	2	9	2.86
LF	L. Piniella	461	.297	11	69	204	13	4	1	2.0	.982	K. Clay	32	78	1	7	2	5.42
C	T. Munson	382	.288	3	39	405	44	10	5	5.2	.978	G. Gossage	36	58	5	3	18	2.64
DH	J. Spencer	295	.288	23	53													
OF	B. Murcer	264	.273	8	33	169	4	3	0	2.5	.983							
DO	R. White	205	.215	3	27	45	3	0	0		1.000							
OD	O. Gamble	113	.389	11	32	47	3	3	2		.943							

Detroit

W-85 L-76

Les Moss
W-27 L-26

Dick Tracewski
W-2 L-0

Sparky Anderson
W-56 L-50

POS	Player	AB	BA	HR	RBI	PO	A	E	DP	TC/G	FA	Pitcher	G	IP	W	L	SV	ERA
1B	J. Thompson	492	.246	20	79	1176	91	8	135	9.1	.994	J. Morris	27	198	17	7	0	3.27
2B	L. Whitaker	423	.286	3	42	280	369	9	103	5.2	.986	M. Wilcox	33	196	12	10	0	4.36
SS	A. Trammell	460	.276	6	50	245	388	26	99	4.6	.961	J. Billingham	35	158	10	7	3	3.30
3B	A. Rodriguez	343	.254	5	36	72	211	13	23	2.8	.956	A. Lopez	61	127	10	5	21	2.41
RF	J. Morales	440	.211	14	56	206	6	3	2	1.8	.986	P. Underwood	27	122	6	4	0	4.57
CF	R. LeFlore	600	.300	9	57	293	6	3	3	2.7	.990	D. Petry	15	98	6	5	0	3.95
LF	S. Kemp	490	.318	26	105	229	12	6	2	2.1	.976	J. Hiller	43	79	4	7	9	5.24
C	L. Parrish	493	.276	19	65	707	79	9	10	5.6	.989	D. Tobik	37	69	3	5	3	4.30
DH	R. Staub	246	.236	9	40													
OF	C. Summers	246	.313	20	51	87	3	1	0	1.3	.989							
UT	J. Wockenfuss	231	.264	15	46	318	26	3	22		.991							
OF	L. Jones	213	.296	4	26	142	3	3	1	1.8	.980							
32	T. Brookens	190	.263	4	21	76	141	11	21		.952							

Cleveland

W-81 L-80

Jeff Torborg
W-43 L-52

Dave Garcia
W-38 L-28

POS	Player	AB	BA	HR	RBI	PO	A	E	DP	TC/G	FA	Pitcher	G	IP	W	L	SV	ERA
1B	A. Thornton	515	.233	26	93	1089	82	7	100	9.1	.994	R. Wise	34	232	15	10	0	3.72
2B	D. Kuiper	479	.255	0	39	345	380	9	89	5.2	**.988**	R. Waits	34	231	16	13	0	4.44
SS	T. Veryzer	449	.220	0	34	238	446	18	90	4.7	.974	M. Paxton	33	160	8	8	0	5.91
3B	T. Harrah	527	.279	20	77	91	160	16	19	2.1	.940	D. Spillner	49	158	9	5	1	4.61
RF	B. Bonds	538	.275	25	85	267	9	6	1	2.4	.979	L. Barker	29	137	6	6	0	4.93
CF	R. Manning	560	.259	3	51	417	9	6	2	3.1	.986	S. Monge	76	131	12	10	19	2.40
LF	J. Norris	353	.246	3	30	214	2	4	0	2.4	.982	W. Garland	18	95	4	10	0	5.21
C	G. Alexander	358	.229	15	54	404	40	**18**	5	5.1	.961	V. Cruz	61	79	3	9	10	4.22
DH	C. Johnson	240	.271	18	61													
01	M. Hargrove	338	.325	10	56	356	16	2	23		.995							
C	R. Hassey	223	.287	4	32	345	29	3	4	5.5	.992							
3B	T. Cox	189	.212	4	22	29	78	4	11	2.1	.964							
OF	P. Dade	170	.282	3	18	73	4	3	1	2.2	.962							
UT	R. Pruitt	166	.283	2	21	66	5	2	1		.973							

Toronto

W-53 L-109

Roy Hartsfield

POS	Player	AB	BA	HR	RBI	PO	A	E	DP	TC/G	FA	Pitcher	G	IP	W	L	SV	ERA
1B	J. Mayberry	464	.274	21	74	1192	74	6	129	9.4	.995	T. Underwood	33	227	9	16	0	3.69
2B	D. Ainge	308	.237	2	19	198	261	11	67	5.5	.977	P. Huffman	31	173	6	**18**	0	5.77
SS	A. Griffin	624	.287	2	31	272	501	**36**	124	5.3	.956	D. Lemanczyk	22	143	8	10	0	3.71
3B	R. Howell	511	.247	15	72	108	290	20	28	3.1	.952	B. Moore	34	139	5	7	0	4.86
RF	B. Bailor	414	.229	1	38	210	16	3	2	1.9	.987	D. Stieb	18	129	8	8	0	4.33
CF	R. Bosetti	619	.260	8	65	466	18	13	4	3.1	.974	J. Jefferson	34	116	2	10	1	5.51
LF	A. Woods	436	.278	5	36	251	10	9	2	2.1	.967	M. Lemongello	18	83	1	9	0	6.29
C	R. Cerone	469	.239	7	61	560	68	13	10	4.7	.980	T. Buskey	44	79	6	10	7	3.42
DH	R. Carty	461	.256	12	55													
OF	O. Velez	274	.288	15	48	130	3	4	1	1.9	.971							
UT	L. Gomez	163	.239	0	11	70	116	3	25		.984							

West

California

W-88 L-74

Jim Fregosi

POS	Player	AB	BA	HR	RBI	PO	A	E	DP	TC/G	FA	Pitcher	G	IP	W	L	SV	ERA
1B	R. Carew	409	.318	3	44	804	55	10	101	8.4	.988	D. Frost	36	239	16	10	1	3.58
2B	B. Grich	534	.294	30	101	340	438	13	111	5.2	.984	N. Ryan	34	223	16	14	0	3.59
SS	B. Campaneris	239	.234	0	15	136	220	16	69	4.5	.957	J. Barr	36	197	10	12	0	4.20
3B	C. Lansford	654	.287	19	79	**135**	263	7	29	2.6	**.983**	D. Aase	37	185	9	10	2	4.82
RF	D. Ford	569	.290	21	101	332	10	8	2	2.5	.977	M. Clear	52	109	11	5	14	3.63
CF	R. Miller	427	.293	2	28	349	3	4	1	3.0	.989	C. Knapp	20	98	5	5	0	5.51
LF	D. Baylor	628	.296	36	**139**	198	3	5	0	2.1	.976	F. Tanana	18	90	7	5	0	3.90
C	B. Downing	509	.326	12	75	669	35	11	5	5.5	.985	D. LaRoche	53	86	7	11	10	5.55
DH	W. Aikens	379	.280	21	81													
OF	J. Rudi	330	.242	11	61	174	5	2	2	2.3	.989							
SS	J. Anderson	234	.248	3	23	126	189	17	42	4.0	.949							

Kansas City

W-85 L-77

Whitey Herzog

POS	Player	AB	BA	HR	RBI	PO	A	E	DP	TC/G	FA	Pitcher	G	IP	W	L	SV	ERA
1B	P. LaCock	408	.277	3	56	829	68	3	79	8.3	**.997**	P. Splittorff	36	240	15	17	0	4.24
2B	F. White	467	.266	10	48	317	332	12	78	5.3	.982	D. Leonard	32	236	14	12	0	4.08
SS	F. Patek	306	.252	1	37	153	249	19	54	4.0	.955	L. Gura	39	234	13	12	0	4.46
3B	G. Brett	645	.329	23	107	129	**373**	**30**	28	**3.6**	.944	R. Gale	34	182	9	10	0	5.64
RF	A. Cowens	516	.295	9	73	288	3	4	0	2.2	.986	M. Pattin	31	94	5	2	3	4.60
CF	A. Otis	577	.295	18	90	385	11	3	5	2.7	.992	S. Busby	22	94	6	6	0	3.64
LF	W. Wilson	588	.315	6	49	384	13	6	0	2.7	.985	A. Hrabosky	58	65	9	4	11	3.74
C	D. Porter	533	.291	20	112	628	68	13	**15**	5.0	.982	D. Quisenberry	32	40	3	2	5	3.15
DH	H. McRae	393	.288	10	74													
S2	U. Washington	268	.254	2	25	174	242	18	68		.959							
UT	J. Wathan	199	.206	2	28	336	24	3	30		.992							
OF	C. Hurdle	171	.240	3	30	88	2	3	0	1.9	.968							
1B	G. Scott	146	.267	1	20	335	21	4	27	8.8	.989							

AMERICAN LEAGUE 1979, *cont.*

Team	POS	Player	AB	BA	HR	RBI	PO	A	E	DP	TC/G	FA	Pitcher	G	IP	W	L	SV	ERA
Texas	1B	P. Putnam	426	.277	18	64	832	62	5	65	9.4	.994	F. Jenkins	37	259	16	14	0	4.07
W-83 L-79	2B	B. Wills	543	.273	5	46	337	468	20	95	5.7	.976	S. Comer	36	242	17	12	0	3.68
Pat Corrales	SS	N. Norman	343	.222	0	21	177	302	24	64	3.5	.952	D. Medich	29	149	10	7	0	4.17
	3B	B. Bell	**670**	.299	18	101	112	364	15	22	3.3	.969	J. Kern	71	143	13	5	29	1.57
	RF	R. Zisk	503	.262	18	64	234	10	7	6	1.9	.972	D. Alexander	23	113	5	7	0	4.46
	CF	A. Oliver	492	.323	12	76	260	9	7	2	2.3	.975	S. Lyle	67	95	5	8	13	3.13
	LF	B. Sample	325	.292	5	35	173	7	0	1	1.7	1.000							
	C	J. Sundberg	495	.275	5	64	**754**	75	4	13	5.6	**.995**							
	DH	J. Ellis	316	.285	12	61													
	OF	J. Grubb	289	.273	10	37	135	8	2	4	1.8	.986							
	OF	M. Rivers	247	.300	6	25	153	4	3	1	2.8	.981							
	DO	O. Gamble	161	.335	8	32	41	2	0	2		1.000							
	1D	W. Montanez	144	.319	8	24	191	16	1	14		.995							
Minnesota	1B	R. Jackson	583	.271	14	68	1447	**137**	9	**175**	10.1	.994	J. Koosman	37	264	20	13	0	3.38
W-82 L-80	2B	R. Wilfong	419	.313	9	59	287	379	14	92	5.1	.979	D. Goltz	36	251	14	13	0	4.16
Gene Mauch	SS	R. Smalley	621	.271	24	95	**296**	**572**	29	**144**	**5.6**	.968	G. Zahn	26	169	13	7	0	3.57
	3B	J. Castino	393	.285	5	52	85	277	14	**31**	2.6	.963	P. Hartzell	28	163	6	10	0	5.36
	RF	H. Powell	338	.293	2	36	165	6	4	3	1.9	.977	M. Marshall	**90**	143	10	15	**32**	2.64
	CF	K. Landreaux	564	.305	15	83	292	10	6	1	2.1	.981	R. Erickson	24	123	3	10	0	5.63
	LF	B. Rivera	263	.281	2	31	169	12	2	0	1.7	.989	P. Redfern	40	108	7	3	1	3.50
	C	B. Wynegar	504	.270	7	57	653	65	6	10	5.0	.992							
	DH	J. Morales	191	.267	2	27													
	DO	G. Adams	326	.301	8	50	66	2	3	0		.958							
	OF	W. Norwood	270	.248	6	30	147	4	4	0	2.2	.974							
	3B	M. Cubbage	243	.276	2	23	34	94	10	9	2.2	.928							
	OF	D. Edwards	229	.249	8	35	165	7	3	0	2.0	.983							
	2B	B. Randall	199	.246	0	14	130	166	5	48	4.2	.983							
	DH	D. Goodwin	159	.289	5	27													
Chicago	1B	M. Squires	295	.264	2	22	741	60	4	62	7.3	.995	K. Kravec	36	250	15	13	1	3.74
W-73 L-87	2B	A. Bannister	506	.285	2	55	150	160	12	32	5.0	.963	R. Wortham	34	204	14	14	0	4.90
Don Kessinger	SS	G. Pryor	476	.275	3	34	161	362	21	54	4.6	.961	R. Baumgarten	28	191	13	8	0	3.53
W-46 L-60	3B	K. Bell	200	.245	4	22	51	153	17	11	3.3	.923	S. Trout	34	155	11	8	4	3.89
Tony LaRussa	RF	C. Washington	471	.280	13	66	256	7	7	3	2.2	.974	R. Scarbery	45	101	2	8	4	4.63
W-27 L-27	CF	C. Lemon	556	.318	17	86	411	10	10	2	2.9	.977	F. Barrios	15	95	8	3	0	3.60
	LF	R. Garr	307	.280	9	39	94	3	5	1	1.5	.951	M. Proly	38	88	3	8	9	3.89
	C	M. May	202	.252	7	28	277	27	6	1	4.8	.981	E. Farmer	42	81	3	7	14	2.44
	DH	J. Orta	325	.262	11	46													
	1B	L. Johnson	479	.309	12	74	748	63	11	62	8.7	.987							
	23	J. Morrison	240	.275	14	35	121	185	9	38		.971							
	3B	E. Soderholm	210	.252	6	34	55	154	3	12	3.8	.986							
	OF	J. Moore	201	.264	1	23	83	3	3	0	1.5	.966							
	DH	W. Nordhagen	193	.280	7	25													
	C	B. Nahorodny	179	.257	6	29	223	25	7	3	4.3	.973							
	OF	R. Torres	170	.253	8	24	117	4	3	0	1.5	.976							
Seattle	1B	B. Bochte	554	.316	16	100	1361	114	**14**	140	10.1	.991	M. Parrott	38	229	14	12	0	3.77
W-67 L-95	2B	J. Cruz	414	.271	1	29	258	361	13	87	5.9	.979	R. Honeycutt	33	194	11	12	0	4.04
Darrell Johnson	SS	M. Mendoza	373	.198	1	29	177	422	20	91	4.2	.968	F. Bannister	30	182	10	15	0	4.05
	3B	D. Meyer	525	.278	20	74	76	201	19	22	2.9	.936	B. McLaughlin	47	124	7	7	14	4.21
	RF	J. Simpson	265	.283	2	27	162	10	6	4	1.7	.966	O. Jones	25	119	3	11	0	6.05
	CF	R. Jones	622	.267	21	78	453	13	5	4	2.9	.989	G. Abbott	23	117	4	10	0	5.15
	LF	L. Roberts	450	.271	15	54	286	6	5	2	2.2	.983	J. Montague	41	116	6	4	1	5.59
	C	L. Cox	293	.215	4	36	408	49	9	6	4.7	.981	R. Dressler	21	104	3	2	0	4.93
	DH	W. Horton	646	.279	29	106							S. Rawley	48	84	5	9	11	3.86
	S2	L. Milbourne	356	.278	2	26	136	250	11	57		.972							
	OF	T. Paciorek	310	.287	6	42	137	2	0	0	1.9	1.000							
	3B	B. Stein	250	.248	7	27	45	120	7	13	2.6	.959							
	C	B. Stinson	247	.243	6	28	376	29	9	2	4.5	.978							
Oakland	1B	D. Revering	472	.288	19	77	828	80	13	77	8.9	.986	R. Langford	34	219	12	16	0	4.27
W-54 L-108	2B	M. Edwards	400	.233	1	23	244	314	**22**	54	5.1	.962	S. McCatty	31	186	11	12	0	4.21
Jim Marshall	SS	R. Picciolo	348	.253	2	27	191	265	17	51	4.5	.964	M. Keough	30	177	2	17	0	5.03
	3B	W. Gross	442	.224	14	50	120	211	20	19	2.9	.943	M. Norris	29	146	5	8	0	4.81
	RF	L. Murray	226	.186	2	20	173	7	7	2	2.1	.963	C. Minetto	36	118	1	5	0	5.57
	CF	D. Murphy	388	.255	11	40	322	10	4	0	2.8	.988	B. Kingman	18	113	8	7	0	4.30
	LF	R. Henderson	351	.274	1	26	215	5	6	0	2.6	.973	D. Heaverlo	62	86	4	11	9	4.19
	C	J. Newman	516	.231	22	71	378	53	10	7	5.4	.977	J. Johnson	14	85	2	8	0	4.34
	DH	M. Page	478	.247	9	42							D. Hamilton	40	83	3	4	5	3.69
	C	J. Essian	313	.243	8	40	348	57	8	5	5.9	.981	M. Morgan	13	77	2	10	0	5.96
	OF	T. Armas	278	.248	11	34	194	7	5	2	2.6	.976	B. Lacey	42	48	1	5	4	5.81
	UT	M. Heath	258	.256	3	27	167	32	5	2		.975							
	UT	D. Chalk	212	.222	2	13	122	151	11	31		.961							
	SS	M. Guerrero	166	.229	0	18	68	129	10	33	4.8	.952							

BATTING AND BASE RUNNING LEADERS

Batting Average		Slugging Average		Home Runs	
F. Lynn, BOS	.333	F. Lynn, BOS	.637	G. Thomas, MIL	45
G. Brett, KC	.329	J. Rice, BOS	.596	F. Lynn, BOS	39
B. Downing, CAL	.326	S. Lezcano, MIL	.573	J. Rice, BOS	39
J. Rice, BOS	.325	G. Brett, KC	.563	D. Baylor, CAL	36
A. Oliver, TEX	.323	R. Jackson, NY	.544	K. Singleton, BAL	35

PITCHING LEADERS

Winning Percentage		Earned Run Average		Wins	
M. Caldwell, MIL	.727	R. Guidry, NY	2.78	M. Flanagan, BAL	23
M. Flanagan, BAL	.719	T. John, NY	2.97	T. John, NY	21
J. Morris, DET	.708	D. Eckersley, BOS	2.99	J. Koosman, MIN	20
T. John, NY	.700	M. Flanagan, BAL	3.08	R. Guidry, NY	18
R. Guidry, NY	.692	J. Morris, DET	3.27		

AMERICAN LEAGUE 1979, *cont.*

BATTING AND BASE RUNNING LEADERS

Total Bases		Runs Batted In		Stolen Bases		Saves	
J. Rice, BOS	369	D. Baylor, CAL	139	W. Wilson, KC	83	M. Marshall, MIN	32
G. Brett, KC	363	J. Rice, BOS	130	R. LeFlore, DET	78	J. Kern, TEX	29
F. Lynn, BOS	338	G. Thomas, MIL	123	J. Cruz, SEA	49	D. Stanhouse, BAL	21
D. Baylor, CAL	333	F. Lynn, BOS	122	A. Bumbry, BAL	37	A. Lopez, DET	21
K. Singleton, BAL	304	D. Porter, KC	112	B. Wills, TEX	35	S. Monge, CLE	19
Hits		**Base on Balls**		**Home Run Percentage**		**Fewest Hits/9 Innings**	
G. Brett, KC	212	D. Porter, KC	121	G. Thomas, MIL	8.1	N. Ryan, CAL	6.82
J. Rice, BOS	201	K. Singleton, BAL	109	F. Lynn, BOS	7.3	K. Kravec, CHI	7.49
B. Bell, TEX	200	G. Thomas, MIL	98	J. Rice, BOS	6.3	R. Guidry, NY	7.74
P. Molitor, MIL	188	W. Randolph, NY	95	R. Jackson, NY	6.2	J. Morris, DET	8.14
C. Lansford, CAL	188						
Runs		**Doubles**		**Triples**		**Most Strikeouts/9 Inn.**	
D. Baylor, CAL	120	C. Lemon, CHI	44	G. Brett, KC	20	N. Ryan, CAL	9.00
G. Brett, KC	119	C. Cooper, MIL	44	P. Molitor, MIL	16	R. Guidry, NY	7.67
J. Rice, BOS	117	F. Lynn, BOS	42	W. Randolph, NY	13	M. Flanagan, BAL	6.43
F. Lynn, BOS	116	G. Brett, KC	42	W. Wilson, KC	13	F. Jenkins, TEX	5.70
		B. Bell, TEX	42				

PITCHING LEADERS

Strikeouts		Complete Games	
N. Ryan, CAL	223	D. Martinez, BAL	18
R. Guidry, NY	201	D. Eckersley, BOS	17
M. Flanagan, BAL	190	N. Ryan, CAL	17
F. Jenkins, TEX	164	T. John, NY	17
J. Koosman, MIN	157		
Shutouts		**Fewest Walks/9 Innings**	
D. Leonard, KC	5	S. McGregor, BAL	1.18
N. Ryan, CAL	5	M. Caldwell, MIL	1.49
M. Flanagan, BAL	5	L. Sorensen, MIL	1.61
M. Caldwell, MIL	4	B. Stanley, BOS	1.82
B. Stanley, BOS	4		
Innings		**Games Pitched**	
D. Martinez, BAL	292	M. Marshall, MIN	90
T. John, NY	276	S. Monge, CLE	76
M. Flanagan, BAL	266	J. Kern, TEX	71
J. Koosman, MIN	264	S. Lyle, TEX	67

		W	L	PCT	GB	R	OR	Batting 2B	3B	HR	BA	SA	SB	Fielding E	DP	FA	Pitching CG	BB	SO	ShO	SV	ERA
East	Baltimore	102	57	.642		757	**582**	258	24	181	.261	.419	99	125	161	.980	52	467	786	**12**	30	**3.26**
	Milwaukee	95	66	.590	8	807	722	291	41	185	.280	.448	100	127	153	.980	**61**	**381**	580	**12**	23	4.03
	Boston	91	69	.569	11.5	841	711	**310**	34	**194**	**.283**	**.456**	60	142	166	.977	47	463	731	11	29	4.03
	New York	89	71	.556	13.5	734	672	226	40	150	.266	.406	65	122	183	**.981**	43	455	731	10	37	3.83
	Detroit	85	76	.528	18	770	738	221	35	164	.269	.415	176	**120**	184	**.981**	25	547	802	5	37	4.28
	Cleveland	81	80	.503	22	760	805	206	29	138	.258	.384	143	134	149	.978	28	570	781	7	32	4.57
	Toronto	53	109	.327	50.5	613	862	253	34	95	.251	.363	75	159	187	.975	44	594	613	7	11	4.82
West	California	88	74	.543		**866**	768	242	43	164	.282	.429	100	135	172	.978	46	573	**820**	9	33	4.34
	Kansas City	85	77	.525	3	851	816	286	**79**	116	.282	.422	**207**	146	160	.977	42	536	640	7	27	4.45
	Texas	83	79	.512	5	750	698	252	26	140	.278	.409	79	130	151	.979	26	532	773	10	**42**	3.86
	Minnesota	82	80	.506	6	764	725	256	46	112	.278	.402	66	134	**203**	.979	31	452	721	6	33	4.13
	Chicago	73	87	.456	14	730	748	290	33	127	.275	.410	97	173	142	.972	28	618	675	9	37	4.10
	Seattle	67	95	.414	21	711	820	250	52	132	.269	.404	126	141	170	.978	37	571	736	7	26	4.58
	Oakland	54	108	.333	34	573	860	188	32	108	.239	.346	104	174	137	.972	41	654	726	4	20	4.75
						10527	10527	3529	548	2006	.269	.408	1497	1962	2318	.978	551	7413	10115	116	417	4.22

NATIONAL LEAGUE 1980

East

Team	POS	Player	AB	BA	HR	RBI	PO	A	E	DP	TC/G	FA	Pitcher	G	IP	W	L	SV	ERA
Philadelphia	1B	P. Rose	655	.282	1	64	1427	**123**	5	113	9.6	**.997**	S. Carlton	38	**304**	**24**	9	0	2.34
W-91 L-71	2B	M. Trillo	531	.292	7	43	**360**	467	11	91	**6.0**	.987	D. Ruthven	33	223	17	10	0	3.55
Dallas Green	SS	L. Bowa	540	.267	2	39	225	449	17	70	4.7	.975	B. Walk	27	152	11	7	0	4.56
	3B	M. Schmidt	548	.286	**48**	**121**	98	**372**	27	**31**	**3.3**	.946	R. Lerch	30	150	4	14	0	5.16
	RF	B. McBride	554	.309	9	87	282	6	3	1	2.2	.990	T. McGraw	57	92	5	4	20	1.47
	CF	G. Maddox	549	.259	11	73	405	7	10	0	3.0	.976	R. Reed	55	91	7	5	9	4.05
	LF	G. Luzinski	368	.228	19	56	137	2	1	0	1.3	.993	D. Noles	48	81	1	4	6	3.89
	C	B. Boone	480	.229	9	55	741	88	**18**	7	6.1	.979	K. Saucier	40	50	7	3	0	3.42
	OF	L. Smith	298	.339	3	20	121	2	4	0	1.5	.969							
	C	K. Moreland	159	.314	4	29	183	21	7	7	5.4	.967							
Montreal	1B	W. Cromartie	597	.288	14	70	1457	93	**14**	104	9.9	.991	S. Rogers	37	281	16	11	0	2.98
W-90 L-72	2B	R. Scott	567	.224	0	46	287	380	12	73	5.3	.982	S. Sanderson	33	211	16	11	0	3.11
Dick Williams	SS	C. Speier	388	.265	1	32	187	396	21	62	4.8	.965	B. Gullickson	24	141	10	5	0	3.00
	3B	L. Parrish	452	.254	15	72	106	231	18	15	2.9	.949	D. Palmer	24	130	8	6	0	2.98
	RF	E. Valentine	311	.315	13	67	154	6	5	1	2.0	.970	B. Lee	24	118	4	6	0	4.96
	CF	A. Dawson	577	.308	17	87	410	14	6	3	2.9	.986	C. Lea	21	104	7	5	0	3.72
	LF	R. LeFlore	521	.257	4	39	233	14	11	1	2.0	.957	F. Norman	48	98	4	4	4	4.13
	C	G. Carter	549	.264	29	101	**822**	**108**	7	8	6.3	**.993**	E. Sosa	67	94	9	6	9	3.06
	OF	R. Office	292	.267	6	30	150	2	2	1	1.6	.987	S. Bahnsen	57	91	7	6	4	3.07
	OF	J. White	214	.262	7	23	101	5	6	1	1.3	.946	W. Fryman	61	80	7	4	17	2.25
	2S	T. Bernazard	183	.224	5	18	82	151	9	25		.963							
Pittsburgh	1B	J. Milner	238	.244	8	34	502	32	5	48	7.7	.991	J. Bibby	35	238	19	6	0	3.33
W-83 L-79	2B	P. Garner	548	.259	5	58	349	**499**	**21**	**116**	5.8	.976	J. Candelaria	35	233	11	14	1	4.02
Chuck Tanner	SS	T. Foli	495	.265	3	38	212	402	12	87	5.0	**.981**	B. Blyleven	34	217	8	13	0	3.82
	3B	B. Madlock	494	.277	10	53	86	214	14	18	2.5	.955	D. Robinson	29	160	7	10	1	3.99
	RF	D. Parker	518	.295	17	79	235	14	9	0	2.0	.965	R. Rhoden	20	127	7	5	0	3.83
	CF	O. Moreno	**676**	.249	2	36	479	15	5	2	3.1	.990	E. Romo	74	124	5	5	11	3.27
	LF	M. Easler	393	.338	21	74	201	6	3	1	1.8	.986	E. Solomon	26	100	7	3	0	2.70
	C	E. Ott	392	.260	8	41	569	73	11	5	5.6	.983	K. Tekulve	78	93	8	12	21	3.39
	OF	L. Lacy	278	.335	7	33	173	7	3	1	2.1	.984	G. Jackson	61	71	8	4	9	2.92
	10	B. Robinson	272	.287	12	36	427	22	7	30		.985							
	3S	D. Berra	245	.220	6	31	82	167	11	23		.958							
	1B	W. Stargell	202	.262	11	38	460	33	4	54	9.2	.992							
	C	S. Nicosia	176	.216	1	22	284	25	5	4	5.4	.984							

NATIONAL LEAGUE 1980, *cont.*

St. Louis

W-74 L-88

Ken Boyer
W-18 L-33

Jack Krol
W-0 L-1

Whitey Herzog
W-38 L-35

Red Schoendienst
W-18 L-19

POS	Player	AB	BA	HR	RBI	PO	A	E	DP	TC/G	FA	Pitcher	G	IP	W	L	SV	ERA
1B	K. Hernandez	595	.321	16	99	1572	115	9	**146**	10.8	.995	P. Vuckovich	32	222	12	9	1	3.41
2B	K. Oberkfell	422	.303	3	46	223	310	6	62	5.3	.989	B. Forsch	31	215	11	10	0	3.77
SS	G. Templeton	504	.319	4	43	223	451	**29**	85	**6.1**	.959	J. Kaat	49	130	8	7	4	3.81
3B	K. Reitz	523	.270	8	58	86	293	8	25	2.6	**.979**	B. Sykes	27	126	6	10	0	4.64
RF	G. Hendrick	572	.302	25	109	322	10	2	2	2.2	.994	S. Martinez	25	120	5	10	0	4.80
CF	T. Scott	415	.251	0	28	324	5	1	2	2.5	.997	J. Fulgham	15	85	4	6	0	3.39
LF	L. Durham	303	.271	8	42	136	14	2	2	1.9	.987	D. Hood	33	82	4	6	0	3.40
C	T. Simmons	495	.303	21	98	520	71	9	12	4.7	.985	J. Littlefield	52	66	5	5	9	3.14
OF	D. Iorg	251	.303	3	36	108	2	1	0	1.8	.991							
CO	T. Kennedy	248	.254	4	34	231	22	7	3		.973							
OF	B. Bonds	231	.203	5	24	114	5	4	2	1.8	.967							
2B	T. Herr	222	.248	0	15	107	136	4	37	4.3	.984							

New York

W-67 L-95

Joe Torre

POS	Player	AB	BA	HR	RBI	PO	A	E	DP	TC/G	FA	Pitcher	G	IP	W	L	SV	ERA
1B	L. Mazzilli	578	.280	16	76	708	49	13	67	8.4	.983	R. Burris	29	170	7	13	0	4.02
2B	D. Flynn	443	.255	0	24	283	370	6	70	5.1	**.991**	P. Zachry	28	165	6	10	0	3.00
SS	F. Taveras	562	.279	0	25	237	347	25	63	4.3	.959	M. Bomback	36	163	10	8	0	4.09
3B	E. Maddox	411	.246	4	34	96	209	14	18	2.8	.956	P. Falcone	37	157	7	10	1	4.53
RF	C. Washington	284	.275	10	42	123	12	3	1	2.0	.978	C. Swan	21	128	5	9	0	3.59
CF	J. Youngblood	514	.276	8	69	292	18	5	6	2.6	.984	T. Hausman	55	122	6	5	1	3.98
LF	S. Henderson	513	.290	8	58	299	7	6	1	2.3	.981	J. Reardon	61	110	8	7	6	2.62
C	A. Trevino	355	.256	0	37	443	63	12	5	6.0	.977	N. Allen	59	97	7	10	22	3.71
10	M. Jorgensen	321	.255	7	43	562	37	4	33		.993							
C	J. Stearns	319	.285	0	45	432	41	7	6	6.5	.985							
OF	J. Morales	193	.254	3	30	107	3	3	1	1.8	.973							

Chicago

W-64 L-98

Preston Gomez
W-38 L-52

Joey Amalfitano
W-26 L-46

POS	Player	AB	BA	HR	RBI	PO	A	E	DP	TC/G	FA	Pitcher	G	IP	W	L	SV	ERA
1B	B. Buckner	578	**.324**	10	68	826	73	6	67	9.6	.993	R. Reuschel	38	257	11	13	0	3.40
2B	M. Tyson	341	.238	3	23	222	329	18	69	4.9	.968	M. Krukcw	34	205	10	15	0	4.39
SS	I. DeJesus	618	.259	3	33	229	529	24	99	5.0	.969	D. Lamp	41	203	10	14	0	5.19
3B	L. Randle	489	.276	5	39	76	225	23	7	2.9	.929	L. McGlothen	39	182	12	14	0	4.80
RF	S. Thompson	226	.212	2	13	100	4	4	2	1.6	.963	B. Caudill	72	128	4	6	1	2.18
CF	J. Martin	494	.227	23	73	262	8	6	0	2.1	.978	D. Tidrow	**84**	116	6	5	6	2.79
LF	D. Kingman	255	.278	18	57	103	8	7	0	1.9	.941	G. Hernandez	53	108	1	9	0	4.42
C	T. Blackwell	320	.272	5	30	572	93	12	**16**	**6.6**	.982	B. Sutter	60	102	5	8	**28**	2.65
OF	M. Vail	312	.298	6	47	126	5	5	1	1.8	.963	D. Capilla	39	90	2	8	0	4.10
10	L. Biittner	273	.249	1	34	305	23	2	16		.994							
32	S. Dillard	244	.225	4	27	89	169	14	19		.949							
C	B. Foote	202	.238	6	28	317	36	3	5	6.5	.992							
OF	J. Figueroa	198	.253	1	11	89	6	2	2	1.7	.979							
1B	C. Johnson	196	.235	10	34	468	16	4	34	10.6	.992							

West

Houston

W-93 L-70

Bill Virdon

POS	Player	AB	BA	HR	RBI	PO	A	E	DP	TC/G	FA	Pitcher	G	IP	W	L	SV	ERA
1B	A. Howe	321	.283	10	46	580	49	9	47	8.3	.986	J. Niekro	37	256	20	12	0	3.55
2B	J. Morgan	461	.243	11	49	244	348	7	68	4.6	.988	N. Ryan	35	234	11	10	0	3.35
SS	C. Reynolds	381	.226	3	28	162	362	17	59	4.0	.969	K. Forsch	32	222	12	13	0	3.20
3B	E. Cabell	604	.276	2	55	118	250	**29**	15	2.6	.927	V. Ruhle	28	159	12	4	0	2.38
RF	T. Puhl	535	.282	13	55	311	14	3	3	2.4	.991	J. Andujar	35	122	3	8	2	3.91
CF	C. Cedeno	499	.309	10	73	338	9	8	3	2.6	.977	J. Richard	17	114	10	4	0	1.89
LF	J. Cruz	612	.302	11	91	323	16	11	1	2.2	.969	D. Smith	57	103	7	5	10	1.92
C	A. Ashby	352	.256	3	48	608	60	6	10	5.9	.991	J. Sambito	64	90	8	4	17	2.20
2S	R. Landestoy	393	.247	1	27	184	291	9	67		.981	F. LaCorte	55	83	8	5	11	2.82
1B	D. Walling	284	.299	3	29	505	31	6	46	8.6	.989							
C	L. Pujols	221	.199	0	20	348	35	4	5	5.2	.990							
OF	J. Leonard	216	.213	3	20	87	6	2	0	1.7	.979							

Los Angeles

W-92 L-71

Tom Lasorda

POS	Player	AB	BA	HR	RBI	PO	A	E	DP	TC/G	FA	Pitcher	G	IP	W	L	SV	ERA
1B	S. Garvey	658	.304	26	106	1502	112	6	122	10.0	.996	J. Reuss	37	229	18	6	3	2.52
2B	D. Lopes	553	.251	10	49	304	416	15	85	5.3	.980	B. Welch	32	214	14	9	0	3.28
SS	B. Russell	466	.264	3	34	179	387	19	57	4.5	.968	D. Sutton	32	212	13	5	1	**2.21**
3B	R. Cey	551	.254	28	77	**127**	317	13	24	2.9	.972	B. Hooton	34	207	14	8	1	3.65
RF	R. Smith	311	.322	15	55	153	15	1	5	2.0	.994	D. Goltz	35	171	7	11	1	4.32
CF	R. Law	388	.260	1	23	233	6	3	3	2.3	.988	R. Sutcliffe	42	110	3	9	5	5.56
LF	D. Baker	579	.294	29	97	308	5	3	3	2.1	.991	B. Castillo	61	98	8	6	5	2.76
C	S. Yeager	227	.211	2	20	382	36	7	5	4.5	.984	S. Howe	59	85	7	9	17	2.65
UT	D. Thomas	297	.266	1	22	203	175	14	39		.964	D. Stanhouse	21	25	2	2	7	5.04
OF	J. Johnstone	251	.307	2	20	100	9	4	0	1.9	.965							
OF	R. Monday	194	.268	10	25	92	1	3	0	1.9	.969							
OF	P. Guerrero	183	.322	7	31	74	1	1	0	1.9	.987							
C	J. Ferguson	172	.238	9	29	297	23	6	4	4.9	.982							

Cincinnati

W-89 L-73

John McNamara

POS	Player	AB	BA	HR	RBI	PO	A	E	DP	TC/G	FA	Pitcher	G	IP	W	L	SV	ERA
1B	D. Driessen	524	.265	14	74	1349	85	7	115	9.5	.995	M. Soto	53	190	10	8	4	3.08
2B	J. Kennedy	337	.261	1	34	200	303	6	53	4.9	.988	F. Pastore	27	185	13	7	0	3.26
SS	D. Concepcion	622	.260	5	77	265	451	16	98	4.7	.978	C. Leibrandt	36	174	10	9	0	4.24
3B	R. Knight	618	.264	14	78	120	291	13	19	2.6	.969	M. LaCoss	34	169	10	12	0	4.63
RF	K. Griffey	544	.294	13	85	266	5	6	3	2.0	.978	T. Seaver	26	168	10	8	0	3.64
CF	D. Collins	551	.303	3	35	337	5	5	1	2.5	.986	P. Moskau	33	153	9	7	2	4.00
LF	G. Foster	528	.273	25	93	295	6	1	1	2.1	.997	T. Hume	78	137	9	10	25	2.56
C	J. Bench	360	.250	24	68	505	39	5	7	5.2	.991	J. Price	24	111	7	3	0	3.57
2B	R. Oester	303	.277	2	20	144	194	7	42	4.4	.980	D. Bair	61	85	3	6	6	4.24
C	J. Nolan	154	.312	3	24	251	23	5	6	5.5	.982							

NATIONAL LEAGUE 1980, *cont.*

Team	POS	Player	AB	BA	HR	RBI	PO	A	E	DP	TC/G	FA	Pitcher	G	IP	W	L	SV	ERA
Atlanta	1B	C. Chambliss	602	.282	18	72	**1626**	101	12	140	**11.0**	.993	P. Niekro	40	275	15	**18**	1	3.63
W-81 L-80	2B	G. Hubbard	431	.248	9	43	268	405	15	91	5.9	.978	D. Alexander	35	232	14	11	0	4.19
Bobby Cox	SS	L. Gomez	278	.191	0	24	135	319	15	55	3.9	.968	T. Boggs	32	192	12	9	0	3.42
	3B	B. Horner	463	.268	35	89	78	251	23	20	2.9	.935	R. Matula	33	177	11	13	0	4.58
	RF	J. Burroughs	278	.263	13	51	129	0	3	0	1.8	.977	L. McWilliams	30	164	9	14	0	4.94
	CF	D. Murphy	569	.281	33	89	374	14	6	4	2.6	.985	R. Camp	77	108	6	4	22	1.92
	LF	G. Matthews	571	.278	19	75	258	8	11	0	1.9	.960	G. Garber	68	82	5	5	7	3.84
	C	B. Benedict	359	.253	2	34	502	76	7	6	4.9	.988	L. Bradford	56	55	3	4	4	2.45
	UT	J. Royster	392	.242	1	20	195	166	18	32		.953							
	S3	L. Blanks	221	.204	2	12	64	189	17	31		.937							
	OF	B. Asselstine	218	.284	3	25	102	0	4	0	1.7	.962							
	SS	R. Ramirez	165	.267	2	11	63	140	11	25	4.7	.949							
San Francisco	1B	M. Ivie	286	.241	4	25	669	32	5	46	9.8	.993	V. Blue	31	224	14	10	0	2.97
W-75 L-86	2B	R. Stennett	397	.244	2	37	244	293	15	53	5.0	.973	B. Knepper	35	215	9	16	0	4.10
Dave Bristol	SS	J. LeMaster	405	.215	3	31	200	372	26	54	4.5	.957	E. Whitson	34	212	11	13	0	3.10
	3B	D. Evans	556	.264	20	78	113	328	25	26	3.3	.946	A. Ripley	23	113	9	10	0	4.14
	RF	J. Clark	437	.284	22	82	229	7	8	1	2.0	.967	J. Montefusco	22	113	4	8	0	4.38
	CF	B. North	415	.251	1	19	313	6	6	1	2.8	.982	T. Griffin	42	108	5	1	0	2.75
	LF	L. Herndon	493	.258	8	49	247	8	11	1	2.2	.959	G. Lavelle	62	100	6	8	9	3.42
	C	M. May	358	.260	6	50	500	59	8	12	5.5	.986	G. Minton	68	91	4	6	19	2.47
	OF	T. Whitfield	321	.296	4	26	140	11	2	1	1.6	.987	A. Holland	54	82	5	3	7	1.76
	1B	R. Murray	194	.216	4	24	508	35	7	32	10.4	.987	A. Hargesheimer	15	75	4	6	0	4.32
	OF	J. Wohlford	193	.280	1	24	89	2	1	0	1.9	.989							
	UT	J. Pettini	190	.232	1	9	66	147	8	24		.964							
	2B	J. Strain	189	.286	0	16	85	102	2	15	4.5	.989							
San Diego	1B	W. Montanez	481	.274	6	63	1185	84	8	105	10.3	.994	J. Curtis	30	187	10	8	0	3.51
W-73 L-89	2B	D. Cash	397	.227	1	23	290	326	8	72	5.1	.987	S. Mura	37	169	8	7	2	3.67
Jerry Coleman	SS	O. Smith	609	.230	0	35	**288**	**621**	24	**113**	5.9	.974	R. Wise	27	154	6	8	0	3.68
	3B	A. Rodriguez	175	.200	2	13	38	128	6	12	2.0	.965	R. Jones	24	154	5	13	0	3.92
	RF	D. Winfield	558	.276	20	87	273	20	4	4	1.9	.987	G. Lucas	46	150	5	8	3	3.24
	CF	J. Mumphrey	564	.298	4	59	398	10	11	1	2.7	.974	B. Shirley	59	137	11	12	7	3.55
	LF	G. Richards	642	.301	4	41	307	21	7	4	2.1	.979	E. Rasmussen	40	111	4	11	1	4.38
	C	G. Tenace	316	.222	17	50	415	46	10	7	4.5	.979	R. Fingers	66	103	11	9	23	2.80
	23	T. Flannery	292	.240	0	25	140	204	8	34		.977	D. Kinney	50	83	4	6	1	4.23
	C	B. Fahey	241	.257	1	22	309	34	8	6	4.1	.977							
	3B	L. Salazar	169	.337	1	25	29	88	7	7	3.0	.944							

BATTING AND BASE RUNNING LEADERS

Batting Average
- B. Buckner, CHI .324
- K. Hernandez, STL .321
- G. Templeton, STL .319
- B. McBride, PHI .309
- C. Cedeno, HOU .309

Slugging Average
- M. Schmidt, PHI .624
- J. Clark, SF .517
- D. Murphy, ATL .510
- T. Simmons, STL .505
- D. Baker, LA .503

Home Runs
- M. Schmidt, PHI 48
- B. Horner, ATL 35
- D. Murphy, ATL 33
- G. Carter, MON 29
- D. Baker, LA 29

Total Bases
- M. Schmidt, PHI 342
- S. Garvey, LA 307
- K. Hernandez, STL 294
- D. Baker, LA 291
- D. Murphy, ATL 290

Runs Batted In
- M. Schmidt, PHI 121
- G. Hendrick, STL 109
- S. Garvey, LA 106
- G. Carter, MON 101
- K. Hernandez, STL 99

Stolen Bases
- R. LeFlore, MON 97
- O. Moreno, PIT 96
- D. Collins, CIN 79
- R. Scott, MON 63
- G. Richards, SD 61

Hits
- S. Garvey, LA 200
- G. Richards, SD 193
- K. Hernandez, STL 191
- B. Buckner, CHI 187

Base on Balls
- J. Morgan, HOU 93
- D. Driessen, CIN 93
- G. Tenace, SD 92
- M. Schmidt, PHI 89

Home Run Percentage
- M. Schmidt, PHI 8.8
- D. Murphy, ATL 5.8
- G. Carter, MON 5.3
- R. Cey, LA 5.1

Runs
- K. Hernandez, STL 111
- M. Schmidt, PHI 104
- D. Murphy, ATL 98
- A. Dawson, MON 96

Doubles
- P. Rose, PHI 42
- A. Dawson, MON 41
- B. Buckner, CHI 41
- K. Hernandez, STL 39
- R. Knight, CIN 39

Triples
- R. Scott, MON 13
- O. Moreno, PIT 13
- L. Herndon, SF 11
- R. LeFlore, MON 11

PITCHING LEADERS

Winning Percentage
- J. Bibby, PIT .760
- J. Reuss, LA .750
- S. Carlton, PHI .727
- D. Ruthven, PHI .630
- J. Niekro, HOU .625

Earned Run Average
- D. Sutton, LA 2.21
- S. Carlton, PHI 2.34
- J. Reuss, LA 2.52
- V. Blue, SF 2.97
- S. Rogers, MON 2.98

Wins
- S. Carlton, PHI 24
- J. Niekro, HOU 20
- J. Bibby, PIT 19
- J. Reuss, LA 18
- D. Ruthven, PHI 17

Saves
- B. Sutter, CHI 28
- T. Hume, CIN 25
- R. Fingers, SD 23
- R. Camp, ATL 22
- N. Allen, NY 22

Strikeouts
- S. Carlton, PHI 286
- N. Ryan, HOU 200
- M. Soto, CIN 182
- P. Niekro, ATL 176
- B. Blyleven, PIT 168

Complete Games
- S. Rogers, MON 14
- S. Carlton, PHI 13
- J. Niekro, HOU 11
- P. Niekro, ATL 11
- J. Reuss, LA 10
- V. Blue, SF 10

Fewest Hits/9 Innings
- M. Soto, CIN 5.97
- D. Sutton, LA 6.92
- S. Carlton, PHI 7.19
- T. Seaver, CIN 7.50

Shutouts
- J. Reuss, LA 6
- J. Richard, HOU 4
- S. Rogers, MON 4

Fewest Walks/9 Innings
- B. Forsch, STL 1.38
- J. Reuss, LA 1.57
- K. Forsch, HOU 1.66
- J. Candelaria, PIT 1.93

Most Strikeouts/9 Inn.
- M. Soto, CIN 8.62
- S. Carlton, PHI 8.47
- N. Ryan, HOU 7.69
- B. Blyleven, PIT 6.97

Innings
- S. Carlton, PHI 304
- S. Rogers, MON 281
- P. Niekro, ATL 275
- R. Reuschel, CHI 257

Games Pitched
- D. Tidrow, CHI 84
- K. Tekulve, PIT 78
- T. Hume, CIN 78
- R. Camp, ATL 77

NATIONAL LEAGUE 1980, *cont.*

								Batting						Fielding			Pitching					
		W	L	PCT	GB	R	OR	2B	3B	HR	BA	SA	SB	E	DP	FA	CG	BB	SO	ShO	SV	ERA
East	Philadelphia	91	71	.562		728	639	272	54	117	.270	**.400**	140	136	136	.979	25	530	889	8	40	3.43
	Montreal	90	72	.556	1	694	629	250	61	114	.257	.388	237	144	126	.977	33	460	823	15	36	3.48
	Pittsburgh	83	79	.512	8	666	646	249	38	116	.266	.388	209	137	154	.978	25	**451**	832	8	**43**	3.58
	St. Louis	74	88	.457	17	**738**	710	**300**	49	101	**.275**	**.400**	117	122	**174**	.981	**34**	495	664	9	27	3.93
	New York	67	95	.414	24	611	702	218	41	61	.257	.345	158	154	132	.975	17	510	886	9	33	3.85
	Chicago	64	98	.395	27	614	728	251	35	107	.251	.365	93	174	149	.974	13	589	923	6	35	3.89
West	*Houston	93	70	.571		637	**589**	231	**67**	75	.261	.367	194	140	145	.978	31	466	**929**	18	41	**3.10**
	Los Angeles	92	71	.564	1	663	591	209	24	**148**	.263	.388	123	123	149	.981	24	480	835	**19**	42	3.24
	Cincinnati	89	73	.549	3.5	707	670	256	45	113	.262	.386	156	**106**	144	**.983**	30	506	833	12	37	3.85
	Atlanta	81	80	.503	11	630	660	226	22	144	.250	.380	73	162	156	.975	29	454	696	9	37	3.77
	San Francisco	75	86	.466	17	573	634	199	44	80	.244	.342	100	159	124	.975	27	492	811	10	35	3.46
	San Diego	73	89	.451	19.5	591	654	195	43	67	.255	.342	**239**	132	157	.980	19	536	728	9	39	3.65
						7852	7852	2856	523	1243	.259	.374	1839	1689	1746	.978	307	5969	9849	132	445	3.60

* Defeated Los Angeles in a 1 game playoff

AMERICAN LEAGUE 1980

		POS	Player	AB	BA	HR	RBI	PO	A	E	DP	TC/G	FA	Pitcher	G	IP	W	L	SV	ERA
East	New York	1B	B. Watson	469	.307	13	68	851	63	9	87	8.9	.990	T. John	36	265	22	9	0	3.43
		2B	W. Randolph	513	.294	7	46	361	401	19	97	5.7	.976	R. Guidry	37	220	17	10	1	3.56
		SS	B. Dent	489	.262	5	52	224	489	13	77	5.1	**.982**	T. Underwood	38	187	13	9	2	3.66
	W-103 L-59	3B	G. Nettles	324	.244	16	45	58	182	10	18	2.8	.960	R. May	41	175	15	5	3	**2.47**
		RF	R. Jackson	514	.300	**41**	111	174	3	7	0	2.0	.962	L. Tiant	25	136	8	9	0	4.90
	Dick Howser	CF	B. Brown	412	.260	14	47	303	7	9	0	2.4	.972	R. Davis	53	131	9	3	7	2.95
		LF	L. Piniella	321	.287	2	27	157	8	5	1	1.6	.971	G. Gossage	64	99	6	2	**33**	2.27
		C	R. Cerone	519	.277	14	85	800	73	9	9	6.0	.990							
		DH	E. Soderholm	275	.287	11	35													
		OF	R. Jones	328	.223	9	42	246	4	3	1	3.1	.988							
		OD	B. Murcer	297	.269	13	57	82	2	4	0		.955							
		1B	J. Spencer	259	.236	13	43	567	41	6	51	8.2	.990							
		OF	O. Gamble	194	.278	14	50	65	2	0	1	1.4	1.000							
		3B	A. Rodriguez	164	.220	3	14	26	77	5	5	2.2	.954							
		OF	J. Lefebvre	150	.227	8	21	75	3	2	1	1.1	.975							
	Baltimore	1B	E. Murray	621	.300	32	116	1369	77	9	158	9.4	.994	S. McGregor	36	252	20	8	0	3.32
		2B	R. Dauer	557	.284	2	63	320	368	6	110	5.1	.991	S. Stone	37	251	**25**	7	0	3.23
		SS	M. Belanger	268	.228	0	22	133	258	10	49	3.7	.975	M. Flanagan	37	251	16	13	0	4.12
	W-100 L-62	3B	D. DeCinces	489	.249	16	64	120	**340**	19	**41**	3.4	.960	J. Palmer	34	224	16	10	0	3.98
		RF	K. Singleton	583	.304	24	104	248	3	4	1	1.7	.984	S. Stewart	33	119	7	7	3	3.55
	Earl Weaver	CF	A. Bumbry	645	.318	9	53	488	7	5	1	3.1	.990	D. Martinez	25	100	6	4	1	3.96
		LF	G. Roenicke	297	.239	10	28	197	8	0	1	1.8	1.000	T. Stoddard	64	86	5	3	26	2.51
		C	R. Dempsey	362	.262	9	40	531	54	8	8	5.3	.987	T. Martinez	53	81	4	4	10	3.00
		DH	T. Crowley	233	.288	12	50													
		SS	K. Garcia	311	.199	1	27	135	240	10	52	4.0	.974							
		C	D. Graham	266	.278	15	54	328	35	7	3	5.1	.981							
		DH	L. May	222	.243	7	31													
		OD	P. Kelly	200	.260	3	26	48	4	0	0		1.000							
		OF	J. Lowenstein	196	.311	4	27	128	3	1	0	1.5	.992							
		DO	B. Ayala	170	.265	10	33	20	2	0	1		1.000							
	Milwaukee	1B	C. Cooper	622	.352	25	**122**	1336	**106**	5	**160**	10.2	**.997**	M. Haas	33	252	16	15	0	3.11
		2B	P. Molitor	450	.304	9	37	240	294	16	80	6.0	.971	M. Caldwell	34	225	13	11	1	4.04
		SS	R. Yount	611	.293	23	87	239	455	28	89	5.4	.961	L. Sorensen	35	196	12	10	1	3.67
		3B	J. Gantner	415	.282	4	40	41	126	11	15	2.6	.938	B. Travers	29	154	12	6	0	3.92
	W-86 L-76	RF	S. Lezcano	411	.229	18	55	228	8	4	4	2.2	.983	R. Cleveland	45	154	11	9	4	3.74
		CF	G. Thomas	628	.239	38	105	455	6	7	1	2.9	.985	B. McClure	52	91	5	8	10	3.07
	Buck Rodgers	LF	B. Oglivie	592	.304	**41**	118	384	18	9	3	2.7	.978	P. Mitchell	17	89	5	5	1	3.54
	W-26 L-21	C	C. Moore	320	.291	2	30	319	28	4	3	3.3	.989	B. Castro	56	84	2	4	8	2.79
	George Bamberger	DH	D. Davis	365	.271	4	30													
	W-47 L-45	UT	D. Money	289	.256	17	46	176	129	12	35		.962							
		3B	S. Bando	254	.197	5	31	46	110	11	12	2.9	.934							
	Buck Rodgers	C	B. Martinez	219	.224	3	17	293	33	5	0	4.4	.985							
	W-13 L-10																			
	Boston	1B	T. Perez	585	.275	25	105	1301	87	10	150	10.2	.993	M. Torrez	36	207	9	16	0	5.09
		2B	D. Stapleton	449	.321	7	45	178	327	11	90	5.5	.979	D. Eckersley	30	198	12	14	0	4.27
		SS	R. Burleson	644	.278	8	51	**301**	**528**	22	**147**	**5.5**	.974	B. Stanley	52	175	10	8	14	3.39
		3B	G. Hoffman	312	.285	4	42	72	193	15	17	2.5	.946	S. Renko	32	165	9	9	0	4.20
	W-83 L-77	RF	D. Evans	463	.266	18	60	268	11	5	7	2.0	.982	D. Drago	43	133	7	7	3	4.13
		CF	F. Lynn	415	.301	12	61	302	11	2	4	2.9	.994	T. Burgmeier	62	99	5	4	24	2.00
	Don Zimmer	LF	J. Rice	504	.294	24	86	233	10	3	2	2.3	.988	J. Tudor	16	92	8	5	0	3.03
	W-82 L-73	C	C. Fisk	478	.289	18	62	522	56	**10**	8	5.1	.983	C. Rainey	16	87	8	3	0	4.86
	Johnny Pesky	DH	C. Yastrzemski	364	.275	15	50													
	W-1 L-4	3D	B. Hobson	324	.228	11	39	52	109	16	5		.910							
		OF	J. Dwyer	260	.285	9	38	111	7	3	2	1.9	.975							
		2B	J. Remy	230	.313	0	9	109	189	7	30	5.1	.977							

AMERICAN LEAGUE 1980, *cont.*

Detroit

W-84 L-78

Sparky Anderson

POS	Player	AB	BA	HR	RBI	PO	A	E	DP	TC/G	FA
1B	R. Hebner	341	.290	12	82	466	35	1	35	8.2	.998
2B	L. Whitaker	477	.233	1	45	340	428	12	93	5.5	.985
SS	A. Trammell	560	.300	9	65	225	412	13	89	4.5	.980
3B	T. Brookens	509	.275	10	66	112	279	**29**	27	3.0	.931
RF	A. Cowens	403	.280	5	42	199	8	3	2	2.0	.986
CF	R. Peters	477	.291	2	42	296	1	7	1	2.8	.977
LF	S. Kemp	508	.293	21	101	197	4	1	3	2.4	.995
C	L. Parrish	553	.286	24	82	557	66	6	8	5.2	.990
DH	C. Summers	347	.297	17	60						
UT	J. Wockenfuss	372	.274	16	65	575	47	11	44		.983
OF	K. Gibson	175	.263	9	16	122	1	1	0	2.5	.992
1B	J. Thompson	126	.214	4	20	328	30	0	33	9.9	1.000

Pitcher	G	IP	W	L	SV	ERA
J. Morris	36	250	16	15	0	4.18
M. Wilcox	32	199	13	11	0	4.48
D. Schatzeder	32	193	11	13	0	4.01
D. Petry	27	165	10	9	0	3.93
D. Rozema	42	145	6	9	4	3.91
A. Lopez	67	124	13	6	21	3.77
P. Underwood	49	113	3	6	5	3.58

Cleveland

W-79 L-81

Dave Garcia

POS	Player	AB	BA	HR	RBI	PO	A	E	DP	TC/G	FA
1B	M. Hargrove	589	.304	11	85	**1391**	88	10	128	9.3	.993
2B	J. Brohamer	142	.225	1	15	77	113	4	27	4.1	.979
SS	T. Veryzer	358	.271	2	28	169	331	15	59	4.8	.971
3B	T. Harrah	561	.267	11	72	120	317	13	27	2.9	.971
RF	J. Orta	481	.291	10	64	269	10	5	1	2.4	.982
CF	R. Manning	471	.234	3	52	379	7	4	1	2.8	.990
LF	M. Dilone	528	.341	0	40	249	7	7	2	2.2	.973
C	R. Hassey	390	.318	8	65	549	52	4	8	5.4	.993
DH	J. Charboneau	453	.289	23	87						
20	A. Bannister	262	.328	1	32	143	108	8	21		.969
S2	J. Dybzinski	248	.230	1	23	142	261	13	45		.969
C	B. Diaz	207	.227	3	32	317	35	4	4	4.7	.989
DH	G. Alexander	178	.225	5	31						
DH	C. Johnson	174	.230	6	28						

Pitcher	G	IP	W	L	SV	ERA
L. Barker	36	246	19	12	0	4.17
R. Waits	33	224	13	14	0	4.46
D. Spillner	34	194	16	11	0	5.29
W. Garland	25	150	6	9	0	4.62
B. Owchinko	29	114	2	9	0	5.29
J. Denny	16	109	8	6	0	4.38
S. Monge	67	94	3	5	14	3.54
V. Cruz	55	86	6	7	12	3.45

Toronto

W-67 L-95

Bobby Mattick

POS	Player	AB	BA	HR	RBI	PO	A	E	DP	TC/G	FA
1B	J. Mayberry	501	.248	30	82	1243	79	8	138	9.8	.994
2B	D. Garcia	543	.278	4	46	316	471	16	112	**5.8**	.980
SS	A. Griffin	653	.254	2	41	295	489	**37**	126	5.3	.955
3B	R. Howell	528	.269	10	57	105	257	16	24	2.7	.958
RF	L. Moseby	389	.229	9	46	208	12	4	1	2.2	.982
CF	B. Bonnell	463	.268	13	56	271	15	8	3	2.4	.973
LF	A. Woods	373	.300	15	47	205	5	2	1	2.4	.991
C	E. Whitt	295	.237	6	34	436	56	7	11	4.8	.986
DH	O. Velez	357	.269	20	62						
OF	B. Bailor	347	.236	1	16	205	16	2	5	2.3	.991
UT	G. Iorg	222	.248	2	14	122	155	3	45		.989
C	B. Davis	218	.216	4	19	317	28	6	6	3.9	.983
OF	R. Bosetti	188	.213	4	18	124	4	2	0	2.5	.985

Pitcher	G	IP	W	L	SV	ERA
J. Clancy	34	251	13	16	0	3.30
D. Stieb	34	243	12	15	0	3.70
J. McLaughlin	55	136	6	9	4	4.50
P. Mirabella	33	131	5	12	0	4.33
J. Jefferson	29	122	4	13	0	5.46
J. Garvin	61	83	4	7	8	2.28
J. Kucek	23	68	3	8	1	6.75

West

Kansas City

W-97 L-65

Jim Frey

POS	Player	AB	BA	HR	RBI	PO	A	E	DP	TC/G	FA
1B	W. Aikens	543	.278	20	98	1081	65	**12**	95	8.4	.990
2B	F. White	560	.264	7	60	395	448	10	103	5.6	.988
SS	U. Washington	549	.273	6	53	237	467	32	86	4.8	.957
3B	G. Brett	449	**.390**	24	118	103	256	17	28	3.4	.955
RF	C. Hurdle	395	.294	10	60	233	8	10	1	2.0	.960
CF	A. Otis	394	.251	10	53	310	6	4	1	3.0	.988
LF	W. Wilson	**705**	.326	3	49	482	9	6	1	3.1	.988
C	D. Porter	418	.249	7	51	322	37	8	6	4.5	.978
DH	H. McRae	489	.297	14	83						
CO	J. Wathan	453	.305	6	58	360	26	7	5		.982
UT	D. Chalk	167	.251	1	20	57	88	6	10		.960
3C	J. Quirk	163	.276	5	21	69	66	8	3		.944

Pitcher	G	IP	W	L	SV	ERA
L. Gura	36	283	18	10	0	2.96
D. Leonard	38	280	20	11	0	3.79
P. Splittorff	34	204	14	11	0	4.15
R. Gale	32	191	13	9	1	3.91
R. Martin	32	137	10	10	2	4.40
D. Quisenberry	**75**	128	12	7	**33**	3.09

Oakland

W-83 L-79

Billy Martin

POS	Player	AB	BA	HR	RBI	PO	A	E	DP	TC/G	FA
1B	D. Revering	376	.290	15	62	724	67	9	56	8.4	.989
2B	D. McKay	295	.244	1	29	99	151	6	24	4.1	.977
SS	M. Guerrero	381	.239	2	23	184	276	18	50	4.1	.962
3B	W. Gross	366	.281	14	61	69	130	11	13	2.1	.948
RF	T. Armas	628	.279	35	109	374	17	10	2	2.5	.975
CF	D. Murphy	573	.274	13	68	507	13	5	0	3.3	.990
LF	R. Henderson	591	.303	9	53	407	15	7	1	2.7	.984
C	J. Essian	285	.232	5	29	333	46	5	5	5.6	.987
DH	M. Page	348	.244	17	51						
1C	J. Newman	438	.233	15	56	675	54	15	28		.980
CD	M. Heath	305	.243	1	33	268	19	4	5		.986
S2	R. Picciolo	271	.240	5	18	163	208	6	39		.984
3B	M. Klutts	197	.269	4	21	46	80	7	3	2.1	.947
2B	J. Cox	169	.213	0	9	107	167	6	28	4.8	.979

Pitcher	G	IP	W	L	SV	ERA
R. Langford	35	**290**	19	12	0	3.26
M. Norris	33	284	22	9	0	2.54
M. Keough	34	250	16	13	0	2.92
S. McCatty	33	222	14	14	0	3.85
B. Kingman	32	211	8	**20**	0	3.84
B. Lacey	47	80	3	2	6	2.92

Minnesota

W-77 L-84

Gene Mauch
W-54 L-71

John Goryl
W-23 L-13

POS	Player	AB	BA	HR	RBI	PO	A	E	DP	TC/G	FA
1B	R. Jackson	396	.265	5	42	983	74	10	105	9.0	.991
2B	R. Wilfong	416	.248	8	45	238	337	3	85	4.8	**.995**
SS	R. Smalley	486	.278	12	63	210	446	17	100	5.4	.975
3B	J. Castino	546	.302	13	64	105	**340**	18	34	3.4	.961
RF	H. Powell	485	.262	6	35	265	11	9	1	2.2	.968
CF	K. Landreaux	484	.281	7	62	231	8	6	0	2.0	.976
LF	R. Sofield	417	.247	9	49	267	7	6	0	2.2	.979
C	B. Wynegar	486	.255	5	57	670	72	9	**13**	5.3	.988
DH	J. Morales	241	.303	8	36						
UT	P. Mackanin	319	.266	4	35	168	285	18	75		.962
13	M. Cubbage	285	.246	8	42	541	98	4	62		.994
DH	G. Adams	262	.286	6	38						
OF	D. Edwards	200	.250	2	20	144	7	**11**	1	2.3	.932

Pitcher	G	IP	W	L	SV	ERA
J. Koosman	38	243	16	13	2	4.04
G. Zahn	38	233	14	18	0	4.40
R. Erickson	32	191	7	13	0	3.25
D. Jackson	32	172	9	9	1	3.87
D. Corbett	73	136	8	6	23	1.99
P. Redfern	23	105	7	7	2	4.54
J. Verhoeven	44	100	3	4	0	3.96
F. Arroyo	21	92	6	6	0	4.70

AMERICAN LEAGUE 1980, *cont.*

Team	POS	Player	AB	BA	HR	RBI	PO	A	E	DP	TC/G	FA	Pitcher	G	IP	W	L	SV	ERA
Texas	1B	P. Putnam	410	.263	13	55	979	80	9	107	7.8	.992	J. Matlack	35	235	10	10	1	3.68
	2B	B. Wills	578	.263	5	58	340	473	13	112	5.7	.984	D. Medich	34	204	14	11	0	3.93
	SS	P. Frias	227	.242	0	10	117	167	16	38	2.8	.947	F. Jenkins	29	198	12	12	0	3.77
W-76 L-85	3B	B. Bell	490	.329	17	83	125	282	8	26	**3.4**	**.981**	G. Perry	24	155	6	9	0	3.43
	RF	J. Grubb	274	.277	9	32	112	6	6	1	1.6	.952	D. Darwin	53	110	13	4	8	2.62
Pat Corrales	CF	M. Rivers	630	.333	7	60	342	19	8	4	2.6	.978	S. Lyle	49	81	3	2	8	4.67
	LF	A. Oliver	656	.319	19	117	314	9	9	2	2.1	.973	J. Kern	38	63	3	11	2	4.86
	C	J. Sundberg	505	.273	10	63	**853**	**76**	7	7	**6.2**	.993							
	DH	R. Zisk	448	.290	19	77													
	UT	R. Staub	340	.300	9	55	262	14	6	28		.979							
	UT	D. Roberts	235	.238	10	30	138	100	11	11		.956							
	OF	B. Sample	204	.260	4	19	105	2	3	0	1.5	.973							
	1D	J. Ellis	182	.236	1	23	240	12	2	22		.992							
	SS	B. Harrelson	180	.272	1	9	118	220	17	57	4.1	.952							
	OF	J. Norris	174	.247	0	16	73	3	0	0	0.9	1.000							
Chicago	1B	M. Squires	343	.283	2	33	904	68	5	79	8.6	.995	B. Burns	34	238	15	13	0	2.84
	2B	J. Morrison	604	.283	15	57	**422**	**481**	**29**	**117**	5.8	.969	S. Trout	32	200	9	16	0	3.69
	SS	T. Cruz	293	.232	2	18	138	298	20	62	5.1	.956	R. Dotson	33	198	12	10	0	4.27
W-70 L-90	3B	K. Bell	191	.178	1	11	35	151	15	12	2.4	.925	M. Proly	62	147	5	10	8	3.06
	RF	H. Baines	491	.255	13	49	229	6	9	1	1.8	.963	R. Baumgarten	24	136	2	12	0	3.44
Tony LaRussa	CF	C. Lemon	514	.292	11	51	347	11	7	2	2.6	.981	L. Hoyt	24	112	9	3	0	4.58
	LF	W. Nordhagen	415	.277	15	59	120	6	4	1	1.8	.969	E. Farmer	64	100	7	9	30	3.33
	C	B. Kimm	251	.243	0	19	375	26	6	2	4.2	.985	R. Wortham	41	92	4	7	1	5.97
	DH	L. Johnson	541	.277	13	81													
	OD	B. Molinaro	344	.291	5	36	85	3	4	0		.957							
	S3	G. Pryor	338	.240	1	29	125	333	16	53		.966							
California	1B	R. Carew	540	.331	3	59	897	57	6	82	9.3	.994	F. Tanana	32	204	11	12	0	4.15
	2B	B. Grich	498	.271	14	62	326	463	9	101	5.5	.989	D. Aase	40	175	8	13	2	4.06
	SS	F. Patek	273	.264	5	34	129	199	16	42	4.2	.953	F. Martinez	30	149	7	9	0	4.53
W-65 L-95	3B	C. Lansford	602	.261	15	80	**151**	250	19	29	2.8	.955	D. LaRoche	52	128	3	5	4	4.08
	RF	L. Harlow	301	.276	4	27	234	11	6	5	2.7	.976	C. Knapp	32	117	2	11	1	6.15
Jim Fregosi	CF	R. Miller	412	.274	2	38	299	11	5	3	2.7	.984	M. Clear	58	106	11	11	9	3.31
	LF	J. Rudi	372	.237	16	53	220	5	2	1	2.5	.991	A. Hassler	41	83	5	1	10	2.49
	C	T. Donohue	218	.188	2	14	330	29	5	5	4.3	.986	D. Frost	15	78	4	8	0	5.31
	DH	J. Thompson	312	.317	17	70													
	OD	D. Baylor	340	.250	5	51	119	4	4	0		.969							
	UT	D. Thon	267	.255	0	15	70	128	10	28		.952							
	OF	B. Clark	261	.230	5	23	213	6	4	2	2.9	.982							
	OF	D. Ford	226	.279	7	26	75	3	5	0	1.8	.940							
	SS	B. Campaneris	210	.252	2	18	108	157	12	41	4.3	.957							
	CD	B. Downing	93	.290	2	25	69	6	0	0		1.000							
Seattle	1B	B. Bochte	520	.300	13	78	1273	98	6	143	**10.4**	.996	F. Bannister	32	218	9	13	0	3.47
	2B	J. Cruz	422	.209	2	16	269	355	11	85	5.5	.983	G. Abbott	31	215	12	12	0	4.10
	SS	M. Mendoza	277	.245	2	14	149	290	19	68	4.0	.959	R. Honeycutt	30	203	10	17	0	3.95
W-59 L-103	3B	T. Cox	247	.243	2	23	47	142	11	20	2.5	.945	J. Beattie	33	187	5	15	0	4.86
	RF	L. Roberts	374	.251	10	33	238	6	4	1	2.4	.984	R. Dressler	30	149	4	10	0	3.99
Darrell Johnson	CF	J. Beniquez	237	.228	6	21	176	3	8	0	2.9	.957	S. Rawley	59	114	7	7	13	3.32
W-39 L-65	LF	D. Meyer	531	.275	11	71	189	10	8	2	1.7	.961	M. Parrott	27	94	1	16	3	7.28
	C	L. Cox	243	.202	4	20	412	45	3	5	4.4	**.993**	B. McLaughlin	45	91	3	6	2	6.82
Maury Wills	DH	W. Horton	335	.221	8	36							D. Heaverlo	60	79	6	3	4	3.87
W-20 L-38	UT	T. Paciorek	418	.273	15	59	360	22	5	25		.987							
	OF	J. Simpson	365	.249	3	34	205	10	5	1	1.8	.977							
	S3	J. Anderson	317	.227	8	30	118	253	22	45		.944							
	UT	L. Milbourne	258	.264	0	26	103	195	8	50		.974							
	OF	R. Craig	240	.237	3	20	155	2	2	1	2.5	.987							
	UT	B. Stein	198	.268	5	27	119	115	4	21		.983							

BATTING AND BASE RUNNING LEADERS

Batting Average		**Slugging Average**		**Home Runs**	
G. Brett, KC	.390	G. Brett, KC	.664	R. Jackson, NY	41
C. Cooper, MIL	.352	R. Jackson, NY	.597	B. Oglivie, MIL	41
M. Dilone, CLE	.341	B. Oglivie, MIL	.563	G. Thomas, MIL	38
M. Rivers, TEX	.333	C. Cooper, MIL	.539	T. Armas, OAK	35
R. Carew, CAL	.331	R. Yount, MIL	.519	E. Murray, BAL	32

Total Bases		**Runs Batted In**		**Stolen Bases**	
C. Cooper, MIL	335	C. Cooper, MIL	122	R. Henderson, OAK	100
B. Oglivie, MIL	333	G. Brett, KC	118	W. Wilson, KC	79
E. Murray, BAL	322	B. Oglivie, MIL	118	M. Dilone, CLE	61
R. Yount, MIL	317	A. Oliver, TEX	117	J. Cruz, SEA	45
A. Oliver, TEX	315	E. Murray, BAL	116	A. Bumbry, BAL	44

Hits		**Base on Balls**		**Home Run Percentage**	
W. Wilson, KC	230	W. Randolph, NY	119	R. Jackson, NY	8.0
C. Cooper, MIL	219	R. Henderson, OAK	117	B. Oglivie, MIL	6.9
M. Rivers, TEX	210	M. Hargrove, CLE	111	G. Thomas, MIL	6.1
A. Oliver, TEX	209	D. Murphy, OAK	102	J. Mayberry, TOR	6.0

PITCHING LEADERS

Winning Percentage		**Earned Run Average**		**Wins**	
S. Stone, BAL	.781	R. May, NY	2.47	S. Stone, BAL	25
R. May, NY	.750	M. Norris, OAK	2.54	T. John, NY	22
S. McGregor, BAL	.714	B. Burns, CHI	2.84	M. Norris, OAK	22
M. Norris, OAK	.710	M. Keough, OAK	2.92	S. McGregor, BAL	20
T. John, NY	.710	L. Gura, KC	2.96	D. Leonard, KC	20

Saves		**Strikeouts**		**Complete Games**	
G. Gossage, NY	33	L. Barker, CLE	187	R. Langford, OAK	28
D. Quisenberry, KC	33	M. Norris, OAK	180	M. Norris, OAK	24
E. Farmer, CHI	30	R. Guidry, NY	166	M. Keough, OAK	20
T. Stoddard, BAL	26	F. Bannister, SEA	155	T. John, NY	16
T. Burgmeier, BOS	24	D. Leonard, KC	155	L. Gura, KC	16

Fewest Hits/9 Innings		**Shutouts**		**Fewest Walks/9 Innings**	
M. Norris, OAK	6.81	T. John, NY	6	J. Matlack, TEX	1.84
R. May, NY	7.41	G. Zahn, MIN	5	P. Splittorff, KC	1.90
J. Clancy, TOR	7.78	D. Stieb, TOR	4	T. John, NY	1.90
T. Underwood, NY	7.84	S. McGregor, BAL	4	F. Tanana, CAL	1.99
		L. Gura, KC	4		

AMERICAN LEAGUE 1980, *cont.*

BATTING AND BASE RUNNING LEADERS

Runs		Doubles		Triples	
W. Wilson, KC	133	R. Yount, MIL	49	A. Griffin, TOR	15
R. Yount, MIL	121	A. Oliver, TEX	43	W. Wilson, KC	15
A. Bumbry, BAL	118	J. Morrison, CHI	40	K. Landreaux, MIN	11
R. Henderson, OAK	111	H. McRae, KC	39	U. Washington, KC	11

PITCHING LEADERS

Most Strikeouts/9 Inn.		Innings		Games Pitched	
L. Barker, CLE	6.84	R. Langford, OAK	290	D. Quisenberry, KC	75
R. May, NY	6.84	M. Norris, OAK	284	D. Corbett, MIN	73
R. Guidry, NY	6.79	L. Gura, KC	283	S. Monge, CLE	67
F. Bannister, SEA	6.40	D. Leonard, KC	280	A. Lopez, DET	67

		W	L	PCT	GB	R	OR	Batting 2B	3B	HR	BA	SA	SB	Fielding E	DP	FA	Pitching CG	BB	SO	ShO	SV	ERA
East	New York	103	59	.636		820	662	239	34	189	.267	.425	86	138	160	.978	29	463	845	**15**	**50**	3.58
	Baltimore	100	62	.617	3	805	**640**	258	29	156	.273	.413	111	**95**	178	**.985**	42	507	789	10	41	3.64
	Milwaukee	86	76	.531	17	811	682	**298**	36	**203**	.275	**.448**	131	147	189	.977	48	**420**	575	14	30	3.71
	Boston	83	77	.519	19	757	767	297	36	162	.283	.436	79	149	**206**	.977	30	481	696	8	43	4.38
	Detroit	84	78	.519	19	**830**	757	232	53	143	.273	.409	75	133	165	.979	40	558	741	9	30	4.25
	Cleveland	79	81	.494	23	738	807	221	40	89	.277	.381	118	105	143	.983	35	552	843	8	32	4.68
	Toronto	67	95	.414	36	624	762	249	53	126	.251	.383	67	133	**206**	.979	39	635	705	9	23	4.19
West	Kansas City	97	65	.599		809	694	266	**59**	115	**.286**	.413	**185**	141	150	.978	37	465	614	10	42	3.83
	Oakland	83	79	.512	14	686	642	212	35	137	.259	.385	175	130	115	.979	**94**	521	769	9	13	**3.46**
	Minnesota	77	84	.478	19.5	670	724	252	46	99	.265	.381	62	148	192	.977	35	468	744	9	30	3.93
	Texas	76	85	.472	20.5	756	752	263	27	124	.284	.405	91	147	169	.977	35	519	**890**	6	25	4.02
	Chicago	70	90	.438	26	587	722	255	38	91	.259	.370	68	171	162	.973	32	563	724	12	42	3.92
	California	65	95	.406	31	698	797	236	32	106	.265	.378	91	134	144	.978	22	529	725	6	30	4.52
	Seattle	59	103	.364	38	610	793	211	35	104	.248	.356	116	149	189	.977	31	540	703	7	26	4.38
						10201	10201	3489	553	1844	.269	.399	1455	1920	2368	.978	549	7221	10363	132	457	4.04

NATIONAL LEAGUE 1981

East

St. Louis

W-59 L-43

Whitey Herzog

POS	Player	AB	BA	HR	RBI	PO	A	E	DP	TC/G	FA	Pitcher	G	IP	W	L	SV	ERA
1B	K. Hernandez	376	.306	8	48	**1054**	86	3	**99**	**11.7**	.997	L. Sorensen	23	140	7	7	0	3.28
2B	T. Herr	411	.268	0	46	211	**374**	5	**74**	**5.7**	**.992**	B. Forsch	20	124	10	5	0	3.19
SS	G. Templeton	333	.288	1	33	160	272	18	54	5.9	.960	J. Martin	17	103	8	5	0	3.41
3B	K. Oberkfell	376	.293	2	45	77	246	15	**23**	3.3	.956	S. Martinez	18	97	2	5	0	3.99
RF	S. Lezcano	214	.266	5	28	103	5	3	1	1.7	.973	B. Sutter	48	82	3	5	**25**	2.63
CF	G. Hendrick	394	.284	18	61	227	6	4	0	2.3	.983	B. Shirley	28	79	6	4	1	4.10
LF	D. Iorg	217	.327	2	39	78	0	3	0	1.4	.963	J. Andujar	11	55	6	1	0	3.74
C	D. Porter	174	.224	6	31	206	31	5	2	4.7	.979	J. Kaat	41	53	6	6	4	3.40
OF	T. Scott	176	.227	2	17	120	2	0	0	2.8	1.000							
C	G. Tenace	129	.233	5	22	126	18	3	1	3.9	.980							
SS	M. Ramsey	124	.258	0	9	52	118	6	20	5.0	.966							
OF	T. Landrum	119	.261	0	10	72	6	0	1	1.2	1.000							

Montreal

W-60 L-48

Dick Williams
W-44 L-37

Jim Fanning
W-16 L-11

POS	Player	AB	BA	HR	RBI	PO	A	E	DP	TC/G	FA	Pitcher	G	IP	W	L	SV	ERA
1B	W. Cromartie	358	.304	6	42	488	32	4	38	8.5	.992	S. Rogers	22	161	12	8	0	3.41
2B	R. Scott	336	.205	0	26	187	278	8	41	5.1	.983	B. Gullickson	22	157	7	9	0	2.81
SS	C. Speier	307	.225	2	25	175	280	17	57	4.9	.964	S. Sanderson	22	137	9	7	0	2.96
3B	L. Parrish	349	.244	8	44	**91**	141	16	7	2.6	.935	R. Burris	22	136	9	7	0	3.04
RF	J. White	119	.218	3	11	58	2	3	1	1.6	.952	B. Lee	31	89	5	6	6	2.93
CF	A. Dawson	394	.302	24	64	327	10	7	1	3.3	.980	C. Lea	16	64	5	4	0	4.64
LF	T. Raines	313	.304	5	37	160	6	4	0	2.1	.976	W. Fryman	35	43	5	3	7	1.88
C	G. Carter	374	.251	16	68	**509**	58	4	11	5.7	.993	J. Reardon	25	42	2	0	6	1.30
UT	T. Wallach	212	.236	4	13	207	31	1	9		.996							

Philadelphia

W-59 L-48

Dallas Green

POS	Player	AB	BA	HR	RBI	PO	A	E	DP	TC/G	FA	Pitcher	G	IP	W	L	SV	ERA
1B	P. Rose	431	.325	0	33	929	91	4	69	9.6	.996	S. Carlton	24	190	13	4	0	2.42
2B	M. Trillo	349	.287	6	36	**245**	286	7	61	5.7	.987	D. Ruthven	23	147	12	7	0	5.14
SS	L. Bowa	360	.283	0	31	117	309	11	50	4.3	.975	L. Christenson	20	107	4	7	1	3.53
3B	M. Schmidt	354	.316	**31**	**91**	74	**249**	15	20	**3.3**	.956	S. Lyle	48	75	9	6	2	4.44
RF	B. McBride	221	.271	2	21	76	2	1	1	1.4	.987	N. Espinosa	14	74	2	5	0	6.08
CF	G. Maddox	323	.263	5	40	251	8	6	4	2.8	.977	R. Reed	39	61	5	3	8	3.10
LF	G. Matthews	359	.301	9	67	170	11	7	1	1.9	.963	M. Bystrom	9	54	4	3	0	3.33
C	B. Boone	227	.211	4	24	365	32	6	1	5.4	.985	T. McGraw	34	44	2	4	10	2.66
C	K. Moreland	196	.255	6	37	256	20	5	2	5.6	.982							
OF	L. Smith	176	.324	2	11	89	10	3	2	2.0	.971							

Pittsburgh

W-46 L-56

Chuck Tanner

POS	Player	AB	BA	HR	RBI	PO	A	E	DP	TC/G	FA	Pitcher	G	IP	W	L	SV	ERA
1B	J. Thompson	223	.242	15	42	590	46	7	65	8.2	.989	R. Rhoden	21	136	9	4	0	3.90
2B	P. Garner	181	.254	1	20	121	148	9	31	5.6	.968	E. Solomon	22	127	8	6	1	3.12
SS	T. Foli	316	.247	0	20	140	247	14	52	5.0	.965	J. Bibby	14	94	6	3	0	2.49
3B	B. Madlock	279	**.341**	6	45	50	147	9	17	2.6	.956	P. Perez	17	86	2	7	0	3.98
RF	D. Parker	240	.258	9	48	110	1	7	0	2.0	.941	R. Scurry	27	74	4	5	7	3.77
CF	O. Moreno	434	.276	1	35	302	6	1	1	3.0	.997	K. Tekulve	45	65	5	5	3	2.49
LF	M. Easler	339	.286	7	42	188	13	4	2	2.3	.980	L. Tiant	9	57	2	5	0	3.95
C	T. Pena	210	.300	2	17	286	41	5	10	5.2	.985	O. Jones	13	54	4	5	0	3.33
UT	D. Berra	232	.241	2	27	89	167	8	27		.970	E. Romo	33	42	1	3	9	4.50
OF	L. Lacy	213	.268	2	10	121	7	3	1	2.1	.977	G. Jackson	35	32	1	2	4	2.51
C	S. Nicosia	169	.231	2	18	257	23	5	2	5.5	.982							

NATIONAL LEAGUE 1981, *cont.*

Team	POS	Player	AB	BA	HR	RBI	PO	A	E	DP	TC/G	FA	Pitcher	G	IP	W	L	SV	ERA
New York	1B	D. Kingman	353	.221	22	59	462	31	13	39	9.0	.974	P. Zachry	24	139	7	**14**	0	4.14
W-41 L-62	2B	D. Flynn	325	.222	1	20	220	301	7	58	5.3	.987	M. Scott	23	136	5	10	0	3.90
Joe Torre	SS	F. Taveras	283	.230	0	11	120	202	24	44	4.4	.931	P. Falcone	35	95	5	3	1	2.56
	3B	H. Brooks	358	.307	4	38	65	192	**21**	14	3.0	.924	E. Lynch	17	80	4	5	0	2.92
	RF	E. Valentine	169	.207	5	21	83	6	4	0	2.0	.957	G. Harris	16	69	3	5	1	4.43
	CF	M. Wilson	328	.271	3	14	226	3	4	2	2.9	.983	N. Allen	43	67	7	6	18	2.96
	LF	L. Mazzilli	324	.228	6	34	192	5	6	1	2.3	.970	R. Jones	13	59	1	8	0	4.88
	C	J. Stearns	273	.271	1	24	302	38	6	7	5.2	.983							
	1B	R. Staub	161	.317	5	21	339	20	4	26	8.9	.989							
	C	A. Trevino	149	.262	0	10	211	22	9	1	5.4	.963							
	OF	J. Youngblood	143	.350	4	25	70	6	3	0	1.9	.962							
	10	M. Jorgensen	122	.205	3	15	143	9	1	8		.993							
Chicago	1B	B. Buckner	421	.311	10	75	996	81	**17**	92	10.4	.984	M. Krukow	25	144	9	9	0	3.69
W-38 L-65	2B	M. Tyson	92	.185	2	8	50	76	8	14	3.7	.940	R. Martz	33	108	5	7	6	3.67
Joey Amalfitano	SS	I. DeJesus	403	.194	0	13	**221**	343	24	**81**	5.5	.959	R. Reuschel	13	86	4	7	0	3.45
	3B	K. Reitz	260	.215	2	28	57	157	5	11	2.7	**.977**	K. Kravec	24	78	1	6	0	5.08
	RF	L. Durham	328	.290	10	35	159	4	5	1	2.0	.970	D. Bird	12	75	4	5	0	3.60
	CF	S. Henderson	287	.293	5	35	152	4	8	2	2.1	.951	D. Tidrow	51	75	3	10	9	5.04
	LF	J. Morales	245	.286	1	25	142	2	2	1	2.0	.986	L. Smith	40	67	3	6	1	3.49
	C	J. Davis	180	.256	4	21	274	44	9	4	5.8	.972	M. Griffin	16	52	2	5	1	4.50
	OF	B. Bonds	163	.215	6	19	108	2	2	0	2.5	.982							
	C	T. Blackwell	158	.234	1	11	268	28	2	1	5.3	.993							
	2B	S. Dillard	119	.218	2	11	54	96	4	21	4.8	.974							
	OF	S. Thompson	115	.165	0	8	49	1	1	0	1.7	.980							
	30	H. Cruz	109	.229	7	15	33	26	3	0		.952							
West																			
Cincinnati	1B	D. Driessen	233	.236	7	33	558	30	3	54	8.0	.995	M. Soto	25	175	12	9	0	3.29
W-66 L-42	2B	R. Oester	354	.271	5	42	202	328	11	61	5.3	.980	T. Seaver	23	166	**14**	2	0	2.55
John McNamara	SS	D. Concepcion	421	.306	5	67	208	322	22	71	5.2	.960	F. Pastore	22	132	4	9	0	4.02
	3B	R. Knight	386	.259	6	34	69	176	11	18	2.4	.957	B. Berenyi	21	126	9	6	0	3.50
	RF	D. Collins	360	.272	3	23	167	4	4	2	1.9	.977	M. LaCoss	20	78	4	7	1	6.12
	CF	K. Griffey	396	.311	2	34	268	8	3	1	2.8	.989	T. Hume	51	68	9	4	13	3.44
	LF	G. Foster	414	.295	22	90	224	8	2	1	2.2	.991	J. Price	41	54	6	1	4	2.50
	C	J. Nolan	236	.309	1	26	393	18	2	2	5.1	**.995**							
	1B	J. Bench	178	.309	8	25	334	23	6	35	9.6	.983							
	C	M. O'Berry	111	.180	1	5	208	22	4	2	4.3	.983							
Los Angeles	1B	S. Garvey	431	.283	10	64	1019	55	1	84	9.8	**.999**	F. Valenzuela	25	**192**	13	7	0	2.48
W-63 L-47	2B	D. Lopes	214	.206	5	17	129	161	2	30	5.3	.993	J. Reuss	22	153	10	4	0	2.29
Tom Lasorda	SS	B. Russell	262	.233	0	22	128	261	14	49	5.0	.965	B. Hooton	23	142	11	6	0	2.28
	3B	R. Cey	312	.288	13	50	71	184	16	15	3.2	.941	B. Welch	23	141	9	5	0	3.45
	RF	P. Guerrero	347	.300	12	48	145	4	4	0	2.0	.974	D. Goltz	26	77	2	7	1	4.09
	CF	K. Landreaux	390	.251	7	41	210	4	0	0	2.3	1.000	S. Howe	41	54	5	3	8	2.50
	LF	D. Baker	400	.320	9	49	181	8	2	1	1.9	.990	B. Castillo	34	51	2	4	5	5.29
	C	M. Scioscia	290	.276	2	29	493	48	7	4	6.0	.987	D. Stewart	32	43	4	3	6	2.51
	UT	D. Thomas	218	.248	4	24	133	144	14	30		.952							
	OF	R. Monday	130	.315	11	25	50	1	2	0	1.3	.962							
	2B	S. Sax	119	.277	2	9	64	93	4	22	5.6	.975							
Houston	1B	C. Cedeno	306	.271	5	34	428	27	4	27	10.0	.991	J. Niekro	24	166	9	9	0	2.82
W-61 L-49	2B	J. Pittman	135	.281	0	7	56	89	3	14	4.2	.980	D. Sutton	23	159	11	9	0	2.60
Bill Virdon	SS	C. Reynolds	323	.260	4	31	139	261	11	36	4.8	.973	B. Knepper	22	157	9	5	0	2.18
	3B	A. Howe	361	.296	3	36	52	206	9	16	2.7	.966	N. Ryan	21	149	11	5	0	**1.69**
	RF	T. Puhl	350	.251	3	28	185	5	0	1	2.2	1.000	V. Ruhle	20	102	4	6	1	2.91
	CF	T. Scott	225	.293	2	22	127	5	2	0	2.4	.985	D. Smith	42	75	5	3	8	2.76
	LF	J. Cruz	409	.267	13	55	237	5	4	2	2.3	.984	J. Sambito	49	64	5	5	10	1.83
	C	A. Ashby	255	.271	4	33	434	58	9	6	**6.2**	.982	F. LaCorte	37	42	4	2	5	3.64
	01	D. Walling	158	.234	5	23	226	9	2	18		.992							
	UT	K. Garcia	136	.272	0	15	58	119	11	14		.941							
	C	L. Pujols	117	.239	1	14	192	14	1	1	5.3	.995							
	2B	P. Garner	113	.239	0	6	62	102	3	17	5.4	.982							
	OF	G. Woods	110	.209	0	12	61	1	1	0	1.6	.984							
San Francisco	1B	E. Cabell	396	.255	2	36	620	63	9	56	10.0	.987	D. Alexander	24	152	11	7	0	2.90
W-56 L-55	2B	J. Morgan	308	.240	8	31	177	258	4	61	5.0	.991	T. Griffin	22	129	8	8	0	3.77
Frank Robinson	SS	J. LeMaster	324	.253	0	28	166	294	17	57	4.6	.964	V. Blue	18	125	8	6	0	2.45
	3B	D. Evans	357	.258	12	48	74	187	13	10	3.1	.953	E. Whitson	22	123	6	9	0	4.02
	RF	J. Clark	385	.268	17	53	193	14	4	4	2.2	.981	A. Holland	47	101	7	5	7	2.41
	CF	J. Martin	241	.241	4	25	138	4	1	1	2.2	.993	A. Ripley	19	91	4	4	0	4.05
	LF	L. Herndon	364	.288	5	41	207	8	5	1	2.4	.977	G. Minton	55	84	4	5	21	2.89
	C	M. May	316	.310	2	33	468	48	6	4	5.6	.989	F. Breining	45	78	5	2	1	2.54
	10	D. Bergman	145	.255	3	13	252	24	3	21		.989	G. Lavelle	34	66	2	6	4	3.82
	OF	B. North	131	.221	1	12	84	1	3	1	2.4	.966							
	1B	J. Leonard	127	.307	4	26	79	2	0	0	2.9	1.000							
Atlanta	1B	C. Chambliss	404	.272	8	51	1046	**94**	4	83	10.7	.997	G. Perry	23	151	8	9	0	3.93
W-50 L-56	2B	G. Hubbard	361	.235	6	33	188	344	5	50	5.5	.991	T. Boggs	25	143	3	13	0	4.09
Bobby Cox	SS	R. Ramirez	307	.218	2	20	181	306	**30**	55	5.4	.942	P. Niekro	22	139	7	7	0	3.11
	3B	B. Horner	300	.277	15	42	51	129	12	6	2.4	.938	R. Mahler	34	112	8	6	2	2.81
	RF	C. Washington	320	.291	5	37	145	5	1	0	1.9	.993	R. Camp	48	76	9	3	17	1.78
	CF	D. Murphy	369	.247	13	50	254	11	5	4	2.6	.981	G. Garber	35	59	4	6	2	2.59
	LF	R. Linares	253	.265	5	25	124	6	5	1	2.3	.963							
	C	B. Benedict	295	.264	5	35	404	**73**	7	7	5.4	.986							
	OF	E. Miller	134	.231	0	7	65	2	1	0	1.9	.985							
	OF	B. Butler	126	.254	0	4	76	2	1	0	2.1	.987							
	3B	B. Pocoroba	122	.180	0	8	15	30	3	4	2.3	.938							

NATIONAL LEAGUE 1981, *cont.*

San Diego

W-41 L-69

Frank Howard

POS	Player	AB	BA	HR	RBI	PO	A	E	DP	TC/G	FA	Pitcher	G	IP	W	L	SV	ERA
1B	B. Perkins	254	.280	2	40	598	38	2	56	8.0	.997	J. Eichelberger	25	141	8	8	0	3.51
2B	J. Bonilla	369	.290	1	25	229	290	**13**	72	5.5	.976	S. Mura	23	139	5	**14**	0	4.27
SS	O. Smith	**450**	.222	0	21	220	**422**	16	72	**6.0**	**.976**	C. Welsh	22	124	6	7	0	3.77
3B	L. Salazar	400	.302	3	38	63	189	12	16	2.8	.955	R. Wise	18	98	4	8	0	3.77
RF	G. Richards	393	.288	3	42	178	14	5	1	1.9	.975	G. Lucas	**57**	90	7	7	13	2.00
CF	R. Jones	397	.249	4	39	295	9	2	3	2.9	.993	T. Lollar	24	77	2	8	1	6.08
LF	J. Lefebvre	246	.256	8	31	167	6	1	2	2.1	.994	J. Curtis	28	67	2	6	0	5.10
C	T. Kennedy	382	.301	2	41	465	63	**20**	**12**	5.5	.964	J. Littlefield	42	64	2	3	2	3.66
1B	R. Bass	176	.210	4	20	390	35	3	38	8.6	.993	E. Show	15	23	1	3	3	3.13
OF	D. Edwards	112	.214	2	13	59	6	2	2	1.4	.970							

BATTING AND BASE RUNNING LEADERS

Batting Average
- B. Madlock, PIT .341
- P. Rose, PHI .325
- D. Baker, LA .320
- M. Schmidt, PHI .316
- B. Buckner, CHI .311

Slugging Average
- M. Schmidt, PHI .644
- A. Dawson, MON .553
- G. Foster, CIN .519
- G. Hendrick, STL .485
- B. Buckner, CHI .480

Home Runs
- M. Schmidt, PHI 31
- A. Dawson, MON 24
- D. Kingman, NY 22
- G. Foster, CIN 22
- G. Hendrick, STL 18

Total Bases
- M. Schmidt, PHI 228
- A. Dawson, MON 218
- G. Foster, CIN 215
- B. Buckner, CHI 202
- G. Hendrick, STL 191

Runs Batted In
- M. Schmidt, PHI 91
- G. Foster, CIN 90
- B. Buckner, CHI 75
- G. Carter, MON 68
- G. Matthews, PHI 67
- D. Concepcion, CIN 67

Stolen Bases
- T. Raines, MON 71
- O. Moreno, PIT 39
- R. Scott, MON 30
- B. North, SF 26
- D. Collins, CIN 26
- A. Dawson, MON 26

Hits
- P. Rose, PHI 140
- B. Buckner, CHI 131
- D. Concepcion, CIN 129
- D. Baker, LA 128

Base on Balls
- M. Schmidt, PHI 73
- J. Morgan, SF 66
- K. Hernandez, STL 61
- J. Thompson, PIT 59
- G. Matthews, PHI 59

Home Run Percentage
- M. Schmidt, PHI 8.8
- D. Kingman, NY 6.2
- A. Dawson, MON 6.1
- G. Foster, CIN 5.3

Runs
- M. Schmidt, PHI 78
- P. Rose, PHI 73
- A. Dawson, MON 71
- G. Hendrick, STL 67

Doubles
- B. Buckner, CHI 35
- R. Jones, SD 34
- D. Concepcion, CIN 28
- K. Hernandez, STL 27

Triples
- C. Reynolds, HOU 12
- G. Richards, SD 12
- T. Herr, STL 9

PITCHING LEADERS

Winning Percentage
- T. Seaver, CIN .875
- S. Carlton, PHI .765
- N. Ryan, HOU .688
- F. Valenzuela, LA .650
- B. Hooton, LA .647

Earned Run Average
- N. Ryan, HOU 1.69
- B. Knepper, HOU 2.18
- B. Hooton, LA 2.28
- J. Reuss, LA 2.29
- S. Carlton, PHI 2.42

Wins
- T. Seaver, CIN 14
- S. Carlton, PHI 13
- F. Valenzuela, LA 13
- D. Ruthven, PHI 12
- S. Rogers, MON 12
- M. Soto, CIN 12

Saves
- B. Sutter, STL 25
- G. Minton, SF 21
- N. Allen, NY 18
- R. Camp, ATL 17
- T. Hume, CIN 13
- G. Lucas, SD 13

Strikeouts
- F. Valenzuela, LA 180
- S. Carlton, PHI 179
- M. Soto, CIN 151
- N. Ryan, HOU 140
- B. Gullickson, MON 115

Complete Games
- F. Valenzuela, LA 11
- S. Carlton, PHI 10
- M. Soto, CIN 10
- J. Reuss, LA 8
- S. Rogers, MON 7

Fewest Hits/9 Innings
- N. Ryan, HOU 5.98
- T. Seaver, CIN 6.51
- F. Valenzuela, LA 6.56
- B. Berenyi, CIN 6.93

Shutouts
- F. Valenzuela, LA 8
- B. Knepper, HOU 5
- B. Hooton, LA 4

Fewest Walks/9 Innings
- G. Perry, ATL 1.43
- J. Reuss, LA 1.59
- D. Sutton, HOU 1.64
- L. Sorensen, STL 1.67

Most Strikeouts/9 Inn.
- S. Carlton, PHI 8.48
- N. Ryan, HOU 8.46
- F. Valenzuela, LA 8.44
- M. Soto, CIN 7.77

Innings
- F. Valenzuela, LA 192
- S. Carlton, PHI 190
- M. Soto, CIN 175
- T. Seaver, CIN 166
- J. Niekro, HOU 166

Games Pitched
- G. Lucas, SD 57
- G. Minton, SF 55
- T. Hume, CIN 51
- D. Tidrow, CHI 51

		W	L	PCT	GB	R	OR	Batting 2B	3B	HR	BA	SA	SB	Fielding E	DP	FA	Pitching CG	BB	SO	ShO	SV	ERA
East	St. Louis	59	43	.578		464	417	158	**45**	50	.265	.377	88	82	108	**.981**	11	290	388	5	**33**	3.63
	Montreal	60	48	.556	2	443	394	146	28	81	.246	.370	**138**	81	88	.980	20	**268**	520	12	23	3.30
	Philadelphia	59	48	.551	2.5	**491**	472	165	25	69	**.273**	**.389**	103	86	90	.980	19	347	580	5	23	4.05
	Pittsburgh	46	56	.451	13	407	425	176	30	55	.257	.369	122	86	106	.979	11	346	492	5	29	3.56
	New York	41	62	.398	18.5	348	432	136	35	57	.248	.356	103	130	89	.968	7	336	490	3	24	3.55
	Chicago	38	65	.369	21.5	370	483	138	29	57	.236	.340	72	113	103	.974	6	388	532	2	20	4.01
West	Cincinnati	66	42	.611		464	440	**190**	24	64	.267	.385	58	**80**	99	**.981**	25	393	593	14	20	3.73
	Los Angeles	63	47	.573	4	450	356	133	20	**82**	.262	.374	73	87	101	.980	**26**	302	603	**19**	24	3.01
	Houston	61	49	.555	6	394	**331**	160	35	45	.257	.356	81	87	81	.980	23	300	**610**	**19**	25	**2.66**
	San Francisco	56	55	.505	11.5	427	414	161	26	63	.250	.357	89	102	102	.977	8	393	561	9	**33**	3.28
	Atlanta	50	56	.472	15	395	416	148	22	64	.243	.349	98	102	93	.976	11	330	471	4	24	3.45
	San Diego	41	69	.373	26	382	455	170	35	32	.256	.346	83	102	**117**	.977	9	414	492	6	23	3.72
						5035	5035	1881	354	719	.255	.364	1108	1138	1177	.978	176	4107	6332	103	301	3.50

National League 1981, *cont.*

First Half

	W	L	PCT	GB
East				
Philadelphia	34	21	.618	
St. Louis	30	20	.600	1.5
Montreal	30	25	.545	4
Pittsburgh	25	23	.521	5.5
New York	17	34	.333	15
Chicago	15	37	.288	17.5

* Defeated Philadelphia in playoff 3 games to 2

	W	L	PCT	GB
West				
*Los Angeles	36	21	.632	
Cincinnati	35	21	.625	0.5
Houston	28	29	.491	8
Atlanta	25	29	.463	9.5
San Francisco	27	32	.458	10
San Diego	23	33	.411	12.5

* Defeated Houston in playoff 3 games to 2

Second Half

	W	L	PCT	GB
East				
*Montreal	30	23	.566	
St. Louis	29	23	.558	0.5
Philadelphia	25	27	.481	4.5
New York	24	28	.462	5.5
Chicago	23	28	.451	6
Pittsburgh	21	33	.389	9.5

	W	L	PCT	GB
West				
Houston	33	20	.623	
Cincinnati	31	21	.596	1.5
San Francisco	29	23	.558	3.5
Los Angeles	27	26	.509	6
Atlanta	25	27	.481	7.5
San Diego	18	36	.333	15.5

AMERICAN LEAGUE 1981

East

Milwaukee

W-62 L-47

Buck Rodgers

POS	Player	AB	BA	HR	RBI	PO	A	E	DP	TC/G	FA	Pitcher	G	IP	W	L	SV	ERA
1B	C. Cooper	416	.320	12	60	**987**	72	**9**	**111**	**10.6**	.992	P. Vuckovich	24	150	**14**	4	0	3.54
2B	J. Gantner	352	.267	2	33	251	352	10	**95**	5.7	.984	M. Caldwell	24	144	11	9	0	3.94
SS	R. Yount	377	.273	10	49	161	370	8	83	**5.8**	**.985**	M. Haas	24	137	11	7	0	4.47
3B	D. Money	185	.216	2	14	27	100	3	8	2.3	.977	J. Slaton	24	117	5	7	0	4.38
RF	G. Thomas	363	.259	21	65	221	8	5	3	2.4	.979	R. Lerch	23	111	7	9	0	4.30
CF	P. Molitor	251	.267	2	19	119	4	3	1	2.7	.976	R. Fingers	47	78	6	3	**28**	1.04
LF	B. Oglivie	400	.242	14	72	211	3	4	1	2.2	.982	J. Easterly	44	62	3	3	4	3.19
C	T. Simmons	380	.216	14	61	300	37	7	3	4.6	.980							
DH	L. Hisle	87	.230	4	11													
3B	R. Howell	244	.238	6	33	38	98	6	9	2.7	.958							
OF	M. Brouhard	186	.274	2	20	92	7	1	2	2.0	.990							
C	C. Moore	156	.301	1	9	147	16	5	0	4.9	.970							

Baltimore

W-59 L-46

Earl Weaver

POS	Player	AB	BA	HR	RBI	PO	A	E	DP	TC/G	FA	Pitcher	G	IP	W	L	SV	ERA
1B	E. Murray	378	.294	**22**	**78**	899	**91**	1	98	10.0	**.999**	D. Martinez	25	179	**14**	5	0	3.32
2B	R. Dauer	369	.263	4	38	201	253	5	71	4.9	**.989**	S. McGregor	24	160	13	5	0	3.26
SS	M. Belanger	139	.165	1	10	86	162	7	21	4.0	.973	J. Palmer	22	127	7	8	0	3.76
3B	D. DeCinces	346	.263	13	55	**86**	191	**17**	**31**	2.9	.942	M. Flanagan	20	116	9	6	0	4.19
RF	K. Singleton	363	.278	13	49	125	2	0	2	1.8	1.000	S. Stewart	29	112	4	8	4	2.33
CF	A. Bumbry	392	.273	1	27	255	6	2	2	2.6	.992	S. Stone	15	63	4	7	0	4.57
LF	G. Roenicke	219	.269	3	20	175	2	3	1	2.2	.983	T. Martinez	37	59	3	3	11	2.90
C	R. Dempsey	251	.215	6	15	384	35	1	6	4.7	**.998**	T. Stoddard	31	37	4	2	7	3.89
DH	T. Crowley	134	.246	4	25													
OF	J. Lowenstein	189	.249	6	20	100	3	1	0	1.4	.990							
S2	L. Sakata	150	.227	5	15	82	148	7	33		.970							
C	D. Graham	142	.176	2	11	138	20	4	1	4.1	.975							
OF	J. Dwyer	134	.224	3	10	84	2	2	0	1.5	.977							

New York

W-59 L-48

Gene Michael
W-48 L-34

Bob Lemon
W-11 L-14

POS	Player	AB	BA	HR	RBI	PO	A	E	DP	TC/G	FA	Pitcher	G	IP	W	L	SV	ERA
1B	B. Watson	156	.212	6	12	367	25	1	42	7.9	.997	R. May	27	148	6	11	1	4.14
2B	W. Randolph	357	.232	2	24	205	268	**11**	74	5.2	.977	T. John	20	140	9	8	0	2.64
SS	B. Dent	227	.238	7	27	104	217	10	49	4.5	.970	R. Guidry	23	127	11	5	0	2.76
3B	G. Nettles	349	.244	15	46	63	214	8	14	2.9	.972	D. Righetti	15	105	8	4	0	2.06
RF	R. Jackson	334	.237	15	54	111	3	3	0	1.9	.974	R. Davis	43	73	4	5	6	2.71
CF	J. Mumphrey	319	.307	6	32	219	5	8	0	2.9	.966	R. Reuschel	12	71	4	4	0	2.66
LF	D. Winfield	388	.294	13	68	196	1	3	0	2.0	.985	G. Gossage	32	47	3	2	20	0.77
C	R. Cerone	234	.244	2	21	353	26	3	1	5.5	.992							
DH	B. Murcer	117	.265	6	24													
OD	O. Gamble	189	.238	10	27	77	0	0	0		1.000							
UT	L. Milbourne	163	.313	1	12	74	121	8	26		.961							
OD	L. Piniella	159	.277	5	18	69	2	1	1		.986							
C	B. Foote	125	.208	6	10	227	14	1	3	7.1	.996							
1B	D. Revering	119	.235	2	7	276	30	2	24	7.0	.994							

Detroit

W-60 L-49

Sparky Anderson

POS	Player	AB	BA	HR	RBI	PO	A	E	DP	TC/G	FA	Pitcher	G	IP	W	L	SV	ERA
1B	R. Hebner	226	.226	5	28	531	29	3	36	9.2	.995	J. Morris	25	198	**14**	7	0	3.05
2B	L. Whitaker	335	.263	5	36	227	**354**	9	77	5.5	.985	M. Wilcox	24	166	12	9	0	3.04
SS	A. Trammell	392	.258	2	31	181	347	9	65	5.1	.983	D. Petry	23	141	10	9	0	3.00
3B	T. Brookens	239	.243	4	25	58	139	10	13	2.9	.952	D. Rozema	28	104	5	5	3	3.63
RF	K. Gibson	290	.328	9	40	142	1	4	0	2.2	.973	A. Lopez	29	82	5	2	3	3.62
CF	A. Cowens	253	.261	1	18	166	3	1	0	2.0	.994	D. Schatzeder	17	71	6	8	0	6.08
LF	S. Kemp	372	.277	9	49	207	4	3	0	2.3	.986	K. Saucier	38	49	4	2	13	1.65
C	L. Parrish	348	.244	10	46	407	40	3	6	5.0	.993							
DH	J. Wockenfuss	172	.215	9	25													
OD	R. Peters	207	.256	0	15	103	3	1	1		.991							
OF	L. Jones	174	.259	2	19	85	5	1	2	1.5	.989							
DO	C. Summers	165	.255	3	21	26	1	1	0		.964							

AMERICAN LEAGUE 1981, *cont.*

Team	POS	Player	AB	BA	HR	RBI	PO	A	E	DP	TC/G	FA	Pitcher	G	IP	W	L	SV	ERA
Boston	1B	T. Perez	306	.252	9	39	519	37	4	63	10.0	.993	D. Eckersley	23	154	9	8	0	4.27
W-59 L-49	2B	J. Remy	358	.307	0	31	162	272	7	58	5.1	.984	F. Tanana	24	141	4	10	0	4.02
Ralph Houk	SS	G. Hoffman	242	.231	1	20	131	233	15	62	4.9	.960	M. Torrez	22	127	10	3	0	3.69
	3B	C. Lansford	399	**.336**	4	52	70	180	13	17	3.1	.951	B. Stanley	35	99	10	8	0	3.82
	RF	D. Evans	412	.296	**22**	71	259	9	2	1	2.5	.993	J. Tudor	18	79	4	3	1	4.56
	CF	R. Miller	316	.291	2	33	219	5	3	0	2.4	.987	M. Clear	34	77	8	3	9	4.09
	LF	J. Rice	**451**	.284	17	62	237	9	3	0	2.3	.988	B. Ojeda	10	66	6	2	0	3.14
	C	R. Gedman	205	.288	5	26	275	30	3	1	5.2	.990	T. Burgmeier	32	60	4	5	6	2.85
	DH	C. Yastrzemski	338	.246	7	53							B. Campbell	30	48	1	1	7	3.19
	UT	D. Stapleton	355	.285	10	42	260	204	17	50		.965							
	C	G. Allenson	139	.223	5	25	235	18	8	3	5.6	.969							
	DH	J. Rudi	122	.180	6	24													
Cleveland	1B	M. Hargrove	322	.317	2	49	766	76	**9**	67	9.7	.989	B. Blyleven	20	159	11	7	0	2.89
W-52 L-51	2B	D. Kuiper	206	.257	0	14	118	174	5	24	4.1	.983	L. Barker	22	154	8	7	0	3.92
Dave Garcia	SS	T. Veryzer	221	.244	0	14	121	207	10	48	4.5	.970	J. Denny	19	146	10	6	0	3.14
	3B	T. Harrah	361	.291	5	44	63	179	13	12	2.5	.949	R. Waits	22	126	8	10	0	4.93
	RF	J. Orta	338	.272	5	34	150	11	1	2	1.9	.994	D. Spillner	32	97	4	4	7	3.15
	CF	R. Manning	360	.244	4	33	305	6	4	3	3.1	.987	S. Monge	31	58	3	5	4	4.34
	LF	M. Dilone	269	.290	0	19	126	7	4	1	2.4	.971	W. Garland	12	56	3	7	0	5.79
	C	R. Hassey	190	.232	1	25	296	38	3	6	**6.0**	.991	M. Stanton	24	43	3	3	2	4.40
	DH	A. Thornton	226	.239	6	30													
	O2	A. Bannister	232	.263	1	17	121	76	2	14		.990							
	C	B. Diaz	182	.313	7	38	247	27	7	0	5.5	.975							
	OD	J. Charboneau	138	.210	4	18	51	1	2	0		.963							
	UT	V. Hayes	109	.257	1	17	30	4	3	1		.919							
Toronto	1B	J. Mayberry	290	.248	17	43	647	36	5	65	8.6	.993	D. Stieb	25	184	11	10	0	3.18
W-37 L-69	2B	D. Garcia	250	.252	1	13	132	181	9	32	5.2	.972	L. Leal	29	130	7	**13**	1	3.67
Bobby Mattick	SS	A. Griffin	388	.209	0	21	186	275	**31**	64	5.1	.937	J. Clancy	22	125	6	12	0	4.90
	3B	D. Ainge	246	.187	0	14	73	133	11	19	2.8	.949	J. Todd	21	98	2	7	0	3.95
	RF	B. Bonnell	227	.220	4	28	148	5	4	1	2.4	.975	M. Bomback	20	90	5	5	0	3.90
	CF	L. Moseby	378	.233	9	43	259	4	3	0	2.7	.989	J. Berenguer	12	71	2	9*	0	4.31
	LF	A. Woods	288	.247	1	21	179	4	5	0	2.4	.973	R. Jackson	39	62	1	2	7	2.61
	C	E. Whitt	195	.236	1	16	297	46	3	5	4.8	.991	J. McLaughlin	40	60	1	5	10	2.85
	DH	O. Velez	240	.212	11	28													
	2B	G. Iorg	215	.242	0	10	82	152	9	29	5.3	.963							
	OF	G. Bell	163	.233	5	12	92	3	3	2	2.2	.969							
	C	B. Martinez	128	.227	4	21	192	22	2	3	4.8	.991							
	UT	W. Upshaw	111	.171	4	10	72	6	0	8		1.000							
West																			
Oakland	1B	J. Spencer	171	.205	2	9	344	36	1	30	7.9	.997	R. Langford	24	195	12	10	0	3.00
W-64 L-45	2B	S. Babitt	156	.256	0	14	84	125	6	12	4.1	.972	S. McCatty	22	186	**14**	7	0	**2.32**
Billy Martin	SS	R. Picciolo	179	.268	4	13	99	157	5	30	3.2	.981	M. Norris	23	173	12	9	0	3.75
	3B	W. Gross	243	.206	10	31	65	127	11	7	2.8	.946	M. Keough	19	140	10	6	0	3.41
	RF	T. Armas	440	.261	**22**	76	259	8	2	2	2.5	.993	B. Kingman	18	100	3	6	0	3.96
	CF	D. Murphy	390	.251	15	60	326	6	5	0	3.2	.985	J. Jones	33	61	4	1	3	3.39
	LF	R. Henderson	423	.319	6	35	327	7	7	0	3.2	.979	B. Owchinko	29	39	4	3	2	3.23
	C	M. Heath	301	.236	8	30	391	45	**10**	6	5.7	.978							
	DH	C. Johnson	273	.260	17	59													
	32	D. McKay	224	.263	4	21	112	167	13	26		.955							
	C1	J. Newman	216	.231	3	15	367	28	2	14		.995							
	SS	F. Stanley	145	.193	0	7	94	118	3	25	3.5	.986							
Texas	1B	P. Putnam	297	.266	8	35	769	64	6	65	8.9	.993	D. Darwin	22	146	9	9	0	3.64
W-57 L-48	2B	B. Wills	410	.251	2	41	**268**	326	10	70	**6.0**	.983	D. Medich	20	143	10	6	0	3.08
Don Zimmer	SS	M. Mendoza	229	.231	0	22	114	270	12	47	4.5	.970	R. Honeycutt	20	128	11	6	0	3.30
	3B	B. Bell	360	.294	10	64	66	**281**	14	18	**3.8**	.961	F. Jenkins	19	106	5	8	0	4.50
	RF	J. Grubb	199	.231	3	26	95	2	1	0	1.7	.990	J. Matlack	17	104	4	7	0	4.15
	CF	M. Rivers	399	.286	3	26	225	12	1	3	2.5	.996	S. Comer	36	77	8	2	6	2.57
	LF	B. Sample	230	.283	3	25	132	4	1	1	2.1	.993	J. Kern	23	30	1	2	6	2.70
	C	J. Sundberg	339	.277	3	28	464	**52**	2	9	5.3	.996							
	DH	A. Oliver	421	.309	4	55													
	OF	L. Roberts	233	.279	4	31	130	2	1	0	1.9	.992							
	UT	B. Stein	115	.330	2	22	166	26	2	10		.990							
Chicago	1B	M. Squires	294	.265	0	25	729	58	6	68	9.0	.992	B. Burns	24	157	10	6	0	2.64
W-54 L-52	2B	T. Bernazard	384	.276	6	34	228	320	7	66	5.3	.987	R. Dotson	24	141	9	8	0	3.77
Tony LaRussa	SS	B. Almon	349	.301	4	41	190	340	17	78	5.3	.969	D. Lamp	27	127	7	6	0	2.41
	3B	J. Morrison	290	.234	10	34	64	199	12	14	3.2	.956	S. Trout	20	125	8	7	0	3.46
	RF	H. Baines	280	.286	10	41	120	10	2	1	1.6	.985	R. Baumgarten	19	102	5	9	0	4.06
	CF	C. Lemon	328	.302	9	50	240	2	4	1	2.6	.984	L. Hoyt	43	91	9	3	10	3.56
	LF	R. LeFlore	337	.246	0	24	162	6	7	2	2.1	.960	E. Farmer	42	53	3	3	10	4.58
	C	C. Fisk	338	.263	7	45	**470**	44	5	**10**	5.6	.990							
	DH	G. Luzinski	378	.265	21	62													
	OF	W. Nordhagen	208	.308	6	33	85	4	5	1	1.6	.947							
	1B	L. Johnson	134	.276	1	15	264	15	3	31	7.8	.989							

AMERICAN LEAGUE 1981, *cont.*

Kansas City

W-50 L-53

Jim Frey
W-30 L-40

Dick Howser
W-20 L-13

POS	Player	AB	BA	HR	RBI	PO	A	E	DP	TC/G	FA	Pitcher	G	IP	W	L	SV	ERA
1B	W. Aikens	349	.266	17	53	844	56	7	79	9.2	.992	D. Leonard	26	**202**	13	11	0	2.99
2B	F. White	364	.250	9	38	226	263	6	70	5.3	.988	L. Gura	23	172	11	8	0	2.72
SS	U. Washington	339	.227	2	29	135	297	12	58	4.5	.973	R. Gale	19	102	6	6	0	5.38
3B	G. Brett	347	.314	6	43	74	170	14	7	2.9	.946	P. Splittorff	21	99	5	5	0	4.36
RF	C. Geronimo	118	.246	2	13	96	1	2	0	1.7	.980	M. Jones	12	76	6	3	0	3.20
CF	A. Otis	372	.269	9	57	294	6	2	1	3.1	.993	R. Martin	29	62	4	5	4	2.76
LF	W. Wilson	439	.303	1	32	299	14	4	3	3.1	.987	D. Quisenberry	40	62	1	4	18	1.74
C	J. Wathan	301	.252	1	19	300	26	7	1	4.6	.979							
DH	H. McRae	389	.272	7	36													
OF	D. Motley	125	.232	2	8	88	3	3	1	2.4	.968							

California

W-51 L-59

Jim Fregosi
W-22 L-25

Gene Mauch
W-29 L-34

POS	Player	AB	BA	HR	RBI	PO	A	E	DP	TC/G	FA	Pitcher	G	IP	W	L	SV	ERA
1B	R. Carew	364	.305	2	21	877	60	5	90	10.5	.995	G. Zahn	25	161	10	11	0	4.42
2B	B. Grich	352	.304	**22**	61	230	349	10	85	5.9	.983	K. Forsch	20	153	11	7	0	2.88
SS	R. Burleson	430	.293	5	33	**208**	**394**	13	**88**	5.6	.979	M. Witt	22	129	8	9	0	3.28
3B	B. Hobson	268	.235	4	36	85	139	**17**	13	2.9	.929	S. Renko	22	102	8	4	1	3.44
RF	D. Ford	375	.277	15	48	188	3	8	0	2.1	.960	A. Hassler	42	76	4	3	5	3.20
CF	F. Lynn	256	.219	5	31	176	4	4	1	2.7	.978	D. Aase	39	65	4	4	11	2.35
LF	B. Downing	317	.249	9	41	97	1	1	0	1.8	.990	D. Frost	12	47	1	8	0	5.55
C	E. Ott	258	.217	2	22	287	36	7	1	4.6	.979							
DH	D. Baylor	377	.239	17	66													
OF	J. Beniquez	166	.181	3	13	117	0	5	0	2.2	.959							

Seattle

W-44 L-65

Maury Wills
W-6 L-18

Rene Lachemann
W-38 L-47

POS	Player	AB	BA	HR	RBI	PO	A	E	DP	TC/G	FA	Pitcher	G	IP	W	L	SV	ERA
1B	B. Bochte	335	.260	6	30	745	49	4	70	9.7	.995	G. Abbott	22	130	4	9	0	3.95
2B	J. Cruz	352	.256	2	24	239	294	10	72	5.9	.982	F. Bannister	21	121	9	9	0	4.46
SS	J. Anderson	162	.204	2	19	88	181	15	44	4.2	.947	K. Clay	22	101	2	7	0	4.63
3B	L. Randle	273	.231	4	25	38	105	2	8	2.5	.986	B. Clark	29	93	2	5	2	4.35
RF	J. Burroughs	319	.254	10	41	127	4	2	1	1.5	.985	M. Parrott	24	85	3	6	1	5.08
CF	J. Simpson	288	.222	2	30	219	5	5	1	2.6	.978	J. Gleaton	20	85	4	7	0	4.76
LF	T. Paciorek	405	.326	14	66	253	10	7	1	2.6	.974	S. Rawley	46	68	4	6	8	3.97
C	J. Narron	203	.222	3	17	248	11	1	3	4.0	.996	L. Andersen	41	68	3	3	5	2.65
DH	R. Zisk	357	.311	16	43							D. Drago	39	54	4	6	5	5.50
3B	D. Meyer	252	.262	3	22	36	87	5	12	2.6	.961							
1D	G. Gray	208	.245	13	31	275	16	2	34		.993							
C	T. Bulling	154	.247	2	15	239	21	6	3	4.3	.977							
OF	D. Henderson	126	.167	6	13	105	4	0	1	1.9	1.000							

Minnesota

W-41 L-68

John Goryl
W-11 L-25

Billy Gardner
W-30 L-43

POS	Player	AB	BA	HR	RBI	PO	A	E	DP	TC/G	FA	Pitcher	G	IP	W	L	SV	ERA
1B	D. Goodwin	151	.225	2	17	341	20	3	27	9.1	.992	A. Williams	23	150	6	10	0	4.08
2B	R. Wilfong	305	.246	3	19	183	268	9	52	4.9	.980	P. Redfern	24	142	9	8	0	4.06
SS	R. Smalley	167	.263	7	22	52	89	8	14	4.0	.946	F. Arroyo	23	128	7	10	0	3.94
3B	J. Castino	381	.268	6	36	**86**	224	8	24	3.2	**.975**	J. Koosman	19	94	3	9*	5	4.21
RF	D. Engle	248	.258	5	32	144	4	3	0	2.0	.980	R. Erickson	14	91	3	8	0	3.86
CF	M. Hatcher	377	.255	3	37	239	3	2	0	2.7	.992	D. Corbett	**54**	88	2	6	17	2.56
LF	G. Ward	295	.264	3	29	185	8	5	4	2.5	.975	B. Havens	14	78	3	6	0	3.58
C	S. Butera	167	.240	0	18	254	41	9	0	5.2	.970							
DH	G. Adams	220	.209	2	24													
OF	H. Powell	264	.239	2	25	122	6	4	1	2.1	.970							
UT	P. Mackanin	225	.231	4	18	171	149	12	40		.964							
UT	R. Jackson	175	.263	4	28	329	30	5	26		.986							
C	B. Wynegar	150	.247	0	10	162	24	1	4	5.1	.995							

BATTING AND BASE RUNNING LEADERS

Batting Average

C. Lansford, BOS	.336
T. Paciorek, SEA	.326
C. Cooper, MIL	.320
R. Henderson, OAK	.319
M. Hargrove, CLE	.317

Slugging Average

B. Grich, CAL	.543
E. Murray, BAL	.534
D. Evans, BOS	.522
T. Paciorek, SEA	.509
C. Cooper, MIL	.495

Home Runs

B. Grich, CAL	22
E. Murray, BAL	22
D. Evans, BOS	22
T. Armas, OAK	22
G. Thomas, MIL	21
G. Luzinski, CHI	21

Total Bases

D. Evans, BOS	215
T. Armas, OAK	211
T. Paciorek, SEA	206
C. Cooper, MIL	206
E. Murray, BAL	202

Runs Batted In

E. Murray, BAL	78
T. Armas, OAK	76
B. Oglivie, MIL	72
D. Evans, BOS	71
D. Winfield, NY	68

Stolen Bases

R. Henderson, OAK	56
J. Cruz, SEA	43
R. LeFlore, CHI	36
W. Wilson, KC	34
M. Dilone, CLE	29

Hits

R. Henderson, OAK	135
C. Lansford, BOS	134
C. Cooper, MIL	133
W. Wilson, KC	133

Base on Balls

D. Evans, BOS	85
D. Murphy, OAK	73
S. Kemp, DET	70
R. Henderson, OAK	64

Home Run Percentage

B. Grich, CAL	6.3
J. Mayberry, TOR	5.9
E. Murray, BAL	5.8
G. Thomas, MIL	5.8

Runs

R. Henderson, OAK	89
D. Evans, BOS	84
C. Cooper, MIL	70
T. Harrah, CLE	64

Doubles

C. Cooper, MIL	35
A. Oliver, TEX	29
T. Paciorek, SEA	28
G. Brett, KC	27
R. Dauer, BAL	27

Triples

J. Castino, MIN	9
H. Baines, CHI	7
G. Brett, KC	7
R. Henderson, OAK	7
W. Wilson, KC	7

PITCHING LEADERS

Winning Percentage

P. Vuckovich, MIL	.778
D. Martinez, BAL	.737
S. McGregor, BAL	.722
R. Guidry, NY	.688
J. Morris, DET	.667
S. McCatty, OAK	.667

Earned Run Average

S. McCatty, OAK	2.32
S. Stewart, BAL	2.33
D. Lamp, CHI	2.41
T. John, NY	2.64
B. Burns, CHI	2.64

Wins

P. Vuckovich, MIL	14
D. Martinez, BAL	14
S. McCatty, OAK	14
J. Morris, DET	14
S. McGregor, BAL	13
D. Leonard, KC	13

Saves

R. Fingers, MIL	28
G. Gossage, NY	20
D. Quisenberry, KC	18
D. Corbett, MIN	17
K. Saucier, DET	13

Strikeouts

L. Barker, CLE	127
B. Burns, CHI	108
B. Blyleven, CLE	107
D. Leonard, KC	107
R. Guidry, NY	104

Complete Games

R. Langford, OAK	18
S. McCatty, OAK	16
J. Morris, DET	15
M. Norris, OAK	12
L. Gura, KC	12

Fewest Hits/9 Innings

S. McCatty, OAK	6.77
J. Morris, DET	6.95
R. Guidry, NY	7.09
D. Darwin, TEX	7.09

Shutouts

K. Forsch, CAL	4
D. Medich, TEX	4
S. McCatty, OAK	4
R. Dotson, CHI	4

Fewest Walks/9 Innings

R. Honeycutt, TEX	1.20
K. Forsch, CAL	1.59
D. Leonard, KC	1.83
L. Gura, KC	1.83

Most Strikeouts/9 Inn.

L. Barker, CLE	7.42
R. Guidry, NY	7.37
F. Bannister, SEA	6.32
B. Burns, CHI	6.19

Innings

D. Leonard, KC	202
J. Morris, DET	198
R. Langford, OAK	195
S. McCatty, OAK	186

Games Pitched

D. Corbett, MIN	54
R. Fingers, MIL	47
S. Rawley, SEA	46
J. Easterly, MIL	44

AMERICAN LEAGUE 1981, *cont.*

		W	L	PCT	GB	R	OR	Batting 2B	3B	HR	BA	SA	SB	Fielding E	DP	FA	Pitching CG	BB	SO	ShO	SV	ERA
East	Milwaukee	62	47	.569		493	459	173	20	96	.257	.391	39	79	**135**	.982	11	352	448	4	**35**	3.91
	Baltimore	59	46	.562	1	429	437	165	11	88	.251	.379	41	68	114	.983	25	347	489	10	23	3.70
	New York	59	48	.551	2	421	**343**	148	22	100	.252	.391	47	72	100	.982	16	287	**606**	**13**	30	**2.90**
	Detroit	60	49	.550	2	427	404	148	29	65	.256	.367	61	**67**	109	**.984**	33	373	476	**13**	22	3.53
	Boston	59	49	.546	2.5	**519**	481	168	17	90	**.275**	**.399**	32	91	108	.979	19	354	536	4	24	3.81
	Cleveland	52	51	.505	7	431	442	150	21	39	.263	.351	**119**	87	91	.978	33	311	569	10	13	3.88
	Toronto	37	69	.349	23.5	329	466	137	23	61	.226	.330	66	105	102	.975	20	377	451	4	18	3.82
West	Oakland	64	45	.587		458	403	119	26	**104**	.247	.379	98	81	74	.980	**60**	370	505	11	10	3.30
	Texas	57	48	.543	5	452	389	**178**	15	49	.270	.369	46	69	102	**.984**	23	322	488	**13**	18	3.40
	Chicago	54	52	.509	8.5	476	423	135	27	76	.272	.387	86	87	113	.979	20	336	529	8	23	3.47
	Kansas City	50	53	.485	11	397	405	169	29	61	.267	.383	100	72	94	.982	24	**273**	404	8	24	3.56
	California	51	59	.464	13.5	476	453	134	16	97	.256	.380	44	101	120	.977	27	323	426	8	19	3.70
	Seattle	44	65	.404	20	426	521	148	13	89	.251	.368	100	91	122	.979	10	360	478	5	23	4.23
	Minnesota	41	68	.376	23	378	486	147	**36**	47	.240	.338	34	96	103	.978	13	376	500	6	22	3.98
						6112	6112	2119	305	1062	.256	.372	913	1166	1487	.980	334	4761	6905	117	304	3.66

First Half

	W	L	PCT	GB
East				
*New York	34	22	.607	
Baltimore	31	23	.574	2
Milwaukee	31	25	.554	3
Detroit	31	26	.544	3.5
Boston	30	26	.536	4
Cleveland	26	24	.520	5
Toronto	16	42	.276	19

* Defeated Milwaukee in playoff 3 games to 2

	W	L	PCT	GB
West				
*Oakland	37	23	.617	
Texas	33	22	.600	1.5
Chicago	31	22	.585	2.5
California	31	29	.517	6
Kansas City	20	30	.400	12
Seattle	21	36	.368	14.5
Minnesota	17	39	.304	18

* Defeated Kansas City in playoff 3 games to 0

Second Half

	W	L	PCT	GB
East				
Milwaukee	31	22	.585	
Boston	29	23	.558	1.5
Detroit	29	23	.558	1.5
Baltimore	28	23	.549	2
Cleveland	26	27	.491	5
New York	25	26	.490	5
Toronto	21	27	.438	7.5
West				
Kansas City	30	23	.566	
Oakland	27	22	.551	1
Texas	24	26	.480	4.5
Minnesota	24	29	.453	6
Seattle	23	29	.442	6.5
Chicago	23	30	.434	7
California	20	30	.400	8.5

NATIONAL LEAGUE 1982

		POS	Player	AB	BA	HR	RBI	PO	A	E	DP	TC/G	FA	Pitcher	G	IP	W	L	SV	ERA
East	St. Louis	1B	K. Hernandez	579	.299	7	94	**1586**	135	11	140	**11.0**	.994	J. Andujar	38	266	15	10	0	2.47
	W-92 L-70	2B	T. Herr	493	.266	0	36	263	427	9	97	5.5	.987	B. Forsch	36	233	15	9	1	3.48
	Whitey Herzog	SS	O. Smith	488	.248	2	43	279	**535**	13	101	**5.9**	**.984**	S. Mura	35	184	12	11	0	4.05
		3B	K. Oberkfell	470	.289	2	34	78	304	11	23	2.9	**.972**	D. LaPoint	42	153	9	3	0	3.42
		RF	G. Hendrick	515	.282	19	104	238	6	5	1	1.9	.980	J. Stuper	23	137	9	7	0	3.36
		CF	W. McGee	422	.296	4	56	245	3	11	0	2.2	.958	B. Sutter	70	102	9	8	**36**	2.90
		LF	L. Smith	592	.307	8	69	303	16	10	3	2.2	.970	D. Bair	63	92	5	3	8	2.55
		C	D. Porter	373	.231	12	48	469	64	9	8	4.9	.983	J. Kaat	62	75	5	3	2	4.08
		UT	M. Ramsey	256	.230	1	21	135	219	10	42		.973							
		OF	D. Iorg	238	.294	0	34	99	2	3	0	1.7	.971							
		OF	D. Green	166	.283	2	23	111	4	1	1	1.7	.991							
	Philadelphia	1B	P. Rose	634	.271	3	54	1428	123	8	114	9.6	.995	S. Carlton	38	**296**	**23**	11	0	3.10
	W-89 L-73	2B	M. Trillo	549	.271	0	39	343	441	5	101	5.3	**.994**	L. Christenson	33	223	9	10	0	3.47
	Pat Corrales	SS	I. DeJesus	536	.239	3	59	216	469	19	80	4.6	.973	M. Krukow	33	208	13	11	0	3.12
		3B	M. Schmidt	514	.280	35	87	110	**324**	23	**28**	3.1	.950	D. Ruthven	33	204	11	11	0	3.79
		RF	G. Vukovich	335	.272	6	42	168	4	4	3	1.7	.977	R. Reed	57	98	5	5	14	2.66
		CF	G. Maddox	412	.284	8	61	253	8	2	4	2.4	.992	M. Bystrom	19	89	5	6	0	4.85
		LF	G. Matthews	616	.281	19	83	268	14	10	2	1.8	.966	E. Farmer	47	76	2	6	6	4.86
		C	B. Diaz	525	.288	18	85	850	80	10	7	6.5	.989	S. Monge	47	72	7	1	2	3.75
		OF	B. Dernier	370	.249	4	21	255	5	5	0	2.2	.981	T. McGraw	34	40	3	3	5	4.31
	Montreal	1B	A. Oliver	617	**.331**	22	**109**	1286	92	**19**	96	8.8	.986	S. Rogers	35	277	19	8	0	**2.40**
	W-86 L-76	2B	D. Flynn	193	.244	0	20	135	157	5	40	5.1	.983	B. Gullickson	34	237	12	14	0	3.57
	Jim Fanning	SS	C. Speier	530	.257	7	60	291	405	13	76	4.6	.982	S. Sanderson	32	224	12	12	0	3.46
		3B	T. Wallach	596	.268	28	97	**132**	287	23	23	2.8	.948	C. Lea	27	178	12	10	0	3.24
		RF	W. Cromartie	497	.254	14	62	275	10	6	1	2.1	.979	R. Burris	37	124	4	14	2	4.73
		CF	A. Dawson	608	.301	23	83	419	8	8	2	3.0	.982	J. Reardon	75	109	7	4	26	2.06
		LF	T. Raines	647	.277	4	43	232	7	2	1	2.0	.992	D. Palmer	13	74	6	4	0	3.18
		C	G. Carter	557	.293	29	97	**954**	**104**	10	6	**7.0**	.991	W. Fryman	60	70	9	4	12	3.75

NATIONAL LEAGUE 1982, *cont.*

		POS	Player	AB	BA	HR	RBI	PO	A	E	DP	TC/G	FA	Pitcher	G	IP	W	L	SV	ERA
	Pittsburgh	1B	J. Thompson	550	.284	31	101	1395	105	10	114	9.7	.993	R. Rhoden	35	230	11	14	0	4.14
	W-84 L-78	2B	J. Ray	647	.281	7	63	**381**	**512**	**21**	89	5.6	.977	D. Robinson	38	227	15	13	0	4.28
	Chuck Tanner	SS	D. Berra	529	.263	10	61	238	498	30	77	5.0	.961	J. Candelaria	31	175	12	7	1	2.94
		3B	B. Madlock	568	.319	19	95	92	266	18	23	2.6	.952	M. Sarmiento	35	165	9	4	1	3.39
		RF	L. Lacy	359	.312	5	31	186	7	7	1	1.8	.965	K. Tekulve	**85**	129	12	8	20	2.87
		CF	O. Moreno	645	.245	3	44	396	10	7	3	2.6	.983	L. McWilliams	19	122	6	5	1	3.11
		LF	M. Easler	475	.276	15	58	243	8	7	2	1.9	.973	R. Scurry	76	104	4	5	14	1.74
		C	T. Pena	497	.296	11	63	763	89	16	6	6.3	.982	E. Romo	45	87	9	3	1	4.36
		OF	D. Parker	244	.270	6	29	108	2	5	1	1.8	.957							
	Chicago	1B	B. Buckner	**657**	.306	15	105	1547	**159**	12	89	10.7	.993	F. Jenkins	34	217	14	15	0	3.15
	W-73 L-89	2B	B. Wills	419	.272	6	38	199	297	19	45	5.0	.963	D. Bird	35	191	9	14	0	5.14
	Lee Elia	SS	L. Bowa	499	.246	0	29	210	396	17	64	4.4	.973	D. Noles	31	171	10	13	0	4.42
		3B	R. Sandberg	635	.271	7	54	79	278	11	19	2.8	.970	R. Martz	28	148	11	10	1	4.21
		RF	J. Johnstone	269	.249	10	43	154	8	3	0	1.9	.982	A. Ripley	28	123	5	7	0	4.26
		CF	L. Durham	539	.312	22	90	301	11	12	1	2.3	.963	L. Smith	72	117	2	5	17	2.69
		LF	K. Moreland	476	.261	15	68	169	9	2	0	2.1	.989	D. Tidrow	65	104	8	3	6	3.39
		C	J. Davis	418	.261	12	52	598	89	11	**11**	5.4	.984	B. Campbell	62	100	3	6	8	3.69
		OF	S. Henderson	257	.233	2	29	126	5	6	0	2.0	.956	G. Hernandez	75	75	4	6	10	3.00
		OF	G. Woods	245	.269	4	30	161	6	0	1	1.6	1.000							
		2S	J. Kennedy	242	.219	2	25	137	220	12	35		.967							
		OF	J. Morales	116	.284	4	30	72	5	0	1	1.9	1.000							
	New York	1B	D. Kingman	535	.204	**37**	99	1232	69	18	88	9.2	.986	P. Falcone	40	171	8	10	2	3.84
	W-65 L-97	2B	W. Backman	261	.272	3	22	169	202	14	30	4.4	.964	C. Puleo	36	171	9	9	1	4.47
	George Bamberger	SS	R. Gardenhire	384	.240	3	33	234	398	29	68	4.9	.956	C. Swan	37	166	11	7	1	3.35
		3B	H. Brooks	457	.249	2	40	89	237	24	17	2.8	.931	M. Scott	37	147	7	13	3	5.14
		RF	E. Valentine	337	.288	8	48	159	10	3	4	1.8	.983	E. Lynch	43	139	4	8	2	3.55
		CF	M. Wilson	639	.279	5	55	415	12	5	4	2.8	.988	P. Zachry	36	138	6	9	1	4.05
		LF	G. Foster	550	.247	13	70	289	12	8	4	2.2	.974	J. Orosco	54	109	4	10	4	2.72
		C	J. Stearns	352	.293	4	28	379	61	6	9	5.5	.987	R. Jones	28	108	7	10	0	4.60
		UT	B. Bailor	376	.277	0	31	166	272	11	42		.976	N. Allen	50	65	3	7	19	3.06
		C	R. Hodges	228	.246	5	27	362	35	8	4	5.5	.980							
		01	R. Staub	219	.242	3	27	172	19	2	12		.990							
		OF	J. Youngblood	202	.257	3	21	88	5	3	1	1.5	.969							
		OF	G. Rajsich	162	.259	2	12	60	0	0	0	1.7	1.000							
West	**Atlanta**	1B	C. Chambliss	534	.270	20	86	1352	138	10	**144**	9.9	.993	P. Niekro	35	234	17	4	0	3.61
	W-89 L-73	2B	G. Hubbard	532	.248	9	59	312	505	14	**111**	**5.8**	.983	R. Mahler	39	205	9	10	0	4.21
	Joe Torre	SS	R. Ramirez	609	.278	10	52	**300**	528	**38**	**130**	5.5	.956	R. Camp	51	177	11	13	5	3.65
		3B	B. Horner	499	.261	32	97	102	217	10	20	2.4	.970	B. Walk	32	164	11	9	0	4.87
		RF	C. Washington	563	.266	16	80	221	9	12	3	1.7	.950	S. Bedrosian	64	138	8	6	11	2.42
		CF	D. Murphy	598	.281	36	**109**	407	6	9	2	2.6	.979	G. Garber	69	119	8	10	30	2.34
		LF	B. Butler	240	.217	0	7	129	2	0	0	1.7	1.000	K. Dayley	20	71	5	6	0	4.54
		C	B. Benedict	386	.246	3	44	602	73	5	9	5.8	**.993**							
		UT	J. Royster	261	.295	2	25	105	112	11	20		.952							
		OF	R. Linares	191	.298	2	17	92	4	0	1	1.8	1.000							
		C	B. Pocoroba	120	.275	2	22	143	16	2	2	4.5	.988							
		1B	B. Watson	114	.246	5	22	206	8	0	18	7.9	1.000							
	Los Angeles	1B	S. Garvey	625	.282	16	86	1539	111	8	132	10.5	.995	F. Valenzuela	37	285	19	13	0	2.87
	W-88 L-74	2B	S. Sax	638	.282	4	47	347	452	19	83	5.5	.977	J. Reuss	39	255	18	11	0	3.11
	Tom Lasorda	SS	B. Russell	497	.274	3	46	216	502	29	64	5.0	.961	B. Welch	36	236	16	11	0	3.36
		3B	R. Cey	556	.254	24	79	93	320	16	23	2.9	.963	D. Stewart	45	146	9	8	1	3.81
		RF	P. Guerrero	575	.304	32	100	269	11	7	6	2.1	.976	B. Hooton	21	121	4	7	0	4.03
		CF	K. Landreaux	461	.284	7	50	281	3	4	1	2.5	.986	S. Howe	66	99	7	5	13	2.08
		LF	D. Baker	570	.300	23	88	226	7	6	1	1.7	.975	T. Forster	56	83	5	6	3	3.04
		C	M. Scioscia	365	.219	5	38	631	57	10	10	5.7	.986	T. Niedenfuer	55	70	3	4	9	2.71
		OF	R. Monday	210	.257	11	42	62	4	4	0	1.2	.943							
		C	S. Yeager	196	.245	2	18	338	42	4	8	5.1	.990							
	San Francisco	1B	R. Smith	349	.284	18	56	792	78	16	61	8.9	.982	B. Laskey	32	189	13	12	0	3.14
	W-87 L-75	2B	J. Morgan	463	.289	14	61	254	364	7	69	5.2	.989	A. Hammaker	29	175	12	8	0	4.11
	Frank Robinson	SS	J. LeMaster	436	.216	2	30	223	382	23	63	4.8	.963	R. Gale	33	170	7	14	0	4.23
		3B	D. Evans	465	.256	16	61	59	150	15	12	2.7	.933	F. Breining	54	143	11	6	0	3.08
		RF	J. Clark	563	.274	27	103	281	10	6	2	1.9	.980	R. Martin	29	141	7	10	0	4.66
		CF	C. Davis	641	.261	19	76	404	16	12	4	2.8	.972	A. Holland	58	130	7	3	5	3.33
		LF	J. Leonard	278	.259	9	49	135	2	6	0	1.9	.958	J. Barr	53	129	4	3	2	3.29
		C	M. May	395	.263	9	39	552	61	8	5	5.6	.987	G. Minton	78	123	10	4	30	1.83
		3B	T. O'Malley	291	.275	2	27	59	160	8	9	2.7	.965	G. Lavelle	68	105	10	7	8	2.67
		OF	J. Wohlford	250	.256	2	25	122	4	1	0	1.8	.992							
		2B	D. Kuiper	218	.280	0	17	101	124	5	24	4.5	.978							
		C	B. Brenly	180	.283	4	15	265	32	12	2	5.1	.961							
	San Diego	1B	B. Perkins	347	.271	2	34	817	64	5	61	9.0	.994	T. Lollar	34	233	16	9	0	3.13
	W-81 L-81	2B	T. Flannery	379	.264	0	30	221	260	13	46	4.8	.974	J. Montefusco	32	184	10	11	0	4.00
	Dick Williams	SS	G. Templeton	563	.247	6	64	220	422	26	70	4.9	.961	J. Eichelberger	31	178	7	14	0	4.20
		3B	L. Salazar	524	.242	8	62	104	291	**26**	**28**	**3.3**	.938	E. Show	47	150	10	6	3	2.64
		RF	S. Lezcano	470	.289	16	84	275	16	3	8	2.2	.990	C. Welsh	28	139	8	8	0	4.91
		CF	R. Jones	424	.283	12	61	314	3	5	1	2.8	.984	J. Curtis	26	116	8	6	0	4.10
		LF	G. Richards	521	.286	3	28	200	8	5	1	2.1	.977	D. Dravecky	31	105	5	3	2	2.57
		C	T. Kennedy	562	.295	21	97	666	56	7	**11**	5.2	.990	L. DeLeon	61	102	9	5	15	2.03
		OF	A. Wiggins	254	.256	1	15	140	8	5	2	2.3	.967	G. Lucas	65	97	1	10	16	3.24
		30	J. Lefebvre	239	.238	4	21	70	74	3	6		.980	F. Chiffer	51	79	4	3	4	2.95
		OF	T. Gwynn	190	.289	1	17	110	1	1	0	2.2	.991							
		2B	J. Bonilla	182	.280	0	8	99	134	6	26	5.3	.975							
		1B	K. Bevacqua	123	.252	0	24	253	16	3	13	9.1	.989							

NATIONAL LEAGUE 1982, *cont.*

Team	POS	Player	AB	BA	HR	RBI	PO	A	E	DP	TC/G	FA	Pitcher	G	IP	W	L	SV	ERA
Houston	1B	R. Knight	609	.294	6	70	945	55	10	76	10.5	.990	J. Niekro	35	270	17	12	0	2.47
	2B	P. Garner	588	.274	13	83	273	429	14	90	5.3	.980	N. Ryan	35	250	16	12	0	3.16
	SS	D. Thon	496	.276	3	36	177	399	15	80	5.0	.975	D. Sutton	27	195	13	8	0	3.00
W-77 L-85	3B	A. Howe	365	.238	5	38	53	153	6	13	2.9	.972	B. Knepper	33	180	5	15	1	4.45
	RF	T. Puhl	507	.262	8	50	257	4	3	3	1.9	.989	V. Ruhle	31	149	9	13	1	3.93
Bill Virdon	CF	T. Scott	460	.239	1	29	262	7	5	0	2.1	.982	M. LaCoss	41	115	6	6	0	2.90
W-49 L-62	LF	J. Cruz	570	.275	9	68	340	9	13	3	2.3	.964	F. LaCorte	55	76	1	5	7	4.48
	C	A. Ashby	339	.257	12	49	530	55	14	5	6.3	.977	D. Smith	49	63	5	4	11	3.84
Bob Lillis	OF	D. Heep	198	.237	4	22	62	2	0	1	1.6	1.000							
W-28 L-23	C	L. Pujols	176	.199	4	15	295	39	3	3	5.3	.991							
Cincinnati	1B	D. Driessen	516	.269	17	57	1239	78	3	123	9.2	**.998**	M. Soto	35	258	14	13	0	2.79
	2B	R. Oester	549	.260	9	47	258	325	17	72	5.1	.972	B. Berenyi	34	222	9	**18**	0	3.36
	SS	D. Concepcion	572	.287	5	53	262	459	17	94	5.1	.977	F. Pastore	31	188	8	13	0	3.97
	3B	J. Bench	399	.258	13	38	54	155	19	10	2.1	.917	B. Shirley	41	153	8	13	0	3.60
W-61 L-101	RF	P. Householder	417	.211	9	34	220	14	2	4	1.8	.992	T. Seaver	21	111	5	13	0	5.50
	CF	C. Cedeno	492	.289	8	57	301	4	3	2	2.4	.990	C. Leibrandt	36	108	5	7	2	5.10
John McNamara	LF	E. Milner	407	.268	4	31	215	8	3	1	2.1	.987	J. Kern	50	76	3	5	2	2.84
W-34 L-58	C	A. Trevino	355	.251	1	33	725	61	**17**	7	6.9	.979	J. Price	59	73	3	4	3	2.85
Russ Nixon	OF	D. Walker	239	.218	5	22	110	7	1	1	1.7	.992	T. Hume	46	64	2	6	17	3.11
W-27 L-43	OF	M. Vail	189	.254	4	29	72	7	1	0	1.5	.988							
	3B	W. Krenchicki	187	.283	2	21	35	93	6	7	1.9	.955							
	01	L. Biittner	184	.310	2	24	170	14	2	13		.989							
	2B	T. Lawless	165	.212	0	4	87	136	5	35	4.9	.978							

BATTING AND BASE RUNNING LEADERS

Batting Average
- A. Oliver, MON .331
- B. Madlock, PIT .319
- L. Durham, CHI .312
- L. Smith, STL .307
- B. Buckner, CHI .306

Slugging Average
- M. Schmidt, PHI .547
- P. Guerrero, LA .536
- L. Durham, CHI .521
- A. Oliver, MON .514
- J. Thompson, PIT .511

Home Runs
- D. Kingman, NY 37
- D. Murphy, ATL 36
- M. Schmidt, PHI 35
- B. Horner, ATL 32
- P. Guerrero, LA 32

Total Bases
- A. Oliver, MON 317
- P. Guerrero, LA 308
- D. Murphy, ATL 303
- A. Dawson, MON 303
- B. Buckner, CHI 290

Runs Batted In
- D. Murphy, ATL 109
- A. Oliver, MON 109
- B. Buckner, CHI 105
- G. Hendrick, STL 104
- J. Clark, SF 103

Stolen Bases
- T. Raines, MON 78
- L. Smith, STL 68
- O. Moreno, PIT 60
- M. Wilson, NY 58
- S. Sax, LA 49

Hits
- A. Oliver, MON 204
- B. Buckner, CHI 201
- A. Dawson, MON 183
- L. Smith, STL 182
- J. Ray, PIT 182

Base on Balls
- M. Schmidt, PHI 107
- J. Thompson, PIT 101
- K. Hernandez, STL 100
- D. Murphy, ATL 93

Home Run Percentage
- D. Kingman, NY 6.9
- M. Schmidt, PHI 6.8
- B. Horner, ATL 6.4
- D. Murphy, ATL 6.0

Runs
- L. Smith, STL 120
- D. Murphy, ATL 113
- M. Schmidt, PHI 108
- A. Dawson, MON 107

Doubles
- A. Oliver, MON 43
- T. Kennedy, SD 42
- A. Dawson, MON 37
- R. Knight, HOU 36

Triples
- D. Thon, HOU 10
- T. Puhl, HOU 9
- M. Wilson, NY 9
- O. Moreno, PIT 9

PITCHING LEADERS

Winning Percentage
- P. Niekro, ATL .810
- S. Rogers, MON .704
- S. Carlton, PHI .676
- T. Lollar, SD .640
- B. Forsch, STL .625

Earned Run Average
- S. Rogers, MON 2.40
- J. Niekro, HOU 2.47
- J. Andujar, STL 2.47
- M. Soto, CIN 2.79
- F. Valenzuela, LA 2.87

Wins
- S. Carlton, PHI 23
- S. Rogers, MON 19
- F. Valenzuela, LA 19
- J. Reuss, LA 18
- P. Niekro, ATL 17
- J. Niekro, HOU 17

Saves
- B. Sutter, STL 36
- G. Minton, SF 30
- G. Garber, ATL 30
- J. Reardon, MON 26
- K. Tekulve, PIT 20

Strikeouts
- S. Carlton, PHI 286
- M. Soto, CIN 274
- N. Ryan, HOU 245
- F. Valenzuela, LA 199
- S. Rogers, MON 179

Complete Games
- S. Carlton, PHI 19
- F. Valenzuela, LA 18
- J. Niekro, HOU 16
- S. Rogers, MON 14
- M. Soto, CIN 13

Fewest Hits/9 Innings
- N. Ryan, HOU 7.05
- M. Soto, CIN 7.06
- C. Lea, MON 7.35
- T. Lollar, SD 7.43

Shutouts
- S. Carlton, PHI 6
- J. Niekro, HOU 5
- J. Andujar, STL 5

Fewest Walks/9 Innings
- D. Bird, CHI 1.41
- A. Hammaker, SF 1.44
- J. Andujar, STL 1.69
- J. Reuss, LA 1.77

Most Strikeouts/9 Inn.
- M. Soto, CIN 9.57
- N. Ryan, HOU 8.81
- S. Carlton, PHI 8.71
- J. Candelaria, PIT 6.85

Innings
- S. Carlton, PHI 296
- F. Valenzuela, LA 285
- S. Rogers, MON 277
- J. Niekro, HOU 270

Games Pitched
- K. Tekulve, PIT 85
- G. Minton, SF 78
- R. Scurry, PIT 76
- G. Hernandez, CHI 75
- J. Reardon, MON 75

								Batting						Fielding				Pitching				
		W	L	PCT	GB	R	OR	2B	3B	HR	BA	SA	SB	E	DP	FA	CG	BB	SO	ShO	SV	ERA
East	St. Louis	92	70	.568		685	**609**	239	**52**	67	.264	.364	**200**	124	169	**.981**	25	502	689	10	47	3.37
	Philadelphia	89	73	.549	3	664	654	245	25	112	.260	.376	128	**121**	138	**.981**	**38**	472	**1002**	13	33	3.61
	Montreal	86	76	.531	6	697	616	270	38	133	.262	.396	156	122	117	.980	34	**448**	936	10	43	3.31
	Pittsburgh	84	78	.519	8	724	696	**272**	40	134	**.273**	**.408**	161	145	133	.977	19	521	933	7	39	3.81
	Chicago	73	89	.451	19	676	709	239	46	102	.260	.375	132	132	110	.979	9	452	764	7	43	3.92
	New York	65	97	.401	27	609	723	227	26	97	.247	.350	137	175	134	.972	15	582	759	5	37	3.88
West	Atlanta	89	73	.549		**739**	702	215	22	**146**	.256	.383	151	137	**186**	.979	15	502	813	11	**51**	3.82
	Los Angeles	88	74	.543	1	691	612	222	32	138	.264	.388	151	139	131	.979	37	468	932	**16**	28	**3.26**
	San Francisco	87	75	.537	2	673	687	213	30	133	.253	.376	130	173	125	.973	18	466	810	4	45	3.64
	San Diego	81	81	.500	8	675	658	217	**52**	81	.257	.359	165	152	142	.976	20	502	765	11	41	3.52
	Houston	77	85	.475	12	569	620	236	48	74	.247	.349	140	136	154	.978	37	479	899	**16**	31	3.41
	Cincinnati	61	101	.377	28	545	661	228	34	82	.251	.350	131	128	158	.980	22	570	998	7	31	3.66
						7947	7947	2823	445	1299	.258	.373	1782	1684	1697	.978	289	5964	10300	117	469	3.60

AMERICAN LEAGUE 1982

East

Milwaukee

W-95 L-67

Buck Rodgers
W-23 L-24

Harvey Kuenn
W-72 L-43

POS	Player	AB	BA	HR	RBI	PO	A	E	DP	TC/G	FA	Pitcher	G	IP	W	L	SV	ERA
1B	C. Cooper	654	.313	32	121	1428	98	5	**156**	9.9	.997	M. Caldwell	35	258	17	13	0	3.91
2B	J. Gantner	447	.295	4	43	307	398	13	104	5.5	.982	P. Vuckovich	30	224	18	6	0	3.34
SS	R. Yount	635	.331	29	114	253	**489**	24	95	5.0	.969	M. Haas	32	193	11	8	1	4.47
3B	P. Molitor	**666**	.302	19	71	128	340	**29**	**48**	3.3	.942	B. McClure	34	173	12	7	0	4.22
RF	C. Moore	456	.254	6	45	231	13	3	6	2.1	.988	J. Slaton	39	118	10	6	6	3.29
CF	G. Thomas	567	.245	**39**	112	427	11	4	4	2.8	.991	R. Lerch	21	109	8	7	0	4.97
LF	B. Oglivie	602	.244	34	102	359	15	7	3	2.4	.982	R. Fingers	50	80	5	6	29	2.60
C	T. Simmons	539	.269	23	97	570	62	3	8	5.2	**.995**	D. Bernard	47	79	3	1	6	3.76
DH	R. Howell	300	.260	4	38													
DH	D. Money	275	.284	16	55													
OF	M. Edwards	178	.247	2	14	119	2	2	1	2.3	.984							

Baltimore

W-94 L-68

Earl Weaver

POS	Player	AB	BA	HR	RBI	PO	A	E	DP	TC/G	FA	Pitcher	G	IP	W	L	SV	ERA
1B	E. Murray	550	.316	32	110	1269	97	4	106	9.2	**.997**	D. Martinez	40	252	16	12	0	4.21
2B	R. Dauer	558	.280	8	57	261	268	7	67	4.4	.987	M. Flanagan	36	236	15	11	0	3.97
SS	C. Ripken	598	.264	28	93	155	289	13	47	4.9	.972	J. Palmer	36	227	15	5	1	3.13
3B	G. Gulliver	145	.200	1	5	34	97	4	6	2.7	.970	S. McGregor	37	226	14	12	0	4.61
RF	D. Ford	421	.235	10	43	263	6	7	2	2.3	.975	S. Stewart	38	139	10	9	5	4.14
CF	A. Bumbry	562	.262	5	40	404	9	6	1	2.9	.986	S. Davis	29	101	8	4	0	3.49
LF	J. Lowenstein	322	.320	24	66	202	2	0	0	1.8	1.000	T. Martinez	76	95	8	8	16	3.41
C	R. Dempsey	344	.256	5	36	491	46	5	8	4.4	.991	T. Stoddard	50	56	3	4	12	4.02
DH	K. Singleton	561	.251	14	77													
OF	G. Roenicke	393	.270	21	74	288	7	3	0	2.4	.990							
2S	L. Sakata	343	.259	6	31	182	299	16	61		.968							
C	J. Nolan	219	.233	6	35	292	22	7	2	4.5	.978							
OD	B. Ayala	128	.305	6	24	35	0	1	0		.972							

Boston

W-89 L-73

Ralph Houk

POS	Player	AB	BA	HR	RBI	PO	A	E	DP	TC/G	FA	Pitcher	G	IP	W	L	SV	ERA
1B	D. Stapleton	538	.264	14	65	964	77	9	98	9.9	.991	D. Eckersley	33	224	13	13	0	3.73
2B	J. Remy	636	.280	0	47	290	432	13	104	4.8	.982	J. Tudor	32	196	13	10	0	3.63
SS	G. Hoffman	469	.209	7	49	246	439	20	93	4.7	.972	M. Torrez	31	176	9	9	0	5.23
3B	C. Lansford	482	.301	11	63	83	216	10	19	2.7	.968	B. Stanley	48	168	12	7	14	3.10
RF	D. Evans	609	.292	32	98	346	9	10	3	2.3	.973	C. Rainey	27	129	7	5	0	5.02
CF	R. Miller	409	.254	4	38	277	6	5	2	2.3	.983	B. Hurst	28	117	3	7	0	5.77
LF	J. Rice	573	.309	24	97	273	10	9	3	2.0	.969	M. Clear	55	105	14	9	14	3.00
C	G. Allenson	264	.205	6	33	454	39	4	8	5.5	.992	T. Burgmeier	40	102	7	0	2	2.29
DH	C. Yastrzemski	459	.275	16	72							B. Ojeda	22	78	4	6	0	5.63
13	W. Boggs	338	.349	5	44	488	168	8	51		.988							
C	R. Gedman	289	.249	4	26	397	29	10	5	5.1	.977							
OF	R. Nichols	245	.302	7	33	169	9	2	4	2.2	.989							
DH	T. Perez	196	.260	6	31													

Detroit

W-83 L-79

Sparky Anderson

POS	Player	AB	BA	HR	RBI	PO	A	E	DP	TC/G	FA	Pitcher	G	IP	W	L	SV	ERA
1B	E. Cabell	464	.261	2	37	548	52	5	62	7.3	.992	J. Morris	37	266	17	16	0	4.06
2B	L. Whitaker	560	.286	15	65	331	**470**	10	**120**	5.4	**.988**	D. Petry	35	246	15	9	0	3.22
SS	A. Trammell	489	.258	9	57	259	459	16	97	4.7	.978	M. Wilcox	29	194	12	10	0	3.62
3B	T. Brookens	398	.231	9	58	72	206	18	20	2.6	.939	J. Ujdur	25	178	10	10	0	3.69
RF	C. Lemon	436	.266	19	52	242	11	4	2	2.1	.984	P. Underwood	33	99	4	8	3	4.73
CF	G. Wilson	322	.292	12	34	215	8	3	1	2.8	.987	D. Tobik	51	99	4	9	9	3.56
LF	L. Herndon	614	.292	23	88	328	11	6	3	2.2	.983	D. Rucker	27	64	5	6	0	3.38
C	L. Parrish	486	.284	32	87	627	76	8	8	5.4	.989	E. Sosa	38	61	3	3	4	4.43
DH	M. Ivie	259	.232	14	38													
OF	K. Gibson	266	.278	8	35	167	4	1	3	2.7	.994							
1B	R. Leach	218	.239	3	12	410	28	2	36	7.9	.995							
DH	J. Turner	210	.248	8	27													
UT	J. Wockenfuss	193	.301	8	32	228	14	2	9		.992							
1D	R. Hebner	179	.274	8	18	286	25	3	15		.990							

New York

W-79 L-83

Bob Lemon
W-6 L-8

Gene Michael
W-44 L-42

Clyde King
W-29 L-33

POS	Player	AB	BA	HR	RBI	PO	A	E	DP	TC/G	FA	Pitcher	G	IP	W	L	SV	ERA
1B	J. Mayberry	215	.209	8	27	455	25	2	49	7.7	.996	R. Guidry	34	222	14	8	0	3.81
2B	W. Randolph	553	.280	3	36	352	380	14	100	5.3	.981	T. John	30	187	10	10	0	3.66
SS	R. Smalley	486	.257	20	67	109	238	8	42	4.0	.977	D. Righetti	33	183	11	10	1	3.79
3B	G. Nettles	405	.232	18	55	73	255	23	23	3.1	.934	S. Rawley	47	164	11	10	3	4.06
RF	K. Griffey	484	.277	12	54	282	8	5	2	2.4	.983	M. Morgan	30	150	7	11	0	4.37
CF	J. Mumphrey	477	.300	9	68	336	5	5	2	2.8	.986	G. Frazier	63	112	4	4	1	3.47
LF	D. Winfield	539	.280	37	106	279	17	8	2	2.3	.974	R. May	41	106	6	6	3	2.89
C	R. Cerone	300	.227	5	28	509	25	6	5	6.1	.989	G. Gossage	56	93	4	5	30	2.23
DH	O. Gamble	316	.272	18	57							R. Erickson	16	71	4	5	1	4.46
01	D. Collins	348	.253	3	25	498	28	7	30		.987							
DO	L. Piniella	261	.307	6	37	68	2	0	1		1.000							
C	B. Wynegar	191	.293	3	20	395	17	3	6	6.7*	.993							
DH	B. Murcer	141	.227	7	30													

Cleveland

W-78 L-84

Dave Garcia

POS	Player	AB	BA	HR	RBI	PO	A	E	DP	TC/G	FA	Pitcher	G	IP	W	L	SV	ERA
1B	M. Hargrove	591	.271	4	65	1293	**123**	5	110	9.3	.996	L. Barker	33	245	15	11	0	3.90
2B	J. Perconte	219	.237	0	15	131	199	8	23	4.1	.976	R. Sutcliffe	34	216	14	8	1	**2.96**
SS	M. Fischlin	276	.268	0	21	136	253	12	42	4.0	.970	L. Sorensen	32	189	10	15	0	5.61
3B	T. Harrah	602	.304	25	78	126	279	12	25	2.6	.971	J. Denny	21	138	6	11	0	5.01
RF	V. Hayes	527	.250	14	82	306	9	6	4	2.3	.981	D. Spillner	65	134	12	10	21	2.49
CF	R. Manning	562	.270	8	44	387	10	9	1	2.7	.978	R. Waits	25	115	2	13	0	5.40
LF	M. Dilone	379	.235	3	25	187	3	7	1	2.0	.964	E. Whitson	40	108	4	2	2	3.26
C	R. Hassey	323	.251	5	34	562	38	4	6	5.8	.993	E. Glynn	47	50	5	2	4	4.17
DH	A. Thornton	589	.273	32	116													
02	A. Bannister	348	.267	4	41	206	124	10	22		.971							
UT	L. Milbourne	291	.275	2	25	149	224	14	41		.964							
SS	J. Dybzinski	212	.231	0	22	118	239	16	39	4.8	.957							
C	C. Bando	184	.212	3	16	268	23	3	1	4.7	.990							

AMERICAN LEAGUE 1982, *cont.*

	Team	POS	Player	AB	BA	HR	RBI	PO	A	E	DP	TC/G	FA	Pitcher	G	IP	W	L	SV	ERA
	Toronto	1B	W. Upshaw	580	.267	21	75	**1438**	101	**17**	123	10.0	.989	D. Stieb	38	**288**	17	14	0	3.25
	W-78 L-84	2B	D. Garcia	597	.310	5	42	273	461	15	94	5.3	.980	J. Clancy	40	267	16	14	0	3.71
	Bobby Cox	SS	A. Griffin	539	.241	1	48	**319**	479	**26**	92	**5.1**	.968	L. Leal	38	250	12	15	0	3.93
		3B	R. Mulliniks	311	.244	4	35	60	137	13	13	2.1	.938	J. Gott	30	136	5	10	0	4.43
		RF	J. Barfield	394	.246	18	58	217	15	9	4	1.8	.963	D. Murray	56	111	8	7	11	3.16
		CF	L. Moseby	487	.236	9	52	361	4	3	0	2.5	.992	R. Jackson	48	97	8	8	6	3.06
		LF	B. Bonnell	437	.293	6	49	232	3	5	0	1.9	.979	J. McLaughlin	44	70	8	6	8	3.21
		C	E. Whitt	284	.261	11	42	406	30	8	0	4.5	.982							
		DH	W. Nordhagen	185	.270	1	20													
		3B	G. Iorg	417	.285	1	36	57	155	12	13	2.2	.946							
		OF	H. Powell	265	.275	3	26	111	2	3	0	1.5	.974							
		C	B. Martinez	260	.242	10	37	382	35	5	8	4.5	.988							
		OF	A. Woods	201	.234	3	24	96	2	3	1	1.6	.970							
West	**California**	1B	R. Carew	523	.319	3	44	1339	94	12	115	**10.8**	.992	G. Zahn	34	229	18	8	0	3.73
	W-93 L-69	2B	B. Grich	506	.261	19	65	338	450	11	112	5.6	.986	K. Forsch	37	228	13	11	0	3.87
	Gene Mauch	SS	T. Foli	480	.252	3	56	235	432	10	87	4.9	**.985**	M. Witt	33	180	8	6	0	3.51
		3B	D. DeCinces	575	.301	30	97	112	**399**	21	41	3.5	.961	S. Renko	31	156	11	6	0	4.44
		RF	R. Jackson	530	.275	**39**	101	200	6	6	1	1.5	.972	B. Kison	33	142	10	5	1	3.17
		CF	F. Lynn	472	.299	21	86	317	6	3	3	2.5	.991	L. Sanchez	46	93	7	4	5	3.21
		LF	B. Downing	623	.281	28	84	321	9	0	0	2.1	1.000	D. Goltz	28	86	8	5	3	4.08
		C	B. Boone	472	.256	7	58	**650**	**87**	8	8	5.2	.989	D. Corbett	33	57	1	7	8	5.05
		DH	D. Baylor	608	.263	24	93							D. Aase	24	52	3	3	4	3.46
		OF	J. Beniquez	196	.265	3	24	113	4	2	1	1.1	.983	A. Moreno	13	49	3	7	1	4.74
	Kansas City	1B	W. Aikens	466	.281	17	74	1048	75	7	95	8.8	.994	L. Gura	37	248	18	12	0	4.03
	W-90 L-72	2B	F. White	524	.298	11	56	**361**	389	**17**	99	5.3	.978	V. Blue	31	181	13	12	0	3.78
	Dick Howser	SS	U. Washington	437	.286	10	60	173	371	22	63	4.8	.961	P. Splittorff	29	162	10	10	0	4.28
		3B	G. Brett	552	.301	21	82	107	294	17	22	3.1	.959	D. Quisenberry	72	137	9	7	**35**	2.57
		RF	J. Martin	519	.266	15	65	333	4	7	2	2.4	.980	D. Leonard	21	131	10	6	0	5.10
		CF	A. Otis	475	.286	11	88	308	5	1	1	2.5	.997	M. Armstrong	52	113	5	5	6	3.20
		LF	W. Wilson	585	**.332**	3	46	376	4	5	0	2.9	.987	B. Black	22	88	4	6	0	4.58
		C	J. Wathan	448	.270	3	51	463	38	10	3	4.3	.980	D. Frost	21	82	6	6	0	5.51
		DH	H. McRae	613	.308	27	**133**													
		S2	O. Concepcion	205	.234	0	15	92	168	11	28		.959							
		OF	C. Geronimo	119	.269	4	23	93	3	0	0	2.2	1.000							
	Chicago	1B	M. Squires	195	.267	1	21	512	48	3	59	5.2	.995	L. Hoyt	39	240	**19**	15	0	3.53
	W-87 L-75	2B	T. Bernazard	540	.256	11	56	353	443	12	116	**5.9**	.985	R. Dotson	34	197	11	15	0	3.84
	Tony LaRussa	SS	B. Almon	308	.256	4	26	164	317	**26**	72	4.7	.949	D. Lamp	44	190	11	8	5	3.99
		3B	A. Rodriguez	257	.241	3	31	78	204	9	19	2.6	.969	J. Koosman	42	173	11	7	3	3.84
		RF	H. Baines	608	.271	25	105	326	10	7	4	2.1	.980	B. Burns	28	169	13	5	0	4.04
		CF	R. Law	336	.318	3	32	215	2	6	0	2.4	.973	S. Trout	25	120	6	9	0	4.26
		LF	S. Kemp	580	.286	19	98	280	6	7	1	1.9	.976	S. Barojas	61	107	6	6	21	3.54
		C	C. Fisk	476	.267	14	65	639	62	4	7	5.3	.994	K. Hickey	60	78	4	4	6	3.00
		DH	G. Luzinski	583	.292	18	102													
		1B	T. Paciorek	382	.312	11	55	833	66	6	85	8.9	.993							
		S3	V. Law	359	.281	5	54	145	294	23	47		.950							
		OF	R. LeFlore	334	.287	4	25	179	7	**12**	1	2.4	.939							
		3B	J. Morrison	166	.223	7	19	19	87	10	10	2.3	.914							
	Seattle	1B	G. Gray	269	.257	7	29	476	31	8	36	8.6	.984	F. Bannister	35	247	12	13	0	3.43
	W-76 L-86	2B	J. Cruz	549	.242	8	49	320	434	10	98	5.1	.987	G. Perry	32	217	10	12	0	4.40
	Rene Lachemann	SS	T. Cruz	492	.230	16	57	215	439	25	**98**	5.0	.963	J. Beattie	28	172	8	12	0	3.34
		3B	M. Castillo	506	.257	3	49	96	209	20	18	2.5	.938	M. Moore	28	144	7	14	0	5.36
		RF	A. Cowens	560	.270	20	78	280	14	4	1	2.1	.987	G. Nelson	22	123	6	9	0	4.62
		CF	D. Henderson	324	.253	14	48	249	11	4	4	2.6	.985	B. Clark	37	115	5	2	0	2.75
		LF	B. Bochte	509	.297	12	70	161	5	2	1	1.7	.988	B. Caudill	70	96	12	9	26	2.35
		C	R. Sweet	258	.256	4	24	431	26	3	6	5.5	.993	E. Vande Berg	**78**	76	9	4	5	2.37
		DH	R. Zisk	503	.292	21	62							M. Stanton	56	71	2	4	7	4.16
		OF	J. Simpson	296	.257	2	23	177	7	3	0	1.9	.984							
		OF	B. Brown	245	.241	4	17	148	5	5	1	2.3	.968							
		1B	J. Maler	221	.226	4	26	529	41	5	45	10.1	.991							
		UT	P. Serna	169	.225	3	8	63	126	9	23		.955							
		C	J. Essian	153	.275	3	20	282	26	2	1	6.5	.994							
	Oakland	1B	D. Meyer	383	.240	8	59	373	31	4	38	7.0	.990	R. Langford	32	237	11	16	0	4.21
	W-68 L-94	2B	D. Lopes	450	.242	11	42	289	338	15	82	5.1	.977	M. Keough	34	209	11	**18**	0	5.72
	Billy Martin	SS	F. Stanley	228	.193	2	17	112	223	13	42	3.6	.963	M. Norris	28	166	7	11	0	4.76
		3B	W. Gross	386	.251	9	41	113	182	9	25	2.8	.970	T. Underwood	56	153	10	6	7	3.29
		RF	T. Armas	536	.233	28	89	333	9	6	1	2.6	.983	S. McCatty	21	129	6	3	0	3.99
		CF	D. Murphy	543	.238	27	94	452	14	8	3	3.2	.983	B. Kingman	23	123	4	12	1	4.48
		LF	R. Henderson	536	.267	10	51	379	2	9	0	2.7	.977	B. Owchinko	54	102	2	4	3	5.21
		C	M. Heath	318	.242	3	39	350	50	11	8	4.6	.973	D. Beard	54	92	10	9	11	3.44
		DH	J. Burroughs	285	.277	16	48													
		C	J. Newman	251	.199	6	30	320	27	4	5	5.2	.989							
		DH	C. Johnson	214	.238	7	31													
		2B	D. McKay	212	.198	4	17	99	116	7	22	3.8	.968							
		1B	J. Rudi	193	.212	5	18	398	20	4	37	8.6	.991							

AMERICAN LEAGUE 1982, *cont.*

Texas

W-64 L-98

Don Zimmer W-38 L-58

Darrell Johnson W-26 L-40

POS	Player	AB	BA	HR	RBI	PO	A	E	DP	TC/G	FA	Pitcher	G	IP	W	L	SV	ERA
1B	D. Hostetler	418	.232	22	67	1099	48	12	102	10.6	.990	C. Hough	34	228	16	13	0	3.95
2B	M. Richardt	402	.241	3	43	234	278	6	68	5.3	.988	F. Tanana	30	194	7	**18**	0	4.21
SS	M. Wagner	179	.240	0	8	77	197	13	32	4.8	.955	R. Honeycutt	30	164	5	17	0	5.27
3B	B. Bell	537	.296	13	67	**131**	396	13	35	**3.7**	**.976**	J. Matlack	33	148	7	7	1	3.53
RF	L. Parrish	440	.264	17	62	190	12	8	4	1.7	.962	D. Medich	21	123	7	11	0	5.06
CF	G. Wright	557	.264	11	50	398	14	8	3	2.8	.981	D. Schmidt	33	110	4	6	6	3.20
LF	B. Sample	360	.261	10	29	196	6	4	1	2.3	.981	S. Comer	37	97	1	6	6	5.10
C	J. Sundberg	470	.251	10	47	607	69	6	**15**	5.2	.991	D. Darwin	56	89	10	8	7	3.44
DH	L. Johnson	324	.259	7	38													
OF	J. Grubb	308	.279	3	26	135	4	5	1	1.9	.965							
2S	D. Flynn	270	.211	0	19	161	254	9	48		.979							
OD	L. Mazzilli	195	.241	4	17	51	1	3	1		.945							
UT	B. Stein	184	.239	1	16	72	122	6	28		.970							

Minnesota

W-60 L-102

Billy Gardner

POS	Player	AB	BA	HR	RBI	PO	A	E	DP	TC/G	FA	Pitcher	G	IP	W	L	SV	ERA
1B	K. Hrbek	532	.301	23	92	1174	88	9	125	9.2	.993	B. Castillo	40	219	13	11	0	3.66
2B	J. Castino	410	.241	6	37	193	228	2	63	4.4	.995	B. Havens	33	209	10	14	0	4.31
SS	R. Washington	451	.271	5	39	127	186	9	38	3.5	.972	A. Williams	26	154	9	7	0	4.22
3B	G. Gaetti	508	.230	25	84	106	286	15	35	2.9	.963	F. Viola	22	126	4	10	0	5.21
RF	T. Brunansky	463	.272	20	46	343	8	5	0	2.8	.986	J. O'Connor	23	126	8	9	0	4.29
CF	B. Mitchell	454	.249	2	28	350	8	1	3	3.0	.997	T. Felton	48	117	0	13	3	4.99
LF	G. Ward	570	.289	28	91	343	13	4	3	2.4	.989	R. Davis	63	106	3	9	22	4.42
C	T. Laudner	306	.255	7	33	454	41	**12**	5	5.5	.976	P. Redfern	27	94	5	11	0	6.58
DH	R. Johnson	234	.248	10	33													
OD	M. Hatcher	277	.249	3	26	78	7	1	0		.988							
SS	L. Faedo	255	.243	3	22	129	218	12	52	4.1	.967							
D1	J. Vega	199	.266	5	29	106	8	3	9		.974							
OD	D. Engle	186	.226	4	16	63	3	1	1		.985							

BATTING AND BASE RUNNING LEADERS

Batting Average
W. Wilson, KC .332
R. Yount, MIL .331
R. Carew, CAL .319
E. Murray, BAL .316
C. Cooper, MIL .313

Slugging Average
R. Yount, MIL .578
D. Winfield, NY .560
E. Murray, BAL .549
D. DeCinces, CAL .548
H. McRae, KC .542

Home Runs
R. Jackson, CAL 39
G. Thomas, MIL 39
D. Winfield, NY 37
B. Oglivie, MIL 34

Total Bases
R. Yount, MIL 367
C. Cooper, MIL 345
H. McRae, KC 332
D. Evans, BOS 325
D. DeCinces, CAL 315

Runs Batted In
H. McRae, KC 133
C. Cooper, MIL 121
A. Thornton, CLE 116
R. Yount, MIL 114
G. Thomas, MIL 112

Stolen Bases
R. Henderson, OAK 130
D. Garcia, TOR 54
J. Cruz, SEA 46
P. Molitor, MIL 41
W. Wilson, KC 37

Hits
R. Yount, MIL 210
C. Cooper, MIL 205
P. Molitor, MIL 201
W. Wilson, KC 194

Base on Balls
R. Henderson, OAK 116
D. Evans, BOS 112
A. Thornton, CLE 109
M. Hargrove, CLE 101

Home Run Percentage
R. Jackson, CAL 7.4
G. Thomas, MIL 6.9
D. Winfield, NY 6.9
L. Parrish, DET 6.6

Runs
P. Molitor, MIL 136
R. Yount, MIL 129
D. Evans, BOS 122
R. Henderson, OAK 119

Doubles
H. McRae, KC 46
R. Yount, MIL 46
F. White, KC 45
D. DeCinces, CAL 42

Triples
W. Wilson, KC 15
L. Herndon, DET 13
R. Yount, MIL 12
J. Mumphrey, NY 10

PITCHING LEADERS

Winning Percentage
J. Palmer, BAL .750
P. Vuckovich, MIL .750
G. Zahn, CAL .692
D. Petry, DET .625
L. Gura, KC .600

Earned Run Average
R. Sutcliffe, CLE 2.96
B. Stanley, BOS 3.10
J. Palmer, BAL 3.13
D. Petry, DET 3.22
D. Stieb, TOR 3.25

Wins
L. Hoyt, CHI 19
P. Vuckovich, MIL 18
G. Zahn, CAL 18
L. Gura, KC 18

Saves
D. Quisenberry, KC 35
G. Gossage, NY 30
R. Fingers, MIL 29
B. Caudill, SEA 26
R. Davis, MIN 22

Strikeouts
F. Bannister, SEA 209
L. Barker, CLE 187
D. Righetti, NY 163
R. Guidry, NY 162
J. Tudor, BOS 146

Complete Games
D. Stieb, TOR 19
J. Morris, DET 17
R. Langford, OAK 15
L. Hoyt, CHI 14

Fewest Hits/9 Innings
R. Sutcliffe, CLE 7.25
J. Ujdur, DET 7.58
D. Righetti, NY 7.62
J. Palmer, BAL 7.73

Shutouts
D. Stieb, TOR 5
G. Zahn, CAL 4
K. Forsch, CAL 4

Fewest Walks/9 Innings
T. John, NY, CAL 1.58
D. Eckersley, BOS 1.73
L. Hoyt, CHI 1.80
M. Haas, MIL 1.82

Most Strikeouts/9 Inn.
D. Righetti, NY 8.02
F. Bannister, SEA 7.62
J. Beattie, SEA 7.31
L. Barker, CLE 6.88

Innings
D. Stieb, TOR 288
J. Clancy, TOR 267
J. Morris, DET 266
M. Caldwell, MIL 258

Games Pitched
E. Vande Berg, SEA 78
T. Martinez, BAL 76
D. Quisenberry, KC 72
B. Caudill, SEA 70

		W	L	PCT	GB	R	OR	Batting						Fielding			Pitching					
								2B	3B	HR	BA	SA	SB	E	DP	FA	CG	BB	SO	ShO	SV	ERA
East	Milwaukee	95	67	.586		**891**	717	277	41	**216**	.279	**.455**	84	125	**184**	.980	34	511	717	6	**47**	3.98
	Baltimore	94	68	.580	1	774	687	259	27	179	.266	.419	49	**101**	140	**.984**	38	488	719	8	34	3.99
	Boston	89	73	.549	6	753	713	271	31	136	.274	.407	42	121	172	.981	23	478	816	11	33	4.03
	Detroit	83	79	.512	12	729	685	237	40	177	.266	.418	93	117	164	.981	**45**	554	740	5	27	**3.80**
	New York	79	83	.488	16	709	716	225	37	161	.256	.398	69	128	157	.979	24	491	939	8	39	3.99
	Cleveland	78	84	.481	17	683	748	225	32	109	.262	.373	151	123	127	.980	31	589	882	9	30	4.11
	Toronto	78	84	.481	17	651	701	262	45	106	.262	.383	118	136	146	.978	41	493	776	**13**	25	3.95
West	California	93	69	.574		814	**670**	268	26	186	.274	.433	55	108	171	.983	40	482	728	10	27	3.82
	Kansas City	90	72	.556	3	784	717	**295**	**58**	132	**.285**	.428	133	127	140	.979	16	471	650	12	45	4.08
	Chicago	87	75	.537	6	786	710	266	52	136	.273	.413	136	154	173	.976	30	**460**	753	10	41	3.87
	Seattle	76	86	.469	17	651	712	259	33	130	.254	.381	131	139	157	.978	23	547	**1002**	11	39	3.88
	Oakland	68	94	.420	25	691	819	211	27	149	.236	.367	**232**	160	135	.974	42	648	697	6	22	4.54
	Texas	64	98	.395	29	590	749	204	26	115	.249	.359	63	121	168	.981	32	483	690	5	24	4.28
	Minnesota	60	102	.370	33	657	819	234	44	148	.257	.396	38	108	162	.982	26	643	812	7	30	4.72
						10163	10163	3493	519	2080	.264	.402	1394	1768	2196	.980	445	7338	10921	121	463	4.07

NATIONAL LEAGUE 1983

East

Philadelphia

W-90 L-72

Pat Corrales
W-43 L-42

Paul Owens
W-47 L-30

POS	Player	AB	BA	HR	RBI	PO	A	E	DP	TC/G	FA	Pitcher	G	IP	W	L	SV	ERA
1B	P. Rose	493	.245	0	45	786	74	9	57	7.8	.990	S. Carlton	37	**284**	15	16	0	3.11
2B	J. Morgan	404	.230	16	59	231	331	17	63	4.9	.971	J. Denny	36	243	**19**	6	0	2.37
SS	I. DeJesus	497	.254	4	45	214	438	23	64	4.3	.966	C. Hudson	26	169	8	8	0	3.35
3B	M. Schmidt	534	.255	**40**	109	107	**332**	19	**29**	3.0	.959	M. Bystrom	24	119	6	9	0	4.60
RF	V. Hayes	351	.265	6	32	165	7	5	0	1.7	.972	K. Gross	17	96	4	6	0	3.56
CF	G. Maddox	324	.275	4	32	216	1	5	0	2.3	.977	R. Reed	61	96	9	1	8	3.48
LF	G. Matthews	446	.258	10	50	174	11	5	2	1.6	.974	G. Hernandez	63	96	8	4	7	3.29
C	B. Diaz	471	.236	15	64	903	97	**14**	7	**7.6**	.986	A. Holland	68	92	8	4	25	2.26
OF	J. Lefebvre	258	.310	8	38	92	4	1	0	1.3	.990							
1B	T. Perez	253	.241	6	43	514	40	1	36	8.0	.998							
OF	G. Gross	245	.302	0	29	104	1	1	0	1.0	.991							
OF	B. Dernier	221	.231	1	15	164	3	2	1	1.6	.988							
C	O. Virgil	140	.214	6	23	228	24	9	2	5.1	.966							

Pittsburgh

W-84 L-78

Chuck Tanner

POS	Player	AB	BA	HR	RBI	PO	A	E	DP	TC/G	FA	Pitcher	G	IP	W	L	SV	ERA
1B	J. Thompson	517	.259	18	76	1266	89	9	131	9.0	.993	R. Rhoden	36	244	13	13	1	3.09
2B	J. Ray	576	.283	5	53	319	452	13	102	5.2	.983	L. McWilliams	35	238	15	8	0	3.25
SS	D. Berra	537	.251	10	52	286	505	30	103	5.1	.963	J. Candelaria	33	198	15	8	0	3.23
3B	B. Madlock	473	**.323**	12	68	59	193	11	20	2.1	.958	L. Tunnell	35	178	11	6	0	3.65
RF	D. Parker	552	.279	12	69	282	3	8	2	2.1	.973	J. DeLeon	15	108	7	3	0	2.83
CF	M. Wynne	366	.243	7	26	223	3	4	2	2.3	.983	C. Guante	49	100	2	6	9	3.32
LF	M. Easler	381	.307	10	54	158	6	6	1	1.6	.965	K. Tekulve	76	99	7	5	18	1.64
C	T. Pena	542	.301	15	70	**976**	90	9	9	7.2	.992	M. Sarmiento	52	84	3	5	4	2.99
OF	L. Lacy	288	.302	4	13	167	2	0	0	1.7	1.000	J. Bibby	29	78	5	12	2	6.69
OF	L. Mazzilli	246	.240	5	24	130	3	2	1	2.4	.985	R. Scurry	61	68	4	9	7	5.56
3B	R. Hebner	162	.265	5	26	16	43	2	1	1.5	.967							
UT	J. Morrison	158	.304	6	25	55	99	7	21		.957							
OF	B. Harper	131	.221	7	20	40	0	0	0	1.1	1.000							

Montreal

W-82 L-80

Bill Virdon

POS	Player	AB	BA	HR	RBI	PO	A	E	DP	TC/G	FA	Pitcher	G	IP	W	L	SV	ERA
1B	A. Oliver	614	.300	8	84	1207	118	**13**	93	8.7	.990	S. Rogers	36	273	17	12	0	3.23
2B	D. Flynn	452	.237	0	26	205	290	7	57	4.7	.986	B. Gullickson	34	242	17	12	0	3.75
SS	C. Speier	261	.257	2	22	107	196	12	31	4.3	.962	C. Lea	33	222	16	11	0	3.12
3B	T. Wallach	581	.269	19	70	**151**	265	19	25	2.8	.956	B. Smith	49	155	6	11	3	2.49
RF	W. Cromartie	360	.278	3	43	208	12	6	2	2.2	.973	R. Burris	40	154	4	7	0	3.68
CF	A. Dawson	633	.299	32	113	435	6	9	2	2.9	.980	J. Reardon	66	92	7	9	21	3.03
LF	T. Raines	615	.298	11	71	307	21	4	3	2.2	.988	S. Sanderson	18	81	6	7	1	4.65
C	G. Carter	541	.270	17	79	847	**107**	5	**14**	6.7	**.995**							
S2	B. Little	350	.260	1	36	181	248	9	44		.979							
O1	T. Francona	230	.257	3	22	172	10	3	10		.984							

St. Louis

W-79 L-83

Whitey Herzog

POS	Player	AB	BA	HR	RBI	PO	A	E	DP	TC/G	FA	Pitcher	G	IP	W	L	SV	ERA
1B	G. Hendrick	529	.318	18	97	819	77	7	72	9.8	.992	J. Andujar	39	225	6	16	1	4.16
2B	T. Herr	313	.323	2	31	178	245	6	60	5.0	.986	J. Stuper	40	198	12	11	1	3.68
SS	O. Smith	552	.243	3	50	**304**	519	21	100	**5.3**	.975	D. LaPoint	37	191	12	9	0	3.95
3B	K. Oberkfell	488	.293	3	38	79	231	13	27	2.5	**.960**	B. Forsch	34	187	10	12	0	4.28
RF	D. Green	422	.284	8	69	214	10	7	2	1.7	.970	N. Allen	25	122	10	6	0	3.70
CF	W. McGee	601	.286	5	75	385	7	5	1	2.7	.987	B. Sutter	60	89	9	10	21	4.23
LF	L. Smith	492	.321	8	45	225	14	15	4	2.0	.941							
C	D. Porter	443	.262	15	66	578	70	7	8	4.9	.989							
O3	A. Van Slyke	309	.262	8	38	132	54	4	3		.979							
1B	K. Hernandez	218	.284	3	26	581*	51	6*	62*	11.8*	.991							
2S	M. Ramsey	175	.263	1	16	91	140	8	31		.967							

Chicago

W-71 L-91

Lee Elia
W-54 L-69

Charlie Fox
W-17 L-22

POS	Player	AB	BA	HR	RBI	PO	A	E	DP	TC/G	FA	Pitcher	G	IP	W	L	SV	ERA
1B	B. Buckner	626	.280	16	66	1366	**161**	**13**	132	10.7	.992	C. Rainey	34	191	14	13	0	4.48
2B	R. Sandberg	633	.261	8	48	330	**571**	13	**126**	**5.8**	**.986**	S. Trout	34	180	10	14	0	4.65
SS	L. Bowa	499	.267	2	43	230	464	11	102	4.9	**.984**	F. Jenkins	33	167	6	9	0	4.30
3B	R. Cey	581	.275	24	90	90	270	17	12	2.4	.955	D. Ruthven	25	149	12	9	0	4.10
RF	K. Moreland	533	.302	16	70	236	7	6	1	1.6	.976	B. Campbell	**82**	122	6	8	8	4.49
CF	M. Hall	410	.283	17	56	239	8	3	2	2.2	.988	D. Noles	24	116	5	10	0	4.72
LF	L. Durham	337	.258	12	55	168	2	6	0	1.9	.966	L. Smith	66	103	4	10	**29**	1.65
C	J. Davis	510	.271	24	84	730	75	13	7	5.5	.984							
OF	G. Woods	190	.242	4	22	97	4	3	0	1.4	.971							
OF	J. Johnstone	140	.257	6	22	55	3	4	1	1.4	.935							

New York

W-68 L-94

George Bamberger
W-16 L-30

Frank Howard
W-52 L-64

POS	Player	AB	BA	HR	RBI	PO	A	E	DP	TC/G	FA	Pitcher	G	IP	W	L	SV	ERA
1B	K. Hernandez	320	.306	9	37	837*	96	7*	85*	10.4*	.993	T. Seaver	34	231	9	14	0	3.55
2B	B. Giles	400	.245	2	27	299	380	14	87	4.9	.980	M. Torrez	39	222	10	**17**	0	4.37
SS	J. Oquendo	328	.213	1	17	182	326	21	65	4.6	.960	E. Lynch	30	175	10	10	0	4.28
3B	H. Brooks	586	.251	5	58	107	289	21	25	2.9	.950	W. Terrell	21	134	8	8	0	3.57
RF	D. Strawberry	420	.257	26	74	232	8	4	0	2.1	.984	J. Orosco	62	110	13	7	17	1.47
CF	M. Wilson	**638**	.276	7	51	422	5	7	1	2.9	.984	D. Sisk	67	104	5	4	11	2.24
LF	G. Foster	601	.241	28	90	314	12	4	3	2.2	.988	S. Holman	35	101	1	7	0	3.74
C	R. Hodges	250	.260	0	21	360	45	12	4	4.3	.971	C. Swan	27	96	2	8	1	5.51
UT	B. Bailor	340	.250	1	30	171	296	16	65		.967	N. Allen	21	54	2	7	2	4.50
OF	D. Heep	253	.253	8	21	90	4	0	1	1.5	1.000							
1B	D. Kingman	248	.198	13	29	443	28	3	43	9.5	.994							
C	J. Ortiz	185	.254	0	12	273	31	11	2	4.7	.965							
PH	R. Staub	115	.296	3	28													

West

Los Angeles

W-91 L-71

Tom Lasorda

POS	Player	AB	BA	HR	RBI	PO	A	E	DP	TC/G	FA	Pitcher	G	IP	W	L	SV	ERA
1B	G. Brock	455	.224	20	66	1162	106	12	94	9.1	.991	F. Valenzuela	35	257	15	10	0	3.75
2B	S. Sax	623	.281	5	41	331	399	**30**	74	5.0	.961	J. Reuss	32	223	12	11	0	2.94
SS	B. Russell	451	.246	1	30	192	392	22	61	4.8	.964	B. Welch	31	204	15	12	0	2.65
3B	P. Guerrero	584	.298	32	103	123	305	**30**	22	2.9	.934	A. Pena	34	177	12	9	1	2.75
RF	M. Marshall	465	.284	17	65	160	3	4	1	1.5	.976	B. Hooton	33	160	9	8	0	4.22
CF	K. Landreaux	481	.281	17	66	299	4	3	1	2.2	.990	T. Niedenfuer	66	95	8	3	11	1.90
LF	D. Baker	531	.260	15	73	249	4	5	2	1.8	.981	D. Stewart	46	76	5	2	8	2.96
C	S. Yeager	335	.203	15	41	579	63	10	10	5.8	.985	S. Howe	46	69	4	7	18	1.44
OF	D. Thomas	192	.250	2	8	97	3	1	0	1.2	.990							
OF	R. Monday	178	.247	6	20	62	1	2	0	1.5	.969							
C	J. Fimple	148	.250	2	22	336	32	4	2	6.9	.989							

NATIONAL LEAGUE 1983, *cont.*

Team	POS	Player	AB	BA	HR	RBI	PO	A	E	DP	TC/G	FA	Pitcher	G	IP	W	L	SV	ERA
Atlanta	1B	C. Chambliss	447	.280	20	78	1092	89	5	117	9.4	.996	C. McMurtry	36	225	15	9	0	3.08
W-88 L-74	2B	G. Hubbard	517	.263	12	70	313	484	12	103	5.5	.985	P. Perez	33	215	15	8	0	3.43
Joe Torre	SS	R. Ramirez	622	.297	7	58	232	490	**39**	**116**	5.0	.949	P. Niekro	34	202	11	10	0	3.97
	3B	B. Horner	386	.303	20	68	76	153	10	18	2.3	.958	R. Camp	40	140	10	9	0	3.79
	RF	C. Washington	496	.278	9	44	218	8	6	3	1.8	.974	S. Bedrosian	70	120	9	10	19	3.60
	CF	D. Murphy	589	.302	36	**121**	373	10	6	0	2.4	.985	P. Falcone	33	107	9	4	0	3.63
	LF	B. Butler	549	.281	5	37	284	13	4	4	2.1	.987	K. Dayley	24	105	5	8	0	4.30
	C	B. Benedict	423	.298	2	43	738	91	7	12	6.2	.992	T. Forster	56	79	3	2	13	2.16
	UT	J. Royster	268	.235	3	30	112	156	10	29		.964	D. Moore	43	69	2	3	6	3.67
	OF	T. Harper	201	.264	3	26	95	5	5	0	1.8	.952	G. Garber	43	61	4	5	9	4.60
	1B	B. Watson	149	.309	6	37	280	19	5	23	8.9	.984							
Houston	1B	R. Knight	507	.304	9	70	1285	73	9	131	9.6	.993	J. Niekro	38	264	15	14	0	3.48
W-85 L-77	2B	B. Doran	535	.271	8	39	**347**	461	17	109	5.4	.979	B. Knepper	35	203	6	13	0	3.19
Bob Lillis	SS	D. Thon	619	.286	20	79	258	**533**	28	114	5.3	.966	N. Ryan	29	196	14	9	0	2.98
	3B	P. Garner	567	.238	14	79	100	311	24	22	2.8	.945	M. Scott	24	145	10	6	0	3.72
	RF	T. Puhl	465	.292	8	44	220	4	2	1	1.8	.991	M. LaCoss	38	138	5	7	1	4.43
	CF	O. Moreno	405	.242	0	25	251	8	6	3	2.7	.977	V. Ruhle	41	115	8	5	3	3.69
	LF	J. Cruz	594	.318	14	92	322	9	7	1	2.1	.979	M. Madden	28	95	9	5	0	3.14
	C	A. Ashby	275	.229	8	34	435	56	13	2	5.9	.974	B. Dawley	48	80	6	6	14	2.82
	OF	K. Bass	195	.236	2	18	68	1	4	1	1.4	.945	D. Smith	42	73	3	1	6	3.10
	OF	T. Scott	186	.226	2	17	89	2	0	1	1.5	1.000	F. DiPino	53	71	3	4	20	2.65
													F. LaCorte	37	53	4	4	3	5.06
San Diego	1B	S. Garvey	388	.294	14	59	888	49	6	69	9.4	.994	E. Show	35	201	15	12	0	4.17
W-81 L-81	2B	J. Bonilla	556	.237	4	45	335	414	11	90	5.1	.986	D. Dravecky	28	184	14	10	0	3.58
Dick Williams	SS	G. Templeton	460	.263	3	40	219	355	24	66	4.9	.960	T. Lollar	30	176	7	12	0	4.61
	3B	L. Salazar	481	.258	14	45	102	250	19	17	**3.1**	.949	E. Whitson	31	144	5	7	1	4.30
	RF	S. Lezcano	317	.233	8	49	171	8	6	1	2.0	.968	A. Hawkins	21	120	5	7	0	2.93
	CF	R. Jones	335	.233	12	49	249	3	5	2	2.3	.981	M. Thurmond	21	115	7	3	0	2.65
	LF	A. Wiggins	503	.276	0	22	242	6	2	1	2.4	.992	L. DeLeon	63	111	6	6	13	2.68
	C	T. Kennedy	549	.284	17	98	782	79	12	8	6.1	.986	J. Montefusco	31	95	9	4	4	3.30
	OF	T. Gwynn	304	.309	1	37	163	9	1	1	2.1	.994	G. Lucas	62	91	5	8	17	2.87
	OF	G. Richards	233	.275	3	22	96	2	2	0	1.9	.980	S. Monge	47	69	7	3	7	3.15
	OF	B. Brown	225	.267	5	22	103	1	4	0	2.0	.963							
	32	T. Flannery	214	.234	3	19	58	148	4	19		.981							
	UT	K. Bevacqua	156	.244	2	24	207	28	2	16		.992							
San Francisco	1B	D. Evans	523	.277	30	82	979	88	7	60	9.5	.993	F. Breining	32	203	11	12	0	3.82
W-79 L-83	2B	B. Wellman	182	.214	1	16	91	160	9	26	3.5	.965	M. Krukow	31	184	11	11	0	3.95
Frank Robinson	SS	J. LeMaster	534	.240	6	30	215	402	23	58	4.6	.964	A. Hammaker	23	172	10	9	0	**2.25**
	3B	T. O'Malley	410	.259	5	45	70	213	18	12	2.6	.940	B. Laskey	25	148	13	10	0	4.19
	RF	J. Clark	492	.268	20	66	249	17	9	3	2.1	.967	A. McGaffigan	43	134	3	9	2	4.29
	CF	C. Davis	486	.233	11	59	357	7	9	1	2.8	.976	M. Davis	20	111	6	4	0	3.49
	LF	J. Leonard	516	.279	21	87	253	17	7	2	2.0	.975	G. Minton	73	107	7	11	22	3.54
	C	B. Brenly	281	.224	7	34	403	70	8	9	5.3	.983	J. Barr	53	93	5	3	2	3.98
	UT	J. Youngblood	373	.292	17	53	147	182	19	28		.945	G. Lavelle	56	87	7	4	20	2.59
	OF	M. Venable	228	.219	6	27	141	5	1	0	2.2	.993							
	C	M. May	186	.247	6	20	285	32	6	5	5.8	.981							
	2B	D. Kuiper	176	.250	0	14	107	140	3	17	3.9	.988							
	1B	D. Bergman	140	.286	6	24	291	27	2	20	6.4	.994							
Cincinnati	1B	D. Driessen	386	.277	12	57	917	71	4	73	8.9	**.996**	M. Soto	34	274	17	13	0	2.70
W-74 L-88	2B	R. Oester	549	.264	11	58	315	413	17	80	4.8	.977	B. Berenyi	32	186	9	14	0	3.86
Russ Nixon	SS	D. Concepcion	528	.233	1	47	225	376	13	67	4.4	.979	F. Pastore	36	184	9	12	0	4.88
	3B	N. Esasky	302	.265	12	46	53	133	13	11	2.4	.935	J. Price	21	144	10	6	0	2.88
	RF	P. Householder	380	.255	6	43	221	5	2	0	2.0	.991	C. Puleo	27	144	6	12	0	4.89
	CF	E. Milner	502	.261	9	33	392	9	4	0	2.9	.990	T. Power	49	111	5	6	2	4.54
	LF	G. Redus	453	.247	17	51	235	11	7	0	2.1	.972	B. Scherrer	73	92	2	3	10	2.74
	C	D. Bilardello	298	.238	9	38	494	72	5	4	5.4	.991	R. Gale	33	90	4	6	1	5.82
	OF	C. Cedeno	332	.232	9	39	138	5	1	1	2.0	.993	B. Hayes	60	69	4	6	7	6.49
	31	J. Bench	310	.255	12	54	275	72	9	26		.975	T. Hume	48	66	3	5	9	4.77
	OF	D. Walker	225	.236	2	29	104	4	5	0	1.9	.956							
	C	A. Trevino	167	.216	1	13	359	28	5	2	6.2	.987							

BATTING AND BASE RUNNING LEADERS

Batting Average		Slugging Average		Home Runs	
B. Madlock, PIT	.323	D. Murphy, ATL	.540	M. Schmidt, PHI	40
L. Smith, STL	.321	A. Dawson, MON	.539	D. Murphy, ATL	36
J. Cruz, HOU	.318	P. Guerrero, LA	.531	P. Guerrero, LA	32
G. Hendrick, STL	.318	M. Schmidt, PHI	.524	A. Dawson, MON	32
R. Knight, HOU	.304	D. Evans, SF	.516	D. Evans, SF	30

Total Bases		Runs Batted In		Stolen Bases	
A. Dawson, MON	341	D. Murphy, ATL	121	T. Raines, MON	90
D. Murphy, ATL	318	A. Dawson, MON	113	A. Wiggins, SD	66
P. Guerrero, LA	310	M. Schmidt, PHI	109	S. Sax, LA	56
D. Thon, HOU	283	P. Guerrero, LA	103	M. Wilson, NY	54
M. Schmidt, PHI	280	T. Kennedy, SD	98	L. Smith, STL	43

PITCHING LEADERS

Winning Percentage		Earned Run Average		Wins	
J. Denny, PHI	.760	A. Hammaker, SF	2.25	J. Denny, PHI	19
L. McWilliams, PIT	.652	J. Denny, PHI	2.37	B. Gullickson, MON	17
P. Perez, ATL	.652	B. Welch, LA	2.65	S. Rogers, MON	17
J. Candelaria, PIT	.652	M. Soto, CIN	2.70	M. Soto, CIN	17
C. McMurtry, ATL	.625	A. Pena, LA	2.75	C. Lea, MON	16

Saves		Strikeouts		Complete Games	
L. Smith, CHI	29	S. Carlton, PHI	275	M. Soto, CIN	18
A. Holland, PHI	25	M. Soto, CIN	242	S. Rogers, MON	13
G. Minton, SF	22	L. McWilliams, PIT	199	B. Gullickson, MON	10
J. Reardon, MON	21	F. Valenzuela, LA	189	D. Dravecky, SD	9
B. Sutter, STL	21	N. Ryan, HOU	183	F. Valenzuela, LA	9
				J. Niekro, HOU	9

NATIONAL LEAGUE 1983, *cont.*

BATTING AND BASE RUNNING LEADERS

Hits		Base on Balls		Home Run Percentage	
J. Cruz, HOU	189	M. Schmidt, PHI	128	M. Schmidt, PHI	7.5
A. Dawson, MON	189	J. Thompson, PIT	99	D. Murphy, ATL	6.1
R. Ramirez, ATL	185	T. Raines, MON	97	D. Evans, SF	5.7
A. Oliver, MON	184	D. Murphy, ATL	90	P. Guerrero, LA	5.5

Runs		Doubles		Triples	
T. Raines, MON	133	J. Ray, PIT	38	B. Butler, ATL	13
D. Murphy, ATL	131	A. Oliver, MON	38	O. Moreno, HOU	11
M. Schmidt, PHI	104	B. Buckner, CHI	38	D. Green, STL	10
A. Dawson, MON	104	G. Carter, MON	37	A. Dawson, MON	10

PITCHING LEADERS

Fewest Hits/9 Innings		Shutouts		Fewest Walks/9 Innings	
N. Ryan, HOU	6.14	S. Rogers, MON	5	A. Hammaker, SF	1.67
M. Soto, CIN	6.81	C. Lea, MON	4	D. Ruthven, PHI, CHI	1.87
B. Welch, LA	7.24	L. McWilliams, PIT	4	J. Denny, PHI	1.97
A. Hammaker, SF	7.68	F. Valenzuela, LA	4	J. Reuss, LA	2.01

Most Strikeouts/9 Inn.		Innings		Games Pitched	
S. Carlton, PHI	8.73	S. Carlton, PHI	284	B. Campbell, CHI	82
N. Ryan, HOU	8.39	M. Soto, CIN	274	K. Tekulve, PIT	76
M. Soto, CIN	7.96	S. Rogers, MON	273	G. Hernandez, CHI, PHI	74
L. McWilliams, PIT	7.53	J. Niekro, HOU	264	G. Minton, SF	73
				B. Scherrer, CIN	73

		W	L	PCT	GB	R	OR	Batting 2B	3B	HR	BA	SA	SB	Fielding E	DP	FA	Pitching CG	BB	SO	ShO	SV	ERA
East	Philadelphia	90	72	.556		696	635	209	45	125	.249	.373	143	152	117	.976	20	**464**	**1092**	10	41	3.34
	Pittsburgh	84	78	.519	6	659	648	238	29	121	.264	.383	124	115	165	**.982**	25	563	1061	14	41	3.55
	Montreal	82	80	.506	8	677	646	**297**	41	102	.264	.386	138	116	130	.981	**38**	479	899	**15**	34	3.58
	St. Louis	79	83	.488	11	679	710	262	**63**	83	.270	.384	**207**	152	173	.976	22	525	709	10	27	3.79
	Chicago	71	91	.438	19	701	719	272	42	140	.261	**.401**	84	115	164	**.982**	9	498	807	10	42	4.07
	New York	68	94	.420	22	575	680	172	26	112	.241	.344	141	151	171	.976	18	615	717	7	33	3.68
West	Los Angeles	91	71	.562		654	**609**	197	34	**146**	.250	.379	166	168	132	.974	27	495	1000	12	40	**3.10**
	Atlanta	88	74	.543	3	**746**	640	218	45	130	**.272**	.400	146	137	**176**	.978	18	540	895	4	**48**	3.67
	Houston	85	77	.525	6	643	646	239	60	97	.257	.375	164	147	165	.977	22	570	904	14	**48**	3.45
	San Diego	81	81	.500	10	653	653	207	34	93	.250	.351	179	129	135	.979	23	528	850	5	44	3.62
	San Francisco	79	83	.488	12	687	697	206	30	142	.247	.375	140	171	109	.973	20	520	881	9	47	3.70
	Cincinnati	74	88	.457	17	623	710	236	35	107	.239	.356	154	**114**	121	.981	34	627	934	5	29	3.98
						7993	7993	2753	484	1398	.255	.376	1786	1667	1758	.978	276	6424	10749	115	474	3.63

AMERICAN LEAGUE 1983

East

Baltimore

W-98 L-64

Joe Altobelli

POS	Player	AB	BA	HR	RBI	PO	A	E	DP	TC/G	FA	Pitcher	G	IP	W	L	SV	ERA
1B	E. Murray	582	.306	33	111	1393	114	10	136	**9.9**	.993	S. McGregor	36	260	18	7	0	3.18
2B	R. Dauer	459	.235	5	41	273	322	7	78	4.6	.988	S. Davis	34	200	13	7	0	3.59
SS	C. Ripken	**663**	.318	27	102	272	**534**	25	**113**	**5.1**	.970	M. Boddicker	27	179	16	8	0	2.77
3B	T. Cruz	221	.208	3	27	49	162	13	19	2.8	.942	D. Martinez	32	153	7	16	0	5.53
RF	D. Ford	407	.280	9	55	218	2	3	0	2.2	.987	S. Stewart	58	144	9	4	7	3.62
CF	J. Shelby	325	.258	5	27	200	9	4	3	1.9	.981	M. Flanagan	20	125	12	4	0	3.30
LF	J. Lowenstein	310	.281	15	60	155	8	3	1	1.6	.982	T. Martinez	65	103	9	3	21	2.35
C	R. Dempsey	347	.231	4	32	591	65	2	7	5.1	**.997**	T. Stoddard	47	58	4	3	9	6.09
DH	K. Singleton	507	.276	18	84													
OF	A. Bumbry	378	.275	3	31	235	3	3	1	2.3	.988							
OF	G. Roenicke	323	.260	19	64	159	7	3	0	1.7	.982							
3B	L. Hernandez	203	.246	6	26	44	109	13	3	2.6	.922							
OF	J. Dwyer	196	.286	8	38	85	1	3	1	1.6	.966							
C	J. Nolan	184	.277	5	24	223	16	5	2	3.8	.980							

Detroit

W-92 L-70

Sparky Anderson

POS	Player	AB	BA	HR	RBI	PO	A	E	DP	TC/G	FA	Pitcher	G	IP	W	L	SV	ERA
1B	E. Cabell	392	.311	5	46	830	79	3	76	8.6	.997	J. Morris	37	**294**	20	13	0	3.34
2B	L. Whitaker	643	.320	12	72	299	447	13	92	4.7	.983	D. Petry	38	266	19	11	0	3.92
SS	A. Trammell	505	.319	14	66	236	367	13	71	4.4	.979	M. Wilcox	26	186	11	10	0	3.97
3B	T. Brookens	332	.214	6	32	54	164	17	21	2.3	.928	J. Berenguer	37	158	9	5	1	3.14
RF	G. Wilson	503	.268	11	65	225	12	3	2	1.7	.988	A. Lopez	57	115	9	8	18	2.81
CF	C. Lemon	491	.255	24	69	406	6	5	3	2.9	.988	D. Rozema	29	105	8	3	2	3.43
LF	L. Herndon	603	.302	20	92	283	6	15	1	2.3	.951	H. Bailey	33	72	5	5	0	4.88
C	L. Parrish	605	.269	27	114	695	73	4	8	**5.9**	.995	D. Bair	27	56	7	3	4	3.88
DH	K. Gibson	401	.227	15	51													
UT	J. Wockenfuss	245	.269	9	44	225	21	2	10		.992							
1B	R. Leach	242	.248	3	26	447	45	3	37	6.8	.994							
OD	J. Grubb	134	.254	4	22	34	1	0	0		1.000							

New York

W-91 L-71

Billy Martin

POS	Player	AB	BA	HR	RBI	PO	A	E	DP	TC/G	FA	Pitcher	G	IP	W	L	SV	ERA
1B	K. Griffey	458	.306	11	46	830	57	7	82	8.9	.992	R. Guidry	31	250	21	9	0	3.42
2B	W. Randolph	420	.279	2	38	265	298	12	77	5.5	.979	S. Rawley	34	238	14	14	1	3.78
SS	R. Smalley	451	.275	18	62	125	230	15	40	4.1	.959	D. Righetti	31	217	14	8	0	3.44
3B	G. Nettles	462	.266	20	75	78	273	16	18	2.9	.956	G. Frazier	61	115	4	4	8	3.43
RF	S. Kemp	373	.241	12	49	215	5	3	3	2.2	.987	B. Shirley	25	108	5	8	0	5.08
CF	J. Mumphrey	267	.262	7	36	227	7	4	1	2.9	.983	R. Fontenot	15	97	8	2	0	3.33
LF	D. Winfield	598	.283	32	116	313	5	7	2	2.2	.978	G. Gossage	57	87	13	5	22	2.27
C	B. Wynegar	301	.296	6	42	480	29	8	4	5.6	.985							
DH	D. Baylor	534	.303	21	85													
SS	A. Robertson	322	.248	1	22	91	242	14	49	4.4	.960							
01	D. Mattingly	279	.283	4	32	350	15	3	31		.992							
C	R. Cerone	246	.220	2	22	412	18	4	2	5.6	.991							
OD	O. Gamble	180	.261	7	26	64	1	4	1		.942							

AMERICAN LEAGUE 1983, *cont.*

Toronto

W-89 L-73

Bobby Cox

POS	Player	AB	BA	HR	RBI	PO	A	E	DP	TC/G	FA	Pitcher	G	IP	W	L	SV	ERA
1B	W. Upshaw	579	.306	27	104	1294	117	**21**	131	9.0	.985	D. Stieb	36	278	17	12	0	3.04
2B	D. Garcia	525	.307	3	38	266	360	12	75	4.9	.981	J. Clancy	34	223	15	11	0	3.91
SS	A. Griffin	528	.250	4	47	**280**	413	25	84	4.6	.965	L. Leal	35	217	13	12	0	4.31
3B	R. Mulliniks	364	.275	10	49	70	161	7	12	2.1	.971	J. Gott	34	177	9	14	0	4.74
RF	J. Barfield	388	.253	27	68	213	16	8	4	2.0	.966	D. Alexander	17	117	7	6	0	3.93
CF	L. Moseby	539	.315	18	81	399	10	7	1	2.8	.983	R. Jackson	49	92	8	3	7	4.50
LF	D. Collins	402	.271	1	34	251	8	3	1	2.3	.989	J. McLaughlin	50	65	7	4	9	4.45
C	E. Whitt	344	.256	17	56	554	50	5	4	5.1	.992	R. Moffitt	45	57	6	2	10	3.77
DH	C. Johnson	407	.265	22	76													
OF	B. Bonnell	377	.318	10	54	212	7	3	0	1.9	.986							
32	G. Iorg	375	.275	2	39	105	223	9	31		.973							
DH	J. Orta	245	.237	10	38													
C	B. Martinez	221	.253	10	33	331	25	4	3	4.2	.989							

Milwaukee

W-87 L-75

Harvey Kuenn

POS	Player	AB	BA	HR	RBI	PO	A	E	DP	TC/G	FA	Pitcher	G	IP	W	L	SV	ERA
1B	C. Cooper	661	.307	30	**126**	**1452**	87	11	**144**	9.8	.993	M. Caldwell	32	228	12	11	0	4.53
2B	J. Gantner	603	.282	11	74	374	**512**	14	**128**	5.7	.984	D. Sutton	31	220	8	13	0	4.08
SS	R. Yount	578	.308	17	80	256	420	19	86	5.0	.973	M. Haas	25	179	13	3	0	3.27
3B	P. Molitor	608	.270	15	47	105	343	16	37	3.2	.966	B. McClure	24	142	9	9	0	4.50
RF	C. Moore	529	.284	2	49	301	9	7	1	2.1	.978	C. Porter	25	134	7	9	0	4.50
CF	R. Manning	375	.229	3	33	325	1	3	0	3.0	.991	J. Slaton	46	112	14	6	5	4.33
LF	B. Oglivie	411	.280	13	66	259	8	4	1	2.4	.985	T. Tellmann	44	100	9	4	8	2.80
C	T. Simmons	600	.308	13	108	395	41	11	4	5.2	.975	P. Ladd	44	49	3	4	25	2.55
DH	R. Howell	194	.278	4	25													
C	N. Yost	196	.224	6	28	252	16	8	2	4.5	.971							
OF	M. Brouhard	185	.276	7	23	112	1	1	0	2.7	.991							
OF	G. Thomas	164	.183	5	18	126	0	1	0	2.8	.992							

Boston

W-78 L-84

Ralph Houk

POS	Player	AB	BA	HR	RBI	PO	A	E	DP	TC/G	FA	Pitcher	G	IP	W	L	SV	ERA
1B	D. Stapleton	542	.247	10	66	1242	95	9	129	9.3	.993	J. Tudor	34	242	13	12	0	4.09
2B	J. Remy	592	.275	0	43	295	376	7	104	4.7	.990	B. Hurst	33	211	12	12	0	4.09
SS	G. Hoffman	473	.260	4	41	240	417	26	82	4.8	.962	D. Eckersley	28	176	9	13	0	5.61
3B	W. Boggs	582	**.361**	5	74	118	368	**27**	40	3.4	.947	B. Ojeda	29	174	12	7	0	4.04
RF	D. Evans	470	.238	22	58	222	6	3	1	2.3	.987	B. Stanley	64	145	8	10	33	2.85
CF	T. Armas	574	.218	36	107	326	5	5	0	2.9	.985	M. Brown	19	104	6	6	0	4.67
LF	J. Rice	626	.305	**39**	**126**	339	21	6	5	2.4	.984	O. Boyd	15	99	4	8	0	3.28
C	G. Allenson	230	.230	3	30	393	29	7	6	5.1	.984	M. Clear	48	96	4	5	4	6.28
DH	C. Yastrzemski	380	.266	10	56							L. Aponte	34	62	5	4	3	3.63
OF	R. Nichols	274	.285	6	22	168	4	1	1	2.4	.994							
OF	R. Miller	262	.286	2	21	141	4	1	1	2.2	.993							
C	R. Gedman	204	.294	2	18	274	26	6	5	4.4	.980							

Cleveland

W-70 L-92

Mike Ferraro
W-40 L-60

Pat Corrales
W-30 L-32

POS	Player	AB	BA	HR	RBI	PO	A	E	DP	TC/G	FA	Pitcher	G	IP	W	L	SV	ERA
1B	M. Hargrove	469	.286	3	57	1098	115	7	131	9.3	.994	R. Sutcliffe	36	243	17	11	0	4.29
2B	M. Trillo	320	.272	1	29	172	269	5	58	5.1	.989	L. Sorensen	36	223	12	11	0	4.24
SS	J. Franco	560	.273	8	80	247	438	28	92	4.8	.961	B. Blyleven	24	156	7	10	0	3.91
3B	T. Harrah	526	.266	9	53	101	273	11	32	2.8	**.971**	L. Barker	24	150	8	13	0	5.11
RF	G. Vukovich	312	.247	3	44	203	3	3	0	1.7	.986	N. Heaton	39	149	11	7	7	4.16
CF	G. Thomas	371	.221	17	51	313	7	6	2	3.1	.982	J. Eichelberger	28	134	4	11	0	4.90
LF	P. Tabler	430	.291	6	65	180	4	10	C	2.4	.948	D. Spillner	60	92	2	9	8	5.07
C	R. Hassey	341	.270	6	42	514	43	3	4	5.0	.995	B. Anderson	39	68	1	6	7	4.08
DH	A. Thornton	508	.281	17	77													
OF	A. Bannister	377	.265	5	45	148	7	5	2	1.8	.969							
OF	B. McBride	230	.291	1	18	81	4	2	1	1.9	.977							
2B	M. Fischlin	225	.209	2	23	151	179	12	46	4.8	.965							
OF	R. Manning	194	.278	1	10	146*	1	2	0	3.0	.987							
UT	B. Perkins	184	.272	0	24	148	6	2	12		.987							

West

Chicago

W-99 L-63

Tony LaRussa

POS	Player	AB	BA	HR	RBI	PO	A	E	DP	TC/G	FA	Pitcher	G	IP	W	L	SV	ERA
1B	M. Squires	153	.222	1	11	515	40	2	55	4.5	**.996**	L. Hoyt	36	261	**24**	10	0	3.66
2B	J. Cruz	334	.251	1	40	213	298	9	71	5.4	.983	R. Dotson	35	240	22	7	0	3.23
SS	J. Dybzinski	256	.230	1	32	140	252	14	47	3.4	.966	F. Bannister	34	217	16	10	0	3.35
3B	V. Law	408	.243	4	42	91	309	14	28	3.0	.966	B. Burns	29	174	10	11	0	3.58
RF	H. Baines	596	.280	20	99	312	10	9	3	2.1	.973	J. Koosman	37	170	11	7	2	4.77
CF	R. Law	501	.283	3	34	302	5	2	2	2.3	.994	D. Lamp	49	116	7	7	15	3.71
LF	R. Kittle	520	.254	35	100	234	7	9	0	1.8	.964	D. Tidrow	50	92	2	4	7	4.22
C	C. Fisk	488	.289	26	86	**709**	46	7	5	5.7	.991	S. Barojas	52	87	3	3	12	2.47
DH	G. Luzinski	502	.255	32	95							J. Agosto	39	42	2	2	7	4.10
10	T. Paciorek	420	.307	9	63	629	38	1	42		.999							
1B	G. Walker	307	.270	10	55	426	19	7	40	7.7	.985							
SS	S. Fletcher	262	.237	3	31	107	275	14	52	4.0	.965							
2B	T. Bernazard	233	.262	2	26	96	189	7	38	4.9	.976							
OF	J. Hairston	126	.294	5	22	29	1	1	0	1.0	.968							

Kansas City

W-79 L-83

Dick Howser

POS	Player	AB	BA	HR	RBI	PO	A	E	DP	TC/G	FA	Pitcher	G	IP	W	L	SV	ERA
1B	W. Aikens	410	.302	23	72	884	64	11	101	8.6	.989	L. Gura	34	200	11	**18**	0	4.90
2B	F. White	549	.260	11	77	**390**	442	8	123	5.8	**.990**	B. Black	24	161	10	7	0	3.79
SS	U. Washington	547	.236	5	41	201	448	**36**	91	4.9	.947	P. Splittorff	27	156	13	8	0	3.63
3B	G. Brett	464	.310	25	93	85	188	24	25	2.9	.919	D. Quisenberry	**69**	139	5	3	**45**	1.94
RF	P. Sheridan	333	.270	7	36	237	6	3	2	2.5	.988	S. Renko	25	121	6	11	1	4.30
CF	A. Otis	356	.261	4	41	233	6	1	1	2.5	.996	M. Armstrong	58	103	10	7	3	3.86
LF	W. Wilson	576	.276	2	33	354	3	9	0	2.7	.975							
C	J. Wathan	437	.245	2	32	360	32	6	5	4.3	.985							
DH	H. McRae	589	.311	12	82													
C	D. Slaught	276	.312	0	28	299	18	12	7	4.2	.964							
UT	O. Concepcion	219	.242	0	20	92	175	15	35		.947							
OF	L. Roberts	213	.258	8	24	139	3	3	0	1.9	.979							

AMERICAN LEAGUE 1983, *cont.*

Team	POS	Player	AB	BA	HR	RBI	PO	A	E	DP	TC/G	FA	Pitcher	G	IP	W	L	SV	ERA
Texas	1B	P. O'Brien	524	.237	8	53	1144	**120**	9	104	9.6	.993	C. Hough	34	252	15	13	0	3.18
W-77 L-85	2B	W. Tolleson	470	.260	3	20	246	315	16	69	5.2	.972	M. Smithson	33	223	10	14	0	3.91
Doug Rader	SS	B. Dent	417	.237	2	34	150	369	11	71	4.1	**.979**	D. Darwin	28	183	8	13	0	3.49
	3B	B. Bell	618	.277	14	66	123	**383**	17	29	**3.4**	.967	R. Honeycutt	25	175	14	8	0	2.42*
	RF	L. Parrish	555	.272	26	88	215	11	9	1	1.8	.962	F. Tanana	29	159	7	9	0	3.16
	CF	G. Wright	634	.276	18	80	460	6	7	1	2.9	.985	J. Butcher	36	123	6	6	5	3.51
	LF	B. Sample	554	.274	12	57	329	8	4	0	2.3	.988	O. Jones	42	67	3	6	10	3.09
	C	J. Sundberg	378	.201	2	28	618	56	5	2	5.2	.993	D. Tobik	27	44	2	1	9	3.68
	DH	D. Hostetler	304	.220	11	46													
	DO	M. Rivers	309	.285	1	20	48	1	1	0		.980							
	UT	B. Stein	232	.310	2	33	222	103	5	40		.985							
	C	B. Johnson	175	.211	5	16	252	15	0	4	4.3	1.000							
Oakland	1B	W. Gross	339	.233	12	44	426	21	2	41	6.1	.996	C. Codiroli	37	206	12	12	1	4.46
W-74 L-88	2B	D. Lopes	494	.277	17	67	254	278	9	81	4.4	.983	S. McCatty	38	167	6	9	5	3.99
Steve Boros	SS	T. Phillips	412	.248	4	35	112	257	23	59	3.9	.941	T. Conroy	39	162	7	10	0	3.94
	3B	C. Lansford	299	.308	10	45	60	163	10	19	3.0	.957	T. Underwood	51	145	9	7	4	4.04
	RF	M. Davis	443	.275	8	62	278	16	8	4	2.5	.974	B. Krueger	17	110	7	6	0	3.61
	CF	D. Murphy	471	.227	17	75	365	7	8	0	3.1	.979	T. Burgmeier	49	96	6	7	4	2.81
	LF	R. Henderson	513	.292	9	48	349	9	3	1	2.5	.992	K. Atherton	29	68	2	5	4	2.77
	C	B. Kearney	298	.255	8	32	437	41	9	5	4.8	.982	D. Beard	43	61	5	5	10	5.61
	DH	J. Burroughs	401	.269	10	56							S. Baker	35	54	3	3	5	4.33
	UT	B. Almon	451	.266	4	63	327	176	20	33		.962							
	C	M. Heath	345	.281	6	33	316	47	10	6	4.7	.973							
	01	G. Hancock	256	.273	8	30	249	10	4	17		.985							
	OF	R. Peters	178	.287	0	20	141	3	2	1	3.1	.986							
	UT	D. Meyer	169	.189	1	13	305	16	4	28		.988							
California	1B	R. Carew	472	.339	2	44	890	42	6	94	10.5	.994	T. John	34	235	11	13	0	4.33
W-70 L-92	2B	B. Grich	387	.292	16	62	270	415	**22**	94	**6.0**	.969	K. Forsch	31	219	11	12	0	4.06
John McNamara	SS	T. Foli	330	.252	2	29	115	274	10	51	5.4	.975	G. Zahn	29	203	9	11	0	3.33
	3B	D. DeCinces	370	.281	18	65	79	216	14	26	3.7	.955	M. Witt	43	154	7	14	5	4.91
	RF	E. Valentine	271	.240	13	43	152	5	6	1	1.9	.963	B. Kison	26	127	11	5	2	4.05
	CF	F. Lynn	437	.272	22	74	274	8	2	4	2.5	.993	L. Sanchez	56	98	10	8	7	3.66
	LF	B. Downing	403	.246	19	53	160	9	1	0	2.0	.994							
	C	B. Boone	468	.256	9	52	606	**83**	**14**	**12**	5.0	.980							
	DH	R. Jackson	397	.194	14	49													
	UT	R. Jackson	348	.230	8	39	402	114	13	43		.975							
	OF	J. Beniquez	315	.305	3	34	174	8	6	1	2.2	.968							
	1D	D. Sconiers	314	.274	8	46	473	23	7	46		.986							
	OF	B. Clark	212	.231	5	21	122	0	0	0	1.7	1.000							
	UT	R. Wilfong	177	.254	2	17	107	144	2	33		.992							
Minnesota	1B	K. Hrbek	515	.297	16	84	1151	89	13	125	9.1	.990	F. Viola	35	210	7	15	0	5.49
W-70 L-92	2B	J. Castino	563	.277	11	57	301	406	7	94	5.4	.990	K. Schrom	33	196	15	8	0	3.71
Billy Gardner	SS	R. Washington	317	.246	4	26	121	204	13	49	4.2	.962	A. Williams	36	193	11	14	1	4.14
	3B	G. Gaetti	584	.245	21	78	**131**	360	17	**46**	3.3	.967	B. Castillo	27	158	8	12	0	4.77
	RF	T. Brunansky	542	.227	28	82	375	16	6	8	2.7	.985	R. Lysander	61	125	5	12	3	3.38
	CF	D. Brown	309	.272	0	22	188	2	1	0	2.4	.995	R. Davis	66	89	5	8	30	3.34
	LF	G. Ward	623	.278	19	88	374	24	9	6	2.7	.978	B. Havens	16	80	5	8	0	8.18
	C	D. Engle	374	.305	8	43	299	26	9	3	4.6	.973	L. Whitehouse	60	74	7	1	2	4.15
	DH	R. Bush	373	.249	11	56													
	OD	M. Hatcher	375	.317	9	47	137	4	3	1		.979							
	SS	L. Faedo	173	.277	1	18	53	133	9	22	3.8	.954							
	C	T. Laudner	168	.185	6	18	259	22	4	5	5.0	.986							
Seattle	1B	P. Putnam	469	.269	19	67	1067	85	7	105	9.3	.994	M. Young	33	204	11	15	0	3.27
W-60 L-102	2B	T. Bernazard	300	.267	6	30	166	233	12	51	5.2	.971	J. Beattie	30	197	10	15	0	3.84
Rene Lachemann	SS	S. Owen	306	.196	2	21	122	233	11	45	4.6	.970	B. Stoddard	35	176	9	17	0	4.41
W-26 L-47	3B	J. Allen	273	.223	4	21	55	155	9	16	2.7	.959	B. Clark	41	162	7	10	0	3.94
Del Crandall	RF	A. Cowens	356	.205	7	35	124	7	2	1	1.9	.985	M. Moore	22	128	6	8	0	4.71
W-34 L-55	CF	D. Henderson	484	.269	17	55	304	17	6	4	2.5	.982	G. Perry	16	102	3	10	0	4.94
	LF	S. Henderson	436	.294	10	54	182	15	6	2	1.8	.970	B. Caudill	63	73	2	8	26	4.71
	C	R. Sweet	249	.221	1	22	413	34	6	6	5.3	.987	M. Stanton	50	65	2	3	7	3.32
	DH	R. Zisk	285	.242	12	36							E. Vande Berg	68	64	2	4	5	3.36
	OF	R. Nelson	291	.254	5	36	122	10	4	1	1.5	.971							
	SS	T. Cruz	216	.190	7	21	97	224	12	42	5.3	.964							
	3B	M. Castillo	203	.207	0	24	35	101	4	9	2.5	.971							
	OF	R. Roenicke	198	.253	4	23	124	12	1	3	2.5	.993							
	2B	J. Cruz	181	.254	2	12	131	173	5	41	5.2	.984							
	C	O. Mercado	178	.197	1	16	342	27	2	2	5.7	.995							

BATTING AND BASE RUNNING LEADERS

Batting Average		Slugging Average		Home Runs	
W. Boggs, BOS	.361	G. Brett, KC	.563	J. Rice, BOS	39
R. Carew, CAL	.339	J. Rice, BOS	.550	T. Armas, BOS	36
L. Whitaker, DET	.320	E. Murray, BAL	.538	R. Kittle, CHI	35
A. Trammell, DET	.319	C. Fisk, CHI	.518	E. Murray, BAL	33
C. Ripken, BAL	.318	C. Ripken, BAL	.517	G. Luzinski, CHI	32
				D. Winfield, NY	32

PITCHING LEADERS

Winning Percentage		Earned Run Average		Wins	
R. Dotson, CHI	.759	R. Honeycutt, TEX	2.42	L. Hoyt, CHI	24
S. McGregor, BAL	.720	M. Boddicker, BAL	2.77	R. Dotson, CHI	22
L. Hoyt, CHI	.706	D. Stieb, TOR	3.04	R. Guidry, NY	21
R. Guidry, NY	.700	C. Hough, TEX	3.18	J. Morris, DET	20
M. Boddicker, BAL	.667	S. McGregor, BAL	3.18	D. Petry, DET	19

AMERICAN LEAGUE 1983, *cont.*

BATTING AND BASE RUNNING LEADERS

Total Bases

J. Rice, BOS	344
C. Ripken, BAL	343
C. Cooper, MIL	336
E. Murray, BAL	313
D. Winfield, NY	307

Runs Batted In

J. Rice, BOS	126
C. Cooper, MIL	126
D. Winfield, NY	116
L. Parrish, DET	114
E. Murray, BAL	111

Stolen Bases

R. Henderson, OAK	108
R. Law, CHI	77
W. Wilson, KC	59
J. Cruz, SEA, CHI	57
B. Sample, TEX	44

Hits

C. Ripken, BAL	211
W. Boggs, BOS	210
L. Whitaker, DET	206
C. Cooper, MIL	203

Base on Balls

R. Henderson, OAK	103
K. Singleton, BAL	99
W. Boggs, BOS	92
A. Thornton, CLE	87

Home Run Percentage

R. Kittle, CHI	6.7
G. Luzinski, CHI	6.4
T. Armas, BOS	6.3
J. Rice, BOS	6.2

Runs

C. Ripken, BAL	121
E. Murray, BAL	115
C. Cooper, MIL	106
R. Henderson, OAK	105

Doubles

C. Ripken, BAL	47
W. Boggs, BOS	44
R. Yount, MIL	42
L. Parrish, DET	42

Triples

R. Yount, MIL	10
K. Gibson, DET	9
A. Griffin, TOR	9
L. Herndon, DET	9

PITCHING LEADERS

Saves

D. Quisenberry, KC	45
B. Stanley, BOS	33
R. Davis, MIN	30
B. Caudill, SEA	26
P. Ladd, MIL	25

Strikeouts

J. Morris, DET	232
F. Bannister, CHI	193
D. Stieb, TOR	187
D. Righetti, NY	169
R. Sutcliffe, CLE	160

Complete Games

R. Guidry, NY	21
J. Morris, DET	20
D. Stieb, TOR	14
S. Rawley, NY	13
S. McGregor, BAL	12

Fewest Hits/9 Innings

M. Boddicker, BAL	7.09
D. Stieb, TOR	7.22
T. Conroy, OAK	7.82
C. Hough, TEX	7.82

Shutouts

M. Boddicker, BAL	5
B. Burns, CHI	4
D. Stieb, TOR	4

Fewest Walks/9 Innings

L. Hoyt, CHI	1.07
S. McGregor, BAL	1.56
T. John, CAL	1.88
R. Honeycutt, TEX	1.91

Most Strikeouts/9 Inn.

F. Bannister, CHI	7.99
J. Morris, DET	7.11
D. Righetti, NY	7.01
T. Conroy, OAK	6.21

Innings

J. Morris, DET	294
D. Stieb, TOR	278
D. Petry, DET	266
L. Hoyt, CHI	261

Games Pitched

D. Quisenberry, KC	69
E. Vande Berg, SEA	68
R. Davis, MIN	66
T. Martinez, BAL	65

								Batting						Fielding			Pitching					
		W	L	PCT	GB	R	OR	2B	3B	HR	BA	SA	SB	E	DP	FA	CG	BB	SO	ShO	SV	ERA
East	Baltimore	98	64	.605		799	652	283	27	**168**	.269	.421	61	121	159	.981	36	452	774	**15**	38	3.63
	Detroit	92	70	.568	6	789	679	283	53	156	.274	.427	93	125	142	.980	42	522	875	9	28	3.80
	New York	91	71	.562	7	770	703	269	40	153	.273	.416	84	139	157	.978	**47**	455	892	12	32	3.85
	Toronto	89	73	.549	9	795	726	268	**58**	167	**.277**	**.436**	131	115	148	.981	43	517	835	8	32	4.12
	Milwaukee	87	75	.537	11	764	708	281	57	132	**.277**	.418	101	**113**	162	**.982**	35	491	689	10	43	4.02
	Boston	78	84	.481	20	724	775	**287**	32	142	.270	.409	30	130	168	.979	29	493	767	7	42	4.34
	Cleveland	70	92	.432	28	704	785	249	31	86	.265	.369	109	122	174	.980	34	529	794	8	25	4.43
West	Chicago	99	63	.611		**800**	650	270	42	157	.262	.413	165	120	158	.981	35	**447**	877	12	48	3.67
	Kansas City	79	83	.488	20	696	767	273	54	109	.271	.397	182	165	178	.974	19	471	593	8	**49**	4.25
	Texas	77	85	.475	22	639	**609**	242	33	106	.255	.366	119	**113**	150	**.982**	43	471	826	11	32	**3.31**
	Oakland	74	88	.457	25	708	782	237	28	121	.262	.381	**235**	157	157	.974	22	626	719	12	33	4.35
	California	70	92	.432	29	722	779	241	22	154	.260	.393	41	154	**190**	.977	39	496	668	7	23	4.31
	Minnesota	70	92	.432	29	709	822	280	41	141	.261	.401	44	121	170	.980	20	580	748	5	39	4.67
	Seattle	60	102	.370	39	558	740	247	31	111	.240	.360	144	136	159	.978	25	544	**910**	9	39	4.12
						10177	10177	3710	549	1903	.265	.401	1539	1831	2272	.979	469	7094	10967	133	503	4.06

NATIONAL LEAGUE 1984

East

Chicago

W-96 L-65

Jim Frey

POS	Player	AB	BA	HR	RBI	PO	A	E	DP	TC/G	FA	Pitcher	G	IP	W	L	SV	ERA
1B	L. Durham	473	.279	23	96	1162	96	7	96	9.7	.994	S. Trout	32	190	13	7	0	3.41
2B	R. Sandberg	636	.314	19	84	314	**550**	6	102	5.6	**.993**	D. Eckersley	24	160	10	8	0	3.03
SS	L. Bowa	391	.223	0	17	217	378	16	64	4.6	.974	R. Sutcliffe	20	150	16	1	0	2.69
3B	R. Cey	505	.240	25	97	97	230	11	22	2.3	**.967**	S. Sanderson	24	141	8	5	0	3.14
RF	K. Moreland	495	.279	16	80	154	6	4	0	1.6	.976	D. Ruthven	23	127	6	10	0	5.04
CF	B. Dernier	536	.278	3	32	355	5	5	1	2.6	.986	L. Smith	69	101	9	7	33	3.65
LF	G. Matthews	491	.291	14	82	224	7	11	0	1.7	.955	R. Reuschel	19	92	5	5	0	5.17
C	J. Davis	523	.256	19	94	811	89	**15**	9	6.3	.984	T. Stoddard	58	92	10	6	7	3.82
OF	M. Hall	150	.280	4	22	69	5	3	2	1.7	.961	C. Rainey	17	88	5	7	0	4.28
												R. Bordi	31	83	5	2	4	3.46
												G. Frazier	37	64	6	3	3	4.10

New York

W-90 L-72

Davey Johnson

POS	Player	AB	BA	HR	RBI	PO	A	E	DP	TC/G	FA	Pitcher	G	IP	W	L	SV	ERA
1B	K. Hernandez	550	.311	15	94	1214	**142**	8	**127**	8.9	.994	D. Gooden	31	218	17	9	0	2.60
2B	W. Backman	436	.280	1	26	218	295	10	72	4.5	.981	W. Terrell	33	215	11	12	0	3.52
SS	J. Oquendo	189	.222	0	10	95	152	7	33	3.8	.972	R. Darling	33	206	12	9	0	3.81
3B	H. Brooks	561	.283	16	73	79	211	22	22	2.4	.929	E. Lynch	40	124	9	8	2	4.50
RF	D. Strawberry	522	.251	26	97	276	11	6	3	2.0	.980	B. Berenyi	19	115	9	6	0	3.76
CF	M. Wilson	587	.276	10	54	396	8	4	6	2.8	.990	S. Fernandez	15	90	6	6	0	3.50
LF	G. Foster	553	.269	24	86	278	6	7	1	2.1	.976	J. Orosco	60	87	10	6	31	2.59
C	M. Fitzgerald	360	.242	2	33	715	47	4	6	**7.2**	**.995**	D. Sisk	50	78	1	3	15	2.09
S2	R. Gardenhire	207	.246	1	10	96	143	10	20		.960							
OF	D. Heep	199	.231	1	12	86	1	3	1	1.9	.967							
2B	K. Chapman	197	.289	3	23	104	130	5	32	4.3	.979							

St. Louis

W-84 L-78

Whitey Herzog

POS	Player	AB	BA	HR	RBI	PO	A	E	DP	TC/G	FA	Pitcher	G	IP	W	L	SV	ERA
1B	D. Green	452	.268	15	65	1088	69	10	98	**10.0**	.991	J. Andujar	36	**261**	**20**	14	0	3.34
2B	T. Herr	558	.276	4	49	328	452	6	**106**	5.5	.992	D. LaPoint	33	193	12	10	0	3.96
SS	O. Smith	412	.257	1	44	233	437	12	**94**	**5.5**	**.982**	D. Cox	29	156	9	11	0	4.03
3B	T. Pendleton	262	.324	1	33	59	155	13	10	3.4	.943	R. Horton	37	126	9	4	1	3.44
RF	G. Hendrick	441	.277	9	69	188	9	2	1	1.7	.990	B. Sutter	71	123	5	7	**45**	1.54
CF	W. McGee	571	.291	6	50	374	10	6	4	2.8	.985	N. Allen	57	119	9	6	3	3.55
LF	L. Smith	504	.250	6	49	184	18	11	0	1.5	.948	K. Kepshire	17	109	6	5	0	3.30
C	D. Porter	422	.232	11	68	620	58	11	6	5.6	.984							
UT	A. Van Slyke	361	.244	7	50	357	82	8	40		.982							
OF	T. Landrum	173	.272	3	26	93	1	2	0	1.1	.979							

NATIONAL LEAGUE 1984, *cont.*

	POS	Player	AB	BA	HR	RBI	PO	A	E	DP	TC/G	FA	Pitcher	G	IP	W	L	SV	ERA
Philadelphia	1B	L. Matuszek	262	.248	12	43	643	55	7	40	8.7	.990	S. Carlton	33	229	13	7	0	3.58
W-81 L-81	2B	J. Samuel	**701**	.272	15	69	388	438	**33**	77	5.4	.962	J. Koosman	36	224	14	15	0	3.25
Paul Owens	SS	I. DeJesus	435	.257	0	35	166	400	29	57	4.2	.951	C. Hudson	30	174	9	11	0	4.04
	3B	M. Schmidt	528	.277	**36**	**106**	85	329	26	19	3.0	.941	J. Denny	22	154	7	7	0	2.45
	RF	S. Lezcano	256	.277	14	40	151	3	3	0	1.8	.981	K. Gross	44	129	8	5	1	4.12
	CF	V. Hayes	561	.292	16	67	341	2	4	1	2.3	.988	S. Rawley	18	120	10	6	0	3.81
	LF	G. Wilson	341	.240	6	31	147	4	5	0	1.4	.968	A. Holland	68	98	5	10	29	3.39
	C	O. Virgil	456	.261	18	68	722	58	6	6	5.7	.992	L. Andersen	64	91	3	7	4	2.38
	OF	G. Maddox	241	.282	5	19	160	3	0	1	2.4	1.000	B. Campbell	57	81	6	5	1	3.43
	1B	T. Corcoran	208	.341	5	36	318	21	1	20	6.7	.997							
	01	G. Gross	202	.322	0	16	195	13	2	9		.990							
	OF	J. Stone	185	.362	1	15	75	1	7	0	1.8	.916							
	1C	J. Wockenfuss	180	.289	6	24	323	20	7	21		.980							
Montreal	1B	T. Francona	214	.346	1	18	427	49	3	43	9.6	.994	B. Gullickson	32	227	12	9	0	3.61
W-78 L-83	2B	D. Flynn	366	.243	0	17	148	223	8	47	4.3	.979	C. Lea	30	224	15	10	0	2.89
Bill Virdon	SS	A. Salazar	174	.155	0	12	88	155	10	35	3.2	.960	B. Smith	28	179	12	13	0	3.32
W-64 L-67	3B	T. Wallach	582	.246	18	72	**162**	**332**	21	**29**	**3.2**	.959	S. Rogers	31	169	6	15	0	4.31
Jim Fanning	RF	A. Dawson	533	.248	17	86	297	11	8	2	2.4	.975	D. Schatzeder	36	136	7	7	1	2.71
W-14 L-16	CF	T. Raines	622	.309	8	60	420	8	5	1	2.7	.988	D. Palmer	20	105	7	3	0	3.84
	LF	J. Wohlford	213	.300	5	29	85	3	1	1	1.5	.989	B. James	62	96	6	6	10	3.66
	C	G. Carter	596	.294	27	**106**	772	65	6	6	5.9	.993	J. Reardon	68	87	7	7	23	2.90
	10	P. Rose	278	.259	0	23	349	44	6	22		.985	G. Lucas	55	53	0	3	8	2.72
	2B	B. Little	266	.244	0	9	137	197	6	44	4.4	.982							
	UT	D. Thomas	243	.255	0	20	118	135	10	33		.962							
	OF	M. Stenhouse	175	.183	4	16	67	4	1	2	1.5	.986							
	1B	D. Driessen	169	.254	9	32	363	23	2	38	8.6	.995							
	OF	M. Dilone	169	.278	1	10	76	1	1	0	1.9	.987							
Pittsburgh	1B	J. Thompson	543	.254	17	74	**1337**	74	**14**	111	9.4	.990	R. Rhoden	33	238	14	9	0	2.72
W-75 L-87	2B	J. Ray	555	.312	6	67	331	400	12	90	5.0	.984	L. McWilliams	34	227	12	11	1	2.93
Chuck Tanner	SS	D. Berra	450	.222	9	52	186	449	**30**	65	4.9	.955	J. Tudor	32	212	12	11	0	3.27
	3B	B. Madlock	403	.253	4	44	66	176	15	17	2.6	.942	J. DeLeon	30	192	7	13	0	3.74
	RF	L. Lacy	474	.321	12	70	268	15	1	4	2.2	.996	J. Candelaria	33	185	12	11	2	2.72
	CF	M. Wynne	653	.266	0	39	373	8	4	1	2.5	.990	D. Robinson	51	122	5	6	10	3.02
	LF	L. Mazzilli	266	.237	4	21	92	2	1	0	1.3	.989	K. Tekulve	72	88	3	9	13	2.66
	C	T. Pena	546	.286	15	78	**895**	**95**	9	**15**	6.8	.991	R. Scurry	43	46	5	6	4	2.53
	32	J. Morrison	304	.286	11	45	81	163	10	21		.961							
	OF	D. Frobel	276	.203	12	28	188	9	9	3	1.8	.956							
West **San Diego**	1B	S. Garvey	617	.284	8	86	1232	87	0	117	8.2	**1.000**	E. Show	32	207	15	9	0	3.40
W-92 L-70	2B	A. Wiggins	596	.258	3	34	**391**	410	32	95	5.3	.962	T. Lollar	31	196	11	13	0	3.91
Dick Williams	SS	G. Templeton	493	.258	2	35	225	407	26	79	4.5	.960	E. Whitson	31	189	14	8	0	3.24
	3B	G. Nettles	395	.228	20	65	93	201	20	14	2.6	.936	M. Thurmond	32	179	14	8	0	2.97
	RF	T. Gwynn	606	**.351**	5	71	345	11	4	4	2.3	.989	D. Dravecky	50	157	9	8	8	2.93
	CF	K. McReynolds	525	.278	20	75	422	10	4	1	3.0	.991	A. Hawkins	36	146	8	9	0	4.68
	LF	C. Martinez	488	.250	13	66	312	15	8	4	2.4	.976	C. Lefferts	62	106	3	4	10	2.13
	C	T. Kennedy	530	.240	14	57	708	54	14	6	5.3	.982	G. Gossage	62	102	10	6	25	2.90
	30	L. Salazar	228	.241	3	17	84	92	6	5		.967							
	OF	B. Brown	171	.251	3	29	100	2	3	0	2.0	.971							
Atlanta	1B	C. Chambliss	389	.257	9	44	996	70	8	84	9.9	.993	R. Mahler	38	222	13	10	0	3.12
W-80 L-82	2B	G. Hubbard	397	.234	9	43	237	405	8	78	5.6	.988	P. Perez	30	212	14	8	0	3.74
Joe Torre	SS	R. Ramirez	591	.266	2	48	**251**	443	**30**	**94**	5.0	.959	C. McMurtry	37	183	9	17	0	4.32
	3B	R. Johnson	294	.279	5	30	44	171	14	14	2.8	.939	R. Camp	31	149	8	6	0	3.27
	RF	C. Washington	416	.286	17	61	170	4	6	0	1.7	.967	L. Barker	21	126	7	8	0	3.85
	CF	D. Murphy	607	.290	**36**	100	369	10	5	1	2.4	.987	P. Falcone	35	120	5	7	2	4.13
	LF	G. Perry	347	.265	7	47	74	2	6	0	1.5	.927	G. Garber	62	106	3	6	11	3.06
	C	B. Benedict	300	.223	4	25	504	37	5	2	5.7	.991	S. Bedrosian	40	84	9	6	11	2.37
	OF	B. Komminsk	301	.203	8	36	135	2	1	0	1.7	.993	J. Dedmon	54	81	4	3	4	3.78
	C	A. Trevino	266	.244	3	28	399	60	5	5	5.9	.989	D. Moore	47	64	4	5	16	2.94
	UT	J. Royster	227	.207	1	21	99	162	9	23		.967							
	3B	K. Oberkfell	172	.233	1	10	31	77	4	8	2.5	.964							
Houston	1B	E. Cabell	436	.310	8	44	971	66	7	97	9.3	.993	J. Niekro	38	248	16	12	0	3.04
W-80 L-82	2B	B. Doran	548	.261	4	41	261	419	10	83	5.0	.986	B. Knepper	35	234	15	10	0	3.20
Bob Lillis	SS	C. Reynolds	527	.260	6	60	212	**472**	25	91	5.0	.965	N. Ryan	30	184	12	11	0	3.04
	3B	P. Garner	374	.278	4	45	71	163	5	16	2.9	.979	M. Scott	31	154	5	11	0	4.68
	RF	T. Puhl	449	.301	9	55	213	6	3	4	1.8	.986	M. LaCoss	39	132	7	5	3	4.02
	CF	J. Mumphrey	524	.290	9	83	317	5	4	2	2.4	.988	B. Dawley	60	98	11	4	5	1.93
	LF	J. Cruz	600	.312	12	95	310	11	8	1	2.1	.976	V. Ruhle	40	90	1	9	2	4.58
	C	M. Bailey	344	.212	9	34	629	56	12	4	6.5	.983	D. Smith	53	77	5	4	5	2.21
	OF	K. Bass	331	.260	2	29	149	4	4	2	1.9	.975	F. DiPino	57	75	4	9	14	3.35
	31	R. Knight	278	.223	2	29	236	95	7	22		.979							
	3B	D. Walling	249	.281	3	31	30	100	6	14	2.6	.956							
	C	A. Ashby	191	.262	4	27	303	42	5	3	5.6	.986							

NATIONAL LEAGUE 1984, *cont.*

Team	POS	Player	AB	BA	HR	RBI	PO	A	E	DP	TC/G	FA	Pitcher	G	IP	W	L	SV	ERA
Los Angeles	1B	G. Brock	271	.225	14	34	703	65	4	61	9.3	.995	F. Valenzuela	34	**261**	12	17	0	3.03
	2B	S. Sax	569	.243	1	35	318	450	21	99	**5.6**	.973	A. Pena	28	199	12	6	0	**2.48**
W-79 L-83	SS	D. Anderson	374	.251	3	34	169	334	18	63	4.7	.965	O. Hershiser	45	190	11	8	2	2.66
	3B	G. Rivera	227	.260	2	17	55	167	15	12	2.6	.937	R. Honeycutt	29	184	10	9	0	2.84
Tom Lasorda	RF	C. Maldonado	254	.268	5	28	124	4	6	0	1.3	.955	B. Welch	31	179	13	13	0	3.78
	CF	K. Landreaux	438	.251	11	47	212	3	3	2	1.7	.986	B. Hooton	54	110	3	6	4	3.44
	LF	M. Marshall	495	.257	21	65	200	9	4	1	1.8	.981	J. Reuss	30	99	5	7	1	3.82
	C	M. Scioscia	341	.273	5	38	701	64	12	8	6.9	.985	P. Zachry	58	83	5	6	2	3.81
	UT	P. Guerrero	535	.303	16	72	271	151	22	24		.950	K. Howell	32	51	5	5	6	3.33
	SS	B. Russell	262	.267	0	19	81	165	9	29	3.9	.965	T. Niedenfuer	33	47	2	5	11	2.47
	OF	R. Reynolds	240	.258	2	24	104	4	3	1	1.8	.973							
	1B	F. Stubbs	217	.194	8	17	395	37	3	31	8.5	.993							
	C	S. Yeager	197	.228	4	29	317	30	2	1	5.4	.994							
	OF	T. Whitfield	180	.244	4	18	76	4	1	0	1.4	.988							

Team	POS	Player	AB	BA	HR	RBI	PO	A	E	DP	TC/G	FA	Pitcher	G	IP	W	L	SV	ERA
Cincinnati	1B	D. Driessen	218	.280	7	28	507	29	5	31	7.7	.991	M. Soto	33	237	18	7	0	3.53
	2B	R. Oester	553	.242	3	38	357	388	15	75	5.2	.980	J. Russell	33	182	6	**18**	0	4.26
	SS	D. Concepcion	531	.245	4	58	156	247	9	41	4.0	.978	J. Price	30	172	7	13	0	4.19
W-70 L-92	3B	N. Esasky	322	.193	10	45	51	130	18	8	2.4	.910	T. Hume	54	113	4	13	3	5.64
	RF	D. Parker	607	.285	16	94	296	6	8	1	2.1	.974	T. Power	**78**	109	9	7	11	2.82
Vern Rapp	CF	E. Milner	336	.232	7	29	285	8	5	4	2.8	.983	J. Tibbs	14	101	6	2	0	2.86
W-51 L-70	LF	G. Redus	394	.254	7	22	200	6	7	3	1.9	.967	F. Pastore	24	98	3	8	0	6.50
	C	B. Gulden	292	.226	4	33	485	53	14	8	5.5	.975	B. Owchinko	49	94	3	5	2	4.12
Pete Rose	01	C. Cedeno	380	.276	10	47	355	21	7	16		.982	J. Franco	54	79	6	2	4	2.61
W-19 L-22	SS	T. Foley	277	.253	5	27	104	197	11	31	3.8	.965	B. Berenyi	13	51	3	7	0	6.00
	OF	D. Walker	195	.292	10	28	110	3	6	0	1.8	.950							
	C	D. Bilardello	182	.209	2	10	323	34	3	3	5.3	.992							
	3B	W. Krenchicki	181	.298	6	22	25	91	4	5	1.9	.967							
	OF	E. Davis	174	.224	10	30	125	4	1	2	2.5	.992							

Team	POS	Player	AB	BA	HR	RBI	PO	A	E	DP	TC/G	FA	Pitcher	G	IP	W	L	SV	ERA
San Francisco	1B	S. Thompson	245	.306	1	31	555	36	1	48	6.8	.998	B. Laskey	35	208	9	14	0	4.33
	2B	M. Trillo	401	.254	4	36	215	287	6	67	5.3	.988	M. Krukow	35	199	11	12	1	4.56
	SS	J. LeMaster	451	.217	4	32	222	391	23	70	4.9	.964	M. Davis	46	175	5	17	0	5.36
W-66 L-96	3B	J. Youngblood	469	.254	10	51	87	195	**36**	11	2.7	.887	J. Robinson	34	172	7	15	0	4.56
	RF	C. Davis	499	.315	21	81	292	9	9	2	2.5	.971	G. Minton	74	124	4	9	19	3.76
Frank Robinson	CF	D. Gladden	342	.351	4	31	232	8	3	1	2.9	.988	F. Williams	61	106	9	4	3	3.55
W-42 L-64	LF	J. Leonard	514	.302	21	86	247	14	8	4	2.1	.970	G. Lavelle	77	101	5	4	12	2.76
	C	B. Brenly	506	.291	20	80	635	69	10	4	5.6	.986	R. Lerch	37	72	5	3	2	4.23
Danny Ozark	1B	A. Oliver	339	.298	0	34	665	55	11	50	8.9	.985							
W-24 L-32	UT	B. Wellman	265	.226	2	25	151	258	11	37		.974							
	OF	D. Baker	243	.292	3	32	112	1	3	0	1.9	.974							
	OF	J. Clark	203	.320	11	44	94	3	1	0	1.8	.990							

BATTING AND BASE RUNNING LEADERS

Batting Average
T. Gwynn, SD .351
L. Lacy, PIT .321
C. Davis, SF .315
R. Sandberg, CHI .314
J. Ray, PIT .312

Slugging Average
D. Murphy, ATL .547
M. Schmidt, PHI .536
R. Sandberg, CHI .520
C. Davis, SF .507
L. Durham, CHI .505

Home Runs
M. Schmidt, PHI 36
D. Murphy, ATL 36
G. Carter, MON 27
D. Strawberry, NY 26
R. Cey, CHI 25

Total Bases
D. Murphy, ATL 332
R. Sandberg, CHI 331
J. Samuel, PHI 310
G. Carter, MON 290
M. Schmidt, PHI 283

Runs Batted In
M. Schmidt, PHI 106
G. Carter, MON 106
D. Murphy, ATL 100
R. Cey, CHI 97
D. Strawberry, NY 97

Stolen Bases
T. Raines, MON 75
J. Samuel, PHI 72
A. Wiggins, SD 70
L. Smith, STL 50
G. Redus, CIN 48
V. Hayes, PHI 48

Hits
T. Gwynn, SD 213
R. Sandberg, CHI 200
T. Raines, MON 192
J. Samuel, PHI 191

Base on Balls
G. Matthews, CHI 103
K. Hernandez, NY 97
M. Schmidt, PHI 92
J. Thompson, PIT 87
T. Raines, MON 87

Home Run Percentage
M. Schmidt, PHI 6.8
D. Murphy, ATL 5.9
D. Strawberry, NY 5.0
R. Cey, CHI 5.0

Runs
R. Sandberg, CHI 114
A. Wiggins, SD 106
T. Raines, MON 106
J. Samuel, PHI 105

Doubles
J. Ray, PIT 38
T. Raines, MON 38
R. Sandberg, CHI 36
J. Samuel, PHI 36

Triples
R. Sandberg, CHI 19
J. Samuel, PHI 19
J. Cruz, HOU 13

PITCHING LEADERS

Winning Percentage
R. Sutcliffe, CHI .941
M. Soto, CIN .720
D. Gooden, NY .654
E. Show, SD .625
B. Knepper, HOU .600
C. Lea, MON .600

Earned Run Average
A. Pena, LA 2.48
D. Gooden, NY 2.60
O. Hershiser, LA 2.66
R. Rhoden, PIT 2.72
J. Candelaria, PIT 2.72

Wins
J. Andujar, STL 20
M. Soto, CIN 18
D. Gooden, NY 17
R. Sutcliffe, CHI 16
J. Niekro, HOU 16

Saves
B. Sutter, STL 45
L. Smith, CHI 33
J. Orosco, NY 31
A. Holland, PHI 29
G. Gossage, SD 25

Strikeouts
D. Gooden, NY 276
F. Valenzuela, LA 240
N. Ryan, HOU 197
M. Soto, CIN 185
S. Carlton, PHI 163

Complete Games
M. Soto, CIN 13
F. Valenzuela, LA 12
J. Andujar, STL 12
B. Knepper, HOU 11
R. Mahler, ATL 9

Fewest Hits/9 Innings
D. Gooden, NY 6.65
M. Soto, CIN 6.86
J. DeLeon, PIT 6.88
N. Ryan, HOU 7.01

Shutouts
O. Hershiser, LA 4
A. Pena, LA 4
J. Andujar, STL 4

Fewest Walks/9 Innings
B. Gullickson, MON 1.47
J. Candelaria, PIT 1.65
E. Whitson, SD 2.00
A. Pena, LA 2.08

Most Strikeouts/9 Inn.
D. Gooden, NY 11.39
N. Ryan, HOU 9.65
F. Valenzuela, LA 8.28
B. Berenyi, CIN, NY 7.27

Innings
F. Valenzuela, LA 261
J. Andujar, STL 261
J. Niekro, HOU 248
R. Rhoden, PIT 238

Games Pitched
T. Power, CIN 78
G. Lavelle, SF 77
G. Minton, SF 74
K. Tekulve, PIT 72

NATIONAL LEAGUE 1984, *cont.*

		W	L	PCT	GB	R	OR	2B	3B	HR	BA	SA	SB	E	DP	FA	CG	BB	SO	ShO	SV	ERA
								Batting						Fielding			Pitching					
East	Chicago	96	65	.596		**762**	658	239	47	136	.260	.397	154	121	137	.981	19	**442**	879	8	50	3.75
	New York	90	72	.556	6.5	652	676	235	25	107	.257	.369	149	129	154	.979	12	573	1028	15	50	3.60
	St. Louis	84	78	.519	12.5	652	645	225	44	75	.252	.351	**220**	**118**	**184**	**.982**	19	494	808	12	**51**	3.58
	Philadelphia	81	81	.500	15.5	720	690	**248**	51	**147**	**.266**	**.407**	186	161	112	.975	11	448	904	6	35	3.62
	Montreal	78	83	.484	18	593	585	242	36	96	.251	.362	131	132	147	.978	19	474	861	10	48	3.31
	Pittsburgh	75	87	.463	21.5	615	**567**	237	33	98	.255	.363	96	128	142	.980	27	502	995	13	34	**3.11**
West	San Diego	92	70	.568		686	634	207	42	109	.259	.371	152	138	144	.978	13	563	812	**17**	44	3.48
	Atlanta	80	82	.494	12	632	655	234	27	111	.247	.361	140	139	153	.978	17	525	859	7	49	3.57
	Houston	80	82	.494	12	693	630	222	**67**	79	.264	.371	105	133	160	.979	24	502	950	13	29	3.32
	Los Angeles	79	83	.488	13	580	600	213	23	102	.244	.348	109	163	146	.975	**39**	499	**1033**	16	27	3.17
	Cincinnati	70	92	.432	22	627	747	238	30	106	.244	.356	160	139	116	.977	25	578	946	6	25	4.16
	San Francisco	66	96	.407	26	682	807	229	26	112	.265	.375	126	173	134	.973	9	549	854	7	38	4.39
						7894	7894	2769	451	1278	.255	.369	1728	1674	1729	.978	234	6149	10929	130	480	3.59

AMERICAN LEAGUE 1984

East

Detroit

W-104 L-58

Sparky Anderson

POS	Player	AB	BA	HR	RBI	PO	A	E	DP	TC/G	FA	Pitcher	G	IP	W	L	SV	ERA
1B	D. Bergman	271	.273	7	44	657	75	8	63	6.5	.989	J. Morris	35	240	19	11	0	3.60
2B	L. Whitaker	558	.289	13	56	290	405	15	83	5.0	.979	D. Petry	35	233	18	8	0	3.24
SS	A. Trammell	555	.314	14	69	180	314	10	71	4.4	.980	M. Wilcox	33	194	17	8	0	4.00
3B	H. Johnson	355	.248	12	50	58	143	12	16	2.0	.944	J. Berenguer	31	168	11	10	0	3.48
RF	K. Gibson	531	.282	27	91	245	4	12	2	1.9	.954	G. Hernandez	**80**	140	9	3	32	1.92
CF	C. Lemon	509	.287	20	76	427	6	2	1	3.1	.995	A. Lopez	71	138	10	1	14	2.94
LF	L. Herndon	407	.280	7	43	199	7	3	0	1.8	.986	D. Rozema	29	101	7	6	0	3.74
C	L. Parrish	578	.237	33	98	720	67	7	**11**	6.3	.991	D. Bair	47	94	5	3	4	3.75
DH	D. Evans	401	.232	16	63													
UT	B. Garbey	327	.287	5	52	411	58	12	53		.975							
UT	T. Brookens	224	.246	5	26	98	187	12	35		.960							
OF	R. Jones	215	.284	12	37	150	4	0	1	2.1	1.000							
OD	J. Grubb	176	.267	8	17	47	0	0	0		1.000							
OF	R. Kuntz	140	.286	2	22	74	2	1	1	1.1	.987							

Toronto

W-89 L-73

Bobby Cox

POS	Player	AB	BA	HR	RBI	PO	A	E	DP	TC/G	FA	Pitcher	G	IP	W	L	SV	ERA
1B	W. Upshaw	569	.278	19	84	1246	103	14	133	9.0	.990	D. Stieb	35	**267**	16	8	0	2.83
2B	D. Garcia	633	.284	5	46	267	427	14	95	4.8	.980	D. Alexander	36	262	17	6	0	3.13
SS	A. Griffin	419	.241	4	30	189	269	18	65	4.1	.962	L. Leal	35	222	13	8	0	3.89
3B	R. Mulliniks	343	.324	3	42	65	148	7	8	1.8	**.968**	J. Clancy	36	220	13	15	0	5.12
RF	G. Bell	606	.292	26	87	289	11	9	1	2.1	.971	J. Gott	35	110	7	6	2	4.02
CF	L. Moseby	592	.280	18	92	473	8	5	2	3.1	.990	R. Jackson	54	86	7	8	10	3.56
LF	D. Collins	441	.308	2	44	203	8	2	3	2.0	.991	D. Lamp	56	85	8	8	9	4.55
C	E. Whitt	315	.238	15	46	583	40	4	8	5.3	.994	J. Key	63	62	4	5	10	4.65
DH	C. Johnson	359	.304	16	61													
OF	J. Barfield	320	.284	14	49	190	9	10	5	2.4	.952							
3B	G. Iorg	247	.227	1	25	62	110	10	15	1.6	.945							
DH	W. Aikens	234	.205	11	26													
SS	T. Fernandez	233	.270	3	19	116	178	8	40	4.1	.974							
C	B. Martinez	232	.220	5	37	360	34	2	5	4.0	.995							

New York

W-87 L-75

Yogi Berra

POS	Player	AB	BA	HR	RBI	PO	A	E	DP	TC/G	FA	Pitcher	G	IP	W	L	SV	ERA
1B	D. Mattingly	603	**.343**	23	110	1107	124	5	135	9.3	**.996**	P. Niekro	32	216	16	8	0	3.09
2B	W. Randolph	564	.287	2	31	334	419	13	**112**	5.4	.983	R. Guidry	29	196	10	11	0	4.51
SS	B. Meacham	360	.253	2	25	136	269	19	52	4.4	.955	R. Fontenot	33	169	8	9	0	3.61
3B	T. Harrah	253	.217	1	27	51	128	6	17	2.5	.968	D. Rasmussen	24	148	9	6	0	4.57
RF	D. Winfield	567	.340	19	100	306	3	2	1	2.2	.994	B. Shirley	41	114	3	3	0	3.38
CF	O. Moreno	355	.259	4	38	262	9	4	2	2.5	.985	J. Howell	61	104	9	4	7	2.69
LF	S. Kemp	313	.291	7	41	138	2	4	0	1.9	.972	D. Righetti	64	96	5	6	31	2.34
C	B. Wynegar	442	.267	6	45	757	59	6	9	6.5	.993	J. Cowley	16	83	9	2	0	3.56
DH	D. Baylor	493	.262	27	89							J. Rijo	24	62	2	8	2	4.76
OF	K. Griffey	399	.273	7	56	181	6	5	0	2.3	.974							
UT	R. Smalley	209	.239	7	26	66	99	12	17		.932							
3B	M. Pagliarulo	201	.239	7	34	44	106	7	16	2.3	.955							
UT	T. Foli	163	.252	0	16	88	122	6	32		.972							
OF	B. Dayett	127	.244	4	23	80	3	1	0	1.4	.988							
DO	O. Gamble	125	.184	10	27	15	1	0	0		1.000							

Boston

W-86 L-76

Ralph Houk

POS	Player	AB	BA	HR	RBI	PO	A	E	DP	TC/G	FA	Pitcher	G	IP	W	L	SV	ERA
1B	B. Buckner	439	.278	11	67	974	96	15*	75	9.6	.986	B. Hurst	33	218	12	12	0	3.92
2B	M. Barrett	475	.303	3	45	245	417	9	67	4.9	**.987**	B. Ojeda	33	217	12	12	0	3.99
SS	J. Gutierrez	449	.263	2	29	228	347	31	60	4.0	.949	O. Boyd	29	198	12	12	0	4.37
3B	W. Boggs	625	.325	6	55	141	330	**20**	**30**	3.2	.959	A. Nipper	29	183	11	6	0	3.89
RF	D. Evans	630	.295	32	104	311	7	2	2	2.0	.994	R. Clemens	21	133	9	4	0	4.32
CF	T. Armas	639	.268	**43**	**123**	329	4	9	2	2.7	.974	B. Stanley	57	107	9	10	22	3.54
LF	J. Rice	657	.280	28	122	336	12	4	3	2.2	.989	M. Clear	47	67	8	3	8	4.03
C	R. Gedman	449	.269	24	72	693	58	**18**	5	6.2	.977							
DH	M. Easler	601	.313	27	91													

AMERICAN LEAGUE 1984, *cont.*

Baltimore

W-85 L-77

Joe Altobelli

POS	Player	AB	BA	HR	RBI	PO	A	E	DP	TC/G	FA
1B	E. Murray	588	.306	29	110	**1538**	**143**	13	**152**	**10.7**	.992
2B	R. Dauer	397	.254	2	24	225	325	11	76	4.6	.980
SS	C. Ripken	641	.304	27	86	**297**	**583**	26	**122**	**5.6**	.971
3B	W. Gross	342	.216	22	64	64	205	18	13	2.5	.937
RF	M. Young	401	.252	17	52	216	4	4	0	1.9	.982
CF	J. Shelby	383	.209	6	30	261	9	2	1	2.2	.993
LF	G. Roenicke	326	.224	10	44	197	6	1	0	1.7	.995
C	R. Dempsey	330	.230	11	34	453	43	4	5	4.6	.992
DH	K. Singleton	363	.215	6	36						
OF	A. Bumbry	344	.270	3	24	230	7	3	1	2.4	.988
OF	J. Lowenstein	270	.237	8	28	94	5	3	0	1.5	.971
C	F. Rayford	250	.256	4	27	287	35	3	2	4.9	.991
OF	J. Dwyer	161	.255	2	21	83	3	3	1	1.7	.966
DH	B. Ayala	118	.212	4	24						

Pitcher	G	IP	W	L	SV	ERA
M. Boddicker	34	261	**20**	11	0	**2.79**
M. Flanagan	34	227	13	13	0	3.53
S. Davis	35	225	14	9	1	3.12
S. McGregor	30	196	15	12	0	3.94
D. Martinez	34	142	6	9	0	5.02
S. Stewart	60	93	7	4	13	3.29
T. Martinez	55	90	4	9	17	3.91

Cleveland

W-75 L-87

Pat Corrales

POS	Player	AB	BA	HR	RBI	PO	A	E	DP	TC/G	FA
1B	M. Hargrove	352	.267	2	44	790	83	8	86	7.1	.991
2B	T. Bernazard	439	.221	2	38	264	397	**20**	85	5.0	.971
SS	J. Franco	**658**	.286	3	79	280	481	**36**	116	5.0	.955
3B	B. Jacoby	439	.264	7	40	86	187	14	17	2.3	.951
RF	G. Vukovich	437	.304	9	60	316	13	2	5	2.5	.994
CF	B. Butler	602	.269	3	49	448	13	4	3	3.0	.991
LF	M. Hall	257	.257	7	30	143	3	1	0	2.1	.993
C	J. Willard	246	.224	10	37	335	35	7	7	5.0	.981
DH	A. Thornton	587	.271	33	99						
UT	P. Tabler	473	.290	10	68	532	89	7	54		.989
OF	J. Carter	244	.275	13	41	122	9	6	0	2.3	.956
C	C. Bando	220	.291	12	41	305	30	6	4	5.4	.982
OF	C. Castillo	211	.261	10	36	123	2	9	0	1.9	.933

Pitcher	G	IP	W	L	SV	ERA
B. Blyleven	33	245	19	7	0	2.87
N. Heaton	38	199	12	15	0	5.21
S. Comer	22	117	4	8	0	5.68
S. Farr	31	116	3	11	1	4.58
E. Camacho	69	100	5	9	23	2.43
T. Waddell	58	97	7	4	6	3.06
R. Smith	22	86	5	5	0	4.59

Milwaukee

W-67 L-94

Rene Lachemann

POS	Player	AB	BA	HR	RBI	PO	A	E	DP	TC/G	FA
1B	C. Cooper	603	.275	11	67	1061	98	10	106	9.6	.991
2B	J. Gantner	613	.282	3	56	**362**	469	13	111	5.5	.985
SS	R. Yount	624	.298	16	80	199	402	18	80	5.2	.971
3B	E. Romero	357	.252	1	31	38	111	9	13	2.7	.943
RF	D. James	387	.295	1	30	252	7	3	1	2.2	.989
CF	R. Manning	341	.249	7	31	231	2	3	2	2.1	.987
LF	B. Oglivie	461	.262	12	60	256	6	8	1	2.2	.970
C	J. Sundberg	348	.261	7	43	556	55	3	6	5.6	**.995**
DH	T. Simmons	497	.221	4	52						
C	B. Schroeder	210	.257	14	25	274	24	4	2	5.2	.987
OF	M. Brouhard	197	.239	6	22	107	6	2	2	2.2	.983
OF	C. Moore	188	.234	2	17	119	2	2	0	2.0	.984
OF	B. Clark	169	.260	2	16	106	0	2	0	1.9	.981
3B	R. Howell	164	.232	4	17	21	67	9	7	2.1	.907
3B	W. Lozado	107	.271	1	20	23	51	6	7	2.2	.925

Pitcher	G	IP	W	L	SV	ERA
D. Sutton	33	213	14	12	0	3.77
M. Haas	31	189	9	11	0	3.99
J. Cocanower	33	175	8	16	0	4.02
B. McClure	39	140	4	8	1	4.38
M. Caldwell	26	126	6	13	0	4.64
P. Ladd	54	91	4	9	3	5.24
C. Porter	17	81	6	4	0	3.87
T. Tellmann	50	81	6	3	4	2.78
R. Fingers	33	46	1	2	23	1.96

West

Kansas City

W-84 L-78

Dick Howser

POS	Player	AB	BA	HR	RBI	PO	A	E	DP	TC/G	FA
1B	S. Balboni	438	.244	28	77	1102	79	**15**	102	9.6	.987
2B	F. White	479	.271	17	56	299	425	11	97	**5.7**	.985
SS	O. Concepcion	287	.282	1	23	105	280	11	53	4.7	.972
3B	G. Pryor	270	.263	4	25	59	138	6	13	1.9	.970
RF	P. Sheridan	481	.283	8	53	273	8	4	1	2.1	.986
CF	W. Wilson	541	.301	2	44	383	6	4	2	3.1	.990
LF	D. Motley	522	.284	15	70	301	7	5	2	2.3	.984
C	D. Slaught	409	.264	4	42	547	44	11	8	4.9	.982
DH	H. McRae	317	.303	3	42						
DH	J. Orta	403	.298	9	50						
3B	G. Brett	377	.284	13	69	59	201	14	18	2.7	.949
10	D. Iorg	235	.255	5	30	399	22	3	33		.993
C1	J. Wathan	171	.181	2	10	304	31	6	10		.982
SS	U. Washington	170	.224	1	10	81	166	10	40	4.2	.961

Pitcher	G	IP	W	L	SV	ERA
B. Black	35	257	17	12	0	3.12
M. Gubicza	29	189	10	14	0	4.05
L. Gura	31	169	12	9	0	5.18
B. Saberhagen	38	158	10	11	1	3.48
C. Leibrandt	23	144	11	7	0	3.63
D. Quisenberry	72	129	6	3	**44**	2.64
J. Beckwith	49	101	8	4	2	3.40

California

W-81 L-81

John McNamara

POS	Player	AB	BA	HR	RBI	PO	A	E	DP	TC/G	FA
1B	R. Carew	329	.295	3	31	724	59	**15**	73	9.6	.981
2B	R. Wilfong	307	.248	6	33	161	266	11	48	4.5	.975
SS	D. Schofield	400	.193	4	21	218	420	12	95	4.6	**.982**
3B	D. DeCinces	547	.269	20	82	107	266	14	22	2.8	.964
RF	F. Lynn	517	.271	23	79	321	12	6	5	2.4	.982
CF	G. Pettis	397	.227	2	29	337	11	6	4	2.6	.983
LF	B. Downing	539	.275	23	91	272	5	0	0	2.1	1.000
C	B. Boone	450	.202	3	32	660	**71**	12	10	5.4	.984
DH	R. Jackson	525	.223	25	81						
UT	B. Grich	363	.256	18	58	311	282	12	84		.980
OF	J. Beniquez	354	.336	8	39	197	5	6	1	2.1	.971
OF	M. Brown	148	.284	7	22	57	4	2	0	1.4	.968

Pitcher	G	IP	W	L	SV	ERA
M. Witt	34	247	15	11	0	3.47
R. Romanick	33	230	12	12	0	3.76
G. Zahn	28	199	13	10	0	3.12
T. John	32	181	7	13	0	4.52
J. Slaton	32	163	7	10	0	4.97
D. Corbett	45	85	5	1	4	2.12
L. Sanchez	49	84	9	7	11	3.33
B. Kison	20	65	4	5	2	5.37
D. Aase	23	39	4	1	8	1.62

Minnesota

W-81 L-81

Billy Gardner

POS	Player	AB	BA	HR	RBI	PO	A	E	DP	TC/G	FA
1B	K. Hrbek	559	.311	27	107	1320	99	14	113	9.7	.990
2B	T. Teufel	568	.262	14	61	315	**485**	13	81	5.2	.984
SS	H. Jimenez	298	.201	0	19	145	273	18	59	4.1	.959
3B	G. Gaetti	588	.262	5	65	**142**	**334**	**20**	26	**3.2**	.960
RF	T. Brunansky	567	.252	32	85	304	13	5	6	2.1	.984
CF	K. Puckett	557	.296	0	31	438	16	3	4	3.6	.993
LF	M. Hatcher	576	.302	5	69	249	11	7	1	2.7	.974
C	D. Engle	391	.266	4	38	376	34	8	3	4.9	.981
DH	R. Bush	311	.225	11	43						
C	T. Laudner	262	.206	10	35	362	38	9	2	5.0	.978
OF	D. Brown	260	.273	1	19	144	4	1	0	2.7	.993
SS	R. Washington	197	.294	3	23	60	114	4	19	2.5	.978

Pitcher	G	IP	W	L	SV	ERA
F. Viola	35	258	18	12	0	3.21
M. Smithson	36	252	15	13	0	3.68
J. Butcher	34	225	13	11	0	3.44
K. Schrom	25	137	5	11	0	4.47
P. Filson	55	119	6	5	1	4.10
E. Hodge	25	100	4	3	0	4.77
R. Davis	64	83	7	11	29	4.55
R. Lysander	36	57	4	3	5	3.65

AMERICAN LEAGUE 1984, *cont.*

Team	POS	Player	AB	BA	HR	RBI	PO	A	E	DP	TC/G	FA	Pitcher	G	IP	W	L	SV	ERA
Oakland	1B	B. Bochte	469	.264	5	52	1048	66	8	119	7.8	.993	R. Burris	34	212	13	10	0	3.15
W-77 L-85	2B	J. Morgan	365	.244	6	43	201	229	10	62	4.4	.977	L. Sorensen	46	183	6	13	1	4.91
Steve Boros	SS	T. Phillips	451	.266	4	37	133	235	23	54	4.3	.941	S. McCatty	33	180	8	14	0	4.76
W-20 L-24	3B	C. Lansford	597	.300	14	74	137	268	18	27	2.8	.957	B. Krueger	26	142	10	10	0	4.75
Jackie Moore	RF	M. Davis	382	.230	9	46	287	6	12	4	2.4	.961	C. Young	20	109	9	4	0	4.06
W-57 L-61	CF	D. Murphy	559	.256	33	88	474	14	6	2	3.2	.988	K. Atherton	57	104	7	6	2	4.33
	LF	R. Henderson	502	.293	16	58	341	7	11	1	2.6	.969	B. Caudill	68	96	9	7	36	2.71
	C	M. Heath	475	.248	13	64	423	54	7	7	4.5	.986	C. Codiroli	28	89	6	4	1	5.84
	DH	D. Kingman	549	.268	35	118													
	UT	D. Lopes	230	.257	9	36	99	47	6	10		.961							
	UT	B. Almon	211	.223	7	16	255	15	2	19		.993							
	SS	D. Hill	174	.230	2	16	99	125	12	28	3.6	.949							

Team	POS	Player	AB	BA	HR	RBI	PO	A	E	DP	TC/G	FA	Pitcher	G	IP	W	L	SV	ERA
Chicago	1B	G. Walker	442	.294	24	75	791	51	4	66	8.4	.995	R. Dotson	32	246	14	15	0	3.59
W-74 L-88	2B	J. Cruz	415	.222	5	43	273	452	18	92	5.3	.976	T. Seaver	34	237	15	11	0	3.95
Tony LaRussa	SS	S. Fletcher	456	.250	3	35	193	381	16	75	4.4	.973	L. Hoyt	34	236	13	**18**	0	4.47
	3B	V. Law	481	.252	17	59	79	199	13	24	2.1	.955	F. Bannister	34	218	14	11	0	4.83
	RF	H. Baines	569	.304	29	94	307	8	6	1	2.2	.981	B. Burns	34	117	4	12	3	5.00
	CF	R. Law	487	.251	6	37	322	5	5	2	2.6	.985	R. Reed	51	73	0	6	12	3.08
	LF	R. Kittle	466	.215	32	74	226	14	7	2	2.0	.972	J. Agosto	49	55	2	1	7	3.09
	C	C. Fisk	359	.231	21	43	421	38	6	4	5.2	.987							
	DH	G. Luzinski	412	.238	13	58													
	10	T. Paciorek	363	.256	4	29	596	25	6	50		.990							
	OD	J. Hairston	227	.260	5	19	57	2	2	0		.967							
	C	M. Hill	193	.233	5	20	308	17	3	4	4.6	.991							

Team	POS	Player	AB	BA	HR	RBI	PO	A	E	DP	TC/G	FA	Pitcher	G	IP	W	L	SV	ERA
Seattle	1B	A. Davis	567	.284	27	116	1271	94	11	108	9.4	.992	M. Langston	35	225	17	10	0	3.40
W-74 L-88	2B	J. Perconte	612	.294	0	31	303	438	14	90	5.0	.981	M. Moore	34	212	7	17	0	4.97
Del Crandall	SS	S. Owen	530	.245	3	43	245	463	17	86	4.8	.977	J. Beattie	32	211	12	16	0	3.41
W-59 L-76	3B	J. Presley	251	.227	10	36	48	113	7	12	2.4	.958	E. Vande Berg	50	130	8	12	7	4.76
Chuck Cottier	RF	A. Cowens	524	.277	15	78	228	8	3	0	1.8	.987	M. Young	22	113	6	8	0	5.72
W-15 L-12	CF	D. Henderson	350	.280	14	43	242	11	3	5	2.6	.988	S. Barojas	19	95	6	5	1	3.98
	LF	S. Henderson	325	.262	10	35	84	4	6	0	1.8	.936	D. Beard	43	76	3	2	5	5.80
	C	B. Kearney	431	.225	7	43	**823**	63	11	9	**6.7**	.988	E. Nunez	37	68	2	2	7	3.18
	DH	K. Phelps	290	.241	24	51							P. Mirabella	52	68	2	5	3	4.37
	OF	B. Bonnell	363	.264	8	48	153	8	1	0	1.7	.994	M. Stanton	54	61	4	4	8	3.54
	OF	P. Bradley	322	.301	0	24	235	3	2	1	2.1	.992							
	UT	L. Milbourne	211	.265	1	22	53	86	12	14		.921							

Team	POS	Player	AB	BA	HR	RBI	PO	A	E	DP	TC/G	FA	Pitcher	G	IP	W	L	SV	ERA
Texas	1B	P. O'Brien	520	.287	18	80	1270	105	11	103	9.8	.992	C. Hough	36	266	16	14	0	3.76
W-69 L-92	2B	W. Tolleson	338	.213	0	9	191	276	10	61	4.4	.979	F. Tanana	35	246	15	15	0	3.25
Doug Rader	SS	C. Wilkerson	484	.248	1	26	151	285	26	50	4.0	.944	D. Darwin	35	224	8	12	0	3.94
	3B	B. Bell	553	.315	11	83	129	323	**20**	28	3.2	.958	D. Stewart	32	192	7	14	0	4.73
	RF	L. Parrish	613	.285	22	101	153	8	3	3	2.0	.982	M. Mason	36	184	9	13	0	3.61
	CF	G. Ward	602	.284	21	79	376	11	5	1	2.6	.987	D. Schmidt	43	70	6	6	12	2.56
	LF	B. Sample	489	.247	5	33	285	3	4	2	2.4	.986	D. Tobik	24	42	1	6	5	3.61
	C	D. Scott	235	.221	3	20	400	41	12	9	5.7	.974							
	DH	M. Rivers	313	.300	4	33													
	OF	G. Wright	383	.243	9	48	175	3	3	0	2.3	.983							
	C	N. Yost	242	.182	6	25	368	20	2	1	5.0	.995							
	01	B. Jones	143	.259	4	22	139	7	1	8		.993							

BATTING AND BASE RUNNING LEADERS

Batting Average
- D. Mattingly, NY .343
- D. Winfield, NY .340
- W. Boggs, BOS .325
- B. Bell, TEX .315
- A. Trammell, DET .314

Slugging Average
- H. Baines, CHI .541
- D. Mattingly, NY .537
- D. Evans, BOS .532
- T. Armas, BOS .531
- K. Hrbek, MIN .522

Home Runs
- T. Armas, BOS 43
- D. Kingman, OAK 35
- D. Murphy, OAK 33
- L. Parrish, DET 33
- A. Thornton, CLE 33

Total Bases
- T. Armas, BOS 339
- D. Evans, BOS 335
- C. Ripken, BAL 327
- D. Mattingly, NY 324
- M. Easler, BOS 310

Runs Batted In
- T. Armas, BOS 123
- J. Rice, BOS 122
- D. Kingman, OAK 118
- A. Davis, SEA 116
- E. Murray, BAL 110
- D. Mattingly, NY 110

Stolen Bases
- R. Henderson, OAK 66
- D. Collins, TOR 60
- B. Butler, CLE 52
- G. Pettis, CAL 48
- W. Wilson, KC 47

Hits
- D. Mattingly, NY 207
- W. Boggs, BOS 203
- C. Ripken, BAL 195
- D. Winfield, NY 193

Base on Balls
- E. Murray, BAL 107
- A. Davis, SEA 97
- D. Evans, BOS 96
- A. Thornton, CLE 91

Home Run Percentage
- R. Kittle, CHI 6.9
- T. Armas, BOS 6.7
- D. Kingman, OAK 6.4
- D. Murphy, OAK 5.9

Runs
- D. Evans, BOS 121
- R. Henderson, OAK 113
- W. Boggs, BOS 109
- B. Butler, CLE 108

Doubles
- D. Mattingly, NY 44
- L. Parrish, TEX 42
- G. Bell, TOR 39
- D. Evans, BOS 37
- C. Ripken, BAL 37

Triples
- D. Collins, TOR 15
- L. Moseby, TOR 15
- K. Gibson, DET 10
- H. Baines, CHI 10

PITCHING LEADERS

Winning Percentage
- D. Alexander, TOR .739
- B. Blyleven, CLE .731
- D. Petry, DET .692
- M. Wilcox, DET .680
- D. Stieb, TOR .667
- P. Niekro, NY .667

Earned Run Average
- M. Boddicker, BAL 2.79
- D. Stieb, TOR 2.83
- B. Blyleven, CLE 2.87
- P. Niekro, NY 3.09
- G. Zahn, CAL 3.12

Wins
- M. Boddicker, BAL 20
- J. Morris, DET 19
- B. Blyleven, CLE 19
- D. Petry, DET 18
- F. Viola, MIN 18

Saves
- D. Quisenberry, KC 44
- B. Caudill, OAK 36
- G. Hernandez, DET 32
- D. Righetti, NY 31
- R. Davis, MIN 29

Strikeouts
- M. Langston, SEA 204
- D. Stieb, TOR 198
- M. Witt, CAL 196
- B. Blyleven, CLE 170
- C. Hough, TEX 165

Complete Games
- C. Hough, TEX 17
- M. Boddicker, BAL 16
- R. Dotson, CHI 14
- B. Blyleven, CLE 12
- J. Beattie, SEA 12

Fewest Hits/9 Innings
- D. Stieb, TOR 7.25
- B. Blyleven, CLE 7.49
- M. Boddicker, BAL 7.51
- M. Langston, SEA 7.52

Shutouts
- G. Zahn, CAL 5
- B. Ojeda, BOS 5

Fewest Walks/9 Innings
- L. Hoyt, CHI 1.64
- M. Smithson, MIN 1.93
- R. Guidry, NY 2.02
- D. Alexander, TOR 2.03

Most Strikeouts/9 Inn.
- M. Langston, SEA 8.16
- M. Witt, CAL 7.15
- M. Moore, SEA 6.71
- D. Stieb, TOR 6.67

Innings
- D. Stieb, TOR 267
- C. Hough, TEX 266
- D. Alexander, TOR 262
- M. Boddicker, BAL 261

Games Pitched
- G. Hernandez, DET 80
- D. Quisenberry, KC 72
- A. Lopez, DET 71
- E. Camacho, CLE 69

AMERICAN LEAGUE 1984, *cont.*

		W	L	PCT	GB	R	OR	Batting 2B	3B	HR	BA	SA	SB	Fielding E	DP	FA	Pitching CG	BB	SO	ShO	SV	ERA
East	Detroit	104	58	.642		**829**	**643**	254	46	**187**	.271	.432	106	127	162	.979	19	489	914	8	**51**	**3.49**
	Toronto	89	73	.549	15	750	696	275	**68**	143	.273	.421	**193**	123	166	.980	34	528	875	10	33	3.86
	New York	87	75	.537	17	758	679	**276**	32	130	.276	.405	62	142	**177**	.977	15	518	**992**	12	43	3.78
	Boston	86	76	.531	18	810	764	259	45	181	**.283**	**.441**	37	143	127	.977	40	517	927	12	32	4.18
	Baltimore	85	77	.525	19	681	667	234	23	160	.252	.391	51	123	166	**.981**	**48**	512	713	**13**	32	3.72
	Cleveland	75	87	.463	29	761	766	222	39	123	.265	.384	126	146	163	.977	21	545	803	7	35	4.25
	Milwaukee	67	94	.416	36.5	641	734	232	36	96	.262	.370	52	136	156	.978	13	480	785	7	41	4.06
West	Kansas City	84	78	.519		673	686	268	52	117	.268	.399	106	131	157	.979	18	**433**	724	9	50	3.92
	California	81	81	.500	3	696	697	211	30	150	.249	.381	79	128	170	.980	36	474	754	12	26	3.96
	Minnesota	81	81	.500	3	673	675	259	33	114	.265	.385	39	**120**	133	.980	32	463	713	9	38	3.85
	Oakland	77	85	.475	7	738	796	257	29	158	.259	.404	145	146	159	.975	15	592	695	6	44	4.48
	Chicago	74	88	.457	10	679	736	225	38	172	.247	.395	109	122	160	**.981**	43	483	840	9	32	4.13
	Seattle	74	88	.457	10	682	774	244	34	129	.258	.384	116	128	141	.979	26	619	972	4	35	4.31
	Texas	69	92	.429	14.5	656	714	227	29	120	.261	.377	80	138	137	.977	38	518	864	6	21	3.91
						10027	10027	3443	534	1980	.264	.398	1301	1853	2174	.979	398	7171	11571	124	513	3.99

NATIONAL LEAGUE 1985

East

St. Louis

W-101 L-61

Whitey Herzog

POS	Player	AB	BA	HR	RBI	PO	A	E	DP	TC/G	FA
1B	J. Clark	442	.281	22	87	1116	66	**14**	102	9.9	.988
2B	T. Herr	596	.302	8	110	337	448	12	120	5.0	.985
SS	O. Smith	537	.276	6	54	264	**549**	14	111	5.2	**.983**
3B	T. Pendleton	559	.240	5	69	129	361	18	26	3.4	.965
RF	A. Van Slyke	424	.259	13	55	234	13	1	4	1.7	.996
CF	W. McGee	612	**.353**	10	82	382	11	9	2	2.7	.978
LF	V. Coleman	636	.267	1	40	305	16	7	1	2.2	.979
C	T. Nieto	253	.225	0	34	384	28	4	3	4.4	.990
C	D. Porter	240	.221	10	36	386	26	4	4	5.1	.990
OF	T. Landrum	161	.280	4	21	91	2	0	1	1.3	1.000

Pitcher	G	IP	W	L	SV	ERA
J. Tudor	36	275	21	8	0	1.93
J. Andujar	38	270	21	12	0	3.40
D. Cox	35	241	18	9	0	2.88
K. Kepshire	32	153	10	9	0	4.75
B. Forsch	34	136	9	6	2	3.90
J. Lahti	52	68	5	2	19	1.84
K. Dayley	57	65	4	4	11	2.76
B. Campbell	50	64	5	3	4	3.50

New York

W-98 L-64

Davey Johnson

POS	Player	AB	BA	HR	RBI	PO	A	E	DP	TC/G	FA
1B	K. Hernandez	593	.309	10	91	1310	**139**	4	113	9.3	**.997**
2B	W. Backman	520	.273	1	38	272	370	7	76	4.6	**.989**
SS	R. Santana	529	.257	1	29	**301**	396	25	81	4.7	.965
3B	H. Johnson	389	.242	11	46	67	171	15	21	2.2	.941
RF	D. Strawberry	393	.277	29	79	211	5	2	2	2.0	.991
CF	M. Wilson	337	.276	6	26	216	0	8	0	2.7	.964
LF	G. Foster	452	.263	21	77	198	7	5	2	1.7	.976
C	G. Carter	555	.281	32	100	**956**	67	8	11	**7.2**	.992
OF	D. Heep	271	.280	7	42	126	1	3	0	1.7	.977
3B	R. Knight	271	.218	6	36	52	109	7	5	2.3	.958
OF	L. Dykstra	236	.254	1	19	165	6	1	2	2.3	.994

Pitcher	G	IP	W	L	SV	ERA
D. Gooden	35	**277**	**24**	4	0	**1.53**
R. Darling	36	248	16	6	0	2.90
E. Lynch	31	191	10	8	0	3.44
S. Fernandez	26	170	9	9	0	2.80
R. McDowell	62	127	6	5	17	2.83
R. Aguilera	21	122	10	7	0	3.24
J. Orosco	54	79	8	6	17	2.73
D. Sisk	42	73	4	5	2	5.30

Montreal

W-84 L-77

Buck Rodgers

POS	Player	AB	BA	HR	RBI	PO	A	E	DP	TC/G	FA
1B	D. Driessen	312	.250	6	25	804	64	3	79	9.9	.997
2B	V. Law	519	.266	10	52	276	367	10	86	5.2	.985
SS	H. Brooks	605	.269	13	100	203	441	28	81	4.3	.958
3B	T. Wallach	569	.260	22	81	**148**	**383**	18	**34**	**3.6**	.967
RF	A. Dawson	529	.255	23	91	248	9	7	1	2.0	.973
CF	H. Winningham	312	.237	3	21	229	6	4	2	2.1	.983
LF	T. Raines	575	.320	11	41	284	8	2	4	2.0	.993
C	M. Fitzgerald	295	.207	5	34	542	46	8	7	5.5	.987
10	T. Francona	281	.267	2	31	431	37	6	32		.987
OF	M. Webster	212	.274	11	30	133	3	1	0	2.1	.993
2B	U. Washington	193	.249	1	17	70	104	4	22	4.1	.978

Pitcher	G	IP	W	L	SV	ERA
B. Smith	32	222	18	5	0	2.91
B. Gullickson	29	181	14	12	0	3.52
J. Hesketh	25	155	10	5	0	2.49
D. Palmer	24	136	7	10	0	3.71
T. Burke	**78**	120	9	4	8	2.39
D. Schatzeder	24	104	3	5	0	3.80
J. Reardon	63	88	2	8	**41**	3.18
G. Lucas	49	68	6	2	2	3.19

Chicago

W-77 L-84

Jim Frey

POS	Player	AB	BA	HR	RBI	PO	A	E	DP	TC/G	FA
1B	L. Durham	542	.282	21	75	1421	107	7	121	**10.2**	.995
2B	R. Sandberg	609	.305	26	83	353	500	12	99	5.7	.986
SS	S. Dunston	250	.260	4	18	144	248	17	39	5.6	.958
3B	R. Cey	500	.232	22	63	75	273	**21**	21	2.6	.943
RF	K. Moreland	587	.307	14	106	233	10	6	2	1.7	.976
CF	B. Dernier	469	.254	1	21	310	4	9	1	2.8	.972
LF	G. Matthews	298	.235	13	40	119	7	3	2	1.5	.977
C	J. Davis	482	.232	17	58	694	84	8	7	5.7	.990
OF	D. Lopes	275	.284	11	44	113	2	1	0	1.5	.991
UT	C. Speier	218	.243	4	24	87	177	11	43		.960
SS	L. Bowa	195	.246	0	13	91	197	9	34	4.5	.970
OF	T. Bosley	180	.328	7	27	84	0	1	0	1.5	.988
OF	B. Hatcher	163	.245	2	10	77	2	1	0	1.8	.988
13	R. Hebner	120	.217	3	22	110	24	4	15		.971

Pitcher	G	IP	W	L	SV	ERA
D. Eckersley	25	169	11	7	0	3.08
R. Fontenot	38	155	6	10	0	4.36
S. Trout	24	141	9	7	0	3.39
R. Sutcliffe	20	130	8	8	0	3.18
S. Sanderson	19	121	5	6	0	3.12
L. Smith	65	98	7	4	33	3.04
D. Ruthven	20	87	4	7	0	4.53
L. Sorensen	45	82	3	7	0	4.26
G. Frazier	51	76	7	8	2	6.39
W. Brusstar	51	74	4	3	4	6.05

Philadelphia

W-75 L-87

John Felske

POS	Player	AB	BA	HR	RBI	PO	A	E	DP	TC/G	FA
1B	M. Schmidt	549	.277	33	93	880	83	7	89	9.2	.993
2B	J. Samuel	**663**	.264	19	74	**389**	463	15	88	5.5	.983
SS	S. Jeltz	196	.189	0	12	106	215	14	38	3.9	.958
3B	R. Schu	416	.252	7	24	86	191	20	19	2.7	.933
RF	G. Wilson	608	.275	14	102	343	18	12	4	2.4	.968
CF	V. Hayes	570	.263	13	70	368	9	6	1	2.6	.984
LF	J. Stone	264	.265	3	11	82	4	3	0	1.3	.966
C	O. Virgil	426	.246	19	55	667	52	4	11	6.0	**.994**
OF	G. Maddox	218	.239	4	23	143	3	3	0	1.6	.980
OF	J. Russell	216	.218	9	23	56	4	0	1	1.2	1.000
1B	T. Corcoran	182	.214	0	22	386	25	3	27	7.0	.993
OF	G. Gross	169	.260	0	14	48	4	0	0	1.0	1.000
SS	L. Aguayo	165	.279	6	21	61	117	8	21	3.1	.957

Pitcher	G	IP	W	L	SV	ERA
J. Denny	33	231	11	14	0	3.82
K. Gross	38	206	15	13	0	3.41
S. Rawley	36	199	13	8	0	3.31
C. Hudson	38	193	8	13	0	3.78
J. Koosman	19	99	6	4	0	4.62
D. Carman	71	86	9	4	7	2.08
K. Tekulve	58	72	4	10	14	2.99

NATIONAL LEAGUE 1985, *cont.*

Pittsburgh

W-57 L-104

Chuck Tanner

POS	Player	AB	BA	HR	RBI	PO	A	E	DP	TC/G	FA	Pitcher	G	IP	W	L	SV	ERA
1B	J. Thompson	402	.241	12	61	995	82	9	69	9.5	.992	R. Rhoden	35	213	10	15	0	4.47
2B	J. Ray	594	.274	7	70	305	423	18	89	4.9	.976	R. Reuschel	31	194	14	8	1	2.27
SS	S. Khalifa	320	.237	2	31	156	316	16	45	5.1	.967	J. DeLeon	31	163	2	**19**	3	4.70
3B	B. Madlock	399	.251	10	41	46	175	14	10	2.4	.940	L. Tunnell	24	132	4	10	0	4.01
RF	G. Hendrick	256	.230	2	25	133	2	4	0	2.1	.971	L. McWilliams	30	126	7	9	0	4.70
CF	M. Wynne	337	.205	2	18	229	7	3	1	2.4	.987	C. Guante	63	109	4	6	5	2.72
LF	S. Kemp	236	.250	2	21	105	1	0	0	1.7	1.000	D. Robinson	44	95	5	11	3	3.87
C	T. Pena	546	.249	10	59	922	**100**	12	9	7.1	.988	J. Candelaria	37	54	2	4	9	3.64
OF	J. Orsulak	397	.300	0	21	229	10	6	1	2.1	.976							
UT	B. Almon	244	.270	6	29	104	108	5	22		.977							
3B	J. Morrison	244	.254	4	22	39	84	5	9	2.2	.961							
OF	M. Brown	205	.332	5	33	87	3	6	1	1.7	.938							

West

Los Angeles

W-95 L-67

Tom Lasorda

POS	Player	AB	BA	HR	RBI	PO	A	E	DP	TC/G	FA	Pitcher	G	IP	W	L	SV	ERA
1B	G. Brock	438	.251	21	66	1113	84	7	86	9.9	.994	F. Valenzuela	35	272	17	10	0	2.45
2B	S. Sax	488	.279	1	42	330	357	**22**	84	5.3	.969	O. Hershiser	36	240	19	3	0	2.03
SS	M. Duncan	562	.244	6	39	174	386	27	57	4.8	.954	J. Reuss	34	213	14	10	0	2.92
3B	D. Anderson	221	.199	4	18	28	107	6	10	2.8	.957	B. Welch	23	167	14	4	0	2.31
RF	M. Marshall	518	.293	28	95	206	9	2	2	1.7	.991	R. Honeycutt	31	142	8	12	1	3.42
CF	K. Landreaux	482	.268	12	50	267	4	7	1	2.0	.975	T. Niedenfuer	64	106	7	9	19	2.71
LF	P. Guerrero	487	.320	33	87	141	7	4	2	1.9	.974	K. Howell	56	86	4	7	12	3.77
C	M. Scioscia	429	.296	7	53	818	66	**13**	8	6.5	.986							
OF	C. Maldonado	213	.225	5	19	121	6	2	0	1.1	.984							
OF	R. Reynolds	207	.266	0	25	94	3	3	0	1.9	.970							
31	E. Cabell	192	.292	0	22	140	75	9	11		.960							
UT	B. Russell	169	.260	0	13	60	82	10	11		.934							

Cincinnati

W-89 L-72

Pete Rose

POS	Player	AB	BA	HR	RBI	PO	A	E	DP	TC/G	FA	Pitcher	G	IP	W	L	SV	ERA
1B	P. Rose	405	.264	2	46	870	73	5	80	8.6	.995	T. Browning	38	261	20	9	0	3.55
2B	R. Oester	526	.295	1	34	366	457	9	100	5.6	.989	M. Soto	36	257	12	15	0	3.58
SS	D. Concepcion	560	.252	7	48	212	404	24	64	4.2	.962	J. Tibbs	35	218	10	16	0	3.92
3B	B. Bell	247	.219	6	36	54	105	9	13	2.5	.946	R. Robinson	33	108	7	7	1	3.99
RF	D. Parker	635	.312	34	**125**	329	12	10	1	2.2	.972	J. Stuper	33	99	8	5	0	4.55
CF	E. Milner	453	.254	3	33	340	12	6	3	2.7	.983	J. Franco	67	99	12	3	12	2.18
LF	N. Esasky	413	.262	21	66	91	4	0	0	1.8	1.000	T. Hume	56	80	3	5	3	3.26
C	D. Van Gorder	151	.238	2	24	255	11	3	2	3.8	.989	T. Power	64	80	8	6	27	2.70
OF	G. Redus	246	.252	6	28	140	3	2	0	1.7	.986							
01	C. Cedeno	220	.241	3	30	206	9	2	11		.991							
1B	T. Perez	183	.328	6	33	340	22	2	34	7.3	.995							
3B	W. Krenchicki	173	.272	4	25	34	84	4	9	2.3	.967							
C	A. Knicely	158	.253	5	26	231	13	8	1	5.5	.968							

Houston

W-83 L-79

Bob Lillis

POS	Player	AB	BA	HR	RBI	PO	A	E	DP	TC/G	FA	Pitcher	G	IP	W	L	SV	ERA
1B	G. Davis	350	.271	20	64	749	57	12	76	9.2	.985	B. Knepper	37	241	15	13	0	3.55
2B	B. Doran	578	.287	14	59	345	440	16	108	5.4	.980	N. Ryan	35	232	10	12	0	3.80
SS	C. Reynolds	379	.272	4	32	158	318	11	65	4.8	.977	M. Scott	36	222	18	8	0	3.29
3B	P. Garner	463	.268	6	51	75	197	20	14	2.4	.932	J. Niekro	32	213	9	12	0	3.72
RF	J. Mumphrey	444	.277	8	61	248	6	8	1	2.1	.969	B. Dawley	49	81	5	3	2	3.56
CF	K. Bass	539	.269	16	68	328	10	1	1	2.4	.997	D. Smith	64	79	9	5	27	2.27
LF	J. Cruz	544	.300	9	79	257	12	8	3	2.0	.971	F. DiPino	54	76	3	7	6	4.03
C	M. Bailey	332	.265	10	45	565	51	**13**	6	5.7	.979	J. Calhoun	44	64	2	5	4	2.54
UT	D. Walling	345	.270	7	45	326	124	12	31		.974							
SS	D. Thon	251	.251	6	29	106	218	11	48	4.2	.967							
OF	T. Puhl	194	.284	2	23	92	3	0	1	1.8	1.000							
C	A. Ashby	189	.280	8	25	312	37	8	1	5.9	.978							
02	J. Pankovits	172	.244	4	14	80	37	1	8		.992							

San Diego

W-83 L-79

Dick Williams

POS	Player	AB	BA	HR	RBI	PO	A	E	DP	TC/G	FA	Pitcher	G	IP	W	L	SV	ERA
1B	S. Garvey	654	.281	17	81	**1442**	92	5	**138**	9.5	.997	E. Show	35	233	12	11	0	3.09
2B	T. Flannery	384	.281	1	40	261	287	13	72	4.6	.977	A. Hawkins	33	229	18	8	0	3.15
SS	G. Templeton	546	.282	6	55	245	460	23	96	4.9	.968	D. Dravecky	34	215	13	11	0	2.93
3B	G. Nettles	440	.261	15	61	122	229	15	16	2.8	.959	L. Hoyt	31	210	16	8	0	3.47
RF	T. Gwynn	622	.317	6	46	337	14	4	2	2.3	.989	M. Thurmond	36	138	7	11	2	3.97
CF	K. McReynolds	564	.234	15	75	430	12	3	3	3.0	.993	C. Lefferts	60	83	7	6	2	3.35
LF	C. Martinez	514	.253	21	72	298	13	7	3	2.1	.978	G. Gossage	50	79	5	3	26	1.82
C	T. Kennedy	532	.261	10	74	654	67	10	**12**	5.2	.986							
23	J. Royster	249	.281	5	31	125	189	8	34		.975							
3B	K. Bevacqua	138	.239	3	25	32	56	5	7	2.8	.946							

Atlanta

W-66 L-96

Eddie Haas
W-50 L-71

Bobby Wine
W-16 L-25

POS	Player	AB	BA	HR	RBI	PO	A	E	DP	TC/G	FA	Pitcher	G	IP	W	L	SV	ERA
1B	B. Horner	483	.267	27	89	892	58	0	105	10.9	1.000	R. Mahler	39	267	17	15	0	3.48
2B	G. Hubbard	439	.232	5	39	339	**539**	10	**127**	**6.3**	.989	S. Bedrosian	37	207	7	15	0	3.83
SS	R. Ramirez	568	.248	5	58	214	451	**32**	**115**	**5.2**	.954	Z. Smith	42	147	9	10	0	3.80
3B	K. Oberkfell	412	.272	3	35	70	220	11	19	2.6	.963	R. Camp	66	128	4	6	3	3.95
RF	C. Washington	398	.276	15	43	122	3	5	1	1.3	.962	G. Garber	59	97	6	6	1	3.61
CF	D. Murphy	616	.300	**37**	111	334	8	7	4	2.2	.980	P. Perez	22	95	1	13	0	6.14
LF	T. Harper	492	.264	17	72	215	10	5	0	1.8	.978	B. Sutter	58	88	7	7	23	4.48
C	R. Cerone	282	.216	3	25	384	48	6	4	4.8	.986	L. Barker	20	74	2	9	0	6.35
OF	B. Komminsk	300	.227	4	21	161	2	7	0	1.8	.959							
1B	G. Perry	238	.214	3	13	541	37	9	48	10.7	.985							
C	B. Benedict	208	.202	0	20	314	35	4	1	5.0	.989							
2S	P. Zuvella	190	.253	0	4	112	169	8	38		.972							
OF	M. Thompson	182	.302	0	6	78	2	3	0	1.7	.964							
1B	C. Chambliss	170	.235	3	21	299	25	1	31	8.3	.997							

NATIONAL LEAGUE 1985, *cont.*

San Francisco

W-62 L-100

Jim Davenport
W-56 L-88

Roger Craig
W-6 L-12

POS	Player	AB	BA	HR	RBI	PO	A	E	DP	TC/G	FA	Pitcher	G	IP	W	L	SV	ERA
1B	D. Green	294	.248	5	20	628	42	9	54	8.7	.987	D. LaPoint	31	207	7	17	0	3.57
2B	M. Trillo	451	.224	3	25	262	357	12	73	5.3	.981	M. Krukow	28	195	8	11	0	3.38
SS	J. Uribe	476	.237	3	26	209	438	26	77	4.6	.961	A. Hammaker	29	171	5	12	0	3.74
3B	C. Brown	432	.271	16	61	94	243	10	15	2.9	**.971**	J. Gott	26	148	7	10	0	3.88
RF	C. Davis	481	.270	13	56	279	10	6	2	2.3	.980	V. Blue	33	131	8	8	0	4.47
CF	D. Gladden	502	.243	7	41	273	3	7	0	2.3	.975	M. Davis	77	114	5	12	7	3.54
LF	J. Leonard	507	.241	17	62	203	10	5	0	1.7	.977	B. Laskey	19	114	5	11	0	3.55
C	B. Brenly	440	.220	19	56	662	62	12	8	6.7	.984	S. Garrelts	74	106	9	6	13	2.30
OF	J. Youngblood	230	.270	4	24	103	4	5	0	2.0	.955	G. Minton	68	97	5	4	4	3.54
1B	D. Driessen	181	.232	3	22	399	27	1	32	8.7	.998							
23	B. Wellman	174	.236	0	16	65	105	8	13		.955							
OF	R. Deer	162	.185	8	20	54	1	1	0	1.5	.982							

BATTING AND BASE RUNNING LEADERS

Batting Average
W. McGee, STL .353
P. Guerrero, LA .320
T. Raines, MON .320
T. Gwynn, SD .317
D. Parker, CIN .312

Slugging Average
P. Guerrero, LA .577
D. Parker, CIN .551
D. Murphy, ATL .539
M. Schmidt, PHI .532
M. Marshall, LA .515

Home Runs
D. Murphy, ATL 37
D. Parker, CIN 34
P. Guerrero, LA 33
M. Schmidt, PHI 33
G. Carter, NY 32

Total Bases
D. Parker, CIN 350
D. Murphy, ATL 332
W. McGee, STL 308
R. Sandberg, CHI 307
M. Schmidt, PHI 292

Runs Batted In
D. Parker, CIN 125
D. Murphy, ATL 111
T. Herr, STL 110
K. Moreland, CHI 106
G. Wilson, PHI 102

Stolen Bases
V. Coleman, STL 110
T. Raines, MON 70
W. McGee, STL 56
R. Sandberg, CHI 54
J. Samuel, PHI 53

Hits
W. McGee, STL 216
D. Parker, CIN 198
T. Gwynn, SD 197
R. Sandberg, CHI 186

Base on Balls
D. Murphy, ATL 90
C. Martinez, SD 87
M. Schmidt, PHI 87
P. Rose, CIN 86
V. Law, MON 86

Home Run Percentage
P. Guerrero, LA 6.8
M. Schmidt, PHI 6.0
D. Murphy, ATL 6.0
G. Carter, NY 5.8

Runs
D. Murphy, ATL 118
T. Raines, MON 115
W. McGee, STL 114
R. Sandberg, CHI 113

Doubles
D. Parker, CIN 42
G. Wilson, PHI 39
T. Herr, STL 38
T. Wallach, MON 36

Triples
W. McGee, STL 18
T. Raines, MON 13
J. Samuel, PHI 13
P. Garner, HOU 10
V. Coleman, STL 10

PITCHING LEADERS

Winning Percentage
O. Hershiser, LA .864
D. Gooden, NY .857
B. Smith, MON .783
R. Darling, NY .727
J. Tudor, STL .724

Earned Run Average
D. Gooden, NY 1.53
J. Tudor, STL 1.93
O. Hershiser, LA 2.03
R. Reuschel, PIT 2.27
B. Welch, LA 2.31

Wins
D. Gooden, NY 24
J. Andujar, STL 21
J. Tudor, STL 21
T. Browning, CIN 20
O. Hershiser, LA 19

Saves
J. Reardon, MON 41
L. Smith, CHI 33
D. Smith, HOU 27
T. Power, CIN 27
G. Gossage, SD 26

Strikeouts
D. Gooden, NY 268
M. Soto, CIN 214
N. Ryan, HOU 209
F. Valenzuela, LA 208
S. Fernandez, NY 180

Complete Games
D. Gooden, NY 16
F. Valenzuela, LA 14
J. Tudor, STL 14
D. Cox, STL 10
J. Andujar, STL 10

Fewest Hits/9 Innings
S. Fernandez, NY 5.71
D. Gooden, NY 6.44
O. Hershiser, LA 6.72
J. Tudor, STL 6.84

Shutouts
J. Tudor, STL 10
D. Gooden, NY 8
O. Hershiser, LA 5
F. Valenzuela, LA 5

Fewest Walks/9 Innings
L. Hoyt, SD 0.86
D. Eckersley, CHI 1.01
E. Lynch, NY 1.27
J. Tudor, STL 1.60

Most Strikeouts/9 Inn.
S. Fernandez, NY 9.51
D. Gooden, NY 8.72
J. DeLeon, PIT 8.24
N. Ryan, HOU 8.11

Innings
D. Gooden, NY 277
J. Tudor, STL 275
F. Valenzuela, LA 272
J. Andujar, STL 270

Games Pitched
T. Burke, MON 78
M. Davis, SF 77
S. Garrelts, SF 74
D. Carman, PHI 71

		W	L	PCT	GB	R	OR	Batting 2B	3B	HR	BA	SA	SB	Fielding E	DP	FA	Pitching CG	BB	SO	ShO	SV	ERA
East	St. Louis	101	61	.623		**747**	572	245	**59**	87	**.264**	.379	**314**	**108**	166	**.983**	**37**	453	798	20	44	3.10
	New York	98	64	.605	3	695	**568**	239	35	134	.257	.385	117	115	138	.982	32	515	**1039**	19	37	3.11
	Montreal	84	77	.522	16.5	633	636	242	49	118	.247	.375	169	121	152	.981	13	509	870	13	**54**	3.55
	Chicago	77	84	.478	23.5	686	729	239	28	**150**	.254	**.390**	182	134	150	.979	20	519	820	8	42	4.16
	Philadelphia	75	87	.463	26	667	673	238	47	141	.245	.383	122	139	142	.978	24	596	899	9	30	3.68
	Pittsburgh	57	104	.354	43.5	568	708	252	28	80	.247	.347	110	133	127	.979	15	584	962	6	29	3.97
West	Los Angeles	95	67	.586		682	579	226	28	129	.261	.382	136	166	131	.974	**37**	462	979	**21**	36	**2.96**
	Cincinnati	89	72	.553	5.5	677	666	249	34	114	.255	.376	159	122	142	.980	24	535	910	11	45	3.71
	Houston	83	79	.512	12	706	691	**261**	42	121	.261	.388	96	152	159	.976	17	543	909	9	42	3.66
	San Diego	83	79	.512	12	650	622	241	28	109	.255	.368	60	124	158	.980	26	**443**	727	19	44	3.41
	Atlanta	66	96	.407	29	632	781	213	28	126	.246	.363	72	159	**197**	.976	9	642	776	9	29	4.19
	San Francisco	62	100	.383	33	556	674	217	31	115	.233	.348	99	148	134	.976	13	572	985	5	24	3.61
						7899	7899	2862	437	1424	.252	.374	1636	1621	1796	.979	267	6373	10674	149	456	3.59

AMERICAN LEAGUE 1985

East

Toronto

W-99 L-62

Bobby Cox

POS	Player	AB	BA	HR	RBI	PO	A	E	DP	TC/G	FA	Pitcher	G	IP	W	L	SV	ERA
1B	W. Upshaw	501	.275	15	65	1157	104	10	111	8.6	.992	D. Stieb	36	265	14	13	0	**2.48**
2B	D. Garcia	600	.282	8	65	302	371	13	88	4.8	.981	D. Alexander	36	261	17	10	0	3.45
SS	T. Fernandez	564	.289	2	51	283	**478**	30	109	**4.9**	.962	J. Key	35	213	14	6	0	3.00
3B	R. Mulliniks	366	.295	10	56	75	162	7	16	2.1	**.971**	J. Clancy	23	129	9	6	0	3.78
RF	J. Barfield	539	.289	27	84	349	22	4	8	2.4	.989	D. Lamp	53	106	11	0	2	3.32
CF	L. Moseby	584	.259	18	71	394	7	8	1	2.7	.980	J. Acker	61	86	7	2	10	3.23
LF	G. Bell	607	.275	28	95	320	13	11	3	2.2	.968	G. Lavelle	69	73	5	7	8	3.10
C	E. Whitt	412	.245	19	64	649	38	8	6	5.2	.988	B. Caudill	67	69	4	6	14	2.99
DH	J. Burroughs	191	.257	6	28							T. Henke	28	40	3	3	13	2.02
3B	G. Iorg	288	.313	7	37	39	137	9	13	1.8	.951							
DH	A. Oliver	187	.251	5	23													

AMERICAN LEAGUE 1985, *cont.*

New York

W-97 L-64

Yogi Berra
W-6 L-10

Billy Martin
W-91 L-54

POS	Player	AB	BA	HR	RBI	PO	A	E	DP	TC/G	FA	Pitcher	G	IP	W	L	SV	ERA
1B	D. Mattingly	652	.324	35	**145**	1318	87	7	**154**	8.9	**.995**	R. Guidry	34	259	**22**	6	0	3.27
2B	W. Randolph	497	.276	5	40	303	425	11	104	5.2	.985	P. Niekro	33	220	16	12	0	4.09
SS	B. Meacham	481	.218	1	47	236	390	24	103	4.2	.963	J. Cowley	30	160	12	6	0	3.95
3B	M. Pagliarulo	380	.239	19	62	67	187	13	15	2.0	.951	E. Whitson	30	159	10	8	0	4.88
RF	D. Winfield	633	.275	26	114	316	13	3	3	2.2	.991	B. Shirley	48	109	5	5	2	2.64
CF	R. Henderson	547	.314	24	72	439	7	9	3	3.2	.980	D. Righetti	74	107	12	7	29	2.78
LF	K. Griffey	438	.274	10	69	222	8	7	3	2.2	.970	D. Rasmussen	22	102	3	5	0	3.98
C	B. Wynegar	309	.223	5	32	547	34	6	7	6.1	.990	B. Fisher	55	98	4	4	14	2.38
DH	D. Baylor	477	.231	23	91							R. Bordi	51	98	6	8	2	3.21
C	R. Hassey	267	.296	13	42	402	20	7	2	6.2	.984							
OF	D. Pasqua	148	.209	9	25	72	2	0	0	2.0	1.000							

Detroit

W-84 L-77

Sparky Anderson

POS	Player	AB	BA	HR	RBI	PO	A	E	DP	TC/G	FA	Pitcher	G	IP	W	L	SV	ERA
1B	D. Evans	505	.248	**40**	94	827	114	15	80	8.5	.984	J. Morris	35	257	16	11	0	3.33
2B	L. Whitaker	608	.280	21	73	314	414	11	101	4.9	.985	D. Petry	34	239	15	13	0	3.36
SS	A. Trammell	605	.258	13	57	225	400	15	89	4.3	.977	W. Terrell	34	229	15	10	0	3.85
3B	T. Brookens	485	.237	7	47	123	261	**23**	26	2.7	.943	F. Tanana	20	137	10	7	0	3.34
RF	K. Gibson	581	.287	29	97	286	1	11	0	2.1	.963	G. Hernandez	74	107	8	10	31	2.70
CF	C. Lemon	517	.265	18	68	411	6	4	3	2.9	.990	J. Berenguer	31	95	5	6	0	5.59
LF	L. Herndon	443	.244	12	37	273	7	7	4	2.1	.976	R. O'Neal	28	94	5	5	1	3.24
C	L. Parrish	549	.273	28	98	695	53	5	9	6.3	.993	A. Lopez	51	86	3	7	5	4.80
DH	J. Grubb	155	.245	5	25													
OD	N. Simmons	251	.239	10	33	67	2	4	1		.945							
UT	B. Garbey	237	.257	6	29	228	20	3	24		.988							

Baltimore

W-83 L-78

Joe Altobelli
W-29 L-26

Cal Ripken
W-1 L-0

Earl Weaver
W-53 L-52

POS	Player	AB	BA	HR	RBI	PO	A	E	DP	TC/G	FA	Pitcher	G	IP	W	L	SV	ERA
1B	E. Murray	583	.297	31	124	1338	152	**19**	**154**	9.8	.987	S. McGregor	35	204	14	14	0	4.81
2B	A. Wiggins	298	.285	0	21	148	186	14	58	4.6	.960	M. Boddicker	32	203	12	17	0	4.07
SS	C. Ripken	642	.282	26	110	**286**	474	26	**123**	4.9	.967	D. Martinez	33	180	13	11	0	5.15
3B	F. Rayford	359	.306	18	48	62	145	6	13	2.7	.972	S. Davis	31	175	10	8	0	4.53
RF	L. Lacy	492	.293	9	48	231	9	4	0	2.1	.984	K. Dixon	34	162	8	4	1	3.67
CF	F. Lynn	448	.263	23	68	314	6	2	2	2.6	.994	S. Stewart	56	130	5	7	9	3.61
LF	M. Young	450	.273	28	81	190	6	5	0	2.2	.975	N. Snell	43	100	3	2	5	2.69
C	R. Dempsey	362	.254	12	52	575	49	8	5	4.8	.987	D. Aase	54	88	10	6	14	3.78
DH	L. Sheets	328	.262	17	50							T. Martinez	49	70	3	3	4	5.40
OF	J. Dwyer	233	.249	7	36	131	4	1	0	1.7	.993							
OF	G. Roenicke	225	.218	15	43	134	6	1	0	1.6	.993							
3B	W. Gross	217	.235	11	18	41	98	10	14	2.2	.933							
2B	R. Dauer	208	.202	2	14	117	181	3	44	4.1	.990							
OF	J. Shelby	205	.283	7	27	148	3	3	0	2.6	.981							

Boston

W-81 L-81

John McNamara

POS	Player	AB	BA	HR	RBI	PO	A	E	DP	TC/G	FA	Pitcher	G	IP	W	L	SV	ERA
1B	B. Buckner	673	.299	16	110	1384	**184**	12	140	9.8	.992	O. Boyd	35	272	15	13	0	3.70
2B	M. Barrett	534	.266	5	56	**355**	479	11	**110**	5.5	.987	B. Hurst	35	229	11	13	0	4.51
SS	J. Gutierrez	275	.218	2	21	143	238	23	47	4.1	.943	A. Nipper	25	162	9	12	0	4.06
3B	W. Boggs	653	**.368**	8	78	134	335	17	30	3.0	.965	B. Ojeda	39	158	9	11	1	4.00
RF	D. Evans	617	.263	29	78	291	9	3	1	2.0	.990	R. Clemens	15	98	7	5	0	3.29
CF	S. Lyons	371	.264	5	30	253	4	7	0	2.3	.973	S. Crawford	44	91	6	5	12	3.76
LF	J. Rice	546	.291	27	103	236	8	9	1	1.9	.964	B. Stanley	48	88	6	6	10	2.87
C	R. Gedman	498	.295	18	80	768	**78**	**15**	13	6.2	.983	T. Lollar	16	67	5	5	1	4.57
DH	M. Easler	568	.262	16	74													
OF	T. Armas	385	.265	23	64	173	3	3	1	2.3	.983							
SS	G. Hoffman	279	.276	6	34	155	231	10	61	4.3	.975							

Milwaukee

W-71 L-90

George Bamberger

POS	Player	AB	BA	HR	RBI	PO	A	E	DP	TC/G	FA	Pitcher	G	IP	W	L	SV	ERA
1B	C. Cooper	631	.293	16	99	1087	94	17	101	9.7	.986	D. Darwin	39	218	8	18	2	3.80
2B	J. Gantner	523	.254	5	44	262	402	8	89	5.4	.988	T. Higuera	32	212	15	8	0	3.90
SS	E. Riles	448	.286	5	45	183	310	22	62	4.5	.957	R. Burris	29	170	9	13	0	4.81
3B	P. Molitor	576	.297	10	48	126	263	19	30	3.0	.953	M. Haas	27	162	8	8	0	3.84
RF	P. Householder	299	.258	11	34	202	5	3	0	2.3	.986	J. Cocanower	24	116	6	8	0	4.33
CF	R. Manning	216	.218	2	18	160	2	4	0	2.2	.976	P. Vuckovich	22	113	6	10	0	5.51
LF	R. Yount	466	.277	15	68	258	4	8	2	2.5	.970	B. Gibson	41	92	6	7	11	3.90
C	C. Moore	349	.232	0	31	504	54	13	7	5.6	.977	R. Fingers	47	55	1	6	17	5.04
DH	T. Simmons	528	.273	12	76													
OF	B. Oglivie	341	.290	10	61	190	4	7	0	2.2	.965							
UT	E. Romero	251	.251	0	21	157	219	8	53		.979							
C	B. Schroeder	194	.242	8	25	211	23	3	4	4.9	.987							
OF	R. Ready	181	.265	1	21	85	5	1	1	2.5	.989							

Cleveland

W-60 L-102

Pat Corrales

POS	Player	AB	BA	HR	RBI	PO	A	E	DP	TC/G	FA	Pitcher	G	IP	W	L	SV	ERA
1B	P. Tabler	404	.275	5	59	739	72	14	77	9.0	.983	N. Heaton	36	208	9	17	0	4.90
2B	T. Bernazard	500	.274	11	59	311	399	16	86	4.9	.978	B. Blyleven	23	180*	9	11	0	3.26
SS	J. Franco	636	.288	6	90	238	419	**35**	95	4.6	.949	V. Ruhle	42	125	2	10	3	4.32
3B	B. Jacoby	606	.274	20	87	114	319	19	26	2.8	.958	T. Waddell	49	113	8	6	9	4.87
RF	G. Vukovich	434	.244	8	45	250	4	3	0	1.9	.988	D. Schulze	19	94	4	10	0	6.01
CF	B. Butler	591	.311	5	50	437	19	1	5	3.0	.998	R. Thompson	57	80	3	8	5	6.30
LF	J. Carter	489	.262	15	59	278	11	5	2	2.2	.983	J. Reed	33	72	3	5	8	4.11
C	J. Willard	300	.270	7	36	427	52	5	11	5.0	.990	C. Wardle	15	66	7	6	0	6.68
DH	A. Thornton	461	.236	22	88													
1B	M. Hargrove	284	.285	1	27	595	66	6	66	7.9	.991							
OF	C. Castillo	184	.245	11	25	101	0	5	0	2.1	.953							
C	C. Bando	173	.139	0	13	251	28	4	3	4.2	.986							
OF	O. Nixon	162	.235	3	9	129	5	4	1	1.7	.971							

AMERICAN LEAGUE 1985, *cont.*

West

Kansas City

W-91 L-71

Dick Howser

POS	Player	AB	BA	HR	RBI	PO	A	E	DP	TC/G	FA	Pitcher	G	IP	W	L	SV	ERA
1B	S. Balboni	600	.243	36	88	**1573**	101	12	138	**10.5**	.993	C. Leibrandt	33	238	17	9	0	2.69
2B	F. White	563	.249	22	69	342	**490**	**17**	101	**5.7**	.980	B. Saberhagen	32	235	20	6	0	2.87
SS	O. Concepcion	314	.204	2	20	127	367	21	63	4.0	.959	D. Jackson	32	208	14	12	0	3.42
3B	G. Brett	550	.335	30	112	107	**339**	15	**33**	3.0	.967	B. Black	33	206	10	15	0	4.33
RF	D. Motley	383	.222	17	49	198	4	7	1	1.8	.967	M. Gubicza	29	177	14	10	0	4.06
CF	W. Wilson	605	.278	4	43	378	4	2	1	2.7	.995	D. Quisenberry	**84**	129	8	9	**37**	2.37
LF	L. Smith	448	.257	6	41	195	10	9	3	1.8	.958							
C	J. Sundberg	367	.245	10	35	572	41	5	10	5.5	.992							
DH	H. McRae	320	.259	14	70													
DH	J. Orta	300	.267	4	45													
OF	P. Sheridan	206	.228	3	17	116	3	2	0	1.8	.983							
OF	D. Iorg	130	.223	1	21	41	0	0	0	1.3	1.000							

California

W-90 L-72

Gene Mauch

POS	Player	AB	BA	HR	RBI	PO	A	E	DP	TC/G	FA	Pitcher	G	IP	W	L	SV	ERA
1B	R. Carew	443	.280	2	39	1055	65	7	121	9.7	.994	M. Witt	35	250	15	9	0	3.56
2B	B. Grich	479	.242	13	53	224	380	2	99	5.2	**.997**	R. Romanick	31	195	14	9	0	4.11
SS	D. Schofield	438	.219	8	41	261	397	25	108	4.6	.963	K. McCaskill	30	190	12	12	0	4.70
3B	D. DeCinces	427	.244	20	78	95	202	13	27	2.8	.958	J. Slaton	29	148	6	10	1	4.37
RF	R. Jackson	460	.252	27	85	112	6	7	1	1.5	.944	D. Moore	65	103	8	8	31	1.92
CF	G. Pettis	443	.257	1	32	368	13	4	5	3.2	.990	S. Cliburn	44	99	9	3	6	2.09
LF	B. Downing	520	.263	20	85	244	5	2	0	2.1	.992	J. Candelaria	13	71	7	3	0	3.80
C	B. Boone	460	.248	5	55	670	71	10	**15**	5.1	.987							
DH	R. Jones	389	.231	21	67													
UT	J. Beniquez	411	.304	8	42	439	26	4	42		.991							
2B	R. Wilfong	217	.189	4	13	124	216	5	45	5.0	.986							
OF	M. Brown	153	.268	4	20	78	3	0	1	1.7	1.000							

Chicago

W-85 L-77

Tony LaRussa

POS	Player	AB	BA	HR	RBI	PO	A	E	DP	TC/G	FA	Pitcher	G	IP	W	L	SV	ERA
1B	G. Walker	601	.258	24	92	1217	97	8	116	8.8	.994	T. Seaver	35	239	16	11	0	3.17
2B	J. Cruz	234	.197	0	15	158	220	7	59	4.4	.982	B. Burns	36	227	18	11	0	3.96
SS	O. Guillen	491	.273	1	33	220	382	12	80	4.1	**.980**	F. Bannister	34	211	10	14	0	4.87
3B	T. Hulett	395	.268	5	36	69	210	**23**	22	2.6	.924	G. Nelson	46	146	10	10	2	4.26
RF	H. Baines	640	.309	22	113	318	8	2	2	2.1	.994	B. James	69	110	8	7	32	2.13
CF	D. Boston	232	.228	3	15	179	7	2	1	2.0	.989							
LF	R. Law	390	.259	4	35	226	7	3	3	2.0	.987							
C	C. Fisk	543	.238	37	107	**801**	60	10	13	**6.7**	.989							
DH	R. Kittle	379	.230	26	58													
UT	L. Salazar	327	.245	10	45	180	57	10	13		.960							
UT	S. Fletcher	301	.256	2	31	123	208	8	36		.976							
2B	B. Little	188	.250	2	27	100	164	3	33	3.9	.989							
DH	O. Gamble	148	.203	4	20													
DH	J. Hairston	140	.243	2	20													

Minnesota

W-77 L-85

Billy Gardner
W-27 L-35

Ray Miller
W-50 L-50

POS	Player	AB	BA	HR	RBI	PO	A	E	DP	TC/G	FA	Pitcher	G	IP	W	L	SV	ERA
1B	K. Hrbek	593	.278	21	93	1339	114	8	114	9.4	.995	M. Smithson	37	257	15	14	0	4.34
2B	T. Teufel	434	.260	10	50	237	352	12	67	4.4	.980	F. Viola	36	251	18	14	0	4.09
SS	G. Gagne	293	.225	2	23	149	269	14	48	4.1	.968	J. Butcher	34	208	11	14	0	4.98
3B	G. Gaetti	560	.246	20	63	**146**	316	18	31	**3.1**	.962	K. Schrom	29	161	9	12	0	4.99
RF	T. Brunansky	567	.242	27	90	300	14	5	2	2.1	.984	B. Blyleven	14	114*	8	5	0	3.00
CF	K. Puckett	**691**	.288	4	74	465	19	8	5	3.1	.984	P. Filson	40	96	4	5	2	3.67
LF	M. Hatcher	444	.282	3	49	215	6	2	2	2.3	.991	R. Davis	57	65	2	6	25	3.48
C	M. Salas	360	.300	9	41	529	39	5	10	5.0	.991							
DH	R. Smalley	388	.258	12	45													
OD	R. Bush	234	.239	10	35	63	0	2	0		.969							
UT	M. Stenhouse	179	.223	5	21	83	10	3	4		.969							
DC	D. Engle	172	.256	7	25	58	3	1	1		.984							
C	T. Laudner	164	.238	7	19	233	19	8	3	3.8	.969							

Oakland

W-77 L-85

Jackie Moore

POS	Player	AB	BA	HR	RBI	PO	A	E	DP	TC/G	FA	Pitcher	G	IP	W	L	SV	ERA
1B	B. Bochte	424	.295	14	60	942	60	10	83	7.9	.990	C. Codiroli	37	226	14	14	0	4.46
2B	D. Hill	393	.285	3	48	228	320	15	56	4.6	.973	D. Sutton	29	194	13	8	0	3.89
SS	A. Griffin	614	.270	2	64	278	440	30	87	4.6	.960	B. Krueger	32	151	9	10	0	4.52
3B	C. Lansford	401	.277	13	46	85	119	5	11	2.2	.976	T. Birtsas	29	141	10	6	0	4.01
RF	M. Davis	547	.287	24	82	370	6	8	1	2.5	.979	K. Atherton	56	105	4	7	3	4.30
CF	D. Murphy	523	.233	20	59	432	6	5	1	3.0	.989	J. Howell	63	98	9	8	29	2.85
LF	D. Collins	379	.251	4	29	221	1	5	0	2.5	.978	S. Ontiveros	39	75	1	3	8	1.93
C	M. Heath	436	.250	13	55	483	44	10	9	4.8	.981	J. Rijo	12	64	6	4	0	3.53
DH	D. Kingman	592	.238	30	91													
UT	D. Baker	343	.268	14	52	465	29	5	33		.990							
C	M. Tettleton	211	.251	3	15	344	24	4	9	4.9	.989							
OF	S. Henderson	193	.301	3	31	79	3	4	0	1.5	.953							

Seattle

W-74 L-88

Chuck Cottier

POS	Player	AB	BA	HR	RBI	PO	A	E	DP	TC/G	FA	Pitcher	G	IP	W	L	SV	ERA
1B	A. Davis	578	.287	18	78	1438	103	13	131	10.1	.992	M. Moore	35	247	17	10	0	3.46
2B	J. Perconte	485	.264	2	23	244	381	9	91	5.1	.986	M. Young	37	218	12	**19**	1	4.91
SS	S. Owen	352	.259	6	37	196	361	14	76	4.9	.975	M. Langston	24	127	7	14	0	5.47
3B	J. Presley	570	.275	28	84	82	335	17	24	2.8	.961	F. Wills	24	123	5	11	1	6.00
RF	A. Cowens	452	.265	14	69	198	10	7	2	2.0	.967	B. Swift	23	121	6	10	0	4.77
CF	D. Henderson	502	.241	14	68	335	8	5	3	2.5	.986	E. Nunez	70	90	7	3	16	3.09
LF	P. Bradley	641	.300	26	88	336	10	5	3	2.2	.986	J. Beattie	18	70	5	6	0	7.29
C	B. Kearney	305	.243	6	27	529	50	3	7	5.4	**.995**							
DH	G. Thomas	484	.215	32	87													
OF	I. Calderon	210	.286	8	28	100	5	2	2	2.0	.981							
C	D. Scott	185	.222	4	23	277	31	6	1	4.2	.981							
UT	D. Ramos	168	.196	1	15	87	119	10	26		.954							
DH	K. Phelps	116	.207	9	24													

AMERICAN LEAGUE 1985, *cont.*

	POS	Player	AB	BA	HR	RBI	PO	A	E	DP	TC/G	FA	Pitcher	G	IP	W	L	SV	ERA
Texas	1B	P. O'Brien	573	.267	22	92	1457	98	8	125	9.8	.995	C. Hough	34	250	14	16	0	3.31
	2B	T. Harrah	396	.270	9	44	212	351	6	71	4.7	.989	M. Mason	38	179	8	15	0	4.83
W-62 L-99	SS	C. Wilkerson	360	.244	0	22	125	274	18	50	3.8	.957	B. Hooton	29	124	5	8	0	5.23
	3B	B. Bell	313	.236	4	32	70	192	16	22	3.3	.942	G. Harris	58	113	5	4	11	2.47
Doug Rader	RF	L. Parrish	346	.249	17	51	111	4	1	0	1.7	.991	D. Noles	28	110	4	8	1	5.06
W-9 L-23	CF	O. McDowell	406	.239	18	42	282	9	2	2	2.8	.993	D. Rozema	34	88	3	7	7	4.19
	LF	G. Ward	593	.287	15	70	304	11	10	2	2.1	.969	D. Schmidt	51	86	7	6	5	3.15
Bobby Valentine	C	D. Slaught	343	.280	8	35	550	33	6	4	5.8	.990	D. Stewart	42	81	0	6	4	5.42
W-53 L-76	DH	C. Johnson	296	.257	12	56													
	OF	G. Wright	363	.190	2	18	213	8	2	2	2.2	.991							
	UT	W. Tolleson	323	.313	1	18	149	255	14	48		.967							
	3B	S. Buechele	219	.219	6	21	52	137	6	17	2.8	.969							
	OD	B. Jones	134	.224	5	23	30	0	0	0		1.000							

BATTING AND BASE RUNNING LEADERS

Batting Average
W. Boggs, BOS .368
G. Brett, KC .335
D. Mattingly, NY .324
R. Henderson, NY .314
B. Butler, CLE .311

Slugging Average
G. Brett, KC .585
D. Mattingly, NY .567
J. Barfield, TOR .536
E. Murray, BAL .523
D. Evans, DET .519

Home Runs
D. Evans, DET 40
C. Fisk, CHI 37
S. Balboni, KC 36
D. Mattingly, NY 35
G. Thomas, SEA 32

Total Bases
D. Mattingly, NY 370
G. Brett, KC 322
P. Bradley, SEA 319
W. Boggs, BOS 312
E. Murray, BAL 305

Runs Batted In
D. Mattingly, NY 145
E. Murray, BAL 124
D. Winfield, NY 114
H. Baines, CHI 113
G. Brett, KC 112

Stolen Bases
R. Henderson, NY 80
G. Pettis, CAL 56
B. Butler, CLE 47
W. Wilson, KC 43
L. Smith, KC 40

Hits
W. Boggs, BOS 240
D. Mattingly, NY 211
B. Buckner, BOS 201
K. Puckett, MIN 199

Base on Balls
D. Evans, BOS 114
T. Harrah, TEX 113
G. Brett, KC 103
R. Henderson, NY 99

Home Run Percentage
D. Evans, DET 7.9
C. Fisk, CHI 6.8
G. Thomas, SEA 6.6
S. Balboni, KC 6.0

Runs
R. Henderson, NY 146
C. Ripken, BAL 116
E. Murray, BAL 111
D. Evans, BOS 110

Doubles
D. Mattingly, NY 48
B. Buckner, BOS 46
W. Boggs, BOS 42
C. Cooper, MIL 39

Triples
W. Wilson, KC 21
B. Butler, CLE 14
K. Puckett, MIN 13
T. Fernandez, TOR 10

PITCHING LEADERS

Winning Percentage
R. Guidry, NY .786
B. Saberhagen, KC .769
C. Leibrandt, KC .654
T. Higuera, MIL .652
D. Alexander, TOR .630
M. Moore, SEA .630

Earned Run Average
D. Stieb, TOR 2.48
C. Leibrandt, KC 2.69
B. Saberhagen, KC 2.87
J. Key, TOR 3.00
B. Blyleven, CLE, MIN 3.16

Wins
R. Guidry, NY 22
B. Saberhagen, KC 20
B. Burns, CHI 18
F. Viola, MIN 18

Saves
D. Quisenberry, KC 37
B. James, CHI 32
D. Moore, CAL 31
G. Hernandez, DET 31
J. Howell, OAK 29
D. Righetti, NY 29

Strikeouts
B. Blyleven, CLE, MIN 206
F. Bannister, CHI 198
J. Morris, DET 191
B. Hurst, BOS 189
M. Witt, CAL 180

Complete Games
B. Blyleven, CLE, MIN 24
C. Hough, TEX 14
M. Moore, SEA 14
J. Morris, DET 13
O. Boyd, BOS 13

Fewest Hits/9 Innings
D. Stieb, TOR 7.00
C. Hough, TEX 7.12
D. Petry, DET 7.16
J. Morris, DET 7.42

Shutouts
B. Blyleven, CLE, MIN 5
B. Burns, CHI 4
J. Morris, DET 4

Fewest Walks/9 Innings
M. Haas, MIL 1.39
B. Saberhagen, KC 1.45
R. Guidry, NY 1.46
J. Butcher, MIN 1.86

Most Strikeouts/9 Inn.
F. Bannister, CHI 8.46
B. Hurst, BOS 7.42
B. Burns, CHI 6.82
J. Morris, DET 6.69

Innings
B. Blyleven, CLE, MIN 294
O. Boyd, BOS 272
D. Stieb, TOR 265
D. Alexander, TOR 261

Games Pitched
D. Quisenberry, KC 84
E. Vande Berg, SEA 76
G. Hernandez, DET 74
D. Righetti, NY 74

								Batting						Fielding				Pitching				
		W	L	PCT	GB	R	OR	2B	3B	HR	BA	SA	SB	E	DP	FA	CG	BB	SO	ShO	SV	ERA
East	Toronto	99	62	.615		759	**588**	281	**53**	158	.269	.425	143	125	164	.980	18	484	823	9	47	**3.31**
	New York	97	64	.602	2	**839**	660	272	31	176	.267	.425	**155**	126	172	.979	25	518	907	9	**49**	3.69
	Detroit	84	77	.522	15	729	688	254	45	202	.253	.424	75	143	152	.977	31	556	943	**11**	40	3.78
	Baltimore	83	78	.516	16	818	764	234	22	**214**	.263	**.430**	69	129	168	.979	32	568	793	6	33	4.38
	Boston	81	81	.500	18.5	800	720	**292**	31	162	**.282**	.429	66	145	161	.977	35	540	913	8	29	4.06
	Milwaukee	71	90	.441	28	690	802	250	44	101	.263	.379	69	142	153	.977	34	499	777	6	37	4.39
	Cleveland	60	102	.370	39.5	729	861	254	31	116	.265	.385	132	141	161	.977	24	547	702	7	28	4.91
West	Kansas City	91	71	.562		687	639	261	49	154	.252	.401	128	127	160	.980	27	463	846	**11**	41	3.49
	California	90	72	.556	1	732	703	215	31	153	.251	.386	106	112	**202**	**.982**	22	514	767	8	41	3.91
	Chicago	85	77	.525	6	736	720	247	37	146	.253	.392	108	**111**	152	**.982**	20	569	**1023**	8	39	4.07
	Minnesota	77	85	.475	14	705	782	282	41	141	.264	.407	68	120	139	.980	**41**	**462**	767	7	34	4.48
	Oakland	77	85	.475	14	757	787	230	34	155	.264	.401	116	140	137	.977	10	607	785	6	41	4.41
	Seattle	74	88	.457	17	719	818	277	38	171	.255	.412	94	122	156	.980	23	637	868	8	30	4.68
	Texas	62	99	.385	28.5	617	785	213	41	129	.253	.381	130	120	145	.980	18	501	863	5	33	4.56
						10317	10317	3562	528	2178	.261	.405	1459	1803	2222	.979	360	7465	11777	109	522	4.15

NATIONAL LEAGUE 1986

		POS	Player	AB	BA	HR	RBI	PO	A	E	DP	TC/G	FA	Pitcher	G	IP	W	L	SV	ERA
East	**New York**	1B	K. Hernandez	551	.310	13	83	1199	149	5	115	9.1	**.996**	D. Gooden	33	250	17	6	0	2.84
		2B	W. Backman	387	.320	1	27	186	290	17	56	4.4	.966	R. Darling	34	237	15	6	0	2.81
	W-108 L-54	SS	R. Santana	394	.218	1	28	203	369	16	68	4.3	.973	B. Ojeda	32	217	18	5	0	2.57
		3B	R. Knight	486	.298	11	76	88	204	16	17	2.3	.948	S. Fernandez	32	204	16	6	1	3.52
	Davey Johnson	RF	D. Strawberry	475	.259	27	93	226	10	6	3	1.8	.975	R. Aguilera	28	142	10	7	0	3.88
		CF	L. Dykstra	431	.295	8	45	283	8	3	2	2.1	.990	R. McDowell	75	128	14	9	22	3.02
		LF	M. Wilson	381	.289	9	45	228	7	5	2	2.1	.979	J. Orosco	58	81	8	6	21	2.33
		C	G. Carter	490	.255	24	105	869	62	8	13	**7.7**	.991							
		OS	K. Mitchell	328	.277	12	43	145	59	8	8		.962							
		2B	T. Teufel	279	.247	4	31	133	173	9	28	3.8	.971							
		OF	G. Foster	233	.227	13	38	96	4	4	1	1.7	.962							
		3S	H. Johnson	220	.245	10	39	50	136	20	24		.903							
		OF	D. Heep	195	.282	5	33	83	2	1	1	1.5	.988							

NATIONAL LEAGUE 1986, *cont.*

Philadelphia

W-86 L-75

John Felske

POS	Player	AB	BA	HR	RBI	PO	A	E	DP	TC/G	FA	Pitcher	G	IP	W	L	SV	ERA
1B	V. Hayes	610	.305	19	98	1182	96	13	105	9.6	.990	K. Gross	37	242	12	12	0	4.02
2B	J. Samuel	591	.266	16	78	290	440	**25**	83	5.3	.967	S. Rawley	23	158	11	7	0	3.54
SS	S. Jeltz	439	.219	0	36	229	406	22	81	4.7	.967	B. Ruffin	21	146	9	4	0	2.46
3B	M. Schmidt	552	.290	**37**	**119**	78	220	6	27	2.5	**.980**	C. Hudson	33	144	7	10	0	4.94
RF	G. Wilson	584	.271	15	84	331	20	4	5	2.3	.989	D. Carman	50	134	10	5	1	3.22
CF	M. Thompson	299	.251	6	23	212	1	2	1	2.4	.991	K. Tekulve	73	110	11	5	4	2.54
LF	G. Redus	340	.247	11	33	185	8	4	2	2.2	.980	S. Bedrosian	68	90	8	6	29	3.39
C	J. Russell	315	.241	13	60	498	39	13	10	6.2	.976	S. Carlton	16	83	4	8	0	6.18
OF	R. Roenicke	275	.247	5	42	181	3	2	0	2.2	.989	M. Maddux	16	78	3	7	0	5.42
OF	J. Stone	249	.277	6	19	103	8	2	1	1.9	.982							
3B	R. Schu	208	.274	8	25	42	94	13	6	2.6	.913							
C	D. Daulton	138	.225	8	21	244	21	4	6	5.6	.985							

St. Louis

W-79 L-82

Whitey Herzog

POS	Player	AB	BA	HR	RBI	PO	A	E	DP	TC/G	FA	Pitcher	G	IP	W	L	SV	ERA
1B	J. Clark	232	.237	9	23	623	35	3	66	10.3	.995	B. Forsch	33	230	14	10	0	3.25
2B	T. Herr	559	.252	2	61	352	414	9	**121**	5.1	.988	D. Cox	32	220	12	13	0	2.90
SS	O. Smith	514	.280	0	54	229	453	15	**96**	4.8	**.978**	J. Tudor	30	219	13	7	0	2.92
3B	T. Pendleton	578	.239	1	59	**133**	**371**	20	**36**	**3.4**	.962	G. Mathews	23	145	11	8	0	3.65
RF	A. Van Slyke	418	.270	13	61	211	11	7	2	2.1	.969	T. Conroy	25	115	5	11	0	5.23
CF	W. McGee	497	.256	7	48	325	9	3	0	2.8	.991	T. Worrell	74	104	9	10	**36**	2.08
LF	V. Coleman	600	.232	0	29	300	12	9	2	2.2	.972	R. Horton	42	100	4	3	3	2.24
C	M. LaValliere	303	.234	3	30	468	47	6	8	4.8	.988							
OF	C. Ford	214	.248	2	29	109	7	3	**5**	1.9	.975							
OF	T. Landrum	205	.210	2	17	131	6	1	1	1.8	.993							
C	M. Heath	190	.205	4	25	259	30	10	4	4.7	.967							

Montreal

W-78 L-83

Buck Rodgers

POS	Player	AB	BA	HR	RBI	PO	A	E	DP	TC/G	FA	Pitcher	G	IP	W	L	SV	ERA
1B	A. Galarraga	321	.271	10	42	805	40	4	59	8.3	.995	F. Youmans	33	219	13	12	0	3.53
2B	V. Law	360	.225	5	44	170	284	3	50	4.9	.993	J. Tibbs	35	190	7	9	0	3.97
SS	H. Brooks	306	.340	14	58	116	222	15	37	4.4	.958	B. Smith	30	187	10	8	0	3.94
3B	T. Wallach	480	.233	18	71	94	270	16	26	2.9	.958	A. McGaffigan	48	143	10	5	2	2.65
RF	A. Dawson	496	.284	20	78	200	11	3	2	1.7	.986	T. Burke	68	101	9	7	4	2.93
CF	M. Webster	576	.290	8	49	325	12	8	3	2.4	.977	B. Sebra	17	91	5	5	0	3.55
LF	T. Raines	580	**.334**	9	62	270	13	6	1	2.0	.979	J. Reardon	62	89	7	9	35	3.94
C	D. Bilardello	191	.194	4	17	391	38	8	3	5.7	.982	J. Hesketh	15	83	6	5	0	5.01
13	W. Krenchicki	221	.240	2	23	325	58	6	26		.985	B. McClure	52	63	2	5	6	3.02
C	M. Fitzgerald	209	.282	6	37	415	35	3	5	6.4	.993							
UT	T. Foley	202	.257	1	18	81	147	4	18		.983							
2B	A. Newman	185	.200	1	8	76	127	7	25	3.6	.967							
OF	H. Winningham	185	.216	4	11	97	2	2	1	1.5	.980							
SS	L. Rivera	166	.205	0	13	64	119	9	24	3.5	.953							

Chicago

W-70 L-90

Jim Frey
W-23 L-33

John Vukovich
W-1 L-1

Gene Michael
W-46 L-56

POS	Player	AB	BA	HR	RBI	PO	A	E	DP	TC/G	FA	Pitcher	G	IP	W	L	SV	ERA
1B	L. Durham	484	.262	20	65	1231	80	7	101	9.3	.995	D. Eckersley	33	201	6	11	0	4.57
2B	R. Sandberg	627	.284	14	76	309	**492**	5	86	5.3	**.994**	R. Sutcliffe	28	177	5	14	0	4.64
SS	S. Dunston	581	.250	17	68	**320**	**465**	**32**	**96**	**5.5**	.961	S. Sanderson	37	170	9	11	1	4.19
3B	R. Cey	256	.273	13	36	41	118	8	7	2.2	.952	S. Trout	37	161	5	7	0	4.75
RF	K. Moreland	586	.271	12	79	181	13	4	3	1.6	.980	E. Lynch	23	100	7	5	0	3.79
CF	B. Dernier	324	.225	4	18	222	3	3	2	2.2	.987	L. Smith	66	90	9	9	31	3.09
LF	G. Matthews	370	.259	21	46	137	5	9	1	1.4	.940	J. Moyer	16	87	7	4	0	5.05
C	J. Davis	528	.250	21	74	**885**	**105**	8	**14**	6.9	.992	R. Fontenot	42	56	3	5	2	3.86
OF	J. Mumphrey	309	.304	5	32	161	3	3	3	1.8	.982	J. Baller	36	54	2	4	5	5.37
30	D. Lopes	157	.299	6	22	51	54	8	3		.929							
3S	C. Speier	155	.284	6	23	53	88	3	14		.979							

Pittsburgh

W-64 L-98

Jim Leyland

POS	Player	AB	BA	HR	RBI	PO	A	E	DP	TC/G	FA	Pitcher	G	IP	W	L	SV	ERA
1B	S. Bream	522	.268	16	77	1320	**166**	**17**	107	9.8	.989	R. Rhoden	34	254	15	12	0	2.84
2B	J. Ray	579	.301	7	78	280	479	5	89	5.1	.993	R. Reuschel	35	216	9	16	0	3.96
SS	R. Belliard	309	.233	0	31	117	269	12	42	4.1	.970	M. Bielecki	31	149	6	11	0	4.66
3B	J. Morrison	537	.274	23	88	92	257	20	12	2.4	.946	B. Walk	44	142	7	8	2	3.75
RF	J. Orsulak	401	.249	2	19	193	11	4	2	1.7	.981	L. McWilliams	49	122	3	11	0	5.15
CF	B. Bonds	413	.223	16	48	280	9	5	2	2.7	.983	B. Kipper	20	114	6	8	0	4.03
LF	R. Reynolds	402	.269	9	48	190	2	9	0	1.8	.955	J. Winn	50	88	3	5	3	3.58
C	T. Pena	510	.288	10	52	810	99	**18**	13	6.7	.981	C. Guante	52	78	5	2	4	3.35
OF	M. Brown	243	.218	4	26	107	3	3	2	1.6	.973	D. Robinson	50	69	3	4	14	3.38
01	M. Diaz	209	.268	12	36	201	6	3	9		.986	B. Jones	26	37	3	4	3	2.89
UT	B. Almon	196	.219	7	27	80	45	8	4		.940							
OF	B. Bonilla	192	.240	1	17	73	3	2	0	1.5	.974							

West

Houston

W-96 L-66

Hal Lanier

POS	Player	AB	BA	HR	RBI	PO	A	E	DP	TC/G	FA	Pitcher	G	IP	W	L	SV	ERA
1B	G. Davis	574	.265	31	101	1253	111	11	90	8.8	.992	M. Scott	37	**275**	18	10	0	**2.22**
2B	B. Doran	550	.276	6	37	262	329	16	62	4.2	.974	B. Knepper	40	258	17	12	0	3.14
SS	D. Thon	278	.248	3	21	142	210	10	39	3.5	.972	N. Ryan	30	178	12	8	0	3.34
3B	D. Walling	382	.312	13	58	59	156	9	6	2.2	.960	J. Deshaies	26	144	12	5	0	3.25
RF	K. Bass	591	.311	20	79	303	12	5	4	2.1	.984	C. Kerfeld	61	94	11	2	7	2.59
CF	B. Hatcher	419	.258	6	36	226	7	4	0	2.0	.983	A. Lopez	45	78	3	3	7	3.46
LF	J. Cruz	479	.278	10	72	237	5	4	1	1.8	.984	D. Smith	54	56	4	7	33	2.73
C	A. Ashby	315	.257	7	38	632	43	10	2	6.7	.985							
3B	P. Garner	313	.265	9	41	58	141	23	13	2.6	.896							
SS	C. Reynolds	313	.249	6	41	106	206	7	38	3.3	.978							
OF	T. Puhl	172	.244	3	14	65	0	0	0	1.4	1.000							

NATIONAL LEAGUE 1986, *cont.*

Cincinnati

W-86 L-76

Pete Rose

POS	Player	AB	BA	HR	RBI	PO	A	E	DP	TC/G	FA
1B	N. Esasky	330	.230	12	41	512	30	5	12	7.8	.991
2B	R. Oester	523	.258	8	44	**367**	475	19	100	**5.7**	.978
SS	K. Stillwell	279	.229	0	26	107	205	16	40	4.1	.951
3B	B. Bell	568	.278	20	75	105	290	10	28	2.7	.975
RF	D. Parker	637	.273	31	116	278	9	9	2	1.9	.970
CF	E. Milner	424	.259	15	47	292	6	3	0	2.4	.990
LF	E. Davis	415	.277	27	71	274	2	7	0	2.3	.975
C	B. Diaz	474	.272	10	56	732	83	13	10	6.2	.984
UT	D. Concepcion	311	.260	3	30	153	223	10	53		.974
1B	P. Rose	237	.219	0	25	523	43	6	54	9.4	.990
1B	T. Perez	200	.255	2	29	398	29	7	46	7.9	.984
OF	K. Daniels	181	.320	6	23	88	0	3	0	1.9	.967

Pitcher	G	IP	W	L	SV	ERA
B. Gullickson	37	245	15	12	0	3.38
T. Browning	39	243	14	13	0	3.81
J. Denny	27	171	11	10	0	4.20
C. Welsh	24	139	6	9	0	4.78
T. Power	56	129	10	6	1	3.70
R. Robinson	70	117	10	3	14	3.24
M. Soto	19	105	5	10	0	4.71
J. Franco	74	101	6	6	29	2.94

San Francisco

W-83 L-79

Roger Craig

POS	Player	AB	BA	HR	RBI	PO	A	E	DP	TC/G	FA
1B	W. Clark	408	.287	11	41	942	72	11	76	10.0	.989
2B	R. Thompson	549	.271	7	47	255	450	17	97	4.8	.976
SS	J. Uribe	453	.223	3	43	249	444	16	95	4.5	.977
3B	C. Brown	416	.317	7	49	73	177	18	17	2.4	.933
RF	C. Davis	526	.278	13	70	303	9	9	2	2.2	.972
CF	D. Gladden	351	.276	4	29	226	7	3	2	2.7	.987
LF	J. Leonard	341	.279	6	42	158	4	5	1	1.9	.970
C	B. Brenly	472	.246	16	62	518	55	3	4	5.7	**.995**
OF	C. Maldonado	405	.252	18	85	161	10	3	0	1.7	.983
C	B. Melvin	268	.224	5	25	442	59	6	7	6.0	.988
1O	M. Aldrete	216	.250	2	25	317	36	1	34		.997
OF	R. Kutcher	186	.237	7	16	99	3	1	1	2.0	.990
OF	J. Youngblood	184	.255	5	28	49	2	0	1	1.1	1.000
1B	H. Spilman	94	.287	2	22	138	15	1	8	8.1	.994

Pitcher	G	IP	W	L	SV	ERA
M. Krukow	34	245	20	9	0	3.05
M. LaCoss	37	204	10	13	0	3.57
S. Garrelts	53	174	13	9	10	3.11
V. Blue	28	157	10	10	0	3.27
J. Robinson	64	104	6	3	8	3.36
M. Davis	67	84	5	7	4	2.99
G. Minton	48	69	4	4	5	3.93

San Diego

W-74 L-88

Steve Boros

POS	Player	AB	BA	HR	RBI	PO	A	E	DP	TC/G	FA
1B	S. Garvey	557	.255	21	81	1160	53	7	94	8.2	.994
2B	T. Flannery	368	.280	3	28	209	246	3	52	4.2	.993
SS	G. Templeton	510	.247	2	44	207	358	20	60	4.1	.966
3B	G. Nettles	354	.218	16	55	83	174	16	14	2.4	.941
RF	T. Gwynn	**642**	.329	14	59	337	19	4	3	2.3	.989
CF	K. McReynolds	560	.287	26	96	332	9	8	4	2.3	.977
LF	J. Kruk	278	.309	4	38	102	4	2	0	1.5	.981
C	T. Kennedy	432	.264	12	57	692	70	8	13	6.3	.990
OF	M. Wynne	288	.264	7	37	203	3	3	2	1.7	.986
UT	J. Royster	257	.257	5	26	87	166	14	23		.948
01	C. Martinez	244	.238	9	25	142	14	2	4		.987
2B	B. Roberts	241	.253	1	12	166	172	10	33	4.0	.971
C	B. Bochy	127	.252	8	22	202	22	2	3	4.7	.991

Pitcher	G	IP	W	L	SV	ERA
A. Hawkins	37	209	10	8	0	4.30
D. Dravecky	26	161	9	11	0	3.07
L. Hoyt	35	159	8	11	0	5.15
E. Show	24	136	9	5	0	2.97
L. McCullers	70	136	10	10	5	2.78
C. Lefferts	**83**	108	9	8	4	3.09
M. Thurmond	17	71	3	7	0	6.50
G. Gossage	45	65	5	7	21	4.45

Los Angeles

W-73 L-89

Tom Lasorda

POS	Player	AB	BA	HR	RBI	PO	A	E	DP	TC/G	FA
1B	G. Brock	325	.234	16	52	726	87	3	46	8.2	.996
2B	S. Sax	633	.332	6	56	**367**	432	16	71	5.3	.980
SS	M. Duncan	407	.229	8	30	172	317	25	46	4.8	.951
3B	B. Madlock	379	.280	10	60	72	170	**24**	7	2.6	.910
RF	M. Marshall	330	.233	19	53	149	8	6	1	1.7	.963
CF	R. Williams	303	.277	4	32	179	5	3	2	1.5	.984
LF	F. Stubbs	420	.226	23	58	206	10	7	2	1.8	.969
C	M. Scioscia	374	.251	5	26	756	64	15	4	7.0	.982
OF	K. Landreaux	283	.261	4	29	145	5	7	0	1.8	.955
1B	E. Cabell	277	.256	2	29	360	32	5	29	6.5	.987
UT	B. Russell	216	.250	0	18	103	84	5	17		.974
3S	D. Anderson	216	.245	1	15	73	152	11	21		.953
C	A. Trevino	202	.262	4	26	304	45	11	4	5.7	.969
01	L. Matuszek	199	.261	9	28	235	22	5	18		.981

Pitcher	G	IP	W	L	SV	ERA
F. Valenzuela	34	269	**21**	11	0	3.14
B. Welch	33	236	7	13	0	3.28
O. Hershiser	35	231	14	14	0	3.85
R. Honeycutt	32	171	11	9	0	3.32
K. Howell	62	98	6	12	12	3.87
T. Niedenfuer	60	80	6	6	11	3.71

Atlanta

W-72 L-89

Chuck Tanner

POS	Player	AB	BA	HR	RBI	PO	A	E	DP	TC/G	FA
1B	B. Horner	517	.273	27	87	**1378**	102	8	**138**	**10.7**	.995
2B	G. Hubbard	408	.230	4	36	282	487	19	120	5.5	.976
SS	A. Thomas	323	.251	6	32	143	290	19	62	4.7	.958
3B	K. Oberkfell	503	.270	5	48	65	258	8	24	2.5	.976
RF	O. Moreno	359	.234	4	27	151	8	5	3	1.7	.970
CF	D. Murphy	614	.265	29	83	303	6	6	1	2.0	.981
LF	K. Griffey	292	.308	12	32	136	1	2	0	1.8	.986
C	O. Virgil	359	.223	15	48	682	93	13	9	7.1	.984
S3	R. Ramirez	496	.240	8	33	155	371	29	68		.948
OF	T. Harper	265	.257	8	30	92	5	3	0	1.2	.970
OF	B. Sample	200	.285	6	14	69	1	1	1	1.3	.986
UT	T. Simmons	127	.252	4	25	167	18	6	13		.969

Pitcher	G	IP	W	L	SV	ERA
R. Mahler	39	238	14	**18**	0	4.88
D. Palmer	35	210	11	10	0	3.65
Z. Smith	38	205	8	16	1	4.05
D. Alexander	17	117	6	6	0	3.84
J. Dedmon	57	100	6	6	3	2.98
J. Acker	21	95	3	8	0	3.79
J. Johnson	17	87	6	7	0	4.97
G. Garber	61	78	5	5	24	2.54
P. Assenmacher	61	68	7	3	7	2.50

BATTING AND BASE RUNNING LEADERS

Batting Average

T. Raines, MON	.334
S. Sax, LA	.332
T. Gwynn, SD	.329
K. Bass, HOU	.311
K. Hernandez, NY	.310

Slugging Average

M. Schmidt, PHI	.547
D. Strawberry, NY	.507
K. McReynolds, SD	.504
G. Davis, HOU	.493
K. Bass, HOU	.486

Home Runs

M. Schmidt, PHI	37
G. Davis, HOU	31
D. Parker, CIN	31
D. Murphy, ATL	29

PITCHING LEADERS

Winning Percentage

B. Ojeda, NY	.783
D. Gooden, NY	.739
S. Fernandez, NY	.727
R. Darling, NY	.714
M. Krukow, SF	.690

Earned Run Average

M. Scott, HOU	2.22
B. Ojeda, NY	2.57
R. Darling, NY	2.81
R. Rhoden, PIT	2.84
D. Gooden, NY	2.84

Wins

F. Valenzuela, LA	21
M. Krukow, SF	20
B. Ojeda, NY	18
M. Scott, HOU	18
D. Gooden, NY	17
B. Knepper, HOU	17

NATIONAL LEAGUE 1986, *cont.*

BATTING AND BASE RUNNING LEADERS

Total Bases

D. Parker, CIN	304
M. Schmidt, PHI	302
T. Gwynn, SD	300
V. Hayes, PHI	293
D. Murphy, ATL	293

Runs Batted In

M. Schmidt, PHI	119
D. Parker, CIN	116
G. Carter, NY	105
G. Davis, HOU	101
V. Hayes, PHI	98

Stolen Bases

V. Coleman, STL	107
E. Davis, CIN	80
T. Raines, MON	70
M. Duncan, LA	48
B. Doran, HOU	42
J. Samuel, PHI	42

Hits

T. Gwynn, SD	211
S. Sax, LA	210
T. Raines, MON	194
V. Hayes, PHI	186

Base on Balls

K. Hernandez, NY	94
M. Schmidt, PHI	89
C. Davis, SF	84
K. Oberkfell, ATL	83

Home Run Percentage

M. Schmidt, PHI	6.7
D. Strawberry, NY	5.7
G. Davis, HOU	5.4
B. Horner, ATL	5.2

Runs

V. Hayes, PHI	107
T. Gwynn, SD	107
E. Davis, CIN	97
M. Schmidt, PHI	97

Doubles

V. Hayes, PHI	46
S. Sax, LA	43
S. Bream, PIT	37
S. Dunston, CHI	36
J. Samuel, PHI	36

Triples

M. Webster, MON	13
J. Samuel, PHI	12
T. Raines, MON	10
V. Coleman, STL	8

PITCHING LEADERS

Saves

T. Worrell, STL	36
J. Reardon, MON	35
D. Smith, HOU	33
L. Smith, CHI	31
J. Franco, CIN	29
S. Bedrosian, PHI	29

Strikeouts

M. Scott, HOU	306
F. Valenzuela, LA	242
F. Youmans, MON	202
S. Fernandez, NY	200
D. Gooden, NY	200

Complete Games

F. Valenzuela, LA	20
D. Gooden, NY	12
R. Rhoden, PIT	12
M. Krukow, SF	10

Fewest Hits/9 Innings

M. Scott, HOU	5.95
F. Youmans, MON	5.96
N. Ryan, HOU	6.02
S. Fernandez, NY	7.09

Shutouts

M. Scott, HOU	5
B. Knepper, HOU	5
B. Welch, LA	3
F. Valenzuela, LA	3

Fewest Walks/9 Innings

D. Eckersley, CHI	1.93
S. Sanderson, CHI	1.96
M. Krukow, SF	2.02
B. Welch, LA	2.10

Most Strikeouts/9 Inn.

M. Scott, HOU	10.00
N. Ryan, HOU	9.81
S. Fernandez, NY	8.81
F. Youmans, MON	8.30

Innings

M. Scott, HOU	275
F. Valenzuela, LA	269
B. Knepper, HOU	258
R. Rhoden, PIT	254

Games Pitched

C. Lefferts, SD	83
R. McDowell, NY	75
J. Franco, CIN	74
T. Worrell, STL	74

		W	L	PCT	GB	R	OR	Batting 2B	3B	HR	BA	SA	SB	Fielding E	DP	FA	Pitching CG	BB	SO	ShO	SV	ERA
East	New York	108	54	.667		**783**	578	261	31	148	**.263**	**.401**	118	138	145	.978	27	509	1083	11	46	**3.11**
	Philadelphia	86	75	.534	21.5	739	713	266	39	154	.253	.400	153	137	157	.978	22	553	874	11	39	3.85
	St. Louis	79	82	.491	28.5	601	611	216	48	58	.236	.327	**262**	**123**	178	**.981**	17	**485**	761	4	46	3.37
	Montreal	78	83	.484	29.5	637	688	255	**50**	110	.254	.379	193	133	132	.979	15	566	1051	9	50	3.78
	Chicago	70	90	.438	37	680	781	257	27	**155**	.256	.397	132	124	147	.980	11	557	962	6	42	4.49
	Pittsburgh	64	98	.395	44	663	700	**273**	33	111	.250	.374	152	143	134	.978	17	570	924	9	30	3.90
West	Houston	96	66	.593		654	**569**	244	32	125	.255	.381	163	130	108	.979	18	523	**1160**	**19**	**51**	3.15
	Cincinnati	86	76	.531	10	732	717	237	35	144	.254	.387	177	140	160	.978	14	524	924	8	45	3.91
	San Francisco	83	79	.512	13	698	618	269	29	114	.253	.375	148	143	149	.977	18	591	992	10	35	3.33
	San Diego	74	88	.457	22	656	723	239	25	136	.261	.388	96	137	135	.978	13	607	934	7	32	3.99
	Los Angeles	73	89	.451	23	638	679	232	14	130	.251	.370	155	181	118	.971	**35**	499	1051	14	25	3.76
	Atlanta	72	89	.447	23.5	615	719	241	24	138	.250	.381	93	141	**181**	.978	17	576	932	5	39	3.97
						8096	8096	2990	387	1523	.253	.380	1842	1670	1744	.978	224	6560	11648	113	480	3.72

AMERICAN LEAGUE 1986

East

Boston

W-95 L-66

John McNamara

POS	Player	AB	BA	HR	RBI	PO	A	E	DP	TC/G	FA
1B	B. Buckner	629	.267	18	102	1067	**157**	14	104	9.0	.989
2B	M. Barrett	625	.286	4	60	303	**450**	14	101	4.9	.982
SS	E. Romero	233	.210	2	23	102	132	10	29	3.3	.959
3B	W. Boggs	580	**.357**	8	71	**121**	267	19	30	2.7	.953
RF	D. Evans	529	.259	26	97	280	10	5	3	2.0	.983
CF	T. Armas	425	.264	11	58	247	4	8	0	2.2	.969
LF	J. Rice	618	.324	20	110	330	16	8	0	2.3	.977
C	R. Gedman	462	.258	16	65	**866**	65	6	10	**7.0**	.994
DH	D. Baylor	585	.238	31	94						
SS	R. Quinones	190	.237	2	15	86	150	15	26	4.0	.940

Pitcher	G	IP	W	L	SV	ERA
R. Clemens	33	254	**24**	4	0	**2.48**
O. Boyd	30	214	16	10	0	3.78
B. Hurst	25	174	13	8	0	2.99
A. Nipper	26	159	10	12	0	5.38
T. Seaver	16	104	5	7	0	3.80
B. Stanley	66	82	6	6	16	4.37
J. Sellers	14	82	3	7	0	4.94
C. Schiraldi	25	51	4	2	9	1.41
J. Sambito	53	45	2	0	12	4.84

New York

W-90 L-72

Lou Piniella

POS	Player	AB	BA	HR	RBI	PO	A	E	DP	TC/G	FA
1B	D. Mattingly	677	.352	31	113	**1377**	100	6	132	9.3	**.996**
2B	W. Randolph	492	.276	5	50	313	381	**20**	94	5.1	.972
SS	W. Tolleson	215	.284	0	14	87	177	5	35	4.8	.981
3B	M. Pagliarulo	504	.238	28	71	103	283	19	25	2.8	.953
RF	D. Winfield	565	.262	24	104	292	9	5	5	2.1	.984
CF	R. Henderson	608	.263	28	74	426	4	6	0	3.0	.986
LF	D. Pasqua	280	.293	16	45	148	4	2	1	1.9	.987
C	B. Wynegar	194	.206	7	29	325	22	2	1	6.1	.994
DH	M. Easler	490	.302	14	78						
OF	K. Griffey	198	.303	9	26	96	5	3	2	2.0	.971
C	R. Hassey	191	.298	6	29	251	9	4	4	5.2	.985
C	J. Skinner	166	.259	1	17	280	22	6	5	5.7	.981

Pitcher	G	IP	W	L	SV	ERA
D. Rasmussen	31	202	18	6	0	3.88
R. Guidry	30	192	9	12	0	3.98
D. Drabek	27	132	7	8	0	4.10
B. Tewksbury	23	130	9	5	0	3.31
J. Niekro	25	126	9	10	0	4.87
D. Righetti	74	107	8	8	**46**	2.45
B. Shirley	39	105	0	4	3	5.04
B. Fisher	62	97	9	5	6	4.93

Detroit

W-87 L-75

Sparky Anderson

POS	Player	AB	BA	HR	RBI	PO	A	E	DP	TC/G	FA
1B	D. Evans	507	.241	29	85	808	108	2	85	8.7	.998
2B	L. Whitaker	584	.269	20	73	276	421	11	98	5.0	.984
SS	A. Trammell	574	.277	21	75	238	445	22	99	4.7	.969
3B	D. Coles	521	.273	20	86	107	242	23	23	2.8	.938
RF	K. Gibson	441	.268	28	86	190	2	2	1	1.7	.990
CF	C. Lemon	403	.251	12	53	316	6	5	1	2.6	.985
LF	D. Collins	419	.270	1	27	211	2	1	1	2.3	.995
C	L. Parrish	327	.257	22	62	483	48	6	5	6.3	.989
DH	J. Grubb	210	.333	13	51						
OF	L. Herndon	283	.247	8	37	156	2	2	0	1.9	.988
UT	T. Brookens	281	.270	3	25	106	144	7	26		.973
OF	P. Sheridan	236	.237	6	19	172	1	4	0	2.0	.977

Pitcher	G	IP	W	L	SV	ERA
J. Morris	35	267	21	8	0	3.27
W. Terrell	34	217	15	12	0	4.56
F. Tanana	32	188	12	9	0	4.16
E. King	33	138	11	4	3	3.51
R. O'Neal	37	123	3	7	2	4.33
D. Petry	20	116	5	10	0	4.66
G. Hernandez	64	89	8	7	24	3.55
B. Campbell	34	56	3	6	3	3.88

AMERICAN LEAGUE 1986, *cont.*

Team	POS	Player	AB	BA	HR	RBI	PO	A	E	DP	TC/G	FA	Pitcher	G	IP	W	L	SV	ERA
Toronto	1B	W. Upshaw	573	.251	9	60	1314	131	12	118	9.5	.992	J. Key	36	232	14	11	0	3.57
W-86 L-76	2B	D. Garcia	424	.281	6	46	224	286	8	66	4.9	.985	J. Clancy	34	219	14	14	0	3.94
Jimy Williams	SS	T. Fernandez	**687**	.310	10	65	**294**	445	13	103	4.6	**.983**	D. Stieb	37	205	7	12	1	4.74
	3B	R. Mulliniks	348	.259	11	45	60	176	6	13	2.2	**.975**	M. Eichhorn	69	157	14	6	10	1.72
	RF	J. Barfield	589	.289	**40**	108	368	20	3	8	2.5	.992	J. Cerutti	34	145	9	4	1	4.15
	CF	L. Moseby	589	.253	21	86	371	6	6	1	2.6	.984	D. Alexander	17	111	5	4	0	4.46
	LF	G. Bell	641	.309	31	108	269	17	10	1	2.0	.966	T. Henke	63	91	9	5	27	3.35
	C	E. Whitt	395	.268	16	56	709	41	7	7	5.9	.991	D. Lamp	40	73	2	6	2	5.05
	DH	C. Johnson	336	.250	15	55													
	32	G. Iorg	327	.260	3	44	91	185	12	16		.958							
	DO	R. Leach	246	.309	5	39	44	0	1	0		.978							
Cleveland	1B	P. Tabler	473	.326	6	48	846	84	9	87	8.8	.990	T. Candiotti	36	252	16	12	0	3.57
W-84 L-78	2B	T. Bernazard	562	.301	17	73	**351**	442	17	95	5.5	.979	P. Niekro	34	210	11	11	0	4.32
Pat Corrales	SS	J. Franco	599	.306	10	74	231	374	18	81	4.6	.971	K. Schrom	34	206	14	7	0	4.54
	3B	B. Jacoby	583	.288	17	80	109	292	25	24	2.7	.941	S. Bailes	62	113	10	10	7	4.95
	RF	J. Carter	663	.302	29	**121**	241	8	6	2	2.5	.976	E. Camacho	51	57	2	4	20	4.08
	CF	B. Butler	587	.278	4	51	434	9	3	3	2.8	.993	F. Wills	26	40	4	4	4	4.91
	LF	M. Hall	442	.296	18	77	233	7	7	1	2.0	.972							
	C	A. Allanson	293	.225	1	29	446	33	**20**	4	5.0	.960							
	DH	A. Thornton	401	.229	17	66													
	OS	C. Snyder	416	.272	24	69	203	70	10	21		.965							
	C	C. Bando	254	.268	2	26	359	30	4	3	4.6	.990							
	OD	C. Castillo	205	.278	8	32	58	4	4	1		.939							
Milwaukee	1B	C. Cooper	542	.258	12	75	697	61	9	78	8.5	.988	T. Higuera	34	248	20	11	0	2.79
W-77 L-84	2B	J. Gantner	497	.274	7	38	304	347	10	87	4.9	.985	B. Wegman	35	198	5	12	0	5.13
George Bamberger	SS	E. Riles	524	.252	9	47	212	327	20	76	3.9	.964	T. Leary	33	188	12	12	0	4.21
W-71 L-81	3B	P. Molitor	437	.281	9	55	82	170	15	25	2.9	.944	J. Nieves	35	185	11	12	0	4.92
Tom Trebelhorn	RF	R. Deer	466	.232	33	86	286	8	8	1	2.3	.974	D. Darwin	27	130	6	8	0	3.52
W-6 L-3	CF	R. Yount	522	.312	9	46	352	9	1	4	2.8	.997	D. Plesac	51	91	10	7	14	2.97
	LF	G. Braggs	215	.237	4	18	116	5	12	0	2.4	.910	M. Clear	59	74	5	5	16	2.20
	C	C. Moore	235	.260	3	39	425	43	4	6	6.6	.992							
	DH	B. Oglivie	346	.283	5	53													
	3B	D. Sveum	317	.246	7	35	45	122	**26**	8	3.0	.865							
	UT	B. Schroeder	217	.212	7	19	307	25	1	13		.997							
	C	R. Cerone	216	.259	4	18	391	44	4	2	6.5	.991							
	OF	R. Manning	205	.254	8	27	155	3	2	0	1.9	.988							
	1B	B. Robidoux	181	.227	1	21	326	29	5	35	8.4	.986							
Baltimore	1B	E. Murray	495	.305	17	84	1045	88	13	100	9.6	.989	M. Boddicker	33	218	14	12	0	4.70
W-73 L-89	2B	J. Bonilla	284	.243	1	18	122	140	5	38	3.8	.981	S. McGregor	34	203	11	15	0	4.52
Earl Weaver	SS	C. Ripken	627	.282	25	81	240	**482**	13	105	4.5	.982	K. Dixon	35	202	11	13	0	4.58
	3B	F. Rayford	210	.176	8	19	40	115	15	15	2.4	.912	M. Flanagan	29	172	7	11	0	4.24
	RF	L. Lacy	491	.287	11	47	239	8	2	4	2.1	.992	S. Davis	25	154	9	12	0	3.62
	CF	F. Lynn	397	.287	23	67	244	2	4	1	2.3	.984	R. Bordi	52	107	6	4	3	4.46
	LF	M. Young	369	.252	9	42	149	1	6	0	2.3	.962	D. Aase	66	82	6	7	34	2.98
	C	R. Dempsey	327	.208	13	29	659	53	7	9	5.9	.990							
	DH	L. Sheets	338	.272	18	60													
	OF	J. Shelby	404	.228	11	49	222	5	5	2	1.9	.978							
	UT	J. Beniquez	343	.300	6	36	211	56	13	15		.954							
	2B	A. Wiggins	239	.251	0	11	121	151	6	40	4.2	.978							
	UT	J. Traber	212	.255	13	44	243	23	5	28		.982							
	3B	T. O'Malley	181	.254	1	18	37	98	9	8	2.6	.938							
	OD	J. Dwyer	160	.244	8	31	33	3	0	1		1.000							
West — **California**	1B	W. Joyner	593	.290	22	100	1222	139	15	128	9.1	.989	M. Witt	34	269	18	10	0	2.84
W-92 L-70	2B	R. Wilfong	288	.219	3	33	135	257	7	48	4.4	.982	K. McCaskill	34	246	17	10	0	3.36
Gene Mauch	SS	D. Schofield	458	.249	13	57	246	389	18	103	4.8	.972	D. Sutton	34	207	15	11	0	3.74
	3B	D. DeCinces	512	.256	26	96	119	216	12	19	2.6	.965	R. Romanick	18	106	5	8	0	5.50
	RF	R. Jones	393	.229	17	49	205	5	4	0	1.8	.981	J. Candelaria	16	92	10	2	0	2.55
	CF	G. Pettis	539	.258	5	58	462	9	7	3	3.1	.985	D. Corbett	46	79	4	2	10	3.66
	LF	B. Downing	513	.267	20	95	267	5	3	0	2.0	.989	J. Slaton	14	73	4	6	0	5.65
	C	B. Boone	442	.222	7	49	812	**84**	11	**16**	6.3	.988	D. Moore	49	73	4	5	21	2.97
	DH	R. Jackson	419	.241	18	58							T. Forster	41	41	4	1	5	3.51
	2B	B. Grich	313	.268	9	30	127	221	7	49	4.1	.980							
	OF	G. Hendrick	283	.272	14	47	144	6	5	2	1.7	.968							
	UT	R. Burleson	271	.284	5	29	62	90	3	15		.981							
	3B	J. Howell	151	.272	4	21	28	56	2	4	2.2	.977							
Texas	1B	P. O'Brien	551	.290	23	90	1224	115	11	123	8.7	.992	C. Hough	33	230	17	10	0	3.79
W-87 L-75	2B	T. Harrah	289	.218	7	41	166	211	7	49	4.1	.982	E. Correa	32	202	12	14	0	4.23
Bobby Valentine	SS	S. Fletcher	530	.300	3	50	196	354	15	86	4.2	.973	J. Guzman	29	172	9	15	0	4.54
	3B	S. Buechele	461	.243	18	54	111	226	11	17	2.5	.968	B. Witt	31	158	11	9	0	5.48
	RF	P. Incaviglia	540	.250	30	88	157	6	14	1	1.6	.921	M. Mason	27	135	7	3	0	4.33
	CF	O. McDowell	572	.266	18	49	325	13	3	3	2.3	.991	G. Harris	73	111	10	8	20	2.83
	LF	G. Ward	380	.316	5	51	237	8	1	3	2.4	.996	M. Williams	**80**	98	8	6	8	3.58
	C	D. Slaught	314	.264	13	46	533	40	4	1	6.3	.993	D. Mohorcic	58	79	2	4	7	2.51
	DH	L. Parrish	464	.276	28	94													
	OF	R. Sierra	382	.264	16	55	200	7	6	1	2.0	.972							
	2S	C. Wilkerson	236	.237	0	15	125	199	13	56		.961							
	UT	T. Paciorek	213	.286	4	22	178	45	4	16		.982							
	CD	D. Porter	155	.265	12	29	165	9	1	2		.994							

AMERICAN LEAGUE 1986, *cont.*

Kansas City

W-76 L-86

Dick Howser
W-40 L-48

Mike Ferraro
W-36 L-38

POS	Player	AB	BA	HR	RBI	PO	A	E	DP	TC/G	FA	Pitcher	G	IP	W	L	SV	ERA
1B	S. Balboni	512	.229	29	88	1236	98	**18**	115	**9.9**	.987	C. Leibrandt	35	231	14	11	0	4.09
2B	F. White	566	.272	22	84	316	439	10	91	5.1	.987	D. Leonard	33	193	8	13	0	4.44
SS	A. Salazar	298	.245	0	24	121	283	9	50	3.6	.978	D. Jackson	32	186	11	12	1	3.20
3B	G. Brett	441	.290	16	73	97	218	16	17	2.9	.952	M. Gubicza	35	181	12	6	0	3.64
RF	D. Motley	217	.203	7	20	92	2	2	1	1.5	.979	B. Saberhagen	30	156	7	12	0	4.15
CF	W. Wilson	631	.269	9	44	408	4	3	2	2.7	.993	B. Black	56	121	5	10	9	3.20
LF	L. Smith	508	.287	8	44	245	5	9	1	2.2	.965	S. Bankhead	24	121	8	9	0	4.61
C	J. Sundberg	429	.212	12	42	686	46	4	11	5.5	**.995**	S. Farr	56	109	8	4	8	3.13
DH	J. Orta	336	.277	9	46							D. Quisenberry	62	81	3	7	12	2.77
OF	R. Law	307	.261	1	36	145	2	2	0	1.9	.987							
DH	H. McRae	278	.252	7	37													
CS	J. Quirk	219	.215	8	26	260	58	4	9		.988							
OF	M. Kingery	209	.258	3	14	102	6	3	2	1.9	.973							
SS	B. Biancalana	190	.242	2	8	102	177	16	40	3.3	.946							

Oakland

W-76 L-86

Jackie Moore
W-29 L-44

Jeff Newman
W-2 L-8

Tony LaRussa
W-45 L-34

POS	Player	AB	BA	HR	RBI	PO	A	E	DP	TC/G	FA	Pitcher	G	IP	W	L	SV	ERA
1B	B. Bochte	407	.256	6	43	912	88	9	79	8.8	.991	C. Young	29	198	13	9	0	3.45
2B	T. Phillips	441	.256	5	52	160	290	11	40	5.2	.976	J. Rijo	39	194	9	11	1	4.65
SS	A. Griffin	594	.285	4	51	282	421	25	85	4.5	.966	J. Andujar	28	155	12	7	1	3.82
3B	C. Lansford	591	.284	19	72	67	147	4	13	2.2	.982	D. Stewart	29	149	9	5	0	3.74
RF	M. Davis	489	.268	19	55	310	9	9	2	2.4	.973	E. Plunk	26	120	4	7	0	5.31
CF	D. Murphy	329	.252	9	39	276	6	2	3	2.9	.993	B. Mooneyham	45	100	4	5	2	4.52
LF	J. Canseco	600	.240	33	117	319	4	14	1	2.2	.958	C. Codiroli	16	92	5	8	0	4.03
C	M. Tettleton	211	.204	10	35	463	32	8	6	5.7	.984	S. Ontiveros	46	73	2	2	10	4.71
DH	D. Kingman	561	.210	35	94							R. Langford	16	55	1	10	0	7.36
23	D. Hill	339	.283	4	29	104	213	9	31		.972	J. Howell	38	53	3	6	16	3.38
OF	D. Baker	242	.240	4	19	80	4	0	1	1.5	1.000							
C	J. Willard	161	.267	4	26	300	12	2	1	4.4	.994							

Chicago

W-72 L-90

Tony LaRussa
W-26 L-38

Doug Rader
W-1 L-1

Jim Fregosi
W-45 L-51

POS	Player	AB	BA	HR	RBI	PO	A	E	DP	TC/G	FA	Pitcher	G	IP	W	L	SV	ERA
1B	G. Walker	282	.277	13	51	670	57	5	57	9.5	.993	R. Dotson	34	197	10	**17**	0	5.48
2B	J. Cruz	209	.215	0	19	132	205	5	45	4.4	.985	F. Bannister	28	165	10	14	0	3.54
SS	O. Guillen	547	.250	2	47	261	459	22	93	4.7	.970	J. Cowley	27	162	11	11	0	3.88
3B	T. Hulett	520	.231	17	44	70	144	11	10	2.5	.951	G. Nelson	54	115	6	6	6	3.85
RF	H. Baines	570	.296	21	88	295	15	5	5	2.2	.984	N. Allen	22	113	7	2	0	3.82
CF	J. Cangelosi	438	.235	2	32	276	7	9	1	2.3	.969	J. Davis	19	105	4	5	0	4.70
LF	B. Bonilla	234	.269	2	26	91	2	1	1	2.2	.989	D. Schmidt	49	92	3	6	8	3.31
C	C. Fisk	457	.221	14	63	389	39	4	3	6.1	.991	B. James	49	58	5	4	14	5.25
DH	R. Kittle	296	.213	17	48													
3B	W. Tolleson	260	.250	3	29	37	113	7	9	2.4	.955							
UT	J. Hairston	225	.271	5	26	132	9	0	11		1.000							
OF	D. Boston	199	.266	5	22	152	3	5	1	3.0	.969							
DH	R. Hassey	150	.353	3	20													
C	J. Skinner	149	.201	4	20	227	15	3	4	4.1	.988							

Minnesota

W-71 L-91

Ray Miller
W-59 L-80

Tom Kelly
W-12 L-11

POS	Player	AB	BA	HR	RBI	PO	A	E	DP	TC/G	FA	Pitcher	G	IP	W	L	SV	ERA
1B	K. Hrbek	550	.267	29	91	1218	104	10	**137**	9.1	.992	B. Blyleven	36	**272**	17	14	0	4.01
2B	S. Lombardozzi	453	.227	8	33	289	407	6	102	4.5	**.991**	F. Viola	37	246	16	13	0	4.51
SS	G. Gagne	472	.250	12	54	228	377	**26**	96	4.1	.959	M. Smithson	34	198	13	14	0	4.77
3B	G. Gaetti	596	.287	34	108	118	**334**	21	**36**	**3.0**	.956	N. Heaton	21	124	4	9	1	3.98
RF	T. Brunansky	593	.256	23	75	315	10	6	1	2.2	.982	M. Portugal	27	113	6	10	1	4.31
CF	K. Puckett	680	.328	31	96	429	8	6	3	2.8	.986	A. Anderson	21	84	3	6	1	5.55
LF	R. Bush	357	.269	7	45	167	2	4	0	1.7	.977	K. Atherton	47	82	5	8	10	3.75
C	M. Salas	258	.233	8	33	358	32	8	5	5.8	.980	R. Davis	36	39	2	6	2	9.08
DH	R. Smalley	459	.246	20	57													
UT	M. Hatcher	317	.278	3	32	220	16	4	16		.983							
C	T. Laudner	193	.244	10	29	299	13	5	3	4.7	.984							
OF	B. Beane	183	.213	3	15	118	0	0	0	1.8	1.000							
C	J. Reed	165	.236	2	9	332	19	2	5	5.5	.994							

Seattle

W-67 L-95

Chuck Cottier
W-9 L-19

Marty Martinez
W-0 L-1

Dick Williams
W-58 L-75

POS	Player	AB	BA	HR	RBI	PO	A	E	DP	TC/G	FA	Pitcher	G	IP	W	L	SV	ERA
1B	A. Davis	479	.271	18	72	880	82	14	112	9.7	.986	M. Moore	38	266	11	13	1	4.30
2B	H. Reynolds	445	.222	1	24	278	415	16	**111**	**5.6**	.977	M. Langston	37	239	12	14	0	4.85
SS	S. Owen	402	.246	0	35	209	372	17	99*	5.3*	.972	M. Morgan	37	216	11	**17**	1	4.53
3B	J. Presley	616	.265	27	107	110	308	15	31	2.8	.965	B. Swift	29	115	2	9	0	5.46
RF	D. Tartabull	511	.270	25	96	157	7	8	0	1.7	.953	M. Young	65	104	8	6	13	3.82
CF	J. Moses	399	.256	3	34	211	9	3	1	2.4	.987	M. Huismann	36	80	3	3	4	3.71
LF	P. Bradley	526	.310	12	50	250	11	1	0	1.9	.996	P. Ladd	52	71	8	6	6	3.82
C	B. Kearney	204	.240	6	25	419	46	5	3	5.9	.989							
DH	K. Phelps	344	.247	24	64													
OF	D. Henderson	337	.276	14	44	182	9	4	1	2.4	.979							
C	S. Bradley	199	.302	5	28	281	21	3	5	5.2	.990							
DH	G. Thomas	170	.194	10	26													

BATTING AND BASE RUNNING LEADERS

Batting Average		Slugging Average		Home Runs	
W. Boggs, BOS	.357	D. Mattingly, NY	.573	J. Barfield, TOR	40
D. Mattingly, NY	.352	J. Barfield, TOR	.559	D. Kingman, OAK	35
K. Puckett, MIN	.328	K. Puckett, MIN	.537	G. Gaetti, MIN	34
P. Tabler, CLE	.326	G. Bell, TOR	.532	R. Deer, MIL	33
J. Rice, BOS	.324	G. Gaetti, MIN	.518	J. Canseco, OAK	33

PITCHING LEADERS

Winning Percentage		Earned Run Average		Wins	
R. Clemens, BOS	.857	R. Clemens, BOS	2.48	R. Clemens, BOS	24
D. Rasmussen, NY	.750	T. Higuera, MIL	2.79	J. Morris, DET	21
J. Morris, DET	.724	M. Witt, CAL	2.84	T. Higuera, MIL	20
T. Higuera, MIL	.645	B. Hurst, BOS	2.99	D. Rasmussen, NY	18
M. Witt, CAL	.643	D. Jackson, KC	3.20	M. Witt, CAL	18

AMERICAN LEAGUE 1986, *cont.*

BATTING AND BASE RUNNING LEADERS

Total Bases
- D. Mattingly, NY 388
- K. Puckett, MIN 365
- G. Bell, TOR 341
- J. Carter, CLE 341
- J. Barfield, TOR 329

Runs Batted In
- J. Carter, CLE 121
- J. Canseco, OAK 117
- D. Mattingly, NY 113
- J. Rice, BOS 110

Stolen Bases
- R. Henderson, NY 87
- J. Cangelosi, CHI 50
- G. Pettis, CAL 50
- K. Gibson, DET 34
- W. Wilson, KC 34

Hits
- D. Mattingly, NY 238
- K. Puckett, MIN 223
- T. Fernandez, TOR 213
- W. Boggs, BOS 207

Base on Balls
- W. Boggs, BOS 105
- D. Evans, BOS 97
- W. Randolph, NY 94
- R. Jackson, CAL 92

Home Run Percentage
- R. Deer, MIL 7.1
- J. Barfield, TOR 6.8
- K. Gibson, DET 6.3
- D. Kingman, OAK 6.2

Runs
- R. Henderson, NY 130
- K. Puckett, MIN 119
- D. Mattingly, NY 117
- J. Carter, CLE 108

Doubles
- D. Mattingly, NY 53
- W. Boggs, BOS 47
- J. Rice, BOS 39
- M. Barrett, BOS 39
- B. Buckner, BOS 39

Triples
- B. Butler, CLE 14
- R. Sierra, TEX 10
- J. Carter, CLE 9
- T. Fernandez, TOR 9

PITCHING LEADERS

Saves
- D. Righetti, NY 46
- D. Aase, BAL 34
- T. Henke, TOR 27
- G. Hernandez, DET 24
- D. Moore, CAL 21

Strikeouts
- M. Langston, SEA 245
- R. Clemens, BOS 238
- J. Morris, DET 223
- B. Blyleven, MIN 215
- M. Witt, CAL 208

Complete Games
- T. Candiotti, CLE 17
- B. Blyleven, MIN 16
- T. Higuera, MIL 15
- J. Morris, DET 15
- M. Witt, CAL 14

Fewest Hits/9 Innings
- R. Clemens, BOS 6.34
- D. Rasmussen, NY 7.13
- M. Witt, CAL 7.29
- C. Hough, TEX 7.35

Shutouts
- J. Morris, DET 6
- B. Hurst, BOS 4
- T. Higuera, MIL 4

Fewest Walks/9 Innings
- R. Guidry, NY 1.78
- O. Boyd, BOS 1.89
- B. Blyleven, MIN 1.92
- B. Wegman, MIL 1.95

Most Strikeouts/9 Inn.
- M. Langston, SEA 9.21
- B. Hurst, BOS 8.62
- R. Clemens, BOS 8.43
- E. Correa, TEX 8.41

Innings
- B. Blyleven, MIN 272
- M. Witt, CAL 269
- J. Morris, DET 267
- M. Moore, SEA 266

Games Pitched
- M. Williams, TEX 80
- D. Righetti, NY 74
- G. Harris, TEX 73
- M. Eichhorn, TOR 69

		W	L	PCT	GB	R	OR	Batting 2B	3B	HR	BA	SA	SB	Fielding E	DP	FA	Pitching CG	BB	SO	ShO	SV	ERA
East	Boston	95	66	.590		794	696	**320**	21	144	.271	.415	41	129	146	.979	36	**474**	1033	6	41	3.93
	New York	90	72	.556	5.5	797	738	275	23	188	.271	**.430**	139	127	153	.979	13	492	878	8	**58**	4.11
	Detroit	87	75	.537	8.5	798	714	234	30	**198**	.263	.424	138	108	163	.982	33	571	880	12	38	4.02
	Toronto	86	76	.531	9.5	809	733	285	35	181	.269	.427	110	**100**	150	**.984**	16	487	1002	12	44	4.08
	Cleveland	84	78	.519	11.5	**831**	841	270	**45**	157	**.284**	**.430**	**141**	157	148	.975	31	605	744	7	34	4.57
	Milwaukee	77	84	.478	18	667	734	255	38	127	.255	.385	100	146	146	.976	29	494	952	12	32	4.01
	Baltimore	73	89	.451	22.5	708	760	223	13	169	.258	.395	64	135	163	.978	17	535	954	6	39	4.30
West	California	92	70	.568		786	684	236	36	167	.255	.404	109	107	156	.983	29	478	955	12	40	3.84
	Texas	87	75	.537	5	771	743	248	43	184	.267	.428	103	122	160	.980	15	736	**1059**	8	41	4.11
	Kansas City	76	86	.469	16	654	**673**	264	**45**	137	.252	.390	97	123	153	.980	24	479	888	**13**	31	**3.82**
	Oakland	76	86	.469	16	731	760	213	25	163	.252	.390	139	135	120	.978	22	667	937	8	37	4.31
	Chicago	72	90	.444	20	644	699	197	34	121	.247	.363	115	117	142	.981	18	561	895	8	38	3.93
	Minnesota	71	91	.438	21	741	839	257	39	196	.261	.428	81	118	168	.980	**39**	503	937	6	24	4.77
	Seattle	67	95	.414	25	718	835	243	41	158	.253	.399	93	156	**191**	.975	33	585	944	5	27	4.65
						10449	10449	3520	468	2290	.261	.408	1470	1780	2159	.979	355	7667	13058	123	524	4.18

NATIONAL LEAGUE 1987

	POS	Player	AB	BA	HR	RBI	PO	A	E	DP	TC/G	FA	Pitcher	G	IP	W	L	SV	ERA
East **St. Louis**	1B	J. Clark	419	.286	35	106	1151	77	14	116	9.9	.989	D. Cox	31	199	11	9	0	3.88
	2B	T. Herr	510	.263	2	83	306	350	7	103	4.8	.989	G. Mathews	32	198	11	11	0	3.73
	SS	O. Smith	600	.303	0	75	245	**516**	10	**111**	4.9	**.987**	B. Forsch	33	179	11	7	0	4.32
	3B	T. Pendleton	583	.286	12	96	117	**369**	26	27	**3.2**	.949	J. Magrane	27	170	9	7	0	3.54
W-95 L-67	RF	C. Ford	228	.285	3	26	157	2	3	0	2.2	.981	R. Horton	67	125	8	3	7	3.82
	CF	W. McGee	620	.285	11	105	353	9	7	1	2.4	.981	B. Dawley	60	97	5	8	2	4.47
Whitey Herzog	LF	V. Coleman	623	.289	3	43	274	16	9	3	2.0	.970	J. Tudor	16	96	10	2	0	3.84
	C	T. Pena	384	.214	5	44	615	51	8	8	6.0	.988	T. Worrell	75	95	8	6	33	2.66
	UT	J. Oquendo	248	.286	1	24	149	133	4	31		.986	K. Dayley	53	61	9	5	4	2.66
	OF	J. Lindeman	207	.208	8	28	78	4	2	3	1.7	.976							
	C	S. Lake	179	.251	2	19	253	21	1	2	4.7	.996							
	OF	J. Morris	157	.261	3	23	86	0	1	0	1.2	.989							
New York	1B	K. Hernandez	587	.290	18	89	1298	**149**	10	110	9.5	.993	R. Darling	32	208	12	8	0	4.29
	2B	T. Teufel	299	.308	14	61	138	213	10	43	3.9	.972	D. Gooden	25	180	15	7	0	3.21
	SS	R. Santana	439	.255	5	44	213	396	17	82	4.5	.973	S. Fernandez	28	156	12	8	0	3.81
	3B	H. Johnson	554	.265	36	99	82	235	21	15	2.4	.938	T. Leach	44	131	11	1	0	3.22
W-92 L-70	RF	D. Strawberry	532	.284	39	104	272	6	8	3	1.9	.972	R. Aguilera	18	115	11	3	0	3.60
	CF	L. Dykstra	431	.285	10	43	239	4	3	1	2.1	.988	J. Mitchell	20	112	3	6	0	4.11
Davey Johnson	LF	K. McReynolds	590	.276	29	95	286	8	4	0	2.0	.987	D. Cone	21	99	5	6	1	3.71
	C	G. Carter	523	.235	20	83	874	70	9	**13**	7.1	.991	R. McDowell	56	89	7	5	25	4.16
	OF	M. Wilson	385	.299	9	34	205	3	8	2	2.0	.963	J. Orosco	58	77	3	9	16	4.44
	2B	W. Backman	300	.250	1	23	131	210	6	44	4.0	.983	R. Myers	54	75	3	6	6	3.96
	3B	D. Magadan	192	.318	3	24	17	85	2	5	2.1	.981							
	C	B. Lyons	130	.254	4	24	223	17	4	0	5.0	.984							
	O1	L. Mazzilli	124	.306	3	24	82	3	0	1		1.000							
Montreal	1B	A. Galarraga	551	.305	13	90	**1300**	103	10	96	9.7	.993	N. Heaton	32	193	13	10	0	4.52
	2B	V. Law	436	.273	12	56	158	276	9	47	4.2	.980	B. Sebra	36	177	6	15	0	4.42
	SS	H. Brooks	430	.263	14	72	131	271	20	53	3.9	.953	B. Smith	26	150	10	9	0	4.37
	3B	T. Wallach	593	.298	26	123	**128**	292	21	21	2.9	.952	D. Martinez	22	145	11	4	0	3.30
W-91 L-71	RF	M. Webster	588	.281	15	63	266	8	5	0	1.8	.982	A. McGaffigan	69	120	5	2	12	2.39
	CF	H. Winningham	347	.239	4	41	225	5	6	1	1.8	.975	F. Youmans	23	116	9	8	0	4.64
Buck Rodgers	LF	T. Raines	530	.330	18	68	297	9	4	1	2.2	.987	T. Burke	55	91	7	0	18	1.19
	C	M. Fitzgerald	287	.240	3	36	602	27	12	2	6.2	.981	R. St. Claire	44	67	3	3	7	4.03
	UT	C. Candaele	449	.272	1	23	237	176	8	28		.981	J. Parrett	45	62	7	6	6	4.21
	S2	T. Foley	280	.293	5	28	133	186	9	43		.973	B. McClure	52	52	6	1	5	3.44
	C	J. Reed	207	.213	1	21	357	36	12	6	5.5	.970							
	OF	R. Nichols	147	.265	4	20	97	4	1	0	1.7	.990							

NATIONAL LEAGUE 1987, *cont.*

Team	POS	Player	AB	BA	HR	RBI	PO	A	E	DP	TC/G	FA	Pitcher	G	IP	W	L	SV	ERA
Philadelphia	1B	V. Hayes	556	.277	21	84	1164	78	12	100	8.7	.990	S. Rawley	36	230	17	11	0	4.39
W-80 L-82	2B	J. Samuel	**655**	.272	28	100	**374**	434	**18**	99	5.2	.978	D. Carman	35	211	13	11	0	4.22
John Felske	SS	S. Jeltz	293	.232	0	12	191	271	14	55	4.2	.971	B. Ruffin	35	205	11	14	0	4.35
W-29 L-32	3B	M. Schmidt	522	.293	35	113	87	315	12	**28**	3.0	.971	K. Gross	34	201	9	16	0	4.35
Lee Elia	RF	G. Wilson	569	.264	14	54	315	18	11	2	2.2	.968	M. Jackson	55	109	3	10	1	4.20
W-51 L-50	CF	M. Thompson	527	.302	7	43	354	4	4	1	2.5	.989	K. Tekulve	**90**	105	6	4	3	3.09
	LF	C. James	358	.293	17	54	198	5	2	1	1.9	.990	S. Bedrosian	65	89	5	3	**40**	2.83
	C	L. Parrish	466	.245	17	67	724	66	9	1	6.3	.989							
	SS	L. Aguayo	209	.206	12	21	81	154	7	29	3.1	.971							
	31	R. Schu	196	.235	7	23	193	71	10	11		.964							

Team	POS	Player	AB	BA	HR	RBI	PO	A	E	DP	TC/G	FA	Pitcher	G	IP	W	L	SV	ERA
Pittsburgh	1B	S. Bream	516	.275	13	65	1236	127	**17**	109	9.6	.988	B. Fisher	37	185	11	9	0	4.52
W-80 L-82	2B	J. Ray	472	.273	5	54	248	358	12	84	5.2	.981	R. Reuschel	25	177	8	6	0	2.75
Jim Leyland	SS	A. Pedrique	246	.301	1	27	115	185	10	43	4.1	.968	D. Drabek	29	176	11	12	0	3.88
	3B	B. Bonilla	466	.300	15	77	53	138	14	12	2.3	.932	M. Dunne	23	163	13	6	0	3.03
	RF	R. Reynolds	335	.260	7	51	134	7	1	2	1.4	.993	B. Walk	39	117	8	2	0	3.31
	CF	A. Van Slyke	564	.293	21	82	328	10	4	6	2.3	.988	B. Kipper	24	111	5	9	0	5.94
	LF	B. Bonds	551	.261	25	59	330	15	5	3	2.4	.986	J. Smiley	63	75	5	5	4	5.76
	C	M. LaValliere	340	.300	1	36	584	70	5	11	5.9	.992	D. Robinson	42	65	6	6	12	3.86
	3B	J. Morrison	348	.264	9	46	46	151	5	11	2.5	.975	J. Gott	25	31	0	2	13	1.45
	UT	M. Diaz	241	.241	16	48	303	23	6	14		.982							
	SS	R. Belliard	203	.207	1	15	104	176	6	29	4.0	.979							
	C	J. Ortiz	192	.271	1	22	313	39	9	2	5.0	.975							
	OF	J. Cangelosi	182	.275	4	18	74	3	3	0	1.7	.963							
	OF	D. Coles	119	.227	6	24	28	1	0	0	1.1	1.000							

Team	POS	Player	AB	BA	HR	RBI	PO	A	E	DP	TC/G	FA	Pitcher	G	IP	W	L	SV	ERA
Chicago	1B	L. Durham	439	.273	27	63	1049	57	11	90	9.1	.990	R. Sutcliffe	34	237	**18**	10	0	3.68
W-76 L-85	2B	R. Sandberg	523	.294	16	59	294	375	10	84	5.2	.985	J. Moyer	35	201	12	15	0	5.10
Gene Michael	SS	S. Dunston	346	.246	5	22	160	271	14	54	4.7	.969	G. Maddux	30	156	6	14	0	5.61
W-68 L-68	3B	K. Moreland	563	.266	27	88	99	300	**28**	27	2.8	.934	S. Sanderson	32	145	8	9	2	4.29
Frank Lucchesi	RF	A. Dawson	621	.287	**49**	**137**	271	12	4	0	1.9	.986	L. Lancaster	27	132	8	3	0	4.90
W-8 L-17	CF	D. Martinez	459	.292	8	36	283	10	6	1	2.2	.980	E. Lynch	58	110	2	9	4	5.38
	LF	J. Mumphrey	309	.333	13	44	124	5	1	0	1.5	.992	L. Smith	62	84	4	10	36	3.12
	C	J. Davis	428	.248	19	51	749	79	9	11	6.8	.989	F. DiPino	69	80	3	3	4	3.15
	OF	R. Palmeiro	221	.276	14	30	64	1	0	1	1.4	1.000							
	UT	M. Trillo	214	.294	8	26	301	53	4	35		.989							
	OF	B. Dernier	199	.317	8	21	86	2	1	1	1.3	.989							
	2S	P. Noce	180	.228	3	14	116	157	5	39		.982							
	OF	B. Dayett	177	.277	5	25	72	2	0	0	0.9	1.000							

West

Team	POS	Player	AB	BA	HR	RBI	PO	A	E	DP	TC/G	FA	Pitcher	G	IP	W	L	SV	ERA
San Francisco	1B	W. Clark	529	.308	35	91	1253	103	13	**130**	9.8	.991	K. Downs	41	186	12	9	1	3.63
W-90 L-72	2B	R. Thompson	420	.262	10	44	246	341	17	99	4.8	.972	M. LaCoss	39	171	13	10	0	3.68
Roger Craig	SS	J. Uribe	309	.291	5	30	145	286	13	62	4.7	.971	A. Hammaker	31	168	10	10	0	3.58
	3B	K. Mitchell	268	.306	15	44	44	131	7	10	2.7	.962	M. Krukow	30	163	5	6	0	4.80
	RF	C. Maldonado	442	.292	20	85	176	7	5	0	1.6	.973	D. Dravecky	18	112	7	5	0	3.20
	CF	C. Davis	500	.250	24	76	265	6	7	2	2.1	.975	S. Garrelts	64	106	11	7	12	3.22
	LF	J. Leonard	503	.280	19	63	193	7	7	2	1.6	.966	J. Robinson	63	97	6	8	10	2.79
	C	B. Brenly	375	.267	18	51	642	**83**	9	10	6.8	.988	C. Lefferts	44	47	3	3	4	3.23
	OF	M. Aldrete	357	.325	9	51	141	3	2	1	1.8	.986	D. Robinson	25	43	5	1	7	2.74
	UT	C. Speier	317	.249	11	39	118	229	4	41		.989							
	C	B. Melvin	246	.199	11	31	407	43	1	7	5.8	.998							
	SS	M. Williams	245	.188	8	21	104	210	8	49	4.6	.975							
	OF	E. Milner	214	.252	4	19	135	0	1	0	1.6	.993							

Team	POS	Player	AB	BA	HR	RBI	PO	A	E	DP	TC/G	FA	Pitcher	G	IP	W	L	SV	ERA
Cincinnati	1B	N. Esasky	346	.272	22	59	772	40	5	72	8.8	.994	T. Power	34	204	10	13	0	4.50
W-84 L-78	2B	R. Oester	237	.253	2	23	183	186	10	37	5.5	.974	T. Browning	32	183	10	13	0	5.02
Pete Rose	SS	B. Larkin	439	.244	12	43	168	358	19	72	4.6	.965	B. Gullickson	27	165	10	11	0	4.85
	3B	B. Bell	522	.284	17	70	93	241	7	17	2.4	**.979**	G. Hoffman	36	159	9	10	0	4.37
	RF	D. Parker	589	.253	26	97	278	13	10	3	2.1	.967	R. Robinson	48	154	7	5	4	3.68
	CF	E. Davis	474	.293	37	100	380	10	4	4	3.1	.990	F. Williams	85	106	4	0	2	2.30
	LF	K. Daniels	368	.334	26	64	178	5	6	0	2.0	.968	R. Murphy	87	101	8	5	3	3.04
	C	B. Diaz	496	.270	15	82	747	70	7	6	6.0	.992	J. Franco	68	82	8	5	32	2.52
	UT	K. Stillwell	395	.258	4	33	144	247	23	38		.944							
	OF	T. Jones	359	.290	10	44	189	2	2	0	2.0	.990							
	UT	D. Concepcion	279	.319	1	33	250	169	5	43		.988							
	1B	T. Francona	207	.227	3	12	373	45	2	38	7.4	.995							
	OF	P. O'Neill	160	.256	7	28	73	2	4	0	1.9	.949							

Team	POS	Player	AB	BA	HR	RBI	PO	A	E	DP	TC/G	FA	Pitcher	G	IP	W	L	SV	ERA
Houston	1B	G. Davis	578	.251	27	93	1283	112	12	89	9.3	.991	M. Scott	36	248	16	13	0	3.23
W-76 L-86	2B	B. Doran	625	.283	16	79	300	431	6	70	4.5	**.992**	N. Ryan	34	212	8	16	0	**2.76**
Hal Lanier	SS	C. Reynolds	374	.254	4	28	160	290	14	43	3.6	.970	D. Darwin	33	196	9	10	0	3.59
	3B	D. Walling	325	.283	5	33	72	109	10	13	2.4	.948	B. Knepper	33	178	8	**17**	0	5.27
	RF	K. Bass	592	.284	19	85	287	11	4	2	1.9	.987	J. Deshaies	26	152	11	6	0	4.62
	CF	B. Hatcher	564	.296	11	63	276	16	4	6	2.1	.986	L. Andersen	67	102	9	5	5	3.45
	LF	J. Cruz	365	.241	11	38	178	5	3	3	1.9	.984	D. Smith	50	60	2	3	24	1.65
	C	A. Ashby	386	.288	14	63	778	46	6	6	**7.5**	**.993**							
	OF	G. Young	274	.321	1	15	143	5	3	1	2.3	.980							
	3B	K. Caminiti	203	.246	3	23	50	98	8	11	2.6	.949							

NATIONAL LEAGUE 1987, *cont.*

Los Angeles

W-73 L-89

Tom Lasorda

POS	Player	AB	BA	HR	RBI	PO	A	E	DP	TC/G	FA	Pitcher	G	IP	W	L	SV	ERA
1B	F. Stubbs	386	.233	16	52	802	78	5	65	8.0	**.994**	O. Hershiser	37	**265**	16	16	1	3.06
2B	S. Sax	610	.280	6	46	342	420	14	92	5.1	.982	B. Welch	35	252	15	9	0	3.22
SS	M. Duncan	261	.215	6	18	90	191	**21**	37	4.5	.930	F. Valenzuela	34	251	14	14	0	3.98
3B	M. Hatcher	287	.282	7	42	37	81	9	7	2.6	.929	R. Honeycutt	27	116	2	12	0	4.59
RF	M. Marshall	402	.294	16	72	147	4	2	0	1.5	.987	T. Leary	39	108	3	11	1	4.76
CF	J. Shelby	476	.277	21	69	269	9	8	3	2.4	.972	A. Pena	37	87	2	7	11	3.50
LF	P. Guerrero	545	.338	27	89	163	6	5	0	1.6	.971	M. Young	47	54	5	8	11	4.47
C	M. Scioscia	461	.265	6	38	**925**	80	11	11	7.4	.989							
S3	D. Anderson	265	.234	1	13	102	202	7	33		.977							
OF	K. Landreaux	182	.203	6	23	72	5	4	3	1.3	.951							

Atlanta

W-69 L-92

Chuck Tanner

POS	Player	AB	BA	HR	RBI	PO	A	E	DP	TC/G	FA	Pitcher	G	IP	W	L	SV	ERA
1B	G. Perry	533	.270	12	74	1288	72	14	118	**10.1**	.990	Z. Smith	36	242	15	10	0	4.09
2B	G. Hubbard	443	.264	5	38	284	**478**	11	**114**	**5.6**	.986	R. Mahler	39	197	8	13	0	4.98
SS	A. Thomas	324	.231	5	39	128	276	20	56	5.2	.953	D. Palmer	28	152	8	11	0	4.90
3B	K. Oberkfell	508	.280	3	48	76	248	7	20	2.6	.979	C. Puleo	35	123	6	8	0	4.23
RF	D. Murphy	566	.295	44	105	325	14	8	1	2.2	.977	D. Alexander	16	118	5	10	0	4.13
CF	D. James	494	.312	10	61	262	4	1	1	2.1	.996	J. Acker	68	115	4	9	14	4.16
LF	K. Griffey	399	.286	14	64	181	7	1	1	1.8	.995	J. Dedmon	53	90	3	4	4	3.91
C	O. Virgil	429	.247	27	72	654	74	8	12	6.0	.989	G. Garber	49	69	8	10	10	4.41
OF	A. Hall	292	.284	3	24	148	5	3	1	2.3	.981							
SS	R. Ramirez	179	.263	1	21	59	99	9	30	4.4	.946							
1C	T. Simmons	177	.277	4	30	280	33	5	25		.984							
3B	G. Nettles	177	.209	5	33	12	46	3	6	1.5	.951							
SS	J. Blauser	165	.242	2	15	65	166	9	28	4.8	.963							
OF	G. Roenicke	151	.219	9	28	60	0	2	0	1.4	.968							

San Diego

W-65 L-97

Larry Bowa

POS	Player	AB	BA	HR	RBI	PO	A	E	DP	TC/G	FA	Pitcher	G	IP	W	L	SV	ERA
1B	J. Kruk	447	.313	20	91	870	75	4	74	9.4	.996	E. Show	34	206	8	16	0	3.84
2B	T. Flannery	276	.228	0	20	139	207	5	40	4.2	.986	E. Whitson	36	206	10	13	0	4.73
SS	G. Templeton	510	.222	5	48	**253**	447	20	77	**4.9**	.972	J. Jones	30	146	9	7	0	4.14
3B	R. Ready	350	.309	12	54	30	95	12	11	2.6	.912	L. McCullers	78	123	8	10	16	3.72
RF	T. Gwynn	589	**.370**	7	54	298	13	6	1	2.0	.981	A. Hawkins	24	118	3	10	0	5.05
CF	S. Jefferson	422	.230	8	29	232	3	3	1	2.2	.987	M. Grant	17	102	6	7	0	4.66
LF	C. Martinez	447	.273	15	70	116	6	4	0	1.6	.968	D. Dravecky	30	79	3	7	0	3.76
C	B. Santiago	546	.300	18	79	817	80	**22**	12	6.3	.976	M. Davis	43	62	5	3	2	3.18
2B	J. Cora	241	.237	0	13	118	192	8	31	4.8	.975	G. Gossage	40	52	5	4	11	3.12
OF	S. Mack	238	.239	4	25	159	1	3	0	1.8	.982							
3B	K. Mitchell	196	.245	7	26	29	108	8	9	2.8	.945							
UT	L. Salazar	189	.254	3	17	56	95	9	11		.944							
OF	M. Wynne	188	.250	2	24	100	2	2	0	1.5	.981							
3B	C. Brown	155	.232	6	23	27	70	6	12	2.4	.942							

BATTING AND BASE RUNNING LEADERS

Batting Average

T. Gwynn, SD	.370
P. Guerrero, LA	.338
T. Raines, MON	.330
J. Kruk, SD	.313
D. James, ATL	.312

Slugging Average

J. Clark, STL	.597
E. Davis, CIN	.593
D. Strawberry, NY	.583
W. Clark, SF	.580
D. Murphy, ATL	.580

Home Runs

A. Dawson, CHI	49
D. Murphy, ATL	44
D. Strawberry, NY	39
E. Davis, CIN	37
H. Johnson, NY	36

Total Bases

A. Dawson, CHI	353
J. Samuel, PHI	329
D. Murphy, ATL	328
D. Strawberry, NY	310
W. Clark, SF	307

Runs Batted In

A. Dawson, CHI	137
T. Wallach, MON	123
M. Schmidt, PHI	113
J. Clark, STL	106
D. Murphy, ATL	105
W. McGee, STL	105

Stolen Bases

V. Coleman, STL	109
T. Gwynn, SD	56
B. Hatcher, HOU	53
E. Davis, CIN	50
T. Raines, MON	50

Hits

T. Gwynn, SD	218
P. Guerrero, LA	184
O. Smith, STL	182
V. Coleman, STL	180

Base on Balls

J. Clark, STL	136
V. Hayes, PHI	121
D. Murphy, ATL	115
D. Strawberry, NY	97

Home Run Percentage

J. Clark, STL	8.4
A. Dawson, CHI	7.9
E. Davis, CIN	7.8
D. Murphy, ATL	7.8

Runs

T. Raines, MON	123
V. Coleman, STL	121
E. Davis, CIN	120
T. Gwynn, SD	119

Doubles

T. Wallach, MON	42
A. Galarraga, MON	40
O. Smith, STL	40

Triples

J. Samuel, PHI	15
T. Gwynn, SD	13
A. Van Slyke, PIT	11
W. McGee, STL	11

PITCHING LEADERS

Winning Percentage

D. Gooden, NY	.682
R. Sutcliffe, CHI	.643
B. Welch, LA	.625
S. Rawley, PHI	.607
Z. Smith, ATL	.600

Earned Run Average

N. Ryan, HOU	2.76
M. Dunne, PIT	3.03
O. Hershiser, LA	3.06
R. Reuschel, PIT, SF	3.09
D. Gooden, NY	3.21

Wins

R. Sutcliffe, CHI	18
S. Rawley, PHI	17
M. Scott, HOU	16
O. Hershiser, LA	16

Saves

S. Bedrosian, PHI	40
L. Smith, CHI	36
T. Worrell, STL	33
J. Franco, CIN	32
R. McDowell, NY	25

Strikeouts

N. Ryan, HOU	270
M. Scott, HOU	233
B. Welch, LA	196
F. Valenzuela, LA	190
O. Hershiser, LA	190

Complete Games

R. Reuschel, PIT, SF	12
F. Valenzuela, LA	12
O. Hershiser, LA	10
Z. Smith, ATL	9
M. Scott, HOU	8

Fewest Hits/9 Innings

N. Ryan, HOU	6.55
M. Scott, HOU	7.23
B. Welch, LA	7.30
M. Dunne, PIT	7.88

Shutouts

R. Reuschel, PIT, SF	4
B. Welch, LA	4

Fewest Walks/9 Innings

R. Reuschel, PIT, SF	1.67
N. Heaton, MON	1.72
B. Gullickson, CIN	2.13
B. Forsch, STL	2.26

Most Strikeouts/9 Inn.

N. Ryan, HOU	11.48
M. Scott, HOU	8.47
B. Sebra, MON	7.92
D. Gooden, NY	7.41

Innings

O. Hershiser, LA	265
B. Welch, LA	252
F. Valenzuela, LA	251
M. Scott, HOU	248

Games Pitched

K. Tekulve, PHI	90
R. Murphy, CIN	87
F. Williams, CIN	85
J. Robinson, SF, PIT	81

NATIONAL LEAGUE 1987, *cont.*

		W	L	PCT	GB	R	OR	Batting 2B	3B	HR	BA	SA	SB	Fielding E	DP	FA	Pitching CG	BB	SO	ShO	SV	ERA
East	St. Louis	95	67	.586		798	693	252	49	94	.263	.378	**248**	**116**	172	**.982**	10	533	873	4	48	3.91
	New York	92	70	.568	3	**823**	698	287	34	192	**.268**	**.434**	159	137	137	.978	16	510	1032	5	**51**	3.84
	Montreal	91	71	.562	4	741	720	**310**	39	120	.265	.401	166	147	122	.976	16	**446**	1012	6	50	3.92
	Philadelphia	80	82	.494	15	702	749	248	**51**	169	.254	.410	111	121	137	.980	13	587	877	5	48	4.18
	Pittsburgh	80	82	.494	15	723	744	282	45	131	.264	.403	140	123	147	.980	25	562	914	**10**	39	4.20
	Chicago	76	85	.472	18.5	720	801	244	33	**209**	.264	.432	109	130	154	.979	11	628	1024	4	48	4.55
West	San Francisco	90	72	.556		783	**669**	274	32	205	.260	.430	126	129	**183**	.980	19	547	1038	8	38	**3.68**
	Cincinnati	84	78	.519	6	783	752	262	29	192	.266	.427	169	130	137	.979	7	485	919	2	44	4.25
	Houston	76	86	.469	14	648	678	238	28	122	.253	.373	162	**116**	113	.981	13	525	**1137**	4	33	3.84
	Los Angeles	73	89	.451	17	635	675	236	23	125	.252	.371	128	155	144	.975	**29**	565	1097	7	32	3.72
	Atlanta	69	92	.429	20.5	747	829	284	24	152	.258	.403	135	**116**	170	**.982**	16	587	837	4	32	4.63
	San Diego	65	97	.401	25	668	763	209	48	113	.260	.378	198	147	135	.976	14	602	897	6	33	4.27
						8771	8771	3126	435	1824	.261	.403	1851	1567	1751	.979	189	6577	11657	65	496	4.08

AMERICAN LEAGUE 1987

East

Detroit

W-98 L-64

Sparky Anderson

POS	Player	AB	BA	HR	RBI	PO	A	E	DP	TC/G	FA	Pitcher	G	IP	W	L	SV	ERA
1B	D. Evans	499	.257	34	99	810	100	3	86	8.7	.997	J. Morris	34	266	18	11	0	3.38
2B	L. Whitaker	604	.265	16	59	275	416	17	99	4.8	.976	W. Terrell	35	245	17	10	0	4.05
SS	A. Trammell	597	.343	28	105	222	421	19	94	4.4	.971	F. Tanana	34	219	15	10	0	3.91
3B	T. Brookens	444	.241	13	59	85	208	14	15	2.5	.954	D. Petry	30	135	9	7	0	5.61
RF	P. Sheridan	421	.259	6	49	236	6	6	1	1.8	.976	J. Robinson	29	127	9	6	0	5.37
CF	C. Lemon	470	.277	20	75	350	4	3	1	2.5	.992	E. King	55	116	6	9	9	4.89
LF	K. Gibson	487	.277	24	79	253	6	7	0	2.2	.974	M. Henneman	55	97	11	3	7	2.98
C	M. Nokes	461	.289	32	87	595	32	5	2	5.8	.992	G. Hernandez	45	49	3	4	8	3.67
DH	B. Madlock	326	.279	14	50													
UT	M. Heath	270	.281	8	33	384	43	5	8		.988							
OF	L. Herndon	225	.324	9	47	82	4	1	1	1.5	.989							
1B	D. Bergman	172	.273	6	22	353	29	3	33	5.9	.992							

Toronto

W-96 L-66

Jimy Williams

POS	Player	AB	BA	HR	RBI	PO	A	E	DP	TC/G	FA	Pitcher	G	IP	W	L	SV	ERA
1B	W. Upshaw	512	.244	15	58	1169	127	9	114	8.9	.993	J. Key	36	261	17	8	0	**2.76**
2B	G. Iorg	310	.210	4	30	139	195	6	33	3.7	.982	J. Clancy	37	241	15	11	0	3.54
SS	T. Fernandez	578	.322	5	67	**270**	396	14	88	4.7	.979	D. Stieb	33	185	13	9	0	4.09
3B	K. Gruber	341	.235	12	36	52	168	12	11	1.9	.948	J. Cerutti	44	151	11	4	0	4.40
RF	J. Barfield	590	.263	28	84	341	17	3	4	2.3	.992	M. Eichhorn	**89**	128	10	6	4	3.17
CF	L. Moseby	592	.282	26	96	294	7	6	1	2.0	.980	T. Henke	72	94	0	6	**34**	2.49
LF	G. Bell	610	.308	47	**134**	248	14	11	1	1.8	.960	J. Musselman	68	89	12	5	3	4.15
C	E. Whitt	446	.269	19	75	**803**	55	5	10	6.6	.994							
DH	F. McGriff	295	.247	20	43													
3B	R. Mulliniks	332	.310	11	44	29	137	13	14	1.9	.927							
OD	R. Leach	195	.282	3	25	51	1	1	0		.981							
DH	C. Fielder	175	.269	14	32													
DO	J. Beniquez	81	.284	5	21	7	0	1	0		.875							

Milwaukee

W-91 L-71

Tom Trebelhorn

POS	Player	AB	BA	HR	RBI	PO	A	E	DP	TC/G	FA	Pitcher	G	IP	W	L	SV	ERA
1B	G. Brock	532	.299	13	85	1065	109	8	111	8.4	.993	T. Higuera	35	262	18	10	0	3.85
2B	J. Castillo	321	.224	3	28	181	219	11	54	4.2	.973	B. Wegman	34	225	12	11	0	4.24
SS	D. Sveum	535	.252	25	95	221	361	21	82	4.2	.965	J. Nieves	34	196	14	8	0	4.88
3B	E. Riles	276	.261	4	38	41	103	10	11	2.4	.935	C. Bosio	46	170	11	8	2	5.24
RF	G. Braggs	505	.269	13	77	301	6	9	1	2.6	.972	C. Crim	53	130	6	8	12	3.67
CF	R. Yount	635	.312	21	103	380	5	5	2	2.6	.987	D. Plesac	57	79	5	6	23	2.61
LF	R. Deer	474	.238	28	80	256	10	7	1	2.2	.974	M. Clear	58	78	8	5	6	4.48
C	B. Surhoff	395	.299	7	68	645	49	11	10	**7.2**	.984							
DH	C. Cooper	250	.248	6	36													
UT	P. Molitor	465	.353	16	75	60	113	5	24		.972							
OF	M. Felder	289	.266	2	31	188	7	5	3	2.0	.975							
23	J. Gantner	265	.272	4	30	119	193	6	44		.981							
C	B. Schroeder	250	.332	14	42	363	26	2	4	5.8	.995							

New York

W-89 L-73

Lou Piniella

POS	Player	AB	BA	HR	RBI	PO	A	E	DP	TC/G	FA	Pitcher	G	IP	W	L	SV	ERA
1B	D. Mattingly	569	.327	30	115	1239	91	5	122	9.5	**.996**	T. John	33	188	13	6	0	4.03
2B	W. Randolph	449	.305	7	67	286	338	12	89	5.3	.981	R. Rhoden	30	182	16	10	0	3.86
SS	W. Tolleson	349	.221	1	22	162	321	15	64	4.2	.970	C. Hudson	35	155	11	7	0	3.61
3B	M. Pagliarulo	522	.234	32	87	96	297	17	35	2.8	.959	D. Rasmussen	26	146	9	7	0	4.75
RF	D. Winfield	575	.275	27	97	253	6	3	1	1.8	.989	R. Guidry	22	118	5	8	0	3.67
CF	C. Washington	312	.279	9	44	166	3	2	1	2.4	.988	D. Righetti	60	95	8	6	31	3.51
LF	G. Ward	529	.248	16	78	200	2	3	0	2.2	.985	T. Stoddard	57	93	4	3	8	3.50
C	R. Cerone	284	.243	4	23	538	38	1	6	5.2	**.998**	P. Clements	55	80	3	3	7	4.95
DH	R. Kittle	159	.277	12	28													
OF	R. Henderson	358	.291	17	37	189	3	4	1	2.8	.980							
UT	D. Pasqua	318	.233	17	42	214	10	2	2		.991							
S2	B. Meacham	203	.271	5	21	110	184	10	36		.967							
DO	M. Easler	167	.281	4	21	24	1	0	0		1.000							
OF	H. Cotto	149	.235	5	20	89	2	1	0	1.6	.989							

AMERICAN LEAGUE 1987, *cont.*

Boston

W-78 L-84

John McNamara

POS	Player	AB	BA	HR	RBI	PO	A	E	DP	TC/G	FA	Pitcher	G	IP	W	L	SV	ERA
1B	B. Buckner	286	.273	2	42	605	58	6	53	9.0	.991	R. Clemens	36	282	**20**	9	0	2.97
2B	M. Barrett	559	.293	3	43	320	438	9	108	**5.6**	**.988**	B. Hurst	33	239	15	13	0	4.41
SS	S. Owen	437	.259	2	48	176	336	13	69	4.0	.975	A. Nipper	30	174	11	12	0	5.43
3B	W. Boggs	551	**.363**	24	89	111	277	14	**37**	2.8	.965	B. Stanley	34	153	4	15	0	5.01
RF	D. Evans	541	.305	34	123	134	5	1	0	1.8	.993	J. Sellers	25	140	7	8	0	5.28
CF	E. Burks	558	.272	20	59	320	15	4	2	2.6	.988	W. Gardner	49	90	3	6	10	5.42
LF	J. Rice	404	.277	13	62	155	12	4	2	1.8	.977	C. Schiraldi	62	84	8	5	6	4.41
C	M. Sullivan	160	.169	2	10	303	29	2	6	5.6	.994							
DH	D. Baylor	339	.239	16	57													
OF	M. Greenwell	412	.328	19	89	162	8	5	0	1.9	.971							
UT	E. Romero	235	.272	0	14	122	151	6	28		.978							
OF	T. Benzinger	223	.278	8	43	146	6	2	2	2.5	.987							
OF	D. Henderson	184	.234	8	25	114	0	5	0	1.9	.958							
C	J. Marzano	168	.244	5	24	337	24	5	7	7.0	.986							
DH	S. Horn	158	.278	14	34													

Baltimore

W-67 L-95

Cal Ripken

POS	Player	AB	BA	HR	RBI	PO	A	E	DP	TC/G	FA	Pitcher	G	IP	W	L	SV	ERA
1B	E. Murray	618	.277	30	91	1371	145	10	**146**	**9.8**	.993	M. Boddicker	33	226	10	12	0	4.18
2B	B. Ripken	234	.308	2	20	133	162	3	53	5.1	.990	E. Bell	33	165	10	13	0	5.45
SS	C. Ripken	624	.252	27	98	240	**480**	20	103	4.6	.973	M. Williamson	61	125	8	9	3	4.03
3B	R. Knight	563	.256	14	65	110	282	18	28	**3.2**	.956	D. Schmidt	35	124	10	5	1	3.77
RF	L. Lacy	258	.244	7	28	135	11	4	2	1.9	.973	J. Habyan	27	116	6	7	1	4.80
CF	F. Lynn	396	.253	23	60	229	2	2	1	2.3	.991	K. Dixon	34	105	7	10	5	6.43
LF	L. Sheets	469	.316	31	94	229	5	6	2	1.9	.975	J. Ballard	14	70	2	8	0	6.59
C	T. Kennedy	512	.250	18	62	750	**58**	6	11	5.7	.993	T. Niedenfuer	45	52	3	5	13	4.99
DH	M. Young	363	.240	16	39													
D2	A. Wiggins	306	.232	1	15	78	98	3	21		.983							
OF	K. Gerhart	284	.243	14	34	174	3	5	0	2.0	.973							
DO	J. Dwyer	241	.274	15	33	57	1	0	0		1.000							
2B	R. Burleson	206	.209	2	14	112	145	6	39	4.8	.977							

Cleveland

W-61 L-101

Pat Corrales
W-31 L-56

Doc Edwards
W-30 L-45

POS	Player	AB	BA	HR	RBI	PO	A	E	DP	TC/G	FA	Pitcher	G	IP	W	L	SV	ERA
1B	J. Carter	588	.264	32	106	644	45	**12**	61	8.3	.983	T. Candiotti	32	202	7	18	0	4.78
2B	T. Bernazard	293	.239	11	30	153	200	6	39	4.6	.983	K. Schrom	32	154	6	13	0	6.50
SS	J. Franco	495	.319	8	52	157	285	17	53	4.1	.963	P. Niekro	22	124	7	11	0	5.89
3B	B. Jacoby	540	.300	32	69	**134**	254	**22**	19	2.8	.946	S. Bailes	39	120	7	8	6	4.64
RF	C. Snyder	577	.236	33	82	283	16	9	3	2.2	.971	S. Carlton	23	109	5	9	1	5.37
CF	B. Butler	522	.295	9	41	393	4	4	2	2.9	.990	G. Swindell	16	102	3	8	0	5.10
LF	M. Hall	485	.280	18	76	264	3	3	2	2.2	.989	R. Yett	37	98	3	9	1	5.25
C	C. Bando	211	.218	5	16	351	34	4	8	4.5	.990	D. Jones	49	91	6	5	8	3.15
DH	P. Tabler	553	.307	11	86													
2B	T. Hinzo	257	.265	3	21	115	204	9	44	4.9	.973							
DO	C. Castillo	220	.250	11	31	29	3	0	0		1.000							

West

Minnesota

W-85 L-77

Tom Kelly

POS	Player	AB	BA	HR	RBI	PO	A	E	DP	TC/G	FA	Pitcher	G	IP	W	L	SV	ERA
1B	K. Hrbek	477	.285	34	90	1179	68	5	112	9.1	.996	B. Blyleven	37	267	15	12	0	4.01
2B	S. Lombardozzi	432	.238	8	38	245	356	14	77	4.6	.977	F. Viola	36	252	17	10	0	2.90
SS	G. Gagne	437	.265	10	40	194	391	18	75	4.4	.970	L. Straker	31	154	8	10	0	4.37
3B	G. Gaetti	584	.257	31	109	**134**	261	11	28	2.7	.973	J. Berenguer	47	112	8	1	4	3.94
RF	T. Brunansky	532	.259	32	85	273	10	3	1	2.1	.990	M. Smithson	21	109	4	7	0	5.94
CF	K. Puckett	624	.332	28	99	341	8	5	2	2.4	.986	J. Niekro	19	96	4	9	0	6.26
LF	D. Gladden	438	.249	8	38	223	9	3	2	2.1	.987	G. Frazier	54	81	5	5	2	4.98
C	T. Laudner	288	.191	16	43	517	28	7	2	5.5	.987	J. Reardon	63	80	8	8	31	4.48
DH	R. Smalley	309	.275	8	34							K. Atherton	59	79	7	5	2	4.54
UT	A. Newman	307	.221	0	29	120	225	5	44		.986							
OF	R. Bush	293	.253	11	46	107	1	2	0	1.5	.982							
D1	G. Larkin	233	.266	4	28	165	10	2	12		.989							

Kansas City

W-83 L-79

Billy Gardner
W-62 L-64

John Wathan
W-21 L-15

POS	Player	AB	BA	HR	RBI	PO	A	E	DP	TC/G	FA	Pitcher	G	IP	W	L	SV	ERA
1B	G. Brett	427	.290	22	78	798	50	6	69	10.3	.993	B. Saberhagen	33	257	18	10	0	3.36
2B	F. White	563	.245	17	78	320	458	10	89	5.2	.987	M. Gubicza	35	242	13	18	0	3.98
SS	A. Salazar	317	.205	2	21	134	332	9	56	4.1	.981	C. Leibrandt	35	240	16	11	0	3.41
3B	K. Seitzer	641	.323	15	83	105	292	**22**	32	3.0	.947	D. Jackson	36	224	9	18	0	4.02
RF	D. Tartabull	582	.309	34	101	228	11	6	1	1.6	.976	B. Black	29	122	8	6	1	3.60
CF	W. Wilson	610	.279	4	30	342	3	1	1	2.4	.997	J. Gleaton	48	51	4	4	5	4.26
LF	B. Jackson	396	.235	22	53	180	9	9	1	1.8	.955	D. Quisenberry	47	49	4	1	8	2.76
C	J. Quirk	296	.236	5	33	532	40	8	3	5.4	.986							
DH	S. Balboni	386	.207	24	60													
UT	J. Beniquez	174	.236	3	26	83	5	1	6		.989							
OD	L. Smith	167	.251	3	8	52	2	5	0		.915							
C	L. Owen	164	.189	5	14	370	38	7	4	5.5	.983							
DH	J. Eisenreich	105	.238	4	21													

Oakland

W-81 L-81

Tony LaRussa

POS	Player	AB	BA	HR	RBI	PO	A	E	DP	TC/G	FA	Pitcher	G	IP	W	L	SV	ERA
1B	M. McGwire	557	.289	**49**	118	1173	90	10	91	8.8	.992	D. Stewart	37	261	**20**	13	0	3.68
2B	T. Phillips	379	.240	10	46	160	260	11	40	5.0	.974	C. Young	31	203	13	7	0	4.08
SS	A. Griffin	494	.263	3	60	245	386	24	72	4.8	.963	S. Ontiveros	35	151	10	8	1	4.00
3B	C. Lansford	554	.289	19	76	98	249	7	15	2.5	**.980**	G. Nelson	54	124	6	5	3	3.93
RF	M. Davis	494	.265	22	72	210	3	13	1	1.8	.942	D. Eckersley	54	116	6	8	16	3.03
CF	D. Murphy	219	.233	8	35	185	1	3	0	2.4	.984	E. Plunk	32	95	4	6	2	4.74
LF	J. Canseco	630	.257	31	113	263	12	7	3	2.2	.975	J. Howell	36	44	3	4	16	5.89
C	T. Steinbach	391	.284	16	56	640	40	10	6	6.4	.986							
DH	R. Jackson	336	.220	15	43													
OF	L. Polonia	435	.287	4	49	235	2	5	1	2.3	.979							
2B	T. Bernazard	214	.266	3	19	90	135	11	22	4.0	.953							
C	M. Tettleton	211	.194	8	26	433	28	6	1	5.8	.987							

AMERICAN LEAGUE 1987, *cont.*

Seattle

W-78 L-84

Dick Williams

POS	Player	AB	BA	HR	RBI	PO	A	E	DP	TC/G	FA	Pitcher	G	IP	W	L	SV	ERA
1B	A. Davis	580	.295	29	100	1386	96	9	133	9.5	.994	M. Langston	35	272	19	13	0	3.84
2B	H. Reynolds	530	.275	1	35	**347**	**507**	**20**	**111**	5.5	.977	M. Moore	33	231	9	**19**	0	4.71
SS	R. Quinones	478	.276	12	56	204	384	**25**	76	4.5	.959	M. Morgan	34	207	12	17	0	4.65
3B	J. Presley	575	.247	24	88	113	**311**	21	28	3.0	.953	S. Bankhead	27	149	9	8	0	5.42
RF	M. Kingery	354	.280	9	52	226	15	2	3	2.1	.992	L. Guetterman	25	113	11	4	0	3.81
CF	J. Moses	390	.246	3	38	220	5	3	0	2.3	.987	J. Reed	39	82	1	2	7	3.42
LF	P. Bradley	603	.297	14	67	273	13	5	1	1.8	.983	B. Wilkinson	56	76	3	4	10	3.66
C	S. Bradley	342	.278	5	43	433	29	8	4	5.7	.983	E. Nunez	48	47	3	4	12	3.80
DH	K. Phelps	332	.259	27	68													
OF	M. Brantley	351	.302	14	54	163	3	3	1	2.1	.982							
C	D. Valle	324	.256	12	53	420	34	5	2	6.1	.989							

Chicago

W-77 L-85

Jim Fregosi

POS	Player	AB	BA	HR	RBI	PO	A	E	DP	TC/G	FA	Pitcher	G	IP	W	L	SV	ERA
1B	G. Walker	566	.256	27	94	**1402**	80	9	135	9.7	.994	F. Bannister	34	229	16	11	0	3.58
2B	F. Manrique	298	.258	4	29	147	234	6	58	4.2	.984	R. Dotson	31	211	11	12	0	4.17
SS	O. Guillen	560	.279	2	51	266	475	19	**105**	**5.1**	.975	J. DeLeon	33	206	11	12	0	4.02
3B	T. Hulett	240	.217	7	28	44	118	8	15	2.8	.953	B. Long	29	169	8	8	1	4.37
RF	I. Calderon	542	.293	28	83	295	8	5	3	2.2	.984	J. Winn	56	94	4	6	6	4.79
CF	K. Williams	391	.281	11	50	303	5	6	2	2.7	.981	B. Thigpen	51	89	7	5	16	2.73
LF	G. Redus	475	.236	12	48	262	13	6	4	2.3	.979	S. Nielsen	19	66	3	5	2	6.24
C	C. Fisk	454	.256	23	71	550	57	6	**15**	5.0	.990	B. James	43	54	4	6	10	4.67
DH	H. Baines	505	.293	20	93													
2B	D. Hill	410	.239	9	46	153	223	5	47	4.5	.987							
OF	D. Boston	337	.258	10	29	207	3	2	3	2.3	.991							
3B	S. Lyons	193	.280	1	19	35	99	4	11	2.7	.971							
UT	J. Royster	154	.240	7	23	56	47	2	5		.981							
UT	J. Hairston	126	.230	5	20	82	5	1	7		.989							

California

W-75 L-87

Gene Mauch

POS	Player	AB	BA	HR	RBI	PO	A	E	DP	TC/G	FA	Pitcher	G	IP	W	L	SV	ERA
1B	W. Joyner	564	.285	34	117	1276	92	10	133	9.2	.993	M. Witt	36	247	16	14	0	4.01
2B	M. McLemore	433	.236	3	41	291	358	17	96	5.0	.974	D. Sutton	35	192	11	11	0	4.70
SS	D. Schofield	479	.251	9	46	204	348	9	76	4.3	**.984**	W. Fraser	36	177	10	10	1	3.92
3B	D. DeCinces	453	.234	16	63	83	226	17	24	2.5	.948	J. Lazorko	26	118	5	6	0	4.59
RF	D. White	639	.263	24	87	424	16	9	3	2.8	.980	J. Candelaria	20	117	8	6	0	4.71
CF	G. Pettis	394	.208	1	17	344	2	7	2	2.7	.980	D. Buice	57	114	6	7	17	3.39
LF	J. Howell	449	.245	23	64	150	4	2	0	1.8	.987	G. Minton	41	76	5	4	10	3.08
C	B. Boone	389	.242	3	33	684	56	**13**	11	5.9	.983	K. McCaskill	14	75	4	6	0	5.67
DH	B. Downing	567	.272	29	77													
OF	R. Jones	192	.245	8	28	81	1	3	0	1.3	.965							
DH	B. Buckner	183	.306	3	32													
OF	G. Hendrick	162	.241	5	25	58	1	2	0	1.4	.967							

Texas

W-75 L-87

Bobby Valentine

POS	Player	AB	BA	HR	RBI	PO	A	E	DP	TC/G	FA	Pitcher	G	IP	W	L	SV	ERA
1B	P. O'Brien	569	.286	23	88	1233	**146**	11	118	8.8	.992	C. Hough	40	**285**	18	13	0	3.79
2B	J. Browne	454	.271	1	38	258	338	12	66	4.7	.980	J. Guzman	37	208	14	14	0	4.67
SS	S. Fletcher	588	.287	5	63	249	413	23	98	4.4	.966	B. Witt	26	143	8	10	0	4.91
3B	S. Buechele	363	.237	13	50	68	175	9	13	2.0	.964	G. Harris	42	141	5	10	0	4.86
RF	R. Sierra	**643**	.263	30	109	272	17	11	6	1.9	.963	M. Williams	85	109	8	6	6	3.23
CF	O. McDowell	407	.241	14	52	263	5	3	1	2.2	.989	D. Mohorcic	74	99	7	6	16	2.99
LF	P. Incaviglia	509	.271	27	80	216	8	13	0	1.8	.945	J. Russell	52	97	5	4	3	4.44
C	D. Slaught	237	.224	8	16	429	39	7	5	5.6	.985							
DH	L. Parrish	557	.268	32	100													
OF	B. Brower	303	.261	14	46	183	2	7	0	1.8	.964							
C	M. Stanley	216	.273	6	37	330	17	7	1	5.8	.980							
UT	G. Petralli	202	.302	7	31	370	34	5	4		.988							
DH	D. Porter	130	.238	7	21													

BATTING AND BASE RUNNING LEADERS

Batting Average

W. Boggs, BOS	.363
P. Molitor, MIL	.353
A. Trammell, DET	.343
K. Puckett, MIN	.332
D. Mattingly, NY	.327

Slugging Average

M. McGwire, OAK	.618
G. Bell, TOR	.605
W. Boggs, BOS	.588
D. Evans, BOS	.569
P. Molitor, MIL	.566

Home Runs

M. McGwire, OAK	49
G. Bell, TOR	47

Total Bases

G. Bell, TOR	369
M. McGwire, OAK	344
K. Puckett, MIN	333
A. Trammell, DET	329
W. Boggs, BOS	324

Runs Batted In

G. Bell, TOR	134
D. Evans, BOS	123
M. McGwire, OAK	118
W. Joyner, CAL	117
D. Mattingly, NY	115

Stolen Bases

H. Reynolds, SEA	60
W. Wilson, KC	59
G. Redus, CHI	52
P. Molitor, MIL	45
R. Henderson, NY	41

Hits

K. Puckett, MIN	207
K. Seitzer, KC	207
A. Trammell, DET	205
W. Boggs, BOS	200

Base on Balls

D. Evans, BOS	106
B. Downing, CAL	106
W. Boggs, BOS	105
D. Evans, DET	100

Home Run Percentage

M. McGwire, OAK	8.8
G. Bell, TOR	7.7
K. Hrbek, MIN	7.1
D. Evans, DET	6.8

Runs

P. Molitor, MIL	114
G. Bell, TOR	111
B. Downing, CAL	110
L. Whitaker, DET	110

Doubles

P. Molitor, MIL	41
W. Boggs, BOS	40

Triples

W. Wilson, KC	15
L. Polonia, OAK	10
P. Bradley, SEA	10
R. Yount, MIL	9

PITCHING LEADERS

Winning Percentage

R. Clemens, BOS	.690
J. Key, TOR	.680
T. Higuera, MIL	.643
B. Saberhagen, KC	.643
F. Viola, MIN	.630
W. Terrell, DET	.630

Earned Run Average

J. Key, TOR	2.76
F. Viola, MIN	2.90
R. Clemens, BOS	2.97
B. Saberhagen, KC	3.36
J. Morris, DET	3.38

Wins

D. Stewart, OAK	20
R. Clemens, BOS	20
M. Langston, SEA	19

Saves

T. Henke, TOR	34
D. Righetti, NY	31
J. Reardon, MIN	31
D. Plesac, MIL	23
D. Buice, CAL	17

Strikeouts

M. Langston, SEA	262
R. Clemens, BOS	256
T. Higuera, MIL	240
C. Hough, TEX	223
J. Morris, DET	208

Complete Games

R. Clemens, BOS	18
B. Hurst, BOS	15
B. Saberhagen, KC	15
M. Langston, SEA	14
T. Higuera, MIL	14

Fewest Hits/9 Innings

J. Key, TOR	7.24
C. Hough, TEX	7.51
J. Morris, DET	7.68
D. Stewart, OAK	7.71

Shutouts

R. Clemens, BOS	7
B. Saberhagen, KC	4

Fewest Walks/9 Innings

B. Long, CHI	1.49
B. Saberhagen, KC	1.86
D. Sutton, CAL	1.93
F. Bannister, CHI	1.93

Most Strikeouts/9 Inn.

M. Langston, SEA	8.67
T. Higuera, MIL	8.25
R. Clemens, BOS	8.18
C. Bosio, MIL	7.94

Innings

C. Hough, TEX	285
R. Clemens, BOS	282
M. Langston, SEA	272
B. Blyleven, MIN	267

Games Pitched

M. Eichhorn, TOR	89
M. Williams, TEX	85
D. Mohorcic, TEX	74
T. Henke, TOR	72

AMERICAN LEAGUE 1987, *cont.*

								Batting						Fielding			Pitching					
		W	L	PCT	GB	R	OR	2B	3B	HR	BA	SA	SB	E	DP	FA	CG	BB	SO	ShO	SV	ERA
East	Detroit	98	64	.605		**896**	735	274	32	**225**	.272	**.451**	106	122	147	.980	33	563	976	8	31	4.02
	Toronto	96	66	.593	2	845	**655**	277	38	215	.269	.446	126	111	148	.982	18	567	1064	3	43	**3.74**
	Milwaukee	91	71	.562	7	862	817	272	46	163	.276	.428	**176**	145	155	.976	28	529	1039	5	45	4.62
	New York	89	73	.549	9	788	758	239	16	196	.262	.418	105	102	155	.983	19	542	900	3	**47**	4.36
	Boston	78	84	.481	20	842	825	273	26	174	**.278**	.430	77	110	158	.982	**47**	517	1034	**13**	16	4.77
	Baltimore	67	95	.414	31	729	880	219	20	211	.258	.418	69	111	**174**	.982	17	547	870	5	30	5.01
	Cleveland	61	101	.377	37	742	957	267	30	187	.263	.422	140	153	128	.975	24	606	849	4	25	5.28
West	Minnesota	85	77	.525		786	806	258	35	196	.261	.430	113	**98**	147	**.984**	16	564	990	2	39	4.63
	Kansas City	83	79	.512	2	715	691	239	40	168	.262	.412	125	131	151	.979	44	548	923	11	26	3.86
	Oakland	81	81	.500	4	806	789	263	33	199	.260	.428	140	142	122	.977	18	531	1042	2	40	4.32
	Seattle	78	84	.481	7	760	801	282	**48**	161	.272	.428	174	122	150	.980	39	**497**	919	6	33	4.48
	Chicago	77	85	.475	8	748	746	**283**	36	173	.258	.415	138	116	**174**	.981	29	537	792	8	37	4.29
	California	75	87	.463	10	770	803	257	26	172	.252	.401	125	117	162	.981	20	504	941	3	36	4.38
	Texas	75	87	.463	10	823	849	264	35	194	.266	.430	120	151	148	.976	20	760	**1103**	0	27	4.63
						11112	11112	3667	461	2634	.265	.425	1734	1731	2119	.980	372	7812	13442	73	475	4.46

NATIONAL LEAGUE 1988

East

New York
W-100 L-60
Davey Johnson

POS	Player	AB	BA	HR	RBI	PO	A	E	DP	TC/G	FA	Pitcher	G	IP	W	L	SV	ERA
1B	K. Hernandez	348	.276	11	55	734	77	2	63	8.7	.998	D. Gooden	34	248	18	9	0	3.19
2B	W. Backman	294	.303	0	17	128	219	4	36	3.8	.989	R. Darling	34	241	17	9	0	3.25
SS	K. Elster	406	.214	9	37	196	345	13	61	3.7	.977	D. Cone	35	231	20	3	0	2.22
3B	H. Johnson	495	.230	24	68	65	187	13	16	2.0	.951	B. Ojeda	29	190	10	13	0	2.88
RF	D. Strawberry	543	.269	**39**	101	297	4	9	3	2.1	.971	S. Fernandez	31	187	12	10	0	3.03
CF	L. Dykstra	429	.270	8	33	270	3	1	0	2.4	.996	T. Leach	52	92	7	2	3	2.54
LF	K. McReynolds	552	.288	27	99	252	18	4	5	1.9	.985	R. McDowell	62	89	5	5	16	2.63
C	G. Carter	455	.242	11	46	**797**	54	9	5	**7.2**	.990	R. Myers	55	68	7	3	26	1.72
OF	M. Wilson	378	.296	8	41	200	4	5	1	2.0	.976							
13	D. Magadan	314	.277	1	35	459	99	10	42		.982							
2B	T. Teufel	273	.234	4	31	153	212	7	48	4.4	.981							

Pittsburgh
W-85 L-75
Jim Leyland

POS	Player	AB	BA	HR	RBI	PO	A	E	DP	TC/G	FA	Pitcher	G	IP	W	L	SV	ERA
1B	S. Bream	462	.264	10	65	1118	**140**	6	88	9.2	.995	D. Drabek	33	219	15	7	0	3.08
2B	J. Lind	611	.262	2	49	333	473	11	73	5.3	.987	B. Walk	32	213	12	10	0	2.71
SS	R. Belliard	286	.213	0	11	131	258	9	50	3.4	**.977**	J. Smiley	34	205	13	11	0	3.25
3B	B. Bonilla	584	.274	24	100	121	**336**	**32**	17	**3.1**	.935	M. Dunne	30	170	7	11	0	3.92
RF	R. Reynolds	323	.248	6	51	142	7	4	2	1.6	.974	B. Fisher	33	146	8	10	1	4.61
CF	A. Van Slyke	587	.288	25	100	406	12	4	2	2.8	.991	J. Robinson	75	125	11	5	9	3.03
LF	B. Bonds	538	.283	24	58	292	5	6	0	2.2	.980	J. Gott	67	77	6	6	34	3.49
C	M. LaValliere	352	.261	2	47	565	55	8	6	5.5	.987							
OF	D. Coles	211	.232	5	36	98	0	1	0	1.8	.990							

Montreal
W-81 L-81
Buck Rodgers

POS	Player	AB	BA	HR	RBI	PO	A	E	DP	TC/G	FA	Pitcher	G	IP	W	L	SV	ERA
1B	A. Galarraga	609	.302	29	92	1464	103	15	124	10.1	.991	D. Martinez	34	235	15	13	0	2.72
2B	T. Foley	377	.265	5	43	164	255	12	46	4.8	.972	B. Smith	32	198	12	10	0	3.00
SS	L. Rivera	371	.224	4	30	160	301	18	69	4.1	.962	P. Perez	27	188	12	8	0	2.44
3B	T. Wallach	592	.257	12	69	**123**	328	18	**31**	3.1	.962	J. Dopson	26	169	3	11	0	3.04
RF	H. Brooks	588	.279	20	90	261	8	9	1	1.9	.968	B. Holman	18	100	4	8	0	3.23
CF	M. Webster	259	.255	2	13	153	2	1	0	2.2	.994	N. Heaton	32	97	3	10	2	4.99
LF	T. Raines	429	.270	12	48	235	5	3	1	2.3	.988	J. Parrett	61	92	12	4	6	2.65
C	N. Santovenia	309	.236	8	41	457	63	9	7	6.2	.983	A. McGaffigan	63	91	6	0	4	2.76
OF	O. Nixon	271	.244	0	15	176	2	1	1	2.2	.994	T. Burke	61	82	3	5	18	3.40
2S	R. Hudler	216	.273	4	14	113	168	10	30		.966	J. Hesketh	60	73	4	3	9	2.85
OF	D. Martinez	191	.257	2	12	119	2	1	1	2.0	.992							
C	M. Fitzgerald	155	.271	5	23	258	21	6	2	6.1	.979							

Chicago
W-77 L-85
Don Zimmer

POS	Player	AB	BA	HR	RBI	PO	A	E	DP	TC/G	FA	Pitcher	G	IP	W	L	SV	ERA
1B	M. Grace	486	.296	7	57	1182	87	**17**	91	9.7	.987	G. Maddux	34	249	18	8	0	3.18
2B	R. Sandberg	618	.264	19	69	291	**522**	11	79	5.4	.987	R. Sutcliffe	32	226	13	14	0	3.86
SS	S. Dunston	575	.249	9	56	**257**	455	20	76	4.8	.973	J. Moyer	34	202	9	15	0	3.48
3B	V. Law	556	.293	11	78	111	272	19	22	2.7	.953	C. Schiraldi	29	166	9	13	1	4.38
RF	A. Dawson	591	.303	24	79	267	7	3	1	1.9	.989	J. Pico	29	113	6	7	1	4.15
CF	D. Martinez	256	.254	4	34	162	2	5	0	2.3	.970	F. DiPino	63	90	2	3	6	4.98
LF	R. Palmeiro	580	.307	8	53	292	6	5	1	2.1	.983	L. Lancaster	44	86	4	6	5	3.78
C	D. Berryhill	309	.259	7	38	448	54	9	5	5.7	.982	G. Gossage	46	44	4	4	13	4.33
OF	M. Webster	264	.265	4	26	169	1	5	0	2.7	.971							
C	J. Davis	249	.229	6	33	383	32	2	1	5.6	.995							
OF	D. Jackson	188	.266	6	20	116	1	2	0	1.6	.983							
UT	M. Trillo	164	.250	1	14	177	81	3	19		.989							

St. Louis
W-76 L-86
Whitey Herzog

POS	Player	AB	BA	HR	RBI	PO	A	E	DP	TC/G	FA	Pitcher	G	IP	W	L	SV	ERA
1B	B. Horner	206	.257	3	33	463	40	5	39	8.9	.990	J. DeLeon	34	225	13	10	0	3.67
2B	L. Alicea	297	.212	1	24	206	240	14	52	5.1	.970	J. Magrane	24	165	5	9	0	**2.18**
SS	O. Smith	575	.270	3	51	234	**519**	22	79	**5.2**	.972	J. Tudor	21	145	6	5	0	2.29
3B	T. Pendleton	391	.253	6	53	75	239	12	13	3.2	.963	L. McWilliams	42	136	6	9	1	3.90
RF	T. Brunansky	523	.245	22	79	267	10	1	0	1.9	.996	S. Terry	51	129	9	6	3	2.92
CF	W. McGee	562	.292	3	50	348	9	9	0	2.7	.975	B. Forsch	30	109	9	4	0	3.73
LF	V. Coleman	616	.260	3	38	290	14	9	1	2.1	.971	T. Worrell	68	90	5	9	32	3.00
C	T. Pena	505	.263	10	51	777	70	5	8	6.0	**.994**	D. Cox	13	86	3	8	0	3.98
UT	J. Oquendo	451	.277	7	46	268	315	11	61		.981	G. Mathews	13	68	4	6	0	4.24
1C	T. Pagnozzi	195	.282	0	15	340	28	4	11		.989	K. Dayley	54	55	2	7	5	2.77
1B	P. Guerrero	149	.268	5	30	348	22	0	18	10.0	1.000							

NATIONAL LEAGUE 1988, *cont.*

Philadelphia

W-65 L-96

Lee Elia
W-60 L-92

John Vukovich
W-5 L-4

POS	Player	AB	BA	HR	RBI	PO	A	E	DP	TC/G	FA
1B	V. Hayes	367	.272	6	45	712	55	8	66	9.1	.990
2B	J. Samuel	629	.243	12	67	**343**	385	16	**92**	4.9	.978
SS	S. Jeltz	379	.187	0	27	195	368	14	73	3.9	.976
3B	M. Schmidt	390	.249	12	62	73	222	19	17	3.0	.939
RF	C. James	566	.242	19	66	256	7	3	3	2.3	.989
CF	M. Thompson	378	.288	2	33	278	5	5	1	2.6	.983
LF	P. Bradley	569	.264	11	56	298	14	3	2	2.1	.990
C	L. Parrish	424	.215	15	60	639	73	9	**11**	6.2	.988
1B	R. Jordan	273	.308	11	43	579	35	5	41	9.0	.992
OF	B. Dernier	166	.289	1	10	98	2	2	0	1.9	.980
OF	R. Jones	124	.290	8	26	70	1	0	0	2.2	1.000

Pitcher	G	IP	W	L	SV	ERA
K. Gross	33	232	12	14	0	3.69
D. Carman	36	201	10	14	0	4.29
S. Rawley	32	198	8	16	0	4.18
B. Ruffin	55	144	6	10	3	4.43
D. Palmer	22	129	7	9	0	4.47
G. Harris	66	107	4	6	1	2.36
K. Tekulve	70	80	3	7	4	3.60
S. Bedrosian	57	74	6	6	28	3.75

West

Los Angeles

W-94 L-67

Tom Lasorda

POS	Player	AB	BA	HR	RBI	PO	A	E	DP	TC/G	FA
1B	F. Stubbs	242	.223	8	34	521	57	13	41	7.0	.978
2B	S. Sax	**632**	.277	5	57	276	429	14	69	4.6	.981
SS	A. Griffin	316	.199	1	27	145	264	15	44	4.6	.965
3B	J. Hamilton	309	.236	6	33	67	157	14	8	2.3	.941
RF	M. Marshall	542	.277	20	82	137	4	5	0	1.6	.966
CF	J. Shelby	494	.263	10	64	329	7	6	1	2.4	.982
LF	K. Gibson	542	.290	25	76	311	6	12	3	2.2	.964
C	M. Scioscia	408	.257	3	35	748	63	7	10	6.7	.991
SS	D. Anderson	285	.249	2	20	128	225	5	49	4.4	.986
OF	M. Davis	281	.196	2	17	121	3	5	2	1.7	.961
3B	P. Guerrero	215	.298	5	35	21	64	10	2	2.1	.895
01	M. Hatcher	191	.293	1	25	188	17	3	7		.986
31	T. Woodson	173	.249	3	15	160	60	6	13		.973
C	R. Dempsey	167	.251	7	30	333	29	4	4	4.9	.989

Pitcher	G	IP	W	L	SV	ERA
O. Hershiser	35	**267**	**23**	8	1	2.26
T. Leary	35	229	17	11	0	2.91
T. Belcher	36	180	12	6	4	2.91
F. Valenzuela	23	142	5	8	1	4.24
A. Pena	60	94	6	7	12	1.91
B. Holton	45	85	7	3	1	1.70
J. Howell	50	65	5	3	21	2.08
J. Orosco	55	53	3	2	9	2.72

Cincinnati

W-87 L-74

Pete Rose
W-11 L-12

Tommy Helms
W-12 L-15

Pete Rose
W-64 L-47

POS	Player	AB	BA	HR	RBI	PO	A	E	DP	TC/G	FA
1B	N. Esasky	391	.243	15	62	982	52	6	70	9.0	.994
2B	J. Treadway	301	.252	2	23	188	252	7	49	4.6	.984
SS	B. Larkin	588	.296	12	56	231	470	**29**	67	4.9	.960
3B	C. Sabo	538	.271	11	44	75	318	14	**31**	3.0	**.966**
RF	P. O'Neill	485	.252	16	73	237	5	4	0	2.1	.984
CF	E. Davis	472	.273	26	93	300	2	6	0	2.4	.981
LF	K. Daniels	495	.291	18	64	256	10	5	2	2.0	.982
C	B. Diaz	315	.219	10	35	468	44	5	9	5.9	.990
UT	D. Concepcion	197	.198	0	8	151	131	2	36		.993
OF	D. Collins	174	.236	0	14	53	2	2	0	1.6	.965

Pitcher	G	IP	W	L	SV	ERA
D. Jackson	35	261	**23**	8	0	2.73
T. Browning	36	251	18	5	0	3.41
J. Rijo	49	162	13	8	0	2.39
M. Soto	14	87	3	7	0	4.66
J. Franco	70	86	6	6	**39**	1.57
R. Robinson	17	79	3	7	0	4.12
J. Armstrong	14	65	4	7	0	5.79

San Diego

W-83 L-78

Larry Bowa
W-16 L-30

Jack McKeon
W-67 L-48

POS	Player	AB	BA	HR	RBI	PO	A	E	DP	TC/G	FA
1B	K. Moreland	511	.256	5	64	637	52	4	55	9.5	.994
2B	R. Alomar	545	.266	9	41	319	459	16	88	5.6	.980
SS	G. Templeton	362	.249	3	36	168	316	16	62	4.8	.968
3B	C. Brown	247	.235	2	19	54	131	10	15	2.7	.949
RF	T. Gwynn	521	**.313**	7	70	264	8	5	1	2.1	.982
CF	M. Wynne	333	.264	11	42	216	5	3	2	2.0	.987
LF	C. Martinez	365	.236	18	65	143	6	1	2	2.3	.993
C	B. Santiago	492	.248	10	46	725	**75**	**12**	**11**	6.0	.985
10	J. Kruk	378	.241	9	44	634	37	3	45		.996
UT	R. Ready	331	.266	7	39	112	153	11	22		.960
SS	D. Thon	258	.264	1	18	82	168	12	28	3.7	.954
3B	T. Flannery	170	.265	0	19	27	76	3	8	2.1	.972

Pitcher	G	IP	W	L	SV	ERA
E. Show	32	235	16	11	0	3.26
A. Hawkins	33	218	14	11	0	3.35
E. Whitson	34	205	13	11	0	3.77
J. Jones	29	179	9	14	0	4.12
D. Rasmussen	20	148	14	4	0	2.55
M. Davis	62	98	5	10	28	2.01
M. Grant	33	98	2	8	0	3.69
L. McCullers	60	98	3	6	10	2.49

San Francisco

W-83 L-79

Roger Craig

POS	Player	AB	BA	HR	RBI	PO	A	E	DP	TC/G	FA
1B	W. Clark	575	.282	29	**109**	**1492**	104	12	**126**	**10.2**	.993
2B	R. Thompson	477	.264	7	48	255	365	14	88	4.7	.978
SS	J. Uribe	493	.252	3	35	212	404	19	77	4.5	.970
3B	K. Mitchell	505	.251	19	80	61	203	16	18	2.7	.943
RF	C. Maldonado	499	.255	12	68	251	5	10	1	1.9	.962
CF	B. Butler	568	.287	6	43	395	3	5	1	2.6	.988
LF	M. Aldrete	389	.267	3	50	211	5	4	1	1.9	.982
C	B. Melvin	273	.234	8	27	403	31	7	4	5.0	.984
C	B. Brenly	206	.189	5	22	334	27	6	2	5.3	.984
UT	E. Riles	187	.294	3	28	46	133	3	17		.984
UT	C. Speier	171	.216	3	18	70	142	3	26		.986
OF	J. Leonard	160	.256	2	20	74	0	1	0	1.7	.987

Pitcher	G	IP	W	L	SV	ERA
R. Reuschel	36	245	19	11	0	3.12
D. Robinson	51	177	10	5	6	2.45
K. Downs	27	168	13	9	0	3.32
A. Hammaker	43	145	9	9	5	3.73
M. Krukow	20	125	7	4	0	3.54
M. LaCoss	19	114	7	7	0	3.62
S. Garrelts	65	98	5	9	13	3.58
C. Lefferts	64	92	3	8	11	2.92
J. Price	38	62	1	6	4	3.94

Houston

W-82 L-80

Hal Lanier

POS	Player	AB	BA	HR	RBI	PO	A	E	DP	TC/G	FA
1B	G. Davis	561	.271	30	99	1355	103	6	104	9.7	**.996**
2B	B. Doran	480	.248	7	53	260	371	8	73	4.9	**.987**
SS	R. Ramirez	566	.276	6	59	232	408	23	68	4.3	.965
3B	B. Bell	269	.253	7	37	31	114	12	8	2.4	.924
RF	K. Bass	541	.255	14	72	267	7	6	2	1.9	.979
CF	G. Young	576	.257	0	37	357	10	3	1	2.6	.992
LF	B. Hatcher	530	.268	7	52	280	7	5	2	2.1	.983
C	A. Trevino	193	.249	2	13	360	24	9	5	5.3	.977
OF	T. Puhl	234	.303	3	19	116	2	2	0	1.5	.983
C	A. Ashby	227	.238	7	33	414	23	4	4	6.7	.991
3B	D. Walling	176	.244	1	20	33	99	7	14	2.7	.950

Pitcher	G	IP	W	L	SV	ERA
N. Ryan	33	220	12	11	0	3.52
M. Scott	32	219	14	8	0	2.92
J. Deshaies	31	207	11	14	0	3.00
D. Darwin	44	192	8	13	3	3.84
B. Knepper	27	175	14	5	0	3.14
J. Agosto	75	92	10	2	4	2.26
L. Andersen	53	83	2	4	5	2.94
D. Smith	51	57	4	5	27	2.67

NATIONAL LEAGUE 1988, *cont.*

Atlanta

W-54 L-106

Chuck Tanner
W-12 L-27

Russ Nixon
W-42 L-79

POS	Player	AB	BA	HR	RBI	PO	A	E	DP	TC/G	FA
1B	G. Perry	547	.300	8	74	1282	106	**17**	102	10.0	.988
2B	R. Gant	563	.259	19	60	295	378	**26**	82	**5.7**	.963
SS	A. Thomas	606	.252	13	68	230	456	**29**	**90**	4.8	.959
3B	K. Oberkfell	422	.277	3	40	83	207	15	21	2.7	.951
RF	D. Murphy	592	.226	24	77	340	15	3	4	2.3	.992
CF	A. Hall	231	.247	1	15	137	7	4	1	2.3	.973
LF	D. James	386	.256	3	30	222	5	3	0	1.9	.987
C	O. Virgil	320	.256	9	31	448	45	5	3	5.2	.990
C	B. Benedict	236	.242	0	19	384	54	5	3	5.0	.989
OF	T. Blocker	198	.212	2	10	164	1	1	0	2.7	.994
OF	K. Griffey	193	.249	2	19	61	2	2	0	1.5	.969

Pitcher	G	IP	W	L	SV	ERA
R. Mahler	39	249	9	16	0	3.69
P. Smith	32	195	7	15	0	3.69
T. Glavine	34	195	7	**17**	0	4.56
Z. Smith	23	140	5	10	0	4.30
C. Puleo	53	106	5	5	1	3.47
J. Alvarez	60	102	5	6	3	2.99
P. Assenmacher	64	79	8	7	5	3.06
B. Sutter	38	45	1	4	14	4.76

BATTING AND BASE RUNNING LEADERS

Batting Average

T. Gwynn, SD	.313
R. Palmeiro, CHI	.307
A. Dawson, CHI	.303
A. Galarraga, MON	.302
G. Perry, ATL	.300

Slugging Average

D. Strawberry, NY	.545
A. Galarraga, MON	.540
W. Clark, SF	.508
A. Van Slyke, PIT	.506
A. Dawson, CHI	.504

Home Runs

D. Strawberry, NY	39
G. Davis, HOU	30
W. Clark, SF	29
A. Galarraga, MON	29
K. McReynolds, NY	27

Total Bases

A. Galarraga, MON	329
A. Dawson, CHI	298
A. Van Slyke, PIT	297
D. Strawberry, NY	296
W. Clark, SF	292

Runs Batted In

W. Clark, SF	109
D. Strawberry, NY	101
B. Bonilla, PIT	100
A. Van Slyke, PIT	100
K. McReynolds, NY	99
G. Davis, HOU	99

Stolen Bases

V. Coleman, STL	81
G. Young, HOU	65
O. Smith, STL	57
O. Nixon, MON	46
C. Sabo, CIN	46

Hits

A. Galarraga, MON	184
A. Dawson, CHI	179
R. Palmeiro, CHI	178
S. Sax, LA	175

Base on Balls

W. Clark, SF	100
B. Butler, SF	97
K. Daniels, CIN	87
H. Johnson, NY	86

Home Run Percentage

D. Strawberry, NY	7.2
E. Davis, CIN	5.5
G. Davis, HOU	5.3
W. Clark, SF	5.0

Runs

B. Butler, SF	109
K. Gibson, LA	106
W. Clark, SF	102
D. Strawberry, NY	101
A. Van Slyke, PIT	101

Doubles

A. Galarraga, MON	42
R. Palmeiro, CHI	41
C. Sabo, CIN	40
S. Bream, PIT	37

Triples

A. Van Slyke, PIT	15
V. Coleman, STL	10
B. Butler, SF	9
G. Young, HOU	9
J. Samuel, PHI	9

PITCHING LEADERS

Winning Percentage

D. Cone, NY	.870
T. Browning, CIN	.783
O. Hershiser, LA	.742
D. Jackson, CIN	.742
G. Maddux, CHI	.692

Earned Run Average

J. Magrane, STL	2.18
D. Cone, NY	2.22
O. Hershiser, LA	2.26
J. Tudor, STL, LA	2.32
J. Rijo, CIN	2.39

Wins

D. Jackson, CIN	23
O. Hershiser, LA	23
D. Cone, NY	20
R. Reuschel, SF	19

Saves

J. Franco, CIN	39
J. Gott, PIT	34
T. Worrell, STL	32
S. Bedrosian, PHI	28
M. Davis, SD	28

Strikeouts

N. Ryan, HOU	228
D. Cone, NY	213
J. DeLeon, STL	208
M. Scott, HOU	190
S. Fernandez, NY	189

Complete Games

O. Hershiser, LA	15
D. Jackson, CIN	15
E. Show, SD	13
R. Sutcliffe, CHI	12
D. Gooden, NY	10

Fewest Hits/9 Innings

S. Fernandez, NY	6.11
P. Perez, MON	6.37
J. Rijo, CIN	6.67
M. Scott, HOU	6.67

Shutouts

O. Hershiser, LA	8
T. Leary, LA	6
D. Jackson, CIN	6
B. Ojeda, NY	5
M. Scott, HOU	5

Fewest Walks/9 Innings

B. Smith, MON	1.45
R. Mahler, ATL	1.52
R. Reuschel, SF	1.54
B. Ojeda, NY	1.56

Most Strikeouts/9 Inn.

N. Ryan, HOU	9.33
S. Fernandez, NY	9.10
J. Rijo, CIN	8.89
J. DeLeon, STL	8.31

Innings

O. Hershiser, LA	267
D. Jackson, CIN	261
T. Browning, CIN	251
R. Mahler, ATL	249
G. Maddux, CHI	249

Games Pitched

R. Murphy, CIN	76
J. Agosto, HOU	75
J. Robinson, PIT	75
K. Tekulve, PHI	70
J. Franco, CIN	70

		W	L	PCT	GB	R	OR	Batting 2B	3B	HR	BA	SA	SB	Fielding E	DP	FA	Pitching CG	BB	SO	ShO	SV	ERA
East	New York	100	60	.625		**703**	**532**	251	24	**152**	.256	**.396**	140	**115**	127	**.981**	31	**404**	**1100**	**17**	46	**2.91**
	Pittsburgh	85	75	.531	15	651	616	240	45	110	.247	.369	119	125	128	.980	12	469	790	4	46	3.47
	Montreal	81	81	.500	20	628	592	260	**48**	107	.251	.373	189	142	145	.978	18	476	923	6	43	3.08
	Chicago	77	85	.475	24	660	694	**262**	46	113	**.261**	.383	120	125	128	.980	30	490	897	9	29	3.84
	St. Louis	76	86	.469	25	578	633	207	33	71	.249	.337	**234**	121	131	**.981**	17	486	881	7	42	3.47
	Philadelphia	65	96	.404	35.5	597	734	246	31	106	.239	.355	112	145	139	.976	16	628	859	3	36	4.14
West	Los Angeles	94	67	.584		628	544	217	25	99	.248	.352	131	142	126	.977	**32**	473	1029	15	**49**	2.97
	Cincinnati	87	74	.540	7	641	596	246	25	122	.246	.368	207	125	131	.980	24	504	934	10	43	3.35
	San Diego	83	78	.516	11	594	583	205	35	94	.247	.351	123	120	**147**	**.981**	30	439	885	4	39	3.28
	San Francisco	83	79	.512	11.5	670	626	227	44	113	.248	.368	121	129	145	.980	25	422	875	11	42	3.39
	Houston	82	80	.506	12.5	617	631	239	31	96	.244	.351	198	138	124	.978	21	478	1049	10	40	3.40
	Atlanta	54	106	.338	39.5	555	741	228	28	96	.242	.348	95	151	138	.976	14	524	810	3	25	4.09
						7522	7522	2828	415	1279	.248	.363	1789	1578	1609	.979	270	5793	11032	99	480	3.45

AMERICAN LEAGUE 1988

East

Boston

W-89 L-73

John McNamara
W-43 L-42

Joe Morgan
W-46 L-31

POS	Player	AB	BA	HR	RBI	PO	A	E	DP	TC/G	FA
1B	T. Benzinger	405	.254	13	70	520	38	5	47	6.6	.991
2B	M. Barrett	612	.283	1	65	312	402	7	97	4.8	.990
SS	J. Reed	338	.293	1	28	123	242	11	49	4.0	.971
3B	W. Boggs	584	**.366**	5	58	**122**	250	11	17	2.5	.971
RF	D. Evans	559	.293	21	111	151	4	2	0	1.8	.987
CF	E. Burks	540	.294	18	92	370	9	9	0	2.7	.977
LF	M. Greenwell	590	.325	22	119	302	6	6	2	2.1	.981
C	R. Gedman	299	.231	9	39	570	40	5	4	6.6	.992
DH	J. Rice	485	.264	15	72						
C	R. Cerone	264	.269	3	27	471	28	0	4	6.0	**1.000**
SS	S. Owen	257	.249	5	18	102	192	10	34	4.0	.967
1B	L. Parrish	158	.259	7	26	221	25	3	18	6.9	.988

Pitcher	G	IP	W	L	SV	ERA
R. Clemens	35	264	18	12	0	2.93
B. Hurst	33	217	18	6	0	3.66
W. Gardner	36	149	8	6	2	3.50
O. Boyd	23	130	9	7	0	5.34
M. Smithson	31	127	9	6	0	5.97
B. Stanley	57	102	6	4	5	3.19
M. Boddicker	15	89	7	3	0	2.63
L. Smith	64	84	4	5	29	2.80
D. Lamp	46	83	7	6	0	3.48

AMERICAN LEAGUE 1988, *cont.*

Detroit

W-88 L-74

Sparky Anderson

POS	Player	AB	BA	HR	RBI	PO	A	E	DP	TC/G	FA
1B	R. Knight	299	.217	3	33	432	33	4	40	7.3	.991
2B	L. Whitaker	403	.275	12	55	218	284	8	53	4.6	.984
SS	A. Trammell	466	.311	15	69	195	355	11	67	4.5	.980
3B	T. Brookens	441	.243	5	38	101	234	17	16	2.6	.952
RF	C. Lemon	512	.264	17	64	296	8	8	3	2.2	.974
CF	G. Pettis	458	.210	3	36	361	5	5	0	2.9	.987
LF	P. Sheridan	347	.254	11	47	203	2	4	0	1.9	.981
C	M. Nokes	382	.251	16	53	574	45	7	8	5.7	.989
DH	D. Evans	437	.208	22	64						
UT	L. Salazar	452	.270	12	62	199	151	10	22		.972
UT	D. Bergman	289	.294	5	35	386	37	4	31		.991
C	M. Heath	219	.247	5	18	357	24	6	3	5.2	.984
2B	J. Walewander	175	.211	0	6	114	144	6	36	4.3	.977
DH	L. Herndon	174	.224	4	20						

Pitcher	G	IP	W	L	SV	ERA
J. Morris	34	235	15	13	0	3.94
D. Alexander	34	229	14	11	0	4.32
W. Terrell	29	206	7	16	0	3.97
F. Tanana	32	203	14	11	0	4.21
J. Robinson	24	172	13	6	0	2.98
M. Henneman	65	91	9	6	22	1.87
G. Hernandez	63	68	6	5	10	3.06

Milwaukee

W-87 L-75

Tom Trebelhorn

POS	Player	AB	BA	HR	RBI	PO	A	E	DP	TC/G	FA
1B	G. Brock	364	.212	6	50	915	102	7	89	9.0	.993
2B	J. Gantner	539	.276	0	47	**325**	428	11	92	5.0	.986
SS	D. Sveum	467	.242	9	51	208	370	**27**	93	4.8	.955
3B	P. Molitor	609	.312	13	60	86	187	17	15	2.8	.941
RF	R. Deer	492	.252	23	85	284	10	3	3	2.2	.990
CF	R. Yount	621	.306	13	91	444	12	2	2	2.9	.996
LF	J. Leonard	374	.235	8	44	191	4	3	1	2.2	.985
C	B. Surhoff	493	.245	5	38	525	42	6	2	5.4	.990
DH	J. Meyer	327	.263	11	45						
OF	G. Braggs	272	.261	10	42	134	1	3	0	2.6	.978

Pitcher	G	IP	W	L	SV	ERA
T. Higuera	31	227	16	9	0	2.45
B. Wegman	32	199	13	13	0	4.12
C. Bosio	38	182	7	15	6	3.36
D. August	24	148	13	7	0	3.09
M. Birkbeck	23	124	10	8	0	4.72
J. Nieves	25	110	7	5	1	4.08
C. Crim	**70**	105	7	6	9	2.91
T. Filer	19	102	5	8	0	4.43
D. Plesac	50	52	1	2	30	2.41

Toronto

W-87 L-75

Jimy Williams

POS	Player	AB	BA	HR	RBI	PO	A	E	DP	TC/G	FA
1B	F. McGriff	536	.282	34	82	1344	93	5	143	9.4	**.997**
2B	M. Lee	381	.291	2	38	221	261	6	64	5.0	.988
SS	T. Fernandez	648	.287	5	70	247	470	14	106	4.7	.981
3B	K. Gruber	569	.278	16	81	114	**349**	14	31	**3.1**	.971
RF	J. Barfield	468	.244	18	56	325	12	4	4	2.5	.988
CF	L. Moseby	472	.239	10	42	304	2	5	1	2.5	.984
LF	G. Bell	614	.269	24	97	253	8	15	1	1.9	.946
C	E. Whitt	398	.251	16	70	643	43	4	10	5.6	.994
DH	R. Mulliniks	337	.300	12	48						
2B	N. Liriano	276	.264	3	23	121	177	12	48	3.9	.961
OD	R. Leach	199	.276	0	23	74	1	0	0		1.000
D1	C. Fielder	174	.230	9	23	99	10	1	10		.991
C	P. Borders	154	.273	5	21	205	14	6	0	5.2	.973

Pitcher	G	IP	W	L	SV	ERA
M. Flanagan	34	211	13	13	0	4.18
D. Stieb	32	207	16	8	0	3.04
J. Clancy	36	196	11	13	1	4.49
J. Key	21	131	12	5	0	3.29
J. Cerutti	46	124	6	7	1	3.13
D. Ward	64	112	9	3	15	3.30
T. Stottlemyre	28	98	4	8	0	5.69
J. Musselman	15	85	8	5	0	3.18
T. Henke	52	68	4	4	25	2.91
D. Wells	41	64	3	5	4	4.62

New York

W-85 L-76

Billy Martin
W-40 L-28

Lou Piniella
W-45 L-48

POS	Player	AB	BA	HR	RBI	PO	A	E	DP	TC/G	FA
1B	D. Mattingly	599	.311	18	88	1250	99	9	131	9.5	.993
2B	W. Randolph	404	.230	2	34	254	339	7	83	**5.5**	.988
SS	R. Santana	480	.240	4	38	202	421	22	96	4.4	.966
3B	M. Pagliarulo	444	.216	15	67	82	232	19	16	2.7	.943
RF	D. Winfield	559	.322	25	107	276	3	3	1	2.0	.989
CF	C. Washington	455	.308	11	64	309	5	5	1	2.7	.984
LF	R. Henderson	554	.305	6	50	320	7	12	5	2.5	.965
C	D. Slaught	322	.283	9	43	496	24	**11**	4	5.6	.979
DH	J. Clark	496	.242	27	93						
C	J. Skinner	251	.227	4	23	395	16	4	5	4.9	.990
OF	G. Ward	231	.225	4	24	130	0	1	0	2.4	.992
DH	K. Phelps	107	.224	10	22						

Pitcher	G	IP	W	L	SV	ERA
R. Rhoden	30	197	12	12	0	4.29
T. John	35	176	9	8	0	4.49
R. Dotson	32	171	12	9	0	5.00
J. Candelaria	25	157	13	7	1	3.38
N. Allen	41	117	5	3	0	3.84
C. Hudson	28	106	6	6	2	4.49
D. Righetti	60	87	5	4	25	3.52
S. Shields	39	82	5	5	0	4.37
C. Guante	56	75	5	6	11	2.88

Cleveland

W-78 L-84

Doc Edwards

POS	Player	AB	BA	HR	RBI	PO	A	E	DP	TC/G	FA
1B	W. Upshaw	493	.245	11	50	1162	102	**12**	93	8.9	.991
2B	J. Franco	613	.303	10	54	310	434	14	87	5.0	.982
SS	J. Bell	211	.218	2	21	103	170	10	37	3.9	.965
3B	B. Jacoby	552	.241	9	49	99	298	10	23	2.7	.975
RF	C. Snyder	511	.272	26	75	314	16	5	0	2.4	.985
CF	J. Carter	621	.271	27	98	444	8	7	3	2.9	.985
LF	M. Hall	515	.280	6	71	288	3	10	1	2.1	.967
C	A. Allanson	434	.263	5	50	**691**	60	**11**	**11**	5.7	.986
DH	R. Kittle	225	.258	18	43						
SS	R. Washington	223	.256	2	21	83	141	16	26	4.4	.933
DH	T. Francona	212	.311	1	12						
OF	C. Castillo	176	.273	4	14	69	1	5	0	1.7	.933

Pitcher	G	IP	W	L	SV	ERA
G. Swindell	33	242	18	14	0	3.20
T. Candiotti	31	217	14	8	0	3.28
J. Farrell	31	210	14	10	0	4.24
S. Bailes	37	145	9	14	0	4.90
R. Yett	23	134	9	6	0	4.62
D. Jones	51	83	3	4	37	2.27

Baltimore

W-54 L-107

Cal Ripken
W-0 L-6

Frank Robinson
W-54 L-101

POS	Player	AB	BA	HR	RBI	PO	A	E	DP	TC/G	FA
1B	E. Murray	603	.284	28	84	867	106	11	101	9.6	.989
2B	B. Ripken	512	.207	2	34	309	440	12	110	5.1	.984
SS	C. Ripken	575	.264	23	81	**284**	480	21	119	4.9	.973
3B	R. Gonzales	237	.215	2	15	45	153	7	19	2.6	.966
RF	J. Orsulak	379	.288	8	27	228	6	5	2	2.0	.979
CF	F. Lynn	301	.252	18	37	216	1	2	0	2.6	.991
LF	P. Stanicek	261	.230	4	17	128	4	2	2	2.1	.985
C	M. Tettleton	283	.261	11	37	361	31	3	1	4.9	.992
DH	L. Sheets	452	.230	10	47						
UT	J. Traber	352	.222	10	45	481	59	6	51		.989
3B	R. Schu	270	.256	4	20	56	108	11	7	2.4	.937
C	T. Kennedy	265	.226	3	16	332	23	2	3	4.5	.994
OF	K. Gerhart	262	.195	9	23	192	3	5	1	2.2	.975
OF	B. Anderson	177	.198	1	9	156	1	3	0	3.3	.981

Pitcher	G	IP	W	L	SV	ERA
J. Bautista	33	172	6	15	0	4.30
J. Tibbs	30	159	4	15	0	5.39
J. Ballard	25	153	8	12	0	4.40
M. Boddicker	21	147	6	12	0	3.86
D. Schmidt	41	130	8	5	2	3.40
M. Williamson	37	118	5	8	2	4.90
O. Peraza	19	86	5	7	0	5.55
M. Thurmond	43	75	1	8	3	4.58
T. Niedenfuer	52	59	3	4	18	3.51

AMERICAN LEAGUE 1988, *cont.*

West

Oakland

W-104 L-58

Tony LaRussa

POS	Player	AB	BA	HR	RBI	PO	A	E	DP	TC/G	FA	Pitcher	G	IP	W	L	SV	ERA
1B	M. McGwire	550	.260	32	99	1228	88	9	118	8.6	.993	D. Stewart	37	**276**	21	12	0	3.23
2B	G. Hubbard	294	.255	3	33	195	267	6	60	4.5	.987	B. Welch	36	245	17	9	0	3.64
SS	W. Weiss	452	.250	3	39	254	431	15	83	4.8	.979	S. Davis	33	202	16	7	0	3.70
3B	C. Lansford	556	.279	7	57	113	220	7	16	2.4	**.979**	C. Young	26	156	11	8	0	4.14
RF	J. Canseco	610	.307	**42**	**124**	304	11	7	3	2.2	.978	G. Nelson	54	112	9	6	3	3.06
CF	D. Henderson	507	.304	24	94	382	5	7	2	2.8	.982	T. Burns	17	103	8	2	1	3.16
LF	L. Polonia	288	.292	2	27	155	3	2	1	2.1	.988	R. Honeycutt	55	80	3	2	7	3.50
C	R. Hassey	323	.257	7	45	465	31	3	7	5.5	.994	E. Plunk	49	78	7	2	5	3.00
DH	D. Baylor	264	.220	7	34							D. Eckersley	60	73	4	2	**45**	2.35
OF	S. Javier	397	.257	2	35	240	6	5	2	2.2	.980	G. Cadaret	58	72	5	2	3	2.89
DO	D. Parker	377	.257	12	55	58	3	3	0		.953							
C	T. Steinbach	351	.265	9	51	484	48	9	5	6.4	.983							
UT	M. Gallego	277	.209	2	20	155	254	8	49		.981							
UT	T. Phillips	212	.203	2	17	84	80	10	18		.943							

Minnesota

W-91 L-71

Tom Kelly

POS	Player	AB	BA	HR	RBI	PO	A	E	DP	TC/G	FA	Pitcher	G	IP	W	L	SV	ERA
1B	K. Hrbek	510	.312	25	76	842	57	3	92	8.6	.997	F. Viola	35	255	**24**	7	0	2.64
2B	S. Lombardozzi	287	.209	3	27	140	211	5	47	4.0	.986	B. Blyleven	33	207	10	**17**	0	5.43
SS	G. Gagne	461	.236	14	48	200	373	18	79	4.0	.970	A. Anderson	30	202	16	9	0	**2.45**
3B	G. Gaetti	468	.301	28	88	105	189	7	24	2.6	.977	C. Lea	24	130	7	7	0	4.85
RF	R. Bush	394	.261	14	51	187	3	4	0	1.8	.979	F. Toliver	21	115	7	6	0	4.24
CF	K. Puckett	**657**	.356	24	121	450	12	3	4	2.9	.994	J. Berenguer	57	100	8	4	2	3.96
LF	D. Gladden	576	.269	11	62	319	12	3	5	2.4	.991	K. Atherton	49	74	7	5	3	3.41
C	T. Laudner	375	.251	13	54	621	35	5	8	6.1	.992	J. Reardon	63	73	2	4	42	2.47
DH	G. Larkin	505	.267	8	70													
2B	T. Herr	304	.263	1	21	140	195	4	54	4.6	.988							
UT	A. Newman	260	.223	0	19	97	155	6	33		.977							
OF	J. Moses	206	.316	2	12	123	1	0	0	1.5	1.000							
C	B. Harper	166	.295	3	20	207	15	2	0	4.7	.991							

Kansas City

W-84 L-77

John Wathan

POS	Player	AB	BA	HR	RBI	PO	A	E	DP	TC/G	FA	Pitcher	G	IP	W	L	SV	ERA
1B	G. Brett	589	.306	24	103	1126	70	10	105	9.7	.992	M. Gubicza	35	270	20	8	0	2.70
2B	F. White	537	.235	8	58	293	426	4	88	4.9	**.994**	B. Saberhagen	35	261	14	16	0	3.80
SS	K. Stillwell	459	.251	10	53	170	349	13	60	4.3	.976	C. Leibrandt	35	243	13	12	0	3.19
3B	K. Seitzer	559	.304	5	60	93	297	**26**	33	2.8	.938	F. Bannister	31	189	12	13	0	4.33
RF	D. Tartabull	507	.274	26	102	227	8	9	1	1.9	.963	S. Farr	62	83	5	4	20	2.50
CF	W. Wilson	591	.262	1	37	365	1	4	0	2.6	.989	T. Power	22	80	5	6	0	5.94
LF	B. Jackson	439	.246	25	68	246	11	7	2	2.2	.973	J. Montgomery	45	63	7	2	1	3.45
C	J. Quirk	196	.240	8	25	409	31	8	5	5.7	.982	G. Garber	26	33	0	4	6	3.58
DH	B. Buckner	242	.256	3	34													
DO	P. Tabler	301	.309	1	49	68	1	1	0		.986							
C	M. Macfarlane	211	.265	4	26	309	18	2	3	4.8	.994							
OF	J. Eisenreich	202	.218	1	19	109	0	4	0	1.8	.965							
UT	B. Pecota	178	.208	1	15	98	145	6	25		.976							

California

W-75 L-87

Cookie Rojas
W-75 L-79

Larry Stubing
W-0 L-8

POS	Player	AB	BA	HR	RBI	PO	A	E	DP	TC/G	FA	Pitcher	G	IP	W	L	SV	ERA
1B	W. Joyner	597	.295	13	85	**1369**	**143**	8	**148**	**9.7**	.995	M. Witt	34	250	13	16	0	4.15
2B	J. Ray	602	.306	6	83	194	328	15	64	5.2	.972	W. Fraser	34	195	12	13	0	5.41
SS	D. Schofield	527	.239	6	34	278	492	13	**125**	5.1	**.983**	C. Finley	31	194	9	15	0	4.17
3B	J. Howell	500	.254	16	63	96	249	17	19	2.4	.953	K. McCaskill	23	146	8	6	0	4.31
RF	C. Davis	600	.268	21	93	299	10	19	1	2.1	.942	D. Petry	22	140	3	9	0	4.38
CF	D. White	455	.259	11	51	364	7	9	2	3.3	.976	T. Clark	15	94	6	6	0	5.07
LF	T. Armas	368	.272	13	49	212	5	3	1	1.9	.986	G. Minton	44	79	4	5	7	2.85
C	B. Boone	352	.295	5	39	506	**66**	8	9	4.8	.986	B. Harvey	50	76	7	5	17	2.13
DH	B. Downing	484	.242	25	64							D. Moore	27	33	5	2	4	4.91
2B	M. McLemore	233	.240	2	16	107	171	6	52	4.5	.979							

Chicago

W-71 L-90

Jim Fregosi

POS	Player	AB	BA	HR	RBI	PO	A	E	DP	TC/G	FA	Pitcher	G	IP	W	L	SV	ERA
1B	G. Walker	377	.247	8	42	935	41	7	93	10.0	.993	M. Perez	32	197	12	10	0	3.79
2B	F. Manrique	345	.235	5	37	228	308	8	77	4.2	.985	J. Reuss	32	183	13	9	0	3.44
SS	O. Guillen	566	.261	0	39	273	**570**	20	115	**5.5**	.977	B. Long	47	174	8	11	2	4.03
3B	S. Lyons	472	.269	5	45	81	238	25	**36**	2.7	.927	D. LaPoint	25	161	10	11	0	3.40
RF	I. Calderon	264	.212	14	35	141	5	7	1	2.3	.954	J. McDowell	26	159	5	10	0	3.97
CF	D. Gallagher	347	.303	5	31	228	5	0	2	2.5	1.000	R. Horton	52	109	6	10	2	4.86
LF	D. Pasqua	422	.227	20	50	258	6	1	2	2.4	.996	B. Thigpen	68	90	5	8	34	3.30
C	C. Fisk	253	.277	19	50	338	36	2	7	5.1	.995							
DH	H. Baines	599	.277	13	81													
OF	D. Boston	281	.217	15	31	190	4	10	2	2.4	.951							
OF	G. Redus	262	.263	6	34	140	7	2	1	2.2	.987							
2B	D. Hill	221	.217	2	20	106	132	6	36	4.1	.975							
03	K. Williams	220	.159	8	28	87	69	17	4		.902							
C	M. Salas	196	.250	3	9	251	35	6	5	4.2	.979							

Texas

W-70 L-91

Bobby Valentine

POS	Player	AB	BA	HR	RBI	PO	A	E	DP	TC/G	FA	Pitcher	G	IP	W	L	SV	ERA
1B	P. O'Brien	547	.272	16	71	1346	140	8	124	9.6	.995	C. Hough	34	252	15	16	0	3.32
2B	C. Wilkerson	338	.293	0	28	153	240	12	52	4.7	.970	J. Guzman	30	207	11	13	0	3.70
SS	S. Fletcher	515	.276	0	47	215	414	11	90	4.6	.983	P. Kilgus	32	203	12	15	0	4.16
3B	S. Buechele	503	.250	16	58	110	297	16	25	2.8	.962	J. Russell	34	189	10	9	0	3.82
RF	R. Sierra	615	.254	23	91	310	11	7	3	2.1	.979	B. Witt	22	174	8	10	0	3.92
CF	O. McDowell	437	.247	6	37	267	2	3	1	2.4	.989	M. Williams	67	68	2	7	18	4.63
LF	P. Incaviglia	418	.249	22	54	172	12	2	1	2.0	.989	R. Hayward	12	63	4	6	0	5.46
C	G. Petralli	351	.282	7	36	409	45	9	7	5.4	.981	D. Mohorcic	43	52	2	6	5	4.85
DH	L. Parrish	248	.190	7	26													
OF	C. Espy	347	.248	2	39	196	10	6	0	2.2	.972							
C	M. Stanley	249	.229	3	27	310	14	3	3	5.1	.991							
2B	J. Browne	214	.229	1	17	112	139	11	27	3.7	.958							
OF	B. Brower	201	.224	1	11	104	2	3	1	1.8	.972							

AMERICAN LEAGUE 1988, *cont.*

Team	POS	Player	AB	BA	HR	RBI	PO	A	E	DP	TC/G	FA	Pitcher	G	IP	W	L	SV	ERA
Seattle	1B	A. Davis	478	.295	18	69	980	65	6	111	9.1	.994	M. Langston	35	261	15	11	0	3.34
	2B	H. Reynolds	598	.283	4	41	303	**471**	**18**	**111**	5.0	.977	M. Moore	37	229	9	15	1	3.78
W-68 L-93	SS	R. Quinones	499	.248	12	52	202	396	23	103	4.6	.963	B. Swift	38	175	8	12	0	4.59
	3B	J. Presley	544	.230	14	62	112	234	22	25	2.5	.940	S. Bankhead	21	135	7	9	0	3.07
Dick Williams	RF	G. Wilson	284	.250	3	17	140	4	3	1	2.0	.980	M. Campbell	20	115	6	10	0	5.89
W-23 L-33	CF	H. Cotto	386	.259	8	33	253	6	2	0	2.2	.992	M. Jackson	62	99	6	5	4	2.63
	LF	M. Brantley	577	.263	15	56	327	5	6	1	2.3	.982	S. Trout	15	56	4	7	0	7.83
Jimmy Snyder	C	S. Bradley	335	.257	4	33	524	37	5	6	**6.7**	.991	M. Schooler	40	48	5	8	15	3.54
W-45 L-60	DH	K. Phelps	190	.284	14	32													
	D1	S. Balboni	350	.251	21	61	334	25	2	34		.994							
	C	D. Valle	290	.231	10	50	484	47	6	7	6.4	.989							
	OF	D. Coles	195	.292	10	34	66	3	1	0	1.5	.986							
	OF	J. Buhner	192	.224	10	25	134	7	1	3	2.4	.993							

BATTING AND BASE RUNNING LEADERS

Batting Average

W. Boggs, BOS	.366
K. Puckett, MIN	.356
M. Greenwell, BOS	.325
D. Winfield, NY	.322
P. Molitor, MIL	.312

Slugging Average

J. Canseco, OAK	.569
F. McGriff, TOR	.552
G. Gaetti, MIN	.551
K. Puckett, MIN	.545
M. Greenwell, BOS	.531

Home Runs

J. Canseco, OAK	42
F. McGriff, TOR	34
M. McGwire, OAK	32
G. Gaetti, MIN	28
E. Murray, BAL	28

Total Bases

K. Puckett, MIN	358
J. Canseco, OAK	347
M. Greenwell, BOS	313
G. Brett, KC	300
J. Carter, CLE	297

Runs Batted In

J. Canseco, OAK	124
K. Puckett, MIN	121
M. Greenwell, BOS	119
D. Evans, BOS	111
D. Winfield, NY	107

Stolen Bases

R. Henderson, NY	93
G. Pettis, DET	44
P. Molitor, MIL	41
J. Canseco, OAK	40
W. Wilson, KC	35
H. Reynolds, SEA	35

Hits

K. Puckett, MIN	234
W. Boggs, BOS	214
M. Greenwell, BOS	192
P. Molitor, MIL	190
R. Yount, MIL	190

Base on Balls

W. Boggs, BOS	125
J. Clark, NY	113
C. Ripken, BAL	102
A. Davis, SEA	95

Home Run Percentage

J. Canseco, OAK	6.9
F. McGriff, TOR	6.3
G. Gaetti, MIN	6.0
M. McGwire, OAK	5.8

Runs

W. Boggs, BOS	128
J. Canseco, OAK	120
R. Henderson, NY	118
P. Molitor, MIL	115

Doubles

W. Boggs, BOS	45
G. Brett, KC	42
J. Ray, CAL	42
K. Puckett, MIN	42

Triples

W. Wilson, KC	11
H. Reynolds, SEA	11
R. Yount, MIL	11
M. Greenwell, BOS	8

PITCHING LEADERS

Winning Percentage

F. Viola, MIN	.774
B. Hurst, BOS	.750
M. Gubicza, KC	.714
S. Davis, OAK	.696
D. Stieb, TOR	.667

Earned Run Average

A. Anderson, MIN	2.45
T. Higuera, MIL	2.45
F. Viola, MIN	2.64
M. Gubicza, KC	2.70
R. Clemens, BOS	2.93

Wins

F. Viola, MIN	24
D. Stewart, OAK	21
M. Gubicza, KC	20
B. Hurst, BOS	18
G. Swindell, CLE	18
R. Clemens, BOS	18

Saves

D. Eckersley, OAK	45
J. Reardon, MIN	42
D. Jones, CLE	37
B. Thigpen, CHI	34
D. Plesac, MIL	30

Strikeouts

R. Clemens, BOS	291
M. Langston, SEA	235
F. Viola, MIN	193
T. Higuera, MIL	192
D. Stewart, OAK	192

Complete Games

R. Clemens, BOS	14
D. Stewart, OAK	14
B. Witt, TEX	13
G. Swindell, CLE	12
M. Witt, CAL	12

Fewest Hits/9 Innings

J. Robinson, DET	6.33
T. Higuera, MIL	6.65
D. Stieb, TOR	6.82
B. Witt, TEX	6.92

Shutouts

R. Clemens, BOS	8
D. Stieb, TOR	4
G. Swindell, CLE	4
M. Gubicza, KC	4

Fewest Walks/9 Innings

A. Anderson, MIN	1.65
G. Swindell, CLE	1.67
D. Alexander, DET	1.81
C. Bosio, MIL	1.88

Most Strikeouts/9 Inn.

R. Clemens, BOS	9.92
M. Langston, SEA	8.09
B. Witt, TEX	7.64
T. Higuera, MIL	7.60

Innings

D. Stewart, OAK	276
M. Gubicza, KC	270
R. Clemens, BOS	264
M. Langston, SEA	261
B. Saberhagen, KC	261

Games Pitched

C. Crim, MIL	70
B. Thigpen, CHI	68
M. Williams, TEX	67
M. Henneman, DET	65

							Batting						Fielding			Pitching					
		W	L	PCT	GB	R	OR	2B	3B	HR	BA	SA	SB	E	DP	FA	CG	BB	SO	ShO	SV	ERA
East	Boston	89	73	.549		**813**	689	**310**	39	124	**.283**	.420	65	93	123	.984	26	493	**1085**	**10**	37	3.97
	Detroit	88	74	.543	1	703	658	213	28	143	.250	.378	87	109	129	.982	34	497	890	6	36	3.71
	Milwaukee	87	75	.537	2	682	**616**	258	26	113	.257	.375	**159**	120	146	.981	30	**437**	832	6	51	3.45
	Toronto	87	75	.537	2	763	680	271	**47**	**158**	.268	.419	107	110	170	.982	16	528	904	7	47	3.80
	New York	85	76	.528	3.5	772	748	272	12	148	.263	.395	146	134	161	.978	16	487	861	3	43	4.26
	Cleveland	78	84	.481	11	666	731	235	28	134	.261	.387	97	124	131	.980	35	442	812	7	46	4.16
	Baltimore	54	107	.335	34.5	550	789	199	20	137	.238	.359	69	119	172	.980	20	523	709	2	26	4.54
West	Oakland	104	58	.642		800	620	251	22	156	.263	.399	129	105	151	.983	22	553	983	4	**64**	**3.44**
	Minnesota	91	71	.562	13	759	672	294	31	151	.274	**.421**	107	**84**	155	**.986**	18	453	897	4	52	3.93
	Kansas City	84	77	.522	19.5	704	648	275	40	121	.259	.391	137	124	147	.980	29	465	886	9	32	3.66
	California	75	87	.463	29	714	771	258	31	124	.261	.385	86	135	175	.979	26	568	817	6	33	4.31
	Chicago	71	90	.441	32.5	631	757	224	35	132	.244	.370	98	154	**177**	.976	11	533	754	2	43	4.12
	Texas	70	91	.435	33.5	637	735	227	39	112	.252	.368	130	131	145	.979	**41**	654	912	8	31	4.05
	Seattle	68	93	.422	35.5	664	744	271	27	148	.257	.398	95	123	168	.980	28	558	981	8	28	4.15
						9858	9858	3558	425	1901	.259	.390	1512	1665	2150	.981	352	7191	12323	82	569	3.97

NATIONAL LEAGUE 1989

	Team	POS	Player	AB	BA	HR	RBI	PO	A	E	DP	TC/G	FA	Pitcher	G	IP	W	L	SV	ERA
East	**Chicago**	1B	M. Grace	510	.314	13	79	1230	126	6	93	9.6	.996	G. Maddux	35	238	19	12	0	2.95
		2B	R. Sandberg	606	.290	30	76	294	466	6	80	4.9	.992	R. Sutcliffe	35	229	16	11	0	3.66
	W-93 L-69	SS	S. Dunston	471	.278	9	60	213	379	17	76	4.4	.972	M. Bielecki	33	212	18	7	0	3.14
		3B	V. Law	408	.235	7	42	76	168	13	13	2.2	.949	S. Sanderson	37	146	11	9	0	3.94
	Don Zimmer	RF	A. Dawson	416	.252	21	77	227	4	3	0	2.1	.987	P. Kilgus	35	146	6	10	2	4.39
		CF	J. Walton	475	.293	5	46	289	2	3	1	2.6	.990	S. Wilson	53	86	6	4	2	4.20
		LF	D. Smith	343	.324	9	52	188	7	5	3	2.0	.975	M. Williams	**76**	82	4	4	36	2.64
		C	D. Berryhill	334	.257	5	41	473	41	4	4	5.8	.992	C. Schiraldi	54	79	3	6	4	3.78
		OF	M. Webster	272	.257	3	19	161	3	6	0	2.3	.965	L. Lancaster	42	73	4	2	8	1.36
		UT	L. McClendon	259	.286	12	40	310	18	6	21		.982							
		S3	D. Ramos	179	.263	1	19	49	142	11	20		.946							

NATIONAL LEAGUE 1989, *cont.*

Team	POS	Player	AB	BA	HR	RBI	PO	A	E	DP	TC/G	FA	Pitcher	G	IP	W	L	SV	ERA
	1B	D. Magadan	374	.286	4	41	574	59	6	50	7.3	.991	D. Cone	34	220	14	8	0	3.52
New York	2B	G. Jefferies	508	.258	12	56	223	254	12	41	4.0	.975	S. Fernandez	35	219	14	5	0	2.83
	SS	K. Elster	458	.231	10	55	**235**	374	15	63	4.2	.976	R. Darling	33	217	14	14	0	3.52
	3B	H. Johnson	571	.287	36	101	63	180	24	15	1.9	.910	B. Ojeda	31	192	13	11	0	3.47
W-87 L-75	RF	D. Strawberry	476	.225	29	77	272	4	8	2	2.2	.972	D. Gooden	19	118	9	4	1	2.89
	CF	J. Samuel	333	.228	3	28	206	4	3	3	2.5	.986	F. Viola	12	85	5	5	0	3.38
Davey Johnson	LF	K. McReynolds	545	.272	22	85	307	10	10	3	2.3	.969	R. Myers	65	84	7	4	24	2.35
	C	B. Lyons	235	.247	3	27	463	29	10	4	6.6	.980	R. Aguilera	36	69	6	6	7	2.34
	OF	M. Wilson	249	.205	3	18	152	2	4	0	2.2	.975	R. McDowell	25	35	1	5	4	3.31
	21	T. Teufel	219	.256	2	15	261	112	10	30		.974							
	1B	K. Hernandez	215	.233	4	19	405	31	4	22	7.6	.991							
	C	M. Sasser	182	.291	1	22	335	19	3	3	5.8	.992							
	1B	P. Guerrero	570	.311	17	117	**1445**	72	**15**	99	9.6	.990	J. DeLeon	36	245	16	12	0	3.05
St. Louis	2B	J. Oquendo	556	.291	1	48	**346**	**500**	5	**106**	**5.5**	**.994**	J. Magrane	34	235	18	9	0	2.91
	SS	O. Smith	593	.273	2	50	209	**483**	17	73	4.6	.976	K. Hill	33	197	7	**15**	0	3.80
	3B	T. Pendleton	613	.264	13	74	113	**392**	15	25	**3.2**	**.971**	S. Terry	31	149	8	10	2	3.57
W-86 L-76	RF	T. Brunansky	556	.239	20	85	291	9	7	2	2.0	.977	T. Power	23	97	7	7	0	3.71
	CF	M. Thompson	545	.290	4	68	348	5	8	1	2.5	.978	D. Quisenberry	63	78	3	1	6	2.64
Whitey Herzog	LF	V. Coleman	563	.254	2	28	247	5	10	1	1.8	.962	K. Dayley	71	75	4	3	12	2.87
	C	T. Pena	424	.259	4	37	674	70	2	**13**	5.6	**.997**	J. Costello	48	62	5	4	3	3.32
	OF	W. McGee	199	.236	3	17	118	2	3	0	2.6	.976	T. Worrell	47	52	3	5	20	2.96
	1B	A. Galarraga	572	.257	23	85	1335	91	11	97	9.8	.992	D. Martinez	34	232	16	7	0	3.18
Montreal	2B	T. Foley	375	.229	7	39	188	295	6	53	4.5	.988	B. Smith	33	216	10	11	0	2.84
	SS	S. Owen	437	.233	6	41	232	388	13	65	4.5	**.979**	K. Gross	31	201	11	12	0	4.38
	3B	T. Wallach	573	.277	13	77	113	302	18	20	2.8	.958	P. Perez	33	198	9	13	0	3.31
W-81 L-81	RF	H. Brooks	542	.268	14	70	234	6	9	2	1.8	.964	M. Langston	24	177	12	9	0	2.39
	CF	D. Martinez	361	.274	3	27	199	7	7	1	1.8	.967	T. Burke	68	85	9	3	28	2.55
Buck Rodgers	LF	T. Raines	517	.286	9	60	253	7	1	0	1.9	.996	A. McGaffigan	57	75	3	5	2	4.68
	C	N. Santovenia	304	.250	5	31	561	66	12	7	**7.2**	.981	J. Hesketh	43	48	6	4	3	5.77
	C	M. Fitzgerald	290	.238	7	42	459	35	8	5	6.5	.984							
	OF	O. Nixon	258	.217	0	21	160	2	2	0	1.7	.988							
	2B	D. Garcia	203	.271	3	18	86	157	7	25	4.0	.972							
	1B	G. Redus	279	.283	6	33	567	54	8	42	8.7	.987	D. Drabek	35	244	14	12	0	2.80
Pittsburgh	2B	J. Lind	578	.232	2	48	309	438	18	81	5.1	.976	J. Smiley	28	205	12	8	0	2.81
	SS	J. Bell	271	.258	2	27	109	197	10	41	4.1	.968	B. Walk	33	196	13	10	0	4.41
	3B	B. Bonilla	616	.281	24	86	125	330	**35**	**31**	3.1	.929	N. Heaton	42	147	6	7	0	3.05
W-74 L-88	RF	G. Wilson	330	.282	9	49	163	4	4	0	2.0	.977	J. Robinson	50	141	7	13	4	4.58
	CF	A. Van Slyke	476	.237	9	53	338	9	4	5	2.9	.989	R. Kramer	35	111	5	9	2	3.96
Jim Leyland	LF	B. Bonds	580	.248	19	58	365	14	6	1	2.5	.984	B. Kipper	52	83	3	4	4	2.93
	C	J. Ortiz	230	.217	1	22	334	32	2	2	4.4	.995	B. Landrum	56	81	2	3	26	1.67
	OF	R. Reynolds	363	.270	6	48	200	6	2	3	2.1	.990							
	SS	R. Quinones	225	.209	3	29	94	174	19	24	4.2	.934							
	UT	J. King	215	.195	5	19	403	59	4	36		.991							
	C	M. LaValliere	190	.316	2	23	306	24	3	3	5.1	.991							
	1B	R. Jordan	523	.285	12	75	1271	61	9	99	9.6	.993	K. Howell	33	204	12	12	0	3.44
Philadelphia	2B	T. Herr	561	.287	2	37	281	415	7	80	4.9	.990	D. Carman	49	149	5	**15**	0	5.24
	SS	D. Thon	435	.271	15	60	174	380	16	65	4.4	.972	B. Ruffin	24	126	6	10	0	4.44
	3B	C. Hayes	299	.258	8	43	49	173	22	15	3.0	.910	L. McWilliams	40	121	2	11	0	4.10
W-67 L-95	RF	V. Hayes	540	.259	26	78	236	9	5	1	2.0	.980	D. Cook	21	106	6	8	0	3.99
	CF	L. Dykstra	352	.222	4	19	208	9	2	0	2.5	.991	J. Parrett	72	106	12	6	6	2.98
Nick Leyva	LF	J. Kruk	281	.331	5	38	111	5	2	2	1.6	.983	T. Mulholland	20	104	4	7	0	5.00
	C	D. Daulton	368	.201	8	44	627	56	11	8	5.5	.984	R. McDowell	44	57	3	3	19	1.11
	UT	S. Jeltz	263	.243	4	25	111	205	6	33		.981	S. Bedrosian	28	34	2	3	6	3.21
	OF	J. Samuel	199	.246	8	20	133	2	1	0	2.7	.993							
	UT	R. Ready	187	.267	8	21	64	36	7	9		.935							
	OF	B. Dernier	187	.171	1	13	95	1	3	0	1.3	.970							
	OF	C. James	179	.207	2	19	61	3	1	0	1.8	.985							
	OF	D. Murphy	156	.218	9	27	69	1	1	1	1.4	.986							
	3B	M. Schmidt	148	.203	6	28	18	71	8	8	2.3	.918							
West																			
	1B	W. Clark	588	.333	23	111	**1445**	111	10	117	**9.9**	.994	R. Reuschel	32	208	17	8	0	2.94
San Francisco	2B	R. Thompson	547	.241	13	50	307	425	8	88	5.0	.989	D. Robinson	34	197	12	11	0	3.43
	SS	J. Uribe	453	.221	1	30	225	436	18	**85**	4.5	.973	S. Garrelts	30	193	14	5	0	**2.28**
	3B	E. Riles	302	.278	7	40	45	107	6	13	1.9	.962	M. LaCoss	45	150	10	10	6	3.17
W-92 L-70	RF	C. Maldonado	345	.217	9	41	181	6	5	1	1.7	.974	C. Lefferts	70	107	2	4	20	2.69
	CF	B. Butler	594	.283	4	36	407	11	6	3	2.8	.986	K. Downs	18	83	4	8	0	4.79
Roger Craig	LF	K. Mitchell	543	.291	**47**	**125**	305	8	7	0	2.2	.978	A. Hammaker	28	77	6	6	0	3.76
	C	T. Kennedy	355	.239	5	34	516	47	8	6	4.7	.986	S. Bedrosian	40	51	1	4	17	2.65
	3B	M. Williams	292	.202	18	50	71	126	8	10	2.8	.961							
	C	K. Manwaring	200	.210	0	18	289	32	6	3	4.0	.982							
	OF	D. Nixon	166	.265	1	15	87	0	3	0	1.4	.967							
	1B	J. Clark	455	.242	26	94	1135	88	**15**	99	9.5	.988	B. Hurst	33	245	15	11	0	2.69
San Diego	2B	R. Alomar	623	.295	7	56	341	472	**28**	91	5.4	.967	E. Whitson	33	227	16	11	0	2.66
	SS	G. Templeton	506	.255	6	40	232	409	20	74	4.7	.970	D. Rasmussen	33	184	10	10	0	4.26
	3B	L. Salazar	246	.268	8	22	37	116	5	10	2.2	.968	G. Harris	56	135	8	9	6	2.60
W-89 L-73	RF	T. Gwynn	604	**.336**	4	62	353	13	6	1	2.4	.984	W. Terrell	19	123	5	13	0	4.01
	CF	M. Wynne	294	.252	6	35	160	7	5	2	1.8	.971	M. Grant	50	116	8	2	2	3.33
Jack McKeon	LF	C. Martinez	267	.221	6	39	103	5	2	1	1.7	.982	E. Show	16	106	8	6	0	4.23
	C	B. Santiago	462	.236	16	62	685	81	**20**	10	6.2	.975	M. Davis	70	93	4	3	**44**	1.85
	UT	B. Roberts	329	.301	3	25	134	113	9	17		.965							
	OF	C. James	303	.264	11	46	145	3	2	0	1.9	.987							
	C	M. Parent	141	.191	7	21	241	17	0	2	6.3	1.000							

NATIONAL LEAGUE 1989, *cont.*

Team	POS	Player	AB	BA	HR	RBI	PO	A	E	DP	TC/G	FA	Pitcher	G	IP	W	L	SV	ERA
Houston	1B	G. Davis	581	.269	34	89	1347	113	12	101	9.4	.992	M. Scott	33	229	**20**	10	0	3.10
	2B	B. Doran	507	.219	8	58	254	345	12	64	4.4	.980	J. Deshaies	34	226	15	10	0	2.91
	SS	R. Ramirez	537	.246	6	54	189	326	**30**	60	3.7	.945	J. Clancy	33	147	7	14	0	5.08
W-86 L-76	3B	K. Caminiti	585	.255	10	72	126	335	22	27	3.0	.954	D. Darwin	68	122	11	4	7	2.36
	RF	T. Puhl	354	.271	0	27	204	3	0	0	2.0	1.000	B. Knepper	22	113	4	10	0	5.89
Art Howe	CF	G. Young	533	.233	0	38	412	15	1	5	3.0	.998	B. Forsch	37	108	4	5	0	5.32
	LF	B. Hatcher	395	.228	3	44	223	1	2	1	2.2	.991	M. Portugal	20	108	7	1	0	2.75
	C	C. Biggio	443	.257	13	60	728	56	8	6	6.3	.990	L. Andersen	60	88	4	4	3	1.54
	OF	K. Bass	313	.300	5	44	186	6	3	0	2.3	.985	J. Agosto	71	83	4	5	1	2.93
	UT	C. Reynolds	189	.201	2	14	86	136	8	24		.965	D. Smith	52	58	3	4	25	2.64
Los Angeles	1B	E. Murray	594	.247	20	88	1316	**137**	6	**122**	9.2	**.996**	O. Hershiser	35	**257**	15	**15**	0	2.31
	2B	W. Randolph	549	.282	2	36	260	412	9	85	4.9	.987	T. Belcher	39	230	15	12	1	2.82
	SS	A. Griffin	506	.247	0	29	208	333	14	69	4.2	.975	F. Valenzuela	31	197	10	13	0	3.43
W-77 L-83	3B	J. Hamilton	548	.245	12	56	**139**	233	19	29	2.7	.951	M. Morgan	40	153	8	11	0	2.53
	RF	M. Marshall	377	.260	11	42	179	2	4	0	1.8	.978	T. Leary	19	117	6	7	0	3.38
Tom Lasorda	CF	J. Shelby	345	.183	1	12	220	3	2	1	2.3	.991	J. Wetteland	31	103	5	8	1	3.77
	LF	K. Gibson	253	.213	9	28	146	3	3	2	2.2	.980	R. Martinez	15	99	6	4	0	3.19
	C	M. Scioscia	408	.250	10	44	**822**	**82**	11	12	7.0	.988	J. Howell	56	80	5	3	28	1.58
	OF	J. Gonzalez	261	.268	3	18	171	8	6	2	2.1	.968	A. Pena	53	76	4	3	5	2.13
	03	M. Hatcher	224	.295	2	25	73	19	4	4		.958							
	OF	M. Davis	173	.249	5	19	74	1	1	1	1.6	.987							
Cincinnati	1B	T. Benzinger	**628**	.245	17	76	1417	73	7	96	9.5	.995	T. Browning	37	250	15	12	0	3.39
	2B	R. Oester	305	.246	1	14	211	239	7	42	4.5	.985	R. Mahler	40	221	9	13	0	3.83
	SS	B. Larkin	325	.342	4	36	142	267	10	31	5.1	.976	D. Jackson	20	116	6	11	0	5.60
W-75 L-87	3B	C. Sabo	304	.260	6	29	36	145	11	12	2.5	.943	J. Rijo	19	111	7	6	0	2.84
	RF	P. O'Neill	428	.276	15	74	223	7	4	1	2.0	.983	S. Scudder	23	100	4	9	0	4.49
Pete Rose	CF	E. Davis	462	.281	34	101	298	2	5	1	2.4	.984	R. Dibble	74	99	10	5	2	2.09
W-59 L-66	LF	K. Griffey	236	.263	8	30	76	2	1	1	1.4	.987	N. Charlton	69	95	8	3	0	2.93
	C	J. Reed	287	.223	3	23	504	50	7	2	5.7	.988	J. Franco	60	81	4	8	32	3.12
Tommy Helms	23	L. Quinones	340	.244	12	34	112	206	10	25		.970							
W-16 L-21	OF	R. Roomes	315	.263	7	34	201	4	4	0	2.1	.981							
	OF	H. Winningham	251	.251	3	13	146	3	3	0	1.8	.980							
	UT	L. Harris	188	.223	2	11	92	134	13	23		.946							
	SS	M. Duncan	174	.247	3	13	65	103	8	17	4.0	.955							
	C	J. Oliver	151	.272	3	23	260	21	4	1	6.1	.986							
Atlanta	1B	G. Perry	266	.252	4	21	618	51	9	49	9.4	.987	J. Smoltz	29	208	12	11	0	2.94
	2B	J. Treadway	473	.277	8	40	271	336	12	80	5.0	.981	T. Glavine	29	186	14	8	0	3.68
	SS	A. Thomas	554	.213	13	57	231	400	29	81	**4.8**	.956	D. Lilliquist	32	166	8	10	0	3.97
W-63 L-97	3B	J. Blauser	456	.270	12	46	42	128	13	9	2.3	.929	P. Smith	28	142	5	14	0	4.75
	RF	T. Gregg	276	.243	6	23	57	1	2	0	1.3	.967	M. Clary	18	109	4	3	0	3.15
Russ Nixon	CF	D. Murphy	574	.228	20	84	331	5	5	0	2.3	.985	Z. Smith	17	99	1	12	0	4.45
	LF	L. Smith	482	.315	21	79	289	3	2	0	2.2	.993	J. Boever	66	82	4	11	21	3.94
	C	J. Davis	231	.169	4	19	364	40	6	1	5.7	.985	M. Eichhorn	45	68	5	5	0	4.35
	OF	O. McDowell	280	.304	7	24	179	2	4	0	2.7	.978							
	13	D. Evans	276	.207	11	39	371	90	10	37		.979							
	3B	R. Gant	260	.177	9	25	23	103	16	8	2.7	.887							
	OF	D. James	170	.259	1	11	87	0	0	0	1.9	1.000							

BATTING AND BASE RUNNING LEADERS

Batting Average	
T. Gwynn, SD	.336
W. Clark, SF	.333
L. Smith, ATL	.315
M. Grace, CHI	.314
P. Guerrero, STL	.311

Slugging Average	
K. Mitchell, SF	.635
H. Johnson, NY	.559
W. Clark, SF	.546
E. Davis, CIN	.541
L. Smith, ATL	.533

Home Runs	
K. Mitchell, SF	47
H. Johnson, NY	36
E. Davis, CIN	34
G. Davis, HOU	34
R. Sandberg, CHI	30

Total Bases	
K. Mitchell, SF	345
W. Clark, SF	321
H. Johnson, NY	319
B. Bonilla, PIT	302
R. Sandberg, CHI	301

Runs Batted In	
K. Mitchell, SF	125
P. Guerrero, STL	117
W. Clark, SF	111
E. Davis, CIN	101
H. Johnson, NY	101

Stolen Bases	
V. Coleman, STL	65
J. Samuel, PHI, NY	42
R. Alomar, SD	42
T. Raines, MON	41
H. Johnson, NY	41

Hits	
T. Gwynn, SD	203
W. Clark, SF	196
R. Alomar, SD	184
P. Guerrero, STL	177

Base on Balls	
J. Clark, SD	132
V. Hayes, PHI	101
T. Raines, MON	93
B. Bonds, PIT	93

Home Run Percentage	
K. Mitchell, SF	8.7
E. Davis, CIN	7.4
H. Johnson, NY	6.3
D. Strawberry, NY	6.1

Runs	
H. Johnson, NY	104
W. Clark, SF	104
R. Sandberg, CHI	104
K. Mitchell, SF	100
B. Butler, SF	100

Doubles	
P. Guerrero, STL	42
T. Wallach, MON	42
H. Johnson, NY	41
W. Clark, SF	38

Triples	
R. Thompson, SF	11
B. Bonilla, PIT	10
A. Van Slyke, PIT	9
V. Coleman, STL	9
W. Clark, SF	9

PITCHING LEADERS

Winning Percentage	
M. Bielecki, CHI	.720
D. Martinez, MON	.696
R. Reuschel, SF	.680
J. Magrane, STL	.667
M. Scott, HOU	.667

Earned Run Average	
S. Garrelts, SF	2.28
O. Hershiser, LA	2.31
M. Langston, MON	2.39
E. Whitson, SD	2.66
B. Hurst, SD	2.69

Wins	
M. Scott, HOU	20
G. Maddux, CHI	19
M. Bielecki, CHI	18
J. Magrane, STL	18
R. Reuschel, SF	17

Saves	
M. Davis, SD	44
M. Williams, CHI	36
J. Franco, CIN	32
J. Howell, LA	28
T. Burke, MON	28

Strikeouts	
J. DeLeon, STL	201
T. Belcher, LA	200
S. Fernandez, NY	198
D. Cone, NY	190
B. Hurst, SD	179

Complete Games	
T. Belcher, LA	10
B. Hurst, SD	10
M. Scott, HOU	9
J. Magrane, STL	9
T. Browning, CIN	9

Fewest Hits/9 Innings	
J. DeLeon, STL	6.36
S. Fernandez, NY	6.44
K. Howell, PHI	6.84
J. Smoltz, ATL	6.92

Shutouts	
T. Belcher, LA	8
D. Drabek, PIT	5
M. Langston, MON	4
T. Glavine, ATL	4
O. Hershiser, LA	4

Fewest Walks/9 Innings	
D. Robinson, SF	1.69
D. Lilliquist, ATL	1.85
D. Martinez, MON	1.90
E. Whitson, SD	1.90

Most Strikeouts/9 Inn.	
M. Langston, MON	8.92
S. Fernandez, NY	8.12
T. Belcher, LA	7.83
D. Cone, NY	7.78

Innings	
O. Hershiser, LA	257
T. Browning, CIN	250
B. Hurst, SD	245
J. DeLeon, STL	245

Games Pitched	
M. Williams, CHI	76
R. Dibble, CIN	74
J. Parrett, PHI	72
J. Agosto, HOU	71
K. Dayley, STL	71

NATIONAL LEAGUE 1989, *cont.*

		W	L	PCT	GB	R	OR	Batting 2B	3B	HR	BA	SA	SB	Fielding E	DP	FA	Pitching CG	BB	SO	ShO	SV	ERA
East	Chicago	93	69	.574		**702**	623	235	45	124	**.261**	.387	136	124	130	.980	18	532	918	5	**55**	3.43
	New York	87	75	.537	6	683	595	**280**	21	**147**	.246	.385	158	144	110	.976	24	532	**1108**	7	38	3.29
	St. Louis	86	76	.531	7	632	608	263	47	73	.258	.363	155	**112**	134	**.982**	18	482	844	8	43	3.36
	Montreal	81	81	.500	12	632	630	267	30	100	.247	.361	**160**	136	126	.979	20	519	1059	10	35	3.48
	Pittsburgh	74	88	.457	19	637	680	263	**53**	95	.241	.359	155	160	130	.975	20	539	827	7	40	3.64
	Philadelphia	67	95	.414	26	629	735	215	36	123	.243	.364	106	133	136	.979	10	613	899	6	33	4.04
West	San Francisco	92	70	.568		699	600	241	52	141	.250	**.390**	87	114	135	**.982**	12	471	802	3	47	3.30
	San Diego	89	73	.549	3	642	626	215	32	120	.251	.369	136	154	147	.976	21	481	933	4	52	3.38
	Houston	86	76	.531	6	647	669	239	28	97	.239	.345	144	142	121	.977	19	551	965	6	38	3.65
	Los Angeles	77	83	.481	14	554	**536**	241	17	89	.240	.339	81	118	**153**	.981	**25**	504	1052	**14**	36	**2.95**
	Cincinnati	75	87	.463	17	632	691	243	28	128	.247	.370	128	121	108	.980	16	559	981	5	37	3.73
	Atlanta	63	97	.394	28	584	680	201	22	128	.234	.350	83	152	124	.976	15	**468**	966	6	33	3.70
						7673	7673	2903	411	1365	.246	.365	1529	1610	1554	.979	218	6251	11354	81	487	3.50

AMERICAN LEAGUE 1989

East

Toronto

W-89 L-73

Jimy Williams
W-12 L-24

Cito Gaston
W-77 L-49

POS	Player	AB	BA	HR	RBI	PO	A	E	DP	TC/G	FA
1B	F. McGriff	551	.269	**36**	92	1460	115	**17**	**148**	**10.0**	.989
2B	N. Liriano	418	.263	5	53	267	330	12	76	5.0	.980
SS	T. Fernandez	573	.257	11	64	260	475	6	93	**5.3**	**.992**
3B	K. Gruber	545	.290	18	73	86	291	**22**	15	**3.4**	.945
RF	J. Felix	415	.258	9	46	243	9	9	0	2.4	.966
CF	L. Moseby	502	.221	11	43	288	3	4	1	2.5	.986
LF	G. Bell	613	.297	18	104	258	4	10	1	2.0	.963
C	E. Whitt	385	.262	11	53	550	43	5	5	5.2	.992
DH	R. Mulliniks	273	.238	3	29						
UT	M. Lee	300	.260	3	34	152	201	11	51		.970
C	P. Borders	241	.257	3	29	261	27	6	1	4.3	.980
OF	M. Wilson	238	.298	2	17	111	2	1	1	2.1	.991

Pitcher	G	IP	W	L	SV	ERA
J. Key	33	216	13	14	0	3.88
D. Stieb	33	207	17	8	0	3.35
J. Cerutti	33	205	11	11	0	3.07
M. Flanagan	30	172	8	10	0	3.93
T. Stottlemyre	27	128	7	7	0	3.88
D. Ward	66	115	4	10	15	3.77
T. Henke	64	89	8	3	20	1.92
D. Wells	54	86	7	4	2	2.40

Baltimore

W-87 L-75

Frank Robinson

POS	Player	AB	BA	HR	RBI	PO	A	E	DP	TC/G	FA
1B	R. Milligan	365	.268	12	45	914	83	5	92	8.6	.995
2B	B. Ripken	318	.239	2	26	255	335	9	81	5.3	.985
SS	C. Ripken	646	.257	21	93	**276**	**531**	8	**119**	5.0	.990
3B	C. Worthington	497	.247	15	70	113	277	20	22	2.8	.951
RF	J. Orsulak	390	.285	7	55	250	10	4	2	2.4	.985
CF	M. Devereaux	391	.266	8	46	288	1	5	0	2.6	.983
LF	P. Bradley	545	.277	11	55	284	4	3	0	2.1	.990
C	M. Tettleton	411	.258	26	65	297	42	2	1	4.5	.994
DH	L. Sheets	304	.243	7	33						
C	B. Melvin	278	.241	1	32	303	20	3	1	4.3	.991
OF	B. Anderson	266	.207	4	16	191	3	3	0	2.5	.985
1B	J. Traber	234	.209	4	26	514	54	1	59	8.2	.998
OF	S. Finley	217	.249	2	25	144	1	2	0	1.9	.986
2B	R. Gonzales	166	.217	1	11	93	125	5	35	4.1	.978
OF	S. Jefferson	127	.260	4	20	79	3	1	1	2.6	.988

Pitcher	G	IP	W	L	SV	ERA
B. Milacki	37	243	14	12	0	3.74
J. Ballard	35	215	18	8	0	3.43
D. Schmidt	38	157	10	13	0	5.69
B. Holton	39	116	5	7	0	4.02
M. Williamson	65	107	10	5	9	2.93
P. Harnisch	18	103	5	9	0	4.62
M. Thurmond	49	90	2	4	4	3.90
D. Johnson	14	89	4	7	0	4.23
G. Olson	64	85	5	2	27	1.69

Boston

W-83 L-79

Joe Morgan

POS	Player	AB	BA	HR	RBI	PO	A	E	DP	TC/G	FA
1B	N. Esasky	564	.277	30	108	1317	107	6	129	9.3	.996
2B	M. Barrett	336	.256	1	27	152	245	10	53	5.1	.975
SS	L. Rivera	323	.257	5	29	126	240	16	59	4.2	.958
3B	W. Boggs	621	.330	3	54	**123**	264	17	**29**	2.7	.958
RF	D. Evans	520	.285	20	100	153	5	3	1	2.1	.981
CF	E. Burks	399	.303	12	61	245	7	6	3	2.7	.977
LF	M. Greenwell	578	.308	14	95	220	11	8	1	1.7	.967
C	R. Cerone	296	.243	4	48	578	41	10	5	**6.5**	.984
DH	J. Rice	209	.234	3	28						
S2	J. Reed	524	.288	3	40	250	422	19	88		.973
OF	D. Heep	320	.300	5	49	92	2	1	1	1.3	.989
OF	K. Romine	274	.274	1	23	157	9	3	4	1.9	.982
C	R. Gedman	260	.212	4	16	486	36	10	6	5.8	.981

Pitcher	G	IP	W	L	SV	ERA
R. Clemens	35	253	17	11	0	3.13
M. Boddicker	34	212	15	11	0	4.00
J. Dopson	29	169	12	8	0	3.99
M. Smithson	40	144	7	14	2	4.95
D. Lamp	42	112	4	2	2	2.32
R. Murphy	74	105	5	7	9	2.74
W. Gardner	22	86	3	7	0	5.97
B. Stanley	43	79	5	2	4	4.88
L. Smith	64	71	6	1	25	3.57

Milwaukee

W-81 L-81

Tom Trebelhorn

POS	Player	AB	BA	HR	RBI	PO	A	E	DP	TC/G	FA
1B	G. Brock	373	.265	12	52	850	58	5	86	9.1	.995
2B	J. Gantner	409	.274	0	34	241	362	8	88	5.4	.987
SS	B. Spiers	345	.255	4	33	138	264	16	57	4.7	.962
3B	P. Molitor	615	.315	11	56	78	243	17	18	3.0	.950
RF	R. Deer	466	.210	26	65	267	10	8	1	2.3	.972
CF	R. Yount	614	.318	21	103	361	8	7	2	2.6	.981
LF	G. Braggs	514	.247	15	66	267	6	8	1	2.1	.972
C	B. Surhoff	436	.248	5	55	526	51	9	6	5.5	.985
DH	J. Meyer	147	.224	7	29						
SS	G. Sheffield	368	.247	5	32	85	194	12	40	4.2	.959
OF	M. Felder	315	.241	3	23	191	8	3	3	2.2	.985
UT	T. Francona	233	.232	3	23	339	26	4	32		.989
C	C. O'Brien	188	.234	6	35	314	36	5	5	5.7	.986
UT	G. Polidor	175	.194	0	14	78	123	12	20		.944
OD	G. Vaughn	113	.265	5	23	32	1	2	0		.943

Pitcher	G	IP	W	L	SV	ERA
C. Bosio	33	235	15	10	0	2.95
D. August	31	142	12	12	0	5.31
T. Higuera	22	135	9	6	0	3.46
M. Knudson	40	124	8	5	0	3.35
C. Crim	**76**	118	9	7	7	2.83
J. Navarro	19	110	7	8	0	3.12
T. Filer	13	72	7	3	0	3.61
D. Plesac	52	61	3	4	33	2.35

AMERICAN LEAGUE 1989, *cont.*

New York

W-74 L-87

Dallas Green
W-56 L-65

Bucky Dent
W-18 L-22

POS	Player	AB	BA	HR	RBI	PO	A	E	DP	TC/G	FA	Pitcher	G	IP	W	L	SV	ERA
1B	D. Mattingly	631	.303	23	113	1274	87	7	143	9.4	.995	A. Hawkins	34	208	15	15	0	4.80
2B	S. Sax	**651**	.315	5	63	312	460	10	**117**	4.9	**.987**	C. Parker	22	120	4	5	0	3.67
SS	A. Espinoza	503	.282	0	41	237	471	22	114	5.0	.970	D. LaPoint	20	114	6	9	0	5.62
3B	M. Pagliarulo	223	.197	4	16	25	122	10	6	2.3	.936	L. Guetterman	70	103	5	5	13	2.45
RF	J. Barfield	441	.240	18	56	297	16	9	3	2.5	.972	G. Cadaret	20	92	5	5	0	4.58
CF	R. Kelly	441	.302	9	48	353	9	6	2	2.7	.984	L. McCullers	52	85	4	3	3	4.57
LF	R. Henderson	235	.247	3	22	144	3	1	0	2.3	.993	W. Terrell	13	83	6	5	0	5.20
C	D. Slaught	350	.251	5	38	493	44	5	8	5.2	.991	E. Plunk	27	76	7	5	0	3.69
DH	S. Balboni	300	.237	17	59							D. Righetti	55	69	2	6	25	3.00
OD	M. Hall	361	.260	17	58	141	3	1	2		.993							
OF	L. Polonia	227	.313	2	29	105	6	2	1	2.1	.982							
C	B. Geren	205	.288	9	27	308	24	3	4	5.6	.991							
DH	K. Phelps	185	.249	7	29													
3B	T. Brookens	168	.226	4	14	17	70	7	4	1.8	.926							

Cleveland

W-73 L-89

Doc Edwards
W-65 L-78

John Hart
W-8 L-11

POS	Player	AB	BA	HR	RBI	PO	A	E	DP	TC/G	FA	Pitcher	G	IP	W	L	SV	ERA
1B	P. O'Brien	554	.260	12	55	1359	114	9	111	9.6	.994	B. Black	33	222	12	11	0	3.36
2B	J. Browne	598	.299	5	45	305	380	15	67	4.6	.979	J. Farrell	31	208	9	14	0	3.63
SS	F. Fermin	484	.238	0	21	247	512	**26**	84	5.1	.967	T. Candiotti	31	206	13	10	0	3.10
3B	B. Jacoby	519	.272	13	64	92	268	17	15	2.6	.955	G. Swindell	28	184	13	6	0	3.37
RF	C. Snyder	489	.215	18	59	291	18	1	5	2.5	.997	S. Bailes	34	114	5	9	0	4.28
CF	J. Carter	**651**	.243	35	105	350	6	8	3	2.5	.978	R. Yett	32	99	5	6	0	5.00
LF	O. McDowell	239	.222	3	22	124	5	1	1	2.0	.992	D. Jones	59	81	7	10	32	2.34
C	A. Allanson	323	.232	3	17	570	53	9	4	5.7	.986	J. Orosco	69	78	3	4	3	2.08
DH	D. Clark	253	.237	8	29							R. Nichols	15	72	4	6	0	4.40
OD	D. James	245	.306	4	29	82	1	2	0		.976							
OF	A. Belle	218	.225	7	37	92	3	2	1	2.2	.979							
OF	B. Komminsk	198	.237	8	33	181	3	1	1	2.7	.995							
C	J. Skinner	178	.230	1	13	280	22	3	1	3.9	.990							

Detroit

W-59 L-103

Sparky Anderson

POS	Player	AB	BA	HR	RBI	PO	A	E	DP	TC/G	FA	Pitcher	G	IP	W	L	SV	ERA
1B	D. Bergman	385	.268	7	37	912	85	7	88	8.2	.993	F. Tanana	33	224	10	14	0	3.58
2B	L. Whitaker	509	.251	28	85	**327**	393	11	99	5.0	.985	D. Alexander	33	223	6	**18**	0	4.44
SS	A. Trammell	449	.243	5	43	188	396	9	71	5.1	.985	J. Morris	24	170	6	14	0	4.86
3B	R. Schu	266	.214	7	21	52	119	12	11	2.2	.934	P. Gibson	45	132	4	8	0	4.64
RF	C. Lemon	414	.237	7	47	189	6	3	0	1.8	.985	M. Henneman	60	90	11	4	8	3.70
CF	G. Pettis	444	.257	1	18	325	1	4	0	2.8	.988	K. Ritz	12	74	4	6	0	4.38
LF	F. Lynn	353	.241	11	46	119	5	1	0	1.8	.992	G. Hernandez	32	31	2	2	15	5.74
C	M. Heath	396	.263	10	43	582	**66**	9	**10**	5.6	.986							
DH	K. Moreland	318	.299	5	35													
UT	G. Ward	275	.251	9	29	227	16	3	15		.988							
CD	M. Nokes	268	.250	9	39	235	26	6	3		.978							
OF	K. Williams	258	.205	6	23	180	11	4	3	2.2	.979							
UT	M. Brumley	212	.198	1	11	80	160	12	24		.952							
3B	D. Strange	196	.214	1	14	33	96	18	11	2.7	.878							
OF	T. Jones	158	.259	3	26	72	0	1	0	2.0	.986							

West

Oakland

W-99 L-63

Tony LaRussa

POS	Player	AB	BA	HR	RBI	PO	A	E	DP	TC/G	FA	Pitcher	G	IP	W	L	SV	ERA
1B	M. McGwire	490	.231	33	95	1170	114	6	122	9.1	.995	D. Stewart	36	258	21	9	0	3.32
2B	T. Phillips	451	.262	4	47	140	252	6	46	4.7	.985	M. Moore	35	242	19	11	0	2.61
SS	M. Gallego	357	.252	3	30	152	255	14	68	4.5	.967	B. Welch	33	210	17	8	0	3.00
3B	C. Lansford	551	.336	2	52	104	183	13	11	2.2	.957	S. Davis	31	169	19	7	0	4.36
RF	S. Javier	310	.248	1	28	219	4	2	0	2.1	.991	C. Young	25	111	5	9	0	3.73
CF	D. Henderson	579	.250	15	80	385	5	9	1	2.7	.977	T. Burns	50	96	6	5	8	2.24
LF	R. Henderson	306	.294	9	35	191	3	3	1	2.4	.985	G. Nelson	50	80	3	5	3	3.26
C	T. Steinbach	454	.273	7	42	529	43	9	6	5.6	.985	R. Honeycutt	64	77	2	2	12	2.35
DH	D. Parker	553	.264	22	97							D. Eckersley	51	58	4	0	33	1.56
C	R. Hassey	268	.228	5	23	421	25	4	4	5.8	.991							
SS	W. Weiss	236	.233	3	21	106	195	15	44	3.8	.953							
OF	J. Canseco	227	.269	17	57	119	5	3	2	2.3	.976							
OF	L. Polonia	206	.286	1	17	126	3	2	1	2.4	.985							

Kansas City

W-92 L-70

John Wathan

POS	Player	AB	BA	HR	RBI	PO	A	E	DP	TC/G	FA	Pitcher	G	IP	W	L	SV	ERA
1B	G. Brett	457	.282	12	80	896	80	2	71	9.4	.998	B. Saberhagen	36	**262**	**23**	6	0	**2.16**
2B	F. White	418	.256	2	36	238	407	10	64	5.0	.985	M. Gubicza	36	255	15	11	0	3.04
SS	K. Stillwell	463	.261	7	54	179	334	16	65	4.1	.970	T. Gordon	49	163	17	9	1	3.64
3B	K. Seitzer	597	.281	4	48	112	272	20	28	2.5	.950	C. Leibrandt	33	161	5	11	0	5.14
RF	D. Tartabull	441	.268	18	62	108	3	2	0	1.6	.982	L. Aquino	34	141	6	8	0	3.50
CF	W. Wilson	383	.253	3	43	252	2	6	0	2.4	.977	J. Montgomery	63	92	7	3	18	1.37
LF	B. Jackson	515	.256	32	105	224	11	8	2	2.2	.967	T. Leach	30	74	5	6	0	4.15
C	B. Boone	405	.274	1	43	**752**	64	7	6	6.4	.991	S. Farr	51	63	2	5	18	4.12
DH	P. Tabler	390	.259	2	42													
OF	J. Eisenreich	475	.293	9	59	273	4	3	0	2.3	.989							
2S	B. Wellman	178	.230	2	12	104	184	2	42		.993							
1D	B. Buckner	176	.216	1	16	181	13	3	19		.985							

California

W-91 L-71

Doug Rader

POS	Player	AB	BA	HR	RBI	PO	A	E	DP	TC/G	FA	Pitcher	G	IP	W	L	SV	ERA
1B	W. Joyner	593	.282	16	79	**1487**	99	4	146	10.0	**.997**	B. Blyleven	33	241	17	5	0	2.73
2B	J. Ray	530	.289	5	62	279	403	11	98	5.3	.984	M. Witt	33	220	9	15	0	4.54
SS	D. Schofield	302	.228	4	26	118	276	7	56	4.5	.983	K. McCaskill	32	212	15	10	0	2.93
3B	J. Howell	474	.228	20	52	95	**322**	11	27	3.0	**.974**	C. Finley	29	200	16	9	0	2.57
RF	C. Washington	418	.273	13	42	187	6	5	2	2.0	.975	J. Abbott	29	181	12	12	0	3.92
CF	D. White	636	.245	12	56	430	10	5	3	2.9	.989	W. Fraser	44	92	4	7	2	3.24
LF	C. Davis	560	.271	22	90	270	5	6	0	1.9	.979	G. Minton	62	90	4	3	8	2.20
C	L. Parrish	433	.238	17	50	638	63	5	7	5.8	.993	B. Harvey	51	55	3	3	25	3.44
DH	B. Downing	544	.283	14	59							B. McClure	48	52	6	1	3	1.55
SS	K. Anderson	223	.229	0	17	96	215	9	52	4.6	.972							
OF	T. Armas	202	.257	11	30	97	4	1	1	2.2	.990							

AMERICAN LEAGUE 1989, *cont.*

Texas

W-83 L-79

Bobby Valentine

POS	Player	AB	BA	HR	RBI	PO	A	E	DP	TC/G	FA	Pitcher	G	IP	W	L	SV	ERA
1B	R. Palmeiro	559	.275	8	64	1167	**119**	12	106	8.8	.991	N. Ryan	32	239	16	10	0	3.20
2B	J. Franco	548	.316	13	92	256	386	13	70	4.7	.980	B. Witt	31	194	12	13	0	5.14
SS	S. Fletcher	314	.239	0	22	124	190	13	45	4.0	.960	K. Brown	28	191	12	9	0	3.35
3B	S. Buechele	486	.235	16	59	106	264	12	22	2.6	.969	C. Hough	30	182	10	13	0	4.35
RF	R. Sierra	634	.306	29	**119**	313	13	9	2	2.1	.973	M. Jeffcoat	22	131	9	6	0	3.58
CF	C. Espy	475	.257	3	31	281	5	3	2	2.2	.990	J. Moyer	15	76	4	9	0	4.86
LF	P. Incaviglia	453	.236	21	81	213	7	6	2	1.8	.973	J. Russell	71	73	6	4	**38**	1.98
C	C. Kreuter	158	.152	5	9	453	26	4	4	5.7	.992	C. Guante	50	69	6	6	2	3.91
DH	H. Baines	172	.285	3	16													
UT	J. Kunkel	293	.270	8	29	143	168	22	27		.934							
DO	R. Leach	239	.272	1	23	57	1	3	0		.951							
S2	F. Manrique	191	.288	2	22	76	112	10	28		.949							
C	G. Petralli	184	.304	4	23	258	15	3	3	5.6	.989							

Minnesota

W-80 L-82

Tom Kelly

POS	Player	AB	BA	HR	RBI	PO	A	E	DP	TC/G	FA	Pitcher	G	IP	W	L	SV	ERA
1B	K. Hrbek	375	.272	25	84	723	60	4	66	8.8	.995	A. Anderson	33	197	17	10	0	3.80
2B	W. Backman	299	.231	1	26	146	187	6	37	4.0	.982	F. Viola	24	176	8	12	0	3.79
SS	G. Gagne	460	.272	9	48	218	389	18	66	4.3	.971	R. Smith	32	172	10	6	1	3.92
3B	G. Gaetti	498	.251	19	75	104	251	10	23	2.9	.973	S. Rawley	27	145	5	12	0	5.21
RF	R. Bush	391	.263	14	54	200	7	3	1	1.9	.986	J. Berenguer	56	106	9	3	3	3.48
CF	K. Puckett	635	**.339**	9	85	438	13	4	3	2.9	.991	J. Reardon	65	73	5	4	31	4.07
LF	D. Gladden	461	.295	8	46	245	8	9	3	2.2	.966	M. Dyer	16	71	4	7	0	4.82
C	B. Harper	385	.325	8	57	456	35	**11**	7	5.0	.978							
DH	J. Dwyer	225	.316	3	23													
UT	A. Newman	446	.253	0	38	191	282	16	58		.967							
UT	G. Larkin	446	.267	6	46	524	28	4	45		.993							
OF	J. Moses	242	.281	1	31	156	3	2	0	1.5	.988							
UT	T. Laudner	239	.222	6	27	347	16	3	5		.992							
OF	C. Castillo	218	.257	8	33	119	3	3	1	1.9	.976							

Seattle

W-73 L-89

Jim Lefebvre

POS	Player	AB	BA	HR	RBI	PO	A	E	DP	TC/G	FA	Pitcher	G	IP	W	L	SV	ERA
1B	A. Davis	498	.305	21	95	1106	81	10	119	9.6	.992	S. Bankhead	33	210	14	6	0	3.34
2B	H. Reynolds	613	.300	0	43	311	**506**	**17**	109	**5.5**	.980	B. Holman	23	160	8	10	0	3.44
SS	O. Vizquel	387	.220	1	20	208	388	18	102	4.3	.971	R. Johnson	22	131	7	9	0	4.40
3B	J. Presley	390	.236	12	41	54	154	17	13	2.5	.924	B. Swift	37	130	7	3	1	4.43
RF	D. Coles	535	.252	10	59	184	9	5	3	2.2	.975	E. Hanson	17	113	9	5	0	3.18
CF	K. Griffey	455	.264	16	61	302	12	10	6	2.6	.969	J. Reed	52	102	7	7	0	3.19
LF	G. Briley	394	.266	13	52	179	5	8	1	1.8	.958	M. Jackson	65	99	4	6	7	3.17
C	D. Valle	316	.237	7	34	496	52	4	3	5.9	.993	M. Dunne	15	85	2	9	0	5.27
DH	J. Leonard	566	.254	24	93							M. Schooler	67	77	1	7	33	2.81
OF	H. Cotto	295	.264	9	33	153	9	2	3	1.8	.988							
C	S. Bradley	270	.274	3	37	388	25	3	4	5.9	.993							
OF	J. Buhner	204	.275	9	33	106	6	4	3	2.0	.966							
3B	E. Martinez	171	.240	2	20	40	72	6	9	1.9	.949							

Chicago

W-69 L-92

Jeff Torborg

POS	Player	AB	BA	HR	RBI	PO	A	E	DP	TC/G	FA	Pitcher	G	IP	W	L	SV	ERA
1B	G. Walker	233	.210	5	26	373	17	5	38	8.2	.987	M. Perez	31	183	11	14	0	5.01
2B	S. Lyons	443	.264	2	50	142	185	6	46	4.8	.982	E. King	25	159	9	10	0	3.39
SS	O. Guillen	597	.253	1	54	272	512	22	106	5.2	.973	S. Rosenberg	38	142	4	13	0	4.94
3B	C. Martinez	350	.300	5	32	45	121	16	12	2.7	.912	G. Hibbard	23	137	6	7	0	3.21
RF	I. Calderon	622	.286	14	87	217	8	5	3	2.2	.978	S. Hillegas	50	120	7	11	3	4.74
CF	D. Gallagher	601	.266	1	46	390	8	3	4	2.5	.993	J. Reuss	23	107	8	5	0	5.06
LF	D. Boston	218	.252	5	23	134	2	4	0	1.9	.971	R. Dotson	17	100	3	7	0	3.88
C	C. Fisk	375	.293	13	68	419	37	3	1	5.1	**.993**	B. Long	30	99	5	5	1	3.92
DH	H. Baines	333	.321	13	56							D. Pall	53	87	4	5	6	3.31
OF	D. Pasqua	246	.248	11	47	149	3	1	2	2.3	.993	B. Thigpen	61	79	2	6	34	3.76
2B	S. Fletcher	232	.272	1	21	108	161	0	38	5.1	1.000							
3B	E. Williams	201	.274	3	10	37	123	16	21	2.7	.909							
2B	F. Manrique	187	.299	2	30	94	127	9	30	4.0	.961							
C	R. Karkovice	182	.264	3	24	299	47	5	6	5.2	.986							
OF	L. Johnson	180	.300	0	16	113	0	2	0	2.6	.983							
UT	R. Kittle	169	.302	11	37	216	12	4	28		.983							

BATTING AND BASE RUNNING LEADERS

Batting Average

K. Puckett, MIN	.339
C. Lansford, OAK	.336
W. Boggs, BOS	.330
R. Yount, MIL	.318
J. Franco, TEX	.316

Slugging Average

R. Sierra, TEX	.543
F. McGriff, TOR	.525
R. Yount, MIL	.511
N. Esasky, BOS	.500
A. Davis, SEA	.496

Home Runs

F. McGriff, TOR	36
J. Carter, CLE	35
M. McGwire, OAK	33
B. Jackson, KC	32
N. Esasky, BOS	30

Total Bases

R. Sierra, TEX	344
R. Yount, MIL	314
J. Carter, CLE	303
D. Mattingly, NY	301
K. Puckett, MIN	295

Runs Batted In

R. Sierra, TEX	119
D. Mattingly, NY	113
N. Esasky, BOS	108
B. Jackson, KC	105
J. Carter, CLE	105

Stolen Bases

R. Henderson, NY, OAK	77
C. Espy, TEX	45
D. White, CAL	44
G. Pettis, DET	43
S. Sax, NY	43

Hits

K. Puckett, MIN	215
W. Boggs, BOS	205
S. Sax, NY	205
R. Yount, MIL	195

Base on Balls

R. Henderson, NY, OAK	126
F. McGriff, TOR	119
W. Boggs, BOS	107
K. Seitzer, KC	102

Home Run Percentage

M. McGwire, OAK	6.7
F. McGriff, TOR	6.5
B. Jackson, KC	6.2
R. Deer, MIL	5.6

PITCHING LEADERS

Winning Percentage

B. Saberhagen, KC	.793
B. Blyleven, CAL	.773
S. Davis, OAK	.731
D. Stewart, OAK	.700
J. Ballard, BAL	.692

Earned Run Average

B. Saberhagen, KC	2.16
C. Finley, CAL	2.57
M. Moore, OAK	2.61
B. Blyleven, CAL	2.73
K. McCaskill, CAL	2.93

Wins

B. Saberhagen, KC	23
D. Stewart, OAK	21
S. Davis, OAK	19
M. Moore, OAK	19
J. Ballard, BAL	18

Saves

J. Russell, TEX	38
B. Thigpen, CHI	34
D. Eckersley, OAK	33
D. Plesac, MIL	33
M. Schooler, SEA	33

Strikeouts

N. Ryan, TEX	301
R. Clemens, BOS	230
B. Saberhagen, KC	193
C. Bosio, MIL	173
M. Gubicza, KC	173

Complete Games

B. Saberhagen, KC	12
J. Morris, DET	10
C. Finley, CAL	9

Fewest Hits/9 Innings

N. Ryan, TEX	6.09
T. Gordon, KC	6.74
D. Stieb, TOR	7.14
B. Saberhagen, KC	7.17

Shutouts

B. Blyleven, CAL	5
K. McCaskill, CAL	4
B. Saberhagen, KC	4

Fewest Walks/9 Innings

J. Key, TOR	1.13
B. Saberhagen, KC	1.48
B. Blyleven, CAL	1.64
C. Bosio, MIL	1.84

AMERICAN LEAGUE 1989, *cont.*

BATTING AND BASE RUNNING LEADERS

Runs		Doubles		Triples	
R. Henderson, NY, OAK	113	W. Boggs, BOS	51	R. Sierra, TEX	14
W. Boggs, BOS	113	K. Puckett, MIN	45	D. White, CAL	13
R. Yount, MIL	101	J. Reed, BOS	42	P. Bradley, BAL	10
R. Sierra, TEX	101	G. Bell, TOR	41		

PITCHING LEADERS

Most Strikeouts/9 Inn.		Innings		Games Pitched	
N. Ryan, TEX	11.32	B. Saberhagen, KC	262	C. Crim, MIL	76
T. Gordon, KC	8.45	D. Stewart, OAK	258	R. Murphy, BOS	74
R. Clemens, BOS	8.17	M. Gubicza, KC	255	K. Rogers, TEX	73
B. Witt, TEX	7.69	R. Clemens, BOS	253	J. Russell, TEX	71

		W	L	PCT	GB	R	OR	Batting 2B	3B	HR	BA	SA	SB	Fielding E	DP	FA	Pitching CG	BB	SO	ShO	SV	ERA
East	Toronto	89	73	.549		731	651	265	40	142	.260	.398	144	127	164	.980	12	478	849	5	38	3.58
	Baltimore	87	75	.537	2	708	686	238	33	129	.252	.379	118	**87**	163	**.986**	16	486	676	3	44	4.00
	Boston	83	79	.512	6	**774**	735	**326**	30	108	**.277**	**.403**	56	127	162	.980	14	548	1054	6	42	4.01
	Milwaukee	81	81	.500	8	707	679	235	32	126	.259	.382	**165**	155	164	.975	16	457	812	4	45	3.80
	New York	74	87	.460	14.5	698	792	229	23	130	.269	.391	137	122	**183**	.980	15	521	787	4	44	4.50
	Cleveland	73	89	.451	16	604	654	221	26	127	.245	.365	74	118	126	.981	23	**452**	844	7	38	3.65
	Detroit	59	103	.364	30	617	816	198	24	116	.242	.351	103	130	153	.979	24	652	831	3	26	4.53
West	Oakland	99	63	.611		712	**576**	220	25	127	.261	.381	157	129	159	.979	17	510	930	3	**57**	**3.09**
	Kansas City	92	70	.568	7	690	635	227	41	101	.261	.373	154	114	139	.982	27	455	978	9	38	3.55
	California	91	71	.562	8	669	578	208	37	**145**	.256	.386	89	96	173	.985	**32**	465	897	**12**	38	3.28
	Texas	83	79	.512	16	695	714	260	**46**	122	.263	.394	101	136	137	.978	26	654	**1112**	6	44	3.91
	Minnesota	80	82	.494	19	740	738	278	35	117	.276	.402	111	107	141	.982	19	500	851	2	38	4.28
	Seattle	73	89	.451	26	694	728	237	29	134	.257	.384	81	143	168	.977	15	560	897	5	44	4.00
	Chicago	69	92	.429	29.5	693	750	262	36	94	.271	.383	97	151	176	.975	9	539	778	2	46	4.23
						9732	9732	3404	457	1718	.261	.384	1587	1742	2208	.980	265	7277	12296	71	582	3.89

NATIONAL LEAGUE 1990

East

Pittsburgh

W-95 L-67

Jim Leyland

POS	Player	AB	BA	HR	RBI	PO	A	E	DP	TC/G	FA	Pitcher	G	IP	W	L	SV	ERA
1B	S. Bream	389	.270	15	67	971	104	8	80	7.6	.993	D. Drabek	33	231	**22**	6	0	2.76
2B	J. Lind	514	.261	1	48	**330**	449	7	74	5.2	.991	J. Smiley	26	149	9	10	0	4.64
SS	J. Bell	583	.254	7	52	**260**	459	22	85	4.7	.970	N. Heaton	30	146	12	9	0	3.45
3B	J. King	371	.245	14	53	58	215	18	15	2.5	.938	B. Walk	26	130	7	5	1	3.75
RF	B. Bonilla	625	.280	32	120	289	8	12	1	2.1	.961	B. Patterson	55	95	8	5	5	2.95
CF	A. Van Slyke	493	.284	17	77	326	6	8	0	2.6	.976	B. Landrum	54	72	7	3	13	2.13
LF	B. Bonds	519	.301	33	114	338	14	6	2	2.4	.983	B. Kipper	41	63	5	2	3	3.02
C	M. LaValliere	279	.258	3	31	478	36	5	6	5.5	.990	S. Belinda	55	58	3	4	8	3.55
3B	W. Backman	315	.292	2	28	34	104	12	5	2.1	.920	T. Power	40	52	1	3	7	3.66
C	D. Slaught	230	.300	4	29	345	36	8	4	5.0	.979							
1B	G. Redus	227	.247	6	23	447	35	6	29	6.8	.988							
OF	R. Reynolds	215	.288	0	19	102	3	3	0	1.8	.972							

New York

W-91 L-71

Davey Johnson
W-20 L-22

Bud Harrelson
W-71 L-49

POS	Player	AB	BA	HR	RBI	PO	A	E	DP	TC/G	FA	Pitcher	G	IP	W	L	SV	ERA
1B	D. Magadan	451	.328	6	72	830	71	2	52	8.0	**.998**	F. Viola	35	**250**	20	12	0	2.67
2B	G. Jefferies	604	.283	15	68	219	278	12	49	4.3	.976	D. Gooden	34	233	19	7	0	3.83
SS	K. Elster	314	.207	9	45	159	251	17	42	4.6	.960	D. Cone	31	212	14	10	0	3.23
3B	H. Johnson	590	.244	23	90	52	159	20	11	2.5	.913	S. Fernandez	30	179	9	14	0	3.46
RF	D. Strawberry	542	.277	37	108	268	10	3	4	1.9	.989	R. Darling	33	126	7	9	0	4.50
CF	D. Boston	366	.273	12	45	203	3	3	1	1.9	.986	B. Ojeda	38	118	7	6	0	3.66
LF	K. McReynolds	521	.269	24	82	237	14	3	2	1.8	.988	A. Pena	52	76	3	3	5	3.20
C	M. Sasser	270	.307	6	41	498	43	**14**	4	6.4	.975	J. Franco	55	68	5	3	**33**	2.53
OF	K. Miller	233	.258	1	12	146	1	3	1	2.5	.980							
OF	M. Carreon	188	.250	10	26	87	1	0	0	1.5	1.000							
UT	T. Teufel	175	.246	10	24	141	58	4	16		.980							
1B	M. Marshall	163	.239	6	27	277	24	2	19	7.2	.993							

Montreal

W-85 L-77

Buck Rodgers

POS	Player	AB	BA	HR	RBI	PO	A	E	DP	TC/G	FA	Pitcher	G	IP	W	L	SV	ERA
1B	A. Galarraga	579	.256	20	87	1300	94	10	93	9.1	.993	D. Martinez	32	226	10	11	0	2.95
2B	D. DeShields	499	.289	4	45	236	371	12	65	4.8	.981	O. Boyd	31	191	10	6	0	2.93
SS	S. Owen	453	.234	5	35	216	340	6	52	3.8	**.989**	K. Gross	31	163	9	12	0	4.57
3B	T. Wallach	626	.296	21	98	128	309	21	23	2.8	.954	M. Gardner	27	153	7	9	0	3.42
RF	L. Walker	419	.241	19	51	249	12	4	5	2.1	.985	Z. Smith	22	139	6	7	0	3.23
CF	D. Martinez	391	.279	11	39	257	6	3	1	2.5	.989	B. Sampen	59	90	12	7	2	2.99
LF	T. Raines	457	.287	9	62	239	3	6	1	2.0	.976	T. Burke	58	75	3	3	20	2.52
C	M. Fitzgerald	313	.243	9	41	560	41	6	**10**	6.2	.990	D. Hall	42	58	4	7	3	5.09
OF	M. Grissom	288	.257	3	29	165	5	2	0	2.0	.988	S. Frey	51	56	8	2	9	2.10
OF	O. Nixon	231	.251	1	20	149	5	1	0	1.8	.994	D. Schmidt	34	48	3	3	13	4.31
UT	T. Foley	164	.213	0	12	80	123	5	26		.976							
C	N. Santovenia	163	.190	6	28	264	24	6	7	5.8	.980							

Chicago

W-77 L-85

Don Zimmer

POS	Player	AB	BA	HR	RBI	PO	A	E	DP	TC/G	FA	Pitcher	G	IP	W	L	SV	ERA
1B	M. Grace	589	.309	9	82	1324	**180**	12	116	9.9	.992	G. Maddux	35	237	15	15	0	3.46
2B	R. Sandberg	615	.306	**40**	100	278	**469**	8	81	4.9	.989	M. Harkey	27	174	12	6	0	3.26
SS	S. Dunston	545	.262	17	66	255	392	20	77	4.6	.970	M. Bielecki	36	168	8	11	1	4.93
3B	L. Salazar	410	.254	12	47	55	136	10	12	2.2	.950	S. Wilson	45	139	4	9	1	4.79
RF	A. Dawson	529	.310	27	100	250	10	5	4	1.9	.981	L. Lancaster	55	109	9	5	6	4.62
CF	J. Walton	392	.263	2	21	247	3	6	0	2.6	.977	P. Assenmacher	74	103	7	2	10	2.80
LF	D. Dascenzo	241	.253	1	26	174	2	0	1	1.6	1.000	S. Boskie	15	98	5	6	0	3.69
C	J. Girardi	419	.270	1	38	653	61	11	5	5.5	.985	J. Pico	31	92	4	4	2	4.79
OF	D. Smith	290	.262	6	27	139	4	2	2	1.8	.986	M. Williams	59	66	1	8	16	3.93
3B	D. Ramos	226	.265	2	17	23	46	5	2	1.1	.932	J. Nunez	21	61	4	7	0	6.53
OF	M. Wynne	186	.204	4	19	108	3	1	2	1.7	.991	B. Long	42	56	6	1	5	4.37
3B	C. Wilkerson	186	.220	0	16	25	62	11	4	1.9	.888							
OF	D. Clark	171	.275	5	20	60	2	0	0	1.6	1.000							

NATIONAL LEAGUE 1990, *cont.*

Philadelphia

W-77 L-85

Nick Leyva

POS	Player	AB	BA	HR	RBI	PO	A	E	DP	TC/G	FA	Pitcher	G	IP	W	L	SV	ERA
1B	R. Jordan	324	.241	5	44	743	37	4	65	9.3	.995	P. Combs	32	183	10	10	0	4.07
2B	T. Herr	447	.264	4	50	240	290	5	79*	4.7	.991	T. Mulholland	33	181	9	10	0	3.34
SS	D. Thon	552	.255	8	48	222	439	25	**86**	4.6	.964	B. Ruffin	32	149	6	13	0	5.38
3B	C. Hayes	561	.258	10	57	121	**324**	20	30	**3.2**	.957	D. Cook	42	142	8	3	1	3.56
RF	V. Hayes	467	.261	17	73	272	8	6	0	2.3	.979	J. DeJesus	22	130	7	8	0	3.74
CF	L. Dykstra	590	.325	9	60	439	7	6	5	3.0	.987	K. Howell	18	107	8	7	0	4.64
LF	J. Kruk	443	.291	7	67	141	2	2	0	1.7	.986	D. Akerfelds	71	93	5	2	3	3.77
C	D. Daulton	459	.268	12	57	683	**70**	8	**10**	5.5	.989	R. McDowell	72	86	6	8	22	3.86
O2	R. Ready	217	.244	1	26	78	86	2	18		.988	J. Parrett	47	82	4	9	1	5.18
OF	D. Murphy	214	.266	7	28	113	4	1	1	2.1	.992	J. Boever	34	46	2	3	6	2.15
1O	C. Martinez	198	.242	8	31	350	25	2	31		.995							

St. Louis

W-70 L-92

Whitey Herzog
W-33 L-47

Red Schoendienst
W-13 L-11

Joe Torre
W-24 L-34

POS	Player	AB	BA	HR	RBI	PO	A	E	DP	TC/G	FA	Pitcher	G	IP	W	L	SV	ERA
1B	P. Guerrero	498	.281	13	80	1083	73	**13**	74	8.9	.989	J. Magrane	31	203	10	17	0	3.59
2B	J. Oquendo	469	.252	1	37	285	393	3	65	4.5	**.996**	J. DeLeon	32	183	7	**19**	0	4.43
SS	O. Smith	512	.254	1	50	212	378	12	66	4.3	.980	J. Tudor	25	146	12	4	0	2.40
3B	T. Pendleton	447	.230	6	58	91	248	19	18	3.1	.947	B. Tewksbury	28	145	10	9	1	3.47
RF	M. Thompson	418	.218	6	30	232	4	7	0	2.1	.971	B. Smith	26	141	9	8	0	4.27
CF	W. McGee	501	.335*	3	62	341	13	16	4	3.0	.957	F. DiPino	62	81	5	2	3	4.56
LF	V. Coleman	497	.292	6	39	244	12	5	2	2.2	.981	K. Hill	17	79	5	6	0	5.49
C	T. Zeile	495	.244	15	57	533	56	7	3	5.7	.988	K. Dayley	58	73	4	4	2	3.56
C	T. Pagnozzi	220	.277	2	23	334	39	4	4	6.0	.989	S. Terry	50	72	2	6	2	4.75
UT	R. Hudler	217	.281	7	22	158	42	5	9		.976	L. Smith	53	69	3	4	27	2.10

West

Cincinnati

W-91 L-71

Lou Piniella

POS	Player	AB	BA	HR	RBI	PO	A	E	DP	TC/G	FA	Pitcher	G	IP	W	L	SV	ERA
1B	T. Benzinger	376	.253	5	46	707	52	6	58	8.1	.992	T. Browning	35	228	15	9	0	3.80
2B	M. Duncan	435	.306	10	55	245	287	15	51	4.8	.973	J. Rijo	29	197	14	8	0	2.70
SS	B. Larkin	614	.301	7	67	254	**469**	17	**86**	**4.7**	.977	J. Armstrong	29	166	12	9	0	3.42
3B	C. Sabo	567	.270	25	71	70	273	12	17	2.4	**.966**	N. Charlton	56	154	12	9	2	2.74
RF	P. O'Neill	503	.270	16	78	271	12	2	0	2.0	.993	R. Mahler	35	135	7	6	4	4.28
CF	E. Davis	453	.260	24	86	257	11	2	1	2.2	.993	D. Jackson	22	117	6	6	0	3.61
LF	B. Hatcher	504	.276	5	25	308	10	1	2	2.4	.997	R. Dibble	68	98	8	3	11	1.74
C	J. Oliver	364	.231	8	52	686	59	6	8	6.4	**.992**	R. Myers	66	87	4	6	31	2.08
1B	H. Morris	309	.340	7	36	589	53	3	50	8.1	.995	T. Layana	55	80	5	3	2	3.49
OF	G. Braggs	201	.299	6	28	110	10	4	3	2.1	.968	S. Scudder	21	72	5	5	0	4.90
C	J. Reed	175	.251	3	16	358	26	5	1	5.6	.987							

Los Angeles

W-86 L-76

Tom Lasorda

POS	Player	AB	BA	HR	RBI	PO	A	E	DP	TC/G	FA	Pitcher	G	IP	W	L	SV	ERA
1B	E. Murray	558	.330	26	95	1180	113	10	88	8.7	.992	R. Martinez	33	234	20	6	0	2.92
2B	J. Samuel	492	.242	13	52	194	258	13	47	4.3	.972	M. Morgan	33	211	11	15	0	3.75
SS	A. Griffin	461	.210	1	35	221	382	**26**	63	4.5	.959	F. Valenzuela	33	204	13	13	0	4.59
3B	M. Sharperson	357	.297	3	36	70	153	12	10	2.2	.949	T. Belcher	24	153	9	9	0	4.00
RF	H. Brooks	568	.266	20	91	255	9	10	2	1.8	.964	T. Crews	66	107	4	5	5	2.77
CF	S. Javier	276	.304	3	24	204	2	0	1	2.4	1.000	M. Hartley	32	79	6	3	1	2.95
LF	K. Daniels	450	.296	27	94	207	13	3	2	1.8	.987	J. Howell	45	66	5	5	16	2.18
C	M. Scioscia	435	.264	12	66	**842**	58	10	9	**6.9**	.989	J. Gott	50	62	3	5	3	2.90
32	L. Harris	431	.304	2	29	139	203	11	24		.969							
OF	K. Gibson	315	.260	8	38	191	4	1	1	2.4	.995							
OF	C. Gwynn	141	.284	5	22	39	1	0	0	0.9	1.000							

San Francisco

W-85 L-77

Roger Craig

POS	Player	AB	BA	HR	RBI	PO	A	E	DP	TC/G	FA	Pitcher	G	IP	W	L	SV	ERA
1B	W. Clark	600	.295	19	95	**1456**	119	12	**118**	**10.4**	.992	J. Burkett	33	204	14	7	1	3.79
2B	R. Thompson	498	.245	15	56	287	441	8	**94**	5.2	.989	S. Garrelts	31	182	12	11	0	4.15
SS	J. Uribe	415	.248	1	24	182	373	20	73	4.3	.965	D. Robinson	26	158	10	7	0	4.57
3B	M. Williams	617	.277	33	**122**	**140**	306	19	**33**	2.9	.959	T. Wilson	27	110	8	7	0	4.00
RF	M. Kingery	207	.295	0	24	126	7	3	2	1.4	.978	R. Reuschel	15	87	3	6	1	3.93
CF	B. Butler	622	.309	3	44	420	4	6	0	2.7	.986	J. Brantley	55	87	5	3	19	1.56
LF	K. Mitchell	524	.290	35	93	295	9	9	3	2.3	.971	S. Bedrosian	68	79	9	9	17	4.20
C	T. Kennedy	303	.277	2	26	390	38	4	3	4.2	.991	M. LaCoss	13	78	6	4	0	3.94
C	G. Carter	244	.254	9	27	323	31	3	2	4.5	.992							
OF	K. Bass	214	.252	7	32	88	2	3	0	1.7	.968							
UT	G. Litton	204	.245	1	24	90	43	1	10		.993							
OF	R. Leach	174	.293	2	16	86	3	1	0	1.7	.989							
UT	E. Riles	155	.200	8	21	53	105	3	14		.981							

Houston

W-75 L-87

Art Howe

POS	Player	AB	BA	HR	RBI	PO	A	E	DP	TC/G	FA	Pitcher	G	IP	W	L	SV	ERA
1B	G. Davis	327	.251	22	64	796	55	4	56	9.4	.995	J. Deshaies	34	209	7	12	0	3.78
2B	B. Doran	344	.288	6	32	170	265	5	43	4.4	.989	M. Scott	32	206	9	13	0	3.81
SS	R. Ramirez	445	.261	2	37	190	321	25	57	4.2	.953	M. Portugal	32	197	11	10	0	3.62
3B	K. Caminiti	541	.242	4	51	118	243	21	22	2.6	.945	B. Gullickson	32	193	10	14	0	3.82
RF	G. Wilson	368	.245	10	55	225	12	6	6	2.3	.975	D. Darwin	48	163	11	4	2	**2.21**
CF	E. Yelding	511	.254	1	28	230	5	7	2	2.6	.971	J. Agosto	**82**	92	9	8	4	4.29
LF	F. Stubbs	448	.261	23	71	112	1	1	0	1.6	.991	J. Clancy	33	76	2	8	1	6.51
C	C. Biggio	555	.276	4	42	546	54	9	4	5.4	.985	L. Andersen	50	74	5	2	6	1.95
UT	C. Candaele	262	.286	3	22	147	120	3	20		.989	D. Smith	49	60	6	6	23	2.39
OF	E. Anthony	239	.192	10	29	124	5	4	0	1.9	.970							

San Diego

W-75 L-87

Jack McKeon
W-37 L-43

Greg Riddoch
W-38 L-44

POS	Player	AB	BA	HR	RBI	PO	A	E	DP	TC/G	FA	Pitcher	G	IP	W	L	SV	ERA
1B	J. Clark	334	.266	25	62	855	69	6	72	8.5	.994	E. Whitson	32	229	14	9	0	2.60
2B	R. Alomar	586	.287	6	60	311	392	**17**	73	**5.3**	.976	B. Hurst	33	224	11	9	0	3.14
SS	G. Templeton	505	.248	9	59	214	367	**26**	74	4.5	.957	A. Benes	32	192	10	11	0	3.60
3B	M. Pagliarulo	398	.254	7	38	79	200	13	16	2.5	.955	D. Rasmussen	32	188	11	15	0	4.51
RF	T. Gwynn	573	.309	4	72	327	11	5	2	2.4	.985	G. Harris	73	117	8	8	9	2.30
CF	J. Carter	**634**	.232	24	115	385	13	5	4	2.7	.988	E. Show	39	106	6	8	1	5.76
LF	B. Roberts	556	.309	9	44	160	8	3	1	2.3	.982	C. Schiraldi	42	104	3	8	1	4.41
C	B. Santiago	344	.270	11	53	538	51	12	6	6.1	.980	C. Lefferts	56	79	7	5	23	2.52
OF	F. Lynn	196	.240	6	23	92	1	0	0	1.7	1.000							
C	M. Parent	189	.222	3	16	324	31	3	6	6.0	.992							
OF	S. Abner	184	.245	1	15	108	1	1	0	1.8	.991							
1B	P. Stephenson	182	.209	4	19	345	36	1	33	6.4	.997							

NATIONAL LEAGUE 1990, *cont.*

Team	POS	Player	AB	BA	HR	RBI	PO	A	E	DP	TC/G	FA	Pitcher	G	IP	W	L	SV	ERA
Atlanta	1B	D. Justice	439	.282	28	78	488	38	10	43	7.8	.981	J. Smoltz	34	231	14	11	0	3.85
	2B	J. Treadway	474	.283	11	59	241	360	15	72	5.0	.976	T. Glavine	33	214	10	12	0	4.28
	SS	J. Blauser	386	.269	8	39	141	257	16	47	4.5	.961	C. Leibrandt	24	162	9	11	0	3.16
W-65 L-97	3B	J. Presley	541	.242	19	72	101	231	**25**	19	2.7	.930	M. Clary	33	102	1	10	0	5.67
	RF	D. Murphy	349	.232	17	55	208	3	4	0	2.2	.981	S. Avery	21	99	3	11	0	5.64
Russ Nixon	CF	R. Gant	575	.303	32	84	357	7	8	2	2.5	.978	P. Smith	13	77	5	6	0	4.79
W-25 L-40	LF	L. Smith	466	.305	9	42	254	6	12	2	2.2	.956	D. Lilliquist	12	62	2	8	0	6.28
	C	G. Olson	298	.262	7	36	501	43	7	3	5.7	.987	K. Mercker	36	48	4	7	7	3.17
Bobby Cox	OF	O. McDowell	305	.243	7	25	134	2	4	0	1.9	.971	J. Boever	33	42	1	3	8	4.68
W-40 L-57	SS	A. Thomas	278	.219	5	30	103	193	10	41	4.3	.967							
	1B	T. Gregg	239	.264	5	32	334	34	5	31	7.5	.987							
	32	M. Lemke	239	.226	0	21	90	192	4	29		.986							
	C	E. Whitt	180	.172	2	10	296	42	3	1	5.8	.991							
	1B	F. Cabrera	137	.277	7	25	264	19	3	15	6.0	.990							

BATTING AND BASE RUNNING LEADERS

Batting Average
- W. McGee, STL .335
- E. Murray, LA .330
- D. Magadan, NY .328
- L. Dykstra, PHI .325
- A. Dawson, CHI .310

Slugging Average
- B. Bonds, PIT .565
- R. Sandberg, CHI .559
- K. Mitchell, SF .544
- R. Gant, ATL .539
- D. Justice, ATL .535

Home Runs
- R. Sandberg, CHI 40
- D. Strawberry, NY 37
- K. Mitchell, SF 35
- B. Bonds, PIT 33
- M. Williams, SF 33

Total Bases
- R. Sandberg, CHI 344
- B. Bonilla, PIT 324
- R. Gant, ATL 310
- M. Williams, SF 301
- T. Wallach, MON 295

Runs Batted In
- M. Williams, SF 122
- B. Bonilla, PIT 120
- J. Carter, SD 115
- B. Bonds, PIT 114
- D. Strawberry, NY 108

Stolen Bases
- V. Coleman, STL 77
- E. Yelding, HOU 64
- B. Bonds, PIT 52
- B. Butler, SF 51
- O. Nixon, MON 50

Hits
- L. Dykstra, PHI 192
- B. Butler, SF 192
- R. Sandberg, CHI 188
- B. Larkin, CIN 185
- T. Wallach, MON 185

Base on Balls
- J. Clark, SD 104
- B. Bonds, PIT 93
- B. Butler, SF 90
- L. Dykstra, PHI 89

Home Run Percentage
- D. Strawberry, NY 6.8
- K. Mitchell, SF 6.7
- R. Sandberg, CHI 6.5
- D. Justice, ATL 6.4

Runs
- R. Sandberg, CHI 116
- B. Bonilla, PIT 112
- B. Butler, SF 108
- R. Gant, ATL 107

Doubles
- G. Jefferies, NY 40
- B. Bonilla, PIT 39
- C. Sabo, CIN 38
- H. Johnson, NY 37
- T. Wallach, MON 37

Triples
- M. Duncan, CIN 11
- T. Gwynn, SD 10
- L. Smith, ATL 9
- V. Coleman, STL 9
- B. Butler, SF 9

PITCHING LEADERS

Winning Percentage
- D. Drabek, PIT .786
- R. Martinez, LA .769
- D. Gooden, NY .731
- F. Viola, NY .625
- T. Browning, CIN .625

Earned Run Average
- D. Darwin, HOU 2.21
- Z. Smith, MON, PIT 2.55
- E. Whitson, SD 2.60
- F. Viola, NY 2.67
- J. Rijo, CIN 2.70

Wins
- D. Drabek, PIT 22
- R. Martinez, LA 20
- F. Viola, NY 20
- D. Gooden, NY 19
- T. Browning, CIN 15
- G. Maddux, CHI 15

Saves
- J. Franco, NY 33
- R. Myers, CIN 31
- L. Smith, STL 27
- D. Smith, HOU 23
- C. Lefferts, SD 23

Strikeouts
- D. Cone, NY 233
- D. Gooden, NY 223
- R. Martinez, LA 223
- F. Viola, NY 182
- S. Fernandez, NY 181

Complete Games
- R. Martinez, LA 12
- B. Hurst, SD 9
- D. Drabek, PIT 9
- G. Maddux, CHI 8

Fewest Hits/9 Innings
- S. Fernandez, NY 6.52
- J. Rijo, CIN 6.90
- R. Martinez, LA 7.34
- D. Drabek, PIT 7.39

Shutouts
- M. Morgan, LA 4
- B. Hurst, SD 4

Fewest Walks/9 Innings
- D. Darwin, HOU 1.72
- E. Whitson, SD 1.85
- C. Leibrandt, ATL 1.94
- D. Martinez, MON 1.95

Most Strikeouts/9 Inn.
- D. Cone, NY 9.91
- S. Fernandez, NY 9.08
- D. Gooden, NY 8.63
- R. Martinez, LA 8.56

Innings
- F. Viola, NY 250
- G. Maddux, CHI 237
- R. Martinez, LA 234
- D. Gooden, NY 233

Games Pitched
- J. Agosto, HOU 82
- P. Assenmacher, CHI 74
- G. Harris, SD 73
- R. McDowell, PHI 72

	Team	W	L	PCT	GB	R	OR	Batting 2B	3B	HR	BA	SA	SB	Fielding E	DP	FA	Pitching CG	BB	SO	ShO	SV	ERA
East	Pittsburgh	95	67	.586		733	619	**288**	42	138	.259	.405	137	134	125	.979	18	**413**	848	8	43	3.40
	New York	91	71	.562	4	**775**	613	278	21	**172**	.256	**.408**	110	132	107	.978	18	444	**1217**	**14**	41	3.42
	Montreal	85	77	.525	10	662	598	227	**43**	114	.250	.370	**235**	110	134	.982	18	510	991	11	**50**	**3.37**
	Chicago	77	85	.475	18	690	774	240	36	136	.263	.392	151	124	136	.980	13	572	877	7	42	4.34
	Philadelphia	77	85	.475	18	646	729	237	27	103	.255	.363	108	117	**150**	.981	18	651	840	7	35	4.07
	St. Louis	70	92	.432	25	599	698	255	41	73	.256	.358	221	130	114	.979	8	475	833	13	39	3.87
West	Cincinnati	91	71	.562		693	**597**	284	40	125	**.265**	.399	166	**102**	126	**.983**	14	543	1029	12	**50**	3.39
	Los Angeles	86	76	.531	5	728	685	222	27	129	.262	.382	141	130	123	.979	**29**	478	1021	12	29	3.72
	San Francisco	85	77	.525	6	719	710	221	35	152	.262	.396	109	107	148	**.983**	14	553	788	6	45	4.08
	Houston	75	87	.463	16	573	656	209	32	94	.242	.345	179	131	124	.978	12	496	854	6	37	3.61
	San Diego	75	87	.463	16	673	673	243	35	123	.257	.380	138	141	141	.977	21	507	928	12	35	3.68
	Atlanta	65	97	.401	26	682	821	263	26	162	.250	.396	92	158	133	.974	17	579	938	8	30	4.58
						8173	8173	2967	405	1521	.256	.383	1787	1516	1561	.979	200	6221	11164	116	476	3.79

AMERICAN LEAGUE 1990

		POS	Player	AB	BA	HR	RBI	PO	A	E	DP	TC/G	FA	Pitcher	G	IP	W	L	SV	ERA
East	**Boston**	1B	C. Quintana	512	.287	7	67	1188	**137**	**17**	116	9.1	.987	R. Clemens	31	228	21	6	0	**1.93**
		2B	J. Reed	598	.289	5	51	215	374	6	82	5.0	.990	M. Boddicker	34	228	17	8	0	3.36
	W-88 L-74	SS	L. Rivera	346	.225	7	45	186	310	18	69	4.6	.965	G. Harris	34	184	13	9	0	4.00
		3B	W. Boggs	619	.302	6	63	108	241	20	18	2.4	.946	D. Kiecker	32	152	8	9	0	3.97
	Joe Morgan	RF	T. Brunansky	461	.267	15	71	267	7	5	1	2.3	.982	T. Bolton	21	120	10	5	0	3.38
		CF	E. Burks	588	.296	21	89	324	7	2	0	2.3	.994	D. Lamp	47	106	3	5	0	4.68
		LF	M. Greenwell	610	.297	14	73	287	13	7	1	1.9	.977	W. Gardner	34	77	3	7	0	4.89
		C	T. Pena	491	.263	7	56	**864**	74	5	13	**6.6**	.995	R. Murphy	68	57	0	6	7	6.32
		DH	D. Evans	445	.249	13	63							J. Reardon	47	51	5	3	21	3.16
														J. Gray	41	51	2	4	9	4.44

AMERICAN LEAGUE 1990, *cont.*

Team	POS	Player	AB	BA	HR	RBI	PO	A	E	DP	TC/G	FA	Pitcher	G	IP	W	L	SV	ERA
Toronto	1B	F. McGriff	557	.300	35	88	1246	126	6	119	9.4	.996	D. Stieb	33	209	18	6	0	2.93
W-86 L-76	2B	M. Lee	391	.243	6	41	259	286	4	65	4.9	**.993**	T. Stottlemyre	33	203	13	17	0	4.34
Cito Gaston	SS	T. Fernandez	635	.276	4	66	**297**	**480**	9	93	**4.9**	.989	D. Wells	43	189	11	6	3	3.14
	3B	K. Gruber	592	.274	31	118	**123**	280	19	21	2.9	.955	J. Key	27	155	13	7	0	4.25
	RF	J. Felix	463	.263	15	65	244	11	9	3	2.1	.966	J. Cerutti	30	140	9	9	0	4.76
	CF	M. Wilson	588	.265	3	51	370	5	3	2	2.7	.992	D. Ward	73	128	2	8	11	3.45
	LF	G. Bell	562	.265	21	86	226	4	5	1	2.2	.979	F. Wills	44	99	6	4	0	4.73
	C	P. Borders	346	.286	15	49	515	46	4	6	4.9	.993	T. Henke	61	75	2	4	32	2.17
	DH	J. Olerud	358	.265	14	48													
	OF	G. Hill	260	.231	12	32	115	4	2	0	2.0	.983							
	C	G. Myers	250	.236	5	22	411	30	3	4	5.1	.993							
	2B	N. Liriano	170	.212	1	15	93	132	4	26	4.7	.983							
Detroit	1B	C. Fielder	573	.277	**51**	**132**	1190	111	14	**137**	9.2	.989	J. Morris	36	250	15	18	0	4.51
W-79 L-83	2B	L. Whitaker	472	.237	18	60	286	372	6	98	5.1	.991	F. Tanana	34	176	9	8	1	5.31
Sparky Anderson	SS	A. Trammell	559	.304	14	89	232	409	14	**102**	4.6	.979	D. Petry	32	150	10	9	0	4.45
	3B	T. Phillips	573	.251	8	55	69	200	20	16	2.8	.931	J. Robinson	27	145	10	9	0	5.96
	RF	C. Lemon	322	.258	5	32	209	7	6	1	2.3	.973	P. Gibson	61	97	5	4	3	3.05
	CF	L. Moseby	431	.248	14	51	288	9	5	5	2.6	.983	M. Henneman	69	94	8	6	22	3.05
	LF	G. Ward	309	.256	9	46	157	2	2	1	1.9	.988	J. Gleaton	57	83	1	3	13	2.94
	C	M. Heath	370	.270	7	38	585	54	13	7	5.6	.980	E. Nunez	42	80	3	1	6	2.24
	DH	D. Bergman	205	.278	2	26							W. Terrell	13	75	6	4	0	4.54
	OD	L. Sheets	360	.261	10	52	98	7	2	1		.981							
	3B	T. Fryman	232	.297	9	27	23	95	11	12	2.7	.915							
	OF	J. Shelby	222	.248	4	20	138	5	4	3	2.2	.973							
	C	M. Salas	164	.232	9	24	227	22	3	3	4.4	.988							
Cleveland	1B	K. Hernandez	130	.200	1	8	340	20	2	28	8.6	.994	G. Swindell	34	215	12	9	0	4.40
W-77 L-85	2B	J. Browne	513	.267	6	50	286	382	10	69	4.9	.985	T. Candiotti	31	202	15	11	0	3.65
John McNamara	SS	F. Fermin	414	.256	1	40	213	421	16	81	4.4	.975	B. Black	29	191	11	10	0	3.53
	3B	B. Jacoby	553	.293	14	75	44	158	4	14	2.1	.981	S. Valdez	24	102	6	6	0	4.75
	RF	C. Snyder	438	.233	14	55	224	11	6	2	2.0	.975	D. Jones	66	84	5	5	43	2.56
	CF	M. Webster	437	.252	12	55	330	1	3	0	2.8	.991	J. Orosco	55	65	5	4	2	3.90
	LF	C. Maldonado	590	.273	22	95	293	9	2	1	2.3	.993							
	C	S. Alomar	445	.290	9	66	686	46	**14**	6	5.8	.981							
	DH	C. James	528	.299	12	70													
	3S	C. Baerga	312	.260	7	47	57	142	12	19		.943							
	UT	D. James	248	.274	1	22	282	17	4	21		.987							
	OF	A. Cole	227	.300	0	13	145	3	6	1	2.6	.961							
	32	T. Brookens	154	.266	1	20	49	99	6	18		.961							
Baltimore	1B	R. Milligan	362	.265	20	60	846	87	9	94	9.6	.990	P. Harnisch	31	189	11	11	0	4.34
W-76 L-85	2B	B. Ripken	406	.291	3	38	250	366	8	84	4.9	.987	D. Johnson	30	180	13	9	0	4.10
Frank Robinson	SS	C. Ripken	600	.250	21	84	242	435	3	94	4.2	**.996**	B. Milacki	27	135	5	8	0	4.46
	3B	C. Worthington	425	.226	8	44	90	218	18	28	2.5	.945	J. Ballard	44	133	2	11	0	4.93
	RF	J. Orsulak	413	.269	11	57	267	5	3	2	2.5	.989	B. McDonald	21	119	8	5	0	2.43
	CF	M. Devereaux	367	.240	12	49	281	4	5	1	2.8	.983	J. Mitchell	24	114	6	6	0	4.64
	LF	P. Bradley	289	.270	4	26	149	3	2	0	2.2	.987	M. Williamson	49	85	8	2	1	2.21
	C	M. Tettleton	444	.223	15	51	425	37	4	3	5.2	.991	G. Olson	64	74	6	5	37	2.42
	DH	S. Horn	246	.248	14	45													
	OF	S. Finley	464	.256	3	37	298	4	7	1	2.3	.977							
	C	B. Melvin	301	.243	5	37	364	25	1	2	5.1	.997							
	OF	B. Anderson	234	.231	3	24	149	3	2	1	2.4	.987							
Milwaukee	1B	G. Brock	367	.248	7	50	885	63	5	89	8.3	.995	T. Higuera	27	170	11	10	0	3.76
W-74 L-88	2B	J. Gantner	323	.263	0	25	164	220	7	54	4.9	.982	M. Knudson	30	168	10	9	0	4.12
Tom Trebelhorn	SS	B. Spiers	363	.242	2	36	159	326	12	72	4.5	.976	J. Navarro	32	149	8	7	1	4.46
	3B	G. Sheffield	487	.294	10	67	98	254	25	16	**3.0**	.934	R. Robinson	22	148	12	5	0	2.91
	RF	R. Deer	440	.209	27	69	243	14	8	7	2.3	.970	C. Bosio	20	133	4	9	0	4.00
	CF	R. Yount	587	.247	17	77	422	3	4	0	2.7	.991	B. Krueger	30	129	6	8	0	3.98
	LF	G. Vaughn	382	.220	17	61	195	8	7	1	2.0	.967	T. Edens	35	89	4	5	2	4.45
	C	B. Surhoff	474	.276	6	59	615	53	10	10	5.4	.985	C. Crim	67	86	3	5	11	3.47
	DH	D. Parker	610	.289	21	92							D. Plesac	66	69	3	7	24	4.43
	21	P. Molitor	418	.285	12	45	461	215	9	64		.987							
	OF	M. Felder	237	.274	3	27	165	8	5	6	1.6	.972							
	SS	E. Diaz	218	.271	0	14	101	163	14	36	4.3	.950							
New York	1B	D. Mattingly	394	.256	5	42	800	78	3	81	9.9	.997	T. Leary	31	208	9	**19**	0	4.11
W-67 L-95	2B	S. Sax	615	.260	4	42	292	457	10	102	4.9	.987	A. Hawkins	28	158	5	12	0	5.37
Bucky Dent	SS	A. Espinoza	438	.224	2	20	268	447	17	100	4.9	.977	D. LaPoint	28	158	7	10	0	4.11
W-18 L-31	3B	R. Velarde	229	.210	5	19	43	128	10	11	2.4	.945	C. Cary	28	157	6	12	0	4.19
Stump Merrill	RF	J. Barfield	476	.246	25	78	305	16	9	3	2.2	.973	G. Cadaret	54	121	5	4	3	4.15
W-49 L-64	CF	R. Kelly	641	.285	15	61	420	5	5	0	2.7	.988	M. Witt	16	97	5	6	0	4.47
	LF	O. Azocar	214	.248	5	19	105	4	1	1	1.9	.991	L. Guetterman	64	93	11	7	2	3.39
	C	B. Geren	277	.213	8	31	487	55	4	5	5.1	.993	D. Righetti	53	53	1	1	36	3.57
	DH	S. Balboni	266	.192	17	34													
	DO	M. Hall	360	.258	12	46	70	2	2	0		.973							
	3B	J. Leyritz	303	.257	5	25	43	101	11	5	2.2	.929							
	1B	K. Maas	254	.252	21	41	486	35	9	45	9.3	.983							
	CD	M. Nokes	240	.237	8	32	181	27	1	5		.995							
	3B	M. Blowers	144	.188	5	21	26	63	10	4	2.2	.899							

AMERICAN LEAGUE 1990, *cont.*

West

Oakland

W-103 L-59

Tony LaRussa

POS	Player	AB	BA	HR	RBI	PO	A	E	DP	TC/G	FA
1B	M. McGwire	523	.235	39	108	**1329**	95	5	126	9.3	.997
2B	W. Randolph	292	.257	1	21	148	240	7	62	4.7	.982
SS	W. Weiss	445	.265	2	35	194	373	12	77	4.2	.979
3B	C. Lansford	507	.268	3	50	100	194	9	22	2.4	**.970**
RF	J. Canseco	481	.274	37	101	182	7	1	2	2.2	.995
CF	D. Henderson	450	.271	20	63	319	5	4	1	2.8	.988
LF	R. Henderson	489	.325	28	61	289	5	5	0	2.5	.983
C	T. Steinbach	379	.251	9	57	396	31	5	1	5.2	.988
DH	H. Baines	94	.266	3	21						
UT	M. Gallego	389	.206	3	34	207	379	13	78		.978
OF	F. Jose	341	.264	8	39	212	5	5	1	2.4	.977
C	R. Hassey	254	.213	5	22	307	18	1	2	5.5	.997
UT	J. Quirk	121	.281	3	26	168	18	5	4		.974

Pitcher	G	IP	W	L	SV	ERA
D. Stewart	36	**267**	22	11	0	2.56
B. Welch	35	238	**27**	6	0	2.95
S. Sanderson	34	206	17	11	0	3.88
M. Moore	33	199	13	15	0	4.65
C. Young	26	124	9	6	0	4.85
G. Nelson	51	75	3	3	5	1.57
D. Eckersley	63	73	4	2	48	0.61
R. Honeycutt	63	63	2	2	7	2.70

Chicago

W-94 L-68

Jeff Torborg

POS	Player	AB	BA	HR	RBI	PO	A	E	DP	TC/G	FA
1B	C. Martinez	272	.224	4	24	632	38	8	50	8.3	.988
2B	S. Fletcher	509	.242	4	56	305	436	9	**115**	5.0	.988
SS	O. Guillen	516	.279	1	58	252	474	17	100	4.7	.977
3B	R. Ventura	493	.249	5	54	116	268	25	32	2.8	.939
RF	S. Sosa	532	.233	15	70	315	14	13	1	2.3	.962
CF	L. Johnson	541	.285	1	51	353	5	10	3	2.5	.973
LF	I. Calderon	607	.273	14	74	268	7	7	1	2.2	.975
C	C. Fisk	452	.285	18	65	660	63	4	14	6.3	.994
DH	D. Pasqua	325	.274	13	58						
D1	R. Kittle	277	.245	16	43	150	5	2	18		.987
1B	F. Thomas	191	.330	7	31	428	26	5	53	9.0	.989
C	R. Karkovice	183	.246	6	20	296	31	2	4	5.1	.994

Pitcher	G	IP	W	L	SV	ERA
G. Hibbard	33	211	14	9	0	3.16
J. McDowell	33	205	14	9	0	3.82
M. Perez	35	197	13	14	0	4.61
E. King	25	151	12	4	0	3.28
W. Edwards	42	95	5	3	2	3.22
B. Thigpen	**77**	89	4	6	**57**	1.83
A. Fernandez	13	88	5	5	0	3.80
D. Pall	56	76	3	5	2	3.32
B. Jones	65	74	11	4	1	2.31
S. Radinsky	62	52	6	1	4	4.82

Texas

W-83 L-79

Bobby Valentine

POS	Player	AB	BA	HR	RBI	PO	A	E	DP	TC/G	FA
1B	R. Palmeiro	598	.319	14	89	1215	91	7	123	9.0	.995
2B	J. Franco	582	.296	11	69	310	444	**19**	101	5.1	.975
SS	J. Huson	396	.240	0	28	157	254	17	69	3.6	.960
3B	S. Buechele	251	.215	7	30	70	157	8	7	2.7	.966
RF	R. Sierra	608	.280	16	96	283	7	10	1	2.0	.967
CF	G. Pettis	423	.239	3	31	285	10	2	4	2.3	.993
LF	P. Incaviglia	529	.233	24	85	290	12	8	2	2.1	.974
C	G. Petralli	325	.255	0	21	599	43	6	5	5.5	.991
DH	H. Baines	321	.290	13	44						
UT	J. Daugherty	310	.300	6	47	225	22	3	21		.988
UT	J. Kunkel	200	.170	3	17	101	172	11	34		.961
UT	M. Stanley	189	.249	2	19	261	25	4	2		.986
3B	S. Coolbaugh	180	.200	2	13	42	118	10	12	2.6	.941

Pitcher	G	IP	W	L	SV	ERA
B. Witt	33	222	17	10	0	3.36
C. Hough	32	219	12	12	0	4.07
N. Ryan	30	204	13	9	0	3.44
K. Brown	26	180	12	10	0	3.60
M. Jeffcoat	44	111	5	6	5	4.47
J. Moyer	33	102	2	6	0	4.66
K. Rogers	69	98	10	6	15	3.13
B. Arnsberg	53	63	6	1	5	2.15
J. Russell	27	25	1	5	10	4.26

California

W-80 L-82

Doug Rader

POS	Player	AB	BA	HR	RBI	PO	A	E	DP	TC/G	FA
1B	W. Joyner	310	.268	8	41	727	62	4	78	9.6	.995
2B	J. Ray	404	.277	5	43	241	295	7	82	5.4	.987
SS	D. Schofield	310	.255	1	18	170	318	17	77	5.1	.966
3B	J. Howell	316	.228	8	33	70	193	17	18	2.7	.939
RF	D. Winfield	414	.275	19	72	165	7	2	1	1.6	.989
CF	D. White	443	.217	11	44	302	11	9	4	2.6	.972
LF	L. Polonia	381	.336	2	32	142	3	3	2	1.7	.980
C	L. Parrish	470	.268	24	70	760	**88**	6	**15**	6.5	.993
DH	B. Downing	330	.273	14	51						
DO	C. Davis	412	.265	12	58	77	5	3	1		.965
UT	D. Hill	352	.264	3	32	194	255	11	64		.976
OF	D. Bichette	349	.255	15	53	183	12	7	5	1.9	.965
1B	L. Stevens	248	.214	7	32	597	36	4	62	9.5	.994
OF	M. Venable	189	.259	4	21	112	3	3	1	1.5	.975

Pitcher	G	IP	W	L	SV	ERA
C. Finley	32	236	18	9	0	2.40
M. Langston	33	223	10	17	0	4.40
J. Abbott	33	212	10	14	0	4.51
K. McCaskill	29	174	12	11	0	3.25
B. Blyleven	23	134	8	7	0	5.24
M. Eichhorn	60	85	2	5	13	3.08
W. Fraser	45	76	5	4	2	3.08
B. Harvey	54	64	4	4	25	3.22

Seattle

W-77 L-85

Jim Lefebvre

POS	Player	AB	BA	HR	RBI	PO	A	E	DP	TC/G	FA
1B	P. O'Brien	366	.224	5	27	850	76	5	68	9.6	.995
2B	H. Reynolds	**642**	.252	5	55	**330**	**499**	**19**	110	**5.3**	.978
SS	O. Vizquel	255	.247	2	18	103	239	7	48	4.3	.980
3B	E. Martinez	487	.302	11	49	89	259	**27**	16	2.6	.928
RF	H. Cotto	355	.259	4	33	194	4	2	1	1.7	.990
CF	K. Griffey	597	.300	22	80	330	8	7	1	2.3	.980
LF	J. Leonard	478	.251	10	75	118	0	2	0	1.5	.983
C	D. Valle	308	.214	7	33	631	44	2	9	6.5	**.997**
DH	A. Davis	494	.283	17	68						
OF	G. Briley	337	.246	5	29	177	4	2	1	1.7	.989
C	S. Bradley	233	.223	1	28	349	24	2	4	6.0	.995
OF	J. Buhner	163	.276	7	33	55	1	2	0	1.5	.966

Pitcher	G	IP	W	L	SV	ERA
E. Hanson	33	236	18	9	0	3.24
M. Young	34	225	8	18	0	3.51
R. Johnson	33	220	14	11	0	3.65
B. Holman	28	190	11	11	0	4.03
B. Swift	55	128	6	4	6	2.39
M. Jackson	63	77	5	7	3	4.54
K. Comstock	60	56	7	4	2	2.89
M. Schooler	49	56	1	4	30	2.25

Kansas City

W-75 L-86

John Wathan

POS	Player	AB	BA	HR	RBI	PO	A	E	DP	TC/G	FA
1B	G. Brett	544	**.329**	14	87	865	66	7	89	9.2	.993
2B	F. White	241	.216	2	21	142	218	8	51	4.7	.978
SS	K. Stillwell	506	.249	3	51	181	350	**24**	79	3.9	.957
3B	K. Seitzer	622	.275	6	38	100	262	18	31	2.5	.953
RF	J. Eisenreich	496	.280	5	51	261	6	1	3	1.9	.996
CF	B. Jackson	405	.272	28	78	230	8	12	2	2.6	.952
LF	W. Wilson	307	.290	2	42	187	2	0	1	1.8	1.000
C	M. Macfarlane	400	.255	6	58	660	23	6	9	6.2	.991
DH	G. Perry	465	.254	8	57						
OD	D. Tartabull	313	.268	15	60	81	1	3	0		.965
UT	B. Pecota	240	.242	5	20	160	195	5	44		.986
UT	P. Tabler	195	.272	1	19	101	10	2	7		.982
OF	B. McRae	168	.286	2	23	120	1	0	0	2.7	1.000

Pitcher	G	IP	W	L	SV	ERA
T. Gordon	32	195	12	11	0	3.73
K. Appier	32	186	12	8	0	2.76
B. Saberhagen	20	135	5	9	0	3.27
S. Farr	57	127	13	7	1	1.98
S. Davis	21	112	7	10	0	4.74
J. Montgomery	73	94	6	5	24	2.39
M. Gubicza	16	94	4	7	0	4.50
S. Crawford	46	80	5	4	1	4.16
M. Davis	53	69	2	7	6	5.11

AMERICAN LEAGUE 1990, *cont.*

Minnesota

W-74 L-88

Tom Kelly

POS	Player	AB	BA	HR	RBI	PO	A	E	DP	TC/G	FA
1B	K. Hrbek	492	.287	22	79	1057	81	3	100	**9.5**	**.997**
2B	A. Newman	388	.242	0	30	118	173	2	48	3.3	.993
SS	G. Gagne	388	.235	7	38	184	377	14	62	4.3	.976
3B	G. Gaetti	577	.229	16	85	102	**318**	18	**36**	2.9	.959
RF	J. Moses	172	.221	1	14	103	2	0	0	1.2	1.000
CF	K. Puckett	551	.298	12	80	354	9	4	3	2.6	.989
LF	D. Gladden	534	.275	5	40	286	12	6	3	2.3	.980
C	B. Harper	479	.294	6	54	672	53	11	5	6.1	.985
DH	G. Larkin	401	.269	5	42						
OF	S. Mack	313	.326	8	44	230	8	3	1	2.2	.988
2B	F. Manrique	228	.237	5	29	104	155	7	40	4.0	.974
2B	N. Liriano	185	.254	0	13	83	128	7	27	4.4	.968
OD	R. Bush	181	.243	6	18	52	1	0	0		1.000
C	J. Ortiz	170	.335	0	18	247	25	0	6	4.0	1.000

Pitcher	G	IP	W	L	SV	ERA
A. Anderson	31	189	7	18	0	4.53
K. Tapani	28	159	12	8	0	4.07
R. Smith	32	153	5	10	0	4.81
D. West	29	146	7	9	0	5.10
M. Guthrie	24	145	7	9	0	3.79
S. Erickson	19	113	8	4	0	2.87
J. Berenguer	51	100	8	5	0	3.41
R. Aguilera	56	65	5	3	32	2.76
J. Candelaria	34	58	7	3	4	3.39

BATTING AND BASE RUNNING LEADERS

Batting Average

G. Brett, KC	.329
R. Henderson, OAK	.325
R. Palmeiro, TEX	.319
A. Trammell, DET	.304
W. Boggs, BOS	.302

Slugging Average

C. Fielder, DET	.592
R. Henderson, OAK	.577
J. Canseco, OAK	.543
F. McGriff, TOR	.530
G. Brett, KC	.515

Home Runs

C. Fielder, DET	51
M. McGwire, OAK	39
J. Canseco, OAK	37
F. McGriff, TOR	35
K. Gruber, TOR	31

Total Bases

C. Fielder, DET	339
K. Gruber, TOR	303
F. McGriff, TOR	295
K. Griffey, SEA	287
E. Burks, BOS	286

Runs Batted In

C. Fielder, DET	132
K. Gruber, TOR	118
M. McGwire, OAK	108
J. Canseco, OAK	101
R. Sierra, TEX	96

Stolen Bases

R. Henderson, OAK	65
S. Sax, NY	43
R. Kelly, NY	42
A. Cole, CLE	40
G. Pettis, TEX	38

Hits

R. Palmeiro, TEX	191
W. Boggs, BOS	187
R. Kelly, NY	183
M. Greenwell, BOS	181

Base on Balls

M. McGwire, OAK	110
M. Tettleton, BAL	106
J. Canseco, OAK	99
T. Phillips, DET	99
R. Henderson, OAK	97

Home Run Percentage

C. Fielder, DET	8.9
J. Canseco, OAK	7.7
M. McGwire, OAK	7.5
F. McGriff, TOR	6.3

Runs

R. Henderson, OAK	119
C. Fielder, DET	104
H. Reynolds, SEA	100
R. Yount, MIL	98

Doubles

G. Brett, KC	45
J. Reed, BOS	45
I. Calderon, CHI	44
W. Boggs, BOS	44

Triples

T. Fernandez, TOR	17
S. Sosa, CHI	10
N. Liriano, TOR, MIN	9
L. Polonia, NY, CAL	9
L. Johnson, CHI	9

PITCHING LEADERS

Winning Percentage

B. Welch, OAK	.818
R. Clemens, BOS	.778
D. Stieb, TOR	.750
M. Boddicker, BOS	.680
D. Stewart, OAK	.667
C. Finley, CAL	.667
E. Hanson, SEA	.667

Earned Run Average

R. Clemens, BOS	1.93
C. Finley, CAL	2.40
D. Stewart, OAK	2.56
K. Appier, KC	2.76
D. Stieb, TOR	2.93

Wins

B. Welch, OAK	27
D. Stewart, OAK	22
R. Clemens, BOS	21
D. Stieb, TOR	18
C. Finley, CAL	18
E. Hanson, SEA	18

Saves

B. Thigpen, CHI	57
D. Eckersley, OAK	48
D. Jones, CLE	43
G. Olson, BAL	37
D. Righetti, NY	36

Strikeouts

N. Ryan, TEX	232
B. Witt, TEX	221
E. Hanson, SEA	211
R. Clemens, BOS	209
M. Langston, CAL	195

Complete Games

J. Morris, DET	11
D. Stewart, OAK	11

Fewest Hits/9 Innings

N. Ryan, TEX	6.04
R. Johnson, SEA	7.13
R. Clemens, BOS	7.61
D. Stewart, OAK	7.62

Shutouts

R. Clemens, BOS	4
D. Stewart, OAK	4
K. Appier, KC	3
M. Perez, CHI	3
J. Morris, DET	3

Fewest Walks/9 Innings

A. Anderson, MIN	1.86
G. Swindell, CLE	1.97
R. Clemens, BOS	2.13
M. Knudson, MIL	2.14

Most Strikeouts/9 Inn.

N. Ryan, TEX	10.24
B. Witt, TEX	8.96
R. Clemens, BOS	8.24
T. Gordon, KC	8.06

Innings

D. Stewart, OAK	267
J. Morris, DET	250
B. Welch, OAK	238
C. Finley, CAL	236
E. Hanson, SEA	236

Games Pitched

B. Thigpen, CHI	77
D. Ward, TOR	73
J. Montgomery, KC	73
M. Henneman, DET	69
K. Rogers, TEX	69

		W	L	PCT	GB	R	OR	Batting 2B	3B	HR	BA	SA	SB	Fielding E	DP	FA	Pitching CG	BB	SO	ShO	SV	ERA
East	Boston	88	74	.543		699	664	298	31	106	**.272**	.395	53	123	154	.980	15	519	997	13	44	3.72
	Toronto	86	76	.531	2	**767**	661	263	**50**	167	.265	**.419**	111	**86**	144	**.986**	6	**445**	892	9	48	3.84
	Detroit	79	83	.488	9	750	754	241	32	**172**	.259	.409	82	131	178	.979	15	661	856	12	45	4.39
	Cleveland	77	85	.475	11	732	737	266	41	110	.267	.391	107	117	146	.981	12	518	860	10	47	4.26
	Baltimore	76	85	.472	11.5	669	698	234	22	132	.245	.370	94	93	151	.985	10	537	776	5	43	4.04
	Milwaukee	74	88	.457	14	732	760	247	36	128	.256	.384	**164**	149	152	.976	23	469	771	13	42	4.08
	New York	67	95	.414	21	603	749	208	19	147	.241	.366	119	126	164	.980	15	618	909	6	41	4.21
West	Oakland	103	59	.636		733	**570**	209	22	164	.254	.391	141	87	152	**.986**	18	494	831	**16**	64	**3.18**
	Chicago	94	68	.580	9	682	633	251	44	106	.258	.379	140	124	169	.980	17	548	914	10	**68**	3.61
	Texas	83	79	.512	20	676	696	257	27	110	.259	.376	115	133	161	.979	**25**	623	997	9	36	3.83
	California	80	82	.494	23	690	706	237	27	147	.260	.391	69	142	**186**	.978	21	544	944	13	42	3.79
	Seattle	77	85	.475	26	640	680	251	26	107	.259	.373	105	130	152	.979	21	606	**1064**	7	41	3.69
	Kansas City	75	86	.466	27.5	707	709	**316**	44	100	.267	.395	107	122	161	.980	18	560	1006	8	33	3.93
	Minnesota	74	88	.457	29	666	729	281	39	100	.265	.385	96	101	161	.983	13	489	872	13	43	4.12
						9746	9746	3559	460	1796	.259	.387	1503	1664	2231	.981	229	7631	12689	144	637	3.91

NATIONAL LEAGUE 1991

	Team	POS	Player	AB	BA	HR	RBI	PO	A	E	DP	TC/G	FA	Pitcher	G	IP	W	L	SV	ERA
East	Pittsburgh	1B	O. Merced	411	.275	10	50	911	60	12	64	9.4	.988	D. Drabek	35	235	15	14	0	3.07
	W-98 L-64	2B	J. Lind	502	.265	3	54	**349**	438	9	79	**5.3**	.989	Z. Smith	35	228	16	10	0	3.20
	Jim Leyland	SS	J. Bell	608	.270	16	67	239	**491**	**24**	78	4.8	.968	J. Smiley	33	208	**20**	8	0	3.08
		3B	J. Wehner	106	.340	0	7	23	65	6	9	2.6	.936	R. Tomlin	31	175	8	7	0	2.98
		RF	B. Bonilla	577	.302	18	100	176	8	2	0	1.8	.989	B. Walk	25	115	9	2	0	3.60
		CF	A. Van Slyke	491	.265	17	83	273	8	1	1	2.1	.996	V. Palacios	36	82	6	3	3	3.75
		LF	B. Bonds	510	.292	25	116	321	13	3	1	2.2	.991	S. Belinda	60	78	7	5	16	3.45
		C	M. LaValliere	336	.289	3	41	565	46	1	4	5.8	**.998**	B. Landrum	61	76	4	4	17	3.18
		10	G. Redus	252	.246	7	24	403	26	6	35		.986							
		C	D. Slaught	220	.295	1	29	338	31	5	4	5.4	.987							
		UT	C. Wilkerson	191	.188	2	18	73	124	2	24		.990							
		OF	G. Varsho	187	.273	4	23	84	2	1	1	1.6	.989							
		01	L. McClendon	163	.288	7	24	158	12	3	13		.983							
	St. Louis	1B	P. Guerrero	427	.272	8	70	953	66	**16**	73	9.2	.985	B. Smith	31	199	12	9	0	3.85
	W-84 L-78	2B	J. Oquendo	366	.240	1	26	244	346	7	60	5.1	.988	B. Tewksbury	30	191	11	12	0	3.25
	Joe Torre	SS	O. Smith	550	.285	3	50	244	387	8	**79**	4.3	**.987**	K. Hill	30	181	11	10	0	3.57
		3B	T. Zeile	565	.280	11	81	124	290	**25**	18	2.9	.943	O. Olivares	28	167	11	7	1	3.71
		RF	F. Jose	568	.305	8	77	268	15	3	2	1.9	.990	J. DeLeon	28	163	5	9	0	2.71
		CF	R. Lankford	566	.251	9	69	367	7	6	2	2.6	.984	J. Agosto	72	86	5	3	2	4.81
		LF	B. Gilkey	268	.216	5	20	164	6	1	1	2.3	.994	L. Smith	67	73	6	3	**47**	2.34
		C	T. Pagnozzi	459	.264	2	57	673	81	7	8	5.5	.991	C. Carpenter	59	66	10	4	0	4.23
		OF	M. Thompson	326	.307	6	34	207	8	2	1	2.4	.991							
		1B	G. Perry	242	.240	6	36	407	28	5	30	7.2	.989							
		OF	R. Hudler	207	.227	1	15	97	4	2	0	1.8	.981							
		2B	G. Pena	185	.243	5	17	95	146	6	28	3.0	.976							
	Chicago	1B	M. Grace	**619**	.273	8	58	**1520**	**167**	8	106	**10.6**	.995	G. Maddux	37	**263**	15	11	0	3.35
	W-77 L-83	2B	R. Sandberg	585	.291	26	100	267	**515**	4	66	5.0	**.995**	M. Bielecki	39	172	13	11	0	4.50
	Don Zimmer	SS	S. Dunston	492	.260	12	50	**261**	383	21	69	4.7	.968	L. Lancaster	64	156	9	7	3	3.52
	W-18 L-19	3B	L. Salazar	333	.258	14	38	46	151	9	5	2.4	.956	S. Boskie	28	129	4	9	0	5.23
	Joe Altobelli	RF	A. Dawson	563	.272	31	104	243	7	3	2	1.8	.988	F. Castillo	18	112	6	7	0	4.35
	W-0 L-1	CF	J. Walton	270	.219	5	17	170	2	3	1	1.7	.983	B. Scanlan	40	111	7	8	1	3.89
	Jim Essian	LF	G. Bell	558	.285	25	86	249	6	10	0	1.8	.962	P. Assenmacher	75	103	7	8	15	3.24
	W-59 L-63	C	R. Wilkins	203	.222	6	22	373	42	3	6	5.1	.993	C. McElroy	71	101	6	2	3	1.95
		30	C. Walker	374	.257	6	34	95	73	8	8		.955	R. Sutcliffe	19	97	6	5	0	4.10
		OF	D. Dascenzo	239	.255	1	18	134	0	2	0	1.6	.985	D. Smith	35	33	0	6	17	6.00
		C	H. Villanueva	192	.276	13	32	259	26	6	2	5.3	.979							
		OF	D. Smith	167	.228	3	21	73	3	3	1	1.9	.962							
	Philadelphia	1B	J. Kruk	538	.294	21	92	735	49	2	54	7.7	.997	T. Mulholland	34	232	16	13	0	3.61
	W-78 L-84	2B	M. Morandini	325	.249	1	20	183	254	6	45	4.6	.986	T. Greene	36	208	13	7	0	3.38
	Nick Leyva	SS	D. Thon	539	.252	9	44	234	412	21	65	4.6	.969	J. DeJesus	31	182	10	9	1	3.42
	W-4 L-9	3B	C. Hayes	460	.230	12	53	85	237	14	25	2.4	.958	B. Ruffin	31	119	4	7	0	3.78
	Jim Fregosi	RF	D. Murphy	544	.252	18	81	287	6	5	0	2.0	.983	D. Cox	23	102	4	6	0	4.57
	W-74 L-75	CF	L. Dykstra	246	.297	3	12	167	3	4	2	2.8	.977	M. Williams	69	88	12	5	30	2.34
		LF	W. Chamberlain	383	.240	13	50	199	4	3	0	2.1	.985	R. McDowell	38	59	3	6	3	3.20
		C	D. Daulton	285	.196	12	42	493	33	8	5	6.1	.985							
		1B	R. Jordan	301	.272	9	49	626	37	9	37	9.3	.987							
		OF	V. Hayes	284	.225	0	21	202	3	2	2	2.9	.990							
		2B	R. Ready	205	.249	1	20	127	145	3	22	4.2	.989							
		23	W. Backman	185	.243	0	15	54	79	4	13		.971							
		3B	D. Hollins	151	.298	6	21	25	58	7	2	2.5	.922							
	New York	1B	D. Magadan	418	.258	4	51	1035	90	5	73	9.3	.996	D. Cone	34	233	14	14	0	3.29
	W-77 L-84	2B	G. Jefferies	486	.272	9	62	144	177	6	15	4.2	.982	F. Viola	35	231	13	15	0	3.97
	Bud Harrelson	SS	K. Elster	348	.241	6	36	149	299	14	39	4.3	.970	D. Gooden	27	190	13	7	0	3.60
	W-74 L-80	3B	H. Johnson	564	.259	**38**	**117**	55	173	18	11	2.4	.927	W. Whitehurst	36	133	7	12	1	4.18
	Mike Cubbage	RF	H. Brooks	357	.238	16	50	166	6	5	0	1.8	.972	R. Darling	17	102	5	6	0	3.87
	W-3 L-4	CF	D. Boston	255	.275	4	21	156	2	3	1	1.4	.981	P. Schourek	35	86	5	4	2	4.27
		LF	K. McReynolds	522	.259	16	74	281	9	2	1	2.1	.993	A. Pena	44	63	6	1	4	2.71
		C	R. Cerone	227	.273	2	16	424	36	6	0	5.8	.987	J. Franco	52	55	5	9	30	2.93
		OF	V. Coleman	278	.255	1	17	132	5	3	0	2.0	.979							
		20	K. Miller	275	.280	4	23	162	150	8	29		.975							
		OF	M. Carreon	254	.260	4	21	96	4	3	1	1.3	.971							
		UT	M. Sasser	228	.272	5	35	271	21	3	6		.990							
		S1	G. Templeton	219	.228	2	20	205	116	7	27		.979							
		C	C. O'Brien	168	.185	2	14	396	37	4	7	6.5	.991							
	Montreal	1B	A. Galarraga	375	.219	9	33	887	80	9	68	9.3	.991	D. Martinez	31	222	14	11	0	**2.39**
	W-71 L-90	2B	D. DeShields	563	.238	10	51	285	405	**27**	72	4.8	.962	M. Gardner	27	168	9	11	0	3.85
	Buck Rodgers	SS	S. Owen	424	.255	3	26	189	376	8	64	4.3	.986	B. Barnes	28	160	5	8	0	4.22
	W-20 L-29	3B	T. Wallach	577	.225	13	73	107	310	14	27	2.9	**.968**	C. Nabholz	24	154	8	7	0	3.63
	Tom Runnells	RF	L. Walker	487	.290	16	64	223	6	2	2	2.3	.991	O. Boyd	19	120	6	8	0	3.52
	W-51 L-61	CF	M. Grissom	558	.267	6	39	350	15	6	2	2.7	.984	B. Sampen	43	92	9	5	0	4.00
		LF	I. Calderon	470	.300	19	75	256	3	7	1	2.2	.974	B. Jones	**77**	89	4	9	13	3.35
		C	G. Reyes	207	.217	0	13	375	61	11	4	5.6	.975	C. Haney	16	85	3	7	0	4.04
		OF	D. Martinez	396	.295	7	42	213	10	4	0	2.0	.982	S. Ruskin	64	64	4	4	6	4.24
		C	M. Fitzgerald	198	.202	4	28	306	24	2	3	6.1	.994	J. Fassero	51	55	2	5	8	2.44
		S1	T. Foley	168	.208	0	15	193	80	5	20		.982	M. Rojas	37	48	3	3	6	3.75
														T. Burke	37	46	3	4	5	4.11

NATIONAL LEAGUE 1991, *cont.*

West

Team	POS	Player	AB	BA	HR	RBI	PO	A	E	DP	TC/G	FA	Pitcher	G	IP	W	L	SV	ERA
Atlanta	1B	S. Bream	265	.253	11	45	668	50	3	53	8.5	.996	T. Glavine	34	247	**20**	11	0	2.55
W-94 L-68	2B	M. Lemke	269	.234	2	23	159	205	8	39	3.4	.978	J. Smoltz	36	230	14	13	0	3.80
Bobby Cox	SS	R. Belliard	353	.249	0	27	168	361	18	53	3.8	.967	C. Leibrandt	36	230	15	13	0	3.49
	3B	T. Pendleton	586	**.319**	22	86	108	**349**	24	**31**	**3.3**	.950	S. Avery	35	210	18	8	0	3.38
	RF	D. Justice	396	.275	21	87	204	9	7	0	2.1	.968	M. Stanton	74	78	5	5	7	2.88
	CF	R. Gant	561	.251	32	105	338	7	6	1	2.4	.983	K. Mercker	50	73	5	3	6	2.58
	LF	L. Smith	353	.275	7	44	134	5	5	2	1.5	.965	J. Berenguer	49	64	0	3	17	2.24
	C	G. Olson	411	.241	6	44	721	48	4	7	6.1	.995	A. Pena	15	19	2	0	11	1.40
	OF	O. Nixon	401	.297	0	26	218	6	3	1	2.0	.987							
	UT	J. Blauser	352	.259	11	54	136	219	17	37		.954							
	2B	J. Treadway	306	.320	3	32	155	206	15	33	4.0	.960							
	1B	B. Hunter	271	.251	12	50	622	46	8	42	8.0	.988							
	C1	F. Cabrera	95	.242	4	23	137	13	3	3		.980							
Los Angeles	1B	E. Murray	576	.260	19	96	1327	128	7	96	9.8	.995	M. Morgan	34	236	14	10	1	2.78
W-93 L-69	2B	J. Samuel	594	.271	12	58	300	442	17	73	5.0	.978	R. Martinez	33	220	17	13	0	3.27
Tom Lasorda	SS	A. Griffin	350	.243	0	27	186	349	22	45	5.1	.961	T. Belcher	33	209	10	9	0	2.62
	3B	L. Harris	429	.287	3	38	77	155	14	16	2.2	.943	B. Ojeda	31	189	12	9	0	3.18
	RF	D. Strawberry	505	.265	28	99	209	11	5	2	1.7	.978	K. Gross	46	116	10	11	3	3.58
	CF	B. Butler	615	.296	2	38	372	8	0	3	2.4	1.000	O. Hershiser	21	112	7	2	0	3.46
	LF	K. Daniels	461	.249	17	73	220	9	5	0	1.8	.979	T. Crews	60	76	2	3	6	3.43
	C	M. Scioscia	345	.264	8	40	677	51	7	8	6.4	.990	J. Howell	44	51	6	5	16	3.18
	C	G. Carter	248	.246	6	26	355	45	5	2	6.0	.988	R. McDowell	33	42	6	3	7	2.55
	UT	M. Sharperson	216	.278	2	20	89	107	4	15		.980							
	OF	S. Javier	176	.205	1	11	70	1	1	0	1.0	.986							
	OF	C. Gwynn	139	.252	5	22	37	2	0	0	1.0	1.000							
San Diego	1B	F. McGriff	528	.278	31	106	1370	87	14	111	9.6	.990	A. Benes	33	223	15	11	0	3.03
W-84 L-78	2B	B. Roberts	424	.281	3	32	128	185	7	35	4.7	.978	B. Hurst	31	222	15	8	0	3.29
Greg Riddoch	SS	T. Fernandez	558	.272	4	38	247	440	20	78	4.9	.972	D. Rasmussen	24	147	6	13	0	3.74
	3B	S. Coolbaugh	180	.217	2	15	32	108	7	8	2.7	.952	G. Harris	20	133	9	5	0	2.23
	RF	T. Gwynn	530	.317	4	62	291	8	3	2	2.3	.990	M. Maddux	64	99	7	2	5	2.46
	CF	D. Jackson	359	.262	21	49	243	2	2	2	2.5	.992	J. Melendez	31	94	8	5	3	3.27
	LF	J. Clark	369	.228	10	47	160	5	1	2	1.7	.994	E. Whitson	13	79	4	6	0	5.03
	C	B. Santiago	580	.267	17	87	830	**100**	**14**	**14**	6.3	.985	C. Lefferts	54	69	1	6	23	3.91
	23	T. Teufel	307	.228	11	42	129	196	9	26		.973	R. Bones	11	54	4	6	0	4.83
	OF	T. Howard	281	.249	4	22	182	4	1	1	2.2	.995	L. Andersen	38	47	3	4	13	2.30
San Francisco	1B	W. Clark	565	.301	29	116	1273	110	4	**115**	9.6	**.997**	B. Black	34	214	12	**16**	0	3.99
W-75 L-87	2B	R. Thompson	492	.262	19	48	320	402	11	**98**	5.1	.985	J. Burkett	36	207	12	11	0	4.18
Roger Craig	SS	J. Uribe	231	.221	1	12	98	218	11	35	3.8	.966	T. Wilson	44	202	13	11	0	3.56
	3B	M. Williams	589	.268	34	98	**131**	293	16	30	2.8	.964	D. Robinson	34	121	5	9	1	4.38
	RF	K. Bass	361	.233	10	40	159	9	4	2	1.7	.977	K. Downs	45	112	10	4	0	4.19
	CF	W. McGee	497	.312	4	43	259	6	6	3	2.1	.978	J. Brantley	67	95	5	2	15	2.45
	LF	K. Mitchell	371	.256	27	69	188	6	6	1	2.0	.970	F. Oliveras	55	79	6	6	3	3.86
	C	S. Decker	233	.206	5	24	385	41	7	5	5.6	.984	D. Righetti	61	72	2	7	24	3.39
	OF	M. Felder	348	.264	0	18	192	3	3	2	1.9	.985							
	UT	D. Anderson	226	.248	2	13	167	127	11	29		.964							
	OF	D. Lewis	222	.248	1	15	159	2	0	0	2.4	1.000							
	C	K. Manwaring	178	.225	0	19	315	28	4	7	5.2	.988							
	C	T. Kennedy	171	.234	3	13	237	36	6	2	4.8	.978							
Cincinnati	1B	H. Morris	478	.318	14	59	979	100	9	87	8.5	.992	T. Browning	36	230	14	14	0	4.18
W-74 L-88	2B	B. Doran	361	.280	6	35	153	208	7	47	4.2	.981	J. Rijo	30	204	15	6	0	2.51
Lou Piniella	SS	B. Larkin	464	.302	20	69	226	372	15	65	**5.2**	.976	J. Armstrong	27	140	7	13	0	5.48
	3B	C. Sabo	582	.301	26	88	86	255	12	24	2.3	.966	R. Myers	58	132	6	13	6	3.55
	RF	P. O'Neill	532	.256	28	91	301	13	2	2	2.1	.994	N. Charlton	39	108	3	5	1	2.91
	CF	E. Davis	285	.235	11	33	190	5	3	2	2.4	.985	S. Scudder	27	101	6	9	1	4.35
	LF	B. Hatcher	442	.262	4	41	248	4	5	0	2.1	.981	C. Hammond	20	100	7	7	0	4.06
	C	J. Oliver	269	.216	11	41	496	40	11	6	6.1	.980	T. Power	68	87	5	3	3	3.62
	2S	M. Duncan	333	.258	12	40	162	212	9	41		.977	K. Gross	29	86	6	4	0	3.47
	C	J. Reed	270	.267	3	31	527	29	5	7	6.3	.991	R. Dibble	67	82	3	5	31	3.17
	OF	G. Braggs	250	.260	11	39	139	2	5	1	2.0	.966							
	23	L. Quinones	212	.222	4	20	57	94	6	18		.962							
	OF	H. Winningham	169	.225	1	4	99	2	5	0	1.6	.953							
Houston	1B	J. Bagwell	554	.294	15	82	1270	106	12	97	9.0	.991	P. Harnisch	33	217	12	9	0	2.70
W-65 L-97	2B	C. Candaele	461	.262	4	50	197	301	9	52	4.7	.982	M. Portugal	32	168	10	12	1	4.49
Art Howe	SS	E. Yelding	276	.243	1	20	113	166	18	31	4.1	.939	J. Deshaies	28	161	5	12	0	4.98
	3B	K. Caminiti	574	.253	13	80	129	293	23	29	2.9	.948	D. Kile	37	154	7	11	0	3.69
	RF	K. Rhodes	136	.213	1	12	87	4	4	1	2.2	.958	J. Jones	26	135	6	8	0	4.39
	CF	S. Finley	596	.285	8	54	323	13	5	2	2.2	.985	A. Osuna	71	82	7	6	12	3.42
	LF	L. Gonzalez	473	.254	13	69	294	6	5	1	2.3	.984	C. Schilling	56	76	3	5	8	3.81
	C	C. Biggio	546	.295	4	46	**889**	64	10	10	**6.9**	.990	R. Bowen	14	72	6	4	0	5.15
	SS	A. Cedeno	251	.243	9	36	88	151	18	36	3.9	.930	X. Hernandez	32	63	2	7	3	4.71
	S2	R. Ramirez	233	.236	1	20	86	123	8	22		.963							

BATTING AND BASE RUNNING LEADERS

Batting Average		Slugging Average		Home Runs	
T. Pendleton, ATL	.319	W. Clark, SF	.536	H. Johnson, NY	38
H. Morris, CIN	.318	H. Johnson, NY	.535	M. Williams, SF	34
T. Gwynn, SD	.317	T. Pendleton, ATL	.517	R. Gant, ATL	32
W. McGee, SF	.312	B. Bonds, PIT	.514	F. McGriff, SD	31
F. Jose, STL	.305	B. Larkin, CIN	.506	A. Dawson, CHI	31

PITCHING LEADERS

Winning Percentage		Earned Run Average		Wins	
J. Smiley, PIT	.714	D. Martinez, MON	2.39	J. Smiley, PIT	20
J. Rijo, CIN	.714	J. Rijo, CIN	2.51	T. Glavine, ATL	20
S. Avery, ATL	.692	T. Glavine, ATL	2.55	S. Avery, ATL	18
B. Hurst, SD	.652	T. Belcher, LA	2.62	R. Martinez, LA	17
T. Glavine, ATL	.645	P. Harnisch, HOU	2.70	Z. Smith, PIT	16
				T. Mulholland, PHI	16

NATIONAL LEAGUE 1991, *cont.*

BATTING AND BASE RUNNING LEADERS

Total Bases

W. Clark, SF	303
T. Pendleton, ATL	303
H. Johnson, NY	302
C. Sabo, CIN	294
M. Williams, SF	294

Runs Batted In

H. Johnson, NY	117
B. Bonds, PIT	116
W. Clark, SF	116
F. McGriff, SD	106
R. Gant, ATL	105

Stolen Bases

M. Grissom, MON	76
O. Nixon, ATL	72
D. DeShields, MON	56
R. Lankford, STL	44
B. Bonds, PIT	43

Hits

T. Pendleton, ATL	187
B. Butler, LA	182
C. Sabo, CIN	175
B. Bonilla, PIT	174

Base on Balls

B. Butler, LA	108
B. Bonds, PIT	107
F. McGriff, SD	105
D. DeShields, MON	95

Home Run Percentage

H. Johnson, NY	6.7
F. McGriff, SD	5.9
M. Williams, SF	5.8
R. Gant, ATL	5.7

Runs

B. Butler, LA	112
H. Johnson, NY	108
R. Sandberg, CHI	104
B. Bonilla, PIT	102

Doubles

B. Bonilla, PIT	44
F. Jose, STL	40
P. O'Neill, CIN	36
T. Zeile, STL	36

Triples

R. Lankford, STL	15
T. Gwynn, SD	11
S. Finley, HOU	10
L. Gonzalez, HOU	9
M. Grissom, MON	9

PITCHING LEADERS

Saves

L. Smith, STL	47
R. Dibble, CIN	31
J. Franco, NY	30
M. Williams, PHI	30
D. Righetti, SF	24

Strikeouts

D. Cone, NY	241
G. Maddux, CHI	198
T. Glavine, ATL	192
J. Rijo, CIN	172
P. Harnisch, HOU	172

Complete Games

D. Martinez, MON	9
T. Glavine, ATL	9
T. Mulholland, PHI	8
G. Maddux, CHI	7
R. Martinez, LA	6
Z. Smith, PIT	6

Fewest Hits/9 Innings

P. Harnisch, HOU	7.02
J. Rijo, CIN	7.27
J. DeJesus, PHI	7.28
K. Hill, STL	7.30

Shutouts

D. Martinez, MON	5
R. Martinez, LA	4
B. Black, SF	3
T. Mulholland, PHI	3
Z. Smith, PIT	3

Fewest Walks/9 Innings

Z. Smith, PIT	1.14
B. Tewksbury, STL	1.79
T. Mulholland, PHI	1.90
J. Smiley, PIT	1.91

Most Strikeouts/9 Inn.

D. Cone, NY	9.32
J. Rijo, CIN	7.58
P. Harnisch, HOU	7.14
D. Gooden, NY	7.11

Innings

G. Maddux, CHI	263
T. Glavine, ATL	247
M. Morgan, LA	236
D. Drabek, PIT	235

Games Pitched

B. Jones, MON	77
P. Assenmacher, CHI	75
M. Stanton, ATL	74
J. Agosto, STL	72
T. Burke, MON, NY	72

								Batting					Fielding			Pitching					
	W	L	PCT	GB	R	OR	2B	3B	HR	BA	SA	SB	E	DP	FA	CG	BB	SO	ShO	SV	ERA
East																					
Pittsburgh	98	64	.605		**768**	632	**259**	50	126	**.263**	.398	124	120	134	.981	**18**	**401**	919	11	**51**	3.44
St. Louis	84	78	.519	14	651	648	239	**53**	68	.255	.357	202	**107**	133	**.982**	9	454	822	5	**51**	3.69
Chicago	77	83	.481	20	695	734	232	26	159	.253	.390	123	113	120	**.982**	12	542	927	3	39	4.03
Philadelphia	78	84	.481	20	629	680	248	33	111	.241	.358	92	119	111	.981	16	670	988	11	35	3.86
New York	77	84	.478	20.5	640	646	250	24	117	.244	.365	153	143	112	.977	12	410	1028	11	39	3.56
Montreal	71	90	.441	26.5	579	655	236	42	95	.246	.357	**221**	133	128	.979	12	584	909	**14**	39	3.64
West																					
Atlanta	94	68	.580		749	644	255	30	141	.258	.393	165	138	122	.978	**18**	481	969	6	48	3.49
Los Angeles	93	69	.574	1	665	**565**	191	29	108	.253	.359	126	123	126	.980	15	500	1028	**14**	40	**3.06**
San Diego	84	78	.519	10	636	646	204	36	121	.244	.362	101	113	130	**.982**	14	457	921	11	47	3.57
San Francisco	75	87	.463	19	649	697	215	48	141	.246	.381	95	109	**151**	**.982**	10	544	905	10	45	4.03
Cincinnati	74	88	.457	20	689	691	250	27	**164**	.258	**.403**	124	125	131	.979	7	560	997	11	43	3.83
Houston	65	97	.401	29	605	717	240	43	79	.244	.347	125	161	129	.974	7	651	**1033**	13	36	4.00
					7955	7955	2819	441	1430	.250	.373	1651	1504	1527	.980	150	6254	11446	120	513	3.68

AMERICAN LEAGUE 1991

		POS	Player	AB	BA	HR	RBI	PO	A	E	DP	TC/G	FA	Pitcher	G	IP	W	L	SV	ERA
East	Toronto	1B	J. Olerud	454	.256	17	68	1120	78	5	77	8.9	.996	T. Stottlemyre	34	219	15	8	0	3.78
		2B	R. Alomar	637	.295	9	69	333	447	15	79	5.0	.981	J. Key	33	209	16	12	0	3.05
	W-91 L-71	SS	M. Lee	445	.234	0	29	194	360	19	52	4.2	.967	D. Wells	40	198	15	10	1	3.72
		3B	K. Gruber	429	.252	20	65	97	231	13	16	3.1	.962	J. Guzman	23	139	10	3	0	2.99
	Cito Gaston	RF	J. Carter	638	.273	33	108	283	13	8	2	2.0	.974	T. Candiotti	19	130	6	7	0	2.98
	W-66 L-54	CF	D. White	642	.282	17	60	439	8	1	2	2.9	.998	M. Timlin	63	108	11	6	3	3.16
		LF	C. Maldonado	177	.277	7	28	98	2	1	0	1.9	.990	D. Ward	**81**	107	7	6	23	2.77
	Gene Tenace	C	G. Myers	309	.262	8	36	484	37	11	5	5.1	.979	T. Henke	49	50	0	2	32	2.32
	W-19 L-14	DH	R. Mulliniks	240	.250	2	24													
		C	P. Borders	291	.244	5	36	505	48	4	4	5.5	.993							
	Cito Gaston	OD	M. Wilson	241	.241	2	28	71	2	2	0		.973							
	W-6 L-3	DH	P. Tabler	185	.216	1	21													
		31	E. Sprague	160	.275	4	20	162	72	12	14		.951							
	Boston	1B	C. Quintana	478	.295	11	71	1026	**101**	8	101	8.2	.993	R. Clemens	35	**271**	18	10	0	**2.62**
		2B	J. Reed	618	.283	5	60	312	444	14	109	5.1	.982	G. Harris	53	173	11	12	2	3.85
		SS	L. Rivera	414	.258	8	40	180	386	**24**	87	4.6	.959	J. Hesketh	39	153	12	4	0	3.29
	W-84 L-78	3B	W. Boggs	546	.332	8	51	89	276	12	34	2.7	.968	M. Gardiner	22	130	9	10	0	4.85
		RF	T. Brunansky	459	.229	16	70	265	5	3	2	2.0	.989	T. Bolton	25	110	8	9	0	5.24
	Joe Morgan	CF	E. Burks	474	.251	14	56	283	2	2	1	2.3	.993	M. Young	19	89	3	7	0	5.18
		LF	M. Greenwell	544	.300	9	83	263	9	3	3	1.9	.989	K. Morton	16	86	6	5	0	4.59
		C	T. Pena	464	.231	5	48	**864**	60	5	**15**	6.6	.995	J. Reardon	57	59	1	4	40	3.03
		DH	J. Clark	481	.249	28	87													
		1B	M. Vaughn	219	.260	4	32	378	26	6	43	8.4	.985							
		UT	S. Lyons	212	.241	4	17	118	43	3	6		.982							
		OF	P. Plantier	148	.331	11	35	80	1	2	0	2.1	.976							
	Detroit	1B	C. Fielder	624	.261	**44**	**133**	1055	83	8	110	9.4	.993	B. Gullickson	35	226	**20**	9	0	3.90
		2B	L. Whitaker	470	.279	23	78	255	361	4	91	4.6	**.994**	W. Terrell	35	219	12	14	0	4.24
		SS	A. Trammell	375	.248	9	55	131	296	9	60	4.7	.979	F. Tanana	33	217	13	12	0	3.77
	W-84 L-78	3B	T. Fryman	557	.259	21	91	45	147	11	13	2.4	.946	M. Leiter	38	135	9	7	1	4.21
		RF	R. Deer	448	.179	25	64	310	8	7	4	2.5	.978	P. Gibson	68	96	5	7	8	4.59
	Sparky Anderson	CF	M. Cuyler	475	.257	3	33	411	7	6	3	2.8	.986	J. Cerutti	38	89	3	6	2	4.57
		LF	L. Moseby	260	.262	6	35	126	1	6	0	2.1	.955	M. Henneman	60	84	10	2	21	2.88
		C	M. Tettleton	501	.263	31	89	558	55	6	2	5.0	.990							
		DH	P. Incaviglia	337	.214	11	38													
		UT	T. Phillips	564	.284	17	72	269	237	8	51		.984							
		1B	D. Bergman	194	.237	7	29	364	29	1	42	8.0	.997							

AMERICAN LEAGUE 1991, *cont.*

Team	POS	Player	AB	BA	HR	RBI	PO	A	E	DP	TC/G	FA	Pitcher	G	IP	W	L	SV	ERA
Milwaukee	1B	F. Stubbs	362	.213	11	38	824	82	8	78	9.9	.991	J. Navarro	34	234	15	12	0	3.92
W-83 L-79	2B	W. Randolph	431	.327	0	54	237	378	**20**	96	**5.2**	.969	C. Bosio	32	205	14	10	0	3.25
Tom Trebelhorn	SS	B. Spiers	414	.283	8	54	201	345	17	93	4.4	.970	B. Wegman	28	193	15	7	0	2.84
	3B	J. Gantner	526	.283	2	47	51	155	5	15	2.3	.976	D. August	28	138	9	8	0	5.47
	RF	D. Bichette	445	.238	15	59	270	14	7	7	2.3	.976	D. Plesac	45	92	2	7	8	4.29
	CF	R. Yount	503	.260	10	77	315	1	2	1	2.7	.994	C. Crim	66	91	8	5	3	4.63
	LF	G. Vaughn	542	.244	27	98	315	5	2	1	2.4	.994	D. Henry	32	36	2	1	15	1.00
	C	B. Surhoff	505	.289	5	68	660	**68**	4	11	5.8	.995	E. Nunez	23	25	2	1	8	6.04
	DH	P. Molitor	**665**	.325	17	75													
	OF	D. Hamilton	405	.311	1	57	234	3	1	0	2.0	.996							
	S3	D. Sveum	266	.241	4	43	82	187	10	33		.964							
	3B	G. Sheffield	175	.194	2	22	29	65	8	7	2.4	.922							
	C	R. Dempsey	147	.231	4	21	246	23	2	4	4.8	.993							
	OF	C. Maldonado	111	.207	5	20	41	0	1	0	1.8	.976							
New York	1B	D. Mattingly	587	.288	9	68	1119	77	5	**135**	9.5	.996	S. Sanderson	34	208	16	10	0	3.81
W-71 L-91	2B	S. Sax	652	.304	10	56	274	443	7	107	4.9	.990	J. Johnson	23	127	6	11	0	5.95
Stump Merrill	SS	A. Espinoza	480	.256	5	33	223	438	21	113	4.6	.969	G. Cadaret	68	122	8	6	3	3.62
	3B	P. Kelly	298	.242	3	23	43	157	16	14	2.7	.926	T. Leary	28	121	4	10	0	6.49
	RF	J. Barfield	284	.225	17	48	178	10	0	3	2.3	1.000	W. Taylor	23	116	7	12	0	6.27
	CF	B. Williams	320	.238	3	34	230	3	5	0	2.8	.979	E. Plunk	43	112	2	5	0	4.76
	LF	M. Hall	492	.285	19	80	221	8	3	2	1.9	.987	L. Guetterman	64	88	3	4	6	3.68
	C	M. Nokes	456	.268	24	77	690	48	6	7	5.7	.992	S. Farr	60	70	5	5	23	2.19
	DH	K. Maas	500	.220	23	63													
	OF	R. Kelly	486	.267	20	69	268	8	4	1	2.2	.986							
	OF	H. Meulens	288	.222	6	29	144	4	5	1	2.1	.967							
	3S	R. Velarde	184	.245	1	15	63	148	15	24		.934							
Baltimore	1B	R. Milligan	483	.263	16	70	929	81	10	92	9.6	.990	B. Milacki	31	184	10	9	0	4.01
W-67 L-95	2B	B. Ripken	287	.216	0	14	201	284	7	75	4.8	.986	B. McDonald	21	126	6	8	0	4.84
Frank Robinson	SS	C. Ripken	650	.323	34	114	**267**	**528**	11	**114**	**5.0**	**.986**	J. Mesa	23	124	6	11	0	5.97
W-13 L-24	3B	L. Gomez	391	.233	16	45	62	184	7	20	2.4	.972	J. Ballard	26	124	6	12	0	5.60
Johnny Oates	RF	D. Evans	270	.270	6	38	116	6	2	2	1.9	.984	J. Robinson	21	104	4	9	0	5.18
W-54 L-71	CF	M. Devereaux	608	.260	19	59	399	10	3	1	2.8	.993	M. Flanagan	64	98	2	7	3	2.38
	LF	J. Orsulak	486	.278	5	43	273	22	1	4	2.2	.997	T. Frohwirth	51	96	7	3	3	1.87
	C	C. Hoiles	341	.243	11	31	433	43	1	5	5.4	**.998**	D. Johnson	22	84	4	8	0	7.07
	DH	S. Horn	317	.233	23	61							M. Williamson	65	80	5	5	4	4.48
	OF	B. Anderson	256	.230	2	27	150	3	3	0	1.5	.981	G. Olson	72	74	4	6	31	3.18
	C	B. Melvin	228	.250	1	23	383	31	1	8	5.8	.998							
	OF	C. Martinez	216	.269	13	33	108	4	2	2	2.1	.982							
	10	D. Segui	212	.278	2	22	264	23	3	22		.990							
	2B	J. Bell	209	.172	1	15	104	189	8	39	3.9	.973							
	UT	T. Hulett	206	.204	7	18	47	96	4	13		.973							
	1B	G. Davis	176	.227	10	28	288	38	8	35	9.3	.976							
Cleveland	1B	B. Jacoby	231	.234	4	24	379	32	5	27	7.6	.988	G. Swindell	33	238	9	16	0	3.48
W-57 L-105	2B	M. Lewis	314	.264	0	30	87	140	8	29	4.7	.966	C. Nagy	33	211	10	15	0	4.13
John McNamara	SS	F. Fermin	424	.262	0	31	214	372	12	74	4.6	.980	E. King	25	151	6	11	0	4.60
W-25 L-52	3B	C. Baerga	593	.288	11	69	54	183	14	14	2.8	.944	R. Nichols	31	137	2	11	1	3.54
Mike Hargrove	RF	M. Whiten	258	.256	7	26	166	11	7	2	2.7	.962	T. Candiotti	15	108	7	6	0	2.24
W-32 L-53	CF	A. Cole	387	.295	0	21	256	6	8	1	2.5	.970	D. Otto	18	100	2	8	0	4.23
	LF	A. Belle	461	.282	28	95	170	8	9	1	2.1	.952	S. Hillegas	51	83	3	4	7	4.34
	C	J. Skinner	284	.243	1	24	504	38	5	4	5.5	.991	D. Jones	36	63	4	8	7	5.54
	DH	C. James	437	.238	5	41							S. Olin	48	56	3	6	17	3.36
	UT	J. Browne	290	.228	1	29	113	141	14	21		.948							
	D1	C. Martinez	257	.284	5	30	229	12	8	30		.968							
	C	S. Alomar	184	.217	0	7	280	19	4	4	6.6	.987							
	10	M. Aldrete	183	.262	1	19	334	23	2	31		.994							

West

Team	POS	Player	AB	BA	HR	RBI	PO	A	E	DP	TC/G	FA	Pitcher	G	IP	W	L	SV	ERA
Minnesota	1B	K. Hrbek	462	.284	20	89	1138	95	8	110	9.7	.994	J. Morris	35	247	18	12	0	3.43
W-95 L-67	2B	C. Knoblauch	565	.281	1	50	249	460	18	94	4.9	.975	K. Tapani	34	244	16	9	0	2.99
Tom Kelly	SS	G. Gagne	408	.265	8	42	181	377	9	69	4.1	.984	S. Erickson	32	204	**20**	8	0	3.18
	3B	M. Pagliarulo	365	.279	6	36	56	248	11	30	2.7	.965	A. Anderson	29	134	5	11	0	4.96
	RF	S. Mack	442	.310	18	74	290	6	7	2	2.2	.977	M. Guthrie	41	98	7	5	2	4.32
	CF	K. Puckett	611	.319	15	89	373	13	6	5	2.6	.985	C. Willis	40	89	8	3	2	2.63
	LF	D. Gladden	461	.247	6	52	240	4	3	1	2.0	.988	S. Bedrosian	56	77	5	3	6	4.42
	C	B. Harper	441	.311	10	69	642	33	8	7	5.7	.988	R. Aguilera	63	69	4	5	42	2.35
	DH	C. Davis	534	.277	29	93													
	01	G. Larkin	255	.286	2	19	340	20	3	23		.992							
	UT	A. Newman	246	.191	0	19	130	184	4	39		.987							
	3B	S. Leius	199	.286	5	20	41	100	7	8	1.9	.953							
	UT	R. Bush	165	.303	6	23	85	5	2	7		.978							
	OF	P. Munoz	138	.283	7	26	89	3	1	2	2.1	.989							
Chicago	1B	D. Pasqua	417	.259	18	66	511	43	5	45	6.7	.991	J. McDowell	35	254	17	10	0	3.41
W-87 L-75	2B	S. Fletcher	248	.206	1	28	177	191	3	49	4.3	.992	C. Hough	31	199	9	10	0	4.02
Jeff Torborg	SS	O. Guillen	524	.273	3	49	249	439	21	88	4.8	.970	G. Hibbard	32	194	11	11	0	4.31
	3B	R. Ventura	606	.284	23	100	**134**	287	**18**	29	2.9	.959	A. Fernandez	34	192	9	13	0	4.51
	RF	S. Sosa	316	.203	10	33	214	6	6	0	2.0	.973	M. Perez	49	136	8	7	1	3.12
	CF	L. Johnson	588	.274	0	49	425	11	2	3	2.8	.995	S. Radinsky	67	71	5	5	8	2.02
	LF	T. Raines	609	.268	5	50	273	12	3	3	2.2	.990	B. Thigpen	67	70	7	5	30	3.49
	C	C. Fisk	460	.241	18	74	535	55	4	5	5.6	.993							
	DH	F. Thomas	559	.318	32	109													
	2B	J. Cora	228	.241	0	18	103	184	9	33	3.7	.970							
	UT	C. Grebeck	224	.281	6	31	104	183	10	34		.966							
	C	R. Karkovice	167	.246	5	22	309	28	4	6	4.9	.988							
	UT	M. Merullo	140	.229	5	21	159	14	2	11		.989							
	OF	W. Newson	132	.295	4	25	48	3	2	0	1.1	.962							

AMERICAN LEAGUE 1991, *cont.*

Texas

W-85 L-77

Bobby Valentine

POS	Player	AB	BA	HR	RBI	PO	A	E	DP	TC/G	FA	Pitcher	G	IP	W	L	SV	ERA
1B	R. Palmeiro	631	.322	26	88	1305	96	**12**	119	9.0	.992	K. Brown	33	211	9	12	0	4.40
2B	J. Franco	589	**.341**	15	78	294	372	14	80	4.7	.979	N. Ryan	27	173	12	6	0	2.91
SS	J. Huson	268	.213	2	26	141	267	15	42	3.6	.965	J. Guzman	25	170	13	7	0	3.08
3B	S. Buechele	416	.267	18	66	87	239	3	20	3.0	.991*	K. Rogers	63	110	10	10	5	5.42
RF	R. Sierra	661	.307	25	116	305	15	7	3	2.0	.979	B. Witt	17	89	3	7	0	6.09
CF	G. Pettis	282	.216	0	19	248	4	6	1	2.0	.977	J. Russell	68	79	6	4	30	3.29
LF	J. Gonzalez	545	.264	27	102	310	6	6	1	2.4	.981							
C	I. Rodriguez	280	.264	3	27	517	62	10	6	**6.7**	.983							
DH	B. Downing	407	.278	17	49													
OD	K. Reimer	394	.269	20	69	110	0	6	0		.948							
30	D. Palmer	268	.187	15	37	69	75	9	6		.941							
C	G. Petralli	199	.271	2	20	293	20	9	3	4.9	.972							
S2	M. Diaz	182	.264	1	22	90	136	7	31		.970							
UT	M. Stanley	181	.249	3	25	288	20	6	2		.981							

Oakland

W-84 L-78

Tony LaRussa

POS	Player	AB	BA	HR	RBI	PO	A	E	DP	TC/G	FA	Pitcher	G	IP	W	L	SV	ERA
1B	M. McGwire	483	.201	22	75	1191	**101**	4	120	8.5	.997	D. Stewart	35	226	11	11	0	5.18
2B	M. Gallego	482	.247	12	49	243	370	7	69	4.6	.989	B. Welch	35	220	12	13	0	4.58
SS	M. Bordick	235	.238	0	21	137	209	10	44	4.2	.972	M. Moore	33	210	17	8	0	2.96
3B	E. Riles	281	.214	5	32	54	101	10	14	2.4	.939	J. Slusarski	20	109	5	7	0	5.27
RF	J. Canseco	572	.266	**44**	122	245	5	9	0	2.0	.965	D. Eckersley	67	76	5	4	43	2.96
CF	D. Henderson	572	.276	25	85	362	10	1	2	2.7	.997	R. Darling	12	75	3	7	0	4.08
LF	R. Henderson	470	.268	18	57	249	10	8	1	2.2	.970	J. Klink	62	62	10	3	2	4.35
C	T. Steinbach	456	.274	6	67	594	48	**13**	7	5.6	.980							
DH	H. Baines	488	.295	20	90													
OF	W. Wilson	294	.238	0	28	176	2	3	0	2.1	.983							
C	J. Quirk	203	.261	1	17	293	32	6	2	6.1	.982							
3B	B. Jacoby	188	.213	0	20	38	72	2	9	2.2	.982							
UT	L. Blankenship	185	.249	3	21	123	122	3	25		.988							

Seattle

W-83 L-79

Jim Lefebvre

POS	Player	AB	BA	HR	RBI	PO	A	E	DP	TC/G	FA	Pitcher	G	IP	W	L	SV	ERA
1B	P. O'Brien	560	.248	17	88	1047	86	3	124	8.6	**.997**	R. Johnson	33	201	13	10	0	3.98
2B	H. Reynolds	631	.254	3	57	**348**	**463**	18	**133**	5.2	.978	B. Holman	30	195	13	14	0	3.69
SS	O. Vizquel	426	.230	1	41	224	422	13	105	4.8	.980	R. DeLucia	32	182	12	13	0	5.09
3B	E. Martinez	544	.307	14	52	84	299	15	25	2.8	.962	B. Krueger	35	175	11	8	0	3.60
RF	J. Buhner	406	.244	27	77	244	15	5	4	2.0	.981	E. Hanson	27	175	8	8	0	3.81
CF	K. Griffey	548	.327	22	100	360	15	4	4	2.5	.989	B. Swift	71	90	1	2	17	1.99
LF	G. Briley	381	.260	2	26	187	5	4	1	1.6	.980	M. Jackson	72	89	7	7	14	3.25
C	D. Valle	324	.194	8	32	669	52	6	9	5.6	.992	R. Swan	63	79	6	2	2	3.43
DH	A. Davis	462	.221	12	69							M. Schooler	34	34	3	3	7	3.67
UT	D. Cochrane	178	.247	2	22	105	25	7	3		.949							
OF	H. Cotto	177	.305	6	23	104	2	2	1	1.9	.981							
DO	T. Jones	175	.251	3	24	49	0	0	0		1.000							
C	S. Bradley	172	.203	0	11	285	16	2	4	4.7	.993							
UT	J. Schaefer	164	.250	1	11	79	120	6	31		.971							

Kansas City

W-82 L-80

John Wathan
W-15 L-22

Bob Schaefer
W-1 L-0

Hal McRae
W-66 L-58

POS	Player	AB	BA	HR	RBI	PO	A	E	DP	TC/G	FA	Pitcher	G	IP	W	L	SV	ERA
1B	T. Benzinger	293	.294	2	40	651	38	3	57	9.2	.996	K. Appier	34	208	13	10	0	3.42
2B	T. Shumpert	369	.217	5	34	249	368	16	81	4.4	.975	B. Saberhagen	28	196	13	8	0	3.07
SS	K. Stillwell	385	.265	6	51	163	263	18	66	3.8	.959	M. Boddicker	30	181	12	12	0	4.08
3B	B. Pecota	398	.286	6	45	69	158	4	14	2.3	.983	T. Gordon	45	158	9	14	1	3.87
RF	D. Tartabull	484	.316	31	100	190	4	7	0	1.6	.965	L. Aquino	38	157	8	4	3	3.44
CF	B. McRae	629	.261	8	64	405	2	3	0	2.7	.993	M. Gubicza	26	133	9	12	0	5.68
LF	K. Gibson	462	.236	16	55	162	3	4	0	1.8	.976	S. Davis	51	114	3	9	2	4.96
C	B. Mayne	231	.251	3	31	425	38	6	4	5.9	.987	J. Montgomery	67	90	4	4	33	2.90
DH	G. Brett	505	.255	10	61							M. Davis	29	63	6	3	1	4.45
OF	J. Eisenreich	375	.301	2	47	143	1	4	0	1.4	.973							
C	M. Macfarlane	267	.277	13	41	391	28	3	4	6.1	.993							
S2	D. Howard	236	.216	1	17	129	248	12	40		.969							
3B	K. Seitzer	234	.265	1	25	45	127	11	8	2.7	.940							
OF	G. Thurman	184	.277	2	13	129	2	4	0	1.9	.970							
1B	W. Cromartie	131	.313	1	20	215	9	1	20	7.8	.996							

California

W-81 L-81

Doug Rader
W-61 L-63

Buck Rodgers
W-20 L-18

POS	Player	AB	BA	HR	RBI	PO	A	E	DP	TC/G	FA	Pitcher	G	IP	W	L	SV	ERA
1B	W. Joyner	551	.301	21	96	**1335**	98	8	124	**10.2**	.994	M. Langston	34	246	19	8	0	3.00
2B	L. Sojo	364	.258	3	20	228	326	11	78	5.3	.981	J. Abbott	34	243	18	11	0	2.89
SS	D. Schofield	427	.225	0	31	186	398	15	83	4.5	.975	C. Finley	34	227	18	9	0	3.80
3B	G. Gaetti	586	.246	18	66	111	**353**	17	**39**	**3.2**	.965	K. McCaskill	30	178	10	**19**	0	4.26
RF	D. Winfield	568	.262	28	86	198	7	2	1	1.8	.990	B. Harvey	67	79	2	4	**46**	1.60
CF	J. Felix	230	.283	2	26	126	1	3	0	2.0	.977	J. Grahe	18	73	3	7	0	4.81
LF	L. Polonia	604	.296	2	50	246	9	5	1	1.8	.981							
C	L. Parrish	402	.216	19	51	658	57	2	11	6.5	.997							
DH	D. Parker	466	.232	11	56													
OF	D. Gallagher	270	.293	1	30	180	8	0	1	2.2	1.000							
2S	D. Hill	209	.239	1	20	112	173	7	34		.976							
OF	M. Venable	187	.246	3	21	86	3	3	0	1.4	.967							

BATTING AND BASE RUNNING LEADERS

Batting Average		Slugging Average		Home Runs	
J. Franco, TEX	.341	D. Tartabull, KC	.593	J. Canseco, OAK	44
W. Boggs, BOS	.332	C. Ripken, BAL	.566	C. Fielder, DET	44
W. Randolph, MIL	.327	J. Canseco, OAK	.556	C. Ripken, BAL	34
K. Griffey, SEA	.327	F. Thomas, CHI	.553	J. Carter, TOR	33
P. Molitor, MIL	.325	R. Palmeiro, TEX	.532	F. Thomas, CHI	32

PITCHING LEADERS

Winning Percentage		Earned Run Average		Wins	
S. Erickson, MIN	.714	R. Clemens, BOS	2.62	S. Erickson, MIN	20
M. Langston, CAL	.704	T. Candiotti, CLE, TOR	2.65	B. Gullickson, DET	20
B. Gullickson, DET	.690	B. Wegman, MIL	2.84	M. Langston, CAL	19
B. Wegman, MIL	.682	J. Abbott, CAL	2.89		
M. Moore, OAK	.680	N. Ryan, TEX	2.91		

AMERICAN LEAGUE 1991, *cont.*

BATTING AND BASE RUNNING LEADERS

Total Bases

C. Ripken, BAL	368
R. Palmeiro, TEX	336
R. Sierra, TEX	332
P. Molitor, MIL	325
J. Carter, TOR	321

Runs Batted In

C. Fielder, DET	133
J. Canseco, OAK	122
R. Sierra, TEX	116
C. Ripken, BAL	114
F. Thomas, CHI	109

Stolen Bases

R. Henderson, OAK	58
R. Alomar, TOR	53
T. Raines, CHI	51
L. Polonia, CAL	48
M. Cuyler, DET	41

Hits

P. Molitor, MIL	216
C. Ripken, BAL	210
R. Palmeiro, TEX	203
R. Sierra, TEX	203

Base on Balls

F. Thomas, CHI	138
M. Tettleton, DET	101
R. Henderson, OAK	98
J. Clark, BOS	96

Home Run Percentage

J. Canseco, OAK	7.7
C. Fielder, DET	7.1
D. Tartabull, KC	6.4
M. Tettleton, DET	6.2

Runs

P. Molitor, MIL	133
J. Canseco, OAK	115
R. Palmeiro, TEX	115
D. White, TOR	110
R. Sierra, TEX	110

Doubles

R. Palmeiro, TEX	49
C. Ripken, BAL	46
R. Sierra, TEX	44

Triples

L. Johnson, CHI	13
P. Molitor, MIL	13
R. Alomar, TOR	11
M. Devereaux, BAL	10
D. White, TOR	10

PITCHING LEADERS

Saves

B. Harvey, CAL	46
D. Eckersley, OAK	43
R. Aguilera, MIN	42
J. Reardon, BOS	40
J. Montgomery, KC	33

Strikeouts

R. Clemens, BOS	241
R. Johnson, SEA	228
N. Ryan, TEX	203
J. McDowell, CHI	191
M. Langston, CAL	183

Complete Games

J. McDowell, CHI	15
R. Clemens, BOS	13
J. Navarro, MIL	10
J. Morris, MIN	10
W. Terrell, DET	8

Fewest Hits/9 Innings

N. Ryan, TEX	5.31
R. Johnson, SEA	6.75
M. Langston, CAL	6.94
R. Clemens, BOS	7.26

Shutouts

R. Clemens, BOS	4
B. Holman, SEA	3
K. Appier, KC	3
S. Erickson, MIN	3
J. McDowell, CHI	3

Fewest Walks/9 Innings

G. Swindell, CLE	1.17
S. Sanderson, NY	1.25
K. Tapani, MIN	1.48
B. Gullickson, DET	1.75

Most Strikeouts/9 Inn.

N. Ryan, TEX	10.56
R. Johnson, SEA	10.19
R. Clemens, BOS	7.99
E. Hanson, SEA	7.37

Innings

R. Clemens, BOS	271
J. McDowell, CHI	254
J. Morris, MIN	247
M. Langston, CAL	246

Games Pitched

D. Ward, TOR	81
M. Jackson, SEA	72
G. Olson, BAL	72
B. Swift, SEA	71

		W	L	PCT	GB	R	OR	Batting 2B	3B	HR	BA	SA	SB	Fielding E	DP	FA	Pitching CG	BB	SO	ShO	SV	ERA
East	Toronto	91	71	.562		684	**622**	295	45	133	.257	.400	148	127	115	.980	10	523	971	**16**	**60**	**3.50**
	Boston	84	78	.519	7	731	712	**305**	25	126	.269	.401	59	116	165	.981	15	530	999	13	45	4.01
	Detroit	84	78	.519	7	817	794	259	26	**209**	.247	.416	109	104	171	.983	18	593	739	8	38	4.51
	Milwaukee	83	79	.512	8	799	744	247	**53**	116	.271	.396	106	118	176	.981	23	527	859	11	41	4.14
	New York	71	91	.438	20	674	777	249	19	147	.256	.387	109	133	181	.979	3	506	936	11	37	4.42
	Baltimore	67	95	.414	24	686	796	256	29	170	.254	.401	50	**91**	172	**.985**	8	504	868	8	42	4.59
	Cleveland	57	105	.352	34	576	759	236	26	79	.254	.350	84	149	150	.976	22	**441**	862	8	33	4.23
West	Minnesota	95	67	.586		776	652	270	42	140	**.280**	.420	107	95	161	**.985**	21	488	876	12	53	3.69
	Chicago	87	75	.537	8	758	681	226	39	139	.262	.391	134	116	151	.982	**28**	601	923	8	40	3.79
	Texas	85	77	.525	10	**829**	814	288	31	177	.270	**.424**	102	134	138	.979	9	662	**1022**	10	41	4.47
	Oakland	84	78	.519	11	760	776	246	19	159	.248	.389	**151**	107	150	.982	14	655	892	10	49	4.57
	Seattle	83	79	.512	12	702	674	268	29	126	.255	.383	97	110	**187**	.983	10	628	1003	13	48	3.79
	Kansas City	82	80	.506	13	727	722	290	41	117	.264	.394	119	125	141	.980	17	529	1004	12	41	3.92
	California	81	81	.500	14	653	649	245	29	115	.255	.374	94	102	156	.984	18	543	990	10	50	3.69
						10172	10172	3680	453	1953	.260	.395	1469	1627	2214	.981	216	7730	12944	150	618	4.09

NATIONAL LEAGUE 1992

	POS	Player	AB	BA	HR	RBI	PO	A	E	DP	TC/G	FA	Pitcher	G	IP	W	L	SV	ERA
East Pittsburgh	1B	O. Merced	405	.247	6	60	882	73	5	73	8.4	.995	D. Drabek	34	257	15	11	0	2.77
	2B	J. Lind	468	.235	0	39	311	428	6	78	5.6	**.992**	R. Tomlin	35	209	14	9	0	3.41
W-96 L-66	SS	J. Bell	632	.264	9	55	**268**	**526**	22	**94**	**5.1**	.973	Z. Smith	23	141	8	8	0	3.06
Jim Leyland	3B	S. Buechele	285	.249	8	43	52	169	10	10	2.9	.957	B. Walk	36	135	10	6	2	3.20
	RF	C. Espy	194	.258	1	20	83	1	4	0	1.1	.955	R. Mason	65	88	5	7	8	4.09
	CF	A. Van Slyke	614	.324	14	89	421	11	5	3	2.8	.989	D. Neagle	55	86	4	6	2	4.48
	LF	B. Bonds	473	.311	34	103	310	4	3	0	2.3	.991	S. Belinda	59	71	6	4	18	3.15
	C	M. LaValliere	293	.256	2	29	421	62	3	6	5.3	.994	B. Patterson	60	65	6	3	9	2.92
	UT	J. King	480	.231	14	65	368	234	12	58		.980							
	C	D. Slaught	255	.345	4	37	365	35	5	4	5.1	.988							
	OF	A. Cole	205	.278	0	10	85	5	1	0	1.7	.989							
	OF	L. McClendon	190	.253	3	20	80	0	3	0	1.4	.964							
	1B	G. Redus	176	.256	3	12	280	16	0	14	8.2	1.000							
	OF	G. Varsho	162	.222	4	22	62	1	1	0	1.5	.984							
Montreal	1B	A. Cianfrocco	232	.241	6	30	375	39	3	25	7.4	.993	D. Martinez	32	226	16	11	0	2.47
	2B	D. DeShields	530	.292	7	56	251	360	15	71	4.7	.976	K. Hill	33	218	16	9	0	2.68
W-87 L-75	SS	S. Owen	386	.269	7	40	188	300	9	44	4.3	.982	C. Nabholz	32	195	11	12	0	3.32
Tom Runnells	3B	T. Wallach	537	.223	9	59	56	184	9	17	2.9	.964	M. Gardner	33	180	12	10	0	4.36
W-17 L-20	RF	L. Walker	528	.301	23	93	269	16	2	2	2.1	.993	M. Rojas	68	101	7	1	10	1.43
Felipe Alou	CF	M. Grissom	**653**	.276	14	66	401	7	7	2	2.6	.983	B. Barnes	21	100	6	6	0	2.97
W-70 L-55	LF	M. Alou	341	.282	9	56	170	6	4	1	1.8	.978	J. Fassero	70	86	8	7	1	2.84*
	C	G. Carter	285	.218	5	29	481	52	6	3	6.3	.989	J. Wetteland	67	83	4	4	37	2.92
	3B	B. Barberie	285	.232	1	24	37	127	12	10	2.8	.932							
	C	D. Fletcher	222	.243	2	26	360	33	2	3	5.7	.995							
	OF	J. Vander Wal	213	.239	4	20	99	2	2	0	1.8	.981							
	OF	I. Calderon	170	.265	3	24	79	2	1	0	1.8	.988							
	1B	G. Colbrunn	168	.268	2	18	363	29	3	24	8.4	.992							

NATIONAL LEAGUE 1992, *cont.*

St. Louis

W-83 L-79

Joe Torre

POS	Player	AB	BA	HR	RBI	PO	A	E	DP	TC/G	FA	Pitcher	G	IP	W	L	SV	ERA
1B	A. Galarraga	325	.243	10	39	777	62	8	71	9.4	.991	B. Tewksbury	33	233	16	5	0	2.16
2B	L. Alicea	265	.245	2	32	130	227	4	36	4.8	.989	O. Olivares	32	197	9	9	0	3.84
SS	O. Smith	518	.295	0	31	232	420	10	82	5.0	.985	R. Cormier	31	186	10	10	0	3.68
3B	T. Zeile	439	.257	7	48	80	235	13	19	2.6	.960	D. Osborne	34	179	11	9	0	3.77
RF	F. Jose	509	.295	14	75	273	11	6	1	2.3	.979	M. Clark	20	113	3	10	0	4.45
CF	R. Lankford	598	.293	20	86	438	5	2	0	2.9	.996	J. DeLeon	29	102	2	7	0	4.57
LF	B. Gilkey	384	.302	7	43	217	9	5	3	2.1	.978	M. Perez	77	93	9	3	0	1.84
C	T. Pagnozzi	485	.249	7	44	688	53	1	10	5.4	**.999**	C. Carpenter	73	88	5	4	1	2.97
OF	M. Thompson	208	.293	4	17	74	1	2	1	1.7	.974	L. Smith	70	75	4	9	**43**	3.12
2B	G. Pena	203	.305	7	31	125	184	5	40	5.5	.984	T. Worrell	67	64	5	3	3	2.11
OF	B. Jordan	193	.207	5	22	101	4	1	0	2.0	.991							
3B	T. Woodson	114	.307	1	22	17	35	3	4	2.1	.945							

Chicago

W-78 L-84

Jim Lefebvre

POS	Player	AB	BA	HR	RBI	PO	A	E	DP	TC/G	FA	Pitcher	G	IP	W	L	SV	ERA
1B	M. Grace	603	.307	9	79	**1580**	**141**	4	119	**11.0**	.998	G. Maddux	35	**268**	**20**	11	0	2.18
2B	R. Sandberg	612	.304	26	87	283	**539**	8	94	5.3	.990	M. Morgan	34	240	16	8	0	2.55
SS	R. Sanchez	255	.251	1	19	143	198	9	52	5.1	.974	F. Castillo	33	205	10	11	0	3.46
3B	S. Buechele	239	.276	1	21	50	119	7	6	2.8	.960	D. Jackson	19	113	4	9	0	4.22
RF	A. Dawson	542	.277	22	90	223	11	2	3	1.7	.992	S. Boskie	23	92	5	11	0	5.01
CF	D. Dascenzo	376	.255	0	20	221	2	5	0	1.9	.978	B. Scanlan	69	87	3	6	14	2.89
LF	D. May	351	.274	8	45	153	3	5	0	1.5	.969	J. Bullinger	39	85	2	8	7	4.66
C	J. Girardi	270	.270	1	12	369	51	4	6	4.9	.991	C. McElroy	72	84	4	7	6	3.55
S3	J. Vizcaino	285	.225	1	17	91	194	9	34		.969	P. Assenmacher	70	68	4	4	8	4.10
OF	S. Sosa	262	.260	8	25	145	4	6	1	2.3	.961							
UT	L. Salazar	255	.208	5	25	114	98	6	16		.972							
C	R. Wilkins	244	.270	8	22	408	47	3	5	6.3	.993							
OF	D. Smith	217	.276	3	24	93	2	2	0	1.5	.979							

New York

W-72 L-90

Jeff Torborg

POS	Player	AB	BA	HR	RBI	PO	A	E	DP	TC/G	FA	Pitcher	G	IP	W	L	SV	ERA
1B	E. Murray	551	.261	16	93	1283	96	**12**	109	9.0	.991	S. Fernandez	32	215	14	11	0	2.73
2B	W. Randolph	286	.252	2	15	149	195	8	53	4.5	.977	D. Gooden	31	206	10	13	0	3.67
SS	D. Schofield	420	.205	4	36	205	391	7	78	4.3	.988*	D. Cone	27	197	13	7	0	2.88
3B	D. Magadan	321	.283	3	28	41	135	11	10	2.0	.941	P. Schourek	22	136	6	8	0	3.64
RF	B. Bonilla	438	.249	19	70	238	7	2	1	2.0	.992	A. Young	52	121	2	14	15	4.17
CF	H. Johnson	350	.223	7	43	206	3	4	0	2.2	.981	W. Whitehurst	44	97	3	9	0	3.62
LF	D. Boston	289	.249	11	35	133	5	1	1	1.5	.993	J. Innis	76	88	6	9	1	2.86
C	T. Hundley	358	.209	7	32	700	48	3	2	6.2	.996	J. Franco	31	33	6	2	15	1.64
UT	B. Pecota	269	.227	2	26	92	218	12	33		.963							
OF	V. Coleman	229	.275	2	21	112	2	1	2	1.9	.991							
UT	C. Walker	227	.308	4	36	42	79	7	6		.945							
OF	D. Gallagher	175	.240	1	21	105	4	2	3	1.5	.982							

Philadelphia

W-70 L-92

Jim Fregosi

POS	Player	AB	BA	HR	RBI	PO	A	E	DP	TC/G	FA	Pitcher	G	IP	W	L	SV	ERA
1B	J. Kruk	507	.323	10	70	979	58	7	76	8.6	.993	T. Mulholland	32	229	13	11	0	3.81
2B	M. Morandini	422	.265	3	30	236	333	5	64	4.6	.991	C. Schilling	42	226	14	11	2	2.35
SS	J. Bell	147	.204	1	8	82	129	6	22	4.7	.972	K. Abbott	31	133	1	14	0	5.13
3B	D. Hollins	586	.270	27	93	120	253	18	22	2.5	.954	B. Rivera	20	102	7	3	0	2.82
RF	R. Amaro	374	.219	7	34	232	5	2	1	2.1	.992	M. Williams	66	81	5	8	29	3.78
CF	L. Dykstra	345	.301	6	39	253	6	3	4	3.1	.989	M. Hartley	46	55	7	6	0	3.44
LF	M. Duncan	574	.267	8	50	123	1	3	0	2.0	.976	B. Jones	44	54	5	6	0	4.64
C	D. Daulton	485	.270	27	**109**	760	69	11	8	6.0	.987							
OF	S. Javier	276	.261	0	24	212	7	3	1	3.0	.986							
1B	R. Jordan	276	.304	4	34	415	27	2	34	8.2	.995							
OF	W. Chamberlain	275	.258	9	41	132	3	4	1	1.9	.971							

West

Atlanta

W-98 L-64

Bobby Cox

POS	Player	AB	BA	HR	RBI	PO	A	E	DP	TC/G	FA	Pitcher	G	IP	W	L	SV	ERA
1B	S. Bream	372	.261	10	61	856	73	10	69	7.8	.989	J. Smoltz	35	247	15	12	0	2.85
2B	M. Lemke	427	.227	6	26	236	325	9	56	3.9	.984	S. Avery	35	234	11	11	0	3.20
SS	R. Belliard	285	.211	0	14	151	289	14	47	3.3	.969	T. Glavine	33	225	**20**	8	0	2.76
3B	T. Pendleton	640	.311	21	105	**133**	**325**	19	27	**3.0**	.960	C. Leibrandt	32	193	15	7	0	3.36
RF	D. Justice	484	.256	21	72	313	8	8	2	2.3	.976	K. Mercker	53	68	3	2	6	3.42
CF	O. Nixon	456	.294	2	22	333	6	3	1	3.1	.991	M. Freeman	58	64	7	5	3	3.22
LF	R. Gant	544	.259	17	80	277	5	4	1	1.9	.986	M. Stanton	65	64	5	4	8	4.10
C	G. Olson	302	.238	3	27	522	43	1	8	6.0	.998	A. Pena	41	42	1	6	15	4.07
SS	J. Blauser	343	.262	14	46	87	182	9	26	2.6	.968							
C	D. Berryhill	307	.228	10	43	426	31	1	5	5.5	.998							
OF	D. Sanders	303	.304	8	28	174	4	3	0	2.4	.983							
1B	B. Hunter	238	.239	14	41	528	49	2	34	6.3	.997							
OF	L. Smith	158	.247	6	33	60	2	3	0	1.9	.954							

Cincinnati

W-90 L-72

Lou Piniella

POS	Player	AB	BA	HR	RBI	PO	A	E	DP	TC/G	FA	Pitcher	G	IP	W	L	SV	ERA
1B	H. Morris	395	.271	6	53	841	86	1	65	8.5	**.999**	T. Belcher	35	228	15	14	0	3.91
2B	B. Doran	387	.235	8	47	170	241	5	55	4.0	.988	G. Swindell	31	214	12	8	0	2.70
SS	B. Larkin	533	.304	12	78	233	408	11	67	4.7	.983	J. Rijo	33	211	15	10	0	2.56
3B	C. Sabo	344	.244	12	43	60	159	9	13	2.5	.961	C. Hammond	28	147	7	10	0	4.21
RF	P. O'Neill	496	.246	14	66	291	12	1	2	2.1	.997	T. Browning	16	87	6	5	0	5.07
CF	D. Martinez	393	.254	3	31	226	7	2	3	2.1	.991	N. Charlton	64	81	4	2	26	2.99
LF	B. Roberts	532	.323	4	45	138	1	1	0	1.8	.993	S. Bankhead	54	71	10	4	1	2.93
C	J. Oliver	485	.270	10	57	**925**	64	8	8	**7.1**	.992	R. Dibble	63	70	3	5	25	3.07
OF	R. Sanders	385	.270	12	36	262	11	6	4	2.5	.978							
OF	G. Braggs	266	.237	8	38	102	3	6	0	1.4	.946							
2S	F. Benavides	173	.231	1	17	80	129	6	26		.972							

NATIONAL LEAGUE 1992, *cont.*

Team	POS	Player	AB	BA	HR	RBI	PO	A	E	DP	TC/G	FA	Pitcher	G	IP	W	L	SV	ERA
San Diego	1B	F. McGriff	531	.286	**35**	104	1219	108	**12**	95	8.9	.991	A. Benes	34	231	13	14	0	3.35
W-82 L-80	2B	K. Stillwell	379	.227	2	24	250	266	**16**	66	4.8	.970	B. Hurst	32	217	14	9	0	3.85
Greg Riddoch	SS	T. Fernandez	622	.275	4	37	240	405	11	65	4.3	.983	C. Lefferts	27	163	13	9	0	3.69
W-78 L-72	3B	G. Sheffield	557	**.330**	33	100	99	299	16	25	2.9	.961	G. Harris	20	118	4	8	0	4.12
Jim Riggleman	RF	T. Gwynn	520	.317	6	41	270	9	5	2	2.2	.982	F. Seminara	19	100	9	4	0	3.68
W-4 L-8	CF	D. Jackson	587	.249	17	70	436	18	2	9	3.0	.996	J. Deshaies	15	96	4	7	0	3.28
	LF	J. Clark	496	.242	12	58	285	10	3	4	2.2	.990	J. Melendez	56	89	6	7	0	2.92
	C	B. Santiago	386	.251	10	42	584	53	**12**	6	6.3	.982	R. Myers	66	80	3	6	38	4.29
	23	T. Teufel	246	.224	6	25	108	159	7	21		.974							
	C	D. Walters	179	.251	4	22	329	25	3	5	6.5	.992							
	OF	O. Azocar	168	.190	0	8	64	1	4	0	1.9	.942							
Houston	1B	J. Bagwell	586	.273	18	96	1334	133	7	110	9.3	.995	P. Harnisch	34	207	9	10	0	3.70
W-81 L-81	2B	C. Biggio	613	.277	6	39	**344**	413	12	81	4.8	.984	B. Henry	28	166	6	9	0	4.02
Art Howe	SS	A. Cedeno	220	.173	2	13	82	175	11	27	3.8	.959	J. Jones	25	139	10	6	0	4.07
	3B	K. Caminiti	506	.294	13	62	102	210	11	19	2.5	.966	D. Kile	22	125	5	10	0	3.95
	RF	E. Anthony	440	.239	19	80	173	6	5	0	1.6	.973	D. Jones	80	112	11	8	36	1.85
	CF	S. Finley	607	.292	5	55	417	8	3	3	2.7	.993	J. Boever	**81**	111	3	6	2	2.51
	LF	L. Gonzalez	387	.243	10	55	261	5	2	1	2.4	.993	X. Hernandez	77	111	9	1	7	2.11
	C	E. Taubensee	297	.222	5	28	557	66	5	6	6.1	.992	M. Portugal	18	101	6	3	0	2.66
	OF	P. Incaviglia	349	.266	11	44	188	8	6	1	2.1	.970	B. Williams	16	96	7	6	0	3.92
	UT	C. Candaele	320	.212	1	18	130	196	11	34		.967	W. Blair	29	79	5	7	0	4.00
	C	S. Servais	205	.239	0	15	386	27	2	5	5.7	.995							
	SS	R. Ramirez	176	.250	1	13	60	113	7	17	3.2	.961							
San Francisco	1B	W. Clark	513	.300	16	73	1275	105	10	**130**	9.9	.993	J. Burkett	32	190	13	9	0	3.84
W-72 L-90	2B	R. Thompson	443	.260	14	49	296	382	15	**101**	**5.8**	.978	B. Black	28	177	10	12	0	3.97
Roger Craig	SS	R. Clayton	321	.224	4	24	141	257	11	51	4.4	.973	B. Swift	30	165	10	4	1	**2.08**
	3B	M. Williams	529	.227	20	66	105	289	**23**	**33**	2.9	.945	T. Wilson	26	154	8	14	0	4.21
	RF	W. McGee	474	.297	1	36	231	11	6	2	2.1	.976	R. Beck	65	92	3	3	17	1.76
	CF	D. Lewis	320	.231	1	18	225	3	0	2	2.4	1.000	J. Brantley	56	92	7	7	7	2.95
	LF	C. James	248	.242	5	32	112	2	3	2	1.9	.974	M. Jackson	67	82	6	6	2	3.73
	C	K. Manwaring	349	.244	4	26	564	68	4	**12**	5.9	.994	D. Righetti	54	78	2	7	3	5.06
	UT	C. Snyder	390	.269	14	57	301	53	6	18		.983							
	OF	M. Felder	322	.286	4	23	159	2	1	0	1.5	.994							
	OF	K. Bass	265	.268	7	30	116	1	2	0	1.7	.983							
	SS	J. Uribe	162	.241	2	13	75	157	7	37	3.9	.971							
Los Angeles	1B	E. Karros	545	.257	20	88	1211	126	9	98	9.4	.993	O. Hershiser	33	211	10	**15**	0	3.67
W-63 L-99	2B	L. Harris	347	.271	0	30	160	206	14	39	4.7	.963	K. Gross	34	205	8	13	0	3.17
Tom Lasorda	SS	J. Offerman	534	.260	1	30	208	398	**42**	74	4.3	.935	T. Candiotti	32	204	11	**15**	0	3.00
	3B	D. Hansen	341	.214	6	22	61	183	8	13	2.3	**.968**	B. Ojeda	29	166	6	9	0	3.63
	RF	M. Webster	262	.267	6	35	130	0	3	0	1.5	.977	R. Martinez	25	151	8	11	0	4.00
	CF	B. Butler	553	.309	3	39	353	9	2	3	2.3	.995	J. Gott	68	88	3	3	6	2.45
	LF	E. Davis	267	.228	5	32	123	0	5	0	1.7	.961	R. McDowell	65	84	6	10	14	4.09
	C	M. Scioscia	348	.221	3	24	641	**74**	9	8	6.7	.988	P. Astacio	11	82	5	5	0	1.98
	23	M. Sharperson	317	.300	3	36	119	220	13	31		.963	J. Candelaria	50	25	2	5	5	2.84
	01	T. Benzinger	293	.239	4	31	263	18	1	17		.996							
	C	C. Hernandez	173	.260	3	17	295	37	7	4	5.4	.979							
	OF	D. Strawberry	156	.237	5	25	67	2	1	0	1.7	.986							

BATTING AND BASE RUNNING LEADERS

Batting Average

G. Sheffield, SD	.330
A. Van Slyke, PIT	.324
J. Kruk, PHI	.323
B. Roberts, CIN	.323
T. Gwynn, SD	.317

Slugging Average

B. Bonds, PIT	.624
G. Sheffield, SD	.580
F. McGriff, SD	.556
D. Daulton, PHI	.524
R. Sandberg, CHI	.510

Home Runs

F. McGriff, SD	35
B. Bonds, PIT	34
G. Sheffield, SD	33
D. Daulton, PHI	27
D. Hollins, PHI	27

Total Bases

G. Sheffield, SD	323
R. Sandberg, CHI	312
A. Van Slyke, PIT	310
T. Pendleton, ATL	303
B. Bonds, PIT	295
F. McGriff, SD	295

Runs Batted In

D. Daulton, PHI	109
T. Pendleton, ATL	105
F. McGriff, SD	104
B. Bonds, PIT	103
G. Sheffield, SD	100

Stolen Bases

M. Grissom, MON	78
D. DeShields, MON	46
B. Roberts, CIN	44
S. Finley, HOU	44
O. Smith, STL	43

Hits

A. Van Slyke, PIT	199
T. Pendleton, ATL	199
R. Sandberg, CHI	186
M. Grace, CHI	185

Base on Balls

B. Bonds, PIT	127
F. McGriff, SD	96
B. Butler, LA	95
C. Biggio, HOU	94

Home Run Percentage

B. Bonds, PIT	7.2
F. McGriff, SD	6.6
G. Sheffield, SD	5.9
D. Daulton, PHI	5.6

Runs

B. Bonds, PIT	109
D. Hollins, PHI	104
A. Van Slyke, PIT	103
R. Sandberg, CHI	100

Doubles

A. Van Slyke, PIT	45
W. Clark, SF	40
M. Duncan, PHI	40
R. Lankford, STL	40

Triples

D. Sanders, ATL	14
S. Finley, HOU	13
A. Van Slyke, PIT	12
L. Alicea, STL	11
B. Butler, LA	11

PITCHING LEADERS

Winning Percentage

B. Tewksbury, STL	.762
T. Glavine, ATL	.714
C. Leibrandt, ATL	.682
M. Morgan, CHI	.667
G. Maddux, CHI	.645

Earned Run Average

B. Swift, SF	2.08
B. Tewksbury, STL	2.16
G. Maddux, CHI	2.18
C. Schilling, PHI	2.35
D. Martinez, MON	2.47

Wins

T. Glavine, ATL	20
G. Maddux, CHI	20
K. Hill, MON	16
D. Martinez, MON	16
B. Tewksbury, STL	16
M. Morgan, CHI	16

Saves

L. Smith, STL	43
R. Myers, SD	38
J. Wetteland, MON	37
D. Jones, HOU	36
M. Williams, PHI	29

Strikeouts

J. Smoltz, ATL	215
D. Cone, NY	214
G. Maddux, CHI	199
S. Fernandez, NY	193
D. Drabek, PIT	177

Complete Games

T. Mulholland, PHI	12
C. Schilling, PHI	10
D. Drabek, PIT	10
G. Maddux, CHI	9
J. Smoltz, ATL	9

Fewest Hits/9 Innings

C. Schilling, PHI	6.56
G. Maddux, CHI	6.75
S. Fernandez, NY	6.79
D. Martinez, MON	6.84

Shutouts

D. Cone, NY	5
T. Glavine, ATL	5

Fewest Walks/9 Innings

B. Tewksbury, STL	0.77
R. Cormier, STL	1.60
G. Swindell, CIN	1.73
T. Mulholland, PHI	1.81

Most Strikeouts/9 Inn.

D. Cone, NY	9.79
S. Fernandez, NY	8.09
J. Smoltz, ATL	7.84
J. Rijo, CIN	7.29

Innings

G. Maddux, CHI	268
D. Drabek, PIT	257
J. Smoltz, ATL	247
M. Morgan, CHI	240

Games Pitched

J. Boever, HOU	81
D. Jones, HOU	80
X. Hernandez, HOU	77
M. Perez, STL	77

NATIONAL LEAGUE 1992, *cont.*

		W	L	PCT	GB	R	OR	Batting 2B	3B	HR	BA	SA	SB	Fielding E	DP	FA	Pitching CG	BB	SO	ShO	SV	ERA
East	Pittsburgh	96	66	.593		**693**	595	272	**54**	106	.255	.381	110	101	144	.984	20	455	844	20	43	3.35
	Montreal	87	75	.537	9	648	581	263	37	102	.252	.370	196	124	113	.980	11	525	1014	14	49	3.25
	St. Louis	83	79	.512	13	631	604	262	44	94	**.262**	.375	**208**	**94**	146	**.985**	10	**400**	842	9	47	3.38
	Chicago	78	84	.481	18	593	624	221	41	104	.254	.364	77	114	142	.982	16	575	901	11	37	3.39
	New York	72	90	.444	24	599	653	259	17	93	.235	.342	129	116	134	.981	17	482	1025	13	34	3.66
	Philadelphia	70	92	.432	26	686	717	255	36	118	.253	.377	127	131	128	.978	**27**	549	851	7	34	4.11
West	Atlanta	98	64	.605		682	**569**	223	48	**138**	.254	**.388**	126	109	121	.982	26	489	948	**24**	41	**3.14**
	Cincinnati	90	72	.556	8	660	609	**281**	44	99	.260	.382	125	96	128	.984	9	470	**1060**	11	**55**	3.46
	San Diego	82	80	.506	16	617	636	255	30	135	.255	.386	69	115	127	.982	9	439	971	11	46	3.56
	Houston	81	81	.500	17	608	668	255	38	96	.246	.359	139	114	125	.981	5	539	978	12	45	3.72
	San Francisco	72	90	.444	26	574	647	220	36	105	.244	.355	112	113	**174**	.982	9	502	927	12	30	3.61
	Los Angeles	63	99	.389	35	548	636	201	34	72	.248	.339	142	174	136	.972	18	553	981	13	29	3.41
						7539	7539	2967	459	1262	.252	.368	1560	1401	1618	.981	177	5978	11342	157	490	3.50

AMERICAN LEAGUE 1992

East

	POS	Player	AB	BA	HR	RBI	PO	A	E	DP	TC/G	FA	Pitcher	G	IP	W	L	SV	ERA
Toronto	1B	J. Olerud	458	.284	16	66	1057	81	7	72	8.6	.994	J. Morris	34	241	**21**	6	0	4.04
W-96 L-66	2B	R. Alomar	571	.310	8	76	287	378	5	66	4.5	.993	J. Key	33	217	13	13	0	3.53
Cito Gaston	SS	M. Lee	396	.263	3	39	187	331	7	67	4.1	.987	J. Guzman	28	181	16	5	0	2.64
	3B	K. Gruber	446	.229	11	43	104	215	17	10	2.8	.949	T. Stottlemyre	28	174	12	11	0	4.50
	RF	J. Carter	622	.264	34	119	257	10	8	2	2.1	.971	D. Wells	41	120	7	9	2	5.40
	CF	D. White	641	.248	17	60	443	8	7	2	3.0	.985	D. Ward	79	101	7	4	12	1.95
	LF	C. Maldonado	489	.272	20	66	260	12	6	1	2.1	.978	D. Stieb	21	96	4	6	0	5.04
	C	P. Borders	480	.242	13	53	784	**88**	8	7	6.4	.991	T. Henke	57	56	3	2	34	2.26
	DH	D. Winfield	583	.290	26	108													
	3B	J. Kent	192	.240	8	35	33	74	10	3	2.4	.915							

	POS	Player	AB	BA	HR	RBI	PO	A	E	DP	TC/G	FA	Pitcher	G	IP	W	L	SV	ERA
Milwaukee	1B	F. Stubbs	288	.229	9	42	525	63	8	44	8.8	.987	B. Wegman	35	262	13	14	0	3.20
W-92 L-70	2B	S. Fletcher	386	.275	3	51	207	319	4	70	5.0	.992	J. Navarro	34	246	17	11	0	3.33
Phil Garner	SS	P. Listach	579	.290	1	47	238	449	24	89	4.8	.966	C. Bosio	33	231	16	6	0	3.62
	3B	K. Seitzer	540	.270	5	71	99	273	12	18	2.6	**.969**	R. Bones	31	163	9	10	0	4.57
	RF	D. Bichette	387	.287	5	41	188	6	2	2	1.9	.990	C. Eldred	14	100	11	2	0	1.79
	CF	R. Yount	557	.264	8	77	371	6	2	0	2.7	.995	D. Plesac	44	79	5	4	1	2.96
	LF	G. Vaughn	501	.228	23	78	288	6	3	0	2.3	.990	D. Henry	68	65	1	4	29	4.02
	C	B. Surhoff	480	.252	4	62	546	59	6	7	5.6	.990	D. Holmes	41	42	4	4	6	2.55
	DH	P. Molitor	609	.320	12	89													
	OF	D. Hamilton	470	.298	5	62	279	10	0	0	2.3	**1.000**							
	23	J. Gantner	256	.246	1	18	153	208	3	45		.992							
	C	D. Nilsson	164	.232	4	25	224	16	2	1	5.3	.992							

	POS	Player	AB	BA	HR	RBI	PO	A	E	DP	TC/G	FA	Pitcher	G	IP	W	L	SV	ERA
Baltimore	1B	R. Milligan	462	.240	11	53	1009	76	7	110	8.5	.994	M. Mussina	32	241	18	5	0	2.54
W-89 L-73	2B	B. Ripken	330	.230	4	36	217	317	4	66	5.0	**.993**	R. Sutcliffe	36	237	16	15	0	4.47
Johnny Oates	SS	C. Ripken	637	.251	14	72	**287**	445	12	**119**	4.6	.984	B. McDonald	35	227	13	13	0	4.24
	3B	L. Gomez	468	.265	17	64	106	246	18	19	2.7	.951	B. Milacki	23	116	6	8	1	5.84
	RF	J. Orsulak	391	.289	4	39	228	9	4	1	2.2	.983	T. Frohwirth	65	106	4	3	4	2.46
	CF	M. Devereaux	653	.276	24	107	431	5	5	3	2.8	.989	A. Mills	35	103	10	4	2	2.61
	LF	B. Anderson	623	.271	21	80	382	10	8	6	2.5	.980	A. Rhodes	15	94	7	5	0	3.63
	C	C. Hoiles	310	.274	20	40	500	31	3	6	5.6	.994	S. Davis	48	89	7	3	4	3.43
	DH	G. Davis	398	.276	13	48							J. Mesa	13	68	3	8	0	5.19
	2B	M. McLemore	228	.246	0	27	126	186	7	47	4.6	.978	G. Olson	60	61	1	5	36	2.05
	OF	C. Martinez	198	.268	5	25	104	4	3	1	2.1	.973							
	1B	D. Segui	189	.233	1	17	375	34	1	42	4.3	.998							
	C	J. Tackett	179	.240	5	24	311	32	1	5	5.4	.997							
	DH	S. Horn	162	.235	5	19													
	UT	T. Hulett	142	.289	2	21	25	92	7	11		.944							

	POS	Player	AB	BA	HR	RBI	PO	A	E	DP	TC/G	FA	Pitcher	G	IP	W	L	SV	ERA
Cleveland	1B	P. Sorrento	458	.269	18	60	996	78	8	108	8.9	.993	C. Nagy	33	252	17	10	0	2.96
W-76 L-86	2B	C. Baerga	657	.312	20	105	**400**	**475**	19	**138**	**5.6**	.979	J. Armstrong	35	167	6	15	0	4.64
Mike Hargrove	SS	M. Lewis	413	.264	5	30	184	333	**25**	71	4.5	.954	D. Cook	32	158	5	7	0	3.82
	3B	B. Jacoby	291	.261	4	36	46	175	10	17	2.1	.957	S. Scudder	23	109	6	10	0	5.28
	RF	M. Whiten	508	.254	9	43	321	14	7	1	2.4	.980	R. Nichols	30	105	4	3	0	4.53
	CF	K. Lofton	576	.285	5	42	420	14	8	3	3.1	.982	T. Power	64	99	3	3	6	2.54
	LF	T. Howard	358	.277	2	32	185	5	2	0	2.0	.990	S. Olin	72	88	8	5	29	2.34
	C	S. Alomar	299	.251	2	26	477	39	2	6	5.9	.996	D. Otto	18	80	5	9	0	7.06
	DH	A. Belle	585	.260	34	112							E. Plunk	58	72	9	6	4	3.64
	OD	G. Hill	369	.241	18	49	126	5	6	1		.956	D. Lilliquist	71	62	5	3	6	1.75
	C	J. Ortiz	244	.250	0	24	402	38	5	2	5.2	.989							
	13	C. Martinez	228	.263	5	35	276	57	4	46		.988							
	UT	F. Fermin	215	.270	0	13	79	168	8	42		.969							

AMERICAN LEAGUE 1992, *cont.*

New York

W-76 L-86

Buck Showalter

POS	Player	AB	BA	HR	RBI	PO	A	E	DP	TC/G	FA	Pitcher	G	IP	W	L	SV	ERA
1B	D. Mattingly	640	.287	14	86	1209	116	4	129	9.3	**.997**	M. Perez	33	248	13	16	0	2.87
2B	P. Kelly	318	.226	7	27	203	296	11	64	5.0	.978	S. Sanderson	33	193	12	11	0	4.93
SS	A. Stankiewicz	400	.268	2	25	133	257	11	54	5.0	.973	S. Kamieniecki	28	188	6	14	0	4.36
3B	C. Hayes	509	.257	18	66	94	249	13	**29**	2.6	.963	G. Cadaret	46	104	4	8	1	4.25
RF	D. Tartabull	421	.266	25	85	142	3	3	1	2.1	.980	T. Leary	18	97	5	6	0	5.57
CF	R. Kelly	580	.272	10	66	389	8	7	3	2.8	.983	R. Monteleone	47	93	7	3	0	3.30
LF	M. Hall	583	.280	15	81	283	10	3	2	2.2	.990	J. Habyan	56	73	5	6	7	3.84
C	M. Nokes	384	.224	22	59	552	47	4	6	5.4	.993	S. Farr	50	52	2	2	30	1.56
DH	K. Maas	286	.248	11	35													
UT	R. Velarde	412	.272	7	46	179	257	15	50		.967							
OF	B. Williams	261	.280	5	26	187	5	1	2	3.1	.995							
C	M. Stanley	173	.249	8	27	266	29	6	3	5.5	.980							
2B	M. Gallego	173	.254	3	14	86	112	2	31	5.0	.990							
UT	J. Leyritz	144	.257	7	26	96	15	1	2		.991							

Detroit

W-75 L-87

Sparky Anderson

POS	Player	AB	BA	HR	RBI	PO	A	E	DP	TC/G	FA	Pitcher	G	IP	W	L	SV	ERA
1B	C. Fielder	594	.244	35	**124**	957	92	10	98	9.3	.991	B. Gullickson	34	222	14	13	0	4.34
2B	L. Whitaker	453	.278	19	71	256	312	9	73	4.8	.984	F. Tanana	32	187	13	11	0	4.39
SS	T. Fryman	**659**	.266	20	96	205	443	20	91	**4.9**	.970	W. Terrell	36	137	7	10	0	5.20
3B	S. Livingstone	354	.282	4	46	67	189	10	15	2.4	.962	J. Doherty	47	116	7	4	3	3.88
RF	R. Deer	393	.247	32	64	229	8	4	1	2.3	.983	M. Leiter	35	112	8	5	0	4.18
CF	M. Cuyler	291	.241	3	28	232	4	4	1	2.7	.983	E. King	17	79	4	6	1	5.22
LF	D. Gladden	417	.254	7	42	227	9	3	2	2.2	.987	M. Henneman	60	77	2	6	24	3.96
C	M. Tettleton	525	.238	32	83	475	47	2	10	4.6	**.996**	K. Knudsen	48	71	2	3	5	4.58
DH	T. Phillips	606	.276	10	64							S. Aldred	16	65	3	8	0	6.78
OF	M. Carreon	336	.232	10	41	178	5	4	2	2.3	.979							
C	C. Kreuter	190	.253	2	16	271	22	5	6	4.8	.983							
1B	D. Bergman	181	.232	1	10	339	22	5	29	6.7	.986							
UT	S. Barnes	165	.273	3	25	127	78	11	16		.949							

Boston

W-73 L-89

Butch Hobson

POS	Player	AB	BA	HR	RBI	PO	A	E	DP	TC/G	FA	Pitcher	G	IP	W	L	SV	ERA
1B	M. Vaughn	355	.234	13	57	741	57	**15**	76	9.6	.982	R. Clemens	32	247	18	11	0	**2.41**
2B	J. Reed	550	.247	3	40	304	472	14	113	5.6	.982	F. Viola	35	238	13	12	0	3.44
SS	L. Rivera	288	.215	0	29	117	286	14	56	4.5	.966	D. Darwin	51	161	9	9	3	3.96
3B	W. Boggs	514	.259	7	50	70	229	15	23	2.7	.952	J. Hesketh	30	149	8	9	1	4.36
RF	T. Brunansky	458	.266	15	74	189	6	4	3	2.2	.980	J. Dopson	25	141	7	11	0	4.08
CF	B. Zupcic	392	.276	3	43	241	11	6	3	2.3	.977	M. Gardiner	28	131	4	10	0	4.75
LF	B. Hatcher	315	.238	1	23	145	5	5	0	2.1	.968	G. Harris	70	108	4	9	4	2.51
C	T. Pena	410	.241	1	38	**786**	57	6	**12**	6.4	.993	J. Reardon	46	42	2	2	27	4.25
DH	J. Clark	257	.210	5	33													
OF	P. Plantier	349	.246	7	30	148	6	4	0	2.1	.975							
13	S. Cooper	337	.276	5	33	472	136	9	49		.985							
OF	E. Burks	235	.255	8	30	120	3	2	0	2.0	.984							
OF	H. Winningham	234	.235	1	14	112	7	3	1	1.8	.975							
UT	T. Naehring	186	.231	3	14	95	170	3	31		.989							
SS	J. Valentin	185	.276	5	25	79	182	10	45	4.7	.963							
OF	M. Greenwell	180	.233	2	18	85	1	0	0	2.1	1.000							

West

Oakland

W-96 L-66

Tony LaRussa

POS	Player	AB	BA	HR	RBI	PO	A	E	DP	TC/G	FA	Pitcher	G	IP	W	L	SV	ERA
1B	M. McGwire	467	.268	42	104	1118	71	6	118	8.6	.995	M. Moore	36	223	17	12	0	4.12
2B	M. Bordick	504	.300	3	48	201	266	6	57	5.0	.987	R. Darling	33	206	15	10	0	3.66
SS	W. Weiss	316	.212	0	21	144	270	19	57	4.2	.956	D. Stewart	31	199	12	10	0	3.66
3B	C. Lansford	496	.262	7	75	86	162	9	10	2.2	.965	B. Welch	20	124	11	7	0	3.27
RF	J. Canseco	366	.246	22	72	163	5	2	3	2.2	.988	J. Parrett	66	98	9	1	0	3.02
CF	W. Wilson	396	.270	0	37	355	2	7	2	3.0	.981	K. Downs	18	82	5	5	0	3.29
LF	R. Henderson	396	.283	15	46	231	9	4	2	2.3	.984	D. Eckersley	69	80	7	1	**51**	1.91
C	T. Steinbach	438	.279	12	53	580	69	10	6	5.3	.985	J. Slusarski	15	76	5	5	0	5.45
DH	H. Baines	478	.253	16	76													
20	L. Blankenship	349	.241	3	34	249	224	5	56		.990							
UT	J. Browne	324	.287	3	40	149	88	5	11		.979							
C	J. Quirk	177	.220	2	11	258	26	8	4	4.9	.973							

Minnesota

W-90 L-72

Tom Kelly

POS	Player	AB	BA	HR	RBI	PO	A	E	DP	TC/G	FA	Pitcher	G	IP	W	L	SV	ERA
1B	K. Hrbek	394	.244	15	58	954	68	3	75	9.9	.997	J. Smiley	34	241	16	9	0	3.21
2B	C. Knoblauch	600	.297	2	56	306	415	6	104	4.7	.992	K. Tapani	34	220	16	11	0	3.97
SS	G. Gagne	439	.246	7	39	208	438	18	83	4.7	.973	S. Erickson	32	212	13	12	0	3.40
3B	S. Leius	409	.249	2	35	58	257	15	12	2.6	.955	B. Krueger	27	161	10	6	0	4.30
RF	P. Munoz	418	.270	12	71	220	8	3	4	1.9	.987	C. Willis	59	79	7	3	1	2.72
CF	K. Puckett	639	.329	19	110	394	9	3	3	2.7	.993	T. Edens	52	76	6	3	3	2.83
LF	S. Mack	600	.315	16	75	322	9	4	2	2.2	.988	M. Guthrie	54	75	2	3	5	2.88
C	B. Harper	502	.307	9	73	744	58	13	8	6.1	.984	R. Aguilera	64	67	2	6	41	2.84
DH	C. Davis	444	.288	12	66													
10	G. Larkin	337	.246	6	42	509	35	5	50		.991							
UT	R. Bush	182	.214	2	22	51	1	0	3		1.000							

Chicago

W-86 L-76

Gene Lamont

POS	Player	AB	BA	HR	RBI	PO	A	E	DP	TC/G	FA	Pitcher	G	IP	W	L	SV	ERA
1B	F. Thomas	573	.323	24	115	**1428**	92	13	112	**9.7**	.992	J. McDowell	34	261	20	10	0	3.18
2B	S. Sax	567	.236	4	47	305	390	**20**	75	5.1	.972	K. McCaskill	34	209	12	13	0	4.18
SS	C. Grebeck	287	.268	3	35	110	277	8	47	4.6	.980	A. Fernandez	29	188	8	11	0	4.27
3B	R. Ventura	592	.282	16	93	**141**	**372**	23	**29**	**3.4**	.957	C. Hough	27	176	7	12	0	3.93
RF	D. Pasqua	265	.211	6	33	153	4	6	0	2.0	.963	G. Hibbard	31	176	10	7	1	4.40
CF	L. Johnson	567	.279	3	47	433	11	6	3	2.9	.987	W. Alvarez	34	100	5	3	1	5.20
LF	T. Raines	551	.294	7	54	312	12	2	0	2.5	.994	T. Leach	51	74	6	5	0	1.95
C	R. Karkovice	342	.237	13	50	533	53	6	8	5.0	.990	R. Hernandez	43	71	7	3	12	1.65
DH	G. Bell	627	.255	25	112							S. Radinsky	68	59	3	7	15	2.73
OF	S. Abner	208	.279	1	16	155	2	0	0	1.7	1.000	B. Thigpen	55	55	1	3	22	4.75
C	C. Fisk	188	.229	3	21	252	26	2	2	5.2	.993							

AMERICAN LEAGUE 1992, *cont.*

Team	POS	Player	AB	BA	HR	RBI	PO	A	E	DP	TC/G	FA	Pitcher	G	IP	W	L	SV	ERA
Texas	1B	R. Palmeiro	608	.268	22	85	1251	**143**	7	131	9.0	.995	K. Brown	35	**266**	**21**	11	0	3.32
W-77 L-85	2B	A. Newman	246	.220	0	12	118	168	5	31	4.0	.983	J. Guzman	33	224	16	11	0	3.66
Bobby Valentine	SS	D. Thon	275	.247	4	37	117	225	15	38	4.1	.958	B. Witt	25	161	9	13	0	4.46
W-45 L-41	3B	D. Palmer	541	.229	26	72	124	254	22	24	2.7	.945	N. Ryan	27	157	5	9	0	3.72
Toby Harrah	RF	R. Sierra	500	.278	14	70	224	6	7	0	2.0	.970	T. Burns	35	103	3	5	1	3.84
W-32 L-44	CF	J. Gonzalez	584	.260	**43**	109	379	9	10	2	2.7	.975	K. Rogers	**81**	79	3	6	6	3.09
	LF	K. Reimer	494	.267	16	58	198	7	11	1	2.0	.949	J. Russell	51	57	2	3	28	1.91
	C	I. Rodriguez	420	.260	8	37	763	85	**15**	10	**7.4**	.983							
	DH	B. Downing	320	.278	10	39													
	S2	J. Huson	318	.261	4	24	178	250	9	66		.979							
	2B	J. Frye	199	.256	1	12	120	196	7	43	4.8	.978							
	C	G. Petralli	192	.198	1	18	263	23	3	6	5.4	.990							
	O2	M. Fariss	166	.217	3	21	71	13	0	5		1.000							
California	1B	L. Stevens	312	.221	7	37	764	49	4	88	9.0	.995	M. Langston	32	229	13	14	0	3.66
W-72 L-90	2B	L. Sojo	368	.272	7	43	187	267	7	72	4.8	.985	J. Abbott	29	211	7	15	0	2.77
Buck Rodgers	SS	G. DiSarcina	518	.247	3	42	250	**486**	**25**	109	4.8	.967	C. Finley	31	204	7	12	0	3.96
W-19 L-20	3B	G. Gaetti	456	.226	12	48	52	163	17	18	3.5	.927	J. Valera	30	188	8	11	0	3.73
John Wathan	RF	V. Hayes	307	.225	4	29	169	1	3	1	2.0	.983	B. Blyleven	25	133	8	12	0	4.74
W-39 L-50	CF	J. Felix	509	.246	9	72	340	9	6	3	2.8	.983	J. Grahe	46	95	5	6	21	3.52
Buck Rodgers	LF	L. Polonia	577	.286	0	35	192	8	4	1	2.1	.980	C. Crim	57	87	7	6	1	5.17
W-14 L-20	C	M. Fitzgerald	189	.212	6	17	290	20	3	4	4.2	.990	S. Frey	51	45	4	2	4	3.57
	DH	H. Brooks	306	.216	8	36							B. Harvey	25	29	0	4	13	2.83
	OF	C. Curtis	441	.259	10	46	250	**16**	6	3	2.0	.978							
	UT	R. Gonzales	329	.277	7	38	191	229	9	49		.979							
Kansas City	1B	W. Joyner	572	.269	9	66	1236	137	10	**138**	9.5	.993	K. Appier	30	208	15	8	0	2.46
W-72 L-90	2B	K. Miller	416	.284	4	38	189	250	13	60	4.9	.971	H. Pichardo	31	144	9	6	0	3.95
Hal McRae	SS	D. Howard	219	.224	1	18	124	204	8	52	4.5	.976	T. Gordon	40	118	6	10	0	4.59
	3B	G. Jefferies	604	.285	10	75	96	304	**26**	22	2.9	.939	M. Gubicza	18	111	7	6	0	3.72
	RF	J. Eisenreich	353	.269	2	28	180	1	1	0	2.1	.995	R. Meacham	64	102	10	4	2	2.74
	CF	B. McRae	533	.223	4	52	419	8	3	2	2.9	.993	R. Reed	19	100	3	7	0	3.68
	LF	K. McReynolds	373	.247	13	49	204	4	3	0	2.0	.986	M. Magnante	44	89	4	9	0	4.94
	C	M. Macfarlane	402	.234	17	48	527	43	4	7	5.5	.993	J. Montgomery	65	83	1	6	39	2.18
	DH	G. Brett	592	.285	7	61													
	S2	C. Wilkerson	296	.250	2	29	144	249	9	55		.978							
	C	B. Mayne	213	.225	0	18	277	23	3	1	4.9	.990							
	OF	G. Thurman	200	.245	0	20	138	5	2	0	2.2	.986							
Seattle	1B	P. O'Brien	396	.222	14	52	623	54	3	72	8.4	.996	D. Fleming	33	228	17	10	0	3.39
W-64 L-98	2B	H. Reynolds	458	.247	3	33	303	362	12	88	5.1	.982	R. Johnson	31	210	12	14	0	3.77
Bill Plummer	SS	O. Vizquel	483	.294	0	21	223	403	7	92	4.7	**.989**	E. Hanson	31	187	8	**17**	0	4.82
	3B	E. Martinez	528	**.343**	18	73	72	209	17	24	2.9	.943	R. Swan	55	104	3	10	9	4.74
	RF	J. Buhner	543	.243	25	79	314	14	2	4	2.2	.994	R. DeLucia	30	84	3	6	1	5.49
	CF	K. Griffey	565	.308	27	103	359	8	1	4	2.7	.997	J. Nelson	66	81	1	7	6	3.44
	LF	K. Mitchell	360	.286	9	67	130	4	0	0	1.9	1.000	M. Schooler	53	52	2	7	13	4.70
	C	D. Valle	367	.240	9	30	606	62	7	10	5.5	.990							
	DH	T. Martinez	460	.257	16	66													
	OF	H. Cotto	294	.259	5	27	170	2	0	0	1.9	1.000							
	UT	G. Briley	200	.275	5	12	65	13	4	3		.951							
	UT	L. Parrish	192	.234	8	21	276	15	3	13		.990							

BATTING AND BASE RUNNING LEADERS

Batting Average
E. Martinez, SEA .343
K. Puckett, MIN .329
F. Thomas, CHI .323
P. Molitor, MIL .320
S. Mack, MIN .315

Slugging Average
M. McGwire, OAK .585
E. Martinez, SEA .544
F. Thomas, CHI .536
K. Griffey, SEA .535
J. Gonzalez, TEX .529

Home Runs
J. Gonzalez, TEX 43
M. McGwire, OAK 42
C. Fielder, DET 35
A. Belle, CLE 34
J. Carter, TOR 34

Total Bases
K. Puckett, MIN 313
J. Carter, TOR 310
J. Gonzalez, TEX 309
F. Thomas, CHI 307
M. Devereaux, BAL 303

Runs Batted In
C. Fielder, DET 124
J. Carter, TOR 119
F. Thomas, CHI 115
A. Belle, CLE 112
G. Bell, CHI 112

Stolen Bases
K. Lofton, CLE 66
P. Listach, MIL 54
B. Anderson, BAL 53
L. Polonia, CAL 51
R. Alomar, TOR 49

Hits
K. Puckett, MIN 210
C. Baerga, CLE 205
P. Molitor, MIL 195
S. Mack, MIN 189

Base on Balls
M. Tettleton, DET 122
F. Thomas, CHI 122
T. Phillips, DET 114
R. Milligan, BAL 106

Home Run Percentage
M. McGwire, OAK 9.0
J. Gonzalez, TEX 7.4
M. Tettleton, DET 6.1
D. Tartabull, NY 5.9

Runs
T. Phillips, DET 114
F. Thomas, CHI 108
R. Alomar, TOR 105
C. Knoblauch, MIN 104
K. Puckett, MIN 104

Doubles
E. Martinez, SEA 46
F. Thomas, CHI 46
R. Yount, MIL 40
D. Mattingly, NY 40

Triples
L. Johnson, CHI 12
M. Devereaux, BAL 11
B. Anderson, BAL 10
T. Raines, CHI 9

PITCHING LEADERS

Winning Percentage
M. Mussina, BAL .783
J. Morris, TOR .778
J. Guzman, TOR .762
C. Bosio, MIL .727
J. McDowell, CHI .667

Earned Run Average
R. Clemens, BOS 2.41
K. Appier, KC 2.46
M. Mussina, BAL 2.54
J. Guzman, TOR 2.64
J. Abbott, CAL 2.77

Wins
J. Morris, TOR 21
K. Brown, TEX 21
J. McDowell, CHI 20
M. Mussina, BAL 18
R. Clemens, BOS 18

Saves
D. Eckersley, OAK 51
R. Aguilera, MIN 41
J. Montgomery, KC 39
G. Olson, BAL 36
T. Henke, TOR 34

Strikeouts
R. Johnson, SEA 241
M. Perez, NY 218
R. Clemens, BOS 208
J. Guzman, TEX 179
J. McDowell, CHI 178

Complete Games
J. McDowell, CHI 13
R. Clemens, BOS 11
K. Brown, TEX 11
M. Perez, NY 10
C. Nagy, CLE 10

Fewest Hits/9 Innings
R. Johnson, SEA 6.59
J. Guzman, TOR 6.73
K. Appier, KC 7.21
R. Clemens, BOS 7.41

Shutouts
R. Clemens, BOS 5
M. Mussina, BAL 4
D. Fleming, SEA 4

Fewest Walks/9 Innings
C. Bosio, MIL 1.71
M. Mussina, BAL 1.79
B. Wegman, MIL 1.89
K. Tapani, MIN 1.96

Most Strikeouts/9 Inn.
R. Johnson, SEA 10.31
J. Guzman, TOR 8.22
M. Perez, NY 7.92
R. Clemens, BOS 7.59

Innings
K. Brown, TEX 266
B. Wegman, MIL 262
J. McDowell, CHI 261
C. Nagy, CLE 252

Games Pitched
K. Rogers, TEX 81
D. Ward, TOR 79
S. Olin, CLE 72
D. Lilliquist, CLE 71

AMERICAN LEAGUE 1992, *cont.*

		W	L	PCT	GB	R	OR	2B	3B	HR	BA	SA	SB	E	DP	FA	CG	BB	SO	ShO	SV	ERA
								Batting						Fielding			Pitching					
East	Toronto	96	66	.593		780	682	265	40	163	.263	**.414**	129	93	109	.985	18	541	954	14	49	3.91
	Milwaukee	92	70	.568	4	740	**604**	272	35	82	.268	.375	**256**	**89**	146	**.986**	19	**435**	793	14	39	**3.43**
	Baltimore	89	73	.549	7	705	656	243	36	148	.259	.398	89	93	168	.985	20	518	846	**16**	48	3.79
	Cleveland	76	86	.469	20	674	746	227	24	127	.266	.383	144	141	**176**	.978	13	566	890	7	46	4.11
	New York	76	86	.469	20	733	746	281	18	163	.261	.406	78	114	165	.982	20	612	851	9	44	4.21
	Detroit	75	87	.463	21	**791**	794	256	16	**182**	.256	.407	66	116	164	.981	10	564	693	4	36	4.60
	Boston	73	89	.451	23	599	669	259	21	84	.246	.347	44	139	170	.978	22	535	943	13	39	3.58
West	Oakland	96	66	.593		745	672	219	24	142	.258	.386	143	125	158	.979	8	601	843	9	**58**	3.73
	Minnesota	90	72	.556	6	747	653	275	27	104	**.277**	.391	123	95	155	.985	16	479	923	13	50	3.70
	Chicago	86	76	.531	10	738	690	269	36	110	.261	.383	160	129	134	.979	21	550	810	5	52	3.82
	Texas	77	85	.475	19	682	753	266	23	159	.250	.393	81	154	153	.975	19	598	**1034**	3	42	4.09
	California	72	90	.444	24	579	671	202	20	88	.243	.338	160	134	172	.979	**26**	532	888	13	42	3.84
	Kansas City	72	90	.444	24	610	667	**284**	**42**	75	.256	.364	131	122	164	.980	9	512	834	12	44	3.81
	Seattle	64	98	.395	32	679	799	278	24	149	.263	.402	100	112	170	.982	21	661	894	9	30	4.55
						9802	9802	3596	386	1776	.259	.385	1704	1656	2204	.981	242	7704	12196	141	619	3.94

NATIONAL LEAGUE 1993

East

Team	POS	Player	AB	BA	HR	RBI	PO	A	E	DP	TC/G	FA	Pitcher	G	IP	W	L	SV	ERA
Philadelphia	1B	J. Kruk	535	.316	14	85	1149	69	8	79	8.5	.993	C. Schilling	34	235	16	7	0	4.02
W-97 L-65	2B	M. Morandini	425	.247	3	33	208	288	5	48	4.5	.990	D. Jackson	32	210	12	11	0	3.77
Jim Fregosi	SS	K. Stocker	259	.324	2	31	118	202	14	44	4.8	.958	T. Greene	31	200	16	4	0	3.42
	3B	D. Hollins	543	.273	18	93	73	215	27	9	2.2	.914	T. Mulholland	29	191	12	9	0	3.25
	RF	J. Eisenreich	362	.318	7	54	218	6	1	0	1.6	.996	B. Rivera	30	163	13	9	0	5.02
	CF	L. Dykstra	**637**	.305	19	66	469	2	10	0	3.0	.979	D. West	76	86	6	4	3	2.92
	LF	M. Thompson	340	.262	4	44	162	6	1	1	1.6	.994	M. Williams	65	62	3	7	43	3.34
	C	D. Daulton	510	.257	24	105	**981**	67	9	**19**	**7.2**	.991	R. Mason	34	50	5	5	0	4.89
	2S	M. Duncan	496	.282	11	73	180	304	21	50		.958							
	OF	P. Incaviglia	368	.274	24	89	164	4	5	1	1.8	.971							
	OF	W. Chamberlain	284	.282	12	45	131	10	1	3	1.9	.993							
	3B	K. Batiste	156	.282	5	29	24	41	3	2	1.2	.956							
Montreal	1B	G. Colbrunn	153	.255	4	23	372	27	2	31	6.6	.995	D. Martinez	35	225	15	9	1	3.85
W-94 L-68	2B	D. DeShields	481	.295	2	29	243	381	11	74	5.2	.983	K. Hill	28	184	9	7	0	3.23
Felipe Alou	SS	W. Cordero	475	.248	10	58	161	370	33	61	4.2	.941	J. Fassero	56	150	12	5	1	2.29
	3B	S. Berry	299	.261	14	49	66	153	15	13	2.4	.936	C. Nabholz	26	117	9	8	0	4.09
	RF	L. Walker	490	.265	22	86	273	13	6	2	2.2	.979	B. Barnes	52	100	2	6	3	4.41
	CF	M. Grissom	630	.298	19	95	416	8	7	3	2.7	.984	M. Rojas	66	88	5	8	10	2.95
	LF	M. Alou	482	.286	18	85	254	11	4	2	2.0	.985	J. Wetteland	70	85	9	3	43	1.37
	C	D. Fletcher	396	.255	9	60	620	41	8	3	5.3	.988							
	UT	M. Lansing	491	.287	3	45	136	336	24	53		.952							
	10	J. Vander Wal	215	.233	5	30	271	14	4	17		.986							
	13	F. Bolick	213	.211	4	24	338	63	8	31		.980							
	OF	L. Frazier	189	.286	1	16	70	3	1	0	1.2	.986							
St. Louis	1B	G. Jefferies	544	.342	16	83	1279	76	9	114	9.7	.993	B. Tewksbury	32	214	17	10	0	3.83
W-87 L-75	2B	L. Alicea	362	.279	3	46	202	280	11	61	5.1	.978	R. Arocha	32	188	11	8	0	3.78
Joe Torre	SS	O. Smith	545	.288	1	53	251	451	19	98	**5.4**	.974	D. Osborne	26	156	10	7	0	3.76
	3B	T. Zeile	571	.277	17	103	83	310	33	26	2.8	.923	R. Cormier	38	145	7	6	0	4.33
	RF	M. Whiten	562	.253	25	99	329	9	10	1	2.4	.971	O. Olivares	58	119	5	3	1	4.17
	CF	R. Lankford	407	.238	7	45	312	6	7	0	2.7	.978	J. Magrane	22	116	8	10	0	4.97
	LF	B. Gilkey	557	.305	16	70	227	19	8	2	1.9	.969	A. Watson	16	86	6	7	0	4.60
	C	T. Pagnozzi	330	.258	7	41	421	44	4	4	5.1	.991	M. Perez	65	73	7	2	7	2.48
	2B	G. Pena	254	.256	5	30	140	200	12	47	5.5	.966	R. Murphy	73	65	5	7	1	4.87
	C	E. Pappas	228	.276	1	28	294	32	6	5	5.3	.982	L. Smith	55	50	2	4	43	4.50
	OF	B. Jordan	223	.309	10	44	140	4	4	0	2.3	.973							
	01	R. Brewer	147	.286	2	20	148	6	3	13		.981							
Chicago	1B	M. Grace	594	.325	14	98	**1456**	112	5	**134**	**10.2**	.997	M. Morgan	32	208	10	15	0	4.03
W-84 L-78	2B	R. Sandberg	456	.309	9	45	209	347	7	76	4.9	.988	J. Guzman	30	191	12	10	0	4.34
Jim Lefebvre	SS	R. Sanchez	344	.282	0	28	158	316	15	60	5.0	.969	G. Hibbard	31	191	15	11	0	3.96
	3B	S. Buechele	460	.272	15	65	79	232	8	24	2.5	**.975**	M. Harkey	28	157	10	10	0	5.26
	RF	S. Sosa	598	.261	33	93	344	17	9	4	2.3	.976	F. Castillo	29	141	5	8	0	4.84
	CF	W. Wilson	221	.258	1	11	109	1	1	0	1.4	.991	J. Bautista	58	112	10	3	2	2.82
	LF	D. May	465	.295	10	77	220	8	7	1	1.9	.970	R. Myers	73	75	2	4	**53**	3.11
	C	R. Wilkins	446	.303	30	73	717	89	3	9	6.1	.996							
	UT	J. Vizcaino	551	.287	4	54	217	410	17	72		.974							
	OF	D. Smith	310	.300	11	35	163	5	8	2	2.0	.955							
	OF	K. Roberson	180	.189	9	27	77	2	3	0	1.6	.963							
	OF	G. Hill	87	.345	10	22	42	2	2	1	2.2	.957							
Pittsburgh	1B	K. Young	449	.236	6	47	1116	101	3	108	9.0	**.998**	S. Cooke	32	211	10	10	0	3.89
W-75 L-87	2B	C. Garcia	546	.269	12	47	296	343	11	84	4.6	.983	B. Walk	32	187	13	14	0	5.68
Jim Leyland	SS	J. Bell	604	.310	9	51	**256**	**527**	11	100	5.2	**.986**	P. Wagner	44	141	8	8	2	4.27
	3B	J. King	611	.295	9	98	105	**353**	17	28	**3.0**	.964	T. Wakefield	24	128	6	11	0	5.61
	RF	O. Merced	447	.313	8	70	209	11	8	4	2.1	.965	R. Tomlin	18	98	4	8	0	4.85
	CF	A. Van Slyke	323	.310	8	50	205	2	1	1	2.7	.995	B. Minor	65	94	8	6	2	4.10
	LF	A. Martin	480	.281	18	64	268	6	7	0	2.1	.975	Z. Smith	14	83	3	7	0	4.55
	C	D. Slaught	377	.300	10	55	539	51	4	10	5.7	.993	S. Belinda	40	42	3	1	19	3.61
	OF	D. Clark	277	.271	11	46	132	3	6	1	1.5	.957	M. Dewey	21	27	1	2	7	2.36
	OF	L. Smith	199	.286	6	24	104	1	2	0	1.8	.981							
	UT	T. Foley	194	.253	3	22	116	105	5	29		.978							
	OF	L. McClendon	181	.221	2	19	84	3	3	1	1.5	.967							
	C	T. Prince	179	.196	2	24	271	31	5	6	5.2	.984							

NATIONAL LEAGUE 1993, *cont.*

Florida

W-64 L-98

Rene Lachemann

POS	Player	AB	BA	HR	RBI	PO	A	E	DP	TC/G	FA	Pitcher	G	IP	W	L	SV	ERA
1B	O. Destrade	569	.255	20	87	1313	90	**19**	109	9.4	.987	C. Hough	34	204	9	16	0	4.27
2B	B. Barberie	375	.277	5	33	201	303	9	62	5.3	.982	J. Armstrong	36	196	9	17	0	4.49
SS	W. Weiss	500	.266	1	39	229	406	15	80	4.2	.977	C. Hammond	32	191	11	12	0	4.66
3B	G. Sheffield	236	.292	10	37	38	123	19*	4	2.7	.894	R. Bowen	27	157	8	12	0	4.42
RF	D. Whitmore	250	.204	4	19	140	3	3	1	2.1	.979	L. Aquino	38	111	6	8	0	3.42
CF	C. Carr	551	.267	4	41	393	7	6	2	2.9	.985	P. Rapp	16	94	4	6	0	4.02
LF	J. Conine	595	.292	12	79	252	11	2	0	1.8	.992	B. Harvey	59	69	1	5	45	1.70
C	B. Santiago	469	.230	13	50	740	64	**11**	4	6.0	.987							
23	R. Renteria	263	.255	2	30	84	151	2	20		.992							
UT	A. Arias	249	.269	2	20	94	144	6	25		.975							
3B	D. Magadan	227	.286	4	29	50	121	7	12	2.8	.961							
OF	J. Felix	214	.238	7	22	91	3	6	0	1.9	.940							
OF	G. Briley	170	.194	3	12	71	2	1	0	1.1	.986							

New York

W-59 L-103

Jeff Torborg
W-13 L-25

Dallas Green
W-46 L-78

POS	Player	AB	BA	HR	RBI	PO	A	E	DP	TC/G	FA	Pitcher	G	IP	W	L	SV	ERA
1B	E. Murray	610	.285	27	100	1319	111	18	118	9.4	.988	D. Gooden	29	209	12	15	0	3.45
2B	J. Kent	496	.270	21	80	250	311	**18**	68	4.6	.969	F. Tanana	29	183	7	15	0	4.48
SS	T. Bogar	205	.244	3	25	88	193	8	34	4.4	.972	E. Hillman	27	145	2	9	0	3.97
3B	H. Johnson	235	.238	7	26	52	135	11	11	3.0	.944	B. Saberhagen	19	139	7	7	0	3.29
RF	B. Bonilla	502	.265	34	87	148	8	5	1	1.9	.969	P. Schourek	41	128	5	12	0	5.96
CF	R. Thompson	288	.250	11	26	228	4	3	0	3.1	.987	S. Fernandez	18	120	5	6	0	2.93
LF	V. Coleman	373	.279	2	25	162	5	3	0	1.9	.982	A. Young	39	100	1	16	3	3.77
C	T. Hundley	417	.228	11	53	592	63	8	6	5.4	.988	M. Maddux	58	75	3	8	5	3.60
OF	J. Orsulak	409	.284	8	35	215	9	5	1	2.0	.978	J. Franco	35	36	4	3	10	5.20
OF	J. Burnitz	263	.243	13	38	165	6	4	2	2.2	.977							
UT	C. Walker	213	.225	5	19	68	82	8	11		.949							
OF	D. Gallagher	201	.274	6	28	117	6	0	1	1.7	1.000							
C	C. O'Brien	188	.255	4	23	325	39	5	5	5.7	.986							
SS	T. Fernandez	173	.225	1	14	83	150	6	28	5.0	.975							
UT	J. McKnight	164	.256	2	13	86	88	10	19		.946							

West

Atlanta

W-104 L-58

Bobby Cox

POS	Player	AB	BA	HR	RBI	PO	A	E	DP	TC/G	FA	Pitcher	G	IP	W	L	SV	ERA
1B	S. Bream	277	.260	9	35	627	62	3	62	7.7	.996	G. Maddux	36	**267**	20	10	0	**2.36**
2B	M. Lemke	493	.252	7	49	**329**	442	14	**100**	5.2	.982	J. Smoltz	35	244	15	11	0	3.62
SS	J. Blauser	597	.305	15	73	189	426	19	86	3.9	.970	T. Glavine	36	239	**22**	6	0	3.20
3B	T. Pendleton	633	.272	17	84	**128**	319	19	32	2.9	.959	S. Avery	35	223	18	6	0	2.94
RF	D. Justice	585	.270	40	120	323	9	5	2	2.1	.985	G. McMichael	74	92	2	3	19	2.06
CF	O. Nixon	461	.269	1	24	308	4	3	1	2.7	.990	P. Smith	20	91	4	8	0	4.37
LF	R. Gant	606	.274	36	117	271	5	11	1	1.9	.962	M. Stanton	63	52	4	6	27	4.67
C	D. Berryhill	335	.245	8	43	570	52	6	2	6.0	.990							
OF	D. Sanders	272	.276	6	28	137	1	2	1	2.3	.986							
C	G. Olson	262	.225	4	24	445	35	6	6	6.0	.988							
1B	F. McGriff	255	.310	19	55	563	45	5	52	9.3	.992							

San Francisco

W-103 L-59

Dusty Baker

POS	Player	AB	BA	HR	RBI	PO	A	E	DP	TC/G	FA	Pitcher	G	IP	W	L	SV	ERA
1B	W. Clark	491	.283	14	73	1078	88	14	113	9.1	.988	B. Swift	34	233	21	8	0	2.82
2B	R. Thompson	494	.312	19	65	273	384	8	95	5.2	.988	J. Burkett	34	232	**22**	7	0	3.65
SS	R. Clayton	549	.282	6	70	251	449	27	**103**	4.8	.963	B. Hickerson	47	120	7	5	0	4.26
3B	M. Williams	579	.294	38	110	117	266	12	**34**	2.7	.970	J. Brantley	53	114	5	6	0	4.28
RF	W. McGee	475	.301	4	46	224	9	5	1	1.9	.979	T. Wilson	22	110	7	5	0	3.60
CF	D. Lewis	522	.253	2	48	344	4	0	3	2.7	1.000	D. Burba	54	95	10	3	0	4.25
LF	B. Bonds	539	.336	**46**	**123**	310	7	5	0	2.1	.984	B. Black	16	94	8	2	0	3.56
C	K. Manwaring	432	.275	5	49	739	70	2	12	6.2	**.998**	R. Beck	76	79	3	1	48	2.16
OF	D. Martinez	241	.241	5	27	131	6	1	2	1.9	.993	M. Jackson	**81**	77	6	6	1	3.03
1B	T. Benzinger	177	.288	6	26	289	15	0	27	7.6	1.000							
OF	M. Carreon	150	.327	7	33	48	2	3	0	1.3	.943							

Houston

W-85 L-77

Art Howe

POS	Player	AB	BA	HR	RBI	PO	A	E	DP	TC/G	FA	Pitcher	G	IP	W	L	SV	ERA
1B	J. Bagwell	535	.320	20	88	1200	113	9	106	9.4	.993	D. Drabek	34	238	9	**18**	0	3.79
2B	C. Biggio	610	.287	21	64	306	**447**	14	90	4.9	.982	P. Harnisch	33	218	16	9	0	2.98
SS	A. Cedeno	505	.283	11	56	153	375	25	78	3.7	.955	M. Portugal	33	208	18	4	0	2.77
3B	K. Caminiti	543	.262	13	75	123	264	24	23	2.9	.942	G. Swindell	31	190	12	13	0	4.16
RF	E. Anthony	486	.249	15	66	233	6	3	0	1.8	.988	D. Kile	32	172	15	8	0	3.51
CF	S. Finley	545	.266	8	44	329	12	4	4	2.5	.988	X. Hernandez	72	97	4	5	9	2.61
LF	L. Gonzalez	540	.300	15	72	347	10	8	2	2.4	.978	D. Jones	71	85	4	10	26	4.54
C	E. Taubensee	288	.250	9	42	551	41	5	5	6.6	.992	B. Williams	42	82	4	4	3	4.83
C	S. Servais	258	.244	11	32	493	40	2	9	6.5	.996							
OF	K. Bass	229	.284	3	37	83	3	1	0	1.4	.989							
31	C. Donnels	179	.257	2	24	168	51	8	19		.965							

Los Angeles

W-81 L-81

Tom Lasorda

POS	Player	AB	BA	HR	RBI	PO	A	E	DP	TC/G	FA	Pitcher	G	IP	W	L	SV	ERA
1B	E. Karros	619	.247	23	80	1335	**147**	12	118	9.5	.992	O. Hershiser	33	216	12	14	0	3.59
2B	J. Reed	445	.276	2	31	280	413	5	76	**5.3**	**.993**	T. Candiotti	33	214	8	10	0	3.12
SS	J. Offerman	590	.269	1	62	250	454	**37**	95	4.7	.950	R. Martinez	32	212	10	12	0	3.44
3B	T. Wallach	477	.222	12	62	112	228	15	14	2.7	.958	K. Gross	33	202	13	13	0	4.14
RF	C. Snyder	516	.266	11	56	172	14	4	1	1.7	.979	P. Astacio	31	186	14	9	0	3.57
CF	B. Butler	607	.298	1	42	369	6	0	0	2.4	1.000	P. Martinez	65	107	10	5	2	2.61
LF	E. Davis	376	.234	14	53	221	7	2	2	2.2	.991	J. Gott	62	78	4	8	25	2.32
C	M. Piazza	547	.318	35	112	899	**98**	**11**	10	6.9	.989	R. McDowell	54	68	5	3	2	2.25
OF	H. Rodriguez	176	.222	8	23	57	3	1	0	1.3	.984							
OF	M. Webster	172	.244	2	14	75	1	4	0	1.4	.950							
3B	D. Hansen	105	.362	4	30	11	27	3	1	2.3	.927							

NATIONAL LEAGUE 1993, *cont.*

Team	POS	Player	AB	BA	HR	RBI	PO	A	E	DP	TC/G	FA	Pitcher	G	IP	W	L	SV	ERA
Cincinnati	1B	H. Morris	379	.317	7	49	746	75	5	61	8.4	.994	J. Rijo	36	257	14	9	0	2.48
	2B	J. Samuel	261	.230	4	26	135	164	9	33	4.4	.971	T. Pugh	31	164	10	15	0	5.26
W-73 L-89	SS	B. Larkin	384	.315	8	51	159	281	16	56	4.6	.965	T. Belcher	22	137	9	6	0	4.47
	3B	C. Sabo	552	.259	21	82	79	242	11	16	2.2	.967	T. Browning	21	114	7	7	0	4.74
Tony Perez	RF	R. Sanders	496	.274	20	83	312	3	8	0	2.4	.975	J. Smiley	18	106	3	9	0	5.62
W-20 L-24	CF	R. Kelly	320	.319	9	35	198	3	1	1	2.6	.995	B. Ayala	43	98	7	10	3	5.60
	LF	K. Mitchell	323	.341	19	64	149	7	7	2	1.9	.957	J. Reardon	58	62	4	6	8	4.09
Davey Johnson	C	J. Oliver	482	.239	14	75	791	68	7	8	6.5	.992	R. Dibble	45	42	1	4	19	6.48
W-53 L-65	UT	J. Branson	381	.241	3	22	185	260	11	56		.976							
	2B	B. Roberts	292	.240	1	18	136	172	5	31	4.9	.984							
	OF	J. Brumfield	272	.268	6	23	172	6	4	1	1.9	.978							
	1B	R. Milligan	234	.274	6	29	468	56	3	47	8.6	.994							
Colorado	1B	A. Galarraga	470	**.370**	22	98	1018	103	11	88	9.5	.990	A. Reynoso	30	189	12	11	0	4.00
	2B	E. Young	490	.269	3	42	153	228	15	43	5.0	.962	W. Blair	46	146	6	10	0	4.75
W-67 L-95	SS	V. Castilla	337	.255	9	30	141	282	11	67	4.2	.975	B. Ruffin	59	140	6	5	2	3.87
Don Baylor	3B	C. Hayes	573	.305	25	98	123	292	20	22	2.8	.954	D. Nied	16	87	5	9	0	5.17
	RF	D. Bichette	538	.310	21	89	308	14	9	3	2.4	.973	B. Henry	20	85	2	8	0	6.59
	CF	A. Cole	348	.256	0	24	219	5	4	1	2.5	.982	S. Reed	64	84	9	5	3	4.48
	LF	J. Clark	478	.282	13	67	192	7	7	1	2.1	.966	D. Holmes	62	67	3	3	25	4.05
	C	J. Girardi	310	.290	3	31	478	46	6	7	6.3	.989							
	OF	D. Boston	291	.261	14	40	124	5	2	1	1.7	.985							
	2B	R. Mejia	229	.231	5	20	126	184	12	38	5.0	.963							
	C	D. Sheaffer	216	.278	4	32	331	28	2	5	5.6	.994							
	S2	F. Benavides	213	.286	3	26	96	152	13	26		.950							
	OF	C. Jones	209	.273	6	31	114	2	2	0	1.7	.983							
San Diego	1B	F. McGriff	302	.275	18	46	640	47	12	50	8.4	.983	A. Benes	34	231	15	15	0	3.78
	2B	J. Gardner	404	.262	1	24	213	294	9	48	3.9	.983	G. Harris	22	152	10	9	0	3.67
W-61 L-101	SS	R. Gutierrez	438	.251	5	26	190	286	14	55	4.2	.971	D. Brocail	24	128	4	13	0	4.56
Jim Riggleman	3B	G. Sheffield	258	.295	10	36	41	102	15*	11	2.4	.905	W. Whitehurst	21	106	4	7	0	3.83
	RF	D. Bell	542	.262	21	72							T. Worrell	21	101	2	7	0	4.92
	LF	P. Plantier	462	.240	34	100	272	14	3	3	2.2	.990	G. Harris	59	59	6	6	23	3.03
	C	K. Higgins	181	.221	0	13	308	31	6	1	5.8	.983							
	OF	T. Gwynn	489	.358	7	59	244	8	5	2	2.1	.981							
	31	A. Cianfrocco	279	.244	11	47	198	95	10	23		.967							
	UT	P. Clark	240	.313	9	33	243	35	8	14		.972							
	UT	C. Shipley	230	.235	4	22	84	121	7	15		.967							
	2B	T. Teufel	200	.250	7	31	85	117	2	22	3.9	.990							
	OF	B. Bean	177	.260	5	32	71	6	1	0	1.4	.987							
	1B	G. Velasquez	143	.210	3	20	221	21	4	20	6.5	.984							

BATTING AND BASE RUNNING LEADERS

Batting Average

A. Galarraga, CLR	.370
T. Gwynn, SD	.358
G. Jefferies, STL	.342
B. Bonds, SF	.336
M. Grace, CHI	.325

Slugging Average

B. Bonds, SF	.677
A. Galarraga, CLR	.602
M. Williams, SF	.561
M. Piazza, LA	.561
F. McGriff, SD, ATL	.549

Home Runs

B. Bonds, SF	46
D. Justice, ATL	40
M. Williams, SF	38
F. McGriff, SD, ATL	37
R. Gant, ATL	36

Total Bases

B. Bonds, SF	365
M. Williams, SF	325
R. Gant, ATL	309
M. Piazza, LA	307
L. Dykstra, PHI	307

Runs Batted In

B. Bonds, SF	123
D. Justice, ATL	120
R. Gant, ATL	117
M. Piazza, LA	112
M. Williams, SF	110

Stolen Bases

C. Carr, FLA	58
M. Grissom, MON	53
O. Nixon, ATL	47
D. Lewis, SF	46
G. Jefferies, STL	46

Hits

L. Dykstra, PHI	194
M. Grace, CHI	193
M. Grissom, MON	188
J. Bell, PIT	187

Base on Balls

L. Dykstra, PHI	129
B. Bonds, SF	126
D. Daulton, PHI	117
J. Kruk, PHI	111

Home Run Percentage

B. Bonds, SF	8.5
P. Plantier, SD	7.4
D. Justice, ATL	6.8
B. Bonilla, NY	6.8

Runs

L. Dykstra, PHI	143
B. Bonds, SF	129
R. Gant, ATL	113
F. McGriff, SD, ATL	111

Doubles

C. Hayes, CLR	45
L. Dykstra, PHI	44
D. Bichette, CLR	43
T. Gwynn, SD	41
C. Biggio, HOU	41

Triples

S. Finley, HOU	13
B. Butler, LA	10
M. Morandini, PHI	9
J. Bell, PIT	9

PITCHING LEADERS

Winning Percentage

M. Portugal, HOU	.818
T. Greene, PHI	.800
T. Glavine, ATL	.786
J. Burkett, SF	.759
S. Avery, ATL	.750

Earned Run Average

G. Maddux, ATL	2.36
J. Rijo, CIN	2.48
M. Portugal, HOU	2.77
B. Swift, SF	2.82
S. Avery, ATL	2.94

Wins

J. Burkett, SF	22
T. Glavine, ATL	22
B. Swift, SF	21
G. Maddux, ATL	20
M. Portugal, HOU	18
S. Avery, ATL	18

Saves

R. Myers, CHI	53
R. Beck, SF	48
B. Harvey, FLA	45
L. Smith, STL	43
M. Williams, PHI	43
J. Wetteland, MON	43

Strikeouts

J. Rijo, CIN	227
J. Smoltz, ATL	208
G. Maddux, ATL	197
C. Schilling, PHI	186
P. Harnisch, HOU	185

Complete Games

G. Maddux, ATL	8
T. Mulholland, PHI	7
D. Gooden, NY	7
T. Greene, PHI	7
D. Drabek, HOU	7
C. Schilling, PHI	7

Fewest Hits/9 Innings

P. Harnisch, HOU	7.07
B. Swift, SF	7.54
J. Rijo, CIN	7.62
J. Smoltz, ATL	7.68

Shutouts

P. Harnisch, HOU	4
R. Martinez, LA	3

Fewest Walks/9 Innings

B. Tewksbury, STL	0.84
R. Arocha, STL	1.48
J. Burkett, SF	1.55
S. Avery, ATL	1.73

Most Strikeouts/9 Inn.

J. Rijo, CIN	7.94
J. Smoltz, ATL	7.68
J. Guzman, CHI	7.68
P. Harnisch, HOU	7.65

Innings

G. Maddux, ATL	267
J. Rijo, CIN	257
J. Smoltz, ATL	244
T. Glavine, ATL	239

Games Pitched

M. Jackson, SF	81
D. West, PHI	76
R. Beck, SF	76
G. McMichael, ATL	74

NATIONAL LEAGUE 1993, *cont.*

								Batting						Fielding			Pitching					
		W	L	PCT	GB	R	OR	2B	3B	HR	BA	SA	SB	E	DP	FA	CG	BB	SO	ShO	SV	ERA
East	Philadelphia	97	65	.599		**877**	740	**297**	51	156	.274	.426	91	141	123	.977	**24**	573	**1117**	11	46	3.95
	Montreal	94	68	.580	3	732	682	270	36	122	.257	.386	**228**	159	144	.975	8	521	934	7	**61**	3.55
	St. Louis	87	75	.537	10	758	744	262	34	118	.272	.395	153	159	157	.975	5	**383**	775	7	54	4.09
	Chicago	84	78	.519	13	738	739	259	32	161	.270	.414	100	115	162	.982	8	470	905	5	56	4.18
	Pittsburgh	75	87	.463	22	707	806	267	50	110	.267	.393	92	105	161	.983	12	485	832	5	34	4.77
	Florida	64	98	.395	33	581	724	197	31	94	.248	.346	117	125	130	.980	4	598	945	5	48	4.13
	New York	59	103	.364	38	672	744	228	37	158	.248	.390	79	156	143	.975	16	434	867	8	22	4.05
West	Atlanta	104	58	.642		767	**559**	239	29	**169**	.262	.408	125	108	146	.983	18	480	1036	**16**	46	**3.14**
	San Francisco	103	59	.636	1	808	636	269	33	168	**.276**	**.427**	120	**101**	**169**	**.984**	4	442	982	9	50	3.61
	Houston	85	77	.525	19	716	630	288	37	138	.267	.409	103	126	141	.979	18	476	1056	14	42	3.49
	Los Angeles	81	81	.500	23	675	662	234	28	130	.261	.383	126	133	141	.979	17	567	1043	9	36	3.50
	Cincinnati	73	89	.451	31	722	785	261	28	137	.264	.396	142	121	133	.980	11	508	996	8	37	4.51
	Colorado	67	95	.414	37	758	967	278	**59**	142	.273	.422	146	167	149	.973	9	609	913	0	35	5.41
	San Diego	61	101	.377	43	679	772	239	28	153	.252	.389	92	160	129	.974	8	558	957	6	32	4.23
						10190	10190	3588	513	1956	.264	.399	1714	1876	2028	.978	162	7104	13358	110	599	4.04

AMERICAN LEAGUE 1993

		POS	Player	AB	BA	HR	RBI	PO	A	E	DP	TC/G	FA	Pitcher	G	IP	W	L	SV	ERA
East	**Toronto**	1B	J. Olerud	551	**.363**	24	107	1160	97	10	107	9.2	.992	J. Guzman	33	221	14	3	0	3.99
		2B	R. Alomar	589	.326	17	93	254	439	14	92	4.7	.980	P. Hentgen	34	216	19	9	0	3.87
	W-95 L-67	SS	T. Fernandez	353	.306	4	50	196	260	7	62	4.9	.985	T. Stottlemyre	30	177	11	12	0	4.84
		3B	E. Sprague	546	.260	12	73	**127**	232	17	21	2.5	.955	D. Stewart	26	162	12	8	0	4.44
	Cito Gaston	RF	J. Carter	603	.254	33	121	289	7	8	0	2.0	.974	J. Morris	27	153	7	12	0	6.19
		CF	D. White	598	.273	15	52	399	6	3	2	2.8	.993	A. Leiter	34	105	9	6	2	4.11
		LF	R. Henderson	163	.215	4	12	76	1	2	0	1.8	.975	D. Cox	44	84	7	6	2	3.12
		C	P. Borders	488	.254	9	55	869	**80**	**13**	12	7.0	.986	D. Ward	71	72	2	3	**45**	2.13
		DH	P. Molitor	636	.332	22	111													
		OF	D. Coles	194	.253	4	26	65	1	3	0	1.6	.957							
		OF	D. Jackson	176	.216	5	19	86	2	1	0	1.9	.989							
		OF	T. Ward	167	.192	4	28	94	2	1	0	1.5	.990							
		C	R. Knorr	101	.248	4	20	168	20	0	4	4.8	1.000							
	New York	1B	D. Mattingly	530	.291	17	86	1258	84	3	123	**10.3**	**.998**	J. Key	34	237	18	6	0	3.00
		2B	P. Kelly	406	.273	7	51	245	369	14	84	5.0	.978	J. Abbott	32	214	11	14	0	4.37
	W-88 L-74	SS	S. Owen	334	.234	2	20	116	312	14	44	4.6	.968	M. Perez	25	163	6	14	0	5.19
		3B	W. Boggs	560	.302	2	59	75	**311**	12	**29**	**3.0**	**.970**	S. Kamieniecki	30	154	10	7	1	4.08
	Buck Showalter	RF	P. O'Neill	498	.311	20	75	230	7	2	1	1.7	.992	B. Wickman	41	140	14	4	4	4.63
		CF	B. Williams	567	.268	12	68	366	5	4	0	2.7	.989	R. Monteleone	42	86	7	4	0	4.94
		LF	D. James	343	.332	7	36	140	4	5	1	1.4	.966	S. Howe	51	51	3	5	4	4.97
		C	M. Stanley	423	.305	26	84	652	46	3	5	5.7	**.996**	S. Farr	49	47	2	2	25	4.21
		DH	D. Tartabull	513	.250	31	102													
		UT	M. Gallego	403	.283	10	54	169	368	13	76		.976							
		UT	J. Leyritz	259	.309	14	53	333	15	2	22		.994							
		UT	R. Velarde	226	.301	7	24	102	92	9	20		.956							
		C	M. Nokes	217	.249	10	35	245	19	2	0	4.8	.992							
		D1	K. Maas	151	.205	9	25	115	5	2	13		.984							
	Baltimore	1B	D. Segui	450	.273	10	60	1152	98	5	122	8.7	.996	B. McDonald	34	220	13	14	0	3.39
		2B	H. Reynolds	485	.252	4	47	306	396	10	**110**	5.0	.986	F. Valenzuela	32	179	8	10	0	4.94
	W-85 L-77	SS	C. Ripken	**641**	.257	24	90	226	**495**	17	101	4.6	.977	M. Mussina	25	168	14	6	0	4.46
		3B	T. Hulett	260	.300	2	23	48	161	8	23	2.9	.963	R. Sutcliffe	29	166	10	10	0	5.75
	Johnny Oates	RF	M. McLemore	581	.284	4	72	282	13	4	4	2.4	.987	J. Moyer	25	152	12	9	0	3.43
		CF	M. Devereaux	527	.250	14	75	311	8	4	3	2.5	.988	A. Mills	45	100	5	4	4	3.23
		LF	B. Anderson	560	.263	13	66	296	7	2	0	2.2	.993	T. Frohwirth	70	96	6	7	3	3.83
		C	C. Hoiles	419	.310	29	82	696	64	5	11	6.2	.993	M. Williamson	48	88	7	5	0	4.91
		DH	H. Baines	416	.313	20	78							A. Rhodes	17	86	5	6	0	6.51
		3B	L. Gomez	244	.197	10	25	48	145	10	16	2.9	.951	G. Olson	50	45	0	2	29	1.60
		OF	J. Voigt	152	.296	6	23	75	3	1	0	1.8	.987							
		3B	M. Pagliarulo	117	.325	6	21	27	47	5	6	2.8	.937							
	Detroit	1B	C. Fielder	573	.267	30	117	971	78	10	84	8.9	.991	M. Moore	36	214	13	9	0	5.22
		2B	L. Whitaker	383	.290	9	67	236	322	11	75	5.2	.981	D. Wells	32	187	11	9	0	4.19
	W-85 L-77	SS	T. Fryman	607	.300	22	97	125	262	19	60	5.0	.953	J. Doherty	32	185	14	11	0	4.44
		3B	S. Livingstone	304	.293	2	39	33	94	6	6	2.1	.955	B. Gullickson	28	159	13	9	0	5.37
	Sparky Anderson	RF	R. Deer	323	.217	14	39	192	5	5	3	2.3	.975	M. Leiter	27	107	6	6	0	4.72
		CF	M. Cuyler	249	.213	0	19	211	2	7	1	2.8	.968	T. Bolton	43	103	6	6	0	4.47
		LF	T. Phillips	566	.313	7	57	215	5	7	1	2.1	.969	B. Krueger	32	82	6	4	0	3.40
		C	C. Kreuter	374	.286	15	51	517	69	7	10	5.3	.988	M. Henneman	63	72	5	3	24	2.64
		DH	K. Gibson	403	.261	13	62													
		UT	M. Tettleton	522	.245	32	110	724	47	6	43		.992							
		UT	A. Trammell	401	.329	12	60	113	238	9	31		.975							
		OF	D. Gladden	356	.267	13	56	196	9	3	1	2.4	.986							
		UT	S. Barnes	160	.281	2	27	158	37	4	7		.980							

AMERICAN LEAGUE 1993, *cont.*

	Team	POS	Player	AB	BA	HR	RBI	PO	A	E	DP	TC/G	FA	Pitcher	G	IP	W	L	SV	ERA
	Boston	1B	M. Vaughn	539	.297	29	101	1110	70	**16**	104	9.1	.987	D. Darwin	34	229	15	11	0	3.26
	W-80 L-82	2B	S. Fletcher	480	.285	5	45	217	371	11	68	5.2	.982	R. Clemens	29	192	11	14	0	4.46
	Butch Hobson	SS	J. Valentin	468	.278	11	66	238	432	20	96	**4.8**	.971	F. Viola	29	184	11	8	0	3.14
		3B	S. Cooper	526	.279	9	63	111	244	24	22	2.5	.937	J. Dopson	34	156	7	11	0	4.97
		RF	B. Zupcic	286	.241	2	26	179	7	4	2	1.6	.979	P. Quantrill	49	138	6	12	1	3.91
		CF	B. Hatcher	508	.287	9	57	284	6	2	2	2.2	.993	G. Harris	**80**	112	6	7	8	3.77
		LF	M. Greenwell	540	.315	13	72	261	6	2	1	2.0	.993	A. Sele	18	112	7	2	0	2.74
		C	T. Pena	304	.181	4	19	698	53	4	6	6.0	.995	K. Ryan	47	50	7	2	1	3.60
		DH	A. Dawson	461	.273	13	67							J. Russell	51	47	1	4	33	2.70
		10	C. Quintana	303	.244	1	19	412	25	3	31		.993							
		OF	I. Calderon	213	.221	1	19	94	2	0	0	2.0	1.000							
		C	B. Melvin	176	.222	3	23	304	18	2	4	4.3	.994							
		UT	E. Riles	143	.189	5	20	26	53	0	8		1.000							
	Cleveland	1B	P. Sorrento	463	.257	18	65	1012	86	6	107	7.7	.995	J. Mesa	34	209	10	12	0	4.92
	W-76 L-86	2B	C. Baerga	624	.321	21	114	**347**	**445**	17	108	**5.4**	.979	T. Kramer	39	121	7	3	0	4.02
	Mike Hargrove	SS	F. Fermin	480	.263	2	45	211	346	**23**	87	4.1	.960	M. Clark	26	109	7	5	0	4.28
		3B	A. Espinoza	263	.278	4	27	42	107	10	9	1.6	.937	J. Hernandez	49	77	6	5	8	3.14
		RF	W. Kirby	458	.269	6	60	273	19	5	5	2.4	.983	E. Plunk	70	71	4	5	15	2.79
		CF	K. Lofton	569	.325	1	42	402	11	9	3	2.9	.979	D. Lilliquist	56	64	4	4	10	2.25
		LF	A. Belle	594	.290	38	**129**	338	16	5	7	2.4	.986	J. DiPoto	46	56	4	4	11	2.40
		C	J. Ortiz	249	.221	0	20	441	58	5	**13**	5.3	.990	D. Cook	25	54	5	5	0	5.67
		DH	R. Jefferson	366	.249	10	34													
		UT	C. Martinez	262	.244	5	31	162	51	9	17		.959							
		32	J. Treadway	221	.303	2	27	46	111	10	13		.940							
		C	S. Alomar	215	.270	6	32	342	25	6	4	5.8	.984							
		OF	T. Howard	178	.236	3	23	81	3	2	1	1.8	.977							
		OD	G. Hill	174	.224	5	25	62	1	4	0		.940							
		3B	J. Thome	154	.266	7	22	29	86	6	10	2.6	.950							
		OF	C. Maldonado	81	.247	5	20	39	1	1	0	1.6	.976							
	Milwaukee	1B	J. Jaha	515	.264	19	70	1186	128	10	116	8.8	.992	C. Eldred	36	**258**	16	16	0	4.01
	W-69 L-93	2B	B. Spiers	340	.238	2	36	209	226	13	53	4.3	.971	J. Navarro	35	214	11	12	0	5.33
	Phil Garner	SS	P. Listach	356	.244	3	30	127	267	10	53	4.3	.975	R. Bones	32	204	11	11	0	4.86
		3B	B. Surhoff	552	.274	7	79	101	216	17	19	2.8	.949	B. Wegman	20	121	4	14	0	4.48
		RF	D. Hamilton	520	.310	9	48	340	10	3	1	2.7	.992	A. Miranda	22	120	4	5	0	3.30
		CF	R. Yount	454	.258	8	51	299	6	1	1	2.7	.997	J. Orosco	57	57	3	5	8	3.18
		LF	G. Vaughn	569	.267	30	97	214	1	3	1	2.3	.986	D. Henry	54	55	4	4	17	5.56
		C	D. Nilsson	296	.257	7	40	430	30	9	3	5.2	.981							
		DH	K. Reimer	437	.249	13	60													
		2S	J. Bell	286	.234	5	29	182	224	11	53		.974							
		UT	D. Thon	245	.269	1	33	80	119	7	19		.966							
		OF	T. Brunansky	224	.183	6	29	146	4	2	0	2.1	.987							
		C	T. Lampkin	162	.198	4	25	242	24	6	2	4.5	.978							
		3B	K. Seitzer	162	.290	7	30	22	59	5	7	2.6	.942							
West	**Chicago**	1B	F. Thomas	549	.317	41	128	1222	83	15	128	8.8	.989	J. McDowell	34	257	**22**	10	0	3.37
	W-94 L-68	2B	J. Cora	579	.268	2	51	295	410	**19**	85	4.8	.974	A. Fernandez	34	247	18	9	0	3.13
	Gene Lamont	SS	O. Guillen	457	.280	4	50	189	361	16	82	4.3	.972	W. Alvarez	31	208	15	8	0	2.95
		3B	R. Ventura	554	.262	22	94	112	278	14	26	2.6	.965	J. Bere	24	143	12	5	0	3.47
		RF	E. Burks	499	.275	17	74	313	6	6	1	2.2	.982	K. McCaskill	30	114	4	8	2	5.23
		CF	L. Johnson	540	.311	0	47	427	7	9	1	3.0	.980	R. Hernandez	70	79	3	4	38	2.29
		LF	T. Raines	415	.306	16	54	200	5	0	1	1.8	1.000	S. Radinsky	73	55	8	2	4	4.28
		C	R. Karkovice	403	.228	20	54	769	63	5	4	6.6	.994							
		DH	G. Bell	410	.217	13	64													
		OD	B. Jackson	284	.232	16	45	89	5	1	1		.989							
		UT	C. Grebeck	190	.226	1	12	91	185	5	40		.982							
		01	D. Pasqua	176	.205	5	20	204	12	3	15		.986							
	Texas	1B	R. Palmeiro	597	.295	37	105	**1388**	**147**	5	**133**	9.6	.997	K. Brown	34	233	15	12	0	3.59
	W-86 L-76	2B	D. Strange	484	.256	7	60	272	362	13	81	4.8	.980	K. Rogers	35	208	16	10	0	4.10
	Kevin Kennedy	SS	M. Lee	205	.220	1	12	96	205	10	35	4.3	.968	R. Pavlik	26	166	12	6	0	3.41
		3B	D. Palmer	519	.245	33	96	85	258	**29**	21	2.5	.922	C. Leibrandt	26	150	9	10	0	4.55
		RF	D. Peltier	160	.269	1	17	72	4	4	2	1.5	.950	C. Lefferts	52	83	3	9	0	6.05
		CF	D. Hulse	407	.290	1	29	244	3	3	1	2.2	.988	T. Henke	66	74	5	5	40	2.91
		LF	J. Gonzalez	536	.310	**46**	118	265	5	4	0	2.1	.985	N. Ryan	13	66	5	5	0	4.88
		C	I. Rodriguez	473	.273	10	66	801	76	8	6	6.6	.991							
		DH	J. Franco	532	.289	14	84													
		OF	J. Canseco	231	.255	10	46	94	4	3	2	2.1	.970							
		OF	G. Redus	222	.288	6	31	103	3	2	0	1.8	.981							
		SS	M. Diaz	205	.273	2	24	81	134	3	28	3.8	.986							
		OF	B. Davis	159	.245	3	20	94	2	4	1	2.3	.960							
	Kansas City	1B	W. Joyner	497	.292	15	65	1116	145	7	116	9.1	.994	D. Cone	34	254	11	14	0	3.33
	W-84 L-78	2B	J. Lind	431	.248	0	37	269	362	4	75	4.7	**.994**	K. Appier	34	239	18	8	0	**2.56**
	Hal McRae	SS	G. Gagne	540	.280	10	57	266	451	10	93	4.6	**.986**	H. Pichardo	30	165	7	8	0	4.04
		3B	G. Gaetti	281	.256	14	46	50	136	5	15	2.7	.974	T. Gordon	48	156	12	6	1	3.58
		RF	F. Jose	499	.253	6	43	237	6	7	3	1.7	.972	C. Haney	23	124	9	9	0	6.02
		CF	B. McRae	627	.282	12	69	394	4	7	3	2.6	.983	M. Gubicza	49	104	5	8	2	4.66
		LF	K. McReynolds	351	.245	11	42	191	5	2	0	1.9	.990	M. Gardner	17	92	4	6	0	6.19
		C	M. Macfarlane	388	.273	20	67	647	68	11	11	6.4	.985	J. Montgomery	69	87	7	5	**45**	2.27
		DH	G. Brett	560	.266	19	75													
		OF	C. Gwynn	287	.300	1	25	149	6	1	0	1.9	.994							
		3B	P. Hiatt	238	.218	7	36	45	114	16	6	2.5	.909							
		C	B. Mayne	205	.254	2	22	356	27	2	1	5.7	.995							
		OF	H. Brooks	168	.286	1	24	53	3	2	1	1.5	.966							

AMERICAN LEAGUE 1993, *cont.*

Seattle

W-82 L-80

Lou Piniella

POS	Player	AB	BA	HR	RBI	PO	A	E	DP	TC/G	FA
1B	T. Martinez	408	.265	17	60	932	60	3	89	9.7	.997
2B	R. Amaral	373	.290	1	44	151	206	9	48	4.8	.975
SS	O. Vizquel	560	.255	2	31	245	475	15	**108**	4.7	.980
3B	M. Blowers	379	.280	15	57	66	225	15	14	2.6	.951
RF	J. Buhner	563	.272	27	98	263	8	6	2	1.9	.978
CF	K. Griffey	582	.309	45	109	316	8	3	3	2.4	.991
LF	M. Felder	342	.211	1	20	143	9	2	0	1.6	.987
C	D. Valle	423	.258	13	63	**881**	71	5	**13**	**7.1**	.995
DH	P. O'Brien	210	.257	7	27						
2B	B. Boone	271	.251	12	38	140	177	3	55	4.3	.991
13	D. Magadan	228	.259	1	21	325	72	5	38		.988
OD	M. Sasser	188	.218	1	21	50	3	3	0		.946
UT	G. Litton	174	.299	3	25	135	52	0	28		1.000

Pitcher	G	IP	W	L	SV	ERA
R. Johnson	35	255	19	8	1	3.24
E. Hanson	31	215	11	12	0	3.47
T. Leary	33	169	11	9	0	5.05
D. Fleming	26	167	12	5	0	4.36
C. Bosio	29	164	9	9	1	3.45
N. Charlton	34	35	1	3	18	2.34
T. Power	25	25	2	2	13	3.91

California

W-71 L-91

Buck Rodgers

POS	Player	AB	BA	HR	RBI	PO	A	E	DP	TC/G	FA
1B	J. Snow	419	.241	16	57	1010	81	6	103	8.5	.995
2B	T. Lovullo	367	.251	6	30	184	220	8	67	4.5	.981
SS	G. DiSarcina	416	.238	3	45	193	362	14	77	4.5	.975
3B	R. Gonzales	335	.251	2	31	63	156	10	20	2.9	.956
RF	T. Salmon	515	.283	31	95	335	12	7	2	2.5	.980
CF	C. Curtis	583	.285	6	59	426	13	9	6	3.0	.980
LF	L. Polonia	576	.271	1	32	286	12	5	3	2.1	.983
C	G. Myers	290	.255	7	40	369	44	6	5	4.3	.986
DH	C. Davis	573	.243	27	112						
OF	S. Javier	237	.291	3	28	101	2	2	0	1.6	.981
2B	D. Easley	230	.313	2	22	101	125	5	26	4.3	.978
3B	E. Perez	180	.250	4	30	24	101	5	7	2.9	.962

Pitcher	G	IP	W	L	SV	ERA
M. Langston	35	256	16	11	0	3.20
C. Finley	35	251	16	14	0	3.15
S. Sanderson	21	135	7	11	0	4.46
J. Farrell	21	91	3	12	0	7.35
P. Leftwich	12	81	4	6	0	3.79
J. Grahe	45	57	4	1	11	2.86
J. Valera	19	53	3	6	4	6.62
S. Frey	55	48	2	3	13	2.98

Minnesota

W-71 L-91

Tom Kelly

POS	Player	AB	BA	HR	RBI	PO	A	E	DP	TC/G	FA
1B	K. Hrbek	392	.242	25	83	940	81	5	98	8.9	.995
2B	C. Knoblauch	602	.277	2	41	298	425	9	98	4.9	.988
SS	P. Meares	346	.251	0	33	165	304	19	70	4.4	.961
3B	M. Pagliarulo	253	.292	3	23	42	137	3	11	2.3	.984
RF	P. Munoz	326	.233	13	38	172	5	3	2	1.8	.983
CF	K. Puckett	622	.296	22	89	312	13	2	2	2.4	.994
LF	S. Mack	503	.276	10	61	347	8	5	1	2.8	.986
C	B. Harper	530	.304	12	73	736	64	10	6	6.0	.988
DH	D. Winfield	547	.271	21	76						
01	D. McCarty	350	.214	2	21	412	38	8	25		.983
UT	J. Reboulet	240	.258	1	15	122	215	6	40		.983
UT	C. Hale	186	.333	3	27	39	63	4	11		.962

Pitcher	G	IP	W	L	SV	ERA
K. Tapani	36	226	12	15	0	4.43
S. Erickson	34	219	8	**19**	0	5.19
W. Banks	31	171	11	12	0	4.04
J. Deshaies	27	167	11	13	0	4.41
M. Trombley	44	114	6	6	2	4.88
E. Guardado	19	95	3	8	0	6.18
R. Aguilera	65	72	4	3	34	3.11

Oakland

W-68 L-94

Tony LaRussa

POS	Player	AB	BA	HR	RBI	PO	A	E	DP	TC/G	FA
1B	M. Aldrete	255	.267	10	33	370	28	2	39	6.8	.995
2B	B. Gates	535	.290	7	69	281	431	14	88	5.2	.981
SS	M. Bordick	546	.249	3	48	**280**	418	13	**108**	4.5	.982
3B	C. Paquette	393	.219	12	46	81	165	13	17	2.5	.950
RF	R. Sierra	630	.233	22	101	291	9	7	3	2.3	.977
CF	D. Henderson	382	.220	20	53	205	7	2	4	2.8	.991
LF	R. Henderson	318	.327	17	47	182	5	5	0	2.6	.974
C	T. Steinbach	389	.285	10	43	422	38	5	9	5.4	.989
DH	T. Neel	427	.290	19	63						
OF	J. Browne	260	.250	2	19	130	1	2	0	2.4	.985
UT	K. Seitzer	255	.255	4	27	206	90	7	31		.977
UT	L. Blankenship	252	.190	2	23	207	65	5	15		.982
C	S. Hemond	215	.256	6	26	395	38	4	5	5.8	.991
UT	S. Brosius	213	.249	6	25	173	29	2	11		.990
1B	M. McGwire	84	.333	9	24	197	14	0	20	8.4	1.000

Pitcher	G	IP	W	L	SV	ERA
B. Witt	35	220	14	13	0	4.21
R. Darling	31	178	5	9	0	5.16
B. Welch	30	167	9	11	0	5.29
K. Downs	42	120	5	10	0	5.64
T. Van Poppel	16	84	6	6	0	5.04
E. Nunez	56	76	3	6	1	3.81
D. Eckersley	64	67	2	4	36	4.16
G. Gossage	39	48	4	5	1	4.53

BATTING AND BASE RUNNING LEADERS

Batting Average

J. Olerud, TOR	.363
P. Molitor, TOR	.332
R. Alomar, TOR	.326
K. Lofton, CLE	.325
C. Baerga, CLE	.321

Slugging Average

J. Gonzalez, TEX	.632
K. Griffey, SEA	.617
F. Thomas, CHI	.607
J. Olerud, TOR	.599
C. Hoiles, BAL	.585

Home Runs

J. Gonzalez, TEX	46
K. Griffey, SEA	45
F. Thomas, CHI	41
A. Belle, CLE	38
R. Palmeiro, TEX	37

Total Bases

K. Griffey, SEA	359
J. Gonzalez, TEX	339
F. Thomas, CHI	333
R. Palmeiro, TEX	331
J. Olerud, TOR	330

Runs Batted In

A. Belle, CLE	129
F. Thomas, CHI	128
J. Carter, TOR	121
J. Gonzalez, TEX	118
C. Fielder, DET	117

Stolen Bases

K. Lofton, CLE	70
L. Polonia, CAL	55
R. Alomar, TOR	55
R. Henderson, OAK, TOR	53
C. Curtis, CAL	48

Hits

P. Molitor, TOR	211
J. Olerud, TOR	200
C. Baerga, CLE	200
R. Alomar, TOR	192

Base on Balls

T. Phillips, DET	132
R. Henderson, OAK, TOR	120
J. Olerud, TOR	114
F. Thomas, CHI	112

Home Run Percentage

J. Gonzalez, TEX	8.6
K. Griffey, SEA	7.7
F. Thomas, CHI	7.5
C. Hoiles, BAL	6.9

Runs

R. Palmeiro, TEX	124
P. Molitor, TOR	121
K. Lofton, CLE	116
D. White, TOR	116

Doubles

J. Olerud, TOR	54
D. White, TOR	42
J. Valentin, BOS	40
R. Palmeiro, TEX	40

Triples

L. Johnson, CHI	14
J. Cora, CHI	13
D. Hulse, TEX	10
T. Fernandez, TOR	9
B. McRae, KC	9

PITCHING LEADERS

Winning Percentage

J. Key, NY	.750
R. Johnson, SEA	.704
K. Appier, KC	.692
J. McDowell, CHI	.688
P. Hentgen, TOR	.679

Earned Run Average

K. Appier, KC	2.56
W. Alvarez, CHI	2.95
J. Key, NY	3.00
A. Fernandez, CHI	3.13
F. Viola, BOS	3.14

Wins

J. McDowell, CHI	22
P. Hentgen, TOR	19
R. Johnson, SEA	19
J. Key, NY	18
K. Appier, KC	18
A. Fernandez, CHI	18

Saves

D. Ward, TOR	45
J. Montgomery, KC	45
T. Henke, TEX	40
R. Hernandez, CHI	38
D. Eckersley, OAK	36

Strikeouts

R. Johnson, SEA	308
M. Langston, CAL	196
J. Guzman, TOR	194
D. Cone, KC	191
C. Finley, CAL	187

Complete Games

C. Finley, CAL	13
K. Brown, TEX	12
J. McDowell, CHI	10
R. Johnson, SEA	10
C. Eldred, MIL	8

Fewest Hits/9 Innings

R. Johnson, SEA	6.52
K. Appier, KC	6.90
D. Cone, KC	7.26
W. Alvarez, CHI	7.28

Shutouts

J. McDowell, CHI	4
K. Brown, TEX	3
R. Johnson, SEA	3
M. Moore, DET	3

Fewest Walks/9 Innings

J. Key, NY	1.64
D. Darwin, BOS	1.92
D. Wells, DET	2.02
K. Tapani, MIN	2.27

Most Strikeouts/9 Inn.

R. Johnson, SEA	10.86
M. Perez, NY	8.17
J. Guzman, TOR	7.90
R. Clemens, BOS	7.51

Innings

C. Eldred, MIL	258
J. McDowell, CHI	257
M. Langston, CAL	256
R. Johnson, SEA	255

Games Pitched

G. Harris, BOS	80
S. Radinsky, CHI	73
D. Ward, TOR	71
T. Fossas, BOS	71
J. Nelson, SEA	71

AMERICAN LEAGUE 1993, *cont.*

		W	L	PCT	GB	R	OR	Batting					SB	Fielding			Pitching					ERA
								2B	3B	HR	BA	SA		E	DP	FA	CG	BB	SO	ShO	SV	
East	Toronto	95	67	.586		847	742	317	42	159	**.279**	**.436**	**170**	107	144	.982	11	620	1023	11	**50**	4.21
	New York	88	74	.543	7	821	761	294	24	178	**.279**	.435	39	105	166	.983	11	552	899	**13**	38	4.35
	Baltimore	85	77	.525	10	786	745	287	24	157	.267	.413	73	100	171	.984	21	579	900	10	42	4.31
	Detroit	85	77	.525	10	**899**	837	282	38	178	.275	.434	104	132	148	.979	11	542	828	7	36	4.65
	Boston	80	82	.494	15	686	698	**319**	29	114	.264	.395	73	122	155	.980	9	552	997	11	44	3.77
	Cleveland	76	86	.469	19	790	813	264	31	141	.275	.409	159	148	**174**	.976	7	591	888	8	45	4.58
	Milwaukee	69	93	.426	26	733	792	240	25	125	.258	.378	138	131	148	.979	**26**	522	810	6	29	4.45
West	Chicago	94	68	.580		776	**664**	228	**44**	162	.265	.411	106	112	153	.982	16	566	974	11	48	**3.70**
	Texas	86	76	.531	8	835	751	284	39	**181**	.267	.431	113	132	145	.979	20	562	957	6	45	4.28
	Kansas City	84	78	.519	10	675	694	294	35	125	.263	.397	100	97	150	.984	16	571	985	6	48	4.04
	Seattle	82	80	.506	12	734	731	272	24	161	.260	.406	91	**90**	173	**.985**	22	605	**1083**	10	41	4.20
	California	71	91	.438	23	684	770	259	24	114	.260	.380	169	120	161	.980	**26**	550	843	6	41	4.34
	Minnesota	71	91	.438	23	693	830	261	27	121	.264	.385	83	100	160	.984	5	**514**	901	3	44	4.71
	Oakland	68	94	.420	26	715	846	260	21	158	.254	.394	131	111	161	.982	8	680	864	2	42	4.90
						10674	10674	3861	427	2074	.266	.407	1549	1607	2209	.981	209	8006	12952	110	593	4.32

NATIONAL LEAGUE 1994

		POS	Player	AB	BA	HR	RBI	PO	A	E	DP	TC/G	FA	Pitcher	G	IP	W	L	SV	ERA
East	Montreal	1B	C. Floyd	334	.281	4	41	527	40	5	43	7.4	.991	K. Hill	23	155	**16**	5	0	3.32
		2B	M. Lansing	394	.266	5	35	144	206	6	46	4.3	.983	P. Martinez	24	145	11	5	1	3.42
	W-74 L-40	SS	W. Cordero	415	.294	15	63	124	316	22	55	4.2	.952	J. Fassero	21	139	8	6	0	2.99
		3B	S. Berry	320	.278	11	41	66	147	14	8	2.3	.938	B. Henry	24	107	8	3	1	2.43
	Felipe Alou	RF	L. Walker	395	.322	19	86	140	5	4	1	2.2	.973	K. Rueter	20	92	7	3	0	5.17
		CF	M. Grissom	475	.288	11	45	321	7	5	0	3.1	.985	M. Rojas	58	84	3	2	16	3.32
		LF	M. Alou	422	.339	22	78	201	4	3	0	2.0	.986	G. Heredia	39	75	6	3	0	3.46
		C	D. Fletcher	285	.260	10	57	479	20	2	2	6.2	.996	J. Shaw	46	67	5	2	1	3.88
		C	L. Webster	143	.273	5	23	237	19	1	0	5.6	.996	J. Wetteland	52	64	4	6	25	2.83
		OF	L. Frazier	140	.271	0	14	55	2	0	1	1.6	1.000	T. Scott	40	53	5	2	1	2.70
	Atlanta	1B	F. McGriff	424	.318	34	94	**1004**	66	7	73	9.6	.994	G. Maddux	25	**202**	**16**	6	0	**1.56**
		2B	M. Lemke	350	.294	3	31	208	300	3	54	5.0	**.994**	T. Glavine	25	165	13	9	0	3.97
	W-68 L-46	SS	J. Blauser	380	.258	6	45	126	289	13	44	4.5	.970	S. Avery	24	152	8	3	0	4.04
		3B	T. Pendleton	309	.252	7	30	60	147	11	12	2.8	.950	J. Smoltz	21	135	6	10	0	4.14
	Bobby Cox	RF	D. Justice	352	.313	19	59	193	6	11	0	2.1	.948	K. Mercker	20	112	9	4	0	3.45
		CF	R. Kelly	255	.286	6	24	128	3	2	0	2.1	.985	G. McMichael	51	59	4	6	21	3.84
		LF	R. Klesko	245	.278	17	47	67	3	6	0	1.0	.921	M. Wohlers	51	51	7	2	1	4.59
		C	J. Lopez	277	.245	13	35	560	35	3	0	**8.0**	.995	M. Stanton	49	46	3	1	3	3.55
		OF	D. Sanders	191	.288	4	21	99	0	2	0	2.2	.980							
		OF	D. Gallagher	152	.224	2	14	87	1	1	0	1.2	.989							
		C	C. O'Brien	152	.243	8	28	308	26	3	1	7.0	.991							
		OF	T. Tarasco	132	.273	5	19	42	1	0	0	0.9	1.000							
		S2	R. Belliard	120	.242	0	9	45	86	1	16		.992							
	New York	1B	D. Segui	336	.241	10	43	665	51	3	65	9.2	**.996**	B. Saberhagen	24	177	14	4	0	2.74
		2B	J. Kent	415	.292	14	68	221	338	**14**	76	5.4	.976	B. Jones	24	160	12	7	0	3.15
	W-55 L-58	SS	J. Vizcaino	410	.256	3	33	137	291	13	55	4.3	.971	P. Smith	21	131	4	10	0	5.55
		3B	B. Bonilla	403	.290	20	67	77	217	**18**	**24**	2.9	.942	M. Gozzo	23	69	3	5	0	4.83
	Dallas Green	RF	J. Orsulak	292	.260	8	42	129	9	3	2	1.6	.979	J. Jacome	8	54	4	3	0	2.67
		CF	R. Thompson	334	.225	18	59	274	5	3	1	2.9	.989	R. Mason	41	51	2	4	1	3.51
		LF	K. McReynolds	180	.256	4	21	91	1	0	1	2.0	1.000	D. Linton	32	50	6	2	0	4.47
		C	T. Hundley	291	.237	16	42	448	28	5	0	5.9	.990	J. Franco	47	50	1	4	**30**	2.70
		C	K. Stinnett	150	.253	2	14	211	20	5	2	5.4	.979	J. Manzanillo	37	47	3	2	2	2.66
		OF	J. Burnitz	143	.238	3	15	63	1	2	0	1.6	.970	D. Gooden	7	41	3	4	0	6.31
		OF	J. Lindeman	137	.270	7	20	54	1	3	0	1.8	.948							
		1B	R. Brogna	131	.351	7	20	308	28	1	29	9.6	.997							
		UT	F. Vina	124	.250	0	6	46	59	4	5		.963							
	Philadelphia	1B	J. Kruk	255	.302	5	38	540	46	3	45	8.5	.995	D. Jackson	25	179	14	6	0	3.26
		2B	M. Morandini	274	.292	2	26	167	216	6	38	4.9	.985	B. Munoz	21	104	7	5	1	2.67
	W-54 L-61	SS	K. Stocker	271	.273	2	28	118	253	16	46	4.7	.959	D. West	31	99	4	10	0	3.55
		3B	D. Hollins	162	.222	4	26	37	47	11	1	2.2	.884	S. Boskie	18	84	4	6	0	5.23
	Jim Fregosi	RF	J. Eisenreich	290	.300	4	43	178	4	2	2	2.0	.989	C. Schilling	13	82	2	8	0	4.48
		CF	L. Dykstra	315	.273	5	24	235	4	4	0	2.9	.984	D. Jones	47	54	2	4	27	2.17
		LF	M. Thompson	220	.273	3	30	119	1	0	1	1.5	1.000	B. Rivera	9	38	3	4	0	6.87
		C	D. Daulton	257	.300	15	56	435	41	3	2	7.0	.994							
		UT	M. Duncan	347	.268	8	48	148	188	12	38		.966							
		OF	P. Incaviglia	244	.230	13	32	90	2	2	0	1.5	.979							
		1B	R. Jordan	220	.282	8	37	430	14	3	41	9.1	.993							
		3B	K. Batiste	209	.234	1	13	31	71	9	3	2.6	.919							
		OF	T. Longmire	139	.237	0	17	45	3	3	1	1.6	.941							
		OF	B. Hatcher	134	.246	2	13	68	4	0	0	1.8	1.000							
	Florida	1B	G. Colbrunn	155	.303	6	31	303	26	4	28	8.1	.988	D. Weathers	24	135	8	12	0	5.27
		2B	B. Barberie	372	.301	5	31	223	320	**14**	61	5.3	.975	P. Rapp	24	133	7	8	0	3.85
		SS	K. Abbott	345	.249	9	33	165	258	15	57	4.4	.966	C. Hough	21	114	5	9	0	5.15
	W-51 L-64	3B	J. Browne	329	.295	3	30	44	87	10	8	2.3	.929	M. Gardner	20	92	4	4	0	4.87
		RF	G. Sheffield	322	.276	27	78	153	7	5	2	1.9	.970	C. Hammond	13	73	4	4	0	3.07
	Rene Lachemann	CF	C. Carr	433	.263	2	30	297	4	6	0	3.0	.980	R. Nen	44	58	5	5	15	2.95
		LF	J. Conine	451	.319	18	82	182	4	5	0	2.0	.974	J. Hernandez	21	23	3	3	9	2.70
		C	B. Santiago	337	.273	11	41	511	**64**	5	3	6.0	.991							
		3B	D. Magadan	211	.275	1	17	21	71	4	5	2.0	.958							
		OF	M. Carrillo	136	.250	0	9	49	5	1	1	1.1	.982							
		1B	O. Destrade	130	.208	5	15	273	19	5	29	8.0	.983							

NATIONAL LEAGUE 1994, *cont.*

		POS	Player	AB	BA	HR	RBI	PO	A	E	DP	TC/G	FA	Pitcher	G	IP	W	L	SV	ERA
Central	Cincinnati	1B	H. Morris	436	.335	10	78	899	77	6	76	8.8	.994	J. Rijo	26	172	9	6	0	3.08
	W-66 L-48	2B	B. Boone	381	.320	12	68	191	267	12	57	4.4	.974	J. Smiley	24	159	11	10	0	3.86
	Davey Johnson	SS	B. Larkin	427	.279	9	52	**178**	312	10	56	4.5	.980	E. Hanson	22	123	5	5	0	4.11
		3B	T. Fernandez	366	.279	8	50	54	165	2	10	2.4	**.991**	J. Roper	16	92	6	2	0	4.50
		RF	R. Sanders	400	.263	17	62	217	12	6	2	2.3	.974	P. Schourek	22	81	7	2	0	4.09
		CF	D. Sanders	184	.277	0	7	110	2	0	0	2.5	1.000	J. Ruffin	51	70	7	2	1	3.09
		LF	K. Mitchell	310	.326	30	77	132	9	4	2	1.6	.972	J. Brantley	50	65	6	6	15	2.48
		C	B. Dorsett	216	.245	5	26	412	34	4	2	6.2	.991	C. McElroy	52	58	1	2	5	2.34
		OF	R. Kelly	179	.302	3	21	119	2	1	0	2.6	.992	H. Carrasco	45	56	5	6	6	2.24
		OF	T. Howard	178	.264	5	24	80	2	3	1	1.5	.965							
		C	E. Taubensee	177	.294	8	21	361	17	4	1	6.3	.990							
		OF	J. Brumfield	122	.311	4	11	74	1	1	0	1.8	.987							
	Houston	1B	J. Bagwell	400	.367	39	**116**	923	**117**	**9**	**93**	9.6	.991	D. Drabek	23	165	12	6	0	2.84
	W-66 L-49	2B	C. Biggio	437	.318	6	56	225	**339**	7	63	5.1	.988	G. Swindell	24	148	8	9	0	4.37
	Terry Collins	SS	A. Cedeno	342	.263	9	49	130	280	**23**	**69**	4.6	.947	D. Kile	24	148	9	6	0	4.57
		3B	K. Caminiti	406	.283	18	75	79	201	9	17	2.7	.969	S. Reynolds	33	124	8	5	0	3.05
		RF	J. Mouton	310	.245	2	16	163	5	3	2	1.8	.982	P. Harnisch	17	95	8	5	0	5.40
		CF	S. Finley	373	.276	11	33	214	9	4	0	2.5	.982	B. Williams	20	78	6	5	0	5.74
		LF	L. Gonzalez	392	.273	8	67	228	5	2	1	2.1	.991	T. Jones	48	73	5	2	5	2.72
		C	S. Servais	251	.195	9	41	481	29	2	1	6.6	.996	D. Veres	32	41	3	3	1	2.41
		OF	K. Bass	203	.310	6	35	82	3	2	1	1.5	.977	J. Hudek	42	39	0	2	16	2.97
		C	T. Eusebio	159	.296	5	30	263	24	2	1	5.6	.993	M. Williams	25	20	1	4	6	7.65
		OF	M. Felder	117	.239	0	13	36	2	1	0	1.2	.974							
	Pittsburgh	1B	B. Hunter	233	.227	11	47	488	38	5	48	9.0	.991	Z. Smith	25	157	10	8	0	3.27
	W-53 L-61	2B	C. Garcia	412	.277	6	28	**226**	316	12	**78**	**5.7**	.978	D. Neagle	24	137	9	10	0	5.12
	Jim Leyland	SS	J. Bell	424	.276	9	45	152	**380**	15	67	**5.0**	.973	S. Cooke	25	134	4	11	0	5.02
		3B	J. King	339	.263	5	42	59	193	12	**24**	2.9	.955	P. Wagner	29	120	7	8	0	4.59
		RF	O. Merced	386	.272	9	51	100	3	2	1	1.5	.981	J. Lieber	17	109	6	7	0	3.73
		CF	A. Van Slyke	374	.246	6	30	238	9	2	1	2.5	.992	R. White	43	75	4	5	6	3.82
		LF	A. Martin	276	.286	9	33	129	8	3	1	1.8	.979	R. Manzanillo	46	50	4	2	1	4.14
		C	D. Slaught	240	.287	2	21	425	36	3	4	6.3	.994	A. Pena	22	29	3	2	7	5.02
		OF	D. Clark	223	.296	10	46	107	5	3	1	2.0	.974							
		C	L. Parrish	126	.270	3	16	225	15	3	1	6.4	.988							
		UT	T. Foley	123	.236	3	15	51	94	3	25		.980							
		13	K. Young	122	.205	1	11	177	45	3	21		.987							
	St. Louis	1B	G. Jefferies	397	.325	12	55	890	52	7	91	9.3	.993	B. Tewksbury	24	156	12	10	0	5.32
	W-53 L-61	2B	G. Pena	213	.254	11	34	119	170	3	42	4.9	.990	V. Palacios	31	118	3	8	1	4.44
	Joe Torre	SS	O. Smith	381	.262	3	30	136	292	8	65	4.5	**.982**	A. Watson	22	116	6	5	0	5.52
		3B	T. Zeile	415	.267	19	75	66	224	12	**24**	2.7	.960	R. Arocha	45	83	4	4	11	4.01
		RF	M. Whiten	334	.293	14	53	234	9	9	0	2.8	.964	T. Urbani	20	80	3	7	0	5.15
		CF	R. Lankford	416	.267	19	57	259	5	6	1	2.6	.978	O. Olivares	14	74	3	4	1	5.74
		LF	B. Gilkey	380	.253	6	45	168	9	3	3	1.8	.983	R. Sutcliffe	16	68	6	4	0	6.52
		C	T. Pagnozzi	243	.272	7	40	369	41	1	3	5.9	**.998**	R. Rodriguez	56	60	3	5	0	4.03
		2B	L. Alicea	205	.278	5	29	124	148	4	38	5.2	.986	R. Murphy	50	40	4	3	2	3.79
		OF	B. Jordan	178	.258	5	15	105	5	1	1	2.4	.991	M. Perez	36	31	2	3	12	8.71
		S2	J. Oquendo	129	.264	0	9	53	98	4	22		.974							
	Chicago	1B	M. Grace	403	.298	6	44	925	76	7	90	9.8	.993	S. Trachsel	22	146	9	7	0	3.21
	W-49 L-64	2B	R. Sandberg	223	.238	5	24	96	202	4	35	5.3	.987	W. Banks	23	138	8	12	0	5.40
	Tom Trebelhorn	SS	S. Dunston	331	.278	11	35	121	219	12	47	4.2	.966	A. Young	20	115	4	6	0	3.92
		3B	S. Buechele	339	.242	14	52	55	136	5	12	2.0	.974	J. Bullinger	33	100	6	2	2	3.60
		RF	S. Sosa	426	.300	25	70	248	5	7	0	2.5	.973	K. Foster	13	81	3	4	0	2.89
		CF	K. Rhodes	269	.234	8	19	142	4	5	1	2.0	.967	M. Morgan	15	81	2	10	0	6.69
		LF	D. May	345	.284	8	51	154	4	1	0	1.7	.994	J. Bautista	58	69	4	5	1	3.89
		C	R. Wilkins	313	.227	7	39	546	51	4	1	6.3	.993	C. Crim	49	64	5	4	2	4.48
		UT	R. Sanchez	291	.285	0	24	152	275	9	52		.979	R. Myers	38	40	1	5	21	3.79
		OF	G. Hill	269	.297	10	38	150	0	2	0	1.9	.987							
		UT	J. Hernandez	132	.242	1	9	46	85	4	15		.970							
		01	E. Zambrano	116	.259	6	18	84	5	2	6		.978							
West	Los Angeles	1B	E. Karros	406	.266	14	46	896	116	**9**	79	9.4	.991	R. Martinez	24	170	12	7	0	3.97
	W-58 L-56	2B	D. DeShields	320	.250	2	33	155	277	6	47	5.0	.986	K. Gross	25	157	9	7	1	3.60
	Tom Lasorda	SS	J. Offerman	243	.210	1	25	123	194	11	45	4.6	.966	T. Candiotti	23	153	7	7	0	4.12
		3B	T. Wallach	414	.280	23	78	**81**	174	11	9	2.4	.959	P. Astacio	23	149	6	8	0	4.29
		RF	R. Mondesi	434	.306	16	56	206	16	8	1	2.1	.965	O. Hershiser	21	135	6	6	0	3.79
		CF	B. Butler	417	.314	8	33	260	8	2	1	2.4	.993	T. Worrell	38	42	6	5	11	4.29
		LF	H. Rodriguez	306	.268	8	49	141	4	2	0	1.7	.986	J. Gott	37	36	5	3	2	5.94
		C	M. Piazza	405	.319	24	92	640	38	**10**	3	6.6	.985	D. Dreifort	27	29	0	5	6	6.21
		UT	C. Snyder	153	.235	6	18	92	23	7	9		.943							
		SS	R. Bournigal	116	.224	0	11	56	97	3	19	3.9	.981							
	San Francisco	1B	T. Benzinger	328	.265	9	31	781	55	5	69	8.5	.994	J. Burkett	25	159	6	8	0	3.62
	W-55 L-60	2B	J. Patterson	240	.237	3	32	120	163	6	32	4.6	.979	M. Portugal	21	137	10	8	0	3.93
	Dusty Baker	SS	R. Clayton	385	.236	3	30	**178**	331	14	62	4.8	.973	B. Swift	17	109	8	7	0	3.38
		3B	M. Williams	445	.267	**43**	96	79	**234**	12	21	**3.0**	.963	B. Hickerson	28	98	4	8	1	5.40
		RF	D. Martinez	235	.247	4	27	86	3	0	1	1.5	1.000	S. Torres	16	84	2	8	0	5.44
		CF	D. Lewis	451	.257	4	29	281	5	2	1	2.5	.993	W. VanLandingham	16	84	8	2	0	3.54
		LF	B. Bonds	391	.312	37	81	198	10	3	0	1.9	.986	D. Burba	57	74	3	6	0	4.38
		C	K. Manwaring	316	.250	1	29	540	53	4	4	6.2	.993	R. Beck	48	49	2	4	28	2.77
		OF	W. McGee	156	.282	5	23	79	2	1	0	2.0	.988	R. Monteleone	39	45	4	3	0	3.18
		2B	R. Thompson	129	.209	2	7	67	121	2	24	5.4	.989	M. Jackson	36	42	3	2	4	1.49
		OF	M. Carreon	100	.270	3	20	44	0	1	0	1.4	.978							

NATIONAL LEAGUE 1994, *cont.*

Team	POS	Player	AB	BA	HR	RBI	PO	A	E	DP	TC/G	FA	Pitcher	G	IP	W	L	SV	ERA
Colorado	1B	A. Galarraga	417	.319	31	85	954	64	8	89	**10.0**	.992	G. Harris	29	130	3	12	1	6.65
W-53 L-64	2B	N. Liriano	255	.255	3	31	144	222	10	42	4.8	.973	D. Nied	22	122	9	7	0	4.80
Don Baylor	SS	W. Weiss	423	.251	1	32	157	318	13	68	4.4	.973	M. Freeman	19	113	10	2	0	2.80
	3B	C. Hayes	423	.288	10	50	72	216	17	19	2.8	.944	M. Harkey	24	92	1	6	0	5.79
	RF	D. Bichette	**484**	.304	27	95	210	10	2	3	1.9	.991	W. Blair	47	78	0	5	3	5.79
	CF	M. Kingery	301	.349	4	41	185	5	4	0	2.0	.979	K. Ritz	15	74	5	6	0	5.62
	LF	H. Johnson	227	.211	10	40	90	2	2	0	1.5	.979	L. Painter	15	74	4	6	0	6.11
	C	J. Girardi	330	.276	4	34	548	55	5	**5**	6.5	.992	S. Reed	**61**	64	3	2	3	3.94
	OF	E. Young	228	.272	7	30	97	4	2	0	1.7	.981	B. Ruffin	56	56	4	5	16	4.04
	OF	E. Burks	149	.322	13	24	79	2	3	0	2.2	.964	A. Reynoso	9	52	3	4	0	4.82
	UT	V. Castilla	130	.331	3	18	67	78	2	23		.986	M. Munoz	57	46	4	2	1	3.74
San Diego	1B	E. Williams	175	.331	11	42	382	29	5	28	9.0	.988	A. Benes	25	172	6	**14**	0	3.86
W-47 L-70	2B	B. Roberts	403	.320	2	31	147	221	9	41	4.2	.976	A. Ashby	24	164	6	11	0	3.40
Jim Riggleman	SS	R. Gutierrez	275	.240	1	28	85	186	22	33	3.8	.925	S. Sanders	23	111	4	8	1	4.78
	3B	C. Shipley	240	.333	4	30	25	63	6	3	1.8	.936	J. Hamilton	16	109	9	6	0	2.98
	RF	T. Gwynn	419	**.394**	12	64	191	6	3	1	1.9	.985	P. Martinez	48	68	3	2	3	2.90
	CF	D. Bell	434	.311	14	54	247	3	10	0	2.4	.962	W. Whitehurst	13	64	4	7	0	4.92
	LF	P. Plantier	341	.220	18	41	159	5	2	0	1.8	.988	T. Hoffman	47	56	4	4	20	2.57
	C	B. Ausmus	327	.251	7	24	**684**	59	7	2	7.6	.991	T. Mauser	35	49	2	4	2	3.49
	S2	L. Lopez	235	.277	2	20	97	169	14	23		.950							
	3B	S. Livingstone	180	.272	2	10	20	78	6	6	2.1	.942							
	UT	P. Clark	149	.215	5	20	148	14	4	14		.976							
	31	A. Cianfrocco	146	.219	4	13	58	65	7	7		.946							
	OF	B. Bean	135	.215	0	14	46	0	0	1	1.2	1.000							
	1B	T. Hyers	118	.254	0	7	258	23	4	19	7.0	.986							

BATTING AND BASE RUNNING LEADERS

Batting Average
T. Gwynn, SD .394
J. Bagwell, HOU .367
M. Alou, MON .339
H. Morris, CIN .335
K. Mitchell, CIN .326

Slugging Average
J. Bagwell, HOU .750
K. Mitchell, CIN .681
B. Bonds, SF .647
F. McGriff, ATL .623
M. Williams, SF .607

Home Runs
M. Williams, SF 43
J. Bagwell, HOU 39
B. Bonds, SF 37
F. McGriff, ATL 34
A. Galarraga, CLR 31

Total Bases
J. Bagwell, HOU 300
M. Williams, SF 270
D. Bichette, CLR 265
F. McGriff, ATL 264
B. Bonds, SF 253

Runs Batted In
J. Bagwell, HOU 116
M. Williams, SF 96
D. Bichette, CLR 95
F. McGriff, ATL 94
M. Piazza, LA 92

Stolen Bases
C. Biggio, HOU 39
D. Sanders, ATL, CIN 38
M. Grissom, MON 36
C. Carr, FLA 32
D. Lewis, SF 30

Hits
T. Gwynn, SD 165
J. Bagwell, HOU 147
D. Bichette, CLR 147
H. Morris, CIN 146

Base on Balls
B. Bonds, SF 74
D. Justice, ATL 69
L. Dykstra, PHI 68
B. Butler, LA 68

Home Run Percentage
J. Bagwell, HOU 9.8
K. Mitchell, CIN 9.7
M. Williams, SF 9.7
B. Bonds, SF 9.5

Runs
J. Bagwell, HOU 104
M. Grissom, MON 96
B. Bonds, SF 89
R. Lankford, STL 89

Doubles
L. Walker, MON 44
C. Biggio, HOU 44
T. Gwynn, SD 35
J. Bell, PIT 35

Triples
B. Butler, LA 9
D. Lewis, SF 9
M. Kingery, CLR 8
R. Sanders, CIN 8
R. Mondesi, LA 8

PITCHING LEADERS

Winning Percentage
B. Saberhagen, NY .778
K. Hill, MON .762
G. Maddux, ATL .727
D. Jackson, PHI .700
P. Martinez, MON .688

Earned Run Average
G. Maddux, ATL 1.56
B. Saberhagen, NY 2.74
D. Drabek, HOU 2.84
J. Fassero, MON 2.99
S. Reynolds, HOU 3.05

Wins
K. Hill, MON 16
G. Maddux, ATL 16
B. Saberhagen, NY 14
D. Jackson, PHI 14
T. Glavine, ATL 13

Saves
J. Franco, NY 30
R. Beck, SF 28
D. Jones, PHI 27
J. Wetteland, MON 25
R. Myers, CHI 21
G. McMichael, ATL 21

Strikeouts
A. Benes, SD 189
J. Rijo, CIN 171
G. Maddux, ATL 156
B. Saberhagen, NY 143
P. Martinez, MON 142

Complete Games
G. Maddux, ATL 10
D. Drabek, HOU 6
T. Candiotti, LA 5

Fewest Hits/9 Innings
G. Maddux, ATL 6.68
P. Martinez, MON 7.15
D. Drabek, HOU 7.21
S. Avery, ATL 7.54

Shutouts
R. Martinez, LA 3
G. Maddux, ATL 3
D. Drabek, HOU 2
A. Benes, SD 2

Fewest Walks/9 Innings
B. Saberhagen, NY 0.66
B. Tewksbury, STL 1.27
G. Maddux, ATL 1.38
S. Reynolds, HOU 1.52

Most Strikeouts/9 Inn.
A. Benes, SD 9.87
J. Rijo, CIN 8.93
P. Martinez, MON 8.83
D. Neagle, PIT 8.01

Innings
G. Maddux, ATL 202
D. Jackson, PHI 179
B. Saberhagen, NY 177
A. Benes, SD 172
J. Rijo, CIN 172

Games Pitched
S. Reed, CLR 61
J. Bautista, CHI 58
M. Rojas, MON 58
M. Munoz, CLR 57
D. Burba, SF 57

		W	L	PCT	GB	R	OR	Batting 2B	3B	HR	BA	SA	SB	Fielding E	DP	FA	Pitching CG	BB	SO	ShO	SV	ERA
East	Montreal	74	40	.649		585	454	246	30	108	.278	.435	**137**	94	86	.979	4	**288**	805	**8**	**46**	**3.56**
	Atlanta	68	46	.596	6	542	**448**	198	18	**137**	.267	.434	48	81	79	.982	**16**	378	**865**	**8**	26	3.57
	New York	55	58	.487	18.5	506	526	164	21	117	.250	.394	25	89	111	.980	7	332	640	3	35	4.13
	Philadelphia	54	61	.470	20.5	521	497	208	28	80	.262	.390	67	94	93	.978	7	377	699	6	30	3.85
	Florida	51	64	.443	23.5	468	576	180	24	94	.266	.396	65	95	101	.978	5	428	649	7	30	4.50
Central	Cincinnati	66	48	.579		**609**	490	211	36	124	**.286**	**.449**	119	73	84	.983	6	339	799	6	27	3.78
	Houston	66	49	.574	0.5	602	503	**252**	25	120	.278	.445	124	76	108	.983	9	367	739	6	29	3.97
	Pittsburgh	53	61	.465	13	466	580	198	23	80	.259	.384	53	91	**124**	.980	8	370	650	2	24	4.64
	St. Louis	53	61	.465	13	535	621	213	27	108	.263	.414	76	80	112	.982	7	355	632	7	29	5.14
	Chicago	49	64	.434	16.5	500	549	189	26	109	.259	.404	69	81	105	.982	5	392	717	5	27	4.47
West	Los Angeles	58	56	.509		532	509	160	29	115	.270	.414	74	88	92	.980	14	354	732	5	20	4.17
	San Francisco	55	60	.478	3.5	504	500	159	32	123	.249	.402	114	**68**	105	**.985**	2	372	655	4	33	3.99
	Colorado	53	64	.453	6.5	573	638	206	**39**	125	.274	.439	91	84	112	.981	4	448	703	5	28	5.15
	San Diego	47	70	.402	12.5	479	531	200	19	92	.275	.401	79	111	81	.975	8	393	862	6	27	4.08
						7422	7422	2784	377	1532	.267	.414	1141	1205	1393	.981	102	5193	10147	78	411	4.21

AMERICAN LEAGUE 1994

East

New York

W-70 L-43

Buck Showalter

POS	Player	AB	BA	HR	RBI	PO	A	E	DP	TC/G	FA	Pitcher	G	IP	W	L	SV	ERA
1B	D. Mattingly	372	.304	6	51	916	66	2	95	**10.1**	**.998**	J. Key	25	168	**17**	4	0	3.27
2B	P. Kelly	286	.280	3	41	182	257	10	69	4.8	.978	J. Abbott	24	160	9	8	0	4.55
SS	M. Gallego	306	.239	6	41	106	245	11	53	5.0	.970	M. Perez	22	151	9	4	0	4.10
3B	W. Boggs	366	.342	11	55	40	213	10	19	**2.8**	.962	T. Mulholland	24	121	6	7	0	6.49
RF	P. O'Neill	368	**.359**	21	83	203	7	1	0	2.1	.995	S. Kamieniecki	22	117	8	6	0	3.76
CF	B. Williams	408	.289	12	57	277	7	3	1	2.7	.990	B. Wickman	**53**	70	5	4	6	3.09
LF	L. Polonia	350	.311	1	36	154	9	4	2	2.0	.976	S. Hitchcock	23	49	4	1	2	4.20
C	M. Stanley	290	.300	17	57	391	30	3	1	5.9	.993	S. Howe	40	40	3	0	15	1.80
DH	D. Tartabull	399	.256	19	67							X. Hernandez	31	40	4	4	6	5.85
UT	R. Velarde	280	.279	9	34	94	188	19	37		.937							
UT	J. Leyritz	249	.265	17	58	282	15	0	6		1.000							

Baltimore

W-63 L-49

Johnny Oates

POS	Player	AB	BA	HR	RBI	PO	A	E	DP	TC/G	FA	Pitcher	G	IP	W	L	SV	ERA
1B	R. Palmeiro	436	.319	23	76	958	67	4	86	9.3	.996	M. Mussina	24	176	16	5	0	3.06
2B	M. McLemore	343	.257	3	29	202	270	9	53	5.0	.981	B. McDonald	24	157	14	7	0	4.06
SS	C. Ripken	444	.315	13	75	130	321	7	**70**	4.1	**.985**	J. Moyer	23	149	5	7	0	4.77
3B	L. Gomez	285	.274	15	56	54	139	5	12	2.5	.975	S. Fernandez	19	115	6	6	0	5.15
RF	J. Hammonds	250	.296	8	31	147	5	6	0	2.4	.962	M. Eichhorn	43	71	6	5	1	2.15
CF	M. Devereaux	301	.203	9	33	203	3	1	1	2.5	.995	A. Rhodes	10	53	3	5	0	5.81
LF	B. Anderson	453	.263	12	48	247	4	1	0	2.3	.996	A. Mills	47	45	3	3	2	5.16
C	C. Hoiles	332	.247	19	53	**615**	36	7	**2**	6.7	.989	L. Smith	41	38	1	4	**33**	3.29
DH	H. Baines	326	.294	16	54													
UT	C. Sabo	258	.256	11	42	52	49	4	5		.962							
OF	J. Voigt	141	.241	3	20	88	2	1	0	1.7	.989							

Toronto

W-55 L-60

Cito Gaston

POS	Player	AB	BA	HR	RBI	PO	A	E	DP	TC/G	FA	Pitcher	G	IP	W	L	SV	ERA
1B	J. Olerud	384	.297	12	67	823	68	6	82	8.6	.993	P. Hentgen	24	175	13	8	0	3.40
2B	R. Alomar	392	.306	8	38	176	275	4	69	4.3	.991	J. Guzman	25	147	12	11	0	5.68
SS	D. Schofield	325	.255	4	32	150	235	11	58	4.2	.972	T. Stottlemyre	26	141	7	7	1	4.22
3B	E. Sprague	405	.240	11	44	**99**	147	14	18	2.4	.946	D. Stewart	22	133	7	8	0	5.87
RF	J. Carter	435	.271	27	103	205	4	2	1	1.9	.991	A. Leiter	20	112	6	7	0	5.08
CF	D. White	403	.270	13	49	267	3	6	1	2.8	.978	T. Castillo	41	68	5	2	1	2.51
LF	M. Huff	207	.304	3	25	126	4	1	1	1.7	.992	D. Hall	30	32	2	3	17	3.41
C	P. Borders	295	.247	3	26	583	**59**	8	**2**	**7.6**	.988							
DH	P. Molitor	454	.341	14	75													
UT	D. Coles	143	.210	4	15	103	9	4	7		.966							
OF	C. Delgado	130	.215	9	24	55	2	2	0	1.4	.966							
C	R. Knorr	124	.242	7	19	247	21	2	1	6.8	.993							

Boston

W-54 L-61

Butch Hobson

POS	Player	AB	BA	HR	RBI	PO	A	E	DP	TC/G	FA	Pitcher	G	IP	W	L	SV	ERA
1B	M. Vaughn	394	.310	26	82	879	57	**10**	**103**	8.8	.989	R. Clemens	24	171	9	7	0	2.85
2B	S. Fletcher	185	.227	3	11	118	163	1	40	5.2	.996	A. Sele	22	143	8	7	0	3.83
SS	J. Valentin	301	.316	9	49	134	239	8	54	4.6	.979	J. Hesketh	25	114	8	5	0	4.26
3B	S. Cooper	369	.282	13	53	51	219	16	20	2.8	.944	D. Darwin	13	76	7	5	0	6.30
RF	B. Hatcher	164	.244	1	18	87	3	3	1	2.2	.968	K. Ryan	42	48	2	3	13	2.44
CF	O. Nixon	398	.274	0	25	254	4	3	1	2.5	.989	G. Harris	35	46	3	4	2	8.28
LF	M. Greenwell	327	.269	11	45	141	10	1	1	1.8	.993	C. Nabholz	8	42	3	4	0	6.64
C	D. Berryhill	255	.263	6	34	409	29	2	**2**	6.6	.995	J. Russell	29	28	0	5	12	5.14
DH	A. Dawson	292	.240	16	48													
UT	T. Naehring	297	.276	7	42	190	182	6	45		.984							
OF	T. Brunansky	177	.237	10	34	84	1	1	1	2.0	.988							
S2	C. Rodriguez	174	.287	1	13	86	129	5	36		.977							
OF	W. Chamberlain	164	.256	4	20	69	5	0	0	2.2	1.000							
OF	L. Tinsley	144	.222	2	14	114	1	1	1	1.9	.991							
C	R. Rowland	118	.229	9	20	195	12	6	0	5.5	.972							

Detroit

W-53 L-62

Sparky Anderson

POS	Player	AB	BA	HR	RBI	PO	A	E	DP	TC/G	FA	Pitcher	G	IP	W	L	SV	ERA
1B	C. Fielder	425	.259	28	90	887	**108**	7	72	9.8	.993	T. Belcher	25	162	7	**15**	0	5.89
2B	L. Whitaker	322	.301	12	43	135	246	12	43	4.7	.969	M. Moore	25	154	11	10	0	5.42
SS	A. Trammell	292	.267	8	28	117	180	10	43	4.9	.967	B. Gullickson	21	115	4	5	0	5.93
3B	T. Fryman	**464**	.263	18	85	78	**222**	14	12	2.8	.955	D. Wells	16	111	5	7	0	3.96
RF	J. Felix	301	.306	13	49	188	4	4	0	2.4	.980	J. Doherty	18	101	6	7	0	6.48
CF	E. Davis	120	.183	3	13	85	1	1	1	2.5	.989	J. Boever	46	81	9	2	3	3.98
LF	T. Phillips	438	.281	19	61	236	6	5	1	2.4	.980	M. Gardiner	38	59	2	2	5	4.14
C	C. Kreuter	170	.224	1	19	278	22	4	1	4.8	.987	M. Henneman	30	35	1	3	8	5.19
DH	K. Gibson	330	.276	23	72													
UT	M. Tettleton	339	.248	17	51	367	30	5	7		.988							
S2	C. Gomez	296	.257	8	53	141	210	8	39		.978							
UT	J. Samuel	136	.309	5	21	82	28	1	4		.991							
OF	M. Cuyler	116	.241	1	11	78	1	2	0	1.8	.975							

Central

Chicago

W-67 L-46

Gene Lamont

POS	Player	AB	BA	HR	RBI	PO	A	E	DP	TC/G	FA	Pitcher	G	IP	W	L	SV	ERA
1B	F. Thomas	399	.353	38	101	735	45	7	74	7.9	.991	J. McDowell	25	181	10	9	0	3.73
2B	J. Cora	312	.276	2	30	161	195	8	47	4.3	.978	A. Fernandez	24	170	11	7	0	3.86
SS	O. Guillen	365	.288	1	39	141	235	16	44	4.0	.959	W. Alvarez	24	162	12	8	0	3.45
3B	R. Ventura	401	.282	18	78	80	176	18	**21**	2.5	.934	J. Bere	24	142	12	2	0	3.81
RF	D. Jackson	369	.312	10	51	225	2	1	1	2.2	.996	S. Sanderson	18	92	8	4	0	5.09
CF	L. Johnson	412	.277	3	54	317	1	0	0	3.1	1.000	J. DeLeon	42	67	3	2	2	3.36
LF	T. Raines	384	.266	10	52	203	3	4	1	2.2	.981	K. McCaskill	40	53	1	4	3	3.42
C	R. Karkovice	207	.213	11	29	417	19	3	1	5.8	.993	R. Hernandez	45	48	4	4	14	4.91
DH	J. Franco	433	.319	20	98													
C	M. LaValliere	139	.281	1	24	305	21	3	1	5.7	.991							
UT	N. Martin	131	.275	1	16	58	77	2	11		.985							

AMERICAN LEAGUE 1994, *cont.*

Cleveland

W-66 L-47

Mike Hargrove

POS	Player	AB	BA	HR	RBI	PO	A	E	DP	TC/G	FA	Pitcher	G	IP	W	L	SV	ERA
1B	P. Sorrento	322	.280	14	62	798	58	4	79	10.0	.995	D. Martinez	24	177	11	6	0	3.52
2B	C. Baerga	442	.314	19	80	205	334	**15**	70	5.4	.973	C. Nagy	23	169	10	8	0	3.45
SS	O. Vizquel	286	.273	1	33	114	204	6	53	4.7	.981	J. Morris	23	141	10	6	0	5.60
3B	J. Thome	321	.268	20	52	62	173	15	12	2.7	.940	M. Clark	20	127	11	3	0	3.82
RF	M. Ramirez	290	.269	17	60	150	7	1	2	1.9	.994	J. Grimsley	14	83	5	2	0	4.57
CF	K. Lofton	459	.349	12	57	276	13	2	3	2.6	.993	J. Mesa	51	73	7	5	2	3.82
LF	A. Belle	412	.357	36	101	205	8	6	0	2.1	.973	E. Plunk	41	71	7	2	3	2.54
C	S. Alomar	292	.288	14	43	453	40	2	0	6.3	.996	J. Russell	13	13	1	1	5	4.97
DH	E. Murray	433	.254	17	76													
UT	A. Espinoza	231	.238	1	19	93	209	10	42		.968							
OF	W. Kirby	191	.293	5	23	92	2	4	1	1.4	.959							

Kansas City

W-64 L-51

Hal McRae

POS	Player	AB	BA	HR	RBI	PO	A	E	DP	TC/G	FA	Pitcher	G	IP	W	L	SV	ERA
1B	W. Joyner	363	.311	8	57	779	64	8	67	9.9	.991	D. Cone	23	172	16	5	0	2.94
2B	J. Lind	290	.269	1	31	149	252	5	44	4.8	.988	T. Gordon	24	155	11	7	0	4.35
SS	G. Gagne	375	.259	7	51	**189**	323	12	63	4.9	.977	K. Appier	23	155	7	6	0	3.83
3B	G. Gaetti	327	.287	12	57	61	162	4	15	2.7	**.982**	M. Gubicza	22	130	7	9	0	4.50
RF	F. Jose	366	.303	11	55	193	7	4	1	2.1	.980	H. Pichardo	45	68	5	3	3	4.92
CF	B. McRae	436	.273	4	40	252	2	3	0	2.3	.988	R. Meacham	36	51	3	3	4	3.73
LF	V. Coleman	438	.240	2	33	163	11	7	1	1.8	.961	J. Montgomery	42	45	2	3	27	4.03
C	M. Macfarlane	314	.255	14	47	498	39	4	**2**	6.7	.993	B. Brewer	50	39	4	1	3	2.56
DH	B. Hamelin	312	.282	24	65													
OF	D. Henderson	198	.247	5	31	72	4	3	0	2.0	.962							
23	T. Shumpert	183	.240	8	24	68	127	8	15		.961							
C	B. Mayne	144	.257	2	20	246	13	1	1	6.2	.996							

Minnesota

W-53 L-60

Tom Kelly

POS	Player	AB	BA	HR	RBI	PO	A	E	DP	TC/G	FA	Pitcher	G	IP	W	L	SV	ERA
1B	K. Hrbek	274	.270	10	53	567	41	2	51	8.5	.997	K. Tapani	24	156	11	7	0	4.62
2B	C. Knoblauch	445	.312	5	51	190	284	3	60	4.4	.994	S. Erickson	23	144	8	11	0	5.44
SS	P. Meares	229	.266	2	24	134	209	13	45	4.5	.963	J. Deshaies	25	130	6	12	0	7.39
3B	S. Leius	350	.246	14	49	63	184	8	13	2.7	.969	P. Mahomes	21	120	9	5	0	4.72
RF	K. Puckett	439	.317	20	**112**	204	13	3	1	2.3	.986	C. Pulido	19	84	3	7	0	5.98
CF	A. Cole	345	.296	4	23	245	4	8	0	2.6	.969	C. Willis	49	59	2	4	3	5.92
LF	S. Mack	303	.333	15	61	201	2	2	0	2.7	.990	M. Guthrie	50	51	4	2	1	6.14
C	M. Walbeck	338	.204	5	35	496	45	4	0	5.7	.993	D. Stevens	24	45	5	2	0	6.80
DH	D. Winfield	294	.252	10	43							R. Aguilera	44	45	1	4	23	3.63
OF	P. Munoz	244	.295	11	36	110	1	4	0	2.0	.965							
UT	J. Reboulet	189	.259	3	23	150	131	7	29		.976							
10	D. McCarty	131	.260	1	12	244	27	5	19		.982							
UT	C. Hale	118	.263	1	11	45	51	3	7		.970							

Milwaukee

W-53 L-62

Phil Garner

POS	Player	AB	BA	HR	RBI	PO	A	E	DP	TC/G	FA	Pitcher	G	IP	W	L	SV	ERA
1B	J. Jaha	291	.241	12	39	660	47	8	60	9.8	.989	C. Eldred	25	179	11	11	0	4.68
2B	J. Reed	399	.271	2	37	**231**	**351**	3	**72**	**5.5**	**.995**	R. Bones	24	171	10	9	0	3.43
SS	J. Valentin	285	.239	11	46	129	285	**20**	60	**5.2**	.954	B. Wegman	19	116	8	4	0	4.51
3B	K. Seitzer	309	.314	5	49	25	72	8	6	2.4	.924	B. Scanlan	30	103	2	6	2	4.11
RF	M. Mieske	259	.259	10	38	155	7	4	1	2.1	.976	J. Navarro	29	90	4	9	0	6.62
CF	A. Diaz	187	.251	1	17	137	5	1	0	2.0	.993	G. Lloyd	43	47	2	3	3	5.17
LF	G. Vaughn	370	.254	19	55	162	5	3	0	2.1	.982	M. Fetters	42	46	1	4	17	2.54
C	D. Nilsson	397	.275	12	69	295	15	2	0	5.2	.994	A. Miranda	8	46	2	5	0	5.28
DH	B. Harper	251	.291	4	32													
OF	T. Ward	367	.232	9	45	260	8	4	1	2.7	.985							
3S	B. Spiers	214	.252	0	17	70	128	8	26		.961							
OF	D. Hamilton	141	.262	1	13	60	2	0	1	1.9	1.000							
UT	B. Surhoff	134	.261	5	22	121	29	4	12		.974							
3B	J. Cirillo	126	.238	3	12	23	59	3	7	2.3	.965							

West

Texas

W-52 L-62

Kevin Kennedy

POS	Player	AB	BA	HR	RBI	PO	A	E	DP	TC/G	FA	Pitcher	G	IP	W	L	SV	ERA
1B	W. Clark	389	.329	13	80	**968**	73	**10**	85	9.8	.990	K. Brown	26	170	7	9	0	4.82
2B	J. Frye	205	.327	0	18	89	135	4	28	4.2	.982	K. Rogers	24	167	11	8	0	4.46
SS	M. Lee	335	.278	2	38	132	255	13	49	4.7	.967	H. Fajardo	18	83	5	7	0	6.91
3B	D. Palmer	342	.246	19	59	50	181	**22**	7	2.8	.913	C. Carpenter	47	59	2	5	5	5.03
RF	R. Greer	277	.314	10	46	159	2	4	2	2.3	.976	R. Pavlik	11	50	2	5	0	7.69
CF	D. Hulse	310	.255	1	19	179	0	4	0	2.4	.978	J. Howell	40	43	4	1	2	5.44
LF	J. Gonzalez	422	.275	19	85	223	9	2	1	2.2	.991	T. Henke	37	38	3	6	15	3.79
C	I. Rodriguez	363	.298	16	57	600	44	5	**2**	6.6	.992							
DH	J. Canseco	429	.282	31	90													
2B	D. Strange	226	.212	5	26	78	146	7	36	4.4	.970							
OF	O. McDowell	183	.262	1	15	113	2	2	0	2.2	.983							
OF	C. James	133	.256	7	19	63	2	0	0	1.4	1.000							
SS	E. Beltre	131	.282	0	12	53	121	7	21	4.4	.961							

Oakland

W-51 L-63

Tony LaRussa

POS	Player	AB	BA	HR	RBI	PO	A	E	DP	TC/G	FA	Pitcher	G	IP	W	L	SV	ERA
1B	T. Neel	278	.266	15	48	295	23	2	34	7.1	.994	R. Darling	25	160	10	11	0	4.50
2B	B. Gates	233	.283	2	24	105	160	7	28	4.3	.974	B. Witt	24	136	8	10	0	5.04
SS	M. Bordick	391	.253	2	37	182	308	13	64	4.5	.974	T. Van Poppel	23	117	7	10	0	6.09
3B	S. Brosius	324	.238	14	49	69	154	13	18	2.5	.945	S. Ontiveros	27	115	6	4	0	**2.65**
RF	R. Sierra	426	.268	23	92	155	8	9	2	1.8	.948	B. Welch	25	69	3	6	0	7.08
CF	S. Javier	419	.272	10	44	270	3	4	0	2.6	.986	J. Briscoe	37	49	4	2	1	4.01
LF	R. Henderson	296	.260	6	20	166	4	4	0	2.5	.977	D. Eckersley	45	44	5	4	19	4.26
C	T. Steinbach	369	.285	11	57	568	**59**	1	**2**	6.8	**.998**							
DH	G. Berroa	340	.306	13	65													
UT	S. Hemond	198	.222	3	20	245	93	6	17		.983							
01	M. Aldrete	178	.242	4	18	207	14	1	15		.995							
1B	M. McGwire	135	.252	9	25	311	17	4	25	8.3	.988							

AMERICAN LEAGUE 1994, *cont.*

Seattle

W-49 L-63

Lou Piniella

POS	Player	AB	BA	HR	RBI	PO	A	E	DP	TC/G	FA	Pitcher	G	IP	W	L	SV	ERA
1B	T. Martinez	329	.261	20	61	705	45	2	62	9.2	.997	R. Johnson	23	172	13	6	0	3.19
2B	R. Amaral	228	.263	4	18	81	102	11	19	4.6	.943	C. Bosio	19	125	4	10	0	4.32
SS	F. Fermin	379	.317	1	35	115	180	8	40	3.9	.974	D. Fleming	23	117	7	11	0	6.46
3B	E. Martinez	326	.285	13	51	44	127	9	8	2.8	.950	R. Salkeld	13	59	2	5	0	7.17
RF	J. Buhner	358	.279	21	68	179	11	2	2	2.0	.990	B. Ayala	46	57	4	3	18	2.86
CF	K. Griffey	433	.323	**40**	90	225	12	4	1	2.3	.983	B. Risley	37	52	9	6	0	3.44
LF	E. Anthony	262	.237	10	30	126	4	2	0	1.9	.985							
C	D. Wilson	282	.216	3	27	602	41	**9**	**2**	7.2	.986							
DH	R. Jefferson	162	.327	8	32													
UT	M. Blowers	270	.289	9	49	141	108	9	15		.965							
2S	L. Sojo	213	.277	6	22	97	185	7	36		.976							
OF	K. Mitchell	128	.227	5	15	49	0	1	0	1.3	.980							
OF	B. Turang	112	.188	1	8	44	1	1	0	1.5	.978							

California

W-47 L-68

Buck Rodgers
W-16 L-23

Bobby Knoop
W-1 L-1

Marcel Lachemann
W-30 L-44

POS	Player	AB	BA	HR	RBI	PO	A	E	DP	TC/G	FA	Pitcher	G	IP	W	L	SV	ERA
1B	J. Snow	223	.220	8	30	489	37	2	56	8.7	.996	C. Finley	25	**183**	10	10	0	4.32
2B	H. Reynolds	207	.232	0	11	116	130	1	24	3.8	.996	M. Langston	18	119	7	8	0	4.68
SS	G. DiSarcina	389	.260	3	33	160	**359**	9	66	4.8	.983	P. Leftwich	20	114	5	10	0	5.68
3B	S. Owen	268	.310	3	37	42	128	8	13	2.5	.955	B. Anderson	18	102	7	5	0	5.22
RF	T. Salmon	373	.287	23	70	219	9	8	1	2.4	.966	M. Leiter	40	95	4	7	2	4.72
CF	C. Curtis	453	.256	11	50	331	9	4	0	3.0	.988	J. Magrane	20	74	2	6	0	7.30
LF	J. Edmonds	289	.273	5	37	145	9	3	0	2.0	.981	J. Grahe	40	43	2	5	13	6.65
C	C. Turner	149	.242	1	12	268	29	1	0	5.2	.997							
DH	C. Davis	392	.311	26	84													
32	D. Easley	316	.215	6	30	122	178	7	34		.977							
OF	B. Jackson	201	.279	13	43	77	3	3	0	1.8	.964							
1B	E. Perez	129	.209	5	16	305	15	1	29	8.4	.997							
C	J. Fabregas	127	.283	0	16	217	16	3	1	5.8	.987							
C	G. Myers	126	.246	2	8	194	28	2	0	5.5	.991							
UT	R. Hudler	124	.298	8	20	71	61	5	20		.964							
OF	D. Smith	122	.262	5	18	50	2	5	1	1.8	.912							

BATTING AND BASE RUNNING LEADERS

Batting Average	
P. O'Neill, NY	.359
A. Belle, CLE	.357
F. Thomas, CHI	.353
K. Lofton, CLE	.349
W. Boggs, NY	.342

Slugging Average	
F. Thomas, CHI	.729
A. Belle, CLE	.714
K. Griffey, SEA	.674
P. O'Neill, NY	.603
B. Hamelin, KC	.599

Home Runs	
K. Griffey, SEA	40
F. Thomas, CHI	38
A. Belle, CLE	36
J. Canseco, TEX	31
C. Fielder, DET	28

Total Bases	
A. Belle, CLE	294
K. Griffey, SEA	292
F. Thomas, CHI	291
K. Lofton, CLE	246
R. Palmeiro, BAL	240

Runs Batted In	
K. Puckett, MIN	112
J. Carter, TOR	103
F. Thomas, CHI	101
A. Belle, CLE	101
J. Franco, CHI	98

Stolen Bases	
K. Lofton, CLE	60
V. Coleman, KC	50
O. Nixon, BOS	42
C. Knoblauch, MIN	35
B. Anderson, BAL	31

Hits	
K. Lofton, CLE	160
P. Molitor, TOR	155
A. Belle, CLE	147
F. Thomas, CHI	141

Base on Balls	
F. Thomas, CHI	109
M. Tettleton, DET	97
T. Phillips, DET	95
R. Henderson, OAK	72
P. O'Neill, NY	72

Home Run Percentage	
F. Thomas, CHI	9.5
K. Griffey, SEA	9.2
A. Belle, CLE	8.7
B. Hamelin, KC	7.7

Runs	
F. Thomas, CHI	106
K. Lofton, CLE	105
K. Griffey, SEA	94
T. Phillips, DET	91

Doubles	
C. Knoblauch, MIN	45
A. Belle, CLE	35
F. Thomas, CHI	34
T. Fryman, DET	34

Triples	
L. Johnson, CHI	14
V. Coleman, KC	12
K. Lofton, CLE	9
A. Diaz, MIL	7

PITCHING LEADERS

Winning Percentage	
J. Bere, CHI	.857
J. Key, NY	.810
M. Clark, CLE	.786
M. Mussina, BAL	.762
D. Cone, KC	.762

Earned Run Average	
S. Ontiveros, OAK	2.65
R. Clemens, BOS	2.85
D. Cone, KC	2.94
M. Mussina, BAL	3.06
R. Johnson, SEA	3.19

Wins	
J. Key, NY	17
D. Cone, KC	16
M. Mussina, BAL	16
B. McDonald, BAL	14
R. Johnson, SEA	13
P. Hentgen, TOR	13

Saves	
L. Smith, BAL	33
J. Montgomery, KC	27
R. Aguilera, MIN	23
D. Eckersley, OAK	19
B. Ayala, SEA	18

Strikeouts	
R. Johnson, SEA	204
R. Clemens, BOS	168
C. Finley, CAL	148
P. Hentgen, TOR	147
K. Appier, KC	145

Complete Games	
R. Johnson, SEA	9
D. Martinez, CLE	7
C. Finley, CAL	7

Fewest Hits/9 Innings	
R. Clemens, BOS	6.54
D. Cone, KC	6.82
R. Johnson, SEA	6.91
S. Ontiveros, OAK	7.26

Shutouts	
R. Johnson, SEA	4
D. Cone, KC	3
D. Martinez, CLE	3
B. Witt, OAK	3
A. Fernandez, CHI	3
P. Hentgen, TOR	3

Fewest Walks/9 Innings	
M. Gubicza, KC	1.80
B. Gullickson, DET	1.95
B. Wegman, MIL	2.02
S. Ontiveros, OAK	2.03

Most Strikeouts/9 Inn.	
R. Johnson, SEA	10.67
R. Clemens, BOS	8.86
K. Appier, KC	8.42
M. Langston, CAL	8.22

Innings	
C. Finley, CAL	183
J. McDowell, CHI	181
C. Eldred, MIL	179
D. Martinez, CLE	177

Games Pitched	
B. Wickman, NY	53
J. Mesa, CLE	51
B. Brewer, KC	50
M. Guthrie, MIN	50

		W	L	PCT	GB	R	OR	Batting						Fielding			Pitching					
								2B	3B	HR	BA	SA	SB	E	DP	FA	CG	BB	SO	ShO	SV	ERA
East	New York	70	43	.619		670	534	238	16	139	**.290**	.462	55	80	119	.982	8	398	656	2	31	4.34
	Baltimore	63	49	.563	6.5	589	**497**	185	20	139	.272	.438	69	**57**	96	**.986**	13	**351**	666	4	37	4.31
	Toronto	55	60	.478	16	566	579	210	30	115	.269	.424	79	81	100	.981	13	482	**832**	4	26	4.70
	Boston	54	61	.470	17	552	621	222	19	120	.263	.421	81	81	121	.981	6	450	729	3	30	4.93
	Detroit	53	62	.461	18	652	671	216	25	161	.265	.454	46	82	88	.981	15	449	560	1	20	5.38
Central	Chicago	67	46	.593		633	498	175	**39**	121	.287	.444	77	79	87	.981	13	377	754	**9**	20	**3.96**
	Cleveland	66	47	.584	1	**679**	562	**240**	20	**167**	**.290**	**.484**	131	90	113	.980	**17**	404	666	5	21	4.36
	Kansas City	64	51	.557	4	574	532	211	38	100	.269	.419	**140**	80	94	.982	5	392	717	6	**38**	4.23
	Minnesota	53	60	.469	14	594	688	239	23	103	.276	.427	94	75	93	.982	6	388	602	4	29	5.68
	Milwaukee	53	62	.461	15	547	586	238	21	99	.263	.408	59	85	**128**	.981	11	421	577	3	23	4.62
West	Texas	52	62	.456		613	697	198	27	124	.280	.436	82	106	102	.976	10	394	683	4	26	5.45
	Oakland	51	63	.447	1	549	589	178	13	113	.260	.399	91	88	100	.979	12	510	732	**9**	23	4.80
	Seattle	49	63	.438	2	569	616	211	18	153	.269	.451	48	95	93	.977	13	486	763	7	21	4.99
	California	47	68	.409	5.5	543	660	178	16	120	.264	.409	65	76	99	.983	11	436	682	4	21	5.42
						8330	8330	2939	325	1774	.273	.434	1117	1155	1433	.981	153	5938	9619	65	366	4.80

NATIONAL LEAGUE 1995

		POS	Player	AB	BA	HR	RBI	PO	A	E	DP	TC/G	FA	Pitcher	G	IP	W	L	SV	ERA
East	Atlanta	1B	F. McGriff	528	.280	27	93	1286	93	5	104	9.6	.996	G. Maddux	28	**210**	**19**	2	0	**1.63**
	W-90 L-54	2B	M. Lemke	399	.253	5	38	205	305	5	61	4.5	.990	T. Glavine	29	199	16	7	0	3.08
	Bobby Cox	SS	J. Blauser	431	.211	12	31	150	335	15	60	4.3	.970	J. Smoltz	29	193	12	7	0	3.18
		3B	C. Jones	524	.265	23	86	80	258	25	19	3.0	.931	S. Avery	29	173	7	13	0	4.67
		RF	D. Justice	411	.253	24	78	233	8	4	0	2.0	.984	K. Mercker	29	143	7	8	0	4.15
		CF	M. Grissom	551	.258	12	42	309	9	2	1	2.4	.994	G. McMichael	67	81	7	2	2	2.79
		LF	R. Klesko	329	.310	23	70	111	2	7	0	1.2	.942	B. Clontz	59	69	8	1	4	3.65
		C	J. Lopez	333	.315	14	51	625	50	8	2	7.3	.988	M. Wohlers	65	65	7	3	25	2.09
		C	C. O'Brien	198	.227	9	23	447	23	4	5	7.4	.992							
		S2	R. Belliard	180	.222	0	7	74	178	1	23		.996							
		OF	D. Smith	131	.252	3	21	24	0	2	0	1.0	.923							
	New York	1B	R. Brogna	495	.289	22	76	1113	92	3	93	9.2	**.998**	B. Jones	30	196	10	10	0	4.19
	W-69 L-75	2B	J. Kent	472	.278	20	65	246	354	10	66	5.0	.984	D. Mlicki	29	161	9	7	0	4.26
	Dallas Green	SS	J. Vizcaino	509	.287	3	56	189	411	10	78	4.6	**.984**	B. Pulsipher	17	127	5	7	0	3.98
		3B	E. Alfonzo	335	.278	4	41	40	110	6	9	2.7	.962	P. Harnisch	18	110	2	8	0	3.68
		RF	C. Everett	289	.260	12	54	147	10	3	1	2.1	.981	B. Saberhagen	16	110	5	5	0	3.35
		CF	B. Butler	367	.311	1	25	207	6	1	1	2.4	.995	J. Isringhausen	14	93	9	2	0	2.81
		LF	J. Orsulak	290	.283	1	37	108	3	4	0	1.3	.965	J. DiPoto	58	79	4	6	2	3.78
		C	T. Hundley	275	.280	15	51	487	28	7	2	5.9	.987	D. Henry	51	67	3	6	4	2.96
		UT	B. Bonilla	317	.325	18	53	164	80	14	11		.946	R. Cornelius	10	58	3	7	0	5.15
		OF	R. Thompson	267	.251	7	31	193	4	3	3	2.7	.985	J. Franco	48	52	5	3	29	2.44
		C	K. Stinnett	196	.219	4	18	380	22	7	1	6.1	.983							
		OF	C. Jones	182	.280	8	31	79	3	2	1	1.6	.976							
		UT	T. Bogar	145	.290	1	21	82	100	6	21		.968							
	Philadelphia	1B	D. Hollins	205	.229	7	25	533	30	7	53	9.3	.988	P. Quantrill	33	179	11	12	0	4.67
	W-69 L-75	2B	M. Morandini	494	.283	6	49	268	336	7	73	5.0	.989	T. Green	26	141	8	9	0	5.31
	Jim Fregosi	SS	K. Stocker	412	.218	1	32	148	383	17	71	4.4	.969	M. Mimbs	35	137	9	7	1	4.15
		3B	C. Hayes	529	.276	11	85	**104**	262	14	**25**	2.7	.963	C. Schilling	17	116	7	5	0	3.57
		RF	J. Eisenreich	377	.316	10	55	205	2	0	1	1.9	1.000	T. Borland	50	74	1	3	6	3.77
		CF	L. Dykstra	254	.264	2	18	152	2	2	1	2.6	.987	H. Slocumb	61	65	5	6	32	2.89
		LF	G. Jefferies	480	.306	11	56	86	3	0	1	1.6	1.000							
		C	D. Daulton	342	.249	9	55	632	45	4	5	7.2	.994							
		OF	A. Van Slyke	214	.243	3	16	117	5	2	1	2.2	.984							
		OF	M. Whiten	212	.269	11	37	105	4	4	0	2.1	.965							
		UT	M. Duncan	196	.286	3	23	156	119	10	36		.965							
		OF	D. Gallagher	157	.318	1	12	89	1	0	0	1.6	1.000							
		C	L. Webster	150	.267	4	14	275	17	3	1	6.9	.990							
	Florida	1B	G. Colbrunn	528	.277	23	89	1070	88	5	107	8.7	.996	J. Burkett	30	188	14	14	0	4.30
	W-67 L-76	2B	Q. Veras	440	.261	5	32	298	315	9	85	5.1	.986	P. Rapp	28	167	14	7	0	3.44
	Rene Lachemann	SS	K. Abbott	420	.255	17	60	149	290	19	64	4.0	.959	C. Hammond	25	161	9	6	0	3.80
		3B	T. Pendleton	513	.290	14	78	**104**	249	18	21	2.9	.951	B. Witt	19	111	2	7	0	3.90
		RF	G. Sheffield	213	.324	16	46	108	5	7	1	2.0	.942	M. Gardner	39	102	5	5	1	4.49
		CF	C. Carr	308	.227	2	20	217	8	3	0	2.2	.987	T. Mathews	57	83	4	4	3	3.38
		LF	J. Conine	483	.302	25	105	195	7	5	1	1.8	.976	R. Nen	62	66	0	7	23	3.29
		C	C. Johnson	315	.251	11	39	641	**63**	6	3	7.3	.992							
		OF	A. Dawson	226	.257	8	37	75	3	8	2	1.5	.907							
		S3	A. Arias	216	.269	3	26	48	108	9	18		.945							
		OF	J. Tavarez	190	.289	2	13	119	1	0	1	2.0	1.000							
		UT	J. Browne	184	.255	1	17	107	78	3	14		.984							
		OF	T. Gregg	156	.237	6	20	63	0	1	0	1.7	.984							
	Montreal	1B	D. Segui	383	.305	10	57	842	68	3	67	9.4	.997	P. Martinez	30	195	14	10	0	3.51
	W-66 L-78	2B	M. Lansing	467	.255	10	62	307	372	6	77	**5.4**	.991	J. Fassero	30	189	13	14	0	4.33
	Felipe Alou	SS	W. Cordero	514	.286	10	49	123	281	17	44	4.0	.960	C. Perez	28	141	10	8	0	3.69
		3B	S. Berry	314	.318	14	55	54	163	12	18	2.8	.948	B. Henry	21	127	7	9	0	2.84
		RF	T. Tarasco	438	.249	14	40	229	7	5	2	2.1	.979	G. Heredia	40	119	5	6	1	4.31
		CF	R. White	474	.295	13	57	268	5	4	2	2.3	.986	M. Rojas	59	68	1	4	30	4.12
		LF	M. Alou	344	.273	14	58	148	5	3	0	1.7	.981	J. Shaw	50	62	1	6	3	4.62
		C	D. Fletcher	350	.286	11	45	612	45	4	5	6.7	.994							
		UT	M. Grudzielanek	269	.245	1	20	94	197	10	25		.967							
		31	S. Andrews	220	.214	8	31	182	97	7	13		.976							
		C	T. Laker	141	.234	3	20	265	27	7	1	4.9	.977							
Central	Cincinnati	1B	H. Morris	359	.279	11	51	755	72	5	79	8.4	.994	P. Schourek	29	190	18	7	0	3.22
	W-85 L-59	2B	B. Boone	513	.267	15	68	**312**	362	4	**106**	4.9	**.994**	J. Smiley	28	177	12	5	0	3.46
	Davey Johnson	SS	B. Larkin	496	.319	15	66	192	342	11	71	4.2	.980	T. Pugh	28	98	6	5	0	3.84
		3B	J. Branson	331	.260	12	45	52	178	7	22	2.4	.970	X. Hernandez	59	90	7	2	3	4.60
		RF	R. Sanders	484	.306	28	99	268	12	5	2	2.2	.982	H. Carrasco	64	87	2	7	5	4.12
		CF	D. Lewis	163	.245	0	8	121	3	1	0	2.2	.992	M. Portugal	14	78	6	5	0	3.82
		LF	R. Gant	410	.276	29	88	191	7	3	0	1.7	.985	D. Wells	11	73	6	5	0	3.59
		C	B. Santiago	266	.286	11	44	462	31	2	4	6.6	**.996**	J. Brantley	56	70	3	2	28	2.82
		OF	T. Howard	281	.302	3	26	127	2	2	0	1.6	.985							
		C	E. Taubensee	218	.284	9	44	326	21	6	0	5.4	.983							
		UT	L. Harris	197	.208	2	16	147	68	4	14		.982							
		3B	M. Lewis	171	.339	3	30	19	104	4	4	1.8	.969							
		OF	J. Walton	162	.290	8	22	107	2	2	0	1.2	.982							
		01	E. Anthony	134	.269	5	23	141	12	4	11		.975							

NATIONAL LEAGUE 1995, *cont.*

Houston

W-76 L-68

Terry Collins

POS	Player	AB	BA	HR	RBI	PO	A	E	DP	TC/G	FA	Pitcher	G	IP	W	L	SV	ERA
1B	J. Bagwell	448	.290	21	87	1004	**129**	7	78	10.0	.994	S. Reynolds	30	189	10	11	0	3.47
2B	C. Biggio	553	.302	22	77	297	**418**	10	74	5.1	.986	D. Drabek	31	185	10	9	0	4.77
SS	O. Miller	324	.262	5	36	133	269	15	49	4.7	.964	G. Swindell	33	153	10	9	0	4.47
3B	D. Magadan	348	.313	2	51	55	161	18	8	2.3	.923	M. Hampton	24	151	9	8	0	3.35
RF	D. Bell	452	.334	8	86	201	10	8	2	2.0	.963	D. Kile	25	127	4	12	0	4.96
CF	B. Hunter	321	.302	2	28	182	8	9	1	2.7	.955	D. Veres	72	103	5	1	1	2.26
LF	D. May	206	.301	8	41	76	0	2	0	1.4	.974	T. Jones	68	100	6	5	15	3.07
C	T. Eusebio	368	.299	6	58	644	50	5	6	6.8	.993	D. Brocail	36	77	6	4	1	4.19
OF	J. Mouton	298	.262	4	27	134	4	0	0	1.5	1.000	J. Dougherty	56	68	8	4	0	4.92
3B	C. Shipley	232	.263	3	24	27	80	2	5	1.7	.982	J. Hudek	19	20	2	2	7	5.40
OF	L. Gonzalez	209	.258	6	35	94	2	2	0	1.8	.980							
OF	J. Cangelosi	201	.318	2	18	92	3	5	0	1.7	.950							
SS	R. Gutierrez	156	.276	0	12	64	107	8	17	4.1	.955							
10	M. Simms	121	.256	9	24	221	18	1	19		.996							

Chicago

W-73 L-71

Jim Riggleman

POS	Player	AB	BA	HR	RBI	PO	A	E	DP	TC/G	FA	Pitcher	G	IP	W	L	SV	ERA
1B	M. Grace	552	.326	16	92	1211	115	7	91	9.3	.995	J. Navarro	29	200	14	6	0	3.28
2B	R. Sanchez	428	.278	3	27	194	342	7	57	4.9	.987	F. Castillo	29	188	11	10	0	3.21
SS	S. Dunston	477	.296	14	69	188	336	17	50	4.3	.969	K. Foster	30	168	12	11	0	4.51
3B	T. Zeile	299	.227	9	30	34	134	11	12	2.4	.939	S. Trachsel	30	161	7	13	0	5.15
RF	S. Sosa	564	.268	36	119	320	13	13	2	2.4	.962	J. Bullinger	24	150	12	8	0	4.14
CF	B. McRae	**580**	.288	12	48	345	4	3	0	2.6	.991	M. Perez	68	71	2	6	2	3.66
LF	L. Gonzalez	262	.290	7	34	172	5	4	0	2.4	.978	R. Myers	57	56	1	2	**38**	3.88
C	S. Servais	175	.286	12	35	328	31	7*	4	7.0	.981							
UT	J. Hernandez	245	.245	13	40	112	189	9	35		.971							
OF	O. Timmons	171	.263	8	28	63	1	2	1	1.2	.970							
UT	H. Johnson	169	.195	7	22	45	64	7	10		.940							
C	R. Wilkins	162	.191	6	14	288	28	4	1	6.5	.988							
OF	S. Bullett	150	.273	3	22	59	1	2	0	1.0	.968							

St. Louis

W-62 L-81

Joe Torre
W-20 L-27

Mike Jorgensen
W-42 L-54

POS	Player	AB	BA	HR	RBI	PO	A	E	DP	TC/G	FA	Pitcher	G	IP	W	L	SV	ERA
1B	J. Mabry	388	.307	5	41	595	51	4	63	8.9	.994	M. Petkovsek	26	137	6	6	0	4.00
2B	J. Oquendo	220	.209	2	17	114	149	5	32	4.3	.981	A. Watson	21	114	7	9	0	4.96
SS	T. Cromer	345	.226	5	18	111	277	16	58	4.3	.960	D. Osborne	19	113	4	6	0	3.81
3B	S. Cooper	374	.230	3	40	65	242	18	22	**3.0**	.945	K. Hill	18	110	6	7	0	5.06
RF	B. Jordan	490	.296	22	81	268	4	1	2	2.2	.996	M. Morgan	17	107	5	6	0	3.88
CF	R. Lankford	483	.277	25	82	300	7	3	1	2.4	.990	D. Jackson	19	101	2	12	0	5.90
LF	B. Gilkey	480	.298	17	69	206	10	3	4	1.9	.986	R. DeLucia	56	82	8	7	0	3.39
C	D. Sheaffer	208	.231	5	30	360	37	3	6	6.0	.993	J. Parrett	59	77	4	7	0	3.64
C	T. Pagnozzi	219	.215	2	15	336	38	2	1	6.2	.995	T. Henke	52	54	1	1	36	1.82
SS	O. Smith	156	.199	0	11	60	128	7	27	4.8	.964							
2B	D. Bell	144	.250	2	19	75	103	6	27	5.0	.967							
1B	T. Zeile	127	.291	5	22	310	29	7	29	10.2	.980							

Pittsburgh

W-58 L-86

Jim Leyland

POS	Player	AB	BA	HR	RBI	PO	A	E	DP	TC/G	FA	Pitcher	G	IP	W	L	SV	ERA
1B	M. Johnson	221	.208	13	28	527	34	8	53	8.1	.986	D. Neagle	31	**210**	13	8	0	3.43
2B	C. Garcia	367	.294	6	50	218	264	9	70	5.3	.982	E. Loaiza	32	173	8	9	0	5.16
SS	J. Bell	530	.262	13	55	205	408	14	89	4.6	.978	P. Wagner	33	165	5	**16**	1	4.80
3B	J. King	445	.265	18	87	47	163	13	13	2.7	.942	J. Ericks	19	106	3	9	0	4.58
RF	O. Merced	487	.300	15	83	200	8	5	2	2.0	.977	S. Parris	15	82	6	6	0	5.38
CF	J. Brumfield	402	.271	4	26	241	8	8	1	2.5	.969	J. Lieber	21	73	4	7	0	6.32
LF	A. Martin	439	.282	13	41	205	8	5	2	1.8	.977	D. Plesac	58	60	4	4	3	3.58
C	M. Parent	233	.232	15	33	365	39	4	1	6.1	.990	D. Miceli	58	58	4	4	21	4.66
2B	N. Liriano	259	.286	5	38	130	132	5	31	4.0	.981							
OF	D. Clark	196	.281	4	24	98	1	4	0	1.7	.961							
3B	K. Young	181	.232	6	22	28	108	12	7	3.1	.919							
OF	S. Pegues	171	.246	6	16	81	2	4	0	1.6	.954							
C	A. Encarnacion	159	.226	2	10	278	42	7	2	5.9	.979							
OF	M. Cummings	152	.243	2	15	79	2	1	0	2.0	.988							

West

Los Angeles

W-78 L-66

Tom Lasorda

POS	Player	AB	BA	HR	RBI	PO	A	E	DP	TC/G	FA	Pitcher	G	IP	W	L	SV	ERA
1B	E. Karros	551	.298	32	105	1234	109	7	100	9.4	.995	R. Martinez	30	206	17	7	0	3.66
2B	D. DeShields	425	.256	8	37	203	330	**11**	54	4.8	.980	I. Valdes	33	198	13	11	1	3.05
SS	J. Offerman	429	.287	4	33	166	312	**35**	56	4.5	.932	H. Nomo	28	191	13	6	0	2.54
3B	T. Wallach	327	.266	9	38	50	156	5	9	2.2	**.976**	T. Candiotti	30	190	7	14	0	3.50
RF	R. Mondesi	536	.285	26	88	281	16	6	2	2.2	.980	P. Astacio	48	104	7	8	0	4.24
CF	R. Kelly	409	.279	6	48	183	2	6	0	1.7	.969	T. Worrell	59	62	4	1	32	2.02
LF	B. Ashley	215	.237	8	27	102	2	3	0	1.6	.972							
C	M. Piazza	434	.346	32	93	**805**	51	9	5	**7.7**	.990							
UT	C. Fonville	308	.276	0	16	125	195	11	28		.967							
3B	D. Hansen	181	.287	1	14	27	70	7	6	1.8	.933							
OF	B. Butler	146	.274	0	13	75	0	1	0	1.9	.987							

Colorado

W-77 L-67

Don Baylor

POS	Player	AB	BA	HR	RBI	PO	A	E	DP	TC/G	FA	Pitcher	G	IP	W	L	SV	ERA
1B	A. Galarraga	554	.280	31	106	**1300**	119	**13**	**128**	**10.1**	.991	K. Ritz	31	173	11	11	2	4.21
2B	J. Bates	322	.267	8	46	134	188	3	47	4.0	.991	B. Swift	19	106	9	3	0	4.94
SS	W. Weiss	427	.260	1	25	202	407	16	**98**	4.6	.974	C. Leskanic	**76**	98	6	3	10	3.40
3B	V. Castilla	527	.309	32	90	86	254	15	20	2.6	.958	M. Freeman	22	95	3	7	0	5.89
RF	L. Walker	494	.306	36	101	225	13	3	0	1.9	.988	A. Reynoso	20	93	7	7	0	5.32
CF	M. Kingery	350	.269	8	37	180	4	4	0	1.7	.979	B. Rekar	15	85	4	6	0	4.98
LF	D. Bichette	579	.340	**40**	**128**	208	9	3	0	1.6	.986	S. Reed	71	84	5	2	3	2.14
C	J. Girardi	462	.262	8	55	729	61	10	3	6.6	.988	R. Bailey	39	81	7	6	0	4.98
2B	E. Young	366	.317	6	36	164	227	**11**	54	5.2	.973	D. Holmes	68	67	6	1	14	3.24
OF	E. Burks	278	.266	14	49	158	3	5	0	2.1	.970	J. Acevedo	17	66	4	6	0	6.44
01	J. Vander Wal	101	.347	5	21	51	4	2	3		.965	B. Ruffin	37	34	0	1	11	2.12

NATIONAL LEAGUE 1995, *cont.*

	POS	Player	AB	BA	HR	RBI	PO	A	E	DP	TC/G	FA	Pitcher	G	IP	W	L	SV	ERA
San Diego	1B	E. Williams	296	.260	12	47	571	48	7	53	7.7	.989	J. Hamilton	31	204	6	9	0	3.08
W-70 L-74	2B	J. Reed	445	.256	4	40	304	363	4	77	5.2	.994	A. Ashby	31	193	12	10	0	2.94
Bruce Bochy	SS	A. Cedeno	390	.210	6	31	139	304	16	58	4.0	.965	A. Benes	19	119	4	7	0	4.17
	3B	K. Caminiti	526	.302	26	94	102	**293**	**27**	24	3.0	.936	W. Blair	40	114	7	5	0	4.34
	RF	T. Gwynn	535	**.368**	9	90	245	8	2	1	1.9	.992	G. Dishman	19	97	4	8	0	5.01
	CF	S. Finley	562	.297	10	44	289	8	7	0	2.2	.977	F. Valenzuela	29	90	8	3	0	4.98
	LF	M. Nieves	234	.205	14	38	95	5	1	1	1.3	.990	S. Sanders	17	90	5	5	0	4.30
	C	B. Ausmus	328	.293	5	34	657	60	6	**8**	7.2	.992	B. Williams	44	72	3	10	0	6.00
	O2	B. Roberts	296	.304	2	25	128	70	3	11		.985	T. Hoffman	55	53	7	4	31	3.88
	C	B. Johnson	207	.251	3	29	394	31	3	2	7.8	.993							
	1B	S. Livingstone	196	.337	5	32	298	17	3	25	7.4	.991							
	OF	P. Plantier	148	.257	5	19	64	5	3	1	1.8	.958							
	UT	A. Cianfrocco	118	.263	5	31	112	50	3	15		.982							
San Francisco	1B	M. Carreon	396	.301	17	65	703	44	5	65	9.3	.993	M. Leiter	30	196	10	12	0	3.82
W-67 L-77	2B	R. Thompson	336	.223	8	23	181	238	3	49	4.6	.993	T. Mulholland	29	149	5	13	0	5.80
Dusty Baker	SS	R. Clayton	509	.244	5	58	**223**	**412**	20	91	**4.8**	.969	W. VanLandingham	18	123	6	3	0	3.67
	3B	M. Williams	283	.336	23	65	49	178	10	10	3.2	.958	M. Portugal	17	104	5	5	0	4.15
	RF	G. Hill	497	.264	24	86	226	10	10	1	2.0	.959	J. Bautista	52	101	3	8	0	6.44
	CF	D. Lewis	309	.252	1	16	200	2	1	0	2.8	.995	J. Brewington	13	75	6	4	0	4.54
	LF	B. Bonds	506	.294	33	104	279	12	6	1	2.1	.980	R. Beck	60	59	5	6	33	4.45
	C	K. Manwaring	379	.251	4	36	607	55	7	5	5.7	.990							
	UT	S. Scarsone	233	.266	11	29	135	112	11	31		.957							
	1B	J. Phillips	231	.195	9	28	535	36	4	45	7.3	.993							
	OF	D. Sanders	214	.285	5	18	127	0	2	0	2.5	.984							
	2B	J. Patterson	205	.205	1	14	114	112	4	30	4.3	.983							
	UT	M. Benjamin	186	.220	3	12	51	121	4	9		.977							

BATTING AND BASE RUNNING LEADERS

Batting Average
T. Gwynn, SD .368
M. Piazza, LA .346
D. Bichette, CLR .340
D. Bell, HOU .334
M. Grace, CHI .326

Slugging Average
D. Bichette, CLR .620
L. Walker, CLR .607
M. Piazza, LA .606
R. Sanders, CIN .579
B. Bonds, SF .577

Home Runs
D. Bichette, CLR 40
L. Walker, CLR 36
S. Sosa, CHI 36
B. Bonds, SF 33

Total Bases
D. Bichette, CLR 359
L. Walker, CLR 300
V. Castilla, CLR 297
E. Karros, LA 295
B. Bonds, SF 292

Runs Batted In
D. Bichette, CLR 128
S. Sosa, CHI 119
A. Galarraga, CLR 106
J. Conine, FLA 105
E. Karros, LA 105

Stolen Bases
Q. Veras, FLA 56
B. Larkin, CIN 51
D. DeShields, LA 39
R. Sanders, CIN 36
S. Finley, SD 36

Hits
T. Gwynn, SD 197
D. Bichette, CLR 197
M. Grace, CHI 180

Base on Balls
B. Bonds, SF 120
W. Weiss, CLR 98
Q. Veras, FLA 80
C. Biggio, HOU 80

Home Run Percentage
M. Piazza, LA 7.4
L. Walker, CLR 7.3
R. Gant, CIN 7.1
D. Bichette, CLR 6.9

Runs
C. Biggio, HOU 123
B. Bonds, SF 109
S. Finley, SD 104
D. Bichette, CLR 102

Doubles
M. Grace, CHI 51
D. Bichette, CLR 38
B. McRae, CHI 38
R. Sanders, CIN 36

Triples
E. Young, CLR 9
B. Butler, NY, LA 9
D. Sanders, CIN, SF 8
L. Gonzalez, HOU, CHI 8
S. Finley, SD 8

PITCHING LEADERS

Winning Percentage
G. Maddux, ATL .905
P. Schourek, CIN .720
R. Martinez, LA .708
T. Glavine, ATL .696

Earned Run Average
G. Maddux, ATL 1.63
H. Nomo, LA 2.54
A. Ashby, SD 2.94
I. Valdes, LA 3.05
T. Glavine, ATL 3.08

Wins
G. Maddux, ATL 19
P. Schourek, CIN 18
R. Martinez, LA 17
T. Glavine, ATL 16

Saves
R. Myers, CHI 38
T. Henke, STL 36
R. Beck, SF 33
T. Worrell, LA 32
H. Slocumb, PHI 32

Strikeouts
H. Nomo, LA 236
J. Smoltz, ATL 193
G. Maddux, ATL 181
S. Reynolds, HOU 175
P. Martinez, MON 174

Complete Games
G. Maddux, ATL 10
M. Leiter, SF 7
I. Valdes, LA 6
D. Neagle, PIT 5

Fewest Hits/9 Innings
H. Nomo, LA 5.83
G. Maddux, ATL 6.31
P. Martinez, MON 7.30
P. Schourek, CIN 7.47

Shutouts
G. Maddux, ATL 3
H. Nomo, LA 3

Fewest Walks/9 Innings
G. Maddux, ATL 0.99
S. Reynolds, HOU 1.76
D. Neagle, PIT 1.93
B. Saberhagen, NY, CLR 1.94

Most Strikeouts/9 Inn.
H. Nomo, LA 11.10
J. Smoltz, ATL 9.02
S. Reynolds, HOU 8.32
P. Martinez, MON 8.04

Innings
G. Maddux, ATL 210
D. Neagle, PIT 210
R. Martinez, LA 206
J. Hamilton, SD 204

Games Pitched
C. Leskanic, CLR 76
D. Veres, HOU 72
S. Reed, CLR 71
Y. Perez, FLA 69

		W	L	PCT	GB	R	OR	Batting 2B	3B	HR	BA	SA	SB	Fielding E	DP	FA	Pitching CG	BB	SO	ShO	SV	ERA
East	Atlanta	90	54	.625		645	**540**	210	27	168	.250	.409	73	100	111	.982	**18**	436	**1087**	11	34	**3.44**
	New York	69	75	.479	21	657	618	218	34	125	.267	.400	58	115	119	.979	9	**401**	901	9	36	3.88
	Philadelphia	69	75	.479	21	615	658	263	30	94	.262	.384	72	97	137	.982	8	538	980	8	41	4.21
	Florida	67	76	.469	22.5	673	673	214	29	144	.262	.406	131	115	135	.979	12	562	994	7	29	4.27
	Montreal	66	78	.458	24	621	638	265	24	118	.259	.394	120	109	112	.980	7	416	950	9	42	4.11
Central	Cincinnati	85	59	.590		747	623	**277**	35	161	.270	.440	**190**	**79**	138	**.985**	8	424	903	10	38	4.03
	Houston	76	68	.528	9	747	674	260	22	109	.275	.399	176	121	114	.979	6	460	1056	8	32	4.06
	Chicago	73	71	.507	12	693	671	267	39	158	.265	.430	105	115	107	.979	6	518	926	**12**	**45**	4.13
	St. Louis	62	81	.434	22.5	563	658	238	24	107	.247	.374	79	113	**147**	.980	4	445	842	6	38	4.09
	Pittsburgh	58	86	.403	27	629	736	245	27	125	.259	.396	84	122	137	.978	11	477	871	7	29	4.70
West	Los Angeles	78	66	.542		634	609	191	31	140	.264	.400	127	130	112	.976	16	462	1060	11	37	3.66
	Colorado	77	67	.535	1	**785**	783	259	**43**	**200**	**.282**	**.471**	125	107	141	.981	1	512	891	1	43	4.97
	San Diego	70	74	.486	8	668	672	231	20	116	.272	.397	124	108	124	.980	6	512	1047	10	35	4.13
	San Francisco	67	77	.465	11	652	776	229	33	152	.253	.404	138	108	134	.980	12	505	801	5	34	4.86
						9329	9329	3367	418	1917	.263	.407	1602	1539	1768	.980	124	6668	13309	114	513	4.18

AMERICAN LEAGUE 1995

		POS	Player	AB	BA	HR	RBI	PO	A	E	DP	TC/G	FA	Pitcher	G	IP	W	L	SV	ERA
East	Boston	1B	M. Vaughn	550	.300	39	**126**	**1262**	94	11	**126**	**9.9**	.992	T. Wakefield	27	195	16	8	0	2.95
		2B	L. Alicea	419	.270	6	44	255	429	16	**98**	**5.3**	.977	E. Hanson	29	187	15	5	0	4.24
		SS	J. Valentin	520	.298	27	102	225	**413**	**18**	94	4.9	.973	R. Clemens	23	140	10	5	0	4.18
	W-86 L-58	3B	T. Naehring	433	.307	10	57	86	244	16	22	2.8	.954	R. Cormier	48	115	7	5	0	4.07
		RF	T. O'Leary	399	.308	10	49	196	6	5	1	2.0	.976	Z. Smith	24	111	8	8	0	5.61
	Kevin Kennedy	CF	L. Tinsley	341	.284	7	41	227	4	5	1	2.4	.979	S. Belinda	63	70	8	1	10	3.10
		LF	M. Greenwell	481	.297	15	76	202	10	6	1	1.8	.972	K. Ryan	28	33	0	4	7	4.96
		C	M. Macfarlane	364	.225	15	51	618	49	5	3	6.1	.993	R. Aguilera	30	30	2	2	20	2.67
		DH	J. Canseco	396	.306	24	81													
		OF	W. McGee	200	.285	2	15	101	7	3	1	1.7	.973							
		C	B. Haselman	152	.243	5	23	257	16	3	0	5.8	.989							
		DH	R. Jefferson	121	.289	5	26													
	New York	1B	D. Mattingly	458	.288	7	49	994	82	7	90	8.7	.994	J. McDowell	30	218	15	10	0	3.93
		2B	P. Kelly	270	.237	4	29	161	255	7	52	4.9	.983	A. Pettitte	31	175	12	9	0	4.17
		SS	T. Fernandez	384	.245	5	45	140	274	10	61	4.1	.976	S. Hitchcock	27	168	11	10	0	4.70
	W-79 L-65	3B	W. Boggs	460	.324	5	63	69	192	5	10	2.3	**.981**	D. Cone	13	99	9	2	0	3.82
		RF	P. O'Neill	460	.300	22	96	218	3	3	0	1.9	.987	S. Kamieniecki	17	90	7	6	0	4.01
	Buck Showalter	CF	B. Williams	563	.307	18	82	431	1	8	0	3.1	.982	M. Perez	13	69	5	5	0	5.58
		LF	G. Williams	182	.247	6	28	138	6	1	0	1.6	.993	J. Wetteland	60	61	1	5	31	2.93
		C	M. Stanley	399	.268	18	83	651	35	5	3	6.5	.993	S. Howe	56	49	6	3	2	4.96
		DH	R. Sierra	215	.260	7	44													
		UT	R. Velarde	367	.278	7	46	170	258	10	48		.977							
		UT	J. Leyritz	264	.269	7	37	418	23	3	12		.993							
		OF	L. Polonia	238	.261	2	15	134	5	0	1	2.2	1.000							
		OD	D. James	209	.287	2	26	30	0	1	0		.968							
		DO	D. Tartabull	192	.224	6	28	27	1	0	1		1.000							
	Baltimore	1B	R. Palmeiro	554	.310	39	104	1178	**123**	4	120	9.2	.997	M. Mussina	32	222	19	9	0	3.29
		2B	M. Alexander	242	.236	3	23	137	165	9	44	3.8	.971	K. Brown	26	172	10	9	0	3.60
		SS	C. Ripken	550	.262	17	88	205	409	7	**99**	4.3	**.989**	J. Moyer	27	116	8	6	0	5.21
	W-71 L-73	3B	J. Manto	254	.256	17	38	40	100	6	11	2.1	.959	S. Erickson	17	109	9	4	0	3.89
		RF	K. Bass	295	.244	5	32	123	3	2	1	1.7	.984	D. Jones	52	47	0	4	22	5.01
	Phil Regan	CF	C. Goodwin	289	.263	1	24	202	1	2	1	2.4	.990							
		LF	B. Anderson	554	.262	16	64	268	1	3	0	1.9	.989							
		C	C. Hoiles	352	.250	19	58	658	34	3	3	6.5	**.996**							
		DH	H. Baines	385	.299	24	63													
		2B	B. Barberie	237	.241	2	25	115	186	7	45	4.2	.977							
		03	B. Bonilla	237	.333	10	46	80	48	5	5		.962							
		OF	J. Hammonds	178	.242	4	23	88	1	1	0	2.0	.989							
		32	J. Huson	161	.248	1	19	59	89	0	19		1.000							
	Detroit	1B	C. Fielder	494	.243	31	82	631	73	5	65	9.2	.993	F. Lira	37	146	9	13	1	4.31
		2B	L. Whitaker	249	.293	14	44	107	162	4	32	4.3	.985	S. Bergman	28	135	7	10	0	5.12
		SS	C. Gomez	431	.223	11	50	155	280	12	59	4.6	.973	M. Moore	25	133	5	15	0	7.53
	W-60 L-84	3B	T. Fryman	567	.275	15	81	106	**335**	14	**38**	**3.2**	.969	D. Wells	18	130	10	3	0	3.04
		RF	D. Bautista	271	.203	7	27	164	3	2	0	2.0	.988	J. Doherty	48	113	5	9	6	5.10
	Sparky Anderson	CF	C. Curtis	586	.268	21	67	361	5	3	0	2.6	.992	B. Bohanon	52	106	1	1	1	5.54
		LF	B. Higginson	410	.224	14	43	247	13	4	2	2.1	.985	J. Boever	60	99	5	7	3	6.39
		C	J. Flaherty	354	.243	11	40	570	33	**11**	4	5.5	.982	J. Lima	15	74	3	9	0	6.11
		DH	K. Gibson	227	.260	9	35							M. Henneman	29	29	0	1	18	1.53
		SS	A. Trammell	223	.269	2	23	86	158	5	34	4.2	.980							
		2B	S. Fletcher	182	.231	1	17	109	161	0	48	4.3	1.000							
		UT	J. Samuel	171	.281	10	34	289	35	9	29		.973							
	Toronto	1B	J. Olerud	492	.291	8	54	1098	90	4	102	9.0	.997	P. Hentgen	30	201	10	14	0	5.11
		2B	R. Alomar	517	.300	13	66	**273**	365	4	84	5.0	**.994**	A. Leiter	28	183	11	11	0	3.64
		SS	A. Gonzalez	367	.243	10	42	158	216	17	44	4.0	.957	J. Guzman	24	135	4	14	0	6.32
	W-56 L-88	3B	E. Sprague	521	.244	18	74	**134**	234	16	20	2.8	.958	D. Cone	17	130	9	6	0	3.38
		RF	S. Green	379	.288	15	54	207	9	6	2	2.0	.973	T. Castillo	55	73	1	5	13	3.22
	Cito Gaston	CF	D. White	427	.283	10	53	260	7	3	0	2.7	.989	M. Timlin	31	42	4	3	5	2.14
		LF	J. Carter	558	.253	25	76	268	9	7	1	2.2	.975							
		C	L. Parrish	178	.202	4	22	346	41	0	6	5.8	1.000							
		DH	P. Molitor	525	.270	15	60													
		C	S. Martinez	191	.241	2	25	329	28	5	5	5.9	.986							
		S2	D. Cedeno	161	.236	4	14	85	131	3	25		.986							
		OF	C. Maldonado	160	.269	7	25	78	2	1	0	1.4	.988							
Central	Cleveland	1B	P. Sorrento	323	.235	25	79	816	57	7	87	9.7	.992	D. Martinez	28	187	12	5	0	3.08
		2B	C. Baerga	557	.314	15	90	230	**444**	19	97	5.2	.973	C. Nagy	29	178	16	6	0	4.55
		SS	O. Vizquel	542	.266	6	56	211	407	9	85	4.6	.986	O. Hershiser	26	167	16	6	0	3.87
	W-100 L-44	3B	J. Thome	452	.314	25	73	75	214	16	19	2.3	.948	M. Clark	22	125	9	7	0	5.27
		RF	M. Ramirez	484	.308	31	107	219	3	5	2	1.7	.978	C. Ogea	20	106	8	3	0	3.05
	Mike Hargrove	CF	K. Lofton	481	.310	7	53	248	11	8	2	2.3	.970	J. Tavarez	57	85	10	2	0	2.44
		LF	A. Belle	546	.317	**50**	**126**	304	7	6	1	2.2	.981	J. Mesa	62	64	3	0	**46**	1.13
		C	T. Pena	263	.262	5	28	508	36	7	2	6.1	.987	E. Plunk	56	64	6	2	2	2.67
		DH	E. Murray	436	.323	21	82													
		C	S. Alomar	203	.300	10	35	364	22	2	3	6.4	.995							
		OF	W. Kirby	188	.207	1	14	95	2	1	1	1.4	.990							
		1B	H. Perry	162	.315	3	23	388	30	0	30	9.3	1.000							

AMERICAN LEAGUE 1995, *cont.*

Kansas City

W-70 L-74

Bob Boone

POS	Player	AB	BA	HR	RBI	PO	A	E	DP	TC/G	FA	Pitcher	G	IP	W	L	SV	ERA
1B	W. Joyner	465	.310	12	83	1111	118	3	119	9.8	**.998**	M. Gubicza	33	213	12	14	0	3.75
2B	K. Lockhart	274	.321	6	33	107	160	7	43	4.5	.974	K. Appier	31	201	15	10	0	3.89
SS	G. Gagne	430	.256	6	49	175	387	**18**	87	4.9	.969	T. Gordon	31	189	12	12	0	4.43
3B	G. Gaetti	514	.261	35	96	90	220	15	20	2.6	.954	J. Jacome	15	84	4	6	0	5.36
RF	J. Nunnally	303	.244	14	42	196	5	6	1	1.9	.971	J. Montgomery	54	66	2	3	31	3.43
CF	T. Goodwin	480	.287	4	28	290	6	3	1	2.3	.990	H. Pichardo	44	64	8	4	1	4.36
LF	V. Coleman	293	.287	4	20	107	7	3	1	1.7	.974							
C	B. Mayne	307	.251	1	27	540	39	3	**8**	5.7	.995							
DH	B. Hamelin	208	.168	7	25													
UT	D. Howard	255	.243	0	19	168	195	6	44		.984							
OF	J. Damon	188	.282	3	23	110	0	1	0	2.4	.991							
OD	M. Tucker	177	.260	4	17	67	3	1	0		.986							
DH	J. Vitiello	130	.254	7	21													

Chicago

W-68 L-76

Gene Lamont
W-11 L-20

Terry Bevington
W-57 L-56

POS	Player	AB	BA	HR	RBI	PO	A	E	DP	TC/G	FA	Pitcher	G	IP	W	L	SV	ERA
1B	F. Thomas	493	.308	40	111	743	35	7	66	8.6	.991	A. Fernandez	30	204	12	8	0	3.80
2B	R. Durham	471	.257	7	51	245	299	15	66	4.6	.973	W. Alvarez	29	175	8	11	0	4.32
SS	O. Guillen	415	.248	1	41	167	318	12	55	4.1	.976	J. Bere	27	138	8	15	0	7.19
3B	R. Ventura	492	.295	26	93	107	206	17	14	2.7	.948	J. Abbott	17	112	6	4	0	3.36
RF	M. Devereaux	333	.306	10	55	188	4	3	1	2.2	.985	B. Keyser	23	92	5	6	0	4.97
CF	L. Johnson	**607**	.306	10	57	335	8	3	2	2.5	.991	K. McCaskill	55	81	6	4	2	4.89
LF	T. Raines	502	.285	12	67	193	7	4	1	1.9	.980	R. Hernandez	60	60	3	7	32	3.92
C	R. Karkovice	323	.217	13	51	629	42	6	1	6.0	.991							
DH	J. Kruk	159	.308	2	23													
01	D. Martinez	303	.307	5	37	392	25	3	38		.993							
OF	L. Mouton	179	.302	5	27	94	5	1	1	1.9	.990							
UT	N. Martin	160	.269	2	17	52	67	7	16		.944							
UT	C. Grebeck	154	.260	1	18	77	127	7	25		.967							

Milwaukee

W-65 L-79

Phil Garner

POS	Player	AB	BA	HR	RBI	PO	A	E	DP	TC/G	FA	Pitcher	G	IP	W	L	SV	ERA
1B	J. Jaha	316	.313	20	65	648	62	2	86	8.8	.997	S. Sparks	33	202	9	11	0	4.63
2B	F. Vina	288	.257	3	29	183	226	7	69	4.2	.983	R. Bones	32	200	10	12	0	4.63
SS	J. Valentin	338	.219	11	49	163	333	15	81	4.9	.971	S. Karl	25	124	6	7	0	4.14
3B	J. Cirillo	328	.277	9	39	47	153	13	21	2.0	.939	B. Givens	19	107	5	7	0	4.95
RF	M. Mieske	267	.251	12	48	177	7	4	0	1.7	.979	S. Roberson	26	84	6	4	0	5.76
CF	D. Hamilton	398	.271	5	44	262	4	3	0	2.5	.989	B. Scanlan	17	83	4	7	0	6.59
LF	D. Hulse	339	.251	3	47	180	2	3	1	1.6	.984	A. Miranda	30	74	4	5	1	5.23
C	J. Oliver	337	.273	12	51	408	40	8	2	5.0	.982	B. Wegman	37	71	5	7	2	5.35
DH	G. Vaughn	392	.224	17	59							M. Fetters	40	35	0	3	22	3.38
UT	K. Seitzer	492	.311	5	69	340	179	10	55		.981							
UT	B. Surhoff	415	.320	13	73	529	44	5	45		.991							
UT	P. Listach	334	.219	0	25	169	273	6	73		.987							
OF	D. Nilsson	263	.278	12	53	99	5	2	0	1.8	.981							
C	M. Matheny	166	.247	0	21	261	18	4	2	3.5	.986							

Minnesota

W-56 L-88

Tom Kelly

POS	Player	AB	BA	HR	RBI	PO	A	E	DP	TC/G	FA	Pitcher	G	IP	W	L	SV	ERA
1B	S. Stahoviak	263	.266	3	23	494	61	1	46	8.1	.998	B. Radke	29	181	11	14	0	5.32
2B	C. Knoblauch	538	.333	11	63	253	400	10	85	4.9	.985	K. Tapani	20	134	6	11	0	4.92
SS	P. Meares	390	.269	12	49	185	317	**18**	67	4.6	.965	M. Trombley	20	98	4	8	0	5.62
3B	S. Leius	372	.247	4	45	60	182	14	21	2.3	.945	P. Mahomes	47	95	4	10	3	6.37
RF	K. Puckett	538	.314	23	99	194	9	4	0	1.9	.981	E. Guardado	51	91	4	9	2	5.12
CF	R. Becker	392	.237	2	33	275	12	4	3	2.8	.986	F. Rodriguez	16	90	5	6	0	5.38
LF	M. Cordova	512	.277	24	84	345	12	5	1	2.6	.986	S. Erickson	15	88	4	6	0	5.95
C	M. Walbeck	393	.257	1	44	604	35	6	3	5.7	.991	D. Stevens	56	66	5	4	10	5.07
DH	P. Munoz	376	.301	18	58							R. Aguilera	22	25	1	1	12	2.52
UT	J. Reboulet	216	.292	4	23	164	159	4	36		.988							
UT	D. Masteller	198	.237	3	21	365	21	2	35		.995							
C	M. Merullo	195	.282	1	27	210	10	3	0	4.8	.987							

West

Seattle

W-79 L-66

Lou Piniella

POS	Player	AB	BA	HR	RBI	PO	A	E	DP	TC/G	FA	Pitcher	G	IP	W	L	SV	ERA
1B	T. Martinez	519	.293	31	111	1043	103	8	86	8.3	.993	R. Johnson	30	214	18	2	0	2.48
2B	J. Cora	427	.297	3	39	206	261	**22**	51	4.4	.955	T. Belcher	28	179	10	12	0	4.52
SS	L. Sojo	339	.289	7	39	110	175	5	33	3.6	.983	C. Bosio	31	170	10	8	0	4.92
3B	M. Blowers	439	.257	23	96	81	167	14	9	2.1	.947	J. Nelson	62	79	7	3	2	2.17
RF	J. Buhner	470	.262	40	121	177	5	2	0	1.5	.989	S. Torres	16	72	3	8	0	6.00
CF	K. Griffey	260	.258	17	42	190	5	2	1	2.8	.990	B. Ayala	63	71	6	5	19	4.44
LF	R. Amaral	238	.282	2	19	121	6	1	0	1.8	.992	N. Charlton	30	48	2	1	14	1.51
C	D. Wilson	399	.278	9	51	**897**	51	5	2	**8.0**	.995							
DH	E. Martinez	511	**.356**	29	113													
OF	A. Diaz	270	.248	3	27	146	4	2	1	1.7	.987							
S2	F. Fermin	200	.195	0	15	107	168	6	41		.979							
OF	V. Coleman	162	.290	1	9	83	2	1	0	2.3	.988							
3B	D. Strange	155	.271	2	21	28	65	5	1	2.4	.949							
OF	D. Bragg	145	.234	3	12	83	7	1	1	1.9	.989							

California

W-78 L-67

Marcel Lachemann

POS	Player	AB	BA	HR	RBI	PO	A	E	DP	TC/G	FA	Pitcher	G	IP	W	L	SV	ERA
1B	J. Snow	544	.289	24	102	1161	56	4	106	8.5	.997	C. Finley	32	203	15	12	0	4.21
2B	D. Easley	357	.216	4	35	145	209	7	41	4.1	.981	M. Langston	31	200	15	7	0	4.63
SS	G. DiSarcina	362	.307	5	41	146	275	6	46	4.4	.986	S. Boskie	20	112	7	7	0	5.64
3B	T. Phillips	525	.261	27	61	53	178	**19**	17	2.8	.924	B. Anderson	18	100	6	8	0	5.87
RF	T. Salmon	537	.330	34	105	319	7	4	0	2.3	.988	M. Bielecki	22	75	4	6	0	5.97
CF	J. Edmonds	558	.290	33	107	402	8	1	2	3.0	.998	L. Smith	52	49	0	5	37	3.47
LF	G. Anderson	374	.321	16	69	213	7	5	0	2.3	.978							
C	J. Fabregas	227	.247	1	22	391	36	6	1	5.9	.986							
DH	C. Davis	424	.318	20	86													
C	G. Myers	273	.260	9	38	340	21	4	5	6.0	.989							
20	R. Hudler	223	.265	6	27	114	114	4	32		.983							
UT	S. Owen	218	.229	1	28	66	95	6	17		.964							

AMERICAN LEAGUE 1995, *cont.*

Texas

W-74 L-70

Johnny Oates

POS	Player	AB	BA	HR	RBI	PO	A	E	DP	TC/G	FA
1B	W. Clark	454	.302	16	92	1077	87	7	120	9.6	.994
2B	J. Frye	313	.278	4	29	172	246	11	51	5.2	.974
SS	B. Gil	415	.219	9	46	228	409	17	92	**5.0**	.974
3B	M. Pagliarulo	241	.232	4	27	42	115	6	12	2.4	.963
RF	R. Greer	417	.271	13	61	212	9	4	0	1.8	.982
CF	O. Nixon	589	.295	0	45	355	4	4	0	2.6	.989
LF	M. McLemore	467	.261	5	41	140	0	2	0	1.9	.986
C	I. Rodriguez	492	.303	12	67	707	**67**	8	3	6.2	.990
DH	J. Gonzalez	352	.295	27	82						
OD	M. Tettleton	429	.238	32	78	100	3	3	1		.972
3B	D. Palmer	119	.336	9	24	19	73	5	7	2.7	.948

Pitcher	G	IP	W	L	SV	ERA
K. Rogers	31	208	17	7	0	3.38
R. Pavlik	31	192	10	10	0	4.37
K. Gross	31	184	9	15	0	5.54
B. Tewksbury	21	130	8	7	0	4.58
R. McDowell	64	85	7	4	4	4.02
M. Whiteside	40	53	5	4	3	4.08
E. Vosberg	44	36	5	5	4	3.00
J. Russell	37	33	1	0	20	3.03

Oakland

W-67 L-77

Tony LaRussa

POS	Player	AB	BA	HR	RBI	PO	A	E	DP	TC/G	FA
1B	M. McGwire	317	.274	39	90	775	63	**12**	64	9.3	.986
2B	B. Gates	524	.254	5	56	232	424	12	79	5.1	.982
SS	M. Bordick	428	.264	8	44	**246**	338	10	92	4.7	.983
3B	C. Paquette	283	.226	13	49	38	77	8	11	1.6	.935
RF	R. Sierra	264	.265	12	42	89	1	4	0	1.5	.957
CF	S. Javier	442	.278	8	56	332	3	0	1	2.7	1.000
LF	R. Henderson	407	.300	9	54	161	5	2	1	1.9	.988
C	T. Steinbach	406	.278	15	65	681	57	5	3	6.7	.993
DH	G. Berroa	546	.278	22	88						
UT	S. Brosius	389	.262	17	46	207	121	15	35		.956
31	J. Giambi	176	.256	6	25	195	55	4	24		.984
10	M. Aldrete	125	.272	4	21	191	10	3	16		.985

Pitcher	G	IP	W	L	SV	ERA
T. Stottlemyre	31	210	14	7	0	4.55
T. Van Poppel	36	138	4	8	0	4.88
S. Ontiveros	22	130	9	6	0	4.37
R. Darling	21	104	4	7	0	6.23
D. Stewart	16	81	3	7	0	6.89
C. Reyes	40	69	4	6	0	5.09
M. Harkey	14	66	4	6	0	6.27
D. Eckersley	52	50	4	6	29	4.83

BATTING AND BASE RUNNING LEADERS

Batting Average
- E. Martinez, SEA .356
- C. Knoblauch, MIN .333
- T. Salmon, CAL .330
- W. Boggs, NY .324
- E. Murray, CLE .323

Slugging Average
- A. Belle, CLE .690
- E. Martinez, SEA .628
- F. Thomas, CHI .606
- T. Salmon, CAL .594
- R. Palmeiro, BAL .583

Home Runs
- A. Belle, CLE 50
- J. Buhner, SEA 40
- F. Thomas, CHI 40
- M. McGwire, OAK 39
- M. Vaughn, BOS 39
- R. Palmeiro, BAL 39

Total Bases
- A. Belle, CLE 377
- R. Palmeiro, BAL 323
- E. Martinez, SEA 321
- T. Salmon, CAL 319
- M. Vaughn, BOS 316

Runs Batted In
- A. Belle, CLE 126
- M. Vaughn, BOS 126
- J. Buhner, SEA 121
- E. Martinez, SEA 113
- F. Thomas, CHI 111
- T. Martinez, SEA 111

Stolen Bases
- K. Lofton, CLE 54
- T. Goodwin, KC 50
- O. Nixon, TEX 50
- C. Knoblauch, MIN 46
- V. Coleman, KC, SEA 42

Hits
- L. Johnson, CHI 186
- E. Martinez, SEA 182
- C. Knoblauch, MIN 179
- T. Salmon, CAL 177

Base on Balls
- F. Thomas, CHI 136
- E. Martinez, SEA 116
- T. Phillips, CAL 113
- M. Tettleton, TEX 107

Home Run Percentage
- M. McGwire, OAK 12.3
- A. Belle, CLE 9.2
- J. Buhner, SEA 8.5
- F. Thomas, CHI 8.1

Runs
- E. Martinez, SEA 121
- A. Belle, CLE 121
- J. Edmonds, CAL 120
- T. Phillips, CAL 119

Doubles
- E. Martinez, SEA 52
- A. Belle, CLE 52
- K. Puckett, MIN 39
- J. Valentin, BOS 37

Triples
- K. Lofton, CLE 13
- L. Johnson, CHI 12
- B. Anderson, BAL 10
- B. Williams, NY 9

PITCHING LEADERS

Winning Percentage
- R. Johnson, SEA .900
- E. Hanson, BOS .750
- C. Nagy, CLE .727
- O. Hershiser, CLE .727
- K. Rogers, TEX .708

Earned Run Average
- R. Johnson, SEA 2.48
- T. Wakefield, BOS 2.95
- D. Martinez, CLE 3.08
- M. Mussina, BAL 3.29
- K. Rogers, TEX 3.38

Wins
- M. Mussina, BAL 19
- R. Johnson, SEA 18
- D. Cone, TOR, NY 18
- K. Rogers, TEX 17

Saves
- J. Mesa, CLE 46
- L. Smith, CAL 37
- R. Aguilera, MIN, BOS 32
- R. Hernandez, CHI 32
- J. Montgomery, KC 31
- J. Wetteland, NY 31

Strikeouts
- R. Johnson, SEA 294
- T. Stottlemyre, OAK 205
- C. Finley, CAL 195
- D. Cone, TOR, NY 191
- K. Appier, KC 185

Complete Games
- J. McDowell, NY 8
- S. Erickson, MIN, BAL 7
- M. Mussina, BAL 7
- T. Wakefield, BOS 6
- D. Cone, TOR, NY 6
- R. Johnson, SEA 6

Fewest Hits/9 Innings
- R. Johnson, SEA 6.68
- K. Appier, KC 7.29
- T. Wakefield, BOS 7.51
- M. Mussina, BAL 7.59

Shutouts
- M. Mussina, BAL 4
- R. Johnson, SEA 3

Fewest Walks/9 Innings
- M. Mussina, BAL 2.03
- D. Martinez, CLE 2.21
- B. Radke, MIN 2.34
- K. Brown, BAL 2.51

Most Strikeouts/9 Inn.
- R. Johnson, SEA 12.35
- T. Stottlemyre, OAK 8.80
- C. Finley, CAL 8.65
- K. Appier, KC 8.27

Innings
- D. Cone, TOR, NY 229
- M. Mussina, BAL 222
- J. McDowell, NY 218
- R. Johnson, SEA 214

Games Pitched
- J. Orosco, BAL 65
- R. McDowell, TEX 64
- S. Belinda, BOS 63
- B. Ayala, SEA 63
- B. Wickman, NY 63

								Batting						Fielding			Pitching					
		W	L	PCT	GB	R	OR	2B	3B	HR	BA	SA	SB	E	DP	FA	CG	BB	SO	ShO	SV	ERA
East	Boston	86	58	.597		791	698	**286**	31	175	.280	.455	99	120	145	.978	7	476	888	9	39	4.39
	New York	79	65	.549	7	749	688	280	34	122	.276	.420	50	74	113	**.986**	18	535	908	5	35	4.56
	Baltimore	71	73	.493	15	704	640	229	27	173	.262	.428	92	**72**	136	**.986**	**19**	523	930	**10**	29	4.31
	Detroit	60	84	.417	26	654	844	228	29	159	.247	.404	73	106	138	.981	5	536	729	3	38	5.49
	Toronto	56	88	.389	30	642	777	275	27	140	.260	.409	75	97	128	.982	16	654	894	8	22	4.88
Central	Cleveland	100	44	.694		**840**	**607**	279	23	**207**	**.291**	**.479**	**132**	101	136	.982	10	**445**	926	**10**	**50**	**3.83**
	Kansas City	70	74	.486	30	629	691	240	35	119	.260	.396	120	90	160	.984	11	503	763	**10**	37	4.49
	Chicago	68	76	.472	32	755	758	252	37	146	.280	.431	110	108	125	.980	12	617	892	4	36	4.85
	Milwaukee	65	79	.451	35	740	747	249	**42**	128	.266	.409	105	105	**179**	.981	7	603	699	4	31	4.82
	Minnesota	56	88	.389	44	703	889	270	34	120	.279	.419	105	100	131	.981	7	533	790	2	27	5.76
West	*Seattle	79	66	.545		796	708	276	20	182	.276	.448	110	104	101	.980	9	591	**1068**	8	39	4.50
	California	78	67	.538	1	801	697	252	25	186	.277	.448	58	95	117	.982	8	486	901	9	42	4.52
	Texas	74	70	.514	4.5	691	720	247	24	138	.265	.410	90	98	147	.982	14	514	838	4	34	4.66
	Oakland	67	77	.465	11.5	730	761	228	18	169	.264	.420	112	102	145	.981	8	556	890	4	34	4.93
						10225	10225	3591	406	2164	.270	.427	1331	1372	1901	.982	151	7572	12116	90	493	4.71

* Defeated California in a 1 game playoff

PART SIX

Home/Road Performance

Year-by-Year Breakdowns of Team Performance
At Home and on the Road for Wins and Losses,
Runs Scored and Allowed, and Home Runs
Hit and Allowed
Seasonal Winning and Losing Streaks
Days in First Place
Date of Clinching Title

Home/Road Performance

The Home/Road Performance section is a chronological listing of team performance at home and on the road for every team since 1900. Categories listed for each team are wins and losses at home and on the road; runs scored and allowed at home and on the road; and home runs hit and allowed at home and on the road.

In the twenty-seven years since the publication of the first edition of *The Baseball Encyclopedia,* a wide range of new methods of analyzing player performance have emerged. Perhaps the most significant of these are the methods examining players in light of the characteristics of the parks in which they play the majority of their games. Baseball fans have known for years that some ballparks are good hitters' parks or good pitchers' parks. Few could have known, until recent research, just how large an effect the park can have on performance. In 1978, to take one example, the Atlanta Braves scored 364 runs in 81 games at home and 236 runs in 81 games on the road: a 54.2% increase in runs scored in their home games. That same year, the Houston Astros allowed 254 runs in 81 games at home, and 380 runs in 81 games on the road: a 33.1% difference. In evaluating the statistics for players on these two teams, it is important to note the advantages given to a hitter in Atlanta and the disadvantages faced by one in Houston.

Historical research has indicated that a normal home-field advantage will be 5% for both hitters and pitchers; in a theoretically neutral home park with no unusual configuration or visibility problems, a team should score 5% more runs in home games and allow 5% fewer. The task facing each organization seeking to construct a team for its particular park is to improve on these theoretical advantages, or to ensure that its club is better able to take advantage of its park's oddities. In examining the statistics that follow, then, it is important to note those parks which have distinct prohitter or propitcher tendencies, like Wrigley Field, Fenway Park, Yankee Stadium, or the Houston Astrodome, but also to note those teams which adapt particularly well to their parks, as reflected in a substantial increase in runs scored and decrease in runs allowed at home.

Finally, the last feature lists the number of days a particular team spent in first place in each season, plus each team's longest winning streak and losing streak.

We are indebted to Bob Tiemann for supplying us with this material.

		Home Games			Road Games			Home Games				Road Games							
	Team	W	L	PCT	W	L	PCT	HR	OHR	R	OR	HR	OHR	R	OR	DIF	LDF	WS	LS
1968 National League (4/10-9/28)	St. Louis	47	34	**.580**	50	31	**.617**	31	35	267	218	42	47	**316**	254	**160**	**9/15**	**9**	5
	San Francisco	42	39	.519	46	35	.568	60	32	299	242	48	54	300	287	11	5/31	5	3
	Chicago	47	34	**.580**	37	44	.457	**83**	**83**	363	332	47	55	249	279	0	—	6	7
	Cincinnati	40	41	.494	43	38	.531	55	66	**377**	**400**	**51**	**48**	313	273	1	4/10	7	7
	Atlanta	41	40	.506	40	41	.494	42	43	241	241	38	44	273	308	1	6/1	6	5
	Pittsburgh	40	41	.494	40	41	.494	33	30	289	268	47	43	294	264	0	—	9	**10**
	Los Angeles	41	40	.506	35	46	.432	25	**24**	212	215	42	41	258	294	0	—	7	8
	Philadelphia	38	43	.469	38	43	.469	52	46	274	297	48	45	269	318	1	4/10	7	9
	New York	32	49	.395	41	40	.506	49	50	224	270	32	37	249	**229**	0	—	4	6
	Houston	42	39	.519	30	51	.370	**22**	30	279	269	44	38	231	319	9	4/18	4	6

ATL	Atlanta	CLE	Cleveland	MIL	Milwaukee	SD	San Diego
BAL	Baltimore	CLR	Colorado	MIN	Minnesota	SEA	Seattle
BOS	Boston	DET	Detroit	MON	Montreal	SF	San Francisco
BKN	Brooklyn	FLA	Florida	NWK	Newark	STL	St. Louis
BUF	Buffalo	HOU	Houston	NY	New York	TEX	Texas
CAL	California	IND	Indianapolis	OAK	Oakland	TOR	Toronto
CHI	Chicago	KC	Kansas City	PHI	Philadelphia	WAS	Washington
CIN	Cincinnati	LA	Los Angeles	PIT	Pittsburgh		

Within each league (or division) teams are listed in their order of standings for the year. For further details on a club's performance in that season, see The Teams and Their Players.

Column Headings Information

W	Wins
L	Losses
PCT	Winning Percentage
HR	Home Runs
OHR	Opposition Home Runs
R	Runs Scored
OR	Opposition Runs Scored
WS	Winning Streak
LS	Losing Streak
DIF	Days in First Place
LDF	Last Day in First Place

League Leaders. For each year, the leaders in a league are indicated, as in The Teams and Their Players, by listing that statistic in boldfaced type. Leaders are listed in the following categories:

Home Game:

Highest Winning Percentage
Most Home Runs
Fewest Home Runs
Most Opposition Home Runs
Fewest Opposition Home Runs
Most Runs
Fewest Runs
Most Opposition Runs
Fewest Opposition Runs

Road Games:

Highest Winning Percentage
Fewest Opposition Runs
Highest Run Factor
Fewest Opposition Home Runs
Most Runs
Highest Opposition Run Factor

Seasonal Leaders:

Longest Winning Streak
Longest Losing Streak
Most Days in First Place

Days in First Place. The DIF listing gives the number of days each club was in first place (either tied or alone) during the regular season, counting the standings at the end of each day's league play from opening day through the pennant winner's final game.

Last Date in First. The LDF listing indicates the latest date each club was in first place (either alone or tied). For the league or division champion, however, the date given in boldface is the date the pennant was mathematically clinched. For the 1981 split season, the clinching date for the champion of each half is given.

Winning and Losing Streaks. WS and LS give the longest winning and losing streaks for each club during each season. Tie games and postponements are not counted, and suspended games are considered to be won or lost on the date the final lead change took place.

For years since 1968, the leading DIF figure and the pennant clinching date are highlighted for each division, while only the longest winning and losing streaks for the league as a whole are highlighted.

	Team	Home Games W	L	PCT	Road Games W	L	PCT	Home Games HR	OHR	R	OR	Road Games HR	OHR	R	OR	DIF	LDF	WS	LS
1900 National League (4/19–10/14)	Brooklyn	43	26	.623	39	28	**.582**	15	15	452	394	11	**15**	364	328	**117**	**10/6**	**9**	5
	Pittsburgh	42	28	.600	37	32	.536	14	7	359	315	12	17	374	**297**			8	7
	Philadelphia	45	23	**.662**	30	40	.429	13	7	434	353	16	22	376	438	61	6/20	6	6
	Boston	42	29	.592	24	43	.358	**40**	**43**	**507**	**420**	8	16	271	319			8	8
	Chicago	45	30	.600	20	45	.308	**12**	**5**	337	329	**21**	16	298	422	2	4/20	**9**	6
	St. Louis	40	31	.563	25	44	.362	23	18	382	316	13	19	361	431	4	4/29	5	8
	Cincinnati	27	34	.443	35	43	.449	**12**	9	**255**	**309**	**21**	19	**447**	436	2	4/28	5	7
	New York	38	31	.551	22	47	.319	13	8	393	375	10	18	320	448			4	**12**
1901 National League (4/18–10/6)	Pittsburgh	45	24	.652	45	25	**.643**	15	8	372	255	13	**12**	**404**	279	**127**	**9/27**	**10**	4
	Philadelphia	46	23	**.667**	37	34	.521	11	**6**	349	**247**	13	13	319	296			**10**	3
	Brooklyn	43	25	.632	36	32	.529	13	**6**	**400**	303	**19**	**12**	344	297	7	5/3	9	5
	St. Louis	40	31	.563	36	33	.522	21	19	392	338	18	19	400	351	2	4/30	6	6
	Boston	41	29	.586	28	40	.412	18	17	297	298	10	**12**	234	**258**	5	4/26	8	5
	Chicago	30	39	.435	23	47	.329	**7**	10	293	357	11	17	285	342	1	4/19	5	8
	New York	30	38	.441	22	47	.319	8	11	**255**	350	11	13	289	405	23	6/14	7	8
	Cincinnati	27	43	.386	25	44	.362	**23**	**33**	279	**409**	15	18	282	409	22	5/22	4	**10**
1901 American League (4/24–9/28)	Chicago	49	21	.700	34	32	**.515**	14	11	**441**	285	18	16	378	346	**122**	**9/23**	10	5
	Boston	49	20	**.710**	30	37	.448	**21**	17	383	**252**	16	16	376	356	14	7/17	9	5
	Detroit	42	27	.609	32	34	.485	15	10	438	369	14	12	303	**325**	26	5/22	7	6
	Philadelphia	42	24	.636	32	38	.457	15	**9**	410	352	**20**	11	**395**	409			9	10
	Baltimore	40	25	.615	28	40	.412	11	11	430	367	13	10	330	383	3	4/28	**11**	6
	Washington	31	35	.470	30	38	.441	17	**36**	333	375	17	15	345	392	6	5/1	6	8
	Cleveland	29	39	.426	26	43	.377	**0**	13	**317**	**399**	12	**9**	346	428			6	**11**
	Milwaukee	32	37	.464	16	52	.235	15	14	342	373	11	19	299	455			5	8
1902 National League (4/17–10/6)	Pittsburgh	56	15	**.789**	47	21	**.691**	9	**2**	**410**	**207**	10	**2**	**365**	**233**	**170**	**9/3**	**10**	2
	Brooklyn	45	23	.662	30	40	.429	8	**2**	277	210	**11**	8	287	309	2	4/18	8	7
	Boston	42	27	.609	31	37	.456	**13**	**11**	283	230	1	4	289	286			9	6
	Cincinnati	35	35	.500	35	35	.500	11	8	353	305	7	8	280	261			6	5
	Chicago	31	38	.449	37	31	.544	**1**	3	228	249	5	7	302	252	6	4/26	6	8
	St. Louis	28	38	.424	28	40	.412	3	7	262	336	7	9	255	359			6	8
	Philadelphia	29	39	.426	27	42	.391	**1**	6	264	**351**	4	6	220	298			6	7
	New York	24	44	.353	24	44	.353	7	7	**214**	297	1	9	187	293	1	4/17	7	**13**
1902 American League (4/19–9/29)	Philadelphia	56	17	**.767**	27	36	.429	19	12	**477**	330	**19**	21	298	**306**	62	**9/24**	**10**	4
	St. Louis	49	21	.700	29	37	.439	16	14	350	289	13	22	269	318	11	8/14	9	6
	Boston	43	27	.614	34	33	**.507**	24	15	348	284	18	**12**	316	316	4	4/22	8	6
	Chicago	48	19	.716	26	41	.388	**5**	**2**	371	**238**	9	28	304	364	**77**	8/12	8	6
	Cleveland	40	25	.615	29	42	.408	15	7	357	257	18	19	**329**	410			7	5
	Washington	40	28	.588	21	47	.309	**35**	**38**	407	341	12	18	300	449	4	4/27	5	6
	Detroit	35	33	.515	17	50	.254	13	8	**312**	286	9	**12**	254	371	18	5/25	5	**11**
	Baltimore	32	31	.508	18	57	.240	17	18	391	**369**	16	**12**	324	479			4	**11**
1903 National League (4/16–9/27)	Pittsburgh	46	24	**.657**	45	25	**.643**	**17**	**5**	393	327	**17**	**3**	**400**	286	**112**	**9/18**	**15**	4
	New York	41	27	.603	43	28	.606	9	10	368	296	11	10	361	271	42	6/18	8	5
	Chicago	45	28	.616	37	28	.569	**2**	7	345	**285**	7	6	350	314	11	6/5	8	4
	Cincinnati	41	35	.539	33	30	.524	12	7	**440**	389	16	8	325	**267**			8	6
	Brooklyn	40	33	.548	30	33	.476	8	9	359	361	7	9	308	321	1	4/17	6	4
	Boston	31	35	.470	27	45	.375	11	**19**	283	314	14	11	295	385	1	4/17	4	7
	Philadelphia	25	33	.431	24	53	.312	9	6	250	298	3	15	367	440			5	10
	St. Louis	22	45	.328	21	49	.300	7	13	**248**	**393**	1	13	257	402	1	4/16	4	**11**
1903 American League (4/20–9/29)	Boston	49	20	**.710**	42	27	**.609**	**35**	12	**395**	266	13	11	**313**	**238**	**118**	**9/16**	**11**	3
	Philadelphia	44	21	.677	31	39	.443	16	8	323	238	15	12	274	281	10	6/22	6	5
	Cleveland	49	25	.662	28	38	.424	11	5	364	256	**20**	11	275	323			8	4
	New York	41	26	.612	31	36	.463	10	6	301	269	8	13	278	304			6	6
	Detroit	37	28	.569	28	43	.394	**5**	7	279	**222**	7	12	288	317	13	5/24	4	6
	St. Louis	38	32	.543	27	42	.391	7	15	**250**	228	5	**10**	250	297			8	**11**
	Chicago	41	28	.594	19	49	.279	**5**	**2**	284	244	9	21	232	369	32	5/31	7	6
	Washington	29	40	.420	14	54	.206	15	**24**	275	**349**	2	14	162	342	1	4/22	4	9
1904 National League (4/14–10/9)	New York	56	26	**.683**	50	21	**.704**	**23**	**30**	397	258	8	**6**	**347**	**218**	**168**	**9/22**	**18**	6
	Chicago	49	27	.645	44	33	.571	6	10	303	**240**	**16**	**6**	296	277	9	6/5	8	6
	Cincinnati	49	27	.645	39	38	.507	12	7	**409**	295	9	7	286	252	8	5/26	8	4
	Pittsburgh	48	30	.615	39	36	.520	5	**2**	338	286	10	11	337	306	1	4/15	7	8
	St. Louis	39	36	.520	36	43	.456	14	15	298	280	10	8	304	315			8	7
	Brooklyn	31	44	.413	25	53	.321	**3**	11	**234**	287	12	16	263	327			5	8
	Boston	34	45	.430	21	53	.284	13	10	269	**363**	11	14	222	386			7	8
	Philadelphia	28	43	.394	24	57	.296	7	7	269	348	**16**	15	302	436	1	4/14	5	**12**
1904 American League (4/14–10/10)	Boston	49	30	.620	46	29	**.613**	18	18	325	240	8	13	283	**226**	**132**	**10/10**	8	6
	New York	46	29	.613	46	30	.605	**22**	**25**	321	288	5	**4**	277	238	39	10/7	6	4
	Chicago	50	27	**.649**	39	38	.507	**0**	**2**	297	**226**	**14**	11	303	256	7	8/21	7	5
	Cleveland	44	31	.587	42	34	.553	14	**2**	**329**	242	13	8	**318**	240	2	4/15	**9**	7
	Philadelphia	47	31	.603	34	39	.466	19	8	308	235	12	5	249	268	5	4/18	8	5
	St. Louis	32	43	.427	33	44	.429	2	14	231	288	8	11	250	316			4	7
	Detroit	34	40	.459	28	50	.359	3	4	237	295	8	12	268	332	3	4/16	6	11
	Washington	23	52	.307	15	61	.197	3	**2**	**221**	**350**	7	17	216	393			3	**13**

	Team	Home Games W	Home Games L	Home Games PCT	Road Games W	Road Games L	Road Games PCT	Home Games HR	Home Games OHR	Home Games R	Home Games OR	Road Games HR	Road Games OHR	Road Games R	Road Games OR	DIF	LDF	WS	LS
1905 National League (4/15–10/7)	New York	54	21	**.720**	51	27	**.654**	**33**	**19**	377	234	6	**6**	**401**	271	**174**	**9/30**	**13**	4
	Pittsburgh	49	28	.636	47	29	.618	**4**	**1**	362	287	**18**	11	330	283	4	4/22	11	5
	Chicago	54	25	.684	38	36	.514	7	4	365	**212**	5	10	302	**230**	1	4/14	7	4
	Philadelphia	39	36	.520	44	33	.571	8	9	353	314	8	12	355	288	7	4/21	9	7
	Cincinnati	50	28	.641	29	46	.387	12	2	**438**	330	15	20	297	368			8	8
	St. Louis	32	45	.416	26	51	.338	13	10	245	342	7	18	290	392			4	**14**
	Boston	29	46	.387	22	57	.278	14	14	**234**	344	3	22	234	387			4	8
	Brooklyn	29	47	.382	19	57	.250	16	16	273	**379**	13	8	233	428			6	10
1905 American League (4/14–10/7)	Philadelphia	50	23	**.685**	42	33	.560	12	12	**337**	247	12	9	286	245	**82**	**10/6**	7	3
	Chicago	50	29	.633	42	31	**.575**	**5**	**2**	300	**207**	6	9	**312**	**244**	24	7/31	7	5
	Detroit	45	30	.600	34	44	.436	**5**	5	267	275	8	**6**	245	327	2	4/26	5	6
	Boston	44	32	.579	34	42	.447	**21**	**20**	296	281	8	13	283	283			8	6
	Cleveland	40	37	.519	36	41	.468	**5**	13	290	284	**13**	10	277	303	73	8/1	8	**10**
	New York	40	35	.533	31	43	.419	15	15	316	302	8	11	270	319	10	5/1	**12**	6
	Washington	33	42	.440	31	45	.408	10	4	289	**340**	12	8	270	283	6	5/11	5	7
	St. Louis	34	42	.447	20	57	.260	**5**	7	**250**	267	11	12	261	341	1	4/14	4	8
1906 National League (4/12–10/7)	Chicago	56	21	**.727**	60	15	**.800**	7	6	**345**	**214**	13	6	**360**	**167**	**147**	**9/19**	**14**	3
	New York	51	24	.680	45	32	.584	9	8	309	239	6	5	316	271	25	5/27	10	4
	Pittsburgh	49	27	.645	44	33	.571	4	8	325	232	8	5	298	238	7	4/21	8	6
	Philadelphia	37	40	.481	34	42	.447	**2**	**5**	226	270	10	13	302	294	3	4/24	5	8
	Brooklyn	31	44	.413	35	42	.455	9	**5**	**191**	287	**16**	10	305	338			6	11
	Cincinnati	36	40	.474	28	47	.373	10	10	316	**333**	6	**4**	217	249			6	6
	St. Louis	28	48	.368	24	50	.324	6	10	241	313	4	7	229	294			6	10
	Boston	28	47	.373	21	55	.276	**11**	**16**	218	329	5	8	190	320	8	4/20	4	**19**
1906 American League (4/14–10/7)	Chicago	54	23	**.701**	39	35	.527	**2**	**1**	275	**180**	5	10	295	280	45	**10/3**	**19**	5
	New York	53	23	.697	37	38	.493	14	8	**395**	296	3	13	245	**247**	48	9/24	15	6
	Cleveland	47	30	.610	42	34	**.553**	4	8	351	229	8	8	**312**	253	22	7/5	6	5
	Philadelphia	48	23	.676	30	44	.405	**21**	4	285	211	11	5	276	331	**78**	8/11	11	8
	St. Louis	40	34	.541	36	39	.480	12	10	272	225	8	**4**	286	273			7	6
	Detroit	42	34	.553	29	44	.397	4	5	315	317	6	9	203	282			9	8
	Washington	33	41	.446	22	54	.289	7	5	260	288	**19**	10	258	376	6	5/6	6	8
	Boston	22	54	.289	27	51	.346	10	**22**	**230**	**364**	3	15	232	342			4	**20**
1907 National League (4/11–10/6)	Chicago	54	19	**.740**	53	26	**.671**	**2**	5	282	**198**	11	**6**	290	**192**	**151**	**9/23**	8	4
	Pittsburgh	47	29	.618	44	34	.564	7	**3**	**330**	258	**12**	9	**304**	252			8	5
	Philadelphia	45	30	.600	38	34	.528	**2**	4	265	247	10	9	247	229	4	4/14	7	5
	New York	45	30	.600	37	41	.474	**19**	19	317	250	4	**6**	257	260	25	5/29	**17**	7
	Brooklyn	37	38	.493	28	45	.384	9	10	**223**	232	9	**6**	223	290			6	12
	Cincinnati	43	36	.544	23	51	.311	3	5	287	227	**12**	11	239	292	5	4/15	7	6
	Boston	31	42	.425	27	48	.360	14	**20**	253	**304**	8	8	249	348	4	4/15	4	**16**
	St. Louis	31	47	.397	21	54	.280	9	10	**223**	289	10	10	196	317			9	12
1907 American League (4/11–10/6)	Detroit	50	27	.649	42	31	**.575**	3	5	**373**	265	8	4	**321**	267	32	**10/5**	**10**	4
	Philadelphia	50	20	**.714**	38	37	.507	**14**	6	324	235	8	6	258	276	45	9/26	7	6
	Chicago	48	29	.623	39	35	.527	**0**	5	316	**222**	5	8	272	**252**	**102**	8/25	6	5
	Cleveland	46	31	.597	39	36	.520	7	**3**	267	226	4	**3**	263	299	1	4/17	8	4
	New York	33	40	.452	37	38	.493	10	7	331	**374**	5	7	274	293	6	4/23	5	6
	St. Louis	36	40	.474	33	43	.434	5	**11**	261	262	4	6	281	293	2	4/12	7	6
	Boston	34	41	.453	25	49	.338	12	**11**	249	270	6	11	215	288	2	4/12	4	**16**
	Washington	27	47	.365	22	55	.286	1	**3**	**228**	310	**11**	7	278	381			4	8
1908 National League (4/14–10/8)	Chicago	47	30	.610	52	25	.675	9	15	294	264	10	**5**	330	**197**	**90**	**10/8**	9	5
	New York	52	25	**.675**	46	31	.597	10	11	**343**	235	10	15	309	221	44	10/7	**11**	4
	Pittsburgh	42	35	.545	56	21	**.727**	12	4	227	255	**13**	12	**358**	214	53	10/3	8	4
	Philadelphia	43	34	.558	40	37	.519	**0**	**3**	251	**213**	11	**5**	253	232			8	7
	Cincinnati	40	37	.519	33	44	.429	8	7	260	272	6	12	229	272			6	6
	Boston	35	42	.455	28	49	.364	13	**20**	295	**328**	4	9	242	294	2	4/15	4	7
	Brooklyn	27	50	.351	26	51	.338	**16**	**3**	**179**	243	12	14	198	273			5	9
	St. Louis	28	49	.364	21	56	.273	9	11	185	295	8	**5**	186	331			4	**11**
1908 American League (4/14–10/8)	Detroit	44	33	.571	46	30	**.605**	6	6	**315**	300	**13**	6	**332**	247	**85**	**10/6**	10	6
	Cleveland	51	26	.662	39	38	.507	8	6	305	223	10	9	263	**234**	17	9/26	9	5
	Chicago	51	25	**.671**	37	39	.487	**1**	4	271	**184**	2	7	266	286	19	6/24	**13**	7
	St. Louis	46	31	.597	37	38	.493	**12**	**2**	292	234	8	**5**	252	249	29	7/14	8	4
	Boston	37	40	.481	38	39	.494	9	9	273	249	5	9	291	264	3	4/16	5	7
	Philadelphia	46	30	.605	22	55	.286	11	5	294	272	10	6	192	290	5	6/6	7	10
	Washington	43	32	.573	24	53	.312	2	8	249	237	6	7	230	302			5	11
	New York	30	47	.390	21	56	.273	11	**16**	**234**	**352**	1	10	226	361	38	6/1	3	**12**
1909 National League (4/14–10/7)	Pittsburgh	56	21	**.727**	54	21	.720	10	6	**354**	237	15	6	345	210	**155**	**9/28**	**16**	4
	Chicago	47	29	.618	57	20	**.740**	8	**0**	281	**199**	12	6	**354**	**191**	6	5/1	10	4
	New York	44	33	.571	48	28	.632	**19**	**23**	298	294	7	6	325	252			9	4
	Cincinnati	39	38	.507	38	38	.500	**5**	2	282	299	**17**	**3**	324	300	6	4/25	7	6
	Philadelphia	40	37	.519	34	42	.447	6	10	266	279	6	13	250	239	3	5/4	7	8
	Brooklyn	34	45	.430	21	53	.284	12	9	238	311	4	22	206	316	1	4/15	4	10
	St. Louis	26	48	.351	28	50	.359	9	12	271	**387**	6	10	312	344			4	**15**
	Boston	27	47	.365	18	61	.228	11	9	**219**	326	4	14	216	357	10	5/3	5	**15**

Season	Team	Home Games W	L	PCT	Road Games W	L	PCT	Home Games HR	OHR	R	OR	Road Games HR	OHR	R	OR	DIF	LDF	WS	LS
1909 American League	Detroit	57	19	.750	41	35	.539	12	9	377	246	7	7	289	247	161	9/30	14	5
(4/12–10/3)	Philadelphia	49	27	.645	46	31	.597	9	4	293	200	12	5	312	208	18	8/24	8	4
	Boston	47	28	.627	41	35	.539	18	13	329	295	2	5	268	255	1	4/13	11	6
	Chicago	42	34	.553	36	40	.474	1	3	256	201	3	5	236	262			8	6
	New York	41	35	.539	33	42	.440	11	9	338	263	5	12	251	324	4	4/25	8	6
	Cleveland	39	37	.513	32	45	.416	2	1	262	259	8	8	231	273	2	4/15	7	11
	St. Louis	40	37	.519	21	52	.288	4	6	242	235	6	10	199	340			4	11
	Washington	27	48	.360	15	62	.195	5	2	197	271	4	10	183	385	2	4/13	3	11
1910 National League	Chicago	58	19	.753	46	31	.597	18	9	354	231	16	9	358	268	144	10/2	11	5
(4/14–10/15)	New York	52	26	.667	39	37	.513	20	17	352	255	11	13	363	312	10	5/7	9	5
	Pittsburgh	46	30	.605	40	37	.519	17	8	365	308	16	12	290	268	21	5/24	8	6
	Philadelphia	40	36	.526	38	39	.494	12	18	333	290	10	18	341	349	14	5/15	7	10
	Cincinnati	39	37	.513	36	42	.462	6	8	320	341	17	19	300	343	3	4/16	4	6
	Brooklyn	39	39	.500	25	51	.329	9	5	255	287	16	12	242	336	1	4/14	7	7
	St. Louis	35	41	.461	28	49	.364	3	14	312	316	12	16	327	402			8	13
	Boston	29	48	.377	24	52	.316	25	25	292	396	6	11	203	305	6	4/19	4	7
1910 American League	Philadelphia	57	19	.750	45	29	.608	9	0	339	211	10	8	334	230	150	9/20	13	4
(4/14–10/9)	New York	49	25	.662	39	38	.507	13	4	343	284	7	10	283	273	12	6/20	9	7
	Detroit	46	31	.597	40	37	.519	17	23	346	306	9	13	333	276	10	5/4	11	5
	Boston	51	28	.646	30	44	.405	32	21	338	262	11	8	300	302	3	4/21	9	6
	Cleveland	39	36	.520	32	45	.416	4	2	278	330	5	7	270	327	8	4/21	7	7
	Chicago	41	37	.526	27	48	.360	2	2	233	198	5	14	224	281	1	4/14	10	11
	Washington	38	35	.521	28	50	.359	3	7	265	252	6	12	236	298	4	4/18	4	10
	St. Louis	26	51	.338	21	56	.273	4	2	229	359	8	12	222	384			3	12
1911 National League	New York	49	25	.662	50	29	.633	25	14	357	267	16	20	399	275	80	10/4	11	4
(4/12–10/12)	Chicago	49	32	.605	43	30	.589	26	14	380	306	28	13	377	301	53	8/24	10	5
	Pittsburgh	48	29	.623	37	40	.481	27	6	393	246	21	30	351	311	4	8/9	13	6
	Philadelphia	42	34	.553	37	39	.487	48	26	352	357	12	17	306	312	51	7/21	6	7
	St. Louis	36	38	.486	39	36	.520	11	12	343	380	16	27	328	365	3	4/16	8	6
	Cincinnati	38	42	.475	32	41	.438	5	6	331	317	16	30	351	389			7	8
	Brooklyn	31	42	.425	33	44	.429	10	11	247	303	18	15	292	356			5	6
	Boston	19	54	.260	25	53	.321	28	47	391	536	9	28	308	485	1	4/12	3	16
1911 American League	Philadelphia	54	20	.730	47	30	.610	11	5	384	253	24	12	477	348	66	9/26	10	6
(4/12–10/8)	Detroit	51	25	.671	38	40	.487	21	15	468	403	9	13	363	373	112	8/3	9	4
	Cleveland	46	30	.605	34	43	.442	7	4	368	344	13	13	323	368			10	5
	Chicago	40	37	.519	37	37	.500	8	13	341	299	12	9	378	325			5	6
	Boston	39	37	.513	39	38	.507	20	15	328	312	15	6	352	331			6	7
	New York	36	40	.474	40	36	.526	14	14	365	422	11	12	319	301	6	4/17	7	6
	Washington	39	38	.507	25	52	.325	11	21	323	356	5	18	302	410	3	4/14	5	8
	St. Louis	25	53	.321	20	54	.270	9	10	296	396	8	18	271	416	2	4/13	4	13
1912 National League	New York	49	25	.662	54	23	.701	31	21	387	302	16	15	436	269	151	9/26	16	4
(4/11–10/6)	Pittsburgh	45	31	.592	48	27	.640	15	10	347	275	24	18	404	290			12	4
	Chicago	46	29	.613	45	30	.600	22	18	394	347	21	15	362	321			7	5
	Cincinnati	45	32	.584	30	46	.395	7	2	309	311	14	26	347	411	29	5/19	6	7
	Philadelphia	34	41	.453	39	38	.507	25	26	318	352	18	17	352	336			5	6
	St. Louis	37	40	.481	26	50	.342	14	9	354	414	13	22	305	416	6	4/17	6	9
	Brooklyn	33	43	.434	25	52	.325	17	20	303	368	15	25	348	386			5	7
	Boston	31	47	.397	21	54	.280	22	28	407	471	13	15	286	390	2	4/12	3	10
1912 American League	Boston	57	20	.740	48	27	.640	10	10	417	286	19	8	382	258	130	9/18	10	5
(4/11–10/6)	Washington	45	33	.577	46	28	.622	13	12	336	295	7	11	362	286			17	4
	Philadelphia	45	32	.584	45	30	.600	11	6	381	342	11	6	398	316	5	4/15	7	4
	Chicago	34	43	.442	44	33	.571	11	11	276	340	6	14	362	306	49	6/9	8	6
	Cleveland	39	35	.527	36	43	.456	3	6	338	326	7	9	338	354	2	4/12	9	8
	Detroit	37	39	.487	32	45	.416	8	6	344	370	11	10	376	407			5	7
	St. Louis	27	50	.351	26	51	.338	6	11	287	379	13	6	265	385			7	7
	New York	31	44	.413	19	58	.247	14	16	352	423	4	12	278	419			5	9
1913 National League	New York	54	23	.701	47	28	.627	23	22	367	250	8	16	317	265	102	9/27	14	5
(4/9–10/5)	Philadelphia	43	33	.566	45	30	.600	51	23	361	366	22	17	332	270	63	6/29	8	9
	Chicago	51	25	.671	37	40	.481	37	19	372	273	22	19	348	352	6	5/3	7	6
	Pittsburgh	41	35	.539	37	36	.507	13	6	324	277	22	20	349	308	1	4/12	8	7
	Boston	34	40	.459	35	42	.455	14	12	298	337	18	26	343	353	7	4/16	5	7
	Brooklyn	29	47	.382	36	37	.493	20	14	296	343	19	19	299	270	1	4/17	7	10
	Cincinnati	32	44	.421	32	45	.416	15	13	307	380	12	27	300	337			5	7
	St. Louis	25	48	.342	26	51	.338	8	20	239	346	6	37	284	409	5	4/17	5	8
1913 American League	Philadelphia	50	26	.658	46	31	.597	19	14	388	271	14	10	406	321	173	9/22	15	6
(4/10–10/5)	Washington	43	35	.551	47	29	.618	10	29	297	318	10	6	299	243	13	4/23	6	3
	Cleveland	45	31	.592	41	35	.539	4	9	336	284	12	11	297	252	1	4/11	9	5
	Boston	41	34	.547	38	37	.507	3	0	328	312	14	6	303	298			5	5
	Chicago	40	37	.519	38	37	.507	6	4	216	233	17	6	272	265			5	7
	Detroit	34	42	.447	32	45	.416	9	4	312	368	15	8	312	348			5	9
	New York	27	47	.365	30	47	.390	5	20	265	339	4	12	264	329			4	13
	St. Louis	31	46	.403	26	50	.342	13	11	247	309	5	10	281	333	3	4/12	3	9

		Home Games			Road Games			Home Games				Road Games							
	Team	W	L	PCT	W	L	PCT	HR	OHR	R	OR	HR	OHR	R	OR	DIF	LDF	WS	LS
1914 National League (4/14–10/6)	Boston	51	25	**.671**	43	34	**.558**	17	16	339	279	18	22	318	269	34	**9/28**	9	7
	New York	43	36	.544	41	34	.547	16	**24**	316	288	14	23	**356**	288	**100**	9/7	6	6
	St. Louis	42	34	.553	39	38	.507	20	14	285	280	13	12	273	**260**	1	4/14	7	7
	Chicago	46	30	.605	32	46	.410	22	20	318	281	**20**	17	287	357			9	7
	Brooklyn	45	34	.570	30	45	.400	17	17	342	306	14	19	280	312	7	4/20	**11**	8
	Philadelphia	48	30	.615	26	50	.342	**50**	16	**377**	321	12	**10**	274	366	7	4/20	8	8
	Pittsburgh	39	36	.520	30	49	.380	**3**	6	**234**	**214**	15	21	269	326	39	5/29	8	12
	Cincinnati	34	42	.447	26	52	.333	4	**5**	290	**328**	12	25	240	323	3	4/17	7	**19**
1914 Federal League (4/13–10/10)	Indianapolis	53	23	**.697**	35	42	.455	14	**8**	**439**	339	19	21	323	**283**	50	**10/7**	**15**	6
	Chicago	41	34	.547	46	33	**.582**	**30**	19	**248**	**208**	22	23	**373**	309	**69**	10/5	6	4
	Baltimore	53	26	.671	31	44	.413	25	15	350	298	7	19	295	330	51	8/7	7	7
	Buffalo	47	29	.618	33	42	.440	21	18	345	300	17	27	275	302	2	6/16	6	4
	Brooklyn	47	32	.595	30	45	.400	27	13	358	335	15	18	304	342	7	4/20	7	**9**
	Kansas City	38	37	.507	29	47	.382	28	21	322	306	11	16	322	377			5	7
	Pittsburgh	37	37	.500	27	49	.355	**11**	10	297	307	**23**	29	308	391			5	6
	St. Louis	31	44	.413	31	45	.408	12	**23**	304	**368**	13	**15**	261	329	13	5/13	8	7
1914 American League (4/14–10/7)	Philadelphia	51	24	**.680**	48	29	**.623**	**17**	13	**354**	247	12	**5**	**395**	282	**130**	**9/27**	**12**	5
	Boston	44	31	.587	47	31	.603	**3**	5	**270**	247	**15**	13	318	**264**			6	5
	Washington	40	33	.548	41	40	.506	8	7	282	**246**	10	13	290	273	6	6/7	7	7
	Detroit	42	35	.545	38	38	.500	11	9	315	318	14	8	300	300	33	5/25	8	7
	St. Louis	42	36	.538	29	46	.387	11	14	271	298	6	6	252	316			6	6
	Chicago	43	37	.538	27	47	.365	7	4	271	285	12	11	216	275	14	4/27	7	**8**
	New York	36	40	.474	34	44	.436	8	**24**	278	259	4	6	259	291	4	4/17	5	6
	Cleveland	32	47	.405	19	55	.257	4	**3**	289	**380**	6	7	249	329			4	**8**
1915 National League (4/14–10/7)	Philadelphia	49	27	.645	41	35	**.539**	**46**	18	313	**235**	12	**8**	276	**228**	**135**	**9/29**	**8**	4
	Boston	49	27	.645	34	42	.447	**3**	**5**	280	263	14	18	302	282			**8**	5
	Brooklyn	51	26	**.662**	29	46	.387	9	14	299	263	5	15	237	297			**8**	**8**
	Chicago	42	34	.553	31	46	.403	31	16	296	**314**	**22**	12	274	306	45	7/12	**8**	**8**
	Pittsburgh	40	37	.519	33	44	.429	8	6	290	241	16	15	267	279	1	4/14	6	6
	St. Louis	42	36	.538	30	45	.400	11	10	**320**	303	9	20	270	298			6	6
	Cincinnati	39	37	.513	32	46	.410	6	7	**265**	295	9	21	251	290			6	7
	New York	37	38	.493	32	45	.416	15	**20**	275	270	9	20	**307**	358	2	4/15	5	7
1915 Federal League (4/10–10/3)	Chicago	44	32	.579	42	34	.553	21	10	310	252	**29**	23	330	286	38	**10/3**	6	6
	St. Louis	43	34	.558	44	33	**.571**	12	15	**334**	280	11	**7**	300	**247**	18	7/14	**12**	4
	Pittsburgh	45	31	.592	41	36	.532	**4**	10	292	269	16	27	300	255	**69**	10/1	7	4
	Kansas City	46	31	**.597**	35	41	.461	15	19	274	**249**	13	10	273	302	45	8/21	5	5
	Newark	40	39	.506	40	33	.548	**4**	**2**	**267**	271	13	13	318	291	17	8/23	8	6
	Buffalo	37	40	.481	37	38	.493	21	21	290	324	19	14	284	310			8	6
	Brooklyn	34	40	.459	36	42	.462	20	11	315	324	16	16	**332**	349	11	4/23	10	8
	Baltimore	24	51	.320	23	56	.291	**29**	**36**	299	**419**	7	16	251	341			4	**9**
1915 American League (4/14–10/7)	Boston	55	20	**.733**	46	30	.605	5	4	323	**221**	9	14	345	278	**84**	**9/30**	8	5
	Detroit	50	26	.658	50	28	**.641**	11	7	**410**	314	12	7	**368**	283	23	6/7	9	4
	Chicago	54	24	.692	39	37	.513	9	4	353	236	**16**	10	364	273	59	7/17	**11**	6
	Washington	48	28	.632	37	40	.481	**2**	**2**	277	235	10	10	292	**256**	2	4/16	7	8
	New York	37	43	.463	32	40	.444	**28**	**32**	306	303	3	9	278	285	11	5/21	7	8
	St. Louis	35	38	.479	28	53	.346	6	7	**237**	315	13	14	284	364			7	8
	Cleveland	27	50	.351	30	45	.400	7	9	277	362	13	10	262	308	2	4/16	6	7
	Philadelphia	20	55	.267	23	54	.299	9	18	285	**457**	7	**3**	260	431	1	4/14	3	**11**
1916 National League (4/12–10/5)	Brooklyn	50	27	**.649**	44	33	.571	19	9	300	233	9	15	285	238	**152**	**10/3**	8	5
	Philadelphia	50	29	.633	41	33	.554	29	17	281	233	13	11	300	256	18	9/8	8	5
	Boston	41	31	.569	48	32	**.600**	6	**4**	**224**	**207**	16	20	**318**	246	10	9/4	6	7
	New York	47	30	.610	39	36	.520	21	**23**	291	229	**21**	18	306	275			**26**	8
	Chicago	37	41	.474	30	45	.400	**34**	22	**309**	**317**	12	**10**	211	**224**	2	4/28	7	8
	Pittsburgh	37	40	.481	28	49	.364	9	5	268	298	11	19	216	288			5	10
	Cincinnati	32	44	.421	28	49	.364	**4**	10	242	312	10	25	263	305			4	8
	St. Louis	36	40	.474	24	53	.312	12	15	251	295	13	16	225	334	1	4/12	5	**14**
1916 American League (4/12–10/4)	Boston	49	28	**.636**	42	35	**.545**	**1**	**1**	252	**205**	**13**	9	298	275	**73**	**10/1**	7	4
	Chicago	49	28	**.636**	40	37	.519	9	5	326	254	8	9	275	**243**	6	8/8	7	8
	Detroit	49	28	**.636**	38	39	.494	7	8	**350**	313	10	**4**	**320**	282	6	9/17	9	5
	New York	46	31	.597	34	43	.442	**22**	**22**	306	277	**13**	15	271	284	35	7/29	7	9
	St. Louis	45	32	.584	34	43	.442	7	10	290	238	7	5	298	307	3	4/14	**14**	7
	Cleveland	44	33	.571	33	44	.429	4	9	323	293	12	7	307	309	47	7/12	8	8
	Washington	49	28	**.636**	27	49	.355	6	**1**	294	248	6	13	242	295	16	6/2	7	7
	Philadelphia	23	53	.303	13	64	.169	15	17	**231**	**399**	4	9	216	377			2	**20**
1917 National League (4/11–10/4)	New York	50	28	**.641**	48	28	**.632**	21	17	294	**220**	**18**	12	**341**	237	**151**	**9/24**	6	3
	Philadelphia	46	29	.613	41	36	.532	**26**	**20**	**297**	270	12	**5**	281	**230**	23	6/26	6	6
	St. Louis	38	38	.500	44	32	.579	15	15	266	302	11	14	265	265	1	5/6	7	4
	Cincinnati	39	38	.507	39	38	.507	10	**3**	279	296	16	17	322	315	2	4/12	7	**8**
	Chicago	35	42	.455	39	38	.507	11	14	273	305	6	20	279	262	10	5/21	**10**	6
	Boston	35	42	.455	37	39	.487	13	**3**	240	269	9	16	296	283	1	4/20	5	5
	Brooklyn	36	38	.486	34	43	.442	14	14	270	288	11	18	241	271			7	7
	Pittsburgh	25	53	.321	26	50	.342	**2**	4	**232**	**307**	7	10	232	288			4	7

1917 American League
(4/11–10/4)

Team	Home Games W	L	PCT	Road Games W	L	PCT	Home Games HR	OHR	R	OR	Road Games HR	OHR	R	OR	DIF	LDF	WS	LS
Chicago	56	21	**.727**	44	33	.571	7	**3**	**327**	**204**	11	7	329	260	**126**	**9/21**	9	4
Boston	45	33	.577	45	29	**.608**	3	4	293	245	11	8	262	**209**	53	8/17	**10**	4
Cleveland	43	34	.558	45	32	.584	5	8	317	314	8	9	267	229	5	4/15	**10**	4
Detroit	34	41	.453	44	34	.564	5	5	285	303	**20**	7	**354**	274			6	7
Washington	42	36	.538	32	43	.427	**1**	**3**	264	255	3	9	279	311	4	4/14	7	**10**
New York	35	40	.467	36	42	.462	**19**	**24**	269	292	8	**4**	255	266	2	5/19	5	8
St. Louis	31	46	.403	26	51	.338	7	11	**252**	**337**	8	8	258	350			3	8
Philadelphia	29	47	.382	26	51	.338	11	17	264	319	6	6	265	372			4	7

1918 National League
(4/15–9/2)

Team	Home Games W	L	PCT	Road Games W	L	PCT	Home Games HR	OHR	R	OR	Road Games HR	OHR	R	OR	DIF	LDF	WS	LS
Chicago	50	26	**.658**	34	19	**.642**	9	5	**300**	235	12	8	238	**158**	**89**	**8/24**	**9**	4
New York	35	21	.625	36	32	.529	9	**13**	204	**181**	4	**7**	**276**	234	51	6/5	**9**	6
Cincinnati	46	24	.657	22	36	.379	9	5	298	256	6	14	232	240	1	4/16	8	**9**
Pittsburgh	41	27	.603	24	33	.421	9	4	270	232	6	9	196	180			8	7
Brooklyn	33	21	.611	24	48	.333	**4**	12	173	185	6	10	187	278			4	**9**
Philadelphia	27	29	.482	28	39	.418	**19**	**13**	220	261	6	9	210	246	1	4/16	5	**9**
Boston	23	29	.442	30	42	.417	5	**2**	**163**	183	8	12	261	286			5	6
St. Louis	32	40	.444	19	38	.333	14	7	241	**280**	**13**	9	213	247	2	4/17	4	6

1918 American League
(4/15–9/2)

Team	Home Games W	L	PCT	Road Games W	L	PCT	Home Games HR	OHR	R	OR	Road Games HR	OHR	R	OR	DIF	LDF	WS	LS
Boston	49	21	**.700**	26	30	.464	2	**3**	272	**165**	**13**	6	202	215	**129**	**8/31**	6	6
Cleveland	38	22	.633	35	32	.522	**1**	4	**274**	219	8	6	230	228	8	7/5	**7**	3
Washington	41	32	.562	31	24	**.564**	2	6	268	238	3	4	193	**174**			**7**	4
New York	37	29	.561	23	34	.404	10	**22**	251	237	10	**3**	242	238	8	7/3	4	7
St. Louis	23	30	.434	35	34	.507	**1**	7	**178**	195	4	4	248	253	2	4/17	6	6
Chicago	30	26	.536	27	41	.397	4	4	216	194	5	5	241	252			5	**8**
Detroit	28	29	.491	27	42	.391	2	7	221	246	11	4	**255**	311			5	7
Philadelphia	35	32	.522	17	44	.279	**15**	8	256	**273**	7	5	156	265			5	**8**

1919 National League
(4/19–9/28)

Team	Home Games W	L	PCT	Road Games W	L	PCT	Home Games HR	OHR	R	OR	Road Games HR	OHR	R	OR	DIF	LDF	WS	LS
Cincinnati	52	19	**.732**	44	25	**.638**	10	**5**	**315**	**189**	10	16	262	**212**	75	**9/16**	**10**	4
New York	46	23	.667	41	30	.577	28	17	310	209	12	17	**295**	261	**76**	7/31	7	4
Chicago	40	31	.563	35	34	.507	11	7	232	190	10	**7**	222	217	1	4/24	7	6
Pittsburgh	40	30	.571	31	38	.449	**8**	7	273	218	9	16	199	248			7	6
Brooklyn	36	33	.522	33	38	.465	12	10	243	227	**13**	11	282	286	21	5/15	6	10
Boston	29	38	.433	28	44	.389	11	9	**231**	265	**13**	20	234	298			4	9
St. Louis	34	35	.493	20	48	.294	9	10	240	244	9	15	223	308			7	9
Philadelphia	26	44	.371	21	46	.313	**29**	**24**	307	**378**	**13**	16	203	321			5	**13**

1919 American League
(4/23–9/29)

Team	Home Games W	L	PCT	Road Games W	L	PCT	Home Games HR	OHR	R	OR	Road Games HR	OHR	R	OR	DIF	LDF	WS	LS
Chicago	48	22	**.686**	40	30	**.571**	5	11	**344**	279	20	14	323	255	**134**	**9/24**	**10**	4
Cleveland	44	25	.638	40	30	**.571**	12	4	340	276	13	15	296	261	2	6/19	**10**	6
New York	46	25	.648	34	34	.500	**33**	30	326	255	12	17	252	**251**	21	7/9	8	6
Detroit	46	24	.657	34	36	.486	10	14	307	243	13	21	311	335	1	4/25	8	6
St. Louis	40	30	.571	27	42	.391	19	23	280	249	12	**12**	253	318			6	9
Boston	35	30	.538	31	41	.431	10	**3**	**233**	**241**	**23**	13	**331**	311	6	4/28	9	6
Washington	32	40	.444	24	44	.353	**2**	5	265	282	22	15	268	288	1	4/23	4	**11**
Philadelphia	21	49	.300	15	55	.214	29	**31**	266	**400**	6	13	191	342			2	9

1920 National League
(4/14–10/3)

Team	Home Games W	L	PCT	Road Games W	L	PCT	Home Games HR	OHR	R	OR	Road Games HR	OHR	R	OR	DIF	LDF	WS	LS
Brooklyn	49	29	**.628**	44	32	**.579**	17	14	**360**	291	11	11	300	**237**	**87**	**9/27**	**10**	6
New York	45	35	.563	41	33	.554	31	**33**	334	282	15	11	348	261			6	5
Cincinnati	42	34	.553	40	37	.519	**5**	**1**	281	**238**	13	25	**358**	331	75	9/8	6	6
Pittsburgh	42	35	.545	37	40	.481	6	4	276	263	10	21	254	289	15	5/27	6	6
Chicago	43	34	.558	32	45	.416	19	15	322	302	15	22	297	333	4	5/31	9	**10**
St. Louis	38	38	.500	37	41	.474	10	10	330	332	**22**	20	345	350			7	7
Boston	36	37	.493	26	53	.329	**5**	11	**271**	292	18	28	252	378	4	4/17	7	**10**
Philadelphia	32	45	.416	30	46	.395	**50**	30	339	**380**	14	**5**	226	334	1	5/3	5	9

1920 American League
(4/14–10/3)

Team	Home Games W	L	PCT	Road Games W	L	PCT	Home Games HR	OHR	R	OR	Road Games HR	OHR	R	OR	DIF	LDF	WS	LS
Cleveland	51	27	.654	47	29	**.618**	20	10	441	330	15	21	**416**	**312**	**134**	**10/2**	7	5
Chicago	52	25	**.675**	44	33	.571	18	10	381	**298**	19	35	413	367	31	8/31	7	7
New York	49	28	.636	46	31	.597	**71**	36	424	308	**44**	**12**	414	321	9	9/15	**10**	4
St. Louis	40	38	.513	36	39	.480	31	33	**473**	415	19	20	324	351			**10**	7
Boston	41	35	.539	31	46	.403	**3**	14	327	300	19	25	323	398	14	5/27	6	5
Washington	37	38	.493	31	46	.403	5	**7**	343	386	31	44	380	416			7	10
Detroit	32	46	.410	29	47	.382	12	24	336	**452**	18	22	316	381			4	13
Philadelphia	25	50	.333	23	56	.291	35	**40**	**254**	401	9	16	304	433	1	4/14	3	**18**

1921 National League
(4/13–10/2)

Team	Home Games W	L	PCT	Road Games W	L	PCT	Home Games HR	OHR	R	OR	Road Games HR	OHR	R	OR	DIF	LDF	WS	LS
New York	53	26	**.671**	41	33	.554	47	46	**407**	321	28	33	**433**	316	32	**9/28**	10	6
Pittsburgh	45	31	.592	45	32	**.584**	13	10	343	295	24	27	349	**300**	**140**	9/10	9	6
St. Louis	48	29	.623	39	37	.513	43	25	397	307	40	36	412	374			10	6
Boston	42	32	.568	37	42	.468	20	18	332	**292**	**41**	36	389	405			8	**7**
Brooklyn	41	37	.526	36	38	.486	32	23	360	361	27	**23**	307	320	1	4/13	**11**	6
Cincinnati	40	36	.526	30	47	.390	**5**	**2**	**321**	306	15	35	297	343	1	4/13	5	6
Chicago	32	44	.421	32	45	.416	23	37	345	434	14	30	323	339	7	4/19	4	**7**
Philadelphia	29	47	.382	22	56	.282	**67**	**49**	326	**485**	21	30	291	434			4	**7**

1921 American League
(4/13–10/2)

Team	Home Games W	L	PCT	Road Games W	L	PCT	Home Games HR	OHR	R	OR	Road Games HR	OHR	R	OR	DIF	LDF	WS	LS
New York	53	25	**.679**	45	30	**.600**	**83**	34	**500**	355	**51**	**17**	448	**353**	54	**10/1**	9	5
Cleveland	51	26	.662	43	34	.558	15	**10**	467	**330**	27	33	**458**	382	**115**	9/19	8	5
St. Louis	43	34	.558	38	39	.494	42	43	423	434	25	28	412	411	1	4/13	8	4
Washington	46	30	.605	34	43	.442	14	13	358	332	28	38	346	406	4	4/30	**11**	10
Boston	41	36	.532	34	43	.442	**3**	16	**332**	333	14	37	336	363	1	4/13	5	8
Detroit	37	40	.481	34	42	.447	19	28	433	412	39	43	450	440	1	4/14	6	9
Chicago	37	40	.481	25	52	.325	13	20	378	399	22	32	305	459			5	**11**
Philadelphia	28	47	.373	25	53	.321	65	**59**	353	**464**	17	26	304	430			4	10

		Home Games			Road Games			Home Games				Road Games							
	Team	**W**	**L**	**PCT**	**W**	**L**	**PCT**	**HR**	**OHR**	**R**	**OR**	**HR**	**OHR**	**R**	**OR**	**DIF**	**LDF**	**WS**	**LS**
1922 National League (4/12–10/1)	New York	51	27	**.654**	42	34	.553	48	38	439	333	32	33	413	**325**	**162**	**9/25**	8	5
	Cincinnati	48	29	.623	38	39	.494	8	**13**	378	**297**	37	36	388	380			7	8
	Pittsburgh	45	33	.577	40	36	.526	22	16	439	390	30	35	426	346			**13**	6
	St. Louis	42	35	.545	43	34	**.558**	59	31	446	414	**48**	30	417	405	11	8/11	8	5
	Chicago	39	37	.513	41	37	.526	22	37	344	382	20	40	**427**	426	6	4/27	8	5
	Brooklyn	44	34	.564	32	44	.421	25	35	380	326	31	39	363	428	1	4/12	8	8
	Philadelphia	35	41	.461	22	55	.286	**94**	**60**	**449**	**517**	21	**29**	289	403	2	4/13	4	**12**
	Boston	32	43	.427	21	57	.269	**6**	15	**287**	373	26	42	309	449			6	9
1922 American League (4/12–10/1)	New York	50	27	.649	44	33	**.571**	53	48	387	**291**	**42**	**25**	371	**327**	**95**	**9/30**	7	8
	St. Louis	54	23	**.701**	39	38	.507	70	41	**471**	314	28	30	396	329	78	9/7	5	3
	Detroit	43	34	.558	36	41	.468	15	32	426	370	39	30	**402**	421			8	6
	Cleveland	44	35	.557	34	41	.453	12	20	423	424	20	38	345	393	10	4/21	**12**	6
	Chicago	43	34	.558	34	43	.442	10	21	351	335	35	36	340	356			8	7
	Washington	40	39	.506	29	46	.387	15	**3**	329	295	30	46	321	411	1	4/12	5	7
	Philadelphia	38	39	.494	27	50	.351	**80**	**82**	388	**437**	31	**25**	317	393	1	4/12	4	7
	Boston	31	42	.425	30	51	.370	**6**	17	**280**	344	39	31	318	425			5	**9**
1923 National League (4/17–10/7)	New York	47	30	**.610**	48	28	**.632**	41	53	408	362	**44**	29	**446**	**317**	**174**	**9/28**	**11**	6
	Cincinnati	46	32	.590	45	31	.592	**6**	**4**	337	**300**	39	24	371	329	1	4/17	9	6
	Pittsburgh	47	30	**.610**	40	37	.519	16	9	381	322	33	44	405	374	1	4/17	7	5
	Chicago	46	31	.597	37	40	.481	63	57	402	354	27	29	354	350			7	6
	St. Louis	42	35	.545	37	39	.487	22	27	335	320	41	43	411	412			6	6
	Brooklyn	37	40	.481	39	38	.507	26	27	348	383	36	28	405	358	1	4/18	5	10
	Boston	22	55	.286	32	45	.416	7	27	**291**	429	25	37	345	369			6	**12**
	Philadelphia	20	55	.267	30	49	.380	**76**	**77**	**418**	**597**	36	**23**	330	411			3	7
1923 American League (4/18–10/7)	New York	46	30	**.605**	52	24	**.684**	**62**	**50**	407	**329**	**43**	18	416	**293**	**161**	**9/20**	**9**	3
	Detroit	45	32	.584	38	39	.494	21	31	400	351	20	27	431	390	5	5/4	5	3
	Cleveland	42	36	.538	40	35	.533	22	16	**455**	393	37	20	**433**	353	15	5/2	6	6
	Washington	43	34	.558	32	44	.421	**7**	16	363	339	19	40	357	408			6	7
	St. Louis	40	36	.526	34	42	.447	50	43	377	364	32	**15**	311	356			6	5
	Philadelphia	34	41	.453	35	42	.455	28	32	345	360	24	36	316	401	3	4/20	6	**12**
	Chicago	30	45	.400	39	40	.494	13	24	**327**	348	29	25	365	393			4	4
	Boston	37	40	.481	24	51	.320	11	**15**	**327**	**402**	23	33	257	407			5	5
1924 National League (4/15–9/29)	New York	51	26	**.662**	42	34	.553	51	40	385	**272**	44	37	**472**	369	**153**	**9/27**	10	5
	Brooklyn	46	31	.597	46	31	**.597**	26	30	342	338	**46**	28	375	337	1	4/15	**15**	3
	Pittsburgh	49	28	.636	41	35	.539	19	17	393	293	24	25	331	**295**			9	4
	Cincinnati	43	33	.566	40	37	.519	**3**	**3**	311	283	33	27	338	296	9	5/20	6	4
	Chicago	46	31	.597	35	41	.461	33	**68**	373	341	33	21	325	358	5	6/14	6	5
	St. Louis	40	37	.519	25	52	.325	32	37	**419**	359	35	32	321	391	1	4/15	7	7
	Philadelphia	26	49	.347	29	47	.382	**58**	64	369	**483**	36	**20**	307	366			5	**10**
	Boston	28	48	.368	25	52	.325	9	8	**254**	366	16	41	266	434	3	4/18	4	**10**
1924 American League (4/15–9/30)	Washington	47	30	**.610**	45	32	.584	**1**	**7**	371	**280**	21	27	384	**333**	52	**9/29**	**10**	6
	New York	45	32	.584	44	31	**.587**	**57**	46	397	324	**41**	**13**	401	343	**97**	9/18	8	6
	Detroit	45	33	.577	41	35	.539	17	28	**427**	393	18	27	**422**	403	27	8/12	8	5
	St. Louis	41	36	.532	33	42	.440	44	**49**	426	**445**	23	19	343	364	1	4/15	6	6
	Philadelphia	36	39	.480	35	42	.455	32	24	**328**	391	31	19	357	387			4	12
	Cleveland	37	38	.493	30	48	.385	13	18	374	375	28	25	381	439			5	9
	Boston	41	36	.532	26	51	.338	8	17	402	391	22	26	335	415	16	6/13	6	9
	Chicago	37	39	.487	29	48	.377	13	23	403	414	28	29	390	444	6	5/2	4	**13**
1925 National League (4/14–10/4)	Pittsburgh	52	25	**.675**	43	33	**.566**	27	31	481	342	51	50	**431**	373	**93**	**9/23**	**9**	4
	New York	47	29	.618	39	37	.513	55	39	362	334	**59**	34	374	368	75	8/1	8	6
	Cincinnati	44	32	.579	36	41	.468	**10**	**5**	334	**285**	34	**30**	356	**358**	6	4/19	**9**	5
	St. Louis	48	28	.632	29	48	.377	66	41	449	359	43	45	379	405			7	7
	Boston	37	39	.487	33	44	.429	15	14	**315**	383	26	53	393	419	2	4/15	5	5
	Brooklyn	40	37	.519	28	48	.368	25	41	383	407	39	34	403	459	2	4/15	6	**12**
	Philadelphia	38	39	.494	30	46	.395	**73**	**74**	**488**	**547**	27	43	324	383			5	11
	Chicago	37	40	.481	31	46	.403	57	63	367	359	29	39	356	414	2	4/17	5	6
1925 American League (4/14–10/4)	Washington	53	22	**.707**	43	33	**.566**	13	**13**	408	**298**	43	36	421	372	76	**9/24**	7	4
	Philadelphia	51	26	.662	37	38	.493	35	37	435	351	41	23	396	**362**	**98**	8/19	9	**12**
	St. Louis	45	32	.584	37	39	.487	**73**	**73**	**503**	**501**	37	26	397	405			6	6
	Detroit	43	34	.558	38	39	.494	18	36	451	399	32	34	**452**	430	1	4/14	**10**	7
	Chicago	44	33	.571	35	42	.455	13	32	366	378	25	37	445	392			7	5
	Cleveland	37	39	.487	33	45	.423	23	19	421	430	29	**22**	361	387	17	5/7	6	8
	New York	42	36	.538	27	49	.355	54	56	354	356	**56**	**22**	352	418	1	4/14	5	5
	Boston	28	47	.373	19	58	.247	**10**	28	**309**	441	31	39	330	481			3	9
1926 National League (4/13–9/29)	St. Louis	47	30	.610	42	35	**.545**	**54**	42	411	359	**36**	34	**406**	319	30	**9/25**	8	5
	Cincinnati	53	23	**.697**	34	44	.436	8	8	372	**259**	27	32	375	392	**75**	9/16	**10**	6
	Pittsburgh	49	28	.636	35	41	.461	17	16	**446**	374	27	35	323	315	38	8/30	5	7
	Chicago	49	28	.636	33	44	.429	38	17	377	295	28	**21**	305	**307**			8	5
	New York	43	33	.566	31	44	.413	45	**43**	333	317	28	27	330	351	11	4/29	7	6
	Brooklyn	38	38	.500	33	44	.429	23	26	314	331	17	24	309	374	16	5/14	6	**9**
	Boston	43	34	.558	23	52	.307	**4**	**5**	**296**	266	12	41	328	453			8	**9**
	Philadelphia	33	42	.440	25	51	.329	51	42	392	**470**	24	26	295	430	5	4/17	5	6

1926 American League
(4/13–9/29)

Team	Home Games W	Home Games L	Home Games PCT	Road Games W	Road Games L	Road Games PCT	Home Games HR	Home Games OHR	Home Games R	Home Games OR	Road Games HR	Road Games OHR	Road Games R	Road Games OR	DIF	LDF	WS	LS
New York	50	25	**.667**	41	38	.519	**58**	33	**417**	326	**63**	23	**430**	387	**158**	**9/25**	**16**	4
Cleveland	49	31	.613	39	35	.527	11	19	376	301	16	30	362	311	13	5/11	9	6
Philadelphia	44	27	.620	39	40	.494	34	27	365	314	27	**11**	312	**256**			9	7
Washington	42	30	.583	39	39	.500	**4**	**15**	373	378	39	30	429	383	4	4/19	10	5
Chicago	47	31	.603	34	41	.453	8	19	332	**294**	24	28	398	371	7	4/19	8	6
Detroit	39	41	.488	40	34	**.541**	16	38	380	**445**	20	20	413	385	1	4/20	7	6
St. Louis	40	39	.506	22	53	.293	53	**64**	375	429	19	22	307	416			5	7
Boston	25	51	.329	21	56	.273	9	16	**288**	438	23	29	274	397			5	**17**

1927 National League
(4/12–10/2)

Team	Home Games W	Home Games L	Home Games PCT	Road Games W	Road Games L	Road Games PCT	Home Games HR	Home Games OHR	Home Games R	Home Games OR	Road Games HR	Road Games OHR	Road Games R	Road Games OR	DIF	LDF	WS	LS
Pittsburgh	48	31	.608	46	29	**.613**	25	23	406	345	29	35	411	314	**104**	**10/1**	11	3
St. Louis	55	25	**.688**	37	36	.507	55	**51**	**433**	354	29	**21**	321	**311**	10	5/10	6	6
New York	49	25	.662	43	37	.538	**62**	49	389	342	**47**	28	**428**	378	19	5/20	10	6
Chicago	50	28	.641	35	40	.467	37	19	398	315	37	31	352	346	49	8/31	**12**	7
Cincinnati	45	35	.563	30	43	.411	**3**	11	348	320	26	25	295	333			8	6
Brooklyn	34	39	.466	31	49	.388	20	35	**266**	**296**	19	28	275	323	1	4/12	5	7
Boston	32	41	.438	28	53	.346	5	**10**	296	339	32	33	355	432			4	**15**
Philadelphia	34	43	.442	17	60	.221	32	46	375	**429**	25	38	303	474			4	14

1927 American League
(4/12–10/2)

Team	Home Games W	Home Games L	Home Games PCT	Road Games W	Road Games L	Road Games PCT	Home Games HR	Home Games OHR	Home Games R	Home Games OR	Road Games HR	Road Games OHR	Road Games R	Road Games OR	DIF	LDF	WS	LS
New York	57	19	**.750**	53	25	**.679**	**83**	30	**479**	**267**	**75**	**12**	**496**	**332**	**173**	**9/13**	9	4
Philadelphia	50	27	.649	41	36	.532	26	36	412	327	30	29	429	399	1	4/30	6	7
Washington	51	28	.646	34	41	.453	10	19	416	308	19	34	366	422	4	4/15	10	12
Detroit	44	32	.579	38	39	.494	25	28	467	433	26	24	378	372	2	4/20	**13**	8
Chicago	38	37	.507	32	46	.410	6	22	337	343	30	33	325	365			7	12
Cleveland	35	42	.455	31	45	.408	10	**11**	333	367	16	26	335	399	1	4/12	7	8
St. Louis	38	38	.500	21	56	.273	42	**57**	440	**457**	13	22	284	447	1	4/16	6	8
Boston	29	49	.372	22	54	.289	**5**	29	**299**	409	23	27	298	447			6	**15**

1928 National League
(4/11–9/30)

Team	Home Games W	Home Games L	Home Games PCT	Road Games W	Road Games L	Road Games PCT	Home Games HR	Home Games OHR	Home Games R	Home Games OR	Road Games HR	Road Games OHR	Road Games R	Road Games OR	DIF	LDF	WS	LS
St. Louis	42	35	.545	53	24	**.688**	62	51	367	336	51	35	**440**	**300**	**107**	**9/29**	8	4
New York	51	26	.662	42	35	.545	**80**	46	411	315	38	**31**	396	338	32	8/21	9	8
Chicago	52	25	**.675**	39	38	.507	40	18	335	**264**	**52**	38	379	351	7	5/21	**13**	5
Pittsburgh	47	30	.610	38	37	.507	16	**14**	**479**	356	36	51	358	348			9	6
Cincinnati	44	33	.571	34	41	.453	**3**	17	324	318	29	41	324	368	30	6/14	7	8
Brooklyn	41	35	.539	36	41	.468	31	25	330	296	35	34	335	344	4	4/30	6	5
Boston	25	51	.329	25	52	.325	24	62	**309**	448	28	38	322	430			4	10
Philadelphia	26	49	.347	17	60	.221	54	**67**	360	**521**	31	42	300	436	2	4/12	4	**12**

1928 American League
(4/10–9/30)

Team	Home Games W	Home Games L	Home Games PCT	Road Games W	Road Games L	Road Games PCT	Home Games HR	Home Games OHR	Home Games R	Home Games OR	Road Games HR	Road Games OHR	Road Games R	Road Games OR	DIF	LDF	WS	LS
New York	52	25	**.675**	49	28	**.636**	**69**	36	400	301	**64**	**23**	**494**	384	**165**	**9/28**	8	3
Philadelphia	52	25	**.675**	46	30	.605	54	33	**430**	**295**	35	33	399	**320**	2	9/8	**10**	6
St. Louis	44	33	.571	38	39	.494	51	**64**	398	389	12	29	374	353	5	4/15	5	9
Washington	37	43	.463	38	36	.514	16	**12**	363	378	24	28	355	327			6	9
Chicago	37	40	.481	35	42	.455	11	28	316	369	13	38	340	356			6	7
Detroit	36	41	.468	32	45	.416	33	26	382	400	29	32	362	404			5	7
Cleveland	29	48	.377	33	44	.429	**10**	15	366	**443**	24	37	308	387	12	4/28	4	**11**
Boston	26	47	.356	31	49	.388	**10**	15	**283**	363	28	34	306	407	1	4/10	6	7

1929 National League
(4/16–10/6)

Team	Home Games W	Home Games L	Home Games PCT	Road Games W	Road Games L	Road Games PCT	Home Games HR	Home Games OHR	Home Games R	Home Games OR	Road Games HR	Road Games OHR	Road Games R	Road Games OR	DIF	LDF	WS	LS
Chicago	52	25	**.675**	46	29	**.613**	76	41	490	374	63	**36**	**492**	384	**102**	**9/18**	**9**	4
Pittsburgh	45	31	.592	43	34	.558	28	37	471	382	32	58	433	398	40	7/23	8	4
New York	39	37	.513	45	30	.600	79	59	418	374	57	43	479	**335**	7	4/25	6	5
St. Louis	43	32	.573	35	42	.455	48	50	414	386	52	51	417	420	19	6/18	7	**11**
Philadelphia	39	37	.513	32	45	.416	**86**	**74**	**503**	**580**	**67**	49	394	452			8	9
Brooklyn	42	35	.545	28	48	.368	53	48	371	413	46	44	384	475			5	9
Cincinnati	38	39	.494	28	49	.364	**7**	**18**	356	**356**	27	43	330	404	1	4/17	5	9
Boston	34	43	.442	22	55	.286	11	39	**318**	403	22	64	339	473	18	5/7	5	**11**

1929 American League
(4/16–10/6)

Team	Home Games W	Home Games L	Home Games PCT	Road Games W	Road Games L	Road Games PCT	Home Games HR	Home Games OHR	Home Games R	Home Games OR	Road Games HR	Road Games OHR	Road Games R	Road Games OR	DIF	LDF	WS	LS
Philadelphia	57	16	**.781**	47	30	**.610**	**72**	47	**484**	**302**	50	**26**	417	**313**	**159**	**9/14**	**11**	4
New York	49	28	.636	39	38	.507	69	55	463	362	**73**	28	436	413	10	5/13	8	5
Cleveland	44	32	.579	37	39	.487	27	21	359	363	35	35	358	373	3	4/24	6	5
St. Louis	41	36	.532	38	37	.507	22	**58**	370	341	24	42	363	372	11	5/4	7	5
Washington	37	40	.481	34	41	.453	**10**	**17**	376	390	38	31	354	386			5	6
Detroit	38	39	.494	32	45	.416	57	33	476	**453**	53	40	**450**	475			6	7
Chicago	35	41	.461	24	52	.316	19	41	**306**	366	18	43	321	426			5	6
Boston	32	45	.416	26	51	.338	11	36	328	399	17	42	277	404			4	**8**

1930 National League
(4/15–9/28)

Team	Home Games W	Home Games L	Home Games PCT	Road Games W	Road Games L	Road Games PCT	Home Games HR	Home Games OHR	Home Games R	Home Games OR	Road Games HR	Road Games OHR	Road Games R	Road Games OR	DIF	LDF	WS	LS
St. Louis	53	24	**.688**	39	38	.507	52	50	541	383	52	**37**	463	**401**	22	**9/26**	9	7
Chicago	51	26	.662	39	38	.507	**93**	62	538	454	**78**	49	460	416	40	9/12	9	4
New York	47	31	.603	40	36	**.526**	91	63	468	395	52	54	**491**	419	28	5/17	9	5
Brooklyn	49	27	.645	37	41	.474	73	66	438	**336**	49	49	433	402	**76**	9/15	**11**	7
Pittsburgh	42	35	.545	38	39	.494	26	51	433	454	60	77	458	474	6	5/3	7	5
Boston	39	38	.507	31	46	.403	29	51	329	401	37	66	364	434			4	7
Cincinnati	37	40	.481	22	55	.286	**20**	**21**	**300**	368	54	54	365	489			7	**13**
Philadelphia	35	42	.455	17	60	.221	72	**72**	**543**	**644**	54	70	401	555	4	4/18	3	11

1930 American League
(4/14–9/28)

Team	Home Games W	Home Games L	Home Games PCT	Road Games W	Road Games L	Road Games PCT	Home Games HR	Home Games OHR	Home Games R	Home Games OR	Road Games HR	Road Games OHR	Road Games R	Road Games OR	DIF	LDF	WS	LS
Philadelphia	58	18	**.763**	44	34	**.564**	**76**	49	485	329	49	35	466	422	**134**	**9/18**	**10**	5
Washington	56	21	.727	38	39	.494	17	**15**	474	**300**	40	37	418	**389**	31	7/12	**10**	5
New York	47	29	.618	39	39	.500	69	54	471	390	**83**	39	**591**	508			6	7
Cleveland	44	33	.571	37	40	.481	34	46	**494**	469	38	39	396	446	6	6/14	7	7
Detroit	45	33	.577	30	46	.395	45	48	441	419	37	38	342	414	3	4/17	6	7
St. Louis	38	40	.487	26	50	.342	35	**72**	432	**475**	40	52	319	411			6	7
Chicago	34	44	.436	28	48	.368	25	42	393	457	38	**32**	336	427	2	4/18	4	6
Boston	30	46	.395	22	56	.282	**15**	31	**287**	354	32	44	325	460	1	4/14	5	**14**

	Team	Home Games			Road Games			Home Games				Road Games							
		W	L	PCT	W	L	PCT	HR	OHR	R	OR	HR	OHR	R	OR	DIF	LDF	WS	LS
1931 National League	St. Louis	54	24	**.692**	47	29	**.618**	31	29	**439**	320	29	36	376	**294**	**164**	**9/16**	**8**	4
(4/14–9/27)	New York	50	27	.649	37	38	.493	**80**	**47**	379	**274**	21	**24**	389	325	5	5/29	**8**	4
	Chicago	50	27	.649	34	43	.442	40	22	414	311	**44**	32	**414**	399	5	4/30	**8**	8
	Brooklyn	46	29	.613	33	44	.429	46	22	363	317	25	34	318	356			6	5
	Pittsburgh	44	33	.571	31	46	.403	25	16	343	327	16	39	293	364			**8**	6
	Philadelphia	40	36	.526	26	52	.333	53	33	391	**423**	28	42	293	405			5	**10**
	Boston	36	41	.468	28	49	.364	16	24	**278**	318	18	42	255	362	7	4/27	4	9
	Cincinnati	38	39	.494	20	57	.260	**6**	**3**	312	328	15	48	280	414			6	7
1931 American League	Philadelphia	60	15	**.800**	47	30	**.610**	61	37	446	**289**	57	36	412	**337**	**140**	**9/15**	**17**	4
(4/14–9/27)	New York	51	25	.671	43	34	.558	**84**	39	**545**	337	**71**	28	**522**	423	14	5/11	10	4
	Washington	55	22	.714	37	40	.481	13	**24**	453	308	36	49	390	383	4	4/21	12	4
	Cleveland	45	31	.592	33	45	.423	38	32	503	405	33	32	382	428	18	5/8	10	**12**
	St. Louis	39	38	.507	24	53	.312	42	**48**	407	425	34	36	315	445	3	4/18	8	9
	Boston	39	40	.494	23	50	.315	**11**	29	**332**	362	26	**25**	293	438			5	8
	Detroit	36	41	.468	25	52	.325	19	43	349	**432**	24	36	302	404			4	8
	Chicago	31	45	.408	25	52	.325	**11**	45	341	421	16	37	363	518			5	10
1932 National League	Chicago	53	24	**.688**	37	40	.481	32	33	390	303	37	**35**	330	**330**	**102**	**9/20**	**14**	4
(4/12–9/25)	Pittsburgh	45	31	.592	41	37	**.526**	22	25	352	338	26	61	349	373	44	8/10	11	**10**
	Brooklyn	44	34	.564	37	39	.487	59	31	378	353	**51**	41	374	394	1		6	5
	Philadelphia	45	32	.584	33	44	.429	**86**	**71**	**507**	**429**	36	36	337	367	7	4/19	5	6
	Boston	44	33	.571	33	44	.429	27	20	299	**285**	36	41	350	370	22	6/10	6	8
	New York	37	40	.481	35	42	.455	78	**71**	362	359	38	41	**393**	347			6	7
	St. Louis	42	35	.545	30	47	.390	36	38	354	357	40	38	330	360	2	4/13	6	8
	Cincinnati	33	44	.429	27	50	.351	**11**	**11**	**270**	344	36	58	305	371	1	4/12	5	**10**
1932 American League	New York	62	15	**.805**	45	32	**.584**	81	44	482	**300**	**79**	49	**520**	424	**141**	**9/13**	**9**	3
(4/11–9/25)	Philadelphia	51	26	.662	43	34	.558	**109**	**80**	**572**	406	63	**32**	409	**346**	1	4/17	7	6
	Washington	51	26	.662	42	35	.545	21	**26**	431	325	40	47	409	391	23	5/15	**9**	4
	Cleveland	43	33	.566	44	32	.579	36	33	460	401	42	37	385	**346**	1	4/13	**9**	6
	Detroit	42	34	.553	34	41	.453	29	50	423	399	51	39	376	388	9	4/26	6	4
	St. Louis	33	42	.440	30	49	.380	47	56	385	428	20	47	351	470			5	**11**
	Chicago	28	49	.364	21	53	.284	**10**	36	300	390	26	52	367	507	3	4/16	4	10
	Boston	27	50	.351	16	61	.208	18	31	**295**	**439**	35	48	271	476			3	**11**
1933 National League	New York	48	27	.640	43	34	**.558**	**55**	44	298	241	27	**17**	338	**274**	**126**	**9/19**	**8**	7
(4/12–10/1)	Pittsburgh	50	27	.649	37	40	.481	12	13	332	272	27	41	335	347	44	5/31	**8**	7
	Chicago	55	24	**.696**	31	44	.413	40	32	334	239	32	19	312	297	1	4/12	**8**	6
	Boston	45	31	.592	38	40	.487	27	26	265	**230**	27	28	287	301			**8**	7
	St. Louis	46	31	.597	36	40	.474	18	25	347	315	**39**	30	**340**	294	4	6/9	7	4
	Brooklyn	36	41	.468	29	47	.382	33	29	306	352	29	22	311	343	2	4/14	5	6
	Philadelphia	32	40	.444	28	52	.350	45	**46**	**355**	**437**	15	41	252	323			7	6
	Cincinnati	37	42	.468	21	52	.288	**5**	**10**	**264**	321	29	37	232	322			5	**10**
1933 American League	Washington	46	30	.605	53	23	**.697**	**14**	**16**	358	338	46	48	492	**327**	**102**	**9/21**	**13**	4
(4/12–10/1)	New York	51	23	**.689**	40	36	.526	79	26	**421**	**324**	**65**	40	**506**	444	76	7/23	9	4
	Philadelphia	46	29	.613	33	43	.434	**82**	50	414	387	57	**27**	461	466			7	6
	Cleveland	45	32	.584	30	44	.405	22	24	353	341	28	36	301	328	9	5/15	7	6
	Detroit	43	35	.551	32	44	.421	27	36	394	382	30	48	328	351			6	8
	Chicago	35	41	.461	32	42	.432	20	42	355	426	23	43	328	388	3	4/14	6	**9**
	Boston	32	40	.444	31	46	.403	23	35	**341**	377	27	40	359	381			6	**9**
	St. Louis	30	46	.395	25	50	.333	43	**68**	389	**480**	21	28	280	340			3	7
1934 National League	St. Louis	48	29	.623	47	29	**.618**	56	43	**451**	363	48	34	348	**293**	13	**9/30**	7	5
(4/17–9/30)	New York	49	26	**.653**	44	34	.564	**75**	43	363	**254**	**51**	**32**	397	329	**127**	9/28	5	5
	Chicago	47	30	.610	39	35	.527	53	44	347	301	48	36	358	338	25	5/21	**8**	5
	Boston	40	35	.533	38	38	.500	36	27	**280**	280	47	51	**403**	434			7	6
	Pittsburgh	45	32	.584	29	44	.397	22	38	421	369	30	40	314	344	10	5/27	7	**9**
	Brooklyn	43	33	.566	28	48	.368	40	38	390	355	39	43	358	440	1	4/17	6	8
	Philadelphia	35	36	.493	21	57	.269	28	**72**	384	400	28	54	291	394			5	7
	Cincinnati	30	47	.390	22	52	.297	**17**	**24**	331	**406**	38	37	259	395			5	8
1934 American League	Detroit	54	26	.675	47	27	**.635**	28	32	**479**	345	46	54	**479**	**363**	**100**	**9/24**	**14**	4
(4/17–9/30)	New York	53	24	**.688**	41	36	.532	75	34	416	**275**	60	37	426	394	61	7/31	8	4
	Cleveland	47	31	.603	38	38	.500	45	34	435	362	55	36	379	401	9	6/2	5	4
	Boston	42	35	.545	34	41	.453	23	**24**	447	405	28	46	373	370			5	4
	Philadelphia	34	40	.459	34	42	.447	**81**	48	371	410	**63**	36	393	428	1	4/17	7	6
	St. Louis	36	39	.480	31	46	.403	35	60	**356**	405	27	**34**	318	395			7	6
	Washington	34	40	.459	32	46	.410	**14**	26	368	397	37	48	361	409	2	4/18	6	5
	Chicago	29	46	.387	24	53	.312	47	**82**	370	**464**	24	57	334	482			4	**10**
1935 National League	Chicago	56	21	**.727**	44	33	**.571**	43	40	426	**264**	45	45	**421**	333	18	**9/27**	**21**	4
(4/16–9/29)	St. Louis	53	24	.688	43	34	.558	39	27	**441**	298	47	41	388	327	20	9/13	14	5
	New York	50	27	.649	41	35	.539	**84**	66	386	302	39	40	384	373	**130**	8/24	7	6
	Pittsburgh	46	31	.597	40	36	.526	32	25	398	340	34	**38**	345	**307**	1	4/16	10	5
	Brooklyn	38	38	.500	32	45	.416	32	43	349	346	27	45	362	421	10	4/26	7	7
	Cincinnati	41	35	.539	27	50	.351	**18**	**18**	331	320	**55**	47	315	452	4	4/22	7	7
	Philadelphia	35	43	.449	29	46	.387	52	**68**	416	**499**	40	**38**	269	372			3	9
	Boston	25	50	.333	13	65	.167	34	41	**309**	381	41	40	266	471	3	4/18	4	**15**

1935 American League (4/16–9/29)

Team	Home Games			Road Games			Home Games				Road Games							
	W	L	PCT	W	L	PCT	HR	OHR	R	OR	HR	OHR	R	OR	DIF	LDF	WS	LS
Detroit	53	25	**.679**	40	33	.548	45	38	**467**	304	**61**	40	452	361	**66**	**9/21**	**10**	6
New York	41	33	.554	48	27	**.640**	60	51	**341**	**294**	44	40	**477**	338	57	7/25	7	4
Cleveland	48	29	.623	34	42	.447	53	30	391	340	40	38	385	399	18	5/10	8	8
Boston	41	37	.526	37	38	.493	26	29	393	404	43	38	325	**328**	6	4/24	4	4
Chicago	42	34	.553	32	44	.421	50	**61**	418	396	24	44	320	354	23	5/29	7	7
Washington	37	39	.487	30	47	.390	**5**	**28**	388	414	27	61	435	489	2	4/18	5	8
St. Louis	31	44	.413	34	43	.442	36	49	374	**513**	37	43	344	417			5	10
Philadelphia	30	42	.417	28	49	.364	**63**	39	369	414	49	**34**	341	455			5	**13**

1936 National League (4/14–9/27)

Team	W	L	PCT	W	L	PCT	HR	OHR	R	OR	HR	OHR	R	OR	DIF	LDF	WS	LS
New York	52	26	**.667**	40	36	.526	68	54	378	296	29	**21**	364	325	55	**9/24**	**15**	6
Chicago	50	27	.649	37	40	.481	34	41	404	**290**	42	35	351	**313**	31	8/11	**15**	6
St. Louis	43	33	.566	44	34	**.564**	38	43	363	386	50	46	**432**	408	**85**	8/24	6	6
Pittsburgh	46	30	.605	38	40	.487	23	25	375	342	37	49	429	376	2	4/15	7	5
Cincinnati	42	34	.553	32	46	.410	24	**21**	358	350	**58**	30	364	410			7	9
Boston	35	43	.449	36	40	.474	26	23	**292**	339	41	46	339	376			5	5
Brooklyn	37	40	.481	30	47	.390	**15**	46	360	397	18	39	302	355			3	9
Philadelphia	30	48	.385	24	52	.316	**69**	**56**	**408**	**499**	34	31	318	375	1	4/14	5	**14**

1936 American League (4/14–9/27)

Team	W	L	PCT	W	L	PCT	HR	OHR	R	OR	HR	OHR	R	OR	DIF	LDF	WS	LS
New York	56	21	**.727**	46	30	**.605**	**82**	41	492	**311**	**100**	43	**573**	420	**141**	**9/9**	7	3
Detroit	44	33	.571	39	38	.507	51	58	448	399	43	42	473	472	1	4/14	**9**	7
Chicago	43	32	.573	38	38	.500	23	55	453	419	37	49	467	454	8	4/22	8	8
Washington	42	35	.545	40	36	.526	**16**	**27**	433	380	46	46	456	419	2	4/15	5	7
Cleveland	49	30	.620	31	44	.413	73	33	**535**	433	50	**40**	386	429	7	4/28	**9**	6
Boston	47	29	.618	27	51	.346	38	31	437	360	48	47	338	**404**	17	5/9	5	7
St. Louis	31	43	.419	26	52	.333	47	63	443	**552**	32	52	361	512			4	**13**
Philadelphia	31	46	.403	22	54	.289	43	**77**	**383**	531	29	54	331	514			4	12

1937 National League (4/19–10/3)

Team	W	L	PCT	W	L	PCT	HR	OHR	R	OR	HR	OHR	R	OR	DIF	LDF	WS	LS
New York	50	25	**.667**	45	32	.584	**76**	57	353	288	35	28	379	**314**	50	**9/30**	8	5
Chicago	46	32	.590	47	29	**.618**	47	48	**412**	361	49	43	**399**	321	**75**	9/1	8	5
Pittsburgh	46	32	.590	40	36	.526	**13**	28	360	332	34	43	344	**314**	42	6/4	**10**	7
St. Louis	45	33	.577	36	40	.474	52	51	406	379	42	44	383	354	9	5/1	6	6
Boston	43	33	.566	36	40	.474	26	15	**252**	**224**	37	45	327	332			7	11
Brooklyn	36	39	.480	26	52	.333	20	30	336	389	17	38	280	383			4	**14**
Philadelphia	29	45	.392	32	47	.405	65	**69**	379	**481**	38	47	345	388	4	4/22	6	7
Cincinnati	28	51	.354	28	47	.373	**13**	**14**	268	347	**60**	**24**	344	360			4	**14**

1937 American League (4/19–10/3)

Team	W	L	PCT	W	L	PCT	HR	OHR	R	OR	HR	OHR	R	OR	DIF	LDF	WS	LS
New York	57	20	**.740**	45	32	**.584**	**94**	41	520	**298**	**80**	51	**459**	373	**143**	**9/23**	9	4
Detroit	49	28	.636	40	37	.519	91	58	**521**	448	59	44	414	393	10	5/8	6	5
Chicago	47	30	.610	39	38	.507	39	62	397	365	28	53	383	**365**	2	6/9	10	7
Cleveland	50	28	.641	33	43	.434	48	**22**	430	329	55	**39**	387	439	4	5/21	7	6
Boston	44	29	.603	36	43	.456	53	43	420	368	47	49	401	407	6	5/7	**12**	5
Washington	43	35	.551	30	45	.400	**14**	30	376	381	33	66	381	460			8	10
Philadelphia	27	50	.351	27	47	.365	51	47	**333**	419	43	58	366	435	14	5/23	5	**15**
St. Louis	25	51	.329	21	57	.269	39	**74**	385	**513**	32	69	330	510	1	4/21	3	12

1938 National League (4/19–10/2)

Team	W	L	PCT	W	L	PCT	HR	OHR	R	OR	HR	OHR	R	OR	DIF	LDF	WS	LS
Chicago	44	33	.571	45	30	**.600**	24	41	349	326	41	30	364	**272**	10	**10/1**	10	6
Pittsburgh	44	33	.571	42	31	.575	22	22	348	330	43	49	359	300	**87**	9/27	**13**	5
New York	43	30	.589	40	37	.519	**89**	**58**	365	297	36	**29**	340	340	74	7/11	11	6
Cincinnati	43	34	.558	39	34	.534	50	31	344	323	**60**	44	379	311			7	6
Boston	45	30	**.600**	32	45	.416	**12**	**19**	**233**	**241**	42	47	328	377			7	7
St. Louis	36	41	.468	35	39	.473	58	45	**414**	425	33	32	311	296			6	8
Brooklyn	31	41	.431	38	39	.494	38	44	319	349	23	44	**385**	361	1	4/19	5	6
Philadelphia	26	48	.351	19	57	.250	18	40	286	**439**	22	36	264	401			3	**9**

1938 American League (4/18–10/2)

Team	W	L	PCT	W	L	PCT	HR	OHR	R	OR	HR	OHR	R	OR	DIF	LDF	WS	LS
New York	55	22	**.714**	44	31	**.587**	**112**	43	**524**	**342**	**62**	**42**	**442**	**368**	**87**	**9/18**	**9**	6
Boston	52	23	.693	36	38	.486	67	52	481	356	31	50	421	395	8	5/18	8	6
Cleveland	46	30	.605	40	36	.526	54	35	425	363	59	65	422	419	72	7/12	**9**	5
Detroit	48	31	.608	36	39	.480	83	60	447	392	54	50	415	403			8	7
Washington	44	33	.571	31	43	.419	33	**27**	412	413	52	65	402	460	10	5/13	7	5
Chicago	33	39	.458	32	44	.421	**24**	41	**326**	364	43	60	383	388	3	4/22	4	**10**
St. Louis	31	43	.419	24	54	.308	52	62	385	**487**	40	70	370	475	1	4/19	4	**10**
Philadelphia	28	47	.373	25	52	.325	55	**64**	378	486	43	78	348	470			5	9

1939 National League (4/17–10/1)

Team	W	L	PCT	W	L	PCT	HR	OHR	R	OR	HR	OHR	R	OR	DIF	LDF	WS	LS
Cincinnati	55	25	**.688**	42	32	**.568**	48	39	404	307	**50**	42	**363**	**288**	**138**	**9/28**	**12**	4
St. Louis	51	27	.654	41	34	.547	63	42	**431**	317	35	34	348	316	19	5/25	10	5
Brooklyn	51	27	.654	33	42	.440	41	49	385	329	37	44	323	316			6	6
Chicago	44	34	.564	40	36	.526	44	35	379	343	47	39	345	335	6	4/27	6	4
New York	41	33	.554	36	41	.468	**84**	**58**	360	315	32	**28**	343	370	2	4/19	9	9
Pittsburgh	35	42	.455	33	43	.434	22	29	339	365	41	41	327	356	1	4/17	5	**12**
Boston	37	35	.514	26	53	.329	**13**	**14**	**254**	**272**	43	49	318	387	9	5/5	6	7
Philadelphia	29	44	.397	16	62	.205	19	49	288	**384**	30	57	265	472			4	11

1939 American League (4/17–10/1)

Team	W	L	PCT	W	L	PCT	HR	OHR	R	OR	HR	OHR	R	OR	DIF	LDF	WS	LS
New York	52	25	**.675**	54	20	**.730**	**84**	48	382	**261**	**82**	**37**	**585**	**295**	**159**	**9/16**	**12**	6
Boston	42	32	.568	47	30	.610	57	39	458	445	67	38	432	350	7	5/10	**12**	6
Cleveland	44	33	.571	43	34	.558	30	33	363	347	55	42	434	353	2	4/22	7	5
Chicago	50	27	.649	35	42	.455	38	51	414	366	26	48	341	371			6	4
Detroit	42	35	.545	39	38	.507	66	65	**461**	434	58	39	388	328	3	4/20	9	7
Washington	37	39	.487	28	48	.368	**11**	**19**	**326**	337	33	56	376	460			8	6
Philadelphia	28	48	.368	27	49	.355	45	**83**	354	523	53	65	357	499	1	4/20	4	8
St. Louis	18	59	.234	25	52	.325	47	80	372	**561**	44	53	361	474	1	4/22	2	**11**

		Home Games			Road Games			Home Games				Road Games							
	Team	W	L	PCT	W	L	PCT	HR	OHR	R	OR	HR	OHR	R	OR	DIF	LDF	WS	LS
1940 National League (4/16–9/29)	Cincinnati	55	21	**.724**	45	32	.584	47	36	352	**240**	42	37	355	288	**139**	**9/18**	**11**	3
	Brooklyn	41	37	.526	47	28	**.627**	40	55	369	358	**53**	46	328	**263**	50	7/6	9	6
	St. Louis	41	36	.532	43	33	.566	**69**	47	368	364	50	36	379	335			9	6
	Pittsburgh	40	34	.541	38	42	.475	26	**22**	**390**	354	50	50	**419**	429	8	4/23	8	9
	Chicago	40	37	.519	35	42	.455	40	32	333	316	46	42	348	320			7	6
	New York	33	43	.434	39	37	.513	61	**75**	323	339	30	**35**	340	320			8	**11**
	Boston	35	40	.467	30	47	.390	**25**	30	328	352	34	53	295	393			6	9
	Philadelphia	24	55	.304	26	48	.351	33	50	**232**	**403**	42	42	262	347	7	4/22	3	9
1940 American League (4/16–9/29)	Detroit	50	29	.633	40	35	**.533**	82	64	**512**	389	52	**38**	376	328	49	**9/27**	6	6
	Cleveland	51	30	.630	38	35	.521	37	**27**	350	**281**	64	59	360	356	**73**	9/19	**8**	6
	New York	52	24	**.684**	36	42	.462	**83**	63	414	284	**72**	56	403	387			**8**	8
	Boston	45	34	.570	37	38	.493	73	64	468	421	**72**	60	**404**	404	57	6/19	6	8
	Chicago	41	36	.532	41	36	.532	36	65	357	363	37	46	378	**309**			**8**	5
	St. Louis	37	39	.487	30	48	.385	68	**68**	419	**460**	50	45	338	422	2	4/17	6	**14**
	Washington	36	41	.468	28	49	.364	**19**	28	**316**	368	33	65	349	443			5	7
	Philadelphia	29	42	.408	25	58	.301	44	62	336	409	61	73	367	523	1	4/16	3	9
1941 National League (4/15–9/28)	Brooklyn	52	25	.675	48	29	**.623**	55	40	**421**	282	46	41	**379**	299	**85**	**9/25**	9	6
	St. Louis	53	24	**.688**	44	32	.579	37	53	405	324	33	32	329	**265**	81	9/3	**11**	5
	Cincinnati	45	34	.570	43	32	.573	27	27	308	**273**	37	34	308	291			8	5
	Pittsburgh	45	32	.584	36	41	.468	20	28	346	336	36	38	344	307			7	5
	New York	38	39	.494	36	40	.474	**68**	**69**	360	358	27	**21**	307	348	12	4/26	5	6
	Chicago	38	39	.494	32	45	.416	37	**20**	311	306	**62**	40	355	364	2	4/16	4	5
	Boston	32	44	.421	30	48	.385	**17**	28	276	321	31	47	316	399			5	8
	Philadelphia	23	52	.307	20	59	.253	34	37	**255**	**384**	30	42	246	409	1	4/15	3	**9**
1941 American League (4/14–9/28)	New York	51	26	**.662**	50	27	**.649**	**76**	44	396	**295**	**75**	37	**434**	**336**	**99**	**9/4**	**14**	5
	Boston	47	30	.610	37	40	.481	70	51	**461**	371	54	37	404	379	9	4/23	8	5
	Chicago	38	39	.494	39	38	.507	17	40	**288**	297	30	49	350	352	2	6/1	9	5
	Cleveland	42	35	.545	33	44	.429	45	35	340	322	58	**36**	337	346	60	6/27	11	8
	Detroit	43	34	.558	32	45	.416	51	43	381	377	30	37	305	366			5	8
	St. Louis	40	37	.519	30	47	.390	49	63	407	408	42	57	358	415	2	4/17	4	6
	Washington	40	37	.519	30	47	.390	**13**	**19**	367	387	39	50	361	411			6	**12**
	Philadelphia	36	41	.468	28	49	.364	43	**75**	373	**432**	42	61	340	408	2	4/16	5	8
1942 National League (4/14–9/27)	St. Louis	60	17	**.779**	46	31	.597	31	24	**419**	**229**	29	25	336	**253**	16	**9/27**	**8**	4
	Brooklyn	57	22	.722	47	28	**.627**	30	35	381	250	32	38	**361**	260	**148**	9/12	**8**	5
	New York	47	31	.603	38	36	.514	**80**	**67**	376	296	29	27	299	304			6	5
	Cincinnati	38	39	.494	38	37	.507	30	23	264	276	36	**24**	263	269			6	6
	Pittsburgh	41	34	.547	25	47	.347	**15**	**21**	333	301	**39**	41	252	330	4	4/19	7	10
	Chicago	36	41	.468	32	45	.416	36	27	298	318	**39**	43	293	347	1	4/14	5	4
	Boston	33	36	.478	26	53	.329	36	34	250	271	32	48	265	374	6	4/19	5	12
	Philadelphia	23	51	.311	19	58	.247	18	31	**182**	**340**	26	30	212	366			3	**13**
1942 American League (4/14–9/27)	New York	58	19	**.753**	45	32	**.584**	**62**	39	394	**226**	46	32	**407**	**281**	**157**	**9/14**	11	5
	Boston	53	24	.688	40	35	.533	54	33	**403**	299	**49**	32	358	295	8	4/22	9	5
	St. Louis	40	37	.519	42	32	.568	55	37	376	350	43	26	354	287	5	4/18	8	**9**
	Cleveland	39	39	.500	36	40	.474	20	24	266	308	30	37	324	351	12	5/5	**13**	6
	Detroit	43	34	.558	30	47	.390	50	40	344	302	26	**20**	245	285			5	7
	Chicago	35	35	.500	31	47	.397	**6**	31	256	275	19	43	282	334			9	7
	Washington	35	42	.455	27	47	.365	13	**11**	339	409	27	39	314	408			5	5
	Philadelphia	25	51	.329	30	48	.385	16	**42**	**249**	**415**	17	47	300	386			5	**9**
1943 National League (4/21–10/3)	St. Louis	58	21	**.734**	47	28	**.627**	33	17	355	**243**	**37**	**16**	324	**232**	**121**	**9/18**	**12**	4
	Cincinnati	48	29	.623	39	38	.507	**17**	**15**	282	280	26	23	326	263	3	4/23	10	5
	Brooklyn	46	31	.597	35	41	.461	21	30	**389**	323	18	29	327	351	44	6/4	10	10
	Pittsburgh	47	30	.610	33	44	.429	20	15	364	296	22	29	305	309	1	4/21	5	5
	Chicago	36	38	.486	38	41	.481	24	19	292	300	28	34	**340**	300			6	**12**
	Boston	38	39	.494	30	46	.395	25	34	**247**	**327**	14	32	218	285			7	6
	Philadelphia	33	43	.434	31	47	.397	29	18	269	314	**37**	41	302	362			7	8
	New York	34	43	.442	21	55	.276	**63**	**52**	291	326	18	28	267	387			4	7
1943 American League (4/20–10/3)	New York	54	23	**.701**	44	33	**.571**	**60**	33	321	**241**	**40**	27	**348**	301	**158**	**9/25**	9	5
	Washington	44	32	.579	40	37	.519	**9**	**14**	**345**	307	38	34	321	288	5	5/29	**10**	5
	Cleveland	44	33	.571	38	38	.500	16	21	269	247	39	31	331	330	7	5/28	8	4
	Chicago	40	36	.526	42	36	.538	20	25	264	311	13	29	309	283			7	6
	Detroit	45	32	.584	33	44	.429	45	26	**345**	284	32	25	287	**276**			5	5
	St. Louis	44	33	.571	28	47	.373	49	**51**	319	290	29	**23**	277	314	3	4/23	7	8
	Boston	39	36	.520	29	48	.377	29	25	293	312	28	36	270	295	1	4/22	4	8
	Philadelphia	27	51	.346	22	54	.289	14	36	**261**	**387**	12	37	236	330			4	**20**
1944 National League (4/18–10/1)	St. Louis	54	22	**.711**	51	27	**.654**	39	**14**	360	**230**	**61**	41	**412**	**260**	**163**	**9/21**	9	5
	Pittsburgh	49	28	.636	41	35	.539	23	31	**399**	357	47	34	345	305			**11**	4
	Cincinnati	45	33	.577	44	32	.579	**14**	23	**253**	252	37	37	320	285	2	5/6	6	4
	Chicago	35	42	.455	40	37	.519	33	40	346	342	38	35	356	327	1	4/18	**11**	13
	New York	39	36	.520	28	51	.354	**75**	**86**	372	382	18	30	310	391	11	4/28	7	13
	Boston	38	40	.487	27	49	.355	51	44	293	307	28	36	300	367			5	8
	Brooklyn	37	39	.487	26	52	.333	27	34	372	**413**	29	41	318	419			5	**16**
	Philadelphia	29	49	.372	32	43	.427	20	21	271	346	35	**28**	268	312	1	4/18	6	12

	Home Games			Road Games			Home Games				Road Games							
Team	W	L	PCT	W	L	PCT	HR	OHR	R	OR	HR	OHR	R	OR	DIF	LDF	WS	LS
1944 American League (4/18–10/1)																		
St. Louis	54	23	**.701**	35	42	.455	45	24	368	272	27	34	316	315	**128**	**10/1**	**10**	4
Detroit	43	34	.558	45	32	**.584**	38	21	325	318	22	**18**	333	**263**	14	9/30	9	5
New York	47	31	.603	36	40	.474	**58**	**45**	388	307	38	37	286	310	32	9/15	6	7
Boston	47	30	.610	30	47	.390	48	34	**389**	311	21	32	**350**	365			9	10
Cleveland	39	38	.507	33	44	.429	27	16	345	**328**	**43**	24	298	349			4	6
Philadelphia	39	37	.513	33	45	.423	18	28	**277**	270	18	30	248	324	2	4/19	6	8
Chicago	41	36	.532	30	47	.390	11	24	302	304	12	44	241	358	2	4/20	8	5
Washington	40	37	.519	24	53	.312	**9**	**13**	286	**268**	24	35	306	396			3	**11**
1945 National League (4/17–9/30)																		
Chicago	49	26	**.653**	49	30	**.620**	24	**17**	330	**253**	33	40	405	**279**	**88**	**9/29**	**11**	6
St. Louis	48	29	.623	47	30	.610	28	29	368	286	36	41	388	297			7	4
Brooklyn	48	30	.615	39	37	.513	29	34	387	347	28	40	**408**	377	22	7/7	**11**	6
Pittsburgh	45	34	.570	37	38	.493	31	25	407	352	**41**	36	346	334	3	6/16	9	5
New York	47	30	.610	31	44	.413	**83**	47	366	325	31	38	302	375	58	6/16	8	6
Boston	36	38	.486	31	47	.397	68	**63**	**411**	395	33	36	310	333			9	10
Cincinnati	36	41	.468	25	52	.325	25	23	267	307	31	47	269	387	2	4/18	9	**13**
Philadelphia	22	55	.286	24	53	.312	**23**	28	**261**	**450**	33	**33**	287	415			5	9
1945 American League (4/17–9/30)																		
Detroit	50	26	**.658**	38	39	.494	43	28	333	285	34	20	300	280	**113**	**9/30**	6	4
Washington	46	31	.597	41	36	**.532**	**1**	**6**	278	**255**	26	36	**344**	307	1	4/17	7	4
St. Louis	47	27	.635	34	43	.442	32	33	353	291	31	26	244	**257**	1	4/17	5	6
New York	48	28	.632	33	43	.434	**65**	**51**	**395**	297	28	**15**	281	309	25	6/27	**8**	9
Cleveland	44	33	.571	29	39	.426	27	15	292	273	**38**	24	265	275			7	5
Chicago	44	29	.603	27	49	.355	8	34	305	277	14	29	291	356	37	5/24	5	6
Boston	42	35	.545	29	48	.377	22	28	306	**299**	28	30	293	375			5	8
Philadelphia	39	35	.527	13	63	.171	16	21	**265**	270	17	34	229	368			5	**14**
1946 National League (4/16–10/3)																		
St. Louis	49	29	.628	49	29	**.628**	39	36	370	288	42	**27**	**342**	**257**	70	**10/3**	7	4
Brooklyn	56	22	**.718**	40	38	.513	20	**22**	**374**	273	35	36	327	297	**122**	9/30	**8**	6
Chicago	44	33	.571	38	38	.500	24	30	291	**260**	32	28	335	321	5	4/20	7	5
Boston	45	31	.592	36	41	.468	**14**	31	300	268	30	45	330	324	1	4/16	6	6
Philadelphia	41	36	.532	28	49	.364	38	34	280	335	42	39	280	370			6	5
Cincinnati	35	42	.455	32	45	.416	37	39	**267**	289	28	31	256	281			4	**9**
Pittsburgh	37	40	.481	26	51	.338	24	23	303	**342**	36	**27**	249	326	1	4/16	6	6
New York	38	39	.494	23	54	.299	**76**	**75**	340	336	**45**	39	272	349	2	4/17	5	7
1946 American League (4/16–9/29)																		
Boston	61	16	**.792**	43	34	.558	65	44	**469**	315	44	45	323	279	**164**	**9/13**	**15**	6
Detroit	48	30	.615	44	32	**.579**	**75**	**68**	391	300	33	**29**	313	**267**	2	4/25	10	7
New York	47	30	.610	40	37	.519	68	34	342	**262**	**68**	32	342	285	5		5	5
Washington	38	38	.500	38	40	.487	**16**	**25**	253	343	44	56	**355**	363			6	6
Chicago	40	38	.513	34	42	.447	17	46	272	290	20	34	290	305			5	9
Cleveland	36	41	.468	32	45	.416	25	36	**231**	264	54	48	306	374	4	4/19	5	7
St. Louis	35	41	.461	31	47	.397	46	29	313	344	38	44	308	366			4	5
Philadelphia	31	46	.403	18	59	.234	21	38	297	**351**	19	45	232	329			4	**10**
1947 National League (4/15–9/28)																		
Brooklyn	52	25	**.675**	42	35	.545	37	57	409	343	46	**47**	365	325	**113**	**9/22**	**13**	5
St. Louis	46	31	.597	43	34	**.558**	45	49	400	331	70	57	380	**303**			9	**9**
Boston	50	27	.649	36	41	.468	29	**39**	332	**289**	56	54	369	333	18	7/5	5	3
New York	45	31	.592	36	42	.462	**131**	75	**417**	380	**90**	**47**	**413**	381	18	6/18	5	8
Cincinnati	42	35	.545	31	46	.403	48	47	318	330	47	55	363	425	1	4/15	4	6
Chicago	36	43	.456	33	42	.440	29	51	**280**	384	42	55	287	338	13	6/14	5	**9**
Philadelphia	38	38	.500	24	54	.308	**24**	43	309	323	36	55	280	364	3	4/17	4	7
Pittsburgh	32	45	.416	30	47	.390	95	**87**	384	**437**	61	68	360	380	11	4/25	4	6
1947 American League (4/15–9/28)																		
New York	55	22	**.714**	42	35	**.545**	54	49	392	**242**	**61**	46	**402**	326	**112**	**9/15**	**19**	3
Detroit	46	31	.597	39	38	.507	**62**	47	370	345	41	**32**	344	297	39	6/14	6	10
Boston	49	30	.620	34	41	.453	61	39	**421**	355	42	45	299	314	6	6/19	8	6
Cleveland	38	39	.494	42	35	**.545**	52	51	314	279	60	43	373	309	1	4/24	5	6
Philadelphia	39	38	.507	39	38	.507	33	41	296	324	28	44	337	**290**	2	4/16	4	7
Chicago	32	43	.427	38	41	.481	20	31	**244**	322	33	45	309	339	19	5/9	6	5
Washington	36	41	.468	28	49	.364	**10**	**20**	**244**	326	32	43	252	349			5	**11**
St. Louis	29	48	.377	30	47	.390	52	**57**	286	**401**	38	46	278	343			6	8
1948 National League (4/19–10/3)																		
Boston	45	31	.592	46	31	.597	**32**	40	349	**297**	63	53	390	287	**109**	**9/26**	**8**	4
St. Louis	44	33	.571	41	36	.532	47	43	359	327	58	60	383	319	26	6/6	6	6
Brooklyn	36	41	.468	48	29	**.623**	43	68	352	386	48	51	392	**281**	8	9/2	7	8
Pittsburgh	47	31	**.603**	36	40	.474	69	64	**384**	370	39	56	322	329	8	6/16	7	6
New York	37	40	.481	41	36	.532	**89**	**82**	366	374	**75**	**40**	**414**	330	23	6/14	7	7
Philadelphia	32	44	.421	34	44	.436	**32**	44	**276**	332	59	51	315	397	5	4/24	5	**10**
Cincinnati	32	45	.416	32	44	.421	68	52	312	**398**	36	52	276	354	1	4/19	5	8
Chicago	35	42	.455	29	48	.377	38	**34**	282	323	49	55	315	383			4	**10**
1948 American League (4/19–10/4)																		
Cleveland	48	30	.615	49	28	**.636**	**77**	41	398	**272**	**78**	41	442	**296**	**115**	**10/4**	8	5
Boston	55	23	**.705**	41	36	.532	60	43	**481**	336	61	40	426	384	40	10/3	**13**	5
New York	50	27	.649	44	33	.571	70	54	413	315	69	40	**444**	318	2	9/24	9	4
Philadelphia	36	41	.468	48	29	.623	33	47	347	396	35	39	382	339	23	8/13	10	8
Detroit	39	38	.507	39	38	.507	39	61	327	355	39	**31**	373	371	3	4/22	7	5
St. Louis	34	42	.447	25	52	.325	29	**64**	363	**451**	34	39	308	398			4	6
Washington	29	48	.377	27	49	.355	**11**	**24**	312	419	20	57	266	377			5	**18**
Chicago	27	48	.360	24	53	.312	21	36	**278**	378	34	53	281	436			3	9

	Team	Home Games W	L	PCT	Road Games W	L	PCT	Home Games HR	OHR	R	OR	Road Games HR	OHR	R	OR	DIF	LDF	WS	LS
1949 National League (4/18–10/2)	Brooklyn	48	29	.623	49	28	**.636**	86	73	**431**	335	**66**	59	**448**	316	**71**	**10/2**	8	4
	St. Louis	51	26	**.662**	45	32	.584	48	**33**	427	**325**	54	**54**	339	**291**	64	9/28	**9**	4
	Philadelphia	40	37	.519	41	36	.532	61	35	336	326	61	69	326	342	1	4/18	7	5
	Boston	43	34	.558	32	45	.416	**40**	40	344	328	63	70	362	391	30	6/4	5	**9**
	New York	43	34	.558	30	47	.390	**94**	**78**	404	331	53	**54**	332	362	23	6/6	7	6
	Pittsburgh	36	41	.468	35	42	.455	77	75	341	**397**	49	67	340	363	2	4/27	8	8
	Cincinnati	35	42	.455	27	50	.351	50	54	326	349	36	70	301	421	4	4/30	4	7
	Chicago	33	44	.429	28	49	.364	53	38	**285**	365	44	66	308	408			3	8
1949 American League (4/18–10/2)	New York	54	23	.701	43	34	**.558**	**72**	53	419	304	43	45	**410**	333	**164**	**10/2**	6	4
	Boston	61	16	**.792**	35	42	.455	71	43	**514**	310	60	**39**	382	357	7	10/1	**11**	8
	Cleveland	49	28	.636	40	37	.519	61	42	319	**263**	51	40	356	311			7	6
	Detroit	50	27	.649	37	40	.481	57	**60**	402	350	31	42	349	**305**	2	4/20	10	6
	Philadelphia	52	25	.675	29	48	.377	42	42	389	326	40	63	337	399			6	6
	Chicago	32	45	.416	31	46	.403	**15**	52	327	353	28	56	321	384			5	6
	St. Louis	36	41	.468	17	60	.221	69	56	394	**426**	48	57	273	487	1	4/19	6	**11**
	Washington	26	51	.338	24	53	.312	20	**14**	**254**	**426**	**61**	65	330	442		4/18	9	**11**
1950 National League (4/18–10/1)	Philadelphia	47	30	.610	44	33	**.571**	58	53	348	**279**	67	69	374	345	**104**	**10/1**	6	5
	Brooklyn	48	30	.615	41	35	.539	**110**	**96**	**458**	386	84	67	389	**338**	41	6/29	**10**	6
	New York	44	32	.579	42	36	.538	84	67	362	290	49	73	373	353			9	7
	Boston	46	31	.597	37	40	.481	59	45	**343**	294	**89**	84	**442**	442	6	7/18	6	5
	St. Louis	47	29	**.618**	31	46	.403	**50**	**43**	389	303	52	76	304	367	30	7/24	7	7
	Cincinnati	38	38	.500	28	49	.364	52	81	355	373	47	**64**	299	361			5	**10**
	Chicago	35	42	.455	29	47	.382	79	63	352	411	82	67	291	361	10	4/27	5	7
	Pittsburgh	33	44	.429	24	52	.316	81	79	370	**447**	57	73	311	410			6	9
1950 American League (4/18–10/1)	New York	53	24	.688	45	32	.584	78	51	440	333	**81**	67	**474**	358	50	**9/29**	9	4
	Detroit	50	30	.625	45	29	**.608**	60	**72**	405	346	54	69	432	367	**120**	9/21	7	4
	Boston	55	22	**.714**	39	38	.507	100	67	**625**	427	61	54	402	377	2	5/10	**11**	5
	Cleveland	49	28	.636	43	34	.558	**102**	57	386	**297**	62	63	420	**357**			8	6
	Washington	35	42	.455	32	45	.416	**18**	**28**	347	407	58	71	343	406	1	4/18	4	7
	Chicago	35	42	.455	25	52	.325	52	55	316	352	41	**52**	309	397			6	7
	St. Louis	27	47	.365	31	49	.388	52	69	368	**484**	54	60	316	432	4	4/21	8	9
	Philadelphia	29	48	.377	23	54	.299	45	67	**314**	406	55	71	356	507			3	**10**
1951 National League (4/16–10/3)	New York	50	28	**.641**	48	31	**.608**	**115**	**89**	399	308	64	**59**	382	**333**	7	**10/3**	**16**	**11**
	Brooklyn	49	29	.628	48	31	**.608**	100	81	**412**	316	**84**	69	**443**	356	**147**	10/2	10	4
	St. Louis	44	34	.564	37	39	.487	44	56	370	323	51	63	313	348	10	5/7	7	5
	Boston	42	35	.545	34	43	.442	59	**37**	367	310	71	**59**	356	352	10	5/12	6	6
	Philadelphia	38	39	.494	35	42	.455	**43**	50	312	**305**	65	60	336	339	2	4/26	5	8
	Cincinnati	35	42	.455	33	44	.429	44	46	**289**	320	44	73	270	347			7	7
	Pittsburgh	32	45	.416	32	45	.416	72	84	388	**465**	65	73	301	380	5	4/20	4	8
	Chicago	32	45	.416	30	47	.390	45	59	304	364	58	66	310	386	3	4/19	3	8
1951 American League (4/17–9/30)	New York	56	22	**.718**	42	34	**.553**	72	43	366	258	**68**	49	**432**	363	**79**	**9/28**	8	4
	Cleveland	53	24	.688	40	37	.519	76	42	324	**249**	64	44	372	345	43	9/15	13	6
	Boston	50	25	.667	37	42	.468	**80**	65	**460**	348	47	**35**	344	377	10	7/21	10	9
	Chicago	39	38	.507	42	35	.545	28	47	334	310	58	62	380	**334**	43	7/11	**14**	5
	Detroit	36	41	.468	37	40	.481	58	60	358	402	46	42	327	339			5	7
	Philadelphia	38	41	.481	32	43	.427	54	59	406	407	48	50	330	338			5	10
	Washington	32	44	.421	30	48	.385	**13**	**35**	**319**	362	41	75	353	402	12	5/3	5	**11**
	St. Louis	24	53	.312	28	49	.364	41	**66**	327	**486**	45	65	284	396			3	9
1952 National League (4/15–9/28)	Brooklyn	45	33	.577	51	24	**.680**	76	**78**	**389**	324	**77**	**43**	**386**	**279**	**152**	**9/23**	9	5
	New York	50	27	**.649**	42	35	.545	**103**	74	369	327	48	47	353	312	20	5/31	7	6
	St. Louis	48	29	.623	40	37	.519	46	59	343	291	51	60	334	339	2	4/16	**10**	6
	Philadelphia	47	29	.618	40	38	.513	**42**	43	318	**269**	51	52	339	283			7	5
	Chicago	42	35	.545	35	42	.455	51	**40**	329	316	56	61	299	315	2	4/16	5	9
	Cincinnati	38	39	.494	31	46	.403	43	43	318	319	61	68	297	340			4	6
	Boston	31	45	.408	33	44	.429	48	44	**257**	314	62	62	312	337			5	**10**
	Pittsburgh	23	54	.299	19	58	.247	45	72	261	**414**	47	61	254	379			2	**10**
1952 American League (4/15–9/28)	New York	49	28	.636	46	31	**.597**	64	48	345	264	65	**46**	382	293	**110**	**9/26**	7	5
	Cleveland	49	28	.636	44	33	.571	**72**	43	333	**260**	**76**	51	**430**	346	37	8/22	**9**	6
	Chicago	44	33	.571	37	40	.481	42	39	305	276	38	47	305	**292**			6	6
	Philadelphia	45	32	.584	34	43	.442	55	**60**	382	**403**	34	53	282	320			6	7
	Washington	42	35	.545	36	41	.468	**13**	**18**	299	292	37	60	299	316			6	5
	Boston	50	27	**.649**	26	51	.338	68	49	**406**	309	45	58	262	349	19	6/13	5	7
	St. Louis	42	35	.545	22	55	.286	47	52	321	346	35	59	283	387	7	4/25	4	**8**
	Detroit	32	45	.416	18	59	.234	65	59	**284**	366	38	52	273	372			4	**8**
1953 National League (4/13–9/27)	Brooklyn	60	17	**.779**	45	32	.584	**110**	82	**517**	333	98	87	**438**	356	**112**	**9/12**	**13**	4
	Milwaukee	45	31	.592	47	31	**.603**	**51**	**44**	**332**	**260**	**105**	**63**	406	**329**	38	6/27	8	8
	Philadelphia	48	29	.623	35	42	.455	63	65	363	304	52	73	353	362	27	5/22	8	5
	St. Louis	48	30	.615	35	41	.461	65	58	420	321	75	81	348	392	1	4/22	5	6
	New York	38	39	.494	32	45	.416	109	81	395	345	67	65	373	402	1	4/14	8	7
	Cincinnati	38	39	.494	30	47	.390	89	**96**	367	391	77	83	347	397			6	8
	Chicago	43	34	.558	22	55	.286	74	69	351	417	63	82	282	418	2	4/15	10	8
	Pittsburgh	26	51	.338	24	53	.312	53	88	338	**460**	46	80	284	427			5	**9**

	Team	Home Games			Road Games			Home Games				Road Games							
		W	L	PCT	W	L	PCT	HR	OHR	R	OR	HR	OHR	R	OR	DIF	LDF	WS	LS
1953 American League (4/14–9/27)	New York	50	27	.649	49	25	**.662**	64	39	347	**255**	**75**	55	**454**	292	**158**	**9/14**	**18**	9
	Cleveland	53	24	**.688**	39	38	.507	**90**	46	**379**	272	70	46	391	355	8	5/10	7	6
	Chicago	41	36	.532	48	29	.623	30	56	349	328	44	57	367	**264**			8	6
	Boston	38	38	.500	46	31	.597	57	59	335	354	44	**33**	321	278	1	4/16	6	8
	Washington	39	36	.520	37	40	.481	**10**	**31**	305	283	59	81	382	331			6	8
	Detroit	30	47	.390	30	47	.390	55	**97**	369	**462**	53	57	326	461			5	13
	Philadelphia	27	50	.351	32	45	.416	49	74	299	447	67	47	333	352	1	4/14	7	8
	St. Louis	23	54	.299	31	46	.403	58	64	**281**	447	54	37	274	331	6	4/20	5	**14**
1954 National League (4/13–9/26)	New York	53	23	**.697**	44	34	.564	**120**	67	**387**	254	66	**46**	345	**296**	**110**	**9/20**	8	6
	Brooklyn	45	32	.584	47	30	**.610**	101	92	380	393	85	72	398	347	26	6/14	**10**	5
	Milwaukee	43	34	.558	46	31	.597	43	**29**	285	**251**	**96**	77	385	305	11	6/1	**10**	5
	Philadelphia	39	39	.500	36	40	.474	47	60	315	305	55	73	344	309	19	5/18	6	8
	Cincinnati	41	36	.532	33	44	.429	94	**105**	380	407	53	64	349	356	15	5/7	6	5
	St. Louis	33	44	.429	39	38	.507	57	90	386	**431**	62	80	**413**	359	4	5/22	5	7
	Chicago	40	37	.519	24	53	.312	86	59	366	385	73	72	334	381	3	4/17	7	**11**
	Pittsburgh	31	46	.403	22	55	.286	**22**	42	**277**	422	54	86	280	423	1	4/13	5	10
1954 American League (4/13–9/26)	Cleveland	59	18	**.766**	52	25	**.675**	**78**	57	376	**252**	**78**	**32**	370	252	**134**	**9/18**	11	4
	New York	54	23	.701	49	28	.636	68	42	**388**	274	65	44	**417**	289	4	4/23	**13**	3
	Chicago	45	32	.584	49	28	.636	39	51	327	294	55	43	384	**227**	22	6/11	8	5
	Boston	38	39	.494	31	46	.403	69	70	357	384	54	48	343	344			6	8
	Detroit	35	42	.455	33	44	.429	44	80	285	336	46	58	299	328	17	5/13	4	5
	Washington	37	41	.474	29	47	.382	27	27	320	335	54	52	312	345	4	4/23	6	6
	Baltimore	32	45	.416	22	55	.286	**19**	**23**	**235**	313	33	55	248	355	2	4/16	5	**14**
	Philadelphia	29	47	.382	22	56	.282	44	**85**	260	**467**	50	56	282	408	2	5/10	5	10
1955 National League (4/11–9/25)	Brooklyn	56	21	**.727**	42	34	**.553**	**119**	85	**461**	318	82	83	396	**332**	**166**	**9/8**	**11**	5
	Milwaukee	46	31	.597	39	38	.507	75	51	342	**297**	**107**	87	**401**	371	2	4/13	7	5
	New York	44	35	.557	36	39	.480	95	91	362	327	74	**64**	340	346			6	6
	Philadelphia	46	31	.597	31	46	.403	76	78	371	309	56	83	304	357	3	4/15	**11**	**13**
	Cincinnati	46	31	.597	29	48	.377	102	91	425	341	79	70	336	343			7	7
	Chicago	43	33	.566	29	48	.377	80	62	348	322	84	91	278	391	5	4/15	6	9
	St. Louis	41	36	.532	27	50	.351	84	**92**	358	**362**	59	93	296	395			5	7
	Pittsburgh	36	39	.480	24	55	.304	**34**	**48**	**298**	337	57	94	262	430			6	11
1955 American League (4/11–9/25)	New York	52	25	**.675**	44	33	**.571**	**89**	44	378	**248**	**86**	64	384	321	**93**	**9/23**	**8**	4
	Cleveland	49	28	.636	44	33	**.571**	84	58	343	318	64	53	355	283	43	9/15	6	4
	Chicago	49	28	.636	42	35	.545	54	47	357	262	62	64	368	295	27	9/3	7	6
	Boston	47	31	.603	37	39	.487	84	79	**470**	395	53	**49**	285	**257**	9	4/21	7	7
	Detroit	46	31	.597	33	44	.429	81	59	386	301	49	67	**389**	357	3	5/5	7	6
	Kansas City	33	43	.434	30	48	.385	70	**110**	333	**477**	51	65	305	434	1	4/12	5	10
	Baltimore	30	47	.390	27	50	.351	**15**	42	**249**	335	39	61	291	419			5	9
	Washington	28	49	.364	25	52	.325	20	**25**	282	357	60	74	316	432	2	4/12	7	**12**
1956 National League (4/17–9/30)	Brooklyn	52	25	**.675**	41	36	.532	102	**89**	369	300	77	82	351	**301**	17	**9/30**	8	5
	Milwaukee	47	29	.618	45	33	**.577**	77	53	344	**265**	**100**	80	**365**	304	**126**	9/28	**11**	5
	Cincinnati	51	26	.662	40	37	.519	**128**	75	**426**	**346**	93	66	349	312	16	7/12	6	4
	St. Louis	43	34	.558	33	44	.429	58	73	358	328	66	82	320	370	4	5/2	6	7
	Philadelphia	40	37	.519	31	46	.403	61	74	337	335	60	98	331	403	2	4/18	6	**10**
	New York	37	40	.481	30	47	.390	94	86	**269**	306	51	**58**	271	344	2	4/18	5	8
	Pittsburgh	35	43	.449	31	45	.408	**49**	**45**	301	328	61	97	287	325	9	6/17	4	8
	Chicago	39	38	.507	21	56	.273	78	77	335	328	64	84	262	380			4	7
1956 American League (4/17–9/30)	New York	49	28	**.636**	48	29	**.623**	**88**	48	**412**	303	**102**	66	**445**	328	**157**	**9/18**	**11**	6
	Cleveland	46	31	.597	42	35	.545	71	61	340	**287**	82	**55**	372	**294**	2	5/15	9	6
	Chicago	46	31	.597	39	38	.507	69	47	403	320	59	71	373	314	11	5/4	9	**11**
	Boston	43	34	.558	41	36	.532	68	64	408	388	71	66	372	363	3	4/19	6	5
	Detroit	37	40	.481	45	32	.584	75	77	359	357	75	63	430	342			7	10
	Baltimore	41	36	.532	28	49	.364	**35**	**39**	**275**	315	56	60	296	390			6	5
	Washington	32	45	.416	27	50	.351	63	95	354	**481**	49	76	298	443			4	**11**
	Kansas City	22	55	.286	30	47	.390	62	**113**	305	449	50	74	314	382	3	4/19	3	6
1957 National League (4/16–9/29)	Milwaukee	45	32	**.584**	50	27	**.649**	75	**51**	312	**289**	**124**	73	**460**	324	**110**	**9/23**	10	3
	St. Louis	42	35	.545	45	32	.584	64	70	356	348	68	70	381	318	26	8/5	8	9
	Brooklyn	43	34	.558	41	36	.532	84	88	383	348	63	**56**	307	**243**	9	6/8	5	4
	Cincinnati	45	32	**.584**	35	42	.455	**118**	**101**	**417**	**410**	69	78	330	371	34	7/4	**12**	**10**
	Philadelphia	38	39	.494	39	38	.507	60	60	299	322	57	79	324	334	2	7/16	5	5
	New York	37	40	.481	32	45	.416	99	86	353	341	58	64	290	360			5	6
	Chicago	31	46	.403	31	46	.403	81	68	301	353	66	76	327	369			6	9
	Pittsburgh	36	41	.468	26	51	.338	**20**	53	**273**	321	72	105	313	375	2	4/18	5	8
1957 American League (4/15–9/29)	New York	48	29	**.623**	50	27	**.649**	60	51	316	**241**	**85**	59	**407**	**293**	**108**	**9/23**	**10**	3
	Chicago	45	32	.584	45	32	.584	40	59	347	263	66	65	360	303	68	6/29	9	5
	Boston	44	33	.571	38	39	.494	72	67	**408**	360	81	**49**	313	308	2	4/17	6	5
	Detroit	45	32	.584	33	44	.429	71	**86**	351	304	45	61	263	310			5	6
	Baltimore	42	33	.560	34	43	.442	**36**	**30**	**283**	248	51	65	314	340	1	4/15	5	5
	Cleveland	40	37	.519	36	40	.474	71	74	348	384	69	56	334	338			5	7
	Kansas City	37	40	.481	22	54	.289	**91**	77	294	344	75	76	269	366	2	4/17	5	**11**
	Washington	28	49	.364	27	50	.351	60	79	304	**415**	51	70	299	393			4	10

1958 National League
(4/15–9/28)

Team	Home Games W	Home Games L	Home Games PCT	Road Games W	Road Games L	Road Games PCT	Home Games HR	Home Games OHR	Home Games R	Home Games OR	Road Games HR	Road Games OHR	Road Games R	Road Games OR	DIF	LDF	WS	LS
Milwaukee	48	29	.623	44	33	**.571**	72	48	**291**	**207**	**95**	77	**384**	334	**119**	**9/21**	**7**	5
Pittsburgh	49	28	**.636**	35	42	.455	**41**	**40**	323	260	93	83	339	347	3	5/4	**7**	**7**
San Francisco	44	33	.571	36	41	.468	85	88	363	354	85	78	364	344	34	7/29	6	6
Cincinnati	40	37	.519	36	41	.468	71	86	**364**	337	52	**62**	331	**284**			6	**7**
Chicago	35	42	.455	37	40	.481	**101**	72	350	381	81	70	359	344	17	5/7	5	**7**
St. Louis	39	38	.507	33	44	.429	62	88	329	381	49	70	290	323			**7**	**7**
Los Angeles	39	38	.507	32	45	.416	92	**101**	359	**405**	80	72	309	356			4	6
Philadelphia	35	42	.455	34	43	.442	59	77	318	397	65	71	346	365	3	4/17	6	**7**

1958 American League
(4/14–9/28)

Team	Home Games W	Home Games L	Home Games PCT	Road Games W	Road Games L	Road Games PCT	Home Games HR	Home Games OHR	Home Games R	Home Games OR	Road Games HR	Road Games OHR	Road Games R	Road Games OR	DIF	LDF	WS	LS
New York	44	33	.571	48	29	**.623**	78	62	362	318	86	**54**	**397**	**259**	**165**	**9/14**	**10**	6
Chicago	47	30	.610	35	42	.455	47	68	318	282	54	84	316	333			7	5
Boston	49	28	**.636**	30	47	.390	73	65	**384**	350	82	56	313	341			6	8
Cleveland	42	34	.553	35	42	.455	72	59	324	293	**89**	64	370	342			7	5
Detroit	43	34	.558	34	43	.442	59	79	348	306	50	**54**	311	300	2	4/16	6	9
Baltimore	46	31	.597	28	48	.368	**46**	**36**	**248**	**256**	62	70	273	319	3	4/17	7	11
Kansas City	43	34	.558	30	47	.390	**88**	**96**	365	363	50	**54**	277	350	2	4/16	6	6
Washington	33	44	.429	28	49	.364	49	80	269	**373**	72	76	284	374	1	4/14	4	**13**

1959 National League
(4/9–9/29)

Team	Home Games W	Home Games L	Home Games PCT	Road Games W	Road Games L	Road Games PCT	Home Games HR	Home Games OHR	Home Games R	Home Games OR	Road Games HR	Road Games OHR	Road Games R	Road Games OR	DIF	LDF	WS	LS
Los Angeles	46	32	.590	42	36	**.538**	82	**90**	363	333	66	67	342	**337**	15	**9/29**	**7**	5
Milwaukee	49	29	**.628**	37	41	.474	83	64	350	274	**94**	**64**	**374**	349	**89**	9/27	**7**	7
San Francisco	42	35	.545	41	36	.532	80	63	339	**271**	87	76	366	342	79	9/19	4	5
Pittsburgh	47	30	.610	31	46	.403	**47**	**53**	348	334	65	81	303	346			5	**9**
Chicago	38	39	.494	36	41	.468	87	76	336	329	76	76	337	359	1	4/11	5	7
Cincinnati	43	34	.558	31	46	.403	**101**	84	**423**	**367**	60	78	341	371	2	5/9	4	6
St. Louis	42	35	.545	29	48	.377	64	64	366	359	54	73	275	366			4	7
Philadelphia	37	40	.481	27	50	.351	55	66	**316**	354	58	84	283	371	4	4/13	5	**9**

1959 American League
(4/9–9/27)

Team	Home Games W	Home Games L	Home Games PCT	Road Games W	Road Games L	Road Games PCT	Home Games HR	Home Games OHR	Home Games R	Home Games OR	Road Games HR	Road Games OHR	Road Games R	Road Games OR	DIF	LDF	WS	LS
Chicago	47	30	**.610**	47	30	**.610**	**44**	61	313	**272**	53	68	356	**316**	87	**9/22**	8	5
Cleveland	43	34	.558	46	31	.597	84	74	346	316	83	74	**399**	330	**90**	7/27	8	7
New York	40	37	.519	39	38	.507	63	**45**	293	305	**90**	75	394	342	4	4/15	6	5
Detroit	41	36	.532	35	42	.455	**95**	**105**	401	**411**	65	72	312	321			5	6
Boston	43	34	.558	32	45	.416	62	66	**404**	356	63	69	322	340			5	7
Baltimore	38	39	.494	36	41	.468	53	50	**260**	299	56	61	291	322	1	6/9	4	6
Kansas City	37	40	.481	29	48	.377	58	80	362	386	59	68	319	374			**11**	13
Washington	34	43	.442	29	48	.377	83	68	307	360	80	**55**	312	341	5	4/13	4	**18**

1960 National League
(4/12–10/2)

Team	Home Games W	Home Games L	Home Games PCT	Road Games W	Road Games L	Road Games PCT	Home Games HR	Home Games OHR	Home Games R	Home Games OR	Road Games HR	Road Games OHR	Road Games R	Road Games OR	DIF	LDF	WS	LS
Pittsburgh	52	25	**.675**	43	34	**.558**	51	36	362	287	69	69	372	306	**146**	**9/25**	**9**	4
Milwaukee	51	26	.662	37	40	.481	**90**	56	342	270	80	74	**382**	388	3	7/24	7	4
St. Louis	51	26	.662	35	42	.455	78	64	361	308	60	63	278	308			7	8
Los Angeles	42	35	.545	40	37	.519	89	**97**	**379**	334	37	**57**	283	**259**	9	4/20	5	4
San Francisco	45	32	.584	34	43	.442	**46**	**34**	**296**	**256**	**84**	73	375	375	30	5/29	7	6
Cincinnati	37	40	.481	30	47	.390	75	68	314	347	65	66	326	345	2	4/13	**9**	6
Chicago	33	44	.429	27	50	.351	52	78	331	**390**	67	74	303	386	2	4/15	4	**9**
Philadelphia	31	46	.403	28	49	.364	54	74	300	373	45	59	246	318			6	7

1960 American League
(4/18–10/2)

Team	Home Games W	Home Games L	Home Games PCT	Road Games W	Road Games L	Road Games PCT	Home Games HR	Home Games OHR	Home Games R	Home Games OR	Road Games HR	Road Games OHR	Road Games R	Road Games OR	DIF	LDF	WS	LS
New York	55	22	**.714**	42	35	.545	**92**	**52**	350	**273**	**101**	71	**396**	354	**99**	**9/25**	**15**	4
Baltimore	44	33	.571	45	32	**.584**	**50**	**52**	332	313	73	65	350	**293**	29	9/9	8	5
Chicago	51	26	.662	36	41	.468	57	54	**379**	298	55	73	362	319	31	8/14	8	5
Cleveland	39	38	.507	37	40	.481	62	84	**315**	351	65	77	352	342	10	6/15	5	5
Washington	32	45	.416	41	36	.532	75	74	336	366	72	**56**	336	330	1	4/18	5	7
Detroit	40	37	.519	31	46	.403	78	**85**	322	323	72	**56**	311	321	11	4/29	7	**10**
Boston	36	41	.468	29	48	.377	65	69	347	**413**	59	58	311	362			7	**10**
Kansas City	34	43	.442	24	53	.312	58	79	327	369	52	81	288	387			5	**10**

1961 National League
(4/11–10/1)

Team	Home Games W	Home Games L	Home Games PCT	Road Games W	Road Games L	Road Games PCT	Home Games HR	Home Games OHR	Home Games R	Home Games OR	Road Games HR	Road Games OHR	Road Games R	Road Games OR	DIF	LDF	WS	LS
Cincinnati	47	30	.610	46	31	**.597**	70	75	345	355	88	72	365	**298**	**113**	**9/26**	8	8
Los Angeles	45	32	.584	44	33	.571	83	**109**	373	358	74	**58**	362	339	28	8/15	8	10
San Francisco	45	32	.584	40	37	.519	97	77	371	316	86	75	**402**	339	37	5/31	6	6
Milwaukee	45	32	.584	38	39	.494	84	72	324	**280**	**104**	81	388	376	1	4/28	**10**	8
St. Louis	48	29	**.623**	32	45	.416	54	69	**413**	362	49	67	290	306	4	4/21	8	6
Pittsburgh	38	39	.494	37	40	.481	49	**54**	338	338	79	67	356	337	4	5/2	4	5
Chicago	40	37	.519	24	53	.312	**102**	81	372	391	74	84	317	409			6	8
Philadelphia	22	55	.286	25	52	.325	**43**	77	**256**	**408**	60	78	328	388			4	**23**

1961 American League
(4/10–10/1)

Team	Home Games W	Home Games L	Home Games PCT	Road Games W	Road Games L	Road Games PCT	Home Games HR	Home Games OHR	Home Games R	Home Games OR	Road Games HR	Road Games OHR	Road Games R	Road Games OR	DIF	LDF	WS	LS
New York	65	16	**.802**	44	37	.543	112	59	411	**251**	**128**	78	416	361	**83**	**9/20**	**13**	4
Detroit	50	31	.617	51	30	**.630**	90	95	389	324	90	75	**452**	347	77	7/24	8	8
Baltimore	48	33	.593	47	34	.580	61	**46**	320	283	88	63	371	**305**			7	5
Chicago	53	28	.654	33	48	.407	80	55	411	320	58	103	354	406	4	4/13	12	7
Cleveland	40	41	.494	38	42	.475	74	98	342	380	76	80	395	372	14	6/16	10	7
Boston	50	31	.617	26	55	.321	63	91	401	386	49	76	328	406			6	6
Minnesota	36	44	.450	34	46	.425	92	89	380	423	75	74	327	355	11	4/27	6	13
Los Angeles	46	36	.561	24	55	.304	**122**	**126**	**447**	421	67	**54**	297	363	4	4/14	6	9
Kansas City	33	47	.413	28	53	.346	**33**	61	365	**434**	57	80	318	429	4	4/14	4	6
Washington	33	46	.418	28	54	.341	34	53	**288**	366	85	78	330	410			5	**14**

1962 National League
(4/9–10/3)

Team	Home Games			Road Games			Home Games				Road Games							
	W	L	PCT	W	L	PCT	HR	OHR	R	OR	HR	OHR	R	OR	DIF	LDF	WS	LS
San Francisco	61	21	**.744**	42	41	.506	**109**	74	**479**	299	**95**	74	399	391	54	**10/3**	10	6
Los Angeles	54	29	.651	48	34	**.585**	47	**39**	409	**289**	93	76	**433**	408	**111**	10/2	**13**	5
Cincinnati	58	23	.716	40	41	.494	95	68	456	294	72	81	346	391			9	4
Pittsburgh	51	30	.630	42	38	.525	48	56	358	315	60	**62**	348	311	19	4/29	10	6
Milwaukee	49	32	.605	37	44	.457	93	74	374	307	88	77	356	358			7	6
St. Louis	44	37	.543	40	41	.494	64	83	407	362	73	66	367	**302**	12	4/28	7	8
Philadelphia	46	34	.575	35	46	.432	70	66	341	346	72	89	364	413	1	4/9	6	8
Houston	32	48	.400	32	48	.400	**44**	41	**268**	340	61	72	324	377	3	4/12	6	9
Chicago	32	49	.395	27	54	.333	71	94	333	456	55	65	299	371			5	10
New York	22	58	.275	18	62	.225	93	**120**	335	**510**	46	72	282	438			3	**17**

1962 American League
(4/9–9/30)

Team	Home Games			Road Games			Home Games				Road Games							
	W	L	PCT	W	L	PCT	HR	OHR	R	OR	HR	OHR	R	OR	DIF	LDF	WS	LS
New York	50	30	**.625**	46	36	.561	92	67	369	306	**107**	79	**448**	374	**130**	**9/25**	**9**	6
Minnesota	45	36	.556	46	35	**.568**	97	97	417	378	88	69	381	335	1	6/11	6	5
Los Angeles	40	41	.494	46	35	**.568**	50	**50**	357	368	87	68	361	338	5	7/5	5	6
Detroit	49	33	.598	36	43	.456	**117**	91	**448**	368	92	78	310	**324**			5	7
Chicago	43	38	.531	42	39	.519	**36**	58	315	319	56	**65**	392	339	5	4/20	6	5
Cleveland	43	38	.531	37	44	.457	103	89	348	350	77	85	334	395	47	7/7	6	9
Baltimore	44	38	.537	33	47	.413	66	65	328	**299**	90	82	324	381			5	6
Boston	39	40	.494	37	44	.457	72	76	369	377	74	83	338	379			5	8
Kansas City	39	42	.481	33	48	.407	64	**118**	387	**423**	52	81	358	414	1	4/10	6	7
Washington	27	53	.338	33	48	.407	65	79	**293**	364	67	72	306	352	6	4/14	5	**13**

1963 National League
(4/8–9/29)

Team	Home Games			Road Games			Home Games				Road Games							
	W	L	PCT	W	L	PCT	HR	OHR	R	OR	HR	OHR	R	OR	DIF	LDF	WS	LS
Los Angeles	53	28	**.654**	46	35	**.568**	42	43	296	**248**	68	68	344	302	**98**	**9/24**	8	5
St. Louis	53	28	**.654**	40	41	.494	79	70	**429**	311	49	54	318	317	32	7/1	**10**	8
San Francisco	50	31	.617	38	43	.469	**101**	64	363	289	**96**	62	**362**	352	47	6/24	9	7
Philadelphia	45	36	.556	42	39	.519	61	60	340	282	65	53	302	296	6	4/15	8	5
Cincinnati	46	35	.568	40	41	.494	65	46	344	300	57	71	304	294	1	4/8	7	4
Milwaukee	45	36	.556	39	42	.481	68	81	341	307	71	68	336	296	2	4/18	7	8
Chicago	43	38	.531	39	42	.481	63	70	298	302	64	**49**	272	**276**	1	6/6	6	6
Pittsburgh	42	39	.519	32	49	.395	47	42	275	295	61	57	292	300	9	5/6	5	6
Houston	44	37	.543	22	59	.272	**25**	**34**	**236**	268	37	61	228	372			6	10
New York	34	47	.420	17	64	.210	61	**93**	276	**381**	35	69	225	393			5	**15**

1963 American League
(4/8–9/29)

Team	Home Games			Road Games			Home Games				Road Games							
	W	L	PCT	W	L	PCT	HR	OHR	R	OR	HR	OHR	R	OR	DIF	LDF	WS	LS
New York	58	22	**.725**	46	35	**.568**	88	55	367	**246**	100	60	347	301	**120**	**9/13**	7	4
Chicago	49	33	.598	45	35	.563	63	46	362	272	51	**54**	321	**272**	19	6/14	7	4
Minnesota	48	33	.593	43	37	.538	**112**	99	377	306	**113**	63	**390**	296			**10**	5
Baltimore	48	33	.593	38	43	.469	72	56	311	268	74	81	333	353	28	6/8	9	5
Cleveland	41	40	.506	38	43	.469	88	87	308	341	81	89	327	361	1	4/9	7	9
Detroit	47	34	.580	32	49	.395	94	**109**	**395**	339	54	86	305	364	4	4/18	8	**10**
Boston	44	36	.550	32	49	.395	95	73	383	346	76	79	283	358	5	5/19	6	9
Kansas City	36	45	.444	37	44	.457	52	87	326	390	43	69	289	314	11	5/6	5	6
Los Angeles	39	42	.481	31	49	.388	**24**	**44**	**264**	306	71	76	333	354	1	4/9	5	**10**
Washington	31	49	.388	25	57	.305	63	82	286	**406**	75	94	292	406			7	**10**

1964 National League
(4/13–10/4)

Team	Home Games			Road Games			Home Games				Road Games							
	W	L	PCT	W	L	PCT	HR	OHR	R	OR	HR	OHR	R	OR	DIF	LDF	WS	LS
St. Louis	48	33	**.593**	45	36	.556	59	81	386	378	50	52	329	274	6	**10/4**	8	5
Cincinnati	47	34	.580	45	36	.556	62	59	331	294	68	53	329	**272**	4	10/3	**9**	4
Philadelphia	46	35	.568	46	35	**.568**	59	61	352	298	71	68	341	334	**133**	9/26	5	**10**
San Francisco	44	37	.543	46	35	**.568**	86	63	314	299	**79**	55	342	288	36	7/15	5	6
Milwaukee	45	36	.556	43	38	.531	**89**	78	**405**	356	70	82	**398**	388			8	7
Los Angeles	41	40	.506	39	42	.481	**26**	38	259	**259**	53	**50**	355	313	1	4/14	4	7
Pittsburgh	42	39	.519	38	43	.469	55	**31**	340	315	66	61	323	321			5	6
Chicago	40	41	.494	36	45	.444	85	**87**	337	**397**	60	57	312	327	1	4/14	4	5
Houston	41	40	.506	25	56	.309	29	44	**246**	290	41	61	249	338	3	4/15	6	8
New York	33	48	.407	20	61	.247	58	61	298	363	45	69	271	413			5	8

1964 American League
(4/13–10/4)

Team	Home Games			Road Games			Home Games				Road Games							
	W	L	PCT	W	L	PCT	HR	OHR	R	OR	HR	OHR	R	OR	DIF	LDF	WS	LS
New York	50	31	.617	49	32	**.605**	69	56	363	290	93	73	**367**	287	33	**10/3**	**11**	6
Chicago	52	29	**.642**	46	35	.568	43	42	306	**213**	63	82	336	288	41	9/16	9	6
Baltimore	49	32	.605	48	33	.593	79	64	351	296	83	**65**	328	**271**	**87**	9/16	7	4
Detroit	46	35	.568	39	42	.481	85	89	340	320	72	75	359	358	3	4/16	7	6
Los Angeles	45	36	.556	37	44	.457	**32**	**31**	**230**	226	70	69	314	325	2	4/14	**11**	5
Cleveland	41	40	.506	38	43	.469	84	82	365	351	80	72	324	342	16	5/16	8	7
Minnesota	40	41	.494	39	42	.481	**115**	88	386	336	**106**	93	351	342	3	4/16	6	**8**
Boston	45	36	.556	27	54	.333	100	87	**393**	382	86	91	295	411	2	4/17	5	7
Washington	31	50	.383	31	50	.383	71	95	294	380	54	77	284	353			4	**8**
Kansas City	26	55	.321	31	50	.383	107	**132**	330	**455**	59	88	291	381			5	7

1965 National League
(4/12–10/3)

Team	Home Games			Road Games			Home Games				Road Games							
	W	L	PCT	W	L	PCT	HR	OHR	R	OR	HR	OHR	R	OR	DIF	LDF	WS	LS
Los Angeles	50	31	.617	47	34	**.580**	26	41	268	**218**	52	86	340	303	**136**	**10/2**	13	4
San Francisco	51	30	**.630**	44	37	.543	81	81	365	327	78	56	317	**266**	21	9/27	**14**	4
Pittsburgh	49	32	.605	41	40	.506	37	38	334	284	74	51	341	296	4	4/20	12	8
Cincinnati	49	32	.605	40	41	.494	**108**	69	**450**	352	75	67	**375**	352	16	9/1	4	6
Milwaukee	44	37	.543	42	39	.519	98	75	366	331	**98**	**48**	342	302	3	8/20	10	6
Philadelphia	45	35	.563	40	41	.494	77	55	312	300	67	61	342	367	3	4/14	6	5
St. Louis	42	39	.519	38	42	.475	68	**103**	379	361	41	63	328	313			7	5
Chicago	40	41	.494	32	49	.395	79	94	330	**380**	55	60	305	343	4	4/17	4	8
Houston	36	45	.444	29	52	.358	**25**	**32**	**250**	313	72	91	319	398			10	8
New York	29	52	.358	21	60	.259	50	81	258	**380**	57	66	237	372			4	**11**

		Home Games			Road Games			Home Games				Road Games							
	Team	W	L	PCT	W	L	PCT	HR	OHR	R	OR	HR	OHR	R	OR	DIF	LDF	WS	LS
1965 American League (4/12–10/3)	Minnesota	51	30	.630	51	30	**.630**	67	**89**	**379**	308	**83**	77	**395**	**292**	**138**	**9/26**	9	4
	Chicago	48	33	.593	47	34	.580	45	51	288	**241**	80	71	359	314	29	6/28	**10**	6
	Baltimore	46	33	.582	48	35	.578	62	71	302	282	63	**49**	339	296			9	3
	Detroit	47	34	.580	42	39	.519	**96**	85	362	310	66	52	318	**292**	8	5/1	8	5
	Cleveland	52	30	**.634**	35	45	.438	90	58	342	287	66	71	321	326	9	7/4	**10**	6
	New York	40	43	.482	37	42	.468	77	63	320	306	72	63	291	298			5	7
	California	46	34	.575	29	53	.354	**36**	**35**	**265**	254	56	56	262	315			5	5
	Washington	36	45	.444	34	47	.420	62	86	302	366	74	74	289	355			4	5
	Boston	34	47	.420	28	53	.346	94	88	375	**433**	71	70	294	358	4	4/20	4	**8**
	Kansas City	33	48	.407	26	55	.321	47	68	301	365	63	93	284	390			4	**8**
1966 National League (4/12–10/2)	Los Angeles	53	28	**.654**	42	39	.519	**43**	**36**	286	**220**	65	48	320	**270**	29	**10/2**	8	4
	San Francisco	47	34	.580	46	34	**.575**	91	77	317	312	90	63	358	314	**87**	9/1	**12**	4
	Pittsburgh	46	35	.568	46	35	.568	48	48	384	317	**110**	77	375	324	69	9/10	6	4
	Philadelphia	48	33	.593	39	42	.481	52	65	354	319	65	72	342	321	3	4/15	7	5
	Atlanta	43	38	.531	42	39	.519	**119**	82	394	335	88	**47**	**388**	348			8	7
	St. Louis	43	38	.531	40	41	.494	48	64	**274**	288	60	66	297	289			7	8
	Cincinnati	46	33	.582	30	51	.370	91	93	**417**	372	58	60	275	330			8	**11**
	Houston	45	36	.556	27	54	.333	48	48	318	317	64	82	294	378			5	9
	New York	32	49	.395	34	46	.425	51	94	276	372	47	72	311	389			7	7
	Chicago	32	49	.395	27	54	.333	80	**100**	342	**410**	60	84	302	399			4	6
1966 American League (4/11–10/2)	Baltimore	48	31	**.608**	49	32	**.605**	85	65	**375**	296	**90**	62	**380**	305	**125**	**9/22**	**10**	4
	Minnesota	49	32	.605	40	41	.494	94	83	**375**	311	50	**56**	288	**270**	3	4/14	6	7
	Detroit	42	39	.519	46	35	.568	**97**	**101**	360	374	82	84	359	324	5	4/16	6	6
	Chicago	45	36	.556	38	43	.469	31	36	**273**	**217**	56	65	301	300	2	4/13	8	5
	Cleveland	41	40	.506	40	41	.494	82	65	283	300	73	64	291	286	56	6/12	**10**	6
	California	42	39	.519	38	43	.469	54	67	303	315	68	69	301	328			7	6
	Kansas City	42	39	.519	32	47	.405	**18**	**27**	284	292	52	79	280	356			8	5
	Washington	42	36	.538	29	52	.358	62	84	**273**	292	64	70	284	367			5	**8**
	Boston	40	41	.494	32	49	.395	80	97	374	**397**	65	67	281	334			6	6
	New York	35	46	.432	35	43	.449	74	63	302	280	88	61	309	332			6	7
1967 National League (4/10–10/1)	St. Louis	49	32	.605	52	28	**.650**	53	54	326	301	62	43	**369**	**256**	**121**	**9/18**	**8**	4
	San Francisco	51	31	**.622**	40	40	.500	65	59	333	271	**75**	54	319	280			7	6
	Chicago	49	34	.590	38	40	.487	70	**90**	366	**332**	58	52	336	292	5	7/24	7	7
	Cincinnati	49	32	.605	38	43	.469	57	66	343	287	52	**35**	261	276	57	6/17	5	4
	Philadelphia	45	35	.563	37	45	.451	48	44	320	292	55	42	292	289			**8**	5
	Pittsburgh	49	32	.605	32	49	.395	43	49	**370**	321	48	59	309	372	2	4/12	5	5
	Atlanta	48	33	.593	29	52	.358	**91**	74	352	316	67	44	279	324			5	6
	Los Angeles	42	39	.519	31	50	.383	36	35	**241**	**230**	46	58	278	365			5	8
	Houston	46	35	.568	23	58	.284	**31**	**32**	337	315	62	88	289	427	2	4/12	7	**10**
	New York	36	42	.462	25	59	.298	44	61	258	307	39	63	240	365			5	7
1967 American League (4/10–10/1)	Boston	49	32	.605	43	38	**.531**	**90**	**88**	**408**	**355**	68	54	314	**259**	18	**10/1**	**10**	5
	Detroit	52	29	**.642**	39	42	.481	83	79	360	272	69	72	323	315	26	9/18	7	7
	Minnesota	52	29	**.642**	39	42	.481	70	63	372	292	61	52	299	298	39	9/30	8	6
	Chicago	49	33	.598	40	40	.500	38	**38**	**243**	**222**	51	**49**	288	269	**89**	9/6	**10**	5
	California	53	30	.639	31	47	.397	56	59	288	276	58	59	279	311	3	4/24	7	7
	Baltimore	35	42	.455	41	43	.488	64	49	283	275	**74**	67	**371**	317	11	4/28	7	6
	Washington	40	40	.500	36	45	.444	57	54	277	332	58	59	273	305			8	6
	Cleveland	36	45	.444	39	42	.481	76	69	274	316	55	51	285	297	1	4/20	4	6
	New York	43	38	.531	29	52	.358	60	47	268	271	40	63	254	350	6	4/29	4	6
	Kansas City	37	44	.457	25	55	.313	**19**	**38**	288	320	50	87	245	340	3	4/13	5	**9**
1968 National League (4/10–9/29)	St. Louis	47	34	**.580**	50	31	**.617**	31	35	267	218	42	47	**316**	254	**160**	**9/15**	**9**	5
	San Francisco	42	39	.519	46	35	.568	60	32	299	242	48	54	300	287	11	5/31	5	3
	Chicago	47	34	**.580**	37	44	.457	**83**	**83**	363	332	47	55	249	279			6	7
	Cincinnati	40	41	.494	43	38	.531	55	66	**377**	**400**	**51**	48	313	273	1	4/10	7	7
	Atlanta	41	40	.506	40	41	.494	42	43	241	241	38	44	273	308	1	6/1	6	5
	Pittsburgh	40	41	.494	40	41	.494	33	30	289	268	47	43	294	264			**9**	**10**
	Los Angeles	41	40	.506	35	46	.432	25	**24**	**212**	**215**	42	41	258	294			7	8
	Philadelphia	38	43	.469	38	43	.469	52	46	274	297	48	45	269	318	1	4/10	7	9
	New York	32	49	.395	41	40	.506	49	50	224	270	32	**37**	249	**229**			4	6
	Houston	42	39	.519	30	51	.370	**22**	30	279	269	44	38	231	319	9	4/18	4	6
1968 American League (4/10–9/29)	Detroit	56	25	**.691**	47	34	**.580**	**107**	**75**	**348**	254	**78**	54	**323**	**238**	**158**	**9/17**	**11**	4
	Baltimore	47	33	.588	44	38	.537	57	54	288	**248**	76	47	291	249	11	5/9	8	7
	Cleveland	43	37	.538	43	38	.531	36	56	246	262	39	42	270	242	1	4/10	6	7
	Boston	46	35	.568	40	41	.494	58	61	325	299	67	54	289	312	1	4/10	8	4
	New York	39	42	.481	44	37	.543	56	50	268	268	53	49	268	263	3	4/12	10	6
	Oakland	44	38	.537	38	42	.475	38	58	296	258	56	66	273	286			4	7
	Minnesota	41	40	.506	38	43	.469	50	51	299	290	55	**41**	263	256	10	4/19	6	6
	California	32	49	.395	35	46	.432	49	66	229	299	34	65	269	316			4	6
	Chicago	36	45	.444	31	50	.383	**29**	**47**	**225**	273	42	50	238	254			4	**10**
	Washington	34	47	.420	31	49	.388	53	53	257	**300**	71	65	267	365			4	9

	Team	Home Games			Road Games			Home Games				Road Games							
		W	L	PCT	W	L	PCT	HR	OHR	R	OR	HR	OHR	R	OR	DIF	LDF	WS	LS
1969 National League (4/8–10/2)	East																		
	New York	52	30	.634	48	32	**.600**	56	59	312	270	53	60	320	271	23	**9/24**	**11**	5
	Chicago	49	32	.605	43	38	.531	84	64	387	321	58	**54**	333	290	**155**	9/9	7	8
	Pittsburgh	47	34	.580	41	40	.506	**41**	**33**	324	322	**78**	63	**401**	330	6	4/13	8	7
	St. Louis	42	38	.525	45	37	.549	**41**	43	273	273	49	56	322	**267**			6	4
	Philadelphia	30	51	.370	33	48	.407	75	64	317	378	62	70	328	367			9	9
	Montreal	24	57	.296	28	53	.346	73	**87**	288	**421**	52	58	294	370	1	4/9	4	**20**
	West																		
	Atlanta	50	31	.617	43	38	.531	77	84	360	321	64	60	331	310	**107**	**9/30**	10	5
	San Francisco	52	29	**.642**	38	43	.469	77	61	362	317	59	59	351	319	29	9/22	9	5
	Cincinnati	50	31	.617	39	42	.481	**97**	74	**407**	373	74	75	391	395	22	9/11	9	5
	Los Angeles	50	31	.617	35	46	.432	**41**	55	325	**258**	56	67	320	303	33	8/20	7	8
	Houston	52	29	**.642**	29	52	.358	47	43	371	313	57	68	305	355			10	8
	San Diego	28	53	.346	24	57	.296	47	47	**239**	358	52	66	229	388	3	4/10	6	11
1969 American League (4/7–10/2)	East																		
	Baltimore	60	21	**.741**	49	32	**.605**	82	**51**	402	251	**93**	66	377	**266**	**169**	**9/13**	8	5
	Detroit	46	35	.568	44	37	.543	104	72	361	305	78	**56**	340	296	3	4/10	7	4
	Boston	46	35	.568	41	40	.506	**105**	78	392	391	92	77	351	345	6	4/15	8	7
	Washington	47	34	.580	39	42	.481	77	62	353	290	71	73	341	354	1	4/11	6	6
	New York	48	32	.600	32	49	.395	44	**51**	284	**245**	50	67	278	342	2	4/8	8	7
	Cleveland	33	48	.407	29	51	.363	56	60	**276**	341	63	74	297	376			5	**10**
	West																		
	Minnesota	57	24	.704	40	41	.494	79	61	**414**	298	84	58	376	320	**138**	**9/22**	**9**	5
	Oakland	49	32	.605	39	42	.481	73	70	330	315	75	93	**410**	363	30	7/4	7	6
	California	43	38	.531	28	53	.346	49	65	277	305	39	61	251	347	2	4/12	6	**10**
	Kansas City	36	45	.444	33	48	.407	**39**	63	301	362	59	73	285	326	12	4/24	4	6
	Chicago	41	40	.506	27	54	.333	61	80	352	387	51	66	273	336	4	4/26	5	8
	Seattle	34	47	.420	30	51	.370	74	**93**	329	**399**	51	79	310	400	3	4/12	5	**10**
1970 National League (4/6–10/1)	East																		
	Pittsburgh	50	32	.610	39	41	.488	43	**41**	356	315	87	65	373	349	**85**	**9/27**	7	7
	Chicago	46	34	.575	38	44	.463	**109**	92	**471**	394	70	**51**	335	**285**	64	6/23	**11**	**12**
	New York	44	38	.537	39	41	.488	63	75	374	**314**	57	60	321	316	25	9/10	7	5
	St. Louis	34	47	.420	42	39	.519	51	44	377	**418**	62	58	367	329	14	4/21	6	8
	Philadelphia	40	40	.500	33	48	.407	48	63	**293**	337	53	69	301	393	7	4/13	6	10
	Montreal	39	41	.488	34	48	.415	77	91	363	385	59	71	324	422			5	11
	West																		
	Cincinnati	57	24	**.704**	45	36	.556	100	58	416	334	91	60	359	347	**178**	**9/17**	8	4
	Los Angeles	39	42	.481	48	32	**.600**	**35**	82	310	316	52	82	**439**	368			7	5
	San Francisco	48	33	.593	38	43	.469	84	77	413	386	81	79	418	440	1	4/11	5	4
	Houston	44	37	.543	35	46	.432	51	64	350	351	78	67	394	412	1	4/7	7	8
	Atlanta	42	39	.519	34	47	.420	92	**119**	395	398	68	66	341	374			**11**	7
	San Diego	31	50	.383	32	49	.395	68	56	312	393	**104**	93	369	395	1	4/7	5	8
1970 American League (4/6–10/1)	East																		
	Baltimore	59	22	**.728**	49	32	**.605**	88	58	386	**256**	**91**	81	**406**	318	**169**	**9/17**	**11**	3
	New York	53	28	.654	40	41	.494	60	**40**	317	257	51	90	363	355			6	5
	Boston	52	29	.642	35	46	.432	117	75	**455**	382	86	81	331	340	2	4/8	7	5
	Detroit	42	39	.519	37	44	.457	86	86	348	379	62	67	318	352	10	4/25	8	7
	Cleveland	43	38	.531	33	48	.407	**133**	**103**	386	370	50	**60**	263	**305**			7	5
	Washington	40	41	.494	30	51	.370	72	61	303	330	66	78	323	359			7	**14**
	West																		
	Minnesota	51	30	.630	47	34	.580	66	53	366	285	87	77	378	320	**171**	**9/22**	7	9
	Oakland	49	32	.605	40	41	.494	83	56	337	265	88	78	341	328	1	4/7	8	6
	California	43	38	.531	43	38	.531	**41**	59	**287**	274	73	95	344	356	16	5/15	5	9
	Kansas City	35	44	.443	30	53	.361	46	48	305	331	51	90	306	374			4	7
	Milwaukee	38	42	.475	27	55	.329	68	72	313	362	58	74	300	389			5	9
	Chicago	31	53	.369	25	53	.321	78	97	346	**469**	45	67	287	353			4	8
1971 National League (4/6–9/30)	East																		
	Pittsburgh	52	28	**.650**	45	37	.549	66	49	**393**	279	**88**	59	**395**	320	**124**	**9/22**	**11**	4
	St. Louis	45	36	.556	45	36	.556	38	49	376	358	57	55	363	341	16	6/8	7	7
	Chicago	44	37	.543	39	42	.481	74	70	363	342	54	62	274	306	1	4/6	7	5
	New York	44	37	.543	39	42	.481	48	50	281	256	50	50	307	**294**	31	6/10	5	6
	Montreal	36	44	.450	35	46	.432	50	68	304	366	38	65	318	363	10	5/1	8	6
	Philadelphia	34	47	.420	33	48	.407	73	80	296	353	50	52	262	335			4	**8**
	West																		
	San Francisco	51	30	.630	39	42	.481	71	58	372	300	69	70	334	344	**176**	**9/30**	9	7
	Los Angeles	42	39	.519	47	34	**.580**	43	56	324	286	52	54	339	301			8	6
	Atlanta	43	39	.524	39	41	.488	**96**	**90**	366	**384**	57	62	277	315	7	4/11	6	5
	Cincinnati	46	35	.568	33	48	.407	69	51	303	**251**	69	61	283	330			5	7
	Houston	39	42	.481	40	41	.494	**18**	**27**	256	263	53	**48**	329	304	1	4/5	8	6
	San Diego	33	48	.407	28	52	.350	42	43	**233**	296	54	50	253	314			4	**8**
1971 American League (4/5–9/30)	East																		
	Baltimore	53	24	**.688**	48	33	.593	78	67	374	**254**	80	58	**368**	276	**142**	**9/24**	**11**	4
	Detroit	54	27	.667	37	44	.457	**90**	70	352	289	**89**	56	349	356	3	4/8	7	3
	Boston	47	33	.588	38	44	.463	88	75	**375**	338	73	61	316	329	39	6/4	7	7
	New York	44	37	.543	38	43	.469	39	61	327	297	58	65	321	344			5	5
	Washington	35	46	.432	28	50	.359	34	59	268	296	52	73	269	364	2	4/6	6	**9**
	Cleveland	29	52	.358	31	50	.383	62	**99**	297	**400**	47	55	246	347			4	7
	West																		
	Oakland	46	35	.568	55	25	**.688**	84	74	325	300	76	57	366	**264**	**164**	**9/15**	7	4
	Kansas City	44	37	.543	41	39	.513	**23**	**36**	296	277	57	48	307	289	1	4/6	6	8
	Chicago	39	42	.481	40	41	.494	60	53	278	310	78	47	339	287	4	4/10	6	7
	California	35	46	.432	41	40	.506	39	55	**233**	297	57	**46**	278	279	3	4/19	7	4
	Minnesota	37	42	.468	37	44	.457	57	71	332	356	59	68	322	314	2	4/13	6	6
	Milwaukee	34	48	.415	35	44	.443	46	64	282	319	58	66	252	290	4	4/15	3	8

1972 National League
(4/15–10/4)

Team	Home Games W	L	PCT	Road Games W	L	PCT	Home Games HR	OHR	R	OR	Road Games HR	OHR	R	OR	DIF	LDF	WS	LS
East																		
Pittsburgh	49	29	**.628**	47	30	.610	53	**34**	351	259	57	56	340	**253**	**113**	**9/21**	9	6
Chicago	46	31	.597	39	39	.500	83	63	**392**	305	50	49	293	262			7	8
New York	41	37	.526	42	36	.538	45	56	254	264	60	62	274	314	50	6/8	**11**	3
St. Louis	40	37	.519	35	44	.443	**31**	38	298	308	39	49	270	292			7	8
Montreal	35	43	.449	35	43	.449	50	56	252	324	41	47	261	285	14	5/1	5	8
Philadelphia	28	51	.354	31	46	.403	49	57	246	316	49	60	257	319	1	4/15	5	**10**
West																		
Cincinnati	42	34	.553	53	25	**.679**	58	59	300	266	66	70	**407**	291	**115**	**9/22**	9	4
Houston	41	36	.532	43	33	.566	58	56	367	355	**76**	58	341	281	31	6/24	9	6
Los Angeles	41	34	.547	44	36	.550	46	37	267	**221**	52	**46**	317	306	29	6/8	6	5
Atlanta	36	41	.468	34	43	.442	**86**	**88**	339	**392**	58	67	289	338			5	7
San Francisco	34	43	.442	35	43	.449	**86**	65	336	321	64	65	326	328	4	4/18	5	8
San Diego	26	54	.325	32	41	.438	41	64	**217**	315	61	57	271	350	2	4/17	5	**10**

1972 American League
(4/15–10/4)

Team	Home Games W	L	PCT	Road Games W	L	PCT	Home Games HR	OHR	R	OR	Road Games HR	OHR	R	OR	DIF	LDF	WS	LS
East																		
Detroit	44	34	.564	42	36	.538	68	67	312	288	54	**34**	246	226	**110**	**10/3**	5	4
Boston	52	26	.667	33	44	.429	**71**	49	**373**	**303**	53	52	267	317	24	10/1	7	5
Baltimore	38	39	.494	42	35	.545	44	40	240	211	56	45	279	**219**	41	9/4	**9**	5
New York	46	31	.597	33	45	.423	53	37	270	219	50	50	287	308			6	5
Cleveland	43	34	.558	29	50	.367	59	**79**	263	261	32	44	209	258	15	5/27	6	8
Milwaukee	37	42	.468	28	49	.364	36	45	243	286	52	71	250	309	3	4/17	6	9
West																		
Oakland	48	29	.623	45	33	**.577**	68	52	287	**210**	**66**	44	**317**	247	**132**	**9/28**	8	4
Chicago	55	23	**.705**	32	44	.421	65	44	341	252	43	50	225	286	14	8/28	7	6
Minnesota	42	32	.568	35	45	.438	52	54	299	255	41	51	238	280	25	5/20	6	8
Kansas City	44	33	.571	32	45	.416	**29**	**28**	309	257	49	57	271	288	4	4/18	5	6
California	44	36	.550	31	44	.413	30	31	**221**	218	48	59	233	315	1	4/15	6	6
Texas	31	46	.403	23	54	.299	33	41	235	288	23	51	226	340			5	**15**

1973 National League
(4/6–10/1)

Team	Home Games W	L	PCT	Road Games W	L	PCT	Home Games HR	OHR	R	OR	Road Games HR	OHR	R	OR	DIF	LDF	WS	LS
East																		
New York	43	38	.531	39	41	.488	39	61	314	283	46	66	294	305	22	**10/1**	7	5
St. Louis	43	38	.531	38	43	.469	**27**	**30**	290	**255**	48	75	353	348	51	9/11	8	7
Pittsburgh	41	40	.506	39	42	.481	72	42	334	301	82	68	370	392	37	9/20	7	6
Montreal	43	38	.531	36	45	.444	63	70	364	353	62	58	304	349			7	7
Chicago	41	39	.513	36	45	.444	66	72	327	356	51	56	287	299	**80**	7/21	7	**11**
Philadelphia	38	43	.469	33	48	.407	78	80	358	381	56	**51**	284	336			5	7
West																		
Cincinnati	50	31	**.617**	49	32	**.605**	47	67	330	287	**90**	68	**411**	334	31	**9/24**	7	4
Los Angeles	50	31	**.617**	45	35	.563	63	62	338	271	47	67	337	**294**	**79**	9/3	7	9
San Francisco	47	34	.580	41	40	.506	85	79	395	363	76	66	344	339	66	6/16	7	5
Houston	41	40	.506	41	40	.506	58	53	315	322	76	58	366	350	9	5/25	**9**	4
Atlanta	40	40	.500	36	45	.444	**118**	**87**	**460**	**437**	88	57	339	337			6	7
San Diego	31	50	.383	29	52	.358	51	80	**273**	355	61	77	275	415	3	4/8	4	10

1973 American League
(4/6–9/30)

Team	Home Games W	L	PCT	Road Games W	L	PCT	Home Games HR	OHR	R	OR	Road Games HR	OHR	R	OR	DIF	LDF	WS	LS
East																		
Baltimore	50	31	**.617**	47	34	**.580**	63	60	408	284	56	64	346	**277**	**77**	**9/22**	**14**	5
Boston	48	33	.593	41	40	.506	83	83	390	339	64	75	348	308	12	7/9	8	5
Detroit	47	34	.580	38	43	.469	86	71	329	332	71	83	313	342	42	8/14	8	8
New York	50	31	**.617**	30	51	.370	74	**42**	359	263	57	67	282	347	46	7/31	8	8
Milwaukee	40	41	.494	34	47	.420	73	52	349	343	72	67	359	388	14	6/19	10	6
Cleveland	34	47	.420	37	44	.457	**92**	**100**	320	**427**	66	72	360	399	1	4/7	4	**10**
West																		
Oakland	50	31	**.617**	44	37	.543	70	70	**313**	**253**	**77**	73	**445**	362	**81**	**9/23**	9	5
Kansas City	48	33	.593	40	41	.494	54	61	**422**	404	60	53	333	348	29	8/15	7	5
Minnesota	37	44	.457	44	37	.543	56	60	357	386	64	55	381	306	10	7/2	5	7
California	43	38	.531	36	45	.444	**41**	49	316	294	52	55	313	363	3	6/27	5	5
Chicago	40	41	.494	37	44	.457	56	58	329	368	55	**52**	323	337	62	6/29	9	5
Texas	35	46	.432	22	59	.272	47	51	321	408	63	79	298	436			6	8

1974 National League
(4/5–10/2)

Team	Home Games W	L	PCT	Road Games W	L	PCT	Home Games HR	OHR	R	OR	Road Games HR	OHR	R	OR	DIF	LDF	WS	LS
East																		
Pittsburgh	52	29	**.642**	36	45	.444	47	**32**	380	303	67	61	371	354	28	**10/2**	8	6
St. Louis	44	37	.543	42	38	.525	45	46	356	329	38	51	321	314	**83**	9/30	6	7
Philadelphia	46	35	.568	34	47	.420	55	56	378	337	40	55	298	364	61	8/2	6	8
Montreal	42	38	.525	37	44	.457	50	49	356	329	36	50	306	328	22	5/16	8	7
New York	36	45	.444	35	46	.432	**43**	49	279	325	53	50	293	321			7	7
Chicago	32	49	.395	34	47	.420	67	**72**	344	**424**	43	50	325	402	2	4/10	6	8
West																		
Los Angeles	52	29	**.642**	50	31	**.617**	68	51	355	**250**	**71**	61	**443**	311	**177**	**10/1**	**9**	6
Cincinnati	50	31	.617	48	33	.593	**74**	62	**389**	295	61	64	387	336	2	4/6	7	4
Atlanta	46	35	.568	42	39	.519	65	44	337	290	55	53	324	**273**			6	4
Houston	46	35	.568	35	46	.432	58	35	330	293	52	**49**	323	339			6	**10**
San Francisco	37	44	.457	35	46	.432	50	61	340	398	43	55	294	325	9	4/13	4	6
San Diego	36	45	.444	24	57	.296	47	54	**272**	381	52	70	269	449			5	**10**

1974 American League
(4/5–10/2)

Team	Home Games W	L	PCT	Road Games W	L	PCT	Home Games HR	OHR	R	OR	Road Games HR	OHR	R	OR	DIF	LDF	WS	LS
East																		
Baltimore	46	35	.568	45	36	**.556**	48	46	**281**	293	68	55	**378**	319	25	**10/1**	**10**	5
New York	47	34	.580	42	39	.519	42	50	315	295	59	54	356	328	37	9/23	6	7
Boston	46	35	.568	38	43	.469	58	66	**375**	348	51	60	321	313	**97**	9/8	6	8
Cleveland	40	41	.494	37	44	.457	72	**92**	338	349	59	**46**	324	345	6	7/12	5	6
Milwaukee	40	41	.494	36	45	.444	58	69	342	329	62	57	305	331	23	6/8	5	6
Detroit	36	45	.444	36	45	.444	**74**	84	335	**412**	57	64	285	356	2	5/18	6	6
West																		
Oakland	49	32	**.605**	41	40	.506	69	43	345	**265**	63	47	344	**286**	**142**	**9/27**	6	4
Texas	42	38	.525	42	38	.525	43	57	321	340	56	69	369	358	17	5/8	5	6
Minnesota	48	33	.593	34	47	.420	60	56	365	317	51	59	308	352	3	4/23	5	4
Chicago	46	34	.575	34	46	.425	66	43	360	365	**69**	60	324	356	9	5/19	7	5
Kansas City	40	41	.494	37	44	.457	**38**	**42**	355	353	51	49	312	309			5	8
California	36	45	.444	32	49	.395	46	47	291	287	49	54	327	370	16	4/22	6	**11**

	Team	Home Games W	L	PCT	Road Games W	L	PCT	Home Games HR	OHR	R	OR	Road Games HR	OHR	R	OR	DIF	LDF	WS	LS
1975 National League (4/7–9/28)	East																		
	Pittsburgh	52	28	.650	40	41	.494	67	41	348	270	**71**	**38**	364	**295**	**121**	**9/22**	6	6
	Philadelphia	51	30	.630	35	46	.432	**72**	47	401	326	53	64	334	368	1	8/18	7	6
	New York	42	39	.519	40	41	.494	52	48	294	301	49	51	352	324	2	4/9	7	7
	St. Louis	45	36	.556	37	44	.457	46	39	351	352	35	59	311	337			7	6
	Chicago	42	39	.519	33	48	.407	54	**71**	392	**427**	41	59	320	400	51	6/5	7	5
	Montreal	39	42	.481	36	45	.444	53	57	326	375	45	45	275	315	2	4/8	6	6
	West																		
	Cincinnati	64	17	**.790**	44	37	**.543**	70	52	**457**	275	54	60	**383**	311	**122**	**9/7**	**10**	6
	Los Angeles	49	32	.605	39	42	.481	64	52	319	**221**	54	52	329	313	40	6/6	8	5
	San Francisco	46	35	.568	34	46	.425	36	**37**	346	335	48	55	313	336			7	8
	San Diego	38	43	.469	33	48	.407	**33**	38	**279**	338	45	61	273	345	13	4/26	5	7
	Atlanta	37	43	.463	30	51	.370	58	63	280	350	49	**38**	303	389	1	4/17	4	6
	Houston	37	44	.457	27	53	.338	40	43	313	338	44	63	351	373	1	4/7	5	**9**
1975 American League (4/8–9/28)	East																		
	Boston	47	34	.580	48	31	**.608**	74	83	**427**	399	60	62	369	**310**	**137**	**9/27**	**10**	5
	Baltimore	44	33	.571	46	36	.561	46	45	**282**	**231**	78	65	**400**	322	2	4/22	7	7
	New York	43	35	.551	40	42	.488	50	56	323	276	60	**48**	358	312	4	6/28	8	7
	Cleveland	41	39	.513	38	41	.481	**79**	85	331	367	74	51	357	336	3	4/10	6	7
	Milwaukee	36	45	.444	32	49	.395	72	63	348	398	74	70	327	394	34	5/22	5	8
	Detroit	31	49	.388	26	53	.329	63	83	301	**421**	62	54	269	365	9	5/1	9	**19**
	West																		
	Oakland	54	27	**.667**	44	37	.543	75	**43**	366	247	76	59	392	359	**161**	**9/24**	8	4
	Kansas City	51	30	.630	40	41	.494	46	45	377	309	72	63	333	340	13	6/3	8	6
	Texas	39	41	.488	40	42	.488	52	70	349	366	**82**	53	365	367	5	5/22	6	6
	Minnesota	39	43	.476	37	40	.481	75	**88**	401	410	46	49	323	326	3	4/11	4	7
	Chicago	42	39	.519	33	47	.413	42	54	350	359	52	53	305	344			9	6
	California	35	46	.432	37	43	.463	**24**	52	294	349	31	71	334	374	3	4/30	4	7
1976 National League (4/9–10/3)	East																		
	Philadelphia	53	28	**.654**	48	33	.593	63	49	424	277	47	49	346	280	**156**	**9/25**	6	9
	Pittsburgh	47	34	.580	45	36	.556	54	44	366	302	56	51	342	328	15	4/25	10	4
	New York	45	37	.549	41	39	.513	43	43	269	**245**	59	54	346	293	9	5/8	10	5
	Chicago	42	39	.519	33	48	.407	71	**84**	355	385	34	39	256	343			5	9
	St. Louis	37	44	.457	35	46	.432	**27**	40	335	346	36	51	294	325	1	4/9	4	5
	Montreal	27	53	.338	28	54	.341	45	41	266	374	49	48	265	360			4	12
	West																		
	Cincinnati	49	32	.605	53	28	**.654**	**73**	46	**426**	337	**68**	54	**431**	296	**155**	**9/21**	7	4
	Los Angeles	49	32	.605	43	38	.531	42	48	296	265	49	49	312	**278**	20	5/28	**12**	6
	Houston	46	36	.561	34	46	.425	30	**27**	277	264	36	55	348	393	3	4/21	7	6
	San Francisco	40	41	.494	34	47	.420	44	32	314	352	41	36	281	334	4	4/24	5	7
	San Diego	42	38	.525	31	51	.378	30	38	**254**	271	34	49	316	391	1	4/9	5	8
	Atlanta	34	47	.420	36	45	.444	43	56	338	**401**	39	**30**	282	299	7	4/26	6	**13**
1976 American League (4/8–10/3)	East																		
	New York	45	35	.563	52	27	**.658**	67	51	349	294	53	46	**381**	**281**	**172**	**9/25**	7	6
	Baltimore	42	39	.519	46	35	.568	58	38	280	306	61	42	339	292	2	4/10	7	9
	Boston	46	35	.568	37	44	.457	**71**	61	**408**	352	**63**	48	308	308			7	**10**
	Cleveland	44	35	.557	37	43	.463	40	43	311	295	45	**37**	304	320			5	5
	Detroit	36	44	.450	38	43	.469	51	**62**	305	**381**	50	39	304	328	3	4/12	4	6
	Milwaukee	36	45	.444	30	50	.375	45	43	292	321	43	56	278	334	5	5/3	5	7
	West																		
	Kansas City	49	32	.605	41	40	.506	37	35	368	287	28	48	345	324	**139**	**10/1**	7	6
	Oakland	51	30	**.630**	36	44	.450	56	57	353	**284**	57	39	333	314	4	4/20	9	8
	Minnesota	44	37	.543	41	40	.506	34	52	368	348	47	**37**	375	356			8	6
	California	38	43	.469	38	43	.469	**24**	35	**249**	**284**	39	60	301	347			4	6
	Texas	39	42	.481	37	44	.457	40	57	319	330	40	49	297	322	36	5/29	8	**10**
	Chicago	35	45	.438	29	52	.358	31	**34**	300	369	42	53	286	376	8	4/19	**10**	**10**
1977 National League (4/7–10/2)	East																		
	Philadelphia	60	21	**.741**	41	40	.506	**101**	63	**453**	299	85	71	**394**	369	59	**9/27**	**13**	5
	Pittsburgh	58	23	.716	38	43	.469	64	76	396	315	69	73	338	350	29	5/27	11	7
	St. Louis	52	31	.627	31	48	.392	41	53	379	314	55	86	358	374	21	5/1	6	7
	Chicago	46	35	.568	35	46	.432	69	82	411	402	42	**46**	281	337	**69**	8/4	8	7
	Montreal	38	43	.469	37	44	.457	66	65	329	362	72	70	336	374	4	4/19	7	11
	New York	35	44	.443	29	54	.349	46	56	**282**	297	42	62	305	366	4	4/12	4	9
	West																		
	Los Angeles	51	30	.630	47	34	**.580**	96	65	386	**273**	95	54	383	**309**	**175**	**9/20**	8	4
	Cincinnati	48	33	.593	40	41	.494	83	83	408	355	**98**	73	**394**	370	3	4/8	7	8
	Houston	46	35	.568	35	46	.432	**40**	**33**	309	291	74	77	371	359	8	4/15	8	8
	San Francisco	38	43	.469	37	44	.457	62	56	353	371	72	58	320	340			6	8
	San Diego	35	46	.432	34	47	.420	53	70	299	368	67	90	393	466			5	8
	Atlanta	40	41	.494	21	60	.259	97	**111**	416	**488**	42	58	262	407			5	**17**

		Home Games			Road Games			Home Games				Road Games							
	Team	**W**	**L**	**PCT**	**W**	**L**	**PCT**	**HR**	**OHR**	**R**	**OR**	**HR**	**OHR**	**R**	**OR**	**DIF**	**LDF**	**WS**	**LS**
1977 American League (4/7–10/2)	East																		
	New York	55	26	**.679**	45	36	.556	84	63	412	305	100	76	**419**	346	**70**	**10/1**	8	5
	Baltimore	54	27	.667	43	37	.538	74	62	356	**269**	74	62	363	384	35	8/1	7	6
	Boston	51	29	.638	46	35	.568	**124**	95	**495**	407	89	63	364	305	47	8/22	11	9
	Detroit	39	42	.481	35	46	.432	81	100	369	401	85	62	345	350			5	6
	Cleveland	37	44	.457	34	46	.425	54	66	339	357	46	70	337	382	8	4/15	9	7
	Milwaukee	37	44	.457	30	51	.370	49	54	305	365	76	82	334	400	21	5/6	5	5
	Toronto	25	55	.313	29	52	.358	**45**	94	**297**	**444**	55	58	308	378	3	4/11	3	11
	West																		
	Kansas City	55	26	**.679**	47	34	.580	56	**50**	408	320	90	60	414	331	52	**9/23**	**16**	4
	Texas	44	37	.543	50	31	**.617**	62	78	369	368	73	**56**	398	**289**	9	8/18	7	4
	Chicago	48	33	.593	42	39	.519	85	58	434	370	**107**	78	410	401	**61**	8/19	9	4
	Minnesota	48	32	.600	36	45	.444	61	79	469	376	62	72	398	400	59	8/16	5	6
	California	39	42	.481	35	46	.432	69	65	320	321	62	71	355	374	2	4/7	6	7
	Seattle	29	52	.358	35	46	.432	75	**103**	303	419	58	91	321	436			5	9
	Oakland	35	46	.432	28	52	.350	58	69	302	347	59	76	303	402	6	4/28	6	**14**
1978 National League (4/7–10/1)	East																		
	Philadelphia	54	28	.659	36	44	.450	80	70	**405**	279	53	48	303	307	**131**	**9/30**	8	5
	Pittsburgh	55	26	**.679**	33	47	.413	57	61	389	310	58	**42**	295	327	2	4/8	**11**	7
	Chicago	44	38	.537	35	45	.438	41	76	393	387	31	49	271	337	29	6/23	8	6
	Montreal	41	39	.513	35	47	.427	46	49	299	283	**75**	68	334	328	9	5/5	6	7
	St. Louis	37	44	.457	32	49	.395	**29**	32	**289**	307	50	62	311	350	3	4/13	5	**11**
	New York	33	47	.413	33	49	.402	37	60	295	340	49	54	312	350	7	4/22	5	6
	West																		
	Los Angeles	54	27	.667	41	40	.506	78	59	361	272	71	48	**366**	**301**	75	**9/24**	7	6
	Cincinnati	49	31	.613	43	38	**.531**	74	61	379	338	62	61	331	350	20	8/6	7	6
	San Francisco	50	31	.617	39	42	.481	47	30	291	**244**	70	54	322	350	**93**	8/15	8	7
	San Diego	50	31	.617	34	47	.420	31	**23**	291	245	44	51	300	353	1	4/7	10	5
	Houston	50	31	.617	24	57	.296	30	29	327	254	40	57	278	380			8	7
	Atlanta	39	42	.481	30	51	.370	**87**	**89**	364	**400**	36	43	236	350			5	7
1978 American League (4/7–10/2)	East																		
	New York	55	26	.679	45	37	**.549**	68	59	358	275	57	**52**	**377**	**307**	21	**10/2**	7	4
	Boston	59	23	**.720**	40	41	.494	**94**	72	445	334	78	65	351	323	**115**	10/1	9	5
	Milwaukee	54	27	.667	39	42	.481	**94**	50	**446**	318	79	59	358	332	9	4/15	10	5
	Baltimore	51	30	.630	39	41	.488	74	42	316	**258**	**80**	65	343	375			**13**	8
	Detroit	47	34	.580	39	42	.481	74	78	395	338	55	57	319	315	39	5/23	5	7
	Cleveland	42	36	.538	27	54	.333	50	**37**	319	287	56	63	320	407	1	4/8	4	6
	Toronto	37	44	.457	22	58	.275	50	75	334	366	48	74	256	409			5	9
	West																		
	Kansas City	56	25	.691	36	45	.444	**43**	44	434	264	55	64	309	370	**100**	**9/26**	10	5
	California	50	31	.617	37	44	.457	56	58	371	316	52	67	320	350	23	8/26	4	7
	Texas	52	30	.634	35	45	.438	62	49	348	289	70	59	344	343	9	7/2	7	8
	Minnesota	38	43	.469	35	46	.432	44	39	322	308	38	63	344	370	1	4/6	8	9
	Chicago	38	42	.475	33	48	.407	56	58	342	349	50	70	292	382	5	4/12	7	9
	Oakland	38	42	.475	31	51	.378	52	51	**281**	330	48	55	251	360	45	7/5	8	**11**
	Seattle	32	49	.395	24	55	.304	58	**93**	343	**423**	39	62	271	411	2	4/6	5	10
1979 National League (4/5–9/30)	East																		
	Pittsburgh	48	33	.593	50	31	**.617**	74	77	399	339	74	48	**376**	**304**	48	**9/30**	9	6
	Montreal	56	25	**.691**	39	40	.494	68	51	378	275	75	65	323	306	**95**	9/24	**10**	5
	St. Louis	42	39	.519	44	37	.543	48	65	379	372	52	62	352	321	10	6/12	7	6
	Philadelphia	43	38	.531	41	40	.506	52	72	332	342	67	63	351	376	32	5/27	7	6
	Chicago	45	36	.556	35	46	.432	79	72	**423**	370	56	55	283	337			6	7
	New York	28	53	.346	35	46	.432	30	58	**267**	354	44	62	326	352	5	4/9	6	**9**
	West																		
	Cincinnati	48	32	.600	42	39	.519	71	53	360	298	61	50	371	346	47	**9/28**	8	4
	Houston	52	29	.642	37	44	.457	**15**	**31**	269	**234**	34	59	314	348	**128**	9/10	7	7
	Los Angeles	46	35	.568	33	48	.407	**106**	55	389	341	**77**	**46**	350	376	1	4/9	8	6
	San Francisco	38	43	.469	33	48	.407	53	61	298	361	72	82	374	390	7	4/14	4	8
	San Diego	39	42	.481	29	51	.363	36	47	287	335	57	61	316	346	1	4/5	5	7
	Atlanta	34	45	.430	32	49	.395	73	**80**	359	**425**	53	52	310	338			6	6
1979 American League (4/5–9/30)	East																		
	Baltimore	55	24	**.696**	47	33	**.588**	74	57	369	**259**	**107**	76	388	**323**	**150**	**9/22**	9	6
	Milwaukee	52	29	.642	43	37	.538	91	81	401	362	94	81	406	360	15	4/19	**10**	5
	Boston	51	29	.638	40	40	.500	**121**	59	**470**	357	73	74	371	354	23	6/5	7	4
	New York	51	30	.630	38	41	.481	77	59	360	308	73	64	374	364			5	8
	Detroit	46	34	.575	39	42	.481	101	74	394	323	63	93	376	415			6	5
	Cleveland	47	34	.580	34	46	.425	87	72	428	409	51	66	332	396			**10**	10
	Toronto	32	49	.395	21	60	.259	50	74	345	**432**	45	91	268	430			4	7
	West																		
	California	49	32	.605	39	42	.481	71	**55**	408	339	93	76	**458**	429	**124**	**9/25**	**10**	7
	Kansas City	46	35	.568	39	42	.481	53	81	462	421	63	84	389	395	7	8/30	6	7
	Texas	44	37	.543	39	42	.481	69	63	382	335	71	72	368	363	27	7/8	8	6
	Minnesota	39	42	.481	43	38	.531	67	61	415	390	45	67	349	335	31	5/26	6	6
	Chicago	33	46	.418	40	41	.494	56	60	349	401	71	**54**	381	347			5	7
	Seattle	36	45	.444	31	50	.383	88	**94**	371	404	44	71	340	416	3	4/6	4	**11**
	Oakland	31	50	.383	23	58	.284	**46**	65	**262**	371	62	82	311	489			4	8

		Home Games			Road Games			Home Games				Road Games							
	Team	**W**	**L**	**PCT**	**W**	**L**	**PCT**	**HR**	**OHR**	**R**	**OR**	**HR**	**OHR**	**R**	**OR**	**DIF**	**LDF**	**WS**	**LS**
1980 National League (4/10–10/5)	East																		
	Philadelphia	49	32	.605	42	39	.519	64	44	**398**	334	53	**43**	330	**305**	19	**10/4**	6	6
	Montreal	51	29	.638	39	43	.476	51	40	357	286	63	60	337	343	**82**	10/2	**10**	4
	Pittsburgh	47	34	.580	36	45	.444	63	53	355	322	53	57	311	324	81	8/31	8	8
	St. Louis	41	40	.506	33	48	.407	41	42	396	357	60	48	342	353	1	4/10	6	10
	New York	38	44	.463	29	51	.363	35	**80**	306	336	26	60	305	366	1	4/10	4	**13**
	Chicago	37	44	.457	27	54	.333	54	62	338	**385**	53	47	276	343	2	5/3	4	7
	West																		
	Houston	55	26	**.679**	38	44	.463	26	**22**	329	**255**	49	47	308	334	**112**	**10/6**	**10**	5
	Los Angeles	55	27	.671	37	44	.457	82	58	327	272	**66**	47	336	319	57	10/5	**10**	4
	Cincinnati	44	37	.543	45	36	**.556**	66	70	356	349	47	**43**	**351**	321	27	8/14	8	5
	Atlanta	50	30	.625	31	50	.383	**84**	79	352	297	60	52	278	363			7	7
	San Francisco	44	37	.543	31	49	.388	**24**	41	**283**	293	56	51	290	341			7	6
	San Diego	45	36	.556	28	53	.346	29	33	295	274	38	64	296	380	3	4/12	8	8
1980 American League (4/9–10/5)	East																		
	New York	53	28	**.654**	50	31	**.617**	**91**	47	409	315	98	55	411	347	**156**	**10/4**	9	3
	Baltimore	50	31	.617	50	31	**.617**	75	81	397	319	81	**53**	408	**321**	2	4/18	10	6
	Milwaukee	40	42	.488	46	34	.575	90	65	368	336	**113**	72	**443**	346	11	4/25	7	7
	Boston	36	45	.444	47	32	.595	79	74	370	**420**	83	55	387	347	7	5/3	9	5
	Detroit	43	38	.531	41	40	.506	77	95	**440**	404	66	57	390	353	1	4/10	9	7
	Cleveland	44	35	.557	35	46	.432	55	66	400	389	34	71	338	418			8	7
	Toronto	35	46	.432	32	49	.395	56	75	311	386	70	60	313	376	15	5/13	6	8
	West																		
	Kansas City	49	32	.605	48	33	.593	47	51	397	335	68	78	412	359	**137**	**9/17**	8	8
	Oakland	46	35	.568	37	44	.457	58	57	337	**277**	79	85	349	365	21	5/17	7	7
	Minnesota	44	36	.550	33	48	.407	51	63	392	361	48	57	278	363	1	4/10	**12**	9
	Texas	39	41	.488	37	44	.457	58	57	380	365	66	62	376	387	7	4/19	5	8
	Chicago	37	42	.468	33	48	.407	**41**	**37**	**281**	350	50	71	306	372	15	5/22	4	6
	California	30	51	.370	35	44	.443	49	76	330	403	57	65	368	394	1	4/11	6	9
	Seattle	36	45	.444	23	58	.284	74	**99**	340	389	30	60	270	404	4	4/14	6	**12**
1981 National League (4/18–6/11) (8/10–10/4)	East																		
	St. Louis	32	21	.604	27	22	.551	22	26	244	218	28	26	220	199	**77**	9/30	8	5
	Montreal	38	18	**.679**	22	30	.423	39	23	255	170	42	35	188	224	29	**10/3**	7	5
	Philadelphia	36	19	.655	23	29	.442	**41**	39	**295**	**261**	28	33	196	211	11	6/10	6	6
	Pittsburgh	22	28	.440	24	28	.462	29	29	189	207	26	31	218	218			4	7
	New York	24	27	.471	17	35	.327	30	38	186	207	27	36	162	225	11	8/18	4	9
	Chicago	27	30	.474	11	35	.239	**41**	38	239	254	16	21	131	229			4	**12**
	West																		
	Cincinnati	32	22	.593	34	20	**.630**	26	**41**	226	230	38	26	**238**	210	2	4/9	8	4
	Los Angeles	33	23	.589	30	24	.556	37	34	221	171	**45**	**20**	229	**185**	**69**	6/10	7	5
	Houston	31	20	.608	30	29	.508	16	**9**	**166**	**106**	29	31	228	225	42	**10/2**	**9**	4
	San Francisco	29	24	.547	27	31	.466	28	19	218	204	35	38	209	210	1	8/30	5	6
	Atlanta	22	27	.449	28	29	.491	37	**41**	182	195	27	21	213	221	18	8/30	6	5
	San Diego	20	35	.364	21	34	.382	**9**	27	168	223	23	37	214	232	2	4/10	5	7
1981 American League (4/9–6/11) (8/10–10/5)	East																		
	Milwaukee	28	21	.571	34	26	**.567**	33	29	203	203	**63**	43	**290**	256	17	**10/3**	6	4
	Baltimore	33	22	.600	26	24	.520	49	47	231	217	39	36	198	220	24	8/29	8	5
	New York	32	19	**.627**	27	29	.482	47	**24**	203	**154**	53	40	218	**189**	12	6/9	9	4
	Detroit	32	23	.582	28	26	.519	43	44	241	196	22	39	186	208	**50**	9/30	9	10
	Boston	30	23	.566	29	26	.527	52	47	**278**	247	38	43	241	234	2	9/25	6	7
	Cleveland	25	29	.463	27	22	.551	19	33	210	216	20	34	221	226	25	5/17	5	5
	Toronto	17	36	.321	20	33	.377	34	41	172	272	27	31	157	194	2	8/15	4	**12**
	West																		
	Oakland	35	21	.625	29	24	.547	**57**	46	234	183	47	34	224	220	**77**	6/11	**11**	8
	Texas	32	24	.571	25	24	.510	21	**24**	232	168	28	43	220	221	1	6/8	5	4
	Chicago	25	24	.510	29	28	.509	31	33	215	198	45	40	261	225	13	8/30	6	6
	Kansas City	19	28	.404	31	25	.554	**17**	27	**163**	197	44	48	234	208	29	**10/5**	6	4
	California	26	28	.481	25	31	.446	48	39	244	233	49	42	232	220	1	4/9	5	8
	Seattle	20	37	.351	24	28	.462	52	**53**	226	271	37	**23**	200	250	8	8/17	5	10
	Minnesota	24	36	.400	17	32	.347	25	47	213	**292**	22	32	165	194	2	8/12	7	8
1982 National League (4/5–10/3)	East																		
	St. Louis	46	35	.568	46	35	.568	**27**	48	338	325	40	46	347	284	**131**	**9/27**	12	4
	Philadelphia	51	30	**.630**	38	43	.469	57	46	301	307	55	**40**	363	347	41	9/13	8	4
	Montreal	40	41	.494	46	35	.568	59	65	335	352	74	45	362	**264**	7	6/24	8	5
	Pittsburgh	42	39	.519	42	39	.519	77	65	**391**	**394**	57	53	333	302	1	4/10	6	4
	Chicago	38	43	.469	35	46	.432	53	62	352	371	49	63	324	338	3	4/9	6	13
	New York	33	48	.407	32	49	.395	48	60	307	357	49	59	302	366	4	4/13	4	**15**
	West																		
	Atlanta	42	39	.519	47	34	**.580**	**95**	**86**	388	387	51	**40**	351	315	**148**	**10/3**	**13**	11
	Los Angeles	43	38	.531	45	36	.556	57	35	321	**283**	**81**	46	**370**	329	36	9/27	8	8
	San Francisco	45	36	.556	42	39	.519	55	54	319	312	78	55	354	375			10	6
	San Diego	43	38	.531	38	43	.469	33	76	316	286	48	63	359	372	1	4/27	11	6
	Houston	43	38	.531	34	47	.420	31	**26**	**290**	294	43	61	279	326			4	6
	Cincinnati	33	48	.407	28	53	.346	37	47	296	325	45	58	249	336			4	9

		Home Games			Road Games			Home Games				Road Games							
	Team	**W**	**L**	**PCT**	**W**	**L**	**PCT**	**HR**	**OHR**	**R**	**OR**	**HR**	**OHR**	**R**	**OR**	**DIF**	**LDF**	**WS**	**LS**
1982 American League (4/5–10/3)	East																		
	Milwaukee	48	34	.585	47	33	**.588**	89	64	431	319	**127**	88	**460**	398	**89**	**10/3**	8	5
	Baltimore	53	28	.654	41	40	.506	87	87	397	330	92	60	377	357	7	10/2	10	9
	Boston	49	32	.605	40	41	.494	67	82	**434**	370	69	73	319	343	68	8/2	8	4
	Detroit	47	34	.580	36	45	.444	**108**	100	378	328	69	72	351	357	25	6/10	8	10
	New York	42	39	.519	37	44	.457	73	55	346	338	88	58	363	378	1	4/16	6	9
	Cleveland	41	40	.506	37	44	.457	49	64	342	377	60	58	341	371	3	4/18	**11**	8
	Toronto	44	37	.543	34	47	.420	62	70	353	379	44	77	298	**322**	2	4/17	6	6
	West																		
	California	52	29	.642	41	40	.506	99	69	414	322	87	**55**	400	348	**104**	**10/2**	7	8
	Kansas City	56	25	**.691**	34	47	.420	61	64	431	**318**	71	99	353	399	52	9/19	8	7
	Chicago	49	31	.613	38	44	.463	51	**43**	383	332	85	56	403	378	29	5/27	8	7
	Seattle	42	39	.519	34	47	.420	78	104	356	388	52	69	295	324	2	4/7	5	7
	Oakland	36	45	.444	32	49	.395	71	83	328	398	78	94	363	421	2	4/7	7	6
	Texas	38	43	.469	26	55	.321	**43**	66	**286**	333	72	62	304	416	1	4/10	4	12
	Minnesota	37	44	.457	23	58	.284	81	**110**	351	**401**	67	98	306	418	3	4/9	4	**14**
1983 National League (4/5–10/2)	East																		
	Philadelphia	50	31	**.617**	40	41	.494	61	61	361	310	64	50	335	325	**68**	**9/28**	**11**	6
	Pittsburgh	41	40	.506	43	38	**.531**	60	63	335	336	61	46	324	**312**	38	9/17	9	6
	Montreal	46	35	.568	36	45	.444	40	56	341	325	62	64	336	321	37	9/13	5	6
	St. Louis	44	37	.543	35	46	.432	38	58	334	350	45	57	345	360	56	7/19	7	8
	Chicago	43	38	.531	28	53	.346	71	69	384	341	69	48	317	378			7	6
	New York	41	41	.500	27	53	.338	63	53	300	329	49	**44**	275	351	4	4/8	4	5
	West																		
	Los Angeles	48	32	.600	43	39	.524	**74**	49	316	296	**72**	48	338	313	**102**	**9/30**	8	5
	Atlanta	46	34	.575	42	40	.512	66	71	**394**	327	64	61	**352**	313	81	8/28	7	6
	Houston	46	36	.561	39	41	.488	**26**	**28**	**294**	**278**	71	66	349	368			6	**9**
	San Diego	47	34	.580	34	47	.420	53	**82**	350	299	40	62	303	354	4	4/8	6	5
	San Francisco	43	38	.531	36	45	.444	73	67	346	356	69	60	341	341			6	4
	Cincinnati	36	45	.444	38	43	.469	52	64	331	**360**	55	71	292	350	6	4/11	4	5
1983 American League (4/4–10/2)	East																		
	Baltimore	50	31	.617	48	33	**.593**	79	66	389	328	**89**	64	410	324	**114**	**9/25**	**8**	7
	Detroit	48	33	.593	44	37	.543	83	87	377	314	73	83	**412**	365	9	8/13	6	4
	New York	51	30	.630	40	41	.494	67	55	398	323	86	61	372	380	3	7/27	7	4
	Toronto	48	33	.593	41	40	.506	**101**	84	**437**	385	66	61	358	341	44	7/25	5	6
	Milwaukee	52	29	.642	35	46	.432	64	57	356	305	68	76	408	403	12	8/25	**8**	**10**
	Boston	38	43	.469	40	41	.494	65	76	373	390	77	82	351	385	18	6/5	5	7
	Cleveland	36	45	.444	34	47	.420	48	71	367	424	38	**49**	337	361	10	4/16	6	5
	West																		
	Chicago	55	26	**.679**	44	37	.543	84	64	432	306	73	64	368	344	**77**	**9/17**	**8**	5
	Kansas City	45	36	.556	34	47	.420	50	66	381	369	59	67	315	398	9	5/3	5	6
	Texas	44	37	.543	33	48	.407	**45**	**33**	326	**294**	61	64	313	**315**	43	7/17	6	8
	Oakland	42	39	.519	32	49	.395	60	54	348	367	61	81	360	415	8	5/2	5	6
	California	35	46	.432	35	46	.432	86	67	368	354	68	63	354	425	59	7/10	7	6
	Minnesota	37	44	.457	33	48	.407	56	**91**	389	**427**	85	72	320	395			5	8
	Seattle	30	51	.370	30	51	.370	64	80	**281**	369	47	65	277	371	2	4/6	4	8
1984 National League (4/2–9/30)	East																		
	Chicago	51	29	**.638**	45	36	**.556**	**86**	70	**414**	360	50	**29**	348	298	**105**	**9/24**	6	5
	New York	48	33	.593	42	39	.519	56	47	336	327	51	57	316	349	65	7/31	8	7
	St. Louis	44	37	.543	40	41	.494	29	42	327	310	46	52	325	335	3	4/6	6	7
	Philadelphia	39	42	.481	42	39	.519	79	45	353	369	**68**	56	367	321	26	6/30	**10**	**9**
	Montreal	39	42	.481	39	41	.488	45	56	**266**	**260**	51	58	327	325	3	4/7	6	6
	Pittsburgh	41	40	.506	34	47	.420	48	44	282	263	50	58	333	304			7	7
	West																		
	San Diego	48	33	.593	44	37	.543	60	61	344	300	49	61	342	334	**145**	**9/20**	6	7
	Atlanta	38	43	.469	42	39	.519	53	72	328	376	58	50	304	**279**	8	6/8	9	5
	Houston	43	38	.531	37	44	.457	**18**	**29**	309	292	61	62	**384**	338			9	5
	Los Angeles	40	41	.494	39	42	.481	49	40	287	321	53	36	293	**279**	29	6/1	6	7
	Cincinnati	39	42	.481	31	50	.383	58	**73**	356	381	48	55	271	366	2	4/3	7	8
	San Francisco	35	46	.432	31	50	.383	55	63	340	**393**	57	62	342	414			6	**9**
1984 American League (4/2–9/30)	East																		
	Detroit	53	29	**.646**	51	29	**.638**	85	69	406	295	**102**	61	**423**	348	**181**	**9/18**	**9**	4
	Toronto	49	32	.605	40	41	.494	59	78	387	339	84	62	363	357			7	6
	New York	51	30	.630	36	45	.444	62	**49**	372	**292**	68	71	386	387			8	5
	Boston	41	40	.506	45	36	.556	100	76	**456**	**413**	81	65	354	351			6	8
	Baltimore	44	37	.543	41	40	.506	82	59	319	306	78	78	362	361			6	5
	Cleveland	41	39	.513	34	48	.415	65	73	411	399	58	68	350	367	5	4/7	8	6
	Milwaukee	38	43	.469	29	51	.363	**42**	68	**286**	344	54	69	355	390			5	**10**
	West																		
	Kansas City	44	37	.543	40	41	.494	48	59	344	326	69	77	329	360	26	**9/28**	6	7
	California	37	44	.457	44	37	.543	79	**83**	341	364	71	60	355	**333**	**77**	8/4	5	7
	Minnesota	47	34	.580	34	47	.420	63	77	372	337	51	82	301	338	58	9/23	6	6
	Oakland	44	37	.543	33	48	.407	77	72	356	344	81	83	382	452	21	5/8	5	9
	Chicago	43	38	.531	31	50	.383	**103**	77	394	389	69	78	285	347	10	7/11	7	6
	Seattle	42	39	.519	32	49	.395	68	82	357	394	61	**56**	325	380	12	4/26	5	6
	Texas	34	46	.425	35	46	.432	55	70	327	357	65	78	329	357			6	7

Season	Team	Home Games W	Home Games L	Home Games PCT	Road Games W	Road Games L	Road Games PCT	Home Games HR	Home Games OHR	Home Games R	Home Games OR	Road Games HR	Road Games OHR	Road Games R	Road Games OR	DIF	LDF	WS	LS
1985 National League (4/8–10/6)	East																		
	St. Louis	54	27	**.667**	47	34	**.580**	**36**	**39**	358	255	51	59	**389**	317	**88**	**10/5**	7	4
	New York	51	30	.630	47	34	**.580**	58	58	344	**254**	76	53	351	314	74	9/15	**9**	6
	Montreal	44	37	.543	40	40	.500	45	45	300	289	73	54	333	347	10	6/28	6	6
	Chicago	41	39	.513	36	45	.444	**98**	**104**	**399**	423	52	52	287	306	35	6/15	6	**13**
	Philadelphia	41	40	.506	34	47	.420	72	57	350	338	69	58	317	335			6	11
	Pittsburgh	35	45	.438	22	59	.272	39	53	314	347	41	54	254	361			3	9
	West																		
	Los Angeles	48	33	.593	47	34	**.580**	47	54	310	258	**82**	**48**	372	321	**91**	**10/2**	8	4
	Cincinnati	47	34	.580	42	38	.525	49	65	347	359	65	66	330	307	8	4/24	7	4
	Houston	44	37	.543	39	42	.481	47	48	333	338	74	71	373	353	2	4/23	**9**	6
	San Diego	44	37	.543	39	42	.481	63	77	321	323	46	50	329	**299**	78	7/12	7	6
	Atlanta	32	49	.395	34	47	.420	65	80	336	**431**	61	54	296	350	8	4/16	5	6
	San Francisco	38	43	.469	24	57	.296	58	67	**265**	307	57	58	291	367	2	4/12	4	10
1985 American League (4/8–10/6)	East																		
	Toronto	54	26	.675	45	36	**.556**	75	78	396	**264**	83	69	363	324	**152**	**10/5**	9	6
	New York	58	22	**.725**	39	42	.481	92	67	411	288	84	90	**428**	372			**11**	8
	Detroit	44	37	.543	40	40	.500	**108**	93	386	368	94	**48**	343	**320**	20	4/29	6	8
	Baltimore	45	36	.556	38	42	.475	103	87	414	374	**111**	73	404	390	21	5/19	6	6
	Boston	43	37	.538	38	44	.463	73	64	**415**	357	89	66	385	363	6	4/13	8	6
	Milwaukee	40	40	.500	31	50	.383	**50**	86	368	**416**	51	89	322	386			5	7
	Cleveland	38	43	.469	22	59	.272	52	76	380	379	64	94	349	482			5	6
	West																		
	Kansas City	50	32	.610	41	39	.513	67	**43**	357	317	87	60	330	322	30	**10/5**	8	5
	California	49	30	.620	41	42	.494	75	93	370	331	78	78	362	372	**142**	10/2	6	5
	Chicago	45	36	.556	40	41	.494	74	83	359	361	72	78	377	359	11	6/20	5	7
	Minnesota	49	35	.583	28	50	.359	71	83	407	393	70	81	298	389	2	4/10	10	**10**
	Oakland	43	36	.544	34	49	.410	66	71	**348**	347	89	101	409	440	6	4/25	5	7
	Seattle	42	41	.506	32	47	.405	92	78	360	389	79	76	359	429	13	4/21	8	8
	Texas	37	43	.463	25	56	.309	76	**102**	356	406	53	71	261	379			5	7
1986 National League (4/7–10/5)	East																		
	New York	55	26	**.679**	53	28	**.654**	77	47	379	**251**	71	56	**404**	327	**170**	**9/17**	**11**	4
	Philadelphia	49	31	.613	37	44	.457	86	49	**413**	344	68	81	326	369			7	5
	St. Louis	42	39	.519	37	43	.463	**27**	63	321	303	31	72	280	308	15	4/22	7	8
	Montreal	36	44	.450	42	39	.519	42	56	**296**	347	68	63	341	341			8	6
	Chicago	42	38	.525	28	52	.350	**89**	**79**	394	**399**	66	64	286	382			5	7
	Pittsburgh	31	50	.383	33	48	.407	49	75	331	357	62	63	332	343			5	6
	West																		
	Houston	52	29	.642	44	37	.543	49	56	327	289	**76**	60	327	**280**	**149**	**9/25**	7	4
	Cincinnati	43	38	.531	43	38	.531	86	73	383	377	58	63	349	340	2	4/8	6	**9**
	San Francisco	46	35	.568	37	44	.457	50	61	345	275	64	60	353	343	37	7/20	6	4
	San Diego	43	38	.531	31	50	.383	80	78	339	319	56	72	317	404	3	4/17	4	5
	Los Angeles	46	35	.568	27	54	.333	57	**46**	326	290	73	69	312	389	1	4/7	8	6
	Atlanta	41	40	.506	31	49	.388	77	71	331	360	61	**46**	284	359	2	4/9	7	6
1986 American League (4/7–10/5)	East																		
	Boston	51	30	**.630**	44	36	.550	55	85	389	350	89	82	405	346	**147**	**9/28**	**11**	4
	New York	41	39	.513	49	33	**.598**	93	96	384	396	95	79	413	**342**	29	5/14	6	5
	Detroit	49	32	.605	38	43	.469	96	83	403	**310**	**102**	100	395	404	4	4/11	5	5
	Toronto	42	39	.519	44	37	.543	87	89	415	389	94	75	394	344	1	4/11	9	5
	Cleveland	45	35	.563	39	43	.476	80	80	403	415	77	87	**428**	426	7	5/8	10	6
	Milwaukee	41	39	.513	36	45	.444	63	79	**338**	375	64	79	329	359	5	4/11	5	8
	Baltimore	37	42	.468	36	47	.434	91	98	348	362	78	79	360	398			6	7
	West																		
	California	50	32	.610	42	38	.525	88	84	371	335	79	**69**	415	349	**131**	**9/26**	7	5
	Texas	51	30	**.630**	36	45	.444	87	61	374	343	97	84	397	400	46	7/6	7	7
	Kansas City	45	36	.556	31	50	.383	60	**46**	342	317	77	75	312	356	3	6/1	4	**11**
	Oakland	47	36	.566	29	50	.367	75	81	363	349	88	85	368	411	4	5/10	7	9
	Chicago	41	40	.506	31	50	.383	**51**	63	341	335	70	80	303	364			7	8
	Minnesota	43	38	.531	28	53	.346	**116**	**107**	**426**	**439**	80	93	315	400	5	4/12	4	7
	Seattle	41	41	.500	26	54	.325	97	99	410	427	61	72	308	408	6	4/15	4	9
1987 National League (4/6–10/4)	East																		
	St. Louis	49	32	**.605**	46	35	**.568**	**42**	60	387	339	52	**69**	411	354	**167**	**10/1**	**9**	7
	New York	49	32	**.605**	43	38	.531	93	63	407	335	**99**	73	**416**	363	15	4/25	7	4
	Montreal	48	33	.593	43	38	.531	62	74	401	371	58	70	340	**349**			8	5
	Philadelphia	43	38	.531	37	44	.457	80	78	385	373	89	89	317	376			5	6
	Pittsburgh	47	34	.580	33	48	.407	71	84	404	363	60	80	319	381			7	7
	Chicago	40	40	.500	36	45	.444	114	90	381	389	95	**69**	339	412	7	5/19	5	5
	West																		
	San Francisco	46	35	.568	44	37	.543	**118**	72	373	312	87	74	410	357	89	**9/28**	7	6
	Cincinnati	42	39	.519	42	39	.519	94	**97**	396	401	98	73	387	351	**111**	8/20	6	7
	Houston	47	34	.580	29	52	.358	51	**46**	334	**268**	71	95	314	410	9	4/23	7	7
	Los Angeles	40	41	.494	33	48	.407	52	56	**280**	306	73	74	355	369			4	**9**
	Atlanta	42	39	.519	27	53	.338	82	88	**421**	**450**	70	75	326	379	3	4/9	5	6
	San Diego	37	44	.457	28	53	.346	60	**97**	338	357	53	78	330	406			7	**9**

	Home Games			Road Games			Home Games				Road Games							
Team	W	L	PCT	W	L	PCT	HR	OHR	R	OR	HR	OHR	R	OR	DIF	LDF	WS	LS
1987 American League (4/6–10/4)																		
East																		
Detroit	54	27	.667	44	37	**.543**	**125**	101	**442**	338	100	79	**454**	397	33	**10/4**	6	5
Toronto	52	29	.642	44	37	**.543**	101	83	425	**319**	**114**	75	420	336	55	10/2	11	9
Milwaukee	48	33	.593	43	38	.531	**72**	79	440	420	91	90	422	397	38	5/13	**13**	**12**
New York	51	30	.630	38	43	.469	98	88	401	346	98	91	387	412	**68**	8/8	10	5
Boston	50	30	.625	28	54	.341	86	75	436	383	88	115	406	442			5	6
Baltimore	31	51	.378	36	44	.450	110	**125**	**351**	456	101	101	378	424	2	4/7	11	10
Cleveland	35	46	.432	26	55	.321	94	118	373	**519**	93	101	369	438			4	8
West																		
Minnesota	56	25	**.691**	29	52	.358	106	92	411	348	90	118	375	458	**138**	**9/28**	7	6
Kansas City	46	35	.568	37	44	.457	73	**57**	375	349	95	**71**	340	342	34	7/5	6	6
Oakland	42	39	.519	39	42	.481	88	75	363	351	111	101	443	438	3	8/29	5	5
Seattle	40	41	.494	38	43	.469	103	115	403	400	58	84	357	401	2	5/14	5	6
Chicago	38	43	.469	39	42	.481	**72**	90	394	414	101	99	354	**332**	2	4/7	7	7
California	38	43	.469	37	44	.457	88	116	377	405	84	96	393	398	13	5/11	8	9
Texas	43	38	.531	32	49	.395	93	111	426	447	101	88	397	402			6	9
1988 National League (4/4–10/2)																		
East																		
New York	56	24	**.700**	44	36	.550	67	**34**	313	**218**	**85**	**44**	**390**	314	**158**	**9/22**	8	5
Pittsburgh	43	38	.531	42	37	.532	56	50	326	298	54	58	325	318	21	5/2	**9**	5
Montreal	43	38	.531	38	43	.469	47	62	333	304	60	60	295	288			8	9
Chicago	39	42	.481	38	43	.469	58	**71**	**346**	373	55	**44**	314	321	9	4/15	5	5
St. Louis	41	40	.506	35	46	.432	**29**	39	314	318	42	52	264	315			7	8
Philadelphia	38	42	.475	27	54	.333	62	64	327	361	44	54	270	373	1	4/9	4	8
West																		
Los Angeles	45	36	.556	49	31	**.613**	49	38	316	297	50	46	312	**247**	**163**	**9/26**	7	3
Cincinnati	45	35	.563	42	39	.519	**75**	**71**	333	312	47	50	308	284	4	4/7	8	6
San Diego	47	34	.580	36	44	.450	56	56	303	267	38	56	291	316			6	6
San Francisco	45	36	.556	38	43	.469	58	42	318	284	55	57	352	342	2	4/9	6	6
Houston	44	37	.543	38	43	.469	33	50	**293**	282	63	73	324	349	19	5/24	6	6
Atlanta	28	51	.354	26	55	.321	48	64	295	**391**	48	**44**	260	350			3	**10**
1988 American League (4/4–10/2)																		
East																		
Boston	53	28	.654	36	45	.444	68	73	**456**	360	56	70	357	329	30	**9/30**	12	4
Detroit	50	31	.617	38	43	.469	83	76	328	303	60	74	375	355	**76**	9/4	5	6
Milwaukee	47	34	.580	40	41	.494	60	65	354	310	53	**60**	328	**306**	4	4/7	10	7
Toronto	45	36	.556	42	39	.519	78	73	371	344	80	70	392	336	3	4/6	6	6
New York	46	34	.575	39	42	.481	77	75	378	345	71	82	394	403	65	7/27	6	6
Cleveland	44	37	.543	34	47	.420	62	52	353	359	72	68	313	372	18	5/2	6	6
Baltimore	34	46	.425	20	61	.247	70	77	**286**	354	67	76	264	435			3	**21**
West																		
Oakland	54	27	**.667**	50	31	**.617**	67	47	362	**294**	**89**	69	**438**	326	**177**	**9/18**	**14**	5
Minnesota	47	34	.580	44	37	.543	76	79	402	354	75	67	357	318			8	6
Kansas City	44	36	.550	40	41	.494	**55**	**37**	359	330	66	65	345	318	6	4/17	7	6
California	35	46	.432	40	41	.494	58	71	333	368	66	64	381	403	1	4/17	7	12
Chicago	40	41	.494	31	49	.388	**55**	64	311	373	77	74	320	384	7	4/19	5	7
Texas	38	43	.469	32	48	.400	58	67	336	368	54	62	301	367	2	4/5	8	6
Seattle	37	44	.457	31	49	.388	**97**	**81**	362	**405**	51	63	302	339			4	9
1989 National League (4/3–10/1)																		
East																		
Chicago	48	33	.593	45	36	**.556**	61	64	**381**	334	63	**42**	321	**289**	**108**	**9/26**	7	7
New York	51	30	.630	36	45	.444	**78**	54	333	275	69	61	**350**	320	25	6/25	6	7
St. Louis	46	35	.568	40	41	.494	**27**	**36**	319	308	46	48	313	300	14	5/12	6	6
Montreal	44	37	.543	37	44	.457	55	60	336	309	45	60	296	321	49	8/6	6	7
Pittsburgh	39	42	.481	35	46	.432	45	60	296	313	50	61	341	367	1	4/5	6	6
Philadelphia	38	42	.475	29	53	.354	63	67	321	376	60	60	308	359	12	4/25	4	**11**
West																		
San Francisco	53	28	**.654**	39	42	.481	62	61	368	255	**79**	59	331	345	**140**	**9/27**	7	3
San Diego	46	35	.568	43	38	.531	66	**82**	324	312	54	51	318	314	1	4/11	6	7
Houston	47	35	.573	39	41	.488	44	50	340	344	53	55	307	325	5	6/16	**10**	5
Los Angeles	44	37	.543	33	46	.418	37	47	**253**	**244**	52	48	301	292			5	5
Cincinnati	38	43	.469	37	44	.457	59	71	312	**377**	69	54	320	314	45	6/10	4	10
Atlanta	33	46	.418	30	51	.370	55	61	309	334	73	53	275	346	4	4/9	7	8
1989 American League (4/3–10/1)																		
East																		
Toronto	46	35	.568	43	38	.531	64	50	330	308	**78**	49	**401**	343	35	**9/30**	6	5
Baltimore	47	34	.580	40	41	.494	61	65	347	338	68	69	361	348	**117**	8/31	8	8
Boston	46	35	.568	37	44	.457	52	70	**419**	374	56	61	355	361	21	5/25	**9**	8
Milwaukee	45	36	.556	36	45	.444	69	54	344	321	57	75	363	358	6	4/28	8	6
New York	41	40	.506	33	47	.413	64	**88**	373	**419**	66	62	325	373	5	5/16	**9**	7
Cleveland	41	40	.506	32	49	.395	56	51	319	332	71	56	285	322	18	5/23	5	6
Detroit	38	43	.469	21	60	.259	74	77	321	389	42	73	296	427			7	**12**
West																		
Oakland	54	27	.667	45	36	**.556**	65	51	370	**284**	62	52	342	**292**	**109**	**9/27**	7	4
Kansas City	55	26	**.679**	37	44	.457	38	**26**	335	388	63	60	355	347	3	5/16	**9**	6
California	52	29	.642	39	42	.481	73	75	317	285	72	**38**	352	293	49	8/20	7	7
Texas	45	36	.556	38	43	.469	**75**	63	352	371	47	56	343	343	29	5/4	8	4
Minnesota	45	36	.556	35	46	.432	59	69	387	404	58	70	353	334	2	4/8	6	8
Seattle	40	41	.494	33	48	.407	68	67	353	386	66	47	341	342			6	**12**
Chicago	35	45	.438	34	47	.420	**36**	58	**301**	365	58	86	392	385	3	4/8	8	7

Season	Team	Home Games W	L	PCT	Road Games W	L	PCT	Home Games HR	OHR	R	OR	Road Games HR	OHR	R	OR	DIF	LDF	WS	LS
1990 National League (4/9–10/3)	East																		
	Pittsburgh	49	32	.605	46	35	**.568**	59	63	351	299	79	72	**382**	320	**152**	**9/30**	7	6
	New York	52	29	**.642**	39	42	.481	**86**	52	**397**	280	**86**	67	378	333	19	9/3	**11**	5
	Montreal	47	34	.580	38	43	.469	48	62	328	**268**	66	65	334	330	6	6/23	7	**8**
	Chicago	39	42	.481	38	43	.469	75	73	372	**437**	61	**48**	318	337	10	4/19	8	6
	Philadelphia	41	40	.506	36	45	.444	47	67	311	367	56	57	335	362	1	5/25	4	6
	St. Louis	34	47	.420	36	45	.444	43	**47**	319	366	30	51	280	332	5	4/13	4	7
	West																		
	Cincinnati	46	35	.568	45	36	.556	70	73	334	312	55	51	359	**285**	**178**	**9/29**	9	**8**
	Los Angeles	47	34	.580	39	42	.481	54	73	351	323	75	64	377	362	2	4/10	6	6
	San Francisco	49	32	.605	36	45	.444	81	70	380	340	71	61	339	370			9	6
	Houston	49	32	.605	26	55	.321	**35**	**47**	**298**	271	59	83	275	385			5	**8**
	San Diego	37	44	.457	38	43	.469	63	**78**	342	348	60	69	331	325			6	7
	Atlanta	37	44	.457	28	53	.346	85	70	352	427	77	58	330	394			6	7
1990 American League (4/9–10/3)	East																		
	Boston	51	30	**.630**	37	44	.457	61	**44**	**394**	318	45	**48**	305	346	**98**	**10/3**	**10**	6
	Toronto	44	37	.543	42	39	.519	**93**	82	385	341	74	61	382	320	49	9/27	6	6
	Detroit	39	42	.481	40	41	.494	92	75	372	**399**	80	79	378	355			7	5
	Cleveland	41	40	.506	36	45	.444	52	**86**	363	373	58	77	369	364			6	8
	Baltimore	40	40	.500	36	45	.444	74	82	320	337	58	79	349	361	2	4/10	6	6
	Milwaukee	39	42	.481	35	46	.432	60	59	356	374	68	62	376	356	32	6/3	4	8
	New York	37	44	.457	30	51	.370	64	78	**296**	361	83	66	307	388	7	4/18	6	8
	West																		
	Oakland	51	30	**.630**	52	29	**.642**	69	52	321	**244**	**95**	71	**412**	326	**169**	**9/25**	7	4
	Chicago	49	31	.613	45	37	.549	**41**	53	345	315	65	53	337	**318**	11	7/8	8	5
	Texas	47	35	.573	36	44	.450	64	59	354	348	46	54	322	348	1	4/9	7	5
	California	42	39	.519	38	43	.469	89	55	360	354	58	51	330	352			7	5
	Seattle	38	43	.469	39	42	.481	49	60	310	341	58	60	330	339	1	4/9	5	5
	Kansas City	45	36	.556	30	50	.375	42	46	370	342	58	70	337	367			5	**9**
	Minnesota	41	40	.506	33	48	.407	46	69	373	380	54	65	293	349			6	**9**
1991 National League (4/8–10/6)	East																		
	Pittsburgh	52	32	.619	46	32	**.590**	61	55	382	314	65	62	**396**	318	**172**	**9/22**	9	8
	St. Louis	52	32	.619	32	46	.410	32	41	345	293	36	73	306	355	1	4/9	5	5
	Philadelphia	47	36	.566	31	48	.392	61	53	341	334	50	58	288	346			**13**	7
	Chicago	46	37	.554	31	46	.403	93	75	386	**396**	66	**42**	309	338	3	4/20	6	9
	New York	40	42	.488	37	42	.468	57	55	332	348	60	53	308	298	14	4/26	10	**11**
	Montreal	33	35	.485	38	55	.409	35	**33**	**216**	**233**	60	78	363	422	1	4/8	7	**11**
	West																		
	Atlanta	48	33	.593	46	35	.568	83	73	**418**	368	58	45	331	**276**	27	**10/5**	8	5
	Los Angeles	54	27	**.667**	39	42	.481	57	46	342	280	51	50	323	285	**132**	10/3	5	7
	San Diego	42	39	.519	42	39	.519	65	72	315	320	56	67	321	326	22	5/8	7	5
	San Francisco	43	38	.531	32	49	.395	69	62	306	305	**72**	81	343	392			11	7
	Cincinnati	39	42	.481	35	46	.432	**104**	**77**	373	376	60	50	316	315	10	5/5	5	10
	Houston	37	44	.457	28	53	.346	**27**	44	302	330	52	85	303	387			9	7
1991 American League (4/8–10/6)	East																		
	Toronto	46	35	.568	45	36	**.556**	75	72	359	344	58	**49**	325	**278**	**134**	**10/2**	6	7
	Boston	43	38	.531	41	40	.506	69	76	378	374	57	71	353	338	46	6/22	7	6
	Detroit	49	32	.605	35	46	.432	**109**	**89**	**437**	**402**	**100**	59	380	392	6	8/26	7	8
	Milwaukee	43	37	.538	40	42	.488	62	73	398	398	54	74	401	346	3	4/10	5	8
	New York	39	42	.481	32	49	.395	82	84	356	380	65	68	318	397			6	8
	Baltimore	33	48	.407	34	47	.420	80	72	329	387	90	75	**457**	409			5	6
	Cleveland	30	52	.366	27	53	.338	**22**	41	**271**	377	57	69	305	382			4	7
	West																		
	Minnesota	51	30	**.630**	44	37	.543	62	75	404	342	78	64	372	310	**108**	**9/29**	**15**	7
	Chicago	46	35	.568	41	40	.506	74	79	378	337	65	75	380	344	18	4/29	8	**9**
	Texas	46	35	.568	39	42	.481	79	77	404	400	98	74	425	414	12	7/10	14	8
	Oakland	47	34	.580	37	44	.457	76	67	357	351	83	88	403	425	40	6/15	7	7
	Seattle	45	36	.556	38	43	.469	69	69	374	319	57	67	328	355	4	5/21	8	7
	Kansas City	40	41	.494	42	39	.519	47	**40**	344	378	70	65	383	344	1	4/8	5	7
	California	40	41	.494	41	40	.506	59	74	291	**303**	56	67	362	346	5	7/3	5	7
1992 National League (4/6–10/4)	East																		
	Pittsburgh	53	28	**.654**	43	38	.531	51	37	363	**277**	55	64	330	318	**172**	**9/27**	11	6
	Montreal	43	38	.531	44	37	.543	50	48	331	**334**	52	**44**	317	**247**	6	7/30	6	4
	St. Louis	45	36	.556	38	43	.469	55	52	328	297	39	66	303	307	10	6/2	6	5
	Chicago	43	38	.531	35	46	.432	59	49	315	297	45	58	278	327	1	4/7	6	8
	New York	41	40	.506	31	50	.383	42	49	288	305	51	49	311	348	1	4/6	7	7
	Philadelphia	41	40	.506	29	52	.358	67	49	**369**	331	51	64	317	386	2	4/11	6	9
	West																		
	Atlanta	51	30	.630	47	34	**.580**	72	45	343	290	**66**	**44**	**339**	279	**77**	**9/29**	**13**	4
	Cincinnati	53	28	**.654**	37	44	.457	60	60	355	289	39	49	305	320	53	8/1	9	7
	San Diego	45	36	.556	37	44	.457	**87**	**64**	339	**334**	48	47	278	302	10	4/29	6	5
	Houston	47	34	.580	34	47	.420	49	41	302	293	47	73	306	375	9	4/27	5	6
	San Francisco	42	39	.519	30	51	.370	57	60	307	294	48	68	267	353	31	5/31	5	9
	Los Angeles	37	44	.457	26	55	.321	**26**	**33**	**277**	281	46	49	271	355	1	4/9	6	**10**

1992 American League
(4/6–10/4)

	Home Games			Road Games			Home Games				Road Games							
Team	**W**	**L**	**PCT**	**W**	**L**	**PCT**	**HR**	**OHR**	**R**	**OR**	**HR**	**OHR**	**R**	**OR**	**DIF**	**LDF**	**WS**	**LS**
East																		
Toronto	53	28	**.654**	43	38	.531	79	60	**390**	334	84	64	390	348	**162**	**10/3**	8	5
Milwaukee	53	28	**.654**	39	42	.481	35	51	339	**254**	47	76	401	350			7	7
Baltimore	43	38	.531	46	35	**.568**	75	69	339	333	73	55	366	**323**			5	6
Cleveland	41	40	.506	35	46	.432	62	**94**	366	397	65	65	308	349			5	6
New York	41	40	.506	35	46	.432	88	70	385	387	75	59	348	359	7	4/13	6	6
Detroit	38	42	.475	37	45	.451	**91**	90	389	**399**	**91**	65	**402**	395			5	6
Boston	44	37	.543	29	52	.358	45	46	328	341	39	61	271	328			4	7
West																		
Oakland	51	30	.630	45	36	.556	76	73	365	326	66	56	380	346	**139**	**9/28**	**10**	5
Minnesota	48	33	.593	42	39	.519	56	56	375	326	48	65	372	327	41	8/4	6	4
Chicago	50	32	.610	36	44	.450	54	62	368	314	56	61	370	376	11	5/17	6	6
Texas	36	45	.444	41	40	.506	71	63	317	376	88	**50**	365	377	8	5/30	7	5
California	41	40	.506	31	50	.383	44	60	**311**	340	44	70	268	331			6	11
Kansas City	44	37	.543	28	53	.346	**24**	**41**	314	336	51	65	296	331			6	9
Seattle	38	43	.469	26	55	.321	78	63	355	398	71	66	324	401			5	**14**

1993 National League
(4/5–10/3)

	Home Games			Road Games			Home Games				Road Games							
Team	**W**	**L**	**PCT**	**W**	**L**	**PCT**	**HR**	**OHR**	**R**	**OR**	**HR**	**OHR**	**R**	**OR**	**DIF**	**LDF**	**WS**	**LS**
East																		
Philadelphia	52	29	.642	45	36	.556	80	57	441	371	76	72	436	369	**181**	**9/28**	6	4
Montreal	55	26	**.679**	39	42	.481	62	50	367	315	60	69	365	367			9	4
St. Louis	49	32	.605	38	43	.469	59	59	376	321	59	93	382	423	1	4/10	5	6
Chicago	43	38	.531	41	40	.506	76	94	381	382	85	59	357	357			6	7
Pittsburgh	40	41	.494	35	46	.432	64	67	372	388	46	86	335	418	4	4/9	5	7
Florida	35	46	.432	29	52	.358	**50**	63	**282**	355	44	72	299	369	1	4/5	4	7
New York	28	53	.346	31	50	.383	75	72	317	376	83	67	355	368	4	4/8	6	8
West																		
Atlanta	51	30	.630	53	28	**.654**	78	52	366	291	**91**	**49**	401	**268**	31	**10/3**	9	5
San Francisco	50	31	.617	53	28	**.654**	82	81	362	293	86	87	**446**	343	**144**	10/2	7	8
Houston	44	37	.543	41	40	.506	62	56	363	**285**	76	61	353	345	11	5/10	5	5
Los Angeles	41	40	.506	40	41	.494	66	**48**	330	318	64	55	345	344	1	4/7	**11**	7
Cincinnati	41	40	.506	32	49	.395	69	81	363	383	68	77	359	402	2	4/6	7	12
Colorado	39	42	.481	28	53	.346	77	**107**	**489**	**551**	65	74	269	416			6	**13**
San Diego	34	47	.420	27	54	.333	**87**	79	345	376	66	69	334	396			5	7

1993 American League
(4/5–10/3)

	Home Games			Road Games			Home Games				Road Games							
Team	**W**	**L**	**PCT**	**W**	**L**	**PCT**	**HR**	**OHR**	**R**	**OR**	**HR**	**OHR**	**R**	**OR**	**DIF**	**LDF**	**WS**	**LS**
East																		
Toronto	48	33	.593	47	34	.580	90	81	437	390	69	**53**	410	352	**96**	**9/27**	9	6
New York	50	31	**.617**	38	43	.469	88	85	389	342	90	85	432	419	18	9/9	6	5
Baltimore	48	33	.593	37	44	.457	87	81	434	371	70	72	434	371	1	7/20	**10**	8
Detroit	44	37	.543	41	40	.506	**103**	**99**	**457**	408	75	89	**442**	429	64	6/25	7	**10**
Boston	43	38	.531	37	44	.457	54	53	393	363	60	74	293	335	22	7/25	**10**	7
Cleveland	46	35	.568	30	51	.370	69	83	387	351	72	99	403	462			8	5
Milwaukee	38	43	.469	31	50	.383	53	65	371	381	72	88	362	411			7	7
West																		
Chicago	45	36	.556	49	32	**.605**	82	70	384	**333**	80	55	392	**331**	**126**	**9/27**	6	6
Texas	50	31	**.617**	36	45	.444	90	72	414	341	**91**	72	421	410	16	4/20	6	6
Kansas City	43	38	.531	41	40	.506	**50**	**49**	370	354	75	56	305	340	25	7/6	5	5
Seattle	46	35	.568	36	45	.444	74	66	380	350	87	69	354	381	1	4/6	6	5
California	44	37	.543	27	54	.333	64	84	363	398	50	69	321	372	26	6/21	6	**10**
Minnesota	36	45	.444	35	46	.432	56	70	360	**433**	65	78	333	397			6	9
Oakland	38	43	.469	30	51	.370	78	78	**333**	387	80	79	382	459	3	4/7	7	9

1994 National League
(4/3–8/11)

	Home Games			Road Games			Home Games				Road Games							
Team	**W**	**L**	**PCT**	**W**	**L**	**PCT**	**HR**	**OHR**	**R**	**OR**	**HR**	**OHR**	**R**	**OR**	**DIF**	**LDF**	**WS**	**LS**
East																		
Montreal	32	20	.615	42	20	**.677**	**42**	47	266	227	66	53	**319**	227	27	**8/7**	8	4
Atlanta	31	24	.564	37	22	.627	**61**	**37**	230	231	**76**	**39**	312	**217**	**104**	7/21	7	4
New York	23	30	.434	32	28	.533	53	60	235	271	64	57	271	255	4	4/7	4	5
Philadelphia	34	26	.567	20	35	.364	45	40	268	243	35	58	253	254	4	4/7	5	6
Florida	25	34	.424	26	30	.464	46	70	245	341	48	50	223	235			5	7
Central																		
Cincinnati	37	22	**.627**	29	26	.527	59	65	306	263	65	52	303	227	**120**	**8/11**	6	5
Houston	37	22	**.627**	29	27	.518	57	56	307	241	63	46	295	262	20	7/28	6	4
Pittsburgh	32	29	.525	21	32	.396	45	61	271	291	36	56	195	289	1	4/16	6	5
St. Louis	23	33	.411	30	28	.517	50	66	248	315	58	68	287	306	7	4/17	5	6
Chicago	20	39	.339	29	25	.537	47	71	**216**	287	62	49	284	262			8	10
West																		
Los Angeles	33	22	.600	25	34	.424	47	49	230	**209**	68	41	302	300	**91**	**8/7**	7	5
San Francisco	29	31	.483	26	29	.473	56	**94**	259	258	67	48	245	242	43	5/17	**9**	6
Colorado	25	32	.439	28	32	.467	59	61	**317**	**356**	66	59	256	282			4	5
San Diego	26	31	.456	21	39	.350	51	57	240	251	41	42	239	280			6	**13**

1994 American League
(4/4–8/11)

	Home Games			Road Games			Home Games				Road Games							
Team	**W**	**L**	**PCT**	**W**	**L**	**PCT**	**HR**	**OHR**	**R**	**OR**	**HR**	**OHR**	**R**	**OR**	**DIF**	**LDF**	**WS**	**LS**
East																		
New York	33	24	.579	37	19	**.661**	63	62	291	260	76	58	**379**	274	**100**	**8/8**	10	4
Baltimore	28	27	.509	35	22	.614	75	70	294	272	64	61	295	**225**	7	4/19	4	4
Toronto	33	26	.559	22	34	.393	63	64	293	275	52	63	273	304	13	5/26	8	10
Boston	31	33	.484	23	28	.451	68	67	320	353	52	53	232	268	30	5/8	7	11
Detroit	34	24	.586	19	38	.333	85	76	**350**	324	76	72	302	347			4	4
Central																		
Chicago	34	19	.642	33	27	.550	62	**43**	296	**206**	59	72	337	292	**68**	**8/10**	7	5
Cleveland	35	16	**.686**	31	31	.500	**87**	44	335	248	80	50	344	314	63	8/5	10	5
Kansas City	35	24	.593	29	27	.518	**41**	48	325	287	59	**47**	249	245			**14**	3
Minnesota	32	27	.542	21	33	.389	48	88	319	339	55	65	275	349			7	5
Milwaukee	24	42	.364	29	30	.492	48	63	275	311	51	64	272	275	10	5/10	5	**14**
West																		
Texas	31	32	.492	21	30	.412	63	67	334	353	61	90	279	344	**89**	**8/11**	4	6
Oakland	24	32	.429	27	31	.466	51	54	**241**	262	62	74	308	327	8	4/20	8	12
Seattle	22	22	.500	27	41	.397	63	44	248	244	**90**	65	321	372	6	5/22	6	7
California	23	40	.365	24	28	.462	74	**93**	286	**389**	46	57	257	271	26	5/29	4	8

1995 National League (4/25–10/1)

Team	Home Games			Road Games			Home Games				Road Games							
	W	L	PCT	W	L	PCT	HR	OHR	R	OR	HR	OHR	R	OR	DIF	LDF	WS	LS
East																		
Atlanta	44	28	**.611**	46	26	**.639**	94	66	322	295	74	**41**	323	**245**	**101**	**9/13**	**9**	5
New York	40	32	.556	29	43	.403	63	68	308	294	62	65	349	324			6	6
Philadelphia	35	37	.486	34	38	.472	51	78	336	359	43	56	279	299	61	7/4	7	8
Florida	37	34	.521	30	42	.417	68	60	331	321	76	79	342	352			8	6
Montreal	31	41	.431	35	37	.486	43	55	303	318	75	73	318	320	3	4/28	4	6
Central																		
Cincinnati	44	28	**.611**	41	31	.569	76	58	358	308	**85**	73	389	315	**124**	**9/22**	**9**	6
Houston	36	36	.500	40	32	.556	**41**	**48**	321	296	68	70	**426**	378	6	5/11	5	**11**
Chicago	34	38	.472	39	33	.542	83	83	339	350	75	79	354	321	37	6/4	8	7
St. Louis	39	33	.542	27	45	.375	54	60	311	316	53	75	252	342	1	4/26	6	6
Pittsburgh	31	41	.431	27	45	.375	69	67	329	396	56	63	300	340			6	6
West																		
Los Angeles	39	33	.542	39	33	.542	62	**48**	**281**	**276**	78	77	353	333	39	**10/1**	6	6
Colorado	44	28	**.611**	33	39	.458	**134**	**107**	**485**	**490**	66	53	300	293	**118**	9/26	6	5
San Diego	40	32	.556	30	42	.417	55	72	304	313	61	70	364	359	1	4/30	4	7
San Francisco	37	35	.514	30	42	.417	76	78	305	364	76	95	347	412	12	6/7	4	5

1995 American League (4/26–10/2)

Team	Home Games			Road Games			Home Games				Road Games							
	W	L	PCT	W	L	PCT	HR	OHR	R	OR	HR	OHR	R	OR	DIF	LDF	WS	LS
East																		
Boston	42	30	.583	44	28	.611	70	63	387	360	105	**64**	404	338	**153**	**9/20**	**12**	5
New York	46	26	.639	33	39	.458	69	76	411	323	53	83	338	365	14	5/12	7	8
Baltimore	36	36	.500	35	37	.486	91	84	357	325	82	65	347	**315**			4	7
Detroit	35	37	.486	25	47	.347	92	93	354	426	67	77	300	418	1	4/26	5	8
Toronto	29	43	.403	27	45	.375	73	78	322	388	67	67	320	389	2	4/27	4	8
Central																		
Cleveland	54	18	**.750**	46	26	**.639**	99	**60**	400	**272**	**108**	75	**440**	335	**146**	**9/8**	9	4
Kansas City	35	37	.486	35	37	.486	**49**	68	**285**	346	70	74	344	345	2	4/27	7	6
Chicago	38	34	.528	30	42	.417	59	73	361	361	87	91	394	397			8	4
Milwaukee	33	39	.458	32	40	.444	56	71	390	426	72	75	350	321	15	5/10	7	6
Minnesota	29	43	.403	27	45	.375	59	**120**	368	**448**	61	90	335	441			5	6
West																		
Seattle	46	27	.630	33	39	.458	**101**	73	**424**	344	81	76	372	364	29	**10/2**	7	5
California	39	33	.542	39	34	.534	90	88	405	322	96	75	396	375	**126**	10/1	8	9
Texas	41	31	.569	33	39	.458	81	73	379	368	57	79	312	352	20	7/13	6	**10**
Oakland	38	34	.528	29	43	.403	80	75	330	343	89	78	400	418			6	9

PART SEVEN

Manager Register

Alphabetical List of Every Man Who Ever
Managed in the Major Leagues
And His Complete Managerial Record

Manager Register

The Manager Register is an alphabetical listing of every man who has managed a major league team from 1876 through today. Included are facts about the managers and their year-by-year managerial records and lifetime totals for the regular season and for Divisional Playoff Series, Championship Series, and World Series. All managers who played in the major leagues can also be found in the Player Register.

Managers included here are defined as men who were in charge of a team while the team was on the field. This definition includes interim managers (those who served between outgoing and incoming managers) but not "acting managers," who took over a team while the regular manager was temporarily absent because of illness, injury, or suspension, unless the "acting manager" served in that capacity for more than thirty days. All information and abbreviations that may appear unfamiliar are explained in the sample format presented below. The man, John Doe, used in the sample is fictitious and serves only to illustrate the information:

John Doe

DOE, JOHN LEE (Slim)
Born John Lee Doughnut
Brother of Bill Doe
B. Jan. 1, 1850, New York, N.Y.
D. July 1, 1955, New York, N.Y.
Hall of Fame 1946.

			G	W	L	T	N	PCT	Standing		
1908	**BOS**	**N**	100	70	30	0	0	.700	4	**1**	
1909	**NY**	**N**	155	90	64	0	0	.584	**3**		
1910			154	96	58	0	0	.623	**1**		
1911			105	60	45	0	0	.571	**5**	6	
1912	**CHI**	**A**	154	101	53	0	0	.656	**1**		
1913	**STL**	**N**	154	90	64	0	0	.584	**2**		
1914	**CHI**	**F**	25	8	17	0	0	.320	4	**6**	5
1915	**NY**	**A**	54	20	34	0	0	.370	**6**	4	
1915	**CLE**	**A**	100	65	35	0	0	.650	5	**2**	
8 yrs.			1001	600	400	0	0	.600			
DIVISIONAL PLAYOFF SERIES											
1995	**NY**	**A**	5	2	3	0	0	.400			
LEAGUE CHAMPIONSHIP SERIES											
1974	**OAK**	**A**	4	3	1	0	0	.750			
1975			3	0	3	0	0	.000			
2 yrs.			7	3	4	0	0	.429			
WORLD SERIES											
1962	**SF**	**N**	7	3	4	0	0	.429			
1974	**OAK**	**A**	5	4	1	0	0	.800			
2 yrs.			12	7	5	0	0	.583			

Manager Information

John Doe

This shortened version of the manager's full name is the name most familiar to the fans. All managers in this section are alphabetically arranged by the last name part of this name.

Doe, John Lee

Manager's full name. The arrangement is last name first, then first and middle name(s).

(Slim)

Nickname. Any name appearing in parentheses is a nickname.

Born John Lee Doughnut

The name the manager was given at birth. A name shown in this form means that the man never used this name while he was a major league manager.

Brother of Bill Doe

The manager's brother. (Relatives indicated here are fathers, sons, and brothers who played or managed in the major leagues and the National Association.)

B. Jan. 1, 1850, New York, N.Y.

Date and place of birth.

D. July 1, 1955, New York, N.Y.

Date and place of death. (Some managers are listed simply as "deceased." Although no certification of death or other information is currently available, it is reasonably certain they are dead.)

Hall of Fame 1946

Doe was elected to the Hall of Fame in 1946.

Column Headings

G	W	L	T	N	PCT	Standing

G	Games Managed
W	Wins
L	Losses
T	Ties
ND	No Decisions
PCT	Winning Percentage
Standing	(explained under Statistical Information)

League and Team Information

1908	**BOS**	**N**	100	70	30	0	0	.700	4	1	
1909	**NY**	**N**	155	90	64	0	0	.584	3		
1910			154	96	58	0	0	.623	1		
1911			105	60	45	0	0	.571	5	6	
1912	**CHI**	**A**	154	101	53	0	0	.656	1		
1913	**STL**	**N**	154	90	64	0	0	.584	2		
1914	**CHI**	**F**	25	8	17	0	0	.320	4	6	5
1915	**NY**	**A**	54	20	34	0	0	.370	6	4	
1915	**CLE**	**A**	100	65	35	0	0	.650	5	2	
8 yrs.			1001	600	400	0	0	.600 3rd			

Although Doe's record does not include managing in each of the six different major leagues that will appear in this section, the symbols for all the leagues are listed below:

N	National League (1876 to date)
A	American League (1901 to date)
F	Federal League (1914–15)
AA	American Association (1882–91)
P	Players' League (1890)
U	Union Association (1884)

BOSThe abbreviation of the city in which the team played. Doe, for example, managed Boston in 1908. All teams in this section are listed by an abbreviation of the city or area in which the team played. The abbreviations follow:

ALT	Altoona	MON	Montreal
ATL	Atlanta	NWK	Newark
BAL	Baltimore	NY	New York
BKN	Brooklyn	OAK	Oakland
BOS	Boston	PHI	Philadelphia
BUF	Buffalo	PIT	Pittsburgh
CAL	California	PRO	Providence
CHI	Chicago	RIC	Richmond
CIN	Cincinnati	ROC	Rochester
CLE	Cleveland	SD	San Diego
CLR	Colorado	SEA	Seattle

COL	Columbus	SF	San Francisco
DET	Detroit	STL	St. Louis
FLA	Florida	STP	St. Paul
HAR	Hartford	SYR	Syracuse
HOU	Houston	TEX	Texas
IND	Indianapolis	TOL	Toledo
KC	Kansas City	TOR	Toronto
LA	Los Angeles	TRO	Troy
LOU	Louisville	WAS	Washington
MIL	Milwaukee	WIL	Wilmington
MIN	Minnesota	WOR	Worcester

Blank space appearing beneath a team and league indicates that the team and league are the same. Doe, for example, managed New York in the National League from 1909 through 1911.

Separate Managerial Records. Whenever a manager served with more than one team in the same year, the information is shown on separate lines. Doe, for example, managed two teams in 1915.

Total Playing Years. This information, which appears directly beneath the last team, indicates the total number of years in which the man managed for at least one game. Doe, for example, managed in at least one game for eight years.

			G	W	L	T	N	PCT	Standing		

John Doe

DOE, JOHN LEE (Slim)
Born John Lee Doughnut
Brother of Bill Doe
B. Jan. 1, 1850, New York, N.Y.
D. July 1, 1955, New York, N.Y.
Hall of Fame 1946.

1908	**BOS**	**N**	100	70	30	0	0	.700	4	**1**	
1909	**NY**	**N**	155	90	64	0	0	.584	**3**		
1910			154	96	58	0	0	.623	**1**		
1911			105	60	45	0	0	.571	**5**	6	
1912	**CHI**	**A**	154	101	53	0	0	.656	**1**		
1913	**STL**	**N**	154	90	64	0	0	.584	**2**		
1914	**CHI**	**F**	25	8	17	0	0	.320	4	**6**	5
1915	**NY**	**A**	54	20	34	0	0	.370	**6**	4	
1915	**CLE**	**A**	100	65	35	0	0	.650	5	**2**	
8 yrs.			1001	600	400	0	0	.600			
DIVISIONAL PLAYOFF SERIES											
1995	**NY**	**A**	5	2	3	0	0	.400			
LEAGUE CHAMPIONSHIP SERIES											
1974	**OAK**	**A**	4	3	1	0	0	.750			
1975			3	0	3	0	0	.000			
2 yrs.			7	3	4	0	0	.429			
WORLD SERIES											
1962	**SF**	**N**	7	3	4	0	0	.429			
1974	**OAK**	**A**	5	4	1	0	0	.800			
2 yrs.			12	7	5	0	0	.583			

Standing. The figures in this column indicate the standing of the team at the end of the season and when there was a managerial change. The four possible cases are as follows:

Only Manager for the Team That Year. Indicated by a single boldfaced figure that appears in the extreme left-hand column and shows the final standing of the team. See Doe in 1909, 1910, 1912, and 1913.

Manager Started Season, but Did Not Finish. Indicated by two figures: the first is boldfaced and shows the standing of the team when this manager left; the second shows the final standing of the team. See Doe in 1911 and 1915, New York.

Manager Finished Season, but Did Not Start. Indicated by two figures: the first shows the standing of the team when this manager started; the second is boldfaced and shows the final standing of the team. See Doe in 1908 and 1915, Cleveland.

Manager Did Not Start or Finish Season. Indicated by three figures: the first shows the standing of the team when this manager started; the second is boldfaced and shows the standing of the team when this manager left; the third shows the final standing of the team. See Doe in 1914.

Split Season Indicator. The 1892 and 1981 seasons divided into two halves. Each half-season is listed separately in the Manager Register. A figure in parentheses to the right of the Standing column indicates whether the record is for the first or second half-season.

Lifetime Leaders. The top ten men are shown for Games, Wins, Losses, and Winning Percentage. Doe has a "3rd"shown below his lifetime winning percentage total. This means that, lifetime, Doe ranks third among major league managers for the highest winning percentage based on a minimum of 1,000 games. Managers who tied for a position receive the same ranking.

Bill Adair

ADAIR, MARION DANNE
B. Feb. 10, 1913, Mobile, Ala.

Year	Team	Lg	G	W	L	T	N	PCT	Standing
1970	CHI	A	10	4	6	0	0	.400	6 **6** 6

Joe Adcock

ADCOCK, JOSEPH WILBUR
B. Oct. 30, 1927, Coushatta, La.

Year	Team	Lg	G	W	L	T	N	PCT	Standing
1967	CLE	A	162	75	87	0	0	.463	**8**

Bob Addy

ADDY, ROBERT EDWARD (The Magnet)
B. Feb. 1845, Rochester, N. Y.
D. Apr. 9, 1910, Pocatello, Ida.

Year	Team	Lg	G	W	L	T	N	PCT	Standing
1877	CIN	N	24	5	19	0	0	.208	6 **6** 6

Bob Allen

ALLEN, ROBERT GILMAN
B. July 10, 1867, Marion, Ohio
D. May 4, 1943, Little Rock, Ark.

Year	Team	Lg	G	W	L	T	N	PCT	Standing
1890	PHI	N	35	25	10	0	0	.714	3 **2** 3
1900	CIN	N	144	62	77	5	0	.446	**7**
2 yrs.			179	87	87	5	0	.500	

Felipe Alou

ALOU, FELIPE
Born Felipe Rojas (Alou).
Brother of Jesus Alou.
Brother of Matty Alou.
Father of Moises Alou.
B. May 12, 1935, Haina, Dominican Republic.

Year	Team	Lg	G	W	L	T	N	PCT	Standing
1992	MON	N	125	70	55	0	0	.560	4 **2**
1993			163	94	68	1	0	.580	**2**
1994			114	74	40	0	0	.649	**1**
1995			144	66	78	0	0	.458	**5**
4 yrs.			546	304	241	1	0	.558	

Walter Alston

ALSTON, WALTER EMMONS (Smokey)
B. Dec. 1, 1911, Venice, Ohio
D. Oct. 1, 1984, Oxford, Ohio.
Hall of Fame 1983.

Year	Team	Lg	G	W	L	T	N	PCT	Standing
1954	BKN	N	154	92	62	0	0	.597	**2**
1955			154	98	55	1	0	.641	**1**
1956			154	93	61	0	0	.604	**1**
1957			154	84	70	0	0	.545	**3**
1958	LA	N	154	71	83	0	0	.461	**7**
1959			156	88	68	0	0	.564	**1**
1960			154	82	72	0	0	.532	**4**
1961			154	89	65	0	0	.578	**2**
1962			165	102	63	0	0	.618	**2**
1963			163	99	63	1	0	.611	**1**
1964			164	80	82	2	0	.494	**6**
1965			162	97	65	0	0	.599	**1**
1966			162	95	67	0	0	.586	**1**
1967			162	73	89	0	0	.451	**8**
1968			162	76	86	0	0	.469	**7**
1969			162	85	77	0	0	.525	**4**
1970			161	87	74	0	0	.540	**2**
1971			162	89	73	0	0	.549	**2**
1972			155	85	70	0	0	.548	**3**
1973			162	95	66	1	0	.590	**2**
1974			162	102	60	0	0	.630	**1**
1975			162	88	74	0	0	.543	**2**
1976			158	90	68	0	0	.570	**2** 2
23 yrs.			3658 **8th**	2040 **6th**	1613 **9th**	5	0	.558	

LEAGUE CHAMPIONSHIP SERIES

Year	Team	Lg	G	W	L	T	N	PCT
1974	LA	N	4	3	1	0	0	.750

WORLD SERIES

Year	Team	Lg	G	W	L	T	N	PCT
1955	BKN	N	7	4	3	0	0	.571
1956			7	3	4	0	0	.429
1959	LA	N	6	4	2	0	0	.667
1963			4	4	0	0	0	1.000
1965			7	4	3	0	0	.571
1966			4	0	4	0	0	.000
1974			5	1	4	0	0	.200
7 yrs.			40 **5th**	20 **5th**	20 **3rd**	0	0	.500 **9th**

Joe Altobelli

ALTOBELLI, JOSEPH SALVATORE
B. May 26, 1932, Detroit, Mich.

Year	Team	Lg	G	W	L	T	N	PCT	Standing
1977	SF	N	162	75	87	0	0	.463	**4**
1978			162	89	73	0	0	.549	**3**
1979			140	61	79	0	0	.436	**4** 4
1983	BAL	A	162	98	64	0	0	.605	**1**
1984			162	85	77	0	0	.525	**5**
1985			55	29	26	0	0	.527	**4** 4
1991	CHI	N	1	0	1	0	0	.000	4 **5** 4
7 yrs.			844	437	407	0	0	.518	

LEAGUE CHAMPIONSHIP SERIES

Year	Team	Lg	G	W	L	T	N	PCT
1983	BAL	A	4	3	1	0	0	.750

WORLD SERIES

Year	Team	Lg	G	W	L	T	N	PCT
1983	BAL	A	5	4	1	0	0	.800

Joey Amalfitano

AMALFITANO, JOHN JOSEPH
B. Jan. 23, 1934, San Pedro, Calif.

Year	Team	Lg	G	W	L	T	N	PCT	Standing
1979	CHI	N	7	2	5	0	0	.286	5 **5**
1980			72	26	46	0	0	.361	6 **6**
1981			54	15	37	2	0	.288	**6** (1st)
1981			52	23	28	1	0	.451	**5** (2nd)
3 yrs.			185	66	116	3	0	.363	

Sparky Anderson

ANDERSON, GEORGE LEE
B. Feb. 22, 1934, Bridgewater, S. D.

Year	Team	Lg	G	W	L	T	N	PCT	Standing
1970	CIN	N	162	102	60	0	0	.630	**1**
1971			162	79	83	0	0	.488	**4**
1972			154	95	59	0	0	.617	**1**
1973			162	99	63	0	0	.611	**1**
1974			163	98	64	1	0	.605	**2**
1975			162	108	54	0	0	.667	**1**
1976			162	102	60	0	0	.630	**1**
1977			162	88	74	0	0	.543	**2**
1978			161	92	69	0	0	.571	**2**
1979	DET	A	106	56	50	0	0	.528	5 **5**
1980			163	84	78	1	0	.519	**4**
1981			57	31	26	0	0	.544	**4** (1st)
1981			52	29	23	0	0	.558	**2** (2nd)
1982			162	83	79	0	0	.512	**4**
1983			162	92	70	0	0	.568	**2**
1984			162	104	58	0	0	.642	**1**
1985			161	84	77	0	0	.522	**3**
1986			162	87	75	0	0	.537	**3**
1987			162	98	64	0	0	.605	**1**
1988			162	88	74	0	0	.543	**2**
1989			162	59	103	0	0	.364	**7**
1990			162	79	83	0	0	.488	**3**
1991			162	84	78	0	0	.519	**2**
1992			162	75	87	0	0	.463	**6**
1993			162	85	77	0	0	.525	**3**
1994			115	53	62	0	0	.461	**5**
1995			144	60	84	0	0	.417	**4**
26 yrs.			4030 **4th**	2194 **3rd**	1834 **6th**	2	0	.545	

LEAGUE CHAMPIONSHIP SERIES

Year	Team	Lg	G	W	L	T	N	PCT
1970	CIN	N	3	3	0	0	0	1.000
1972			5	3	2	0	0	.600
1973			5	2	3	0	0	.400
1975			3	3	0	0	0	1.000
1976			3	3	0	0	0	1.000
1984	DET	A	3	3	0	0	0	1.000
1987			5	1	4	0	0	.200
7 yrs.			27 **4th**	18 **1st**	9	0	0	.667 **2nd**

WORLD SERIES

Year	Team	Lg	G	W	L	T	N	PCT
1970	CIN	N	5	1	4	0	0	.200
1972			7	3	4	0	0	.429
1975			7	4	3	0	0	.571
1976			4	4	0	0	0	1.000
1984	DET	A	5	4	1	0	0	.800
5 yrs.			28 **7th**	16 **7th**	12	0	0	.571 **3rd**

Cap Anson

ANSON, ADRIAN CONSTANTINE (Pops, Old Anse)
B. Apr. 11, 1852, Marshalltown, Iowa
D. Apr. 14, 1922, Chicago, Ill.
Hall of Fame 1939.

Year	Team	Lg	G	W	L	T	N	PCT	Standing
1879	CHI	N	64	41	21	2	0	.661	**2** 4
1880			86	67	17	2	0	.798	**1**
1881			84	56	28	0	0	.667	**1**
1882			84	55	29	0	0	.655	**1**
1883			98	59	39	0	0	.602	**2**
1884			113	62	50	1	0	.554	**4**
1885			113	87	25	1	0	.777	**1**
1886			126	90	34	2	0	.726	**1**
1887			127	71	50	3	3	.587	**3**
1888			136	77	58	1	0	.570	**2**
1889			136	67	65	4	0	.508	**3**
1890			139	84	53	2	0	.613	**2**
1891			137	82	53	2	0	.607	**2**
1892			71	31	39	1	0	.443	**8** (1st)
1892			76	39	37	0	0	.513	**7** (2nd)
1893			128	56	71	1	0	.441	**9**
1894			137	57	75	3	2	.432	**8**
1895			133	72	58	3	0	.554	**4**
1896			132	71	57	4	0	.555	**5**
1897			138	59	73	6	0	.447	**9**
1898	NY	N	22	9	13	0	0	.409	6 **7** 7
20 yrs.			2280	1292	945	38	5	.578 **10th**	

Luke Appling

APPLING, LUCIUS BENJAMIN (Old Aches and Pains)
B. Apr. 2, 1907, High Point, N. C.
D. Jan. 3, 1991, Cumming, Ga.
Hall of Fame 1964.

Year	Team	Lg	G	W	L	T	N	PCT	Standing
1967	KC	A	40	10	30	0	0	.250	10 **10**

Bill Armour

ARMOUR, WILLIAM R.
B. Sept. 3, 1869, Homestead, Pa.
D. Dec. 2, 1922, Minneapolis, Minn.

Year	Team	Lg	G	W	L	T	N	PCT	Standing
1902	CLE	A	137	69	67	1	0	.507	**5**
1903			140	77	63	0	0	.550	**3**
1904			154	86	65	3	0	.570	**4**
1905	DET	A	154	79	74	1	0	.516	**3**
1906			151	71	78	2	0	.477	**6**
5 yrs.			736	382	347	7	0	.524	

Ken Aspromonte

ASPROMONTE, KENNETH JOSEPH
Brother of Bob Aspromonte.
B. Sept. 22, 1931, Brooklyn, N. Y.

Year	Team	Lg	G	W	L	T	N	PCT	Standing
1972	CLE	A	156	72	84	0	0	.462	**5**
1973			162	71	91	0	0	.438	**6**
1974			162	77	85	0	0	.475	**4**
3 yrs.			480	220	260	0	0	.458	

Jimmy Austin

AUSTIN, JAMES PHILIP (Pepper)
B. Dec. 8, 1879, Swansea, Wales
D. Mar. 6, 1965, Laguna Beach, Calif.

Year	Team	Lg	G	W	L	T	N	PCT	Standing
1913	STL	A	8	2	6	0	0	.250	7 **8** 8
1918			16	7	9	0	0	.438	5 **6** 5
1923			51	22	29	0	0	.431	3 **5**
3 yrs.			75	31	44	0	0	.413	

Del Baker

BAKER, DELMAR DAVID
B. May 3, 1892, Sherwood, Ore.
D. Sept. 11, 1973, San Antonio, Tex.

Year	Team	Lg	G	W	L	T	N	PCT	Standing
1933	DET	A	2	2	0	0	0	1.000	5 **5**
1936			34	18	16	0	0	.529	3 **4** 2
1937			54	34	20	0	0	.630	3 **3** 2
1938			57	37	19	1	0	.661	5 **4**
1939			155	81	73	1	0	.526	**5**
1940			155	90	64	1	0	.584	**1**
1941			155	75	79	1	0	.487	**4**

Del Baker *continued*

			G	W	L	T	N	PCT	Standing
1942			156	73	81	2	0	.474	5
1960	BOS	A	7	2	5	0	0	.286	8 8 7
9 yrs.			775	412	357	6	0	.536	
WORLD SERIES									
1940	DET	A	7	3	4	0	0	.429	

Dusty Baker

BAKER, JOHNNIE B., JR.
B. June 15, 1949, Riverside, Calif.

			G	W	L	T	N	PCT	Standing
1993	SF	N	162	103	59	0	0	.636	2
1994			115	55	60	0	0	.478	2
1995			144	67	77	0	0	.465	4
3 yrs.			421	225	196	0	0	.534	

George Bamberger

BAMBERGER, GEORGE IRVIN
B. Aug. 1, 1925, Staten Island, N. Y.

			G	W	L	T	N	PCT	Standing
1978	MIL	A	162	93	69	0	0	.574	3
1979			161	95	66	0	0	.590	2
1980			92	47	45	0	0	.511	2 4 3
1982	NY	N	162	65	97	0	0	.401	6
1983			46	16	30	0	0	.348	6 6
1985	MIL	A	161	71	90	0	0	.441	6
1986			152	71	81	0	0	.467	6 6
7 yrs.			936	458	478	0	0	.489	

Dave Bancroft

BANCROFT, DAVID JAMES (Beauty)
B. Apr. 20, 1891, Sioux City, Iowa
D. Oct. 9, 1972, Superior, Wis.
Hall of Fame 1971.

			G	W	L	T	N	PCT	Standing
1924	BOS	N	66	27	38	1	0	.415	6 8
1924			50	15	35	0	0	.300	8 8
1925			153	70	83	0	0	.458	5
1926			153	66	86	1	0	.434	7
1927			155	60	94	1	0	.390	7
4 yrs.			577	238	336	3	0	.415	

Frank Bancroft

BANCROFT, FRANK CARTER
B. May 9, 1846, Lancaster, Mass.
D. Mar. 30, 1921, Cincinnati, Ohio.

			G	W	L	T	N	PCT	Standing
1880	WOR	N	85	40	43	2	0	.482	5
1881	DET	N	84	41	43	0	0	.488	4
1882			86	42	41	3	0	.506	6
1883	CLE	N	100	55	42	3	0	.567	4
1884	PRO	N	114	84	28	2	0	.750	1
1885			110	53	57	0	0	.482	4
1887	PHI	AA	55	26	29	0	0	.473	5 5
1889	IND	N	68	25	43	0	0	.368	7 7
1902	CIN	N	16	9	7	0	0	.563	7 5 4
9 yrs.			718	375	333	10	0	.530	

Sam Barkley

BARKLEY, SAMUEL E.
B. May 24, 1858, Wheeling, W. Va.
D. Apr. 20, 1912, Wheeling, W. Va.

			G	W	L	T	N	PCT	Standing
1888	KC	AA	57	21	36	0	0	.368	8 8 8

Billy Barnie

BARNIE, WILLIAM HARRISON (Bald Billy)
B. Jan. 26, 1853, New York, N. Y.
D. July 15, 1900, Hartford, Conn.

			G	W	L	T	N	PCT	Standing
1883	BAL	AA	96	28	68	0	0	.292	8
1884			108	63	43	2	0	.594	6
1885			110	41	68	1	0	.376	8
1886			139	48	83	8	0	.366	8
1887			141	77	58	6	0	.570	3
1888			138	57	80	0	1	.416	5
1889			139	70	65	4	0	.519	5
1890			38	15	19	4	0	.441	6
1891			139	71	64	4	0	.526	4
1892	WAS	N	2	0	2	0	0	.000	11 7 (1st)
1893	LOU	N	126	50	75	1	0	.400	11
1894			131	36	94	0	1	.277	12

Billy Barnie *continued*

			G	W	L	T	N	PCT	Standing
1897	BKN	N	136	61	71	4	0	.462	6
1898			35	15	20	0	0	.429	9 10
14 yrs.			1478	632	810	34	2	.438	

Ed Barrow

BARROW, EDWARD GRANT (Cousin Ed)
B. May 10, 1868, Springfield, Ill.
D. Dec. 15, 1953, Port Chester, N. Y.
Hall of Fame 1953.

			G	W	L	T	N	PCT	Standing
1903	DET	A	137	65	71	1	0	.478	5
1904			84	32	46	6	0	.410	7 7
1918	BOS	A	126	75	51	0	0	.595	1
1919			138	66	71	1	0	.482	6
1920			154	72	81	1	0	.471	5
5 yrs.			639	310	320	9	0	.492	
WORLD SERIES									
1918	BOS	A	6	4	2	0	0	.667	

Jack Barry

BARRY, JOHN JOSEPH
B. Apr. 26, 1887, Meriden, Conn.
D. Apr. 23, 1961, Shrewsbury, Mass.

			G	W	L	T	N	PCT	Standing
1917	BOS	A	157	90	62	5	0	.592	2

Joe Battin

BATTIN, JOSEPH V.
B. Nov. 11, 1851, Philadelphia, Pa.
D. Dec. 10, 1937, Akron, Ohio.

			G	W	L	T	N	PCT	Standing
1883	PIT	AA	13	2	11	0	0	.154	7 7
1884			13	6	7	0	0	.462	9 10 11
1884	PIT	U	6	1	5	0	0	.167	8 8
2 yrs.			32	9	23	0	0	.281	

Hank Bauer

BAUER, HENRY ALBERT
B. July 31, 1922, East St. Louis, Ill.

			G	W	L	T	N	PCT	Standing
1961	KC	A	102	35	67	0	0	.343	8 9
1962			162	72	90	0	0	.444	9
1964	BAL	A	163	97	65	1	0	.599	3
1965			162	94	68	0	0	.580	3
1966			160	97	63	0	0	.606	1
1967			161	76	85	0	0	.472	6
1968			80	43	37	0	0	.538	3 2
1969	OAK	A	149	80	69	0	0	.537	2 2
8 yrs.			1139	594	544	1	0	.522	
WORLD SERIES									
1966	BAL	A	4	4	0	0	0	1.000	

Don Baylor

BAYLOR, DON EDWARD
B. June 28, 1949, Austin, Tex.

			G	W	L	T	N	PCT	Standing
1993	CLR	N	162	67	95	0	0	.414	6
1994			117	53	64	0	0	.453	3
1995			144	77	67	0	0	.535	2
3 yrs.			423	197	226	0	0	.466	
DIVISIONAL PLAYOFF SERIES									
1995	CLR	N	4	1	3	0	0	.250	

Vern Benson

BENSON, VERNON ADAIR
B. Sept. 19, 1924, Granite Quarry, N. C.

			G	W	L	T	N	PCT	Standing
1977	ATL	N	1	1	0	0	0	1.000	6 6 6

Yogi Berra

BERRA, LAWRENCE PETER
Father of Dale Berra.
B. May 12, 1925, St. Louis, Mo.
Hall of Fame 1972.

			G	W	L	T	N	PCT	Standing
1964	NY	A	164	99	63	2	0	.611	1
1972	NY	N	156	83	73	0	0	.532	3
1973			161	82	79	0	0	.509	1
1974			162	71	91	0	0	.438	5
1975			109	56	53	0	0	.514	3 3
1984	NY	A	162	87	75	0	0	.537	3
1985			16	6	10	0	0	.375	7 2
7 yrs.			930	484	444	2	0	.522	

Yogi Berra *continued*

			G	W	L	T	N	PCT	Standing
LEAGUE CHAMPIONSHIP SERIES									
1973	NY	N	5	3	2	0	0	.600	
WORLD SERIES									
1964	NY	A	7	3	4	0	0	.429	
1973	NY	N	7	3	4	0	0	.429	
2 yrs.			14	6	8	0	0	.429	

Terry Bevington

BEVINGTON, TERRY PAUL
B. July 7, 1956, Akron, Ohio

			G	W	L	T	N	PCT	Standing
1995	CHI	A	113	57	56	0	0	.504	4 3

Hugo Bezdek

BEZDEK, HUGO FRANCIS
B. Apr. 1, 1883, Prague, Austria-Hungary
D. Sept. 19, 1952, Atlantic City, N. J.

			G	W	L	T	N	PCT	Standing
1917	PIT	N	91	30	59	2	0	.337	8 8
1918			126	65	60	1	0	.520	4
1919			139	71	68	0	0	.511	4
3 yrs.			356	166	187	3	0	.470	

Bickerson

BICKERSON,
Deceased.

			G	W	L	T	N	PCT	Standing
1884	WAS	AA	1	0	1	0	0	.000	13 13

Joe Birmingham

BIRMINGHAM, JOSEPH LEO (Dode)
B. Aug. 6, 1884, Elmira, N. Y.
D. Apr. 24, 1946, Tampico, Mexico.

			G	W	L	T	N	PCT	Standing
1912	CLE	A	28	21	7	0	0	.750	6 5
1913			155	86	66	3	0	.566	3
1914			157	51	102	4	0	.333	8
1915			28	12	16	0	0	.429	6 7
4 yrs.			368	170	191	7	0	.471	

Del Bissonette

BISSONETTE, DELPHIA LOUIS
B. Sept. 6, 1899, Winthrop, Me.
D. June 9, 1972, Augusta, Me.

			G	W	L	T	N	PCT	Standing
1945	BOS	N	60	25	34	1	0	.424	7 6

Lena Blackburne

BLACKBURNE, RUSSELL AUBREY (Slats)
B. Oct. 23, 1886, Clifton Heights, Pa.
D. Feb. 29, 1968, Riverside, N. J.

			G	W	L	T	N	PCT	Standing
1928	CHI	A	80	40	40	0	0	.500	6 5
1929			152	59	93	0	0	.388	7
2 yrs.			232	99	133	0	0	.427	

Ray Blades

BLADES, FRANCIS RAYMOND
B. Aug. 6, 1896, Mt. Vernon, Ill.
D. May 18, 1979, Lincoln, Ill.

			G	W	L	T	N	PCT	Standing
1939	STL	N	155	92	61	2	0	.601	2
1940			39	14	24	1	0	.368	6 3
1948	BKN	N	1	1	0	0	0	1.000	5 5 3
3 yrs.			195	107	85	3	0	.557	

Walter Blair

BLAIR, WALTER ALLEN (Heavy)
B. Oct. 13, 1883, Landrus, Pa.
D. Aug. 20, 1948, Lewisburg, Pa.

			G	W	L	T	N	PCT	Standing
1915	BUF	F	2	1	1	0	0	.500	8 8 6

Ossie Bluege

BLUEGE, OSWALD LOUIS
Brother of Otto Bluege.
B. Oct. 24, 1900, Chicago, Ill.
D. Oct. 14, 1985, Edina, Minn.

			G	W	L	T	N	PCT	Standing
1943	WAS	A	153	84	69	0	0	.549	2
1944			154	64	90	0	0	.416	8
1945			156	87	67	2	0	.565	2
1946			155	76	78	1	0	.494	4
1947			154	64	90	0	0	.416	7
5 yrs.			772	375	394	3	0	.488	

Bruce Bochy

BOCHY, BRUCE DOUGLAS
B. Apr. 16, 1955, Landes De Bussac, France

			G	W	L	T	N	PCT	Standing
1995	SD	N	144	70	74	0	0	.486	3

Tommy Bond

BOND, THOMAS HENRY
B. Apr. 2, 1856, Granard, Ireland
D. Jan. 24, 1941, Boston, Mass.

			G	W	L	T	N	PCT	Standing
1882	WOR	N	6	2	4	0	0	.333	8 8 8

Bob Boone

BOONE, ROBERT RAYMOND
Son of Ray Boone.
Father of Bret Boone.
B. Nov. 19, 1947, San Diego, Calif.

			G	W	L	T	N	PCT	Standing
1995	KC	A	144	70	74	0	0	.486	2

Steve Boros

BOROS, STEPHEN
B. Sept. 3, 1936, Flint, Mich.

			G	W	L	T	N	PCT	Standing
1983	OAK	A	162	74	88	0	0	.457	4
1984			44	20	24	0	0	.455	4 4
1986	SD	N	162	74	88	0	0	.457	4
3 yrs.			368	168	200	0	0	.457	

Jim Bottomley

BOTTOMLEY, JAMES LeROY (Sunny Jim)
B. Apr. 23, 1900, Oglesby, Ill.
D. Dec. 11, 1959, St. Louis, Mo.
Hall of Fame 1974.

			G	W	L	T	N	PCT	Standing
1937	STL	A	78	21	56	1	0	.273	7 8

Lou Boudreau

BOUDREAU, LOUIS
B. July 17, 1917, Harvey, Ill.
Hall of Fame 1970.

			G	W	L	T	N	PCT	Standing
1942	CLE	A	156	75	79	2	0	.487	4
1943			153	82	71	0	0	.536	3
1944			155	72	82	1	0	.468	5
1945			147	73	72	2	0	.503	5
1946			156	68	86	2	0	.442	6
1947			157	80	74	3	0	.519	4
1948			156	97	58	1	0	.626	1
1949			154	89	65	0	0	.578	3
1950			155	92	62	1	0	.597	4
1952	BOS	A	154	76	78	0	0	.494	6
1953			153	84	69	0	0	.549	4
1954			156	69	85	2	0	.448	4
1955	KC	A	155	63	91	1	0	.409	6
1956			154	52	102	0	0	.338	8
1957			104	36	67	1	0	.350	8 7
1960	CHI	N	139	54	83	2	0	.394	8 7
16 yrs.			2404	1162	1224	18	0	.487	
WORLD SERIES									
1948	CLE	A	6	4	2	0	0	.667	

Larry Bowa

BOWA, LAWRENCE ROBERT
B. Dec. 6, 1945, Sacramento, Calif.

			G	W	L	T	N	PCT	Standing
1987	SD	N	162	65	97	0	0	.401	6
1988			46	16	30	0	0	.348	5 3
2 yrs.			208	81	127	0	0	.389	

Frank Bowerman

BOWERMAN, FRANK EUGENE (Mike)
B. Dec. 5, 1868, Romeo, Mich.
D. Nov. 30, 1948, Romeo, Mich.

			G	W	L	T	N	PCT	Standing
1909	BOS	N	76	22	54	0	0	.289	8 8

Ken Boyer

BOYER, KENTON LLOYD
Brother of Clete Boyer.
Brother of Cloyd Boyer.
B. May 20, 1931, Liberty, Mo.
D. Sept. 7, 1982, St. Louis, Mo.

			G	W	L	T	N	PCT	Standing
1978	STL	N	143	62	81	0	0	.434	6 5
1979			163	86	76	1	0	.531	3
1980			51	18	33	0	0	.353	6 4
3 yrs.			357	166	190	1	0	.466	

Bill Bradley

BRADLEY, WILLIAM JOSEPH
B. Feb. 13, 1878, Cleveland, Ohio
D. Mar. 11, 1954, Cleveland, Ohio.

			G	W	L	T	N	PCT	Standing
1905	CLE	A	41	20	21	0	0	.488	1 2 5
1914	BKN	F	157	77	77	3	0	.500	5
2 yrs.			198	97	98	3	0	.497	

Bobby Bragan

BRAGAN, ROBERT RANDALL
B. Oct. 30, 1917, Birmingham, Ala.

			G	W	L	T	N	PCT	Standing
1956	PIT	N	157	66	88	3	0	.429	7
1957			104	36	67	1	0	.350	8 7
1958	CLE	A	67	31	36	0	0	.463	5 4
1963	MIL	N	163	84	78	1	0	.519	6
1964			162	88	74	0	0	.543	5
1965			162	86	76	0	0	.531	5
1966	ATL	N	112	52	59	1	0	.468	5 5
7 yrs.			927	443	478	6	0	.481	

Roger Bresnahan

BRESNAHAN, ROGER PHILIP (The Duke of Tralee)
B. June 11, 1879, Toledo, Ohio
D. Dec. 4, 1944, Toledo, Ohio.
Hall of Fame 1945.

			G	W	L	T	N	PCT	Standing
1909	STL	N	154	54	98	2	0	.355	7
1910			153	63	90	0	0	.412	7
1911			158	75	74	9	0	.503	5
1912			153	63	90	0	0	.412	6
1915	CHI	N	157	73	80	3	1	.477	4
5 yrs.			775	328	432	14	1	.432	

Dave Bristol

BRISTOL, JAMES DAVID
B. June 23, 1933, Macon, Ga.

			G	W	L	T	N	PCT	Standing
1966	CIN	N	77	39	38	0	0	.506	8 7
1967			162	87	75	0	0	.537	4
1968			163	83	79	1	0	.512	4
1969			163	89	73	1	0	.549	3
1970	MIL	A	163	65	97	1	0	.401	5
1971			161	69	92	0	0	.429	6
1972			30	10	20	0	0	.333	6 6
1976	ATL	N	162	70	92	0	0	.432	6
1977			29	8	21	0	0	.276	6 6
1977			131	52	79	0	0	.397	6 6
1979	SF	N	22	10	12	0	0	.455	4 4
1980			161	75	86	0	0	.466	5
11 yrs.			1424	657	764	3	0	.462	

Freeman Brown

BROWN, FREEMAN
B. Jan. 31, 1845, Hubbardstown, Mass.
D. Dec. 27, 1916, Worcester, Mass.

			G	W	L	T	N	PCT	Standing
1882	WOR	N	41	9	32	0	0	.220	8 8

Three Finger Brown

BROWN, MORDECAI PETER CENTENNIAL (Miner)
B. Oct. 19, 1876, Nyesville, Ind.
D. Feb. 14, 1948, Terre Haute, Ind.
Hall of Fame 1949.

			G	W	L	T	N	PCT	Standing
1914	STL	F	114	50	63	1	0	.442	7 8

Tom Brown

BROWN, THOMAS TARLTON (Handsome)
B. Sept. 21, 1860, Liverpool, England
D. Oct. 25, 1927, Washington, D. C.

			G	W	L	T	N	PCT	Standing
1897	WAS	N	99	52	46	1	0	.531	11 6
1898			38	12	26	0	0	.316	11 11
2 yrs.			137	64	72	1	0	.471	

Earle Brucker

BRUCKER, EARLE FRANCIS, SR.
Father of Earle Brucker.
B. May 6, 1901, Albany, N. Y.
D. May 8, 1981, San Diego, Calif.

			G	W	L	T	N	PCT	Standing
1952	CIN	N	5	3	2	0	0	.600	7 7 6

Al Buckenberger

BUCKENBERGER, ALBERT C.
B. Jan. 31, 1861, Detroit, Mich.
D. July 1, 1917, Syracuse, N. Y.

			G	W	L	T	N	PCT	Standing
1889	COL	AA	140	60	78	2	0	.435	6
1890			80	39	41	0	0	.488	5 2
1892	PIT	N	29	15	14	0	0	.517	7 6 (1st)
1892			66	38	27	1	0	.585	10 4 (2nd)
1893			131	81	48	2	0	.628	2
1894			110	53	55	1	1	.491	7 7
1895	STL	N	50	16	34	0	0	.320	11 11
1902	BOS	N	142	73	64	5	0	.533	3
1903			140	58	80	2	0	.420	6
1904			155	55	98	2	0	.359	7
9 yrs.			1043	488	539	15	1	.475	

Charlie Buffinton

BUFFINTON, CHARLES G.
B. June 14, 1861, Fall River, Mass.
D. Sept. 23, 1907, Fall River, Mass.

			G	W	L	T	N	PCT	Standing
1890	PHI	P	116	61	54	1	0	.530	5 5

Jack Burdock

BURDOCK, JOHN JOSEPH (Black Jack)
B. Apr. 1852, Brooklyn, N. Y.
D. Nov. 27, 1931, Brooklyn, N. Y.

			G	W	L	T	N	PCT	Standing
1883	BOS	N	54	30	24	0	0	.556	4 1

Jimmy Burke

BURKE, JAMES TIMOTHY (Sunset Jimmy)
B. Oct. 12, 1874, St. Louis, Mo.
D. Mar. 26, 1942, St. Louis, Mo.

			G	W	L	T	N	PCT	Standing
1905	STL	N	90	34	56	0	0	.378	7 6 6
1918	STL	A	61	29	31	1	0	.483	6 5
1919			140	67	72	1	0	.482	5
1920			154	76	77	1	0	.497	4
4 yrs.			445	206	236	3	0	.466	

Watch Burnham

BURNHAM, GEORGE WALTER
B. May 20, 1860, Albion, Mich.
D. Nov. 18, 1902, Detroit, Mich.

			G	W	L	T	N	PCT	Standing
1887	IND	N	28	6	22	0	0	.214	8 8

Tom Burns

BURNS, THOMAS EVERETT
B. Mar. 30, 1857, Honesdale, Pa.
D. Mar. 19, 1902, Jersey City, N. J.

			G	W	L	T	N	PCT	Standing
1892	PIT	N	48	22	25	1	0	.468	7 6 (1st)
1892			13	5	7	1	0	.417	10 4 (2nd)
1898	CHI	N	152	85	65	2	0	.567	4
1899			152	75	73	4	0	.507	8
3 yrs.			365	187	170	8	0	.524	

Bill Burwell

BURWELL, WILLIAM EDWIN
B. Mar. 27, 1895, Jarbalo, Kans.
D. June 11, 1973, Ormond Beach, Fla.

			G	W	L	T	N	PCT	Standing
1947	PIT	N	1	1	0	0	0	1.000	8 7

Donie Bush

BUSH, OWEN JOSEPH
B. Oct. 8, 1887, Indianapolis, Ind.
D. Mar. 28, 1972, Indianapolis, Ind.

			G	W	L	T	N	PCT	Standing
1923	**WAS**	**A**	155	75	78	2	0	.490	**4**
1927	**PIT**	**N**	156	94	60	2	0	.610	**1**
1928			152	85	67	0	0	.559	**4**
1929			119	67	51	1	0	.568	**2** 2
1930	**CHI**	**A**	154	62	92	0	0	.403	**7**
1931			156	56	97	3	0	.366	**8**
1933	**CIN**	**N**	153	58	94	1	0	.382	**8**
7 yrs.			1045	497	539	9	0	.480	
WORLD SERIES									
1927	**PIT**	**N**	4	0	4	0	0	.000	

Ormond Butler

BUTLER, ORMOND HOOK
B. Nov. 18, 1854, West Virginia
D. Sept. 12, 1915, Mount Hope, Md.

			G	W	L	T	N	PCT	Standing
1883	**PIT**	**AA**	53	17	36	0	0	.321	6 **7** 7

Charlie Byrne

BYRNE, CHARLES H.
B. Sept. 1843, New York, N. Y.
D. Jan. 4, 1898, New York, N. Y.

			G	W	L	T	N	PCT	Standing
1885	**BKN**	**AA**	75	38	37	0	0	.507	7 **5**
1886			141	76	61	4	0	.555	**3**
1887			138	60	74	4	0	.448	**6**
3 yrs.			354	174	172	8	0	.503	

Nixey Callahan

CALLAHAN, JAMES JOSEPH (Cal)
B. Mar. 18, 1874, Fitchburg, Mass.
D. Oct. 4, 1934, Boston, Mass.

			G	W	L	T	N	PCT	Standing
1903	**CHI**	**A**	138	60	77	1	0	.438	**7**
1904			42	23	18	1	0	.561	**4** 3
1912			158	78	76	4	0	.506	**4**
1913			153	78	74	1	0	.513	**5**
1914			157	70	84	3	0	.455	**6**
1916	**PIT**	**N**	157	65	89	3	0	.422	**6**
1917			61	20	40	1	0	.333	**8** 8
7 yrs.			866	394	458	14	0	.462	

Count Campau

CAMPAU, CHARLES COLUMBUS
B. Oct. 17, 1863, Detroit, Mich.
D. Apr. 3, 1938, New Orleans, La.

			G	W	L	T	N	PCT	Standing
1890	**STL**	**AA**	42	26	14	1	1	.650	5 **2** 3

Joe Cantillon

CANTILLON, JOSEPH D. (Pongo)
B. Aug. 19, 1861, Janesville, Wis.
D. Jan. 31, 1930, Hickman, Ky.

			G	W	L	T	N	PCT	Standing
1907	**WAS**	**A**	154	49	102	3	0	.325	**8**
1908			155	67	85	3	0	.441	**7**
1909			156	42	110	4	0	.276	**8**
3 yrs.			465	158	297	10	0	.347	

Max Carey

CAREY, MAX (Scoops)
Born Maximilian Carnarius.
B. Jan. 11, 1890, Terre Haute, Ind.
D. May 30, 1976, Miami, Fla.
Hall of Fame 1961.

			G	W	L	T	N	PCT	Standing
1932	**BKN**	**N**	154	81	73	0	0	.526	**3**
1933			157	65	88	4	0	.425	**6**
2 yrs.			311	146	161	4	0	.476	

Bill Carrigan

CARRIGAN, WILLIAM FRANCIS (Rough)
B. Oct. 22, 1883, Lewiston, Me.
D. July 8, 1969, Lewiston, Me.

			G	W	L	T	N	PCT	Standing
1913	**BOS**	**A**	70	40	30	0	0	.571	5 **4**
1914			159	91	62	6	0	.595	**2**
1915			155	101	50	4	0	.669	**1**
1916			156	91	63	2	0	.591	**1**
1927			154	51	103	0	0	.331	**8**

Bill Carrigan *continued*

			G	W	L	T	N	PCT	Standing
1928			154	57	96	1	0	.373	**8**
1929			155	58	96	1	0	.377	**8**
7 yrs.			1003	489	500	14	0	.494	
WORLD SERIES									
1915	**BOS**	**A**	5	4	1	0	0	.800	
1916			5	4	1	0	0	.800	
2 yrs.			10	8	2	0	0	.800	

Bob Caruthers

CARUTHERS, ROBERT LEE (Parisian Bob)
B. Jan. 5, 1864, Memphis, Tenn.
D. Aug. 5, 1911, Peoria, Ill.

			G	W	L	T	N	PCT	Standing
1892	**STL**	**N**	50	16	32	2	0	.333	12 **11** (2nd)

Phil Cavarretta

CAVARRETTA, PHILIP JOSEPH
B. July 19, 1916, Chicago, Ill.

			G	W	L	T	N	PCT	Standing
1951	**CHI**	**N**	74	27	47	0	0	.365	7 **8**
1952			155	77	77	1	0	.500	**5**
1953			155	65	89	1	0	.422	**7**
3 yrs.			384	169	213	2	0	.442	

Ollie Caylor

CAYLOR, OLIVER PERRY
B. Dec. 14, 1849, Dayton, Ohio
D. Oct. 19, 1897, Winona, Minn.

			G	W	L	T	N	PCT	Standing
1885	**CIN**	**AA**	112	63	49	0	0	.563	**2**
1886			141	65	73	3	0	.471	**5**
1887	**NY**	**AA**	100	35	60	5	0	.368	7 **7**
3 yrs.			353	163	182	8	0	.472	

Frank Chance

CHANCE, FRANK LEROY (Husk, The Peerless Leader)
B. Sept. 9, 1877, Fresno, Calif.
D. Sept. 15, 1924, Los Angeles, Calif.
Hall of Fame 1946.

			G	W	L	T	N	PCT	Standing
1905	**CHI**	**N**	90	55	33	2	0	.625	4 **3**
1906			155	116	36	3	0	.763	**1**
1907			155	107	45	3	0	.704	**1**
1908			158	99	55	4	0	.643	**1**
1909			155	104	49	2	0	.680	**2**
1910			154	104	50	0	0	.675	**1**
1911			158	92	62	3	1	.597	**2**
1912			153	91	59	2	1	.607	**3**
1913	**NY**	**A**	153	57	94	2	0	.377	**7**
1914			137	60	74	3	0	.448	**7** 6
1923	**BOS**	**A**	154	61	91	2	0	.401	**8**
11 yrs.			1622	946	648	26	2	.593 **6th**	
WORLD SERIES									
1906	**CHI**	**N**	6	2	4	0	0	.333	
1907			5	4	0	1	0	1.000	
1908			5	4	1	0	0	.800	
1910			5	1	4	0	0	.200	
4 yrs.			21	11	9	1	0	.550 **5th**	

Ben Chapman

CHAPMAN, WILLIAM BENJAMIN
B. Dec. 25, 1908, Nashville, Tenn.
D. July 7, 1993, Hoover, Ala.

			G	W	L	T	N	PCT	Standing
1945	**PHI**	**N**	85	28	57	0	0	.329	8 **8**
1946			155	69	85	1	0	.448	**5**
1947			155	62	92	1	0	.403	**7**
1948			79	37	42	0	0	.468	**7** 6
4 yrs.			474	196	276	2	0	.415	

Jack Chapman

CHAPMAN, JOHN CURTIS
B. May 8, 1843, Brooklyn, N. Y.
D. June 10, 1916, Brooklyn, N. Y.

			G	W	L	T	N	PCT	Standing
1876	**LOU**	**N**	69	30	36	3	0	.455	**5**
1877			61	35	25	1	0	.583	**2**
1878	**MIL**	**N**	61	15	45	1	0	.250	**6**
1882	**WOR**	**N**	37	7	30	0	0	.189	8 **8**
1883	**DET**	**N**	101	40	58	3	0	.408	**7**

Jack Chapman *continued*

			G	W	L	T	N	PCT	Standing
1884			114	28	84	2	0	.250	**8**
1885	**BUF**	**N**	88	31	57	0	0	.352	7 **6**
1889	**LOU**	**AA**	7	1	6	0	0	.143	8 **8**
1890			136	88	44	4	0	.667	**1**
1891			139	54	83	2	0	.394	**7**
1892	**LOU**	**N**	54	21	33	0	0	.389	**10** 11 (1st)
11 yrs.			867	350	501	16	0	.411	

Hal Chase

CHASE, HAROLD HOMER (Prince Hal)
B. Feb. 13, 1883, Los Gatos, Calif.
D. May 18, 1947, Colusa, Calif.

			G	W	L	T	N	PCT	Standing
1910	**NY**	**A**	14	10	4	0	0	.714	3 **2**
1911			153	76	76	1	0	.500	**6**
2 yrs.			167	86	80	1	0	.518	

John Clapp

CLAPP, JOHN EDGAR
Brother of Aaron Clapp.
B. July 17, 1851, Ithaca, N. Y.
D. Dec. 18, 1904, Ithaca, N. Y.

			G	W	L	T	N	PCT	Standing
1878	**IND**	**N**	63	24	36	3	0	.400	**5**
1879	**BUF**	**N**	79	46	32	1	0	.590	**3**
1880	**CIN**	**N**	83	21	59	3	0	.262	**8**
1881	**CLE**	**N**	74	32	41	1	0	.438	7 **7**
1883	**NY**	**N**	98	46	50	2	0	.479	**6**
5 yrs.			397	169	218	10	0	.437	

Fred Clarke

CLARKE, FRED CLIFFORD (Cap)
Brother of Josh Clarke.
B. Oct. 3, 1872, Winterset, Iowa
D. Aug. 14, 1960, Winfield, Kans.
Hall of Fame 1945.

			G	W	L	T	N	PCT	Standing
1897	**LOU**	**N**	92	35	54	2	1	.393	9 **11**
1898			154	70	81	3	0	.464	**9**
1899			156	75	77	3	1	.493	**9**
1900	**PIT**	**N**	140	79	60	1	0	.568	**2**
1901			140	90	49	1	0	.647	**1**
1902			142	103	36	3	0	.741	**1**
1903			141	91	49	1	0	.650	**1**
1904			156	87	66	3	0	.569	**4**
1905			155	96	57	2	0	.627	**2**
1906			154	93	60	1	0	.608	**3**
1907			157	91	63	3	0	.591	**2**
1908			155	98	56	1	0	.636	**2**
1909			154	110	42	1	1	.724	**1**
1910			154	86	67	1	0	.562	**3**
1911			156	85	69	1	1	.552	**3**
1912			153	93	58	1	1	.616	**5**
1913			155	78	71	6	0	.523	**4**
1914			158	69	85	4	0	.448	**7**
1915			157	73	81	2	1	.474	**5**
19 yrs.			2829	1602	1181	40	6	.576	
WORLD SERIES									
1903	**PIT**	**N**	8	3	5	0	0	.375	
1909			7	4	3	0	0	.571	
2 yrs.			15	7	8	0	0	.467	

Jack Clements

CLEMENTS, JOHN J.
B. June 24, 1864, Philadelphia, Pa.
D. May 23, 1941, Philadelphia, Pa.

			G	W	L	T	N	PCT	Standing
1890	**PHI**	**N**	19	13	6	0	0	.684	1 **2** 3

Ty Cobb

COBB, TYRUS RAYMOND (The Georgia Peach)
B. Dec. 18, 1886, Narrows, Ga.
D. July 17, 1961, Atlanta, Ga.
Hall of Fame 1936.

			G	W	L	T	N	PCT	Standing
1921	**DET**	**A**	154	71	82	1	0	.464	**6**
1922			155	79	75	1	0	.513	**3**
1923			155	83	71	1	0	.539	**2**

Ty Cobb *continued*

Year	Team	Lg	G	W	L	T	N	PCT	Standing
1924			156	86	68	2	0	.558	3
1925			156	81	73	2	0	.526	4
1926			157	79	75	3	0	.513	6
6 yrs.			933	479	444	10	0	.519	

Mickey Cochrane

COCHRANE, GORDON STANLEY (Black Mike)
B. Apr. 6, 1903, Bridgewater, Mass.
D. June 28, 1962, Lake Forest, Ill.
Hall of Fame 1947.

Year	Team	Lg	G	W	L	T	N	PCT	Standing
1934	DET	A	154	101	53	0	0	.656	1
1935			152	93	58	1	0	.616	1
1936			53	29	24	0	0	.547	3 2
1936			67	36	31	0	0	.537	4 2
1937			29	16	13	0	0	.552	3 2
1937			72	39	32	1	0	.549	3 2
1938			98	47	51	0	0	.480	5 4
5 yrs.			625	361	262	2	0	.579	

WORLD SERIES

Year	Team	Lg	G	W	L	T	N	PCT	Standing
1934	DET	A	7	3	4	0	0	.429	
1935			6	4	2	0	0	.667	
2 yrs.			13	7	6	0	0	.538	

Andy Cohen

COHEN, ANDREW HOWARD
Brother of Syd Cohen.
B. Oct. 25, 1904, Baltimore, Md.
D. Oct. 29, 1988, El Paso, Tex.

Year	Team	Lg	G	W	L	T	N	PCT	Standing
1960	PHI	N	1	1	0	0	0	1.000	8 4 8

Bob Coleman

COLEMAN, ROBERT HUNTER
B. Sept. 26, 1890, Huntingburg, Ind.
D. July 16, 1959, Boston, Mass.

Year	Team	Lg	G	W	L	T	N	PCT	Standing
1943	BOS	N	46	21	25	0	0	.457	6 6
1944			155	65	89	1	0	.422	6
1945			94	42	51	1	0	.452	7 6
3 yrs.			295	128	165	2	0	.437	

Jerry Coleman

COLEMAN, GERALD FRANCIS
B. Sept. 14, 1924, San Jose, Calif.

Year	Team	Lg	G	W	L	T	N	PCT	Standing
1980	SD	N	163	73	89	1	0	.451	6

Eddie Collins

COLLINS, EDWARD TROWBRIDGE, SR. (Cocky)
Played as Eddie Sullivan in 1906.
Father of Eddie Collins.
B. May 2, 1887, Millerton, N. Y.
D. Mar. 25, 1951, Boston, Mass.
Hall of Fame 1939.

Year	Team	Lg	G	W	L	T	N	PCT	Standing
1924	CHI	A	27	14	13	0	0	.519	6 6 8
1925			154	79	75	0	0	.513	5
1926			155	81	72	2	0	.529	5
3 yrs.			336	174	160	2	0	.521	

Jimmy Collins

COLLINS, JAMES JOSEPH
B. Jan. 16, 1870, Buffalo, N. Y.
D. Mar. 6, 1943, Buffalo, N. Y.
Hall of Fame 1945.

Year	Team	Lg	G	W	L	T	N	PCT	Standing
1901	BOS	A	138	79	57	2	0	.581	2
1902			138	77	60	1	0	.562	3
1903			141	91	47	3	0	.659	1
1904			157	95	59	3	0	.617	1
1905			153	78	74	1	0	.513	4
1906			115	35	79	1	0	.307	8 8
6 yrs.			842	455	376	11	0	.548	

WORLD SERIES

Year	Team	Lg	G	W	L	T	N	PCT	Standing
1903	BOS	A	8	5	3	0	0	.625	

Shano Collins

COLLINS, JOHN FRANCIS
B. Dec. 4, 1885, Charlestown, Mass.
D. Sept. 10, 1955, Newton, Mass.

Year	Team	Lg	G	W	L	T	N	PCT	Standing
1931	BOS	A	153	62	90	1	0	.408	6
1932			55	11	44	0	0	.200	8 8
2 yrs.			208	73	134	1	0	.353	

Terry Collins

COLLINS, TERRY LEE
B. May 27, 1949, Midland, Mich.

Year	Team	Lg	G	W	L	T	N	PCT	Standing
1994	HOU	N	115	66	49	0	0	.574	2
1995			144	76	68	0	0	.528	2
2 yrs.			259	142	117	0	0	.548	

Charlie Comiskey

COMISKEY, CHARLES ALBERT (Commy, The Old Roman)
B. Aug. 15, 1859, Chicago, Ill.
D. Oct. 26, 1931, Eagle River, Wis.
Hall of Fame 1939.

Year	Team	Lg	G	W	L	T	N	PCT	Standing
1883	STL	AA	19	12	7	0	0	.632	2 2
1884			25	16	7	2	0	.696	5 4
1885			112	79	33	0	0	.705	1
1886			139	93	46	0	0	.669	1
1887			138	95	40	3	0	.704	1
1888			137	92	43	2	0	.681	1
1889			141	90	45	6	0	.667	2
1890	CHI	P	138	75	62	1	0	.547	4
1891	STL	AA	139	85	51	2	1	.625	2
1892	CIN	N	77	44	31	2	0	.587	4 (1st)
1892			78	38	37	3	0	.507	8 (2nd)
1893			131	65	63	3	0	.508	6
1894			134	55	75	2	2	.423	10
12 yrs.			1408	839	540	26	3	.608	
								3rd	

Roger Connor

CONNOR, ROGER
Brother of Joe Connor.
B. July 1, 1857, Waterbury, Conn.
D. Jan. 4, 1931, Waterbury, Conn.
Hall of Fame 1976.

Year	Team	Lg	G	W	L	T	N	PCT	Standing
1896	STL	N	46	8	37	1	0	.178	11 11 11

Dusty Cooke

COOKE, ALLEN LINDSEY
B. June 23, 1907, Swepsonville, N. C.
D. Nov. 21, 1987, Raleigh, N. C.

Year	Team	Lg	G	W	L	T	N	PCT	Standing
1948	PHI	N	13	6	6	1	0	.500	7 6 6

Jack Coombs

COOMBS, JOHN WESLEY (Cy)
B. Nov. 18, 1882, LeGrand, Iowa
D. Apr. 15, 1957, Palestine, Tex.

Year	Team	Lg	G	W	L	T	N	PCT	Standing
1919	PHI	N	63	18	44	1	0	.290	8 8

Johnny Cooney

COONEY, JOHN WALTER
Brother of Jimmy Cooney.
Son of Jimmy Cooney.
B. Mar. 18, 1901, Cranston, R. I.
D. July 8, 1986, Sarasota, Fla.

Year	Team	Lg	G	W	L	T	N	PCT	Standing
1949	BOS	N	46	20	25	1	0	.444	4 4

Pat Corrales

CORRALES, PATRICK (Ike)
B. Mar. 20, 1941, Los Angeles, Calif.

Year	Team	Lg	G	W	L	T	N	PCT	Standing
1978	TEX	A	1	1	0	0	0	1.000	2 2
1979			162	83	79	0	0	.512	3
1980			163	76	85	2	0	.472	4
1982	PHI	N	162	89	73	0	0	.549	2
1983			86	43	42	1	0	.506	1 1
1983	CLE	A	62	30	32	0	0	.484	7 7
1984			163	75	87	1	0	.463	6
1985			162	60	102	0	0	.370	7
1986			163	84	78	1	0	.519	5
1987			87	31	56	0	0	.356	7 7
9 yrs.			1211	572	634	5	0	.474	

Red Corriden

CORRIDEN, JOHN MICHAEL, SR.
Father of John Corriden.
B. Sept. 4, 1887, Logansport, Ind.
D. Sept. 28, 1959, Indianapolis, Ind.

Year	Team	Lg	G	W	L	T	N	PCT	Standing
1950	CHI	A	125	52	72	1	0	.419	8 6

Chuck Cottier

COTTIER, CHARLES KEITH
B. Jan. 8, 1936, Delta, Colo.

Year	Team	Lg	G	W	L	T	N	PCT	Standing
1984	SEA	A	27	15	12	0	0	.556	7 6
1985			162	74	88	0	0	.457	6
1986			28	9	19	0	0	.321	6 7
3 yrs.			217	98	119	0	0	.452	

Bobby Cox

COX, ROBERT JOE
B. May 21, 1941, Tulsa, Okla.

Year	Team	Lg	G	W	L	T	N	PCT	Standing
1978	ATL	N	162	69	93	0	0	.426	6
1979			160	66	94	0	0	.412	6
1980			161	81	80	0	0	.503	4
1981			55	25	29	1	0	.463	4 (1st)
1981			52	25	27	0	0	.481	5 (2nd)
1982	TOR	A	162	78	84	0	0	.481	6
1983			162	89	73	0	0	.549	4
1984			163	89	73	1	0	.549	2
1985			161	99	62	0	0	.615	1
1990	ATL	N	97	40	57	0	0	.412	6 6
1991			162	94	68	0	0	.580	1
1992			162	98	64	0	0	.605	1
1993			162	104	58	0	0	.642	1
1994			114	68	46	0	0	.596	2
1995			144	90	54	0	0	.625	1
14 yrs.			2079	1115	962	2	0	.537	

DIVISIONAL PLAYOFF SERIES

Year	Team	Lg	G	W	L	T	N	PCT	Standing
1995	ATL	N	4	3	1	0	0	.750	

LEAGUE CHAMPIONSHIP SERIES

Year	Team	Lg	G	W	L	T	N	PCT	Standing
1985	TOR	A	7	3	4	0	0	.429	
1991	ATL	N	7	4	3	0	0	.571	
1992			7	4	3	0	0	.571	
1993			6	2	4	0	0	.333	
1995			4	4	0	0	0	1.000	
5 yrs.			31	17	14	0	0	.548	
			1st	2nd	1st			5th	

WORLD SERIES

Year	Team	Lg	G	W	L	T	N	PCT	Standing
1991	ATL	N	7	3	4	0	0	.429	
1992			6	2	4	0	0	.333	
1995			6	4	2	0	0	.667	
3 yrs.			19	9	10	0	0	.474	

Harry Craft

CRAFT, HARRY FRANCIS
B. Apr. 19, 1915, Ellisville, Miss.
D. Aug. 3, 1995, Conroe, Tex.

Year	Team	Lg	G	W	L	T	N	PCT	Standing
1957	KC	A	50	23	27	0	0	.460	8 7
1958			156	73	81	2	0	.474	7
1959			154	66	88	0	0	.429	7
1961	CHI	N	12	4	8	0	0	.333	6 7 7
1961			4	3	1	0	0	.750	7 7 7
1962	HOU	N	162	64	96	2	0	.400	8
1963			162	66	96	0	0	.407	9
1964			149	61	88	0	0	.409	9 9
7 yrs.			849	360	485	4	0	.426	

Roger Craig

CRAIG, ROGER LEE
B. Feb. 17, 1930, Durham, N. C.

Year	Team	Lg	G	W	L	T	N	PCT	Standing
1978	SD	N	162	84	78	0	0	.519	4
1979			161	68	93	0	0	.422	5
1985	SF	N	18	6	12	0	0	.333	6 6
1986			162	83	79	0	0	.512	3
1987			162	90	72	0	0	.556	1
1988			162	83	79	0	0	.512	4
1989			162	92	70	0	0	.568	1
1990			162	85	77	0	0	.525	3
1991			162	75	87	0	0	.463	4
1992			162	72	90	0	0	.444	5
10 yrs.			1475	738	737	0	0	.500	

Roger Craig *continued*

LEAGUE CHAMPIONSHIP SERIES

			G	W	L	T	N	PCT	Standing
1987	**SF**	**N**	7	3	4	0	0	.429	
1989			5	4	1	0	0	.800	
2 yrs.			12	7	5	0	0	.583 **4th**	

WORLD SERIES

			G	W	L	T	N	PCT	Standing
1989	**SF**	**N**	4	0	4	0	0	.000	

Del Crandall

CRANDALL, DELMAR WESLEY
B. Mar. 5, 1930, Ontario, Calif.

			G	W	L	T	N	PCT	Standing
1972	**MIL**	**A**	124	54	70	0	0	.435	6 **6**
1973			162	74	88	0	0	.457	**5**
1974			162	76	86	0	0	.469	**5**
1975			161	67	94	0	0	.416	**5** 5
1983	**SEA**	**A**	89	34	55	0	0	.382	7 **7**
1984			135	59	76	0	0	.437	**7** 6
6 yrs.			833	364	469	0	0	.437	

Sam Crane

CRANE, SAMUEL NEWHALL
B. Jan. 2, 1854, Springfield, Mass.
D. June 26, 1925, New York, N. Y.

			G	W	L	T	N	PCT	Standing
1880	**BUF**	**N**	85	24	58	3	0	.293	**7**
1884	**CIN**	**U**	70	49	21	0	0	.700	5 **3**
2 yrs.			155	73	79	3	0	.480	

Gavvy Cravath

CRAVATH, CLIFFORD CARLTON (Cactus)
B. Mar. 23, 1881, Escondido, Calif.
D. May 23, 1963, Laguna Beach, Calif.

			G	W	L	T	N	PCT	Standing
1919	**PHI**	**N**	75	29	46	0	0	.387	8 **8**
1920			153	62	91	0	0	.405	**8**
2 yrs.			228	91	137	0	0	.399	

Bill Craver

CRAVER, WILLIAM H.
B. June 1844, Troy, N. Y.
D. June 17, 1901, Troy, N. Y.

			G	W	L	T	N	PCT	Standing
1876	**NY**	**N**	57	21	35	1	0	.375	**6**

George Creamer

CREAMER, GEORGE W.
Born George W. Triebel.
B. 1855, Philadelphia, Pa.
D. June 27, 1886, Philadelphia, Pa.

			G	W	L	T	N	PCT	Standing
1884	**PIT**	**AA**	8	0	8	0	0	.000	12 **12** 11

Joe Cronin

CRONIN, JOSEPH EDWARD
B. Oct. 12, 1906, San Francisco, Calif.
D. Sept. 7, 1984, Osterville, Mass.
Hall of Fame 1956.

			G	W	L	T	N	PCT	Standing
1933	**WAS**	**A**	153	99	53	1	0	.651	**1**
1934			155	66	86	3	0	.434	**7**
1935	**BOS**	**A**	154	78	75	1	0	.510	**4**
1936			155	74	80	1	0	.481	**6**
1937			154	80	72	2	0	.526	**5**
1938			150	88	61	1	0	.591	**2**
1939			152	89	62	1	0	.589	**2**
1940			154	82	72	0	0	.532	**4**
1941			155	84	70	1	0	.545	**2**
1942			152	93	59	0	0	.612	**2**
1943			155	68	84	3	0	.447	**7**
1944			156	77	77	2	0	.500	**4**
1945			157	71	83	3	0	.461	**7**
1946			156	104	50	2	0	.675	**1**
1947			157	83	71	3	0	.539	**3**
15 yrs.			2315	1236	1055	24	0	.540	

WORLD SERIES

			G	W	L	T	N	PCT	Standing
1933	**WAS**	**A**	5	1	4	0	0	.200	
1946	**BOS**	**A**	7	3	4	0	0	.429	
2 yrs.			12	4	8	0	0	.333	

Jack Crooks

CROOKS, JOHN CHARLES
B. Nov. 9, 1866, St. Paul, Minn.
D. Jan. 29, 1918, St. Louis, Mo.

			G	W	L	T	N	PCT	Standing
1892	**STL**	**N**	47	24	22	1	0	.522	11 **9** (1st)
1892			15	3	11	1	0	.214	**12** 11 (2nd)

Lave Cross

CROSS, LAFAYETTE NAPOLEON
Brother of Amos Cross.
Brother of Frank Cross.
B. May 12, 1866, Milwaukee, Wis.
D. Sept. 6, 1927, Toledo, Ohio.

			G	W	L	T	N	PCT	Standing
1899	**CLE**	**N**	38	8	30	0	0	.211	**12** 12

Mike Cubbage

CUBBAGE, MICHAEL LEE
B. July 21, 1950, Charlottesville, Va.

			G	W	L	T	N	PCT	Standing
1991	**NY**	**N**	7	3	4	0	0	.429	3 **5**

Ed Curtis

CURTIS, EDWIN R.
Deceased.

			G	W	L	T	N	PCT	Standing
1884	**ALT**	**U**	25	6	19	0	0	.240	**11**

Charlie Cushman

CUSHMAN, CHARLES H.
B. May 25, 1850, New York, N. Y.
D. June 29, 1909, Milwaukee, Wis.

			G	W	L	T	N	PCT	Standing
1891	**MIL**	**AA**	36	21	15	0	0	.583	**3**

Ned Cuthbert

CUTHBERT, EDGAR EDWARD
B. June 20, 1845, Philadelphia, Pa.
D. Feb. 6, 1905, St. Louis, Mo.

			G	W	L	T	N	PCT	Standing
1882	**STL**	**AA**	80	37	43	0	0	.463	**5**

Bill Dahlen

DAHLEN, WILLIAM FREDERICK (Bad Bill)
B. Jan. 5, 1870, Nelliston, N. Y.
D. Dec. 5, 1950, Brooklyn, N. Y.

			G	W	L	T	N	PCT	Standing
1910	**BKN**	**N**	156	64	90	2	0	.416	**6**
1911			154	64	86	4	0	.427	**7**
1912			153	58	95	0	0	.379	**7**
1913			152	65	84	3	0	.436	**6**
4 yrs.			615	251	355	9	0	.414	

Alvin Dark

DARK, ALVIN RALPH (Blackie)
B. Jan. 7, 1922, Comanche, Okla.

			G	W	L	T	N	PCT	Standing
1961	**SF**	**N**	155	85	69	1	0	.552	**3**
1962			165	103	62	0	0	.624	**1**
1963			162	88	74	0	0	.543	**3**
1964			162	90	72	0	0	.556	**4**
1966	**KC**	**A**	160	74	86	0	0	.463	**7**
1967			121	52	69	0	0	.430	**10** 10
1968	**CLE**	**A**	162	86	75	1	0	.534	**3**
1969			161	62	99	0	0	.385	**6**
1970			162	76	86	0	0	.469	**5**
1971			103	42	61	0	0	.408	**6** 6
1974	**OAK**	**A**	162	90	72	0	0	.556	**1**
1975			162	98	64	0	0	.605	**1**
1977	**SD**	**N**	113	48	65	0	0	.425	5 **5**
13 yrs.			1950	994	954	2	0	.510	

LEAGUE CHAMPIONSHIP SERIES

			G	W	L	T	N	PCT	Standing
1974	**OAK**	**A**	4	3	1	0	0	.750	
1975			3	0	3	0	0	.000	
2 yrs.			7	3	4	0	0	.429	

WORLD SERIES

			G	W	L	T	N	PCT	Standing
1962	**SF**	**N**	7	3	4	0	0	.429	
1974	**OAK**	**A**	5	4	1	0	0	.800	
2 yrs.			12	7	5	0	0	.583	

Jim Davenport

DAVENPORT, JAMES HOUSTON
B. Aug. 17, 1933, Siluria, Ala.

			G	W	L	T	N	PCT	Standing
1985	**SF**	**N**	144	56	88	0	0	.389	**6** 6

Mordecai Davidson

DAVIDSON, MORDECAI H.
B. Nov. 30, 1846, Port Washington, Ohio
D. Sept. 6, 1940, Louisville, Ky.

			G	W	L	T	N	PCT	Standing
1888	**LOU**	**AA**	3	1	2	0	0	.333	8 **8** 7
1888			90	34	52	4	0	.395	8 **7**

George Davis

DAVIS, GEORGE STACEY
B. Aug. 23, 1870, Cohoes, N. Y.
D. Oct. 17, 1940, Philadelphia, Pa.

			G	W	L	T	N	PCT	Standing
1895	**NY**	**N**	33	16	17	0	0	.485	**8** 9
1900			78	39	37	2	0	.513	8 **8**
1901			141	52	85	4	0	.380	**7**
3 yrs.			252	107	139	6	0	.435	

Harry Davis

DAVIS, HARRY H. (Jasper)
B. July 19, 1873, Philadelphia, Pa.
D. Aug. 11, 1947, Philadelphia, Pa.

			G	W	L	T	N	PCT	Standing
1912	**CLE**	**A**	127	54	71	2	0	.432	**6** 5

Spud Davis

DAVIS, VIRGIL LAWRENCE
B. Dec. 20, 1904, Birmingham, Ala.
D. Aug. 14, 1984, Birmingham, Ala.

			G	W	L	T	N	PCT	Standing
1946	**PIT**	**N**	3	1	2	0	0	.333	7 **7**

John Day

DAY, JOHN B.
B. Sept. 23, 1847, Colchester, Mass.
D. Jan. 25, 1925, Cliffside, N. J.

			G	W	L	T	N	PCT	Standing
1899	**NY**	**N**	66	29	35	1	1	.453	**9** 10

Bucky Dent

DENT, RUSSELL EARL
Born Russell Earl O'Dey.
B. Nov. 25, 1951, Savannah, Ga.

			G	W	L	T	N	PCT	Standing
1989	**NY**	**A**	40	18	22	0	0	.450	6 **5**
1990			49	18	31	0	0	.367	**7** 7
2 yrs.			89	36	53	0	0	.404	

Bill Dickey

DICKEY, WILLIAM MALCOLM
Brother of George Dickey.
B. June 6, 1907, Bastrop, La.
D. Nov. 12, 1993, Little Rock, Ark.
Hall of Fame 1954.

			G	W	L	T	N	PCT	Standing
1946	**NY**	**A**	105	57	48	0	0	.543	2 **3** 3

Harry Diddlebock

DIDDLEBOCK, HENRY H.
B. June 27, 1854, Philadelphia, Pa.
D. Feb. 5, 1900, Philadelphia, Pa.

			G	W	L	T	N	PCT	Standing
1896	**STL**	**N**	17	7	10	0	0	.412	**10** 11

Larry Doby

DOBY, LAWRENCE EUGENE
B. Dec. 13, 1924, Camden, S. C.

			G	W	L	T	N	PCT	Standing
1978	**CHI**	**A**	87	37	50	0	0	.425	5 **5**

Patsy Donovan

DONOVAN, PATRICK JOSEPH
B. Mar. 16, 1865, Queenstown, Ireland
D. Dec. 25, 1953, Lawrence, Mass.

			G	W	L	T	N	PCT	Standing
1897	**PIT**	**N**	135	60	71	4	0	.458	**8**
1899			131	69	58	4	0	.543	10 **7**
1901	**STL**	**N**	142	76	64	2	0	.543	**4**
1902			140	56	78	6	0	.418	**6**
1903			139	43	94	2	0	.314	**8**
1904	**WAS**	**A**	139	37	97	5	0	.276	8 **8**
1906	**BKN**	**N**	153	66	86	1	0	.434	**5**
1907			153	65	83	5	0	.439	**5**
1908			154	53	101	0	0	.344	**7**
1910	**BOS**	**A**	158	81	72	5	0	.529	**4**
1911			153	78	75	0	0	.510	**5**
11 yrs.			1597	684	879	34	0	.438	

Wild Bill Donovan

DONOVAN, WILLIAM EDWARD
B. Oct. 13, 1876, Lawrence, Mass.
D. Dec. 9, 1923, Forsyth, N. Y.

			G	W	L	T	N	PCT	Standing		
1915	NY	A	154	69	83	2	0	.454	**5**		
1916			156	80	74	2	0	.519	**4**		
1917			155	71	82	2	0	.464	**6**		
1921	PHI	N	87	25	62	0	0	.287	**8**	8	
4 yrs.			552	245	301	6	0	.449			

Red Dooin

DOOIN, CHARLES SEBASTIAN
B. June 12, 1879, Cincinnati, Ohio
D. May 12, 1952, Rochester, N. Y.

			G	W	L	T	N	PCT	Standing		
1910	PHI	N	157	78	75	4	0	.510	**4**		
1911			153	79	73	1	0	.520	**4**		
1912			152	73	79	0	0	.480	**5**		
1913			159	88	63	8	0	.583	**2**		
1914			154	74	80	0	0	.481	**6**		
5 yrs.			775	392	370	13	0	.514			

Mike Dorgan

DORGAN, MICHAEL CORNELIUS
Brother of Jerry Dorgan.
B. Oct. 2, 1853, Middletown, Conn.
D. Apr. 26, 1909, Hartford, Conn.

			G	W	L	T	N	PCT	Standing		
1879	SYR	N	43	17	26	0	0	.395	**6**	7	
1880	PRO	N	39	26	12	1	0	.684	3	**2**	
1881	WOR	N	56	24	32	0	0	.429	**7**	8	
3 yrs.			138	67	70	1	0	.489			

Tommy Dowd

DOWD, THOMAS JEFFERSON (Buttermilk Tommy)
B. Apr. 20, 1869, Holyoke, Mass.
D. July 2, 1933, Holyoke, Mass.

			G	W	L	T	N	PCT	Standing		
1896	STL	N	63	25	38	0	0	.397	11	**11**	
1897			29	6	22	1	0	.214	**12**	12	
2 yrs.			92	31	60	1	0	.341			

Jack Doyle

DOYLE, JOHN JOSEPH (Dirty Jack)
B. Oct. 25, 1869, Killorglin, Ireland
D. Dec. 31, 1958, Holyoke, Mass.

			G	W	L	T	N	PCT	Standing		
1895	NY	N	64	32	31	1	0	.508	8	**9**	9
1898	WAS	N	17	8	9	0	0	.471	11	**10**	11
2 yrs.			81	40	40	1	0	.500			

Chuck Dressen

DRESSEN, CHARLES WALTER
B. Sept. 20, 1898, Decatur, Ill.
D. Aug. 10, 1966, Detroit, Mich.

			G	W	L	T	N	PCT	Standing		
1934	CIN	N	60	21	39	0	0	.350	8	**8**	
1935			154	68	85	1	0	.444	**6**		
1936			154	74	80	0	0	.481	**5**		
1937			130	51	78	1	0	.395	**8**	8	
1951	BKN	N	158	97	60	1	0	.618	**2**		
1952			155	96	57	2	0	.627	**1**		
1953			155	105	49	1	0	.682	**1**		
1955	WAS	A	154	53	101	0	0	.344	**8**		
1956			155	59	95	1	0	.383	**7**		
1957			20	4	16	0	0	.200	**8**	8	
1960	MIL	N	154	88	66	0	0	.571	**2**		
1961			130	71	58	1	0	.550	**3**	4	
1963	DET	A	102	55	47	0	0	.539	9	**5**	
1964			163	85	77	1	0	.525	**4**		
1965			120	65	55	0	0	.542	3	**4**	
1966			26	16	10	0	0	.615	**3**	3	
16 yrs.			1990	1008	973	9	0	.509			
WORLD SERIES											
1952	BKN	N	7	3	4	0	0	.429			
1953			6	2	4	0	0	.333			
2 yrs.			13	5	8	0	0	.385			

Hugh Duffy

DUFFY, HUGH
B. Nov. 26, 1866, Cranston, R. I.
D. Oct. 19, 1954, Boston, Mass.
Hall of Fame 1945.

			G	W	L	T	N	PCT	Standing		
1901	MIL	A	139	48	89	2	0	.350	**8**		
1904	PHI	N	155	52	100	3	0	.342	**8**		
1905			155	83	69	3	0	.546	**4**		
1906			154	71	82	1	0	.464	**4**		
1910	CHI	A	156	68	85	3	0	.444	**6**		
1911			154	77	74	3	0	.510	**4**		
1921	BOS	A	154	75	79	0	0	.487	**5**		
1922			154	61	93	0	0	.396	**8**		
8 yrs.			1221	535	671	15	0	.444			

Fred Dunlap

DUNLAP, FREDERICK C. (Sure Shot)
B. May 21, 1859, Philadelphia, Pa.
D. Dec. 1, 1902, Philadelphia, Pa.

			G	W	L	T	N	PCT	Standing		
1882	CLE	N	80	42	36	2	0	.538	8	**5**	
1884	STL	U	83	66	16	1	0	.805	1	**1**	
1885	STL	N	50	21	29	0	0	.420	**5**	8	
1885			22	9	11	2	0	.450	8	**8**	
1889	PIT	N	17	7	10	0	0	.412	7	**7**	5
4 yrs.			252	145	102	5	0	.587			

Leo Durocher

DUROCHER, LEO ERNEST (The Lip)
B. July 27, 1905, W. Springfield, Mass.
D. Oct. 7, 1991, Palm Springs, Calif.
Hall of Fame 1994.

			G	W	L	T	N	PCT	Standing		
1939	BKN	N	157	84	69	4	0	.549	**3**		
1940			156	88	65	3	0	.575	**2**		
1941			157	100	54	3	0	.649	**1**		
1942			155	104	50	1	0	.675	**2**		
1943			153	81	72	0	0	.529	**3**		
1944			155	63	91	1	0	.409	**7**		
1945			155	87	67	1	0	.565	**3**		
1946			157	96	60	1	0	.615	**2**		
1948			73	35	37	1	0	.486	**5**	3	
1948	NY	N	79	41	38	0	0	.519	4	**5**	
1949			156	73	81	2	0	.474	**5**		
1950			154	86	68	0	0	.558	**3**		
1951			157	98	59	0	0	.624	**1**		
1952			154	92	62	0	0	.597	**2**		
1953			155	70	84	1	0	.455	**5**		
1954			154	97	57	0	0	.630	**1**		
1955			154	80	74	0	0	.519	**3**		
1966	CHI	N	162	59	103	0	0	.364	**10**		
1967			162	87	74	1	0	.540	**3**		
1968			163	84	78	1	0	.519	**3**		
1969			163	92	70	1	0	.568	**2**		
1970			162	84	78	0	0	.519	**2**		
1971			162	83	79	0	0	.512	**3**		
1972			91	46	44	1	0	.511	**4**	2	
1972	HOU	N	31	16	15	0	0	.516	2	**2**	
1973			162	82	80	0	0	.506	**4**		
24 yrs.			3739	2008	1709	22	0	.540			
			7th	**7th**	**8th**						
WORLD SERIES											
1941	BKN	N	5	1	4	0	0	.200			
1951	NY	N	6	2	4	0	0	.333			
1954			4	4	0	0	0	1.000			
3 yrs.			15	7	8	0	0	.467			

Frank Dwyer

DWYER, JOHN FRANCIS
B. Mar. 25, 1868, Lee, Mass.
D. Feb. 4, 1943, Pittsfield, Mass.

			G	W	L	T	N	PCT	Standing
1902	DET	A	137	52	83	2	0	.385	**7**

Eddie Dyer

DYER, EDWIN HAWLEY
B. Oct. 11, 1900, Morgan City, La.
D. Apr. 20, 1964, Houston, Tex.

			G	W	L	T	N	PCT	Standing
1946	STL	N	156	98	58	0	0	.628	**1**
1947			156	89	65	2	0	.578	**2**
1948			155	85	69	1	0	.552	**2**

Eddie Dyer *continued*

			G	W	L	T	N	PCT	Standing
1949			157	96	58	3	0	.623	**2**
1950			153	78	75	0	0	.510	**5**
5 yrs.			777	446	325	6	0	.578	
WORLD SERIES									
1946	STL	N	7	4	3	0	0	.571	

Jimmy Dykes

DYKES, JAMES JOSEPH
B. Nov. 10, 1896, Philadelphia, Pa.
D. June 15, 1976, Philadelphia, Pa.

			G	W	L	T	N	PCT	Standing	
1934	CHI	A	138	49	88	1	0	.358	8	**8**
1935			153	74	78	1	0	.487	**5**	
1936			153	81	70	2	0	.536	**3**	
1937			154	86	68	0	0	.558	**3**	
1938			149	65	83	1	0	.439	**6**	
1939			155	85	69	0	1	.552	**4**	
1940			155	82	72	0	1	.532	**4**	
1941			156	77	77	2	0	.500	**3**	
1942			148	66	82	0	0	.446	**6**	
1943			155	82	72	1	0	.532	**4**	
1944			154	71	83	0	0	.461	**7**	
1945			150	71	78	1	0	.477	**6**	
1946			30	10	20	0	0	.333	**7**	5
1951	PHI	A	154	70	84	0	0	.455	**6**	
1952			155	79	75	1	0	.513	**4**	
1953			157	59	95	3	0	.383	**7**	
1954	BAL	A	154	54	100	0	0	.351	**7**	
1958	CIN	N	41	24	17	0	0	.585	7	**4**
1959	DET	A	137	74	63	0	0	.540	8	**4**
1960			96	44	52	0	0	.458	**6**	6
1960	CLE	A	58	26	32	0	0	.448	4	**4**
1961			160	77	83	0	0	.481	**5**	5
21 yrs.			2962	1406	1541	13	2	.477		
					10th					

Charlie Ebbets

EBBETS, CHARLES HERCULES
B. Oct. 29, 1859, New York, N. Y.
D. Apr. 18, 1925, New York, N. Y.

			G	W	L	T	N	PCT	Standing	
1898	BKN	N	110	38	68	4	0	.358	9	**10**

Doc Edwards

EDWARDS, HOWARD RODNEY
B. Dec. 10, 1936, Red Jacket, W. Va.

			G	W	L	T	N	PCT	Standing	
1987	CLE	A	75	30	45	0	0	.400	7	**7**
1988			162	78	84	0	0	.481	**6**	
1989			143	65	78	0	0	.455	**6**	6
3 yrs.			380	173	207	0	0	.455		

Kid Elberfeld

ELBERFELD, NORMAN ARTHUR (The Tabasco Kid)
B. Apr. 13, 1875, Pomeroy, Ohio
D. Jan. 13, 1944, Chattanooga, Tenn.

			G	W	L	T	N	PCT	Standing	
1908	NY	A	98	27	71	0	0	.276	6	**8**

Lee Elia

ELIA, LEE CONSTANTINE
B. July 16, 1937, Philadelphia, Pa.

			G	W	L	T	N	PCT	Standing	
1982	CHI	N	162	73	89	0	0	.451	**5**	
1983			123	54	69	0	0	.439	**5**	5
1987	PHI	N	101	51	50	0	0	.505	5	**4**
1988			153	60	92	1	0	.395	**6**	6
4 yrs.			539	238	300	1	0	.442		

Joe Ellick

ELLICK, JOSEPH J.
B. Apr. 3, 1854, Cincinnati, Ohio
D. Apr. 21, 1923, Kansas City, Mo.

			G	W	L	T	N	PCT	Standing	
1884	PIT	U	13	6	6	1	0	.500	**8**	8

Bob Elliott

ELLIOTT, ROBERT IRVING
B. Nov. 26, 1916, San Francisco, Calif.
D. May 4, 1966, San Diego, Calif.

			G	W	L	T	N	PCT	Standing
1960	KC	A	155	58	96	1	0	.377	**8**

Jewel Ens

ENS, JEWEL WINKLEMEYER
Brother of Mutz Ens.
B. Aug. 24, 1889, St. Louis, Mo.
D. Jan. 17, 1950, Syracuse, N. Y.

			G	W	L	T	N	PCT	Standing
1929	**PIT**	**N**	35	21	14	0	0	.600	2 **2**
1930			154	80	74	0	0	.519	**5**
1931			155	75	79	1	0	.487	**5**
3 yrs.			344	176	167	1	0	.513	

Cal Ermer

ERMER, CALVIN COOLIDGE
B. Nov. 10, 1923, Baltimore, Md.

			G	W	L	T	N	PCT	Standing
1967	**MIN**	**A**	114	66	46	2	0	.589	6 **2**
1968			162	79	83	0	0	.488	**7**
2 yrs.			276	145	129	2	0	.529	

Jim Essian

ESSIAN, JAMES SARKIS
B. Jan. 2, 1951, Detroit, Mich.

			G	W	L	T	N	PCT	Standing
1991	**CHI**	**N**	122	59	63	0	0	.484	5 **4**

Dude Esterbrook

ESTERBROOK, THOMAS JOHN
B. June 9, 1857, Staten Island, N. Y.
D. Apr. 30, 1901, Middletown, N. Y.

			G	W	L	T	N	PCT	Standing
1889	**LOU**	**AA**	10	2	8	0	0	.200	**8** 8

Johnny Evers

EVERS, JOHN JOSEPH (The Crab, The Trojan)
Brother of Joe Evers.
B. July 21, 1881, Troy, N. Y.
D. Mar. 28, 1947, Albany, N. Y.
Hall of Fame 1946.

			G	W	L	T	N	PCT	Standing
1913	**CHI**	**N**	155	88	65	2	0	.575	**3**
1921			96	41	55	0	0	.427	**6** 7
1924	**CHI**	**A**	21	10	11	0	0	.476	**6** 8
1924			103	41	61	1	0	.402	6 **8**
3 yrs.			375	180	192	3	0	.484	

Buck Ewing

EWING, WILLIAM
Brother of John Ewing.
B. Oct. 17, 1859, Hoagland, Ohio
D. Oct. 20, 1906, Cincinnati, Ohio.
Hall of Fame 1939.

			G	W	L	T	N	PCT	Standing
1890	**NY**	**P**	132	74	57	1	0	.565	**3**
1895	**CIN**	**N**	132	66	64	2	0	.508	**8**
1896			128	77	50	1	0	.606	**3**
1897			134	76	56	2	0	.576	**4**
1898			157	92	60	5	0	.605	**3**
1899			157	83	67	6	1	.553	**6**
1900	**NY**	**N**	63	21	41	1	0	.339	**8** 8
7 yrs.			903	489	395	18	1	.553	

Jay Faatz

FAATZ, JAYSON S.
B. Oct. 24, 1860, Weedsport, N. Y.
D. Apr. 10, 1923, Syracuse, N. Y.

			G	W	L	T	N	PCT	Standing
1890	**BUF**	**P**	34	9	24	1	0	.273	8 **8** 8

Bibb Falk

FALK, BIBB AUGUST (Jockey)
Brother of Chet Falk.
B. Jan. 27, 1899, Austin, Tex.
D. June 8, 1989, Austin, Tex.

			G	W	L	T	N	PCT	Standing
1933	**CLE**	**A**	1	1	0	0	0	1.000	5 **5** 4

Jim Fanning

FANNING, WILLIAM JAMES
B. Sept. 14, 1927, Chicago, Ill.

			G	W	L	T	N	PCT	Standing
1981	**MON**	**N**	27	16	11	0	0	.593	6 **1** (2nd)
1982			162	86	76	0	0	.531	**3**
1984			30	14	16	0	0	.467	5 **5**
3 yrs.			219	116	103	0	0	.530	

DIVISIONAL PLAYOFF SERIES

			G	W	L	T	N	PCT	Standing
1981	**MON**	**N**	5	3	2	0	0	.600	

Jim Fanning *continued*

LEAGUE CHAMPIONSHIP SERIES

			G	W	L	T	N	PCT	Standing
1981	**MON**	**N**	5	2	3	0	0	.400	

Jack Farrell

FARRELL, JOHN A. (Moose)
B. July 5, 1857, Newark, N. J.
D. Feb. 10, 1914, Overbrook, N. J.

			G	W	L	T	N	PCT	Standing
1881	**PRO**	**N**	51	24	27	0	0	.471	**4** 2

Kerby Farrell

FARRELL, MAJOR KERBY
B. Sept. 3, 1913, Leapwood, Tenn.
D. Dec. 17, 1975, Nashville, Tenn.

			G	W	L	T	N	PCT	Standing
1957	**CLE**	**A**	153	76	77	0	0	.497	**6**

John Felske

FELSKE, JOHN FREDERICK
B. May 30, 1942, Chicago, Ill.

			G	W	L	T	N	PCT	Standing
1985	**PHI**	**N**	162	75	87	0	0	.463	**5**
1986			161	86	75	0	0	.534	**2**
1987			61	29	32	0	0	.475	**5** 4
3 yrs.			384	190	194	0	0	.495	

Bob Ferguson

FERGUSON, ROBERT VAVASOUR (Death to Flying Things)
B. Jan. 31, 1845, Brooklyn, N. Y.
D. May 3, 1894, Brooklyn, N. Y.

			G	W	L	T	N	PCT	Standing
1876	**HAR**	**N**	69	47	21	1	0	.691	**3**
1877			60	31	27	2	0	.534	**3**
1878	**CHI**	**N**	61	30	30	1	0	.500	**4**
1879	**TRO**	**N**	30	7	22	1	0	.241	8 **8**
1880			83	41	42	0	0	.494	**4**
1881			85	39	45	1	0	.464	**5**
1882			85	35	48	2	0	.422	**7**
1883	**PHI**	**N**	17	4	13	0	0	.235	**8** 8
1884	**PIT**	**AA**	42	11	31	0	0	.262	10 **12** 11
1886	**NY**	**AA**	120	48	70	2	0	.407	8 **7**
1887			30	6	24	0	0	.200	**8** 7
11 yrs.			682	299	373	10	0	.445	

Mike Ferraro

FERRARO, MICHAEL DENNIS
B. Aug. 14, 1944, Kingston, N. Y.

			G	W	L	T	N	PCT	Standing
1983	**CLE**	**A**	100	40	60	0	0	.400	**7** 7
1986	**KC**	**A**	74	36	38	0	0	.486	4 **3**
2 yrs.			174	76	98	0	0	.437	

Wally Fessenden

FESSENDEN, WALLACE CLIFTON
B. Oct. 5, 1860, Windham, N. H.
D. 1933

			G	W	L	T	N	PCT	Standing
1890	**SYR**	**AA**	11	4	7	0	0	.364	7 **6** 6

Freddie Fitzsimmons

FITZSIMMONS, FREDERICK LANDIS (Fat Freddie)
B. July 26, 1901, Mishawaka, Ind.
D. Nov. 18, 1979, Yucca Valley, Calif.

			G	W	L	T	N	PCT	Standing
1943	**PHI**	**N**	65	26	38	1	0	.406	5 **7**
1944			154	61	92	1	0	.399	**8**
1945			69	18	51	0	0	.261	**8** 8
3 yrs.			288	105	181	2	0	.367	

Art Fletcher

FLETCHER, ARTHUR
B. Jan. 5, 1885, Collinsville, Ill.
D. Feb. 6, 1950, Los Angeles, Calif.

			G	W	L	T	N	PCT	Standing
1923	**PHI**	**N**	155	50	104	1	0	.325	**8**
1924			152	55	96	1	0	.364	**7**
1925			153	68	85	0	0	.444	**6**
1926			152	58	93	1	0	.384	**8**
1929	**NY**	**A**	11	6	5	0	0	.545	2 **2**
5 yrs.			623	237	383	3	0	.382	

Silver Flint

FLINT, FRANK SYLVESTER
B. Aug. 3, 1855, Philadelphia, Pa.
D. Jan. 14, 1892, Chicago, Ill.

			G	W	L	T	N	PCT	Standing
1879	**CHI**	**N**	19	5	12	2	0	.294	2 **4**

Jim Fogarty

FOGARTY, JAMES G.
Brother of Joe Fogarty.
B. Feb. 12, 1864, San Francisco, Calif.
D. May 20, 1891, Philadelphia, Pa.

			G	W	L	T	N	PCT	Standing
1890	**PHI**	**P**	16	7	9	0	0	.438	**5** 5

Horace Fogel

FOGEL, HORACE S.
B. Mar. 2, 1861, Macungie, Pa.
D. Nov. 15, 1928, Philadelphia, Pa.

			G	W	L	T	N	PCT	Standing
1887	**IND**	**N**	70	20	49	1	0	.290	8 **8**
1902	**NY**	**N**	44	18	23	1	2	.439	**4** 8
2 yrs.			114	38	72	2	2	.345	

Lee Fohl

FOHL, LEO ALEXANDER
B. Nov. 28, 1870, Pittsburgh, Pa.
D. Oct. 30, 1965, Cleveland, Ohio.

			G	W	L	T	N	PCT	Standing
1915	**CLE**	**A**	127	45	79	2	1	.363	6 **7**
1916			157	77	77	3	0	.500	**6**
1917			156	88	66	2	0	.571	**3**
1918			129	73	54	2	0	.575	**2**
1919			78	44	34	0	0	.564	**3** 2
1921	**STL**	**A**	154	81	73	0	0	.526	**3**
1922			154	93	61	0	0	.604	**2**
1923			103	52	49	2	0	.515	**3** 5
1924	**BOS**	**A**	157	67	87	2	1	.435	**7**
1925			152	47	105	0	0	.309	**8**
1926			154	46	107	1	0	.301	**8**
11 yrs.			1521	713	792	14	2	.474	

Lew Fonseca

FONSECA, LEWIS ALBERT
B. Jan. 21, 1899, Oakland, Calif.
D. Nov. 26, 1989, Ely, Iowa.

			G	W	L	T	N	PCT	Standing
1932	**CHI**	**A**	152	49	102	1	0	.325	**7**
1933			151	67	83	1	0	.447	**6**
1934			15	4	11	0	0	.267	**8** 8
3 yrs.			318	120	196	2	0	.380	

Dave Foutz

FOUTZ, DAVID LUTHER (Scissors)
Brother of Frank Foutz.
B. Sept. 7, 1856, Carroll County, Md.
D. Mar. 5, 1897, Waverly, Md.

			G	W	L	T	N	PCT	Standing
1893	**BKN**	**N**	130	65	63	2	0	.508	**6**
1894			135	70	61	3	1	.534	**5**
1895			134	71	60	2	1	.542	**5**
1896			133	58	73	2	0	.443	**9**
4 yrs.			532	264	257	9	2	.507	

Charlie Fox

FOX, CHARLES FRANCIS (Irish)
B. Oct. 7, 1921, New York, N. Y.

			G	W	L	T	N	PCT	Standing
1970	**SF**	**N**	120	67	53	0	0	.558	4 **3**
1971			162	90	72	0	0	.556	**1**
1972			155	69	86	0	0	.445	**5**
1973			162	88	74	0	0	.543	**3**
1974			76	34	42	0	0	.447	**5** 5
1976	**MON**	**N**	34	12	22	0	0	.353	6 **6**
1983	**CHI**	**N**	39	17	22	0	0	.436	5 **5**
7 yrs.			748	377	371	0	0	.504	

LEAGUE CHAMPIONSHIP SERIES

			G	W	L	T	N	PCT	Standing
1971	**SF**	**N**	4	1	3	0	0	.250	

Herman Franks

FRANKS, HERMAN LOUIS
B. Jan. 4, 1914, Price, Utah

			G	W	L	T	N	PCT	Standing
1965	**SF**	**N**	163	95	67	1	0	.586	**2**
1966			161	93	68	0	0	.578	**2**
1967			162	91	71	0	0	.562	**2**

Herman Franks *continued*

Year	Team	Lg	G	W	L	T	N	PCT	Standing	
1968			163	88	74	1	0	.543	2	
1977	CHI	N	162	81	81	0	0	.500	4	
1978			162	79	83	0	0	.488	3	
1979			155	78	77	0	0	.503	5 5	
7 yrs.			1128	605	521	2	0	.537		

George Frazer

FRAZER, GEORGE KASSON
B. Jan. 7, 1861, Syracuse, N. Y.
D. Feb. 5, 1913, Philadelphia, Pa.

Year	Team	Lg	G	W	L	T	N	PCT	Standing	
1890	SYR	AA	71	31	40	0	0	.437	7 6	
1890			46	20	25	1	0	.444	6 6	

Joe Frazier

FRAZIER, JOSEPH FILMORE (Cobra Joe)
B. Oct. 6, 1922, Liberty, N. C.

Year	Team	Lg	G	W	L	T	N	PCT	Standing	
1976	NY	N	162	86	76	0	0	.531	3	
1977			45	15	30	0	0	.333	6 6	
2 yrs.			207	101	106	0	0	.488		

Jim Fregosi

FREGOSI, JAMES LOUIS
B. Apr. 4, 1942, San Francisco, Calif.

Year	Team	Lg	G	W	L	T	N	PCT	Standing	
1978	CAL	A	117	62	55	0	0	.530	3 2	
1979			162	88	74	0	0	.543	1	
1980			160	65	95	0	0	.406	6	
1981			48	22	25	0	1	.468	4 4	(1st)
1986	CHI	A	96	45	51	0	0	.469	5 5	
1987			162	77	85	0	0	.475	5	
1988			161	71	90	0	0	.441	5	
1991	PHI	N	149	74	75	0	0	.497	6 3	
1992			162	70	92	0	0	.432	6	
1993			162	97	65	0	0	.599	1	
1994			115	54	61	0	0	.470	4	
1995			144	69	75	0	0	.479	2	
12 yrs.			1638	794	843	0	1	.485		

LEAGUE CHAMPIONSHIP SERIES

Year	Team	Lg	G	W	L	T	N	PCT
1979	CAL	A	4	1	3	0	0	.250
1993	PHI	N	6	4	2	0	0	.667
2 yrs.			10	5	5	0	0	.500

WORLD SERIES

Year	Team	Lg	G	W	L	T	N	PCT
1993	PHI	N	6	2	4	0	0	.333

Jim Frey

FREY, JAMES GOTTFRIED
B. May 26, 1931, Cleveland, Ohio

Year	Team	Lg	G	W	L	T	N	PCT	Standing	
1980	KC	A	162	97	65	0	0	.599	1	
1981			50	20	30	0	0	.400	5	(1st)
1981			20	10	10	0	0	.500	2 1	(2nd)
1984	CHI	N	161	96	65	0	0	.596	1	
1985			162	77	84	1	0	.478	4	
1986			56	23	33	0	0	.411	5 5	
5 yrs.			611	323	287	1	0	.530		

LEAGUE CHAMPIONSHIP SERIES

Year	Team	Lg	G	W	L	T	N	PCT
1980	KC	A	3	3	0	0	0	1.000
1984	CHI	N	5	2	3	0	0	.400
2 yrs.			8	5	3	0	0	.625

WORLD SERIES

Year	Team	Lg	G	W	L	T	N	PCT
1980	KC	A	6	2	4	0	0	.333

Frankie Frisch

FRISCH, FRANK FRANCIS (The Fordham Flash)
B. Sept. 9, 1898, Bronx, N. Y.
D. Mar. 12, 1973, Wilmington, Del.
Hall of Fame 1947.

Year	Team	Lg	G	W	L	T	N	PCT	Standing	
1933	STL	N	63	36	26	1	0	.581	5 5	
1934			154	95	58	1	0	.621	1	
1935			154	96	58	0	0	.623	2	
1936			155	87	67	1	0	.565	2	
1937			157	81	73	3	0	.526	4	
1938			139	63	72	4	0	.467	6 6	
1940	PIT	N	156	78	76	2	0	.506	4	
1941			156	81	73	2	0	.526	4	
1942			151	66	81	4	0	.449	5	
1943			157	80	74	3	0	.519	4	

Frankie Frisch *continued*

Year	Team	Lg	G	W	L	T	N	PCT	Standing	
1944			158	90	63	5	0	.588	2	
1945			155	82	72	1	0	.532	4	
1946			152	62	89	1	0	.411	7 7	
1949	CHI	N	104	42	62	0	0	.404	8 8	
1950			154	64	89	1	0	.418	7	
1951			81	35	45	1	0	.438	7 8	
16 yrs.			2246	1138	1078	30	0	.514		

WORLD SERIES

Year	Team	Lg	G	W	L	T	N	PCT
1934	STL	N	7	4	3	0	0	.571

Judge Fuchs

FUCHS, EMIL EDWIN
B. Apr. 17, 1878, Hamburg, Germany
D. Dec. 5, 1961, Boston, Mass.

Year	Team	Lg	G	W	L	T	N	PCT	Standing	
1929	BOS	N	154	56	98	0	0	.364	8	

John Gaffney

GAFFNEY, JOHN H. (Honest John, King of the Umpires)
B. June 29, 1855, Roxbury, Mass.
D. Aug. 8, 1913, New York, N. Y.

Year	Team	Lg	G	W	L	T	N	PCT	Standing	
1886	WAS	N	43	15	25	3	0	.375	8 8	
1887			126	46	76	4	0	.377	7	
2 yrs.			169	61	101	7	0	.377		

Pud Galvin

GALVIN, JAMES FRANCIS (Gentle Jeems, The Little Steam Engine)
B. Dec. 25, 1856, St. Louis, Mo.
D. Mar. 7, 1902, Pittsburgh, Pa.
Hall of Fame 1965.

Year	Team	Lg	G	W	L	T	N	PCT	Standing	
1885	BUF	N	24	7	17	0	0	.292	7 6	

John Ganzel

GANZEL, JOHN HENRY
Brother of Charlie Ganzel.
B. Apr. 7, 1874, Kalamazoo, Mich.
D. Jan. 14, 1959, Orlando, Fla.

Year	Team	Lg	G	W	L	T	N	PCT	Standing	
1908	CIN	N	155	73	81	1	0	.474	5	
1915	BKN	F	35	17	18	0	0	.486	7 7	
2 yrs.			190	90	99	1	0	.476		

Dave Garcia

GARCIA, DAVID
B. Sept. 15, 1920, East St. Louis, Ill.

Year	Team	Lg	G	W	L	T	N	PCT	Standing	
1977	CAL	A	81	35	46	0	0	.432	5 5	
1978			45	25	20	0	0	.556	3 2	
1979	CLE	A	66	38	28	0	0	.576	6 6	
1980			160	79	81	0	0	.494	6	
1981			50	26	24	0	0	.520	6	(1st)
1981			53	26	27	0	0	.491	5	(2nd)
1982			162	78	84	0	0	.481	6	
6 yrs.			617	307	310	0	0	.498		

Billy Gardner

GARDNER, WILLIAM FREDERICK (Shotgun)
B. July 19, 1927, Waterford, Conn.

Year	Team	Lg	G	W	L	T	N	PCT	Standing	
1981	MIN	A	20	6	14	0	0	.300	5 7	(1st)
1981			53	24	29	0	0	.453	4	(2nd)
1982			162	60	102	0	0	.370	7	
1983			162	70	92	0	0	.432	5	
1984			162	81	81	0	0	.500	2	
1985			62	27	35	0	0	.435	6 4	
1987	KC	A	126	62	64	0	0	.492	4 2	
6 yrs.			747	330	417	0	0	.442		

Phil Garner

GARNER, PHILIP MASON (Scrap Iron)
B. Apr. 30, 1949, Jefferson City, Tenn.

Year	Team	Lg	G	W	L	T	N	PCT	Standing	
1992	MIL	A	162	92	70	0	0	.568	2	
1993			162	69	93	0	0	.426	7	
1994			115	53	62	0	0	.461	5	
1995			144	65	79	0	0	.451	4	
4 yrs.			583	279	304	0	0	.479		

Cito Gaston

GASTON, CLARENCE EDWIN
B. Mar. 17, 1944, San Antonio, Tex.

Year	Team	Lg	G	W	L	T	N	PCT	Standing	
1989	TOR	A	126	77	49	0	0	.611	6 1	
1990			162	86	76	0	0	.531	2	
1991			120	66	54	0	0	.550	1 1	
1991			9	6	3	0	0	.667	1 1	
1992			162	96	66	0	0	.593	1	
1993			162	95	67	0	0	.586	1	
1994			115	55	60	0	0	.478	3	
1995			144	56	88	0	0	.389	5	
7 yrs.			1000	537	463	0	0	.537		

LEAGUE CHAMPIONSHIP SERIES

Year	Team	Lg	G	W	L	T	N	PCT
1989	TOR	A	5	1	4	0	0	.200
1991			5	1	4	0	0	.200
1992			6	4	2	0	0	.667
1993			6	4	2	0	0	.667
4 yrs.			22	10	12	0	0	.455
			6th	7th	5th			10th

WORLD SERIES

Year	Team	Lg	G	W	L	T	N	PCT
1992	TOR	A	6	4	2	0	0	.667
1993			6	4	2	0	0	.667
2 yrs.			12	8	4	0	0	.667

Joe Gerhardt

GERHARDT, JOHN JOSEPH (Move Up Joe)
B. Feb. 14, 1855, Washington, D. C.
D. Mar. 11, 1922, Middletown, N. Y.

Year	Team	Lg	G	W	L	T	N	PCT	Standing	
1883	LOU	AA	98	52	45	1	0	.536	5	
1890	STL	AA	38	20	16	2	0	.556	2 3	
2 yrs.			136	72	61	3	0	.541		

Doc Gessler

GESSLER, HARRY HOMER (Brownie)
B. Dec. 23, 1880, Greensburg, Pa.
D. Dec. 25, 1924, Pittsburgh, Pa.

Year	Team	Lg	G	W	L	T	N	PCT	Standing	
1914	PIT	F	11	3	8	0	0	.273	8 7	

George Gibson

GIBSON, GEORGE C. (Moon)
B. July 22, 1880, London, Ont., Canada
D. Jan. 25, 1967, London, Ont., Canada.

Year	Team	Lg	G	W	L	T	N	PCT	Standing	
1920	PIT	N	155	79	75	1	0	.513	4	
1921			154	90	63	1	0	.588	2	
1922			65	32	33	0	0	.492	5 3	
1925	CHI	N	26	12	14	0	0	.462	8 8	
1932	PIT	N	154	86	68	0	0	.558	2	
1933			154	87	67	0	0	.565	2	
1934			51	27	24	0	0	.529	4 5	
7 yrs.			759	413	344	2	0	.546		

Jim Gifford

GIFFORD, JAMES H.
B. Oct. 18, 1845, Warren, N. Y.
D. Dec. 19, 1901, Columbus, Ohio.

Year	Team	Lg	G	W	L	T	N	PCT	Standing	
1884	IND	AA	87	25	60	2	0	.294	10 11	
1885	NY	AA	108	44	64	0	0	.407	7	
1886			17	5	12	0	0	.294	8 7	
3 yrs.			212	74	136	2	0	.352		

Jack Glasscock

GLASSCOCK, JOHN WESLEY (Old Battle Ax)
B. July 22, 1859, Wheeling, W. Va.
D. Feb. 24, 1947, Wheeling, W. Va.

Year	Team	Lg	G	W	L	T	N	PCT	Standing	
1889	IND	N	67	34	32	1	0	.515	7 7	
1892	STL	N	4	1	3	0	0	.250	10 9	(1st)
2 yrs.			71	35	35	1	0	.500		

Kid Gleason

GLEASON, WILLIAM J. (Youngster)
Brother of Harry Gleason.
B. Oct. 26, 1866, Camden, N. J.
D. Jan. 2, 1933, Philadelphia, Pa.

Year	Team	Lg	G	W	L	T	N	PCT	Standing	
1919	CHI	A	140	88	52	0	0	.629	1	
1920			154	96	58	0	0	.623	2	
1921			154	62	92	0	0	.403	7	
1922			155	77	77	1	0	.500	5	
1923			156	69	85	2	0	.448	7	
5 yrs.			759	392	364	3	0	.519		

Kid Gleason *continued*

WORLD SERIES

			G	W	L	T	N	PCT	Standing
1919	**CHI**	**A**	8	3	5	0	0	.375	

Preston Gomez

GOMEZ, PEDRO
Born Pedro Gomez (Martinez).
B. Apr. 20, 1923, Central Preston, Cuba.

			G	W	L	T	N	PCT	Standing
1969	**SD**	**N**	162	52	110	0	0	.321	**6**
1970			162	63	99	0	0	.389	**6**
1971			161	61	100	0	0	.379	**6**
1972			11	4	7	0	0	.364	**4** 6
1974	**HOU**	**N**	162	81	81	0	0	.500	**4**
1975			127	47	80	0	0	.370	**6** 6
1980	**CHI**	**N**	90	38	52	0	0	.422	**6** 6
7 yrs.			875	346	529	0	0	.395	

Mike Gonzalez

GONZALEZ, MIGUEL ANGEL
Born Miguel Angel Gonzalez (Cordero).
B. Sept. 24, 1890, Havana, Cuba
D. Feb. 19, 1977, Havana, Cuba.

			G	W	L	T	N	PCT	Standing
1938	**STL**	**N**	17	8	8	1	0	.500	6 **6**
1940			6	1	5	0	0	.167	6 **7** 3
2 yrs.			23	9	13	1	0	.409	

Joe Gordon

GORDON, JOSEPH LOWELL (Flash)
B. Feb. 18, 1915, Los Angeles, Calif.
D. Apr. 14, 1978, Sacramento, Calif.

			G	W	L	T	N	PCT	Standing
1958	**CLE**	**A**	86	46	40	0	0	.535	5 **4**
1959			154	89	65	0	0	.578	**2**
1960			95	49	46	0	0	.516	**4** 4
1960	**DET**	**A**	57	26	31	0	0	.456	6 **6**
1961	**KC**	**A**	60	26	33	1	0	.441	**8** 9
1969			163	69	93	1	0	.426	**4**
5 yrs.			615	305	308	2	0	.498	

George Gore

GORE, GEORGE F.
B. May 3, 1857, Saccarappa, Me.
D. Sept. 16, 1933, Utica, N. Y.

			G	W	L	T	N	PCT	Standing
1892	**STL**	**N**	16	6	9	1	0	.400	12 **12** 11 (2nd)

John Goryl

GORYL, JOHN ALBERT
B. Oct. 21, 1933, Cumberland, R. I.

			G	W	L	T	N	PCT	Standing
1980	**MIN**	**A**	36	23	13	0	0	.639	6 **3**
1981			37	11	25	0	1	.306	**5** 7 (1st)
2 yrs.			73	34	38	0	1	.472	

Charlie Gould

GOULD, CHARLES HARVEY
B. Aug. 21, 1847, Cincinnati, Ohio
D. Apr. 10, 1917, Flushing, N. Y.

			G	W	L	T	N	PCT	Standing
1876	**CIN**	**N**	65	9	56	0	0	.138	**8**

Hank Gowdy

GOWDY, HENRY MORGAN
B. Aug. 24, 1889, Columbus, Ohio
D. Aug. 1, 1966, Columbus, Ohio.

			G	W	L	T	N	PCT	Standing
1946	**CIN**	**N**	4	3	1	0	0	.750	6 **6**

Mase Graffen

GRAFFEN, SAMUEL MASON
B. 1845, Philadelphia, Pa.
D. Nov. 18, 1883, Silver City, N. M.

			G	W	L	T	N	PCT	Standing
1876	**STL**	**N**	56	39	17	0	0	.696	**2** 2

Alex Grammas

GRAMMAS, ALEXANDER PETER
B. Apr. 3, 1926, Birmingham, Ala.

			G	W	L	T	N	PCT	Standing
1969	**PIT**	**N**	5	4	1	0	0	.800	3 **3**
1976	**MIL**	**A**	161	66	95	0	0	.410	**6**
1977			162	67	95	0	0	.414	**6**
3 yrs.			328	137	191	0	0	.418	

Dallas Green

GREEN, GEORGE DALLAS
B. Aug. 4, 1934, Newport, Del.

			G	W	L	T	N	PCT	Standing
1979	**PHI**	**N**	30	19	11	0	0	.633	5 **4**
1980			162	91	71	0	0	.562	**1**
1981			56	34	21	1	0	.618	**1** (1st)
1981			53	25	27	1	0	.481	**3** (2nd)
1989	**NY**	**A**	121	56	65	0	0	.463	**6** 5
1993	**NY**	**N**	124	46	78	0	0	.371	7 **7**
1994			113	55	58	0	0	.487	**3**
1995			144	69	75	0	0	.479	**2**
7 yrs.			803	395	406	2	0	.493	

DIVISIONAL PLAYOFF SERIES

			G	W	L	T	N	PCT	Standing
1981	**PHI**	**N**	5	2	3	0	0	.400	

LEAGUE CHAMPIONSHIP SERIES

			G	W	L	T	N	PCT	Standing
1980	**PHI**	**N**	5	3	2	0	0	.600	

WORLD SERIES

			G	W	L	T	N	PCT	Standing
1980	**PHI**	**N**	6	4	2	0	0	.667	

Mike Griffin

GRIFFIN, MICHAEL JOSEPH
B. Mar. 20, 1865, Utica, N. Y.
D. Apr. 10, 1908, Utica, N. Y.

			G	W	L	T	N	PCT	Standing
1898	**BKN**	**N**	4	1	3	0	0	.250	9 **9** 10

Sandy Griffin

GRIFFIN, TOBIAS CHARLES
B. July 19, 1858, Fayetteville, N. Y.
D. June 5, 1926, Fayetteville, N. Y.

			G	W	L	T	N	PCT	Standing
1891	**WAS**	**AA**	6	2	4	0	0	.333	9 **9**

Clark Griffith

GRIFFITH, CLARK CALVIN (General, Griff)
B. Nov. 20, 1869, Clear Creek, Mo.
D. Oct. 27, 1955, Washington, D. C.
Hall of Fame 1946.

			G	W	L	T	N	PCT	Standing
1901	**CHI**	**A**	137	83	53	1	0	.610	**1**
1902			138	74	60	4	0	.552	**4**
1903	**NY**	**A**	136	72	62	2	0	.537	**4**
1904			155	92	59	4	0	.609	**2**
1905			152	71	78	3	0	.477	**6**
1906			155	90	61	4	0	.596	**2**
1907			152	70	78	4	0	.473	**5**
1908			57	24	32	1	0	.429	**6** 8
1909	**CIN**	**N**	157	77	76	3	1	.503	**4**
1910			156	75	79	2	0	.487	**5**
1911			159	70	83	6	0	.458	**6**
1912	**WAS**	**A**	154	91	61	2	0	.599	**2**
1913			155	90	64	1	0	.584	**2**
1914			158	81	73	4	0	.526	**3**
1915			155	85	68	2	0	.556	**4**
1916			159	76	77	6	0	.497	**7**
1917			158	74	79	4	1	.484	**5**
1918			130	72	56	2	0	.563	**3**
1919			142	56	84	2	0	.400	**7**
1920			153	68	84	1	0	.447	**6**
20 yrs.			2918	1491	1367	58	2	.522	

Burleigh Grimes

GRIMES, BURLEIGH ARLAND (Ol' Stubblebeard)
B. Aug. 18, 1893, Emerald, Wis.
D. Dec. 6, 1985, Clear Lake, Wis.
Hall of Fame 1964.

			G	W	L	T	N	PCT	Standing
1937	**BKN**	**N**	155	62	91	2	0	.405	**6**
1938			151	69	80	2	0	.463	**7**
2 yrs.			306	131	171	4	0	.434	

Charlie Grimm

GRIMM, CHARLES JOHN (Jolly Cholly)
B. Aug. 28, 1898, St. Louis, Mo.
D. Nov. 15, 1983, Scottsdale, Ariz.

			G	W	L	T	N	PCT	Standing
1932	**CHI**	**N**	55	37	18	0	0	.673	2 **1**
1933			154	86	68	0	0	.558	**3**
1934			152	86	65	1	0	.570	**3**
1935			154	100	54	0	0	.649	**1**
1936			154	87	67	0	0	.565	**2**

Charlie Grimm *continued*

			G	W	L	T	N	PCT	Standing
1937			154	93	61	0	0	.604	**2**
1938			81	45	36	0	0	.556	**3** 1
1944			146	74	69	3	0	.517	8 **4**
1945			155	98	56	1	0	.636	**1**
1946			155	82	71	2	0	.536	**3**
1947			155	69	85	1	0	.448	**6**
1948			155	64	90	1	0	.416	**8**
1949			50	19	31	0	0	.380	**8** 8
1952	**BOS**	**N**	120	51	67	2	0	.432	6 **7**
1953	**MIL**	**N**	157	92	62	3	0	.597	**2**
1954			154	89	65	0	0	.578	**3**
1955			154	85	69	0	0	.552	**2**
1956			46	24	22	0	0	.522	**5** 2
1960	**CHI**	**N**	17	6	11	0	0	.353	**8** 7
19 yrs.			2368	1287	1067	14	0	.547	

WORLD SERIES

			G	W	L	T	N	PCT	Standing
1932	**CHI**	**N**	4	0	4	0	0	.000	
1935			6	2	4	0	0	.333	
1945			7	3	4	0	0	.429	
3 yrs.			17	5	12	0	0	.294	

Heinie Groh

GROH, HENRY KNIGHT
Brother of Lew Groh.
B. Sept. 18, 1889, Rochester, N. Y.
D. Aug. 22, 1968, Cincinnati, Ohio.

			G	W	L	T	N	PCT	Standing
1918	**CIN**	**N**	10	7	3	0	0	.700	4 **3**

Don Gutteridge

GUTTERIDGE, DONALD JOSEPH
B. June 19, 1912, Pittsburg, Kans.

			G	W	L	T	N	PCT	Standing
1969	**CHI**	**A**	145	60	85	0	0	.414	4 **5**
1970			136	49	87	0	0	.360	**6** 6
2 yrs.			281	109	172	0	0	.388	

Eddie Haas

HAAS, GEORGE EDWIN
B. May 26, 1935, Paducah, Ky.

			G	W	L	T	N	PCT	Standing
1985	**ATL**	**N**	121	50	71	0	0	.413	**5** 5

Stan Hack

HACK, STANLEY CAMFIELD (Smiling Stan)
B. Dec. 6, 1909, Sacramento, Calif.
D. Dec. 15, 1979, Dixon, Ill.

			G	W	L	T	N	PCT	Standing
1954	**CHI**	**N**	154	64	90	0	0	.416	**7**
1955			154	72	81	1	0	.471	**6**
1956			157	60	94	3	0	.390	**8**
1958	**STL**	**N**	10	3	7	0	0	.300	5 **5**
4 yrs.			475	199	272	4	0	.423	

Charlie Hackett

HACKETT, CHARLES M.
B. Holyoke, Mass.
D. Aug. 1, 1898, Holyoke, Mass.

			G	W	L	T	N	PCT	Standing
1884	**CLE**	**N**	113	35	77	1	0	.313	**7**
1885	**BKN**	**AA**	37	15	22	0	0	.405	**7** 5
2 yrs.			150	50	99	1	0	.336	

Bill Hallman

HALLMAN, WILLIAM WILSON
B. Mar. 31, 1867, Pittsburgh, Pa.
D. Sept. 11, 1920, Philadelphia, Pa.

			G	W	L	T	N	PCT	Standing
1897	**STL**	**N**	50	13	36	0	1	.265	12 **12** 12

Fred Haney

HANEY, FRED GIRARD (Pudge)
B. Apr. 25, 1898, Albuquerque, N. M.
D. Nov. 9, 1977, Beverly Hills, Calif.

			G	W	L	T	N	PCT	Standing
1939	**STL**	**A**	156	43	111	2	0	.279	**8**
1940			156	67	87	2	0	.435	**6**
1941			44	15	29	0	0	.341	**7** 6
1953	**PIT**	**N**	154	50	104	0	0	.325	**8**
1954			154	53	101	0	0	.344	**8**
1955			154	60	94	0	0	.390	**8**
1956	**MIL**	**N**	109	68	40	1	0	.630	5 **2**
1957			155	95	59	1	0	.617	**1**

Fred Haney *continued*

			G	W	L	T	N	PCT	Standing
1958			154	92	62	0	0	.597	**1**
1959			157	86	70	1	0	.551	**2**
10 yrs.			1393	629	757	7	0	.454	
WORLD SERIES									
1957	**MIL**	**N**	7	4	3	0	0	.571	
1958			7	3	4	0	0	.429	
2 yrs.			14	7	7	0	0	.500	

Ned Hanlon

HANLON, EDWARD HUGH
B. Aug. 22, 1857, Montville, Conn.
D. Apr. 14, 1937, Baltimore, Md.
Hall of Fame 1996.

			G	W	L	T	N	PCT	Standing
1889	**PIT**	**N**	46	26	18	2	0	.591	7 **5**
1890	**PIT**	**P**	131	60	68	0	3	.469	**6**
1891	**PIT**	**N**	78	31	47	0	0	.397	**8** 8
1892	**BAL**	**N**	56	17	39	0	0	.304	12 **12** (1st)
1892			77	26	46	5	0	.361	**10** (2nd)
1893			130	60	70	0	0	.462	**8**
1894			129	89	39	1	0	.695	**1**
1895			132	87	43	2	0	.669	**1**
1896			132	90	39	3	0	.698	**1**
1897			136	90	40	6	0	.692	**2**
1898			154	96	53	5	0	.644	**2**
1899	**BKN**	**N**	150	101	47	2	0	.682	**1**
1900			142	82	54	6	0	.603	**1**
1901			137	79	57	1	0	.581	**3**
1902			141	75	63	3	0	.543	**2**
1903			139	70	66	3	0	.515	**5**
1904			154	56	97	1	0	.366	**6**
1905			155	48	104	3	0	.316	**8**
1906	**CIN**	**N**	155	64	87	4	0	.424	**6**
1907			156	66	87	3	0	.431	**6**
19 yrs.			2530	1313	1164	50	3	.530	

Mel Harder

HARDER, MELVIN LeROY (Chief, Wimpy)
B. Oct. 15, 1909, Beemer, Neb.

			G	W	L	T	N	PCT	Standing
1961	**CLE**	**A**	1	1	0	0	0	1.000	5 **5**
1962			2	2	0	0	0	1.000	6 **6**
2 yrs.			3	3	0	0	0	1.000	

Mike Hargrove

HARGROVE, DUDLEY MICHAEL
(The Human Rain Delay)
B. Oct. 26, 1949, Perryton, Tex.

			G	W	L	T	N	PCT	Standing
1991	**CLE**	**A**	85	32	53	0	0	.376	7 **7**
1992			162	76	86	0	0	.469	**4**
1993			162	76	86	0	0	.469	**6**
1994			113	66	47	0	0	.584	**2**
1995			144	100	44	0	0	.694	**1**
5 yrs.			666	350	316	0	0	.526	
DIVISIONAL PLAYOFF SERIES									
1995	**CLE**	**A**	3	3	0	0	0	1.000	
LEAGUE CHAMPIONSHIP SERIES									
1995	**CLE**	**A**	6	4	2	0	0	.667	
WORLD SERIES									
1995	**CLE**	**A**	6	2	4	0	0	.333	

Toby Harrah

HARRAH, COLBERT DALE
B. Oct. 26, 1948, Sissonville, W. Va.

			G	W	L	T	N	PCT	Standing
1992	**TEX**	**A**	76	32	44	0	0	.421	3 **4**

Bud Harrelson

HARRELSON, DERREL McKINLEY
B. June 6, 1944, Niles, Calif.

			G	W	L	T	N	PCT	Standing
1990	**NY**	**N**	120	71	49	0	0	.592	4 **2**
1991			154	74	80	0	0	.481	**3** 5
2 yrs.			274	145	129	0	0	.529	

Bucky Harris

HARRIS, STANLEY RAYMOND
B. Nov. 8, 1896, Port Jervis, N. Y.
D. Nov. 8, 1977, Bethesda, Md.
Hall of Fame 1975.

			G	W	L	T	N	PCT	Standing
1924	**WAS**	**A**	156	92	62	2	0	.597	**1**
1925			152	96	55	1	0	.636	**1**
1926			152	81	69	2	0	.540	**4**
1927			157	85	69	3	0	.552	**3**
1928			155	75	79	1	0	.487	**4**
1929	**DET**	**A**	155	70	84	1	0	.455	**6**
1930			154	75	79	0	0	.487	**5**
1931			154	61	93	0	0	.396	**7**
1932			153	76	75	1	1	.503	**5**
1933			153	73	79	1	0	.480	**5** 5
1934	**BOS**	**A**	153	76	76	1	0	.500	**4**
1935	**WAS**	**A**	154	67	86	1	0	.438	**6**
1936			153	82	71	0	0	.536	**4**
1937			158	73	80	5	0	.477	**6**
1938			152	75	76	1	0	.497	**5**
1939			153	65	87	0	1	.428	**6**
1940			154	64	90	0	0	.416	**7**
1941			156	70	84	2	0	.455	**6**
1942			151	62	89	0	0	.411	**7**
1943	**PHI**	**N**	92	38	52	2	0	.422	**5** 7
1947	**NY**	**A**	155	97	57	1	0	.630	**1**
1948			154	94	60	0	0	.610	**3**
1950	**WAS**	**A**	155	67	87	1	0	.435	**5**
1951			154	62	92	0	0	.403	**7**
1952			157	78	76	3	0	.506	**5**
1953			152	76	76	0	0	.500	**5**
1954			155	66	88	1	0	.429	**6**
1955	**DET**	**A**	154	79	75	0	0	.513	**5**
1956			155	82	72	1	0	.532	**5**
29 yrs.			4408 **3rd**	2157 **4th**	2218 **2nd**	31	2	.493	
WORLD SERIES									
1924	**WAS**	**A**	7	4	3	0	0	.571	
1925			7	3	4	0	0	.429	
1947	**NY**	**A**	7	4	3	0	0	.571	
3 yrs.			21	11	10	0	0	.524 **7th**	

Lum Harris

HARRIS, CHALMER LUMAN
B. Jan. 17, 1915, New Castle, Ala.

			G	W	L	T	N	PCT	Standing
1961	**BAL**	**A**	27	17	10	0	0	.630	3 **3**
1964	**HOU**	**N**	13	5	8	0	0	.385	9 **9**
1965			162	65	97	0	0	.401	**9**
1968	**ATL**	**N**	163	81	81	1	0	.500	**5**
1969			162	93	69	0	0	.574	**1**
1970			162	76	86	0	0	.469	**5**
1971			162	82	80	0	0	.506	**3**
1972			105	47	57	1	0	.452	**5** 4
8 yrs.			956	466	488	2	0	.488	
LEAGUE CHAMPIONSHIP SERIES									
1969	**ATL**	**N**	3	0	3	0	0	.000	

Jim Hart

HART, JAMES ARISTOTLE
B. July 10, 1855, Fairview, Pa.
D. July 18, 1919, Chicago, Ill.

			G	W	L	T	N	PCT	Standing
1885	**LOU**	**AA**	112	53	59	0	0	.473	**5**
1886			138	66	70	2	0	.485	**4**
1889	**BOS**	**N**	133	83	45	5	0	.648	**2**
3 yrs.			383	202	174	7	0	.537	

John Hart

HART, JOHN HENRY
Born John Henry Reen.
B. July 21, 1948, Tampa, Fla.

			G	W	L	T	N	PCT	Standing
1989	**CLE**	**A**	19	8	11	0	0	.421	6 **6**

Gabby Hartnett

HARTNETT, CHARLES LEO
B. Dec. 20, 1900, Woonsocket, R. I.
D. Dec. 20, 1972, Park Ridge, Ill.
Hall of Fame 1955.

			G	W	L	T	N	PCT	Standing
1938	**CHI**	**N**	73	44	27	2	0	.620	3 **1**
1939			156	84	70	2	0	.545	**4**
1940			154	75	79	0	0	.487	**5**
3 yrs.			383	203	176	4	0	.536	
WORLD SERIES									
1938	**CHI**	**N**	4	0	4	0	0	.000	

Roy Hartsfield

HARTSFIELD, ROY THOMAS
B. Oct. 25, 1925, Chattahoochee, Ga.

			G	W	L	T	N	PCT	Standing
1977	**TOR**	**A**	161	54	107	0	0	.335	**7**
1978			161	59	102	0	0	.366	**7**
1979			162	53	109	0	0	.327	**7**
3 yrs.			484	166	318	0	0	.343	

Grady Hatton

HATTON, GRADY EDGEBERT
B. Oct. 7, 1922, Beaumont, Tex.

			G	W	L	T	N	PCT	Standing
1966	**HOU**	**N**	163	72	90	1	0	.444	**8**
1967			162	69	93	0	0	.426	**9**
1968			61	23	38	0	0	.377	**10** 10
3 yrs.			386	164	221	1	0	.426	

Guy Hecker

HECKER, GUY JACKSON (Blond Guy)
B. Apr. 3, 1856, Youngsville, Pa.
D. Dec. 3, 1938, Wooster, Ohio.

			G	W	L	T	N	PCT	Standing
1890	**PIT**	**N**	138	23	113	2	0	.169	**8**

Don Heffner

HEFFNER, DONALD HENRY (Jeep)
B. Feb. 8, 1911, Rouzerville, Pa.
D. Aug. 1, 1989, Pasadena, Calif.

			G	W	L	T	N	PCT	Standing
1966	**CIN**	**N**	83	37	46	0	0	.446	**8** 7

Louie Heilbroner

HEILBRONER, LOUIS WILBUR
B. July 4, 1861, Ft. Wayne, Ind.
D. Dec. 21, 1933, Ft. Wayne, Ind.

			G	W	L	T	N	PCT	Standing
1900	**STL**	**N**	50	23	25	2	0	.479	7 **5**

Tommy Helms

HELMS, TOMMY VANN
B. May 5, 1941, Charlotte, N. C.

			G	W	L	T	N	PCT	Standing
1988	**CIN**	**N**	27	12	15	0	0	.444	4 **4** 2
1989			37	16	21	0	0	.432	4 **5**
2 yrs.			64	28	36	0	0	.438	

Solly Hemus

HEMUS, SOLOMON JOSEPH
B. Apr. 17, 1923, Phoenix, Ariz.

			G	W	L	T	N	PCT	Standing
1959	**STL**	**N**	154	71	83	0	0	.461	**7**
1960			155	86	68	1	0	.558	**3**
1961			75	33	41	1	0	.446	**6** 5
3 yrs.			384	190	192	2	0	.497	

Bill Henderson

HENDERSON, WILLIAM C.
Deceased.

			G	W	L	T	N	PCT	Standing
1884	**BAL**	**U**	106	58	47	1	0	.552	**4**

Jack Hendricks

HENDRICKS, JOHN CHARLES
B. Apr. 9, 1875, Joliet, Ill.
D. May 13, 1943, Chicago, Ill.

			G	W	L	T	N	PCT	Standing
1918	**STL**	**N**	133	51	78	2	2	.395	**8**
1924	**CIN**	**N**	153	83	70	0	0	.542	**4**
1925			153	80	73	0	0	.523	**3**
1926			157	87	67	3	0	.565	**2**
1927			153	75	78	0	0	.490	**5**
1928			153	78	74	1	0	.513	**5**
1929			155	66	88	1	0	.429	**7**
7 yrs.			1057	520	528	7	2	.496	

Ed Hengle

HENGLE, EDWARD SIEGFRIED
Brother of Moxie Hengle.
B. Chicago, Ill.
D. Nov. 4, 1927, Norwich, England.

			G	W	L	T	N	PCT	Standing	
1884	**CHI**	**U**	74	34	39	1	0	.466	**6**	

Billy Herman

HERMAN, WILLIAM JENNINGS BRYAN
B. July 7, 1909, New Albany, Ind.
D. Sept. 5, 1992, West Palm Beach, Fla.
Hall of Fame 1975.

			G	W	L	T	N	PCT	Standing	
1947	**PIT**	**N**	155	61	92	2	0	.399	**8** 7	
1964	**BOS**	**A**	2	2	0	0	0	1.000	8 **8**	
1965			162	62	100	0	0	.383	**9**	
1966			146	64	82	0	0	.438	**10** 9	
4 yrs.			465	189	274	2	0	.408		

Buck Herzog

HERZOG, CHARLES LINCOLN
B. July 9, 1885, Baltimore, Md.
D. Sept. 4, 1953, Baltimore, Md.

			G	W	L	T	N	PCT	Standing	
1914	**CIN**	**N**	157	60	94	3	0	.390	**8**	
1915			160	71	83	6	0	.461	**7**	
1916			84	34	49	1	0	.410	**8** 7	
3 yrs.			401	165	226	10	0	.422		

Whitey Herzog

HERZOG, DORREL NORMAN ELVERT
(The White Rat)
B. Nov. 9, 1931, New Athens, Ill.

			G	W	L	T	N	PCT	Standing	
1973	**TEX**	**A**	138	47	91	0	0	.341	**6** 6	
1974	**CAL**	**A**	4	2	2	0	0	.500	6 **6** 6	
1975	**KC**	**A**	66	41	25	0	0	.621	2 **2**	
1976			162	90	72	0	0	.556	**1**	
1977			162	102	60	0	0	.630	**1**	
1978			162	92	70	0	0	.568	**1**	
1979			162	85	77	0	0	.525	**2**	
1980	**STL**	**N**	73	38	35	0	0	.521	6 **5** 4	
1981			51	30	20	1	0	.600	**2**	(1st)
1981			52	29	23	0	0	.558	**2**	(2nd)
1982			162	92	70	0	0	.568	**1**	
1983			162	79	83	0	0	.488	**4**	
1984			162	84	78	0	0	.519	**3**	
1985			162	101	61	0	0	.623	**1**	
1986			161	79	82	0	0	.491	**3**	
1987			162	95	67	0	0	.586	**1**	
1988			162	76	86	0	0	.469	**5**	
1989			162	86	76	0	0	.531	**3**	
1990			80	33	47	0	0	.412	**6** 6	
18 yrs.			2407	1281	1125	1	0	.532		

LEAGUE CHAMPIONSHIP SERIES

			G	W	L	T	N	PCT	Standing	
1976	**KC**	**A**	5	2	3	0	0	.400		
1977			5	2	3	0	0	.400		
1978			4	1	3	0	0	.250		
1982	**STL**	**N**	3	3	0	0	0	1.000		
1985			6	4	2	0	0	.667		
1987			7	4	3	0	0	.571		
6 yrs.			30	16	14	0	0	.533		
			2nd	**3rd**	**1st**			**6th**		

WORLD SERIES

			G	W	L	T	N	PCT	Standing	
1982	**STL**	**N**	7	4	3	0	0	.571		
1985			7	3	4	0	0	.429		
1987			7	3	4	0	0	.429		
3 yrs.			21	10	11	0	0	.476		

Walter Hewett

HEWETT, WALTER F.
B. 1861, Washington, D. C.
D. Oct. 7, 1944, Washington, D. C.

			G	W	L	T	N	PCT	Standing	
1888	**WAS**	**N**	40	10	29	1	0	.256	**8** 8	

Pinky Higgins

HIGGINS, MICHAEL FRANKLIN
B. May 27, 1909, Red Oak, Tex.
D. Mar. 21, 1969, Dallas, Tex.

			G	W	L	T	N	PCT	Standing	
1955	**BOS**	**A**	154	84	70	0	0	.545	**4**	
1956			155	84	70	1	0	.545	**4**	
1957			154	82	72	0	0	.532	**3**	

Pinky Higgins *continued*

			G	W	L	T	N	PCT	Standing	
1958			155	79	75	1	0	.513	**3**	
1959			73	31	42	0	0	.425	**8** 5	
1960			105	48	57	0	0	.457	8 **7**	
1961			163	76	86	1	0	.469	**6**	
1962			160	76	84	0	0	.475	**8**	
8 yrs.			1119	560	556	3	0	.502		

Vedie Himsl

HIMSL, AVITUS BERNARD
B. Apr. 2, 1917, Plevna, Mont.

			G	W	L	T	N	PCT	Standing	
1961	**CHI**	**N**	11	5	6	0	0	.455	**6** 7	
1961			17	5	12	0	0	.294	7 **7** 7	
1961			4	0	3	1	0	.000	7 **7** 7	

Billy Hitchcock

HITCHCOCK, WILLIAM CLYDE
Brother of Jim Hitchcock.
B. July 31, 1916, Inverness, Ala.

			G	W	L	T	N	PCT	Standing	
1960	**DET**	**A**	1	1	0	0	0	1.000	6 **6** 6	
1962	**BAL**	**A**	162	77	85	0	0	.475	**7**	
1963			162	86	76	0	0	.531	**4**	
1966	**ATL**	**N**	51	33	18	0	0	.647	5 **5**	
1967			159	77	82	0	0	.484	**7** 7	
5 yrs.			535	274	261	0	0	.512		

Butch Hobson

HOBSON, CLELL LAVERN, JR.
B. Aug. 17, 1951, Tuscaloosa, Ala.

			G	W	L	T	N	PCT	Standing	
1992	**BOS**	**A**	162	73	89	0	0	.451	**7**	
1993			162	80	82	0	0	.494	**5**	
1994			115	54	61	0	0	.470	**4**	
3 yrs.			439	207	232	0	0	.472		

Gil Hodges

HODGES, GILBERT RAYMOND
Born Gilbert Ray Hodge.
B. Apr. 4, 1924, Princeton, Ind.
D. Apr. 2, 1972, West Palm Beach, Fla.

			G	W	L	T	N	PCT	Standing	
1963	**WAS**	**A**	121	42	79	0	0	.347	10 **10**	
1964			162	62	100	0	0	.383	**9**	
1965			162	70	92	0	0	.432	**8**	
1966			159	71	88	0	0	.447	**8**	
1967			161	76	85	0	0	.472	**6**	
1968	**NY**	**N**	163	73	89	1	0	.451	**9**	
1969			162	100	62	0	0	.617	**1**	
1970			162	83	79	0	0	.512	**3**	
1971			162	83	79	0	0	.512	**3**	
9 yrs.			1414	660	753	1	0	.467		

LEAGUE CHAMPIONSHIP SERIES

			G	W	L	T	N	PCT	Standing	
1969	**NY**	**N**	3	3	0	0	0	1.000		

WORLD SERIES

			G	W	L	T	N	PCT	Standing	
1969	**NY**	**N**	5	4	1	0	0	.800		

Fred Hoey

HOEY, FREDERICK CHAMBERLAIN
B. 1866, New York, N. Y.
D. Dec. 7, 1933, Paris, France.

			G	W	L	T	N	PCT	Standing	
1899	**NY**	**N**	87	31	55	1	0	.360	9 **10**	

Bill Holbert

HOLBERT, WILLIAM HENRY
B. Mar. 14, 1855, Baltimore, Md.
D. Mar. 20, 1935, Laurel, Md.

			G	W	L	T	N	PCT	Standing	
1879	**SYR**	**N**	1	0	1	0	0	.000	6 **6** 7	

Holly Hollingshead

HOLLINGSHEAD, JOHN SAMUEL
B. Jan. 17, 1853, Washington, D. C.
D. Oct. 6, 1926, Washington, D. C.

			G	W	L	T	N	PCT	Standing	
1884	**WAS**	**AA**	62	12	50	0	0	.194	**13** 13	

Tommy Holmes

HOLMES, THOMAS FRANCIS (Kelly)
B. Mar. 29, 1917, Brooklyn, N. Y.

			G	W	L	T	N	PCT	Standing	
1951	**BOS**	**N**	95	48	47	0	0	.505	5 **4**	
1952			35	13	22	0	0	.371	**6** 7	
2 yrs.			130	61	69	0	0	.469		

Rogers Hornsby

HORNSBY, ROGERS (Rajah)
B. Apr. 27, 1896, Winters, Tex.
D. Jan. 5, 1963, Chicago, Ill.
Hall of Fame 1942.

			G	W	L	T	N	PCT	Standing	
1925	**STL**	**N**	115	64	51	0	0	.557	8 **4**	
1926			156	89	65	2	0	.578	**1**	
1927	**NY**	**N**	33	22	10	1	0	.688	4 **3**	
1928	**BOS**	**N**	122	39	83	0	0	.320	7 **7**	
1930	**CHI**	**N**	4	4	0	0	0	1.000	2 **2**	
1931			156	84	70	2	0	.545	**3**	
1932			99	53	46	0	0	.535	**2** 1	
1933	**STL**	**A**	54	19	33	2	0	.365	8 **8**	
1934			154	67	85	2	0	.441	**6**	
1935			155	65	87	3	0	.428	**7**	
1936			155	57	95	3	0	.375	**7**	
1937			78	25	52	1	0	.325	**7** 8	
1952			51	22	29	0	0	.431	**8** 7	
1952	**CIN**	**N**	51	27	24	0	0	.529	7 **6**	
1953			147	64	82	1	0	.438	**6** 6	
14 yrs.			1530	701	812	17	0	.463		

WORLD SERIES

			G	W	L	T	N	PCT	Standing	
1926	**STL**	**N**	7	4	3	0	0	.571		

Ralph Houk

HOUK, RALPH GEORGE (Major)
B. Aug. 9, 1919, Lawrence, Kans.

			G	W	L	T	N	PCT	Standing	
1961	**NY**	**A**	163	109	53	1	0	.673	**1**	
1962			162	96	66	0	0	.593	**1**	
1963			161	104	57	0	0	.646	**1**	
1966			140	66	73	1	0	.475	10 **10**	
1967			163	72	90	1	0	.444	**9**	
1968			164	83	79	2	0	.512	**5**	
1969			162	80	81	1	0	.497	**5**	
1970			163	93	69	1	0	.574	**2**	
1971			162	82	80	0	0	.506	**4**	
1972			155	79	76	0	0	.510	**4**	
1973			162	80	82	0	0	.494	**4**	
1974	**DET**	**A**	162	72	90	0	0	.444	**6**	
1975			159	57	102	0	0	.358	**6**	
1976			161	74	87	0	0	.460	**5**	
1977			162	74	88	0	0	.457	**4**	
1978			162	86	76	0	0	.531	**5**	
1981	**BOS**	**A**	56	30	26	0	0	.536	**5**	(1st)
1981			52	29	23	0	0	.558	**2**	(2nd)
1982			162	89	73	0	0	.549	**3**	
1983			162	78	84	0	0	.481	**6**	
1984			162	86	76	0	0	.531	**4**	
20 yrs.			3157	1619	1531	7	0	.514		

WORLD SERIES

			G	W	L	T	N	PCT	Standing	
1961	**NY**	**A**	5	4	1	0	0	.800		
1962			7	4	3	0	0	.571		
1963			4	0	4	0	0	.000		
3 yrs.			16	8	8	0	0	.500		
								9th		

Frank Howard

HOWARD, FRANK OLIVER (Hondo,
The Capitol Punisher)
B. Aug. 8, 1936, Columbus, Ohio

			G	W	L	T	N	PCT	Standing	
1981	**SD**	**N**	56	23	33	0	0	.411	**6**	(1st)
1981			54	18	36	0	0	.333	**6**	(2nd)
1983	**NY**	**N**	116	52	64	0	0	.448	6 **6**	
2 yrs.			226	93	133	0	0	.412		

Art Howe

HOWE, ARTHUR HENRY, JR.
B. Dec. 15, 1946, Pittsburgh, Pa.

			G	W	L	T	N	PCT	Standing	
1989	**HOU**	**N**	162	86	76	0	0	.531	**3**	
1990			162	75	87	0	0	.463	**4**	
1991			162	65	97	0	0	.401	**6**	
1992			162	81	81	0	0	.500	**4**	
1993			162	85	77	0	0	.525	**3**	
5 yrs.			810	392	418	0	0	.484		

Dan Howley

HOWLEY, DANIEL PHILIP (Dapper Dan)
B. Oct. 16, 1885, Weymouth, Mass.
D. Mar. 10, 1944, Weymouth, Mass.

			G	W	L	T	N	PCT	Standing
1927	STL	A	155	59	94	2	0	.386	**7**
1928			154	82	72	0	0	.532	**3**
1929			154	79	73	2	0	.520	**4**
1930	CIN	N	154	59	95	0	0	.383	**7**
1931			154	58	96	0	0	.377	**8**
1932			155	60	94	1	0	.390	**8**
6 yrs.			926	397	524	5	0	.431	

Dick Howser

HOWSER, RICHARD DALTON
B. May 14, 1936, Miami, Fla.
D. June 17, 1987, Kansas City, Mo.

			G	W	L	T	N	PCT	Standing
1978	NY	A	1	0	1	0	0	.000	3 **3** 1
1980			162	103	59	0	0	.636	**1**
1981	KC	A	33	20	13	0	0	.606	2 **1** (2nd)
1982			162	90	72	0	0	.556	**2**
1983			163	79	83	1	0	.488	**2**
1984			162	84	78	0	0	.519	**1**
1985			162	91	71	0	0	.562	**1**
1986			88	40	48	0	0	.455	**4** 3
8 yrs.			933	507	425	1	0	.544	

DIVISIONAL PLAYOFF SERIES

			G	W	L	T	N	PCT
1981	KC	A	3	0	3	0	0	.000

LEAGUE CHAMPIONSHIP SERIES

			G	W	L	T	N	PCT
1980	NY	A	3	0	3	0	0	.000
1984	KC	A	3	0	3	0	0	.000
1985			7	4	3	0	0	.571
3 yrs.			13	4	9	0	0	.308

WORLD SERIES

			G	W	L	T	N	PCT
1985	KC	A	7	4	3	0	0	.571

George Huff

HUFF, GEORGE A.
B. June 11, 1872, Champaign, Ill.
D. Oct. 1, 1936, Champaign, Ill.

			G	W	L	T	N	PCT	Standing
1907	BOS	A	8	2	6	0	0	.250	4 **6** 7

Miller Huggins

HUGGINS, MILLER JAMES (Hug, The Mighty Mite)
B. Mar. 27, 1879, Cincinnati, Ohio
D. Sept. 25, 1929, New York, N. Y.
Hall of Fame 1964.

			G	W	L	T	N	PCT	Standing
1913	STL	N	153	51	99	3	0	.340	**8**
1914			157	81	72	4	0	.529	**3**
1915			157	72	81	4	0	.471	**6**
1916			153	60	93	0	0	.392	**7**
1917			154	82	70	2	0	.539	**3**
1918	NY	A	126	60	63	3	0	.488	**4**
1919			141	80	59	2	0	.576	**3**
1920			154	95	59	0	0	.617	**3**
1921			153	98	55	0	0	.641	**1**
1922			154	94	60	0	0	.610	**1**
1923			152	98	54	0	0	.645	**1**
1924			153	89	63	1	0	.586	**2**
1925			156	69	85	2	0	.448	**7**
1926			155	91	63	1	0	.591	**1**
1927			155	110	44	1	0	.714	**1**
1928			154	101	53	0	0	.656	**1**
1929			143	82	61	0	0	.573	**2** 2
17 yrs.			2570	1413	1134	23	0	.555	

WORLD SERIES

			G	W	L	T	N	PCT
1921	NY	A	8	3	5	0	0	.375
1922			5	0	4	1	0	.000
1923			6	4	2	0	0	.667
1926			7	3	4	0	0	.429
1927			4	4	0	0	0	1.000
1928			4	4	0	0	0	1.000
6 yrs.			34	18	15	1	0	.545
			6th	**6th**	**5th**			**6th**

Billy Hunter

HUNTER, GORDON WILLIAM
B. June 4, 1928, Punxsutawney, Pa.

			G	W	L	T	N	PCT	Standing
1977	TEX	A	93	60	33	0	0	.645	4 **2**
1978			161	86	75	0	0	.534	**2** 2
2 yrs.			254	146	108	0	0	.575	

Tim Hurst

HURST, TIMOTHY CARROLL
B. June 30, 1865, Ashland, Pa.
D. June 4, 1915, Pottsville, Pa.

			G	W	L	T	N	PCT	Standing
1898	STL	N	154	39	111	4	0	.260	**12**

Fred Hutchinson

HUTCHINSON, FREDERICK CHARLES
B. Aug. 12, 1919, Seattle, Wash.
D. Nov. 12, 1964, Bradenton, Fla.

			G	W	L	T	N	PCT	Standing
1952	DET	A	83	27	55	1	0	.329	8 **8**
1953			158	60	94	4	0	.390	**6**
1954			155	68	86	1	0	.442	**5**
1956	STL	N	156	76	78	2	0	.494	**4**
1957			154	87	67	0	0	.565	**2**
1958			144	69	75	0	0	.479	**5** 5
1959	CIN	N	74	39	35	0	0	.527	7 **5**
1960			154	67	87	0	0	.435	**6**
1961			154	93	61	0	0	.604	**1**
1962			162	98	64	0	0	.605	**3**
1963			162	86	76	0	0	.531	**5**
1964			100	54	45	1	0	.545	**3** 2
1964			10	6	4	0	0	.600	4 **3** 2
12 yrs.			1666	830	827	9	0	.501	

WORLD SERIES

			G	W	L	T	N	PCT
1961	CIN	N	5	1	4	0	0	.200

Arthur Irwin

IRWIN, ARTHUR ALBERT
Brother of John Irwin.
B. Feb. 14, 1858, Toronto, Ont., Canada
D. July 16, 1921, Atlantic Ocean.

			G	W	L	T	N	PCT	Standing
1889	WAS	N	76	28	45	3	0	.384	8 **8**
1891	BOS	AA	139	93	42	4	0	.689	**1**
1892	WAS	N	74	35	39	0	0	.473	11 **7** (1st)
1892			34	11	21	2	0	.344	**11** 12 (2nd)
1894	PHI	N	132	71	57	1	3	.555	**4**
1895			133	78	53	2	0	.595	**3**
1896	NY	N	90	36	53	1	0	.404	**10** 7
1898	WAS	N	30	10	19	1	0	.345	11 **11**
1899			155	54	98	3	0	.355	**11**
8 yrs.			863	416	427	17	3	.493	

Hughie Jennings

JENNINGS, HUGH AMBROSE (Hustling Hughie)
B. Apr. 2, 1869, Pittston, Pa.
D. Feb. 1, 1928, Scranton, Pa.
Hall of Fame 1945.

			G	W	L	T	N	PCT	Standing
1907	DET	A	153	92	58	3	0	.613	**1**
1908			154	90	63	1	0	.588	**1**
1909			158	98	54	6	0	.645	**1**
1910			155	86	68	1	0	.558	**3**
1911			154	89	65	0	0	.578	**2**
1912			154	69	84	1	0	.451	**6**
1913			153	66	87	0	0	.431	**6**
1914			157	80	73	4	0	.523	**4**
1915			156	100	54	2	0	.649	**2**
1916			155	87	67	1	0	.565	**3**
1917			155	78	75	1	1	.510	**4**
1918			128	55	71	2	0	.437	**7**
1919			140	80	60	0	0	.571	**4**
1920			155	61	93	1	0	.396	**7**
1924	NY	N	44	32	12	0	0	.727	3 **1** 1
1925			32	21	11	0	0	.656	1 **1** 2
16 yrs.			2203	1184	995	23	1	.543	

WORLD SERIES

			G	W	L	T	N	PCT
1907	DET	A	4	0	4	0	0	.000
1908			5	1	4	0	0	.200
1909			7	3	4	0	0	.429
3 yrs.			16	4	12	0	0	.250

Darrell Johnson

JOHNSON, DARRELL DEAN
B. Aug. 25, 1928, Horace, Neb.

			G	W	L	T	N	PCT	Standing
1974	BOS	A	162	84	78	0	0	.519	**3**
1975			160	95	65	0	0	.594	**1**
1976			86	41	45	0	0	.477	**3** 3
1977	SEA	A	162	64	98	0	0	.395	**6**
1978			160	56	104	0	0	.350	**7**
1979			162	67	95	0	0	.414	**6**
1980			105	39	65	1	0	.375	**7** 7
1982	TEX	A	66	26	40	0	0	.394	6 **6**
8 yrs.			1063	472	590	1	0	.444	

LEAGUE CHAMPIONSHIP SERIES

			G	W	L	T	N	PCT
1975	BOS	A	3	3	0	0	0	1.000

WORLD SERIES

			G	W	L	T	N	PCT
1975	BOS	A	7	3	4	0	0	.429

Davey Johnson

JOHNSON, DAVID ALLEN
B. Jan. 30, 1943, Orlando, Fla.

			G	W	L	T	N	PCT	Standing
1984	NY	N	162	90	72	0	0	.556	**2**
1985			162	98	64	0	0	.605	**2**
1986			162	108	54	0	0	.667	**1**
1987			162	92	70	0	0	.568	**2**
1988			160	100	60	0	0	.625	**1**
1989			162	87	75	0	0	.537	**2**
1990			42	20	22	0	0	.476	**4** 2
1993	CIN	N	118	53	65	0	0	.449	5 **5**
1994			115	66	48	1	0	.579	**1**
1995			144	85	59	0	0	.590	**1**
10 yrs.			1389	799	589	1	0	.576	

DIVISIONAL PLAYOFF SERIES

			G	W	L	T	N	PCT
1995	CIN	N	3	3	0	0	0	1.000

LEAGUE CHAMPIONSHIP SERIES

			G	W	L	T	N	PCT
1986	NY	N	6	4	2	0	0	.667
1988			7	3	4	0	0	.429
1995	CIN	N	4	0	4	0	0	.000
3 yrs.			17	7	10	0	0	.412
					7th			

WORLD SERIES

			G	W	L	T	N	PCT
1986	NY	N	7	4	3	0	0	.571

Roy Johnson

JOHNSON, ROY J. (Hardrock)
B. Oct. 1, 1895, Madill, Okla.
D. Jan. 10, 1986, Scottsdale, Ariz.

			G	W	L	T	N	PCT	Standing
1944	CHI	N	1	0	1	0	0	.000	8 **8** 4

Walter Johnson

JOHNSON, WALTER PERRY (Barney, The Big Train)
B. Nov. 6, 1887, Humboldt, Kans.
D. Dec. 10, 1946, Washington, D. C.
Hall of Fame 1936.

			G	W	L	T	N	PCT	Standing
1929	WAS	A	153	71	81	1	0	.467	**5**
1930			154	94	60	0	0	.610	**2**
1931			156	92	62	2	0	.597	**3**
1932			154	93	61	0	0	.604	**3**
1933	CLE	A	99	48	51	0	0	.485	5 **4**
1934			154	85	69	0	0	.552	**3**
1935			96	46	48	2	0	.489	**5** 3
7 yrs.			966	529	432	5	0	.550	

Fielder Jones

JONES, FIELDER ALLISON
B. Aug. 13, 1871, Shinglehouse, Pa.
D. Mar. 13, 1934, Portland, Ore.

			G	W	L	T	N	PCT	Standing
1904	CHI	A	114	66	47	1	0	.584	4 **3**
1905			158	92	60	6	0	.605	**2**
1906			154	93	58	3	0	.616	**1**
1907			157	87	64	6	0	.576	**3**
1908			156	88	64	4	0	.579	**3**
1914	STL	F	40	12	26	2	0	.316	7 **8**
1915			159	87	67	5	0	.565	**2**
1916	STL	A	158	79	75	4	0	.513	**5**

Fielder Jones *continued*

			G	W	L	T	N	PCT	Standing
1917			155	57	97	1	0	.370	**7**
1918			46	22	24	0	0	.478	**5** 5
10 yrs.			1297	683	582	32	0	.540	
WORLD SERIES									
1906	CHI	A	6	4	2	0	0	.667	

Eddie Joost

JOOST, EDWIN DAVID
B. June 5, 1916, San Francisco, Calif.

			G	W	L	T	N	PCT	Standing
1954	PHI	A	156	51	103	2	0	.331	**8**

Mike Jorgensen

JORGENSEN, MICHAEL
B. Aug. 16, 1948, Passaic, N. J.

			G	W	L	T	N	PCT	Standing
1995	STL	N	96	42	54	0	0	.438	4 **4**

Bill Joyce

JOYCE, WILLIAM MICHAEL (Scrappy Bill)
B. Sept. 21, 1865, St. Louis, Mo.
D. May 8, 1941, St. Louis, Mo.

			G	W	L	T	N	PCT	Standing
1896	NY	N	43	28	14	1	0	.667	10 **7**
1897			138	83	48	6	1	.634	**3**
1898			43	22	21	0	0	.512	**6** 7
1898			92	46	39	7	0	.541	7 **7**
3 yrs.			316	179	122	14	1	.595	

Bill Jurges

JURGES, WILLIAM FREDERICK
B. May 9, 1908, Bronx, N. Y.

			G	W	L	T	N	PCT	Standing
1959	BOS	A	80	44	36	0	0	.550	8 **5**
1960			42	15	27	0	0	.357	**8** 7
2 yrs.			122	59	63	0	0	.484	

Eddie Kasko

KASKO, EDWARD MICHAEL
B. June 27, 1932, Linden, N. J.

			G	W	L	T	N	PCT	Standing
1970	BOS	A	162	87	75	0	0	.537	**3**
1971			162	85	77	0	0	.525	**3**
1972			155	85	70	0	0	.548	**2**
1973			161	88	73	0	0	.547	**2** 2
4 yrs.			640	345	295	0	0	.539	

Johnny Keane

KEANE, JOHN JOSEPH
B. Nov. 3, 1911, St. Louis, Mo.
D. Jan. 6, 1967, Houston, Tex.

			G	W	L	T	N	PCT	Standing
1961	STL	N	80	47	33	0	0	.587	6 **5**
1962			163	84	78	1	0	.519	**6**
1963			162	93	69	0	0	.574	**2**
1964			162	93	69	0	0	.574	**1**
1965	NY	A	162	77	85	0	0	.475	**6**
1966			20	4	16	0	0	.200	**10** 10
6 yrs.			749	398	350	1	0	.532	
WORLD SERIES									
1964	STL	N	7	4	3	0	0	.571	

Joe Kelley

KELLEY, JOSEPH JAMES
B. Dec. 9, 1871, Cambridge, Mass.
D. Aug. 14, 1943, Baltimore, Md.
Hall of Fame 1971.

			G	W	L	T	N	PCT	Standing
1902	CIN	N	60	34	26	0	0	.567	5 **4**
1903			141	74	65	2	0	.532	**4**
1904			157	88	65	4	0	.575	**3**
1905			155	79	74	2	0	.516	**5**
1908	BOS	N	156	63	91	2	0	.409	**6**
5 yrs.			669	338	321	10	0	.513	

Honest John Kelly

KELLY, JOHN O.
B. Oct. 31, 1856, New York, N. Y.
D. Mar. 27, 1926, Malba, N. Y.

			G	W	L	T	N	PCT	Standing
1887	LOU	AA	139	76	60	3	0	.559	**4**
1888			39	10	29	0	0	.256	**8** 7
2 yrs.			178	86	89	3	0	.491	

King Kelly

KELLY, MICHAEL JOSEPH
B. Dec. 31, 1857, Troy, N. Y.
D. Nov. 8, 1894, Boston, Mass.
Hall of Fame 1945.

			G	W	L	T	N	PCT	Standing
1887	BOS	N	94	49	43	2	0	.533	**5** 5
1890	BOS	P	133	81	48	1	3	.628	**1**
1891	CIN	AA	102	43	57	1	1	.430	**7**
3 yrs.			329	173	148	4	4	.539	

Tom Kelly

KELLY, JAY THOMAS
B. Aug. 15, 1950, Graceville, Minn.

			G	W	L	T	N	PCT	Standing
1986	MIN	A	23	12	11	0	0	.522	7 **6**
1987			162	85	77	0	0	.525	**1**
1988			162	91	71	0	0	.562	**2**
1989			162	80	82	0	0	.494	**5**
1990			162	74	88	0	0	.457	**7**
1991			162	95	67	0	0	.586	**1**
1992			162	90	72	0	0	.556	**2**
1993			162	71	91	0	0	.438	**5**
1994			113	53	60	0	0	.469	**4**
1995			144	56	88	0	0	.389	**5**
10 yrs.			1414	707	707	0	0	.500	
LEAGUE CHAMPIONSHIP SERIES									
1987	MIN	A	5	4	1	0	0	.800	
1991			5	4	1	0	0	.800	
2 yrs.			10	8 **9th**	2	0	0	.800	
WORLD SERIES									
1987	MIN	A	7	4	3	0	0	.571	
1991			7	4	3	0	0	.571	
2 yrs.			14	8	6	0	0	.571	

Bob Kennedy

KENNEDY, ROBERT DANIEL
Father of Terry Kennedy.
B. Aug. 18, 1920, Chicago, Ill.

			G	W	L	T	N	PCT	Standing
1963	CHI	N	162	82	80	0	0	.506	**7**
1964			162	76	86	0	0	.469	**8**
1965			58	24	32	2	0	.429	**9** 8
1968	OAK	A	163	82	80	1	0	.506	**6**
4 yrs.			545	264	278	3	0	.487	

Jim Kennedy

KENNEDY, JAMES C.
B. 1867, New York, N. Y.
D. Apr. 20, 1904, Brighton Beach, N. Y.

			G	W	L	T	N	PCT	Standing
1890	BKN	AA	100	26	72	1	1	.265	**9**

Kevin Kennedy

KENNEDY, KEVIN CURTIS
B. May 26, 1954, Los Angeles, Calif.

			G	W	L	T	N	PCT	Standing
1993	TEX	A	162	86	76	0	0	.531	**2**
1994			114	52	62	0	0	.456	**1**
1995	BOS	A	144	86	58	0	0	.597	**1**
3 yrs.			420	224	196	0	0	.533	
DIVISIONAL PLAYOFF SERIES									
1995	BOS	A	3	0	3	0	0	.000	

John Kerins

KERINS, JOHN NELSON
B. July 15, 1858, Indianapolis, Ind.
D. Sept. 8, 1919, Louisville, Ky.

			G	W	L	T	N	PCT	Standing
1888	LOU	AA	7	3	4	0	0	.429	8 **8** 7

Don Kessinger

KESSINGER, DONALD EULON
Father of Keith Kessinger.
B. July 17, 1942, Forrest City, Ark.

			G	W	L	T	N	PCT	Standing
1979	CHI	A	106	46	60	0	0	.434	**5** 5

Bill Killefer

KILLEFER, WILLIAM LAVIER (Reindeer Bill)
Brother of Red Killefer.
B. Oct. 10, 1887, Bloomingdale, Mich.
D. July 3, 1960, Elsmere, Del.

			G	W	L	T	N	PCT	Standing
1921	CHI	N	57	23	34	0	0	.404	6 **7**
1922			156	80	74	2	0	.519	**5**

Bill Killefer *continued*

			G	W	L	T	N	PCT	Standing
1923			154	83	71	0	0	.539	**4**
1924			154	81	72	0	1	.529	**5**
1925			75	33	42	0	0	.440	**7** 8
1930	STL	A	154	64	90	0	0	.416	**6**
1931			154	63	91	0	0	.409	**5**
1932			154	63	91	0	0	.409	**6**
1933			91	34	57	0	0	.374	**8** 8
9 yrs.			1149	524	622	2	1	.457	

Clyde King

KING, CLYDE EDWARD
B. May 23, 1925, Goldsboro, N. C.

			G	W	L	T	N	PCT	Standing
1969	SF	N	162	90	72	0	0	.556	**2**
1970			42	19	23	0	0	.452	**4** 3
1974	ATL	N	64	38	25	1	0	.603	4 **3**
1975			134	58	76	0	0	.433	**5** 5
1982	NY	A	62	29	33	0	0	.468	5 **5**
5 yrs.			464	234	229	1	0	.505	

Mal Kittridge

KITTRIDGE, MALACHI JEDDIDAH
B. Oct. 12, 1869, Clinton, Mass.
D. June 23, 1928, Gary, Ind.

			G	W	L	T	N	PCT	Standing
1904	WAS	A	18	1	16	1	0	.059	**8** 8

Lou Klein

KLEIN, LOUIS FRANK
B. Oct. 22, 1918, New Orleans, La.
D. June 20, 1976, Metairie, La.

			G	W	L	T	N	PCT	Standing
1961	CHI	N	11	5	6	0	0	.455	7 **7** 7
1962			30	12	18	0	0	.400	9 **9** 9
1965			106	48	58	0	0	.453	9 **8**
3 yrs.			147	65	82	0	0	.442	

Johnny Kling

KLING, JOHN (Noisy)
Brother of Bill Kling.
B. Feb. 25, 1875, Kansas City, Mo.
D. Jan. 31, 1947, Kansas City, Mo.

			G	W	L	T	N	PCT	Standing
1912	BOS	N	155	52	101	2	0	.340	**8**

Otto Knabe

KNABE, FRANZ OTTO (Dutch)
B. June 12, 1884, Carrick, Pa.
D. May 17, 1961, Philadelphia, Pa.

			G	W	L	T	N	PCT	Standing
1914	BAL	F	160	84	70	6	0	.545	**3**
1915			155	47	107	0	1	.305	**8**
2 yrs.			315	131	177	6	1	.425	

Lon Knight

KNIGHT, ALONZO P.
B. June 16, 1853, Philadelphia, Pa.
D. Apr. 23, 1932, Philadelphia, Pa.

			G	W	L	T	N	PCT	Standing
1883	PHI	AA	98	66	32	0	0	.673	**1**
1884			108	61	46	1	0	.570	**7**
2 yrs.			206	127	78	1	0	.620	

Bobby Knoop

KNOOP, ROBERT FRANK
B. Oct. 18, 1938, Sioux City, Iowa.

			G	W	L	T	N	PCT	Standing
1994	CAL	A	2	1	1	0	0	.500	3 **2** 4

Jack Krol

KROL, JOHN THOMAS
B. July 5, 1936, Chicago, Ill.
D. May 30, 1994, Winston-Salem, N. C.

			G	W	L	T	N	PCT	Standing
1978	STL	N	2	1	1	0	0	.500	6 **6** 5
1980			1	0	1	0	0	.000	6 **6** 4
2 yrs.			3	1	2	0	0	.333	

Karl Kuehl

KUEHL, KARL OTTO
B. Sept. 5, 1937, Monterey Park, Calif.

			G	W	L	T	N	PCT	Standing
1976	MON	N	128	43	85	0	0	.336	**6** 6

Harvey Kuenn
KUENN, HARVEY EDWARD
B. Dec. 4, 1930, West Allis, Wis.
D. Feb. 28, 1988, Peoria, Ariz.

			G	W	L	T	N	PCT	Standing
1975	MIL	A	1	1	0	0	0	1.000	5 5
1982			116	72	43	1	0	.626	5 1
1983			162	87	75	0	0	.537	5
3 yrs.			279	160	118	1	0	.576	

LEAGUE CHAMPIONSHIP SERIES

			G	W	L	T	N	PCT
1982	MIL	A	5	3	2	0	0	.600

WORLD SERIES

			G	W	L	T	N	PCT
1982	MIL	A	7	3	4	0	0	.429

Joe Kuhel
KUHEL, JOSEPH ANTHONY
B. June 25, 1906, Cleveland, Ohio
D. Feb. 26, 1984, Kansas City, Kans.

			G	W	L	T	N	PCT	Standing
1948	WAS	A	154	56	97	1	0	.366	7
1949			154	50	104	0	0	.325	8
2 yrs.			308	106	201	1	0	.345	

Marcel Lachemann
LACHEMANN, MARCEL ERNEST
Brother of Rene Lachemann.
B. June 13, 1941, Los Angeles, Calif.

			G	W	L	T	N	PCT	Standing
1994	CAL	A	74	30	44	0	0	.405	2 4
1995			145	78	67	0	0	.538	2
2 yrs.			219	108	111	0	0	.493	

Rene Lachemann
LACHEMANN, RENE GEORGE
Brother of Marcel Lachemann.
B. May 4, 1945, Los Angeles, Calif.

			G	W	L	T	N	PCT	Standing
1981	SEA	A	33	15	18	0	0	.455	7 6 (1st)
1981			52	23	29	0	0	.442	5 (2nd)
1982			162	76	86	0	0	.469	4
1983			73	26	47	0	0	.356	7 7
1984	MIL	A	161	67	94	0	0	.416	7
1993	FLA	N	162	64	98	0	0	.395	6
1994			115	51	64	0	0	.443	5
1995			143	67	76	0	0	.469	4
7 yrs.			901	389	512	0	0	.432	

Nap Lajoie
LAJOIE, NAPOLEON (Larry)
B. Sept. 5, 1874, Woonsocket, R. I.
D. Feb. 7, 1959, Daytona Beach, Fla.
Hall of Fame 1937.

			G	W	L	T	N	PCT	Standing
1905	CLE	A	58	37	21	0	0	.638	1 5
1905			56	19	36	1	0	.345	2 5
1906			157	89	64	4	0	.582	3
1907			158	85	67	6	0	.559	4
1908			157	90	64	3	0	.584	2
1909			114	57	57	0	0	.500	6 6
5 yrs.			700	377	309	14	0	.550	

Fred Lake
LAKE, FREDERICK LOVETT
B. Oct. 16, 1866, Nova Scotia, Canada
D. Nov. 24, 1931, Boston, Mass.

			G	W	L	T	N	PCT	Standing
1908	BOS	A	40	22	17	1	0	.564	6 5
1909			152	88	63	1	0	.583	3
1910	BOS	N	157	53	100	4	0	.346	8
3 yrs.			349	163	180	6	0	.475	

Gene Lamont
LAMONT, GENE WILLIAM
B. Dec. 25, 1946, Rockford, Ill.

			G	W	L	T	N	PCT	Standing
1992	CHI	A	162	86	76	0	0	.531	3
1993			162	94	68	0	0	.580	1
1994			113	67	46	0	0	.593	1
1995			31	11	20	0	0	.355	4 3
4 yrs.			468	258	210	0	0	.551	

LEAGUE CHAMPIONSHIP SERIES

			G	W	L	T	N	PCT
1993	CHI	A	6	2	4	0	0	.333

Hal Lanier
LANIER, HAROLD CLIFTON
Son of Max Lanier.
B. July 4, 1942, Denton, N. C.

			G	W	L	T	N	PCT	Standing
1986	HOU	N	162	96	66	0	0	.593	1
1987			162	76	86	0	0	.469	3
1988			162	82	80	0	0	.506	5
3 yrs.			486	254	232	0	0	.523	

LEAGUE CHAMPIONSHIP SERIES

			G	W	L	T	N	PCT
1986	HOU	N	6	2	4	0	0	.333

Henry Larkin
LARKIN, HENRY E. (Ted)
B. Jan. 12, 1860, Reading, Pa.
D. Jan. 31, 1942, Reading, Pa.

			G	W	L	T	N	PCT	Standing
1890	CLE	P	79	34	45	0	0	.430	7 7

Tony LaRussa
LaRUSSA, ANTHONY
B. Oct. 4, 1944, Tampa, Fla.

			G	W	L	T	N	PCT	Standing
1979	CHI	A	54	27	27	0	0	.500	5 5
1980			162	70	90	2	0	.438	5
1981			53	31	22	0	0	.585	3 (1st)
1981			53	23	30	0	0	.434	6 (2nd)
1982			162	87	75	0	0	.537	3
1983			162	99	63	0	0	.611	1
1984			162	74	88	0	0	.457	5
1985			163	85	77	1	0	.525	3
1986			64	26	38	0	0	.406	6 5
1986	OAK	A	79	45	34	0	0	.570	7 3
1987			162	81	81	0	0	.500	3
1988			162	104	58	0	0	.642	1
1989			162	99	63	0	0	.611	1
1990			162	103	59	0	0	.636	1
1991			162	84	78	0	0	.519	4
1992			162	96	66	0	0	.593	1
1993			162	68	94	0	0	.420	7
1994			114	51	63	0	0	.447	2
1995			144	67	77	0	0	.465	4
17 yrs.			2506	1320	1183	3	0	.527	

LEAGUE CHAMPIONSHIP SERIES

			G	W	L	T	N	PCT
1983	CHI	A	4	1	3	0	0	.250
1988	OAK	A	4	4	0	0	0	1.000
1989			5	4	1	0	0	.800
1990			4	4	0	0	0	1.000
1992			6	2	4	0	0	.333
5 yrs.			23	15	8	0	0	.652
			5th	5th				3rd

WORLD SERIES

			G	W	L	T	N	PCT
1988	OAK	A	5	1	4	0	0	.200
1989			4	4	0	0	0	1.000
1990			4	0	4	0	0	.000
3 yrs.			13	5	8	0	0	.385

Tom Lasorda
LASORDA, THOMAS CHARLES
B. Sept. 22, 1927, Norristown, Pa.

			G	W	L	T	N	PCT	Standing
1976	LA	N	4	2	2	0	0	.500	2 2
1977			162	98	64	0	0	.605	1
1978			162	95	67	0	0	.586	1
1979			162	79	83	0	0	.488	3
1980			163	92	71	0	0	.564	2
1981			57	36	21	0	0	.632	1 (1st)
1981			53	27	26	0	0	.509	4 (2nd)
1982			162	88	74	0	0	.543	2
1983			163	91	71	1	0	.562	1
1984			162	79	83	0	0	.488	4
1985			162	95	67	0	0	.586	1
1986			162	73	89	0	0	.451	5
1987			162	73	89	0	0	.451	4
1988			162	94	67	1	0	.584	1
1989			160	77	83	0	0	.481	4
1990			162	86	76	0	0	.531	2
1991			162	93	69	0	0	.574	2
1992			162	63	99	0	0	.389	6

Tom Lasorda *continued*

			G	W	L	T	N	PCT	Standing
1993			162	81	81	0	0	.500	4
1994			114	58	56	0	0	.509	1
1995			144	78	66	0	0	.542	1
20 yrs.			2964	1558	1404	2	0	.526	

DIVISIONAL PLAYOFF SERIES

			G	W	L	T	N	PCT
1981	LA	N	5	3	2	0	0	.600
1995			3	0	3	0	0	.000
2 yrs.			8	3	5	0	0	.375

LEAGUE CHAMPIONSHIP SERIES

			G	W	L	T	N	PCT
1977	LA	N	4	3	1	0	0	.750
1978			4	3	1	0	0	.750
1981			5	3	2	0	0	.600
1983			4	1	3	0	0	.250
1985			6	2	4	0	0	.333
1988			7	4	3	0	0	.571
6 yrs.			30	16	14	0	0	.533
			2nd	3rd	1st			6th

WORLD SERIES

			G	W	L	T	N	PCT
1977	LA	N	6	2	4	0	0	.333
1978			6	2	4	0	0	.333
1981			6	4	2	0	0	.667
1988			5	4	1	0	0	.800
4 yrs.			23	12	11	0	0	.522
			10th	8th				8th

Arlie Latham
LATHAM, WALTER ARLINGTON (The Freshest Man on Earth)
B. Mar. 15, 1860, W. Lebanon, N. H.
D. Nov. 29, 1952, Garden City, N. Y.

			G	W	L	T	N	PCT	Standing
1896	STL	N	3	0	3	0	0	.000	10 10 11

Juice Latham
LATHAM, GEORGE WARREN (Jumbo)
B. Sept. 6, 1852, Utica, N. Y.
D. May 26, 1914, Utica, N. Y.

			G	W	L	T	N	PCT	Standing
1882	PHI	AA	75	41	34	0	0	.547	2

Cookie Lavagetto
LAVAGETTO, HARRY ARTHUR
B. Dec. 1, 1912, Oakland, Calif.
D. Aug. 10, 1990, Orinda, Calif.

			G	W	L	T	N	PCT	Standing
1957	WAS	A	134	51	83	0	0	.381	8 8
1958			156	61	93	2	0	.396	8
1959			154	63	91	0	0	.409	8
1960			154	73	81	0	0	.474	5
1961	MIN	A	49	19	30	0	0	.388	8 7
1961			10	4	6	0	0	.400	9 9 7
5 yrs.			657	271	384	2	0	.414	

Bob Leadley
LEADLEY, ROBERT H.
B. 1858, Brooklyn, N. Y.
Deceased.

			G	W	L	T	N	PCT	Standing
1888	DET	N	40	19	19	2	0	.500	3 5
1890	CLE	N	58	23	33	2	0	.411	7 7
1891			68	34	34	0	0	.500	6 5
3 yrs.			166	76	86	4	0	.469	

Jim Lefebvre
LEFEBVRE, JAMES KENNETH (Frenchy)
B. Jan. 7, 1942, Inglewood, Calif.

			G	W	L	T	N	PCT	Standing
1989	SEA	A	162	73	89	0	0	.451	6
1990			162	77	85	0	0	.475	5
1991			162	83	79	0	0	.512	5
1992	CHI	N	162	78	84	0	0	.481	4
1993			163	84	78	1	0	.519	4
5 yrs.			811	395	415	1	0	.488	

Bob Lemon
LEMON, ROBERT GRANVILLE
B. Sept. 22, 1920, San Bernardino, Calif.
Hall of Fame 1976.

			G	W	L	T	N	PCT	Standing
1970	KC	A	110	46	64	0	0	.418	5 4
1971			161	85	76	0	0	.528	2
1972			154	76	78	0	0	.494	4

Bob Lemon *continued*

Year	Team	Lg	G	W	L	T	N	PCT	Standing
1977	**CHI**	**A**	162	90	72	0	0	.556	**3**
1978			74	34	40	0	0	.459	**5** 5
1978	**NY**	**A**	68	48	20	0	0	.706	3 **1**
1979			65	34	31	0	0	.523	**4** 4
1981			25	11	14	0	0	.440	5 **6** (2nd)
1982			14	6	8	0	0	.429	**4** 5
8 yrs.			833	430	403	0	0	.516	

DIVISIONAL PLAYOFF SERIES

Year	Team	Lg	G	W	L	T	N	PCT
1981	**NY**	**A**	5	3	2	0	0	.600

LEAGUE CHAMPIONSHIP SERIES

Year	Team	Lg	G	W	L	T	N	PCT
1978	**NY**	**A**	4	3	1	0	0	.750
1981			3	3	0	0	0	1.000
2 yrs.			7	6	1	0	0	.857

WORLD SERIES

Year	Team	Lg	G	W	L	T	N	PCT
1978	**NY**	**A**	6	4	2	0	0	.667
1981			6	2	4	0	0	.333
2 yrs.			12	6	6	0	0	.500

Jim Lemon

LEMON, JAMES ROBERT
B. Mar. 23, 1928, Covington, Va.

Year	Team	Lg	G	W	L	T	N	PCT	Standing
1968	**WAS**	**A**	161	65	96	0	0	.404	**10**

Jim Leyland

LEYLAND, JAMES RICHARD
B. Dec. 15, 1944, Toledo, Ohio

Year	Team	Lg	G	W	L	T	N	PCT	Standing
1986	**PIT**	**N**	162	64	98	0	0	.395	**6**
1987			162	80	82	0	0	.494	**4**
1988			160	85	75	0	0	.531	**2**
1989			164	74	88	2	0	.457	**5**
1990			162	95	67	0	0	.586	**1**
1991			162	98	64	0	0	.605	**1**
1992			162	96	66	0	0	.593	**1**
1993			162	75	87	0	0	.463	**5**
1994			114	53	61	0	0	.465	**3**
1995			143	58	85	0	0	.406	**5**
10 yrs.			1553	778	773	2	0	.502	

LEAGUE CHAMPIONSHIP SERIES

Year	Team	Lg	G	W	L	T	N	PCT
1990	**PIT**	**N**	6	2	4	0	0	.333
1991			7	3	4	0	0	.429
1992			7	3	4	0	0	.429
3 yrs.			20	8	12	0	0	.400
			9th	**9th**	**5th**			

Nick Leyva

LEYVA, NICHOLAS TOMAS
B. Aug. 16, 1953, Ontario, Calif.

Year	Team	Lg	G	W	L	T	N	PCT	Standing
1989	**PHI**	**N**	162	67	95	0	0	.414	**6**
1990			162	77	85	0	0	.475	**4**
1991			13	4	9	0	0	.308	**6** 3
3 yrs.			337	148	189	0	0	.439	

Bob Lillis

LILLIS, ROBERT PERRY (Flea)
B. June 2, 1930, Altadena, Calif.

Year	Team	Lg	G	W	L	T	N	PCT	Standing
1982	**HOU**	**N**	51	28	23	0	0	.549	5 **5**
1983			162	85	77	0	0	.525	**3**
1984			162	80	82	0	0	.494	**2**
1985			162	83	79	0	0	.512	**3**
4 yrs.			537	276	261	0	0	.514	

Johnny Lipon

LIPON, JOHN JOSEPH (Skids)
B. Nov. 10, 1922, Martins Ferry, Ohio.

Year	Team	Lg	G	W	L	T	N	PCT	Standing
1971	**CLE**	**A**	59	18	41	0	0	.305	6 **6**

Hans Lobert

LOBERT, JOHN BERNARD (Honus)
Brother of Frank Lobert.
B. Oct. 18, 1881, Wilmington, Del.
D. Sept. 14, 1968, Philadelphia, Pa.

Year	Team	Lg	G	W	L	T	N	PCT	Standing
1938	**PHI**	**N**	2	0	2	0	0	.000	8 **8**
1942			151	42	109	0	0	.278	**8**
2 yrs.			153	42	111	0	0	.275	

Whitey Lockman

LOCKMAN, CARROLL WALTER
B. July 25, 1926, Lowell, N. C.

Year	Team	Lg	G	W	L	T	N	PCT	Standing
1972	**CHI**	**N**	65	39	26	0	0	.600	4 **2**
1973			161	77	84	0	0	.478	**5**
1974			93	41	52	0	0	.441	**5** 6
3 yrs.			319	157	162	0	0	.492	

Tom Loftus

LOFTUS, THOMAS JOSEPH
B. Nov. 15, 1856, St. Louis, Mo.
D. Apr. 16, 1910, Dubuque, Iowa.

Year	Team	Lg	G	W	L	T	N	PCT	Standing
1884	**MIL**	**U**	12	8	4	0	0	.667	**2**
1888	**CLE**	**AA**	71	30	38	3	0	.441	7 **6**
1889	**CLE**	**N**	136	61	72	3	0	.459	**6**
1890	**CIN**	**N**	134	77	55	2	0	.583	**4**
1891			138	56	81	1	0	.409	**7**
1900	**CHI**	**N**	146	65	75	6	0	.464	**5**
1901			140	53	86	1	0	.381	**6**
1902	**WAS**	**A**	138	61	75	2	0	.449	**6**
1903			140	43	94	3	0	.314	**8**
9 yrs.			1055	454	580	21	0	.439	

Ed Lopat

LOPAT, EDMUND WALTER (Steady Eddie)
Born Edmund Walter Lopatynski.
B. June 21, 1918, New York, N. Y.
D. June 15, 1992, Darien, Conn.

Year	Team	Lg	G	W	L	T	N	PCT	Standing
1963	**KC**	**A**	162	73	89	0	0	.451	**8**
1964			52	17	35	0	0	.327	**10** 10
2 yrs.			214	90	124	0	0	.421	

Al Lopez

LOPEZ, ALFONSO RAYMOND
B. Aug. 20, 1908, Tampa, Fla.
Hall of Fame 1977.

Year	Team	Lg	G	W	L	T	N	PCT	Standing
1951	**CLE**	**A**	155	93	61	1	0	.604	**2**
1952			155	93	61	1	0	.604	**2**
1953			155	92	62	1	0	.597	**2**
1954			156	111	43	2	0	.721	**1**
1955			154	93	61	0	0	.604	**2**
1956			155	88	66	1	0	.571	**2**
1957	**CHI**	**A**	155	90	64	1	0	.584	**2**
1958			155	82	72	1	0	.532	**2**
1959			156	94	60	2	0	.610	**1**
1960			154	87	67	0	0	.565	**3**
1961			163	86	76	1	0	.531	**4**
1962			162	85	77	0	0	.525	**5**
1963			162	94	68	0	0	.580	**2**
1964			162	98	64	0	0	.605	**2**
1965			162	95	67	0	0	.586	**2**
1968			11	6	5	0	0	.545	9 **9** 8
1968			36	15	21	0	0	.417	9 **8**
1969			17	8	9	0	0	.471	**4** 5
17 yrs.			2425	1410	1004	11	0	.584	
								8th	

WORLD SERIES

Year	Team	Lg	G	W	L	T	N	PCT
1954	**CLE**	**A**	4	0	4	0	0	.000
1959	**CHI**	**A**	6	2	4	0	0	.333
2 yrs.			10	2	8	0	0	.200

Harry Lord

LORD, HARRY DONALD
B. Mar. 8, 1882, Porter, Me.
D. Aug. 9, 1948, Westbrook, Me.

Year	Team	Lg	G	W	L	T	N	PCT	Standing
1915	**BUF**	**F**	110	60	49	1	0	.550	8 **6**

Bobby Lowe

LOWE, ROBERT LINCOLN (Link)
B. July 10, 1868, Pittsburgh, Pa.
D. Dec. 8, 1951, Detroit, Mich.

Year	Team	Lg	G	W	L	T	N	PCT	Standing
1904	**DET**	**A**	78	30	44	4	0	.405	7 **7**

Frank Lucchesi

LUCCHESI, FRANK JOSEPH
B. Apr. 24, 1927, San Francisco, Calif.

Year	Team	Lg	G	W	L	T	N	PCT	Standing
1970	**PHI**	**N**	161	73	88	0	0	.453	**5**
1971			162	67	95	0	0	.414	**6**
1972			76	26	50	0	0	.342	**6** 6

Frank Lucchesi *continued*

Year	Team	Lg	G	W	L	T	N	PCT	Standing
1975	**TEX**	**A**	67	35	32	0	0	.522	4 **3**
1976			162	76	86	0	0	.469	**5**
1977			62	31	31	0	0	.500	**4** 2
1987	**CHI**	**N**	25	8	17	0	0	.320	5 **6**
7 yrs.			715	316	399	0	0	.442	

Harry Lumley

LUMLEY, HARRY G
B. Sept. 29, 1880, Forest City, Pa.
D. May 22, 1938, Binghamton, N. Y.

Year	Team	Lg	G	W	L	T	N	PCT	Standing
1909	**BKN**	**N**	155	55	98	2	0	.359	**6**

Ted Lyons

LYONS, THEODORE AMAR
B. Dec. 28, 1900, Lake Charles, La.
D. July 25, 1986, Sulphur, La.
Hall of Fame 1955.

Year	Team	Lg	G	W	L	T	N	PCT	Standing
1946	**CHI**	**A**	125	64	60	1	0	.516	7 **5**
1947			155	70	84	1	0	.455	**6**
1948			154	51	101	2	0	.336	**8**
3 yrs.			434	185	245	4	0	.430	

Connie Mack

MACK, CORNELIUS ALEXANDER (The Tall Tactician)
Born Cornelius Alexander McGillicuddy.
Father of Earle Mack.
B. Dec. 22, 1862, E. Brookfield, Mass.
D. Feb. 8, 1956, Philadelphia, Pa.
Hall of Fame 1937.

Year	Team	Lg	G	W	L	T	N	PCT	Standing
1894	**PIT**	**N**	23	12	10	1	0	.545	7 **7**
1895			135	71	61	2	1	.538	**7**
1896			131	66	63	2	0	.512	**6**
1901	**PHI**	**A**	137	74	62	1	0	.544	**4**
1902			137	83	53	1	0	.610	**1**
1903			137	75	60	2	0	.556	**2**
1904			155	81	70	4	0	.536	**5**
1905			152	92	56	4	0	.622	**1**
1906			149	78	67	4	0	.538	**4**
1907			150	88	57	5	0	.607	**2**
1908			157	68	85	4	0	.444	**6**
1909			153	95	58	0	0	.621	**2**
1910			155	102	48	5	0	.680	**1**
1911			152	101	50	1	0	.669	**1**
1912			153	90	62	1	0	.592	**3**
1913			153	96	57	0	0	.627	**1**
1914			158	99	53	6	0	.651	**1**
1915			154	43	109	2	0	.283	**8**
1916			154	36	117	1	0	.235	**8**
1917			154	55	98	1	0	.359	**8**
1918			130	52	76	2	0	.406	**8**
1919			140	36	104	0	0	.257	**8**
1920			156	48	106	2	0	.312	**8**
1921			155	53	100	2	0	.346	**8**
1922			155	65	89	1	0	.422	**7**
1923			153	69	83	1	0	.454	**6**
1924			152	71	81	0	0	.467	**5**
1925			153	88	64	1	0	.579	**2**
1926			150	83	67	0	0	.553	**3**
1927			155	91	63	1	0	.591	**2**
1928			153	98	55	0	0	.641	**2**
1929			151	104	46	1	0	.693	**1**
1930			154	102	52	0	0	.662	**1**
1931			153	107	45	1	0	.704	**1**
1932			154	94	60	0	0	.610	**2**
1933			152	79	72	1	0	.523	**3**
1934			153	68	82	3	0	.453	**5**
1935			149	58	91	0	0	.389	**8**
1936			154	53	100	1	0	.346	**8**
1937			120	39	80	1	0	.328	**7** 7
1938			154	53	99	2	0	.349	**8**
1939			62	25	37	0	0	.403	**6** 7
1940			154	54	100	0	0	.351	**8**
1941			154	64	90	0	0	.416	**8**
1942			154	55	99	0	0	.357	**8**

Connie Mack *continued*

			G	W	L	T	N	PCT	Standing
1943			155	49	105	1	0	.318	8
1944			155	72	82	1	0	.468	5
1945			153	52	98	3	0	.347	8
1946			155	49	105	1	0	.318	8
1947			156	78	76	2	0	.506	5
1948			154	84	70	0	0	.545	4
1949			154	81	73	0	0	.526	5
1950			154	52	102	0	0	.338	8
53 yrs.			7755	3731	3948	75	1	.486	
			1st	1st	1st				

WORLD SERIES

			G	W	L	T	N	PCT	Standing
1905	PHI	A	5	1	4	0	0	.200	
1910			5	4	1	0	0	.800	
1911			6	4	2	0	0	.667	
1913			5	4	1	0	0	.800	
1914			4	0	4	0	0	.000	
1929			5	4	1	0	0	.800	
1930			6	4	2	0	0	.667	
1931			7	3	4	0	0	.429	
8 yrs.			43	24	19	0	0	.558	
			3rd	4th	4th			4th	

Denny Mack
MACK, DENNIS JOSEPH
Born Dennis Joseph McGee.
B. 1851, Easton, Pa.
D. Apr. 10, 1888, Wilkes-Barre, Pa.

			G	W	L	T	N	PCT	Standing
1882	LOU	AA	80	42	38	0	0	.525	3

Earle Mack
MACK, EARLE THADDEUS
Born Earle Thaddeus McGillicuddy.
Son of Connie Mack.
B. Feb. 1, 1890, Spencer, Mass.
D. Feb. 4, 1967, Upper Darby, Pa.

			G	W	L	T	N	PCT	Standing
1937	PHI	A	34	15	17	2	0	.469	7 7
1939			91	30	60	1	0	.333	6 7
2 yrs.			125	45	77	3	0	.369	

Jimmy Macullar
MACULLAR, JAMES F. (Little Mac)
B. Jan. 16, 1855, Boston, Mass.
D. Apr. 8, 1924, Baltimore, Md.

			G	W	L	T	N	PCT	Standing
1879	SYR	N	27	5	21	1	0	.192	6 7

Lee Magee
MAGEE, LEO CHRISTOPHER
Born Leopold Christopher Hoernschemeyer.
B. June 4, 1889, Cincinnati, Ohio
D. Mar. 14, 1966, Columbus, Ohio.

			G	W	L	T	N	PCT	Standing
1915	BKN	F	118	53	64	1	0	.453	7 7

Fergy Malone
MALONE, FERGUSON G.
B. 1842, Ireland
D. Jan. 1, 1905, Seattle, Wash.

			G	W	L	T	N	PCT	Standing
1884	PHI	U	67	21	46	0	0	.313	9

Jack Manning
MANNING, JOHN E.
B. Dec. 20, 1853, Braintree, Mass.
D. Aug. 15, 1929, Boston, Mass.

			G	W	L	T	N	PCT	Standing
1877	CIN	N	20	7	12	1	0	.368	6 6

Jimmy Manning
MANNING, JAMES H.
B. Jan. 31, 1862, Fall River, Mass.
D. Oct. 22, 1929, Edinburg, Tex.

			G	W	L	T	N	PCT	Standing
1901	WAS	A	138	61	73	4	0	.455	6

Rabbit Maranville
MARANVILLE, WALTER JAMES VINCENT
B. Nov. 11, 1891, Springfield, Mass.
D. Jan. 5, 1954, New York, N. Y.
Hall of Fame 1954.

			G	W	L	T	N	PCT	Standing
1925	CHI	N	53	23	30	0	0	.434	7 8 8

Marty Marion
MARION, MARTIN WHITEFORD (Slats, The Octopus)
Brother of Red Marion.
B. Dec. 1, 1917, Richburg, S. C.

			G	W	L	T	N	PCT	Standing
1951	STL	N	155	81	73	1	0	.526	3
1952	STL	A	104	42	61	1	0	.408	8 7
1953			154	54	100	0	0	.351	8
1954	CHI	A	9	3	6	0	0	.333	3 3
1955			155	91	63	1	0	.591	3
1956			154	85	69	0	0	.552	3
6 yrs.			731	356	372	3	0	.489	

Jim Marshall
MARSHALL, RUFUS JAMES
B. May 25, 1931, Danville, Ill.

			G	W	L	T	N	PCT	Standing
1974	CHI	N	69	25	44	0	0	.362	5 6
1975			162	75	87	0	0	.463	5
1976			162	75	87	0	0	.463	4
1979	OAK	A	162	54	108	0	0	.333	7
4 yrs.			555	229	326	0	0	.413	

Billy Martin
MARTIN, ALFRED MANUEL (The Kid)
B. May 16, 1928, Berkeley, Calif.
D. Dec. 25, 1989, Johnson City, N. Y.

			G	W	L	T	N	PCT	Standing
1969	MIN	A	162	97	65	0	0	.599	1
1971	DET	A	162	91	71	0	0	.562	2
1972			156	86	70	0	0	.551	1
1973			134	71	63	0	0	.530	3 3
1973	TEX	A	23	9	14	0	0	.391	6 6
1974			161	84	76	1	0	.525	2
1975			95	44	51	0	0	.463	4 3
1975	NY	A	56	30	26	0	0	.536	3 3
1976			159	97	62	0	0	.610	1
1977			162	100	62	0	0	.617	1
1978			94	52	42	0	0	.553	3 1
1979			95	55	40	0	0	.579	4 4
1980	OAK	A	162	83	79	0	0	.512	2
1981			60	37	23	0	0	.617	1 (1st)
1981			49	27	22	0	0	.551	2 (2nd)
1982			162	68	94	0	0	.420	5
1983	NY	A	162	91	71	0	0	.562	3
1985			145	91	54	0	0	.628	7 2
1988			68	40	28	0	0	.588	2 5
16 yrs.			2267	1253	1013	1	0	.553	

DIVISIONAL PLAYOFF SERIES

			G	W	L	T	N	PCT	Standing
1981	OAK	A	3	3	0	0	0	1.000	

LEAGUE CHAMPIONSHIP SERIES

			G	W	L	T	N	PCT	Standing
1969	MIN	A	3	0	3	0	0	.000	
1972	DET	A	5	2	3	0	0	.400	
1976	NY	A	5	3	2	0	0	.600	
1977			5	3	2	0	0	.600	
1981	OAK	A	3	0	3	0	0	.000	
5 yrs.			21	8	13	0	0	.381	
			8th	9th	4th				

WORLD SERIES

			G	W	L	T	N	PCT	Standing
1976	NY	A	4	0	4	0	0	.000	
1977			6	4	2	0	0	.667	
2 yrs.			10	4	6	0	0	.400	

Marty Martinez
MARTINEZ, ORLANDO
Born Orlando Martinez Oliva.
B. Aug. 23, 1941, Havana, Cuba.

			G	W	L	T	N	PCT	Standing
1986	SEA	A	1	0	1	0	0	.000	6 6 7

Charlie Mason
MASON, CHARLES E.
B. June 25, 1853, New Orleans, La.
D. Oct. 21, 1936, Philadelphia, Pa.

			G	W	L	T	N	PCT	Standing
1887	PHI	AA	82	38	40	4	0	.487	5 5

Eddie Mathews
MATHEWS, EDWIN LEE
B. Oct. 13, 1931, Texarkana, Tex.
Hall of Fame 1978.

			G	W	L	T	N	PCT	Standing
1972	ATL	N	50	23	27	0	0	.460	5 4
1973			162	76	85	1	0	.472	5
1974			99	50	49	0	0	.505	4 3
3 yrs.			311	149	161	1	0	.481	

Christy Mathewson
MATHEWSON, CHRISTOPHER (Big Six, Matty)
Brother of Henry Mathewson.
B. Aug. 12, 1880, Factoryville, Pa.
D. Oct. 7, 1925, Saranac Lake, N. Y.
Hall of Fame 1936.

			G	W	L	T	N	PCT	Standing
1916	CIN	N	69	25	43	1	0	.368	8 7
1917			157	78	76	3	0	.506	4
1918			120	61	57	1	1	.517	4 3
3 yrs.			346	164	176	5	1	.482	

Bobby Mattick
MATTICK, ROBERT JAMES
Son of Wally Mattick.
B. Dec. 5, 1915, Sioux City, Iowa

			G	W	L	T	N	PCT	Standing
1980	TOR	A	162	67	95	0	0	.414	7
1981			58	16	42	0	0	.276	7 (1st)
1981			48	21	27	0	0	.438	7 (2nd)
2 yrs.			268	104	164	0	0	.388	

Gene Mauch
MAUCH, GENE WILLIAM (Skip)
B. Nov. 18, 1925, Salina, Kans.

			G	W	L	T	N	PCT	Standing
1960	PHI	N	152	58	94	0	0	.382	4 8
1961			155	47	107	1	0	.305	8
1962			161	81	80	0	0	.503	7
1963			162	87	75	0	0	.537	4
1964			162	92	70	0	0	.568	2
1965			162	85	76	1	0	.528	6
1966			162	87	75	0	0	.537	4
1967			162	82	80	0	0	.506	5
1968			54	27	27	0	0	.500	6 8
1969	MON	N	162	52	110	0	0	.321	6
1970			162	73	89	0	0	.451	6
1971			162	71	90	1	0	.441	5
1972			156	70	86	0	0	.449	5
1973			162	79	83	0	0	.488	4
1974			161	79	82	0	0	.491	4
1975			162	75	87	0	0	.463	5
1976	MIN	A	162	85	77	0	0	.525	3
1977			161	84	77	0	0	.522	4
1978			162	73	89	0	0	.451	4
1979			162	82	80	0	0	.506	4
1980			125	54	71	0	0	.432	6 3
1981	CAL	A	13	9	4	0	0	.692	4 4 (1st)
1981			50	20	30	0	0	.400	7 (2nd)
1982			162	93	69	0	0	.574	1
1985			162	90	72	0	0	.556	2
1986			162	92	70	0	0	.568	1
1987			162	75	87	0	0	.463	6
26 yrs.			3942	1902	2037	3	0	.483	
			5th	9th	3rd				

LEAGUE CHAMPIONSHIP SERIES

			G	W	L	T	N	PCT	Standing
1982	CAL	A	5	2	3	0	0	.400	
1986			7	3	4	0	0	.429	
2 yrs.			12	5	7	0	0	.417	

Jimmy McAleer
McALEER, JAMES ROBERT
B. July 10, 1864, Youngstown, Ohio
D. Apr. 29, 1931, Youngstown, Ohio.

			G	W	L	T	N	PCT	Standing
1901	CLE	A	138	55	82	1	0	.401	7
1902	STL	A	140	78	58	4	0	.574	2
1903			139	65	74	0	0	.468	6
1904			156	65	87	4	0	.428	6
1905			156	54	99	3	0	.353	8
1906			154	76	73	5	0	.510	5
1907			155	69	83	3	0	.454	6
1908			155	83	69	3	0	.546	4

Jimmy McAleer *continued*

			G	W	L	T	N	PCT	Standing		
1909			154	61	89	4	0	.407	**7**		
1910	**WAS**	**A**	157	66	85	6	0	.437	**7**		
1911			154	64	90	0	0	.416	**7**		
11 yrs.			1658	736	889	33	0	.453			

George McBride

McBRIDE, GEORGE FLORIAN
B. Nov. 20, 1880, Milwaukee, Wis.
D. July 2, 1973, Milwaukee, Wis.

			G	W	L	T	N	PCT	Standing		
1921	**WAS**	**A**	154	80	73	1	0	.523	**4**		

Jack McCallister

McCALLISTER, JOHN
B. Jan. 19, 1879, Marietta, Ohio
D. Oct. 18, 1946, Columbus, Ohio.

			G	W	L	T	N	PCT	Standing		
1927	**CLE**	**A**	153	66	87	0	0	.431	**6**		

Joe McCarthy

McCARTHY, JOSEPH VINCENT (Marse Joe)
B. Apr. 21, 1887, Philadelphia, Pa.
D. Jan. 3, 1978, Buffalo, N. Y.
Hall of Fame 1957.

			G	W	L	T	N	PCT	Standing		
1926	**CHI**	**N**	155	82	72	1	0	.532	**4**		
1927			153	85	68	0	0	.556	**4**		
1928			154	91	63	0	0	.591	**3**		
1929			156	98	54	4	0	.645	**1**		
1930			152	86	64	2	0	.573	**2**	2	
1931	**NY**	**A**	155	94	59	2	0	.614	**2**		
1932			156	107	47	1	1	.695	**1**		
1933			152	91	59	2	0	.607	**2**		
1934			154	94	60	0	0	.610	**2**		
1935			149	89	60	0	0	.597	**2**		
1936			155	102	51	2	0	.667	**1**		
1937			157	102	52	2	1	.662	**1**		
1938			157	99	53	5	0	.651	**1**		
1939			152	106	45	1	0	.702	**1**		
1940			155	88	66	0	1	.571	**3**		
1941			156	101	53	2	0	.656	**1**		
1942			154	103	51	0	0	.669	**1**		
1943			155	98	56	1	0	.636	**1**		
1944			154	83	71	0	0	.539	**3**		
1945			152	81	71	0	0	.533	**4**		
1946			35	22	13	0	0	.629	**2**	3	
1948	**BOS**	**A**	155	96	59	0	0	.619	**2**		
1949			155	96	58	1	0	.623	**2**		
1950			59	31	28	0	0	.525	**4**	3	
24 yrs.			3487	2125	1333	26	3	.615			
			10th	**5th**				**1st**			
WORLD SERIES											
1929	**CHI**	**N**	5	1	4	0	0	.200			
1932	**NY**	**A**	4	4	0	0	0	1.000			
1936			6	4	2	0	0	.667			
1937			5	4	1	0	0	.800			
1938			4	4	0	0	0	1.000			
1939			4	4	0	0	0	1.000			
1941			5	4	1	0	0	.800			
1942			5	1	4	0	0	.200			
1943			5	4	1	0	0	.800			
9 yrs.			43	30	13	0	0	.698			
			3rd	**2nd**	**8th**			**1st**			

Tommy McCarthy

McCARTHY, THOMAS FRANCIS MICHAEL
B. July 24, 1863, Boston, Mass.
D. Aug. 5, 1922, Boston, Mass.
Hall of Fame 1946.

			G	W	L	T	N	PCT	Standing		
1890	**STL**	**AA**	18	10	8	0	0	.556	**4**	3	
1890			5	4	1	0	0	.800	2	**2**	3

John McCloskey

McCLOSKEY, JOHN JAMES (Honest John)
B. Apr. 4, 1862, Louisville, Ky.
D. Nov. 17, 1940, Louisville, Ky.

			G	W	L	T	N	PCT	Standing		
1895	**LOU**	**N**	133	35	96	2	0	.267	**12**		
1896			19	2	17	0	0	.105	**12**	12	
1906	**STL**	**N**	154	52	98	4	0	.347	**7**		

John McCloskey *continued*

			G	W	L	T	N	PCT	Standing		
1907			155	52	101	2	0	.340	**8**		
1908			154	49	105	0	0	.318	**8**		
5 yrs.			615	190	417	8	0	.313			

Jim McCormick

McCORMICK, JAMES
B. Nov. 3, 1856, Glasgow, Scotland
D. Mar. 10, 1918, Paterson, N. J.

			G	W	L	T	N	PCT	Standing		
1879	**CLE**	**N**	82	27	55	0	0	.329	**6**		
1880			85	47	37	1	0	.560	**3**		
1882			4	0	4	0	0	.000	**8**	5	
3 yrs.			171	74	96	1	0	.435			

Mel McGaha

McGAHA, FRED MELVIN
B. Sept. 26, 1926, Bastrop, La.

			G	W	L	T	N	PCT	Standing		
1962	**CLE**	**A**	160	78	82	0	0	.488	**6**	6	
1964	**KC**	**A**	111	40	70	1	0	.364	10	**10**	
1965			26	5	21	0	0	.192	**10**	10	
3 yrs.			297	123	173	1	0	.416			

Mike McGeary

McGEARY, MICHAEL HENRY
B. 1851, Philadelphia, Pa.
Deceased.

			G	W	L	T	N	PCT	Standing		
1880	**PRO**	**N**	16	8	7	1	0	.533	**4**	2	
1881	**CLE**	**N**	11	4	7	0	0	.364	**7**	7	
2 yrs.			27	12	14	1	0	.462			

John McGraw

McGRAW, JOHN JOSEPH (Little Napoleon)
B. Apr. 7, 1873, Truxton, N. Y.
D. Feb. 25, 1934, New Rochelle, N. Y.
Hall of Fame 1937.

			G	W	L	T	N	PCT	Standing		
1899	**BAL**	**N**	152	86	62	4	0	.581	**4**		
1901	**BAL**	**A**	135	68	65	2	0	.511	**5**		
1902			58	26	31	1	0	.456	**7**	8	
1902	**NY**	**N**	65	25	38	2	0	.397	8	**8**	
1903			142	84	55	3	0	.604	**2**		
1904			158	106	47	5	0	.693	**1**		
1905			155	105	48	2	0	.686	**1**		
1906			153	96	56	1	0	.632	**2**		
1907			155	82	71	2	0	.536	**4**		
1908			157	98	56	3	0	.636	**2**		
1909			158	92	61	5	0	.601	**3**		
1910			155	91	63	1	0	.591	**2**		
1911			154	99	54	1	0	.647	**1**		
1912			154	103	48	3	0	.682	**1**		
1913			156	101	51	4	0	.664	**1**		
1914			156	84	70	2	0	.545	**2**		
1915			155	69	83	3	0	.454	**8**		
1916			155	86	66	3	0	.566	**4**		
1917			158	98	56	4	0	.636	**1**		
1918			124	71	53	0	0	.573	**2**		
1919			140	87	53	0	0	.621	**2**		
1920			155	86	68	1	0	.558	**2**		
1921			153	94	59	0	0	.614	**1**		
1922			156	93	61	2	0	.604	**1**		
1923			153	95	58	0	0	.621	**1**		
1924			29	16	13	0	0	.552	**3**	1	
1924			81	45	35	0	1	.563	1	**1**	
1925			14	10	4	0	0	.714	**1**	2	
1925			106	55	51	0	0	.519	1	**2**	
1926			151	74	77	0	0	.490	**5**		
1927			122	70	52	0	0	.574	**4**	3	
1928			155	93	61	1	0	.604	**2**		
1929			152	84	67	1	0	.556	**3**		
1930			154	87	67	0	0	.565	**3**		
1931			153	87	65	1	0	.572	**2**		
1932			40	17	23	0	0	.425	**8**	6	
33 yrs.			4769	2763	1948	57	1	.586			
			2nd	**2nd**	**4th**			**7th**			
WORLD SERIES											
1905	**NY**	**N**	5	4	1	0	0	.800			
1911			6	2	4	0	0	.333			
1912			7	3	4	0	0	.429			

John McGraw *continued*

			G	W	L	T	N	PCT	Standing		
1913			5	1	4	0	0	.200			
1917			6	2	4	0	0	.333			
1921			8	5	3	0	0	.625			
1922			5	4	0	1	0	1.000			
1923			6	2	4	0	0	.333			
1924			7	3	4	0	0	.429			
9 yrs.			55	26	28	1	0	.481			
			2nd	**3rd**	**1st**						

Deacon McGuire

McGUIRE, JAMES THOMAS
B. Nov. 18, 1863, Youngstown, Ohio
D. Oct. 31, 1936, Duck Lake, Mich.

			G	W	L	T	N	PCT	Standing		
1898	**WAS**	**N**	70	21	47	2	0	.309	10	**11**	11
1907	**BOS**	**A**	112	45	61	6	0	.425	8	**7**	
1908			115	53	62	0	0	.461	**6**	5	
1909	**CLE**	**A**	41	14	25	2	0	.359	6	**6**	
1910			161	71	81	9	0	.467	**5**		
1911			17	6	11	0	0	.353	**7**	3	
6 yrs.			516	210	287	19	0	.423			

Bill McGunnigle

McGUNNIGLE, WILLIAM HENRY (Gunner)
B. Jan. 1, 1855, Boston, Mass.
D. Mar. 9, 1899, Brockton, Mass.

			G	W	L	T	N	PCT	Standing		
1888	**BKN**	**AA**	143	88	52	3	0	.629	**2**		
1889			140	93	44	3	0	.679	**1**		
1890	**BKN**	**N**	129	86	43	0	0	.667	**1**		
1891	**PIT**	**N**	59	24	33	2	0	.421	8	**8**	
1896	**LOU**	**N**	115	36	76	3	0	.321	12	**12**	
5 yrs.			586	327	248	11	0	.569			

Stuffy McInnis

McINNIS, JOHN PHALEN
B. Sept. 19, 1890, Gloucester, Mass.
D. Feb. 16, 1960, Ipswich, Mass.

			G	W	L	T	N	PCT	Standing		
1927	**PHI**	**N**	155	51	103	1	0	.331	**8**		

Bill McKechnie

McKECHNIE, WILLIAM BOYD (Deacon)
B. Aug. 7, 1886, Wilkinsburg, Pa.
D. Oct. 29, 1965, Bradenton, Fla.
Hall of Fame 1962.

			G	W	L	T	N	PCT	Standing		
1915	**NWK**	**F**	102	54	45	3	0	.545	6	**5**	
1922	**PIT**	**N**	90	53	36	1	0	.596	5	**3**	
1923			154	87	67	0	0	.565	**3**		
1924			153	90	63	0	0	.588	**3**		
1925			153	95	58	0	0	.621	**1**		
1926			157	84	69	4	0	.549	**3**		
1928	**STL**	**N**	154	95	59	0	0	.617	**1**		
1929			63	34	29	0	0	.540	4	**4**	
1930	**BOS**	**N**	154	70	84	0	0	.455	**6**		
1931			156	64	90	2	0	.416	**7**		
1932			155	77	77	1	0	.500	**5**		
1933			156	83	71	2	0	.539	**4**		
1934			152	78	73	1	0	.517	**4**		
1935			153	38	115	0	0	.248	**8**		
1936			157	71	83	3	0	.461	**6**		
1937			152	79	73	0	0	.520	**5**		
1938	**CIN**	**N**	151	82	68	1	0	.547	**4**		
1939			156	97	57	2	0	.630	**1**		
1940			155	100	53	2	0	.654	**1**		
1941			154	88	66	0	0	.571	**3**		
1942			154	76	76	2	0	.500	**4**		
1943			155	87	67	1	0	.565	**2**		
1944			155	89	65	1	0	.578	**3**		
1945			154	61	93	0	0	.396	**7**		
1946			152	64	86	2	0	.427	**6**	6	
25 yrs.			3647	1896	1723	28	0	.524			
			9th	**10th**	**7th**						
WORLD SERIES											
1925	**PIT**	**N**	7	4	3	0	0	.571			
1928	**STL**	**N**	4	0	4	0	0	.000			
1939	**CIN**	**N**	4	0	4	0	0	.000			
1940			7	4	3	0	0	.571			
4 yrs.			22	8	14	0	0	.364			
					6th						

Jack McKeon

McKEON, JOHN ALOYSIUS
B. Nov. 23, 1930, South Amboy, N. J.

Year	Team	Lg	G	W	L	T	N	PCT	Standing
1973	**KC**	**A**	162	88	74	0	0	.543	**2**
1974			162	77	85	0	0	.475	**5**
1975			96	50	46	0	0	.521	**2** 2
1977	**OAK**	**A**	53	26	27	0	0	.491	**7** 7
1978			123	45	78	0	0	.366	6 **6**
1988	**SD**	**N**	115	67	48	0	0	.583	5 **3**
1989			162	89	73	0	0	.549	**2**
1990			80	37	43	0	0	.463	**4** 4
8 yrs.			953	479	474	0	0	.503	

Alex McKinnon

McKINNON, ALEXANDER J.
B. Aug. 14, 1856, Boston, Mass.
D. July 24, 1887, Charlestown, Mass.

Year	Team	Lg	G	W	L	T	N	PCT	Standing
1885	**STL**	**N**	39	6	32	1	0	.158	5 **8** 8

Denny McKnight

McKNIGHT, HENRY DENNIS
B. 1847, Pittsburgh, Pa.
D. May 5, 1900, Pittsburgh, Pa.

Year	Team	Lg	G	W	L	T	N	PCT	Standing
1884	**PIT**	**AA**	12	4	8	0	0	.333	**9** 11

George McManus

McMANUS, GEORGE
B. Oct. 1846
D. Oct. 2, 1918, New York, N. Y.

Year	Team	Lg	G	W	L	T	N	PCT	Standing
1876	**STL**	**N**	8	6	2	0	0	.750	2 **2**
1877			60	28	32	0	0	.467	**4**
2 yrs.			68	34	34	0	0	.500	

Marty McManus

McMANUS, MARTIN JOSEPH
B. Mar. 14, 1900, Chicago, Ill.
D. Feb. 18, 1966, St. Louis, Mo.

Year	Team	Lg	G	W	L	T	N	PCT	Standing
1932	**BOS**	**A**	99	32	67	0	0	.323	8 **8**
1933			149	63	86	0	0	.423	**7**
2 yrs.			248	95	153	0	0	.383	

Roy McMillan

McMILLAN, ROY DAVID
B. July 17, 1930, Bonham, Tex.

Year	Team	Lg	G	W	L	T	N	PCT	Standing
1972	**MIL**	**A**	2	1	1	0	0	.500	6 **6** 6
1975	**NY**	**N**	53	26	27	0	0	.491	3 **3**
2 yrs.			55	27	28	0	0	.491	

John McNamara

McNAMARA, JOHN FRANCIS
B. June 4, 1932, Sacramento, Calif.

Year	Team	Lg	G	W	L	T	N	PCT	Standing	
1969	**OAK**	**A**	13	8	5	0	0	.615	2 **2**	
1970			162	89	73	0	0	.549	**2**	
1974	**SD**	**N**	162	60	102	0	0	.370	**6**	
1975			162	71	91	0	0	.438	**4**	
1976			162	73	89	0	0	.451	**5**	
1977			48	20	28	0	0	.417	**5** 5	
1979	**CIN**	**N**	161	90	71	0	0	.559	**1**	
1980			163	89	73	1	0	.549	**3**	
1981			56	35	21	0	0	.625	**2**	(1st)
1981			52	31	21	0	0	.596	**2**	(2nd)
1982			92	34	58	0	0	.370	**6** 6	
1983	**CAL**	**A**	162	70	92	0	0	.432	**5**	
1984			162	81	81	0	0	.500	**2**	
1985	**BOS**	**A**	163	81	81	1	0	.500	**5**	
1986			161	95	66	0	0	.590	**1**	
1987			162	78	84	0	0	.481	**5**	
1988			85	43	42	0	0	.506	**4** 1	
1990	**CLE**	**A**	162	77	85	0	0	.475	**4**	
1991			77	25	52	0	0	.325	**7** 7	
18 yrs.			2367	1150	1215	2	0	.486		

LEAGUE CHAMPIONSHIP SERIES

Year	Team	Lg	G	W	L	T	N	PCT
1979	**CIN**	**N**	3	0	3	0	0	.000
1986	**BOS**	**A**	7	4	3	0	0	.571
2 yrs.			10	4	6	0	0	.400

WORLD SERIES

Year	Team	Lg	G	W	L	T	N	PCT
1986	**BOS**	**A**	7	3	4	0	0	.429

Bid McPhee

McPHEE, JOHN ALEXANDER
B. Nov. 1, 1859, Massena, N. Y.
D. Jan. 3, 1943, San Diego, Calif.

Year	Team	Lg	G	W	L	T	N	PCT	Standing
1901	**CIN**	**N**	142	52	87	3	0	.374	**8**
1902			65	27	37	1	0	.422	**7** 4
2 yrs.			207	79	124	4	0	.389	

Hal McRae

McRAE, HAROLD ABRAHAM
Father of Brian McRae.
B. July 10, 1945, Avon Park, Fla.

Year	Team	Lg	G	W	L	T	N	PCT	Standing
1991	**KC**	**A**	124	66	58	0	0	.532	7 **6**
1992			162	72	90	0	0	.444	**5**
1993			162	84	78	0	0	.519	**3**
1994			115	64	51	0	0	.557	**3**
4 yrs.			563	286	277	0	0	.508	

Cal McVey

McVEY, CALVIN ALEXANDER
B. Aug. 30, 1850, Montrose, Iowa
D. Aug. 20, 1926, San Francisco, Calif.

Year	Team	Lg	G	W	L	T	N	PCT	Standing
1878	**CIN**	**N**	61	37	23	1	0	.617	**2**
1879			63	34	28	1	0	.548	5 **5**
2 yrs.			124	71	51	2	0	.582	

Sam Mele

MELE, SABATH ANTHONY
B. Jan. 21, 1923, Astoria, N. Y.

Year	Team	Lg	G	W	L	T	N	PCT	Standing
1961	**MIN**	**A**	7	2	5	0	0	.286	8 **9** 7
1961			95	45	49	1	0	.479	9 **7**
1962			163	91	71	1	0	.562	**2**
1963			161	91	70	0	0	.565	**3**
1964			163	79	83	1	0	.488	**6**
1965			162	102	60	0	0	.630	**1**
1966			162	89	73	0	0	.549	**2**
1967			50	25	25	0	0	.500	**6** 2
7 yrs.			963	524	436	3	0	.546	

WORLD SERIES

Year	Team	Lg	G	W	L	T	N	PCT
1965	**MIN**	**A**	7	3	4	0	0	.429

Oscar Melillo

MELILLO, OSCAR DONALD (Ski, Spinach)
B. Aug. 4, 1899, Chicago, Ill.
D. Nov. 14, 1963, Chicago, Ill.

Year	Team	Lg	G	W	L	T	N	PCT	Standing
1938	**STL**	**A**	10	2	7	1	0	.222	7 **7**

Stump Merrill

MERRILL, CARL HARRISON
B. Feb. 25, 1944, Brunswick, Me.

Year	Team	Lg	G	W	L	T	N	PCT	Standing
1990	**NY**	**A**	113	49	64	0	0	.434	7 **7**
1991			162	71	91	0	0	.438	**5**
2 yrs.			275	120	155	0	0	.436	

Charlie Metro

METRO, CHARLES
Born Charles Moreskonich.
B. Apr. 28, 1919, Nanty Glo, Pa.

Year	Team	Lg	G	W	L	T	N	PCT	Standing
1962	**CHI**	**N**	112	43	69	0	0	.384	9 **9**
1970	**KC**	**A**	52	19	33	0	0	.365	**5** 4
2 yrs.			164	62	102	0	0	.378	

Billy Meyer

MEYER, WILLIAM ADAM
B. Jan. 14, 1892, Knoxville, Tenn.
D. Mar. 31, 1957, Knoxville, Tenn.

Year	Team	Lg	G	W	L	T	N	PCT	Standing
1948	**PIT**	**N**	156	83	71	2	0	.539	**4**
1949			154	71	83	0	0	.461	**6**
1950			154	57	96	1	0	.373	**8**
1951			155	64	90	1	0	.416	**7**
1952			155	42	112	1	0	.273	**8**
5 yrs.			774	317	452	5	0	.412	

Gene Michael

MICHAEL, EUGENE RICHARD (Stick)
B. June 2, 1938, Kent, Ohio

Year	Team	Lg	G	W	L	T	N	PCT	Standing	
1981	**NY**	**A**	56	34	22	0	0	.607	**1**	(1st)
1981			26	14	12	0	0	.538	**5** 6	(2nd)
1982			86	44	42	0	0	.512	4 **5** 5	

Gene Michael *continued*

Year	Team	Lg	G	W	L	T	N	PCT	Standing
1986	**CHI**	**N**	102	46	56	0	0	.451	5 **5**
1987			136	68	68	0	0	.500	**5** 6
4 yrs.			406	206	200	0	0	.507	

Clyde Milan

MILAN, JESSE CLYDE (Deerfoot)
Brother of Horace Milan.
B. Mar. 25, 1887, Linden, Tenn.
D. Mar. 3, 1953, Orlando, Fla.

Year	Team	Lg	G	W	L	T	N	PCT	Standing
1922	**WAS**	**A**	154	69	85	0	0	.448	**6**

Doggie Miller

MILLER, GEORGE FREDERICK (Calliope, Foghorn)
B. Aug. 15, 1864, Brooklyn, N. Y.
D. Apr. 6, 1909, Brooklyn, N. Y.

Year	Team	Lg	G	W	L	T	N	PCT	Standing
1894	**STL**	**N**	133	56	76	1	0	.424	**9**

Ray Miller

MILLER, RAYMOND ROGER
B. Apr. 30, 1945, Takoma Park, Md.

Year	Team	Lg	G	W	L	T	N	PCT	Standing
1985	**MIN**	**A**	100	50	50	0	0	.500	6 **4**
1986			139	59	80	0	0	.424	**7** 6
2 yrs.			239	109	130	0	0	.456	

Buster Mills

MILLS, COLONEL BUSTER
B. Sept. 16, 1908, Ranger, Tex.
D. Dec. 1, 1991, Arlington, Tex.

Year	Team	Lg	G	W	L	T	N	PCT	Standing
1953	**CIN**	**N**	8	4	4	0	0	.500	6 **6**

Fred Mitchell

MITCHELL, FREDERICK FRANCIS
Born Frederick Francis Yapp.
B. June 5, 1878, Cambridge, Mass.
D. Oct. 13, 1970, Newton, Mass.

Year	Team	Lg	G	W	L	T	N	PCT	Standing
1917	**CHI**	**N**	157	74	80	3	0	.481	**5**
1918			131	84	45	2	0	.651	**1**
1919			140	75	65	0	0	.536	**3**
1920			154	75	79	0	0	.487	**5**
1921	**BOS**	**N**	153	79	74	0	0	.516	**4**
1922			154	53	100	1	0	.346	**8**
1923			155	54	100	1	0	.351	**7**
7 yrs.			1044	494	543	7	0	.476	

WORLD SERIES

Year	Team	Lg	G	W	L	T	N	PCT
1918	**CHI**	**N**	6	2	4	0	0	.333

Jackie Moore

MOORE, JACKIE SPENCER
B. Feb. 19, 1939, Jay, Fla.

Year	Team	Lg	G	W	L	T	N	PCT	Standing
1984	**OAK**	**A**	118	57	61	0	0	.483	4 **4**
1985			162	77	85	0	0	.475	**4**
1986			73	29	44	0	0	.397	**6** 3
3 yrs.			353	163	190	0	0	.462	

Terry Moore

MOORE, TERRY BLUFORD
B. May 27, 1912, Vernon, Ala.
D. Mar. 29, 1995, Collinsville, Ill.

Year	Team	Lg	G	W	L	T	N	PCT	Standing
1954	**PHI**	**N**	77	35	42	0	0	.455	3 **4**

Pat Moran

MORAN, PATRICK JOSEPH
B. Feb. 7, 1876, Fitchburg, Mass.
D. Mar. 7, 1924, Orlando, Fla.

Year	Team	Lg	G	W	L	T	N	PCT	Standing
1915	**PHI**	**N**	153	90	62	1	0	.592	**1**
1916			154	91	62	1	0	.595	**2**
1917			155	87	65	2	1	.572	**2**
1918			125	55	68	2	0	.447	**6**
1919	**CIN**	**N**	140	96	44	0	0	.686	**1**
1920			154	82	71	1	0	.536	**3**
1921			153	70	83	0	0	.458	**6**
1922			156	86	68	2	0	.558	**2**
1923			154	91	63	0	0	.591	**2**
9 yrs.			1344	748	586	9	1	.561	

Pat Moran *continued*

WORLD SERIES

Year	Team	Lg	G	W	L	T	N	PCT	Standing
1915	**PHI**	**N**	5	1	4	0	0	.200	
1919	**CIN**	**N**	8	5	3	0	0	.625	
2 yrs.			13	6	7	0	0	.462	

Joe Morgan

MORGAN, JOSEPH MICHAEL
B. Nov. 19, 1930, Walpole, Mass.

Year	Team	Lg	G	W	L	T	N	PCT	Standing
1988	**BOS**	**A**	77	46	31	0	0	.597	4 **1**
1989			162	83	79	0	0	.512	**3**
1990			162	88	74	0	0	.543	**1**
1991			162	84	78	0	0	.519	**2**
4 yrs.			563	301	262	0	0	.535	

LEAGUE CHAMPIONSHIP SERIES

Year	Team	Lg	G	W	L	T	N	PCT	Standing
1988	**BOS**	**A**	4	0	4	0	0	.000	
1990			4	0	4	0	0	.000	
2 yrs.			8	0	8	0	0	.000	

George Moriarty

MORIARTY, GEORGE JOSEPH
Brother of Bill Moriarty.
B. July 7, 1884, Chicago, Ill.
D. Apr. 8, 1964, Miami, Fla.

Year	Team	Lg	G	W	L	T	N	PCT	Standing
1927	**DET**	**A**	156	82	71	3	0	.536	**4**
1928			154	68	86	0	0	.442	**6**
2 yrs.			310	150	157	3	0	.489	

John Morrill

MORRILL, JOHN FRANCIS (Honest John)
B. Feb. 19, 1855, Boston, Mass.
D. Apr. 2, 1932, Boston, Mass.

Year	Team	Lg	G	W	L	T	N	PCT	Standing
1882	**BOS**	**N**	85	45	39	1	0	.536	**3**
1883			44	33	11	0	0	.750	4 **1**
1884			116	73	38	5	0	.658	**2**
1885			113	46	66	1	0	.411	**5**
1886			118	56	61	1	0	.479	**5**
1887			32	12	17	0	3	.414	5 **5**
1888			137	70	64	3	0	.522	**4**
1889	**WAS**	**N**	51	13	38	0	0	.255	**8** 8
8 yrs.			696	348	334	11	3	.510	

Charlie Morton

MORTON, CHARLES HAZEN
B. Oct. 12, 1854, Kingsville, Ohio
D. Dec. 9, 1921, Massillon, Ohio.

Year	Team	Lg	G	W	L	T	N	PCT	Standing
1884	**TOL**	**AA**	110	46	58	6	0	.442	**8**
1885	**DET**	**N**	38	7	31	0	0	.184	**7** 6
1890	**TOL**	**AA**	134	68	64	2	0	.515	**4**
3 yrs.			282	121	153	8	0	.442	

Felix Moses

MOSES, FELIX I.
B. Richmond, Va.
Deceased.

Year	Team	Lg	G	W	L	T	N	PCT	Standing
1884	**RIC**	**AA**	46	12	30	4	0	.286	**10**

Les Moss

MOSS, JOHN LESTER
B. May 14, 1925, Tulsa, Okla.

Year	Team	Lg	G	W	L	T	N	PCT	Standing
1968	**CHI**	**A**	2	0	2	0	0	.000	9 **9** 8
1968			34	12	22	0	0	.353	9 **9** 8
1979	**DET**	**A**	53	27	26	0	0	.509	**5** 5
2 yrs.			89	39	50	0	0	.438	

Tim Murnane

MURNANE, TIMOTHY HAYES
B. June 4, 1852, Naugatuck, Conn.
D. Feb. 7, 1917, Boston, Mass.

Year	Team	Lg	G	W	L	T	N	PCT	Standing
1884	**BOS**	**U**	111	58	51	2	0	.532	**5**

Billy Murray

MURRAY, WILLIAM JEREMIAH
B. Apr. 13, 1864, Peabody, Mass.
D. Mar. 25, 1937, Youngstown, Ohio.

Year	Team	Lg	G	W	L	T	N	PCT	Standing
1907	**PHI**	**N**	149	83	64	2	0	.565	**3**
1908			155	83	71	1	0	.539	**4**
1909			154	74	79	1	0	.484	**5**
3 yrs.			458	240	214	4	0	.529	

Danny Murtaugh

MURTAUGH, DANIEL EDWARD
B. Oct. 8, 1917, Chester, Pa.
D. Dec. 2, 1976, Chester, Pa.

Year	Team	Lg	G	W	L	T	N	PCT	Standing
1957	**PIT**	**N**	51	26	25	0	0	.510	8 **7**
1958			154	84	70	0	0	.545	**2**
1959			155	78	76	1	0	.506	**4**
1960			155	95	59	1	0	.617	**1**
1961			154	75	79	0	0	.487	**6**
1962			161	93	68	0	0	.578	**4**
1963			162	74	88	0	0	.457	**8**
1964			162	80	82	0	0	.494	**6**
1967			79	39	39	1	0	.500	6 **6**
1970			162	89	73	0	0	.549	**1**
1971			162	97	65	0	0	.599	**1**
1973			26	13	13	0	0	.500	2 **3**
1974			162	88	74	0	0	.543	**1**
1975			161	92	69	0	0	.571	**1**
1976			162	92	70	0	0	.568	**2**
15 yrs.			2068	1115	950	3	0	.540	

LEAGUE CHAMPIONSHIP SERIES

Year	Team	Lg	G	W	L	T	N	PCT	Standing
1970	**PIT**	**N**	3	0	3	0	0	.000	
1971			4	3	1	0	0	.750	
1974			4	1	3	0	0	.250	
1975			3	0	3	0	0	.000	
4 yrs.			14	4	10 **7th**	0	0	.286	

WORLD SERIES

Year	Team	Lg	G	W	L	T	N	PCT	Standing
1960	**PIT**	**N**	7	4	3	0	0	.571	
1971			7	4	3	0	0	.571	
2 yrs.			14	8	6	0	0	.571	

Jim Mutrie

MUTRIE, JAMES J. (Truthful Jim)
B. June 13, 1851, Chelsea, Mass.
D. Jan. 24, 1938, New York, N. Y.

Year	Team	Lg	G	W	L	T	N	PCT	Standing
1883	**NY**	**AA**	97	54	42	1	0	.563	**4**
1884			112	75	32	5	0	.701	**1**
1885	**NY**	**N**	112	85	27	0	0	.759	**2**
1886			124	75	44	5	0	.630	**3**
1887			129	68	55	6	0	.553	**4**
1888			138	84	47	7	0	.641	**1**
1889			131	83	43	5	0	.659	**1**
1890			135	63	68	4	0	.481	**6**
1891			136	71	61	4	0	.538	**3**
9 yrs.			1114	658	419	37	0	.611 **2nd**	

George Myatt

MYATT, GEORGE EDWARD (Foghorn, Mercury, Stud)
B. June 14, 1914, Denver, Colo.

Year	Team	Lg	G	W	L	T	N	PCT	Standing
1968	**PHI**	**N**	1	1	0	0	0	1.000	6 **5** 8
1969			54	19	35	0	0	.352	5 **5**
2 yrs.			55	20	35	0	0	.364	

Henry Myers

MYERS, HENRY C.
B. May 1858, Philadelphia, Pa.
D. Apr. 18, 1895, Philadelphia, Pa.

Year	Team	Lg	G	W	L	T	N	PCT	Standing
1882	**BAL**	**AA**	74	19	54	1	0	.260	**6**

Billy Nash

NASH, WILLIAM MITCHELL
B. June 24, 1865, Richmond, Va.
D. Nov. 15, 1929, East Orange, N. J.

Year	Team	Lg	G	W	L	T	N	PCT	Standing
1896	**PHI**	**N**	130	62	68	0	0	.477	**8**

Johnny Neun

NEUN, JOHN HENRY
B. Oct. 28, 1900, Baltimore, Md.
D. Mar. 28, 1990, Baltimore, Md.

Year	Team	Lg	G	W	L	T	N	PCT	Standing
1946	**NY**	**A**	14	8	6	0	0	.571	3 **3**
1947	**CIN**	**N**	154	73	81	0	0	.474	**5**
1948			100	44	56	0	0	.440	**7** 7
3 yrs.			268	125	143	0	0	.466	

Jeff Newman

NEWMAN, JEFFREY LYNN
B. Sept. 11, 1948, Ft. Worth, Tex.

Year	Team	Lg	G	W	L	T	N	PCT	Standing
1986	**OAK**	**A**	10	2	8	0	0	.200	6 **7** 3

Kid Nichols

NICHOLS, CHARLES AUGUSTUS (Nick)
B. Sept. 14, 1869, Madison, Wis.
D. Apr. 11, 1953, Kansas City, Mo.
Hall of Fame 1949.

Year	Team	Lg	G	W	L	T	N	PCT	Standing
1904	**STL**	**N**	155	75	79	1	0	.487	**5**
1905			14	5	9	0	0	.357	**7** 6
2 yrs.			169	80	88	1	0	.476	

Hugh Nicol

NICOL, HUGH N.
B. Jan. 1, 1858, Campsie, Scotland
D. June 27, 1921, Lafayette, Ind.

Year	Team	Lg	G	W	L	T	N	PCT	Standing
1897	**STL**	**N**	40	8	32	0	0	.200	12 **12** 12

Russ Nixon

NIXON, RUSSELL EUGENE
B. Feb. 19, 1935, Cleves, Ohio.

Year	Team	Lg	G	W	L	T	N	PCT	Standing
1982	**CIN**	**N**	70	27	43	0	0	.386	6 **6**
1983			162	74	88	0	0	.457	**6**
1988	**ATL**	**N**	121	42	79	0	0	.347	6 **6**
1989			160	63	97	0	0	.394	**6**
1990			65	25	40	0	0	.385	**6** 6
5 yrs.			578	231	347	0	0	.400	

Bill Norman

NORMAN, HENRY WILLIS PATRICK
B. July 16, 1910, St. Louis, Mo.
D. Apr. 21, 1962, Milwaukee, Wis.

Year	Team	Lg	G	W	L	T	N	PCT	Standing
1958	**DET**	**A**	105	56	49	0	0	.533	5 **5**
1959			17	2	15	0	0	.118	**8** 4
2 yrs.			122	58	64	0	0	.475	

Rebel Oakes

OAKES, ENNIS TELFAIR
B. Dec. 17, 1886, Homer, La.
D. Feb. 29, 1948, Rocky Springs, La.

Year	Team	Lg	G	W	L	T	N	PCT	Standing
1914	**PIT**	**F**	143	61	78	4	0	.439	8 **7**
1915			156	86	67	3	0	.562	**3**
2 yrs.			299	147	145	7	0	.503	

Johnny Oates

OATES, JOHNNY LANE
B. Jan. 21, 1946, Sylva, N. C.

Year	Team	Lg	G	W	L	T	N	PCT	Standing
1991	**BAL**	**A**	125	54	71	0	0	.432	7 **6**
1992			162	89	73	0	0	.549	**3**
1993			162	85	77	0	0	.525	**3**
1994			112	63	49	0	0	.563	**2**
1995	**TEX**	**A**	144	74	70	0	0	.514	**3**
5 yrs.			705	365	340	0	0	.518	

Jack O'Connor

O'CONNOR, JOHN JOSEPH (Peach Pie)
B. June 2, 1869, St. Louis, Mo.
D. Nov. 14, 1937, St. Louis, Mo.

Year	Team	Lg	G	W	L	T	N	PCT	Standing
1910	**STL**	**A**	158	47	107	4	0	.305	**8**

Hank O'Day

O'DAY, HENRY FRANCIS (Peep)
B. July 8, 1862, Chicago, Ill.
D. July 2, 1935, Chicago, Ill.

Year	Team	Lg	G	W	L	T	N	PCT	Standing
1912	**CIN**	**N**	155	75	78	2	0	.490	**4**
1914	**CHI**	**N**	156	78	76	2	0	.506	**4**
2 yrs.			311	153	154	4	0	.498	

Bob O'Farrell

O'FARRELL, ROBERT ARTHUR
B. Oct. 19, 1896, Waukegan, Ill.
D. Feb. 20, 1988, Waukegan, Ill.

			G	W	L	T	N	PCT	Standing		
1927	**STL**	**N**	153	92	61	0	0	.601	**2**		
1934	**CIN**	**N**	91	30	60	1	0	.333	**8**	8	
2 yrs.			244	122	121	1	0	.502			

Dan O'Leary

O'LEARY, DANIEL (Hustling Dan)
B. Oct. 22, 1856, Detroit, Mich.
D. June 24, 1922, Chicago, Ill.

			G	W	L	T	N	PCT	Standing		
1884	**CIN**	**U**	35	20	15	0	0	.571	**5**	3	

Steve O'Neill

O'NEILL, STEPHEN FRANCIS
Brother of Jim O'Neill.
Brother of Jack O'Neill.
Brother of Mike O'Neill.
B. July 6, 1891, Minooka, Pa.
D. Jan. 26, 1962, Cleveland, Ohio.

			G	W	L	T	N	PCT	Standing		
1935	**CLE**	**A**	60	36	23	1	0	.610	5	**3**	
1936			157	80	74	3	0	.519	**5**		
1937			156	83	71	1	1	.539	**4**		
1943	**DET**	**A**	155	78	76	1	0	.506	**5**		
1944			156	88	66	2	0	.571	**2**		
1945			155	88	65	2	0	.575	**1**		
1946			155	92	62	1	0	.597	**2**		
1947			158	85	69	4	0	.552	**2**		
1948			154	78	76	0	0	.506	**5**		
1950	**BOS**	**A**	95	63	32	0	0	.663	4	**3**	
1951			154	87	67	0	0	.565	**3**		
1952	**PHI**	**N**	91	59	32	0	0	.648	6	**4**	
1953			156	83	71	2	0	.539	**3**		
1954			77	40	37	0	0	.519	**3**	4	
14 yrs.			1879	1040	821	17	1	.559			

WORLD SERIES

			G	W	L	T	N	PCT
1945	**DET**	**A**	7	4	3	0	0	.571

Jack Onslow

ONSLOW, JOHN JAMES
Brother of Eddie Onslow.
B. Oct. 13, 1888, Scottdale, Pa.
D. Dec. 22, 1960, Concord, Mass.

			G	W	L	T	N	PCT	Standing		
1949	**CHI**	**A**	154	63	91	0	0	.409	**6**		
1950			31	8	22	1	0	.267	**8**	6	
2 yrs.			185	71	113	1	0	.386			

Jim O'Rourke

O'ROURKE, JAMES HENRY (Orator Jim)
Father of Queenie O'Rourke.
Brother of John O'Rourke.
B. Sept. 1, 1850, Bridgeport, Conn.
D. Jan. 8, 1919, Bridgeport, Conn.
Hall of Fame 1945.

			G	W	L	T	N	PCT	Standing		
1881	**BUF**	**N**	83	45	38	0	0	.542	**3**		
1882			84	45	39	0	0	.536	**3**		
1883			98	52	45	1	0	.536	**5**		
1884			114	64	47	3	0	.577	**3**		
1893	**WAS**	**N**	130	40	89	1	0	.310	**12**		
5 yrs.			509	246	258	5	0	.488			

Dave Orr

ORR, DAVID L.
B. Sept. 29, 1859, New York, N. Y.
D. June 3, 1915, Brooklyn, N. Y.

			G	W	L	T	N	PCT	Standing		
1887	**NY**	**AA**	8	3	5	0	0	.375	8	**7**	7

Mel Ott

OTT, MELVIN THOMAS (Master Melvin)
B. Mar. 2, 1909, Gretna, La.
D. Nov. 21, 1958, New Orleans, La.
Hall of Fame 1951.

			G	W	L	T	N	PCT	Standing		
1942	**NY**	**N**	154	85	67	2	0	.559	**3**		
1943			156	55	98	3	0	.359	**8**		
1944			155	67	87	1	0	.435	**5**		
1945			154	78	74	2	0	.513	**5**		
1946			154	61	93	0	0	.396	**8**		

Mel Ott *continued*

			G	W	L	T	N	PCT	Standing		
1947			155	81	73	1	0	.526	**4**		
1948			76	37	38	1	0	.493	**4**	5	
7 yrs.			1004	464	530	10	0	.467			

Paul Owens

OWENS, PAUL FRANCIS (The Pope)
B. Feb. 7, 1924, Salamanca, N. Y.

			G	W	L	T	N	PCT	Standing		
1972	**PHI**	**N**	80	33	47	0	0	.412	6	**6**	
1983			77	47	30	0	0	.610	1	**1**	
1984			162	81	81	0	0	.500	**4**		
3 yrs.			319	161	158	0	0	.505			

LEAGUE CHAMPIONSHIP SERIES

			G	W	L	T	N	PCT
1983	**PHI**	**N**	4	3	1	0	0	.750

WORLD SERIES

			G	W	L	T	N	PCT
1983	**PHI**	**N**	5	1	4	0	0	.200

Danny Ozark

OZARK, DANIEL LEONARD (Ozark Ike)
Born Daniel Leonard Orzechowski.
B. Nov. 24, 1923, Buffalo, N. Y.

			G	W	L	T	N	PCT	Standing		
1973	**PHI**	**N**	162	71	91	0	0	.438	**6**		
1974			162	80	82	0	0	.494	**3**		
1975			162	86	76	0	0	.531	**2**		
1976			162	101	61	0	0	.623	**1**		
1977			162	101	61	0	0	.623	**1**		
1978			162	90	72	0	0	.556	**1**		
1979			133	65	67	1	0	.492	**5**	4	
1984	**SF**	**N**	56	24	32	0	0	.429	6	**6**	
8 yrs.			1161	618	542	1	0	.533			

LEAGUE CHAMPIONSHIP SERIES

			G	W	L	T	N	PCT
1976	**PHI**	**N**	3	0	3	0	0	.000
1977			4	1	3	0	0	.250
1978			4	1	3	0	0	.250
3 yrs.			11	2	9	0	0	.182

Salty Parker

PARKER, FRANCIS JAMES
B. July 8, 1913, East St. Louis, Ill.
D. July 27, 1992, Houston, Tex.

			G	W	L	T	N	PCT	Standing		
1967	**NY**	**N**	11	4	7	0	0	.364	10	**10**	
1972	**HOU**	**N**	1	1	0	0	0	1.000	3	**2**	2
2 yrs.			12	5	7	0	0	.417			

Roger Peckinpaugh

PECKINPAUGH, ROGER THORPE
B. Feb. 5, 1891, Wooster, Ohio
D. Nov. 17, 1977, Cleveland, Ohio.

			G	W	L	T	N	PCT	Standing		
1914	**NY**	**A**	20	10	10	0	0	.500	7	**6**	
1928	**CLE**	**A**	155	62	92	1	0	.403	**7**		
1929			152	81	71	0	0	.533	**3**		
1930			154	81	73	0	0	.526	**4**		
1931			155	78	76	1	0	.506	**4**		
1932			153	87	65	1	0	.572	**4**		
1933			51	26	25	0	0	.510	**5**	4	
1941			155	75	79	1	0	.487	**4**		
8 yrs.			995	500	491	4	0	.505			

Tony Perez

PEREZ, ATANASIO
Father of Eduardo Perez.
B. May 14, 1942, Camaguey, Cuba

			G	W	L	T	N	PCT	Standing		
1993	**CIN**	**N**	44	20	24	0	0	.455	**5**	5	

Johnny Pesky

PESKY, JOHN MICHAEL
Born John Michael Paveskovich.
B. Sept. 27, 1919, Portland, Ore.

			G	W	L	T	N	PCT	Standing		
1963	**BOS**	**A**	161	76	85	0	0	.472	**7**		
1964			160	70	90	0	0	.438	**8**	8	
1980			5	1	4	0	0	.200	4	**4**	
3 yrs.			326	147	179	0	0	.451			

Fred Pfeffer

PFEFFER, NATHANIEL FREDERICK (Dandelion, Fritz)
B. Mar. 17, 1860, Louisville, Ky.
D. Apr. 10, 1932, Chicago, Ill.

			G	W	L	T	N	PCT	Standing		
1892	**LOU**	**N**	23	9	14	0	0	.391	10	**11**	(1st)
1892			77	33	42	2	0	.440	**9**		(2nd)

Lew Phelan

PHELAN, LEWIS G.
Deceased.

			G	W	L	T	N	PCT	Standing		
1895	**STL**	**N**	45	11	30	4	0	.268	11	**11**	

Bill Phillips

PHILLIPS, WILLIAM CORCORAN (Silver Bill, Whoa Bill)
B. Nov. 9, 1868, Allenport, Pa.
D. Oct. 25, 1941, Charleroi, Pa.

			G	W	L	T	N	PCT	Standing		
1914	**IND**	**F**	157	88	65	4	0	.575	**1**		
1915	**NWK**	**F**	53	26	27	0	0	.491	**6**	5	
2 yrs.			210	114	92	4	0	.553			

Horace Phillips

PHILLIPS, HORACE B. (Hustling Horace)
B. May 14, 1853, Salem, Ohio
Deceased.

			G	W	L	T	N	PCT	Standing		
1879	**TRO**	**N**	47	12	34	1	0	.261	**8**	8	
1883	**COL**	**AA**	97	32	65	0	0	.330	**6**		
1884	**PIT**	**AA**	35	9	24	2	0	.273	12	**11**	
1885			111	56	55	0	0	.505	**3**		
1886			140	80	57	3	0	.584	**2**		
1887	**PIT**	**N**	125	55	69	1	0	.444	**6**		
1888			139	66	68	4	1	.493	**6**		
1889			71	28	43	0	0	.394	**7**	5	
8 yrs.			765	338	415	11	1	.449			

Lefty Phillips

PHILLIPS, HAROLD ROSS
B. May 16, 1919, Los Angeles, Calif.
D. June 10, 1972, Fullerton, Calif.

			G	W	L	T	N	PCT	Standing		
1969	**CAL**	**A**	124	60	63	1	0	.488	6	**3**	
1970			162	86	76	0	0	.531	**3**		
1971			162	76	86	0	0	.469	**4**		
3 yrs.			448	222	225	1	0	.497			

Lip Pike

PIKE, LIPMAN EMANUEL (The Iron Batter)
Brother of Jay Pike.
B. May 25, 1845, New York, N. Y.
D. Oct. 10, 1893, Brooklyn, N. Y.

			G	W	L	T	N	PCT	Standing		
1877	**CIN**	**N**	14	3	11	0	0	.214	**6**	6	

Lou Piniella

PINIELLA, LOUIS VICTOR (Sweet Lou)
B. Aug. 28, 1943, Tampa, Fla.

			G	W	L	T	N	PCT	Standing		
1986	**NY**	**A**	162	90	72	0	0	.556	**2**		
1987			162	89	73	0	0	.549	**4**		
1988			93	45	48	0	0	.484	2	**5**	
1990	**CIN**	**N**	162	91	71	0	0	.562	**1**		
1991			162	74	88	0	0	.457	**5**		
1992			162	90	72	0	0	.556	**2**		
1993	**SEA**	**A**	162	82	80	0	0	.506	**4**		
1994			112	49	63	0	0	.438	**3**		
1995			145	79	66	0	0	.545	**1**		
9 yrs.			1322	689	633	0	0	.521			

DIVISIONAL PLAYOFF SERIES

			G	W	L	T	N	PCT
1995	**SEA**	**A**	5	3	2	0	0	.600

LEAGUE CHAMPIONSHIP SERIES

			G	W	L	T	N	PCT
1990	**CIN**	**N**	6	4	2	0	0	.667
1995	**SEA**	**A**	6	2	4	0	0	.333
2 yrs.			12	6	6	0	0	.500
								8th

WORLD SERIES

			G	W	L	T	N	PCT
1990	**CIN**	**N**	4	4	0	0	0	1.000

Bill Plummer

PLUMMER, WILLIAM FRANCIS
B. Mar. 21, 1947, Oakland, Calif.

			G	W	L	T	N	PCT	Standing
1992	SEA	A	162	64	98	0	0	.395	**7**

Eddie Popowski

POPOWSKI, EDWARD JOSEPH (Pop)
B. Aug. 20, 1913, Sayreville, N. J.

			G	W	L	T	N	PCT	Standing
1969	BOS	A	9	5	4	0	0	.556	3 **3**
1973			1	1	0	0	0	1.000	2 **2**
2 yrs.			10	6	4	0	0	.600	

Matt Porter

PORTER, MATTHEW SHELDON
B. 1859, N. Y.
Deceased.

			G	W	L	T	N	PCT	Standing
1884	KC	U	16	3	13	0	0	.188	12 **12** 12

Pat Powers

POWERS, PATRICK THOMAS
B. June 27, 1860, Trenton, N. J.
D. Aug. 29, 1925, Belmar, N. J.

			G	W	L	T	N	PCT	Standing	
1890	ROC	AA	133	63	63	7	0	.500	**5**	
1892	NY	N	74	31	43	0	0	.419	**10**	(1st)
1892			79	40	37	2	0	.519	**6**	(2nd)
2 yrs.			286	134	143	9	0	.484		

Al Pratt

PRATT, ALBERT G. (Uncle Al)
B. Nov. 19, 1847, Pittsburgh, Pa.
D. Nov. 21, 1937, Pittsburgh, Pa.

			G	W	L	T	N	PCT	Standing
1882	PIT	AA	79	39	39	1	0	.500	**4**
1883			32	12	20	0	0	.375	**6** 7
2 yrs.			111	51	59	1	0	.464	

Jim Price

PRICE, JAMES LYMAN
B. 1847, New York, N. Y.
D. Oct. 6, 1931, Chicago, Ill.

			G	W	L	T	N	PCT	Standing
1884	NY	N	100	56	42	2	0	.571	**4** 4

Doc Prothro

PROTHRO, JAMES THOMPSON
B. July 16, 1893, Memphis, Tenn.
D. Oct. 14, 1971, Memphis, Tenn.

			G	W	L	T	N	PCT	Standing
1939	PHI	N	152	45	106	1	0	.298	**8**
1940			153	50	103	0	0	.327	**8**
1941			155	43	111	1	0	.279	**8**
3 yrs.			460	138	320	2	0	.301	

Blondie Purcell

PURCELL, WILLIAM ALOYSIUS
B. Mar. 16, 1854, Paterson, N. J.
D. Feb. 20, 1912, Trenton, N. J.

			G	W	L	T	N	PCT	Standing
1883	PHI	N	82	13	68	1	0	.160	8 **8**

Frank Quilici

QUILICI, FRANCIS RALPH (Guido)
B. May 11, 1939, Chicago, Ill.

			G	W	L	T	N	PCT	Standing
1972	MIN	A	84	41	43	0	0	.488	3 **3**
1973			162	81	81	0	0	.500	**3**
1974			163	82	80	1	0	.506	**3**
1975			159	76	83	0	0	.478	**4**
4 yrs.			568	280	287	1	0	.494	

Joe Quinn

QUINN, JOSEPH J. (Ol' Reliable, Uncle Joe)
B. Dec. 25, 1864, Sydney, Australia
D. Nov. 12, 1940, St. Louis, Mo.

			G	W	L	T	N	PCT	Standing
1895	STL	N	40	11	28	0	1	.282	11 **11** 11
1899	CLE	N	116	12	104	0	0	.103	12 **12**
2 yrs.			156	23	132	0	1	.148	

Doug Rader

RADER, DOUGLAS LEE (Rojo, The Red Rooster)
B. July 30, 1944, Chicago, Ill.

			G	W	L	T	N	PCT	Standing
1983	TEX	A	163	77	85	1	0	.475	**3**
1984			161	69	92	0	0	.429	**7**
1985			32	9	23	0	0	.281	**7** 7

Doug Rader *continued*

			G	W	L	T	N	PCT	Standing
1986	CHI	A	2	1	1	0	0	.500	6 **5** 5
1989	CAL	A	162	91	71	0	0	.562	**3**
1990			162	80	82	0	0	.494	**4**
1991			124	61	63	0	0	.492	**7** 7
7 yrs.			806	388	417	1	0	.482	

Vern Rapp

RAPP, VERNON FRED
B. May 11, 1928, St. Louis, Mo.

			G	W	L	T	N	PCT	Standing
1977	STL	N	162	83	79	0	0	.512	**3**
1978			17	6	11	0	0	.353	**6** 5
1984	CIN	N	121	51	70	0	0	.421	**5** 5
3 yrs.			300	140	160	0	0	.467	

Al Reach

REACH, ALFRED JAMES
Brother of Bob Reach.
B. May 25, 1840, London, England
D. Jan. 14, 1928, Atlantic City, N. J.

			G	W	L	T	N	PCT	Standing
1890	PHI	N	11	4	7	0	0	.364	2 **3** 3

Phil Regan

REGAN, PHILIP RAYMOND (The Vulture)
B. Apr. 6, 1937, Otsego, Mich.

			G	W	L	T	N	PCT	Standing
1995	BAL	A	144	71	73	0	0	.493	**3**

Del Rice

RICE, DELBERT W.
B. Oct. 27, 1922, Portsmouth, Ohio
D. Jan. 26, 1983, Buena Park, Calif.

			G	W	L	T	N	PCT	Standing
1972	CAL	A	155	75	80	0	0	.484	**5**

Paul Richards

RICHARDS, PAUL RAPIER
B. Nov. 21, 1908, Waxahachie, Tex.
D. May 4, 1986, Waxahachie, Tex.

			G	W	L	T	N	PCT	Standing
1951	CHI	A	155	81	73	1	0	.526	**4**
1952			156	81	73	2	0	.526	**3**
1953			156	89	65	2	0	.578	**3**
1954			146	91	54	1	0	.628	**3** 3
1955	BAL	A	156	57	97	2	0	.370	**7**
1956			154	69	85	0	0	.448	**6**
1957			154	76	76	2	0	.500	**5**
1958			154	74	79	1	0	.484	**6**
1959			155	74	80	1	0	.481	**6**
1960			154	89	65	0	0	.578	**2**
1961			136	78	57	1	0	.578	**3** 3
1976	CHI	A	161	64	97	0	0	.398	**6**
12 yrs.			1837	923	901	13	0	.506	

Danny Richardson

RICHARDSON, DANIEL
B. Jan. 25, 1863, Elmira, N. Y.
D. Sept. 12, 1926, New York, N. Y.

			G	W	L	T	N	PCT	Standing	
1892	WAS	N	43	12	31	0	0	.279	11 **12**	(2nd)

Branch Rickey

RICKEY, WESLEY BRANCH (The Mahatma)
B. Dec. 20, 1881, Flat, Ohio
D. Dec. 9, 1965, Columbia, Mo.
Hall of Fame 1967.

			G	W	L	T	N	PCT	Standing
1913	STL	A	12	5	6	1	0	.455	8 **8**
1914			159	71	82	6	0	.464	**5**
1915			159	63	91	5	0	.409	**6**
1919	STL	N	138	54	83	1	0	.394	**7**
1920			155	75	79	1	0	.487	**5**
1921			154	87	66	1	0	.569	**3**
1922			154	85	69	0	0	.552	**3**
1923			154	79	74	1	0	.516	**5**
1924			154	65	89	0	0	.422	**6**
1925			38	13	25	0	0	.342	**8** 4
10 yrs.			1277	597	664	16	0	.473	

Greg Riddoch

RIDDOCH, GREGORY LEE
B. July 15, 1945, Greeley, Colo.

			G	W	L	T	N	PCT	Standing
1990	SD	N	82	38	44	0	0	.463	4 **4**
1991			162	84	78	0	0	.519	**3**
1992			150	78	72	0	0	.520	**3** 3
3 yrs.			394	200	194	0	0	.508	

Jim Riggleman

RIGGLEMAN, JAMES DAVID
B. Nov. 9, 1952, Ft. Dix, N. J.

			G	W	L	T	N	PCT	Standing
1992	SD	N	12	4	8	0	0	.333	3 **3**
1993			162	61	101	0	0	.377	**7**
1994			117	47	70	0	0	.402	**4**
1995	CHI	N	144	73	71	0	0	.507	**3**
4 yrs.			435	185	250	0	0	.425	

Bill Rigney

RIGNEY, WILLIAM JOSEPH (Specs, The Cricket)
B. Jan. 29, 1918, Alameda, Calif.

			G	W	L	T	N	PCT	Standing
1956	NY	N	154	67	87	0	0	.435	**6**
1957			154	69	85	0	0	.448	**6**
1958	SF	N	154	80	74	0	0	.519	**3**
1959			154	83	71	0	0	.539	**3**
1960			58	33	25	0	0	.569	**2** 5
1961	LA	A	162	70	91	1	0	.435	**8**
1962			162	86	76	0	0	.531	**3**
1963			161	70	91	0	0	.435	**9**
1964			162	82	80	0	0	.506	**5**
1965	CAL	A	162	75	87	0	0	.463	**7**
1966			162	80	82	0	0	.494	**6**
1967			161	84	77	0	0	.522	**5**
1968			162	67	95	0	0	.414	**8**
1969			39	11	28	0	0	.282	**6** 3
1970	MIN	A	162	98	64	0	0	.605	**1**
1971			160	74	86	0	0	.463	**5**
1972			70	36	34	0	0	.514	**3** 3
1976	SF	N	162	74	88	0	0	.457	**4**
18 yrs.			2561	1239	1321	1	0	.484	

LEAGUE CHAMPIONSHIP SERIES

			G	W	L	T	N	PCT
1970	MIN	A	3	0	3	0	0	.000

Cal Ripken

RIPKEN, CALVIN EDWIN, SR.
Father of Cal Ripken.
Father of Billy Ripken.
B. Dec. 17, 1935, Aberdeen, Md.

			G	W	L	T	N	PCT	Standing
1985	BAL	A	1	1	0	0	0	1.000	4 **4** 4
1987			162	67	95	0	0	.414	**6**
1988			6	0	6	0	0	.000	**6** 7
3 yrs.			169	68	101	0	0	.402	

Frank Robinson

ROBINSON, FRANK
B. Aug. 31, 1935, Beaumont, Tex.
Hall of Fame 1982.

			G	W	L	T	N	PCT	Standing	
1975	CLE	A	159	79	80	0	0	.497	**4**	
1976			159	81	78	0	0	.509	**4**	
1977			57	26	31	0	0	.456	**6** 5	
1981	SF	N	59	27	32	0	0	.458	**5**	(1st)
1981			52	29	23	0	0	.558	**3**	(2nd)
1982			162	87	75	0	0	.537	**3**	
1983			162	79	83	0	0	.488	**5**	
1984			106	42	64	0	0	.396	**6** 6	
1988	BAL	A	155	54	101	0	0	.348	6 **7**	
1989			162	87	75	0	0	.537	**2**	
1990			161	76	85	0	0	.472	**5**	
1991			37	13	24	0	0	.351	**7** 6	
11 yrs.			1431	680	751	0	0	.475		

Wilbert Robinson

ROBINSON, WILBERT (Uncle Robbie)
Brother of Fred Robinson.
B. June 29, 1863, Bolton, Mass.
D. Aug. 8, 1934, Atlanta, Ga.
Hall of Fame 1945.

			G	W	L	T	N	PCT	Standing
1902	BAL	A	83	24	57	2	0	.296	7 **8**
1914	BKN	N	154	75	79	0	0	.487	**5**

Wilbert Robinson *continued*

			G	W	L	T	N	PCT	Standing
1915			154	80	72	2	0	.526	**3**
1916			156	94	60	2	0	.610	**1**
1917			156	70	81	5	0	.464	**7**
1918			127	57	69	0	1	.452	**5**
1919			141	69	71	1	0	.493	**5**
1920			155	93	61	1	0	.604	**1**
1921			152	77	75	0	0	.507	**5**
1922			155	76	78	1	0	.494	**6**
1923			155	76	78	1	0	.494	**6**
1924			154	92	62	0	0	.597	**2**
1925			153	68	85	0	0	.444	**6**
1926			155	71	82	2	0	.464	**6**
1927			154	65	88	1	0	.425	**6**
1928			155	77	76	2	0	.503	**6**
1929			153	70	83	0	0	.458	**6**
1930			154	86	68	0	0	.558	**4**
1931			153	79	73	1	0	.520	**4**
19 yrs.			2819	1399	1398	21	1	.500	

WORLD SERIES

			G	W	L	T	N	PCT
1916	**BKN**	**N**	5	1	4	0	0	.200
1920			7	2	5	0	0	.286
2 yrs.			12	3	9	0	0	.250

Matt Robison

ROBISON, MATTHEW STANLEY
B. Mar. 30, 1859, Pittsburgh, Pa.
D. Mar. 24, 1911, Cleveland, Ohio.

			G	W	L	T	N	PCT	Standing
1905	**STL**	**N**	50	19	31	0	0	.380	6 **6**

Buck Rodgers

RODGERS, ROBERT LEROY
B. Aug. 16, 1938, Delaware, Ohio.

			G	W	L	T	N	PCT	Standing	
1980	**MIL**	**A**	47	26	21	0	0	.553	**2** 3	
1980			23	13	10	0	0	.565	4 **3**	
1981			56	31	25	0	0	.554	**3**	(1st)
1981			53	31	22	0	0	.585	**1**	(2nd)
1982			47	23	24	0	0	.489	**5** 1	
1985	**MON**	**N**	161	84	77	0	0	.522	**3**	
1986			161	78	83	0	0	.484	**4**	
1987			162	91	71	0	0	.562	**3**	
1988			163	81	81	1	0	.500	**3**	
1989			162	81	81	0	0	.500	**4**	
1990			162	85	77	0	0	.525	**3**	
1991			49	20	29	0	0	.408	**6** 6	
1991	**CAL**	**A**	38	20	18	0	0	.526	7 **7**	
1992			39	19	20	0	0	.487	**5** 5	
1992			34	14	20	0	0	.412	5 **5**	
1993			162	71	91	0	0	.438	**5**	
1994			39	16	23	0	0	.410	**3** 4	
13 yrs.			1558	784	773	1	0	.504		

DIVISIONAL PLAYOFF SERIES

			G	W	L	T	N	PCT
1981	**MIL**	**A**	5	2	3	0	0	.400

Jim Rogers

ROGERS, JAMES F.
B. Apr. 9, 1872, Hartford, Conn.
D. Jan. 21, 1900, Bridgeport, Conn.

			G	W	L	T	N	PCT	Standing
1897	**LOU**	**N**	44	17	24	2	1	.415	**9** 11

Cookie Rojas

ROJAS, OCTAVIO VICTOR
Born Octavio Victor Rojas (Rivas).
B. Mar. 6, 1939, Havana, Cuba.

			G	W	L	T	N	PCT	Standing
1988	**CAL**	**A**	154	75	79	0	0	.487	**4** 4

Red Rolfe

ROLFE, ROBERT ABIAL
B. Oct. 17, 1908, Penacook, N. H.
D. July 8, 1969, Gifford, N. H.

			G	W	L	T	N	PCT	Standing
1949	**DET**	**A**	155	87	67	1	0	.565	**4**
1950			157	95	59	3	0	.617	**2**
1951			154	73	81	0	0	.474	**5**
1952			73	23	49	1	0	.319	**8** 8
4 yrs.			539	278	256	5	0	.521	

Pete Rose

ROSE, PETER EDWARD (Charlie Hustle)
B. Apr. 14, 1941, Cincinnati, Ohio

			G	W	L	T	N	PCT	Standing
1984	**CIN**	**N**	41	19	22	0	0	.463	5 **5**
1985			162	89	72	1	0	.553	**2**
1986			162	86	76	0	0	.531	**2**
1987			162	84	78	0	0	.519	**2**
1988			23	11	12	0	0	.478	**4** 2
1988			111	64	47	0	0	.577	4 **2**
1989			125	59	66	0	0	.472	**4** 5
6 yrs.			786	412	373	1	0	.525	

Chief Roseman

ROSEMAN, JAMES JOHN
B. July 4, 1856, Brooklyn, N. Y.
D. July 4, 1938, Brooklyn, N. Y.

			G	W	L	T	N	PCT	Standing
1890	**STL**	**AA**	36	17	19	0	0	.472	4 **5** 3

Dave Rowe

ROWE, DAVID ELWOOD (Eli)
Brother of Jack Rowe.
B. Oct. 9, 1854, Harrisburg, Pa.
D. Dec. 9, 1930, Glendale, Calif.

			G	W	L	T	N	PCT	Standing
1886	**KC**	**N**	126	30	91	5	0	.248	**7**
1888	**KC**	**AA**	50	14	36	0	0	.280	**8** 8
2 yrs.			176	44	127	5	0	.257	

Jack Rowe

ROWE, JOHN CHARLES
Brother of Dave Rowe.
B. Dec. 18, 1857, Harrisburg, Pa.
D. Apr. 25, 1911, St. Louis, Mo.

			G	W	L	T	N	PCT	Standing
1890	**BUF**	**P**	81	22	58	1	0	.275	**8** 8
1890			19	5	14	0	0	.263	8 **8**

Pants Rowland

ROWLAND, CLARENCE HENRY
B. Feb. 12, 1879, Platteville, Wis.
D. May 17, 1969, Chicago, Ill.

			G	W	L	T	N	PCT	Standing
1915	**CHI**	**A**	156	93	61	1	1	.604	**3**
1916			155	89	65	1	0	.578	**2**
1917			156	100	54	2	0	.649	**1**
1918			124	57	67	0	0	.460	**6**
4 yrs.			591	339	247	4	1	.578	

WORLD SERIES

			G	W	L	T	N	PCT
1917	**CHI**	**A**	6	4	2	0	0	.667

Dick Rudolph

RUDOLPH, RICHARD (Baldy)
B. Aug. 25, 1887, New York, N. Y.
D. Oct. 20, 1949, Bronx, N. Y.

			G	W	L	T	N	PCT	Standing
1924	**BOS**	**N**	38	11	27	0	0	.289	6 **8** 8

Muddy Ruel

RUEL, HEROLD DOMINIC
B. Feb. 20, 1896, St. Louis, Mo.
D. Nov. 13, 1963, Palo Alto, Calif.

			G	W	L	T	N	PCT	Standing
1947	**STL**	**A**	154	59	95	0	0	.383	**8**

Tom Runnells

RUNNELLS, THOMAS WILLIAM
B. Apr. 17, 1955, Greeley, Colo.

			G	W	L	T	N	PCT	Standing
1991	**MON**	**N**	112	51	61	0	0	.455	6 **6**
1992			37	17	20	0	0	.459	**4** 2
2 yrs.			149	68	81	0	0	.456	

Pete Runnels

RUNNELS, JAMES EDWARD
Born James Edward Runnells.
B. Jan. 28, 1928, Lufkin, Tex.
D. May 20, 1991, Pasadena, Tex.

			G	W	L	T	N	PCT	Standing
1966	**BOS**	**A**	16	8	8	0	0	.500	10 **9**

Connie Ryan

RYAN, CORNELIUS JOSEPH
B. Feb. 27, 1920, New Orleans, La.
D. Jan. 3, 1996, Metairie, La.

			G	W	L	T	N	PCT	Standing
1975	**ATL**	**N**	27	9	18	0	0	.333	5 **5**
1977	**TEX**	**A**	6	2	4	0	0	.333	2 **4** 2
2 yrs.			33	11	22	0	0	.333	

Eddie Sawyer

SAWYER, EDWIN MILBY
B. Sept. 10, 1910, Westerly, R. I.

			G	W	L	T	N	PCT	Standing
1948	**PHI**	**N**	63	23	40	0	0	.365	6 **6**
1949			154	81	73	0	0	.526	**3**
1950			157	91	63	3	0	.591	**1**
1951			154	73	81	0	0	.474	**5**
1952			63	28	35	0	0	.444	**6** 4
1958			70	30	40	0	0	.429	7 **8**
1959			155	64	90	1	0	.416	**8**
1960			1	0	1	0	0	.000	**8** 8
8 yrs.			817	390	423	4	0	.480	

WORLD SERIES

			G	W	L	T	N	PCT
1950	**PHI**	**N**	4	0	4	0	0	.000

Mike Scanlon

SCANLON, MICHAEL B.
B. Nov. 1843, Cork, Ireland
D. Jan. 18, 1929, Washington, D. C.

			G	W	L	T	N	PCT	Standing
1884	**WAS**	**U**	114	47	65	2	0	.420	**7**
1886	**WAS**	**N**	82	13	67	2	0	.162	**8** 8
2 yrs.			196	60	132	4	0	.313	

Bob Schaefer

SCHAEFER, ROBERT WALDEN
B. May 22, 1944, Putnam, Conn.

			G	W	L	T	N	PCT	Standing
1991	**KC**	**A**	1	1	0	0	0	1.000	7 **7** 6

Ray Schalk

SCHALK, RAYMOND WILLIAM (Cracker)
B. Aug. 12, 1892, Harvel, Ill.
D. May 19, 1970, Chicago, Ill.
Hall of Fame 1955.

			G	W	L	T	N	PCT	Standing
1927	**CHI**	**A**	153	70	83	0	0	.458	**5**
1928			75	32	42	1	0	.432	**6** 5
2 yrs.			228	102	125	1	0	.449	

Bob Scheffing

SCHEFFING, ROBERT BODEN
B. Aug. 11, 1913, Overland, Mo.
D. Oct. 26, 1985, Phoenix, Ariz.

			G	W	L	T	N	PCT	Standing
1957	**CHI**	**N**	156	62	92	2	0	.403	**7**
1958			154	72	82	0	0	.468	**5**
1959			155	74	80	1	0	.481	**5**
1961	**DET**	**A**	163	101	61	1	0	.623	**2**
1962			161	85	76	0	0	.528	**4**
1963			60	24	36	0	0	.400	**9** 5
6 yrs.			849	418	427	4	0	.495	

Harry Schlafly

SCHLAFLY, HARRY LINTON
B. Sept. 20, 1878, Port Washington, Ohio
D. June 27, 1919, Canton, Ohio.

			G	W	L	T	N	PCT	Standing
1914	**BUF**	**F**	156	80	71	4	1	.530	**4**
1915			41	13	28	0	0	.317	**8** 6
2 yrs.			197	93	99	4	1	.484	

Gus Schmelz

SCHMELZ, GUSTAVUS HEINRICH
B. Sept. 26, 1850, Columbus, Ohio
D. Oct. 14, 1925, Columbus, Ohio.

			G	W	L	T	N	PCT	Standing
1884	**COL**	**AA**	110	69	39	2	0	.639	**2**
1886	**STL**	**N**	126	43	79	4	0	.352	**6**
1887	**CIN**	**AA**	136	81	54	1	0	.600	**2**
1888			137	80	54	3	0	.597	**4**
1889			141	76	63	2	0	.547	**4**
1890	**CLE**	**N**	78	21	55	2	0	.276	**7** 7
1890	**COL**	**AA**	57	38	13	6	0	.745	5 **2** 2
1891			138	61	76	1	0	.445	**6**

Gus Schmelz *continued*

			G	W	L	T	N	PCT	Standing
1894	**WAS**	**N**	132	45	87	0	0	.341	**11**
1895			133	43	85	4	1	.336	**10**
1896			133	58	73	2	0	.443	**9**
1897			36	9	25	2	0	.265	**11** 6
11 yrs.			1357	624	703	29	1	.470	

Red Schoendienst

SCHOENDIENST, ALBERT FRED
B. Feb. 2, 1923, Germantown, Ill.
Hall of Fame 1989.

			G	W	L	T	N	PCT	Standing
1965	**STL**	**N**	162	80	81	1	0	.497	**7**
1966			162	83	79	0	0	.512	**6**
1967			161	101	60	0	0	.627	**1**
1968			162	97	65	0	0	.599	**1**
1969			162	87	75	0	0	.537	**4**
1970			162	76	86	0	0	.469	**4**
1971			163	90	72	1	0	.556	**2**
1972			156	75	81	0	0	.481	**4**
1973			162	81	81	0	0	.500	**2**
1974			161	86	75	0	0	.534	**2**
1975			163	82	80	1	0	.506	**3**
1976			162	72	90	0	0	.444	**5**
1980			37	18	19	0	0	.486	5 **4**
1990			24	13	11	0	0	.542	6 **6** 6
14 yrs.			1999	1041	955	3	0	.522	

WORLD SERIES

			G	W	L	T	N	PCT	Standing
1967	**STL**	**N**	7	4	3	0	0	.571	
1968			7	3	4	0	0	.429	
2 yrs.			14	7	7	0	0	.500	

Joe Schultz

SCHULTZ, JOSEPH CHARLES, JR. (Dode)
Son of Joe Schultz.
B. Aug. 29, 1918, Chicago, Ill.
D. Jan. 10, 1996, St. Louis, Mo.

			G	W	L	T	N	PCT	Standing
1969	**SEA**	**A**	163	64	98	1	0	.395	**6**
1973	**DET**	**A**	28	14	14	0	0	.500	3 **3**
2 yrs.			191	78	112	1	0	.411	

Frank Selee

SELEE, FRANK GIBSON
B. Oct. 26, 1859, Amherst, N. H.
D. July 5, 1909, Denver, Colo.

			G	W	L	T	N	PCT	Standing	
1890	**BOS**	**N**	134	76	57	1	0	.571	**5**	
1891			140	87	51	2	0	.630	**1**	
1892			75	52	22	1	0	.703	**1**	(1st)
1892			77	50	26	1	0	.658	**2**	(2nd)
1893			131	86	43	2	0	.667	**1**	
1894			133	83	49	1	0	.629	**3**	
1895			133	71	60	1	1	.542	**5**	
1896			132	74	57	1	0	.565	**4**	
1897			135	93	39	3	0	.705	**1**	
1898			152	102	47	3	0	.685	**1**	
1899			153	95	57	1	0	.625	**2**	
1900			142	66	72	4	0	.478	**4**	
1901			140	69	69	2	0	.500	**5**	
1902	**CHI**	**N**	143	68	69	4	2	.496	**5**	
1903			139	82	56	1	0	.594	**3**	
1904			156	93	60	3	0	.608	**2**	
1905			65	37	28	0	0	.569	**4** 3	
16 yrs.			2180	1284	862	31	3	.598 **4th**		

Luke Sewell

SEWELL, JAMES LUTHER
Brother of Joe Sewell.
Brother of Tommy Sewell.
B. Jan. 5, 1901, Titus, Ala.
D. May 14, 1987, Akron, Ohio.

			G	W	L	T	N	PCT	Standing
1941	**STL**	**A**	113	55	55	3	0	.500	7 **6**
1942			151	82	69	0	0	.543	**3**
1943			153	72	80	1	0	.474	**6**
1944			154	89	65	0	0	.578	**1**
1945			154	81	70	3	0	.536	**3**
1946			125	53	71	1	0	.427	**7** 7
1949	**CIN**	**N**	3	1	2	0	0	.333	7 **7**
1950			153	66	87	0	0	.431	**6**

Luke Sewell *continued*

			G	W	L	T	N	PCT	Standing
1951			155	68	86	1	0	.442	**6**
1952			98	39	59	0	0	.398	**7** 6
10 yrs.			1259	606	644	9	0	.485	

WORLD SERIES

			G	W	L	T	N	PCT	Standing
1944	**STL**	**A**	6	2	4	0	0	.333	

Dan Shannon

SHANNON, DANIEL WEBSTER
B. Mar. 23, 1865, Bridgeport, Conn.
D. Oct. 25, 1913, Bridgeport, Conn.

			G	W	L	T	N	PCT	Standing
1889	**LOU**	**AA**	58	10	46	2	0	.179	8 **8** 8
1891	**WAS**	**AA**	51	15	34	2	0	.306	7 **9** 9
2 yrs.			109	25	80	4	0	.238	

Bill Sharsig

SHARSIG, WILLIAM A.
B. 1855, Philadelphia, Pa.
D. Feb. 1, 1902, Philadelphia, Pa.

			G	W	L	T	N	PCT	Standing
1886	**PHI**	**AA**	41	22	17	2	0	.564	6 **6**
1888			137	81	52	3	1	.609	**3**
1889			138	75	58	5	0	.564	**3**
1890			132	54	78	0	0	.409	**8**
1891			18	6	11	1	0	.353	**7** 5
5 yrs.			466	238	216	11	1	.524	

Bob Shawkey

SHAWKEY, JAMES ROBERT
B. Dec. 4, 1890, Sigel, Pa.
D. Dec. 31, 1980, Syracuse, N. Y.

			G	W	L	T	N	PCT	Standing
1930	**NY**	**A**	154	86	68	0	0	.558	**3**

Tom Sheehan

SHEEHAN, THOMAS CLANCY
B. Mar. 31, 1894, Grand Ridge, Ill.
D. Oct. 29, 1982, Chillicothe, Ohio.

			G	W	L	T	N	PCT	Standing
1960	**SF**	**N**	98	46	50	2	0	.479	2 **5**

Larry Shepard

SHEPARD, LAWRENCE WILLIAM
B. Apr. 3, 1919, Lakewood, Ohio

			G	W	L	T	N	PCT	Standing
1968	**PIT**	**N**	163	80	82	1	0	.494	**6**
1969			157	84	73	0	0	.535	**3** 3
2 yrs.			320	164	155	1	0	.514	

Norm Sherry

SHERRY, NORMAN BURT
Brother of Larry Sherry.
B. July 16, 1931, New York, N. Y.

			G	W	L	T	N	PCT	Standing
1976	**CAL**	**A**	66	37	29	0	0	.561	4 **4**
1977			81	39	42	0	0	.481	**5** 5
2 yrs.			147	76	71	0	0	.517	

Bill Shettsline

SHETTSLINE, WILLIAM JOSEPH (Shetts)
B. Oct. 25, 1863, Philadelphia, Pa.
D. Feb. 22, 1933, Philadelphia, Pa.

			G	W	L	T	N	PCT	Standing
1898	**PHI**	**N**	104	59	44	1	0	.573	8 **6**
1899			154	94	58	2	0	.618	**3**
1900			141	75	63	3	0	.543	**3**
1901			140	83	57	0	0	.593	**2**
1902			138	56	81	1	0	.409	**7**
5 yrs.			677	367	303	7	0	.548	

Burt Shotton

SHOTTON, BURTON EDWIN (Barney)
B. Oct. 18, 1884, Brownhelm, Ohio
D. July 29, 1962, Lake Wales, Fla.

			G	W	L	T	N	PCT	Standing
1928	**PHI**	**N**	152	43	109	0	0	.283	**8**
1929			154	71	82	1	0	.464	**5**
1930			156	52	102	2	0	.338	**8**
1931			155	66	88	1	0	.429	**6**
1932			154	78	76	0	0	.506	**4**
1933			152	60	92	0	0	.395	**7**
1934	**CIN**	**N**	1	1	0	0	0	1.000	8 **8** 8
1947	**BKN**	**N**	153	92	60	1	0	.605	1 **1**

Burt Shotton *continued*

			G	W	L	T	N	PCT	Standing
1948			81	48	33	0	0	.593	5 **3**
1949			156	97	57	2	0	.630	**1**
1950			155	89	65	1	0	.578	**2**
11 yrs.			1469	697	764	8	0	.477	

WORLD SERIES

			G	W	L	T	N	PCT	Standing
1947	**BKN**	**N**	7	3	4	0	0	.429	
1949			5	1	4	0	0	.200	
2 yrs.			12	4	8	0	0	.333	

Buck Showalter

SHOWALTER, WILLIAM NATHANIEL III
B. May 23, 1956, DeFuniak, Fla.

			G	W	L	T	N	PCT	Standing
1992	**NY**	**A**	162	76	86	0	0	.469	**4**
1993			162	88	74	0	0	.543	**2**
1994			113	70	43	0	0	.619	**1**
1995			144	79	65	0	0	.549	**2**
4 yrs.			581	313	268	0	0	.539	

DIVISIONAL PLAYOFF SERIES

			G	W	L	T	N	PCT	Standing
1995	**NY**	**A**	5	2	3	0	0	.400	

Ken Silvestri

SILVESTRI, KENNETH JOSEPH (Hawk)
B. May 3, 1916, Chicago, Ill.
D. Mar. 31, 1992, Tallahassee, Fla.

			G	W	L	T	N	PCT	Standing
1967	**ATL**	**N**	3	0	3	0	0	.000	7 **7**

Joe Simmons

SIMMONS, JOSEPH S.
B. June 13, 1845, New York, N. Y.
Deceased.

			G	W	L	T	N	PCT	Standing
1884	**WIL**	**U**	18	2	16	0	0	.111	**13**

Lew Simmons

SIMMONS, LEWIS
B. Aug. 27, 1838, New Castle, Pa.
D. Sept. 2, 1911, Jamestown, Pa.

			G	W	L	T	N	PCT	Standing
1886	**PHI**	**AA**	98	41	55	2	0	.427	**6** 6

Dick Sisler

SISLER, RICHARD ALLAN
Brother of Dave Sisler.
Son of George Sisler.
B. Nov. 2, 1920, St. Louis, Mo.

			G	W	L	T	N	PCT	Standing
1964	**CIN**	**N**	6	3	3	0	0	.500	3 **4** 2
1964			47	29	18	0	0	.617	3 **2**
1965			162	89	73	0	0	.549	**4**
2 yrs.			215	121	94	0	0	.563	

George Sisler

SISLER, GEORGE HAROLD (Gorgeous George)
Father of Dave Sisler.
Father of Dick Sisler.
B. Mar. 24, 1893, Manchester, Ohio
D. Mar. 26, 1973, Richmond Heights, Mo.
Hall of Fame 1939.

			G	W	L	T	N	PCT	Standing
1924	**STL**	**A**	153	74	78	0	1	.487	**4**
1925			154	82	71	1	0	.536	**3**
1926			155	62	92	1	0	.403	**7**
3 yrs.			462	218	241	2	1	.475	

Frank Skaff

SKAFF, FRANCIS MICHAEL
B. Sept. 30, 1913, LaCrosse, Wis.
D. Apr. 12, 1988, Towson, Md.

			G	W	L	T	N	PCT	Standing
1966	**DET**	**A**	79	40	39	0	0	.506	3 **3**

Bob Skinner

SKINNER, ROBERT RALPH
Father of Joel Skinner.
B. Oct. 3, 1931, La Jolla, Calif.

			G	W	L	T	N	PCT	Standing
1968	**PHI**	**N**	107	48	59	0	0	.449	5 **8**
1969			108	44	64	0	0	.407	**5** 5
1977	**SD**	**N**	1	1	0	0	0	1.000	5 **5** 5
3 yrs.			216	93	123	0	0	.431	

Jack Slattery

SLATTERY, JOHN TERRENCE
B. Jan. 6, 1878, South Boston, Mass.
D. July 17, 1949, Boston, Mass.

			G	W	L	T	N	PCT	Standing
1928	BOS	N	31	11	20	0	0	.355	**7** 7

Harry Smith

SMITH, HARRY THOMAS
B. Oct. 31, 1874, Yorkshire, England
D. Feb. 17, 1933, Salem, N. J.

			G	W	L	T	N	PCT	Standing
1909	BOS	N	79	23	54	2	0	.299	**8** 8

Heinie Smith

SMITH, GEORGE HENRY
B. Oct. 24, 1871, Pittsburgh, Pa.
D. June 25, 1939, Buffalo, N. Y.

			G	W	L	T	N	PCT	Standing
1902	NY	N	32	5	27	0	0	.156	4 **8** 8

Mayo Smith

SMITH, EDWARD MAYO
B. Jan. 17, 1915, New London, Mo.
D. Nov. 24, 1977, Boynton Beach, Fla.

			G	W	L	T	N	PCT	Standing
1955	PHI	N	154	77	77	0	0	.500	**4**
1956			154	71	83	0	0	.461	**5**
1957			156	77	77	2	0	.500	**5**
1958			84	39	45	0	0	.464	**7** 8
1959	CIN	N	80	35	45	0	0	.438	**7** 5
1967	DET	A	163	91	71	1	0	.562	**2**
1968			164	103	59	2	0	.636	**1**
1969			162	90	72	0	0	.556	**2**
1970			162	79	83	0	0	.488	**4**
9 yrs.			1279	662	612	5	0	.520	

WORLD SERIES

			G	W	L	T	N	PCT
1968	DET	A	7	4	3	0	0	.571

Jimmy Snyder

SNYDER, JAMES ROBERT
B. Aug. 15, 1932, Dearborn, Mich.

			G	W	L	T	N	PCT	Standing
1988	SEA	A	105	45	60	0	0	.429	6 **7**

Pop Snyder

SNYDER, CHARLES N.
B. Oct. 6, 1854, Washington, D. C.
D. Oct. 29, 1924, Washington, D. C.

			G	W	L	T	N	PCT	Standing
1882	CIN	AA	80	55	25	0	0	.688	**1**
1883			98	61	37	0	0	.622	**3**
1884			40	24	14	2	0	.632	5 **5**
1891	WAS	AA	70	23	46	1	0	.333	6 **7** 9
4 yrs.			288	163	122	3	0	.572	

Allen Sothoron

SOTHORON, ALLEN SUTTON
B. Apr. 27, 1893, Bradford, Ohio
D. June 17, 1939, St. Louis, Mo.

			G	W	L	T	N	PCT	Standing
1933	STL	A	8	2	6	0	0	.250	8 **8** 8

Billy Southworth

SOUTHWORTH, WILLIAM HARRISON
B. Mar. 9, 1893, Harvard, Neb.
D. Nov. 15, 1969, Columbus, Ohio.

			G	W	L	T	N	PCT	Standing
1929	STL	N	90	43	45	2	0	.489	**4** 4
1940			111	69	40	2	0	.633	7 **3**
1941			155	97	56	2	0	.634	**2**
1942			156	106	48	2	0	.688	**1**
1943			157	105	49	3	0	.682	**1**
1944			157	105	49	3	0	.682	**1**
1945			155	95	59	1	0	.617	**2**
1946	BOS	N	154	81	72	1	0	.529	**4**
1947			154	86	68	0	0	.558	**3**
1948			154	91	62	1	0	.595	**1**
1949			111	55	54	2	0	.505	**4** 4
1950			156	83	71	2	0	.539	**4**
1951			60	28	31	1	0	.475	**5** 4
13 yrs.			1770	1044	704	22	0	.597 **5th**	

WORLD SERIES

			G	W	L	T	N	PCT
1942	STL	N	5	4	1	0	0	.800
1943			5	1	4	0	0	.200

Billy Southworth *continued*

			G	W	L	T	N	PCT
1944			6	4	2	0	0	.667
1948	BOS	N	6	2	4	0	0	.333
4 yrs.			22	11	11	0	0	.500 **9th**

Al Spalding

SPALDING, ALBERT GOODWILL
B. Sept. 2, 1850, Byron, Ill.
D. Sept. 9, 1915, San Diego, Calif.
Hall of Fame 1939.

			G	W	L	T	N	PCT	Standing
1876	CHI	N	66	52	14	0	0	.788	**1**
1877			60	26	33	1	0	.441	**5**
2 yrs.			126	78	47	1	0	.624	

Tris Speaker

SPEAKER, TRISTRAM E. (Spoke, The Grey Eagle)
B. Apr. 4, 1888, Hubbard, Tex.
D. Dec. 8, 1958, Lake Whitney, Tex.
Hall of Fame 1937.

			G	W	L	T	N	PCT	Standing
1919	CLE	A	61	40	21	0	0	.656	3 **2**
1920			154	98	56	0	0	.636	**1**
1921			154	94	60	0	0	.610	**2**
1922			155	78	76	1	0	.506	**4**
1923			153	82	71	0	0	.536	**3**
1924			153	67	86	0	0	.438	**6**
1925			155	70	84	1	0	.455	**6**
1926			154	88	66	0	0	.571	**2**
8 yrs.			1139	617	520	2	0	.543	

WORLD SERIES

			G	W	L	T	N	PCT
1920	CLE	A	7	5	2	0	0	.714

Harry Spence

SPENCE, HARRISON L.
B. Feb. 22, 1856, New York, N. Y.
D. May 17, 1908, Chicago, Ill.

			G	W	L	T	N	PCT	Standing
1888	IND	N	136	50	85	1	0	.370	**7**

Chick Stahl

STAHL, CHARLES SYLVESTER
B. Jan. 10, 1873, Avila, Ind.
D. Mar. 28, 1907, West Baden, Ind.

			G	W	L	T	N	PCT	Standing
1906	BOS	A	40	14	26	0	0	.350	8 **8**

Jake Stahl

STAHL, GARLAND
B. Apr. 13, 1879, Elkhart, Ill.
D. Sept. 18, 1922, Monrovia, Calif.

			G	W	L	T	N	PCT	Standing
1905	WAS	A	154	64	87	3	0	.424	**7**
1906			151	55	95	1	0	.367	**7**
1912	BOS	A	154	105	47	2	0	.691	**1**
1913			81	39	41	1	0	.488	**5** 4
4 yrs.			540	263	270	7	0	.493	

WORLD SERIES

			G	W	L	T	N	PCT
1912	BOS	A	8	4	3	1	0	.571

George Stallings

STALLINGS, GEORGE TWEEDY (The Miracle Man)
B. Nov. 17, 1867, Augusta, Ga.
D. May 13, 1929, Haddock, Ga.

			G	W	L	T	N	PCT	Standing
1897	PHI	N	134	55	77	2	0	.417	**10**
1898			46	19	27	0	0	.413	**8** 6
1901	DET	A	136	74	61	1	0	.548	**3**
1909	NY	A	153	74	77	2	0	.490	**5**
1910			142	78	59	5	0	.569	**3** 2
1913	BOS	N	154	69	82	3	0	.457	**5**
1914			158	94	59	5	0	.614	**1**
1915			157	83	69	5	0	.546	**2**
1916			158	89	63	6	0	.586	**3**
1917			158	72	81	4	1	.471	**6**
1918			124	53	71	0	0	.427	**7**
1919			140	57	82	1	0	.410	**6**
1920			153	62	90	1	0	.408	**7**
13 yrs.			1813	879	898	35	1	.495	

WORLD SERIES

			G	W	L	T	N	PCT
1914	BOS	N	4	4	0	0	0	1.000

Eddie Stanky

STANKY, EDWARD RAYMOND (Muggsy, The Brat)
B. Sept. 3, 1916, Philadelphia, Pa.

			G	W	L	T	N	PCT	Standing
1952	STL	N	154	88	66	0	0	.571	**3**
1953			157	83	71	3	0	.539	**3**
1954			154	72	82	0	0	.468	**6**
1955			36	17	19	0	0	.472	**5** 7
1966	CHI	A	163	83	79	1	0	.512	**4**
1967			162	89	73	0	0	.549	**4**
1968			79	34	45	0	0	.430	**9** 8
1977	TEX	A	1	1	0	0	0	1.000	4 **2** 2
8 yrs.			906	467	435	4	0	.518	

Casey Stengel

STENGEL, CHARLES DILLON (The Old Professor)
B. July 30, 1890, Kansas City, Mo.
D. Sept. 29, 1975, Glendale, Calif.
Hall of Fame 1966.

			G	W	L	T	N	PCT	Standing
1934	BKN	N	153	71	81	1	0	.467	**6**
1935			154	70	83	1	0	.458	**5**
1936			156	67	87	2	0	.435	**7**
1938	BOS	N	153	77	75	1	0	.507	**5**
1939			152	63	88	1	0	.417	**7**
1940			152	65	87	0	0	.428	**7**
1941			156	62	92	2	0	.403	**7**
1942			150	59	89	2	0	.399	**7**
1943			107	47	60	0	0	.439	6 **6**
1949	NY	A	155	97	57	1	0	.630	**1**
1950			155	98	56	1	0	.636	**1**
1951			154	98	56	0	0	.636	**1**
1952			154	95	59	0	0	.617	**1**
1953			151	99	52	0	0	.656	**1**
1954			155	103	51	1	0	.669	**2**
1955			154	96	58	0	0	.623	**1**
1956			154	97	57	0	0	.630	**1**
1957			154	98	56	0	0	.636	**1**
1958			155	92	62	1	0	.597	**1**
1959			155	79	75	1	0	.513	**3**
1960			155	97	57	1	0	.630	**1**
1962	NY	N	161	40	120	1	0	.250	**10**
1963			162	51	111	0	0	.315	**10**
1964			163	53	109	1	0	.327	**10**
1965			96	31	64	1	0	.326	**10** 10
25 yrs.			3766 **6th**	1905 **8th**	1842 **5th**	19	0	.508	

WORLD SERIES

			G	W	L	T	N	PCT
1949	NY	A	5	4	1	0	0	.800
1950			4	4	0	0	0	1.000
1951			6	4	2	0	0	.667
1952			7	4	3	0	0	.571
1953			6	4	2	0	0	.667
1955			7	3	4	0	0	.429
1956			7	4	3	0	0	.571
1957			7	3	4	0	0	.429
1958			7	4	3	0	0	.571
1960			7	3	4	0	0	.429
10 yrs.			63 **1st**	37 **1st**	26 **2nd**	0	0	.587 **2nd**

George Stovall

STOVALL, GEORGE THOMAS (Firebrand)
Brother of Jesse Stovall.
B. Nov. 23, 1878, Independence, Mo.
D. Nov. 5, 1951, Burlington, Iowa.

			G	W	L	T	N	PCT	Standing
1911	CLE	A	139	74	62	3	0	.544	7 **3**
1912	STL	A	117	41	74	2	0	.357	8 **7**
1913			135	50	84	1	0	.373	**7** 8
1914	KC	F	154	67	84	3	0	.444	**6**
1915			153	81	72	0	0	.529	**4**
5 yrs.			698	313	376	9	0	.454	

Harry Stovey

STOVEY, HARRY DUFFIELD
Born Harry Duffield Stowe.
B. Dec. 20, 1856, Philadelphia, Pa.
D. Sept. 20, 1937, New Bedford, Mass.

			G	W	L	T	N	PCT	Standing
1881	WOR	N	27	8	18	1	0	.308	7 **8**
1885	PHI	AA	113	55	57	1	0	.491	**4**
2 yrs.			140	63	75	2	0	.457	

Gabby Street

STREET, CHARLES EVARD (Old Sarge)
B. Sept. 30, 1882, Huntsville, Ala.
D. Feb. 6, 1951, Joplin, Mo.

Year	Team	Lg	G	W	L	T	N	PCT	Standing
1929	**STL**	**N**	1	1	0	0	0	1.000	4 **4** 4
1930			154	92	62	0	0	.597	**1**
1931			154	101	53	0	0	.656	**1**
1932			156	72	82	2	0	.468	**6**
1933			91	46	45	0	0	.505	**5** 5
1938	**STL**	**A**	146	53	90	3	0	.371	**7** 7
6 yrs.			702	365	332	5	0	.524	
WORLD SERIES									
1930	**STL**	**N**	6	2	4	0	0	.333	
1931			7	4	3	0	0	.571	
2 yrs.			13	6	7	0	0	.462	

Cub Stricker

STRICKER, JOHN A.
Born John A. Streaker.
B. June 8, 1859, Philadelphia, Pa.
D. Nov. 19, 1937, Philadelphia, Pa.

Year	Team	Lg	G	W	L	T	N	PCT	Standing
1892	**STL**	**N**	23	6	17	0	0	.261	10 **11** 9 (1st)

George Strickland

STRICKLAND, GEORGE BEVAN (Bo)
B. Jan. 10, 1926, New Orleans, La.

Year	Team	Lg	G	W	L	T	N	PCT	Standing
1964	**CLE**	**A**	73	33	39	1	0	.458	**8** 6
1966			39	15	24	0	0	.385	5 **5**
2 yrs.			112	48	63	1	0	.432	

Larry Stubing

STUBING, LAWRENCE GEORGE (Moose)
B. Mar. 31, 1938, Bronx, N. Y.

Year	Team	Lg	G	W	L	T	N	PCT	Standing
1988	**CAL**	**A**	8	0	8	0	0	.000	4 **4**

Clyde Sukeforth

SUKEFORTH, CLYDE LeROY (Sukey)
B. Nov. 30, 1901, Washington, Me.

Year	Team	Lg	G	W	L	T	N	PCT	Standing
1947	**BKN**	**N**	2	2	0	0	0	1.000	**1** 1

Billy Sullivan

SULLIVAN, WILLIAM JOSEPH, SR.
Father of Billy Sullivan.
B. Feb. 1, 1875, Oakland, Wis.
D. Jan. 28, 1965, Newberg, Ore.

Year	Team	Lg	G	W	L	T	N	PCT	Standing
1909	**CHI**	**A**	159	78	74	7	0	.513	**4**

Haywood Sullivan

SULLIVAN, HAYWOOD COOPER
Father of Marc Sullivan.
B. Dec. 15, 1930, Donalsonville, Ga.

Year	Team	Lg	G	W	L	T	N	PCT	Standing
1965	**KC**	**A**	136	54	82	0	0	.397	10 **10**

Pat Sullivan

SULLIVAN, JAMES PATRICK
D. May 22, 1898

Year	Team	Lg	G	W	L	T	N	PCT	Standing
1890	**COL**	**AA**	3	2	1	0	0	.667	2 **2**

Ted Sullivan

SULLIVAN, THEODORE PAUL
B. 1851, County Clare, Ireland
D. July 5, 1929, Washington, D. C.

Year	Team	Lg	G	W	L	T	N	PCT	Standing
1883	**STL**	**AA**	79	53	26	0	0	.671	**2** 2
1884	**STL**	**U**	31	28	3	0	0	.903	**1** 1
1884	**KC**	**U**	62	13	46	3	0	.220	12 **12**
1888	**WAS**	**N**	96	38	57	1	0	.400	8 **8**
3 yrs.			268	132	132	4	0	.500	

Bob Swift

SWIFT, ROBERT VIRGIL
B. Mar. 6, 1915, Salina, Kans.
D. Oct. 17, 1966, Detroit, Mich.

Year	Team	Lg	G	W	L	T	N	PCT	Standing
1965	**DET**	**A**	42	24	18	0	0	.571	**3** 4
1966			57	32	25	0	0	.561	3 **3** 3
2 yrs.			99	56	43	0	0	.566	

Chuck Tanner

TANNER, CHARLES WILLIAM
Father of Bruce Tanner.
B. July 4, 1929, New Castle, Pa.

Year	Team	Lg	G	W	L	T	N	PCT	Standing
1970	**CHI**	**A**	16	3	13	0	0	.188	6 **6**
1971			162	79	83	0	0	.488	**3**
1972			154	87	67	0	0	.565	**2**
1973			162	77	85	0	0	.475	**5**
1974			163	80	80	3	0	.500	**4**
1975			161	75	86	0	0	.466	**5**
1976	**OAK**	**A**	161	87	74	0	0	.540	**2**
1977	**PIT**	**N**	162	96	66	0	0	.593	**2**
1978			161	88	73	0	0	.547	**2**
1979			163	98	64	1	0	.605	**1**
1980			162	83	79	0	0	.512	**3**
1981			49	25	23	1	0	.521	**4** (1st)
1981			54	21	33	0	0	.389	**6** (2nd)
1982			162	84	78	0	0	.519	**4**
1983			162	84	78	0	0	.519	**2**
1984			162	75	87	0	0	.463	**6**
1985			161	57	104	0	0	.354	**6**
1986	**ATL**	**N**	161	72	89	0	0	.447	**6**
1987			161	69	92	0	0	.429	**5**
1988			39	12	27	0	0	.308	**6** 6
19 yrs.			2738	1352	1381	5	0	.495	
LEAGUE CHAMPIONSHIP SERIES									
1979	**PIT**	**N**	3	3	0	0	0	1.000	
WORLD SERIES									
1979	**PIT**	**N**	7	4	3	0	0	.571	

El Tappe

TAPPE, ELVIN WALTER
B. May 21, 1927, Quincy, Ill.

Year	Team	Lg	G	W	L	T	N	PCT	Standing
1961	**CHI**	**N**	2	2	0	0	0	1.000	7 **7** 7
1961			79	35	43	1	0	.449	7 **7** 7
1961			16	5	11	0	0	.313	7 **7**
1962			20	4	16	0	0	.200	**9** 9
2 yrs.			117	46	70	1	0	.397	

George Taylor

TAYLOR, GEORGE J.
B. Nov. 22, 1853, New York, N. Y.
Deceased.

Year	Team	Lg	G	W	L	T	N	PCT	Standing
1884	**BKN**	**AA**	109	40	64	5	0	.385	**9**

Zack Taylor

TAYLOR, JAMES WREN
B. July 27, 1898, Yulee, Fla.
D. Sept. 19, 1974, Orlando, Fla.

Year	Team	Lg	G	W	L	T	N	PCT	Standing
1946	**STL**	**A**	31	13	17	1	0	.433	7 **7**
1948			155	59	94	2	0	.386	**6**
1949			155	53	101	1	0	.344	**7**
1950			154	58	96	0	0	.377	**7**
1951			154	52	102	0	0	.338	**8**
5 yrs.			649	235	410	4	0	.364	

Birdie Tebbetts

TEBBETTS, GEORGE ROBERT
B. Nov. 10, 1912, Burlington, Vt.

Year	Team	Lg	G	W	L	T	N	PCT	Standing
1954	**CIN**	**N**	154	74	80	0	0	.481	**5**
1955			154	75	79	0	0	.487	**5**
1956			155	91	63	1	0	.591	**3**
1957			154	80	74	0	0	.519	**4**
1958			113	52	61	0	0	.460	**7** 4
1961	**MIL**	**N**	25	12	13	0	0	.480	3 **4**
1962			162	86	76	0	0	.531	**5**
1963	**CLE**	**A**	162	79	83	0	0	.488	**5**
1964			91	46	44	1	0	.511	8 **6**
1965			162	87	75	0	0	.537	**5**
1966			123	66	57	0	0	.537	**5** 5
11 yrs.			1455	748	705	2	0	.515	

Patsy Tebeau

TEBEAU, OLIVER WENDELL
Brother of White Wings Tebeau.
B. Dec. 5, 1864, St. Louis, Mo.
D. May 15, 1918, St. Louis, Mo.

Year	Team	Lg	G	W	L	T	N	PCT	Standing
1890	**CLE**	**P**	52	21	30	1	0	.412	7 **7**
1891	**CLE**	**N**	73	31	40	2	0	.459	6 **5**

Patsy Tebeau *continued*

Year	Team	Lg	G	W	L	T	N	PCT	Standing
1892			74	40	33	1	0	.548	**5** (1st)
1892			79	53	23	3	0	.697	**1** (2nd)
1893			129	73	55	1	0	.570	**3**
1894			130	68	61	1	0	.527	**6**
1895			132	84	46	1	1	.646	**2**
1896			135	80	48	7	0	.625	**2**
1897			132	69	62	1	0	.527	**5**
1898			156	81	68	7	0	.544	**5**
1899	**STL**	**N**	155	84	67	4	0	.556	**5**
1900			92	42	50	0	0	.457	**7** 5
11 yrs.			1339	726	583	29	1	.555	

Gene Tenace

TENACE, FURY GENE
Born Fiore Gino Tennaci.
B. Oct. 10, 1946, Russellton, Pa.

Year	Team	Lg	G	W	L	T	N	PCT	Standing
1991	**TOR**	**A**	33	19	14	0	0	.576	1 **1** 1

Fred Tenney

TENNEY, FREDERICK
B. Nov. 26, 1871, Georgetown, Mass.
D. July 3, 1952, Boston, Mass.

Year	Team	Lg	G	W	L	T	N	PCT	Standing
1905	**BOS**	**N**	156	51	103	2	0	.331	**7**
1906			152	49	102	1	0	.325	**8**
1907			152	58	90	4	0	.392	**7**
1911			156	44	107	5	0	.291	**8**
4 yrs.			616	202	402	12	0	.334	

Bill Terry

TERRY, WILLIAM HAROLD (Memphis Bill)
B. Oct. 30, 1896, Atlanta, Ga.
D. Jan. 9, 1989, Jacksonville, Fla.
Hall of Fame 1954.

Year	Team	Lg	G	W	L	T	N	PCT	Standing
1932	**NY**	**N**	114	55	59	0	0	.482	8 **6**
1933			156	91	61	4	0	.599	**1**
1934			153	93	60	0	0	.608	**2**
1935			156	91	62	3	0	.595	**3**
1936			154	92	62	0	0	.597	**1**
1937			152	95	57	0	0	.625	**1**
1938			152	83	67	2	0	.553	**3**
1939			151	77	74	0	0	.510	**5**
1940			152	72	80	0	0	.474	**6**
1941			156	74	79	3	0	.484	**5**
10 yrs.			1496	823	661	12	0	.555	
WORLD SERIES									
1933	**NY**	**N**	5	4	1	0	0	.800	
1936			6	2	4	0	0	.333	
1937			5	1	4	0	0	.200	
3 yrs.			16	7	9	0	0	.438	

Fred Thomas

THOMAS, FREDERICK L.
B. Ind.
Deceased.

Year	Team	Lg	G	W	L	T	N	PCT	Standing
1887	**IND**	**N**	29	11	18	0	0	.379	8 **8** 8

Andrew Thompson

THOMPSON, ANDREW M.
B. 1846, Ill.
Deceased.

Year	Team	Lg	G	W	L	T	N	PCT	Standing
1884	**STP**	**U**	9	2	6	1	0	.250	**10**

Jack Tighe

TIGHE, JOHN THOMAS
B. Aug. 9, 1913, Kearny, N. J.

Year	Team	Lg	G	W	L	T	N	PCT	Standing
1957	**DET**	**A**	154	78	76	0	0	.506	**4**
1958			49	21	28	0	0	.429	**5** 5
2 yrs.			203	99	104	0	0	.488	

Joe Tinker

TINKER, JOSEPH BERT
B. July 27, 1880, Muscotah, Kans.
D. July 27, 1948, Orlando, Fla.
Hall of Fame 1946.

Year	Team	Lg	G	W	L	T	N	PCT	Standing
1913	**CIN**	**N**	156	64	89	3	0	.418	**7**
1914	**CHI**	**F**	158	87	67	3	1	.565	**2**

Joe Tinker *continued*

Year	Team	Lg	G	W	L	T	N	PCT	Standing
1915			156	86	66	3	1	.566	**1**
1916	CHI	N	156	67	86	3	0	.438	**5**
4 yrs.			626	304	308	12	2	.497	

Jeff Torborg

TORBORG, JEFFREY ALLEN
B. Nov. 26, 1941, Plainfield, N. J.

Year	Team	Lg	G	W	L	T	N	PCT	Standing
1977	CLE	A	104	45	59	0	0	.433	6 **5**
1978			159	69	90	0	0	.434	**6**
1979			95	43	52	0	0	.453	**6** 6
1989	CHI	A	161	69	92	0	0	.429	**7**
1990			162	94	68	0	0	.580	**2**
1991			162	87	75	0	0	.537	**2**
1992	NY	N	162	72	90	0	0	.444	**5**
1993			38	13	25	0	0	.342	**7** 7
8 yrs.			1043	492	551	0	0	.472	

Joe Torre

TORRE, JOSEPH PAUL
Brother of Frank Torre.
B. July 18, 1940, Brooklyn, N. Y.

Year	Team	Lg	G	W	L	T	N	PCT	Standing
1977	NY	N	117	49	68	0	0	.419	6 **6**
1978			162	66	96	0	0	.407	**6**
1979			163	63	99	1	0	.389	**6**
1980			162	67	95	0	0	.414	**5**
1981			52	17	34	1	0	.333	**5** (1st)
1981			53	24	28	1	0	.462	**4** (2nd)
1982	ATL	N	162	89	73	0	0	.549	**1**
1983			162	88	74	0	0	.543	**2**
1984			162	80	82	0	0	.494	**2**
1990	STL	N	58	24	34	0	0	.414	6 **6**
1991			162	84	78	0	0	.519	**2**
1992			162	83	79	0	0	.512	**3**
1993			162	87	75	0	0	.537	**3**
1994			115	53	61	1	0	.465	**3**
1995			47	20	27	0	0	.426	**4** 4
14 yrs.			1901	894	1003	4	0	.471	

LEAGUE CHAMPIONSHIP SERIES

Year	Team	Lg	G	W	L	T	N	PCT
1982	ATL	N	3	0	3	0	0	.000

Dick Tracewski

TRACEWSKI, RICHARD JOSEPH
B. Feb. 3, 1935, Eynon, Pa.

Year	Team	Lg	G	W	L	T	N	PCT	Standing
1979	DET	A	2	2	0	0	0	1.000	5 **5** 5

Pie Traynor

TRAYNOR, HAROLD JOSEPH
B. Nov. 11, 1899, Framingham, Mass.
D. Mar. 16, 1972, Pittsburgh, Pa.
Hall of Fame 1948.

Year	Team	Lg	G	W	L	T	N	PCT	Standing
1934	PIT	N	100	47	52	1	0	.475	4 **5**
1935			153	86	67	0	0	.562	**4**
1936			156	84	70	2	0	.545	**4**
1937			154	86	68	0	0	.558	**3**
1938			152	86	64	2	0	.573	**2**
1939			153	68	85	0	0	.444	**6**
6 yrs.			868	457	406	5	0	.530	

Tom Trebelhorn

TREBELHORN, THOMAS LYNN
B. Jan. 27, 1948, Portland, Ore.

Year	Team	Lg	G	W	L	T	N	PCT	Standing
1986	MIL	A	9	6	3	0	0	.667	6 **6**
1987			162	91	71	0	0	.562	**3**
1988			162	87	75	0	0	.537	**3**
1989			162	81	81	0	0	.500	**4**
1990			162	74	88	0	0	.457	**6**
1991			162	83	79	0	0	.512	**4**
1994	CHI	N	113	49	64	0	0	.434	**5**
7 yrs.			932	471	461	0	0	.505	

Sam Trott

TROTT, SAMUEL W.
B. Mar. 1859, Washington, D. C.
D. June 5, 1925, Catonsville, Md.

Year	Team	Lg	G	W	L	T	N	PCT	Standing
1891	WAS	AA	12	4	7	1	0	.364	**6** 9

Ted Turner

TURNER, ROBERT EDWARD
B. Nov. 19, 1938, Cincinnati, Ohio

Year	Team	Lg	G	W	L	T	N	PCT	Standing
1977	ATL	N	1	0	1	0	0	.000	6 **6** 6

Bob Unglaub

UNGLAUB, ROBERT ALEXANDER
B. July 31, 1881, Baltimore, Md.
D. Nov. 29, 1916, Baltimore, Md.

Year	Team	Lg	G	W	L	T	N	PCT	Standing
1907	BOS	A	29	9	20	0	0	.310	6 **8** 7

Bobby Valentine

VALENTINE, ROBERT JOHN
B. May 13, 1950, Stamford, Conn.

Year	Team	Lg	G	W	L	T	N	PCT	Standing
1985	TEX	A	129	53	76	0	0	.411	7 **7**
1986			162	87	75	0	0	.537	**2**
1987			162	75	87	0	0	.463	**6**
1988			161	70	91	0	0	.435	**6**
1989			162	83	79	0	0	.512	**4**
1990			162	83	79	0	0	.512	**3**
1991			162	85	77	0	0	.525	**3**
1992			86	45	41	0	0	.523	**3** 4
8 yrs.			1186	581	605	0	0	.490	

George Van Haltren

VAN HALTREN, GEORGE EDWARD MARTIN
B. Mar. 30, 1866, St. Louis, Mo.
D. Sept. 29, 1945, Oakland, Calif.

Year	Team	Lg	G	W	L	T	N	PCT	Standing
1892	BAL	N	11	1	10	0	0	.091	**12** 12 (1st)

Mickey Vernon

VERNON, JAMES BARTON
B. Apr. 22, 1918, Marcus Hook, Pa.

Year	Team	Lg	G	W	L	T	N	PCT	Standing
1961	WAS	A	161	61	100	0	0	.379	**9**
1962			162	60	101	1	0	.373	**10**
1963			40	14	26	0	0	.350	**10** 10
3 yrs.			363	135	227	1	0	.373	

Bill Virdon

VIRDON, WILLIAM CHARLES
B. June 9, 1931, Hazel Park, Mich.

Year	Team	Lg	G	W	L	T	N	PCT	Standing
1972	PIT	N	155	96	59	0	0	.619	**1**
1973			136	67	69	0	0	.493	**2** 3
1974	NY	A	162	89	73	0	0	.549	**2**
1975			104	53	51	0	0	.510	**3** 3
1975	HOU	N	35	17	17	1	0	.500	6 **6**
1976			162	80	82	0	0	.494	**3**
1977			162	81	81	0	0	.500	**3**
1978			162	74	88	0	0	.457	**5**
1979			162	89	73	0	0	.549	**2**
1980			163	93	70	0	0	.571	**1**
1981			57	28	29	0	0	.491	**3** (1st)
1981			53	33	20	0	0	.623	**1** (2nd)
1982			111	49	62	0	0	.441	**5** 5
1983	MON	N	163	82	80	1	0	.506	**3**
1984			131	64	67	0	0	.489	**5** 5
13 yrs.			1918	995	921	2	0	.519	

DIVISIONAL PLAYOFF SERIES

Year	Team	Lg	G	W	L	T	N	PCT
1981	HOU	N	5	2	3	0	0	.400

LEAGUE CHAMPIONSHIP SERIES

Year	Team	Lg	G	W	L	T	N	PCT
1972	PIT	N	5	2	3	0	0	.400
1980	HOU	N	5	2	3	0	0	.400
2 yrs.			10	4	6	0	0	.400

Ossie Vitt

VITT, OSCAR JOSEPH
B. Jan. 4, 1890, San Francisco, Calif.
D. Jan. 31, 1963, Oakland, Calif.

Year	Team	Lg	G	W	L	T	N	PCT	Standing
1938	CLE	A	153	86	66	1	0	.566	**3**
1939			154	87	67	0	0	.565	**3**
1940			155	89	65	1	0	.578	**2**
3 yrs.			462	262	198	2	0	.570	

Chris Von Der Ahe

VON DER AHE, CHRISTIAN FREDERICK WILHELM
B. Oct. 7, 1851, Hille, Germany
D. June 7, 1913, St. Louis, Mo.

Year	Team	Lg	G	W	L	T	N	PCT	Standing
895	STL	N	1	1	0	0	0	1.000	11 **11** 11
1895	STL	N	1	1	0	0	0	1.000	11 **11** 11
1896			2	0	2	0	0	.000	10 **11** 11
1897			14	2	12	0	0	.143	12 **12**
3 yrs.			17	3	14	0	0	.176	

John Vukovich

VUKOVICH, JOHN CHRISTOPHER
B. July 31, 1947, Sacramento, Calif.

Year	Team	Lg	G	W	L	T	N	PCT	Standing
1986	CHI	N	2	1	1	0	0	.500	5 **5** 5
1988	PHI	N	9	5	4	0	0	.556	6 **6**
2 yrs.			11	6	5	0	0	.545	

Heinie Wagner

WAGNER, CHARLES F.
B. Sept. 23, 1880, New York, N. Y.
D. Mar. 20, 1943, New Rochelle, N. Y.

Year	Team	Lg	G	W	L	T	N	PCT	Standing
1930	BOS	A	154	52	102	0	0	.338	**8**

Honus Wagner

WAGNER, JOHN PETER (The Flying Dutchman)
Brother of Butts Wagner.
B. Feb. 24, 1874, Chartiers, Pa.
D. Dec. 6, 1955, Carnegie, Pa.
Hall of Fame 1936.

Year	Team	Lg	G	W	L	T	N	PCT	Standing
1917	PIT	N	5	1	4	0	0	.200	8 **8** 8

Harry Walker

WALKER, HARRY WILLIAM (The Hat)
Son of Dixie Walker.
Brother of Dixie Walker.
B. Oct. 22, 1916, Pascagoula, Miss.

Year	Team	Lg	G	W	L	T	N	PCT	Standing
1955	STL	N	118	51	67	0	0	.432	5 **7**
1965	PIT	N	163	90	72	1	0	.556	**3**
1966			162	92	70	0	0	.568	**3**
1967			84	42	42	0	0	.500	**6** 6
1968	HOU	N	101	49	52	0	0	.485	10 **10**
1969			162	81	81	0	0	.500	**5**
1970			162	79	83	0	0	.488	**4**
1971			162	79	83	0	0	.488	**4**
1972			121	67	54	0	0	.554	**3** 2
9 yrs.			1235	630	604	1	0	.511	

Bobby Wallace

WALLACE, RHODERICK JOHN (Rhody)
B. Nov. 4, 1873, Pittsburgh, Pa.
D. Nov. 3, 1960, Torrance, Calif.
Hall of Fame 1953.

Year	Team	Lg	G	W	L	T	N	PCT	Standing
1911	STL	A	152	45	107	0	0	.296	**8**
1912			40	12	27	1	0	.308	**8** 7
1937	CIN	N	25	5	20	0	0	.200	8 **8**
3 yrs.			217	62	154	1	0	.287	

Ed Walsh

WALSH, EDWARD AUGUSTINE (Big Ed)
Father of Ed Walsh.
B. May 14, 1881, Plains, Pa.
D. May 26, 1959, Pompano Beach, Fla.
Hall of Fame 1946.

Year	Team	Lg	G	W	L	T	N	PCT	Standing
1924	CHI	A	3	1	2	0	0	.333	6 **6** 8

Mike Walsh

WALSH, MICHAEL JOHN
B. Apr. 29, 1850, Ireland
D. Feb. 2, 1929, Louisville, Ky.

Year	Team	Lg	G	W	L	T	N	PCT	Standing
1884	LOU	AA	110	68	40	2	0	.630	**3**

Bucky Walters

WALTERS, WILLIAM HENRY
B. Apr. 19, 1909, Philadelphia, Pa.
D. Apr. 20, 1991, Abington, Pa.

			G	W	L	T	N	PCT	Standing			
1948	**CIN**	**N**	53	20	33	0	0	.377	7	**7**		
1949			153	61	90	2	0	.404	**7**	7		
2 yrs.			206	81	123	2	0	.397				

John Waltz

WALTZ, JOHN J.
Deceased.

			G	W	L	T	N	PCT	Standing			
1892	**BAL**	**N**	8	2	6	0	0	.250	12	**12**	12	(1st)

Monte Ward

WARD, JOHN MONTGOMERY
B. Mar. 3, 1860, Bellefonte, Pa.
D. Mar. 4, 1925, Augusta, Ga.
Hall of Fame 1964.

			G	W	L	T	N	PCT	Standing			
1880	**PRO**	**N**	32	18	13	1	0	.581	4	**3**	2	
1884	**NY**	**N**	16	6	8	2	0	.429	4	**4**		
1890	**BKN**	**P**	133	76	56	1	0	.576	**2**			
1891	**BKN**	**N**	137	61	76	0	0	.445	**6**			
1892			78	51	26	1	0	.662	**2**			(1st)
1892			80	44	33	3	0	.571	**3**			(2nd)
1893	**NY**	**N**	136	68	64	4	0	.515	**5**			
1894			139	88	44	5	2	.667	**2**			
7 yrs.			751	412	320	17	2	.563				

John Wathan

WATHAN, JOHN DAVID (Duke)
B. Oct. 4, 1949, Cedar Rapids, Iowa

			G	W	L	T	N	PCT	Standing			
1987	**KC**	**A**	36	21	15	0	0	.583	4	**2**		
1988			161	84	77	0	0	.522	**3**			
1989			162	92	70	0	0	.568	**2**			
1990			161	75	86	0	0	.466	**6**			
1991			37	15	22	0	0	.405	**7**	6		
1992	**CAL**	**A**	89	39	50	0	0	.438	5	**5**	5	
6 yrs.			646	326	320	0	0	.505				

Bill Watkins

WATKINS, WILLIAM HENRY
B. May 5, 1858, Brantford, Ont., Canada
D. June 9, 1937, Port Huron, Mich.

			G	W	L	T	N	PCT	Standing			
1884	**IND**	**AA**	23	4	18	1	0	.182	10	**11**		
1885	**DET**	**N**	70	34	36	0	0	.486	7	**6**		
1886			126	87	36	3	0	.707	**2**			
1887			127	79	45	3	0	.637	**1**			
1888			94	49	44	1	0	.527	**3**	5		
1888	**KC**	**AA**	25	8	17	0	0	.320	8	**8**		
1889			139	55	82	2	0	.401	**7**			
1893	**STL**	**N**	135	57	75	3	0	.432	**10**			
1898	**PIT**	**N**	152	72	76	4	0	.486	**8**			
1899			24	7	15	1	1	.318	**10**	7		
9 yrs.			915	452	444	18	1	.504				

Harvey Watkins

WATKINS, HARVEY L.
Deceased.

			G	W	L	T	N	PCT	Standing			
1895	**NY**	**N**	35	18	17	0	0	.514	9	**9**		

Earl Weaver

WEAVER, EARL SIDNEY
B. Aug. 14, 1930, St. Louis, Mo.
Hall of Fame 1996.

			G	W	L	T	N	PCT	Standing			
1968	**BAL**	**A**	82	48	34	0	0	.585	3	**2**		
1969			162	109	53	0	0	.673	**1**			
1970			162	108	54	0	0	.667	**1**			
1971			158	101	57	0	0	.639	**1**			
1972			154	80	74	0	0	.519	**3**			
1973			162	97	65	0	0	.599	**1**			
1974			162	91	71	0	0	.562	**1**			
1975			159	90	69	0	0	.566	**2**			
1976			162	88	74	0	0	.543	**2**			
1977			161	97	64	0	0	.602	**2**			
1978			161	90	71	0	0	.559	**4**			
1979			159	102	57	0	0	.642	**1**			
1980			162	100	62	0	0	.617	**2**			

Earl Weaver *continued*

			G	W	L	T	N	PCT	Standing			
1981			54	31	23	0	0	.574	**2**			(1st)
1981			51	28	23	0	0	.549	**4**			(2nd)
1982			163	94	68	1	0	.580	**2**			
1985			105	53	52	0	0	.505	4	**4**		
1986			162	73	89	0	0	.451	**7**			
17 yrs.			2541	1480	1060	1	0	.583				
								9th				

LEAGUE CHAMPIONSHIP SERIES

			G	W	L	T	N	PCT
1969	**BAL**	**A**	3	3	0	0	0	1.000
1970			3	3	0	0	0	1.000
1971			3	3	0	0	0	1.000
1973			5	2	3	0	0	.400
1974			4	1	3	0	0	.250
1979			4	3	1	0	0	.750
6 yrs.			22	15	7	0	0	.682
			6th	**5th**				**1st**

WORLD SERIES

			G	W	L	T	N	PCT
1969	**BAL**	**A**	5	1	4	0	0	.200
1970			5	4	1	0	0	.800
1971			7	3	4	0	0	.429
1979			7	3	4	0	0	.429
4 yrs.			24	11	13	0	0	.458
			9th		**8th**			

Wes Westrum

WESTRUM, WESLEY NOREEN
B. Nov. 28, 1922, Clearbrook, Minn.

			G	W	L	T	N	PCT	Standing			
1965	**NY**	**N**	68	19	48	1	0	.284	10	**10**		
1966			161	66	95	0	0	.410	**9**			
1967			151	57	94	0	0	.377	**10**	10		
1974	**SF**	**N**	86	38	48	0	0	.442	5	**5**		
1975			161	80	81	0	0	.497	**3**			
5 yrs.			627	260	366	1	0	.415				

Harry Wheeler

WHEELER, HARRY EUGENE
B. Mar. 3, 1858, Versailles, Ind.
D. Oct. 9, 1900, Cincinnati, Ohio.

			G	W	L	T	N	PCT	Standing			
1884	**KC**	**U**	4	0	4	0	0	.000	**12**	12		

Deacon White

WHITE, JAMES LAURIE
Brother of Will White.
B. Dec. 7, 1847, Caton, N. Y.
D. July 7, 1939, Aurora, Ill.

			G	W	L	T	N	PCT	Standing			
1879	**CIN**	**N**	18	9	9	0	0	.500	**5**	5		

Jo-Jo White

WHITE, JOYNER CLIFFORD
Father of Mike White.
B. June 1, 1909, Red Oak, Ga.
D. Oct. 9, 1986, Tacoma, Wash.

			G	W	L	T	N	PCT	Standing			
1960	**CLE**	**A**	1	1	0	0	0	1.000	4	**4**	4	

Will White

WHITE, WILLIAM HENRY (Whoop-La)
Brother of Deacon White.
B. Oct. 11, 1854, Caton, N. Y.
D. Aug. 31, 1911, Port Carling, Ont., Canada.

			G	W	L	T	N	PCT	Standing			
1884	**CIN**	**AA**	72	44	27	1	0	.620	**5**	5		

Del Wilber

WILBER, DELBERT QUENTIN (Babe)
B. Feb. 24, 1919, Lincoln Park, Mich.

			G	W	L	T	N	PCT	Standing			
1973	**TEX**	**A**	1	1	0	0	0	1.000	6	**6**	6	

Kaiser Wilhelm

WILHELM, IRVIN KEY
B. Jan. 26, 1874, Wooster, Ohio
D. May 21, 1936, Rochester, N. Y.

			G	W	L	T	N	PCT	Standing			
1921	**PHI**	**N**	67	26	41	0	0	.388	8	**8**		
1922			154	57	96	1	0	.373	**7**			
2 yrs.			221	83	137	1	0	.377				

Dick Williams

WILLIAMS, RICHARD HIRSCHFELD
B. May 7, 1929, St. Louis, Mo.

			G	W	L	T	N	PCT	Standing			
1967	**BOS**	**A**	162	92	70	0	0	.568	**1**			
1968			162	86	76	0	0	.531	**4**			
1969			153	82	71	0	0	.536	**3**	3		
1971	**OAK**	**A**	161	101	60	0	0	.627	**1**			
1972			155	93	62	0	0	.600	**1**			
1973			162	94	68	0	0	.580	**1**			
1974	**CAL**	**A**	84	36	48	0	0	.429	6	**6**		
1975			161	72	89	0	0	.447	**6**			
1976			96	39	57	0	0	.406	**4**	4		
1977	**MON**	**N**	162	75	87	0	0	.463	**5**			
1978			162	76	86	0	0	.469	**4**			
1979			160	95	65	0	0	.594	**2**			
1980			162	90	72	0	0	.556	**2**			
1981			55	30	25	0	0	.545	**3**			(1st)
1981			26	14	12	0	0	.538	**6**	1		(2nd)
1982	**SD**	**N**	162	81	81	0	0	.500	**4**			
1983			163	81	81	1	0	.500	**4**			
1984			162	92	70	0	0	.568	**1**			
1985			162	83	79	0	0	.512	**3**			
1986	**SEA**	**A**	133	58	75	0	0	.436	6	**7**		
1987			162	78	84	0	0	.481	**4**			
1988			56	23	33	0	0	.411	**6**	7		
21 yrs.			3023	1571	1451	1	0	.520				

LEAGUE CHAMPIONSHIP SERIES

			G	W	L	T	N	PCT
1971	**OAK**	**A**	3	0	3	0	0	.000
1972			5	3	2	0	0	.600
1973			5	3	2	0	0	.600
1984	**SD**	**N**	5	3	2	0	0	.600
4 yrs.			18	9	9	0	0	.500
			10th	**8th**				**8th**

WORLD SERIES

			G	W	L	T	N	PCT
1967	**BOS**	**A**	7	3	4	0	0	.429
1972	**OAK**	**A**	7	4	3	0	0	.571
1973			7	4	3	0	0	.571
1984	**SD**	**N**	5	1	4	0	0	.200
4 yrs.			26	12	14	0	0	.462
			8th	**8th**	**6th**			

Jimmy Williams

WILLIAMS, JAMES ANDREWS
B. Jan. 3, 1848, Columbus, Ohio
D. Oct. 24, 1918, North Hempstead, N. Y.

			G	W	L	T	N	PCT	Standing			
1884	**STL**	**AA**	85	51	33	1	0	.607	**5**	4		
1887	**CLE**	**AA**	133	39	92	2	0	.298	**8**			
1888			64	20	44	0	0	.313	**7**	6		
3 yrs.			282	110	169	3	0	.394				

Jimy Williams

WILLIAMS, JAMES FRANCIS
B. Oct. 4, 1943, Santa Maria, Calif.

			G	W	L	T	N	PCT	Standing			
1986	**TOR**	**A**	163	86	76	1	0	.531	**4**			
1987			162	96	66	0	0	.593	**2**			
1988			162	87	75	0	0	.537	**3**			
1989			36	12	24	0	0	.333	**6**	1		
4 yrs.			523	281	241	1	0	.538				

Ted Williams

WILLIAMS, THEODORE SAMUEL
(The Splendid Splinter, The Thumper)
B. Aug. 30, 1918, San Diego, Calif.
Hall of Fame 1966.

			G	W	L	T	N	PCT	Standing			
1969	**WAS**	**A**	162	86	76	0	0	.531	**4**			
1970			162	70	92	0	0	.432	**6**			
1971			159	63	96	0	0	.396	**5**			
1972	**TEX**	**A**	154	54	100	0	0	.351	**6**			
4 yrs.			637	273	364	0	0	.429				

Maury Wills

WILLS, MAURICE MORNING
Father of Bump Wills.
B. Oct. 2, 1932, Washington, D. C.

			G	W	L	T	N	PCT	Standing			
1980	**SEA**	**A**	58	20	38	0	0	.345	7	**7**		
1981			25	6	18	1	0	.250	**7**	6		(1st)
2 yrs.			83	26	56	1	0	.317				

Jimmie Wilson

WILSON, JAMES (Ace)
B. July 23, 1900, Philadelphia, Pa.
D. May 31, 1947, Bradenton, Fla.

Year	Team	Lg	G	W	L	T	N	PCT	Standing
1934	**PHI**	**N**	149	56	93	0	0	.376	**7**
1935			156	64	89	3	0	.418	**7**
1936			154	54	100	0	0	.351	**8**
1937			155	61	92	2	0	.399	**7**
1938			149	45	103	1	0	.304	**8** 8
1941	**CHI**	**N**	155	70	84	1	0	.455	**6**
1942			155	68	86	1	0	.442	**6**
1943			154	74	79	1	0	.484	**5**
1944			10	1	9	0	0	.100	**8** 4
9 yrs.			1237	493	735	9	0	.401	

Bobby Wine

WINE, ROBERT PAUL, SR.
Father of Robbie Wine.
B. Sept. 17, 1938, New York, N. Y.

Year	Team	Lg	G	W	L	T	N	PCT	Standing
1985	**ATL**	**N**	41	16	25	0	0	.390	5 **5**

Ivy Wingo

WINGO, IVEY BROWN
Brother of Al Wingo.
B. July 8, 1890, Gainesville, Ga.
D. Mar. 1, 1941, Norcross, Ga.

Year	Team	Lg	G	W	L	T	N	PCT	Standing
1916	**CIN**	**N**	2	1	1	0	0	.500	8 **8** 7

Bobby Winkles

WINKLES, BOBBY BROOKS (Winks)
B. Mar. 11, 1930, Tuckerman, Ark.

Year	Team	Lg	G	W	L	T	N	PCT	Standing
1973	**CAL**	**A**	162	79	83	0	0	.488	**4**
1974			75	30	44	1	0	.405	**6** 6
1977	**OAK**	**A**	108	37	71	0	0	.343	7 **7**
1978			39	24	15	0	0	.615	**6** 6
4 yrs.			384	170	213	1	0	.444	

Chicken Wolf

WOLF, WILLIAM VAN WINKLE
B. May 12, 1862, Louisville, Ky.
D. May 16, 1903, Louisville, Ky.

Year	Team	Lg	G	W	L	T	N	PCT	Standing
1889	**LOU**	**AA**	65	14	51	0	0	.215	8 **8** 8

Harry Wolverton

WOLVERTON, HARRY STERLING
B. Dec. 6, 1873, Mt. Vernon, Ohio
D. Feb. 4, 1937, Oakland, Calif.

Year	Team	Lg	G	W	L	T	N	PCT	Standing
1912	**NY**	**A**	153	50	102	1	0	.329	**8**

George Wood

WOOD, GEORGE A. (Dandy)
B. Nov. 9, 1858, Boston, Mass.
D. Apr. 4, 1924, Harrisburg, Pa.

Year	Team	Lg	G	W	L	T	N	PCT	Standing
1891	**PHI**	**AA**	125	67	55	3	0	.549	7 **5**

Al Wright

WRIGHT, ALFRED HECTOR
B. Mar. 30, 1842, Cedar Grove, N. J.
D. Apr. 20, 1905

Year	Team	Lg	G	W	L	T	N	PCT	Standing
1876	**PHI**	**N**	60	14	45	1	0	.237	**7**

George Wright

WRIGHT, GEORGE
Brother of Sam Wright.
Brother of Harry Wright.
B. Jan. 28, 1847, Yonkers, N. Y.
D. Aug. 21, 1937, Boston, Mass.
Hall of Fame 1937.

Year	Team	Lg	G	W	L	T	N	PCT	Standing
1879	**PRO**	**N**	85	59	25	1	0	.702	**1**

Harry Wright

WRIGHT, WILLIAM HENRY
Brother of George Wright.
Brother of Sam Wright.
B. Jan. 10, 1835, Sheffield, England
D. Oct. 3, 1895, Atlantic City, N. J.
Hall of Fame 1953.

Year	Team	Lg	G	W	L	T	N	PCT	Standing	
1876	**BOS**	**N**	70	39	31	0	0	.557	**4**	
1877			61	42	18	1	0	.700	**1**	
1878			60	41	19	0	0	.683	**1**	
1879			84	54	30	0	0	.643	**2**	
1880			86	40	44	2	0	.476	**6**	
1881			83	38	45	0	0	.458	**6**	
1882	**PRO**	**N**	84	52	32	0	0	.619	**2**	
1883			98	58	40	0	0	.592	**3**	
1884	**PHI**	**N**	113	39	73	1	0	.348	**6**	
1885			111	56	54	1	0	.509	**3**	
1886			119	71	43	5	0	.623	**4**	
1887			128	75	48	5	0	.610	**2**	
1888			132	69	61	1	1	.531	**3**	
1889			130	63	64	3	0	.496	**4**	
1890			22	14	8	0	0	.636	**1** 3	
1890			46	22	23	1	0	.489	2 **3**	
1891			138	68	69	1	0	.496	**4**	
1892			77	46	30	1	0	.605	**3**	(1st)
1892			78	41	36	1	0	.532	**5**	(2nd)
1893			133	72	57	4	0	.558	**4**	
18 yrs.			1853	1000	825	27	1	.548		

Rudy York

YORK, RUDOLPH PRESTON
B. Aug. 17, 1913, Ragland, Ala.
D. Feb. 5, 1970, Rome, Ga.

Year	Team	Lg	G	W	L	T	N	PCT	Standing
1959	**BOS**	**A**	1	0	1	0	0	.000	8 **8** 5

Tom York

YORK, THOMAS JEFFERSON
B. July 13, 1851, Brooklyn, N. Y.
D. Feb. 17, 1936, New York, N. Y.

Year	Team	Lg	G	W	L	T	N	PCT	Standing
1878	**PRO**	**N**	62	33	27	2	0	.550	**3**
1881			34	23	10	1	0	.697	4 **2**
2 yrs.			96	56	37	3	0	.602	

Eddie Yost

YOST, EDWARD FREDERICK (The Walking Man)
B. Oct. 13, 1926, Brooklyn, N. Y.

Year	Team	Lg	G	W	L	T	N	PCT	Standing
1963	**WAS**	**A**	1	0	1	0	0	.000	10 **10** 10

Cy Young

YOUNG, DENTON TRUE (Foxy Grandpa)
B. Mar. 29, 1867, Gilmore, Ohio
D. Nov. 4, 1955, Newcomerstown, Ohio.
Hall of Fame 1937.

Year	Team	Lg	G	W	L	T	N	PCT	Standing
1907	**BOS**	**A**	6	3	3	0	0	.500	**4** 7

Chief Zimmer

ZIMMER, CHARLES LOUIS
B. Nov. 23, 1860, Marietta, Ohio
D. Aug. 22, 1949, Cleveland, Ohio.

Year	Team	Lg	G	W	L	T	N	PCT	Standing
1903	**PHI**	**N**	139	49	86	4	0	.363	**7**

Don Zimmer

ZIMMER, DONALD WILLIAM (Popeye)
B. Jan. 17, 1931, Cincinnati, Ohio

Year	Team	Lg	G	W	L	T	N	PCT	Standing	
1972	**SD**	**N**	142	54	88	0	0	.380	4 **6**	
1973			162	60	102	0	0	.370	**6**	
1976	**BOS**	**A**	76	42	34	0	0	.553	3 **3**	
1977			161	97	64	0	0	.602	**2**	
1978			163	99	64	0	0	.607	**2**	
1979			160	91	69	0	0	.569	**3**	
1980			155	82	73	0	0	.529	**4** 4	
1981	**TEX**	**A**	55	33	22	0	0	.600	**2**	(1st)
1981			50	24	26	0	0	.480	**3**	(2nd)
1982			96	38	58	0	0	.396	**6** 6	
1988	**CHI**	**N**	163	77	85	1	0	.475	**4**	
1989			162	93	69	0	0	.574	**1**	
1990			162	77	85	0	0	.475	**4**	
1991			37	18	19	0	0	.486	**4** 4	
13 yrs.			1744	885	858	1	0	.508		

LEAGUE CHAMPIONSHIP SERIES

Year	Team	Lg	G	W	L	T	N	PCT
1989	**CHI**	**N**	5	1	4	0	0	.200

PART EIGHT

Player Register

Alphabetical List of Every Man
(Except Certain Pitchers)
Who Ever Played in the Major Leagues
With His Complete Batting and Fielding Records

Player Register

The Player Register is an alphabetical listing of every man who has played in the major leagues from 1876 through today, except those players who were primarily pitchers. However, pitchers who pinch hit and played in other positions for a total of 25 games or more are listed in this Player Register. Included are facts about the players and their year-by-year batting and fielding records and lifetime totals for the regular season, divisional playoff series, League Championship Series, and World Series.

Much of this information has never been compiled, especially for the period 1876 through 1919. For certain other years some statistics are still missing or incomplete. Research in this area is still in progress, and the years that lack complete information are indicated. In fact, all information and abbreviations that may appear unfamiliar are explained in the sample format presented below. John Doe, the player used in the sample, is fictitious and serves only to illustrate the information.

John Doe

DOE, JOHN LEE (Slim)
Played as John Cherry part of 1900.
Born John Lee Doughnut. Brother of Bill Doe.
B. Jan. 1, 1850, New York, N.Y. D. July 1, 1955, New York, N.Y.
Manager 1908–15.
Hall of Fame 1946.

BR TR 6′2″ 165 lbs.
BB 1884 BL 1906

Year	Team	Games	BA	SA	AB	H	2B	3B	HR	HR%	R	RBI	BB	SO	SB	Pinch Hit AB	Pinch Hit H	PO	A	E	DP	TC/G	FA	G by Pos
1884	STL U	125	.278	.345	435	121	18	1	3	0.7		44	37	42	7	9	2	118	267	46	16	3.4	.893	SS-99, P-26
1885	LOU AA	155	.252	.320	557	138	22	3	3	0.6	50	58	42	48	8	8	4	94	266	44	23	2.6	.891	SS-115, P-40
1886	CLE N	147	.276	.375	485	134	38	5	0	0.0	66	54	48	50	8	7	1	120	277	51	25	3.0	.886	SS-107, P-40
1887	BOS N	129	.280	.337	418	117	15	3	1	0.2	38	52	32	37	1	1	0	136	310	59	29	3.9	.883	SS-102, P-27
1888	NY N	144	.267	.362	506	135	26	2	6	1.2	50	63	43	50	1	10	8	136	245	72	20	3.1	.841	SS-105, P-39
1889	3 teams	DET N (10G - .300)	PIT N (32G - .241)	PHI N (31G - .364)																				
"	total	83	.316	.671	237	75	31	16	7	3.0	90	42	25	35	3	6	3	91	156	35	14	4.3	.876	SS-61, P-22
1890	NY P	123	.277	.370	430	119	27	5	1	0.2	63	59	39	39	2	12	10	137	331	65	44	3.5	.878	SS-85, P-38
1900	CHI N	146	.233	.325	498	116	29	4	3	0.6	51	46	59	53	1	13	8	161	307	48	32	4.5	.907	SS-111, P-35
1901	NY N	149	.272	.352	540	147	19	6	4	0.7	57	74	49	58	3	23	15	202	405	59	47	4.8	.911	SS-114, P-35
1906	BOS N	144	.252	.333	567	143	26	4	4	0.7	70	43	37	54	1	7	1	244	393	54	35	4.8	.922	SS-113, P-31
1907		134	.272	.369	515	140	31	2	5	1.0	61	70	37	42	0	13	8	215	390	39	45	4.8	.939	SS-97, P-37
1908		106	.242	.317	372	92	10	2	4	1.1	36	40	4	55	1	1	0	227	352	35	33	5.8	.943	SS-105, P-1
1914	CHI F	6	.000	.000	6	0	0	0	0	0.0	0	0	0	1	0	0	0	2	4	0	1	1.0	1.000	P-6
1915	NY A	1	—	—	0	0	0	0	0	—	0	0	0	0	0	0	0	2	3	1	2	6.0	.833	SS-1
14 yrs.		1592	.266	.360	5556	1927	292	53 4th	41	0.7	676	601	452	564	36	110	60	1185	3706	608	366	3.5	.889	SS-1215, P-377
DIVISIONAL PLAYOFF SERIES																								
1908	BOS N	5	.300	.350	20	6	1	0	0	0.0	0	0	1	3	1	0	0	12	9	1	0	4.4	.955	SS-5
LEAGUE CHAMPIONSHIP SERIES																								
1908	BOS N	3	.357	1.143	14	5	2	0	3	21.4	3	7	0	1	0	0	0	4	4	0	1	2.0	1.000	SS-3
WORLD SERIES																								
1906	BOS N	7	.321	1.000	28	9	1	0	6	21.4	12	14	3	4	0	0	0	4	8	2	2	2.0	.857	SS-5, P-2
1908		5	.500	.900	10	5	1	0	1	10.0	3	2	0	2	0	2	0	8	6	1	2	2.0	.900	P-4, SS-1
2 yrs.		12	.368	.974	38	14	2	0	7 5th	18.4	15	16 9th	3	6	0	2	0	18	14	3	4	2.0	.875	SS-6, P-6

Player Information

John Doe

This shortened version of the player's full name is the name most familiar to the fans. All players in this section are alphabetically arranged by the last name part of this name.

Doe, John Lee

Player's full name. The arrangement is last name first, then first and middle name(s).

(Slim)

Player's nickname. Any name appearing in parentheses is a nickname.

BR TR BB 1884 BL 1906

The player's main batting and throwing style. Doe, for instance, batted and threw right-handed. The information listed directly below the main batting information indicates that at various times in a player's career he changed his batting style. The "BB" for Doe in 1884 means he was a switch hitter that year, and the

"BL" means he batted left-handed in 1906. For the years that are not shown it can be assumed that Doe batted right, as his main batting information indicates.

6'2"

Player's height.

165 lbs

Player's average playing weight.

Played as John Cherry part of 1900

The player at one time in his major league career played under another name and can be found in box scores or newspaper stories only under that name.

Born John Lee Doughnut

The name the player was given at birth. (For the most part, the player never used this name while playing in the major leagues, but, if he did, it would be listed as "played as," which is explained above under the heading "Played as John Cherry part of 1900.")

Brother of Bill Doe

The player's brother. (Relatives indicated here are fathers, sons, and brothers who played or managed in the major leagues and the National Association.)

B. Jan. 1, 1850, New York, N.Y.

Date and place of birth.

D. July 1, 1955, New York, N.Y.

Date and place of death. (Some players are listed simply as "deceased." Although no certification of death or other information is available, it is reasonably certain they are dead.)

Manager 1908–15

Doe also served as a major league manager. All men who were managers can be found also in the Manager Register, where their complete managerial record is shown.

Hall of Fame 1946

Doe was elected to the Baseball Hall of Fame in 1946.

Column Headings Information

																Pinch Hit								
Year	Team	Games	BA	SA	AB	H	2B	3B	HR	HR%	R	RBI	BB	SO	SB	AB	H	PO	A	E	DP	TC/G	FA	G by Pos

G	Games
AB	At Bats
BA	Batting Average
SA	Slugging Average
H	Hits
2B	Doubles
3B	Triples
HR	Home Runs
HR %	Home Run Percentage (the number of home runs per 100 times at bat)
R	Runs Scored
RBI	Runs Batted In
BB	Bases on Balls
SO	Strikeouts
SB	Stolen Bases

Pinch Hit

AB	Pinch Hit At Bats
H	Pinch Hits

Fielding

PO	Putouts
A	Assists
E	Errors
DP	Double Plays
TC/G	Total Chances Per Game
FA	Fielding Average
G by POS	Games by Position. (All fielding positions a man played within the given year are shown. The position where the most games were played is listed first. Any man who pitched, as Doe did, is listed also in the alphabetically arranged Pitcher Register, where his complete pitching record can be found.) If no fielding positions are shown in a particular year, it means the player only pinch hit or pinch ran. In the case of a designated hitter, the number of games he has played as a designated hitter will be shown alongside the letters DH.

Team and League Information

1884	**STL**	**U**																					
1885	**LOU**	**AA**																					
1886	**CLE**	**N**																					
1887	**BOS**	**N**																					
1888	**NY**	**N**																					
1889	**3 teams**		**DET N** (10G-.300)	**PIT N** (32G-.241)	**PHI N** (31G-.364)																		
"	**total**		83	.316	.671	237	75	31	16	7	3.0	90	42	25	35	3	6	3	91	156	35	14	4.3 .876 SS-61, P-22
1890	**NY**	**P**																					
1900	**CHI**	**N**																					
1901	**NY**	**N**																					
1906	**BOS**	**N**																					
1907																							
1908																							
1914	**CHI**	**F**																					
1915	**NY**	**A**																					
14 yrs.																							

Doe's record has been exaggerated so that his playing career spans all the years of the six different major leagues. Directly alongside the year and team information is the symbol for the league:

N	National League (1876 to date)
A	American League (1901 to date)
F	Federal League (1914–15)
AA	American Association (1882–91)
P	Players' League (1890)
U	Union Association (1884)

STL— The abbreviation of the city in which the team played. Doe, for example, played for St. Louis in 1884. All teams in this section are listed by an abbreviation of the city or area in which the team played. The abbreviations follow:

ALT	Altoona
ATL	Atlanta
BAL	Baltimore
BOS	Boston
BKN	Brooklyn
BUF	Buffalo
CAL	California
CHI	Chicago
CIN	Cincinnati
CLE	Cleveland
CLR	Colorado
COL	Columbus
DET	Detroit
FLA	Florida
HAR	Hartford
HOU	Houston
IND	Indianapolis
KC	Kansas City
LA	Los Angeles
LOU	Louisville
MIL	Milwauke
MIN	Minnesota
MON	Montreal
NWK	Newark
NY	New York
OAK	Oakland
PHI	Philadelphia
PIT	Pittsburgh
PRO	Providence
RIC	Richmond
ROC	Rochester
SD	San Diego
SEA	Seattle
SF	San Francisco
STL	St. Louis
STP	St. Paul
SYR	Syracuse
TEX	Texas
TOL	Toledo
TOR	Toronto
TRO	Troy
WAS	Washington
WIL	Wilmington
WOR	Worcester

Blank space appearing beneath a team and league indicates that the team and league are the same. Doe, for example, played for Boston in the National League from 1906 through 1908.

3 Teams Total. Indicates a player played for more than one team in the same year. Doe played for three teams in 1889. The number of games he played and his batting average for each team are also shown. Directly beneath this line, following the word "total," is Doe's combined record for all three teams for 1889.

Total Playing Years. This information, which appears as the first item on the player's lifetime total line, indicates the total number of years in which he played at least one game. Doe, for example, played in at least one game for 14 years.

Statistical Information

Year	Team	Games	BA	SA	AB	H	2B	3B	HR	HR%	R	RBI	BB	SO	SB	Pinch Hit AB	Pinch Hit H	PO	A	E	DP	TC/G	FA	G by Pos

John Doe

DOE, JOHN LEE (Slim)
Played as John Cherry part of 1900.
Born John Lee Doughnut. Brother of Bill Doe.
B. Jan. 1, 1850, New York, N.Y. D. July 1, 1955, New York, N.Y.
Manager 1908–15.
Hall of Fame 1946.

BR TR 6'2" 165 lbs.
BB 1884 BL 1906

Year	Team	Games	BA	SA	AB	H	2B	3B	HR	HR%	R	RBI	BB	SO	SB	Pinch Hit AB	Pinch Hit H	PO	A	E	DP	TC/G	FA	G by Pos
1884	STL U	125	.278	.345	435	121	18	1	3	0.7		44	37	42	7	9	2	118	267	46	16	3.4	.893	SS-99, P-26
1885	LOU AA	155	.252	.320	557	138	22	3	3	0.6	50	58	42	48	8	8	4	94	266	44	23	2.6	.891	SS-115, P-40
1886	CLE N	147	.276	.375	485	134	38	5	0	0.0	66	54	48	50	8	7	1	120	277	51	25	3.0	.886	SS-107, P-40
1887	BOS N	129	.280	.337	418	117	15	3	1	0.2	38	52	32	37	1	1	0	136	310	59	29	3.9	.883	SS-102, P-27
1888	NY N	144	.267	.362	506	135	26	2	6	1.2	50	63	43	50	1	10	8	136	245	72	20	3.1	.841	SS-105, P-39
1889	3 teams	DET N (10G - .300)	PIT N (32G - .241)	PHI N (31G - .364)																				
"	total	83	.316	.671	237	75	31	16	7	3.0	90	42	25	35	3	6	3	91	156	35	14	4.3	.876	SS-61, P-22
1890	NY P	123	.277	.370	430	119	27	5	1	0.2	63	59	39	39	2	12	10	137	331	65	44	3.5	.878	SS-85, P-38
1900	CHI N	146	.233	.325	498	116	29	4	3	0.6	51	46	59	53	1	13	8	161	307	48	32	4.5	.907	SS-111, P-35
1901	NY N	149	.272	.352	540	147	19	6	4	0.7	57	74	49	58	3	23	15	202	405	59	47	4.8	.911	SS-114, P-35
1906	BOS N	144	.252	.333	567	143	26	4	4	0.7	70	43	37	54	1	7	1	244	393	54	35	4.8	.922	SS-113, P-31
1907		134	.272	.369	515	140	31	2	5	1.0	61	70	37	42	0	13	8	215	390	39	45	4.8	.939	SS-97, P-37
1908		106	.242	.317	372	92	10	2	4	1.1	36	40	4	55	1	1	0	227	352	35	33	5.8	.943	SS-105, P-1
1914	CHI F	6	.000	.000	6	0	0	0	0	0.0	0	0	0	1	0	0	0	2	4	0	1	1.0	1.000	P-6
1915	NY A	1	—	—	0	0	0	0	0	—	0	0	0	0	0	0	0	2	3	1	2	6.0	.833	SS-1
14 yrs.		1592	.266	.360	5556	1927	292	53 4th	41	0.7	676	601	452	564	36	110	60	1185	3706	608	366	3.5	.889	SS-1215, P-377

League Leaders. Statistics that appear in boldfaced print indicate the player led his league that year in a particular statistical category. Doe, for example, led the National League in doubles in 1886. When there is a tie for league lead, the figures for all the men who tied are shown in boldface.

All-Time Single Season Leaders. Indicated by the small number that appears next to the statistic. Doe, for example, is shown by a small number "1" next to his doubles total in 1886. This means he is first on the all-time major league list for hitting the most doubles in a single season. All players who tied for first are shown by the same number.

Lifetime Leaders. Indicated by the figure that appears beneath the line showing the player's lifetime totals. Doe has a "4th" shown below his lifetime triples total. This means that, lifetime, Doe ranks fourth among major league players for hitting the most triples. Once again, only the top ten are indicated, and players who are tied receive the same number.

Unavailable Information. Any time a blank space is shown in a particular statistical column, such as in Doe's 1884 runs scored total, it indicates the information was unavailable or incomplete.

Meaningless Averages. Indicated by use of a dash (—). In the case of Doe, a dash is shown for his 1915 batting average. This means that, although he played one game, he had no official at bats. A batting average of .000 would mean he had at least one at bat with no hits.

League Leaders Qualifications. Throughout baseball there have been different rules used to determine the minimum appearances necessary to qualify for league leader in categories concerning averages (Batting Average, Earned Run Average, etc.). For the rules and the years they were in effect, see Appendix C.

World Series and Championship Playoffs

Year	Team	Games	BA	SA	AB	H	2B	3B	HR	HR%	R	RBI	BB	SO	SB	Pinch Hit AB	Pinch Hit H	PO	A	E	DP	TC/G	FA	G by Pos
DIVISIONAL PLAYOFF SERIES																								
1908	BOS N	5	.300	.350	20	6	1	0	0	0.0	0	0	1	3	1	0	0	12	9	1	0	4.4	.955	SS-5
LEAGUE CHAMPIONSHIP SERIES																								
1908	BOS N	3	.357	1.143	14	5	2	0	3	21.4	3	7	0	1	0	0	0	4	4	0	1	2.0	1.000	SS-3
WORLD SERIES																								
1906	BOS N	7	.321	1.000	28	9	1	0	6	21.4	12	14	3	4	0	0	0	4	8	2	2	2.0	.857	SS-5, P-2
1908		5	.500	.900	10	5	1	0	1	10.0	3	2	0	2	0	2	0	8	6	1	2	2.0	.900	P-4, SS-1
2 yrs.		12	.368	.974	38	14	2	0	7 5th	18.4	15	16 9th	3	6	0	2	0	18	14	3	4	2.0	.875	SS-6, P-6

World Series and League Championship Series Lifetime Leaders. Indicated by the figure that appears beneath the player's lifetime totals. Doe has a "5th" shown below his lifetime home run total. This means that, lifetime, Doe ranks fifth among major league players for hitting the most home runs in total World Series play. Players who tied for a position in the top ten are shown by the same number, so that, if two men tied for fourth and fifth place, the appropriate information for both men would be followed by the small number "4," and the next man would be considered sixth in the ranking.

Hank Aaron

AARON, HENRY LOUIS (Hammerin' Hank) BR TR 6′ 180 lbs.
Brother of Tommie Aaron.
B. Feb. 5, 1934, Mobile, Ala.
Hall of Fame 1982.

Year	Team	Games	BA	SA	AB	H	2B	3B	HR	HR%	R	RBI	BB	SO	SB	Pinch Hit AB	Pinch Hit H	PO	A	E	DP	TC/G	FA	G by Pos
1954	MIL N	122	.280	.447	468	131	27	6	13	2.8	58	69	28	39	2	6	1	223	5	7	0	2.0	.970	OF-116
1955		153	.314	.540	602	189	**37**	9	27	4.5	105	106	49	61	3	2	1	340	93	15	25	2.9	.967	OF-126, 2B-27
1956		153	**.328**	.558	609	**200**	**34**	14	26	4.3	106	92	37	54	2	1	0	316	17	13	4	2.3	.962	OF-152
1957		151	.322	.600	615	198	27	6	**44**	7.2	**118**	**132**	57	58	1	0	0	346	9	6	0	2.4	.983	OF-150
1958		153	.326	.546	601	196	34	4	30	5.0	109	95	59	49	4	0	0	305	12	5	0	2.1	.984	OF-153
1959		154	**.355**	**.636**	629	**223**	46	7	39	6.2	116	123	51	54	8	0	0	263	22	5	3	1.8	.983	OF-152, 3B-5
1960		153	.292	.566	590	172	20	11	40	6.8	102	**126**	60	63	16	0	0	321	13	6	6	2.2	.982	OF-153, 2B-2
1961		155	.327	.594	603	197	**39**	10	34	5.6	115	120	56	64	21	1	0	379	15	7	3	2.6	.983	OF-154, 3B-2
1962		156	.323	.618	592	191	28	6	45	7.6	127	128	66	73	15	2	1	341	11	7	1	2.3	.981	OF-153, 1B-1
1963		161	.319	**.586**	631	201	29	4	**44**	7.0	**121**	**130**	78	94	31	0	0	267	10	6	1	1.8	.979	OF-161
1964		145	.328	.514	570	187	30	2	24	4.2	103	95	62	46	22	1	0	284	28	6	7	2.1	.981	OF-139, 2B-11
1965		150	.318	.560	570	181	**40**	1	32	5.6	109	89	60	81	24	2	1	298	9	4	2	2.1	.987	OF-148
1966	ATL N	158	.279	.539	603	168	23	1	**44**	7.3	117	**127**	76	96	21	1	1	315	12	4	5	2.1	.988	OF-158, 2B-2
1967		155	.307	**.573**	600	184	37	3	**39**	6.5	**113**	109	63	97	17	3	0	322	12	7	3	2.2	.979	OF-152, 2B-1
1968		160	.287	.498	606	174	33	4	29	4.8	84	86	64	62	28	2	0	418	20	5	10	2.7	.989	OF-151, 1B-14
1969		147	.300	.607	547	164	30	3	44	8.0	100	97	87	47	9	0	0	299	13	5	6	2.1	.984	OF-144, 1B-4
1970		150	.298	.574	516	154	26	1	38	7.4	103	118	74	63	9	9	1	319	10	7	7	2.5	.979	OF-125, 1B-11
1971		139	.327	**.669**	495	162	22	3	47	**9.5**	95	118	71	58	1	8	2	733	40	5	56	5.9	.994	1B-71, OF-60
1972		129	.265	.514	449	119	10	0	34	**7.6**	75	77	92	55	4	5	2	996	70	17	75	8.7	.984	1B-109, OF-15
1973		120	.301	.643	392	118	12	1	40	**10.2**	84	96	68	51	1	11	3	206	5	5	0	2.1	.977	OF-105
1974		112	.268	.491	340	91	16	0	20	5.9	47	69	39	29	1	17	1	142	3	2	0	1.7	.986	OF-89
1975	MIL A	137	.234	.355	465	109	16	2	12	2.6	45	60	70	51	0	5	1	2	0	0	0	0.0	1.000	DH-128, OF-3
1976		85	.229	.369	271	62	8	0	10	3.7	22	35	35	38	0	10	2	1	0	0	0	0.0	1.000	DH-74, OF-1
23 yrs.		3298	.305	.555	12364	3771	624	98	755	6.1	2174	2297	1402	1383	240	86	17	7436	429	144	214	2.5	.982	OF-2760, 1B-210, DH-202, 2B-43, 3B-7
		3rd			**2nd**	**3rd**	**9th**		**1st**		**2nd**	**1st**												
LEAGUE CHAMPIONSHIP SERIES																								
1969	ATL N	3	.357	1.143	14	5	2	0	3	21.4	3	7	0	1	0	0	0	5	1	1	0	2.3	.857	OF-3
WORLD SERIES																								
1957	MIL N	7	.393	.786	28	11	0	1	3	10.7	5	7	1	6	0	0	0	11	0	0	0	1.6	1.000	OF-7
1958		7	.333	.407	27	9	2	0	0	0.0	3	2	4	6	0	0	0	14	0	0	0	2.0	1.000	OF-7
2 yrs.		14	.364	.600	55	20	2	1	3	5.5	8	9	5	12	0	0	0	25	0	0	0	1.8	1.000	OF-14
			7th																					

Tommie Aaron

AARON, TOMMIE LEE BR TR 6′ 3″ 190 lbs.
Brother of Hank Aaron.
B. Aug. 5, 1939, Mobile, Ala. D. Aug. 16, 1984, Atlanta, Ga.

Year	Team	Games	BA	SA	AB	H	2B	3B	HR	HR%	R	RBI	BB	SO	SB	Pinch Hit AB	Pinch Hit H	PO	A	E	DP	TC/G	FA	G by Pos
1962	MIL N	141	.231	.374	334	77	20	2	8	2.4	54	38	41	58	6	11	3	572	48	10	56	4.1	.984	1B-110, OF-42, 3B-1, 2B-1
1963		72	.200	.281	135	27	6	1	1	0.7	6	15	11	27	0	16	2	221	18	1	28	3.6	.996	1B-45, OF-14, 2B-6, 3B-1
1965		8	.188	.188	16	3	0	0	0	0.0	1	1	1	2	0	2	1	45	4	2	3	8.5	.961	1B-6
1968	ATL N	98	.244	.311	283	69	10	3	1	0.4	21	25	21	37	3	18	3	287	20	5	13	3.4	.984	OF-62, 1B-28, 3B-1
1969		49	.250	.333	60	15	2	0	1	1.7	13	5	6	6	0	23	4	65	2	0	5	2.8	1.000	1B-16, OF-8
1970		44	.206	.333	63	13	2	0	2	3.2	3	7	3	10	0	16	2	53	2	2	1	2.0	.965	1B-16, OF-12
1971		25	.226	.264	53	12	2	0	0	0.0	4	3	3	5	0	6	2	74	19	2	18	5.3	.979	1B-11, 3B-7
7 yrs.		437	.229	.327	944	216	42	6	13	1.4	102	94	86	145	9	92	17	1317	113	22	124	3.8	.985	1B-232, OF-138, 3B-10, 2B-7
LEAGUE CHAMPIONSHIP SERIES																								
1969	ATL N	1	.000	.000	1	0	0	0	0	0.0	0	0	0	0	0	1	0	0	0	0	0	0.0	—	

Ed Abbaticchio

ABBATICCHIO, EDWARD JAMES BR TR 5′11″ 170 lbs.
B. Apr. 15, 1877, Latrobe, Pa. D. Jan. 6, 1957, Fort Lauderdale, Fla.

Year	Team	Games	BA	SA	AB	H	2B	3B	HR	HR%	R	RBI	BB	SO	SB	Pinch Hit AB	Pinch Hit H	PO	A	E	DP	TC/G	FA	G by Pos
1897	PHI N	3	.300	.300	10	3	0	0	0	0.0	0	0	1		0	0	0	0	7	1	0	2.7	.875	2B-3
1898		25	.228	.272	92	21	4	0	0	0.0	9	14	7		4	0	0	36	25	12	0	2.9	.836	3B-20, 2B-4, OF-1
1903	BOS N	136	.227	.290	489	111	18	5	1	0.2	61	46	52		23	3	1	361	367	58	43	5.9	.926	2B-116, SS-17
1904		154	.256	.337	579	148	18	10	3	0.5	76	54	40		24	0	0	367	473	78	47	6.0	.915	SS-154
1905		153	.279	.374	**610**	170	25	12	3	0.5	70	41	35		30	0	0	387	468	75	53	6.1	.919	SS-152, OF-1
1907	PIT N	147	.262	.331	496	130	14	7	2	0.4	63	82	65		35	0	0	320	380	36	37	5.0	.951	2B-147
1908		146	.250	.316	500	125	16	7	1	0.2	43	61	58		22	2	0	268	423	22	42	5.0	.969	2B-144
1909		36	.230	.264	87	20	0	0	1	1.1	13	16	19		2	11	2	57	74	10	6	6.1	.929	SS-18, 2B-4, OF-1
1910	2 teams PIT N (3G –.000) BOS N (52G –.247)																							
″	total	55	.243	.287	181	44	4	2	0	0.0	20	10	12	16	2	7	0	77	151	23	19	5.2	.908	SS-47, 2B-1
9 yrs.		855	.254	.325	3044	772	99	43	11	0.4	355	324	289	16	142	23	3	1873	2368	315	247	5.5	.931	2B-419, SS-388, 3B-20, OF-3
WORLD SERIES																								
1909	PIT N	1	.000	.000	1	0	0	0	0	0.0	0	0	0	1	0	1	0	0	0	0	0	0.0	—	

Charlie Abbey

ABBEY, CHARLES S. BL 5′ 8½″ 169 lbs.
B. Oct. 14, 1866, Falls City, Neb. D. Apr. 27, 1926, San Francisco, Calif.

Year	Team	Games	BA	SA	AB	H	2B	3B	HR	HR%	R	RBI	BB	SO	SB	Pinch Hit AB	Pinch Hit H	PO	A	E	DP	TC/G	FA	G by Pos
1893	WAS N	31	.259	.336	116	30	1	4	0	0.0	11	12	12	6	9	0	0	68	6	5	1	2.5	.937	OF-31
1894		129	.314	.472	523	164	26	18	7	1.3	95	101	58	38	31	0	0	344	26	37	6	3.2	.909	OF-129
1895		132	.276	.389	511	141	14	10	8	1.6	102	84	43	41	28	0	0	275	32	33	7	2.6	.903	OF-132
1896		79	.262	.352	301	79	12	6	1	0.3	47	49	27	20	16	2	1	105	10	16	0	1.7	.878	OF-78, P-1
1897		80	.260	.390	300	78	14	8	3	1.0	52	34	27		9	0	0	126	14	8	1	1.9	.946	OF-80
5 yrs.		451	.281	.404	1751	492	67	46	19	1.1	307	280	167	105	93	2	1	918	88	99	15	2.5	.910	OF-450, P-1

Fred Abbott

ABBOTT, HARRY FREDERICK (Faithful Fred) BR TR 5′10″ 180 lbs.
Born Harry Frederick Winbigler.
B. Oct. 22, 1874, Versailles, Ohio D. June 11, 1935, Los Angeles, Calif.

Year	Team	Games	BA	SA	AB	H	2B	3B	HR	HR%	R	RBI	BB	SO	SB	Pinch Hit AB	Pinch Hit H	PO	A	E	DP	TC/G	FA	G by Pos
1903	CLE A	77	.235	.314	255	60	11	3	1	0.4	25	25	7		8	3	0	357	101	19	10	6.4	.960	C-71, 1B-3
1904		41	.169	.231	130	22	4	2	0	0.0	14	12	6		2	1	0	216	41	10	5	6.7	.963	C-33, 1B-7
1905	PHI N	42	.195	.258	128	25	6	1	0	0.0	9	12	6		4	2	0	195	43	11	11	6.4	.956	C-34, 1B-5
3 yrs.		160	.209	.279	513	107	21	6	1	0.2	48	49	19		14	6	0	768	185	40	26	6.5	.960	C-138, 1B-15

Kurt Abbott

ABBOTT, KURT THOMAS
B. June 2, 1969, Zanesville, Ohio.
BR TR 5′11″ 180 lbs.

Year	Team	Games	BA	SA	AB	H	2B	3B	HR	HR%	R	RBI	BB	SO	SB	Pinch Hit AB	Pinch Hit H	PO	A	E	DP	TC/G	FA	G by Pos
1993	OAK A	20	.246	.410	61	15	1	0	3	4.9	11	9	3	20	2	2	1	36	13	2	2	2.4	.961	OF-13, SS-6, 2B-2
1994	FLA N	101	.249	.394	345	86	17	3	9	2.6	41	33	16	98	3	3	2	165	258	15	57	4.4	.966	SS-99
1995		120	.255	.452	420	107	18	7	17	4.0	60	60	36	110	4	5	0	149	290	19	64	4.0	.959	SS-115
3 yrs.		241	.252	.425	826	208	36	10	29	3.5	112	102	55	228	9	10	3	350	561	36	123	4.0	.962	SS-220, OF-13, 2B-2

Ody Abbott

ABBOTT, ODY CLEON (Toby)
B. Sept. 5, 1888, New Eagle, Pa. D. Apr. 13, 1933, Washington, D. C.
BR TR 6′ 2″ 180 lbs.

Year	Team	Games	BA	SA	AB	H	2B	3B	HR	HR%	R	RBI	BB	SO	SB	Pinch Hit AB	Pinch Hit H	PO	A	E	DP	TC/G	FA	G by Pos
1910	STL N	22	.186	.243	70	13	2	1	0	0.0	2	6	6	20	3	1	0	52	2	1	2	2.6	.982	OF-21

Cliff Aberson

ABERSON, CLIFFORD ALEXANDER
B. Aug. 28, 1921, Chicago, Ill. D. June 23, 1973, Vallejo, Calif.
BR TR 6′ 200 lbs.

Year	Team	Games	BA	SA	AB	H	2B	3B	HR	HR%	R	RBI	BB	SO	SB	Pinch Hit AB	Pinch Hit H	PO	A	E	DP	TC/G	FA	G by Pos
1947	CHI N	47	.279	.450	140	39	6	3	4	2.9	24	20	20	32	0	6	2	62	7	6	1	1.9	.920	OF-40
1948		12	.188	.313	32	6	1	0	1	3.1	1	6	5	10	0	3	1	12	1	2	1	1.9	.867	OF-8
1949		4	.000	.000	7	0	0	0	0	0.0	0	0	0	2	0	3	0	2	0	0	0	2.0	1.000	OF-1
3 yrs.		63	.251	.408	179	45	7	3	5	2.8	25	26	25	44	0	12	3	76	8	8	2	1.9	.913	OF-49

Shawn Abner

ABNER, SHAWN WESLEY
B. June 17, 1966, Hamilton, Ohio.
BR TR 6′ 1″ 190 lbs.

Year	Team	Games	BA	SA	AB	H	2B	3B	HR	HR%	R	RBI	BB	SO	SB	Pinch Hit AB	Pinch Hit H	PO	A	E	DP	TC/G	FA	G by Pos
1987	SD N	16	.277	.511	47	13	3	1	2	4.3	5	7	2	8	1	3	1	23	2	2	1	1.9	.926	OF-14
1988		37	.181	.289	83	15	3	0	2	2.4	6	5	4	19	0	0	0	55	1	1	1	1.6	.982	OF-35
1989		57	.176	.275	102	18	4	0	2	2.0	13	14	5	20	1	8	1	67	0	0	0	1.3	1.000	OF-51
1990		91	.245	.310	184	45	9	0	1	0.5	17	15	9	28	2	27	5	108	1	1	1	1.8	.991	OF-62
1991	2 teams	SD N (53G –.165) CAL A (41G –.228)																						
″	total	94	.194	.301	216	42	10	2	3	1.4	27	14	11	43	1	15	2	158	4	0	1	2.1	1.000	OF-77
1992	CHI A	97	.279	.351	208	58	10	1	1	0.5	21	16	12	35	1	19	6	155	2	0	0	1.7	1.000	OF-94, DH-1
6 yrs.		392	.227	.323	840	191	39	4	11	1.3	89	71	43	153	6	72	15	566	10	4	3	1.7	.993	OF-333, DH-1

Cal Abrams

ABRAMS, CALVIN ROSS (Abie)
B. Mar. 2, 1924, Philadelphia, Pa.
BL TL 6′ 185 lbs.

Year	Team	Games	BA	SA	AB	H	2B	3B	HR	HR%	R	RBI	BB	SO	SB	Pinch Hit AB	Pinch Hit H	PO	A	E	DP	TC/G	FA	G by Pos
1949	BKN N	8	.083	.125	24	2	1	0	0	0.0	6	0	7	6	1	1	0	9	1	2	0	1.7	.833	OF-7
1950		38	.205	.227	44	9	1	0	0	0.0	5	4	9	13	0	20	4	17	0	0	0	1.1	1.000	OF-15
1951		67	.280	.393	150	42	8	0	3	2.0	27	19	36	26	3	22	5	64	3	4	1	2.1	.944	OF-34
1952	2 teams	BKN N (10G –.200) CIN N (71G –.278)																						
″	total	81	.274	.387	168	46	9	2	2	1.2	24	13	21	29	1	35	6	87	1	0	1	1.9	1.000	OF-46
1953	PIT N	119	.286	.435	448	128	10	6	15	3.3	66	43	58	70	4	7	2	205	13	6	3	2.0	.973	OF-112
1954	2 teams	PIT N (17G –.143) BAL A (115G –.293)																						
″	total	132	.280	.402	465	130	23	8	6	1.3	73	27	82	76	1	5	1	271	8	6	1	2.2	.979	OF-128
1955	BAL A	118	.243	.359	309	75	12	3	6	1.9	56	32	89	69	2	16	2	195	7	3	1	2.0	.985	OF-96, 1B-4
1956	CHI A	4	.333	.333	3	1	0	0	0	0.0	0	0	2	1	0	2	1	2	0	0	0	1.0	1.000	OF-2
8 yrs.		567	.269	.392	1611	433	64	19	32	2.0	257	138	304	290	12	108	21	850	33	21	7	2.0	.977	OF-440, 1B-4

Joe Abreu

ABREU, JOSEPH LAWRENCE (The Magician)
B. May 24, 1913, Oakland, Calif. D. Mar. 17, 1993, Hayward, Calif.
BR TR 5′ 8″ 160 lbs.

Year	Team	Games	BA	SA	AB	H	2B	3B	HR	HR%	R	RBI	BB	SO	SB	Pinch Hit AB	Pinch Hit H	PO	A	E	DP	TC/G	FA	G by Pos
1942	CIN N	9	.214	.357	28	6	1	0	1	3.6	4	3	4	4	0	1	0	9	15	1	0	3.1	.960	3B-6, 2B-2

Bill Abstein

ABSTEIN, WILLIAM HENRY (Big Bill)
B. Feb. 2, 1883, St. Louis, Mo. D. Apr. 8, 1940, St. Louis, Mo.
BR TR 6′ 185 lbs.

Year	Team	Games	BA	SA	AB	H	2B	3B	HR	HR%	R	RBI	BB	SO	SB	Pinch Hit AB	Pinch Hit H	PO	A	E	DP	TC/G	FA	G by Pos
1906	PIT N	8	.200	.200	20	4	0	0	0	0.0	2	3	0		2	3	0	5	8	3	0	3.2	.813	2B-3, OF-2
1909		137	.260	.344	512	133	20	10	1	0.2	51	70	27		16	2	0	1412	65	27	70	11.1	.982	1B-135
1910	STL A	25	.149	.172	87	13	2	0	0	0.0	1	3	2		3	2	0	268	20	11	13	13.0	.963	1B-23
3 yrs.		170	.242	.315	619	150	22	10	1	0.2	54	76	29		21	7	0	1685	93	41	83	11.2	.977	1B-158, 2B-3, OF-2
WORLD SERIES																								
1909	PIT N	7	.231	.308	26	6	2	0	0	0.0	3	2	3	10	1	0	0	70	4	5	3	11.3	.937	1B-7

Merito Acosta

ACOSTA, BALDOMERO PEDRO
Born Baldomero Pedro Acosta (Fernandez).
Brother of Jose Acosta.
B. May 19, 1896, Bauta, Cuba D. Nov. 17, 1963, Miami, Fla.
BL TL 5′ 7″ 140 lbs.

Year	Team	Games	BA	SA	AB	H	2B	3B	HR	HR%	R	RBI	BB	SO	SB	Pinch Hit AB	Pinch Hit H	PO	A	E	DP	TC/G	FA	G by Pos
1913	WAS A	9	.300	.400	20	6	0	1	0	0.0	3	1	4	2	2	2	1	5	0	2	0	1.0	.714	OF-7
1914		38	.257	.338	74	19	2	2	0	0.0	10	4	11	18	3	12	2	24	6	5	1	1.5	.857	OF-24
1915		72	.209	.245	163	34	4	1	0	0.0	20	18	28	15	8	15	4	75	4	3	2	1.5	.963	OF-53
1916		4	.143	.143	7	1	0	0	0	0.0	0	0	2	0	0	0	0	10	1	0	0	2.8	1.000	OF-4
1918	2 teams	WAS A (3G –.000) PHI A (49G –.302)																						
″	total	52	.298	.351	171	51	3	3	0	0.0	23	14	18	11	4	6	1	77	7	5	2	2.0	.944	OF-45
5 yrs.		175	.255	.308	435	111	9	7	0	0.0	56	37	63	46	17	35	8	191	18	15	5	1.7	.933	OF-133

Jerry Adair

ADAIR, KENNETH JERRY
B. Dec. 17, 1936, Sand Springs, Okla. D. May 31, 1987, Tulsa, Okla.
BR TR 6′ 175 lbs.

Year	Team	Games	BA	SA	AB	H	2B	3B	HR	HR%	R	RBI	BB	SO	SB	Pinch Hit AB	Pinch Hit H	PO	A	E	DP	TC/G	FA	G by Pos
1958	BAL A	11	.105	.105	19	2	0	0	0	0.0	1	0	1	7	0	0	0	11	23	2	5	3.3	.944	SS-10, 2B-1
1959		12	.314	.371	35	11	0	1	0	0.0	3	2	1	5	0	0	0	26	19	4	5	4.1	.918	2B-11, SS-1
1960		3	.200	.800	5	1	0	0	1	20.0	1	1	0	0	0	0	0	3	4	0	2	2.3	1.000	2B-3
1961		133	.264	.394	386	102	21	1	9	2.3	41	37	35	51	5	0	0	259	299	11	62	4.2	.981	2B-107, SS-27, 3B-2
1962		139	.284	.414	538	153	29	4	11	2.0	67	48	27	77	7	4	0	295	362	20	89	4.6	.970	SS-113, 2B-34, 3B-1
1963		109	.228	.346	382	87	21	3	6	1.6	34	30	9	51	3	5	2	242	268	8	67	5.0	.985	2B-103
1964		155	.248	.341	569	141	20	3	9	1.6	56	47	28	72	3	2	1	395	422	5	107	5.4	.994	2B-153
1965		157	.259	.351	582	151	26	3	7	1.2	51	66	35	65	6	0	0	395	446	12	99	5.4	.986	2B-157
1966	2 teams	BAL A (17G –.288) CHI A (105G –.243)																						
″	total	122	.249	.332	422	105	19	2	4	0.9	30	39	21	52	3	4	1	228	361	14	61	4.4	.977	SS-75, 2B-63
1967	2 teams	CHI A (28G –.204) BOS A (89G –.291)																						
″	total	117	.271	.338	414	112	17	1	3	0.7	47	35	17	52	1	8	2	175	236	10	51	3.7	.976	2B-50, 3B-35, SS-30

Jerry Adair *continued*

Year	Team	Games	BA	SA	AB	H	2B	3B	HR	HR%	R	RBI	BB	SO	SB	Pinch Hit AB	Pinch Hit H	PO	A	E	DP	TC/G	FA	G by Pos
1968	BOS A	74	.216	.250	208	45	1	0	2	1.0	18	12	9	28	0	13	3	90	139	8	22	3.6	.966	SS-46, 2B-12, 3B-7, 1B-1
1969	KC A	126	.250	.310	432	108	9	1	5	1.2	29	48	20	36	1	6	1	237	279	9	42	4.4	.983	2B-109, SS-8, 3B-1
1970		7	.148	.148	27	4	0	0	0	0.0	0	1	5	3	0	0	0	24	20	0	6	6.3	1.000	2B-7
13 yrs.		1165	.254	.347	4019	1022	163	19	57	1.4	378	366	208	499	29	42	10	2380	2878	103	618	4.6	.981	2B-810, SS-310, 3B-46, 1B-1
WORLD SERIES																								
1967	BOS A	5	.125	.125	16	2	0	0	0	0.0	0	1	0	3	1	0	0	7	11	0	1	4.5	1.000	2B-4

Jimmy Adair

ADAIR, JAMES AUDREY (Choppy) BR TR 5′10½″ 154 lbs.
B. Jan. 25, 1907, Waxahachie, Tex. D. Dec. 9, 1982, Dallas, Tex.

Year	Team	Games	BA	SA	AB	H	2B	3B	HR	HR%	R	RBI	BB	SO	SB	Pinch Hit AB	Pinch Hit H	PO	A	E	DP	TC/G	FA	G by Pos
1931	CHI N	18	.276	.342	76	21	3	1	0	0.0	9	3	1	8	1	0	0	37	55	5	9	5.4	.948	SS-18

Bert Adams

ADAMS, JOHN BERTRAM BB TR 6′ 1″ 185 lbs.
B. June 21, 1891, Wharton, Tex. D. June 24, 1940, Los Angeles, Calif.

Year	Team	Games	BA	SA	AB	H	2B	3B	HR	HR%	R	RBI	BB	SO	SB	Pinch Hit AB	Pinch Hit H	PO	A	E	DP	TC/G	FA	G by Pos
1910	CLE A	5	.231	.231	13	3	0	0	0	0.0	1	0	0		0	0	0	12	15	1	1	5.6	.964	C-5
1911		2	.200	.200	5	1	0	0	0	0.0	0	0	1		0	0	0	6	3	1	0	5.0	.900	C-2
1912		20	.204	.278	54	11	2	1	0	0.0	5	6	4		0	0	0	85	28	7	3	6.0	.942	C-20
1915	PHI N	24	.111	.111	27	3	0	0	0	0.0	1	2	2	3	0	0	0	34	6	2	0	1.8	.952	C-23, 1B-1
1916		11	.231	.231	13	3	0	0	0	0.0	2	1	0	3	0	1	0	20	6	2	1	2.5	.929	C-11
1917		43	.206	.290	107	22	4	1	1	0.9	4	7	0	20	0	4	1	135	40	1	4	4.5	.994	C-38, 1B-1
1918		84	.176	.194	227	40	4	0	0	0.0	10	12	10	26	5	8	3	261	69	8	8	4.4	.976	C-76
1919		78	.233	.293	232	54	7	2	1	0.4	14	17	6	27	4	4	0	249	90	12	15	4.8	.966	C-73
8 yrs.		267	.202	.248	678	137	17	4	2	0.3	37	45	23	79	9	17	4	802	257	34	32	4.4	.969	C-248, 1B-2

Bob Adams

ADAMS, ROBERT MELVIN BR TR 6′ 2″ 200 lbs.
B. Jan. 6, 1952, Pittsburgh, Pa.

Year	Team	Games	BA	SA	AB	H	2B	3B	HR	HR%	R	RBI	BB	SO	SB	Pinch Hit AB	Pinch Hit H	PO	A	E	DP	TC/G	FA	G by Pos
1977	DET A	15	.250	.542	24	6	1	0	2	8.3	2	2	0	5	0	12	4	26	1	0	1	9.0	1.000	1B-2, C-1

Bobby Adams

ADAMS, ROBERT HENRY BR TR 5′10½″ 160 lbs.
Father of Mike Adams. Brother of Dick Adams.
B. Dec. 14, 1921, Tuolumne, Calif.

Year	Team	Games	BA	SA	AB	H	2B	3B	HR	HR%	R	RBI	BB	SO	SB	Pinch Hit AB	Pinch Hit H	PO	A	E	DP	TC/G	FA	G by Pos
1946	CIN N	94	.244	.344	311	76	13	3	4	1.3	35	24	18	32	16	13	4	192	252	15	67	6.0	.967	2B-74, OF-2, 3B-1
1947		81	.272	.396	217	59	11	2	4	1.8	39	20	25	23	9	1	1	172	177	12	46	5.2	.967	2B-69
1948		87	.298	.408	262	78	20	3	1	0.4	33	21	25	23	6	14	5	167	155	11	34	4.7	.967	2B-64, 3B-7
1949		107	.253	.325	277	70	16	2	0	0.0	32	25	26	36	4	23	6	176	160	7	29	4.5	.980	2B-63, 3B-14
1950		115	.282	.414	348	98	21	8	3	0.9	57	25	43	29	7	9	1	170	200	14	34	4.0	.964	2B-53, 3B-42
1951		125	.266	.357	403	107	12	5	5	1.2	57	24	43	40	4	30	10	184	215	18	33	4.0	.957	3B-60, 2B-42, OF-1
1952		154	.283	.363	**637**	180	25	4	6	0.9	85	48	49	67	11	0	0	176	328	20	28	3.4	.962	3B-154
1953		150	.275	.357	607	167	14	6	8	1.3	99	49	58	67	3	0	0	159	324	25	39	3.4	.951	3B-150
1954		110	.269	.387	390	105	25	6	3	0.8	69	23	55	46	2	11	4	134	189	16	25	3.6	.953	3B-93, 2B-2
1955	**2 teams**	**CIN N** (64G –.273) **CHI A** (28G –.095)																						
″	**total**	92	.251	.386	171	43	11	3	2	1.2	31	23	24	25	2	20	5	47	105	5	13	2.8	.968	3B-51, 2B-6
1956	BAL A	41	.225	.297	111	25	6	1	0	0.0	19	7	25	15	1	0	0	62	65	5	12	3.1	.962	3B-24, 2B-18
1957	CHI N	60	.251	.342	187	47	10	2	1	0.5	21	10	17	28	0	8	1	44	68	6	5	2.5	.949	3B-47, 2B-1
1958		62	.281	.406	96	27	4	4	0	0.0	14	4	6	15	2	35	9	63	24	3	6	3.3	.967	1B-11, 3B-9, 2B-7
1959		3	.000	.000	2	0	0	0	0	0.0	0	0	0	1	0	2	0	2	0	1	0	3.0	.667	1B-1
14 yrs.		1281	.269	.368	4019	1082	188	49	37	0.9	591	303	414	447	67	166	46	1748	2262	158	371	3.9	.962	3B-652, 2B-399, 1B-12, OF-3

Buster Adams

ADAMS, ELVIN CLARK BR TR 6′ 180 lbs.
B. June 24, 1915, Trinidad, Colo. D. Sept. 1, 1990, Rancho Mirage, Calif.

Year	Team	Games	BA	SA	AB	H	2B	3B	HR	HR%	R	RBI	BB	SO	SB	Pinch Hit AB	Pinch Hit H	PO	A	E	DP	TC/G	FA	G by Pos
1939	STL N	2	.000	.000	1	0	0	0	0	0.0	1	0	0	0	0	1	0	0	0	0	0	0.0	—	
1943	**2 teams**	**STL N** (8G –.091) **PHI N** (111G –.256)																						
″	**total**	119	.252	.347	429	108	15	7	4	0.9	49	39	43	71	2	2	1	309	6	5	8	2.8	.984	OF-113
1944	PHI N	151	.283	.440	584	165	35	3	17	2.9	86	64	74	74	2	0	0	449	14	10	1	3.1	.979	OF-151
1945	**2 teams**	**PHI N** (14G –.232) **STL N** (140G –.292)																						
″	**total**	154	.287	.440	634	182	29	1	22	3.5	104	109	62	80	3	0	0	408	9	9	3	2.8	.979	OF-153
1946	STL N	81	.185	.306	173	32	6	0	5	2.9	21	22	29	27	3	21	6	95	1	1	1	1.7	.990	OF-58
1947	PHI N	69	.247	.352	182	45	11	1	2	1.1	21	15	26	29	2	15	6	78	5	4	2	1.7	.954	OF-51
6 yrs.		576	.266	.400	2003	532	96	12	50	2.5	282	249	234	281	12	39	13	1339	35	29	15	2.7	.979	OF-526

Dick Adams

ADAMS, RICHARD LEROY BR TL 6′ 185 lbs.
Brother of Bobby Adams.
B. Apr. 8, 1920, Tuolumne, Calif.

Year	Team	Games	BA	SA	AB	H	2B	3B	HR	HR%	R	RBI	BB	SO	SB	Pinch Hit AB	Pinch Hit H	PO	A	E	DP	TC/G	FA	G by Pos
1947	PHI A	37	.202	.360	89	18	2	3	2	2.2	9	11	2	18	0	10	1	171	17	1	19	7.0	.995	1B-24, OF-3

Doug Adams

ADAMS, HAROLD DOUGLAS BL TR 6′ 3″ 185 lbs.
B. Jan. 27, 1943, Blue River, Wis.

Year	Team	Games	BA	SA	AB	H	2B	3B	HR	HR%	R	RBI	BB	SO	SB	Pinch Hit AB	Pinch Hit H	PO	A	E	DP	TC/G	FA	G by Pos
1969	CHI A	8	.214	.214	14	3	0	0	0	0.0	1	1	1	3	0	5	2	9	2	0	0	2.8	1.000	C-4

George Adams

ADAMS, GEORGE (Partridge) BR TR 5′ 6″ 175 lbs.
B. Grafton, Mass. Deceased.

Year	Team	Games	BA	SA	AB	H	2B	3B	HR	HR%	R	RBI	BB	SO	SB	Pinch Hit AB	Pinch Hit H	PO	A	E	DP	TC/G	FA	G by Pos
1879	SYR N	4	.231	.231	13	3	0	0	0	0.0	0	0	1	1		0	0	21	0	4	0	6.3	.840	OF-2, 1B-2

Glenn Adams

ADAMS, GLENN CHARLES BL TR 6′ 1″ 180 lbs.
B. Oct. 4, 1947, Northbridge, Mass.

Year	Team	Games	BA	SA	AB	H	2B	3B	HR	HR%	R	RBI	BB	SO	SB	Pinch Hit AB	Pinch Hit H	PO	A	E	DP	TC/G	FA	G by Pos
1975	SF N	61	.300	.478	90	27	2	1	4	4.4	10	15	11	25	1	33	12	31	1	2	0	1.4	.941	OF-25
1976		69	.243	.297	74	18	4	0	0	0.0	2	3	1	12	1	59	13	3	0	0	0	0.5	1.000	OF-6
1977	MIN A	95	.338	.468	269	91	17	0	6	2.2	32	49	18	30	0	11	6	60	3	2	1	0.7	.969	DH-47, OF-44
1978		116	.258	.390	310	80	18	1	7	2.3	27	35	17	32	0	23	8	5	0	0	0	0.0	1.000	DH-101, OF-5
1979		119	.301	.420	326	98	13	1	8	2.5	34	50	25	27	2	21	2	66	2	3	0	0.7	.958	DH-55, OF-53

Glenn Adams *continued*

Year	Team	Games	BA	SA	AB	H	2B	3B	HR	HR%	R	RBI	BB	SO	SB	Pinch Hit AB	Pinch Hit H	PO	A	E	DP	TC/G	FA	G by Pos
1980		99	.286	.412	262	75	11	2	6	2.3	32	38	15	26	2	16	2	18	0	1	0	0.2	.947	DH-81, OF-12
1981		72	.209	.282	220	46	10	0	2	0.9	13	24	20	26	0	13	6	0	0	0	0	0.0	.000	DH-62
1982	TOR A	30	.258	.364	66	17	4	0	1	1.5	2	11	4	5	0	9	2	0	0	0	0	0.0	.000	DH-27
8 yrs.		661	.280	.398	1617	452	79	5	34	2.1	152	225	111	183	6	185	51	183	6	8	1	0.4	.959	DH-373, OF-145

Herb Adams

ADAMS, HERBERT LOREN BL TL 5′ 9″ 160 lbs.
B. Apr. 14, 1928, Hollywood, Calif.

Year	Team	Games	BA	SA	AB	H	2B	3B	HR	HR%	R	RBI	BB	SO	SB	Pinch Hit AB	Pinch Hit H	PO	A	E	DP	TC/G	FA	G by Pos
1948	CHI A	5	.273	.364	11	3	1	0	0	0.0	1	0	1	1	0	0	0	10	2	0	0	3.0	1.000	OF-4
1949		56	.293	.346	208	61	5	3	0	0.0	26	16	9	16	1	5	1	112	4	3	1	2.5	.975	OF-48
1950		34	.203	.271	118	24	2	3	0	0.0	12	2	12	7	3	1	0	90	1	2	0	2.8	.978	OF-33
3 yrs.		95	.261	.320	337	88	8	6	0	0.0	39	18	22	24	4	6	1	212	7	5	1	2.6	.978	OF-85

Jim Adams

ADAMS, JAMES J. TR
B. 1868, East St. Louis, Ill. Deceased.

Year	Team	Games	BA	SA	AB	H	2B	3B	HR	HR%	R	RBI	BB	SO	SB	Pinch Hit AB	Pinch Hit H	PO	A	E	DP	TC/G	FA	G by Pos
1890	STL AA	1	.250	.250	4	1	0	0	0	0.0	0		0		0	0	0	4	1	0	0	5.0	1.000	C-1

Mike Adams

ADAMS, ROBERT MICHAEL BR TR 5′ 9″ 180 lbs.
Son of Bobby Adams.
B. July 22, 1948, Cincinnati, Ohio.

Year	Team	Games	BA	SA	AB	H	2B	3B	HR	HR%	R	RBI	BB	SO	SB	Pinch Hit AB	Pinch Hit H	PO	A	E	DP	TC/G	FA	G by Pos
1972	MIN A	3	.333	.333	6	2	0	0	0	0.0	0	0	0	1	0	1	0	1	0	0	0	1.0	1.000	OF-1
1973		55	.212	.379	66	14	2	0	3	4.5	21	6	17	18	2	1	0	45	0	1	0	1.8	.978	OF-24, DH-2
1976	CHI N	25	.138	.207	29	4	2	0	0	0.0	1	2	8	7	0	16	1	4	2	0	0	0.8	1.000	OF-4, 3B-3, 2B-1
1977		2	.000	.000	2	0	0	0	0	0.0	0	0	0	1	0	1	0	0	0	0	0	0.0	.000	OF-2
1978	OAK A	15	.200	.267	15	3	1	0	0	0.0	5	1	7	2	0	5	0	7	6	0	2	1.1	1.000	2B-6, 3B-3, DH-3
5 yrs.		100	.195	.314	118	23	5	0	3	2.5	27	9	32	29	2	24	1	57	8	1	2	1.3	.985	OF-31, 2B-7, 3B-6, DH-5

Ricky Adams

ADAMS, RICKY LEE BR TR 6′ 2″ 180 lbs.
B. Jan. 21, 1959, Upland, Calif.

Year	Team	Games	BA	SA	AB	H	2B	3B	HR	HR%	R	RBI	BB	SO	SB	Pinch Hit AB	Pinch Hit H	PO	A	E	DP	TC/G	FA	G by Pos
1982	CAL A	8	.143	.143	14	2	0	0	0	0.0	1	0	0	2	1	1	1	6	12	1	4	2.4	.947	SS-8
1983		58	.250	.321	112	28	2	0	2	1.8	22	6	5	12	1	0	0	58	141	8	29	3.6	.961	SS-38, 3B-16, 2B-4
1985	SF N	54	.190	.281	121	23	3	1	2	1.7	12	10	5	23	1	4	1	35	101	5	13	3.0	.965	SS-25, 3B-16, 2B-6
3 yrs.		120	.215	.291	247	53	5	1	4	1.6	35	16	10	37	3	5	2	99	254	14	46	3.2	.962	SS-71, 3B-32, 2B-10

Sparky Adams

ADAMS, EARL JOHN BR TR 5′ 5½″ 151 lbs.
B. Aug. 26, 1894, Zerbe, Pa. D. Feb. 24, 1989, Pottsville, Pa.

Year	Team	Games	BA	SA	AB	H	2B	3B	HR	HR%	R	RBI	BB	SO	SB	Pinch Hit AB	Pinch Hit H	PO	A	E	DP	TC/G	FA	G by Pos
1922	CHI N	11	.250	.295	44	11	0	1	0	0.0	5	3	4	3	1	0	0	18	35	5	5	5.3	.914	2B-11
1923		95	.289	.367	311	90	12	0	4	1.3	40	35	26	10	20	10	4	156	249	28	45	5.4	.935	SS-79, OF-1
1924		117	.280	.337	418	117	11	5	1	0.2	66	27	40	20	15	7	2	224	343	31	79	5.6	.948	SS-88, 2B-19
1925		149	.287	.368	**627**	180	29	8	2	0.3	95	48	44	15	26	0	0	367	573	16	95	6.4	.983	2B-144, SS-5
1926		154	.309	.375	**624**	193	35	3	0	0.0	95	39	52	27	27	2	0	338	523	31	97	5.7	.965	2B-136, 3B-19, SS-2
1927		146	.292	.340	**647**	189	17	7	0	0.0	100	49	42	26	26	0	0	276	443	18	69	4.8	.976	2B-60, 3B-53, SS-40
1928	PIT N	135	.276	.325	539	149	14	6	0	0.0	91	38	64	18	8	1	0	317	440	19	68	5.7	.976	2B-107, SS-27, OF-1
1929		74	.260	.311	196	51	8	1	0	0.0	37	11	15	5	3	4	2	75	130	17	14	3.3	.923	SS-30, 2B-20, 3B-15, OF-2
1930	STL N	137	.314	.409	570	179	36	9	0	0.0	98	55	45	27	7	2	1	140	264	16	46	3.1	.962	3B-104, 2B-25, SS-7
1931		143	.293	.390	608	178	**46**	5	1	0.2	97	40	42	24	16	1	0	127	239	18	30	2.7	.953	3B-138, SS-6
1932		31	.276	.315	127	35	3	1	0	0.0	22	13	14	5	0	0	0	25	42	5	11	2.4	.931	3B-30
1933	2 teams	STL N (8G –.167) CIN N (137G –.262)																						
″	total	145	.257	.305	568	146	22	1	1	0.2	60	22	45	33	3	0	0	132	311	18	19	3.1	.961	3B-135, SS-13
1934	CIN N	87	.252	.317	278	70	16	1	0	0.0	38	14	20	10	2	12	4	92	156	8	21	3.8	.969	3B-38, 2B-29
13 yrs.		1424	.286	.353	5557	1588	249	48	9	0.2	844	394	453	223	154	39	13	2287	3748	230	599	4.5	.963	2B-551, 3B-532, SS-297, OF-4
WORLD SERIES																								
1930	STL N	6	.143	.143	21	3	0	0	0	0.0	0	1	0	4	0	0	0	4	7	0	1	1.8	1.000	3B-6
1931		2	.250	.250	4	1	0	0	0	0.0	0	0	0	1	0	0	0	0	1	0	0	0.5	1.000	3B-2
2 yrs.		8	.160	.160	25	4	0	0	0	0.0	0	1	0	5	0	0	0	4	8	0	1	1.5	1.000	3B-8

Spencer Adams

ADAMS, SPENCER DEWEY BL TR 5′ 9″ 158 lbs.
B. July 21, 1898, Layton, Utah D. Nov. 24, 1970, Salt Lake City, Utah.

Year	Team	Games	BA	SA	AB	H	2B	3B	HR	HR%	R	RBI	BB	SO	SB	Pinch Hit AB	Pinch Hit H	PO	A	E	DP	TC/G	FA	G by Pos
1923	PIT N	25	.250	.286	56	14	0	1	0	0.0	11	4	6	6	2	1	1	25	33	7	5	3.8	.892	2B-11, SS-6
1925	WAS A	39	.273	.382	55	15	4	1	0	0.0	11	4	5	4	1	1	0	30	30	6	4	2.5	.909	2B-15, SS-8, 3B-3
1926	NY A	28	.120	.160	25	3	1	0	0	0.0	7	1	3	7	1	10	0	11	10	0	2	4.2	1.000	2B-4, 3B-1
1927	STL A	88	.266	.332	259	69	11	3	0	0.0	32	29	24	33	1	5	0	159	190	21	35	4.5	.943	2B-54, 3B-28
4 yrs.		180	.256	.322	395	101	16	5	0	0.0	61	38	38	50	5	17	1	225	263	34	46	4.0	.935	2B-84, 3B-32, SS-14
WORLD SERIES																								
1925	WAS A	2	.000	.000	1	0	0	0	0	0.0	0	0	0	0	0	1	0	0	0	0	0	0.0	.000	2B-1
1926	NY A	2	—	—	0	0	0	0	0	—	0	0	0	0	0	0	0	0	0	0	0	0.0	—	
2 yrs.		4	.000	.000	1	0	0	0	0	0.0	0	0	0	0	0	1	0	0	0	0	0	0.0		2B-1

Joe Adcock

ADCOCK, JOSEPH WILBUR BR TR 6′ 4″ 210 lbs.
B. Oct. 30, 1927, Coushatta, La.
Manager 1967.

Year	Team	Games	BA	SA	AB	H	2B	3B	HR	HR%	R	RBI	BB	SO	SB	Pinch Hit AB	Pinch Hit H	PO	A	E	DP	TC/G	FA	G by Pos
1950	CIN N	102	.293	.406	372	109	16	1	8	2.2	46	55	24	24	2	4	0	346	17	8	16	3.7	.978	OF-75, 1B-24
1951		113	.243	.380	395	96	16	4	10	2.5	40	47	24	29	1	5	2	221	8	4	2	2.2	.983	OF-107
1952		117	.278	.460	378	105	22	4	13	3.4	43	52	23	38	1	14	4	306	8	3	8	3.1	.991	OF-85, 1B-17
1953	MIL N	157	.285	.453	590	168	33	6	18	3.1	71	80	42	82	3	0	0	1389	96	13	146	9.5	.991	1B-157
1954		133	.308	.520	500	154	27	5	23	4.6	73	87	44	58	1	1	1	1229	67	6	125	9.8	.995	1B-133
1955		84	.264	.469	288	76	14	0	15	5.2	40	45	31	44	0	5	1	725	44	8	68	10.0	.990	1B-78
1956		137	.291	.597	454	132	23	1	38	**8.4**	76	103	32	86	1	8	2	1086	75	6	109	9.0	.995	1B-129
1957		65	.287	.541	209	60	13	2	12	5.7	31	38	20	51	0	6	1	477	30	2	60	9.1	.996	1B-56
1958		105	.275	.506	320	88	15	1	19	5.9	40	54	21	63	0	14	3	564	37	7	55	6.5	.988	1B-71, OF-22
1959		115	.292	.535	404	118	19	2	25	6.2	53	76	32	77	0	10	3	807	81	7	67	8.1	.992	1B-89, OF-21
1960		138	.298	.500	514	153	21	4	25	4.9	55	91	46	86	2	2	1	1229	104	9	105	9.9	.993	1B-136
1961		152	.285	.507	562	160	20	0	35	6.2	77	108	59	94	2	4	1	1471	102	11	133	10.7	.993	1B-148

Year	Team	Lg	Games	BA	SA	AB	H	2B	3B	HR	HR%	R	RBI	BB	SO	SB	Pinch Hit AB	Pinch Hit H	PO	A	E	DP	TC/G	FA	G by Pos

Joe Adcock *continued*

Year	Team	Lg	Games	BA	SA	AB	H	2B	3B	HR	HR%	R	RBI	BB	SO	SB	Pinch Hit AB	Pinch Hit H	PO	A	E	DP	TC/G	FA	G by Pos
1962			121	.248	.506	391	97	12	1	29	7.4	48	78	50	91	2	8	3	907	57	3	72	8.6	.997	1B-112
1963	CLE	A	97	.251	.420	283	71	7	1	13	4.6	28	49	30	53	1	22	5	608	36	3	46	8.3	.995	1B-78
1964	LA	A	118	.268	.475	366	98	13	0	21	5.7	39	64	48	61	0	11	4	959	54	7	94	9.7	.993	1B-105
1965	CAL	A	122	.241	.401	349	84	14	0	14	4.0	30	47	37	74	2	23	4	789	45	3	68	8.6	.996	1B-97
1966			83	.273	.576	231	63	10	3	18	7.8	33	48	31	48	2	16	4	565	39	2	60	8.5	.997	1B-71
17 yrs.			1959	.277	.485	6606	1832	295	35	336	5.1	823	1122	594	1059	20	153	39	13678	900	102	1234	8.1	.993	1B-1501, OF-310
WORLD SERIES																									
1957	MIL	N	5	.200	.200	15	3	0	0	0	0.0	1	2	0	2	0	1	0	38	2	1	2	8.2	.976	1B-5
1958			4	.308	.308	13	4	0	0	0	0.0	1	0	1	3	0	1	1	23	2	0	0	6.3	1.000	1B-4
2 yrs.			9	.250	.250	28	7	0	0	0	0.0	2	2	1	5	0	2	1	61	4	1	2	7.3	.985	1B-9

Bob Addis

ADDIS, ROBERT GORDON BL TR 6′ 175 lbs.
B. Nov. 6, 1925, Mineral, Ohio.

Year	Team	Lg	Games	BA	SA	AB	H	2B	3B	HR	HR%	R	RBI	BB	SO	SB	Pinch Hit AB	Pinch Hit H	PO	A	E	DP	TC/G	FA	G by Pos
1950	BOS	N	16	.250	.286	28	7	1	0	0	0.0	7	2	3	5	1	10	1	7	0	0	0	1.0	1.000	OF-7
1951			85	.276	.327	199	55	7	0	1	0.5	23	24	9	10	3	36	**12**	107	1	2	1	2.4	.982	OF-46
1952	CHI	N	93	.295	.363	292	86	13	2	1	0.3	38	20	23	30	4	15	4	160	8	2	2	2.2	.988	OF-76
1953	2 teams		CHI N (10G –.167) PIT N (4G –.000)																						
″	total		14	.133	.200	15	2	1	0	0	0.0	2	1	2	2	0	8	1	7	1	0	1	2.7	1.000	OF-3
4 yrs.			208	.281	.341	534	150	22	2	2	0.4	70	47	37	47	8	69	18	281	10	4	4	2.2	.986	OF-132

Jim Adduci

ADDUCI, JAMES DAVID BL TL 6′ 5″ 200 lbs.
B. Aug. 9, 1959, Chicago, Ill.

Year	Team	Lg	Games	BA	SA	AB	H	2B	3B	HR	HR%	R	RBI	BB	SO	SB	Pinch Hit AB	Pinch Hit H	PO	A	E	DP	TC/G	FA	G by Pos
1983	STL	N	10	.050	.050	20	1	0	0	0	0.0	0	0	1	6	0	3	0	47	4	0	3	7.3	1.000	1B-6, OF-1
1986	MIL	A	3	.091	.182	11	1	1	0	0	0.0	2	0	1	2	0	0	0	25	3	0	1	9.3	1.000	1B-3
1988			44	.266	.383	94	25	6	1	1	1.1	8	15	0	15	0	3	0	40	3	1	1	1.1	.977	OF-24, DH-12, 1B-3
1989	PHI	N	13	.368	.421	19	7	1	0	0	0.0	1	0	0	4	0	8	3	25	3	0	1	5.6	1.000	1B-4, OF-1
4 yrs.			70	.236	.326	144	34	8	1	1	0.7	11	15	2	27	0	14	3	137	13	1	6	2.8	.993	OF-26, 1B-16, DH-12

Bob Addy

ADDY, ROBERT EDWARD (The Magnet) BL TL 5′ 8″ 160 lbs.
B. Feb. 1845, Rochester, N. Y. D. Apr. 9, 1910, Pocatello, Ida.
Manager 1877.

Year	Team	Lg	Games	BA	SA	AB	H	2B	3B	HR	HR%	R	RBI	BB	SO	SB	Pinch Hit AB	Pinch Hit H	PO	A	E	DP	TC/G	FA	G by Pos
1876	CHI	N	32	.282	.324	142	40	4	1	0	0.0	36	16	5	0		0	0	46	6	13	0	2.0	.800	OF-32
1877	CIN	N	57	.278	.310	245	68	2	3	0	0.0	27	31	6	5	0	0	0	74	17	22	5	2.0	.805	OF-57
2 yrs.			89	.279	.315	387	108	6	4	0	0.0	63	47	11	5	0	0	0	120	23	35	5	2.0	.803	OF-89

Morrie Aderholt

ADERHOLT, MORRIS WOODROW BL TR 6′ 1″ 188 lbs.
B. Sept. 13, 1915, Mt. Olive, N. C. D. Mar. 18, 1955, Sarasota, Fla.

Year	Team	Lg	Games	BA	SA	AB	H	2B	3B	HR	HR%	R	RBI	BB	SO	SB	Pinch Hit AB	Pinch Hit H	PO	A	E	DP	TC/G	FA	G by Pos
1939	WAS	A	7	.200	.320	25	5	0	0	1	4.0	5	4	2	6	0	1	0	22	19	6	3	6.7	.872	2B-7
1940			1	.000	.000	2	0	0	0	0	0.0	0	0	0	0	0	0	0	2	1	0	1	3.0	1.000	2B-1
1941			11	.143	.143	14	2	0	0	0	0.0	3	1	1	3	0	5	1	8	4	3	1	5.0	.800	2B-2, 3B-1
1944	BKN	N	17	.271	.407	59	16	2	3	0	0.0	9	10	4	4	0	3	0	26	1	4	0	2.4	.871	OF-13
1945	2 teams		BKN N (39G –.217) BOS N (31G –.333)																						
″	total		70	.290	.358	162	47	5	0	2	1.2	19	17	12	16	3	36	8	67	1	1	0	2.1	.986	OF-32, 2B-1
5 yrs.			106	.267	.351	262	70	7	3	3	1.1	36	32	19	29	3	45	9	125	26	14	5	2.9	.915	OF-45, 2B-11, 3B-1

Dick Adkins

ADKINS, RICHARD EARL BR TR 5′10″ 165 lbs.
B. Mar. 3, 1920, Electra, Tex. D. Sept. 12, 1955, Electra, Tex.

Year	Team	Lg	Games	BA	SA	AB	H	2B	3B	HR	HR%	R	RBI	BB	SO	SB	Pinch Hit AB	Pinch Hit H	PO	A	E	DP	TC/G	FA	G by Pos
1942	PHI	A	3	.143	.143	7	1	0	0	0	0.0	2	0	0	2	0	0	0	2	5	1	1	2.7	.875	SS-3

Henry Adkinson

ADKINSON, HENRY MAGEE
B. Sept. 1, 1874, Chicago, Ill. D. May 1, 1923, Salt Lake City, Utah.

Year	Team	Lg	Games	BA	SA	AB	H	2B	3B	HR	HR%	R	RBI	BB	SO	SB	Pinch Hit AB	Pinch Hit H	PO	A	E	DP	TC/G	FA	G by Pos
1895	STL	N	1	.400	.400	5	2	0	0	0	0.0	1	0	0	2	0	0	0	2	0	1	0	3.0	.667	OF-1

Dave Adlesh

ADLESH, DAVID GEORGE BR TR 6′ 187 lbs.
B. July 15, 1943, Long Beach, Calif.

Year	Team	Lg	Games	BA	SA	AB	H	2B	3B	HR	HR%	R	RBI	BB	SO	SB	Pinch Hit AB	Pinch Hit H	PO	A	E	DP	TC/G	FA	G by Pos
1963	HOU	N	6	.000	.000	8	0	0	0	0	0.0	0	0	0	4	0	2	0	8	0	1	0	1.5	.889	C-6
1964			3	.200	.200	10	2	0	0	0	0.0	0	0	0	5	0	0	0	11	2	0	0	4.3	1.000	C-3
1965			15	.147	.176	34	5	1	0	0	0.0	2	3	2	12	0	2	1	51	5	0	1	4.3	1.000	C-13
1966			3	.000	.000	6	0	0	0	0	0.0	0	0	0	4	0	3	0	11	0	0	0	11.0	1.000	C-1
1967			39	.181	.223	94	17	1	0	1	1.1	4	4	11	28	0	8	2	179	8	1	1	6.1	.995	C-31
1968			40	.183	.212	104	19	1	1	0	0.0	3	4	5	27	0	4	2	193	11	2	0	5.7	.990	C-36
6 yrs.			106	.168	.199	256	43	3	1	1	0.4	9	11	18	80	0	19	5	453	26	4	2	5.4	.992	C-90

Troy Afenir

AFENIR, MICHAEL TROY BR TR 6′ 4″ 185 lbs.
B. Sept. 21, 1963, Escondido, Calif.

Year	Team	Lg	Games	BA	SA	AB	H	2B	3B	HR	HR%	R	RBI	BB	SO	SB	Pinch Hit AB	Pinch Hit H	PO	A	E	DP	TC/G	FA	G by Pos
1987	HOU	N	10	.300	.350	20	6	1	0	0	0.0	1	1	0	12	0	1	0	35	2	1	1	3.8	.974	C-10
1990	OAK	A	14	.143	.143	14	2	0	0	0	0.0	0	2	0	6	0	6	1	13	0	0	0	1.0	1.000	C-12, DH-1
1991			5	.091	.091	11	1	0	0	0	0.0	0	0	0	2	0	1	0	18	1	0	1	3.8	1.000	C-4, DH-1
1992	CIN	N	16	.176	.324	34	6	1	2	0	0.0	3	4	5	12	0	1	1	57	2	0	1	3.9	1.000	C-15
4 yrs.			45	.190	.266	79	15	2	2	0	0.0	4	7	5	32	0	9	2	123	5	1	3	3.0	.992	C-41, DH-2

Tommie Agee

AGEE, TOMMIE LEE BR TR 5′11″ 195 lbs.
B. Aug. 9, 1942, Magnolia, Ala.

Year	Team	Lg	Games	BA	SA	AB	H	2B	3B	HR	HR%	R	RBI	BB	SO	SB	Pinch Hit AB	Pinch Hit H	PO	A	E	DP	TC/G	FA	G by Pos
1962	CLE	A	5	.214	.214	14	3	0	0	0	0.0	0	2	0	4	0	2	0	4	0	0	0	1.3	1.000	OF-3
1963			13	.148	.296	27	4	1	0	1	3.7	3	3	2	9	0	0	0	10	2	0	1	0.9	1.000	OF-13
1964			13	.167	.167	12	2	0	0	0	0.0	0	0	0	3	0	0	0	5	0	0	0	0.4	1.000	OF-12
1965	CHI	A	10	.158	.211	19	3	1	0	0	0.0	2	3	2	6	0	1	0	13	0	0	0	1.4	1.000	OF-9
1966			160	.273	.447	629	172	27	8	22	3.5	98	86	41	127	44	0	0	376	12	7	7	2.5	.982	OF-159
1967			158	.234	.371	529	124	26	2	14	2.6	73	52	44	129	28	2	1	337	6	11	2	2.3	.969	OF-152
1968	NY	N	132	.217	.307	368	80	12	3	5	1.4	30	17	15	103	13	3	1	216	6	5	2	1.8	.978	OF-127
1969			149	.271	.464	565	153	23	4	26	4.6	97	76	59	137	12	3	1	334	7	5	0	2.4	.986	OF-146
1970			153	.286	.469	636	182	30	7	24	3.8	107	75	55	156	31	3	1	374	4	13	3	2.6	.967	OF-150
1971			113	.285	.428	425	121	19	0	14	3.3	58	50	50	84	28	6	3	265	7	6	0	2.6	.978	OF-107

Tommie Agee *continued*

Year	Team	Games	BA	SA	AB	H	2B	3B	HR	HR%	R	RBI	BB	SO	SB	Pinch Hit AB	Pinch Hit H	PO	A	E	DP	TC/G	FA	G by Pos
1972		114	.227	.374	422	96	23	0	13	3.1	52	47	53	92	8	4	0	273	6	11	1	2.7	.962	OF-109
1973	2 teams	HOU N (83G –.235) STL N (26G –.177)																						
"	total	109	.222	.398	266	59	8	3	11	4.1	38	22	21	68	3	19	4	164	3	3	2	2.0	.982	OF-86
12 yrs.		1129	.255	.412	3912	999	170	27	130	3.3	558	433	342	918	167	43	11	2371	53	61	18	2.3	.975	OF-1073
LEAGUE CHAMPIONSHIP SERIES																								
1969	NY N	3	.357	.857	14	5	1	0	2	14.3	4	4	2	5	2	0	0	9	0	0	0	3.0	1.000	OF-3
WORLD SERIES																								
1969	NY N	5	.167	.333	18	3	0	0	1	5.6	1	1	2	5	1	0	0	19	0	0	0	3.8	1.000	OF-5

Harry Agganis

AGGANIS, HARRY (The Golden Greek) BL TL 6′ 2″ 200 lbs.
B. Apr. 20, 1929, Lynn, Mass. D. June 27, 1955, Cambridge, Mass.

Year	Team	Games	BA	SA	AB	H	2B	3B	HR	HR%	R	RBI	BB	SO	SB	Pinch Hit AB	Pinch Hit H	PO	A	E	DP	TC/G	FA	G by Pos
1954	BOS A	132	.251	.394	434	109	13	8	11	2.5	54	57	47	57	6	11	3	1064	89	12	101	9.8	.990	1B-119
1955		25	.313	.458	83	26	10	1	0	0.0	11	10	10	10	2	3	0	208	14	3	15	11.3	.987	1B-20
2 yrs.		157	.261	.404	517	135	23	9	11	2.1	65	67	57	67	8	14	3	1272	103	15	116	10.0	.989	1B-139

Joe Agler

AGLER, JOSEPH ABRAM BL TL 5′11″ 165 lbs.
B. June 12, 1887, Coshocton, Ohio D. Apr. 26, 1971, Massillon, Ohio.

Year	Team	Games	BA	SA	AB	H	2B	3B	HR	HR%	R	RBI	BB	SO	SB	Pinch Hit AB	Pinch Hit H	PO	A	E	DP	TC/G	FA	G by Pos
1912	WAS A	1	.000	.000	1	0	0	0	0	0.0	0	0	0		0	1	0	0	0	0	0	0.0	—	
1914	BUF F	135	.272	.335	463	126	17	6	0	0.0	82	20	77		21	3	1	831	57	16	47	7.0	.982	1B-76, OF-54
1915	2 teams	BUF F (25G –.178) BAL F (72G –.215)																						
"	total	97	.206	.251	287	59	5	4	0	0.0	39	16	54		17	7	0	626	54	15	44	8.1	.978	1B-59, OF-24, 2B-3
3 yrs.		233	.246	.302	751	185	22	10	0	0.0	121	36	131		38	11	1	1457	111	31	91	7.4	.981	1B-135, OF-78, 2B-3

Sam Agnew

AGNEW, SAMUEL LESTER BR TR 5′11″ 185 lbs.
B. Apr. 12, 1887, Farmington, Mo. D. July 19, 1951, Sonoma, Calif.

Year	Team	Games	BA	SA	AB	H	2B	3B	HR	HR%	R	RBI	BB	SO	SB	Pinch Hit AB	Pinch Hit H	PO	A	E	DP	TC/G	FA	G by Pos
1913	STL A	104	.208	.290	307	64	9	5	2	0.7	27	24	20	49	11	0	0	383	170	28	17	5.6	.952	C-103
1914		113	.212	.254	311	66	5	4	0	0.0	22	16	24	63	10	0	0	451	163	25	10	5.7	.961	C-113
1915		104	.203	.231	295	60	4	2	0	0.0	18	19	12	36	5	1	0	398	153	39	16	5.8	.934	C-102
1916	BOS A	40	.209	.269	67	14	2	1	0	0.0	4	7	6	4	0	2	0	110	47	8	4	4.3	.952	C-38
1917		85	.208	.246	260	54	6	2	0	0.0	17	16	19	30	2	0	0	297	88	14	5	4.7	.965	C-85
1918		72	.166	.206	199	33	8	0	0	0.0	11	6	11	26	0	0	0	254	104	13	10	5.2	.965	C-72
1919	WAS A	42	.235	.306	98	23	7	0	0	0.0	6	10	10	8	1	5	1	141	48	5	5	5.4	.974	C-36
7 yrs.		560	.204	.253	1537	314	41	14	2	0.1	105	98	102	216	29	8	1	2034	773	132	67	5.4	.955	C-549
WORLD SERIES																								
1918	BOS A	4	.000	.000	9	0	0	0	0	0.0	0	0	0	0	0	0	0	12	6	0	0	4.5	1.000	C-4

Luis Aguayo

AGUAYO, LUIS BR TR 5′ 9″ 173 lbs.
Born Luis Aguayo (Muriel).
B. Mar. 13, 1959, Vega Baja, Puerto Rico.

Year	Team	Games	BA	SA	AB	H	2B	3B	HR	HR%	R	RBI	BB	SO	SB	Pinch Hit AB	Pinch Hit H	PO	A	E	DP	TC/G	FA	G by Pos
1980	PHI N	20	.277	.447	47	13	1	2	1	2.1	7	8	2	3	1	1	0	44	44	3	10	4.8	.967	2B-14, SS-5
1981		45	.214	.298	84	18	4	0	1	1.2	11	7	6	15	1	3	1	39	63	5	15	2.4	.953	2B-21, SS-21, 3B-3
1982		50	.268	.518	56	15	1	2	3	5.4	11	7	5	7	1	5	1	27	49	4	5	2.0	.950	2B-21, SS-15, 3B-5
1983		2	.250	.250	4	1	0	0	0	0.0	1	0	1	2	0	0	0	3	0	0	0	1.5	1.000	SS-2
1984		58	.278	.458	72	20	4	0	3	4.2	15	11	8	16	0	16	3	18	55	3	7	2.1	.961	3B-14, 2B-12, SS-10
1985		91	.279	.467	165	46	7	3	6	3.6	27	21	22	26	1	8	3	92	158	9	27	3.1	.965	SS-60, 2B-17, 3B-7
1986		62	.211	.361	133	28	6	1	4	3.0	17	13	8	26	1	14	7	57	90	5	19	2.9	.967	2B-31, SS-20, 3B-1
1987		94	.206	.431	209	43	9	1	12	5.7	25	21	15	56	0	18	2	86	172	7	30	3.1	.974	SS-78, 2B-6, 3B-2
1988	2 teams	PHI N (49G –.247) NY A (50G –.250)																						
"	total	99	.249	.354	237	59	7	0	6	2.5	21	13	20	50	2	13	4	83	156	13	24	2.7	.948	3B-46, SS-33, 2B-15
1989	CLE A	47	.175	.268	97	17	4	1	1	1.0	7	8	7	19	0	5	0	34	80	5	11	2.6	.958	3B-19, SS-15, 2B-10, DH-2
10 yrs.		568	.236	.393	1104	260	43	10	37	3.4	142	109	94	220	7	83	21	483	867	54	148	2.8	.962	SS-259, 2B-147, 3B-97, DH-2
DIVISIONAL PLAYOFF SERIES																								
1981	PHI N	2	—	—	0	0	0	0	0	—	1	0	0	0	0	0	0	0	0	0	0	0.0	—	

Charlie Ahearn

AHEARN, CHARLES
B. Troy, N. Y. Deceased.

Year	Team	Games	BA	SA	AB	H	2B	3B	HR	HR%	R	RBI	BB	SO	SB	Pinch Hit AB	Pinch Hit H	PO	A	E	DP	TC/G	FA	G by Pos
1880	TRO N	1	.250	.250	4	1	0	0	0	0.0	1	0	0	0		0	0	2	5	2	0	9.0	.778	C-1

Willie Aikens

AIKENS, WILLIE MAYS BL TR 6′ 3″ 220 lbs.
B. Oct. 14, 1954, Seneca, S. C.

Year	Team	Games	BA	SA	AB	H	2B	3B	HR	HR%	R	RBI	BB	SO	SB	Pinch Hit AB	Pinch Hit H	PO	A	E	DP	TC/G	FA	G by Pos
1977	CAL A	42	.198	.242	91	18	4	0	0	0.0	5	6	10	23	1	15	1	94	8	3	10	4.0	.971	1B-13, DH-13
1979		116	.280	.493	379	106	18	0	21	5.5	59	81	61	79	1	11	3	462	31	2	49	4.7	.996	1B-55, DH-51
1980	KC A	151	.278	.433	543	151	24	0	20	3.7	70	98	64	88	1	0	0	1081	65	12	95	7.7	.990	1B-138, DH-13
1981		101	.266	.458	349	93	16	0	17	4.9	45	53	62	47	0	2	0	844	56	7	79	9.2	.992	1B-99
1982		134	.281	.457	466	131	29	1	17	3.6	50	74	45	70	0	10	4	1048	75	7	95	8.8	.994	1B-128
1983		125	.302	.539	410	124	26	1	23	5.6	49	72	45	75	0	8	2	884	64	11	101	8.1	.989	1B-112, DH-6
1984	TOR A	93	.205	.376	234	48	7	0	11	4.7	21	26	29	56	0	15	3	12	1	0	1	0.2	1.000	DH-81, 1B-2
1985		12	.200	.400	20	4	1	0	1	5.0	2	5	3	6	0	6	1	0	0	0	0	0.0	.000	DH-11
8 yrs.		774	.271	.455	2492	675	125	2	110	4.4	301	415	319	444	3	67	14	4425	300	42	430	6.6	.991	1B-547, DH-175
DIVISIONAL PLAYOFF SERIES																								
1981	KC A	3	.333	.333	9	3	0	0	0	0.0	0	0	3	2	0	0	0	27	1	0	0	9.3	1.000	1B-3
LEAGUE CHAMPIONSHIP SERIES																								
1980	KC A	3	.364	.364	11	4	0	0	0	0.0	0	2	0	1	0	0	0	22	1	0	2	7.7	1.000	1B-3
WORLD SERIES																								
1980	KC A	6	.400	1.100	20	8	0	1	4	20.0	5	8	6	8	0	0	0	55	2	2	6	9.8	.966	1B-6

Danny Ainge

AINGE, DANIEL RAE
B. Mar. 17, 1959, Eugene, Ore.
BR TR 6′ 4″ 175 lbs.

Year	Team	Games	BA	SA	AB	H	2B	3B	HR	HR%	R	RBI	BB	SO	SB	Pinch Hit AB	Pinch Hit H	PO	A	E	DP	TC/G	FA	G by Pos
1979	TOR A	87	.237	.286	308	73	7	1	2	0.6	26	19	12	58	1	0	0	198	261	11	67	5.4	.977	2B-86, DH-1
1980		38	.243	.315	111	27	6	1	0	0.0	11	4	2	29	3	3	0	69	12	1	3	2.3	.988	OF-29, 3B-3, DH-2, 2B-1
1981		86	.187	.228	246	46	6	2	0	0.0	20	14	23	41	8	0	0	88	146	12	20	2.7	.951	3B-77, SS-6, OF-4, 2B-2, DH-1
3 yrs.		211	.220	.269	665	146	19	4	2	0.3	57	37	37	128	12	3	0	355	419	24	90	3.8	.970	2B-89, 3B-80, OF-33, SS-6, DH-4

Eddie Ainsmith

AINSMITH, EDWARD WILBUR
B. Feb. 4, 1892, Cambridge, Mass. D. Sept. 6, 1981, Fort Lauderdale, Fla.
BR TR 5′11″ 180 lbs.

Year	Team	Games	BA	SA	AB	H	2B	3B	HR	HR%	R	RBI	BB	SO	SB	Pinch Hit AB	Pinch Hit H	PO	A	E	DP	TC/G	FA	G by Pos
1910	WAS A	33	.192	.240	104	20	1	2	0	0.0	4	9	6		0	0	0	131	52	7	4	6.3	.963	C-30
1911		61	.221	.275	149	33	2	3	0	0.0	12	14	10		5	7	1	208	71	14	2	6.0	.952	C-49
1912		60	.226	.285	186	42	7	2	0	0.0	22	22	14		4	2	0	415	85	22	5	9.0	.958	C-58
1913		79	.214	.293	229	49	4	4	2	0.9	26	20	12	41	17	0	0	418	82	17	10	6.5	.967	C-79, P-1
1914		58	.225	.272	151	34	7	0	0	0.0	11	13	9	28	8	3	2	290	55	11	5	7.0	.969	C-51
1915		47	.200	.267	120	24	4	2	0	0.0	13	6	10	18	7	3	0	209	47	3	2	6.2	.988	C-42
1916		51	.170	.210	100	17	4	0	0	0.0	11	8	8	14	3	1	0	207	50	11	9	5.8	.959	C-46
1917		125	.191	.263	350	67	17	4	0	0.0	38	42	40	48	16	5	0	580	154	22	15	6.4	.971	C-119
1918		96	.212	.308	292	62	10	9	0	0.0	22	20	29	44	6	4	1	413	131	14	13	6.3	.975	C-89
1919	DET A	114	.272	.409	364	99	17	12	3	0.8	42	32	45	30	9	8	1	456	107	22	7	5.5	.962	C-106
1920		69	.231	.306	186	43	5	3	1	0.5	19	19	14	19	4	7	2	219	55	13	4	4.7	.955	C-61
1921	2 teams DET A (35G –.276) STL N (27G –.290)																							
″	total	62	.281	.350	160	45	5	3	0	0.0	11	17	16	11	1	4	0	177	42	11	2	4.0	.952	C-57, 1B-1
1922	STL N	119	.293	.454	379	111	14	4	13	3.4	46	59	28	43	2	2	1	428	99	20	14	4.7	.963	C-116
1923	2 teams STL N (82G –.213) BKN N (2G –.200)																							
″	total	84	.212	.330	273	58	11	6	3	1.1	22	36	22	19	4	2	1	251	58	6	4	3.8	.981	C-82
1924	NY N	10	.600	.600	5	3	0	0	0	0.0	0	0	0	0	0	1	1	5	0	0	0	0.6	1.000	C-9
15 yrs.		1068	.232	.324	3048	707	108	54	22	0.7	299	317	263	315	86	49	10	4407	1088	193	96	5.7	.966	C-994, 1B-1, P-1

George Aiton

AITON, GEORGE WILSON (Bill)
B. Dec. 29, 1890, Kingman, Kans. D. Aug. 16, 1976, Van Nuys, Calif.
BB TR 5′11½″ 175 lbs.

Year	Team	Games	BA	SA	AB	H	2B	3B	HR	HR%	R	RBI	BB	SO	SB	Pinch Hit AB	Pinch Hit H	PO	A	E	DP	TC/G	FA	G by Pos
1912	STL A	8	.235	.235	17	4	0	0	0	0.0	1	1	4		0	1	0	10	1	1	0	2.0	.917	OF-6

John Ake

AKE, JOHN LECKIE
B. Aug. 29, 1861, Altoona, Pa. D. May 11, 1887, La Crosse, Wis.
BR TR 6′ 1″ 180 lbs.

Year	Team	Games	BA	SA	AB	H	2B	3B	HR	HR%	R	RBI	BB	SO	SB	Pinch Hit AB	Pinch Hit H	PO	A	E	DP	TC/G	FA	G by Pos
1884	BAL AA	13	.192	.231	52	10	0	1	0	0.0	1		0			0	0	10	15	10	2	2.7	.714	3B-9, OF-3, SS-1

Bill Akers

AKERS, WILLIAM G.
B. Dec. 25, 1904, Chattanooga, Tenn. D. Apr. 13, 1962, Chattanooga, Tenn.
BR TR 5′11″ 178 lbs.

Year	Team	Games	BA	SA	AB	H	2B	3B	HR	HR%	R	RBI	BB	SO	SB	Pinch Hit AB	Pinch Hit H	PO	A	E	DP	TC/G	FA	G by Pos
1929	DET A	24	.265	.373	83	22	4	1	1	1.2	15	9	10	9	2	0	0	43	57	7	13	4.5	.935	SS-24
1930		85	.279	.472	233	65	8	5	9	3.9	36	40	36	34	5	5	2	119	184	20	43	4.3	.938	SS-49, 3B-26
1931		29	.197	.288	66	13	2	2	0	0.0	5	3	7	6	0	5	2	46	42	7	8	4.1	.926	SS-21, 2B-2
1932	BOS N	36	.258	.344	93	24	3	1	1	1.1	8	17	10	15	0	6	1	27	46	7	4	2.7	.913	3B-20, SS-5, 2B-5
4 yrs.		174	.261	.404	475	124	17	9	11	2.3	64	69	63	64	7	16	5	235	329	41	68	4.0	.932	SS-99, 3B-46, 2B-7

Butch Alberts

ALBERTS, FRANCIS BURT
B. May 4, 1950, Williamsport, Pa.
BR TR 6′ 2″ 205 lbs.

Year	Team	Games	BA	SA	AB	H	2B	3B	HR	HR%	R	RBI	BB	SO	SB	Pinch Hit AB	Pinch Hit H	PO	A	E	DP	TC/G	FA	G by Pos
1978	TOR A	6	.278	.333	18	5	1	0	0	0.0	1	0	0	2	0	2	0	0	0	0	0	0.0	.000	DH-4

Gus Alberts

ALBERTS, AUGUSTUS PETER
B. 1861, Reading, Pa. D. May 7, 1912, Idaho Springs, Colo.
BR TR 5′ 6½″ 180 lbs.

Year	Team	Games	BA	SA	AB	H	2B	3B	HR	HR%	R	RBI	BB	SO	SB	Pinch Hit AB	Pinch Hit H	PO	A	E	DP	TC/G	FA	G by Pos
1884	2 teams PIT AA (2G –.200) WAS U (4G –.250)																							
″	total	6	.238	.238	21	5	0	0	0	0.0	5		4			0	0	5	18	6	1	4.8	.793	SS-6
1888	CLE AA	102	.206	.275	364	75	10	6	1	0.3	51	48	41		26	0	0	126	277	57	24	4.5	.876	SS-53, 3B-49
1891	MIL AA	12	.098	.098	41	4	0	0	0	0.0	6	2	7	5	1	0	0	14	21	8	2	3.6	.814	3B-12
3 yrs.		120	.197	.256	426	84	10	6	1	0.2	62	50	52	5	27	0	0	145	316	71	27	4.4	.867	3B-61, SS-59

Jack Albright

ALBRIGHT, HAROLD JOHN
B. June 30, 1921, St. Petersburg, Fla. D. July 22, 1991, San Diego, Calif.
BR TR 5′ 9″ 175 lbs.

Year	Team	Games	BA	SA	AB	H	2B	3B	HR	HR%	R	RBI	BB	SO	SB	Pinch Hit AB	Pinch Hit H	PO	A	E	DP	TC/G	FA	G by Pos
1947	PHI N	41	.232	.333	99	23	4	0	2	2.0	9	5	10	11	1	2	0	48	85	8	15	4.3	.943	SS-33

Luis Alcaraz

ALCARAZ, ANGEL LUIS
Born Angel Luis Alcaraz (Acosta).
B. June 20, 1941, Humacao, Puerto Rico.
BR TR 5′ 9″ 165 lbs.

Year	Team	Games	BA	SA	AB	H	2B	3B	HR	HR%	R	RBI	BB	SO	SB	Pinch Hit AB	Pinch Hit H	PO	A	E	DP	TC/G	FA	G by Pos
1967	LA N	17	.233	.250	60	14	1	0	0	0.0	1	3	1	13	1	0	0	44	51	1	18	5.6	.990	2B-17
1968		41	.151	.217	106	16	1	0	2	1.9	4	5	9	23	1	5	1	57	71	7	9	4.0	.948	2B-20, 3B-13, SS-1
1969	KC A	22	.253	.342	79	20	2	1	1	1.3	15	7	7	9	0	1	0	43	50	1	5	4.3	.989	2B-19, 3B-2, SS-1
1970		35	.167	.250	120	20	5	1	1	0.8	10	14	4	13	0	3	1	65	68	1	12	4.3	.993	2B-31
4 yrs.		115	.192	.260	365	70	9	2	4	1.1	30	29	21	58	2	9	2	209	240	10	44	4.4	.978	2B-87, 3B-15, SS-2

Scotty Alcock

ALCOCK, JOHN FORBES
B. Nov. 29, 1885, Wooster, Ohio D. Jan. 30, 1973, Wooster, Ohio.
BR TR 5′ 9½″ 160 lbs.

Year	Team	Games	BA	SA	AB	H	2B	3B	HR	HR%	R	RBI	BB	SO	SB	Pinch Hit AB	Pinch Hit H	PO	A	E	DP	TC/G	FA	G by Pos
1914	CHI A	54	.173	.224	156	27	4	2	0	0.0	12	7	7	14	4	3	0	61	96	16	11	3.5	.908	3B-48, 2B-1

Mike Aldrete

ALDRETE, MICHAEL PETER
B. Jan. 29, 1961, Carmel, Calif.
BL TL 5′11″ 180 lbs.

Year	Team	Games	BA	SA	AB	H	2B	3B	HR	HR%	R	RBI	BB	SO	SB	Pinch Hit AB	Pinch Hit H	PO	A	E	DP	TC/G	FA	G by Pos
1986	SF N	84	.250	.389	216	54	18	3	2	0.9	27	25	33	34	1	16	4	317	36	1	34	5.2	.997	1B-37, OF-31
1987		126	.325	.462	357	116	18	2	9	2.5	50	51	43	50	6	25	6	328	18	3	21	3.1	.991	OF-79, 1B-33
1988		139	.267	.329	389	104	15	0	3	0.8	44	50	56	65	6	29	11	272	8	4	3	2.3	.986	OF-115, 1B-10
1989	MON N	76	.221	.316	136	30	8	1	1	0.7	12	12	19	30	1	26	8	109	9	1	8	2.5	.992	OF-37, 1B-10
1990		96	.242	.317	161	39	7	1	1	0.6	22	18	37	31	1	36	9	160	12	1	16	3.1	.994	OF-38, 1B-18
1991	2 teams SD N (12G –.000) CLE A (85G –.262)																							
″	total	97	.242	.298	198	48	6	1	1	0.5	24	20	39	41	1	20	2	341	24	2	31	4.9	.995	1B-47, OF-21, DH-7
1993	OAK A	95	.267	.443	255	68	13	1	10	3.9	40	33	34	45	1	17	7	407	28	2	39	5.1	.995	1B-59, OF-20, DH-6

Mike Aldrete *continued*

Year	Team	Games	BA	SA	AB	H	2B	3B	HR	HR%	R	RBI	BB	SO	SB	Pinch Hit AB	Pinch Hit H	PO	A	E	DP	TC/G	FA	G by Pos
1994		76	.242	.337	178	43	5	0	4	2.2	23	18	20	35	2	25	3	207	14	1	15	3.5	.995	OF-35, 1B-27, DH-1
1995	2 teams OAK A (60G –.272) CAL A (18G –.250)																							
″	total	78	.268	.403	149	40	8	0	4	2.7	19	24	19	31	0	31	11	199	10	3	16	3.8	.986	1B-36, OF-18, DH-2
9 yrs.		867	.266	.374	2039	542	98	9	35	1.7	261	251	300	362	19	225	61	2340	159	18	183	3.7	.993	OF-394, 1B-277, DH-16
LEAGUE CHAMPIONSHIP SERIES																								
1987	SF N	5	.100	.100	10	1	0	0	0	0.0	0	1	0	2	0	2	0	5	0	0	0	1.7	1.000	OF-3

Chuck Aleno

ALENO, CHARLES
B. Feb. 19, 1917, St. Louis, Mo.
BR TR 6′ 1½″ 215 lbs.

Year	Team	Games	BA	SA	AB	H	2B	3B	HR	HR%	R	RBI	BB	SO	SB	Pinch Hit AB	Pinch Hit H	PO	A	E	DP	TC/G	FA	G by Pos
1941	CIN N	54	.243	.337	169	41	7	3	1	0.6	23	18	11	16	3	11	2	56	77	3	6	3.2	.978	3B-40, 1B-2
1942		7	.143	.214	14	2	1	0	0	0.0	1	0	3	3	0	3	0	4	11	3	2	6.0	.833	3B-2, 2B-1
1943		7	.300	.300	10	3	0	0	0	0.0	0	1	2	1	0	4	2	2	0	0	0	1.0	1.000	OF-2
1944		50	.165	.213	127	21	3	0	1	0.8	10	15	15	15	0	2	0	75	65	6	9	3.0	.959	3B-42, SS-3, 1B-3
4 yrs.		118	.209	.281	320	67	11	3	2	0.6	34	34	31	35	3	20	4	137	153	12	17	3.2	.960	3B-84, 1B-5, SS-3, OF-2, 2B-1

Dale Alexander

ALEXANDER, DAVID DALE (Moose)
B. Apr. 26, 1903, Greeneville, Tenn. D. Mar. 2, 1979, Greeneville, Tenn.
BR TR 6′ 3″ 210 lbs.

Year	Team	Games	BA	SA	AB	H	2B	3B	HR	HR%	R	RBI	BB	SO	SB	Pinch Hit AB	Pinch Hit H	PO	A	E	DP	TC/G	FA	G by Pos
1929	DET A	155	.343	.580	626	**215**	43	15	25	4.0	110	137	56	63	5	0	0	1443	90	18	129	10.0	.988	1B-155
1930		154	.326	.507	602	196	33	8	20	3.3	86	135	42	56	6	0	0	1338	71	22	132	9.3	.985	1B-154
1931		135	.325	.445	517	168	47	3	3	0.6	75	87	64	35	5	6	0	1205	53	16	91	9.8	.987	1B-126, OF-4
1932	2 teams DET A (23G –.250) BOS A (101G –.372)																							
″	total	124	**.367**	.513	392	144	27	3	8	2.0	58	60	61	21	4	15	4	1055	67	9	93	11.0	.992	1B-103
1933	BOS A	94	.281	.380	313	88	14	1	5	1.6	40	40	25	22	0	15	4	728	47	6	51	9.9	.992	1B-79
5 yrs.		662	.331	.497	2450	811	164	30	61	2.5	369	459	248	197	20	36	8	5769	328	71	496	9.9	.988	1B-617, OF-4

Gary Alexander

ALEXANDER, GARY WAYNE
B. Mar. 27, 1953, Los Angeles, Calif.
BR TR 6′ 2″ 195 lbs.

Year	Team	Games	BA	SA	AB	H	2B	3B	HR	HR%	R	RBI	BB	SO	SB	Pinch Hit AB	Pinch Hit H	PO	A	E	DP	TC/G	FA	G by Pos
1975	SF N	3	.000	.000	3	0	0	0	0	0.0	1	0	1	2	0	3	0	2	0	0	0	1.0	1.000	C-2
1976		23	.178	.301	73	13	1	1	2	2.7	12	7	10	16	1	0	0	92	16	4	0	4.9	.964	C-23
1977		51	.303	.496	119	36	4	2	5	4.2	17	20	20	33	3	17	7	174	8	6	0	5.5	.968	C-33, OF-1
1978	2 teams OAK A (58G –.207) CLE A (90G –.235)																							
″	total	148	.225	.444	498	112	20	4	27	5.4	57	84	57	**166**	0	10	1	321	34	6	3	2.5	.983	DH-71, C-66, OF-6, 1B-1
1979	CLE A	110	.229	.391	358	82	9	2	15	4.2	54	54	46	100	4	6	2	404	40	18	5	4.4	.961	C-91, DH-13, OF-2
1980		76	.225	.360	178	40	7	1	5	2.8	22	31	17	52	0	23	7	34	2	1	0	0.7	.973	DH-40, C-13, OF-2
1981	PIT N	21	.213	.404	47	10	4	1	1	2.1	6	6	3	12	0	5	0	64	6	3	4	4.3	.959	1B-9, OF-8
7 yrs.		432	.230	.411	1276	293	45	11	55	4.3	169	202	154	381	8	64	17	1091	106	38	12	3.2	.969	C-228, DH-124, OF-19, 1B-10

Hugh Alexander

ALEXANDER, HUGH
B. July 10, 1917, Buffalo, Mo.
BR TR 6′ 190 lbs.

Year	Team	Games	BA	SA	AB	H	2B	3B	HR	HR%	R	RBI	BB	SO	SB	Pinch Hit AB	Pinch Hit H	PO	A	E	DP	TC/G	FA	G by Pos
1937	CLE A	7	.091	.091	11	1	0	0	0	0.0	0	0	0	5	1	3	0	2	0	1	0	1.0	.667	OF-3

Manny Alexander

ALEXANDER, MANUEL
Born Manuel DeJesus (Alexander).
B. Mar. 20, 1971, San Pedro de Macoris, Dominican Republic.
BR TR 5′10″ 150 lbs.

Year	Team	Games	BA	SA	AB	H	2B	3B	HR	HR%	R	RBI	BB	SO	SB	Pinch Hit AB	Pinch Hit H	PO	A	E	DP	TC/G	FA	G by Pos
1992	BAL A	4	.200	.200	5	1	0	0	0	0.0	1	0	0	3	0	0	0	3	3	0	1	2.0	1.000	SS-3
1993		3	—	—	0	0	0	0	0	—	1	0	0	0	0	0	0	0	0	0	0	0.0	.000	DH-1
1995		94	.236	.318	242	57	9	1	3	1.2	35	23	20	30	11	7	1	140	170	10	45	3.5	.969	2B-82, SS-7, 3B-2, DH-1
3 yrs.		101	.235	.316	247	58	9	1	3	1.2	37	23	20	33	11	7	1	143	173	10	46	3.4	.969	2B-82, SS-10, 3B-2, DH-2

Matt Alexander

ALEXANDER, MATTHEW
B. Jan. 30, 1947, Shreveport, La.
BB TR 5′11″ 168 lbs.

Year	Team	Games	BA	SA	AB	H	2B	3B	HR	HR%	R	RBI	BB	SO	SB	Pinch Hit AB	Pinch Hit H	PO	A	E	DP	TC/G	FA	G by Pos
1973	CHI N	12	.200	.200	5	1	0	0	0	0.0	4	1	1	1	2	1	0	2	0	0	0	0.7	1.000	OF-3
1974		45	.204	.278	54	11	2	1	0	0.0	15	0	12	12	8	11	3	13	24	3	3	1.6	.925	3B-19, OF-4, 2B-2
1975	OAK A	63	.100	.100	10	1	0	0	0	0.0	16	0	1	1	17	2	0	7	2	1	1	0.3	.900	DH-17, OF-11, 2B-3, 3B-2
1976		61	.033	.033	30	1	0	0	0	0.0	16	0	0	5	20	1	0	23	0	0	0	0.5	1.000	OF-23, DH-19
1977		90	.238	.262	42	10	1	0	0	0.0	24	2	4	6	26	0	0	21	2	0	0	0.4	1.000	OF-31, DH-12, SS-12, 2B-4, 3B-1
1978	PIT N	7	—	—	0	0	0	0	0	—	2	0	0	0	4	0	0	0	0	0	0	0.0	—	
1979		44	.538	.692	13	7	0	1	0	0.0	16	1	0	0	13	1	0	8	1	0	0	0.8	1.000	OF-11, SS-1
1980		37	.333	.667	3	1	1	0	0	0.0	13	0	0	0	10	0	0	6	0	0	0	1.2	1.000	OF-4, 2B-1
1981		15	.364	.364	11	4	0	0	0	0.0	5	0	0	1	3	4	0	8	0	0	0	1.3	1.000	OF-6
9 yrs.		374	.214	.262	168	36	4	2	0	0.0	111	4	18	26	103	20	3	88	29	4	4	0.7	.967	OF-93, DH-48, 3B-22, SS-13, 2B-10
LEAGUE CHAMPIONSHIP SERIES																								
1979	PIT N	1	—	—	0	0	0	0	0	—	1	0	0	0	0	0	0	0	0	0	0	0.0	—	
WORLD SERIES																								
1979	PIT N	1	—	—	0	0	0	0	0	—	0	0	0	0	0	0	0	0	0	0	0	0.0	.000	OF-1

Nin Alexander

ALEXANDER, WILLIAM HENRY
B. Nov. 24, 1858, Pana, Ill. D. Dec. 22, 1933, Pana, Ill.
BR TR 5′ 4½″ 163 lbs.

Year	Team	Games	BA	SA	AB	H	2B	3B	HR	HR%	R	RBI	BB	SO	SB	Pinch Hit AB	Pinch Hit H	PO	A	E	DP	TC/G	FA	G by Pos
1884	2 teams KC U (19G –.138) STL AA (1G –.000)																							
″	total	20	.130	.130	69	9	0	0	0	0.0	2		1			0	0	81	43	14	0	6.0	.899	C-18, OF-3, SS-2

Walt Alexander

ALEXANDER, WALTER ERNEST
B. Mar. 5, 1891, Atlanta, Ga. D. Dec. 29, 1978, Ft. Worth, Tex.
BR TR 5′10½″ 165 lbs.

Year	Team	Games	BA	SA	AB	H	2B	3B	HR	HR%	R	RBI	BB	SO	SB	Pinch Hit AB	Pinch Hit H	PO	A	E	DP	TC/G	FA	G by Pos
1912	STL A	37	.175	.216	97	17	4	0	0	0.0	5	5	8		1	0	0	140	46	6	2	5.2	.969	C-37
1913		43	.136	.173	110	15	2	1	0	0.0	5	7	4	36	1	0	0	128	71	11	7	4.9	.948	C-43
1915	2 teams STL A (1G –.000) NY A (25G –.250)																							
″	total	26	.246	.348	69	17	4	0	1	1.4	7	5	13	16	2	0	0	132	44	6	5	7.3	.967	C-25
1916	NY A	36	.256	.359	78	20	6	1	0	0.0	8	3	13	20	0	8	2	100	43	6	2	5.5	.960	C-27
1917		20	.137	.216	51	7	2	1	0	0.0	1	4	4	11	1	0	0	82	16	5	2	5.2	.951	C-20
5 yrs.		162	.188	.254	405	76	18	3	1	0.2	26	24	42	83	5	8	2	582	220	34	18	5.5	.959	C-152

Edgardo Alfonzo

ALFONZO, EDGARDO ANTONIO
B. Aug. 11, 1973, Santa Teresa, Venezuela.

BR TR 5′11″ 185 lbs.

Year	Team	Games	BA	SA	AB	H	2B	3B	HR	HR%	R	RBI	BB	SO	SB	Pinch Hit AB	Pinch Hit H	PO	A	E	DP	TC/G	FA	G by Pos
1995	NY N	101	.278	.382	335	93	13	5	4	1.2	26	41	12	37	1	10	2	81	170	7	19	2.8	.973	3B-58, 2B-29, SS-6

Luis Alicea

ALICEA, LUIS RENE
Born Luis Rene Alicea (DeJesus).
B. July 29, 1965, Santurce, Puerto Rico.

BB TR 5′ 9″ 165 lbs.

Year	Team	Games	BA	SA	AB	H	2B	3B	HR	HR%	R	RBI	BB	SO	SB	Pinch Hit AB	Pinch Hit H	PO	A	E	DP	TC/G	FA	G by Pos
1988	STL N	93	.212	.283	297	63	10	4	1	0.3	20	24	25	32	1	5	1	206	240	14	52	5.1	.970	2B-91
1991		56	.191	.235	68	13	3	0	0	0.0	5	0	8	19	0	39	8	19	23	0	4	3.0	1.000	2B-11, 3B-2, SS-1
1992		85	.245	.385	265	65	9	11	2	0.8	26	32	27	40	2	6	0	136	233	7	38	4.8	.981	2B-75, SS-4
1993		115	.279	.373	362	101	19	3	3	0.8	50	46	47	54	11	17	6	210	281	11	61	5.0	.978	2B-96, OF-4, 3B-1
1994		88	.278	.459	205	57	12	5	5	2.4	32	29	30	38	4	34	8	126	148	4	38	5.1	.986	2B-53, OF-2
1995	BOS A	132	.270	.375	419	113	20	3	6	1.4	64	44	63	61	13	0	0	255	429	16	98	5.3	.977	2B-132
6 yrs.		569	.255	.364	1616	412	73	26	17	1.1	197	175	200	244	31	101	23	952	1354	52	291	5.0	.978	2B-458, OF-6, SS-5, 3B-3
DIVISIONAL PLAYOFF SERIES																								
1995	BOS A	3	.600	1.000	10	6	1	0	1	10.0	1	1	2	2	1	0	0	6	11	1	0	6.0	.944	2B-3

Andy Allanson

ALLANSON, ANDREW NEAL
B. Dec. 22, 1961, Richmond, Va.

BR TR 6′ 5″ 220 lbs.

Year	Team	Games	BA	SA	AB	H	2B	3B	HR	HR%	R	RBI	BB	SO	SB	Pinch Hit AB	Pinch Hit H	PO	A	E	DP	TC/G	FA	G by Pos
1986	CLE A	101	.225	.280	293	66	7	3	1	0.3	30	29	14	36	10	0	0	446	33	20	4	5.0	.960	C-99
1987		50	.266	.364	154	41	6	0	3	1.9	17	16	9	30	1	0	0	252	22	4	3	5.6	.986	C-50
1988		133	.263	.323	434	114	11	0	5	1.2	44	50	25	63	5	0	0	691	60	11	11	5.7	.986	C-133
1989		111	.232	.294	323	75	9	1	3	0.9	30	17	23	47	4	0	0	570	53	9	4	5.7	.986	C-111
1991	DET A	60	.232	.318	151	35	10	0	1	0.7	10	16	7	31	0	3	1	219	22	5	3	4.2	.980	C-56, 1B-2, DH-1
1992	MIL A	9	.320	.360	25	8	1	0	0	0.0	6	0	1	2	3	0	0	30	3	2	0	3.9	.943	C-9
1993	SF N	13	.167	.208	24	4	1	0	0	0.0	3	2	1	2	0	4	1	38	0	0	0	3.8	1.000	C-8, 1B-2
1995	CAL A	35	.171	.317	82	14	3	0	3	3.7	5	10	7	12	0	1	0	164	16	1	1	5.2	.994	C-35
8 yrs.		512	.240	.310	1486	357	48	4	16	1.1	145	140	87	223	23	8	2	2410	209	52	26	5.3	.981	C-501, 1B-4, DH-1

Bernie Allen

ALLEN, BERNARD KEITH
B. Apr. 16, 1939, East Liverpool, Ohio.

BL TR 6′ 175 lbs.

Year	Team	Games	BA	SA	AB	H	2B	3B	HR	HR%	R	RBI	BB	SO	SB	Pinch Hit AB	Pinch Hit H	PO	A	E	DP	TC/G	FA	G by Pos
1962	MIN A	159	.269	.403	573	154	27	7	12	2.1	79	64	62	82	0	1	1	357	394	13	109	4.8	.983	2B-158
1963		139	.240	.356	421	101	20	1	9	2.1	52	43	38	52	0	5	2	236	256	12	65	3.9	.976	2B-128
1964		74	.214	.329	243	52	8	1	6	2.5	28	20	33	30	1	3	0	161	173	7	40	4.8	.979	2B-71
1965		19	.231	.282	39	9	2	0	0	0.0	2	6	6	8	0	8	3	18	22	0	6	3.6	1.000	2B-10, 3B-1
1966		101	.238	.348	319	76	18	1	5	1.6	34	30	26	40	2	6	0	191	216	11	47	4.6	.974	2B-89, 3B-2
1967	WAS A	87	.193	.256	254	49	5	1	3	1.2	13	18	18	43	1	12	1	177	200	4	57	5.1	.990	2B-75
1968		120	.241	.343	373	90	12	4	6	1.6	31	40	28	35	2	15	3	263	272	5	63	4.8	.991	2B-110, 3B-2
1969		122	.247	.389	365	90	17	4	9	2.5	33	45	50	35	5	13	5	243	286	15	70	4.7	.972	2B-110, 3B-6
1970		104	.234	.360	261	61	7	1	8	3.1	31	29	43	21	0	23	3	176	204	11	49	4.3	.972	2B-80, 3B-12
1971		97	.266	.376	229	61	11	1	4	1.7	18	22	33	27	2	32	7	85	126	10	16	2.9	.955	2B-41, 3B-34
1972	NY A	84	.227	.391	220	50	9	0	9	4.1	26	21	23	42	0	20	0	75	132	9	26	3.4	.958	3B-44, 2B-20
1973	2 teams NY A (16G –.180) MON N (16G –.180)																							
″	total	32	.180	.320	100	18	2	0	4	4.0	10	18	10	8	0	2	0	38	62	4	6	2.9	.962	2B-18, 3B-16, DH-2
12 yrs.		1138	.239	.358	3397	811	138	21	75	2.2	357	356	370	423	13	140	25	2020	2343	101	554	4.3	.977	2B-910, 3B-117, DH-2

Bob Allen

ALLEN, ROBERT
Born Alvah Charles Allen.
B. Oct. 13, 1894, Muscoda, Wis. D. Dec. 18, 1975, Naperville, Ill.

BR TR 5′10″ 180 lbs.

Year	Team	Games	BA	SA	AB	H	2B	3B	HR	HR%	R	RBI	BB	SO	SB	Pinch Hit AB	Pinch Hit H	PO	A	E	DP	TC/G	FA	G by Pos
1919	PHI A	9	.136	.182	22	3	1	0	0	0.0	3	0	3	7	0	2	1	8	0	1	0	1.5	.889	OF-6

Bob Allen

ALLEN, ROBERT GILMAN
B. July 10, 1867, Marion, Ohio D. May 4, 1943, Little Rock, Ark.
Manager 1890, 1900.

BR TR 5′11″ 175 lbs.

Year	Team	Games	BA	SA	AB	H	2B	3B	HR	HR%	R	RBI	BB	SO	SB	Pinch Hit AB	Pinch Hit H	PO	A	E	DP	TC/G	FA	G by Pos
1890	PHI N	133	.226	.320	456	103	15	11	2	0.4	69	57	87	54	13	0	0	337	500	69	68	6.8	.924	SS-133
1891		118	.221	.263	438	97	7	4	1	0.2	46	51	43	44	12	0	0	258	426	79	50	6.5	.896	SS-118
1892		152	.227	.323	563	128	20	14	2	0.4	77	64	61	60	15	0	0	331	537	77	67	6.2	.919	SS-152
1893		124	.268	.410	471	126	19	12	8	1.7	86	90	71	40	8	0	0	302	447	66	65	6.6	.919	SS-124
1894		40	.255	.362	149	38	10	3	0	0.0	26	19	17	11	4	0	0	87	129	20	15	5.9	.915	SS-40
1897	BOS N	34	.319	.387	119	38	5	0	1	0.8	33	24	18		1	0	0	82	119	16	12	6.4	.926	SS-32, OF-1, 2B-1
1900	CIN N	5	.133	.200	15	2	1	0	0	0.0	0	1	0		0	0	0	6	13	3	1	4.4	.864	SS-5
7 yrs.		606	.241	.334	2211	532	77	44	14	0.6	337	306	297	209	53	0	0	1403	2171	330	278	6.4	.915	SS-604, OF-1, 2B-1

Dick Allen

ALLEN, RICHARD ANTHONY (Richie)
Brother of Ron Allen. Brother of Hank Allen.
B. Mar. 8, 1942, Wampum, Pa.

BR TR 5′11″ 187 lbs.

Year	Team	Games	BA	SA	AB	H	2B	3B	HR	HR%	R	RBI	BB	SO	SB	Pinch Hit AB	Pinch Hit H	PO	A	E	DP	TC/G	FA	G by Pos
1963	PHI N	10	.292	.458	24	7	2	1	0	0.0	6	2	0	5	0	2	0	10	0	2	0	1.5	.833	OF-7, 3B-1
1964		162	.318	.557	632	201	38	**13**	29	4.6	**125**	91	67	**138**	3	0	0	154	325	41	30	3.2	.921	3B-162
1965		161	.302	.494	619	187	31	14	20	3.2	93	85	74	**150**	15	1	0	130	305	26	29	2.8	.944	3B-160, SS-2
1966		141	.317	**.632**	524	166	25	10	40	**7.6**	112	110	68	136	10	4	1	146	182	14	15	2.5	.959	3B-91, OF-47
1967		122	.307	.566	463	142	31	10	23	5.0	89	77	75	117	20	1	0	95	249	35	23	3.1	.908	3B-121, SS-1, 2B-1
1968		152	.263	.520	521	137	17	9	33	6.3	87	90	74	161	7	8	0	215	20	12	4	1.7	.951	OF-139, 3B-10
1969		118	.288	.573	438	126	23	3	32	7.3	79	89	64	144	9	1	1	1024	54	16	100	9.4	.985	1B-117
1970	STL N	122	.279	.560	459	128	17	5	34	7.4	88	101	71	118	5	3	1	708	109	18	70	7.0	.978	1B-79, 3B-38, OF-3
1971	LA N	155	.295	.468	549	162	24	1	23	4.2	82	90	93	113	8	3	0	382	151	21	38	3.6	.962	3B-67, OF-60, 1B-28
1972	CHI A	148	.308	**.603**	506	156	28	5	**37**	**7.3**	90	**113**	**99**	126	19	7	1	1235	69	7	94	9.0	.995	1B-143, 3B-2
1973		72	.316	.612	250	79	20	3	16	6.4	39	41	33	51	7	3	0	601	46	4	55	9.3	.994	1B-67, 2B-2, DH-1
1974		128	.301	**.563**	462	139	23	1	**32**	**6.9**	84	88	57	89	7	4	0	998	50	16	112	8.4	.985	1B-125, 2B-1, DH-1
1975	PHI N	119	.233	.385	416	97	21	3	12	2.9	54	62	58	109	11	5	0	900	70	18	79	8.7	.982	1B-113
1976		85	.268	.480	298	80	16	1	15	5.0	52	49	37	63	11	2	1	671	44	8	71	8.5	.989	1B-85
1977	OAK A	54	.240	.351	171	41	4	0	5	2.9	19	31	24	36	1	2	0	389	37	7	36	8.5	.984	1B-50, DH-1
15 yrs.		1749	.292	.534	6332	1848	320	79	351	5.5	1099	1119	894	1556	133	46	5	7658	1711	245	756	5.6	.975	1B-807, 3B-652, OF-256, 2B-4, DH-3, SS-3

Dick Allen *continued*

Year	Team	Games	BA	SA	AB	H	2B	3B	HR	HR%	R	RBI	BB	SO	SB	Pinch Hit AB	Pinch Hit H	PO	A	E	DP	TC/G	FA	G by Pos
LEAGUE CHAMPIONSHIP SERIES																								
1976	PHI N	3	.222	.222	9	2	0	0	0	0.0	1	0	3	2	0	0	0	28	0	1	1	9.7	.966	1B-3

Ethan Allen

ALLEN, ETHAN NATHAN BR TR 6′ 1″ 180 lbs.
B. Jan. 1, 1904, Cincinnati, Ohio D. Sept. 15, 1993, Brookings, Ore.

Year	Team	Games	BA	SA	AB	H	2B	3B	HR	HR%	R	RBI	BB	SO	SB	Pinch Hit AB	Pinch Hit H	PO	A	E	DP	TC/G	FA	G by Pos
1926	CIN N	18	.308	.385	13	4	1	0	0	0.0	3	0	0	3	0	2	0	9	0	0	0	1.0	1.000	OF-9
1927		111	.295	.407	359	106	26	4	2	0.6	54	20	14	23	12	2	1	250	6	3	3	2.6	.988	OF-98
1928		129	.305	.402	485	148	30	7	1	0.2	55	62	27	29	6	0	0	348	12	7	4	2.8	.981	OF-129
1929		143	.292	.416	538	157	27	11	6	1.1	69	64	20	21	21	2	0	393	12	5	2	3.0	.988	OF-137
1930	2 teams	CIN N (21G –.217) NY N (76G –.307)																						
″	total	97	.292	.447	284	83	10	2	10	3.5	58	38	17	25	6	18	5	153	6	3	0	2.1	.981	OF-77
1931	NY N	94	.329	.453	298	98	18	2	5	1.7	58	43	15	15	6	14	8	151	2	4	1	2.0	.975	OF-77
1932		54	.175	.301	103	18	6	2	1	1.0	13	7	1	12	0	22	1	44	1	2	0	2.0	.957	OF-24
1933	STL N	91	.241	.291	261	63	7	3	0	0.0	25	36	13	22	3	21	3	179	8	3	1	2.8	.984	OF-67
1934	PHI N	145	.330	.468	581	192	**42**	4	10	1.7	87	85	33	47	6	0	0	337	19	8	3	2.5	.978	OF-145
1935		156	.307	.419	645	198	46	1	8	1.2	90	63	43	54	5	0	0	412	26	9	6	2.9	.980	OF-156
1936	2 teams	PHI N (30G –.296) CHI N (91G –.295)																						
″	total	121	.295	.390	498	147	21	7	4	0.8	68	48	17	38	16	0	0	273	3	8	2	2.4	.972	OF-119
1937	STL A	103	.316	.378	320	101	18	1	0	0.0	39	31	21	17	3	23	8	186	8	4	1	2.5	.980	OF-78
1938		19	.303	.455	33	10	3	1	0	0.0	4	4	2	4	0	12	3	11	0	0	0	1.6	1.000	OF-7
13 yrs.		1281	.300	.410	4418	1325	255	45	47	1.1	623	501	223	310	84	116	29	2746	103	56	23	2.6	.981	OF-1123

Hank Allen

ALLEN, HAROLD ANDREW BR TR 6′ 190 lbs.
Brother of Ron Allen. Brother of Dick Allen.
B. July 23, 1940, Wampum, Pa.

Year	Team	Games	BA	SA	AB	H	2B	3B	HR	HR%	R	RBI	BB	SO	SB	Pinch Hit AB	Pinch Hit H	PO	A	E	DP	TC/G	FA	G by Pos
1966	WAS A	9	.387	.484	31	12	0	0	1	3.2	2	6	3	6	0	0	0	22	0	2	0	2.7	.917	OF-9
1967		116	.233	.318	292	68	8	4	3	1.0	34	17	13	53	3	21	7	148	1	3	1	1.5	.980	OF-99
1968		68	.219	.289	128	28	2	2	1	0.8	16	9	7	16	0	22	5	51	41	7	6	1.9	.929	OF-25, 3B-16, 2B-11
1969		109	.277	.343	271	75	9	3	1	0.4	42	17	13	28	12	23	5	128	14	10	3	1.5	.934	OF-91, 3B-6, 2B-3
1970	2 teams	WAS A (22G –.211) MIL A (28G –.230)																						
″	total	50	.222	.283	99	22	6	0	0	0.0	7	8	12	14	0	14	2	65	12	0	4	1.9	1.000	OF-31, 2B-5, 1B-4
1972	CHI A	9	.143	.143	21	3	0	0	0	0.0	1	0	0	2	0	0	0	4	15	2	5	3.5	.905	3B-6
1973		28	.103	.154	39	4	2	0	0	0.0	2	0	1	9	0	5	0	42	12	1	1	2.3	.982	3B-9, 1B-8, OF-5, C-1, 2B-1
7 yrs.		389	.241	.312	881	212	27	9	6	0.7	104	57	49	128	15	85	19	460	95	25	20	1.8	.957	OF-260, 3B-37, 2B-20, 1B-12, C-1

Hezekiah Allen

ALLEN, HEZEKIAH (Ki) 5′11″ 160 lbs.
B. Feb. 25, 1863, Westport, Conn. D. Sept. 21, 1916, Saugatuck, Conn.

Year	Team	Games	BA	SA	AB	H	2B	3B	HR	HR%	R	RBI	BB	SO	SB	Pinch Hit AB	Pinch Hit H	PO	A	E	DP	TC/G	FA	G by Pos
1884	PHI N	1	.667	.667	3	2	0	0	0	0.0	0		0	0		0	0	2	0	0	1	2.0	1.000	C-1

Horace Allen

ALLEN, HORACE TANNER (Pug) BL TR 6′ 187 lbs.
B. June 11, 1899, DeLand, Fla. D. July 5, 1981, Canton, N. C.

Year	Team	Games	BA	SA	AB	H	2B	3B	HR	HR%	R	RBI	BB	SO	SB	Pinch Hit AB	Pinch Hit H	PO	A	E	DP	TC/G	FA	G by Pos
1919	BKN N	4	.000	.000	7	0	0	0	0	0.0	0	0	0	2	0	1	0	2	1	0	0	1.5	1.000	OF-2

Jack Allen

ALLEN, CYRUS ALBAN BR TR 160 lbs.
B. Oct. 2, 1855, Woodstock, Ill. D. Apr. 21, 1915, Girard, Pa.

Year	Team	Games	BA	SA	AB	H	2B	3B	HR	HR%	R	RBI	BB	SO	SB	Pinch Hit AB	Pinch Hit H	PO	A	E	DP	TC/G	FA	G by Pos
1879	2 teams	SYR N (11G –.188) CLE N (16G –.117)																						
″	total	27	.148	.213	108	16	3	2	0	0.0	14	7	2	14		0	0	48	37	21	2	3.9	.802	3B-22, OF-5

Jamie Allen

ALLEN, JAMES BRADLEY BR TR 6′ 205 lbs.
B. May 29, 1958, Yakima, Wash.

Year	Team	Games	BA	SA	AB	H	2B	3B	HR	HR%	R	RBI	BB	SO	SB	Pinch Hit AB	Pinch Hit H	PO	A	E	DP	TC/G	FA	G by Pos
1983	SEA A	86	.223	.304	273	61	10	0	4	1.5	23	21	33	52	6	3	2	55	155	9	16	2.6	.959	3B-82, DH-2

Kim Allen

ALLEN, KIM BRYANT BR TR 5′11″ 175 lbs.
B. Apr. 5, 1953, Fontana, Calif.

Year	Team	Games	BA	SA	AB	H	2B	3B	HR	HR%	R	RBI	BB	SO	SB	Pinch Hit AB	Pinch Hit H	PO	A	E	DP	TC/G	FA	G by Pos
1980	SEA A	23	.235	.294	51	12	3	0	0	0.0	9	3	8	3	10	0	0	26	42	2	8	3.5	.971	2B-15, OF-4, SS-1
1981		19	.000	.000	3	0	0	0	0	0.0	1	0	0	2	2	2	0	1	0	0	0	0.2	1.000	DH-2, OF-2, 2B-2
2 yrs.		42	.222	.278	54	12	3	0	0	0.0	10	3	8	5	12	2	0	27	42	2	8	2.7	.972	2B-17, OF-6, DH-2, SS-1

Myron Allen

ALLEN, MYRON SMITH BR TR 5′ 8″ 150 lbs.
B. Mar. 22, 1854, Kingston, N. Y. D. Mar. 8, 1924, Kingston, N. Y.

Year	Team	Games	BA	SA	AB	H	2B	3B	HR	HR%	R	RBI	BB	SO	SB	Pinch Hit AB	Pinch Hit H	PO	A	E	DP	TC/G	FA	G by Pos
1883	NY N	1	.000	.000	4	0	0	0	0	0.0	0		0	2		0	0	1	1	0	0	2.0	1.000	P-1
1886	BOS N	1	.000	.000	3	0	0	0	0	0.0	0	0	0	1		0	0	2	2	0	0	4.0	1.000	2B-1
1887	CLE AA	117	.276	.393	463	128	22	10	4	0.9	66		36		26	0	0	230	32	31	7	2.4	.894	OF-115, 3B-3, SS-2, P-2
1888	KC AA	37	.213	.316	136	29	6	4	0	0.0	23	10	9		4	0	0	73	17	7	1	2.6	.928	OF-35, P-2
4 yrs.		156	.259	.371	606	157	28	14	4	0.7	89	10	45	3	30	0	0	306	52	38	8	2.5	.904	OF-150, P-5, 3B-3, SS-2, 2B-1

Nick Allen

ALLEN, ARTEMUS WARD BR TR 6′ 180 lbs.
B. Sept. 14, 1888, Norton, Kans. D. Oct. 16, 1939, Hines, Ill.

Year	Team	Games	BA	SA	AB	H	2B	3B	HR	HR%	R	RBI	BB	SO	SB	Pinch Hit AB	Pinch Hit H	PO	A	E	DP	TC/G	FA	G by Pos
1914	BUF F	32	.238	.254	63	15	1	0	0	0.0	3	4	3		4	5	2	93	30	4	5	4.9	.969	C-26
1915		84	.205	.247	215	44	7	1	0	0.0	14	17	18		4	4	1	347	110	21	8	6.0	.956	C-80
1916	CHI N	5	.063	.063	16	1	0	0	0	0.0	1	1	0	3	0	1	0	19	4	1	1	6.0	.958	C-4
1918	CIN N	37	.260	.323	96	25	2	2	0	0.0	6	5	4	7	0	4	3	105	47	8	7	5.2	.950	C-31
1919		15	.320	.400	25	8	0	1	0	0.0	7	5	2	6	0	2	0	36	10	2	2	4.0	.958	C-12
1920		43	.271	.329	85	23	3	1	0	0.0	10	4	6	11	0	6	2	107	39	6	5	4.2	.961	C-36
6 yrs.		216	.232	.278	500	116	13	5	0	0.0	41	36	33	27	8	22	8	707	240	42	28	5.2	.958	C-189

Pete Allen

ALLEN, JESSE HALL BR TR 5′ 8½″ 185 lbs.
B. May 1, 1868, Columbiana, Ohio D. Apr. 16, 1946, Philadelphia, Pa.

Year	Team	Games	BA	SA	AB	H	2B	3B	HR	HR%	R	RBI	BB	SO	SB	Pinch Hit AB	Pinch Hit H	PO	A	E	DP	TC/G	FA	G by Pos
1893	CLE N	1	.000	.000	4	0	0	0	0	0.0	0	0	0	0	0	0	0	1	0	0	0	1.0	1.000	C-1

Rod Allen

ALLEN, RODERICK BERNET
B. Oct. 5, 1959, Los Angeles, Calif.
BR TR 6′ 1″ 185 lbs.

Year	Team	Lg	Games	BA	SA	AB	H	2B	3B	HR	HR%	R	RBI	BB	SO	SB	Pinch Hit AB	Pinch Hit H	PO	A	E	DP	TC/G	FA	G by Pos
1983	SEA	A	11	.167	.167	12	2	0	0	0	0.0	1	0	0	1	0	4	1	5	0	0	0	1.0	1.000	DH-3, OF-2
1984	DET	A	15	.296	.333	27	8	1	0	0	0.0	6	3	2	8	1	3	1	2	0	0	0	0.2	1.000	DH-11, OF-2
1988	CLE	A	5	.091	.182	11	1	1	0	0	0.0	1	0	0	2	0	2	1	0	0	0	0	0.0	.000	DH-4
3 yrs.			31	.220	.260	50	11	2	0	0	0.0	8	3	2	11	1	9	3	7	0	0	0	0.3	1.000	DH-18, OF-4

Ron Allen

ALLEN, RONALD FREDERICK
Brother of Dick Allen. Brother of Hank Allen.
B. Dec. 23, 1943, Wampum, Pa.
BB TR 6′ 3″ 205 lbs.

Year	Team	Lg	Games	BA	SA	AB	H	2B	3B	HR	HR%	R	RBI	BB	SO	SB	Pinch Hit AB	Pinch Hit H	PO	A	E	DP	TC/G	FA	G by Pos
1972	STL	N	7	.091	.364	11	1	0	0	1	9.1	2	1	3	5	0	0	0	29	1	1	1	6.2	.968	1B-5

Sled Allen

ALLEN, FLETCHER MANSON
B. Aug. 23, 1886, West Plains, Mo. D. Oct. 16, 1959, Lubbock, Tex.
BR TR 6′ 1″ 180 lbs.

Year	Team	Lg	Games	BA	SA	AB	H	2B	3B	HR	HR%	R	RBI	BB	SO	SB	Pinch Hit AB	Pinch Hit H	PO	A	E	DP	TC/G	FA	G by Pos
1910	STL	A	14	.130	.174	23	3	1	0	0	0.0	3	1	1		0	1	0	21	7	3	0	2.4	.903	C-12, 1B-1

Gary Allenson

ALLENSON, GARY MARTIN (Hardrock)
B. Feb. 4, 1955, Culver City, Calif.
BR TR 5′11″ 185 lbs.

Year	Team	Lg	Games	BA	SA	AB	H	2B	3B	HR	HR%	R	RBI	BB	SO	SB	Pinch Hit AB	Pinch Hit H	PO	A	E	DP	TC/G	FA	G by Pos
1979	BOS	A	108	.203	.299	241	49	10	2	3	1.2	27	22	20	42	1	0	0	410	42	9	4	4.3	.980	C-104, 3B-3
1980			36	.357	.443	70	25	6	0	0	0.0	9	10	13	11	2	1	0	100	8	2	1	3.1	.982	C-24, DH-6, 3B-5
1981			47	.223	.388	139	31	8	0	5	3.6	23	25	23	33	0	0	0	235	18	8	3	5.6	.969	C-47
1982			92	.205	.314	264	54	11	0	6	2.3	25	33	38	39	0	1	0	454	39	4	8	5.5	.992	C-91
1983			84	.230	.317	230	53	11	0	3	1.3	19	30	27	43	0	1	0	393	29	7	6	5.1	.984	C-84
1984			35	.229	.325	83	19	2	0	2	2.4	9	8	9	14	0	0	0	135	12	2	4	4.3	.987	C-35
1985	TOR	A	14	.118	.147	34	4	1	0	0	0.0	2	3	0	10	0	0	0	39	2	0	0	2.9	1.000	C-14
7 yrs.			416	.221	.325	1061	235	49	2	19	1.8	114	131	130	192	3	3	0	1766	150	32	26	4.7	.984	C-399, 3B-8, DH-6

Gene Alley

ALLEY, LEONARD EUGENE
B. July 10, 1940, Richmond, Va.
BR TR 5′10″ 160 lbs.

Year	Team	Lg	Games	BA	SA	AB	H	2B	3B	HR	HR%	R	RBI	BB	SO	SB	Pinch Hit AB	Pinch Hit H	PO	A	E	DP	TC/G	FA	G by Pos
1963	PIT	N	17	.216	.235	51	11	1	0	0	0.0	3	0	2	12	0	1	0	20	35	3	7	3.9	.948	3B-7, SS-4, 2B-4
1964			81	.211	.321	209	44	3	1	6	2.9	30	13	21	56	0	9	1	102	213	11	45	5.0	.966	SS-61, 3B-3, 2B-1
1965			153	.252	.348	500	126	21	6	5	1.0	47	47	32	82	7	2	0	243	516	26	113	5.2	.967	SS-110, 2B-40, 3B-1
1966			147	.299	.418	579	173	28	10	7	1.2	88	43	27	83	8	1	0	235	472	15	128	5.0	.979	SS-143
1967			152	.287	.391	550	158	25	7	6	1.1	59	55	36	70	10	4	0	257	500	26	105	5.4	.967	SS-146
1968			133	.245	.321	474	116	20	2	4	0.8	48	39	39	78	13	4	0	209	475	16	97	5.3	.977	SS-109, 2B-24
1969			82	.246	.354	285	70	3	2	8	2.8	28	32	19	48	4	1	0	146	220	12	56	4.6	.968	2B-53, SS-25, 3B-5
1970			121	.244	.362	426	104	16	5	8	1.9	46	41	31	70	7	5	0	216	412	15	88	5.4	.977	SS-108, 2B-8, 3B-2
1971			114	.227	.342	348	79	8	7	6	1.7	38	28	35	43	9	4	2	187	317	22	55	4.8	.958	SS-108, 3B-1
1972			119	.248	.320	347	86	12	2	3	0.9	30	36	38	52	4	5	3	181	340	16	88	4.6	.970	SS-114, 3B-4
1973			76	.203	.285	158	32	3	2	2	1.3	25	8	20	28	1	12	0	83	141	4	23	4.0	.982	SS-49, 3B-8
11 yrs.			1195	.254	.354	3927	999	140	44	55	1.4	442	342	300	622	63	48	6	1879	3641	166	805	5.0	.971	SS-977, 2B-130, 3B-31
LEAGUE CHAMPIONSHIP SERIES																									
1970	PIT	N	2	.000	.000	7	0	0	0	0	0.0	0	0	1	2	0	0	0	6	7	0	3	6.5	1.000	SS-2
1971			1	.500	.500	2	1	0	0	0	0.0	1	0	0	0	0	0	0	1	1	0	1	2.0	1.000	SS-1
1972			5	.000	.000	16	0	0	0	0	0.0	1	0	0	3	0	0	0	10	4	2	0	3.2	.875	SS-5
3 yrs.			8	.040	.040	25	1	0	0	0	0.0	2	0	1	5	0	0	0	17	12	2	4	3.9	.935	SS-8
WORLD SERIES																									
1971	PIT	N	2	.000	.000	2	0	0	0	0	0.0	0	0	1	0	0	0	0	1	4	0	0	2.5	1.000	SS-2

Gair Allie

ALLIE, GAIR ROOSEVELT
B. Oct. 29, 1931, Statesville, N. C.
BR TR 6′ 1″ 190 lbs.

Year	Team	Lg	Games	BA	SA	AB	H	2B	3B	HR	HR%	R	RBI	BB	SO	SB	Pinch Hit AB	Pinch Hit H	PO	A	E	DP	TC/G	FA	G by Pos
1954	PIT	N	121	.199	.268	418	83	8	6	3	0.7	38	30	56	84	1	4	0	211	295	26	59	4.7	.951	SS-95, 3B-19

Bob Allietta

ALLIETTA, ROBERT GEORGE
B. May 1, 1952, New Bedford, Mass.
BR TR 6′ 190 lbs.

Year	Team	Lg	Games	BA	SA	AB	H	2B	3B	HR	HR%	R	RBI	BB	SO	SB	Pinch Hit AB	Pinch Hit H	PO	A	E	DP	TC/G	FA	G by Pos
1975	CAL	A	21	.178	.267	45	8	1	0	1	2.2	4	2	1	6	0	0	0	92	6	0	0	4.7	1.000	C-21

Art Allison

ALLISON, ARTHUR ALGERNON
Brother of Doug Allison.
B. Jan. 29, 1849, Philadelphia, Pa. D. Feb. 25, 1916, Washington, D. C.
5′ 8″ 150 lbs.

Year	Team	Lg	Games	BA	SA	AB	H	2B	3B	HR	HR%	R	RBI	BB	SO	SB	Pinch Hit AB	Pinch Hit H	PO	A	E	DP	TC/G	FA	G by Pos
1876	LOU	N	31	.208	.238	130	27	2	1	0	0.0	9	10	2	6		0	0	124	12	16	3	4.9	.895	OF-23, 1B-8

Bob Allison

ALLISON, WILLIAM ROBERT
B. July 11, 1934, Raytown, Mo. D. Apr. 9, 1995, Rio Verde, Ariz.
BR TR 6′ 3″ 205 lbs.

Year	Team	Lg	Games	BA	SA	AB	H	2B	3B	HR	HR%	R	RBI	BB	SO	SB	Pinch Hit AB	Pinch Hit H	PO	A	E	DP	TC/G	FA	G by Pos
1958	WAS	A	11	.200	.229	35	7	1	0	0	0.0	1	0	2	5	0	0	0	24	0	0	0	2.2	1.000	OF-11
1959			150	.261	.482	570	149	18	**9**	30	5.3	83	85	60	92	13	1	0	333	8	9	1	2.3	.974	OF-149
1960			144	.251	.413	501	126	30	3	15	3.0	79	69	92	94	11	4	0	311	13	11	4	2.3	.967	OF-140, 1B-4
1961	MIN	A	159	.245	.450	556	136	21	3	29	5.2	83	105	103	100	2	0	0	417	18	10	12	2.6	.978	OF-150, 1B-18
1962			149	.266	.511	519	138	24	8	29	5.6	102	102	84	115	8	0	0	287	10	7	1	2.1	.977	OF-147
1963			148	.271	.533	527	143	25	4	35	6.6	**99**	91	90	109	6	1	0	326	11	10	4	2.4	.971	OF-147
1964			149	.287	.553	492	141	27	4	32	6.5	90	86	92	99	10	8	1	829	58	12	64	5.8	.987	1B-93, OF-61
1965			135	.233	.445	438	102	14	5	23	5.3	71	78	73	114	10	14	2	247	12	7	5	2.1	.974	OF-122, 1B-3
1966			70	.220	.411	168	37	6	1	8	4.8	34	19	30	34	6	11	5	86	3	3	0	1.6	.967	OF-56
1967			153	.258	.470	496	128	21	6	24	4.8	73	75	74	114	6	6	4	220	6	5	0	1.6	.978	OF-145
1968			145	.247	.456	469	116	16	8	22	4.7	63	52	52	98	9	13	2	316	16	8	14	2.5	.976	OF-117, 1B-17
1969			81	.228	.418	189	43	8	2	8	4.2	18	27	29	39	2	20	4	96	3	0	1	1.6	1.000	OF-58, 1B-3
1970			47	.208	.319	72	15	5	0	1	1.4	15	7	14	20	1	20	7	54	4	2	2	2.5	.967	OF-17, 1B-7
13 yrs.			1541	.255	.471	5032	1281	216	53	256	5.1	811	796	795	1033	84	98	25	3546	162	84	108	2.6	.978	OF-1320, 1B-145
LEAGUE CHAMPIONSHIP SERIES																									
1969	MIN	A	2	.000	.000	8	0	0	0	0	0.0	0	1	0	0	0	0	0	6	0	0	0	3.0	1.000	OF-2
1970			3	.000	.000	2	0	0	0	0	0.0	0	0	1	1	0	2	0	0	0	0	0	0.0	—	
2 yrs.			5	.000	.000	10	0	0	0	0	0.0	0	1	1	1	0	2	0	6	0	0	0	3.0	1.000	OF-2

Bob Allison *continued*

Year	Team	Games	BA	SA	AB	H	2B	3B	HR	HR%	R	RBI	BB	SO	SB	Pinch Hit AB	Pinch Hit H	PO	A	E	DP	TC/G	FA	G by Pos
WORLD SERIES																								
1965	MIN A	5	.125	.375	16	2	1	0	1	6.3	3	2	2	9	1	0	0	11	0	0	0	2.2	1.000	OF-5

Doug Allison

ALLISON, DOUGLAS L. BR TR 5′10½″ 160 lbs.
Brother of Art Allison.
B. July 1845, Philadelphia, Pa. D. Dec. 19, 1916, Washington, D. C.

Year	Team	Games	BA	SA	AB	H	2B	3B	HR	HR%	R	RBI	BB	SO	SB	Pinch Hit AB	Pinch Hit H	PO	A	E	DP	TC/G	FA	G by Pos
1876	HAR N	44	.264	.288	163	43	4	0	0	0.0	19	15	3	9		0	0	206	43	34	2	6.2	.880	C-40, OF-6
1877		29	.148	.165	115	17	2	0	0	0.0	14	6	3	7		0	0	127	36	19	4	6.3	.896	C-29
1878	PRO N	19	.289	.316	76	22	2	0	0	0.0	9	7	1	8		0	0	96	27	12	1	6.8	.911	C-19, P-1
1879		1	.000	.000	5	0	0	0	0	0.0	0	0	0	1		0	0	9	1	2	0	12.0	.833	C-1
1883	BAL AA	1	.667	.667	3	2	0	0	0	0.0	2		0			0	0	1	2	0	0	1.5	1.000	C-1, OF-1
5 yrs.		94	.232	.254	362	84	8	0	0	0.0	44	28	7	25		0	0	439	109	67	7	6.3	.891	C-90, OF-7, P-1

Milo Allison

ALLISON, MILO HENRY (Pete) BL TR 6′ 163 lbs.
B. Oct. 16, 1890, Elk Rapids, Mich. D. June 18, 1957, Kenosha, Wis.

Year	Team	Games	BA	SA	AB	H	2B	3B	HR	HR%	R	RBI	BB	SO	SB	Pinch Hit AB	Pinch Hit H	PO	A	E	DP	TC/G	FA	G by Pos
1913	CHI N	2	.333	.333	6	2	0	0	0	0.0	1	0	0	1	1	0	0	3	0	0	0	3.0	1.000	OF-1
1914		1	1.000	1.000	1	1	0	0	0	0.0	0	0	0	0	0	1	1	0	0	0	0	0.0	—	
1916	CLE A	14	.278	.278	18	5	0	0	0	0.0	10	0	6	1	0	1	0	5	0	0	0	1.0	1.000	OF-5
1917		32	.143	.143	35	5	0	0	0	0.0	4	0	9	7	3	14	0	12	1	0	0	1.2	1.000	OF-11
4 yrs.		49	.217	.217	60	13	0	0	0	0.0	15	0	15	9	4	16	1	20	1	0	0	1.2	1.000	OF-17

Beau Allred

ALLRED, DALE LeBEAU BL TL 6′ 190 lbs.
B. June 4, 1965, Mesa, Ariz.

Year	Team	Games	BA	SA	AB	H	2B	3B	HR	HR%	R	RBI	BB	SO	SB	Pinch Hit AB	Pinch Hit H	PO	A	E	DP	TC/G	FA	G by Pos
1989	CLE A	13	.250	.375	24	6	3	0	0	0.0	0	1	2	10	0	8	2	11	1	0	1	1.7	1.000	OF-5, DH-2
1990		4	.188	.438	16	3	1	0	1	6.3	2	2	2	3	0	0	0	5	0	1	0	1.5	.833	OF-4
1991		48	.232	.328	125	29	3	0	3	2.4	17	12	25	35	2	6	0	105	1	3	0	2.5	.972	OF-42, DH-1
3 yrs.		65	.230	.345	165	38	7	0	4	2.4	19	15	29	48	2	14	2	121	2	4	1	2.4	.969	OF-51, DH-3

Mel Almada

ALMADA, BALDOMERO MELO BL TL 6′ 170 lbs.
Born Baldomero Melo Almada (Quiros).
B. Feb. 7, 1913, Huatabampo, Mexico D. Aug. 13, 1988, Hermosillo, Mexico.

Year	Team	Games	BA	SA	AB	H	2B	3B	HR	HR%	R	RBI	BB	SO	SB	Pinch Hit AB	Pinch Hit H	PO	A	E	DP	TC/G	FA	G by Pos
1933	BOS A	14	.341	.409	44	15	0	0	1	2.3	11	3	11	3	3	1	0	27	1	0	0	2.2	1.000	OF-13
1934		23	.233	.278	90	21	2	1	0	0.0	7	10	6	8	3	0	0	60	4	1	0	2.8	.985	OF-23
1935		151	.290	.379	607	176	27	9	3	0.5	85	59	55	34	20	0	0	354	23	12	4	2.6	.969	OF-149, 1B-3
1936		96	.253	.338	320	81	16	4	1	0.3	40	21	24	15	2	13	5	144	9	2	2	1.9	.987	OF-81
1937	2 teams	BOS A (32G –.236) WAS A (100G –.309)																						
″	total	132	.295	.394	543	160	27	6	5	0.9	91	42	53	27	12	0	0	376	17	17	6	3.1	.959	OF-127, 1B-4
1938	2 teams	WAS A (47G –.244) STL A (102G –.342)																						
″	total	149	.311	.395	633	197	29	6	4	0.6	101	52	46	38	13	1	0	394	16	14	2	2.9	.967	OF-148
1939	2 teams	STL A (42G –.239) BKN N (39G –.214)																						
″	total	81	.228	.272	246	56	6	1	1	0.4	28	10	19	25	3	8	3	159	4	3	1	2.5	.982	OF-66
7 yrs.		646	.284	.367	2483	706	107	27	15	0.6	363	197	214	150	56	23	8	1514	74	49	15	2.7	.970	OF-607, 1B-7

Rafael Almeida

ALMEIDA, RAFAEL D. BR TR 5′ 9″ 164 lbs.
B. July 30, 1887, Havana, Cuba D. Mar. 1968, Havana, Cuba.

Year	Team	Games	BA	SA	AB	H	2B	3B	HR	HR%	R	RBI	BB	SO	SB	Pinch Hit AB	Pinch Hit H	PO	A	E	DP	TC/G	FA	G by Pos
1911	CIN N	36	.313	.385	96	30	5	1	0	0.0	9	15	9	16	3	4	1	36	45	10	2	3.1	.890	3B-27, 2B-1, SS-1
1912		16	.220	.390	59	13	4	3	0	0.0	9	10	5	8	0	1	0	13	28	5	2	2.9	.891	3B-16
1913		50	.262	.392	130	34	4	2	3	2.3	14	21	11	16	4	7	1	49	72	11	8	3.1	.917	3B-37, OF-3, SS-2, 2B-1
3 yrs.		102	.270	.389	285	77	13	6	3	1.1	32	46	25	40	7	12	2	98	145	26	12	3.1	.903	3B-80, OF-3, SS-3, 2B-2

Bill Almon

ALMON, WILLIAM FRANCIS BR TR 6′ 3″ 180 lbs.
B. Nov. 21, 1952, Providence, R. I.

Year	Team	Games	BA	SA	AB	H	2B	3B	HR	HR%	R	RBI	BB	SO	SB	Pinch Hit AB	Pinch Hit H	PO	A	E	DP	TC/G	FA	G by Pos
1974	SD N	16	.316	.342	38	12	1	0	0	0.0	4	3	2	9	1	0	0	13	30	4	4	3.4	.915	SS-14
1975		6	.400	.400	10	4	0	0	0	0.0	0	0	0	1	0	1	0	6	5	0	0	5.5	1.000	SS-2
1976		14	.246	.351	57	14	3	0	1	1.8	6	6	2	9	3	0	0	23	52	3	8	5.6	.962	SS-14
1977		155	.261	.336	613	160	18	11	2	0.3	75	43	37	114	20	0	0	303	538	41	87	5.7	.954	SS-155
1978		138	.252	.309	405	102	19	2	0	0.0	39	21	33	74	17	4	1	102	255	23	26	2.8	.939	3B-114, SS-15, 2B-7
1979		100	.227	.258	198	45	3	0	1	0.5	20	8	21	48	6	3	0	142	193	7	48	3.9	.980	2B-61, SS-25, OF-1
1980	2 teams	MON N (18G –.263) NY N (48G –.170)																						
″	total	66	.193	.260	150	29	4	3	0	0.0	15	7	9	32	2	4	0	79	134	12	25	3.6	.947	SS-34, 2B-19, 3B-9
1981	CHI A	103	.301	.375	349	105	10	2	4	1.1	46	41	21	60	16	0	0	190	340	17	78	5.3	.969	SS-103
1982		111	.256	.354	308	79	10	4	4	1.3	40	26	25	49	10	1	0	164	317	26	72	4.7	.949	SS-108, DH-1
1983	OAK A	143	.266	.361	451	120	29	1	4	0.9	45	63	26	67	26	14	3	327	176	20	33	3.2	.962	SS-52, 3B-40, 1B-38, OF-23, 2B-5, DH-4
1984		106	.223	.374	211	47	11	0	7	3.3	24	16	10	42	5	15	3	255	15	2	19	2.5	.993	OF-48, 1B-44, DH-12, 3B-4, SS-1, C-1
1985	PIT N	88	.270	.414	244	66	17	0	6	2.5	33	29	22	61	10	14	5	104	108	5	22	2.4	.977	SS-43, OF-32, 3B-7, 1B-7
1986		102	.219	.383	196	43	7	2	7	3.6	29	27	30	38	11	28	5	80	45	8	4	1.3	.940	OF-54, 3B-28, SS-19, 1B-4
1987	2 teams	PIT N (19G –.200) NY N (49G –.241)																						
″	total	68	.230	.284	74	17	4	0	0	0.0	13	5	9	21	1	22	4	26	42	3	7	1.7	.958	SS-26, 2B-10, OF-3, 1B-2, 3B-1
1988	PHI N	20	.115	.192	26	3	2	0	0	0.0	1	1	3	11	0	6	0	20	15	2	2	2.5	.946	3B-9, SS-5, 1B-1
15 yrs.		1236	.254	.343	3330	846	138	25	36	1.1	390	296	250	636	128	112	21	1834	2265	173	435	3.5	.960	SS-616, 3B-212, OF-161, 2B-102, 1B-96, DH-17, C-1

Roberto Alomar

ALOMAR, ROBERTO BB TR 6′ 184 lbs.
Born Roberto Alomar (Velazquez).
Brother of Sandy Alomar. Son of Sandy Alomar.
B. Feb. 5, 1968, Ponce, Puerto Rico.

Year	Team	Games	BA	SA	AB	H	2B	3B	HR	HR%	R	RBI	BB	SO	SB	Pinch Hit AB	Pinch Hit H	PO	A	E	DP	TC/G	FA	G by Pos
1988	SD N	143	.266	.382	545	145	24	6	9	1.7	84	41	47	83	24	0	0	319	459	16	88	5.6	.980	2B-143
1989		158	.295	.376	623	184	27	1	7	1.1	82	56	53	76	42	1	0	341	472	28	91	5.4	.967	2B-157
1990		147	.287	.381	586	168	27	5	6	1.0	80	60	48	72	24	3	0	316	404	19	77	5.2	.974	2B-137, SS-5
1991	TOR A	161	.295	.436	637	188	41	11	9	1.4	88	69	57	86	53	1	0	333	447	15	79	5.0	.981	2B-160
1992		152	.310	.427	571	177	27	8	8	1.4	105	76	87	52	49	0	0	287	378	5	66	4.4	.993	2B-150, DH-1

Roberto Alomar *continued*

Year	Team	Games	BA	SA	AB	H	2B	3B	HR	HR%	R	RBI	BB	SO	SB	Pinch Hit AB	Pinch Hit H	PO	A	E	DP	TC/G	FA	G by Pos
1993		153	.326	.492	589	192	35	6	17	2.9	109	93	80	67	55	2	1	254	439	14	92	4.7	.980	2B-151
1994		107	.306	.452	392	120	25	4	8	2.0	78	38	51	41	19	4	0	176	275	4	69	4.3	.991	2B-106
1995		130	.300	.449	517	155	24	7	13	2.5	71	66	47	45	30	2	0	273	365	4	84	5.0	.994	2B-128
8 yrs.		1151	.298	.423	4460	1329	230	48	77	1.7	697	499	470	522	296	13	1	2299	3239	105	646	5.0	.981	2B-1132, SS-5, DH-1
LEAGUE CHAMPIONSHIP SERIES																								
1991	TOR A	5	.474	.474	19	9	0	0	0	0.0	3	4	2	3	2	0	0	14	9	0	2	4.6	1.000	2B-5
1992		6	.423	.692	26	11	1	0	2	7.7	4	4	2	1	5	0	0	16	15	0	5	5.2	1.000	2B-6
1993		6	.292	.333	24	7	1	0	0	0.0	3	4	4	3	4	0	0	14	19	0	5	5.5	1.000	2B-6
3 yrs.		17	.391	.507	69	27	2	0	2	2.9	10	12	8	7	11	0	0	44	43	0	12	5.1	1.000	2B-17
			3rd			**8th**									**2nd**									
WORLD SERIES																								
1992	TOR A	6	.208	.250	24	5	1	0	0	0.0	3	0	3	3	3	0	0	5	12	0	0	2.8	1.000	2B-6
1993		6	.480	.640	25	12	2	1	0	0.0	5	6	2	3	4	0	0	9	21	2	2	5.3	.938	2B-6
2 yrs.		12	.347	.449	49	17	3	1	0	0.0	8	6	5	6	7	0	0	14	33	2	2	4.1	.959	2B-12
															9th									

Sandy Alomar

ALOMAR, SANTOS, JR.
Born Santos Alomar (Velazquez).
Brother of Roberto Alomar. Son of Sandy Alomar.
B. June 18, 1966, Salinas, Puerto Rico.

BR TR 6′ 5″ 200 lbs.

Year	Team	Games	BA	SA	AB	H	2B	3B	HR	HR%	R	RBI	BB	SO	SB	Pinch Hit AB	Pinch Hit H	PO	A	E	DP	TC/G	FA	G by Pos
1988	SD N	1	.000	.000	1	0	0	0	0	0.0	0	0	0	1	0	1	0	0	0	0	0	0.0	—	
1989		7	.211	.421	19	4	1	0	1	5.3	1	6	3	3	0	1	0	33	1	0	1	5.7	1.000	C-6
1990	CLE A	132	.290	.418	445	129	26	2	9	2.0	60	66	25	46	4	9	2	686	46	14	6	5.8	.981	C-129
1991		51	.217	.266	184	40	9	0	0	0.0	10	7	8	24	0	1	0	280	19	4	4	6.1	.987	C-46, DH-4
1992		89	.251	.324	299	75	16	0	2	0.7	22	26	13	32	3	1	0	477	39	2	6	5.8	.996	C-88, DH-1
1993		64	.270	.395	215	58	7	1	6	2.8	24	32	11	28	3	2	1	342	25	6	4	5.8	.984	C-64
1994		80	.288	.490	292	84	15	1	14	4.8	44	43	25	31	8	2	0	453	40	2	0	6.3	.996	C-78
1995		66	.300	.478	203	61	6	0	10	4.9	32	35	7	26	3	10	1	364	22	2	3	6.4	.995	C-61
8 yrs.		490	.272	.401	1658	451	80	4	42	2.5	193	215	92	191	21	27	4	2635	192	30	24	6.0	.989	C-472, DH-5
DIVISIONAL PLAYOFF SERIES																								
1995	CLE A	3	.182	.273	11	2	1	0	0	0.0	1	1	0	1	0	0	0	22	1	0	0	7.7	1.000	C-3
LEAGUE CHAMPIONSHIP SERIES																								
1995	CLE A	5	.267	.467	15	4	1	1	0	0.0	0	1	1	1	0	0	0	30	3	1	0	6.8	.971	C-5
WORLD SERIES																								
1995	CLE A	5	.200	.333	15	3	2	0	0	0.0	0	1	0	2	0	0	0	28	0	0	0	5.6	1.000	C-5

Sandy Alomar

ALOMAR, SANTOS, SR.
Born Sandy Alomar (Conde).
Father of Sandy Alomar. Father of Roberto Alomar.
B. Oct. 19, 1943, Salinas, Puerto Rico.

BB TR 5′ 9″ 140 lbs.
BR 1965–1966

Year	Team	Games	BA	SA	AB	H	2B	3B	HR	HR%	R	RBI	BB	SO	SB	Pinch Hit AB	Pinch Hit H	PO	A	E	DP	TC/G	FA	G by Pos
1964	MIL N	19	.245	.264	53	13	1	0	0	0.0	3	6	0	11	1	0	0	27	60	3	8	4.7	.967	SS-19
1965		67	.241	.269	108	26	1	1	0	0.0	16	8	4	12	12	0	0	68	114	5	19	3.2	.973	SS-39, 2B-19
1966	ATL N	31	.091	.114	44	4	1	0	0	0.0	4	2	1	10	0	1	0	30	34	1	11	2.5	.985	2B-21, SS-5
1967	2 teams	NY N (15G –.000) CHI A (12G –.200)																						
″	total	27	.081	.081	37	3	0	0	0	0.0	5	0	2	6	2	1	0	27	32	1	9	2.4	.983	SS-18, 2B-4, 3B-3
1968	CHI A	133	.253	.287	363	92	8	2	0	0.0	41	12	20	42	21	4	2	210	264	20	55	3.6	.960	2B-99, 3B-27, SS-9, OF-1
1969	2 teams	CHI A (22G –.224) CAL A (134G –.250)																						
″	total	156	.248	.279	617	153	12	2	1	0.2	68	34	40	54	20	0	0	344	401	23	109	4.9	.970	2B-156
1970	CAL A	162	.251	.293	672	169	18	2	2	0.3	82	36	49	65	35	0	0	391	481	20	124	5.4	.978	2B-153, SS-10, 3B-1
1971		162	.260	.321	**689**	179	24	3	4	0.6	77	42	41	60	39	0	0	393	530	17	115	5.7	.982	2B-137, SS-28
1972		155	.239	.287	610	146	20	3	1	0.2	65	25	47	55	20	0	0	353	394	17	93	4.8	.978	2B-154, SS-4
1973		136	.238	.257	470	112	7	1	0	0.0	45	28	34	44	25	0	0	290	355	17	86	4.7	.974	2B-110, SS-31
1974	2 teams	CAL A (46G –.222) NY A (76G –.269)																						
″	total	122	.261	.300	333	87	8	1	1	0.3	47	28	15	33	8	3	1	222	241	11	56	4.1	.977	2B-91, SS-19, 3B-5, OF-1, DH-1
1975	NY A	151	.239	.305	489	117	18	4	2	0.4	61	39	26	58	28	0	0	341	370	11	94	4.8	.985	2B-150, SS-1
1976		67	.239	.282	163	39	4	0	1	0.6	20	10	13	12	12	2	0	95	114	7	18	3.7	.968	2B-38, DH-9, SS-6, 3B-3, 1B-1, OF-1
1977	TEX A	69	.265	.337	83	22	3	0	1	1.2	21	11	8	13	4	7	2	52	52	3	13	1.8	.972	DH-26, 2B-18, SS-6, OF-5, 1B-4, 3B-1
1978		24	.207	.241	29	6	1	0	0	0.0	3	1	1	7	0	0	0	45	21	2	7	3.0	.971	1B-9, 2B-6, DH-3, 3B-3, SS-2
15 yrs.		1481	.245	.288	4760	1168	126	19	13	0.3	558	282	301	482	227	18	5	2888	3463	158	817	4.5	.976	2B-1156, SS-197, 3B-43, DH-39, 1B-14, OF-8
LEAGUE CHAMPIONSHIP SERIES																								
1976	NY A	2	.000	.000	1	0	0	0	0	0.0	0	0	0	0	0	1	0	0	0	0	0	0.0	.000	DH-1

Felipe Alou

ALOU, FELIPE
Born Felipe Rojas (Alou).
Father of Moises Alou. Brother of Matty Alou. Brother of Jesus Alou.
B. May 12, 1935, Haina, Dominican Republic.
Manager 1992–95.

BR TR 6′ 195 lbs.

Year	Team	Games	BA	SA	AB	H	2B	3B	HR	HR%	R	RBI	BB	SO	SB	Pinch Hit AB	Pinch Hit H	PO	A	E	DP	TC/G	FA	G by Pos
1958	SF N	75	.253	.390	182	46	9	2	4	2.2	21	16	19	34	4	5	1	126	2	2	1	1.9	.985	OF-70
1959		95	.275	.466	247	68	13	2	10	4.0	38	33	17	38	5	21	5	111	2	3	0	1.7	.974	OF-69
1960		106	.264	.410	322	85	17	3	8	2.5	48	44	16	42	10	9	0	156	5	7	0	1.8	.958	OF-95
1961		132	.289	.465	415	120	19	0	18	4.3	59	52	26	41	11	11	2	196	10	2	1	1.7	.990	OF-122
1962		154	.316	.513	561	177	30	3	25	4.5	96	98	33	66	10	4	0	262	7	8	3	1.8	.971	OF-150
1963		157	.281	.474	565	159	31	9	20	3.5	75	82	27	87	11	8	4	279	9	4	2	1.9	.986	OF-153
1964	MIL N	121	.253	.395	415	105	26	3	9	2.2	60	51	30	41	5	18	5	329	12	5	12	3.1	.986	OF-92, 1B-18
1965		143	.297	.481	555	165	29	2	23	4.1	80	78	31	63	8	9	3	626	43	6	39	4.1	.991	OF-91, 1B-69, 3B-2, SS-1
1966	ATL N	154	.327	.533	**666**	**218**	32	6	31	4.7	**122**	74	24	51	5	0	0	935	64	13	63	5.8	.987	1B-90, OF-79, 3B-3, SS-1
1967		140	.274	.408	574	157	26	3	15	2.6	76	43	32	50	6	3	1	864	34	9	67	6.4	.990	1B-85, OF-56
1968		160	.317	.438	**662**	**210**	37	5	11	1.7	72	57	48	56	12	3	0	379	8	8	2	2.5	.980	OF-158
1969		123	.282	.345	476	134	13	1	5	1.1	54	32	23	23	4	2	2	260	4	3	1	2.3	.989	OF-116
1970	OAK A	154	.271	.367	575	156	25	3	8	1.4	70	55	32	31	10	9	1	290	11	7	4	2.1	.977	OF-145, 1B-1

Felipe Alou *continued*

Year	Team	Games	BA	SA	AB	H	2B	3B	HR	HR%	R	RBI	BB	SO	SB	Pinch Hit AB	Pinch Hit H	PO	A	E	DP	TC/G	FA	G by Pos
1971	2 teams	OAK A (2G –.250)	NY A (131G –.289)																					
″	total	133	.288	.409	469	135	21	6	8	1.7	52	69	32	25	5	19	7	513	23	4	23	4.4	.993	OF-82, 1B-42
1972	NY A	120	.278	.395	324	90	18	1	6	1.9	33	37	22	27	1	29	**10**	669	54	7	69	6.6	.990	1B-95, OF-15
1973	2 teams	NY A (93G –.236)	MON N (19G –.208)																					
″	total	112	.232	.317	328	76	13	0	5	1.5	29	31	11	29	0	21	5	542	34	7	43	5.6	.988	1B-68, OF-37
1974	MIL A	3	.000	.000	3	0	0	0	0	0.0	0	0	0	2	0	3	0	0	0	1	0	1.0	.000	OF-1
17 yrs.		2082	.286	.433	7339	2101	359	49	206	2.8	985	852	423	706	107	174	46	6537	322	96	330	3.5	.986	OF-1531, 1B-468, 3B-5, SS-2
LEAGUE CHAMPIONSHIP SERIES																								
1969	ATL N	1	.000	.000	1	0	0	0	0	0.0	0	0	0	0	0	1	0	0	0	0	0	0.0	—	
WORLD SERIES																								
1962	SF N	7	.269	.385	26	7	1	1	0	0.0	2	1	1	4	0	0	0	8	0	1	0	1.3	.889	OF-7

Jesus Alou

ALOU, JESUS MARIA (Jay) BR TR 6′ 2″ 190 lbs.
Born Jesus Maria Rojas (Alou).
Brother of Matty Alou. Brother of Felipe Alou.
B. Mar. 24, 1942, Haina, Dominican Republic.

Year	Team	Games	BA	SA	AB	H	2B	3B	HR	HR%	R	RBI	BB	SO	SB	Pinch Hit AB	Pinch Hit H	PO	A	E	DP	TC/G	FA	G by Pos
1963	SF N	16	.250	.292	24	6	1	0	0	0.0	3	5	0	3	0	4	0	7	0	1	0	0.7	.875	OF-12
1964		115	.274	.327	376	103	11	0	3	0.8	42	28	13	35	6	13	4	172	8	5	2	1.7	.973	OF-108
1965		143	.298	.398	543	162	19	4	9	1.7	76	52	13	40	8	8	4	238	7	5	0	1.8	.980	OF-136
1966		110	.259	.308	370	96	13	1	1	0.3	41	20	9	22	5	13	3	141	4	5	1	1.5	.967	OF-100
1967		129	.292	.367	510	149	15	4	5	1.0	55	30	14	39	1	6	2	195	5	11	2	1.7	.948	OF-123
1968		120	.263	.317	419	110	15	4	0	0.0	26	39	9	23	1	18	4	175	10	2	2	1.8	.989	OF-105
1969	HOU N	115	.248	.341	452	112	19	4	5	1.1	49	34	15	30	4	0	0	173	8	14	1	1.7	.928	OF-112
1970		117	.306	.384	458	140	27	3	1	0.2	59	44	21	15	3	11	2	169	6	7	2	1.7	.962	OF-108
1971		122	.279	.360	433	121	21	4	2	0.5	41	40	13	17	3	17	5	229	7	4	3	2.2	.983	OF-109
1972		52	.312	.376	93	29	4	1	0	0.0	8	11	7	5	0	31	8	32	0	1	0	1.4	.970	OF-23
1973	2 teams	HOU N (28G –.236)	OAK A (36G –.306)																					
″	total	64	.282	.350	163	46	5	0	2	1.2	17	19	3	12	0	22	5	56	1	1	1	1.4	.983	OF-35, DH-6
1974	OAK A	96	.268	.332	220	59	8	0	2	0.9	13	15	5	9	0	41	7	35	3	0	1	0.6	1.000	DH-41, OF-25
1975	NY N	62	.265	.294	102	27	3	0	0	0.0	8	11	4	5	0	39	14	23	3	1	0	1.4	.963	OF-20
1978	HOU N	77	.324	.417	139	45	5	1	2	1.4	7	19	6	5	0	44	16	40	1	1	0	1.5	.976	OF-28
1979		42	.256	.349	43	11	4	0	0	0.0	3	10	6	7	0	34	8	8	0	0	1	1.1	1.000	OF-6, 1B-1
15 yrs.		1380	.280	.353	4345	1216	170	26	32	0.7	448	377	138	267	31	301	82	1693	63	58	16	1.7	.968	OF-1050, DH-47, 1B-1
LEAGUE CHAMPIONSHIP SERIES																								
1973	OAK A	4	.333	.333	6	2	0	0	0	0.0	0	1	0	1	0	3	1	0	0	0	0	0.0	.000	DH-1
1974		1	1.000	1.000	1	1	0	0	0	0.0	0	0	0	0	0	1	1	0	0	0	0	0.0	—	
2 yrs.		5	.429	.429	7	3	0	0	0	0.0	0	1	0	1	0	4	2	0	0	0	0	0.0		DH-1
WORLD SERIES																								
1973	OAK A	7	.158	.211	19	3	1	0	0	0.0	0	3	0	0	0	1	0	5	0	0	0	0.8	1.000	OF-6
1974		1	.000	.000	1	0	0	0	0	0.0	0	0	0	1	0	1	0	0	0	0	0	0.0	—	
2 yrs.		8	.150	.200	20	3	1	0	0	0.0	0	3	0	1	0	2	0	5	0	0	0	0.8	1.000	OF-6

Matty Alou

ALOU, MATEO BL TL 5′ 9″ 160 lbs.
Born Mateo Rojas (Alou).
Brother of Jesus Alou. Brother of Felipe Alou.
B. Dec. 22, 1938, Haina, Dominican Republic.

Year	Team	Games	BA	SA	AB	H	2B	3B	HR	HR%	R	RBI	BB	SO	SB	Pinch Hit AB	Pinch Hit H	PO	A	E	DP	TC/G	FA	G by Pos
1960	SF N	4	.333	.333	3	1	0	0	0	0.0	1	0	0	0	0	3	1	1	0	0	0	1.0	1.000	OF-1
1961		81	.310	.455	200	62	7	2	6	3.0	38	24	15	18	3	22	5	85	2	2	0	1.5	.978	OF-58
1962		78	.292	.390	195	57	8	1	3	1.5	28	14	14	17	3	24	9	80	3	2	0	1.5	.976	OF-57
1963		63	.145	.158	76	11	1	0	0	0.0	4	2	2	13	0	**45**	8	19	1	1	0	1.0	.952	OF-20
1964		110	.264	.308	250	66	4	2	1	0.4	28	14	11	25	5	30	4	120	2	3	1	1.6	.976	OF-80
1965		117	.231	.299	324	75	12	2	2	0.6	37	18	17	28	10	19	1	139	6	2	1	1.4	.986	OF-103, P-1
1966	PIT N	141	**.342**	.421	535	183	18	9	2	0.4	86	27	24	44	23	7	4	264	11	8	3	2.1	.972	OF-136
1967		139	.338	.413	550	186	21	7	2	0.4	87	28	24	42	16	10	2	252	9	3	3	2.0	.989	OF-134, 1B-1
1968		146	.332	.396	558	185	28	4	0	0.0	59	52	27	26	18	2	1	298	8	5	0	2.2	.984	OF-144
1969		162	.331	.411	**698**	**231**	**41**	6	1	0.1	105	48	42	35	22	0	0	327	10	8	4	2.1	.977	OF-162
1970		155	.297	.356	**677**	201	21	8	1	0.1	97	47	30	18	19	2	0	297	15	8	1	2.1	.975	OF-153
1971	STL N	149	.315	.415	609	192	28	6	7	1.1	85	74	34	27	19	6	2	710	35	9	42	5.0	.988	OF-94, 1B-57
1972	2 teams	STL N (108G –.314)	OAK A (32G –.281)																					
″	total	140	.307	.379	525	161	22	2	4	0.8	57	47	35	35	13	9	1	644	47	7	54	5.1	.990	OF-71, 1B-67
1973	2 teams	NY A (123G –.296)	STL N (11G –.273)																					
″	total	134	.295	.354	508	150	22	1	2	0.4	60	29	31	43	5	10	3	525	27	12	46	4.4	.979	OF-86, 1B-41, DH-1
1974	SD N	48	.198	.235	81	16	3	0	0	0.0	8	3	5	6	0	30	5	33	0	1	0	2.3	.971	OF-13, 1B-2
15 yrs.		1667	.307	.381	5789	1777	236	50	31	0.5	780	427	311	377	156	219	46	3794	176	71	155	2.7	.982	OF-1312, 1B-168, DH-1, P-1
LEAGUE CHAMPIONSHIP SERIES																								
1970	PIT N	3	.250	.333	12	3	1	0	0	0.0	1	0	2	1	0	0	0	6	0	0	0	2.0	1.000	OF-3
1972	OAK A	5	.381	.571	21	8	4	0	0	0.0	2	2	0	2	1	0	0	8	0	0	0	1.6	1.000	OF-5
2 yrs.		8	.333	.485	33	11	5	0	0	0.0	3	2	2	3	1	0	0	14	0	0	0	1.8	1.000	OF-8
WORLD SERIES																								
1962	SF N	6	.333	.417	12	4	1	0	0	0.0	2	1	0	1	0	3	2	3	0	0	0	0.8	1.000	OF-4
1972	OAK A	7	.042	.042	24	1	0	0	0	0.0	0	0	3	0	1	0	0	11	1	1	1	1.9	.923	OF-7
2 yrs.		13	.139	.167	36	5	1	0	0	0.0	2	1	3	1	1	3	2	14	1	1	1	1.5	.938	OF-11

Moises Alou

ALOU, MOISES ROJAS BR TR 6′ 3″ 185 lbs.
Son of Felipe Alou.
B. July 3, 1966, Atlanta, Ga.

Year	Team	Games	BA	SA	AB	H	2B	3B	HR	HR%	R	RBI	BB	SO	SB	Pinch Hit AB	Pinch Hit H	PO	A	E	DP	TC/G	FA	G by Pos
1990	2 teams	PIT N (2G –.200)	MON N (14G –.200)																					
″	total	16	.200	.300	20	4	0	1	0	0.0	4	0	0	3	0	15	1	9	1	0	0	1.4	1.000	OF-7
1992	MON N	115	.282	.455	341	96	28	2	9	2.6	53	56	25	46	16	15	7	170	6	4	1	1.8	.978	OF-100
1993		136	.286	.483	482	138	29	6	18	3.7	70	85	38	53	17	3	1	254	11	4	2	2.0	.985	OF-136

Moises Alou *continued*

Year	Team	Games	BA	SA	AB	H	2B	3B	HR	HR%	R	RBI	BB	SO	SB	Pinch Hit AB	Pinch Hit H	PO	A	E	DP	TC/G	FA	G by Pos
1994		107	.339	.592	422	143	31	5	22	5.2	81	78	42	63	7	1	0	201	4	3	0	2.0	.986	OF-106
1995		93	.273	.459	344	94	22	0	14	4.1	48	58	29	56	4	0	0	148	5	3	0	1.7	.981	OF-92
5 yrs.		467	.295	.498	1609	475	110	14	63	3.9	256	277	134	221	44	24	9	782	27	14	3	1.9	.983	OF-441

Whitey Alperman

ALPERMAN, CHARLES AUGUSTUS
B. Nov. 11, 1879, Etna, Pa. D. Dec. 25, 1942, Pittsburgh, Pa.
BR TR 5′10″ 180 lbs.

Year	Team	Games	BA	SA	AB	H	2B	3B	HR	HR%	R	RBI	BB	SO	SB	Pinch Hit AB	Pinch Hit H	PO	A	E	DP	TC/G	FA	G by Pos
1906	BKN N	128	.252	.338	441	111	15	7	3	0.7	38	46	6		13	1	0	312	388	47	29	5.8	.937	2B-104, SS-24, 3B-1
1907		141	.233	.342	558	130	23	**16**	2	0.4	44	39	13		5	3	1	339	437	45	45	5.8	.945	2B-115, 3B-14, SS-12
1908		70	.197	.235	213	42	3	1	1	0.5	17	15	9		2	11	1	96	135	22	8	4.4	.913	2B-42, 3B-9, OF-5, SS-2
1909		111	.248	.357	420	104	19	12	1	0.2	35	41	2		7	3	0	266	297	42	32	5.6	.931	2B-108
4 yrs.		450	.237	.331	1632	387	60	36	7	0.4	134	141	30		27	18	2	1013	1257	156	114	5.6	.936	2B-369, SS-38, 3B-24, OF-5

Dell Alston

ALSTON, WENDELL
B. Sept. 22, 1952, Valhalla, N. Y.
BL TR 6′ 180 lbs.

Year	Team	Games	BA	SA	AB	H	2B	3B	HR	HR%	R	RBI	BB	SO	SB	Pinch Hit AB	Pinch Hit H	PO	A	E	DP	TC/G	FA	G by Pos
1977	NY A	22	.325	.500	40	13	4	0	1	2.5	10	4	3	4	3	8	3	2	1	0	0	0.3	1.000	DH-10, OF-2
1978	2 teams	NY A (3G –.000) OAK A (58G –.208)																						
″	total	61	.205	.233	176	36	2	0	1	0.6	17	10	10	23	11	7	1	106	0	4	2	1.8	.964	OF-50, 1B-9, DH-3
1979	CLE A	54	.290	.403	62	18	0	2	1	1.6	10	12	10	10	4	11	1	29	2	1	0	0.9	.969	OF-30, DH-7
1980		52	.222	.315	54	12	1	2	0	0.0	11	9	5	7	2	7	1	35	1	2	0	1.2	.947	OF-26, DH-6
4 yrs.		189	.238	.310	332	79	7	4	3	0.9	48	35	28	44	20	33	6	172	4	7	2	1.3	.962	OF-108, DH-26, 1B-9

Tom Alston

ALSTON, THOMAS EDISON
B. Jan. 31, 1926, Greensboro, N. C. D. Dec. 30, 1993, Winston-Salem, N. C.
BL TR 6′ 5″ 210 lbs.

Year	Team	Games	BA	SA	AB	H	2B	3B	HR	HR%	R	RBI	BB	SO	SB	Pinch Hit AB	Pinch Hit H	PO	A	E	DP	TC/G	FA	G by Pos
1954	STL N	66	.246	.369	244	60	14	2	4	1.6	28	34	24	41	3	2	1	552	72	7	57	9.7	.989	1B-65
1955		13	.125	.125	8	1	0	0	0	0.0	0	0	0	0	0	6	1	14	1	0	1	2.1	1.000	1B-7
1956		3	.000	.000	2	0	0	0	0	0.0	0	0	0	0	0	0	0	4	1	0	1	1.7	1.000	1B-3
1957		9	.294	.353	17	5	1	0	0	0.0	2	2	1	5	0	3	2	35	1	2	4	6.3	.947	1B-6
4 yrs.		91	.244	.358	271	66	15	2	4	1.5	30	36	25	46	3	11	4	605	75	9	63	8.5	.987	1B-81

Walter Alston

ALSTON, WALTER EMMONS (Smokey)
B. Dec. 1, 1911, Venice, Ohio D. Oct. 1, 1984, Oxford, Ohio.
Manager 1954–76.
Hall of Fame 1983.
BR TR 6′ 2″ 195 lbs.

Year	Team	Games	BA	SA	AB	H	2B	3B	HR	HR%	R	RBI	BB	SO	SB	Pinch Hit AB	Pinch Hit H	PO	A	E	DP	TC/G	FA	G by Pos
1936	STL N	1	.000	.000	1	0	0	0	0	0.0	0	0	0	1	0	0	0	1	0	1	0	2.0	.500	1B-1

Jesse Altenburg

ALTENBURG, JESSE HOWARD (Chip)
B. Jan. 2, 1893, Ashley, Mich. D. Mar. 12, 1973, Lansing, Mich.
BL TR 5′ 9″ 158 lbs.

Year	Team	Games	BA	SA	AB	H	2B	3B	HR	HR%	R	RBI	BB	SO	SB	Pinch Hit AB	Pinch Hit H	PO	A	E	DP	TC/G	FA	G by Pos
1916	PIT N	8	.429	.643	14	6	1	1	0	0.0	2	0	1	1	0	1	0	5	0	0	0	0.6	1.000	OF-8
1917		11	.176	.176	17	3	0	0	0	0.0	1	3	0	4	0	6	0	4	0	0	0	1.0	1.000	OF-4
2 yrs.		19	.290	.387	31	9	1	1	0	0.0	3	3	1	5	0	7	0	9	0	0	0	0.8	1.000	OF-12

Dave Altizer

ALTIZER, DAVID TILDEN (Filipino)
B. Nov. 6, 1876, Pearl, Ill. D. May 14, 1964, Pleasant Hill, Ill.
BL TR 5′10½″ 160 lbs.

Year	Team	Games	BA	SA	AB	H	2B	3B	HR	HR%	R	RBI	BB	SO	SB	Pinch Hit AB	Pinch Hit H	PO	A	E	DP	TC/G	FA	G by Pos
1906	WAS A	115	.256	.307	433	111	9	5	1	0.2	56	27	35		37	0	0	263	324	43	31	5.5	.932	SS-113, OF-2
1907		147	.269	.320	540	145	15	5	1	0.2	60	42	34		38	0	0	790	297	50	41	7.7	.956	SS-71, 1B-50, OF-26
1908	2 teams	WAS A (67G –.224) CLE A (29G –.213)																						
″	total	96	.221	.248	294	65	2	3	0	0.0	30	23	20		15	7	1	169	162	19	15	4.1	.946	2B-38, OF-24, 3B-16, SS-4, 1B-4
1909	CHI A	116	.233	.293	382	89	6	7	1	0.3	47	20	39		27	7	1	540	45	10	25	5.6	.983	OF-62, 1B-45
1910	CIN N	3	.600	.600	10	6	0	0	0	0.0	3	0	3	0	0	0	0	7	7	1	1	5.0	.933	SS-3
1911		37	.227	.307	75	17	4	1	0	0.0	8	4	9	5	2	4	1	43	61	10	6	4.4	.912	SS-23, 2B-1, OF-1, 1B-1
6 yrs.		514	.250	.300	1734	433	36	21	3	0.2	204	116	140	5	119	18	3	1812	896	133	119	5.9	.953	SS-214, OF-115, 1B-100, 2B-39, 3B-16

George Altman

ALTMAN, GEORGE LEE
B. Mar. 20, 1933, Goldsboro, N. C.
BL TR 6′ 4″ 200 lbs.

Year	Team	Games	BA	SA	AB	H	2B	3B	HR	HR%	R	RBI	BB	SO	SB	Pinch Hit AB	Pinch Hit H	PO	A	E	DP	TC/G	FA	G by Pos
1959	CHI N	135	.245	.383	420	103	14	4	12	2.9	54	47	34	80	1	15	4	278	7	3	2	2.4	.990	OF-121
1960		119	.266	.455	334	89	16	4	13	3.9	50	51	32	67	4	20	8	308	16	2	15	3.3	.994	OF-79, 1B-21
1961		138	.303	.560	518	157	28	**12**	27	5.2	77	96	40	92	6	6	0	278	12	6	5	2.2	.980	OF-130, 1B-3
1962		147	.318	.511	534	170	27	5	22	4.1	74	74	62	89	19	6	1	355	16	7	16	2.6	.981	OF-129, 1B-16
1963	STL N	135	.274	.401	464	127	18	7	9	1.9	62	47	47	93	13	12	3	220	8	5	1	1.9	.979	OF-124
1964	NY N	124	.230	.332	422	97	14	1	9	2.1	48	47	18	70	4	18	6	202	12	7	3	2.0	.968	OF-109
1965	CHI N	90	.235	.342	196	46	7	1	4	2.0	24	23	19	36	3	43	6	78	0	4	1	1.7	.951	OF-45, 1B-2
1966		88	.222	.335	185	41	6	0	5	2.7	19	17	14	37	2	44	9	69	6	2	1	1.7	.974	OF-42, 1B-4
1967		15	.111	.222	18	2	2	0	0	0.0	1	1	2	8	0	9	2	4	0	0	1	0.8	1.000	OF-4, 1B-1
9 yrs.		991	.269	.432	3091	832	132	34	101	3.3	409	403	268	572	52	173	39	1792	77	36	45	2.3	.981	OF-783, 1B-47

Joe Altobelli

ALTOBELLI, JOSEPH SALVATORE
B. May 26, 1932, Detroit, Mich.
Manager 1977–79, 1983–85, 1991.
BL TL 6′ 185 lbs.

Year	Team	Games	BA	SA	AB	H	2B	3B	HR	HR%	R	RBI	BB	SO	SB	Pinch Hit AB	Pinch Hit H	PO	A	E	DP	TC/G	FA	G by Pos
1955	CLE A	42	.200	.320	75	15	3	0	2	2.7	8	5	5	14	0	1	0	224	11	2	14	5.9	.992	1B-40
1957		83	.207	.287	87	18	3	2	0	0.0	9	9	5	14	3	22	4	158	9	1	16	2.7	.994	1B-56, OF-7
1961	MIN A	41	.221	.358	95	21	2	1	3	3.2	10	14	13	14	0	12	4	54	1	2	0	2.1	.965	OF-25, 1B-2
3 yrs.		166	.210	.323	257	54	8	3	5	1.9	27	28	23	42	3	35	8	436	21	5	30	3.6	.989	1B-98, OF-32

George Alusik

ALUSIK, GEORGE JOSEPH (Glider, Turk)
B. Feb. 11, 1935, Ashley, Pa.
BR TR 6′ 3½″ 175 lbs.

Year	Team	Games	BA	SA	AB	H	2B	3B	HR	HR%	R	RBI	BB	SO	SB	Pinch Hit AB	Pinch Hit H	PO	A	E	DP	TC/G	FA	G by Pos
1958	DET A	2	.000	.000	2	0	0	0	0	0.0	0	0	0	1	0	1	0	1	0	0	0	1.0	1.000	OF-1
1961		15	.143	.143	14	2	0	0	0	0.0	0	2	1	4	0	12	2	0	0	0	0	0.0	.000	OF-1
1962	2 teams	DET A (2G –.000) KC A (90G –.273)																						
″	total	92	.270	.483	211	57	10	1	11	5.2	29	35	16	29	1	38	11	89	3	3	0	1.9	.968	OF-50, 1B-1
1963	KC A	87	.267	.439	221	59	11	0	9	4.1	28	37	26	33	0	19	9	98	5	0	1	1.6	1.000	OF-63
1964		102	.240	.343	204	49	10	1	3	1.5	18	19	30	36	0	40	6	150	6	2	10	2.8	.987	OF-44, 1B-12
5 yrs.		298	.256	.416	652	167	31	2	23	3.5	75	93	73	103	1	110	28	338	14	5	11	2.1	.986	OF-159, 1B-13

Luis Alvarado

ALVARADO, LUIS CESAR (Pimba)
Born Luis Cesar Alvarado (Martinez).
B. Jan. 15, 1949, La Jas, Puerto Rico.
BR TR 5′ 9″ 162 lbs.

Year	Team	Games	BA	SA	AB	H	2B	3B	HR	HR%	R	RBI	BB	SO	SB	Pinch Hit AB	Pinch Hit H	PO	A	E	DP	TC/G	FA	G by Pos
1968	BOS A	11	.130	.174	46	6	2	0	0	0.0	3	1	1	11	0	0	0	14	26	1	6	3.7	.976	SS-11
1969		6	.000	.000	5	0	0	0	0	0.0	0	0	0	2	0	1	0	4	6	0	2	2.0	1.000	SS-5
1970		59	.224	.301	183	41	11	0	1	0.5	19	10	9	30	1	1	0	45	134	8	17	3.3	.957	3B-29, SS-27
1971	CHI A	99	.216	.277	264	57	14	1	0	0.0	22	8	11	34	1	9	0	120	238	13	46	4.3	.965	SS-71, 2B-16
1972		103	.213	.283	254	54	4	1	4	1.6	30	29	13	36	2	7	2	107	234	15	30	3.6	.958	SS-81, 2B-16, 3B-2
1973		80	.232	.286	203	47	7	2	0	0.0	21	20	4	20	6	7	4	120	158	9	31	3.9	.969	2B-45, SS-18, 3B-10
1974	3 teams CHI A (8G –.100) CLE A (61G –.219) STL N (17G –.139)																							
″	total	86	.194	.219	160	31	4	0	0	0.0	16	13	8	21	1	5	1	104	147	11	34	3.3	.958	2B-47, SS-28, DH-3, 3B-1
1976	STL N	16	.286	.310	42	12	1	0	0	0.0	5	3	3	6	0	0	0	22	22	3	3	2.9	.936	2B-16
1977	2 teams NY N (1G –.000) DET A (2G –.000)																							
″	total	3	.000	.000	3	0	0	0	0	0.0	0	0	0	0	0	0	0	1	2	0	0	1.0	1.000	3B-2, 2B-1
9 yrs.		463	.214	.271	1160	248	43	4	5	0.4	116	84	49	160	11	30	7	537	967	60	169	3.6	.962	SS-241, 2B-141, 3B-44, DH-3

Orlando Alvarez

ALVAREZ, JESUS MANUEL ORLANDO
Born Jesus Manuel Orlando Alvarez (Monge).
B. Feb. 28, 1952, Rio Grande, Puerto Rico.
BR TR 6′ 165 lbs.

Year	Team	Games	BA	SA	AB	H	2B	3B	HR	HR%	R	RBI	BB	SO	SB	Pinch Hit AB	Pinch Hit H	PO	A	E	DP	TC/G	FA	G by Pos
1973	LA N	4	.250	.500	4	1	1	0	0	0.0	0	0	0	1	0	4	1	0	0	0	0	0.0	—	
1974		2	.000	.000	1	0	0	0	0	0.0	0	0	0	0	0	1	0	1	0	0	0	1.0	1.000	OF-1
1975		4	.000	.000	4	0	0	0	0	0.0	0	0	0	1	0	4	0	0	0	0	0	0.0	—	
1976	CAL A	15	.167	.333	42	7	1	0	2	4.8	4	8	0	3	0	5	0	12	1	0	1	1.0	1.000	OF-11, DH-2
4 yrs.		25	.157	.314	51	8	2	0	2	3.9	4	8	0	5	0	14	1	13	1	0	1	1.0	1.000	OF-12, DH-2

Ossie Alvarez

ALVAREZ, OSWALDO
Born Oswaldo Alvarez (Gonzalez).
B. Oct. 19, 1933, Matanzas, Cuba.
BR TR 5′10″ 165 lbs.

Year	Team	Games	BA	SA	AB	H	2B	3B	HR	HR%	R	RBI	BB	SO	SB	Pinch Hit AB	Pinch Hit H	PO	A	E	DP	TC/G	FA	G by Pos
1958	WAS A	87	.209	.224	196	41	3	0	0	0.0	20	5	16	26	1	3	0	126	183	10	38	3.9	.969	SS-64, 2B-14, 3B-3
1959	DET A	8	.500	.500	2	1	0	0	0	0.0	0	0	0	1	0	2	1	0	0	0	0	0.0	—	
2 yrs.		95	.212	.227	198	42	3	0	0	0.0	20	5	16	27	1	5	1	126	183	10	38	3.9	.969	SS-64, 2B-14, 3B-3

Rogelio Alvarez

ALVAREZ, ROGELIO (Borrego)
Born Rogelio Alvarez (Hernandez).
B. Apr. 18, 1938, Pinar Del Rio, Cuba.
BR TR 5′11″ 183 lbs.

Year	Team	Games	BA	SA	AB	H	2B	3B	HR	HR%	R	RBI	BB	SO	SB	Pinch Hit AB	Pinch Hit H	PO	A	E	DP	TC/G	FA	G by Pos
1960	CIN N	3	.111	.111	9	1	0	0	0	0.0	1	0	0	3	0	1	0	21	0	0	1	10.5	1.000	1B-2
1962		14	.214	.214	28	6	0	0	0	0.0	1	2	1	10	0	2	0	69	4	2	8	5.8	.973	1B-13
2 yrs.		17	.189	.189	37	7	0	0	0	0.0	2	2	1	13	0	3	0	90	4	2	9	6.4	.979	1B-15

Max Alvis

ALVIS, ROY MAXWELL
B. Feb. 2, 1938, Jasper, Tex.
BR TR 5′11″ 185 lbs.

Year	Team	Games	BA	SA	AB	H	2B	3B	HR	HR%	R	RBI	BB	SO	SB	Pinch Hit AB	Pinch Hit H	PO	A	E	DP	TC/G	FA	G by Pos
1962	CLE A	12	.216	.255	51	11	2	0	0	0.0	1	3	2	13	3	0	0	13	16	2	1	2.6	.935	3B-12
1963		158	.274	.460	602	165	32	7	22	3.7	81	67	36	109	9	0	0	170	285	28	32	3.1	.942	3B-158
1964		107	.252	.446	381	96	14	3	18	4.7	51	53	29	77	5	1	1	83	191	13	18	2.7	.955	3B-105
1965		159	.247	.397	604	149	24	2	21	3.5	88	61	47	121	12	2	1	169	264	19	17	2.9	.958	3B-156
1966		157	.245	.378	596	146	22	3	17	2.9	67	55	50	98	4	0	0	180	280	20	24	3.1	.958	3B-157
1967		161	.256	.403	637	163	23	4	21	3.3	66	70	38	107	3	0	0	169	304	17	20	3.0	.965	3B-161
1968		131	.223	.327	452	101	17	3	8	1.8	38	37	41	91	5	6	1	114	202	13	18	2.6	.960	3B-128
1969		66	.225	.272	191	43	6	0	1	0.5	13	15	14	26	1	9	0	49	96	4	10	2.5	.973	3B-58, SS-1
1970	MIL A	62	.183	.278	115	21	2	0	3	2.6	16	12	5	20	1	15	3	15	55	7	4	2.1	.909	3B-36
9 yrs.		1013	.247	.390	3629	895	142	22	111	3.1	421	373	262	662	43	33	6	962	1693	123	144	2.9	.956	3B-971, SS-1

Billy Alvord

ALVORD, WILLIAM CHARLES (Uncle Bill)
B. Aug. 1863, St. Louis, Mo. Deceased.
5′10″ 187 lbs.

Year	Team	Games	BA	SA	AB	H	2B	3B	HR	HR%	R	RBI	BB	SO	SB	Pinch Hit AB	Pinch Hit H	PO	A	E	DP	TC/G	FA	G by Pos
1885	STL N	2	.000	.000	5	0	0	0	0	0.0	0	0	1	2		0	0	4	1	2	0	3.5	.714	3B-2
1889	KC AA	50	.231	.371	186	43	8	9	0	0.0	23	18	10	35	3	0	0	66	140	43	17	5.0	.827	3B-34, SS-8, 2B-8
1890	TOL AA	116	.273	.376	495	135	13	16	2	0.4	69		22		21	0	0	203	252	67	13	4.5	.872	3B-116
1891	2 teams CLE N (13G –.288) WAS AA (81G –.234)																							
″	total	94	.243	.305	371	90	10	5	1	0.3	35	37	11	45	3	0	0	167	238	68	11	5.0	.856	3B-94
1893	CLE N	3	.167	.167	12	2	0	0	0	0.0	2	2	0	1	0	0	0	5	2	1	0	2.7	.875	3B-3
5 yrs.		265	.253	.346	1069	270	31	30	3	0.3	129	57	44	83	27	0	0	445	633	181	41	4.8	.856	3B-249, SS-8, 2B-8

Brant Alyea

ALYEA, GARRABRANT RYERSON
B. Dec. 8, 1940, Passaic, N. J.
BR TR 6′ 3″ 215 lbs.

Year	Team	Games	BA	SA	AB	H	2B	3B	HR	HR%	R	RBI	BB	SO	SB	Pinch Hit AB	Pinch Hit H	PO	A	E	DP	TC/G	FA	G by Pos
1965	WAS A	8	.231	.692	13	3	0	0	2	15.4	3	6	1	4	0	5	1	17	0	0	0	4.3	1.000	1B-3, OF-1
1968		53	.267	.473	150	40	11	1	6	4.0	18	23	10	39	0	18	3	76	0	0	0	1.9	1.000	OF-39
1969		104	.249	.405	237	59	4	0	11	4.6	29	40	34	67	1	41	8	90	6	6	0	1.4	.941	OF-69, 1B-3
1970	MIN A	94	.291	.531	258	75	12	1	16	6.2	34	61	28	51	3	18	7	93	4	2	0	1.3	.980	OF-75
1971		79	.177	.241	158	28	4	0	2	1.3	13	15	24	38	1	25	4	47	3	2	0	1.1	.962	OF-48
1972	2 teams OAK A (20G –.194) STL N (13G –.158)																							
″	total	33	.180	.280	50	9	2	0	1	2.0	3	3	3	11	0	20	3	25	4	0	1	2.6	1.000	OF-11
6 yrs.		371	.247	.421	866	214	33	2	38	4.4	100	148	100	210	5	127	26	348	17	10	1	1.5	.973	OF-243, 1B-6
LEAGUE CHAMPIONSHIP SERIES																								
1970	MIN A	3	.000	.000	7	0	0	0	0	0.0	1	0	2	3	0	1	0	0	0	0	0	0.0	.000	OF-2

Joey Amalfitano

AMALFITANO, JOHN JOSEPH
B. Jan. 23, 1934, San Pedro, Calif.
Manager 1979–81.
BR TR 5′11″ 175 lbs.

Year	Team	Games	BA	SA	AB	H	2B	3B	HR	HR%	R	RBI	BB	SO	SB	Pinch Hit AB	Pinch Hit H	PO	A	E	DP	TC/G	FA	G by Pos
1954	NY N	9	.000	.000	5	0	0	0	0	0.0	2	0	0	4	0	0	0	2	5	0	1	1.4	1.000	3B-4, 2B-1
1955		36	.227	.364	22	5	1	1	0	0.0	8	1	2	2	0	4	0	12	19	3	3	4.9	.912	SS-5, 3B-2
1960	SF N	106	.277	.351	328	91	15	3	1	0.3	47	27	26	31	2	13	5	103	187	14	24	3.0	.954	3B-63, 2B-33, SS-3, OF-1
1961		109	.255	.320	384	98	11	4	2	0.5	64	23	44	59	7	12	4	204	236	13	48	4.5	.971	2B-95, 3B-6
1962	HOU N	117	.237	.303	380	90	12	5	1	0.3	44	27	45	43	4	2	1	231	270	18	72	4.5	.965	2B-110, 3B-5
1963	SF N	54	.175	.219	137	24	3	0	1	0.7	11	7	12	18	2	18	1	61	92	3	13	3.5	.981	2B-37, 3B-7
1964	CHI N	100	.241	.373	324	78	19	6	4	1.2	51	27	40	42	2	10	3	201	254	17	47	5.4	.964	2B-86, SS-1, 1B-1

Joey Amalfitano *continued*

Year	Team	Games	BA	SA	AB	H	2B	3B	HR	HR%	R	RBI	BB	SO	SB	Pinch Hit AB	Pinch Hit H	PO	A	E	DP	TC/G	FA	G by Pos
1965		67	.271	.313	96	26	4	0	0	0.0	13	8	12	14	2	37	8	31	67	2	9	3.6	.980	2B-24, SS-4
1966		41	.158	.211	38	6	2	0	0	0.0	8	3	4	10	0	9	2	23	19	1	5	2.5	.977	2B-12, 3B-3, SS-2
1967		4	.000	.000	1	0	0	0	0	0.0	0	0	0	1	0	1	0	0	0	0	0	0.0	—	
10 yrs.		643	.244	.321	1715	418	67	19	9	0.5	248	123	185	224	19	106	24	868	1149	71	222	4.1	.966	2B-398, 3B-90, SS-15, 1B-1, OF-1

Rich Amaral

AMARAL, RICHARD LOUIS
B. Apr. 1, 1962, Visalia, Calif.
BR TR 6′ 175 lbs.

Year	Team	Games	BA	SA	AB	H	2B	3B	HR	HR%	R	RBI	BB	SO	SB	Pinch Hit AB	Pinch Hit H	PO	A	E	DP	TC/G	FA	G by Pos
1991	SEA A	14	.063	.063	16	1	0	0	0	0.0	2	0	1	5	0	2	0	13	16	2	6	2.6	.935	2B-5, 3B-2, SS-2, DH-2, 1B-1
1992		35	.240	.300	100	24	3	0	1	1.0	9	7	5	16	4	2	0	33	68	3	10	2.6	.971	SS-17, 3B-17, OF-3, 1B-2, 2B-1
1993		110	.290	.367	373	108	24	1	1	0.3	53	44	33	54	19	5	3	180	270	10	71	3.8	.978	2B-77, 3B-19, SS-14, DH-9, 1B-3
1994		77	.263	.377	228	60	10	2	4	1.8	37	18	24	28	5	6	2	108	117	15	24	3.3	.938	2B-42, OF-16, SS-7, DH-5, 1B-2
1995		90	.282	.382	238	67	14	2	2	0.8	45	19	21	33	21	10	2	121	6	1	0	1.7	.992	OF-73, DH-1
5 yrs.		326	.272	.361	955	260	51	5	8	0.8	146	88	84	136	49	25	7	455	477	31	111	3.0	.968	2B-125, OF-92, SS-40, 3B-38, DH-17, 1B-8
LEAGUE CHAMPIONSHIP SERIES																								
1995	SEA A	2	.000	.000	2	0	0	0	0	0.0	0	0	0	1	0	2	0	0	0	0	0	0.0	—	

Ruben Amaro

AMARO, RUBEN
Born Ruben Amaro (Mora).
Father of Ruben Amaro.
B. Jan. 6, 1936, Veracruz, Mexico.
BR TR 5′11″ 170 lbs.

Year	Team	Games	BA	SA	AB	H	2B	3B	HR	HR%	R	RBI	BB	SO	SB	Pinch Hit AB	Pinch Hit H	PO	A	E	DP	TC/G	FA	G by Pos
1958	STL N	40	.224	.276	76	17	2	1	0	0.0	8	0	5	8	0	1	0	45	66	6	18	3.2	.949	SS-36, 2B-1
1960	PHI N	92	.231	.273	264	61	9	1	0	0.0	25	16	21	32	0	0	0	153	230	14	47	4.3	.965	SS-92
1961		135	.257	.349	381	98	14	9	1	0.3	34	32	53	59	1	0	0	254	380	19	92	4.8	.971	SS-132, 1B-3, 2B-1
1962		79	.243	.288	226	55	10	0	0	0.0	24	19	30	28	5	0	0	144	224	12	50	4.8	.968	SS-78, 1B-1
1963		115	.217	.304	217	47	9	2	2	0.9	25	19	19	31	0	7	0	111	169	13	29	2.6	.956	SS-63, 3B-45, 1B-5
1964		129	.264	.341	299	79	11	0	4	1.3	31	34	16	37	1	9	1	298	203	11	55	3.6	.979	SS-79, 1B-58, 2B-3, 3B-3, OF-1
1965		118	.212	.250	184	39	7	0	0	0.0	26	15	27	22	1	7	0	187	134	11	34	2.6	.967	1B-60, SS-60, 2B-6
1966	NY A	14	.217	.217	23	5	0	0	0	0.0	0	3	0	2	0	0	0	17	25	1	8	3.1	.977	SS-14
1967		130	.223	.259	417	93	12	0	1	0.2	31	17	43	49	3	2	0	228	379	18	75	4.9	.971	SS-123, 3B-3, 1B-2
1968		47	.122	.146	41	5	1	0	0	0.0	3	0	9	6	0	1	0	54	37	2	11	2.1	.978	SS-23, 1B-22
1969	CAL A	41	.222	.222	27	6	0	0	0	0.0	4	1	4	6	0	5	1	41	17	1	2	1.7	.983	1B-18, 2B-9, SS-5, 3B-2
11 yrs.		940	.234	.292	2155	505	75	13	8	0.4	211	156	227	280	11	32	2	1532	1864	108	421	3.7	.969	SS-705, 1B-169, 3B-53, 2B-20, OF-1

Ruben Amaro

AMARO, RUBEN, JR.
Son of Ruben Amaro.
B. Feb. 12, 1965, Philadelphia, Pa.
BB TR 5′10″ 170 lbs.

Year	Team	Games	BA	SA	AB	H	2B	3B	HR	HR%	R	RBI	BB	SO	SB	Pinch Hit AB	Pinch Hit H	PO	A	E	DP	TC/G	FA	G by Pos
1991	CAL A	10	.217	.261	23	5	1	0	0	0.0	0	2	3	3	0	2	0	9	6	1	1	1.6	.938	OF-5, 2B-4, DH-1
1992	PHI N	126	.219	.348	374	82	15	6	7	1.9	43	34	37	54	11	14	2	232	5	2	1	2.1	.992	OF-113
1993		25	.333	.521	48	16	2	2	1	2.1	7	6	6	5	0	8	0	25	1	1	1	1.7	.963	OF-16
1994	CLE A	26	.217	.522	23	5	1	0	2	8.7	5	5	2	3	2	11	1	10	0	1	0	0.7	.909	OF-12, DH-3
1995		28	.200	.300	60	12	3	0	1	1.7	5	7	4	6	1	9	2	35	0	0	0	1.4	1.000	OF-22, DH-3
5 yrs.		215	.227	.362	528	120	22	8	11	2.1	60	54	52	71	14	44	5	311	12	5	3	1.8	.985	OF-168, DH-7, 2B-4
LEAGUE CHAMPIONSHIP SERIES																								
1995	CLE A	3	.000	.000	1	0	0	0	0	0.0	1	0	0	0	0	0	0	0	0	0	0	0.0	.000	DH-1
WORLD SERIES																								
1995	CLE A	2	.000	.000	2	0	0	0	0	0.0	0	0	0	1	0	1	0	0	0	0	0	0.0	.000	OF-1

Wayne Ambler

AMBLER, WAYNE HARPER
B. Nov. 8, 1915, Abington, Pa.
BR TR 5′ 8½″ 165 lbs.

Year	Team	Games	BA	SA	AB	H	2B	3B	HR	HR%	R	RBI	BB	SO	SB	Pinch Hit AB	Pinch Hit H	PO	A	E	DP	TC/G	FA	G by Pos
1937	PHI A	56	.216	.247	162	35	5	0	0	0.0	3	11	13	8	1	0	0	107	149	12	34	4.8	.955	2B-56
1938		120	.234	.298	393	92	21	2	0	0.0	42	38	48	31	2	0	0	221	326	32	58	4.8	.945	SS-116, 2B-4
1939		95	.211	.269	227	48	13	0	0	0.0	15	24	22	25	1	0	0	150	208	18	34	3.9	.952	SS-77, 2B-19
3 yrs.		271	.224	.279	782	175	39	2	0	0.0	60	73	83	64	4	0	0	478	683	62	126	4.5	.949	SS-193, 2B-79

Ed Amelung

AMELUNG, EDWARD ALLEN
B. Apr. 13, 1959, Fullerton, Calif.
BL TL 5′11″ 180 lbs.

Year	Team	Games	BA	SA	AB	H	2B	3B	HR	HR%	R	RBI	BB	SO	SB	Pinch Hit AB	Pinch Hit H	PO	A	E	DP	TC/G	FA	G by Pos
1984	LA N	34	.217	.217	46	10	0	0	0	0.0	7	4	2	4	3	11	1	31	0	0	0	1.3	1.000	OF-23
1986		8	.091	.091	11	1	0	0	0	0.0	0	0	0	4	0	4	0	5	0	0	0	1.3	1.000	OF-4
2 yrs.		42	.193	.193	57	11	0	0	0	0.0	7	4	2	8	3	15	1	36	0	0	0	1.3	1.000	OF-27

Sandy Amoros

AMOROS, EDMUNDO
Born Edmundo Amoros (Isasi).
B. Jan. 30, 1930, Havana, Cuba D. June 27, 1992, Miami, Fla.
BL TL 5′ 7½″ 170 lbs.

Year	Team	Games	BA	SA	AB	H	2B	3B	HR	HR%	R	RBI	BB	SO	SB	Pinch Hit AB	Pinch Hit H	PO	A	E	DP	TC/G	FA	G by Pos
1952	BKN N	20	.250	.364	44	11	3	1	0	0.0	10	3	5	14	1	11	0	18	0	0	0	1.8	1.000	OF-10
1954		79	.274	.490	263	72	18	6	9	3.4	44	34	31	24	1	8	2	149	6	2	1	2.2	.987	OF-70
1955		119	.247	.402	388	96	16	7	10	2.6	59	51	55	45	10	9	3	201	10	6	1	2.0	.972	OF-109
1956		114	.260	.517	292	76	11	8	16	5.5	53	58	59	51	3	22	3	123	3	6	0	1.5	.955	OF-86
1957		106	.277	.403	238	66	7	1	7	2.9	40	26	46	42	3	28	4	122	2	2	0	1.9	.984	OF-66
1959	LA N	5	.200	.200	5	1	0	0	0	0.0	1	1	0	1	0	5	1	0	0	0	0	0.0	—	
1960	2 teams	LA N (9G –.143) DET A (65G –.149)																						
″	total	74	.148	.185	81	12	0	0	1	1.2	8	7	15	12	0	48	8	22	1	0	0	1.8	1.000	OF-13
7 yrs.		517	.255	.430	1311	334	55	23	43	3.3	215	180	211	189	18	131	21	635	22	16	2	1.9	.976	OF-354
WORLD SERIES																								
1952	BKN N	1	—	—	0	0	0	0	0	—	0	0	0	0	0	0	0	0	0	0	0	0.0	—	
1955		5	.333	.583	12	4	0	0	1	8.3	3	3	4	4	0	0	0	9	2	0	1	2.2	1.000	OF-5
1956		6	.053	.053	19	1	0	0	0	0.0	1	1	2	4	0	0	0	10	0	0	0	1.7	1.000	OF-6
3 yrs.		12	.161	.258	31	5	0	0	1	3.2	4	4	6	8	0	0	0	19	2	0	1	1.9	1.000	OF-11

Alf Anderson

ANDERSON, ALFRED WALTON BR TR 5′11″ 165 lbs.
B. Jan. 28, 1914, Gainesville, Ga. D. June 23, 1985, Albany, Ga.

Year	Team	Lg	Games	BA	SA	AB	H	2B	3B	HR	HR%	R	RBI	BB	SO	SB	Pinch Hit AB	Pinch Hit H	PO	A	E	DP	TC/G	FA	G by Pos
1941	PIT	N	70	.215	.278	223	48	7	2	1	0.4	32	10	14	30	2	5	1	97	161	19	29	4.8	.931	SS-58
1942			54	.271	.307	166	45	4	1	0	0.0	24	7	18	19	4	4	1	77	103	11	17	4.0	.942	SS-48
1946			2	.000	.000	1	0	0	0	0	0.0	0	0	1	0	0	1	0	0	0	0	0	0.0	—	
3 yrs.			126	.238	.290	390	93	11	3	1	0.3	56	17	33	49	6	10	2	174	264	30	46	4.4	.936	SS-106

Andy Anderson

ANDERSON, ANDY HOLM BR TR 5′11″ 172 lbs.
B. Nov. 13, 1922, Bremerton, Wash. D. July 18, 1982, Seattle, Wash.

Year	Team	Lg	Games	BA	SA	AB	H	2B	3B	HR	HR%	R	RBI	BB	SO	SB	Pinch Hit AB	Pinch Hit H	PO	A	E	DP	TC/G	FA	G by Pos
1948	STL	A	51	.276	.391	87	24	5	1	1	1.1	13	12	8	15	0	21	5	44	54	9	14	3.2	.916	2B-21, SS-10, 1B-2
1949			71	.125	.169	136	17	3	0	1	0.7	10	5	14	21	0	12	1	74	98	6	24	3.0	.966	SS-44, 3B-8, 2B-8
2 yrs.			122	.184	.256	223	41	8	1	2	0.9	23	17	22	36	0	33	6	118	152	15	38	3.1	.947	SS-54, 2B-29, 3B-8, 1B-2

Brady Anderson

ANDERSON, BRADY KEVIN BL TL 6′1″ 170 lbs.
B. Jan. 18, 1964, Silver Spring, Md.

Year	Team	Lg	Games	BA	SA	AB	H	2B	3B	HR	HR%	R	RBI	BB	SO	SB	Pinch Hit AB	Pinch Hit H	PO	A	E	DP	TC/G	FA	G by Pos
1988	2 teams	BOS A (41G –.230) BAL A (53G –.198)																							
″	total		94	.212	.286	325	69	13	4	1	0.3	31	21	23	75	10	7	0	243	4	4	1	2.8	.984	OF-90
1989	BAL	A	94	.207	.312	266	55	12	2	4	1.5	44	16	43	45	16	6	1	191	3	3	0	2.3	.985	OF-79, DH-8
1990			89	.231	.308	234	54	5	2	3	1.3	24	24	31	46	15	18	6	149	3	2	1	2.1	.987	OF-63, DH-11
1991			113	.230	.324	256	59	12	3	2	0.8	40	27	38	44	12	14	4	150	3	3	0	1.5	.981	OF-101, DH-3
1992			159	.271	.449	623	169	28	10	21	3.4	100	80	98	98	53	1	0	382	10	8	6	2.5	.980	OF-158
1993			142	.263	.425	560	147	36	8	13	2.3	87	66	82	99	24	1	0	296	7	2	0	2.1	.993	OF-140, DH-2
1994			111	.263	.419	453	119	25	5	12	2.6	78	48	57	75	31	1	0	247	4	1	0	2.3	.996	OF-109
1995			143	.262	.444	554	145	33	10	16	2.9	108	64	87	111	26	0	0	268	1	3	0	1.9	.989	OF-142
8 yrs.			945	.250	.393	3271	817	164	44	72	2.2	512	346	459	593	187	48	11	1926	35	26	8	2.2	.987	OF-882, DH-24

Dave Anderson

ANDERSON, DAVID CARTER BR TR 6′2″ 185 lbs.
B. Aug. 1, 1960, Louisville, Ky.

Year	Team	Lg	Games	BA	SA	AB	H	2B	3B	HR	HR%	R	RBI	BB	SO	SB	Pinch Hit AB	Pinch Hit H	PO	A	E	DP	TC/G	FA	G by Pos
1983	LA	N	61	.165	.261	115	19	4	2	1	0.9	12	2	12	15	6	2	1	56	100	5	19	3.0	.969	SS-53, 3B-1
1984			121	.251	.329	374	94	16	2	3	0.8	51	34	45	55	15	5	0	176	359	19	67	4.5	.966	SS-111, 3B-11
1985			77	.199	.281	221	44	6	0	4	1.8	24	18	35	42	5	4	2	61	187	9	20	3.3	.965	3B-51, SS-25, 2B-2
1986			92	.245	.301	216	53	9	0	1	0.5	31	15	22	39	5	4	1	77	159	11	21	2.7	.955	3B-51, SS-34, 2B-5
1987			108	.234	.313	265	62	12	3	1	0.4	32	13	24	43	9	6	2	103	207	7	33	3.0	.978	SS-65, 3B-35, 2B-5
1988			116	.249	.319	285	71	10	2	2	0.7	31	20	32	45	4	7	2	139	244	5	53	3.7	.987	SS-82, 3B-12, 2B-11
1989			87	.229	.264	140	32	2	0	1	0.7	15	14	17	26	2	25	4	61	73	1	15	2.3	.993	SS-33, 3B-18, 2B-7
1990	SF	N	60	.350	.450	100	35	5	1	1	1.0	14	6	3	20	1	13	6	33	59	1	10	2.0	.989	SS-29, 2B-13, 1B-3, 3B-2
1991			100	.248	.314	226	56	5	2	2	0.9	24	13	12	35	2	29	4	167	127	11	29	3.2	.964	SS-63, 1B-16, 3B-11, 2B-6
1992	LA	N	51	.286	.440	84	24	4	0	3	3.6	10	8	4	11	0	14	6	21	41	4	7	2.0	.939	3B-26, SS-7
10 yrs.			873	.242	.318	2026	490	73	12	19	0.9	244	143	206	331	49	109	28	894	1556	73	274	3.2	.971	SS-502, 3B-218, 2B-49, 1B-19
LEAGUE CHAMPIONSHIP SERIES																									
1985	LA	N	4	.000	.000	5	0	0	0	0	0.0	1	0	3	1	0	0	0	3	4	0	0	1.8	1.000	SS-3, 3B-1
WORLD SERIES																									
1988	LA	N	1	.000	.000	1	0	0	0	0	0.0	0	0	0	1	0	1	0	0	0	0	0	0.0	.000	DH-1

Dwain Anderson

ANDERSON, DWAIN CLEAVEN BR TR 5′11″ 165 lbs.
B. Nov. 23, 1947, Oakland, Calif.

Year	Team	Lg	Games	BA	SA	AB	H	2B	3B	HR	HR%	R	RBI	BB	SO	SB	Pinch Hit AB	Pinch Hit H	PO	A	E	DP	TC/G	FA	G by Pos
1971	OAK	A	16	.270	.378	37	10	2	1	0	0.0	3	3	5	9	0	0	0	20	26	4	4	3.1	.920	SS-10, 2B-5, 3B-1
1972	2 teams	OAK A (3G –.000) STL N (57G –.267)																							
″	total		60	.254	.317	142	36	4	1	1	0.7	14	8	9	27	0	1	0	71	101	8	18	3.1	.956	SS-44, 3B-14, 2B-1
1973	2 teams	STL N (18G –.118) SD N (53G –.121)																							
″	total		71	.121	.121	124	15	0	0	0	0.0	16	3	18	33	2	15	1	46	93	13	15	3.0	.914	SS-42, 3B-6, OF-2
1974	CLE	A	2	.333	.333	3	1	0	0	0	0.0	0	0	0	1	0	0	0	1	0	0	0	1.0	1.000	2B-1
4 yrs.			149	.203	.245	306	62	6	2	1	0.3	33	14	32	70	2	16	1	138	220	25	37	3.0	.935	SS-96, 3B-21, 2B-7, OF-2

Ferrell Anderson

ANDERSON, FERRELL JACK BR TR 6′1″ 200 lbs.
B. Jan. 9, 1918, Maple City, Kans. D. Mar. 12, 1978, Joplin, Mo.

Year	Team	Lg	Games	BA	SA	AB	H	2B	3B	HR	HR%	R	RBI	BB	SO	SB	Pinch Hit AB	Pinch Hit H	PO	A	E	DP	TC/G	FA	G by Pos
1946	BKN	N	79	.256	.337	199	51	10	0	2	1.0	19	14	18	21	1	8	2	258	35	11	5	4.3	.964	C-70
1953	STL	N	18	.286	.343	35	10	2	0	0	0.0	1	1	0	4	0	7	0	32	4	0	0	3.0	1.000	C-12
2 yrs.			97	.261	.338	234	61	12	0	2	0.9	20	15	18	25	1	15	2	290	39	11	5	4.1	.968	C-82

Garret Anderson

ANDERSON, GARRET JOSEPH BL TL 6′3″ 190 lbs.
B. June 30, 1972, Los Angeles, Calif.

Year	Team	Lg	Games	BA	SA	AB	H	2B	3B	HR	HR%	R	RBI	BB	SO	SB	Pinch Hit AB	Pinch Hit H	PO	A	E	DP	TC/G	FA	G by Pos
1994	CAL	A	5	.385	.385	13	5	0	0	0	0.0	0	1	0	2	0	1	1	10	0	0	0	2.5	1.000	OF-4
1995			106	.321	.505	374	120	19	1	16	4.3	50	69	19	65	6	6	1	213	7	5	0	2.2	.978	OF-100, DH-1
2 yrs.			111	.323	.501	387	125	19	1	16	4.1	50	70	19	67	6	7	2	223	7	5	0	2.2	.979	OF-104, DH-1

George Anderson

ANDERSON, GEORGE JENDRUS BL TR 5′8½″ 160 lbs.
Born George Andrew Jendrus.
B. Sept. 26, 1889, Cleveland, Ohio D. May 28, 1962, Cleveland, Ohio.

Year	Team	Lg	Games	BA	SA	AB	H	2B	3B	HR	HR%	R	RBI	BB	SO	SB	Pinch Hit AB	Pinch Hit H	PO	A	E	DP	TC/G	FA	G by Pos
1914	BKN	F	98	.316	.393	364	115	13	3	3	0.8	58	24	31		16	5	0	176	15	11	2	2.2	.946	OF-92
1915			136	.264	.356	511	135	23	9	2	0.4	70	39	52		20	1	0	200	16	10	5	1.7	.956	OF-134
1918	STL	N	35	.295	.402	132	39	4	5	0	0.0	20	6	15	7	0	0	0	62	3	3	1	1.9	.956	OF-35
3 yrs.			269	.287	.375	1007	289	40	17	5	0.5	148	69	98	7	36	6	0	438	34	24	8	1.9	.952	OF-261

Goat Anderson

ANDERSON, EDWARD JOHN BL TR
B. Jan. 13, 1880, Cleveland, Ohio D. Mar. 15, 1923, South Bend, Ind.

Year	Team	Lg	Games	BA	SA	AB	H	2B	3B	HR	HR%	R	RBI	BB	SO	SB	Pinch Hit AB	Pinch Hit H	PO	A	E	DP	TC/G	FA	G by Pos
1907	PIT	N	127	.206	.225	413	85	3	1	1	0.2	73	12	80		27	5	1	215	23	13	5	2.1	.948	OF-117, 2B-5

Hal Anderson

ANDERSON, HAROLD BR TR 5′11″ 160 lbs.
B. Feb. 10, 1904, St. Louis, Mo. D. May 1, 1974, St. Louis, Mo.

Year	Team	Lg	Games	BA	SA	AB	H	2B	3B	HR	HR%	R	RBI	BB	SO	SB	Pinch Hit AB	Pinch Hit H	PO	A	E	DP	TC/G	FA	G by Pos
1932	CHI	A	9	.250	.250	32	8	0	0	0	0.0	4	2	0	1	0	0	0	21	1	0	1	2.4	1.000	OF-9

Harry Anderson

ANDERSON, HARRY WALTER
B. Sept. 10, 1931, North East, Md.
BL TR 6′ 3″ 205 lbs.

Year	Team	Games	BA	SA	AB	H	2B	3B	HR	HR%	R	RBI	BB	SO	SB	Pinch Hit AB	Pinch Hit H	PO	A	E	DP	TC/G	FA	G by Pos
1957	PHI N	118	.268	.453	400	107	15	4	17	4.3	53	61	36	61	2	11	3	213	5	3	1	2.0	.986	OF-109
1958		140	.301	.524	515	155	34	6	23	4.5	80	97	59	**95**	0	10	1	552	33	13	40	4.4	.978	OF-87, 1B-49
1959		142	.240	.402	508	122	28	6	14	2.8	50	63	43	95	1	6	1	283	17	6	4	2.2	.980	OF-137
1960	2 teams	PHI N (38G –.247) CIN N (42G –.167)																						
″	total	80	.214	.358	159	34	5	0	6	3.8	16	21	21	39	0	29	1	203	14	2	9	4.7	.991	1B-27, OF-20
1961	CIN N	4	.250	.250	4	1	0	0	0	0.0	0	0	0	1	0	4	1	0	0	0	0	0.0	—	
5 yrs.		484	.264	.450	1586	419	82	16	60	3.8	199	242	159	291	3	60	7	1251	69	24	54	3.1	.982	OF-353, 1B-76

Jim Anderson

ANDERSON, JAMES LEA
B. Feb. 23, 1957, Los Angeles, Calif.
BR TR 6′ 170 lbs.

Year	Team	Games	BA	SA	AB	H	2B	3B	HR	HR%	R	RBI	BB	SO	SB	Pinch Hit AB	Pinch Hit H	PO	A	E	DP	TC/G	FA	G by Pos
1978	CAL A	48	.194	.259	108	21	7	0	0	0.0	6	7	11	16	0	0	0	72	99	8	21	3.7	.955	SS-47, 2B-1
1979		96	.248	.350	234	58	13	1	3	1.3	33	23	17	31	3	0	0	141	205	17	44	3.6	.953	SS-82, 3B-10, 2B-6, C-3
1980	SEA A	116	.227	.325	317	72	7	0	8	2.5	46	30	27	39	2	8	2	120	255	22	45	3.7	.945	SS-65, 3B-33, DH-5, 2B-2, C-1
1981		70	.204	.284	162	33	7	0	2	1.2	12	19	17	29	3	0	0	88	183	15	45	4.1	.948	SS-68, 3B-2
1983	TEX A	50	.216	.245	102	22	1	1	0	0.0	8	6	5	8	1	0	0	46	102	5	13	2.9	.967	SS-27, 2B-17, OF-3, 3B-3, DH-2, C-1
1984		39	.106	.106	47	5	0	0	0	0.0	2	1	4	7	0	0	0	37	58	1	13	2.5	.990	SS-31, 3B-6, 2B-1
6 yrs.		419	.218	.298	970	211	35	2	13	1.3	107	86	81	130	9	8	2	504	902	68	181	3.5	.954	SS-320, 3B-54, 2B-27, DH-7, C-5, OF-3
LEAGUE CHAMPIONSHIP SERIES																								
1979	CAL A	4	.091	.091	11	1	0	0	0	0.0	0	0	0	1	0	0	0	4	11	0	2	3.8	1.000	SS-4

John Anderson

ANDERSON, JOHN JOSEPH (Terrible Swede)
B. Dec. 14, 1873, Sarpsborg, Norway D. July 23, 1949, Worcester, Mass.
BB TR 6′ 2″ 180 lbs.

Year	Team	Games	BA	SA	AB	H	2B	3B	HR	HR%	R	RBI	BB	SO	SB	Pinch Hit AB	Pinch Hit H	PO	A	E	DP	TC/G	FA	G by Pos
1894	BKN N	17	.302	.460	63	19	1	3	1	1.6	14	19	3	3	7	0	0	22	1	6	0	1.7	.793	OF-16, 3B-1
1895		102	.286	.444	419	120	11	14	9	2.1	76	87	12	29	24	0	0	205	11	29	4	2.4	.882	OF-101
1896		108	.314	.453	430	135	23	17	1	0.2	70	55	18	23	37	1	0	538	28	16	30	5.3	.973	OF-68, 1B-42
1897		117	.325	.455	492	160	28	12	4	0.8	93	85	17		29	0	0	279	12	21	3	2.6	.933	OF-115, 1B-3
1898	2 teams	BKN N (25G –.244) WAS N (110G –.305)																						
″	total	135	.294	**.494**	520	153	33	**22**	9	1.7	82	81	29	0	20	1	0	407	33	22	19	3.4	.952	OF-115, 1B-19
1899	BKN N	117	.269	.362	439	118	18	7	3	0.7	65	92	27		25	3	0	537	30	19	27	5.0	.968	OF-76, 1B-41
1901	MIL A	138	.330	.476	576	190	46	7	8	1.4	90	99	24		35	0	0	1350	67	26	81	10.5	.982	1B-125, OF-13
1902	STL A	126	.284	.385	524	149	29	6	4	0.8	60	85	21		15	0	0	1363	47	22	78	11.1	.985	1B-126, OF-3
1903		138	.284	.385	550	156	34	8	2	0.4	65	78	23		16	0	0	1423	92	22	71	11.0	.986	1B-133, OF-7
1904	NY A	143	.278	.385	558	155	27	12	3	0.5	62	82	23		20	1	1	554	42	15	22	4.2	.975	OF-111, 1B-33
1905	2 teams	NY A (32G –.232) WAS A (93G –.290)																						
″	total	125	.279	.361	499	139	24	7	1	0.2	62	52	30		31	7	1	266	15	13	1	2.5	.956	OF-111, 1B-7
1906	WAS A	151	.271	.343	583	158	25	4	3	0.5	62	70	19		**39**	0	0	286	19	15	2	2.1	.953	OF-151
1907		87	.288	.348	333	96	12	4	0	0.0	33	44	34		19	0	0	671	34	13	13	8.3	.982	1B-61, OF-26
1908	CHI A	123	.262	.315	355	93	17	1	0	0.0	36	47	30		21	25	5	176	13	5	11	2.0	.974	OF-90, 1B-9
14 yrs.		1627	.290	.404	6341	1841	328	124	48	0.8	870	976	310	55	338	38	7	8077	444	244	362	5.5	.972	OF-1003, 1B-599, 3B-1

Kent Anderson

ANDERSON, KENT McKAY
Brother of Mike Anderson.
B. Aug. 12, 1963, Florence, S. C.
BR TR 6′ 1″ 180 lbs.

Year	Team	Games	BA	SA	AB	H	2B	3B	HR	HR%	R	RBI	BB	SO	SB	Pinch Hit AB	Pinch Hit H	PO	A	E	DP	TC/G	FA	G by Pos
1989	CAL A	86	.229	.265	223	51	6	1	0	0.0	27	17	17	42	1	3	0	102	233	10	56	4.1	.971	SS-70, 2B-7, 3B-5, OF-2, DH-1
1990		49	.308	.385	143	44	6	1	1	0.7	16	5	13	19	0	0	0	75	129	9	26	4.3	.958	SS-28, 3B-16, 2B-5
2 yrs.		135	.260	.311	366	95	12	2	1	0.3	43	22	30	61	1	3	0	177	362	19	82	4.2	.966	SS-98, 3B-21, 2B-12, OF-2, DH-1

Mike Anderson

ANDERSON, MICHAEL ALLEN
Brother of Kent Anderson.
B. June 22, 1951, Florence, S. C.
BR TR 6′ 2″ 200 lbs.

Year	Team	Games	BA	SA	AB	H	2B	3B	HR	HR%	R	RBI	BB	SO	SB	Pinch Hit AB	Pinch Hit H	PO	A	E	DP	TC/G	FA	G by Pos
1971	PHI N	26	.247	.393	89	22	5	1	2	2.2	11	5	13	28	0	0	0	67	1	1	0	2.7	.986	OF-26
1972		36	.194	.320	103	20	5	1	2	1.9	8	5	19	36	1	0	0	68	6	1	1	2.1	.987	OF-35
1973		87	.254	.451	193	49	9	1	9	4.7	32	28	19	53	0	26	4	99	4	2	1	1.6	.981	OF-67
1974		145	.251	.354	395	99	22	2	5	1.3	35	34	37	75	2	19	5	240	12	5	3	1.9	.981	OF-133, 1B-1
1975		115	.259	.372	247	64	10	3	4	1.6	24	28	17	66	1	16	5	170	6	4	1	1.7	.978	OF-105, 1B-3
1976	STL N	86	.291	.357	199	58	8	1	1	0.5	17	12	26	30	1	21	7	136	7	3	4	2.3	.979	OF-58, 1B-5
1977		94	.221	.338	154	34	4	1	4	2.6	18	17	14	31	2	20	5	96	4	2	0	1.3	.980	OF-77
1978	BAL A	53	.094	.156	32	3	0	1	0	0.0	2	3	3	10	0	6	0	25	0	1	0	0.6	.962	OF-47
1979	PHI N	79	.231	.321	78	18	4	0	1	1.3	12	2	13	14	1	11	0	68	3	2	1	1.0	.973	OF-70, P-1
9 yrs.		721	.246	.362	1490	367	67	11	28	1.9	159	134	161	343	8	119	26	969	43	21	11	1.6	.980	OF-618, 1B-9, P-1

Sparky Anderson

ANDERSON, GEORGE LEE
B. Feb. 22, 1934, Bridgewater, S. D.
Manager 1970–95.
BR TR 5′ 9″ 170 lbs.

Year	Team	Games	BA	SA	AB	H	2B	3B	HR	HR%	R	RBI	BB	SO	SB	Pinch Hit AB	Pinch Hit H	PO	A	E	DP	TC/G	FA	G by Pos
1959	PHI N	152	.218	.249	477	104	9	3	0	0.0	42	34	42	53	6	0	0	343	403	12	70	5.0	.984	2B-152

Ernie Andres

ANDRES, ERNEST HENRY (Junie)
B. Jan. 11, 1918, Jeffersonville, Ind.
BR TR 6′ 1″ 200 lbs.

Year	Team	Games	BA	SA	AB	H	2B	3B	HR	HR%	R	RBI	BB	SO	SB	Pinch Hit AB	Pinch Hit H	PO	A	E	DP	TC/G	FA	G by Pos
1946	BOS A	15	.098	.146	41	4	2	0	0	0.0	0	1	3	5	0	0	0	8	25	0	1	2.2	1.000	3B-15

Kim Andrew

ANDREW, KIM DARNELL
B. Nov. 14, 1953, Glendale, Calif.
BR TR 5′10″ 160 lbs.

Year	Team	Games	BA	SA	AB	H	2B	3B	HR	HR%	R	RBI	BB	SO	SB	Pinch Hit AB	Pinch Hit H	PO	A	E	DP	TC/G	FA	G by Pos
1975	BOS A	2	.500	.500	2	1	0	0	0	0.0	0	0	0	0	0	0	0	1	1	0	0	1.0	1.000	2B-2

Ed Andrews

ANDREWS, GEORGE EDWARD
B. Apr. 5, 1859, Painesville, Ohio D. Aug. 12, 1934, West Palm Beach, Fla.
BR TR 5′ 8″ 160 lbs.

Year	Team	Games	BA	SA	AB	H	2B	3B	HR	HR%	R	RBI	BB	SO	SB	Pinch Hit AB	Pinch Hit H	PO	A	E	DP	TC/G	FA	G by Pos
1884	PHI N	109	.221	.281	420	93	21	2	0	0.0	74		9	42		0	0	239	326	69	37	5.8	.891	2B-109
1885		103	.266	.316	421	112	15	3	0	0.0	77		32	25		0	0	184	24	22	4	2.2	.904	OF-99, 2B-5
1886		107	.249	.316	437	109	15	4	2	0.5	93	28	31	35		0	0	196	31	26	3	2.4	.897	OF-104, 2B-3
1887		104	.325	.422	464	151	19	7	4	0.9	110	67	21	21	57	0	0	221	28	31	2	2.6	.889	OF-99, 2B-7, 1B-1
1888		124	.239	.297	528	126	14	4	3	0.6	75	44	21	41	35	0	0	210	23	25	5	2.1	.903	OF-124

Ed Andrews *continued*

Year	Team	Games	BA	SA	AB	H	2B	3B	HR	HR%	R	RBI	BB	SO	SB	Pinch Hit AB	Pinch Hit H	PO	A	E	DP	TC/G	FA	G by Pos
1889	2 teams	PHI N (10G –.282)	IND N (40G –.306)																					
"	total	50	.302	.358	212	64	12	0	0	0.0	42	29	7	14	14	0	0	91	12	16	1	2.3	.866	OF-49, 2B-2
1890	BKN P	94	.253	.322	395	100	14	2	3	0.8	84	38	40	32	21	0	0	220	17	23	3	2.8	.912	OF-94
1891	CIN AA	83	.211	.253	356	75	7	4	0	0.0	47	26	33	35	22	0	0	173	25	8	4	2.5	.961	OF-83
8 yrs.		774	.257	.320	3233	830	117	26	12	0.4	602	232	194	245	149	0	0	1534	486	220	59	2.9	.902	OF-652, 2B-126, 1B-1

Fred Andrews

ANDREWS, FRED
B. May 4, 1952, Lafayette, La.
BR TR 5′ 8″ 163 lbs.

Year	Team	Games	BA	SA	AB	H	2B	3B	HR	HR%	R	RBI	BB	SO	SB	Pinch Hit AB	Pinch Hit H	PO	A	E	DP	TC/G	FA	G by Pos
1976	PHI N	4	.667	.667	6	4	0	0	0	0.0	1	0	2	0	1	0	0	7	3	0	1	2.5	1.000	2B-4
1977		12	.174	.261	23	4	0	1	0	0.0	3	2	1	5	1	5	2	16	18	0	6	4.9	1.000	2B-7
2 yrs.		16	.276	.345	29	8	0	1	0	0.0	4	2	3	5	2	5	2	23	21	0	7	4.0	1.000	2B-11

Jim Andrews

ANDREWS, JAMES PRATT
B. June 5, 1865, Shelburne Falls, Mass. D. Dec. 27, 1907, Chicago, Ill.

Year	Team	Games	BA	SA	AB	H	2B	3B	HR	HR%	R	RBI	BB	SO	SB	Pinch Hit AB	Pinch Hit H	PO	A	E	DP	TC/G	FA	G by Pos
1890	CHI N	53	.188	.272	202	38	4	2	3	1.5	32	17	23	41	11	0	0	80	10	10	1	1.9	.900	OF-53

Mike Andrews

ANDREWS, MICHAEL JAY
Brother of Rob Andrews.
B. July 9, 1943, Los Angeles, Calif.
BR TR 6′ 3″ 195 lbs.

Year	Team	Games	BA	SA	AB	H	2B	3B	HR	HR%	R	RBI	BB	SO	SB	Pinch Hit AB	Pinch Hit H	PO	A	E	DP	TC/G	FA	G by Pos
1966	BOS A	5	.167	.167	18	3	0	0	0	0.0	1	0	0	2	0	0	0	11	18	0	2	5.8	1.000	2B-5
1967		142	.263	.352	494	130	20	0	8	1.6	79	40	62	72	7	2	0	305	346	17	63	4.6	.975	2B-139, SS-6
1968		147	.271	.354	536	145	22	1	7	1.3	77	45	81	57	3	5	1	339	383	18	94	5.1	.976	2B-139, SS-4, 3B-1
1969		121	.293	.455	464	136	26	2	15	3.2	79	59	71	53	1	1	0	297	334	18	82	5.4	.972	2B-120
1970		151	.253	.390	589	149	28	1	17	2.9	91	65	81	63	2	3	0	342	350	19	74	4.8	.973	2B-148
1971	CHI A	109	.282	.439	330	93	16	0	12	3.6	45	47	67	36	3	12	4	374	202	21	68	5.9	.965	2B-76, 1B-25
1972		148	.220	.297	505	111	18	0	7	1.4	58	50	70	78	2	1	1	387	327	19	76	4.9	.974	2B-145, 1B-5
1973	2 teams	CHI A (52G –.201)	OAK A (18G –.190)																					
"	total	70	.200	.256	180	36	10	0	0	0.0	11	10	26	29	0	15	1	92	18	1	5	1.8	.991	DH-32, 2B-15, 1B-9, 3B-5
8 yrs.		893	.258	.369	3116	803	140	4	66	2.1	441	316	458	390	18	39	7	2147	1978	113	464	4.8	.973	2B-787, 1B-39, DH-32, SS-10, 3B-6
LEAGUE CHAMPIONSHIP SERIES																								
1973	OAK A	2	.000	.000	1	0	0	0	0	0.0	0	0	0	0	0	0	0	1	0	0	0	0.5	1.000	1B-1, DH-1
WORLD SERIES																								
1967	BOS A	5	.308	.308	13	4	0	0	0	0.0	2	1	0	1	0	2	1	2	6	0	0	2.7	1.000	2B-3
1973	OAK A	2	.000	.000	3	0	0	0	0	0.0	0	0	1	1	0	2	0	1	0	2	0	3.0	.333	2B-1
2 yrs.		7	.250	.250	16	4	0	0	0	0.0	2	1	1	2	0	4	1	3	6	2	0	2.8	.818	2B-4

Rob Andrews

ANDREWS, ROBERT PATRICK
Brother of Mike Andrews.
B. Dec. 11, 1952, Santa Monica, Calif.
BR TR 6′ 185 lbs.

Year	Team	Games	BA	SA	AB	H	2B	3B	HR	HR%	R	RBI	BB	SO	SB	Pinch Hit AB	Pinch Hit H	PO	A	E	DP	TC/G	FA	G by Pos
1975	HOU N	103	.238	.285	277	66	5	4	0	0.0	29	19	31	34	12	1	0	193	249	10	67	4.5	.978	2B-94, SS-6
1976		109	.256	.300	410	105	8	5	0	0.0	42	23	33	27	7	0	0	228	356	14	66	5.4	.977	2B-107, SS-3
1977	SF N	127	.264	.303	436	115	11	3	0	0.0	60	25	56	33	5	9	1	225	314	20	66	4.9	.964	2B-115
1978		79	.220	.288	177	39	3	3	1	0.6	21	11	20	18	5	12	2	123	135	6	23	4.2	.977	2B-62, SS-1
1979		75	.260	.318	154	40	3	0	2	1.3	22	13	8	9	4	22	5	97	102	9	21	3.7	.957	2B-53, 3B-3
5 yrs.		493	.251	.298	1454	365	30	15	3	0.2	174	91	148	121	33	44	8	866	1156	59	243	4.7	.972	2B-431, SS-10, 3B-3

Shane Andrews

ANDREWS, DARRELL SHANE
B. Aug. 28, 1971, Dallas, Tex.
BR TR 6′ 1″ 215 lbs.

Year	Team	Games	BA	SA	AB	H	2B	3B	HR	HR%	R	RBI	BB	SO	SB	Pinch Hit AB	Pinch Hit H	PO	A	E	DP	TC/G	FA	G by Pos
1995	MON N	84	.214	.377	220	47	10	1	8	3.6	27	31	17	68	1	11	1	182	97	7	13	3.6	.976	3B-51, 1B-29

Stan Andrews

ANDREWS, STANLEY JOSEPH (Polo)
Born Stanley Joseph Andruskewicz.
B. Apr. 17, 1917, Lynn, Mass. D. June 10, 1995, Bradenton, Fla.
BR TR 5′11″ 178 lbs.

Year	Team	Games	BA	SA	AB	H	2B	3B	HR	HR%	R	RBI	BB	SO	SB	Pinch Hit AB	Pinch Hit H	PO	A	E	DP	TC/G	FA	G by Pos
1939	BOS N	13	.231	.231	26	6	0	0	0	0.0	1	1	1	2	0	3	1	22	2	4	0	2.8	.857	C-10
1940		19	.182	.182	33	6	0	0	0	0.0	1	2	0	3	1	5	1	29	5	2	0	2.6	.944	C-14
1944	BKN N	4	.125	.125	8	1	0	0	0	0.0	1	1	1	2	0	0	0	10	1	0	0	2.8	1.000	C-4
1945	2 teams	BKN N (21G –.163)	PHI N (13G –.333)																					
"	total	34	.232	.317	82	19	2	1	1	1.2	8	8	6	9	1	1	0	93	18	6	2	3.5	.949	C-33
4 yrs.		70	.215	.262	149	32	2	1	1	0.7	11	12	8	16	2	9	2	154	26	12	2	3.1	.938	C-61

Wally Andrews

ANDREWS, WILLIAM WALTER
B. Sept. 18, 1859, Philadelphia, Pa. D. Jan. 20, 1940, Indianapolis, Ind.
BR TR 6′ 3″ 170 lbs.

Year	Team	Games	BA	SA	AB	H	2B	3B	HR	HR%	R	RBI	BB	SO	SB	Pinch Hit AB	Pinch Hit H	PO	A	E	DP	TC/G	FA	G by Pos
1884	LOU AA	14	.204	.347	49	10	5	1	0	0.0	10		4			0	0	98	12	10	3	8.6	.917	1B-9, 3B-3, OF-1, SS-1
1888		26	.194	.323	93	18	6	3	0	0.0	12	6	13		5	0	0	283	10	1	16	11.3	.997	1B-26
2 yrs.		40	.197	.331	142	28	11	4	0	0.0	22	6	17		5	0	0	381	22	11	19	10.4	.973	1B-35, 3B-3, OF-1, SS-1

Bill Andrus

ANDRUS, WILLIAM MORGAN
B. July 25, 1907, Beaumont, Tex. D. Mar. 12, 1982, Washington, D. C.
BR TR 6′ 185 lbs.

Year	Team	Games	BA	SA	AB	H	2B	3B	HR	HR%	R	RBI	BB	SO	SB	Pinch Hit AB	Pinch Hit H	PO	A	E	DP	TC/G	FA	G by Pos
1931	WAS A	3	.000	.000	7	0	0	0	0	0.0	0	1	0	1	0	1	0	1	2	1	1	2.0	.750	3B-2
1937	PHI N	3	.000	.000	2	0	0	0	0	0.0	0	0	0	2	0	2	0	0	0	0	0	0.0	.000	3B-1
2 yrs.		6	.000	.000	9	0	0	0	0	0.0	0	1	0	3	0	3	0	1	2	1	1	1.3	.750	3B-3

Bill Andrus

ANDRUS, WILLIAM WIMAN
B. Oct. 14, 1858, Orono, Ont., Canada D. June 17, 1935, Miles City, Mont.

Year	Team	Games	BA	SA	AB	H	2B	3B	HR	HR%	R	RBI	BB	SO	SB	Pinch Hit AB	Pinch Hit H	PO	A	E	DP	TC/G	FA	G by Pos
1885	PRO N	1	.000	.000	4	0	0	0	0	0.0	0	0	0	0		0	0	2	3	0	0	5.0	1.000	3B-1

Fred Andrus

ANDRUS, FREDERICK HOTHAM
B. Aug. 23, 1850, Washington, Mich. D. Nov. 10, 1937, Detroit, Mich.
BR TR 6′ 2″ 185 lbs.

Year	Team	Games	BA	SA	AB	H	2B	3B	HR	HR%	R	RBI	BB	SO	SB	Pinch Hit AB	Pinch Hit H	PO	A	E	DP	TC/G	FA	G by Pos
1876	CHI N	8	.306	.389	36	11	3	0	0	0.0	6	2	0	5		0	0	5	0	2	0	0.9	.714	OF-8
1884		1	.200	.200	5	1	0	0	0	0.0	3		1	0		0	0	0	3	0	0	3.0	1.000	P-1
2 yrs.		9	.293	.366	41	12	3	0	0	0.0	9	2	1	5		0	0	5	3	2	0	1.1	.800	OF-8, P-1

Tom Angley

ANGLEY, THOMAS SAMUEL
B. Oct. 2, 1904, Baltimore, Md. D. Oct. 26, 1952, Wichita, Kans.
BL TR 5′ 8″ 190 lbs.

Year	Team	Games	BA	SA	AB	H	2B	3B	HR	HR%	R	RBI	BB	SO	SB	Pinch Hit AB	Pinch Hit H	PO	A	E	DP	TC/G	FA	G by Pos
1929	CHI N	5	.250	.313	16	4	1	0	0	0.0	1	6	2	2	0	0	0	23	7	1	0	6.2	.968	C-5

Pat Ankenman

ANKENMAN, FREDERICK NORMAN
B. Dec. 23, 1912, Houston, Tex. D. Jan. 13, 1989, Houston, Tex.
BR TR 5′ 4″ 125 lbs.

Year	Team	Games	BA	SA	AB	H	2B	3B	HR	HR%	R	RBI	BB	SO	SB	Pinch Hit AB	Pinch Hit H	PO	A	E	DP	TC/G	FA	G by Pos
1936	STL N	1	.000	.000	3	0	0	0	0	0.0	0	0	0	3	0	0	0	2	1	2	0	5.0	.600	SS-1
1943	BKN N	1	.500	.500	2	1	0	0	0	0.0	1	0	0	0	0	0	0	2	2	0	1	4.0	1.000	SS-1
1944		13	.250	.292	24	6	1	0	0	0.0	1	3	0	2	0	0	0	11	23	1	2	2.7	.971	2B-11, SS-2
3 yrs.		15	.241	.276	29	7	1	0	0	0.0	2	3	0	5	0	1	0	15	26	3	3	2.9	.932	2B-11, SS-4

Bill Annis

ANNIS, WILLIAM PERLEY
B. May 24, 1857, Stoneham, Mass. D. June 10, 1923, Kennebunkport, Me.
BR 5′ 7″ 150 lbs.

Year	Team	Games	BA	SA	AB	H	2B	3B	HR	HR%	R	RBI	BB	SO	SB	Pinch Hit AB	Pinch Hit H	PO	A	E	DP	TC/G	FA	G by Pos
1884	BOS N	27	.177	.198	96	17	2	0	0	0.0	17		0	8		0	0	22	5	3	1	1.1	.900	OF-27

Cap Anson

ANSON, ADRIAN CONSTANTINE (Pops, Old Anse)
B. Apr. 11, 1852, Marshalltown, Iowa D. Apr. 14, 1922, Chicago, Ill.
Manager 1879–98.
Hall of Fame 1939.
BR TR 6′ 227 lbs.

Year	Team	Games	BA	SA	AB	H	2B	3B	HR	HR%	R	RBI	BB	SO	SB	Pinch Hit AB	Pinch Hit H	PO	A	E	DP	TC/G	FA	G by Pos
1876	CHI N	66	.356	.440	309	110	9	7	1	0.3	63	59	12	8		0	0	137	147	50	8	4.9	.850	3B-66, C-2
1877		59	.337	.420	255	86	**19**	1	0	0.0	52	32	9	3		0	0	177	118	42	14	4.7	.875	3B-40, C-31
1878		60	.341	.402	261	89	12	2	0	0.0	55	40	13	1		0	0	94	42	25	7	2.6	.845	OF-48, 2B-9, 3B-3, C-3
1879		51	.317	.414	227	72	20	1	0	0.0	40	34	2	2		0	0	620	8	16	26	12.6	.975	1B-51
1880		86	.337	.419	356	120	24	1	1	0.3	54	**74**	14	12		0	0	849	30	25	29	9.8	.972	1B-81, 3B-9, 2B-1, SS-1
1881		84	**.399**	.510	343	**137**	21	7	1	0.3	67	**82**	26	4		0	0	894	43	24	48	11.0	.975	1B-84, C-2, SS-1
1882		82	.362	.500	348	126	29	8	1	0.3	69	**83**	20	7		0	0	813	27	46	42	10.7	.948	1B-82, C-1
1883		98	.308	.419	413	127	36	5	0	0.0	70		18	9		0	0	1034	42	42	59	11.0	.962	1B-98, P-2, OF-1, C-1
1884		112	.335	.543	475	159	30	3	21	4.4	108		29	13		0	0	1216	48	62	86	11.3	.953	1B-112, C-3, P-1, SS-1
1885		112	.310	.461	464	144	**35**	7	7	1.5	100	**114**	34	13		0	0	1255	39	57	62	12.0	.958	1B-112, C-1
1886		125	.371	.544	504	187	35	11	10	2.0	117	**147**	55	19	**29**	0	0	1220	84	53	70	9.9	.961	1B-125, C-12
1887		122	.347	.517	472	164	33	13	7	1.5	107	102	60	18	27	0	0	1233	70	37	75	10.9	.972	1B-122, C-1
1888		134	**.344**	.499	515	177	20	12	12	2.3	101	**84**	47	24	28	0	0	1314	65	20	85	10.4	.986	1B-134
1889		134	.311	.440	518	161	32	7	7	1.4	100	117	86	19	27	0	0	1409	79	27	73	11.3	.982	1B-134
1890		139	.312	.401	504	157	14	5	7	1.4	95	107	**113**	23	29	0	0	1361	56	32	61	10.4	.978	1B-135, C-3, 2B-2
1891		136	.291	.409	540	157	24	8	8	1.5	81	**120**	75	29	17	0	0	1409	80	29	86	11.0	.981	1B-136, C-2
1892		146	.272	.354	559	152	25	9	1	0.2	62	74	67	30	13	0	0	1491	67	44	62	11.0	.973	1B-146
1893		103	.314	.384	398	125	24	2	0	0.0	70	91	68	12	13	1	1	997	44	20	59	10.5	.981	1B-101
1894		83	.395	.542	347	137	28	4	5	1.4	82	99	40	15	17	0	0	743	48	8	52	9.6	.990	1B-82, 2B-1
1895		122	.335	.422	474	159	23	6	2	0.4	87	91	55	23	12	0	0	1176	60	19	82	10.3	.985	1B-122
1896		108	.331	.400	402	133	18	2	2	0.5	72	90	49	10	24	1	0	901	62	20	67	9.1	.980	1B-98, C-10
1897		114	.285	.361	424	121	17	3	3	0.7	67	75	60		11	0	0	969	75	27	69	9.4	.975	1B-103, C-11
22 yrs.		2276	.329	.446	9108	3000	528	124	96	1.1	1719	1715	952	294	247	2	1	21312	1334	725	1222	10.0	.969	1B-2058, 3B-118, C-83, OF-49, 2B-13, P-3, SS-3

Eric Anthony

ANTHONY, ERIC TODD
B. Nov. 8, 1967, San Diego, Calif.
BL TL 6′ 2″ 195 lbs.

Year	Team	Games	BA	SA	AB	H	2B	3B	HR	HR%	R	RBI	BB	SO	SB	Pinch Hit AB	Pinch Hit H	PO	A	E	DP	TC/G	FA	G by Pos
1989	HOU N	25	.180	.410	61	11	2	0	4	6.6	7	7	9	16	0	5	2	34	1	0	0	1.7	1.000	OF-21
1990		84	.192	.351	239	46	8	0	10	4.2	26	29	29	78	5	11	1	124	5	4	0	1.9	.970	OF-71
1991		39	.153	.229	118	18	6	0	1	0.8	11	7	12	41	1	2	0	64	5	1	1	1.9	.986	OF-37
1992		137	.239	.407	440	105	15	1	19	4.3	45	80	38	98	5	22	5	173	6	5	0	1.6	.973	OF-115
1993		145	.249	.397	486	121	19	4	15	3.1	70	66	49	88	3	16	2	233	6	3	0	1.8	.988	OF-131
1994	SEA A	79	.237	.412	262	62	14	1	10	3.8	31	30	23	66	6	9	1	126	4	2	0	1.8	.985	OF-71, DH-4
1995	CIN N	47	.269	.425	134	36	6	0	5	3.7	19	23	13	30	2	9	3	141	12	4	11	3.8	.975	OF-24, 1B-17
7 yrs.		556	.229	.387	1740	399	70	6	64	3.7	209	242	173	417	22	74	14	895	39	19	12	1.9	.980	OF-470, 1B-17, DH-4
LEAGUE CHAMPIONSHIP SERIES																								
1995	CIN N	2	.000	.000	1	0	0	0	0	0.0	0	0	1	1	0	1	0	0	0	0	0	0.0	—	

Joe Antolick

ANTOLICK, JOSEPH
B. Apr. 11, 1916, Hokendauqua, Pa.
BR TR 6′ 185 lbs.

Year	Team	Games	BA	SA	AB	H	2B	3B	HR	HR%	R	RBI	BB	SO	SB	Pinch Hit AB	Pinch Hit H	PO	A	E	DP	TC/G	FA	G by Pos
1944	PHI N	4	.333	.333	6	2	0	0	0	0.0	1	0	1	0	0	1	0	9	1	0	1	3.3	1.000	C-3

John Antonelli

ANTONELLI, JOHN LAWRENCE
B. July 15, 1915, Memphis, Tenn. D. Apr. 18, 1990, Memphis, Tenn.
BR TR 5′10½″ 165 lbs.

Year	Team	Games	BA	SA	AB	H	2B	3B	HR	HR%	R	RBI	BB	SO	SB	Pinch Hit AB	Pinch Hit H	PO	A	E	DP	TC/G	FA	G by Pos
1944	STL N	8	.190	.238	21	4	1	0	0	0.0	0	1	0	4	0	0	0	28	10	0	2	4.8	1.000	1B-3, 3B-3, 2B-2
1945	2 teams STL N (2G –.000) PHI N (125G –.256)																							
″	total	127	.254	.321	507	129	27	2	1	0.2	50	28	24	25	1	2	0	181	251	20	32	3.4	.956	3B-109, 2B-23, SS-1, 1B-1
2 yrs.		135	.252	.318	528	133	28	2	1	0.2	50	29	24	29	1	2	0	209	261	20	34	3.5	.959	3B-112, 2B-25, 1B-4, SS-1

Bill Antonello

ANTONELLO, WILLIAM JAMES
B. May 19, 1927, Brooklyn, N. Y. D. Mar. 4, 1993, Fridley, Minn.
BR TR 5′11″ 185 lbs.

Year	Team	Games	BA	SA	AB	H	2B	3B	HR	HR%	R	RBI	BB	SO	SB	Pinch Hit AB	Pinch Hit H	PO	A	E	DP	TC/G	FA	G by Pos
1953	BKN N	40	.163	.302	43	7	1	1	1	2.3	9	4	2	11	0	8	0	27	0	1	0	1.1	.964	OF-25

Luis Aparicio

APARICIO, LUIS ERNESTO (Little Looie)
Born Luis Ernesto Aparicio (Montiel).
B. Apr. 29, 1934, Maracaibo, Venezuela.
Hall of Fame 1984.
BR TR 5′ 9″ 160 lbs.

Year	Team	Games	BA	SA	AB	H	2B	3B	HR	HR%	R	RBI	BB	SO	SB	Pinch Hit AB	Pinch Hit H	PO	A	E	DP	TC/G	FA	G by Pos
1956	CHI A	152	.266	.341	533	142	19	6	3	0.6	69	56	34	63	**21**	0	0	250	474	35	91	5.0	.954	SS-152
1957		143	.257	.332	575	148	22	6	3	0.5	82	41	52	55	**28**	1	0	246	449	20	85	5.0	.972	SS-142
1958		145	.266	.345	557	148	20	9	2	0.4	76	40	35	38	**29**	0	0	289	463	21	90	5.3	.973	SS-145
1959		152	.257	.332	612	157	18	5	6	1.0	98	51	53	40	**56**	0	0	282	460	23	87	5.0	.970	SS-152
1960		153	.277	.343	600	166	20	7	2	0.3	86	61	43	39	**51**	0	0	305	551	18	117	5.7	.979	SS-153
1961		156	.272	.352	625	170	24	4	6	1.0	90	45	38	33	**53**	0	0	264	487	30	86	5.0	.962	SS-156
1962		153	.241	.334	581	140	23	5	7	1.2	72	40	32	36	**31**	1	0	280	452	20	102	4.9	.973	SS-152

Luis Aparicio *continued*

Year	Team	Games	BA	SA	AB	H	2B	3B	HR	HR%	R	RBI	BB	SO	SB	Pinch Hit AB	Pinch Hit H	PO	A	E	DP	TC/G	FA	G by Pos
1963	BAL A	146	.250	.331	601	150	18	8	5	0.8	73	45	36	35	**40**	0	0	275	403	12	76	4.8	.983	SS-145
1964		146	.266	.363	578	154	20	3	10	1.7	93	37	49	51	**57**	1	0	260	437	15	98	4.9	.979	SS-145
1965		144	.225	.339	564	127	20	10	8	1.4	67	40	46	56	26	1	0	238	439	20	87	4.9	.971	SS-141
1966		151	.276	.366	**659**	182	25	8	6	0.9	97	41	33	42	25	0	0	303	441	17	104	5.0	.978	SS-151
1967		134	.233	.313	546	127	22	5	4	0.7	55	31	29	44	18	2	0	221	333	25	67	4.4	.957	SS-131
1968	CHI A	155	.264	.334	622	164	24	4	4	0.6	55	36	33	43	17	2	0	269	535	19	92	5.3	.977	SS-154
1969		156	.280	.362	599	168	24	5	5	0.8	77	51	66	29	24	1	0	248	563	20	94	5.4	.976	SS-154
1970		146	.313	.404	552	173	29	3	5	0.9	86	43	53	34	8	3	2	251	483	18	99	5.2	.976	SS-146
1971	BOS A	125	.232	.303	491	114	23	0	4	0.8	56	45	35	43	6	2	1	194	338	16	56	4.5	.971	SS-121
1972		110	.257	.351	436	112	26	3	3	0.7	47	39	26	28	3	1	0	183	304	16	54	4.6	.968	SS-109
1973		132	.271	.309	499	135	17	1	0	0.0	56	49	43	33	13	0	0	190	404	21	68	4.7	.966	SS-132
18 yrs.		2599	.262	.343	10230	2677	394	92	83	0.8	1335	791	736	742	506	15	3	4548	8016	366	1553	5.0	.972	SS-2581
WORLD SERIES																								
1959	CHI A	6	.308	.346	26	8	1	0	0	0.0	1	0	2	3	1	0	0	10	16	2	2	4.7	.929	SS-6
1966	BAL A	4	.250	.313	16	4	1	0	0	0.0	0	2	0	0	0	0	0	9	8	0	2	4.3	1.000	SS-4
2 yrs.		10	.286	.333	42	12	2	0	0	0.0	1	2	2	3	1	0	0	19	24	2	4	4.5	.956	SS-10

Luke Appling

APPLING, LUCIUS BENJAMIN (Old Aches and Pains) BR TR 5′10″ 183 lbs.
B. Apr. 2, 1907, High Point, N. C. D. Jan. 3, 1991, Cumming, Ga.
Manager 1967.
Hall of Fame 1964.

Year	Team	Games	BA	SA	AB	H	2B	3B	HR	HR%	R	RBI	BB	SO	SB	Pinch Hit AB	Pinch Hit H	PO	A	E	DP	TC/G	FA	G by Pos
1930	CHI A	6	.308	.385	26	8	2	0	0	0.0	2	2	0	0	2	0	0	12	17	4	1	5.5	.879	SS-6
1931		96	.232	.313	297	69	13	4	1	0.3	36	28	29	27	9	12	3	151	233	43	39	5.5	.899	SS-76, 2B-1
1932		139	.274	.374	489	134	20	10	3	0.6	66	63	40	36	9	7	3	270	419	49	84	5.7	.934	SS-85, 2B-30, 3B-14
1933		151	.322	.443	612	197	36	10	6	1.0	90	85	56	29	6	0	0	314	534	55	107	6.0	.939	SS-151
1934		118	.303	.405	452	137	28	6	2	0.4	75	61	59	27	3	0	0	264	357	35	59	5.6	.947	SS-110, 2B-8
1935		153	.307	.389	525	161	28	6	1	0.2	94	71	122	40	12	0	0	335	556	39	93	6.1	.958	SS-153
1936		138	**.388**	.508	526	204	31	7	6	1.1	111	128	85	25	10	1	0	320	471	41	119	6.1	.951	SS-137
1937		154	.317	.439	574	182	42	8	4	0.7	98	77	86	28	18	0	0	280	541	49	111	5.6	.944	SS-154
1938		81	.303	.350	294	89	14	0	0	0.0	41	44	42	17	1	2	1	149	258	20	37	5.5	.953	SS-78
1939		148	.314	.368	516	162	16	6	0	0.0	82	56	105	37	16	0	0	289	461	39	78	5.3	.951	SS-148
1940		150	.348	.442	566	197	27	13	0	0.0	96	79	69	35	3	0	0	307	436	37	83	5.2	.953	SS-150
1941		154	.314	.390	592	186	26	8	1	0.2	93	57	82	32	12	0	0	294	473	42	95	5.3	.948	SS-154
1942		142	.262	.341	543	142	26	4	3	0.6	78	53	63	23	17	0	0	269	418	38	77	5.1	.948	SS-141
1943		155	**.328**	.407	585	192	33	2	3	0.5	63	80	90	29	27	0	0	300	500	36	115	5.4	.957	SS-155
1945		18	.362	.517	58	21	2	2	1	1.7	12	10	12	7	1	1	0	37	56	7	7	5.9	.930	SS-17
1946		149	.309	.378	582	180	27	5	1	0.2	59	55	71	41	6	0	0	252	505	39	99	5.3	.951	SS-149
1947		139	.306	.412	503	154	29	0	8	1.6	67	49	64	28	8	7	0	233	423	35	86	5.3	.949	SS-129, 3B-2
1948		139	.314	.354	497	156	16	2	0	0.0	63	47	94	35	10	3	1	217	373	35	63	4.6	.944	3B-72, SS-64
1949		142	.301	.394	492	148	21	5	5	1.0	82	58	121	24	7	1	0	253	450	26	95	5.2	.964	SS-141
1950		50	.234	.320	128	30	3	4	0	0.0	11	13	12	8	2	15	1	128	62	3	29	5.7	.984	SS-20, 1B-13, 2B-1
20 yrs.		2422	.310	.398	8857	2749	440	102	45	0.5	1319	1116	1302	528	179	49	9	4674	7543	672	1477	5.5	.948	SS-2218, 3B-88, 2B-40, 1B-13

Angel Aragon

ARAGON, ANGEL (Bing, Pete) BR TR 5′ 5″ 150 lbs.
Born Angel Aragon (Valdes).
Father of Jack Aragon.
B. Aug. 2, 1890, Havana, Cuba D. Jan. 24, 1952, New York, N. Y.

Year	Team	Games	BA	SA	AB	H	2B	3B	HR	HR%	R	RBI	BB	SO	SB	Pinch Hit AB	Pinch Hit H	PO	A	E	DP	TC/G	FA	G by Pos
1914	NY A	6	.143	.143	7	1	0	0	0	0.0	1	0	1	2	0	5	1	0	0	0	0	0.0	.000	OF-1
1916		13	.185	.185	27	5	0	0	0	0.0	3	3	2	2	2	1	0	7	18	3	0	2.5	.893	3B-8, OF-3
1917		14	.067	.089	45	3	1	0	0	0.0	2	2	2	2	0	2	0	22	13	1	2	3.0	.972	OF-6, 3B-4, SS-2
3 yrs.		33	.114	.127	79	9	1	0	0	0.0	6	5	5	6	2	8	1	29	31	4	2	2.7	.938	3B-12, OF-10, SS-2

Jack Aragon

ARAGON, ANGEL VALDES BR TR 5′10″ 176 lbs.
Born Angel Valdes Aragon (Reyes).
Son of Angel Aragon.
B. Nov. 20, 1915, Havana, Cuba D. Apr. 4, 1988, Clearwater, Fla.

Year	Team	Games	BA	SA	AB	H	2B	3B	HR	HR%	R	RBI	BB	SO	SB	Pinch Hit AB	Pinch Hit H	PO	A	E	DP	TC/G	FA	G by Pos
1941	NY N	1	—	—	0	0	0	0	0	—	0	0	0	0	0	0	0	0	0	0	0	0.0	—	

Maurice Archdeacon

ARCHDEACON, MAURICE JOHN (Comet, Flash) BL TL 5′ 8″ 153 lbs.
B. Dec. 14, 1898, St. Louis, Mo. D. Sept. 5, 1954, St. Louis, Mo.

Year	Team	Games	BA	SA	AB	H	2B	3B	HR	HR%	R	RBI	BB	SO	SB	Pinch Hit AB	Pinch Hit H	PO	A	E	DP	TC/G	FA	G by Pos
1923	CHI A	22	.402	.483	87	35	5	1	0	0.0	23	4	6	8	2	1	0	44	1	4	0	2.5	.918	OF-20
1924		95	.319	.372	288	92	9	3	0	0.0	59	25	40	30	11	14	5	173	8	8	2	2.5	.958	OF-77
1925		10	.111	.111	9	1	0	0	0	0.0	2	0	2	1	0	8	1	2	0	0	0	2.0	1.000	OF-1
3 yrs.		127	.333	.391	384	128	14	4	0	0.0	84	29	48	39	13	23	6	219	9	12	2	2.4	.950	OF-98

Jimmy Archer

ARCHER, JAMES PETER BR TR 5′10″ 168 lbs.
B. May 13, 1883, Dublin, Ireland D. Mar. 29, 1958, Milwaukee, Wis.

Year	Team	Games	BA	SA	AB	H	2B	3B	HR	HR%	R	RBI	BB	SO	SB	Pinch Hit AB	Pinch Hit H	PO	A	E	DP	TC/G	FA	G by Pos
1904	PIT N	7	.150	.150	20	3	0	0	0	0.0	1	1	0		0	0	0	25	9	3	0	4.6	.919	C-7, OF-1
1907	DET A	18	.119	.119	42	5	0	0	0	0.0	6	0	4		0	0	0	64	20	3	0	4.8	.966	C-17, 2B-1
1909	CHI N	80	.230	.291	261	60	9	2	1	0.4	31	30	12		5	0	0	408	97	21	7	6.6	.960	C-80
1910		98	.259	.371	313	81	17	6	2	0.6	36	41	14	49	6	8	3	620	97	20	31	8.3	.973	C-49, 1B-40
1911		116	.253	.357	387	98	18	5	4	1.0	41	41	18	43	5	3	0	560	128	15	17	6.2	.979	C-102, 1B-10, 2B-1
1912		120	.283	.384	385	109	20	2	5	1.3	35	58	22	36	7	1	0	504	149	23	15	5.7	.966	C-118
1913		110	.267	.360	367	98	14	7	2	0.5	38	44	19	27	4	3	1	512	143	21	10	6.1	.969	C-103, 1B-8
1914		79	.258	.310	248	64	9	2	0	0.0	17	19	9	9	1	3	1	367	105	13	8	6.4	.973	C-76
1915		97	.243	.320	309	75	11	5	1	0.3	21	27	11	38	5	5	2	447	126	13	11	6.7	.978	C-88
1916		77	.220	.283	205	45	6	2	1	0.5	11	30	12	24	3	16	2	236	84	7	5	5.0	.979	C-65, 3B-1
1917		2	.000	.000	2	0	0	0	0	0.0	0	0	0	1	0	2	0	0	0	0	0	0.0	—	
1918	3 teams	PIT N (24G –.155)	BKN N (9G –.273)	CIN N (9G –.269)																				
"	total	42	.208	.283	106	22	2	3	0	0.0	10	5	3	14	0	5	1	117	54	3	8	4.7	.983	C-35, 1B-2
12 yrs.		846	.250	.333	2645	660	106	34	16	0.6	247	296	124	241	36	46	10	3860	1012	142	112	6.2	.972	C-740, 1B-60, 2B-2, 3B-1, OF-1

Jimmy Archer *continued*

WORLD SERIES

Year	Team	Games	BA	SA	AB	H	2B	3B	HR	HR%	R	RBI	BB	SO	SB	Pinch Hit AB	Pinch Hit H	PO	A	E	DP	TC/G	FA	G by Pos
1907	DET A	1	.000	.000	3	0	0	0	0	0.0	0	0	0	1	0	0	0	4	1	0	0	5.0	1.000	C-1
1910	CHI N	3	.182	.273	11	2	1	0	0	0.0	1	0	0	4	0	0	0	36	7	0	2	14.3	1.000	C-2, 1B-1
2 yrs.		4	.143	.214	14	2	1	0	0	0.0	1	0	0	5	0	0	0	40	8	0	2	12.0	1.000	C-3, 1B-1

George Archie

ARCHIE, GEORGE ALBERT
B. Apr. 27, 1914, Nashville, Tenn.
BR TR 6′ 170 lbs.

Year	Team	Games	BA	SA	AB	H	2B	3B	HR	HR%	R	RBI	BB	SO	SB	Pinch Hit AB	Pinch Hit H	PO	A	E	DP	TC/G	FA	G by Pos
1938	DET A	3	.000	.000	2	0	0	0	0	0.0	0	0	0	1	0	2	0	0	0	0	0	0.0	—	
1941	2 teams	WAS A (105G –.269)	STL A (9G –.379)																					
″	total	114	.277	.375	408	113	23	4	3	0.7	48	53	37	45	10	9	1	341	174	19	36	5.1	.964	3B-73, 1B-31
1946	STL A	4	.182	.273	11	2	1	0	0	0.0	1	0	0	1	0	0	0	34	6	0	6	13.3	1.000	1B-3
3 yrs.		121	.273	.371	421	115	24	4	3	0.7	49	53	37	47	10	11	1	375	180	19	42	5.4	.967	3B-73, 1B-34

Jose Arcia

ARCIA, JOSE RAIMUNDO (Flaco)
Born Jose Raimundo Arcia (Orta).
B. Aug. 22, 1943, Havana, Cuba.
BR TR 6′ 3″ 170 lbs.

Year	Team	Games	BA	SA	AB	H	2B	3B	HR	HR%	R	RBI	BB	SO	SB	Pinch Hit AB	Pinch Hit H	PO	A	E	DP	TC/G	FA	G by Pos
1968	CHI N	59	.190	.274	84	16	4	0	1	1.2	15	8	3	24	0	5	1	49	34	2	3	2.4	.976	OF-17, 2B-10, SS-7, 3B-1
1969	SD N	120	.215	.272	302	65	11	3	0	0.0	35	10	14	47	14	0	0	194	237	15	44	3.8	.966	2B-68, SS-37, 3B-8, OF-4, 1B-1
1970		114	.223	.288	229	51	9	3	0	0.0	28	17	12	36	3	1	0	137	189	15	47	3.3	.956	SS-67, 2B-20, 3B-9, OF-7
3 yrs.		293	.215	.278	615	132	24	6	1	0.2	78	35	29	107	17	6	1	380	460	32	94	3.4	.963	SS-111, 2B-98, OF-28, 3B-18, 1B-1

Dan Ardell

ARDELL, DANIEL MIERS
B. May 27, 1941, Seattle, Wash.
BL TL 6′ 2″ 190 lbs.

Year	Team	Games	BA	SA	AB	H	2B	3B	HR	HR%	R	RBI	BB	SO	SB	Pinch Hit AB	Pinch Hit H	PO	A	E	DP	TC/G	FA	G by Pos
1961	LA A	7	.250	.250	4	1	0	0	0	0.0	1	0	1	2	0	2	1	13	0	0	1	13.0	1.000	1B-1

Joe Ardner

ARDNER, JOSEPH A. (Old Hoss)
B. Feb. 27, 1858, Mt. Vernon, Ohio D. Sept. 15, 1935, Cleveland, Ohio.
BR TR 160 lbs.

Year	Team	Games	BA	SA	AB	H	2B	3B	HR	HR%	R	RBI	BB	SO	SB	Pinch Hit AB	Pinch Hit H	PO	A	E	DP	TC/G	FA	G by Pos
1884	CLE N	26	.174	.207	92	16	1	1	0	0.0	6	4	1	24		0	0	55	71	20	6	5.6	.863	2B-25, 3B-1
1890		84	.223	.269	323	72	13	1	0	0.0	28	35	17	40	9	0	0	205	257	40	42	6.0	.920	2B-84
2 yrs.		110	.212	.255	415	88	14	2	0	0.0	34	39	18	64	9	0	0	260	328	60	48	5.9	.907	2B-109, 3B-1

Hank Arft

ARFT, HENRY IRVEN (Bow Wow)
B. Jan. 28, 1922, Manchester, Mo.
BL TL 5′10½″ 190 lbs.

Year	Team	Games	BA	SA	AB	H	2B	3B	HR	HR%	R	RBI	BB	SO	SB	Pinch Hit AB	Pinch Hit H	PO	A	E	DP	TC/G	FA	G by Pos
1948	STL A	69	.238	.363	248	59	10	3	5	2.0	25	38	45	43	1	0	0	598	43	3	81	9.3	.995	1B-69
1949		6	.200	.400	5	1	1	0	0	0.0	1	2	0	1	0	5	1	0	0	0	0	0.0	—	
1950		98	.268	.364	280	75	16	4	1	0.4	45	32	46	48	3	13	3	701	51	4	59	9.0	.995	1B-84
1951		112	.261	.397	345	90	16	5	7	2.0	44	42	41	34	4	15	5	820	86	10	100	9.4	.989	1B-97
1952		15	.143	.321	28	4	3	1	0	0.0	1	4	5	7	0	5	0	63	4	1	11	6.8	.985	1B-10
5 yrs.		300	.253	.375	906	229	46	13	13	1.4	116	118	137	133	8	38	9	2182	184	18	251	9.2	.992	1B-260

Alex Arias

ARIAS, ALEJANDRO
B. Nov. 20, 1967, New York, N. Y.
BR TR 6′ 3″ 185 lbs.

Year	Team	Games	BA	SA	AB	H	2B	3B	HR	HR%	R	RBI	BB	SO	SB	Pinch Hit AB	Pinch Hit H	PO	A	E	DP	TC/G	FA	G by Pos
1992	CHI N	32	.293	.354	99	29	6	0	0	0.0	14	7	11	13	0	0	0	43	74	4	8	4.0	.967	SS-30
1993	FLA N	96	.269	.321	249	67	5	1	2	0.8	27	20	27	18	1	25	4	94	144	6	25	3.5	.975	2B-30, 3B-22, SS-18
1994		59	.239	.283	113	27	5	0	0	0.0	4	15	9	19	0	27	9	37	52	2	9	2.6	.978	SS-20, 3B-15
1995		94	.269	.370	216	58	9	2	3	1.4	22	26	22	20	1	38	12	57	127	9	21	3.1	.953	SS-36, 3B-21, 2B-6
4 yrs.		281	.267	.335	677	181	25	3	5	0.7	67	68	69	70	2	90	25	231	397	21	63	3.3	.968	SS-104, 3B-58, 2B-36

Buzz Arlett

ARLETT, RUSSELL LORIS
B. Jan. 3, 1899, Elmhurst, Calif. D. May 16, 1964, Minneapolis, Minn.
BB TR 6′ 3½″ 225 lbs.

Year	Team	Games	BA	SA	AB	H	2B	3B	HR	HR%	R	RBI	BB	SO	SB	Pinch Hit AB	Pinch Hit H	PO	A	E	DP	TC/G	FA	G by Pos
1931	PHI N	121	.313	.538	418	131	26	7	18	4.3	65	72	45	39	3	14	4	303	21	13	11	3.1	.961	OF-94, 1B-13

Marcos Armas

ARMAS, MARCOS RAFAEL
Born Marcos Rafael Armas (Ruiz).
Brother of Tony Armas.
B. Aug. 5, 1969, Puerto Piritu, Venezuela.
BR TR 6′ 5″ 190 lbs.

Year	Team	Games	BA	SA	AB	H	2B	3B	HR	HR%	R	RBI	BB	SO	SB	Pinch Hit AB	Pinch Hit H	PO	A	E	DP	TC/G	FA	G by Pos
1993	OAK A	15	.194	.355	31	6	2	0	1	3.2	7	1	1	12	1	2	0	77	4	0	4	5.4	1.000	1B-12, DH-2, OF-1

Tony Armas

ARMAS, ANTONIO RAFAEL
Born Antonio Rafael Armas (Machado).
Brother of Marcos Armas.
B. July 2, 1953, Anzoatequi, Venezuela.
BR TR 5′11″ 182 lbs.

Year	Team	Games	BA	SA	AB	H	2B	3B	HR	HR%	R	RBI	BB	SO	SB	Pinch Hit AB	Pinch Hit H	PO	A	E	DP	TC/G	FA	G by Pos
1976	PIT N	4	.333	.333	6	2	0	0	0	0.0	0	1	0	2	0	2	0	3	0	0	0	1.5	1.000	OF-2
1977	OAK A	118	.240	.380	363	87	8	2	13	3.6	26	53	20	99	1	7	0	294	9	6	4	2.7	.981	OF-112, SS-1
1978		91	.213	.272	239	51	6	1	2	0.8	17	13	10	62	1	4	0	214	3	2	0	2.5	.991	OF-85, DH-3
1979		80	.248	.421	278	69	9	3	11	4.0	29	34	16	67	1	0	0	194	7	5	2	2.6	.976	OF-80
1980		158	.279	.500	628	175	18	8	35	5.6	87	109	29	128	5	0	0	374	17	10	2	2.5	.975	OF-158
1981		109	.261	.480	440	115	24	3	**22**	5.0	51	76	19	**115**	5	0	0	259	8	2	2	2.5	.993	OF-109
1982		138	.233	.433	536	125	19	2	28	5.2	58	89	33	128	2	2	0	333	9	6	1	2.6	.983	OF-135, DH-1
1983	BOS A	145	.218	.453	574	125	23	2	36	6.3	77	107	29	131	0	2	0	326	5	5	0	2.3	.985	OF-116, DH-27
1984		157	.268	.531	639	171	29	5	**43**	6.7	107	**123**	32	**156**	1	0	0	329	4	9	2	2.2	.974	OF-126, DH-31
1985		103	.265	.514	385	102	17	5	23	6.0	50	64	18	90	0	5	1	173	3	3	1	1.8	.983	OF-79, DH-19
1986		121	.264	.409	425	112	21	4	11	2.6	40	58	24	77	0	4	1	247	4	8	0	2.2	.969	OF-117, DH-1
1987	CAL A	28	.198	.370	81	16	3	1	3	3.7	8	9	1	11	1	6	2	36	0	0	0	1.3	1.000	OF-27
1988		120	.272	.443	368	100	20	2	13	3.5	42	49	22	87	1	9	2	212	5	3	1	1.9	.986	OF-113, DH-5
1989		60	.257	.465	202	52	7	1	11	5.4	22	30	7	48	0	9	2	101	5	2	3	2.0	.981	OF-47, DH-6, 1B-2
14 yrs.		1432	.252	.453	5164	1302	204	39	251	4.9	614	815	260	1201	18	50	8	3095	79	61	18	2.3	.981	OF-1306, DH-93, 1B-2, SS-1

DIVISIONAL PLAYOFF SERIES

Year	Team	Games	BA	SA	AB	H	2B	3B	HR	HR%	R	RBI	BB	SO	SB	Pinch Hit AB	Pinch Hit H	PO	A	E	DP	TC/G	FA	G by Pos
1981	OAK A	3	.545	.727	11	6	2	0	0	0.0	1	3	1	1	0	0	0	6	0	1	0	2.3	.857	OF-3

Tony Armas *continued*

Year	Team	Games	BA	SA	AB	H	2B	3B	HR	HR%	R	RBI	BB	SO	SB	Pinch Hit AB	Pinch Hit H	PO	A	E	DP	TC/G	FA	G by Pos
LEAGUE CHAMPIONSHIP SERIES																								
1981	OAK A	3	.167	.167	12	2	0	0	0	0.0	0	0	0	5	0	0	0	5	2	0	0	2.3	1.000	OF-3
1986	BOS A	5	.125	.188	16	2	1	0	0	0.0	1	0	0	2	0	0	0	12	0	0	0	2.4	1.000	OF-5
2 yrs.		8	.143	.179	28	4	1	0	0	0.0	1	0	0	7	0	0	0	17	2	0	0	2.4	1.000	OF-8
WORLD SERIES																								
1986	BOS A	1	.000	.000	1	0	0	0	0	0.0	0	0	0	1	0	1	0	0	0	0	0	0.0	—	

Ed Armbrister

ARMBRISTER, EDISON ROSANDA BR TR 5′11″ 160 lbs.
B. July 4, 1948, Nassau, Bahamas.

Year	Team	Games	BA	SA	AB	H	2B	3B	HR	HR%	R	RBI	BB	SO	SB	Pinch Hit AB	Pinch Hit H	PO	A	E	DP	TC/G	FA	G by Pos
1973	CIN N	18	.216	.432	37	8	3	1	1	2.7	5	5	2	8	0	5	1	21	1	2	0	1.7	.917	OF-14
1974		9	.286	.286	7	2	0	0	0	0.0	0	0	1	1	0	5	2	1	0	0	0	0.3	1.000	OF-4
1975		59	.185	.200	65	12	1	0	0	0.0	9	2	5	19	3	28	7	13	0	2	0	0.8	.867	OF-19
1976		73	.295	.462	78	23	3	2	2	2.6	20	7	6	22	7	27	7	31	4	1	1	1.1	.972	OF-32
1977		65	.256	.423	78	20	4	3	1	1.3	12	5	10	21	5	24	5	25	3	3	1	1.1	.903	OF-27
5 yrs.		224	.245	.377	265	65	11	6	4	1.5	46	19	24	71	15	89	22	91	8	8	2	1.1	.925	OF-96
LEAGUE CHAMPIONSHIP SERIES																								
1973	CIN N	3	.167	.167	6	1	0	0	0	0.0	0	0	0	5	0	2	0	3	0	0	0	3.0	1.000	OF-1
1975		1	—	—	0	0	0	0	0	—	0	1	0	0	0	0	0	0	0	0	0	0.0	—	
1976		1	—	—	0	0	0	0	0	—	0	0	0	0	0	0	0	0	0	0	0	0.0	—	
3 yrs.		5	.167	.167	6	1	0	0	0	0.0	0	1	0	5	0	2	0	3	0	0	0	3.0	1.000	OF-1
WORLD SERIES																								
1975	CIN N	5	.000	.000	1	0	0	0	0	0.0	1	0	2	0	0	1	0	0	0	0	0	0.0	—	

Charlie Armbruster

ARMBRUSTER, CHARLES A. BR TR 5′ 9″ 180 lbs.
B. Aug. 30, 1880, Cincinnati, Ohio D. Oct. 7, 1964, Grants Pass, Ore.

Year	Team	Games	BA	SA	AB	H	2B	3B	HR	HR%	R	RBI	BB	SO	SB	Pinch Hit AB	Pinch Hit H	PO	A	E	DP	TC/G	FA	G by Pos
1905	BOS A	35	.198	.242	91	18	4	0	0	0.0	13	6	18		3	0	0	154	30	11	0	5.6	.944	C-35
1906		72	.144	.184	201	29	6	1	0	0.0	9	6	25		2	4	0	270	100	17	6	5.8	.956	C-66, 1B-1
1907	2 teams	BOS A (23G –.100) CHI A (1G –.000)																						
″	total	24	.095	.111	63	6	1	0	0	0.0	2	0	9		1	1	0	89	37	8	4	6.1	.940	C-22
3 yrs.		131	.149	.186	355	53	11	1	0	0.0	24	12	52		6	5	0	513	167	36	10	5.8	.950	C-123, 1B-1

Harry Armbruster

ARMBRUSTER, HARRY (Buster) BL TL 5′10″ 190 lbs.
B. Mar. 2, 1882, Cincinnati, Ohio D. Dec. 10, 1953, Cincinnati, Ohio.

Year	Team	Games	BA	SA	AB	H	2B	3B	HR	HR%	R	RBI	BB	SO	SB	Pinch Hit AB	Pinch Hit H	PO	A	E	DP	TC/G	FA	G by Pos
1906	PHI A	91	.238	.306	265	63	6	3	2	0.8	40	24	43		13	12	3	124	9	4	1	1.9	.971	OF-74

George Armstrong

ARMSTRONG, NOBLE GEORGE (Dodo) BR TR 5′10″ 190 lbs.
B. June 3, 1924, Orange, N. J. D. July 24, 1993, Orange, New Jersey.

Year	Team	Games	BA	SA	AB	H	2B	3B	HR	HR%	R	RBI	BB	SO	SB	Pinch Hit AB	Pinch Hit H	PO	A	E	DP	TC/G	FA	G by Pos
1946	PHI A	8	.167	.333	6	1	1	0	0	0.0	0	0	1	1	0	4	1	4	1	0	1	1.3	1.000	C-4

Harry Arndt

ARNDT, HARRY J. TR
B. Feb. 12, 1879, South Bend, Ind. D. Mar. 25, 1921, South Bend, Ind.

Year	Team	Games	BA	SA	AB	H	2B	3B	HR	HR%	R	RBI	BB	SO	SB	Pinch Hit AB	Pinch Hit H	PO	A	E	DP	TC/G	FA	G by Pos
1902	2 teams	DET A (10G –.147) BAL A (68G –.254)																						
″	total	78	.241	.323	282	68	7	5	2	0.7	45	35	41		9	0	0	136	25	18	1	2.2	.899	OF-72, 2B-4, 3B-2, 1B-1, SS-1
1905	STL N	113	.243	.313	415	101	11	6	2	0.5	41	36	24		13	2	1	206	285	23	26	4.6	.955	2B-90, OF-9, 3B-7, SS-5
1906		69	.270	.391	256	69	7	9	2	0.8	30	26	19		5	1	0	116	139	9	16	3.9	.966	3B-65, 1B-1, OF-1
1907		11	.188	.219	32	6	1	0	0	0.0	3	2	1		0	4	1	36	9	1	3	6.6	.978	1B-4, 3B-3
4 yrs.		271	.248	.333	985	244	26	20	6	0.6	119	99	85		27	7	2	494	458	51	46	3.8	.949	2B-94, OF-82, 3B-77, 1B-6, SS-6

Larry Arndt

ARNDT, LARRY WAYNE BR TR 6′ 1″ 195 lbs.
B. Feb. 25, 1963, Fremont, Ohio.

Year	Team	Games	BA	SA	AB	H	2B	3B	HR	HR%	R	RBI	BB	SO	SB	Pinch Hit AB	Pinch Hit H	PO	A	E	DP	TC/G	FA	G by Pos
1989	OAK A	2	.167	.167	6	1	0	0	0	0.0	1	0	0	1	0	0	0	8	2	0	3	5.0	1.000	3B-1, 1B-1

Chris Arnold

ARNOLD, CHRISTOPHER PAUL BR TR 5′10″ 160 lbs.
B. Nov. 6, 1947, Long Beach, Calif.

Year	Team	Games	BA	SA	AB	H	2B	3B	HR	HR%	R	RBI	BB	SO	SB	Pinch Hit AB	Pinch Hit H	PO	A	E	DP	TC/G	FA	G by Pos
1971	SF N	6	.231	.462	13	3	0	0	1	7.7	2	3	1	2	0	4	1	4	7	1	0	4.0	.917	2B-3
1972		51	.226	.321	84	19	3	1	1	1.2	8	4	8	12	0	21	4	24	50	2	5	2.7	.974	3B-17, 2B-7, SS-4
1973		49	.296	.389	54	16	2	0	1	1.9	7	13	8	11	0	36	12	16	2	1	0	1.7	.947	C-9, 2B-1, 3B-1
1974		78	.241	.333	174	42	7	3	1	0.6	22	26	15	27	1	38	9	72	94	5	19	4.4	.971	2B-31, 3B-7, SS-1
1975		29	.195	.195	41	8	0	0	0	0.0	4	0	4	8	0	17	3	10	8	1	5	2.4	.947	OF-4, 2B-4
1976		60	.217	.246	69	15	0	1	0	0.0	4	5	6	16	0	45	12	14	29	1	4	3.1	.977	2B-8, 3B-4, SS-1, 1B-1
6 yrs.		273	.237	.315	435	103	12	5	4	0.9	47	51	42	76	1	161	41	140	190	11	33	3.3	.968	2B-54, 3B-29, C-9, SS-6, OF-4, 1B-1

Morrie Arnovich

ARNOVICH, MORRIS (Snooker) BR TR 5′10″ 168 lbs.
B. Nov. 16, 1910, Superior, Wis. D. July 20, 1959, Superior, Wis.

Year	Team	Games	BA	SA	AB	H	2B	3B	HR	HR%	R	RBI	BB	SO	SB	Pinch Hit AB	Pinch Hit H	PO	A	E	DP	TC/G	FA	G by Pos
1936	PHI N	13	.313	.438	48	15	3	0	1	2.1	4	7	1	3	0	0	0	37	1	0	0	2.9	1.000	OF-13
1937		117	.290	.449	410	119	27	4	10	2.4	60	60	34	32	5	9	2	237	10	7	5	2.4	.972	OF-107
1938		139	.275	.357	502	138	29	0	4	0.8	47	72	42	37	2	6	0	327	18	6	0	2.6	.983	OF-133
1939		134	.324	.413	491	159	25	2	5	1.0	68	67	58	28	7	2	1	335	10	6	0	2.7	.983	OF-132
1940	2 teams	PHI N (39G –.199) CIN N (62G –.284)																						
″	total	101	.250	.301	352	88	12	3	0	0.0	30	33	27	25	1	4	1	220	8	4	0	2.4	.983	OF-97
1941	NY N	85	.280	.377	207	58	8	3	2	1.0	25	22	23	14	2	20	5	103	5	2	0	1.8	.982	OF-61
1946		1	.000	.000	3	0	0	0	0	0.0	0	0	0	0	0	0	0	1	0	0	0	1.0	1.000	OF-1
7 yrs.		590	.287	.383	2013	577	104	12	22	1.1	234	261	185	139	17	41	9	1260	52	25	5	2.5	.981	OF-544
WORLD SERIES																								
1940	CIN N	1	.000	.000	1	0	0	0	0	0.0	0	0	0	0	0	1	0	2	0	0	0	2.0	1.000	OF-1

Tug Arundel

ARUNDEL, JOHN THOMAS
B. June 30, 1862, Auburn, N. Y. D. Sept. 5, 1912, Auburn, N. Y.

Year	Team	Games	BA	SA	AB	H	2B	3B	HR	HR%	R	RBI	BB	SO	SB	Pinch Hit AB	Pinch Hit H	PO	A	E	DP	TC/G	FA	G by Pos
1882	PHI AA	1	.000	.000	5	0	0	0	0	0.0	0		0			0	0	6	2	2	0	10.0	.800	C-1
1884	TOL AA	15	.085	.085	47	4	0	0	0	0.0	6		3			0	0	113	26	8	2	9.8	.946	C-15

Tug Arundel *continued*

Year	Team		Games	BA	SA	AB	H	2B	3B	HR	HR%	R	RBI	BB	SO	SB	Pinch Hit AB	Pinch Hit H	PO	A	E	DP	TC/G	FA	G by Pos
1887	IND	N	43	.197	.223	157	31	4	0	0	0.0	13	13	8	12	8	0	0	157	66	36	5	5.8	.861	C-42, OF-2, 1B-1
1888	WAS	N	17	.196	.235	51	10	0	1	0	0.0	2	3	5	10	1	0	0	63	16	15	1	5.5	.840	C-17
4 yrs.			76	.173	.196	260	45	4	1	0	0.0	21	16	16	22	9	0	0	339	110	61	8	6.5	.880	C-75, OF-2, 1B-1

Randy Asadoor

ASADOOR, RANDALL CARL
B. Oct. 20, 1962, Fresno, Calif.

BR TR 6′ 1″ 185 lbs.

Year	Team		Games	BA	SA	AB	H	2B	3B	HR	HR%	R	RBI	BB	SO	SB	Pinch Hit AB	Pinch Hit H	PO	A	E	DP	TC/G	FA	G by Pos
1986	SD	N	15	.364	.455	55	20	5	0	0	0.0	9	7	3	13	1	0	0	12	31	5	1	2.8	.896	3B-15, 2B-2

Jim Asbell

ASBELL, JAMES MARION
B. June 22, 1914, Dallas, Tex. D. July 6, 1967, San Mateo, Calif.

BR TR 6′ 195 lbs.

Year	Team		Games	BA	SA	AB	H	2B	3B	HR	HR%	R	RBI	BB	SO	SB	Pinch Hit AB	Pinch Hit H	PO	A	E	DP	TC/G	FA	G by Pos
1938	CHI	N	17	.182	.242	33	6	2	0	0	0.0	6	3	3	9	0	6	3	14	1	0	1	0.9	1.000	OF-17

Asby Asbjornson

ASBJORNSON, ROBERT ANTHONY
B. June 19, 1909, Concord, Mass. D. Jan. 21, 1970, Williamsport, Pa.

BR TR 6′ 1″ 196 lbs.

Year	Team		Games	BA	SA	AB	H	2B	3B	HR	HR%	R	RBI	BB	SO	SB	Pinch Hit AB	Pinch Hit H	PO	A	E	DP	TC/G	FA	G by Pos
1928	BOS	A	6	.188	.250	16	3	1	0	0	0.0	0	1	1	1	0	0	0	8	3	1	0	2.0	.917	C-6
1929			17	.103	.103	29	3	0	0	0	0.0	1	0	1	6	0	1	0	21	5	3	1	1.9	.897	C-15
1931	CIN	N	45	.305	.381	118	36	7	1	0	0.0	13	22	7	23	0	14	3	82	24	2	2	3.5	.981	C-31
1932			29	.172	.259	58	10	2	0	1	1.7	5	4	0	15	0	13	0	45	4	2	2	3.2	.961	C-16
4 yrs.			97	.235	.303	221	52	10	1	1	0.5	19	27	9	45	0	28	3	156	36	8	5	2.9	.960	C-68

Richie Ashburn

ASHBURN, RICH (Whitey)
B. Mar. 19, 1927, Tilden, Neb.
Hall of Fame 1995.

BL TR 5′10″ 170 lbs.

Year	Team		Games	BA	SA	AB	H	2B	3B	HR	HR%	R	RBI	BB	SO	SB	Pinch Hit AB	Pinch Hit H	PO	A	E	DP	TC/G	FA	G by Pos
1948	PHI	N	117	.333	.400	463	154	17	4	2	0.4	78	40	60	22	**32**	1	0	344	14	7	2	3.1	.981	OF-116
1949			154	.284	.349	**662**	188	18	11	1	0.2	84	37	58	38	9	0	0	514	13	11	3	3.5	.980	OF-154
1950			151	.303	.402	594	180	25	**14**	2	0.3	84	41	63	32	14	2	0	405	8	5	2	2.8	.988	OF-147
1951			154	.344	.426	643	**221**	31	5	4	0.6	92	63	50	37	29	0	0	538	15	7	6	3.6	.988	OF-154
1952			154	.282	.357	613	173	31	6	1	0.2	93	42	75	30	16	1	1	428	23	9	5	3.0	.980	OF-154
1953			156	.330	.408	622	**205**	25	9	2	0.3	110	57	61	35	14	0	0	496	18	5	4	3.3	.990	OF-156
1954			153	.313	.376	559	175	16	8	1	0.2	111	41	**125**	46	11	0	0	483	12	8	2	3.3	.984	OF-153
1955			140	**.338**	.448	533	180	32	9	3	0.6	91	42	105	36	12	1	1	387	10	7	3	2.9	.983	OF-140
1956			154	.303	.384	628	190	26	8	3	0.5	94	50	79	45	10	0	0	503	11	9	3	3.4	.983	OF-154
1957			156	.297	.364	626	186	26	8	0	0.0	93	33	**94**	44	13	0	0	502	18	7	7	3.4	.987	OF-156
1958			152	**.350**	.441	615	**215**	24	**13**	2	0.3	98	33	**97**	48	30	0	0	495	8	8	2	3.4	.984	OF-152
1959			153	.266	.307	564	150	16	2	1	0.2	86	20	79	42	9	4	1	359	4	11	1	2.5	.971	OF-149
1960	CHI	N	151	.291	.338	547	159	16	5	0	0.0	99	40	**116**	50	16	6	1	317	11	8	2	2.3	.976	OF-146
1961			109	.257	.306	307	79	7	4	0	0.0	49	19	55	27	7	34	10	131	4	3	0	1.8	.978	OF-76
1962	NY	N	135	.306	.393	389	119	7	3	7	1.8	60	28	81	39	12	31	13	192	13	6	2	2.1	.972	OF-97, 2B-2
15 yrs.			2189	.308	.382	8365	2574	317	109	29	0.3	1322	586	1198	571	234	80	27	6094	182	111	44	3.0	.983	OF-2104, 2B-2
WORLD SERIES																									
1950	PHI	N	4	.176	.235	17	3	1	0	0	0.0	0	1	0	4	0	0	0	9	0	0	0	2.3	1.000	OF-4

Alan Ashby

ASHBY, ALAN DEAN
B. July 8, 1951, Long Beach, Calif.

BB TR 6′ 2″ 185 lbs.

Year	Team		Games	BA	SA	AB	H	2B	3B	HR	HR%	R	RBI	BB	SO	SB	Pinch Hit AB	Pinch Hit H	PO	A	E	DP	TC/G	FA	G by Pos
1973	CLE	A	11	.172	.310	29	5	1	0	1	3.4	4	3	2	11	0	1	0	45	0	1	0	4.2	.978	C-11
1974			10	.143	.143	7	1	0	0	0	0.0	1	0	1	2	0	1	1	12	0	0	0	1.3	1.000	C-9
1975			90	.224	.331	254	57	10	1	5	2.0	32	32	30	42	3	1	0	450	43	6	7	5.5	.988	C-87, 1B-2, DH-1, 3B-1
1976			89	.239	.316	247	59	5	1	4	1.6	26	32	27	49	0	5	0	476	52	7	7	6.0	.987	C-86, 1B-2, 3B-1
1977	TOR	A	124	.210	.280	396	83	16	3	2	0.5	25	29	50	51	0	0	0	619	71	11	11	5.7	.984	C-124
1978			81	.261	.420	264	69	15	0	9	3.4	27	29	28	32	1	0	0	399	38	6	6	5.5	.986	C-81
1979	HOU	N	108	.202	.277	336	68	15	2	2	0.6	25	35	26	70	0	3	1	548	57	8	5	5.8	.987	C-105
1980			116	.256	.347	352	90	19	2	3	0.9	30	48	35	40	0	5	1	608	60	6	10	5.9	.991	C-114
1981			83	.271	.369	255	69	13	0	4	1.6	20	33	35	33	0	4	2	434	58	9	6	6.2	.982	C-81
1982			100	.257	.416	339	87	14	2	12	3.5	40	49	27	53	2	6	3	530	55	14	5	6.3	.977	C-95
1983			87	.229	.389	275	63	18	1	8	2.9	31	34	31	38	0	5	2	435	56	13	2	5.9	.974	C-85
1984			66	.262	.361	191	50	7	0	4	2.1	16	27	20	22	0	4	2	303	42	5	3	5.6	.986	C-63
1985			65	.280	.450	189	53	8	0	8	4.2	20	25	24	27	0	4	1	312	37	8	1	5.9	.978	C-60
1986			120	.257	.371	315	81	15	0	7	2.2	24	38	39	56	1	20	3	632	43	10	2	6.7	.985	C-103
1987			125	.288	.438	386	111	16	0	14	3.6	53	63	50	52	0	16	1	778	46	6	6	7.5	.993	C-110
1988			73	.238	.374	227	54	10	0	7	3.1	19	33	29	36	0	10	2	414	23	4	4	6.7	.991	C-66
1989			22	.164	.213	61	10	1	1	0	0.0	4	3	7	8	0	2	1	101	4	0	0	5.5	1.000	C-19
17 yrs.			1370	.245	.361	4123	1010	183	13	90	2.2	397	513	461	622	7	87	20	7096	685	114	75	6.0	.986	C-1299, 1B-4, 3B-2, DH-1
DIVISIONAL PLAYOFF SERIES																									
1981	HOU	N	3	.111	.444	9	1	0	0	1	11.1	1	2	2	0	0	0	0	24	2	0	0	8.7	1.000	C-3
LEAGUE CHAMPIONSHIP SERIES																									
1980	HOU	N	2	.125	.125	8	1	0	0	0	0.0	0	1	0	0	0	1	1	11	2	0	0	6.5	1.000	C-2
1986			6	.130	.304	23	3	1	0	1	4.3	2	2	2	1	0	0	0	58	1	0	0	9.8	1.000	C-6
2 yrs.			8	.129	.258	31	4	1	0	1	3.2	2	3	2	1	0	1	1	69	3	0	0	9.0	1.000	C-8

Tucker Ashford

ASHFORD, THOMAS STEVEN
B. Dec. 4, 1954, Memphis, Tenn.

BR TR 6′ 1″ 195 lbs.

Year	Team		Games	BA	SA	AB	H	2B	3B	HR	HR%	R	RBI	BB	SO	SB	Pinch Hit AB	Pinch Hit H	PO	A	E	DP	TC/G	FA	G by Pos
1976	SD	N	4	.600	.800	5	3	1	0	0	0.0	0	0	1	0	2	2	1	1	2	0	0	3.0	1.000	3B-1
1977			81	.217	.325	249	54	18	0	3	1.2	25	24	21	35	2	1	0	49	159	15	16	2.5	.933	3B-74, SS-10, 2B-4
1978			75	.245	.374	155	38	11	0	3	1.9	11	26	14	31	1	18	7	108	53	6	22	2.6	.964	3B-32, 2B-18, 1B-14
1980	TEX	A	15	.125	.125	32	4	0	0	0	0.0	2	3	3	3	0	0	0	10	25	2	1	2.6	.946	3B-12, SS-2
1981	NY	A	3	—	—	0	0	0	0	0	—	0	0	0	0	0	0	0	0	0	0	0	0.0	.000	2B-2
1983	NY	N	35	.179	.214	56	10	0	1	0	0.0	3	2	7	4	0	10	1	14	31	1	6	1.6	.978	3B-15, 2B-13, C-1
1984	KC	A	9	.154	.231	13	2	1	0	0	0.0	1	0	1	2	0	0	0	2	8	1	1	1.2	.909	3B-9
7 yrs.			222	.218	.318	510	111	31	1	6	1.2	42	55	47	75	5	31	9	184	278	25	46	2.4	.949	3B-143, 2B-37, 1B-14, SS-12, C-1

Year	Team	Games	BA	SA	AB	H	2B	3B	HR	HR%	R	RBI	BB	SO	SB	Pinch Hit AB	Pinch Hit H	PO	A	E	DP	TC/G	FA	G by Pos

Billy Ashley

ASHLEY, BILLY MANUAL BR TR 6′ 7″ 220 lbs.
B. July 11, 1970, Trenton, Mich.

Year	Team	Games	BA	SA	AB	H	2B	3B	HR	HR%	R	RBI	BB	SO	SB	Pinch Hit AB	Pinch Hit H	PO	A	E	DP	TC/G	FA	G by Pos
1992	LA N	29	.221	.337	95	21	5	0	2	2.1	6	6	5	34	0	4	2	34	2	6	0	1.6	.857	OF-27
1993		14	.243	.243	37	9	0	0	0	0.0	0	0	2	11	0	3	1	11	3	0	0	1.3	1.000	OF-11
1994		2	.333	.500	6	2	1	0	0	0.0	0	0	0	2	0	0	0	3	0	0	0	1.5	1.000	OF-2
1995		81	.237	.372	215	51	5	0	8	3.7	17	27	25	88	0	14	2	102	2	3	0	1.6	.972	OF-69
4 yrs.		126	.235	.351	353	83	11	0	10	2.8	23	33	32	135	0	21	5	150	7	9	0	1.5	.946	OF-109
DIVISIONAL PLAYOFF SERIES																								
1995	LA N	1	—	—	0	0	0	0	0	—	0	0	1	0	0	0	0	0	0	0	0	0.0	—	

Tom Asmussen

ASMUSSEN, THOMAS WILLIAM TR
B. Sept. 26, 1876, Chicago, Ill. D. Aug. 21, 1963, Arlington Heights, Ill.

Year	Team	Games	BA	SA	AB	H	2B	3B	HR	HR%	R	RBI	BB	SO	SB	Pinch Hit AB	Pinch Hit H	PO	A	E	DP	TC/G	FA	G by Pos
1907	BOS N	2	.000	.000	5	0	0	0	0	0.0	0	0	0		0	0	0	3	2	0	0	2.5	1.000	C-2

Bob Aspromonte

ASPROMONTE, ROBERT THOMAS BR TR 6′ 2″ 170 lbs.
Brother of Ken Aspromonte.
B. June 19, 1938, Brooklyn, N. Y.

Year	Team	Games	BA	SA	AB	H	2B	3B	HR	HR%	R	RBI	BB	SO	SB	Pinch Hit AB	Pinch Hit H	PO	A	E	DP	TC/G	FA	G by Pos
1956	BKN N	1	.000	.000	1	0	0	0	0	0.0	0	0	0	1	0	1	0	0	0	0	0	0.0	—	
1960	LA N	21	.182	.255	55	10	1	0	1	1.8	1	6	0	6	1	5	1	16	25	4	5	2.4	.911	SS-15, 3B-4
1961		47	.241	.293	58	14	3	0	0	0.0	7	2	4	12	0	31	9	8	18	1	0	1.8	.963	3B-9, SS-4, 2B-2
1962	HOU N	149	.266	.376	534	142	18	4	11	2.1	59	59	46	54	4	1	0	168	257	15	25	2.9	.966	3B-142, SS-11, 2B-1
1963		136	.214	.306	468	100	9	5	8	1.7	42	49	40	57	3	5	0	137	213	23	4	2.8	.938	3B-131, 1B-1
1964		157	.280	.392	553	155	20	3	12	2.2	51	69	35	54	6	2	0	133	261	11	10	2.6	.973	3B-155
1965		152	.263	.322	578	152	15	2	5	0.9	53	52	38	54	2	1	1	178	292	18	30	3.1	.963	3B-146, 1B-6, SS-4
1966		152	.252	.334	560	141	16	3	8	1.4	55	52	35	63	0	3	0	154	264	18	19	2.8	.959	3B-149, SS-2, 1B-2
1967		137	.294	.401	486	143	24	5	6	1.2	51	58	45	44	2	4	2	130	237	14	17	2.9	.963	3B-133
1968		124	.225	.264	409	92	9	2	1	0.2	25	46	35	57	1	12	3	116	155	10	9	2.5	.964	3B-75, OF-36, 1B-1, SS-1
1969	ATL N	82	.253	.348	198	50	8	1	3	1.5	16	24	13	19	0	26	5	74	46	8	2	1.9	.938	OF-24, 3B-23, SS-18, 2B-2
1970		62	.213	.236	127	27	3	0	0	0.0	5	7	13	13	0	27	5	29	53	5	5	2.4	.943	3B-30, SS-4, 1B-1, OF-1
1971	NY N	104	.225	.301	342	77	9	1	5	1.5	21	33	29	25	0	7	1	76	145	8	10	2.4	.965	3B-97
13 yrs.		1324	.252	.336	4369	1103	135	26	60	1.4	386	457	333	459	19	125	27	1219	1966	135	136	2.7	.959	3B-1094, OF-61, SS-59, 1B-11, 2B-5
LEAGUE CHAMPIONSHIP SERIES																								
1969	ATL N	3	.000	.000	3	0	0	0	0	0.0	0	0	0	0	0	3	0	0	0	0	0	0.0	—	

Ken Aspromonte

ASPROMONTE, KENNETH JOSEPH BR TR 6′ 180 lbs.
Brother of Bob Aspromonte.
B. Sept. 22, 1931, Brooklyn, N. Y.
Manager 1972–74.

Year	Team	Games	BA	SA	AB	H	2B	3B	HR	HR%	R	RBI	BB	SO	SB	Pinch Hit AB	Pinch Hit H	PO	A	E	DP	TC/G	FA	G by Pos
1957	BOS A	24	.269	.333	78	21	5	0	0	0.0	9	4	17	10	0	0	0	46	65	4	14	4.8	.965	2B-24
1958	2 teams BOS A (6G –.125) WAS A (92G –.225)																							
″	total	98	.219	.316	269	59	9	1	5	1.9	15	27	28	29	1	9	2	159	204	13	53	4.2	.965	2B-78, 3B-11, SS-1
1959	WAS A	70	.244	.324	225	55	12	0	2	0.9	31	14	26	39	2	5	0	127	164	13	30	4.6	.957	2B-52, SS-12, OF-1, 1B-1
1960	2 teams WAS A (4G –.000) CLE A (117G –.290)																							
″	total	121	.288	.400	462	133	20	1	10	2.2	65	48	53	34	4	6	0	238	268	22	71	4.6	.958	2B-80, 3B-36
1961	2 teams LA A (66G –.223) CLE A (22G –.229)																							
″	total	88	.224	.302	308	69	16	1	2	0.6	34	19	39	24	0	3	1	185	246	14	63	5.4	.969	2B-83
1962	2 teams CLE A (20G –.143) MIL N (34G –.291)																							
″	total	54	.252	.290	107	27	4	0	0	0.0	15	8	12	10	0	21	5	46	52	2	10	3.7	.980	2B-18, 3B-9
1963	CHI N	20	.147	.235	34	5	3	0	0	0.0	2	4	4	4	0	8	0	19	26	2	4	5.2	.957	2B-7, 1B-2
7 yrs.		475	.249	.338	1483	369	69	3	19	1.3	171	124	179	150	7	52	8	820	1025	70	245	4.6	.963	2B-342, 3B-56, SS-13, 1B-3, OF-1

Brian Asselstine

ASSELSTINE, BRIAN HANLY BL TR 6′ 1″ 175 lbs.
B. Sept. 23, 1953, Santa Barbara, Calif.

Year	Team	Games	BA	SA	AB	H	2B	3B	HR	HR%	R	RBI	BB	SO	SB	Pinch Hit AB	Pinch Hit H	PO	A	E	DP	TC/G	FA	G by Pos
1976	ATL N	11	.212	.303	33	7	0	0	1	3.0	2	3	1	2	0	2	0	19	0	0	0	2.1	1.000	OF-9
1977		83	.210	.355	124	26	6	0	4	3.2	12	17	9	10	1	47	10	57	1	1	0	1.7	.983	OF-35
1978		39	.272	.417	103	28	3	3	2	1.9	11	13	11	16	2	6	1	60	1	2	0	1.8	.968	OF-35
1979		8	.100	.100	10	1	0	0	0	0.0	1	0	1	2	0	6	0	1	0	0	0	1.0	1.000	OF-1
1980		87	.284	.394	218	62	13	1	3	1.4	18	25	11	37	1	22	3	102	0	4	0	1.7	.962	OF-61
1981		56	.256	.384	86	22	5	0	2	2.3	8	10	5	7	1	36	9	22	1	1	1	1.5	.958	OF-16
6 yrs.		284	.254	.378	574	146	27	4	12	2.1	52	68	38	74	5	119	23	261	3	8	1	1.7	.971	OF-157

Joe Astroth

ASTROTH, JOSEPH HENRY BR TR 5′ 9″ 187 lbs.
B. Sept. 1, 1922, East Alton, Ill.

Year	Team	Games	BA	SA	AB	H	2B	3B	HR	HR%	R	RBI	BB	SO	SB	Pinch Hit AB	Pinch Hit H	PO	A	E	DP	TC/G	FA	G by Pos
1945	PHI A	10	.059	.059	17	1	0	0	0	0.0	1	1	0	1	0	2	0	20	4	4	0	3.5	.857	C-8
1946		4	.143	.143	7	1	0	0	0	0.0	0	0	0	2	0	0	0	7	1	1	0	2.3	.889	C-4
1949		55	.243	.284	148	36	4	1	0	0.0	18	12	21	13	1	8	2	163	24	4	4	4.3	.979	C-44
1950		39	.327	.400	110	36	3	1	1	0.9	11	18	18	3	0	0	0	123	9	2	3	3.5	.985	C-38
1951		64	.246	.353	187	46	10	2	2	1.1	30	19	18	13	0	6	1	228	18	2	2	4.4	.992	C-57
1952		104	.249	.291	337	84	7	2	1	0.3	24	36	25	27	2	1	0	436	36	4	9	4.7	.992	C-102
1953		82	.296	.404	260	77	15	2	3	1.2	28	24	27	12	1	3	0	341	47	5	13	5.0	.987	C-79
1954		77	.221	.279	226	50	8	1	1	0.4	22	23	21	19	0	6	2	300	39	4	5	4.8	.988	C-71
1955	KC A	101	.252	.328	274	69	4	1	5	1.8	29	23	47	33	2	2	1	420	50	5	9	4.8	.989	C-100
1956		8	.077	.077	13	1	0	0	0	0.0	0	0	0	1	0	0	0	19	5	0	1	3.0	1.000	C-8
10 yrs.		544	.254	.324	1579	401	51	10	13	0.8	163	156	177	124	6	28	6	2057	233	31	46	4.5	.987	C-511

Charlie Atherton

ATHERTON, CHARLES MORGAN HERBERT (Prexy) BR TR 5′10″ 160 lbs.
B. Oct. 19, 1873, New Brunswick, N. J. D. Dec. 19, 1934, Vienna, Austria.

Year	Team	Games	BA	SA	AB	H	2B	3B	HR	HR%	R	RBI	BB	SO	SB	Pinch Hit AB	Pinch Hit H	PO	A	E	DP	TC/G	FA	G by Pos
1899	WAS N	65	.248	.318	242	60	5	6	0	0.0	28	23	21		2	1	1	91	119	26	7	3.7	.890	3B-63, OF-1

Lefty Atkinson

ATKINSON, HUBERT BURLEY BL TL 5′ 6½″ 149 lbs.
B. June 4, 1904, Chicago, Ill. D. Feb. 12, 1961, Chicago, Ill.

Year	Team	Games	BA	SA	AB	H	2B	3B	HR	HR%	R	RBI	BB	SO	SB	Pinch Hit AB	Pinch Hit H	PO	A	E	DP	TC/G	FA	G by Pos
1927	WAS A	1	.000	.000	1	0	0	0	0	0.0	1	0	0	0	0	0	0	0	0	0	0	0.0	—	

Dick Attreau

ATTREAU, RICHARD GILBERT BL TL 6′ 160 lbs.
B. Apr. 8, 1897, Chicago, Ill. D. July 5, 1964, Chicago, Ill.

Year	Team	Games	BA	SA	AB	H	2B	3B	HR	HR%	R	RBI	BB	SO	SB	Pinch Hit AB	Pinch Hit H	PO	A	E	DP	TC/G	FA	G by Pos
1926	PHI N	17	.230	.279	61	14	1	1	0	0.0	9	5	6	5	0	0	0	173	6	2	12	10.6	.989	1B-17
1927		44	.205	.277	83	17	1	1	1	1.2	17	11	14	18	1	10	0	174	8	2	13	7.1	.989	1B-26
2 yrs.		61	.215	.278	144	31	2	2	1	0.7	26	16	20	23	1	10	0	347	14	4	25	8.5	.989	1B-43

Toby Atwell

ATWELL, MAURICE DAILEY BL TR 5′ 9½″ 185 lbs.
B. Mar. 8, 1924, Leesburg, Va.

Year	Team	Games	BA	SA	AB	H	2B	3B	HR	HR%	R	RBI	BB	SO	SB	Pinch Hit AB	Pinch Hit H	PO	A	E	DP	TC/G	FA	G by Pos
1952	CHI N	107	.290	.367	362	105	16	3	2	0.6	36	31	40	22	2	5	0	451	50	12	2	5.1	.977	C-101
1953	2 teams	CHI N (24G –.230) PIT N (53G –.245)																						
"	total	77	.239	.291	213	51	8	0	1	0.5	21	25	33	19	0	11	2	295	37	15	2	5.1	.957	C-68
1954	PIT N	96	.289	.376	287	83	8	4	3	1.0	36	26	43	21	2	8	4	360	39	4	4	4.6	.990	C-88
1955		71	.213	.266	207	44	8	0	1	0.5	21	18	40	16	0	6	0	334	24	3	3	5.4	.992	C-67
1956	2 teams	PIT N (12G –.111) MIL N (15G –.167)																						
"	total	27	.146	.292	48	7	1	0	2	4.2	2	10	5	6	0	7	0	59	6	0	1	3.4	1.000	C-19
5 yrs.		378	.260	.333	1117	290	41	7	9	0.8	116	110	161	84	4	37	6	1499	156	34	12	4.9	.980	C-343

Bill Atwood

ATWOOD, WILLIAM FRANKLIN BR TR 5′11½″ 190 lbs.
B. Sept. 25, 1911, Rome, Ga. D. Sept. 14, 1993, Snyder, Tex.

Year	Team	Games	BA	SA	AB	H	2B	3B	HR	HR%	R	RBI	BB	SO	SB	Pinch Hit AB	Pinch Hit H	PO	A	E	DP	TC/G	FA	G by Pos
1936	PHI N	71	.302	.401	192	58	9	2	2	1.0	21	29	11	15	0	15	4	184	27	6	3	4.1	.972	C-53
1937		87	.244	.326	279	68	15	1	2	0.7	27	32	30	27	3	6	1	290	48	11	5	4.4	.968	C-80
1938		102	.196	.263	281	55	8	1	3	1.1	27	28	25	26	0	5	2	350	53	13	12	4.4	.969	C-94
1939		4	.000	.000	6	0	0	0	0	0.0	0	1	2	3	1	0	0	7	0	0	1	3.5	1.000	C-2
1940		78	.192	.236	203	39	9	0	0	0.0	7	22	25	18	0	6	1	238	43	3	3	4.1	.989	C-69
5 yrs.		342	.229	.302	961	220	41	4	7	0.7	82	112	93	89	4	32	8	1069	171	33	24	4.3	.974	C-298

Jake Atz

ATZ, JOHN JACOB BR TR 5′ 9½″ 160 lbs.
Born John Jacob Zimmerman.
B. July 1, 1879, Washington, D. C. D. May 22, 1945, New Orleans, La.

Year	Team	Games	BA	SA	AB	H	2B	3B	HR	HR%	R	RBI	BB	SO	SB	Pinch Hit AB	Pinch Hit H	PO	A	E	DP	TC/G	FA	G by Pos
1902	WAS A	3	.100	.100	10	1	0	0	0	0.0	1	0	0		0	0	0	2	11	0	1	4.3	1.000	2B-3
1907	CHI A	3	.143	.143	7	1	0	0	0	0.0	0	0	0		0	1	0	0	8	0	1	4.0	1.000	3B-2
1908		83	.194	.209	206	40	3	0	0	0.0	24	27	31		9	17	4	100	188	17	15	4.7	.944	2B-46, SS-18, 3B-1
1909		119	.236	.299	381	90	18	3	0	0.0	39	22	38		14	1	0	208	315	25	41	4.5	.954	2B-118, OF-3, SS-1
4 yrs.		208	.219	.263	604	132	21	3	0	0.0	64	49	69		23	19	4	310	522	42	58	4.6	.952	2B-167, SS-19, OF-3, 3B-3

Harry Aubrey

AUBREY, HARRY HERBERT TR
B. July 5, 1880, St. Joseph, Mo. D. Sept. 18, 1953, Baltimore, Md.

Year	Team	Games	BA	SA	AB	H	2B	3B	HR	HR%	R	RBI	BB	SO	SB	Pinch Hit AB	Pinch Hit H	PO	A	E	DP	TC/G	FA	G by Pos
1903	BOS N	96	.212	.249	325	69	8	2	0	0.0	26	27	18		7	0	0	185	301	74	20	5.8	.868	SS-94, OF-1, 2B-1

Rich Aude

AUDE, RICHARD THOMAS BR TR 6′ 5″ 180 lbs.
B. July 13, 1971, Van Nuys, Calif.

Year	Team	Games	BA	SA	AB	H	2B	3B	HR	HR%	R	RBI	BB	SO	SB	Pinch Hit AB	Pinch Hit H	PO	A	E	DP	TC/G	FA	G by Pos
1993	PIT N	13	.115	.154	26	3	1	0	0	0.0	1	4	1	7	0	6	1	47	3	1	6	6.4	.980	1B-7, OF-1
1995		42	.248	.376	109	27	8	0	2	1.8	10	19	6	20	1	14	4	223	11	1	27	7.3	.996	1B-32
2 yrs.		55	.222	.333	135	30	9	0	2	1.5	11	23	7	27	1	20	5	270	14	2	33	7.2	.993	1B-39, OF-1

Rick Auerbach

AUERBACH, FREDERICK STEVEN BR TR 6′ 165 lbs.
B. Feb. 15, 1950, Woodland Hills, Calif.

Year	Team	Games	BA	SA	AB	H	2B	3B	HR	HR%	R	RBI	BB	SO	SB	Pinch Hit AB	Pinch Hit H	PO	A	E	DP	TC/G	FA	G by Pos
1971	MIL A	79	.203	.258	236	48	10	0	1	0.4	22	9	20	40	3	0	0	120	193	12	31	4.2	.963	SS-78
1972		153	.218	.269	554	121	16	3	2	0.4	50	30	43	62	24	1	0	256	452	30	90	4.8	.959	SS-153
1973		6	.100	.200	10	1	1	0	0	0.0	2	0	0	1	0	1	0	4	6	2	0	6.0	.833	SS-2
1974	LA N	45	.342	.384	73	25	0	0	1	1.4	12	4	8	9	4	4	1	38	60	8	6	2.8	.925	SS-19, 2B-16, 3B-3
1975		85	.224	.276	170	38	9	0	0	0.0	18	12	18	22	3	0	0	82	137	9	18	2.7	.961	SS-81, 1B-1, 3B-1
1976		36	.128	.128	47	6	0	0	0	0.0	7	1	6	6	0	2	0	41	50	6	13	3.6	.938	SS-12, 3B-8, 2B-7
1977	CIN N	33	.156	.200	45	7	2	0	0	0.0	5	3	4	7	0	2	0	37	46	5	7	2.8	.943	2B-19, SS-12
1978		63	.327	.545	55	18	6	0	2	3.6	17	5	7	12	1	13	7	29	47	3	9	2.0	.962	SS-26, 2B-10, 3B-3
1979		62	.210	.340	100	21	8	1	1	1.0	17	12	14	19	0	23	5	31	54	5	7	2.4	.944	3B-18, SS-16, 2B-3
1980		24	.333	.515	33	11	1	1	1	3.0	5	4	3	5	0	17	3	4	14	1	1	2.7	.947	3B-3, SS-3, 2B-1
1981	SEA A	38	.155	.226	84	13	3	0	1	1.2	12	6	4	15	1	0	0	44	99	3	26	3.8	.979	SS-38
11 yrs.		624	.220	.286	1407	309	56	5	9	0.6	167	86	127	198	36	63	16	686	1158	84	208	3.6	.956	SS-440, 2B-56, 3B-36, 1B-1
LEAGUE CHAMPIONSHIP SERIES																								
1974	LA N	1	1.000	2.000	1	1	1	0	0	0.0	0	0	0	0	0	1	1	0	0	0	0	0.0	—	
1979	CIN N	2	.000	.000	2	0	0	0	0	0.0	0	0	0	1	0	2	0	0	0	0	0	0.0	—	
2 yrs.		3	.333	.667	3	1	1	0	0	0.0	0	0	0	1	0	3	1							
WORLD SERIES																								
1974	LA N	1	—	—	0	0	0	0	0	—	0	0	0	0	0	0	0	0	0	0	0	0.0	—	

Dave Augustine

AUGUSTINE, DAVID RALPH BR TR 6′ 2″ 174 lbs.
B. Nov. 28, 1949, Follansbee, W. Va.

Year	Team	Games	BA	SA	AB	H	2B	3B	HR	HR%	R	RBI	BB	SO	SB	Pinch Hit AB	Pinch Hit H	PO	A	E	DP	TC/G	FA	G by Pos
1973	PIT N	11	.286	.429	7	2	1	0	0	0.0	1	0	0	1	0	0	0	4	1	0	0	0.6	1.000	OF-9
1974		18	.182	.182	22	4	0	0	0	0.0	3	0	0	5	0	0	0	20	2	0	0	2.0	1.000	OF-11
2 yrs.		29	.207	.241	29	6	1	0	0	0.0	4	0	0	6	0	0	0	24	3	0	0	1.4	1.000	OF-20

Doyle Aulds

AULDS, LEYCESTER DOYLE (Tex) BR TR 6′ 2″ 185 lbs.
B. Dec. 28, 1920, Farmerville, La.

Year	Team	Games	BA	SA	AB	H	2B	3B	HR	HR%	R	RBI	BB	SO	SB	Pinch Hit AB	Pinch Hit H	PO	A	E	DP	TC/G	FA	G by Pos
1947	BOS A	3	.250	.250	4	1	0	0	0	0.0	0	0	0	1	0	0	0	7	0	0	0	2.3	1.000	C-3

Doug Ault

AULT, DOUGLAS REAGAN BR TL 6′ 3″ 200 lbs.
B. Mar. 9, 1950, Beaumont, Tex.

Year	Team	Games	BA	SA	AB	H	2B	3B	HR	HR%	R	RBI	BB	SO	SB	Pinch Hit AB	Pinch Hit H	PO	A	E	DP	TC/G	FA	G by Pos
1976	TEX A	9	.300	.350	20	6	1	0	0	0.0	0	0	1	3	0	3	1	23	0	0	1	3.3	1.000	1B-4, DH-3
1977	TOR A	129	.245	.382	445	109	22	3	11	2.5	44	64	39	68	4	8	4	1113	103	16	91	9.8	.987	1B-122, DH-4
1978		54	.240	.356	104	25	1	1	3	2.9	10	7	17	14	0	20	5	190	10	6	13	5.6	.971	1B-25, OF-7, DH-5
1980		64	.194	.306	144	28	5	1	3	2.1	12	15	14	23	0	14	5	200	20	0	21	4.1	1.000	1B-32, DH-21, OF-1
4 yrs.		256	.236	.362	713	168	29	5	17	2.4	66	86	71	108	4	45	15	1526	133	22	126	7.5	.987	1B-183, DH-33, OF-8

Rich Aurilia

AURILIA, RICHARD SANTO — BR TR 6′ 170 lbs.
B. Sept. 2, 1971, Brooklyn, N. Y.

Year	Team	Games	BA	SA	AB	H	2B	3B	HR	HR%	R	RBI	BB	SO	SB	Pinch Hit AB	Pinch Hit H	PO	A	E	DP	TC/G	FA	G by Pos
1995	SF N	9	.474	.947	19	9	3	0	2	10.5	4	4	1	2	1	2	0	8	16	0	4	4.0	1.000	SS-6

Brad Ausmus

AUSMUS, BRADLEY DAVID — BR TR 5′11″ 190 lbs.
B. Apr. 14, 1969, New Haven, Conn.

Year	Team	Games	BA	SA	AB	H	2B	3B	HR	HR%	R	RBI	BB	SO	SB	Pinch Hit AB	Pinch Hit H	PO	A	E	DP	TC/G	FA	G by Pos
1993	SD N	49	.256	.412	160	41	8	1	5	3.1	18	12	6	28	2	0	0	272	34	8	5	6.4	.975	C-49
1994		101	.251	.358	327	82	12	1	7	2.1	45	24	30	63	5	0	0	687	59	7	2	7.5	.991	C-99, 1B-1
1995		103	.293	.412	328	96	16	4	5	1.5	44	34	31	56	16	1	0	657	60	6	8	7.2	.992	C-100, 1B-1
3 yrs.		253	.269	.390	815	219	36	6	17	2.1	107	70	67	147	23	1	0	1616	153	21	15	7.2	.988	C-248, 1B-2

Jimmy Austin

AUSTIN, JAMES PHILIP (Pepper) — BB TR 5′ 7½″ 155 lbs.
B. Dec. 8, 1879, Swansea, Wales D. Mar. 6, 1965, Laguna Beach, Calif.
Manager 1913, 1918, 1923.

Year	Team	Games	BA	SA	AB	H	2B	3B	HR	HR%	R	RBI	BB	SO	SB	Pinch Hit AB	Pinch Hit H	PO	A	E	DP	TC/G	FA	G by Pos
1909	NY A	136	.231	.286	437	101	11	5	1	0.2	37	39	32		30	1	1	225	301	44	27	4.2	.923	3B-111, SS-23, 2B-1
1910		133	.218	.275	432	94	11	4	2	0.5	46	36	47		22	0	0	204	284	30	10	3.9	.942	3B-133
1911	STL A	148	.261	.359	541	141	25	11	2	0.4	84	45	69		26	0	0	228	337	42	27	4.1	.931	3B-148
1912		149	.252	.319	536	135	14	8	2	0.4	57	44	38		28	0	0	219	292	50	22	3.8	.911	3B-149
1913		142	.266	.339	489	130	18	6	2	0.4	56	42	45	51	37	0	0	216	288	30	21	3.8	.944	3B-142
1914		130	.238	.290	466	111	16	4	0	0.0	55	30	40	59	20	2	0	183	249	30	18	3.6	.935	3B-127
1915		141	.266	.310	477	127	6	6	1	0.2	61	30	64	60	18	0	0	188	264	41	32	3.5	.917	3B-141
1916		129	.207	.280	411	85	15	6	1	0.2	55	28	74	59	19	3	0	128	274	26	21	3.5	.939	3B-124
1917		127	.240	.314	455	109	18	8	0	0.0	61	19	50	46	13	0	0	169	273	26	25	3.7	.944	3B-121, SS-6
1918		110	.264	.324	367	97	14	4	0	0.0	42	20	53	32	18	4	2	173	241	30	20	4.2	.932	SS-57, 3B-48
1919		106	.237	.313	396	94	9	9	1	0.3	54	21	42	31	8	6	2	161	207	24	15	4.0	.939	3B-98
1920		83	.271	.343	280	76	11	3	1	0.4	38	32	31	15	2	7	1	108	171	17	14	3.9	.943	3B-75
1921		27	.273	.333	66	18	2	1	0	0.0	8	2	4	7	2	2	1	43	46	4	4	4.2	.957	SS-14, 2B-6, 3B-2
1922		15	.290	.452	31	9	3	1	0	0.0	6	1	3	2	0	4	0	13	9	1	1	1.8	.957	3B-11, 2B-2
1923		1	—	—	0	0	0	0	0	—	0	0	0	0	0	0	0	0	0	0	0	0.0	.000	C-1
1925		1	.000	.000	1	0	0	0	0	0.0	0	0	0	0	0	0	0	1	0	0	0	1.0	1.000	3B-1
1926		1	.500	1.000	2	1	1	0	0	0.0	1	1	0	0	1	0	0	1	1	0	1	2.0	1.000	3B-1
1929		1	.000	.000	1	0	0	0	0	0.0	0	0	0	1	0	0	0	0	2	0	0	2.0	1.000	3B-1
18 yrs.		1580	.246	.314	5388	1328	174	76	13	0.2	661	390	592	363	244	29	7	2260	3239	395	258	3.8	.933	3B-1433, SS-100, 2B-9, C-1

Chick Autry

AUTRY, WILLIAM ASKEW — BL TL 5′11″ 168 lbs.
B. Jan. 2, 1885, Humboldt, Tenn. D. Jan. 16, 1976, Santa Rosa, Calif.

Year	Team	Games	BA	SA	AB	H	2B	3B	HR	HR%	R	RBI	BB	SO	SB	Pinch Hit AB	Pinch Hit H	PO	A	E	DP	TC/G	FA	G by Pos
1907	CIN N	7	.200	.200	25	5	0	0	0	0.0	3	0	1		0	0	0	13	0	1	0	2.0	.929	OF-7
1909	2 teams	CIN N (9G –.182) BOS N (65G –.196)																						
″	total	74	.194	.220	232	45	6	0	0	0.0	19	17	23		6	0	0	701	45	8	30	10.2	.989	1B-70, OF-4
2 yrs.		81	.195	.218	257	50	6	0	0	0.0	22	17	24		6	0	0	714	45	9	30	9.5	.988	1B-70, OF-11

Martin Autry

AUTRY, MARTIN GORDON (Chick) — BR TR 6′ 180 lbs.
B. Mar. 5, 1903, Martindale, Tex. D. Jan. 26, 1950, Savannah, Ga.

Year	Team	Games	BA	SA	AB	H	2B	3B	HR	HR%	R	RBI	BB	SO	SB	Pinch Hit AB	Pinch Hit H	PO	A	E	DP	TC/G	FA	G by Pos
1924	NY A	2	—	—	0	0	0	0	0	—	1	0	0	0	0	0	0	1	0	0	0	0.5	1.000	C-2
1926	CLE A	3	.143	.143	7	1	0	0	0	0.0	1	0	1	0	0	0	0	4	2	0	0	2.0	1.000	C-3
1927		16	.256	.395	43	11	4	1	0	0.0	5	7	0	6	0	1	0	42	14	4	1	4.3	.933	C-14
1928		22	.300	.483	60	18	6	1	1	1.7	6	1	9	7	0	4	0	61	8	2	3	3.9	.972	C-18
1929	CHI A	43	.208	.302	96	20	6	0	1	1.0	7	12	1	8	0	11	3	64	14	5	1	2.8	.940	C-30
1930		34	.254	.296	71	18	1	1	0	0.0	1	5	4	8	0	5	1	96	22	1	1	4.1	.992	C-29
6 yrs.		120	.245	.350	277	68	17	3	2	0.7	21	25	15	29	0	21	4	268	60	12	6	3.5	.965	C-96

Earl Averill

AVERILL, EARL DOUGLAS — BR TR 5′10″ 185 lbs.
Son of Earl Averill.
B. Sept. 9, 1931, Cleveland, Ohio.

Year	Team	Games	BA	SA	AB	H	2B	3B	HR	HR%	R	RBI	BB	SO	SB	Pinch Hit AB	Pinch Hit H	PO	A	E	DP	TC/G	FA	G by Pos
1956	CLE A	42	.237	.398	93	22	6	0	3	3.2	12	14	14	25	0	8	2	157	15	1	2	5.1	.994	C-34
1958		17	.182	.309	55	10	1	0	2	3.6	2	7	4	7	1	0	0	10	34	7	3	3.0	.863	3B-17
1959	CHI N	74	.237	.452	186	44	10	0	10	5.4	22	34	15	39	0	25	10	197	49	13	4	5.0	.950	C-32, 3B-13, OF-5, 2B-2
1960	2 teams	CHI N (52G –.235) CHI A (10G –.214)																						
″	total	62	.233	.293	116	27	4	0	1	0.9	16	15	15	18	1	30	6	155	10	3	1	4.1	.982	C-39, OF-1, 3B-1
1961	LA A	115	.266	.489	323	86	9	0	21	6.5	56	59	62	70	1	21	7	548	38	5	6	6.0	.992	C-88, OF-9, 2B-1
1962		92	.219	.332	187	41	9	0	4	2.1	21	22	43	47	0	34	7	85	7	0	0	1.7	1.000	OF-49, C-6
1963	PHI N	47	.268	.423	71	19	2	0	3	4.2	8	8	9	14	0	24	4	89	12	5	0	3.5	.953	C-20, OF-8, 3B-1, 1B-1
7 yrs.		449	.242	.409	1031	249	41	0	44	4.3	137	159	162	220	3	142	36	1241	165	34	16	4.4	.976	C-219, OF-72, 3B-32, 2B-3, 1B-1

Earl Averill

AVERILL, HOWARD EARL — BL TR 5′ 9½″ 172 lbs.
Father of Earl Averill.
B. May 21, 1902, Snohomish, Wash. D. Aug. 16, 1983, Everett, Wash.
Hall of Fame 1975.

Year	Team	Games	BA	SA	AB	H	2B	3B	HR	HR%	R	RBI	BB	SO	SB	Pinch Hit AB	Pinch Hit H	PO	A	E	DP	TC/G	FA	G by Pos
1929	CLE A	152	.331	.535	602	199	43	13	18	3.0	110	97	64	53	13	0	0	388	14	14	3	2.7	.966	OF-152
1930		139	.339	.537	534	181	33	8	19	3.6	102	119	56	48	10	5	2	345	11	19	5	2.8	.949	OF-134
1931		155	.333	.576	**627**	209	36	10	32	5.1	140	143	68	38	9	0	0	398	9	10	3	2.7	.976	OF-155
1932		153	.314	.569	631	198	37	14	32	5.1	116	124	75	40	5	0	0	412	12	16	3	2.9	.964	OF-153
1933		151	.301	.474	599	180	39	16	11	1.8	83	92	54	29	3	2	1	390	8	12	3	2.8	.971	OF-149
1934		154	.313	.569	598	187	48	6	31	5.2	128	113	99	44	4	0	0	410	12	13	3	2.8	.970	OF-154
1935		140	.288	.496	563	162	34	13	19	3.4	109	79	70	58	8	1	0	371	6	7	2	2.8	.982	OF-139
1936		152	.378	.627	614	**232**	39	**15**	28	4.6	136	126	65	35	3	2	1	369	11	12	2	2.6	.969	OF-150
1937		156	.299	.493	609	182	33	11	21	3.4	121	92	88	65	5	0	0	362	11	9	3	2.4	.976	OF-156
1938		134	.330	.535	482	159	27	15	14	2.9	101	93	81	48	5	3	0	331	14	9	2	2.7	.975	OF-131
1939	2 teams	CLE A (24G –.273) DET A (87G –.262)																						
″	total	111	.264	.464	364	96	28	6	11	3.0	66	65	49	42	4	19	6	169	3	4	0	1.9	.977	OF-91
1940	DET A	64	.280	.381	118	33	4	1	2	1.7	10	20	5	14	0	38	12	23	2	1	0	1.2	.962	OF-22
1941	BOS N	8	.118	.118	17	2	0	0	0	0.0	2	2	1	4	0	3	0	5	2	0	0	1.8	1.000	OF-4
13 yrs.		1669	.318	.533	6358	2020	401	128	238	3.7	1224	1165	775	518	69	73	22	3973	115	126	29	2.7	.970	OF-1590

Earl Averill *continued*

Year	Team	Games	BA	SA	AB	H	2B	3B	HR	HR%	R	RBI	BB	SO	SB	Pinch Hit AB	Pinch Hit H	PO	A	E	DP	TC/G	FA	G by Pos
WORLD SERIES																								
1940	DET A	3	.000	.000	3	0	0	0	0	0.0	0	0	0	0	0	3	0	0	0	0	0	0.0	—	

Bobby Avila

AVILA, ROBERTO FRANCISCO (Beto)
Born Roberto Francisco Avila (Gonzalez).
B. Apr. 2, 1924, Veracruz, Mexico.
BR TR 5′10″ 175 lbs.

Year	Team	Games	BA	SA	AB	H	2B	3B	HR	HR%	R	RBI	BB	SO	SB	Pinch Hit AB	Pinch Hit H	PO	A	E	DP	TC/G	FA	G by Pos
1949	CLE A	31	.214	.214	14	3	0	0	0	0.0	3	3	1	3	0	9	2	5	7	0	1	2.4	1.000	2B-5
1950		80	.299	.383	201	60	10	2	1	0.5	39	21	29	17	5	6	2	157	137	5	47	4.7	.983	2B-62, SS-2
1951		141	.304	.410	542	165	21	3	10	1.8	76	58	60	31	14	4	1	349	417	14	87	5.7	.982	2B-136
1952		150	.300	.415	597	179	26	**11**	7	1.2	102	45	67	36	12	1	0	355	431	28	81	5.5	.966	2B-149
1953		141	.286	.379	559	160	22	3	8	1.4	85	55	58	27	10	2	0	346	445	11	114	5.7	.986	2B-140
1954		143	**.341**	.477	555	189	27	2	15	2.7	112	67	59	31	9	1	0	361	410	21	102	5.4	.973	2B-141, SS-7
1955		141	.272	.400	537	146	22	4	13	2.4	83	61	82	47	1	1	1	348	342	13	108	5.0	.982	2B-141
1956		138	.224	.318	513	115	14	2	10	1.9	74	54	70	68	17	5	1	322	351	16	83	5.1	.977	2B-135
1957		129	.268	.354	463	124	19	3	5	1.1	60	48	46	47	2	8	1	293	270	11	74	4.7	.981	2B-107, 3B-16
1958		113	.253	.365	375	95	21	3	5	1.3	54	30	56	45	5	15	5	193	225	9	68	3.7	.979	2B-82, 3B-33
1959	3 teams	BAL A (20G –.170)	BOS A (22G –.244)	MIL N (51G –.238)																				
″	total	93	.227	.322	264	60	3	2	6	2.3	37	23	34	47	3	14	2	143	162	10	31	3.9	.968	2B-70, OF-10, 3B-1
11 yrs.		1300	.281	.388	4620	1296	185	35	80	1.7	725	465	562	399	78	66	15	2872	3197	138	796	5.0	.978	2B-1168, 3B-50, OF-10, SS-9
WORLD SERIES																								
1954	CLE A	4	.133	.133	15	2	0	0	0	0.0	1	0	2	1	0	0	0	12	10	0	1	5.5	1.000	2B-4

Ramon Aviles

AVILES, RAMON ANTONIO
Born Ramon Antonio Aviles (Miranda).
B. Jan. 22, 1952, Manati, Puerto Rico.
BR TR 5′ 9″ 155 lbs.

Year	Team	Games	BA	SA	AB	H	2B	3B	HR	HR%	R	RBI	BB	SO	SB	Pinch Hit AB	Pinch Hit H	PO	A	E	DP	TC/G	FA	G by Pos
1977	BOS A	1	—	—	0	0	0	0	0	—	0	0	0	0	0	0	0	0	1	0	0	1.0	1.000	2B-1
1979	PHI N	27	.279	.311	61	17	2	0	0	0.0	7	12	8	8	0	3	1	40	44	2	8	3.2	.977	2B-27
1980		51	.277	.396	101	28	6	0	2	2.0	12	9	10	9	0	6	2	60	74	8	21	3.2	.944	SS-29, 2B-15
1981		38	.214	.250	28	6	1	0	0	0.0	2	3	3	5	0	4	0	16	30	1	4	1.2	.979	2B-20, 3B-13, SS-5
4 yrs.		117	.268	.347	190	51	9	0	2	1.1	21	24	21	22	0	13	3	116	149	11	33	2.5	.960	2B-63, SS-34, 3B-13
DIVISIONAL PLAYOFF SERIES																								
1981	PHI N	1	—	—	0	0	0	0	0	—	0	0	1	0	0	0	0	0	0	0	0	0.0	—	
LEAGUE CHAMPIONSHIP SERIES																								
1980	PHI N	1	—	—	0	0	0	0	0	—	1	0	0	0	0	0	0	0	0	0	0	0.0	—	

Benny Ayala

AYALA, BENIGNO
Born Benigno Ayala (Felix).
B. Feb. 7, 1951, Yauco, Puerto Rico.
BR TR 6′ 1″ 185 lbs.

Year	Team	Games	BA	SA	AB	H	2B	3B	HR	HR%	R	RBI	BB	SO	SB	Pinch Hit AB	Pinch Hit H	PO	A	E	DP	TC/G	FA	G by Pos
1974	NY N	23	.235	.338	68	16	1	0	2	2.9	9	8	7	17	0	4	0	37	1	3	1	2.0	.927	OF-20
1976		22	.115	.231	26	3	0	0	1	3.8	2	2	2	6	0	15	2	7	1	1	0	1.3	.889	OF-7
1977	STL N	1	.333	.333	3	1	0	0	0	0.0	0	0	0	1	0	0	0	6	1	0	1	7.0	1.000	OF-1
1979	BAL A	42	.256	.523	86	22	5	0	6	7.0	15	13	6	9	0	13	3	38	0	1	0	1.1	.974	OF-24, DH-10
1980		76	.265	.500	170	45	8	1	10	5.9	28	33	19	21	0	28	5	20	2	0	1	0.4	1.000	DH-41, OF-19
1981		44	.279	.407	86	24	2	0	3	3.5	12	13	11	9	0	16	5	3	2	0	0	0.2	1.000	DH-27, OF-4
1982		64	.305	.492	128	39	6	0	6	4.7	17	24	5	14	1	24	9	59	0	1	2	1.3	.983	OF-25, DH-17, 1B-3
1983		47	.221	.404	104	23	7	0	4	3.8	12	13	9	18	0	14	4	41	0	2	0	1.2	.953	OF-24, DH-11
1984		60	.212	.364	118	25	6	0	4	3.4	9	24	8	24	1	29	9	10	0	0	0	0.2	1.000	DH-34, OF-13
1985	CLE A	46	.250	.421	76	19	7	0	2	2.6	10	15	4	17	0	22	4	21	1	2	0	1.0	.917	OF-20, DH-3
10 yrs.		425	.251	.434	865	217	42	1	38	4.4	114	145	71	136	2	165	41	242	8	10	5	0.9	.962	OF-157, DH-143, 1B-3
LEAGUE CHAMPIONSHIP SERIES																								
1983	BAL A	1	—	—	0	0	0	0	0	—	0	1	0	0	0	0	0	0	0	0	0	0.0	.000	DH-1
WORLD SERIES																								
1979	BAL A	4	.333	.833	6	2	0	0	1	16.7	1	2	1	0	0	0	0	4	0	0	0	1.3	1.000	OF-3
1983		1	1.000	1.000	1	1	0	0	0	0.0	1	1	0	0	0	1	1	0	0	0	0	0.0	—	
2 yrs.		5	.429	.857	7	3	0	0	1	14.3	2	3	1	0	0	1	1	4	0	0	0	1.3	1.000	OF-3

Dick Aylward

AYLWARD, RICHARD JOHN
B. June 4, 1925, Baltimore, Md. D. June 11, 1983, Spring Valley, Calif.
BR TR 6′ 190 lbs.

Year	Team	Games	BA	SA	AB	H	2B	3B	HR	HR%	R	RBI	BB	SO	SB	Pinch Hit AB	Pinch Hit H	PO	A	E	DP	TC/G	FA	G by Pos
1953	CLE A	4	.000	.000	3	0	0	0	0	0.0	0	0	0	1	0	0	0	4	0	0	0	1.0	1.000	C-4

Joe Azcue

AZCUE, JOSE JOAQUIN (The Immortal Azcue)
Born Jose Joaquin Azcue (Lopez).
B. Aug. 18, 1939, Cienfuegos, Cuba.
BR TR 6′ 190 lbs.

Year	Team	Games	BA	SA	AB	H	2B	3B	HR	HR%	R	RBI	BB	SO	SB	Pinch Hit AB	Pinch Hit H	PO	A	E	DP	TC/G	FA	G by Pos
1960	CIN N	14	.097	.097	31	3	0	0	0	0.0	1	3	2	6	0	2	0	66	6	0	0	5.1	1.000	C-14
1962	KC A	72	.229	.305	223	51	9	1	2	0.9	18	25	17	27	1	2	2	363	42	6	5	5.9	.985	C-70
1963	2 teams	KC A (2G –.000)	CLE A (94G –.284)																					
″	total	96	.281	.460	324	91	16	0	14	4.3	26	46	15	47	1	8	2	569	42	5	13	6.7	.992	C-92
1964	CLE A	83	.273	.358	271	74	9	1	4	1.5	20	34	16	38	0	7	1	510	36	4	2	7.2	.993	C-76
1965		111	.230	.269	335	77	7	0	2	0.6	16	35	27	54	2	10	3	714	53	5	2	7.1	.994	C-108
1966		98	.275	.404	302	83	10	1	9	3.0	22	37	20	22	0	3	1	588	40	7	3	6.5	.989	C-97
1967		86	.251	.437	295	74	12	5	11	3.7	33	34	22	35	0	2	1	636	57	1	4	8.1	.999	C-86
1968		115	.280	.342	357	100	10	0	4	1.1	23	42	28	33	1	17	4	699	50	3	11	7.8	.996	C-97
1969	3 teams	CLE A (7G –.292)	BOS A (19G –.216)	CAL A (80G –.218)																				
″	total	106	.223	.266	323	72	8	0	2	0.6	23	23	35	36	0	4	0	573	70	7	15	6.2	.989	C-105
1970	CAL A	114	.242	.302	351	85	13	1	2	0.6	19	25	24	40	0	4	1	587	51	6	10	5.8	.991	C-112
1972	2 teams	CAL A (3G –.000)	MIL A (11G –.143)																					
″	total	14	.125	.125	16	2	0	0	0	0.0	0	0	1	6	0	3	1	24	5	0	2	2.6	1.000	C-11
11 yrs.		909	.252	.344	2828	712	94	9	50	1.8	201	304	207	344	5	62	16	5329	452	44	67	6.7	.992	C-868

Oscar Azocar

AZOCAR, OSCAR GREGORIO
Born Oscar Gregorio Azocar (Azocar).
B. Feb. 21, 1965, Soro, Venezuela.

BL TL 6′ 1″ 170 lbs.

Year	Team	Games	BA	SA	AB	H	2B	3B	HR	HR%	R	RBI	BB	SO	SB	Pinch Hit AB	Pinch Hit H	PO	A	E	DP	TC/G	FA	G by Pos
1990	NY A	65	.248	.355	214	53	8	0	5	2.3	18	19	2	15	7	8	3	105	4	1	1	1.9	.991	OF-57, DH-1
1991	SD N	38	.246	.281	57	14	2	0	0	0.0	5	9	1	9	2	25	5	19	0	2	0	1.5	.905	OF-13, 1B-1
1992		99	.190	.226	168	32	6	0	0	0.0	15	8	9	12	1	56	10	64	1	4	0	1.9	.942	OF-37
3 yrs.		202	.226	.296	439	99	16	0	5	1.1	38	36	12	36	10	89	18	188	5	7	1	1.8	.965	OF-107, 1B-1, DH-1

Charlie Babb

BABB, CHARLES AMOS
B. Feb. 20, 1873, Milwaukie, Ore. D. Mar. 20, 1954, Portland, Ore.

BB TR 5′10½″ 165 lbs.

Year	Team	Games	BA	SA	AB	H	2B	3B	HR	HR%	R	RBI	BB	SO	SB	Pinch Hit AB	Pinch Hit H	PO	A	E	DP	TC/G	FA	G by Pos
1903	NY N	121	.248	.321	424	105	15	8	0	0.0	68	46	45		22	0	0	250	363	60	37	5.6	.911	SS-113, 3B-8
1904	BKN N	151	.265	.311	521	138	18	3	0	0.0	49	53	53		34	0	0	370	459	65	44	5.9	.927	SS-151
1905		75	.187	.238	235	44	8	2	0	0.0	27	17	27		10	1	0	401	141	27	34	7.7	.953	SS-36, 1B-31, 3B-5, 2B-2
3 yrs.		347	.243	.300	1180	287	41	13	0	0.0	144	116	125		66	1	0	1021	963	152	115	6.2	.929	SS-300, 1B-31, 3B-13, 2B-2

Loren Babe

BABE, LOREN ROLLAND (Bee Bee)
B. Jan. 11, 1928, Pisgah, Iowa D. Feb. 14, 1984, Omaha, Neb.

BL TR 5′10″ 180 lbs.

Year	Team	Games	BA	SA	AB	H	2B	3B	HR	HR%	R	RBI	BB	SO	SB	Pinch Hit AB	Pinch Hit H	PO	A	E	DP	TC/G	FA	G by Pos
1952	NY A	12	.095	.143	21	2	1	0	0	0.0	1	0	4	4	1	2	0	4	16	2	3	2.4	.909	3B-9
1953	2 teams	NY A (5G –.333) PHI A (103G –.224)																						
″	total	108	.230	.305	361	83	17	2	2	0.6	36	26	35	22	0	12	3	122	207	18	27	3.5	.948	3B-98, SS-1
2 yrs.		120	.223	.296	382	85	18	2	2	0.5	37	26	39	26	1	14	3	126	223	20	30	3.4	.946	3B-107, SS-1

Charlie Babington

BABINGTON, CHARLES PERCY
B. May 4, 1895, Cranston, R. I. D. Mar. 22, 1957, Providence, R. I.

BR TR 6′ 170 lbs.

Year	Team	Games	BA	SA	AB	H	2B	3B	HR	HR%	R	RBI	BB	SO	SB	Pinch Hit AB	Pinch Hit H	PO	A	E	DP	TC/G	FA	G by Pos
1915	NY N	28	.242	.394	33	8	3	1	0	0.0	5	2	0	4	1	10	2	10	0	1	0	0.8	.909	OF-12, 1B-1

Shooty Babitt

BABITT, MACK NEAL II
B. Mar. 9, 1959, Oakland, Calif.

BR TR 5′ 8″ 174 lbs.

Year	Team	Games	BA	SA	AB	H	2B	3B	HR	HR%	R	RBI	BB	SO	SB	Pinch Hit AB	Pinch Hit H	PO	A	E	DP	TC/G	FA	G by Pos
1981	OAK A	54	.256	.301	156	40	1	3	0	0.0	10	14	13	13	5	2	0	84	125	6	12	4.1	.972	2B-52

Wally Backman

BACKMAN, WALTER WAYNE
B. Sept. 22, 1959, Hillsboro, Ore.

BB TR 5′ 9″ 160 lbs.

Year	Team	Games	BA	SA	AB	H	2B	3B	HR	HR%	R	RBI	BB	SO	SB	Pinch Hit AB	Pinch Hit H	PO	A	E	DP	TC/G	FA	G by Pos
1980	NY N	27	.323	.355	93	30	1	1	0	0.0	12	9	11	14	2	0	0	62	55	1	11	4.2	.992	2B-20, SS-8
1981		26	.278	.333	36	10	2	0	0	0.0	5	0	4	7	1	15	3	14	21	2	2	3.1	.946	2B-11, 3B-1
1982		96	.272	.372	261	71	13	2	3	1.1	37	22	49	47	8	5	0	173	209	16	30	4.2	.960	2B-88, 3B-6, SS-1
1983		26	.167	.214	42	7	0	1	0	0.0	6	3	2	8	0	16	3	16	15	2	2	2.1	.939	2B-14, 3B-2
1984		128	.280	.339	436	122	19	2	1	0.2	68	26	56	63	32	11	3	223	307	10	73	4.4	.981	2B-115, SS-7
1985		145	.273	.344	520	142	24	5	1	0.2	77	38	36	72	30	15	6	273	370	7	76	4.6	.989	2B-140, SS-1
1986		124	.320	.385	387	124	18	2	1	0.3	67	27	36	32	13	15	5	186	290	17	56	4.4	.966	2B-113
1987		94	.250	.287	300	75	6	1	1	0.3	43	23	25	43	11	12	2	131	210	6	44	4.0	.983	2B-87
1988		99	.303	.344	294	89	12	0	0	0.0	44	17	41	49	9	6	1	128	219	4	36	3.8	.989	2B-92
1989	MIN A	87	.231	.284	299	69	9	2	1	0.3	33	26	32	45	1	4	0	146	187	6	37	4.0	.982	2B-84, DH-1
1990	PIT N	104	.292	.397	315	92	21	3	2	0.6	62	28	42	53	6	15	3	56	136	12	10	2.4	.941	3B-71, 2B-15
1991	PHI N	94	.243	.308	185	45	12	0	0	0.0	20	15	30	30	3	38	7	54	79	4	13	2.4	.971	2B-36, 3B-20
1992		42	.271	.292	48	13	1	0	0	0.0	6	6	6	9	1	29	10	10	20	1	4	2.6	.968	2B-10, 3B-2
1993	SEA A	10	.138	.138	29	4	0	0	0	0.0	2	0	1	8	0	1	0	4	15	3	0	2.2	.864	3B-9, 2B-1
14 yrs.		1102	.275	.339	3245	893	138	19	10	0.3	482	240	371	480	117	182	43	1476	2133	91	394	3.9	.975	2B-826, 3B-111, SS-17, DH-1
LEAGUE CHAMPIONSHIP SERIES																								
1986	NY N	6	.238	.238	21	5	0	0	0	0.0	5	2	2	4	1	0	0	9	18	0	4	4.5	1.000	2B-6
1988		7	.273	.318	22	6	1	0	0	0.0	2	2	2	5	1	0	0	7	19	2	1	4.0	.929	2B-7
1990	PIT N	3	.143	.286	7	1	1	0	0	0.0	1	0	1	3	1	1	0	1	3	0	0	2.0	1.000	3B-2
3 yrs.		16	.240	.280	50	12	2	0	0	0.0	8	4	5	12	3	1	0	17	40	2	5	3.9	.966	2B-13, 3B-2
WORLD SERIES																								
1986	NY N	6	.333	.333	18	6	0	0	0	0.0	4	1	4	2	1	0	0	9	13	0	1	3.7	1.000	2B-6

Eddie Bacon

BACON, EDGAR SUTER
B. Apr. 8, 1895, Franklin County, Ky. D. Oct. 2, 1963, Louisville, Ky.

Year	Team	Games	BA	SA	AB	H	2B	3B	HR	HR%	R	RBI	BB	SO	SB	Pinch Hit AB	Pinch Hit H	PO	A	E	DP	TC/G	FA	G by Pos
1917	PHI A	4	.500	.667	6	3	1	0	0	0.0	1	2	0	0	0	3	1	1	7	0	0	8.0	1.000	P-1

Art Bader

BADER, ARTHUR HERMAN
B. Sept. 21, 1886, St. Louis, Mo. D. Apr. 5, 1957, St. Louis, Mo.

BR TR 5′10″ 170 lbs.

Year	Team	Games	BA	SA	AB	H	2B	3B	HR	HR%	R	RBI	BB	SO	SB	Pinch Hit AB	Pinch Hit H	PO	A	E	DP	TC/G	FA	G by Pos
1904	STL A	2	.000	.000	3	0	0	0	0	0.0	0	0	1		0	1	0	1	1	0	0	2.0	1.000	OF-1

Red Badgro

BADGRO, MORRIS HIRAM
B. Dec. 1, 1902, Orilla, Wash.

BL TR 6′ 190 lbs.

Year	Team	Games	BA	SA	AB	H	2B	3B	HR	HR%	R	RBI	BB	SO	SB	Pinch Hit AB	Pinch Hit H	PO	A	E	DP	TC/G	FA	G by Pos
1929	STL A	54	.284	.385	148	42	12	0	1	0.7	27	18	11	15	1	15	4	58	1	1	1	1.6	.983	OF-37
1930		89	.239	.355	234	56	18	3	1	0.4	30	27	13	27	3	24	9	112	8	6	3	2.1	.952	OF-61
2 yrs.		143	.257	.366	382	98	30	3	2	0.5	57	45	24	42	4	39	13	170	9	7	4	1.9	.962	OF-98

Carlos Baerga

BAERGA, CARLOS OBED
Born Carlos Obed Baerga (Ortiz).
B. Nov. 4, 1968, Santurce, Puerto Rico.

BB TR 5′11″ 165 lbs.

Year	Team	Games	BA	SA	AB	H	2B	3B	HR	HR%	R	RBI	BB	SO	SB	Pinch Hit AB	Pinch Hit H	PO	A	E	DP	TC/G	FA	G by Pos
1990	CLE A	108	.260	.394	312	81	17	2	7	2.2	46	47	16	57	0	31	11	79	164	17	27	2.5	.935	3B-50, SS-48, 2B-8
1991		158	.288	.398	593	171	28	2	11	1.9	80	69	48	74	3	4	1	217	421	27	73	4.0	.959	3B-89, 2B-75, SS-2
1992		161	.312	.455	657	205	32	1	20	3.0	92	105	35	76	10	0	0	400	475	19	138	5.6	.979	2B-160, DH-1
1993		154	.321	.486	624	200	28	6	21	3.4	105	114	34	68	15	1	0	347	445	17	108	5.3	.979	2B-150, DH-4
1994		103	.314	.525	442	139	32	2	19	4.3	81	80	10	45	8	0	0	205	334	15	70	5.4	.973	2B-102, DH-1
1995		135	.314	.452	557	175	28	2	15	2.7	87	90	35	31	11	0	0	230	444	19	97	5.1	.973	2B-134, DH-1
6 yrs.		819	.305	.454	3185	971	165	15	93	2.9	491	505	178	351	47	36	12	1478	2283	114	513	4.7	.971	2B-629, 3B-139, SS-50, DH-7
DIVISIONAL PLAYOFF SERIES																								
1995	CLE A	3	.286	.357	14	4	1	0	0	0.0	2	1	0	1	0	0	0	8	5	1	1	4.7	.929	2B-3
LEAGUE CHAMPIONSHIP SERIES																								
1995	CLE A	6	.400	.520	25	10	0	0	1	4.0	3	4	2	3	0	0	0	12	22	0	2	5.7	1.000	2B-6

Carlos Baerga *continued*

WORLD SERIES

Year	Team	Games	BA	SA	AB	H	2B	3B	HR	HR%	R	RBI	BB	SO	SB	Pinch Hit AB	Pinch Hit H	PO	A	E	DP	TC/G	FA	G by Pos
1995	CLE A	6	.192	.269	26	5	2	0	0	0.0	1	4	1	1	0	0	0	15	24	1	7	6.7	.975	2B-6

Jose Baez

BAEZ, JOSE ANTONIO BR TR 5′8″ 160 lbs.
Born Jose Antonio Mota (Baez).
B. Dec. 31, 1953, San Cristobal, Dominican Republic.

Year	Team	Games	BA	SA	AB	H	2B	3B	HR	HR%	R	RBI	BB	SO	SB	Pinch Hit AB	Pinch Hit H	PO	A	E	DP	TC/G	FA	G by Pos
1977	SEA A	91	.259	.321	305	79	14	1	1	0.3	39	17	19	20	6	7	1	152	253	11	54	5.1	.974	2B-77, DH-3, 3B-1
1978		23	.160	.200	50	8	0	1	0	0.0	8	2	6	7	1	3	0	39	55	2	17	5.3	.979	2B-14, 3B-3, DH-1
2 yrs.		114	.245	.304	355	87	14	2	1	0.3	47	19	25	27	7	10	1	191	308	13	71	5.2	.975	2B-91, 3B-4, DH-4

Kevin Baez

BAEZ, KEVIN RICHARD BR TR 6′ 160 lbs.
B. Jan. 10, 1967, Brooklyn, N. Y.

Year	Team	Games	BA	SA	AB	H	2B	3B	HR	HR%	R	RBI	BB	SO	SB	Pinch Hit AB	Pinch Hit H	PO	A	E	DP	TC/G	FA	G by Pos
1990	NY N	5	.167	.250	12	2	1	0	0	0.0	0	0	0	0	0	0	0	5	7	0	1	3.0	1.000	SS-4
1992		6	.154	.154	13	2	0	0	0	0.0	0	0	0	0	0	0	0	5	11	2	2	3.6	.889	SS-5
1993		52	.183	.254	126	23	9	0	0	0.0	10	7	13	17	0	1	0	57	117	6	24	3.5	.967	SS-52
3 yrs.		63	.179	.245	151	27	10	0	0	0.0	10	7	13	17	0	1	0	67	135	8	27	3.4	.962	SS-61

Bill Bagwell

BAGWELL, WILLIAM MALLORY (Big Bill) BL TL 6′1″ 175 lbs.
B. Feb. 24, 1896, Choudrant, La. D. Oct. 5, 1976, Choudrant, La.

Year	Team	Games	BA	SA	AB	H	2B	3B	HR	HR%	R	RBI	BB	SO	SB	Pinch Hit AB	Pinch Hit H	PO	A	E	DP	TC/G	FA	G by Pos
1923	BOS N	56	.290	.441	93	27	4	2	2	2.2	8	10	6	12	0	32	6	33	1	0	1	1.5	1.000	OF-22
1925	PHI A	36	.300	.380	50	15	2	1	0	0.0	4	10	2	2	0	31	7	2	0	1	0	0.8	.667	OF-4
2 yrs.		92	.294	.420	143	42	6	3	2	1.4	12	20	8	14	0	63	13	35	1	1	1	1.4	.973	OF-26

Jeff Bagwell

BAGWELL, JEFFREY ROBERT BR TR 6′ 195 lbs.
B. May 27, 1968, Boston, Mass.

Year	Team	Games	BA	SA	AB	H	2B	3B	HR	HR%	R	RBI	BB	SO	SB	Pinch Hit AB	Pinch Hit H	PO	A	E	DP	TC/G	FA	G by Pos
1991	HOU N	156	.294	.437	554	163	26	4	15	2.7	79	82	75	116	7	4	2	1270	106	12	97	9.0	.991	1B-155
1992		162	.273	.444	586	160	34	6	18	3.1	87	96	84	97	10	4	2	1334	133	7	110	9.3	.995	1B-159
1993		142	.320	.516	535	171	37	4	20	3.7	76	88	62	73	13	2	1	1200	113	9	106	9.4	.993	1B-140
1994		110	.367	**.750**	400	147	32	2	39	**9.8**	**104**	**116**	65	65	15	1	0	924	118	9	93	9.6	.991	1B-109, OF-1
1995		114	.290	.496	448	130	29	0	21	4.7	88	87	79	102	12	0	0	1004	129	7	78	10.0	.994	1B-114
5 yrs.		684	.306	.515	2523	771	158	16	113	4.5	434	469	365	453	57	11	5	5732	599	44	484	9.4	.993	1B-677, OF-1

Frank Bahret

BAHRET, FRANK J. 6′1″ 184 lbs.
B. Poughkeepsie, N. Y. Deceased.

Year	Team	Games	BA	SA	AB	H	2B	3B	HR	HR%	R	RBI	BB	SO	SB	Pinch Hit AB	Pinch Hit H	PO	A	E	DP	TC/G	FA	G by Pos
1884	BAL U	2	.000	.000	8	0	0	0	0	0.0	0		0			0	0	4	0	0	0	2.0	1.000	OF-2

Bill Bailey

BAILEY, HARRY LEWIS BL TR 5′10½″ 170 lbs.
B. Nov. 19, 1881, Shawnee, Ohio D. Oct. 27, 1967, Seattle, Wash.

Year	Team	Games	BA	SA	AB	H	2B	3B	HR	HR%	R	RBI	BB	SO	SB	Pinch Hit AB	Pinch Hit H	PO	A	E	DP	TC/G	FA	G by Pos
1911	NY A	5	.111	.111	9	1	0	0	0	0.0	1	0	0		0	2	0	0	3	0	0	1.0	1.000	OF-2, 3B-1

Bob Bailey

BAILEY, ROBERT SHERWOOD BR TR 6′1″ 180 lbs.
B. Oct. 13, 1942, Long Beach, Calif.

Year	Team	Games	BA	SA	AB	H	2B	3B	HR	HR%	R	RBI	BB	SO	SB	Pinch Hit AB	Pinch Hit H	PO	A	E	DP	TC/G	FA	G by Pos
1962	PIT N	14	.167	.262	42	7	2	1	0	0.0	6	6	6	10	1	2	0	10	25	3	2	3.2	.921	3B-12
1963		154	.228	.328	570	130	15	3	12	2.1	60	45	58	98	10	1	1	118	337	33	40	3.1	.932	3B-153, SS-3
1964		143	.281	.404	530	149	26	3	11	2.1	73	51	44	78	10	13	3	117	224	23	19	2.6	.937	3B-105, OF-35, SS-2
1965		159	.256	.363	626	160	28	3	11	1.8	87	49	70	93	10	2	0	119	247	23	25	2.3	.941	3B-142, OF-28
1966		126	.279	.447	380	106	19	3	13	3.4	51	46	47	65	5	11	4	81	202	12	20	2.5	.959	3B-96, OF-22
1967	LA N	116	.227	.301	322	73	8	2	4	1.2	21	28	40	50	5	19	3	94	154	16	12	2.7	.939	3B-65, OF-27, 1B-4, SS-1
1968		105	.227	.348	322	73	9	3	8	2.5	24	39	38	69	1	16	2	81	164	13	14	2.8	.950	3B-90, SS-1, OF-1
1969	MON N	111	.265	.419	358	95	16	6	9	2.5	46	53	40	76	3	15	4	715	67	8	77	8.1	.990	1B-85, OF-12, 3B-1
1970		131	.287	.597	352	101	19	3	28	8.0	77	84	72	70	5	36	12	179	86	8	18	2.5	.971	3B-48, OF-44, 1B-18
1971		157	.251	.382	545	137	21	4	14	2.6	65	83	97	105	13	0	0	177	204	14	16	2.2	.965	3B-120, OF-51, 1B-9
1972		143	.233	.368	489	114	10	4	16	3.3	55	57	59	112	6	7	3	95	251	22	21	2.6	.940	3B-134, OF-5, 1B-3
1973		151	.273	.489	513	140	25	4	26	5.1	77	86	88	99	5	5	0	94	275	17	25	2.6	.956	3B-146, OF-2
1974		152	.280	.446	507	142	20	2	20	3.9	69	73	100	107	4	8	2	139	125	10	10	1.9	.964	OF-78, 3B-68
1975		106	.273	.361	227	62	5	0	5	2.2	23	30	46	38	4	40	11	89	10	2	2	1.6	.980	OF-61, 3B-3
1976	CIN N	69	.298	.508	124	37	6	1	6	4.8	17	23	16	26	0	27	10	39	14	3	2	1.4	.946	OF-31, 3B-10
1977	2 teams	CIN N (49G –.253) BOS A (2G –.000)																						
"	total	51	.247	.370	81	20	2	1	2	2.5	9	11	12	11	1	27	6	109	10	3	11	5.5	.975	1B-19, OF-3
1978	BOS A	43	.191	.351	94	18	3	0	4	4.3	12	9	19	19	2	13	1	2	2	0	0	0.1	1.000	DH-34, OF-1, 3B-1
17 yrs.		1931	.257	.403	6082	1564	234	43	189	3.1	772	773	852	1126	85	242	62	2258	2397	210	314	2.7	.957	3B-1194, OF-401, 1B-138, DH-34, SS-7

Ed Bailey

BAILEY, LONAS EDGAR BL TR 6′2″ 205 lbs.
Brother of Jim Bailey.
B. Apr. 15, 1931, Strawberry Plains, Tenn.

Year	Team	Games	BA	SA	AB	H	2B	3B	HR	HR%	R	RBI	BB	SO	SB	Pinch Hit AB	Pinch Hit H	PO	A	E	DP	TC/G	FA	G by Pos
1953	CIN N	2	.375	.500	8	3	1	0	0	0.0	1	1	1	3	0	0	0	6	0	0	0	3.0	1.000	C-2
1954		73	.197	.388	183	36	2	3	9	4.9	21	20	35	34	1	12	0	194	20	6	2	3.6	.973	C-61
1955		21	.205	.359	39	8	1	1	1	2.6	3	4	4	10	0	9	3	42	8	2	3	4.7	.962	C-11
1956		118	.300	.551	383	115	8	2	28	7.3	59	75	52	50	2	13	8	511	52	9	10	5.4	.984	C-106
1957		122	.261	.463	391	102	15	2	20	5.1	54	48	73	69	5	6	2	542	41	5	5	5.1	.991	C-115
1958		112	.250	.411	360	90	23	1	11	3.1	39	59	47	61	2	11	1	438	44	6	6	4.9	.988	C-99
1959		121	.264	.393	379	100	13	0	12	3.2	43	40	62	53	2	8	2	549	64	6	6	5.3	.990	C-117
1960		133	.261	.406	441	115	19	3	13	2.9	52	67	59	70	1	9	2	621	52	7	8	5.3	.990	C-129
1961	2 teams	CIN N (12G –.302) SF N (107G –.238)																						
"	total	119	.245	.386	383	94	13	1	13	3.4	43	53	45	46	1	9	5	684	45	12	4	6.4	.984	C-115, OF-1
1962	SF N	96	.232	.476	254	59	9	1	17	6.7	32	45	42	42	1	18	6	419	25	6	3	6.0	.987	C-75
1963		105	.263	.494	308	81	8	0	21	6.8	41	68	50	64	0	16	3	560	44	8	3	7.0	.987	C-88
1964	MIL N	95	.262	.362	271	71	10	1	5	1.8	30	34	34	39	2	14	3	416	28	8	3	5.7	.982	C-80

Ed Bailey *continued*

Year	Team	Games	BA	SA	AB	H	2B	3B	HR	HR%	R	RBI	BB	SO	SB	Pinch Hit AB	Pinch Hit H	PO	A	E	DP	TC/G	FA	G by Pos
1965	2 teams	SF N (24G –.107) CHI N (66G –.253)																						
″	total	90	.230	.348	178	41	6	0	5	2.8	14	26	40	35	0	22	2	302	29	6	5	4.7	.982	C-66, 1B-5
1966	CAL A	5	.000	.000	3	0	0	0	0	0.0	0	0	1	1	0	3	0	0	0	0	0	0.0	—	
14 yrs.		1212	.256	.429	3581	915	128	15	155	4.3	432	540	545	577	17	150	37	5284	452	81	58	5.4	.986	C-1064, 1B-5, OF-1
WORLD SERIES																								
1962	SF N	6	.071	.286	14	1	0	0	1	7.1	1	2	0	3	0	2	0	15	0	0	0	5.0	1.000	C-3

Fred Bailey

BAILEY, FREDERICK MIDDLETON (Penny) BL TL 5′11″ 150 lbs.
B. Aug. 16, 1895, Mt. Hope, W. Va. D. Aug. 16, 1972, Huntington, W. Va.

Year	Team	Games	BA	SA	AB	H	2B	3B	HR	HR%	R	RBI	BB	SO	SB	Pinch Hit AB	Pinch Hit H	PO	A	E	DP	TC/G	FA	G by Pos
1916	BOS N	6	.100	.100	10	1	0	0	0	0.0	0	1	0	3	0	5	1	1	0	0	0	0.5	1.000	OF-2
1917		50	.191	.255	110	21	2	1	1	0.9	9	5	9	25	3	18	4	46	5	2	0	1.7	.962	OF-31
1918		4	.250	.250	4	1	0	0	0	0.0	1	0	0	1	0	4	1	0	0	0	0	0.0	—	
3 yrs.		60	.185	.242	124	23	2	1	1	0.8	10	6	9	29	3	27	6	47	5	2	0	1.6	.963	OF-33

Gene Bailey

BAILEY, ARTHUR EUGENE BR TR 5′ 8″ 160 lbs.
B. Nov. 25, 1893, Pearsall, Tex. D. Nov. 14, 1973, Houston, Tex.

Year	Team	Games	BA	SA	AB	H	2B	3B	HR	HR%	R	RBI	BB	SO	SB	Pinch Hit AB	Pinch Hit H	PO	A	E	DP	TC/G	FA	G by Pos
1917	PHI A	5	.083	.083	12	1	0	0	0	0.0	1	0	1	1	0	0	0	5	0	1	0	1.5	.833	OF-4
1919	BOS N	4	.333	.333	6	2	0	0	0	0.0	0	1	0	2	1	1	1	5	0	0	0	1.7	1.000	OF-3
1920	2 teams	BOS N (13G –.083) BOS A (46G –.230)																						
″	total	59	.208	.220	159	33	2	0	0	0.0	16	5	12	18	2	3	0	79	4	2	0	1.8	.976	OF-48
1923	BKN N	127	.265	.333	411	109	11	7	1	0.2	71	42	43	34	9	12	3	291	14	12	2	3.0	.962	OF-100, 1B-5
1924		18	.239	.370	46	11	3	0	1	2.2	7	4	7	6	1	0	0	39	2	0	1	2.4	1.000	OF-17
5 yrs.		213	.246	.303	634	156	16	7	2	0.3	95	52	63	61	13	16	4	419	20	15	3	2.6	.967	OF-172, 1B-5

Mark Bailey

BAILEY, JOHN MARK BB TR 6′ 5″ 195 lbs.
B. Nov. 4, 1961, Springfield, Mo.

Year	Team	Games	BA	SA	AB	H	2B	3B	HR	HR%	R	RBI	BB	SO	SB	Pinch Hit AB	Pinch Hit H	PO	A	E	DP	TC/G	FA	G by Pos
1984	HOU N	108	.212	.343	344	73	16	1	9	2.6	38	34	53	71	0	0	0	629	56	12	4	6.5	.983	C-108
1985		114	.265	.398	332	88	14	0	10	3.0	47	45	67	70	0	2	1	566	52	13	6	5.6	.979	C-110, 1B-2
1986		57	.176	.288	153	27	5	0	4	2.6	9	15	28	45	1	5	2	322	33	4	3	6.6	.989	C-53, 1B-1
1987		35	.203	.219	64	13	1	0	0	0.0	5	3	10	21	1	8	3	126	7	2	0	5.0	.985	C-27
1988		8	.130	.130	23	3	0	0	0	0.0	1	0	5	6	0	0	0	48	3	1	0	6.5	.981	C-8
1990	SF N	5	.143	.571	7	1	0	0	1	14.3	1	3	0	2	0	5	0	3	0	0	0	3.0	1.000	C-1
1992		13	.154	.192	26	4	1	0	0	0.0	0	1	3	7	0	5	0	33	2	0	0	5.0	1.000	C-7
7 yrs.		340	.220	.337	949	209	37	1	24	2.5	101	101	166	222	2	25	6	1727	153	32	13	6.0	.983	C-314, 1B-3

Bob Bailor

BAILOR, ROBERT MICHAEL BR TR 5′11″ 170 lbs.
B. July 10, 1951, Connellsville, Pa.

Year	Team	Games	BA	SA	AB	H	2B	3B	HR	HR%	R	RBI	BB	SO	SB	Pinch Hit AB	Pinch Hit H	PO	A	E	DP	TC/G	FA	G by Pos
1975	BAL A	5	.143	.143	7	1	0	0	0	0.0	0	0	1	0	0	0	0	5	9	0	1	4.7	1.000	SS-2, 2B-1
1976		9	.333	.667	6	2	0	1	0	0.0	2	0	0	0	0	1	0	0	0	0	0	0.0		SS-1, DH-1
1977	TOR A	122	.310	.403	496	154	21	5	5	1.0	62	32	17	26	15	3	2	235	165	12	27	3.3	.971	OF-63, SS-53, DH-7
1978		154	.264	.338	621	164	29	7	1	0.2	74	52	38	21	5	3	2	329	82	15	15	2.7	.965	OF-125, 3B-28, SS-4
1979		130	.229	.287	414	95	11	5	1	0.2	50	38	36	27	14	4	1	217	32	3	2	2.0	.988	OF-118, 2B-9, DH-1
1980		117	.236	.297	347	82	14	2	1	0.3	44	16	36	33	12	1	0	233	61	2	14	2.3	.993	OF-98, SS-12, 3B-11, P-3, DH-1, 2B-1
1981	NY N	51	.284	.346	81	23	3	1	0	0.0	11	8	8	11	2	3	0	43	60	4	9	2.2	.963	SS-22, 2B-13, OF-13, 3B-1
1982		110	.277	.319	376	104	14	1	0	0.0	44	31	20	17	20	13	6	166	272	11	42	3.2	.976	SS-60, 2B-56, 3B-21, OF-4
1983		118	.250	.282	340	85	8	0	1	0.3	33	30	20	23	18	9	1	171	296	16	65	3.5	.967	SS-75, 2B-50, 3B-11, OF-3
1984	LA N	65	.275	.305	131	36	4	0	0	0.0	11	8	8	1	3	7	2	59	117	6	19	3.3	.967	2B-23, 3B-17, SS-16
1985		74	.246	.288	118	29	3	1	0	0.0	8	7	3	5	1	6	3	35	103	3	12	2.1	.979	3B-45, 2B-16, SS-5, OF-1
11 yrs.		955	.264	.325	2937	775	107	23	9	0.3	339	222	187	164	90	50	17	1493	1197	72	206	2.8	.974	OF-425, SS-250, 2B-169, 3B-134, DH-10, P-3
LEAGUE CHAMPIONSHIP SERIES																								
1985	LA N	2	.000	.000	1	0	0	0	0	0.0	0	0	0	0	0	0	0	0	1	0	0	0.5	1.000	3B-2

Harold Baines

BAINES, HAROLD DOUGLAS BL TL 6′ 2″ 175 lbs.
B. Mar. 15, 1959, Easton, Md.

Year	Team	Games	BA	SA	AB	H	2B	3B	HR	HR%	R	RBI	BB	SO	SB	Pinch Hit AB	Pinch Hit H	PO	A	E	DP	TC/G	FA	G by Pos
1980	CHI A	141	.255	.405	491	125	23	6	13	2.6	55	49	19	65	2	9	1	229	6	9	1	1.8	.963	OF-137, DH-1
1981		82	.286	.482	280	80	11	7	10	3.6	42	41	12	41	6	5	1	120	10	2	1	1.6	.985	OF-80, DH-1
1982		161	.271	.469	608	165	29	8	25	4.1	89	105	49	95	10	1	0	326	10	7	4	2.1	.980	OF-161
1983		156	.280	.443	596	167	33	2	20	3.4	76	99	49	85	7	1	1	312	10	9	3	2.1	.973	OF-155
1984		147	.304	**.541**	569	173	28	10	29	5.1	72	94	54	75	1	1	0	307	8	6	1	2.2	.981	OF-147
1985		160	.309	.467	640	198	29	3	22	3.4	86	113	42	89	1	1	0	318	8	2	2	2.0	.994	OF-159, DH-1
1986		145	.296	.465	570	169	29	2	21	3.7	72	88	38	89	2	1	0	295	15	5	5	2.2	.984	OF-141, DH-3
1987		132	.293	.479	505	148	26	4	20	4.0	59	93	46	82	0	9	3	13	0	0	0	0.1	1.000	DH-117, OF-8
1988		158	.277	.411	599	166	39	1	13	2.2	55	81	67	109	0	4	2	14	1	2	0	0.1	.882	DH-147, OF-9
1989	2 teams	CHI A (96G –.321) TEX A (50G –.285)																						
″	total	146	.309	.465	505	156	29	1	16	3.2	73	72	73	79	0	8	1	54	0	2	0	0.4	.964	DH-116, OF-26
1990	2 teams	TEX A (103G –.290) OAK A (32G –.266)																						
″	total	135	.284	.441	415	118	15	1	16	3.9	52	65	67	80	0	13	4	5	0	1	0	0.0	.833	DH-125, OF-2
1991	OAK A	141	.295	.473	488	144	25	1	20	4.1	76	90	72	67	0	11	5	11	1	1	0	0.1	.923	DH-125, OF-12
1992		140	.253	.391	478	121	18	0	16	3.3	58	76	59	61	1	9	3	27	0	1	0	0.2	.964	DH-116, OF-23
1993	BAL A	118	.313	.510	416	130	22	0	20	4.8	64	78	57	52	0	6	2	0	0	0	0	0.0	.000	DH-116
1994		94	.294	.485	326	96	12	1	16	4.9	44	54	30	49	0	10	4	0	0	0	0	0.0	.000	DH-91
1995		127	.299	.540	385	115	19	1	24	6.2	60	63	70	45	0	9	5	0	0	0	0	0.0	.000	DH-122
16 yrs.		2183	.289	.465	7871	2271	387	48	301	3.8	1033	1261	804	1163	30	98	32	2031	69	47	17	1.0	.978	DH-1081, OF-1060
LEAGUE CHAMPIONSHIP SERIES																								
1983	CHI A	4	.125	.125	16	2	0	0	0	0.0	0	0	1	3	0	0	0	6	1	0	0	1.8	1.000	OF-4
1990	OAK A	4	.357	.429	14	5	1	0	0	0.0	2	3	2	1	1	0	0	0	0	0	0	0.0	.000	DH-4
1992		6	.440	.640	25	11	2	0	1	4.0	6	4	0	3	0	0	0	0	0	0	0	0.0	.000	DH-6
3 yrs.		14	.327	.436	55	18	3	0	1	1.8	8	7	3	7	1	0	0	6	1	0	0	0.5	1.000	DH-10, OF-4

Harold Baines *continued*

Year	Team	Games	BA	SA	AB	H	2B	3B	HR	HR%	R	RBI	BB	SO	SB	Pinch Hit AB	Pinch Hit H	PO	A	E	DP	TC/G	FA	G by Pos
WORLD SERIES																								
1990	OAK A	3	.143	.571	7	1	0	0	1	14.3	1	2	1	2	0	1	0	0	0	0	0	0.0	.000	DH-2

Al Baird

BAIRD, ALBERT WELLS
B. June 2, 1895, Cleburne, Tex. D. Nov. 27, 1976, Shreveport, La.
BR TR 5′ 9″ 160 lbs.

Year	Team	Games	BA	SA	AB	H	2B	3B	HR	HR%	R	RBI	BB	SO	SB	Pinch Hit AB	Pinch Hit H	PO	A	E	DP	TC/G	FA	G by Pos
1917	NY N	10	.292	.292	24	7	0	0	0	0.0	1	4	2	2	2	0	0	20	22	1	1	4.3	.977	2B-7, SS-3
1919		38	.241	.253	83	20	1	0	0	0.0	8	5	5	9	3	0	0	42	94	13	11	3.9	.913	2B-24, SS-9, 3B-5
2 yrs.		48	.252	.262	107	27	1	0	0	0.0	9	9	7	11	5	0	0	62	116	14	12	4.0	.927	2B-31, SS-12, 3B-5

Doug Baird

BAIRD, HOWARD DOUGLAS
B. Sept. 27, 1891, St. Charles, Mo. D. June 13, 1967, Thomasville, Ga.
BR TR 5′ 9½″ 148 lbs.

Year	Team	Games	BA	SA	AB	H	2B	3B	HR	HR%	R	RBI	BB	SO	SB	Pinch Hit AB	Pinch Hit H	PO	A	E	DP	TC/G	FA	G by Pos
1915	PIT N	145	.219	.322	512	112	26	12	1	0.2	49	53	37	**88**	29	2	0	196	235	25	13	3.0	.945	3B-131, OF-20, 2B-3
1916		128	.216	.279	430	93	10	7	1	0.2	41	28	24	49	20	3	0	183	215	27	22	3.4	.936	3B-80, 2B-29, OF-16
1917	2 teams	PIT N (43G –.259) STL N (104G –.253)																						
″	total	147	.255	.357	499	127	25	13	0	0.0	55	42	43	71	26	0	0	167	334	33	27	3.6	.938	3B-144, OF-2, 2B-2
1918	STL N	82	.247	.354	316	78	12	8	2	0.6	41	25	25	42	25	0	0	101	219	11	12	4.0	.967	3B-81, OF-1, SS-1
1919	3 teams	PHI N (66G –.252) STL N (16G –.212) BKN N (20G –.183)																						
″	total	102	.236	.322	335	79	13	5	2	0.6	43	42	25	41	18	5	1	122	195	19	19	3.6	.943	3B-91, 2B-1, OF-1
1920	2 teams	BKN N (6G –.333) NY N (7G –.125)																						
″	total	13	.214	.214	14	3	0	0	0	0.0	1	1	3	4	0	3	1	5	8	1	1	2.3	.929	3B-6
6 yrs.		617	.234	.326	2106	492	86	45	6	0.3	230	191	157	295	118	13	2	774	1206	116	94	3.4	.945	3B-533, OF-40, 2B-35, SS-1

Bill Baker

BAKER, WILLIAM PRESLEY
B. Feb. 22, 1911, Paw Creek, N. C.
BR TR 6′ 200 lbs.

Year	Team	Games	BA	SA	AB	H	2B	3B	HR	HR%	R	RBI	BB	SO	SB	Pinch Hit AB	Pinch Hit H	PO	A	E	DP	TC/G	FA	G by Pos
1940	CIN N	27	.217	.261	69	15	1	1	0	0.0	5	7	4	8	2	3	0	87	9	0	1	4.0	1.000	C-24
1941	2 teams	CIN N (2G –.000) PIT N (35G –.224)																						
″	total	37	.221	.265	68	15	3	0	0	0.0	5	6	12	1	0	3	0	75	14	3	1	2.7	.967	C-34
1942	PIT N	18	.118	.118	17	2	0	0	0	0.0	1	2	1	0	0	7	2	19	1	0	0	1.8	1.000	C-11
1943		63	.273	.360	172	47	6	3	1	0.6	12	26	22	6	3	7	1	157	29	4	3	3.4	.979	C-56
1946		53	.239	.301	113	27	4	0	1	0.9	7	8	12	6	0	9	2	97	14	4	3	2.7	.965	C-41, 1B-1
1948	STL N	45	.294	.395	119	35	10	1	0	0.0	13	15	15	7	1	7	2	152	15	1	2	4.7	.994	C-36
1949		20	.133	.167	30	4	1	0	0	0.0	2	4	2	2	0	10	0	16	1	0	1	1.7	1.000	C-10
7 yrs.		263	.247	.316	588	145	25	5	2	0.3	45	68	68	30	6	46	7	603	83	12	11	3.3	.983	C-212, 1B-1
WORLD SERIES																								
1940	CIN N	3	.250	.250	4	1	0	0	0	0.0	1	0	0	1	0	1	0	7	0	1	1	2.7	.875	C-3

Charlie Baker

BAKER, CHARLES A.
B. Jan. 15, 1856, Sterling, Mass. D. Jan. 15, 1937, Manchester, N. H.

Year	Team	Games	BA	SA	AB	H	2B	3B	HR	HR%	R	RBI	BB	SO	SB	Pinch Hit AB	Pinch Hit H	PO	A	E	DP	TC/G	FA	G by Pos
1884	2 teams	CHI U (12G –.156) PIT U (3G –.083)																						
″	total	15	.140	.228	57	8	2	0	1	1.8	5		0			0	0	15	10	9	1	2.3	.735	OF-11, SS-3, 2B-1

Chuck Baker

BAKER, CHARLES JOSEPH
B. Dec. 6, 1952, Seattle, Wash.
BR TR 5′11″ 180 lbs.

Year	Team	Games	BA	SA	AB	H	2B	3B	HR	HR%	R	RBI	BB	SO	SB	Pinch Hit AB	Pinch Hit H	PO	A	E	DP	TC/G	FA	G by Pos
1978	SD N	44	.207	.224	58	12	1	0	0	0.0	8	3	2	15	0	6	1	42	70	6	16	3.3	.949	2B-24, SS-12
1980		9	.136	.182	22	3	1	0	0	0.0	0	0	0	4	0	1	0	3	23	1	3	3.4	.963	SS-8
1981	MIN A	40	.182	.273	66	12	0	3	0	0.0	6	6	1	8	0	5	2	35	72	4	13	3.1	.964	SS-31, 2B-3, DH-1, 3B-1
3 yrs.		93	.185	.240	146	27	2	3	0	0.0	14	9	3	27	0	12	3	80	165	11	32	3.2	.957	SS-51, 2B-27, DH-1, 3B-1

Dave Baker

BAKER, DAVID GLENN
B. Nov. 25, 1956, Lacona, Iowa.
BL TR 6′ 185 lbs.

Year	Team	Games	BA	SA	AB	H	2B	3B	HR	HR%	R	RBI	BB	SO	SB	Pinch Hit AB	Pinch Hit H	PO	A	E	DP	TC/G	FA	G by Pos
1982	TOR A	9	.250	.300	20	5	1	0	0	0.0	3	2	3	3	0	0	0	5	16	5	2	3.3	.808	3B-8

Del Baker

BAKER, DELMAR DAVID
B. May 3, 1892, Sherwood, Ore. D. Sept. 11, 1973, San Antonio, Tex.
Manager 1933, 1936–42, 1960.
BR TR 5′11½″ 176 lbs.

Year	Team	Games	BA	SA	AB	H	2B	3B	HR	HR%	R	RBI	BB	SO	SB	Pinch Hit AB	Pinch Hit H	PO	A	E	DP	TC/G	FA	G by Pos
1914	DET A	43	.214	.271	70	15	2	1	0	0.0	4	1	6	9	0	3	0	79	25	9	3	3.0	.920	C-38
1915		68	.246	.313	134	33	3	3	0	0.0	16	15	15	15	3	3	0	184	53	15	8	4.1	.940	C-61
1916		61	.153	.194	98	15	4	0	0	0.0	7	6	11	8	2	1	0	164	29	5	4	3.4	.975	C-59
3 yrs.		172	.209	.265	302	63	9	4	0	0.0	27	22	32	32	5	7	0	427	107	29	15	3.6	.948	C-158

Doug Baker

BAKER, DOUGLAS LEE
B. Apr. 3, 1961, Fullerton, Calif.
BB TR 5′ 9″ 160 lbs.

Year	Team	Games	BA	SA	AB	H	2B	3B	HR	HR%	R	RBI	BB	SO	SB	Pinch Hit AB	Pinch Hit H	PO	A	E	DP	TC/G	FA	G by Pos
1984	DET A	43	.185	.241	108	20	4	1	0	0.0	15	11	7	22	3	1	1	56	86	5	20	3.3	.966	SS-39, 2B-5
1985		15	.185	.222	27	5	1	0	0	0.0	4	1	0	9	0	3	0	12	12	1	2	1.9	.960	SS-12, 2B-1
1986		13	.125	.167	24	3	1	0	0	0.0	1	0	2	7	0	1	0	17	21	1	5	3.0	.974	SS-10, 2B-2, DH-1
1987		8	.000	.000	1	0	0	0	0	0.0	0	0	0	1	0	1	0	2	8	0	1	1.3	1.000	SS-6, 3B-1, 2B-1
1988	MIN A	11	.000	.000	7	0	0	0	0	0.0	1	0	0	5	0	0	0	5	7	0	3	1.1	1.000	SS-9, 3B-1, 2B-1
1989		43	.295	.385	78	23	5	1	0	0.0	17	9	9	18	0	4	1	42	63	2	9	2.4	.981	2B-25, SS-19, DH-1
1990		3	.000	.000	1	0	0	0	0	0.0	0	0	0	0	0	0	0	1	2	0	0	1.0	1.000	2B-3
7 yrs.		136	.207	.268	246	51	11	2	0	0.0	38	21	18	62	3	10	2	135	199	9	40	2.5	.974	SS-95, 2B-38, 3B-2, DH-2
LEAGUE CHAMPIONSHIP SERIES																								
1984	DET A	1	—	—	0	0	0	0	0	—	0	0	0	0	0	0	0	0	0	0	0	0.0	.000	SS-1

Dusty Baker

BAKER, JOHNNIE B., JR.
B. June 15, 1949, Riverside, Calif.
Manager 1993–95.
BR TR 6′ 2″ 183 lbs.

Year	Team	Games	BA	SA	AB	H	2B	3B	HR	HR%	R	RBI	BB	SO	SB	Pinch Hit AB	Pinch Hit H	PO	A	E	DP	TC/G	FA	G by Pos
1968	ATL N	6	.400	.400	5	2	0	0	0	0.0	0	0	0	1	0	3	1	0	0	0	0	0.0	.000	OF-3
1969		3	.000	.000	7	0	0	0	0	0.0	0	0	0	3	0	0	0	2	0	0	0	0.7	1.000	OF-3
1970		13	.292	.292	24	7	0	0	0	0.0	3	4	2	4	0	1	0	11	1	3	0	1.4	.800	OF-11
1971		29	.226	.258	62	14	2	0	0	0.0	2	4	1	14	0	13	2	29	1	0	0	1.7	1.000	OF-18
1972		127	.321	.504	446	143	27	2	17	3.8	62	76	45	68	4	4	1	344	8	4	1	2.9	.989	OF-123

Dusty Baker *continued*

Year	Team	Games	BA	SA	AB	H	2B	3B	HR	HR%	R	RBI	BB	SO	SB	Pinch Hit AB	Pinch Hit H	PO	A	E	DP	TC/G	FA	G by Pos
1973		159	.288	.454	604	174	29	4	21	3.5	101	99	67	72	24	4	1	390	10	7	1	2.6	.983	OF-156
1974		149	.256	.422	574	147	35	0	20	3.5	80	69	71	87	18	1	0	359	10	7	2	2.5	.981	OF-148
1975		142	.261	.421	494	129	18	2	19	3.8	63	72	67	57	12	6	2	287	10	3	0	2.2	.990	OF-136
1976	**LA N**	112	.242	.307	384	93	13	0	4	1.0	36	39	31	54	2	8	4	254	3	1	1	2.4	.996	OF-106
1977		153	.291	.512	533	155	26	1	30	5.6	86	86	58	89	2	2	0	227	8	3	2	1.6	.987	OF-152
1978		149	.262	.375	522	137	24	1	11	2.1	62	66	47	66	12	5	0	250	13	4	1	1.8	.985	OF-145
1979		151	.274	.455	554	152	29	1	23	4.2	86	88	56	70	11	2	0	289	14	3	4	2.0	.990	OF-150
1980		153	.294	.503	579	170	26	4	29	5.0	80	97	43	66	12	3	0	308	5	3	3	2.1	.991	OF-151
1981		103	.320	.445	400	128	17	3	9	2.3	48	49	29	43	10	1	1	181	8	2	1	1.9	.990	OF-101
1982		147	.300	.458	570	171	19	1	23	4.0	80	88	56	62	17	4	1	226	7	6	1	1.7	.975	OF-144
1983		149	.260	.395	531	138	25	1	15	2.8	71	73	72	59	7	6	1	249	4	5	2	1.8	.981	OF-143
1984	**SF N**	100	.292	.374	243	71	7	2	3	1.2	31	32	40	27	4	30	7	112	1	3	0	1.9	.974	OF-62
1985	**OAK A**	111	.268	.440	343	92	15	1	14	4.1	48	52	50	47	2	17	7	465	29	5	33	4.7	.990	1B-58, OF-35, DH-13
1986		83	.240	.322	242	58	8	0	4	1.7	25	19	27	37	0	15	3	90	4	0	1	1.3	1.000	OF-55, DH-15, 1B-3
19 yrs.		2039	.278	.432	7117	1981	320	23	242	3.4	964	1013	762	926	137	125	31	4073	136	59	53	2.2	.986	OF-1842, 1B-61, DH-28
DIVISIONAL PLAYOFF SERIES																								
1981	**LA N**	5	.167	.222	18	3	1	0	0	0.0	2	1	2	0	0	0	0	12	0	0	0	2.4	1.000	OF-5
LEAGUE CHAMPIONSHIP SERIES																								
1977	**LA N**	4	.357	.857	14	5	1	0	2	14.3	4	8	2	3	0	0	0	3	0	0	0	0.8	1.000	OF-4
1978		4	.467	.600	15	7	2	0	0	0.0	1	1	3	0	0	0	0	5	0	0	0	1.3	1.000	OF-4
1981		5	.316	.368	19	6	1	0	0	0.0	3	3	1	0	0	0	0	10	0	1	0	2.2	.909	OF-5
1983		4	.357	.643	14	5	1	0	1	7.1	4	1	2	0	0	0	0	9	0	0	0	2.3	1.000	OF-4
4 yrs.		17	.371	.597	62	23	5	0	3	4.8	12	13	8	3	0	0	0	27	0	1	0	1.6	.964	OF-17
			6th	**5th**								**9th**												
WORLD SERIES																								
1977	**LA N**	6	.292	.417	24	7	0	0	1	4.2	4	5	0	2	0	0	0	11	0	1	0	2.0	.917	OF-6
1978		6	.238	.381	21	5	0	0	1	4.8	2	1	1	3	0	0	0	12	0	0	0	2.0	1.000	OF-6
1981		6	.167	.167	24	4	0	0	0	0.0	3	1	1	6	0	0	0	13	0	0	0	2.2	1.000	OF-6
3 yrs.		18	.232	.319	69	16	0	0	2	2.9	9	7	2	11	0	0	0	36	0	1	0	2.1	.973	OF-18

Floyd Baker

BAKER, FLOYD WILSON
B. Oct. 10, 1916, Luray, Va.

BL TR 5′ 9″ 160 lbs.

Year	Team	Games	BA	SA	AB	H	2B	3B	HR	HR%	R	RBI	BB	SO	SB	Pinch Hit AB	Pinch Hit H	PO	A	E	DP	TC/G	FA	G by Pos
1943	**STL A**	22	.174	.217	46	8	2	0	0	0.0	5	4	6	4	0	11	2	24	27	2	7	4.8	.962	SS-10, 3B-1
1944		44	.175	.206	97	17	3	0	0	0.0	10	5	11	5	2	11	4	41	68	5	9	3.5	.956	2B-17, SS-16
1945	**CHI A**	82	.250	.288	208	52	8	0	0	0.0	22	19	23	12	3	16	1	51	127	5	10	2.7	.973	3B-58, 2B-11
1946		9	.250	.292	24	6	1	0	0	0.0	2	3	2	3	0	3	0	10	15	1	1	4.3	.962	3B-6
1947		105	.264	.313	371	98	12	3	0	0.0	61	22	66	28	9	0	0	88	258	7	29	3.4	.980	3B-101, SS-1, 2B-1
1948		104	.215	.257	335	72	8	3	0	0.0	47	18	73	26	4	11	4	131	226	13	34	4.1	.965	3B-71, 2B-18, SS-1
1949		125	.260	.327	388	101	15	4	1	0.3	38	40	84	32	3	0	0	111	280	9	32	3.2	.978	3B-122, SS-3, 2B-1
1950		83	.317	.355	186	59	7	0	0	0.0	26	11	32	10	1	24	6	53	105	2	9	2.8	.988	3B-53, 2B-3, OF-2
1951		82	.263	.323	133	35	6	1	0	0.0	24	14	25	12	0	33	**9**	40	58	6	8	2.0	.942	3B-44, 2B-5, SS-3
1952	**WAS A**	79	.262	.293	263	69	8	0	0	0.0	27	33	30	17	1	4	0	166	196	6	42	4.8	.984	2B-68, SS-7, 3B-1
1953	**2 teams**	**WAS A** (9G –.000)	**BOS A** (81G –.273)																					
″	**total**	90	.263	.307	179	47	4	2	0	0.0	22	24	25	10	0	31	3	67	93	5	18	3.1	.970	3B-38, 2B-16
1954	**2 teams**	**BOS A** (21G –.200)	**PHI N** (23G –.227)																					
″	**total**	44	.214	.262	42	9	2	0	0	0.0	1	3	5	5	0	25	7	15	18	1	2	2.0	.971	3B-14, 2B-3
1955	**PHI N**	5	.000	.000	8	0	0	0	0	0.0	0	0	0	1	0	4	0	5	3	0	0	8.0	1.000	3B-1
13 yrs.		874	.251	.297	2280	573	76	13	1	0.0	285	196	382	165	23	173	36	802	1474	62	201	3.4	.973	3B-510, 2B-143, SS-41, OF-2
WORLD SERIES																								
1944	**STL A**	2	.000	.000	2	0	0	0	0	0.0	0	0	0	2	0	2	0	1	0	0	0	0.5	1.000	2B-2

Frank Baker

BAKER, FRANK
B. Jan. 11, 1944, Bartow, Fla.

BL TR 5′10″ 180 lbs.

Year	Team	Games	BA	SA	AB	H	2B	3B	HR	HR%	R	RBI	BB	SO	SB	Pinch Hit AB	Pinch Hit H	PO	A	E	DP	TC/G	FA	G by Pos
1969	**CLE A**	52	.256	.372	172	44	5	3	3	1.7	21	15	14	34	2	7	1	71	5	4	0	1.7	.950	OF-46
1971		73	.210	.304	181	38	12	1	1	0.6	18	23	12	34	1	23	3	65	2	1	1	1.3	.985	OF-51
2 yrs.		125	.232	.337	353	82	17	4	4	1.1	39	38	26	68	3	30	4	136	7	5	1	1.5	.966	OF-97

Frank Baker

BAKER, FRANK WATTS
B. Oct. 29, 1946, Meridian, Miss.

BL TR 6′ 2″ 178 lbs.

Year	Team	Games	BA	SA	AB	H	2B	3B	HR	HR%	R	RBI	BB	SO	SB	Pinch Hit AB	Pinch Hit H	PO	A	E	DP	TC/G	FA	G by Pos
1970	**NY A**	35	.231	.282	117	27	4	1	0	0.0	6	11	14	26	1	0	0	62	118	5	22	5.3	.973	SS-35
1971		43	.139	.165	79	11	2	0	0	0.0	9	2	16	22	3	1	0	53	97	8	28	4.2	.949	SS-38
1973	**BAL A**	44	.190	.317	63	12	1	2	1	1.6	10	11	7	7	0	2	1	44	65	5	17	2.8	.956	SS-32, 2B-7, 1B-1, 3B-1
1974		24	.172	.207	29	5	1	0	0	0.0	3	0	3	5	0	0	0	16	31	9	5	2.7	.839	SS-17, 2B-3, 3B-1
4 yrs.		146	.191	.250	288	55	8	3	1	0.3	28	24	40	60	4	3	1	175	311	27	72	3.8	.947	SS-122, 2B-10, 3B-2, 1B-1
LEAGUE CHAMPIONSHIP SERIES																								
1973	**BAL A**	2	—	—	0	0	0	0	0	—	0	0	0	0	0	0	0	0	0	0	0	0.0	.000	SS-2
1974		2	—	—	0	0	0	0	0	—	0	0	0	0	0	0	0	1	1	1	0	1.5	.667	SS-2
2 yrs.		4			0	0	0	0	0		0	0	0	0	0	0	0	1	1	1	0	0.8	.667	SS-4

Frank Baker

BAKER, JOHN FRANKLIN (Home Run)
B. Mar. 13, 1886, Trappe, Md. D. June 28, 1963, Trappe, Md.
Hall of Fame 1955.

BL TR 5′11″ 173 lbs.

Year	Team	Games	BA	SA	AB	H	2B	3B	HR	HR%	R	RBI	BB	SO	SB	Pinch Hit AB	Pinch Hit H	PO	A	E	DP	TC/G	FA	G by Pos
1908	**PHI A**	9	.290	.387	31	9	3	0	0	0.0	5	2	0		0	0	0	12	22	0	0	3.8	1.000	3B-9
1909		148	.305	.447	541	165	27	**19**	4	0.7	73	85	26		20	2	0	209	277	42	16	3.6	.920	3B-146
1910		146	.283	.392	561	159	25	15	2	0.4	83	74	34		21	0	0	207	313	45	35	3.9	.920	3B-146
1911		148	.334	.505	592	198	40	14	**11**	**1.9**	96	115	40		38	0	0	217	274	30	26	3.5	.942	3B-148
1912		149	.347	.541	577	200	40	21	**10**	**1.7**	116	**133**	50		40	0	0	217	321	34	25	3.8	.941	3B-149
1913		149	.336	.492	565	190	34	9	**12**	**2.1**	116	**126**	63	31	34	0	0	233	280	44	19	3.7	.921	3B-149
1914		150	.319	.442	570	182	23	10	**9**	1.6	84	97	53	37	19	1	0	221	292	24	20	3.6	.955	3B-149
1916	**NY A**	100	.269	.428	360	97	23	2	10	**2.8**	46	52	36	30	15	3	0	133	210	22	16	3.8	.940	3B-96
1917		146	.282	.365	553	156	24	2	6	1.1	57	71	48	27	18	0	0	202	317	28	21	3.7	.949	3B-146
1918		126	.306	.409	504	154	24	5	6	1.2	65	68	38	13	8	0	0	175	282	13	30	3.7	.972	3B-126

Frank Baker *continued*

Year	Team	Games	BA	SA	AB	H	2B	3B	HR	HR%	R	RBI	BB	SO	SB	Pinch Hit AB	Pinch Hit H	PO	A	E	DP	TC/G	FA	G by Pos
1919		141	.293	.388	567	166	22	1	10	1.8	70	83	44	18	13	0	0	176	286	22	28	3.4	.955	3B-141
1921		94	.294	.436	330	97	16	2	9	2.7	46	71	26	12	8	9	0	84	173	11	16	3.2	.959	3B-83
1922		69	.278	.444	234	65	12	3	7	3.0	30	36	15	14	1	8	1	68	108	7	7	3.0	.962	3B-60
13 yrs.		1575	.307	.442	5985	1838	313	103	96	1.6	887	1013	473	182	235	23	1	2154	3155	322	259	3.6	.943	3B-1548
WORLD SERIES																								
1910	PHI A	5	.409	.545	22	9	3	0	0	0.0	6	4	2	1	0	0	0	9	11	3	2	4.6	.870	3B-5
1911		6	.375	.708	24	9	2	0	2	8.3	7	5	1	5	0	0	0	10	10	2	2	3.7	.909	3B-6
1913		5	.450	.600	20	9	0	0	1	5.0	2	7	0	2	1	0	0	6	6	1	0	2.6	.923	3B-5
1914		4	.250	.375	16	4	2	0	0	0.0	0	2	1	3	0	0	0	10	15	0	1	6.3	1.000	3B-4
1921	NY A	4	.250	.250	8	2	0	0	0	0.0	0	0	1	0	0	2	0	2	3	0	0	2.5	1.000	3B-2
1922		1	.000	.000	1	0	0	0	0	0.0	0	0	0	0	0	1	0	0	0	0	0	0.0	—	
6 yrs.		25	.363 8th	.538	91	33	7	0	3	3.3	15	18	5	11	1	3	0	37	45	6	5	4.0	.932	3B-22

Gene Baker

BAKER, EUGENE WALTER
B. June 15, 1925, Davenport, Iowa.
BR TR 6′ 1″ 170 lbs.

Year	Team	Games	BA	SA	AB	H	2B	3B	HR	HR%	R	RBI	BB	SO	SB	Pinch Hit AB	Pinch Hit H	PO	A	E	DP	TC/G	FA	G by Pos
1953	CHI N	7	.227	.273	22	5	1	0	0	0.0	1	0	1	4	1	1	0	11	11	2	3	4.0	.917	2B-6
1954		135	.275	.425	541	149	32	5	13	2.4	68	61	47	55	4	0	0	355	385	25	102	5.7	.967	2B-134
1955		154	.268	.392	609	163	29	7	11	1.8	82	52	49	57	9	0	0	432	444	30	114	5.9	.967	2B-154
1956		140	.258	.377	546	141	23	3	12	2.2	65	57	39	54	4	0	0	362	426	25	99	5.8	.969	2B-140
1957	2 teams	CHI N (12G –.250) PIT N (111G –.266)																						
″	total	123	.264	.364	409	108	22	5	3	0.7	40	46	35	32	3	16	3	140	234	24	36	3.5	.940	3B-72, SS-28, 2B-13
1958	PIT N	29	.250	.321	56	14	2	1	0	0.0	3	7	8	6	0	14	6	19	28	0	2	3.4	1.000	3B-11, 2B-3
1960		33	.243	.243	37	9	0	0	0	0.0	5	4	2	9	0	18	4	7	9	0	2	2.0	1.000	3B-7, 2B-1
1961		9	.100	.100	10	1	0	0	0	0.0	1	0	3	2	0	3	0	0	6	0	0	2.0	1.000	3B-3
8 yrs.		630	.265	.385	2230	590	109	21	39	1.7	265	227	184	219	21	52	13	1326	1543	106	358	5.2	.964	2B-451, 3B-93, SS-28
WORLD SERIES																								
1960	PIT N	3	.000	.000	3	0	0	0	0	0.0	0	0	0	1	0	3	0	0	0	0	0	0.0	—	

George Baker

BAKER, GEORGE F.
B. 1859, St. Louis, Mo. Deceased.

Year	Team	Games	BA	SA	AB	H	2B	3B	HR	HR%	R	RBI	BB	SO	SB	Pinch Hit AB	Pinch Hit H	PO	A	E	DP	TC/G	FA	G by Pos
1883	BAL AA	7	.227	.227	22	5	0	0	0	0.0	0		0			0	0	13	6	7	2	3.3	.731	SS-4, C-3, OF-1
1884	STL U	80	.164	.183	317	52	6	0	0	0.0	39		5			0	0	451	138	73	14	8.1	.890	C-68, OF-5, 2B-4, 3B-3, SS-2
1885	STL N	38	.122	.122	131	16	0	0	0	0.0	5	5	9	28		0	0	153	34	32	2	5.8	.854	C-32, 3B-3, OF-2, 2B-1
1886	KC N	1	.250	.250	4	1	0	0	0	0.0	1	0	0	1		0	0	5	3	1	0	9.0	.889	C-1
4 yrs.		126	.156	.169	474	74	6	0	0	0.0	45	5	14	29		0	0	622	181	113	18	7.1	.877	C-104, OF-8, 3B-6, SS-6, 2B-5

Howard Baker

BAKER, HOWARD FRANCIS
B. Mar. 1, 1888, Bridgeport, Conn. D. Jan. 16, 1964, Bridgeport, Conn.
BR TR 5′11″ 175 lbs.

Year	Team	Games	BA	SA	AB	H	2B	3B	HR	HR%	R	RBI	BB	SO	SB	Pinch Hit AB	Pinch Hit H	PO	A	E	DP	TC/G	FA	G by Pos
1912	CLE A	11	.167	.167	30	5	0	0	0	0.0	1	2	5		0	1	0	15	12	1	0	2.8	.964	3B-10
1914	CHI A	15	.277	.340	47	13	1	1	0	0.0	4	5	3	8	2	0	0	7	22	4	1	2.2	.879	3B-15
1915	2 teams	CHI A (2G –.000) NY N (1G –.000)																						
″	total	3	.000	.000	5	0	0	0	0	0.0	0	0	0	2	0	2	0	1	2	0	0	3.0	1.000	3B-1
3 yrs.		29	.220	.256	82	18	1	1	0	0.0	5	7	8	10	2	3	0	23	36	5	1	2.5	.922	3B-26

Jack Baker

BAKER, JACK EDWARD
B. May 4, 1950, Birmingham, Ala.
BR TR 6′ 5″ 225 lbs.

Year	Team	Games	BA	SA	AB	H	2B	3B	HR	HR%	R	RBI	BB	SO	SB	Pinch Hit AB	Pinch Hit H	PO	A	E	DP	TC/G	FA	G by Pos
1976	BOS A	12	.130	.261	23	3	0	0	1	4.3	1	2	1	5	0	4	0	48	3	1	6	5.8	.981	1B-8, DH-1
1977		2	.000	.000	3	0	0	0	0	0.0	0	0	0	1	0	1	0	5	1	1	0	7.0	.857	1B-1
2 yrs.		14	.115	.231	26	3	0	0	1	3.8	1	2	1	6	0	5	0	53	4	2	6	5.9	.966	1B-9, DH-1

Jesse Baker

BAKER, JESSE (Tiny)
Born Michael Myron Silverman.
B. Mar. 4, 1895, Cleveland, Ohio D. July 29, 1976, West Los Angeles, Calif.
BR TR 5′ 4″ 140 lbs.

Year	Team	Games	BA	SA	AB	H	2B	3B	HR	HR%	R	RBI	BB	SO	SB	Pinch Hit AB	Pinch Hit H	PO	A	E	DP	TC/G	FA	G by Pos
1919	WAS A	1	—	—	0	0	0	0	0	—	0	0	0	0	0	0	0	0	1	0	0	1.0	1.000	SS-1

Phil Baker

BAKER, PHILIP
B. Sept. 19, 1856, Philadelphia, Pa. D. June 4, 1940, Washington, D. C.
BL TL 5′ 8″ 152 lbs.

Year	Team	Games	BA	SA	AB	H	2B	3B	HR	HR%	R	RBI	BB	SO	SB	Pinch Hit AB	Pinch Hit H	PO	A	E	DP	TC/G	FA	G by Pos
1883	BAL AA	28	.273	.331	121	33	2	1	1	0.8	22		8			0	0	113	14	21	2	4.4	.858	C-19, OF-14, SS-1
1884	WAS U	86	.288	.356	371	107	12	5	1	0.3	75		11			0	0	515	40	34	16	6.0	.942	1B-39, OF-32, C-27
1886	WAS N	81	.222	.280	325	72	6	5	1	0.3	37	34	20	32		0	0	602	15	21	30	6.9	.967	1B-56, OF-21, C-16
3 yrs.		195	.259	.322	817	212	20	11	3	0.4	134	34	39	32		0	0	1230	69	76	48	6.1	.945	1B-95, OF-67, C-62, SS-1

Tracy Baker

BAKER, TRACY LEE
B. Nov. 7, 1891, Pendleton, Ore. D. Mar. 14, 1975, Placerville, Calif.
BR TR 6′ 1″ 180 lbs.

Year	Team	Games	BA	SA	AB	H	2B	3B	HR	HR%	R	RBI	BB	SO	SB	Pinch Hit AB	Pinch Hit H	PO	A	E	DP	TC/G	FA	G by Pos
1911	BOS A	1	—	—	0	0	0	0	0	—	0	0	0		0	0	0	4	0	0	0	4.0	1.000	1B-1

John Balaz

BALAZ, JOHN LAWRENCE
B. Nov. 24, 1950, Toronto, Ont., Canada.
BR TR 6′ 3″ 180 lbs.

Year	Team	Games	BA	SA	AB	H	2B	3B	HR	HR%	R	RBI	BB	SO	SB	Pinch Hit AB	Pinch Hit H	PO	A	E	DP	TC/G	FA	G by Pos
1974	CAL A	14	.238	.310	42	10	0	0	1	2.4	4	5	2	10	0	1	1	17	0	0	0	1.4	1.000	OF-12
1975		45	.242	.350	120	29	8	1	1	0.8	10	10	5	25	0	7	2	40	3	0	1	1.1	1.000	OF-27, DH-11
2 yrs.		59	.241	.340	162	39	8	1	2	1.2	14	15	7	35	0	8	3	57	3	0	1	1.2	1.000	OF-39, DH-11

Steve Balboni

BALBONI, STEPHEN CHARLES (Bye-Bye)
B. Jan. 16, 1957, Brockton, Mass.
BR TR 6′ 3″ 225 lbs.

Year	Team	Games	BA	SA	AB	H	2B	3B	HR	HR%	R	RBI	BB	SO	SB	Pinch Hit AB	Pinch Hit H	PO	A	E	DP	TC/G	FA	G by Pos
1981	NY A	4	.286	.714	7	2	1	1	0	0.0	2	2	1	4	0	1	0	14	1	0	2	3.8	1.000	1B-3, DH-1
1982		33	.187	.280	107	20	2	1	2	1.9	8	4	6	34	0	5	1	194	13	2	23	6.7	.990	1B-26, DH-5
1983		32	.233	.430	86	20	2	0	5	5.8	8	17	8	23	0	3	1	178	9	3	19	7.0	.984	1B-23, DH-4
1984	KC A	126	.244	.498	438	107	23	2	28	6.4	58	77	45	139	0	1	0	1102	79	15	102	9.5	.987	1B-125, DH-1
1985		160	.243	.477	600	146	28	2	36	6.0	74	88	52	**166**	1	1	0	1573	101	12	138	10.5	.993	1B-160
1986		138	.229	.451	512	117	25	1	29	5.7	54	88	43	146	0	2	0	1236	98	18	115	9.9	.987	1B-137
1987		121	.207	.427	386	80	11	1	24	6.2	44	60	34	97	0	15	4	521	41	6	39	5.3	.989	1B-55, DH-52

Steve Balboni *continued*

Year	Team	Games	BA	SA	AB	H	2B	3B	HR	HR%	R	RBI	BB	SO	SB	Pinch Hit AB	Pinch Hit H	PO	A	E	DP	TC/G	FA	G by Pos
1988	2 teams	KC A (21G –.143) SEA A (97G –.251)																						
"	total	118	.235	.448	413	97	17	1	23	5.6	46	66	24	87	0	9	2	428	30	4	45	4.0	.991	DH-62, 1B-53
1989	NY A	110	.237	.460	300	71	12	2	17	5.7	33	59	25	67	0	25	6	150	7	1	15	1.5	.994	DH-82, 1B-20
1990		116	.192	.406	266	51	6	0	17	6.4	24	34	35	91	0	40	8	183	7	3	23	1.9	.984	DH-72, 1B-28
1993	TEX A	2	.600	.600	5	3	0	0	0	0.0	0	0	0	2	0	1	0	0	0	0	0	0.0	.000	DH-2
11 yrs.		960	.229	.451	3120	714	127	11	181	5.8	351	495	273	856	1	103	22	5579	386	64	521	6.6	.989	1B-630, DH-281
LEAGUE CHAMPIONSHIP SERIES																								
1984	KC A	3	.100	.100	10	1	0	0	0	0.0	0	0	1	4	0	0	0	20	3	1	2	8.0	.958	1B-3
1985		7	.120	.120	25	3	0	0	0	0.0	1	1	2	8	0	0	0	71	7	2	5	11.4	.975	1B-7
2 yrs.		10	.114	.114	35	4	0	0	0	0.0	1	1	3	12	0	0	0	91	10	3	7	10.4	.971	1B-10
WORLD SERIES																								
1985	KC A	7	.320	.320	25	8	0	0	0	0.0	2	3	5	4	0	0	0	70	3	0	1	10.4	1.000	1B-7

Bobby Balcena

BALCENA, ROBERT RUDOLPH BR TL 5′ 7″ 160 lbs.
B. Aug. 1, 1925, San Pedro, Calif. D. Jan. 4, 1990, San Pedro, Calif.

Year	Team	Games	BA	SA	AB	H	2B	3B	HR	HR%	R	RBI	BB	SO	SB	Pinch Hit AB	Pinch Hit H	PO	A	E	DP	TC/G	FA	G by Pos
1956	CIN N	7	.000	.000	2	0	0	0	0	0.0	2	0	0	1	0	2	0	1	0	0	0	0.5	1.000	OF-2

Billy Baldwin

BALDWIN, ROBERT HARVEY BL TL 6′ 175 lbs.
B. June 9, 1951, Tazewell, Va.

Year	Team	Games	BA	SA	AB	H	2B	3B	HR	HR%	R	RBI	BB	SO	SB	Pinch Hit AB	Pinch Hit H	PO	A	E	DP	TC/G	FA	G by Pos
1975	DET A	30	.221	.379	95	21	3	0	4	4.2	8	8	5	14	2	0	0	53	4	1	1	2.2	.983	OF-25, DH-1
1976	NY N	9	.273	.545	22	6	1	1	1	4.5	4	5	1	2	0	3	1	12	1	1	1	2.8	.929	OF-5
2 yrs.		39	.231	.410	117	27	4	1	5	4.3	12	13	6	16	2	3	1	65	5	2	2	2.3	.972	OF-30, DH-1

Frank Baldwin

BALDWIN, FRANK DeWITT BR TR 5′11″ 195 lbs.
B. Dec. 25, 1928, High Bridge, N. J.

Year	Team	Games	BA	SA	AB	H	2B	3B	HR	HR%	R	RBI	BB	SO	SB	Pinch Hit AB	Pinch Hit H	PO	A	E	DP	TC/G	FA	G by Pos
1953	CIN N	16	.100	.100	20	2	0	0	0	0.0	0	0	1	9	0	11	1	9	0	0	0	1.5	1.000	C-6

Henry Baldwin

BALDWIN, HENRY CLAY (Ted) BR TR 5′11″ 180 lbs.
B. June 13, 1894, Chadds Ford, Pa. D. Feb. 24, 1964, West Chester, Pa.

Year	Team	Games	BA	SA	AB	H	2B	3B	HR	HR%	R	RBI	BB	SO	SB	Pinch Hit AB	Pinch Hit H	PO	A	E	DP	TC/G	FA	G by Pos
1927	PHI N	6	.313	.313	16	5	0	0	0	0.0	1	1	1	2	0	1	1	4	6	1	1	2.2	.909	SS-3, 3B-2

Jeff Baldwin

BALDWIN, JEFFREY ALLEN BL TL 6′ 1″ 180 lbs.
B. Sept. 5, 1965, Milford, Del.

Year	Team	Games	BA	SA	AB	H	2B	3B	HR	HR%	R	RBI	BB	SO	SB	Pinch Hit AB	Pinch Hit H	PO	A	E	DP	TC/G	FA	G by Pos
1990	HOU N	7	.000	.000	8	0	0	0	0	0.0	1	0	1	2	0	6	0	1	0	0	0	0.3	1.000	OF-3

Kid Baldwin

BALDWIN, CLARENCE GEOGHAN BR TR 5′ 6″ 147 lbs.
B. Nov. 1, 1864, Newport, Ky. D. July 10, 1897, Cincinnati, Ohio.

Year	Team	Games	BA	SA	AB	H	2B	3B	HR	HR%	R	RBI	BB	SO	SB	Pinch Hit AB	Pinch Hit H	PO	A	E	DP	TC/G	FA	G by Pos
1884	2 teams	KC U (50G –.194) PIT U (1G –1.000)																						
"	total	51	.198	.271	192	38	5	3	1	0.5	19		4			0	0	220	92	41	4	6.2	.884	C-45, OF-10, 3B-1, 2B-1
1885	CIN AA	34	.135	.167	126	17	1	0	1	0.8	9		3			0	0	142	37	34	4	5.9	.840	C-25, OF-6, P-2, 2B-2, 3B-1
1886		87	.229	.327	315	72	8	7	3	1.0	41		8			0	0	369	118	67	13	6.2	.879	C-71, 3B-13, OF-6
1887		96	.253	.351	388	98	15	10	1	0.3	46		6		13	0	0	381	165	79	9	6.4	.874	C-96, OF-2
1888		67	.218	.292	271	59	11	3	1	0.4	27	25	3		4	0	0	355	108	41	6	7.4	.919	C-65, OF-2, 1B-1
1889		60	.247	.341	223	55	14	2	1	0.4	34	34	5	32	7	0	0	288	93	38	5	6.9	.909	C-55, OF-4, 3B-1, 1B-1
1890	2 teams	CIN N (22G –.153) PHI AA (24G –.233)																						
"	total	46	.198	.228	162	32	1	2	0	0.0	10	10	7	6	4	0	0	201	75	35	7	6.8	.887	C-39, 3B-5, OF-2
7 yrs.		441	.221	.301	1677	371	55	27	8	0.5	186	69	36	38	28	0	0	1956	688	335	48	6.5	.888	C-396, OF-32, 3B-21, 2B-3, 1B-2, P-2

Reggie Baldwin

BALDWIN, REGINALD CONRAD BR TR 6′ 1″ 195 lbs.
B. Aug. 19, 1954, River Rouge, Mich.

Year	Team	Games	BA	SA	AB	H	2B	3B	HR	HR%	R	RBI	BB	SO	SB	Pinch Hit AB	Pinch Hit H	PO	A	E	DP	TC/G	FA	G by Pos
1978	HOU N	38	.254	.373	67	17	5	0	1	1.5	5	11	3	3	0	18	5	76	8	4	1	5.2	.955	C-17
1979		14	.200	.250	20	4	1	0	0	0.0	0	1	0	1	0	12	3	10	1	0	0	2.8	1.000	C-3, 1B-1
2 yrs.		52	.241	.345	87	21	6	0	1	1.1	5	12	3	4	0	30	8	86	9	4	1	4.7	.960	C-20, 1B-1

Mike Balenti

BALENTI, MICHAEL RICHARD BR TR 5′11″ 175 lbs.
B. July 3, 1886, Calumet, Okla. D. Aug. 4, 1955, Altus, Okla.

Year	Team	Games	BA	SA	AB	H	2B	3B	HR	HR%	R	RBI	BB	SO	SB	Pinch Hit AB	Pinch Hit H	PO	A	E	DP	TC/G	FA	G by Pos
1911	CIN N	8	.250	.250	8	2	0	0	0	0.0	2	0	0	1	3	0	0	2	4	1	1	2.3	.857	SS-2, OF-1
1913	STL A	70	.180	.227	211	38	2	4	0	0.0	17	11	6	32	3	4	1	124	170	23	26	5.0	.927	SS-56, OF-8
2 yrs.		78	.183	.228	219	40	2	4	0	0.0	19	11	6	33	6	4	1	126	174	24	27	4.8	.926	SS-58, OF-9

Lee Bales

BALES, WESLEY OWEN BB TR 5′10½″ 165 lbs.
B. Dec. 4, 1944, Los Angeles, Calif.

Year	Team	Games	BA	SA	AB	H	2B	3B	HR	HR%	R	RBI	BB	SO	SB	Pinch Hit AB	Pinch Hit H	PO	A	E	DP	TC/G	FA	G by Pos
1966	ATL N	12	.063	.063	16	1	0	0	0	0.0	4	0	0	5	0	0	0	12	17	0	2	2.9	1.000	2B-7, 3B-3
1967	HOU N	19	.111	.111	27	3	0	0	0	0.0	4	2	8	7	1	6	0	9	13	1	2	3.3	.957	2B-6, SS-1
2 yrs.		31	.093	.093	43	4	0	0	0	0.0	8	2	8	12	1	6	0	21	30	1	4	3.1	.981	2B-13, 3B-3, SS-1

Art Ball

BALL, ARTHUR TR 168 lbs.
B. Apr. 1876, Ky. D. Dec. 26, 1915, Chicago, Ill.

Year	Team	Games	BA	SA	AB	H	2B	3B	HR	HR%	R	RBI	BB	SO	SB	Pinch Hit AB	Pinch Hit H	PO	A	E	DP	TC/G	FA	G by Pos
1894	STL N	1	.333	.333	3	1	0	0	0	0.0	0	0	0	1	0	0	0	2	0	1	0	3.0	.667	2B-1
1898	BAL N	32	.185	.210	81	15	2	0	0	0.0	7	8	7		2	0	0	38	74	8	6	3.8	.933	3B-15, SS-14, 2B-2, OF-1
2 yrs.		33	.190	.214	84	16	2	0	0	0.0	7	8	7	1	2	0	0	40	74	9	6	3.7	.927	3B-15, SS-14, 2B-3, OF-1

Jim Ball

BALL, JAMES CHANDLER BR TR 5′11″ 175 lbs.
B. Feb. 22, 1884, Harford County, Md. D. Apr. 7, 1963, Glendale, Calif.

Year	Team	Games	BA	SA	AB	H	2B	3B	HR	HR%	R	RBI	BB	SO	SB	Pinch Hit AB	Pinch Hit H	PO	A	E	DP	TC/G	FA	G by Pos
1907	BOS N	10	.167	.222	36	6	2	0	0	0.0	3	3	2		0	0	0	37	15	2	2	5.4	.963	C-10
1908		6	.067	.067	15	1	0	0	0	0.0	1	0	1		0	0	0	14	8	2	0	4.0	.917	C-6
2 yrs.		16	.137	.176	51	7	2	0	0	0.0	4	3	3		0	0	0	51	23	4	2	4.9	.949	C-16

Neal Ball

BALL, CORNELIUS
B. Apr. 22, 1881, Grand Haven, Mich. D. Oct. 15, 1957, Bridgeport, Conn.
BR TR 5′ 7″ 145 lbs.

Year	Team	Games	BA	SA	AB	H	2B	3B	HR	HR%	R	RBI	BB	SO	SB	Pinch Hit AB	Pinch Hit H	PO	A	E	DP	TC/G	FA	G by Pos
1907	NY A	15	.205	.273	44	9	1	1	0	0.0	5	4	1		1	0	0	29	36	13	3	4.9	.833	SS-11, 2B-5
1908		132	.247	.291	446	110	16	2	0	0.0	34	38	21		32	1	1	270	438	81	28	6.0	.897	SS-130, 2B-1
1909	2 teams	NY A (8G –.207) CLE A (96G –.256)																						
″	total	104	.252	.317	353	89	14	3	1	0.3	34	28	20		19	0	0	213	307	49	43	5.5	.914	SS-95, 2B-8
1910	CLE A	53	.210	.252	119	25	3	1	0	0.0	12	12	9		4	3	0	73	95	11	10	4.3	.939	SS-27, OF-6, 2B-6, 3B-3
1911		116	.296	.396	412	122	14	9	3	0.7	45	45	27		21	1	0	228	329	36	41	5.2	.939	2B-95, 3B-17, SS-1
1912	2 teams	CLE A (37G –.227) BOS A (18G –.200)																						
″	total	55	.220	.266	177	39	6	1	0	0.0	22	20	12		12	1	1	106	113	15	13	4.3	.936	2B-54
1913	BOS A	21	.172	.207	58	10	2	0	0	0.0	9	4	9	13	3	2	0	30	49	11	5	4.7	.878	2B-10, SS-8, 3B-1
7 yrs.		496	.251	.314	1609	404	56	17	4	0.2	161	151	99	13	92	8	2	949	1367	216	143	5.3	.915	SS-272, 2B-179, 3B-21, OF-6
WORLD SERIES																								
1912	BOS A	1	.000	.000	1	0	0	0	0	0.0	0	0	0	1	0	1	0	0	0	0	0	0.0	—	

Pelham Ballenger

BALLENGER, PELHAM ASHBY
B. Feb. 6, 1894, Gilreath Mill, S. C. D. Dec. 8, 1948, Greenville County, S. C.
BR TR 5′11″ 160 lbs.

Year	Team	Games	BA	SA	AB	H	2B	3B	HR	HR%	R	RBI	BB	SO	SB	Pinch Hit AB	Pinch Hit H	PO	A	E	DP	TC/G	FA	G by Pos
1928	WAS A	3	.111	.111	9	1	0	0	0	0.0	0	0	0	1	0	0	0	1	8	0	1	3.0	1.000	3B-3

Hal Bamberger

BAMBERGER, HAROLD EARL (Dutch)
B. Oct. 29, 1924, Lebanon, Pa.
BL TR 6′ 173 lbs.

Year	Team	Games	BA	SA	AB	H	2B	3B	HR	HR%	R	RBI	BB	SO	SB	Pinch Hit AB	Pinch Hit H	PO	A	E	DP	TC/G	FA	G by Pos
1948	NY N	7	.083	.083	12	1	0	0	0	0.0	0	0	1	2	0	3	0	6	0	0	0	2.0	1.000	OF-3

Dave Bancroft

BANCROFT, DAVID JAMES (Beauty)
B. Apr. 20, 1891, Sioux City, Iowa D. Oct. 9, 1972, Superior, Wis.
Manager 1924–27.
Hall of Fame 1971.
BB TR 5′ 9½″ 160 lbs.

Year	Team	Games	BA	SA	AB	H	2B	3B	HR	HR%	R	RBI	BB	SO	SB	Pinch Hit AB	Pinch Hit H	PO	A	E	DP	TC/G	FA	G by Pos
1915	PHI N	153	.254	.330	563	143	18	2	7	1.2	85	30	77	62	15	0	0	336	492	64	60	5.8	.928	SS-153
1916		142	.212	.252	477	101	10	0	3	0.6	53	33	74	57	15	0	0	326	510	60	64	6.3	.933	SS-142
1917		127	.243	.335	478	116	22	5	4	0.8	56	43	44	42	14	1	0	289	445	52	58	6.3	.934	SS-120, 2B-3, OF-2
1918		125	.265	.319	499	132	19	4	0	0.0	69	26	54	36	11	0	0	371	457	64	57	7.1	.928	SS-125
1919		92	.272	.352	335	91	13	7	0	0.0	45	25	31	30	8	4	1	242	306	28	43	6.5	.951	SS-88
1920	2 teams	PHI N (42G –.298) NY N (108G –.299)																						
″	total	150	.299	.387	613	183	36	9	0	0.0	102	36	42	44	8	0	0	362	598	45	95	6.7	.955	SS-150
1921	NY N	153	.318	.441	606	193	26	15	6	1.0	121	67	66	23	17	0	0	396	546	39	105	6.4	.960	SS-153
1922		156	.321	.418	651	209	41	5	4	0.6	117	60	79	27	16	0	0	405	579	62	93	6.7	.941	SS-156
1923		107	.304	.399	444	135	33	3	1	0.2	80	31	62	23	8	0	0	280	416	46	62	6.9	.938	SS-96, 2B-11
1924	BOS N	79	.279	.339	319	89	11	1	2	0.6	49	21	37	24	4	0	0	186	259	18	57	5.9	.961	SS-79
1925		128	.319	.426	479	153	29	8	2	0.4	75	49	64	22	7	3	1	300	459	44	81	6.4	.945	SS-125
1926		127	.311	.384	453	141	18	6	1	0.2	70	44	64	29	3	1	0	318	400	33	75	6.0	.956	SS-123, 3B-2
1927		111	.243	.307	375	91	13	4	1	0.3	44	31	43	36	5	5	1	275	329	39	66	6.1	.939	SS-104, 3B-1
1928	BKN N	149	.247	.303	515	127	19	5	0	0.0	47	51	59	20	7	0	0	350	484	46	66	5.9	.948	SS-149
1929		104	.277	.332	358	99	11	3	1	0.3	35	44	29	11	7	2	0	224	309	25	45	5.5	.955	SS-102
1930	NY N	10	.059	.118	17	1	1	0	0	0.0	0	0	2	1	0	1	0	13	15	1	0	3.6	.966	SS-8
16 yrs.		1913	.279	.358	7182	2004	320	77	32	0.4	1048	591	827	487	145	17	3	4673	6604	666	1027	6.3	.944	SS-1873, 2B-14, 3B-3, OF-2
WORLD SERIES																								
1915	PHI N	5	.294	.294	17	5	0	0	0	0.0	2	1	2	2	0	0	0	13	10	1	2	4.8	.958	SS-5
1921	NY N	8	.152	.182	33	5	1	0	0	0.0	3	3	1	5	0	0	0	16	17	1	1	4.3	.971	SS-8
1922		5	.211	.211	19	4	0	0	0	0.0	4	2	2	1	0	0	0	9	17	1	2	5.4	.963	SS-5
1923		6	.083	.083	24	2	0	0	0	0.0	1	1	1	2	1	0	0	11	24	0	6	5.8	1.000	SS-6
4 yrs.		24	.172	.183	93	16	1	0	0	0.0	10	7	6	10	1	0	0	49	68	3	11	5.0	.975	SS-24

Chris Bando

BANDO, CHRISTOPHER MICHAEL
Brother of Sal Bando.
B. Feb. 4, 1956, Cleveland, Ohio.
BB TR 6′ 195 lbs.

Year	Team	Games	BA	SA	AB	H	2B	3B	HR	HR%	R	RBI	BB	SO	SB	Pinch Hit AB	Pinch Hit H	PO	A	E	DP	TC/G	FA	G by Pos
1981	CLE A	21	.213	.277	47	10	3	0	0	0.0	3	6	2	2	0	9	0	53	5	2	0	3.5	.967	C-15, DH-2
1982		66	.212	.304	184	39	6	1	3	1.6	13	16	24	30	0	12	4	268	23	3	1	4.5	.990	C-63, 3B-2
1983		48	.256	.380	121	31	3	0	4	3.3	15	15	15	19	0	9	2	170	19	1	2	4.4	.995	C-43
1984		75	.291	.505	220	64	11	0	12	5.5	38	41	33	35	1	11	2	307	30	6	4	5.2	.983	C-63, 1B-1, DH-1, 3B-1
1985		73	.139	.173	173	24	4	1	0	0.0	11	13	22	21	0	8	2	251	28	4	3	4.2	.986	C-67
1986		92	.268	.327	254	68	9	0	2	0.8	28	26	22	49	0	13	2	359	30	4	3	4.6	.990	C-86
1987		89	.218	.332	211	46	9	0	5	2.4	20	16	12	28	0	5	0	351	34	4	8	4.5	.990	C-86
1988	2 teams	CLE A (32G –.125) DET A (1G –.000)																						
″	total	33	.125	.181	72	9	1	0	1	1.4	6	8	8	12	0	2	0	123	14	3	2	4.2	.979	C-33
1989	OAK A	1	.500	.500	2	1	0	0	0	0.0	0	1	0	1	0	0	0	8	0	0	0	8.0	1.000	C-1
9 yrs.		498	.227	.329	1284	292	46	2	27	2.1	134	142	138	197	1	69	12	1890	183	27	23	4.5	.987	C-457, 3B-3, DH-3, 1B-1

Sal Bando

BANDO, SALVATORE LEONARD
Brother of Chris Bando.
B. Feb. 13, 1944, Cleveland, Ohio.
BR TR 6′ 195 lbs.

Year	Team	Games	BA	SA	AB	H	2B	3B	HR	HR%	R	RBI	BB	SO	SB	Pinch Hit AB	Pinch Hit H	PO	A	E	DP	TC/G	FA	G by Pos
1966	KC A	11	.292	.417	24	7	1	1	0	0.0	1	1	1	3	0	4	2	5	23	2	1	4.3	.933	3B-7
1967		47	.192	.246	130	25	3	2	0	0.0	11	6	16	24	1	4	0	43	96	6	7	3.3	.959	3B-44
1968	OAK A	162	.251	.354	605	152	25	5	9	1.5	67	67	51	78	13	0	0	188	272	17	27	2.9	.964	3B-162, OF-1
1969		162	.281	.484	609	171	25	3	31	5.1	106	113	111	82	1	0	0	178	321	24	36	3.2	.954	3B-162
1970		155	.263	.430	502	132	20	2	20	4.0	93	75	118	88	6	1	0	158	258	20	22	2.9	.954	3B-152
1971		153	.271	.452	538	146	23	1	24	4.5	75	94	86	55	3	0	0	141	267	12	22	2.7	.971	3B-153
1972		152	.236	.368	535	126	20	3	15	2.8	64	77	78	55	3	1	0	124	337	20	29	3.2	.958	3B-151, 2B-1
1973		162	.287	.498	592	170	**32**	3	29	4.9	97	98	82	84	4	0	0	126	281	22	24	2.6	.949	3B-159, DH-3
1974		146	.243	.426	498	121	21	2	22	4.4	84	103	86	79	2	4	2	113	287	23	28	2.9	.946	3B-141, DH-3
1975		160	.230	.356	562	129	24	1	15	2.7	64	78	87	80	7	1	0	122	314	15	36	2.8	.967	3B-160
1976		158	.240	.427	550	132	18	2	27	4.9	75	84	76	74	20	0	0	127	310	17	27	2.8	.963	3B-155, SS-5, DH-2
1977	MIL A	159	.250	.395	580	145	27	3	17	2.9	65	82	75	89	4	0	0	98	283	13	32	2.4	.967	3B-135, DH-24, 2B-1, SS-1
1978		152	.285	.439	540	154	20	6	17	3.1	85	78	72	52	3	4	0	132	332	15	29	3.2	.969	3B-134, DH-12, 1B-5

Sal Bando *continued*

Year	Team	Games	BA	SA	AB	H	2B	3B	HR	HR%	R	RBI	BB	SO	SB	Pinch Hit AB	Pinch Hit H	PO	A	E	DP	TC/G	FA	G by Pos
1979		130	.246	.345	476	117	14	3	9	1.9	57	43	57	42	2	1	1	106	225	12	19	2.6	.965	3B-109, DH-19, 1B-4, P-1, 2B-1
1980		78	.197	.311	254	50	12	1	5	2.0	28	31	29	35	5	6	0	62	112	12	14	2.4	.935	3B-57, DH-15, 1B-7
1981		32	.200	.354	65	13	4	0	2	3.1	10	9	6	3	1	6	1	65	25	1	9	3.5	.989	3B-15, 1B-9, DH-2
16 yrs.		2019	.254	.408	7060	1790	289	38	242	3.4	982	1039	1031	923	75	32	6	1788	3743	231	362	2.9	.960	3B-1896, DH-80, 1B-25, SS-6, 2B-3, P-1, OF-1
DIVISIONAL PLAYOFF SERIES																								
1981	**MIL A**	5	.294	.471	17	5	3	0	0	0.0	1	1	2	3	0	0	0	3	5	0	0	1.6	1.000	3B-5
LEAGUE CHAMPIONSHIP SERIES																								
1971	**OAK A**	3	.364	.818	11	4	2	0	1	9.1	3	1	1	0	0	0	0	6	2	0	2	2.7	1.000	3B-3
1972		5	.200	.200	20	4	0	0	0	0.0	0	0	0	3	0	0	0	6	16	0	1	4.4	1.000	3B-5
1973		5	.167	.500	18	3	0	0	2	11.1	2	3	3	6	0	0	0	7	10	0	0	3.4	1.000	3B-5
1974		4	.231	.692	13	3	0	0	2	15.4	4	2	4	0	0	0	0	3	8	0	2	2.8	1.000	3B-4
1975		3	.500	.667	12	6	2	0	0	0.0	1	2	0	3	0	0	0	3	11	1	0	5.0	.933	3B-3
5 yrs.		20	.270	.527	74	20	4	0	5 **4th**	6.8 **6th**	10	8	8	12	0	0	0	25	47	1	5	3.7	.986	3B-20
WORLD SERIES																								
1972	**OAK A**	7	.269	.308	26	7	1	0	0	0.0	2	1	2	5	0	0	0	3	12	1	0	2.3	.938	3B-7
1973		7	.231	.346	26	6	1	1	0	0.0	5	1	4	7	0	0	0	6	14	1	2	3.0	.952	3B-7
1974		5	.063	.063	16	1	0	0	0	0.0	3	2	2	5	0	0	0	2	10	0	0	2.4	1.000	3B-5
3 yrs.		19	.206	.265	68	14	2	1	0	0.0	10	4	8	17	0	0	0	11	36	2	2	2.6	.959	3B-19

Jeff Banister

BANISTER, JEFFERY TODD
B. Jan. 15, 1965, Weatherford, Okla.

BR TR 6′ 2″ 200 lbs.

Year	Team	Games	BA	SA	AB	H	2B	3B	HR	HR%	R	RBI	BB	SO	SB	Pinch Hit AB	Pinch Hit H	PO	A	E	DP	TC/G	FA	G by Pos
1991	**PIT N**	1	1.000	1.000	1	1	0	0	0	0.0	0	0	0	0	0	1	1	0	0	0	0	0.0	—	

Ernie Banks

BANKS, ERNEST (Mr. Cub)
B. Jan. 31, 1931, Dallas, Tex.
Hall of Fame 1977.

BR TR 6′ 1″ 180 lbs.

Year	Team	Games	BA	SA	AB	H	2B	3B	HR	HR%	R	RBI	BB	SO	SB	Pinch Hit AB	Pinch Hit H	PO	A	E	DP	TC/G	FA	G by Pos
1953	**CHI N**	10	.314	.571	35	11	1	1	2	5.7	3	6	4	5	0	0	0	19	33	1	9	5.3	.981	SS-10
1954		154	.275	.427	593	163	19	7	19	3.2	70	79	40	50	6	0	0	312	475	34	105	5.3	.959	SS-154
1955		154	.295	.596	596	176	29	9	44	7.4	98	117	45	72	9	0	0	290	482	22	102	5.2	.972	SS-154
1956		139	.297	.530	538	160	25	8	28	5.2	82	85	52	62	6	0	0	279	357	25	92	4.8	.962	SS-139
1957		156	.285	.579	594	169	34	6	43	7.2	113	102	70	85	8	0	0	241	348	14	71	3.8	.977	SS-100, 3B-58
1958		154	.313	**.614**	**617**	193	23	11	**47**	**7.6**	119	**129**	52	87	4	0	0	292	468	32	100	5.1	.960	SS-154
1959		155	.304	.596	589	179	25	6	45	7.6	97	**143**	64	72	2	1	0	271	519	12	95	5.2	.985	SS-154
1960		156	.271	.554	597	162	32	7	**41**	6.9	94	117	71	69	1	0	0	283	488	18	94	5.1	.977	SS-156
1961		138	.278	.507	511	142	22	4	29	5.7	75	80	54	75	1	4	1	273	370	21	76	5.0	.968	SS-104, OF-23, 1B-7
1962		154	.269	.503	610	164	20	6	37	6.1	87	104	30	71	5	4	2	1462	107	11	135	10.4	.993	1B-149, 3B-3
1963		130	.227	.403	432	98	20	1	18	4.2	41	64	39	73	0	5	1	1178	78	9	97	10.1	.993	1B-125
1964		157	.264	.450	591	156	29	6	23	3.9	67	95	36	84	1	0	0	1565	132	10	122	10.9	.994	1B-157
1965		163	.265	.453	612	162	25	3	28	4.6	79	106	55	64	3	2	1	1682	93	15	143	11.0	.992	1B-162
1966		141	.272	.432	511	139	23	7	15	2.9	52	75	29	59	0	8	1	1183	92	13	88	9.3	.990	1B-130, 3B-8
1967		151	.276	.455	573	158	26	4	23	4.0	68	95	27	93	2	5	1	1383	91	10	111	10.1	.993	1B-147
1968		150	.246	.469	552	136	27	0	32	5.8	71	83	27	67	2	4	1	1379	88	6	118	10.0	.996	1B-147
1969		155	.253	.416	565	143	19	2	23	4.1	60	106	42	101	0	2	2	1419	87	4	116	9.9	.997	1B-153
1970		72	.252	.459	222	56	6	2	12	5.4	25	44	20	33	0	9	2	528	35	4	53	9.1	.993	1B-62
1971		39	.193	.325	83	16	2	0	3	3.6	4	6	6	14	0	18	2	167	12	0	15	8.9	1.000	1B-20
19 yrs.		2528	.274	.500	9421	2583	407	90	512	5.4	1305	1636	763	1236	50	62	14	14206	4355	261	1742	7.6	.986	1B-1259, SS-1125, 3B-69, OF-23

George Banks

BANKS, GEORGE EDWARD
B. Sept. 24, 1938, Pacolet Mills, S. C. D. Mar. 1, 1985, Spartanburg, S. C.

BR TR 5′11″ 185 lbs.

Year	Team	Games	BA	SA	AB	H	2B	3B	HR	HR%	R	RBI	BB	SO	SB	Pinch Hit AB	Pinch Hit H	PO	A	E	DP	TC/G	FA	G by Pos
1962	**MIN A**	63	.252	.408	103	26	0	2	4	3.9	22	15	21	27	0	28	5	26	11	2	1	1.7	.949	OF-17, 3B-6
1963		25	.155	.338	71	11	4	0	3	4.2	5	8	9	21	0	3	0	22	39	6	4	3.2	.910	3B-21
1964	**2 teams**	**MIN A** (1G –.000)	**CLE A** (9G –.294)																					
″	**total**	10	.278	.667	18	5	1	0	2	11.1	6	3	6	7	0	5	1	7	2	0	0	1.8	1.000	OF-3, 3B-1, 2B-1
1965	**CLE A**	4	.200	.400	5	1	1	0	0	0.0	0	0	1	3	0	3	0	0	2	0	1	2.0	1.000	3B-1
1966		4	.250	.250	4	1	0	0	0	0.0	0	1	0	1	0	4	1	0	0	0	0	0.0	—	
5 yrs.		106	.219	.403	201	44	6	2	9	4.5	33	27	37	59	0	43	7	55	54	8	6	2.3	.932	3B-29, OF-20, 2B-1

Bill Bankston

BANKSTON, WILBORN EVERETT
B. May 25, 1893, Barnesville, Ga. D. Feb. 26, 1970, Griffin, Ga.

BL TR 5′11″ 180 lbs.

Year	Team	Games	BA	SA	AB	H	2B	3B	HR	HR%	R	RBI	BB	SO	SB	Pinch Hit AB	Pinch Hit H	PO	A	E	DP	TC/G	FA	G by Pos
1915	**PHI A**	11	.139	.306	36	5	1	1	1	2.8	6	2	2	5	1	2	1	14	1	2	0	2.1	.882	OF-8

Jim Banning

BANNING, JAMES M.
B. 1866, New York, N. Y.

BL TR 5′ 6″ 150 lbs.

Year	Team	Games	BA	SA	AB	H	2B	3B	HR	HR%	R	RBI	BB	SO	SB	Pinch Hit AB	Pinch Hit H	PO	A	E	DP	TC/G	FA	G by Pos
1888	**WAS N**	1	—	—	0	0	0	0	0	—	0	0	0	0	0	0	0	1	0	0	0	1.0	1.000	C-1
1889		2	.000	.000	1	0	0	0	0	0.0	0	0	0	0	0	0	0	2	2	0	0	2.0	1.000	C-2
2 yrs.		3	.000	.000	1	0	0	0	0	0.0	0	0	0	0	0	0	0	3	2	0	0	1.7	1.000	C-3

Alan Bannister

BANNISTER, ALAN
B. Sept. 3, 1951, Montebello, Calif.

BR TR 5′11″ 170 lbs.

Year	Team	Games	BA	SA	AB	H	2B	3B	HR	HR%	R	RBI	BB	SO	SB	Pinch Hit AB	Pinch Hit H	PO	A	E	DP	TC/G	FA	G by Pos
1974	**PHI N**	26	.120	.120	25	3	0	0	0	0.0	4	1	3	7	0	7	0	10	0	0	0	1.0	1.000	OF-8, SS-2
1975		24	.262	.344	61	16	3	1	0	0.0	10	0	1	9	2	1	0	54	4	2	0	3.0	.967	OF-18, SS-1, 2B-1
1976	**CHI A**	73	.248	.317	145	36	6	2	0	0.0	19	8	14	21	12	2	0	92	36	5	7	2.0	.962	OF-43, SS-14, DH-4, 2B-4, 3B-1
1977		139	.275	.338	560	154	20	3	3	0.5	87	57	54	49	4	1	0	265	331	40	52	4.6	.937	SS-133, OF-3, 2B-3
1978		49	.224	.290	107	24	3	2	0	0.0	16	8	11	12	3	10	0	34	16	2	3	1.2	.962	DH-19, OF-15, SS-8, 2B-2
1979		136	.285	.383	506	144	28	8	2	0.4	71	55	43	40	22	0	0	250	187	21	37	3.4	.954,	2B-65, OF-47, 3B-12, DH-9, 1B-1
1980	**2 teams**	**CHI A** (45G –.192)	**CLE A** (81G –.328)																					
″	**total**	126	.283	.370	392	111	23	4	1	0.3	57	41	40	41	14	12	0	189	153	14	27	2.8	.961	OF-63, 2B-41, 3B-20, SS-2
1981	**CLE A**	68	.263	.332	232	61	11	1	1	0.4	36	17	16	19	16	11	4	129	76	3	14	3.1	.986	OF-35, 2B-30, 1B-2, SS-1

Alan Bannister *continued*

Year	Team	Games	BA	SA	AB	H	2B	3B	HR	HR%	R	RBI	BB	SO	SB	Pinch Hit AB	Pinch Hit H	PO	A	E	DP	TC/G	FA	G by Pos
1982		101	.267	.353	348	93	16	1	4	1.1	40	41	42	41	18	6	1	207	124	10	22	3.2	.971	OF-55, 2B-48, SS-2, DH-1, 3B-1
1983		117	.265	.393	377	100	25	4	5	1.3	51	45	31	43	6	10	5	186	66	7	14	2.1	.973	OF-91, 2B-27, DH-3, 1B-3
1984	2 teams	HOU N (9G –.200) TEX A (47G –.300)																						
"	total	56	.285	.377	130	37	4	1	2	1.5	22	9	23	19	2	17	4	71	38	5	5	2.6	.956	2B-25, DH-9, SS-4, OF-4, 3B-1, 1B-1
1985	TEX A	57	.262	.336	122	32	4	1	1	0.8	17	6	14	17	8	14	6	46	18	1	4	1.2	.985	DH-21, OF-14, 2B-10, 3B-5, 1B-4
12 yrs.		972	.270	.355	3005	811	143	28	19	0.6	430	288	292	318	107	91	20	1533	1049	110	185	2.9	.959	OF-396, 2B-256, SS-167, DH-66, 3B-40, 1B-11

Jimmy Bannon

BANNON, JAMES HENRY (Foxy Grandpa) BR TR 5′ 5″ 160 lbs.
Brother of Tom Bannon.
B. May 5, 1871, Amesbury, Mass. D. Mar. 24, 1948, Glen Rock, N. J.

Year	Team	Games	BA	SA	AB	H	2B	3B	HR	HR%	R	RBI	BB	SO	SB	Pinch Hit AB	Pinch Hit H	PO	A	E	DP	TC/G	FA	G by Pos
1893	STL N	26	.336	.439	107	36	3	4	0	0.0	9	15	4	5	8	0	0	31	10	15	2	2.1	.732	OF-24, SS-2, P-1
1894	BOS N	128	.336	.514	494	166	29	10	13	2.6	130	114	62	42	47	0	0	241	43	41	12	2.5	.874	OF-128, P-1
1895		123	.350	.479	489	171	35	5	6	1.2	101	74	54	31	28	1	0	209	31	33	3	2.2	.879	OF-122, P-1
1896		89	.251	.306	343	86	9	5	0	0.0	52	50	32	23	16	1	0	164	57	29	7	2.8	.884	OF-76, 2B-6, SS-5, 3B-3
4 yrs.		366	.320	.447	1433	459	76	24	19	1.3	292	253	152	101	99	2	0	645	141	118	24	2.4	.869	OF-350, SS-7, 2B-6, 3B-3, P-3

Tom Bannon

BANNON, THOMAS EDWARD (Uncle Tom) BR TR 5′ 8″ 175 lbs.
Brother of Jimmy Bannon.
B. May 8, 1869, Amesbury, Mass. D. Jan. 26, 1950, Lynn, Mass.

Year	Team	Games	BA	SA	AB	H	2B	3B	HR	HR%	R	RBI	BB	SO	SB	Pinch Hit AB	Pinch Hit H	PO	A	E	DP	TC/G	FA	G by Pos
1895	NY N	37	.270	.333	159	43	6	2	0	0.0	33	8	7	8	20	0	0	198	18	19	16	6.4	.919	OF-21, 1B-16
1896		2	.143	.286	7	1	1	0	0	0.0	1	0	1	1	0	0	0	1	0	1	0	1.0	.500	OF-2
2 yrs.		39	.265	.331	166	44	7	2	0	0.0	34	8	8	9	20	0	0	199	18	20	16	6.1	.916	OF-23, 1B-16

Walter Barbare

BARBARE, WALTER LAWRENCE (Dinty) BR TR 6′ 162 lbs.
B. Aug. 11, 1891, Greenville, S. C. D. Oct. 28, 1965, Greenville, S. C.

Year	Team	Games	BA	SA	AB	H	2B	3B	HR	HR%	R	RBI	BB	SO	SB	Pinch Hit AB	Pinch Hit H	PO	A	E	DP	TC/G	FA	G by Pos
1914	CLE A	15	.308	.423	52	16	2	2	0	0.0	6	5	2	5	1	0	0	13	31	4	4	3.2	.917	3B-14, SS-1
1915		77	.191	.211	246	47	3	1	0	0.0	15	11	10	27	6	5	1	101	141	10	12	3.7	.960	3B-68, 1B-1
1916		13	.229	.250	48	11	1	0	0	0.0	3	3	4	9	0	1	0	12	30	1	2	3.6	.977	3B-12
1918	BOS A	13	.172	.276	29	5	3	0	0	0.0	2	2	0	1	1	1	0	6	14	4	1	2.0	.833	3B-11, SS-1
1919	PIT N	85	.273	.355	293	80	11	5	1	0.3	34	34	18	18	11	3	1	111	137	10	11	3.2	.961	3B-80, 2B-1
1920		57	.274	.323	186	51	5	2	0	0.0	9	12	9	11	5	7	2	79	161	13	21	5.0	.949	SS-34, 2B-12, 3B-5
1921	BOS N	134	.302	.367	550	166	22	7	0	0.0	66	49	24	28	11	2	2	311	421	32	63	5.8	.958	SS-121, 2B-8, 3B-2
1922		106	.231	.265	373	86	5	4	0	0.0	38	40	21	22	2	11	3	241	238	14	44	5.1	.972	2B-45, 3B-38, 1B-14
8 yrs.		500	.260	.315	1777	462	52	21	1	0.1	173	156	88	121	37	30	9	874	1173	88	158	4.6	.959	3B-230, SS-157, 2B-66, 1B-15

Red Barbary

BARBARY, DONALD ODELL BR TR 6′ 3″ 190 lbs.
B. June 20, 1920, Simpsonville, S. C.

Year	Team	Games	BA	SA	AB	H	2B	3B	HR	HR%	R	RBI	BB	SO	SB	Pinch Hit AB	Pinch Hit H	PO	A	E	DP	TC/G	FA	G by Pos
1943	WAS A	1	.000	.000	1	0	0	0	0	0.0	0	0	0	0	0	1	0	0	0	0	0	0.0	—	

Jap Barbeau

BARBEAU, WILLIAM JOSEPH BR TR 5′ 5″ 140 lbs.
B. June 10, 1882, New York, N. Y. D. Sept. 10, 1969, Milwaukee, Wis.

Year	Team	Games	BA	SA	AB	H	2B	3B	HR	HR%	R	RBI	BB	SO	SB	Pinch Hit AB	Pinch Hit H	PO	A	E	DP	TC/G	FA	G by Pos
1905	CLE A	11	.270	.351	37	10	1	1	0	0.0	1	2	1		1	0	0	24	33	6	6	5.7	.905	2B-11
1906		42	.194	.279	129	25	5	3	0	0.0	8	12	9		5	3	0	41	68	21	5	3.4	.838	3B-32, SS-6
1909	2 teams	PIT N (91G –.220) STL N (47G –.251)																						
"	total	138	.230	.278	525	121	19	3	0	0.0	83	30	65		33	7	0	155	211	43	15	3.1	.895	3B-131
1910	STL N	7	.190	.286	21	4	0	1	0	0.0	4	2	3	3	0	0	0	6	19	2	1	3.9	.926	3B-6, 2B-1
4 yrs.		198	.225	.282	712	160	25	8	0	0.0	96	46	78	3	39	10	0	226	331	72	27	3.4	.886	3B-169, 2B-12, SS-6

Dave Barbee

BARBEE, DAVID MONROE BR TR 5′11½″ 178 lbs.
B. May 7, 1905, Greensboro, N. C. D. July 1, 1968, Albemarle, N. C.

Year	Team	Games	BA	SA	AB	H	2B	3B	HR	HR%	R	RBI	BB	SO	SB	Pinch Hit AB	Pinch Hit H	PO	A	E	DP	TC/G	FA	G by Pos
1926	PHI A	19	.170	.298	47	8	1	1	1	2.1	7	5	2	4	0	8	0	18	1	0	0	1.9	1.000	OF-10
1932	PIT N	97	.257	.407	327	84	22	6	5	1.5	37	55	18	38	1	19	8	190	5	5	2	2.6	.975	OF-78
2 yrs.		116	.246	.393	374	92	23	7	6	1.6	44	60	20	42	1	27	8	208	6	5	2	2.5	.977	OF-88

Charlie Barber

BARBER, CHARLES D. BR TR
B. 1854, Philadelphia, Pa. D. Nov. 23, 1910, Philadelphia, Pa.

Year	Team	Games	BA	SA	AB	H	2B	3B	HR	HR%	R	RBI	BB	SO	SB	Pinch Hit AB	Pinch Hit H	PO	A	E	DP	TC/G	FA	G by Pos
1884	CIN U	55	.201	.245	204	41	1	4	0	0.0	38		11			0	0	68	112	35	4	3.9	.837	3B-55

Turner Barber

BARBER, TYRUS TURNER BL TR 5′11″ 170 lbs.
B. July 9, 1893, Lavinia, Tenn. D. Oct. 20, 1968, Milan, Tenn.

Year	Team	Games	BA	SA	AB	H	2B	3B	HR	HR%	R	RBI	BB	SO	SB	Pinch Hit AB	Pinch Hit H	PO	A	E	DP	TC/G	FA	G by Pos
1915	WAS A	20	.302	.358	53	16	1	1	0	0.0	9	6	6	7	0	1	0	17	3	1	1	1.1	.952	OF-19
1916		15	.212	.364	33	7	0	1	1	3.0	3	5	2	3	0	3	1	10	0	2	0	1.3	.833	OF-9
1917	CHI N	7	.214	.250	28	6	1	0	0	0.0	2	2	2	8	1	0	0	13	2	0	0	2.1	1.000	OF-7
1918		55	.236	.293	123	29	3	2	0	0.0	11	10	9	16	3	20	4	82	5	4	3	2.9	.956	OF-27, 1B-4
1919		76	.313	.387	230	72	9	4	0	0.0	26	21	14	17	7	6	1	123	7	7	1	2.0	.949	OF-68
1920		94	.265	.324	340	90	10	5	0	0.0	27	50	9	26	5	5	2	767	32	10	40	9.2	.988	1B-69, OF-17, 2B-2
1921		127	.314	.369	452	142	14	4	1	0.2	73	54	41	24	5	2	1	234	23	8	4	2.2	.970	OF-123
1922		84	.310	.376	226	70	7	4	0	0.0	35	29	30	9	7	19	2	242	8	4	12	4.0	.984	OF-47, 1B-16
1923	BKN N	13	.217	.261	46	10	2	0	0	0.0	3	8	2	2	0	1	1	20	1	0	1	1.8	1.000	OF-12
9 yrs.		491	.289	.351	1531	442	47	21	2	0.1	189	185	115	112	28	57	12	1508	81	36	62	3.9	.978	OF-329, 1B-89, 2B-2
WORLD SERIES																								
1918	CHI N	3	.000	.000	2	0	0	0	0	0.0	0	0	0	0	0	2	0	0	0	0	0	0.0	—	

Bret Barberie

BARBERIE, BRET EDWARD BB TR 5′11″ 185 lbs.
B. Aug. 16, 1967, Long Beach, Calif.

Year	Team	Games	BA	SA	AB	H	2B	3B	HR	HR%	R	RBI	BB	SO	SB	Pinch Hit AB	Pinch Hit H	PO	A	E	DP	TC/G	FA	G by Pos
1991	MON N	57	.353	.515	136	48	12	2	2	1.5	16	18	20	22	0	16	1	53	90	5	15	3.7	.966	SS-19, 3B-10, 2B-10, 1B-1
1992		111	.232	.281	285	66	11	0	1	0.4	26	24	47	62	9	22	8	66	188	13	18	3.0	.951	3B-63, 2B-26, SS-1
1993	FLA N	99	.277	.371	375	104	16	2	5	1.3	45	33	33	58	2	2	0	201	303	9	62	5.3	.982	2B-97

Bret Barberie *continued*

Year	Team	Games	BA	SA	AB	H	2B	3B	HR	HR%	R	RBI	BB	SO	SB	Pinch Hit AB	Pinch Hit H	PO	A	E	DP	TC/G	FA	G by Pos
1994		107	.301	.406	372	112	20	2	5	1.3	40	31	23	65	2	5	2	223	320	14	61	5.3	.975	2B-106
1995	**BAL A**	90	.241	.325	237	57	14	0	2	0.8	32	25	36	50	3	15	5	115	187	7	45	3.8	.977	2B-74, DH-5, 3B-3
5 yrs.		464	.275	.368	1405	387	73	6	15	1.1	159	131	159	257	16	60	16	658	1088	48	201	4.3	.973	2B-313, 3B-76, SS-20, DH-5, 1B-1

Jim Barbieri

BARBIERI, JAMES PATRICK BL TR 5′ 7″ 155 lbs.
B. Sept. 15, 1941, Schenectady, N. Y.

Year	Team	Games	BA	SA	AB	H	2B	3B	HR	HR%	R	RBI	BB	SO	SB	Pinch Hit AB	Pinch Hit H	PO	A	E	DP	TC/G	FA	G by Pos
1966	**LA N**	39	.280	.341	82	23	5	0	0	0.0	9	3	9	7	2	17	4	29	2	2	1	1.6	.939	OF-20
WORLD SERIES																								
1966	**LA N**	1	.000	.000	1	0	0	0	0	0.0	0	0	0	1	0	1	0	0	0	0	0	0.0	—	

George Barclay

BARCLAY, GEORGE OLIVER (Deerfoot) TR 5′10″ 162 lbs.
B. May 16, 1876, Millville, Pa. D. Apr. 3, 1909, Philadelphia, Pa.

Year	Team	Games	BA	SA	AB	H	2B	3B	HR	HR%	R	RBI	BB	SO	SB	Pinch Hit AB	Pinch Hit H	PO	A	E	DP	TC/G	FA	G by Pos
1902	**STL N**	137	.300	.350	543	163	14	2	3	0.6	79	53	31		30	0	0	247	16	28	3	2.1	.904	OF-137
1903		108	.248	.310	419	104	10	8	0	0.0	37	42	15		12	0	0	187	13	22	0	2.1	.901	OF-107
1904	**2 teams** **STL N** (103G –.200) **BOS N** (24G –.226)																							
″	**total**	127	.205	.254	468	96	10	5	1	0.2	46	38	14		17	0	0	197	9	12	3	1.7	.945	OF-127
1905	**BOS N**	29	.176	.185	108	19	1	0	0	0.0	5	7	2		2	1	0	39	2	7	1	1.7	.854	OF-28
4 yrs.		401	.248	.298	1538	382	35	15	4	0.3	167	140	62		61	1	0	670	40	69	7	2.0	.911	OF-399

Jesse Barfield

BARFIELD, JESSE LEE BR TR 6′ 1″ 200 lbs.
B. Oct. 29, 1959, Joliet, Ill.

Year	Team	Games	BA	SA	AB	H	2B	3B	HR	HR%	R	RBI	BB	SO	SB	Pinch Hit AB	Pinch Hit H	PO	A	E	DP	TC/G	FA	G by Pos
1981	**TOR A**	25	.232	.368	95	22	3	2	2	2.1	7	9	4	19	4	0	0	71	2	0	1	2.9	1.000	OF-25
1982		139	.246	.426	394	97	13	2	18	4.6	54	58	42	79	1	21	6	217	15	9	4	1.7	.963	OF-137, DH-1
1983		128	.253	.510	388	98	13	3	27	7.0	58	68	22	110	2	16	6	213	16	8	4	1.9	.966	OF-120, DH-5
1984		110	.284	.466	320	91	14	1	14	4.4	51	49	35	81	8	20	8	190	9	10	5	2.2	.952	OF-88, DH-9
1985		155	.289	.536	539	156	34	9	27	5.0	94	84	66	143	22	1	0	349	22	4	8	2.4	.989	OF-154
1986		158	.289	.559	589	170	35	2	**40**	6.8	107	108	69	146	8	1	0	368	20	3	8	2.5	.992	OF-157
1987		159	.263	.458	590	155	25	3	28	4.7	89	84	58	141	3	4	1	341	17	3	4	2.3	.992	OF-158
1988		137	.244	.425	468	114	21	5	18	3.8	62	56	41	108	7	4	1	325	12	4	4	2.5	.988	OF-136, DH-1
1989	**2 teams** **TOR A** (21G –.200) **NY A** (129G –.240)																							
″	**total**	150	.234	.415	521	122	23	1	23	4.4	79	67	87	150	5	2	0	340	20	10	4	2.5	.973	OF-150
1990	**NY A**	153	.246	.456	476	117	21	2	25	5.3	69	78	82	150	4	13	3	305	16	9	3	2.2	.973	OF-151
1991		84	.225	.447	284	64	12	0	17	6.0	37	48	36	80	1	4	2	178	10	0	3	2.3	1.000	OF-81
1992		30	.137	.221	95	13	2	0	2	2.1	8	7	9	27	1	3	0	54	3	2	0	2.0	.966	OF-30
12 yrs.		1428	.256	.466	4759	1219	216	30	241	5.1	715	716	551	1234	66	89	27	2951	162	62	48	2.3	.980	OF-1387, DH-16
LEAGUE CHAMPIONSHIP SERIES																								
1985	**TOR A**	7	.280	.440	25	7	1	0	1	4.0	3	4	3	7	1	0	0	21	0	1	0	3.1	.955	OF-7

Cy Barger

BARGER, EROS BOLIVAR BL TR 6′ 160 lbs.
B. May 18, 1885, Jamestown, Ky. D. Sept. 23, 1964, Columbia, Ky.

Year	Team	Games	BA	SA	AB	H	2B	3B	HR	HR%	R	RBI	BB	SO	SB	Pinch Hit AB	Pinch Hit H	PO	A	E	DP	TC/G	FA	G by Pos
1906	**NY A**	2	.333	.333	3	1	0	0	0	0.0	0	0	0		0	0	0	0	1	0	0	0.5	1.000	P-2
1907		1	.000	.000	2	0	0	0	0	0.0	0	0	0		0	0	0	0	0	1	0	1.0	.000	P-1
1910	**BKN N**	35	.231	.298	104	24	3	2	0	0.0	7	7	5	14	0	6	3	9	87	1	2	2.8	.990	P-35
1911		57	.228	.248	145	33	1	1	0	0.0	16	9	5	20	2	10	2	34	68	5	2	2.5	.953	P-30, OF-11, 1B-1
1912		17	.189	.216	37	7	1	0	0	0.0	3	3	3	7	1	1	0	2	29	2	0	2.1	.939	P-16
1914	**PIT F**	38	.205	.265	83	17	1	2	0	0.0	4	9	2		0	0	0	9	61	2	0	2.1	.972	P-33, SS-1
1915		36	.278	.315	54	15	2	0	0	0.0	3	3	1		0	0	0	4	42	0	1	1.4	1.000	P-34
7 yrs.		186	.227	.269	428	97	8	5	0	0.0	33	31	16	41	3	17	5	58	288	11	5	2.2	.969	P-151, OF-11, SS-1, 1B-1

Ray Barker

BARKER, RAYMOND HERRELL (Buddy) BL TR 6′ 192 lbs.
B. Mar. 12, 1936, Martinsburg, W. Va.

Year	Team	Games	BA	SA	AB	H	2B	3B	HR	HR%	R	RBI	BB	SO	SB	Pinch Hit AB	Pinch Hit H	PO	A	E	DP	TC/G	FA	G by Pos
1960	**BAL A**	5	.000	.000	6	0	0	0	0	0.0	0	0	0	3	0	5	0	0	0	0	0	0.0	.000	OF-1
1965	**2 teams** **CLE A** (11G –.000) **NY A** (98G –.254)																							
″	**total**	109	.246	.398	211	52	11	0	7	3.3	21	31	22	48	1	44	11	400	49	4	41	6.8	.991	1B-64, 3B-3
1966	**NY A**	61	.187	.373	75	14	5	0	3	4.0	11	13	4	20	0	11	0	196	25	3	11	4.8	.987	1B-47
1967		17	.077	.077	26	2	0	0	0	0.0	2	0	3	5	0	4	0	66	8	3	5	5.9	.961	1B-13
4 yrs.		192	.214	.358	318	68	16	0	10	3.1	34	44	29	76	1	64	11	662	82	10	57	5.9	.987	1B-124, 3B-3, OF-1

Red Barkley

BARKLEY, JOHN DUNCAN BR TR 5′11″ 160 lbs.
B. Sept. 19, 1913, Childress, Tex.

Year	Team	Games	BA	SA	AB	H	2B	3B	HR	HR%	R	RBI	BB	SO	SB	Pinch Hit AB	Pinch Hit H	PO	A	E	DP	TC/G	FA	G by Pos
1937	**STL A**	31	.267	.327	101	27	6	0	0	0.0	9	14	14	17	1	0	0	75	81	5	20	5.2	.969	2B-31
1939	**BOS N**	12	.000	.000	11	0	0	0	0	0.0	1	0	1	2	0	1	0	4	18	3	2	2.3	.880	SS-7, 3B-4
1943	**BKN N**	20	.314	.373	51	16	3	0	0	0.0	6	7	4	7	1	0	0	22	37	7	9	3.7	.894	SS-18
3 yrs.		63	.264	.319	163	43	9	0	0	0.0	16	21	19	26	2	1	0	101	136	15	31	4.2	.940	2B-31, SS-25, 3B-4

Sam Barkley

BARKLEY, SAMUEL E. BR TR 5′11½″ 180 lbs.
B. May 24, 1858, Wheeling, W. Va. D. Apr. 20, 1912, Wheeling, W. Va.
Manager 1888.

Year	Team	Games	BA	SA	AB	H	2B	3B	HR	HR%	R	RBI	BB	SO	SB	Pinch Hit AB	Pinch Hit H	PO	A	E	DP	TC/G	FA	G by Pos
1884	**TOL AA**	104	.306	.444	435	133	**39**	9	1	0.2	71		22			0	0	326	358	53	46	7.0	.928	2B-103, C-2
1885	**STL AA**	106	.268	.373	418	112	18	10	2	0.5	67		25			0	0	411	331	55	46	7.4	.931	2B-96, 1B-11
1886	**PIT AA**	122	.266	.366	478	127	32	8	0	0.0	77		58			0	0	391	329	47	53	6.3	.939	2B-112, OF-8, 1B-2
1887	**PIT N**	89	.224	.285	340	76	10	4	1	0.3	44	35	30	24	6	0	0	664	129	37	38	9.3	.955	1B-53, 2B-36
1888	**KC AA**	116	.216	.303	482	104	21	6	3	0.6	67	51	26		15	0	0	341	314	43	44	6.0	.938	2B-116
1889		45	.284	.341	176	50	6	2	0	0.0	36	23	15	20	8	0	0	116	104	17	21	5.3	.928	2B-41, 1B-4
6 yrs.		582	.258	.355	2329	602	126	39	7	0.3	362	109	176	44	29	0	0	2249	1565	252	248	7.0	.938	2B-504, 1B-70, OF-8, C-2

Bruce Barmes

BARMES, BRUCE RAYMOND (Squeaky) BL TR 5′ 8″ 165 lbs.
B. Oct. 23, 1929, Vincennes, Ind.

Year	Team	Games	BA	SA	AB	H	2B	3B	HR	HR%	R	RBI	BB	SO	SB	Pinch Hit AB	Pinch Hit H	PO	A	E	DP	TC/G	FA	G by Pos
1953	**WAS A**	5	.200	.200	5	1	0	0	0	0.0	1	0	0	0	0	4	1	2	0	0	0	2.0	1.000	OF-1

Babe Barna

BARNA, HERBERT PAUL
B. Mar. 2, 1915, Clarksburg, W. Va. D. May 18, 1972, Charleston, W. Va.
BL TR 6′ 2″ 210 lbs.

Year	Team	Games	BA	SA	AB	H	2B	3B	HR	HR%	R	RBI	BB	SO	SB	Pinch Hit AB	Pinch Hit H	PO	A	E	DP	TC/G	FA	G by Pos
1937	PHI A	14	.389	.611	36	14	2	0	2	5.6	10	9	2	6	1	3	1	17	2	2	3	2.1	.905	OF-9, 1B-1
1938		9	.133	.133	30	4	0	0	0	0.0	4	2	3	5	0	2	0	10	1	1	0	1.7	.917	OF-7
1941	NY N	10	.214	.357	42	9	3	0	1	2.4	5	5	2	6	0	0	0	16	2	0	1	1.8	1.000	OF-10
1942		104	.257	.378	331	85	8	7	6	1.8	39	58	38	48	3	13	5	169	4	3	0	2.0	.983	OF-89
1943	2 teams	NY N (40G –.204) BOS A (30G –.170)																						
″	total	70	.187	.284	225	42	9	2	3	1.3	30	22	31	33	5	9	2	102	5	4	1	1.9	.964	OF-60
5 yrs.		207	.232	.346	664	154	22	9	12	1.8	88	96	76	98	9	27	8	314	14	10	5	1.9	.970	OF-175, 1B-1

Bill Barnes

BARNES, WILLIAM H.
B. Indianapolis, Ind. Deceased.

Year	Team	Games	BA	SA	AB	H	2B	3B	HR	HR%	R	RBI	BB	SO	SB	Pinch Hit AB	Pinch Hit H	PO	A	E	DP	TC/G	FA	G by Pos
1884	STP U	8	.200	.233	30	6	1	0	0	0.0	2		0			0	0	8	0	3	1	1.4	.727	OF-8

Eppie Barnes

BARNES, EVERETT DUANE
B. Dec. 1, 1900, Ossining, N. Y. D. Nov. 17, 1980, Mineola, N. Y.
BL TL 5′ 9″ 175 lbs.

Year	Team	Games	BA	SA	AB	H	2B	3B	HR	HR%	R	RBI	BB	SO	SB	Pinch Hit AB	Pinch Hit H	PO	A	E	DP	TC/G	FA	G by Pos
1923	PIT N	2	.500	.500	2	1	0	0	0	0.0	0	0	0	1	0	0	0	2	1	0	1	3.0	1.000	1B-1
1924		2	.000	.000	5	0	0	0	0	0.0	0	0	0	1	0	1	0	8	1	0	0	9.0	1.000	1B-1
2 yrs.		4	.143	.143	7	1	0	0	0	0.0	0	0	0	2	0	1	0	10	2	0	1	6.0	1.000	1B-2

Honey Barnes

BARNES, JOHN FRANCIS
B. Jan. 29, 1900, Fulton, N. Y. D. June 18, 1981, Lockport, N. Y.
BL TR 5′10″ 175 lbs.

Year	Team	Games	BA	SA	AB	H	2B	3B	HR	HR%	R	RBI	BB	SO	SB	Pinch Hit AB	Pinch Hit H	PO	A	E	DP	TC/G	FA	G by Pos
1926	NY A	1	—	—	0	0	0	0	0	—	0	0	1	0	0	0	0	0	0	0	0	0.0	.000	C-1

Lute Barnes

BARNES, LUTHER OWENS
B. Apr. 28, 1947, Forest City, Iowa.
BR TR 5′10″ 160 lbs.

Year	Team	Games	BA	SA	AB	H	2B	3B	HR	HR%	R	RBI	BB	SO	SB	Pinch Hit AB	Pinch Hit H	PO	A	E	DP	TC/G	FA	G by Pos
1972	NY N	24	.236	.319	72	17	2	2	0	0.0	5	6	6	4	0	3	0	40	50	3	13	4.7	.968	2B-14, SS-6
1973		3	.500	.500	2	1	0	0	0	0.0	2	1	0	1	0	2	1	0	0	0	0	0.0	—	
2 yrs.		27	.243	.324	74	18	2	2	0	0.0	7	7	6	5	0	5	1	40	50	3	13	4.7	.968	2B-14, SS-6

Red Barnes

BARNES, EMILE DEERING
B. Dec. 25, 1903, Suggsville, Ala. D. July 3, 1959, Mobile, Ala.
BL TR 5′10½″ 158 lbs.

Year	Team	Games	BA	SA	AB	H	2B	3B	HR	HR%	R	RBI	BB	SO	SB	Pinch Hit AB	Pinch Hit H	PO	A	E	DP	TC/G	FA	G by Pos
1927	WAS A	3	.364	.455	11	4	1	0	0	0.0	5	0	1	3	0	0	0	3	1	0	1	1.3	1.000	OF-3
1928		114	.302	.470	417	126	22	15	6	1.4	82	51	55	38	7	7	2	255	16	6	2	2.7	.978	OF-104
1929		72	.200	.292	130	26	5	2	1	0.8	16	15	13	12	1	36	8	48	2	7	0	1.9	.877	OF-30
1930	2 teams	WAS A (12G –.167) CHI A (85G –.248)																						
″	total	97	.245	.353	278	68	13	7	1	0.4	49	31	26	23	4	22	3	179	6	12	3	2.7	.939	OF-72
4 yrs.		286	.268	.403	836	224	41	24	8	1.0	152	97	95	76	12	65	13	485	25	25	6	2.6	.953	OF-209

Ross Barnes

BARNES, ROSCOE CHARLES
B. May 8, 1850, Mount Morris, Ill. D. Feb. 5, 1915, Chicago, Ill.
BR TR 5′ 8½″ 145 lbs.

Year	Team	Games	BA	SA	AB	H	2B	3B	HR	HR%	R	RBI	BB	SO	SB	Pinch Hit AB	Pinch Hit H	PO	A	E	DP	TC/G	FA	G by Pos
1876	CHI N	66	**.429**	**.590**	322	**138**	**21**	**14**	1	0.3	**126**	59	**20**	8		0	0	167	199	36	22	6.0	.910	2B-66, P-1
1877		22	.272	.283	92	25	1	0	0	0.0	16	5	7	4		0	0	49	70	23	5	6.5	.838	2B-22
1879	CIN N	77	.266	.316	323	86	9	2	1	0.3	55	30	16	25		0	0	137	261	71	19	6.1	.849	SS-61, 2B-16
1881	BOS N	69	.271	.325	295	80	14	1	0	0.0	42	17	16	16		0	0	110	235	59	20	5.8	.854	SS-63, 2B-7
4 yrs.		234	.319	.401	1032	329	45	17	2	0.2	239	111	59	53		0	0	463	765	189	66	6.0	.867	SS-124, 2B-111, P-1

Sam Barnes

BARNES, SAMUEL THOMAS
B. Dec. 18, 1899, Suggsville, Ala. D. Feb. 19, 1981, Montgomery, Ala.
BL TR 5′ 8″ 150 lbs.

Year	Team	Games	BA	SA	AB	H	2B	3B	HR	HR%	R	RBI	BB	SO	SB	Pinch Hit AB	Pinch Hit H	PO	A	E	DP	TC/G	FA	G by Pos
1921	DET A	7	.182	.273	11	2	1	0	0	0.0	2	0	2	1	0	2	0	6	11	1	0	9.0	.944	2B-2

Skeeter Barnes

BARNES, WILLIAM HENRY
B. Mar. 3, 1957, Cincinnati, Ohio.
BR TR 5′11″ 170 lbs.

Year	Team	Games	BA	SA	AB	H	2B	3B	HR	HR%	R	RBI	BB	SO	SB	Pinch Hit AB	Pinch Hit H	PO	A	E	DP	TC/G	FA	G by Pos
1983	CIN N	15	.206	.294	34	7	0	0	1	2.9	5	4	7	3	2	2	0	45	11	1	7	4.1	.982	3B-7, 1B-7
1984		32	.119	.190	42	5	0	0	1	2.4	5	3	4	6	0	16	1	7	15	0	0	1.6	1.000	3B-11, OF-3
1985	MON N	19	.154	.192	26	4	1	0	0	0.0	0	0	0	2	0	10	1	13	6	0	1	2.4	1.000	3B-4, OF-3, 1B-1
1987	STL N	4	.250	1.000	4	1	0	0	1	25.0	1	3	0	0	0	3	0	0	0	0	0	0.0	.000	3B-1
1989	CIN N	5	.000	.000	3	0	0	0	0	0.0	1	0	0	0	0	3	0	0	0	0	0	0.0	—	
1991	DET A	75	.289	.491	159	46	13	2	5	3.1	28	17	9	24	10	11	0	92	38	2	4	1.9	.985	OF-33, 3B-17, 1B-9, 2B-7, DH-3
1992		95	.273	.388	165	45	8	1	3	1.8	27	25	10	18	3	16	3	127	78	11	16	2.5	.949	3B-39, 1B-17, OF-15, 2B-7, DH-7
1993		84	.281	.381	160	45	8	1	2	1.3	24	27	11	19	5	17	6	158	37	4	7	2.4	.980	1B-27, OF-18, 3B-13, DH-13, 2B-10, SS-2
1994		24	.286	.429	21	6	0	0	1	4.8	4	4	0	2	0	5	1	20	2	1	2	1.1	.957	1B-15, OF-4, DH-1
9 yrs.		353	.259	.389	614	159	30	4	14	2.3	95	83	41	74	20	83	12	462	187	19	37	2.3	.972	3B-92, OF-76, 1B-76, 2B-24, DH-24, SS-2

Ed Barney

BARNEY, EDMUND J.
B. Jan. 23, 1890, Amery, Wis. D. Oct. 4, 1967, Rice Lake, Wis.
BL TR 5′10½″ 178 lbs.

Year	Team	Games	BA	SA	AB	H	2B	3B	HR	HR%	R	RBI	BB	SO	SB	Pinch Hit AB	Pinch Hit H	PO	A	E	DP	TC/G	FA	G by Pos
1915	2 teams	NY A (11G –.194) PIT N (32G –.273)																						
″	total	43	.252	.289	135	34	1	2	0	0.0	17	13	14	18	9	6	2	88	3	2	2	2.6	.978	OF-36
1916	PIT N	45	.197	.226	137	27	4	0	0	0.0	16	9	23	15	8	4	1	103	5	4	3	2.8	.964	OF-40
2 yrs.		88	.224	.257	272	61	5	2	0	0.0	33	22	37	33	17	10	3	191	8	6	5	2.7	.971	OF-76

Clyde Barnhart

BARNHART, CLYDE LEE (Pooch)
Father of Vic Barnhart.
B. Dec. 29, 1895, Buck Valley, Pa. D. Jan. 21, 1980, Hagerstown, Md.
BR TR 5′10″ 155 lbs.

Year	Team	Games	BA	SA	AB	H	2B	3B	HR	HR%	R	RBI	BB	SO	SB	Pinch Hit AB	Pinch Hit H	PO	A	E	DP	TC/G	FA	G by Pos
1920	PIT N	12	.326	.500	46	15	4	2	0	0.0	5	5	1	2	1	0	0	10	23	1	3	2.8	.971	3B-12
1921		124	.258	.370	449	116	15	13	3	0.7	66	62	32	36	3	6	1	101	204	14	19	2.7	.956	3B-118
1922		75	.330	.426	209	69	7	5	1	0.5	30	38	25	7	3	16	4	76	34	8	4	2.1	.932	3B-30, OF-26
1923		114	.324	.563	327	106	25	13	9	2.8	60	72	47	21	5	17	4	179	14	3	1	2.1	.985	OF-92
1924		102	.276	.384	344	95	6	11	3	0.9	49	51	30	17	8	12	2	186	8	6	3	2.3	.970	OF-88
1925		142	.325	.447	539	175	32	11	4	0.7	85	114	59	25	9	3	1	295	11	12	2	2.3	.962	OF-138
1926		76	.192	.207	203	39	3	0	0	0.0	26	10	23	13	1	15	2	101	5	1	1	1.8	.991	OF-61

Clyde Barnhart *continued*

Year	Team	Games	BA	SA	AB	H	2B	3B	HR	HR%	R	RBI	BB	SO	SB	Pinch Hit AB	Pinch Hit H	PO	A	E	DP	TC/G	FA	G by Pos
1927		108	.319	.442	360	115	25	5	3	0.8	66	54	37	19	2	11	1	222	5	5	2	2.5	.978	OF-94
1928		61	.296	.408	196	58	6	2	4	2.0	18	30	11	9	3	10	2	96	3	3	0	2.1	.971	OF-48, 3B-1
9 yrs.		814	.295	.418	2673	788	123	62	27	1.0	405	436	265	149	35	90	17	1266	307	53	35	2.3	.967	OF-547, 3B-161
WORLD SERIES																								
1925	PIT N	7	.250	.286	28	7	1	0	0	0.0	1	5	3	5	1	0	0	12	1	0	0	1.9	1.000	OF-7
1927		4	.313	.375	16	5	1	0	0	0.0	0	4	0	0	0	0	0	6	1	0	0	1.8	1.000	OF-4
2 yrs.		11	.273	.318	44	12	2	0	0	0.0	1	9	3	5	1	0	0	18	2	0	0	1.8	1.000	OF-11

Vic Barnhart

BARNHART, VICTOR DEE BR TR 6′ 188 lbs.
Son of Clyde Barnhart.
B. Sept. 1, 1922, Hagerstown, Md.

Year	Team	Games	BA	SA	AB	H	2B	3B	HR	HR%	R	RBI	BB	SO	SB	Pinch Hit AB	Pinch Hit H	PO	A	E	DP	TC/G	FA	G by Pos
1944	PIT N	1	.500	.500	2	1	0	0	0	0.0	0	0	1	1	0	0	0	2	6	1	0	9.0	.889	SS-1
1945		71	.269	.303	201	54	7	0	0	0.0	21	19	9	11	2	2	2	108	174	22	32	4.8	.928	SS-60, 3B-4
1946		2	.000	.000	1	0	0	0	0	0.0	0	0	0	0	0	1	0	0	0	0	0	0.0	—	
3 yrs.		74	.270	.304	204	55	7	0	0	0.0	21	19	10	12	2	3	2	110	180	23	32	4.8	.927	SS-61, 3B-4

Billy Barnie

BARNIE, WILLIAM HARRISON (Bald Billy) 5′ 7″ 157 lbs.
B. Jan. 26, 1853, New York, N. Y. D. July 15, 1900, Hartford, Conn.
Manager 1883–94, 1897–98.

Year	Team	Games	BA	SA	AB	H	2B	3B	HR	HR%	R	RBI	BB	SO	SB	Pinch Hit AB	Pinch Hit H	PO	A	E	DP	TC/G	FA	G by Pos
1883	BAL AA	17	.200	.200	55	11	0	0	0	0.0	7		2			0	0	71	23	18	2	5.6	.839	C-13, OF-6, SS-1
1886		2	.000	.000	6	0	0	0	0	0.0	0		1			0	0	5	2	1	0	4.0	.875	C-1, OF-1
2 yrs.		19	.180	.180	61	11	0	0	0	0.0	7		3			0	0	76	25	19	2	5.5	.842	C-14, OF-7, SS-1

Dick Barone

BARONE, RICHARD ANTHONY BR TR 5′ 9″ 165 lbs.
B. Oct. 13, 1932, San Jose, Calif.

Year	Team	Games	BA	SA	AB	H	2B	3B	HR	HR%	R	RBI	BB	SO	SB	Pinch Hit AB	Pinch Hit H	PO	A	E	DP	TC/G	FA	G by Pos
1960	PIT N	3	.000	.000	6	0	0	0	0	0.0	0	0	0	1	0	0	0	4	3	1	0	4.0	.875	SS-2

Bob Barr

BARR, ROBERT McCLELLAND BR TR 6′ 1″ 192 lbs.
B. Dec. 1856, Washington, D. C. D. Mar. 11, 1930, Washington, D. C.

Year	Team	Games	BA	SA	AB	H	2B	3B	HR	HR%	R	RBI	BB	SO	SB	Pinch Hit AB	Pinch Hit H	PO	A	E	DP	TC/G	FA	G by Pos
1883	PIT AA	37	.246	.317	142	35	4	3	0	0.0	12		5			0	0	62	43	17	2	2.7	.861	P-26, OF-14, 1B-4, 3B-1
1884	2 teams	WAS AA (39G –.148) IND AA (18G –.185)																						
"	total	57	.160	.250	200	32	6	3	2	1.0	21		8			0	0	33	80	36	3	2.6	.758	P-48, OF-7, 1B-2
1886	WAS N	22	.165	.190	79	13	2	0	0	0.0	6	2	4	23		0	0	6	36	9	1	2.3	.824	P-22
1890	ROC AA	57	.179	.219	201	36	2	0	2	1.0	22		13		1	0	0	20	111	10	2	2.5	.929	P-57
1891	NY N	5	.091	.091	11	1	0	0	0	0.0	0	0	2	3	0	0	0	1	6	1	1	1.6	.875	P-5
5 yrs.		178	.185	.245	633	117	14	6	4	0.6	61	2	32	26	1	0	0	122	276	73	9	2.5	.845	P-158, OF-21, 1B-6, 3B-1

Scotty Barr

BARR, HYDER EDWARD BR TR 6′ 175 lbs.
B. Oct. 6, 1886, Bristol, Tenn. D. Dec. 2, 1934, Fort Worth, Tex.

Year	Team	Games	BA	SA	AB	H	2B	3B	HR	HR%	R	RBI	BB	SO	SB	Pinch Hit AB	Pinch Hit H	PO	A	E	DP	TC/G	FA	G by Pos
1908	PHI A	19	.143	.179	56	8	2	0	0	0.0	4	1	3		0	1	0	30	27	5	1	3.3	.919	2B-11, 3B-4, OF-2, 1B-2
1909		22	.078	.098	51	4	1	0	0	0.0	5	1	11		2	0	0	69	1	6	0	3.5	.921	OF-15, 1B-7
2 yrs.		41	.112	.140	107	12	3	0	0	0.0	9	2	14		2	1	0	99	28	11	1	3.4	.920	OF-17, 2B-11, 1B-9, 3B-4

Cuno Barragan

BARRAGAN, FACUNDO ANTHONY BR TR 5′11″ 180 lbs.
B. June 20, 1932, Sacramento, Calif.

Year	Team	Games	BA	SA	AB	H	2B	3B	HR	HR%	R	RBI	BB	SO	SB	Pinch Hit AB	Pinch Hit H	PO	A	E	DP	TC/G	FA	G by Pos
1961	CHI N	10	.214	.321	28	6	0	0	1	3.6	3	2	2	7	0	0	0	35	4	0	1	3.9	1.000	C-10
1962		58	.201	.261	134	27	6	1	0	0.0	11	12	21	28	0	7	0	207	27	7	2	4.4	.971	C-55
1963		1	.000	.000	1	0	0	0	0	0.0	0	0	0	1	0	0	0	1	0	0	0	1.0	1.000	C-1
3 yrs.		69	.202	.270	163	33	6	1	1	0.6	14	14	23	36	0	7	0	243	31	7	3	4.3	.975	C-66

German Barranca

BARRANCA, GERMAN BL TR 6′ 160 lbs.
Born German Barranca (Costales).
B. Oct. 19, 1956, Veracruz, Mexico.

Year	Team	Games	BA	SA	AB	H	2B	3B	HR	HR%	R	RBI	BB	SO	SB	Pinch Hit AB	Pinch Hit H	PO	A	E	DP	TC/G	FA	G by Pos
1979	KC A	5	.600	.800	5	3	1	0	0	0.0	3	0	0	0	3	0	0	4	7	0	3	3.7	1.000	DH-1, 2B-1, 3B-1
1980		7	—	—	0	0	0	0	0	—	3	0	0	0	0	0	0	0	0	0	0	0.0	—	
1981	CIN N	9	.333	.333	6	2	0	0	0	0.0	2	1	0	0	0	6	2	0	0	0	0	0.0	—	
1982		46	.255	.392	51	13	1	3	0	0.0	11	2	2	9	2	39	9	5	9	3	1	2.8	.824	2B-6
4 yrs.		67	.290	.419	62	18	2	3	0	0.0	19	3	2	9	5	45	11	9	16	3	4	3.1	.893	2B-7, DH-1, 3B-1

Bill Barrett

BARRETT, WILLIAM JOSEPH (Whispering Bill) BR TR 6′ 175 lbs.
B. May 28, 1900, Cambridge, Mass. D. Jan. 26, 1951, Cambridge, Mass.

Year	Team	Games	BA	SA	AB	H	2B	3B	HR	HR%	R	RBI	BB	SO	SB	Pinch Hit AB	Pinch Hit H	PO	A	E	DP	TC/G	FA	G by Pos
1921	PHI A	14	.233	.367	30	7	2	1	0	0.0	3	3	0	5	0	0	0	13	32	3	1	3.4	.938	SS-7, P-4, 3B-2, 1B-1
1923	CHI A	42	.272	.377	162	44	7	2	2	1.2	17	23	9	24	12	1	0	91	8	6	1	2.6	.943	OF-40, 3B-1
1924		119	.271	.355	406	110	18	5	2	0.5	52	56	30	38	15	7	2	223	220	45	42	4.4	.908	SS-77, OF-27, 3B-8
1925		81	.363	.518	245	89	23	3	3	1.2	44	40	24	27	5	7	1	132	131	19	24	3.7	.933	2B-41, OF-27, SS-4, 3B-4
1926		111	.307	.462	368	113	31	4	6	1.6	46	61	25	26	9	6	3	190	9	8	3	2.0	.961	OF-102, 1B-2
1927		147	.286	.403	556	159	35	9	4	0.7	62	83	52	46	20	0	0	289	22	12	6	2.2	.963	OF-147
1928		76	.277	.379	235	65	11	2	3	1.3	34	26	14	30	8	9	2	122	62	5	7	3.0	.974	OF-37, 2B-26
1929	2 teams	CHI A (3G –.000) BOS A (111G –.270)																						
"	total	114	.270	.377	371	100	23	4	3	0.8	57	35	55	38	11	1	0	204	17	6	4	2.1	.974	OF-109, 3B-1
1930	2 teams	BOS A (6G –.167) WAS A (6G –.000)																						
"	total	12	.136	.182	22	3	1	0	0	0.0	3	1	2	5	0	5	0	6	0	0	0	1.0	1.000	OF-6
9 yrs.		716	.288	.405	2395	690	151	30	23	1.0	318	328	211	239	80	36	8	1270	501	104	88	2.8	.945	OF-495, SS-88, 2B-67, 3B-16, P-4, 1B-3

Bob Barrett

BARRETT, ROBERT SCHLEY (Jumbo) BR TR 5′11″ 175 lbs.
B. Jan. 27, 1899, Atlanta, Ga. D. Jan. 18, 1982, Atlanta, Ga.

Year	Team	Games	BA	SA	AB	H	2B	3B	HR	HR%	R	RBI	BB	SO	SB	Pinch Hit AB	Pinch Hit H	PO	A	E	DP	TC/G	FA	G by Pos
1923	CHI N	3	.333	.333	3	1	0	0	0	0.0	0	0	0	0	0	3	1	0	0	0	0	0.0	—	
1924		54	.241	.414	133	32	2	3	5	3.8	12	21	7	29	1	10	2	123	80	13	20	5.0	.940	2B-25, 1B-10, 3B-8
1925	2 teams	CHI N (14G –.313) BKN N (1G –.000)																						
"	total	15	.303	.333	33	10	1	0	0	0.0	1	8	1	4	1	5	2	13	9	0	3	2.2	1.000	3B-6, 2B-4
1927	BKN N	99	.259	.341	355	92	10	2	5	1.4	29	38	14	22	1	3	0	76	167	21	12	2.8	.920	3B-96
1929	BOS A	68	.270	.349	126	34	10	0	0	0.0	15	19	10	6	3	23	7	53	64	6	4	3.0	.951	3B-34, 1B-4, 2B-2, OF-1
5 yrs.		239	.260	.357	650	169	23	5	10	1.5	57	86	32	61	6	44	12	265	320	40	39	3.3	.936	3B-144, 2B-31, 1B-14, OF-1

Jimmy Barrett

BARRETT, JAMES ERIGENA BL TR 5′ 9″ 170 lbs.
B. Mar. 28, 1875, Athol, Mass. D. Oct. 24, 1921, Detroit, Mich.

Year	Team	Games	BA	SA	AB	H	2B	3B	HR	HR%	R	RBI	BB	SO	SB	Pinch Hit AB	Pinch Hit H	PO	A	E	DP	TC/G	FA	G by Pos
1899	CIN N	26	.370	.478	92	34	2	4	0	0.0	30	10	18		4	0	0	42	2	3	0	1.8	.936	OF-26
1900		137	.316	.389	545	172	11	7	5	0.9	114	42	72		44	0	0	287	25	24	6	2.5	.929	OF-137
1901	DET A	135	.293	.378	542	159	16	9	4	0.7	110	65	76		26	0	0	300	31	21	7	2.6	.940	OF-135
1902		136	.303	.387	509	154	19	6	4	0.8	93	44	74		24	0	0	326	22	14	6	2.7	.961	OF-136
1903		136	.315	.391	517	163	13	10	2	0.4	95	31	**74**		27	0	0	303	19	15	7	2.5	.955	OF-136
1904		162	.268	.300	624	167	10	5	0	0.0	83	31	**79**		15	0	0	339	29	11	6	2.3	.971	OF-162
1905		20	.254	.269	67	17	1	0	0	0.0	2	3	6		0	2	0	29	0	0	0	1.6	1.000	OF-18
1906	CIN N	5	.000	.000	12	0	0	0	0	0.0	1	0	2		0	1	0	3	1	0	1	1.0	1.000	OF-4
1907	BOS A	106	.244	.310	390	95	11	6	1	0.3	52	28	38		3	7	3	183	14	7	5	2.1	.966	OF-99
1908		2	.125	.125	8	1	0	0	0	0.0	0	1	1		0	0	0	2	0	0	0	1.0	1.000	OF-2
10 yrs.		865	.291	.359	3306	962	83	47	16	0.5	580	255	440		143	10	3	1814	143	95	38	2.4	.954	OF-855

Johnny Barrett

BARRETT, JOHN JOSEPH BL TL 5′10½″ 170 lbs.
B. Dec. 18, 1915, Lowell, Mass. D. Aug. 17, 1974, Seabrook Beach, N. H.

Year	Team	Games	BA	SA	AB	H	2B	3B	HR	HR%	R	RBI	BB	SO	SB	Pinch Hit AB	Pinch Hit H	PO	A	E	DP	TC/G	FA	G by Pos
1942	PIT N	111	.247	.316	332	82	11	6	0	0.0	56	26	48	42	10	13	4	202	11	6	4	2.3	.973	OF-94
1943		130	.231	.303	290	67	12	3	1	0.3	41	32	32	23	5	27	11	165	6	2	0	1.7	.988	OF-99
1944		149	.269	.415	568	153	24	**19**	7	1.2	99	83	86	56	**28**	2	1	373	12	11	4	2.7	.972	OF-147
1945		142	.256	.418	507	130	29	4	15	3.0	97	67	79	68	25	6	3	318	8	8	0	2.5	.976	OF-132
1946	2 teams	PIT N (32G –.169) BOS N (24G –.233)																						
″	total	56	.193	.246	114	22	6	0	0	0.0	10	12	20	12	1	16	4	57	2	4	1	1.7	.937	OF-38
5 yrs.		588	.251	.369	1811	454	82	32	23	1.3	303	220	265	201	69	64	23	1115	39	31	9	2.3	.974	OF-510

Marty Barrett

BARRETT, MARTIN F. BR TR 5′ 9″ 170 lbs.
B. Nov. 1860, Port Henry, N. Y. D. Jan. 29, 1910, Holyoke, Mass.

Year	Team	Games	BA	SA	AB	H	2B	3B	HR	HR%	R	RBI	BB	SO	SB	Pinch Hit AB	Pinch Hit H	PO	A	E	DP	TC/G	FA	G by Pos
1884	2 teams	BOS N (3G –.000) IND AA (5G –.077)																						
″	total	8	.053	.105	19	1	1	0	0	0.0	1		1	4		0	0	23	7	6	0	4.5	.833	C-7, OF-1

Marty Barrett

BARRETT, MARTIN GLENN BR TR 5′11″ 175 lbs.
Brother of Tom Barrett.
B. June 23, 1958, Arcadia, Calif.

Year	Team	Games	BA	SA	AB	H	2B	3B	HR	HR%	R	RBI	BB	SO	SB	Pinch Hit AB	Pinch Hit H	PO	A	E	DP	TC/G	FA	G by Pos
1982	BOS A	8	.056	.056	18	1	0	0	0	0.0	0	0	0	1	0	0	0	11	21	0	4	4.6	1.000	2B-7
1983		33	.227	.295	44	10	1	1	0	0.0	7	2	3	1	0	0	0	32	28	1	8	2.2	.984	2B-23, DH-5
1984		139	.303	.383	475	144	23	3	3	0.6	56	45	42	25	4	1	0	245	417	9	67	4.9	.987	2B-136
1985		156	.266	.343	534	142	26	0	5	0.9	59	56	56	50	7	0	0	355	479	11	110	5.5	.987	2B-155
1986		158	.286	.381	625	179	39	4	4	0.6	94	60	65	31	15	0	0	303	450	14	101	4.9	.982	2B-158
1987		137	.293	.351	559	164	23	0	3	0.5	72	43	51	38	15	0	0	320	438	9	108	5.6	.988	2B-137
1988		150	.283	.337	612	173	28	1	1	0.2	83	65	40	35	7	1	0	312	402	7	97	4.8	.990	2B-150
1989		86	.256	.318	336	86	18	0	1	0.3	31	27	32	12	4	2	1	152	245	10	53	4.8	.975	2B-80, DH-4
1990		62	.226	.252	159	36	4	0	0	0.0	15	13	15	13	4	0	0	90	148	2	28	3.9	.992	2B-60, 3B-1, DH-1
1991	SD N	12	.188	.438	16	3	1	0	1	6.3	1	3	0	3	0	8	3	7	6	0	2	3.3	1.000	3B-2, 2B-2
10 yrs.		941	.278	.347	3378	938	163	9	18	0.5	418	314	304	209	56	12	4	1827	2634	63	578	4.9	.986	2B-908, DH-10, 3B-3
LEAGUE CHAMPIONSHIP SERIES																								
1986	BOS A	7	.367	.433	30	11	2	0	0	0.0	4	5	2	2	0	0	0	19	21	0	4	5.7	1.000	2B-7
1988		4	.067	.067	15	1	0	0	0	0.0	2	0	1	0	0	0	0	6	8	0	1	3.5	1.000	2B-4
1990		3	—	—	0	0	0	0	0	—	0	0	0	0	0	0	0	2	0	0	0	0.7	1.000	2B-3
3 yrs.		14	.267	.311	45	12	2	0	0	0.0	6	5	3	2	0	0	0	27	29	0	5	4.0	1.000	2B-14
WORLD SERIES																								
1986	BOS A	7	.433	.500	30	13	2	0	0	0.0	1	4	5	2	0	0	0	13	25	0	5	5.4	1.000	2B-7

Tom Barrett

BARRETT, THOMAS LOREN BB TR 5′ 9″ 157 lbs.
Brother of Marty Barrett.
B. Apr. 2, 1960, San Fernando, Calif.

Year	Team	Games	BA	SA	AB	H	2B	3B	HR	HR%	R	RBI	BB	SO	SB	Pinch Hit AB	Pinch Hit H	PO	A	E	DP	TC/G	FA	G by Pos
1988	PHI N	36	.204	.222	54	11	1	0	0	0.0	5	3	7	8	0	21	8	16	31	2	6	4.9	.959	2B-10
1989		14	.222	.222	27	6	0	0	0	0.0	3	1	1	7	0	2	0	26	18	1	9	5.0	.978	2B-9
1992	BOS A	4	.000	.000	3	0	0	0	0	0.0	1	0	2	0	0	0	0	3	4	0	0	3.5	1.000	2B-2
3 yrs.		54	.202	.214	84	17	1	0	0	0.0	9	4	10	15	0	23	8	45	53	3	15	4.8	.970	2B-21

Jose Barrios

BARRIOS, JOSE MANUEL BR TR 6′ 4″ 195 lbs.
B. June 26, 1957, New York, N. Y.

Year	Team	Games	BA	SA	AB	H	2B	3B	HR	HR%	R	RBI	BB	SO	SB	Pinch Hit AB	Pinch Hit H	PO	A	E	DP	TC/G	FA	G by Pos
1982	SF N	19	.158	.158	19	3	0	0	0	0.0	2	0	1	4	0	3	0	47	0	0	4	6.7	1.000	1B-7

Red Barron

BARRON, DAVID IRENUS BR TR 5′11½″ 185 lbs.
B. June 21, 1900, Clarksville, Ga. D. Oct. 4, 1982, Atlanta, Ga.

Year	Team	Games	BA	SA	AB	H	2B	3B	HR	HR%	R	RBI	BB	SO	SB	Pinch Hit AB	Pinch Hit H	PO	A	E	DP	TC/G	FA	G by Pos
1929	BOS N	10	.190	.238	21	4	1	0	0	0.0	3	1	1	4	2	1	0	12	1	1	1	2.3	.929	OF-6

Cuke Barrows

BARROWS, ROLAND BR TL 5′ 8″ 158 lbs.
B. Oct. 20, 1883, Gray, Me. D. Feb. 10, 1955, Gorham, Me.

Year	Team	Games	BA	SA	AB	H	2B	3B	HR	HR%	R	RBI	BB	SO	SB	Pinch Hit AB	Pinch Hit H	PO	A	E	DP	TC/G	FA	G by Pos
1909	CHI A	5	.150	.150	20	3	0	0	0	0.0	1	2	0		0	0	0	10	2	1	1	2.6	.923	OF-5
1910		6	.200	.200	20	4	0	0	0	0.0	0	1	3		0	0	0	7	0	1	0	1.3	.875	OF-6
1911		13	.196	.239	46	9	2	0	0	0.0	5	4	7		2	0	0	17	0	1	0	1.4	.944	OF-13
1912		8	.231	.231	13	3	0	0	0	0.0	0	2	2		1	4	1	1	1	0	0	0.7	1.000	OF-3
4 yrs.		32	.192	.212	99	19	2	0	0	0.0	6	9	12		3	4	1	35	3	3	1	1.5	.927	OF-27

Jack Barry

BARRY, JOHN JOSEPH BR TR 5′ 9″ 158 lbs.
B. Apr. 26, 1887, Meriden, Conn. D. Apr. 23, 1961, Shrewsbury, Mass.
Manager 1917.

Year	Team	Games	BA	SA	AB	H	2B	3B	HR	HR%	R	RBI	BB	SO	SB	Pinch Hit AB	Pinch Hit H	PO	A	E	DP	TC/G	FA	G by Pos
1908	PHI A	40	.222	.296	135	30	4	3	0	0.0	13	8	10		5	3	1	54	86	10	3	4.1	.933	2B-20, SS-14, 3B-3
1909		124	.215	.259	409	88	11	2	1	0.2	56	23	44		17	0	0	196	351	43	40	4.8	.927	SS-124
1910		145	.259	.337	487	126	19	5	3	0.6	64	60	52		14	0	0	279	406	63	54	5.2	.916	SS-145
1911		127	.265	.344	442	117	18	7	1	0.2	73	63	38		30	0	0	268	384	39	49	5.4	.944	SS-127
1912		139	.261	.337	483	126	19	9	0	0.0	76	55	47		22	0	0	238	438	55	55	5.3	.925	SS-139
1913		134	.275	.365	455	125	20	6	3	0.7	62	85	44	32	15	0	0	248	403	32	60	5.1	.953	SS-134
1914		140	.242	.268	467	113	12	0	0	0.0	57	42	53	34	22	0	0	244	447	39	61	5.2	.947	SS-140

Jack Barry *continued*

Year	Team	Games	BA	SA	AB	H	2B	3B	HR	HR%	R	RBI	BB	SO	SB	Pinch Hit AB	Pinch Hit H	PO	A	E	DP	TC/G	FA	G by Pos
1915	2 teams	PHI A (54G –.222) BOS A (78G –.262)																						
"	total	132	.244	.305	442	108	19	4	0	0.0	46	41	39	20	6	0	0	249	366	27	40	4.9	.958	2B-78, SS-54
1916	BOS A	94	.203	.227	330	67	6	1	0	0.0	28	20	17	24	8	0	0	200	282	13	30	5.3	.974	2B-94
1917		116	.214	.253	388	83	9	0	2	0.5	45	30	47	27	12	0	0	196	339	14	40	4.7	.974	2B-116
1919		31	.241	.306	108	26	5	1	0	0.0	13	2	5	5	2	0	0	54	88	12	13	5.0	.922	2B-31
11 yrs.		1222	.243	.303	4146	1009	142	38	10	0.2	533	429	396	142	153	3	1	2226	3590	347	445	5.1	.944	SS-877, 2B-339, 3B-3
WORLD SERIES																								
1910	PHI A	5	.235	.353	17	4	2	0	0	0.0	3	3	1	3	0	0	0	8	12	0	1	4.0	1.000	SS-5
1911		6	.368	.579	19	7	4	0	0	0.0	2	2	0	1	2	0	0	9	13	3	0	4.2	.880	SS-6
1913		5	.300	.450	20	6	3	0	0	0.0	3	2	0	0	0	0	0	9	16	1	5	5.2	.962	SS-5
1914		4	.071	.071	14	1	0	0	0	0.0	1	0	1	3	1	0	0	5	21	0	2	6.5	1.000	SS-4
1915	BOS A	5	.176	.176	17	3	0	0	0	0.0	1	1	1	2	0	0	0	10	9	1	1	4.0	.950	2B-5
5 yrs.		25	.241	.345	87	21	9	0	0	0.0	10	8	3	9	3	0	0	41	71	5	9	4.7	.957	SS-20, 2B-5
							3rd																	

Jeff Barry

BARRY, JEFFREY FINAS BB TR 6′ 1″ 190 lbs.
B. Sept. 22, 1969, Medford, Ore.

Year	Team	Games	BA	SA	AB	H	2B	3B	HR	HR%	R	RBI	BB	SO	SB	Pinch Hit AB	Pinch Hit H	PO	A	E	DP	TC/G	FA	G by Pos
1995	NY N	15	.133	.200	15	2	1	0	0	0.0	2	0	1	8	0	12	1	2	0	0	0	1.0	1.000	OF-2

Rich Barry

BARRY, RICHARD DONOVAN BR TR 6′ 4″ 205 lbs.
B. Sept. 12, 1940, Berkeley, Calif.

Year	Team	Games	BA	SA	AB	H	2B	3B	HR	HR%	R	RBI	BB	SO	SB	Pinch Hit AB	Pinch Hit H	PO	A	E	DP	TC/G	FA	G by Pos
1969	PHI N	20	.188	.219	32	6	1	0	0	0.0	4	0	5	6	0	11	2	15	0	1	0	1.8	.938	OF-9

Shad Barry

BARRY, JOHN C. BR TR
B. Oct. 27, 1878, Newburgh, N. Y. D. Nov. 27, 1936, Los Angeles, Calif.

Year	Team	Games	BA	SA	AB	H	2B	3B	HR	HR%	R	RBI	BB	SO	SB	Pinch Hit AB	Pinch Hit H	PO	A	E	DP	TC/G	FA	G by Pos
1899	WAS N	78	.287	.368	247	71	7	5	1	0.4	31	33	12		11	3	0	254	65	19	13	4.3	.944	OF-23, 1B-22, SS-13, 3B-13, 2B-7
1900	BOS N	81	.260	.366	254	66	10	7	1	0.4	40	37	13		9	**14**	3	199	82	23	13	4.4	.924	OF-24, SS-18, 2B-16, 1B-10, 3B-1
1901	2 teams	BOS N (11G –.175) PHI N (67G –.246)																						
"	total	78	.236	.288	292	69	12	0	1	0.3	38	28	17		14	4	0	146	124	33	8	4.0	.891	2B-35, OF-24, 3B-16, SS-1
1902	PHI N	138	.287	.363	543	156	20	6	3	0.6	65	57	44		14	0	0	193	15	13	3	1.6	.941	OF-137, 1B-1
1903		138	.276	.344	550	152	24	5	1	0.2	75	60	30		26	0	0	503	28	16	12	4.0	.971	OF-107, 1B-30, 3B-1
1904	2 teams	PHI N (35G –.205) CHI N (73G –.262)																						
"	total	108	.244	.286	385	94	9	2	1	0.3	44	29	28		14	3	0	350	89	25	21	4.3	.946	OF-62, 1B-18, 3B-17, SS-8, 2B-2
1905	2 teams	CHI N (27G –.212) CIN N (125G –.324)																						
"	total	152	.304	.371	598	182	13	12	1	0.2	100	66	38		21	1	0	1474	79	28	17	10.5	.982	1B-149, OF-2
1906	2 teams	CIN N (73G –.287) STL N (62G –.249)																						
"	total	135	.269	.335	516	139	19	6	1	0.2	64	45	41		17	0	0	746	61	20	33	6.1	.976	OF-65, 1B-64, 3B-6
1907	STL N	81	.247	.277	292	72	5	2	0	0.0	30	19	28		4	0	0	94	11	4	0	1.3	.963	OF-81
1908	2 teams	STL N (74G –.228) NY N (37G –.149)																						
"	total	111	.212	.251	335	71	9	2	0	0.0	29	16	28		10	7	1	146	12	8	1	1.6	.952	OF-100, SS-2
10 yrs.		1100	.267	.330	4012	1072	128	47	10	0.2	516	390	279		140	32	4	4105	566	189	121	4.5	.961	OF-625, 1B-294, 2B-60, 3B-54, SS-42

Dick Bartell

BARTELL, RICHARD WILLIAM (Rowdy Richard) BR TR 5′ 9″ 160 lbs.
B. Nov. 22, 1907, Chicago, Ill. D. Aug. 4, 1995, Alameda, Calif.

Year	Team	Games	BA	SA	AB	H	2B	3B	HR	HR%	R	RBI	BB	SO	SB	Pinch Hit AB	Pinch Hit H	PO	A	E	DP	TC/G	FA	G by Pos
1927	PIT N	1	.000	.000	2	0	0	0	0	0.0	0	0	2	0	0	0	0	3	2	0	1	5.0	1.000	SS-1
1928		72	.305	.386	233	71	8	4	1	0.4	27	36	21	18	4	2	0	158	199	16	40	5.6	.957	2B-39, SS-27, 3B-1
1929		143	.302	.420	610	184	40	13	2	0.3	101	57	40	29	11	0	0	392	458	33	66	5.3	.963	SS-97, 2B-70
1930		129	.320	.467	475	152	32	13	4	0.8	69	75	39	34	8	3	0	304	458	48	111	6.4	.941	SS-126
1931	PHI N	135	.289	.392	554	160	43	7	0	0.0	88	34	27	38	6	0	0	319	442	42	98	5.9	.948	SS-133, 2B-3
1932		154	.308	.414	614	189	48	7	1	0.2	118	53	64	47	8	0	0	359	529	34	83	6.0	.963	SS-154
1933		152	.271	.336	587	159	25	5	1	0.2	78	37	56	46	6	0	0	381	493	45	100	6.0	.951	SS-152
1934		146	.310	.373	604	187	30	4	0	0.0	102	37	64	59	13	0	0	350	483	40	93	6.0	.954	SS-146
1935	NY N	137	.262	.406	539	141	28	4	14	2.6	60	53	37	52	5	0	0	339	424	37	71	5.8	.954	SS-137
1936		145	.298	.418	510	152	31	3	8	1.6	71	42	40	36	6	0	0	317	559	40	106	6.4	.956	SS-144
1937		128	.306	.469	516	158	38	2	14	2.7	91	62	40	38	5	0	0	281	476	33	96	6.2	.958	SS-128
1938		127	.262	.376	481	126	26	1	9	1.9	67	49	55	60	4	0	0	288	447	37	85	6.1	.952	SS-127
1939	CHI N	105	.238	.348	336	80	24	2	3	0.9	37	34	42	25	6	3	1	241	307	33	62	5.7	.943	SS-101, 3B-1
1940	DET A	139	.233	.330	528	123	24	3	7	1.3	76	53	76	53	12	0	0	295	394	34	74	5.2	.953	SS-139
1941	2 teams	DET A (5G –.167) NY N (104G –.303)																						
"	total	109	.299	.392	385	115	21	0	5	1.3	44	36	54	31	6	3	0	134	225	15	23	3.4	.960	3B-84, SS-26
1942	NY N	90	.244	.342	316	77	10	3	5	1.6	53	24	44	34	4	8	1	135	191	14	27	4.1	.959	3B-52, SS-31
1943		99	.270	.356	337	91	14	0	5	1.5	48	28	47	27	5	10	1	128	258	11	19	4.6	.972	3B-54, SS-33
1946		5	.000	.000	2	0	0	0	0	0.0	0	0	0	0	0	0	0	1	3	0	1	0.7	1.000	3B-4, 2B-2
18 yrs.		2016	.284	.391	7629	2165	442	71	79	1.0	1130	710	748	627	109	29	3	4425	6348	512	1156	5.6	.955	SS-1702, 3B-196, 2B-114
WORLD SERIES																								
1936	NY N	6	.381	.667	21	8	3	0	1	4.8	5	3	4	4	0	0	0	8	13	1	4	3.7	.955	SS-6
1937		5	.238	.286	21	5	1	0	0	0.0	3	1	0	3	0	0	0	13	11	3	3	5.4	.889	SS-5
1940	DET A	7	.269	.346	26	7	2	0	0	0.0	2	3	3	3	0	0	0	12	12	1	2	3.6	.960	SS-7
3 yrs.		18	.294	.426	68	20	6	0	1	1.5	10	7	7	10	0	0	0	33	36	5	9	4.1	.932	SS-18

Tony Bartirome

BARTIROME, ANTHONY JOSEPH BL TL 5′10″ 155 lbs.
B. May 9, 1932, Pittsburgh, Pa.

Year	Team	Games	BA	SA	AB	H	2B	3B	HR	HR%	R	RBI	BB	SO	SB	Pinch Hit AB	Pinch Hit H	PO	A	E	DP	TC/G	FA	G by Pos
1952	PIT N	124	.220	.265	355	78	10	3	0	0.0	32	16	26	37	3	1	0	909	72	11	91	8.4	.989	1B-118

Boyd Bartley

BARTLEY, BOYD OWEN BR TR 5′ 8½″ 165 lbs.
B. Feb. 11, 1920, Chicago, Ill.

Year	Team	Games	BA	SA	AB	H	2B	3B	HR	HR%	R	RBI	BB	SO	SB	Pinch Hit AB	Pinch Hit H	PO	A	E	DP	TC/G	FA	G by Pos
1943	BKN N	9	.048	.048	21	1	0	0	0	0.0	0	1	1	3	0	0	0	14	21	4	3	4.3	.897	SS-9

Irv Bartling
BARTLING, HENRY IRVING BR TR 6′ 175 lbs.
B. June 27, 1914, Bay City, Mich. D. June 12, 1973, Westland, Mich.

Year	Team	Games	BA	SA	AB	H	2B	3B	HR	HR%	R	RBI	BB	SO	SB	Pinch Hit AB	Pinch Hit H	PO	A	E	DP	TC/G	FA	G by Pos
1938	PHI A	14	.174	.239	46	8	1	1	0	0.0	5	5	3	7	0	0	0	29	35	6	8	5.0	.914	SS-13, 3B-1

Bob Barton
BARTON, ROBERT WILBUR BR TR 6′ 175 lbs.
B. July 30, 1941, Norwood, Ohio.

Year	Team	Games	BA	SA	AB	H	2B	3B	HR	HR%	R	RBI	BB	SO	SB	Pinch Hit AB	Pinch Hit H	PO	A	E	DP	TC/G	FA	G by Pos
1965	SF N	4	.571	.571	7	4	0	0	0	0.0	1	1	0	0	0	2	1	13	0	0	0	6.5	1.000	C-2
1966		43	.176	.220	91	16	2	1	0	0.0	1	3	5	5	0	4	0	161	19	1	4	4.6	.994	C-39
1967		7	.211	.211	19	4	0	0	0	0.0	0	1	0	2	0	0	0	33	3	0	0	5.1	1.000	C-7
1968		46	.261	.283	92	24	2	0	0	0.0	4	5	7	18	0	2	0	194	23	1	4	4.8	.995	C-45
1969		49	.170	.189	106	18	2	0	0	0.0	5	1	9	19	0	0	0	186	9	3	3	4.0	.985	C-49
1970	SD N	61	.218	.314	188	41	6	0	4	2.1	15	16	15	37	1	2	0	347	28	2	5	6.4	.995	C-59
1971		121	.250	.346	376	94	17	2	5	1.3	23	23	35	49	0	3	1	698	67	15	10	6.6	.981	C-119
1972		29	.193	.205	88	17	1	0	0	0.0	1	9	2	19	2	0	0	170	13	2	1	6.4	.989	C-29
1973	CIN N	3	.000	.000	1	0	0	0	0	0.0	0	0	1	0	0	1	0	5	0	0	0	2.5	1.000	C-2
1974	SD N	30	.235	.247	81	19	1	0	0	0.0	4	7	13	19	0	1	1	179	23	4	3	7.1	.981	C-29
10 yrs.		393	.226	.287	1049	237	31	3	9	0.9	54	66	87	168	3	15	3	1986	185	28	30	5.8	.987	C-380

Harry Barton
BARTON, HARRY LAMB BB TR 5′ 6½″ 155 lbs.
B. Jan. 20, 1875, Chester, Pa. D. Jan. 25, 1955, Upland, Pa.

Year	Team	Games	BA	SA	AB	H	2B	3B	HR	HR%	R	RBI	BB	SO	SB	Pinch Hit AB	Pinch Hit H	PO	A	E	DP	TC/G	FA	G by Pos
1905	PHI A	29	.167	.233	60	10	2	1	0	0.0	5	3	3		2	10	1	56	16	4	0	4.2	.947	C-13, 3B-2, 1B-2, OF-1

Vince Barton
BARTON, VINCENT DAVID BL TR 6′ 180 lbs.
B. Feb. 1, 1908, Edmonton, Alta., Canada D. Sept. 13, 1973, Toronto, Ont., Canada.

Year	Team	Games	BA	SA	AB	H	2B	3B	HR	HR%	R	RBI	BB	SO	SB	Pinch Hit AB	Pinch Hit H	PO	A	E	DP	TC/G	FA	G by Pos
1931	CHI N	66	.238	.452	239	57	10	1	13	5.4	45	50	21	40	1	4	1	133	2	5	0	2.3	.964	OF-61
1932		36	.224	.351	134	30	2	3	3	2.2	19	15	8	22	0	2	0	64	3	0	1	2.0	1.000	OF-34
2 yrs.		102	.233	.416	373	87	12	4	16	4.3	64	65	29	62	1	6	1	197	5	5	1	2.2	.976	OF-95

Dave Bartosch
BARTOSCH, DAVID ROBERT BR TR 6′ 1″ 190 lbs.
B. Mar. 24, 1917, St. Louis, Mo.

Year	Team	Games	BA	SA	AB	H	2B	3B	HR	HR%	R	RBI	BB	SO	SB	Pinch Hit AB	Pinch Hit H	PO	A	E	DP	TC/G	FA	G by Pos
1945	STL N	24	.255	.277	47	12	1	0	0	0.0	9	1	6	3	0	13	5	26	1	1	0	2.5	.964	OF-11

Monty Basgall
BASGALL, ROMANUS BR TR 5′10½″ 175 lbs.
B. Feb. 8, 1922, Pfeifer, Kans.

Year	Team	Games	BA	SA	AB	H	2B	3B	HR	HR%	R	RBI	BB	SO	SB	Pinch Hit AB	Pinch Hit H	PO	A	E	DP	TC/G	FA	G by Pos
1948	PIT N	38	.216	.353	51	11	1	0	2	3.9	12	6	3	5	0	5	1	37	35	0	4	3.3	1.000	2B-22
1949		107	.218	.273	308	67	9	1	2	0.6	25	26	31	32	1	4	1	224	225	13	58	4.6	.972	2B-98, 3B-3
1951		55	.209	.268	153	32	5	2	0	0.0	15	9	12	14	0	0	0	140	144	9	39	5.3	.969	2B-55
3 yrs.		200	.215	.279	512	110	15	3	4	0.8	52	41	46	51	1	9	2	401	404	22	101	4.6	.973	2B-175, 3B-3

Al Bashang
BASHANG, ALBERT C. BB TR 5′ 8″ 150 lbs.
B. Aug. 22, 1888, Cincinnati, Ohio D. June 23, 1967, Cincinnati, Ohio.

Year	Team	Games	BA	SA	AB	H	2B	3B	HR	HR%	R	RBI	BB	SO	SB	Pinch Hit AB	Pinch Hit H	PO	A	E	DP	TC/G	FA	G by Pos
1912	DET A	5	.083	.083	12	1	0	0	0	0.0	3	0	3		0	0	0	6	0	0	0	1.2	1.000	OF-5
1918	BKN N	2	.200	.200	5	1	0	0	0	0.0	0	0	0	0	0	1	0	0	1	0	0	1.0	1.000	OF-1
2 yrs.		7	.118	.118	17	2	0	0	0	0.0	3	0	3	0	0	1	0	6	1	0	0	1.2	1.000	OF-6

Walt Bashore
BASHORE, WALTER FRANKLIN BR TR 6′ 170 lbs.
Born Walter Franklin Beshore.
B. Oct. 6, 1909, Harrisburg, Pa. D. Sept. 26, 1984, Sebring, Fla.

Year	Team	Games	BA	SA	AB	H	2B	3B	HR	HR%	R	RBI	BB	SO	SB	Pinch Hit AB	Pinch Hit H	PO	A	E	DP	TC/G	FA	G by Pos
1936	PHI N	10	.200	.200	10	2	0	0	0	0.0	1	0	1	3	0	2	0	2	0	0	0	0.3	1.000	OF-6, 3B-1

Eddie Basinski
BASINSKI, EDWIN FRANK (Fiddler) BR TR 6′ 1″ 172 lbs.
B. Nov. 4, 1922, Buffalo, N. Y.

Year	Team	Games	BA	SA	AB	H	2B	3B	HR	HR%	R	RBI	BB	SO	SB	Pinch Hit AB	Pinch Hit H	PO	A	E	DP	TC/G	FA	G by Pos
1944	BKN N	39	.257	.314	105	27	4	1	0	0.0	13	9	6	10	1	1	0	86	87	8	15	4.5	.956	2B-37, SS-3
1945		108	.262	.313	336	88	9	4	0	0.0	30	33	11	33	0	2	0	177	267	35	62	4.5	.927	SS-101, 2B-6
1947	PIT N	56	.199	.335	161	32	6	2	4	2.5	15	17	18	27	0	0	0	116	130	7	34	4.5	.972	2B-56
3 yrs.		203	.244	.319	602	147	19	7	4	0.7	58	59	35	70	1	3	0	379	484	50	111	4.5	.945	SS-104, 2B-99

Doc Bass
BASS, WILLIAM CAPERS 5′10″ 165 lbs.
B. Dec. 4, 1899, Macon, Ga. D. Jan. 12, 1970, Macon, Ga.

Year	Team	Games	BA	SA	AB	H	2B	3B	HR	HR%	R	RBI	BB	SO	SB	Pinch Hit AB	Pinch Hit H	PO	A	E	DP	TC/G	FA	G by Pos
1918	BOS N	1	1.000	1.000	1	1	0	0	0	0.0	1	0	0	0	1	1	1	0	0	0	0	0.0	—	

John Bass
BASS, JOHN E. 5′ 6″ 150 lbs.
B. 1850, Baltimore, Md. Deceased.

Year	Team	Games	BA	SA	AB	H	2B	3B	HR	HR%	R	RBI	BB	SO	SB	Pinch Hit AB	Pinch Hit H	PO	A	E	DP	TC/G	FA	G by Pos
1877	HAR N	1	.250	.250	4	1	0	0	0	0.0	1	0	0	0		0	0	0	0	0	0	0.0	.000	OF-1

Kevin Bass
BASS, KEVIN CHARLES BB TR 6′ 183 lbs.
B. May 12, 1959, Redwood City, Calif.

Year	Team	Games	BA	SA	AB	H	2B	3B	HR	HR%	R	RBI	BB	SO	SB	Pinch Hit AB	Pinch Hit H	PO	A	E	DP	TC/G	FA	G by Pos
1982	2 teams	MIL A (18G –.000) HOU N (12G –.042)																						
″	total	30	.030	.030	33	1	0	0	0	0.0	6	1	1	9	0	1	0	18	0	1	0	0.8	.947	OF-21, DH-2
1983	HOU N	88	.236	.333	195	46	7	3	2	1.0	25	18	6	27	2	43	11	68	1	4	1	1.4	.945	OF-52
1984		121	.260	.360	331	86	17	5	2	0.6	33	29	6	57	5	44	13	149	4	4	2	1.9	.975	OF-81
1985		150	.269	.427	539	145	27	5	16	3.0	72	68	31	63	19	12	4	328	10	1	1	2.4	.997	OF-141
1986		157	.311	.486	591	184	33	5	20	3.4	83	79	38	72	22	2	2	303	12	5	4	2.1	.984	OF-155
1987		157	.284	.449	592	168	31	5	19	3.2	83	85	53	77	21	2	1	287	11	4	2	1.9	.987	OF-155
1988		157	.255	.390	541	138	27	2	14	2.6	57	72	42	65	31	16	6	267	7	6	2	1.9	.979	OF-147
1989		87	.300	.435	313	94	19	4	5	1.6	42	44	29	44	11	2	1	186	6	3	0	2.3	.985	OF-84
1990	SF N	61	.252	.402	214	54	9	1	7	3.3	25	32	14	26	2	5	1	88	2	3	0	1.7	.968	OF-55
1991		124	.233	.366	361	84	10	4	10	2.8	43	40	36	56	7	24	3	159	9	4	2	1.7	.977	OF-101
1992	2 teams	SF N (89G –.268) NY N (46G –.270)																						
″	total	135	.269	.418	402	108	23	5	9	2.2	40	39	23	70	14	29	7	191	2	3	0	1.8	.985	OF-111
1993	HOU N	111	.284	.402	229	65	18	0	3	1.3	31	37	26	31	7	52	14	83	3	1	0	1.4	.989	OF-64
1994		82	.310	.483	203	63	15	1	6	3.0	37	35	28	24	2	26	9	82	3	2	1	1.5	.977	OF-57
1995	BAL A	111	.244	.336	295	72	12	0	5	1.7	32	32	24	47	8	31	9	123	3	2	1	1.3	.984	OF-77, DH-19
14 yrs.		1571	.270	.411	4839	1308	248	40	118	2.4	609	611	357	668	151	289	81	2332	73	43	16	1.9	.982	OF-1301, DH-21

Kevin Bass *continued*

Year	Team	Games	BA	SA	AB	H	2B	3B	HR	HR%	R	RBI	BB	SO	SB	Pinch Hit AB	Pinch Hit H	PO	A	E	DP	TC/G	FA	G by Pos
LEAGUE CHAMPIONSHIP SERIES																								
1986	**HOU N**	6	.292	.375	24	7	2	0	0	0.0	0	0	4	4	2	0	0	16	0	1	0	2.8	.941	OF-6

Randy Bass

BASS, RANDY WILLIAM
B. Mar. 13, 1954, Lawton, Okla.
BL TR 6′ 1″ 210 lbs.

Year	Team	Games	BA	SA	AB	H	2B	3B	HR	HR%	R	RBI	BB	SO	SB	Pinch Hit AB	Pinch Hit H	PO	A	E	DP	TC/G	FA	G by Pos
1977	**MIN A**	9	.105	.105	19	2	0	0	0	0.0	0	0	0	5	0	4	0	0	0	0	0	0.0	.000	DH-6
1978	**KC A**	2	.000	.000	2	0	0	0	0	0.0	0	0	0	0	0	2	0	0	0	0	0	0.0	—	
1979	**MON N**	2	.000	.000	1	0	0	0	0	0.0	0	0	0	0	0	1	0	1	0	0	0	1.0	1.000	1B-1
1980	**SD N**	19	.286	.510	49	14	0	1	3	6.1	5	8	7	7	0	3	0	127	6	2	10	9.0	.985	1B-15
1981		69	.210	.313	176	37	4	1	4	2.3	13	20	20	28	0	19	5	390	35	3	38	8.6	.993	1B-50
1982	**2 teams**	**SD N** (13G –.200) **TEX A** (16G –.208)																						
″	**total**	29	.205	.308	78	16	2	0	2	2.6	6	14	3	11	0	5	1	121	7	0	16	5.8	1.000	1B-15, DH-7
6 yrs.		130	.212	.326	325	69	6	2	9	2.8	24	42	30	51	0	34	6	639	48	5	64	7.4	.993	1B-81, DH-13

Charley Bassett

BASSETT, CHARLES EDWIN
B. Feb. 9, 1863, Central Falls, R. I. D. May 28, 1942, Pawtucket, R. I.
BR TR 5′10″ 150 lbs.

Year	Team	Games	BA	SA	AB	H	2B	3B	HR	HR%	R	RBI	BB	SO	SB	Pinch Hit AB	Pinch Hit H	PO	A	E	DP	TC/G	FA	G by Pos
1884	**PRO N**	27	.139	.190	79	11	2	1	0	0.0	10		4	15		0	0	23	47	15	1	3.7	.824	3B-13, SS-7, OF-2, 2B-1
1885		82	.144	.186	285	41	8	2	0	0.0	21	16	19	60		0	0	141	248	39	24	5.2	.909	2B-39, SS-23, 3B-20, C-1
1886	**KC N**	90	.260	.380	342	89	19	8	2	0.6	41	32	36	43		0	0	131	290	55	25	5.3	.884	SS-82, 3B-8
1887	**IND N**	119	.230	.294	452	104	14	6	1	0.2	41	47	25	31	25	0	0	273	444	53	62	6.5	.931	2B-119
1888		128	.241	.308	481	116	20	3	2	0.4	58	60	32	41	24	0	0	250	423	57	44	5.7	.922	2B-128
1889		127	.245	.317	477	117	12	5	4	0.8	64	68	37	38	15	0	0	322	451	52	67	6.5	.937	2B-127
1890	**NY N**	100	.239	.310	410	98	13	8	0	0.0	52	54	29	25	14	0	0	201	332	27	43	5.6	.952	2B-100
1891		130	.260	.349	524	136	19	8	4	0.8	60	68	36	29	16	0	0	166	308	47	23	4.0	.910	3B-121, 2B-9
1892	**2 teams**	**NY N** (35G –.208) **LOU N** (79G –.214)																						
″	**total**	114	.212	.278	443	94	7	8	2	0.5	45	51	21	29	16	0	0	162	313	59	24	4.7	.890	3B-78, 2B-36
9 yrs.		917	.231	.304	3493	806	114	49	15	0.4	392	396	239	311	110	0	0	1669	2856	404	313	5.4	.918	2B-559, 3B-240, SS-112, OF-2, C-1

Johnny Bassler

BASSLER, JOHN LANDIS
B. June 3, 1895, Lancaster, Pa. D. June 29, 1979, Santa Monica, Calif.
BL TR 5′ 9″ 170 lbs.

Year	Team	Games	BA	SA	AB	H	2B	3B	HR	HR%	R	RBI	BB	SO	SB	Pinch Hit AB	Pinch Hit H	PO	A	E	DP	TC/G	FA	G by Pos
1913	**CLE A**	1	.000	.000	2	0	0	0	0	0.0	0	0	0	0	0	0	0	1	0	1	0	2.0	.500	C-1
1914		43	.182	.221	77	14	1	1	0	0.0	5	6	15	8	3	10	1	99	42	8	3	5.5	.946	C-25, OF-1, 3B-1
1921	**DET A**	119	.307	.379	388	119	18	5	0	0.0	37	56	58	16	2	3	1	433	113	14	7	4.9	.975	C-115
1922		121	.323	.360	372	120	14	0	0	0.0	41	41	62	12	2	2	0	421	113	11	12	4.6	.980	C-118
1923		135	.298	.345	383	114	12	3	0	0.0	45	49	76	13	2	5	2	447	133	7	8	4.6	.988	C-128
1924		124	.346	.422	379	131	20	3	1	0.3	43	68	62	11	2	3	1	402	103	11	11	4.2	.979	C-122
1925		121	.279	.352	344	96	19	3	0	0.0	40	52	74	6	1	3	0	375	87	8	14	4.0	.983	C-118
1926		66	.305	.362	174	53	8	1	0	0.0	20	22	45	6	0	2	0	223	61	0	6	4.5	1.000	C-63
1927		81	.285	.320	200	57	7	0	0	0.0	19	24	45	9	1	12	2	206	56	7	8	4.0	.974	C-67
9 yrs.		811	.304	.361	2319	704	99	16	1	0.0	250	318	437	81	13	40	7	2607	708	67	69	4.5	.980	C-757, OF-1, 3B-1

Charlie Bastian

BASTIAN, CHARLES J.
B. July 4, 1860, Philadelphia, Pa. D. Jan. 18, 1932, Pennsauken, N. J.
BR TR 5′ 6½″ 145 lbs.

Year	Team	Games	BA	SA	AB	H	2B	3B	HR	HR%	R	RBI	BB	SO	SB	Pinch Hit AB	Pinch Hit H	PO	A	E	DP	TC/G	FA	G by Pos
1884	**2 teams**	**WIL U** (17G –.200) **KC U** (11G –.196)																						
″	**total**	28	.198	.377	106	21	4	3	3	2.8	12		7			0	0	67	95	14	9	6.1	.920	2B-27, SS-1, P-1
1885	**PHI N**	103	.167	.252	389	65	11	5	4	1.0	63		35	**82**		0	0	164	337	62	34	5.5	.890	SS-103
1886		105	.217	.316	373	81	9	11	2	0.5	46	38	33	73		0	0	175	326	34	23	5.1	.936	2B-87, SS-10, 3B-8
1887		60	.213	.285	221	47	11	1	1	0.5	33	21	19	29	11	0	0	110	170	25	21	5.0	.918	2B-39, SS-18, 3B-4
1888		80	.193	.225	275	53	4	1	1	0.4	30	17	27	41	12	0	0	162	277	27	16	5.8	.942	2B-65, 3B-14, SS-1
1889	**CHI N**	46	.135	.135	155	21	0	0	0	0.0	19	10	25	46	1	0	0	67	163	19	10	5.4	.924	SS-45, 2B-1
1890	**CHI P**	80	.191	.261	283	54	10	5	0	0.0	38	29	33	37	4	0	0	129	231	44	28	5.1	.891	SS-64, 2B-12, 3B-4
1891	**2 teams**	**CIN AA** (1G –.000) **PHI N** (1G –.000)																						
″	**total**	2	.000	.000	4	0	0	0	0	0.0	0	0	0	0	0	0	0	4	5	0	1	4.5	1.000	SS-1, 2B-1
8 yrs.		504	.189	.264	1806	342	49	26	11	0.6	241	115	179	308	28	0	0	878	1604	225	142	5.3	.917	SS-243, 2B-232, 3B-30, P-1

Emil Batch

BATCH, EMIL (Heinie)
B. Jan. 21, 1880, Brooklyn, N. Y. D. Aug. 23, 1926, Brooklyn, N. Y.
BR TR 5′ 7″ 170 lbs.

Year	Team	Games	BA	SA	AB	H	2B	3B	HR	HR%	R	RBI	BB	SO	SB	Pinch Hit AB	Pinch Hit H	PO	A	E	DP	TC/G	FA	G by Pos
1904	**BKN N**	28	.255	.372	94	24	1	2	2	2.1	9	7	1		6	0	0	26	55	11	3	3.3	.880	3B-28
1905		145	.252	.352	568	143	20	11	5	0.9	64	49	26		21	0	0	203	246	57	22	3.5	.887	3B-145
1906		59	.256	.350	203	52	7	6	0	0.0	23	11	15		3	6	1	104	7	5	0	2.2	.957	OF-50, 3B-2
1907		116	.247	.289	388	96	10	3	0	0.0	38	31	23		7	8	1	182	17	15	4	2.0	.930	OF-102, 3B-2, SS-1, 2B-1
4 yrs.		348	.251	.334	1253	315	38	22	7	0.6	134	98	65		37	14	2	515	325	88	29	2.8	.905	3B-177, OF-152, SS-1, 2B-1

John Bateman

BATEMAN, JOHN ALVIN
B. July 21, 1942, Killeen, Tex.
BR TR 6′ 3″ 210 lbs.

Year	Team	Games	BA	SA	AB	H	2B	3B	HR	HR%	R	RBI	BB	SO	SB	Pinch Hit AB	Pinch Hit H	PO	A	E	DP	TC/G	FA	G by Pos
1963	**HOU N**	128	.210	.334	404	85	8	6	10	2.5	23	59	13	103	0	13	2	690	81	23	7	6.9	.971	C-115
1964		74	.190	.294	221	42	8	0	5	2.3	18	19	17	48	0	2	0	400	43	6	4	6.2	.987	C-72
1965		45	.197	.380	142	28	3	1	7	4.9	15	14	12	37	0	5	0	234	26	4	3	6.8	.985	C-39
1966		131	.279	.467	433	121	24	3	17	3.9	39	70	20	74	0	11	2	731	63	15	14	6.7	.981	C-121
1967		76	.190	.250	252	48	9	0	2	0.8	16	17	17	53	0	4	1	483	46	6	5	7.5	.989	C-71
1968		111	.249	.337	350	87	19	0	4	1.1	28	33	23	46	1	2	1	690	49	11	6	6.9	.985	C-108
1969	**MON N**	74	.209	.328	235	49	4	0	8	3.4	16	19	12	44	0	7	2	433	26	7	5	7.1	.985	C-66
1970		139	.237	.383	520	123	21	5	15	2.9	51	68	28	75	8	2	0	824	62	15	19	6.6	.983	C-137
1971		139	.242	.350	492	119	17	3	10	2.0	34	56	19	87	1	4	1	726	56	12	12	5.8	.985	C-137
1972	**2 teams**	**MON N** (18G –.241) **PHI N** (82G –.222)																						
″	**total**	100	.224	.292	281	63	10	0	3	1.1	10	20	11	43	0	14	2	475	39	14	6	6.1	.973	C-87
10 yrs.		1017	.230	.350	3330	765	123	18	81	2.4	250	375	172	610	10	64	11	5686	491	113	81	6.6	.982	C-953

Billy Bates

BATES, WILLIAM DERRICK
B. Dec. 7, 1963, Houston, Tex.
BL TR 5′ 7″ 155 lbs.

Year	Team	Games	BA	SA	AB	H	2B	3B	HR	HR%	R	RBI	BB	SO	SB	Pinch Hit AB	Pinch Hit H	PO	A	E	DP	TC/G	FA	G by Pos
1989	MIL A	7	.214	.214	14	3	0	0	0	0.0	3	0	0	1	2	1	1	14	16	2	7	4.6	.938	2B-7
1990	2 teams	MIL A (14G –.103) CIN N (8G –.000)																						
″	total	22	.088	.118	34	3	1	0	0	0.0	8	2	4	9	6	1	0	18	34	2	6	3.6	.963	2B-15
2 yrs.		29	.125	.146	48	6	1	0	0	0.0	11	2	4	10	8	2	1	32	50	4	13	3.9	.953	2B-22
LEAGUE CHAMPIONSHIP SERIES																								
1990	CIN N	2	—	—	0	0	0	0	0	—	1	0	0	0	0	0	0	0	0	0	0	0.0	—	
WORLD SERIES																								
1990	CIN N	1	1.000	1.000	1	1	0	0	0	0.0	1	0	0	0	0	1	1	0	0	0	0	0.0	—	

Bud Bates

BATES, HUBERT EDGAR
B. Mar. 16, 1912, Los Angeles, Calif. D. Apr. 29, 1987, Long Beach, Calif.
BR TR 6′ 165 lbs.

Year	Team	Games	BA	SA	AB	H	2B	3B	HR	HR%	R	RBI	BB	SO	SB	Pinch Hit AB	Pinch Hit H	PO	A	E	DP	TC/G	FA	G by Pos
1939	PHI N	15	.259	.345	58	15	2	0	1	1.7	8	2	2	8	1	0	0	44	1	1	1	3.3	.978	OF-14

Charlie Bates

BATES, CHARLES WILLIAM
B. Sept. 17, 1907, Philadelphia, Pa. D. Jan. 29, 1980, Topeka, Kans.
BR TR 5′10″ 165 lbs.

Year	Team	Games	BA	SA	AB	H	2B	3B	HR	HR%	R	RBI	BB	SO	SB	Pinch Hit AB	Pinch Hit H	PO	A	E	DP	TC/G	FA	G by Pos
1927	PHI A	9	.237	.395	38	9	2	2	0	0.0	5	2	3	5	3	0	0	17	1	3	0	2.3	.857	OF-9

Del Bates

BATES, DELBERT OAKLEY, JR.
B. June 12, 1940, Seattle, Wash.
BL TR 6′ 2″ 195 lbs.

Year	Team	Games	BA	SA	AB	H	2B	3B	HR	HR%	R	RBI	BB	SO	SB	Pinch Hit AB	Pinch Hit H	PO	A	E	DP	TC/G	FA	G by Pos
1970	PHI N	22	.133	.167	60	8	2	0	0	0.0	1	1	6	15	0	5	0	116	8	1	0	6.3	.992	C-20

Jason Bates

BATES, JASON CHARLES
B. Jan. 5, 1971, Downey, Calif.
BB TR 5′11″ 170 lbs.

Year	Team	Games	BA	SA	AB	H	2B	3B	HR	HR%	R	RBI	BB	SO	SB	Pinch Hit AB	Pinch Hit H	PO	A	E	DP	TC/G	FA	G by Pos
1995	CLR N	116	.267	.419	322	86	17	4	8	2.5	42	46	42	70	3	9	3	168	255	5	53	3.7	.988	2B-81, SS-20, 3B-15
DIVISIONAL PLAYOFF SERIES																								
1995	CLR N	4	.250	.250	4	1	0	0	0	0.0	0	0	0	0	0	2	1	1	3	0	0	2.0	1.000	3B-1, 2B-1

Johnny Bates

BATES, JOHN WILLIAM
B. Aug. 21, 1882, Steubenville, Ohio D. Feb. 10, 1949, Steubenville, Ohio.
BL TL 5′ 7″ 168 lbs.

Year	Team	Games	BA	SA	AB	H	2B	3B	HR	HR%	R	RBI	BB	SO	SB	Pinch Hit AB	Pinch Hit H	PO	A	E	DP	TC/G	FA	G by Pos
1906	BOS N	140	.252	.349	504	127	21	5	6	1.2	52	54	36		9	0	0	238	12	11	4	1.9	.958	OF-140
1907		126	.260	.367	447	116	18	12	2	0.4	52	49	39		11	5	1	171	18	4	5	1.6	.979	OF-120
1908		127	.258	.324	445	115	14	6	1	0.2	48	29	35		25	10	0	205	15	12	2	2.0	.948	OF-117
1909	2 teams	BOS N (63G –.288) PHI N (77G –.293)																						
″	total	140	.291	.371	502	146	26	4	2	0.4	70	38	48		37	5	1	253	27	14	3	2.2	.952	OF-133
1910	PHI N	135	.305	.420	498	152	26	11	3	0.6	91	61	61	49	31	4	0	308	24	16	8	2.7	.954	OF-131
1911	CIN N	148	.292	.394	518	151	24	13	1	0.2	89	61	103	59	33	1	0	352	21	13	4	2.6	.966	OF-147
1912		81	.289	.410	239	69	12	7	1	0.4	45	29	47	16	10	12	3	157	15	9	4	2.8	.950	OF-65
1913		131	.278	.388	407	113	13	7	6	1.5	63	51	67	30	21	17	6	192	19	12	6	2.0	.946	OF-112
1914	3 teams	CIN N (67G –.245) CHI N (9G –.125) BAL F (59G –.305)																						
″	total	135	.274	.380	361	99	13	8	3	0.8	55	45	68	19	10	8	1	204	11	15	1	1.9	.935	OF-119
9 yrs.		1163	.277	.376	3921	1088	167	73	25	0.6	565	417	504	173	187	62	12	2080	162	106	37	2.2	.955	OF-1084

Ray Bates

BATES, RAYMOND
B. Feb. 8, 1890, Paterson, N. J. D. Aug. 15, 1970, Tucson, Ariz.
BR TR 6′ 165 lbs.

Year	Team	Games	BA	SA	AB	H	2B	3B	HR	HR%	R	RBI	BB	SO	SB	Pinch Hit AB	Pinch Hit H	PO	A	E	DP	TC/G	FA	G by Pos
1913	CLE A	20	.167	.300	30	5	0	2	0	0.0	4	4	3	9	3	1	0	6	13	2	2	1.5	.905	3B-12, OF-2
1917	PHI A	127	.237	.320	485	115	20	7	2	0.4	47	66	21	39	12	3	0	168	267	31	17	3.8	.933	3B-124
2 yrs.		147	.233	.318	515	120	20	9	2	0.4	51	70	24	48	15	4	0	174	280	33	19	3.5	.932	3B-136, OF-2

Bill Bathe

BATHE, WILLIAM DAVID
B. Oct. 14, 1960, Downey, Calif.
BR TR 6′ 2″ 200 lbs.

Year	Team	Games	BA	SA	AB	H	2B	3B	HR	HR%	R	RBI	BB	SO	SB	Pinch Hit AB	Pinch Hit H	PO	A	E	DP	TC/G	FA	G by Pos
1986	OAK A	39	.184	.359	103	19	3	0	5	4.9	9	11	2	20	0	0	0	211	11	2	1	5.7	.991	C-39
1989	SF N	30	.281	.313	32	9	1	0	0	0.0	3	6	0	7	0	26	6	13	0	0	0	1.9	1.000	C-7
1990		52	.229	.458	48	11	0	1	3	6.3	3	12	7	12	0	39	9	10	1	0	1	1.4	1.000	C-8
3 yrs.		121	.213	.377	183	39	4	1	8	4.4	15	29	9	39	0	65	15	234	12	2	2	4.6	.992	C-54
LEAGUE CHAMPIONSHIP SERIES																								
1989	SF N	2	.000	.000	1	0	0	0	0	0.0	0	0	0	1	0	1	0	0	0	0	0	0.0	—	
WORLD SERIES																								
1989	SF N	2	.500	2.000	2	1	0	0	1	50.0	1	3	0	0	0	2	1	0	0	0	0	0.0	—	

Rafael Batista

BATISTA, RAFAEL
Born Rafael Batista (Sanchez).
B. Oct. 20, 1947, San Pedro de Macoris, Dominican Republic.
BL TL 6′ 1″ 195 lbs.

Year	Team	Games	BA	SA	AB	H	2B	3B	HR	HR%	R	RBI	BB	SO	SB	Pinch Hit AB	Pinch Hit H	PO	A	E	DP	TC/G	FA	G by Pos
1973	HOU N	12	.267	.267	15	4	0	0	0	0.0	2	2	1	6	0	6	0	26	1	0	1	3.4	1.000	1B-8
1975		10	.300	.400	10	3	1	0	0	0.0	0	0	0	4	0	10	3	0	0	0	0	0.0	—	
2 yrs.		22	.280	.320	25	7	1	0	0	0.0	2	2	1	10	0	16	3	26	1	0	1	3.4	1.000	1B-8

Kevin Batiste

BATISTE, KEVIN WADE
B. Oct. 21, 1966, Galveston, Tex.
BR TR 6′ 2″ 178 lbs.

Year	Team	Games	BA	SA	AB	H	2B	3B	HR	HR%	R	RBI	BB	SO	SB	Pinch Hit AB	Pinch Hit H	PO	A	E	DP	TC/G	FA	G by Pos
1989	TOR A	6	.250	.250	8	2	0	0	0	0.0	1	0	0	5	0	0	0	7	0	0	0	1.4	1.000	OF-5

Kim Batiste

BATISTE, KIMOTHY EMIL
B. Mar. 15, 1968, New Orleans, La.
BR TR 6′ 175 lbs.

Year	Team	Games	BA	SA	AB	H	2B	3B	HR	HR%	R	RBI	BB	SO	SB	Pinch Hit AB	Pinch Hit H	PO	A	E	DP	TC/G	FA	G by Pos
1991	PHI N	10	.222	.222	27	6	0	0	0	0.0	2	1	1	8	0	2	0	10	22	1	4	4.7	.970	SS-7
1992		44	.206	.257	136	28	4	0	1	0.7	9	10	4	18	0	2	0	69	85	13	17	4.1	.922	SS-41
1993		79	.282	.436	156	44	7	1	5	3.2	14	29	3	29	0	0	0	72	108	10	15	2.3	.947	3B-58, SS-24
1994		64	.234	.278	209	49	6	0	1	0.5	17	13	1	32	1	7	2	52	116	12	13	3.1	.933	3B-42, SS-17
4 yrs.		197	.241	.316	528	127	17	1	7	1.3	42	53	9	87	1	11	2	203	331	36	49	3.0	.937	3B-100, SS-89
LEAGUE CHAMPIONSHIP SERIES																								
1993	PHI N	4	1.000	1.000	1	1	0	0	0	0.0	0	1	0	0	0	0	0	2	0	2	0	1.0	.500	3B-4
WORLD SERIES																								
1993	PHI N	3	—	—	0	0	0	0	0	—	0	0	0	0	0	0	0	0	1	0	0	0.3	1.000	3B-3

Bill Batsch

BATSCH, WILLIAM McKINLEY BR TR 5'10½" 168 lbs.
B. May 18, 1892, Mingo Junction, Ohio D. Dec. 31, 1963, Canton, Ohio.

Year	Team	Games	BA	SA	AB	H	2B	3B	HR	HR%	R	RBI	BB	SO	SB	Pinch Hit AB	Pinch Hit H	PO	A	E	DP	TC/G	FA	G by Pos
1916	PIT N	1	—	—	0	0	0	0	0	—	0	0	1	0	0	0	0	0	0	0	0	0.0	—	

Larry Battam

BATTAM, LAWRENCE 5'11"
B. May 1, 1878, Brooklyn, N. Y. D. Jan. 27, 1938, Brooklyn, N. Y.

Year	Team	Games	BA	SA	AB	H	2B	3B	HR	HR%	R	RBI	BB	SO	SB	Pinch Hit AB	Pinch Hit H	PO	A	E	DP	TC/G	FA	G by Pos
1895	NY N	2	.250	.250	4	1	0	0	0	0.0	0	0	2	1	0	0	0	0	2	1	0	1.5	.667	3B-2

George Batten

BATTEN, GEORGE BURNETT BR TR 5'11" 165 lbs.
B. Oct. 7, 1891, Haddonfield, N. J. D. Aug. 4, 1972, New Port Ritchey, Fla.

Year	Team	Games	BA	SA	AB	H	2B	3B	HR	HR%	R	RBI	BB	SO	SB	Pinch Hit AB	Pinch Hit H	PO	A	E	DP	TC/G	FA	G by Pos
1912	NY A	1	.000	.000	3	0	0	0	0	0.0	0	0	0		0	0	0	1	1	1	0	3.0	.667	2B-1

Earl Battey

BATTEY, EARL JESSE BR TR 6' 1" 205 lbs.
B. Jan. 5, 1935, Los Angeles, Calif.

Year	Team	Games	BA	SA	AB	H	2B	3B	HR	HR%	R	RBI	BB	SO	SB	Pinch Hit AB	Pinch Hit H	PO	A	E	DP	TC/G	FA	G by Pos
1955	CHI A	5	.286	.286	7	2	0	0	0	0.0	1	0	1	1	0	1	0	19	2	0	0	4.2	1.000	C-5
1956		4	.250	.250	4	1	0	0	0	0.0	1	0	1	1	0	0	0	4	0	1	0	1.7	.800	C-3
1957		48	.174	.322	115	20	2	3	3	2.6	12	6	11	38	0	4	3	165	19	2	2	4.3	.989	C-43
1958		68	.226	.417	168	38	8	0	8	4.8	24	26	24	34	1	17	1	220	27	3	6	5.1	.988	C-49
1959		26	.219	.391	64	14	1	2	2	3.1	9	7	8	13	0	5	0	92	10	1	1	5.2	.990	C-20
1960	WAS A	137	.270	.427	466	126	24	2	15	3.2	49	60	48	68	4	4	2	749	65	15	10	6.1	.982	C-136
1961	MIN A	133	.302	.470	460	139	24	1	17	3.7	70	55	53	66	3	2	0	812	60	6	9	6.7	.993	C-131
1962		148	.280	.393	522	146	20	3	11	2.1	58	57	57	48	0	1	0	872	82	9	9	6.6	.991	C-147
1963		147	.285	.476	508	145	17	1	26	5.1	64	84	61	75	0	2	0	861	66	6	11	6.4	.994	C-146
1964		131	.272	.407	405	110	17	1	12	3.0	33	52	51	49	1	8	2	813	52	9	4	7.0	.990	C-125
1965		131	.297	.409	394	117	22	2	6	1.5	36	60	50	23	0	5	0	652	56	10	10	5.6	.986	C-128
1966		115	.255	.327	364	93	12	1	4	1.1	30	34	43	30	4	2	1	705	45	4	9	6.7	.995	C-113
1967		48	.165	.211	109	18	3	1	0	0.0	6	8	13	24	0	9	3	212	17	3	2	5.7	.987	C-41
13 yrs.		1141	.270	.409	3586	969	150	17	104	2.9	393	449	421	470	13	60	12	6176	501	69	73	6.2	.990	C-1087
WORLD SERIES																								
1965	MIN A	7	.120	.200	25	3	0	1	0	0.0	1	2	0	5	0	0	0	31	6	0	2	5.3	1.000	C-7

Joe Battin

BATTIN, JOSEPH V. BR TR
B. Nov. 11, 1851, Philadelphia, Pa. D. Dec. 10, 1937, Akron, Ohio.
Manager 1883–84.

Year	Team	Games	BA	SA	AB	H	2B	3B	HR	HR%	R	RBI	BB	SO	SB	Pinch Hit AB	Pinch Hit H	PO	A	E	DP	TC/G	FA	G by Pos
1876	STL N	64	.300	.367	283	85	11	4	0	0.0	34	46	6	6		0	0	118	146	40	8	4.8	.868	3B-63, 2B-1
1877		57	.199	.288	226	45	3	7	1	0.4	28	22	6	17		0	0	117	136	55	10	5.2	.821	3B-32, 2B-21, OF-5, P-1
1882	PIT AA	34	.211	.286	133	28	5	1	1	0.8	13		3			0	0	62	108	24	5	5.7	.876	3B-34
1883		98	.214	.276	388	83	9	6	1	0.3	42		11			0	0	151	258	50	12	4.6	.891	3B-98, P-2
1884	3 teams PIT AA (43G –.177) PIT U (18G –.188) BAL U (17G –.102)																							
"	total	78	.164	.192	286	47	4	2	0	0.0	21		3			0	0	101	178	33	8	4.0	.894	3B-78
1890	SYR AA	29	.210	.244	119	25	2	1	0	0.0	15		8		8	0	0	44	60	27	2	4.5	.794	3B-29
6 yrs.		360	.218	.277	1435	313	34	21	3	0.2	153	68	37	23	8	0	0	593	886	229	45	4.7	.866	3B-334, 2B-22, OF-5, P-3

Allen Battle

BATTLE, ALLEN ZELMO BR TR 6' 170 lbs.
B. Nov. 29, 1968, Grantham, N. C.

Year	Team	Games	BA	SA	AB	H	2B	3B	HR	HR%	R	RBI	BB	SO	SB	Pinch Hit AB	Pinch Hit H	PO	A	E	DP	TC/G	FA	G by Pos
1995	STL N	61	.271	.314	118	32	5	0	0	0.0	13	2	15	26	3	21	3	60	0	1	0	1.9	.984	OF-32

Howard Battle

BATTLE, HOWARD DION BR TR 6' 210 lbs.
B. Mar. 25, 1972, Biloxi, Miss.

Year	Team	Games	BA	SA	AB	H	2B	3B	HR	HR%	R	RBI	BB	SO	SB	Pinch Hit AB	Pinch Hit H	PO	A	E	DP	TC/G	FA	G by Pos
1995	TOR A	9	.200	.200	15	3	0	0	0	0.0	3	0	4	8	1	1	0	1	6	0	0	1.0	1.000	3B-6, DH-1

Jim Battle

BATTLE, JAMES MILTON BR TR 6' 1" 170 lbs.
B. Mar. 26, 1901, Bailey, Tex. D. Sept. 30, 1965, Chico, Calif.

Year	Team	Games	BA	SA	AB	H	2B	3B	HR	HR%	R	RBI	BB	SO	SB	Pinch Hit AB	Pinch Hit H	PO	A	E	DP	TC/G	FA	G by Pos
1927	CHI A	6	.375	.625	8	3	0	1	0	0.0	1	0	0	1	0	0	0	5	2	0	0	1.2	1.000	3B-4, SS-2

Matt Batts

BATTS, MATTHEW DANIEL BR TR 5'11" 200 lbs.
B. Oct. 16, 1921, San Antonio, Tex.

Year	Team	Games	BA	SA	AB	H	2B	3B	HR	HR%	R	RBI	BB	SO	SB	Pinch Hit AB	Pinch Hit H	PO	A	E	DP	TC/G	FA	G by Pos
1947	BOS A	7	.500	.750	16	8	1	0	1	6.3	3	5	1	1	0	1	0	15	2	0	1	2.8	1.000	C-6
1948		46	.314	.441	118	37	12	0	1	0.8	13	24	15	9	0	6	1	118	18	2	3	3.4	.986	C-41
1949		60	.242	.369	157	38	9	1	3	1.9	23	31	25	22	1	11	1	193	23	5	2	4.4	.977	C-50
1950		75	.273	.412	238	65	15	3	4	1.7	27	34	18	19	0	2	1	306	29	2	3	4.6	.994	C-73
1951	2 teams BOS A (11G –.138) STL A (79G –.302)																							
"	total	90	.285	.412	277	79	18	1	5	1.8	27	33	22	23	2	11	1	291	37	13	6	4.5	.962	C-75
1952	DET A	56	.237	.324	173	41	4	1	3	1.7	11	13	14	22	1	2	0	262	36	5	4	5.5	.983	C-55
1953		116	.278	.406	374	104	24	3	6	1.6	38	42	24	36	2	12	4	463	44	7	7	5.0	.986	C-103
1954	2 teams DET A (12G –.286) CHI A (55G –.228)																							
"	total	67	.235	.341	179	42	8	1	3	1.7	17	24	19	19	0	17	4	249	24	3	4	5.5	.989	C-50
1955	CIN N	26	.254	.338	71	18	4	1	0	0.0	4	13	4	11	0	5	1	65	8	1	2	3.5	.986	C-21
1956		3	.000	.000	2	0	0	0	0	0.0	0	0	1	1	0	2	0	0	0	0	0	0.0	—	
10 yrs.		546	.269	.391	1605	432	95	11	26	1.6	163	219	143	163	6	69	13	1962	221	38	32	4.7	.983	C-474

Hank Bauer

BAUER, HENRY ALBERT BR TR 6' 192 lbs.
B. July 31, 1922, East St. Louis, Ill.
Manager 1961–62, 1964–69.

Year	Team	Games	BA	SA	AB	H	2B	3B	HR	HR%	R	RBI	BB	SO	SB	Pinch Hit AB	Pinch Hit H	PO	A	E	DP	TC/G	FA	G by Pos
1948	NY A	19	.180	.300	50	9	1	1	1	2.0	6	9	6	13	1	2	0	26	1	1	0	2.0	.964	OF-14
1949		103	.272	.432	301	82	6	6	10	3.3	56	45	37	42	2	5	2	156	11	4	3	1.8	.977	OF-95
1950		113	.320	.463	415	133	16	2	13	3.1	72	70	35	41	2	2	1	228	8	3	3	2.2	.987	OF-110
1951		118	.296	.454	348	103	19	3	10	2.9	53	54	42	39	5	13	5	188	7	2	1	1.8	.990	OF-107
1952		141	.293	.463	553	162	31	6	17	3.1	86	74	50	61	6	2	1	233	16	4	2	1.8	.984	OF-139
1953		133	.304	.446	437	133	20	6	10	2.3	77	57	59	45	2	16	3	230	13	2	3	1.9	.992	OF-126
1954		114	.294	.459	377	111	16	5	12	3.2	73	54	40	42	4	9	4	179	6	2	1	1.7	.989	OF-108
1955		139	.278	.461	492	137	20	5	20	4.1	97	53	56	65	8	6	1	248	13	5	3	2.0	.981	OF-133, C-1
1956		147	.241	.445	539	130	18	7	26	4.8	96	84	59	72	4	7	4	242	10	8	2	1.8	.969	OF-146
1957		137	.259	.455	479	124	22	**9**	18	3.8	70	65	42	64	7	4	1	200	7	3	1	1.6	.986	OF-135

Hank Bauer *continued*

Year	Team	Games	BA	SA	AB	H	2B	3B	HR	HR%	R	RBI	BB	SO	SB	Pinch Hit AB	Pinch Hit H	PO	A	E	DP	TC/G	FA	G by Pos
1958		128	.268	.423	452	121	22	6	12	2.7	62	50	32	56	3	6	2	186	7	4	0	1.6	.980	OF-123
1959		114	.238	.375	341	81	20	0	9	2.6	44	39	33	54	4	7	1	139	2	4	0	1.3	.972	OF-111
1960	KC A	95	.275	.369	255	70	15	0	3	1.2	30	31	21	36	1	33	10	85	4	2	1	1.4	.978	OF-67
1961		43	.264	.396	106	28	3	1	3	2.8	11	18	9	8	1	9	1	44	2	2	0	1.4	.958	OF-35
14 yrs.		1544	.277	.439	5145	1424	229	57	164	3.2	833	703	521	638	50	121	36	2384	107	46	20	1.7	.982	OF-1449, C-1
WORLD SERIES																								
1949	NY A	3	.167	.167	6	1	0	0	0	0.0	0	0	0	0	0	1	0	3	0	0	0	1.0	1.000	OF-3
1950		4	.133	.133	15	2	0	0	0	0.0	0	1	0	0	0	0	0	8	0	0	0	2.0	1.000	OF-4
1951		6	.167	.278	18	3	0	1	0	0.0	0	3	1	1	0	0	0	7	0	0	0	1.2	1.000	OF-6
1952		7	.056	.056	18	1	0	0	0	0.0	2	1	4	3	0	1	0	10	0	0	0	1.4	1.000	OF-7
1953		6	.261	.348	23	6	0	1	0	0.0	6	1	2	4	0	0	0	14	0	0	0	2.3	1.000	OF-6
1955		6	.429	.429	14	6	0	0	0	0.0	1	1	0	1	0	1	0	7	0	0	0	1.4	1.000	OF-5
1956		7	.281	.375	32	9	0	0	1	3.1	3	3	0	5	1	0	0	14	1	1	0	2.3	.938	OF-7
1957		7	.258	.581	31	8	2	1	2	6.5	3	6	1	6	0	0	0	10	0	0	0	1.4	1.000	OF-7
1958		7	.323	.710	31	10	0	0	4	12.9	6	8	0	5	0	0	0	7	0	0	0	1.0	1.000	OF-7
9 yrs.		53	.245	.399	188	46	2	3	7	3.7	21	24	8	25	1	3	0	80	1	1	0	1.6	.988	OF-52
		4th			6th	5th		4th	10th		10th	8th		7th										

Paddy Baumann

BAUMANN, CHARLES JOHN BR TR 5′ 9″ 160 lbs.
B. Dec. 20, 1885, Indianapolis, Ind. D. Nov. 20, 1969, Indianapolis, Ind.

Year	Team	Games	BA	SA	AB	H	2B	3B	HR	HR%	R	RBI	BB	SO	SB	Pinch Hit AB	Pinch Hit H	PO	A	E	DP	TC/G	FA	G by Pos
1911	DET A	26	.255	.362	94	24	2	4	0	0.0	8	11	6		1	0	0	68	71	6	6	5.6	.959	2B-23, OF-3
1912		13	.262	.286	42	11	1	0	0	0.0	3	7	6		4	1	0	19	23	9	1	4.3	.824	3B-6, 2B-5, OF-1
1913		49	.298	.393	191	57	7	4	1	0.5	31	22	16	18	4	0	0	97	136	14	15	5.0	.943	2B-49
1914		3	.000	.000	11	0	0	0	0	0.0	1	0	2	1	0	0	0	5	8	0	1	4.3	1.000	2B-3
1915	NY A	76	.292	.388	219	64	13	1	2	0.9	30	28	28	32	9	10	2	129	140	6	20	4.4	.978	2B-43, 3B-19
1916		79	.287	.346	237	68	5	3	1	0.4	35	25	19	16	10	14	5	93	64	8	8	2.6	.952	OF-28, 3B-26, 2B-9
1917		49	.218	.255	110	24	2	1	0	0.0	10	8	4	9	2	21	6	37	32	4	8	2.8	.945	2B-18, OF-7, 3B-1
7 yrs.		295	.274	.350	904	248	30	13	4	0.4	118	101	81	76	30	46	13	448	474	47	59	4.0	.951	2B-150, 3B-52, OF-39

Jim Baumer

BAUMER, JAMES SLOAN BR TR 6′ 2″ 185 lbs.
B. Jan. 29, 1931, Tulsa, Okla.

Year	Team	Games	BA	SA	AB	H	2B	3B	HR	HR%	R	RBI	BB	SO	SB	Pinch Hit AB	Pinch Hit H	PO	A	E	DP	TC/G	FA	G by Pos
1949	CHI A	8	.400	.700	10	4	1	1	0	0.0	2	2	2	1	0	0	0	3	12	1	4	2.3	.938	SS-7
1961	CIN N	10	.125	.125	24	3	0	0	0	0.0	0	0	0	9	0	0	0	18	14	0	2	3.6	1.000	2B-9
2 yrs.		18	.206	.294	34	7	1	1	0	0.0	2	2	2	10	0	0	0	21	26	1	6	3.0	.979	2B-9, SS-7

John Baumgartner

BAUMGARTNER, JOHN EDWARD BR TR 6′ 1″ 190 lbs.
B. May 29, 1931, Birmingham, Ala.

Year	Team	Games	BA	SA	AB	H	2B	3B	HR	HR%	R	RBI	BB	SO	SB	Pinch Hit AB	Pinch Hit H	PO	A	E	DP	TC/G	FA	G by Pos
1953	DET A	7	.185	.185	27	5	0	0	0	0.0	3	2	0	5	0	0	0	10	11	2	2	3.3	.913	3B-7

Frankie Baumholtz

BAUMHOLTZ, FRANK CONRAD BL TL 5′10½″ 175 lbs.
B. Oct. 7, 1918, Midvale, Ohio.

Year	Team	Games	BA	SA	AB	H	2B	3B	HR	HR%	R	RBI	BB	SO	SB	Pinch Hit AB	Pinch Hit H	PO	A	E	DP	TC/G	FA	G by Pos
1947	CIN N	151	.283	.384	643	182	32	9	5	0.8	96	45	56	53	6	1	1	282	18	7	2	2.0	.977	OF-150
1948		128	.296	.395	415	123	19	5	4	1.0	57	30	27	32	8	15	7	216	11	3	2	2.1	.987	OF-110
1949	2 teams	CIN N (27G –.235)			CHI N (58G –.226)																			
"	total	85	.229	.331	245	56	9	5	2	0.8	27	23	15	29	2	20	6	120	4	3	3	2.0	.976	OF-63
1951	CHI N	146	.284	.380	560	159	28	10	2	0.4	62	50	49	36	5	4	2	307	6	8	2	2.3	.975	OF-140
1952		103	.325	.416	409	133	17	4	4	1.0	59	35	27	27	5	2	0	248	10	7	3	2.6	.974	OF-101
1953		133	.306	.419	520	159	36	7	3	0.6	75	25	42	36	3	3	0	290	6	6	0	2.3	.980	OF-130
1954		90	.297	.416	303	90	12	6	4	1.3	38	28	20	15	1	17	2	168	2	2	0	2.4	.988	OF-71
1955		105	.289	.379	280	81	12	5	1	0.4	23	27	16	24	0	37	**15**	131	3	1	1	2.1	.993	OF-63
1956	PHI N	76	.270	.270	100	27	0	0	0	0.0	13	9	6	6	0	52	**14**	23	2	1	0	1.7	.962	OF-15
1957		2	.000	.000	2	0	0	0	0	0.0	0	0	0	0	0	2	0	0	0	0	0	0.0	—	
10 yrs.		1019	.290	.389	3477	1010	165	51	25	0.7	450	272	258	258	30	153	47	1785	62	38	13	2.2	.980	OF-843

Danny Bautista

BAUTISTA, DANIEL BR TR 5′11″ 170 lbs.
Born Daniel Bautista (Alcantara).
B. May 24, 1972, Santo Domingo, Dominican Republic.

Year	Team	Games	BA	SA	AB	H	2B	3B	HR	HR%	R	RBI	BB	SO	SB	Pinch Hit AB	Pinch Hit H	PO	A	E	DP	TC/G	FA	G by Pos
1993	DET A	17	.311	.410	61	19	3	0	1	1.6	6	9	1	10	3	0	0	38	2	0	0	2.4	1.000	OF-16, DH-1
1994		31	.232	.414	99	23	4	1	4	4.0	12	15	3	18	1	3	1	66	0	0	0	2.1	1.000	OF-30, DH-1
1995		89	.203	.314	271	55	9	0	7	2.6	28	27	12	68	4	6	3	164	3	2	0	2.0	.988	OF-86
3 yrs.		137	.225	.350	431	97	16	1	12	2.8	46	51	16	96	8	9	4	268	5	2	0	2.1	.993	OF-132, DH-2

Jim Baxes

BAXES, DIMITRIOS SPEROS BR TR 6′ 1″ 190 lbs.
Brother of Mike Baxes.
B. July 5, 1928, San Francisco, Calif.

Year	Team	Games	BA	SA	AB	H	2B	3B	HR	HR%	R	RBI	BB	SO	SB	Pinch Hit AB	Pinch Hit H	PO	A	E	DP	TC/G	FA	G by Pos
1959	2 teams	LA N (11G –.303)			CLE A (77G –.239)																			
"	total	88	.246	.471	280	69	12	0	17	6.1	39	39	25	54	1	12	3	134	177	17	33	4.1	.948	2B-48, 3B-32

Mike Baxes

BAXES, MICHAEL BR TR 5′10″ 175 lbs.
Brother of Jim Baxes.
B. Dec. 18, 1930, San Francisco, Calif.

Year	Team	Games	BA	SA	AB	H	2B	3B	HR	HR%	R	RBI	BB	SO	SB	Pinch Hit AB	Pinch Hit H	PO	A	E	DP	TC/G	FA	G by Pos
1956	KC A	73	.226	.302	106	24	3	1	1	0.9	9	5	18	15	0	9	1	57	113	11	17	2.9	.939	SS-62, 2B-1
1958		73	.212	.264	231	49	10	1	0	0.0	31	8	21	24	1	4	0	135	157	9	40	4.6	.970	2B-61, SS-4
2 yrs.		146	.217	.276	337	73	13	2	1	0.3	40	13	39	39	1	13	1	192	270	20	57	3.8	.959	SS-66, 2B-62

John Baxter

BAXTER, JOHN MORRIS 6′ 3″
B. July 27, 1876, Chippawa Falls, Wis. D. Aug. 7, 1926, Portland, Ore.

Year	Team	Games	BA	SA	AB	H	2B	3B	HR	HR%	R	RBI	BB	SO	SB	Pinch Hit AB	Pinch Hit H	PO	A	E	DP	TC/G	FA	G by Pos
1907	STL N	6	.190	.190	21	4	0	0	0	0.0	1	0	0		0	0	0	54	4	5	1	10.5	.921	1B-6

Harry Bay

BAY, HARRY ELBERT (Deerfoot)
B. Jan. 17, 1878, Pontiac, Ill. D. Mar. 20, 1952, Peoria, Ill.
BL TL 5′ 8″ 138 lbs.

Year	Team	Games	BA	SA	AB	H	2B	3B	HR	HR%	R	RBI	BB	SO	SB	Pinch Hit AB	Pinch Hit H	PO	A	E	DP	TC/G	FA	G by Pos
1901	CIN N	41	.210	.261	157	33	1	2	1	0.6	25	3	13		4	1	1	78	3	4	3	2.1	.953	OF-40
1902	2 teams	CIN N (6G –.375)	CLE A (108G –.290)																					
″	total	114	.293	.335	471	138	10	5	0	0.0	74	24	38		22	4	0	248	14	9	3	2.5	.967	OF-110
1903	CLE A	140	.292	.364	579	169	15	12	1	0.2	94	35	29		**45**	0	0	293	13	16	3	2.3	.950	OF-140
1904		132	.261	.338	506	132	12	9	3	0.6	69	36	43		38	0	0	281	15	4	6	2.3	.987	OF-132
1905		143	.298	.367	550	164	18	10	0	0.0	90	22	36		36	0	0	303	14	10	4	2.3	.969	OF-143
1906		68	.275	.325	280	77	8	3	0	0.0	47	14	26		17	0	0	131	8	3	2	2.1	.979	OF-68
1907		34	.179	.211	95	17	1	1	0	0.0	14	7	10		7	3	1	55	5	2	1	2.0	.968	OF-31
1908		1	—	—	0	0	0	0	0	—	0	0	0		0	0	0	0	0	0	0	0.0	—	
8 yrs.		673	.277	.339	2638	730	65	42	5	0.2	413	141	195		169	8	2	1389	72	48	22	2.3	.968	OF-664

Dick Bayless

BAYLESS, HARRY OWEN
B. Sept. 6, 1883, Joplin, Mo. D. Dec. 16, 1920, Santa Rita, N. M.
BL TR 5′ 9″ 178 lbs.

Year	Team	Games	BA	SA	AB	H	2B	3B	HR	HR%	R	RBI	BB	SO	SB	Pinch Hit AB	Pinch Hit H	PO	A	E	DP	TC/G	FA	G by Pos
1908	CIN N	19	.225	.282	71	16	1	0	1	1.4	7	3	6		0	0	0	29	6	2	2	1.9	.946	OF-19

Don Baylor

BAYLOR, DON EDWARD
B. June 28, 1949, Austin, Tex.
Manager 1993–95.
BR TR 6′ 1″ 190 lbs.

Year	Team	Games	BA	SA	AB	H	2B	3B	HR	HR%	R	RBI	BB	SO	SB	Pinch Hit AB	Pinch Hit H	PO	A	E	DP	TC/G	FA	G by Pos
1970	BAL A	8	.235	.235	17	4	0	0	0	0.0	4	4	2	3	1	0	0	15	0	0	0	2.5	1.000	OF-6
1971		1	.000	.000	2	0	0	0	0	0.0	0	1	2	1	0	0	0	4	0	0	0	4.0	1.000	OF-1
1972		102	.253	.416	320	81	13	3	11	3.4	33	38	29	50	24	16	5	206	4	5	5	2.3	.977	OF-84, 1B-9
1973		118	.286	.437	405	116	20	4	11	2.7	64	51	35	48	32	12	2	228	10	6	2	2.1	.975	OF-110, 1B-6, DH-1
1974		137	.272	.382	489	133	22	1	10	2.0	66	59	43	56	29	5	3	260	2	5	2	1.9	.981	OF-129, 1B-8, DH-1
1975		145	.282	.489	524	148	21	6	25	4.8	79	76	53	64	32	1	1	286	8	5	1	2.1	.983	OF-135, DH-7, 1B-2
1976	OAK A	157	.247	.368	595	147	25	1	15	2.5	85	68	58	72	52	2	0	781	45	12	40	5.0	.986	OF-76, 1B-69, DH-23
1977	CAL A	154	.251	.433	561	141	27	0	25	4.5	87	75	62	76	26	1	0	280	16	7	14	1.9	.977	OF-77, DH-61, 1B-18
1978		158	.255	.472	591	151	26	0	34	5.8	103	99	56	71	22	0	0	194	9	6	6	1.3	.971	DH-100, OF-39, 1B-17
1979		162	.296	.530	628	186	33	3	36	5.7	**120**	**139**	71	51	22	0	0	203	3	5	1	1.3	.976	OF-97, DH-65, 1B-1
1980		90	.250	.341	340	85	12	2	5	1.5	39	51	24	32	6	0	0	119	4	4	0	1.4	.969	OF-54, DH-36
1981		103	.239	.427	377	90	18	1	17	4.5	52	66	42	51	3	1	1	38	3	0	2	0.4	1.000	DH-97, 1B-4, OF-1
1982		157	.263	.424	608	160	24	1	24	3.9	80	93	57	69	10	0	0	0	0	0	0	0.0	.000	DH-155
1983	NY A	144	.303	.494	534	162	33	3	21	3.9	82	85	40	53	17	9	2	23	2	1	0	0.2	.962	DH-136, OF-5, 1B-1
1984		134	.262	.489	493	129	29	1	27	5.5	84	89	39	67	1	10	2	8	0	1	0	0.1	.889	DH-127, 1B-5
1985		142	.231	.430	477	110	24	1	23	4.8	70	91	52	90	0	13	5	0	0	0	0	0.0	.000	DH-140
1986	BOS A	160	.238	.439	585	139	23	1	31	5.3	93	94	62	111	3	0	0	71	4	1	7	0.5	.987	DH-143, 1B-13, OF-3
1987	2 teams	BOS A (108G –.239)	MIN A (20G –.286)																					
″	total	128	.245	.392	388	95	9	0	16	4.1	67	63	45	59	5	17	6	0	0	0	0	0.0		DH-117
1988	OAK A	92	.220	.326	264	58	7	0	7	2.7	28	34	34	44	0	12	1	0	0	0	0	0.0	.000	DH-80
19 yrs.		2292	.260	.436	8198	2135	366	28	338	4.1	1236	1276	806	1068	285	99	28	2716	110	58	80	1.3	.980	DH-1289, OF-817, 1B-153

LEAGUE CHAMPIONSHIP SERIES

Year	Team	Games	BA	SA	AB	H	2B	3B	HR	HR%	R	RBI	BB	SO	SB	Pinch Hit AB	Pinch Hit H	PO	A	E	DP	TC/G	FA	G by Pos
1973	BAL A	4	.273	.273	11	3	0	0	0	0.0	3	1	3	5	0	0	0	7	0	0	0	2.3	1.000	OF-3
1974		4	.267	.267	15	4	0	0	0	0.0	0	0	0	2	0	0	0	9	0	0	0	2.3	1.000	OF-4
1979	CAL A	4	.188	.375	16	3	0	0	1	6.3	2	2	1	2	0	0	0	4	0	0	0	1.0	1.000	DH-3, OF-1
1982		5	.294	.647	17	5	1	1	1	5.9	2	10	2	0	0	0	0	0	0	0	0	0.0	.000	DH-5
1986	BOS A	7	.346	.577	26	9	3	0	1	3.8	6	2	4	5	0	0	0	0	0	0	0	0.0	.000	DH-7
1987	MIN A	2	.400	.400	5	2	0	0	0	0.0	0	1	0	0	0	1	1	0	0	0	0	0.0	.000	DH-2
1988	OAK A	2	.000	.000	6	0	0	0	0	0.0	0	1	1	2	0	0	0	0	0	0	0	0.0	.000	DH-2
7 yrs.		28	.271	.427	96	26	4	1	3	3.1	13	17	11	16	0	1	1	20	0	0	0	0.7	1.000	DH-19, OF-8
		3rd			**5th**	**9th**					**10th**	**5th**	**9th**											

WORLD SERIES

Year	Team	Games	BA	SA	AB	H	2B	3B	HR	HR%	R	RBI	BB	SO	SB	Pinch Hit AB	Pinch Hit H	PO	A	E	DP	TC/G	FA	G by Pos
1986	BOS A	4	.182	.273	11	2	1	0	0	0.0	1	1	1	3	0	1	0	0	0	0	0	0.0	.000	DH-3
1987	MIN A	5	.385	.615	13	5	0	0	1	7.7	3	3	1	1	0	2	1	0	0	0	0	0.0	.000	DH-3
1988	OAK A	1	.000	.000	1	0	0	0	0	0.0	0	0	0	1	0	1	0	0	0	0	0	0.0	—	
3 yrs.		10	.280	.440	25	7	1	0	1	4.0	4	4	2	5	0	4	1	0	0	0	0	0.0		DH-6

Jack Beach

BEACH, STONEWALL JACKSON
B. 1862, Alexandria, Va. D. July 23, 1896, Alexandria, Va.

Year	Team	Games	BA	SA	AB	H	2B	3B	HR	HR%	R	RBI	BB	SO	SB	Pinch Hit AB	Pinch Hit H	PO	A	E	DP	TC/G	FA	G by Pos
1884	WAS AA	8	.097	.161	31	3	2	0	0	0.0	3		0			0	0	10	2	6	1	2.3	.667	OF-8

Bob Beall

BEALL, ROBERT BROOKS
B. Apr. 24, 1948, Portland, Ore.
BB TL 5′11″ 180 lbs.

Year	Team	Games	BA	SA	AB	H	2B	3B	HR	HR%	R	RBI	BB	SO	SB	Pinch Hit AB	Pinch Hit H	PO	A	E	DP	TC/G	FA	G by Pos
1975	ATL N	20	.226	.290	31	7	2	0	0	0.0	2	1	6	9	0	9	0	57	4	1	6	7.8	.984	1B-8
1978		108	.243	.303	185	45	8	0	1	0.5	29	16	36	27	4	50	10	282	24	4	23	6.5	.987	1B-40, OF-8
1979		17	.133	.267	15	2	2	0	0	0.0	1	1	3	4	0	9	1	9	1	0	0	3.3	1.000	1B-3
1980	PIT N	3	.000	.000	3	0	0	0	0	0.0	0	0	0	1	0	3	0	0	0	0	0	0.0	—	
4 yrs.		148	.231	.295	234	54	12	0	1	0.4	32	18	45	41	4	71	11	348	29	5	29	6.5	.987	1B-51, OF-8

Johnny Beall

BEALL, JOHN WOOLF
B. Mar. 12, 1882, Beltsville, Md. D. June 14, 1926, Beltsville, Md.
BL TR 6′ 180 lbs.

Year	Team	Games	BA	SA	AB	H	2B	3B	HR	HR%	R	RBI	BB	SO	SB	Pinch Hit AB	Pinch Hit H	PO	A	E	DP	TC/G	FA	G by Pos
1913	2 teams	CLE A (6G –.167)	CHI A (17G –.267)																					
″	total	23	.258	.379	66	17	0	1	2	3.0	10	4	0	2	1	6	1	38	3	2	0	2.5	.953	OF-17
1915	CIN N	10	.235	.265	34	8	1	0	0	0.0	3	3	5	10	0	0	0	22	2	1	1	2.5	.960	OF-10
1916		6	.333	.571	21	7	2	0	1	4.8	3	4	3	7	1	1	0	9	2	0	0	1.8	1.000	OF-6
1918	STL N	19	.224	.245	49	11	1	0	0	0.0	2	6	3	6	0	5	2	26	2	0	1	1.6	1.000	OF-18
4 yrs.		58	.253	.341	170	43	4	1	3	1.8	18	17	11	25	2	12	3	95	9	3	2	2.1	.972	OF-51

Tommy Beals

BEALS, THOMAS L.
B. Aug. 1850, New York, N. Y. D. Oct. 2, 1915, San Francisco, Calif.
BR 5′ 5″ 144 lbs.

Year	Team	Games	BA	SA	AB	H	2B	3B	HR	HR%	R	RBI	BB	SO	SB	Pinch Hit AB	Pinch Hit H	PO	A	E	DP	TC/G	FA	G by Pos
1880	CHI N	13	.152	.152	46	7	0	0	0	0.0	4	3	1	6		0	0	14	3	5	1	1.7	.773	OF-10, 2B-3

Charlie Beamon

BEAMON, CHARLES ALFONZO, JR.
Son of Charlie Beamon.
B. Dec. 4, 1953, Oakland, Calif.
BL TL 6′ 1″ 183 lbs.

Year	Team	Games	BA	SA	AB	H	2B	3B	HR	HR%	R	RBI	BB	SO	SB	Pinch Hit AB	Pinch Hit H	PO	A	E	DP	TC/G	FA	G by Pos
1978	SEA A	10	.182	.182	11	2	0	0	0	0.0	2	0	1	1	0	1	0	20	4	0	2	3.0	1.000	DH-6, 1B-2
1979		27	.200	.240	25	5	1	0	0	0.0	5	0	0	5	1	14	3	15	2	0	0	1.2	1.000	1B-7, DH-5, OF-2
1981	TOR A	8	.200	.267	15	3	1	0	0	0.0	1	0	2	2	0	3	0	6	0	0	0	1.2	1.000	DH-4, 1B-1
3 yrs.		45	.196	.235	51	10	2	0	0	0.0	8	0	3	8	1	18	3	41	6	0	2	1.7	1.000	DH-15, 1B-10, OF-2

Billy Bean

BEAN, WILLIAM DARO
B. May 11, 1964, Santa Ana, Calif.
BL TL 6′ 185 lbs.

Year	Team	Games	BA	SA	AB	H	2B	3B	HR	HR%	R	RBI	BB	SO	SB	Pinch Hit AB	Pinch Hit H	PO	A	E	DP	TC/G	FA	G by Pos
1987	DET A	26	.258	.288	66	17	2	0	0	0.0	6	4	5	11	1	5	0	54	1	0	0	2.3	1.000	OF-24
1988		10	.182	.364	11	2	0	1	0	0.0	2	0	0	2	0	4	2	8	1	0	2	1.3	1.000	OF-4, 1B-2, DH-1
1989	2 teams	DET A (9G –.000) LA N (51G –.197)																						
″	total	60	.171	.220	82	14	4	0	0	0.0	7	3	6	13	0	7	1	61	0	2	1	1.2	.968	OF-50, 1B-2
1993	SD N	88	.260	.395	177	46	9	0	5	2.8	19	32	6	29	2	27	6	122	9	1	5	2.0	.992	OF-54, 1B-12
1994		84	.215	.267	135	29	5	1	0	0.0	7	14	7	25	0	33	12	96	5	0	4	1.8	1.000	OF-39, 1B-16
1995		4	.000	.000	7	0	0	0	0	0.0	1	0	1	4	0	1	0	3	0	1	0	1.0	.750	OF-4
6 yrs.		272	.226	.308	478	108	20	2	5	1.0	42	53	25	84	3	77	21	344	16	4	12	1.8	.989	OF-175, 1B-32, DH-1

Joe Bean

BEAN, JOSEPH WILLIAM
B. Mar. 18, 1874, Boston, Mass. D. Feb. 15, 1961, Atlanta, Ga.
BR TR 5′ 8″ 138 lbs.

Year	Team	Games	BA	SA	AB	H	2B	3B	HR	HR%	R	RBI	BB	SO	SB	Pinch Hit AB	Pinch Hit H	PO	A	E	DP	TC/G	FA	G by Pos
1902	NY N	48	.222	.244	176	39	2	1	0	0.0	13	5	5		9	0	0	71	153	28	19	5.3	.889	SS-48

Billy Beane

BEANE, WILLIAM LAMAR
B. Mar. 29, 1962, Orlando, Fla.
BR TR 6′ 4″ 195 lbs.

Year	Team	Games	BA	SA	AB	H	2B	3B	HR	HR%	R	RBI	BB	SO	SB	Pinch Hit AB	Pinch Hit H	PO	A	E	DP	TC/G	FA	G by Pos
1984	NY N	5	.100	.100	10	1	0	0	0	0.0	0	0	0	2	0	2	0	2	0	0	0	0.4	1.000	OF-5
1985		8	.250	.375	8	2	1	0	0	0.0	0	1	0	3	0	4	2	1	0	0	0	0.5	1.000	OF-2
1986	MIN A	80	.213	.295	183	39	6	0	3	1.6	20	15	11	54	2	11	1	118	0	0	0	1.6	1.000	OF-67, DH-5
1987		12	.267	.400	15	4	2	0	0	0.0	1	1	0	6	0	3	0	8	0	0	0	1.1	1.000	OF-7
1988	DET A	6	.167	.167	6	1	0	0	0	0.0	1	1	0	2	0	0	0	5	0	0	0	0.8	1.000	OF-6
1989	OAK A	37	.241	.304	79	19	5	0	0	0.0	8	11	0	13	3	7	3	58	3	1	1	1.8	.984	OF-25, 1B-4, DH-4, 3B-1, C-1
6 yrs.		148	.219	.296	301	66	14	0	3	1.0	30	29	11	80	5	27	6	192	3	1	1	1.5	.995	OF-112, DH-9, 1B-4, 3B-1, C-1

Ollie Beard

BEARD, OLIVER PERRY
B. May 2, 1862, Lexington, Ky. D. May 28, 1929, Cincinnati, Ohio.
BR TR 5′11″ 180 lbs.

Year	Team	Games	BA	SA	AB	H	2B	3B	HR	HR%	R	RBI	BB	SO	SB	Pinch Hit AB	Pinch Hit H	PO	A	E	DP	TC/G	FA	G by Pos
1889	CIN AA	141	.285	.364	558	159	13	14	1	0.2	96	77	35	39	36	0	0	214	537	87	63	5.9	.896	SS-141
1890	CIN N	122	.268	.382	492	132	17	15	3	0.6	64	72	44	13	30	0	0	155	445	71	45	5.5	.894	SS-113, 3B-9
1891	LOU AA	68	.241	.296	257	62	4	5	0	0.0	35	24	33	9	7	0	0	91	172	36	17	4.4	.880	3B-61, SS-7
3 yrs.		331	.270	.357	1307	353	34	34	4	0.3	195	173	112	61	73	0	0	460	1154	194	125	5.5	.893	SS-261, 3B-70

Ted Beard

BEARD, CRAMER THEODORE
B. Jan. 7, 1921, Woodsboro, Md.
BL TL 5′ 8″ 165 lbs.

Year	Team	Games	BA	SA	AB	H	2B	3B	HR	HR%	R	RBI	BB	SO	SB	Pinch Hit AB	Pinch Hit H	PO	A	E	DP	TC/G	FA	G by Pos
1948	PIT N	25	.198	.284	81	16	1	3	0	0.0	15	7	12	18	5	2	1	66	0	0	0	3.0	1.000	OF-22
1949		14	.083	.083	24	2	0	0	0	0.0	1	1	2	2	0	3	0	9	0	1	0	1.0	.900	OF-10
1950		61	.232	.356	177	41	6	2	4	2.3	32	12	27	45	3	12	3	112	4	2	0	2.4	.983	OF-49
1951		22	.188	.271	48	9	1	0	1	2.1	7	3	6	14	0	6	2	23	2	0	0	1.1	1.000	OF-22
1952		15	.182	.273	44	8	2	1	0	0.0	5	3	7	9	2	1	0	27	1	0	0	2.2	1.000	OF-13
1957	CHI A	38	.205	.218	78	16	1	0	0	0.0	15	7	18	14	3	3	1	33	5	1	0	1.4	.974	OF-28
1958		19	.091	.227	22	2	0	0	1	4.5	5	2	6	5	3	3	0	15	0	0	0	1.0	1.000	OF-15
7 yrs.		194	.198	.285	474	94	11	6	6	1.3	80	35	78	107	16	30	7	285	12	4	0	1.9	.987	OF-159

Lew Beasley

BEASLEY, LEWIS PAIGE
B. Aug. 27, 1948, Sparta, Va.
BL TR 5′10″ 172 lbs.

Year	Team	Games	BA	SA	AB	H	2B	3B	HR	HR%	R	RBI	BB	SO	SB	Pinch Hit AB	Pinch Hit H	PO	A	E	DP	TC/G	FA	G by Pos
1977	TEX A	25	.219	.250	32	7	1	0	0	0.0	5	3	2	2	1	2	0	10	0	2	0	0.6	.833	OF-18, SS-1, DH-1

Dave Beatle

BEATLE, DAVID
B. 1861, New York, N. Y. Deceased.
6′ 2″ 200 lbs.

Year	Team	Games	BA	SA	AB	H	2B	3B	HR	HR%	R	RBI	BB	SO	SB	Pinch Hit AB	Pinch Hit H	PO	A	E	DP	TC/G	FA	G by Pos
1884	DET N	1	.000	.000	3	0	0	0	0	0.0	0		0	2		0	0	3	1	3	0	3.5	.571	OF-1, C-1

Des Beatty

BEATTY, ALOYSIUS DESMOND (Desperate)
B. Apr. 7, 1893, Baltimore, Md. D. Oct. 6, 1969, Norway, Me.
BR TR 5′ 8½″ 158 lbs.

Year	Team	Games	BA	SA	AB	H	2B	3B	HR	HR%	R	RBI	BB	SO	SB	Pinch Hit AB	Pinch Hit H	PO	A	E	DP	TC/G	FA	G by Pos
1914	NY N	2	.000	.000	3	0	0	0	0	0.0	0	1	0	0	0	0	0	2	3	3	0	4.0	.625	SS-1, 3B-1

Jim Beauchamp

BEAUCHAMP, JAMES EDWARD
B. Aug. 21, 1939, Vinita, Okla.
BR TR 6′ 2″ 190 lbs.

Year	Team	Games	BA	SA	AB	H	2B	3B	HR	HR%	R	RBI	BB	SO	SB	Pinch Hit AB	Pinch Hit H	PO	A	E	DP	TC/G	FA	G by Pos
1963	STL N	4	.000	.000	3	0	0	0	0	0.0	0	0	0	2	0	3	0	0	0	0	0	0.0	—	
1964	HOU N	23	.164	.309	55	9	2	0	2	3.6	6	4	5	16	0	6	1	27	1	2	1	1.8	.933	OF-15, 1B-2
1965	2 teams	HOU N (24G –.189) MIL N (4G –.000)																						
″	total	28	.179	.196	56	10	1	0	0	0.0	5	4	6	12	0	13	2	49	7	1	2	4.1	.982	OF-9, 1B-5
1967	ATL N	4	.000	.000	3	0	0	0	0	0.0	0	1	0	0	0	3	0	0	0	0	0	0.0	—	
1968	CIN N	31	.263	.404	57	15	2	0	2	3.5	10	14	4	19	0	17	4	34	1	0	1	2.5	1.000	OF-13, 1B-1
1969		43	.250	.317	60	15	1	0	1	1.7	8	8	5	13	0	32	7	38	2	1	2	3.4	.976	OF-9, 1B-3
1970	2 teams	HOU N (31G –.192) STL N (44G –.259)																						
″	total	75	.238	.333	84	20	2	0	2	2.4	11	10	11	18	2	37	9	49	4	0	2	1.7	1.000	OF-26, 1B-5
1971	STL N	77	.235	.358	162	38	8	3	2	1.2	24	16	9	26	3	32	8	311	19	6	27	7.5	.982	1B-44, OF-1
1972	NY N	58	.242	.375	120	29	1	0	5	4.2	10	19	7	33	0	21	6	188	9	5	16	5.3	.975	1B-35, OF-3
1973		50	.279	.328	61	17	1	1	0	0.0	5	14	7	11	1	34	9	59	3	2	7	5.8	.969	1B-11
10 yrs.		393	.231	.334	661	153	18	4	14	2.1	79	90	54	150	6	198	46	755	46	17	58	4.5	.979	1B-106, OF-76
WORLD SERIES																								
1973	NY N	4	.000	.000	4	0	0	0	0	0.0	0	0	0	1	0	4	0	0	0	0	0	0.0	—	

Ginger Beaumont

BEAUMONT, CLARENCE HOWETH BL TR 5′ 8″ 190 lbs.
B. July 23, 1876, Rochester, Wis. D. Apr. 10, 1956, Burlington, Wis.

Year	Team	Games	BA	SA	AB	H	2B	3B	HR	HR%	R	RBI	BB	SO	SB	Pinch Hit AB	Pinch Hit H	PO	A	E	DP	TC/G	FA	G by Pos
1899	PIT N	111	.352	.444	437	154	15	8	3	0.7	90	38	41		31	6	**3**	250	21	23	7	2.8	.922	OF-102, 1B-2
1900		138	.279	.356	567	158	14	9	4	0.7	107	50	40		27	0	0	274	10	17	3	2.2	.944	OF-138
1901		133	.332	.418	558	185	14	5	8	1.4	120	72	44		36	0	0	289	8	18	2	2.4	.943	OF-133
1902		131	**.357**	.417	544	**194**	21	6	0	0.0	101	67	39		33	0	0	260	15	7	8	2.2	.975	OF-130
1903		141	.341	.444	**613**	**209**	30	6	7	1.1	**137**	68	44		23	0	0	258	15	15	2	2.0	.948	OF-141
1904		153	.301	.374	**615**	**185**	12	12	3	0.5	97	54	34		28	0	0	287	14	10	6	2.0	.968	OF-153
1905		103	.328	.424	384	126	12	8	3	0.8	60	40	22		21	4	1	200	12	6	5	2.2	.972	OF-97
1906		80	.265	.332	310	82	9	3	2	0.6	48	32	19		1	1	0	148	6	9	2	2.1	.945	OF-78
1907	BOS N	150	.322	.424	580	**187**	19	14	4	0.7	67	62	37		25	1	1	296	30	13	12	2.3	.962	OF-149
1908		125	.267	.347	476	127	20	6	2	0.4	66	52	42		13	4	1	259	17	10	3	2.4	.965	OF-121
1909		123	.263	.310	407	107	11	4	0	0.0	35	60	35		12	14	5	234	15	8	3	2.3	.969	OF-111
1910	CHI N	56	.267	.343	172	46	5	1	2	1.2	30	22	28	14	4	13	3	107	5	5	0	2.1	.957	OF-56
12 yrs.		1444	.311	.392	5663	1760	182	82	38	0.7	958	617	425	14	254	43	14	2862	168	141	53	2.2	.956	OF-1409, 1B-2
WORLD SERIES																								
1903	PIT N	8	.265	.324	34	9	0	1	0	0.0	6	0	2	4	2	0	0	22	0	0	0	2.8	1.000	OF-8
1910	CHI N	3	.000	.000	2	0	0	0	0	0.0	1	0	1	1	0	2	0	0	0	0	0	0.0	—	
2 yrs.		11	.250	.306	36	9	0	1	0	0.0	7	0	3	5	2	2	0	22	0	0	0	2.8	1.000	OF-8

George Bechtel

BECHTEL, GEORGE A. 5′11″ 165 lbs.
B. Sept. 2, 1848, Philadelphia, Pa. Deceased.

Year	Team	Games	BA	SA	AB	H	2B	3B	HR	HR%	R	RBI	BB	SO	SB	Pinch Hit AB	Pinch Hit H	PO	A	E	DP	TC/G	FA	G by Pos
1876	2 teams LOU N (14G –.182) NY N (2G –.300)																							
″	total	16	.200	.215	65	13	1	0	0	0.0	4	2	0	1		0	0	17	1	7	0	1.6	.720	OF-16

Clyde Beck

BECK, CLYDE EUGENE (Jersey) BR TR 5′10″ 150 lbs.
B. Jan. 6, 1900, Bassett, Calif. D. July 15, 1988, Temple City, Calif.

Year	Team	Games	BA	SA	AB	H	2B	3B	HR	HR%	R	RBI	BB	SO	SB	Pinch Hit AB	Pinch Hit H	PO	A	E	DP	TC/G	FA	G by Pos
1926	CHI N	30	.198	.235	81	16	0	0	1	1.2	10	4	7	15	0	0	0	68	80	1	19	5.5	.993	2B-27
1927		117	.258	.350	391	101	20	5	2	0.5	44	44	43	37	0	0	0	267	402	24	67	5.9	.965	2B-99, 3B-17, SS-1
1928		131	.257	.329	483	124	18	4	3	0.6	72	52	58	58	3	1	1	167	299	18	53	3.6	.963	3B-87, SS-47, 2B-1
1929		54	.211	.247	190	40	7	0	0	0.0	28	9	19	24	3	5	1	42	118	6	20	3.5	.964	3B-33, SS-14
1930		83	.213	.316	244	52	7	0	6	2.5	32	34	36	32	2	0	0	149	236	20	54	4.9	.951	SS-57, 2B-24, 3B-2
1931	CIN N	53	.154	.213	136	21	4	2	0	0.0	17	19	21	14	1	8	2	41	65	5	12	2.5	.955	3B-38, SS-6
6 yrs.		468	.232	.307	1525	354	56	11	12	0.8	203	162	184	180	9	14	4	734	1200	74	225	4.4	.963	3B-177, 2B-151, SS-125

Erve Beck

BECK, ERVIN THOMAS (Dutch) BR TR 5′10″ 168 lbs.
B. July 19, 1878, Toledo, Ohio D. Dec. 23, 1916, Toledo, Ohio.

Year	Team	Games	BA	SA	AB	H	2B	3B	HR	HR%	R	RBI	BB	SO	SB	Pinch Hit AB	Pinch Hit H	PO	A	E	DP	TC/G	FA	G by Pos
1899	BKN N	8	.167	.250	24	4	2	0	0	0.0	2	2	0		0	0	0	8	22	4	1	4.3	.882	2B-6, SS-2
1901	CLE A	135	.289	.401	539	156	26	8	6	1.1	78	79	23		7	3	1	310	404	56	44	5.8	.927	2B-132
1902	2 teams CIN N (48G –.305) DET A (41G –.296)																							
″	total	89	.301	.384	349	105	14	3	3	0.9	42	42	7		5	4	1	491	124	24	40	7.5	.962	1B-42, 2B-32, OF-11
3 yrs.		232	.291	.390	912	265	42	11	9	1.0	122	123	30		12	7	2	809	550	84	85	6.4	.942	2B-170, 1B-42, OF-11, SS-2

Fred Beck

BECK, FREDERICK THOMAS BL TL 6′ 1″ 180 lbs.
B. Nov. 17, 1886, Havana, Ill. D. Mar. 12, 1962, Havana, Ill.

Year	Team	Games	BA	SA	AB	H	2B	3B	HR	HR%	R	RBI	BB	SO	SB	Pinch Hit AB	Pinch Hit H	PO	A	E	DP	TC/G	FA	G by Pos
1909	BOS N	96	.198	.272	334	66	4	6	3	0.9	20	27	17		5	8	0	464	26	14	18	5.6	.972	OF-57, 1B-33
1910		154	.275	.415	571	157	32	9	**10**	1.8	52	64	19	55	8	1	0	479	28	17	20	3.4	.968	OF-134, 1B-19
1911	2 teams CIN N (41G –.184) PHI N (66G –.281)																							
″	total	107	.253	.367	297	75	9	5	5	1.7	33	45	18	34	5	21	4	129	10	5	6	1.7	.965	OF-77, 1B-6
1914	CHI F	157	.279	.395	555	155	23	4	11	2.0	51	77	44		9	0	0	1614	55	31	86	10.8	.982	1B-157
1915		121	.223	.303	373	83	9	3	5	1.3	35	38	24		4	4	0	1073	42	9	57	9.6	.992	1B-117
5 yrs.		635	.252	.361	2130	536	77	27	34	1.6	191	251	122	89	31	34	4	3759	161	76	187	6.7	.981	1B-332, OF-268

Zinn Beck

BECK, ZINN BERTRAM BR TR 5′10½″ 160 lbs.
B. Sept. 30, 1885, Steubenville, Ohio D. Mar. 19, 1981, West Palm Beach, Fla.

Year	Team	Games	BA	SA	AB	H	2B	3B	HR	HR%	R	RBI	BB	SO	SB	Pinch Hit AB	Pinch Hit H	PO	A	E	DP	TC/G	FA	G by Pos
1913	STL N	10	.167	.200	30	5	1	0	0	0.0	4	2	4	10	1	0	0	11	29	5	2	4.5	.889	SS-5, 3B-5
1914		137	.232	.333	457	106	15	11	3	0.7	42	45	28	32	14	0	0	182	318	35	30	3.9	.935	3B-122, SS-16
1915		70	.233	.309	223	52	9	4	0	0.0	21	15	12	31	3	2	0	63	137	16	10	3.3	.926	3B-60, SS-4, 2B-2
1916		62	.223	.272	184	41	7	1	0	0.0	8	10	14	21	3	9	2	46	86	13	8	2.7	.910	3B-52, 1B-1, 2B-1
1918	NY A	11	.000	.000	8	0	0	0	0	0.0	0	1	0	1	0	4	0	16	2	0	2	3.6	1.000	1B-5
5 yrs.		290	.226	.307	902	204	32	16	3	0.3	75	73	58	95	21	15	2	318	572	69	52	3.5	.928	3B-239, SS-25, 1B-6, 2B-3

Heinie Beckendorf

BECKENDORF, HENRY WARD BR TR 5′ 9″ 174 lbs.
B. June 15, 1884, New York, N. Y. D. Sept. 15, 1949, Jackson Heights, N. Y.

Year	Team	Games	BA	SA	AB	H	2B	3B	HR	HR%	R	RBI	BB	SO	SB	Pinch Hit AB	Pinch Hit H	PO	A	E	DP	TC/G	FA	G by Pos
1909	DET A	15	.259	.296	27	7	1	0	0	0.0	1	1	2		0	0	0	36	9	2	4	3.1	.957	C-15
1910	2 teams DET A (3G –.231) WAS A (37G –.155)																							
″	total	40	.164	.173	110	18	1	0	0	0.0	8	12	6		0	2	1	206	37	3	3	6.5	.988	C-38
2 yrs.		55	.182	.197	137	25	2	0	0	0.0	9	13	8		0	2	1	242	46	5	7	5.5	.983	C-53

Beals Becker

BECKER, DAVID BEALS BL TL 5′ 9″ 170 lbs.
B. July 5, 1886, El Dorado, Kans. D. Aug. 16, 1943, Huntington Park, Calif.

Year	Team	Games	BA	SA	AB	H	2B	3B	HR	HR%	R	RBI	BB	SO	SB	Pinch Hit AB	Pinch Hit H	PO	A	E	DP	TC/G	FA	G by Pos
1908	2 teams PIT N (20G –.154) BOS N (43G –.275)																							
″	total	63	.242	.271	236	57	3	2	0	0.0	17	7	9		9	3	0	57	12	3	1	1.2	.958	OF-60
1909	BOS N	152	.246	.326	562	138	15	6	6	1.1	60	24	47		21	0	0	222	26	18	8	1.8	.932	OF-152
1910	NY N	80	.286	.437	126	36	2	4	3	2.4	18	24	14	25	11	30	5	68	7	2	0	1.7	.974	OF-45, 1B-1
1911		88	.262	.355	172	45	11	1	1	0.6	28	20	26	22	19	**26**	3	72	7	2	0	1.5	.975	OF-55
1912		125	.264	.393	402	106	18	8	6	1.5	66	58	54	35	30	5	1	230	20	11	4	2.2	.958	OF-117
1913	2 teams CIN N (30G –.296) PHI N (88G –.324)																							
″	total	118	.316	.502	414	131	24	13	9	2.2	64	58	28	42	11	11	4	243	11	6	3	2.5	.977	OF-105, 1B-1
1914	PHI N	138	.325	.446	514	167	25	5	9	1.8	76	66	37	59	16	12	3	270	17	16	3	2.4	.947	OF-126
1915		112	.246	.414	338	83	16	4	11	3.3	38	35	26	48	12	13	2	177	5	11	0	2.0	.943	OF-95
8 yrs.		876	.276	.397	2764	763	114	43	45	1.6	367	292	241	231	129	100	18	1339	105	69	19	2.0	.954	OF-755, 1B-2

Beals Becker *continued*

Year	Team	Games	BA	SA	AB	H	2B	3B	HR	HR%	R	RBI	BB	SO	SB	Pinch Hit AB	Pinch Hit H	PO	A	E	DP	TC/G	FA	G by Pos
WORLD SERIES																								
1911	NY N	3	.000	.000	3	0	0	0	0	0.0	0	0	0	0	0	3	0	0	0	0	0	0.0	—	
1912		2	.000	.000	4	0	0	0	0	0.0	1	0	2	0	0	0	0	0	1	0	0	1.0	1.000	OF-1
1915	PHI N	2	—	—	0	0	0	0	0	—	0	0	0	0	0	0	0	0	0	0	0	0.0	.000	OF-2
3 yrs.		7	.000	.000	7	0	0	0	0	0.0	1	0	2	0	0	3	0	0	1	0	0	0.3	1.000	OF-3

Heinz Becker

BECKER, HEINZ REINHARD (Dutch)
B. Aug. 26, 1915, Berlin, Germany D. Nov. 11, 1991, Dallas, Tex.

BB TR 6′ 2″ 200 lbs.
BL 1946

Year	Team	Games	BA	SA	AB	H	2B	3B	HR	HR%	R	RBI	BB	SO	SB	Pinch Hit AB	Pinch Hit H	PO	A	E	DP	TC/G	FA	G by Pos
1943	CHI N	24	.145	.145	69	10	0	0	0	0.0	5	2	9	6	0	3	0	161	15	3	9	9.9	.983	1B-18
1945		67	.286	.421	133	38	8	2	2	1.5	25	27	17	16	0	36	5	222	12	0	21	8.4	1.000	1B-28
1946	2 teams	CHI N (9G –.286)	CLE A (50G –.299)																					
″	total	59	.299	.377	154	46	10	1	0	0.0	15	18	24	19	1	11	3	347	26	2	34	8.5	.995	1B-44
1947	CLE A	2	.000	.000	2	0	0	0	0	0.0	0	0	0	1	0	2	0	0	0	0	0	0.0	—	
4 yrs.		152	.263	.346	358	94	18	3	2	0.6	45	47	50	42	1	52	8	730	53	5	64	8.8	.994	1B-90
WORLD SERIES																								
1945	CHI N	3	.500	.500	2	1	0	0	0	0.0	0	0	1	1	0	2	1	0	0	0	0	0.0	—	

Joe Becker

BECKER, JOSEPH EDWARD
B. June 25, 1908, St. Louis, Mo.

BR TR 6′ 1″ 180 lbs.

Year	Team	Games	BA	SA	AB	H	2B	3B	HR	HR%	R	RBI	BB	SO	SB	Pinch Hit AB	Pinch Hit H	PO	A	E	DP	TC/G	FA	G by Pos
1936	CLE A	22	.180	.340	50	9	3	1	1	2.0	5	11	5	4	0	7	0	40	3	1	0	2.9	.977	C-15
1937		18	.333	.455	33	11	2	1	0	0.0	3	2	3	4	0	6	2	29	8	2	0	3.3	.949	C-12
2 yrs.		40	.241	.386	83	20	5	2	1	1.2	8	13	8	8	0	13	2	69	11	3	0	3.1	.964	C-27

Marty Becker

BECKER, MARTIN HENRY
B. Dec. 25, 1893, Tiffin, Ohio D. Sept. 25, 1957, Cincinnati, Ohio.

BB TL 5′ 8½″ 155 lbs.

Year	Team	Games	BA	SA	AB	H	2B	3B	HR	HR%	R	RBI	BB	SO	SB	Pinch Hit AB	Pinch Hit H	PO	A	E	DP	TC/G	FA	G by Pos
1915	NY N	17	.250	.288	52	13	2	0	0	0.0	5	3	2	9	3	1	0	29	4	3	1	2.3	.917	OF-16

Rich Becker

BECKER, RICHARD GODHARD
B. Feb. 1, 1972, Aurora, Ill.

BB TL 5′10″ 180 lbs.

Year	Team	Games	BA	SA	AB	H	2B	3B	HR	HR%	R	RBI	BB	SO	SB	Pinch Hit AB	Pinch Hit H	PO	A	E	DP	TC/G	FA	G by Pos
1993	MIN A	3	.286	.571	7	2	2	0	0	0.0	3	0	5	4	1	0	0	7	0	1	0	2.7	.875	OF-3
1994		28	.265	.327	98	26	3	0	1	1.0	12	8	13	25	6	2	1	87	2	1	1	3.3	.989	OF-26, DH-1
1995		106	.237	.296	392	93	15	1	2	0.5	45	33	34	95	8	1	1	275	12	4	3	2.8	.986	OF-105
3 yrs.		137	.243	.306	497	121	20	1	3	0.6	60	41	52	124	15	3	2	369	14	6	4	2.9	.985	OF-134, DH-1

Glenn Beckert

BECKERT, GLENN ALFRED
B. Oct. 12, 1940, Pittsburgh, Pa.

BR TR 6′ 1″ 190 lbs.

Year	Team	Games	BA	SA	AB	H	2B	3B	HR	HR%	R	RBI	BB	SO	SB	Pinch Hit AB	Pinch Hit H	PO	A	E	DP	TC/G	FA	G by Pos
1965	CHI N	154	.239	.298	614	147	21	3	3	0.5	73	30	28	52	6	2	2	326	494	23	101	5.5	.973	2B-153
1966		153	.287	.348	656	188	23	7	1	0.2	73	59	26	36	10	1	0	373	403	24	89	5.2	.970	2B-152, SS-1
1967		146	.280	.369	597	167	32	3	5	0.8	91	40	30	25	10	1	0	327	422	25	89	5.4	.968	2B-144
1968		155	.294	.369	643	189	28	4	4	0.6	**98**	37	31	20	8	0	0	356	461	19	107	5.4	.977	2B-155
1969		131	.291	.341	543	158	22	1	1	0.2	69	37	24	24	6	1	0	262	401	24	71	5.3	.965	2B-129
1970		143	.288	.349	591	170	15	6	3	0.5	99	36	32	22	4	3	0	303	412	22	88	5.3	.970	2B-138, OF-1
1971		131	.342	.406	530	181	18	5	2	0.4	80	42	24	24	3	2	1	275	382	9	76	5.2	.986	2B-129
1972		120	.270	.344	474	128	22	2	3	0.6	51	43	23	17	2	2	1	256	396	16	71	5.7	.976	2B-118
1973		114	.255	.290	372	95	13	0	0	0.0	38	29	30	15	0	25	6	163	262	7	50	4.9	.984	2B-88
1974	SD N	64	.256	.262	172	44	1	0	0	0.0	11	7	11	8	0	26	4	71	80	10	17	4.4	.938	2B-36, 3B-1
1975		9	.375	.438	16	6	1	0	0	0.0	2	0	1	0	0	5	1	0	6	0	0	1.5	1.000	3B-4
11 yrs.		1320	.283	.345	5208	1473	196	31	22	0.4	685	360	260	243	49	68	15	2712	3719	179	759	5.3	.973	2B-1242, 3B-5, OF-1, SS-1

Jake Beckley

BECKLEY, JACOB PETER (St. Jacob)
B. Aug. 4, 1867, Hannibal, Mo. D. June 25, 1918, Kansas City, Mo.
Hall of Fame 1971.

BL TL 5′10″ 200 lbs.

Year	Team	Games	BA	SA	AB	H	2B	3B	HR	HR%	R	RBI	BB	SO	SB	Pinch Hit AB	Pinch Hit H	PO	A	E	DP	TC/G	FA	G by Pos
1888	PIT N	71	.343	.417	283	97	15	3	0	0.0	35	27	7	22	20	0	0	744	19	16	38	11.0	.979	1B-71
1889		123	.301	.437	522	157	24	10	9	1.7	91	97	29	29	11	0	0	1236	54	24	73	10.7	.982	1B-122, OF-1
1890	PIT P	121	.324	.541	516	167	38	**22**	10	1.9	109	120	42	32	18	0	0	1256	58	32	61	11.1	.976	1B-121
1891	PIT N	133	.292	.419	554	162	20	19	4	0.7	94	73	44	46	13	0	0	1250	87	24	63	10.2	.982	1B-133
1892		151	.236	.381	614	145	21	19	10	1.6	102	96	31	44	30	0	0	1523	132	38	88	11.2	.978	1B-151
1893		131	.303	.459	542	164	32	19	5	0.9	108	106	54	26	15	0	0	1360	95	21	83	11.3	.986	1B-131
1894		131	.343	.520	533	183	36	17	8	1.5	121	120	43	16	21	0	0	1227	84	30	80	10.2	.978	1B-131
1895		129	.328	.487	530	174	31	19	5	0.9	104	110	24	20	20	0	0	1340	54	31	76	11.0	.978	1B-129
1896	2 teams	PIT N (59G –.253)	NY N (46G –.302)																					
″	total	105	.276	.419	399	110	15	9	8	2.0	81	70	31	35	19	0	0	981	53	20	60	9.9	.981	1B-101, OF-5, 2B-1
1897	2 teams	NY N (17G –.250)	CIN N (97G –.345)																					
″	total	114	.330	.485	433	143	19	12	8	1.8	84	87	20		25	0	0	996	60	24	68	9.5	.978	1B-114
1898	CIN N	118	.294	.416	459	135	20	12	4	0.9	86	72	28		6	0	0	1167	53	21	76	10.5	.983	1B-118
1899		134	.333	.466	513	171	27	16	3	0.6	87	99	40		20	0	0	1291	72	19	74	10.3	.986	1B-134
1900		141	.341	.434	558	190	26	10	2	0.4	98	94	40		23	1	0	1389	93	30	91	10.8	.980	1B-140
1901		140	.307	.434	580	178	**39**	13	3	0.5	78	79	28		4	0	0	1366	71	34	79	10.5	.977	1B-140
1902		129	.331	.429	532	176	23	7	5	0.9	82	69	34		15	0	0	1269	66	23	84	10.4	.983	1B-129, P-1
1903		120	.327	.447	459	150	29	10	2	0.4	85	81	42		23	1	1	1127	78	30	56	10.4	.976	1B-119
1904	STL N	142	.325	.403	551	179	22	9	1	0.2	72	67	35		17	0	0	1526	64	20	65	11.3	.988	1B-142
1905		134	.286	.370	514	147	20	10	1	0.2	48	57	30		12	0	0	1442	69	28	56	11.5	.982	1B-134
1906		87	.247	.334	320	79	16	6	0	0.0	29	44	13		3	2	1	928	43	13	38	11.6	.987	1B-85
1907		32	.209	.235	115	24	3	0	0	0.0	6	7	1		0	0	0	303	13	4	17	10.0	.988	1B-32
20 yrs.		2386	.308	.436	9527	2931	476	242	88	0.9	1600	1575	616	270	315	4	2	23721	1318	482	1326	10.7	.981	1B-2377, OF-6, P-1, 2B-1
								4th																

Julio Becquer

BECQUER, JULIO
Born Julio Becquer (Villegas).
B. Dec. 20, 1931, Havana, Cuba.
BL TL 5′11½″ 178 lbs.

Year	Team	Games	BA	SA	AB	H	2B	3B	HR	HR%	R	RBI	BB	SO	SB	Pinch Hit AB	Pinch Hit H	PO	A	E	DP	TC/G	FA	G by Pos
1955	WAS A	10	.214	.214	14	3	0	0	0	0.0	1	1	0	1	0	8	3	15	2	0	2	8.5	1.000	1B-2
1957		105	.226	.312	186	42	6	2	2	1.1	14	22	10	29	3	**65**	**18**	300	19	0	29	7.4	1.000	1B-43
1958		86	.238	.256	164	39	3	0	0	0.0	10	12	8	21	1	41	11	320	34	2	26	8.3	.994	1B-42, OF-1
1959		108	.268	.382	220	59	12	5	1	0.5	20	26	8	17	3	**56**	**12**	454	32	5	38	9.3	.990	1B-53
1960		110	.252	.389	298	75	15	7	4	1.3	41	35	12	35	1	39	8	611	38	7	59	8.4	.989	1B-77, P-1
1961	2 teams	LA A (11G –.000)	MIN A (57G –.238)																					
″	total	68	.217	.435	92	20	1	2	5	5.4	13	18	3	17	0	47	11	73	5	0	8	2.7	1.000	1B-23, OF-5, P-1
1963	MIN A	1	—	—	0	0	0	0	0	—	1	0	0	0	0	0	0	0	0	0	0	0.0	—	
7 yrs.		488	.244	.352	974	238	37	16	12	1.2	100	114	41	120	8	256	63	1773	130	14	162	7.7	.993	1B-240, OF-6, P-2

Howie Bedell

BEDELL, HOWARD WILLIAM
B. Sept. 29, 1935, Clearfield, Pa.
BL TR 6′ 1″ 185 lbs.

Year	Team	Games	BA	SA	AB	H	2B	3B	HR	HR%	R	RBI	BB	SO	SB	Pinch Hit AB	Pinch Hit H	PO	A	E	DP	TC/G	FA	G by Pos
1962	MIL N	58	.196	.232	138	27	1	2	0	0.0	15	2	11	22	1	11	1	63	0	3	0	1.5	.955	OF-45
1968	PHI N	9	.143	.143	7	1	0	0	0	0.0	0	1	1	0	0	7	1	0	0	0	0	0.0	—	
2 yrs.		67	.193	.228	145	28	1	2	0	0.0	15	3	12	22	1	18	2	63	0	3	0	1.5	.955	OF-45

Gene Bedford

BEDFORD, WILLIAM EUGENE
B. Dec. 2, 1896, Dallas, Tex. D. Oct. 6, 1977, San Antonio, Tex.
BB TR 5′ 8″ 170 lbs.

Year	Team	Games	BA	SA	AB	H	2B	3B	HR	HR%	R	RBI	BB	SO	SB	Pinch Hit AB	Pinch Hit H	PO	A	E	DP	TC/G	FA	G by Pos
1925	CLE A	2	.000	.000	3	0	0	0	0	0.0	1	0	0	1	0	0	0	0	1	0	0	0.5	1.000	2B-2

Ed Beecher

BEECHER, EDWARD (Scrap Iron)
B. May 1876, Ind. Deceased.

Year	Team	Games	BA	SA	AB	H	2B	3B	HR	HR%	R	RBI	BB	SO	SB	Pinch Hit AB	Pinch Hit H	PO	A	E	DP	TC/G	FA	G by Pos
1897	STL N	3	.333	.333	12	4	0	0	0	0.0	1	1	0		1	0	0	6	0	0	0	2.0	1.000	OF-3
1898	CLE N	8	.200	.280	25	5	2	0	0	0.0	1	0	0		0	0	0	10	1	2	0	1.6	.846	OF-8
2 yrs.		11	.243	.297	37	9	2	0	0	0.0	2	1	0		1	0	0	16	1	2	0	1.7	.895	OF-11

Harry Beecher

BEECHER, EDWARD HARRY
B. July 2, 1860, Guilford, Conn. D. Sept. 12, 1935, Hartford, Conn.
BL TL 5′10″ 185 lbs.

Year	Team	Games	BA	SA	AB	H	2B	3B	HR	HR%	R	RBI	BB	SO	SB	Pinch Hit AB	Pinch Hit H	PO	A	E	DP	TC/G	FA	G by Pos
1887	PIT N	41	.243	.325	169	41	8	0	2	1.2	15	22	7	8	8	0	0	85	12	9	1	2.6	.915	OF-41
1889	WAS N	42	.296	.346	179	53	9	0	0	0.0	20	30	5	4	3	0	0	88	7	13	3	2.6	.880	OF-39, 1B-3
1890	BUF P	126	.297	.392	536	159	22	10	3	0.6	69	90	29	23	14	0	0	211	24	55	4	2.3	.810	OF-126, P-1
1891	2 teams	WAS AA (58G –.243)	PHI AA (16G –.211)																					
″	total	74	.235	.343	306	72	13	7	2	0.7	44	35	30	13	24	0	0	127	15	26	4	2.3	.845	OF-74
4 yrs.		283	.273	.363	1190	325	52	17	7	0.6	148	177	71	48	49	0	0	511	58	103	12	2.4	.847	OF-280, 1B-3, P-1

Jodie Beeler

BEELER, JOSEPH SAM
B. Nov. 26, 1921, Dallas, Tex.
BR TR 6′ 170 lbs.

Year	Team	Games	BA	SA	AB	H	2B	3B	HR	HR%	R	RBI	BB	SO	SB	Pinch Hit AB	Pinch Hit H	PO	A	E	DP	TC/G	FA	G by Pos
1944	CIN N	3	.000	.000	3	0	0	0	0	0.0	0	0	0	2	0	0	0	0	0	2	0	1.0	.000	3B-1, 2B-1

Gene Begley

BEGLEY, EUGENE T.
B. June 7, 1861, Brooklyn, N. Y. Deceased.

Year	Team	Games	BA	SA	AB	H	2B	3B	HR	HR%	R	RBI	BB	SO	SB	Pinch Hit AB	Pinch Hit H	PO	A	E	DP	TC/G	FA	G by Pos
1886	NY N	5	.125	.125	16	2	0	0	0	0.0	1	1	1	3		0	0	14	7	3	0	4.8	.875	C-3, OF-2

Jim Begley

BEGLEY, JAMES LAWRENCE (Imp)
B. Sept. 19, 1902, San Francisco, Calif. D. Feb. 20, 1957, San Francisco, Calif.
BR TR 5′ 6″ 145 lbs.

Year	Team	Games	BA	SA	AB	H	2B	3B	HR	HR%	R	RBI	BB	SO	SB	Pinch Hit AB	Pinch Hit H	PO	A	E	DP	TC/G	FA	G by Pos
1924	CIN N	2	.200	.200	5	1	0	0	0	0.0	1	0	2	0	0	0	0	5	9	1	0	7.5	.933	2B-2

Steve Behel

BEHEL, STEPHEN ARNOLD DOUGLAS
B. Nov. 6, 1860, Earlville, Ill. D. Feb. 15, 1945, Los Angeles, Calif.

Year	Team	Games	BA	SA	AB	H	2B	3B	HR	HR%	R	RBI	BB	SO	SB	Pinch Hit AB	Pinch Hit H	PO	A	E	DP	TC/G	FA	G by Pos
1884	MIL U	9	.242	.273	33	8	1	0	0	0.0	5		3			0	0	4	1	0	0	0.6	1.000	OF-9
1886	NY AA	59	.205	.246	224	46	5	2	0	0.0	32		22			0	0	84	7	15	0	1.8	.858	OF-59
2 yrs.		68	.210	.249	257	54	6	2	0	0.0	37		25			0	0	88	8	15	0	1.6	.865	OF-68

Ollie Bejma

BEJMA, ALOYSIUS FRANK
Born Alojzy Frank Bejma.
B. Sept. 12, 1907, South Bend, Ind. D. Jan. 3, 1995, South Bend, Ind.
BR TR 5′10″ 115 lbs.

Year	Team	Games	BA	SA	AB	H	2B	3B	HR	HR%	R	RBI	BB	SO	SB	Pinch Hit AB	Pinch Hit H	PO	A	E	DP	TC/G	FA	G by Pos
1934	STL A	95	.271	.378	262	71	16	3	2	0.8	39	29	40	36	3	22	6	129	145	11	27	4.2	.961	SS-32, 2B-14, 3B-13, OF-9
1935		64	.192	.283	198	38	8	2	2	1.0	18	26	27	21	1	7	2	122	178	15	34	5.5	.952	2B-47, SS-8, 3B-2
1936		67	.259	.360	139	36	2	3	2	1.4	19	18	27	21	0	21	6	74	82	8	9	4.1	.951	2B-32, 3B-7, SS-1
1939	CHI A	90	.251	.378	307	77	9	3	8	2.6	52	44	36	27	1	6	1	174	201	7	36	4.6	.982	2B-81, SS-1, 3B-1
4 yrs.		316	.245	.354	906	222	35	11	14	1.5	128	117	130	105	5	56	15	499	606	41	106	4.6	.964	2B-174, SS-42, 3B-23, OF-9

Mark Belanger

BELANGER, MARK HENRY
B. June 8, 1944, Pittsfield, Mass.
BR TR 6′ 1″ 170 lbs.

Year	Team	Games	BA	SA	AB	H	2B	3B	HR	HR%	R	RBI	BB	SO	SB	Pinch Hit AB	Pinch Hit H	PO	A	E	DP	TC/G	FA	G by Pos
1965	BAL A	11	.333	.333	3	1	0	0	0	0.0	1	0	0	0	0	0	0	1	1	0	2	0.5	1.000	SS-4
1966		8	.158	.211	19	3	1	0	0	0.0	2	0	0	3	0	0	0	9	20	0	3	4.8	1.000	SS-6
1967		69	.174	.217	184	32	5	0	1	0.5	19	10	12	46	6	2	0	100	138	9	24	3.7	.964	SS-38, 2B-26, 3B-2
1968		145	.208	.248	472	98	13	0	2	0.4	40	21	40	114	10	0	0	248	444	22	73	4.9	.969	SS-145
1969		150	.287	.345	530	152	17	4	2	0.4	76	50	53	54	14	3	1	251	449	23	79	4.9	.968	SS-148
1970		145	.218	.259	459	100	6	5	1	0.2	53	36	52	65	13	3	0	212	412	19	78	4.5	.970	SS-143
1971		150	.266	.320	500	133	19	4	0	0.0	67	35	73	48	10	1	0	280	443	16	77	5.0	.978	SS-149
1972		113	.186	.246	285	53	9	1	2	0.7	36	16	18	53	6	1	0	180	285	12	53	4.5	.975	SS-105
1973		154	.226	.262	470	106	15	1	0	0.0	60	27	49	54	13	0	0	241	530	23	100	5.2	.971	SS-154
1974		155	.225	.300	493	111	14	4	5	1.0	54	36	51	69	17	0	0	243	552	13	100	5.2	.984	SS-155
1975		152	.226	.276	442	100	11	1	3	0.7	44	27	36	53	16	0	0	259	508	17	105	5.2	.978	SS-152
1976		153	.270	.326	522	141	22	2	1	0.2	66	40	51	64	27	0	0	239	545	14	97	5.2	.982	SS-153
1977		144	.206	.274	402	83	13	4	2	0.5	39	30	43	68	15	0	0	244	417	10	82	4.7	.985	SS-142
1978		135	.213	.250	348	74	13	0	0	0.0	39	16	40	55	6	1	0	184	409	9	76	4.5	.985	SS-134
1979		101	.167	.217	198	33	6	2	0	0.0	28	9	29	33	5	1	1	110	195	3	38	3.1	.990	SS-98
1980		113	.228	.276	268	61	7	3	0	0.0	37	22	12	25	6	2	0	133	258	10	49	3.7	.975	SS-109
1981		64	.165	.237	139	23	3	2	1	0.7	9	10	12	25	2	1	0	86	162	7	21	4.0	.973	SS-63
1982	LA N	54	.240	.260	50	12	1	0	0	0.0	6	4	5	10	1	4	1	20	63	4	4	1.9	.954	SS-44, 2B-1
18 yrs.		2016	.228	.280	5784	1316	175	33	20	0.3	676	389	576	839	167	19	3	3040	5831	211	1061	4.6	.977	SS-1942, 2B-27, 3B-2

Mark Belanger *continued*

Year	Team	Games	BA	SA	AB	H	2B	3B	HR	HR%	R	RBI	BB	SO	SB	Pinch Hit AB	Pinch Hit H	PO	A	E	DP	TC/G	FA	G by Pos
LEAGUE CHAMPIONSHIP SERIES																								
1969	BAL A	3	.267	.600	15	4	0	1	1	6.7	4	1	0	0	0	0	0	4	9	0	1	4.3	1.000	SS-3
1970		3	.333	.333	12	4	0	0	0	0.0	5	1	1	0	0	0	0	6	14	0	3	6.7	1.000	SS-3
1971		3	.250	.250	8	2	0	0	0	0.0	1	1	3	2	0	0	0	6	11	0	3	5.7	1.000	SS-3
1973		5	.125	.125	16	2	0	0	0	0.0	0	1	1	1	0	0	0	8	17	0	1	5.0	1.000	SS-5
1974		4	.000	.000	9	0	0	0	0	0.0	0	0	1	3	0	0	0	7	12	1	2	5.0	.950	SS-4
1979		3	.200	.200	5	1	0	0	0	0.0	0	1	0	2	0	0	0	0	6	0	0	2.0	1.000	SS-3
6 yrs.		21	.200	.277	65	13	0	1	1	1.5	10	5	6	8	0	0	0	31	69	1	10	4.8	.990	SS-21
WORLD SERIES																								
1969	BAL A	5	.200	.200	15	3	0	0	0	0.0	2	1	2	1	0	0	0	8	14	0	3	4.4	1.000	SS-5
1970		5	.105	.105	19	2	0	0	0	0.0	0	1	1	2	0	0	0	11	14	1	1	5.2	.962	SS-5
1971		7	.238	.333	21	5	0	1	0	0.0	4	0	5	2	1	0	0	10	20	3	1	4.7	.909	SS-7
1979		5	.000	.000	6	0	0	0	0	0.0	1	0	1	1	0	0	0	3	7	1	2	2.8	.909	SS-4
4 yrs.		22	.164	.197	61	10	0	1	0	0.0	7	2	9	6	1	0	0	32	55	5	7	4.4	.946	SS-21

Wayne Belardi

BELARDI, CARROLL WAYNE (Footsie) BL TL 6′ 1″ 185 lbs.
B. Sept. 5, 1930, St. Helena, Calif. D. Oct. 21, 1993, Santa Cruz, Calif.

Year	Team	Games	BA	SA	AB	H	2B	3B	HR	HR%	R	RBI	BB	SO	SB	Pinch Hit AB	Pinch Hit H	PO	A	E	DP	TC/G	FA	G by Pos
1950	BKN N	10	.000	.000	10	0	0	0	0	0.0	0	0	0	4	0	9	0	2	0	0	0	2.0	1.000	1B-1
1951		3	.333	1.000	3	1	0	1	0	0.0	1	0	0	2	0	3	1	0	0	0	0	0.0	—	
1953		69	.239	.485	163	39	3	2	11	6.7	19	34	16	40	0	28	9	283	23	5	34	8.2	.984	1B-38
1954	2 teams	BKN N (11G –.222) DET A (88G –.232)																						
″	total	99	.232	.394	259	60	7	1	11	4.2	27	25	35	37	1	21	4	636	51	8	54	8.8	.988	1B-79
1955	DET A	3	.000	.000	3	0	0	0	0	0.0	0	0	0	1	0	3	0	0	0	0	0	0.0	—	
1956		79	.279	.429	154	43	3	1	6	3.9	24	15	15	13	0	37	8	243	17	5	21	8.0	.981	1B-31, OF-2
6 yrs.		263	.242	.422	592	143	13	5	28	4.7	71	74	66	97	1	101	22	1164	91	18	109	8.4	.986	1B-149, OF-2
WORLD SERIES																								
1953	BKN N	2	.000	.000	2	0	0	0	0	0.0	0	0	0	1	0	2	0	0	0	0	0	0.0	—	

Kevin Belcher

BELCHER, KEVIN DONNELL BR TR 6′ 195 lbs.
B. Aug. 8, 1967, Waco, Tex.

Year	Team	Games	BA	SA	AB	H	2B	3B	HR	HR%	R	RBI	BB	SO	SB	Pinch Hit AB	Pinch Hit H	PO	A	E	DP	TC/G	FA	G by Pos
1990	TEX A	16	.133	.200	15	2	1	0	0	0.0	4	0	2	6	0	1	0	12	0	0	0	1.3	1.000	OF-9

Ira Belden

BELDEN, IRA ALLISON BL TR 5′11″ 175 lbs.
B. Apr. 16, 1874, Cleveland, Ohio D. July 15, 1916, Lakewood, Ohio.

Year	Team	Games	BA	SA	AB	H	2B	3B	HR	HR%	R	RBI	BB	SO	SB	Pinch Hit AB	Pinch Hit H	PO	A	E	DP	TC/G	FA	G by Pos
1897	CLE N	8	.267	.400	30	8	0	2	0	0.0	5	4	2		0	0	0	17	2	0	0	2.4	1.000	OF-8

Beau Bell

BELL, ROY CHESTER BR TR 6′ 2″ 185 lbs.
B. Aug. 20, 1907, Bellville, Tex. D. Sept. 14, 1977, College Station, Tex.

Year	Team	Games	BA	SA	AB	H	2B	3B	HR	HR%	R	RBI	BB	SO	SB	Pinch Hit AB	Pinch Hit H	PO	A	E	DP	TC/G	FA	G by Pos
1935	STL A	76	.250	.345	220	55	8	2	3	1.4	20	17	16	16	1	24	4	187	9	10	11	3.7	.951	OF-37, 1B-15, 3B-3
1936		155	.344	.502	616	212	40	12	11	1.8	100	123	60	55	4	0	0	425	19	13	20	2.9	.972	OF-142, 1B-17
1937		156	.340	.509	642	**218**	**51**	8	14	2.2	82	117	53	54	2	0	0	462	42	10	24	3.2	.981	OF-131, 1B-26, 3B-2
1938		147	.262	.414	526	138	35	3	13	2.5	91	84	71	46	1	8	3	290	12	6	7	2.3	.981	OF-132, 1B-4
1939	2 teams	STL A (11G –.219) DET A (54G –.239)																						
″	total	65	.235	.307	166	39	5	2	1	0.6	18	29	28	19	0	17	3	93	4	0	1	2.1	1.000	OF-46
1940	CLE A	120	.279	.365	444	124	22	2	4	0.9	55	58	34	41	2	9	0	309	13	8	17	3.0	.976	OF-97, 1B-14
1941		48	.192	.288	104	20	4	3	0	0.0	12	9	10	8	1	23	3	106	4	0	9	4.6	1.000	OF-14, 1B-10
7 yrs.		767	.297	.432	2718	806	165	32	46	1.7	378	437	272	239	11	81	13	1872	103	47	89	2.9	.977	OF-599, 1B-86, 3B-5

Buddy Bell

BELL, DAVID GUS BR TR 6′ 1″ 180 lbs.
Father of David Bell. Son of Gus Bell.
B. Aug. 27, 1951, Pittsburgh, Pa.

Year	Team	Games	BA	SA	AB	H	2B	3B	HR	HR%	R	RBI	BB	SO	SB	Pinch Hit AB	Pinch Hit H	PO	A	E	DP	TC/G	FA	G by Pos
1972	CLE A	132	.255	.363	466	119	21	1	9	1.9	49	36	34	29	5	3	1	284	23	3	6	2.4	.990	OF-123, 3B-6
1973		156	.268	.393	631	169	23	7	14	2.2	86	59	49	47	7	1	0	146	363	22	44	3.4	.959	3B-154, OF-2
1974		116	.262	.352	423	111	15	1	7	1.7	51	46	35	29	1	0	0	112	274	15	31	3.5	.963	3B-115, DH-1
1975		153	.271	.376	553	150	20	4	10	1.8	66	59	51	72	6	0	0	146	330	25	29	3.3	.950	3B-153
1976		159	.281	.366	604	170	26	2	7	1.2	75	60	44	49	3	1	1	109	331	20	23	2.9	.957	3B-158, 1B-2
1977		129	.292	.426	479	140	23	4	11	2.3	64	64	45	63	1	3	1	134	253	16	23	3.1	.960	3B-118, OF-11
1978		142	.282	.392	556	157	27	8	6	1.1	71	62	39	43	1	3	1	125	355	15	30	3.5	.970	3B-139, DH-1
1979	TEX A	162	.299	.451	**670**	200	42	3	18	2.7	89	101	30	45	5	0	0	147	429	17	31	3.3	.971	3B-147, SS-33
1980		129	.329	.498	490	161	24	4	17	3.5	76	83	40	39	3	9	2	125	282	8	26	3.3	.981	3B-123, SS-3
1981		97	.294	.428	360	106	16	1	10	2.8	44	64	42	30	3	1	0	67	284	14	19	3.8	.962	3B-96, SS-1
1982		148	.296	.426	537	159	27	2	13	2.4	62	67	70	50	5	1	0	131	397	13	35	3.6	.976	3B-145, SS-4
1983		156	.277	.411	618	171	35	3	14	2.3	75	66	50	48	3	2	0	123	383	17	29	3.4	.967	3B-154
1984		148	.315	.458	553	174	36	5	11	2.0	87	83	63	54	2	0	0	129	323	20	28	3.2	.958	3B-147
1985	2 teams	TEX A (84G –.236) CIN N (67G –.219)																						
″	total	151	.229	.350	560	128	28	5	10	1.8	61	68	67	48	3	2	1	124	297	25	35	3.0	.944	3B-150
1986	CIN N	155	.278	.445	568	158	29	3	20	3.5	89	75	73	49	2	4	2	105	291	10	28	2.7	.975	3B-151, 2B-1
1987		143	.284	.425	522	148	19	2	17	3.3	74	70	71	39	4	1	0	93	241	7	17	2.4	.979	3B-142
1988	2 teams	CIN N (21G –.185) HOU N (74G –.253)																						
″	total	95	.241	.344	323	78	10	1	7	2.2	27	40	26	32	1	9	0	88	140	15	14	2.8	.938	3B-79, 1B-9
1989	TEX A	34	.183	.232	82	15	4	0	0	0.0	4	3	7	10	0	8	1	10	13	0	0	0.7	1.000	DH-22, 3B-9, 1B-1
18 yrs.		2405	.279	.406	8995	2514	425	56	201	2.2	1150	1106	836	776	55	48	10	2198	5009	262	448	3.1	.965	3B-2186, OF-136, SS-41, DH-24, 1B-12, 2B-1

David Bell

BELL, DAVID MICHAEL BR TR 5′10″ 170 lbs.
Son of Buddy Bell.
B. Sept. 14, 1972, Cincinnati, Ohio.

Year	Team	Games	BA	SA	AB	H	2B	3B	HR	HR%	R	RBI	BB	SO	SB	Pinch Hit AB	Pinch Hit H	PO	A	E	DP	TC/G	FA	G by Pos
1995	2 teams	CLE A (2G –.000) STL N (39G –.250)																						
″	total	41	.247	.363	146	36	7	2	2	1.4	13	19	4	25	1	2	0	77	110	7	27	4.6	.964	2B-37, 3B-5

Derek Bell

BELL, DEREK NATHANIEL BR TR 6′ 2″ 200 lbs.
B. Dec. 11, 1968, Tampa, Fla.

Year	Team	Lg	Games	BA	SA	AB	H	2B	3B	HR	HR%	R	RBI	BB	SO	SB	Pinch Hit AB	Pinch Hit H	PO	A	E	DP	TC/G	FA	G by Pos
1991	TOR	A	18	.143	.143	28	4	0	0	0	0.0	5	1	6	5	3	0	0	16	0	2	0	1.4	.889	OF-13
1992			61	.242	.354	161	39	6	3	2	1.2	23	15	15	34	7	2	0	105	4	0	1	1.9	1.000	OF-56, DH-1
1993	SD	N	150	.262	.417	542	142	19	1	21	3.9	73	72	23	122	26	8	0	334	37	17	7	2.7	.956	OF-125, 3B-19
1994			108	.311	.454	434	135	20	0	14	3.2	54	54	29	88	24	1	0	247	3	10	0	2.4	.962	OF-108
1995	HOU	N	112	.334	.442	452	151	21	2	8	1.8	63	86	33	71	27	2	1	201	10	8	2	2.0	.963	OF-110
5 yrs.			449	.291	.423	1617	471	66	6	45	2.8	218	228	106	320	87	13	1	903	54	37	10	2.3	.963	OF-412, 3B-19, DH-1
LEAGUE CHAMPIONSHIP SERIES																									
1992	TOR	A	2	—	—	0	0	0	0	0	—	1	0	1	0	0	0	0	1	0	0	0	0.5	1.000	OF-2
WORLD SERIES																									
1992	TOR	A	2	.000	.000	1	0	0	0	0	0.0	1	0	1	0	0	1	0	0	0	0	0	0.0	—	

Fern Bell

BELL, FERNANDO JEROME LEE (Danny) BR TR 6′ 180 lbs.
B. Jan. 21, 1913, Ada, Okla.

Year	Team	Lg	Games	BA	SA	AB	H	2B	3B	HR	HR%	R	RBI	BB	SO	SB	Pinch Hit AB	Pinch Hit H	PO	A	E	DP	TC/G	FA	G by Pos
1939	PIT	N	83	.286	.389	262	75	5	8	2	0.8	44	34	42	18	2	8	1	154	7	7	0	2.5	.958	OF-67, 3B-1
1940			6	.000	.000	3	0	0	0	0	0.0	0	1	1	1	0	3	0	0	0	0	0	0.0	—	
2 yrs.			89	.283	.385	265	75	5	8	2	0.8	44	35	43	19	2	11	1	154	7	7	0	2.5	.958	OF-67, 3B-1

Frank Bell

BELL, FRANK GUSTAV 6′
Brother of Charlie Bell.
B. 1863, Cincinnati, Ohio D. Apr. 14, 1891, Cincinnati, Ohio.

Year	Team	Lg	Games	BA	SA	AB	H	2B	3B	HR	HR%	R	RBI	BB	SO	SB	Pinch Hit AB	Pinch Hit H	PO	A	E	DP	TC/G	FA	G by Pos
1885	BKN	AA	10	.172	.241	29	5	0	1	0	0.0	5		0			0	0	27	5	9	0	3.7	.780	C-5, OF-4, 3B-2

George Bell

BELL, GEORGE ANTONIO BR TR 6′ 1″ 190 lbs.
Born George Antonio Bell (Mathey).
Brother of Juan Bell.
B. Oct. 21, 1959, San Pedro de Macoris, Dominican Republic.

Year	Team	Lg	Games	BA	SA	AB	H	2B	3B	HR	HR%	R	RBI	BB	SO	SB	Pinch Hit AB	Pinch Hit H	PO	A	E	DP	TC/G	FA	G by Pos
1981	TOR	A	60	.233	.350	163	38	2	1	5	3.1	19	12	5	27	3	5	3	92	3	3	2	1.9	.969	OF-44, DH-8
1983			39	.268	.438	112	30	5	4	2	1.8	5	17	4	17	1	3	1	61	1	3	0	1.8	.954	OF-34, DH-2
1984			159	.292	.498	606	177	39	4	26	4.3	85	87	24	86	11	8	3	289	13	9	1	2.0	.971	OF-147, DH-7, 3B-3
1985			157	.275	.479	607	167	28	6	28	4.6	87	95	43	90	21	0	0	320	14	11	3	2.2	.968	OF-157, 3B-2
1986			159	.309	.532	641	198	38	6	31	4.8	101	108	41	62	7	1	1	270	17	10	1	1.9	.966	OF-147, DH-11, 3B-1
1987			156	.308	.605	610	188	32	4	47	7.7	111	**134**	39	75	5	1	0	249	14	11	1	1.8	.960	OF-148, 2B-1, 3B-1
1988			156	.269	.446	614	165	27	5	24	3.9	78	97	34	66	4	2	0	253	8	15	1	1.8	.946	OF-149, DH-7
1989			153	.297	.458	613	182	41	2	18	2.9	88	104	33	60	4	0	0	258	4	10	1	1.8	.963	OF-134, DH-19
1990			142	.265	.422	562	149	25	0	21	3.7	67	86	32	80	3	0	0	226	4	5	1	1.7	.979	OF-106, DH-36
1991	CHI	N	149	.285	.468	558	159	27	0	25	4.5	63	86	32	62	2	4	2	249	6	10	0	1.8	.962	OF-146
1992	CHI	A	155	.255	.418	627	160	27	0	25	4.0	74	112	31	97	5	0	0	27	0	1	0	0.2	.964	DH-140, OF-15
1993			102	.217	.363	410	89	17	2	13	3.2	36	64	13	49	1	0	0	0	0	0	0	0.0	.000	DH-102
12 yrs.			1587	.278	.469	6123	1702	308	34	265	4.3	814	1002	331	771	67	24	10	2294	84	88	11	1.6	.964	OF-1227, DH-332, 3B-7, 2B-1
LEAGUE CHAMPIONSHIP SERIES																									
1985	TOR	A	7	.321	.429	28	9	3	0	0	0.0	4	1	0	4	0	0	0	13	0	0	0	1.9	1.000	OF-7
1989			5	.200	.350	20	4	0	0	1	5.0	2	2	0	3	0	0	0	3	1	0	0	0.8	1.000	DH-3, OF-2
2 yrs.			12	.271	.396	48	13	3	0	1	2.1	6	3	0	7	0	0	0	16	1	0	0	1.4	1.000	OF-9, DH-3

Gus Bell

BELL, DAVID RUSSELL BL TR 6′ 1½″ 190 lbs.
Father of Buddy Bell.
B. Nov. 15, 1928, Louisville, Ky. D. May 7, 1995, Montgomery, Ohio.

Year	Team	Lg	Games	BA	SA	AB	H	2B	3B	HR	HR%	R	RBI	BB	SO	SB	Pinch Hit AB	Pinch Hit H	PO	A	E	DP	TC/G	FA	G by Pos
1950	PIT	N	111	.282	.443	422	119	22	11	8	1.9	62	53	28	46	4	6	1	203	10	5	3	2.1	.977	OF-104
1951			149	.278	.443	600	167	27	**12**	16	2.7	80	89	42	41	1	2	1	267	18	4	4	2.0	.986	OF-145
1952			131	.250	.419	468	117	21	5	16	3.4	53	59	36	72	1	8	0	202	8	6	2	1.8	.972	OF-123
1953	CIN	N	151	.300	.525	610	183	37	5	30	4.9	102	105	48	72	0	1	1	447	16	11	5	3.1	.977	OF-151
1954			153	.299	.465	619	185	38	7	17	2.7	104	101	48	58	5	1	0	406	12	6	2	2.8	.986	OF-153
1955			154	.308	.510	610	188	30	6	27	4.4	88	104	54	57	4	0	0	364	4	5	0	2.4	.987	OF-154
1956			150	.292	.501	603	176	31	4	29	4.8	82	84	50	66	6	1	0	330	12	5	4	2.3	.986	OF-149
1957			121	.292	.420	510	149	20	3	13	2.5	65	61	30	54	0	1	0	311	7	4	1	2.7	.988	OF-121
1958			112	.252	.382	385	97	16	2	10	2.6	42	46	36	40	2	7	1	235	7	1	2	2.3	.996	OF-107
1959			148	.293	.445	580	170	27	2	19	3.3	59	115	29	44	2	5	2	269	15	1	1	2.0	.996	OF-145
1960			143	.262	.388	515	135	19	5	12	2.3	65	62	29	40	4	13	3	239	13	3	1	1.9	.988	OF-131
1961			103	.255	.345	235	60	10	1	3	1.3	27	33	18	21	1	36	11	112	1	1	0	1.5	.991	OF-75
1962	2 teams		NY N (30G –.149)			MIL N (79G –.285)																			
″	total		109	.241	.359	315	76	13	3	6	1.9	36	30	22	24	0	26	4	115	10	2	3	1.5	.984	OF-84
1963	MIL	N	3	.333	.333	3	1	0	0	0	0.0	0	0	0	0	0	3	1	0	0	0	0	0.0	—	
1964			3	.000	.000	3	0	0	0	0	0.0	0	0	0	1	0	3	0	0	0	0	0	0.0	—	
15 yrs.			1741	.281	.445	6478	1823	311	66	206	3.2	865	942	470	636	30	112	25	3500	133	54	28	2.2	.985	OF-1642
WORLD SERIES																									
1961	CIN	N	3	.000	.000	3	0	0	0	0	0.0	0	0	0	0	0	3	0	0	0	0	0	0.0	—	

Jay Bell

BELL, JAY STUART BR TR 6′ 1″ 180 lbs.
B. Dec. 11, 1965, Eglin Air Force Base, Fla.

Year	Team	Lg	Games	BA	SA	AB	H	2B	3B	HR	HR%	R	RBI	BB	SO	SB	Pinch Hit AB	Pinch Hit H	PO	A	E	DP	TC/G	FA	G by Pos
1986	CLE	A	5	.357	.714	14	5	2	0	1	7.1	3	4	2	3	0	1	0	1	6	2	1	2.3	.778	2B-2, DH-2
1987			38	.216	.352	125	27	9	1	2	1.6	14	13	8	31	2	0	0	67	93	9	22	4.4	.947	SS-38
1988			73	.218	.280	211	46	5	1	2	0.9	23	21	21	53	4	0	0	103	170	10	37	3.9	.965	SS-72
1989	PIT	N	78	.258	.351	271	70	13	3	2	0.7	33	27	19	47	5	3	1	109	197	10	41	4.1	.968	SS-78
1990			159	.254	.362	583	148	28	7	7	1.2	93	52	65	109	10	2	1	260	459	22	85	4.7	.970	SS-159
1991			157	.270	.428	608	164	32	8	16	2.6	96	67	52	99	10	2	0	239	491	24	78	4.8	.968	SS-156
1992			159	.264	.383	632	167	36	6	9	1.4	87	55	55	103	7	0	0	268	526	22	94	5.1	.973	SS-159
1993			154	.310	.437	604	187	32	9	9	1.5	102	51	77	122	16	0	0	256	527	11	100	5.2	.986	SS-154
1994			110	.276	.441	424	117	35	4	9	2.1	68	45	49	82	2	1	0	152	380	15	67	5.0	.973	SS-110
1995			138	.262	.404	530	139	28	4	13	2.5	79	55	55	110	2	1	0	206	414	14	90	4.6	.978	SS-136, 3B-3
10 yrs.			1071	.267	.396	4002	1070	220	43	70	1.7	598	390	403	759	58	10	2	1661	3263	139	615	4.7	.973	SS-1062, 3B-3, 2B-2, DH-2

Jay Bell *continued*

LEAGUE CHAMPIONSHIP SERIES

Year	Team	Games	BA	SA	AB	H	2B	3B	HR	HR%	R	RBI	BB	SO	SB	Pinch Hit AB	Pinch Hit H	PO	A	E	DP	TC/G	FA	G by Pos
1990	PIT N	6	.250	.450	20	5	1	0	1	5.0	3	1	4	3	0	0	0	4	22	1	2	4.5	.963	SS-6
1991		7	.414	.586	29	12	2	0	1	3.4	2	1	0	10	0	0	0	13	19	1	2	4.7	.970	SS-7
1992		7	.172	.345	29	5	2	0	1	3.4	3	4	3	4	0	0	0	6	8	1	0	2.1	.933	SS-7
3 yrs.		20	.282	.462	78	22	5	0	3	3.8	8	6	7	17 10th	0	0	0	23	49	3	4	3.8	.960	SS-20

John Bell

BELL, JOHN
Born Rudolph Fred Baerwald.
B. Jan. 1, 1881, Wausau, Wis. D. July 28, 1955, Albuquerque, N. M.
BR TR 5′ 8½″ 158 lbs.

Year	Team	Games	BA	SA	AB	H	2B	3B	HR	HR%	R	RBI	BB	SO	SB	Pinch Hit AB	Pinch Hit H	PO	A	E	DP	TC/G	FA	G by Pos
1907	NY A	17	.212	.288	52	11	2	1	0	0.0	4	3	3		4	0	0	35	0	4	0	2.3	.897	OF-17

Juan Bell

BELL, JUAN
Born Juan Bell (Mathey).
Brother of George Bell.
B. Mar. 29, 1968, San Pedro de Macoris, Dominican Republic.
BR TR 5′11″ 172 lbs.

Year	Team	Games	BA	SA	AB	H	2B	3B	HR	HR%	R	RBI	BB	SO	SB	Pinch Hit AB	Pinch Hit H	PO	A	E	DP	TC/G	FA	G by Pos
1989	BAL A	8	.000	.000	4	0	0	0	0	0.0	2	0	0	1	1	0	0	2	6	0	1	1.0	1.000	DH-4, SS-2, 2B-2
1990		5	.000	.000	2	0	0	0	0	0.0	1	0	0	1	0	0	0	1	1	0	0	1.0	1.000	SS-1, DH-1
1991		100	.172	.249	209	36	9	2	1	0.5	26	15	8	51	0	5	0	107	199	9	40	3.2	.971	2B-77, SS-15, DH-4, OF-1
1992	PHI N	46	.204	.259	147	30	3	1	1	0.7	12	8	18	29	5	1	0	82	129	6	22	4.7	.972	SS-46
1993	2 teams	PHI N (24G –.200) MIL A (91G –.234)																						
″	total	115	.228	.322	351	80	12	3	5	1.4	47	36	41	76	6	2	0	218	281	21	64	4.6	.960	SS-62, 2B-47, OF-3, DH-2
1994	MON N	38	.278	.381	97	27	4	0	2	2.1	12	10	15	21	4	9	2	43	72	2	15	4.0	.983	2B-25, 3B-3, SS-1
1995	BOS A	17	.154	.346	26	4	2	0	1	3.8	7	2	2	10	0	1	0	15	24	3	5	3.5	.929	SS-6, 2B-5, 3B-1
7 yrs.		329	.212	.298	836	177	30	6	10	1.2	107	71	84	189	16	18	2	468	712	41	147	4.0	.966	2B-156, SS-133, DH-11, 3B-4, OF-4

Kevin Bell

BELL, KEVIN ROBERT
B. July 13, 1955, Los Angeles, Calif.
BR TR 6′ 195 lbs.

Year	Team	Games	BA	SA	AB	H	2B	3B	HR	HR%	R	RBI	BB	SO	SB	Pinch Hit AB	Pinch Hit H	PO	A	E	DP	TC/G	FA	G by Pos
1976	CHI A	68	.248	.396	230	57	7	6	5	2.2	24	20	18	56	2	1	0	70	124	6	10	2.9	.970	3B-67, DH-1
1977		9	.179	.321	28	5	1	0	1	3.6	4	6	3	8	0	0	0	12	21	2	8	3.5	.943	SS-5, 3B-4, OF-1
1978		54	.191	.279	68	13	0	0	2	2.9	9	5	5	19	1	2	0	23	64	5	6	1.7	.946	3B-52, DH-1
1979		70	.245	.355	200	49	8	1	4	2.0	20	22	15	43	2	2	0	51	154	17	11	3.2	.923	3B-68, SS-2
1980		92	.178	.241	191	34	5	2	1	0.5	16	11	29	37	0	3	2	36	153	16	13	2.3	.922	3B-83, SS-3, DH-3
1982	OAK A	4	.333	.444	9	3	1	0	0	0.0	1	0	0	2	0	0	0	3	3	1	1	1.8	.857	3B-3, DH-1
6 yrs.		297	.222	.331	726	161	22	9	13	1.8	74	64	70	165	5	8	2	195	519	47	49	2.6	.938	3B-277, SS-10, DH-6, OF-1

Les Bell

BELL, LESTER ROWLAND
B. Dec. 14, 1901, Harrisburg, Pa. D. Dec. 26, 1985, Hershey, Pa.
BR TR 5′11″ 165 lbs.

Year	Team	Games	BA	SA	AB	H	2B	3B	HR	HR%	R	RBI	BB	SO	SB	Pinch Hit AB	Pinch Hit H	PO	A	E	DP	TC/G	FA	G by Pos
1923	STL N	15	.373	.451	51	19	2	1	0	0.0	5	9	9	7	1	0	0	35	53	8	9	6.4	.917	SS-15
1924		17	.246	.421	57	14	3	2	1	1.8	5	5	3	7	0	0	0	44	42	9	8	5.6	.905	SS-17
1925		153	.285	.422	586	167	29	9	11	1.9	80	88	43	47	4	0	0	151	285	36	39	3.1	.924	3B-153, SS-1
1926		155	.325	.518	581	189	33	14	17	2.9	85	100	54	62	9	0	0	165	254	22	25	2.8	.950	3B-155
1927		115	.259	.426	390	101	26	6	9	2.3	48	65	34	63	5	5	0	101	183	30	21	2.9	.904	3B-100, SS-10
1928	BOS N	153	.277	.413	591	164	36	7	10	1.7	58	91	40	45	1	0	0	177	314	27	37	3.4	.948	3B-153
1929		139	.298	.422	483	144	23	5	9	1.9	58	72	50	42	4	9	2	111	201	17	15	2.6	.948	3B-127, SS-1, 2B-1
1930	CHI N	74	.278	.431	248	69	15	4	5	2.0	35	47	24	27	1	2	0	81	105	9	15	2.7	.954	3B-70, 1B-2
1931		75	.282	.405	252	71	17	1	4	1.6	30	32	19	22	0	5	1	66	118	11	18	2.8	.944	3B-70
9 yrs.		896	.290	.438	3239	938	184	49	66	2.0	404	509	276	322	25	21	3	931	1555	169	187	3.0	.936	3B-828, SS-44, 1B-2, 2B-1

WORLD SERIES

Year	Team	Games	BA	SA	AB	H	2B	3B	HR	HR%	R	RBI	BB	SO	SB	Pinch Hit AB	Pinch Hit H	PO	A	E	DP	TC/G	FA	G by Pos
1926	STL N	7	.259	.407	27	7	1	0	1	3.7	4	6	2	5	0	0	0	7	17	2	0	3.7	.923	3B-7

Mike Bell

BELL, MICHAEL ALLEN
B. Apr. 22, 1968, Lewiston, N. J.
BL TL 6′ 1″ 175 lbs.

Year	Team	Games	BA	SA	AB	H	2B	3B	HR	HR%	R	RBI	BB	SO	SB	Pinch Hit AB	Pinch Hit H	PO	A	E	DP	TC/G	FA	G by Pos
1990	ATL N	36	.244	.467	45	11	5	1	1	2.2	8	5	2	9	0	11	2	97	9	2	6	4.5	.981	1B-24
1991		17	.133	.233	30	4	0	0	1	3.3	4	1	2	7	1	4	0	72	5	2	7	5.6	.975	1B-14
2 yrs.		53	.200	.373	75	15	5	1	2	2.7	12	6	4	16	1	15	2	169	14	4	13	4.9	.979	1B-38

Terry Bell

BELL, TERENCE WILLIAM
B. Oct. 27, 1962, Dayton, Ohio.
BR TR 6′ 195 lbs.

Year	Team	Games	BA	SA	AB	H	2B	3B	HR	HR%	R	RBI	BB	SO	SB	Pinch Hit AB	Pinch Hit H	PO	A	E	DP	TC/G	FA	G by Pos
1986	KC A	8	.000	.000	3	0	0	0	0	0.0	0	0	2	1	0	0	0	7	0	0	0	0.9	1.000	C-8
1987	ATL N	1	.000	.000	1	0	0	0	0	0.0	0	0	0	1	0	1	0	0	0	0	0	0.0	—	
2 yrs.		9	.000	.000	4	0	0	0	0	0.0	0	0	2	2	0	1	0	7	0	0	0	0.9	1.000	C-8

Zeke Bella

BELLA, JOHN
B. Aug. 23, 1930, Greenwich, Conn.
BR TL 5′11″ 185 lbs.

Year	Team	Games	BA	SA	AB	H	2B	3B	HR	HR%	R	RBI	BB	SO	SB	Pinch Hit AB	Pinch Hit H	PO	A	E	DP	TC/G	FA	G by Pos
1957	NY A	5	.100	.100	10	1	0	0	0	0.0	0	0	1	2	0	1	0	7	1	0	0	2.0	1.000	OF-4
1959	KC A	47	.207	.293	82	17	2	1	1	1.2	10	9	9	14	0	22	5	23	2	0	1	1.0	1.000	OF-25, 1B-1
2 yrs.		52	.196	.272	92	18	2	1	1	1.1	10	9	10	16	0	23	5	30	3	0	1	1.1	1.000	OF-29, 1B-1

Albert Belle

BELLE, ALBERT JOJUAN
B. Aug. 25, 1966, Shreveport, La.
BR TR 6′ 1″ 190 lbs.

Year	Team	Games	BA	SA	AB	H	2B	3B	HR	HR%	R	RBI	BB	SO	SB	Pinch Hit AB	Pinch Hit H	PO	A	E	DP	TC/G	FA	G by Pos
1989	CLE A	62	.225	.394	218	49	8	4	7	3.2	22	37	12	55	2	2	1	92	3	2	1	1.6	.979	OF-44, DH-17
1990		9	.174	.304	23	4	0	0	1	4.3	1	3	1	6	0	2	0	0	0	0	0	0.0		DH-6, OF-1
1991		123	.282	.540	461	130	31	2	28	6.1	60	95	25	99	3	4	1	170	8	9	1	1.5	.952	OF-89, DH-32
1992		153	.260	.477	585	152	23	1	34	5.8	81	112	52	128	8	1	0	94	1	3	0	0.6	.969	DH-100, OF-52
1993		159	.290	.552	594	172	36	3	38	6.4	93	**129**	76	96	23	1	0	338	16	5	7	2.3	.986	OF-150, DH-9
1994		106	.357	.714	412	147	35	2	36	8.7	90	101	58	71	9	0	0	205	8	6	0	2.1	.973	OF-104, DH-2
1995		143	.317	**.690**	546	173	**52**	1	**50**	9.2	**121**	**126**	73	80	5	0	0	304	7	6	1	2.2	.981	OF-142, DH-1
7 yrs.		755	.291	.571	2839	827	185	13	194	6.8	468	603	297	535	50	10	2	1203	43	31	10	1.7	.976	OF-582, DH-167

Albert Belle *continued*

Year	Team	Games	BA	SA	AB	H	2B	3B	HR	HR%	R	RBI	BB	SO	SB	Pinch Hit AB	Pinch Hit H	PO	A	E	DP	TC/G	FA	G by Pos
DIVISIONAL PLAYOFF SERIES																								
1995	CLE A	3	.273	.636	11	3	1	0	1	9.1	3	3	4	3	0	0	0	7	0	1	0	2.7	.875	OF-3
LEAGUE CHAMPIONSHIP SERIES																								
1995	CLE A	5	.222	.444	18	4	1	0	1	5.6	1	1	3	5	0	0	0	4	0	2	0	1.2	.667	OF-5
WORLD SERIES																								
1995	CLE A	6	.235	.588	17	4	0	0	2	11.8	4	4	7	5	0	0	0	10	0	1	0	1.8	.909	OF-6

Rafael Belliard

BELLIARD, RAFAEL LEONIDAS
Born Rafael Leonidas Belliard (Matias).
B. Oct. 24, 1961, Puerto Nuevo Mao, Dominican Republic.

BR TR 5′ 6″ 160 lbs.
BB 1982–1982

Year	Team	Games	BA	SA	AB	H	2B	3B	HR	HR%	R	RBI	BB	SO	SB	Pinch Hit AB	Pinch Hit H	PO	A	E	DP	TC/G	FA	G by Pos
1982	PIT N	9	.500	.500	2	1	0	0	0	0.0	3	0	0	0	1	1	1	2	2	0	0	1.0	1.000	SS-4
1983		4	.000	.000	1	0	0	0	0	0.0	1	0	0	1	0	0	0	1	3	0	1	1.3	1.000	SS-3
1984		20	.227	.227	22	5	0	0	0	0.0	3	0	0	1	4	0	0	12	13	3	4	2.2	.893	SS-12, 2B-1
1985		17	.200	.200	20	4	0	0	0	0.0	1	1	0	5	0	2	0	13	23	2	3	3.2	.947	SS-12
1986		117	.233	.262	309	72	5	2	0	0.0	33	31	26	54	12	4	0	147	317	12	50	4.0	.975	SS-96, 2B-23
1987		81	.207	.271	203	42	4	3	1	0.5	26	15	20	25	5	1	0	113	191	6	31	4.0	.981	SS-71, 2B-7
1988		122	.213	.241	286	61	0	4	0	0.0	28	11	26	47	7	1	0	134	261	9	51	3.4	.978	SS-117, 2B-3
1989		67	.214	.240	154	33	4	0	0	0.0	10	8	8	22	5	1	0	71	138	3	20	3.2	.986	SS-40, 2B-20, 3B-6
1990		47	.204	.259	54	11	3	0	0	0.0	10	6	5	13	1	10	2	37	36	2	8	2.1	.973	2B-21, SS-10, 3B-5
1991	ATL N	149	.249	.286	353	88	9	2	0	0.0	36	27	22	63	3	3	0	168	361	18	53	3.8	.967	SS-145
1992		144	.211	.239	285	60	6	1	0	0.0	20	14	14	43	0	1	0	152	291	14	48	3.3	.969	SS-139, 2B-1
1993		91	.228	.291	79	18	5	0	0	0.0	6	6	4	13	0	4	2	53	99	1	18	1.9	.993	SS-58, 2B-24
1994		46	.242	.317	120	29	7	1	0	0.0	9	9	2	29	0	3	0	45	86	1	16	3.0	.992	SS-26, 2B-18
1995		75	.222	.244	180	40	2	1	0	0.0	12	7	6	28	2	0	0	74	178	1	23	3.5	.996	SS-40, 2B-32
14 yrs.		989	.224	.261	2068	464	45	14	1	0.0	198	135	133	344	40	31	5	1022	1999	72	326	3.3	.977	SS-773, 2B-150, 3B-11
DIVISIONAL PLAYOFF SERIES																								
1995	ATL N	4	.000	.000	5	0	0	0	0	0.0	1	0	0	1	0	0	0	2	5	0	1	1.8	1.000	SS-4
LEAGUE CHAMPIONSHIP SERIES																								
1991	ATL N	7	.211	.211	19	4	0	0	0	0.0	0	1	3	3	0	0	0	9	15	1	4	3.6	.960	SS-7
1992		4	.000	.000	2	0	0	0	0	0.0	1	0	1	0	0	0	0	2	3	0	0	1.3	1.000	SS-3, 2B-1
1993		2	.000	.000	1	0	0	0	0	0.0	1	0	0	1	0	0	0	0	0	0	0	0.0		SS-1, 2B-1
1995		4	.273	.273	11	3	0	0	0	0.0	1	0	0	3	0	0	0	6	7	1	3	3.5	.929	SS-4
4 yrs.		17	.212	.212	33	7	0	0	0	0.0	3	1	4	7	0	0	0	17	25	2	7	2.6	.955	SS-15, 2B-2
WORLD SERIES																								
1991	ATL N	7	.375	.438	16	6	1	0	0	0.0	0	4	1	2	0	0	0	8	21	0	4	4.1	1.000	SS-7
1992		4	—	—	0	0	0	0	0	—	0	0	0	0	0	0	0	2	2	0	1	1.0	1.000	SS-3, 2B-1
1995		6	.000	.000	16	0	0	0	0	0.0	0	1	0	4	0	0	0	3	11	2	0	2.7	.875	SS-6
3 yrs.		17	.188	.219	32	6	1	0	0	0.0	0	5	1	6	0	0	0	13	34	2	5	2.9	.959	SS-16, 2B-1

John Bellman

BELLMAN, JOHN HUTCHINS
B. Mar. 4, 1864, Louisville, Ky. D. Dec. 8, 1931, Louisville, Ky.

Year	Team	Games	BA	SA	AB	H	2B	3B	HR	HR%	R	RBI	BB	SO	SB	Pinch Hit AB	Pinch Hit H	PO	A	E	DP	TC/G	FA	G by Pos
1889	STL AA	1	.500	.500	2	1	0	0	0	0.0	1	0	1	0	0	0	0	1	1	0	0	2.0	1.000	C-1

Rob Belloir

BELLOIR, ROBERT EDWARD
B. July 13, 1948, Heidelberg, Germany.

BR TR 5′10″ 155 lbs.

Year	Team	Games	BA	SA	AB	H	2B	3B	HR	HR%	R	RBI	BB	SO	SB	Pinch Hit AB	Pinch Hit H	PO	A	E	DP	TC/G	FA	G by Pos
1975	ATL N	43	.219	.257	105	23	2	1	0	0.0	11	9	7	8	0	2	0	39	106	13	17	4.1	.918	SS-38, 2B-1
1976		30	.200	.233	60	12	2	0	0	0.0	5	4	5	7	0	3	0	25	41	4	8	2.6	.943	SS-12, 3B-10, 2B-5
1977		6	.000	.000	1	0	0	0	0	0.0	2	0	0	0	0	1	0	1	2	0	0	1.0	1.000	SS-3
1978		2	1.000	2.000	1	1	1	0	0	0.0	0	0	0	0	0	1	1	0	1	0	0	0.5	1.000	SS-1, 3B-1
4 yrs.		81	.216	.257	167	36	5	1	0	0.0	18	13	12	15	0	7	1	65	150	17	25	3.3	.927	SS-54, 3B-11, 2B-6

Esteban Beltre

BELTRE, ESTEBAN
Born Esteban Beltre (Valera).
B. Dec. 26, 1967, Ingenio Quesqueya, Dominican Republic.

BR TR 5′10″ 155 lbs.

Year	Team	Games	BA	SA	AB	H	2B	3B	HR	HR%	R	RBI	BB	SO	SB	Pinch Hit AB	Pinch Hit H	PO	A	E	DP	TC/G	FA	G by Pos
1991	CHI A	8	.167	.167	6	1	0	0	0	0.0	0	0	1	1	1	0	0	1	5	0	1	0.8	1.000	SS-8
1992		49	.191	.236	110	21	2	0	1	0.9	21	10	3	18	1	0	0	53	92	12	12	3.3	.924	SS-43, DH-4
1994	TEX A	48	.282	.321	131	37	5	0	0	0.0	12	12	16	25	2	1	0	59	132	9	23	4.3	.955	SS-41, 3B-5, 2B-1
1995		54	.217	.304	92	20	8	0	0	0.0	7	7	4	15	0	2	2	55	79	5	19	2.7	.964	SS-36, 2B-15, 3B-1
4 yrs.		159	.233	.286	339	79	15	0	1	0.3	40	29	24	59	4	3	2	168	308	26	55	3.3	.948	SS-128, 2B-16, 3B-6, DH-4

Harry Bemis

BEMIS, HARRY PARKER
B. Feb. 1, 1874, Farmington, N. H. D. May 23, 1947, Cleveland, Ohio.

BR TR 5′ 6½″ 155 lbs.

Year	Team	Games	BA	SA	AB	H	2B	3B	HR	HR%	R	RBI	BB	SO	SB	Pinch Hit AB	Pinch Hit H	PO	A	E	DP	TC/G	FA	G by Pos
1902	CLE A	93	.312	.404	317	99	12	7	1	0.3	42	29	19		3	3	1	334	121	17	2	5.2	.964	C-87, OF-2, 2B-1
1903		92	.261	.354	314	82	20	3	1	0.3	31	41	8		5	8	3	414	86	6	9	6.0	.988	C-74, 1B-10, 2B-1
1904		97	.226	.295	336	76	11	6	0	0.0	35	25	8		6	4	1	497	90	26	14	6.6	.958	C-79, 1B-13, 2B-1
1905		69	.292	.376	226	66	13	3	0	0.0	27	28	13		3	4	1	268	72	9	4	5.4	.974	C-58, 2B-4, 3B-2, 1B-1
1906		93	.276	.374	297	82	13	5	2	0.7	28	30	12		8	12	2	340	73	16	7	5.3	.963	C-81
1907		65	.250	.291	172	43	7	0	0	0.0	12	19	7		5	12	4	206	42	10	6	4.9	.961	C-51, 1B-2
1908		91	.224	.264	277	62	9	1	0	0.0	23	33	7		14	12	1	337	75	15	5	5.5	.965	C-76, 1B-2
1909		42	.187	.252	123	23	2	3	0	0.0	4	13	0		2	5	2	167	33	6	0	5.7	.971	C-36
1910		61	.216	.275	167	36	5	1	1	0.6	11	16	5		3	12	3	186	63	10	4	5.6	.961	C-46
9 yrs.		703	.255	.329	2229	569	92	29	5	0.2	213	234	79		49	72	18	2749	655	115	51	5.6	.967	C-588, 1B-28, 2B-7, 3B-2, OF-2

Marvin Benard

BENARD, MARVIN LARRY
B. Jan. 20, 1971, Bluefields, Nicaragua.

BL TL 5′10″ 180 lbs.

Year	Team	Games	BA	SA	AB	H	2B	3B	HR	HR%	R	RBI	BB	SO	SB	Pinch Hit AB	Pinch Hit H	PO	A	E	DP	TC/G	FA	G by Pos
1995	SF N	13	.382	.529	34	13	2	0	1	2.9	5	4	1	7	1	5	1	19	0	0	0	2.7	1.000	OF-7

Freddie Benavides

BENAVIDES, ALFREDO
B. Apr. 7, 1966, Laredo, Tex.

BR TR 6′ 2″ 180 lbs.

Year	Team	Games	BA	SA	AB	H	2B	3B	HR	HR%	R	RBI	BB	SO	SB	Pinch Hit AB	Pinch Hit H	PO	A	E	DP	TC/G	FA	G by Pos
1991	CIN N	24	.286	.302	63	18	1	0	0	0.0	11	3	1	15	1	2	0	33	53	2	6	3.8	.977	SS-20, 2B-3
1992		74	.231	.318	173	40	10	1	1	0.6	14	17	10	34	0	11	3	80	129	6	26	3.0	.972	2B-37, SS-34, 3B-1

Freddie Benavides *continued*

Year	Team	Games	BA	SA	AB	H	2B	3B	HR	HR%	R	RBI	BB	SO	SB	Pinch Hit AB	Pinch Hit H	PO	A	E	DP	TC/G	FA	G by Pos
1993	CLR N	74	.286	.404	213	61	10	3	3	1.4	20	26	6	27	3	5	1	98	158	13	27	3.7	.952	SS-48, 2B-19, 3B-5, 1B-1
1994	MON N	47	.188	.271	85	16	5	1	0	0.0	8	6	3	15	0	8	3	52	47	2	12	2.1	.980	2B-36, 3B-5, SS-3, 1B-3
4 yrs.		219	.253	.343	534	135	26	5	4	0.7	53	52	20	91	4	26	7	263	387	23	71	3.1	.966	SS-105, 2B-95, 3B-11, 1B-4

Johnny Bench

BENCH, JOHNNY LEE
B. Dec. 7, 1947, Oklahoma City, Okla.
Hall of Fame 1989.

BR TR 6′ 1″ 197 lbs.

Year	Team	Games	BA	SA	AB	H	2B	3B	HR	HR%	R	RBI	BB	SO	SB	Pinch Hit AB	Pinch Hit H	PO	A	E	DP	TC/G	FA	G by Pos
1967	CIN N	26	.163	.256	86	14	3	1	1	1.2	7	6	5	19	0	0	0	175	16	1	0	7.4	.995	C-26
1968		154	.275	.433	564	155	40	2	15	2.7	67	82	31	96	1	2	0	942	102	9	10	6.8	.991	C-154
1969		148	.293	.487	532	156	23	1	26	4.9	83	90	49	86	6	10	2	793	76	7	10	6.0	.992	C-147
1970		158	.293	.587	605	177	35	4	**45**	7.4	97	**148**	54	102	5	4	1	854	78	15	19	5.4	.984	C-139, OF-24, 1B-12, 3B-1
1971		149	.238	.423	562	134	19	2	27	4.8	80	61	49	83	2	2	0	735	67	10	16	4.8	.988	C-141, OF-12, 1B-12, 3B-3
1972		147	.270	.541	538	145	22	2	**40**	7.4	87	**125**	100	84	6	0	0	791	63	10	10	5.5	.988	C-129, OF-17, 1B-7, 3B-4
1973		152	.253	.429	557	141	17	3	25	4.5	83	104	83	83	4	1	0	757	63	6	10	5.1	.993	C-134, OF-23, 1B-4, 3B-1
1974		160	.280	.507	621	174	38	2	33	5.3	108	**129**	80	90	5	1	0	794	123	9	18	5.2	.990	C-137, 3B-36, 1B-5
1975		142	.283	.519	530	150	39	1	28	5.3	83	110	65	108	11	5	1	646	52	8	11	4.7	.989	C-121, OF-19, 1B-9
1976		135	.234	.394	465	109	24	1	16	3.4	62	74	81	95	13	8	1	655	60	4	11	5.4	.994	C-128, OF-5, 1B-1
1977		142	.275	.540	494	136	34	2	31	6.3	67	109	58	95	2	2	0	735	69	12	13	5.5	.985	C-135, OF-8, 1B-4, 3B-1
1978		120	.260	.483	393	102	17	1	23	5.9	52	73	50	83	4	11	2	680	53	9	13	6.2	.988	C-107, 1B-11, OF-2
1979		130	.276	.459	464	128	19	0	22	4.7	73	80	67	73	4	4	0	632	69	10	12	5.6	.986	C-126, 1B-2
1980		114	.250	.483	360	90	12	0	24	6.7	52	68	41	64	4	13	2	505	39	5	7	5.2	.991	C-105
1981		52	.309	.489	178	55	8	0	8	4.5	14	25	17	21	0	8	3	375	28	7	35	9.1	.983	1B-38, C-7
1982		119	.258	.396	399	103	16	0	13	3.3	44	38	37	58	1	9	1	108	159	19	17	2.5	.934	3B-107, 1B-8, C-1
1983		110	.255	.432	310	79	15	2	12	3.9	32	54	24	38	0	34	9	292	74	10	26	4.7	.973	3B-42, 1B-32, C-5, OF-1
17 yrs.		2158	.267	.476	7658	2048	381	24	389	5.1	1091	1376	891	1278	68	114	22	10469	1191	151	238	5.4	.987	C-1742, 3B-195, 1B-145, OF-111

LEAGUE CHAMPIONSHIP SERIES

Year	Team	Games	BA	SA	AB	H	2B	3B	HR	HR%	R	RBI	BB	SO	SB	Pinch Hit AB	Pinch Hit H	PO	A	E	DP	TC/G	FA	G by Pos
1970	CIN N	3	.222	.556	9	2	0	0	1	11.1	2	1	3	1	0	0	0	20	3	0	0	7.7	1.000	C-3
1972		5	.333	.667	18	6	1	1	1	5.6	3	2	1	3	2	0	0	28	3	1	1	6.4	.969	C-5
1973		5	.263	.526	19	5	2	0	1	5.3	1	1	2	2	0	0	0	31	2	0	0	6.6	1.000	C-5
1975		3	.077	.077	13	1	0	0	0	0.0	1	0	1	6	1	0	0	18	4	0	0	7.3	1.000	C-3
1976		3	.333	.667	12	4	1	0	1	8.3	3	1	1	2	1	0	0	11	4	0	1	5.0	1.000	C-3
1979		3	.250	.667	12	3	0	1	1	8.3	1	1	2	2	0	0	0	17	2	0	0	6.3	1.000	C-3
6 yrs.		22	.253	.530	83	21	4	2	5	6.0	11	6	10	16	4	0	0	125	18	1	2	6.5	.993	C-22
				10th				**4th**	**4th**															

WORLD SERIES

Year	Team	Games	BA	SA	AB	H	2B	3B	HR	HR%	R	RBI	BB	SO	SB	Pinch Hit AB	Pinch Hit H	PO	A	E	DP	TC/G	FA	G by Pos
1970	CIN N	5	.211	.368	19	4	0	0	1	5.3	3	3	1	2	0	0	0	36	3	0	1	7.8	1.000	C-5
1972		7	.261	.435	23	6	1	0	1	4.3	4	1	5	5	2	0	0	41	7	1	2	7.0	.980	C-7
1975		7	.207	.379	29	6	2	0	1	3.4	5	4	2	4	0	0	0	44	6	0	3	7.1	1.000	C-7
1976		4	.533	1.133	15	8	1	1	2	13.3	4	6	0	1	0	0	0	18	2	0	0	5.0	1.000	C-4
4 yrs.		23	.279	.523	86	24	4	1	5	5.8	16	14	8	12	2	0	0	139	18	1	6	6.9	.994	C-23

Chief Bender

BENDER, CHARLES ALBERT
B. May 5, 1884, Crow Wing County, Minn. D. May 22, 1954, Philadelphia, Pa.
Hall of Fame 1953.

BR TR 6′ 2″ 185 lbs.

Year	Team	Games	BA	SA	AB	H	2B	3B	HR	HR%	R	RBI	BB	SO	SB	Pinch Hit AB	Pinch Hit H	PO	A	E	DP	TC/G	FA	G by Pos
1903	PHI A	43	.183	.233	120	22	4	1	0	0.0	10	8	3		3	3	2	37	80	10	2	3.2	.921	P-36, 1B-3, OF-1
1904		31	.228	.316	79	18	3	2	0	0.0	8	5	5		3	1	0	13	48	7	0	2.3	.897	P-29
1905		38	.217	.293	92	20	3	2	0	0.0	11	14	3		3	3	0	14	77	3	2	2.7	.968	P-35
1906		44	.253	.384	99	25	4	0	3	3.0	9	13	9		2	2	0	32	54	8	1	2.3	.915	P-36, OF-4
1907		45	.230	.310	100	23	6	1	0	0.0	10	8	5		2	7	1	32	57	8	2	2.6	.918	P-33, 1B-2, 2B-1, OF-1
1908		20	.220	.240	50	11	1	0	0	0.0	5	2	10		1	1	0	25	31	3	1	3.1	.949	P-18, 1B-1
1909		40	.215	.269	93	20	5	0	0	0.0	6	9	5		1	5	1	13	78	4	1	2.8	.958	P-34
1910		36	.269	.344	93	25	3	2	0	0.0	6	16	6		0	6	1	13	85	3	3	3.4	.970	P-30
1911		32	.165	.165	79	13	0	0	0	0.0	9	8	2		2	1	0	11	58	0	4	2.2	1.000	P-31
1912		27	.150	.200	60	9	1	1	0	0.0	5	4	6		2	0	0	6	36	2	2	1.6	.955	P-27
1913		48	.154	.218	78	12	3	1	0	0.0	7	10	6	17	1	0	0	8	55	2	1	1.4	.969	P-48
1914		28	.145	.210	62	9	1	0	1	1.6	4	8	4	13	0	0	0	7	47	2	0	2.0	.964	P-28
1915	BAL F	26	.267	.350	60	16	2	0	1	1.7	7	2	6		0	0	0	12	45	4	3	2.3	.934	P-26
1916	PHI N	28	.279	.372	43	12	4	0	0	0.0	2	5	3	9	0	0	0	9	40	2	1	1.8	.961	P-27, 3B-1
1917		20	.205	.282	39	8	0	0	1	2.6	3	4	2	3	0	0	0	5	22	1	4	1.4	.964	P-20
1925	CHI A	1	—	—	0	0	0	0	0	—	0	0	0	0	0	0	0	0	0	0	0	0.0	.000	P-1
16 yrs.		507	.212	.280	1147	243	40	10	6	0.5	102	116	75	42	20	29	5	237	813	59	27	2.3	.947	P-459, 1B-6, OF-6, 3B-1, 2B-1

WORLD SERIES

Year	Team	Games	BA	SA	AB	H	2B	3B	HR	HR%	R	RBI	BB	SO	SB	Pinch Hit AB	Pinch Hit H	PO	A	E	DP	TC/G	FA	G by Pos
1905	PHI A	2	.000	.000	5	0	0	0	0	0.0	0	0	0	1	0	0	0	1	6	0	0	3.5	1.000	P-2
1910		2	.333	.333	6	2	0	0	0	0.0	1	1	1	1	0	0	0	1	2	0	1	1.5	1.000	P-2
1911		3	.091	.091	11	1	0	0	0	0.0	0	0	0	1	0	0	0	1	6	0	0	2.3	1.000	P-3
1913		2	.000	.000	8	0	0	0	0	0.0	0	1	0	1	0	0	0	0	5	0	0	2.5	1.000	P-2
1914		1	.000	.000	2	0	0	0	0	0.0	0	0	0	0	0	0	0	1	3	0	2	4.0	1.000	P-1
5 yrs.		10	.094	.094	32	3	0	0	0	0.0	1	2	1	4	0	0	0	4	22	0	3	2.6	1.000	P-10

Art Benedict

BENEDICT, ARTHUR MELVILLE
B. Mar. 31, 1862, Cornwall, Ill. D. Jan. 20, 1948, Blue Rapids, Kans.

BR TR

Year	Team	Games	BA	SA	AB	H	2B	3B	HR	HR%	R	RBI	BB	SO	SB	Pinch Hit AB	Pinch Hit H	PO	A	E	DP	TC/G	FA	G by Pos
1883	PHI N	3	.267	.333	15	4	1	0	0	0.0	3		0	4		0	0	3	5	6	0	4.7	.571	2B-3

Bruce Benedict

BENEDICT, BRUCE EDWIN
B. Aug. 18, 1955, Birmingham, Ala.

BR TR 6′ 1″ 175 lbs.

Year	Team	Games	BA	SA	AB	H	2B	3B	HR	HR%	R	RBI	BB	SO	SB	Pinch Hit AB	Pinch Hit H	PO	A	E	DP	TC/G	FA	G by Pos
1978	ATL N	22	.250	.288	52	13	2	0	0	0.0	3	1	6	6	0	0	0	81	14	1	1	4.4	.990	C-22
1979		76	.225	.279	204	46	11	0	0	0.0	14	15	33	18	1	1	0	344	35	6	3	5.1	.984	C-76
1980		120	.253	.315	359	91	14	1	2	0.6	18	34	28	36	3	0	0	502	76	7	6	4.9	.988	C-120

Bruce Benedict *continued*

Year	Team	Games	BA	SA	AB	H	2B	3B	HR	HR%	R	RBI	BB	SO	SB	Pinch Hit AB	Pinch Hit H	PO	A	E	DP	TC/G	FA	G by Pos
1981		90	.264	.363	295	78	12	1	5	1.7	26	35	33	21	1	0	0	404	73	7	7	5.4	.986	C-90
1982		118	.246	.303	386	95	11	1	3	0.8	34	44	37	40	4	1	0	602	73	5	9	5.8	.993	C-118
1983		134	.298	.348	423	126	13	1	2	0.5	43	43	61	24	1	0	0	738	91	7	12	6.2	.992	C-134
1984		95	.223	.297	300	67	8	1	4	1.3	26	25	34	25	1	0	0	504	37	5	2	5.7	.991	C-95
1985		70	.202	.231	208	42	6	0	0	0.0	12	20	22	12	0	0	0	314	35	4	1	5.0	.989	C-70
1986		64	.225	.300	160	36	10	1	0	0.0	11	13	15	10	1	7	4	252	28	2	1	4.9	.993	C-57
1987		37	.147	.189	95	14	1	0	1	1.1	4	5	17	15	0	2	0	165	21	2	3	5.4	.989	C-35
1988		90	.242	.271	236	57	7	0	0	0.0	11	19	19	26	0	3	1	384	54	5	3	5.0	.989	C-89
1989		66	.194	.231	160	31	3	0	1	0.6	12	6	23	18	0	1	0	361	40	2	2	6.2	.995	C-65
12 yrs.		982	.242	.299	2878	696	98	6	18	0.6	214	260	328	251	12	15	5	4651	577	53	50	5.4	.990	C-971
LEAGUE CHAMPIONSHIP SERIES																								
1982	ATL N	3	.250	.375	8	2	1	0	0	0.0	1	0	2	1	0	0	0	16	2	0	0	6.0	1.000	C-3

Joe Benes

BENES, JOSEPH ANTHONY (Bananas) BR TR 5′ 8½″ 158 lbs.
B. Jan. 8, 1901, Long Island City, N. Y. D. Mar. 7, 1975, Elmhurst, N. Y.

Year	Team	Games	BA	SA	AB	H	2B	3B	HR	HR%	R	RBI	BB	SO	SB	Pinch Hit AB	Pinch Hit H	PO	A	E	DP	TC/G	FA	G by Pos
1931	STL N	10	.167	.167	12	2	0	0	0	0.0	1	0	2	1	0	0	0	8	13	1	1	2.4	.955	SS-6, 2B-2, 3B-1

Benny Bengough

BENGOUGH, BERNARD OLIVER BR TR 5′ 7½″ 168 lbs.
B. July 27, 1898, Niagara Falls, N. Y. D. Dec. 22, 1968, Philadelphia, Pa.

Year	Team	Games	BA	SA	AB	H	2B	3B	HR	HR%	R	RBI	BB	SO	SB	Pinch Hit AB	Pinch Hit H	PO	A	E	DP	TC/G	FA	G by Pos
1923	NY A	19	.132	.170	53	7	2	0	0	0.0	1	3	4	2	0	0	0	58	14	2	2	3.9	.973	C-19
1924		11	.313	.500	16	5	1	1	0	0.0	4	3	2	0	0	0	0	34	3	0	3	3.4	1.000	C-11
1925		95	.258	.322	283	73	14	2	0	0.0	17	23	19	9	0	1	0	325	83	3	12	4.4	.993	C-94
1926		36	.381	.452	84	32	6	0	0	0.0	9	14	7	4	1	1	0	107	36	4	2	4.2	.973	C-35
1927		31	.247	.353	85	21	3	3	0	0.0	6	10	4	4	0	1	0	114	31	2	0	4.9	.986	C-30
1928		58	.267	.298	161	43	3	1	0	0.0	12	9	7	8	0	0	0	206	37	2	7	4.2	.992	C-58
1929		23	.194	.258	62	12	2	1	0	0.0	5	7	0	2	0	0	0	47	8	1	1	2.4	.982	C-23
1930		44	.235	.314	102	24	4	2	0	0.0	10	12	3	8	1	0	0	171	18	2	2	4.3	.990	C-44
1931	STL A	40	.250	.293	140	35	4	1	0	0.0	6	12	4	4	0	3	0	119	26	2	6	4.0	.986	C-37
1932		54	.252	.317	139	35	7	1	0	0.0	13	15	12	4	0	5	1	153	30	2	7	3.9	.989	C-47
10 yrs.		411	.255	.317	1125	287	46	12	0	0.0	83	108	62	45	2	11	1	1334	286	20	42	4.1	.988	C-398
WORLD SERIES																								
1927	NY A	2	.000	.000	4	0	0	0	0	0.0	1	0	1	0	0	0	0	4	0	0	0	2.0	1.000	C-2
1928		4	.231	.231	13	3	0	0	0	0.0	1	1	1	1	0	0	0	33	2	0	0	8.8	1.000	C-4
2 yrs.		6	.176	.176	17	3	0	0	0	0.0	2	1	2	1	0	0	0	37	2	0	0	6.5	1.000	C-6

Juan Beniquez

BENIQUEZ, JUAN JOSE BR TR 5′11″ 150 lbs.
Born Juan Jose Beniquez (Torres).
B. May 13, 1950, San Sebastian, Puerto Rico.

Year	Team	Games	BA	SA	AB	H	2B	3B	HR	HR%	R	RBI	BB	SO	SB	Pinch Hit AB	Pinch Hit H	PO	A	E	DP	TC/G	FA	G by Pos
1971	BOS A	16	.298	.333	57	17	2	0	0	0.0	8	4	3	4	3	0	0	24	27	6	5	3.8	.895	SS-15
1972		33	.242	.333	99	24	4	1	1	1.0	10	8	7	11	2	3	1	38	88	14	19	5.2	.900	SS-27
1974		106	.267	.357	389	104	14	3	5	1.3	60	33	25	61	19	8	0	264	4	6	2	2.7	.978	OF-97, DH-4
1975		78	.291	.402	254	74	14	4	2	0.8	43	17	25	26	7	8	5	110	17	1	2	1.6	.992	OF-44, DH-20, 3B-14
1976	TEX A	145	.255	.301	478	122	14	4	0	0.0	49	33	39	56	17	4	1	411	18	7	3	3.1	.984	OF-141, 2B-1
1977		123	.269	.413	424	114	19	6	10	2.4	56	50	43	43	26	0	0	311	10	4	1	2.6	.988	OF-123
1978		127	.260	.378	473	123	17	3	11	2.3	61	50	20	59	10	2	0	309	8	9	1	2.6	.972	OF-126
1979	NY A	62	.254	.394	142	36	6	1	4	2.8	19	17	9	17	3	1	0	100	15	2	0	1.9	.983	OF-60, 3B-3
1980	SEA A	70	.228	.346	237	54	10	0	6	2.5	26	21	17	25	2	5	0	176	3	8	0	2.8	.957	OF-65, DH-1
1981	CAL A	58	.181	.265	166	30	5	0	3	1.8	18	13	15	16	2	2	0	117	0	5	0	2.2	.959	OF-55, DH-1
1982		112	.265	.388	196	52	11	2	3	1.5	25	24	15	21	3	3	1	113	4	2	1	1.1	.983	OF-107
1983		92	.305	.381	315	96	15	0	3	1.0	44	34	15	29	4	3	1	174	8	6	1	2.1	.968	OF-84, DH-6
1984		110	.336	.452	354	119	17	0	8	2.3	60	39	18	43	0	10	3	197	5	6	1	2.1	.971	OF-98
1985		132	.304	.418	411	125	13	5	8	1.9	54	42	34	47	4	24	5	439	26	4	42	3.5	.991	OF-71, 1B-46, DH-14, SS-1, 3B-1
1986	BAL A	113	.300	.397	343	103	15	0	6	1.7	48	36	40	49	2	19	9	211	56	13	15	2.6	.954	OF-54, 3B-25, DH-16, 1B-14
1987	2 teams	KC A (57G –.236)	TOR A (39G –.284)																					
″	total	96	.251	.400	255	64	12	1	8	3.1	20	47	16	39	0	23	6	97	5	2	6	1.8	.981	OF-29, DH-15, 1B-8, 3B-6
1988	TOR A	27	.293	.379	58	17	2	0	1	1.7	9	8	8	6	0	8	2	0	0	0	0	0.0		DH-19, OF-1
17 yrs.		1500	.274	.379	4651	1274	190	30	79	1.7	610	476	349	552	104	123	34	3091	294	95	99	2.5	.973	OF-1155, DH-96, 1B-68, 3B-49, SS-43, 2B-1
LEAGUE CHAMPIONSHIP SERIES																								
1975	BOS A	3	.250	.250	12	3	0	0	0	0.0	2	1	0	1	2	0	0	0	0	0	0	0.0	.000	DH-3
1982	CAL A	2	—	—	0	0	0	0	0	—	0	0	0	0	0	0	0	1	0	0	0	0.5	1.000	OF-2
2 yrs.		5	.250	.250	12	3	0	0	0	0.0	2	1	0	1	2	0	0	1	0	0	0	0.2	1.000	DH-3, OF-2
WORLD SERIES																								
1975	BOS A	3	.125	.125	8	1	0	0	0	0.0	0	1	1	1	0	1	0	6	1	0	0	3.5	1.000	OF-2

Yamil Benitez

BENITEZ, YAMIL ANTONIO BR TR 6′ 2″ 195 lbs.
B. Oct. 5, 1972, San Juan, Puerto Rico.

Year	Team	Games	BA	SA	AB	H	2B	3B	HR	HR%	R	RBI	BB	SO	SB	Pinch Hit AB	Pinch Hit H	PO	A	E	DP	TC/G	FA	G by Pos
1995	MON N	14	.385	.641	39	15	2	1	2	5.1	8	7	1	7	0	2	0	18	1	1	0	1.4	.950	OF-14

Mike Benjamin

BENJAMIN, MICHAEL PAUL BR TR 6′ 3″ 195 lbs.
B. Nov. 22, 1965, Euclid, Ohio.

Year	Team	Games	BA	SA	AB	H	2B	3B	HR	HR%	R	RBI	BB	SO	SB	Pinch Hit AB	Pinch Hit H	PO	A	E	DP	TC/G	FA	G by Pos
1989	SF N	14	.167	.167	6	1	0	0	0	0.0	6	0	0	1	0	1	1	4	4	0	0	1.0	1.000	SS-8
1990		22	.214	.411	56	12	3	1	2	3.6	7	3	3	10	1	2	0	29	53	1	10	4.0	.988	SS-21
1991		54	.123	.208	106	13	3	0	2	1.9	12	8	7	26	3	2	1	64	123	3	23	3.7	.984	SS-51, 3B-1
1992		40	.173	.267	75	13	2	1	1	1.3	4	3	4	15	1	2	0	34	71	1	13	3.0	.991	SS-33, 3B-2
1993		63	.199	.329	146	29	7	0	4	2.7	22	16	9	23	0	0	0	74	133	5	33	3.4	.976	2B-23, SS-23, 3B-16
1994		38	.258	.419	62	16	5	1	1	1.6	9	9	5	16	5	0	0	33	69	3	14	3.2	.971	SS-18, 2B-10, 3B-5
1995		68	.220	.301	186	41	6	0	3	1.6	19	12	8	51	11	4	0	51	121	4	9	2.6	.977	3B-43, SS-16, 2B-8
7 yrs.		299	.196	.308	637	125	26	3	13	2.0	79	51	36	142	21	11	2	289	574	17	102	3.2	.981	SS-170, 3B-67, 2B-41

Stan Benjamin

BENJAMIN, ALFRED STANLEY
B. May 20, 1914, Framingham, Mass.

BR TR 6′ 2″ 194 lbs.

Year	Team	Games	BA	SA	AB	H	2B	3B	HR	HR%	R	RBI	BB	SO	SB	Pinch Hit AB	Pinch Hit H	PO	A	E	DP	TC/G	FA	G by Pos
1939	PHI N	13	.140	.220	50	7	2	1	0	0.0	4	2	1	6	1	0	0	18	12	4	1	2.8	.882	OF-7, 3B-5
1940		8	.222	.222	9	2	0	0	0	0.0	1	1	1	1	0	4	1	3	1	0	0	2.0	1.000	OF-2
1941		129	.235	.325	480	113	20	7	3	0.6	47	27	20	81	17	9	1	254	18	5	8	2.3	.982	OF-110, 1B-8, 2B-2, 3B-1
1942		78	.224	.319	210	47	8	3	2	1.0	24	8	10	27	5	15	4	174	13	5	12	3.2	.974	OF-45, 1B-15
1945	CLE A	14	.333	.429	21	7	2	0	0	0.0	1	3	0	0	0	10	3	9	2	0	0	2.8	1.000	OF-4
5 yrs.		242	.229	.318	770	176	32	11	5	0.6	77	41	32	115	23	38	9	458	46	14	21	2.6	.973	OF-168, 1B-23, 3B-6, 2B-2

Ike Benners

BENNERS, ISAAC B. (Windy)
B. June 7, 1856, Philadelphia, Pa. D. Apr. 18, 1932, Philadelphia, Pa.

BL 175 lbs.

Year	Team	Games	BA	SA	AB	H	2B	3B	HR	HR%	R	RBI	BB	SO	SB	Pinch Hit AB	Pinch Hit H	PO	A	E	DP	TC/G	FA	G by Pos
1884	2 teams	BKN AA (49G –.201) WIL U (6G –.045)																						
″	total	55	.185	.299	211	39	11	5	1	0.5	25		8			0	0	76	2	18	1	1.7	.813	OF-54, 1B-1

Charlie Bennett

BENNETT, CHARLES WESLEY
B. Nov. 21, 1854, New Castle, Pa. D. Feb. 24, 1927, Detroit, Mich.

BR TR 5′11″ 180 lbs.

Year	Team	Games	BA	SA	AB	H	2B	3B	HR	HR%	R	RBI	BB	SO	SB	Pinch Hit AB	Pinch Hit H	PO	A	E	DP	TC/G	FA	G by Pos
1878	MIL N	49	.245	.310	184	45	9	0	1	0.5	16	12	10	26		0	0	197	33	51	4	5.1	.819	C-35, OF-20
1880	WOR N	51	.228	.306	193	44	9	3	0	0.0	20	18	10	30		0	0	291	47	32	4	7.1	.914	C-46, OF-6
1881	DET N	76	.301	.478	299	90	18	7	7	2.3	44	64	18	37		0	0	432	102	25	8	7.2	.955	C-70, 3B-5, OF-3
1882		84	.301	.450	342	103	16	10	5	1.5	43	51	20	33		0	0	493	111	39	12	7.6	.939	C-65, 3B-11, 2B-7, 1B-1, SS-1
1883		92	.305	.474	371	113	34	7	5	1.3	56		26	59		0	0	382	124	38	17	5.5	.930	C-72, 2B-15, OF-12
1884		89	.264	.380	337	89	18	6	3	0.9	36		36	40		0	0	463	113	60	10	7.0	.906	C-79, OF-5, SS-4, 3B-1, 2B-1, 1B-1
1885		91	.269	.456	349	94	24	13	5	1.4	49	60	47	37		0	0	379	106	49	13	5.9	.908	C-62, OF-19, 3B-10
1886		72	.243	.396	235	57	13	4	5	2.1	37	34	48	29		0	0	432	86	24	14	7.3	.956	C-69, OF-4, SS-1
1887		46	.244	.400	160	39	6	5	3	1.9	26	20	30	22	7	0	0	201	58	13	11	5.8	.952	C-45, 1B-1, OF-1
1888		74	.264	.399	258	68	12	4	5	1.9	32	29	31	40	4	0	0	428	94	18	10	7.3	.967	C-73, 1B-1
1889	BOS N	82	.231	.328	247	57	8	2	4	1.6	42	28	21	43	7	0	0	419	74	23	9	6.3	.955	C-82
1890		85	.214	.320	281	60	17	2	3	1.1	59	40	72	56	6	0	0	448	90	23	8	6.6	.959	C-85
1891		75	.215	.332	256	55	9	3	5	2.0	35	39	42	61	3	0	0	383	75	19	10	6.4	.960	C-75
1892		35	.202	.263	114	23	4	0	1	0.9	19	16	27	23	6	0	0	169	31	11	3	6.0	.948	C-35
1893		60	.209	.304	191	40	6	0	4	2.1	34	27	40	36	5	0	0	204	40	12	1	4.3	.953	C-60
15 yrs.		1061	.256	.388	3817	977	203	66	56	1.5	548	438	478	572	38	0	0	5321	1184	437	134	6.4	.937	C-953, OF-70, 3B-27, 2B-23, SS-6, 1B-4

Fred Bennett

BENNETT, JAMES FRED (Red)
B. Mar. 15, 1902, Atkins, Ark. D. May 12, 1957, Atkins, Ark.

BR TR 5′ 9″ 185 lbs.

Year	Team	Games	BA	SA	AB	H	2B	3B	HR	HR%	R	RBI	BB	SO	SB	Pinch Hit AB	Pinch Hit H	PO	A	E	DP	TC/G	FA	G by Pos
1928	STL A	7	.250	.375	8	2	1	0	0	0.0	0	0	0	2	0	6	1	2	0	0	0	2.0	1.000	OF-1
1931	PIT N	32	.281	.371	89	25	5	0	1	1.1	6	7	7	4	0	9	2	36	3	2	0	2.0	.951	OF-21
2 yrs.		39	.278	.371	97	27	6	0	1	1.0	6	7	7	6	0	15	3	38	3	2	0	2.0	.953	OF-22

Gary Bennett

BENNETT, GARY DAVID
B. Apr. 17, 1972, Waukegan, Ill.

BR TR 6′ 190 lbs.

Year	Team	Games	BA	SA	AB	H	2B	3B	HR	HR%	R	RBI	BB	SO	SB	Pinch Hit AB	Pinch Hit H	PO	A	E	DP	TC/G	FA	G by Pos
1995	PHI N	1	.000	.000	1	0	0	0	0	0.0	0	0	0	1	0	1	0	0	0	0	0	0.0	—	

Herschel Bennett

BENNETT, HERSCHEL EMMETT
B. Sept. 21, 1896, Elwood, Mo. D. Sept. 9, 1964, Springfield, Mo.

BL TR 5′ 9½″ 160 lbs.

Year	Team	Games	BA	SA	AB	H	2B	3B	HR	HR%	R	RBI	BB	SO	SB	Pinch Hit AB	Pinch Hit H	PO	A	E	DP	TC/G	FA	G by Pos
1923	STL A	5	.000	.000	4	0	0	0	0	0.0	0	0	1	1	0	3	0	1	0	0	0	1.0	1.000	OF-1
1924		41	.330	.468	94	31	4	3	1	1.1	16	11	3	6	1	18	6	26	2	1	0	1.4	.966	OF-21
1925		98	.279	.376	298	83	11	6	2	0.7	46	37	18	16	4	16	9	140	12	14	1	2.3	.916	OF-73
1926		80	.267	.360	225	60	14	2	1	0.4	33	26	22	21	2	28	**12**	106	9	6	3	2.4	.950	OF-50
1927		93	.266	.363	256	68	12	2	3	1.2	40	30	14	21	6	30	5	118	5	7	1	2.4	.946	OF-55
5 yrs.		317	.276	.376	877	242	41	13	7	0.8	135	104	58	65	13	95	32	391	28	28	5	2.2	.937	OF-200

Joe Bennett

BENNETT, JOSEPH ROSENBLUM
B. July 2, 1900, New York, N. Y. D. July 11, 1987, Morro Bay, Calif.

BR TR 5′ 9″ 168 lbs.

Year	Team	Games	BA	SA	AB	H	2B	3B	HR	HR%	R	RBI	BB	SO	SB	Pinch Hit AB	Pinch Hit H	PO	A	E	DP	TC/G	FA	G by Pos
1923	PHI N	1	—	—	0	0	0	0	0	—	0	0	0	0	0	0	0	0	1	0	0	1.0	1.000	3B-1

Pug Bennett

BENNETT, JUSTIN TITUS
B. Feb. 20, 1874, Ponca, Neb. D. Sept. 12, 1935, Kirkland, Wash.

BR TR 5′11″ 165 lbs.

Year	Team	Games	BA	SA	AB	H	2B	3B	HR	HR%	R	RBI	BB	SO	SB	Pinch Hit AB	Pinch Hit H	PO	A	E	DP	TC/G	FA	G by Pos
1906	STL N	153	.262	.318	**595**	156	16	7	1	0.2	66	34	56		20	0	0	295	447	41	43	5.1	.948	2B-153
1907		87	.222	.259	324	72	8	2	0	0.0	20	21	21		7	1	0	178	214	25	27	4.8	.940	2B-83, 3B-3
2 yrs.		240	.248	.297	919	228	24	9	1	0.1	86	55	77		27	1	0	473	661	66	70	5.0	.945	2B-236, 3B-3

Vern Benson

BENSON, VERNON ADAIR
B. Sept. 19, 1924, Granite Quarry, N. C.
Manager 1977.

BL TR 5′10″ 160 lbs.

Year	Team	Games	BA	SA	AB	H	2B	3B	HR	HR%	R	RBI	BB	SO	SB	Pinch Hit AB	Pinch Hit H	PO	A	E	DP	TC/G	FA	G by Pos
1943	PHI A	2	.000	.000	2	0	0	0	0	0.0	0	0	0	0	0	2	0	0	0	0	0	0.0	—	
1946		7	.000	.000	5	0	0	0	0	0.0	1	0	1	3	0	0	0	4	0	0	0	2.0	1.000	OF-2
1951	STL N	13	.261	.435	46	12	3	1	1	2.2	8	7	6	8	0	0	0	10	19	2	3	2.4	.935	3B-9, OF-4
1952		20	.191	.362	47	9	2	0	2	4.3	6	5	5	9	0	5	2	5	27	4	3	2.4	.889	3B-15
1953		13	.000	.000	4	0	0	0	0	0.0	2	0	1	2	0	4	0	0	0	0	0	0.0	—	
5 yrs.		55	.202	.356	104	21	5	1	3	2.9	17	12	13	22	0	11	2	19	46	6	6	2.4	.915	3B-24, OF-6

Jack Bentley

BENTLEY, JOHN NEEDLES
B. Mar. 8, 1895, Sandy Spring, Md. D. Oct. 24, 1969, Olney, Md.

BL TL 5′11½″ 200 lbs.

Year	Team	Games	BA	SA	AB	H	2B	3B	HR	HR%	R	RBI	BB	SO	SB	Pinch Hit AB	Pinch Hit H	PO	A	E	DP	TC/G	FA	G by Pos
1913	WAS A	3	.000	.000	3	0	0	0	0	0.0	0	0	0	0	0	0	0	0	5	0	0	1.7	1.000	P-3
1914		30	.275	.325	40	11	2	0	0	0.0	7	4	0	5	0	0	0	9	33	3	1	1.5	.933	P-30
1915		4	.000	.000	2	0	0	0	0	0.0	0	0	0	1	0	0	0	1	2	1	0	1.0	.750	P-4
1916		2	—	—	0	0	0	0	0	—	0	0	0	0	0	0	0	0	1	0	0	0.5	1.000	P-2
1923	NY N	52	.427	.573	89	38	6	2	1	1.1	9	14	3	4	0	20	**10**	5	38	1	1	1.4	.977	P-31
1924		46	.265	.337	98	26	5	1	0	0.0	12	6	3	13	0	18	4	3	43	1	3	1.7	.979	P-28
1925		64	.303	.485	99	30	5	2	3	3.0	10	18	9	11	0	**28**	**9**	13	33	3	2	1.5	.939	P-28, OF-3, 1B-1

Jack Bentley *continued*

Year	Team	Games	BA	SA	AB	H	2B	3B	HR	HR%	R	RBI	BB	SO	SB	Pinch Hit AB	Pinch Hit H	PO	A	E	DP	TC/G	FA	G by Pos
1926	2 teams	PHI N (75G –.258) NY N (3G –.250)																						
"	total	78	.258	.357	244	63	12	3	2	0.8	19	27	5	4	0	16	2	516	33	4	41	8.6	.993	1B-56, P-8
1927	NY N	8	.222	.556	9	2	0	0	1	11.1	1	2	1	1	0	1	0	10	2	1	0	2.2	.923	P-4, 1B-2
9 yrs.		287	.291	.406	584	170	30	8	7	1.2	58	71	21	39	0	83	25	557	190	14	48	3.8	.982	P-138, 1B-59, OF-3
WORLD SERIES																								
1923	NY N	5	.600	.800	5	3	1	0	0	0.0	0	0	0	0	0	3	2	0	2	0	0	1.0	1.000	P-2
1924		5	.286	.714	7	2	0	0	1	14.3	1	2	1	1	0	1	0	1	3	0	0	1.3	1.000	P-3
2 yrs.		10	.417	.750	12	5	1	0	1	8.3	1	2	1	1	0	4	2	1	5	0	0	1.2	1.000	P-5

Butch Benton

BENTON, ALFRED LEE BR TR 6′ 1″ 190 lbs.
B. Aug. 24, 1957, Tampa, Fla.

Year	Team	Games	BA	SA	AB	H	2B	3B	HR	HR%	R	RBI	BB	SO	SB	Pinch Hit AB	Pinch Hit H	PO	A	E	DP	TC/G	FA	G by Pos
1978	NY N	4	.500	.500	4	2	0	0	0	0.0	1	2	0	0	0	1	0	4	0	0	0	4.0	1.000	C-1
1980		12	.048	.048	21	1	0	0	0	0.0	0	0	2	4	0	4	0	27	2	2	0	3.9	.935	C-8
1982	CHI N	4	.143	.143	7	1	0	0	0	0.0	0	1	0	1	0	0	0	20	1	0	0	5.3	1.000	C-4
1985	CLE A	31	.179	.239	67	12	4	0	0	0.0	5	7	3	9	0	4	1	75	13	4	1	3.5	.957	C-26
4 yrs.		51	.162	.202	99	16	4	0	0	0.0	6	10	5	14	0	9	1	126	16	6	1	3.8	.959	C-39

Stan Benton

BENTON, STANLEY W. (Rabbit) BR TR 5′ 7″ 150 lbs.
B. Sept. 29, 1901, Cannel City, Ky. D. June 7, 1984, Mesquite, Tex.

Year	Team	Games	BA	SA	AB	H	2B	3B	HR	HR%	R	RBI	BB	SO	SB	Pinch Hit AB	Pinch Hit H	PO	A	E	DP	TC/G	FA	G by Pos
1922	PHI N	6	.211	.263	19	4	1	0	0	0.0	1	3	2	1	0	1	0	14	18	4	0	7.2	.889	2B-5

Todd Benzinger

BENZINGER, TODD ERIC BB TR 6′ 1″ 185 lbs.
B. Feb. 11, 1963, Dayton, Ky.

Year	Team	Games	BA	SA	AB	H	2B	3B	HR	HR%	R	RBI	BB	SO	SB	Pinch Hit AB	Pinch Hit H	PO	A	E	DP	TC/G	FA	G by Pos
1987	BOS A	73	.278	.444	223	62	11	1	8	3.6	36	43	22	41	5	8	2	155	7	2	2	2.6	.988	OF-61, 1B-2
1988		120	.254	.425	405	103	28	1	13	3.2	47	70	22	80	2	7	3	602	38	6	47	4.8	.991	1B-85, OF-48, DH-1
1989	CIN N	161	.245	.381	**628**	154	28	3	17	2.7	79	76	44	120	3	3	1	1417	73	7	96	9.5	.995	1B-158
1990		118	.253	.340	376	95	14	2	5	1.3	35	46	19	69	3	15	0	733	52	6	58	7.5	.992	1B-95, OF-10
1991	2 teams	CIN N (51G –.187) KC A (78G –.294)																						
"	total	129	.262	.351	416	109	18	5	3	0.7	36	51	27	66	4	22	3	797	51	5	64	7.6	.994	1B-96, OF-15, DH-1
1992	LA N	121	.239	.348	293	70	16	2	4	1.4	24	31	15	54	2	48	13	263	18	1	17	3.0	.996	OF-51, 1B-42
1993	SF N	86	.288	.452	177	51	7	2	6	3.4	25	26	13	35	0	41	8	299	15	0	27	6.5	1.000	1B-40, OF-7, 3B-1
1994		107	.265	.399	328	87	13	2	9	2.7	32	31	17	84	2	14	5	781	55	5	69	8.5	.994	1B-99
1995		9	.200	.500	10	2	0	0	1	10.0	2	2	2	3	0	6	1	15	0	0	2	3.0	1.000	1B-5
9 yrs.		924	.257	.386	2856	733	135	18	66	2.3	316	376	181	552	21	164	36	5062	309	32	382	6.6	.994	1B-622, OF-192, DH-2, 3B-1
LEAGUE CHAMPIONSHIP SERIES																								
1988	BOS A	4	.091	.091	11	1	0	0	0	0.0	0	0	1	3	0	1	0	21	1	0	2	7.3	1.000	1B-3
1990	CIN N	5	.333	.333	9	3	0	0	0	0.0	0	0	2	0	0	2	2	17	0	0	0	8.5	1.000	1B-2
2 yrs.		9	.200	.200	20	4	0	0	0	0.0	0	0	3	3	0	3	2	38	1	0	2	7.8	1.000	1B-5
WORLD SERIES																								
1990	CIN N	4	.182	.182	11	2	0	0	0	0.0	1	0	0	0	0	1	0	24	0	0	1	8.0	1.000	1B-3

Johnny Berardino

BERARDINO, JOHN BR TR 5′11½″ 175 lbs.
B. May 1, 1917, Los Angeles, Calif.

Year	Team	Games	BA	SA	AB	H	2B	3B	HR	HR%	R	RBI	BB	SO	SB	Pinch Hit AB	Pinch Hit H	PO	A	E	DP	TC/G	FA	G by Pos
1939	STL A	126	.256	.361	468	120	24	5	5	1.1	42	58	37	36	6	2	1	325	363	33	71	5.8	.954	2B-114, 3B-8, SS-2
1940		142	.258	.424	523	135	31	4	16	3.1	71	85	32	46	6	8	2	297	399	42	96	5.5	.943	SS-112, 2B-13, 3B-9
1941		128	.271	.384	469	127	30	4	5	1.1	48	89	41	27	3	4	0	262	305	27	81	4.8	.955	SS-123, 3B-1
1942		29	.284	.405	74	21	6	0	1	1.4	11	10	4	2	3	8	1	65	32	4	13	4.8	.960	3B-6, SS-6, 1B-5, 2B-4
1946		144	.265	.357	582	154	29	5	5	0.9	70	68	34	58	2	1	0	374	414	23	96	5.7	.972	2B-143
1947		90	.261	.350	306	80	22	1	1	0.3	29	20	44	26	6	2	0	242	221	11	61	5.5	.977	2B-86
1948	CLE A	66	.190	.279	147	28	5	1	2	1.4	19	10	27	16	0	11	2	199	85	3	34	5.4	.990	2B-20, 1B-18, SS-12, 3B-3
1949		50	.198	.267	116	23	6	1	0	0.0	11	13	14	14	0	14	2	38	68	6	7	3.1	.946	3B-25, 2B-8, SS-3
1950	2 teams	CLE A (4G –.400) PIT N (40G –.206)																						
"	total	44	.213	.272	136	29	3	1	1	0.7	13	15	20	11	0	3	2	94	118	7	29	5.3	.968	2B-37, 3B-4
1951	STL A	39	.227	.303	119	27	7	1	0	0.0	13	13	17	18	1	3	0	47	47	9	6	2.9	.913	3B-31, 2B-2, 1B-1, OF-1
1952	2 teams	CLE A (35G –.094) PIT N (19G –.143)																						
"	total	54	.125	.170	88	11	4	0	0	0.0	7	6	14	14	0	8	0	50	83	5	15	3.5	.964	2B-26, SS-8, 3B-4, 1B-2
11 yrs.		912	.249	.355	3028	755	167	23	36	1.2	334	387	284	268	27	64	10	1993	2135	170	509	5.1	.960	2B-453, SS-266, 3B-91, 1B-26, OF-1

Lou Berberet

BERBERET, LOUIS JOSEPH BL TR 5′11″ 200 lbs.
B. Nov. 20, 1929, Long Beach, Calif.

Year	Team	Games	BA	SA	AB	H	2B	3B	HR	HR%	R	RBI	BB	SO	SB	Pinch Hit AB	Pinch Hit H	PO	A	E	DP	TC/G	FA	G by Pos
1954	NY A	5	.400	.400	5	2	0	0	0	0.0	1	3	1	1	0	2	1	12	0	0	0	4.0	1.000	C-3
1955		2	.400	.400	5	2	0	0	0	0.0	1	2	1	0	0	1	1	10	0	0	0	10.0	1.000	C-1
1956	WAS A	95	.261	.377	207	54	6	3	4	1.9	25	27	46	33	0	33	6	266	28	1	6	5.0	.997	C-59
1957		99	.261	.398	264	69	11	2	7	2.7	24	36	41	38	0	16	3	349	48	0	8	5.2	1.000	C-77
1958	2 teams	WAS A (5G –.167) BOS A (57G –.210)																						
"	total	62	.208	.306	173	36	5	3	2	1.2	11	18	35	33	0	8	0	242	21	5	3	5.3	.981	C-51
1959	DET A	100	.216	.367	338	73	8	2	13	3.8	38	44	35	59	0	3	0	511	39	6	4	5.9	.989	C-95
1960		85	.194	.276	232	45	4	0	5	2.2	18	23	41	31	2	4	1	396	36	3	4	5.4	.993	C-81
7 yrs.		448	.230	.350	1224	281	34	10	31	2.5	118	153	200	195	2	67	12	1786	172	15	25	5.4	.992	C-367

Moe Berg

BERG, MORRIS BR TR 6′ 1″ 185 lbs.
B. Mar. 2, 1902, New York, N. Y. D. May 29, 1972, Belleville, N. J.

Year	Team	Games	BA	SA	AB	H	2B	3B	HR	HR%	R	RBI	BB	SO	SB	Pinch Hit AB	Pinch Hit H	PO	A	E	DP	TC/G	FA	G by Pos
1923	BKN N	49	.186	.240	129	24	3	2	0	0.0	9	6	2	5	1	0	0	86	126	22	20	4.9	.906	SS-47, 2B-1
1926	CHI A	41	.221	.274	113	25	6	0	0	0.0	4	7	6	9	0	6	1	60	89	8	21	4.6	.949	SS-31, 2B-2, 3B-1
1927		35	.246	.304	69	17	4	0	0	0.0	4	4	4	10	0	6	1	39	41	9	4	3.1	.899	2B-10, C-10, SS-6, 3B-3
1928		76	.246	.317	224	55	16	0	0	0.0	25	29	14	25	2	3	1	256	52	3	8	4.3	.990	C-73
1929		106	.288	.308	351	101	7	0	0	0.0	32	47	17	16	5	0	0	290	86	7	12	3.6	.982	C-106
1930		20	.115	.164	61	7	3	0	0	0.0	4	7	1	5	0	0	0	55	14	1	1	3.5	.986	C-20
1931	CLE A	10	.077	.154	13	1	1	0	0	0.0	1	0	1	1	0	1	0	12	4	2	0	2.3	.889	C-8
1932	WAS A	75	.236	.303	195	46	8	1	1	0.5	16	26	8	13	1	0	0	229	35	0	9	3.5	1.000	C-75

Moe Berg *continued*

Year	Team	Games	BA	SA	AB	H	2B	3B	HR	HR%	R	RBI	BB	SO	SB	Pinch Hit AB	Pinch Hit H	PO	A	E	DP	TC/G	FA	G by Pos
1933		40	.185	.323	65	12	3	0	2	3.1	8	9	4	5	0	4	0	76	10	0	3	2.5	1.000	C-35
1934	2 teams	WAS A (33G –.244) CLE A (29G –.258)																						
"	total	62	.251	.301	183	46	7	1	0	0.0	9	15	7	11	2	3	0	214	21	4	2	3.9	.983	C-62
1935	BOS A	38	.286	.398	98	28	5	0	2	2.0	13	12	5	3	0	1	0	99	15	1	2	3.1	.991	C-37
1936		39	.240	.288	125	30	4	1	0	0.0	9	19	2	6	0	0	0	175	29	3	3	5.3	.986	C-39
1937		47	.255	.291	141	36	3	1	0	0.0	13	20	5	4	0	0	0	208	24	5	2	5.0	.979	C-47
1938		10	.333	.333	12	4	0	0	0	0.0	0	0	0	1	0	3	2	14	1	0	2	1.9	1.000	C-7, 1B-1
1939		14	.273	.394	33	9	1	0	1	3.0	3	5	2	3	0	1	0	45	10	2	1	4.4	.965	C-13
15 yrs.		662	.243	.299	1812	441	71	6	6	0.3	150	206	78	117	11	28	5	1858	557	67	90	3.9	.973	C-532, SS-84, 2B-13, 3B-4, 1B-1

Augie Bergamo

BERGAMO, AUGUST SAMUEL
B. Feb. 14, 1917, Detroit, Mich. D. Aug. 19, 1974, Grosse Pointe, Mich.
BL TL 5′ 9″ 165 lbs.

Year	Team	Games	BA	SA	AB	H	2B	3B	HR	HR%	R	RBI	BB	SO	SB	Pinch Hit AB	Pinch Hit H	PO	A	E	DP	TC/G	FA	G by Pos
1944	STL N	80	.286	.380	192	55	6	3	2	1.0	35	19	35	23	0	26	4	87	0	1	0	1.7	.989	OF-50, 1B-2
1945		94	.316	.414	304	96	17	2	3	1.0	51	44	43	21	0	15	4	160	9	5	4	2.2	.971	OF-77, 1B-2
2 yrs.		174	.304	.401	496	151	23	5	5	1.0	86	63	78	44	0	41	8	247	9	6	4	2.0	.977	OF-127, 1B-4
WORLD SERIES																								
1944	STL N	3	.000	.000	6	0	0	0	0	0.0	0	1	2	3	0	0	0	1	0	0	0	0.5	1.000	OF-2

Bill Bergen

BERGEN, WILLIAM ALOYSIUS
Brother of Marty Bergen.
B. June 13, 1878, N. Brookfield, Mass. D. Dec. 19, 1943, Worcester, Mass.
BR TR 6′ 184 lbs.

Year	Team	Games	BA	SA	AB	H	2B	3B	HR	HR%	R	RBI	BB	SO	SB	Pinch Hit AB	Pinch Hit H	PO	A	E	DP	TC/G	FA	G by Pos
1901	CIN N	87	.179	.234	308	55	6	4	1	0.3	15	17	8		2	0	0	406	117	16	8	6.2	.970	C-87
1902		89	.180	.224	322	58	8	3	0	0.0	19	36	14		2	0	0	406	137	23	13	6.4	.959	C-89
1903		58	.227	.266	207	47	4	2	0	0.0	21	19	7		2	0	0	251	85	7	3	5.9	.980	C-58
1904	BKN N	96	.182	.207	329	60	4	2	0	0.0	17	12	9		3	0	0	415	151	24	10	6.3	.959	C-93, 1B-1
1905		79	.190	.219	247	47	3	2	0	0.0	12	22	7		4	3	0	371	127	24	8	6.9	.954	C-76
1906		103	.159	.184	353	56	3	3	0	0.0	9	19	7		2	0	0	485	149	15	9	6.3	.977	C-103
1907		51	.159	.181	138	22	3	0	0	0.0	2	14	1		1	0	0	175	67	8	3	4.9	.968	C-51
1908		99	.175	.215	302	53	8	2	0	0.0	8	15	5		1	0	0	470	137	7	9	6.2	.989	C-99
1909		112	.139	.156	346	48	1	1	1	0.3	16	15	10		4	0	0	536	202	18	18	6.8	.976	C-112
1910		89	.161	.177	249	40	2	1	0	0.0	11	14	6	39	0	0	0	373	151	10	15	6.0	.981	C-89
1911		84	.132	.154	227	30	3	1	0	0.0	8	10	14	42	2	0	0	346	121	9	10	5.7	.981	C-84
11 yrs.		947	.170	.201	3028	516	45	21	2	0.1	138	193	88	81	23	3	0	4234	1444	161	106	6.2	.972	C-941, 1B-1

Marty Bergen

BERGEN, MARTIN
Brother of Bill Bergen.
B. Oct. 25, 1871, N. Brookfield, Mass. D. Jan. 19, 1900, N. Brookfield, Mass.
TR 5′10″ 170 lbs.

Year	Team	Games	BA	SA	AB	H	2B	3B	HR	HR%	R	RBI	BB	SO	SB	Pinch Hit AB	Pinch Hit H	PO	A	E	DP	TC/G	FA	G by Pos
1896	BOS N	65	.269	.376	245	66	6	4	4	1.6	39	37	11	22	6	1	0	213	70	25	6	4.8	.919	C-63, 1B-1
1897		87	.248	.318	327	81	11	3	2	0.6	47	45	18		5	0	0	353	66	17	4	5.1	.961	C-85, OF-1
1898		120	.280	.359	446	125	16	5	3	0.7	62	60	13		9	1	1	511	109	24	6	5.4	.963	C-117, 1B-2
1899		72	.258	.335	260	67	11	3	1	0.4	32	34	10		4	0	0	253	89	16	4	5.0	.955	C-72
4 yrs.		344	.265	.347	1278	339	44	15	10	0.8	180	176	52	22	24	2	1	1330	334	82	20	5.1	.953	C-337, 1B-3, OF-1

Boze Berger

BERGER, LOUIS WILLIAM
B. May 13, 1910, Baltimore, Md. D. Nov. 3, 1992, Bethesda, Md.
BR TR 6′ 2″ 180 lbs.

Year	Team	Games	BA	SA	AB	H	2B	3B	HR	HR%	R	RBI	BB	SO	SB	Pinch Hit AB	Pinch Hit H	PO	A	E	DP	TC/G	FA	G by Pos
1932	CLE A	1	.000	.000	1	0	0	0	0	0.0	0	0	0	1	0	0	0	0	0	0	0	0.0	.000	SS-1
1935		124	.258	.371	461	119	27	5	5	1.1	62	43	34	97	7	0	0	325	425	29	93	6.2	.963	2B-120, SS-3, 1B-2, 3B-1
1936		28	.173	.212	52	9	2	0	0	0.0	1	3	1	14	0	1	0	67	33	9	11	4.4	.917	1B-8, 2B-8, 3B-7, SS-2
1937	CHI A	52	.238	.392	130	31	5	0	5	3.8	19	13	15	24	1	6	2	37	76	10	9	2.9	.919	3B-40, SS-1, 2B-1
1938		118	.217	.281	470	102	15	3	3	0.6	60	36	43	80	4	0	0	239	353	39	79	5.3	.938	SS-67, 2B-42, 3B-9
1939	BOS A	20	.300	.367	30	9	2	0	0	0.0	4	2	1	10	0	3	1	12	21	1	2	2.0	.971	SS-10, 3B-5, 2B-2
6 yrs.		343	.236	.329	1144	270	51	8	13	1.1	146	97	94	226	12	10	3	680	908	88	194	5.1	.947	2B-173, SS-84, 3B-62, 1B-10

Clarence Berger

BERGER, CLARENCE EDWARD
B. Nov. 1, 1894, East Cleveland, Ohio D. June 30, 1959, Washington, D. C.
BL TR 6′ 185 lbs.

Year	Team	Games	BA	SA	AB	H	2B	3B	HR	HR%	R	RBI	BB	SO	SB	Pinch Hit AB	Pinch Hit H	PO	A	E	DP	TC/G	FA	G by Pos
1914	PIT N	6	.077	.077	13	1	0	0	0	0.0	2	0	1	4	0	1	0	2	0	0	0	0.4	1.000	OF-5

Joe Berger

BERGER, JOSEPH AUGUST (Fats)
B. Dec. 20, 1886, St. Louis, Mo. D. Mar. 5, 1956, Rock Island, Ill.
BR TR 5′10½″ 170 lbs.

Year	Team	Games	BA	SA	AB	H	2B	3B	HR	HR%	R	RBI	BB	SO	SB	Pinch Hit AB	Pinch Hit H	PO	A	E	DP	TC/G	FA	G by Pos
1913	CHI A	77	.215	.287	223	48	6	2	2	0.9	27	20	36	28	5	2	0	114	223	15	19	4.8	.957	2B-69, SS-4, 3B-1
1914		47	.155	.189	148	23	3	1	0	0.0	11	3	13	9	2	1	0	76	113	15	11	4.4	.926	SS-27, 2B-12, 3B-7
2 yrs.		124	.191	.248	371	71	9	3	2	0.5	38	23	49	37	7	3	0	190	336	30	30	4.6	.946	2B-81, SS-31, 3B-8

Johnny Berger

BERGER, JOHN HENNE
B. Aug. 27, 1901, Philadelphia, Pa. D. May 7, 1979, Lake Charles, La.
BR TR 5′ 9″ 165 lbs.

Year	Team	Games	BA	SA	AB	H	2B	3B	HR	HR%	R	RBI	BB	SO	SB	Pinch Hit AB	Pinch Hit H	PO	A	E	DP	TC/G	FA	G by Pos
1922	PHI A	2	1.000	1.000	1	1	0	0	0	0.0	0	0	0	0	1	0	0	4	0	0	0	2.0	1.000	C-2
1927	WAS A	9	.267	.267	15	4	0	0	0	0.0	1	1	2	3	0	0	0	25	0	2	1	3.0	.926	C-9
2 yrs.		11	.313	.313	16	5	0	0	0	0.0	1	1	2	3	1	0	0	29	0	2	1	2.8	.935	C-11

Tun Berger

BERGER, JOHN HENRY
B. Dec. 6, 1867, Pittsburgh, Pa. D. June 10, 1907, Pittsburgh, Pa.
TR 204 lbs.

Year	Team	Games	BA	SA	AB	H	2B	3B	HR	HR%	R	RBI	BB	SO	SB	Pinch Hit AB	Pinch Hit H	PO	A	E	DP	TC/G	FA	G by Pos
1890	PIT N	104	.266	.332	391	104	18	4	0	0.0	64	40	35	23	11	0	0	224	168	56	11	4.4	.875	OF-41, SS-33, C-21, 2B-6, 3B-1
1891		43	.239	.291	134	32	2	1	1	0.7	15	14	12	10	4	0	0	116	64	30	2	4.9	.857	C-18, 2B-17, SS-6, OF-2
1892	WAS N	26	.144	.186	97	14	2	1	0	0.0	9	3	7	9	3	0	0	56	52	14	3	4.5	.885	SS-18, C-9
3 yrs.		173	.241	.301	622	150	22	6	1	0.2	88	57	54	42	18	0	0	396	284	100	16	4.5	.872	SS-57, C-48, OF-43, 2B-23, 3B-1

Wally Berger

BERGER, WALTER ANTONE BR TR 6′ 2″ 198 lbs.
B. Oct. 10, 1905, Chicago, Ill. D. Nov. 30, 1988, Redondo Beach, Calif.

Year	Team	Games	BA	SA	AB	H	2B	3B	HR	HR%	R	RBI	BB	SO	SB	Pinch Hit AB	Pinch Hit H	PO	A	E	DP	TC/G	FA	G by Pos
1930	BOS N	151	.310	.614	555	172	27	14	38	6.8	98	119	54	69	3	6	1	307	10	11	3	2.3	.966	OF-145
1931		156	.323	.512	617	199	44	8	19	3.1	94	84	55	70	13	0	0	459	16	11	5	3.1	.977	OF-156, 1B-1
1932		145	.307	.468	602	185	34	6	17	2.8	90	73	33	66	5	1	0	498	14	3	11	3.6	.994	OF-134, 1B-11
1933		137	.313	.566	528	165	37	8	27	**5.1**	84	106	41	**77**	2	1	1	382	6	9	4	2.9	.977	OF-136
1934		150	.298	.546	615	183	35	8	34	5.5	92	121	49	65	2	0	0	385	9	9	2	2.7	.978	OF-150
1935		150	.295	.548	589	174	39	4	**34**	**5.8**	91	**130**	50	80	3	1	0	458	8	17	1	3.2	.965	OF-149
1936		138	.288	.483	534	154	23	3	25	4.7	88	91	53	84	1	5	1	384	10	14	1	3.1	.966	OF-133
1937	2 teams	BOS N (30G –.274) NY N (59G –.291)																						
″	total	89	.285	.532	312	89	20	3	17	5.4	54	65	29	63	3	9	1	158	5	4	0	2.1	.976	OF-80
1938	2 teams	NY N (16G –.188) CIN N (99G –.307)																						
″	total	115	.298	.478	439	131	23	4	16	3.6	76	60	31	48	2	5	2	221	7	7	2	2.2	.970	OF-107
1939	CIN N	97	.258	.438	329	85	15	1	14	4.3	36	44	36	63	1	2	0	158	6	5	0	1.8	.970	OF-95
1940	2 teams	CIN N (2G –.000) PHI N (20G –.317)																						
″	total	22	.302	.419	43	13	2	0	1	2.3	3	5	4	9	1	9	0	20	0	1	0	1.8	.952	OF-11, 1B-1
11 yrs.		1350	.300	.522	5163	1550	299	59	242	4.7	806	898	435	694	36	39	6	3430	91	91	29	2.8	.975	OF-1296, 1B-13
WORLD SERIES																								
1937	NY N	3	.000	.000	3	0	0	0	0	0.0	0	0	0	1	0	3	0	0	0	0	0	0.0	—	
1939	CIN N	4	.000	.000	15	0	0	0	0	0.0	0	1	0	4	0	0	0	8	0	0	0	2.0	1.000	OF-4
2 yrs.		7	.000	.000	18	0	0	0	0	0.0	0	1	0	5	0	3	0	8	0	0	0	2.0	1.000	OF-4

John Bergh

BERGH, JOHN BAPTIST
B. Oct. 8, 1857, Boston, Mass. D. Apr. 16, 1883, Boston, Mass.

Year	Team	Games	BA	SA	AB	H	2B	3B	HR	HR%	R	RBI	BB	SO	SB	Pinch Hit AB	Pinch Hit H	PO	A	E	DP	TC/G	FA	G by Pos
1876	PHI N	1	.000	.000	4	0	0	0	0	0.0	0	0	0	2		0	0	3	2	1	0	3.0	.833	OF-1, C-1
1880	BOS N	11	.200	.275	40	8	3	0	0	0.0	2	0	2	5		0	0	54	11	12	0	7.0	.844	C-11
2 yrs.		12	.182	.250	44	8	3	0	0	0.0	2	0	2	7		0	0	57	13	13	0	6.4	.843	C-12, OF-1

Marty Berghammer

BERGHAMMER, MARTIN ANDREW BL TR 5′ 9″ 172 lbs.
B. Jan. 18, 1888, Elliot, Pa. D. Dec. 21, 1957, Pittsburgh, Pa.

Year	Team	Games	BA	SA	AB	H	2B	3B	HR	HR%	R	RBI	BB	SO	SB	Pinch Hit AB	Pinch Hit H	PO	A	E	DP	TC/G	FA	G by Pos
1911	CHI A	2	.000	.000	5	0	0	0	0	0.0	0	0	0		0	0	0	5	2	0	0	3.5	1.000	2B-2
1913	CIN N	74	.218	.266	188	41	4	1	1	0.5	25	13	10	29	16	0	0	111	172	29	20	4.7	.907	SS-53, 2B-13
1914		77	.223	.241	112	25	2	0	0	0.0	15	6	10	18	4	13	2	45	88	10	9	3.1	.930	SS-33, 2B-13
1915	PIT F	132	.243	.290	469	114	10	6	0	0.0	96	33	83		26	0	0	286	359	39	55	5.2	.943	SS-132
4 yrs.		285	.233	.275	774	180	16	7	1	0.1	136	52	103	47	46	13	2	447	621	78	84	4.7	.932	SS-218, 2B-28

Al Bergman

BERGMAN, ALFRED HENRY (Dutch) BR TR 5′ 7″ 155 lbs.
B. Sept. 27, 1890, Peru, Ind. D. June 20, 1961, Fort Wayne, Ind.

Year	Team	Games	BA	SA	AB	H	2B	3B	HR	HR%	R	RBI	BB	SO	SB	Pinch Hit AB	Pinch Hit H	PO	A	E	DP	TC/G	FA	G by Pos
1916	CLE A	8	.214	.357	14	3	0	1	0	0.0	2	0	2	4	0	3	0	2	6	1	0	3.0	.889	2B-3

Dave Bergman

BERGMAN, DAVID BRUCE BL TL 6′ 1½″ 185 lbs.
B. June 6, 1953, Evanston, Ill.

Year	Team	Games	BA	SA	AB	H	2B	3B	HR	HR%	R	RBI	BB	SO	SB	Pinch Hit AB	Pinch Hit H	PO	A	E	DP	TC/G	FA	G by Pos
1975	NY A	7	.000	.000	17	0	0	0	0	0.0	0	0	2	4	0	0	0	10	1	1	1	2.0	.917	OF-6
1977		5	.250	.250	4	1	0	0	0	0.0	1	1	0	0	0	0	0	8	0	0	0	1.6	1.000	OF-3, 1B-2
1978	HOU N	104	.231	.269	186	43	5	1	0	0.0	15	12	39	32	2	16	2	328	16	4	26	3.7	.989	1B-66, OF-29
1979		13	.400	.600	15	6	0	0	1	6.7	4	2	0	3	0	10	5	8	0	0	1	2.0	1.000	1B-4
1980		90	.256	.359	78	20	6	1	0	0.0	12	3	10	10	1	24	4	187	16	1	23	3.2	.995	1B-59, OF-5
1981	2 teams	HOU N (6G –.167) SF N (63G –.255)																						
″	total	69	.252	.391	151	38	9	0	4	2.6	17	14	19	18	2	23	4	255	25	3	21	5.8	.989	1B-34, OF-15
1982	SF N	100	.273	.413	121	33	3	1	4	3.3	22	14	18	11	3	21	5	321	20	4	18	4.6	.988	1B-69, OF-6
1983		90	.286	.457	140	40	4	1	6	4.3	16	24	24	21	2	31	11	299	27	2	20	5.9	.994	1B-50, OF-6
1984	DET A	120	.273	.417	271	74	8	5	7	2.6	42	44	33	40	3	21	6	658	75	8	63	6.4	.989	1B-114, OF-2
1985		69	.179	.257	140	25	2	0	3	2.1	8	7	14	15	0	24	6	306	25	3	25	6.7	.991	1B-44, DH-5, OF-1
1986		65	.231	.315	130	30	6	1	1	0.8	14	9	21	16	0	22	5	255	29	4	30	5.6	.986	1B-41, DH-8, OF-2
1987		91	.273	.453	172	47	7	3	6	3.5	25	22	30	23	0	21	4	357	29	3	33	4.9	.992	1B-65, OF-7, DH-7
1988		116	.294	.394	289	85	14	0	5	1.7	37	35	38	34	0	24	3	386	37	4	31	4.0	.991	1B-64, DH-30, OF-13
1989		137	.268	.361	385	103	13	1	7	1.8	38	37	44	44	1	18	1	912	85	7	88	7.7	.993	1B-123, DH-7, OF-1
1990		100	.278	.366	205	57	10	1	2	1.0	21	26	33	17	3	33	6	203	13	1	19	2.6	.995	DH-51, 1B-27, OF-5
1991		86	.237	.407	194	46	10	1	7	3.6	23	29	35	40	1	25	3	365	29	1	42	6.0	.997	1B-49, DH-13, OF-4
1992		87	.232	.265	181	42	3	0	1	0.6	17	10	20	19	1	22	6	339	22	5	29	5.4	.986	1B-55, DH-12, OF-1
17 yrs.		1349	.258	.367	2679	690	100	16	54	2.0	312	289	380	347	19	335	71	5197	449	51	470	5.2	.991	1B-866, DH-133, OF-106
LEAGUE CHAMPIONSHIP SERIES																								
1980	HOU N	4	.333	1.000	3	1	0	1	0	0.0	0	2	0	0	0	0	0	8	2	1	0	2.8	.909	1B-4
1984	DET A	2	1.000	1.000	1	1	0	0	0	0.0	1	0	0	0	1	0	0	5	0	0	0	5.0	1.000	1B-1
1987		4	.250	.250	4	1	0	0	0	0.0	0	2	0	1	0	2	1	6	0	0	0	3.0	1.000	1B-1, DH-1
3 yrs.		10	.375	.625	8	3	0	1	0	0.0	1	4	0	1	1	2	1	19	2	1	0	3.1	.955	1B-6, DH-1
WORLD SERIES																								
1984	DET A	5	.000	.000	5	0	0	0	0	0.0	0	0	0	1	0	0	0	22	4	0	0	5.2	1.000	1B-5

Frank Berkelbach

BERKELBACH, FRANCIS P. 6′ 182 lbs.
B. Philadelphia, Pa. Deceased.

Year	Team	Games	BA	SA	AB	H	2B	3B	HR	HR%	R	RBI	BB	SO	SB	Pinch Hit AB	Pinch Hit H	PO	A	E	DP	TC/G	FA	G by Pos
1884	CIN AA	6	.240	.320	25	6	0	1	0	0.0	3		0			0	0	6	0	3	0	1.5	.667	OF-6

Bob Berman

BERMAN, ROBERT LEON BR TR 5′ 8″ 147 lbs.
B. Jan. 24, 1899, New York, N. Y. D. Aug. 2, 1988, Bridgeport, Conn.

Year	Team	Games	BA	SA	AB	H	2B	3B	HR	HR%	R	RBI	BB	SO	SB	Pinch Hit AB	Pinch Hit H	PO	A	E	DP	TC/G	FA	G by Pos
1918	WAS A	2	—	—	0	0	0	0	0	—	0	0	0	0	0	0	0	2	0	0	0	2.0	1.000	C-1

Curt Bernard

BERNARD, CURTIS HENRY BL TR 5′10½″ 150 lbs.
B. Feb. 18, 1878, Parkersburg, W. Va. D. Apr. 10, 1955, Culver City, Calif.

Year	Team	Games	BA	SA	AB	H	2B	3B	HR	HR%	R	RBI	BB	SO	SB	Pinch Hit AB	Pinch Hit H	PO	A	E	DP	TC/G	FA	G by Pos
1900	NY N	20	.254	.282	71	18	2	0	0	0.0	9	8	6		1	0	0	26	6	2	0	1.7	.941	OF-19, SS-1
1901		23	.224	.276	76	17	0	2	0	0.0	11	6	7		2	1	0	31	14	11	1	2.5	.804	OF-15, 2B-4, SS-2, 3B-1
2 yrs.		43	.238	.279	147	35	2	2	0	0.0	20	14	13		3	1	0	57	20	13	1	2.1	.856	OF-34, 2B-4, SS-3, 3B-1

Tony Bernazard

BERNAZARD, ANTONIO
Born Antonio Bernazard (Garcia).
B. Aug. 24, 1956, Caguas, Puerto Rico.

BB TR 5′ 9″ 150 lbs.

Year	Team	Games	BA	SA	AB	H	2B	3B	HR	HR%	R	RBI	BB	SO	SB	Pinch Hit AB	Pinch Hit H	PO	A	E	DP	TC/G	FA	G by Pos
1979	MON N	22	.300	.425	40	12	2	0	1	2.5	11	8	15	12	1	2	0	22	34	1	4	4.1	.982	2B-14
1980		82	.224	.355	183	41	7	1	5	2.7	26	18	17	41	9	22	4	82	151	9	25	4.0	.963	2B-39, SS-22
1981	CHI A	106	.276	.380	384	106	14	4	6	1.6	53	34	54	66	4	2	0	228	321	7	66	5.3	.987	2B-104, SS-1
1982		137	.256	.396	540	138	25	9	11	2.0	90	56	67	88	11	0	0	353	443	12	116	5.9	.985	2B-137
1983	2 teams	CHI A (59G –.262)	SEA A (80G –.267)																					
″	total	139	.265	.385	533	141	34	3	8	1.5	65	56	55	97	23	2	0	262	422	19	89	5.1	.973	2B-138
1984	CLE A	140	.221	.287	439	97	15	4	2	0.5	44	38	43	70	20	3	0	264	397	20	85	5.0	.971	2B-136, DH-1
1985		153	.274	.404	500	137	26	3	11	2.2	73	59	69	72	17	9	4	313	399	16	87	4.9	.978	2B-147, SS-1
1986		146	.301	.456	562	169	28	4	17	3.0	88	73	53	77	17	1	1	351	442	17	95	5.5	.979	2B-146
1987	2 teams	CLE A (79G –.239)	OAK A (61G –.266)																					
″	total	140	.250	.393	507	127	26	2	14	2.8	73	49	55	79	11	3	1	243	335	17	61	4.3	.971	2B-137, DH-3
1991	DET A	6	.167	.167	12	2	0	0	0	0.0	0	0	0	4	0	3	0	3	6	1	3	2.5	.900	2B-2, DH-2
10 yrs.		1071	.262	.387	3700	970	177	30	75	2.0	523	391	428	606	113	47	10	2121	2950	119	631	5.0	.977	2B-1000, SS-24, DH-6

Juan Bernhardt

BERNHARDT, JUAN RAMON
Born Juan Ramon Bernhardt (Coradin).
B. Aug. 31, 1953, San Pedro de Macoris, Dominican Republic.

BR TR 5′11″ 160 lbs.

Year	Team	Games	BA	SA	AB	H	2B	3B	HR	HR%	R	RBI	BB	SO	SB	Pinch Hit AB	Pinch Hit H	PO	A	E	DP	TC/G	FA	G by Pos
1976	NY A	10	.190	.238	21	4	1	0	0	0.0	1	1	0	4	0	5	0	4	1	1	0	0.9	.833	OF-4, DH-2, 3B-1
1977	SEA A	89	.243	.354	305	74	9	2	7	2.3	32	30	5	26	2	12	2	69	42	2	7	1.4	.982	DH-54, 3B-21, 1B-8
1978		54	.230	.321	165	38	9	0	2	1.2	13	12	9	10	1	5	1	263	63	6	21	6.8	.982	1B-25, 3B-22, DH-2
1979		1	1.000	1.000	1	1	0	0	0	0.0	0	0	0	0	0	1	1	0	0	0	0	0.0	—	
4 yrs.		154	.238	.339	492	117	19	2	9	1.8	46	43	14	40	3	23	4	336	106	9	28	3.2	.980	DH-58, 3B-44, 1B-33, OF-4

Carlos Bernier

BERNIER, CARLOS
Born Carlos Bernier (Rodriguez).
B. Jan. 28, 1927, Juana Diaz, Puerto Rico D. Apr. 6, 1989, Juana Diaz, Puerto Rico.

BR TR 5′ 9″ 180 lbs.

Year	Team	Games	BA	SA	AB	H	2B	3B	HR	HR%	R	RBI	BB	SO	SB	Pinch Hit AB	Pinch Hit H	PO	A	E	DP	TC/G	FA	G by Pos
1953	PIT N	105	.213	.316	310	66	7	8	3	1.0	48	31	51	53	15	16	3	220	8	7	1	2.7	.970	OF-87

Johnny Bero

BERO, JOHN GEORGE
B. Dec. 22, 1922, Gary, W. Va. D. May 11, 1985, Gardena, Calif.

BL TR 6′ 170 lbs.

Year	Team	Games	BA	SA	AB	H	2B	3B	HR	HR%	R	RBI	BB	SO	SB	Pinch Hit AB	Pinch Hit H	PO	A	E	DP	TC/G	FA	G by Pos
1948	DET A	4	.000	.000	9	0	0	0	0	0.0	2	0	1	1	0	1	0	5	3	0	0	4.0	1.000	2B-2
1951	STL A	61	.212	.338	160	34	5	0	5	3.1	24	17	26	30	1	7	2	91	137	11	30	4.3	.954	SS-55, 2B-1
2 yrs.		65	.201	.320	169	34	5	0	5	3.0	26	17	27	31	1	8	2	96	140	11	30	4.3	.955	SS-55, 2B-3

Dale Berra

BERRA, DALE ANTHONY
Son of Yogi Berra.
B. Dec. 13, 1956, Ridgewood, N. J.

BR TR 6′ 180 lbs.

Year	Team	Games	BA	SA	AB	H	2B	3B	HR	HR%	R	RBI	BB	SO	SB	Pinch Hit AB	Pinch Hit H	PO	A	E	DP	TC/G	FA	G by Pos
1977	PIT N	17	.175	.200	40	7	1	0	0	0.0	0	3	1	8	0	2	0	14	22	1	1	2.6	.973	3B-14
1978		56	.207	.356	135	28	2	0	6	4.4	16	14	13	20	3	0	0	31	84	11	11	2.2	.913	3B-55, SS-2
1979		44	.211	.325	123	26	5	0	3	2.4	11	15	11	17	0	0	0	43	86	12	14	3.2	.915	SS-22, 3B-22
1980		93	.220	.343	245	54	8	2	6	2.4	21	31	16	52	2	4	1	88	171	11	23	2.8	.959	3B-48, SS-45, 2B-4
1981		81	.241	.319	232	56	12	0	2	0.9	21	27	17	34	11	3	0	89	167	8	27	2.9	.970	3B-42, SS-30, 2B-18
1982		156	.263	.386	529	139	25	5	10	1.9	64	61	33	83	6	0	0	241	505	30	77	4.9	.961	SS-153, 3B-6
1983		161	.251	.358	537	135	25	1	10	1.9	51	52	61	84	8	0	0	286	505	30	103	5.1	.963	SS-161
1984		136	.222	.318	450	100	16	0	9	2.0	31	52	34	78	1	1	1	186	449	30	65	4.9	.955	SS-135, 3B-1
1985	NY A	48	.229	.321	109	25	5	1	1	0.9	8	8	7	20	1	7	2	22	74	9	9	2.2	.914	3B-41, SS-6
1986		42	.231	.352	108	25	7	0	2	1.9	10	13	9	14	0	3	1	40	67	4	11	2.7	.964	SS-19, 3B-18, DH-4
1987	HOU N	19	.178	.244	45	8	3	0	0	0.0	3	2	8	12	0	1	0	14	40	2	4	2.7	.964	SS-18, 2B-3
11 yrs.		853	.236	.344	2553	603	109	9	49	1.9	236	278	210	422	32	21	5	1054	2170	148	345	3.9	.956	SS-591, 3B-247, 2B-25, DH-4

Yogi Berra

BERRA, LAWRENCE PETER
Father of Dale Berra.
B. May 12, 1925, St. Louis, Mo.
Manager 1964, 1972–75, 1984–85.
Hall of Fame 1972.

BL TR 5′ 7½″ 185 lbs.

Year	Team	Games	BA	SA	AB	H	2B	3B	HR	HR%	R	RBI	BB	SO	SB	Pinch Hit AB	Pinch Hit H	PO	A	E	DP	TC/G	FA	G by Pos
1946	NY A	7	.364	.682	22	8	1	0	2	9.1	3	4	1	1	0	1	0	28	6	0	2	5.7	1.000	C-6
1947		83	.280	.464	293	82	15	3	11	3.8	41	54	13	12	0	8	2	307	18	9	5	4.5	.973	C-51, OF-24
1948		125	.305	.488	469	143	24	10	14	3.0	70	98	25	24	3	10	5	390	40	9	7	3.6	.979	C-71, OF-50
1949		116	.277	.480	415	115	20	2	20	4.8	59	91	22	25	2	7	3	544	60	7	18	5.6	.989	C-109
1950		151	.322	.533	597	192	30	6	28	4.7	116	124	55	12	4	3	1	777	64	13	16	5.8	.985	C-148
1951		141	.294	.492	547	161	19	4	27	4.9	92	88	44	20	5	0	0	693	82	13	25	5.6	.984	C-141
1952		142	.273	.478	534	146	17	1	30	5.6	97	98	66	24	2	3	0	700	73	6	10	5.6	.992	C-140
1953		137	.296	.523	503	149	23	5	27	5.4	80	108	50	32	0	10	4	566	64	9	9	4.8	.986	C-133
1954		151	.307	.488	584	179	28	6	22	3.8	88	125	56	29	0	1	0	718	64	8	14	5.3	.990	C-149, 3B-1
1955		147	.272	.470	541	147	20	3	27	5.0	84	108	60	20	1	4	1	721	54	13	10	5.4	.984	C-145
1956		140	.298	.534	521	155	29	2	30	5.8	93	105	65	29	3	4	0	733	57	11	15	5.9	.986	C-135, OF-1
1957		134	.251	.438	482	121	14	2	24	5.0	74	82	57	25	1	10	1	707	61	4	12	6.1	.995	C-121, OF-6
1958		122	.266	.471	433	115	17	3	22	5.1	60	90	35	35	3	10	3	558	44	2	11	5.6	.997	C-85, OF-21, 1B-2
1959		131	.284	.462	472	134	25	1	19	4.0	64	69	43	38	1	11	3	706	62	4	10	6.3	.995	C-116, OF-7
1960		120	.276	.446	359	99	14	1	15	4.2	46	62	38	23	2	24	5	312	24	5	6	3.4	.985	C-63, OF-36
1961		119	.271	.466	395	107	11	0	22	5.6	62	61	35	28	2	19	5	237	15	2	2	2.5	.992	OF-87, C-15
1962		86	.224	.388	232	52	8	0	10	4.3	25	35	24	18	0	23	6	238	17	6	6	4.4	.977	C-31, OF-28
1963		64	.293	.497	147	43	6	0	8	5.4	20	28	15	17	1	28	5	244	13	3	5	7.4	.988	C-35
1965	NY N	4	.222	.222	9	2	0	0	0	0.0	1	0	0	3	0	2	0	15	1	1	0	8.5	.941	C-2
19 yrs.		2120	.285	.482	7555	2150	321	49	358	4.7	1175	1430	704	415	30	178	44	9194	819	125	183	5.2	.988	C-1696, OF-260, 1B-2, 3B-1
WORLD SERIES																								
1947	NY A	6	.158	.316	19	3	0	0	1	5.3	2	2	1	2	0	1	1	21	2	2	0	4.2	.920	C-4, OF-2
1949		4	.063	.063	16	1	0	0	0	0.0	2	1	1	3	0	0	0	37	3	0	1	10.0	1.000	C-4
1950		4	.200	.400	15	3	0	0	1	6.7	2	2	2	1	0	0	0	30	1	0	1	7.8	1.000	C-4
1951		6	.261	.304	23	6	1	0	0	0.0	4	0	2	1	0	0	0	27	3	1	0	5.2	.968	C-6
1952		7	.214	.464	28	6	1	0	2	7.1	2	3	2	4	0	0	0	59	7	1	1	9.6	.985	C-7

Year	Team	Games	BA	SA	AB	H	2B	3B	HR	HR%	R	RBI	BB	SO	SB	Pinch Hit AB	Pinch Hit H	PO	A	E	DP	TC/G	FA	G by Pos

Yogi Berra *continued*

1953		6	.429	.619	21	9	1	0	1	4.8	3	4	3	3	0	0	0	36	3	0	1	6.5	1.000	C-6
1955		7	.417	.583	24	10	1	0	1	4.2	5	2	3	1	0	0	0	40	4	0	1	6.3	1.000	C-7
1956		7	.360	.800	25	9	2	0	3	12.0	5	10	4	1	0	0	0	50	3	0	0	7.6	1.000	C-7
1957		7	.320	.480	25	8	1	0	1	4.0	5	2	4	0	0	0	0	44	2	1	0	6.7	.979	C-7
1958		7	.222	.333	27	6	3	0	0	0.0	3	2	1	0	0	0	0	60	6	0	1	9.4	1.000	C-7
1960		7	.318	.455	22	7	0	0	1	4.5	6	8	2	0	0	1	0	10	0	0	0	1.4	1.000	OF-4, C-3
1961		4	.273	.545	11	3	0	0	1	9.1	2	3	5	1	0	0	0	11	0	1	0	3.0	.917	OF-4
1962		2	.000	.000	2	0	0	0	0	0.0	0	0	2	0	0	0	0	6	1	0	0	7.0	1.000	C-1
1963		1	.000	.000	1	0	0	0	0	0.0	0	0	0	0	0	1	0	0	0	0	0	0.0	—	
14 yrs.		75	.274	.452	259	71	10	0	12	4.6	41	39	32	17	0	3	1	431	35	6	6	6.5	.987	C-63, OF-10
		1st			**1st**	**1st**	**1st**		**3rd**		**2nd**	**2nd**	**3rd**											

Denny Berran

BERRAN, DENNIS MARTIN — BL TL
B. Oct. 8, 1887, Merrimac, Mass. D. Apr. 28, 1943, Boston, Mass.

1912	CHI A	2	.250	.250	4	1	0	0	0	0.0	1	0	0		0	0	0	1	0	0	0	0.5	1.000	OF-2

Ray Berres

BERRES, RAYMOND FREDERICK — BR TR 5′9″ 170 lbs.
B. Aug. 31, 1907, Kenosha, Wis.

1934	BKN N	39	.215	.266	79	17	4	0	0	0.0	7	3	1	16	0	1	0	79	14	3	0	2.6	.969	C-37
1936		105	.240	.296	267	64	10	1	1	0.4	16	13	14	35	1	0	0	436	59	6	7	4.8	.988	C-105
1937	PIT N	2	.167	.167	6	1	0	0	0	0.0	0	0	0	0	0	0	0	9	2	0	0	5.5	1.000	C-2
1938		40	.230	.250	100	23	2	0	0	0.0	7	6	8	10	0	0	0	128	21	1	0	3.8	.993	C-40
1939		81	.229	.264	231	53	6	1	0	0.0	22	16	11	25	1	1	1	269	36	2	4	3.8	.993	C-80
1940	2 teams	PIT N (21G –.188)	BOS N (85G –.192)																					
"	total	106	.192	.215	261	50	4	1	0	0.0	14	16	19	20	0	0	0	294	65	7	8	3.5	.981	C-106
1941	BOS N	120	.201	.247	279	56	10	0	1	0.4	21	19	17	20	2	0	0	356	64	2	3	3.5	.995	C-120
1942	NY N	12	.188	.188	32	6	0	0	0	0.0	0	1	2	3	0	0	0	34	2	1	1	3.1	.973	C-12
1943		20	.143	.179	28	4	1	0	0	0.0	1	0	1	2	0	3	1	43	9	1	1	3.1	.981	C-17
1944		16	.471	.647	17	8	0	0	1	5.9	4	2	1	0	0	0	0	13	4	0	1	1.4	1.000	C-12
1945		20	.167	.167	30	5	0	0	0	0.0	4	2	2	3	0	0	0	43	2	0	0	2.3	1.000	C-20
11 yrs.		561	.216	.255	1330	287	37	3	3	0.2	96	78	76	134	4	5	2	1704	278	23	25	3.6	.989	C-551

Geronimo Berroa

BERROA, GERONIMO EMILIANO — BR TR 6′ 165 lbs.
Born Geronimo Emiliano Letta (Berroa).
B. Mar. 18, 1965, Santo Domingo, Dominican Republic.

1989	ATL N	81	.265	.338	136	36	4	0	2	1.5	7	9	7	32	0	47	11	67	1	2	0	2.1	.971	OF-34
1990		7	.000	.000	4	0	0	0	0	0.0	0	0	1	1	0	3	0	1	0	0	0	0.3	1.000	OF-3
1992	CIN N	13	.267	.333	15	4	1	0	0	0.0	2	0	2	1	0	9	1	2	1	0	0	1.0	1.000	OF-3
1993	FLA N	14	.118	.147	34	4	1	0	0	0.0	3	0	2	7	0	5	0	9	1	2	0	1.3	.833	OF-9
1994	OAK A	96	.306	.485	340	104	18	2	13	3.8	55	65	41	62	7	8	1	131	5	1	6	1.4	.993	DH-44, OF-42, 1B-9
1995		141	.278	.451	546	152	22	3	22	4.0	87	88	63	98	7	2	0	130	5	4	1	1.0	.971	DH-72, OF-71
6 yrs.		352	.279	.434	1075	300	46	5	37	3.4	154	162	116	201	14	74	13	340	13	9	7	1.3	.975	OF-162, DH-116, 1B-9

Charlie Berry

BERRY, CHARLES FRANCIS — BR TR 6′ 185 lbs.
Son of Charlie Berry.
B. Oct. 18, 1902, Phillipsburg, N. J. D. Sept. 6, 1972, Evanston, Ill.

1925	PHI A	10	.214	.286	14	3	1	0	0	0.0	1	3	0	2	0	6	1	9	0	1	0	2.5	.900	C-4
1928	BOS A	80	.260	.350	177	46	7	3	1	0.6	18	19	21	19	1	14	4	153	34	8	2	3.1	.959	C-63
1929		77	.242	.348	207	50	11	4	1	0.5	19	21	15	29	2	4	3	236	51	5	8	4.1	.983	C-72
1930		88	.289	.441	256	74	9	6	6	2.3	31	35	16	22	2	3	2	279	56	4	4	4.0	.988	C-85
1931		111	.283	.389	357	101	16	2	6	1.7	41	49	29	38	4	9	2	312	78	6	8	3.9	.985	C-102
1932	2 teams	BOS A (10G –.188)	CHI A (72G –.305)																					
"	total	82	.291	.453	258	75	18	6	4	1.6	33	37	24	25	3	2	0	240	58	7	8	3.8	.977	C-80
1933	CHI A	86	.255	.328	271	69	8	3	2	0.7	25	28	17	16	0	3	0	260	39	4	1	3.7	.987	C-83
1934	PHI A	99	.268	.320	269	72	10	2	0	0.0	14	34	22	23	1	0	0	339	48	5	9	4.0	.987	C-99
1935		62	.253	.368	190	48	7	3	3	1.6	14	29	10	20	0	6	1	189	37	3	7	4.1	.987	C-56
1936		13	.059	.118	17	1	1	0	0	0.0	0	1	6	2	0	1	0	29	4	1	0	2.8	.971	C-12
1938		1	.000	.000	2	0	0	0	0	0.0	0	0	0	0	0	0	0	1	1	0	1	2.0	1.000	C-1
11 yrs.		709	.267	.374	2018	539	88	29	23	1.1	196	256	160	196	13	48	13	2047	406	44	48	3.8	.982	C-657

Charlie Berry

BERRY, CHARLES JOSEPH — BR TR 5′11″ 175 lbs.
Father of Charlie Berry.
B. Sept. 6, 1860, Elizabeth, N. J. D. Feb. 16, 1940, Phillipsburg, N. J.

1884	4 teams	ALT U (7G –.240)	KC U (29G –.246)	CHI U (5G –.118)	PIT U (2G –.100)																			
"	total	43	.224	.300	170	38	8	1	1	0.6	21		1			0	0	115	89	30	7	5.2	.872	2B-36, OF-8, 3B-1

Claude Berry

BERRY, CLAUDE ELZY (Admiral) — BR TR 5′7″ 165 lbs.
B. Feb. 14, 1880, Losantville, Ind. D. Feb. 1, 1974, Richmond, Ind.

1904	CHI A	3	.000	.000	1	0	0	0	0	0.0	1	0	1		0	0	0	5	1	0	0	2.0	1.000	C-3
1906	PHI A	10	.233	.233	30	7	0	0	0	0.0	2	2	2		1	0	0	52	24	5	0	8.1	.938	C-10
1907		8	.211	.316	19	4	2	0	0	0.0	2	1	2		0	0	0	29	5	2	0	4.5	.944	C-8
1914	PIT F	124	.238	.341	411	98	18	9	2	0.5	35	36	26		6	1	0	550	202	23	18	6.4	.970	C-122
1915		100	.192	.247	292	56	11	1	1	0.3	32	26	29		7	0	0	384	144	11	8	5.4	.980	C-99
5 yrs.		245	.219	.299	753	165	31	10	3	0.4	72	65	60		14	1	0	1020	376	41	26	5.9	.971	C-242

Joe Berry

BERRY, JOSEPH HOWARD, JR. (Nig) — BR TR 5′10½″ 159 lbs.
Son of Joe Berry.
B. Dec. 31, 1894, Philadelphia, Pa. D. Apr. 29, 1976, Philadelphia, Pa.

1921	NY N	9	.333	.667	6	2	0	1	0	0.0	0	2	1	1	0	0	0	0	7	1	0	1.1	.875	2B-7
1922		6	—	—	0	0	0	0	0	—	0	0	0	0	0	0	0	0	0	0	0	0.0	.000	2B-6
2 yrs.		15	.333	.667	6	2	0	1	0	0.0	0	2	1	1	0	0	0	0	7	1	0	0.6	.875	2B-13

Joe Berry

BERRY, JOSEPH HOWARD, SR. (Hodge)
Father of Joe Berry.
B. Sept. 10, 1872, Wheeling, W. Va. D. Mar. 13, 1961, Allenwood, N. J.
BB TR 5′ 9″ 172 lbs.

Year	Team	Games	BA	SA	AB	H	2B	3B	HR	HR%	R	RBI	BB	SO	SB	Pinch Hit AB	Pinch Hit H	PO	A	E	DP	TC/G	FA	G by Pos
1902	PHI N	1	.250	.250	4	1	0	0	0	0.0	0	1	1		1	0	0	3	0	0	0	3.0	1.000	C-1

Ken Berry

BERRY, ALLEN KENT
B. May 10, 1941, Kansas City, Mo.
BR TR 6′ 175 lbs.

Year	Team	Games	BA	SA	AB	H	2B	3B	HR	HR%	R	RBI	BB	SO	SB	Pinch Hit AB	Pinch Hit H	PO	A	E	DP	TC/G	FA	G by Pos
1962	CHI A	3	.333	.333	6	2	0	0	0	0.0	2	0	0	0	0	1	1	4	1	0	1	2.5	1.000	OF-2
1963		4	.200	.200	5	1	0	0	0	0.0	2	0	1	1	0	0	0	6	0	1	0	2.3	.857	OF-2, 2B-1
1964		12	.375	.500	32	12	1	0	1	3.1	4	4	5	3	0	0	0	15	0	0	0	1.3	1.000	OF-12
1965		157	.218	.347	472	103	17	4	12	2.5	51	42	28	96	4	1	0	331	6	7	1	2.2	.980	OF-156
1966		147	.271	.379	443	120	20	2	8	1.8	50	34	28	63	7	3	0	208	10	2	1	1.6	.991	OF-141
1967		147	.241	.330	485	117	14	4	7	1.4	49	41	46	68	9	4	0	233	9	2	1	1.7	.992	OF-143
1968		153	.252	.343	504	127	21	2	7	1.4	49	32	25	64	6	2	1	352	11	7	2	2.5	.981	OF-151
1969		130	.232	.327	297	69	12	2	4	1.3	25	18	24	50	1	2	0	215	7	0	1	1.9	1.000	OF-120
1970		141	.276	.356	463	128	12	2	7	1.5	45	50	43	61	6	2	1	331	9	4	2	2.5	.988	OF-138
1971	CAL A	111	.221	.309	298	66	17	0	3	1.0	29	22	18	33	3	10	5	237	5	3	0	2.4	.988	OF-101
1972		119	.289	.377	409	118	15	3	5	1.2	41	39	35	47	5	4	1	272	13	0	5	2.5	1.000	OF-116
1973		136	.284	.342	415	118	11	2	3	0.7	48	36	26	50	1	3	0	309	5	1	0	2.4	.997	OF-129
1974	MIL A	98	.240	.300	267	64	9	2	1	0.4	21	24	18	26	3	9	1	187	8	1	1	2.1	.995	OF-82, DH-13
1975	CLE A	25	.200	.225	40	8	1	0	0	0.0	6	1	1	7	0	1	0	24	1	2	0	1.2	.926	OF-18, DH-5
14 yrs.		1383	.255	.344	4136	1053	150	23	58	1.4	422	343	298	569	45	42	10	2724	85	30	15	2.1	.989	OF-1311, DH-18, 2B-1

Neil Berry

BERRY, CORNELIUS JOHN
B. Jan. 11, 1922, Kalamazoo, Mich.
BR TR 5′10″ 168 lbs.

Year	Team	Games	BA	SA	AB	H	2B	3B	HR	HR%	R	RBI	BB	SO	SB	Pinch Hit AB	Pinch Hit H	PO	A	E	DP	TC/G	FA	G by Pos
1948	DET A	87	.266	.305	256	68	8	1	0	0.0	46	16	37	23	1	5	1	138	199	17	46	5.3	.952	SS-41, 2B-26
1949		109	.237	.271	329	78	9	1	0	0.0	38	18	27	24	4	4	0	227	237	14	56	4.8	.971	2B-95, SS-4
1950		39	.250	.275	40	10	1	0	0	0.0	9	7	6	11	0	4	0	21	35	3	14	4.2	.949	SS-11, 2B-2, 3B-1
1951		67	.229	.287	157	36	5	2	0	0.0	17	9	10	15	4	4	0	78	127	12	22	3.9	.945	SS-38, 2B-10, 3B-7
1952		73	.228	.280	189	43	4	3	0	0.0	22	13	22	19	1	1	1	91	160	9	26	3.8	.965	SS-66, 3B-2
1953	2 teams	STL A (57G –.283) CHI A (5G –.125)																						
″	total	62	.271	.318	107	29	1	2	0	0.0	15	11	10	11	1	6	1	50	69	10	12	3.1	.922	2B-18, 3B-18, SS-6
1954	BAL A	5	.111	.111	9	1	0	0	0	0.0	1	0	1	2	0	0	0	6	7	0	2	2.6	1.000	SS-5
7 yrs.		442	.244	.286	1087	265	28	9	0	0.0	148	74	113	105	11	24	3	611	834	65	178	4.3	.957	SS-171, 2B-151, 3B-28

Sean Berry

BERRY, SEAN ROBERT
B. Mar. 22, 1966, Santa Monica, Calif.
BR TR 5′11″ 200 lbs.

Year	Team	Games	BA	SA	AB	H	2B	3B	HR	HR%	R	RBI	BB	SO	SB	Pinch Hit AB	Pinch Hit H	PO	A	E	DP	TC/G	FA	G by Pos
1990	KC A	8	.217	.348	23	5	1	1	0	0.0	2	4	2	5	0	0	0	7	10	1	2	2.3	.944	3B-8
1991		31	.133	.183	60	8	3	0	0	0.0	5	1	5	23	0	1	0	13	52	2	3	2.2	.970	3B-30
1992	MON N	24	.333	.404	57	19	1	0	1	1.8	5	4	1	11	2	5	3	10	19	4	1	1.6	.879	3B-20
1993		122	.261	.465	299	78	15	2	14	4.7	50	49	41	70	12	30	7	66	153	15	13	2.4	.936	3B-96
1994		103	.278	.453	320	89	19	2	11	3.4	43	41	32	50	14	3	0	66	147	14	8	2.3	.938	3B-100
1995		103	.318	.529	314	100	22	1	14	4.5	38	55	25	53	3	18	5	76	167	12	18	3.0	.953	3B-83, 1B-3
6 yrs.		391	.279	.459	1073	299	61	6	40	3.7	143	154	106	212	31	57	15	238	548	48	45	2.5	.942	3B-337, 1B-3

Damon Berryhill

BERRYHILL, DAMON SCOTT
B. Dec. 3, 1963, South Laguna, Calif.
BB TR 6′ 205 lbs.

Year	Team	Games	BA	SA	AB	H	2B	3B	HR	HR%	R	RBI	BB	SO	SB	Pinch Hit AB	Pinch Hit H	PO	A	E	DP	TC/G	FA	G by Pos
1987	CHI N	12	.179	.214	28	5	1	0	0	0.0	2	1	3	5	0	1	0	37	3	4	0	4.0	.909	C-11
1988		95	.259	.395	309	80	19	1	7	2.3	19	38	17	56	1	6	1	448	54	9	5	5.7	.982	C-90
1989		91	.257	.341	334	86	13	0	5	1.5	37	41	16	54	1	6	2	473	41	4	4	5.8	.992	C-89
1990		17	.189	.321	53	10	4	0	1	1.9	6	9	5	14	0	1	0	87	3	2	0	6.1	.978	C-15
1991	2 teams	CHI N (62G –.189) ATL N (1G –.000)																						
″	total	63	.188	.325	160	30	7	0	5	3.1	13	14	11	42	1	17	2	214	24	8	2	5.0	.967	C-49
1992	ATL N	101	.228	.384	307	70	16	1	10	3.3	21	43	17	67	0	16	4	426	31	1	5	5.5	.998	C-84
1993		115	.245	.382	335	82	18	2	8	2.4	24	43	21	64	0	12	2	570	52	6	2	6.0	.990	C-105
1994	BOS A	82	.263	.416	255	67	17	2	6	2.4	30	34	19	59	0	13	4	409	29	2	2	6.0	.995	C-67, DH-6
1995	CIN N	34	.183	.293	82	15	3	0	2	2.4	6	11	10	19	0	6	1	153	12	2	0	5.6	.988	C-29, 1B-1
9 yrs.		610	.239	.369	1863	445	98	6	44	2.4	158	234	119	380	3	78	16	2817	249	38	20	5.7	.988	C-539, DH-6, 1B-1
LEAGUE CHAMPIONSHIP SERIES																								
1992	ATL N	7	.167	.208	24	4	1	0	0	0.0	1	1	3	2	0	0	0	43	5	0	0	6.9	1.000	C-7
1993		6	.211	.368	19	4	0	0	1	5.3	2	3	1	5	0	0	0	42	0	0	0	7.0	1.000	C-6
2 yrs.		13	.186	.279	43	8	1	0	1	2.3	3	4	4	7	0	0	0	85	5	0	0	6.9	1.000	C-13
WORLD SERIES																								
1992	ATL N	6	.091	.227	22	2	0	0	1	4.5	1	3	1	11	0	0	0	33	2	0	0	5.8	1.000	C-6

Harry Berte

BERTE, HARRY THOMAS
B. May 10, 1872, Covington, Ky. D. May 6, 1952, Los Angeles, Calif.
TR

Year	Team	Games	BA	SA	AB	H	2B	3B	HR	HR%	R	RBI	BB	SO	SB	Pinch Hit AB	Pinch Hit H	PO	A	E	DP	TC/G	FA	G by Pos
1903	STL N	4	.333	.333	15	5	0	0	0	0.0	1	1	1		0	0	0	3	6	4	1	3.3	.692	2B-3, SS-1

Dick Bertell

BERTELL, RICHARD GEORGE
B. Nov. 21, 1935, Oak Park, Ill.
BR TR 6′½″ 200 lbs.

Year	Team	Games	BA	SA	AB	H	2B	3B	HR	HR%	R	RBI	BB	SO	SB	Pinch Hit AB	Pinch Hit H	PO	A	E	DP	TC/G	FA	G by Pos
1960	CHI N	5	.133	.133	15	2	0	0	0	0.0	0	2	3	1	0	0	0	18	6	0	0	4.8	1.000	C-5
1961		92	.273	.330	267	73	7	1	2	0.7	20	33	15	33	0	6	2	396	49	8	10	5.0	.982	C-90
1962		77	.302	.377	215	65	6	2	2	0.9	19	18	13	30	0	5	1	306	36	5	0	4.6	.986	C-76
1963		100	.233	.286	322	75	7	2	2	0.6	15	14	24	41	0	1	0	549	84	8	15	6.5	.988	C-99
1964		112	.238	.320	353	84	11	3	4	1.1	29	35	33	67	2	3	0	531	52	11	3	5.4	.981	C-110
1965	2 teams	CHI N (34G –.214) SF N (22G –.188)																						
″	total	56	.205	.227	132	27	3	0	0	0.0	7	10	18	15	0	0	0	241	35	4	4	5.0	.986	C-56
1967	CHI N	2	.167	.500	6	1	0	1	0	0.0	1	0	0	1	0	0	0	12	1	0	0	6.5	1.000	C-2
7 yrs.		444	.250	.312	1310	327	34	9	10	0.8	91	112	106	188	2	15	3	2053	263	36	32	5.4	.985	C-438

Reno Bertoia

BERTOIA, RENO PETER
B. Jan. 8, 1935, St. Vito Udine, Italy.
BR TR 5′11½″ 185 lbs.

Year	Team	Games	BA	SA	AB	H	2B	3B	HR	HR%	R	RBI	BB	SO	SB	Pinch Hit AB	Pinch Hit H	PO	A	E	DP	TC/G	FA	G by Pos
1953	DET A	1	.000	.000	1	0	0	0	0	0.0	0	0	0	1	0	0	0	1	0	1	0	2.0	.500	2B-1
1954		54	.162	.297	37	6	2	0	1	2.7	13	2	5	9	1	2	0	27	41	3	7	2.7	.958	2B-15, 3B-8, SS-3

Reno Bertoia *continued*

Year	Team	Games	BA	SA	AB	H	2B	3B	HR	HR%	R	RBI	BB	SO	SB	Pinch Hit AB	Pinch Hit H	PO	A	E	DP	TC/G	FA	G by Pos
1955		38	.206	.309	68	14	2	1	1	1.5	13	10	5	11	0	6	0	23	52	4	8	3.2	.949	3B-14, 2B-6, SS-5
1956		22	.182	.258	66	12	2	0	1	1.5	7	5	6	12	0	0	0	54	61	2	19	5.8	.983	2B-18, 3B-2
1957		97	.275	.383	295	81	16	2	4	1.4	28	28	19	43	2	9	0	79	128	10	8	2.4	.954	3B-83, SS-7, 2B-2
1958		86	.233	.333	240	56	6	0	6	2.5	28	27	20	35	5	5	0	72	142	12	13	3.1	.947	3B-68, SS-5, OF-1
1959	WAS A	90	.237	.347	308	73	10	0	8	2.6	33	29	29	48	2	14	3	145	207	10	41	4.7	.972	2B-71, 3B-5, SS-1
1960		121	.265	.359	460	122	17	7	4	0.9	44	45	26	58	3	5	3	120	247	14	27	2.9	.963	3B-112, 2B-21
1961	3 teams	MIN A (35G –.212) KC A (39G –.242) DET A (24G –.217)																						
"	total	98	.226	.267	270	61	5	0	2	0.7	35	25	32	35	3	6	2	78	166	17	19	3.0	.935	3B-74, 2B-13, SS-1
1962	DET A	5	—	—	0	0	0	0	0	—	3	0	0	0	0	0	0	0	2	0	0	0.7	1.000	2B-1, 3B-1, SS-1
10 yrs.		612	.244	.336	1745	425	60	10	27	1.5	204	171	142	252	16	47	8	599	1046	73	142	3.2	.958	3B-367, 2B-148, SS-23, OF-1

Bob Bescher

BESCHER, ROBERT HENRY BB TL 6′ 1″ 200 lbs.
B. Feb. 25, 1884, London, Ohio D. Nov. 29, 1942, London, Ohio.

1908	CIN N	32	.272	.404	114	31	5	5	0	0.0	16	17	9		10	0	0	84	2	0	2	2.7	1.000	OF-32
1909		124	.240	.312	446	107	17	6	1	0.2	73	34	56		**54**	6	1	247	14	13	4	2.3	.953	OF-117
1910		150	.250	.338	589	147	20	10	4	0.7	95	48	81	75	**70**	0	0	339	16	20	4	2.5	.947	OF-150
1911		153	.275	.367	599	165	32	10	1	0.2	106	45	102	**78**	**81**	0	0	267	21	14	2	2.0	.954	OF-153
1912		145	.281	.396	548	154	29	11	4	0.7	**120**	38	83	61	**67**	2	1	347	15	14	4	2.6	.963	OF-143
1913		141	.258	.350	511	132	22	11	1	0.2	86	37	**94**	68	38	2	0	283	22	10	2	2.3	.968	OF-138
1914	NY N	135	.270	.365	512	138	23	4	6	1.2	82	35	45	48	36	8	3	298	14	13	7	2.6	.960	OF-126
1915	STL N	130	.263	.348	486	128	15	7	4	0.8	71	34	52	53	27	0	0	257	12	8	1	2.1	.971	OF-130
1916		151	.235	.339	561	132	24	8	6	1.1	78	43	60	50	39	0	0	284	18	15	2	2.1	.953	OF-151
1917		42	.155	.209	110	17	1	1	1	0.9	10	8	20	13	3	8	0	61	0	1	0	1.9	.984	OF-32
1918	CLE A	25	.333	.400	60	20	2	1	0	0.0	12	6	17	5	3	4	3	28	3	1	0	1.9	.969	OF-17
11 yrs.		1228	.258	.351	4536	1171	190	74	28	0.6	749	345	619	451	428	30	8	2495	137	109	28	2.3	.960	OF-1189

Jim Beswick

BESWICK, JAMES WILLIAM BB TR 6′ 1″ 180 lbs.
B. Feb. 12, 1958, Wilkensburg, Pa.

1978	SD N	17	.050	.050	20	1	0	0	0	0.0	2	0	1	7	0	7	1	8	0	0	0	1.3	1.000	OF-6

Frank Betcher

BETCHER, FRANKLIN LYLE BB TR 5′11″ 173 lbs.
Born Franklin Lyle Bettger.
B. Feb. 15, 1888, Philadelphia, Pa. D. Nov. 27, 1981, Wynnewood, Pa.

1910	STL N	35	.202	.225	89	18	2	0	0	0.0	7	6	7	14	1	8	2	37	61	8	5	3.9	.925	SS-12, 3B-7, 2B-6, OF-2

Bill Bethea

BETHEA, WILLIAM LAMAR (Spot) BR TR 6′ 175 lbs.
B. Jan. 1, 1942, Houston, Tex.

1964	MIN A	10	.167	.200	30	5	1	0	0	0.0	4	2	4	4	0	0	0	16	16	0	6	3.2	1.000	2B-7, SS-3

Larry Bettencourt

BETTENCOURT, LAWRENCE JOSEPH BR TR 5′11″ 195 lbs.
B. Sept. 22, 1905, Newark, Calif. D. Sept. 15, 1978, New Orleans, La.

1928	STL A	67	.283	.465	159	45	9	4	4	2.5	30	24	22	19	2	17	2	42	68	6	4	2.6	.948	3B-41, OF-2, C-1
1931		74	.257	.364	206	53	9	2	3	1.5	27	26	31	35	4	14	2	99	6	4	1	1.9	.963	OF-58
1932		27	.133	.267	30	4	1	0	1	3.3	4	3	7	6	1	17	2	9	2	0	0	1.8	1.000	OF-4, 3B-2
3 yrs.		168	.258	.397	395	102	19	6	8	2.0	61	53	60	60	7	48	6	150	76	10	5	2.2	.958	OF-64, 3B-43, C-1

Bruno Betzel

BETZEL, CHRISTIAN FREDERICK ALBERT JOHN HENRY DAVID BR TR 5′ 9″ 158 lbs.
B. Dec. 6, 1894, Chattanooga, Ohio D. Feb. 7, 1965, West Hollywood, Fla.

1914	STL N	7	.000	.000	9	0	0	0	0	0.0	2	0	1	1	0	2	0	4	11	0	0	3.0	1.000	2B-4, 3B-1
1915		117	.251	.305	367	92	12	4	0	0.0	42	27	18	48	10	3	1	109	228	25	11	3.3	.931	3B-105, 2B-3, SS-2
1916		142	.233	.312	510	119	15	11	1	0.2	49	37	39	77	22	0	0	319	435	40	67	5.2	.950	2B-113, 3B-33, OF-7
1917		106	.216	.256	328	71	4	3	1	0.3	24	17	20	47	9	3	2	193	225	17	42	4.3	.961	2B-75, OF-23, 3B-4
1918		76	.222	.309	230	51	6	7	0	0.0	18	13	12	16	8	6	2	100	103	17	10	3.4	.923	3B-34, OF-21, 2B-10
5 yrs.		448	.231	.295	1444	333	37	25	2	0.1	135	94	90	189	49	14	5	725	1002	99	130	4.2	.946	2B-205, 3B-177, OF-51, SS-2

Kurt Bevacqua

BEVACQUA, KURT ANTHONY BR TR 6′ 180 lbs.
B. Jan. 23, 1947, Miami Beach, Fla.

1971	CLE A	55	.204	.307	137	28	3	1	3	2.2	9	13	4	28	0	15	3	77	72	5	11	3.3	.968	2B-36, OF-5, 3B-3, SS-2
1972		19	.114	.200	35	4	0	0	1	2.9	2	1	3	10	0	6	1	11	5	1	1	1.4	.941	OF-11, 3B-1
1973	KC A	99	.257	.330	276	71	8	3	2	0.7	39	40	25	42	2	14	6	120	90	9	20	2.9	.959	3B-40, 2B-16, OF-10, 1B-9
1974	2 teams	PIT N (18G –.114) KC A (39G –.211)																						
"	total	57	.184	.192	125	23	1	0	0	0.0	11	3	11	30	1	15	2	98	42	6	20	3.0	.959	3B-21, 1B-14, 2B-7, DH-3, SS-2, OF-1
1975	MIL A	104	.229	.306	258	59	14	0	2	0.8	30	24	26	45	3	5	1	157	168	13	35	3.3	.962	3B-60, 2B-32, SS-5, 1B-3, DH-1
1976		12	.143	.143	7	1	0	0	0	0.0	3	0	0	0	0	2	0	0	6	0	0	3.0	1.000	2B-2
1977	TEX A	39	.333	.604	96	32	7	2	5	5.2	13	28	6	13	0	14	5	42	31	1	4	1.9	.986	OF-14, 3B-11, 1B-5, 2B-5, DH-3
1978		90	.222	.343	248	55	12	0	6	2.4	21	30	18	31	1	16	1	62	116	18	12	2.5	.908	3B-49, DH-16, 2B-13, 1B-1
1979	SD N	114	.253	.330	297	75	12	4	1	0.3	23	34	38	25	2	29	6	115	156	11	21	2.9	.961	3B-64, 2B-16, OF-8, 1B-8
1980	2 teams	SD N (62G –.268) PIT N (22G –.163)																						
"	total	84	.228	.307	114	26	7	1	0	0.0	5	16	12	8	1	**56**	**17**	32	31	2	2	2.1	.969	3B-22, OF-4, 1B-3, 2B-2
1981	PIT N	29	.259	.407	27	7	1	0	1	3.7	2	4	4	6	0	19	5	7	10	1	3	3.0	.944	2B-4, 3B-2
1982	SD N	64	.252	.325	123	31	9	0	0	0.0	15	24	17	22	2	26	9	256	16	3	13	8.1	.989	1B-30, OF-3, 3B-1
1983		74	.244	.327	156	38	7	0	2	1.3	17	24	18	33	0	34	14	207	28	2	16	4.6	.992	1B-27, OF-12, 3B-12
1984		59	.200	.275	80	16	3	0	1	1.3	7	9	14	19	0	30	7	73	15	1	10	2.7	.989	1B-20, 3B-10, OF-3
1985		71	.239	.348	138	33	6	0	3	2.2	17	25	25	17	0	26	5	49	60	7	8	2.7	.940	3B-33, 1B-9, OF-1
15 yrs.		970	.236	.327	2117	499	90	11	27	1.3	214	275	221	329	12	307	82	1306	846	80	176	3.2	.964	3B-329, 2B-133, 1B-129, OF-72, DH-23, SS-9
LEAGUE CHAMPIONSHIP SERIES																								
1984	SD N	2	.000	.000	2	0	0	0	0	0.0	0	0	0	0	0	2	0	0	0	0	0	0.0	—	
WORLD SERIES																								
1984	SD N	5	.412	.882	17	7	2	0	2	11.8	4	4	1	2	0	0	0	0	0	0	0	0.0	.000	DH-5

Hal Bevan

BEVAN, JOSEPH HAROLD
B. Nov. 15, 1930, New Orleans, La. D. Oct. 5, 1968, New Orleans, La.
BR TR 6' 2" 198 lbs.

Year	Team	Games	BA	SA	AB	H	2B	3B	HR	HR%	R	RBI	BB	SO	SB	Pinch Hit AB	Pinch Hit H	PO	A	E	DP	TC/G	FA	G by Pos
1952	2 teams	BOS A (1G –.000)	PHI A (8G –.353)																					
"	total	9	.333	.333	18	6	0	0	0	0.0	1	4	0	1	2	0	0	5	9	0	0	2.0	1.000	3B-7
1955	KC A	3	.000	.000	3	0	0	0	0	0.0	0	0	0	0	0	2	0	1	0	0	0	1.0	1.000	3B-1
1961	CIN N	3	.333	1.333	3	1	0	0	1	33.3	1	1	0	2	0	3	1	0	0	0	0	0.0	—	
3 yrs.		15	.292	.417	24	7	0	0	1	4.2	2	5	0	3	2	5	1	6	9	0	0	1.9	1.000	3B-8

Monte Beville

BEVILLE, HENRY MONTE
B. Feb. 24, 1875, Dublin, Ind. D. Jan. 24, 1955, Grand Rapids, Mich.
BL TR 5'11" 180 lbs.

Year	Team	Games	BA	SA	AB	H	2B	3B	HR	HR%	R	RBI	BB	SO	SB	Pinch Hit AB	Pinch Hit H	PO	A	E	DP	TC/G	FA	G by Pos
1903	NY A	82	.194	.256	258	50	14	1	0	0.0	23	29	16		4	4	1	314	69	15	7	5.1	.962	C-75, 1B-3
1904	2 teams	NY A (9G –.273)	DET A (54G –.207)																					
"	total	63	.214	.260	196	42	7	1	0	0.0	16	15	10		2	4	0	394	45	21	11	7.5	.954	C-33, 1B-28
2 yrs.		145	.203	.258	454	92	21	2	0	0.0	39	44	26		6	8	1	708	114	36	18	6.2	.958	C-108, 1B-31

Buddy Biancalana

BIANCALANA, ROLAND AMERICO
B. Feb. 2, 1960, Greenbrae, Calif.
BB TR 5'11" 155 lbs.

Year	Team	Games	BA	SA	AB	H	2B	3B	HR	HR%	R	RBI	BB	SO	SB	Pinch Hit AB	Pinch Hit H	PO	A	E	DP	TC/G	FA	G by Pos
1982	KC A	3	.500	1.500	2	1	0	1	0	0.0	0	0	1	0	0	0	0	2	8	0	1	3.3	1.000	SS-3
1983		6	.200	.200	15	3	0	0	0	0.0	2	0	0	7	1	0	0	11	21	3	3	5.8	.914	SS-6
1984		66	.194	.299	134	26	6	1	2	1.5	18	9	6	44	1	2	2	62	144	8	28	3.4	.963	SS-33, 2B-29, DH-1
1985		81	.188	.261	138	26	5	1	1	0.7	21	6	17	34	1	0	0	83	169	10	32	3.3	.962	SS-74, 2B-4, DH-2
1986		100	.242	.337	190	46	4	4	2	1.1	24	8	15	50	5	0	0	108	190	16	41	3.1	.949	SS-89, 2B-12
1987	2 teams	KC A (37G –.213)	HOU N (18G –.042)																					
"	total	55	.155	.211	71	11	1	0	1	1.4	5	7	2	22	0	3	0	30	63	8	13	1.9	.921	SS-38, 2B-15
6 yrs.		311	.205	.293	550	113	16	7	6	1.1	70	30	41	157	8	5	2	296	595	45	118	3.1	.952	SS-243, 2B-60, DH-3
LEAGUE CHAMPIONSHIP SERIES																								
1984	KC A	2	.000	.000	1	0	0	0	0	0.0	0	0	0	1	0	0	0	1	2	0	0	1.5	1.000	SS-2
1985		7	.222	.278	18	4	1	0	0	0.0	2	1	1	6	0	0	0	10	20	0	5	4.3	1.000	SS-7
2 yrs.		9	.211	.263	19	4	1	0	0	0.0	2	1	1	7	0	0	0	11	22	0	5	3.7	1.000	SS-9
WORLD SERIES																								
1985	KC A	7	.278	.278	18	5	0	0	0	0.0	2	2	5	4	0	0	0	6	20	0	1	3.7	1.000	SS-7

Tommy Bianco

BIANCO, THOMAS ANTHONY
B. Dec. 16, 1952, Rockville Centre, N. Y.
BB TR 5'11" 190 lbs.

Year	Team	Games	BA	SA	AB	H	2B	3B	HR	HR%	R	RBI	BB	SO	SB	Pinch Hit AB	Pinch Hit H	PO	A	E	DP	TC/G	FA	G by Pos
1975	MIL A	18	.176	.206	34	6	1	0	0	0.0	6	0	3	7	0	5	0	16	13	1	0	2.1	.967	3B-7, 1B-5, DH-2

Hank Biasetti

BIASETTI, HENRY ARCADO
B. Jan. 14, 1922, Beano, Italy.
BL TL 5'11" 175 lbs.

Year	Team	Games	BA	SA	AB	H	2B	3B	HR	HR%	R	RBI	BB	SO	SB	Pinch Hit AB	Pinch Hit H	PO	A	E	DP	TC/G	FA	G by Pos
1949	PHI A	21	.083	.167	24	2	2	0	0	0.0	6	2	8	5	0	9	0	44	2	1	4	5.9	.979	1B-8

Dante Bichette

BICHETTE, ALPHONSE DANTE
B. Nov. 18, 1963, West Palm Beach, Fla.
BR TR 6' 3" 215 lbs.

Year	Team	Games	BA	SA	AB	H	2B	3B	HR	HR%	R	RBI	BB	SO	SB	Pinch Hit AB	Pinch Hit H	PO	A	E	DP	TC/G	FA	G by Pos
1988	CAL A	21	.261	.304	46	12	2	0	0	0.0	1	8	0	7	0	0	0	44	2	1	0	2.2	.979	OF-21
1989		48	.210	.326	138	29	7	0	3	2.2	13	15	6	24	3	9	0	95	6	1	2	2.5	.990	OF-40, DH-1
1990		109	.255	.433	349	89	15	1	15	4.3	40	53	16	79	5	8	2	183	12	7	5	1.9	.965	OF-105
1991	MIL A	134	.238	.393	445	106	18	3	15	3.4	53	59	22	107	14	10	4	270	14	7	7	2.3	.976	OF-127, 3B-1
1992		112	.287	.406	387	111	27	2	5	1.3	37	41	16	74	18	10	1	188	6	2	2	1.9	.990	OF-101, DH-4
1993	CLR N	141	.310	.526	538	167	43	5	21	3.9	93	89	28	99	14	4	0	308	14	9	3	2.4	.973	OF-137
1994		116	.304	.548	**484**	147	33	2	27	5.6	74	95	19	70	21	2	1	210	10	2	3	1.9	.991	OF-116
1995		139	.340	**.620**	579	**197**	38	2	**40**	6.9	102	**128**	22	96	13	3	1	208	9	3	0	1.6	.986	OF-136
8 yrs.		820	.289	.489	2966	858	183	15	126	4.2	413	488	129	556	88	46	9	1506	73	32	22	2.0	.980	OF-783, DH-5, 3B-1
DIVISIONAL PLAYOFF SERIES																								
1995	CLR N	4	.588	.941	17	10	3	0	1	5.9	6	3	1	3	0	0	0	9	0	0	0	2.3	1.000	OF-4

Oscar Bielaski

BIELASKI, OSCAR
B. Mar. 21, 1847, Washington, D. C. D. Nov. 8, 1911, Washington, D. C.
BR TR 5'10½" 170 lbs.

Year	Team	Games	BA	SA	AB	H	2B	3B	HR	HR%	R	RBI	BB	SO	SB	Pinch Hit AB	Pinch Hit H	PO	A	E	DP	TC/G	FA	G by Pos
1876	CHI N	32	.209	.230	139	29	3	0	0	0.0	24	10	2	3		0	0	41	4	14	1	1.8	.763	OF-32

Lou Bierbauer

BIERBAUER, LOUIS W.
Also appeared in box score as Bauer.
B. Sept. 28, 1865, Erie, Pa. D. Jan. 31, 1926, Erie, Pa.
BL TR 5' 8" 140 lbs.

Year	Team	Games	BA	SA	AB	H	2B	3B	HR	HR%	R	RBI	BB	SO	SB	Pinch Hit AB	Pinch Hit H	PO	A	E	DP	TC/G	FA	G by Pos
1886	PHI AA	137	.226	.289	522	118	17	5	2	0.4	56		21			0	0	406	435	89	55	6.6	.904	2B-133, C-4, P-2, SS-2
1887		126	.272	.340	530	144	19	7	1	0.2	74		13		40	0	0	332	378	61	45	6.1	.921	2B-126, P-1
1888		134	.267	.338	535	143	20	9	0	0.0	83	80	25		34	0	0	364	423	70	41	6.3	.918	2B-121, 3B-13, P-1
1889		130	.304	.417	549	167	27	7	7	1.3	80	105	29	30	17	0	0	472	406	55	80	7.1	.941	2B-130, C-1
1890	BKN P	133	.306	.431	589	180	31	11	7	1.2	128	99	40	15	16	0	0	372	468	62	77	6.8	.931	2B-133
1891	PIT N	121	.206	.262	500	103	13	6	1	0.2	60	47	28	19	12	0	0	331	384	55	42	6.4	.929	2B-121
1892		152	.236	.331	649	153	20	9	8	1.2	81	65	25	29	11	0	0	385	555	49	66	6.5	.950	2B-152
1893		128	.284	.384	528	150	19	11	4	0.8	84	94	36	12	11	0	0	352	441	34	71	6.5	.959	2B-128
1894		130	.303	.406	525	159	19	13	3	0.6	86	107	26	9	19	0	0	309	453	50	58	6.2	.938	2B-130
1895		117	.258	.333	466	120	13	11	0	0.0	53	69	19	8	18	0	0	284	400	39	52	6.2	.946	2B-117
1896		59	.287	.372	258	74	10	6	0	0.0	33	39	5	7	7	0	0	140	206	12	32	6.1	.966	2B-59
1897	STL N	12	.217	.217	46	10	0	0	0	0.0	1	1	0		2	0	0	25	33	5	4	5.3	.921	2B-12
1898		4	.000	.000	9	0	0	0	0	0.0	0	0	1		0	0	0	3	10	4	0	4.3	.765	2B-2, SS-1, 3B-1
13 yrs.		1383	.267	.354	5706	1521	208	95	33	0.6	819	706	268	129	187	0	0	3775	4592	585	623	6.4	.935	2B-1364, 3B-14, C-5, P-4, SS-3

Carson Bigbee

BIGBEE, CARSON LEE (Skeeter)
Brother of Lyle Bigbee.
B. Mar. 31, 1895, Waterloo, Ore. D. Oct. 17, 1964, Portland, Ore.
BL TR 5' 9" 157 lbs.

Year	Team	Games	BA	SA	AB	H	2B	3B	HR	HR%	R	RBI	BB	SO	SB	Pinch Hit AB	Pinch Hit H	PO	A	E	DP	TC/G	FA	G by Pos
1916	PIT N	43	.250	.341	164	41	3	6	0	0.0	17	3	7	14	8	0	0	81	55	10	7	3.4	.932	2B-23, OF-19, 3B-1
1917		133	.239	.288	469	112	11	6	0	0.0	46	21	37	16	19	5	2	272	56	15	10	2.7	.956	OF-107, 2B-16, SS-2
1918		92	.255	.319	310	79	11	3	1	0.3	47	19	42	10	19	4	2	168	13	8	1	2.1	.958	OF-92

Carson Bigbee *continued*

Year	Team	Games	BA	SA	AB	H	2B	3B	HR	HR%	R	RBI	BB	SO	SB	Pinch Hit AB	Pinch Hit H	PO	A	E	DP	TC/G	FA	G by Pos
1919		125	.276	.328	478	132	11	4	2	0.4	61	27	37	26	31	1	0	343	21	11	5	3.0	.971	OF-124
1920		137	.280	.391	550	154	19	15	4	0.7	78	32	45	28	31	0	0	289	16	9	4	2.4	.971	OF-133
1921		147	.323	.427	632	204	23	17	3	0.5	100	42	41	19	21	1	0	351	27	9	6	2.7	.977	OF-146
1922		150	.350	.471	614	215	29	15	5	0.8	113	99	56	13	24	0	0	345	27	17	5	2.6	.956	OF-150
1923		123	.299	.363	499	149	18	7	0	0.0	79	54	43	15	10	1	1	283	12	3	3	2.4	.990	OF-122
1924		89	.262	.284	282	74	4	1	0	0.0	42	15	26	12	15	8	4	155	9	10	2	2.3	.943	OF-75
1925		66	.238	.294	126	30	7	0	0	0.0	31	8	7	8	2	13	3	62	3	4	1	1.6	.942	OF-42
1926		42	.221	.382	68	15	3	1	2	2.9	15	4	3	0	2	10	3	26	2	1	0	1.4	.966	OF-21
11 yrs.		1147	.287	.369	4192	1205	139	75	17	0.4	629	324	344	161	182	43	15	2375	241	97	44	2.5	.964	OF-1031, 2B-39, SS-2, 3B-1
WORLD SERIES																								
1925	PIT N	4	.333	.667	3	1	1	0	0	0.0	1	1	0	0	1	3	1	0	0	0	0	0.0	.000	OF-1

Lyle Bigbee

BIGBEE, LYLE RANDOLPH (Al) BL TR 6′ 180 lbs.
Brother of Carson Bigbee.
B. Aug. 22, 1893, Sweet Home, Ore. D. Aug. 5, 1942, Portland, Ore.

Year	Team	Games	BA	SA	AB	H	2B	3B	HR	HR%	R	RBI	BB	SO	SB	Pinch Hit AB	Pinch Hit H	PO	A	E	DP	TC/G	FA	G by Pos
1920	PHI A	37	.186	.243	70	13	1	0	1	1.4	4	8	8	10	1	10	3	23	12	4	0	1.6	.897	OF-13, P-12
1921	PIT N	5	.000	.000	2	0	0	0	0	0.0	0	0	0	1	0	0	0	0	2	0	0	0.4	1.000	P-5
2 yrs.		42	.181	.236	72	13	1	0	1	1.4	4	8	8	11	1	10	3	23	14	4	0	1.4	.902	P-17, OF-13

Elliott Bigelow

BIGELOW, ELLIOTT ALLARDICE (Gilly) BL TL 5′11″ 185 lbs.
B. Oct. 13, 1897, Tarpon Springs, Fla. D. Aug. 10, 1933, Tampa, Fla.

Year	Team	Games	BA	SA	AB	H	2B	3B	HR	HR%	R	RBI	BB	SO	SB	Pinch Hit AB	Pinch Hit H	PO	A	E	DP	TC/G	FA	G by Pos
1929	BOS A	100	.284	.374	211	60	16	0	1	0.5	23	26	23	18	1	35	6	63	5	4	1	1.2	.944	OF-58

Craig Biggio

BIGGIO, CRAIG ALAN BR TR 5′11″ 185 lbs.
B. Dec. 14, 1965, Smithtown, N. Y.

Year	Team	Games	BA	SA	AB	H	2B	3B	HR	HR%	R	RBI	BB	SO	SB	Pinch Hit AB	Pinch Hit H	PO	A	E	DP	TC/G	FA	G by Pos
1988	HOU N	50	.211	.350	123	26	6	1	3	2.4	14	5	7	29	6	0	0	292	28	3	0	6.5	.991	C-50
1989		134	.257	.402	443	114	21	2	13	2.9	64	60	49	64	21	4	3	742	56	9	6	6.2	.989	C-125, OF-5
1990		150	.276	.348	555	153	24	2	4	0.7	53	42	53	79	25	3	2	657	60	13	4	4.5	.982	C-113, OF-50
1991		149	.295	.374	546	161	23	4	4	0.7	79	46	53	71	19	9	3	894	73	11	11	6.8	.989	C-139, 2B-3, OF-2
1992		162	.277	.369	613	170	32	3	6	1.0	96	39	94	95	38	1	0	344	413	12	81	4.8	.984	2B-161
1993		155	.287	.474	610	175	41	5	21	3.4	98	64	77	93	15	0	0	306	447	14	90	4.9	.982	2B-155
1994		114	.318	.483	437	139	**44**	5	6	1.4	88	56	62	58	**39**	2	0	225	339	7	63	5.1	.988	2B-113
1995		141	.302	.483	553	167	30	2	22	4.0	**123**	77	80	85	33	1	0	297	418	10	74	5.1	.986	2B-141
8 yrs.		1055	.285	.415	3880	1105	221	24	79	2.0	615	389	475	574	196	20	8	3757	1834	79	329	5.4	.986	2B-573, C-427, OF-57

Ivan Bigler

BIGLER, IVAN EDWARD BR TR 5′ 9″ 150 lbs.
B. Dec. 13, 1892, Bradford, Ohio D. Apr. 1, 1975, Coldwater, Mich.

Year	Team	Games	BA	SA	AB	H	2B	3B	HR	HR%	R	RBI	BB	SO	SB	Pinch Hit AB	Pinch Hit H	PO	A	E	DP	TC/G	FA	G by Pos
1917	STL A	1	—	—	0	0	0	0	0	—	0	0	0	0	0	0	0	0	0	0	0	0.0	—	

George Bignell

BIGNELL, GEORGE WILLIAM 5′ 9″ 160 lbs.
B. July 18, 1858, Taunton, Mass. D. Jan. 16, 1925, Providence, R. I.

Year	Team	Games	BA	SA	AB	H	2B	3B	HR	HR%	R	RBI	BB	SO	SB	Pinch Hit AB	Pinch Hit H	PO	A	E	DP	TC/G	FA	G by Pos
1884	MIL U	4	.222	.222	9	2	0	0	0	0.0	4		1			0	0	47	11	3	2	15.3	.951	C-4

Larry Biittner

BIITTNER, LAWRENCE DAVID BL TL 6′ 2″ 205 lbs.
B. July 27, 1945, Pocahontas, Iowa.

Year	Team	Games	BA	SA	AB	H	2B	3B	HR	HR%	R	RBI	BB	SO	SB	Pinch Hit AB	Pinch Hit H	PO	A	E	DP	TC/G	FA	G by Pos
1970	WAS A	2	.000	.000	2	0	0	0	0	0.0	0	0	0	0	0	2	0	0	0	0	0	0.0	—	
1971		66	.257	.292	171	44	4	1	0	0.0	12	16	16	20	1	19	7	83	7	6	1	2.2	.938	OF-41, 1B-3
1972	TEX A	137	.259	.335	382	99	18	1	3	0.8	34	31	29	37	1	17	4	503	41	8	37	4.2	.986	OF-65, 1B-65
1973		83	.252	.310	258	65	8	2	1	0.4	19	12	20	21	1	7	1	234	20	2	17	3.2	.992	OF-57, 1B-20, DH-3
1974	MON N	18	.269	.308	26	7	1	0	0	0.0	2	3	0	2	0	15	4	7	1	0	0	2.0	1.000	1B-4
1975		121	.315	.408	346	109	13	5	3	0.9	34	28	34	33	2	27	8	166	8	5	0	1.9	.972	OF-93
1976	2 teams	MON N (11G –.188)	CHI N (78G –.245)																					
″	total	89	.237	.308	224	53	14	1	0	0.0	23	18	10	9	0	32	6	283	35	5	20	5.0	.985	1B-33, OF-31
1977	CHI N	138	.298	.432	493	147	28	1	12	2.4	74	62	35	36	2	15	5	792	65	11	51	6.5	.987	1B-80, OF-52, P-1
1978		120	.257	.341	343	88	15	1	4	1.2	32	50	23	37	0	33	11	601	53	9	53	7.3	.986	1B-62, OF-29
1979		111	.290	.393	272	79	13	3	3	1.1	35	50	21	23	1	42	13	282	23	6	24	4.1	.981	OF-44, 1B-32
1980		127	.249	.319	273	68	12	2	1	0.4	21	34	18	33	1	52	11	305	23	2	16	4.2	.994	1B-41, OF-38
1981	CIN N	42	.213	.279	61	13	4	0	0	0.0	1	8	4	4	0	29	7	57	5	0	3	5.6	1.000	1B-8, OF-3
1982		97	.310	.413	184	57	9	2	2	1.1	18	24	17	16	1	49	10	170	14	2	13	4.0	.989	OF-31, 1B-15
1983	TEX A	66	.276	.336	116	32	5	1	0	0.0	5	18	9	16	0	31	8	140	15	2	13	4.8	.987	1B-22, DH-9, OF-2
14 yrs.		1217	.273	.359	3151	861	144	20	29	0.9	310	354	236	287	10	370	95	3623	310	58	248	4.5	.985	OF-486, 1B-385, DH-12, P-1

Dann Bilardello

BILARDELLO, DANN JAMES BR TR 6′ 185 lbs.
B. May 26, 1959, Santa Cruz, Calif.

Year	Team	Games	BA	SA	AB	H	2B	3B	HR	HR%	R	RBI	BB	SO	SB	Pinch Hit AB	Pinch Hit H	PO	A	E	DP	TC/G	FA	G by Pos
1983	CIN N	109	.238	.389	298	71	18	0	9	3.0	27	38	15	49	2	5	0	494	72	5	4	5.4	.991	C-105
1984		68	.209	.280	182	38	7	0	2	1.1	16	10	19	34	0	5	2	323	34	3	3	5.3	.992	C-68
1985		42	.167	.196	102	17	0	0	1	1.0	6	9	4	15	0	1	0	198	20	3	1	5.3	.986	C-42
1986	MON N	79	.194	.283	191	37	5	0	4	2.1	12	17	14	32	1	2	1	391	38	8	3	5.7	.982	C-77
1989	PIT N	33	.225	.375	80	18	6	0	2	2.5	11	8	2	18	1	0	0	150	14	5	1	5.1	.970	C-33
1990		19	.054	.054	37	2	0	0	0	0.0	1	3	4	10	0	0	0	69	9	0	0	4.1	1.000	C-19
1991	SD N	15	.269	.423	26	7	2	1	0	0.0	4	5	3	4	0	2	0	59	6	0	1	5.0	1.000	C-13
1992		17	.121	.152	33	4	1	0	0	0.0	2	1	4	8	0	4	1	73	9	0	2	5.9	1.000	C-14
8 yrs.		382	.204	.305	949	194	39	1	18	1.9	79	91	65	170	4	19	4	1757	202	24	15	5.3	.988	C-371

Steve Bilko

BILKO, STEVEN THOMAS BR TR 6′ 1″ 230 lbs.
B. Nov. 13, 1928, Nanticoke, Pa. D. Mar. 7, 1978, Wilkes-Barre, Pa.

Year	Team	Games	BA	SA	AB	H	2B	3B	HR	HR%	R	RBI	BB	SO	SB	Pinch Hit AB	Pinch Hit H	PO	A	E	DP	TC/G	FA	G by Pos
1949	STL N	6	.294	.412	17	5	2	0	0	0.0	3	2	5	6	0	1	0	42	3	0	1	9.0	1.000	1B-5
1950		10	.182	.212	33	6	1	0	0	0.0	1	2	4	10	0	1	1	81	7	1	8	9.9	.989	1B-9
1951		21	.222	.361	72	16	4	0	2	2.8	5	12	9	10	0	2	1	170	13	3	18	9.8	.984	1B-19

Steve Bilko *continued*

Year	Team	Games	BA	SA	AB	H	2B	3B	HR	HR%	R	RBI	BB	SO	SB	Pinch Hit AB	Pinch Hit H	PO	A	E	DP	TC/G	FA	G by Pos
1952		20	.264	.417	72	19	6	1	1	1.4	7	6	4	15	0	0	0	177	24	1	14	10.1	.995	1B-20
1953		154	.251	.412	570	143	23	3	21	3.7	72	84	70	**125**	0	0	0	1446	124	15	145	10.3	.991	1B-154
1954	**2 teams**	**STL N** (8G –.143) **CHI N** (47G –.239)																						
″	**total**	55	.226	.434	106	24	8	1	4	3.8	12	13	14	25	0	24	6	203	35	0	20	8.5	1.000	1B-28
1958	**2 teams**	**CIN N** (31G –.264) **LA N** (47G –.208)																						
″	**total**	78	.234	.479	188	44	5	4	11	5.9	25	35	18	57	0	27	5	345	28	2	39	8.2	.995	1B-46
1960	**DET A**	78	.207	.396	222	46	11	2	9	4.1	20	25	27	31	0	17	1	501	36	5	47	8.7	.991	1B-62
1961	**LA A**	114	.279	.544	294	82	16	1	20	6.8	49	59	58	81	1	24	8	579	61	7	56	7.3	.989	1B-86, OF-3
1962		64	.287	.500	164	47	9	1	8	4.9	26	38	25	35	1	14	3	371	28	2	36	8.0	.995	1B-50
10 yrs.		600	.249	.444	1738	432	85	13	76	4.4	220	276	234	395	2	110	25	3915	359	36	384	8.9	.992	1B-479, OF-3

Dick Billings

BILLINGS, RICHARD ARLIN BR TR 6′ 1″ 195 lbs.
B. Dec. 4, 1942, Detroit, Mich.

Year	Team	Games	BA	SA	AB	H	2B	3B	HR	HR%	R	RBI	BB	SO	SB	Pinch Hit AB	Pinch Hit H	PO	A	E	DP	TC/G	FA	G by Pos
1968	**WAS A**	12	.182	.303	33	6	1	0	1	3.0	3	3	5	13	0	3	1	14	6	1	0	1.8	.952	OF-8, 3B-4
1969		27	.135	.135	37	5	0	0	0	0.0	3	0	6	8	0	15	1	9	4	0	1	1.9	1.000	OF-6, 3B-1
1970		11	.250	.458	24	6	2	0	1	4.2	3	1	2	3	0	3	0	25	3	0	0	3.5	1.000	C-8
1971		116	.246	.338	349	86	14	0	6	1.7	32	48	21	54	2	24	8	379	37	4	5	4.4	.990	C-62, OF-32, 3B-2
1972	**TEX A**	133	.254	.322	469	119	15	1	5	1.1	41	58	29	77	1	10	1	547	64	16	13	4.5	.974	C-92, OF-41, 3B-5, 1B-1
1973		81	.179	.250	280	50	11	0	3	1.1	17	32	20	43	1	5	1	376	34	13	4	5.2	.969	C-72, OF-4, 1B-3, DH-2
1974	**2 teams**	**TEX A** (16G –.226) **STL N** (1G –.200)																						
″	**total**	17	.222	.250	36	8	1	0	0	0.0	2	0	4	7	2	1	0	64	2	0	1	4.1	1.000	C-14, OF-1, DH-1
1975	**STL N**	3	.000	.000	3	0	0	0	0	0.0	0	0	0	2	0	3	0	0	0	0	0	0.0	—	
8 yrs.		400	.227	.304	1231	280	44	1	16	1.3	101	142	87	207	6	64	12	1414	150	34	24	4.5	.979	C-248, OF-92, 3B-12, 1B-4, DH-3

Josh Billings

BILLINGS, JOHN AUGUSTUS BR TR 5′11″ 165 lbs.
B. Nov. 30, 1891, Grantville, Kans. D. Dec. 30, 1981, Santa Monica, Calif.

Year	Team	Games	BA	SA	AB	H	2B	3B	HR	HR%	R	RBI	BB	SO	SB	Pinch Hit AB	Pinch Hit H	PO	A	E	DP	TC/G	FA	G by Pos
1913	**CLE A**	1	.000	.000	3	0	0	0	0	0.0	0	0	0	3	0	0	0	4	2	1	0	7.0	.857	C-1
1914		8	.250	.375	8	2	1	0	0	0.0	2	0	1	1	1	2	0	10	3	3	0	5.3	.813	C-3
1915		8	.190	.238	21	4	1	0	0	0.0	2	0	0	6	1	0	0	30	6	0	0	4.5	1.000	C-7, OF-1
1916		22	.161	.161	31	5	0	0	0	0.0	2	1	2	11	0	9	1	38	13	1	3	4.3	.981	C-12
1917		66	.178	.233	129	23	3	2	0	0.0	8	9	8	21	2	17	4	134	51	5	2	4.0	.974	C-48
1918		2	.333	.333	3	1	0	0	0	0.0	0	0	0	0	0	1	0	2	0	0	0	2.0	1.000	C-1
1919	**STL A**	38	.197	.237	76	15	1	1	0	0.0	9	3	1	12	0	7	1	76	35	4	2	4.1	.965	C-27, 1B-1
1920		66	.277	.335	155	43	5	2	0	0.0	19	11	11	10	1	22	9	138	36	6	1	4.5	.967	C-40
1921		20	.217	.217	46	10	0	0	0	0.0	2	4	0	7	0	7	0	45	9	1	0	4.6	.982	C-12
1922		5	.429	.571	7	3	1	0	0	0.0	0	1	0	0	0	1	0	5	1	0	0	2.0	1.000	C-3
1923		4	.000	.000	9	0	0	0	0	0.0	0	0	0	2	0	0	0	8	3	1	1	3.0	.917	C-4
11 yrs.		240	.217	.262	488	106	12	5	0	0.0	44	29	23	73	5	66	15	490	159	22	9	4.2	.967	C-158, 1B-1, OF-1

George Binks

BINKS, GEORGE ALVIN (Bingo) BL TL 6′ 175 lbs.
Born George Alvin Binkowski.
B. July 11, 1916, Chicago, Ill.

Year	Team	Games	BA	SA	AB	H	2B	3B	HR	HR%	R	RBI	BB	SO	SB	Pinch Hit AB	Pinch Hit H	PO	A	E	DP	TC/G	FA	G by Pos
1944	**WAS A**	5	.250	.250	12	3	0	0	0	0.0	0	0	0	1	0	1	0	4	0	0	0	1.3	1.000	OF-3
1945		145	.278	.391	550	153	32	6	6	1.1	62	81	34	52	11	1	1	485	25	9	17	3.5	.983	OF-128, 1B-20
1946		65	.194	.216	134	26	3	0	0	0.0	13	12	6	16	1	**35**	7	68	1	0	0	2.5	1.000	OF-28
1947	**PHI A**	104	.258	.357	333	86	19	4	2	0.6	33	34	23	36	8	15	4	239	15	7	5	3.0	.973	OF-75, 1B-13
1948	**2 teams**	**PHI A** (17G –.098) **STL A** (15G –.217)																						
″	**total**	32	.141	.156	64	9	1	0	0	0.0	4	3	4	3	1	9	1	35	1	0	1	1.6	1.000	OF-19, 1B-4
5 yrs.		351	.253	.344	1093	277	55	10	8	0.7	112	130	67	108	21	61	13	831	42	16	23	3.1	.982	OF-253, 1B-37

Steve Biras

BIRAS, STEPHEN ALEXANDER BR TR 5′11″ 185 lbs.
B. Feb. 26, 1922, East St. Louis, Ill. D. Apr. 21, 1965, St. Louis, Mo.

Year	Team	Games	BA	SA	AB	H	2B	3B	HR	HR%	R	RBI	BB	SO	SB	Pinch Hit AB	Pinch Hit H	PO	A	E	DP	TC/G	FA	G by Pos
1944	**CLE A**	2	1.000	1.000	2	2	0	0	0	0.0	0	2	0	0	0	1	1	1	1	1	0	3.0	.667	2B-1

Jud Birchall

BIRCHALL, ADONIRAM JUDSON
B. 1858, Germantown, Pa. D. Dec. 22, 1887, Philadelphia, Pa.

Year	Team	Games	BA	SA	AB	H	2B	3B	HR	HR%	R	RBI	BB	SO	SB	Pinch Hit AB	Pinch Hit H	PO	A	E	DP	TC/G	FA	G by Pos
1882	**PHI AA**	75	.263	.305	338	89	12	1	0	0.0	65		8			0	0	138	18	24	0	2.4	.867	OF-74, 2B-1
1883		96	.241	.274	**449**	108	10	1	1	0.2	95		19			0	0	168	22	45	0	2.4	.809	OF-96
1884		54	.258	.285	221	57	2	2	0	0.0	36		4			0	0	82	15	17	1	2.1	.851	OF-52, 3B-2
3 yrs.		225	.252	.287	1008	254	24	4	1	0.1	196		31			0	0	388	55	86	1	2.4	.837	OF-222, 3B-2, 2B-1

Frank Bird

BIRD, FRANK ZEPHERIN (Dodo) BR TR 5′10″ 195 lbs.
B. Mar. 10, 1869, Spencer, Mass. D. May 20, 1958, Worcester, Mass.

Year	Team	Games	BA	SA	AB	H	2B	3B	HR	HR%	R	RBI	BB	SO	SB	Pinch Hit AB	Pinch Hit H	PO	A	E	DP	TC/G	FA	G by Pos
1892	**STL N**	17	.200	.360	50	10	3	1	1	2.0	9	1	6	11	2	0	0	52	17	6	1	4.4	.920	C-17

Joe Birmingham

BIRMINGHAM, JOSEPH LEO (Dode) BR TR 5′10″ 185 lbs.
B. Aug. 6, 1884, Elmira, N. Y. D. Apr. 24, 1946, Tampico, Mexico.
Manager 1912–15.

Year	Team	Games	BA	SA	AB	H	2B	3B	HR	HR%	R	RBI	BB	SO	SB	Pinch Hit AB	Pinch Hit H	PO	A	E	DP	TC/G	FA	G by Pos
1906	**CLE A**	10	.297	.432	37	11	3	1	0	0.0	4	6	1		2	0	0	16	3	0	0	1.9	1.000	OF-10
1907		138	.235	.300	476	112	10	9	1	0.2	55	33	16		23	1	0	277	35	17	11	2.4	.948	OF-134, SS-3
1908		122	.213	.257	413	88	10	1	2	0.5	32	38	19		15	0	0	250	23	12	6	2.3	.958	OF-121, SS-1
1909		100	.289	.356	343	99	10	5	1	0.3	29	38	19		12	2	1	203	15	12	2	2.3	.948	OF-98
1910		104	.231	.272	364	84	11	2	0	0.0	41	35	23		18	0	0	224	29	10	8	2.5	.962	OF-103, 3B-1
1911		125	.304	.380	447	136	18	5	2	0.4	55	51	15		16	6	1	253	55	14	10	2.8	.957	OF-101, 3B-16
1912		107	.255	.322	369	94	19	3	0	0.0	49	45	26		15	2	0	264	27	14	11	2.9	.954	OF-96, 1B-9
1913		47	.282	.366	131	37	9	1	0	0.0	16	15	8	22	7	10	0	73	2	2	0	2.1	.974	OF-37
1914		19	.128	.128	47	6	0	0	0	0.0	2	4	2	5	0	4	0	14	1	0	0	1.1	1.000	OF-14
9 yrs.		772	.254	.316	2627	667	90	27	6	0.2	283	265	129	27	108	25	2	1574	190	81	48	2.5	.956	OF-714, 3B-17, 1B-9, SS-4

John Bischoff

BISCHOFF, JOHN GEORGE (Smiley) BR TR 5′ 7″ 165 lbs.
B. Oct. 28, 1894, Edwardsville, Ill. D. Dec. 28, 1981, Granite City, Ill.

Year	Team	Games	BA	SA	AB	H	2B	3B	HR	HR%	R	RBI	BB	SO	SB	Pinch Hit AB	Pinch Hit H	PO	A	E	DP	TC/G	FA	G by Pos
1925	2 teams	CHI A (7G –.091) BOS A (41G –.278)																						
″	total	48	.264	.361	144	38	9	1	1	0.7	14	16	7	16	1	3	0	108	39	7	1	3.5	.955	C-44
1926	BOS A	59	.260	.378	127	33	11	2	0	0.0	6	19	15	16	1	12	2	121	27	4	8	3.3	.974	C-46
2 yrs.		107	.262	.369	271	71	20	3	1	0.4	20	35	22	32	2	15	2	229	66	11	9	3.4	.964	C-90

Frank Bishop

BISHOP, FRANK H.
B. Sept. 21, 1860, Belvedere, Ill. D. June 18, 1929, Chicago, Ill.

Year	Team	Games	BA	SA	AB	H	2B	3B	HR	HR%	R	RBI	BB	SO	SB	Pinch Hit AB	Pinch Hit H	PO	A	E	DP	TC/G	FA	G by Pos
1884	CHI U	4	.188	.250	16	3	1	0	0	0.0	1		0			0	0	6	4	5	0	3.8	.667	3B-3, SS-1

Max Bishop

BISHOP, MAX FREDERICK (Camera Eye, Tilly) BL TR 5′ 8½″ 165 lbs.
B. Sept. 5, 1899, Waynesboro, Pa. D. Feb. 24, 1962, Waynesboro, Pa.

Year	Team	Games	BA	SA	AB	H	2B	3B	HR	HR%	R	RBI	BB	SO	SB	Pinch Hit AB	Pinch Hit H	PO	A	E	DP	TC/G	FA	G by Pos
1924	PHI A	91	.255	.333	294	75	13	2	2	0.7	52	21	54	30	4	5	1	189	273	15	50	6.0	.969	2B-80
1925		105	.280	.383	368	103	18	4	4	1.1	66	27	87	37	5	1	0	233	352	26	53	5.9	.957	2B-104
1926		122	.265	.325	400	106	20	2	0	0.0	77	33	116	41	4	2	0	235	365	8	55	5.1	.987	2B-119
1927		117	.277	.323	372	103	15	1	0	0.0	80	22	105	28	8	7	1	211	342	19	48	5.4	.967	2B-106
1928		126	.316	.432	472	149	27	5	6	1.3	104	50	97	36	9	0	0	284	371	15	62	5.4	.978	2B-125
1929		129	.232	.316	475	110	19	6	3	0.6	102	36	**128**	44	1	0	0	301	371	21	58	5.4	.970	2B-129
1930		130	.252	.408	441	111	27	6	10	2.3	117	38	128	60	3	3	2	267	418	17	61	5.5	.976	2B-127
1931		130	.294	.400	497	146	30	4	5	1.0	115	37	112	51	3	0	0	314	414	12	84	5.7	.984	2B-130
1932		114	.254	.359	409	104	24	2	5	1.2	89	37	110	43	2	6	0	232	340	7	68	5.5	.988	2B-106
1933		117	.294	.399	391	115	27	1	4	1.0	80	42	106	46	1	2	0	254	359	16	52	5.6	.975	2B-113
1934	BOS A	97	.261	.332	253	66	13	1	1	0.4	65	22	82	22	3	20	2	293	164	4	48	6.4	.991	2B-57, 1B-15
1935		60	.230	.295	122	28	3	1	1	0.8	19	14	28	14	0	8	1	114	94	4	12	4.5	.981	2B-34, 1B-11, SS-2
12 yrs.		1338	.271	.366	4494	1216	236	35	41	0.9	966	379	1153	452	43	54	7	2927	3863	164	651	5.5	.976	2B-1230, 1B-26, SS-2
WORLD SERIES																								
1929	PHI A	5	.190	.190	21	4	0	0	0	0.0	2	1	2	3	0	0	0	9	12	0	2	4.2	1.000	2B-5
1930		6	.222	.222	18	4	0	0	0	0.0	5	0	7	3	0	0	0	8	9	0	0	2.8	1.000	2B-6
1931		7	.148	.148	27	4	0	0	0	0.0	4	0	3	5	0	0	0	12	18	0	4	4.3	1.000	2B-7
3 yrs.		18	.182	.182	66	12	0	0	0	0.0	11	1	12	11	0	0	0	29	39	0	6	3.8	1.000	2B-18

Mike Bishop

BISHOP, MICHAEL DAVID BR TR 6′ 2″ 185 lbs.
B. Nov. 5, 1958, Santa Maria, Calif.

Year	Team	Games	BA	SA	AB	H	2B	3B	HR	HR%	R	RBI	BB	SO	SB	Pinch Hit AB	Pinch Hit H	PO	A	E	DP	TC/G	FA	G by Pos
1983	NY N	3	.125	.250	8	1	1	0	0	0.0	2	0	3	4	0	0	0	16	1	1	0	6.0	.944	C-3

Rivington Bisland

BISLAND, RIVINGTON MARTIN BR TR 5′ 9″ 155 lbs.
B. Feb. 17, 1890, New York, N. Y. D. Jan. 11, 1973, Salzburg, Austria.

Year	Team	Games	BA	SA	AB	H	2B	3B	HR	HR%	R	RBI	BB	SO	SB	Pinch Hit AB	Pinch Hit H	PO	A	E	DP	TC/G	FA	G by Pos
1912	PIT N	1	.000	.000	1	0	0	0	0	0.0	0	0	0	0	0	1	0	0	0	0	0	0.0	—	
1913	STL A	12	.136	.136	44	6	0	0	0	0.0	3	3	2	5	0	0	0	21	31	2	3	4.5	.963	SS-12
1914	CLE A	18	.105	.123	57	6	1	0	0	0.0	9	2	6	2	2	1	0	31	45	3	6	4.9	.962	SS-15, 3B-1
3 yrs.		31	.118	.127	102	12	1	0	0	0.0	12	5	8	7	2	2	0	52	76	5	9	4.8	.962	SS-27, 3B-1

Del Bissonette

BISSONETTE, DELPHIA LOUIS BL TL 5′11″ 180 lbs.
B. Sept. 6, 1899, Winthrop, Me. D. June 9, 1972, Augusta, Me.
Manager 1945.

Year	Team	Games	BA	SA	AB	H	2B	3B	HR	HR%	R	RBI	BB	SO	SB	Pinch Hit AB	Pinch Hit H	PO	A	E	DP	TC/G	FA	G by Pos
1928	BKN N	155	.320	.543	587	188	30	13	25	4.3	90	106	70	75	5	0	0	1482	77	20	95	10.2	.987	1B-155
1929		116	.281	.476	431	121	28	10	12	2.8	68	75	46	58	2	3	0	1093	47	15	70	10.2	.987	1B-113
1930		146	.336	.523	572	192	33	13	16	2.8	102	113	56	66	4	0	0	1427	72	20	142	10.4	.987	1B-146
1931		152	.290	.431	587	170	19	14	12	2.0	90	87	59	53	4	0	0	1460	66	16	136	10.1	.990	1B-152
1933		35	.246	.333	114	28	7	0	1	0.9	9	10	2	17	2	3	1	298	19	4	25	10.0	.988	1B-32
5 yrs.		604	.305	.486	2291	699	117	50	66	2.9	359	391	233	269	17	6	1	5760	281	75	468	10.2	.988	1B-598

Red Bittmann

BITTMANN, HENRY PETER
B. July 22, 1862, Cincinnati, Ohio D. Nov. 8, 1929, Cincinnati, Ohio.

Year	Team	Games	BA	SA	AB	H	2B	3B	HR	HR%	R	RBI	BB	SO	SB	Pinch Hit AB	Pinch Hit H	PO	A	E	DP	TC/G	FA	G by Pos
1889	KC AA	4	.286	.286	14	4	0	0	0	0.0	2	2	1	1	1	0	0	9	12	0	2	5.3	1.000	2B-4

George Bjorkman

BJORKMAN, GEORGE ANTON BR TR 6′ 2″ 190 lbs.
B. Aug. 26, 1956, Ontario, Calif.

Year	Team	Games	BA	SA	AB	H	2B	3B	HR	HR%	R	RBI	BB	SO	SB	Pinch Hit AB	Pinch Hit H	PO	A	E	DP	TC/G	FA	G by Pos
1983	HOU N	29	.227	.360	75	17	4	0	2	2.7	8	14	16	29	0	0	0	136	16	1	0	5.3	.993	C-29

Bill Black

BLACK, JOHN WILLIAM (Jigger) BL TR 5′11″ 168 lbs.
B. Aug. 12, 1899, Philadelphia, Pa. D. Jan. 14, 1968, Philadelphia, Pa.

Year	Team	Games	BA	SA	AB	H	2B	3B	HR	HR%	R	RBI	BB	SO	SB	Pinch Hit AB	Pinch Hit H	PO	A	E	DP	TC/G	FA	G by Pos
1924	CHI A	6	.200	.200	5	1	0	0	0	0.0	0	0	0	0	0	0	0	0	0	0	0	0.0	.000	2B-1

Bob Black

BLACK, ROBERT BENJAMIN
B. Dec. 10, 1862, Cincinnati, Ohio D. Mar. 21, 1933, Sioux City, Iowa.

Year	Team	Games	BA	SA	AB	H	2B	3B	HR	HR%	R	RBI	BB	SO	SB	Pinch Hit AB	Pinch Hit H	PO	A	E	DP	TC/G	FA	G by Pos
1884	KC U	38	.247	.390	146	36	14	2	1	0.7	25		10			0	0	58	50	20	4	3.0	.844	OF-19, P-16, 2B-6, SS-1

Jack Black

BLACK, JOHN FALCONER BR TR 6′ 1″ 185 lbs.
Born John Falconer Haddow.
B. Feb. 23, 1890, Covington, Ky. D. Mar. 20, 1962, Rutherford, N. J.

Year	Team	Games	BA	SA	AB	H	2B	3B	HR	HR%	R	RBI	BB	SO	SB	Pinch Hit AB	Pinch Hit H	PO	A	E	DP	TC/G	FA	G by Pos
1911	STL A	54	.151	.172	186	28	4	0	0	0.0	13	7	10		4	0	0	519	37	16	31	10.6	.972	1B-54

Ethan Blackaby

BLACKABY, ETHAN ALLAN BL TL 5′11″ 190 lbs.
B. July 24, 1940, Cincinnati, Ohio.

Year	Team	Games	BA	SA	AB	H	2B	3B	HR	HR%	R	RBI	BB	SO	SB	Pinch Hit AB	Pinch Hit H	PO	A	E	DP	TC/G	FA	G by Pos
1962	MIL N	6	.154	.231	13	2	1	0	0	0.0	0	0	1	8	0	3	1	3	0	0	0	1.0	1.000	OF-3
1964		9	.083	.083	12	1	0	0	0	0.0	0	1	1	2	0	4	0	1	0	1	0	0.4	.500	OF-5
2 yrs.		15	.120	.160	25	3	1	0	0	0.0	0	1	2	10	0	7	1	4	0	1	0	0.6	.800	OF-8

Earl Blackburn

BLACKBURN, EARL STUART BR TR 5′11″ 180 lbs.
B. Nov. 1, 1892, Leesville, Ohio D. Aug. 3, 1966, Mansfield, Ohio.

Year	Team	Games	BA	SA	AB	H	2B	3B	HR	HR%	R	RBI	BB	SO	SB	Pinch Hit AB	Pinch Hit H	PO	A	E	DP	TC/G	FA	G by Pos
1912	2 teams	PIT N (1G –.000) CIN N (1G –.000)																						
″	total	2			0	0	0	0	0		0	0	1	0	0	0	0	6	0	0	0	3.0	1.000	C-2
1913	CIN N	17	.259	.259	27	7	0	0	0	0.0	1	3	2	5	2	5	1	30	9	7	1	3.8	.848	C-12
1915	BOS N	3	.167	.167	6	1	0	0	0	0.0	0	0	2	1	0	0	0	8	3	0	1	3.7	1.000	C-3

Earl Blackburn *continued*

Year	Team	Games	BA	SA	AB	H	2B	3B	HR	HR%	R	RBI	BB	SO	SB	Pinch Hit AB	Pinch Hit H	PO	A	E	DP	TC/G	FA	G by Pos
1916		47	.273	.382	110	30	4	4	0	0.0	12	7	9	21	2	3	1	166	45	6	2	4.9	.972	C-44
1917	CHI N	2	.000	.000	2	0	0	0	0	0.0	0	0	0	0	0	2	0	0	0	0	0	0.0	—	
5 yrs.		71	.262	.345	145	38	4	4	0	0.0	13	10	14	27	4	10	2	210	57	13	4	4.6	.954	C-61

Lena Blackburne

BLACKBURNE, RUSSELL AUBREY (Slats) BR TR 5′11″ 160 lbs.
B. Oct. 23, 1886, Clifton Heights, Pa. D. Feb. 29, 1968, Riverside, N. J.
Manager 1928–29.

Year	Team	Games	BA	SA	AB	H	2B	3B	HR	HR%	R	RBI	BB	SO	SB	Pinch Hit AB	Pinch Hit H	PO	A	E	DP	TC/G	FA	G by Pos
1910	CHI A	75	.174	.194	242	42	3	1	0	0.0	16	10	19		4	0	0	173	265	43	29	6.5	.911	SS-74
1912		3	.000	.000	1	0	0	0	0	0.0	0	0	1		1	0	0	3	2	1	1	2.0	.833	SS-2, 3B-1
1914		144	.222	.270	474	105	10	5	1	0.2	52	35	66	58	25	1	0	239	433	26	28	4.9	.963	2B-143
1915		96	.216	.240	283	61	5	1	0	0.0	33	25	35	34	13	2	1	99	153	15	16	2.9	.944	3B-83, SS-9
1918	CIN N	125	.228	.299	435	99	8	10	1	0.2	35	45	25	30	6	0	0	319	413	48	69	6.2	.938	SS-125
1919	2 teams	BOS N (31G –.263)			PHI N (72G –.199)																			
″	total	103	.213	.296	371	79	13	6	2	0.5	37	23	16	29	5	4	1	129	213	22	15	3.6	.940	3B-96, 1B-2, 2B-2, SS-2
1927	CHI A	1	1.000	1.000	1	1	0	0	0	0.0	1	1	0	0	0	1	1	0	0	0	0	0.0	—	
1929		1	—	—	0	0	0	0	0	—	0	0	0	0	0	0	0	0	0	0	0	0.0	.000	P-1
8 yrs.		548	.214	.268	1807	387	39	23	4	0.2	174	139	162	151	54	8	3	962	1479	155	158	4.8	.940	SS-212, 3B-180, 2B-145, 1B-2, P-1

George Blackerby

BLACKERBY, GEORGE FRANKLIN BR TR 6′ 1″ 176 lbs.
B. Nov. 18, 1903, Luther, Okla. D. May 30, 1987, Wichita Falls, Tex.

Year	Team	Games	BA	SA	AB	H	2B	3B	HR	HR%	R	RBI	BB	SO	SB	Pinch Hit AB	Pinch Hit H	PO	A	E	DP	TC/G	FA	G by Pos
1928	CHI A	30	.253	.253	83	21	0	0	0	0.0	8	12	4	10	2	10	4	40	1	2	0	2.2	.953	OF-20

Fred Blackwell

BLACKWELL, FREDERICK WILLIAM BL TR 5′10½″ 160 lbs.
B. Sept. 7, 1891, Bowling Green, Ky. D. Dec. 8, 1975, Morgantown, Ky.

Year	Team	Games	BA	SA	AB	H	2B	3B	HR	HR%	R	RBI	BB	SO	SB	Pinch Hit AB	Pinch Hit H	PO	A	E	DP	TC/G	FA	G by Pos
1917	PIT N	3	.200	.200	10	2	0	0	0	0.0	1	2	0	3	0	0	0	14	3	0	0	5.7	1.000	C-3
1918		8	.154	.154	13	2	0	0	0	0.0	1	4	3	4	0	0	0	19	6	2	0	3.4	.926	C-8
1919		24	.215	.262	65	14	3	0	0	0.0	3	4	3	9	0	2	1	87	19	4	1	5.0	.964	C-22
3 yrs.		35	.205	.239	88	18	3	0	0	0.0	5	10	6	16	0	2	1	120	28	6	1	4.7	.961	C-33

Tim Blackwell

BLACKWELL, TIMOTHY P. BB TR 5′11″ 170 lbs.
B. Aug. 19, 1952, San Diego, Calif.

Year	Team	Games	BA	SA	AB	H	2B	3B	HR	HR%	R	RBI	BB	SO	SB	Pinch Hit AB	Pinch Hit H	PO	A	E	DP	TC/G	FA	G by Pos
1974	BOS A	44	.246	.270	122	30	1	1	0	0.0	9	8	10	21	1	0	0	182	21	6	5	4.8	.971	C-44
1975		59	.197	.250	132	26	3	2	0	0.0	15	6	19	13	0	0	0	230	23	4	3	4.4	.984	C-57, DH-2
1976	PHI N	4	.250	.250	8	2	0	0	0	0.0	0	1	0	1	0	2	1	17	0	0	0	4.3	1.000	C-4
1977	2 teams	PHI N (1G –.000)			MON N (16G –.091)																			
″	total	17	.091	.136	22	2	1	0	0	0.0	4	0	2	7	0	2	0	37	2	3	1	2.8	.929	C-15
1978	CHI N	49	.223	.252	103	23	3	0	0	0.0	8	7	23	17	0	0	0	213	20	3	3	4.8	.987	C-49
1979		63	.164	.205	122	20	3	1	0	0.0	8	12	32	25	0	1	0	245	28	7	3	4.4	.975	C-63
1980		103	.272	.394	320	87	16	4	5	1.6	24	30	41	62	0	0	0	572	93	12	16	6.6	.982	C-103
1981		58	.234	.342	158	37	10	2	1	0.6	21	11	23	23	2	2	0	268	28	2	1	5.3	.993	C-56
1982	MON N	23	.190	.286	42	8	2	1	0	0.0	2	3	3	11	0	6	1	58	9	1	1	3.8	.985	C-18
1983		6	.200	.267	15	3	1	0	0	0.0	0	2	1	3	0	1	0	28	1	2	0	6.2	.935	C-5
10 yrs.		426	.228	.305	1044	238	40	11	6	0.6	91	80	154	183	3	14	2	1850	225	40	33	5.1	.981	C-414, DH-2

Ray Blades

BLADES, FRANCIS RAYMOND BR TR 5′ 7½″ 163 lbs.
B. Aug. 6, 1896, Mt. Vernon, Ill. D. May 18, 1979, Lincoln, Ill.
Manager 1939–40, 1948.

Year	Team	Games	BA	SA	AB	H	2B	3B	HR	HR%	R	RBI	BB	SO	SB	Pinch Hit AB	Pinch Hit H	PO	A	E	DP	TC/G	FA	G by Pos
1922	STL N	37	.300	.446	130	39	2	4	3	2.3	27	21	25	21	3	0	0	67	20	11	2	2.9	.888	OF-29, SS-4, 3B-1
1923		98	.246	.391	317	78	21	5	5	1.6	48	44	37	46	4	4	1	194	12	7	2	2.4	.967	OF-83, 3B-4
1924		131	.311	.487	456	142	21	13	11	2.4	86	68	35	38	7	2	1	275	30	13	3	2.6	.959	OF-109, 3B-7, 2B-7
1925		122	.342	.535	462	158	37	8	12	2.6	112	57	59	47	6	4	2	267	13	6	4	2.5	.979	OF-114, 3B-1
1926		107	.305	.462	416	127	17	12	8	1.9	81	43	62	57	6	1	0	229	10	5	1	2.3	.980	OF-105
1927		61	.317	.450	180	57	8	5	2	1.1	33	29	28	22	3	9	4	64	0	6	0	1.4	.914	OF-50
1928		51	.235	.376	85	20	7	1	1	1.2	9	19	20	26	0	24	4	34	1	1	1	1.9	.972	OF-19
1930		45	.396	.614	101	40	6	2	4	4.0	26	25	21	15	1	7	2	66	1	3	0	2.2	.957	OF-32
1931		35	.284	.388	67	19	4	0	1	1.5	10	5	10	7	1	14	4	26	1	4	0	1.5	.871	OF-20
1932		80	.229	.333	201	46	10	1	3	1.5	35	29	34	31	2	16	2	117	2	3	0	1.9	.975	OF-62, 3B-1
10 yrs.		767	.301	.460	2415	726	133	51	50	2.1	467	340	331	310	33	81	20	1339	90	59	13	2.3	.960	OF-623, 3B-14, 2B-7, SS-4
WORLD SERIES																								
1928	STL N	1	.000	.000	1	0	0	0	0	0.0	0	0	0	1	0	1	0	0	0	0	0	0.0	—	
1930		5	.111	.111	9	1	0	0	0	0.0	2	0	2	2	0	1	0	10	0	0	0	3.3	1.000	OF-3
1931		2	.000	.000	2	0	0	0	0	0.0	0	0	0	2	0	2	0	0	0	0	0	0.0	—	
3 yrs.		8	.083	.083	12	1	0	0	0	0.0	2	0	2	5	0	4	0	10	0	0	0	3.3	1.000	OF-3

Rick Bladt

BLADT, RICHARD ALAN BR TR 6′ 1″ 160 lbs.
B. Dec. 9, 1946, Santa Cruz, Calif.

Year	Team	Games	BA	SA	AB	H	2B	3B	HR	HR%	R	RBI	BB	SO	SB	Pinch Hit AB	Pinch Hit H	PO	A	E	DP	TC/G	FA	G by Pos
1969	CHI N	10	.154	.154	13	2	0	0	0	0.0	1	1	0	5	0	1	0	12	1	0	0	1.9	1.000	1B-7
1975	NY A	52	.222	.291	117	26	3	1	1	0.9	13	11	11	8	6	1	1	103	4	3	1	2.2	.973	OF-51
2 yrs.		62	.215	.277	130	28	3	1	1	0.8	14	12	11	13	6	2	1	115	5	3	1	2.1	.976	OF-51, 1B-7

Rae Blaemire

BLAEMIRE, RAE BERTRUM BR TR 6′ 178 lbs.
B. Feb. 8, 1911, Gary, Ind. D. Dec. 23, 1975, Champaign, Ill.

Year	Team	Games	BA	SA	AB	H	2B	3B	HR	HR%	R	RBI	BB	SO	SB	Pinch Hit AB	Pinch Hit H	PO	A	E	DP	TC/G	FA	G by Pos
1941	NY N	2	.400	.400	5	2	0	0	0	0.0	0	0	0	0	0	0	0	5	0	0	0	2.5	1.000	C-2

Buddy Blair

BLAIR, LOUIS NATHAN BL TR 6′ 186 lbs.
B. Sept. 10, 1910, Columbia, Miss.

Year	Team	Games	BA	SA	AB	H	2B	3B	HR	HR%	R	RBI	BB	SO	SB	Pinch Hit AB	Pinch Hit H	PO	A	E	DP	TC/G	FA	G by Pos
1942	PHI A	137	.279	.397	484	135	26	8	5	1.0	48	66	30	30	1	12	2	143	234	28	21	3.2	.931	3B-126

Footsie Blair

BLAIR, CLARENCE VICK
B. July 13, 1900, Enterprise, Okla. D. July 1, 1982, Texarkana, Tex.
BL TR 6' 1" 180 lbs.

Year	Team	Games	BA	SA	AB	H	2B	3B	HR	HR%	R	RBI	BB	SO	SB	Pinch Hit AB	Pinch Hit H	PO	A	E	DP	TC/G	FA	G by Pos
1929	CHI N	26	.319	.431	72	23	5	0	1	1.4	10	8	3	4	1	3	2	82	23	3	6	6.4	.972	3B-8, 1B-7, 2B-2
1930		134	.273	.388	578	158	24	12	6	1.0	97	59	20	58	9	6	1	266	456	34	85	5.9	.955	2B-115, 3B-13
1931		86	.258	.404	240	62	19	5	2	0.8	31	29	14	26	1	16	2	245	120	13	28	5.6	.966	2B-44, 1B-23, 3B-1
3 yrs.		246	.273	.396	890	243	48	17	9	1.0	138	96	37	88	11	25	5	593	599	50	119	5.8	.960	2B-161, 1B-30, 3B-22
WORLD SERIES																								
1929	CHI N	1	.000	.000	1	0	0	0	0	0.0	0	0	0	0	0	1	0	0	0	0	0	0.0	—	

Paul Blair

BLAIR, PAUL L. D. (Motormouth)
B. Feb. 1, 1944, Cushing, Okla.
BR TR 6' 168 lbs.
BB 1971

Year	Team	Games	BA	SA	AB	H	2B	3B	HR	HR%	R	RBI	BB	SO	SB	Pinch Hit AB	Pinch Hit H	PO	A	E	DP	TC/G	FA	G by Pos
1964	BAL A	8	.000	.000	1	0	0	0	0	0.0	0	0	0	1	0	0	0	2	0	0	0	0.3	1.000	OF-6
1965		119	.234	.338	364	85	19	2	5	1.4	49	25	32	52	8	0	0	241	5	2	0	2.1	.992	OF-116
1966		133	.277	.416	303	84	20	2	6	2.0	35	33	15	36	5	5	1	204	4	2	2	1.7	.990	OF-127
1967		151	.293	.446	552	162	27	**12**	11	2.0	72	64	50	68	8	5	1	369	13	6	3	2.7	.985	OF-146
1968		141	.211	.318	421	89	22	1	7	1.7	48	38	37	60	4	11	2	272	11	3	3	2.2	.990	OF-132, 3B-1
1969		150	.285	.477	625	178	32	5	26	4.2	102	76	40	72	20	1	0	407	14	5	5	2.8	.988	OF-150
1970		133	.267	.438	480	128	24	2	18	3.8	79	65	56	93	24	6	0	368	10	5	3	3.0	.987	OF-128, 3B-1
1971		141	.262	.397	516	135	24	8	10	1.9	75	44	32	94	14	4	1	331	4	3	1	2.4	.991	OF-138
1972		142	.233	.358	477	111	20	8	8	1.7	47	49	25	78	7	11	3	337	10	3	1	2.5	.991	OF-139
1973		146	.280	.402	500	140	25	3	10	2.0	73	64	43	72	18	8	0	369	14	4	4	2.7	.990	OF-144, DH-1
1974		151	.261	.417	552	144	27	4	17	3.1	77	62	43	59	27	4	0	447	7	7	2	3.1	.985	OF-151
1975		140	.218	.300	440	96	13	4	5	1.1	51	31	25	82	17	5	2	327	8	3	1	2.4	.991	OF-138, DH-1, 1B-1
1976		145	.197	.264	375	74	16	0	3	0.8	29	16	22	49	15	11	2	327	6	7	1	2.4	.979	OF-139, DH-1
1977	NY A	83	.262	.396	164	43	4	3	4	2.4	20	25	9	16	3	3	1	125	1	4	0	1.6	.969	OF-79, DH-1
1978		75	.176	.264	125	22	5	0	2	1.6	10	13	9	17	1	16	5	90	5	2	1	1.3	.979	OF-64, 2B-5, SS-4, 3B-3
1979	2 teams	NY A (26G –.200) CIN N (75G –.150)																						
"	total	77	.152	.234	145	22	4	1	2	1.4	7	15	11	28	0	8	0	123	3	1	0	1.8	.992	OF-69
1980	NY A	12	.000	.000	2	0	0	0	0	0.0	2	0	0	0	0	0	0	8	0	0	0	0.7	1.000	OF-12
17 yrs.		1947	.250	.382	6042	1513	282	55	134	2.2	776	620	449	877	171	98	18	4347	115	57	27	2.4	.987	OF-1878, 2B-5, 3B-5, SS-4, DH-4, 1B-1
LEAGUE CHAMPIONSHIP SERIES																								
1969	BAL A	3	.400	.733	15	6	2	0	1	6.7	1	6	2	2	0	0	0	8	0	0	0	2.7	1.000	OF-3
1970		3	.077	.077	13	1	0	0	0	0.0	0	0	1	4	0	0	0	4	0	0	0	1.3	1.000	OF-3
1971		3	.333	.444	9	3	1	0	0	0.0	1	2	0	3	0	0	0	5	0	0	0	1.7	1.000	OF-3
1973		5	.167	.167	18	3	0	0	0	0.0	2	0	1	5	0	0	0	8	0	0	0	1.6	1.000	OF-5
1974		4	.286	.500	14	4	0	0	1	7.1	3	2	2	2	0	0	0	7	0	0	0	1.8	1.000	OF-4
1977	NY A	3	.400	.400	5	2	0	0	0	0.0	1	0	0	0	0	0	0	2	0	0	0	0.7	1.000	OF-3
1978		4	.000	.000	6	0	0	0	0	0.0	1	0	0	1	0	2	0	8	0	0	0	2.0	1.000	OF-3, 2B-1
7 yrs.		25	.237	.350	80	19	3	0	2	2.5	9	10	6	17 10th	0	2	0	42	0	0	0	1.7	1.000	OF-24, 2B-1
WORLD SERIES																								
1966	BAL A	4	.167	.667	6	1	0	0	1	16.7	2	1	1	0	0	0	0	9	0	0	0	2.3	1.000	OF-4
1969		5	.100	.100	20	2	0	0	0	0.0	1	0	2	5	1	0	0	7	0	0	0	1.4	1.000	OF-5
1970		5	.474	.526	19	9	1	0	0	0.0	5	3	2	4	0	0	0	18	0	1	0	3.8	.947	OF-5
1971		4	.333	.444	9	3	1	0	0	0.0	2	0	0	1	0	0	0	6	2	1	0	3.0	.889	OF-3
1977	NY A	4	.250	.250	4	1	0	0	0	0.0	0	1	0	0	0	1	0	1	0	0	0	0.3	1.000	OF-3
1978		6	.375	.500	8	3	1	0	0	0.0	2	0	1	4	0	1	1	5	0	0	0	0.8	1.000	OF-6
6 yrs.		28	.288	.379	66	19	3	0	1	1.5	12	5	6	14	1	2	1	46	2	2	0	1.9	.960	OF-26

Walter Blair

BLAIR, WALTER ALLEN (Heavy)
B. Oct. 13, 1883, Landrus, Pa. D. Aug. 20, 1948, Lewisburg, Pa.
Manager 1915.
BR TR 6' 185 lbs.

Year	Team	Games	BA	SA	AB	H	2B	3B	HR	HR%	R	RBI	BB	SO	SB	Pinch Hit AB	Pinch Hit H	PO	A	E	DP	TC/G	FA	G by Pos
1907	NY A	7	.182	.182	22	4	0	0	0	0.0	1	1	2		0	0	0	36	11	4	0	7.3	.922	C-7
1908		76	.190	.237	211	40	5	1	1	0.5	9	13	11		4	3	1	246	59	15	4	4.4	.953	C-60, OF-9, 1B-3
1909		42	.209	.264	110	23	2	2	0	0.0	5	11	7		2	0	0	151	37	7	2	4.6	.964	C-42
1910		6	.227	.318	22	5	0	1	0	0.0	2	2	0		0	0	0	22	10	1	2	5.5	.970	C-6
1911		85	.194	.252	222	43	9	2	0	0.0	18	26	16		2	0	0	386	102	16	12	5.9	.968	C-84, 1B-1
1914	BUF F	128	.243	.283	378	92	11	2	0	0.0	22	33	32		6	0	0	604	194	13	17	6.3	.984	C-128
1915		98	.224	.317	290	65	15	3	2	0.7	23	20	18		4	1	0	404	150	11	15	5.8	.981	C-97
7 yrs.		442	.217	.275	1255	272	42	11	3	0.2	80	106	86		18	4	1	1849	563	67	52	5.7	.973	C-424, OF-9, 1B-4

Harry Blake

BLAKE, HARRY COOPER (Dude)
B. June 16, 1874, Portsmouth, Ohio D. Oct. 14, 1919, Chicago, Ill.
BR TR 5' 7" 165 lbs.

Year	Team	Games	BA	SA	AB	H	2B	3B	HR	HR%	R	RBI	BB	SO	SB	Pinch Hit AB	Pinch Hit H	PO	A	E	DP	TC/G	FA	G by Pos
1894	CLE N	73	.264	.351	296	78	15	4	1	0.3	51	51	30	22	1	0	0	120	16	10	4	2.0	.932	OF-73
1895		84	.276	.343	315	87	10	1	3	1.0	50	45	30	33	11	1	0	119	13	15	3	1.8	.898	OF-83
1896		104	.240	.305	383	92	12	5	1	0.3	66	43	46	30	10	0	0	186	21	15	5	2.1	.932	OF-103, SS-1
1897		32	.256	.325	117	30	3	1	1	0.9	17	15	12		5	0	0	87	3	1	2	2.8	.989	OF-32
1898		136	.245	.312	474	116	18	7	0	0.0	65	58	69		12	0	0	239	25	13	4	2.0	.953	OF-136, 1B-2
1899	STL N	97	.240	.318	292	70	9	4	2	0.7	50	41	43		16	4	2	203	27	10	6	2.6	.958	OF-87, 2B-4, 1B-1, SS-1, C-1
6 yrs.		526	.252	.324	1877	473	67	22	8	0.4	299	253	230	85	55	5	2	954	105	64	24	2.1	.943	OF-514, 2B-4, 1B-3, SS-2, C-1

Link Blakely

BLAKELY, LINCOLN HOWARD
B. Feb. 12, 1912, Oakland, Calif. D. Sept. 28, 1976, Oakland, Calif.
BR TR 6' 180 lbs.

Year	Team	Games	BA	SA	AB	H	2B	3B	HR	HR%	R	RBI	BB	SO	SB	Pinch Hit AB	Pinch Hit H	PO	A	E	DP	TC/G	FA	G by Pos
1934	CIN N	34	.225	.255	102	23	1	1	0	0.0	11	10	5	14	1	1	0	72	4	1	2	2.8	.987	OF-28

Bob Blakiston

BLAKISTON, ROBERT J.
Born Robert J. Blackstone.
B. Oct. 2, 1855, San Francisco, Calif. D. Dec. 25, 1918, San Francisco, Calif.

5′ 8½″ 180 lbs.

Year	Team	Games	BA	SA	AB	H	2B	3B	HR	HR%	R	RBI	BB	SO	SB	Pinch Hit AB	Pinch Hit H	PO	A	E	DP	TC/G	FA	G by Pos
1882	PHI AA	72	.228	.249	281	64	4	1	0	0.0	40		9			0	0	84	94	45	3	3.1	.798	OF-38, 3B-34, 2B-1
1883		44	.246	.299	167	41	3	3	0	0.0	26		9			0	0	77	17	15	0	2.3	.862	OF-37, 1B-6, 3B-5
1884	2 teams	PHI AA (32G –.258)	IND AA (6G –.222)																					
″	total	38	.253	.301	146	37	7	0	0	0.0	21		12			0	0	101	13	16	1	3.3	.877	OF-29, 1B-6, 3B-2, 2B-1, SS-1
3 yrs.		154	.239	.276	594	142	14	4	0	0.0	87		30			0	0	262	124	76	4	2.9	.835	OF-104, 3B-41, 1B-12, 2B-2, SS-1

Johnny Blanchard

BLANCHARD, JOHN EDWIN
B. Feb. 26, 1933, Minneapolis, Minn.

BL TR 6′ 1″ 193 lbs.

Year	Team	Games	BA	SA	AB	H	2B	3B	HR	HR%	R	RBI	BB	SO	SB	Pinch Hit AB	Pinch Hit H	PO	A	E	DP	TC/G	FA	G by Pos
1955	NY A	1	.000	.000	3	0	0	0	0	0.0	0	0	1	0	0	0	0	7	0	0	0	7.0	1.000	C-1
1959		49	.169	.288	59	10	1	0	2	3.4	6	4	7	12	0	28	2	36	1	2	1	1.9	.949	C-12, OF-8, 1B-1
1960		53	.242	.414	99	24	3	1	4	4.0	8	14	6	17	0	23	4	151	7	2	0	5.7	.988	C-28
1961		93	.305	.613	243	74	10	1	21	8.6	38	54	27	28	1	26	7	292	18	3	2	5.0	.990	C-48, OF-15
1962		93	.232	.419	246	57	7	0	13	5.3	33	39	28	32	0	25	3	159	3	6	0	2.6	.964	OF-47, C-15, 1B-2
1963		76	.225	.463	218	49	4	0	16	7.3	22	45	26	30	0	14	1	76	2	1	0	1.2	.987	OF-64
1964		77	.255	.435	161	41	8	0	7	4.3	18	28	24	24	1	31	8	166	11	2	6	4.3	.989	C-25, OF-14, 1B-3
1965	3 teams	NY A (12G –.147)	KC A (52G –.200)	MIL N (10G –.100)																				
″	total	74	.183	.274	164	30	3	0	4	2.4	12	16	17	20	0	30	4	144	12	4	1	3.4	.975	C-26, OF-21
8 yrs.		516	.239	.441	1193	285	36	2	67	5.6	137	200	136	163	2	177	29	1031	54	20	10	3.3	.982	OF-169, C-155, 1B-6
WORLD SERIES																								
1960	NY A	5	.455	.636	11	5	2	0	0	0.0	2	2	0	0	0	3	1	5	2	0	1	3.5	1.000	C-2
1961		4	.400	1.100	10	4	1	0	2	20.0	4	3	2	0	0	2	1	2	1	0	0	1.5	1.000	OF-2
1962		1	.000	.000	1	0	0	0	0	0.0	0	0	0	1	0	1	0	0	0	0	0	0.0	—	
1963		1	.000	.000	3	0	0	0	0	0.0	0	0	0	0	0	0	0	1	0	0	0	1.0	1.000	OF-1
1964		4	.250	.500	4	1	1	0	0	0.0	0	0	0	1	0	4	1	0	0	0	0	0.0	—	
5 yrs.		15	.345	.690	29	10	4	0	2	6.9	6	5	2	2	0	10	3	8	3	0	1	2.2	1.000	OF-3, C-2

Damaso Blanco

BLANCO, DAMASO
Born Damaso Blanco (Caripe).
B. Dec. 11, 1941, Curiepe, Venezuela.

BR TR 5′10″ 165 lbs.

Year	Team	Games	BA	SA	AB	H	2B	3B	HR	HR%	R	RBI	BB	SO	SB	Pinch Hit AB	Pinch Hit H	PO	A	E	DP	TC/G	FA	G by Pos
1972	SF N	39	.350	.400	20	7	1	0	0	0.0	5	2	4	3	2	0	0	14	22	2	3	1.3	.947	3B-19, SS-8, 2B-3
1973		28	.000	.000	12	0	0	0	0	0.0	4	0	1	2	0	6	0	6	4	0	0	0.7	1.000	3B-7, SS-5, 2B-3
1974		5	.000	.000	1	0	0	0	0	0.0	0	0	0	1	1	1	0	0	0	0	0	0.0	—	
3 yrs.		72	.212	.242	33	7	1	0	0	0.0	9	2	5	6	3	7	0	20	26	2	3	1.1	.958	3B-26, SS-13, 2B-6

Ossie Blanco

BLANCO, OSWALDO CARLOS
Born Oswaldo Carlos Blanco (Diaz).
B. Sept. 8, 1945, Caracas, Venezuela.

BR TR 6′ 185 lbs.

Year	Team	Games	BA	SA	AB	H	2B	3B	HR	HR%	R	RBI	BB	SO	SB	Pinch Hit AB	Pinch Hit H	PO	A	E	DP	TC/G	FA	G by Pos
1970	CHI A	34	.197	.197	66	13	0	0	0	0.0	4	8	3	14	0	16	3	144	8	1	9	6.7	.993	1B-22, OF-1
1974	CLE A	18	.194	.194	36	7	0	0	0	0.0	1	2	7	4	0	0	0	127	4	1	11	7.8	.992	1B-16, DH-1
2 yrs.		52	.196	.196	102	20	0	0	0	0.0	5	10	10	18	0	16	3	271	12	2	20	7.1	.993	1B-38, DH-1, OF-1

Coonie Blank

BLANK, FRANK IGNATZ
B. Oct. 18, 1892, St. Louis, Mo. D. Dec. 8, 1961, St. Louis, Mo.

BR TR 5′11″ 165 lbs.

Year	Team	Games	BA	SA	AB	H	2B	3B	HR	HR%	R	RBI	BB	SO	SB	Pinch Hit AB	Pinch Hit H	PO	A	E	DP	TC/G	FA	G by Pos
1909	STL N	1	.000	.000	2	0	0	0	0	0.0	0	0	0		0	0	0	2	0	0	0	2.0	1.000	C-1

Cliff Blankenship

BLANKENSHIP, CLIFFORD DOUGLAS
B. Apr. 10, 1880, Columbus, Ga. D. Apr. 26, 1956, Oakland, Calif.

BR TR 5′10½″ 165 lbs.

Year	Team	Games	BA	SA	AB	H	2B	3B	HR	HR%	R	RBI	BB	SO	SB	Pinch Hit AB	Pinch Hit H	PO	A	E	DP	TC/G	FA	G by Pos
1905	CIN N	19	.196	.250	56	11	1	1	0	0.0	8	7	4		1	3	0	139	4	6	7	9.9	.960	1B-15
1907	WAS A	37	.225	.245	102	23	2	0	0	0.0	4	6	3		3	5	2	167	35	8	3	6.8	.962	C-24, 1B-7
1909		39	.250	.250	60	15	0	0	0	0.0	4	9	0		2	16	3	38	12	6	1	2.7	.893	C-17, OF-4
3 yrs.		95	.225	.248	218	49	3	1	0	0.0	16	22	7		6	24	5	344	51	20	11	6.2	.952	C-41, 1B-22, OF-4

Lance Blankenship

BLANKENSHIP, LANCE ROBERT
B. Dec. 6, 1963, Portland, Ore.

BR TR 6′ 190 lbs.

Year	Team	Games	BA	SA	AB	H	2B	3B	HR	HR%	R	RBI	BB	SO	SB	Pinch Hit AB	Pinch Hit H	PO	A	E	DP	TC/G	FA	G by Pos
1988	OAK A	10	.000	.000	3	0	0	0	0	0.0	1	0	0	1	0	2	0	1	1	0	0	0.5	1.000	2B-4
1989		58	.232	.312	125	29	5	1	1	0.8	22	4	8	31	5	4	0	69	49	1	11	2.0	.992	OF-25, 2B-24, DH-10
1990		86	.191	.213	136	26	3	0	0	0.0	18	10	20	23	3	12	2	66	69	5	9	1.7	.964	3B-28, OF-28, 2B-20, DH-6, 1B-1
1991		90	.249	.341	185	46	8	0	3	1.6	33	21	23	42	12	8	0	123	122	3	25	2.7	.988	2B-45, OF-28, 3B-14, DH-6
1992		123	.241	.341	349	84	24	1	3	0.9	59	34	82	57	21	4	0	286	226	6	60	3.7	.988	2B-78, OF-51, 1B-7, DH-3
1993		94	.190	.254	252	48	8	1	2	0.8	43	23	67	64	13	5	2	207	65	5	15	2.8	.982	OF-66, 2B-19, 1B-6, DH-5, SS-2
6 yrs.		461	.222	.299	1050	233	48	3	9	0.9	176	92	200	218	54	35	4	752	532	20	120	2.7	.985	OF-198, 2B-190, 3B-42, DH-30, 1B-14, SS-2
LEAGUE CHAMPIONSHIP SERIES																								
1989	OAK A	1	—	—	0	0	0	0	0	—	0	0	0	0	0	0	0	0	1	0	0	1.0	1.000	2B-1
1990		3	—	—	0	0	0	0	0	—	1	0	0	0	1	0	0	0	0	0	0	0.0	—	
1992		5	.231	.231	13	3	0	0	0	0.0	2	0	3	4	1	0	0	11	13	2	3	5.2	.923	2B-5
3 yrs.		9	.231	.231	13	3	0	0	0	0.0	3	0	3	4	2	0	0	11	14	2	3	4.5	.926	2B-6
WORLD SERIES																								
1989	OAK A	1	.500	.500	2	1	0	0	0	0.0	1	0	0	0	0	1	1	1	0	0	0	1.0	1.000	2B-1
1990		1	.000	.000	1	0	0	0	0	0.0	0	0	0	1	0	1	0	0	0	0	0	0.0	—	
2 yrs.		2	.333	.333	3	1	0	0	0	0.0	1	0	0	1	0	2	1	1	0	0	0	1.0	1.000	2B-1

Larvell Blanks

BLANKS, LARVELL (Sugar Bear)
B. Jan. 28, 1950, Del Rio, Tex.

BR TR 5′ 8″ 167 lbs.

Year	Team	Games	BA	SA	AB	H	2B	3B	HR	HR%	R	RBI	BB	SO	SB	Pinch Hit AB	Pinch Hit H	PO	A	E	DP	TC/G	FA	G by Pos
1972	ATL N	33	.329	.424	85	28	5	0	1	1.2	10	7	7	12	0	7	3	49	74	0	12	5.1	1.000	2B-18, SS-4, 3B-2
1973		17	.222	.222	18	4	0	0	0	0.0	1	0	1	3	0	10	3	1	3	0	0	0.6	1.000	3B-3, SS-2, 2B-2

Larvell Blanks *continued*

Year	Team	Games	BA	SA	AB	H	2B	3B	HR	HR%	R	RBI	BB	SO	SB	Pinch Hit AB	Pinch Hit H	PO	A	E	DP	TC/G	FA	G by Pos
1974		3	.250	.250	8	2	0	0	0	0.0	0	1	0	0	0	1	1	1	7	1	0	4.5	.889	SS-2
1975		141	.234	.293	471	110	13	3	3	0.6	49	38	38	43	4	2	0	212	438	27	75	4.8	.960	SS-129, 2B-12
1976	CLE A	104	.280	.393	328	92	8	7	5	1.5	45	41	30	31	1	14	4	152	214	11	53	3.6	.971	SS-56, 2B-46, 3B-2
1977		105	.286	.398	322	92	10	4	6	1.9	43	38	19	37	3	24	6	100	181	11	27	2.9	.962	SS-66, 3B-18, 2B-12, DH-6
1978		70	.254	.337	193	49	10	0	2	1.0	19	20	10	16	0	12	2	83	144	13	25	3.8	.946	SS-43, 2B-17, 3B-3, DH-1
1979	TEX A	68	.200	.267	120	24	5	0	1	0.8	13	15	11	9	0	12	2	65	90	3	22	2.4	.981	SS-49, 2B-16, DH-1
1980	ATL N	88	.204	.258	221	45	6	0	2	0.9	23	12	16	27	1	10	1	65	189	17	31	2.7	.937	SS-56, 3B-43, 2B-1
9 yrs.		629	.253	.335	1766	446	57	14	20	1.1	203	172	132	178	9	92	22	728	1340	83	245	3.5	.961	SS-407, 2B-124, 3B-71, DH-8

Don Blasingame

BLASINGAME, DON LEE (The Blazer) BL TR 5′10″ 160 lbs.
B. Mar. 16, 1932, Corinth, Miss.

Year	Team	Games	BA	SA	AB	H	2B	3B	HR	HR%	R	RBI	BB	SO	SB	Pinch Hit AB	Pinch Hit H	PO	A	E	DP	TC/G	FA	G by Pos
1955	STL N	5	.375	.438	16	6	1	0	0	0.0	4	0	6	0	1	0	0	10	19	2	2	6.2	.935	2B-3, SS-2
1956		150	.261	.322	587	153	22	7	0	0.0	94	27	72	52	8	2	0	373	442	21	120	5.6	.975	2B-98, SS-49, 3B-2
1957		154	.271	.368	**650**	176	25	7	8	1.2	108	58	71	49	21	0	0	372	512	14	128	5.8	.984	2B-154
1958		143	.274	.356	547	150	19	10	2	0.4	71	36	57	47	20	4	0	312	380	26	97	5.2	.964	2B-137
1959		150	.289	.359	615	178	26	7	1	0.2	90	24	67	42	15	1	0	362	439	17	104	5.5	.979	2B-150
1960	SF N	136	.235	.300	523	123	12	8	2	0.4	72	31	49	53	14	3	0	318	329	14	66	5.0	.979	2B-133
1961	2 teams	SF N (3G –.000) CIN N (123G –.222)																						
″	total	126	.222	.286	451	100	18	4	1	0.2	60	21	41	39	4	8	2	277	304	17	53	5.2	.972	2B-116
1962	CIN N	141	.281	.340	494	139	9	7	2	0.4	77	35	63	44	4	6	2	334	352	17	66	5.1	.976	2B-137
1963	2 teams	CIN N (18G –.161) WAS A (69G –.256)																						
″	total	87	.246	.323	285	70	12	2	2	0.7	33	12	31	23	3	9	2	184	194	4	58	5.0	.990	2B-75, 3B-2
1964	WAS A	143	.267	.314	506	135	17	2	1	0.2	56	34	40	44	8	17	0	259	336	14	70	4.5	.977	2B-135
1965		129	.223	.290	403	90	8	8	1	0.2	47	18	35	45	5	13	2	235	248	8	68	4.5	.984	2B-110
1966	2 teams	WAS A (68G –.215) KC A (12G –.158)																						
″	total	80	.210	.265	219	46	9	0	1	0.5	19	12	20	24	2	10	1	124	141	4	34	4.3	.985	2B-62, SS-1
12 yrs.		1444	.258	.327	5296	1366	178	62	21	0.4	731	308	552	462	105	73	9	3160	3696	158	866	5.1	.977	2B-1310, SS-52, 3B-4
WORLD SERIES																								
1961	CIN N	3	.143	.143	7	1	0	0	0	0.0	1	0	0	3	0	0	0	5	4	0	0	3.0	1.000	2B-3

Johnny Blatnik

BLATNIK, JOHN LOUIS (Chief) BR TR 6′ 195 lbs.
B. Mar. 10, 1921, Bridgeport, Ohio.

Year	Team	Games	BA	SA	AB	H	2B	3B	HR	HR%	R	RBI	BB	SO	SB	Pinch Hit AB	Pinch Hit H	PO	A	E	DP	TC/G	FA	G by Pos
1948	PHI N	121	.260	.407	415	108	27	8	6	1.4	56	45	31	77	3	15	4	220	9	13	1	2.3	.946	OF-105
1949		6	.125	.125	8	1	0	0	0	0.0	3	0	4	1	0	3	1	3	0	0	0	1.5	1.000	OF-2
1950	2 teams	PHI N (4G –.250) STL N (7G –.150)																						
″	total	11	.167	.167	24	4	0	0	0	0.0	0	1	5	5	0	4	1	8	1	1	0	1.3	.900	OF-8
3 yrs.		138	.253	.389	447	113	27	8	6	1.3	59	46	40	83	3	22	6	231	10	14	1	2.2	.945	OF-115

Buddy Blattner

BLATTNER, ROBERT GARNETT BR TR 6′½″ 180 lbs.
B. Feb. 8, 1920, St. Louis, Mo.

Year	Team	Games	BA	SA	AB	H	2B	3B	HR	HR%	R	RBI	BB	SO	SB	Pinch Hit AB	Pinch Hit H	PO	A	E	DP	TC/G	FA	G by Pos
1942	STL N	19	.043	.043	23	1	0	0	0	0.0	3	1	3	6	0	2	0	14	18	3	3	2.2	.914	SS-13, 2B-3
1946	NY N	126	.255	.405	420	107	18	6	11	2.6	63	49	56	52	12	2	0	286	315	15	62	5.4	.976	2B-114, 1B-1
1947		55	.261	.346	153	40	9	2	0	0.0	28	13	21	19	4	2	0	86	106	11	15	5.3	.946	2B-34, 3B-4
1948		8	.200	.250	20	4	1	0	0	0.0	3	0	3	2	2	0	0	8	22	0	4	4.3	1.000	2B-7
1949	PHI N	64	.247	.464	97	24	6	0	5	5.2	15	21	19	17	0	29	7	35	38	2	7	0.9	.973	3B-62, 2B-15, SS-7
5 yrs.		272	.247	.384	713	176	34	8	16	2.2	112	84	102	96	18	35	7	429	499	31	91	3.7	.968	2B-173, 3B-66, SS-20, 1B-1

Jeff Blauser

BLAUSER, JEFFREY MICHAEL BR TR 6′ 170 lbs.
B. Nov. 8, 1965, Los Gatos, Calif.

Year	Team	Games	BA	SA	AB	H	2B	3B	HR	HR%	R	RBI	BB	SO	SB	Pinch Hit AB	Pinch Hit H	PO	A	E	DP	TC/G	FA	G by Pos
1987	ATL N	51	.242	.352	165	40	6	3	2	1.2	11	15	18	34	7	1	0	65	166	9	28	4.8	.963	SS-50
1988		18	.239	.403	67	16	3	1	2	3.0	7	7	2	11	0	1	0	35	59	4	8	5.8	.959	2B-9, SS-8
1989		142	.270	.410	456	123	24	2	12	2.6	63	46	38	101	5	9	4	137	254	21	28	2.8	.949	3B-78, 2B-39, SS-30, OF-2
1990		115	.269	.409	386	104	24	3	8	2.1	46	39	35	70	3	4	2	169	288	16	54	4.0	.966	SS-93, 2B-14, 3B-9, OF-1
1991		129	.259	.409	352	91	14	3	11	3.1	49	54	54	59	5	26	6	136	219	17	37	2.8	.954	SS-85, 2B-32, 3B-18
1992		123	.262	.458	343	90	19	3	14	4.1	61	46	46	82	5	16	2	119	225	14	34	2.8	.961	SS-106, 2B-21, 3B-1
1993		161	.305	.436	597	182	29	2	15	2.5	110	73	85	109	16	2	0	189	426	19	86	3.9	.970	SS-161
1994		96	.258	.382	380	98	21	4	6	1.6	56	45	38	64	1	0	0	126	289	13	44	4.5	.970	SS-96
1995		115	.211	.341	431	91	16	2	12	2.8	60	31	57	107	8	0	0	150	335	15	60	4.3	.970	SS-115
9 yrs.		950	.263	.404	3177	835	156	23	82	2.6	463	356	373	637	50	59	14	1126	2261	128	379	3.6	.964	SS-744, 2B-115, 3B-106, OF-3
DIVISIONAL PLAYOFF SERIES																								
1995	ATL N	3	.000	.000	6	0	0	0	0	0.0	0	0	1	3	0	0	0	5	11	1	3	5.7	.941	SS-3
LEAGUE CHAMPIONSHIP SERIES																								
1991	ATL N	2	.000	.000	2	0	0	0	0	0.0	0	0	0	0	0	1	0	0	1	1	0	1.0	.500	SS-2
1992		7	.208	.417	24	5	0	1	1	4.2	3	4	3	2	0	0	0	7	15	2	1	3.4	.917	SS-7
1993		6	.280	.560	25	7	1	0	2	8.0	5	4	4	7	0	0	0	6	14	0	0	3.3	1.000	SS-6
1995		1	.000	.000	4	0	0	0	0	0.0	0	0	1	2	0	0	0	4	6	0	3	10.0	1.000	SS-1
4 yrs.		16	.218	.436	55	12	1	1	3	5.5	8	8	8	11	0	1	0	17	36	3	4	3.5	.946	SS-16
WORLD SERIES																								
1991	ATL N	5	.167	.167	6	1	0	0	0	0.0	0	0	1	1	0	4	0	3	3	0	1	1.2	1.000	SS-5
1992		6	.250	.250	24	6	0	0	0	0.0	2	0	1	9	2	0	0	7	22	0	5	4.8	1.000	SS-6
2 yrs.		11	.233	.233	30	7	0	0	0	0.0	2	0	2	10	2	4	0	10	25	0	6	3.2	1.000	SS-11

Marv Blaylock

BLAYLOCK, MARVIN EDWARD BL TL 6′1½″ 175 lbs.
B. Sept. 30, 1929, Fort Smith, Ark. D. Oct. 23, 1993, Conway, Ark.

Year	Team	Games	BA	SA	AB	H	2B	3B	HR	HR%	R	RBI	BB	SO	SB	Pinch Hit AB	Pinch Hit H	PO	A	E	DP	TC/G	FA	G by Pos
1950	NY N	1	.000	.000	1	0	0	0	0	0.0	0	0	0	0	0	1	0	0	0	0	0	0.0	—	
1955	PHI N	113	.208	.324	259	54	7	7	3	1.2	30	24	31	43	6	27	5	537	48	5	36	7.1	.992	1B-77, OF-6
1956		136	.254	.385	460	117	14	8	10	2.2	61	50	50	86	5	8	0	950	72	8	86	8.2	.992	1B-124, OF-1
1957		37	.154	.385	26	4	0	0	2	7.7	5	4	3	8	0	19	4	22	1	0	0	1.8	1.000	1B-12, OF-1
4 yrs.		287	.235	.363	746	175	21	15	15	2.0	96	78	84	137	11	55	9	1509	121	13	122	7.4	.992	1B-213, OF-8

Curt Blefary

BLEFARY, CURTIS LeROY
B. July 5, 1943, Brooklyn, N. Y.
BL TR 6′ 2″ 195 lbs.

Year	Team	Games	BA	SA	AB	H	2B	3B	HR	HR%	R	RBI	BB	SO	SB	Pinch Hit AB	Pinch Hit H	PO	A	E	DP	TC/G	FA	G by Pos
1965	BAL A	144	.260	.470	462	120	23	4	22	4.8	72	70	88	73	4	9	1	227	10	5	3	1.8	.979	OF-136
1966		131	.255	.468	419	107	14	3	23	5.5	73	64	73	56	1	13	3	274	17	5	9	2.3	.983	OF-109, 1B-20
1967		155	.242	.413	554	134	19	5	22	4.0	69	81	73	94	4	6	1	583	63	11	39	4.2	.983	OF-103, 1B-52
1968		137	.200	.322	451	90	8	1	15	3.3	50	39	65	66	6	6	2	437	35	11	11	3.4	.977	OF-92, C-40, 1B-12
1969	HOU N	155	.253	.393	542	137	26	7	12	2.2	66	67	77	79	8	2	0	1238	103	17	117	8.9	.987	1B-152, OF-1
1970	NY A	99	.212	.335	269	57	6	0	9	3.3	34	37	43	37	1	12	3	159	3	3	9	1.9	.982	OF-79, 1B-6
1971	2 teams	NY A (21G –.194) OAK A (50G –.218)																						
″	total	71	.212	.365	137	29	3	0	6	4.4	19	14	18	20	0	27	4	135	22	4	1	3.6	.975	OF-20, C-14, 3B-5, 1B-4, 2B-2
1972	2 teams	OAK A (8G –.455) SD N (74G –.196)																						
″	total	82	.221	.345	113	25	5	0	3	2.7	11	10	19	19	0	56	11	89	8	2	3	3.7	.980	C-12, 1B-7, OF-4, 3B-3, 2B-1
8 yrs.		974	.237	.400	2947	699	104	20	112	3.8	394	382	456	444	24	131	25	3142	261	58	192	4.0	.983	OF-544, 1B-253, C-66, 3B-8, 2B-3
LEAGUE CHAMPIONSHIP SERIES																								
1971	OAK A	1	.000	.000	1	0	0	0	0	0.0	0	0	0	1	0	1	0	0	0	0	0	0.0	—	
WORLD SERIES																								
1966	BAL A	4	.077	.077	13	1	0	0	0	0.0	0	0	2	3	0	0	0	7	0	0	0	1.8	1.000	OF-4

Ike Blessitt

BLESSITT, ISAIAH
B. Sept. 30, 1949, Detroit, Mich.
BR TR 5′11″ 185 lbs.

Year	Team	Games	BA	SA	AB	H	2B	3B	HR	HR%	R	RBI	BB	SO	SB	Pinch Hit AB	Pinch Hit H	PO	A	E	DP	TC/G	FA	G by Pos
1972	DET A	4	.000	.000	5	0	0	0	0	0.0	0	0	0	2	0	3	0	2	0	0	0	2.0	1.000	OF-1

Ned Bligh

BLIGH, EDWIN FORREST
B. June 30, 1864, Brooklyn, N. Y. D. Apr. 18, 1892, Brooklyn, N. Y.
BR TR 5′11″ 172 lbs.

Year	Team	Games	BA	SA	AB	H	2B	3B	HR	HR%	R	RBI	BB	SO	SB	Pinch Hit AB	Pinch Hit H	PO	A	E	DP	TC/G	FA	G by Pos
1886	BAL AA	3	.000	.000	9	0	0	0	0	0.0	0		1			0	0	10	5	3	0	6.0	.833	C-3
1888	CIN AA	3	.000	.000	5	0	0	0	0	0.0	0	0	0		0	0	0	5	1	0	1	2.0	1.000	C-2, OF-1
1889	COL AA	28	.140	.172	93	13	1	1	0	0.0	6	5	4	14	2	0	0	121	45	13	2	6.4	.927	C-28
1890	2 teams	COL AA (8G –.207) LOU AA (24G –.205)																						
″	total	32	.206	.255	102	21	2	0	1	1.0	11		11		1	0	0	152	44	16	2	6.6	.925	C-32
4 yrs.		66	.163	.201	209	34	3	1	1	0.5	17	5	16	14	3	0	0	288	95	32	5	6.3	.923	C-65, OF-1

Elmer Bliss

BLISS, ELMER WARD
B. Mar. 9, 1875, Penfield, Pa. D. Mar. 18, 1962, Bradford, Pa.
BL TR 6′ 180 lbs.

Year	Team	Games	BA	SA	AB	H	2B	3B	HR	HR%	R	RBI	BB	SO	SB	Pinch Hit AB	Pinch Hit H	PO	A	E	DP	TC/G	FA	G by Pos
1903	NY A	1	.000	.000	3	0	0	0	0	0.0	0	0	0		0	0	0	0	0	0	0	0.0	.000	P-1
1904		1	.000	.000	1	0	0	0	0	0.0	0	0	0		0	0	0	0	0	0	0	0.0	.000	OF-1
2 yrs.		2	.000	.000	4	0	0	0	0	0.0	0	0	0		0	0	0	0	0	0	0	0.0		OF-1, P-1

Frank Bliss

BLISS, FRANK EUGENE
B. Dec. 10, 1852, Chicago, Ill. D. Jan. 8, 1929, Nashville, Tenn.
5′ 9″ 155 lbs.

Year	Team	Games	BA	SA	AB	H	2B	3B	HR	HR%	R	RBI	BB	SO	SB	Pinch Hit AB	Pinch Hit H	PO	A	E	DP	TC/G	FA	G by Pos
1878	MIL N	2	.125	.125	8	1	0	0	0	0.0	1	0	0	0		0	0	9	3	1	0	6.5	.923	3B-1, C-1

Jack Bliss

BLISS, JOHN JOSEPH ALBERT
B. Jan. 9, 1882, Vancouver, Wash. D. Oct. 23, 1968, Temple City, Calif.
BR TR 5′ 9″ 185 lbs.

Year	Team	Games	BA	SA	AB	H	2B	3B	HR	HR%	R	RBI	BB	SO	SB	Pinch Hit AB	Pinch Hit H	PO	A	E	DP	TC/G	FA	G by Pos
1908	STL N	44	.213	.265	136	29	4	0	1	0.7	9	5	8		3	2	1	194	59	2	6	5.9	.992	C-43
1909		35	.221	.283	113	25	2	1	1	0.9	12	8	12		2	9	1	138	37	9	10	5.8	.951	C-32
1910		16	.061	.061	33	2	0	0	0	0.0	2	3	4	8	0	3	0	39	10	1	0	3.8	.980	C-13
1911		97	.229	.295	258	59	6	4	1	0.4	36	27	42	25	5	8	1	332	104	22	9	5.4	.952	C-84, SS-1
1912		49	.246	.289	114	28	3	1	0	0.0	11	18	19	14	3	6	3	140	42	5	7	4.6	.973	C-41
5 yrs.		241	.219	.274	654	143	15	6	3	0.5	70	61	85	47	13	28	6	843	252	39	32	5.3	.966	C-213, SS-1

Bruno Block

BLOCK, JOHN JAMES
Born John James Blochowitz.
B. Mar. 13, 1885, Wisconsin Rapids, Wis. D. Aug. 6, 1937, S. Milwaukee, Wis.
BR TR 5′ 9″ 185 lbs.

Year	Team	Games	BA	SA	AB	H	2B	3B	HR	HR%	R	RBI	BB	SO	SB	Pinch Hit AB	Pinch Hit H	PO	A	E	DP	TC/G	FA	G by Pos
1907	WAS A	24	.140	.211	57	8	2	1	0	0.0	3	2	2		0	3	0	59	16	4	1	3.8	.949	C-21
1910	CHI A	55	.211	.230	152	32	1	1	0	0.0	12	9	13		3	6	0	244	77	12	8	7.1	.964	C-47
1911		39	.304	.400	115	35	6	1	1	0.9	11	18	6		0	1	0	201	40	7	2	6.5	.972	C-38
1912		46	.257	.382	136	35	5	6	0	0.0	8	26	7		1	0	0	222	65	6	4	6.4	.980	C-46
1914	CHI F	43	.190	.250	100	19	4	1	0	0.0	8	13	11		1	10	2	126	37	6	7	5.1	.964	C-33
5 yrs.		207	.230	.304	560	129	18	10	1	0.2	42	68	39		5	20	2	852	235	35	22	6.1	.969	C-185

Cy Block

BLOCK, SEYMOUR
B. May 4, 1919, Brooklyn, N. Y.
BR TR 6′ 180 lbs.

Year	Team	Games	BA	SA	AB	H	2B	3B	HR	HR%	R	RBI	BB	SO	SB	Pinch Hit AB	Pinch Hit H	PO	A	E	DP	TC/G	FA	G by Pos
1942	CHI N	9	.364	.455	33	12	1	1	0	0.0	6	4	3	3	2	0	0	12	15	2	2	3.2	.931	3B-8, 2B-1
1945		2	.143	.143	7	1	0	0	0	0.0	1	1	0	0	0	0	0	3	7	0	0	5.0	1.000	3B-1, 2B-1
1946		6	.231	.231	13	3	0	0	0	0.0	2	0	4	0	0	1	0	4	7	0	3	2.8	1.000	3B-4
3 yrs.		17	.302	.358	53	16	1	1	0	0.0	9	5	7	3	2	1	0	19	29	2	5	3.3	.960	3B-13, 2B-2
WORLD SERIES																								
1945	CHI N	1	—	—	0	0	0	0	0	—	0	0	0	0	0	0	0	0	0	0	0	0.0	—	

Terry Blocker

BLOCKER, TERRY FENNELL
B. Aug. 18, 1959, Columbia, S. C.
BL TL 6′ 2″ 195 lbs.

Year	Team	Games	BA	SA	AB	H	2B	3B	HR	HR%	R	RBI	BB	SO	SB	Pinch Hit AB	Pinch Hit H	PO	A	E	DP	TC/G	FA	G by Pos
1985	NY N	18	.067	.067	15	1	0	0	0	0.0	1	0	1	2	0	5	0	4	0	0	0	0.8	1.000	OF-5
1988	ATL N	66	.212	.283	198	42	4	2	2	1.0	13	10	10	20	1	4	0	164	1	1	0	2.7	.994	OF-61
1989		26	.226	.258	31	7	1	0	0	0.0	1	1	1	5	1	18	3	7	0	0	0	0.8	1.000	OF-8, P-1
3 yrs.		110	.205	.266	244	50	5	2	2	0.8	15	11	12	27	2	27	3	175	1	1	0	2.4	.994	OF-74, P-1

Wes Blogg

BLOGG, WESLEY COLLINS
B. 1855, Norfolk, Va. D. Mar. 10, 1897, Baltimore, Md.

Year	Team	Games	BA	SA	AB	H	2B	3B	HR	HR%	R	RBI	BB	SO	SB	Pinch Hit AB	Pinch Hit H	PO	A	E	DP	TC/G	FA	G by Pos
1883	PIT AA	9	.147	.147	34	5	0	0	0	0.0	0	0	0	0		0	0	36	6	7	0	5.4	.857	C-6, OF-3

Ron Blomberg

BLOMBERG, RONALD MARK (Boomer) BL TR 6′ 1½″ 195 lbs.
B. Aug. 23, 1948, Atlanta, Ga.

Year	Team	Games	BA	SA	AB	H	2B	3B	HR	HR%	R	RBI	BB	SO	SB	Pinch Hit AB	Pinch Hit H	PO	A	E	DP	TC/G	FA	G by Pos
1969	NY A	4	.500	.500	6	3	0	0	0	0.0	0	0	1	0	0	1	1	2	0	0	0	1.0	1.000	OF-2
1971		64	.322	.477	199	64	6	2	7	3.5	30	31	14	23	2	11	2	96	1	3	1	1.8	.970	OF-57
1972		107	.268	.488	299	80	22	1	14	4.7	36	49	38	26	0	15	5	813	32	13	88	9.0	.985	1B-95
1973		100	.329	.498	301	99	13	1	12	4.0	45	57	34	25	2	6	2	359	28	8	38	4.1	.980	DH-55, 1B-41
1974		90	.311	.481	264	82	11	2	10	3.8	39	48	29	33	2	10	5	32	2	0	0	0.4	1.000	DH-58, OF-19
1975		34	.255	.481	106	27	8	2	4	3.8	18	17	13	10	0	5	2	2	0	0	0	0.1	1.000	DH-27, OF-1
1976		1	.000	.000	2	0	0	0	0	0.0	0	0	0	0	0	1	0	0	0	0	0	0.0	.000	DH-1
1978	CHI A	61	.231	.372	156	36	7	0	5	3.2	16	22	11	17	0	16	2	70	3	1	2	1.7	.986	DH-36, 1B-7
8 yrs.		461	.293	.473	1333	391	67	8	52	3.9	184	224	140	134	6	65	19	1374	66	25	129	3.7	.983	DH-177, 1B-143, OF-79

Joe Blong

BLONG, JOSEPH MYLES BR TR
B. Sept. 17, 1853, St. Louis, Mo. D. Sept. 16, 1892, St. Louis, Mo.

Year	Team	Games	BA	SA	AB	H	2B	3B	HR	HR%	R	RBI	BB	SO	SB	Pinch Hit AB	Pinch Hit H	PO	A	E	DP	TC/G	FA	G by Pos
1876	STL N	62	.235	.292	264	62	7	4	0	0.0	30	30	2	9		0	0	64	15	9	2	1.4	.898	OF-62, P-1
1877		58	.216	.280	218	47	8	3	0	0.0	17	13	4	22		0	0	73	30	18	0	1.9	.851	OF-40, P-25
2 yrs.		120	.226	.286	482	109	15	7	0	0.0	47	43	6	31		0	0	137	45	27	2	1.6	.871	OF-102, P-26

Jimmy Bloodworth

BLOODWORTH, JAMES HENRY BR TR 5′11″ 180 lbs.
B. July 26, 1917, Tallahassee, Fla.

Year	Team	Games	BA	SA	AB	H	2B	3B	HR	HR%	R	RBI	BB	SO	SB	Pinch Hit AB	Pinch Hit H	PO	A	E	DP	TC/G	FA	G by Pos
1937	WAS A	15	.220	.300	50	11	2	1	0	0.0	3	8	5	8	0	1	0	28	42	4	9	5.3	.946	2B-14
1939		83	.289	.409	318	92	24	1	4	1.3	34	40	10	26	3	5	2	237	220	13	66	6.0	.972	2B-73, OF-5
1940		119	.245	.386	469	115	17	8	11	2.3	47	70	16	71	3	0	0	456	304	15	94	6.5	.981	2B-96, 1B-17, 3B-6
1941		142	.245	.346	506	124	24	3	7	1.4	59	66	41	58	1	4	0	386	446	25	108	6.2	.971	2B-132, 3B-6, SS-1
1942	DET A	137	.242	.362	533	129	23	1	13	2.4	62	57	35	63	2	1	0	336	431	22	66	5.8	.972	2B-134, SS-2
1943		129	.241	.344	474	114	23	4	6	1.3	41	52	29	59	4	0	0	349	393	21	74	5.9	.972	2B-129
1946		76	.245	.345	249	61	8	1	5	2.0	25	36	12	26	3	4	0	157	184	9	46	4.9	.974	2B-71
1947	PIT N	88	.250	.345	316	79	9	0	7	2.2	27	48	16	39	1	1	0	222	206	9	56	5.0	.979	2B-87
1949	CIN N	134	.261	.385	452	118	27	1	9	2.0	40	59	27	36	1	14	8	447	262	11	75	5.9	.985	2B-92, 1B-23, 3B-8
1950	2 teams	CIN N (4G –.214)	PHI N (54G –.229)																					
″	total	58	.227	.255	110	25	3	0	0	0.0	7	14	8	12	0	16	4	79	59	0	14	3.5	1.000	2B-31, 1B-7, 3B-2
1951	PHI N	21	.143	.143	42	6	0	0	0	0.0	2	3	1	9	1	7	3	38	26	0	4	4.6	1.000	2B-8, 1B-6
11 yrs.		1002	.248	.358	3519	874	160	20	62	1.8	347	453	200	407	19	53	17	2735	2573	129	612	5.7	.976	2B-867, 1B-53, 3B-22, OF-5, SS-3
WORLD SERIES																								
1950	PHI N	1	—	—	0	0	0	0	0	—	0	0	0	0	0	0	0	0	0	0	0	0.0	.000	2B-1

Clyde Bloomfield

BLOOMFIELD, CLYDE STALCUP (Bud) BR TR 5′11½″ 175 lbs.
B. Jan. 5, 1936, Oklahoma City, Okla.

Year	Team	Games	BA	SA	AB	H	2B	3B	HR	HR%	R	RBI	BB	SO	SB	Pinch Hit AB	Pinch Hit H	PO	A	E	DP	TC/G	FA	G by Pos
1963	STL N	1	—	—	0	0	0	0	0	—	0	0	0	0	0	0	0	0	0	0	0	0.0	.000	3B-1
1964	MIN A	7	.143	.143	7	1	0	0	0	0.0	1	0	0	0	0	0	0	5	5	0	2	2.0	1.000	2B-3, SS-2
2 yrs.		8	.143	.143	7	1	0	0	0	0.0	1	0	0	0	0	0	0	5	5	0	2	1.7	1.000	2B-3, SS-2, 3B-1

Greg Blosser

BLOSSER, GREGORY BRENT BL TL 6′ 3″ 200 lbs.
B. June 26, 1971, Manatee, Fla.

Year	Team	Games	BA	SA	AB	H	2B	3B	HR	HR%	R	RBI	BB	SO	SB	Pinch Hit AB	Pinch Hit H	PO	A	E	DP	TC/G	FA	G by Pos
1993	BOS A	17	.071	.107	28	2	1	0	0	0.0	1	1	2	7	1	7	0	11	1	0	0	1.2	1.000	OF-9, DH-1
1994		5	.091	.091	11	1	0	0	0	0.0	2	1	4	4	0	1	0	8	0	3	0	2.8	.727	OF-3, DH-1
2 yrs.		22	.077	.103	39	3	1	0	0	0.0	3	2	6	11	1	8	0	19	1	3	0	1.6	.870	OF-12, DH-2

Jack Blott

BLOTT, JOHN LEONARD BR TR 6′ 210 lbs.
B. Aug. 24, 1902, Girard, Ohio D. June 11, 1964, Ann Arbor, Mich.

Year	Team	Games	BA	SA	AB	H	2B	3B	HR	HR%	R	RBI	BB	SO	SB	Pinch Hit AB	Pinch Hit H	PO	A	E	DP	TC/G	FA	G by Pos
1924	CIN N	2	.000	.000	1	0	0	0	0	0.0	0	0	0	0	0	1	0	1	0	0	0	1.0	1.000	C-1

Mike Blowers

BLOWERS, MICHAEL ROY BR TR 6′ 2″ 190 lbs.
B. Apr. 24, 1965, Wurzburg, West Germany.

Year	Team	Games	BA	SA	AB	H	2B	3B	HR	HR%	R	RBI	BB	SO	SB	Pinch Hit AB	Pinch Hit H	PO	A	E	DP	TC/G	FA	G by Pos
1989	NY A	13	.263	.263	38	10	0	0	0	0.0	2	3	3	13	0	1	0	9	14	4	3	2.1	.852	3B-13
1990		48	.188	.319	144	27	4	0	5	3.5	16	21	12	50	1	3	0	26	63	10	4	2.1	.899	3B-45, DH-2
1991		15	.200	.286	35	7	0	0	1	2.9	3	1	4	3	0	1	0	4	16	3	1	1.6	.870	3B-14
1992	SEA A	31	.192	.274	73	14	3	0	1	1.4	7	2	6	20	0	1	0	28	44	1	8	2.3	.986	3B-29, 1B-3
1993		127	.280	.475	379	106	23	3	15	4.0	55	57	44	98	1	6	2	70	225	15	14	2.5	.952	3B-117, OF-2, DH-2, 1B-1, C-1
1994		85	.289	.437	270	78	13	0	9	3.3	37	49	25	60	2	14	4	141	108	9	15	3.0	.965	3B-48, 1B-20, OF-9, DH-9
1995		134	.257	.474	439	113	24	1	23	5.2	59	96	53	128	2	10	2	117	172	16	16	2.2	.948	3B-126, 1B-7, OF-5
7 yrs.		453	.258	.430	1378	355	67	4	54	3.9	179	229	147	372	6	36	8	395	642	58	61	2.4	.947	3B-392, 1B-31, OF-16, DH-13, C-1
DIVISIONAL PLAYOFF SERIES																								
1995	SEA A	5	.167	.167	18	3	0	0	0	0.0	0	1	3	7	0	0	0	2	6	0	0	1.3	1.000	3B-5, 1B-1
LEAGUE CHAMPIONSHIP SERIES																								
1995	SEA A	6	.222	.389	18	4	0	0	1	5.6	1	2	0	4	0	0	0	5	9	0	0	2.3	1.000	3B-6

Bert Blue

BLUE, BIRD WAYNE BR TR 6′ 3″ 200 lbs.
B. Oct. 9, 1877, Bettsville, Ohio D. Sept. 2, 1929, Detroit, Mich.

Year	Team	Games	BA	SA	AB	H	2B	3B	HR	HR%	R	RBI	BB	SO	SB	Pinch Hit AB	Pinch Hit H	PO	A	E	DP	TC/G	FA	G by Pos
1908	2 teams	STL A (11G –.360)	PHI A (6G –.158)																					
″	total	17	.273	.455	44	12	1	2	1	2.3	4	2	3		0	3	0	74	15	3	1	6.6	.967	C-14

Lu Blue

BLUE, LUZERNE ATWELL BB TL 5′10″ 165 lbs.
B. Mar. 5, 1897, Washington, D. C. D. July 28, 1958, Alexandria, Va.

Year	Team	Games	BA	SA	AB	H	2B	3B	HR	HR%	R	RBI	BB	SO	SB	Pinch Hit AB	Pinch Hit H	PO	A	E	DP	TC/G	FA	G by Pos
1921	DET A	153	.308	.427	585	180	33	11	5	0.9	103	75	103	47	13	1	0	1478	85	16	75	10.4	.990	1B-152
1922		145	.300	.414	584	175	31	9	6	1.0	131	45	82	48	8	1	1	1506	75	15	107	11.1	.991	1B-144
1923		129	.284	.371	504	143	27	7	1	0.2	100	46	96	40	9	0	0	1347	93	12	74	11.3	.992	1B-129
1924		108	.311	.428	395	123	26	7	2	0.5	81	50	64	26	9	0	0	1099	85	17	72	11.1	.986	1B-108
1925		150	.306	.391	532	163	18	9	3	0.6	91	94	83	29	19	2	0	1480	101	19	115	10.8	.988	1B-148
1926		128	.287	.415	429	123	24	14	1	0.2	92	52	90	18	13	12	5	1156	57	19	95	11.2	.985	1B-109, OF-1
1927		112	.260	.364	365	95	17	9	1	0.3	71	42	71	28	13	5	2	1019	68	18	99	10.6	.984	1B-104

Lu Blue *continued*

Year	Team	Games	BA	SA	AB	H	2B	3B	HR	HR%	R	RBI	BB	SO	SB	Pinch Hit AB	Pinch Hit H	PO	A	E	DP	TC/G	FA	G by Pos
1928	STL A	154	.281	.455	549	154	32	11	14	2.6	116	80	105	43	12	0	0	1472	107	17	121	10.4	.989	1B-154
1929		151	.293	.429	573	168	40	10	6	1.0	111	61	126	32	12	0	0	1491	88	10	127	10.5	.994	1B-151
1930		117	.235	.351	425	100	27	5	4	0.9	85	42	81	44	12	4	1	1110	68	16	91	10.8	.987	1B-111
1931	CHI A	155	.304	.399	589	179	23	15	1	0.2	119	62	127	60	13	0	0	1452	81	16	105	10.0	.990	1B-155
1932		112	.249	.316	373	93	21	2	0	0.0	51	43	64	21	17	6	1	1014	88	16	106	10.6	.986	1B-105
1933	BKN N	1	.000	.000	1	0	0	0	0	0.0	0	0	0	0	0	0	0	2	0	0	0	2.0	1.000	1B-1
13 yrs.		1615	.287	.401	5904	1696	319	109	44	0.7	1151	692	1092	436	150	31	10	15626	996	191	1187	10.7	.989	1B-1571, OF-1

Ossie Bluege

BLUEGE, OSWALD LOUIS BR TR 5′11″ 162 lbs.
Brother of Otto Bluege.
B. Oct. 24, 1900, Chicago, Ill. D. Oct. 14, 1985, Edina, Minn.
Manager 1943–47.

Year	Team	Games	BA	SA	AB	H	2B	3B	HR	HR%	R	RBI	BB	SO	SB	Pinch Hit AB	Pinch Hit H	PO	A	E	DP	TC/G	FA	G by Pos
1922	WAS A	19	.197	.213	61	12	1	0	0	0.0	5	2	7	7	1	1	0	18	33	4	3	2.9	.927	3B-17, SS-2
1923		109	.245	.338	379	93	15	7	2	0.5	48	42	48	53	5	0	0	131	251	25	31	3.7	.939	3B-107, 2B-2
1924		117	.281	.353	402	113	15	4	2	0.5	59	49	39	36	7	1	1	118	231	20	15	3.2	.946	3B-102, 2B-10, SS-4
1925		145	.287	.377	522	150	27	4	4	0.8	77	79	59	56	16	0	0	160	290	22	29	3.2	.953	3B-144, SS-4
1926		139	.271	.361	487	132	19	8	3	0.6	69	65	70	46	12	0	0	146	270	22	18	3.1	.950	3B-134, SS-8
1927		146	.274	.362	503	138	21	10	1	0.2	71	66	57	47	15	0	0	185	337	21	20	3.7	.961	3B-146
1928		146	.297	.400	518	154	33	7	2	0.4	78	75	46	27	18	1	1	150	330	20	34	3.5	.960	3B-144
1929		64	.295	.400	220	65	6	1	5	2.3	35	31	19	15	6	4	0	74	145	6	24	3.9	.973	3B-34, 2B-14, SS-10
1930		134	.290	.395	476	138	27	7	3	0.6	64	69	51	40	15	0	0	138	258	15	20	3.1	.964	3B-134
1931		152	.272	.382	570	155	25	7	8	1.4	82	98	50	39	16	0	0	151	286	18	24	3.0	.960	3B-152, SS-1
1932		149	.258	.347	507	131	22	4	5	1.0	64	64	84	41	9	0	0	158	295	14	28	3.1	.970	3B-149
1933		140	.261	.325	501	131	14	0	6	1.2	63	71	55	34	6	2	1	116	247	13	25	2.7	.965	3B-138
1934		99	.246	.291	285	70	9	2	0	0.0	39	11	23	15	2	13	4	114	202	10	28	4.0	.969	3B-41, SS-30, OF-5, 2B-5
1935		100	.263	.325	320	84	14	3	0	0.0	44	34	37	21	2	7	2	148	238	17	39	4.6	.958	SS-58, 3B-25, 2B-4
1936		90	.288	.342	319	92	12	1	1	0.3	43	55	38	16	5	0	0	177	258	5	46	4.9	.989	2B-52, SS-23, 3B-15
1937		42	.283	.370	127	36	4	2	1	0.8	12	13	13	19	1	7	2	78	95	8	19	5.7	.956	SS-28, 3B-2, 1B-2
1938		58	.261	.337	184	48	12	1	0	0.0	25	21	21	11	3	8	1	100	144	5	33	5.0	.980	2B-38, SS-10, 3B-1, 1B-1
1939		18	.153	.153	59	9	0	0	0	0.0	5	3	7	2	1	1	0	103	22	3	13	7.5	.977	1B-11, 3B-2, SS-2, 2B-2
18 yrs.		1867	.272	.356	6440	1751	276	68	43	0.7	883	848	724	525	140	45	12	2265	3932	248	449	3.6	.962	3B-1487, SS-180, 2B-127, 1B-14, OF-5
WORLD SERIES																								
1924	WAS A	7	.192	.192	26	5	0	0	0	0.0	2	3	3	4	1	0	0	8	24	3	6	3.9	.914	SS-5, 3B-4
1925		5	.278	.333	18	5	1	0	0	0.0	2	2	1	4	0	0	0	1	14	0	1	3.0	1.000	3B-5
1933		5	.125	.188	16	2	1	0	0	0.0	1	0	1	6	0	0	0	3	13	0	0	3.2	1.000	3B-5
3 yrs.		17	.200	.233	60	12	2	0	0	0.0	5	5	5	14	1	0	0	12	51	3	7	3.5	.955	3B-14, SS-5

Otto Bluege

BLUEGE, OTTO ADAM (Squeaky) BR TR 5′10″ 154 lbs.
Brother of Ossie Bluege.
B. July 20, 1909, Chicago, Ill. D. June 28, 1977, Chicago, Ill.

Year	Team	Games	BA	SA	AB	H	2B	3B	HR	HR%	R	RBI	BB	SO	SB	Pinch Hit AB	Pinch Hit H	PO	A	E	DP	TC/G	FA	G by Pos
1932	CIN N	1	—	—	0	0	0	0	0	—	1	0	0	0	0	0	0	0	0	0	0	0.0	—	
1933		108	.213	.247	291	62	6	2	0	0.0	17	18	26	29	0	0	0	176	272	29	50	4.5	.939	SS-95, 2B-10, 3B-1
2 yrs.		109	.213	.247	291	62	6	2	0	0.0	18	18	26	29	0	0	0	176	272	29	50	4.5	.939	SS-95, 2B-10, 3B-1

Red Bluhm

BLUHM, HARVEY FRED BR TR 5′11″ 165 lbs.
B. June 27, 1894, Cleveland, Ohio D. May 7, 1952, Flint, Mich.

Year	Team	Games	BA	SA	AB	H	2B	3B	HR	HR%	R	RBI	BB	SO	SB	Pinch Hit AB	Pinch Hit H	PO	A	E	DP	TC/G	FA	G by Pos
1918	BOS A	1	.000	.000	1	0	0	0	0	0.0	0	0	0	0	0	1	0	0	0	0	0	0.0	—	

Chet Boak

BOAK, CHESTER ROBERT BR TR 6′ 180 lbs.
B. June 19, 1935, New Castle, Pa. D. Nov. 28, 1983, Emporium, Pa.

Year	Team	Games	BA	SA	AB	H	2B	3B	HR	HR%	R	RBI	BB	SO	SB	Pinch Hit AB	Pinch Hit H	PO	A	E	DP	TC/G	FA	G by Pos
1960	KC A	5	.154	.154	13	2	0	0	0	0.0	1	1	0	2	0	0	0	11	11	1	4	4.6	.957	2B-5
1961	WAS A	5	.000	.000	7	0	0	0	0	0.0	0	0	1	1	1	4	0	1	2	0	0	3.0	1.000	2B-1
2 yrs.		10	.100	.100	20	2	0	0	0	0.0	1	1	1	3	1	4	0	12	13	1	4	4.3	.962	2B-6

Randy Bobb

BOBB, MARK RANDALL BR TR 6′ 1″ 195 lbs.
B. Jan. 1, 1948, Los Angeles, Calif. D. June 13, 1982, Carnelian Bay, Calif.

Year	Team	Games	BA	SA	AB	H	2B	3B	HR	HR%	R	RBI	BB	SO	SB	Pinch Hit AB	Pinch Hit H	PO	A	E	DP	TC/G	FA	G by Pos
1968	CHI N	7	.125	.125	8	1	0	0	0	0.0	0	0	1	2	0	0	0	14	2	0	0	2.3	1.000	C-7
1969		3	.000	.000	2	0	0	0	0	0.0	0	0	0	1	0	0	0	4	0	0	0	2.0	1.000	C-2
2 yrs.		10	.100	.100	10	1	0	0	0	0.0	0	0	1	3	0	0	0	18	2	0	0	2.2	1.000	C-9

John Boccabella

BOCCABELLA, JOHN DOMINIC BR TR 6′ 1″ 195 lbs.
B. June 29, 1941, San Francisco, Calif.

Year	Team	Games	BA	SA	AB	H	2B	3B	HR	HR%	R	RBI	BB	SO	SB	Pinch Hit AB	Pinch Hit H	PO	A	E	DP	TC/G	FA	G by Pos
1963	CHI N	24	.189	.311	74	14	4	1	1	1.4	7	5	6	21	0	1	0	234	12	1	29	10.3	.996	1B-24
1964		9	.391	.565	23	9	2	1	0	0.0	4	6	0	3	0	3	1	41	3	0	3	6.3	1.000	1B-5, OF-2
1965		6	.333	.833	12	4	0	0	2	16.7	2	4	1	2	0	2	1	12	1	1	0	4.7	.929	1B-2, OF-1
1966		75	.228	.359	206	47	9	0	6	2.9	22	25	14	39	0	16	2	255	20	1	13	4.1	.996	OF-33, 1B-30, C-5
1967		25	.171	.257	35	6	1	1	0	0.0	0	8	3	7	0	11	2	35	1	0	3	2.8	1.000	OF-9, 1B-3, C-1
1968		7	.071	.071	14	1	0	0	0	0.0	0	1	2	2	0	2	0	27	0	0	0	5.4	1.000	C-4, OF-1
1969	MON N	40	.105	.163	86	9	2	0	1	1.2	4	6	6	30	1	7	1	137	19	0	0	4.9	1.000	C-32
1970		61	.269	.407	145	39	3	1	5	3.4	18	17	11	24	0	8	2	314	44	3	25	6.2	.992	1B-33, C-24, 3B-1
1971		74	.220	.333	177	39	11	0	3	1.7	15	15	14	26	0	5	0	335	33	4	30	4.9	.989	1B-37, C-37, 3B-2
1972		83	.227	.290	207	47	8	1	1	0.5	14	10	9	29	1	3	0	367	39	6	12	5.1	.985	C-73, 1B-7, 3B-1
1973		118	.233	.318	403	94	13	0	7	1.7	25	46	26	57	1	1	0	610	65	14	10	5.8	.980	C-117, 1B-1
1974	SF N	29	.138	.175	80	11	3	0	0	0.0	6	5	4	6	0	4	0	110	6	1	1	4.5	.991	C-26
12 yrs.		551	.219	.317	1462	320	56	5	26	1.8	117	148	96	246	3	63	9	2477	243	31	126	5.4	.989	C-319, 1B-142, OF-46, 3B-4

Milt Bocek

BOCEK, MILTON FRANK
B. July 16, 1912, Chicago, Ill.
BR TR 6′ 1″ 185 lbs.

Year	Team	Games	BA	SA	AB	H	2B	3B	HR	HR%	R	RBI	BB	SO	SB	Pinch Hit AB	Pinch Hit H	PO	A	E	DP	TC/G	FA	G by Pos
1933	CHI A	11	.364	.545	22	8	1	0	1	4.5	3	3	4	6	0	5	1	6	0	0	0	1.0	1.000	OF-6
1934		19	.211	.237	38	8	1	0	0	0.0	3	3	5	5	0	6	0	25	2	0	1	2.7	1.000	OF-10
2 yrs.		30	.267	.350	60	16	2	0	1	1.7	6	6	9	11	0	11	1	31	2	0	1	2.1	1.000	OF-16

Bruce Bochte

BOCHTE, BRUCE ANTON
B. Nov. 12, 1950, Pasadena, Calif.
BL TL 6′ 3″ 195 lbs.

Year	Team	Games	BA	SA	AB	H	2B	3B	HR	HR%	R	RBI	BB	SO	SB	Pinch Hit AB	Pinch Hit H	PO	A	E	DP	TC/G	FA	G by Pos
1974	CAL A	57	.270	.378	196	53	4	1	5	2.6	24	26	18	23	6	1	0	248	9	5	16	4.2	.981	OF-39, 1B-24
1975		107	.285	.376	375	107	19	3	3	0.8	41	48	45	43	3	3	1	850	51	12	90	8.6	.987	1B-105, DH-1
1976		146	.258	.311	466	120	17	1	2	0.4	53	49	64	53	4	8	3	651	42	7	38	4.8	.990	OF-86, 1B-59, DH-1
1977	2 teams	CAL A (25G –.290) CLE A (112G –.304)																						
″	total	137	.301	.394	492	148	23	1	7	1.4	64	51	47	42	6	1	0	486	33	9	19	3.8	.983	OF-100, 1B-36, DH-2
1978	SEA A	140	.263	.395	486	128	25	3	11	2.3	58	51	60	47	3	5	3	180	7	3	2	1.4	.984	OF-91, DH-43, 1B-1
1979		150	.316	.493	554	175	38	6	16	2.9	81	100	67	64	2	4	2	1361	114	14	140	10.1	.991	1B-147
1980		148	.300	.456	520	156	34	4	13	2.5	62	78	72	81	2	6	1	1273	98	6	143	9.6	.996	1B-133, DH-11
1981		99	.260	.361	335	87	16	0	6	1.8	39	30	47	53	1	8	2	766	49	4	70	8.4	.995	1B-82, OF-14, DH-1
1982		144	.297	.409	509	151	21	0	12	2.4	58	70	67	71	8	4	2	428	26	3	39	3.2	.993	OF-99, 1B-34, DH-12
1984	OAK A	148	.264	.345	469	124	23	0	5	1.1	58	52	52	59	2	11	4	1048	66	8	119	7.7	.993	1B-144, DH-2
1985		137	.295	.439	424	125	17	1	14	3.3	48	60	49	58	3	9	3	942	60	10	83	7.9	.990	1B-128
1986		125	.256	.337	407	104	13	1	6	1.5	57	43	65	68	3	9	4	912	88	9	79	8.7	.991	1B-115, DH-1
12 yrs.		1538	.282	.396	5233	1478	250	21	100	1.9	643	658	653	662	43	69	25	9145	643	90	838	6.5	.991	1B-1008, OF-429, DH-74

Bruce Bochy

BOCHY, BRUCE DOUGLAS
B. Apr. 16, 1955, Landes De Bussac, France.
Manager 1995.
BR TR 6′ 3″ 205 lbs.

Year	Team	Games	BA	SA	AB	H	2B	3B	HR	HR%	R	RBI	BB	SO	SB	Pinch Hit AB	Pinch Hit H	PO	A	E	DP	TC/G	FA	G by Pos
1978	HOU N	54	.266	.377	154	41	8	0	3	1.9	8	15	11	35	0	3	0	268	35	8	5	5.9	.974	C-53
1979		56	.217	.271	129	28	4	0	1	0.8	11	6	13	25	0	3	0	198	29	7	4	4.3	.970	C-55
1980		22	.182	.227	22	4	1	0	0	0.0	0	0	5	7	0	9	1	19	1	0	0	1.8	1.000	C-10, 1B-1
1982	NY N	17	.306	.510	49	15	4	0	2	4.1	4	8	4	6	0	0	0	92	8	4	1	6.1	.962	C-16, 1B-1
1983	SD N	23	.214	.286	42	9	1	1	0	0.0	2	3	0	9	0	12	4	51	5	0	0	5.1	1.000	C-11
1984		37	.228	.435	92	21	5	1	4	4.3	10	15	3	21	0	1	0	147	12	2	2	4.5	.988	C-36
1985		48	.268	.446	112	30	2	0	6	5.4	16	13	6	30	0	8	1	148	11	2	2	3.5	.988	C-46
1986		63	.252	.512	127	32	9	0	8	6.3	16	22	14	23	1	20	7	202	22	2	3	4.7	.991	C-48
1987		38	.160	.280	75	12	3	0	2	2.7	8	11	11	21	0	12	1	95	7	4	0	4.6	.962	C-23
9 yrs.		358	.239	.388	802	192	37	2	26	3.2	75	93	67	177	1	68	14	1220	130	29	17	4.6	.979	C-298, 1B-2
LEAGUE CHAMPIONSHIP SERIES																								
1980	HOU N	1	.000	.000	1	0	0	0	0	0.0	0	0	0	0	0	0	0	5	1	0	1	6.0	1.000	C-1
WORLD SERIES																								
1984	SD N	1	1.000	1.000	1	1	0	0	0	0.0	0	0	0	0	0	1	1	0	0	0	0	0.0	—	

Eddie Bockman

BOCKMAN, JOSEPH EDWARD
B. July 26, 1920, Santa Ana, Calif.
BR TR 5′ 9″ 175 lbs.

Year	Team	Games	BA	SA	AB	H	2B	3B	HR	HR%	R	RBI	BB	SO	SB	Pinch Hit AB	Pinch Hit H	PO	A	E	DP	TC/G	FA	G by Pos
1946	NY A	4	.083	.167	12	1	1	0	0	0.0	2	0	1	4	0	0	0	8	6	1	3	3.8	.933	3B-4
1947	CLE A	96	.258	.394	66	17	2	2	1	1.5	8	14	5	17	0	20	5	22	33	3	8	3.2	.948	3B-12, 2B-4, OF-1, SS-1
1948	PIT N	70	.239	.358	176	42	7	1	4	2.3	23	23	17	35	2	11	2	51	100	6	9	3.0	.962	3B-51, 2B-1
1949		79	.223	.341	220	49	6	1	6	2.7	21	19	23	31	3	5	2	62	128	8	14	2.7	.960	3B-68, 2B-5
4 yrs.		249	.230	.350	474	109	16	4	11	2.3	54	56	46	87	5	36	9	143	267	18	34	2.9	.958	3B-135, 2B-10, OF-1, SS-1

Ping Bodie

BODIE, FRANK STEPHAN
Born Francesco Stephano Pezzolo.
B. Oct. 8, 1887, San Francisco, Calif. D. Dec. 17, 1961, San Francisco, Calif.
BR TR 5′ 8″ 195 lbs.

Year	Team	Games	BA	SA	AB	H	2B	3B	HR	HR%	R	RBI	BB	SO	SB	Pinch Hit AB	Pinch Hit H	PO	A	E	DP	TC/G	FA	G by Pos
1911	CHI A	145	.289	.407	551	159	27	13	4	0.7	75	97	49		14	1	0	287	64	16	13	2.5	.956	OF-128, 2B-16
1912		137	.294	.407	472	139	24	7	5	1.1	58	72	43		12	7	3	208	11	7	3	1.7	.969	OF-130
1913		127	.264	.397	406	107	14	8	8	2.0	43	48	35	57	5	6	0	226	14	8	1	2.1	.968	OF-119
1914		107	.229	.315	327	75	9	5	3	0.9	21	29	21	35	12	10	2	175	14	8	2	2.1	.959	OF-95
1917	PHI A	148	.291	.418	557	162	28	11	7	1.3	51	74	53	40	13	2	0	267	32	11	8	2.1	.965	OF-145, 1B-1
1918	NY A	91	.256	.358	324	83	12	6	3	0.9	36	46	27	24	6	1	0	181	17	6	3	2.3	.971	OF-90
1919		134	.278	.406	475	132	27	8	6	1.3	45	59	36	46	15	0	0	293	19	13	6	2.4	.960	OF-134
1920		129	.295	.446	471	139	26	12	7	1.5	63	79	40	30	6	0	0	264	12	9	2	2.2	.968	OF-129
1921		31	.172	.241	87	15	2	2	0	0.0	5	12	8	8	0	6	0	32	2	2	1	1.4	.944	OF-25
9 yrs.		1049	.275	.396	3670	1011	169	72	43	1.2	397	516	312	240	83	33	5	1933	185	80	39	2.2	.964	OF-995, 2B-16, 1B-1

Tony Boeckel

BOECKEL, NORMAN DOXIE (Elmer)
B. Aug. 25, 1892, Los Angeles, Calif. D. Feb. 16, 1924, Torrey Pines, Calif.
BR TR 5′10½″ 175 lbs.

Year	Team	Games	BA	SA	AB	H	2B	3B	HR	HR%	R	RBI	BB	SO	SB	Pinch Hit AB	Pinch Hit H	PO	A	E	DP	TC/G	FA	G by Pos
1917	PIT N	64	.265	.324	219	58	11	1	0	0.0	16	23	8	31	6	2	0	71	116	13	9	3.2	.935	3B-62
1919	2 teams	PIT N (45G –.250) BOS N (95G –.249)																						
″	total	140	.250	.321	517	129	20	7	1	0.2	60	42	53	33	21	2	1	141	265	21	13	3.1	.951	3B-138
1920	BOS N	153	.268	.349	582	156	28	5	3	0.5	70	62	38	50	18	0	0	229	273	33	31	3.5	.938	3B-151, SS-3, 2B-1
1921		153	.313	.441	592	185	20	13	10	1.7	93	84	52	41	20	0	0	184	276	33	19	3.2	.933	3B-153
1922		119	.289	.410	402	116	19	6	6	1.5	61	47	35	32	14	13	4	128	168	15	13	2.9	.952	3B-106
1923		148	.298	.405	568	169	32	4	7	1.2	72	79	51	31	11	0	0	170	267	28	27	3.1	.940	3B-147, SS-1
6 yrs.		777	.282	.381	2880	813	130	36	27	0.9	372	337	237	218	90	17	5	923	1365	143	112	3.2	.941	3B-757, SS-4, 2B-1

Len Boehmer

BOEHMER, LEONARD JOSEPH STEPHEN
B. June 28, 1941, Flinthill, Mo.
BR TR 6′ 1″ 192 lbs.

Year	Team	Games	BA	SA	AB	H	2B	3B	HR	HR%	R	RBI	BB	SO	SB	Pinch Hit AB	Pinch Hit H	PO	A	E	DP	TC/G	FA	G by Pos
1967	CIN N	2	.000	.000	3	0	0	0	0	0.0	0	0	0	0	0	0	0	0	1	0	0	1.0	1.000	2B-1
1969	NY A	45	.176	.213	108	19	4	0	0	0.0	5	7	8	10	0	15	1	194	32	3	16	7.4	.987	1B-21, 3B-8, 2B-1, SS-1
1971		3	.000	.000	5	0	0	0	0	0.0	0	0	0	0	0	2	0	1	1	0	0	2.0	1.000	3B-1
3 yrs.		50	.164	.198	116	19	4	0	0	0.0	5	7	8	10	0	17	1	195	34	3	16	7.0	.987	1B-21, 3B-9, 2B-2, SS-1

Tim Bogar

BOGAR, TIMOTHY PAUL
B. Oct. 28, 1966, Indianapolis, Ind.
BR TR 6′ 2″ 198 lbs.

Year	Team	Games	BA	SA	AB	H	2B	3B	HR	HR%	R	RBI	BB	SO	SB	Pinch Hit AB	Pinch Hit H	PO	A	E	DP	TC/G	FA	G by Pos
1993	NY N	78	.244	.351	205	50	13	0	3	1.5	19	25	14	29	0	4	0	105	217	9	42	4.2	.973	SS-66, 3B-7, 2B-6
1994		50	.154	.269	52	8	0	0	2	3.8	5	5	4	11	1	5	1	77	37	1	16	2.6	.991	3B-22, 1B-14, SS-7, 2B-1, OF-1
1995		78	.290	.359	145	42	7	0	1	0.7	17	21	9	25	1	12	3	82	100	6	21	2.7	.968	SS-27, 3B-25, 1B-10, 2B-7, OF-1
3 yrs.		206	.249	.343	402	100	20	0	6	1.5	41	51	27	65	2	21	4	264	354	16	79	3.3	.975	SS-100, 3B-54, 1B-24, 2B-14, OF-2

Terry Bogener

BOGENER, TERRY WAYNE
B. Sept. 28, 1955, Hannibal, Mo.
BL TL 6′ 193 lbs.

Year	Team	Games	BA	SA	AB	H	2B	3B	HR	HR%	R	RBI	BB	SO	SB	Pinch Hit AB	Pinch Hit H	PO	A	E	DP	TC/G	FA	G by Pos
1982	TEX A	24	.217	.333	60	13	2	1	1	1.7	6	4	4	8	2	3	0	22	0	0	0	1.1	1.000	OF-16, DH-4

Wade Boggs

BOGGS, WADE ANTHONY
B. June 15, 1958, Omaha, Neb.
BL TR 6′ 2″ 190 lbs.

Year	Team	Games	BA	SA	AB	H	2B	3B	HR	HR%	R	RBI	BB	SO	SB	Pinch Hit AB	Pinch Hit H	PO	A	E	DP	TC/G	FA	G by Pos
1982	BOS A	104	.349	.441	338	118	14	1	5	1.5	51	44	35	21	1	13	4	489	168	8	51	6.9	.988	1B-49, 3B-44, DH-3, OF-1
1983		153	**.361**	.486	582	210	44	7	5	0.9	100	74	92	36	3	0	0	118	368	27	40	3.4	.947	3B-153
1984		158	.325	.416	625	203	31	4	6	1.0	109	55	89	44	3	1	0	141	330	20	30	3.1	.959	3B-155, DH-2
1985		161	**.368**	.478	653	**240**	42	3	8	1.2	107	78	96	61	2	0	0	134	335	17	30	3.0	.965	3B-161
1986		149	**.357**	.486	580	207	47	2	8	1.4	107	71	**105**	44	0	0	0	121	267	19	30	2.7	.953	3B-149
1987		147	**.363**	.588	551	200	40	6	24	4.4	108	89	105	48	1	1	0	112	277	14	37	2.7	.965	3B-145, 1B-1, DH-1
1988		155	**.366**	.490	584	214	**45**	6	5	0.9	**128**	58	**125**	34	2	1	1	122	250	11	17	2.5	.971	3B-151, DH-3
1989		156	.330	.449	621	205	**51**	7	3	0.5	**113**	54	107	51	2	1	0	123	264	17	29	2.6	.958	3B-152, DH-3
1990		155	.302	.418	619	187	44	5	6	1.0	89	63	87	68	0	0	0	108	241	20	18	2.4	.946	3B-152, DH-3
1991		144	.332	.460	546	181	42	2	8	1.5	93	51	89	32	1	3	2	89	276	12	34	2.7	.968	3B-140
1992		143	.259	.358	514	133	22	4	7	1.4	62	50	74	31	1	4	0	70	229	15	23	2.3	.952	3B-117, DH-21
1993	NY A	143	.302	.362	560	169	26	1	2	0.4	83	59	74	49	0	6	1	75	311	12	29	2.8	.970	3B-134, DH-8
1994		97	.342	.489	366	125	19	1	11	3.0	61	55	61	29	2	5	1	66	217	10	21	3.0	.966	3B-93, 1B-4
1995		126	.324	.422	460	149	22	4	5	1.1	76	63	74	50	1	11	4	114	197	5	14	2.5	.984	3B-117, 1B-9
14 yrs.		1991	.334	.453	7599	2541	489	53	103	1.4	1287	864	1213	598	19	46	13	1882	3730	207	403	3.0	.964	3B-1863, 1B-63, DH-44, OF-1
DIVISIONAL PLAYOFF SERIES																								
1995	NY A	4	.263	.526	19	5	2	0	1	5.3	4	3	3	5	0	0	0	4	8	0	1	3.0	1.000	3B-4
LEAGUE CHAMPIONSHIP SERIES																								
1986	BOS A	7	.233	.333	30	7	1	1	0	0.0	3	2	4	1	0	0	0	7	14	2	1	3.3	.913	3B-7
1988		4	.385	.385	13	5	0	0	0	0.0	2	3	3	4	0	0	0	6	6	0	1	3.0	1.000	3B-4
1990		4	.438	.688	16	7	1	0	1	6.3	1	1	0	3	0	0	0	6	10	0	2	4.0	1.000	3B-4
3 yrs.		15	.322	.441	59	19	2	1	1	1.7	6	6	7	8	0	0	0	19	30	2	4	3.4	.961	3B-15
WORLD SERIES																								
1986	BOS A	7	.290	.387	31	9	3	0	0	0.0	3	3	3	2	0	0	0	4	15	0	1	2.7	1.000	3B-7

Charlie Bohn

BOHN, CHARLES (Sir Charles)
B. 1857, Cleveland, Ohio D. Aug. 1, 1903, Cleveland, Ohio.
BR TR 5′ 9″ 165 lbs.

Year	Team	Games	BA	SA	AB	H	2B	3B	HR	HR%	R	RBI	BB	SO	SB	Pinch Hit AB	Pinch Hit H	PO	A	E	DP	TC/G	FA	G by Pos
1882	LOU AA	4	.154	.154	13	2	0	0	0	0.0	0		0			0	0	5	9	4	0	4.5	.778	OF-2, P-2

Sammy Bohne

BOHNE, SAMUEL ARTHUR
Born Samuel Arthur Cohen.
B. Oct. 22, 1896, San Francisco, Calif. D. May 23, 1977, Palo Alto, Calif.
BR TR 5′ 8½″ 175 lbs.

Year	Team	Games	BA	SA	AB	H	2B	3B	HR	HR%	R	RBI	BB	SO	SB	Pinch Hit AB	Pinch Hit H	PO	A	E	DP	TC/G	FA	G by Pos
1916	STL N	14	.237	.237	38	9	0	0	0	0.0	3	0	4	6	3	0	0	15	32	7	3	3.9	.870	SS-14
1921	CIN N	153	.285	.398	613	175	28	16	3	0.5	98	44	54	38	26	0	0	313	450	26	73	5.1	.967	2B-102, 3B-53
1922		112	.274	.360	383	105	14	5	3	0.8	53	51	39	18	13	2	0	226	391	31	60	6.1	.952	2B-85, SS-22
1923		139	.252	.340	539	136	18	10	3	0.6	77	47	48	37	16	0	0	299	442	25	55	5.4	.967	2B-96, 3B-35, SS-9, 1B-1
1924		100	.255	.384	349	89	15	9	4	1.1	42	46	18	24	9	0	0	194	294	23	40	5.1	.955	2B-48, SS-40, 3B-12
1925		73	.257	.336	214	55	9	1	2	0.9	24	24	14	14	6	3	1	131	163	16	27	4.6	.948	SS-49, 2B-10, OF-4, 3B-2, 1B-2
1926	**2 teams**	**CIN N** (25G –.204) **BKN N** (47G –.200)																						
″	**total**	72	.201	.279	179	36	3	4	1	0.6	12	16	16	17	2	0	0	104	167	12	17	4.3	.958	2B-31, SS-20, 3B-15
7 yrs.		663	.261	.359	2315	605	87	45	16	0.7	309	228	193	154	75	5	1	1282	1939	140	275	5.2	.958	2B-372, SS-154, 3B-117, OF-4, 1B-3

Bruce Boisclair

BOISCLAIR, BRUCE ARMAND
B. Dec. 9, 1952, Putnam, Conn.
BL TL 6′ 2″ 185 lbs.

Year	Team	Games	BA	SA	AB	H	2B	3B	HR	HR%	R	RBI	BB	SO	SB	Pinch Hit AB	Pinch Hit H	PO	A	E	DP	TC/G	FA	G by Pos
1974	NY N	7	.250	.333	12	3	1	0	0	0.0	0	1	1	4	0	0	0	10	2	1	0	2.6	.923	OF-5
1976		110	.287	.374	286	82	13	3	2	0.7	42	13	28	55	9	21	12	156	3	3	1	1.9	.981	OF-87
1977		127	.293	.407	307	90	21	1	4	1.3	41	44	31	57	6	30	9	159	2	6	1	1.7	.964	OF-91, 1B-9
1978		107	.224	.322	214	48	7	1	4	1.9	24	15	23	43	3	47	12	115	3	2	0	1.7	.983	OF-69, 1B-1
1979		59	.184	.255	98	18	5	1	0	0.0	7	4	3	24	0	35	5	36	2	0	0	1.5	1.000	OF-24, 1B-1
5 yrs.		410	.263	.360	917	241	47	6	10	1.1	114	77	86	183	18	133	38	476	12	12	2	1.7	.976	OF-276, 1B-11

Bob Boken

BOKEN, ROBERT ANTHONY
B. Feb. 23, 1908, Maryville, Ill. D. Oct. 6, 1988, Las Vegas, Nev.
BR TR 6′ 2″ 165 lbs.

Year	Team	Games	BA	SA	AB	H	2B	3B	HR	HR%	R	RBI	BB	SO	SB	Pinch Hit AB	Pinch Hit H	PO	A	E	DP	TC/G	FA	G by Pos
1933	WAS A	55	.278	.414	133	37	5	2	3	2.3	19	26	9	16	0	7	2	72	91	7	13	2.8	.959	2B-31, 3B-19, SS-10
1934	**2 teams**	**WAS A** (11G –.222) **CHI A** (81G –.236)																						
″	**total**	92	.235	.306	324	76	10	2	3	0.9	35	46	18	33	4	5	2	173	259	37	47	5.5	.921	2B-58, SS-22, 3B-6
2 yrs.		147	.247	.337	457	113	15	4	6	1.3	54	72	27	49	4	12	4	245	350	44	60	4.4	.931	2B-89, SS-32, 3B-25

Ed Boland

BOLAND, EDWARD JOHN
B. Apr. 18, 1908, Long Island City, N. Y.
BL TL 5′10″ 165 lbs.

Year	Team	Games	BA	SA	AB	H	2B	3B	HR	HR%	R	RBI	BB	SO	SB	Pinch Hit AB	Pinch Hit H	PO	A	E	DP	TC/G	FA	G by Pos
1934	PHI N	8	.300	.400	30	9	1	1	0	0.0	2	5	0	2	1	1	0	6	1	2	0	1.3	.778	OF-7
1935		30	.213	.213	47	10	0	0	0	0.0	5	4	4	6	1	17	2	15	0	3	0	1.8	.833	OF-10
1944	WAS A	19	.271	.339	59	16	4	0	0	0.0	4	14	0	6	0	5	1	22	2	3	0	1.9	.889	OF-14
3 yrs.		57	.257	.309	136	35	5	1	0	0.0	11	23	4	14	2	23	3	43	3	8	0	1.7	.852	OF-31

Charlie Bold

BOLD, CHARLES DICKENS (Dutch)
B. Oct. 27, 1894, Karlskrona, Sweden D. July 29, 1978, Chelsea, Mass.
BR TR 6′ 2″ 185 lbs.

Year	Team	Games	BA	SA	AB	H	2B	3B	HR	HR%	R	RBI	BB	SO	SB	Pinch Hit AB	Pinch Hit H	PO	A	E	DP	TC/G	FA	G by Pos
1914	STL A	2	.000	.000	1	0	0	0	0	0.0	0	0	0	1	0	0	0	1	0	1	0	2.0	.500	1B-1

Carl Boles

BOLES, CARL THEODORE
B. Oct. 31, 1934, Center Point, Ark.
BR TR 5′11″ 185 lbs.

Year	Team	Lg	Games	BA	SA	AB	H	2B	3B	HR	HR%	R	RBI	BB	SO	SB	Pinch Hit AB	Pinch Hit H	PO	A	E	DP	TC/G	FA	G by Pos
1962	SF	N	19	.375	.375	24	9	0	0	0	0.0	4	1	0	6	0	11	4	5	0	1	0	0.9	.833	OF-7

Joe Boley

BOLEY, JOHN PETER
Born John Peter Bolinsky.
B. July 19, 1896, Mahanoy City, Pa. D. Dec. 30, 1962, Mahanoy City, Pa.
BR TR 5′11″ 170 lbs.

Year	Team	Lg	Games	BA	SA	AB	H	2B	3B	HR	HR%	R	RBI	BB	SO	SB	Pinch Hit AB	Pinch Hit H	PO	A	E	DP	TC/G	FA	G by Pos
1927	PHI	A	116	.311	.411	370	115	18	8	1	0.3	49	52	26	14	8	1	0	182	318	26	49	4.6	.951	SS-114
1928			132	.264	.325	425	112	20	3	0	0.0	49	49	32	11	5	0	0	244	320	30	51	4.5	.949	SS-132
1929			91	.251	.366	303	76	17	6	2	0.7	36	47	24	16	1	0	0	162	229	15	50	4.6	.963	SS-88, 3B-1
1930			121	.276	.367	420	116	22	2	4	1.0	41	55	32	26	0	1	0	221	296	16	62	4.4	.970	SS-120
1931			67	.228	.295	224	51	9	3	0	0.0	26	20	15	13	1	4	1	102	150	12	31	4.2	.955	SS-62, 2B-1
1932	2 teams	PHI A (10G –.206) CLE A (1G –.250)																							
″	total		11	.211	.263	38	8	2	0	0	0.0	2	4	1	4	0	0	0	11	20	3	2	3.1	.912	SS-11
6 yrs.			538	.269	.354	1780	478	88	22	7	0.4	203	227	130	84	15	6	1	922	1333	102	245	4.5	.957	SS-527, 2B-1, 3B-1
WORLD SERIES																									
1929	PHI	A	5	.235	.235	17	4	0	0	0	0.0	1	1	0	3	0	0	0	4	13	0	1	3.4	1.000	SS-5
1930			6	.095	.095	21	2	0	0	0	0.0	1	1	0	1	0	0	0	9	13	1	0	3.8	.957	SS-6
1931			1	.000	.000	1	0	0	0	0	0.0	0	0	0	1	0	1	0	0	0	0	0	0.0	—	
3 yrs.			12	.154	.154	39	6	0	0	0	0.0	2	2	0	5	0	1	0	13	26	1	1	3.6	.975	SS-11

Jim Bolger

BOLGER, JAMES CYRIL (Dutch)
B. Feb. 23, 1932, Cincinnati, Ohio.
BR TR 6′2″ 180 lbs.

Year	Team	Lg	Games	BA	SA	AB	H	2B	3B	HR	HR%	R	RBI	BB	SO	SB	Pinch Hit AB	Pinch Hit H	PO	A	E	DP	TC/G	FA	G by Pos
1950	CIN	N	2	.000	.000	1	0	0	0	0	0.0	0	0	0	0	0	0	0	0	0	0	0	0.0	.000	OF-2
1951			2	—	—	0	0	0	0	0	—	1	0	0	0	1	0	0	0	0	0	0	0.0	—	
1954			5	.333	.333	3	1	0	0	0	0.0	1	0	0	1	0	2	0	0	0	0	0	0.0	.000	OF-2
1955	CHI	N	64	.206	.287	160	33	5	4	0	0.0	19	7	9	17	2	1	1	125	1	6	0	2.6	.955	OF-51
1957			112	.275	.352	273	75	4	1	5	1.8	28	29	10	36	0	**48**	**17**	154	7	4	1	2.5	.976	OF-63, 3B-3
1958			84	.225	.300	120	27	4	1	1	0.8	15	11	9	20	0	51	10	46	1	3	0	1.4	.940	OF-37
1959	2 teams	CLE A (8G –.000) PHI N (35G –.083)																							
″	total		43	.073	.091	55	4	1	0	0	0.0	1	1	4	9	0	32	4	15	0	1	0	1.8	.938	OF-9
7 yrs.			312	.229	.301	612	140	14	6	6	1.0	65	48	32	83	3	134	32	340	9	14	1	2.2	.961	OF-164, 3B-3

Frank Bolick

BOLICK, FRANK CHARLES
B. June 28, 1966, Ashland, Pa.
BB TR 5′10″ 190 lbs.

Year	Team	Lg	Games	BA	SA	AB	H	2B	3B	HR	HR%	R	RBI	BB	SO	SB	Pinch Hit AB	Pinch Hit H	PO	A	E	DP	TC/G	FA	G by Pos
1993	MON	N	95	.211	.329	213	45	13	0	4	1.9	25	24	23	37	1	33	7	338	63	8	31	5.5	.980	1B-51, 3B-24

Frank Bolling

BOLLING, FRANK ELMORE
Brother of Milt Bolling.
B. Nov. 16, 1931, Mobile, Ala.
BR TR 6′1″ 175 lbs.

Year	Team	Lg	Games	BA	SA	AB	H	2B	3B	HR	HR%	R	RBI	BB	SO	SB	Pinch Hit AB	Pinch Hit H	PO	A	E	DP	TC/G	FA	G by Pos
1954	DET	A	117	.236	.337	368	87	15	2	6	1.6	46	38	36	51	3	3	0	248	232	13	54	4.4	.974	2B-113
1956			102	.281	.434	366	103	21	7	7	1.9	53	45	42	51	6	0	0	223	260	11	72	4.8	.978	2B-102
1957			146	.259	.405	576	149	27	6	15	2.6	72	40	57	64	4	0	0	394	401	16	112	5.6	.980	2B-146
1958			154	.269	.392	610	164	25	4	14	2.3	91	75	54	54	6	0	0	342	445	12	109	5.2	.985	2B-154
1959			127	.266	.403	459	122	18	3	13	2.8	56	55	45	37	2	1	0	281	340	8	81	5.0	.987	2B-126
1960			139	.254	.356	536	136	20	4	9	1.7	64	59	40	48	7	1	0	375	377	17	93	5.6	.978	2B-138
1961	MIL	N	148	.262	.379	585	153	16	4	15	2.6	86	56	57	62	7	0	0	326	489	10	112	5.6	.988	2B-148
1962			122	.271	.399	406	110	17	4	9	2.2	45	43	35	45	2	5	1	252	298	6	70	4.7	.989	2B-119
1963			142	.244	.312	542	132	18	2	5	0.9	73	43	41	47	2	0	0	326	379	14	107	5.1	.981	2B-141
1964			120	.199	.278	352	70	11	1	5	1.4	35	34	21	44	0	7	0	212	255	7	68	4.1	.985	2B-117
1965			148	.264	.363	535	141	26	3	7	1.3	55	50	24	41	0	1	0	310	393	17	90	4.9	.976	2B-147
1966	ATL	N	75	.211	.256	227	48	7	0	1	0.4	16	18	10	14	1	11	1	134	150	5	35	4.3	.983	2B-67
12 yrs.			1540	.254	.366	5562	1415	221	40	106	1.9	692	556	462	558	40	29	2	3423	4019	136	1003	5.0	.982	2B-1518

Jack Bolling

BOLLING, JOHN EDWARD
B. Feb. 20, 1917, Mobile, Ala.
BL TL 5′11″ 168 lbs.

Year	Team	Lg	Games	BA	SA	AB	H	2B	3B	HR	HR%	R	RBI	BB	SO	SB	Pinch Hit AB	Pinch Hit H	PO	A	E	DP	TC/G	FA	G by Pos
1939	PHI	N	69	.289	.384	211	61	11	0	3	1.4	27	13	11	10	6	17	4	392	38	8	35	9.1	.982	1B-48
1944	BKN	N	56	.351	.496	131	46	14	1	1	0.8	21	25	14	4	0	24	6	206	20	2	7	8.4	.991	1B-27
2 yrs.			125	.313	.427	342	107	25	1	4	1.2	48	38	25	14	6	41	10	598	58	10	42	8.9	.985	1B-75

Milt Bolling

BOLLING, MILTON JOSEPH
Brother of Frank Bolling.
B. Aug. 9, 1930, Mississippi City, Miss.
BR TR 6′1″ 177 lbs.

Year	Team	Lg	Games	BA	SA	AB	H	2B	3B	HR	HR%	R	RBI	BB	SO	SB	Pinch Hit AB	Pinch Hit H	PO	A	E	DP	TC/G	FA	G by Pos
1952	BOS	A	11	.222	.333	36	8	1	0	1	2.8	4	3	3	5	0	0	0	22	41	1	6	5.8	.984	SS-11
1953			109	.263	.353	323	85	12	1	5	1.5	30	28	24	41	1	1	0	174	321	23	71	4.8	.956	SS-109
1954			113	.249	.368	370	92	20	3	6	1.6	42	36	47	55	2	1	0	191	377	33	73	5.4	.945	SS-107, 3B-5
1955			6	.200	.200	5	1	0	0	0	0.0	0	0	0	1	0	2	0	1	3	1	0	2.5	.800	SS-2
1956			45	.212	.347	118	25	3	2	3	2.5	19	8	18	20	0	5	2	38	81	9	13	3.4	.930	SS-26, 3B-11, 2B-1
1957	2 teams	BOS A (1G –.000) WAS A (91G –.227)																							
″	total		92	.227	.320	278	63	12	1	4	1.4	29	19	18	59	2	4	0	168	232	12	53	4.5	.971	2B-53, SS-37, 3B-1
1958	DET	A	24	.194	.258	31	6	2	0	0	0.0	3	0	5	7	0	4	0	15	24	2	7	2.7	.951	SS-13, 3B-1, 2B-1
7 yrs.			400	.241	.345	1161	280	50	7	19	1.6	127	94	115	188	5	17	2	609	1079	81	223	4.7	.954	SS-305, 2B-55, 3B-18

Don Bollweg

BOLLWEG, DONALD RAYMOND
B. Feb. 12, 1921, Wheaton, Ill.
BL TL 6′1″ 190 lbs.

Year	Team	Lg	Games	BA	SA	AB	H	2B	3B	HR	HR%	R	RBI	BB	SO	SB	Pinch Hit AB	Pinch Hit H	PO	A	E	DP	TC/G	FA	G by Pos
1950	STL	N	4	.182	.182	11	2	0	0	0	0.0	1	1	1	1	0	0	0	26	0	0	3	6.5	1.000	1B-4
1951			6	.111	.222	9	1	1	0	0	0.0	1	2	0	1	0	4	1	16	0	1	2	8.5	.941	1B-2
1953	NY	A	70	.297	.503	155	46	6	4	6	3.9	24	24	21	31	1	21	5	323	15	6	37	8.0	.983	1B-43
1954	PHI	A	103	.224	.358	268	60	15	3	5	1.9	35	24	35	33	1	29	6	530	51	13	55	8.4	.978	1B-71
1955	KC	A	12	.111	.111	9	1	0	0	0	0.0	1	2	3	2	0	9	1	8	0	0	3	2.7	1.000	1B-3
5 yrs.			195	.243	.396	452	110	22	7	11	2.4	62	53	60	68	2	63	13	903	66	20	100	8.0	.980	1B-123
WORLD SERIES																									
1953	NY	A	3	.000	.000	2	0	0	0	0	0.0	0	0	0	2	0	2	0	0	0	0	0	0.0	.000	1B-1

Cecil Bolton

BOLTON, CECIL GLANFORD (Lefty)
B. Feb. 13, 1904, Booneville, Miss. D. Aug. 25, 1993, Jackson, Miss.
BL TL 6′ 4″ 195 lbs.

Year	Team	Lg	Games	BA	SA	AB	H	2B	3B	HR	HR%	R	RBI	BB	SO	SB	Pinch Hit AB	Pinch Hit H	PO	A	E	DP	TC/G	FA	G by Pos
1928	CLE	A	4	.154	.462	13	2	0	2	0	0.0	1	0	2	2	0	0	0	41	1	2	3	11.0	.955	1B-4

Cliff Bolton

BOLTON, WILLIAM CLIFTON
B. Apr. 10, 1907, High Point, N. C. D. Apr. 21, 1979, Lexington, N. C.
BL TR 5′ 9″ 160 lbs.

Year	Team	Lg	Games	BA	SA	AB	H	2B	3B	HR	HR%	R	RBI	BB	SO	SB	Pinch Hit AB	Pinch Hit H	PO	A	E	DP	TC/G	FA	G by Pos
1931	WAS	A	23	.256	.326	43	11	1	1	0	0.0	3	6	1	5	0	10	6	15	3	1	0	1.5	.947	C-13
1933			33	.410	.487	39	16	1	1	0	0.0	4	6	6	3	0	22	9	16	2	2	1	2.0	.900	C-9, OF-1
1934			42	.270	.365	148	40	9	1	1	0.7	12	17	11	9	2	3	2	134	20	3	4	4.0	.981	C-39
1935			110	.304	.427	375	114	18	11	2	0.5	47	55	56	13	0	3	0	356	52	12	8	4.0	.971	C-106
1936			86	.291	.401	289	84	18	4	2	0.7	41	51	25	12	1	5	1	287	44	7	4	4.1	.979	C-83
1937	DET	A	27	.263	.351	57	15	2	0	1	1.8	6	7	8	6	0	13	3	47	9	1	2	4.4	.982	C-13
1941	WAS	A	14	.000	.000	11	0	0	0	0	0.0	0	1	1	2	0	10	0	2	0	0	0	0.7	1.000	C-3
7 yrs.			335	.291	.398	962	280	49	18	6	0.6	113	143	108	50	3	66	21	857	130	26	19	3.8	.974	C-266, OF-1
WORLD SERIES																									
1933	WAS	A	2	.000	.000	2	0	0	0	0	0.0	0	0	0	0	0	2	0	0	0	0	0	0.0	—	

Tommy Bond

BOND, THOMAS HENRY
B. Apr. 2, 1856, Granard, Ireland D. Jan. 24, 1941, Boston, Mass.
Manager 1882.
BR TR 5′ 7½″ 160 lbs.

Year	Team	Lg	Games	BA	SA	AB	H	2B	3B	HR	HR%	R	RBI	BB	SO	SB	Pinch Hit AB	Pinch Hit H	PO	A	E	DP	TC/G	FA	G by Pos
1876	HAR	N	45	.275	.319	182	50	8	0	0	0.0	18	21	0	4		0	0	25	93	15	0	3.0	.887	P-45
1877	BOS	N	61	.228	.266	259	59	4	3	0	0.0	32	30	1	15		0	0	30	104	9	2	2.3	.937	P-58, OF-3
1878			59	.212	.237	236	50	4	1	0	0.0	22	23	0	9		0	0	27	117	9	4	2.5	.941	P-59, OF-2
1879			65	.241	.261	257	62	3	1	0	0.0	35	21	6	8		0	0	36	144	9	7	2.7	.952	P-64, OF-5, 1B-1
1880			76	.220	.241	282	62	4	1	0	0.0	27	24	8	14		0	0	61	153	16	8	2.5	.930	P-63, OF-26, 1B-1, 3B-1
1881			3	.200	.200	10	2	0	0	0	0.0	0	0	0	0		0	0	2	7	0	0	3.0	1.000	P-3
1882	WOR	N	8	.133	.133	30	4	0	0	0	0.0	1	2	2	3		0	0	11	1	4	0	1.6	.750	OF-8, P-2
1884	2 teams		BOS U (37G –.296) IND AA (7G –.130)																						
″	total		44	.276	.335	185	51	9	1	0	0.0	21		4			0	0	27	62	17	3	2.2	.840	P-28, OF-19, 3B-1
8 yrs.			361	.236	.268	1441	340	32	7	0	0.0	156	121	21	53		0	0	219	681	79	24	2.5	.919	P-322, OF-63, 3B-2, 1B-2

Walt Bond

BOND, WALTER FRANKLIN
B. Oct. 19, 1937, Denmark, Tenn. D. Sept. 14, 1967, Houston, Tex.
BL TR 6′ 7″ 228 lbs.

Year	Team	Lg	Games	BA	SA	AB	H	2B	3B	HR	HR%	R	RBI	BB	SO	SB	Pinch Hit AB	Pinch Hit H	PO	A	E	DP	TC/G	FA	G by Pos
1960	CLE	A	40	.221	.366	131	29	2	1	5	3.8	19	18	13	14	4	5	0	76	2	0	1	2.2	1.000	OF-36
1961			38	.173	.346	52	9	1	1	2	3.8	7	7	6	10	1	23	2	17	1	0	0	1.5	1.000	OF-12
1962			12	.380	.800	50	19	3	0	6	12.0	10	17	4	9	1	0	0	25	0	0	0	2.1	1.000	OF-12
1964	HOU	N	148	.254	.420	543	138	16	7	20	3.7	63	85	38	90	2	2	0	796	41	13	46	5.8	.985	1B-76, OF-71
1965			117	.263	.366	407	107	17	2	7	1.7	46	47	42	51	2	7	1	704	49	14	52	6.8	.982	1B-74, OF-38
1967	MIN	A	10	.313	.563	16	5	1	0	1	6.3	4	5	3	1	0	5	2	7	0	1	0	2.7	.875	OF-3
6 yrs.			365	.256	.410	1199	307	40	11	41	3.4	149	179	106	175	10	42	5	1625	93	28	99	5.4	.984	OF-172, 1B-150

Barry Bonds

BONDS, BARRY LAMAR
Son of Bobby Bonds.
B. July 24, 1964, Riverside, Calif.
BL TL 6′ 1″ 185 lbs.

Year	Team	Lg	Games	BA	SA	AB	H	2B	3B	HR	HR%	R	RBI	BB	SO	SB	Pinch Hit AB	Pinch Hit H	PO	A	E	DP	TC/G	FA	G by Pos
1986	PIT	N	113	.223	.416	413	92	26	3	16	3.9	72	48	65	102	36	3	1	280	9	5	2	2.7	.983	OF-110
1987			150	.261	.492	551	144	34	9	25	4.5	99	59	54	88	32	7	1	330	15	5	3	2.4	.986	OF-145
1988			144	.283	.491	538	152	30	5	24	4.5	97	58	72	82	17	11	2	292	5	6	0	2.2	.980	OF-136
1989			159	.248	.426	580	144	34	6	19	3.3	96	58	93	93	32	8	3	365	14	6	1	2.5	.984	OF-156
1990			151	.301	**.565**	519	156	32	3	33	6.4	104	114	93	83	52	2	0	338	14	6	2	2.4	.983	OF-150
1991			153	.292	.514	510	149	28	5	25	4.9	95	116	107	73	43	3	1	321	13	3	1	2.2	.991	OF-150
1992			140	.311	**.624**	473	147	36	5	34	**7.2**	**109**	103	**127**	69	39	2	0	310	4	3	0	2.3	.991	OF-139
1993	SF	N	159	.336	**.677**	539	181	38	4	**46**	**8.5**	129	**123**	126	79	29	3	0	310	7	5	0	2.1	.984	OF-157
1994			112	.312	.647	391	122	18	1	37	9.5	89	81	**74**	43	29	0	0	198	10	3	0	1.9	.986	OF-112
1995			144	.294	.577	506	149	30	7	33	6.5	109	104	**120**	83	31	1	0	279	12	6	1	2.1	.980	OF-143
10 yrs.			1425	.286	.541	5020	1436	306	48	292	5.8	999	864	931	795	340	40	8	3023	103	48	10	2.3	.985	OF-1398
LEAGUE CHAMPIONSHIP SERIES																									
1990	PIT	N	6	.167	.167	18	3	0	0	0	0.0	4	1	6	5	2	0	0	13	0	0	0	2.2	1.000	OF-6
1991			7	.148	.185	27	4	1	0	0	0.0	1	0	2	4	3	0	0	14	1	1	0	2.3	.938	OF-7
1992			7	.261	.435	23	6	1	0	1	4.3	5	2	6	4	1	0	0	17	0	0	0	2.4	1.000	OF-7
3 yrs.			20	.191	.265	68	13	2	0	1	1.5	10	3	14	13	6	0	0	44	1	1	0	2.3	.978	OF-20
														5th		**8th**									

Bobby Bonds

BONDS, BOBBY LEE
Father of Barry Bonds.
B. Mar. 15, 1946, Riverside, Calif.
BR TR 6′ 1″ 190 lbs.

Year	Team	Lg	Games	BA	SA	AB	H	2B	3B	HR	HR%	R	RBI	BB	SO	SB	Pinch Hit AB	Pinch Hit H	PO	A	E	DP	TC/G	FA	G by Pos
1968	SF	N	81	.254	.407	307	78	10	5	9	2.9	55	35	38	84	16	0	0	169	6	4	1	2.2	.978	OF-80
1969			158	.259	.473	622	161	25	6	32	5.1	**120**	90	81	**187**	45	1	0	339	9	8	2	2.3	.978	OF-155
1970			157	.302	.504	663	200	36	10	26	3.9	134	78	77	**189**[1]	48	2	0	326	14	11	7	2.2	.969	OF-157
1971			155	.288	.512	619	178	32	4	33	5.3	110	102	62	137	26	3	1	329	10	2	1	2.2	.994	OF-154
1972			153	.259	.446	626	162	29	5	26	4.2	118	80	60	137	44	0	0	345	8	8	3	2.4	.978	OF-153
1973			160	.283	.530	643	182	34	4	39	6.1	**131**	96	87	**148**	43	2	1	346	12	11	5	2.3	.970	OF-158
1974			150	.256	.434	567	145	22	8	21	3.7	97	71	95	134	41	3	1	305	11	11	3	2.2	.966	OF-148
1975	NY	A	145	.270	.512	529	143	26	3	32	6.0	93	85	89	137	30	4	1	287	12	4	6	2.1	.987	OF-129, DH-12
1976	CAL	A	99	.265	.386	378	100	10	3	10	2.6	48	54	41	90	30	1	0	199	9	5	3	2.2	.977	OF-98, DH-1
1977			158	.264	.520	592	156	23	9	37	6.3	103	115	74	141	41	1	0	272	5	4	0	1.8	.986	OF-140, DH-18
1978	2 teams		CHI A (26G –.278) TEX A (130G –.265)																						
″	total		156	.267	.480	565	151	19	4	31	5.5	93	90	79	120	43	2	1	253	16	9	6	1.8	.968	OF-133, DH-21
1979	CLE	A	146	.275	.463	538	148	24	1	25	4.6	93	85	74	135	34	1	0	267	9	6	1	1.9	.979	OF-116, DH-29
1980	STL	N	86	.203	.316	231	47	5	3	5	2.2	37	24	33	74	15	15	2	114	5	4	2	1.8	.967	OF-70
1981	CHI	N	45	.215	.380	163	35	7	1	6	3.7	26	19	24	44	5	0	0	108	2	2	0	2.5	.982	OF-45
14 yrs.			1849	.268	.471	7043	1886	302	66	332	4.7	1258	1024	914	1757	461	35	7	3659	128	89	40	2.1	.977	OF-1736, DH-81
															6th										

Bobby Bonds *continued*

Year	Team	Games	BA	SA	AB	H	2B	3B	HR	HR%	R	RBI	BB	SO	SB	Pinch Hit AB	Pinch Hit H	PO	A	E	DP	TC/G	FA	G by Pos
LEAGUE CHAMPIONSHIP SERIES																								
1971	**SF N**	3	.250	.250	8	2	0	0	0	0.0	0	0	2	4	0	0	0	3	0	1	0	1.3	.750	OF-3

George Bone

BONE, GEORGE DRUMMOND BB TR 5′ 7″ 152 lbs.
B. Aug. 28, 1876, New Haven, Conn. D. May 26, 1918, West Haven, Conn.

Year	Team	Games	BA	SA	AB	H	2B	3B	HR	HR%	R	RBI	BB	SO	SB	Pinch Hit AB	Pinch Hit H	PO	A	E	DP	TC/G	FA	G by Pos
1901	**MIL A**	12	.302	.349	43	13	2	0	0	0.0	6	6	4		0	0	0	24	29	8	6	5.1	.869	SS-12

Nino Bongiovanni

BONGIOVANNI, ANTHONY THOMAS BL TL 5′10″ 175 lbs.
B. Dec. 21, 1911, Pike's Peak, La.

Year	Team	Games	BA	SA	AB	H	2B	3B	HR	HR%	R	RBI	BB	SO	SB	Pinch Hit AB	Pinch Hit H	PO	A	E	DP	TC/G	FA	G by Pos
1938	**CIN N**	2	.286	.429	7	2	1	0	0	0.0	0	0	0	0	0	0	0	6	0	0	0	3.0	1.000	OF-2
1939		66	.258	.296	159	41	6	0	0	0.0	17	16	9	8	0	27	7	89	1	1	1	2.3	.989	OF-39
2 yrs.		68	.259	.301	166	43	7	0	0	0.0	17	16	9	8	0	27	7	95	1	1	1	2.4	.990	OF-41
WORLD SERIES																								
1939	**CIN N**	1	.000	.000	1	0	0	0	0	0.0	0	0	0	0	0	1	0	0	0	0	0	0.0	—	

Bobby Bonilla

BONILLA, ROBERTO MARTIN ANTONIO BB TR 6′ 3″ 210 lbs.
B. Feb. 23, 1963, Bronx, N. Y.

Year	Team	Games	BA	SA	AB	H	2B	3B	HR	HR%	R	RBI	BB	SO	SB	Pinch Hit AB	Pinch Hit H	PO	A	E	DP	TC/G	FA	G by Pos
1986	**2 teams**	**CHI A** (75G –.269) **PIT N** (63G –.240)																						
″	**total**	138	.256	.333	426	109	16	4	3	0.7	55	43	62	88	8	19	2	451	38	5	29	3.7	.990	OF-94, 1B-34, 3B-4
1987	**PIT N**	141	.300	.481	466	140	33	3	15	3.2	58	77	39	64	3	17	6	142	139	16	13	2.1	.946	3B-89, OF-46, 1B-6
1988		159	.274	.476	584	160	32	7	24	4.1	87	100	85	82	3	0	0	121	336	32	17	3.1	.935	3B-159
1989		163	.281	.490	616	173	37	10	24	3.9	96	86	76	93	8	1	0	190	334	35	37	3.4	.937	3B-156, 1B-8, OF-1
1990		160	.280	.518	625	175	39	7	32	5.1	112	120	45	103	4	1	0	315	35	15	2	2.2	.959	OF-149, 3B-14, 1B-3
1991		157	.302	.492	577	174	**44**	6	18	3.1	102	100	90	67	2	2	0	247	144	15	19	2.3	.963	OF-104, 3B-67, 1B-4
1992	**NY N**	128	.249	.432	438	109	23	0	19	4.3	62	70	66	73	4	5	2	277	9	4	3	2.3	.986	OF-121, 1B-6
1993		139	.265	.522	502	133	21	3	34	6.8	81	87	72	96	3	0	0	238	112	17	11	2.6	.954	OF-85, 3B-52, 1B-6
1994		108	.290	.504	403	117	24	1	20	5.0	60	67	55	101	1	0	0	77	217	18	24	2.9	.942	3B-107
1995	**2 teams**	**NY N** (80G –.325) **BAL A** (61G –.333)																						
″	**total**	141	.329	.576	554	182	37	8	28	5.1	96	99	54	79	0	1	0	244	128	19	16	2.6	.951	OF-70, 3B-70, 1B-10
10 yrs.		1434	.284	.487	5191	1472	306	49	217	4.2	809	849	644	846	36	46	10	2302	1492	176	171	2.7	.956	3B-718, OF-670, 1B-77
LEAGUE CHAMPIONSHIP SERIES																								
1990	**PIT N**	6	.190	.238	21	4	1	0	0	0.0	0	1	3	1	0	0	0	4	5	1	1	1.3	.900	OF-5, 3B-3
1991		7	.304	.391	23	7	2	0	0	0.0	2	1	6	2	0	0	0	12	1	0	0	1.9	1.000	OF-7
2 yrs.		13	.250	.318	44	11	3	0	0	0.0	2	2	9	3	0	0	0	16	6	1	1	1.5	.957	OF-12, 3B-3

Juan Bonilla

BONILLA, JUAN GUILLERMO BR TR 5′ 9″ 170 lbs.
Born Juan Guillermo Bonilla (Urania).
B. Jan. 12, 1956, Santurce, Puerto Rico.

Year	Team	Games	BA	SA	AB	H	2B	3B	HR	HR%	R	RBI	BB	SO	SB	Pinch Hit AB	Pinch Hit H	PO	A	E	DP	TC/G	FA	G by Pos
1981	**SD N**	99	.290	.344	369	107	13	2	1	0.3	30	25	25	23	4	0	0	229	290	13	72	5.5	.976	2B-97
1982		45	.280	.335	182	51	6	2	0	0.0	21	8	11	15	0	0	0	99	134	6	26	5.3	.975	2B-45
1983		152	.237	.304	556	132	17	4	4	0.7	55	45	50	40	3	4	1	335	414	11	90	5.1	.986	2B-149
1985	**NY A**	8	.125	.188	16	2	1	0	0	0.0	0	2	0	3	0	2	0	7	14	1	3	3.1	.955	2B-7
1986	**BAL A**	102	.243	.296	284	69	10	1	1	0.4	33	18	25	21	0	7	2	143	175	10	48	3.1	.970	2B-70, 3B-33, DH-2
1987	**NY A**	23	.255	.364	55	14	3	0	1	1.8	6	3	5	6	0	1	1	40	44	3	10	3.8	.966	2B-22, 3B-1
6 yrs.		429	.256	.317	1462	375	50	9	7	0.5	145	101	116	108	7	14	4	853	1071	44	249	4.6	.978	2B-390, 3B-34, DH-2

Luther Bonin

BONIN, ERNEST LUTHER BL TR 5′ 9½″ 178 lbs.
B. Jan. 13, 1888, Green Hill, Ind. D. Jan. 3, 1965, Sycamore, Ohio.

Year	Team	Games	BA	SA	AB	H	2B	3B	HR	HR%	R	RBI	BB	SO	SB	Pinch Hit AB	Pinch Hit H	PO	A	E	DP	TC/G	FA	G by Pos
1913	**STL A**	1	.000	.000	1	0	0	0	0	0.0	0	0	0	0	0	1	0	0	0	0	0	0.0	—	
1914	**BUF F**	20	.184	.263	76	14	4	1	0	0.0	6	4	7		3	0	0	28	4	1	1	1.6	.970	OF-20
2 yrs.		21	.182	.260	77	14	4	1	0	0.0	6	4	7	0	3	1	0	28	4	1	1	1.6	.970	OF-20

Barry Bonnell

BONNELL, ROBERT BARRY BR TR 6′ 3″ 190 lbs.
B. Oct. 27, 1953, Clermont County, Ohio.

Year	Team	Games	BA	SA	AB	H	2B	3B	HR	HR%	R	RBI	BB	SO	SB	Pinch Hit AB	Pinch Hit H	PO	A	E	DP	TC/G	FA	G by Pos
1977	**ATL N**	100	.300	.339	360	108	11	0	1	0.3	41	45	37	32	7	7	1	203	65	8	1	2.6	.971	OF-75, 3B-32
1978		117	.240	.306	304	73	11	3	1	0.3	36	16	20	30	12	1	0	187	35	6	3	1.9	.974	OF-105, 3B-15
1979		127	.259	.424	375	97	20	3	12	3.2	47	45	26	55	8	4	1	221	8	4	2	1.9	.983	OF-124, 3B-1
1980	**TOR A**	130	.268	.417	463	124	22	4	13	2.8	55	56	37	59	3	5	1	271	15	8	3	2.4	.973	OF-122, DH-3
1981		66	.220	.339	227	50	7	4	4	1.8	21	28	12	25	4	2	0	148	5	4	1	2.4	.975	OF-66
1982		140	.293	.407	437	128	26	3	6	1.4	59	49	32	51	14	22	4	234	7	5	1	1.8	.980	OF-125, 3B-9, DH-6
1983		121	.318	.469	377	120	21	3	10	2.7	49	54	33	52	9	7	2	213	13	3	1	1.9	.987	OF-117, 3B-4, DH-1
1984	**SEA A**	110	.264	.394	363	96	15	4	8	2.2	42	48	25	51	5	8	1	171	23	6	1	1.8	.970	OF-94, 3B-10, 1B-5
1985		48	.243	.342	111	27	8	0	1	0.9	9	10	6	19	1	18	4	61	2	1	3	2.2	.984	OF-22, 1B-5, DH-2
1986		17	.196	.235	51	10	2	0	0	0.0	4	4	1	13	0	3	0	46	6	2	1	2.8	.963	OF-9, 1B-8, DH-2
10 yrs.		976	.272	.389	3068	833	143	24	56	1.8	363	355	229	387	63	77	14	1755	179	47	17	2.1	.976	OF-859, 3B-71, 1B-18, DH-14

Bob Bonner

BONNER, ROBERT AVERILL BR TR 6′ 185 lbs.
B. Aug. 12, 1956, Uvalde, Tex.

Year	Team	Games	BA	SA	AB	H	2B	3B	HR	HR%	R	RBI	BB	SO	SB	Pinch Hit AB	Pinch Hit H	PO	A	E	DP	TC/G	FA	G by Pos
1980	**BAL A**	4	.000	.000	4	0	0	0	0	0.0	1	1	0	0	0	0	0	2	6	1	1	3.0	.889	SS-3
1981		10	.296	.370	27	8	2	0	0	0.0	6	2	1	4	1	0	0	15	26	1	8	4.7	.976	2B-9
1982		41	.169	.234	77	13	3	1	0	0.0	8	5	3	12	0	0	0	33	61	4	9	2.4	.959	SS-38, 2B-3
1983		6	—	—	0	0	0	0	0	—	0	0	0	0	0	0	0	1	0	0	0	0.2	1.000	2B-5, DH-1
4 yrs.		61	.194	.259	108	21	5	1	0	0.0	15	8	4	16	1	0	0	51	93	6	18	2.5	.960	SS-41, 2B-17, DH-1

Frank Bonner

BONNER, FRANK J. (The Human Flea)
B. Aug. 20, 1869, Lowell, Mass. D. Dec. 31, 1905, Kansas City, Mo.
BR TR 5′ 7½″ 169 lbs.

Year	Team	Games	BA	SA	AB	H	2B	3B	HR	HR%	R	RBI	BB	SO	SB	Pinch Hit AB	Pinch Hit H	PO	A	E	DP	TC/G	FA	G by Pos
1894	BAL N	33	.322	.441	118	38	10	2	0	0.0	27	24	17	5	12	1	0	67	65	14	9	4.3	.904	2B-27, OF-4, 3B-2, SS-1
1895	2 teams	BAL N (11G –.333) STL N (15G –.136)																						
″	total	26	.218	.297	101	22	1	2	1	1.0	12	15	6	9	6	0	0	27	28	19	2	2.7	.743	3B-21, OF-5, C-1
1896	BKN N	9	.176	.235	34	6	2	0	0	0.0	8	5	2	8	1	0	0	8	35	4	3	5.2	.915	2B-9
1899	WAS N	85	.274	.372	347	95	20	4	2	0.6	41	44	18		6	0	0	192	264	29	34	5.7	.940	2B-85
1902	2 teams	CLE A (34G –.280) PHI A (11G –.182)																						
″	total	45	.256	.290	176	45	6	0	0	0.0	16	17	5		1	0	0	92	123	20	9	5.2	.915	2B-45
1903	BOS N	48	.220	.266	173	38	5	0	1	0.6	11	10	7		2	2	1	104	116	15	19	5.1	.936	2B-24, SS-22
6 yrs.		246	.257	.333	949	244	44	8	4	0.4	115	115	55	22	28	3	1	490	631	101	76	5.0	.917	2B-190, SS-23, 3B-23, OF-9, C-1

Zeke Bonura

BONURA, HENRY JOHN
B. Sept. 20, 1908, New Orleans, La. D. Mar. 9, 1987, New Orleans, La.
BR TR 6′ 210 lbs.

Year	Team	Games	BA	SA	AB	H	2B	3B	HR	HR%	R	RBI	BB	SO	SB	Pinch Hit AB	Pinch Hit H	PO	A	E	DP	TC/G	FA	G by Pos
1934	CHI A	127	.302	.545	510	154	35	4	27	5.3	86	110	64	31	0	0	0	1239	77	5	94	10.4	.996	1B-127
1935		138	.295	.485	550	162	34	4	21	3.8	107	92	57	28	4	0	0	1421	83	9	109	11.0	.994	1B-138
1936		148	.330	.482	587	194	39	7	12	2.0	120	137	94	29	4	1	0	1500	107	7	150	11.1	.996	1B-146
1937		116	.345	.573	447	154	41	2	19	4.3	79	100	49	24	5	1	0	1114	63	13	123	10.3	.989	1B-115
1938	WAS A	137	.289	.472	540	156	27	3	22	4.1	72	114	44	29	2	8	2	1209	93	9	132	10.2	.993	1B-129
1939	NY N	123	.321	.477	455	146	26	6	11	2.4	75	85	46	22	1	0	0	1205	90	11	110	10.7	.992	1B-122
1940	2 teams	WAS A (79G –.273) CHI N (49G –.264)																						
″	total	128	.270	.385	493	133	30	3	7	1.4	61	65	50	17	3	5	1	1120	82	18	104	9.9	.985	1B-123
7 yrs.		917	.307	.487	3582	1099	232	29	119	3.3	600	703	404	180	19	15	3	8808	595	72	822	10.5	.992	1B-900

Everitt Booe

BOOE, EVERITT LITTLE
B. Sept. 28, 1891, Mocksville, N. C. D. Mar. 21, 1969, Kenedy, Tex.
BL TR 5′ 8½″ 165 lbs.

Year	Team	Games	BA	SA	AB	H	2B	3B	HR	HR%	R	RBI	BB	SO	SB	Pinch Hit AB	Pinch Hit H	PO	A	E	DP	TC/G	FA	G by Pos
1913	PIT N	29	.200	.250	80	16	0	2	0	0.0	9	2	6	9	2	6	1	37	4	0	1	1.9	1.000	OF-22
1914	2 teams	IND F (20G –.226) BUF F (76G –.224)																						
″	total	96	.224	.276	272	61	10	2	0	0.0	34	20	28		12	14	3	107	45	17	9	2.2	.899	OF-63, SS-11, 3B-2, 2B-1
2 yrs.		125	.219	.270	352	77	10	4	0	0.0	43	22	34	9	14	20	4	144	49	17	10	2.1	.919	OF-85, SS-11, 3B-2, 2B-1

Buddy Booker

BOOKER, RICHARD LEE
B. May 28, 1942, Lynchburg, Va.
BL TR 5′10″ 170 lbs.

Year	Team	Games	BA	SA	AB	H	2B	3B	HR	HR%	R	RBI	BB	SO	SB	Pinch Hit AB	Pinch Hit H	PO	A	E	DP	TC/G	FA	G by Pos
1966	CLE A	18	.214	.464	28	6	1	0	2	7.1	6	5	2	6	0	8	0	25	2	1	0	2.3	.964	C-12
1968	CHI A	5	.000	.000	5	0	0	0	0	0.0	0	0	1	2	0	4	0	2	0	0	0	0.7	1.000	C-3
2 yrs.		23	.182	.394	33	6	1	0	2	6.1	6	5	3	8	0	12	0	27	2	1	0	2.0	.967	C-15

Rod Booker

BOOKER, RODERICK STEWART
B. Sept. 4, 1958, Los Angeles, Calif.
BL TR 6′ 175 lbs.

Year	Team	Games	BA	SA	AB	H	2B	3B	HR	HR%	R	RBI	BB	SO	SB	Pinch Hit AB	Pinch Hit H	PO	A	E	DP	TC/G	FA	G by Pos
1987	STL N	44	.277	.340	47	13	1	1	0	0.0	9	8	7	7	2	18	4	25	28	2	5	2.4	.964	2B-18, 3B-4, SS-1
1988		18	.343	.429	35	12	3	0	0	0.0	6	3	4	3	2	6	2	3	15	2	0	1.4	.900	3B-13, 2B-1
1989		10	.250	.250	8	2	0	0	0	0.0	1	0	0	1	0	2	0	4	9	2	2	2.5	.867	2B-5, 3B-1
1990	PHI N	73	.221	.290	131	29	5	2	0	0.0	19	10	15	26	3	13	2	57	74	4	15	2.3	.970	SS-27, 2B-23, 3B-10
1991		28	.226	.245	53	12	1	0	0	0.0	3	7	1	7	0	3	1	17	33	0	2	2.2	1.000	SS-20, 3B-3
5 yrs.		173	.248	.307	274	68	10	3	0	0.0	38	28	27	44	7	42	9	106	159	10	24	2.2	.964	SS-48, 2B-47, 3B-31

Al Bool

BOOL, ALBERT J.
B. Aug. 24, 1897, Lincoln, Neb. D. Sept. 27, 1981, Lincoln, Neb.
BR TR 5′11″ 180 lbs.

Year	Team	Games	BA	SA	AB	H	2B	3B	HR	HR%	R	RBI	BB	SO	SB	Pinch Hit AB	Pinch Hit H	PO	A	E	DP	TC/G	FA	G by Pos
1928	WAS A	2	.143	.143	7	1	0	0	0	0.0	0	1	0	0	0	0	0	8	2	0	0	5.0	1.000	C-2
1930	PIT N	78	.259	.449	216	56	12	4	7	3.2	30	46	25	29	0	11	3	190	42	8	4	3.7	.967	C-65
1931	BOS N	49	.188	.200	85	16	1	0	0	0.0	5	6	9	13	0	11	1	73	14	1	4	2.4	.989	C-37
3 yrs.		129	.237	.373	308	73	13	4	7	2.3	35	53	34	42	0	22	4	271	58	9	8	3.3	.973	C-104

Bob Boone

BOONE, ROBERT RAYMOND
Father of Bret Boone. Son of Ray Boone.
B. Nov. 19, 1947, San Diego, Calif.
Manager 1995.
BR TR 6′ 2½″ 195 lbs.

Year	Team	Games	BA	SA	AB	H	2B	3B	HR	HR%	R	RBI	BB	SO	SB	Pinch Hit AB	Pinch Hit H	PO	A	E	DP	TC/G	FA	G by Pos
1972	PHI N	16	.275	.353	51	14	1	0	1	2.0	4	4	5	7	1	3	0	66	7	5	1	5.6	.936	C-14
1973		145	.261	.365	521	136	20	2	10	1.9	42	61	41	36	3	0	0	868	89	10	16	6.7	.990	C-145
1974		146	.242	.322	488	118	24	3	3	0.6	41	52	35	29	3	1	1	825	77	22	7	6.3	.976	C-146
1975		97	.246	.329	289	71	14	2	2	0.7	28	20	32	14	1	6	1	459	48	5	7	5.4	.990	C-92, 3B-3
1976		121	.271	.366	361	98	18	2	4	1.1	40	54	45	44	2	12	4	587	39	6	5	5.6	.991	C-108, 1B-4
1977		132	.284	.436	440	125	26	4	11	2.5	55	66	42	54	5	1	0	654	83	8	9	5.6	.989	C-131, 3B-2
1978		132	.283	.425	435	123	18	4	12	2.8	48	62	46	37	2	5	1	650	55	8	7	5.4	.989	C-129, 1B-3, OF-1
1979		119	.286	.422	398	114	21	3	9	2.3	38	58	49	33	1	1	0	527	66	8	8	5.1	.987	C-117, 3B-2
1980		141	.229	.338	480	110	23	1	9	1.9	34	55	48	41	3	4	1	741	88	18	7	6.1	.979	C-138
1981		76	.211	.295	227	48	7	0	4	1.8	19	24	22	16	2	4	0	365	32	6	1	5.4	.985	C-75
1982	CAL A	143	.256	.337	472	121	17	0	7	1.5	42	58	39	34	0	0	0	650	87	8	8	5.2	.989	C-143
1983		142	.256	.353	468	120	18	0	9	1.9	46	52	24	42	4	0	0	606	83	14	12	5.0	.980	C-142
1984		139	.202	.262	450	91	16	1	3	0.7	33	32	25	45	3	2	2	660	71	12	10	5.4	.984	C-137
1985		150	.248	.317	460	114	17	0	5	1.1	37	55	37	35	1	2	2	670	71	10	15	5.1	.987	C-147
1986		144	.222	.305	442	98	12	2	7	1.6	48	49	43	30	1	0	0	812	84	11	16	6.3	.988	C-144
1987		128	.242	.311	389	94	18	0	3	0.8	42	33	35	36	0	1	1	684	56	13	11	5.9	.983	C-127, DH-1
1988		122	.295	.386	352	104	17	0	5	1.4	38	39	29	26	2	1	1	506	66	8	9	4.8	.986	C-121
1989	KC A	131	.274	.323	405	111	13	2	1	0.2	33	43	49	37	3	1	0	752	64	7	6	6.4	.991	C-129
1990		40	.239	.265	117	28	3	0	0	0.0	11	9	17	12	1	0	0	243	19	4	0	6.7	.985	C-40
19 yrs.		2264	.254	.346	7245	1838	303	26	105	1.4	679	826	663	608	38	44	14	11325	1185	183	155	5.7	.986	C-2225, 1B-7, 3B-7, DH-1, OF-1
DIVISIONAL PLAYOFF SERIES																								
1981	PHI N	3	.000	.000	5	0	0	0	0	0.0	0	0	0	0	0	0	0	10	2	0	0	4.0	1.000	C-3

Bob Boone *continued*

Year	Team	Games	BA	SA	AB	H	2B	3B	HR	HR%	R	RBI	BB	SO	SB	Pinch Hit AB	Pinch Hit H	PO	A	E	DP	TC/G	FA	G by Pos
LEAGUE CHAMPIONSHIP SERIES																								
1976	**PHI N**	3	.286	.286	7	2	0	0	0	0.0	0	1	1	0	0	0	0	8	2	0	0	3.3	1.000	C-3
1977		4	.400	.400	10	4	0	0	0	0.0	1	0	0	0	0	0	0	18	2	0	1	5.0	1.000	C-4
1978		3	.182	.182	11	2	0	0	0	0.0	0	0	0	1	0	0	0	16	2	1	0	6.3	.947	C-3
1980		5	.222	.222	18	4	0	0	0	0.0	1	2	1	2	0	0	0	22	3	0	1	5.0	1.000	C-5
1982	**CAL A**	5	.250	.438	16	4	0	0	1	6.3	3	4	0	2	0	0	0	30	3	0	0	6.6	1.000	C-5
1986		7	.455	.591	22	10	0	0	1	4.5	4	2	1	3	0	0	0	35	4	0	0	5.6	1.000	C-7
6 yrs.		27 **6th**	.310	.381	84	26 **9th**	0	0	2	2.4	9	9	3	8	0	0	0	129	16	1	2	5.4	.993	C-27
WORLD SERIES																								
1980	**PHI N**	6	.412	.529	17	7	2	0	0	0.0	3	4	4	0	0	0	0	49	3	0	0	8.7	1.000	C-6

Bret Boone

BOONE, BRET ROBERT BR TR 5′10″ 180 lbs.
Son of Bob Boone.
B. Apr. 6, 1969, El Cajon, Calif.

Year	Team	Games	BA	SA	AB	H	2B	3B	HR	HR%	R	RBI	BB	SO	SB	Pinch Hit AB	Pinch Hit H	PO	A	E	DP	TC/G	FA	G by Pos
1992	**SEA A**	33	.194	.318	129	25	4	0	4	3.1	15	15	4	34	1	1	0	72	96	6	22	4.6	.966	2B-32, 3B-6
1993		76	.251	.443	271	68	12	2	12	4.4	31	38	17	52	2	0	0	140	177	3	55	4.3	.991	2B-74, DH-1
1994	**CIN N**	108	.320	.491	381	122	25	2	12	3.1	59	68	24	74	3	2	1	192	269	12	57	4.4	.975	2B-106, 3B-2
1995		138	.267	.429	513	137	34	2	15	2.9	63	68	41	84	5	0	0	312	362	4	106	4.9	.994	2B-138
4 yrs.		355	.272	.439	1294	352	75	6	43	3.3	168	189	86	244	11	3	1	716	904	25	240	4.6	.985	2B-350, 3B-8, DH-1
DIVISIONAL PLAYOFF SERIES																								
1995	**CIN N**	3	.300	.700	10	3	1	0	1	10.0	4	1	1	3	1	0	0	7	5	0	0	4.0	1.000	2B-3
LEAGUE CHAMPIONSHIP SERIES																								
1995	**CIN N**	4	.214	.214	14	3	0	0	0	0.0	1	0	1	2	0	0	0	9	13	0	3	5.5	1.000	2B-4

Ike Boone

BOONE, ISAAC MORGAN BL TR 6′ 195 lbs.
Brother of Danny Boone.
B. Feb. 17, 1897, Samantha, Ala. D. Aug. 1, 1958, Northport, Ala.

Year	Team	Games	BA	SA	AB	H	2B	3B	HR	HR%	R	RBI	BB	SO	SB	Pinch Hit AB	Pinch Hit H	PO	A	E	DP	TC/G	FA	G by Pos
1922	**NY N**	2	.500	.500	2	1	0	0	0	0.0	0	0	0	1	0	2	1	0	0	0	0	0.0	—	
1923	**BOS A**	5	.267	.400	15	4	0	1	0	0.0	1	2	1	0	0	1	0	13	0	1	0	3.5	.929	OF-4
1924		128	.333	.486	486	162	29	3	13	2.7	71	96	55	32	2	4	1	189	17	5	3	1.7	.976	OF-123
1925		133	.330	.479	476	157	34	5	9	1.9	79	68	60	19	1	11	3	198	9	13	1	1.9	.941	OF-118
1927	**CHI A**	29	.226	.358	53	12	4	0	1	1.9	10	11	3	4	0	16	3	15	0	0	0	1.4	1.000	OF-11
1930	**BKN N**	40	.297	.495	101	30	9	1	3	3.0	13	13	14	8	0	9	3	47	1	2	0	1.9	.960	OF-27
1931		6	.200	.200	5	1	0	0	0	0.0	0	0	2	2	0	5	1	0	0	0	0	0.0	—	
1932		13	.143	.190	21	3	1	0	0	0.0	2	2	5	2	0	5	0	8	1	0	1	1.1	1.000	OF-8
8 yrs.		356	.319	.470	1159	370	77	10	26	2.2	176	192	140	68	3	53	12	470	28	21	5	1.8	.960	OF-291

Luke Boone

BOONE, LUTE JOSEPH (Danny) BR TR 5′ 9″ 160 lbs.
B. May 6, 1890, Pittsburgh, Pa. D. July 29, 1982, Pittsburgh, Pa.

Year	Team	Games	BA	SA	AB	H	2B	3B	HR	HR%	R	RBI	BB	SO	SB	Pinch Hit AB	Pinch Hit H	PO	A	E	DP	TC/G	FA	G by Pos
1913	**NY A**	5	.333	.333	12	4	0	0	0	0.0	3	1	3	1	0	1	0	8	10	3	0	5.3	.857	SS-4
1914		106	.222	.254	370	82	8	2	0	0.0	34	21	31	41	10	5	0	249	310	25	33	5.9	.957	2B-90, 3B-9
1915		130	.204	.276	431	88	12	2	5	1.2	44	43	41	53	14	0	0	271	419	24	61	5.5	.966	2B-115, SS-12, 3B-3
1916		46	.185	.242	124	23	4	0	1	0.8	14	8	8	10	7	0	0	58	108	13	11	4.1	.927	3B-25, SS-12, 2B-7
1918	**PIT N**	27	.198	.231	91	18	3	0	0	0.0	7	3	8	6	1	0	0	56	85	12	6	5.7	.922	SS-26, 2B-1
5 yrs.		314	.209	.261	1028	215	27	4	6	0.6	102	76	91	111	32	6	0	642	932	77	111	5.4	.953	2B-213, SS-54, 3B-37

Ray Boone

BOONE, RAYMOND OTIS (Ike) BR TR 6′ 172 lbs.
Father of Bob Boone.
B. July 27, 1923, San Diego, Calif.

Year	Team	Games	BA	SA	AB	H	2B	3B	HR	HR%	R	RBI	BB	SO	SB	Pinch Hit AB	Pinch Hit H	PO	A	E	DP	TC/G	FA	G by Pos
1948	**CLE A**	6	.400	.600	5	2	1	0	0	0.0	0	1	0	1	0	1	0	3	5	1	0	2.3	.889	SS-4
1949		86	.252	.345	258	65	4	4	4	1.6	39	26	38	17	0	7	1	162	210	21	58	5.2	.947	SS-76
1950		109	.301	.430	365	110	14	6	7	1.9	53	58	56	27	4	6	0	178	267	26	64	4.6	.945	SS-102
1951		151	.233	.329	544	127	14	1	12	2.2	65	51	48	36	5	0	0	311	425	33	108	5.1	.957	SS-151
1952		103	.263	.367	316	83	8	2	7	2.2	57	45	53	33	0	4	0	180	254	28	57	4.7	.939	SS-96, 3B-2, 2B-1
1953	**2 teams**	**CLE A** (34G –.241) **DET A** (101G –.312)																						
″	**total**	135	.296	.519	497	147	17	8	26	5.2	94	114	72	68	3	4	1	179	313	23	58	3.9	.955	3B-97, SS-34
1954	**DET A**	148	.295	.466	543	160	19	7	20	3.7	76	85	71	53	4	0	0	170	332	19	22	3.5	.964	3B-148, SS-1
1955		135	.284	.476	500	142	22	7	20	4.0	61	**116**	50	49	1	8	2	135	252	19	33	3.2	.953	3B-126
1956		131	.308	.518	481	148	14	6	25	5.2	77	81	77	46	0	0	0	151	243	17	23	3.2	.959	3B-130
1957		129	.273	.418	462	126	25	3	12	2.6	48	65	57	47	1	5	1	977	57	12	103	8.6	.989	1B-117, 3B-4
1958	**2 teams**	**DET A** (39G –.237) **CHI A** (77G –.244)																						
″	**total**	116	.242	.406	360	87	16	2	13	3.6	41	61	32	46	1	21	2	747	49	11	71	8.5	.986	1B-95
1959	**3 teams**	**CHI A** (9G –.238) **KC A** (61G –.273) **MIL N** (13G –.200)																						
″	**total**	83	.262	.369	168	44	6	0	4	2.4	25	19	38	24	2	37	11	333	35	7	26	7.5	.981	1B-47, 3B-3
1960	**2 teams**	**MIL N** (7G –.250) **BOS A** (34G –.205)																						
″	**total**	41	.211	.267	90	19	2	0	1	1.1	9	15	16	16	0	15	3	199	14	1	22	8.2	.995	1B-26
13 yrs.		1373	.275	.429	4589	1260	162	46	151	3.3	645	737	608	463	21	108	21	3725	2456	218	645	5.1	.966	3B-510, SS-464, 1B-285, 2B-1
WORLD SERIES																								
1948	**CLE A**	1	.000	.000	1	0	0	0	0	0.0	0	0	0	1	0	1	0	0	0	0	0	0.0	—	

Amos Booth

BOOTH, AMOS SMITH (The Darling) BR TR 5′ 9″ 159 lbs.
B. Sept. 4, 1852, Cincinnati, Ohio D. July 1, 1921, Miamisburg, Ohio.

Year	Team	Games	BA	SA	AB	H	2B	3B	HR	HR%	R	RBI	BB	SO	SB	Pinch Hit AB	Pinch Hit H	PO	A	E	DP	TC/G	FA	G by Pos
1876	**CIN N**	63	.261	.272	272	71	3	0	0	0.0	31	14	9	11		0	0	138	117	76	10	4.4	.770	3B-24, C-24, SS-22, OF-3, P-3
1877		44	.172	.197	157	27	2	1	0	0.0	16	13	12	10		0	0	77	101	36	6	4.2	.832	SS-13, P-12, C-12, 2B-10, 3B-3, OF-1

Amos Booth *continued*

Year	Team	Games	BA	SA	AB	H	2B	3B	HR	HR%	R	RBI	BB	SO	SB	Pinch Hit AB	Pinch Hit H	PO	A	E	DP	TC/G	FA	G by Pos
1880		1	.000	.000	2	0	0	0	0	0.0	0	0	0	0		0	0	0	0	0	0	0.0	.000	3B-1
1882	2 teams BAL AA (1G –.000) LOU AA (1G –.000)																							
″	total	2	.000	.000	7	0	0	0	0	0.0	0		0			0	0	3	3	0	0	3.0	1.000	2B-1, 3B-1
4 yrs.		110	.224	.240	438	98	5	1	0	0.0	47	27	21	21		0	0	218	221	112	16	4.2	.797	C-36, SS-35, 3B-29, P-15, 2B-11, OF-4

Eddie Booth

BOOTH, EDWARD H.
B. Brooklyn, N. Y. Deceased.

Year	Team	Games	BA	SA	AB	H	2B	3B	HR	HR%	R	RBI	BB	SO	SB	Pinch Hit AB	Pinch Hit H	PO	A	E	DP	TC/G	FA	G by Pos
1876	NY N	57	.215	.232	228	49	2	1	0	0.0	17	7	2	4		0	0	88	18	31	1	2.3	.774	OF-53, 2B-5, P-1

Frenchy Bordagaray

BORDAGARAY, STANLEY GEORGE
B. Jan. 3, 1910, Coalinga, Calif.
BR TR 5′ 7½″ 175 lbs.

Year	Team	Games	BA	SA	AB	H	2B	3B	HR	HR%	R	RBI	BB	SO	SB	Pinch Hit AB	Pinch Hit H	PO	A	E	DP	TC/G	FA	G by Pos
1934	CHI A	29	.322	.379	87	28	3	1	0	0.0	12	2	3	8	1	12	8	28	2	2	0	1.9	.938	OF-17
1935	BKN N	120	.282	.363	422	119	19	6	1	0.2	69	39	17	29	18	9	2	227	14	5	2	2.3	.980	OF-105
1936		125	.315	.419	372	117	21	3	4	1.1	63	31	17	42	12	6	2	227	36	6	3	2.6	.978	OF-92, 2B-11
1937	STL N	96	.293	.367	300	88	11	4	1	0.3	43	37	15	25	11	16	1	105	72	9	2	2.4	.952	3B-50, OF-28
1938		81	.282	.327	156	44	5	1	0	0.0	19	21	8	9	2	**43**	**20**	72	9	6	0	2.6	.931	OF-29, 3B-4
1939	CIN N	63	.197	.254	122	24	5	1	0	0.0	19	12	9	10	3	11	0	67	7	1	2	1.7	.987	OF-43, 2B-2
1941	NY A	36	.260	.274	73	19	1	0	0	0.0	10	4	6	8	1	13	4	28	1	1	1	1.6	.967	OF-19
1942	BKN N	48	.241	.276	58	14	2	0	0	0.0	11	5	3	3	2	15	4	22	0	0	0	1.3	1.000	OF-17
1943		89	.302	.384	268	81	18	2	0	0.0	47	19	30	15	6	6	2	115	32	8	2	2.0	.948	OF-53, 3B-25
1944		130	.281	.385	501	141	26	4	6	1.2	85	51	36	22	2	10	3	180	151	17	14	2.8	.951	3B-98, OF-25
1945		113	.256	.355	273	70	9	6	2	0.7	32	49	29	15	7	32	8	86	93	19	7	2.5	.904	3B-57, OF-22
11 yrs.		930	.283	.366	2632	745	120	28	14	0.5	410	270	173	186	65	173	54	1157	417	74	33	2.4	.955	OF-450, 3B-234, 2B-13
WORLD SERIES																								
1939	CIN N	2	—	—	0	0	0	0	0	—	0	0	0	0	0	0	0	0	0	0	0	0.0	—	
1941	NY A	1	—	—	0	0	0	0	0	—	0	0	0	0	0	0	0	0	0	0	0	0.0	—	
2 yrs.		3			0	0	0	0	0		0	0	0	0	0	0	0							

Pat Borders

BORDERS, PATRICK LANCE
B. May 14, 1963, Columbus, Ohio.
BR TR 6′ 2″ 190 lbs.

Year	Team	Games	BA	SA	AB	H	2B	3B	HR	HR%	R	RBI	BB	SO	SB	Pinch Hit AB	Pinch Hit H	PO	A	E	DP	TC/G	FA	G by Pos
1988	TOR A	56	.273	.448	154	42	6	3	5	3.2	15	21	3	24	0	15	5	205	19	7	0	5.1	.970	C-43, 3B-1, 2B-1
1989		94	.257	.349	241	62	11	1	3	1.2	22	29	11	45	2	20	5	261	27	6	1	3.4	.980	C-68, DH-18
1990		125	.286	.497	346	99	24	2	15	4.3	36	49	18	57	0	25	5	515	46	4	6	4.9	.993	C-115, DH-1
1991		105	.244	.354	291	71	17	0	5	1.7	22	36	11	45	0	18	5	505	48	4	4	5.5	.993	C-102
1992		138	.242	.385	480	116	26	2	13	2.7	47	53	33	75	1	3	3	784	88	8	7	6.4	.991	C-137
1993		138	.254	.371	488	124	30	0	9	1.8	38	55	20	66	2	0	0	869	80	13	12	7.0	.986	C-138
1994		85	.247	.329	295	73	13	1	3	1.0	24	26	15	50	1	0	0	583	59	8	2	7.6	.988	C-85
1995	2 teams KC A (52G –.231) HOU N (11G –.114)																							
″	total	63	.208	.331	178	37	8	1	4	2.2	15	13	9	29	0	8	2	252	23	1	4	4.7	.996	C-56, DH-3
8 yrs.		804	.252	.384	2473	624	135	10	57	2.3	219	282	120	391	6	89	25	3974	390	51	36	5.7	.988	C-744, DH-22, 3B-1, 2B-1
LEAGUE CHAMPIONSHIP SERIES																								
1989	TOR A	1	1.000	1.000	1	1	0	0	0	0.0	0	1	0	0	0	1	1	1	0	0	0	1.0	1.000	C-1
1991		5	.263	.316	19	5	1	0	0	0.0	0	2	0	0	0	0	0	38	3	2	0	8.6	.953	C-5
1992		6	.318	.455	22	7	0	0	1	4.5	3	3	1	1	0	0	0	38	3	1	1	7.0	.976	C-6
1993		6	.250	.292	24	6	1	0	0	0.0	1	3	0	6	1	0	0	41	4	0	1	7.5	1.000	C-6
4 yrs.		18	.288	.364	66	19	2	0	1	1.5	4	9	1	7	1	1	1	118	10	3	2	7.3	.977	C-18
WORLD SERIES																								
1992	TOR A	6	.450	.750	20	9	3	0	1	5.0	2	3	2	1	0	0	0	48	5	1	2	9.0	.981	C-6
1993		6	.304	.304	23	7	0	0	0	0.0	2	1	2	1	0	0	0	50	2	1	0	8.8	.981	C-6
2 yrs.		12	.372	.512	43	16	3	0	1	2.3	4	4	4	2	0	0	0	98	7	2	2	8.9	.981	C-12

Mike Bordick

BORDICK, MICHAEL TODD
B. July 21, 1965, Marquette, Mich.
BR TR 5′11″ 170 lbs.

Year	Team	Games	BA	SA	AB	H	2B	3B	HR	HR%	R	RBI	BB	SO	SB	Pinch Hit AB	Pinch Hit H	PO	A	E	DP	TC/G	FA	G by Pos
1990	OAK A	25	.071	.071	14	1	0	0	0	0.0	0	0	1	4	0	4	1	9	8	0	0	0.7	1.000	3B-10, SS-9, 2B-7
1991		90	.238	.268	235	56	5	1	0	0.0	21	21	14	37	3	2	0	146	213	11	46	4.1	.970	SS-84, 2B-5, 3B-1
1992		154	.300	.371	504	151	19	4	3	0.6	62	48	40	59	12	1	0	311	449	16	107	4.7	.979	2B-95, SS-70
1993		159	.249	.311	546	136	21	2	3	0.5	60	48	60	58	10	2	0	285	420	13	110	4.5	.982	SS-159, 2B-1
1994		114	.253	.335	391	99	18	4	2	0.5	38	37	38	44	7	0	0	190	320	14	67	4.5	.973	SS-112, 2B-4
1995		126	.264	.350	428	113	13	0	8	1.9	46	44	35	48	11	1	0	246	338	10	92	4.7	.983	SS-126, DH-1
6 yrs.		668	.263	.331	2118	556	76	11	16	0.8	227	198	188	250	43	10	1	1187	1748	64	422	4.4	.979	SS-560, 2B-112, 3B-11, DH-1
LEAGUE CHAMPIONSHIP SERIES																								
1992	OAK A	6	.053	.053	19	1	0	0	0	0.0	1	0	1	2	1	0	0	15	14	0	4	4.8	1.000	SS-4, 2B-2
WORLD SERIES																								
1990	OAK A	3	—	—	0	0	0	0	0	—	0	0	0	0	0	0	0	0	2	0	0	0.7	1.000	SS-3

Glenn Borgmann

BORGMANN, GLENN DENNIS
B. May 25, 1950, Paterson, N. J.
BR TR 6′ 4″ 210 lbs.

Year	Team	Games	BA	SA	AB	H	2B	3B	HR	HR%	R	RBI	BB	SO	SB	Pinch Hit AB	Pinch Hit H	PO	A	E	DP	TC/G	FA	G by Pos
1972	MIN A	56	.234	.309	175	41	4	0	3	1.7	11	14	25	25	0	0	0	304	31	12	4	6.2	.965	C-56
1973		12	.265	.324	34	9	2	0	0	0.0	7	9	6	10	0	0	0	55	2	0	0	4.8	1.000	C-12
1974		128	.252	.307	345	87	8	1	3	0.9	33	45	39	44	2	4	0	652	52	2	4	5.5	.997	C-128
1975		125	.207	.278	352	73	15	2	2	0.6	34	33	47	59	0	2	0	618	81	8	6	5.7	.989	C-125
1976		24	.246	.338	65	16	3	0	1	1.5	10	6	19	7	1	1	1	110	13	3	1	5.3	.976	C-24
1977		17	.256	.419	43	11	1	0	2	4.7	12	7	11	9	0	0	0	70	8	0	1	4.6	1.000	C-17
1978		49	.211	.333	123	26	4	1	3	2.4	16	15	18	17	0	3	1	185	20	2	6	4.4	.990	C-46, DH-1
1979		31	.200	.243	70	14	3	0	0	0.0	4	8	12	11	1	0	0	129	11	1	0	4.5	.993	C-31
1980	CHI A	32	.218	.310	87	19	2	0	2	2.3	10	14	14	9	0	1	0	134	18	0	1	4.8	1.000	C-32
9 yrs.		474	.229	.304	1294	296	42	4	16	1.2	137	151	191	191	4	11	2	2257	236	28	23	5.3	.989	C-471, DH-1

Bob Borkowski

BORKOWSKI, ROBERT VILARIAN (Bush) BR TR 6′ 182 lbs.
B. Jan. 27, 1926, Dayton, Ohio.

Year	Team	Games	BA	SA	AB	H	2B	3B	HR	HR%	R	RBI	BB	SO	SB	Pinch Hit AB	Pinch Hit H	PO	A	E	DP	TC/G	FA	G by Pos
1950	CHI N	85	.273	.379	256	70	7	4	4	1.6	27	29	16	30	1	14	2	155	4	4	1	2.5	.975	OF-65, 1B-1
1951		58	.157	.169	89	14	1	0	0	0.0	9	10	3	16	0	23	3	41	1	3	0	1.8	.933	OF-25
1952	CIN N	126	.252	.334	377	95	11	4	4	1.1	42	24	26	53	1	18	3	258	8	3	4	2.5	.989	OF-103, 1B-5
1953		94	.269	.406	249	67	11	1	7	2.8	32	29	21	41	0	27	9	114	3	3	1	1.7	.975	OF-67, 1B-2
1954		73	.265	.370	162	43	12	1	1	0.6	13	19	8	18	0	33	8	82	3	0	1	2.2	1.000	OF-36, 1B-3
1955	2 teams CIN N (25G –.167) BKN N (9G –.105)																							
″	total	34	.135	.162	37	5	1	0	0	0.0	3	1	2	8	0	9	2	18	1	1	1	1.0	.950	OF-20, 1B-1
6 yrs.		470	.251	.346	1170	294	43	10	16	1.4	126	112	76	166	2	124	27	668	20	14	8	2.1	.980	OF-316, 1B-12

Red Borom

BOROM, EDWARD JONES BL TR 5′11″ 180 lbs.
B. Oct. 30, 1915, Spartanburg, S. C.

Year	Team	Games	BA	SA	AB	H	2B	3B	HR	HR%	R	RBI	BB	SO	SB	Pinch Hit AB	Pinch Hit H	PO	A	E	DP	TC/G	FA	G by Pos
1944	DET A	7	.071	.071	14	1	0	0	0	0.0	1	1	2	2	0	2	0	6	14	2	1	4.4	.909	2B-4, SS-1
1945		55	.269	.300	130	35	4	0	0	0.0	19	9	7	8	4	12	2	66	93	6	16	4.9	.964	2B-28, 3B-4, SS-2
2 yrs.		62	.250	.278	144	36	4	0	0	0.0	20	10	9	10	4	14	2	72	107	8	17	4.8	.957	2B-32, 3B-4, SS-3
WORLD SERIES																								
1945	DET A	2	.000	.000	1	0	0	0	0	0.0	0	0	0	0	0	1	0	0	0	0	0	0.0	—	

Steve Boros

BOROS, STEPHEN BR TR 6′ 185 lbs.
B. Sept. 3, 1936, Flint, Mich.
Manager 1983–84, 1986.

Year	Team	Games	BA	SA	AB	H	2B	3B	HR	HR%	R	RBI	BB	SO	SB	Pinch Hit AB	Pinch Hit H	PO	A	E	DP	TC/G	FA	G by Pos
1957	DET A	24	.146	.171	41	6	1	0	0	0.0	4	2	1	8	0	4	0	8	27	3	1	2.7	.921	3B-9, SS-5
1958		6	.000	.000	2	0	0	0	0	0.0	0	0	0	0	0	0	0	2	0	0	0	2.0	1.000	2B-1
1961		116	.270	.364	396	107	18	2	5	1.3	51	62	68	42	4	0	0	115	192	15	15	2.8	.953	3B-116
1962		116	.228	.407	356	81	14	1	16	4.5	46	47	53	62	3	8	0	118	163	21	19	2.7	.930	3B-105, 2B-6
1963	CHI N	41	.211	.389	90	19	5	1	3	3.3	9	7	12	19	0	17	2	126	7	4	7	5.5	.971	1B-14, OF-11
1964	CIN N	117	.257	.322	370	95	12	3	2	0.5	31	31	47	43	4	1	0	95	204	12	18	2.7	.961	3B-114
1965		2	—	—	0	0	0	0	0	—	0	0	0	0	0	0	0	0	1	0	0	0.5	1.000	3B-2
7 yrs.		422	.245	.359	1255	308	50	7	26	2.1	141	149	181	174	11	30	2	464	594	55	60	2.9	.951	3B-346, 1B-14, OF-11, 2B-7, SS-5

Babe Borton

BORTON, WILLIAM BAKER BL TL 6′ 178 lbs.
B. Aug. 14, 1888, Marion, Ill. D. July 29, 1954, Berkeley, Calif.

Year	Team	Games	BA	SA	AB	H	2B	3B	HR	HR%	R	RBI	BB	SO	SB	Pinch Hit AB	Pinch Hit H	PO	A	E	DP	TC/G	FA	G by Pos
1912	CHI A	31	.371	.419	105	39	3	1	0	0.0	15	17	8		1	1	1	312	16	1	14	11.0	.997	1B-30
1913	2 teams CHI A (28G –.275) NY A (33G –.130)																							
″	total	61	.191	.239	188	36	6	0	1	0.5	17	24	41	24	2	2	0	632	44	11	35	11.6	.984	1B-59
1915	STL F	159	.286	.390	549	157	20	14	3	0.5	**97**	83	**92**		17	0	0	1571	58	12	91	10.3	.993	1B-159
1916	STL A	66	.224	.306	98	22	1	2	1	1.0	10	12	19	13	1	35	6	205	8	2	7	9.8	.991	1B-22
4 yrs.		317	.270	.354	940	254	30	17	5	0.5	139	136	160	37	21	38	7	2720	126	26	147	10.6	.991	1B-270

Don Bosch

BOSCH, DONALD JOHN BB TR 5′10″ 160 lbs.
B. July 15, 1942, San Francisco, Calif.

Year	Team	Games	BA	SA	AB	H	2B	3B	HR	HR%	R	RBI	BB	SO	SB	Pinch Hit AB	Pinch Hit H	PO	A	E	DP	TC/G	FA	G by Pos
1966	PIT N	3	.000	.000	2	0	0	0	0	0.0	0	0	0	0	0	1	0	0	0	0	0	0.0	.000	OF-1
1967	NY N	44	.140	.161	93	13	0	1	0	0.0	7	2	5	24	3	3	0	55	2	0	0	1.5	1.000	OF-39
1968		50	.171	.261	111	19	1	0	3	2.7	14	7	9	33	0	9	1	73	3	2	1	2.4	.974	OF-33
1969	MON N	49	.179	.250	112	20	5	0	1	0.9	13	4	8	20	1	15	2	52	1	2	0	1.7	.964	OF-32
4 yrs.		146	.164	.226	318	52	6	1	4	1.3	34	13	22	77	4	28	3	180	6	4	1	1.8	.979	OF-105

Rick Bosetti

BOSETTI, RICHARD ALAN BR TR 5′11″ 185 lbs.
B. Aug. 5, 1953, Redding, Calif.

Year	Team	Games	BA	SA	AB	H	2B	3B	HR	HR%	R	RBI	BB	SO	SB	Pinch Hit AB	Pinch Hit H	PO	A	E	DP	TC/G	FA	G by Pos
1976	PHI N	13	.278	.333	18	5	1	0	0	0.0	6	0	1	3	3	1	0	9	1	0	0	1.7	1.000	OF-6
1977	STL N	41	.232	.232	69	16	0	0	0	0.0	12	3	6	11	4	2	0	42	3	0	0	1.3	1.000	OF-35
1978	TOR A	136	.259	.347	568	147	25	5	5	0.9	61	42	30	65	6	0	0	417	17	6	1	3.3	.986	OF-135
1979		162	.260	.362	619	161	35	2	8	1.3	59	65	22	70	13	0	0	466	18	13	4	3.1	.974	OF-162
1980		53	.213	.324	188	40	7	1	4	2.1	24	18	15	29	4	1	0	124	4	2	0	2.5	.985	OF-51
1981	2 teams TOR A (25G –.234) OAK A (9G –.105)																							
″	total	34	.197	.227	66	13	2	0	0	0.0	9	5	5	9	0	3	1	52	0	0	0	1.9	1.000	OF-24, DH-3
1982	OAK A	6	.200	.200	15	3	0	0	0	0.0	1	0	0	1	0	0	0	14	2	0	0	2.7	1.000	OF-6
7 yrs.		445	.250	.338	1543	385	70	8	17	1.1	172	133	79	188	30	7	1	1124	45	21	5	2.8	.982	OF-419, DH-3
DIVISIONAL PLAYOFF SERIES																								
1981	OAK A	1	—	—	0	0	0	0	0	—	0	0	0	0	0	0	0	0	0	0	0	0.0	.000	OF-1
LEAGUE CHAMPIONSHIP SERIES																								
1981	OAK A	2	.250	.500	4	1	1	0	0	0.0	1	0	0	1	0	1	0	2	0	0	0	1.0	1.000	OF-1, DH-1

Thad Bosley

BOSLEY, THADDIS BL TL 6′ 3″ 175 lbs.
B. Sept. 17, 1956, Oceanside, Calif.

Year	Team	Games	BA	SA	AB	H	2B	3B	HR	HR%	R	RBI	BB	SO	SB	Pinch Hit AB	Pinch Hit H	PO	A	E	DP	TC/G	FA	G by Pos
1977	CAL A	58	.297	.363	212	63	10	2	0	0.0	19	19	16	32	5	4	2	130	1	5	0	2.5	.963	OF-55
1978	CHI A	66	.269	.329	219	59	5	1	2	0.9	25	13	13	32	12	1	0	155	3	4	0	2.5	.975	OF-64
1979		36	.312	.390	77	24	1	1	1	1.3	13	8	9	14	4	7	1	57	2	2	1	2.1	.967	OF-28, DH-1
1980		70	.224	.279	147	33	2	0	2	1.4	12	14	10	27	3	25	8	91	1	4	0	1.8	.958	OF-52
1981	MIL A	42	.229	.248	105	24	2	0	0	0.0	11	3	6	13	2	4	0	55	1	2	0	1.5	.966	OF-37, DH-1
1982	SEA A	22	.174	.196	46	8	1	0	0	0.0	3	2	4	8	3	3	0	12	1	0	0	0.7	1.000	OF-19
1983	CHI N	43	.292	.458	72	21	4	1	2	2.8	12	12	10	12	1	18	4	27	1	0	1	1.4	1.000	OF-20
1984		55	.296	.418	98	29	2	2	2	2.0	17	14	13	22	5	23	6	39	2	1	0	1.3	.976	OF-33
1985		108	.328	.511	180	59	6	3	7	3.9	25	27	20	29	5	60	**20**	84	0	1	0	1.5	.988	OF-55
1986		87	.275	.350	120	33	4	1	1	0.8	15	9	18	24	3	51	16	31	0	1	0	0.8	.969	OF-41
1987	KC A	80	.279	.357	140	39	6	1	1	0.7	13	16	9	26	0	**42**	**12**	28	0	1	0	0.7	.966	OF-28, DH-13
1988	2 teams KC A (15G –.190) CAL A (35G –.280)																							
″	total	50	.260	.313	96	25	5	0	0	0.0	10	9	8	18	1	10	3	59	0	2	0	1.6	.967	OF-32, DH-6
1989	TEX A	37	.225	.350	40	9	2	0	1	2.5	5	9	3	11	2	28	7	12	1	0	1	1.0	1.000	OF-8, DH-5
1990		30	.138	.241	29	4	0	0	1	3.4	3	3	4	7	1	19	3	4	0	0	0	0.3	1.000	OF-9, DH-4
14 yrs.		784	.272	.357	1581	430	50	12	20	1.3	183	158	143	275	47	295	82	784	13	23	3	1.6	.972	OF-481, DH-30

Thad Bosley *continued*

Year	Team	Games	BA	SA	AB	H	2B	3B	HR	HR%	R	RBI	BB	SO	SB	Pinch Hit AB	Pinch Hit H	PO	A	E	DP	TC/G	FA	G by Pos
DIVISIONAL PLAYOFF SERIES																								
1981	MIL A	1	—	—	0	0	0	0	0	—	0	0	0	0	0	0	0	0	0	0	0	0.0	.000	DH-1
LEAGUE CHAMPIONSHIP SERIES																								
1984	CHI N	2	.000	.000	2	0	0	0	0	0.0	0	0	0	2	0	2	0	0	0	0	0	0.0	—	

Harley Boss

BOSS, ELMER HARLEY (Lefty)
B. Nov. 19, 1908, Hodge, La. D. May 15, 1964, Nashville, Tenn.
BL TL 5′11½″ 185 lbs.

Year	Team	Games	BA	SA	AB	H	2B	3B	HR	HR%	R	RBI	BB	SO	SB	Pinch Hit AB	Pinch Hit H	PO	A	E	DP	TC/G	FA	G by Pos
1928	WAS A	12	.250	.250	12	3	0	0	0	0.0	1	2	3	1	0	4	0	32	0	1	2	6.6	.970	1B-5
1929		28	.273	.333	66	18	2	1	0	0.0	9	6	2	6	0	9	1	119	9	3	13	7.3	.977	1B-18
1930		3	.000	.000	3	0	0	0	0	0.0	0	0	0	0	0	2	0	2	0	0	0	2.0	1.000	1B-1
1933	CLE A	112	.269	.347	438	118	17	7	1	0.2	54	53	25	27	2	3	0	1062	71	7	89	10.4	.994	1B-110
4 yrs.		155	.268	.341	519	139	19	8	1	0.2	64	61	30	34	2	18	1	1215	80	11	104	9.7	.992	1B-134

Henry Bostick

BOSTICK, HENRY LANDERS
Born Henry Landers Lifsit.
B. Jan. 12, 1895, Boston, Mass. D. Sept. 16, 1968, Denver, Colo.
BR TR

Year	Team	Games	BA	SA	AB	H	2B	3B	HR	HR%	R	RBI	BB	SO	SB	Pinch Hit AB	Pinch Hit H	PO	A	E	DP	TC/G	FA	G by Pos
1915	PHI A	2	.000	.000	7	0	0	0	0	0.0	0	2	1	1	0	0	0	0	2	0	0	1.0	1.000	3B-2

Lyman Bostock

BOSTOCK, LYMAN WESLEY
B. Nov. 22, 1950, Birmingham, Ala. D. Sept. 23, 1978, Gary, Ind.
BL TR 6′ 1″ 180 lbs.

Year	Team	Games	BA	SA	AB	H	2B	3B	HR	HR%	R	RBI	BB	SO	SB	Pinch Hit AB	Pinch Hit H	PO	A	E	DP	TC/G	FA	G by Pos
1975	MIN A	98	.282	.366	369	104	21	5	0	0.0	52	29	28	42	2	2	0	188	3	3	0	2.1	.985	OF-92, DH-1
1976		128	.323	.430	474	153	21	9	4	0.8	75	60	33	37	12	9	4	320	10	4	2	2.7	.988	OF-124
1977		153	.336	.508	593	199	36	12	14	2.4	104	90	51	59	16	10	1	349	10	4	0	2.4	.989	OF-149
1978	CAL A	147	.296	.379	568	168	24	4	5	0.9	74	71	59	36	15	1	0	366	7	4	2	2.6	.989	OF-146, DH-1
4 yrs.		526	.311	.427	2004	624	102	30	23	1.1	305	250	171	174	45	22	5	1223	30	15	4	2.5	.988	OF-511, DH-2

Daryl Boston

BOSTON, DARYL LAMONT
B. Jan. 4, 1963, Cincinnati, Ohio.
BL TL 6′ 3″ 185 lbs.

Year	Team	Games	BA	SA	AB	H	2B	3B	HR	HR%	R	RBI	BB	SO	SB	Pinch Hit AB	Pinch Hit H	PO	A	E	DP	TC/G	FA	G by Pos
1984	CHI A	35	.169	.229	83	14	3	1	0	0.0	8	3	4	20	6	2	1	59	2	6	1	1.9	.910	OF-34, DH-1
1985		95	.228	.332	232	53	13	1	3	1.3	20	15	14	44	8	5	1	179	7	2	1	2.0	.989	OF-93, DH-2
1986		56	.266	.427	199	53	11	3	5	2.5	29	22	21	33	9	1	0	152	3	5	1	3.0	.969	OF-53, DH-1
1987		103	.258	.421	337	87	21	2	10	3.0	51	29	25	68	12	10	2	207	3	2	3	2.2	.991	OF-92, DH-5
1988		105	.217	.434	281	61	12	2	15	5.3	37	31	21	44	9	13	3	190	4	10	2	2.3	.951	OF-85, DH-5
1989		101	.252	.372	218	55	3	4	5	2.3	34	23	24	31	7	16	4	134	2	4	0	1.7	.971	OF-75, DH-9
1990	2 teams	CHI A (5G –.000) NY N (115G –.273)																						
″	total	120	.272	.439	367	100	21	2	12	3.3	65	45	28	50	19	18	3	203	3	3	1	1.8	.986	OF-110, DH-3
1991	NY N	137	.275	.416	255	70	16	4	4	1.6	40	21	30	42	15	27	6	156	2	3	1	1.4	.981	OF-115
1992		130	.249	.426	289	72	14	2	11	3.8	37	35	38	60	12	40	7	133	5	1	1	1.5	.993	OF-95
1993	CLR N	124	.261	.464	291	76	15	1	14	4.8	46	40	26	57	1	37	9	124	5	2	1	1.7	.985	OF-79
1994	NY A	52	.182	.364	77	14	2	0	4	5.2	11	14	6	20	0	25	5	15	1	0	0	0.7	1.000	OF-16, DH-8
11 yrs.		1058	.249	.410	2629	655	131	22	83	3.2	378	278	237	469	98	194	41	1552	37	38	12	1.8	.977	OF-847, DH-34

Ken Boswell

BOSWELL, KENNETH GEORGE
B. Feb. 23, 1946, Austin, Tex.
BL TR 6′ 170 lbs.

Year	Team	Games	BA	SA	AB	H	2B	3B	HR	HR%	R	RBI	BB	SO	SB	Pinch Hit AB	Pinch Hit H	PO	A	E	DP	TC/G	FA	G by Pos
1967	NY N	11	.225	.375	40	9	3	0	1	2.5	2	4	1	5	0	1	0	12	34	1	5	4.7	.979	2B-6, 3B-4
1968		75	.261	.342	284	74	7	2	4	1.4	37	11	16	27	7	6	1	154	203	13	37	5.4	.965	2B-69
1969		102	.279	.381	362	101	14	7	3	0.8	48	32	36	47	7	10	1	190	229	18	51	4.6	.959	2B-96
1970		105	.254	.345	351	89	13	2	5	1.4	32	44	41	32	5	7	2	204	244	2	49	4.5	.996	2B-101
1971		116	.273	.367	392	107	20	1	5	1.3	46	40	36	31	5	7	0	191	234	12	56	4.0	.973	2B-109
1972		100	.211	.318	355	75	9	1	9	2.5	35	33	32	35	2	7	1	208	183	4	53	4.2	.990	2B-94
1973		76	.227	.318	110	25	2	1	2	1.8	12	14	12	11	0	**51**	12	15	33	2	3	2.5	.960	3B-17, 2B-3
1974		96	.216	.279	222	48	6	1	2	0.9	19	15	18	19	0	42	9	94	113	6	18	3.9	.972	2B-28, 3B-20, OF-7
1975	HOU N	86	.242	.309	178	43	8	2	0	0.0	16	21	30	12	0	35	6	54	103	6	13	3.0	.963	2B-31, 3B-23
1976		91	.262	.341	126	33	8	1	0	0.0	12	18	8	8	1	65	20	8	21	2	4	1.5	.935	3B-16, 2B-3, OF-1
1977		72	.216	.247	97	21	1	1	0	0.0	7	12	10	12	0	53	14	33	35	0	9	2.4	1.000	2B-26, 3B-2
11 yrs.		930	.248	.337	2517	625	91	19	31	1.2	266	244	240	239	27	284	66	1163	1432	66	298	4.1	.975	2B-566, 3B-82, OF-8
LEAGUE CHAMPIONSHIP SERIES																								
1969	NY N	3	.333	.833	12	4	0	0	2	16.7	4	5	1	2	0	0	0	3	2	1	1	2.0	.833	2B-3
1973		1	.000	.000	1	0	0	0	0	0.0	0	0	0	0	0	1	0	0	0	0	0	0.0	—	
2 yrs.		4	.308	.769	13	4	0	0	2	15.4	4	5	1	2	0	1	0	3	2	1	1	2.0	.833	2B-3
WORLD SERIES																								
1969	NY N	1	.333	.333	3	1	0	0	0	0.0	1	0	0	0	0	0	0	0	1	0	0	1.0	1.000	2B-1
1973		3	1.000	1.000	3	3	0	0	0	0.0	1	0	0	0	0	3	3	0	0	0	0	0.0	—	
2 yrs.		4	.667	.667	6	4	0	0	0	0.0	2	0	0	0	0	3	3	0	1	0	0	1.0	1.000	2B-1

John Bottarini

BOTTARINI, JOHN CHARLES
B. Sept. 14, 1908, Crockett, Calif. D. Oct. 8, 1976, Jemez Springs, N. M.
BR TR 6′ 190 lbs.

Year	Team	Games	BA	SA	AB	H	2B	3B	HR	HR%	R	RBI	BB	SO	SB	Pinch Hit AB	Pinch Hit H	PO	A	E	DP	TC/G	FA	G by Pos
1937	CHI N	26	.275	.425	40	11	3	0	1	2.5	3	7	5	10	0	7	2	44	9	0	0	2.8	1.000	C-18, OF-1

Jim Bottomley

BOTTOMLEY, JAMES LeROY (Sunny Jim)
B. Apr. 23, 1900, Oglesby, Ill. D. Dec. 11, 1959, St. Louis, Mo.
Manager 1937.
Hall of Fame 1974.
BL TL 6′ 180 lbs.

Year	Team	Games	BA	SA	AB	H	2B	3B	HR	HR%	R	RBI	BB	SO	SB	Pinch Hit AB	Pinch Hit H	PO	A	E	DP	TC/G	FA	G by Pos
1922	STL N	37	.325	.543	151	49	8	5	5	3.3	29	35	6	13	3	3	1	346	12	5	20	10.7	.986	1B-34
1923		134	.371	.535	523	194	34	14	8	1.5	79	94	45	44	4	4	1	1264	43	18	95	10.2	.986	1B-130
1924		137	.316	.500	528	167	31	12	14	2.7	87	111	35	35	5	3	1	1297	49	24	110	10.2	.982	1B-133, 2B-1
1925		153	.367	.578	619	**227**	**44**	12	21	3.4	92	128	47	36	3	0	0	1466	74	21	133	10.2	.987	1B-153
1926		154	.299	.506	603	180	**40**	14	19	3.2	98	**120**	58	52	4	0	0	1607	54	19	118	10.9	.989	1B-154

Jim Bottomley *continued*

Year	Team	Games	BA	SA	AB	H	2B	3B	HR	HR%	R	RBI	BB	SO	SB	Pinch Hit AB	Pinch Hit H	PO	A	E	DP	TC/G	FA	G by Pos
1927		152	.303	.509	574	174	31	15	19	3.3	95	124	74	49	8	0	0	1656	70	20	149	11.5	.989	1B-152
1928		149	.325	.628	576	187	42	**20**	**31**	5.4	123	**136**	71	54	10	0	0	1454	52	20	113	10.3	.987	1B-148
1929		146	.314	.568	560	176	31	12	29	5.2	108	137	70	54	3	1	0	1347	75	13	122	9.9	.991	1B-145
1930		131	.304	.493	487	148	33	7	15	3.1	92	97	44	36	5	7	2	1164	41	12	127	9.8	.990	1B-124
1931		108	.348	.534	382	133	34	5	9	2.4	73	75	34	24	3	14	3	897	43	12	95	10.2	.987	1B-93
1932		91	.296	.473	311	92	16	3	11	3.5	45	48	25	32	2	16	7	662	41	10	67	9.6	.986	1B-74
1933	CIN N	145	.250	.395	549	137	23	9	13	2.4	57	83	42	28	3	0	0	1511	72	15	112	11.0	.991	1B-145
1934		142	.284	.439	556	158	31	11	11	2.0	72	78	33	40	1	3	0	1303	77	15	106	10.0	.989	1B-139
1935		107	.258	.323	399	103	21	1	1	0.3	44	49	18	24	3	10	5	934	53	8	74	10.3	.992	1B-97
1936	STL A	140	.298	.476	544	162	39	11	12	2.2	72	95	44	55	0	0	0	1250	47	10	103	9.3	.992	1B-140
1937		65	.239	.330	109	26	7	0	1	0.9	11	12	18	15	1	**38**	7	179	12	1	16	8.0	.995	1B-24
16 yrs.		1991	.310	.500	7471	2313	465	151	219	2.9	1177	1422	664	591	58	99	27	18337	815	223	1560	10.3	.988	1B-1885, 2B-1
WORLD SERIES																								
1926	STL N	7	.345	.448	29	10	3	0	0	0.0	4	5	1	2	0	0	0	79	1	0	5	11.4	1.000	1B-7
1928		4	.214	.571	14	3	0	1	1	7.1	1	3	2	6	0	0	0	36	2	0	2	9.5	1.000	1B-4
1930		6	.045	.091	22	1	1	0	0	0.0	1	0	2	9	0	0	0	58	2	0	3	10.0	1.000	1B-6
1931		7	.160	.200	25	4	1	0	0	0.0	2	2	2	5	0	0	0	61	2	1	7	9.1	.984	1B-7
4 yrs.		24	.200	.311	90	18	5	1	1	1.1	8	10	7	22	0	0	0	234	7	1	17	10.1	.996	1B-24

Ed Bouchee

BOUCHEE, EDWARD FRANCIS
B. Mar. 7, 1933, Livingston, Mont.

BL TL 6′ 200 lbs.

Year	Team	Games	BA	SA	AB	H	2B	3B	HR	HR%	R	RBI	BB	SO	SB	Pinch Hit AB	Pinch Hit H	PO	A	E	DP	TC/G	FA	G by Pos
1956	PHI N	9	.273	.364	22	6	2	0	0	0.0	0	1	5	6	0	2	0	54	3	0	6	9.5	1.000	1B-6
1957		154	.293	.470	574	168	35	8	17	3.0	78	76	84	91	1	0	0	1182	125	16	93	8.6	.988	1B-154
1958		89	.257	.425	334	86	19	5	9	2.7	55	39	51	74	1	0	0	690	58	5	59	8.5	.993	1B-89
1959		136	.285	.449	499	142	29	4	15	3.0	75	74	70	74	0	2	1	1127	95	17	96	9.2	.986	1B-134
1960	2 teams	PHI N (22G –.262) CHI N (98G –.237)																						
″	total	120	.242	.330	364	88	15	1	5	1.4	34	52	54	62	2	17	1	867	71	8	68	9.3	.992	1B-102
1961	CHI N	112	.248	.417	319	79	12	3	12	3.8	49	38	58	77	1	12	1	852	76	16	97	8.8	.983	1B-107
1962	NY N	50	.161	.287	87	14	2	0	3	3.4	7	10	18	17	0	28	5	137	23	4	16	8.6	.976	1B-19
7 yrs.		670	.265	.419	2199	583	114	21	61	2.8	298	290	340	401	5	61	8	4909	451	66	435	8.9	.988	1B-611

Al Boucher

BOUCHER, ALEXANDER FRANCIS (Bo)
B. Nov. 13, 1881, Franklin, Mass. D. June 23, 1974, Torrance, Calif.

BR TR 5′ 8½″ 156 lbs.

Year	Team	Games	BA	SA	AB	H	2B	3B	HR	HR%	R	RBI	BB	SO	SB	Pinch Hit AB	Pinch Hit H	PO	A	E	DP	TC/G	FA	G by Pos
1914	STL F	147	.231	.308	516	119	26	4	2	0.4	62	49	52		13	0	0	193	263	42	18	3.4	.916	3B-147

Medric Boucher

BOUCHER, MEDRIC CHARLES FRANCIS (Bush)
B. Mar. 12, 1886, St. Louis, Mo. D. Mar. 12, 1974, Martinez, Calif.

BR TR 5′10″ 165 lbs.

Year	Team	Games	BA	SA	AB	H	2B	3B	HR	HR%	R	RBI	BB	SO	SB	Pinch Hit AB	Pinch Hit H	PO	A	E	DP	TC/G	FA	G by Pos
1914	2 teams	BAL F (16G –.313) PIT F (1G –.000)																						
″	total	17	.294	.471	17	5	1	1	0	0.0	2	2	1		0	6	2	24	2	1	1	3.0	.963	C-7, 1B-1, OF-1

Lou Boudreau

BOUDREAU, LOUIS
B. July 17, 1917, Harvey, Ill.
Manager 1942–50, 1952–57, 1960.
Hall of Fame 1970.

BR TR 5′11″ 185 lbs.

Year	Team	Games	BA	SA	AB	H	2B	3B	HR	HR%	R	RBI	BB	SO	SB	Pinch Hit AB	Pinch Hit H	PO	A	E	DP	TC/G	FA	G by Pos
1938	CLE A	1	.000	.000	1	0	0	0	0	0.0	0	0	1	0	0	0	0	0	0	0	0	0.0	.000	3B-1
1939		53	.258	.360	225	58	15	4	0	0.0	42	19	28	24	2	0	0	103	184	14	31	5.7	.953	SS-53
1940		155	.295	.443	627	185	46	10	9	1.4	97	101	73	39	6	0	0	277	454	24	116	4.9	.968	SS-155
1941		148	.257	.415	579	149	**45**	8	10	1.7	95	56	85	57	9	0	0	296	444	26	97	5.2	.966	SS-147
1942		147	.283	.370	506	143	18	10	2	0.4	57	58	75	39	7	1	0	281	426	26	107	5.0	.965	SS-146
1943		152	.286	.388	539	154	32	7	3	0.6	69	67	90	31	4	1	0	331	489	25	122	5.5	.970	SS-152, C-1
1944		150	**.327**	.437	584	191	**45**	5	3	0.5	91	67	73	39	11	1	0	340	517	19	134	5.8	.978	SS-149, C-1
1945		97	.306	.408	346	106	24	1	3	0.9	50	48	35	20	0	0	0	217	289	9	73	5.3	.983	SS-97
1946		140	.293	.410	515	151	30	6	6	1.2	51	62	40	14	6	1	0	315	405	22	94	5.3	.970	SS-139
1947		150	.307	.424	538	165	**45**	3	4	0.7	79	67	67	10	1	1	1	305	475	14	120	5.4	.982	SS-148
1948		152	.355	.534	560	199	34	6	18	3.2	116	106	98	9	3	1	1	297	483	20	119	5.3	.975	SS-151, C-1
1949		134	.284	.364	475	135	20	3	4	0.8	53	60	70	10	0	4	1	253	353	12	95	4.6	.981	SS-88, 3B-38, 1B-6, 2B-1
1950		81	.269	.346	260	70	13	2	1	0.4	23	29	31	5	1	9	2	156	176	4	46	4.6	.988	SS-61, 1B-8, 3B-2, 2B-2
1951	BOS A	82	.267	.396	273	73	18	1	5	1.8	37	47	30	12	1	11	1	94	181	15	51	4.2	.948	SS-52, 3B-15, 1B-2
1952		4	.000	.000	2	0	0	0	0	0.0	1	2	0	0	0	2	0	0	1	0	0	0.5	1.000	SS-1, 3B-1
15 yrs.		1646	.295	.415	6030	1779	385	66	68	1.1	861	789	796	309	51	32	6	3265	4877	230	1205	5.2	.973	SS-1539, 3B-57, 1B-16, 2B-3, C-3
WORLD SERIES																								
1948	CLE A	6	.273	.455	22	6	4	0	0	0.0	1	3	1	1	0	0	0	11	14	0	5	4.2	1.000	SS-6

Chris Bourjos

BOURJOS, CHRISTOPHER
B. Oct. 16, 1954, Chicago, Ill.

BR TR 6′ 185 lbs.

Year	Team	Games	BA	SA	AB	H	2B	3B	HR	HR%	R	RBI	BB	SO	SB	Pinch Hit AB	Pinch Hit H	PO	A	E	DP	TC/G	FA	G by Pos
1980	SF N	13	.227	.409	22	5	1	0	1	4.5	4	2	2	7	0	7	2	5	0	0	0	0.8	1.000	OF-6

Rafael Bournigal

BOURNIGAL, RAFAEL ANTONIO
Born Rafael Antonio Bournigal (Pelletier).
B. May 12, 1966, Azua, Dominican Republic.

BR TR 5′11″ 160 lbs.

Year	Team	Games	BA	SA	AB	H	2B	3B	HR	HR%	R	RBI	BB	SO	SB	Pinch Hit AB	Pinch Hit H	PO	A	E	DP	TC/G	FA	G by Pos
1992	LA N	10	.150	.200	20	3	1	0	0	0.0	1	0	1	2	0	1	0	12	17	1	6	3.3	.967	SS-9
1993		8	.500	.556	18	9	1	0	0	0.0	0	3	0	2	0	2	1	5	14	0	3	2.4	1.000	SS-4, 2B-4
1994		40	.224	.267	116	26	3	1	0	0.0	2	11	9	5	0	0	0	56	97	3	19	3.9	.981	SS-40
3 yrs.		58	.247	.292	154	38	5	1	0	0.0	3	14	10	9	0	3	1	73	128	4	28	3.6	.980	SS-53, 2B-4

Pat Bourque

BOURQUE, PATRICK DANIEL
B. Mar. 23, 1947, Worcester, Mass.
BL TL 6′ 210 lbs.

Year	Team	Games	BA	SA	AB	H	2B	3B	HR	HR%	R	RBI	BB	SO	SB	Pinch Hit AB	Pinch Hit H	PO	A	E	DP	TC/G	FA	G by Pos
1971	CHI N	14	.189	.324	37	7	0	1	1	2.7	3	3	3	9	0	3	1	75	13	4	6	8.4	.957	1B-11
1972		11	.259	.296	27	7	1	0	0	0.0	3	5	2	2	0	4	0	57	6	0	8	9.0	1.000	1B-7
1973	2 teams CHI N (57G –.209) OAK A (23G –.190)																							
″	total	80	.204	.420	181	37	10	1	9	5.0	19	29	31	31	1	20	4	348	35	5	34	6.7	.987	1B-43, DH-15
1974	2 teams OAK A (73G –.229) MIN A (23G –.219)																							
″	total	96	.225	.300	160	36	6	0	2	1.3	11	24	22	31	0	35	7	291	26	4	33	4.7	.988	1B-60, DH-8
4 yrs.		201	.215	.356	405	87	17	2	12	3.0	36	61	58	73	1	62	12	771	80	13	81	6.0	.985	1B-121, DH-23
LEAGUE CHAMPIONSHIP SERIES																								
1973	OAK A	2	.000	.000	1	0	0	0	0	0.0	0	0	1	1	0	0	0	0	0	0	0	0.0	.000	DH-2
WORLD SERIES																								
1973	OAK A	2	.500	.500	2	1	0	0	0	0.0	0	0	0	0	0	1	0	3	1	0	0	2.0	1.000	1B-2

Larry Bowa

BOWA, LAWRENCE ROBERT
B. Dec. 6, 1945, Sacramento, Calif.
Manager 1987–88.
BB TR 5′10″ 155 lbs.

Year	Team	Games	BA	SA	AB	H	2B	3B	HR	HR%	R	RBI	BB	SO	SB	Pinch Hit AB	Pinch Hit H	PO	A	E	DP	TC/G	FA	G by Pos
1970	PHI N	145	.250	.303	547	137	17	6	0	0.0	50	34	21	48	24	0	0	202	418	13	69	4.4	.979	SS-143, 2B-1
1971		159	.249	.292	**650**	162	18	5	0	0.0	74	25	36	61	28	0	0	272	560	11	97	5.4	.987	SS-157
1972		152	.250	.320	579	145	11	**13**	1	0.2	67	31	32	51	17	0	0	212	494	9	88	4.8	.987	SS-150
1973		122	.211	.249	446	94	11	3	0	0.0	42	23	24	31	10	0	0	191	361	12	87	4.6	.979	SS-122
1974		162	.275	.338	669	184	19	10	1	0.1	97	36	23	52	39	0	0	256	462	12	104	4.5	.984	SS-162
1975		136	.305	.377	583	178	18	9	2	0.3	79	38	24	32	24	0	0	227	403	25	82	4.9	.962	SS-135
1976		156	.248	.301	624	155	15	9	0	0.0	71	49	32	31	30	0	0	180	492	17	90	4.4	.975	SS-156
1977		154	.280	.340	624	175	19	3	4	0.6	93	41	32	32	32	0	0	222	518	13	94	4.9	.983	SS-154
1978		156	.294	.370	654	192	31	5	3	0.5	78	43	24	40	27	0	0	224	502	10	87	4.7	.986	SS-156
1979		147	.241	.314	539	130	17	11	0	0.0	74	31	61	32	20	0	0	229	448	6	80	4.7	.991	SS-146
1980		147	.267	.322	540	144	16	4	2	0.4	57	39	24	28	21	0	0	225	449	17	70	4.7	.975	SS-147
1981		103	.283	.339	360	102	14	3	0	0.0	34	31	26	17	16	1	0	117	309	11	50	4.3	.975	SS-102
1982	CHI N	142	.246	.305	499	123	15	7	0	0.0	50	29	39	38	8	2	1	210	396	17	64	4.4	.973	SS-140
1983		147	.267	.339	499	133	20	5	2	0.4	73	43	35	30	7	4	1	230	464	11	102	4.9	.984	SS-145
1984		133	.223	.269	391	87	14	2	0	0.0	33	17	28	24	10	2	1	217	378	16	64	4.6	.974	SS-132
1985	2 teams CHI N (72G –.246) NY N (14G –.105)																							
″	total	86	.234	.304	214	50	7	4	0	0.0	15	15	13	22	5	3	0	109	210	11	39	4.2	.967	SS-75, 2B-4
16 yrs.		2247	.260	.320	8418	2191	262	99	15	0.2	987	525	474	569	318	12	3	3323	6864	211	1267	4.7	.980	SS-2222, 2B-5
DIVISIONAL PLAYOFF SERIES																								
1981	PHI N	5	.176	.235	17	3	1	0	0	0.0	0	1	0	0	0	0	0	12	9	1	0	4.4	.955	SS-5
LEAGUE CHAMPIONSHIP SERIES																								
1976	PHI N	3	.125	.250	8	1	1	0	0	0.0	1	1	3	0	0	0	0	2	11	0	1	4.3	1.000	SS-3
1977		4	.118	.118	17	2	0	0	0	0.0	2	1	1	0	0	0	0	0	17	0	2	4.3	1.000	SS-4
1978		4	.333	.333	18	6	0	0	0	0.0	2	0	1	2	0	0	0	5	16	0	4	5.3	1.000	SS-4
1980		5	.316	.316	19	6	0	0	0	0.0	2	0	3	3	1	0	0	4	11	1	4	3.2	.938	SS-5
1984	CHI N	5	.200	.267	15	3	1	0	0	0.0	1	1	1	0	0	0	0	8	15	0	6	4.6	1.000	SS-5
5 yrs.		21	.234	.260	77	18	2	0	0	0.0	8	3	9	5	1	0	0	19	70	1	17	4.3	.989	SS-21
WORLD SERIES																								
1980	PHI N	6	.375	.417	24	9	1	0	0	0.0	3	2	0	0	3	0	0	5	18	0	7	3.8	1.000	SS-6

Benny Bowcock

BOWCOCK, BENJAMIN JAMES
B. Oct. 28, 1879, Fall River, Mass. D. June 16, 1961, New Bedford, Mass.
BR TR 5′ 7″ 150 lbs.

Year	Team	Games	BA	SA	AB	H	2B	3B	HR	HR%	R	RBI	BB	SO	SB	Pinch Hit AB	Pinch Hit H	PO	A	E	DP	TC/G	FA	G by Pos
1903	STL A	14	.320	.480	50	16	3	1	1	2.0	7	10	3		1	0	0	22	32	7	4	4.4	.885	2B-14

Tim Bowden

BOWDEN, DAVID TIMON
B. Aug. 15, 1891, McDonough, Ga. D. Oct. 25, 1949, Emory, Ga.
BL TR 5′10″ 175 lbs.

Year	Team	Games	BA	SA	AB	H	2B	3B	HR	HR%	R	RBI	BB	SO	SB	Pinch Hit AB	Pinch Hit H	PO	A	E	DP	TC/G	FA	G by Pos
1914	STL A	7	.222	.222	9	2	0	0	0	0.0	0	0	1	6	0	3	1	4	0	0	0	1.0	1.000	OF-4

Chick Bowen

BOWEN, EMMONS JOSEPH
B. July 26, 1897, New Haven, Conn. D. Aug. 9, 1948, New Haven, Conn.
BR TR 5′ 7″ 165 lbs.

Year	Team	Games	BA	SA	AB	H	2B	3B	HR	HR%	R	RBI	BB	SO	SB	Pinch Hit AB	Pinch Hit H	PO	A	E	DP	TC/G	FA	G by Pos
1919	NY N	3	.200	.200	5	1	0	0	0	0.0	0	1	1	2	0	0	0	4	0	0	0	2.0	1.000	OF-2

Sam Bowen

BOWEN, SAMUEL THOMAS
B. Sept. 18, 1952, Brunswick, Ga.
BR TR 5′ 9″ 170 lbs.

Year	Team	Games	BA	SA	AB	H	2B	3B	HR	HR%	R	RBI	BB	SO	SB	Pinch Hit AB	Pinch Hit H	PO	A	E	DP	TC/G	FA	G by Pos
1977	BOS A	3	.000	.000	2	0	0	0	0	0.0	0	0	0	2	0	0	0	3	0	0	0	1.0	1.000	OF-3
1978		6	.143	.571	7	1	0	0	1	14.3	3	1	1	2	0	0	0	2	0	0	0	0.5	1.000	OF-4
1980		7	.154	.154	13	2	0	0	0	0.0	0	0	2	3	1	0	0	17	1	0	0	3.0	1.000	OF-6
3 yrs.		16	.136	.273	22	3	0	0	1	4.5	3	1	3	7	1	0	0	22	1	0	0	1.8	1.000	OF-13

Sam Bowens

BOWENS, SAMUEL EDWARD
B. Mar. 23, 1939, Wilmington, N. C.
BR TR 6′ 1½″ 188 lbs.

Year	Team	Games	BA	SA	AB	H	2B	3B	HR	HR%	R	RBI	BB	SO	SB	Pinch Hit AB	Pinch Hit H	PO	A	E	DP	TC/G	FA	G by Pos
1963	BAL A	15	.333	.500	48	16	3	1	1	2.1	8	9	4	5	1	2	0	20	0	1	0	1.6	.952	OF-13
1964		139	.263	.453	501	132	25	2	22	4.4	58	71	42	99	4	5	0	249	8	5	1	1.9	.981	OF-135
1965		84	.163	.296	203	33	4	1	7	3.4	16	20	10	41	7	13	2	108	3	2	1	1.7	.982	OF-68
1966		89	.210	.329	243	51	9	1	6	2.5	26	20	17	52	9	22	6	114	7	5	2	1.9	.960	OF-68
1967		62	.183	.342	120	22	2	1	5	4.2	13	12	11	43	3	26	6	41	2	1	0	1.4	.977	OF-32
1968	WAS A	57	.191	.330	115	22	4	0	4	3.5	14	7	11	39	0	29	6	42	2	2	0	1.7	.957	OF-27
1969		33	.193	.211	57	11	1	0	0	0.0	6	4	5	14	1	3	0	32	1	1	0	1.1	.971	OF-30
7 yrs.		479	.223	.375	1287	287	48	6	45	3.5	141	143	100	293	25	100	20	606	23	17	4	1.7	.974	OF-373

Frank Bowerman

BOWERMAN, FRANK EUGENE (Mike) BR TR 6′ 2″ 190 lbs.
B. Dec. 5, 1868, Romeo, Mich. D. Nov. 30, 1948, Romeo, Mich.
Manager 1909.

Year	Team	Games	BA	SA	AB	H	2B	3B	HR	HR%	R	RBI	BB	SO	SB	Pinch Hit AB	Pinch Hit H	PO	A	E	DP	TC/G	FA	G by Pos
1895	BAL N	1	.000	.000	1	0	0	0	0	0.0	0	0	0	0	0	0	0	2	0	0	0	2.0	1.000	C-1
1896		4	.125	.125	16	2	0	0	0	0.0	0	4	1	0	0	0	0	21	6	2	1	7.3	.931	C-3, 1B-1
1897		38	.315	.377	130	41	5	0	1	0.8	16	21	1		3	2	0	155	29	10	1	5.4	.948	C-36
1898	2 teams	BAL N (5G –.438)	PIT N (69G –.274)																					
″	total	74	.284	.335	257	73	7	3	0	0.0	22	30	9		5	2	0	300	86	18	14	5.6	.955	C-63, 1B-9
1899	PIT N	109	.259	.366	424	110	16	10	3	0.7	49	53	11		10	2	0	535	144	32	21	6.6	.955	C-79, 1B-28
1900	NY N	80	.241	.293	270	65	5	3	1	0.4	25	42	6		10	2	0	235	144	33	17	5.4	.920	C-75, SS-2
1901		59	.199	.257	191	38	5	3	0	0.0	20	14	7		3	4	1	281	95	24	6	7.1	.940	C-46, SS-3, 3B-3, 2B-3, 1B-1
1902		107	.253	.322	367	93	13	6	0	0.0	38	26	13		12	5	0	445	144	26	10	6.1	.958	C-98, 1B-3
1903		64	.276	.338	210	58	6	2	1	0.5	22	31	6		5	4	3	348	67	9	9	7.1	.979	C-55, 1B-4, OF-1
1904		93	.232	.318	289	67	11	4	2	0.7	38	27	16		7	3	0	495	103	13	14	6.7	.979	C-79, 1B-9, 2B-2, P-1
1905		98	.269	.333	297	80	8	1	3	1.0	37	41	12		6	7	3	528	76	13	12	6.9	.979	C-72, 1B-17, 2B-1
1906		103	.228	.284	285	65	7	3	1	0.4	23	42	15		5	5	2	477	92	8	10	6.6	.986	C-67, 1B-20
1907		96	.260	.299	311	81	8	2	0	0.0	31	32	17		11	5	1	606	79	6	14	7.6	.991	C-62, 1B-29
1908	BOS N	86	.228	.280	254	58	8	1	1	0.4	16	25	13		4	12	4	329	77	12	14	5.6	.971	C-63, 1B-11
1909		33	.212	.232	99	21	2	0	0	0.0	6	4	2		0	6	0	122	33	12	6	6.2	.928	C-27
15 yrs.		1045	.251	.314	3401	852	101	38	13	0.4	343	392	129	0	81	59	14	4879	1175	218	149	6.4	.965	C-826, 1B-132, 2B-6, SS-5, 3B-3, P-1, OF-1

Billy Bowers

BOWERS, GROVER BILL BL TR 5′ 9½″ 176 lbs.
B. Mar. 25, 1923, Parkin, Ark.

Year	Team	Games	BA	SA	AB	H	2B	3B	HR	HR%	R	RBI	BB	SO	SB	Pinch Hit AB	Pinch Hit H	PO	A	E	DP	TC/G	FA	G by Pos
1949	CHI A	26	.192	.244	78	15	2	1	0	0.0	5	6	4	5	1	6	0	46	2	1	0	2.5	.980	OF-20

Frank Bowes

BOWES, FRANK M. TR 5′ 9″ 160 lbs.
B. 1865, Bath, N. Y. D. Jan. 21, 1895, Brooklyn, N. Y.

Year	Team	Games	BA	SA	AB	H	2B	3B	HR	HR%	R	RBI	BB	SO	SB	Pinch Hit AB	Pinch Hit H	PO	A	E	DP	TC/G	FA	G by Pos
1890	BKN AA	61	.220	.259	232	51	5	2	0	0.0	28		7		11	0	0	164	67	35	8	4.3	.868	C-25, OF-19, 3B-13, 1B-3, SS-2

Jim Bowie

BOWIE, JIM BL TL 6′ 205 lbs.
B. Feb. 17, 1965, Tokyo, Japan.

Year	Team	Games	BA	SA	AB	H	2B	3B	HR	HR%	R	RBI	BB	SO	SB	Pinch Hit AB	Pinch Hit H	PO	A	E	DP	TC/G	FA	G by Pos
1994	OAK A	6	.214	.214	14	3	0	0	0	0.0	0	0	0	2	0	1	0	44	2	0	5	7.7	1.000	1B-6

Hoss Bowlin

BOWLIN, LOIS WELDON BR TR 5′ 9″ 155 lbs.
B. Dec. 10, 1940, Paragould, Ark.

Year	Team	Games	BA	SA	AB	H	2B	3B	HR	HR%	R	RBI	BB	SO	SB	Pinch Hit AB	Pinch Hit H	PO	A	E	DP	TC/G	FA	G by Pos
1967	KC A	2	.200	.200	5	1	0	0	0	0.0	0	0	0	0	0	0	0	0	4	0	0	2.0	1.000	3B-2

Steve Bowling

BOWLING, STEPHEN SHADDON BR TR 6′ 185 lbs.
B. June 26, 1952, Tulsa, Okla.

Year	Team	Games	BA	SA	AB	H	2B	3B	HR	HR%	R	RBI	BB	SO	SB	Pinch Hit AB	Pinch Hit H	PO	A	E	DP	TC/G	FA	G by Pos
1976	MIL A	14	.167	.214	42	7	2	0	0	0.0	4	2	2	5	0	1	0	38	1	1	1	2.9	.975	OF-13, DH-1
1977	TOR A	89	.206	.273	194	40	8	1	1	0.5	19	13	37	42	2	2	0	139	14	2	0	1.8	.987	OF-87
2 yrs.		103	.199	.263	236	47	10	1	1	0.4	23	15	39	47	2	3	0	177	15	3	1	1.9	.985	OF-100, DH-1

Bill Bowman

BOWMAN, WILLIAM GEORGE 5′11″ 180 lbs.
B. 1869, Chicago, Ill. Deceased.

Year	Team	Games	BA	SA	AB	H	2B	3B	HR	HR%	R	RBI	BB	SO	SB	Pinch Hit AB	Pinch Hit H	PO	A	E	DP	TC/G	FA	G by Pos
1891	CHI N	15	.089	.111	45	4	1	0	0	0.0	2	5	5	9	0	0	0	41	13	5	1	3.9	.915	C-15

Bob Bowman

BOWMAN, ROBERT LEROY BR TR 6′ 1″ 195 lbs.
B. May 10, 1931, Laytonville, Calif.

Year	Team	Games	BA	SA	AB	H	2B	3B	HR	HR%	R	RBI	BB	SO	SB	Pinch Hit AB	Pinch Hit H	PO	A	E	DP	TC/G	FA	G by Pos
1955	PHI N	3	.000	.000	3	0	0	0	0	0.0	0	0	0	0	0	0	0	3	0	0	0	1.5	1.000	OF-2
1956		6	.188	.500	16	3	0	1	1	6.3	2	2	0	6	0	1	0	5	0	1	0	1.2	.833	OF-5
1957		99	.266	.392	237	63	8	2	6	2.5	31	23	27	50	0	15	1	123	8	10	2	1.7	.929	OF-81
1958		91	.288	.500	184	53	11	2	8	4.3	31	24	16	30	0	31	13	82	1	1	0	1.5	.988	OF-57
1959		57	.127	.203	79	10	0	0	2	2.5	7	5	5	23	0	32	7	30	2	0	1	1.3	1.000	OF-20, P-5
5 yrs.		256	.249	.403	519	129	19	5	17	3.3	71	54	48	109	0	79	21	243	11	12	3	1.6	.955	OF-165, P-5

El Bowman

BOWMAN, ELMARI WILHELM (Big Bow) BR TR 6′½″ 193 lbs.
B. Mar. 19, 1897, Proctor, Vt. D. Dec. 17, 1985, Los Angeles, Calif.

Year	Team	Games	BA	SA	AB	H	2B	3B	HR	HR%	R	RBI	BB	SO	SB	Pinch Hit AB	Pinch Hit H	PO	A	E	DP	TC/G	FA	G by Pos
1920	WAS A	2	.000	.000	1	0	0	0	0	0.0	1	0	1	0	0	1	0	0	0	0	0	0.0	—	

Ernie Bowman

BOWMAN, ERNEST FERRELL BR TR 5′10″ 160 lbs.
B. July 28, 1935, Johnson City, Tenn.

Year	Team	Games	BA	SA	AB	H	2B	3B	HR	HR%	R	RBI	BB	SO	SB	Pinch Hit AB	Pinch Hit H	PO	A	E	DP	TC/G	FA	G by Pos
1961	SF N	38	.211	.316	38	8	0	2	0	0.0	10	2	1	8	2	3	1	19	32	5	3	1.8	.911	2B-13, SS-12, 3B-7
1962		46	.190	.286	42	8	1	0	1	2.4	9	4	1	10	0	3	0	22	30	0	2	1.4	1.000	2B-17, 3B-11, SS-10
1963		81	.184	.208	125	23	3	0	0	0.0	10	4	0	15	1	1	0	70	101	8	17	2.3	.955	SS-40, 2B-26, 3B-12
3 yrs.		165	.190	.244	205	39	4	2	1	0.5	29	10	2	33	3	7	1	111	163	13	22	1.9	.955	SS-62, 2B-56, 3B-30
WORLD SERIES																								
1962	SF N	2	.000	.000	1	0	0	0	0	0.0	1	0	0	0	0	0	0	0	5	0	0	5.0	1.000	SS-1

Joe Bowman

BOWMAN, JOSEPH EMIL BL TR 6′ 2″ 190 lbs.
B. June 17, 1910, Argentine, Kans. D. Nov. 22, 1990, Kansas City, Mo.

Year	Team	Games	BA	SA	AB	H	2B	3B	HR	HR%	R	RBI	BB	SO	SB	Pinch Hit AB	Pinch Hit H	PO	A	E	DP	TC/G	FA	G by Pos
1932	PHI A	7	1.000	1.000	1	1	0	0	0	0.0	0	0	0	0	0	0	0	1	6	1	0	1.1	.875	P-7
1934	NY N	31	.172	.241	29	5	0	1	0	0.0	4	4	2	3	0	0	0	6	20	0	0	0.9	1.000	P-30
1935	PHI N	49	.194	.284	67	13	1	1	1	1.5	6	7	4	7	1	13	3	9	28	2	2	1.1	.949	P-33, OF-1
1936		44	.195	.208	77	15	1	0	0	0.0	9	6	6	14	0	4	2	7	32	5	4	1.1	.886	P-40
1937	PIT N	35	.213	.234	47	10	1	0	0	0.0	3	4	5	9	0	2	0	14	24	0	3	1.3	1.000	P-30
1938		18	.333	.429	21	7	0	1	0	0.0	5	1	1	3	0	0	0	2	8	1	2	0.6	.909	P-17
1939		70	.344	.448	96	33	8	1	0	0.0	9	18	5	9	0	29	6	6	39	0	3	1.2	1.000	P-37
1940		57	.244	.356	90	22	5	1	1	1.1	11	14	14	14	0	17	4	15	36	1	0	1.6	.981	P-32

Joe Bowman *continued*

Year	Team	Games	BA	SA	AB	H	2B	3B	HR	HR%	R	RBI	BB	SO	SB	Pinch Hit AB	Pinch Hit H	PO	A	E	DP	TC/G	FA	G by Pos
1941		22	.258	.290	31	8	1	0	0	0.0	4	1	1	2	0	4	1	5	13	0	0	1.0	1.000	P-18
1944	BOS A	59	.200	.290	100	20	5	2	0	0.0	7	16	5	19	1	31	7	9	20	2	3	1.2	.935	P-26
1945	2 teams	BOS A (9G –.222)	CIN N (29G –.070)																					
"	total	38	.087	.138	80	7	2	1	0	0.0	4	4	3	10	1	9	1	12	28	3	0	1.5	.930	P-28
11 yrs.		430	.221	.293	639	141	24	8	2	0.3	62	75	46	90	3	109	24	86	254	15	17	1.2	.958	P-298, OF-1

Red Bowser

BOWSER, JAMES HARVEY
B. Sept. 20, 1881, Freeport, Pa. D. May 22, 1943, Moundsville, W. Va.

Year	Team	Games	BA	SA	AB	H	2B	3B	HR	HR%	R	RBI	BB	SO	SB	Pinch Hit AB	Pinch Hit H	PO	A	E	DP	TC/G	FA	G by Pos
1910	CHI A	1	.000	.000	2	0	0	0	0	0.0	0	0	0		0	0	0	0	0	0	0	0.0	.000	OF-1

Bob Boyd

BOYD, ROBERT RICHARD (The Rope)
B. Oct. 1, 1925, Potts Camp, Miss.
BL TL 5′10″ 170 lbs.

Year	Team	Games	BA	SA	AB	H	2B	3B	HR	HR%	R	RBI	BB	SO	SB	Pinch Hit AB	Pinch Hit H	PO	A	E	DP	TC/G	FA	G by Pos
1951	CHI A	12	.167	.278	18	3	0	1	0	0.0	3	4	3	3	0	5	1	36	1	0	8	6.2	1.000	1B-6
1953		55	.297	.412	165	49	6	2	3	1.8	20	23	13	11	1	8	4	301	16	1	25	7.1	.997	1B-29, OF-16
1954		29	.179	.232	56	10	3	0	0	0.0	10	5	4	3	2	2	0	71	3	2	3	3.0	.974	OF-13, 1B-12
1956	BAL A	70	.311	.400	225	70	8	3	2	0.9	28	11	30	14	0	10	3	474	24	5	46	7.4	.990	1B-60, OF-8
1957		141	.318	.408	485	154	16	8	4	0.8	73	34	55	31	2	15	6	1073	70	10	107	8.7	.991	1B-132, OF-1
1958		125	.309	.439	401	124	21	5	7	1.7	58	36	25	24	1	32	4	757	53	5	85	8.2	.994	1B-99
1959		128	.265	.345	415	110	20	2	3	0.7	42	41	29	14	3	20	4	927	46	15	88	9.1	.985	1B-109
1960		71	.317	.427	82	26	5	2	0	0.0	9	9	6	5	0	56	17	64	4	0	9	4.0	1.000	1B-17
1961	2 teams	KC A (26G –.229)	MIL N (36G –.244)																					
"	total	62	.236	.258	89	21	2	0	0	0.0	10	12	2	9	0	49	9	64	7	0	7	6.5	1.000	1B-11
9 yrs.		693	.293	.388	1936	567	81	23	19	1.0	253	175	167	114	9	197	48	3767	224	38	378	7.9	.991	1B-475, OF-38

Frank Boyd

BOYD, FRANK JAY
B. Apr. 2, 1868, West Middletown, Pa. D. Dec. 16, 1937, Oil City, Pa.
BR TR

Year	Team	Games	BA	SA	AB	H	2B	3B	HR	HR%	R	RBI	BB	SO	SB	Pinch Hit AB	Pinch Hit H	PO	A	E	DP	TC/G	FA	G by Pos
1893	CLE N	2	.200	.400	5	1	1	0	0	0.0	3	3	1	0	0	0	0	2	2	0	0	2.0	1.000	C-2

Jake Boyd

BOYD, JACOB HENRY
B. Jan. 19, 1874, Martinsburg, W. Va. D. Aug. 12, 1932, Gettysburg, Pa.
TL 160 lbs.

Year	Team	Games	BA	SA	AB	H	2B	3B	HR	HR%	R	RBI	BB	SO	SB	Pinch Hit AB	Pinch Hit H	PO	A	E	DP	TC/G	FA	G by Pos
1894	WAS N	6	.143	.143	21	3	0	0	0	0.0	1	1	1	4	2	0	0	4	8	2	0	2.3	.857	OF-3, P-3
1895		51	.268	.331	157	42	5	1	1	0.6	29	16	20	28	2	0	0	50	55	24	5	2.4	.814	OF-21, P-14, 2B-10, SS-8, 3B-1
1896		4	.077	.077	13	1	0	0	0	0.0	1	1	1	1	0	0	0	1	9	1	0	2.8	.909	P-4
3 yrs.		61	.241	.293	191	46	5	1	1	0.5	31	18	22	33	4	0	0	55	72	27	5	2.4	.825	OF-24, P-21, 2B-10, SS-8, 3B-1

Clete Boyer

BOYER, CLETIS LEROY
Brother of Ken Boyer. Brother of Cloyd Boyer.
B. Feb. 8, 1937, Cassville, Mo.
BR TR 6′ 165 lbs.

Year	Team	Games	BA	SA	AB	H	2B	3B	HR	HR%	R	RBI	BB	SO	SB	Pinch Hit AB	Pinch Hit H	PO	A	E	DP	TC/G	FA	G by Pos
1955	KC A	47	.241	.253	79	19	1	0	0	0.0	3	6	3	17	0	9	0	32	41	3	6	2.3	.961	SS-12, 3B-11, 2B-10
1956		67	.217	.279	129	28	3	1	1	0.8	15	4	11	24	1	5	1	100	124	6	34	4.0	.974	2B-51, 3B-7
1957		10	—	—	0	0	0	0	0	—	0	0	0	0	0	0	0	0	0	0	0	0.0		3B-1, 2B-1
1959	NY A	47	.175	.193	114	20	2	0	0	0.0	4	3	6	23	1	6	0	49	90	2	14	3.4	.986	SS-26, 3B-16
1960		124	.242	.405	393	95	20	1	14	3.6	54	46	23	85	2	2	0	157	297	17	44	3.6	.964	3B-99, SS-33
1961		148	.224	.347	504	113	19	5	11	2.2	61	55	63	83	1	0	0	170	373	17	41	3.6	.970	3B-141, SS-12, OF-1
1962		158	.272	.413	566	154	24	1	18	3.2	85	68	51	106	3	0	0	187	396	22	41	3.9	.964	3B-157
1963		152	.251	.363	557	140	20	3	12	2.2	59	54	33	91	4	0	0	184	344	25	40	3.7	.955	3B-141, SS-9, 2B-1
1964		147	.218	.304	510	111	10	5	8	1.6	43	52	36	93	6	3	0	164	339	16	41	3.6	.969	3B-123, SS-21
1965		148	.251	.424	514	129	23	6	18	3.5	69	58	39	79	4	1	0	137	354	16	46	3.4	.968	3B-147, SS-2
1966		144	.240	.384	500	120	22	4	14	2.8	59	57	46	48	6	0	0	201	396	18	38	4.3	.971	3B-85, SS-59
1967	ATL N	154	.245	.423	572	140	18	3	26	4.5	63	96	39	81	6	2	0	177	309	15	35	3.2	.970	3B-150, SS-6
1968		71	.227	.311	273	62	7	2	4	1.5	19	17	16	32	2	2	0	74	135	4	17	3.1	.981	3B-69
1969		144	.250	.371	496	124	16	1	14	2.8	57	57	55	87	3	3	0	139	275	15	18	3.0	.965	3B-141
1970		134	.246	.381	475	117	14	1	16	3.4	44	62	41	71	2	2	1	113	280	19	22	3.1	.954	3B-126, SS-5
1971		30	.245	.439	98	24	1	0	6	6.1	10	19	8	11	0	3	1	18	57	3	6	3.0	.962	3B-25, SS-1
16 yrs.		1725	.242	.372	5780	1396	200	33	162	2.8	645	654	470	931	41	38	3	1902	3810	198	443	3.5	.966	3B-1439, SS-186, 2B-63, OF-1
LEAGUE CHAMPIONSHIP SERIES																								
1969	ATL N	3	.111	.111	9	1	0	0	0	0.0	0	3	2	3	0	0	0	4	8	1	1	4.3	.923	3B-3
WORLD SERIES																								
1960	NY A	4	.250	.583	12	3	2	1	0	0.0	1	1	0	1	0	0	0	0	8	0	2	1.6	1.000	3B-4, SS-1
1961		5	.267	.400	15	4	2	0	0	0.0	0	3	4	0	0	0	0	6	12	1	0	3.8	.947	3B-5
1962		7	.318	.500	22	7	1	0	1	4.5	2	4	1	3	0	0	0	9	16	2	2	3.9	.926	3B-7
1963		4	.077	.077	13	1	0	0	0	0.0	0	0	1	6	0	0	0	2	8	0	0	2.5	1.000	3B-4
1964		7	.208	.375	24	5	1	0	1	4.2	2	3	1	5	1	0	0	5	22	2	0	4.1	.931	3B-7
5 yrs.		27	.233	.395	86	20	6	1	2	2.3	5	11	7	15	1	0	0	22	66	5	4	3.3	.946	3B-27, SS-1

Ken Boyer

BOYER, KENTON LLOYD
Brother of Cloyd Boyer. Brother of Clete Boyer.
B. May 20, 1931, Liberty, Mo. D. Sept. 7, 1982, St. Louis, Mo.
Manager 1978–80.
BR TR 6′ 1½″ 190 lbs.

Year	Team	Games	BA	SA	AB	H	2B	3B	HR	HR%	R	RBI	BB	SO	SB	Pinch Hit AB	Pinch Hit H	PO	A	E	DP	TC/G	FA	G by Pos
1955	STL N	147	.264	.425	530	140	27	2	18	3.4	78	62	37	67	22	1	0	155	295	21	34	3.0	.955	3B-139, SS-18
1956		150	.306	.494	595	182	30	2	26	4.4	91	98	38	65	8	1	0	130	309	18	37	3.1	.961	3B-149
1957		142	.265	.414	544	144	18	3	19	3.5	79	62	44	77	12	1	0	316	95	14	8	2.9	.967	OF-105, 3B-41
1958		150	.307	.496	570	175	21	9	23	4.0	101	90	49	53	11	1	0	168	350	20	41	3.6	.963	3B-144, OF-6, SS-1
1959		149	.309	.508	563	174	18	5	28	5.0	86	94	67	77	12	1	0	143	310	22	33	3.1	.954	3B-143, SS-12
1960		151	.304	.562	552	168	26	10	32	5.8	95	97	56	77	8	5	1	140	300	19	37	3.1	.959	3B-146
1961		153	.329	.533	589	194	26	11	24	4.1	109	95	68	91	6	0	0	117	346	24	23	3.2	.951	3B-153
1962		160	.291	.470	611	178	27	5	24	3.9	92	98	75	104	12	0	0	158	318	22	34	3.1	.956	3B-160

Ken Boyer *continued*

Year	Team	Games	BA	SA	AB	H	2B	3B	HR	HR%	R	RBI	BB	SO	SB	Pinch Hit AB	Pinch Hit H	PO	A	E	DP	TC/G	FA	G by Pos
1963		159	.285	.454	617	176	28	2	24	3.9	86	111	70	90	1	0	0	129	293	34	23	2.9	.925	3B-159
1964		162	.295	.489	628	185	30	10	24	3.8	100	**119**	70	85	3	0	0	131	337	24	30	3.0	.951	3B-162
1965		144	.260	.374	535	139	18	2	13	2.4	71	75	57	73	2	3	0	113	250	12	18	2.6	.968	3B-143
1966	NY N	136	.266	.415	496	132	28	2	14	2.8	62	61	30	64	4	7	3	125	294	21	34	3.3	.952	3B-130, 1B-2
1967	2 teams	NY N (56G –.235) CHI A (57G –.261)																						
"	total	113	.249	.361	346	86	12	3	7	2.0	34	34	33	47	2	15	4	233	166	11	28	4.0	.973	3B-77, 1B-26
1968	2 teams	CHI A (10G –.125) LA N (83G –.271)																						
"	total	93	.257	.376	245	63	7	2	6	2.4	20	41	17	40	2	29	6	287	72	11	31	5.1	.970	3B-39, 1B-33
1969	LA N	25	.206	.265	34	7	2	0	0	0.0	0	4	2	7	0	19	4	31	2	1	6	8.5	.971	1B-4
15 yrs.		2034	.287	.462	7455	2143	318	68	282	3.8	1104	1141	713	1017	105	83	18	2376	3737	274	417	3.2	.957	3B-1785, OF-111, 1B-65, SS-31
WORLD SERIES																								
1964	STL N	7	.222	.481	27	6	1	0	2	7.4	5	6	1	5	0	0	0	9	16	1	0	3.7	.962	3B-7

Doe Boyland

BOYLAND, DORIAN SCOTT
B. Jan. 6, 1955, Chicago, Ill.

BL TL 6′ 4″ 200 lbs.

Year	Team	Games	BA	SA	AB	H	2B	3B	HR	HR%	R	RBI	BB	SO	SB	Pinch Hit AB	Pinch Hit H	PO	A	E	DP	TC/G	FA	G by Pos
1978	PIT N	6	.250	.250	8	2	0	0	0	0.0	1	1	0	1	0	5	1	8	0	0	0	8.0	1.000	1B-1
1979		4	.000	.000	3	0	0	0	0	0.0	0	0	0	2	0	3	0	0	0	0	0	0.0	—	
1981		11	.000	.000	8	0	0	0	0	0.0	0	0	1	3	0	8	0	0	0	0	0	0.0	—	
3 yrs.		21	.105	.105	19	2	0	0	0	0.0	1	1	1	6	0	16	1	8	0	0	0	8.0	1.000	1B-1

Buzz Boyle

BOYLE, RALPH FRANCIS
Brother of Jim Boyle.
B. Feb. 9, 1908, Cincinnati, Ohio D. Nov. 12, 1978, Cincinnati, Ohio.

BL TL 5′11½″ 170 lbs.

Year	Team	Games	BA	SA	AB	H	2B	3B	HR	HR%	R	RBI	BB	SO	SB	Pinch Hit AB	Pinch Hit H	PO	A	E	DP	TC/G	FA	G by Pos
1929	BOS N	17	.263	.386	57	15	2	1	1	1.8	8	2	6	11	2	0	0	32	1	0	0	1.9	1.000	OF-17
1930		1	.000	.000	1	0	0	0	0	0.0	0	0	0	1	0	0	0	0	0	0	0	0.0	.000	OF-1
1933	BKN N	93	.299	.361	338	101	13	4	0	0.0	38	31	16	24	7	3	1	195	2	5	0	2.2	.975	OF-90
1934		128	.305	.447	472	144	26	10	7	1.5	88	48	51	44	8	6	2	275	20	9	1	2.5	.970	OF-121
1935		127	.272	.371	475	129	17	9	4	0.8	51	44	43	45	7	2	0	244	18	10	5	2.2	.963	OF-124
5 yrs.		366	.290	.395	1343	389	58	24	12	0.9	185	125	116	125	24	11	3	746	41	24	6	2.3	.970	OF-353

Eddie Boyle

BOYLE, EDWARD J.
Brother of Jack Boyle.
B. May 8, 1874, Cincinnati, Ohio D. Feb. 9, 1941, Cincinnati, Ohio.

BR TR 6′ 3″ 200 lbs.

Year	Team	Games	BA	SA	AB	H	2B	3B	HR	HR%	R	RBI	BB	SO	SB	Pinch Hit AB	Pinch Hit H	PO	A	E	DP	TC/G	FA	G by Pos
1896	2 teams	LOU N (3G –.000) PIT N (2G –.000)																						
"	total	5	.000	.000	14	0	0	0	0	0.0	0	0	2	3	0	0	0	16	4	2	0	4.4	.909	C-5

Henry Boyle

BOYLE, HENRY J. (Handsome Henry)
B. Sept. 20, 1860, Philadelphia, Pa. D. May 25, 1932, Philadelphia, Pa.

TR

Year	Team	Games	BA	SA	AB	H	2B	3B	HR	HR%	R	RBI	BB	SO	SB	Pinch Hit AB	Pinch Hit H	PO	A	E	DP	TC/G	FA	G by Pos
1884	STL U	65	.260	.366	262	68	10	3	4	1.5	41		9			0	0	85	49	19	7	2.2	.876	OF-43, P-19, 3B-4, SS-1, 1B-1, 2B-1
1885	STL N	72	.202	.256	258	52	9	1	1	0.4	24	21	13	38		0	0	94	76	19	4	2.5	.899	P-42, OF-31, 2B-2
1886		30	.250	.333	108	27	2	2	1	0.9	8	13	5	19		0	0	18	39	9	1	2.1	.864	P-25, OF-6
1887	IND N	41	.191	.312	141	27	9	1	2	1.4	17	13	9	18	2	0	0	12	42	10	2	1.5	.844	P-38, OF-4
1888		37	.144	.184	125	18	2	0	1	0.8	13	6	6	31	1	0	0	14	84	7	1	2.8	.933	P-37, 1B-1
1889		46	.245	.329	155	38	10	0	1	0.6	17	17	9	23	4	0	0	17	51	3	0	1.5	.958	P-46, 3B-1
6 yrs.		291	.219	.301	1049	230	42	7	10	1.0	120	70	51	129	7	0	0	240	341	67	15	2.1	.897	P-207, OF-84, 3B-5, 2B-3, 1B-2, SS-1

Jack Boyle

BOYLE, JOHN ANTHONY (Honest Jack)
Brother of Eddie Boyle.
B. Mar. 22, 1866, Cincinnati, Ohio D. Jan. 7, 1913, Cincinnati, Ohio.

BR TR 6′ 4″ 190 lbs.

Year	Team	Games	BA	SA	AB	H	2B	3B	HR	HR%	R	RBI	BB	SO	SB	Pinch Hit AB	Pinch Hit H	PO	A	E	DP	TC/G	FA	G by Pos
1886	CIN AA	1	.200	.200	5	1	0	0	0	0.0	0		0			0	0	8	2	3	0	13.0	.769	C-1
1887	STL AA	88	.189	.220	350	66	3	1	2	0.6	48		20		7	0	0	352	116	57	8	5.8	.891	C-86, OF-2, 1B-2, 3B-1
1888		71	.241	.292	257	62	8	1	1	0.4	33	23	13		11	0	0	382	123	37	11	7.6	.932	C-70, OF-1
1889		99	.245	.334	347	85	11	4	4	1.2	54	42	21	42	5	0	0	409	135	33	14	5.7	.943	C-80, 3B-12, OF-5, 1B-4, 2B-1
1890	CHI P	100	.260	.320	369	96	9	5	1	0.3	56	49	44	29	11	0	0	335	154	61	16	5.2	.889	C-50, 3B-30, SS-16, 1B-7, OF-2
1891	STL AA	121	.281	.394	434	122	18	8	5	1.2	76	79	44	35	18	0	0	494	161	53	17	5.4	.925	C-91, SS-25, 3B-7, 2B-3, OF-3, 1B-3
1892	NY N	120	.183	.239	436	80	8	8	0	0.0	52	32	36	40	10	0	0	787	152	60	34	8.1	.940	C-79, 1B-40, SS-2, OF-2
1893	PHI N	116	.286	.403	504	144	29	9	4	0.8	105	81	41	30	22	0	0	1085	82	15	71	9.9	.987	1B-112, C-6, 2B-2
1894		114	.301	.408	495	149	21	10	4	0.8	98	88	45	26	21	0	0	952	63	19	76	8.9	.982	1B-114, 3B-1, 2B-1
1895		133	.253	.297	**565**	143	17	4	0	0.0	90	67	35	23	13	0	0	1245	61	36	69	10.1	.973	1B-133
1896		40	.297	.359	145	43	4	1	1	0.7	17	28	6	7	3	0	0	196	22	12	10	5.8	.948	C-28, 1B-12
1897		75	.253	.313	288	73	9	1	2	0.7	37	36	19		3	2	1	373	51	12	10	5.9	.972	1B-50, C-24
1898		6	.091	.182	22	2	0	1	0	0.0	0	3	1		0	0	0	40	6	6	3	7.4	.885	1B-4, C-3
13 yrs.		1084	.253	.327	4217	1066	137	53	24	0.6	666	528	325	232	124	2	1	6658	1128	404	339	7.3	.951	C-518, 1B-481, 3B-51, SS-43, OF-15, 2B-7

Jack Boyle

BOYLE, JOHN BELLEW
B. July 9, 1889, Morris, Ill. D. Apr. 3, 1971, Ft. Lauderdale, Fla.

BL TR 5′11½″ 165 lbs.

Year	Team	Games	BA	SA	AB	H	2B	3B	HR	HR%	R	RBI	BB	SO	SB	Pinch Hit AB	Pinch Hit H	PO	A	E	DP	TC/G	FA	G by Pos
1912	PHI N	15	.280	.320	25	7	1	0	0	0.0	4	2	1	5	0	5	2	6	23	2	2	3.9	.935	3B-6, SS-2

Jim Boyle

BOYLE, JAMES JOHN
Brother of Buzz Boyle.
B. Jan. 19, 1904, Cincinnati, Ohio D. Dec. 24, 1958, Cincinnati, Ohio.

BR TR 6′ 180 lbs.

Year	Team	Games	BA	SA	AB	H	2B	3B	HR	HR%	R	RBI	BB	SO	SB	Pinch Hit AB	Pinch Hit H	PO	A	E	DP	TC/G	FA	G by Pos
1926	NY N	1	—	—	0	0	0	0	0	—	0	0	0	0	0	0	0	0	0	0	0	0.0	.000	C-1

Gib Brack

BRACK, GILBERT HERMAN (Gibby)
B. Mar. 29, 1908, Chicago, Ill. D. Jan. 20, 1960, Greenville, Tex.
BR TR 5′ 9″ 170 lbs.

Year	Team	Games	BA	SA	AB	H	2B	3B	HR	HR%	R	RBI	BB	SO	SB	Pinch Hit AB	Pinch Hit H	PO	A	E	DP	TC/G	FA	G by Pos
1937	BKN N	112	.274	.435	372	102	27	9	5	1.3	60	38	44	93	9	6	1	208	10	7	0	2.2	.969	OF-101
1938	2 teams	BKN N (40G –.214) PHI N (72G –.287)																						
″	total	112	.275	.414	338	93	22	5	5	1.5	50	34	22	44	3	14	6	182	8	6	3	2.4	.969	OF-81
1939	PHI N	91	.289	.463	270	78	21	4	6	2.2	40	41	26	49	1	19	5	247	11	8	12	4.0	.970	OF-48, 1B-19
3 yrs.		315	.279	.436	980	273	70	18	16	1.6	150	113	92	186	13	39	12	637	29	21	15	2.8	.969	OF-230, 1B-19

Buddy Bradford

BRADFORD, CHARLES WILLIAM
B. July 25, 1944, Mobile, Ala.
BR TR 5′11″ 170 lbs.

Year	Team	Games	BA	SA	AB	H	2B	3B	HR	HR%	R	RBI	BB	SO	SB	Pinch Hit AB	Pinch Hit H	PO	A	E	DP	TC/G	FA	G by Pos
1966	CHI A	14	.143	.143	28	4	0	0	0	0.0	3	0	2	6	0	0	0	5	0	1	0	0.7	.833	OF-9
1967		24	.100	.150	20	2	1	0	0	0.0	6	1	1	7	1	3	1	9	0	1	0	0.7	.900	OF-14
1968		103	.217	.310	281	61	11	0	5	1.8	32	24	23	67	8	6	1	162	4	6	0	1.7	.965	OF-99
1969		93	.256	.421	273	70	8	2	11	4.0	36	27	34	75	5	5	0	141	5	6	1	1.7	.961	OF-88
1970	2 teams	CHI A (32G –.187) CLE A (75G –.196)																						
″	total	107	.193	.343	254	49	9	1	9	3.5	33	31	31	73	1	18	3	163	2	3	0	1.8	.982	OF-91, 3B-1
1971	2 teams	CLE A (20G –.158) CIN N (79G –.200)																						
″	total	99	.188	.283	138	26	5	1	2	1.4	21	15	20	33	4	14	2	106	3	4	1	1.3	.965	OF-84
1972	CHI A	35	.271	.438	48	13	2	0	2	4.2	13	8	4	13	3	10	4	32	1	0	0	1.2	1.000	OF-28
1973		53	.238	.411	168	40	3	1	8	4.8	24	15	17	43	4	5	0	114	9	1	2	2.4	.992	OF-51
1974		39	.333	.510	96	32	2	0	5	5.2	16	10	13	11	1	7	2	47	2	1	0	1.5	.980	OF-32, DH-1
1975	2 teams	CHI A (25G –.155) STL N (50G –.272)																						
″	total	75	.223	.396	139	31	4	1	6	4.3	20	30	20	46	3	27	6	69	2	4	0	1.6	.947	OF-43, DH-4
1976	CHI A	55	.219	.350	160	35	5	2	4	2.5	20	14	19	37	6	9	0	91	0	2	0	1.8	.978	OF-48, DH-3
11 yrs.		697	.226	.364	1605	363	50	8	52	3.2	224	175	184	411	36	104	19	939	28	29	4	1.7	.971	OF-587, DH-8, 3B-1

Vic Bradford

BRADFORD, HENRY VICTOR
B. Mar. 5, 1915, Brownsville, Tenn.
BR TR 6′ 2″ 190 lbs.

Year	Team	Games	BA	SA	AB	H	2B	3B	HR	HR%	R	RBI	BB	SO	SB	Pinch Hit AB	Pinch Hit H	PO	A	E	DP	TC/G	FA	G by Pos
1943	NY N	6	.200	.200	5	1	0	0	0	0.0	1	1	1	1	0	1	0	3	0	0	0	3.0	1.000	OF-1

Al Bradley

BRADLEY, AL
Deceased.
5′10″ 185 lbs.

Year	Team	Games	BA	SA	AB	H	2B	3B	HR	HR%	R	RBI	BB	SO	SB	Pinch Hit AB	Pinch Hit H	PO	A	E	DP	TC/G	FA	G by Pos
1884	WAS U	1	.000	.000	3	0	0	0	0	0.0	0		2			0	0	3	0	0	0	3.0	1.000	OF-1

Bill Bradley

BRADLEY, WILLIAM JOSEPH
B. Feb. 13, 1878, Cleveland, Ohio D. Mar. 11, 1954, Cleveland, Ohio.
Manager 1905, 1914.
BR TR 6′ 185 lbs.

Year	Team	Games	BA	SA	AB	H	2B	3B	HR	HR%	R	RBI	BB	SO	SB	Pinch Hit AB	Pinch Hit H	PO	A	E	DP	TC/G	FA	G by Pos
1899	CHI N	35	.310	.419	129	40	6	1	2	1.6	26	18	12		4	0	0	61	82	23	8	4.7	.861	3B-30, SS-5
1900		122	.282	.399	444	125	21	8	5	1.1	63	49	27		14	1	1	292	304	63	21	5.4	.904	3B-106, 1B-15
1901	CLE A	133	.293	.403	516	151	28	13	1	0.2	95	55	26		15	0	0	192	298	37	25	3.9	.930	3B-133, P-1
1902		137	.340	.515	550	187	39	12	11	2.0	104	77	27		11	0	0	188	324	43	21	4.1	.923	3B-137
1903		137	.315	.495	543	171	36	22	6	1.1	103	68	25		21	0	0	151	299	37	18	3.6	.924	3B-137
1904		154	.300	.402	607	182	31	8	5	0.8	94	83	26		27	0	0	178	308	23	18	3.3	.955	3B-154
1905		145	.268	.354	537	144	34	6	0	0.0	63	51	27		22	0	0	187	312	29	17	3.6	.945	3B-145
1906		82	.275	.358	302	83	15	2	2	0.7	32	25	18		13	0	0	107	177	10	6	3.6	.966	3B-82
1907		139	.223	.267	498	111	20	1	0	0.0	48	34	35		20	0	0	164	278	29	18	3.4	.938	3B-139
1908		148	.243	.318	548	133	24	7	1	0.2	70	46	29		18	0	0	192	296	30	16	3.5	.942	3B-116, SS-32
1909		95	.186	.222	334	62	6	3	0	0.0	30	22	19		8	2	1	126	162	13	17	3.2	.957	3B-87, 2B-3, 1B-3
1910		61	.196	.210	214	42	3	0	0	0.0	12	12	10		6	0	0	89	126	10	8	3.7	.956	3B-61
1914	BKN F	7	.500	.667	6	3	1	0	0	0.0	1	3	0		0	6	3	0	0	0	0	0.0	—	
1915	KC F	66	.187	.241	203	38	9	1	0	0.0	15	9	9		6	5	0	55	95	8	4	2.6	.949	3B-61
14 yrs.		1461	.271	.370	5431	1472	273	84	33	0.6	756	552	290		185	14	5	1982	3061	355	197	3.7	.934	3B-1388, SS-37, 1B-18, 2B-3, P-1

George Bradley

BRADLEY, GEORGE WASHINGTON
B. Apr. 1, 1914, Greenwood, Ark. D. Oct. 19, 1982, Lawrenceburg, Tenn.
BR TR 6′ 1½″ 185 lbs.

Year	Team	Games	BA	SA	AB	H	2B	3B	HR	HR%	R	RBI	BB	SO	SB	Pinch Hit AB	Pinch Hit H	PO	A	E	DP	TC/G	FA	G by Pos
1946	STL A	4	.167	.250	12	2	1	0	0	0.0	2	3	0	1	0	0	0	5	0	0	0	1.7	1.000	OF-3

George Bradley

BRADLEY, GEORGE WASHINGTON (Grin)
B. July 13, 1852, Reading, Pa. D. Oct. 2, 1931, Philadelphia, Pa.
BR TR 5′10½″ 175 lbs.

Year	Team	Games	BA	SA	AB	H	2B	3B	HR	HR%	R	RBI	BB	SO	SB	Pinch Hit AB	Pinch Hit H	PO	A	E	DP	TC/G	FA	G by Pos
1876	STL N	64	.249	.321	265	66	7	6	0	0.0	29	28	3	12		0	0	50	87	12	4	2.3	.919	P-64
1877	CHI N	55	.243	.304	214	52	7	3	0	0.0	31	12	6	19		0	0	48	89	18	2	2.2	.884	P-50, 3B-16, 1B-3, OF-1
1879	TRO N	63	.247	.323	251	62	9	5	0	0.0	36	23	1	20		0	0	62	154	33	1	3.9	.867	P-54, 3B-5, 1B-3, SS-1, OF-1
1880	PRO N	82	.227	.288	309	70	7	6	0	0.0	32	23	5	38		0	0	104	214	55	10	4.0	.853	3B-57, P-28, OF-7, 1B-2
1881	2 teams	DET N (1G –.000) CLE N (60G –.249)																						
″	total	61	.245	.318	245	60	10	1	2	0.8	21	18	4	25		0	0	89	106	39	9	3.8	.833	3B-48, SS-7, P-6, OF-1
1882	CLE N	30	.183	.226	115	21	5	0	0	0.0	16	6	4	16		0	0	82	47	13	8	4.3	.908	P-18, OF-9, 1B-6
1883	2 teams	CLE N (4G –.313) PHI AA (76G –.234)																						
″	total	80	.238	.308	328	78	8	6	1	0.3	47		8	1		0	0	92	160	68	10	3.7	.788	3B-44, P-26, OF-11, SS-4, 1B-2
1884	CIN U	58	.190	.270	226	43	4	7	0	0.0	31		7			0	0	82	94	24	4	3.1	.880	P-41, OF-16, SS-5, 1B-2
1886	PHI AA	13	.083	.125	48	4	0	1	0	0.0	1		1			0	0	14	48	11	2	5.6	.849	SS-13
1888	BAL AA	1	.000	.000	3	0	0	0	0	0.0	0	0	0		0	0	0	2	1	2	0	5.0	.600	SS-1
10 yrs.		507	.228	.295	2004	456	57	35	3	0.1	244	110	39	131	0	0	0	625	1000	275	50	3.4	.855	P-287, 3B-170, OF-46, SS-31, 1B-18

Hugh Bradley

BRADLEY, HUGH FREDERICK (Corns)
B. May 23, 1885, Grafton, Mass. D. Jan. 26, 1949, Worcester, Mass.
BR TR 5′10″ 175 lbs.

Year	Team	Games	BA	SA	AB	H	2B	3B	HR	HR%	R	RBI	BB	SO	SB	Pinch Hit AB	Pinch Hit H	PO	A	E	DP	TC/G	FA	G by Pos
1910	BOS A	32	.169	.289	83	14	6	2	0	0.0	8	7	5		2	7	2	196	7	1	9	8.2	.995	1B-21, C-3, OF-1
1911		12	.317	.439	41	13	2	0	1	2.4	9	4	2		1	0	0	128	8	1	7	11.4	.993	1B-12
1912		40	.190	.307	137	26	11	1	1	0.7	16	19	15		3	0	0	354	21	4	13	9.5	.989	1B-40
1914	PIT F	118	.307	.382	427	131	20	6	0	0.0	41	61	27		7	0	0	1132	60	12	52	10.2	.990	1B-118
1915	3 teams	PIT F (26G –.273) BKN F (37G –.246) NWK F (12G –.152)																						
″	total	75	.240	.298	225	54	7	3	0	0.0	10	26	10		10	18	3	347	23	3	11	6.5	.992	1B-34, OF-22, C-1
5 yrs.		277	.261	.344	913	238	46	12	2	0.2	84	117	59		23	25	5	2157	119	21	92	9.1	.991	1B-225, OF-23, C-4

Jack Bradley

BRADLEY, JOHN THOMAS BR TR 5′11″ 175 lbs.
B. Sept. 20, 1893, Denver, Colo. D. Mar. 18, 1969, Tulsa, Okla.

Year	Team	Games	BA	SA	AB	H	2B	3B	HR	HR%	R	RBI	BB	SO	SB	Pinch Hit AB	Pinch Hit H	PO	A	E	DP	TC/G	FA	G by Pos
1916	CLE A	2	.000	.000	3	0	0	0	0	0.0	0	0	0	1	0	1	0	2	0	0	0	2.0	1.000	C-1

Mark Bradley

BRADLEY, MARK ALLEN BR TR 6′ 1″ 180 lbs.
B. Dec. 3, 1956, Elizabethtown, Ky.

Year	Team	Games	BA	SA	AB	H	2B	3B	HR	HR%	R	RBI	BB	SO	SB	Pinch Hit AB	Pinch Hit H	PO	A	E	DP	TC/G	FA	G by Pos
1981	LA N	9	.167	.333	6	1	1	0	0	0.0	2	0	0	1	0	2	0	3	1	0	0	0.7	1.000	OF-6
1982		8	.333	.333	3	1	0	0	0	0.0	1	0	0	0	0	1	0	1	0	0	0	0.3	1.000	OF-3
1983	NY N	73	.202	.327	104	21	4	0	3	2.9	10	5	11	35	4	34	6	41	2	0	1	1.2	1.000	OF-35
3 yrs.		90	.204	.327	113	23	5	0	3	2.7	13	5	11	36	4	37	6	45	3	0	1	1.1	1.000	OF-44

Phil Bradley

BRADLEY, PHILIP POOLE BR TR 6′ 185 lbs.
B. Mar. 11, 1959, Bloomington, Ind.

Year	Team	Games	BA	SA	AB	H	2B	3B	HR	HR%	R	RBI	BB	SO	SB	Pinch Hit AB	Pinch Hit H	PO	A	E	DP	TC/G	FA	G by Pos
1983	SEA A	23	.269	.299	67	18	2	0	0	0.0	8	5	8	5	3	3	0	36	1	1	0	1.7	.974	OF-21, DH-1
1984		124	.301	.363	322	97	12	4	0	0.0	49	24	34	61	21	3	0	235	3	2	1	2.0	.992	OF-117, DH-3
1985		159	.300	.498	641	192	33	8	26	4.1	100	88	55	129	22	0	0	336	10	5	3	2.2	.986	OF-159
1986		143	.310	.445	526	163	27	4	12	2.3	88	50	77	134	21	2	0	250	11	1	0	1.9	.996	OF-140
1987		158	.297	.463	603	179	38	10	14	2.3	101	67	84	119	40	0	0	273	13	5	1	1.8	.983	OF-158
1988	PHI N	154	.264	.392	569	150	30	5	11	1.9	77	56	54	106	11	2	0	298	14	3	2	2.1	.990	OF-153
1989	BAL A	144	.277	.417	545	151	23	10	11	2.0	83	55	70	103	20	4	0	284	4	3	0	2.0	.990	OF-140, DH-2
1990	2 teams	BAL A (72G –.270) CHI A (45G –.226)																						
″	total	117	.256	.327	422	108	14	2	4	0.9	59	31	50	61	17	6	1	219	4	4	0	1.9	.982	OF-108, DH-9
8 yrs.		1022	.286	.421	3695	1058	179	43	78	2.1	565	376	432	718	155	20	1	1931	60	24	7	2.0	.988	OF-996, DH-15

Scott Bradley

BRADLEY, SCOTT WILLIAM BL TR 5′11″ 175 lbs.
B. Mar. 22, 1960, Glen Ridge, N. J.

Year	Team	Games	BA	SA	AB	H	2B	3B	HR	HR%	R	RBI	BB	SO	SB	Pinch Hit AB	Pinch Hit H	PO	A	E	DP	TC/G	FA	G by Pos
1984	NY A	9	.286	.333	21	6	1	0	0	0.0	3	2	1	1	0	1	0	10	0	0	0	1.3	1.000	OF-5, C-3
1985		19	.163	.245	49	8	2	1	0	0.0	4	1	1	5	0	7	1	12	0	1	0	1.1	.923	DH-9, C-3
1986	2 teams	CHI A (9G –.286) SEA A (68G –.302)																						
″	total	77	.300	.432	220	66	8	3	5	2.3	20	28	13	7	1	17	5	281	21	3	5	4.4	.990	C-59, DH-9, OF-1
1987	SEA A	102	.278	.371	342	95	15	1	5	1.5	34	43	15	18	0	12	4	438	39	8	4	5.3	.984	C-82, 3B-8, OF-2
1988		103	.257	.349	335	86	17	1	4	1.2	45	33	17	16	1	12	2	543	42	6	7	6.0	.990	C-85, DH-4, OF-4, 3B-3, 1B-2
1989		103	.274	.367	270	74	16	0	3	1.1	21	37	21	23	1	25	9	400	26	4	6	5.4	.991	C-70, DH-6, 1B-2, OF-1
1990		101	.223	.275	233	52	9	0	1	0.4	11	28	15	20	0	35	10	354	30	2	4	5.1	.995	C-63, DH-6, 3B-5, 1B-1
1991		83	.203	.244	172	35	7	0	0	0.0	10	11	19	19	0	25	3	288	18	4	4	4.3	.987	C-65, 3B-4, DH-2, 1B-1
1992	2 teams	SEA A (2G –.000) CIN N (5G –.400)																						
″	total	7	.333	.333	6	2	0	0	0	0.0	1	1	2	1	0	5	2	3	2	0	0	1.7	1.000	C-3
9 yrs.		604	.257	.343	1648	424	75	6	18	1.1	149	184	104	110	3	139	36	2329	178	28	30	5.0	.989	C-433, DH-36, 3B-20, OF-13, 1B-6

Dallas Bradshaw

BRADSHAW, DALLAS CARL (Rabbit, Windy) BL TR 5′ 7″ 145 lbs.
B. Nov. 23, 1895, Wolf Creek, Ill. D. Dec. 11, 1939, Herrin, Ill.

Year	Team	Games	BA	SA	AB	H	2B	3B	HR	HR%	R	RBI	BB	SO	SB	Pinch Hit AB	Pinch Hit H	PO	A	E	DP	TC/G	FA	G by Pos
1917	PHI A	2	.000	.000	4	0	0	0	0	0.0	0	0	0	1	0	1	0	5	2	0	1	7.0	1.000	2B-1

George Bradshaw

BRADSHAW, GEORGE THOMAS BR TR 6′ 2″ 185 lbs.
B. Sept. 12, 1924, Salisbury, N. C.

Year	Team	Games	BA	SA	AB	H	2B	3B	HR	HR%	R	RBI	BB	SO	SB	Pinch Hit AB	Pinch Hit H	PO	A	E	DP	TC/G	FA	G by Pos
1952	WAS A	10	.217	.304	23	5	2	0	0	0.0	3	6	1	2	0	1	0	21	1	2	0	2.7	.917	C-9

Terry Bradshaw

BRADSHAW, TERRY LEON BL TR 6′ 180 lbs.
B. Feb. 3, 1969, Franklin, Va.

Year	Team	Games	BA	SA	AB	H	2B	3B	HR	HR%	R	RBI	BB	SO	SB	Pinch Hit AB	Pinch Hit H	PO	A	E	DP	TC/G	FA	G by Pos
1995	STL N	19	.227	.295	44	10	1	1	0	0.0	6	2	2	10	1	8	3	19	1	1	0	2.1	.952	OF-10

Bob Brady

BRADY, ROBERT JAY BL TR 6′ 1″ 175 lbs.
B. Nov. 8, 1922, Lewistown, Pa.

Year	Team	Games	BA	SA	AB	H	2B	3B	HR	HR%	R	RBI	BB	SO	SB	Pinch Hit AB	Pinch Hit H	PO	A	E	DP	TC/G	FA	G by Pos
1946	BOS N	3	.200	.200	5	1	0	0	0	0.0	0	0	1	1	0	2	1	4	2	1	0	7.0	.857	C-1
1947		1	.000	.000	1	0	0	0	0	0.0	0	0	0	0	0	1	0	0	0	0	0	0.0	—	
2 yrs.		4	.167	.167	6	1	0	0	0	0.0	0	0	1	1	0	3	1	4	2	1	0	7.0	.857	C-1

Brian Brady

BRADY, BRIAN PHELAN BL TL 5′11″ 185 lbs.
B. July 11, 1962, Elmhurst, N. Y.

Year	Team	Games	BA	SA	AB	H	2B	3B	HR	HR%	R	RBI	BB	SO	SB	Pinch Hit AB	Pinch Hit H	PO	A	E	DP	TC/G	FA	G by Pos
1989	CAL A	2	.500	1.000	2	1	1	0	0	0.0	0	1	0	1	0	2	1	0	0	0	0	0.0	.000	OF-1

Cliff Brady

BRADY, CLIFFORD FRANCIS BR TR 5′ 5½″ 140 lbs.
B. Mar. 6, 1897, St. Louis, Mo. D. Sept. 25, 1974, Belleville, Ill.

Year	Team	Games	BA	SA	AB	H	2B	3B	HR	HR%	R	RBI	BB	SO	SB	Pinch Hit AB	Pinch Hit H	PO	A	E	DP	TC/G	FA	G by Pos
1920	BOS A	53	.228	.267	180	41	5	1	0	0.0	16	12	13	12	0	0	0	111	193	8	21	5.9	.974	2B-53

Doug Brady

BRADY, STEPHEN DOUGLAS BB TR 5′11″ 165 lbs.
B. Nov. 23, 1969, Jacksonville, Ill.

Year	Team	Games	BA	SA	AB	H	2B	3B	HR	HR%	R	RBI	BB	SO	SB	Pinch Hit AB	Pinch Hit H	PO	A	E	DP	TC/G	FA	G by Pos
1995	CHI A	12	.190	.238	21	4	1	0	0	0.0	4	3	2	4	0	3	1	14	21	0	4	4.4	1.000	2B-6, DH-2

Fred Brady

Playing record listed under Larry Kopf.

Steve Brady

BRADY, STEPHEN A. 5′ 9½″ 165 lbs.
B. July 14, 1851, Worcester, Mass. D. Nov. 1, 1917, Hartford, Conn.

Year	Team	Games	BA	SA	AB	H	2B	3B	HR	HR%	R	RBI	BB	SO	SB	Pinch Hit AB	Pinch Hit H	PO	A	E	DP	TC/G	FA	G by Pos
1883	NY AA	97	.271	.326	432	117	12	6	0	0.0	69		11			0	0	844	31	37	32	9.4	.959	1B-81, OF-16
1884		112	.252	.287	485	122	11	3	0	0.0	102		21			0	0	189	27	18	2	2.0	.923	OF-110, 1B-5, 2B-1

Steve Brady *continued*

Year	Team	Games	BA	SA	AB	H	2B	3B	HR	HR%	R	RBI	BB	SO	SB	Pinch Hit AB	Pinch Hit H	PO	A	E	DP	TC/G	FA	G by Pos
1885		108	.295	.371	434	128	14	5	3	0.7	60		25			0	0	198	18	29	5	2.2	.882	OF-105, 1B-4, 2B-2, 3B-1
1886		124	.240	.279	466	112	8	5	0	0.0	56		35			0	0	177	26	38	2	1.9	.842	OF-123, 1B-1
4 yrs.		441	.264	.314	1817	479	45	19	3	0.2	287		92			0	0	1408	102	122	41	3.6	.925	OF-354, 1B-91, 2B-3, 3B-1

Bobby Bragan

BRAGAN, ROBERT RANDALL
B. Oct. 30, 1917, Birmingham, Ala.
Manager 1956–58, 1963–66.
BR TR 5′10½″ 175 lbs.

Year	Team	Games	BA	SA	AB	H	2B	3B	HR	HR%	R	RBI	BB	SO	SB	Pinch Hit AB	Pinch Hit H	PO	A	E	DP	TC/G	FA	G by Pos
1940	PHI N	132	.222	.300	474	105	14	1	7	1.5	36	44	28	34	2	0	0	268	443	49	83	5.7	.936	SS-132, 3B-2
1941		154	.251	.318	557	140	19	3	4	0.7	37	69	26	29	7	0	0	324	438	45	86	5.1	.944	SS-154, 2B-2, 3B-1
1942		109	.218	.284	335	73	12	2	2	0.6	17	15	20	21	0	2	0	242	263	27	55	5.0	.949	SS-78, C-22, 2B-4, 3B-3
1943	BKN N	74	.264	.341	220	58	7	2	2	0.9	17	24	15	16	0	1	0	264	55	10	9	4.4	.970	C-57, 3B-12, SS-5
1944		94	.267	.327	266	71	8	4	0	0.0	26	17	13	14	2	3	1	207	130	12	21	4.0	.966	SS-51, C-35, 2B-1
1947		25	.194	.250	36	7	2	0	0	0.0	3	3	7	3	1	4	1	56	5	0	1	2.5	1.000	C-24
1948		9	.167	.167	12	2	0	0	0	0.0	0	0	1	0	0	4	0	11	1	0	0	2.4	1.000	C-5
7 yrs.		597	.240	.309	1900	456	62	12	15	0.8	136	172	110	117	12	14	2	1372	1335	143	255	4.8	.950	SS-420, C-143, 3B-18, 2B-7
WORLD SERIES																								
1947	BKN N	1	1.000	2.000	1	1	1	0	0	0.0	0	1	0	0	0	1	1	0	0	0	0	0.0	—	

Darren Bragg

BRAGG, DARREN WILLIAM
B. Sept. 7, 1969, Waterbury, Conn.
BL TR 5′ 9″ 180 lbs.

Year	Team	Games	BA	SA	AB	H	2B	3B	HR	HR%	R	RBI	BB	SO	SB	Pinch Hit AB	Pinch Hit H	PO	A	E	DP	TC/G	FA	G by Pos
1994	SEA A	8	.158	.211	19	3	1	0	0	0.0	4	2	2	5	0	1	0	1	0	0	0	0.2	1.000	OF-3, DH-3
1995		52	.234	.345	145	34	5	1	3	2.1	20	12	18	37	9	6	2	83	7	1	1	1.9	.989	OF-47, DH-1
2 yrs.		60	.226	.329	164	37	6	1	3	1.8	24	14	20	42	9	7	2	84	7	1	1	1.7	.989	OF-50, DH-4

Glenn Braggs

BRAGGS, GLENN ERICK
B. Oct. 17, 1962, San Bernardino, Calif.
BR TR 6′ 3″ 210 lbs.

Year	Team	Games	BA	SA	AB	H	2B	3B	HR	HR%	R	RBI	BB	SO	SB	Pinch Hit AB	Pinch Hit H	PO	A	E	DP	TC/G	FA	G by Pos
1986	MIL A	58	.237	.349	215	51	8	2	4	1.9	19	18	11	47	1	0	0	116	5	12	0	2.3	.910	OF-56, DH-2
1987		132	.269	.430	505	136	28	7	13	2.6	67	77	47	96	12	3	0	301	6	9	1	2.4	.972	OF-123, DH-8
1988		72	.261	.423	272	71	14	0	10	3.7	30	42	14	60	6	0	0	134	1	3	0	1.9	.978	OF-54, DH-18
1989		144	.247	.370	514	127	12	3	15	2.9	77	66	42	111	17	1	0	267	6	8	1	1.9	.972	OF-132, DH-13
1990	2 teams	MIL A (37G –.248) CIN N (72G –.299)																						
″	total	109	.280	.417	314	88	14	1	9	2.9	39	41	38	64	8	14	4	191	11	7	3	2.2	.967	OF-92, DH-2
1991	CIN N	85	.260	.432	250	65	10	0	11	4.4	36	39	23	46	11	15	4	139	2	5	1	2.0	.966	OF-74
1992		92	.237	.410	266	63	16	3	8	3.0	40	38	36	48	3	18	4	102	3	6	0	1.4	.946	OF-79
7 yrs.		692	.257	.405	2336	601	102	16	70	3.0	308	321	211	472	58	51	12	1250	34	50	6	2.0	.963	OF-610, DH-43
LEAGUE CHAMPIONSHIP SERIES																								
1990	CIN N	2	.200	.200	5	1	0	0	0	0.0	0	0	0	1	0	0	0	2	0	0	0	1.0	1.000	OF-2
WORLD SERIES																								
1990	CIN N	2	.000	.000	4	0	0	0	0	0.0	0	2	1	0	0	2	0	0	0	0	0	0.0	.000	OF-1

Dave Brain

BRAIN, DAVID LEONARD
B. Jan. 24, 1879, Hereford, England D. May 25, 1959, Los Angeles, Calif.
BR TR 5′10″ 170 lbs.

Year	Team	Games	BA	SA	AB	H	2B	3B	HR	HR%	R	RBI	BB	SO	SB	Pinch Hit AB	Pinch Hit H	PO	A	E	DP	TC/G	FA	G by Pos
1901	CHI A	5	.350	.400	20	7	1	0	0	0.0	2	5	1		0	0	0	14	16	3	4	6.6	.909	2B-5
1903	STL N	119	.231	.319	464	107	8	15	1	0.2	44	60	25		21	0	0	233	350	63	43	5.5	.902	SS-72, 3B-46
1904		127	.266	.408	488	130	24	12	7	1.4	57	72	17		18	2	0	259	308	45	26	4.9	.926	SS-59, 3B-30, OF-19, 2B-13, 1B-4
1905	2 teams	STL N (44G –.228) PIT N (85G –.257)																						
″	total	129	.247	.366	465	115	21	11	4	0.9	42	63	23		12	3	1	170	274	35	19	3.9	.927	3B-84, SS-33, OF-6
1906	BOS N	139	.250	.333	525	131	19	5	5	1.0	43	45	29		11	0	0	208	321	48	26	4.2	.917	3B-139
1907		133	.279	.420	509	142	24	9	**10**	2.0	60	56	29		10	0	0	198	325	47	27	4.3	.918	3B-130, OF-3
1908	2 teams	CIN N (16G –.109) NY N (11G –.176)																						
″	total	27	.125	.125	72	9	0	0	0	0.0	6	2	10		1	2	0	44	10	6	0	2.4	.900	OF-19, 2B-3, 3B-2, SS-1
7 yrs.		679	.252	.363	2543	641	97	52	27	1.1	254	303	134		73	7	1	1126	1604	247	145	4.5	.917	3B-431, SS-165, OF-47, 2B-21, 1B-4

Fred Brainerd

BRAINERD, FREDERICK F.
B. Feb. 17, 1892, Champaign, Ill. D. Apr. 17, 1959, Galveston, Tex.
BR TR 6′ 176 lbs.

Year	Team	Games	BA	SA	AB	H	2B	3B	HR	HR%	R	RBI	BB	SO	SB	Pinch Hit AB	Pinch Hit H	PO	A	E	DP	TC/G	FA	G by Pos
1914	NY N	2	.200	.200	5	1	0	0	0	0.0	1	0	1	0	0	0	0	6	6	1	1	6.5	.923	2B-2
1915		91	.201	.257	249	50	7	2	1	0.4	31	21	21	44	6	20	3	443	94	18	37	7.7	.968	1B-45, 3B-16, SS-9, OF-1, 2B-1
1916		2	.000	.000	7	0	0	0	0	0.0	0	0	0	0	0	0	0	3	2	3	0	4.0	.625	3B-2
3 yrs.		95	.195	.249	261	51	7	2	1	0.4	32	21	22	44	6	20	3	452	102	22	38	7.6	.962	1B-45, 3B-18, SS-9, 2B-3, OF-1

Erv Brame

BRAME, ERVIN BECKHAM
B. Oct. 12, 1901, Big Rock, Tenn. D. Nov. 22, 1949, Hopkinsville, Ky.
BL TR 6′ 2″ 190 lbs.

Year	Team	Games	BA	SA	AB	H	2B	3B	HR	HR%	R	RBI	BB	SO	SB	Pinch Hit AB	Pinch Hit H	PO	A	E	DP	TC/G	FA	G by Pos
1928	PIT N	35	.265	.408	49	13	4	0	1	2.0	6	11	4	3	0	9	1	2	18	1	0	0.9	.952	P-24
1929		59	.310	.500	116	36	8	1	4	3.4	9	25	2	7	0	21	10	7	36	3	0	1.2	.935	P-37
1930		50	.353	.474	116	41	5	0	3	2.6	20	22	0	2	0	16	6	1	39	2	0	1.3	.952	P-32
1931		48	.274	.337	95	26	4	1	0	0.0	6	15	4	16	0	21	7	1	34	1	2	1.4	.972	P-26
1932		26	.250	.250	20	5	0	0	0	0.0	2	2	0	4	0	3	1	0	9	0	1	0.4	1.000	P-23
5 yrs.		218	.306	.429	396	121	21	2	8	2.0	43	75	10	32	0	70	25	11	136	7	3	1.1	.955	P-142

Art Bramhall

BRAMHALL, ARTHUR WASHINGTON
B. Feb. 22, 1909, Oak Park, Ill. D. Sept. 4, 1985, Madison, Wis.
BR TR 5′11″ 170 lbs.

Year	Team	Games	BA	SA	AB	H	2B	3B	HR	HR%	R	RBI	BB	SO	SB	Pinch Hit AB	Pinch Hit H	PO	A	E	DP	TC/G	FA	G by Pos
1935	PHI N	2	.000	.000	1	0	0	0	0	0.0	0	0	0	0	0	0	0	2	2	0	0	2.0	1.000	SS-1, 3B-1

Al Brancato

BRANCATO, ALBERT
B. May 29, 1919, Philadelphia, Pa.
BR TR 5′ 9½″ 188 lbs.

Year	Team	Games	BA	SA	AB	H	2B	3B	HR	HR%	R	RBI	BB	SO	SB	Pinch Hit AB	Pinch Hit H	PO	A	E	DP	TC/G	FA	G by Pos
1939	PHI A	21	.206	.324	68	14	5	0	1	1.5	12	8	8	4	1	0	0	20	42	4	2	3.1	.939	3B-20, SS-1
1940		107	.191	.252	298	57	11	2	1	0.3	42	23	28	36	3	2	0	160	231	23	39	3.9	.944	SS-80, 3B-25

Al Brancato *continued*

Year	Team	Games	BA	SA	AB	H	2B	3B	HR	HR%	R	RBI	BB	SO	SB	Pinch Hit AB	Pinch Hit H	PO	A	E	DP	TC/G	FA	G by Pos
1941		144	.234	.317	530	124	20	9	2	0.4	60	49	59	49	1	1	0	267	403	61	82	5.0	.917	SS-139, 3B-7
1945		10	.118	.147	34	4	1	0	0	0.0	3	0	1	3	0	0	0	22	25	2	5	4.9	.959	SS-10
4 yrs.		282	.214	.290	930	199	37	11	4	0.4	117	80	96	92	5	3	0	469	701	90	128	4.5	.929	SS-230, 3B-52

Ron Brand

BRAND, RONALD GEORGE BR TR 5′ 7½″ 167 lbs.
B. Jan. 13, 1940, Los Angeles, Calif.

Year	Team	Games	BA	SA	AB	H	2B	3B	HR	HR%	R	RBI	BB	SO	SB	Pinch Hit AB	Pinch Hit H	PO	A	E	DP	TC/G	FA	G by Pos
1963	PIT N	46	.288	.364	66	19	2	0	1	1.5	8	7	10	11	0	5	0	141	13	5	4	4.3	.969	C-33, 3B-2, 2B-2
1965	HOU N	117	.235	.281	391	92	6	3	2	0.5	27	37	19	34	10	6	0	598	60	8	11	5.9	.988	C-102, 3B-6, OF-5
1966		56	.244	.260	123	30	2	0	0	0.0	12	10	9	13	0	20	3	150	29	3	6	4.8	.984	C-25, 2B-9, OF-3, 3B-1
1967		84	.242	.288	215	52	8	1	0	0.0	22	18	23	17	4	14	2	397	37	1	3	6.3	.998	C-67, 2B-1, OF-1
1968		43	.160	.185	81	13	2	0	0	0.0	7	4	9	11	1	7	1	154	14	0	3	5.4	1.000	C-29, OF-1, 3B-1
1969	MON N	103	.258	.300	287	74	12	0	0	0.0	19	20	30	19	2	13	3	492	44	8	7	6.3	.985	C-84, OF-2
1970		72	.238	.302	126	30	2	3	0	0.0	10	9	9	16	2	35	7	60	57	7	8	2.6	.944	SS-19, 3B-12, C-9, OF-5, 2B-3
1971		47	.214	.214	56	12	0	0	0	0.0	3	1	3	5	1	15	3	28	44	3	10	2.3	.960	SS-22, OF-4, 3B-4, C-1, 2B-1
8 yrs.		568	.239	.282	1345	322	34	7	3	0.2	108	106	112	126	20	115	19	2020	298	35	52	5.2	.985	C-350, SS-41, 3B-26, OF-21, 2B-16

Jackie Brandt

BRANDT, JOHN GEORGE BR TR 5′11″ 165 lbs.
B. Apr. 28, 1934, Omaha, Neb.

Year	Team	Games	BA	SA	AB	H	2B	3B	HR	HR%	R	RBI	BB	SO	SB	Pinch Hit AB	Pinch Hit H	PO	A	E	DP	TC/G	FA	G by Pos
1956	2 teams	STL N (27G –.286) NY N (98G –.299)																						
″	total	125	.298	.478	393	117	19	8	12	3.1	54	50	21	36	3	4	2	198	9	2	1	1.7	.990	OF-122
1958	SF N	18	.250	.269	52	13	1	0	0	0.0	7	3	6	5	1	5	1	28	0	0	0	2.0	1.000	OF-14
1959		137	.270	.415	429	116	16	5	12	2.8	63	57	35	69	11	16	4	204	39	12	4	1.8	.953	OF-116, 3B-18, 1B-3, 2B-1
1960	BAL A	145	.254	.413	511	130	24	6	15	2.9	73	65	47	69	5	4	0	285	10	6	2	2.1	.980	OF-142, 3B-2, 1B-1
1961		139	.297	.444	516	153	18	5	16	3.1	93	72	62	51	10	0	0	293	6	8	2	2.2	.974	OF-136, 3B-1
1962		143	.255	.446	505	129	29	5	19	3.8	76	75	55	64	9	6	1	310	10	8	2	2.3	.976	OF-138, 3B-2
1963		142	.248	.404	451	112	15	5	15	3.3	49	61	34	85	4	8	1	272	11	4	1	2.1	.986	OF-134, 3B-1
1964		137	.243	.369	523	127	25	1	13	2.5	66	47	45	104	1	4	0	345	14	7	2	2.7	.981	OF-134
1965		96	.243	.412	243	59	17	0	8	3.3	35	24	21	40	1	14	2	143	6	6	0	1.8	.961	OF-84
1966	PHI N	82	.250	.317	164	41	6	1	1	0.6	16	15	17	36	0	15	4	78	3	1	0	1.2	.988	OF-71
1967	2 teams	PHI N (16G –.105) HOU N (41G –.236)																						
″	total	57	.213	.306	108	23	5	1	1	0.9	8	16	8	15	0	33	9	106	7	1	5	4.8	.991	1B-14, OF-9, 3B-1
11 yrs.		1221	.262	.412	3895	1020	175	37	112	2.9	540	485	351	574	45	109	24	2262	115	55	19	2.1	.977	OF-1100, 3B-25, 1B-18, 2B-1

Otis Brannan

BRANNAN, OTIS OWEN BL TR 5′ 9″ 160 lbs.
B. Mar. 13, 1899, Greenbrier, Ark. D. June 6, 1967, Little Rock, Ark.

Year	Team	Games	BA	SA	AB	H	2B	3B	HR	HR%	R	RBI	BB	SO	SB	Pinch Hit AB	Pinch Hit H	PO	A	E	DP	TC/G	FA	G by Pos
1928	STL A	135	.244	.356	483	118	18	3	10	2.1	68	66	60	19	3	0	0	272	434	26	74	5.4	.964	2B-135
1929		23	.275	.353	51	14	1	0	1	2.0	4	8	4	4	0	4	1	31	47	2	6	4.2	.975	2B-19
2 yrs.		158	.247	.356	534	132	19	3	11	2.1	72	74	64	23	3	4	1	303	481	28	80	5.3	.966	2B-154

Dudley Branom

BRANOM, EDGAR DUDLEY BL TL 6′ 1″ 190 lbs.
B. Nov. 30, 1897, Sulphur Springs, Tex. D. Feb. 4, 1980, Sun City, Ariz.

Year	Team	Games	BA	SA	AB	H	2B	3B	HR	HR%	R	RBI	BB	SO	SB	Pinch Hit AB	Pinch Hit H	PO	A	E	DP	TC/G	FA	G by Pos
1927	PHI A	30	.234	.245	94	22	1	0	0	0.0	8	13	2	5	2	4	2	231	17	7	18	9.8	.973	1B-26

Kitty Bransfield

BRANSFIELD, WILLIAM EDWARD BR TR 5′11″ 207 lbs.
B. Jan. 7, 1875, Worcester, Mass. D. May 1, 1947, Worcester, Mass.

Year	Team	Games	BA	SA	AB	H	2B	3B	HR	HR%	R	RBI	BB	SO	SB	Pinch Hit AB	Pinch Hit H	PO	A	E	DP	TC/G	FA	G by Pos
1898	BOS N	5	.222	.444	9	2	0	1	0	0.0	2	1	0		0	0	0	12	0	1	0	2.6	.923	C-4, 1B-1
1901	PIT N	139	.295	.398	566	167	26	16	0	0.0	92	91	29		23	0	0	1374	52	28	72	10.5	.981	1B-139
1902		102	.305	.396	417	127	21	7	1	0.2	50	69	17		23	1	0	1064	41	18	40	11.1	.984	1B-101
1903		127	.265	.350	505	134	23	7	2	0.4	69	57	33		13	0	0	1347	88	28	82	11.5	.981	1B-127
1904		139	.223	.290	520	116	17	9	0	0.0	47	60	22		11	0	0	1454	89	30	70	11.3	.981	1B-139
1905	PHI N	151	.259	.345	580	150	23	9	3	0.5	55	76	27		27	0	0	1398	92	23	75	10.0	.985	1B-151
1906		140	.275	.353	524	144	28	5	1	0.2	47	60	16		12	1	0	1318	88	29	57	10.3	.980	1B-139
1907		94	.233	.287	348	81	15	2	0	0.0	25	38	14		8	2	0	862	53	21	46	10.2	.978	1B-92
1908		144	.304	.395	527	160	25	7	3	0.6	53	71	23		30	1	1	1472	89	22	67	11.1	.986	1B-143
1909		140	.292	.372	527	154	27	6	1	0.2	47	59	18		17	2	0	1377	89	16	71	10.7	.989	1B-138
1910		123	.239	.319	427	102	17	4	3	0.7	39	52	20	34	10	12	2	1026	51	20	82	10.0	.982	1B-110
1911	2 teams	PHI N (23G –.256) CHI N (3G –.400)																						
″	total	26	.283	.377	53	15	3	1	0	0.0	4	3	2	7	1	15	1	101	5	1	8	9.7	.991	1B-11
12 yrs.		1330	.270	.353	5003	1352	225	74	14	0.3	530	637	221	41	175	34	4	12805	737	237	670	10.6	.983	1B-1291, C-4
WORLD SERIES																								
1903	PIT N	8	.200	.333	30	6	0	2	0	0.0	3	1	1	6	1	0	0	80	6	2	5	11.0	.977	1B-8

Jeff Branson

BRANSON, JEFFERY GLENN BL TR 6′ 180 lbs.
B. Jan. 26, 1967, Waynesboro, Miss.

Year	Team	Games	BA	SA	AB	H	2B	3B	HR	HR%	R	RBI	BB	SO	SB	Pinch Hit AB	Pinch Hit H	PO	A	E	DP	TC/G	FA	G by Pos
1992	CIN N	72	.296	.374	115	34	7	1	0	0.0	12	15	5	16	0	34	13	46	63	7	19	2.8	.940	2B-33, 3B-8, SS-1
1993		125	.241	.310	381	92	15	1	3	0.8	40	22	19	73	4	17	6	185	260	11	56	3.8	.976	SS-59, 2B-45, 3B-14, 1B-1
1994		58	.284	.505	109	31	4	1	6	5.5	18	16	5	16	0	19	5	39	52	1	6	2.0	.989	2B-19, 3B-18, SS-8, 1B-2
1995		122	.260	.435	331	86	18	2	12	3.6	43	45	44	69	2	11	1	84	241	9	37	2.4	.973	3B-98, SS-32, 2B-6, 1B-1
4 yrs.		377	.260	.385	936	243	44	5	21	2.2	113	98	73	174	6	81	25	354	616	28	118	2.9	.972	3B-138, 2B-103, SS-100, 1B-4
DIVISIONAL PLAYOFF SERIES																								
1995	CIN N	3	.286	.429	7	2	1	0	0	0.0	0	2	2	0	0	0	0	1	8	0	0	3.0	1.000	3B-3
LEAGUE CHAMPIONSHIP SERIES																								
1995	CIN N	4	.111	.222	9	1	1	0	0	0.0	2	0	0	2	1	2	0	1	3	0	1	1.0	1.000	3B-4

Marshall Brant

BRANT, MARSHALL LEE BR TR 6′ 5″ 185 lbs.
B. Sept. 17, 1955, Garberville, Calif.

Year	Team	Games	BA	SA	AB	H	2B	3B	HR	HR%	R	RBI	BB	SO	SB	Pinch Hit AB	Pinch Hit H	PO	A	E	DP	TC/G	FA	G by Pos
1980	NY A	3	.000	.000	6	0	0	0	0	0.0	0	0	0	3	0	1	0	9	1	0	1	3.3	1.000	1B-2, DH-1
1983	OAK A	5	.143	.143	14	2	0	0	0	0.0	2	2	0	3	0	2	0	19	0	2	4	5.3	.905	1B-3, DH-1
2 yrs.		8	.100	.100	20	2	0	0	0	0.0	2	2	0	6	0	3	0	28	1	2	5	4.4	.935	1B-5, DH-2

Mickey Brantley

BRANTLEY, MICHAEL CHARLES
B. June 17, 1961, Catskill, N. Y.
BR TR 5′10″ 180 lbs.

Year	Team	Games	BA	SA	AB	H	2B	3B	HR	HR%	R	RBI	BB	SO	SB	Pinch Hit AB	Pinch Hit H	PO	A	E	DP	TC/G	FA	G by Pos
1986	SEA A	27	.196	.353	102	20	3	2	3	2.9	12	7	10	21	1	2	0	54	3	1	1	2.3	.983	OF-25
1987		92	.302	.499	351	106	23	2	14	4.0	52	54	24	44	13	4	1	163	3	3	1	1.9	.982	OF-82, DH-8
1988		149	.263	.399	577	152	25	4	15	2.6	76	56	26	64	18	1	1	327	5	6	1	2.3	.982	OF-147
1989		34	.157	.204	108	17	5	0	0	0.0	14	8	7	7	2	3	0	50	1	0	0	1.7	1.000	OF-23, DH-7
4 yrs.		302	.259	.407	1138	295	56	8	32	2.8	154	125	67	136	34	10	2	594	12	10	3	2.1	.984	OF-277, DH-15

Roy Brashear

BRASHEAR, ROY PARKS
Brother of Kitty Brashear.
B. Jan. 3, 1874, Ashtabula, Ohio D. Apr. 20, 1951, Los Angeles, Calif.
BR TR

Year	Team	Games	BA	SA	AB	H	2B	3B	HR	HR%	R	RBI	BB	SO	SB	Pinch Hit AB	Pinch Hit H	PO	A	E	DP	TC/G	FA	G by Pos
1902	STL N	110	.276	.314	388	107	8	2	1	0.3	36	40	32		9	3	1	828	97	24	54	8.9	.975	1B-67, 2B-21, OF-16, SS-3
1903	PHI N	20	.227	.267	75	17	3	0	0	0.0	9	4	6		2	0	0	60	40	9	8	5.4	.917	2B-18, 1B-2
2 yrs.		130	.268	.307	463	124	11	2	1	0.2	45	44	38		11	3	1	888	137	33	62	8.3	.969	1B-69, 2B-39, OF-16, SS-3

Joe Bratcher

BRATCHER, JOSEPH WARWICK (Goobers)
B. July 22, 1898, Grand Saline, Tex. D. Oct. 13, 1977, Fort Worth, Tex.
BL TR 5′ 8½″ 140 lbs.

Year	Team	Games	BA	SA	AB	H	2B	3B	HR	HR%	R	RBI	BB	SO	SB	Pinch Hit AB	Pinch Hit H	PO	A	E	DP	TC/G	FA	G by Pos
1924	STL N	4	.000	.000	1	0	0	0	0	0.0	1	0	0	0	0	1	0	0	0	0	0	0.0	.000	OF-1

Fritz Bratschi

BRATSCHI, FREDERICK OSCAR
B. Jan. 16, 1892, Alliance, Ohio D. Jan. 10, 1962, Massillon, Ohio.
BR TR 5′10″ 170 lbs.

Year	Team	Games	BA	SA	AB	H	2B	3B	HR	HR%	R	RBI	BB	SO	SB	Pinch Hit AB	Pinch Hit H	PO	A	E	DP	TC/G	FA	G by Pos
1921	CHI A	16	.286	.321	28	8	1	0	0	0.0	0	3	0	2	0	10	3	7	2	0	0	1.8	1.000	OF-5
1926	BOS A	72	.275	.347	167	46	10	1	0	0.0	12	19	14	15	0	30	7	55	1	3	0	1.6	.949	OF-37
1927		1	.000	.000	1	0	0	0	0	0.0	0	0	0	0	0	1	0	0	0	0	0	0.0	—	
3 yrs.		89	.276	.342	196	54	11	1	0	0.0	12	22	14	17	0	41	10	62	3	3	0	1.6	.956	OF-42

Steve Braun

BRAUN, STEPHEN RUSSELL
B. May 8, 1948, Trenton, N. J.
BL TR 5′10″ 180 lbs.

Year	Team	Games	BA	SA	AB	H	2B	3B	HR	HR%	R	RBI	BB	SO	SB	Pinch Hit AB	Pinch Hit H	PO	A	E	DP	TC/G	FA	G by Pos
1971	MIN A	128	.254	.344	343	87	12	2	5	1.5	51	35	48	50	8	26	7	107	193	13	24	2.8	.958	3B-73, 2B-28, SS-10, OF-2
1972		121	.289	.356	402	116	21	0	2	0.5	40	50	45	38	4	14	4	110	207	13	26	2.9	.961	3B-74, 2B-20, SS-11, OF-9
1973		115	.283	.438	361	102	28	5	6	1.7	46	42	74	48	4	5	1	86	175	16	21	2.6	.942	3B-102, OF-6
1974		129	.280	.364	453	127	12	1	8	1.8	53	40	56	51	4	6	1	195	47	12	8	2.0	.953	OF-108, 3B-17
1975		136	.302	.428	453	137	18	3	11	2.4	70	45	66	55	0	11	6	271	14	10	4	2.3	.966	OF-106, 1B-9, DH-9, 3B-2, 2B-1
1976		122	.288	.353	417	120	12	3	3	0.7	73	61	67	43	12	9	5	71	32	6	3	0.9	.945	DH-71, OF-32, 3B-16
1977	SEA A	139	.235	.315	451	106	19	1	5	1.1	51	31	80	59	8	11	0	186	11	6	3	1.5	.970	OF-100, DH-32, 3B-1
1978	2 teams	SEA A (32G –.230) KC A (64G –.263)																						
″	total	96	.251	.370	211	53	14	1	3	1.4	27	29	37	21	4	38	11	68	9	4	2	1.3	.951	OF-37, DH-14, 3B-11
1979	KC A	58	.267	.388	116	31	2	0	4	3.4	15	10	22	11	0	28	8	26	4	0	1	1.0	1.000	OF-18, DH-11, 3B-2
1980	2 teams	KC A (14G –.043) TOR A (37G –.273)																						
″	total	51	.205	.269	78	16	2	0	1	1.3	4	10	10	7	0	35	10	2	1	0	0	0.2	1.000	DH-14, OF-5, 3B-1
1981	STL N	44	.196	.283	46	9	2	1	0	0.0	9	2	15	7	1	25	5	15	2	0	1	1.3	1.000	OF-12, 3B-1
1982		58	.274	.339	62	17	4	0	0	0.0	6	4	11	10	0	41	12	6	5	1	0	0.9	.917	OF-8, 3B-5
1983		78	.272	.413	92	25	2	1	3	3.3	8	7	21	7	0	48	15	26	4	0	1	1.2	1.000	OF-22, 3B-4
1984		86	.276	.327	98	27	3	1	0	0.0	6	16	17	17	0	60	17	10	1	0	0	0.6	1.000	OF-19, 3B-1
1985		64	.239	.343	67	16	4	0	1	1.5	7	6	10	9	0	45	11	14	1	0	0	1.1	1.000	OF-14
15 yrs.		1425	.271	.367	3650	989	155	19	52	1.4	466	388	579	433	45	402	113 7th	1193	706	81	94	1.9	.959	OF-498, 3B-310, DH-151, 2B-49, SS-21, 1B-9

LEAGUE CHAMPIONSHIP SERIES

Year	Team	Games	BA	SA	AB	H	2B	3B	HR	HR%	R	RBI	BB	SO	SB	Pinch Hit AB	Pinch Hit H	PO	A	E	DP	TC/G	FA	G by Pos
1978	KC A	2	.000	.000	5	0	0	0	0	0.0	0	0	1	1	0	1	0	5	0	0	0	5.0	1.000	OF-1
1982	STL N	1	.000	.000	1	0	0	0	0	0.0	0	0	0	0	0	1	0	0	0	0	0	0.0	—	
1985		2	.000	.000	2	0	0	0	0	0.0	0	0	0	0	0	2	0	0	0	0	0	0.0	—	
3 yrs.		5	.000	.000	8	0	0	0	0	0.0	0	0	1	1	0	4	0	5	0	0	0	5.0	1.000	OF-1

WORLD SERIES

Year	Team	Games	BA	SA	AB	H	2B	3B	HR	HR%	R	RBI	BB	SO	SB	Pinch Hit AB	Pinch Hit H	PO	A	E	DP	TC/G	FA	G by Pos
1982	STL N	2	.500	.500	2	1	0	0	0	0.0	0	2	1	0	0	1	0	0	0	0	0	0.0	.000	DH-2
1985		1	.000	.000	1	0	0	0	0	0.0	0	0	0	0	0	1	0	0	0	0	0	0.0	—	
2 yrs.		3	.333	.333	3	1	0	0	0	0.0	0	2	1	0	0	2	0	0	0	0	0	0.0		DH-2

Angel Bravo

BRAVO, ANGEL ALFONSO
Born Angel Alfonso Bravo (Urdaneta).
B. Aug. 4, 1942, Maracaibo, Venezuela.
BL TL 5′ 8″ 150 lbs.

Year	Team	Games	BA	SA	AB	H	2B	3B	HR	HR%	R	RBI	BB	SO	SB	Pinch Hit AB	Pinch Hit H	PO	A	E	DP	TC/G	FA	G by Pos
1969	CHI A	27	.289	.411	90	26	4	2	1	1.1	10	3	3	5	2	2	0	44	0	1	0	1.8	.978	OF-25
1970	CIN N	65	.277	.323	65	18	1	1	0	0.0	10	3	9	13	0	42	13	17	1	1	0	0.9	.947	OF-22
1971	2 teams	CIN N (5G –.200) SD N (52G –.155)																						
″	total	57	.159	.190	63	10	2	0	0	0.0	6	6	8	13	0	40	7	5	0	1	0	0.7	.833	OF-9
3 yrs.		149	.248	.321	218	54	7	3	1	0.5	26	12	20	31	2	84	20	66	1	3	0	1.3	.957	OF-56

LEAGUE CHAMPIONSHIP SERIES

Year	Team	Games	BA	SA	AB	H	2B	3B	HR	HR%	R	RBI	BB	SO	SB	Pinch Hit AB	Pinch Hit H	PO	A	E	DP	TC/G	FA	G by Pos
1970	CIN N	1	.000	.000	1	0	0	0	0	0.0	0	0	0	0	0	1	0	0	0	0	0	0.0	—	

WORLD SERIES

Year	Team	Games	BA	SA	AB	H	2B	3B	HR	HR%	R	RBI	BB	SO	SB	Pinch Hit AB	Pinch Hit H	PO	A	E	DP	TC/G	FA	G by Pos
1970	CIN N	4	.000	.000	2	0	0	0	0	0.0	0	0	1	1	0	2	0	0	0	0	0	0.0	—	

Buster Bray

BRAY, CLARENCE WILBUR
B. Apr. 1, 1913, Birmingham, Ala. D. Sept. 4, 1982, Evansville, Ind.
BL TL 6′ 170 lbs.

Year	Team	Games	BA	SA	AB	H	2B	3B	HR	HR%	R	RBI	BB	SO	SB	Pinch Hit AB	Pinch Hit H	PO	A	E	DP	TC/G	FA	G by Pos
1941	BOS N	4	.091	.182	11	1	1	0	0	0.0	2	1	1	2	0	0	0	6	0	0	0	2.0	1.000	OF-3

Frank Brazill

BRAZILL, FRANK LEO
B. Aug. 11, 1899, Spangler, Pa. D. Nov. 3, 1976, Oakland, Calif.
BL TR 5′11½″ 175 lbs.

Year	Team	Games	BA	SA	AB	H	2B	3B	HR	HR%	R	RBI	BB	SO	SB	Pinch Hit AB	Pinch Hit H	PO	A	E	DP	TC/G	FA	G by Pos
1921	PHI A	66	.271	.299	177	48	3	1	0	0.0	17	19	23	21	2	19	5	350	42	9	30	8.9	.978	1B-36, 3B-9
1922		6	.077	.077	13	1	0	0	0	0.0	0	1	0	1	0	4	0	1	2	1	0	2.0	.750	3B-2
2 yrs.		72	.258	.284	190	49	3	1	0	0.0	17	20	23	22	2	23	5	351	44	10	30	8.6	.975	1B-36, 3B-11

Sid Bream

BREAM, SIDNEY EUGENE
B. Aug. 3, 1960, Carlisle, Pa.
BL TL 6′ 4″ 215 lbs.

Year	Team	Games	BA	SA	AB	H	2B	3B	HR	HR%	R	RBI	BB	SO	SB	Pinch Hit AB	Pinch Hit H	PO	A	E	DP	TC/G	FA	G by Pos
1983	LA N	15	.182	.182	11	2	0	0	0	0.0	0	2	2	2	0	10	2	8	0	0	1	2.0	1.000	1B-4
1984		27	.184	.245	49	9	3	0	0	0.0	2	6	6	9	1	11	1	95	11	0	9	7.6	1.000	1B-14

Sid Bream *continued*

Year	Team	Games	BA	SA	AB	H	2B	3B	HR	HR%	R	RBI	BB	SO	SB	Pinch Hit AB	Pinch Hit H	PO	A	E	DP	TC/G	FA	G by Pos
1985	2 teams LA N (24G –.132) PIT N (26G –.284)																							
″	total	50	.230	.399	148	34	7	0	6	4.1	18	21	18	24	0	10	2	367	35	3	29	9.9	.993	1B-41
1986	PIT N	154	.268	.450	522	140	37	5	16	3.1	73	77	60	73	13	5	1	1320	166	17	107	9.7	.989	1B-153, OF-2
1987		149	.275	.411	516	142	25	3	13	2.5	64	65	49	69	9	7	2	1236	127	17	109	9.6	.988	1B-144
1988		148	.264	.409	462	122	37	0	10	2.2	50	65	47	64	9	16	6	1118	140	6	88	9.2	.995	1B-138
1989		19	.222	.306	36	8	3	0	0	0.0	3	4	12	10	0	2	0	111	7	1	5	9.2	.992	1B-13
1990		147	.270	.455	389	105	23	2	15	3.9	39	67	48	65	8	14	2	971	104	8	80	7.6	.993	1B-142
1991	ATL N	91	.253	.423	265	67	12	0	11	4.2	32	45	25	31	0	9	5	668	50	3	53	8.5	.996	1B-85
1992		125	.261	.414	372	97	25	1	10	2.7	30	61	46	51	6	12	4	856	73	10	69	7.8	.989	1B-120
1993		117	.260	.415	277	72	14	1	9	3.2	33	35	31	43	4	29	10	627	62	3	62	7.7	.996	1B-90
1994	HOU N	46	.344	.426	61	21	5	0	0	0.0	7	7	9	9	0	32	13	60	11	1	8	7.2	.986	1B-10
12 yrs.		1088	.264	.420	3108	819	191	12	90	2.9	351	455	353	450	50	157	48	7437	786	69	620	8.7	.992	1B-954, OF-2
LEAGUE CHAMPIONSHIP SERIES																								
1990	PIT N	4	.500	1.000	8	4	1	0	1	12.5	1	3	2	3	0	1	0	26	3	0	3	7.3	1.000	1B-4
1991	ATL N	4	.300	.600	10	3	0	0	1	10.0	1	3	0	1	0	1	0	19	3	0	2	5.5	1.000	1B-4
1992		7	.273	.545	22	6	3	0	1	4.5	5	2	3	0	0	0	0	53	3	0	3	8.0	1.000	1B-7
1993		1	1.000	1.000	1	1	0	0	0	0.0	1	0	0	0	0	0	0	1	0	0	0	1.0	1.000	1B-1
4 yrs.		16	.341	.659	41	14	4	0	3	7.3	8	8	5	4	0	2	0	99	9	0	8	6.8	1.000	1B-16
WORLD SERIES																								
1991	ATL N	7	.125	.208	24	3	2	0	0	0.0	0	0	3	4	0	0	0	69	7	0	6	10.9	1.000	1B-7
1992		5	.200	.200	15	3	0	0	0	0.0	1	0	4	0	0	0	0	41	1	1	4	8.6	.977	1B-5
2 yrs.		12	.154	.205	39	6	2	0	0	0.0	1	0	7	4	0	0	0	110	8	1	10	9.9	.992	1B-12

Jim Breazeale

BREAZEALE, JAMES LEO
B. Oct. 3, 1949, Houston, Tex.

BL TR 6′ 2″ 210 lbs.

Year	Team	Games	BA	SA	AB	H	2B	3B	HR	HR%	R	RBI	BB	SO	SB	Pinch Hit AB	Pinch Hit H	PO	A	E	DP	TC/G	FA	G by Pos
1969	ATL N	2	.000	.000	1	0	0	0	0	0.0	1	0	2	0	0	0	0	5	0	1	0	6.0	.833	1B-1
1971		10	.190	.333	21	4	0	0	1	4.8	1	3	0	3	0	5	3	31	2	0	3	8.3	1.000	1B-4
1972		52	.247	.447	85	21	2	0	5	5.9	10	17	6	12	0	33	10	121	3	0	11	7.3	1.000	1B-16, 3B-1
1978	CHI A	25	.208	.375	72	15	3	0	3	4.2	8	13	8	10	0	2	1	124	3	1	10	5.6	.992	1B-19, DH-4
4 yrs.		89	.223	.402	179	40	5	0	9	5.0	20	33	16	25	0	40	14	281	8	2	24	6.5	.993	1B-40, DH-4, 3B-1

Danny Breeden

BREEDEN, DANNY RICHARD
Brother of Hal Breeden.
B. June 27, 1942, Albany, Ga.

BR TR 5′11½″ 185 lbs.

Year	Team	Games	BA	SA	AB	H	2B	3B	HR	HR%	R	RBI	BB	SO	SB	Pinch Hit AB	Pinch Hit H	PO	A	E	DP	TC/G	FA	G by Pos
1969	CIN N	3	.125	.125	8	1	0	0	0	0.0	0	1	0	3	0	0	0	12	4	1	0	5.7	.941	C-3
1971	CHI N	25	.154	.169	65	10	1	0	0	0.0	3	4	9	18	0	0	0	150	7	4	2	6.4	.975	C-25
2 yrs.		28	.151	.164	73	11	1	0	0	0.0	3	5	9	21	0	0	0	162	11	5	2	6.4	.972	C-28

Hal Breeden

BREEDEN, HAROLD NOEL
Brother of Danny Breeden.
B. June 28, 1944, Albany, Ga.

BR TL 6′ 2″ 200 lbs.

Year	Team	Games	BA	SA	AB	H	2B	3B	HR	HR%	R	RBI	BB	SO	SB	Pinch Hit AB	Pinch Hit H	PO	A	E	DP	TC/G	FA	G by Pos
1971	CHI N	23	.139	.250	36	5	1	0	1	2.8	1	2	2	7	0	14	0	48	7	1	2	7.0	.982	1B-8
1972	MON N	42	.230	.356	87	20	2	0	3	3.4	6	10	7	15	0	17	5	159	10	1	12	4.7	.994	1B-26, OF-10
1973		105	.275	.535	258	71	10	6	15	5.8	36	43	29	45	0	43	12	515	45	5	50	8.6	.991	1B-66
1974		79	.247	.347	190	47	13	0	2	1.1	14	20	24	35	0	25	6	422	31	6	43	8.2	.987	1B-56
1975		24	.135	.189	37	5	2	0	0	0.0	4	1	7	5	0	12	3	84	4	1	5	7.4	.989	1B-12
5 yrs.		273	.243	.413	608	148	28	6	21	3.5	61	76	69	107	0	111	26	1228	97	14	112	7.5	.990	1B-168, OF-10

Marv Breeding

BREEDING, MARVIN EUGENE
B. Mar. 8, 1934, Decatur, Ala.

BR TR 6′ 175 lbs.

Year	Team	Games	BA	SA	AB	H	2B	3B	HR	HR%	R	RBI	BB	SO	SB	Pinch Hit AB	Pinch Hit H	PO	A	E	DP	TC/G	FA	G by Pos
1960	BAL A	152	.267	.336	551	147	25	2	3	0.5	69	43	35	80	10	0	0	359	422	18	116	5.3	.977	2B-152
1961		90	.209	.254	244	51	8	0	1	0.4	32	16	14	33	5	3	0	179	179	11	53	4.6	.970	2B-80
1962		95	.246	.321	240	59	10	1	2	0.8	27	18	8	41	2	10	1	146	196	9	47	4.7	.974	2B-73, 3B-1, SS-1
1963	2 teams WAS A (58G –.274) LA N (20G –.167)																							
″	total	78	.258	.318	233	60	7	2	1	0.4	26	15	9	26	2	10	4	92	134	13	15	3.3	.946	2B-39, 3B-30, SS-3
4 yrs.		415	.250	.314	1268	317	50	5	7	0.6	154	92	66	180	19	23	5	776	931	51	231	4.6	.971	2B-344, 3B-31, SS-4

Ted Breitenstein

BREITENSTEIN, THEODORE P.
B. June 1, 1869, St. Louis, Mo. D. May 3, 1935, St. Louis, Mo.

BL TL 5′ 9″ 167 lbs.

Year	Team	Games	BA	SA	AB	H	2B	3B	HR	HR%	R	RBI	BB	SO	SB	Pinch Hit AB	Pinch Hit H	PO	A	E	DP	TC/G	FA	G by Pos
1891	STL AA	6	.000	.000	12	0	0	0	0	0.0	2	0	2	0	1	0	0	2	3	0	0	0.7	1.000	P-6, OF-1
1892	STL N	47	.122	.145	131	16	1	1	0	0.0	16	6	16	20	4	0	0	33	69	6	3	2.2	.944	P-39, OF-10
1893		49	.181	.219	160	29	1	1	1	0.6	20	14	18	15	3	0	0	43	82	8	4	2.7	.940	P-48, OF-2
1894		63	.220	.280	182	40	7	2	0	0.0	27	13	31	19	3	0	0	47	83	10	4	2.2	.929	P-56, OF-7
1895		72	.193	.202	218	42	2	0	0	0.0	25	18	29	22	5	1	1	63	98	17	1	2.5	.904	P-54, OF-16
1896		51	.259	.315	162	42	5	2	0	0.0	21	12	13	26	8	1	1	46	89	8	4	2.8	.944	P-44, OF-8
1897	CIN N	41	.266	.395	124	33	4	6	0	0.0	16	23	6		5	1	0	16	65	3	3	2.1	.964	P-40
1898		41	.215	.248	121	26	2	1	0	0.0	16	17	16		0	0	0	22	89	4	3	2.8	.965	P-39, OF-2
1899		33	.352	.438	105	37	4	1	1	1.0	18	11	10		1	0	0	25	50	5	1	2.4	.938	P-26, OF-7
1900		41	.190	.262	126	24	1	1	2	1.6	12	12	9		0	5	1	29	62	7	0	2.7	.929	P-24, OF-12
1901	STL N	3	.333	.333	6	2	0	0	0	0.0	1	0	0		0	0	0	2	7	0	2	3.0	1.000	P-3
11 yrs.		447	.216	.267	1347	291	27	15	4	0.3	174	126	150	102	30	8	3	328	697	68	25	2.5	.938	P-379, OF-65

Herb Bremer

BREMER, HERBERT FREDERICK (Butch)
B. Oct. 25, 1913, Chicago, Ill. D. Nov. 28, 1979, Columbus, Ga.

BR TR 6′ 195 lbs.

Year	Team	Games	BA	SA	AB	H	2B	3B	HR	HR%	R	RBI	BB	SO	SB	Pinch Hit AB	Pinch Hit H	PO	A	E	DP	TC/G	FA	G by Pos
1937	STL N	11	.212	.242	33	7	1	0	0	0.0	2	3	2	4	0	0	0	40	6	1	2	4.7	.979	C-10
1938		50	.219	.305	151	33	5	1	2	1.3	14	14	9	36	1	0	0	186	30	5	2	4.4	.977	C-50
1939		9	.111	.111	9	1	0	0	0	0.0	0	1	0	2	0	1	0	13	0	0	0	1.6	1.000	C-8
3 yrs.		70	.212	.285	193	41	6	1	2	1.0	16	18	11	42	1	1	0	239	36	6	4	4.1	.979	C-68

Sam Brenegan

BRENEGAN, OLAF SELMER
B. Sept. 1, 1890, Galesville, Wis. D. Apr. 20, 1956, Galesville, Wis.

BL TR 6′ 2″ 185 lbs.

Year	Team	Games	BA	SA	AB	H	2B	3B	HR	HR%	R	RBI	BB	SO	SB	Pinch Hit AB	Pinch Hit H	PO	A	E	DP	TC/G	FA	G by Pos
1914	PIT N	1	—	—	0	0	0	0	0	—	0	0	0	0	0	0	0	0	0	0	0	0.0	.000	C-1

Bob Brenly

BRENLY, ROBERT EARL
B. Feb. 25, 1954, Coshocton, Ohio.
BR TR 6′ 2″ 210 lbs.

Year	Team		Games	BA	SA	AB	H	2B	3B	HR	HR%	R	RBI	BB	SO	SB	Pinch Hit AB	Pinch Hit H	PO	A	E	DP	TC/G	FA	G by Pos
1981	SF	N	19	.333	.489	45	15	2	1	1	2.2	5	4	6	4	0	1	0	52	6	4	2	3.4	.935	C-14, 3B-3, OF-1
1982			65	.283	.383	180	51	4	1	4	2.2	26	15	18	26	6	9	3	265	32	12	2	5.0	.961	C-61, 3B-1
1983			104	.224	.356	281	63	12	2	7	2.5	36	34	37	48	10	13	2	465	73	9	15	5.4	.984	C-90, 1B-10, OF-2
1984			145	.291	.464	506	147	28	0	20	4.0	74	80	48	52	6	6	1	807	76	13	21	5.9	.985	C-127, 1B-22, OF-3
1985			133	.220	.391	440	97	16	1	19	4.3	41	56	57	62	1	7	1	719	85	17	16	6.0	.979	C-110, 3B-17, 1B-10
1986			149	.246	.403	472	116	26	0	16	3.4	60	62	74	97	10	8	0	688	118	16	20	5.0	.981	C-101, 3B-45, 1B-19
1987			123	.267	.467	375	100	19	1	18	4.8	55	51	47	85	10	8	2	685	86	9	14	6.7	.988	C-108, 1B-6, 3B-2
1988			73	.189	.296	206	39	7	0	5	2.4	13	22	20	40	1	5	0	334	27	6	2	5.3	.984	C-69
1989	2 teams		TOR A (48G –.170)	SF N (12G –.182)																					
″	total		60	.173	.264	110	19	5	1	1	0.9	11	9	11	24	1	16	6	92	10	1	1	1.8	.990	DH-28, C-25, 1B-5
9 yrs.			871	.247	.403	2615	647	119	7	91	3.5	321	333	318	438	45	73	15	4107	513	87	93	5.4	.982	C-705, 1B-72, 3B-68, DH-28, OF-6
LEAGUE CHAMPIONSHIP SERIES																									
1987	SF	N	6	.235	.471	17	4	1	0	1	5.9	3	2	3	7	0	1	0	28	2	0	0	5.0	1.000	C-6

Jim Brennan

BRENNAN, JAMES AUGUSTUS (Old Sport)
B. 1862, St. Louis, Mo. D. Oct. 18, 1904, Philadelphia, Pa.

Year	Team		Games	BA	SA	AB	H	2B	3B	HR	HR%	R	RBI	BB	SO	SB	Pinch Hit AB	Pinch Hit H	PO	A	E	DP	TC/G	FA	G by Pos
1884	STL	U	56	.216	.251	231	50	6	1	0	0.0	38		12			0	0	172	92	40	4	5.3	.868	C-33, OF-16, 3B-7, SS-1
1885	STL	N	3	.100	.100	10	1	0	0	0	0.0	0	1	1	1		0	0	3	1	3	0	2.3	.571	OF-2, 3B-1
1888	KC	AA	34	.169	.186	118	20	2	0	0	0.0	5	6	3		3	0	0	111	62	27	5	5.7	.865	C-25, OF-5, 3B-5
1889	PHI	AA	31	.221	.257	113	25	4	0	0	0.0	12	15	10	15	1	0	0	53	55	22	5	4.2	.831	C-13, 2B-7, OF-7, 3B-4
1890	CLE	P	59	.253	.326	233	59	3	7	0	0.0	32	26	13	29	8	0	0	153	77	47	8	4.5	.830	C-42, 3B-14, OF-6
5 yrs.			183	.220	.264	705	155	15	8	0	0.0	87	48	39	45	12	0	0	492	287	139	22	4.9	.849	C-113, OF-36, 3B-31, 2B-7, SS-1

Bill Brenzel

BRENZEL, WILLIAM RICHARD
B. Mar. 3, 1910, Oakland, Calif. D. June 12, 1979, Oakland, Calif.
BR TR 5′10″ 173 lbs.

Year	Team		Games	BA	SA	AB	H	2B	3B	HR	HR%	R	RBI	BB	SO	SB	Pinch Hit AB	Pinch Hit H	PO	A	E	DP	TC/G	FA	G by Pos
1932	PIT	N	9	.042	.083	24	1	1	0	0	0.0	0	2	0	4	0	0	0	35	2	0	1	4.1	1.000	C-9
1934	CLE	A	15	.216	.275	51	11	3	0	0	0.0	4	3	2	1	0	0	0	67	10	0	1	5.1	1.000	C-15
1935			52	.218	.268	142	31	5	1	0	0.0	12	14	6	10	2	0	0	135	18	4	3	3.1	.975	C-51
3 yrs.			76	.198	.249	217	43	9	1	0	0.0	16	19	8	15	2	0	0	237	30	4	5	3.6	.985	C-75

Roger Bresnahan

BRESNAHAN, ROGER PHILIP (The Duke of Tralee)
B. June 11, 1879, Toledo, Ohio D. Dec. 4, 1944, Toledo, Ohio.
Manager 1909–12, 1915.
Hall of Fame 1945.
BR TR 5′ 9″ 200 lbs.

Year	Team		Games	BA	SA	AB	H	2B	3B	HR	HR%	R	RBI	BB	SO	SB	Pinch Hit AB	Pinch Hit H	PO	A	E	DP	TC/G	FA	G by Pos
1897	WAS	N	6	.375	.375	16	6	0	0	0	0.0	1	3	1		0	0	0	2	7	0	0	1.3	1.000	P-6, OF-1
1900	CHI	N	2	.000	.000	2	0	0	0	0	0.0	0	0	0		0	0	0	0	0	0	0	0.0	.000	C-1
1901	BAL	A	86	.268	.369	295	79	9	9	1	0.3	40	32	23		10	1	0	219	71	27	4	3.7	.915	C-69, OF-8, 3B-4, 2B-2, P-2
1902	2 teams		BAL A (65G –.272)	NY N (51G –.292)																					
″	total		116	.281	.414	413	116	22	9	5	1.2	47	56	37		18	2	2	290	120	35	12	3.7	.921	OF-42, C-38, 3B-31, SS-4, 1B-4
1903	NY	N	113	.350	.493	406	142	30	8	4	1.0	87	55	61		34	1	1	300	46	21	11	3.3	.943	OF-84, 1B-13, C-11, 3B-4
1904			109	.284	.410	402	114	22	7	5	1.2	81	33	58		13	3	1	241	30	15	13	2.6	.948	OF-93, 1B-10, SS-4, 3B-1, 2B-1
1905			104	.302	.375	331	100	18	3	0	0.0	58	46	50		11	6	0	503	115	19	15	6.7	.970	C-87, OF-8
1906			124	.281	.356	405	114	22	4	0	0.0	69	43	81		25	0	0	478	131	17	8	5.1	.973	C-82, OF-40
1907			110	.253	.360	328	83	9	7	4	1.2	57	38	61		15	6	2	547	101	13	12	6.4	.980	C-95, 1B-6, OF-2, 3B-1
1908			140	.283	.359	449	127	25	3	1	0.2	70	54	**83**		14	1	1	657	140	12	12	5.8	.985	C-139
1909	STL	N	72	.244	.269	234	57	4	1	0	0.0	27	23	46		11	2	0	224	105	16	9	5.0	.954	C-59, 2B-9, 3B-1
1910			88	.278	.368	234	65	15	3	0	0.0	35	27	55	17	13	5	0	296	103	16	12	5.2	.961	C-77, OF-2, P-1
1911			81	.278	.463	227	63	17	8	3	1.3	22	41	45	19	4	3	1	325	103	14	9	5.6	.968	C-77, 2B-2
1912			48	.333	.463	108	36	7	2	1	0.9	8	15	14	9	4	14	7	138	49	5	4	6.9	.974	C-28
1913	CHI	N	68	.230	.304	161	37	5	2	1	0.6	20	21	21	11	7	9	4	194	67	10	2	4.7	.963	C-58
1914			86	.278	.351	248	69	10	4	0	0.0	42	24	49	20	14	4	1	377	131	12	6	5.2	.977	C-85, 2B-14, OF-1
1915			77	.204	.262	221	45	8	1	1	0.5	19	19	29	23	19	6	0	345	95	8	9	6.6	.982	C-68
17 yrs.			1430	.280	.379	4480	1253	223	71	26	0.6	683	530	714	99	212	63	20	5136	1414	240	138	4.9	.965	C-974, OF-281, 3B-42, 1B-33, 2B-28, P-9, SS-8
WORLD SERIES																									
1905	NY	N	5	.313	.438	16	5	2	0	0	0.0	3	1	4	0	1	0	0	27	7	0	0	6.8	1.000	C-5

Rube Bressler

BRESSLER, RAYMOND BLOOM
B. Oct. 23, 1894, Coder, Pa. D. Nov. 7, 1966, Mt. Washington, Ohio.
BR TL 6′ 187 lbs.

Year	Team		Games	BA	SA	AB	H	2B	3B	HR	HR%	R	RBI	BB	SO	SB	Pinch Hit AB	Pinch Hit H	PO	A	E	DP	TC/G	FA	G by Pos
1914	PHI	A	29	.216	.275	51	11	1	1	0	0.0	6	4	6	7	0	0	0	6	26	2	2	1.2	.941	P-29
1915			33	.145	.236	55	8	0	1	1	1.8	9	4	9	13	0	1	0	7	56	7	0	2.2	.900	P-32
1916			4	.200	.600	5	1	0	1	0	0.0	1	1	0	0	0	0	0	0	2	0	0	0.5	1.000	P-4
1917	CIN	N	3	.200	.200	5	1	0	0	0	0.0	0	0	0	2	0	1	0	1	1	0	0	1.0	1.000	P-2
1918			23	.274	.355	62	17	5	0	0	0.0	10	6	5	4	0	1	0	10	51	1	2	3.1	.984	P-17, OF-3
1919			61	.206	.309	165	34	3	4	2	1.2	22	17	23	15	2	1	0	107	19	5	1	2.1	.962	OF-48, P-13
1920			21	.267	.300	30	8	1	0	0	0.0	4	3	1	4	1	6	0	25	7	4	2	2.4	.889	P-10, OF-3, 1B-2
1921			109	.307	.409	323	99	18	6	1	0.3	41	54	39	20	5	12	4	202	7	8	5	2.4	.963	OF-85, 1B-6
1922			52	.264	.340	53	14	0	2	0	0.0	7	8	4	4	1	**43**	**13**	16	0	1	0	3.4	.941	1B-3, OF-2
1923			54	.277	.319	119	33	3	1	0	0.0	25	18	20	4	3	24	9	227	9	4	12	8.6	.983	1B-22, OF-6
1924			115	.347	.483	383	133	14	13	4	1.0	41	49	22	20	9	16	3	561	35	9	36	6.1	.985	1B-50, OF-49
1925			97	.348	.476	319	111	17	6	4	1.3	43	61	40	16	9	6	3	602	23	12	46	7.1	.981	1B-52, OF-38
1926			86	.357	.478	297	106	15	9	1	0.3	58	51	37	20	3	4	0	183	5	5	2	2.3	.974	OF-80, 1B-4
1927			124	.291	.375	467	136	14	8	3	0.6	43	77	32	22	4	3	0	261	15	8	5	2.4	.972	OF-120
1928	BKN	N	145	.295	.429	501	148	29	13	4	0.8	78	70	80	33	2	7	3	254	7	4	0	1.9	.985	OF-137
1929			136	.318	.461	456	145	22	8	9	2.0	72	77	67	27	4	12	3	263	7	13	0	2.3	.954	OF-122
1930			109	.299	.409	335	100	12	8	3	0.9	53	52	51	19	4	8	0	262	11	1	8	2.8	.996	OF-90, 1B-7

Rube Bressler *continued*

Year	Team	Games	BA	SA	AB	H	2B	3B	HR	HR%	R	RBI	BB	SO	SB	Pinch Hit AB	Pinch Hit H	PO	A	E	DP	TC/G	FA	G by Pos
1931		67	.281	.373	153	43	4	5	0	0.0	22	26	11	10	0	29	2	66	2	1	0	1.9	.986	OF-35, 1B-1
1932	**2 teams**	**PHI N** (27G –.229)	**STL N** (10G –.158)																					
"	**total**	37	.216	.294	102	22	6	1	0	0.0	9	8	2	6	0	14	5	51	4	0	1	2.5	1.000	OF-22
19 yrs.		1305	.301	.413	3881	1170	164	87	32	0.8	544	586	449	246	47	188	45	3104	287	85	122	3.2	.976	OF-840, 1B-147, P-107

Ed Bressoud

BRESSOUD, EDWARD FRANCIS
B. May 2, 1932, Los Angeles, Calif.
BR TR 6′ 1″ 175 lbs.

Year	Team	Games	BA	SA	AB	H	2B	3B	HR	HR%	R	RBI	BB	SO	SB	Pinch Hit AB	Pinch Hit H	PO	A	E	DP	TC/G	FA	G by Pos
1956	**NY N**	49	.227	.276	163	37	4	2	0	0.0	15	9	12	20	1	1	0	67	125	10	26	4.2	.950	SS-48
1957		49	.268	.433	127	34	2	2	5	3.9	11	10	4	19	0	2	0	67	97	13	16	3.9	.927	SS-33, 3B-12
1958	**SF N**	66	.263	.343	137	36	5	3	0	0.0	19	8	14	22	0	0	0	105	106	8	26	3.3	.963	2B-57, 3B-6, SS-4
1959		104	.251	.403	315	79	17	2	9	2.9	36	26	28	55	0	5	0	153	270	13	38	4.6	.970	SS-92, 2B-1, 3B-1, 1B-1
1960		116	.225	.376	386	87	19	6	9	2.3	37	43	35	72	1	1	0	191	339	22	53	4.8	.960	SS-115
1961		59	.211	.342	114	24	6	0	3	2.6	14	11	11	23	1	20	4	51	61	4	12	3.1	.966	SS-34, 3B-3, 2B-1
1962	**BOS A**	153	.277	.444	599	166	40	9	14	2.3	79	68	46	118	2	0	0	291	482	28	107	5.2	.965	SS-153
1963		140	.260	.451	497	129	23	6	20	4.0	61	60	52	93	1	2	0	260	351	24	76	4.6	.962	SS-137
1964		158	.293	.456	566	166	41	3	15	2.7	86	55	72	99	1	0	0	248	411	19	78	4.3	.972	SS-158
1965		107	.226	.351	296	67	11	1	8	2.7	29	25	29	77	0	21	7	147	196	13	46	4.0	.963	SS-86, 3B-2, OF-1
1966	**NY N**	133	.225	.360	405	91	15	5	10	2.5	48	49	47	107	2	12	2	213	343	23	67	4.1	.960	SS-94, 3B-32, 1B-9, 2B-7
1967	**STL N**	52	.134	.224	67	9	1	1	1	1.5	8	1	9	18	0	3	1	34	58	7	12	2.0	.929	SS-48, 3B-1
12 yrs.		1186	.252	.401	3672	925	184	40	94	2.6	443	365	359	723	9	67	14	1827	2839	184	557	4.3	.962	SS-1002, 2B-66, 3B-57, 1B-10, OF-1
WORLD SERIES																								
1967	**STL N**	2	—	—	0	0	0	0	0	—	0	0	0	0	0	0	0	0	0	0	0	0.0	.000	SS-2

Jim Breton

BRETON, JOHN FREDERICK
B. July 15, 1891, Chicago, Ill. D. May 30, 1973, Beloit, Wis.
BR TR 5′10½″ 178 lbs.

Year	Team	Games	BA	SA	AB	H	2B	3B	HR	HR%	R	RBI	BB	SO	SB	Pinch Hit AB	Pinch Hit H	PO	A	E	DP	TC/G	FA	G by Pos
1913	**CHI A**	10	.167	.267	30	5	1	1	0	0.0	1	2	1	5	0	0	0	8	30	3	2	4.1	.927	SS-7, 3B-3
1914		81	.212	.260	231	49	7	2	0	0.0	21	24	24	42	9	0	0	84	159	24	6	3.4	.910	3B-79
1915		16	.139	.167	36	5	1	0	0	0.0	3	1	5	9	2	0	0	15	19	4	2	2.4	.895	3B-14, SS-1, 2B-1
3 yrs.		107	.199	.249	297	59	9	3	0	0.0	25	27	30	56	11	0	0	107	208	31	10	3.3	.910	3B-96, SS-8, 2B-1

George Brett

BRETT, GEORGE HOWARD
Brother of Ken Brett.
B. May 15, 1953, Glen Dale, W. Va.
BL TR 6′ 185 lbs.

Year	Team	Games	BA	SA	AB	H	2B	3B	HR	HR%	R	RBI	BB	SO	SB	Pinch Hit AB	Pinch Hit H	PO	A	E	DP	TC/G	FA	G by Pos
1973	**KC A**	13	.125	.175	40	5	2	0	0	0.0	2	0	0	5	0	1	0	9	28	1	2	2.9	.974	3B-13
1974		133	.282	.363	457	129	21	5	2	0.4	49	47	21	38	8	2	0	102	279	21	16	3.0	.948	3B-132, SS-1
1975		159	.308	.456	**634**	**195**	35	**13**	11	1.7	84	89	46	49	13	0	0	132	356	26	27	3.2	.949	3B-159, SS-1
1976		159	**.333**	.462	**645**	**215**	34	**14**	7	1.1	94	67	49	36	21	0	0	146	350	26	23	3.2	.950	3B-157, SS-4
1977		139	.312	.532	564	176	32	13	22	3.9	105	88	55	24	14	3	1	115	325	21	33	3.3	.954	3B-135, DH-3, SS-1
1978		128	.294	.467	510	150	**45**	8	9	1.8	79	62	39	35	23	0	0	104	289	16	25	3.2	.961	3B-128, SS-1
1979		154	.329	.563	645	**212**	42	**20**	23	3.6	119	107	51	36	17	0	0	176	378	31	34	3.7	.947	3B-149, 1B-8, DH-1
1980		117	**.390**	**.664**	449	175	33	9	24	5.3	87	118	58	22	15	3	1	107	256	17	29	3.4	.955	3B-112, 1B-1
1981		89	.314	.484	347	109	27	7	6	1.7	42	43	27	23	14	0	0	74	170	14	7	2.9	.946	3B-88
1982		144	.301	.505	552	166	32	9	21	3.8	101	82	71	51	6	0	0	130	295	17	23	3.0	.962	3B-134, OF-12
1983		123	.310	**.563**	464	144	38	2	25	5.4	90	93	57	39	0	1	1	210	192	25	34	3.3	.941	3B-102, 1B-14, OF-13, DH-1
1984		104	.284	.459	377	107	21	3	13	3.4	42	69	38	37	0	3	1	59	201	14	18	2.7	.949	3B-101
1985		155	.335	**.585**	550	184	38	5	30	5.5	108	112	103	49	9	2	0	107	339	15	33	3.0	.967	3B-152, DH-1
1986		124	.290	.481	441	128	28	4	16	3.6	70	73	80	45	1	1	0	97	218	16	17	2.7	.952	3B-115, DH-7, SS-2
1987		115	.290	.496	427	124	18	2	22	5.2	71	78	72	47	6	0	0	805	69	9	72	7.7	.990	1B-83, DH-21, 3B-11
1988		157	.306	.509	589	180	42	3	24	4.1	90	103	82	51	14	0	0	1126	70	10	105	7.6	.992	1B-124, DH-33, SS-1
1989		124	.282	.431	457	129	26	3	12	2.6	67	80	59	47	14	3	0	898	80	2	71	8.0	.998	1B-104, DH-17, OF-2
1990		142	**.329**	.515	544	179	**45**	7	14	2.6	82	87	56	63	9	1	0	880	67	7	89	6.6	.993	1B-102, DH-32, OF-9, 3B-1
1991		131	.255	.402	505	129	40	2	10	2.0	77	61	58	75	2	3	1	87	5	1	6	0.7	.989	DH-118, 1B-10
1992		152	.285	.397	592	169	35	5	7	1.2	55	61	35	69	8	3	0	139	17	3	10	1.1	.981	DH-132, 1B-15, 3B-3
1993		145	.266	.434	560	149	31	3	19	3.4	69	75	39	67	7	6	2	0	0	0	0	0.0	.000	DH-140
21 yrs.		2707	.305	.487	10349	3154	665	137	317	3.1	1583	1595	1096	908	201	32	7	5503	3984	292	674	3.6	.970	3B-1692, DH-506, 1B-461, OF-36, SS-11
							5th																	
DIVISIONAL PLAYOFF SERIES																								
1981	**KC A**	3	.167	.167	12	2	0	0	0	0.0	0	0	0	0	0	0	0	1	6	1	0	2.7	.875	3B-3
LEAGUE CHAMPIONSHIP SERIES																								
1976	**KC A**	5	.444	.778	18	8	1	1	1	5.6	4	5	2	1	0	0	0	3	7	3	1	2.6	.769	3B-5
1977		5	.300	.500	20	6	0	2	0	0.0	2	2	1	0	0	0	0	5	12	2	2	3.8	.895	3B-5
1978		4	.389	1.056	18	7	1	1	3	16.7	7	3	0	1	0	0	0	3	8	1	1	3.0	.917	3B-4
1980		3	.273	.909	11	3	1	0	2	18.2	3	4	1	0	0	0	0	2	7	0	0	3.0	1.000	3B-3
1984		3	.231	.231	13	3	0	0	0	0.0	0	0	0	2	0	0	0	2	7	0	1	3.0	1.000	3B-3
1985		7	.348	.826	23	8	2	0	3	13.0	6	5	7	5	0	0	0	7	8	2	0	2.4	.882	3B-7
6 yrs.		27	.340	.728	103	35	5	4	9	8.7	22	19	11	9	0	0	0	22	49	8	5	2.9	.899	3B-27
		6th		**2nd**	**4th**	**3rd**		**1st**	**1st**	**2nd**	**1st**	**3rd**	**9th**											
WORLD SERIES																								
1980	**KC A**	6	.375	.667	24	9	2	1	1	4.2	3	3	2	4	1	0	0	4	17	1	1	3.7	.955	3B-6
1985		7	.370	.407	27	10	1	0	0	0.0	5	1	4	7	1	0	0	10	19	1	1	4.3	.967	3B-7
2 yrs.		13	.373	.529	51	19	3	1	1	2.0	8	4	6	11	2	0	0	14	36	2	2	4.0	.962	3B-13
			6th																					

Ken Brett

BRETT, KENNETH ALVEN
Brother of George Brett.
B. Sept. 18, 1948, Brooklyn, N. Y.
BL TL 6′ 190 lbs.

Year	Team	Games	BA	SA	AB	H	2B	3B	HR	HR%	R	RBI	BB	SO	SB	Pinch Hit AB	Pinch Hit H	PO	A	E	DP	TC/G	FA	G by Pos
1967	**BOS A**	1	—	—	0	0	0	0	0	—	0	0	0	0	0	0	0	0	0	0	0	0.0	.000	P-1
1969		8	.300	.700	10	3	1	0	1	10.0	1	3	1	1	0	0	0	2	6	0	0	1.0	1.000	P-8
1970		41	.317	.537	41	13	3	0	2	4.9	8	3	2	7	0	0	0	9	20	2	0	0.8	.935	P-41
1971		29	.200	.200	10	2	0	0	0	0.0	0	0	0	2	0	0	0	0	8	0	0	0.3	1.000	P-29
1972	**MIL A**	31	.227	.250	44	10	1	0	0	0.0	6	1	2	10	0	1	0	6	15	3	1	0.9	.875	P-26

Ken Brett *continued*

Year	Team	Games	BA	SA	AB	H	2B	3B	HR	HR%	R	RBI	BB	SO	SB	Pinch Hit AB	Pinch Hit H	PO	A	E	DP	TC/G	FA	G by Pos
1973	PHI N	37	.250	.463	80	20	5	0	4	5.0	6	16	4	17	0	2	0	13	39	0	4	1.7	1.000	P-31
1974	PIT N	43	.310	.448	87	27	4	1	2	2.3	13	15	4	20	0	15	3	12	28	0	1	1.5	1.000	P-27
1975		26	.231	.365	52	12	4	0	1	1.9	5	4	1	7	0	3	0	13	18	1	0	1.4	.969	P-23
1976	2 teams	NY A (2G –.000) CHI A (33G –.083)																						
"	total	35	.083	.083	12	1	0	0	0	0.0	0	0	0	1	0	6	1	11	35	3	0	1.7	.939	P-29
1977	2 teams	CHI A (13G –.000) CAL A (21G –.000)																						
"	total	34			0	0	0	0	0		0	0	0	0	0	0	0	11	48	2	6	1.8	.967	P-34
1978	CAL A	31	—	—	0	0	0	0	0	—	0	0	0	0	0	0	0	12	20	2	4	1.1	.941	P-31
1979	2 teams	MIN A (9G –.000) LA N (30G –.273)																						
"	total	39	.273	.273	11	3	0	0	0	0.0	0	2	0	2	0	0	0	10	17	0	1	0.7	1.000	P-39
1980	KC A	8	—	—	0	0	0	0	0	—	0	0	0	0	0	0	0	0	3	0	0	0.4	1.000	P-8
1981		22	—	—	0	0	0	0	0	—	0	0	0	0	0	0	0	5	6	0	1	0.5	1.000	P-22
14 yrs.		385	.262	.406	347	91	18	1	10	2.9	39	44	14	67	0	27	4	104	263	13	18	1.1	.966	P-349
LEAGUE CHAMPIONSHIP SERIES																								
1974	PIT N	1	.000	.000	1	0	0	0	0	0.0	0	0	0	1	0	0	0	0	1	0	0	1.0	1.000	P-1
1975		2	—	—	0	0	0	0	0	—	0	0	0	0	0	0	0	0	0	0	0	0.0	.000	P-2
2 yrs.		3	.000	.000	1	0	0	0	0	0.0	0	0	0	1	0	0	0	0	1	0	0	0.3	1.000	P-3
WORLD SERIES																								
1967	BOS A	2	—	—	0	0	0	0	0	—	0	0	0	0	0	0	0	0	0	0	0	0.0	.000	P-2

Mike Brewer

BREWER, MICHAEL QUINN BR TR 6′ 5″ 190 lbs.
Brother of Tony Brewer.
B. Oct. 24, 1959, Shreveport, La.

Year	Team	Games	BA	SA	AB	H	2B	3B	HR	HR%	R	RBI	BB	SO	SB	Pinch Hit AB	Pinch Hit H	PO	A	E	DP	TC/G	FA	G by Pos
1986	KC A	12	.167	.222	18	3	1	0	0	0.0	0	0	2	6	0	1	0	9	0	0	0	0.9	1.000	OF-9, DH-1

Rod Brewer

BREWER, RODNEY LEE BL TL 6′ 3″ 210 lbs.
B. Feb. 24, 1966, Eustis, Fla.

Year	Team	Games	BA	SA	AB	H	2B	3B	HR	HR%	R	RBI	BB	SO	SB	Pinch Hit AB	Pinch Hit H	PO	A	E	DP	TC/G	FA	G by Pos
1990	STL N	14	.240	.280	25	6	1	0	0	0.0	4	2	0	4	0	5	0	46	6	1	5	5.9	.981	1B-9
1991		19	.077	.077	13	1	0	0	0	0.0	0	1	0	5	0	1	0	30	3	1	2	1.9	.971	1B-15, OF-3
1992		29	.301	.359	103	31	6	0	0	0.0	11	10	8	12	0	1	0	220	19	0	17	7.7	1.000	1B-27, OF-4
1993		110	.286	.381	147	42	8	0	2	1.4	15	20	17	26	1	42	12	148	6	3	13	2.4	.981	OF-33, 1B-32, P-1
4 yrs.		172	.278	.351	288	80	15	0	2	0.7	30	33	25	47	1	49	12	444	34	5	37	3.9	.990	1B-83, OF-40, P-1

Tony Brewer

BREWER, ANTHONY BRUCE BR TR 5′11″ 190 lbs.
Brother of Mike Brewer.
B. Nov. 25, 1957, Coushatta, La.

Year	Team	Games	BA	SA	AB	H	2B	3B	HR	HR%	R	RBI	BB	SO	SB	Pinch Hit AB	Pinch Hit H	PO	A	E	DP	TC/G	FA	G by Pos
1984	LA N	24	.108	.216	37	4	1	0	1	2.7	3	4	4	9	1	14	1	9	0	0	0	0.9	1.000	OF-10

Charlie Brewster

BREWSTER, CHARLES LAWRENCE BR TR 5′ 8½″ 175 lbs.
B. Dec. 27, 1916, Marthaville, La.

Year	Team	Games	BA	SA	AB	H	2B	3B	HR	HR%	R	RBI	BB	SO	SB	Pinch Hit AB	Pinch Hit H	PO	A	E	DP	TC/G	FA	G by Pos
1943	2 teams	CIN N (7G –.125) PHI N (49G –.220)																						
"	total	56	.216	.228	167	36	2	0	0	0.0	13	12	10	20	1	2	0	76	112	20	19	4.3	.904	SS-46, 2B-2
1944	CHI N	10	.250	.295	44	11	2	0	0	0.0	4	2	5	7	0	0	0	27	29	6	9	6.2	.903	SS-10
1946	CLE A	3	.000	.000	2	0	0	0	0	0.0	0	0	1	1	0	1	0	0	1	0	0	1.0	1.000	SS-1
3 yrs.		69	.221	.239	213	47	4	0	0	0.0	17	14	16	28	1	3	0	103	142	26	28	4.6	.904	SS-57, 2B-2

Fred Brickell

BRICKELL, GEORGE FREDERICK BL TR 5′ 7″ 160 lbs.
Father of Fritzie Brickell.
B. Nov. 9, 1906, Saffordville, Kans. D. Apr. 8, 1961, Wichita, Kans.

Year	Team	Games	BA	SA	AB	H	2B	3B	HR	HR%	R	RBI	BB	SO	SB	Pinch Hit AB	Pinch Hit H	PO	A	E	DP	TC/G	FA	G by Pos
1926	PIT N	24	.345	.436	55	19	3	1	0	0.0	11	4	3	6	0	4	2	20	3	2	1	1.8	.920	OF-14
1927		32	.286	.476	21	6	1	0	1	4.8	6	4	1	0	0	15	4	5	0	0	0	1.7	1.000	OF-3
1928		81	.322	.426	202	65	4	4	3	1.5	34	41	20	18	5	24	7	107	6	5	1	2.4	.958	OF-50
1929		60	.314	.381	118	37	4	2	0	0.0	13	17	7	12	3	29	6	54	3	0	0	2.1	1.000	OF-27
1930	2 teams	PIT N (68G –.297) PHI N (53G –.246)																						
"	total	121	.270	.362	459	124	21	9	1	0.2	69	31	28	41	4	5	2	285	9	13	1	2.7	.958	OF-114
1931	PHI N	130	.253	.305	514	130	14	5	1	0.2	77	31	42	39	5	5	2	341	8	8	2	2.9	.978	OF-122
1932		45	.333	.455	66	22	6	1	0	0.0	9	2	4	5	2	20	5	27	2	2	1	2.6	.935	OF-12
1933		8	.308	.538	13	4	1	1	0	0.0	2	1	1	0	0	2	0	10	1	0	0	2.8	1.000	OF-4
8 yrs.		501	.281	.363	1448	407	54	23	6	0.4	221	131	106	121	19	104	28	849	32	30	6	2.6	.967	OF-346
WORLD SERIES																								
1927	PIT N	2	.000	.000	2	0	0	0	0	0.0	1	0	0	0	0	2	0	0	0	0	0	0.0	—	

Fritzie Brickell

BRICKELL, FRITZ DARRELL BR TR 5′ 5½″ 157 lbs.
Son of Fred Brickell.
B. Mar. 19, 1935, Wichita, Kans. D. Oct. 15, 1965, Wichita, Kans.

Year	Team	Games	BA	SA	AB	H	2B	3B	HR	HR%	R	RBI	BB	SO	SB	Pinch Hit AB	Pinch Hit H	PO	A	E	DP	TC/G	FA	G by Pos
1958	NY A	2	—	—	0	0	0	0	0	—	0	0	0	0	0	0	0	0	1	0	0	0.5	1.000	2B-2
1959		18	.256	.359	39	10	1	0	1	2.6	4	4	1	10	0	0	0	16	35	4	3	3.1	.927	SS-15, 2B-3
1961	LA A	21	.122	.122	49	6	0	0	0	0.0	3	3	6	9	0	3	0	30	34	7	11	4.2	.901	SS-17
3 yrs.		41	.182	.227	88	16	1	0	1	1.1	7	7	7	19	0	3	0	46	70	11	14	3.4	.913	SS-32, 2B-5

George Brickley

BRICKLEY, GEORGE VINCENT BR TR 5′ 9″ 180 lbs.
B. July 19, 1894, Everett, Mass. D. Feb. 23, 1947, Everett, Mass.

Year	Team	Games	BA	SA	AB	H	2B	3B	HR	HR%	R	RBI	BB	SO	SB	Pinch Hit AB	Pinch Hit H	PO	A	E	DP	TC/G	FA	G by Pos
1913	PHI A	5	.167	.333	12	2	0	1	0	0.0	0	0	0	4	0	1	0	2	0	0	0	0.5	1.000	OF-4

Jim Bridewesser

BRIDEWESER, JAMES EHRENFELD BR TR 6′ 165 lbs.
B. Feb. 13, 1927, Lancaster, Ohio D. Aug. 25, 1989, El Toro, Calif.

Year	Team	Games	BA	SA	AB	H	2B	3B	HR	HR%	R	RBI	BB	SO	SB	Pinch Hit AB	Pinch Hit H	PO	A	E	DP	TC/G	FA	G by Pos
1951	NY A	2	.375	.375	8	3	0	0	0	0.0	1	0	0	1	0	0	0	4	5	2	3	5.5	.818	SS-2
1952		42	.263	.263	38	10	0	0	0	0.0	12	2	3	5	0	9	1	13	23	4	4	1.5	.900	SS-22, 2B-4, 3B-1
1953		7	1.000	1.667	3	3	0	1	0	0.0	3	3	1	0	0	2	2	5	0	1	0	2.0	.833	SS-3
1954	BAL A	73	.265	.319	204	54	7	2	0	0.0	18	12	15	27	1	11	2	106	140	16	30	3.9	.939	SS-48, 2B-19
1955	CHI A	34	.207	.328	58	12	3	2	0	0.0	6	4	3	7	0	1	0	30	51	4	13	2.7	.953	SS-26, 3B-3, 2B-2

Jim Brideweser *continued*

Year	Team	Games	BA	SA	AB	H	2B	3B	HR	HR%	R	RBI	BB	SO	SB	Pinch Hit AB	Pinch Hit H	PO	A	E	DP	TC/G	FA	G by Pos
1956	2 teams	CHI A (10G –.182) DET A (70G –.218)																						
″	total	80	.216	.246	167	36	5	0	0	0.0	23	11	20	22	3	1	1	117	150	6	34	3.5	.978	SS-42, 2B-31, 3B-4
1957	BAL A	91	.268	.345	142	38	6	1	1	0.7	16	18	21	16	2	5	1	93	146	14	33	3.2	.945	SS-74, 3B-3, 2B-1
7 yrs.		329	.252	.310	620	156	21	6	1	0.2	79	50	63	78	6	29	7	368	515	47	117	3.3	.949	SS-217, 2B-57, 3B-11

Rocky Bridges

BRIDGES, EVERETT LAMAR BR TR 5′ 8″ 170 lbs.
B. Aug. 7, 1927, Refugio, Tex.

Year	Team	Games	BA	SA	AB	H	2B	3B	HR	HR%	R	RBI	BB	SO	SB	Pinch Hit AB	Pinch Hit H	PO	A	E	DP	TC/G	FA	G by Pos
1951	BKN N	63	.254	.328	134	34	7	0	1	0.7	13	15	10	10	0	2	0	48	94	15	15	2.7	.904	3B-40, 2B-10, SS-9
1952		51	.196	.250	56	11	3	0	0	0.0	9	2	7	9	0	3	1	44	53	3	12	2.3	.970	2B-24, SS-13, 3B-6
1953	CIN N	122	.227	.273	432	98	13	2	1	0.2	52	21	37	42	6	4	0	335	328	16	95	5.5	.976	2B-115, SS-6, 3B-3
1954		53	.231	.250	52	12	1	0	0	0.0	4	2	7	7	0	1	0	45	60	2	13	2.1	.981	SS-20, 2B-19, 3B-13
1955		95	.286	.327	168	48	4	0	1	0.6	20	18	15	19	1	0	0	69	117	6	14	2.0	.969	3B-59, SS-26, 2B-9
1956		71	.211	.211	19	4	0	0	0	0.0	9	1	4	3	1	2	0	25	24	1	1	0.7	.980	3B-51, 2B-8, SS-7, OF-1
1957	2 teams	CIN N (5G –.000) WAS A (120G –.228)																						
″	total	125	.227	.304	392	89	17	2	3	0.8	41	47	41	33	0	0	0	261	422	20	84	5.5	.972	SS-109, 2B-16, 3B-2
1958	WAS A	116	.263	.355	377	99	14	3	5	1.3	38	28	27	32	0	4	0	194	333	13	73	4.6	.976	SS-112, 3B-3, 2B-3
1959	DET A	116	.268	.349	381	102	16	3	3	0.8	38	35	30	35	1	2	0	195	308	24	70	4.6	.954	SS-110, 2B-5
1960	3 teams	DET A (10G –.200) CLE A (10G –.333) STL N (3G –.000)																						
″	total	23	.313	.313	32	10	0	0	0	0.0	1	3	1	2	0	0	0	20	36	3	6	2.6	.949	3B-10, SS-10, 2B-3
1961	LA A	84	.240	.297	229	55	5	1	2	0.9	20	15	26	37	1	1	0	145	197	6	35	4.0	.983	2B-58, SS-25, 3B-4
11 yrs.		919	.247	.313	2272	562	80	11	16	0.7	245	187	205	229	10	19	1	1381	1972	109	418	3.8	.969	SS-447, 2B-270, 3B-191, OF-1

Al Bridwell

BRIDWELL, ALBERT HENRY BL TR 5′ 9″ 170 lbs.
B. Jan. 4, 1884, Friendship, Ohio D. Jan. 23, 1969, Portsmouth, Ohio.

Year	Team	Games	BA	SA	AB	H	2B	3B	HR	HR%	R	RBI	BB	SO	SB	Pinch Hit AB	Pinch Hit H	PO	A	E	DP	TC/G	FA	G by Pos
1905	CIN N	82	.252	.272	254	64	3	1	0	0.0	17	17	19		8	7	3	104	118	17	15	3.2	.929	3B-43, OF-18, 2B-7, SS-5, 1B-1
1906	BOS N	120	.227	.251	459	104	9	1	0	0.0	41	22	44		6	0	0	322	390	54	43	6.4	.930	SS-119, OF-1
1907		140	.218	.242	509	111	8	2	0	0.0	49	26	61		17	0	0	325	437	47	57	5.8	.942	SS-140
1908	NY N	147	.285	.319	467	133	14	1	0	0.0	53	46	52		20	0	0	277	486	55	39	5.6	.933	SS-147
1909		145	.294	.338	476	140	11	5	0	0.0	59	55	67		32	0	0	268	439	45	55	5.2	.940	SS-144
1910		142	.276	.335	492	136	15	7	0	0.0	74	48	73	23	14	1	0	304	417	41	52	5.4	.946	SS-141
1911	2 teams	NY N (76G –.270) BOS N (51G –.291)																						
″	total	127	.279	.317	445	124	15	1	0	0.0	57	41	66	18	10	0	0	207	398	46	45	5.1	.929	SS-127
1912	BOS N	31	.236	.302	106	25	5	1	0	0.0	6	14	7	6	2	0	0	52	80	9	14	4.5	.936	SS-31
1913	CHI N	135	.240	.291	405	97	6	6	1	0.2	35	37	74	28	12	0	0	282	399	37	46	5.3	.948	SS-135
1914	STL F	117	.236	.286	381	90	6	5	1	0.3	46	33	71		9	3	0	240	316	31	37	5.1	.947	SS-103, 2B-11
1915		65	.229	.269	175	40	3	2	0	0.0	20	9	25		6	6	2	77	130	12	10	3.8	.945	2B-42, 3B-15, 1B-1
11 yrs.		1251	.255	.295	4169	1064	95	32	2	0.0	457	348	559	75	136	17	5	2458	3610	394	413	5.2	.939	SS-1092, 2B-60, 3B-58, OF-19, 1B-2

Bunny Brief

BRIEF, ANTHONY VINCENT BR TR 6′ 185 lbs.
Born Antonio Bordetzki.
B. July 3, 1892, Remus, Mich. D. Feb. 10, 1963, Milwaukee, Wis.

Year	Team	Games	BA	SA	AB	H	2B	3B	HR	HR%	R	RBI	BB	SO	SB	Pinch Hit AB	Pinch Hit H	PO	A	E	DP	TC/G	FA	G by Pos
1912	STL A	15	.310	.381	42	13	3	0	0	0.0	9	5	6		2	2	0	48	2	4	3	4.2	.926	OF-9, 1B-4
1913		84	.217	.318	258	56	11	6	1	0.4	24	26	21	46	3	14	1	640	35	10	41	9.8	.985	1B-62, OF-8
1915	CHI A	48	.214	.318	154	33	6	2	2	1.3	13	17	16	28	8	2	0	458	23	7	21	10.6	.986	1B-46
1917	PIT N	36	.217	.330	115	25	5	1	2	1.7	15	11	15	21	4	2	2	309	22	4	23	9.9	.988	1B-34
4 yrs.		183	.223	.325	569	127	25	9	5	0.9	61	59	58	95	17	20	3	1455	82	25	88	9.6	.984	1B-146, OF-17

Charlie Briggs

BRIGGS, CHARLES R. 5′ 7″ 170 lbs.
B. 1861, Batavia, Ill. Deceased.

Year	Team	Games	BA	SA	AB	H	2B	3B	HR	HR%	R	RBI	BB	SO	SB	Pinch Hit AB	Pinch Hit H	PO	A	E	DP	TC/G	FA	G by Pos
1884	CHI U	49	.170	.253	182	31	8	2	1	0.5	29		11			0	0	68	30	24	6	2.4	.803	OF-37, 2B-12, SS-2

Dan Briggs

BRIGGS, DAN LEE BL TL 6′ 180 lbs.
B. Nov. 18, 1952, Scotia, Calif.

Year	Team	Games	BA	SA	AB	H	2B	3B	HR	HR%	R	RBI	BB	SO	SB	Pinch Hit AB	Pinch Hit H	PO	A	E	DP	TC/G	FA	G by Pos
1975	CAL A	13	.226	.355	31	7	1	0	1	3.2	3	3	2	6	0	1	0	49	1	2	4	4.0	.962	1B-6, OF-5, DH-2
1976		77	.214	.294	248	53	13	2	1	0.4	19	14	13	47	0	4	2	358	26	5	33	4.6	.987	1B-44, OF-40, DH-1
1977		59	.162	.230	74	12	2	0	1	1.4	6	4	8	14	0	3	0	154	14	2	10	2.9	.988	1B-45, OF-13
1978	CLE A	15	.163	.265	49	8	0	1	1	2.0	4	1	4	9	0	0	0	38	1	0	1	2.6	1.000	OF-15
1979	SD N	104	.207	.357	227	47	4	3	8	3.5	34	30	18	45	2	29	3	393	31	7	21	4.6	.984	1B-50, OF-44
1981	MON N	9	.091	.091	11	1	0	0	0	0.0	0	0	0	3	0	3	0	16	2	0	1	3.0	1.000	OF-3, 1B-3
1982	CHI N	48	.125	.125	48	6	0	0	0	0.0	1	1	0	9	0	37	4	14	2	1	1	1.2	.941	OF-10, 1B-4
7 yrs.		325	.195	.294	688	134	20	6	12	1.7	67	53	45	133	2	77	9	1022	77	17	71	3.9	.985	1B-152, OF-130, DH-3

Grant Briggs

BRIGGS, GRANT 5′11″ 170 lbs.
B. Mar. 16, 1865, Pittsburgh, Pa. D. May 31, 1928, Pittsburgh, Pa.

Year	Team	Games	BA	SA	AB	H	2B	3B	HR	HR%	R	RBI	BB	SO	SB	Pinch Hit AB	Pinch Hit H	PO	A	E	DP	TC/G	FA	G by Pos
1890	SYR AA	86	.180	.231	316	57	6	5	0	0.0	44		16		7	0	0	273	94	27	8	4.5	.931	C-46, OF-33, 3B-5, SS-4
1891	LOU AA	1	.250	.250	4	1	0	0	0	0.0	0	0	0	0	0	0	0	3	1	0	0	4.0	1.000	C-1
1892	STL N	22	.073	.091	55	4	1	0	0	0.0	2	1	5	14	2	0	0	45	13	9	0	2.9	.866	C-15, OF-8
1895	LOU N	1	.000	.000	3	0	0	0	0	0.0	0	0	0	1	0	0	0	1	0	0	0	1.0	1.000	C-1
4 yrs.		110	.164	.209	378	62	7	5	0	0.0	46	1	21	15	9	0	0	322	108	36	8	4.1	.923	C-63, OF-41, 3B-5, SS-4

John Briggs

BRIGGS, JOHN EDWARD BL TL 6′ 1″ 190 lbs.
B. Mar. 10, 1944, Paterson, N. J.

Year	Team	Games	BA	SA	AB	H	2B	3B	HR	HR%	R	RBI	BB	SO	SB	Pinch Hit AB	Pinch Hit H	PO	A	E	DP	TC/G	FA	G by Pos
1964	PHI N	61	.258	.333	66	17	2	0	1	1.5	16	6	9	12	1	29	7	22	1	1	0	1.2	.958	OF-19, 1B-1
1965		93	.236	.362	229	54	9	4	4	1.7	47	23	42	44	3	32	7	110	2	2	0	1.7	.982	OF-66
1966		81	.282	.490	255	72	13	5	10	3.9	43	23	41	55	3	17	2	126	3	3	0	1.9	.977	OF-69
1967		106	.232	.373	332	77	12	4	9	2.7	47	30	41	72	3	13	2	182	2	4	0	2.0	.979	OF-94
1968		110	.254	.361	338	86	13	1	7	2.1	36	31	58	72	8	14	7	423	23	7	33	4.5	.985	OF-65, 1B-36
1969		124	.238	.410	361	86	20	3	12	3.3	51	46	64	78	9	16	3	213	6	6	2	2.0	.973	OF-108, 1B-2
1970		110	.270	.434	341	92	15	7	9	2.6	43	47	39	65	5	15	6	188	7	4	1	2.1	.980	OF-95

John Briggs *continued*

Year	Team	Games	BA	SA	AB	H	2B	3B	HR	HR%	R	RBI	BB	SO	SB	Pinch Hit AB	Pinch Hit H	PO	A	E	DP	TC/G	FA	G by Pos
1971	2 teams	PHI N (10G –.182) MIL A (125G –.264)																						
"	total	135	.259	.453	397	103	12	1	21	5.3	54	62	77	81	1	10	1	578	45	12	54	4.8	.981	OF-73, 1B-60
1972	MIL A	135	.266	.455	418	111	14	1	21	5.0	58	65	54	67	1	10	4	414	18	5	21	3.3	.989	OF-106, 1B-28
1973		142	.246	.426	488	120	20	7	18	3.7	78	57	87	83	15	2	0	294	9	10	1	2.3	.968	OF-137, DH-1
1974		154	.253	.428	554	140	30	8	17	3.1	72	73	71	102	9	4	1	309	10	9	2	2.2	.973	OF-149, DH-2
1975	2 teams	MIL A (28G –.297) MIN A (87G –.231)																						
"	total	115	.246	.376	338	83	10	2	10	3.0	56	44	80	54	6	8	1	530	58	10	38	5.5	.983	OF-56, 1B-49, DH-3
12 yrs.		1366	.253	.416	4117	1041	170	43	139	3.4	601	507	663	785	64	170	41	3389	184	73	152	3.0	.980	OF-1037, 1B-176, DH-6

Harry Bright

BRIGHT, HARRY JAMES
B. Sept. 22, 1929, Kansas City, Mo.
BR TR 6′ 190 lbs.

Year	Team	Games	BA	SA	AB	H	2B	3B	HR	HR%	R	RBI	BB	SO	SB	Pinch Hit AB	Pinch Hit H	PO	A	E	DP	TC/G	FA	G by Pos
1958	PIT N	15	.250	.417	24	6	1	0	1	4.2	4	3	1	6	0	4	1	4	11	0	0	2.1	1.000	3B-7
1959		40	.250	.458	48	12	1	0	3	6.3	4	8	5	10	0	31	7	6	5	0	0	1.4	1.000	OF-4, 3B-3, 2B-1
1960		4	.000	.000	4	0	0	0	0	0.0	0	0	0	2	0	4	0	0	0	0	0	0.0	—	
1961	WAS A	72	.240	.339	183	44	6	0	4	2.2	20	21	19	23	0	23	3	71	101	11	15	3.7	.940	3B-40, C-8, 2B-1
1962		113	.273	.462	392	107	15	4	17	4.3	55	67	26	51	2	15	4	802	72	11	83	8.6	.988	1B-99, C-3, 3B-1
1963	2 teams	CIN N (1G –.000) NY A (60G –.236)																						
"	total	61	.234	.411	158	37	7	0	7	4.4	15	23	13	32	0	12	2	284	29	6	33	6.6	.981	1B-36, 3B-12
1964	NY A	4	.200	.200	5	1	0	0	0	0.0	0	0	1	1	0	1	0	9	0	0	0	4.5	1.000	1B-2
1965	CHI N	27	.280	.320	25	7	1	0	0	0.0	1	4	0	8	0	25	7	0	0	0	0	0.0	—	
8 yrs.		336	.255	.416	839	214	31	4	32	3.8	99	126	65	133	2	115	24	1176	218	28	131	6.6	.980	1B-137, 3B-63, C-11, OF-4, 2B-2
WORLD SERIES																								
1963	NY A	2	.000	.000	2	0	0	0	0	0.0	0	0	0	2	0	2	0	0	0	0	0	0.0	—	

Greg Briley

BRILEY, GREGORY
B. May 24, 1965, Greenville, N. C.
BL TR 5′ 9″ 175 lbs.

Year	Team	Games	BA	SA	AB	H	2B	3B	HR	HR%	R	RBI	BB	SO	SB	Pinch Hit AB	Pinch Hit H	PO	A	E	DP	TC/G	FA	G by Pos
1988	SEA A	13	.250	.389	36	9	2	0	1	2.8	6	4	5	6	0	3	0	13	0	1	0	1.3	.929	OF-11
1989		115	.266	.442	394	105	22	4	13	3.3	52	52	39	82	11	11	3	197	38	9	7	2.1	.963	OF-105, 2B-10, DH-2
1990		125	.246	.356	337	83	18	2	5	1.5	40	29	37	48	16	18	4	177	4	2	1	1.6	.989	OF-107, DH-4
1991		139	.260	.336	381	99	17	3	2	0.5	39	26	27	51	23	24	7	187	5	4	1	1.5	.980	OF-125, DH-2, 3B-1, 2B-1
1992		86	.275	.400	200	55	10	0	5	2.5	18	12	4	31	9	29	8	65	13	4	3	1.3	.951	OF-42, DH-12, 3B-4, 2B-4
1993	FLA N	120	.194	.282	170	33	6	0	3	1.8	17	12	12	42	6	56	11	71	2	1	0	1.1	.986	OF-67
6 yrs.		598	.253	.372	1518	384	75	9	29	1.9	172	135	124	260	65	141	33	710	62	21	12	1.6	.974	OF-457, DH-20, 2B-15, 3B-5

Bill Brinker

BRINKER, WILLIAM HUTCHINSON (Dode)
B. Aug. 30, 1883, Warrensburg, Mo. D. Feb. 5, 1965, Arcadia, Calif.
BB TR 6′ 1″ 190 lbs.

Year	Team	Games	BA	SA	AB	H	2B	3B	HR	HR%	R	RBI	BB	SO	SB	Pinch Hit AB	Pinch Hit H	PO	A	E	DP	TC/G	FA	G by Pos
1912	PHI N	9	.222	.278	18	4	1	0	0	0.0	1	2	2	3	0	3	0	7	4	2	0	3.3	.846	OF-2, 3B-2

Chuck Brinkman

BRINKMAN, CHARLES ERNEST
Brother of Ed Brinkman.
B. Sept. 16, 1944, Cincinnati, Ohio.
BR TR 6′ 1″ 185 lbs.

Year	Team	Games	BA	SA	AB	H	2B	3B	HR	HR%	R	RBI	BB	SO	SB	Pinch Hit AB	Pinch Hit H	PO	A	E	DP	TC/G	FA	G by Pos
1969	CHI A	14	.067	.067	15	1	0	0	0	0.0	2	0	1	5	0	1	0	28	2	0	1	2.1	1.000	C-14
1970		9	.250	.300	20	5	1	0	0	0.0	4	0	3	3	0	0	0	32	5	1	1	4.2	.974	C-9
1971		15	.200	.200	20	4	0	0	0	0.0	0	1	3	5	0	1	0	45	4	0	0	3.5	1.000	C-14
1972		35	.135	.135	52	7	0	0	0	0.0	1	0	4	7	0	3	1	118	11	2	3	4.0	.985	C-33
1973		63	.187	.252	139	26	6	0	1	0.7	13	10	11	37	0	0	0	262	36	4	5	4.8	.987	C-63
1974	2 teams	CHI A (8G –.143) PIT N (4G –.143)																						
"	total	12	.143	.143	21	3	0	0	0	0.0	2	1	1	3	0	0	0	28	1	0	0	2.4	1.000	C-12
6 yrs.		148	.172	.210	267	46	7	0	1	0.4	22	12	23	60	0	5	1	513	59	7	10	4.0	.988	C-145

Ed Brinkman

BRINKMAN, EDWIN ALBERT
Brother of Chuck Brinkman.
B. Dec. 8, 1941, Cincinnati, Ohio.
BR TR 6′ 170 lbs.

Year	Team	Games	BA	SA	AB	H	2B	3B	HR	HR%	R	RBI	BB	SO	SB	Pinch Hit AB	Pinch Hit H	PO	A	E	DP	TC/G	FA	G by Pos
1961	WAS A	4	.091	.091	11	1	0	0	0	0.0	0	0	1	1	0	1	0	2	6	1	1	3.0	.889	3B-3
1962		54	.165	.233	133	22	7	1	0	0.0	8	4	11	28	1	0	0	71	96	9	22	3.7	.949	SS-38, 3B-10
1963		145	.228	.319	514	117	20	3	7	1.4	44	45	31	86	5	2	1	241	462	37	97	5.2	.950	SS-143
1964		132	.224	.336	447	100	20	3	8	1.8	54	34	26	99	2	7	1	234	364	19	75	4.9	.969	SS-125
1965		154	.185	.257	444	82	13	2	5	1.1	35	35	38	82	1	3	0	292	369	25	76	4.6	.964	SS-150
1966		158	.229	.326	582	133	18	9	7	1.2	42	48	29	105	7	0	0	263	501	28	83	5.0	.965	SS-158
1967		109	.188	.237	320	60	9	2	1	0.3	21	18	24	58	1	0	0	160	309	10	54	4.4	.979	SS-109
1968		77	.187	.202	193	36	3	0	0	0.0	12	6	19	31	0	2	0	97	198	11	28	4.0	.964	SS-74, 2B-2, OF-1
1969		151	.266	.325	576	153	18	5	2	0.3	71	43	50	42	2	1	1	248	511	19	92	5.2	.976	SS-150
1970		158	.262	.301	625	164	17	2	1	0.2	63	40	60	41	8	2	1	301	569	23	103	5.7	.974	SS-157
1971	DET A	159	.228	.275	527	120	18	2	1	0.2	40	37	44	54	1	0	0	235	513	15	91	4.8	.980	SS-159
1972		156	.203	.279	516	105	19	1	6	1.2	42	49	38	51	0	0	0	233	495	7	81	4.7	.990	SS-156
1973		162	.237	.324	515	122	16	4	7	1.4	55	40	34	79	0	0	0	249	480	24	89	4.6	.968	SS-162
1974		153	.221	.347	502	111	15	3	14	2.8	55	54	29	71	2	0	0	239	498	21	89	5.0	.972	SS-151, 3B-2
1975	3 teams	STL N (28G –.240) TEX A (1G –.000) NY A (44G –.175)																						
"	total	73	.207	.300	140	29	8	1	1	0.7	8	8	10	17	0	4	1	71	129	12	28	3.0	.943	SS-63, 3B-4, 2B-3
15 yrs.		1845	.224	.300	6045	1355	201	38	60	1.0	550	461	444	845	30	22	5	2936	5500	261	1009	4.8	.970	SS-1795, 3B-19, 2B-5, OF-1
LEAGUE CHAMPIONSHIP SERIES																								
1972	DET A	1	.250	.500	4	1	1	0	0	0.0	0	0	0	0	0	0	0	1	2	0	0	3.0	1.000	SS-1

Leon Brinkopf

BRINKOPF, LEON CLARENCE
B. Oct. 20, 1926, Cape Girardeau, Mo.
BR TR 5′11½″ 185 lbs.

Year	Team	Games	BA	SA	AB	H	2B	3B	HR	HR%	R	RBI	BB	SO	SB	Pinch Hit AB	Pinch Hit H	PO	A	E	DP	TC/G	FA	G by Pos
1952	CHI N	9	.182	.182	22	4	0	0	0	0.0	1	2	4	5	0	2	1	4	17	1	1	3.7	.955	SS-6

Fatty Briody

BRIODY, CHARLES F. (Alderman, Fallstaff)
B. Aug. 13, 1858, Lansingburg, N. Y. D. June 22, 1903, Chicago, Ill.
TR 5′ 8½″ 190 lbs.

Year	Team	Games	BA	SA	AB	H	2B	3B	HR	HR%	R	RBI	BB	SO	SB	Pinch Hit AB	Pinch Hit H	PO	A	E	DP	TC/G	FA	G by Pos
1880	TRO N	1	.000	.000	4	0	0	0	0	0.0	0	0	0	0		0	0	4	3	3	0	10.0	.700	C-1
1882	CLE N	53	.258	.325	194	50	13	0	0	0.0	30	13	9	13		0	0	251	89	37	6	7.1	.902	C-53

Fatty Briody *continued*

Year	Team		Games	BA	SA	AB	H	2B	3B	HR	HR%	R	RBI	BB	SO	SB	Pinch Hit AB	Pinch Hit H	PO	A	E	DP	TC/G	FA	G by Pos
1883			40	.234	.283	145	34	5	1	0	0.0	23		3	13		0	0	191	56	25	8	6.8	.908	C-33, 2B-4, 1B-2, 3B-1
1884	2 teams	CLE N (43G –.169) CIN U (22G –.337)																							
"	total		65	.232	.295	237	55	8	2	1	0.4	28	12	7	19		0	0	437	112	41	6	9.1	.931	C-64, OF-1
1885	STL	N	62	.195	.251	215	42	9	0	1	0.5	14	17	12	23		0	0	245	87	39	3	5.9	.895	C-60, 3B-1, OF-1, 2B-1
1886	KC	N	56	.237	.312	215	51	10	3	0	0.0	14	29	3	35		0	0	269	95	32	4	6.9	.919	C-54, OF-2, 1B-1
1887	DET	N	33	.227	.336	128	29	6	1	2	1.6	24	26	9	10	6	0	0	144	61	21	4	6.8	.907	C-33
1888	KC	AA	13	.208	.229	48	10	1	0	0	0.0	1	8	1		0	0	0	52	17	8	3	5.9	.896	C-13
8 yrs.			323	.228	.294	1186	271	52	7	4	0.3	134	105	44	113	6	0	0	1593	520	206	34	7.1	.911	C-311, 2B-5, OF-4, 1B-3, 3B-2

George Bristow

BRISTOW, GEORGE T. BR TR 5′10″ 170 lbs.
B. May 1870, Paw Paw, Ill. Deceased.

Year	Team		Games	BA	SA	AB	H	2B	3B	HR	HR%	R	RBI	BB	SO	SB	Pinch Hit AB	Pinch Hit H	PO	A	E	DP	TC/G	FA	G by Pos
1899	CLE	N	3	.125	.250	8	1	1	0	0	0.0	0	0	0		0	0	0	4	1	0	0	1.7	1.000	OF-3

Bernardo Brito

BRITO, BERNARDO BR TR 6′ 1″ 190 lbs.
Born Bernardo Brito (Perez).
B. Dec. 4, 1963, San Cristobal, Dominican Republic.

Year	Team		Games	BA	SA	AB	H	2B	3B	HR	HR%	R	RBI	BB	SO	SB	Pinch Hit AB	Pinch Hit H	PO	A	E	DP	TC/G	FA	G by Pos
1992	MIN	A	8	.143	.214	14	2	1	0	0	0.0	1	2	0	4	0	4	0	3	0	1	0	1.0	.750	OF-3, DH-1
1993			27	.241	.500	54	13	2	0	4	7.4	8	9	1	20	0	12	1	12	1	0	0	0.8	1.000	OF-10, DH-7
1995			5	.200	.800	5	1	0	0	1	20.0	1	1	0	3	0	2	0	0	0	0	0	0.0	.000	DH-3
3 yrs.			40	.219	.466	73	16	3	0	5	6.8	10	12	1	27	0	18	1	15	1	1	0	0.7	.941	OF-13, DH-11

Jorge Brito

BRITO, JORGE MANUEL BR TR 6′ 1″ 190 lbs.
Born Jorge Manuel Brito (Uceta).
B. June 22, 1966, Moncion, Dominican Republic.

Year	Team		Games	BA	SA	AB	H	2B	3B	HR	HR%	R	RBI	BB	SO	SB	Pinch Hit AB	Pinch Hit H	PO	A	E	DP	TC/G	FA	G by Pos
1995	CLR	N	18	.216	.275	51	11	3	0	0	0.0	5	7	2	17	1	0	0	109	6	1	0	6.4	.991	C-18

Gus Brittain

BRITTAIN, AUGUST SCHUSTER BR TR 5′10″ 192 lbs.
B. Nov. 29, 1909, Wilmington, N. C. D. Feb. 16, 1974, Wilmington, N. C.

Year	Team		Games	BA	SA	AB	H	2B	3B	HR	HR%	R	RBI	BB	SO	SB	Pinch Hit AB	Pinch Hit H	PO	A	E	DP	TC/G	FA	G by Pos
1937	CIN	N	3	.167	.167	6	1	0	0	0	0.0	0	0	0	3	0	2	0	3	1	0	0	4.0	1.000	C-1

Gil Britton

BRITTON, STEPHEN GILBERT BR TR 5′10″ 160 lbs.
B. Sept. 21, 1891, Parsons, Kans. D. June 20, 1983, Parsons, Kans.

Year	Team		Games	BA	SA	AB	H	2B	3B	HR	HR%	R	RBI	BB	SO	SB	Pinch Hit AB	Pinch Hit H	PO	A	E	DP	TC/G	FA	G by Pos
1913	PIT	N	3	.000	.000	12	0	0	0	0	0.0	0	0	0	2	0	0	0	5	9	3	2	5.7	.824	SS-3

Greg Brock

BROCK, GREGORY ALLEN BL TR 6′ 3″ 200 lbs.
B. June 14, 1957, McMinnville, Ore.

Year	Team		Games	BA	SA	AB	H	2B	3B	HR	HR%	R	RBI	BB	SO	SB	Pinch Hit AB	Pinch Hit H	PO	A	E	DP	TC/G	FA	G by Pos
1982	LA	N	18	.118	.176	17	2	1	0	0	0.0	1	1	1	5	0	13	2	9	0	0	0	3.0	1.000	1B-3
1983			146	.224	.396	455	102	14	2	20	4.4	64	66	83	81	5	6	1	1162	106	12	94	9.1	.991	1B-140
1984			88	.225	.402	271	61	6	0	14	5.2	33	34	39	37	8	8	0	703	65	4	61	9.3	.995	1B-83
1985			129	.251	.438	438	110	19	0	21	4.8	64	66	54	72	4	9	2	1113	84	7	86	9.9	.994	1B-122
1986			115	.234	.422	325	76	13	0	16	4.9	33	52	37	60	2	23	4	726	87	3	46	8.2	.996	1B-99
1987	MIL	A	141	.299	.438	532	159	29	3	13	2.4	81	85	57	63	5	0	0	1065	109	8	111	8.4	.993	1B-141
1988			115	.212	.310	364	77	16	1	6	1.6	53	50	63	48	6	1	0	915	102	7	89	8.9	.993	1B-114, DH-1
1989			107	.265	.405	373	99	16	0	12	3.2	40	52	43	49	6	1	1	850	58	5	86	8.5	.995	1B-100, DH-7
1990			123	.248	.368	367	91	23	0	7	1.9	42	50	43	45	4	8	1	885	63	5	89	8.3	.995	1B-115
1991			31	.283	.400	60	17	4	0	1	1.7	9	6	14	9	1	4	0	150	10	0	18	6.4	1.000	1B-25
10 yrs.			1013	.248	.399	3202	794	141	6	110	3.4	420	462	434	469	41	73	11	7578	684	51	680	8.8	.994	1B-942, DH-8
LEAGUE CHAMPIONSHIP SERIES																									
1983	LA	N	3	.000	.000	9	0	0	0	0	0.0	1	0	0	3	0	0	0	13	0	0	3	4.3	1.000	1B-3
1985			5	.083	.333	12	1	0	0	1	8.3	2	2	2	2	0	1	0	35	4	0	2	9.8	1.000	1B-4
2 yrs.			8	.048	.190	21	1	0	0	1	4.8	3	2	2	5	0	1	0	48	4	0	5	7.4	1.000	1B-7

John Brock

BROCK, JOHN ROY BR TR 5′ 6½″ 165 lbs.
B. Oct. 16, 1896, Hamilton, Ill. D. Oct. 27, 1951, Clayton, Mo.

Year	Team		Games	BA	SA	AB	H	2B	3B	HR	HR%	R	RBI	BB	SO	SB	Pinch Hit AB	Pinch Hit H	PO	A	E	DP	TC/G	FA	G by Pos
1917	STL	N	7	.400	.467	15	6	1	0	0	0.0	4	2	0	2	2	3	1	13	4	1	0	4.5	.944	C-4
1918			27	.212	.250	52	11	2	0	0	0.0	9	4	3	10	5	7	2	38	20	3	1	3.2	.951	C-18, OF-1
2 yrs.			34	.254	.299	67	17	3	0	0	0.0	13	6	3	12	7	10	3	51	24	4	1	3.4	.949	C-22, OF-1

Lou Brock

BROCK, LOUIS CLARK BL TL 5′11½″ 170 lbs.
B. June 18, 1939, El Dorado, Ark.
Hall of Fame 1985.

Year	Team		Games	BA	SA	AB	H	2B	3B	HR	HR%	R	RBI	BB	SO	SB	Pinch Hit AB	Pinch Hit H	PO	A	E	DP	TC/G	FA	G by Pos
1961	CHI	N	4	.091	.091	11	1	0	0	0	0.0	1	0	1	3	0	0	0	6	0	2	0	2.7	.750	OF-3
1962			123	.263	.412	434	114	24	7	9	2.1	73	35	35	96	16	15	2	243	7	9	2	2.4	.965	OF-106
1963			148	.258	.382	547	141	19	11	9	1.6	79	37	31	122	24	10	2	269	17	8	7	2.1	.973	OF-140
1964	2 teams	CHI N (52G –.251) STL N (103G –.348)																							
"	total		155	.315	.464	634	200	30	11	14	2.2	111	58	40	127	43	1	0	266	15	14	1	1.9	.953	OF-154
1965	STL	N	155	.288	.445	631	182	35	8	16	2.5	107	69	45	116	63	1	0	272	11	12	1	1.9	.959	OF-153
1966			156	.285	.429	643	183	24	12	15	2.3	94	46	31	134	**74**	1	0	269	9	19	1	1.9	.936	OF-154
1967			159	.299	.472	**689**	206	32	12	21	3.0	**113**	76	24	109	**52**	4	0	272	12	13	2	1.9	.956	OF-157
1968			159	.279	.418	660	184	**46**	**14**	6	0.9	92	51	46	124	**62**	3	1	269	9	14	1	1.9	.952	OF-156
1969			157	.298	.434	655	195	33	10	12	1.8	97	47	50	115	**53**	2	1	255	7	14	2	1.8	.949	OF-157
1970			155	.304	.422	664	202	29	5	13	2.0	114	57	60	99	51	3	2	247	9	10	2	1.8	.962	OF-152
1971			157	.313	.425	640	200	37	7	7	1.1	**126**	61	76	107	**64**	2	1	262	7	14	3	1.8	.951	OF-157
1972			153	.311	.393	621	193	26	8	3	0.5	81	42	47	93	**63**	4	1	253	6	13	1	1.8	.952	OF-149
1973			160	.297	.398	650	193	29	8	7	1.1	110	63	71	112	**70**	1	0	310	3	12	1	2.0	.963	OF-159
1974			153	.306	.381	635	194	25	7	3	0.5	105	48	61	88	**118**	3	1	283	8	10	2	2.0	.967	OF-152
1975			136	.309	.400	528	163	27	6	3	0.6	78	47	38	64	56	8	3	247	5	9	0	2.0	.966	OF-128
1976			133	.301	.394	498	150	24	5	4	0.8	73	67	35	75	56	12	3	221	6	4	0	1.9	.983	OF-123
1977			141	.272	.354	489	133	22	6	2	0.4	69	46	30	74	35	18	7	184	2	9	1	1.5	.954	OF-130
1978			92	.221	.252	298	66	9	0	0	0.0	31	12	17	29	17	15	4	114	2	3	0	1.5	.975	OF-79
1979			120	.304	.398	405	123	15	4	5	1.2	56	38	23	43	21	22	5	152	7	7	2	1.7	.958	OF-98
19 yrs.			2616	.293	.410	10332	3023	486	141	149	1.4	1610	900	761	1730	938	125	33	4394	142	196	29	1.9	.959	OF-2507
															8th	**2nd**									

Lou Brock *continued*

Year	Team	Lg	Games	BA	SA	AB	H	2B	3B	HR	HR%	R	RBI	BB	SO	SB	Pinch Hit AB	Pinch Hit H	PO	A	E	DP	TC/G	FA	G by Pos
WORLD SERIES																									
1964	STL	N	7	.300	.467	30	9	2	0	1	3.3	2	5	0	3	0	0	0	8	1	1	0	1.4	.900	OF-7
1967			7	.414	.655	29	12	2	1	1	3.4	8	3	2	3	7	0	0	13	0	0	0	1.9	1.000	OF-7
1968			7	.464	.857	28	13	3	1	2	7.1	6	5	3	4	7	0	0	13	0	1	0	2.0	.929	OF-7
3 yrs.			21	.391	.655	87	34	7	2	4	4.6	16	13	5	10	14	0	0	34	1	2	0	1.8	.946	OF-21
				4th	**6th**											**1st**									

Matt Broderick

BRODERICK, MATTHEW THOMAS
B. Dec. 1, 1877, Lattimer, Pa. D. Feb. 22, 1941, Freeland, Pa.
BR TR 5′ 6½″ 135 lbs.

Year	Team	Lg	Games	BA	SA	AB	H	2B	3B	HR	HR%	R	RBI	BB	SO	SB	Pinch Hit AB	Pinch Hit H	PO	A	E	DP	TC/G	FA	G by Pos
1903	BKN	N	2	.000	.000	2	0	0	0	0	0.0	0	0	0		0	1	0	1	0	0	1	1.0	1.000	2B-1

Steve Brodie

BRODIE, WALTER SCOTT
B. Sept. 11, 1868, Warrenton, Va. D. Oct. 30, 1935, Baltimore, Md.
BL TR 5′11″ 180 lbs.

Year	Team	Lg	Games	BA	SA	AB	H	2B	3B	HR	HR%	R	RBI	BB	SO	SB	Pinch Hit AB	Pinch Hit H	PO	A	E	DP	TC/G	FA	G by Pos
1890	BOS	N	132	.296	.368	514	152	19	9	0	0.0	77	67	66	20	29	0	0	225	19	12	6	1.9	.953	OF-132
1891			133	.260	.319	523	136	13	6	2	0.4	84	78	63	39	25	0	0	268	25	15	9	2.3	.951	OF-133
1892	STL	N	154	.252	.319	602	152	10	9	4	0.7	85	60	52	31	28	0	0	326	59	26	12	2.7	.937	OF-137, 2B-16, 3B-2
1893	2 teams		STL N (107G –.318) BAL N (25G –.361)																						
″	total		132	.325	.412	566	184	23	10	2	0.4	89	98	45	18	49	0	0	323	23	17	7	2.8	.953	OF-132
1894	BAL	N	129	.366	.464	573	210	25	11	3	0.5	134	113	18	8	42	0	0	310	14	17	4	2.6	.950	OF-129
1895			131	.348	.449	528	184	27	10	2	0.4	85	134	26	15	35	0	0	307	23	12	2	2.6	.965	OF-131
1896			132	.297	.388	516	153	19	11	2	0.4	98	87	36	17	25	0	0	320	22	10	6	2.7	.972	OF-132
1897	PIT	N	100	.292	.392	370	108	7	12	2	0.5	47	53	25		11	0	0	218	11	4	1	2.3	.983	OF-100
1898	2 teams		PIT N (42G –.263) BAL N (23G –.306)																						
″	total		65	.280	.327	254	71	8	2	0	0.0	27	40	11		6	0	0	165	9	10	1	2.8	.946	OF-65
1899	BAL	N	137	.309	.379	531	164	26	1	3	0.6	82	87	31		19	0	0	310	15	7	5	2.4	.979	OF-137
1901	BAL	A	83	.310	.389	306	95	6	6	2	0.7	41	41	25		9	0	0	178	4	7	0	2.3	.963	OF-83
1902	NY	N	109	.281	.332	416	117	8	2	3	0.7	37	42	22		11	0	0	219	22	12	7	2.3	.953	OF-109
12 yrs.			1437	.303	.381	5699	1726	191	89	25	0.4	886	900	420	148	289	0	0	3169	246	149	60	2.5	.958	OF-1420, 2B-16, 3B-2

Rico Brogna

BROGNA, RICO JOSEPH
B. Apr. 18, 1970, Turners Falls, Mass.
BL TL 6′ 2″ 190 lbs.

Year	Team	Lg	Games	BA	SA	AB	H	2B	3B	HR	HR%	R	RBI	BB	SO	SB	Pinch Hit AB	Pinch Hit H	PO	A	E	DP	TC/G	FA	G by Pos
1992	DET	A	9	.192	.346	26	5	1	0	1	3.8	3	3	3	5	0	0	0	48	6	1	9	5.5	.982	1B-8, DH-2
1994	NY	N	39	.351	.626	131	46	11	2	7	5.3	16	20	6	29	1	4	1	308	28	1	29	9.6	.997	1B-35
1995			134	.289	.485	495	143	27	2	22	4.4	72	76	39	111	0	9	2	1113	92	3	93	9.2	.998	1B-131
3 yrs.			182	.298	.508	652	194	39	4	30	4.6	91	99	48	145	1	13	3	1469	126	5	131	9.1	.997	1B-174, DH-2

Jack Brohamer

BROHAMER, JOHN ANTHONY
B. Feb. 26, 1950, Maywood, Calif.
BL TR 5′10″ 165 lbs.
BB 1972

Year	Team	Lg	Games	BA	SA	AB	H	2B	3B	HR	HR%	R	RBI	BB	SO	SB	Pinch Hit AB	Pinch Hit H	PO	A	E	DP	TC/G	FA	G by Pos
1972	CLE	A	136	.233	.294	527	123	13	2	5	0.9	49	35	27	46	3	6	1	285	395	16	87	5.2	.977	2B-132, 3B-1
1973			102	.220	.307	300	66	12	1	4	1.3	29	29	32	23	0	10	3	215	279	15	67	5.2	.971	2B-97
1974			101	.270	.330	315	85	11	1	2	0.6	33	30	26	22	2	9	4	203	269	6	67	4.8	.987	2B-99
1975			69	.244	.350	217	53	5	0	6	2.8	15	16	14	14	2	3	1	166	162	8	52	5.1	.976	2B-66
1976	CHI	A	119	.251	.356	354	89	12	2	7	2.0	33	40	44	28	1	1	0	265	338	10	75	5.2	.984	2B-117, 3B-1
1977			59	.257	.401	152	39	10	3	2	1.3	26	20	21	8	0	2	0	54	100	8	15	2.8	.951	3B-38, 2B-18, DH-1
1978	BOS	A	81	.234	.311	244	57	14	1	1	0.4	34	25	25	13	1	11	3	64	103	5	18	2.2	.971	3B-30, DH-25, 2B-23
1979			64	.266	.328	192	51	7	1	1	0.5	25	11	15	15	0	8	1	74	140	5	27	3.8	.977	2B-36, 3B-22
1980	2 teams		BOS A (21G –.316) CLE A (53G –.225)																						
″	total		74	.251	.327	199	50	7	1	2	1.0	18	21	18	9	0	15	3	89	142	7	30	3.5	.971	2B-51, 3B-13, DH-4
9 yrs.			805	.245	.327	2500	613	91	12	30	1.2	262	227	222	178	9	65	16	1415	1928	80	438	4.4	.977	2B-639, 3B-105, DH-30

Herman Bronkie

BRONKIE, HERMAN CHARLES (Dutch)
B. Mar. 30, 1885, S. Manchester, Conn. D. May 27, 1968, Somers, Conn.
BR TR 5′ 9″ 165 lbs.

Year	Team	Lg	Games	BA	SA	AB	H	2B	3B	HR	HR%	R	RBI	BB	SO	SB	Pinch Hit AB	Pinch Hit H	PO	A	E	DP	TC/G	FA	G by Pos
1910	CLE	A	4	.222	.222	9	2	0	0	0	0.0	1	0	1		1	0	0	4	4	4	0	3.0	.667	3B-3, SS-1
1911			2	.167	.167	6	1	0	0	0	0.0	0	0	0		0	0	0	3	1	0	0	2.0	1.000	3B-2
1912			6	.000	.000	16	0	0	0	0	0.0	1	0	1		0	0	0	7	15	2	1	4.0	.917	3B-6
1914	CHI	N	1	1.000	2.000	1	1	1	0	0	0.0	1	1	0	0	0	0	0	0	0	1	0	1.0	.000	3B-1
1918	STL	N	18	.221	.309	68	15	3	0	1	1.5	7	7	2	4	0	0	0	18	43	1	2	3.4	.984	3B-18
1919	STL	A	67	.255	.327	196	50	6	4	0	0.0	23	14	23	23	2	12	3	90	115	12	16	4.2	.945	3B-34, 2B-16, 1B-2
1922			23	.281	.375	64	18	4	1	0	0.0	7	2	6	7	0	4	1	24	31	5	7	3.3	.917	3B-18
7 yrs.			121	.242	.317	360	87	14	5	1	0.3	40	24	33	34	3	16	4	146	209	25	26	3.8	.934	3B-82, 2B-16, 1B-2, SS-1

Tom Brookens

BROOKENS, THOMAS DALE
B. Aug. 10, 1953, Chambersburg, Pa.
BR TR 5′10″ 165 lbs.

Year	Team	Lg	Games	BA	SA	AB	H	2B	3B	HR	HR%	R	RBI	BB	SO	SB	Pinch Hit AB	Pinch Hit H	PO	A	E	DP	TC/G	FA	G by Pos
1979	DET	A	60	.263	.374	190	50	5	2	4	2.1	23	21	11	40	10	0	0	76	141	11	21	3.7	.952	3B-42, 2B-19, DH-1
1980			151	.275	.418	509	140	25	9	10	2.0	64	66	32	71	13	4	1	127	307	29	38	3.1	.937	3B-138, 2B-9, DH-1, SS-1
1981			71	.243	.343	239	58	10	1	4	1.7	19	25	14	43	5	1	0	58	139	10	13	2.9	.952	3B-71
1982			140	.231	.352	398	92	15	3	9	2.3	40	58	27	63	5	6	2	119	276	20	27	2.8	.952	3B-113, 2B-26, SS-9, OF-1
1983			138	.214	.325	332	71	13	3	6	1.8	50	32	29	46	10	10	1	97	254	22	34	2.6	.941	3B-103, SS-30, 2B-10, DH-1
1984			113	.246	.397	224	55	11	4	5	2.2	32	26	19	33	6	3	2	98	187	12	35	2.4	.960	3B-68, SS-28, 2B-26, DH-1
1985			156	.237	.375	485	115	34	6	7	1.4	54	47	27	78	14	1	1	135	277	24	28	2.7	.945	3B-151, SS-8, 2B-3, C-1, DH-1
1986			98	.270	.356	281	76	11	2	3	1.1	42	25	20	42	11	7	1	106	144	7	26	2.6	.973	3B-35, 2B-31, DH-14, SS-14, OF-3
1987			143	.241	.376	444	107	15	3	13	2.9	59	59	33	63	7	2	0	119	256	19	33	2.6	.952	3B-122, SS-16, 2B-11
1988			136	.243	.351	441	107	23	5	5	1.1	62	38	44	74	4	5	1	101	235	17	16	2.5	.952	3B-136, SS-3, 2B-1
1989	NY	A	66	.226	.333	168	38	6	0	4	2.4	14	14	11	27	1	11	3	27	85	7	7	1.7	.941	3B-51, SS-7, 2B-5, OF-3, DH-3
1990	CLE	A	64	.266	.357	154	41	7	2	1	0.6	18	20	14	25	0	9	0	57	104	6	20	2.7	.964	3B-35, 2B-21, SS-3, 1B-2, DH-1
12 yrs.			1336	.246	.367	3865	950	175	40	71	1.8	477	431	281	605	86	59	12	1120	2405	184	298	2.7	.950	3B-1065, 2B-162, SS-119, DH-23, OF-7, 1B-2, C-1

Tom Brookens *continued*

Year	Team	Games	BA	SA	AB	H	2B	3B	HR	HR%	R	RBI	BB	SO	SB	Pinch Hit AB	Pinch Hit H	PO	A	E	DP	TC/G	FA	G by Pos
LEAGUE CHAMPIONSHIP SERIES																								
1984	DET A	2	.000	.000	2	0	0	0	0	0.0	0	0	0	1	0	0	0	0	2	1	0	1.5	.667	3B-1, 2B-1
1987		5	.000	.000	13	0	0	0	0	0.0	0	0	0	3	0	0	0	3	15	0	0	3.6	1.000	3B-5
2 yrs.		7	.000	.000	15	0	0	0	0	0.0	0	0	0	4	0	0	0	3	17	1	0	3.0	.952	3B-6, 2B-1
WORLD SERIES																								
1984	DET A	3	.000	.000	3	0	0	0	0	0.0	0	0	0	1	0	2	0	0	3	0	0	1.0	1.000	3B-3

Bobby Brooks

BROOKS, ROBERT, JR. BR TR 5′ 8½″ 165 lbs.
B. Nov. 1, 1945, Los Angeles, Calif. D. Oct. 11, 1994, Harbor City, Calif.

Year	Team	Games	BA	SA	AB	H	2B	3B	HR	HR%	R	RBI	BB	SO	SB	Pinch Hit AB	Pinch Hit H	PO	A	E	DP	TC/G	FA	G by Pos
1969	OAK A	29	.241	.418	79	19	5	0	3	3.8	13	10	20	24	0	4	1	35	2	0	0	1.8	1.000	OF-21
1970		7	.333	.722	18	6	1	0	2	11.1	2	5	1	7	0	3	0	4	0	0	0	0.8	1.000	OF-5
1972		15	.179	.179	39	7	0	0	0	0.0	4	5	8	8	0	4	1	40	0	3	0	3.9	.930	OF-11
1973	CAL A	4	.143	.143	7	1	0	0	0	0.0	0	0	0	3	0	3	0	0	0	0	0	0.0	.000	OF-1
4 yrs.		55	.231	.378	143	33	6	0	5	3.5	19	20	29	42	0	14	2	79	2	3	0	2.2	.964	OF-38

Harry Brooks

BROOKS, HARRY FRANK
B. Nov. 30, 1865, Philadelphia, Pa. D. Dec. 5, 1945, Philadelphia, Pa.

Year	Team	Games	BA	SA	AB	H	2B	3B	HR	HR%	R	RBI	BB	SO	SB	Pinch Hit AB	Pinch Hit H	PO	A	E	DP	TC/G	FA	G by Pos
1886	NY AA	1	.000	.000	1	0	0	0	0	0.0	0		0			0	0	1	0	5	0	3.0	.167	OF-1, P-1

Hubie Brooks

BROOKS, HUBERT, JR. BR TR 6′ 178 lbs.
B. Sept. 24, 1956, Los Angeles, Calif.

Year	Team	Games	BA	SA	AB	H	2B	3B	HR	HR%	R	RBI	BB	SO	SB	Pinch Hit AB	Pinch Hit H	PO	A	E	DP	TC/G	FA	G by Pos
1980	NY N	24	.309	.395	81	25	2	1	1	1.2	8	10	5	9	1	1	0	16	40	2	2	2.5	.966	3B-23
1981		98	.307	.411	358	110	21	2	4	1.1	34	38	23	65	9	2	0	67	193	21	14	2.9	.925	3B-93, OF-3, SS-1
1982		126	.249	.317	457	114	21	2	2	0.4	40	40	28	76	6	1	0	89	237	24	17	2.8	.931	3B-126
1983		150	.251	.321	586	147	18	4	5	0.9	53	58	24	96	6	2	1	116	303	21	28	2.9	.952	3B-145, 2B-7
1984		153	.283	.417	561	159	23	2	16	2.9	61	73	48	79	6	0	0	112	284	29	41	2.7	.932	3B-129, SS-26
1985	MON N	156	.269	.413	605	163	34	7	13	2.1	67	100	34	79	6	2	1	203	441	28	81	4.3	.958	SS-155
1986		80	.340	.569	306	104	18	5	14	4.6	50	58	25	60	4	0	0	116	222	15	37	4.4	.958	SS-80
1987		112	.263	.426	430	113	22	3	14	3.3	57	72	24	72	4	3	2	131	271	20	53	3.9	.953	SS-109
1988		151	.279	.447	588	164	35	2	20	3.4	61	90	35	108	7	2	1	261	8	9	1	1.9	.968	OF-149
1989		148	.268	.404	542	145	30	1	14	2.6	56	70	39	108	6	8	0	234	6	9	2	1.8	.964	OF-140
1990	LA N	153	.266	.424	568	151	28	1	20	3.5	74	91	33	108	2	1	0	255	9	10	2	1.8	.964	OF-150
1991	NY N	103	.238	.409	357	85	11	1	16	4.5	48	50	44	62	3	4	0	166	6	5	0	1.8	.972	OF-100
1992	CAL A	82	.216	.337	306	66	13	0	8	2.6	28	36	12	46	3	8	2	64	4	1	4	0.9	.986	DH-70, 1B-6
1993	KC A	75	.286	.375	168	48	12	0	1	0.6	14	24	11	27	0	33	**10**	72	6	2	2	1.5	.975	OF-40, DH-9, 1B-3
1994		34	.230	.311	61	14	2	0	1	1.6	5	14	2	10	1	20	5	33	1	0	3	1.5	1.000	DH-19, 1B-4
15 yrs.		1645	.269	.403	5974	1608	290	31	149	2.5	656	824	387	1005	64	87	22	1935	2031	196	287	2.6	.953	OF-582, 3B-516, SS-371, DH-98, 1B-13, 2B-7

Jerry Brooks

BROOKS, JEROME EDWARD BR TR 6′ 195 lbs.
B. Mar. 23, 1967, Syracuse, N. Y.

Year	Team	Games	BA	SA	AB	H	2B	3B	HR	HR%	R	RBI	BB	SO	SB	Pinch Hit AB	Pinch Hit H	PO	A	E	DP	TC/G	FA	G by Pos
1993	LA N	9	.222	.667	9	2	1	0	1	11.1	2	1	0	2	0	8	1	0	0	0	0	0.0	.000	OF-2

Mandy Brooks

BROOKS, JONATHAN JOSEPH BR TR 5′ 9″ 165 lbs.
Born Jonathan Joseph Brozek.
B. Aug. 18, 1897, Milwaukee, Wis. D. June 17, 1962, Kirkwood, Mo.

Year	Team	Games	BA	SA	AB	H	2B	3B	HR	HR%	R	RBI	BB	SO	SB	Pinch Hit AB	Pinch Hit H	PO	A	E	DP	TC/G	FA	G by Pos
1925	CHI N	90	.281	.504	349	98	25	7	13	3.7	55	72	19	28	10	1	0	249	9	6	2	3.0	.977	OF-89
1926		26	.188	.271	48	9	1	0	1	2.1	7	6	5	5	0	6	1	23	2	0	2	1.4	1.000	OF-18
2 yrs.		116	.270	.476	397	107	26	7	14	3.5	62	78	24	33	10	7	1	272	11	6	4	2.7	.979	OF-107

Scott Brosius

BROSIUS, SCOTT DAVID BR TR 6′ 1″ 185 lbs.
B. Aug. 15, 1966, Hillsboro, Ore.

Year	Team	Games	BA	SA	AB	H	2B	3B	HR	HR%	R	RBI	BB	SO	SB	Pinch Hit AB	Pinch Hit H	PO	A	E	DP	TC/G	FA	G by Pos
1991	OAK A	36	.235	.397	68	16	5	0	2	2.9	9	4	3	11	3	4	2	31	16	0	3	1.2	1.000	2B-18, OF-13, 3B-7, DH-1
1992		38	.218	.379	87	19	2	0	4	4.6	13	13	3	13	3	2	0	68	15	1	2	2.3	.988	OF-20, 3B-12, 1B-3, SS-1, DH-1
1993		70	.249	.390	213	53	10	1	6	2.8	26	25	14	37	6	6	2	173	29	2	11	2.7	.990	OF-46, 1B-11, 3B-10, SS-6, DH-2
1994		96	.238	.417	324	77	14	1	14	4.3	31	49	24	57	2	0	0	81	154	13	19	2.5	.948	3B-93, OF-7, 1B-1
1995		123	.262	.452	389	102	19	2	17	4.4	69	46	41	67	4	4	0	207	121	15	35	2.5	.956	3B-60, OF-49, 1B-18, SS-3, 2B-3, DH-2
5 yrs.		363	.247	.420	1081	267	50	4	43	4.0	148	137	85	185	18	16	4	560	335	31	70	2.4	.967	3B-182, OF-135, 1B-33, 2B-21, SS-10, DH-6

Siggy Broskie

BROSKIE, SIGMUND THEODORE (Chops) BR TR 5′11½″ 200 lbs.
B. Mar. 23, 1911, Iselin, Pa. D. May 17, 1975, Canton, Ohio.

Year	Team	Games	BA	SA	AB	H	2B	3B	HR	HR%	R	RBI	BB	SO	SB	Pinch Hit AB	Pinch Hit H	PO	A	E	DP	TC/G	FA	G by Pos
1940	BOS N	11	.273	.318	22	6	1	0	0	0.0	1	4	1	2	0	0	0	23	6	2	1	2.8	.935	C-11

Tony Brottem

BROTTEM, ANTON CHRISTIAN BR TR 6′½″ 176 lbs.
B. Apr. 30, 1892, Halstad, Minn. D. Aug. 5, 1929, Chicago, Ill.

Year	Team	Games	BA	SA	AB	H	2B	3B	HR	HR%	R	RBI	BB	SO	SB	Pinch Hit AB	Pinch Hit H	PO	A	E	DP	TC/G	FA	G by Pos
1916	STL N	26	.182	.212	33	6	1	0	0	0.0	3	4	3	10	1	7	4	25	13	2	1	2.4	.950	C-15, OF-2
1918		2	.000	.000	4	0	0	0	0	0.0	0	0	1	0	0	1	0	11	3	0	0	7.0	1.000	1B-2
1921	2 teams	WAS A (4G –.143) PIT N (30G –.242)																						
"	total	34	.235	.255	98	23	2	0	0	0.0	7	9	5	12	0	1	0	101	29	2	1	4.0	.985	C-33
3 yrs.		62	.215	.237	135	29	3	0	0	0.0	10	13	9	22	1	9	4	137	45	4	2	3.6	.978	C-48, 1B-2, OF-2

Cal Broughton

BROUGHTON, CECIL CALVERT BR TR
B. Dec. 28, 1860, Magnolia, Wis. D. Mar. 15, 1939, Evansville, Wis.

Year	Team	Games	BA	SA	AB	H	2B	3B	HR	HR%	R	RBI	BB	SO	SB	Pinch Hit AB	Pinch Hit H	PO	A	E	DP	TC/G	FA	G by Pos
1883	2 teams	CLE N (4G –.200) BAL AA (9G –.188)																						
"	total	13	.190	.190	42	8	0	0	0	0.0	3		3	2		0	0	56	16	12	0	6.5	.857	C-12, OF-1
1884	MIL U	11	.308	.436	39	12	5	0	0	0.0	5		0			0	0	72	12	5	0	7.4	.944	C-7, OF-5
1885	2 teams	STL AA (4G –.059) NY AA (11G –.146)																						
"	total	15	.121	.138	58	7	1	0	0	0.0	2		1			0	0	80	24	16	1	8.0	.867	C-15
1888	DET N	1	.000	.000	4	0	0	0	0	0.0	0	0	0	0	0	0	0	6	3	0	0	9.0	1.000	C-1
4 yrs.		40	.189	.231	143	27	6	0	0	0.0	10	0	4	2	0	0	0	214	55	33	1	7.4	.891	C-35, OF-6

Mark Brouhard

BROUHARD, MARK STEVEN BR TR 6′ 1″ 210 lbs.
B. May 22, 1956, Burbank, Calif.

Year	Team	Games	BA	SA	AB	H	2B	3B	HR	HR%	R	RBI	BB	SO	SB	Pinch Hit AB	Pinch Hit H	PO	A	E	DP	TC/G	FA	G by Pos
1980	**MIL A**	45	.232	.400	125	29	6	0	5	4.0	17	16	7	24	1	8	0	77	4	1	3	1.9	.988	DH-21, OF-12, 1B-10
1981		60	.274	.371	186	51	6	3	2	1.1	19	20	7	41	1	4	1	92	7	1	2	1.7	.990	OF-51, DH-7
1982		40	.269	.435	108	29	4	1	4	3.7	16	10	9	17	0	7	0	69	2	1	0	1.9	.986	OF-30, DH-7
1983		56	.276	.454	185	51	10	1	7	3.8	25	23	9	39	0	6	2	112	1	1	0	2.2	.991	OF-42, DH-11
1984		66	.239	.365	197	47	7	0	6	3.0	20	22	16	37	0	7	0	107	6	2	2	1.9	.983	OF-52, DH-8
1985		37	.259	.389	108	28	7	2	1	0.9	11	13	5	26	0	7	0	53	0	2	0	1.8	.964	OF-29, DH-1
6 yrs.		304	.259	.400	909	235	40	7	25	2.8	108	104	53	184	2	39	3	510	20	8	7	1.9	.985	OF-216, DH-55, 1B-10
LEAGUE CHAMPIONSHIP SERIES																								
1982	**MIL A**	1	.750	1.750	4	3	1	0	1	25.0	4	3	0	0	0	0	0	1	0	0	0	1.0	1.000	OF-1

Art Brouthers

BROUTHERS, ARTHUR H. TR 6′ 1″
B. Nov. 25, 1882, Montgomery, Ala. D. Sept. 28, 1959, Charleston, S. C.

Year	Team	Games	BA	SA	AB	H	2B	3B	HR	HR%	R	RBI	BB	SO	SB	Pinch Hit AB	Pinch Hit H	PO	A	E	DP	TC/G	FA	G by Pos
1906	**PHI A**	36	.208	.257	144	30	5	1	0	0.0	18	14	5		4	1	0	42	57	11	3	3.3	.900	3B-33

Dan Brouthers

BROUTHERS, DENNIS JOSEPH (Big Dan) BL TL 6′ 2″ 207 lbs.
B. May 8, 1858, Sylvan Lake, N. Y. D. Aug. 2, 1932, East Orange, N. J.
Hall of Fame 1945.

Year	Team	Games	BA	SA	AB	H	2B	3B	HR	HR%	R	RBI	BB	SO	SB	Pinch Hit AB	Pinch Hit H	PO	A	E	DP	TC/G	FA	G by Pos
1879	**TRO N**	39	.274	.429	168	46	12	1	4	2.4	17	17	1	18		0	0	406	7	34	11	11.2	.924	1B-37, P-3
1880		3	.167	.167	12	2	0	0	0	0.0	0	1	1	0		0	0	25	0	3	1	9.3	.893	1B-3
1881	**BUF N**	65	.319	**.541**	270	86	18	9	**8**	**3.0**	60	45	18	22		0	0	377	18	33	18	6.6	.923	OF-35, 1B-30
1882		84	**.368**	**.547**	351	**129**	23	11	6	1.7	71		21	7		0	0	882	19	24	35	11.0	.974	1B-84
1883		98	**.374**	**.572**	425	**159**	41	**17**	3	0.7	85		16	17		0	0	1041	40	44	40	11.4	.961	1B-97, 3B-1, P-1
1884		94	.327	**.563**	398	130	22	15	14	3.5	82		33	20		0	0	958	30	39	38	10.9	.962	1B-93, 3B-1
1885		98	.359	**.543**	407	146	32	11	7	1.7	87	60	34	10		0	0	996	25	26	54	10.7	.975	1B-98
1886	**DET N**	121	.370	**.581**	489	181	**40**	15	**11**	**2.2**	139	72	66	16		0	0	1256	27	42	64	11.0	.968	1B-121
1887		123	.338	.562	500	169	**36**	20	12	2.4	**153**	101	71	9	34	0	0	1141	35	38	67	9.9	.969	1B-123
1888		129	.307	.464	522	160	**33**	11	9	1.7	**118**	66	68	13	34	0	0	1345	48	42	56	11.1	.971	1B-129
1889	**BOS N**	126	**.373**	.507	485	181	26	9	7	1.4	105	118	66	6	22	0	0	1243	58	35	78	10.6	.974	1B-126
1890	**BOS P**	123	.330	.454	460	152	36	9	1	0.2	117	97	99	17	28	0	0	1187	73	49	78	10.6	.963	1B-123
1891	**BOS AA**	130	**.350**	**.512**	486	170	26	19	5	1.0	117	109	87	20	31	0	0	1313	34	30	82	10.6	.978	1B-130
1892	**BKN N**	152	**.335**	.480	588	**197**	30	20	5	0.9	121	**124**	84	30	31	0	0	1498	105	29	69	10.7	.982	1B-152
1893		77	.337	.511	282	95	21	11	2	0.7	57	59	52	10	9	0	0	736	47	11	51	10.3	.986	1B-77
1894	**BAL N**	123	.347	.560	525	182	39	23	9	1.7	137	128	67	9	38	0	0	1184	65	31	83	10.4	.976	1B-123
1895	**2 teams**	**BAL N** (5G –.261) **LOU N** (24G –.309)																						
″	**total**	29	.300	.467	120	36	12	1	2	1.7	15	20	12	3	1	0	0	254	13	11	22	9.6	.960	1B-29
1896	**PHI N**	57	.344	.445	218	75	13	3	1	0.5	42	41	44	11	7	0	0	566	23	10	44	10.5	.983	1B-57
1904	**NY N**	2	.000	.000	5	0	0	0	0	0.0	0	0	0		0	1	0	6	0	0	0	6.0	1.000	1B-1
19 yrs.		1673	.342 **9th**	.519	6711	2296	460	205 **8th**	106	1.6	1523	1058	840	238	235	1	0	16414	667	531	891	10.5	.970	1B-1633, OF-35, P-4, 3B-2

Joe Brovia

BROVIA, JOSEPH JOHN (Ox) BL TR 6′ 3″ 195 lbs.
B. Feb. 18, 1922, Davenport, Calif. D. Aug. 15, 1994, Santa Cruz, Calif.

Year	Team	Games	BA	SA	AB	H	2B	3B	HR	HR%	R	RBI	BB	SO	SB	Pinch Hit AB	Pinch Hit H	PO	A	E	DP	TC/G	FA	G by Pos
1955	**CIN N**	21	.111	.111	18	2	0	0	0	0.0	0	4	1	6	0	18	2	0	0	0	0	0.0	—	

Bob Brower

BROWER, ROBERT RICHARD BR TR 5′11″ 185 lbs.
B. Jan. 10, 1960, Jamaica, N. Y.

Year	Team	Games	BA	SA	AB	H	2B	3B	HR	HR%	R	RBI	BB	SO	SB	Pinch Hit AB	Pinch Hit H	PO	A	E	DP	TC/G	FA	G by Pos
1986	**TEX A**	21	.111	.222	9	1	1	0	0	0.0	3	0	0	3	1	1	0	9	0	0	0	0.5	1.000	OF-17, DH-1
1987		127	.261	.452	303	79	10	3	14	4.6	63	46	36	66	15	9	1	183	2	7	0	1.7	.964	OF-106, DH-7
1988		82	.224	.274	201	45	7	0	1	0.5	29	11	27	38	10	6	1	104	2	3	1	1.5	.972	OF-59, DH-13
1989	**NY A**	26	.232	.362	69	16	3	0	2	2.9	9	3	6	11	3	1	1	62	2	2	1	2.5	.970	OF-25, DH-1
4 yrs.		256	.242	.376	582	141	21	3	17	2.9	104	60	69	118	29	17	3	358	6	12	2	1.6	.968	OF-207, DH-22

Frank Brower

BROWER, FRANK WILLARD (Turkeyfoot) BL TR 6′ 2″ 180 lbs.
B. Mar. 26, 1893, Gainesville, Va. D. Nov. 20, 1960, Baltimore, Md.

Year	Team	Games	BA	SA	AB	H	2B	3B	HR	HR%	R	RBI	BB	SO	SB	Pinch Hit AB	Pinch Hit H	PO	A	E	DP	TC/G	FA	G by Pos
1920	**WAS A**	36	.311	.429	119	37	7	2	1	0.8	21	13	9	11	1	5	2	131	10	5	7	4.9	.966	OF-20, 1B-9, 3B-1
1921		83	.261	.365	203	53	12	3	1	0.5	31	35	18	7	1	27	6	108	12	9	4	2.6	.930	OF-46, 1B-4
1922		139	.293	.418	471	138	20	6	9	1.9	61	71	52	25	8	9	1	269	14	5	5	2.3	.983	OF-121, 1B-7
1923	**CLE A**	126	.285	.509	397	113	25	8	16	4.0	77	66	62	32	6	6	2	1047	66	13	87	9.9	.988	1B-112, OF-2
1924		66	.280	.477	107	30	10	1	3	2.8	16	20	27	9	1	24	5	188	18	2	11	6.3	.990	1B-26, P-4, OF-3
5 yrs.		450	.286	.443	1297	371	74	20	30	2.3	206	205	168	84	17	71	16	1743	120	34	114	5.3	.982	OF-192, 1B-158, P-4, 3B-1

Lou Brower

BROWER, LOUIS LESTER BR TR 5′10″ 155 lbs.
B. July 1, 1900, Cincinnati, Ohio D. Mar. 4, 1994, Tyler, Tex.

Year	Team	Games	BA	SA	AB	H	2B	3B	HR	HR%	R	RBI	BB	SO	SB	Pinch Hit AB	Pinch Hit H	PO	A	E	DP	TC/G	FA	G by Pos
1931	**DET A**	21	.161	.177	62	10	1	0	0	0.0	3	6	8	5	1	0	0	40	40	10	11	4.1	.889	SS-20, 2B-2

Bill Brown

BROWN, WILLIAM VERNA BL TL 5′ 8″ 185 lbs.
B. July 8, 1893, Coleman, Tex. D. May 13, 1965, Lubbock, Tex.

Year	Team	Games	BA	SA	AB	H	2B	3B	HR	HR%	R	RBI	BB	SO	SB	Pinch Hit AB	Pinch Hit H	PO	A	E	DP	TC/G	FA	G by Pos
1912	**STL A**	9	.200	.200	20	4	0	0	0	0.0	0	1	0		0	2	1	10	0	1	0	1.6	.909	OF-7

Bobby Brown

BROWN, ROBERT WILLIAM BL TR 6′ 1″ 180 lbs.
B. Oct. 25, 1924, Seattle, Wash.

Year	Team	Games	BA	SA	AB	H	2B	3B	HR	HR%	R	RBI	BB	SO	SB	Pinch Hit AB	Pinch Hit H	PO	A	E	DP	TC/G	FA	G by Pos
1946	**NY A**	7	.333	.375	24	8	1	0	0	0.0	1	1	4	0	0	0	0	9	12	0	1	3.0	1.000	SS-5, 3B-2
1947		69	.300	.373	150	45	6	1	1	0.7	21	18	21	9	0	27	**9**	35	54	7	8	2.3	.927	3B-27, SS-11, OF-3
1948		113	.300	.405	363	109	19	5	3	0.8	62	48	48	16	0	22	4	130	173	18	33	3.6	.944	3B-41, SS-26, 2B-17, OF-4
1949		104	.283	.399	343	97	14	4	6	1.7	61	61	38	18	4	16	5	89	158	13	17	2.9	.950	3B-86, OF-3
1950		95	.267	.339	277	74	4	2	4	1.4	33	37	39	18	3	14	3	63	140	9	13	2.6	.958	3B-82

Bobby Brown *continued*

Year	Team	Games	BA	SA	AB	H	2B	3B	HR	HR%	R	RBI	BB	SO	SB	Pinch Hit AB	Pinch Hit H	PO	A	E	DP	TC/G	FA	G by Pos
1951		103	.268	.387	313	84	15	2	6	1.9	44	51	47	18	1	10	1	80	151	11	14	2.7	.955	3B-90
1952		29	.247	.303	89	22	2	0	1	1.1	6	14	9	6	1	4	0	23	61	10	4	3.9	.894	3B-24
1954		28	.217	.283	60	13	1	0	1	1.7	5	7	8	3	0	9	3	15	31	0	2	2.7	1.000	3B-17
8 yrs.		548	.279	.376	1619	452	62	14	22	1.4	233	237	214	88	9	102	25	444	780	68	92	2.9	.947	3B-369, SS-42, 2B-17, OF-10
WORLD SERIES																								
1947	NY A	4	1.000	1.667	3	3	2	0	0	0.0	2	3	1	0	0	3	3	0	0	0	0	0.0	—	
1949		4	.500	.917	12	6	1	2	0	0.0	4	5	2	2	0	1	0	0	6	0	0	2.0	1.000	3B-3
1950		4	.333	.583	12	4	1	1	0	0.0	2	1	0	0	0	1	0	0	1	1	0	0.5	.500	3B-4
1951		5	.357	.429	14	5	1	0	0	0.0	1	0	2	1	0	1	0	1	8	0	0	2.3	1.000	3B-4
4 yrs.		17	.439	.707	41	18	5	3 **4th**	0	0.0	9	9	5	3	0	6	3	1	15	1	0	1.5	.941	3B-11

Bobby Brown

BROWN, ROGERS LEE
B. May 25, 1954, Norfolk, Va.

BB TR 6′ 2″ 190 lbs.
BL 1979

Year	Team	Games	BA	SA	AB	H	2B	3B	HR	HR%	R	RBI	BB	SO	SB	Pinch Hit AB	Pinch Hit H	PO	A	E	DP	TC/G	FA	G by Pos
1979	**2 teams**	TOR A (4G –.000) NY A (30G –.250)																						
″	**total**	34	.218	.282	78	17	3	1	0	0.0	8	3	4	18	2	2	0	64	0	3	0	2.1	.955	OF-31, DH-1
1980	NY A	137	.260	.415	412	107	12	5	14	3.4	65	47	29	82	27	5	0	303	7	9	0	2.4	.972	OF-131, DH-1
1981		31	.226	.242	62	14	1	0	0	0.0	5	6	5	15	4	1	0	54	2	3	4	1.9	.949	OF-29, DH-2
1982	SEA A	79	.241	.327	245	59	7	1	4	1.6	29	17	17	32	28	7	2	148	5	5	1	2.2	.968	OF-68, DH-3
1983	SD N	57	.267	.382	225	60	5	3	5	2.2	40	22	23	38	27	2	1	103	1	4	0	2.0	.963	OF-54
1984		85	.251	.368	171	43	7	2	3	1.8	28	29	11	33	16	24	9	100	2	3	0	2.0	.971	OF-53
1985		79	.155	.190	84	13	3	0	0	0.0	8	6	5	20	6	44	8	20	2	0	2	0.8	1.000	OF-28
7 yrs.		502	.245	.355	1277	313	38	12	26	2.0	183	130	94	238	110	85	20	792	19	27	7	2.1	.968	OF-394, DH-7
DIVISIONAL PLAYOFF SERIES																								
1981	NY A	1	—	—	0	0	0	0	0	—	0	0	0	0	0	0	0	0	0	0	0	0.0	—	
LEAGUE CHAMPIONSHIP SERIES																								
1980	NY A	3	.000	.000	10	0	0	0	0	0.0	1	0	1	2	0	0	0	7	0	0	0	2.3	1.000	OF-3
1981		3	1.000	1.000	1	1	0	0	0	0.0	2	0	0	0	0	0	0	0	0	0	0	0.0	.000	OF-2
1984	SD N	3	.000	.000	4	0	0	0	0	0.0	1	0	1	2	1	1	0	3	0	0	0	1.0	1.000	OF-3
3 yrs.		9	.067	.067	15	1	0	0	0	0.0	4	0	2	4	1	1	0	10	0	0	0	1.3	1.000	OF-8
WORLD SERIES																								
1981	NY A	4	.000	.000	1	0	0	0	0	0.0	1	0	0	1	0	1	0	1	0	0	0	0.5	1.000	OF-2
1984	SD N	5	.067	.067	15	1	0	0	0	0.0	1	2	0	4	0	0	0	13	0	0	0	2.6	1.000	OF-5
2 yrs.		9	.063	.063	16	1	0	0	0	0.0	2	2	0	5	0	1	0	14	0	0	0	2.0	1.000	OF-7

Chris Brown

BROWN, JOHN CHRISTOPHER
B. Aug. 15, 1961, Jackson, Miss.

BR TR 6′ 185 lbs.

Year	Team	Games	BA	SA	AB	H	2B	3B	HR	HR%	R	RBI	BB	SO	SB	Pinch Hit AB	Pinch Hit H	PO	A	E	DP	TC/G	FA	G by Pos
1984	SF N	23	.286	.405	84	24	7	0	1	1.2	6	11	9	19	2	0	0	23	40	7	3	3.0	.900	3B-23
1985		131	.271	.442	432	117	20	3	16	3.7	50	61	38	78	2	9	3	94	243	10	15	2.9	.971	3B-120
1986		116	.317	.421	416	132	16	3	7	1.7	57	49	33	43	13	1	0	73	181	18	17	2.4	.934	3B-111, SS-2
1987	**2 teams**	SF N (38G –.242) SD N (44G –.232)																						
″	**total**	82	.237	.394	287	68	9	0	12	4.2	34	40	20	46	4	3	2	60	132	16	17	2.6	.923	3B-80, SS-1
1988	SD N	80	.235	.283	247	58	6	0	2	0.8	14	19	19	49	0	5	0	54	131	10	15	2.7	.949	3B-72
1989	DET A	17	.193	.246	57	11	3	0	0	0.0	3	4	1	17	0	0	0	15	25	4	4	2.6	.909	3B-17
6 yrs.		449	.269	.392	1523	410	61	6	38	2.5	164	184	120	252	21	18	5	319	752	65	71	2.7	.943	3B-423, SS-3

Curt Brown

BROWN, CURTIS, JR.
Brother of Leon Brown.
B. Sept. 14, 1945, Sacramento, Calif.

BR TR 5′11″ 180 lbs.

Year	Team	Games	BA	SA	AB	H	2B	3B	HR	HR%	R	RBI	BB	SO	SB	Pinch Hit AB	Pinch Hit H	PO	A	E	DP	TC/G	FA	G by Pos
1973	MON N	1	.000	.000	4	0	0	0	0	0.0	0	0	0	0	0	0	0	3	0	0	0	3.0	1.000	OF-1

Darrell Brown

BROWN, DARRELL WAYNE
B. Oct. 29, 1955, Oklahoma City, Okla.

BB TR 6′ 180 lbs.

Year	Team	Games	BA	SA	AB	H	2B	3B	HR	HR%	R	RBI	BB	SO	SB	Pinch Hit AB	Pinch Hit H	PO	A	E	DP	TC/G	FA	G by Pos
1981	DET A	16	.250	.250	4	1	0	0	0	0.0	4	0	0	1	1	2	1	2	0	0	0	0.2	1.000	OF-6, DH-4
1982	OAK A	8	.333	.444	18	6	0	1	0	0.0	2	3	1	2	1	0	0	9	0	0	0	1.1	1.000	OF-7, DH-1
1983	MIN A	91	.272	.304	309	84	6	2	0	0.0	40	22	10	28	3	6	0	188	2	1	0	2.3	.995	OF-81, DH-3
1984		95	.273	.342	260	71	9	3	1	0.4	36	19	14	16	4	35	10	144	4	1	0	2.2	.993	OF-55, DH-13
4 yrs.		210	.274	.325	591	162	15	6	1	0.2	82	44	25	47	9	43	11	343	6	2	0	2.1	.994	OF-149, DH-21

Delos Brown

BROWN, DELOS HIGHT
B. Oct. 4, 1892, Anna, Ill. D. Dec. 21, 1964, Carbondale, Ill.

BR TR 5′ 9″ 160 lbs.

Year	Team	Games	BA	SA	AB	H	2B	3B	HR	HR%	R	RBI	BB	SO	SB	Pinch Hit AB	Pinch Hit H	PO	A	E	DP	TC/G	FA	G by Pos
1914	CHI A	1	.000	.000	1	0	0	0	0	0.0	0	0	0	1	0	1	0	0	0	0	0	0.0	—	

Dick Brown

BROWN, RICHARD ERNEST
Brother of Larry Brown.
B. Jan. 17, 1935, Shinnston, W. Va. D. Apr. 12, 1970, Baltimore, Md.

BR TR 6′ 2″ 176 lbs.

Year	Team	Games	BA	SA	AB	H	2B	3B	HR	HR%	R	RBI	BB	SO	SB	Pinch Hit AB	Pinch Hit H	PO	A	E	DP	TC/G	FA	G by Pos
1957	CLE A	34	.263	.404	114	30	4	0	4	3.5	10	22	4	23	1	1	0	190	18	3	4	6.4	.986	C-33
1958		68	.237	.387	173	41	5	0	7	4.0	20	20	12	27	1	6	0	278	23	4	6	4.9	.987	C-62
1959		48	.220	.376	141	31	7	0	5	3.5	15	16	11	39	0	2	0	245	20	1	5	5.5	.996	C-48
1960	CHI A	16	.163	.372	43	7	0	0	3	7.0	4	5	3	11	0	2	1	66	7	1	1	5.3	.986	C-14
1961	DET A	98	.266	.474	308	82	12	2	16	5.2	32	45	22	57	0	3	2	460	38	5	7	5.5	.990	C-91
1962		134	.241	.353	431	104	12	0	12	2.8	40	40	21	66	0	3	1	742	42	5	8	6.0	.994	C-132
1963	BAL A	59	.246	.322	171	42	7	0	2	1.2	13	13	15	35	1	1	1	317	23	5	7	5.9	.986	C-58
1964		88	.257	.387	230	59	6	0	8	3.5	24	32	12	45	2	7	0	380	29	5	4	4.9	.988	C-84
1965		96	.231	.333	255	59	9	1	5	2.0	17	30	17	53	2	7	1	466	40	9	6	5.6	.983	C-92
9 yrs.		641	.244	.380	1866	455	62	3	62	3.3	175	223	117	356	7	32	6	3144	240	38	48	5.6	.989	C-614

Don Brown

BROWN, JAMES DONALDSON (Moose)
B. Mar. 31, 1897, Laurel, Md.
BR TR 6′ 178 lbs.

Year	Team	Games	BA	SA	AB	H	2B	3B	HR	HR%	R	RBI	BB	SO	SB	Pinch Hit AB	Pinch Hit H	PO	A	E	DP	TC/G	FA	G by Pos
1915	**STL N**	1	.500	.500	2	1	0	0	0	0.0	0	0	2	1	0	0	0	1	0	0	0	1.0	1.000	OF-1
1916	**PHI A**	14	.238	.405	42	10	2	1	1	2.4	6	5	4	9	0	2	0	15	2	2	0	1.6	.895	OF-12
2 yrs.		15	.250	.409	44	11	2	1	1	2.3	6	5	6	10	0	2	0	16	2	2	0	1.5	.900	OF-13

Drummond Brown

BROWN, DRUMMOND NICOL
B. Jan. 31, 1885, Los Angeles, Calif. D. Jan. 27, 1927, Platte County, Mo.
BR TR 6′ 180 lbs.

Year	Team	Games	BA	SA	AB	H	2B	3B	HR	HR%	R	RBI	BB	SO	SB	Pinch Hit AB	Pinch Hit H	PO	A	E	DP	TC/G	FA	G by Pos
1913	**BOS N**	15	.324	.441	34	11	1	0	1	2.9	3	2	2	9	0	3	0	41	17	2	0	5.0	.967	C-12
1914	**KC F**	31	.190	.241	58	11	3	0	0	0.0	4	5	7		1	4	0	94	33	6	5	5.3	.955	C-23, 1B-2
1915		77	.242	.308	227	55	10	1	1	0.4	13	26	12		3	11	2	276	104	15	4	6.0	.962	C-65, 1B-1
3 yrs.		123	.241	.310	319	77	14	1	2	0.6	20	33	21	9	4	18	2	411	154	23	9	5.7	.961	C-100, 1B-3

Ed Brown

BROWN, EDWARD P.
B. Chicago, Ill. Deceased.
TR 178 lbs.

Year	Team	Games	BA	SA	AB	H	2B	3B	HR	HR%	R	RBI	BB	SO	SB	Pinch Hit AB	Pinch Hit H	PO	A	E	DP	TC/G	FA	G by Pos
1882	**STL AA**	17	.183	.183	60	11	0	0	0	0.0	4		4			0	0	21	6	6	0	1.8	.818	OF-15, 2B-2, P-1
1884	**TOL AA**	42	.176	.196	153	27	3	0	0	0.0	13		2			0	0	45	56	24	1	2.8	.808	3B-39, OF-2, 2B-1, P-1, C-1
2 yrs.		59	.178	.192	213	38	3	0	0	0.0	17		6			0	0	66	62	30	1	2.5	.810	3B-39, OF-17, 2B-3, P-2, C-1

Eddie Brown

BROWN, EDWARD WILLIAM (Glass Arm Eddie)
B. July 17, 1891, Milligan, Neb. D. Sept. 10, 1956, Vallejo, Calif.
BR TR 6′ 3″ 190 lbs.

Year	Team	Games	BA	SA	AB	H	2B	3B	HR	HR%	R	RBI	BB	SO	SB	Pinch Hit AB	Pinch Hit H	PO	A	E	DP	TC/G	FA	G by Pos
1920	**NY N**	3	.125	.250	8	1	1	0	0	0.0	1	0	0	3	0	1	0	6	0	0	0	3.0	1.000	OF-2
1921		70	.281	.359	128	36	6	2	0	0.0	16	12	4	11	1	37	11	63	2	3	0	2.3	.956	OF-30
1924	**BKN N**	114	.308	.424	455	140	30	4	5	1.1	56	78	26	15	3	0	0	311	3	8	0	2.8	.975	OF-114
1925		153	.306	.429	618	189	39	11	5	0.8	88	99	22	18	3	0	0	449	7	13	3	3.1	.972	OF-153
1926	**BOS N**	153	.328	.415	612	**201**	31	8	2	0.3	71	84	23	20	5	0	0	401	10	15	2	2.8	.965	OF-153
1927		155	.306	.401	558	171	35	6	2	0.4	64	75	28	20	11	4	2	347	10	7	1	2.4	.981	OF-150, 1B-1
1928		142	.268	.340	523	140	28	2	2	0.4	45	59	24	22	6	10	4	309	6	13	3	2.5	.960	OF-129, 1B-1
7 yrs.		790	.303	.400	2902	878	170	33	16	0.6	341	407	127	109	29	52	17	1886	38	59	9	2.7	.970	OF-731, 1B-2

Fred Brown

BROWN, FRED HERBERT
B. Apr. 12, 1879, Ossipee, N. H. D. Feb. 3, 1955, Somersworth, N. H.
BR TR 5′10½″ 190 lbs.

Year	Team	Games	BA	SA	AB	H	2B	3B	HR	HR%	R	RBI	BB	SO	SB	Pinch Hit AB	Pinch Hit H	PO	A	E	DP	TC/G	FA	G by Pos
1901	**BOS N**	7	.143	.143	14	2	0	0	0	0.0	1	2	0		0	2	1	8	1	0	0	1.8	1.000	OF-5
1902		2	.333	.500	6	2	1	0	0	0.0	1	0	0		0	0	0	0	1	0	0	0.5	1.000	OF-2
2 yrs.		9	.200	.250	20	4	1	0	0	0.0	2	2	0		0	2	1	8	2	0	0	1.4	1.000	OF-7

Gates Brown

BROWN, WILLIAM JAMES
B. May 2, 1939, Crestline, Ohio.
BL TR 5′11″ 220 lbs.

Year	Team	Games	BA	SA	AB	H	2B	3B	HR	HR%	R	RBI	BB	SO	SB	Pinch Hit AB	Pinch Hit H	PO	A	E	DP	TC/G	FA	G by Pos
1963	**DET A**	55	.268	.402	82	22	3	1	2	2.4	16	14	8	13	2	30	6	35	3	0	1	2.4	1.000	OF-16
1964		123	.272	.458	426	116	22	6	15	3.5	65	54	31	53	11	19	4	205	4	4	0	2.0	.981	OF-106
1965		96	.256	.467	227	58	14	2	10	4.4	33	43	17	33	6	34	9	108	1	3	0	2.0	.973	OF-56
1966		88	.266	.432	169	45	5	1	7	4.1	27	27	18	19	3	40	13	46	4	1	1	1.2	.980	OF-43
1967		51	.187	.286	91	17	1	1	2	2.2	17	9	13	15	0	26	4	22	1	0	0	1.1	1.000	OF-20
1968		67	.370	.685	92	34	7	2	6	6.5	15	15	12	4	0	39	**18**	21	1	0	0	1.2	1.000	OF-17, 1B-1
1969		60	.204	.290	93	19	1	2	1	1.1	13	6	5	17	0	39	8	28	1	3	0	2.3	.906	OF-14
1970		81	.226	.323	124	28	3	0	3	2.4	18	24	20	14	0	41	10	37	1	2	0	1.5	.950	OF-26
1971		82	.338	.549	195	66	2	3	11	5.6	37	29	21	17	4	26	9	68	2	1	0	1.3	.986	OF-56
1972		103	.230	.369	252	58	5	0	10	4.0	33	31	26	28	3	28	4	122	5	3	1	1.8	.977	OF-72
1973		125	.236	.366	377	89	11	1	12	3.2	48	50	52	41	1	4	0	1	0	0	0	0.0	1.000	DH-119, OF-2
1974		73	.242	.384	99	24	2	0	4	4.0	7	17	10	15	0	**53**	**16**	0	0	0	0	0.0	.000	DH-13
1975		47	.171	.314	35	6	2	0	1	2.9	1	3	9	6	0	35	6	0	0	0	0	0.0	—	
13 yrs.		1051	.257	.420	2262	582	78	19	84	3.7	330	322	242	275	30	414	107	693	23	17	3	1.3	.977	OF-428, DH-132, 1B-1
																	10th							
LEAGUE CHAMPIONSHIP SERIES																								
1972	**DET A**	3	.000	.000	2	0	0	0	0	0.0	1	0	1	0	0	2	0	0	0	0	0	0.0	—	
WORLD SERIES																								
1968	**DET A**	1	.000	.000	1	0	0	0	0	0.0	0	0	0	0	0	1	0	0	0	0	0	0.0	—	

Ike Brown

BROWN, ISAAC
B. Apr. 13, 1942, Memphis, Tenn.
BR TR 6′ 190 lbs.

Year	Team	Games	BA	SA	AB	H	2B	3B	HR	HR%	R	RBI	BB	SO	SB	Pinch Hit AB	Pinch Hit H	PO	A	E	DP	TC/G	FA	G by Pos
1969	**DET A**	70	.229	.376	170	39	4	3	5	2.9	24	12	26	43	2	12	0	87	116	9	18	3.5	.958	2B-45, 3B-12, OF-3, SS-1
1970		56	.287	.468	94	27	5	0	4	4.3	17	15	13	26	0	21	7	49	33	8	8	3.2	.911	2B-23, OF-4, 3B-1
1971		59	.255	.482	110	28	1	0	8	7.3	20	19	19	25	0	19	6	133	27	3	10	4.2	.982	1B-17, OF-9, 2B-8, 3B-4, SS-1
1972		51	.250	.357	84	21	3	0	2	2.4	12	10	17	23	1	12	1	122	11	1	7	3.3	.993	OF-22, 1B-13, 2B-3, SS-1, 3B-1
1973		42	.289	.382	76	22	2	1	1	1.3	12	9	15	13	0	7	1	117	12	2	9	3.5	.985	1B-21, OF-12, DH-2, 3B-2
1974		2	.000	.000	2	0	0	0	0	0.0	0	0	0	0	0	0	0	2	1	0	0	1.5	1.000	3B-2
6 yrs.		280	.256	.410	536	137	15	4	20	3.7	85	65	90	130	3	71	15	510	200	23	52	3.5	.969	2B-79, 1B-51, OF-50, 3B-22, SS-3, DH-2
LEAGUE CHAMPIONSHIP SERIES																								
1972	**DET A**	1	.500	.500	2	1	0	0	0	0.0	0	2	0	1	0	0	0	2	0	0	0	2.0	1.000	1B-1

Jake Brown

BROWN, JERALD RAY
B. Mar. 3, 1948, Sumrall, Miss. D. Dec. 18, 1981, Houston, Tex.
BR TR 6′ 2″ 200 lbs.

Year	Team	Games	BA	SA	AB	H	2B	3B	HR	HR%	R	RBI	BB	SO	SB	Pinch Hit AB	Pinch Hit H	PO	A	E	DP	TC/G	FA	G by Pos
1975	**SF N**	41	.209	.279	43	9	3	0	0	0.0	6	4	5	13	0	22	4	11	1	2	0	1.0	.857	OF-14

Jarvis Brown

BROWN, JARVIS ARDEL
B. Mar. 26, 1967, Waukegan, Ill.
BR TR 5′ 7″ 165 lbs.

Year	Team	Games	BA	SA	AB	H	2B	3B	HR	HR%	R	RBI	BB	SO	SB	Pinch Hit AB	Pinch Hit H	PO	A	E	DP	TC/G	FA	G by Pos
1991	**MIN A**	38	.216	.216	37	8	0	0	0	0.0	10	0	2	8	7	2	0	21	0	1	0	0.6	.955	OF-32, DH-4
1992		35	.067	.067	15	1	0	0	0	0.0	8	0	2	4	2	0	0	20	0	1	0	0.7	.952	OF-31, DH-1
1993	**SD N**	47	.233	.331	133	31	9	2	0	0.0	21	8	15	26	3	5	1	109	2	2	0	2.6	.982	OF-43

Jarvis Brown *continued*

Year	Team		Games	BA	SA	AB	H	2B	3B	HR	HR%	R	RBI	BB	SO	SB	Pinch Hit AB	Pinch Hit H	PO	A	E	DP	TC/G	FA	G by Pos
1994	ATL	N	17	.133	.400	15	2	1	0	1	6.7	3	1	0	2	0	4	1	10	0	0	0	1.1	1.000	OF-9
1995	BAL	A	18	.148	.185	27	4	1	0	0	0.0	2	1	7	9	1	1	0	16	0	0	0	0.9	1.000	OF-17
5 yrs.			155	.203	.282	227	46	11	2	1	0.4	44	10	26	49	13	12	2	176	2	4	0	1.3	.978	OF-132, DH-5
LEAGUE CHAMPIONSHIP SERIES																									
1991	MIN	A	1	—	—	0	0	0	0	0	—	1	0	0	0	0	0	0	0	0	0	0	0.0	.000	DH-1
WORLD SERIES																									
1991	MIN	A	3	.000	.000	2	0	0	0	0	0.0	0	0	0	0	0	1	0	0	0	0	0	0.0		OF-2, DH-1

Jimmy Brown

BROWN, JAMES ROBERTSON
B. Apr. 25, 1910, Jamesville, N. C. D. Dec. 29, 1977, Bath, N. C.
BB TR 5′ 8½″ 165 lbs.

Year	Team		Games	BA	SA	AB	H	2B	3B	HR	HR%	R	RBI	BB	SO	SB	Pinch Hit AB	Pinch Hit H	PO	A	E	DP	TC/G	FA	G by Pos
1937	STL	N	138	.276	.360	525	145	20	9	2	0.4	86	53	27	29	10	6	1	277	415	31	67	5.2	.957	2B-112, SS-25, 3B-1
1938			108	.301	.364	382	115	12	6	0	0.0	50	38	27	9	7	9	3	195	264	21	55	4.7	.956	2B-49, SS-30, 3B-24
1939			147	.298	.384	**645**	192	31	8	3	0.5	88	51	32	18	4	1	0	328	492	35	92	5.6	.959	SS-104, 2B-50
1940			107	.280	.335	454	127	17	4	0	0.0	56	30	24	15	9	1	0	198	243	22	42	4.0	.952	2B-48, 3B-41, SS-28
1941			132	.306	.406	549	168	28	9	3	0.5	81	56	45	22	2	1	1	157	304	17	31	3.6	.964	3B-123, 2B-11
1942			145	.256	.320	**606**	155	28	4	1	0.2	75	71	52	11	4	0	0	299	329	26	66	4.1	.960	2B-82, 3B-66, SS-12
1943			34	.182	.255	110	20	4	2	0	0.0	6	8	6	1	0	1	0	65	76	2	14	4.2	.986	2B-19, 3B-9, SS-6
1946	PIT	N	79	.241	.266	241	58	6	0	0	0.0	23	12	18	5	3	20	**7**	127	168	16	28	5.2	.949	SS-30, 2B-21, 3B-9
8 yrs.			890	.279	.352	3512	980	146	42	9	0.3	465	319	231	110	39	39	12	1646	2291	170	395	4.6	.959	2B-392, 3B-273, SS-235
WORLD SERIES																									
1942	STL	N	5	.300	.300	20	6	0	0	0	0.0	2	1	3	0	0	0	0	6	16	3	2	5.0	.880	2B-5

Joe Brown

BROWN, JOSEPH E.
B. Apr. 4, 1859, Warren, Pa. D. June 28, 1888, Warren, Pa.
5′10″ 162 lbs.

Year	Team		Games	BA	SA	AB	H	2B	3B	HR	HR%	R	RBI	BB	SO	SB	Pinch Hit AB	Pinch Hit H	PO	A	E	DP	TC/G	FA	G by Pos
1884	CHI	N	15	.213	.230	61	13	1	0	0	0.0	6		0	15		0	0	11	13	4	0	1.6	.857	OF-9, P-7, 1B-1, C-1
1885	BAL	AA	5	.158	.158	19	3	0	0	0	0.0	2		0			0	0	5	8	0	2	2.6	1.000	P-4, 2B-1
2 yrs.			20	.200	.213	80	16	1	0	0	0.0	8		0	15		0	0	16	21	4	2	1.8	.902	P-11, OF-9, 1B-1, 2B-1, C-1

Larry Brown

BROWN, LARRY LESLIE
Brother of Dick Brown.
B. Mar. 1, 1940, Shinnston, W. Va.
BR TR 5′10″ 160 lbs.

Year	Team		Games	BA	SA	AB	H	2B	3B	HR	HR%	R	RBI	BB	SO	SB	Pinch Hit AB	Pinch Hit H	PO	A	E	DP	TC/G	FA	G by Pos
1963	CLE	A	74	.255	.340	247	63	6	0	5	2.0	28	18	22	27	4	5	1	113	176	14	25	4.2	.954	SS-46, 2B-27
1964			115	.230	.379	335	77	12	1	12	3.6	33	40	24	55	1	12	1	189	275	9	56	4.4	.981	2B-103, SS-4
1965			124	.253	.368	438	111	22	2	8	1.8	52	40	38	62	5	5	1	195	310	15	66	4.3	.971	SS-95, 2B-26
1966			105	.229	.291	340	78	12	0	3	0.9	29	17	36	58	0	6	2	153	264	19	52	4.4	.956	SS-90, 2B-10
1967			152	.227	.311	485	110	16	2	7	1.4	38	37	53	62	4	1	0	233	414	22	90	4.5	.967	SS-150
1968			154	.234	.319	495	116	18	3	6	1.2	43	35	43	46	1	1	0	255	371	22	70	4.2	.966	SS-154
1969			132	.239	.294	469	112	10	2	4	0.9	48	24	44	43	5	6	2	200	315	20	63	4.0	.963	SS-101, 3B-29, 2B-5
1970			72	.258	.316	155	40	5	2	0	0.0	17	15	20	14	1	22	5	72	105	8	23	3.1	.957	SS-27, 3B-17, 2B-16
1971	2 teams		CLE A (13G –.220)		OAK A (70G –.196)																				
″	total		83	.201	.234	239	48	3	1	1	0.4	18	14	10	22	1	8	0	106	166	7	35	3.6	.975	SS-44, 2B-23, 3B-10
1972	OAK	A	47	.183	.197	142	26	2	0	0	0.0	11	4	13	8	0	0	0	110	112	6	31	4.9	.974	2B-46, 3B-1
1973	BAL	A	17	.250	.357	28	7	0	0	1	3.6	4	5	5	4	0	3	0	10	13	3	2	1.6	.885	3B-15, 2B-1
1974	TEX	A	54	.197	.224	76	15	2	0	0	0.0	10	5	9	13	0	2	1	29	64	5	12	1.8	.949	3B-47, 2B-8, SS-1
12 yrs.			1129	.233	.313	3449	803	108	13	47	1.4	331	254	317	414	22	71	13	1665	2585	150	525	4.0	.966	SS-712, 2B-265, 3B-119
LEAGUE CHAMPIONSHIP SERIES																									
1973	BAL	A	1	—	—	0	0	0	0	0	—	0	0	0	0	0	0	0	0	0	0	0	0.0	.000	3B-1

Leon Brown

BROWN, LEON (Brownie)
Brother of Curt Brown.
B. Nov. 16, 1949, Sacramento, Calif.
BR TR 6′ 185 lbs.

Year	Team		Games	BA	SA	AB	H	2B	3B	HR	HR%	R	RBI	BB	SO	SB	Pinch Hit AB	Pinch Hit H	PO	A	E	DP	TC/G	FA	G by Pos
1976	NY	N	64	.214	.257	70	15	3	0	0	0.0	11	2	4	4	2	7	1	46	3	0	1	1.1	1.000	OF-43

Lew Brown

BROWN, LEWIS J. (Blower)
B. Feb. 1, 1858, Leominster, Mass. D. Jan. 16, 1889, Boston, Mass.
BR TR 5′10½″ 185 lbs.

Year	Team		Games	BA	SA	AB	H	2B	3B	HR	HR%	R	RBI	BB	SO	SB	Pinch Hit AB	Pinch Hit H	PO	A	E	DP	TC/G	FA	G by Pos
1876	BOS	N	45	.210	.333	195	41	6	6	2	1.0	23	21	3	22		0	0	193	45	40	4	6.0	.856	C-45, OF-1
1877			58	.253	.394	221	56	12	8	1	0.5	27	31	6	**33**		0	0	387	67	49	5	8.5	.903	C-55, 1B-4
1878	PRO	N	58	.305	.453	243	74	21	6	1	0.4	44	43	7	37		0	0	410	88	54	18	8.9	.902	C-45, 1B-15, P-1, OF-1
1879	2 teams		PRO N (53G –.258)		CHI N (6G –.286)																				
″	total		59	.260	.372	250	65	14	4	2	0.8	25	41	5	28		0	0	362	66	68	10	8.3	.863	C-48, 1B-6, OF-6
1881	2 teams		DET N (27G –.241)		PRO N (18G –.240)																				
″	total		45	.240	.344	183	44	6	2	3	1.6	25	24	7	29		0	0	313	10	15	24	7.5	.956	1B-32, OF-13
1883	2 teams		BOS N (14G –.241)		LOU AA (14G –.183)																				
″	total		28	.211	.298	114	24	6	2	0	0.0	11	9	4	6		0	0	281	7	26	13	10.8	.917	1B-28, C-1
1884	BOS	U	85	.231	.314	325	75	18	3	1	0.3	50		13			0	0	737	128	72	15	10.4	.923	C-54, 1B-33, OF-2, P-1
7 yrs.			378	.248	.362	1531	379	83	31	10	0.7	205	169	45	155		0	0	2683	411	324	89	8.7	.905	C-248, 1B-118, OF-23, P-2

Lindsay Brown

BROWN, JOHN LINDSAY (Red)
B. July 22, 1911, Mason, Tex. D. Jan. 1, 1967, San Antonio, Tex.
BR TR 5′10″ 160 lbs.

Year	Team		Games	BA	SA	AB	H	2B	3B	HR	HR%	R	RBI	BB	SO	SB	Pinch Hit AB	Pinch Hit H	PO	A	E	DP	TC/G	FA	G by Pos
1937	BKN	N	48	.270	.313	115	31	3	1	0	0.0	16	6	3	17	1	1	0	73	106	12	26	4.2	.937	SS-45

Marty Brown

BROWN, MARTY LEO
B. Jan. 23, 1963, Lawton, Okla.
BR TR 6′ 1″ 190 lbs.

Year	Team		Games	BA	SA	AB	H	2B	3B	HR	HR%	R	RBI	BB	SO	SB	Pinch Hit AB	Pinch Hit H	PO	A	E	DP	TC/G	FA	G by Pos
1988	CIN	N	10	.188	.250	16	3	1	0	0	0.0	0	2	1	2	0	4	1	1	9	0	0	1.3	1.000	3B-8
1989			16	.167	.200	30	5	1	0	0	0.0	2	4	4	9	0	3	0	2	19	2	2	2.1	.913	3B-11
1990	BAL	A	9	.200	.200	15	3	0	0	0	0.0	1	0	1	7	0	2	1	1	3	0	0	0.4	1.000	DH-4, 2B-3, 3B-2
3 yrs.			35	.180	.213	61	11	2	0	0	0.0	3	6	6	18	0	9	2	4	31	2	2	1.3	.946	3B-21, DH-4, 2B-3

Mike Brown

BROWN, MICHAEL CHARLES
B. Dec. 29, 1959, San Francisco, Calif.
BR TR 6′ 2″ 190 lbs.

Year	Team	Games	BA	SA	AB	H	2B	3B	HR	HR%	R	RBI	BB	SO	SB	Pinch Hit AB	Pinch Hit H	PO	A	E	DP	TC/G	FA	G by Pos
1983	**CAL A**	31	.231	.385	104	24	5	1	3	2.9	12	9	7	20	1	0	0	52	4	3	1	1.9	.949	OF-31
1984		62	.284	.520	148	42	8	3	7	4.7	19	22	13	23	0	14	3	57	4	2	0	1.3	.968	OF-44, DH-3
1985	**2 teams**	**CAL A** (60G –.268) **PIT N** (57G –.332)																						
″	**total**	117	.304	.472	358	109	27	3	9	2.5	52	53	29	48	2	11	3	165	6	6	2	1.6	.966	OF-104, DH-7
1986	**PIT N**	87	.218	.296	243	53	7	0	4	1.6	18	26	27	32	2	20	4	107	3	3	2	1.6	.973	OF-71
1988	**CAL A**	18	.220	.260	50	11	2	0	0	0.0	4	3	1	12	0	2	0	33	2	2	0	2.1	.946	OF-18
5 yrs.		315	.265	.411	903	239	49	7	23	2.5	105	113	77	135	5	47	10	414	19	16	5	1.6	.964	OF-268, DH-10

Ollie Brown

BROWN, OLLIE LEE (Downtown)
Brother of Oscar Brown.
B. Feb. 11, 1944, Tuscaloosa, Ala.
BR TR 6′ 2″ 178 lbs.

Year	Team	Games	BA	SA	AB	H	2B	3B	HR	HR%	R	RBI	BB	SO	SB	Pinch Hit AB	Pinch Hit H	PO	A	E	DP	TC/G	FA	G by Pos
1965	**SF N**	6	.200	.300	10	2	1	0	0	0.0	0	0	0	2	0	1	0	4	0	0	0	1.0	1.000	OF-4
1966		115	.233	.319	348	81	7	1	7	2.0	32	33	33	66	2	3	0	163	12	4	1	1.6	.978	OF-114
1967		120	.267	.396	412	110	12	1	13	3.2	44	53	25	65	0	4	1	190	5	3	0	1.7	.985	OF-115
1968		40	.232	.274	95	22	4	0	0	0.0	7	11	3	23	1	6	1	32	1	0	0	0.9	1.000	OF-35
1969	**SD N**	151	.264	.412	568	150	18	3	20	3.5	76	61	44	97	10	1	1	269	14	7	4	2.0	.976	OF-148
1970		139	.292	.489	534	156	34	1	23	4.3	79	89	34	78	5	3	0	258	12	10	3	2.0	.964	OF-137
1971		145	.273	.362	484	132	16	0	9	1.9	36	55	52	74	3	11	3	263	9	5	2	2.1	.982	OF-134
1972	**3 teams**	**SD N** (23G –.171) **OAK A** (20G –.241) **MIL A** (66G –.279)																						
″	**total**	109	.248	.323	303	75	11	0	4	1.3	29	32	28	47	1	24	1	181	9	1	3	2.1	.995	OF-89, 3B-1
1973	**MIL A**	97	.280	.392	296	83	10	1	7	2.4	28	32	33	53	4	9	0	1	0	0	0	0.0	1.000	DH-82, OF-4
1974	**2 teams**	**HOU N** (27G –.217) **PHI N** (43G –.242)																						
″	**total**	70	.232	.417	168	39	6	2	7	4.2	19	19	10	35	0	29	11	73	1	3	0	1.5	.961	OF-53
1975	**PHI N**	84	.303	.510	145	44	12	0	6	4.1	19	26	15	29	1	30	8	67	0	0	0	1.8	1.000	OF-38
1976		92	.254	.383	209	53	10	1	5	2.4	30	30	33	33	2	26	9	105	7	6	2	1.6	.949	OF-75
1977		50	.243	.357	70	17	3	1	1	1.4	5	13	4	14	1	31	7	16	1	0	0	0.8	1.000	OF-21
13 yrs.		1218	.265	.394	3642	964	144	11	102	2.8	404	454	314	616	30	178	42	1622	71	39	15	1.6	.977	OF-967, DH-82, 3B-1
LEAGUE CHAMPIONSHIP SERIES																								
1976	**PHI N**	1	.000	.000	2	0	0	0	0	0.0	0	0	1	1	0	0	0	2	0	0	0	2.0	1.000	OF-1
1977		2	.000	.000	2	0	0	0	0	0.0	0	0	0	1	0	2	0	0	0	0	0	0.0	—	
2 yrs.		3	.000	.000	4	0	0	0	0	0.0	0	0	1	2	0	2	0	2	0	0	0	2.0	1.000	OF-1

Oscar Brown

BROWN, OSCAR LEE
Brother of Ollie Brown.
B. Feb. 8, 1946, Long Beach, Calif.
BR TR 6′ 175 lbs.

Year	Team	Games	BA	SA	AB	H	2B	3B	HR	HR%	R	RBI	BB	SO	SB	Pinch Hit AB	Pinch Hit H	PO	A	E	DP	TC/G	FA	G by Pos
1969	**ATL N**	7	.250	.250	4	1	0	0	0	0.0	2	0	0	1	0	1	0	2	0	0	0	0.7	1.000	OF-3
1970		28	.383	.532	47	18	2	1	1	2.1	6	7	7	7	0	3	2	24	0	1	0	1.0	.960	OF-25
1971		27	.209	.302	43	9	4	0	0	0.0	4	5	3	8	0	10	1	20	1	0	0	1.4	1.000	OF-15
1972		76	.226	.323	164	37	5	1	3	1.8	19	16	4	29	0	15	1	82	7	10	2	1.7	.899	OF-59
1973		22	.207	.259	58	12	3	0	0	0.0	3	0	3	10	0	9	1	32	1	0	0	2.5	1.000	OF-13
5 yrs.		160	.244	.339	316	77	14	2	4	1.3	34	28	17	55	0	38	5	160	9	11	2	1.6	.939	OF-115

Randy Brown

BROWN, EDWIN RANDOLPH
B. Aug. 29, 1944, Leesburg, Fla.
BL TR 5′ 7″ 170 lbs.

Year	Team	Games	BA	SA	AB	H	2B	3B	HR	HR%	R	RBI	BB	SO	SB	Pinch Hit AB	Pinch Hit H	PO	A	E	DP	TC/G	FA	G by Pos
1969	**CAL A**	13	.160	.200	25	4	1	0	0	0.0	3	0	6	1	0	3	0	41	4	0	2	4.1	1.000	C-10, OF-1
1970		5	.000	.000	4	0	0	0	0	0.0	0	0	0	0	0	0	0	5	1	0	0	1.2	1.000	C-5
2 yrs.		18	.138	.172	29	4	1	0	0	0.0	3	0	6	1	0	3	0	46	5	0	2	3.2	1.000	C-15, OF-1

Sam Brown

BROWN, SAMUEL WAKEFIELD
B. May 21, 1878, Webster, Pa. D. Nov. 8, 1931, Mount Pleasant, Pa.
BR TR

Year	Team	Games	BA	SA	AB	H	2B	3B	HR	HR%	R	RBI	BB	SO	SB	Pinch Hit AB	Pinch Hit H	PO	A	E	DP	TC/G	FA	G by Pos
1906	**BOS N**	71	.208	.242	231	48	6	1	0	0.0	12	20	13		4	5	1	235	88	13	5	5.2	.961	C-35, OF-13, 3B-12, 1B-3, 2B-2
1907		70	.192	.221	208	40	6	0	0	0.0	17	14	12		0	4	1	288	93	11	14	6.0	.972	C-63, 1B-2
2 yrs.		141	.200	.232	439	88	12	1	0	0.0	29	34	25		4	9	2	523	181	24	19	5.6	.967	C-98, OF-13, 3B-12, 1B-5, 2B-2

Tom Brown

BROWN, THOMAS TARLTON (Handsome)
B. Sept. 21, 1860, Liverpool, England D. Oct. 25, 1927, Washington, D. C.
Manager 1897–98.
BL TR 5′10″ 168 lbs.

Year	Team	Games	BA	SA	AB	H	2B	3B	HR	HR%	R	RBI	BB	SO	SB	Pinch Hit AB	Pinch Hit H	PO	A	E	DP	TC/G	FA	G by Pos
1882	**BAL AA**	45	.304	.370	181	55	5	2	1	0.6	30		6			0	0	59	16	28	1	2.2	.728	OF-45, P-2
1883	**COL AA**	97	.274	.371	420	115	12	7	5	1.2	69		20			0	0	153	22	49	3	2.3	.781	OF-96, P-3
1884		107	.273	.375	451	123	9	11	5	1.1	93		24			0	0	165	18	35	5	2.0	.839	OF-107, P-4
1885	**PIT AA**	108	.307	.426	437	134	16	12	4	0.9	81		34			0	0	186	21	44	2	2.3	.825	OF-108, P-2
1886		115	.285	.363	460	131	11	11	1	0.2	106		56			0	0	185	32	42	12	2.2	.838	OF-115, P-1
1887	**2 teams**	**PIT N** (47G –.245) **IND N** (36G –.179)																						
″	**total**	83	.217	.277	332	72	6	4	2	0.6	50	15	19	65	25	0	0	188	17	36	2	2.9	.851	OF-83
1888	**BOS N**	107	.248	.369	420	104	10	7	9	2.1	62	49	30	68	46	0	0	172	18	22	3	2.0	.896	OF-107
1889		90	.232	.304	362	84	10	5	2	0.6	93	24	59	56	63	0	0	169	13	20	1	2.2	.901	OF-90
1890	**BOS P**	128	.276	.392	543	150	23	14	4	0.7	146	61	86	**84**	79	0	0	276	32	30	8	2.6	.911	OF-128
1891	**BOS AA**	137	.321	.469	**589**	**189**	30	**21**	5	0.8	**177**	71	70	**96**	**106**	0	0	228	23	35	7	2.1	.878	OF-137
1892	**LOU N**	153	.227	.285	**660**	150	16	8	2	0.3	105	45	47	**94**	78	0	0	351	37	34	8	2.8	.919	OF-153
1893		122	.240	.323	529	127	15	7	5	0.9	104	54	56	63	**66**	0	0	339	39	29	13	3.3	.929	OF-122
1894		129	.254	.397	536	136	22	14	9	1.7	122	57	60	**73**	66	0	0	331	21	34	8	3.0	.912	OF-129
1895	**2 teams**	**STL N** (83G –.217) **WAS N** (34G –.239)																						
″	**total**	117	.223	.310	484	108	19	7	3	0.6	97	47	66	**60**	42	0	0	274	16	18	5	2.6	.942	OF-117
1896	**WAS N**	116	.294	.375	435	128	17	6	2	0.5	87	59	58	49	28	0	0	262	7	21	2	2.5	.928	OF-116
1897		116	.292	.369	469	137	17	2	5	1.1	91	45	52		25	0	0	252	17	21	5	2.5	.928	OF-115
1898		16	.164	.182	55	9	1	0	0	0.0	8	2	5		3	0	0	36	1	3	0	2.7	.925	OF-15
17 yrs.		1786	.265	.361	7363	1952	239	138	64	0.9	1521	529	748	708	627	0	0	3626	350	501	85	2.5	.888	OF-1783, P-12

Tom Brown

BROWN, THOMAS WILLIAM
B. Dec. 12, 1940, Laureldale, Pa.
BB TL 6′ 1″ 190 lbs.

Year	Team	Games	BA	SA	AB	H	2B	3B	HR	HR%	R	RBI	BB	SO	SB	Pinch Hit AB	Pinch Hit H	PO	A	E	DP	TC/G	FA	G by Pos
1963	**WAS A**	61	.147	.207	116	17	4	0	1	0.9	8	4	11	45	2	22	4	120	7	0	9	4.2	1.000	OF-16, 1B-14

Tommy Brown

BROWN, THOMAS MICHAEL (Buckshot) BR TR 6' 1" 170 lbs.
B. Dec. 6, 1927, Brooklyn, N. Y.

Year	Team	Games	BA	SA	AB	H	2B	3B	HR	HR%	R	RBI	BB	SO	SB	Pinch Hit AB	Pinch Hit H	PO	A	E	DP	TC/G	FA	G by Pos
1944	BKN N	46	.164	.192	146	24	4	0	0	0.0	17	8	8	17	0	0	0	89	109	16	24	4.7	.925	SS-46
1945		57	.245	.332	196	48	3	4	2	1.0	13	19	6	16	3	1	0	93	164	23	27	5.0	.918	SS-55, OF-1
1947		15	.235	.265	34	8	1	0	0	0.0	3	2	1	6	0	4	1	12	15	2	2	2.9	.931	3B-6, OF-3, SS-1
1948		54	.241	.310	145	35	4	0	2	1.4	18	20	7	17	1	9	1	44	60	7	7	2.5	.937	3B-43, 1B-1
1949		41	.303	.427	89	27	2	0	3	3.4	14	18	6	8	0	13	4	53	1	4	0	2.1	.931	OF-27
1950		48	.291	.616	86	25	2	1	8	9.3	15	20	11	9	0	29	7	31	2	3	0	2.3	.917	OF-16
1951	2 teams	BKN N (11G –.160)			PHI N (78G –.219)																			
"	total	89	.213	.376	221	47	4	1	10	4.5	26	33	17	25	1	26	4	183	37	9	15	3.6	.961	OF-37, 2B-14, 1B-12, 3B-1
1952	2 teams	PHI N (18G –.160)			CHI N (61G –.320)																			
"	total	79	.302	.409	225	68	12	0	4	1.8	26	26	16	27	1	15	3	144	112	17	24	4.6	.938	SS-39, 2B-10, 1B-8, OF-3
1953	CHI N	65	.196	.304	138	27	7	1	2	1.4	19	13	13	17	1	30	5	48	70	13	13	4.2	.901	SS-25, OF-6
9 yrs.		494	.241	.355	1280	309	39	7	31	2.4	151	159	85	142	7	127	25	697	570	94	112	3.8	.931	SS-166, OF-93, 3B-50, 2B-24, 1B-21
WORLD SERIES																								
1949	BKN N	2	.000	.000	2	0	0	0	0	0.0	0	0	0	1	0	2	0	0	0	0	0	0.0	—	

Willard Brown

BROWN, WILLARD (Big Bill, California Brown) BR TR 6' 2" 190 lbs.
B. 1866, San Francisco, Calif. D. Dec. 20, 1897, San Francisco, Calif.

Year	Team	Games	BA	SA	AB	H	2B	3B	HR	HR%	R	RBI	BB	SO	SB	Pinch Hit AB	Pinch Hit H	PO	A	E	DP	TC/G	FA	G by Pos
1887	NY N	49	.218	.259	170	37	3	2	0	0.0	17	25	10	15	10	0	0	231	71	31	5	6.5	.907	C-46, 3B-3, OF-2
1888		20	.271	.288	59	16	1	0	0	0.0	4	6	1	8	1	0	0	134	24	19	0	8.9	.893	C-20
1889		40	.259	.353	139	36	10	0	1	0.7	16	29	9	9	6	0	0	146	39	32	3	5.4	.853	C-37, OF-3
1890	NY P	60	.278	.400	230	64	8	4	4	1.7	47	43	13	13	5	0	0	241	49	26	5	5.2	.918	C-34, OF-13, 1B-9, 3B-3, 2B-2
1891	PHI N	115	.243	.306	441	107	20	4	0	0.0	62	50	34	35	7	0	0	1059	68	18	62	9.7	.984	1B-97, C-19, OF-2
1893	2 teams	BAL N (7G –.125)			LOU N (111G –.304)																			
"	total	118	.292	.379	493	144	26	7	1	0.2	85	90	51	35	9	0	0	1145	54	14	79	10.2	.988	1B-118, C-1
1894	2 teams	LOU N (13G –.208)			STL N (3G –.111)																			
"	total	16	.193	.228	57	11	2	0	0	0.0	5	9	5	9	1	0	0	141	19	3	8	10.2	.982	1B-16
7 yrs.		418	.261	.338	1589	415	70	17	6	0.4	236	252	123	124	39	0	0	3097	324	143	162	8.4	.960	1B-240, C-157, OF-20, 3B-6, 2B-2

Willard Brown

BROWN, WILLARD JESSIE BR TR 5'11½" 200 lbs.
B. June 26, 1913, Shreveport, La.

Year	Team	Games	BA	SA	AB	H	2B	3B	HR	HR%	R	RBI	BB	SO	SB	Pinch Hit AB	Pinch Hit H	PO	A	E	DP	TC/G	FA	G by Pos
1947	STL A	21	.179	.269	67	12	3	0	1	1.5	4	6	0	7	2	3	1	41	0	0	0	2.3	1.000	OF-18

Byron Browne

BROWNE, BYRON ELLIS BR TR 6' 2" 190 lbs.
B. Dec. 27, 1942, St. Joseph, Mo.

Year	Team	Games	BA	SA	AB	H	2B	3B	HR	HR%	R	RBI	BB	SO	SB	Pinch Hit AB	Pinch Hit H	PO	A	E	DP	TC/G	FA	G by Pos
1965	CHI N	4	.000	.000	6	0	0	0	0	0.0	0	0	0	2	0	1	0	2	0	1	0	0.8	.667	OF-4
1966		120	.243	.427	419	102	15	7	16	3.8	46	51	40	**143**	3	5	0	200	3	7	0	1.8	.967	OF-114
1967		10	.158	.263	19	3	2	0	0	0.0	3	2	4	5	1	2	0	12	0	0	0	1.5	1.000	OF-8
1968	HOU N	10	.231	.231	13	3	0	0	0	0.0	0	1	4	6	0	6	1	7	1	0	1	4.0	1.000	OF-2
1969	STL N	22	.226	.321	53	12	0	1	1	1.9	9	7	11	14	0	7	0	35	3	0	1	2.4	1.000	OF-16
1970	PHI N	104	.248	.437	270	67	17	2	10	3.7	29	36	33	72	1	18	4	150	4	4	1	1.8	.975	OF-88
1971		58	.206	.382	68	14	3	0	3	4.4	5	5	8	23	0	27	7	21	0	0	0	0.7	1.000	OF-30
1972		21	.190	.190	21	4	0	0	0	0.0	2	0	1	8	0	14	3	2	0	0	0	0.2	1.000	OF-9
8 yrs.		349	.236	.405	869	205	37	10	30	3.5	94	102	101	273	5	80	15	429	11	12	3	1.7	.973	OF-271

Earl Browne

BROWNE, EARL JAMES (Snitz) BL TL 6' 175 lbs.
B. Mar. 5, 1911, Louisville, Ky. D. Jan. 12, 1993, Whittier, Calif.

Year	Team	Games	BA	SA	AB	H	2B	3B	HR	HR%	R	RBI	BB	SO	SB	Pinch Hit AB	Pinch Hit H	PO	A	E	DP	TC/G	FA	G by Pos
1935	PIT N	9	.250	.313	32	8	2	0	0	0.0	6	6	2	8	0	0	0	76	5	0	4	9.0	1.000	1B-9
1936		8	.304	.522	23	7	1	2	0	0.0	7	3	1	4	0	3	1	16	2	1	1	3.8	.947	OF-4, 1B-1
1937	PHI N	105	.292	.422	332	97	19	3	6	1.8	42	52	21	41	4	26	7	305	29	5	31	4.4	.985	OF-54, 1B-23
1938		21	.257	.311	74	19	4	0	0	0.0	4	8	5	11	0	3	1	131	10	3	11	8.0	.979	1B-16, OF-2
4 yrs.		143	.284	.401	461	131	26	5	6	1.3	59	69	29	64	4	32	9	528	46	9	47	5.3	.985	OF-60, 1B-49

George Browne

BROWNE, GEORGE EDWARD BL TR 5'10½" 160 lbs.
B. Jan. 12, 1876, Richmond, Va. D. Dec. 9, 1920, Hyde Park, N. Y.

Year	Team	Games	BA	SA	AB	H	2B	3B	HR	HR%	R	RBI	BB	SO	SB	Pinch Hit AB	Pinch Hit H	PO	A	E	DP	TC/G	FA	G by Pos
1901	PHI N	8	.192	.231	26	5	1	0	0	0.0	2	4	1		2	0	0	13	0	0	0	1.6	1.000	OF-8
1902	2 teams	PHI N (70G –.260)			NY N (53G –.319)																			
"	total	123	.286	.342	497	142	16	6	0	0.0	71	40	25		24	0	0	262	21	30	3	2.5	.904	OF-123
1903	NY N	141	.313	.372	591	185	20	3	3	0.5	105	45	43		27	0	0	212	13	20	4	1.7	.918	OF-141
1904		150	.284	.347	596	169	16	5	4	0.7	**99**	39	39		24	1	0	201	20	18	7	1.6	.925	OF-149
1905		127	.293	.397	536	157	16	14	4	0.7	95	43	20		26	0	0	175	9	17	1	1.6	.915	OF-127
1906		122	.264	.302	477	126	10	4	0	0.0	61	38	27		32	1	0	153	17	12	3	1.5	.934	OF-121
1907		127	.260	.360	458	119	11	10	5	1.1	54	37	31		15	4	0	146	14	10	5	1.4	.941	OF-121
1908	BOS N	138	.228	.274	536	122	10	6	1	0.2	61	34	36		17	3	1	248	20	14	8	2.0	.950	OF-138
1909	2 teams	CHI N (12G –.205)			WAS A (103G –.272)																			
"	total	115	.266	.336	432	115	15	6	1	0.2	47	17	22		16	2	0	163	13	12	3	1.7	.936	OF-113
1910	2 teams	WAS A (7G –.182)			CHI A (30G –.241)																			
"	total	37	.231	.276	134	31	4	1	0	0.0	18	4	13		5	3	0	42	2	4	1	1.4	.917	OF-34
1911	BKN N	8	.333	.333	12	4	0	0	0	0.0	1	2	1	1	2	4	0	4	0	0	0	2.0	1.000	OF-2
1912	PHI N	6	.200	.200	5	1	0	0	0	0.0	0	0	1	0	0	4	1	0	0	0	0	0.0	.000	3B-1
12 yrs.		1102	.273	.339	4300	1176	119	55	18	0.4	614	303	259	1	190	22	2	1619	129	137	35	1.7	.927	OF-1077, 3B-1
WORLD SERIES																								
1905	NY N	5	.182	.182	22	4	0	0	0	0.0	2	1	0	2	2	0	0	3	0	0	0	0.6	1.000	OF-5

Jerry Browne

BROWNE, JEROME AUSTIN BB TR 5'10" 140 lbs.
B. Feb. 13, 1966, Christiansted, Virgin Islands.

Year	Team	Games	BA	SA	AB	H	2B	3B	HR	HR%	R	RBI	BB	SO	SB	Pinch Hit AB	Pinch Hit H	PO	A	E	DP	TC/G	FA	G by Pos
1986	TEX A	11	.417	.500	24	10	2	0	0	0.0	6	3	1	4	0	1	0	9	15	2	4	3.3	.923	2B-8
1987		132	.271	.339	454	123	16	6	1	0.2	63	38	61	50	27	5	0	258	338	12	66	4.6	.980	2B-130, DH-1
1988		73	.229	.304	214	49	9	2	1	0.5	26	17	25	32	7	3	0	112	139	11	27	3.7	.958	2B-70, DH-1
1989	CLE A	153	.299	.390	598	179	31	4	5	0.8	83	45	68	64	14	2	0	305	380	15	67	4.6	.979	2B-151, DH-2
1990		140	.267	.372	513	137	26	5	6	1.2	92	50	72	46	12	3	1	286	382	10	69	4.9	.985	2B-139

Jerry Browne *continued*

Year	Team	Games	BA	SA	AB	H	2B	3B	HR	HR%	R	RBI	BB	SO	SB	Pinch Hit AB	Pinch Hit H	PO	A	E	DP	TC/G	FA	G by Pos
1991		107	.228	.269	290	66	5	2	1	0.3	28	29	27	29	2	34	11	113	141	14	21	3.1	.948	2B-47, OF-17, 3B-15, DH-7
1992	OAK A	111	.287	.364	324	93	12	2	3	0.9	43	40	40	40	3	15	7	149	88	5	11	2.0	.979	3B-58, OF-43, 2B-19, SS-1, DH-1
1993		76	.250	.323	260	65	13	0	2	0.8	27	19	22	17	4	10	1	149	28	6	6	2.5	.967	OF-56, 3B-13, 2B-3, 1B-2
1994	FLA N	101	.295	.398	329	97	17	4	3	0.9	42	30	52	23	3	8	2	117	125	15	12	2.4	.942	3B-62, OF-30, 2B-15
1995		77	.255	.293	184	47	4	0	1	0.5	21	17	25	20	1	23	6	107	78	3	14	3.0	.984	OF-29, 2B-27, 3B-7
10 yrs.		981	.271	.351	3190	866	135	25	23	0.7	431	288	393	325	73	104	28	1605	1714	93	297	3.6	.973	2B-609, OF-175, 3B-155, DH-12, 1B-2, SS-1
LEAGUE CHAMPIONSHIP SERIES																								
1992	OAK A	4	.400	.400	10	4	0	0	0	0.0	3	2	2	0	0	0	0	6	0	0	0	2.0	1.000	3B-2, OF-1

Pidge Browne

BROWNE, PRENTICE ALMONT
B. Mar. 21, 1929, Peekskill, N. Y.
BL TL 6' 1" 190 lbs.

Year	Team	Games	BA	SA	AB	H	2B	3B	HR	HR%	R	RBI	BB	SO	SB	Pinch Hit AB	Pinch Hit H	PO	A	E	DP	TC/G	FA	G by Pos
1962	HOU N	65	.210	.320	100	21	4	2	1	1.0	8	10	13	9	0	36	8	155	15	3	11	6.7	.983	1B-26

Pete Browning

BROWNING, LOUIS ROGERS (The Louisville Slugger, The Gladiator)
B. June 17, 1861, Louisville, Ky. D. Sept. 10, 1905, Louisville, Ky.
BR TR 6' 180 lbs.

Year	Team	Games	BA	SA	AB	H	2B	3B	HR	HR%	R	RBI	BB	SO	SB	Pinch Hit AB	Pinch Hit H	PO	A	E	DP	TC/G	FA	G by Pos
1882	LOU AA	69	**.378**	**.510**	288	109	17	3	5	1.7	67		26			0	0	200	221	63	31	6.6	.870	2B-42, SS-18, 3B-13
1883		84	.338	.458	358	121	15	11	2	0.6	95		23			0	0	137	94	48	9	3.2	.828	OF-48, SS-26, 3B-10, 2B-3, 1B-1
1884		103	.336	.472	447	150	33	8	4	0.9	101		13			0	0	393	86	52	23	5.1	.902	3B-52, OF-24, 1B-23, 2B-4, P-1
1885		112	**.362**	.530	481	**174**	34	10	9	1.9	98		25			0	0	214	20	26	4	2.3	.900	OF-112
1886		112	**.340**	.441	467	159	29	6	2	0.4	86		30			0	0	153	14	44	1	1.9	.791	OF-112
1887		134	.402	.547	547	220	35	16	4	0.7	137		55		103	0	0	281	21	46	7	2.6	.868	OF-134
1888		99	.313	.436	383	120	22	8	3	0.8	58	72	37		36	0	0	174	16	24	8	2.2	.888	OF-99
1889		83	.256	.364	324	83	19	5	2	0.6	39	32	34	30	21	0	0	152	12	22	4	2.2	.882	OF-83
1890	CLE P	118	**.373**	.517	493	184	**40**	8	5	1.0	112	93	75	36	35	0	0	248	18	32	4	2.5	.893	OF-118
1891	2 teams	PIT N (50G –.291)	CIN N (55G –.343)																					
"	total	105	.317	.422	419	133	24	4	4	1.0	64	61	51	54	16	0	0	218	14	22	2	2.4	.913	OF-105
1892	2 teams	LOU N (21G –.247)	CIN N (83G –.303)																					
"	total	104	.292	.383	384	112	16	5	3	0.8	57	56	52	32	13	0	0	203	14	19	2	2.2	.919	OF-103, 1B-2
1893	LOU N	57	.355	.445	220	78	11	3	1	0.5	38	37	44	15	8	0	0	114	5	16	1	2.4	.881	OF-57
1894	2 teams	STL N (2G –.143)	BKN N (1G –1.000)																					
"	total	3	.333	.333	9	3	0	0	0	0.0	2	2	1	0	0	0	0	3	0	0	0	1.0	1.000	OF-3
13 yrs.		1183	.341	.466	4820	1646	295	87	44	0.9	954	353	466	167	232	0	0	2490	535	414	96	2.9	.880	OF-998, 3B-75, 2B-49, SS-44, 1B-26, P-1

Bill Brubaker

BRUBAKER, WILBUR LEE
B. Nov. 7, 1910, Cleveland, Ohio D. Dec. 2, 1978, Laguna Beach, Calif.
BR TR 6' 2" 185 lbs.

Year	Team	Games	BA	SA	AB	H	2B	3B	HR	HR%	R	RBI	BB	SO	SB	Pinch Hit AB	Pinch Hit H	PO	A	E	DP	TC/G	FA	G by Pos
1932	PIT N	7	.417	.542	24	10	3	0	0	0.0	3	4	3	4	1	0	0	7	13	2	2	3.1	.909	3B-7
1933		2	.000	.000	2	0	0	0	0	0.0	0	0	0	0	0	1	0	0	1	0	0	1.0	1.000	3B-1
1934		3	.333	.500	6	2	1	0	0	0.0	0	1	1	0	0	0	0	1	5	0	1	2.0	1.000	3B-3
1935		6	.000	.000	11	0	0	0	0	0.0	1	0	2	5	0	1	0	3	5	1	0	1.8	.889	3B-5
1936		145	.289	.384	554	160	27	4	6	1.1	77	102	50	**96**	5	0	0	134	209	22	8	2.5	.940	3B-145
1937		120	.254	.366	413	105	20	4	6	1.5	57	48	47	51	2	0	0	108	225	17	17	2.9	.951	3B-115, SS-3, 1B-1
1938		45	.295	.420	112	33	5	0	3	2.7	18	19	9	14	2	9	3	111	36	9	10	5.0	.942	3B-18, 1B-9, SS-3, OF-1
1939		100	.232	.365	345	80	23	1	7	2.0	41	43	29	51	3	5	1	183	290	27	47	5.1	.946	2B-65, 3B-32, SS-1
1940		38	.192	.256	78	15	3	1	0	0.0	8	7	8	16	0	4	1	52	46	3	5	3.3	.970	3B-19, SS-8, 1B-4
1943	BOS N	13	.421	.579	19	8	3	0	0	0.0	3	1	2	2	0	3	2	9	6	2	2	2.1	.882	3B-5, 1B-3
10 yrs.		479	.264	.373	1564	413	85	10	22	1.4	208	225	151	239	13	23	7	608	836	83	92	3.4	.946	3B-350, 2B-65, 1B-17, SS-15, OF-1

Lou Bruce

BRUCE, LOUIS R.
B. Jan. 16, 1877, St. Regis, N. Y. D. Feb. 9, 1968, Ilion, N. Y.
BL TR 5' 5" 145 lbs.

Year	Team	Games	BA	SA	AB	H	2B	3B	HR	HR%	R	RBI	BB	SO	SB	Pinch Hit AB	Pinch Hit H	PO	A	E	DP	TC/G	FA	G by Pos
1904	PHI A	30	.267	.297	101	27	3	0	0	0.0	9	8	5		2	3	1	30	11	3	2	1.5	.932	OF-25, P-2, 2B-1, 3B-1

Earle Brucker

BRUCKER, EARLE FRANCIS, SR.
Father of Earle Brucker.
B. May 6, 1901, Albany, N. Y. D. May 8, 1981, San Diego, Calif.
Manager 1952.
BR TR 5'11" 175 lbs.

Year	Team	Games	BA	SA	AB	H	2B	3B	HR	HR%	R	RBI	BB	SO	SB	Pinch Hit AB	Pinch Hit H	PO	A	E	DP	TC/G	FA	G by Pos
1937	PHI A	102	.259	.397	317	82	16	5	6	1.9	40	37	48	30	1	9	0	323	48	11	13	4.2	.971	C-92
1938		53	.374	.561	171	64	21	1	3	1.8	26	35	19	16	1	7	2	188	20	3	1	4.7	.986	C-44, 1B-1
1939		62	.291	.442	172	50	15	1	3	1.7	18	31	24	16	0	13	4	150	18	0	5	3.6	1.000	C-47
1940		23	.196	.261	46	9	1	1	0	0.0	3	2	6	3	0	9	2	47	9	2	1	4.5	.966	C-13
1943		1	.000	.000	1	0	0	0	0	0.0	0	0	0	0	0	1	0	0	0	0	0	0.0	—	
5 yrs.		241	.290	.438	707	205	53	8	12	1.7	87	105	97	65	2	39	8	708	95	16	20	4.2	.980	C-196, 1B-1

Earle Brucker

BRUCKER, EARLE FRANCIS, JR.
Son of Earle Brucker.
B. Aug. 29, 1925, Los Angeles, Calif.
BL TR 6' 2" 210 lbs.

Year	Team	Games	BA	SA	AB	H	2B	3B	HR	HR%	R	RBI	BB	SO	SB	Pinch Hit AB	Pinch Hit H	PO	A	E	DP	TC/G	FA	G by Pos
1948	PHI A	2	.167	.333	6	1	1	0	0	0.0	0	0	1	1	0	0	0	6	1	0	0	3.5	1.000	C-2

J. T. Bruett

BRUETT, JOSEPH TIMOTHY
B. Oct. 8, 1967, Milwaukee, Wis.
BL TL 5'11" 175 lbs.

Year	Team	Games	BA	SA	AB	H	2B	3B	HR	HR%	R	RBI	BB	SO	SB	Pinch Hit AB	Pinch Hit H	PO	A	E	DP	TC/G	FA	G by Pos
1992	MIN A	56	.250	.303	76	19	4	0	0	0.0	7	2	6	12	6	8	3	46	1	1	0	1.0	.979	OF-45, DH-2
1993		17	.250	.350	20	5	2	0	0	0.0	2	1	1	4	0	4	1	12	0	2	0	1.1	.857	OF-13
2 yrs.		73	.250	.313	96	24	6	0	0	0.0	9	3	7	16	6	12	4	58	1	3	0	1.0	.952	OF-58, DH-2

Frank Bruggy

BRUGGY, FRANK LEO
B. May 4, 1891, Elizabeth, N. J. D. Apr. 5, 1959, Elizabeth, N. J.
BR TR 5'11" 195 lbs.

Year	Team	Games	BA	SA	AB	H	2B	3B	HR	HR%	R	RBI	BB	SO	SB	Pinch Hit AB	Pinch Hit H	PO	A	E	DP	TC/G	FA	G by Pos
1921	PHI N	86	.310	.419	277	86	11	2	5	1.8	28	28	23	37	6	12	4	236	73	15	16	3.7	.954	C-86, 1B-2
1922	PHI A	53	.279	.342	111	31	7	0	0	0.0	10	9	6	11	1	21	4	73	25	8	2	3.4	.925	C-31
1923		54	.210	.267	105	22	3	0	1	1.0	4	6	4	9	1	13	1	88	24	5	2	3.0	.957	C-34, 1B-5

Frank Bruggy *continued*

Year	Team	Games	BA	SA	AB	H	2B	3B	HR	HR%	R	RBI	BB	SO	SB	Pinch Hit AB	Pinch Hit H	PO	A	E	DP	TC/G	FA	G by Pos
1924		50	.265	.319	113	30	6	0	0	0.0	9	8	8	15	4	7	0	91	25	9	0	2.8	.928	C-44
1925	CIN N	6	.214	.214	14	3	0	0	0	0.0	2	1	2	0	0	0	0	17	3	3	0	3.8	.870	C-6
5 yrs.		249	.277	.356	620	172	27	2	6	1.0	53	52	43	72	12	53	9	505	150	40	20	3.3	.942	C-201, 1B-7

Jacob Brumfield

BRUMFIELD, JACOB DONNELL
B. May 27, 1965, Bogalusa, La.
BR TR 6′ 170 lbs.

Year	Team	Games	BA	SA	AB	H	2B	3B	HR	HR%	R	RBI	BB	SO	SB	Pinch Hit AB	Pinch Hit H	PO	A	E	DP	TC/G	FA	G by Pos
1992	CIN N	24	.133	.133	30	4	0	0	0	0.0	6	2	2	4	6	5	1	20	1	0	0	1.3	1.000	OF-16
1993		103	.268	.419	272	73	17	3	6	2.2	40	23	21	47	20	5	0	178	16	7	4	2.0	.965	OF-96, 2B-4
1994		68	.311	.525	122	38	10	2	4	3.3	36	11	15	18	6	19	2	74	1	1	0	1.8	.987	OF-43
1995	PIT N	116	.271	.368	402	109	23	2	4	1.0	64	26	37	71	22	18	7	241	8	8	1	2.5	.969	OF-104
4 yrs.		311	.271	.400	826	224	50	7	14	1.7	146	62	75	140	54	47	10	513	26	16	5	2.1	.971	OF-259, 2B-4

Mike Brumley

BRUMLEY, ANTHONY MICHAEL
Son of Mike Brumley.
B. Apr. 9, 1963, Oklahoma City, Okla.
BB TR 5′10″ 165 lbs.

Year	Team	Games	BA	SA	AB	H	2B	3B	HR	HR%	R	RBI	BB	SO	SB	Pinch Hit AB	Pinch Hit H	PO	A	E	DP	TC/G	FA	G by Pos
1987	CHI N	39	.202	.288	104	21	2	2	1	1.0	8	9	10	30	7	3	0	43	93	5	24	4.0	.965	SS-34, 2B-1
1989	DET A	92	.198	.255	212	42	5	2	1	0.5	33	11	14	45	8	3	0	80	160	12	24	2.8	.952	SS-42, 2B-24, 3B-11, DH-8, OF-4
1990	SEA A	62	.224	.313	147	33	5	4	0	0.0	19	7	10	22	2	7	2	63	123	5	26	3.2	.974	SS-47, 2B-6, 3B-3, OF-2, DH-1
1991	BOS A	63	.212	.254	118	25	5	0	0	0.0	16	5	10	22	2	4	0	46	116	7	20	2.8	.959	SS-31, 3B-17, 2B-7, OF-4, DH-2
1992		2	.000	.000	1	0	0	0	0	0.0	0	0	0	0	0	1	0	0	0	0	0	0.0	—	
1993	HOU N	8	.300	.300	10	3	0	0	0	0.0	1	2	1	3	0	7	2	1	1	0	0	0.7	1.000	OF-1, SS-1, 3B-1
1994	OAK A	11	.240	.240	25	6	0	0	0	0.0	0	2	1	8	0	2	0	10	9	2	2	1.8	.905	2B-4, 3B-4, OF-3, SS-1
1995	HOU N	18	.056	.222	18	1	0	0	1	5.6	1	2	0	6	1	8	1	3	2	1	0	0.8	.833	OF-3, SS-3, 3B-1, 1B-1
8 yrs.		295	.206	.272	635	131	17	8	3	0.5	78	38	46	136	20	35	5	246	504	32	96	2.9	.959	SS-159, 2B-42, 3B-37, OF-17, DH-11, 1B-1

Mike Brumley

BRUMLEY, TONY MIKE
Father of Mike Brumley.
B. July 10, 1938, Granite, Okla.
BL TR 5′10″ 195 lbs.

Year	Team	Games	BA	SA	AB	H	2B	3B	HR	HR%	R	RBI	BB	SO	SB	Pinch Hit AB	Pinch Hit H	PO	A	E	DP	TC/G	FA	G by Pos
1964	WAS A	136	.244	.312	426	104	19	2	2	0.5	36	35	40	54	1	14	3	628	44	6	4	5.1	.991	C-132
1965		79	.208	.269	216	45	4	0	3	1.4	15	15	20	33	1	15	3	376	25	4	2	6.1	.990	C-66
1966		9	.111	.167	18	2	1	0	0	0.0	1	0	0	2	0	2	0	19	4	0	0	3.3	1.000	C-7
3 yrs.		224	.229	.294	660	151	24	2	5	0.8	52	50	60	89	2	31	6	1023	73	10	6	5.4	.991	C-205

Glenn Brummer

BRUMMER, GLENN EDWARD
B. Nov. 23, 1954, Olney, Ill.
BR TR 6′ 200 lbs.

Year	Team	Games	BA	SA	AB	H	2B	3B	HR	HR%	R	RBI	BB	SO	SB	Pinch Hit AB	Pinch Hit H	PO	A	E	DP	TC/G	FA	G by Pos
1981	STL N	21	.200	.233	30	6	1	0	0	0.0	2	2	1	2	0	2	0	43	3	0	1	2.4	1.000	C-19
1982		35	.234	.297	64	15	4	0	0	0.0	4	8	0	12	2	1	1	88	8	3	1	3.1	.970	C-32
1983		45	.276	.356	87	24	7	0	0	0.0	7	9	10	11	1	5	0	122	11	3	2	3.3	.978	C-41
1984		28	.207	.259	58	12	0	0	1	1.7	3	3	3	7	0	2	0	101	9	3	0	4.3	.973	C-26
1985	TEX A	49	.278	.315	108	30	4	0	0	0.0	7	5	11	22	1	1	0	183	5	2	2	3.9	.989	C-47, OF-1, DH-1
5 yrs.		178	.251	.305	347	87	16	0	1	0.3	23	27	25	54	4	11	1	537	36	11	6	3.5	.981	C-165, OF-1, DH-1
WORLD SERIES																								
1982	STL N	1	—	—	0	0	0	0	0	—	0	0	0	0	0	0	0	0	0	0	0	0.0	.000	C-1

Tom Brunansky

BRUNANSKY, THOMAS ANDREW (Bruno)
B. Aug. 20, 1960, Covina, Calif.
BR TR 6′ 4″ 205 lbs.

Year	Team	Games	BA	SA	AB	H	2B	3B	HR	HR%	R	RBI	BB	SO	SB	Pinch Hit AB	Pinch Hit H	PO	A	E	DP	TC/G	FA	G by Pos
1981	CAL A	11	.152	.424	33	5	0	0	3	9.1	7	6	8	10	1	0	0	27	3	2	1	2.9	.938	OF-11
1982	MIN A	127	.272	.471	463	126	30	1	20	4.3	77	46	71	101	1	0	0	343	8	5	0	2.8	.986	OF-127
1983		151	.227	.445	542	123	24	5	28	5.2	70	82	61	95	2	2	0	375	16	6	8	2.6	.985	OF-146, DH-4
1984		155	.252	.459	567	143	21	0	32	5.6	75	85	57	94	4	2	0	304	13	5	6	2.1	.984	OF-153, DH-1
1985		157	.242	.448	567	137	28	4	27	4.8	71	90	71	86	5	3	1	300	14	5	2	2.1	.984	OF-155
1986		157	.256	.423	593	152	28	1	23	3.9	69	75	53	98	12	5	1	315	10	6	1	2.1	.982	OF-152, DH-2
1987		155	.259	.489	532	138	22	2	32	6.0	83	85	74	104	11	1	1	273	10	3	1	1.8	.990	OF-138, DH-17
1988	2 teams	MIN A (14G –.184)	STL N (143G –.245)																					
″	total	157	.240	.414	572	137	23	4	23	4.0	74	85	86	93	17	0	0	286	10	4	0	1.9	.987	OF-156, DH-1
1989	STL N	158	.239	.410	556	133	29	3	20	3.6	67	85	59	107	5	6	0	291	9	7	2	2.0	.977	OF-155, 1B-1
1990	2 teams	STL N (19G –.158)	BOS A (129G –.267)																					
″	total	148	.255	.419	518	132	27	5	16	3.1	66	73	66	115	5	6	2	304	8	7	2	2.2	.978	OF-138, DH-7
1991	BOS A	142	.229	.390	459	105	24	1	16	3.5	54	70	49	72	1	5	2	265	5	3	2	2.0	.989	OF-137, DH-1
1992		138	.266	.445	458	122	31	3	15	3.3	47	74	66	96	2	7	2	373	16	6	22	2.9	.985	OF-92, 1B-28, DH-17
1993	MIL A	80	.183	.321	224	41	7	3	6	2.7	20	29	25	59	3	8	0	146	4	2	0	2.0	.987	OF-71, DH-6
1994	2 teams	MIL A (16G –.214)	BOS A (48G –.237)																					
″	total	64	.234	.449	205	48	12	1	10	4.9	24	34	24	57	0	7	1	142	2	1	8	2.4	.993	OF-49, 1B-7, DH-5
14 yrs.		1800	.245	.434	6289	1542	306	33	271	4.3	804	919	770	1187	69	52	10	3744	128	62	55	2.2	.984	OF-1680, DH-61, 1B-36
LEAGUE CHAMPIONSHIP SERIES																								
1987	MIN A	5	.412	1.000	17	7	4	0	2	11.8	5	9	4	3	0	0	0	10	0	0	0	2.0	1.000	OF-5
1990	BOS A	4	.083	.083	12	1	0	0	0	0.0	0	1	1	3	0	0	0	13	0	0	0	3.3	1.000	OF-4
2 yrs.		9	.276	.621	29	8	4	0	2	6.9	5	10	5	6	0	0	0	23	0	0	0	2.6	1.000	OF-9
WORLD SERIES																								
1987	MIN A	7	.200	.200	25	5	0	0	0	0.0	5	2	4	4	1	0	0	14	0	0	0	2.0	1.000	OF-7

Arlo Brunsberg

BRUNSBERG, ARLO ADOLPH
B. Aug. 15, 1940, Fertile, Minn.
BL TR 6′ 195 lbs.

Year	Team	Games	BA	SA	AB	H	2B	3B	HR	HR%	R	RBI	BB	SO	SB	Pinch Hit AB	Pinch Hit H	PO	A	E	DP	TC/G	FA	G by Pos
1966	DET A	2	.333	.667	3	1	1	0	0	0.0	1	0	0	0	0	0	0	4	0	0	0	2.0	1.000	C-2

Bob Brush

BRUSH, ROBERT
B. Mar. 8, 1875, Osage, Iowa D. Apr. 2, 1944, San Bernardino, Calif.

Year	Team	Games	BA	SA	AB	H	2B	3B	HR	HR%	R	RBI	BB	SO	SB	Pinch Hit AB	Pinch Hit H	PO	A	E	DP	TC/G	FA	G by Pos
1907	BOS N	2	.000	.000	2	0	0	0	0	0.0	0	0	0		0	1	0	2	0	0	0	2.0	1.000	1B-1

Bill Bruton

BRUTON, WILLIAM HARON BL TR 6′½″ 169 lbs.
B. Dec. 22, 1925, Panola, Ala. D. Dec. 5, 1995, Marshallton, Del.

Year	Team	Games	BA	SA	AB	H	2B	3B	HR	HR%	R	RBI	BB	SO	SB	Pinch Hit AB	Pinch Hit H	PO	A	E	DP	TC/G	FA	G by Pos
1953	MIL N	151	.250	.330	613	153	18	14	1	0.2	82	41	44	100	**26**	1	0	397	15	9	5	2.8	.979	OF-150
1954		142	.284	.365	567	161	20	7	4	0.7	89	30	40	78	**34**	3	2	350	14	7	3	2.6	.981	OF-141
1955		149	.275	.403	**636**	175	30	12	9	1.4	106	47	43	72	**25**	2	0	412	17	14	6	3.0	.968	OF-149
1956		147	.272	.419	525	143	23	**15**	8	1.5	73	56	26	63	8	4	0	391	10	13	1	2.9	.969	OF-145
1957		79	.278	.438	306	85	16	9	5	1.6	41	30	19	35	11	1	0	206	5	4	2	2.7	.981	OF-79
1958		100	.280	.360	325	91	11	3	3	0.9	47	28	27	37	4	5	0	203	6	5	0	2.2	.977	OF-96
1959		133	.289	.397	478	138	22	6	6	1.3	72	41	35	54	13	6	2	309	6	3	2	2.4	.991	OF-133
1960		151	.286	.428	629	180	27	**13**	12	1.9	**112**	54	41	97	22	3	0	351	10	5	3	2.5	.986	OF-149
1961	DET A	160	.257	.384	596	153	15	5	17	2.9	99	63	61	66	22	6	1	410	4	5	2	2.7	.988	OF-155
1962		147	.278	.430	561	156	27	5	16	2.9	90	74	55	67	14	5	1	394	5	7	2	2.8	.983	OF-145
1963		145	.256	.372	524	134	21	8	8	1.5	84	48	59	70	14	11	6	339	6	3	3	2.5	.991	OF-138
1964		106	.277	.399	296	82	11	5	5	1.7	42	33	32	54	14	26	6	143	7	2	3	1.9	.987	OF-81
12 yrs.		1610	.273	.393	6056	1651	241	102	94	1.6	937	545	482	793	207	73	18	3905	105	77	32	2.6	.981	OF-1561
WORLD SERIES																								
1958	MIL N	7	.412	.588	17	7	0	0	1	5.9	2	2	5	5	0	1	0	12	0	1	0	1.9	.923	OF-7

Ed Bruyette

BRUYETTE, EDWARD T. BL TR 5′10″ 170 lbs.
B. Aug. 31, 1874, Manawa, Wis. D. Aug. 5, 1940, Peshastin, Wash.

Year	Team	Games	BA	SA	AB	H	2B	3B	HR	HR%	R	RBI	BB	SO	SB	Pinch Hit AB	Pinch Hit H	PO	A	E	DP	TC/G	FA	G by Pos
1901	MIL A	26	.183	.220	82	15	3	0	0	0.0	7	4	12		1	0	0	35	14	9	1	2.2	.845	OF-21, 2B-3, SS-1, 3B-1

Billy Bryan

BRYAN, WILLIAM RONALD BL TR 6′ 4″ 200 lbs.
B. Dec. 4, 1938, Morgan, Ga.

Year	Team	Games	BA	SA	AB	H	2B	3B	HR	HR%	R	RBI	BB	SO	SB	Pinch Hit AB	Pinch Hit H	PO	A	E	DP	TC/G	FA	G by Pos
1961	KC A	9	.158	.316	19	3	0	0	1	5.3	2	2	2	7	0	5	1	16	1	0	0	4.3	1.000	C-4
1962		25	.149	.284	74	11	2	1	2	2.7	5	7	5	32	0	3	0	117	4	3	0	5.6	.976	C-22
1963		24	.169	.354	65	11	1	1	3	4.6	11	7	9	22	0	0	0	147	4	3	0	6.4	.981	C-24
1964		93	.241	.477	220	53	9	2	13	5.9	19	36	16	69	0	36	11	317	22	3	5	5.3	.991	C-65
1965		108	.252	.446	325	82	11	5	14	4.3	36	51	29	87	0	14	1	527	44	9	6	6.1	.984	C-95
1966	2 teams	KC A (32G –.132) NY A (27G –.217)																						
″	total	59	.172	.297	145	25	6	0	4	2.8	5	12	11	36	0	22	3	214	23	6	8	5.9	.975	C-35, 1B-6
1967	NY A	16	.167	.417	12	2	0	0	1	8.3	1	2	5	3	0	10	1	5	1	0	1	6.0	1.000	C-1
1968	WAS A	40	.204	.315	108	22	3	0	3	2.8	7	8	14	27	0	12	1	155	15	3	1	6.2	.983	C-28
8 yrs.		374	.216	.395	968	209	32	9	41	4.2	86	125	91	283	0	102	18	1498	114	27	21	5.9	.984	C-274, 1B-6

Derek Bryant

BRYANT, DEREK ROSZELL BR TR 5′11″ 185 lbs.
B. Oct. 9, 1951, Lexington, Ky.

Year	Team	Games	BA	SA	AB	H	2B	3B	HR	HR%	R	RBI	BB	SO	SB	Pinch Hit AB	Pinch Hit H	PO	A	E	DP	TC/G	FA	G by Pos
1979	OAK A	39	.179	.217	106	19	2	1	0	0.0	8	13	10	10	0	2	0	55	2	0	0	1.6	1.000	OF-33, DH-2

Don Bryant

BRYANT, DONALD RAY BR TR 6′ 5″ 200 lbs.
B. July 13, 1941, Jasper, Fla.

Year	Team	Games	BA	SA	AB	H	2B	3B	HR	HR%	R	RBI	BB	SO	SB	Pinch Hit AB	Pinch Hit H	PO	A	E	DP	TC/G	FA	G by Pos
1966	CHI N	13	.308	.385	26	8	2	0	0	0.0	2	4	1	4	1	3	0	42	3	1	2	4.6	.978	C-10
1969	HOU N	31	.186	.254	59	11	1	0	1	1.7	2	6	4	13	0	2	1	141	7	1	2	5.3	.993	C-28
1970		15	.208	.208	24	5	0	0	0	0.0	2	3	1	8	0	3	0	42	2	2	0	3.5	.957	C-13
3 yrs.		59	.220	.275	109	24	3	0	1	0.9	6	13	6	25	1	8	1	225	12	4	4	4.7	.983	C-51

George Bryant

BRYANT, GEORGE F.
B. Feb. 10, 1857, Bridgeport, Conn. D. Mar. 14, 1898, Martinsville, Ind.

Year	Team	Games	BA	SA	AB	H	2B	3B	HR	HR%	R	RBI	BB	SO	SB	Pinch Hit AB	Pinch Hit H	PO	A	E	DP	TC/G	FA	G by Pos
1885	DET N	1	.000	.000	4	0	0	0	0	0.0	0	1	0	2		0	0	1	1	0	1	2.0	1.000	2B-1

Ralph Bryant

BRYANT, RALPH WENDELL BL TR 6′ 2″ 200 lbs.
B. May 20, 1961, Fort Gaines, Ga.

Year	Team	Games	BA	SA	AB	H	2B	3B	HR	HR%	R	RBI	BB	SO	SB	Pinch Hit AB	Pinch Hit H	PO	A	E	DP	TC/G	FA	G by Pos
1985	LA N	6	.333	.333	6	2	0	0	0	0.0	0	1	0	2	0	4	1	0	0	0	0	0.0	.000	OF-3
1986		27	.253	.600	75	19	4	2	6	8.0	15	13	5	25	0	3	2	39	2	2	0	1.7	.953	OF-26
1987		46	.246	.391	69	17	2	1	2	2.9	7	10	10	24	2	29	6	22	0	2	0	1.3	.917	OF-19
3 yrs.		79	.253	.493	150	38	6	3	8	5.3	22	24	15	51	2	36	9	61	2	4	0	1.4	.940	OF-48

Steve Brye

BRYE, STEPHEN ROBERT BR TR 6′ 190 lbs.
B. Feb. 4, 1949, Alameda, Calif.

Year	Team	Games	BA	SA	AB	H	2B	3B	HR	HR%	R	RBI	BB	SO	SB	Pinch Hit AB	Pinch Hit H	PO	A	E	DP	TC/G	FA	G by Pos
1970	MIN A	9	.182	.273	11	2	1	0	0	0.0	1	2	2	4	0	1	0	4	0	0	0	0.7	1.000	OF-6
1971		28	.224	.318	107	24	1	0	3	2.8	10	11	7	15	3	0	0	53	4	2	0	2.1	.966	OF-28
1972		100	.241	.300	253	61	9	3	0	0.0	18	12	17	38	3	10	5	170	9	1	1	1.9	.994	OF-93
1973		92	.263	.396	278	73	9	5	6	2.2	39	33	35	43	3	2	0	209	4	3	1	2.5	.986	OF-87, DH-1
1974		135	.283	.365	488	138	32	1	2	0.4	52	41	22	59	1	5	1	301	10	1	2	2.4	.997	OF-129
1975		86	.252	.423	246	62	13	1	9	3.7	41	34	21	37	2	10	5	112	7	2	0	1.6	.983	OF-72, DH-6
1976		87	.264	.329	258	68	11	0	2	0.8	33	23	13	31	1	12	2	147	1	2	0	1.9	.987	OF-78, DH-3
1977	MIL A	94	.249	.419	241	60	14	3	7	2.9	27	28	16	39	1	14	1	166	8	0	1	2.0	1.000	OF-83, DH-6
1978	PIT N	66	.235	.322	115	27	7	0	1	0.9	16	9	11	10	2	21	3	57	2	1	0	1.3	.983	OF-47
9 yrs.		697	.258	.365	1997	515	97	13	30	1.5	237	193	144	276	16	75	17	1219	45	12	5	2.0	.991	OF-623, DH-16

Hal Bubser

BUBSER, HAROLD FRED BR TR 5′11″ 170 lbs.
B. Sept. 28, 1895, Chicago, Ill. D. June 22, 1959, Melrose Park, Ill.

Year	Team	Games	BA	SA	AB	H	2B	3B	HR	HR%	R	RBI	BB	SO	SB	Pinch Hit AB	Pinch Hit H	PO	A	E	DP	TC/G	FA	G by Pos
1922	CHI A	3	.000	.000	3	0	0	0	0	0.0	0	0	0	2	0	3	0	0	0	0	0	0.0	—	

Johnny Bucha

BUCHA, JOHN GEORGE BR TR 5′11″ 190 lbs.
B. Jan. 22, 1925, Allentown, Pa.

Year	Team	Games	BA	SA	AB	H	2B	3B	HR	HR%	R	RBI	BB	SO	SB	Pinch Hit AB	Pinch Hit H	PO	A	E	DP	TC/G	FA	G by Pos
1948	STL N	2	.000	.000	1	0	0	0	0	0.0	0	0	1	0	0	1	0	1	0	0	0	1.0	1.000	C-1
1950		22	.139	.167	36	5	1	0	0	0.0	1	1	4	7	0	5	2	42	5	2	0	2.9	.959	C-17
1953	DET A	60	.222	.297	158	35	9	0	1	0.6	17	14	20	14	1	2	0	218	22	4	4	4.4	.984	C-56
3 yrs.		84	.205	.272	195	40	10	0	1	0.5	18	15	25	21	1	8	2	261	27	6	4	4.0	.980	C-74

Jerry Buchek

BUCHEK, GERALD PETER BR TR 5′11″ 185 lbs.
B. May 9, 1942, St. Louis, Mo.

Year	Team	Games	BA	SA	AB	H	2B	3B	HR	HR%	R	RBI	BB	SO	SB	Pinch Hit AB	Pinch Hit H	PO	A	E	DP	TC/G	FA	G by Pos
1961	STL N	31	.133	.156	90	12	2	0	0	0.0	6	9	0	28	0	0	0	42	62	10	20	3.7	.912	SS-31
1963		3	.250	.250	4	1	0	0	0	0.0	0	0	0	2	0	2	0	1	1	0	1	2.0	1.000	SS-1

Jerry Buchek *continued*

Year	Team	Games	BA	SA	AB	H	2B	3B	HR	HR%	R	RBI	BB	SO	SB	Pinch Hit AB	Pinch Hit H	PO	A	E	DP	TC/G	FA	G by Pos
1964		35	.200	.333	30	6	0	2	0	0.0	7	1	3	11	0	2	0	24	35	5	5	2.1	.922	SS-20, 2B-9, 3B-1
1965		55	.247	.386	166	41	8	3	3	1.8	17	21	13	46	1	5	0	93	154	5	38	4.8	.980	2B-33, SS-18, 3B-1
1966		100	.236	.342	284	67	10	4	4	1.4	23	25	23	71	0	9	1	151	228	19	52	3.9	.952	2B-49, SS-48, 3B-4
1967	NY N	124	.236	.375	411	97	11	2	14	3.4	35	41	26	101	3	9	2	226	300	12	59	4.4	.978	2B-95, 3B-17, SS-9
1968		73	.182	.219	192	35	4	0	1	0.5	8	11	10	53	1	18	3	57	91	7	11	2.7	.955	3B-37, 2B-12, OF-9
7 yrs.		421	.220	.325	1177	259	35	11	22	1.9	96	108	75	312	5	45	6	594	871	58	186	3.9	.962	2B-198, SS-127, 3B-60, OF-9
WORLD SERIES																								
1964	STL N	4	1.000	1.000	1	1	0	0	0	0.0	1	0	0	0	0	0	0	0	1	0	0	0.3	1.000	2B-4

Jim Bucher

BUCHER, JAMES QUINTER BL TR 5′11″ 170 lbs.
B. Mar. 11, 1911, Manassas, Va.

Year	Team	Games	BA	SA	AB	H	2B	3B	HR	HR%	R	RBI	BB	SO	SB	Pinch Hit AB	Pinch Hit H	PO	A	E	DP	TC/G	FA	G by Pos
1934	BKN N	47	.226	.333	84	19	5	2	0	0.0	12	8	4	7	1	18	8	38	48	9	10	3.7	.905	2B-20, 3B-6
1935		123	.302	.397	473	143	22	1	7	1.5	72	58	10	33	4	12	0	194	188	18	29	3.4	.955	2B-41, 3B-39, OF-37
1936		110	.251	.343	370	93	12	8	2	0.5	49	41	29	27	5	10	3	145	138	19	15	3.0	.937	3B-39, 2B-32, OF-30
1937		125	.253	.324	380	96	11	2	4	1.1	44	37	20	18	5	23	3	173	192	23	35	4.0	.941	2B-49, 3B-43, OF-6
1938	STL N	17	.228	.316	57	13	3	1	0	0.0	7	7	2	2	0	2	1	33	31	3	9	4.5	.955	2B-14, 3B-1
1944	BOS A	80	.274	.365	277	76	9	2	4	1.4	39	31	19	13	3	15	5	99	138	11	25	3.8	.956	3B-44, 2B-21
1945		52	.225	.291	151	34	4	3	0	0.0	19	11	7	13	1	17	2	27	69	6	8	3.0	.941	3B-32, 2B-2
7 yrs.		554	.265	.351	1792	474	66	19	17	0.9	242	193	91	113	19	97	22	709	804	89	131	3.5	.944	3B-204, 2B-179, OF-73

Dick Buckley

BUCKLEY, RICHARD D. TR 5′10″ 195 lbs.
B. Sept. 21, 1858, Troy, N. Y. D. Dec. 12, 1929, Pittsburgh, Pa.

Year	Team	Games	BA	SA	AB	H	2B	3B	HR	HR%	R	RBI	BB	SO	SB	Pinch Hit AB	Pinch Hit H	PO	A	E	DP	TC/G	FA	G by Pos
1888	IND N	71	.273	.388	260	71	9	3	5	1.9	28	22	6	24	4	0	0	238	89	43	9	4.9	.884	C-51, 3B-22, OF-1, 1B-1
1889		68	.258	.392	260	67	11	0	8	3.1	35	41	15	32	5	0	0	194	82	38	4	4.6	.879	C-55, 3B-12, OF-1, 1B-1
1890	NY N	70	.256	.320	266	68	11	0	2	0.8	39	26	23	35	3	0	0	368	104	39	4	7.3	.924	C-62, 3B-8
1891		75	.217	.308	253	55	9	1	4	1.6	23	31	11	30	3	0	0	447	85	23	7	7.4	.959	C-74, 3B-1
1892	STL N	121	.227	.324	410	93	17	4	5	1.2	43	52	22	34	7	0	0	535	124	43	15	5.8	.939	C-119, 1B-2
1893		9	.174	.217	23	4	1	0	0	0.0	2	1	0	0	0	0	0	26	6	3	2	3.9	.914	C-9
1894	2 teams	STL N (29G –.180) PHI N (43G –.294)																						
″	total	72	.253	.349	249	63	8	5	2	0.8	23	29	12	16	1	1	0	258	69	15	4	4.8	.956	C-69, 1B-2
1895	PHI N	38	.250	.321	112	28	6	1	0	0.0	20	14	9	17	2	0	0	152	29	16	5	5.2	.919	C-38
8 yrs.		524	.245	.342	1833	449	72	14	26	1.4	213	216	98	188	25	1	0	2218	588	220	50	5.7	.927	C-477, 3B-43, 1B-6, OF-2

Kevin Buckley

BUCKLEY, KEVIN JOHN BR TR 6′ 1″ 195 lbs.
B. Jan. 16, 1959, Quincy, Mass.

Year	Team	Games	BA	SA	AB	H	2B	3B	HR	HR%	R	RBI	BB	SO	SB	Pinch Hit AB	Pinch Hit H	PO	A	E	DP	TC/G	FA	G by Pos
1984	TEX A	5	.286	.429	7	2	1	0	0	0.0	1	0	2	4	0	2	0	0	0	0	0	0.0	.000	DH-3

Bill Buckner

BUCKNER, WILLIAM JOSEPH (Billy Bucks) BL TL 6′ 185 lbs.
B. Dec. 14, 1949, Vallejo, Calif.

Year	Team	Games	BA	SA	AB	H	2B	3B	HR	HR%	R	RBI	BB	SO	SB	Pinch Hit AB	Pinch Hit H	PO	A	E	DP	TC/G	FA	G by Pos
1969	LA N	1	.000	.000	1	0	0	0	0	0.0	0	0	0	0	0	1	0	0	0	0	0	0.0	—	
1970		28	.191	.265	68	13	3	1	0	0.0	6	4	3	7	0	8	2	37	1	0	1	1.8	1.000	OF-20, 1B-1
1971		108	.277	.366	358	99	15	1	5	1.4	37	41	11	18	4	17	3	235	11	1	4	2.5	.996	OF-86, 1B-11
1972		105	.319	.410	383	122	14	3	5	1.3	47	37	17	13	10	11	3	434	22	4	28	4.8	.991	OF-61, 1B-35
1973		140	.275	.351	575	158	20	0	8	1.4	68	46	17	34	12	9	2	981	50	3	93	7.3	.997	1B-93, OF-48
1974		145	.314	.412	580	182	30	3	7	1.2	83	58	30	24	31	9	1	284	5	7	2	2.1	.976	OF-137, 1B-6
1975		92	.243	.358	288	70	11	2	6	2.1	30	31	17	15	8	19	3	138	4	2	0	2.0	.986	OF-72
1976		154	.301	.389	642	193	28	4	7	1.1	76	60	26	26	28	1	1	315	7	5	0	2.1	.985	OF-153, 1B-1
1977	CHI N	122	.284	.425	426	121	27	0	11	2.6	40	60	21	23	7	22	7	966	58	10	75	10.4	.990	1B-99
1978		117	.323	.419	446	144	26	1	5	1.1	47	74	18	17	7	12	2	1075	83	6	85	11.1	.995	1B-105
1979		149	.284	.437	591	168	34	7	14	2.4	72	66	30	28	9	8	3	1258	124	7	118	9.9	.995	1B-140
1980		145	**.324**	.457	578	187	41	3	10	1.7	69	68	30	18	1	6	0	916	78	8	69	7.0	.992	1B-94, OF-50
1981		106	.311	.480	421	131	**35**	3	10	2.4	45	75	26	16	5	2	1	996	81	17	92	10.4	.984	1B-105
1982		161	.306	.441	**657**	201	34	5	15	2.3	93	105	36	26	15	0	0	1547	159	12	89	10.7	.993	1B-161
1983		153	.280	.436	626	175	**38**	6	16	2.6	79	66	25	30	12	2	1	1391	161	13	132	9.8	.992	1B-144, OF-15
1984	2 teams	CHI N (21G –.209) BOS A (114G –.278)																						
″	total	135	.272	.392	482	131	21	2	11	2.3	54	69	25	39	2	12	3	1045	102	15	80	9.5	.987	1B-120, OF-2
1985	BOS A	162	.299	.447	673	201	46	3	16	2.4	89	110	30	36	18	0	0	1384	184	12	140	9.8	.992	1B-162
1986		153	.267	.421	629	168	39	2	18	2.9	73	102	40	25	6	0	0	1067	157	14	104	8.1	.989	1B-138, DH-15
1987	2 teams	BOS A (75G –.273) CAL A (57G –.306)																						
″	total	132	.286	.365	469	134	18	2	5	1.1	39	74	22	26	2	15	8	640	60	6	54	6.0	.992	1B-79, DH-39
1988	2 teams	CAL A (19G –.209) KC A (89G –.256)																						
″	total	108	.249	.330	285	71	14	0	3	1.1	19	43	17	19	5	28	**8**	161	13	1	12	2.3	.994	DH-53, 1B-22
1989	KC A	79	.216	.267	176	38	4	1	1	0.6	7	16	6	11	1	**38**	10	181	13	3	19	4.6	.985	1B-24, DH-19
1990	BOS A	22	.186	.256	43	8	0	0	1	2.3	4	3	3	2	0	11	2	75	6	0	6	5.4	1.000	1B-15
22 yrs.		2517	.289	.408	9397	2715	498	49	174	1.9	1077	1208	450	453	183	231	60	15126	1379	146	1203	7.2	.991	1B-1555, OF-644, DH-126
LEAGUE CHAMPIONSHIP SERIES																								
1974	LA N	4	.167	.222	18	3	1	0	0	0.0	0	0	0	2	0	0	0	6	0	0	0	1.5	1.000	OF-4
1986	BOS A	7	.214	.250	28	6	1	0	0	0.0	3	3	0	2	0	0	0	51	5	0	4	8.0	1.000	1B-7
2 yrs.		11	.196	.239	46	9	2	0	0	0.0	3	3	0	4	0	0	0	57	5	0	4	5.6	1.000	1B-7, OF-4
WORLD SERIES																								
1974	LA N	5	.250	.450	20	5	1	0	1	5.0	1	1	0	1	0	0	0	11	0	0	0	2.2	1.000	OF-5
1986	BOS A	7	.188	.188	32	6	0	0	0	0.0	2	1	1	3	0	0	0	53	7	1	5	8.7	.984	1B-7
2 yrs.		12	.212	.288	52	11	1	0	1	1.9	3	2	1	4	0	0	0	64	7	1	5	6.0	.986	1B-7, OF-5

Mark Budaska

BUDASKA, MARK DAVID BB TL 6′ 180 lbs.
B. Dec. 27, 1952, Sharon, Pa.

Year	Team	Games	BA	SA	AB	H	2B	3B	HR	HR%	R	RBI	BB	SO	SB	Pinch Hit AB	Pinch Hit H	PO	A	E	DP	TC/G	FA	G by Pos
1978	OAK A	4	.250	.500	4	1	1	0	0	0.0	0	0	1	2	0	2	1	1	0	1	0	1.0	.500	OF-2
1981		9	.156	.188	32	5	1	0	0	0.0	3	2	4	10	0	0	0	0	0	0	0	0.0	.000	DH-9
2 yrs.		13	.167	.222	36	6	2	0	0	0.0	3	2	5	12	0	2	1	1	0	1	0	0.2	.500	DH-9, OF-2

Budd

BUDD
B. Cleveland, Ohio Deceased.

Year	Team	Games	BA	SA	AB	H	2B	3B	HR	HR%	R	RBI	BB	SO	SB	Pinch Hit AB	Pinch Hit H	PO	A	E	DP	TC/G	FA	G by Pos
1890	CLE P	1	.000	.000	4	0	0	0	0	0.0	0	0	0	3	0	0	0	2	0	0	0	2.0	1.000	OF-1

Don Buddin

BUDDIN, DONALD THOMAS
B. May 5, 1934, Turbeville, S. C. BR TR 5′11″ 178 lbs.

Year	Team	Games	BA	SA	AB	H	2B	3B	HR	HR%	R	RBI	BB	SO	SB	Pinch Hit AB	Pinch Hit H	PO	A	E	DP	TC/G	FA	G by Pos
1956	BOS A	114	.239	.342	377	90	24	0	5	1.3	49	37	65	62	2	1	0	213	370	29	98	5.4	.953	SS-113
1958		136	.237	.368	497	118	25	2	12	2.4	74	43	82	106	0	0	0	269	445	31	102	5.5	.958	SS-136
1959		151	.241	.357	485	117	24	1	10	2.1	75	53	92	99	6	0	0	235	412	35	89	4.5	.949	SS-150
1960		124	.245	.360	428	105	21	5	6	1.4	62	36	62	59	4	0	0	230	356	30	79	5.0	.951	SS-124
1961		115	.263	.398	339	89	22	3	6	1.8	58	42	72	45	2	4	1	204	294	23	70	4.8	.956	SS-109
1962	2 teams	HOU N (40G –.163)	DET A (31G –.229)																					
″	total	71	.196	.288	163	32	7	1	2	1.2	24	14	37	33	1	12	3	92	128	10	28	3.7	.957	SS-46, 3B-11, 2B-5
6 yrs.		711	.241	.359	2289	551	123	12	41	1.8	342	225	410	404	15	17	4	1243	2005	158	466	4.9	.954	SS-678, 3B-11, 2B-5

Steve Buechele

BUECHELE, STEVEN BERNARD
B. Sept. 26, 1961, Lancaster, Calif. BR TR 6′2″ 190 lbs.

Year	Team	Games	BA	SA	AB	H	2B	3B	HR	HR%	R	RBI	BB	SO	SB	Pinch Hit AB	Pinch Hit H	PO	A	E	DP	TC/G	FA	G by Pos
1985	TEX A	69	.219	.356	219	48	6	3	6	2.7	22	21	14	38	3	0	0	52	138	6	17	2.8	.969	3B-69, 2B-1
1986		153	.243	.410	461	112	19	2	18	3.9	54	54	35	98	5	2	1	174	292	12	42	2.8	.975	3B-137, 2B-33, OF-2
1987		136	.237	.399	363	86	20	0	13	3.6	45	50	28	66	2	2	1	89	211	9	20	2.2	.971	3B-123, 2B-18, OF-2
1988		155	.250	.404	503	126	21	4	16	3.2	68	58	65	79	2	2	0	114	300	16	25	2.8	.963	3B-153, 2B-2
1989		155	.235	.387	486	114	22	2	16	3.3	60	59	36	107	1	1	0	128	288	12	29	2.6	.972	3B-145, 2B-18, SS-1, DH-1
1990		91	.215	.339	251	54	10	0	7	2.8	30	30	27	63	1	2	0	72	160	8	7	2.6	.967	3B-88, 2B-4
1991	2 teams	TEX A (121G –.267)	PIT N (31G –.246)																					
″	total	152	.262	.440	530	139	22	3	22	4.2	74	85	49	97	0	5	2	121	339	7	28	2.9	.985	3B-142, 2B-13, SS-4
1992	2 teams	PIT N (80G –.249)	CHI N (65G –.276)																					
″	total	145	.261	.372	524	137	23	4	9	1.7	52	64	52	105	1	1	1	103	289	17	16	2.8	.958	3B-143, 2B-2
1993	CHI N	133	.272	.437	460	125	27	2	15	3.3	53	65	48	87	1	3	0	97	232	8	27	2.5	.976	3B-129, 1B-6
1994		104	.242	.404	339	82	11	1	14	4.1	33	52	39	80	1	2	0	101	144	5	13	2.4	.980	3B-99, 1B-6, 2B-1
1995	2 teams	CHI N (32G –.189)	TEX A (9G –.125)																					
″	total	41	.177	.215	130	23	2	0	1	0.8	10	9	15	22	0	2	0	33	66	5	4	2.5	.952	3B-41
11 yrs.		1334	.245	.394	4266	1046	183	21	137	3.2	501	547	408	842	17	22	5	1084	2459	105	228	2.6	.971	3B-1269, 2B-92, 1B-12, SS-5, OF-4, DH-1

LEAGUE CHAMPIONSHIP SERIES

Year	Team	Games	BA	SA	AB	H	2B	3B	HR	HR%	R	RBI	BB	SO	SB	Pinch Hit AB	Pinch Hit H	PO	A	E	DP	TC/G	FA	G by Pos
1991	PIT N	7	.304	.391	23	7	2	0	0	0.0	2	0	4	6	0	0	0	8	14	0	1	3.1	1.000	3B-7

Charlie Buelow

BUELOW, CHARLES JOHN
B. Jan. 12, 1877, Dubuque, Iowa D. May 4, 1951, Dubuque, Iowa. BR TR

Year	Team	Games	BA	SA	AB	H	2B	3B	HR	HR%	R	RBI	BB	SO	SB	Pinch Hit AB	Pinch Hit H	PO	A	E	DP	TC/G	FA	G by Pos
1901	NY N	22	.111	.167	72	8	4	0	0	0.0	3	4	2		0	3	0	20	43	11	2	3.9	.851	3B-17, 2B-2

Fritz Buelow

BUELOW, FREDERICK WILLIAM ALEXANDER
B. Feb. 13, 1876, Berlin, Germany D. Dec. 27, 1933, Detroit, Mich. BR TR 5′10½″ 170 lbs.

Year	Team	Games	BA	SA	AB	H	2B	3B	HR	HR%	R	RBI	BB	SO	SB	Pinch Hit AB	Pinch Hit H	PO	A	E	DP	TC/G	FA	G by Pos
1899	STL N	7	.467	.733	15	7	0	2	0	0.0	4	2	2		0	1	0	12	1	1	0	2.3	.929	C-4, OF-2
1900		6	.235	.235	17	4	0	0	0	0.0	2	3	0		0	1	1	13	6	3	0	4.4	.864	C-4, OF-1
1901	DET A	70	.225	.316	231	52	5	5	2	0.9	28	29	11		2	1	0	213	84	10	4	4.4	.967	C-69
1902		66	.223	.290	224	50	5	2	2	0.9	23	29	9		3	0	0	190	81	20	7	4.5	.931	C-63, 1B-2
1903		63	.214	.307	192	41	3	6	1	0.5	24	13	6		4	0	0	278	67	13	7	5.8	.964	C-60, 1B-2
1904	2 teams	DET A (42G –.110)	CLE A (42G –.176)																					
″	total	84	.141	.176	255	36	5	2	0	0.0	17	10	19		4	0	0	378	88	11	5	5.7	.977	C-84
1905	CLE A	74	.174	.212	236	41	4	1	1	0.4	11	18	6		7	2	1	294	76	13	5	5.3	.966	C-59, OF-8, 1B-3, 3B-2
1906		34	.163	.186	86	14	2	0	0	0.0	7	7	9		0	0	0	122	39	10	5	5.0	.942	C-33, 1B-1
1907	STL A	26	.147	.160	75	11	1	0	0	0.0	9	1	7		0	1	0	77	36	2	4	4.6	.983	C-25
9 yrs.		430	.192	.252	1331	256	25	18	6	0.5	125	112	69		20	6	2	1577	478	83	37	5.1	.961	C-401, OF-11, 1B-8, 3B-2

Art Bues

BUES, ARTHUR FREDERICK
B. Mar. 3, 1888, Milwaukee, Wis. D. Nov. 7, 1954, Whitefish Bay, Wis. BR TR 5′11″ 184 lbs.

Year	Team	Games	BA	SA	AB	H	2B	3B	HR	HR%	R	RBI	BB	SO	SB	Pinch Hit AB	Pinch Hit H	PO	A	E	DP	TC/G	FA	G by Pos
1913	BOS N	2	.000	.000	1	0	0	0	0	0.0	0	0	0	1	0	0	0	0	0	0	0	0.0		3B-1, 2B-1
1914	CHI N	14	.222	.289	45	10	1	1	0	0.0	3	4	5	6	1	2	0	14	16	1	0	2.6	.968	3B-12
2 yrs.		16	.217	.283	46	10	1	1	0	0.0	3	4	5	7	1	2	0	14	16	1	0	2.2	.968	3B-13, 2B-1

Charlie Buffinton

BUFFINTON, CHARLES G.
B. June 14, 1861, Fall River, Mass. D. Sept. 23, 1907, Fall River, Mass. BR TR 6′1″ 180 lbs.
Manager 1890.

Year	Team	Games	BA	SA	AB	H	2B	3B	HR	HR%	R	RBI	BB	SO	SB	Pinch Hit AB	Pinch Hit H	PO	A	E	DP	TC/G	FA	G by Pos
1882	BOS N	15	.260	.280	50	13	1	0	0	0.0	5	4	2	3		0	0	34	12	7	0	3.3	.868	OF-7, P-5, 1B-4
1883		86	.238	.287	341	81	8	3	1	0.3	28	26	6	24		0	0	84	69	33	6	1.9	.823	OF-51, P-43, 1B-2
1884		87	.267	.344	352	94	18	3	1	0.3	48		16	12		0	0	146	118	24	6	3.2	.917	P-67, OF-13, 1B-11
1885		82	.240	.302	338	81	12	3	1	0.3	26	33	3	26		0	0	196	121	27	11	4.1	.922	P-51, OF-18, 1B-15
1886		44	.290	.341	176	51	4	1	1	0.6	27	30	6	12		0	0	181	35	11	8	6.1	.952	1B-19, P-18
1887	PHI N	66	.268	.331	269	72	12	1	1	0.4	34	46	11	3	8	0	0	124	93	23	8	3.3	.904	P-40, OF-22, 1B-10
1888		46	.181	.219	160	29	4	1	0	0.0	14	12	7	5	1	0	0	31	122	10	3	3.5	.939	P-46, OF-1
1889		47	.208	.221	154	32	2	0	0	0.0	16	21	9	5	0	0	0	18	80	9	4	2.2	.916	P-47, OF-1
1890	PHI P	42	.273	.340	150	41	3	2	1	0.7	24	24	9	3	1	0	0	50	81	16	6	3.3	.891	P-36, OF-5, 1B-3
1891	BOS AA	58	.188	.227	181	34	2	1	1	0.6	16	16	19	15	0	0	0	43	119	13	5	2.8	.926	P-48, OF-10, 1B-4
1892	BAL N	13	.349	.419	43	15	1	1	0	0.0	7	4	3	6	1	0	0	3	30	4	1	2.8	.892	P-13
11 yrs.		586	.245	.299	2214	543	67	16	7	0.3	245	216	91	114	11	0	0	910	880	177	58	3.2	.910	P-414, OF-128, 1B-68

Damon Buford

BUFORD, DAMON JACKSON
Son of Don Buford.
B. June 12, 1970, Baltimore, Md. BR TR 5′10″ 170 lbs.

Year	Team	Games	BA	SA	AB	H	2B	3B	HR	HR%	R	RBI	BB	SO	SB	Pinch Hit AB	Pinch Hit H	PO	A	E	DP	TC/G	FA	G by Pos
1993	BAL A	53	.228	.367	79	18	5	0	2	2.5	18	9	9	19	2	3	1	61	2	1	2	1.4	.984	OF-30, DH-16
1994		4	.500	.500	2	1	0	0	0	0.0	2	0	0	1	0	0	0	0	0	0	0	0.0		OF-1, DH-1
1995	2 teams	BAL A (24G –.063)	NY N (44G –.235)																					
″	total	68	.202	.304	168	34	5	0	4	2.4	30	14	25	35	10	4	2	107	2	2	0	1.8	.982	OF-63
3 yrs.		125	.213	.325	249	53	10	0	6	2.4	50	23	34	55	12	7	3	168	4	3	2	1.6	.983	OF-94, DH-17

Don Buford

BUFORD, DONALD ALVIN BB TR 5′ 7″ 160 lbs.
Father of Damon Buford.
B. Feb. 2, 1937, Linden, Tex.

Year	Team	Games	BA	SA	AB	H	2B	3B	HR	HR%	R	RBI	BB	SO	SB	Pinch Hit AB	Pinch Hit H	PO	A	E	DP	TC/G	FA	G by Pos
1963	CHI A	12	.286	.405	42	12	1	2	0	0.0	9	5	5	7	1	1	0	13	12	2	1	2.5	.926	3B-9, 2B-2
1964		135	.262	.348	442	116	14	6	4	0.9	62	30	46	62	12	10	1	226	261	16	65	3.9	.968	2B-92, 3B-37
1965		155	.283	.389	586	166	22	5	10	1.7	93	47	67	76	17	8	2	339	416	14	102	4.3	.982	2B-139, 3B-41
1966		163	.244	.349	607	148	26	7	8	1.3	85	52	69	71	51	1	0	199	383	34	42	3.4	.945	3B-133, 2B-37, OF-11
1967		156	.241	.316	535	129	10	9	4	0.7	61	32	65	51	34	3	1	198	349	27	46	3.3	.953	3B-121, 2B-51, OF-1
1968	BAL A	130	.282	.437	426	120	13	4	15	3.5	65	46	57	46	27	20	6	239	111	8	22	2.9	.978	OF-65, 2B-58, 3B-2
1969		144	.291	.417	554	161	31	3	11	2.0	99	64	96	62	19	5	1	255	38	6	5	2.1	.980	OF-128, 2B-10, 3B-6
1970		144	.272	.411	504	137	15	2	17	3.4	99	66	109	55	16	10	2	224	19	4	3	1.8	.984	OF-130, 3B-3, 2B-3
1971		122	.290	.477	449	130	19	4	19	4.2	**99**	54	89	62	15	8	2	217	6	3	0	2.0	.987	OF-115
1972		125	.206	.267	408	84	6	2	5	1.2	46	22	69	83	8	19	2	173	6	2	1	1.7	.989	OF-105
10 yrs.		1286	.264	.379	4553	1203	157	44	93	2.0	718	418	672	575	200	85	17	2083	1601	116	287	2.9	.969	OF-555, 2B-392, 3B-352
LEAGUE CHAMPIONSHIP SERIES																								
1969	BAL A	3	.286	.357	14	4	1	0	0	0.0	3	1	3	0	0	0	0	8	0	0	0	2.7	1.000	OF-3
1970		2	.429	1.000	7	3	1	0	1	14.3	2	3	2	0	0	0	0	2	0	0	0	1.0	1.000	OF-2
1971		2	.429	.714	7	3	0	1	0	0.0	1	0	2	1	0	0	0	1	0	0	0	0.5	1.000	OF-2
3 yrs.		7	.357	.607	28	10	2	1	1	3.6	6	4	7	1	0	0	0	11	0	0	0	1.6	1.000	OF-7
WORLD SERIES																								
1969	BAL A	5	.100	.300	20	2	1	0	1	5.0	1	2	2	4	0	0	0	8	0	0	0	1.6	1.000	OF-5
1970		4	.267	.467	15	4	0	0	1	6.7	3	1	3	2	0	0	0	6	0	0	0	1.5	1.000	OF-4
1971		6	.261	.565	23	6	1	0	2	8.7	3	4	3	3	0	0	0	13	1	0	0	2.3	1.000	OF-6
3 yrs.		15	.207	.448	58	12	2	0	4	6.9	7	7	8	9	0	0	0	27	1	0	0	1.9	1.000	OF-15

Jay Buhner

BUHNER, JAY CAMPBELL BR TR 6′ 3″ 205 lbs.
B. Aug. 13, 1964, Louisville, Ky.

Year	Team	Games	BA	SA	AB	H	2B	3B	HR	HR%	R	RBI	BB	SO	SB	Pinch Hit AB	Pinch Hit H	PO	A	E	DP	TC/G	FA	G by Pos
1987	NY A	7	.227	.318	22	5	2	0	0	0.0	0	1	1	6	0	0	0	11	1	0	1	1.7	1.000	OF-7
1988	2 teams	NY A (25G –.188) SEA A (60G –.224)																						
"	total	85	.215	.421	261	56	13	1	13	5.0	36	38	28	93	1	4	1	186	9	3	3	2.4	.985	OF-81
1989	SEA A	58	.275	.490	204	56	15	1	9	4.4	27	33	19	55	1	0	0	106	6	4	3	2.0	.966	OF-57
1990		51	.276	.479	163	45	12	0	7	4.3	16	33	17	50	2	3	0	55	1	2	0	1.2	.966	OF-40, DH-10
1991		137	.244	.498	406	99	14	4	27	6.7	64	77	53	117	0	10	1	244	15	5	4	2.0	.981	OF-131
1992		152	.243	.422	543	132	16	3	25	4.6	69	79	71	146	0	3	1	314	14	2	4	2.2	.994	OF-150
1993		158	.272	.476	563	153	28	3	27	4.8	91	98	100	144	2	2	1	263	8	6	2	1.8	.978	OF-148, DH-10
1994		101	.279	.542	358	100	23	4	21	5.9	74	68	66	63	0	3	1	179	11	2	2	1.9	.990	OF-96, DH-4
1995		126	.262	.566	470	123	23	0	40	8.5	86	121	60	120	0	0	0	177	5	2	0	1.5	.989	OF-120, DH-4
9 yrs.		875	.257	.486	2990	769	146	16	169	5.7	463	548	415	794	6	25	5	1535	70	26	19	1.9	.984	OF-830, DH-28
DIVISIONAL PLAYOFF SERIES																								
1995	SEA A	5	.458	.625	24	11	1	0	1	4.2	2	3	2	4	0	0	0	11	1	0	0	2.4	1.000	OF-5
LEAGUE CHAMPIONSHIP SERIES																								
1995	SEA A	6	.304	.783	23	7	2	0	3	13.0	5	5	2	8	0	0	0	15	0	1	0	2.7	.938	OF-6

Harry Buker

BUKER, HENRY L. (Happy)
B. 1859, Chicago, Ill. D. Aug. 10, 1899, Chicago, Ill.

Year	Team	Games	BA	SA	AB	H	2B	3B	HR	HR%	R	RBI	BB	SO	SB	Pinch Hit AB	Pinch Hit H	PO	A	E	DP	TC/G	FA	G by Pos
1884	DET N	30	.135	.144	111	15	1	0	0	0.0	5		4	15		0	0	35	65	14	5	3.8	.877	SS-19, OF-11

George Bullard

BULLARD, GEORGE DONALD (Curly) BR TR 5′ 9½″ 165 lbs.
B. Oct. 24, 1928, Lynn, Mass.

Year	Team	Games	BA	SA	AB	H	2B	3B	HR	HR%	R	RBI	BB	SO	SB	Pinch Hit AB	Pinch Hit H	PO	A	E	DP	TC/G	FA	G by Pos
1954	DET A	4	.000	.000	1	0	0	0	0	0.0	0	0	0	0	0	0	0	2	2	1	0	5.0	.800	SS-1

Sim Bullas

BULLAS, SIMEON EDWARD (Derby) BR TR 5′ 7½″ 150 lbs.
B. Apr. 10, 1861, Cleveland, Ohio D. Jan. 14, 1908, Cleveland, Ohio.

Year	Team	Games	BA	SA	AB	H	2B	3B	HR	HR%	R	RBI	BB	SO	SB	Pinch Hit AB	Pinch Hit H	PO	A	E	DP	TC/G	FA	G by Pos
1884	TOL AA	13	.089	.133	45	4	0	1	0	0.0	4		1			0	0	55	17	7	0	5.6	.911	C-12, OF-2

Scott Bullett

BULLETT, SCOTT DOUGLAS BB TL 6′ 2″ 200 lbs.
B. Dec. 25, 1968, Martinsburg, W. Va.

Year	Team	Games	BA	SA	AB	H	2B	3B	HR	HR%	R	RBI	BB	SO	SB	Pinch Hit AB	Pinch Hit H	PO	A	E	DP	TC/G	FA	G by Pos
1991	PIT N	11	.000	.000	4	0	0	0	0	0.0	2	0	0	3	1	1	0	2	0	0	0	0.7	1.000	OF-3
1993		23	.200	.273	55	11	0	2	0	0.0	2	4	3	15	3	4	2	35	1	0	0	1.9	1.000	OF-19
1995	CHI N	104	.273	.460	150	41	5	7	3	2.0	19	22	12	30	8	37	12	59	1	2	0	1.0	.968	OF-64
3 yrs.		138	.249	.402	209	52	5	9	3	1.4	23	26	15	48	12	42	14	96	2	2	0	1.2	.980	OF-86

Terry Bulling

BULLING, TERRY CHARLES (Bud) BR TR 6′ 1″ 200 lbs.
B. Dec. 15, 1952, Lynwood, Calif.

Year	Team	Games	BA	SA	AB	H	2B	3B	HR	HR%	R	RBI	BB	SO	SB	Pinch Hit AB	Pinch Hit H	PO	A	E	DP	TC/G	FA	G by Pos
1977	MIN A	15	.156	.188	32	5	1	0	0	0.0	2	5	5	5	0	1	0	37	3	2	0	3.2	.952	C-10, DH-3
1981	SEA A	62	.247	.305	154	38	3	0	2	1.3	15	15	21	20	0	4	0	239	21	6	3	4.3	.977	C-62
1982		56	.221	.286	154	34	7	0	1	0.6	17	8	19	16	2	1	0	304	24	3	5	5.9	.991	C-56
1983		5	.000	.000	5	0	0	0	0	0.0	0	0	0	0	0	0	0	17	0	0	0	3.4	1.000	C-5
4 yrs.		138	.223	.281	345	77	11	0	3	0.9	34	28	45	41	2	6	0	597	48	11	8	4.8	.983	C-133, DH-3

Eric Bullock

BULLOCK, ERIC GERALD BL TL 5′11″ 185 lbs.
B. Feb. 16, 1960, Los Angeles, Calif.

Year	Team	Games	BA	SA	AB	H	2B	3B	HR	HR%	R	RBI	BB	SO	SB	Pinch Hit AB	Pinch Hit H	PO	A	E	DP	TC/G	FA	G by Pos
1985	HOU N	18	.280	.360	25	7	2	0	0	0.0	3	2	1	3	0	12	3	6	0	2	0	1.1	.750	OF-7
1986		6	.048	.048	21	1	0	0	0	0.0	0	1	0	3	2	0	0	7	0	1	0	1.3	.875	OF-6
1988	MIN A	16	.294	.294	17	5	0	0	0	0.0	3	3	3	1	1	10	3	7	0	1	0	1.3	.875	OF-4, DH-2
1989	PHI N	6	.000	.000	4	0	0	0	0	0.0	1	0	0	2	0	3	0	2	0	0	0	0.7	1.000	OF-3
1990	MON N	4	.500	.500	2	1	0	0	0	0.0	0	0	0	0	0	2	1	0	0	0	0	0.0	—	
1991		73	.222	.319	72	16	4	0	1	1.4	6	6	9	13	6	48	10	22	3	1	0	2.2	.962	OF-9, 1B-3
1992		8	.000	.000	5	0	0	0	0	0.0	0	0	0	1	0	5	0	0	0	0	0	0.0	—	
7 yrs.		131	.205	.267	146	30	6	0	1	0.7	13	12	13	23	9	80	17	44	3	5	0	1.5	.904	OF-29, 1B-3, DH-2

Al Bumbry

BUMBRY, ALONZA BENJAMIN
Born Alonza Benjamin Bumbrey.
B. Apr. 21, 1947, Fredericksburg, Va.
BL TR 5′ 8″ 170 lbs.

Year	Team	Games	BA	SA	AB	H	2B	3B	HR	HR%	R	RBI	BB	SO	SB	Pinch Hit AB	Pinch Hit H	PO	A	E	DP	TC/G	FA	G by Pos
1972	BAL A	9	.364	.545	11	4	0	1	0	0.0	5	0	0	0	1	3	0	4	0	0	0	2.0	1.000	OF-2
1973		110	.337	.500	356	120	15	**11**	7	2.0	73	34	34	49	23	8	5	134	2	3	0	1.5	.978	OF-86, DH-7
1974		94	.233	.304	270	63	10	3	1	0.4	35	19	21	46	12	7	1	115	7	6	0	1.7	.953	OF-67, DH-7
1975		114	.269	.364	349	94	19	4	2	0.6	47	32	32	81	16	20	4	70	2	0	1	0.8	1.000	DH-48, OF-39, 3B-1
1976		133	.251	.376	450	113	15	7	9	2.0	71	36	43	76	42	7	1	251	9	3	2	2.1	.989	OF-116, DH-10
1977		133	.317	.411	518	164	31	3	4	0.8	74	41	45	88	19	2	2	329	7	3	0	2.6	.991	OF-130
1978		33	.237	.368	114	27	5	2	2	1.8	21	6	17	15	5	5	1	62	2	1	0	2.3	.985	OF-28
1979		148	.285	.376	569	162	29	1	7	1.2	80	49	43	74	37	8	3	367	7	7	1	2.6	.982	OF-146
1980		160	.318	.433	645	205	29	9	9	1.4	118	53	78	75	44	1	0	488	7	5	1	3.1	.990	OF-160
1981		101	.273	.337	392	107	18	2	1	0.3	61	27	51	51	22	2	0	255	6	2	2	2.6	.992	OF-100
1982		150	.262	.338	562	147	20	4	5	0.9	77	40	44	77	10	7	0	404	9	6	1	2.8	.986	OF-147, DH-1
1983		124	.275	.357	378	104	14	4	3	0.8	63	31	31	33	12	12	3	235	3	3	1	2.1	.988	OF-104, DH-11
1984		119	.270	.337	344	93	12	1	3	0.9	47	24	25	35	9	12	2	230	7	3	1	2.2	.988	OF-99, DH-9
1985	SD N	68	.200	.263	95	19	3	0	1	1.1	6	10	7	9	2	47	5	31	0	2	0	1.9	.939	OF-17
14 yrs.		1496	.281	.378	5053	1422	220	52	54	1.1	778	402	471	709	254	141	27	2975	68	44	10	2.3	.986	OF-1241, DH-93, 3B-1
LEAGUE CHAMPIONSHIP SERIES																								
1973	BAL A	2	.000	.000	7	0	0	0	0	0.0	1	0	2	2	0	0	0	4	1	1	0	3.0	.833	OF-2
1974		2	.000	.000	1	0	0	0	0	0.0	0	0	0	1	0	1	0	0	0	0	0	0.0	—	
1979		4	.250	.375	16	4	0	1	0	0.0	5	0	4	3	2	0	0	10	0	1	0	2.8	.909	OF-4
1983		3	.125	.250	8	1	1	0	0	0.0	0	1	0	2	0	0	0	3	0	0	0	1.0	1.000	OF-3
4 yrs.		11	.156	.250	32	5	1	1	0	0.0	6	1	6	8	2	1	0	17	1	2	0	2.2	.900	OF-9
WORLD SERIES																								
1979	BAL A	7	.143	.143	21	3	0	0	0	0.0	3	1	2	1	0	2	0	14	1	1	0	2.3	.938	OF-7
1983		4	.091	.182	11	1	1	0	0	0.0	0	1	0	1	0	0	0	12	0	0	0	3.0	1.000	OF-4
2 yrs.		11	.125	.156	32	4	1	0	0	0.0	3	2	2	2	0	2	0	26	1	1	0	2.5	.964	OF-11

Josh Bunce

BUNCE, JOSHUA
B. May 10, 1847, Brooklyn, N. Y. D. Apr. 28, 1912, Brooklyn, N. Y.

Year	Team	Games	BA	SA	AB	H	2B	3B	HR	HR%	R	RBI	BB	SO	SB	Pinch Hit AB	Pinch Hit H	PO	A	E	DP	TC/G	FA	G by Pos
1877	HAR N	1	.000	.000	4	0	0	0	0	0.0	0	0	0	0		0	0	1	0	0	0	1.0	1.000	OF-1

Nels Burbrink

BURBRINK, NELSON EDWARD
B. Dec. 28, 1921, Cincinnati, Ohio.
BR TR 5′10″ 195 lbs.

Year	Team	Games	BA	SA	AB	H	2B	3B	HR	HR%	R	RBI	BB	SO	SB	Pinch Hit AB	Pinch Hit H	PO	A	E	DP	TC/G	FA	G by Pos
1955	STL N	58	.276	.335	170	47	8	1	0	0.0	11	15	14	13	1	3	2	261	24	6	4	5.3	.979	C-55

Al Burch

BURCH, ALBERT WILLIAM
B. Oct. 7, 1883, Albany, N. Y. D. Oct. 5, 1926, Brooklyn, N. Y.
BL TR 5′ 8½″ 160 lbs.

Year	Team	Games	BA	SA	AB	H	2B	3B	HR	HR%	R	RBI	BB	SO	SB	Pinch Hit AB	Pinch Hit H	PO	A	E	DP	TC/G	FA	G by Pos
1906	STL N	91	.266	.287	335	89	5	1	0	0.0	40	11	37		15	0	0	155	15	12	6	2.0	.934	OF-91
1907	2 teams STL N (48G –.227) BKN N (40G –.292)																							
"	total	88	.255	.296	274	70	5	3	0	0.0	30	17	28		12	3	0	150	24	17	4	2.2	.911	OF-84, 2B-1
1908	BKN N	123	.243	.292	456	111	8	4	2	0.4	45	18	33		15	6	1	242	24	8	6	2.4	.971	OF-116
1909		152	.271	.329	601	163	20	6	1	0.2	80	30	51		38	0	0	335	23	16	5	2.5	.957	OF-151, 1B-1
1910		103	.236	.284	352	83	8	3	1	0.3	41	20	22	30	13	18	7	246	18	10	15	3.3	.964	OF-70, 1B-13
1911		54	.228	.275	167	38	2	3	0	0.0	18	7	15	22	3	6	0	104	14	3	3	2.6	.975	OF-43, 2B-3
6 yrs.		611	.254	.299	2185	554	48	20	4	0.2	254	103	186	52	96	33	8	1232	118	66	39	2.5	.953	OF-555, 1B-14, 2B-4

Ernie Burch

BURCH, EARNEST W.
B. 1856, DeKalb County, Ill.
BL

Year	Team	Games	BA	SA	AB	H	2B	3B	HR	HR%	R	RBI	BB	SO	SB	Pinch Hit AB	Pinch Hit H	PO	A	E	DP	TC/G	FA	G by Pos
1884	CLE N	32	.210	.242	124	26	4	0	0	0.0	9	7	5	24		0	0	52	10	7	1	2.2	.899	OF-32
1886	BKN AA	113	.261	.349	456	119	22	6	2	0.4	78		39			0	0	142	10	20	3	1.5	.884	OF-113
1887		49	.293	.388	188	55	4	4	2	1.1	47		29		15	0	0	90	8	11	1	2.2	.899	OF-49
3 yrs.		194	.260	.341	768	200	30	10	4	0.5	134	7	73	24	15	0	0	284	28	38	5	1.8	.891	OF-194

Bob Burda

BURDA, EDWARD ROBERT
B. July 16, 1938, St. Louis, Mo.
BL TL 5′11″ 174 lbs.

Year	Team	Games	BA	SA	AB	H	2B	3B	HR	HR%	R	RBI	BB	SO	SB	Pinch Hit AB	Pinch Hit H	PO	A	E	DP	TC/G	FA	G by Pos
1962	STL N	7	.071	.071	14	1	0	0	0	0.0	0	0	3	1	1	1	0	11	0	1	0	2.0	.917	OF-6
1965	SF N	31	.111	.111	27	3	0	0	0	0.0	0	5	5	6	0	12	1	34	0	1	1	2.9	.971	1B-11, OF-1
1966		37	.163	.233	43	7	3	0	0	0.0	3	2	2	5	0	25	4	28	2	0	0	2.7	1.000	1B-7, OF-4
1969		97	.230	.391	161	37	8	0	6	3.7	20	27	21	12	0	35	8	234	14	3	15	3.9	.988	1B-45, OF-19
1970	2 teams SF N (28G –.261) MIL A (78G –.248)																							
"	total	106	.249	.335	245	61	9	0	4	1.6	20	23	21	19	1	27	8	111	4	2	4	1.5	.983	OF-65, 1B-15
1971	STL N	65	.296	.338	71	21	0	0	1	1.4	6	12	10	11	0	**48**	**14**	62	6	0	4	4.9	1.000	1B-13, OF-1
1972	BOS A	45	.164	.260	73	12	1	0	2	2.7	4	9	8	11	0	27	2	124	7	1	13	8.3	.992	1B-15, OF-1
7 yrs.		388	.224	.319	634	142	21	0	13	2.1	53	78	70	65	2	175	37	604	33	8	37	3.2	.988	1B-106, OF-97

Jack Burdock

BURDOCK, JOHN JOSEPH (Black Jack)
B. Apr. 1852, Brooklyn, N. Y. D. Nov. 27, 1931, Brooklyn, N. Y.
Manager 1883.
BR TR 5′ 9½″ 158 lbs.

Year	Team	Games	BA	SA	AB	H	2B	3B	HR	HR%	R	RBI	BB	SO	SB	Pinch Hit AB	Pinch Hit H	PO	A	E	DP	TC/G	FA	G by Pos
1876	HAR N	69	.259	.294	309	80	9	1	0	0.0	66	23	13	16		0	0	211	175	45	19	6.2	.896	2B-69, 3B-1
1877		58	.260	.282	277	72	6	0	0	0.0	35	9	2	16		0	0	190	201	44	25	7.5	.899	2B-55, 3B-3
1878	BOS N	60	.260	.358	246	64	12	6	0	0.0	37	25	3	17		0	0	245	212	41	34	8.3	.918	2B-60
1879		84	.240	.284	359	86	10	3	0	0.0	64	36	9	28		0	0	303	300	59	43	7.9	.911	2B-84
1880		86	.253	.340	356	90	17	4	2	0.6	58	35	8	26		0	0	328	275	50	39	7.6	.923	2B-86
1881		73	.238	.319	282	67	12	4	1	0.4	36	24	7	18		0	0	202	208	40	35	6.2	.911	2B-72, SS-1
1882		83	.238	.301	319	76	6	7	0	0.0	36	27	9	24		0	0	223	256	35	28	6.2	.932	2B-83
1883		96	.330	.475	400	132	27	8	5	1.3	80	**88**	14	35		0	0	224	290	44	39	5.8	.921	2B-96
1884		87	.269	.380	361	97	14	4	6	1.7	65		15	52		0	0	183	278	39	23	5.7	.922	2B-87, 3B-1
1885		45	.142	.172	169	24	5	0	0	0.0	18	7	8	18		0	0	99	134	21	16	5.6	.917	2B-45
1886		59	.217	.253	221	48	6	1	0	0.0	26	25	11	27		0	0	145	165	33	22	5.8	.904	2B-59
1887		65	.257	.283	237	61	6	0	0	0.0	36	29	18	22	19	0	0	117	188	41	34	5.3	.882	2B-65

Jack Burdock *continued*

Year	Team	Games	BA	SA	AB	H	2B	3B	HR	HR%	R	RBI	BB	SO	SB	Pinch Hit AB	Pinch Hit H	PO	A	E	DP	TC/G	FA	G by Pos
1888	2 teams	BOS N (22G –.203) BKN AA (70G –.122)																						
"	total	92	.142	.166	325	46	1	2	1	0.3	20	12	10	5	10	0	0	225	291	55	32	6.2	.904	2B-92
1891	BKN N	3	.083	.083	12	1	0	0	0	0.0	1	1	1	1	0	0	0	4	9	0	1	4.3	1.000	2B-3
14 yrs.		960	.244	.310	3873	944	131	40	15	0.4	578	341	128	305	29	0	0	2699	2982	547	390	6.5	.912	2B-956, 3B-5, SS-1

Pete Burg

BURG, JOSEPH PETER BR TR 5′10″ 150 lbs.
B. June 4, 1882, Chicago, Ill. D. Apr. 28, 1969, Joliet, Ill.

Year	Team	Games	BA	SA	AB	H	2B	3B	HR	HR%	R	RBI	BB	SO	SB	Pinch Hit AB	Pinch Hit H	PO	A	E	DP	TC/G	FA	G by Pos
1910	BOS N	13	.326	.370	46	15	0	1	0	0.0	7	10	7	12	5	0	0	16	33	8	3	4.4	.860	3B-11, SS-2

Smoky Burgess

BURGESS, FORREST HARRILL BL TR 5′ 8½″ 185 lbs.
B. Feb. 6, 1927, Caroleen, N. C. D. Sept. 15, 1991, Asheville, N. C.

Year	Team	Games	BA	SA	AB	H	2B	3B	HR	HR%	R	RBI	BB	SO	SB	Pinch Hit AB	Pinch Hit H	PO	A	E	DP	TC/G	FA	G by Pos
1949	CHI N	46	.268	.321	56	15	0	0	1	1.8	4	12	4	4	0	37	12	21	6	0	2	3.4	1.000	C-8
1951		94	.251	.315	219	55	4	2	2	0.9	21	20	21	12	2	30	5	210	35	5	6	3.9	.980	C-64
1952	PHI N	110	.296	.429	371	110	27	2	6	1.6	49	56	49	21	3	6	3	439	47	11	6	4.8	.978	C-104
1953		102	.292	.417	312	91	17	5	4	1.3	31	36	37	17	3	9	3	395	23	3	8	4.4	.993	C-95
1954		108	.368	.510	345	127	27	5	4	1.2	41	46	42	11	1	17	6	356	30	10	4	4.4	.975	C-91
1955	2 teams	PHI N (7G –.190) CIN N (116G –.306)																						
"	total	123	.301	.495	442	133	17	3	21	4.8	71	78	50	36	1	9	3	492	36	7	6	4.7	.987	C-113
1956	CIN N	90	.275	.476	229	63	10	0	12	5.2	28	39	26	18	0	29	7	257	18	0	2	5.0	1.000	C-55
1957		90	.283	.566	205	58	14	1	14	6.8	29	39	24	16	0	39	11	223	15	3	0	5.4	.988	C-45
1958		99	.283	.410	251	71	12	1	6	2.4	28	31	22	20	0	40	11	297	21	4	2	5.6	.988	C-58
1959	PIT N	114	.297	.485	377	112	28	5	11	2.9	41	59	31	16	0	17	7	441	39	8	4	4.8	.984	C-101
1960		110	.294	.412	337	99	15	2	7	2.1	33	39	35	13	0	20	9	485	38	3	7	5.9	.994	C-89
1961		100	.303	.486	323	98	17	3	12	3.7	37	52	30	16	1	14	4	426	27	4	4	5.0	.991	C-92
1962		130	.328	.500	360	118	19	2	13	3.6	38	61	31	19	0	5	1	550	45	7	5	6.0	.988	C-101
1963		91	.280	.394	264	74	10	1	6	2.3	20	37	24	14	0	18	6	364	40	4	4	5.7	.990	C-72
1964	2 teams	PIT N (68G –.246) CHI A (7G –.200)																						
"	total	75	.244	.324	176	43	3	1	3	1.7	10	18	15	14	2	26	8	237	18	2	3	5.8	.992	C-44
1965	CHI A	80	.286	.416	77	22	4	0	2	2.6	2	24	11	7	0	**65**	**20**	17	3	0	0	4.0	1.000	C-5
1966		79	.313	.388	67	21	5	0	0	0.0	0	15	11	8	0	**66**	**21**	4	0	0	0	2.0	1.000	C-2
1967		77	.133	.250	60	8	1	0	2	3.3	2	11	14	8	0	**60**	8	0	0	0	0	0.0	—	
18 yrs.		1718	.295	.446	4471	1318	230	33	126	2.8	485	673	477	270	13	507	145 **2nd**	5214	441	71	63	5.0	.988	C-1139
WORLD SERIES																								
1960	PIT N	5	.333	.389	18	6	1	0	0	0.0	2	0	2	1	0	0	0	27	2	0	0	5.8	1.000	C-5

Tom Burgess

BURGESS, THOMAS ROLAND (Tim) BL TL 6′ 180 lbs.
B. Sept. 1, 1927, London, Ont., Canada.

Year	Team	Games	BA	SA	AB	H	2B	3B	HR	HR%	R	RBI	BB	SO	SB	Pinch Hit AB	Pinch Hit H	PO	A	E	DP	TC/G	FA	G by Pos
1954	STL N	17	.048	.095	21	1	1	0	0	0.0	2	1	3	9	0	11	0	3	0	1	0	1.0	.750	OF-4
1962	LA A	87	.196	.301	143	28	7	1	2	1.4	17	13	36	20	2	43	7	286	15	1	27	8.2	.997	1B-35, OF-2
2 yrs.		104	.177	.274	164	29	8	1	2	1.2	19	14	39	29	2	54	7	289	15	2	27	7.5	.993	1B-35, OF-6

Bill Burgo

BURGO, WILLIAM ROSS BR TR 5′ 8″ 185 lbs.
B. Nov. 5, 1919, Johnstown, Pa. D. Oct. 19, 1988, Morgan City, La.

Year	Team	Games	BA	SA	AB	H	2B	3B	HR	HR%	R	RBI	BB	SO	SB	Pinch Hit AB	Pinch Hit H	PO	A	E	DP	TC/G	FA	G by Pos
1943	PHI A	17	.371	.529	70	26	4	2	1	1.4	12	9	4	1	0	0	0	45	2	1	1	2.8	.979	OF-17
1944		27	.239	.295	88	21	2	0	1	1.1	6	3	7	3	1	3	0	62	1	3	0	3.0	.955	OF-22
2 yrs.		44	.297	.399	158	47	6	2	2	1.3	18	12	11	4	1	3	0	107	3	4	1	2.9	.965	OF-39

Bill Burich

BURICH, WILLIAM MAX BR TR 6′ 180 lbs.
B. May 29, 1918, Calumet, Mich.

Year	Team	Games	BA	SA	AB	H	2B	3B	HR	HR%	R	RBI	BB	SO	SB	Pinch Hit AB	Pinch Hit H	PO	A	E	DP	TC/G	FA	G by Pos
1942	PHI N	25	.287	.300	80	23	1	0	0	0.0	3	7	6	13	2	3	0	49	49	8	6	4.8	.925	SS-19, 3B-3
1946		2	.000	.000	1	0	0	0	0	0.0	1	0	0	0	0	0	0	0	0	0	0	0.0	.000	3B-1
2 yrs.		27	.284	.296	81	23	1	0	0	0.0	4	7	6	13	2	3	0	49	49	8	6	4.6	.925	SS-19, 3B-4

Mack Burk

BURK, MACK EDWIN BR TR 6′ 4″ 180 lbs.
B. Apr. 21, 1935, Nacogdoches, Tex.

Year	Team	Games	BA	SA	AB	H	2B	3B	HR	HR%	R	RBI	BB	SO	SB	Pinch Hit AB	Pinch Hit H	PO	A	E	DP	TC/G	FA	G by Pos
1956	PHI N	15	1.000	1.000	1	1	0	0	0	0.0	3	0	0	0	0	1	1	1	0	0	0	1.0	1.000	C-1
1958		1	.000	.000	1	0	0	0	0	0.0	0	0	0	1	0	1	0	0	0	0	0	0.0	—	
2 yrs.		16	.500	.500	2	1	0	0	0	0.0	3	0	0	1	0	2	1	1	0	0	0	1.0	1.000	C-1

Bob Burkam

BURKAM, CHAUNCEY DePEW (Chris) BL TR 5′11″ 175 lbs.
B. Oct. 13, 1892, Benton Harbor, Mich. D. May 9, 1964, Kalamazoo, Mich.

Year	Team	Games	BA	SA	AB	H	2B	3B	HR	HR%	R	RBI	BB	SO	SB	Pinch Hit AB	Pinch Hit H	PO	A	E	DP	TC/G	FA	G by Pos
1915	STL A	1	.000	.000	1	0	0	0	0	0.0	0	0	0	1	0	1	0	0	0	0	0	0.0	—	

Dan Burke

BURKE, DANIEL L. BR TR 5′10″ 190 lbs.
B. Oct. 25, 1868, Abington, Mass. D. Mar. 20, 1933, Taunton, Mass.

Year	Team	Games	BA	SA	AB	H	2B	3B	HR	HR%	R	RBI	BB	SO	SB	Pinch Hit AB	Pinch Hit H	PO	A	E	DP	TC/G	FA	G by Pos
1890	2 teams	ROC AA (32G –.216) SYR AA (9G –.000)																						
"	total	41	.180	.189	122	22	1	0	0	0.0	15		22		2	0	0	105	18	13	2	3.1	.904	OF-29, C-13, 1B-2
1892	BOS N	1	.000	.000	4	0	0	0	0	0.0	0	0	0	2	0	0	0	8	1	1	1	10.0	.900	C-1
2 yrs.		42	.175	.183	126	22	1	0	0	0.0	15	0	22	2	2	0	0	113	19	14	3	3.2	.904	OF-29, C-14, 1B-2

Eddie Burke

BURKE, EDWARD D. BL TR 5′ 6″ 161 lbs.
B. Oct. 6, 1866, Northumberland, Pa. D. Nov. 26, 1907, Utica, N. Y.

Year	Team	Games	BA	SA	AB	H	2B	3B	HR	HR%	R	RBI	BB	SO	SB	Pinch Hit AB	Pinch Hit H	PO	A	E	DP	TC/G	FA	G by Pos
1890	2 teams	PHI N (100G –.263) PIT N (31G –.210)																						
"	total	131	.251	.363	554	139	21	13	5	0.9	102	57	63	49	44	0	0	294	34	36	7	2.8	.901	OF-127, 2B-4
1891	MIL AA	35	.236	.319	144	34	9	0	1	0.7	31	21	12	19	7	0	0	70	8	7	3	2.4	.918	OF-35
1892	2 teams	CIN N (15G –.146) NY N (89G –.259)																						
"	total	104	.248	.344	404	100	11	5	6	1.5	87	45	55	41	44	0	0	206	188	61	20	4.4	.866	2B-59, OF-44, 3B-1
1893	NY N	135	.279	.410	537	150	23	10	9	1.7	122	80	51	32	54	0	0	278	19	29	2	2.4	.911	OF-135
1894		136	.304	.410	566	172	23	11	5	0.9	121	77	37	35	34	0	0	260	17	20	3	2.2	.933	OF-136

Eddie Burke *continued*

Year	Team	Games	BA	SA	AB	H	2B	3B	HR	HR%	R	RBI	BB	SO	SB	Pinch Hit AB	Pinch Hit H	PO	A	E	DP	TC/G	FA	G by Pos
1895	2 teams	NY N (40G –.257) CIN N (56G –.268)																						
"	total	96	.263	.354	395	104	14	8	2	0.5	90	40	29	23	33	0	0	212	16	24	4	2.7	.905	OF-95
1896	CIN N	122	.340	.426	521	177	24	9	1	0.2	120	52	41	29	53	0	0	290	13	21	3	2.7	.935	OF-122
1897		95	.266	.323	387	103	17	1	1	0.3	71	41	29		22	0	0	224	11	15	4	2.6	.940	OF-95
8 yrs.		854	.279	.378	3508	979	142	57	30	0.9	744	413	317	228	291	0	0	1834	306	213	46	2.8	.909	OF-789, 2B-63, 3B-1

Frank Burke

BURKE, FRANK ALOYSIUS
B. Feb. 16, 1880, Carbon County, Pa. D. Sept. 17, 1946, Los Angeles, Calif.
TR

Year	Team	Games	BA	SA	AB	H	2B	3B	HR	HR%	R	RBI	BB	SO	SB	Pinch Hit AB	Pinch Hit H	PO	A	E	DP	TC/G	FA	G by Pos
1906	NY N	8	.333	.667	9	3	1	1	0	0.0	2	1	1		1	3	1	2	0	1	0	0.8	.667	OF-4
1907	BOS N	43	.178	.194	129	23	0	1	0	0.0	6	8	11		3	6	1	60	3	3	0	1.8	.955	OF-36
2 yrs.		51	.188	.225	138	26	1	2	0	0.0	8	9	12		4	9	2	62	3	4	0	1.7	.942	OF-40

Glenn Burke

BURKE, GLENN LAWRENCE
B. Nov. 16, 1952, Oakland, Calif. D. May 30, 1995, San Leandro, Calif.
BR TR 6′ 195 lbs.

Year	Team	Games	BA	SA	AB	H	2B	3B	HR	HR%	R	RBI	BB	SO	SB	Pinch Hit AB	Pinch Hit H	PO	A	E	DP	TC/G	FA	G by Pos
1976	LA N	25	.239	.283	46	11	2	0	0	0.0	9	5	3	8	3	1	0	33	0	1	0	1.7	.971	OF-20
1977		83	.254	.320	169	43	8	0	1	0.6	16	13	5	22	13	9	0	98	1	3	0	1.4	.971	OF-74
1978	2 teams	LA N (16G –.211) OAK A (78G –.235)																						
"	total	94	.233	.283	219	51	6	1	1	0.5	21	16	10	30	16	2	0	163	1	2	0	2.0	.988	OF-82, DH-2, 1B-1
1979	OAK A	23	.213	.258	89	19	2	1	0	0.0	4	4	4	10	3	0	0	46	2	0	0	2.1	1.000	OF-23
4 yrs.		225	.237	.291	523	124	18	2	2	0.4	50	38	22	70	35	12	0	340	4	6	0	1.7	.983	OF-199, DH-2, 1B-1
LEAGUE CHAMPIONSHIP SERIES																								
1977	LA N	4	.000	.000	7	0	0	0	0	0.0	0	0	0	3	0	0	0	3	0	0	0	0.8	1.000	OF-4
WORLD SERIES																								
1977	LA N	3	.200	.200	5	1	0	0	0	0.0	0	0	0	1	0	0	0	10	0	0	0	3.3	1.000	OF-3

Jimmy Burke

BURKE, JAMES TIMOTHY (Sunset Jimmy)
B. Oct. 12, 1874, St. Louis, Mo. D. Mar. 26, 1942, St. Louis, Mo.
Manager 1905, 1918–20.
BR TR 5′ 7″ 160 lbs.

Year	Team	Games	BA	SA	AB	H	2B	3B	HR	HR%	R	RBI	BB	SO	SB	Pinch Hit AB	Pinch Hit H	PO	A	E	DP	TC/G	FA	G by Pos
1898	CLE N	13	.105	.132	38	4	1	0	0	0.0	1	1	2		1	0	0	8	21	5	0	2.6	.853	3B-13
1899	STL N	2	.333	.333	6	2	0	0	0	0.0	1	0	1		0	0	0	4	8	1	2	6.5	.923	2B-2
1901	3 teams	MIL A (64G –.206) CHI A (42G –.264) PIT N (14G –.196)																						
"	total	120	.225	.255	432	97	13	0	0	0.0	48	51	33		17	0	0	172	291	73	18	4.5	.864	3B-89, SS-31
1902	PIT N	60	.296	.374	203	60	12	2	0	0.0	24	26	17		9	2	0	90	120	23	8	4.0	.901	2B-27, OF-18, 3B-9, SS-4
1903	STL N	115	.285	.329	431	123	13	3	0	0.0	55	42	23		28	1	0	170	257	40	14	4.1	.914	3B-93, 2B-15, OF-5
1904		118	.227	.266	406	92	10	3	0	0.0	37	37	15		17	0	0	148	217	42	10	3.4	.897	3B-118
1905		122	.225	.276	431	97	9	5	1	0.2	34	30	21		15	0	0	174	238	34	13	3.7	.924	3B-122
7 yrs.		550	.244	.289	1947	475	58	13	1	0.1	200	187	112		87	3	0	766	1152	218	65	3.9	.898	3B-444, 2B-44, SS-35, OF-23

Joe Burke

BURKE, JOSEPH A.
B. Cincinnati, Ohio Deceased.
5′ 7″ 160 lbs.

Year	Team	Games	BA	SA	AB	H	2B	3B	HR	HR%	R	RBI	BB	SO	SB	Pinch Hit AB	Pinch Hit H	PO	A	E	DP	TC/G	FA	G by Pos
1890	STL AA	2	.667	.667	6	4	0	0	0	0.0	3		1		0	0	0	0	6	2	0	4.0	.750	3B-2
1891	CIN AA	1	.250	.250	4	1	0	0	0	0.0	0	1	0	2	0	0	0	4	5	0	0	9.0	1.000	2B-1
2 yrs.		3	.500	.500	10	5	0	0	0	0.0	3	1	1	2	0	0	0	4	11	2	0	5.7	.882	3B-2, 2B-1

John Burke

BURKE, JOHN PATRICK
B. Jan. 27, 1877, Hazleton, Pa. D. Aug. 4, 1950, Jersey City, N. J.
BR TR

Year	Team	Games	BA	SA	AB	H	2B	3B	HR	HR%	R	RBI	BB	SO	SB	Pinch Hit AB	Pinch Hit H	PO	A	E	DP	TC/G	FA	G by Pos
1902	NY N	4	.154	.154	13	2	0	0	0	0.0	0	0	0		0	0	0	5	3	0	0	2.0	1.000	OF-2, P-2

Leo Burke

BURKE, LEO PATRICK
B. May 6, 1934, Hagerstown, Md.
BR TR 5′11″ 185 lbs.

Year	Team	Games	BA	SA	AB	H	2B	3B	HR	HR%	R	RBI	BB	SO	SB	Pinch Hit AB	Pinch Hit H	PO	A	E	DP	TC/G	FA	G by Pos
1958	BAL A	7	.455	.818	11	5	1	0	1	9.1	4	4	1	2	0	3	1	2	0	1	0	0.8	.667	OF-3, 3B-1
1959		5	.200	.200	10	2	0	0	0	0.0	0	1	0	5	0	2	0	4	4	0	0	2.0	1.000	3B-2, 2B-2
1961	LA A	6	.000	.000	5	0	0	0	0	0.0	0	0	0	1	0	5	0	0	0	0	0	0.0	—	
1962		19	.266	.469	64	17	1	0	4	6.3	8	14	5	11	0	2	0	27	8	4	2	2.3	.897	OF-12, 3B-4, SS-1
1963	2 teams	STL N (30G –.204) CHI N (27G –.184)																						
"	total	57	.194	.327	98	19	2	1	3	3.1	10	12	8	25	0	28	8	72	35	7	7	3.8	.939	OF-11, 2B-10, 3B-5, 1B-4
1964	CHI N	59	.262	.340	103	27	3	1	1	1.0	11	14	7	31	0	34	10	46	11	2	2	2.0	.966	OF-18, 2B-5, 3B-4, 1B-2, C-1
1965		12	.200	.200	10	2	0	0	0	0.0	0	0	0	4	0	9	1	2	0	0	0	0.7	1.000	C-2, OF-1
7 yrs.		165	.239	.365	301	72	7	2	9	3.0	33	45	21	79	0	83	20	153	58	14	11	2.6	.938	OF-45, 2B-17, 3B-16, 1B-6, C-3, SS-1

Les Burke

BURKE, LESLIE KINGSTON (Buck)
B. Dec. 18, 1902, Lynn, Mass. D. May 6, 1975, Danvers, Mass.
BL TR 5′ 9″ 168 lbs.

Year	Team	Games	BA	SA	AB	H	2B	3B	HR	HR%	R	RBI	BB	SO	SB	Pinch Hit AB	Pinch Hit H	PO	A	E	DP	TC/G	FA	G by Pos
1923	DET A	7	.100	.100	10	1	0	0	0	0.0	2	2	0	1	0	1	0	1	3	2	0	1.5	.667	3B-2, 2B-1, C-1
1924		72	.253	.328	241	61	10	4	0	0.0	30	17	22	20	2	7	4	133	184	15	32	5.2	.955	2B-58, SS-6
1925		77	.289	.356	180	52	6	3	0	0.0	32	24	17	8	4	22	4	100	130	9	27	4.6	.962	2B-52
1926		38	.227	.240	75	17	1	0	0	0.0	9	4	7	3	1	13	1	35	54	6	8	4.1	.937	2B-15, 3B-7, SS-1
4 yrs.		194	.259	.320	506	131	17	7	0	0.0	73	47	46	32	7	43	9	269	371	32	67	4.7	.952	2B-126, 3B-9, SS-7, C-1

Mike Burke

BURKE, MICHAEL E.
B. 1855, Cincinnati, Ohio D. June 9, 1889, Albany, N. Y.
BR TR 6′ 190 lbs.

Year	Team	Games	BA	SA	AB	H	2B	3B	HR	HR%	R	RBI	BB	SO	SB	Pinch Hit AB	Pinch Hit H	PO	A	E	DP	TC/G	FA	G by Pos
1879	CIN N	28	.222	.248	117	26	3	0	0	0.0	13	8	2	5		0	0	36	62	32	3	4.5	.754	SS-19, OF-5, 3B-5

Pat Burke

BURKE, PATRICK EDWARD
B. May 13, 1901, St. Louis, Mo. D. July 7, 1965, St. Louis, Mo.
BR TR 5′10½″ 170 lbs.

Year	Team	Games	BA	SA	AB	H	2B	3B	HR	HR%	R	RBI	BB	SO	SB	Pinch Hit AB	Pinch Hit H	PO	A	E	DP	TC/G	FA	G by Pos
1924	STL A	1	.000	.000	3	0	0	0	0	0.0	0	1	0	0	0	0	0	0	0	0	0	0.0	.000	3B-1

Jesse Burkett

BURKETT, JESSE CAIL (The Crab)
B. Dec. 4, 1868, Wheeling, W. Va. D. May 27, 1953, Worcester, Mass.
Hall of Fame 1946.
BL TL 5′ 8″ 155 lbs.

Year	Team	Games	BA	SA	AB	H	2B	3B	HR	HR%	R	RBI	BB	SO	SB	Pinch Hit AB	Pinch Hit H	PO	A	E	DP	TC/G	FA	G by Pos
1890	NY N	101	.309	.461	401	124	23	13	4	1.0	67	60	33	52	14	0	0	111	56	36	5	1.8	.823	OF-90, P-21
1891	CLE N	42	.269	.359	167	45	7	4	0	0.0	29	13	23	19	1	0	0	53	5	7	1	1.5	.892	OF-42
1892		145	.275	.375	608	167	15	14	6	1.0	119	66	67	59	36	0	0	271	20	31	7	2.2	.904	OF-145

Jesse Burkett *continued*

Year	Team		Games	BA	SA	AB	H	2B	3B	HR	HR%	R	RBI	BB	SO	SB	Pinch Hit AB	Pinch Hit H	PO	A	E	DP	TC/G	FA	G by Pos
1893			125	.348	.491	511	178	25	15	6	1.2	145	82	98	23	39	0	0	239	19	46	5	2.4	.849	OF-125
1894			125	.358	.509	523	187	27	14	8	1.5	138	94	84	27	28	0	0	242	17	24	5	2.2	.915	OF-125, P-1
1895			131	**.409**	.524	550	**225**	22	13	5	0.9	153	83	74	31	41	0	0	273	17	38	4	2.5	.884	OF-132
1896			133	**.410**	.541	**586**	**240**	27	16	6	1.0	**160**	72	49	19	34	0	0	269	18	23	4	2.3	.926	OF-133
1897			128	.383	.476	517	198	28	7	2	0.4	129	60	76		28	0	0	226	18	13	3	2.0	.949	OF-127
1898			150	.341	.399	624	213	18	9	0	0.0	114	42	69		19	0	0	268	17	19	3	2.0	.938	OF-150
1899	STL	N	141	.396	.500	558	221	21	8	7	1.3	116	71	67		25	0	0	298	23	23	3	2.4	.933	OF-140, 2B-1
1900			141	.363	.474	559	203	11	15	7	1.3	88	68	62		32	0	0	337	17	25	6	2.7	.934	OF-141
1901			142	**.382**	.524	**597**	**228**	21	17	10	1.7	**139**	75	59		27	0	0	307	17	27	4	2.5	.923	OF-142
1902	STL	A	137	.306	.419	549	168	29	9	5	0.9	97	52	71		23	0	0	301	20	26	6	2.5	.925	OF-137, 3B-1, SS-1, P-1
1903			133	.296	.379	514	152	20	7	3	0.6	74	40	52		17	0	0	230	10	15	4	1.9	.941	OF-132
1904			147	.273	.340	576	157	15	9	2	0.3	72	27	78		12	0	0	266	24	18	4	2.1	.942	OF-147
1905	BOS	A	149	.257	.346	573	147	13	13	4	0.7	78	47	67		13	0	0	276	11	22	0	2.1	.929	OF-149
16 yrs.			2070	.339	.448	8413	2853	322	183	75	0.9	1718	952	1029	230	389	0	0	3967	309	393	64	2.2	.916	OF-2057, P-23, 3B-1, SS-1, 2B-1

Ellis Burks

BURKS, ELLIS RENA
B. Sept. 11, 1964, Vicksburg, Miss.

BR TR 6′ 2″ 175 lbs.

Year	Team		Games	BA	SA	AB	H	2B	3B	HR	HR%	R	RBI	BB	SO	SB	Pinch Hit AB	Pinch Hit H	PO	A	E	DP	TC/G	FA	G by Pos
1987	BOS	A	133	.272	.441	558	152	30	2	20	3.6	94	59	41	98	27	0	0	320	15	4	2	2.6	.988	OF-132
1988			144	.294	.481	540	159	37	5	18	3.3	93	92	62	89	25	0	0	370	9	9	0	2.7	.977	OF-142, DH-2
1989			97	.303	.471	399	121	19	6	12	3.0	73	61	36	52	21	0	0	245	7	6	3	2.7	.977	OF-95, DH-1
1990			152	.296	.486	588	174	33	8	21	3.6	89	89	48	82	9	3	1	324	7	2	0	2.2	.994	OF-143, DH-6
1991			130	.251	.422	474	119	33	3	14	3.0	56	56	39	81	6	2	0	283	2	2	1	2.2	.993	OF-126, DH-2
1992			66	.255	.417	235	60	8	3	8	3.4	35	30	25	48	5	3	0	120	3	2	0	2.0	.984	OF-63, DH-1
1993	CHI	A	146	.275	.441	499	137	24	4	17	3.4	75	74	60	97	6	5	2	313	6	6	1	2.2	.982	OF-146
1994	CLR	N	42	.322	.678	149	48	8	3	13	8.7	33	24	16	39	3	3	0	79	2	3	0	2.2	.964	OF-39
1995			103	.266	.496	278	74	10	6	14	5.0	41	49	39	72	7	29	6	158	3	5	0	2.1	.970	OF-80
9 yrs.			1013	.281	.467	3720	1044	202	40	137	3.7	589	534	366	658	109	45	9	2212	54	39	7	2.4	.983	OF-966, DH-12
DIVISIONAL PLAYOFF SERIES																									
1995	CLR	N	2	.333	.500	6	2	1	0	0	0.0	1	2	0	1	0	0	0	4	0	1	0	2.5	.800	OF-2
LEAGUE CHAMPIONSHIP SERIES																									
1988	BOS	A	4	.235	.294	17	4	1	0	0	0.0	2	1	0	3	0	0	0	10	0	0	0	2.5	1.000	OF-4
1990			4	.267	.400	15	4	2	0	0	0.0	1	0	1	1	1	0	0	9	1	0	0	2.5	1.000	OF-4
1993	CHI	A	6	.304	.478	23	7	1	0	1	4.3	4	3	3	5	0	0	0	15	0	0	0	2.5	1.000	OF-6
3 yrs.			14	.273	.400	55	15	4	0	1	1.8	7	4	4	9	1	0	0	34	1	0	0	2.5	1.000	OF-14

Rick Burleson

BURLESON, RICHARD PAUL (Rooster)
B. Apr. 29, 1951, Lynwood, Calif.

BR TR 5′10″ 165 lbs.

Year	Team		Games	BA	SA	AB	H	2B	3B	HR	HR%	R	RBI	BB	SO	SB	Pinch Hit AB	Pinch Hit H	PO	A	E	DP	TC/G	FA	G by Pos
1974	BOS	A	114	.284	.372	384	109	22	0	4	1.0	36	44	21	34	3	1	0	209	329	21	65	4.6	.962	SS-88, 2B-31, 3B-2
1975			158	.252	.329	580	146	25	1	6	1.0	66	62	45	44	8	0	0	267	498	29	102	5.0	.963	SS-158
1976			152	.291	.383	540	157	27	1	7	1.3	75	42	60	37	14	0	0	274	478	34	88	5.2	.957	SS-152
1977			154	.293	.382	**663**	194	36	7	3	0.5	80	52	47	69	13	0	0	285	482	24	111	5.1	.970	SS-154
1978			145	.248	.339	626	155	32	5	5	0.8	75	49	40	71	8	0	0	285	482	15	100	5.4	.981	SS-144
1979			153	.278	.368	627	174	32	5	5	0.8	93	60	35	54	9	1	0	272	523	16	109	5.3	.980	SS-153
1980			155	.278	.366	644	179	29	2	8	1.2	89	51	62	51	12	0	0	301	528	22	147	5.5	.974	SS-155
1981	CAL	A	109	.293	.372	430	126	17	1	5	1.2	53	33	42	38	4	0	0	208	394	13	88	5.6	.979	SS-109
1982			11	.156	.178	45	7	1	0	0	0.0	4	2	6	3	0	0	0	19	51	1	12	6.5	.986	SS-11
1983			33	.286	.345	119	34	7	0	0	0.0	22	11	12	12	0	2	1	54	102	5	16	5.2	.969	SS-31
1984			7	.000	.000	4	0	0	0	0	0.0	2	0	0	2	0	4	0	0	0	0	0	0.0	—	
1986			93	.284	.391	271	77	14	0	5	1.8	35	29	33	32	1	11	3	62	90	3	15	1.8	.981	DH-38, SS-37, 2B-6, 3B-4
1987	BAL	A	62	.209	.316	206	43	14	1	2	1.0	26	14	17	30	0	2	0	112	145	6	39	4.2	.977	2B-55, DH-7
13 yrs.			1346	.273	.361	5139	1401	256	23	50	1.0	656	449	420	477	72	21	4	2348	4102	189	892	5.0	.972	SS-1192, 2B-92, DH-45, 3B-6
LEAGUE CHAMPIONSHIP SERIES																									
1975	BOS	A	3	.444	.667	9	4	2	0	0	0.0	2	1	1	0	0	0	0	4	12	1	1	5.7	.941	SS-3
1986	CAL	A	4	.273	.273	11	3	0	0	0	0.0	0	0	0	0	0	1	0	3	5	0	0	2.7	1.000	2B-2, DH-1
2 yrs.			7	.350	.450	20	7	2	0	0	0.0	2	1	1	0	0	1	0	7	17	1	1	4.2	.960	SS-3, 2B-2, DH-1
WORLD SERIES																									
1975	BOS	A	7	.292	.333	24	7	1	0	0	0.0	1	2	4	2	0	0	0	9	19	1	4	4.1	.966	SS-7

Hercules Burnett

BURNETT, HERCULES H.
B. Aug. 13, 1869, Louisville, Ky. D. Oct. 4, 1936, Louisville, Ky.

BR 177 lbs.

Year	Team		Games	BA	SA	AB	H	2B	3B	HR	HR%	R	RBI	BB	SO	SB	Pinch Hit AB	Pinch Hit H	PO	A	E	DP	TC/G	FA	G by Pos
1888	LOU	AA	1	.000	.000	4	0	0	0	0	0.0	1	0	1		1	0	0	2	0	1	0	3.0	.667	OF-1
1895	LOU	N	5	.412	.882	17	7	0	1	2	11.8	6	3	2	2	2	0	0	18	1	3	1	4.4	.864	OF-4, 1B-1
2 yrs.			6	.333	.714	21	7	0	1	2	9.5	7	3	3	2	3	0	0	20	1	4	1	4.2	.840	OF-5, 1B-1

Jack Burnett

BURNETT, JOHN P.
B. Dec. 2, 1889, Mo. D. Sept. 8, 1929, Taft, Calif.

Year	Team		Games	BA	SA	AB	H	2B	3B	HR	HR%	R	RBI	BB	SO	SB	Pinch Hit AB	Pinch Hit H	PO	A	E	DP	TC/G	FA	G by Pos
1907	STL	N	59	.238	.316	206	49	8	4	0	0.0	18	12	15		5	0	0	98	8	5	1	1.9	.955	OF-59

Johnny Burnett

BURNETT, JOHN HENDERSON
B. Nov. 1, 1904, Bartow, Fla. D. Aug. 13, 1959, Tampa, Fla.

BL TR 5′11″ 175 lbs.

Year	Team		Games	BA	SA	AB	H	2B	3B	HR	HR%	R	RBI	BB	SO	SB	Pinch Hit AB	Pinch Hit H	PO	A	E	DP	TC/G	FA	G by Pos
1927	CLE	A	17	.000	.000	8	0	0	0	0	0.0	5	0	0	3	1	6	0	2	3	1	1	3.0	.833	2B-2
1928			3	.500	.500	10	5	0	0	0	0.0	3	1	0	1	0	1	1	6	7	2	3	7.5	.867	SS-2
1929			19	.152	.182	33	5	1	0	0	0.0	2	2	1	2	0	1	0	30	38	6	3	5.3	.919	SS-10, 2B-4
1930			54	.312	.388	170	53	13	0	0	0.0	28	20	17	8	2	8	3	44	105	11	14	3.5	.931	3B-27, SS-19
1931			111	.300	.389	427	128	25	5	1	0.2	85	52	39	25	5	2	1	194	296	34	52	4.4	.935	SS-63, 2B-35, 3B-21, OF-1
1932			129	.297	.385	512	152	23	5	4	0.8	81	53	46	27	2	1	1	232	373	37	62	5.0	.942	SS-103, 2B-26
1933			83	.272	.341	261	71	11	2	1	0.4	39	29	23	14	3	12	1	124	198	23	31	4.9	.933	SS-41, 2B-17, 3B-12

Johnny Burnett *continued*

Year	Team		Games	BA	SA	AB	H	2B	3B	HR	HR%	R	RBI	BB	SO	SB	Pinch Hit AB	Pinch Hit H	PO	A	E	DP	TC/G	FA	G by Pos
1934			72	.293	.409	208	61	11	2	3	1.4	28	30	18	11	1	14	3	73	93	9	12	3.1	.949	3B-42, SS-9, 2B-3, OF-2
1935	**STL**	**A**	70	.223	.282	206	46	10	1	0	0.0	17	26	19	16	1	16	4	71	136	13	18	3.6	.941	3B-31, SS-18, 2B-12
9 yrs.			558	.284	.366	1835	521	94	15	9	0.5	288	213	163	107	15	61	14	776	1249	136	196	4.3	.937	SS-265, 3B-133, 2B-99, OF-3

Jeromy Burnitz

BURNITZ, JEROMY NEAL
B. Apr. 15, 1969, Westminster, Calif.
BL TR 6′ 190 lbs.

Year	Team		Games	BA	SA	AB	H	2B	3B	HR	HR%	R	RBI	BB	SO	SB	Pinch Hit AB	Pinch Hit H	PO	A	E	DP	TC/G	FA	G by Pos
1993	**NY**	**N**	86	.243	.475	263	64	10	6	13	4.9	49	38	38	66	3	10	3	165	6	4	2	2.2	.977	OF-79
1994			45	.238	.329	143	34	4	0	3	2.1	26	15	23	45	1	3	1	63	1	2	0	1.6	.970	OF-42
1995	**CLE**	**A**	9	.571	.714	7	4	1	0	0	0.0	4	0	0	0	0	0	0	10	0	0	0	1.3	1.000	OF-6, DH-2
3 yrs.			140	.247	.429	413	102	15	6	16	3.9	79	53	61	111	4	13	4	238	7	6	2	1.9	.976	OF-127, DH-2

Charlie Burns

BURNS, CHARLES BIRMINGHAM
B. May 15, 1879, Bayview, Md. D. June 6, 1968, Havre de Grace, Md.
BR TR 6′ 175 lbs.

Year	Team		Games	BA	SA	AB	H	2B	3B	HR	HR%	R	RBI	BB	SO	SB	Pinch Hit AB	Pinch Hit H	PO	A	E	DP	TC/G	FA	G by Pos
1902	**BAL**	**A**	1	1.000	1.000	1	1	0	0	0	0.0	0	0	0		0	1	1	0	0	0	0	0.0	—	

Dick Burns

BURNS, RICHARD SIMON
B. Dec. 26, 1863, Holyoke, Mass. D. Nov. 16, 1937, Holyoke, Mass.
BB TL 5′ 7″ 140 lbs.

Year	Team		Games	BA	SA	AB	H	2B	3B	HR	HR%	R	RBI	BB	SO	SB	Pinch Hit AB	Pinch Hit H	PO	A	E	DP	TC/G	FA	G by Pos
1883	**DET**	**N**	37	.186	.250	140	26	7	1	0	0.0	11		2	22		0	0	22	32	14	2	1.7	.794	OF-24, P-17
1884	**CIN**	**U**	79	.306	.457	350	107	17	**12**	4	1.1	84		5			0	0	87	81	26	1	2.3	.866	OF-44, P-40, SS-2
1885	**STL**	**N**	14	.222	.296	54	12	2	1	0	0.0	2	4	3	8		0	0	13	5	7	1	1.7	.720	OF-14, P-1
3 yrs.			130	.267	.388	544	145	26	14	4	0.7	97	4	10	30		0	0	122	118	47	4	2.0	.836	OF-82, P-58, SS-2

Ed Burns

BURNS, EDWARD JAMES
B. Oct. 31, 1888, San Francisco, Calif. D. June 1, 1942, Monterey, Calif.
BR TR 5′ 6″ 165 lbs.

Year	Team		Games	BA	SA	AB	H	2B	3B	HR	HR%	R	RBI	BB	SO	SB	Pinch Hit AB	Pinch Hit H	PO	A	E	DP	TC/G	FA	G by Pos
1912	**STL**	**N**	1	.000	.000	1	0	0	0	0	0.0	0	1	0	0	0	0	0	0	0	0	0	0.0	.000	C-1
1913	**PHI**	**N**	17	.200	.300	30	6	3	0	0	0.0	3	3	6	3	2	1	0	38	10	1	2	3.3	.980	C-15
1914			70	.259	.338	139	36	3	4	0	0.0	8	16	20	12	5	14	3	180	72	14	5	4.8	.947	C-55
1915			67	.241	.270	174	42	5	0	0	0.0	11	16	20	12	1	5	2	241	61	6	6	4.6	.981	C-67
1916			78	.233	.279	219	51	8	1	0	0.0	14	14	16	18	3	2	0	285	87	8	5	4.9	.979	C-75, SS-1, OF-1
1917			20	.204	.224	49	10	1	0	0	0.0	2	6	1	5	2	5	0	47	20	2	0	4.6	.971	C-15
1918			68	.207	.223	184	38	1	1	0	0.0	10	9	20	9	1	0	0	184	77	5	3	3.9	.981	C-68
7 yrs.			321	.230	.271	796	183	21	6	0	0.0	48	65	83	59	14	27	5	975	327	36	21	4.5	.973	C-296, SS-1, OF-1
WORLD SERIES																									
1915	**PHI**	**N**	5	.188	.188	16	3	0	0	0	0.0	1	0	1	2	0	0	0	27	9	1	2	7.4	.973	C-5

George Burns

BURNS, GEORGE HENRY (Tioga George)
B. Jan. 31, 1893, Niles, Ohio D. Jan. 7, 1978, Kirkland, Wash.
BR TR 6′ 1½″ 180 lbs.

Year	Team		Games	BA	SA	AB	H	2B	3B	HR	HR%	R	RBI	BB	SO	SB	Pinch Hit AB	Pinch Hit H	PO	A	E	DP	TC/G	FA	G by Pos
1914	**DET**	**A**	137	.291	.389	478	139	22	5	5	1.0	55	57	32	56	23	0	0	1576	79	30	72	12.3	.982	1B-137
1915			105	.253	.352	392	99	18	3	5	1.3	49	50	22	51	9	1	0	1155	57	17	65	11.8	.986	1B-104
1916			135	.286	.382	479	137	22	6	4	0.8	60	73	22	30	12	11	3	1355	54	22	71	11.5	.985	1B-124
1917			119	.226	.317	407	92	14	10	1	0.2	42	40	15	33	3	15	2	1127	57	12	44	11.5	.990	1B-104
1918	**PHI**	**A**	130	.352	.467	505	**178**	22	9	6	1.2	61	70	23	25	8	0	0	1389	104	27	109	11.7	.982	1B-128, OF-2
1919			126	.296	.447	470	139	29	9	8	1.7	63	57	19	18	15	5	0	971	75	24	46	8.9	.978	1B-86, OF-34
1920	**2 teams**		**PHI A** (22G –.233)		**CLE A** (44G –.268)																				
″	**total**		66	.250	.353	116	29	7	1	1	0.9	8	20	10	10	5	39	11	104	12	3	1	4.8	.975	OF-13, 1B-12
1921	**CLE**	**A**	84	.361	.480	244	88	21	4	0	0.0	52	48	13	19	2	10	2	534	41	6	40	8.0	.990	1B-73
1922	**BOS**	**A**	147	.306	.446	558	171	32	5	12	2.2	71	73	20	28	8	6	2	1412	94	20	103	10.9	.987	1B-140
1923			146	.328	.470	551	181	47	5	7	1.3	91	82	45	33	9	0	0	1485	92	16	103	10.9	.990	1B-146
1924	**CLE**	**A**	129	.310	.437	462	143	37	5	4	0.9	64	66	29	27	14	2	0	1227	110	18	85	10.7	.987	1B-127
1925			127	.336	.473	488	164	41	4	6	1.2	69	79	24	24	16	1	1	1195	82	14	94	10.2	.989	1B-126
1926			151	.358	.494	603	**216**	**64**	3	4	0.7	97	114	28	33	13	0	0	1499	99	19	122	10.7	.988	1B-151
1927			140	.319	.435	549	175	51	2	3	0.5	84	78	42	27	13	1	0	1362	102	15	111	10.6	.990	1B-139
1928	**2 teams**		**CLE A** (82G –.249)		**NY A** (4G –.500)																				
″	**total**		86	.254	.390	213	54	12	1	5	2.3	30	30	17	12	2	30	6	477	38	8	44	9.5	.985	1B-55
1929	**2 teams**		**NY A** (9G –.000)		**PHI A** (29G –.265)																				
″	**total**		38	.224	.362	58	13	5	0	1	1.7	5	11	2	7	1	17	0	99	5	0	9	5.5	1.000	1B-19
16 yrs.			1866	.307	.429	6573	2018	444	72	72	1.1	901	948	363	433	153	138	27	16967	1101	251	1119	10.7	.986	1B-1671, OF-49
WORLD SERIES																									
1920	**CLE**	**A**	5	.300	.400	10	3	1	0	0	0.0	1	3	3	3	0	1	1	38	1	1	2	10.0	.975	1B-4
1929	**PHI**	**A**	1	.000	.000	2	0	0	0	0	0.0	0	0	0	1	0	2	0	0	0	0	0	0.0	—	
2 yrs.			6	.250	.333	12	3	1	0	0	0.0	1	3	3	4	0	3	1	38	1	1	2	10.0	.975	1B-4

George Burns

BURNS, GEORGE JOSEPH
B. Nov. 24, 1889, Utica, N. Y. D. Aug. 15, 1966, Gloversville, N. Y.
BR TR 5′ 7″ 160 lbs.

Year	Team		Games	BA	SA	AB	H	2B	3B	HR	HR%	R	RBI	BB	SO	SB	Pinch Hit AB	Pinch Hit H	PO	A	E	DP	TC/G	FA	G by Pos
1911	**NY**	**N**	6	.059	.059	17	1	0	0	0	0.0	2	0	1	0	0	0	0	7	0	0	0	1.2	1.000	OF-6
1912			29	.294	.373	51	15	4	0	0	0.0	11	3	8	8	7	2	1	24	3	0	1	1.2	1.000	OF-23
1913			150	.286	.370	605	173	37	4	2	0.3	81	54	58	**74**	40	0	0	321	22	13	2	2.4	.963	OF-150
1914			154	.303	.417	561	170	35	10	3	0.5	**100**	60	89	53	**62**	0	0	326	19	18	5	2.4	.950	OF-154
1915			155	.272	.375	**622**	169	27	14	3	0.5	83	51	56	57	27	0	0	278	13	12	4	2.0	.960	OF-155
1916			155	.279	.368	**623**	174	24	8	5	0.8	**105**	41	63	47	37	0	0	289	19	12	3	2.1	.963	OF-155
1917			152	.302	.412	597	180	25	13	5	0.8	**103**	45	**75**	55	40	0	0	325	16	9	4	2.3	.974	OF-152
1918			119	.290	.389	465	135	22	6	4	0.9	80	51	43	37	40	0	0	292	10	11	1	2.6	.965	OF-119
1919			139	.303	.404	534	162	30	9	2	0.4	**86**	46	**82**	37	**40**	0	0	290	15	3	4	2.2	.990	OF-139
1920			154	.287	.399	631	181	35	9	6	1.0	**115**	46	**76**	48	22	0	0	336	11	6	5	2.3	.983	OF-154
1921			149	.299	.395	605	181	28	9	4	0.7	111	61	**80**	24	19	0	0	360	17	11	2	2.6	.972	OF-149, 3B-1
1922	**CIN**	**N**	156	.285	.353	631	180	20	10	1	0.2	104	53	78	38	30	0	0	386	20	10	3	2.7	.976	OF-156
1923			154	.274	.375	614	168	27	13	3	0.5	99	45	**101**	46	12	0	0	327	11	14	3	2.3	.960	OF-154
1924			93	.256	.342	336	86	19	2	2	0.6	43	33	29	21	3	3	2	168	13	7	4	2.1	.963	OF-90
1925	**PHI**	**N**	88	.292	.390	349	102	29	1	1	0.3	65	22	33	20	4	0	0	189	9	2	2	2.3	.990	OF-88
15 yrs.			1853	.287	.384	7241	2077	362	108	41	0.6	1188	611	872	565	383	5	3	3918	198	128	43	2.3	.970	OF-1844, 3B-1

George Burns *continued*

Year	Team	Games	BA	SA	AB	H	2B	3B	HR	HR%	R	RBI	BB	SO	SB	Pinch Hit AB	Pinch Hit H	PO	A	E	DP	TC/G	FA	G by Pos
WORLD SERIES																								
1913	NY N	5	.158	.263	19	3	2	0	0	0.0	2	1	1	5	1	0	0	14	0	1	0	3.0	.933	OF-5
1917		6	.227	.227	22	5	0	0	0	0.0	3	2	3	6	1	0	0	10	0	0	0	1.7	1.000	OF-6
1921		8	.333	.515	33	11	4	1	0	0.0	2	2	3	5	1	0	0	9	0	0	0	1.1	1.000	OF-8
3 yrs.		19	.257	.365	74	19	6	1	0	0.0	7	5	7	16	3	0	0	33	0	1	0	1.8	.971	OF-19

Jack Burns

BURNS, JOHN IRVING (Slug) BL TL 5′10½″ 175 lbs.
B. Aug. 31, 1907, Cambridge, Mass. D. Apr. 18, 1975, Brighton, Mass.

Year	Team	Games	BA	SA	AB	H	2B	3B	HR	HR%	R	RBI	BB	SO	SB	Pinch Hit AB	Pinch Hit H	PO	A	E	DP	TC/G	FA	G by Pos
1930	STL A	8	.300	.400	30	9	3	0	0	0.0	5	2	5	5	0	0	0	70	6	0	10	9.5	1.000	1B-8
1931		144	.260	.353	570	148	27	7	4	0.7	75	70	42	58	19	1	0	1346	125	11	131	10.4	.993	1B-143
1932		150	.305	.438	617	188	33	8	11	1.8	111	70	61	43	17	0	0	1399	101	12	130	10.1	.992	1B-150
1933		144	.288	.417	556	160	43	4	7	1.3	89	71	56	51	11	1	0	1336	81	12	129	10.0	.992	1B-143
1934		154	.257	.392	612	157	28	8	13	2.1	86	73	62	47	9	0	0	1365	81	12	132	9.5	.992	1B-154
1935		143	.286	.368	549	157	28	1	5	0.9	77	67	68	49	3	0	0	1239	57	11	115	9.3	.992	1B-141
1936	2 teams	STL A (9G –.214) DET A (138G –.283)																						
″	total	147	.281	.378	572	161	37	3	4	0.7	98	64	82	46	4	6	3	1308	74	8	129	9.9	.994	1B-140
7 yrs.		890	.280	.392	3506	980	199	31	44	1.3	541	417	376	299	63	8	3	8063	525	66	776	9.8	.992	1B-879

Jim Burns

BURNS, JAMES M. 5′ 7″ 168 lbs.
B. Quincy, Ill. Deceased.

Year	Team	Games	BA	SA	AB	H	2B	3B	HR	HR%	R	RBI	BB	SO	SB	Pinch Hit AB	Pinch Hit H	PO	A	E	DP	TC/G	FA	G by Pos
1888	KC AA	15	.303	.303	66	20	0	0	0	0.0	13	4	1		6	0	0	25	4	5	2	2.3	.853	OF-15
1889		134	.304	.408	579	176	23	11	5	0.9	103	97	20	68	56	0	0	323	12	33	4	2.7	.910	OF-134, 3B-1
1891	WAS AA	20	.317	.390	82	26	6	0	0	0.0	15	10	6	10	2	0	0	27	6	11	0	2.1	.750	OF-20, SS-1
3 yrs.		169	.305	.396	727	222	29	11	5	0.7	131	111	27	78	64	0	0	375	22	49	6	2.6	.890	OF-169, SS-1, 3B-1

Joe Burns

BURNS, JOSEPH FRANCIS BL TL 5′11″ 170 lbs.
B. Mar. 26, 1889, Ipswich, Mass. D. July 12, 1987, Beverly, Mass.

Year	Team	Games	BA	SA	AB	H	2B	3B	HR	HR%	R	RBI	BB	SO	SB	Pinch Hit AB	Pinch Hit H	PO	A	E	DP	TC/G	FA	G by Pos
1910	CIN N	1	1.000	1.000	1	1	0	0	0	0.0	0	0	0	0	1	1	1	0	0	0	0	0.0	—	
1913	DET A	4	.385	.385	13	5	0	0	0	0.0	0	1	2	4	0	0	0	7	0	0	0	1.8	1.000	OF-4
2 yrs.		5	.429	.429	14	6	0	0	0	0.0	0	1	2	4	1	1	1	7	0	0	0	1.8	1.000	OF-4

Joe Burns

BURNS, JOSEPH FRANCIS BR TR 6′ 175 lbs.
B. Feb. 25, 1900, Trenton, N. J. D. Jan. 7, 1986, Trenton, N. J.

Year	Team	Games	BA	SA	AB	H	2B	3B	HR	HR%	R	RBI	BB	SO	SB	Pinch Hit AB	Pinch Hit H	PO	A	E	DP	TC/G	FA	G by Pos
1924	CHI A	8	.105	.105	19	2	0	0	0	0.0	1	0	0	2	0	2	0	12	2	1	1	2.5	.933	C-6

Joe Burns

BURNS, JOSEPH JAMES BR TR 5′10½″ 175 lbs.
B. June 17, 1916, Bryn Mawr, Pa. D. June 24, 1974, Bryn Mawr, Pa.

Year	Team	Games	BA	SA	AB	H	2B	3B	HR	HR%	R	RBI	BB	SO	SB	Pinch Hit AB	Pinch Hit H	PO	A	E	DP	TC/G	FA	G by Pos
1943	BOS N	52	.207	.252	135	28	3	0	1	0.7	12	5	8	25	2	10	1	37	66	7	6	2.9	.936	3B-34, OF-4
1944	PHI A	28	.240	.307	75	18	2	0	1	1.3	5	8	4	8	0	2	1	28	37	7	5	2.8	.903	3B-17, 2B-9
1945		31	.256	.289	90	23	1	1	0	0.0	7	3	4	17	0	6	2	32	7	2	1	1.6	.951	OF-19, 3B-5, 1B-1
3 yrs.		111	.230	.277	300	69	6	1	2	0.7	24	16	16	50	2	18	4	97	110	16	12	2.5	.928	3B-56, OF-23, 2B-9, 1B-1

John Burns

BURNS, JOHN JOSEPH BR TR 5′10″ 160 lbs.
B. May 13, 1880, Avoca, Pa. D. June 24, 1957, Waterford, Conn.

Year	Team	Games	BA	SA	AB	H	2B	3B	HR	HR%	R	RBI	BB	SO	SB	Pinch Hit AB	Pinch Hit H	PO	A	E	DP	TC/G	FA	G by Pos
1903	DET A	11	.270	.270	37	10	0	0	0	0.0	2	3	1		0	0	0	19	33	1	5	4.8	.981	2B-11
1904		4	.125	.125	16	2	0	0	0	0.0	3	1	1		1	0	0	11	9	1	1	5.3	.952	2B-4
2 yrs.		15	.226	.226	53	12	0	0	0	0.0	5	4	2		1	0	0	30	42	2	6	4.9	.973	2B-15

Oyster Burns

BURNS, THOMAS P. BR TR 5′ 8″ 183 lbs.
B. Sept. 6, 1864, Philadelphia, Pa. D. Nov. 11, 1928, Brooklyn, N. Y.

Year	Team	Games	BA	SA	AB	H	2B	3B	HR	HR%	R	RBI	BB	SO	SB	Pinch Hit AB	Pinch Hit H	PO	A	E	DP	TC/G	FA	G by Pos
1884	2 teams	WIL U (2G –.143) BAL AA (35G –.298)																						
″	total	37	.290	.536	138	40	2	7	6	4.3	34		8			0	0	51	41	15	2	2.7	.860	OF-24, 2B-10, SS-2, P-2, 3B-1
1885	BAL AA	78	.231	.349	321	74	11	6	5	1.6	47		16			0	0	121	83	27	12	2.8	.883	OF-45, P-15, SS-10, 2B-6, 3B-6, 1B-1
1887		140	.341	.519	551	188	33	**19**	9	1.6	122		63		58	0	0	205	326	101	23	4.4	.840	SS-98, 3B-42, P-3, 2B-1
1888	2 teams	BAL AA (79G –.298) BKN AA (52G –.284)																						
″	total	131	.293	.435	529	155	27	15	6	1.1	94	67	38		44	0	0	226	182	69	16	3.4	.855	OF-70, SS-59, P-5, 2B-4, 3B-2
1889	BKN AA	131	.304	.423	504	153	19	13	5	1.0	105	100	68	26	32	0	0	160	83	24	9	2.0	.910	OF-113, SS-19
1890	BKN N	119	.284	.464	472	134	22	12	13	**2.8**	102	**128**	51	42	21	0	0	142	28	10	5	1.5	.944	OF-116, 3B-3
1891		123	.285	.417	470	134	24	13	4	0.9	75	83	53	30	21	0	0	187	49	30	6	2.1	.887	OF-113, SS-6, 3B-5
1892		141	.315	.454	542	171	27	18	4	0.7	88	96	65	42	33	0	0	183	34	23	6	1.7	.904	OF-129, 3B-7, SS-5
1893		109	.270	.412	415	112	22	8	7	1.7	68	60	36	16	14	0	0	159	20	14	5	1.8	.927	OF-108, SS-1
1894		126	.361	.507	513	185	32	14	5	1.0	107	109	44	18	30	0	0	208	15	12	4	1.9	.949	OF-125
1895	2 teams	BKN N (20G –.184) NY N (33G –.307)																						
″	total	53	.258	.342	190	49	5	4	1	0.5	28	32	22	8	10	1	0	94	9	11	3	2.2	.904	OF-51, 1B-1
11 yrs.		1188	.300	.446	4645	1395	224	129	65	1.4	870	675	464	182	263	1	0	1736	870	336	91	2.4	.886	OF-894, SS-200, 3B-66, P-25, 2B-21, 1B-2

Pat Burns

BURNS, PATRICK
Deceased.

Year	Team	Games	BA	SA	AB	H	2B	3B	HR	HR%	R	RBI	BB	SO	SB	Pinch Hit AB	Pinch Hit H	PO	A	E	DP	TC/G	FA	G by Pos
1884	2 teams	BAL AA (6G –.200) BAL U (1G –.500)																						
″	total	7	.241	.379	29	7	2	1	0	0.0	3		3			0	0	71	1	4	3	10.9	.947	1B-7

Tom Burns

BURNS, THOMAS EVERETT BR TR 5′ 7″ 152 lbs.
B. Mar. 30, 1857, Honesdale, Pa. D. Mar. 19, 1902, Jersey City, N. J.
Manager 1892, 1898–99.

Year	Team	Games	BA	SA	AB	H	2B	3B	HR	HR%	R	RBI	BB	SO	SB	Pinch Hit AB	Pinch Hit H	PO	A	E	DP	TC/G	FA	G by Pos
1880	CHI N	85	.309	.378	333	103	17	3	0	0.0	47	43	12	23		0	0	73	202	46	9	3.5	.857	SS-79, 3B-9, C-2, P-1
1881		84	.278	.389	342	95	20	3	4	1.2	41	42	14	22		0	0	116	263	56	22	5.1	.871	SS-80, 3B-3, 2B-3
1882		84	.248	.346	355	88	23	6	0	0.0	55	48	15	28		0	0	189	258	65	30	6.1	.873	2B-43, SS-41
1883		97	.294	.435	405	119	37	7	2	0.5	69		13	31		0	0	180	317	84	30	5.9	.855	SS-79, 2B-19, OF-1
1884		83	.245	.359	343	84	14	2	7	2.0	54		13	50		0	0	102	259	69	21	5.2	.840	SS-80, 3B-3
1885		111	.272	.411	445	121	23	9	7	1.6	82	70	16	48		0	0	151	370	96	35	5.5	.844	SS-111, 2B-1
1886		112	.276	.382	445	123	18	10	3	0.7	64	65	14	40		0	0	149	247	49	12	4.0	.890	3B-112

Tom Burns *continued*

Year	Team	Games	BA	SA	AB	H	2B	3B	HR	HR%	R	RBI	BB	SO	SB	Pinch Hit AB	Pinch Hit H	PO	A	E	DP	TC/G	FA	G by Pos
1887		115	.264	.380	424	112	20	10	3	0.7	57	60	34	32	32	0	0	184	248	61	25	4.3	.876	3B-107, OF-8
1888		134	.238	.306	483	115	12	6	3	0.6	60	70	26	49	34	0	0	194	273	49	16	3.9	.905	3B-134
1889		136	.242	.339	525	127	27	6	4	0.8	64	66	32	57	18	0	0	225	301	72	30	4.4	.880	3B-136
1890		139	.277	.362	538	149	16	6	6	1.1	86	86	57	45	44	0	0	188	290	54	25	3.8	.898	3B-139
1891		59	.226	.280	243	55	8	1	1	0.4	36	17	21	21	18	0	0	106	118	28	12	4.3	.889	3B-53, SS-4, OF-2
1892	PIT N	12	.205	.205	39	8	0	0	0	0.0	7	4	3	8	1	1	0	11	11	10	0	2.9	.688	3B-8, OF-3
13 yrs.		1251	.264	.364	4920	1299	235	69	40	0.8	722	571	270	454	147	1	0	1868	3157	739	267	4.6	.872	3B-704, SS-474, 2B-66, OF-14, C-2, P-1

Alex Burr

BURR, ALEXANDER THOMSON — BR TR 6′ 3½″ 190 lbs.
B. Nov. 1, 1893, Chicago, Ill. D. Oct. 12, 1918, Cazaux, France.

Year	Team	Games	BA	SA	AB	H	2B	3B	HR	HR%	R	RBI	BB	SO	SB	Pinch Hit AB	Pinch Hit H	PO	A	E	DP	TC/G	FA	G by Pos
1914	NY A	1	—	—	0	0	0	0	0	—	0	0	0	0	0	0	0	0	0	0	0	0.0	.000	OF-1

Buster Burrell

BURRELL, FRANK ANDREW — BR TR 5′10″ 165 lbs.
B. Dec. 22, 1866, Weymouth, Mass. D. May 8, 1962, Weymouth, Mass.

Year	Team	Games	BA	SA	AB	H	2B	3B	HR	HR%	R	RBI	BB	SO	SB	Pinch Hit AB	Pinch Hit H	PO	A	E	DP	TC/G	FA	G by Pos
1891	NY N	15	.094	.094	53	5	0	0	0	0.0	1	1	3	12	2	0	0	67	16	15	1	6.1	.847	C-15, OF-1
1895	BKN N	12	.143	.250	28	4	0	0	1	3.6	7	5	4	3	0	0	0	24	7	6	1	3.1	.838	C-12
1896		62	.301	.383	206	62	11	3	0	0.0	19	23	15	13	1	2	0	176	42	17	3	3.9	.928	C-60
1897		33	.243	.320	103	25	2	0	2	1.9	15	18	10		1	2	1	117	25	13	1	5.0	.916	C-27, 1B-4
4 yrs.		122	.246	.318	390	96	13	3	3	0.8	42	47	32	28	4	4	1	384	90	51	6	4.4	.903	C-114, 1B-4, OF-1

Larry Burright

BURRIGHT, LARRY ALLEN (Possum) — BR TR 5′11″ 170 lbs.
B. July 10, 1937, Roseville, Ill.

Year	Team	Games	BA	SA	AB	H	2B	3B	HR	HR%	R	RBI	BB	SO	SB	Pinch Hit AB	Pinch Hit H	PO	A	E	DP	TC/G	FA	G by Pos
1962	LA N	115	.205	.317	249	51	6	5	4	1.6	35	30	21	67	4	1	0	176	207	15	35	3.6	.962	2B-109, SS-1
1963	NY N	41	.220	.260	100	22	2	1	0	0.0	9	3	8	25	1	2	0	70	111	9	21	5.4	.953	SS-19, 2B-15, 3B-1
1964		3	.000	.000	7	0	0	0	0	0.0	0	0	0	0	0	0	0	10	12	0	3	7.3	1.000	2B-3
3 yrs.		159	.205	.295	356	73	8	6	4	1.1	44	33	29	92	5	3	0	256	330	24	59	4.1	.961	2B-127, SS-20, 3B-1

Paul Burris

BURRIS, PAUL ROBERT — BR TR 6′ 190 lbs.
B. July 21, 1923, Hickory, N. C.

Year	Team	Games	BA	SA	AB	H	2B	3B	HR	HR%	R	RBI	BB	SO	SB	Pinch Hit AB	Pinch Hit H	PO	A	E	DP	TC/G	FA	G by Pos
1948	BOS N	2	.500	.500	4	2	0	0	0	0.0	0	0	0	0	0	0	0	6	1	0	0	3.5	1.000	C-2
1950		10	.174	.217	23	4	1	0	0	0.0	1	3	1	2	0	2	1	39	0	0	0	4.9	1.000	C-8
1952		55	.220	.280	168	37	4	0	2	1.2	14	21	7	19	0	5	1	208	16	0	3	4.5	1.000	C-50
1953	MIL N	2	.000	.000	1	0	0	0	0	0.0	0	0	0	0	0	0	0	1	0	0	0	0.5	1.000	C-2
4 yrs.		69	.219	.276	196	43	5	0	2	1.0	15	24	8	21	0	7	2	254	17	0	3	4.4	1.000	C-62

Jeff Burroughs

BURROUGHS, JEFFREY ALAN — BR TR 6′ 1″ 200 lbs.
B. Mar. 7, 1951, Long Beach, Calif.

Year	Team	Games	BA	SA	AB	H	2B	3B	HR	HR%	R	RBI	BB	SO	SB	Pinch Hit AB	Pinch Hit H	PO	A	E	DP	TC/G	FA	G by Pos
1970	WAS A	6	.167	.167	12	2	0	0	0	0.0	1	1	2	5	0	4	1	5	0	0	0	1.7	1.000	OF-3
1971		59	.232	.365	181	42	9	0	5	2.8	20	25	22	55	1	8	2	82	3	3	0	1.8	.966	OF-50
1972	TEX A	22	.185	.246	65	12	1	0	1	1.5	4	3	5	22	0	5	1	33	2	2	1	1.9	.946	OF-19, 1B-1
1973		151	.279	.487	526	147	17	1	30	5.7	71	85	67	88	0	5	0	320	14	8	3	2.3	.977	OF-148, 1B-3, DH-1
1974		152	.301	.504	554	167	33	2	25	4.5	84	**118**	91	104	2	0	0	242	11	8	6	1.7	.969	OF-150, 1B-2, DH-1
1975		152	.226	.409	585	132	20	0	29	5.0	81	94	79	**155**	4	2	1	249	10	9	2	1.8	.966	OF-148, DH-3
1976		158	.237	.369	604	143	22	2	18	3.0	71	86	69	93	0	0	0	289	12	4	3	1.9	.987	OF-155, DH-3
1977	ATL N	154	.271	.520	579	157	19	1	41	7.1	91	114	86	126	4	0	0	249	9	7	3	1.7	.974	OF-154
1978		153	.301	.529	488	147	30	6	23	4.7	72	77	**117**	92	1	3	1	224	13	6	2	1.7	.975	OF-147
1979		116	.224	.348	397	89	14	1	11	2.8	49	47	73	75	2	5	1	175	8	7	1	1.7	.963	OF-110
1980		99	.263	.453	278	73	14	0	13	4.7	35	51	35	57	1	24	9	129	0	3	0	1.8	.977	OF-73
1981	SEA A	89	.254	.395	319	81	13	1	10	3.1	32	41	41	64	0	1	0	127	4	2	1	1.5	.985	OF-87, DH-1
1982	OAK A	113	.277	.505	285	79	13	2	16	5.6	42	48	45	61	1	33	11	52	0	1	0	0.6	.981	DH-48, OF-34
1983		121	.269	.387	401	108	15	1	10	2.5	43	56	47	79	0	13	5	0	0	0	0	0.0	.000	DH-114
1984		58	.211	.310	71	15	1	0	2	2.8	5	8	18	23	0	33	4	1	0	0	0	0.0	1.000	DH-23, OF-4
1985	TOR A	86	.257	.429	191	49	9	3	6	3.1	19	28	34	36	0	29	3	0	0	0	0	0.0	.000	DH-75
16 yrs.		1689	.261	.439	5536	1443	230	20	240	4.3	720	882	831	1135	16	165	39	2177	86	60	22	1.5	.974	OF-1282, DH-269, 1B-6
LEAGUE CHAMPIONSHIP SERIES																								
1985	TOR A	1	.000	.000	1	0	0	0	0	0.0	0	0	0	0	0	1	0	0	0	0	0	0.0	—	

Dick Burrus

BURRUS, MAURICE LENNON — BL TL 5′11″ 175 lbs.
B. Jan. 29, 1898, Hatteras, N. C. D. Feb. 2, 1972, Elizabeth City, N. C.

Year	Team	Games	BA	SA	AB	H	2B	3B	HR	HR%	R	RBI	BB	SO	SB	Pinch Hit AB	Pinch Hit H	PO	A	E	DP	TC/G	FA	G by Pos
1919	PHI A	70	.258	.314	194	50	3	4	0	0.0	17	8	9	25	2	21	4	347	22	10	17	7.9	.974	1B-38, OF-10
1920		71	.185	.244	135	25	8	0	0	0.0	11	10	5	7	0	37	7	252	16	4	22	8.2	.985	1B-31, OF-2
1925	BOS N	152	.340	.449	588	200	41	4	5	0.9	82	87	51	29	8	1	0	1416	85	15	110	10.0	.990	1B-151
1926		131	.270	.335	486	131	21	1	3	0.6	59	61	37	16	4	3	0	1153	103	12	97	9.8	.991	1B-130
1927		72	.318	.382	220	70	8	3	0	0.0	22	32	17	10	3	10	4	505	44	16	51	9.3	.972	1B-61
1928		64	.270	.380	137	37	6	0	3	2.2	15	13	19	8	1	23	7	286	15	7	29	9.6	.977	1B-32
6 yrs.		560	.291	.373	1760	513	87	12	11	0.6	206	211	138	95	18	95	22	3959	285	64	326	9.5	.985	1B-443, OF-12

Frank Burt

BURT, FRANK J.
B. Camden, N. J. Deceased.

Year	Team	Games	BA	SA	AB	H	2B	3B	HR	HR%	R	RBI	BB	SO	SB	Pinch Hit AB	Pinch Hit H	PO	A	E	DP	TC/G	FA	G by Pos
1882	BAL AA	10	.111	.222	36	4	2	1	0	0.0	2		1			0	0	21	1	5	1	2.7	.815	OF-10

Ellis Burton

BURTON, ELLIS NARRINGTON — BB TR 5′11″ 160 lbs.
B. Aug. 12, 1936, Los Angeles, Calif.

Year	Team	Games	BA	SA	AB	H	2B	3B	HR	HR%	R	RBI	BB	SO	SB	Pinch Hit AB	Pinch Hit H	PO	A	E	DP	TC/G	FA	G by Pos
1958	STL N	8	.233	.500	30	7	0	1	2	6.7	5	4	3	8	0	1	0	12	0	0	0	1.7	1.000	OF-7
1960		29	.214	.250	28	6	1	0	0	0.0	5	2	4	14	0	5	2	8	0	0	0	0.3	1.000	OF-23
1963	2 teams	CLE A (26G –.194) CHI N (93G –.230)																						
"	total	119	.227	.397	353	80	19	1	13	3.7	51	42	40	63	6	9	2	159	7	4	2	1.6	.976	OF-106
1964	CHI N	42	.190	.314	105	20	3	2	2	1.9	12	7	17	22	4	12	2	51	0	1	0	1.8	.981	OF-29
1965		17	.175	.200	40	7	1	0	0	0.0	6	4	1	10	1	8	2	19	1	0	0	1.7	1.000	OF-12
5 yrs.		215	.216	.365	556	120	24	4	17	3.1	79	59	65	117	11	35	8	249	8	5	2	1.5	.981	OF-177

Jim Busby

BUSBY, JAMES FRANKLIN
B. Jan. 8, 1927, Kenedy, Tex.

BR TR 6′ 1″ 175 lbs.

Year	Team	Games	BA	SA	AB	H	2B	3B	HR	HR%	R	RBI	BB	SO	SB	Pinch Hit AB	Pinch Hit H	PO	A	E	DP	TC/G	FA	G by Pos
1950	CHI A	18	.208	.208	48	10	0	0	0	0.0	5	4	1	5	0	0	0	25	2	1	1	2.3	.964	OF-12
1951		143	.283	.354	477	135	15	2	5	1.0	59	68	40	46	26	3	0	360	16	7	4	2.8	.982	OF-139
1952	2 teams	CHI A (16G –.128) WAS A (129G –.244)																						
″	total	145	.236	.305	551	130	24	4	2	0.4	63	47	24	55	5	1	0	472	4	3	0	3.3	.994	OF-144
1953	WAS A	150	.312	.415	586	183	28	7	6	1.0	68	82	38	45	13	0	0	482	15	6	4	3.4	.988	OF-150
1954		155	.298	.389	628	187	22	7	7	1.1	83	80	43	56	17	0	0	491	6	6	1	3.2	.988	OF-155
1955	2 teams	WAS A (47G –.230) CHI A (99G –.243)																						
″	total	146	.239	.337	528	126	19	6	7	1.3	61	41	38	59	12	0	0	375	7	5	3	2.7	.987	OF-146
1956	CLE A	135	.235	.354	494	116	17	3	12	2.4	72	50	43	47	8	5	1	344	3	4	0	2.6	.989	OF-133
1957	2 teams	CLE A (30G –.189) BAL A (86G –.250)																						
″	total	116	.238	.323	362	86	12	2	5	1.4	40	23	24	44	6	8	2	277	9	5	2	2.6	.983	OF-111
1958	BAL A	113	.237	.330	215	51	7	2	3	1.4	32	19	24	37	6	6	1	196	1	1	0	1.9	.995	OF-103, 3B-1
1959	BOS A	61	.225	.333	102	23	8	0	1	1.0	16	5	5	18	0	18	1	49	1	1	0	1.5	.980	OF-34
1960	2 teams	BOS A (1G –.000) BAL A (79G –.258)																						
″	total	80	.258	.314	159	41	7	1	0	0.0	25	12	20	14	2	3	1	133	2	2	1	1.9	.985	OF-72
1961	BAL A	75	.258	.315	89	23	3	1	0	0.0	15	6	8	10	2	4	1	76	2	1	0	1.1	.987	OF-71
1962	HOU N	15	.182	.182	11	2	0	0	0	0.0	2	1	2	3	0	3	1	4	0	0	0	0.4	1.000	OF-10, C-1
13 yrs.		1352	.262	.350	4250	1113	162	35	48	1.1	541	438	310	439	97	51	8	3284	68	42	16	2.6	.988	OF-1280, C-1, 3B-1

Paul Busby

BUSBY, PAUL MILLER (Red)
B. Aug. 25, 1918, Waynesboro, Miss.

BL TR 6′ 1″ 175 lbs.

Year	Team	Games	BA	SA	AB	H	2B	3B	HR	HR%	R	RBI	BB	SO	SB	Pinch Hit AB	Pinch Hit H	PO	A	E	DP	TC/G	FA	G by Pos
1941	PHI N	10	.313	.313	16	5	0	0	0	0.0	3	2	0	1	0	6	1	3	0	0	0	1.0	1.000	OF-3
1943		26	.250	.275	40	10	1	0	0	0.0	13	5	2	1	2	11	3	25	0	0	0	2.5	1.000	OF-10
2 yrs.		36	.268	.286	56	15	1	0	0	0.0	16	7	2	2	2	17	4	28	0	0	0	2.2	1.000	OF-13

Ed Busch

BUSCH, EDGAR JOHN
B. Nov. 16, 1917, Lebanon, Ill. D. Jan. 17, 1987, St. Clair County, Ill.

BR TR 5′10″ 175 lbs.

Year	Team	Games	BA	SA	AB	H	2B	3B	HR	HR%	R	RBI	BB	SO	SB	Pinch Hit AB	Pinch Hit H	PO	A	E	DP	TC/G	FA	G by Pos
1943	PHI A	4	.294	.294	17	5	0	0	0	0.0	2	0	1	2	0	1	0	10	6	1	1	4.3	.941	SS-4
1944		140	.271	.306	484	131	11	3	0	0.0	41	40	29	17	5	1	0	257	393	41	62	4.9	.941	SS-111, 2B-27, 3B-4
1945		126	.250	.288	416	104	10	3	0	0.0	37	35	32	9	2	2	0	221	379	31	70	5.1	.951	SS-116, 3B-5, 2B-2, 1B-1
3 yrs.		270	.262	.298	917	240	21	6	0	0.0	80	75	62	28	7	3	0	488	778	73	133	5.0	.945	SS-231, 2B-29, 3B-9, 1B-1

Mike Busch

BUSCH, MICHAEL ANTHONY
B. July 7, 1968, Davenport, Iowa.

BR TR 6′ 5″ 241 lbs.

Year	Team	Games	BA	SA	AB	H	2B	3B	HR	HR%	R	RBI	BB	SO	SB	Pinch Hit AB	Pinch Hit H	PO	A	E	DP	TC/G	FA	G by Pos
1995	LA N	13	.235	.765	17	4	0	0	3	17.6	3	6	0	7	0	7	2	10	6	1	2	1.4	.941	3B-10, 1B-2

Donie Bush

BUSH, OWEN JOSEPH
B. Oct. 8, 1887, Indianapolis, Ind. D. Mar. 28, 1972, Indianapolis, Ind.
Manager 1923, 1927–31, 1933.

BB TR 5′ 6″ 140 lbs.

Year	Team	Games	BA	SA	AB	H	2B	3B	HR	HR%	R	RBI	BB	SO	SB	Pinch Hit AB	Pinch Hit H	PO	A	E	DP	TC/G	FA	G by Pos
1908	DET A	20	.294	.338	68	20	1	1	0	0.0	13	4	7		2	0	0	42	63	7	9	5.6	.938	SS-20
1909		157	.273	.314	532	145	18	2	0	0.0	114	33	**88**		53	0	0	308	567	71	38	6.0	.925	SS-157
1910		142	.262	.323	496	130	13	4	3	0.6	90	34	**78**		49	0	0	310	489	51	31	6.0	.940	SS-141, 3B-1
1911		150	.232	.287	561	130	18	5	1	0.2	126	36	**98**		40	0	0	372	556	75	42	6.7	.925	SS-150
1912		144	.231	.301	511	118	14	8	2	0.4	107	38	**117**		35	0	0	317	547	66	45	6.5	.929	SS-144
1913		153	.251	.322	593	149	19	10	1	0.2	98	40	80	32	44	0	0	331	510	56	61	5.9	.938	SS-153
1914		157	.252	.295	596	150	18	4	0	0.0	97	32	**112**	54	35	0	0	425	544	58	64	6.5	.944	SS-157
1915		155	.228	.283	561	128	12	8	1	0.2	99	44	118	44	35	0	0	340	504	57	61	5.8	.937	SS-155
1916		145	.225	.267	550	124	5	9	0	0.0	73	34	75	42	19	0	0	278	435	34	41	5.2	.954	SS-144
1917		147	.281	.322	581	163	18	3	0	0.0	**112**	24	80	40	34	0	0	281	423	51	41	5.1	.932	SS-147
1918		128	.234	.266	500	117	10	3	0	0.0	74	22	79	31	9	0	0	280	364	48	29	5.4	.931	SS-128
1919		129	.244	.289	509	124	11	6	0	0.0	82	26	75	36	22	0	0	290	376	40	38	5.5	.943	SS-129
1920		141	.263	.324	506	133	18	5	1	0.2	85	33	73	32	15	1	1	258	421	45	39	5.2	.938	SS-140
1921	2 teams	DET A (104G –.281) WAS A (23G –.214)																						
″	total	127	.270	.305	486	131	7	5	0	0.0	87	29	57	27	10	2	1	251	391	37	46	5.4	.946	SS-102, 2B-23
1922	WAS A	41	.239	.284	134	32	4	1	0	0.0	17	7	21	7	1	3	0	31	81	5	12	3.1	.957	3B-37, 2B-1
1923		10	.409	.409	22	9	0	0	0	0.0	6	0	0	1	0	1	0	5	15	3	0	3.3	.870	3B-6, 2B-1
16 yrs.		1946	.250	.300	7206	1803	186	74	9	0.1	1280	436	1158	346	403	7	2	4119	6286	704	597	5.7	.937	SS-1867, 3B-44, 2B-25
WORLD SERIES																								
1909	DET A	7	.261	.304	23	6	1	0	0	0.0	5	2	5	3	1	0	0	10	18	5	3	4.7	.848	SS-7

Joe Bush

BUSH, LESLIE AMBROSE (Bullet Joe)
B. Nov. 27, 1892, Brainerd, Minn. D. Nov. 1, 1974, Ft. Lauderdale, Fla.

BR TR 5′ 9″ 173 lbs.

Year	Team	Games	BA	SA	AB	H	2B	3B	HR	HR%	R	RBI	BB	SO	SB	Pinch Hit AB	Pinch Hit H	PO	A	E	DP	TC/G	FA	G by Pos
1912	PHI A	1	.500	1.000	4	2	0	1	0	0.0	1	3	0		0	0	0	1	1	1	1	3.0	.667	P-1
1913		39	.157	.229	70	11	3	1	0	0.0	8	1	2	21	0	0	0	15	75	2	4	2.4	.978	P-39
1914		38	.189	.284	74	14	4	0	1	1.4	6	8	2	25	0	0	0	8	55	3	1	1.7	.955	P-38
1915		25	.143	.143	49	7	0	0	0	0.0	2	0	1	22	0	0	0	7	39	3	3	2.0	.939	P-25
1916		41	.140	.180	100	14	4	0	0	0.0	4	6	0	23	0	0	0	19	94	6	8	3.0	.950	P-40
1917		37	.200	.250	80	16	2	1	0	0.0	9	4	5	12	0	0	0	20	61	6	0	2.4	.931	P-37
1918	BOS A	36	.276	.347	98	27	3	2	0	0.0	8	14	6	11	0	0	0	16	81	2	5	2.8	.980	P-36
1919		6	.400	.400	5	2	0	0	0	0.0	1	2	0	1	0	1	0	0	2	0	1	0.7	1.000	P-3
1920		45	.245	.265	102	25	2	0	0	0.0	14	7	9	15	0	5	1	25	66	4	7	2.6	.958	P-35, OF-2
1921		51	.325	.433	120	39	5	4	0	0.0	19	14	3	14	2	8	2	15	64	1	0	2.0	.988	P-37, OF-4
1922	NY A	39	.326	.432	95	31	6	2	0	0.0	15	12	3	11	0	0	0	16	61	0	4	2.0	1.000	P-39
1923		38	.274	.425	113	31	5	3	2	1.8	12	19	3	8	0	1	0	15	74	3	3	2.5	.967	P-37
1924		60	.339	.484	124	42	9	3	1	0.8	13	14	7	6	0	16	8	24	60	1	4	2.2	.988	P-39
1925	STL A	57	.255	.431	102	26	12	0	2	2.0	10	18	6	8	2	21	2	17	54	0	5	2.1	1.000	P-33, OF-1
1926	2 teams	WAS A (17G –.233) PIT N (28G –.265)																						
″	total	45	.253	.342	79	20	4	0	1	1.3	6	10	4	12	0	10	1	9	39	2	3	1.6	.960	P-31, OF-1
1927	2 teams	PIT N (7G –.600) NY N (3G –.500)																						
″	total	10	.556	.556	9	5	0	0	0	0.0	0	2	1	1	0	1	1	0	4	0	0	0.5	1.000	P-8
1928	PHI A	15	.067	.067	15	1	0	0	0	0.0	0	0	1	2	0	1	0	5	10	0	1	1.3	1.000	P-11, OF-1
17 yrs.		583	.253	.345	1239	313	59	17	7	0.6	128	134	53	192	4	64	15	212	840	34	50	2.2	.969	P-489, OF-9

Joe Bush *continued*

Year	Team	Games	BA	SA	AB	H	2B	3B	HR	HR%	R	RBI	BB	SO	SB	Pinch Hit AB	Pinch Hit H	PO	A	E	DP	TC/G	FA	G by Pos
WORLD SERIES																								
1913	PHI A	1	.250	.250	4	1	0	0	0	0.0	0	0	0	1	0	0	0	0	1	0	1	1.0	1.000	P-1
1914		1	.000	.000	5	0	0	0	0	0.0	0	0	0	2	0	0	0	0	5	1	0	6.0	.833	P-1
1918	BOS A	2	.000	.000	2	0	0	0	0	0.0	0	0	1	0	0	0	0	0	3	0	0	1.5	1.000	P-2
1922	NY A	2	.167	.167	6	1	0	0	0	0.0	0	1	0	0	0	0	0	1	3	0	2	2.0	1.000	P-2
1923		4	.429	.571	7	3	1	0	0	0.0	2	1	1	1	0	0	0	2	3	0	0	1.7	1.000	P-3
5 yrs.		10	.208	.250	24	5	1	0	0	0.0	2	2	2	4	0	0	0	3	15	1	3	2.1	.947	P-9

Randy Bush

BUSH, ROBERT RANDALL
B. Oct. 5, 1958, Dover, Del.
BL TL 6′ 1″ 190 lbs.

Year	Team	Games	BA	SA	AB	H	2B	3B	HR	HR%	R	RBI	BB	SO	SB	Pinch Hit AB	Pinch Hit H	PO	A	E	DP	TC/G	FA	G by Pos
1982	MIN A	55	.244	.412	119	29	6	1	4	3.4	13	13	8	28	0	25	3	7	0	0	0	0.2	1.000	DH-26, 1B-6
1983		124	.249	.418	373	93	24	3	11	2.9	43	56	34	51	0	19	4	21	3	0	1	0.2	1.000	DH-103, 1B-3
1984		113	.225	.392	311	70	17	1	11	3.5	46	43	31	60	1	20	8	5	0	0	1	0.1	1.000	DH-89, 1B-2
1985		97	.239	.449	234	56	13	3	10	4.3	26	35	24	30	3	32	4	79	0	2	1	1.2	.975	OF-41, DH-28, 1B-1
1986		130	.269	.420	357	96	19	7	7	2.0	50	45	39	63	5	30	13	182	2	4	2	1.7	.979	OF-102, DH-6, 1B-3
1987		122	.253	.413	293	74	10	2	11	3.8	46	46	43	49	10	30	7	164	5	4	4	1.9	.977	OF-75, 1B-9, DH-9
1988		136	.261	.434	394	103	20	3	14	3.6	51	51	58	49	8	19	6	206	5	4	1	1.6	.981	OF-109, DH-17, 1B-6
1989		141	.263	.435	391	103	17	4	14	3.6	60	54	48	73	5	18	1	339	14	3	14	2.6	.992	OF-109, 1B-25, DH-5
1990		73	.243	.387	181	44	8	0	6	3.3	17	18	21	27	0	12	2	64	3	0	1	1.0	1.000	OF-32, DH-29, 1B-6
1991		93	.303	.485	165	50	10	1	6	3.6	21	23	24	25	0	34	**13**	85	5	2	7	1.5	.978	OF-38, 1B-12, DH-10
1992		100	.214	.302	182	39	8	1	2	1.1	14	22	11	37	1	**48**	9	51	1	0	3	0.9	1.000	OF-24, DH-24, 1B-8
1993		35	.156	.200	45	7	2	0	0	0.0	1	3	7	13	0	19	4	13	0	0	2	1.3	1.000	DH-5, 1B-4, OF-1
12 yrs.		1219	.251	.413	3045	764	154	26	96	3.2	388	409	348	505	33	306	74	1216	38	19	37	1.3	.985	OF-531, DH-351, 1B-85
LEAGUE CHAMPIONSHIP SERIES																								
1987	MIN A	4	.250	.417	12	3	0	1	0	0.0	4	2	3	2	3	0	0	0	0	0	0	0.0	.000	DH-4
WORLD SERIES																								
1987	MIN A	4	.167	.333	6	1	1	0	0	0.0	1	2	0	1	0	3	0	0	0	0	0	0.0	.000	DH-2
1991		3	.250	.250	4	1	0	0	0	0.0	0	0	0	1	0	3	1	0	0	0	0	0.0	.000	OF-2
2 yrs.		7	.200	.300	10	2	1	0	0	0.0	1	2	0	2	0	6	1	0	0	0	0	0.0		OF-2, DH-2

Doc Bushong

BUSHONG, ALBERT JOHN
B. Sept. 15, 1856, Philadelphia, Pa. D. Aug. 19, 1908, Brooklyn, N. Y.
BR TR 5′11″ 165 lbs.

Year	Team	Games	BA	SA	AB	H	2B	3B	HR	HR%	R	RBI	BB	SO	SB	Pinch Hit AB	Pinch Hit H	PO	A	E	DP	TC/G	FA	G by Pos
1876	PHI N	5	.048	.048	21	1	0	0	0	0.0	4	1	0	0		0	0	24	6	9	0	7.8	.769	C-5
1880	WOR N	41	.171	.192	146	25	3	0	0	0.0	13	19	1	16		0	0	261	76	30	6	8.7	.918	C-40, OF-1, 3B-1
1881		76	.233	.287	275	64	7	4	0	0.0	35	21	21	23		0	0	368	124	44	10	7.1	.918	C-76
1882		69	.158	.194	253	40	4	1	1	0.4	20	15	5	17		0	0	308	101	47	8	6.6	.897	C-69
1883	CLE N	63	.172	.195	215	37	5	0	0	0.0	15		7	19		0	0	370	88	46	5	8.0	.909	C-63
1884		62	.236	.276	203	48	6	1	0	0.0	24	10	17	11		0	0	356	98	58	11	8.1	.887	C-62, OF-1
1885	STL AA	85	.267	.343	300	80	13	5	0	0.0	42		11			0	0	429	122	40	10	6.9	.932	C-85, 3B-1
1886		107	.223	.251	386	86	8	0	1	0.3	56		31			0	0	653	134	48	14	7.8	.943	C-106, 1B-1
1887		53	.254	.274	201	51	4	0	0	0.0	35		11		14	0	0	204	93	23	3	5.7	.928	C-52, OF-2, 3B-2
1888	BKN AA	69	.209	.237	253	53	5	1	0	0.0	23	16	5		9	0	0	347	105	42	8	7.2	.915	C-69
1889		25	.155	.167	84	13	1	0	0	0.0	15	8	9	7	2	0	0	85	41	15	5	5.6	.894	C-25
1890	BKN N	16	.236	.273	55	13	2	0	0	0.0	5	7	6	4	2	0	0	82	13	9	1	6.5	.913	C-15, OF-1
12 yrs.		671	.214	.250	2392	511	58	12	2	0.1	287	97	124	97	27	0	0	3487	1001	411	81	7.2	.916	C-667, OF-5, 3B-4, 1B-1

Joe Buskey

BUSKEY, JOSEPH HENRY (Jazzbow)
B. Dec. 18, 1902, Cumberland, Md. D. Apr. 11, 1949, Cumberland, Md.
BR TR 5′10″ 175 lbs.

Year	Team	Games	BA	SA	AB	H	2B	3B	HR	HR%	R	RBI	BB	SO	SB	Pinch Hit AB	Pinch Hit H	PO	A	E	DP	TC/G	FA	G by Pos
1926	PHI N	5	.000	.000	8	0	0	0	0	0.0	1	0	1	1	0	0	0	8	9	4	1	4.2	.810	SS-5

Mike Buskey

BUSKEY, MICHAEL THOMAS
B. Jan. 13, 1949, San Francisco, Calif.
BR TR 5′11″ 160 lbs.

Year	Team	Games	BA	SA	AB	H	2B	3B	HR	HR%	R	RBI	BB	SO	SB	Pinch Hit AB	Pinch Hit H	PO	A	E	DP	TC/G	FA	G by Pos
1977	PHI N	6	.286	.571	7	2	0	1	0	0.0	1	1	0	1	0	0	0	7	8	2	3	2.8	.882	SS-6

Ray Busse

BUSSE, RAYMOND EDWARD
B. Sept. 25, 1948, Daytona Beach, Fla.
BR TR 6′ 4″ 175 lbs.

Year	Team	Games	BA	SA	AB	H	2B	3B	HR	HR%	R	RBI	BB	SO	SB	Pinch Hit AB	Pinch Hit H	PO	A	E	DP	TC/G	FA	G by Pos
1971	HOU N	10	.147	.235	34	5	3	0	0	0.0	2	4	2	9	0	2	0	7	15	2	0	3.0	.917	SS-5, 3B-3
1973	2 teams	STL N (24G –.143) HOU N (15G –.059)																						
″	total	39	.126	.287	87	11	4	2	2	2.3	7	5	6	33	0	6	0	35	75	11	18	3.9	.909	SS-28, 3B-3
1974	HOU N	19	.206	.235	34	7	1	0	0	0.0	3	0	3	12	0	11	1	2	17	3	1	2.8	.864	3B-8
3 yrs.		68	.148	.265	155	23	8	2	2	1.3	12	9	11	54	0	19	1	44	107	16	19	3.6	.904	SS-33, 3B-14

Hank Butcher

BUTCHER, HENRY JOSEPH
B. July 12, 1886, Chicago, Ill. D. Dec. 28, 1979, Hazel Crest, Ill.
BR TR 5′10″ 180 lbs.

Year	Team	Games	BA	SA	AB	H	2B	3B	HR	HR%	R	RBI	BB	SO	SB	Pinch Hit AB	Pinch Hit H	PO	A	E	DP	TC/G	FA	G by Pos
1911	CLE A	38	.241	.361	133	32	7	3	1	0.8	21	11	11		9	4	1	57	5	1	2	1.9	.984	OF-34
1912		24	.195	.305	82	16	4	1	1	1.2	9	10	6		1	4	0	43	3	4	1	2.5	.920	OF-20
2 yrs.		62	.223	.340	215	48	11	4	2	0.9	30	21	17		10	8	1	100	8	5	3	2.1	.956	OF-54

Sal Butera

BUTERA, SALVATORE PHILIP
B. Sept. 25, 1952, Richmond Hill, N. Y.
BR TR 6′ 190 lbs.

Year	Team	Games	BA	SA	AB	H	2B	3B	HR	HR%	R	RBI	BB	SO	SB	Pinch Hit AB	Pinch Hit H	PO	A	E	DP	TC/G	FA	G by Pos
1980	MIN A	34	.271	.282	85	23	1	0	0	0.0	4	2	3	6	0	2	0	106	9	6	0	3.6	.950	C-32, DH-2
1981		62	.240	.293	167	40	7	1	0	0.0	13	18	22	14	0	1	0	256	41	9	0	5.0	.971	C-59, 1B-1, DH-1
1982		54	.254	.270	126	32	2	0	0	0.0	9	8	17	12	0	1	0	230	26	3	5	4.9	.988	C-53
1983	DET A	4	.200	.200	5	1	0	0	0	0.0	1	0	0	0	0	0	0	12	1	1	0	3.5	.929	C-4
1984	MON N	3	.000	.000	3	0	0	0	0	0.0	0	0	1	0	0	0	0	9	0	0	0	4.5	1.000	C-2
1985		67	.200	.283	120	24	1	0	3	2.5	11	12	13	12	0	0	0	227	20	4	5	3.7	.984	C-66, P-1
1986	CIN N	56	.239	.363	113	27	6	1	2	1.8	14	16	21	10	0	2	0	215	17	5	2	4.4	.979	C-53, P-1
1987	2 teams	CIN N (5G –.182) MIN A (51G –.171)																						
″	total	56	.172	.262	122	21	5	0	2	1.6	8	14	8	22	0	0	0	232	25	6	3	4.7	.977	C-56
1988	TOR A	23	.233	.350	60	14	2	1	1	1.7	3	6	1	9	0	1	0	97	10	1	1	4.7	.991	C-23
9 yrs.		359	.227	.295	801	182	24	3	8	1.0	63	76	86	85	0	7	0	1384	149	35	16	4.4	.978	C-348, DH-3, P-2, 1B-1

Sal Butera *continued*

Year	Team	Games	BA	SA	AB	H	2B	3B	HR	HR%	R	RBI	BB	SO	SB	Pinch Hit AB	Pinch Hit H	PO	A	E	DP	TC/G	FA	G by Pos
LEAGUE CHAMPIONSHIP SERIES																								
1987	MIN A	1	.667	.667	3	2	0	0	0	0.0	0	0	0	0	0	0	0	6	0	0	0	6.0	1.000	C-1
WORLD SERIES																								
1987	MIN A	1	—	—	0	0	0	0	0	—	0	0	0	0	0	0	0	0	0	0	0	0.0	.000	C-1

Ed Butka

BUTKA, EDWARD LUKE (Babe)
B. Jan. 7, 1916, Canonsburg, Pa.
BR TR 6′ 3″ 193 lbs.

Year	Team	Games	BA	SA	AB	H	2B	3B	HR	HR%	R	RBI	BB	SO	SB	Pinch Hit AB	Pinch Hit H	PO	A	E	DP	TC/G	FA	G by Pos
1943	WAS A	3	.333	.444	9	3	1	0	0	0.0	0	1	0	3	0	1	1	17	3	0	1	6.7	1.000	1B-3
1944		15	.195	.220	41	8	1	0	0	0.0	1	1	2	11	0	1	0	98	7	3	8	7.7	.972	1B-14
2 yrs.		18	.220	.260	50	11	2	0	0	0.0	1	2	2	14	0	2	1	115	10	3	9	7.5	.977	1B-17

Art Butler

BUTLER, ARTHUR EDWARD
Born Arthur Edward Bouthillier.
B. Dec. 19, 1887, Fall River, Mass. D. Oct. 7, 1984, Fall River, Mass.
BR TR 5′ 9″ 160 lbs.

Year	Team	Games	BA	SA	AB	H	2B	3B	HR	HR%	R	RBI	BB	SO	SB	Pinch Hit AB	Pinch Hit H	PO	A	E	DP	TC/G	FA	G by Pos
1911	BOS N	27	.176	.206	68	12	2	0	0	0.0	11	2	6	6	0	7	1	19	32	7	1	3.1	.879	3B-14, 2B-4, SS-1
1912	PIT N	43	.273	.344	154	42	4	2	1	0.6	19	17	15	11	2	0	0	71	99	7	12	4.1	.960	2B-43
1913		82	.280	.350	214	60	9	3	0	0.0	40	20	32	14	9	18	6	127	144	26	14	5.4	.912	2B-27, SS-24, OF-2, 3B-2
1914	STL N	86	.201	.277	274	55	12	3	1	0.4	29	24	39	23	14	2	0	155	228	30	24	4.9	.927	SS-84, OF-1
1915		130	.254	.307	469	119	12	5	1	0.2	73	31	47	34	26	2	0	235	351	53	43	4.9	.917	SS-130
1916		86	.209	.255	110	23	5	0	0	0.0	9	7	7	12	3	**54**	**13**	23	10	3	3	1.4	.917	OF-15, 2B-8, 3B-1, SS-1
6 yrs.		454	.241	.303	1289	311	44	13	3	0.2	181	101	146	100	54	83	20	630	864	126	97	4.5	.922	SS-240, 2B-82, OF-18, 3B-17

Bill Butler

BUTLER, WILLIAM J.
B. 1861, New Orleans, La. Deceased.

Year	Team	Games	BA	SA	AB	H	2B	3B	HR	HR%	R	RBI	BB	SO	SB	Pinch Hit AB	Pinch Hit H	PO	A	E	DP	TC/G	FA	G by Pos
1884	IND AA	9	.226	.452	31	7	3	2	0	0.0	7		1			0	0	5	2	3	0	1.1	.700	OF-9

Brett Butler

BUTLER, BRETT MORGAN
B. June 15, 1957, Los Angeles, Calif.
BL TL 5′10″ 160 lbs.

Year	Team	Games	BA	SA	AB	H	2B	3B	HR	HR%	R	RBI	BB	SO	SB	Pinch Hit AB	Pinch Hit H	PO	A	E	DP	TC/G	FA	G by Pos
1981	ATL N	40	.254	.317	126	32	2	3	0	0.0	17	4	19	17	9	2	1	76	2	1	0	2.1	.987	OF-37
1982		89	.217	.225	240	52	2	0	0	0.0	35	7	25	35	21	6	1	129	2	0	0	1.7	1.000	OF-77
1983		151	.281	.393	549	154	21	**13**	5	0.9	84	37	54	56	39	6	1	284	13	4	4	2.1	.987	OF-143
1984	CLE A	159	.269	.355	602	162	25	9	3	0.5	108	49	86	62	52	3	0	448	13	4	3	3.0	.991	OF-156
1985		152	.311	.431	591	184	28	14	5	0.8	106	50	63	42	47	1	0	437	19	1	5	3.0	.998	OF-150, DH-1
1986		161	.278	.375	587	163	17	**14**	4	0.7	92	51	70	65	32	1	0	434	9	3	3	2.8	.993	OF-159
1987		137	.295	.425	522	154	25	8	9	1.7	91	41	91	55	33	0	0	393	4	4	2	2.9	.990	OF-136
1988	SF N	157	.287	.398	568	163	27	9	6	1.1	**109**	43	97	64	43	2	0	395	3	5	1	2.6	.988	OF-155
1989		154	.283	.354	594	168	22	4	4	0.7	100	36	59	69	31	0	0	407	11	6	3	2.8	.986	OF-152
1990		160	.309	.384	622	**192**	20	9	3	0.5	108	44	90	62	51	1	0	420	4	6	0	2.7	.986	OF-159
1991	LA N	161	.296	.343	615	182	13	5	2	0.3	**112**	38	**108**	79	38	1	0	372	8	0	3	2.4	1.000	OF-161
1992		157	.309	.391	553	171	14	11	3	0.5	86	39	95	67	41	3	1	353	9	2	3	2.3	.995	OF-155
1993		156	.298	.371	607	181	21	10	1	0.2	80	42	86	69	39	1	0	369	6	0	0	2.4	1.000	OF-155
1994		111	.314	.446	417	131	13	**9**	8	1.9	79	33	68	52	27	0	0	260	8	2	1	2.4	.993	OF-111
1995	2 teams	NY N (90G –.311) LA N (39G –.274)																						
″	total	129	.300	.376	513	154	18	**9**	1	0.2	78	38	67	51	32	1	1	282	6	2	1	2.2	.993	OF-129
15 yrs.		2074	.291	.380	7706	2243	268	127	54	0.7	1285	552	1078	845	535	28	5	5059	117	40	29	2.6	.992	OF-2035, DH-1
DIVISIONAL PLAYOFF SERIES																								
1995	LA N	3	.267	.267	15	4	0	0	0	0.0	1	1	0	3	0	0	0	7	0	0	0	2.3	1.000	OF-3
LEAGUE CHAMPIONSHIP SERIES																								
1982	ATL N	2	.000	.000	1	0	0	0	0	0.0	0	0	0	0	0	1	0	0	0	0	0	0.0	.000	OF-1
1989	SF N	5	.211	.211	19	4	0	0	0	0.0	6	0	3	3	0	0	0	9	0	0	0	1.8	1.000	OF-5
2 yrs.		7	.200	.200	20	4	0	0	0	0.0	6	0	3	3	0	1	0	9	0	0	0	1.5	1.000	OF-6
WORLD SERIES																								
1989	SF N	4	.286	.357	14	4	1	0	0	0.0	1	1	2	1	2	0	0	9	0	0	0	2.3	1.000	OF-4

Dick Butler

BUTLER, RICHARD H.
B. Brooklyn, N. Y. Deceased.

Year	Team	Games	BA	SA	AB	H	2B	3B	HR	HR%	R	RBI	BB	SO	SB	Pinch Hit AB	Pinch Hit H	PO	A	E	DP	TC/G	FA	G by Pos
1897	LOU N	10	.184	.184	38	7	0	0	0	0.0	3	2	0		1	0	0	25	11	8	0	4.4	.818	C-10
1899	WAS N	12	.278	.333	36	10	0	1	0	0.0	4	1	2		1	1	0	19	14	4	0	3.4	.892	C-11
2 yrs.		22	.230	.257	74	17	0	1	0	0.0	7	3	2		2	1	0	44	25	12	0	3.9	.852	C-21

Frank Butler

BUTLER, FRANK DEAN (Stuffy)
B. July 18, 1860, Savannah, Ga. D. July 18, 1945, Jacksonville, Fla.
BL TL

Year	Team	Games	BA	SA	AB	H	2B	3B	HR	HR%	R	RBI	BB	SO	SB	Pinch Hit AB	Pinch Hit H	PO	A	E	DP	TC/G	FA	G by Pos
1895	NY N	5	.273	.318	22	6	1	0	0	0.0	5	2	1	1	0	0	0	9	0	0	0	1.8	1.000	OF-5

Frank Butler

BUTLER, FRANK EDWARD (Kid)
B. May 1861, Boston, Mass. D. Apr. 9, 1921, South Boston, Mass.
5′ 6″ 140 lbs.

Year	Team	Games	BA	SA	AB	H	2B	3B	HR	HR%	R	RBI	BB	SO	SB	Pinch Hit AB	Pinch Hit H	PO	A	E	DP	TC/G	FA	G by Pos
1884	BOS U	71	.169	.227	255	43	15	0	0	0.0	36		12			0	0	99	45	29	1	2.4	.832	OF-53, 2B-12, SS-6, 3B-2

John Butler

BUTLER, JOHN ALBERT
Played as Fred King in 1901.
B. July 26, 1879, Boston, Mass. D. Feb. 2, 1950, Boston, Mass.
BR TR 5′ 7″ 170 lbs.

Year	Team	Games	BA	SA	AB	H	2B	3B	HR	HR%	R	RBI	BB	SO	SB	Pinch Hit AB	Pinch Hit H	PO	A	E	DP	TC/G	FA	G by Pos
1901	MIL A	1	.000	.000	3	0	0	0	0	0.0	0	0	0		0	0	0	2	0	0	0	2.0	1.000	C-1
1904	STL N	12	.162	.189	37	6	1	0	0	0.0	0	1	4		0	0	0	49	11	2	2	5.2	.968	C-12
1906	BKN N	1	—	—	0	0	0	0	0	—	0	0	0		0	0	0	1	1	0	0	2.0	1.000	C-1
1907		30	.127	.139	79	10	1	0	0	0.0	6	2	9		0	1	0	106	34	8	4	5.1	.946	C-28, OF-1
4 yrs.		44	.134	.151	119	16	2	0	0	0.0	6	3	13		0	1	0	158	46	10	6	5.0	.953	C-42, OF-1

Johnny Butler

BUTLER, JOHN STEPHEN (Trolley Line)
B. Mar. 20, 1893, Fall River, Kans. D. Apr. 29, 1967, Seal Beach, Calif.
BR TR 6′ 175 lbs.

Year	Team	Games	BA	SA	AB	H	2B	3B	HR	HR%	R	RBI	BB	SO	SB	Pinch Hit AB	Pinch Hit H	PO	A	E	DP	TC/G	FA	G by Pos
1926	BKN N	147	.269	.349	501	135	27	5	1	0.2	54	68	54	44	6	0	0	298	407	34	48	4.9	.954	SS-102, 3B-42, 2B-8
1927		149	.238	.298	521	124	13	6	2	0.4	39	57	34	33	9	1	0	279	356	27	56	4.4	.959	SS-90, 3B-60

Johnny Butler *continued*

Year	Team	Games	BA	SA	AB	H	2B	3B	HR	HR%	R	RBI	BB	SO	SB	Pinch Hit AB	Pinch Hit H	PO	A	E	DP	TC/G	FA	G by Pos
1928	CHI N	62	.270	.310	174	47	7	0	0	0.0	17	16	19	7	2	1	0	53	124	10	10	3.1	.947	3B-59, SS-2
1929	STL N	17	.164	.218	55	9	1	1	0	0.0	5	5	4	5	0	0	0	30	33	2	2	3.8	.969	3B-9, SS-8
4 yrs.		375	.252	.317	1251	315	48	12	3	0.2	115	146	111	89	17	2	0	660	920	73	116	4.3	.956	SS-202, 3B-170, 2B-8

Kid Butler

BUTLER, WILLIS EVERETT
B. Aug. 9, 1887, Franklin, Pa. D. Feb. 22, 1964, Richmond, Calif.
BR TR 5′11″ 155 lbs.

Year	Team	Games	BA	SA	AB	H	2B	3B	HR	HR%	R	RBI	BB	SO	SB	Pinch Hit AB	Pinch Hit H	PO	A	E	DP	TC/G	FA	G by Pos
1907	STL A	20	.220	.254	59	13	2	0	0	0.0	4	6	2		1	3	0	18	43	3	3	3.8	.953	2B-11, 3B-5, SS-1

Rob Butler

BUTLER, ROBERT FRANK JOHN
B. Apr. 10, 1970, East York, Ont., Canada.
BL TL 5′11″ 185 lbs.

Year	Team	Games	BA	SA	AB	H	2B	3B	HR	HR%	R	RBI	BB	SO	SB	Pinch Hit AB	Pinch Hit H	PO	A	E	DP	TC/G	FA	G by Pos
1993	TOR A	17	.271	.354	48	13	4	0	0	0.0	8	2	7	12	2	1	0	32	0	1	0	2.1	.970	OF-16
1994		41	.176	.203	74	13	0	1	0	0.0	13	5	7	8	0	4	0	43	0	1	0	1.4	.977	OF-31, DH-1
2 yrs.		58	.213	.262	122	26	4	1	0	0.0	21	7	14	20	2	5	0	75	0	2	0	1.6	.974	OF-47, DH-1
WORLD SERIES																								
1993	TOR A	2	.500	.500	2	1	0	0	0	0.0	1	0	0	0	0	2	1	0	0	0	0	0.0	—	

Joe Buzas

BUZAS, JOSEPH JOHN
B. Oct. 2, 1919, Alpha, N. J.
BR TR 6′ 1″ 180 lbs.

Year	Team	Games	BA	SA	AB	H	2B	3B	HR	HR%	R	RBI	BB	SO	SB	Pinch Hit AB	Pinch Hit H	PO	A	E	DP	TC/G	FA	G by Pos
1945	NY A	30	.262	.323	65	17	2	1	0	0.0	8	6	2	5	2	16	3	17	36	6	6	4.9	.898	SS-12

Bill Byers

BYERS, JAMES WILLIAM (Big Bill)
B. Oct. 3, 1877, Bridgetown, Ind. D. Sept. 8, 1948, Baltimore, Md.
BR TR 5′ 7″

Year	Team	Games	BA	SA	AB	H	2B	3B	HR	HR%	R	RBI	BB	SO	SB	Pinch Hit AB	Pinch Hit H	PO	A	E	DP	TC/G	FA	G by Pos
1904	STL N	19	.217	.217	60	13	0	0	0	0.0	3	4	1		0	2	1	90	15	4	1	6.4	.963	C-16, 1B-1

Burley Byers

BYERS, BURLEY
Born Christopher A. Bayer.
B. Dec. 19, 1875, Louisville, Ky. D. May 30, 1933, Louisville, Ky.
175 lbs.

Year	Team	Games	BA	SA	AB	H	2B	3B	HR	HR%	R	RBI	BB	SO	SB	Pinch Hit AB	Pinch Hit H	PO	A	E	DP	TC/G	FA	G by Pos
1899	LOU N	1	.000	.000	3	0	0	0	0	0.0	0	0	0		0	0	0	2	1	2	0	5.0	.600	SS-1

Randell Byers

BYERS, RANDELL PARKER
B. Oct. 2, 1964, Bridgeton, N. J.
BL TR 6′ 2″ 180 lbs.

Year	Team	Games	BA	SA	AB	H	2B	3B	HR	HR%	R	RBI	BB	SO	SB	Pinch Hit AB	Pinch Hit H	PO	A	E	DP	TC/G	FA	G by Pos
1987	SD N	10	.313	.375	16	5	1	0	0	0.0	1	1	1	5	1	3	0	6	1	0	0	1.4	1.000	OF-5
1988		11	.200	.300	10	2	1	0	0	0.0	0	0	0	5	0	10	2	0	0	0	0	0.0	.000	OF-2
2 yrs.		21	.269	.346	26	7	2	0	0	0.0	1	1	1	10	1	13	2	6	1	0	0	1.0	1.000	OF-7

Jim Byrd

BYRD, JAMES EDWARD
B. Oct. 3, 1968, WeWahitchka, Fla.
BR TR 6′ 1″ 185 lbs.

Year	Team	Games	BA	SA	AB	H	2B	3B	HR	HR%	R	RBI	BB	SO	SB	Pinch Hit AB	Pinch Hit H	PO	A	E	DP	TC/G	FA	G by Pos
1993	BOS A	2	—	—	0	0	0	0	0	—	0	0	0	0	0	0	0	0	0	0	0	0.0	.000	DH-1

Sammy Byrd

BYRD, SAMUEL DEWEY (Babe Ruth's Legs)
B. Oct. 15, 1907, Bremen, Ga. D. May 11, 1981, Mesa, Ariz.
BR TR 5′10½″ 175 lbs.

Year	Team	Games	BA	SA	AB	H	2B	3B	HR	HR%	R	RBI	BB	SO	SB	Pinch Hit AB	Pinch Hit H	PO	A	E	DP	TC/G	FA	G by Pos
1929	NY A	62	.312	.471	170	53	12	0	5	2.9	32	28	28	18	1	8	0	108	6	6	2	2.2	.950	OF-54
1930		92	.284	.440	218	62	12	2	6	2.8	46	31	30	18	5	4	2	119	2	1	0	1.4	.992	OF-85
1931		115	.270	.395	248	67	18	2	3	1.2	51	32	29	26	5	25	5	148	3	4	1	1.8	.974	OF-88
1932		104	.297	.478	209	62	12	1	8	3.8	49	30	30	20	1	9	4	129	4	5	1	1.5	.964	OF-90
1933		85	.280	.411	107	30	6	1	2	1.9	26	11	15	12	0	9	2	75	1	1	0	1.1	.987	OF-71
1934		106	.246	.335	191	47	8	0	3	1.6	32	23	18	22	1	1	0	156	2	2	1	1.5	.988	OF-104
1935	CIN N	121	.262	.406	416	109	25	4	9	2.2	51	52	37	51	4	6	4	284	10	9	1	2.6	.970	OF-115
1936		59	.248	.348	141	35	8	0	2	1.4	17	13	11	11	0	19	4	86	1	1	1	2.4	.989	OF-37
8 yrs.		744	.274	.412	1700	465	101	10	38	2.2	304	220	198	178	17	81	21	1105	29	29	7	1.8	.975	OF-644
WORLD SERIES																								
1932	NY A	1	—	—	0	0	0	0	0	—	0	0	0	0	0	0	0	0	0	0	0	0.0	.000	OF-1

Bobby Byrne

BYRNE, ROBERT MATTHEW
B. Dec. 31, 1884, St. Louis, Mo. D. Dec. 31, 1964, Wayne, Pa.
BR TR 5′ 7½″ 145 lbs.

Year	Team	Games	BA	SA	AB	H	2B	3B	HR	HR%	R	RBI	BB	SO	SB	Pinch Hit AB	Pinch Hit H	PO	A	E	DP	TC/G	FA	G by Pos
1907	STL N	148	.256	.294	558	143	11	5	0	0.0	55	29	35		21	0	0	215	353	50	24	4.1	.919	3B-148, SS-1
1908		127	.191	.212	439	84	7	1	0	0.0	27	14	23		16	1	0	187	258	40	15	3.8	.918	3B-122, SS-4
1909	2 teams	STL N (105G –.214) PIT N (46G –.256)																						
″	total	151	.226	.290	589	133	19	8	1	0.2	92	40	78		29	0	0	214	359	37	14	4.0	.939	3B-151
1910	PIT N	148	.296	.417	602	**178**	**43**	12	2	0.3	101	52	66	27	36	0	0	167	289	35	11	3.3	.929	3B-148
1911		153	.259	.366	598	155	24	17	2	0.3	96	52	67	41	23	1	0	181	282	35	21	3.3	.930	3B-152
1912		130	.288	.405	528	152	31	11	3	0.6	99	35	54	40	20	0	0	144	187	18	14	2.7	.948	3B-130
1913	2 teams	PIT N (113G –.270) PHI N (19G –.224)																						
″	total	132	.265	.322	506	134	23	0	2	0.4	63	51	34	31	12	5	1	174	208	23	14	3.2	.943	3B-125
1914	PHI N	126	.272	.302	467	127	12	1	0	0.0	61	26	45	44	9	4	2	222	349	43	23	5.0	.930	2B-101, 3B-22
1915		105	.209	.245	387	81	6	4	0	0.0	50	21	39	28	4	0	0	98	183	9	9	2.8	.969	3B-105
1916		48	.234	.319	141	33	10	1	0	0.0	22	9	14	7	6	6	1	46	79	9	8	3.3	.933	3B-40
1917	2 teams	PHI N (13G –.357) CHI A (1G –.000)																						
″	total	14	.333	.333	15	5	0	0	0	0.0	1	0	1	2	0	9	2	2	2	0	0	0.8	1.000	3B-4, 2B-1
11 yrs.		1282	.254	.323	4830	1225	186	60	10	0.2	667	329	456	220	176	26	6	1650	2549	299	153	3.6	.934	3B-1147, 2B-102, SS-5
WORLD SERIES																								
1909	PIT N	7	.250	.292	24	6	1	0	0	0.0	5	0	1	4	1	0	0	11	17	1	1	4.1	.966	3B-7
1915	PHI N	1	.000	.000	1	0	0	0	0	0.0	0	0	0	0	0	1	0	0	0	0	0	0.0	—	
2 yrs.		8	.240	.280	25	6	1	0	0	0.0	5	0	1	4	1	1	0	11	17	1	1	4.1	.966	3B-7

Tommy Byrne

BYRNE, THOMAS JOSEPH
B. Dec. 31, 1919, Baltimore, Md.
BL TL 6′ 1″ 182 lbs.

Year	Team	Games	BA	SA	AB	H	2B	3B	HR	HR%	R	RBI	BB	SO	SB	Pinch Hit AB	Pinch Hit H	PO	A	E	DP	TC/G	FA	G by Pos
1943	NY A	13	.091	.091	11	1	0	0	0	0.0	0	0	2	3	0	1	0	2	8	1	0	1.0	.909	P-11
1946		14	.222	.222	9	2	0	0	0	0.0	2	0	1	0	0	6	1	1	2	0	0	0.8	1.000	P-4
1947		4	—	—	0	0	0	0	0	—	0	0	1	0	0	0	0	0	1	0	0	0.3	1.000	P-4
1948		31	.326	.500	46	15	3	1	1	2.2	8	7	1	7	0	0	0	2	17	0	2	0.6	1.000	P-31
1949		35	.193	.289	83	16	4	2	0	0.0	8	13	2	20	0	1	0	7	19	3	4	0.9	.897	P-32

Tommy Byrne *continued*

Year	Team	Games	BA	SA	AB	H	2B	3B	HR	HR%	R	RBI	BB	SO	SB	Pinch Hit AB	Pinch Hit H	PO	A	E	DP	TC/G	FA	G by Pos
1950		34	.272	.407	81	22	3	1	2	2.5	14	16	4	15	1	1	0	9	23	0	2	1.0	1.000	P-31
1951	**2 teams**	**NY A** (9G –.222)	**STL A** (34G –.281)																					
"	**total**	43	.273	.409	66	18	3	0	2	3.0	9	15	4	10	0	13	2	6	20	1	2	1.0	.963	P-28
1952	**STL A**	40	.250	.369	84	21	5	1	1	1.2	9	12	5	18	0	9	0	10	15	2	1	0.9	.926	P-29
1953	**2 teams**	**CHI A** (18G –.167)	**WAS A** (14G –.059)																					
"	**total**	32	.114	.200	35	4	0	0	1	2.9	2	5	5	13	0	18	1	4	11	2	0	1.4	.882	P-12
1954	**NY A**	7	.368	.684	19	7	4	1	0	0.0	2	6	0	3	0	2	0	0	8	1	1	1.8	.889	P-5
1955		45	.205	.282	78	16	1	1	1	1.3	6	6	8	15	0	14	0	4	22	2	3	1.0	.929	P-27
1956		44	.269	.500	52	14	1	1	3	5.8	8	10	2	11	0	8	0	8	18	1	4	0.7	.963	P-37
1957		35	.189	.486	37	7	2	0	3	8.1	5	8	3	11	0	7	2	6	9	1	0	0.5	.938	P-30
13 yrs.		377	.238	.378	601	143	26	8	14	2.3	73	98	38	126	1	80	6	59	173	14	19	0.9	.943	P-281
WORLD SERIES																								
1949	**NY A**	1	1.000	1.000	1	1	0	0	0	0.0	0	0	0	0	0	0	0	0	0	0	0	0.0	.000	P-1
1955		3	.167	.167	6	1	0	0	0	0.0	0	2	0	2	0	1	0	0	2	0	0	1.0	1.000	P-2
1956		2	.000	.000	1	0	0	0	0	0.0	0	0	0	0	0	1	0	0	0	0	0	0.0	.000	P-1
1957		2	.500	.500	2	1	0	0	0	0.0	0	0	0	1	0	0	0	0	0	0	0	0.0	.000	P-2
4 yrs.		8	.300	.300	10	3	0	0	0	0.0	0	2	0	3	0	2	0	0	2	0	0	0.3	1.000	P-6

Jim Byrnes

BYRNES, JAMES JOSEPH BR TR 5′ 9″ 150 lbs.
B. Jan. 5, 1880, San Francisco, Calif. D. July 31, 1941, San Francisco, Calif.

Year	Team	Games	BA	SA	AB	H	2B	3B	HR	HR%	R	RBI	BB	SO	SB	Pinch Hit AB	Pinch Hit H	PO	A	E	DP	TC/G	FA	G by Pos
1906	**PHI A**	9	.174	.261	23	4	0	1	0	0.0	2	0	0		0	1	0	30	10	5	1	5.6	.889	C-8

Milt Byrnes

BYRNES, MILTON JOHN (Skippy) BL TL 5′10½″ 170 lbs.
B. Nov. 15, 1916, St. Louis, Mo. D. Feb. 1, 1979, St. Louis, Mo.

Year	Team	Games	BA	SA	AB	H	2B	3B	HR	HR%	R	RBI	BB	SO	SB	Pinch Hit AB	Pinch Hit H	PO	A	E	DP	TC/G	FA	G by Pos
1943	**STL A**	129	.280	.406	429	120	28	7	4	0.9	58	50	54	49	1	14	1	289	13	1	3	2.7	.997	OF-114
1944		128	.295	.393	407	120	20	4	4	1.0	63	45	68	50	1	5	3	282	7	7	1	2.4	.976	OF-122
1945		133	.249	.387	442	110	29	4	8	1.8	53	59	78	84	1	7	2	333	13	4	0	2.8	.989	OF-125, 1B-2
3 yrs.		390	.274	.395	1278	350	77	15	16	1.3	174	154	200	183	3	26	6	904	33	12	4	2.6	.987	OF-361, 1B-2
WORLD SERIES																								
1944	**STL A**	3	.000	.000	2	0	0	0	0	0.0	0	0	1	2	0	2	0	0	0	0	0	0.0	—	

Putsy Caballero

CABALLERO, RALPH JOSEPH BR TR 5′10″ 170 lbs.
B. Nov. 5, 1927, New Orleans, La.

Year	Team	Games	BA	SA	AB	H	2B	3B	HR	HR%	R	RBI	BB	SO	SB	Pinch Hit AB	Pinch Hit H	PO	A	E	DP	TC/G	FA	G by Pos
1944	**PHI N**	4	.000	.000	4	0	0	0	0	0.0	0	0	0	1	0	0	0	4	4	1	0	4.5	.889	3B-2
1945		9	.000	.000	1	0	0	0	0	0.0	1	1	0	0	0	0	0	4	2	1	1	1.4	.857	3B-5
1947		2	.143	.143	7	1	0	0	0	0.0	2	0	1	0	0	0	0	3	6	0	1	3.0	1.000	2B-2, 3B-1
1948		113	.245	.285	351	86	12	1	0	0.0	33	19	24	18	7	11	3	145	200	18	23	3.6	.950	3B-79, 2B-23
1949		29	.279	.324	68	19	3	0	0	0.0	8	3	0	3	0	4	1	60	48	2	13	5.0	.982	2B-21, SS-1
1950		46	.167	.167	24	4	0	0	0	0.0	12	0	2	2	1	5	2	14	8	1	2	2.1	.957	2B-5, 3B-4, SS-2
1951		84	.186	.248	161	30	3	2	1	0.6	15	11	12	7	1	3	0	133	124	4	37	4.1	.985	2B-57, SS-3, 3B-3
1952		35	.238	.310	42	10	3	0	0	0.0	10	6	2	3	1	1	1	24	23	4	5	2.3	.922	SS-8, 3B-7, 2B-7
8 yrs.		322	.228	.274	658	150	21	3	1	0.2	81	40	41	34	10	24	7	387	415	31	82	3.6	.963	2B-115, 3B-101, SS-14
WORLD SERIES																								
1950	**PHI N**	3	.000	.000	1	0	0	0	0	0.0	0	0	0	1	0	1	0	0	0	0	0	0.0	—	

Enos Cabell

CABELL, ENOS MILTON BR TR 6′ 4″ 170 lbs.
B. Oct. 8, 1949, Fort Riley, Kans.

Year	Team	Games	BA	SA	AB	H	2B	3B	HR	HR%	R	RBI	BB	SO	SB	Pinch Hit AB	Pinch Hit H	PO	A	E	DP	TC/G	FA	G by Pos
1972	**BAL A**	3	.000	.000	5	0	0	0	0	0.0	0	1	0	0	0	1	0	7	0	0	1	7.0	1.000	1B-1
1973		32	.213	.319	47	10	2	0	1	2.1	12	3	3	7	1	4	1	111	4	1	14	4.8	.991	1B-23, 3B-1
1974		80	.241	.339	174	42	4	2	3	1.7	24	17	7	20	5	4	0	223	45	4	18	3.9	.985	1B-28, OF-22, 3B-19, 2B-1
1975	**HOU N**	117	.264	.365	348	92	17	6	2	0.6	43	43	18	53	12	17	7	197	58	6	17	2.3	.977	OF-67, 1B-25, 3B-22
1976		144	.273	.329	586	160	13	7	2	0.3	85	43	29	79	35	1	0	131	263	17	24	2.8	.959	3B-143, 1B-3
1977		150	.282	.438	625	176	36	7	16	2.6	101	68	27	55	42	3	0	176	288	24	19	3.2	.951	3B-144, 1B-8, SS-1
1978		162	.295	.398	**660**	195	31	8	7	1.1	92	71	22	80	33	0	0	211	277	18	19	3.0	.964	3B-153, 1B-14, SS-1
1979		155	.272	.368	603	164	30	5	6	1.0	60	67	21	68	37	0	0	396	199	14	31	3.3	.977	3B-132, 1B-51
1980		152	.276	.351	604	167	23	8	2	0.3	69	55	26	84	21	1	1	118	250	29	15	2.6	.927	3B-150, 1B-1
1981	**SF N**	96	.255	.326	396	101	20	1	2	0.5	41	36	10	47	6	6	1	634	90	16	58	8.1	.978	1B-69, 3B-22
1982	**DET A**	125	.261	.323	464	121	17	3	2	0.4	45	37	15	48	15	10	2	592	143	16	69	5.2	.979	1B-83, 3B-59, OF-3
1983		121	.311	.434	392	122	23	5	5	1.3	62	46	16	41	4	11	4	830	79	3	76	7.7	.997	1B-106, DH-8, 3B-4, SS-1
1984	**HOU N**	127	.310	.417	436	135	17	3	8	1.8	52	44	21	47	8	17	5	971	66	7	97	9.3	.993	1B-112
1985	**2 teams**	**HOU N** (60G –.245)	**LA N** (57G –.292)																					
"	**total**	117	.272	.352	335	91	19	1	2	0.6	40	36	30	36	9	31	10	456	97	11	41	5.3	.980	1B-70, 3B-32, OF-4
1986	**LA N**	107	.256	.318	277	71	11	0	2	0.7	27	29	14	26	10	34	4	389	49	9	31	5.3	.980	1B-61, OF-16, 3B-7
15 yrs.		1688	.277	.370	5952	1647	263	56	60	1.0	753	596	259	691	238	140	35	5442	1908	175	530	4.5	.977	3B-888, 1B-655, OF-112, DH-8, SS-3, 2B-1
LEAGUE CHAMPIONSHIP SERIES																								
1974	**BAL A**	3	.250	.250	4	1	0	0	0	0.0	0	0	0	2	0	1	0	2	0	0	0	2.0	1.000	OF-1
1980	**HOU N**	5	.238	.286	21	5	1	0	0	0.0	1	0	1	3	0	0	0	1	9	0	1	2.0	1.000	3B-5
1985	**LA N**	5	.077	.077	13	1	0	0	0	0.0	1	0	0	3	0	3	0	19	3	0	1	7.3	1.000	1B-3
3 yrs.		13	.184	.211	38	7	1	0	0	0.0	2	0	1	8	0	4	0	22	12	0	2	3.8	1.000	3B-5, 1B-3, OF-1

Al Cabrera

CABRERA, ALFREDO A. TR
B. 1883, Canary Islands, Spain D. Havana, Cuba.

Year	Team	Games	BA	SA	AB	H	2B	3B	HR	HR%	R	RBI	BB	SO	SB	Pinch Hit AB	Pinch Hit H	PO	A	E	DP	TC/G	FA	G by Pos
1913	**STL N**	1	.000	.000	2	0	0	0	0	0.0	0	0	0	0	0	0	0	0	0	0	0	0.0	.000	SS-1

Francisco Cabrera

CABRERA, FRANCISCO BR TR 6′ 4″ 195 lbs.
Born Francisco Cabrera (Paulino).
B. Oct. 10, 1966, Santo Domingo, Dominican Republic.

Year	Team	Games	BA	SA	AB	H	2B	3B	HR	HR%	R	RBI	BB	SO	SB	Pinch Hit AB	Pinch Hit H	PO	A	E	DP	TC/G	FA	G by Pos
1989	**2 teams**	**TOR A** (3G –.167)	**ATL N** (4G –.214)																					
"	**total**	7	.192	.308	26	5	3	0	0	0.0	1	0	1	6	0	1	0	27	1	1	1	4.8	.966	DH-3, 1B-2, C-1
1990	**ATL N**	63	.277	.482	137	38	5	1	7	5.1	14	25	5	21	1	21	6	269	19	3	15	5.7	.990	1B-48, C-3
1991		44	.242	.432	95	23	6	0	4	4.2	7	23	6	20	1	18	3	137	13	3	3	4.9	.980	C-17, 1B-14

Francisco Cabrera *continued*

Year	Team	Games	BA	SA	AB	H	2B	3B	HR	HR%	R	RBI	BB	SO	SB	Pinch Hit AB	Pinch Hit H	PO	A	E	DP	TC/G	FA	G by Pos
1992		12	.300	.900	10	3	0	0	2	20.0	2	3	1	1	0	10	3	0	0	0	0	0.0	.000	C-1
1993		70	.241	.422	83	20	3	0	4	4.8	8	11	8	21	0	51	9	65	10	0	4	5.4	1.000	1B-12, C-2
5 yrs.		196	.254	.453	351	89	17	1	17	4.8	32	62	21	69	2	101	21	498	43	7	23	5.3	.987	1B-76, C-24, DH-3
LEAGUE CHAMPIONSHIP SERIES																								
1992	ATL N	2	.500	.500	2	1	0	0	0	0.0	0	2	0	0	0	2	1	0	0	0	0	0.0	—	
1993		3	.667	.667	3	2	0	0	0	0.0	0	1	0	1	0	3	2	1	0	0	0	1.0	1.000	C-1
2 yrs.		5	.600	.600	5	3	0	0	0	0.0	0	3	0	1	0	5	3	1	0	0	0	1.0	1.000	C-1
WORLD SERIES																								
1991	ATL N	3	.000	.000	1	0	0	0	0	0.0	0	0	0	0	0	1	0	0	0	0	0	0.0	.000	C-1
1992		1	.000	.000	1	0	0	0	0	0.0	0	0	0	0	0	1	0	0	0	0	0	0.0	—	
2 yrs.		4	.000	.000	2	0	0	0	0	0.0	0	0	0	0	0	2	0	0	0	0	0	0.0		C-1

Craig Cacek

CACEK, CRAIG THOMAS BR TR 6′ 1″ 200 lbs.
B. Sept. 10, 1954, Hollywood, Calif.

Year	Team	Games	BA	SA	AB	H	2B	3B	HR	HR%	R	RBI	BB	SO	SB	Pinch Hit AB	Pinch Hit H	PO	A	E	DP	TC/G	FA	G by Pos
1977	HOU N	7	.050	.050	20	1	0	0	0	0.0	0	1	1	3	0	2	0	52	1	1	6	9.0	.981	1B-6

Edgar Caceres

CACERES, EDGAR F. BB TR 6′ 1″ 170 lbs.
B. June 6, 1964, Barquismeto, Venezuela.

Year	Team	Games	BA	SA	AB	H	2B	3B	HR	HR%	R	RBI	BB	SO	SB	Pinch Hit AB	Pinch Hit H	PO	A	E	DP	TC/G	FA	G by Pos
1995	KC A	55	.239	.350	117	28	6	2	1	0.9	13	17	8	15	2	8	3	73	92	1	17	3.0	.994	2B-36, SS-8, 1B-6, 3B-3, DH-3

Charlie Cady

CADY, CHARLES B. 5′11″ 180 lbs.
B. Dec. 1865, Chicago, Ill. D. June 7, 1909, Kankakee, Ill.

Year	Team	Games	BA	SA	AB	H	2B	3B	HR	HR%	R	RBI	BB	SO	SB	Pinch Hit AB	Pinch Hit H	PO	A	E	DP	TC/G	FA	G by Pos
1883	CLE N	3	.000	.000	11	0	0	0	0	0.0	0		1	5		0	0	1	1	0	0	0.7	1.000	OF-2, P-1
1884	2 teams	CHI U (6G –.100) KC U (2G –.000)																						
″	total	8	.087	.217	23	2	1	1	0	0.0	4		1			0	0	7	8	7	0	2.8	.682	P-4, OF-2, 2B-1, C-1
2 yrs.		11	.059	.147	34	2	1	1	0	0.0	4		2	5		0	0	8	9	7	0	2.2	.708	P-5, OF-4, 2B-1, C-1

Hick Cady

CADY, FORREST LeROY BR TR 6′ 2″ 179 lbs.
B. Jan. 26, 1886, Bishop Hill, Ill. D. Mar. 3, 1946, Cedar Rapids, Iowa.

Year	Team	Games	BA	SA	AB	H	2B	3B	HR	HR%	R	RBI	BB	SO	SB	Pinch Hit AB	Pinch Hit H	PO	A	E	DP	TC/G	FA	G by Pos
1912	BOS A	47	.259	.385	135	35	13	2	0	0.0	19	9	10		0	0	0	280	57	3	6	7.2	.991	C-43, 1B-4
1913		39	.250	.344	96	24	5	2	0	0.0	10	6	5	14	1	1	0	198	44	2	3	6.4	.992	C-38
1914		61	.258	.308	159	41	6	1	0	0.0	14	8	12	22	2	3	0	217	80	9	1	5.3	.971	C-58
1915		78	.278	.346	205	57	10	2	0	0.0	25	17	19	25	0	1	0	313	79	8	12	5.2	.980	C-77
1916		78	.191	.265	162	31	6	3	0	0.0	5	13	15	16	0	12	4	195	51	8	4	3.8	.969	C-63, 1B-3
1917		17	.152	.217	46	7	1	1	0	0.0	4	2	1	6	0	3	1	54	17	3	2	5.3	.959	C-14
1919	PHI N	34	.214	.306	98	21	6	0	1	1.0	6	19	4	8	1	5	2	85	35	2	2	4.2	.984	C-29
7 yrs.		354	.240	.320	901	216	47	11	1	0.1	83	74	66	91	4	25	7	1342	363	35	30	5.3	.980	C-322, 1B-7
WORLD SERIES																								
1912	BOS A	7	.136	.136	22	3	0	0	0	0.0	1	1	0	3	0	0	0	35	9	1	0	6.4	.978	C-7
1915		4	.333	.333	6	2	0	0	0	0.0	0	0	1	2	0	0	0	14	4	0	0	4.5	1.000	C-4
1916		2	.250	.250	4	1	0	0	0	0.0	1	0	3	0	0	0	0	11	1	0	1	6.0	1.000	C-2
3 yrs.		13	.188	.188	32	6	0	0	0	0.0	2	1	4	5	0	0	0	60	14	1	1	5.8	.987	C-13

Tom Cafego

CAFEGO, THOMAS BL TR 5′10″ 160 lbs.
B. Aug. 21, 1911, Whipple, W. Va. D. Oct. 29, 1961, Detroit, Mich.

Year	Team	Games	BA	SA	AB	H	2B	3B	HR	HR%	R	RBI	BB	SO	SB	Pinch Hit AB	Pinch Hit H	PO	A	E	DP	TC/G	FA	G by Pos
1937	STL A	4	.000	.000	4	0	0	0	0	0.0	1	0	0	1	0	1	0	1	0	1	0	2.0	.500	OF-1

Joe Caffie

CAFFIE, JOSEPH CLIFFORD (Rabbit) BL TR 5′10½″ 180 lbs.
B. Feb. 14, 1931, Ramer, Ala.

Year	Team	Games	BA	SA	AB	H	2B	3B	HR	HR%	R	RBI	BB	SO	SB	Pinch Hit AB	Pinch Hit H	PO	A	E	DP	TC/G	FA	G by Pos
1956	CLE A	12	.342	.342	38	13	0	0	0	0.0	7	1	4	8	3	1	1	21	1	0	0	2.2	1.000	OF-10
1957		32	.270	.416	89	24	2	1	3	3.4	14	10	4	11	0	9	0	40	0	1	0	2.2	.976	OF-19
2 yrs.		44	.291	.394	127	37	2	1	3	2.4	21	11	8	19	3	10	1	61	1	1	0	2.2	.984	OF-29

Caffrey

CAFFREY
Deceased.

Year	Team	Games	BA	SA	AB	H	2B	3B	HR	HR%	R	RBI	BB	SO	SB	Pinch Hit AB	Pinch Hit H	PO	A	E	DP	TC/G	FA	G by Pos
1890	PHI AA	1	.250	.250	4	1	0	0	0	0.0	0		0		0	0	0	1	2	1	0	4.0	.750	SS-1

Ben Caffyn

CAFFYN, BENJAMIN THOMAS BL TL
B. Feb. 10, 1880, Peoria, Ill. D. Nov. 22, 1942, Peoria, Ill.

Year	Team	Games	BA	SA	AB	H	2B	3B	HR	HR%	R	RBI	BB	SO	SB	Pinch Hit AB	Pinch Hit H	PO	A	E	DP	TC/G	FA	G by Pos
1906	CLE A	30	.194	.233	103	20	4	0	0	0.0	16	3	12		2	1	0	38	2	4	2	1.5	.909	OF-29

Wayne Cage

CAGE, WAYNE LEVELL BL TL 6′ 4″ 205 lbs.
B. Nov. 23, 1951, Monroe, La.

Year	Team	Games	BA	SA	AB	H	2B	3B	HR	HR%	R	RBI	BB	SO	SB	Pinch Hit AB	Pinch Hit H	PO	A	E	DP	TC/G	FA	G by Pos
1978	CLE A	36	.245	.449	98	24	6	1	4	4.1	11	13	9	28	1	6	0	73	8	1	10	2.6	.988	DH-20, 1B-11
1979		29	.232	.321	56	13	2	0	1	1.8	6	6	5	16	0	12	1	37	4	0	3	2.6	1.000	DH-9, 1B-7
2 yrs.		65	.240	.403	154	37	8	1	5	3.2	17	19	14	44	1	18	1	110	12	1	13	2.6	.992	DH-29, 1B-18

John Cahill

CAHILL, JOHN PATRICK PARNELL (Patsy) BR TR 5′ 7½″ 168 lbs.
B. Apr. 30, 1865, San Francisco, Calif. D. Oct. 31, 1901, Pleasanton, Calif.

Year	Team	Games	BA	SA	AB	H	2B	3B	HR	HR%	R	RBI	BB	SO	SB	Pinch Hit AB	Pinch Hit H	PO	A	E	DP	TC/G	FA	G by Pos
1884	COL AA	59	.219	.262	210	46	3	3	0	0.0	28		6			0	0	71	28	19	2	1.9	.839	OF-54, SS-5, P-2
1886	STL N	125	.199	.268	463	92	17	6	1	0.2	43	32	9	79		0	0	166	39	36	5	1.9	.851	OF-124, P-2, SS-1, 3B-1
1887	IND N	68	.205	.243	263	54	4	3	0	0.0	22	26	9	5	34	0	0	90	28	28	3	2.0	.808	OF-56, 3B-9, P-6, SS-1
3 yrs.		252	.205	.260	936	192	24	12	1	0.1	93	58	24	84	34	0	0	327	95	83	10	1.9	.836	OF-234, 3B-10, P-10, SS-7

Tom Cahill

CAHILL, THOMAS H.
B. Oct. 1868, Fall River, Mass. D. Dec. 25, 1894, Scranton, Pa.

Year	Team	Games	BA	SA	AB	H	2B	3B	HR	HR%	R	RBI	BB	SO	SB	Pinch Hit AB	Pinch Hit H	PO	A	E	DP	TC/G	FA	G by Pos
1891	LOU AA	119	.253	.347	430	109	17	7	3	0.7	68	44	41	51	38	0	0	385	242	69	31	5.6	.901	C-55, SS-49, OF-12, 2B-6, 3B-2

George Caithamer

CAITHAMER, GEORGE THEODORE BR TR 5′ 7½″ 160 lbs.
B. July 22, 1910, Chicago, Ill. D. June 1, 1954, Chicago, Ill.

Year	Team	Games	BA	SA	AB	H	2B	3B	HR	HR%	R	RBI	BB	SO	SB	Pinch Hit AB	Pinch Hit H	PO	A	E	DP	TC/G	FA	G by Pos
1934	CHI A	5	.316	.368	19	6	1	0	0	0.0	1	3	1	5	0	0	0	21	2	1	1	4.8	.958	C-5

Ivan Calderon

CALDERON, IVAN BR TR 6′ 1″ 220 lbs.
Born Ivan Calderon (Perez).
B. Mar. 19, 1962, Fajardo, Puerto Rico.

Year	Team	Games	BA	SA	AB	H	2B	3B	HR	HR%	R	RBI	BB	SO	SB	Pinch Hit AB	Pinch Hit H	PO	A	E	DP	TC/G	FA	G by Pos
1984	SEA A	11	.208	.375	24	5	1	0	1	4.2	2	1	2	5	1	0	0	22	0	0	0	2.0	1.000	OF-11
1985		67	.286	.514	210	60	16	4	8	3.8	37	28	19	45	4	10	3	108	5	2	3	2.0	.983	OF-53, DH-3, 1B-2
1986	2 teams	SEA A (37G –.237) CHI A (13G –.303)																						
″	total	50	.250	.341	164	41	7	1	2	1.2	16	15	9	39	3	7	2	64	4	5	1	1.7	.932	OF-37, DH-6
1987	CHI A	144	.293	.526	542	159	38	2	28	5.2	93	83	60	109	10	1	0	295	8	5	3	2.2	.984	OF-139, DH-3
1988		73	.212	.424	264	56	14	0	14	5.3	40	35	34	66	4	1	0	141	5	7	1	2.2	.954	OF-67, DH-3
1989		157	.286	.437	622	178	34	9	14	2.3	83	87	43	94	7	2	0	384	17	9	24	2.5	.978	OF-103, DH-36, 1B-26
1990		158	.273	.422	607	166	44	2	14	2.3	85	74	51	79	32	2	1	269	7	7	1	1.8	.975	OF-130, DH-27, 1B-2
1991	MON N	134	.300	.481	470	141	22	3	19	4.0	69	75	53	64	31	10	4	284	5	7	5	2.3	.976	OF-122, 1B-4
1992		48	.265	.424	170	45	14	2	3	1.8	19	24	14	22	1	2	1	79	2	1	0	1.8	.988	OF-46
1993	2 teams	BOS A (73G –.221) CHI A (9G –.115)																						
″	total	82	.209	.280	239	50	10	2	1	0.4	26	22	21	33	4	14	1	94	2	0	0	1.4	1.000	OF-47, DH-24
10 yrs.		924	.272	.442	3312	901	200	25	104	3.1	470	444	306	556	97	49	12	1740	55	43	38	2.1	.977	OF-755, DH-102, 1B-34

Sammy Calderone

CALDERONE, SAMUEL FRANCIS BR TR 5′10½″ 185 lbs.
B. Feb. 6, 1926, Beverly, N. J.

Year	Team	Games	BA	SA	AB	H	2B	3B	HR	HR%	R	RBI	BB	SO	SB	Pinch Hit AB	Pinch Hit H	PO	A	E	DP	TC/G	FA	G by Pos
1950	NY N	34	.299	.358	67	20	1	0	1	1.5	9	12	2	5	0	1	0	63	6	2	1	2.2	.972	C-33
1953		35	.222	.267	45	10	2	0	0	0.0	4	8	1	4	0	6	0	50	6	2	2	1.9	.966	C-31
1954	MIL N	22	.379	.448	29	11	2	0	0	0.0	3	5	4	4	0	7	2	45	4	0	3	3.1	1.000	C-16
3 yrs.		91	.291	.348	141	41	5	0	1	0.7	16	25	7	13	0	14	2	158	16	4	6	2.2	.978	C-80

Bruce Caldwell

CALDWELL, BRUCE BR TR 6′ 195 lbs.
B. Feb. 8, 1906, Ashton, R. I. D. Feb. 15, 1959, West Haven, Conn.

Year	Team	Games	BA	SA	AB	H	2B	3B	HR	HR%	R	RBI	BB	SO	SB	Pinch Hit AB	Pinch Hit H	PO	A	E	DP	TC/G	FA	G by Pos
1928	CLE A	18	.222	.333	27	6	1	1	0	0.0	2	3	2	2	1	7	0	15	1	0	1	1.5	1.000	OF-10, 1B-1
1932	BKN N	7	.091	.091	11	1	0	0	0	0.0	2	2	2	2	0	1	1	14	0	2	1	2.7	.875	1B-6
2 yrs.		25	.184	.263	38	7	1	1	0	0.0	4	5	4	4	1	8	1	29	1	2	2	1.9	.938	OF-10, 1B-7

Ray Caldwell

CALDWELL, RAYMOND BENJAMIN (Slim) BL TR 6′ 2″ 190 lbs.
B. Apr. 26, 1888, Croydon, Pa. D. Aug. 17, 1967, Salamanca, N. Y.

Year	Team	Games	BA	SA	AB	H	2B	3B	HR	HR%	R	RBI	BB	SO	SB	Pinch Hit AB	Pinch Hit H	PO	A	E	DP	TC/G	FA	G by Pos
1910	NY A	6	.000	.000	6	0	0	0	0	0.0	0	0	0		0	0	0	1	4	0	0	0.8	1.000	P-6
1911		58	.272	.313	147	40	4	1	0	0.0	14	17	11	0	5	4	1	27	56	6	2	1.7	.933	P-41, OF-11
1912		41	.237	.303	76	18	1	2	0	0.0	18	6	5		4	7	2	2	59	4	2	2.2	.938	P-30
1913		55	.289	.361	97	28	3	2	0	0.0	10	11	3	15	3	19	4	8	42	0	1	1.7	1.000	P-27, OF-3
1914		59	.195	.230	113	22	4	0	0	0.0	9	10	7	24	2	21	4	56	46	6	3	2.9	.944	P-31, 1B-6
1915		72	.243	.368	144	35	4	1	4	2.8	27	20	9	32	4	**33**	9	12	72	1	5	2.4	.988	P-36
1916		45	.204	.226	93	19	2	0	0	0.0	6	4	2	17	1	19	3	4	45	3	2	2.2	.942	P-21, OF-3
1917		63	.258	.371	124	32	6	1	2	1.6	12	12	16	16	2	15	5	23	60	2	1	2.1	.976	P-32, OF-8
1918		65	.291	.377	151	44	10	0	1	0.7	14	18	13	23	2	19	6	52	38	3	2	2.2	.968	P-24, OF-19
1919	2 teams	BOS A (33G –.271) CLE A (6G –.348)																						
″	total	39	.296	.394	71	21	5	1	0	0.0	9	6	0	13	0	12	2	6	26	2	0	1.3	.941	P-24, OF-2
1920	CLE A	41	.213	.247	89	19	3	0	0	0.0	17	7	10	13	0	4	0	6	49	5	0	1.8	.917	P-34
1921		38	.208	.340	53	11	4	0	1	1.9	2	3	2	5	0	1	0	5	35	3	1	1.2	.930	P-37
12 yrs.		582	.248	.322	1164	289	46	8	8	0.7	138	114	78	158	23	154	36	202	532	35	19	1.9	.954	P-343, OF-46, 1B-6
WORLD SERIES																								
1920	CLE A	1	—	—	0	0	0	0	0	—	0	0	0	0	0	0	0	0	0	0	0	0.0	.000	P-1

Bill Calhoun

CALHOUN, WILLIAM DAVITTE (Mary) BL TL 6′ 180 lbs.
B. June 23, 1890, Rockmart, Ga. D. Jan. 28, 1955, Sandersville, Ga.

Year	Team	Games	BA	SA	AB	H	2B	3B	HR	HR%	R	RBI	BB	SO	SB	Pinch Hit AB	Pinch Hit H	PO	A	E	DP	TC/G	FA	G by Pos
1913	BOS N	6	.077	.077	13	1	0	0	0	0.0	0	0	0	3	0	3	1	31	1	1	1	11.0	.970	1B-3

John Calhoun

CALHOUN, JOHN CHARLES (Red) BR TR 6′ 185 lbs.
B. Dec. 14, 1879, Pittsburgh, Pa. D. Feb. 27, 1947, Cincinnati, Ohio.

Year	Team	Games	BA	SA	AB	H	2B	3B	HR	HR%	R	RBI	BB	SO	SB	Pinch Hit AB	Pinch Hit H	PO	A	E	DP	TC/G	FA	G by Pos
1902	STL N	20	.156	.219	64	10	2	1	0	0.0	3	8	8		1	2	0	60	22	4	4	4.8	.953	3B-12, 1B-5, OF-1

Marty Callaghan

CALLAGHAN, MARTIN FRANCIS BL TL 5′10″ 157 lbs.
B. June 9, 1900, Norwood, Mass. D. June 23, 1975, Norfolk, Mass.

Year	Team	Games	BA	SA	AB	H	2B	3B	HR	HR%	R	RBI	BB	SO	SB	Pinch Hit AB	Pinch Hit H	PO	A	E	DP	TC/G	FA	G by Pos
1922	CHI N	74	.257	.343	175	45	7	4	0	0.0	31	20	17	17	2	17	3	85	2	5	0	1.7	.946	OF-53
1923		61	.225	.279	129	29	1	3	0	0.0	18	14	8	18	2	16	3	60	3	2	0	1.7	.969	OF-38
1928	CIN N	81	.290	.370	238	69	11	4	0	0.0	29	24	27	10	5	7	1	140	5	3	2	2.1	.980	OF-69
1930		79	.276	.333	225	62	9	2	0	0.0	28	16	19	25	1	23	3	142	3	2	1	2.7	.986	OF-54
4 yrs.		295	.267	.338	767	205	28	13	0	0.0	106	74	71	70	10	63	10	427	13	12	3	2.1	.973	OF-214

Dave Callahan

CALLAHAN, DAVID JOSEPH BL TR 5′10″ 165 lbs.
B. July 20, 1888, Ottawa, Ill. D. Oct. 28, 1969, Ottawa, Ill.

Year	Team	Games	BA	SA	AB	H	2B	3B	HR	HR%	R	RBI	BB	SO	SB	Pinch Hit AB	Pinch Hit H	PO	A	E	DP	TC/G	FA	G by Pos
1910	CLE A	13	.182	.205	44	8	1	0	0	0.0	6	2	4		5	1	0	28	0	0	0	2.3	1.000	OF-12
1911		5	.333	.500	12	4	0	1	0	0.0	1	0	1		0	2	1	4	2	0	1	2.0	1.000	OF-3
2 yrs.		18	.214	.268	56	12	1	1	0	0.0	7	2	5		5	3	1	32	2	0	1	2.3	1.000	OF-15

Ed Callahan

CALLAHAN, EDWARD JOSEPH
B. Dec. 11, 1857, Boston, Mass. D. Feb. 5, 1947, New York, N. Y.

Year	Team	Games	BA	SA	AB	H	2B	3B	HR	HR%	R	RBI	BB	SO	SB	Pinch Hit AB	Pinch Hit H	PO	A	E	DP	TC/G	FA	G by Pos
1884	3 teams	STL U (1G –.000) KC U (3G –.364) BOS U (4G –.385)																						
″	total	8	.333	.333	27	9	0	0	0	0.0	2		1			0	0	7	12	5	1	3.0	.792	OF-5, SS-3

Leo Callahan

CALLAHAN, LEO DAVID BL TL 5′ 8″ 142 lbs.
B. Aug. 9, 1890, Jamaica Plain, Mass. D. May 2, 1982, Erie, Pa.

Year	Team	Games	BA	SA	AB	H	2B	3B	HR	HR%	R	RBI	BB	SO	SB	Pinch Hit AB	Pinch Hit H	PO	A	E	DP	TC/G	FA	G by Pos
1913	BKN N	33	.171	.293	41	7	3	1	0	0.0	6	3	4	5	0	24	5	12	0	2	0	1.8	.857	OF-8
1919	PHI N	81	.230	.336	235	54	14	4	1	0.4	26	9	29	19	5	21	3	102	13	6	1	2.1	.950	OF-58
2 yrs.		114	.221	.330	276	61	17	5	1	0.4	32	12	33	24	5	45	8	114	13	8	1	2.0	.941	OF-66

Nixey Callahan

CALLAHAN, JAMES JOSEPH (Cal) BR TR 5′10½″ 180 lbs.
B. Mar. 18, 1874, Fitchburg, Mass. D. Oct. 4, 1934, Boston, Mass.
Manager 1903–04, 1912–14, 1916–17.

Year	Team		Games	BA	SA	AB	H	2B	3B	HR	HR%	R	RBI	BB	SO	SB	Pinch Hit AB	Pinch Hit H	PO	A	E	DP	TC/G	FA	G by Pos
1894	PHI	N	9	.238	.238	21	5	0	0	0	0.0	4	0	0	7	0	0	0	4	8	1	0	1.4	.923	P-9
1897	CHI	N	94	.292	.400	360	105	18	6	3	0.8	60	47	10		12	2	0	147	201	42	25	4.1	.892	2B-30, P-23, OF-21, SS-18, 3B-2
1898			43	.262	.366	164	43	7	5	0	0.0	27	22	4		3	0	0	42	67	11	3	2.8	.908	P-31, OF-9, SS-1, 2B-1, 1B-1
1899			47	.260	.327	150	39	4	3	0	0.0	21	18	8		9	1	0	40	103	14	4	3.3	.911	P-35, OF-9, SS-2, 2B-1
1900			32	.235	.296	115	27	3	2	0	0.0	16	9	6		5	0	0	21	94	3	2	3.7	.975	P-32
1901	CHI	A	45	.331	.466	118	39	7	3	1	0.8	15	19	10		10	**10**	**3**	27	93	10	5	3.7	.923	P-27, 3B-6, 2B-2
1902			70	.234	.284	218	51	7	2	0	0.0	27	13	6		4	**12**	2	57	108	9	7	2.9	.948	P-35, OF-23, SS-1
1903			118	.292	.387	439	128	26	5	2	0.5	47	56	20		24	5	3	131	216	38	5	3.4	.901	3B-102, OF-8, P-3
1904			132	.261	.317	482	126	23	2	0	0.0	66	54	39		29	1	0	207	79	14	5	2.3	.953	OF-104, 2B-28
1905			96	.272	.368	345	94	18	6	1	0.3	50	43	29		26	3	1	120	10	6	0	1.5	.956	OF-93
1911			120	.281	.350	466	131	13	5	3	0.6	64	60	15		45	5	1	173	10	7	2	1.7	.963	OF-114
1912			111	.272	.336	408	111	9	7	1	0.2	45	52	12		19	4	1	166	3	11	0	1.7	.939	OF-107
1913			6	.222	.222	9	2	0	0	0	0.0	0	1	0	2	0	5	1	2	0	0	0	2.0	1.000	OF-1
13 yrs.			923	.273	.352	3295	901	135	46	11	0.3	442	394	159	9	186	48	12	1137	992	166	58	2.6	.928	OF-489, P-195, 3B-110, 2B-62, SS-22, 1B-1

Pat Callahan

CALLAHAN, PATRICK HENRY
B. Oct. 15, 1866, Cleveland, Ohio D. Feb. 4, 1940, Louisville, Ky.

Year	Team		Games	BA	SA	AB	H	2B	3B	HR	HR%	R	RBI	BB	SO	SB	Pinch Hit AB	Pinch Hit H	PO	A	E	DP	TC/G	FA	G by Pos
1884	IND	AA	61	.260	.353	258	67	8	5	2	0.8	38		8			0	0	66	94	37	5	3.2	.812	3B-61

Red Callahan

CALLAHAN, JAMES TIMOTHY (Red) BR TR 5′ 9″ 145 lbs.
Born James Timothy Callaghan.
B. Jan. 12, 1879, Allegheny County, Pa. D. Mar. 9, 1968, Carnegie, Pa.

Year	Team		Games	BA	SA	AB	H	2B	3B	HR	HR%	R	RBI	BB	SO	SB	Pinch Hit AB	Pinch Hit H	PO	A	E	DP	TC/G	FA	G by Pos
1902	NY	N	1	.000	.000	4	0	0	0	0	0.0	0	0	1		0	0	0	0	0	0	0	0.0	.000	OF-1

Wes Callahan

CALLAHAN, WESLEY LeROY BR TR 5′ 7½″ 155 lbs.
B. July 3, 1888, Lyons, Ind. D. Sept. 13, 1953, Dayton, Ohio.

Year	Team		Games	BA	SA	AB	H	2B	3B	HR	HR%	R	RBI	BB	SO	SB	Pinch Hit AB	Pinch Hit H	PO	A	E	DP	TC/G	FA	G by Pos
1913	STL	N	7	.286	.286	14	4	0	0	0	0.0	0	1	2	2	1	1	0	8	15	2	2	4.2	.920	SS-6

Frank Callaway

CALLAWAY, FRANK BURNETT BR TR 6′ 170 lbs.
B. Feb. 26, 1898, Knoxville, Tenn. D. Aug. 21, 1987, Knoxville, Tenn.

Year	Team		Games	BA	SA	AB	H	2B	3B	HR	HR%	R	RBI	BB	SO	SB	Pinch Hit AB	Pinch Hit H	PO	A	E	DP	TC/G	FA	G by Pos
1921	PHI	A	14	.240	.300	50	12	1	1	0	0.0	7	2	2	11	1	0	0	22	43	9	2	5.3	.878	SS-14
1922			29	.271	.354	48	13	0	2	0	0.0	5	4	0	13	0	4	0	19	38	6	5	3.2	.905	2B-11, 3B-5, SS-4
2 yrs.			43	.255	.327	98	25	1	3	0	0.0	12	6	2	24	1	4	0	41	81	15	7	4.0	.891	SS-18, 2B-11, 3B-5

Johnny Callison

CALLISON, JOHN WESLEY BL TR 5′10″ 175 lbs.
B. Mar. 12, 1939, Qualls, Okla.

Year	Team		Games	BA	SA	AB	H	2B	3B	HR	HR%	R	RBI	BB	SO	SB	Pinch Hit AB	Pinch Hit H	PO	A	E	DP	TC/G	FA	G by Pos
1958	CHI	A	18	.297	.469	64	19	4	2	1	1.6	10	12	6	14	1	0	0	39	2	1	1	2.3	.976	OF-18
1959			49	.173	.288	104	18	3	0	3	2.9	12	12	13	20	0	4	0	54	3	1	0	1.4	.983	OF-41
1960	PHI	N	99	.260	.427	288	75	11	5	9	3.1	36	30	45	70	0	15	3	176	7	2	4	2.2	.989	OF-86
1961			138	.266	.418	455	121	20	11	9	2.0	74	47	69	76	10	14	3	227	10	8	2	2.0	.967	OF-124
1962			157	.300	.491	603	181	26	**10**	23	3.8	107	83	54	96	10	9	4	327	24	7	7	2.4	.980	OF-152
1963			157	.284	.502	626	178	36	11	26	4.2	96	78	50	111	8	2	0	298	26	2	4	2.1	.994	OF-157
1964			162	.274	.492	654	179	30	10	31	4.7	101	104	36	95	6	2	1	319	19	4	3	2.1	.988	OF-162
1965			160	.262	.509	619	162	25	**16**	32	5.2	93	101	57	117	6	6	0	313	21	6	2	2.1	.982	OF-159
1966			155	.276	.418	612	169	**40**	7	11	1.8	93	55	56	83	8	3	1	275	12	3	2	1.9	.990	OF-154
1967			149	.261	.408	556	145	30	5	14	2.5	62	64	55	63	6	3	0	286	12	7	1	2.1	.977	OF-147
1968			121	.244	.415	398	97	18	4	14	3.5	46	40	42	70	4	11	3	187	10	0	1	1.8	1.000	OF-109
1969			134	.265	.440	495	131	29	5	16	3.2	66	64	49	73	2	6	1	273	12	3	3	2.2	.990	OF-129
1970	CHI	N	147	.264	.440	477	126	23	2	19	4.0	65	68	60	63	7	3	1	244	8	7	3	1.8	.973	OF-144
1971			103	.210	.341	290	61	12	1	8	2.8	27	38	36	55	2	14	1	158	3	3	0	1.8	.982	OF-89
1972	NY	A	92	.258	.393	275	71	10	0	9	3.3	28	34	18	34	3	19	4	127	4	1	1	1.8	.992	OF-74
1973			45	.176	.228	136	24	4	0	1	0.7	10	10	4	24	1	5	2	46	2	2	0	1.2	.960	OF-32, DH-10
16 yrs.			1886	.264	.441	6652	1757	321	89	226	3.4	926	840	650	1064	74	116	24	3349	175	57	34	2.0	.984	OF-1777, DH-10

Jack Calvo

CALVO, JACINTO BL TL 5′10″ 156 lbs.
Born Jacinto Calvo (Gonzalez).
B. June 11, 1894, Havana, Cuba D. June 15, 1965, Miami, Fla.

Year	Team		Games	BA	SA	AB	H	2B	3B	HR	HR%	R	RBI	BB	SO	SB	Pinch Hit AB	Pinch Hit H	PO	A	E	DP	TC/G	FA	G by Pos
1913	WAS	A	16	.242	.333	33	8	0	0	1	3.0	5	2	1	4	0	2	0	7	2	1	0	0.8	.900	OF-12
1920			17	.043	.130	23	1	0	1	0	0.0	5	2	2	2	0	7	1	6	0	0	0	0.6	1.000	OF-10
2 yrs.			33	.161	.250	56	9	0	1	1	1.8	10	4	3	6	0	9	1	13	2	1	0	0.7	.938	OF-22

Hank Camelli

CAMELLI, HENRY RICHARD BR TR 5′11″ 190 lbs.
B. Dec. 12, 1914, Gloucester, Mass.

Year	Team		Games	BA	SA	AB	H	2B	3B	HR	HR%	R	RBI	BB	SO	SB	Pinch Hit AB	Pinch Hit H	PO	A	E	DP	TC/G	FA	G by Pos
1943	PIT	N	1	.000	.000	3	0	0	0	0	0.0	1	0	1	0	0	0	0	4	1	0	0	5.0	1.000	C-1
1944			63	.296	.376	125	37	5	1	1	0.8	14	10	18	12	0	1	1	170	16	8	0	3.2	.959	C-61
1945			1	.000	.000	2	0	0	0	0	0.0	0	0	1	0	0	0	0	4	0	0	0	4.0	1.000	C-1
1946			42	.208	.271	96	20	2	2	0	0.0	8	5	8	9	0	2	0	117	18	4	2	4.1	.971	C-34
1947	BOS	N	52	.193	.280	150	29	8	1	1	0.7	10	11	18	18	0	1	1	194	20	5	3	4.3	.977	C-51
5 yrs.			159	.229	.306	376	86	15	4	2	0.5	33	26	46	39	0	4	2	489	55	17	5	3.8	.970	C-148

John Cameron

CAMERON, JOHN S. (Happy Jack)
B. Sept. 1884, Nova Scotia, Canada D. Aug. 17, 1951, Boston, Mass.

Year	Team		Games	BA	SA	AB	H	2B	3B	HR	HR%	R	RBI	BB	SO	SB	Pinch Hit AB	Pinch Hit H	PO	A	E	DP	TC/G	FA	G by Pos
1906	BOS	N	18	.180	.180	61	11	0	0	0	0.0	3	4	2		0	0	0	20	5	4	1	1.6	.862	OF-16, P-2

Mike Cameron

CAMERON, MICHAEL TERRANCE BR TR 6′ 1″ 170 lbs.
B. Jan. 8, 1973, La Grange, Ga.

Year	Team		Games	BA	SA	AB	H	2B	3B	HR	HR%	R	RBI	BB	SO	SB	Pinch Hit AB	Pinch Hit H	PO	A	E	DP	TC/G	FA	G by Pos
1995	CHI	A	28	.184	.316	38	7	2	0	1	2.6	4	2	3	15	0	0	0	33	1	0	0	1.2	1.000	OF-28

Dolf Camilli

CAMILLI, ADOLF LOUIS BL TL 5′10″ 185 lbs.
Father of Doug Camilli.
B. Apr. 23, 1907, San Francisco, Calif.

Year	Team	Games	BA	SA	AB	H	2B	3B	HR	HR%	R	RBI	BB	SO	SB	Pinch Hit AB	Pinch Hit H	PO	A	E	DP	TC/G	FA	G by Pos
1933	CHI N	16	.224	.397	58	13	2	1	2	3.4	8	7	4	11	3	0	0	163	14	1	21	11.1	.994	1B-16
1934	2 teams	CHI N (32G –.275)	PHI N (102G –.265)																					
"	total	134	.267	.432	498	133	28	3	16	3.2	69	87	53	**94**	4	0	0	1176	79	18	129	9.5	.986	1B-134
1935	PHI N	156	.261	.440	602	157	23	5	25	4.2	88	83	65	**113**	9	0	0	1442	96	20	118	10.0	.987	1B-156
1936		151	.315	.577	530	167	29	13	28	5.3	106	102	116	84	5	1	1	1446	79	18	122	10.3	.988	1B-150
1937		131	.339	.587	475	161	23	7	27	5.7	101	80	90	82	6	0	0	1256	99	8	104	10.4	.994	1B-131
1938	BKN N	146	.251	.485	509	128	25	11	24	4.7	106	100	**119**	101	6	0	0	1356	95	8	129	10.1	.995	1B-145
1939		157	.290	.524	565	164	30	12	26	4.6	105	104	**110**	**107**	1	0	0	1515	129	17	138	10.6	.990	1B-157
1940		142	.287	.529	512	147	29	13	23	4.5	92	96	89	83	9	1	0	1299	79	11	85	9.9	.992	1B-140
1941		149	.285	.556	529	151	29	6	**34**	**6.4**	92	**120**	104	**115**	3	1	0	1379	98	16	107	10.1	.989	1B-148
1942		150	.252	.471	524	132	23	7	26	5.0	89	109	97	85	10	0	0	1334	85	12	123	9.5	.992	1B-150
1943		95	.246	.374	353	87	15	6	6	1.7	56	43	65	48	2	0	0	853	60	7	78	9.7	.992	1B-95
1945	BOS A	63	.212	.288	198	42	5	2	2	1.0	24	19	35	38	2	8	1	505	44	5	62	10.3	.991	1B-54
12 yrs.		1490	.277	.492	5353	1482	261	86	239	4.5	936	950	947	961	60	11	2	13724	957	141	1216	10.0	.990	1B-1476
WORLD SERIES																								
1941	BKN N	5	.167	.222	18	3	1	0	0	0.0	1	1	1	6	0	0	0	45	5	0	4	10.0	1.000	1B-5

Doug Camilli

CAMILLI, DOUGLAS JOSEPH BR TR 5′11″ 195 lbs.
Son of Dolf Camilli.
B. Sept. 22, 1936, Philadelphia, Pa.

Year	Team	Games	BA	SA	AB	H	2B	3B	HR	HR%	R	RBI	BB	SO	SB	Pinch Hit AB	Pinch Hit H	PO	A	E	DP	TC/G	FA	G by Pos
1960	LA N	6	.333	.542	24	8	2	0	1	4.2	4	3	1	4	0	1	0	46	3	1	1	8.3	.980	C-6
1961		13	.133	.433	30	4	0	0	3	10.0	3	4	1	9	0	4	0	64	5	1	1	5.8	.986	C-12
1962		45	.284	.523	88	25	5	2	4	4.5	16	22	12	21	0	6	3	162	8	3	1	4.4	.983	C-39
1963		49	.162	.265	117	19	1	1	3	2.6	9	10	11	22	0	3	1	285	15	7	1	6.5	.977	C-47
1964		50	.179	.203	123	22	3	0	0	0.0	1	10	8	19	0	3	0	266	19	3	0	6.3	.990	C-46
1965	WAS A	75	.192	.280	193	37	6	1	3	1.6	13	18	16	34	0	14	2	319	23	7	2	5.9	.980	C-59
1966		44	.206	.299	107	22	4	0	2	1.9	5	8	3	19	0	3	1	180	21	2	2	5.2	.990	C-39
1967		30	.183	.268	82	15	1	0	2	2.4	5	5	4	16	0	6	2	128	10	1	2	5.8	.993	C-24
1969		1	.333	.333	3	1	0	0	0	0.0	0	0	0	2	0	0	0	2	1	0	0	3.0	1.000	C-1
9 yrs.		313	.199	.309	767	153	22	4	18	2.3	56	80	56	146	0	40	9	1452	105	25	10	5.8	.984	C-273

Lou Camilli

CAMILLI, LOUIS STEVEN BB TR 5′10″ 170 lbs.
B. Sept. 24, 1946, El Paso, Tex.

Year	Team	Games	BA	SA	AB	H	2B	3B	HR	HR%	R	RBI	BB	SO	SB	Pinch Hit AB	Pinch Hit H	PO	A	E	DP	TC/G	FA	G by Pos
1969	CLE A	13	.000	.000	14	0	0	0	0	0.0	0	0	0	3	0	0	0	13	11	0	1	1.8	1.000	3B-13
1970		16	.000	.000	15	0	0	0	0	0.0	0	0	2	2	0	12	0	4	4	0	0	1.3	1.000	SS-3, 2B-2, 3B-1
1971		39	.198	.222	81	16	2	0	0	0.0	5	0	8	10	0	4	0	39	74	4	9	3.0	.966	SS-23, 2B-16
1972		39	.146	.195	41	6	2	0	0	0.0	2	3	3	8	0	29	5	6	10	0	2	1.6	1.000	SS-8, 2B-2
4 yrs.		107	.146	.172	151	22	4	0	0	0.0	7	3	13	23	0	45	5	62	99	4	12	2.4	.976	SS-34, 2B-20, 3B-14

Ken Caminiti

CAMINITI, KENNETH GENE BB TR 6′ 200 lbs.
B. Apr. 21, 1963, Hanford, Calif.

Year	Team	Games	BA	SA	AB	H	2B	3B	HR	HR%	R	RBI	BB	SO	SB	Pinch Hit AB	Pinch Hit H	PO	A	E	DP	TC/G	FA	G by Pos
1987	HOU N	63	.246	.335	203	50	7	1	3	1.5	10	23	12	44	0	9	2	50	98	8	11	2.6	.949	3B-61
1988		30	.181	.241	83	15	2	0	1	1.2	5	7	5	18	0	5	0	12	43	3	2	2.1	.948	3B-28
1989		161	.255	.369	585	149	31	3	10	1.7	71	72	51	93	4	2	0	126	335	22	27	3.0	.954	3B-160
1990		153	.242	.309	541	131	20	2	4	0.7	52	51	48	97	9	10	1	118	243	21	22	2.6	.945	3B-149
1991		152	.253	.383	574	145	30	3	13	2.3	65	80	46	85	4	2	0	129	293	23	29	2.9	.948	3B-152
1992		135	.294	.441	506	149	31	2	13	2.6	68	62	44	68	10	6	1	102	210	11	19	2.5	.966	3B-129
1993		143	.262	.390	543	142	31	0	13	2.4	75	75	49	88	8	1	0	123	264	24	23	2.9	.942	3B-143
1994		111	.283	.495	406	115	28	2	18	4.4	63	75	43	71	4	6	0	79	201	9	17	2.7	.969	3B-108
1995	SD N	143	.302	.513	526	159	33	0	26	4.9	74	94	69	94	12	0	0	102	293	27	24	3.0	.936	3B-143
9 yrs.		1091	.266	.403	3967	1055	213	13	101	2.5	483	539	367	658	51	41	4	841	1980	148	174	2.8	.950	3B-1073

Howie Camp

CAMP, HOWARD LEE (Red) BL TR 5′ 9″ 169 lbs.
B. July 1, 1893, Munford, Ala. D. May 8, 1960, Eastaboga, Ala.

Year	Team	Games	BA	SA	AB	H	2B	3B	HR	HR%	R	RBI	BB	SO	SB	Pinch Hit AB	Pinch Hit H	PO	A	E	DP	TC/G	FA	G by Pos
1917	NY A	5	.286	.333	21	6	1	0	0	0.0	3	0	1	2	0	0	0	10	2	2	0	2.8	.857	OF-5

Llewellan Camp

CAMP, LLEWELLAN ROBERT BL TR 6′ 175 lbs.
Brother of Kid Camp.
B. Feb. 22, 1868, Columbus, Ohio D. Oct. 1, 1948, Omaha, Neb.

Year	Team	Games	BA	SA	AB	H	2B	3B	HR	HR%	R	RBI	BB	SO	SB	Pinch Hit AB	Pinch Hit H	PO	A	E	DP	TC/G	FA	G by Pos
1892	STL N	42	.207	.283	145	30	3	1	2	1.4	19	13	17	27	12	0	0	42	62	30	4	3.2	.776	3B-39, OF-3
1893	CHI N	38	.263	.436	156	41	7	7	2	1.3	37	17	19	19	30	0	0	55	66	18	7	3.6	.871	3B-16, OF-11, 2B-9, SS-3
1894		8	.182	.242	33	6	2	0	0	0.0	1	1	1	6	0	0	0	26	18	9	4	6.6	.830	2B-8
3 yrs.		88	.231	.350	334	77	12	8	4	1.2	57	31	37	52	42	0	0	123	146	57	15	3.7	.825	3B-55, 2B-17, OF-14, SS-3

Roy Campanella

CAMPANELLA, ROY (Campy) BR TR 5′ 9½″ 190 lbs.
B. Nov. 19, 1921, Philadelphia, Pa. D. June 26, 1993, Woodland Hills, Calif.
Hall of Fame 1969.

Year	Team	Games	BA	SA	AB	H	2B	3B	HR	HR%	R	RBI	BB	SO	SB	Pinch Hit AB	Pinch Hit H	PO	A	E	DP	TC/G	FA	G by Pos
1948	BKN N	83	.258	.416	279	72	11	3	9	3.2	32	45	36	45	3	4	1	413	45	9	12	6.0	.981	C-78
1949		130	.287	.498	436	125	22	2	22	5.0	65	82	67	36	3	3	1	684	55	11	5	5.9	.985	C-127
1950		126	.281	.551	437	123	19	3	31	7.1	70	89	55	51	1	3	2	683	54	11	14	6.1	.985	C-123
1951		143	.325	.590	505	164	33	1	33	6.5	90	108	53	51	1	5	2	722	72	11	12	5.8	.986	C-140
1952		128	.269	.453	468	126	18	1	22	4.7	73	97	57	59	8	6	1	662	55	4	7	5.9	.994	C-122
1953		144	.312	.611	519	162	26	3	41	7.9	103	**142**	67	58	4	9	5	807	57	10	9	6.2	.989	C-140
1954		111	.207	.401	397	82	14	3	19	4.8	43	51	42	49	1	1	0	600	58	7	7	6.0	.989	C-111
1955		123	.318	.583	446	142	20	1	32	7.2	81	107	56	41	2	3	2	672	54	6	8	6.0	.992	C-121
1956		124	.219	.394	388	85	6	1	20	5.2	39	73	66	61	1	7	0	659	49	11	3	5.9	.985	C-121
1957		103	.242	.388	330	80	9	0	13	3.9	31	62	34	50	1	4	1	618	51	5	5	6.7	.993	C-100
10 yrs.		1215	.276	.500	4205	1161	178	18	242	5.8	627	856	533	501	25	45	15	6520	550	85	82	6.0	.988	C-1183
WORLD SERIES																								
1949	BKN N	5	.267	.533	15	4	1	0	1	6.7	2	2	3	1	0	0	0	32	2	0	1	6.8	1.000	C-5
1952		7	.214	.214	28	6	0	0	0	0.0	0	1	1	6	0	0	0	39	5	0	0	6.3	1.000	C-7

Roy Campanella *continued*

Year	Team	Games	BA	SA	AB	H	2B	3B	HR	HR%	R	RBI	BB	SO	SB	Pinch Hit AB	Pinch Hit H	PO	A	E	DP	TC/G	FA	G by Pos
1953		6	.273	.409	22	6	0	0	1	4.5	6	2	2	3	0	0	0	47	9	0	1	9.3	1.000	C-6
1955		7	.259	.593	27	7	3	0	2	7.4	4	4	3	3	0	0	0	42	3	1	1	6.6	.978	C-7
1956		7	.182	.227	22	4	1	0	0	0.0	2	3	3	7	0	0	0	49	3	0	1	7.4	1.000	C-7
5 yrs.		32	.237	.386	114	27	5	0	4	3.5	14	12	12	20	0	0	0	209	22	1	4	7.3	.996	C-32

Bert Campaneris

CAMPANERIS, DAGOBERTO (Campy)
Born Dagoberto Campaneris (Blanco).
B. Mar. 9, 1942, Pueblo Nuevo, Cuba.

BR TR 5′10″ 160 lbs.

Year	Team	Games	BA	SA	AB	H	2B	3B	HR	HR%	R	RBI	BB	SO	SB	Pinch Hit AB	Pinch Hit H	PO	A	E	DP	TC/G	FA	G by Pos
1964	**KC A**	67	.257	.375	269	69	14	3	4	1.5	27	22	15	41	10	1	0	102	108	8	16	3.1	.963	SS-38, OF-27, 3B-6
1965		144	.270	.382	578	156	23	**12**	6	1.0	67	42	41	71	**51**	2	1	258	276	35	53	3.7	.938	SS-109, OF-39, C-1, 2B-1, 1B-1, P-1, 3B-1
1966		142	.267	.379	573	153	29	10	5	0.9	82	42	25	72	**52**	2	0	283	350	19	80	4.7	.971	SS-138
1967		147	.248	.331	601	149	29	6	3	0.5	85	32	36	82	**55**	1	0	259	365	30	75	4.5	.954	SS-145
1968	**OAK A**	159	.276	.361	**642**	**177**	25	9	4	0.6	87	38	50	69	**62**	1	0	283	458	34	86	4.9	.956	SS-155, OF-3
1969		135	.260	.305	547	142	15	2	2	0.4	71	25	30	62	62	4	1	220	391	21	72	5.1	.967	SS-125
1970		147	.279	.448	603	168	28	4	22	3.6	97	64	36	73	**42**	5	2	267	414	19	92	4.9	.973	SS-143
1971		134	.251	.323	569	143	18	4	5	0.9	80	47	29	64	34	1	1	231	303	26	85	4.2	.954	SS-133
1972		149	.240	.325	**625**	150	25	2	8	1.3	85	32	32	88	**52**	0	0	283	494	18	93	5.4	.977	SS-148
1973		151	.250	.318	601	150	17	6	4	0.7	89	46	50	79	34	0	0	228	496	23	87	5.0	.969	SS-149
1974		134	.290	.366	527	153	18	8	2	0.4	77	41	47	81	34	0	0	207	423	22	76	4.9	.966	SS-133, DH-1
1975		137	.265	.330	509	135	15	3	4	0.8	69	46	50	71	24	0	0	199	378	23	58	4.4	.962	SS-137
1976		149	.256	.291	536	137	14	1	1	0.2	67	52	63	80	54	0	0	231	490	23	66	5.0	.969	SS-149
1977	**TEX A**	150	.254	.341	552	140	19	7	5	0.9	77	46	47	86	27	1	0	269	483	25	91	5.2	.968	SS-149
1978		98	.186	.238	269	50	5	3	1	0.4	30	17	20	36	22	1	0	151	263	20	44	4.7	.954	SS-89, DH-4
1979	**2 teams**	**TEX A** (8G –.111) **CAL A** (85G –.234)																						
"	**total**	93	.230	.278	248	57	4	4	0	0.0	29	15	20	35	13	0	0	148	233	17	74	4.4	.957	SS-90, DH-1
1980	**CAL A**	77	.252	.329	210	53	8	1	2	1.0	32	18	14	33	10	3	0	108	157	12	41	4.1	.957	SS-64, DH-2, 2B-1
1981		55	.256	.341	82	21	2	1	1	1.2	11	10	5	10	5	1	1	10	49	6	7	1.3	.908	3B-45, SS-3, 2B-2
1983	**NY A**	60	.322	.357	143	46	5	0	0	0.0	19	11	8	9	6	2	0	52	96	7	19	2.8	.955	2B-32, 3B-24
19 yrs.		2328	.259	.342	8684	2249	313	86	79	0.9	1181	646	618	1142	649	25	6	3789	6227	388	1215	4.5	.963	SS-2097, 3B-76, OF-69, 2B-36, DH-8, P-1, C-1, 1B-1

LEAGUE CHAMPIONSHIP SERIES

Year	Team	Games	BA	SA	AB	H	2B	3B	HR	HR%	R	RBI	BB	SO	SB	Pinch Hit AB	Pinch Hit H	PO	A	E	DP	TC/G	FA	G by Pos
1971	**OAK A**	3	.167	.250	12	2	1	0	0	0.0	0	0	0	1	0	0	0	3	6	0	1	3.0	1.000	SS-3
1972		2	.429	.429	7	3	0	0	0	0.0	3	0	1	0	2	0	0	3	7	0	1	5.0	1.000	SS-2
1973		5	.333	.667	21	7	1	0	2	9.5	3	3	2	2	3	0	0	6	15	1	1	4.4	.955	SS-5
1974		4	.176	.176	17	3	0	0	0	0.0	0	3	0	3	1	0	0	3	17	0	1	5.0	1.000	SS-4
1975		3	.000	.000	11	0	0	0	0	0.0	1	0	1	1	0	0	0	2	10	0	3	4.0	1.000	SS-3
1979	**CAL A**	1	—	—	0	0	0	0	0	—	0	0	0	0	0	0	0	0	0	0	0	0.0	.000	SS-1
6 yrs.		18	.221	.338	68	15	2	0	2	2.9	7	6	4	7	6 **8th**	0	0	17	55	1	7	4.1	.986	SS-18

WORLD SERIES

Year	Team	Games	BA	SA	AB	H	2B	3B	HR	HR%	R	RBI	BB	SO	SB	Pinch Hit AB	Pinch Hit H	PO	A	E	DP	TC/G	FA	G by Pos
1972	**OAK A**	7	.179	.179	28	5	0	0	0	0.0	1	0	1	4	0	0	0	17	15	1	2	4.7	.970	SS-7
1973		7	.290	.452	31	9	0	1	1	3.2	6	3	1	7	3	0	0	10	28	1	3	5.6	.974	SS-7
1974		5	.353	.471	17	6	2	0	0	0.0	1	2	0	2	1	0	0	6	16	2	5	4.8	.917	SS-5
3 yrs.		19	.263	.355	76	20	2	1	1	1.3	8	5	2	13	4	0	0	33	59	4	10	5.1	.958	SS-19

Al Campanis

CAMPANIS, ALEXANDER SEBASTIAN
Born Alessandro Campani.
Father of Jim Campanis.
B. Nov. 2, 1916, Kos, Greece.

BB TR 6′ 185 lbs.

Year	Team	Games	BA	SA	AB	H	2B	3B	HR	HR%	R	RBI	BB	SO	SB	Pinch Hit AB	Pinch Hit H	PO	A	E	DP	TC/G	FA	G by Pos
1943	**BKN N**	7	.100	.100	20	2	0	0	0	0.0	3	0	4	5	0	0	0	25	20	0	5	6.4	1.000	2B-7

Jim Campanis

CAMPANIS, JAMES ALEXANDER
Son of Al Campanis.
B. Feb. 9, 1944, New York, N. Y.

BR TR 6′ 195 lbs.

Year	Team	Games	BA	SA	AB	H	2B	3B	HR	HR%	R	RBI	BB	SO	SB	Pinch Hit AB	Pinch Hit H	PO	A	E	DP	TC/G	FA	G by Pos
1966	**LA N**	1	.000	.000	1	0	0	0	0	0.0	0	0	0	0	0	1	0	2	0	0	0	2.0	1.000	C-1
1967		41	.161	.274	62	10	1	0	2	3.2	3	2	9	14	0	24	5	90	6	1	2	4.2	.990	C-23
1968		4	.091	.091	11	1	0	0	0	0.0	0	0	1	2	0	0	0	18	6	1	0	6.3	.960	C-4
1969	**KC A**	30	.157	.217	83	13	5	0	0	0.0	4	5	5	19	0	7	1	155	7	3	2	6.3	.982	C-26
1970		31	.130	.241	54	7	0	0	2	3.7	6	2	4	14	0	16	1	64	7	1	1	5.1	.986	C-13, OF-1
1973	**PIT N**	6	.167	.167	6	1	0	0	0	0.0	0	0	0	0	0	6	1	0	0	0	0	0.0	—	
6 yrs.		113	.147	.230	217	32	6	0	4	1.8	13	9	19	49	0	54	8	329	26	6	5	5.3	.983	C-67, OF-1

Count Campau

CAMPAU, CHARLES COLUMBUS
B. Oct. 17, 1863, Detroit, Mich. D. Apr. 3, 1938, New Orleans, La.
Manager 1890.

BL TR 5′11″ 160 lbs.

Year	Team	Games	BA	SA	AB	H	2B	3B	HR	HR%	R	RBI	BB	SO	SB	Pinch Hit AB	Pinch Hit H	PO	A	E	DP	TC/G	FA	G by Pos
1888	**DET N**	70	.203	.259	251	51	5	3	1	0.4	28	18	19	36	27	0	0	101	10	8	3	1.7	.933	OF-70
1890	**STL AA**	75	.322	.516	314	101	9	11	**10**	3.2	68		26		36	0	0	118	16	9	1	1.9	.937	OF-74, 3B-1, 1B-1
1894	**WAS N**	2	.143	.143	7	1	0	0	0	0.0	1	0	1	4	0	0	0	4	0	0	0	2.0	1.000	OF-2
3 yrs.		147	.267	.399	572	153	14	14	11	1.9	97	18	46	40	63	0	0	223	26	17	4	1.8	.936	OF-146, 3B-1, 1B-1

Bruce Campbell

CAMPBELL, BRUCE DOUGLAS
B. Oct. 20, 1909, Chicago, Ill. D. June 17, 1995, Fort Myers Beach, Fla.

BL TR 6′1″ 185 lbs.

Year	Team	Games	BA	SA	AB	H	2B	3B	HR	HR%	R	RBI	BB	SO	SB	Pinch Hit AB	Pinch Hit H	PO	A	E	DP	TC/G	FA	G by Pos
1930	**CHI A**	5	.500	.800	10	5	1	1	0	0.0	4	5	1	2	0	1	1	8	0	0	0	2.0	1.000	OF-4
1931		4	.412	.882	17	7	2	0	2	11.8	4	5	0	4	0	0	0	9	0	1	0	2.5	.900	OF-4
1932	**2 teams**	**CHI A** (7G –.222) **STL A** (139G –.285)																						
"	**total**	146	.283	.447	611	173	36	11	14	2.3	86	87	40	**104**	7	3	0	306	13	22	4	2.4	.935	OF-143
1933	**STL A**	148	.277	.457	567	157	38	8	16	2.8	87	106	69	77	10	4	1	250	18	14	4	2.0	.950	OF-144
1934		138	.279	.412	481	134	25	6	9	1.9	62	74	51	64	5	14	4	230	14	17	3	2.1	.935	OF-123
1935	**CLE A**	80	.325	.497	308	100	26	3	7	2.3	56	54	31	33	2	4	1	129	2	1	1	1.8	.992	OF-75
1936		76	.372	.587	172	64	15	2	6	3.5	35	30	19	17	2	25	9	68	4	3	2	1.6	.960	OF-47
1937		134	.301	.471	448	135	42	11	4	0.9	82	61	67	49	4	11	5	204	14	5	5	1.8	.978	OF-123

Bruce Campbell *continued*

Year	Team	Games	BA	SA	AB	H	2B	3B	HR	HR%	R	RBI	BB	SO	SB	Pinch Hit AB	Pinch Hit H	PO	A	E	DP	TC/G	FA	G by Pos
1938		133	.290	.460	511	148	27	12	12	2.3	90	72	53	57	11	11	2	220	13	8	3	2.0	.967	OF-122
1939		130	.287	.449	450	129	23	13	8	1.8	84	72	67	48	7	14	2	200	12	13	3	2.0	.942	OF-115
1940	DET A	103	.283	.448	297	84	15	5	8	2.7	56	44	45	28	2	23	9	133	6	6	0	2.0	.959	OF-74
1941		141	.275	.457	512	141	28	10	15	2.9	72	93	68	67	3	5	2	241	5	6	1	1.9	.976	OF-133
1942	WAS A	122	.278	.389	378	105	17	5	5	1.3	41	63	37	34	0	29	5	188	4	9	1	2.3	.955	OF-87
13 yrs.		1360	.290	.455	4762	1382	295	87	106	2.2	759	766	548	584	53	144	41	2186	105	105	27	2.0	.956	OF-1194
WORLD SERIES																								
1940	DET A	7	.360	.520	25	9	1	0	1	4.0	4	5	4	4	0	0	0	17	0	0	0	2.4	1.000	OF-7

Dave Campbell

CAMPBELL, DAVID WILSON — BR TR 6′ 1″ 180 lbs.
B. Jan. 14, 1942, Manistee, Mich.

Year	Team	Games	BA	SA	AB	H	2B	3B	HR	HR%	R	RBI	BB	SO	SB	Pinch Hit AB	Pinch Hit H	PO	A	E	DP	TC/G	FA	G by Pos
1967	DET A	2	.000	.000	2	0	0	0	0	0.0	0	0	0	1	0	1	0	1	0	1	0	2.0	.500	1B-1
1968		9	.125	.500	8	1	0	0	1	12.5	1	2	1	3	0	3	0	4	3	0	1	1.4	1.000	2B-5
1969		32	.103	.128	39	4	1	0	0	0.0	4	2	4	15	0	14	2	38	9	2	5	2.6	.959	1B-13, 2B-5, 3B-1
1970	SD N	154	.219	.336	581	127	28	2	12	2.1	71	40	40	115	18	1	0	359	455	22	96	5.5	.974	2B-153
1971		108	.227	.334	365	83	14	2	7	1.9	38	29	37	75	9	1	0	179	264	18	50	3.9	.961	2B-69, 3B-40, SS-4, OF-2, 1B-2
1972		33	.240	.290	100	24	5	0	0	0.0	6	3	11	12	0	0	0	25	67	1	3	2.9	.989	3B-31, 2B-1
1973	3 teams	SD N (33G –.224) STL N (13G –.000) HOU N (9G –.267)																						
″	total	55	.194	.231	134	26	5	0	0	0.0	4	11	8	25	1	10	0	88	106	5	22	4.3	.975	2B-33, 3B-7, 1B-5, OF-1
1974	HOU N	35	.087	.130	23	2	1	0	0	0.0	4	2	1	8	1	13	0	20	17	2	5	2.2	.949	2B-9, 1B-6, 3B-2, OF-1
8 yrs.		428	.213	.311	1252	267	54	4	20	1.6	128	89	102	254	29	43	2	714	921	51	182	4.3	.970	2B-275, 3B-81, 1B-27, OF-4, SS-4

Gilly Campbell

CAMPBELL, WILLIAM GILTHORPE — BL TR 5′ 7½″ 182 lbs.
B. Feb. 13, 1908, Kansas City, Kans. D. Feb. 21, 1973, Los Angeles, Calif.

Year	Team	Games	BA	SA	AB	H	2B	3B	HR	HR%	R	RBI	BB	SO	SB	Pinch Hit AB	Pinch Hit H	PO	A	E	DP	TC/G	FA	G by Pos
1933	CHI N	46	.281	.371	89	25	3	1	1	1.1	11	10	7	4	0	23	6	66	9	4	1	4.0	.949	C-20
1935	CIN N	88	.257	.330	218	56	7	0	3	1.4	26	30	42	7	3	15	4	278	37	4	4	4.4	.987	C-66, 1B-5, OF-1
1936		89	.268	.345	235	63	13	1	1	0.4	28	40	43	14	2	14	3	260	49	5	11	4.4	.984	C-71, 1B-1
1937		18	.275	.325	40	11	2	0	0	0.0	3	2	5	1	0	1	0	51	7	2	0	3.5	.967	C-17
1938	BKN N	54	.246	.286	126	31	5	0	0	0.0	10	11	19	9	0	10	2	139	22	7	2	3.8	.958	C-44
5 yrs.		295	.263	.332	708	186	30	2	5	0.7	78	93	116	35	5	63	15	794	124	22	18	4.2	.977	C-218, 1B-6, OF-1

Jim Campbell

CAMPBELL, JAMES ROBERT — BR TR 6′ 190 lbs.
B. June 24, 1937, Palo Alto, Calif.

Year	Team	Games	BA	SA	AB	H	2B	3B	HR	HR%	R	RBI	BB	SO	SB	Pinch Hit AB	Pinch Hit H	PO	A	E	DP	TC/G	FA	G by Pos
1962	HOU N	27	.221	.372	86	19	4	0	3	3.5	6	6	6	23	0	2	1	174	20	6	1	8.0	.970	C-25
1963		55	.222	.316	158	35	3	0	4	2.5	9	19	10	40	0	12	2	246	28	6	4	6.7	.979	C-42
2 yrs.		82	.221	.336	244	54	7	0	7	2.9	15	25	16	63	0	14	3	420	48	12	5	7.2	.975	C-67

Jim Campbell

CAMPBELL, JAMES ROBERT, JR. — BL TR 6′ 205 lbs.
B. Jan. 10, 1943, Hartsville, S. C.

Year	Team	Games	BA	SA	AB	H	2B	3B	HR	HR%	R	RBI	BB	SO	SB	Pinch Hit AB	Pinch Hit H	PO	A	E	DP	TC/G	FA	G by Pos
1970	STL N	13	.231	.231	13	3	0	0	0	0.0	0	1	0	3	0	13	3	0	0	0	0	0.0	—	

Joe Campbell

CAMPBELL, JOSEPH EARL — BR TR 6′ 1″ 175 lbs.
B. Mar. 10, 1944, Louisville, Ky.

Year	Team	Games	BA	SA	AB	H	2B	3B	HR	HR%	R	RBI	BB	SO	SB	Pinch Hit AB	Pinch Hit H	PO	A	E	DP	TC/G	FA	G by Pos
1967	CHI N	1	.000	.000	3	0	0	0	0	0.0	0	0	0	3	0	0	0	0	0	0	0	0.0	.000	OF-1

Marc Campbell

CAMPBELL, MARC THADDEUS (Hutch) — BL TR 5′10″ 155 lbs.
B. Nov. 29, 1884, Punxsutawney, Pa. D. Feb. 13, 1946, New Bethlehem, Pa.

Year	Team	Games	BA	SA	AB	H	2B	3B	HR	HR%	R	RBI	BB	SO	SB	Pinch Hit AB	Pinch Hit H	PO	A	E	DP	TC/G	FA	G by Pos
1907	PIT N	2	.250	.250	4	1	0	0	0	0.0	0	1	1		0	0	0	2	6	1	0	4.5	.889	SS-2

Paul Campbell

CAMPBELL, PAUL McLAUGHLIN — BL TL 5′10″ 185 lbs.
B. Sept. 1, 1917, Paw Creek, N. C.

Year	Team	Games	BA	SA	AB	H	2B	3B	HR	HR%	R	RBI	BB	SO	SB	Pinch Hit AB	Pinch Hit H	PO	A	E	DP	TC/G	FA	G by Pos
1941	BOS A	1	—	—	0	0	0	0	0	—	0	0	0	0	0	0	0	0	0	0	0	0.0	—	
1942		26	.067	.067	15	1	0	0	0	0.0	4	0	1	5	1	13	1	1	0	0	0	0.3	1.000	OF-4
1946		28	.115	.154	26	3	1	0	0	0.0	3	0	2	7	0	14	2	34	1	0	2	7.0	1.000	1B-5
1948	DET A	59	.265	.337	83	22	1	1	1	1.2	15	11	1	10	0	13	1	172	18	6	11	7.3	.969	1B-27
1949		87	.278	.404	255	71	15	4	3	1.2	38	30	24	32	3	9	5	461	38	7	67	6.8	.986	1B-74
1950		3	.000	.000	1	0	0	0	0	0.0	1	0	0	0	0	1	0	0	0	0	0	0.0	—	
6 yrs.		204	.255	.358	380	97	17	5	4	1.1	61	41	28	54	4	50	9	668	57	13	80	6.7	.982	1B-106, OF-4
WORLD SERIES																								
1946	BOS A	1	—	—	0	0	0	0	0	—	0	0	0	0	0	0	0	0	0	0	0	0.0	—	

Ron Campbell

CAMPBELL, RONALD THOMAS — BR TR 6′ 1″ 180 lbs.
B. Apr. 5, 1940, Chattanooga, Tenn.

Year	Team	Games	BA	SA	AB	H	2B	3B	HR	HR%	R	RBI	BB	SO	SB	Pinch Hit AB	Pinch Hit H	PO	A	E	DP	TC/G	FA	G by Pos
1964	CHI N	26	.272	.391	92	25	6	1	1	1.1	7	10	1	21	0	0	0	64	95	10	15	6.5	.941	2B-26
1965		2	.000	.000	2	0	0	0	0	0.0	0	0	0	0	0	2	0	0	0	0	0	0.0	—	
1966		24	.217	.233	60	13	1	0	0	0.0	4	4	6	5	1	5	1	17	53	2	9	4.0	.972	SS-11, 3B-7
3 yrs.		52	.247	.325	154	38	7	1	1	0.6	11	14	7	26	1	7	1	81	148	12	24	5.5	.950	2B-26, SS-11, 3B-7

Sam Campbell

CAMPBELL, SAMUEL
B. Philadelphia, Pa. Deceased.

Year	Team	Games	BA	SA	AB	H	2B	3B	HR	HR%	R	RBI	BB	SO	SB	Pinch Hit AB	Pinch Hit H	PO	A	E	DP	TC/G	FA	G by Pos
1890	PHI AA	2	.000	.000	5	0	0	0	0	0.0	0		1		0	0	0	4	1	1	0	3.0	.833	2B-2

Soup Campbell

CAMPBELL, CLARENCE — BL TR 6′ 1″ 188 lbs.
B. Mar. 7, 1915, Sparta, Va.

Year	Team	Games	BA	SA	AB	H	2B	3B	HR	HR%	R	RBI	BB	SO	SB	Pinch Hit AB	Pinch Hit H	PO	A	E	DP	TC/G	FA	G by Pos
1940	CLE A	35	.226	.242	62	14	1	0	0	0.0	8	2	7	12	0	19	5	32	0	0	0	2.0	1.000	OF-16
1941		104	.250	.332	328	82	10	4	3	0.9	36	35	31	21	1	24	4	202	6	4	0	2.7	.981	OF-78
2 yrs.		139	.246	.318	390	96	11	4	3	0.8	44	37	38	33	1	43	9	234	6	4	0	2.6	.984	OF-94

Vin Campbell

CAMPBELL, ARTHUR VINCENT BL TR 6′ 185 lbs.
B. Jan. 30, 1888, St. Louis, Mo. D. Nov. 16, 1969, Towson, Md.

Year	Team	Games	BA	SA	AB	H	2B	3B	HR	HR%	R	RBI	BB	SO	SB	Pinch Hit AB	Pinch Hit H	PO	A	E	DP	TC/G	FA	G by Pos
1908	CHI N	1	.000	.000	1	0	0	0	0	0.0	0	0	0		0	1	0	0	0	0	0	0.0	—	
1910	PIT N	97	.326	.436	282	92	9	5	4	1.4	42	21	26	23	17	18	5	145	8	18	2	2.3	.895	OF-74
1911		42	.312	.366	93	29	3	1	0	0.0	12	10	8	7	6	17	4	35	1	3	0	1.9	.923	OF-21
1912	BOS N	145	.296	.391	**624**	185	32	9	3	0.5	102	48	32	44	19	1	0	340	20	24	6	2.7	.938	OF-144
1914	IND F	134	.318	.439	544	173	23	11	7	1.3	92	44	37		26	1	0	218	18	19	6	1.9	.925	OF-132
1915	NWK F	127	.310	.389	525	163	18	10	1	0.2	78	44	29		24	1	0	200	15	12	3	1.8	.947	OF-126
6 yrs.		546	.310	.408	2069	642	85	36	15	0.7	326	167	132	74	92	39	9	938	62	76	17	2.2	.929	OF-497

Frank Campos

CAMPOS, FRANCISCO JOSE BL TL 5′11″ 180 lbs.
Born Francisco Jose Campos (Lopez).
B. May 11, 1924, Havana, Cuba.

Year	Team	Games	BA	SA	AB	H	2B	3B	HR	HR%	R	RBI	BB	SO	SB	Pinch Hit AB	Pinch Hit H	PO	A	E	DP	TC/G	FA	G by Pos
1951	WAS A	8	.423	.615	26	11	3	1	0	0.0	4	3	0	1	0	1	0	6	0	0	0	0.9	1.000	OF-7
1952		53	.259	.330	112	29	6	1	0	0.0	9	8	1	13	0	27	2	45	0	1	0	2.0	.978	OF-23
1953		10	.111	.111	9	1	0	0	0	0.0	0	2	1	0	0	9	1	0	0	0	0	0.0	—	
3 yrs.		71	.279	.367	147	41	9	2	0	0.0	13	13	2	14	0	37	3	51	0	1	0	1.7	.981	OF-30

Sil Campusano

CAMPUSANO, SILVESTRE BR TR 6′ 160 lbs.
Born Silvestre Campusano (Diaz).
B. Dec. 31, 1965, Santo Domingo, Dominican Republic.

Year	Team	Games	BA	SA	AB	H	2B	3B	HR	HR%	R	RBI	BB	SO	SB	Pinch Hit AB	Pinch Hit H	PO	A	E	DP	TC/G	FA	G by Pos
1988	TOR A	73	.218	.359	142	31	10	2	2	1.4	14	12	9	33	0	2	0	111	2	8	0	1.7	.934	OF-69, DH-2
1990	PHI N	66	.212	.318	85	18	1	1	2	2.4	10	9	6	16	1	16	2	40	1	1	0	0.9	.976	OF-47
1991		15	.114	.200	35	4	0	0	1	2.9	2	2	1	10	0	3	1	27	1	0	0	1.9	1.000	OF-15
3 yrs.		154	.202	.324	262	53	11	3	5	1.9	26	23	16	59	1	21	3	178	4	9	0	1.4	.953	OF-131, DH-2

George Canale

CANALE, GEORGE ANTHONY BL TR 6′ 1″ 190 lbs.
B. Aug. 11, 1965, Memphis, Tenn.

Year	Team	Games	BA	SA	AB	H	2B	3B	HR	HR%	R	RBI	BB	SO	SB	Pinch Hit AB	Pinch Hit H	PO	A	E	DP	TC/G	FA	G by Pos
1989	MIL A	13	.192	.346	26	5	1	0	1	3.8	5	3	2	3	0	0	0	86	4	1	4	8.3	.989	1B-11
1990		10	.077	.154	13	1	1	0	0	0.0	4	0	2	6	0	1	1	32	4	0	1	4.0	1.000	1B-6, DH-3
1991		21	.176	.500	34	6	2	0	3	8.8	6	10	8	6	0	1	0	101	15	2	9	6.2	.983	1B-19
3 yrs.		44	.164	.384	73	12	4	0	4	5.5	15	13	12	15	0	2	1	219	23	3	14	6.3	.988	1B-36, DH-3

Willie Canate

CANATE, EMISAEL WILLIAM BR TR 6′ 170 lbs.
Born Emisael William Canate (Librada).
B. Dec. 11, 1971, Maracaibo, Venezuela.

Year	Team	Games	BA	SA	AB	H	2B	3B	HR	HR%	R	RBI	BB	SO	SB	Pinch Hit AB	Pinch Hit H	PO	A	E	DP	TC/G	FA	G by Pos
1993	TOR A	38	.213	.277	47	10	0	0	1	2.1	12	3	6	15	1	3	0	38	2	0	1	1.3	1.000	OF-31, DH-1
WORLD SERIES																								
1993	TOR A	1	—	—	0	0	0	0	0	—	0	0	0	0	0	0	0	0	0	0	0	0.0	—	

Jimmy Canavan

CANAVAN, JAMES EDWARD BR TR 5′ 8″ 160 lbs.
B. Nov. 26, 1866, New Bedford, Mass. D. May 27, 1949, New Bedford, Mass.

Year	Team	Games	BA	SA	AB	H	2B	3B	HR	HR%	R	RBI	BB	SO	SB	Pinch Hit AB	Pinch Hit H	PO	A	E	DP	TC/G	FA	G by Pos
1891	2 teams	CIN AA (101G –.228)		MIL AA (35G –.268)																				
″	total	136	.238	.380	568	135	15	18	10	1.8	107	87	43	54	28	0	0	282	415	113	36	6.0	.860	SS-112, 2B-24
1892	CHI N	118	.166	.239	439	73	10	11	0	0.0	48	32	48	48	33	0	0	294	355	54	41	6.0	.923	2B-112, OF-4, SS-2
1893	CIN N	121	.226	.317	461	104	13	7	5	1.1	65	64	51	20	31	1	0	255	33	21	0	2.5	.932	OF-116, 2B-5, 3B-1
1894		101	.272	.478	356	97	16	9	13	3.7	77	70	62	25	13	1	0	205	29	27	8	2.6	.897	OF-95, SS-3, 3B-2, 2B-1, 1B-1
1897	BKN N	63	.217	.304	240	52	9	3	2	0.8	25	34	26		9	0	0	157	162	32	18	5.6	.909	2B-63
5 yrs.		539	.223	.344	2064	461	63	48	30	1.5	322	287	230	147	114	2	0	1193	994	247	103	4.5	.899	OF-215, 2B-205, SS-117, 3B-3, 1B-1

Casey Candaele

CANDAELE, CASEY TODD BB TR 5′ 9″ 160 lbs.
B. Jan. 12, 1961, Lompoc, Calif.

Year	Team	Games	BA	SA	AB	H	2B	3B	HR	HR%	R	RBI	BB	SO	SB	Pinch Hit AB	Pinch Hit H	PO	A	E	DP	TC/G	FA	G by Pos
1986	MON N	30	.231	.288	104	24	4	1	0	0.0	9	6	5	15	3	3	1	45	74	2	13	4.3	.983	2B-24, 3B-4
1987		138	.272	.347	449	122	23	4	1	0.2	62	23	38	28	7	12	3	237	176	8	28	2.6	.981	2B-68, OF-67, SS-25, 1B-1
1988	2 teams	MON N (36G –.172)		HOU N (21G –.161)																				
″	total	57	.170	.238	147	25	8	1	0	0.0	11	5	11	17	1	7	1	79	126	2	21	4.1	.990	2B-45, OF-5, 3B-1
1990	HOU N	130	.286	.397	262	75	8	6	3	1.1	30	22	31	42	7	30	10	147	120	3	20	2.2	.989	OF-58, 2B-49, SS-13, 3B-1
1991		151	.262	.362	461	121	20	7	4	0.9	44	50	40	49	9	19	3	244	318	10	53	3.9	.983	2B-109, OF-26, 3B-11
1992		135	.212	.266	320	68	12	1	1	0.3	19	18	24	36	7	25	3	130	196	11	34	2.7	.967	SS-65, 3B-29, OF-21, 2B-9
1993		75	.240	.331	121	29	8	0	1	0.8	18	7	10	14	2	36	7	46	40	3	4	1.6	.966	2B-19, OF-17, SS-14, 3B-4
7 yrs.		716	.249	.331	1864	464	83	20	10	0.5	193	131	159	201	36	132	28	928	1050	39	173	2.9	.981	2B-323, OF-194, SS-117, 3B-50, 1B-1

John Cangelosi

CANGELOSI, JOHN ANTHONY BB TL 5′ 8″ 150 lbs.
B. Mar. 10, 1963, Brooklyn, N. Y.

Year	Team	Games	BA	SA	AB	H	2B	3B	HR	HR%	R	RBI	BB	SO	SB	Pinch Hit AB	Pinch Hit H	PO	A	E	DP	TC/G	FA	G by Pos
1985	CHI A	5	.000	.000	2	0	0	0	0	0.0	2	0	0	1	0	0	0	1	0	0	0	0.2	1.000	OF-3, DH-2
1986		137	.235	.299	438	103	16	3	2	0.5	65	32	71	61	50	1	0	276	7	9	1	2.2	.969	OF-129, DH-3
1987	PIT N	104	.275	.418	182	50	8	3	4	2.2	44	18	46	33	21	50	10	74	3	3	0	1.7	.963	OF-47
1988		75	.254	.305	118	30	4	1	0	0.0	18	8	17	16	9	42	12	52	0	2	0	2.2	.963	OF-24, P-1
1989		112	.219	.269	160	35	4	2	0	0.0	18	9	35	20	11	**68**	12	71	1	2	0	1.6	.973	OF-46
1990		58	.197	.224	76	15	2	0	0	0.0	13	1	11	12	7	36	8	24	0	0	0	2.0	1.000	OF-12
1992	TEX A	73	.188	.247	85	16	2	0	1	1.2	12	6	18	16	6	5	2	76	4	3	1	1.2	.964	OF-65, DH-6
1994	NY N	62	.252	.288	111	28	4	0	0	0.0	14	4	19	20	5	19	5	64	5	0	1	1.4	1.000	OF-50
1995	HOU N	90	.318	.393	201	64	5	2	2	1.0	46	18	48	42	21	29	8	92	4	5	0	1.7	.950	OF-59, P-1
9 yrs.		716	.248	.317	1373	341	45	11	9	0.7	232	96	265	221	130	250	57	730	24	24	3	1.7	.969	OF-435, DH-11, P-2

Rip Cannell

CANNELL, VIRGIN WIRT BL TR 5′10½″ 180 lbs.
B. Jan. 23, 1880, S. Bridgton, Me. D. Aug. 26, 1948, Bridgton, Me.

Year	Team	Games	BA	SA	AB	H	2B	3B	HR	HR%	R	RBI	BB	SO	SB	Pinch Hit AB	Pinch Hit H	PO	A	E	DP	TC/G	FA	G by Pos
1904	BOS N	100	.234	.254	346	81	5	1	0	0.0	32	18	23		10	6	1	135	5	16	1	1.7	.897	OF-93
1905		154	.247	.286	567	140	14	4	0	0.0	52	36	51		17	0	0	315	14	23	6	2.3	.935	OF-154
2 yrs.		254	.242	.274	913	221	19	5	0	0.0	84	54	74		27	6	1	450	19	39	7	2.1	.923	OF-247

Chris Cannizzaro

CANNIZZARO, CHRISTOPHER JOHN — BR TR 6′ 190 lbs.
B. May 3, 1938, Oakland, Calif.

Year	Team	Games	BA	SA	AB	H	2B	3B	HR	HR%	R	RBI	BB	SO	SB	Pinch Hit AB	Pinch Hit H	PO	A	E	DP	TC/G	FA	G by Pos
1960	STL N	7	.222	.222	9	2	0	0	0	0.0	0	1	1	3	0	0	0	19	3	0	1	3.7	1.000	C-6
1961		6	.500	.500	2	1	0	0	0	0.0	0	0	0	0	0	1	1	5	0	0	0	1.0	1.000	C-5
1962	NY N	59	.241	.271	133	32	2	1	0	0.0	9	9	19	26	1	3	1	219	34	7	3	4.6	.973	C-56, OF-1
1963		16	.242	.273	33	8	1	0	0	0.0	4	4	1	8	0	1	1	49	6	0	0	3.7	1.000	C-15
1964		60	.311	.372	164	51	10	0	0	0.0	11	10	14	28	0	5	1	225	28	3	6	4.8	.988	C-53
1965		114	.183	.231	251	46	8	2	0	0.0	17	7	28	60	0	2	0	435	69	12	8	4.6	.977	C-112
1968	PIT N	25	.241	.397	58	14	2	2	1	1.7	5	7	9	13	0	0	0	111	10	3	1	5.0	.976	C-25
1969	SD N	134	.220	.297	418	92	14	3	4	1.0	23	33	42	81	0	2	0	644	69	9	8	5.5	.988	C-132
1970		111	.279	.378	341	95	13	3	5	1.5	27	42	48	49	2	2	0	559	44	12	5	5.6	.980	C-110
1971	2 teams	SD N (21G –.190) CHI N (71G –.213)																						
″	total	92	.208	.319	260	54	9	1	6	2.3	20	31	39	34	0	2	0	425	32	7	4	5.2	.985	C-89
1972	LA N	73	.240	.300	200	48	6	0	2	1.0	14	18	31	38	0	5	2	312	26	6	4	4.8	.983	C-72
1973		17	.190	.190	21	4	0	0	0	0.0	0	3	3	3	0	3	0	33	0	0	0	2.5	1.000	C-13
1974	SD N	26	.183	.200	60	11	1	0	0	0.0	2	4	6	11	0	0	0	126	12	3	2	5.4	.979	C-26
13 yrs.		740	.235	.309	1950	458	66	12	18	0.9	132	169	241	354	3	26	6	3162	333	62	42	5.0	.983	C-714, OF-1

Joe Cannon

CANNON, JOSEPH JEROME (J. J.) — BL TR 6′ 3″ 193 lbs.
B. July 13, 1953, Camp Lejeune, N. C.

Year	Team	Games	BA	SA	AB	H	2B	3B	HR	HR%	R	RBI	BB	SO	SB	Pinch Hit AB	Pinch Hit H	PO	A	E	DP	TC/G	FA	G by Pos
1977	HOU N	9	.118	.235	17	2	2	0	0	0.0	3	1	0	5	1	4	1	7	0	0	0	2.3	1.000	OF-3
1978		8	.222	.222	18	4	0	0	0	0.0	1	1	0	1	0	3	0	7	0	2	0	1.8	.778	OF-5
1979	TOR A	61	.211	.254	142	30	1	1	1	0.7	14	5	1	34	12	0	0	81	5	0	1	1.7	1.000	OF-50
1980		70	.080	.080	50	4	0	0	0	0.0	16	4	0	14	2	4	0	29	1	1	0	0.9	.968	OF-33, DH-1
4 yrs.		148	.176	.211	227	40	3	1	1	0.4	34	11	1	54	15	11	1	124	6	3	1	1.4	.977	OF-91, DH-1

Jose Canseco

CANSECO, JOSE — BR TR 6′ 3″ 185 lbs.
Born Jose Canseco (Capas).
Brother of Ozzie Canseco.
B. July 2, 1964, Havana, Cuba.

Year	Team	Games	BA	SA	AB	H	2B	3B	HR	HR%	R	RBI	BB	SO	SB	Pinch Hit AB	Pinch Hit H	PO	A	E	DP	TC/G	FA	G by Pos
1985	OAK A	29	.302	.490	96	29	3	0	5	5.2	16	13	4	31	1	4	1	56	2	3	1	2.3	.951	OF-26
1986		157	.240	.457	600	144	29	1	33	5.5	85	117	65	175	15	1	1	319	4	14	1	2.2	.958	OF-155, DH-1
1987		159	.257	.470	630	162	35	3	31	4.9	81	113	50	157	15	1	0	263	12	7	3	1.8	.975	OF-130, DH-30
1988		158	.307	**.569**	610	187	34	0	**42**	**6.9**	120	**124**	78	128	40	1	0	304	11	7	3	2.1	.978	OF-144, DH-13
1989		65	.269	.542	227	61	9	1	17	7.5	40	57	23	69	6	3	1	119	5	3	2	2.1	.976	OF-56, DH-5
1990		131	.274	.543	481	132	14	2	37	7.7	83	101	72	158	19	2	1	182	7	1	2	1.5	.995	OF-88, DH-43
1991		154	.266	.556	572	152	32	1	**44**	**7.7**	115	122	78	152	26	6	2	245	5	9	0	1.7	.965	OF-131, DH-24
1992	2 teams	OAK A (97G –.246) TEX A (22G –.233)																						
″	total	119	.244	.456	439	107	15	0	26	5.9	74	87	63	128	6	3	0	195	5	3	3	1.7	.985	OF-90, DH-28
1993	TEX A	60	.255	.455	231	59	14	1	10	4.3	30	46	16	62	6	3	0	94	4	3	2	1.7	.970	OF-49, DH-9, P-1
1994		111	.282	.552	429	121	19	2	31	7.2	88	90	69	114	15	0	0	0	0	0	0	0.0	.000	DH-111
1995	BOS A	102	.306	.556	396	121	25	1	24	6.1	64	81	42	93	4	0	0	1	0	0	0	0.0	1.000	DH-101, OF-1
11 yrs.		1245	.271	.515	4711	1275	229	12	300	6.4	796	951	560	1267	153	24	6	1778	55	50	17	1.5	.973	OF-870, DH-365, P-1
DIVISIONAL PLAYOFF SERIES																								
1995	BOS A	3	.000	.000	13	0	0	0	0	0.0	0	0	2	2	0	0	0	4	0	0	0	1.3	1.000	DH-2, OF-1
LEAGUE CHAMPIONSHIP SERIES																								
1988	OAK A	4	.313	.938	16	5	1	0	3	18.8	4	4	1	2	1	0	0	6	0	0	0	1.5	1.000	OF-4
1989		5	.294	.471	17	5	0	0	1	5.9	1	3	3	7	0	1	0	6	1	1	0	1.6	.875	OF-5
1990		4	.182	.182	11	2	0	0	0	0.0	3	1	5	5	2	0	0	14	0	0	0	3.5	1.000	OF-4
3 yrs.		13	.273	.568	44	12	1	0	4	9.1	8	8	9	14	3	1	0	26	1	1	0	2.2	.964	OF-13
WORLD SERIES																								
1988	OAK A	5	.053	.211	19	1	0	0	1	5.3	1	5	2	5	1	0	0	8	0	0	0	1.6	1.000	OF-5
1989		4	.357	.571	14	5	0	0	1	7.1	5	3	4	3	1	0	0	6	0	0	0	1.5	1.000	OF-4
1990		4	.083	.333	12	1	0	0	1	8.3	1	2	2	3	0	1	0	4	0	0	0	1.3	1.000	OF-3
3 yrs.		13	.156	.356	45	7	0	0	3	6.7	7	10	8	11	2	1	0	18	0	0	0	1.5	1.000	OF-12

Ozzie Canseco

CANSECO, OSVALDO — BR TR 6′ 2″ 220 lbs.
Born Osvaldo Canseco (Capas).
Brother of Jose Canseco.
B. July 2, 1964, Havana, Cuba.

Year	Team	Games	BA	SA	AB	H	2B	3B	HR	HR%	R	RBI	BB	SO	SB	Pinch Hit AB	Pinch Hit H	PO	A	E	DP	TC/G	FA	G by Pos
1990	OAK A	9	.105	.158	19	2	1	0	0	0.0	1	1	1	10	0	5	1	3	0	0	0	0.5	1.000	DH-4, OF-2
1992	STL N	9	.276	.448	29	8	5	0	0	0.0	7	3	7	4	0	1	1	8	0	1	0	1.1	.889	OF-8
1993		6	.176	.176	17	3	0	0	0	0.0	0	0	1	3	0	0	0	1	0	1	0	0.4	.500	OF-5
3 yrs.		24	.200	.292	65	13	6	0	0	0.0	8	4	9	17	0	6	2	12	0	2	0	0.7	.857	OF-15, DH-4

Bart Cantz

CANTZ, BARTHOLOMEW L. — TR
B. Jan. 29, 1860, Philadelphia, Pa. D. Feb. 12, 1943, Philadelphia, Pa.

Year	Team	Games	BA	SA	AB	H	2B	3B	HR	HR%	R	RBI	BB	SO	SB	Pinch Hit AB	Pinch Hit H	PO	A	E	DP	TC/G	FA	G by Pos
1888	BAL AA	37	.167	.198	126	21	2	1	0	0.0	7	9	2		0	0	0	158	50	23	1	6.2	.900	C-33, OF-4
1889		20	.174	.203	69	12	2	0	0	0.0	6	8	4	14	2	0	0	80	15	15	2	5.5	.864	C-18, OF-2
1890	PHI AA	5	.045	.045	22	1	0	0	0	0.0	1		0		0	0	0	15	10	3	1	5.6	.893	C-5
3 yrs.		62	.157	.184	217	34	4	1	0	0.0	14	17	6	14	2	0	0	253	75	41	4	6.0	.889	C-56, OF-6

Nick Capra

CAPRA, NICK LEE — BR TR 5′ 8″ 164 lbs.
B. Mar. 8, 1958, Denver, Colo.

Year	Team	Games	BA	SA	AB	H	2B	3B	HR	HR%	R	RBI	BB	SO	SB	Pinch Hit AB	Pinch Hit H	PO	A	E	DP	TC/G	FA	G by Pos
1982	TEX A	13	.267	.467	15	4	0	0	1	6.7	2	1	3	4	2	0	0	14	2	0	1	1.8	1.000	OF-9
1983		8	.000	.000	2	0	0	0	0	0.0	2	0	0	0	0	2	0	0	0	0	0	0.0	.000	OF-4
1985		8	.125	.125	8	1	0	0	0	0.0	1	0	0	0	0	0	0	11	0	0	0	1.4	1.000	OF-8
1988	KC A	14	.138	.172	29	4	1	0	0	0.0	3	0	2	3	1	1	0	15	0	0	0	1.4	1.000	OF-11
1991	TEX A	2	—	—	0	0	0	0	0	—	1	0	1	0	0	0	0	4	0	0	0	2.0	1.000	OF-2
5 yrs.		45	.167	.241	54	9	1	0	1	1.9	9	1	6	7	3	3	0	44	2	0	1	1.4	1.000	OF-34

Pat Capri

CAPRI, PATRICK NICHOLAS — BR TR 6′½″ 170 lbs.
B. Nov. 27, 1918, New York, N. Y. D. June 14, 1989, New York, N. Y.

Year	Team	Games	BA	SA	AB	H	2B	3B	HR	HR%	R	RBI	BB	SO	SB	Pinch Hit AB	Pinch Hit H	PO	A	E	DP	TC/G	FA	G by Pos
1944	BOS N	7	.000	.000	1	0	0	0	0	0.0	1	0	0	1	0	0	0	0	2	0	1	2.0	1.000	2B-1

Ralph Capron

CAPRON, RALPH EARL (Cape) BL TR 5′11½″ 165 lbs.
B. June 16, 1889, Minneapolis, Minn. D. Sept. 19, 1980, Los Angeles, Calif.

Year	Team	Games	BA	SA	AB	H	2B	3B	HR	HR%	R	RBI	BB	SO	SB	Pinch Hit AB	Pinch Hit H	PO	A	E	DP	TC/G	FA	G by Pos
1912	PIT N	1	—	—	0	0	0	0	0	—	0	0	0	0	0	0	0	0	0	0	0	0.0	—	
1913	PHI N	2	.000	.000	1	0	0	0	0	0.0	1	0	0	0	0	0	0	0	0	0	0	0.0	.000	OF-1
2 yrs.		3	.000	.000	1	0	0	0	0	0.0	1	0	0	0	0	0	0	0	0	0	0	0.0		OF-1

Ramon Caraballo

CARABALLO, RAMON BB TR 5′ 7″ 150 lbs.
Born Ramon Caraballo (Sanchez).
B. May 23, 1969, Rio San Juan, Dominican Republic.

Year	Team	Games	BA	SA	AB	H	2B	3B	HR	HR%	R	RBI	BB	SO	SB	Pinch Hit AB	Pinch Hit H	PO	A	E	DP	TC/G	FA	G by Pos
1993	ATL N	6	—	—	0	0	0	0	0	—	0	0	0	0	0	0	0	4	3	0	0	1.4	1.000	2B-5
1995	STL N	34	.202	.323	99	20	4	1	2	2.0	10	3	6	33	3	10	3	56	73	6	20	5.6	.956	2B-24
2 yrs.		40	.202	.323	99	20	4	1	2	2.0	10	3	6	33	3	10	3	60	76	6	20	4.9	.958	2B-29

Jack Carbine

CARBINE, JOHN C. 6′ 187 lbs.
B. Oct. 12, 1855, Syracuse, N. Y. D. Sept. 11, 1915, Forest Park, Ill.

Year	Team	Games	BA	SA	AB	H	2B	3B	HR	HR%	R	RBI	BB	SO	SB	Pinch Hit AB	Pinch Hit H	PO	A	E	DP	TC/G	FA	G by Pos
1876	LOU N	7	.160	.160	25	4	0	0	0	0.0	3	1	0	0		0	0	72	2	10	5	12.0	.881	1B-6, OF-1

Bernie Carbo

CARBO, BERNARDO BL TR 5′11″ 173 lbs.
B. Aug. 5, 1947, Detroit, Mich.

Year	Team	Games	BA	SA	AB	H	2B	3B	HR	HR%	R	RBI	BB	SO	SB	Pinch Hit AB	Pinch Hit H	PO	A	E	DP	TC/G	FA	G by Pos
1969	CIN N	4	.000	.000	3	0	0	0	0	0.0	0	0	0	2	0	3	0	0	0	0	0	0.0	—	
1970		125	.310	.551	365	113	19	3	21	5.8	54	63	94	77	10	7	3	177	8	4	2	1.6	.979	OF-119
1971		106	.219	.339	310	68	20	1	5	1.6	33	20	54	56	2	12	3	154	7	3	0	1.8	.982	OF-90
1972	2 teams	CIN N (19G –.143) STL N (99G –.258)																						
″	total	118	.251	.362	323	81	13	1	7	2.2	44	34	63	59	0	17	1	171	16	6	3	2.0	.969	OF-96, 3B-1
1973	STL N	111	.286	.422	308	88	18	0	8	2.6	42	40	58	52	2	17	5	171	11	4	3	2.0	.978	OF-94
1974	BOS A	117	.249	.414	338	84	20	0	12	3.6	40	61	58	90	4	12	6	164	5	1	1	1.7	.994	OF-87, DH-15
1975		107	.257	.483	319	82	21	3	15	4.7	64	50	83	69	2	8	2	157	7	4	1	1.7	.976	OF-85, DH-13
1976	2 teams	BOS A (17G –.236) MIL A (69G –.235)																						
″	total	86	.235	.345	238	56	11	0	5	2.1	25	21	41	72	2	12	2	72	5	0	1	1.1	1.000	DH-39, OF-34
1977	BOS A	86	.289	.522	228	66	6	1	15	6.6	36	34	47	72	1	14	4	131	5	7	1	1.9	.951	OF-67, DH-7
1978	2 teams	BOS A (17G –.261) CLE A (60G –.287)																						
″	total	77	.282	.400	220	62	11	0	5	2.3	28	22	28	39	2	8	0	27	0	0	0	0.4	1.000	DH-57, OF-13
1979	STL N	52	.281	.438	64	18	1	0	3	4.7	6	12	10	22	1	32	6	10	0	0	0	0.6	1.000	OF-17
1980	2 teams	STL N (14G –.182) PIT N (7G –.333)																						
″	total	21	.235	.235	17	4	0	0	0	0.0	0	1	2	1	0	17	4	0	0	0	0	0.0	—	
12 yrs.		1010	.264	.427	2733	722	140	9	96	3.5	372	358	538	611	26	159	36	1234	64	29	12	1.6	.978	OF-702, DH-131, 3B-1
LEAGUE CHAMPIONSHIP SERIES																								
1970	CIN N	2	.000	.000	6	0	0	0	0	0.0	0	0	1	3	0	0	0	0	0	0	0	0.0	.000	OF-2
WORLD SERIES																								
1970	CIN N	4	.000	.000	8	0	0	0	0	0.0	0	0	2	3	0	2	0	4	0	0	0	2.0	1.000	OF-2
1975	BOS A	4	.429	1.429	7	3	1	0	2	28.6	3	4	1	1	0	3	2	1	1	0	0	1.0	1.000	OF-2
2 yrs.		8	.200	.667	15	3	1	0	2	13.3	3	4	3	4	0	5	2	5	1	0	0	1.5	1.000	OF-4

Jose Cardenal

CARDENAL, JOSE ROSARIO BR TR 5′10″ 150 lbs.
Born Jose Rosario Domec (Cardenal).
B. Oct. 7, 1943, Matanzas, Cuba.

Year	Team	Games	BA	SA	AB	H	2B	3B	HR	HR%	R	RBI	BB	SO	SB	Pinch Hit AB	Pinch Hit H	PO	A	E	DP	TC/G	FA	G by Pos
1963	SF N	9	.200	.200	5	1	0	0	0	0.0	1	2	1	1	0	4	1	0	0	0	0	0.0	.000	OF-2
1964		20	.000	.000	15	0	0	0	0	0.0	3	0	2	3	2	2	0	8	2	1	0	0.7	.909	OF-16
1965	CAL A	134	.250	.367	512	128	23	2	11	2.1	58	57	27	72	37	1	1	287	13	11	2	2.4	.965	OF-129, 3B-2, 2B-1
1966		154	.276	.399	561	155	15	3	16	2.9	67	48	34	69	24	10	2	351	10	3	4	2.5	.992	OF-146
1967		108	.236	.344	381	90	13	5	6	1.6	40	27	15	63	10	8	0	195	10	3	0	2.1	.986	OF-101
1968	CLE A	157	.257	.353	583	150	21	7	7	1.2	78	44	39	74	40	7	1	367	12	10	7	2.5	.974	OF-153
1969		146	.257	.373	557	143	26	3	11	2.0	75	45	49	58	36	4	1	329	12	6	2	2.4	.983	OF-142, 3B-5
1970	STL N	148	.293	.428	552	162	32	6	10	1.8	73	74	45	70	26	16	8	276	6	9	0	2.2	.969	OF-134
1971	2 teams	STL N (89G –.243) MIL A (53G –.258)																						
″	total	142	.248	.369	499	124	22	4	10	2.0	57	80	42	55	21	9	5	314	15	9	1	2.5	.973	OF-135
1972	CHI N	143	.291	.454	533	155	24	6	17	3.2	96	70	55	58	25	5	2	223	11	7	1	1.8	.971	OF-137
1973		145	.303	.437	522	158	33	2	11	2.1	80	68	58	62	19	2	1	234	13	5	2	1.8	.980	OF-142
1974		143	.293	.441	542	159	35	3	13	2.4	75	72	56	67	23	8	2	262	15	10	4	2.1	.965	OF-136
1975		154	.317	.423	574	182	30	2	9	1.6	85	68	77	50	34	5	1	313	14	8	3	2.2	.976	OF-151
1976		136	.299	.401	521	156	25	2	8	1.5	64	47	32	39	23	8	1	246	10	5	1	2.0	.981	OF-128
1977		100	.239	.341	226	54	12	1	3	1.3	33	18	28	30	5	31	10	85	1	2	0	1.4	.977	OF-62, 2B-1, 3B-1
1978	PHI N	87	.249	.368	201	50	12	0	4	2.0	27	33	23	16	2	33	9	365	17	5	39	6.1	.987	1B-50, OF-13
1979	2 teams	PHI N (29G –.208) NY N (11G –.297)																						
″	total	40	.247	.400	85	21	7	0	2	2.4	12	13	14	11	2	17	4	49	0	0	3	2.0	1.000	OF-21, 1B-3
1980	2 teams	NY N (26G –.167) KC A (25G –.340)																						
″	total	51	.263	.295	95	25	3	0	0	0.0	12	9	11	9	0	17	1	60	3	1	1	1.9	.984	OF-29, 1B-5
18 yrs.		2017	.275	.395	6964	1913	333	46	138	2.0	936	775	608	807	329	187	50	3964	164	95	70	2.3	.978	OF-1777, 1B-58, 3B-8, 2B-2
LEAGUE CHAMPIONSHIP SERIES																								
1978	PHI N	2	.167	.167	6	1	0	0	0	0.0	0	0	1	1	0	0	0	21	0	0	1	10.5	1.000	1B-2
WORLD SERIES																								
1980	KC A	4	.200	.200	10	2	0	0	0	0.0	0	0	0	3	0	1	0	7	0	0	0	1.8	1.000	OF-4

Leo Cardenas

CARDENAS, LEONARDO LAZARO (Chico) BR TR 5′11″ 150 lbs.
Born Leonardo Lazaro Cardenas (Alfonso).
B. Dec. 17, 1938, Matanzas, Cuba.

Year	Team	Games	BA	SA	AB	H	2B	3B	HR	HR%	R	RBI	BB	SO	SB	Pinch Hit AB	Pinch Hit H	PO	A	E	DP	TC/G	FA	G by Pos
1960	CIN N	48	.232	.324	142	33	2	4	1	0.7	13	12	6	32	0	1	0	76	128	9	32	4.5	.958	SS-47
1961		74	.308	.485	198	61	18	1	5	2.5	23	24	15	39	1	12	1	83	133	6	21	3.5	.973	SS-63
1962		153	.294	.411	589	173	31	4	10	1.7	77	60	39	99	2	3	1	273	443	21	84	4.9	.972	SS-149
1963		158	.235	.326	565	133	22	4	7	1.2	42	48	23	101	3	2	1	270	420	20	84	4.5	.972	SS-157
1964		163	.251	.357	597	150	32	2	9	1.5	61	69	41	110	4	0	0	336	436	32	87	4.9	.960	SS-163

Leo Cardenas *continued*

Year	Team	Games	BA	SA	AB	H	2B	3B	HR	HR%	R	RBI	BB	SO	SB	Pinch Hit AB	Pinch Hit H	PO	A	E	DP	TC/G	FA	G by Pos
1965		156	.287	.431	557	160	25	11	11	2.0	65	57	60	100	1	1	0	292	440	19	92	4.8	.975	SS-155
1966		160	.255	.419	568	145	25	4	20	3.5	59	81	45	87	9	0	0	279	446	15	87	4.6	.980	SS-160
1967		108	.256	.325	379	97	14	3	2	0.5	30	21	34	77	4	0	0	190	316	15	57	4.8	.971	SS-108
1968		137	.235	.319	452	106	13	2	7	1.5	45	41	36	83	2	1	0	221	388	29	66	4.7	.955	SS-136
1969	**MIN A**	160	.280	.388	578	162	24	4	10	1.7	67	70	66	96	5	0	0	310	570	32	126	5.7	.965	SS-160
1970		160	.247	.374	588	145	34	4	11	1.9	67	65	42	101	2	0	0	280	487	17	91	4.9	.978	SS-160
1971		153	.264	.421	554	146	25	4	18	3.2	59	75	51	69	3	1	0	266	445	11	89	4.7	.985	SS-153
1972	**CAL A**	150	.223	.283	551	123	11	2	6	1.1	25	42	35	73	1	0	0	241	471	22	82	4.9	.970	SS-150
1973	**CLE A**	72	.215	.236	195	42	4	0	0	0.0	9	12	13	42	1	0	0	90	167	11	37	3.7	.959	SS-67, 3B-5
1974	**TEX A**	34	.272	.304	92	25	3	0	0	0.0	5	7	2	14	1	1	0	26	54	2	3	2.3	.976	3B-21, SS-10, DH-4
1975		55	.235	.284	102	24	2	0	1	1.0	15	5	14	12	0	9	1	38	85	5	12	2.5	.961	3B-43, SS-5, 2B-3
16 yrs.		1941	.257	.367	6707	1725	285	49	118	1.8	662	689	522	1135	39	31	4	3271	5429	266	1050	4.7	.970	SS-1843, 3B-69, DH-4, 2B-3
LEAGUE CHAMPIONSHIP SERIES																								
1969	**MIN A**	3	.154	.308	13	2	0	1	0	0.0	0	0	0	7	0	0	0	14	12	1	3	9.0	.963	SS-3
1970		3	.182	.182	11	2	0	0	0	0.0	1	1	1	1	0	0	0	6	11	2	3	6.3	.895	SS-3
2 yrs.		6	.167	.250	24	4	0	1	0	0.0	1	1	1	8	0	0	0	20	23	3	6	7.7	.935	SS-6
WORLD SERIES																								
1961	**CIN N**	3	.333	.667	3	1	1	0	0	0.0	0	0	0	1	0	3	1	0	0	0	0	0.0	—	

Rod Carew

CAREW, RODNEY CLINE
Born Rodney Cline Carew (Scott).
B. Oct. 1, 1945, Gatun, Canal Zone.
Hall of Fame 1991.

BL TR 6′ 170 lbs.

Year	Team	Games	BA	SA	AB	H	2B	3B	HR	HR%	R	RBI	BB	SO	SB	Pinch Hit AB	Pinch Hit H	PO	A	E	DP	TC/G	FA	G by Pos
1967	**MIN A**	137	.292	.409	514	150	22	7	8	1.6	66	51	37	91	5	1	1	289	314	15	60	4.6	.976	2B-134
1968		127	.273	.347	461	126	27	2	1	0.2	46	42	26	71	12	9	2	266	285	18	50	4.7	.968	2B-117, SS-4
1969		123	**.332**	.467	458	152	30	4	8	1.7	79	56	37	72	19	7	4	244	302	17	80	4.8	.970	2B-118
1970		51	.366	.524	191	70	12	3	4	2.1	27	28	11	28	4	5	0	79	122	8	26	4.5	.962	2B-45, 1B-1
1971		147	.307	.380	577	177	16	10	2	0.3	88	48	45	81	6	3	1	324	331	16	76	4.7	.976	2B-142, 3B-2
1972		142	**.318**	.379	535	170	21	6	0	0.0	61	51	43	60	12	5	1	331	378	16	85	5.2	.978	2B-139
1973		149	**.350**	.471	580	**203**	30	**11**	6	1.0	98	62	62	55	41	3	0	383	413	13	96	5.5	.984	2B-147
1974		153	**.364**	.446	599	**218**	30	5	3	0.5	86	55	74	49	38	5	1	375	416	33	114	5.6	.960	2B-148
1975		143	**.359**	.497	535	192	24	4	14	2.6	89	80	64	40	35	5	2	408	377	21	89	5.8	.974	2B-123, 1B-14, DH-2
1976		156	.331	.463	605	200	29	12	9	1.5	97	90	67	52	49	5	3	1398	110	16	149	9.6	.990	1B-152, 2B-7
1977		155	**.388**	.570	616	**239**	38	**16**	14	2.3	**128**	100	69	55	23	6	3	1463	124	10	161	10.2	.994	1B-151, 2B-4, DH-1
1978		152	**.333**	.441	564	188	26	10	5	0.9	85	70	78	62	27	10	4	1363	105	16	134	9.7	.989	1B-148, 2B-4, OF-1
1979	**CAL A**	110	.318	.391	409	130	15	3	3	0.7	78	44	73	46	18	0	0	804	55	10	101	8.0	.988	1B-103, DH-6
1980		144	.331	.437	540	179	34	7	3	0.6	74	59	59	38	23	11	4	897	57	6	82	7.1	.994	1B-103, DH-32
1981		93	.305	.374	364	111	17	1	2	0.5	57	21	45	45	16	2	1	877	60	5	90	10.2	.995	1B-90, DH-2
1982		138	.319	.403	523	167	25	5	3	0.6	88	44	67	49	10	5	1	1339	94	12	115	10.8	.992	1B-134
1983		129	.339	.411	472	160	24	2	2	0.4	66	44	57	48	6	17	6	891	42	6	94	8.2	.994	1B-89, DH-24, 2B-2
1984		93	.295	.353	329	97	8	1	3	0.9	42	31	40	39	4	12	4	724	59	15	73	9.5	.981	1B-83, DH-1
1985		127	.280	.345	443	124	17	3	2	0.5	69	39	64	47	5	13	2	1055	65	7	121	9.7	.994	1B-116
19 yrs.		2469	.328	.429	9315	3053	445	112	92	1.0	1424	1015	1018	1028	353	124	40	13510	3709	260	1796	7.3	.985	1B-1184, 2B-1130, DH-68, SS-4, 3B-2, OF-1
LEAGUE CHAMPIONSHIP SERIES																								
1969	**MIN A**	3	.071	.071	14	1	0	0	0	0.0	0	0	1	4	0	0	0	5	3	1	1	3.0	.889	2B-3
1970		2	.000	.000	2	0	0	0	0	0.0	0	0	0	1	0	2	0	0	0	0	0	0.0	—	
1979	**CAL A**	4	.412	.588	17	7	3	0	0	0.0	4	1	0	0	1	0	0	34	1	0	6	8.8	1.000	1B-4
1982		5	.176	.235	17	3	1	0	0	0.0	2	0	4	4	1	0	0	43	4	0	3	9.4	1.000	1B-5
4 yrs.		14	.220	.300	50	11	4	0	0	0.0	6	1	5	9	2	2	0	82	8	1	10	7.6	.989	1B-9, 2B-3

Andy Carey

CAREY, ANDREW ARTHUR
B. Oct. 18, 1931, Oakland, Calif.

BR TR 6′ 1½″ 190 lbs.

Year	Team	Games	BA	SA	AB	H	2B	3B	HR	HR%	R	RBI	BB	SO	SB	Pinch Hit AB	Pinch Hit H	PO	A	E	DP	TC/G	FA	G by Pos
1952	**NY A**	16	.150	.150	40	6	0	0	0	0.0	6	1	3	10	0	0	0	13	23	6	4	2.8	.857	3B-14, SS-1
1953		51	.321	.531	81	26	5	0	4	4.9	14	8	9	12	2	7	1	34	56	2	8	2.1	.978	3B-40, SS-2, 2B-1
1954		122	.302	.423	411	124	14	6	8	1.9	60	65	43	38	5	3	0	154	283	15	32	3.8	.967	3B-120
1955		135	.257	.378	510	131	19	**11**	7	1.4	73	47	44	51	3	0	0	154	301	22	37	3.5	.954	3B-135
1956		132	.237	.339	422	100	18	2	7	1.7	54	50	45	53	9	1	0	114	265	21	26	3.1	.948	3B-131
1957		85	.255	.393	247	63	6	5	6	2.4	30	33	15	42	2	6	1	66	147	5	9	2.7	.977	3B-81
1958		102	.286	.486	315	90	19	4	12	3.8	39	45	34	43	1	7	2	99	195	12	22	3.1	.961	3B-99
1959		41	.257	.356	101	26	1	0	3	3.0	11	9	7	17	1	8	3	39	48	8	10	2.8	.916	3B-34
1960	**2 teams**	**NY A** (4G –.333) **KC A** (102G –.233)																						
″	**total**	106	.234	.402	346	81	14	4	12	3.5	31	54	26	53	0	15	1	95	181	7	26	3.0	.975	3B-93, OF-1
1961	**2 teams**	**KC A** (39G –.244) **CHI A** (56G –.266)																						
″	**total**	95	.256	.395	266	68	18	5	3	1.1	41	25	26	47	0	1	0	58	143	10	16	2.3	.953	3B-93
1962	**LA N**	53	.234	.351	111	26	5	1	2	1.8	12	13	16	23	0	13	2	28	54	6	4	2.1	.932	3B-42
11 yrs.		938	.260	.396	2850	741	119	38	64	2.2	371	350	268	389	23	61	10	854	1696	114	194	3.0	.957	3B-882, SS-3, OF-1, 2B-1
WORLD SERIES																								
1955	**NY A**	2	.500	1.500	2	1	0	1	0	0.0	0	1	0	0	0	2	1	0	0	0	0	0.0	—	
1956		7	.158	.158	19	3	0	0	0	0.0	2	0	1	6	0	0	0	6	10	2	0	2.6	.889	3B-7
1957		2	.286	.429	7	2	1	0	0	0.0	0	1	1	0	0	0	0	3	6	0	0	4.5	1.000	3B-2
1958		5	.083	.083	12	1	0	0	0	0.0	1	0	0	3	0	0	0	2	6	0	0	1.6	1.000	3B-5
4 yrs.		16	.175	.250	40	7	1	1	0	0.0	3	2	2	9	0	2	1	11	22	2	0	2.5	.943	3B-14

Max Carey

CAREY, MAX (Scoops) — BB TR 5′11½″ 170 lbs.
Born Maximilian Carnarius.
B. Jan. 11, 1890, Terre Haute, Ind. D. May 30, 1976, Miami, Fla.
Manager 1932–33.
Hall of Fame 1961.

Year	Team	Games	BA	SA	AB	H	2B	3B	HR	HR%	R	RBI	BB	SO	SB	Pinch Hit AB	Pinch Hit H	PO	A	E	DP	TC/G	FA	G by Pos
1910	PIT N	2	.500	.833	6	3	0	1	0	0.0	2	2	2	1	0	0	0	10	1	0	0	5.5	1.000	OF-2
1911		129	.258	.375	427	110	15	10	5	1.2	77	43	44	75	27	5	1	304	11	8	5	2.6	.975	OF-122
1912		150	.302	.394	587	177	23	8	5	0.9	114	66	61	79	45	0	0	369	19	13	10	2.7	.968	OF-150
1913		154	.277	.371	**620**	172	23	10	5	0.8	**99**	49	55	67	**61**	0	0	363	28	16	6	2.6	.961	OF-154
1914		156	.243	.347	**593**	144	25	**17**	1	0.2	76	31	59	56	38	1	1	318	23	12	3	2.3	.966	OF-154
1915		140	.254	.333	564	143	26	5	3	0.5	76	27	57	58	**36**	1	0	307	21	6	5	2.4	.982	OF-140
1916		154	.264	.374	599	158	23	11	7	1.2	90	42	59	58	**63**	0	0	419	32	8	10	3.0	.983	OF-154
1917		155	.296	.378	588	174	21	12	1	0.2	82	51	58	38	**46**	2	2	440	28	10	8	3.1	.979	OF-153
1918		126	.274	.348	468	128	14	6	3	0.6	70	48	**62**	25	**58**	0	0	359	25	17	9	3.2	.958	OF-126
1919		66	.307	.365	244	75	10	2	0	0.0	41	9	25	24	18	2	1	173	5	10	1	3.0	.947	OF-63
1920		130	.289	.348	485	140	18	4	1	0.2	74	35	59	31	**52**	2	1	345	10	12	0	2.8	.967	OF-129
1921		140	.309	.430	521	161	34	4	7	1.3	85	56	70	30	37	1	0	431	15	20	6	3.4	.957	OF-139
1922		155	.329	.459	629	207	28	12	10	1.6	140	70	**80**	26	**51**	0	0	449	22	15	4	3.1	.969	OF-155
1923		153	.308	.452	610	188	32	**19**	6	1.0	120	63	73	28	**51**	0	0	450	28	19	4	3.2	.962	OF-153
1924		149	.297	.412	599	178	30	9	7	1.2	113	55	58	17	**49**	0	0	428	16	16	3	3.1	.965	OF-149
1925		133	.343	.491	542	186	39	13	5	0.9	109	44	66	19	**46**	2	0	363	20	20	2	3.1	.950	OF-130
1926	2 teams	PIT N (86G –.222)	BKN N (27G –.260)																					
″	total	113	.231	.300	424	98	17	6	0	0.0	64	35	38	19	10	3	3	295	8	19	3	3.0	.941	OF-109
1927	BKN N	144	.266	.364	538	143	30	10	1	0.2	70	54	64	18	32	2	1	331	19	11	6	2.6	.970	OF-141
1928		108	.247	.304	296	73	11	0	2	0.7	41	19	47	24	18	10	3	202	8	3	1	2.2	.986	OF-95
1929		19	.304	.304	23	7	0	0	0	0.0	2	1	3	2	0	11	4	7	0	0	0	1.8	1.000	OF-4
20 yrs.		2476	.285	.385	9363	2665	419	159	69	0.7	1545	800	1040	695	738 **7th**	42	17	6363	339	235	86	2.9	.966	OF-2422
WORLD SERIES																								
1925	PIT N	7	.458	.625	24	11	4	0	0	0.0	6	2	2	3	3	0	0	14	0	1	0	2.1	.933	OF-7

Paul Carey

CAREY, PAUL STEPHEN — BL TR 6′ 4″ 220 lbs.
B. Jan. 8, 1968, Boston, Mass.

Year	Team	Games	BA	SA	AB	H	2B	3B	HR	HR%	R	RBI	BB	SO	SB	Pinch Hit AB	Pinch Hit H	PO	A	E	DP	TC/G	FA	G by Pos
1993	BAL A	18	.213	.234	47	10	1	0	0	0.0	1	3	5	14	0	6	0	64	1	2	7	4.8	.970	1B-9, DH-5

Roger Carey

CAREY, ROGER J.
Deceased.

Year	Team	Games	BA	SA	AB	H	2B	3B	HR	HR%	R	RBI	BB	SO	SB	Pinch Hit AB	Pinch Hit H	PO	A	E	DP	TC/G	FA	G by Pos
1887	NY N	1	.000	.000	4	0	0	0	0	0.0	0	2	0	1	0	0	0	2	6	2	1	10.0	.800	2B-1

Scoops Carey

CAREY, GEORGE C. — BR TR 175 lbs.
B. Dec. 4, 1870, Pittsburgh, Pa. D. Dec. 17, 1916, East Liverpool, Ohio.

Year	Team	Games	BA	SA	AB	H	2B	3B	HR	HR%	R	RBI	BB	SO	SB	Pinch Hit AB	Pinch Hit H	PO	A	E	DP	TC/G	FA	G by Pos
1895	BAL N	123	.261	.335	490	128	21	6	1	0.2	59	75	27	32	2	0	0	1137	46	15	73	9.5	.987	1B-123, SS-1, OF-1, 3B-1
1898	LOU N	8	.188	.281	32	6	1	1	0	0.0	1	1	1		0	0	0	94	5	4	5	12.9	.961	1B-8
1902	WAS A	120	.314	.440	452	142	35	11	0	0.0	46	60	20		3	0	0	1190	69	14	54	10.6	.989	1B-120
1903		48	.202	.240	183	37	3	2	0	0.0	8	23	4		0	1	0	435	23	11	18	10.0	.977	1B-47
4 yrs.		299	.271	.360	1157	313	60	20	1	0.1	114	159	52	32	5	1	0	2856	143	44	150	10.1	.986	1B-298, SS-1, OF-1, 3B-1

Tom Carey

CAREY, THOMAS FRANCIS ALOYSIUS (Scoops) — BR TR 5′ 8½″ 170 lbs.
B. Oct. 11, 1906, Hoboken, N. J. D. Feb. 21, 1970, Rochester, N. Y.

Year	Team	Games	BA	SA	AB	H	2B	3B	HR	HR%	R	RBI	BB	SO	SB	Pinch Hit AB	Pinch Hit H	PO	A	E	DP	TC/G	FA	G by Pos
1935	STL A	76	.291	.378	296	86	18	4	0	0.0	29	42	13	11	0	0	0	189	253	18	52	6.1	.961	2B-76
1936		134	.273	.359	488	133	27	6	1	0.2	58	57	27	25	2	6	2	308	435	25	82	6.0	.967	2B-128, SS-1
1937		130	.275	.335	487	134	24	1	1	0.2	54	40	21	26	1	0	0	293	397	15	83	5.3	.979	2B-87, SS-44, 3B-1
1939	BOS A	54	.242	.304	161	39	6	2	0	0.0	17	20	3	9	0	7	2	93	116	2	22	4.7	.991	2B-35, SS-10
1940		43	.323	.387	62	20	4	0	0	0.0	4	7	2	1	0	10	3	24	49	3	14	2.7	.961	SS-20, 3B-4, 2B-4
1941		24	.200	.200	20	4	0	0	0	0.0	7	2	0	2	0	3	1	14	14	0	3	1.6	1.000	2B-9, SS-8
1942		1	1.000	1.000	1	1	0	0	0	0.0	0	1	0	0	0	0	0	1	0	0	0	1.0	1.000	2B-1
1946		3	.200	.200	5	1	0	0	0	0.0	0	0	0	1	0	0	0	3	6	1	2	3.3	.900	2B-3
8 yrs.		465	.275	.348	1520	418	79	13	2	0.1	169	169	66	75	3	26	8	925	1270	64	258	5.2	.972	2B-343, SS-83, 3B-5

Tom Carey

CAREY, THOMAS JOHN — BR TR 5′ 8″ 145 lbs.
Born J. J. Norton.
B. 1849, Brooklyn, N. Y. D. Feb. 13, 1899, Los Angeles, Calif.

Year	Team	Games	BA	SA	AB	H	2B	3B	HR	HR%	R	RBI	BB	SO	SB	Pinch Hit AB	Pinch Hit H	PO	A	E	DP	TC/G	FA	G by Pos
1876	HAR N	68	.270	.294	289	78	7	0	0	0.0	51	26	3	4		0	0	74	218	39	9	4.9	.882	SS-68
1877		60	.255	.292	274	70	3	2	1	0.4	38	20	0	9		0	0	49	203	53	11	5.1	.826	SS-60
1878	PRO N	61	.237	.300	253	60	10	3	0	0.0	33	24	0	14		0	0	56	207	38	8	4.9	.874	SS-61
1879	CLE N	80	.239	.287	335	80	14	1	0	0.0	30	32	5	20		0	0	79	263	54	13	4.9	.864	SS-80
4 yrs.		269	.250	.293	1151	288	34	6	1	0.1	152	102	8	47		0	0	258	891	184	41	5.0	.862	SS-269

Bobby Cargo

CARGO, ROBERT J. — BR TR
B. Oct. 1868, Pittsburgh, Pa. D. Apr. 27, 1904, Atlanta, Ga.

Year	Team	Games	BA	SA	AB	H	2B	3B	HR	HR%	R	RBI	BB	SO	SB	Pinch Hit AB	Pinch Hit H	PO	A	E	DP	TC/G	FA	G by Pos
1892	PIT N	2	.250	.250	4	1	0	0	0	0.0	0	0	0	0	0	0	0	2	5	4	2	5.5	.636	SS-2

Fred Carisch

CARISCH, FREDERICK BEHLMER — BR TR 5′10½″ 174 lbs.
B. Nov. 14, 1881, Fountain City, Wis. D. Apr. 19, 1977, San Gabriel, Calif.

Year	Team	Games	BA	SA	AB	H	2B	3B	HR	HR%	R	RBI	BB	SO	SB	Pinch Hit AB	Pinch Hit H	PO	A	E	DP	TC/G	FA	G by Pos
1903	PIT N	5	.333	.722	18	6	4	0	1	5.6	4	5	0		0	1	0	24	7	1	0	8.0	.969	C-4
1904		37	.248	.288	125	31	3	1	0	0.0	9	8	9		3	1	0	237	44	5	6	7.9	.983	C-22, 1B-14
1905		32	.206	.262	107	22	0	3	0	0.0	7	8	2		1	2	0	137	42	5	3	6.1	.973	C-30
1906		4	.083	.083	12	1	0	0	0	0.0	0	0	1		1	0	0	15	5	2	0	5.5	.909	C-4
1912	CLE A	26	.271	.343	70	19	3	1	0	0.0	4	5	1		3	2	0	100	40	7	5	6.4	.952	C-23
1913		81	.216	.252	222	48	4	2	0	0.0	11	26	21	19	6	2	0	391	114	15	10	6.6	.971	C-79
1914		40	.216	.284	102	22	3	2	0	0.0	8	5	12	18	2	2	0	183	44	9	5	6.2	.962	C-38
1923	DET A	2	—	—	0	0	0	0	0	—	0	0	0	0	0	0	0	1	0	0	0	0.5	1.000	C-2
8 yrs.		227	.227	.285	656	149	17	9	1	0.2	43	57	46	37	16	10	0	1088	296	44	29	6.6	.969	C-202, 1B-14

Fred Carl

CARL, FREDERICK E. TL 5′ 6″ 158 lbs.
B. Sept. 8, 1858, Baltimore, Md. D. May 4, 1919, Washington, D. C.

Year	Team	Games	BA	SA	AB	H	2B	3B	HR	HR%	R	RBI	BB	SO	SB	Pinch Hit AB	Pinch Hit H	PO	A	E	DP	TC/G	FA	G by Pos
1889	LOU AA	25	.202	.263	99	20	2	2	0	0.0	13	13	16	22	0	0	0	38	29	13	9	3.2	.837	OF-18, 2B-6, 3B-1

Jim Carlin

CARLIN, JAMES ARTHUR BR TR 5′11″ 165 lbs.
B. Feb. 23, 1918, Wylam, Ala.

Year	Team	Games	BA	SA	AB	H	2B	3B	HR	HR%	R	RBI	BB	SO	SB	Pinch Hit AB	Pinch Hit H	PO	A	E	DP	TC/G	FA	G by Pos
1941	PHI N	16	.143	.333	21	3	1	0	1	4.8	2	2	3	4	0	4	0	4	1	0	0	0.5	1.000	OF-9, 3B-2

Walter Carlisle

CARLISLE, WALTER G. (Rosy) BB TR 5′ 9″ 154 lbs.
B. July 6, 1883, Yorkshire, England D. May 27, 1945, Los Angeles, Calif.

Year	Team	Games	BA	SA	AB	H	2B	3B	HR	HR%	R	RBI	BB	SO	SB	Pinch Hit AB	Pinch Hit H	PO	A	E	DP	TC/G	FA	G by Pos
1908	BOS A	3	.100	.100	10	1	0	0	0	0.0	0	0	1		1	0	0	5	1	0	0	2.0	1.000	OF-3

Swede Carlstrom

CARLSTROM, ALBIN OSCAR BR TR 6′ 167 lbs.
B. Oct. 26, 1886, Elizabeth, N. J. D. Apr. 23, 1935, Elizabeth, N. J.

Year	Team	Games	BA	SA	AB	H	2B	3B	HR	HR%	R	RBI	BB	SO	SB	Pinch Hit AB	Pinch Hit H	PO	A	E	DP	TC/G	FA	G by Pos
1911	BOS A	2	.167	.167	6	1	0	0	0	0.0	0	0	0		0	0	0	3	6	0	1	4.5	1.000	SS-2

Cleo Carlyle

CARLYLE, HIRAM CLEO BL TR 6′ 170 lbs.
Brother of Roy Carlyle.
B. Sept. 7, 1902, Fairburn, Ga. D. Nov. 12, 1967, Los Angeles, Calif.

Year	Team	Games	BA	SA	AB	H	2B	3B	HR	HR%	R	RBI	BB	SO	SB	Pinch Hit AB	Pinch Hit H	PO	A	E	DP	TC/G	FA	G by Pos
1927	BOS A	95	.234	.345	278	65	12	8	1	0.4	31	28	36	40	4	10	3	127	10	5	0	1.7	.965	OF-83

Roy Carlyle

CARLYLE, ROY EDWARD (Dizzy) BL TR 6′ 2½″ 195 lbs.
Brother of Cleo Carlyle.
B. Dec. 10, 1900, Buford, Ga. D. Nov. 22, 1956, Norcross, Ga.

Year	Team	Games	BA	SA	AB	H	2B	3B	HR	HR%	R	RBI	BB	SO	SB	Pinch Hit AB	Pinch Hit H	PO	A	E	DP	TC/G	FA	G by Pos
1925	2 teams	WAS A (1G –.000) BOS A (93G –.326)																						
″	total	94	.325	.495	277	90	20	3	7	2.5	36	49	16	30	1	22	8	122	5	13	0	2.1	.907	OF-67
1926	2 teams	BOS A (45G –.287) NY A (35G –.377)																						
″	total	80	.309	.415	217	67	11	3	2	0.9	25	27	8	27	0	25	10	77	5	8	0	1.7	.911	OF-53
2 yrs.		174	.318	.460	494	157	31	6	9	1.8	61	76	24	57	1	47	18	199	10	21	0	1.9	.909	OF-120

George Carman

CARMAN, GEORGE WARTMAN
B. Mar. 29, 1866, Philadelphia, Pa. D. June 16, 1929, Lancaster, Pa.

Year	Team	Games	BA	SA	AB	H	2B	3B	HR	HR%	R	RBI	BB	SO	SB	Pinch Hit AB	Pinch Hit H	PO	A	E	DP	TC/G	FA	G by Pos
1890	PHI AA	27	.172	.194	93	16	2	0	0	0.0	9		8		5	0	0	33	46	25	4	3.9	.760	SS-14, OF-10, 2B-2, 3B-1

Duke Carmel

CARMEL, LEON JAMES BL TL 6′ 3″ 202 lbs.
B. Apr. 23, 1937, New York, N. Y.

Year	Team	Games	BA	SA	AB	H	2B	3B	HR	HR%	R	RBI	BB	SO	SB	Pinch Hit AB	Pinch Hit H	PO	A	E	DP	TC/G	FA	G by Pos
1959	STL N	10	.130	.174	23	3	1	0	0	0.0	2	3	1	6	0	0	0	15	0	0	0	1.5	1.000	OF-10
1960		4	.000	.000	3	0	0	0	0	0.0	0	0	1	1	1	0	0	10	2	0	1	4.0	1.000	1B-2, OF-1
1963	2 teams	STL N (57G –.227) NY N (47G –.235)																						
″	total	104	.233	.358	193	45	6	3	4	2.1	20	20	25	48	2	19	4	270	11	6	13	3.7	.979	OF-59, 1B-19
1965	NY A	6	.000	.000	8	0	0	0	0	0.0	0	0	0	5	0	4	0	7	1	0	0	4.0	1.000	1B-2
4 yrs.		124	.211	.322	227	48	7	3	4	1.8	22	23	27	60	3	23	4	302	14	6	14	3.5	.981	OF-70, 1B-23

Eddie Carnett

CARNETT, EDWIN ELLIOTT (Lefty) BL TL 6′ 185 lbs.
B. Oct. 21, 1916, Springfield, Mo.

Year	Team	Games	BA	SA	AB	H	2B	3B	HR	HR%	R	RBI	BB	SO	SB	Pinch Hit AB	Pinch Hit H	PO	A	E	DP	TC/G	FA	G by Pos
1941	BOS N	2	—	—	0	0	0	0	0	—	0	0	0	0	0	0	0	0	0	0	0	0.0	.000	P-2
1944	CHI A	126	.276	.357	457	126	18	8	1	0.2	51	60	26	35	5	10	1	425	17	12	16	3.9	.974	OF-88, 1B-25, P-2
1945	CLE A	30	.219	.315	73	16	7	0	0	0.0	5	7	2	9	0	11	3	33	1	1	1	1.9	.971	OF-16, P-2
3 yrs.		158	.268	.351	530	142	25	8	1	0.2	56	67	28	44	5	21	4	458	18	13	17	3.6	.973	OF-104, 1B-25, P-6

Bill Carney

CARNEY, WILLIAM JOHN BB TR 5′10″
B. Mar. 25, 1874, St. Paul, Minn. D. July 31, 1938, Hopkins, Minn.

Year	Team	Games	BA	SA	AB	H	2B	3B	HR	HR%	R	RBI	BB	SO	SB	Pinch Hit AB	Pinch Hit H	PO	A	E	DP	TC/G	FA	G by Pos
1904	CHI N	2	.000	.000	7	0	0	0	0	0.0	0	0	1		0	0	0	0	1	0	0	0.5	1.000	OF-2

Jack Carney

CARNEY, JOHN JOSEPH (Handsome Jack) BR TR 5′10″ 175 lbs.
B. Nov. 10, 1866, Salem, Mass. D. Oct. 19, 1925, Litchfield, N. H.

Year	Team	Games	BA	SA	AB	H	2B	3B	HR	HR%	R	RBI	BB	SO	SB	Pinch Hit AB	Pinch Hit H	PO	A	E	DP	TC/G	FA	G by Pos
1889	WAS N	69	.231	.267	273	63	7	0	1	0.4	25	29	14	14	12	0	0	541	18	30	30	8.5	.949	1B-53, OF-16
1890	2 teams	BUF P (28G –.271) CLE P (25G –.348)																						
″	total	53	.306	.378	196	60	8	3	0	0.0	26	34	21	19	8	0	0	296	14	15	22	6.1	.954	1B-30, OF-23
1891	2 teams	CIN AA (99G –.278) MIL AA (31G –.300)																						
″	total	130	.283	.394	477	135	15	10	6	1.3	69	66	48	26	20	0	0	1308	65	33	58	10.8	.977	1B-130
3 yrs.		252	.273	.354	946	258	30	13	7	0.7	120	129	83	59	40	0	0	2145	97	78	110	9.2	.966	1B-213, OF-39

Pat Carney

CARNEY, PATRICK JOSEPH (Doc) BL TL 6′ 200 lbs.
B. Aug. 7, 1876, Holyoke, Mass. D. Jan. 9, 1953, Worcester, Mass.

Year	Team	Games	BA	SA	AB	H	2B	3B	HR	HR%	R	RBI	BB	SO	SB	Pinch Hit AB	Pinch Hit H	PO	A	E	DP	TC/G	FA	G by Pos
1901	BOS N	13	.291	.364	55	16	2	1	0	0.0	6	6	3		0	0	0	14	0	1	0	1.2	.933	OF-13
1902		137	.270	.330	522	141	17	4	2	0.4	75	65	42		27	0	0	153	19	13	7	1.3	.930	OF-137, P-2
1903		110	.240	.298	392	94	12	4	1	0.3	37	49	28		10	8	0	116	29	7	4	1.5	.954	OF-92, P-10, 1B-1
1904		78	.204	.237	279	57	5	2	0	0.0	24	11	12		6	1	0	92	18	5	5	1.5	.957	OF-71, P-4, 1B-1
4 yrs.		338	.247	.300	1248	308	36	11	3	0.2	142	131	85		43	9	0	375	66	26	16	1.4	.944	OF-313, P-16, 1B-2

Hick Carpenter

CARPENTER, WARREN WILLIAM BR TL 5′11″ 186 lbs.
B. Aug. 16, 1855, Grafton, Mass. D. Apr. 18, 1937, San Diego, Calif.

Year	Team	Games	BA	SA	AB	H	2B	3B	HR	HR%	R	RBI	BB	SO	SB	Pinch Hit AB	Pinch Hit H	PO	A	E	DP	TC/G	FA	G by Pos
1879	SYR N	65	.203	.226	261	53	6	0	0	0.0	30	20	2	15		0	0	355	49	39	12	6.7	.912	1B-34, 3B-18, OF-11, 2B-3
1880	CIN N	77	.240	.287	300	72	6	4	0	0.0	32	23	2	15		0	0	213	128	50	12	5.1	.872	3B-67, 1B-9, SS-1
1881	WOR N	83	.216	.280	347	75	12	2	2	0.6	40	31	3	19		0	0	141	172	56	14	4.4	.848	3B-83
1882	CIN AA	80	.342	.422	351	**120**	15	5	1	0.3	78		10			0	0	137	167	60	7	4.6	.835	3B-80
1883		95	.296	.376	436	129	18	4	3	0.7	99		18			0	0	133	181	47	6	3.8	.870	3B-95
1884		108	.255	.323	474	121	16	2	4	0.8	80		6			0	0	157	168	44	16	3.4	.881	3B-108, OF-1
1885		112	.277	.349	473	131	12	8	2	0.4	89		9			0	0	153	191	56	17	3.6	.860	3B-112
1886		111	.221	.273	458	101	8	5	2	0.4	67		18			0	0	127	221	66	23	3.7	.841	3B-111
1887		127	.249	.303	498	124	12	6	1	0.2	70		19		44	0	0	144	242	70	17	3.6	.846	3B-127
1888		136	.267	.327	551	147	14	5	3	0.5	68	67	5		59	0	0	142	286	66	15	3.6	.866	3B-136

Hick Carpenter *continued*

Year	Team		Games	BA	SA	AB	H	2B	3B	HR	HR%	R	RBI	BB	SO	SB	Pinch Hit AB	Pinch Hit H	PO	A	E	DP	TC/G	FA	G by Pos
1889			123	.261	.333	486	127	23	6	0	0.0	67	63	18	41	47	0	0	161	208	69	19	3.6	.842	3B-121, 1B-2
1892	STL	N	1	.333	.333	3	1	0	0	0	0.0	0	0	1	1	0	0	0	2	3	2	0	7.0	.714	3B-1
12 yrs.			1118	.259	.321	4638	1201	142	47	18	0.4	720	204	111	91	150	0	0	1865	2016	625	158	4.0	.861	3B-1059, 1B-45, OF-12, 2B-3, SS-1

Charlie Carr

CARR, CHARLES CARBITT
B. Dec. 27, 1876, Coatesville, Pa. D. Nov. 25, 1932, Memphis, Tenn.
BR TR 6′ 4″ 195 lbs.

Year	Team		Games	BA	SA	AB	H	2B	3B	HR	HR%	R	RBI	BB	SO	SB	Pinch Hit AB	Pinch Hit H	PO	A	E	DP	TC/G	FA	G by Pos
1898	WAS	N	20	.192	.219	73	14	2	0	0	0.0	6	4	2		2	0	0	200	8	11	15	10.9	.950	1B-20
1901	PHI	A	2	.125	.125	8	1	0	0	0	0.0	0	0	0		0	0	0	23	2	2	0	13.5	.926	1B-2
1903	DET	A	135	.281	.374	548	154	23	11	2	0.4	59	79	10		10	0	0	1276	111	25	60	10.5	.982	1B-135
1904	2 teams		DET A (92G –.214) CLE A (32G –.225)																						
″	total		124	.217	.271	480	104	18	4	0	0.0	38	47	18		6	0	0	1233	121	27	59	11.1	.980	1B-124
1905	CLE	A	89	.235	.310	306	72	12	4	1	0.3	29	31	13		12	2	1	940	50	9	33	11.5	.991	1B-87
1906	CIN	N	22	.191	.277	94	18	2	3	0	0.0	9	10	2		0	0	0	221	16	4	16	11.0	.983	1B-22
1914	IND	F	115	.293	.383	441	129	11	10	3	0.7	44	69	26		19	0	0	1088	59	11	67	10.1	.991	1B-115
7 yrs.			507	.252	.329	1950	492	68	32	6	0.3	185	240	71		49	2	1	4981	367	89	250	10.8	.984	1B-505

Chuck Carr

CARR, CHARLES LEE GLENN
B. Aug. 10, 1968, San Bernardino, Calif.
BB TR 5′10″ 155 lbs.

Year	Team		Games	BA	SA	AB	H	2B	3B	HR	HR%	R	RBI	BB	SO	SB	Pinch Hit AB	Pinch Hit H	PO	A	E	DP	TC/G	FA	G by Pos
1990	NY	N	4	.000	.000	2	0	0	0	0	0.0	0	0	0	2	1	2	0	0	0	0	0	0.0	.000	OF-1
1991			12	.182	.182	11	2	0	0	0	0.0	1	1	0	2	1	3	0	9	0	0	0	1.0	1.000	OF-9
1992	STL	N	22	.219	.266	64	14	3	0	0	0.0	8	3	9	6	10	0	0	39	1	0	0	2.1	1.000	OF-19
1993	FLA	N	142	.267	.330	551	147	19	2	4	0.7	75	41	49	74	**58**	1	0	393	7	6	2	2.9	.985	OF-139
1994			106	.263	.330	433	114	19	2	2	0.5	61	30	22	71	32	3	1	297	4	6	0	3.0	.980	OF-104
1995			105	.227	.312	308	70	20	0	2	0.6	54	20	46	49	25	2	0	217	8	3	0	2.2	.987	OF-103
6 yrs.			391	.253	.321	1369	347	61	4	8	0.6	199	95	126	204	127	11	1	955	20	15	2	2.6	.985	OF-375

Lew Carr

CARR, LEWIS SMITH
B. Aug. 15, 1872, Union Springs, N. Y. D. June 15, 1954, Moravia, N. Y.
BR TR 6′ 2″ 200 lbs.

Year	Team		Games	BA	SA	AB	H	2B	3B	HR	HR%	R	RBI	BB	SO	SB	Pinch Hit AB	Pinch Hit H	PO	A	E	DP	TC/G	FA	G by Pos
1901	PIT	N	9	.250	.357	28	7	1	1	0	0.0	2	4	2		0	0	0	12	19	5	3	3.6	.861	SS-9, 3B-1

Chico Carrasquel

CARRASQUEL, ALFONSO
Born Alfonso Carrasquel (Colon).
B. Jan. 23, 1926, Caracas, Venezuela.
BR TR 6′ 170 lbs.

Year	Team		Games	BA	SA	AB	H	2B	3B	HR	HR%	R	RBI	BB	SO	SB	Pinch Hit AB	Pinch Hit H	PO	A	E	DP	TC/G	FA	G by Pos
1950	CHI	A	141	.282	.365	524	148	21	5	4	0.8	72	46	66	46	0	0	0	234	458	28	113	5.1	.961	SS-141
1951			147	.264	.331	538	142	22	4	2	0.4	41	58	46	39	14	0	0	306	477	20	107	5.5	.975	SS-147
1952			100	.248	.298	359	89	7	4	1	0.3	36	42	33	27	2	1	1	176	248	16	50	4.4	.964	SS-99
1953			149	.279	.359	552	154	30	4	2	0.4	72	47	38	47	5	0	0	278	462	18	87	5.1	.976	SS-149
1954			155	.255	.368	620	158	28	3	12	1.9	106	62	85	67	7	0	0	280	492	20	102	5.1	.975	SS-155
1955			145	.256	.348	523	134	11	2	11	2.1	83	52	61	59	1	4	1	222	424	18	81	4.6	.973	SS-144
1956	CLE	A	141	.243	.323	474	115	15	1	7	1.5	60	48	52	61	0	0	0	240	354	20	70	4.3	.967	SS-141, 3B-1
1957			125	.276	.378	392	108	14	1	8	2.0	37	57	41	53	0	3	1	212	357	24	75	4.9	.960	SS-122
1958	2 teams		CLE A (49G –.256) KC A (59G –.212)																						
″	total		108	.234	.313	316	74	11	1	4	1.3	33	34	35	27	0	11	4	107	181	12	33	3.0	.960	SS-54, 3B-46
1959	BAL	A	114	.223	.295	346	77	13	0	4	1.2	28	28	34	41	2	6	2	157	271	13	68	3.9	.971	SS-89, 2B-22, 3B-2, 1B-1
10 yrs.			1325	.258	.342	4644	1199	172	25	55	1.2	568	474	491	467	31	25	9	2212	3724	189	786	4.7	.969	SS-1241, 3B-49, 2B-22, 1B-1

Camilo Carreon

CARREON, CAMILO
Father of Mark Carreon.
B. Aug. 6, 1937, Colton, Calif. D. Sept. 2, 1987, Tucson, Ariz.
BR TR 6′ 1½″ 190 lbs.

Year	Team		Games	BA	SA	AB	H	2B	3B	HR	HR%	R	RBI	BB	SO	SB	Pinch Hit AB	Pinch Hit H	PO	A	E	DP	TC/G	FA	G by Pos
1959	CHI	A	1	.000	.000	1	0	0	0	0	0.0	0	0	0	0	0	0	0	3	0	0	0	3.0	1.000	C-1
1960			8	.235	.235	17	4	0	0	0	0.0	2	2	1	3	0	1	0	22	2	0	0	3.4	1.000	C-7
1961			78	.271	.354	229	62	5	1	4	1.7	32	27	21	24	0	7	2	395	25	2	6	5.9	.995	C-71
1962			106	.256	.361	313	80	19	1	4	1.3	31	37	33	37	1	11	5	519	30	3	5	5.9	.995	C-93
1963			101	.274	.341	270	74	10	1	2	0.7	28	35	23	32	1	7	3	429	36	6	7	5.1	.987	C-92
1964			37	.274	.326	95	26	5	0	0	0.0	12	4	7	13	0	3	0	134	13	2	2	4.4	.987	C-34
1965	CLE	A	19	.231	.365	52	12	2	1	1	1.9	6	7	9	6	1	0	0	122	9	0	1	6.9	1.000	C-19
1966	BAL	A	4	.222	.444	9	2	2	0	0	0.0	2	2	3	2	0	1	1	24	0	0	0	8.0	1.000	C-3
8 yrs.			354	.264	.349	986	260	43	4	11	1.1	113	114	97	117	3	30	11	1648	115	13	21	5.6	.993	C-320

Mark Carreon

CARREON, MARK STEVEN
Son of Camilo Carreon.
B. July 19, 1963, Chicago, Ill.
BR TL 6′ 170 lbs.

Year	Team		Games	BA	SA	AB	H	2B	3B	HR	HR%	R	RBI	BB	SO	SB	Pinch Hit AB	Pinch Hit H	PO	A	E	DP	TC/G	FA	G by Pos
1987	NY.	N	9	.250	.250	12	3	0	0	0	0.0	0	1	1	1	0	5	1	4	0	1	0	1.0	.800	OF-5
1988			7	.556	1.111	9	5	2	0	1	11.1	5	1	2	1	0	2	0	1	0	0	0	0.3	1.000	OF-4
1989			68	.308	.489	133	41	6	0	6	4.5	20	16	12	17	2	27	10	57	0	1	0	1.5	.983	OF-39
1990			82	.250	.473	188	47	12	0	10	5.3	30	26	15	29	1	24	4	87	1	0	0	1.5	1.000	OF-60
1991			106	.260	.331	254	66	6	0	4	1.6	18	21	12	26	2	35	12	96	4	3	1	1.3	.971	OF-77
1992	DET	A	101	.232	.360	336	78	11	1	10	3.0	34	41	22	57	3	8	2	178	5	4	2	1.9	.979	OF-83, DH-13
1993	SF	N	78	.327	.540	150	49	9	1	7	4.7	22	33	13	16	1	35	10	54	4	3	1	1.4	.951	OF-41, 1B-3
1994			51	.270	.400	100	27	4	0	3	3.0	8	20	7	20	0	21	6	44	0	1	0	1.4	.978	OF-33
1995			117	.301	.490	396	119	24	0	17	4.3	53	65	23	37	0	15	4	732	45	7	65	7.6	.991	1B-81, OF-22
9 yrs.			619	.276	.435	1578	435	74	2	58	3.7	190	224	107	204	9	172	49	1253	59	20	69	2.9	.985	OF-364, 1B-84, DH-13

Bill Carrigan

CARRIGAN, WILLIAM FRANCIS (Rough)
B. Oct. 22, 1883, Lewiston, Me. D. July 8, 1969, Lewiston, Me.
Manager 1913–16, 1927–29.
BR TR 5′ 9″ 175 lbs.

Year	Team		Games	BA	SA	AB	H	2B	3B	HR	HR%	R	RBI	BB	SO	SB	Pinch Hit AB	Pinch Hit H	PO	A	E	DP	TC/G	FA	G by Pos
1906	BOS	A	37	.211	.211	109	23	0	0	0	0.0	5	10	5		3	2	1	139	48	12	2	5.7	.940	C-35
1908			57	.235	.295	149	35	5	2	0	0.0	13	14	3		1	7	2	223	75	13	6	6.2	.958	C-47, 1B-3
1909			94	.296	.368	280	83	13	2	1	0.4	27	36	17		2	6	0	411	118	13	14	6.4	.976	C-77, 1B-8
1910			114	.249	.313	342	85	11	1	3	0.9	36	53	23		10	4	0	495	134	25	12	5.9	.962	C-110
1911			72	.289	.336	232	67	6	1	1	0.4	29	30	26		5	4	2	374	94	13	13	7.1	.973	C-62, 1B-6

Bill Carrigan *continued*

Year	Team	Lg	Games	BA	SA	AB	H	2B	3B	HR	HR%	R	RBI	BB	SO	SB	Pinch Hit AB	Pinch Hit H	PO	A	E	DP	TC/G	FA	G by Pos
1912			87	.263	.297	266	70	7	1	0	0.0	34	24	38		7	0	0	413	102	16	7	6.1	.970	C-87
1913			85	.242	.340	256	62	15	5	0	0.0	17	28	27	26	6	4	0	383	127	11	8	6.4	.979	C-81
1914			81	.253	.309	178	45	5	1	1	0.6	18	22	40	18	1	2	0	350	84	7	8	5.7	.984	C-78
1915			46	.200	.232	95	19	3	0	0	0.0	10	7	16	12	0	2	0	183	54	6	3	5.5	.975	C-44
1916			33	.270	.333	63	17	2	1	0	0.0	7	11	11	3	2	5	1	122	27	0	1	5.5	1.000	C-27
10 yrs.			706	.257	.314	1970	506	67	14	6	0.3	196	235	206	59	37	36	6	3093	863	116	74	6.1	.972	C-648, 1B-17
WORLD SERIES																									
1912	BOS	A	2	.000	.000	7	0	0	0	0	0.0	0	0	0	0	0	0	0	9	5	0	0	7.0	1.000	C-2
1915			1	.000	.000	2	0	0	0	0	0.0	0	0	1	1	0	0	0	8	0	0	0	8.0	1.000	C-1
1916			1	.667	.667	3	2	0	0	0	0.0	0	1	0	1	0	0	0	3	1	0	0	4.0	1.000	C-1
3 yrs.			4	.167	.167	12	2	0	0	0	0.0	0	1	1	2	0	0	0	20	6	0	0	6.5	1.000	C-4

Matias Carrillo

CARRILLO, MATIAS BL TL 5′11″ 190 lbs.
Born Matias Carrillo (Garcia).
B. Feb. 24, 1963, Los Mochis, Mexico.

Year	Team	Lg	Games	BA	SA	AB	H	2B	3B	HR	HR%	R	RBI	BB	SO	SB	Pinch Hit AB	Pinch Hit H	PO	A	E	DP	TC/G	FA	G by Pos
1991	MIL	A	3	—	—	0	0	0	0	0	—	0	0	0	0	0	0	0	0	0	0	0	0.0	.000	OF-3
1993	FLA	N	24	.255	.364	55	14	6	0	0	0.0	4	3	1	7	0	9	0	21	0	0	0	1.3	1.000	OF-16
1994			80	.250	.301	136	34	7	0	0	0.0	13	9	9	31	3	27	6	49	5	1	1	1.1	.982	OF-49
3 yrs.			107	.251	.319	191	48	13	0	0	0.0	17	12	10	38	3	36	6	70	5	1	1	1.1	.987	OF-68

Chick Carroll

CARROLL, EDWARD
B. 1868, Arkansas D. July 13, 1908, Chicago, Ill.

Year	Team	Lg	Games	BA	SA	AB	H	2B	3B	HR	HR%	R	RBI	BB	SO	SB	Pinch Hit AB	Pinch Hit H	PO	A	E	DP	TC/G	FA	G by Pos
1884	WAS	U	4	.250	.250	16	4	0	0	0	0.0	1		0			0	0	3	1	4	0	2.0	.500	OF-4

Cliff Carroll

CARROLL, SAMUEL CLIFFORD BB TR 5′8″ 163 lbs.
B. Oct. 18, 1859, Clay Grove, Iowa D. June 12, 1923, Portland, Ore.

Year	Team	Lg	Games	BA	SA	AB	H	2B	3B	HR	HR%	R	RBI	BB	SO	SB	Pinch Hit AB	Pinch Hit H	PO	A	E	DP	TC/G	FA	G by Pos
1882	PRO	N	10	.122	.122	41	5	0	0	0	0.0	4		0	4		0	0	17	2	0	2	1.9	1.000	OF-10
1883			58	.265	.353	238	63	12	3	1	0.4	37		4	28		0	0	109	11	13	4	2.3	.902	OF-58
1884			113	.261	.334	452	118	16	4	3	0.7	90		29	39		0	0	206	11	23	1	2.1	.904	OF-113
1885			104	.232	.282	426	99	12	3	1	0.2	62	40	29	29		0	0	207	10	28	2	2.4	.886	OF-104
1886	WAS	N	111	.229	.296	433	99	11	6	2	0.5	73	22	44	26		0	0	153	22	28	4	1.8	.862	OF-111
1887			103	.248	.336	420	104	17	4	4	1.0	79	37	17	30	40	0	0	146	19	18	6	1.8	.902	OF-103
1888	PIT	N	5	.000	.000	20	0	0	0	0	0.0	1	0	0	8	2	0	0	5	1	3	0	1.8	.667	OF-5
1890	CHI	N	136	.285	.369	**582**	166	16	6	7	1.2	134	65	53	34	34	0	0	265	28	20	7	2.3	.936	OF-136
1891			130	.256	.367	515	132	20	8	7	1.4	87	80	50	42	31	0	0	168	15	17	5	1.5	.915	OF-130
1892	STL	N	101	.273	.376	407	111	14	8	4	1.0	82	49	47	22	30	0	0	181	19	22	1	2.2	.901	OF-101
1893	BOS	N	120	.224	.276	438	98	7	5	2	0.5	80	54	88	28	29	0	0	226	18	22	5	2.2	.917	OF-120
11 yrs.			991	.251	.329	3972	995	125	47	31	0.8	729	347	361	290	166	0	0	1683	156	194	37	2.1	.905	OF-991

Dixie Carroll

CARROLL, DORSEY LEE BL TR 5′11″ 165 lbs.
B. May 9, 1891, Paducah, Ky. D. Oct. 13, 1984, Jacksonville, Fla.

Year	Team	Lg	Games	BA	SA	AB	H	2B	3B	HR	HR%	R	RBI	BB	SO	SB	Pinch Hit AB	Pinch Hit H	PO	A	E	DP	TC/G	FA	G by Pos
1919	BOS	N	15	.265	.367	49	13	3	1	0	0.0	10	7	7	1	5	1	1	30	5	3	1	2.9	.921	OF-13

Doc Carroll

CARROLL, RALPH ARTHUR (Red) BR TR 6′ 170 lbs.
B. Dec. 28, 1891, Worcester, Mass. D. June 27, 1983, Worcester, Mass.

Year	Team	Lg	Games	BA	SA	AB	H	2B	3B	HR	HR%	R	RBI	BB	SO	SB	Pinch Hit AB	Pinch Hit H	PO	A	E	DP	TC/G	FA	G by Pos
1916	PHI	A	10	.091	.091	22	2	0	0	0	0.0	1	0	1	8	0	0	0	35	14	3	1	5.2	.942	C-10

Fred Carroll

CARROLL, FREDERICK HERBERT BR TR 5′11″ 185 lbs.
B. July 2, 1864, Sacramento, Calif. D. Nov. 7, 1904, San Rafael, Calif.

Year	Team	Lg	Games	BA	SA	AB	H	2B	3B	HR	HR%	R	RBI	BB	SO	SB	Pinch Hit AB	Pinch Hit H	PO	A	E	DP	TC/G	FA	G by Pos
1884	COL	AA	69	.278	.440	252	70	13	5	6	2.4	46		13			0	0	406	92	37	3	7.8	.931	C-54, OF-15
1885	PIT	AA	71	.268	.371	280	75	13	8	0	0.0	45		7			0	0	348	102	43	3	6.8	.913	C-60, OF-12
1886			122	.288	.422	486	140	28	11	5	1.0	92		52			0	0	753	106	68	26	7.5	.927	C-70, OF-27, 1B-25, SS-1
1887	PIT	N	102	.328	.499	421	138	24	15	6	1.4	71	54	36	21	23	0	0	451	56	62	9	5.5	.891	OF-46, C-40, 1B-17, SS-1
1888			97	.249	.331	366	91	14	5	2	0.5	62	48	32	31	18	0	0	366	68	50	10	4.9	.897	C-54, OF-38, 1B-5, 3B-1
1889			91	.330	.484	318	105	21	11	2	0.6	80	51	85	26	19	0	0	299	61	28	6	4.2	.928	C-43, OF-41, 1B-7, 3B-1
1890	PIT	P	111	.298	.394	416	124	20	7	2	0.5	95	71	75	22	35	0	0	380	55	56	7	4.4	.886	C-56, OF-49, 1B-7
1891	PIT	N	91	.218	.312	353	77	13	4	4	1.1	55	48	48	36	22	0	0	160	12	16	2	2.1	.915	OF-91
8 yrs.			754	.284	.408	2892	820	146	66	27	0.9	546	272	348	136	117	0	0	3163	552	360	66	5.4	.912	C-377, OF-319, 1B-61, 3B-2, SS-2

Pat Carroll

CARROLL, PATRICK
B. Mar. 1853, Philadelphia, Pa. D. Feb. 14, 1916, Philadelphia, Pa.

Year	Team	Lg	Games	BA	SA	AB	H	2B	3B	HR	HR%	R	RBI	BB	SO	SB	Pinch Hit AB	Pinch Hit H	PO	A	E	DP	TC/G	FA	G by Pos
1884	2 teams		ALT U (11G –.265) PHI U (5G –.158)																						
″	total		16	.235	.265	68	16	2	0	0	0.0	5		1			0	0	64	21	13	0	6.1	.867	C-13, OF-3

Scrappy Carroll

CARROLL, JOHN E. 5′ 7½″
B. Aug. 27, 1860, Buffalo, N. Y. D. Nov. 14, 1942, Buffalo, N. Y.

Year	Team	Lg	Games	BA	SA	AB	H	2B	3B	HR	HR%	R	RBI	BB	SO	SB	Pinch Hit AB	Pinch Hit H	PO	A	E	DP	TC/G	FA	G by Pos
1884	STP	U	9	.097	.129	31	3	1	0	0	0.0	3		2			0	0	11	7	5	1	2.3	.783	OF-8, 3B-2
1885	BUF	N	13	.075	.075	40	3	0	0	0	0.0	1	1	2	8		0	0	18	4	2	0	1.8	.917	OF-13
1887	CLE	AA	57	.199	.231	216	43	5	1	0	0.0	30		15		19	0	0	81	14	19	1	2.0	.833	OF-54, 3B-3, 2B-1
3 yrs.			79	.171	.199	287	49	6	1	0	0.0	34	1	19	8	19	0	0	110	25	26	2	2.0	.839	OF-75, 3B-5, 2B-1

Tommy Carroll

CARROLL, THOMAS EDWARD BR TR 6′ 3″ 186 lbs.
B. Sept. 17, 1936, Jamaica, N. Y.

Year	Team	Lg	Games	BA	SA	AB	H	2B	3B	HR	HR%	R	RBI	BB	SO	SB	Pinch Hit AB	Pinch Hit H	PO	A	E	DP	TC/G	FA	G by Pos
1955	NY	A	14	.333	.333	6	2	0	0	0	0.0	3	0	0	2	0	0	0	2	5	1	0	2.0	.875	SS-4
1956			36	.353	.353	17	6	0	0	0	0.0	11	0	1	3	1	3	2	0	13	2	3	1.3	.867	3B-11, SS-1
1959	KC	A	14	.143	.143	7	1	0	0	0	0.0	1	1	0	1	0	0	0	7	11	1	1	1.6	.947	SS-9, 3B-3
3 yrs.			64	.300	.300	30	9	0	0	0	0.0	15	1	1	6	1	3	2	9	29	4	4	1.5	.905	3B-14, SS-14
WORLD SERIES																									
1955	NY	A	2	—	—	0	0	0	0	0	—	0	0	0	0	0	0	0	0	0	0	0	0.0	—	

Kid Carsey

CARSEY, WILFRED
B. Oct. 22, 1870, New York, N. Y. D. Mar. 29, 1960, Miami, Fla.
BL TR 5′ 7″ 168 lbs.

Year	Team	Games	BA	SA	AB	H	2B	3B	HR	HR%	R	RBI	BB	SO	SB	Pinch Hit AB	Pinch Hit H	PO	A	E	DP	TC/G	FA	G by Pos
1891	WAS AA	61	.150	.198	187	28	5	2	0	0.0	25	15	19	38	2	0	0	25	126	14	5	2.6	.915	P-54, OF-7, SS-2
1892	PHI N	44	.153	.206	131	20	2	1	1	0.8	8	10	9	24	1	0	0	20	85	14	3	2.6	.882	P-43, OF-2
1893		39	.186	.207	145	27	1	1	0	0.0	12	10	5	14	2	0	0	17	81	8	1	2.7	.925	P-39
1894		35	.272	.320	125	34	2	2	0	0.0	30	18	16	11	3	0	0	15	59	5	4	2.3	.937	P-35
1895		44	.291	.305	141	41	2	0	0	0.0	24	20	15	12	2	0	0	9	77	12	2	2.2	.878	P-44
1896		27	.222	.296	81	18	2	2	0	0.0	13	7	11	12	1	0	0	9	50	6	3	2.4	.908	P-27
1897	2 teams	PHI N (4G –.231) STL N (13G –.302)																						
″	total	17	.286	.393	56	16	2	2	0	0.0	3	6	1		1	1	1	8	32	3	0	2.7	.930	P-16
1898	STL N	38	.200	.248	105	21	0	1	1	1.0	8	10	10		3	0	0	29	65	13	3	2.8	.879	P-20, 2B-10, OF-8
1899	3 teams	CLE N (11G –.278) WAS N (4G –.000) NY N (5G –.333)																						
″	total	20	.246	.262	65	16	1	0	0	0.0	8	5	5		2	0	0	18	53	10	4	4.1	.877	P-14, 3B-3, SS-3
1901	BKN N	2	.000	.000	2	0	0	0	0	0.0	0	0	0		0	0	0	0	1	0	0	0.5	1.000	P-2
10 yrs.		327	.213	.256	1038	221	17	11	2	0.2	131	101	91	111	17	1	1	150	629	85	25	2.6	.902	P-294, OF-17, 2B-10, SS-5, 3B-3

Kit Carson

CARSON, WALTER LLOYD
B. Nov. 15, 1912, Colton, Calif. D. June 21, 1983, Long Beach, Calif.
BL TL 6′ 180 lbs.

Year	Team	Games	BA	SA	AB	H	2B	3B	HR	HR%	R	RBI	BB	SO	SB	Pinch Hit AB	Pinch Hit H	PO	A	E	DP	TC/G	FA	G by Pos
1934	CLE A	5	.278	.500	18	5	2	1	0	0.0	4	1	2	3	0	1	1	2	0	0	0	0.5	1.000	OF-4
1935		16	.227	.318	22	5	2	0	0	0.0	1	1	2	6	0	10	2	7	0	0	0	1.8	1.000	OF-4
2 yrs.		21	.250	.400	40	10	4	1	0	0.0	5	2	4	9	0	11	3	9	0	0	0	1.1	1.000	OF-8

Frank Carswell

CARSWELL, FRANK WILLIS (Tex, Wheels)
B. Nov. 6, 1919, Palestine, Tex.
BR TR 6′ 195 lbs.

Year	Team	Games	BA	SA	AB	H	2B	3B	HR	HR%	R	RBI	BB	SO	SB	Pinch Hit AB	Pinch Hit H	PO	A	E	DP	TC/G	FA	G by Pos
1953	DET A	16	.267	.267	15	4	0	0	0	0.0	2	2	3	1	0	12	4	1	0	0	0	0.3	1.000	OF-3

Blackie Carter

CARTER, OTIS LEONARD
B. Sept. 30, 1902, Langley, S. C. D. Sept. 10, 1976, Greenville, S. C.
BR TR 5′10″ 175 lbs.

Year	Team	Games	BA	SA	AB	H	2B	3B	HR	HR%	R	RBI	BB	SO	SB	Pinch Hit AB	Pinch Hit H	PO	A	E	DP	TC/G	FA	G by Pos
1925	NY N	1	.000	.000	4	0	0	0	0	0.0	0	0	0	1	0	0	0	1	1	0	0	2.0	1.000	OF-1
1926		5	.235	.471	17	4	1	0	1	5.9	4	1	1	0	0	1	0	11	0	1	0	3.0	.917	OF-4
2 yrs.		6	.190	.381	21	4	1	0	1	4.8	4	1	1	1	0	1	0	12	1	1	0	2.8	.929	OF-5

Gary Carter

CARTER, GARY EDMUND (Kid)
B. Apr. 8, 1954, Culver City, Calif.
BR TR 6′ 2″ 205 lbs.

Year	Team	Games	BA	SA	AB	H	2B	3B	HR	HR%	R	RBI	BB	SO	SB	Pinch Hit AB	Pinch Hit H	PO	A	E	DP	TC/G	FA	G by Pos
1974	MON N	9	.407	.593	27	11	0	1	1	3.7	5	6	1	2	2	1	1	28	4	0	1	4.0	1.000	C-6, OF-2
1975		144	.270	.416	503	136	20	1	17	3.4	58	68	72	83	5	5	1	430	38	9	7	3.0	.981	OF-92, C-66, 3B-1
1976		91	.219	.309	311	68	8	1	6	1.9	31	38	30	43	0	2	0	364	42	2	8	4.3	.995	C-60, OF-36
1977		154	.284	.525	522	148	29	2	31	5.9	86	84	58	103	5	6	3	813	101	9	14	6.3	.990	C-146, OF-1
1978		157	.255	.422	533	136	27	1	20	3.8	76	72	62	70	10	6	0	787	83	10	9	5.8	.989	C-152, 1B-1
1979		141	.283	.485	505	143	26	5	22	4.4	74	75	40	62	3	3	0	751	88	9	12	6.1	.989	C-138
1980		154	.264	.486	549	145	25	5	29	5.3	76	101	58	78	3	4	0	822	108	7	8	6.3	.993	C-149
1981		100	.251	.444	374	94	20	2	16	4.3	48	68	35	35	1	0	0	515	58	4	12	5.7	.993	C-100, 1B-1
1982		154	.293	.510	557	163	32	1	29	5.2	91	97	78	64	2	3	0	954	104	10	6	7.0	.991	C-153
1983		145	.270	.444	541	146	37	3	17	3.1	63	79	51	57	1	2	0	855	108	5	15	6.7	.995	C-144, 1B-1
1984		159	.294	.487	596	175	32	1	27	4.5	75	**106**	64	57	2	2	0	990	78	7	25	6.4	.993	C-143, 1B-25
1985	NY N	149	.281	.488	555	156	17	1	32	5.8	83	100	69	46	1	2	0	987	70	8	13	7.1	.992	C-143, 1B-6, OF-1
1986		132	.255	.439	490	125	14	2	24	4.9	81	105	62	63	1	1	0	943	70	9	18	7.5	.991	C-122, 1B-9, OF-4, 3B-1
1987		139	.235	.392	523	123	18	2	20	3.8	55	83	42	73	0	4	0	886	70	9	14	6.9	.991	C-135, 1B-4, OF-1
1988		130	.242	.358	455	110	16	2	11	2.4	39	46	34	52	0	7	4	842	58	10	8	7.0	.989	C-119, 1B-10, 3B-1
1989		50	.183	.275	153	28	8	0	2	1.3	14	15	12	15	0	4	1	266	31	6	6	6.3	.980	C-47, 1B-1
1990	SF N	92	.254	.406	244	62	10	0	9	3.7	24	27	25	31	1	19	4	348	31	3	5	4.6	.992	C-80, 1B-3
1991	LA N	101	.246	.375	248	61	14	0	6	2.4	22	26	22	26	2	27	2	402	52	5	5	5.9	.989	C-68, 1B-10
1992	MON N	95	.218	.340	285	62	18	1	5	1.8	24	29	33	37	0	10	2	507	53	6	5	6.3	.989	C-85, 1B-5
19 yrs.		2296	.262	.439	7971	2092	371	31	324	4.1	1025	1225	848	997	39	108	18	12490	1247	128	191	6.1	.991	C-2056, OF-137, 1B-76, 3B-3
DIVISIONAL PLAYOFF SERIES																								
1981	MON N	5	.421	.895	19	8	3	0	2	10.5	3	6	1	1	0	0	0	21	5	0	0	5.2	1.000	C-5
LEAGUE CHAMPIONSHIP SERIES																								
1981	MON N	5	.438	.500	16	7	1	0	0	0.0	3	0	4	2	0	0	0	27	3	0	0	6.0	1.000	C-5
1986	NY N	6	.148	.185	27	4	1	0	0	0.0	1	2	2	5	0	0	0	42	5	0	0	7.8	1.000	C-6
1988		7	.222	.333	27	6	1	1	0	0.0	0	4	1	3	0	0	0	58	1	0	0	8.4	1.000	C-7
3 yrs.		18	.243	.314	70	17	3	1	0	0.0	4	6	7	10	0	0	0	127	9	0	0	7.6	1.000	C-18
WORLD SERIES																								
1986	NY N	7	.276	.552	29	8	2	0	2	6.9	4	9	0	4	0	0	0	57	1	0	0	8.3	1.000	C-7

Howard Carter

CARTER, JOHN HOWARD (Nick)
B. Oct. 13, 1904, New York, N. Y. D. July 24, 1991, New York, N. Y.
BR TR 5′10″ 154 lbs.

Year	Team	Games	BA	SA	AB	H	2B	3B	HR	HR%	R	RBI	BB	SO	SB	Pinch Hit AB	Pinch Hit H	PO	A	E	DP	TC/G	FA	G by Pos
1926	CIN N	5	.000	.000	1	0	0	0	0	0.0	0	0	0	0	0	0	0	0	3	0	0	0.8	1.000	2B-3, SS-1

Joe Carter

CARTER, JOSEPH CHRIS
B. Mar. 7, 1960, Oklahoma City, Okla.
BR TR 6′ 3″ 210 lbs.

Year	Team	Games	BA	SA	AB	H	2B	3B	HR	HR%	R	RBI	BB	SO	SB	Pinch Hit AB	Pinch Hit H	PO	A	E	DP	TC/G	FA	G by Pos
1983	CHI N	23	.176	.235	51	9	1	1	0	0.0	6	1	0	21	1	5	1	26	0	0	0	1.6	1.000	OF-16
1984	CLE A	66	.275	.467	244	67	6	1	13	5.3	32	41	11	48	2	7	5	169	11	6	4	2.8	.968	OF-59, 1B-7
1985		143	.262	.409	489	128	27	0	15	3.1	64	59	25	74	24	4	0	311	17	6	4	2.2	.982	OF-135, 1B-11, DH-7, 2B-1, 3B-1
1986		162	.302	.514	663	200	36	9	29	4.4	108	**121**	32	95	29	1	1	800	55	10	52	5.0	.988	OF-104, 1B-70
1987		149	.264	.480	588	155	27	2	32	5.4	83	106	27	105	31	2	0	782	46	17	61	5.6	.980	1B-84, OF-62, DH-5
1988		157	.271	.478	621	168	36	6	27	4.3	85	98	35	82	27	1	0	444	8	7	3	2.9	.985	OF-156
1989		162	.243	.465	**651**	158	32	4	35	5.4	84	105	39	112	13	0	0	443	20	9	7	2.9	.981	OF-146, 1B-11, DH-8
1990	SD N	162	.232	.391	**634**	147	27	1	24	3.8	79	115	48	93	22	1	0	492	16	11	19	3.2	.979	OF-150, 1B-14
1991	TOR A	162	.273	.503	638	174	42	3	33	5.2	89	108	49	112	20	0	0	283	13	8	2	1.9	.974	OF-151, DH-11
1992		158	.264	.498	622	164	30	7	34	5.5	97	119	36	109	12	1	0	284	13	9	3	1.9	.971	OF-129, DH-24, 1B-4

Joe Carter *continued*

Year	Team	Games	BA	SA	AB	H	2B	3B	HR	HR%	R	RBI	BB	SO	SB	Pinch Hit AB	Pinch Hit H	PO	A	E	DP	TC/G	FA	G by Pos
1993		155	.254	.489	603	153	33	5	33	5.5	92	121	47	113	8	1	0	289	7	8	0	2.0	.974	OF-151, DH-3
1994		111	.271	.524	435	118	25	2	27	6.2	70	103	33	64	11	0	0	205	4	2	1	1.9	.991	OF-110, DH-1
1995		139	.253	.428	558	141	23	0	25	4.5	70	76	37	87	12	0	0	315	12	7	3	2.4	.979	OF-128, 1B-7, DH-5
13 yrs.		1749	.262	.469	6797	1782	345	41	327	4.8	959	1173	419	1115	212	23	7	4843	222	100	159	2.9	.981	OF-1497, 1B-208, DH-64, 2B-1, 3B-1
LEAGUE CHAMPIONSHIP SERIES																								
1991	TOR A	5	.263	.526	19	5	2	0	1	5.3	3	4	1	5	0	0	0	4	1	0	0	1.0	1.000	OF-3, DH-2
1992		6	.192	.308	26	5	0	0	1	3.8	2	3	2	4	2	0	0	16	1	1	1	2.3	.944	OF-6, 1B-2
1993		6	.259	.259	27	7	0	0	0	0.0	2	2	1	5	0	0	0	12	1	0	0	2.2	1.000	OF-6
3 yrs.		17	.236	.347	72	17	2	0	2	2.8	7	9	4	14	2	0	0	32	3	1	1	1.9	.972	OF-15, 1B-2, DH-2
WORLD SERIES																								
1992	TOR A	6	.273	.636	22	6	2	0	2	9.1	2	3	3	2	0	0	0	27	1	0	0	4.7	1.000	OF-4, 1B-2
1993		6	.280	.560	25	7	1	0	2	8.0	6	8	0	4	0	0	0	13	0	2	0	2.5	.867	OF-6
2 yrs.		12	.277	.596	47	13	3	0	4	8.5 **5th**	8	11	3	6	0	0	0	40	1	2	0	3.6	.953	OF-10, 1B-2

Steve Carter

CARTER, STEVEN JEROME BL TR 6′ 4″ 201 lbs.
B. Dec. 3, 1964, Charlottesville, Va.

Year	Team	Games	BA	SA	AB	H	2B	3B	HR	HR%	R	RBI	BB	SO	SB	Pinch Hit AB	Pinch Hit H	PO	A	E	DP	TC/G	FA	G by Pos
1989	PIT N	9	.125	.375	16	2	1	0	1	6.3	2	3	2	5	0	2	0	4	0	0	0	0.8	1.000	OF-5
1990		5	.200	.200	5	1	0	0	0	0.0	0	0	0	1	0	2	0	4	0	0	0	1.3	1.000	OF-3
2 yrs.		14	.143	.333	21	3	1	0	1	4.8	2	3	2	6	0	4	0	8	0	0	0	1.0	1.000	OF-8

Ed Cartwright

CARTWRIGHT, EDWARD CHARLES (Jumbo) BR TR 5′10″ 220 lbs.
B. Oct. 6, 1859, Johnstown, Pa. D. Sept. 3, 1933, St. Petersburg, Fla.

Year	Team	Games	BA	SA	AB	H	2B	3B	HR	HR%	R	RBI	BB	SO	SB	Pinch Hit AB	Pinch Hit H	PO	A	E	DP	TC/G	FA	G by Pos
1890	STL AA	75	.300	.447	300	90	12	4	8	2.7	70		29		26	0	0	706	25	18	37	10.0	.976	1B-75
1894	WAS N	132	.294	.485	507	149	35	13	12	2.4	88	106	57	43	31	0	0	1219	71	36	63	10.0	.973	1B-132
1895		122	.331	.494	472	156	34	17	3	0.6	95	90	54	41	50	0	0	1102	95	19	69	10.0	.984	1B-122
1896		133	.277	.353	499	138	15	10	1	0.2	76	62	54	44	28	0	0	1276	71	30	76	10.4	.978	1B-133
1897		33	.234	.266	124	29	4	0	0	0.0	19	15	8		9	0	0	285	26	12	17	9.8	.963	1B-33
5 yrs.		495	.295	.432	1902	562	100	44	24	1.3	348	273	202	128	144	0	0	4588	288	115	262	10.1	.977	1B-495

Rico Carty

CARTY, RICARDO ADOLFO BR TR 6′ 3″ 200 lbs.
Born Ricardo Adolfo Jacobo (Carty).
B. Sept. 1, 1939, San Pedro de Macoris, Dominican Republic.

Year	Team	Games	BA	SA	AB	H	2B	3B	HR	HR%	R	RBI	BB	SO	SB	Pinch Hit AB	Pinch Hit H	PO	A	E	DP	TC/G	FA	G by Pos
1963	MIL N	2	.000	.000	2	0	0	0	0	0.0	0	0	0	2	0	2	0	0	0	0	0	0.0	—	
1964		133	.330	.554	455	150	28	4	22	4.8	72	88	43	78	1	12	3	176	5	4	1	1.5	.978	OF-121
1965		83	.310	.494	271	84	18	1	10	3.7	37	35	17	44	1	11	3	112	3	5	1	1.6	.958	OF-73
1966	ATL N	151	.326	.468	521	170	25	2	15	2.9	73	76	60	74	4	12	2	318	16	10	1	2.4	.971	OF-126, C-17, 1B-2, 3B-1
1967		134	.255	.401	444	113	16	2	15	3.4	41	64	49	70	4	14	2	267	9	11	6	2.4	.962	OF-112, 1B-9
1969		104	.342	.549	304	104	15	0	16	5.3	47	58	32	28	0	22	9	118	0	6	0	1.6	.952	OF-79
1970		136	**.366**	.584	478	175	23	3	25	5.2	84	101	77	46	1	3	1	219	5	6	0	1.7	.974	OF-133
1972		86	.277	.402	271	75	12	2	6	2.2	31	29	44	33	0	8	2	139	3	3	1	1.9	.979	OF-78
1973	**3 teams**	**TEX A** (86G –.232) **CHI N** (22G –.214) **OAK A** (7G –.250)																						
″	**total**	115	.229	.302	384	88	13	0	5	1.3	29	42	44	50	2	7	2	123	2	2	0	1.2	.984	OF-72, DH-32
1974	CLE A	33	.363	.451	91	33	5	0	1	1.1	6	16	5	9	0	11	2	64	1	1	9	3.0	.985	DH-14, 1B-8
1975		118	.308	.504	383	118	19	1	18	4.7	57	64	45	31	2	8	6	209	15	3	21	2.1	.987	DH-72, 1B-26, OF-12
1976		152	.310	.442	552	171	34	0	13	2.4	67	83	67	45	1	1	1	81	3	0	8	0.6	1.000	DH-137, 1B-12, OF-1
1977		127	.280	.432	461	129	23	1	15	3.3	50	80	56	51	1	2	1	20	3	0	4	0.2	1.000	DH-123, 1B-2
1978	**2 teams**	**TOR A** (104G –.284) **OAK A** (41G –.277)																						
″	**total**	145	.282	.502	528	149	21	1	31	5.9	70	99	57	57	1	4	0	0	0	0	0	0.0		DH-142
1979	TOR A	132	.256	.390	461	118	26	0	12	2.6	48	55	46	45	3	9	4	0	0	0	0	0.0	.000	DH-129
15 yrs.		1651	.299	.464	5606	1677	278	17	204	3.6	712	890	642	663	21	126	38	1846	65	51	52	1.3	.974	OF-807, DH-649, 1B-59, C-17, 3B-1
LEAGUE CHAMPIONSHIP SERIES																								
1969	ATL N	3	.300	.500	10	3	2	0	0	0.0	4	0	3	1	0	0	0	2	0	0	0	0.7	1.000	OF-3

Bob Caruthers

CARUTHERS, ROBERT LEE (Parisian Bob) BL TR 5′ 7″ 138 lbs.
B. Jan. 5, 1864, Memphis, Tenn. D. Aug. 5, 1911, Peoria, Ill.
Manager 1892.

Year	Team	Games	BA	SA	AB	H	2B	3B	HR	HR%	R	RBI	BB	SO	SB	Pinch Hit AB	Pinch Hit H	PO	A	E	DP	TC/G	FA	G by Pos
1884	STL AA	23	.256	.354	82	21	2	0	2	2.4	15		4			0	0	14	10	5	0	1.0	.828	OF-16, P-13
1885		60	.225	.302	222	50	10	2	1	0.5	37		20			0	0	33	86	15	4	2.2	.888	P-53, OF-7
1886		87	.334	.527	317	106	21	14	4	1.3	91		64			0	0	72	76	19	5	1.9	.886	P-44, OF-43, 2B-2
1887		98	.357	.547	364	130	23	11	8	2.2	102		66		49	0	0	182	105	18	4	3.0	.941	OF-54, P-39, 1B-7
1888	BKN AA	94	.230	.334	335	77	10	5	5	1.5	58	53	45		23	0	0	127	97	26	5	2.6	.896	OF-51, P-44
1889		59	.250	.366	172	43	8	3	2	1.2	45	31	44	17	9	0	0	33	95	6	4	2.2	.955	P-56, OF-3, 1B-2
1890	BKN N	71	.265	.340	238	63	7	4	1	0.4	46	29	47	18	13	0	0	65	83	20	2	2.2	.881	OF-39, P-37
1891		56	.281	.380	171	48	5	3	2	1.2	24	23	25	13	4	**1**	0	29	69	11	2	1.9	.899	P-38, OF-17, 2B-1
1892	STL N	143	.277	.357	513	142	16	8	3	0.6	76	69	86	29	24	0	0	209	61	29	10	2.0	.903	OF-122, P-16, 2B-6, 1B-4
1893	**2 teams**	**CHI N** (1G –.000) **CIN N** (13G –.292)																						
″	**total**	14	.275	.373	51	14	2	0	1	2.0	14	8	16	2	4	0	0	24	1	4	0	2.1	.862	OF-14
10 yrs.		705	.282	.400	2465	694	104	50	29	1.2	508	213	417	79	126	1	0	788	683	153	36	2.2	.906	OF-366, P-340, 1B-13, 2B-9

Paul Casanova

CASANOVA, PAULINO BR TR 6′ 4″ 180 lbs.
Born Paulino Casanova (Ortiz).
B. Dec. 21, 1941, Colon, Cuba.

Year	Team	Games	BA	SA	AB	H	2B	3B	HR	HR%	R	RBI	BB	SO	SB	Pinch Hit AB	Pinch Hit H	PO	A	E	DP	TC/G	FA	G by Pos
1965	WAS A	5	.308	.385	13	4	1	0	0	0.0	2	1	1	3	0	0	0	15	0	1	0	4.0	.938	C-4
1966		122	.254	.406	429	109	16	5	13	3.0	45	44	14	78	1	3	0	674	53	14	12	6.2	.981	C-119
1967		141	.248	.339	528	131	19	1	9	1.7	47	53	17	65	1	8	1	827	70	15	19	6.7	.984	C-137
1968		96	.196	.252	322	63	6	0	4	1.2	19	25	7	52	0	7	1	472	46	6	3	5.7	.989	C-92
1969		124	.216	.282	379	82	9	2	4	1.1	26	37	18	52	0	5	1	583	59	5	5	5.3	.992	C-122
1970		104	.229	.354	328	75	17	3	6	1.8	25	30	10	47	0	9	1	461	48	6	12	5.2	.988	C-100
1971		94	.203	.286	311	63	9	1	5	1.6	19	26	14	52	0	8	1	416	40	7	4	5.6	.985	C-83

Paul Casanova *continued*

Year	Team		Games	BA	SA	AB	H	2B	3B	HR	HR%	R	RBI	BB	SO	SB	Pinch Hit AB	Pinch Hit H	PO	A	E	DP	TC/G	FA	G by Pos
1972	ATL	N	49	.206	.272	136	28	3	0	2	1.5	8	10	4	28	0	6	0	139	16	4	3	3.7	.975	C-43
1973			82	.216	.335	236	51	7	0	7	3.0	18	18	11	36	0	4	1	330	48	9	3	5.0	.977	C-78
1974			42	.202	.202	104	21	0	0	0	0.0	5	8	5	17	0	9	4	123	15	2	4	4.2	.986	C-33
10 yrs.			859	.225	.319	2786	627	87	12	50	1.8	214	252	101	430	2	59	10	4040	395	69	65	5.6	.985	C-811

George Case

CASE, GEORGE WASHINGTON BR TR 6′ 183 lbs.
B. Nov. 11, 1915, Trenton, N. J. D. Jan. 23, 1989, Trenton, N. J.

Year	Team		Games	BA	SA	AB	H	2B	3B	HR	HR%	R	RBI	BB	SO	SB	Pinch Hit AB	Pinch Hit H	PO	A	E	DP	TC/G	FA	G by Pos
1937	WAS	A	22	.289	.400	90	26	6	2	0	0.0	14	11	3	5	2	0	0	51	1	3	0	2.5	.945	OF-22
1938			107	.305	.395	433	132	27	3	2	0.5	69	40	39	28	11	8	1	207	7	8	2	2.2	.964	OF-101
1939			128	.302	.377	530	160	20	7	2	0.4	103	35	56	36	**51**	2	0	332	7	16	2	2.9	.955	OF-123
1940			154	.293	.375	656	192	29	5	5	0.8	109	56	52	39	**35**	0	0	384	10	12	0	2.6	.970	OF-154
1941			153	.271	.354	649	176	32	8	2	0.3	95	53	51	37	**33**	2	0	362	21	10	3	2.6	.975	OF-151
1942			125	.320	.407	513	164	26	2	5	1.0	101	43	44	30	**44**	1	0	270	4	14	1	2.4	.951	OF-120
1943			141	.294	.374	613	180	36	5	1	0.2	**102**	52	40	27	**61**	0	0	318	8	5	2	2.4	.985	OF-140
1944			119	.249	.301	465	116	14	2	2	0.4	63	32	49	22	49	0	0	288	7	9	2	2.7	.970	OF-114
1945			123	.294	.357	504	148	19	5	1	0.2	72	31	49	27	30	0	0	316	17	7	3	2.8	.979	OF-123
1946	CLE	A	118	.225	.295	484	109	23	4	1	0.2	46	22	34	38	**28**	0	0	226	5	4	0	2.0	.983	OF-118
1947	WAS	A	36	.150	.163	80	12	1	0	0	0.0	11	2	8	8	5	3	0	51	1	2	0	2.6	.963	OF-21
11 yrs.			1226	.282	.358	5017	1415	233	43	21	0.4	785	377	425	297	349	16	1	2805	88	90	15	2.5	.970	OF-1187

Bob Casey

CASEY, ORRIN ROBINSON 5′11″ 190 lbs.
B. Jan. 26, 1859, Adolphustown, Ont., Canada D. Nov. 28, 1936, Syracuse, N. Y.

Year	Team		Games	BA	SA	AB	H	2B	3B	HR	HR%	R	RBI	BB	SO	SB	Pinch Hit AB	Pinch Hit H	PO	A	E	DP	TC/G	FA	G by Pos
1882	DET	N	9	.231	.410	39	9	2	1	1	2.6	5	7	0	15		0	0	10	10	12	0	3.6	.625	3B-8, 2B-1

Dennis Casey

CASEY, DENNIS PATRICK BL TR 5′ 9″ 164 lbs.
Brother of Dan Casey.
B. Mar. 30, 1858, Binghamton, N. Y. D. Jan. 19, 1909, Binghamton, N. Y.

Year	Team		Games	BA	SA	AB	H	2B	3B	HR	HR%	R	RBI	BB	SO	SB	Pinch Hit AB	Pinch Hit H	PO	A	E	DP	TC/G	FA	G by Pos
1884	2 teams		WIL U (2G –.250) BAL AA (37G –.248)																						
″	total		39	.248	.408	157	39	8	4	3	1.9	21		5			0	0	51	5	6	2	1.6	.903	OF-39
1885	BAL	AA	63	.288	.398	264	76	10	5	3	1.1	50		21			0	0	100	10	24	0	2.1	.821	OF-63
2 yrs.			102	.273	.401	421	115	18	9	6	1.4	71		26			0	0	151	15	30	2	1.9	.847	OF-102

Doc Casey

CASEY, JAMES PATRICK BB TR 5′ 6″ 157 lbs.
B. Mar. 15, 1870, Lawrence, Mass. D. Dec. 30, 1936, Detroit, Mich. BL 1898–1901

Year	Team		Games	BA	SA	AB	H	2B	3B	HR	HR%	R	RBI	BB	SO	SB	Pinch Hit AB	Pinch Hit H	PO	A	E	DP	TC/G	FA	G by Pos
1898	WAS	N	28	.277	.295	112	31	2	0	0	0.0	13	15	3		15	0	0	38	62	14	5	3.9	.877	3B-22, SS-4, C-3
1899	2 teams		WAS N (9G –.118) BKN N (134G –.269)																						
″	total		143	.259	.322	559	145	16	8	1	0.2	78	45	27		28	0	0	174	275	56	23	3.5	.889	3B-143
1900	BKN	N	1	.333	.333	3	1	0	0	0	0.0	0	1	0		0	0	0	1	2	0	0	3.0	1.000	3B-1
1901	DET	A	128	.283	.357	540	153	16	9	2	0.4	105	46	32		34	1	0	133	324	58	25	4.1	.887	3B-127
1902			132	.273	.352	520	142	18	7	3	0.6	69	55	44		22	0	0	174	309	51	17	4.0	.904	3B-132
1903	CHI	N	112	.290	.329	435	126	8	3	1	0.2	56	40	19		11	0	0	143	190	31	5	3.3	.915	3B-112
1904			136	.268	.325	548	147	20	4	1	0.2	71	43	18		21	0	0	163	244	39	11	3.3	.913	3B-134, C-2
1905			144	.232	.316	526	122	21	10	1	0.2	66	56	41		22	2	0	162	254	22	7	3.1	.950	3B-142, SS-1
1906	BKN	N	149	.233	.291	571	133	17	8	0	0.0	71	34	52		22	0	0	172	272	39	11	3.2	.919	3B-149
1907			141	.231	.279	527	122	19	3	0	0.0	55	19	34		16	3	0	176	274	21	16	3.4	.955	3B-138
10 yrs.			1114	.258	.320	4341	1122	137	52	9	0.2	584	354	270		191	6	0	1336	2206	331	120	3.5	.915	3B-1100, SS-5, C-5

Joe Casey

CASEY, JOSEPH FELIX BR TR 5′ 9″ 180 lbs.
B. Aug. 15, 1887, Boston, Mass. D. June 2, 1966, Melrose, Mass.

Year	Team		Games	BA	SA	AB	H	2B	3B	HR	HR%	R	RBI	BB	SO	SB	Pinch Hit AB	Pinch Hit H	PO	A	E	DP	TC/G	FA	G by Pos
1909	DET	A	3	.000	.000	5	0	0	0	0	0.0	1	0	1		0	0	0	9	5	0	1	4.7	1.000	C-3
1910			23	.194	.242	62	12	3	0	0	0.0	3	2	2		1	0	0	101	33	5	2	6.3	.964	C-22
1911			15	.152	.152	33	5	0	0	0	0.0	2	3	3		0	0	0	35	10	3	1	3.2	.938	C-12, OF-3
1918	WAS	A	9	.235	.235	17	4	0	0	0	0.0	3	2	2	2	0	0	0	34	5	0	0	4.9	1.000	C-8
4 yrs.			50	.179	.205	117	21	3	0	0	0.0	9	7	8	2	1	0	0	179	53	8	4	5.0	.967	C-45, OF-3

Dave Cash

CASH, DAVID, JR. BR TR 5′11″ 170 lbs.
B. June 11, 1948, Utica, N. Y.

Year	Team		Games	BA	SA	AB	H	2B	3B	HR	HR%	R	RBI	BB	SO	SB	Pinch Hit AB	Pinch Hit H	PO	A	E	DP	TC/G	FA	G by Pos
1969	PIT	N	18	.279	.361	61	17	3	1	0	0.0	8	4	9	9	2	0	0	37	60	1	9	5.8	.990	2B-17
1970			64	.314	.419	210	66	7	6	1	0.5	30	28	17	25	5	4	1	147	156	8	46	5.7	.974	2B-55
1971			123	.289	.354	478	138	17	4	2	0.4	79	34	46	33	13	4	2	254	333	10	82	4.5	.983	2B-105, 3B-24, SS-3
1972			99	.282	.374	425	120	22	4	3	0.7	58	30	22	31	9	3	1	260	342	5	81	6.3	.992	2B-97
1973			116	.271	.342	436	118	21	2	2	0.5	59	31	38	36	2	14	4	244	311	12	49	5.2	.979	2B-92, 3B-17
1974	PHI	N	162	.300	.378	**687**	206	26	11	2	0.3	89	58	46	33	20	0	0	396	519	22	141	5.8	.977	2B-162
1975			162	.305	.388	**699**	**213**	40	3	4	0.6	111	57	56	34	13	0	0	400	481	17	126	5.5	.981	2B-162
1976			160	.284	.345	**666**	189	14	**12**	1	0.2	92	56	54	13	10	1	0	407	424	10	118	5.3	.988	2B-158
1977	MON	N	153	.289	.375	650	188	42	7	0	0.0	91	43	52	33	21	0	0	343	443	11	73	5.2	.986	2B-153
1978			159	.252	.315	658	166	26	3	3	0.5	66	43	37	29	12	0	0	362	400	11	91	4.9	.986	2B-159
1979			76	.321	.422	187	60	11	1	2	1.1	24	19	12	12	7	30	10	88	110	6	18	4.3	.971	2B-47
1980	SD	N	130	.227	.280	397	90	14	2	1	0.3	25	23	35	21	6	7	1	290	326	8	72	5.1	.987	2B-123
12 yrs.			1422	.283	.358	5554	1571	243	56	21	0.4	732	426	424	309	120	63	19	3228	3905	121	906	5.3	.983	2B-1330, 3B-41, SS-3
LEAGUE CHAMPIONSHIP SERIES																									
1970	PIT	N	2	.125	.250	8	1	1	0	0	0.0	1	0	1	1	0	0	0	6	8	0	3	7.0	1.000	2B-2
1971			4	.421	.526	19	8	2	0	0	0.0	5	1	0	1	1	0	0	11	11	1	3	5.8	.957	2B-4
1972			5	.211	.211	19	4	0	0	0	0.0	0	3	0	0	0	0	0	5	10	1	1	3.2	.938	2B-5
1976	PHI	N	3	.308	.385	13	4	1	0	0	0.0	1	1	0	0	0	0	0	8	8	0	2	5.3	1.000	2B-3
4 yrs.			14	.288	.356	59	17	4	0	0	0.0	7	5	1	2	1	0	0	30	37	2	9	4.9	.971	2B-14
WORLD SERIES																									
1971	PIT	N	7	.133	.167	30	4	1	0	0	0.0	2	1	3	1	1	0	0	20	23	0	6	6.1	1.000	2B-7

Norm Cash

CASH, NORMAN DALTON BL TL 6′ 185 lbs.
B. Nov. 10, 1934, Justiceburg, Tex. D. Oct. 12, 1986, Beaver Island, Mich.

Year	Team	Games	BA	SA	AB	H	2B	3B	HR	HR%	R	RBI	BB	SO	SB	Pinch Hit AB	Pinch Hit H	PO	A	E	DP	TC/G	FA	G by Pos
1958	CHI A	13	.250	.250	8	2	0	0	0	0.0	2	0	0	1	0	5	1	2	0	0	0	0.5	1.000	OF-4
1959		58	.240	.375	104	25	0	1	4	3.8	16	16	18	9	1	19	5	231	14	4	19	8.0	.984	1B-31
1960	DET A	121	.286	.501	353	101	16	3	18	5.1	64	63	65	58	4	23	9	743	59	7	68	7.9	.991	1B-99, OF-4
1961		159	**.361**	.662	535	**193**	22	8	41	7.7	119	132	124	85	11	1	0	1231	127	11	121	8.7	.992	1B-157
1962		148	.243	.513	507	123	16	2	39	7.7	94	89	104	82	6	2	1	1091	116	10	94	8.2	.992	1B-146, OF-3
1963		147	.270	.471	493	133	19	1	26	5.3	67	79	89	76	2	7	0	1161	99	7	93	8.9	.994	1B-142
1964		144	.257	.453	479	123	15	5	23	4.8	63	83	70	66	2	10	1	1105	92	4	97	8.8	.997	1B-137
1965		142	.266	.512	467	124	23	1	30	**6.4**	79	82	77	62	6	5	0	1091	97	9	96	8.6	.992	1B-139
1966		160	.279	.478	603	168	18	3	32	5.3	98	93	66	91	2	3	1	1271	114	17	118	8.9	.988	1B-158
1967		152	.242	.430	488	118	16	5	22	4.5	64	72	81	100	3	7	1	1135	112	6	89	8.6	.995	1B-146
1968		127	.263	.487	411	108	15	1	25	6.1	50	63	39	70	1	15	2	924	88	8	66	8.7	.992	1B-117
1969		142	.280	.464	483	135	15	4	22	4.6	81	74	63	80	2	9	2	1016	96	7	99	8.4	.994	1B-134
1970		130	.259	.441	370	96	18	2	15	4.1	58	53	72	58	0	17	6	868	70	10	76	8.3	.989	1B-114
1971		135	.283	.531	452	128	10	3	32	**7.1**	72	91	59	86	1	7	1	1020	75	9	105	8.4	.992	1B-131
1972		137	.259	.445	440	114	16	0	22	5.0	51	61	50	64	0	11	0	1060	70	8	102	8.5	.993	1B-134
1973		121	.262	.471	363	95	19	0	19	5.2	51	40	47	73	1	8	2	856	64	8	72	7.9	.991	1B-114, DH-3
1974		53	.228	.416	149	34	3	2	7	4.7	17	12	19	30	1	9	3	368	24	6	32	9.0	.985	1B-44
17 yrs.		2089	.271	.488	6705	1820	241	41	377	5.6	1046	1103	1043	1091	43	158	35	15173	1317	131	1347	8.5	.992	1B-1943, OF-11, DH-3
LEAGUE CHAMPIONSHIP SERIES																								
1972	DET A	5	.267	.467	15	4	0	0	1	6.7	1	2	2	3	0	1	0	39	3	0	2	8.4	1.000	1B-5
WORLD SERIES																								
1959	CHI A	4	.000	.000	4	0	0	0	0	0.0	0	0	0	2	0	4	0	0	0	0	0	0.0	—	
1968	DET A	7	.385	.500	26	10	0	0	1	3.8	5	5	3	5	0	0	0	59	6	2	3	9.6	.970	1B-7
2 yrs.		11	.333	.433	30	10	0	0	1	3.3	5	5	3	7	0	4	0	59	6	2	3	9.6	.970	1B-7

Ron Cash

CASH, RONALD FORREST BR TR 6′ 180 lbs.
B. Nov. 20, 1949, Atlanta, Ga.

Year	Team	Games	BA	SA	AB	H	2B	3B	HR	HR%	R	RBI	BB	SO	SB	Pinch Hit AB	Pinch Hit H	PO	A	E	DP	TC/G	FA	G by Pos
1973	DET A	14	.410	.487	39	16	1	1	0	0.0	8	6	5	5	0	0	0	13	10	1	0	1.8	.958	OF-7, 3B-6
1974		20	.226	.258	62	14	2	0	0	0.0	6	5	0	11	0	1	0	139	9	4	12	8.0	.974	1B-15, 3B-4
2 yrs.		34	.297	.347	101	30	3	1	0	0.0	14	11	5	16	0	1	0	152	19	5	12	5.5	.972	1B-15, 3B-10, OF-7

Jay Cashion

CASHION, JAY CARL BL TR 6′ 2″ 200 lbs.
B. June 6, 1891, Mecklenburg, N. C. D. Nov. 17, 1935, Lake Millicent, Wis.

Year	Team	Games	BA	SA	AB	H	2B	3B	HR	HR%	R	RBI	BB	SO	SB	Pinch Hit AB	Pinch Hit H	PO	A	E	DP	TC/G	FA	G by Pos
1911	WAS A	21	.324	.351	37	12	1	0	0	0.0	3	4	1		0	9	2	3	22	0	0	2.3	1.000	P-11
1912		43	.214	.340	103	22	5	1	2	1.9	7	12	8		2	8	1	27	41	1	1	2.0	.986	P-26, OF-9
1913		7	.250	.250	12	3	0	0	0	0.0	1	2	1	1	0	0	0	4	5	2	1	1.6	.818	P-4, OF-3
1914		2	.000	.000	1	0	0	0	0	0.0	0	0	0	1	0	0	0	1	3	1	1	2.5	.800	P-2
4 yrs.		73	.242	.333	153	37	6	1	2	1.3	11	18	10	2	2	17	3	35	71	4	3	2.0	.964	P-43, OF-12

Ed Caskin

CASKIN, EDWARD JAMES BR TR 5′ 9½″ 165 lbs.
B. Dec. 30, 1851, Danvers, Mass. D. Oct. 9, 1924, Danvers, Mass.

Year	Team	Games	BA	SA	AB	H	2B	3B	HR	HR%	R	RBI	BB	SO	SB	Pinch Hit AB	Pinch Hit H	PO	A	E	DP	TC/G	FA	G by Pos
1879	TRO N	70	.257	.313	304	78	13	2	0	0.0	32	21	2	14		0	0	170	225	50	12	6.4	.888	SS-42, C-22, 2B-6
1880		82	.225	.264	333	75	5	4	0	0.0	36	28	7	24		0	0	97	297	51	16	5.3	.885	SS-82, C-2
1881		63	.226	.265	234	53	7	1	0	0.0	33	21	13	29		0	0	85	205	30	18	5.1	.906	SS-63
1883	NY N	95	.238	.285	383	91	11	2	1	0.3	47		14	25		0	0	194	277	80	19	5.8	.855	SS-81, 2B-13, C-1
1884		100	.231	.282	351	81	10	1	2	0.6	49		34	55		0	0	149	293	59	28	4.9	.882	SS-96, C-6
1885	STL N	71	.179	.191	262	47	3	0	0	0.0	31	12	12	22		0	0	88	146	35	5	3.7	.870	3B-69, C-2, SS-1
1886	NY N	1	.500	.500	4	2	0	0	0	0.0	1	1	0	1		0	0	3	0	0	0	3.0	1.000	SS-1
7 yrs.		482	.228	.270	1871	427	49	10	3	0.2	229	83	82	170		0	0	786	1443	305	98	5.2	.880	SS-366, 3B-69, C-33, 2B-19

Harry Cassady

CASSADY, HARRY DELBERT BL TL 5′ 8″ 145 lbs.
B. July 20, 1880, Bellflower, Ill. D. Apr. 22, 1969, Fresno, Calif.

Year	Team	Games	BA	SA	AB	H	2B	3B	HR	HR%	R	RBI	BB	SO	SB	Pinch Hit AB	Pinch Hit H	PO	A	E	DP	TC/G	FA	G by Pos
1904	PIT N	12	.205	.205	44	9	0	0	0	0.0	8	3	2		2	0	0	10	3	2	0	1.3	.867	OF-12
1905	WAS A	9	.133	.133	30	4	0	0	0	0.0	2	1	0		0	0	0	14	1	0	0	1.7	1.000	OF-9
2 yrs.		21	.176	.176	74	13	0	0	0	0.0	10	4	2		2	0	0	24	4	2	0	1.4	.933	OF-21

Joe Cassidy

CASSIDY, JOSEPH PHILLIP BR TR
B. Feb. 8, 1883, Chester, Pa. D. Mar. 25, 1906, Chester, Pa.

Year	Team	Games	BA	SA	AB	H	2B	3B	HR	HR%	R	RBI	BB	SO	SB	Pinch Hit AB	Pinch Hit H	PO	A	E	DP	TC/G	FA	G by Pos
1904	WAS A	152	.241	.332	581	140	12	**19**	1	0.2	63	33	15		17	0	0	336	362	51	42	4.9	.932	SS-99, OF-32, 3B-23
1905		151	.215	.262	576	124	16	4	1	0.2	67	43	25		23	0	0	308	520	66	50	5.9	.926	SS-151
2 yrs.		303	.228	.297	1157	264	28	23	2	0.2	130	76	40		40	0	0	644	882	117	92	5.4	.929	SS-250, OF-32, 3B-23

John Cassidy

CASSIDY, JOHN P. BR TL 5′ 8″ 168 lbs.
B. 1855, Brooklyn, N. Y. D. July 3, 1891, Brooklyn, N. Y.

Year	Team	Games	BA	SA	AB	H	2B	3B	HR	HR%	R	RBI	BB	SO	SB	Pinch Hit AB	Pinch Hit H	PO	A	E	DP	TC/G	FA	G by Pos
1876	HAR N	12	.277	.319	47	13	2	0	0	0.0	6	8	1	0		0	0	41	4	2	3	3.9	.957	OF-8, 1B-4
1877		60	.378	.458	251	95	10	5	0	0.0	43	27	3	3		0	0	42	18	23	2	1.4	.723	OF-58, P-2
1878	CHI N	60	.266	.301	256	68	7	1	0	0.0	33	29	9	11		0	0	91	31	28	6	2.5	.813	OF-60, C-1
1879	TRO N	9	.189	.216	37	7	1	0	0	0.0	4	1	2	4		0	0	24	2	4	2	3.0	.867	OF-8, 1B-2
1880		83	.253	.338	352	89	14	8	0	0.0	40	29	12	34		0	0	130	18	22	1	2.0	.871	OF-82, 2B-1
1881		85	.222	.281	370	82	13	3	1	0.3	57	11	18	21		0	0	144	24	25	1	2.3	.870	OF-84, SS-1
1882		29	.174	.215	121	21	3	1	0	0.0	14	9	3	16		0	0	35	23	25	1	2.9	.699	OF-16, 3B-13
1883	PRO N	89	.238	.309	366	87	16	5	0	0.0	46		9	38		0	0	132	29	26	2	2.1	.861	OF-88, 2B-1, 1B-1
1884	BKN AA	106	.252	.319	433	109	11	6	2	0.5	57		19			0	0	131	31	34	5	1.8	.827	OF-100, 3B-5, SS-1
1885		54	.213	.271	221	47	6	2	1	0.5	36		8			0	0	62	7	12	3	1.5	.852	OF-54
10 yrs.		587	.252	.316	2454	618	83	31	4	0.2	336	114	84	127		0	0	832	187	201	26	2.1	.835	OF-558, 3B-18, 1B-7, 2B-2, SS-2, P-2, C-1

Pete Cassidy

CASSIDY, PETER FRANCIS BR TR 5′10″ 165 lbs.
B. Apr. 8, 1873, Wilmington, Del. D. July 9, 1929, Wilmington, Del.

Year	Team	Games	BA	SA	AB	H	2B	3B	HR	HR%	R	RBI	BB	SO	SB	Pinch Hit AB	Pinch Hit H	PO	A	E	DP	TC/G	FA	G by Pos
1896	**LOU N**	49	.212	.228	184	39	1	1	0	0.0	16	12	7	7	5	0	0	368	48	24	18	9.0	.945	1B-38, SS-11
1899	**2 teams**	**BKN N** (6G –.150) **WAS N** (46G –.315)																						
″	**total**	52	.298	.414	198	59	14	0	3	1.5	23	36	10		6	1	0	360	45	21	26	8.4	.951	1B-37, 3B-9, SS-5
2 yrs.		101	.257	.325	382	98	15	1	3	0.8	39	48	17	7	11	1	0	728	93	45	44	8.7	.948	1B-75, SS-16, 3B-9

Jack Cassini

CASSINI, JACK DEMPSEY (Scat) BR TR 5′10″ 175 lbs.
B. Oct. 26, 1919, Dearborn, Mich.

Year	Team	Games	BA	SA	AB	H	2B	3B	HR	HR%	R	RBI	BB	SO	SB	Pinch Hit AB	Pinch Hit H	PO	A	E	DP	TC/G	FA	G by Pos
1949	**PIT N**	8	—	—	0	0	0	0	0	—	3	0	0	0	0	0	0	0	0	0	0	0.0	—	

Pedro Castellano

CASTELLANO, PEDRO ORLANDO BR TR 6′ 1″ 194 lbs.
Born Pedro Orlando Castellano (Arrieta).
B. Mar. 11, 1970, Barquisimeto, Venezuela.

Year	Team	Games	BA	SA	AB	H	2B	3B	HR	HR%	R	RBI	BB	SO	SB	Pinch Hit AB	Pinch Hit H	PO	A	E	DP	TC/G	FA	G by Pos
1993	**CLR N**	34	.183	.338	71	13	2	0	3	4.2	12	7	8	16	1	6	1	55	33	4	10	2.9	.957	3B-13, 1B-10, SS-5, 2B-4
1995		4	.000	.000	5	0	0	0	0	0.0	0	0	2	3	0	1	0	1	0	0	0	0.3	1.000	3B-3
2 yrs.		38	.171	.316	76	13	2	0	3	3.9	12	7	10	19	1	7	1	56	33	4	10	2.7	.957	3B-16, 1B-10, SS-5, 2B-4

Jim Castiglia

CASTIGLIA, JAMES VINCENT BL TR 5′11″ 200 lbs.
B. Sept. 30, 1918, Passaic, N. J.

Year	Team	Games	BA	SA	AB	H	2B	3B	HR	HR%	R	RBI	BB	SO	SB	Pinch Hit AB	Pinch Hit H	PO	A	E	DP	TC/G	FA	G by Pos
1942	**PHI A**	16	.389	.389	18	7	0	0	0	0.0	2	2	1	3	0	13	4	6	1	1	0	2.7	.875	C-3

Pete Castiglione

CASTIGLIONE, PETER PAUL BR TR 5′11″ 175 lbs.
B. Feb. 13, 1921, Greenwich, Conn.

Year	Team	Games	BA	SA	AB	H	2B	3B	HR	HR%	R	RBI	BB	SO	SB	Pinch Hit AB	Pinch Hit H	PO	A	E	DP	TC/G	FA	G by Pos
1947	**PIT N**	13	.280	.280	50	14	0	0	0	0.0	6	1	2	5	0	0	0	26	39	2	6	5.2	.970	SS-13
1948		4	.000	.000	2	0	0	0	0	0.0	0	0	0	0	1	1	0	0	1	0	0	1.0	1.000	SS-1
1949		118	.268	.362	448	120	20	2	6	1.3	57	43	20	43	2	5	1	115	236	14	32	3.1	.962	3B-98, SS-17, OF-2
1950		94	.255	.350	263	67	10	3	3	1.1	29	22	23	23	1	22	7	116	125	10	23	3.3	.960	3B-35, SS-29, 2B-9, 1B-3
1951		132	.261	.361	482	126	19	4	7	1.5	62	42	34	28	2	9	2	148	292	21	36	3.6	.954	3B-99, SS-28
1952		67	.266	.374	214	57	9	1	4	1.9	27	18	17	8	3	9	2	69	129	10	7	3.5	.952	3B-57, 1B-1, OF-1
1953	**2 teams**	**PIT N** (45G –.208) **STL N** (67G –.173)																						
″	**total**	112	.199	.284	211	42	4	1	4	1.9	23	24	7	19	1	8	4	68	132	7	14	2.0	.966	3B-94, 2B-9, SS-3
1954	**STL N**	5	—	—	0	0	0	0	0	—	1	0	0	0	0	0	0	0	1	0	0	0.2	1.000	3B-5
8 yrs.		545	.255	.349	1670	426	62	11	24	1.4	205	150	103	126	10	54	16	542	955	64	118	3.1	.959	3B-388, SS-91, 2B-18, 1B-4, OF-3

Vinny Castilla

CASTILLA, VINICIO BR TR 6′ 1″ 175 lbs.
Born Vinicio Castilla (Soria).
B. July 4, 1967, Oaxaca, Mexico.

Year	Team	Games	BA	SA	AB	H	2B	3B	HR	HR%	R	RBI	BB	SO	SB	Pinch Hit AB	Pinch Hit H	PO	A	E	DP	TC/G	FA	G by Pos
1991	**ATL N**	12	.200	.200	5	1	0	0	0	0.0	1	0	0	2	0	0	0	6	6	0	0	1.0	1.000	SS-12
1992		9	.250	.313	16	4	1	0	0	0.0	1	1	1	4	0	0	0	2	12	1	1	1.9	.933	SS-4, 3B-4
1993	**CLR N**	105	.255	.404	337	86	9	7	9	2.7	36	30	13	45	2	2	0	141	282	11	67	4.2	.975	SS-104
1994		52	.331	.500	130	43	11	1	3	2.3	16	18	7	23	2	10	3	67	78	2	23	3.4	.986	SS-18, 2B-14, 3B-9, 1B-2
1995		139	.309	.564	527	163	34	2	32	6.1	82	90	30	87	2	1	0	89	262	15	21	2.6	.959	3B-136, SS-5
5 yrs.		317	.293	.497	1015	297	55	10	44	4.3	136	139	51	161	6	13	3	305	640	29	112	3.2	.970	3B-149, SS-143, 2B-14, 1B-2
DIVISIONAL PLAYOFF SERIES																								
1995	**CLR N**	4	.467	1.133	15	7	1	0	3	20.0	3	6	0	1	0	0	0	3	13	1	1	4.3	.941	3B-4

Alberto Castillo

CASTILLO, ALBERTO TERRERO BR TR 6′ 184 lbs.
B. Feb. 10, 1970, San Juan de la Maguana, Dominican Republic.

Year	Team	Games	BA	SA	AB	H	2B	3B	HR	HR%	R	RBI	BB	SO	SB	Pinch Hit AB	Pinch Hit H	PO	A	E	DP	TC/G	FA	G by Pos
1995	**NY N**	13	.103	.103	29	3	0	0	0	0.0	2	0	3	9	1	0	0	66	10	2	0	6.5	.974	C-12

Braulio Castillo

CASTILLO, BRAULIO ROBINSON BR TR 6′ 160 lbs.
Born Braulio Robinson Medrano (Castillo).
B. May 13, 1968, Elias Pina, Dominican Republic.

Year	Team	Games	BA	SA	AB	H	2B	3B	HR	HR%	R	RBI	BB	SO	SB	Pinch Hit AB	Pinch Hit H	PO	A	E	DP	TC/G	FA	G by Pos
1991	**PHI N**	28	.173	.231	52	9	3	0	0	0.0	3	2	1	15	1	0	0	40	2	1	1	1.7	.977	OF-26
1992		28	.197	.342	76	15	3	1	2	2.6	12	7	4	15	1	5	0	43	0	2	0	1.9	.956	OF-24
2 yrs.		56	.188	.297	128	24	6	1	2	1.6	15	9	5	30	2	5	0	83	2	3	1	1.8	.966	OF-50

Carmen Castillo

CASTILLO, MONTE CARMELO BR TR 6′ 1″ 180 lbs.
B. June 8, 1958, San Pedro de Macoris, Dominican Republic.

Year	Team	Games	BA	SA	AB	H	2B	3B	HR	HR%	R	RBI	BB	SO	SB	Pinch Hit AB	Pinch Hit H	PO	A	E	DP	TC/G	FA	G by Pos
1982	**CLE A**	47	.208	.292	120	25	4	0	2	1.7	11	11	6	17	0	3	0	91	0	2	0	2.1	.978	OF-43, DH-2
1983		23	.278	.472	36	10	2	1	1	2.8	9	3	4	6	1	2	0	23	3	2	1	1.4	.929	OF-19, DH-1
1984		87	.261	.464	211	55	9	2	10	4.7	36	36	21	32	1	18	3	123	2	9	0	1.9	.933	OF-70, DH-2
1985		67	.245	.462	184	45	5	1	11	6.0	27	25	11	40	3	9	1	101	0	5	0	1.8	.953	OF-51, DH-9
1986		85	.278	.439	205	57	9	0	8	3.9	34	32	9	48	2	21	3	58	4	4	1	0.9	.939	OF-37, DH-35
1987		89	.250	.477	220	55	17	0	11	5.0	27	31	16	52	1	29	5	29	3	0	0	0.5	1.000	DH-43, OF-23
1988		66	.273	.386	176	48	8	0	4	2.3	12	14	5	31	6	16	4	69	1	5	0	1.4	.933	OF-45, DH-9
1989	**MIN A**	94	.257	.454	218	56	13	3	8	3.7	23	33	15	40	1	29	8	119	3	3	1	1.5	.976	OF-67, DH-16
1990		64	.219	.248	137	30	4	0	0	0.0	11	12	3	23	0	22	5	24	0	2	0	0.5	.923	DH-35, OF-21
1991		9	.167	.333	12	2	0	1	0	0.0	0	0	0	2	0	6	1	3	0	0	0	0.5	1.000	OF-4, DH-2
10 yrs.		631	.252	.418	1519	383	71	8	55	3.6	190	197	90	291	15	155	30	640	16	32	3	1.3	.953	OF-380, DH-154

Juan Castillo

CASTILLO, JUAN BB TR 5′11″ 162 lbs.
Born Juan Castillo (Brayas). BR 1988–1989
B. Jan. 25, 1962, San Pedro de Macoris, Dominican Republic.

Year	Team	Games	BA	SA	AB	H	2B	3B	HR	HR%	R	RBI	BB	SO	SB	Pinch Hit AB	Pinch Hit H	PO	A	E	DP	TC/G	FA	G by Pos
1986	**MIL A**	26	.167	.204	54	9	0	1	0	0.0	6	5	5	12	1	0	0	41	46	4	10	3.5	.956	2B-17, SS-4, DH-2, 3B-2, OF-1
1987		116	.224	.312	321	72	11	4	3	0.9	44	28	33	76	15	7	2	190	251	12	59	3.9	.974	2B-97, SS-13, 3B-7
1988		54	.222	.222	90	20	0	0	0	0.0	10	2	3	14	2	0	0	24	82	7	13	2.2	.938	2B-18, 3B-17, SS-13, DH-3, OF-1
1989		3	.000	.000	4	0	0	0	0	0.0	0	3	0	2	0	0	0	6	5	0	1	3.7	1.000	2B-3
4 yrs.		199	.215	.279	469	101	11	5	3	0.6	60	38	41	104	18	7	2	261	384	23	83	3.4	.966	2B-135, SS-30, 3B-26, DH-5, OF-2

Manny Castillo

CASTILLO, ESTEBAN MANUEL ANTONIO
Born Esteban Manuel Antonio Castillo (Cabrera).
B. Apr. 1, 1957, Santo Domingo, Dominican Republic.

BB TR 5′ 9″ 160 lbs.

Year	Team	Lg	Games	BA	SA	AB	H	2B	3B	HR	HR%	R	RBI	BB	SO	SB	Pinch Hit AB	Pinch Hit H	PO	A	E	DP	TC/G	FA	G by Pos
1980	KC	A	7	.200	.200	10	2	0	0	0	0.0	1	0	0	0	0	2	1	2	8	0	0	1.7	1.000	3B-3, DH-2, 2B-1
1982	SEA	A	138	.257	.336	506	130	29	1	3	0.6	49	49	22	35	2	11	1	109	220	21	24	2.5	.940	3B-130, 2B-9
1983			91	.207	.266	203	42	6	3	0	0.0	13	24	7	20	1	29	7	78	118	6	17	2.6	.970	3B-55, 1B-11, DH-6, 2B-5, P-1
3 yrs.			236	.242	.314	719	174	35	4	3	0.4	63	73	29	55	3	42	9	189	346	27	41	2.5	.952	3B-188, 2B-15, 1B-11, DH-8, P-1

Marty Castillo

CASTILLO, MARTIN HORACE
B. Jan. 16, 1957, Long Beach, Calif.

BR TR 6′ 1″ 190 lbs.

Year	Team	Lg	Games	BA	SA	AB	H	2B	3B	HR	HR%	R	RBI	BB	SO	SB	Pinch Hit AB	Pinch Hit H	PO	A	E	DP	TC/G	FA	G by Pos
1981	DET	A	6	.125	.125	8	1	0	0	0	0.0	1	0	0	2	0	0	0	5	8	0	3	2.2	1.000	3B-4, OF-1, C-1
1982			1	—	—	0	0	0	0	0	—	0	0	0	0	0	0	0	1	0	0	0	1.0	1.000	C-1
1983			67	.193	.277	119	23	4	0	2	1.7	10	10	7	22	2	2	0	73	69	1	6	2.1	.993	3B-58, C-10
1984			70	.234	.383	141	33	5	2	4	2.8	16	17	10	33	1	1	0	161	37	7	3	2.9	.966	C-36, 3B-33, DH-1
1985			57	.119	.214	84	10	2	0	2	2.4	4	5	2	19	0	0	0	123	31	4	2	2.8	.975	C-32, 3B-25
5 yrs.			201	.190	.301	352	67	11	2	8	2.3	31	32	19	76	3	3	0	363	145	12	14	2.6	.977	3B-120, C-80, DH-1, OF-1
LEAGUE CHAMPIONSHIP SERIES																									
1984	DET	A	3	.250	.250	8	2	0	0	0	0.0	0	2	0	3	1	0	0	3	4	0	0	2.3	1.000	3B-3
WORLD SERIES																									
1984	DET	A	3	.333	.667	9	3	0	0	1	11.1	2	2	2	1	0	0	0	3	3	0	0	2.0	1.000	3B-3

Tony Castillo

CASTILLO, ANTHONY
B. June 14, 1957, San Jose, Calif.

BR TR 6′ 4″ 190 lbs.

Year	Team	Lg	Games	BA	SA	AB	H	2B	3B	HR	HR%	R	RBI	BB	SO	SB	Pinch Hit AB	Pinch Hit H	PO	A	E	DP	TC/G	FA	G by Pos
1978	SD	N	5	.125	.125	8	1	0	0	0	0.0	0	1	0	2	0	0	0	16	3	1	0	4.0	.950	C-5

John Castino

CASTINO, JOHN ANTHONY
B. Oct. 23, 1954, Evanston, Ill.

BR TR 5′11″ 175 lbs.

Year	Team	Lg	Games	BA	SA	AB	H	2B	3B	HR	HR%	R	RBI	BB	SO	SB	Pinch Hit AB	Pinch Hit H	PO	A	E	DP	TC/G	FA	G by Pos
1979	MIN	A	148	.285	.397	393	112	13	8	5	1.3	49	52	27	72	5	8	3	91	286	15	34	2.6	.962	3B-143, SS-5
1980			150	.302	.430	546	165	17	7	13	2.4	67	64	29	67	7	1	0	128	395	22	48	3.5	.960	3B-138, SS-18
1981			101	.268	.396	381	102	13	**9**	6	1.6	41	36	18	52	4	0	0	96	236	9	29	3.3	.974	3B-98, 2B-4
1982			117	.241	.344	410	99	12	6	6	1.5	48	37	36	51	2	0	0	230	278	4	69	4.1	.992	2B-96, 3B-21, OF-6, DH-1
1983			142	.277	.403	563	156	30	4	11	2.0	83	57	62	54	4	2	0	316	430	8	95	5.3	.989	2B-132, 3B-8, DH-1
1984			8	.444	.481	27	12	1	0	0	0.0	5	3	5	2	0	0	0	8	12	0	1	2.5	1.000	3B-8
6 yrs.			666	.278	.398	2320	646	86	34	41	1.8	293	249	177	298	22	11	3	869	1637	58	276	3.8	.977	3B-416, 2B-232, SS-23, OF-6, DH-2

Vince Castino

CASTINO, VINCENT CHARLES
B. Oct. 11, 1917, Willisville, Ill. D. Mar. 6, 1967, Sacramento, Calif.

BR TR 5′ 9″ 175 lbs.

Year	Team	Lg	Games	BA	SA	AB	H	2B	3B	HR	HR%	R	RBI	BB	SO	SB	Pinch Hit AB	Pinch Hit H	PO	A	E	DP	TC/G	FA	G by Pos
1943	CHI	A	33	.228	.297	101	23	1	0	2	2.0	14	16	12	11	0	3	0	90	9	3	3	3.4	.971	C-30
1944			29	.231	.295	78	18	5	0	0	0.0	8	3	10	13	0	2	1	85	16	1	4	3.9	.990	C-26
1945			26	.216	.243	37	8	1	0	0	0.0	2	4	3	7	0	1	0	32	7	2	1	1.6	.951	C-25
3 yrs.			88	.227	.287	216	49	7	0	2	0.9	24	23	25	31	0	6	1	207	32	6	8	3.0	.976	C-81

Don Castle

CASTLE, DONALD HARDY
B. Feb. 1, 1950, Kokomo, Ind.

BL TL 6′ 1″ 205 lbs.

Year	Team	Lg	Games	BA	SA	AB	H	2B	3B	HR	HR%	R	RBI	BB	SO	SB	Pinch Hit AB	Pinch Hit H	PO	A	E	DP	TC/G	FA	G by Pos
1973	TEX	A	4	.308	.385	13	4	1	0	0	0.0	0	2	1	3	0	1	0	0	0	0	0	0.0	.000	DH-3

John Castle

CASTLE, JOHN FRANCIS
B. June 1, 1883, Honey Brook, Pa. D. Apr. 13, 1929, Philadelphia, Pa.

5′10½″

Year	Team	Lg	Games	BA	SA	AB	H	2B	3B	HR	HR%	R	RBI	BB	SO	SB	Pinch Hit AB	Pinch Hit H	PO	A	E	DP	TC/G	FA	G by Pos
1910	PHI	N	3	.250	.250	4	1	0	0	0	0.0	1	0	0	0	1	0	0	0	0	0	0	0.0	.000	OF-2

Foster Castleman

CASTLEMAN, FOSTER EPHRAIM
B. Jan. 1, 1931, Nashville, Tenn.

BR TR 6′ 175 lbs.

Year	Team	Lg	Games	BA	SA	AB	H	2B	3B	HR	HR%	R	RBI	BB	SO	SB	Pinch Hit AB	Pinch Hit H	PO	A	E	DP	TC/G	FA	G by Pos
1954	NY	N	13	.250	.250	12	3	0	0	0	0.0	0	1	0	3	0	11	3	0	0	0	0	0.0	.000	2B-2
1955			15	.214	.464	28	6	1	0	2	7.1	3	4	2	4	0	7	1	14	10	0	2	3.4	1.000	2B-6, 3B-1
1956			124	.226	.392	385	87	16	3	14	3.6	33	45	15	50	2	17	3	91	213	17	10	2.9	.947	3B-107, SS-2, 2B-1
1957			18	.162	.297	37	6	2	0	1	2.7	7	1	2	8	0	9	1	6	12	2	1	2.2	.900	3B-7, SS-1, 2B-1
1958	BAL	A	98	.170	.240	200	34	5	0	3	1.5	15	14	16	34	2	2	0	113	174	11	40	3.0	.963	SS-91, 3B-4, 2B-4, OF-1
5 yrs.			268	.205	.341	662	136	24	3	20	3.0	58	65	35	99	4	46	8	224	409	30	53	2.9	.955	3B-119, SS-94, 2B-14, OF-1

Juan Castro

CASTRO, JUAN GABRIEL
B. June 20, 1972, Los Mochis, Mexico.

BR TR 5′10″ 163 lbs.

Year	Team	Lg	Games	BA	SA	AB	H	2B	3B	HR	HR%	R	RBI	BB	SO	SB	Pinch Hit AB	Pinch Hit H	PO	A	E	DP	TC/G	FA	G by Pos
1995	LA	N	11	.250	.250	4	1	0	0	0	0.0	0	0	1	1	0	0	0	3	7	0	2	0.9	1.000	3B-7, SS-4

Louis Castro

CASTRO, LOUIS R. (Jud)
B. 1877, Cartagena, Colombia.

BR TR 5′ 7″

Year	Team	Lg	Games	BA	SA	AB	H	2B	3B	HR	HR%	R	RBI	BB	SO	SB	Pinch Hit AB	Pinch Hit H	PO	A	E	DP	TC/G	FA	G by Pos
1902	PHI	A	42	.245	.336	143	35	8	1	1	0.7	18	15	4		2	2	0	75	86	17	10	4.4	.904	2B-36, OF-3, SS-1

Danny Cater

CATER, DANNY ANDERSON
B. Feb. 25, 1940, Austin, Tex.

BR TR 6′ 170 lbs.

Year	Team	Lg	Games	BA	SA	AB	H	2B	3B	HR	HR%	R	RBI	BB	SO	SB	Pinch Hit AB	Pinch Hit H	PO	A	E	DP	TC/G	FA	G by Pos
1964	PHI	N	60	.296	.388	152	45	9	1	1	0.7	13	13	7	15	1	18	6	110	7	3	7	2.6	.975	OF-39, 1B-7, 3B-1
1965	CHI	A	142	.270	.403	514	139	18	4	14	2.7	74	55	33	65	3	7	2	189	21	6	3	1.5	.972	OF-127, 3B-11, 1B-3
1966	2 teams		CHI A (21G –.183) KC A (116G –.292)																						
″	total		137	.278	.373	485	135	17	4	7	1.4	50	56	28	47	4	5	1	565	104	11	55	5.0	.984	1B-53, 3B-42, OF-40
1967	KC	A	142	.270	.340	529	143	17	4	4	0.8	55	46	34	56	4	2	1	424	109	13	35	3.5	.976	3B-56, OF-55, 1B-44
1968	OAK	A	147	.290	.393	504	146	28	3	6	1.2	53	62	35	43	8	11	4	1007	69	5	89	7.6	.995	1B-121, OF-20, 2B-1
1969			152	.262	.361	584	153	24	2	10	1.7	64	76	28	40	1	8	1	1125	108	9	113	8.0	.993	1B-132, OF-20, 2B-4
1970	NY	A	155	.301	.393	582	175	26	5	6	1.0	64	76	34	44	4	3	0	1016	153	16	89	6.6	.986	1B-131, 3B-42, OF-7
1971			121	.276	.364	428	118	16	5	4	0.9	39	50	19	25	0	10	3	605	173	13	61	6.1	.984	1B-78, 3B-52
1972	BOS	A	92	.237	.372	317	75	17	1	8	2.5	32	39	15	33	0	6	1	656	61	5	65	8.0	.993	1B-90
1973			63	.313	.390	195	61	12	0	1	0.5	30	24	10	22	0	7	2	303	56	6	45	6.0	.984	1B-37, 3B-21, DH-3

Danny Cater *continued*

Year	Team	Games	BA	SA	AB	H	2B	3B	HR	HR%	R	RBI	BB	SO	SB	Pinch Hit AB	Pinch Hit H	PO	A	E	DP	TC/G	FA	G by Pos
1974		56	.246	.405	126	31	5	0	5	4.0	14	20	10	13	1	18	5	126	10	0	9	3.7	1.000	1B-23, DH-14
1975	STL N	22	.229	.286	35	8	2	0	0	0.0	3	2	1	3	0	13	2	49	4	1	4	4.5	.981	1B-12
12 yrs.		1289	.276	.377	4451	1229	191	29	66	1.5	491	519	254	406	26	108	28	6175	875	88	575	5.6	.988	1B-731, OF-308, 3B-225, DH-17, 2B-5

Eli Cates

CATES, ELI ELDO BR TR 5′ 9½″ 175 lbs.
B. Jan. 26, 1877, Greensfork, Ind. D. May 29, 1964, Anderson, Ind.

Year	Team	Games	BA	SA	AB	H	2B	3B	HR	HR%	R	RBI	BB	SO	SB	Pinch Hit AB	Pinch Hit H	PO	A	E	DP	TC/G	FA	G by Pos
1908	WAS A	40	.186	.237	59	11	1	1	0	0.0	5	3	6		0	16	1	8	38	5	1	2.3	.902	P-19, 2B-3

Ted Cather

CATHER, THEODORE PHYSICK BR TR 5′10½″ 178 lbs.
B. May 20, 1889, Chester, Pa. D. Apr. 9, 1945, Elkton, Md.

Year	Team	Games	BA	SA	AB	H	2B	3B	HR	HR%	R	RBI	BB	SO	SB	Pinch Hit AB	Pinch Hit H	PO	A	E	DP	TC/G	FA	G by Pos
1912	STL N	5	.421	.579	19	8	1	1	0	0.0	4	2	0	4	1	0	0	15	2	1	0	3.6	.944	OF-5
1913		67	.213	.301	183	39	8	4	0	0.0	16	12	9	24	7	7	3	71	8	7	0	1.5	.919	OF-57, 1B-1, P-1
1914	2 teams	STL N (39G –.273) BOS N (50G –.297)																						
″	total	89	.287	.377	244	70	18	2	0	0.0	30	40	10	43	11	12	1	106	8	4	2	1.6	.966	OF-76
1915	BOS N	40	.206	.314	102	21	3	1	2	2.0	10	18	15	19	2	7	1	35	2	4	0	1.0	.902	OF-40
4 yrs.		201	.252	.347	548	138	30	8	2	0.4	60	72	34	90	21	26	5	227	20	16	2	1.5	.939	OF-178, 1B-1, P-1
WORLD SERIES																								
1914	BOS N	1	.000	.000	5	0	0	0	0	0.0	0	0	0	1	0	0	0	2	0	0	0	2.0	1.000	OF-1

Buster Caton

CATON, JAMES HOWARD BR TR 5′ 6″ 165 lbs.
B. July 16, 1896, Zanesville, Ohio D. Jan. 8, 1948, Zanesville, Ohio.

Year	Team	Games	BA	SA	AB	H	2B	3B	HR	HR%	R	RBI	BB	SO	SB	Pinch Hit AB	Pinch Hit H	PO	A	E	DP	TC/G	FA	G by Pos
1917	PIT N	14	.211	.298	57	12	1	2	0	0.0	6	4	6	7	0	0	0	21	47	8	5	5.4	.895	SS-14
1918		80	.234	.297	303	71	5	7	0	0.0	37	17	32	16	12	1	0	136	276	32	35	5.6	.928	SS-79
1919		39	.176	.225	102	18	1	2	0	0.0	13	5	12	10	2	6	1	38	52	6	3	3.3	.938	SS-17, 3B-11, OF-1
1920		98	.236	.295	352	83	11	5	0	0.0	29	27	33	19	4	1	1	191	296	37	40	5.5	.929	SS-96
4 yrs.		231	.226	.287	814	184	18	16	0	0.0	85	53	83	52	18	8	2	386	671	83	83	5.2	.927	SS-206, 3B-11, OF-1

Tom Catterson

CATTERSON, THOMAS HENRY BL TL 5′10″ 170 lbs.
B. Aug. 25, 1884, Warwick, R. I. D. Feb. 5, 1920, Portland, Me.

Year	Team	Games	BA	SA	AB	H	2B	3B	HR	HR%	R	RBI	BB	SO	SB	Pinch Hit AB	Pinch Hit H	PO	A	E	DP	TC/G	FA	G by Pos
1908	BKN N	19	.191	.279	68	13	1	1	1	1.5	5	2	5		0	1	0	39	1	1	0	2.3	.976	OF-18
1909		9	.222	.222	18	4	0	0	0	0.0	0	1	3		0	1	0	5	0	1	0	1.0	.833	OF-6
2 yrs.		28	.198	.267	86	17	1	1	1	1.2	5	3	8		0	2	0	44	1	2	0	2.0	.957	OF-24

John Caulfield

CAULFIELD, JOHN JOSEPH (Jake) BR TR 5′11″ 170 lbs.
B. Nov. 23, 1917, Los Angeles, Calif. D. Dec. 16, 1986, San Francisco, Calif.

Year	Team	Games	BA	SA	AB	H	2B	3B	HR	HR%	R	RBI	BB	SO	SB	Pinch Hit AB	Pinch Hit H	PO	A	E	DP	TC/G	FA	G by Pos
1946	PHI A	44	.277	.362	94	26	8	0	0	0.0	13	10	4	11	0	2	0	49	55	8	13	3.5	.929	SS-31, 3B-1

Wayne Causey

CAUSEY, JAMES WAYNE BL TR 5′10½″ 175 lbs.
B. Dec. 26, 1936, Ruston, La.

Year	Team	Games	BA	SA	AB	H	2B	3B	HR	HR%	R	RBI	BB	SO	SB	Pinch Hit AB	Pinch Hit H	PO	A	E	DP	TC/G	FA	G by Pos
1955	BAL A	68	.194	.234	175	34	2	1	1	0.6	14	9	17	25	0	8	0	30	85	12	11	2.0	.906	3B-55, 2B-7, SS-1
1956		53	.170	.227	88	15	0	1	1	1.1	7	4	8	23	0	16	5	26	52	2	4	2.2	.975	3B-30, 2B-7
1957		14	.200	.200	10	2	0	0	0	0.0	2	1	5	2	0	3	0	14	13	1	2	2.5	.964	2B-6, 3B-5
1961	KC A	104	.276	.404	312	86	14	1	8	2.6	37	49	37	28	0	2	0	133	228	16	25	3.5	.958	3B-88, SS-11, 2B-9
1962		117	.252	.344	305	77	14	1	4	1.3	40	38	41	30	2	28	9	143	200	14	25	4.2	.961	SS-51, 3B-26, 2B-9
1963		139	.280	.395	554	155	32	4	8	1.4	72	44	56	54	4	1	1	267	405	15	81	5.0	.978	SS-135, 3B-2
1964		157	.281	.386	604	170	31	4	8	1.3	82	49	88	65	0	3	2	323	423	25	92	4.9	.968	SS-131, 2B-17, 3B-9
1965		144	.261	.343	513	134	17	8	3	0.6	48	34	61	48	1	8	1	221	313	15	60	3.9	.973	SS-62, 2B-45, 3B-35
1966	2 teams	KC A (28G –.228) CHI A (78G –.244)																						
″	total	106	.239	.288	243	58	8	2	0	0.0	24	18	31	19	3	19	7	115	150	11	21	3.2	.960	2B-60, 3B-16, SS-11
1967	CHI A	124	.226	.291	292	66	10	3	1	0.3	21	28	32	35	2	34	10	153	200	8	36	3.7	.978	2B-96, SS-2
1968	3 teams	CHI A (59G –.180) CAL A (4G –.000) ATL N (16G –.108)																						
″	total	79	.149	.196	148	22	2	1	1	0.7	10	11	14	12	0	36	6	62	76	4	17	2.6	.972	2B-51, SS-2, 3B-2
11 yrs.		1105	.252	.341	3244	819	130	26	35	1.1	357	285	390	341	12	158	41	1487	2145	123	374	3.8	.967	SS-406, 2B-307, 3B-268

John Cavanaugh

CAVANAUGH, JOHN J. BR TR 5′ 9″ 158 lbs.
B. June 5, 1900, Reading, Pa. D. Jan. 14, 1961, New Brunswick, N. J.

Year	Team	Games	BA	SA	AB	H	2B	3B	HR	HR%	R	RBI	BB	SO	SB	Pinch Hit AB	Pinch Hit H	PO	A	E	DP	TC/G	FA	G by Pos
1919	PHI N	1	.000	.000	1	0	0	0	0	0.0	0	0	0	1	0	0	0	0	0	0	0	0.0	.000	3B-1

Phil Cavarretta

CAVARRETTA, PHILIP JOSEPH BL TL 5′11½″ 175 lbs.
B. July 19, 1916, Chicago, Ill.
Manager 1951–53.

Year	Team	Games	BA	SA	AB	H	2B	3B	HR	HR%	R	RBI	BB	SO	SB	Pinch Hit AB	Pinch Hit H	PO	A	E	DP	TC/G	FA	G by Pos
1934	CHI N	7	.381	.619	21	8	0	1	1	4.8	5	6	2	3	1	2	0	53	5	0	6	11.6	1.000	1B-5
1935		146	.275	.404	589	162	28	12	8	1.4	85	82	39	61	4	1	0	1347	98	20	129	10.1	.986	1B-145
1936		124	.273	.376	458	125	18	1	9	2.0	55	56	17	36	8	8	4	980	71	14	93	9.3	.987	1B-115
1937		106	.286	.429	329	94	18	7	5	1.5	43	56	32	35	7	11	4	454	40	10	28	5.3	.980	OF-53, 1B-43
1938		92	.239	.321	268	64	11	4	1	0.4	29	28	14	27	4	13	1	277	21	4	14	3.8	.987	OF-52, 1B-28
1939		22	.273	.364	55	15	3	1	0	0.0	4	0	4	3	2	7	3	106	6	1	10	8.1	.991	1B-13, OF-1
1940		65	.280	.409	193	54	11	4	2	1.0	34	22	31	18	3	10	0	524	30	5	57	10.8	.991	1B-52
1941		107	.286	.413	346	99	18	4	6	1.7	46	40	53	28	2	5	2	463	15	5	20	4.9	.990	OF-66, 1B-33
1942		136	.270	.363	482	130	28	4	3	0.6	59	54	71	42	7	6	0	744	49	7	49	6.1	.991	OF-70, 1B-61
1943		143	.291	.421	530	154	27	9	8	1.5	93	73	75	42	3	2	0	1305	67	18	103	9.9	.987	1B-134, OF-7
1944		152	.321	.451	614	**197**	35	15	5	0.8	106	82	67	42	4	0	0	1363	78	13	121	9.6	.991	1B-139, OF-13
1945		132	**.355**	.500	498	177	34	10	6	1.2	94	97	81	34	5	0	0	1172	78	9	83	9.6	.993	1B-120, OF-11
1946		139	.294	.435	510	150	28	10	8	1.6	89	78	88	54	2	2	0	646	47	11	28	5.1	.984	OF-86, 1B-51
1947		127	.314	.397	459	144	22	5	2	0.4	56	63	58	35	2	3	2	420	24	8	26	3.6	.982	OF-100, 1B-24
1948		111	.278	.383	334	93	16	5	3	0.9	41	40	35	29	4	23	3	446	32	3	46	5.9	.994	1B-41, OF-40
1949		105	.294	.444	360	106	22	4	8	2.2	46	49	45	31	2	9	2	712	67	5	59	8.3	.994	1B-70, OF-25
1950		82	.273	.441	256	70	11	1	10	3.9	49	31	40	31	1	9	2	609	47	9	55	9.5	.986	1B-67, OF-3
1951		89	.311	.442	206	64	7	1	6	2.9	24	28	27	28	0	33	**12**	444	42	3	51	9.2	.994	1B-53
1952		41	.238	.333	63	15	1	1	1	1.6	7	8	9	3	0	26	5	98	10	1	13	8.4	.991	1B-13
1953		27	.286	.429	21	6	3	0	0	0.0	3	3	6	3	0	21	6	0	0	0	0	0.0	—	

Phil Cavarretta *continued*

Year	Team	Games	BA	SA	AB	H	2B	3B	HR	HR%	R	RBI	BB	SO	SB	Pinch Hit AB	Pinch Hit H	PO	A	E	DP	TC/G	FA	G by Pos
1954	CHI A	71	.316	.411	158	50	6	0	3	1.9	21	24	26	12	4	16	2	269	17	3	29	5.5	.990	1B-44, OF-9
1955		6	.000	.000	4	0	0	0	0	0.0	1	0	0	1	0	2	0	3	0	0	0	1.0	1.000	1B-3
22 yrs.		2030	.293	.416	6754	1977	347	99	95	1.4	990	920	820	598	65	209	48	12435	844	149	1020	7.5	.989	1B-1254, OF-536
WORLD SERIES																								
1935	CHI N	6	.125	.125	24	3	0	0	0	0.0	1	0	0	5	0	0	0	58	3	1	3	10.3	.984	1B-6
1938		4	.462	.538	13	6	1	0	0	0.0	1	0	0	1	0	1	1	4	1	0	0	1.7	1.000	OF-3
1945		7	.423	.615	26	11	2	0	1	3.8	7	5	4	3	0	0	0	71	3	0	5	10.6	1.000	1B-7
3 yrs.		17	.317	.413	63	20	3	0	1	1.6	9	5	4	9	0	1	1	133	7	1	8	8.8	.993	1B-13, OF-3

Ike Caveney

CAVENEY, JAMES CHRISTOPHER BR TR 5′ 9″ 168 lbs.
B. Dec. 10, 1894, San Francisco, Calif. D. July 6, 1949, San Francisco, Calif.

Year	Team	Games	BA	SA	AB	H	2B	3B	HR	HR%	R	RBI	BB	SO	SB	Pinch Hit AB	Pinch Hit H	PO	A	E	DP	TC/G	FA	G by Pos
1922	CIN N	118	.239	.338	394	94	12	9	3	0.8	41	54	29	33	6	0	0	256	404	47	74	6.0	.934	SS-118
1923		138	.277	.381	488	135	21	9	4	0.8	58	63	26	41	5	0	0	313	477	49	86	6.1	.942	SS-138
1924		95	.273	.371	337	92	19	1	4	1.2	36	32	14	21	2	1	0	210	326	44	61	6.1	.924	SS-90, 2B-5
1925		115	.249	.318	358	89	9	5	2	0.6	38	47	28	31	2	4	0	209	349	35	72	5.3	.941	SS-111
4 yrs.		466	.260	.354	1577	410	61	24	13	0.8	173	196	97	126	15	5	0	988	1556	175	293	5.9	.936	SS-457, 2B-5

Andujar Cedeno

CEDENO, ANDUJAR BR TR 6′ 1″ 170 lbs.
Born Andujar Cedeno (Donastorg).
Brother of Domingo Cedeno.
B. Aug. 21, 1969, La Romana, Dominican Republic.

Year	Team	Games	BA	SA	AB	H	2B	3B	HR	HR%	R	RBI	BB	SO	SB	Pinch Hit AB	Pinch Hit H	PO	A	E	DP	TC/G	FA	G by Pos
1990	HOU N	7	.000	.000	8	0	0	0	0	0.0	0	0	0	5	0	2	0	3	2	1	0	2.0	.833	SS-3
1991		67	.243	.418	251	61	13	2	9	3.6	27	36	9	74	4	1	0	88	151	18	36	3.9	.930	SS-66
1992		71	.173	.277	220	38	13	2	2	0.9	15	13	14	71	2	1	0	82	175	11	27	3.8	.959	SS-70
1993		149	.283	.412	505	143	24	4	11	2.2	69	56	48	97	9	1	1	155	376	25	78	3.7	.955	SS-149, 3B-1
1994		98	.263	.418	342	90	26	0	9	2.6	38	49	29	79	1	3	1	130	280	23	69	4.6	.947	SS-95
1995	SD N	120	.210	.308	390	82	16	2	6	1.5	42	31	28	92	5	1	1	139	305	17	58	3.9	.963	SS-116, 3B-1
6 yrs.		512	.241	.371	1716	414	92	10	37	2.2	191	185	128	418	21	9	3	597	1289	95	268	4.0	.952	SS-499, 3B-2

Cesar Cedeno

CEDENO, CESAR BR TR 6′ 2″ 175 lbs.
Born Cesar Cedeno (Encarnacion).
B. Feb. 25, 1951, Santo Domingo, Dominican Republic.

Year	Team	Games	BA	SA	AB	H	2B	3B	HR	HR%	R	RBI	BB	SO	SB	Pinch Hit AB	Pinch Hit H	PO	A	E	DP	TC/G	FA	G by Pos
1970	HOU N	90	.310	.451	355	110	21	4	7	2.0	46	42	15	57	17	2	1	211	1	7	0	2.4	.968	OF-90
1971		161	.264	.398	611	161	**40**	6	10	1.6	85	81	25	102	20	4	0	348	6	4	0	2.3	.989	OF-157, 1B-2
1972		139	.320	.537	559	179	**39**	8	22	3.9	103	82	56	62	55	1	0	345	9	7	1	2.6	.981	OF-137
1973		139	.320	.537	525	168	35	2	25	4.8	86	70	41	79	56	4	0	357	10	7	2	2.8	.981	OF-136
1974		160	.269	.461	610	164	29	5	26	4.3	95	102	64	103	57	2	0	446	11	3	4	2.9	.993	OF-157
1975		131	.288	.440	500	144	31	3	13	2.6	93	63	62	52	50	0	0	322	8	6	2	2.6	.982	OF-131
1976		150	.297	.454	575	171	26	5	18	3.1	89	83	55	51	58	4	0	377	11	8	5	2.7	.980	OF-146
1977		141	.279	.457	530	148	36	8	14	2.6	92	71	47	50	61	3	0	335	14	1	2	2.6	.997	OF-137
1978		50	.281	.453	192	54	8	2	7	3.6	31	23	15	24	23	0	0	149	2	2	1	3.1	.987	OF-50
1979		132	.262	.374	470	123	27	4	6	1.3	57	54	64	52	30	11	2	948	35	17	79	7.6	.983	1B-91, OF-40
1980		137	.309	.465	499	154	32	8	10	2.0	71	73	66	72	48	1	0	338	9	8	3	2.6	.977	OF-136
1981		82	.271	.382	306	83	19	0	5	1.6	42	34	24	31	12	2	0	510	28	5	27	6.8	.991	1B-46, OF-34
1982	CIN N	138	.289	.413	492	142	35	1	8	1.6	52	57	41	41	16	7	2	301	5	3	2	2.3	.990	OF-131, 1B-1
1983		98	.232	.361	332	77	16	0	9	2.7	40	39	33	53	13	10	2	258	10	1	8	3.0	.996	OF-73, 1B-17
1984		110	.276	.429	380	105	24	2	10	2.6	59	47	25	54	19	14	2	355	21	7	16	3.2	.982	OF-77, 1B-44
1985	2 teams	CIN N (83G –.241)			STL N (28G –.434)																			
″	total	111	.291	.443	296	86	16	1	9	3.0	38	49	24	42	14	25	10	351	14	3	27	3.3	.992	1B-57, OF-55
1986	LA N	37	.231	.282	78	18	2	1	0	0.0	5	6	7	13	1	13	3	33	1	2	0	1.2	.944	OF-31
17 yrs.		2006	.285	.443	7310	2087	436	60	199	2.7	1084	976	664	938	550	103	22	5984	195	91	179	3.2	.985	OF-1718, 1B-258
DIVISIONAL PLAYOFF SERIES																								
1981	HOU N	4	.231	.308	13	3	1	0	0	0.0	0	0	2	2	2	0	0	36	2	1	0	9.8	.974	1B-4
LEAGUE CHAMPIONSHIP SERIES																								
1980	HOU N	3	.182	.182	11	2	0	0	0	0.0	1	1	1	0	0	0	0	5	0	0	0	1.7	1.000	OF-3
1985	STL N	5	.167	.250	12	2	1	0	0	0.0	2	0	2	3	0	2	0	5	0	0	0	1.3	1.000	OF-4
2 yrs.		8	.174	.217	23	4	1	0	0	0.0	3	1	3	3	0	2	0	10	0	0	0	1.4	1.000	OF-7
WORLD SERIES																								
1985	STL N	5	.133	.200	15	2	1	0	0	0.0	1	1	2	2	0	0	0	9	0	0	0	1.8	1.000	OF-5

Domingo Cedeno

CEDENO, DOMINGO ANTONIO BB TR 6′ 1″ 170 lbs.
Born Domingo Antonio Cedeno (Donastorg).
Brother of Andujar Cedeno.
B. Nov. 4, 1968, La Romana, Dominican Republic.

Year	Team	Games	BA	SA	AB	H	2B	3B	HR	HR%	R	RBI	BB	SO	SB	Pinch Hit AB	Pinch Hit H	PO	A	E	DP	TC/G	FA	G by Pos
1993	TOR A	15	.174	.174	46	8	0	0	0	0.0	5	7	1	10	1	1	0	10	39	1	5	3.3	.980	SS-10, 2B-5
1994		47	.196	.278	97	19	2	3	0	0.0	14	10	10	31	1	3	0	40	64	8	11	2.6	.929	2B-28, SS-8, 3B-6, OF-1
1995		51	.236	.360	161	38	6	1	4	2.5	18	14	10	35	0	1	0	85	131	3	25	4.3	.986	SS-30, 2B-20, 3B-1
3 yrs.		113	.214	.306	304	65	8	4	4	1.3	37	31	21	76	2	5	0	135	234	12	41	3.5	.969	2B-53, SS-48, 3B-7, OF-1

Roger Cedeno

CEDENO, ROGER LEANDRO BB TR 6′ 1″ 165 lbs.
B. Aug. 16, 1974, Valencia, Venezuela.

Year	Team	Games	BA	SA	AB	H	2B	3B	HR	HR%	R	RBI	BB	SO	SB	Pinch Hit AB	Pinch Hit H	PO	A	E	DP	TC/G	FA	G by Pos
1995	LA N	40	.238	.286	42	10	2	0	0	0.0	4	3	3	10	1	5	1	43	0	1	0	1.2	.977	OF-36

Orlando Cepeda

CEPEDA, ORLANDO MANUEL (Cha-Cha, The Baby Bull) BR TR 6′ 2″ 210 lbs.
Born Orlando Manuel Cepeda (Penne).
B. Sept. 17, 1937, Ponce, Puerto Rico.

Year	Team	Games	BA	SA	AB	H	2B	3B	HR	HR%	R	RBI	BB	SO	SB	Pinch Hit AB	Pinch Hit H	PO	A	E	DP	TC/G	FA	G by Pos
1958	SF N	148	.312	.512	603	188	**38**	4	25	4.1	88	96	29	84	15	1	0	1322	97	16	131	9.8	.989	1B-147
1959		151	.317	.522	605	192	35	4	27	4.5	92	105	33	100	23	0	0	995	74	22	74	6.4	.980	1B-122, OF-44, 3B-4
1960		151	.297	.497	569	169	36	3	24	4.2	81	96	34	91	15	4	0	681	37	13	40	4.7	.982	OF-91, 1B-63
1961		152	.311	.609	585	182	28	4	**46**	**7.9**	105	**142**	39	91	12	1	0	774	51	5	50	5.2	.994	1B-81, OF-80
1962		162	.306	.518	625	191	26	1	35	5.6	105	114	37	97	10	4	1	1356	88	14	125	9.0	.990	1B-160, OF-2

Orlando Cepeda *continued*

Year	Team	Games	BA	SA	AB	H	2B	3B	HR	HR%	R	RBI	BB	SO	SB	Pinch Hit AB	Pinch Hit H	PO	A	E	DP	TC/G	FA	G by Pos
1963		156	.316	.563	579	183	33	4	34	5.9	100	97	37	70	8	8	2	1262	83	21	91	8.9	.985	1B-150, OF-3
1964		142	.304	.539	529	161	27	2	31	5.9	75	97	43	83	9	2	0	1211	80	18	89	9.4	.986	1B-139, OF-1
1965		33	.176	.294	34	6	1	0	1	2.9	1	5	3	9	0	21	4	28	2	0	1	5.0	1.000	1B-4, OF-2
1966	**2 teams**	**SF N** (19G –.286) **STL N** (123G –.303)																						
″	**total**	142	.301	.473	501	151	26	0	20	4.0	70	73	38	79	9	7	4	1171	63	15	116	9.3	.988	1B-126, OF-8
1967	**STL N**	151	.325	.524	563	183	37	0	25	4.4	91	**111**	62	75	11	1	1	1304	90	10	103	9.3	.993	1B-151
1968		157	.248	.378	600	149	26	2	16	2.7	71	73	43	96	8	3	1	1362	90	17	109	9.5	.988	1B-154
1969	**ATL N**	154	.257	.428	573	147	28	2	22	3.8	74	88	55	76	12	1	0	1318	101	9	91	9.3	.994	1B-153
1970		148	.305	.543	567	173	33	0	34	6.0	87	111	47	75	6	1	1	1288	112	12	100	9.5	.992	1B-148
1971		71	.276	.492	250	69	10	1	14	5.6	31	44	22	29	3	8	1	586	49	5	60	10.2	.992	1B-63
1972	**2 teams**	**ATL N** (28G –.298) **OAK A** (3G –.000)																						
″	**total**	31	.287	.460	87	25	3	0	4	4.6	6	9	7	17	0	8	0	171	13	0	15	8.4	1.000	1B-22
1973	**BOS A**	142	.289	.444	550	159	25	0	20	3.6	51	86	50	81	0	0	0	0	0	0	0	0.0	.000	DH-142
1974	**KC A**	33	.215	.290	107	23	5	0	1	0.9	3	18	9	16	1	7	2	0	0	0	0	0.0	.000	DH-26
17 yrs.		2124	.297	.499	7927	2351	417	27	379	4.8	1131	1365	588	1169	142	77	17	14829	1030	177	1195	7.7	.989	1B-1683, OF-231, DH-168, 3B-4
LEAGUE CHAMPIONSHIP SERIES																								
1969	**ATL N**	3	.455	.909	11	5	2	0	1	9.1	2	3	1	2	1	0	0	29	1	2	2	10.7	.938	1B-3
WORLD SERIES																								
1962	**SF N**	5	.158	.211	19	3	1	0	0	0.0	1	2	0	4	0	0	0	39	4	0	6	8.6	1.000	1B-5
1967	**STL N**	7	.103	.172	29	3	2	0	0	0.0	1	1	0	4	0	0	0	52	4	0	3	8.0	1.000	1B-7
1968		7	.250	.464	28	7	0	0	2	7.1	2	6	2	3	0	0	0	48	4	0	7	7.4	1.000	1B-7
3 yrs.		19	.171	.289	76	13	3	0	2	2.6	4	9	2	11	0	0	0	139	12	0	16	7.9	1.000	1B-19

Ed Cermak

CERMAK, EDWARD HUGO BR TR 5′11″ 170 lbs.
B. Mar. 10, 1882, Cleveland, Ohio D. Nov. 22, 1911, Cleveland, Ohio.

Year	Team	Games	BA	SA	AB	H	2B	3B	HR	HR%	R	RBI	BB	SO	SB	Pinch Hit AB	Pinch Hit H	PO	A	E	DP	TC/G	FA	G by Pos
1901	**CLE A**	1	.000	.000	4	0	0	0	0	0.0	0	0	0		0	0	0	4	1	0	1	5.0	1.000	OF-1

Rick Cerone

CERONE, RICHARD ALDO BR TR 5′11″ 192 lbs.
B. May 19, 1954, Newark, N. J.

Year	Team	Games	BA	SA	AB	H	2B	3B	HR	HR%	R	RBI	BB	SO	SB	Pinch Hit AB	Pinch Hit H	PO	A	E	DP	TC/G	FA	G by Pos
1975	**CLE A**	7	.250	.333	12	3	1	0	0	0.0	1	0	1	0	0	0	0	18	1	0	0	2.7	1.000	C-7
1976		7	.125	.125	16	2	0	0	0	0.0	1	1	0	2	0	1	1	25	1	1	1	3.9	.963	C-6, DH-1
1977	**TOR A**	31	.200	.270	100	20	4	0	1	1.0	7	10	6	12	0	0	0	146	15	1	1	5.2	.994	C-31
1978		88	.223	.298	282	63	8	2	3	1.1	25	20	23	32	0	4	1	426	44	4	7	5.5	.992	C-84, DH-2
1979		136	.239	.358	469	112	27	4	7	1.5	47	61	37	40	1	2	0	560	68	13	10	4.7	.980	C-136
1980	**NY A**	147	.277	.432	519	144	30	4	14	2.7	70	85	32	56	1	0	0	800	73	9	9	6.0	.990	C-147
1981		71	.244	.342	234	57	13	2	2	0.9	23	21	12	24	0	2	2	353	26	3	1	5.5	.992	C-69
1982		89	.227	.310	300	68	10	0	5	1.7	29	28	19	27	0	0	0	509	25	6	5	6.1	.989	C-89
1983		80	.220	.272	246	54	7	0	2	0.8	18	22	15	29	0	2	0	412	18	4	2	5.5	.991	C-78, 3B-1
1984		38	.208	.283	120	25	3	0	2	1.7	8	13	9	15	1	0	0	230	9	1	1	6.3	.996	C-38
1985	**ATL N**	96	.216	.280	282	61	9	0	3	1.1	15	25	29	25	0	7	1	384	48	6	4	4.8	.986	C-91
1986	**MIL A**	68	.259	.380	216	56	14	0	4	1.9	22	18	15	28	1	0	0	391	44	4	2	6.5	.991	C-68
1987	**NY A**	113	.243	.335	284	69	12	1	4	1.4	28	23	30	46	0	6	2	542	38	1	6	5.1	.998	C-111, 1B-2, P-2
1988	**BOS A**	84	.269	.360	264	71	13	1	3	1.1	31	27	20	32	0	4	1	471	28	0	4	5.9	1.000	C-83, DH-1
1989		102	.243	.345	296	72	16	1	4	1.4	28	48	34	40	0	7	3	579	41	10	5	6.4	.984	C-97, OF-1, DH-1
1990	**NY A**	49	.302	.388	139	42	6	0	2	1.4	12	11	5	13	0	14	2	179	14	1	1	4.6	.995	C-35, DH-6, 2B-1
1991	**NY N**	90	.273	.357	227	62	13	0	2	0.9	18	16	30	24	1	14	4	424	36	6	0	5.8	.987	C-81
1992	**MON N**	33	.270	.381	63	17	4	0	1	1.6	10	7	3	5	1	6	0	106	7	0	0	4.0	1.000	C-28
18 yrs.		1329	.245	.343	4069	998	190	15	59	1.4	393	436	320	450	6	69	17	6555	536	70	59	5.5	.990	C-1279, DH-11, P-2, 1B-2, OF-1, 2B-1, 3B-1
DIVISIONAL PLAYOFF SERIES																								
1981	**NY A**	5	.333	.611	18	6	2	0	1	5.6	1	5	0	2	0	0	0	42	1	1	0	8.8	.977	C-5
LEAGUE CHAMPIONSHIP SERIES																								
1980	**NY A**	3	.333	.583	12	4	0	0	1	8.3	1	2	0	1	0	0	0	14	4	0	0	6.0	1.000	C-3
1981		3	.100	.100	10	1	0	0	0	0.0	1	0	0	0	0	0	0	23	2	0	1	8.3	1.000	C-3
2 yrs.		6	.227	.364	22	5	0	0	1	4.5	2	2	0	1	0	0	0	37	6	0	1	7.2	1.000	C-6
WORLD SERIES																								
1981	**NY A**	6	.190	.381	21	4	1	0	1	4.8	2	3	4	2	0	0	0	42	4	0	0	7.7	1.000	C-6

Bob Cerv

CERV, ROBERT HENRY BR TR 6′ 200 lbs.
B. May 5, 1926, Weston, Neb.

Year	Team	Games	BA	SA	AB	H	2B	3B	HR	HR%	R	RBI	BB	SO	SB	Pinch Hit AB	Pinch Hit H	PO	A	E	DP	TC/G	FA	G by Pos
1951	**NY A**	12	.214	.250	28	6	1	0	0	0.0	4	2	4	6	0	3	0	14	0	2	0	1.8	.875	OF-9
1952		36	.241	.356	87	21	3	2	1	1.1	11	8	9	22	0	9	2	52	1	0	0	2.0	1.000	OF-27
1953		8	.000	.000	6	0	0	0	0	0.0	0	0	1	1	0	6	0	0	0	0	0	0.0	—	
1954		56	.260	.470	100	26	6	0	5	5.0	14	13	11	17	0	28	9	25	1	3	0	1.2	.897	OF-24
1955		55	.341	.541	85	29	4	2	3	3.5	17	22	7	16	4	33	11	25	1	0	0	1.3	1.000	OF-20
1956		54	.304	.530	115	35	5	6	3	2.6	16	25	18	13	0	10	0	59	4	1	2	1.5	.984	OF-44
1957	**KC A**	124	.272	.420	345	94	14	2	11	3.2	35	44	20	57	1	41	9	157	6	6	1	1.9	.964	OF-89
1958		141	.305	.592	515	157	20	7	38	7.4	93	104	50	82	3	6	2	311	13	5	3	2.4	.985	OF-136
1959		125	.285	.479	463	132	22	4	20	4.3	61	87	35	87	3	5	2	231	8	5	2	2.1	.980	OF-119
1960	**2 teams**	**KC A** (23G –.256) **NY A** (87G –.250)																						
″	**total**	110	.252	.449	294	74	12	2	14	4.8	46	40	40	53	0	30	8	162	12	4	4	2.4	.978	OF-72, 1B-3
1961	**2 teams**	**LA A** (18G –.158) **NY A** (57G –.271)																						
″	**total**	75	.234	.429	175	41	8	1	8	4.6	20	26	13	25	1	22	8	96	5	2	2	2.1	.981	OF-45, 1B-3
1962	**2 teams**	**NY A** (14G –.118) **HOU N** (19G –.226)																						
″	**total**	33	.188	.333	48	9	1	0	2	4.2	3	3	4	13	0	20	4	8	1	1	0	1.1	.900	OF-9
12 yrs.		829	.276	.481	2261	624	96	26	105	4.6	320	374	212	392	12	213	55	1140	52	29	14	2.0	.976	OF-594, 1B-6

Bob Cerv *continued*

Year	Team	Games	BA	SA	AB	H	2B	3B	HR	HR%	R	RBI	BB	SO	SB	Pinch Hit AB	Pinch Hit H	PO	A	E	DP	TC/G	FA	G by Pos
WORLD SERIES																								
1955	NY A	5	.125	.313	16	2	0	0	1	6.3	1	1	0	4	0	1	1	10	0	0	0	2.5	1.000	OF-4
1956		1	1.000	1.000	1	1	0	0	0	0.0	0	0	0	0	0	1	1	0	0	0	0	0.0	—	
1960		4	.357	.357	14	5	0	0	0	0.0	1	0	0	3	0	1	1	8	0	1	0	3.0	.889	OF-3
3 yrs.		10	.258	.355	31	8	0	0	1	3.2	2	1	0	7	0	3	3	18	0	1	0	2.7	.947	OF-7

Ron Cey

CEY, RONALD CHARLES (Penguin) BR TR 5′10″ 185 lbs.
B. Feb. 15, 1948, Tacoma, Wash.

Year	Team	Games	BA	SA	AB	H	2B	3B	HR	HR%	R	RBI	BB	SO	SB	Pinch Hit AB	Pinch Hit H	PO	A	E	DP	TC/G	FA	G by Pos
1971	LA N	2	.000	.000	2	0	0	0	0	0.0	0	0	0	2	0	2	0	0	0	0	0	0.0	—	
1972		11	.270	.378	37	10	1	0	1	2.7	3	3	7	10	0	0	0	7	20	3	1	2.7	.900	3B-11
1973		152	.245	.385	507	124	18	4	15	3.0	60	80	74	77	1	7	1	111	328	18	39	3.1	.961	3B-146
1974		159	.262	.397	577	151	20	2	18	3.1	88	97	76	68	1	0	0	155	365	22	25	3.4	.959	3B-158
1975		158	.283	.473	566	160	29	2	25	4.4	72	101	78	74	5	0	0	144	309	19	23	3.0	.960	3B-158
1976		145	.277	.462	502	139	18	3	23	4.6	69	80	89	74	0	1	0	111	334	16	22	3.2	.965	3B-144
1977		153	.241	.450	564	136	22	3	30	5.3	77	110	93	106	3	0	0	138	346	18	29	3.3	.964	3B-153
1978		159	.270	.452	555	150	32	0	23	4.1	84	84	96	96	2	1	0	116	336	16	26	3.0	.966	3B-158
1979		150	.281	.499	487	137	20	1	28	5.7	77	81	86	85	3	0	0	123	265	9	25	2.6	.977	3B-150
1980		157	.254	.452	551	140	25	0	28	5.1	81	77	69	92	2	0	0	127	317	13	24	2.9	.972	3B-157
1981		85	.288	.474	312	90	15	2	13	4.2	42	50	40	55	0	1	1	71	184	16	15	3.2	.941	3B-84
1982		150	.254	.428	556	141	23	1	24	4.3	62	79	57	99	3	1	0	93	320	16	23	2.9	.963	3B-149
1983	CHI N	159	.275	.460	581	160	33	1	24	4.1	73	90	62	85	0	1	0	90	270	17	12	2.4	.955	3B-157
1984		146	.240	.442	505	121	27	0	25	5.0	71	97	61	108	3	2	1	97	230	11	22	2.3	.967	3B-144
1985		145	.232	.408	500	116	18	2	22	4.4	64	63	58	106	1	7	2	75	273	21	21	2.6	.943	3B-140
1986		97	.273	.508	256	70	21	0	13	5.1	42	36	44	66	0	13	3	41	118	8	7	2.2	.952	3B-77
1987	OAK A	45	.221	.394	104	23	6	0	4	3.8	12	11	22	32	0	7	2	56	4	1	4	1.5	.984	DH-30, 1B-7, 3B-3
17 yrs.		2073	.261	.445	7162	1868	328	21	316	4.4	977	1139	1012	1235	24	43	10	1555	4019	224	318	2.9	.961	3B-1989, DH-30, 1B-7
LEAGUE CHAMPIONSHIP SERIES																								
1974	LA N	4	.313	.688	16	5	3	0	1	6.3	2	1	3	2	0	0	0	2	4	2	1	2.0	.750	3B-4
1977		4	.308	.615	13	4	1	0	1	7.7	4	4	2	4	1	0	0	7	14	1	0	5.5	.955	3B-4
1978		4	.313	.563	16	5	1	0	1	6.3	4	3	2	4	0	0	0	2	13	0	1	3.8	1.000	3B-4
1981		5	.278	.333	18	5	1	0	0	0.0	1	3	3	2	0	0	0	5	16	1	1	4.4	.955	3B-5
1984	CHI N	5	.158	.368	19	3	1	0	1	5.3	3	3	3	3	0	0	0	1	7	0	0	1.6	1.000	3B-5
5 yrs.		22	.268	.500	82	22	7	0	4	4.9	14	14	13	15	1	0	0	17	54	4	3	3.4	.947	3B-22
							1st				7th	7th	7th											
WORLD SERIES																								
1974	LA N	5	.176	.176	17	3	0	0	0	0.0	1	0	3	3	0	0	0	5	9	1	0	3.0	.933	3B-5
1977		6	.190	.381	21	4	1	0	1	4.8	2	3	3	5	0	0	0	5	7	0	0	2.0	1.000	3B-6
1978		6	.286	.429	21	6	0	0	1	4.8	2	4	3	3	0	0	0	2	12	0	1	2.3	1.000	3B-6
1981		6	.350	.500	20	7	0	0	1	5.0	3	6	3	3	0	0	0	4	11	0	1	2.5	1.000	3B-6
4 yrs.		23	.253	.380	79	20	1	0	3	3.8	8	13	12	14	0	0	0	16	39	1	2	2.4	.982	3B-23

Elio Chacon

CHACON, ELIO BR TR 5′ 9″ 160 lbs.
Born Elio Chacon (Rodriguez).
B. Oct. 26, 1936, Caracas, Venezuela D. Apr. 24, 1992, Caracas, Venezuela.

Year	Team	Games	BA	SA	AB	H	2B	3B	HR	HR%	R	RBI	BB	SO	SB	Pinch Hit AB	Pinch Hit H	PO	A	E	DP	TC/G	FA	G by Pos
1960	CIN N	49	.181	.190	116	21	1	0	0	0.0	14	7	14	23	7	3	0	100	95	4	25	4.4	.980	2B-43, OF-2
1961		61	.265	.371	132	35	4	2	2	1.5	26	5	21	22	1	1	0	85	104	2	22	3.8	.990	2B-42, OF-8
1962	NY N	118	.236	.296	368	87	10	3	2	0.5	49	27	76	64	12	3	0	206	333	22	64	5.0	.961	SS-110, 2B-2, 3B-1
3 yrs.		228	.232	.292	616	143	15	5	4	0.6	89	39	111	109	20	7	0	391	532	28	111	4.6	.971	SS-110, 2B-87, OF-10, 3B-1
WORLD SERIES																								
1961	CIN N	4	.250	.250	12	3	0	0	0	0.0	2	0	1	2	0	1	0	12	9	0	4	7.0	1.000	2B-3

Chet Chadbourne

CHADBOURNE, CHESTER JAMES (Pop) BL TR 5′ 9″ 170 lbs.
B. Oct. 26, 1884, Parkman, Me. D. June 21, 1943, Los Angeles, Calif.

Year	Team	Games	BA	SA	AB	H	2B	3B	HR	HR%	R	RBI	BB	SO	SB	Pinch Hit AB	Pinch Hit H	PO	A	E	DP	TC/G	FA	G by Pos
1906	BOS A	11	.302	.326	43	13	1	0	0	0.0	7	3	3		1	0	0	23	48	6	4	6.4	.922	2B-11, SS-1
1907		10	.289	.289	38	11	0	0	0	0.0	0	1	7		1	0	0	16	1	0	0	1.7	1.000	OF-10
1914	KC F	147	.277	.348	581	161	22	8	1	0.2	92	37	69		42	1	0	238	34	10	6	1.9	.965	OF-146
1915		152	.227	.290	587	133	16	9	1	0.2	75	35	62		29	0	0	308	24	7	7	2.2	.979	OF-152
1918	BOS N	27	.260	.298	104	27	2	1	0	0.0	9	6	5	5	5	0	0	60	2	5	1	2.5	.925	OF-27
5 yrs.		347	.255	.316	1353	345	41	18	2	0.1	183	82	146	5	78	1	0	645	109	28	18	2.3	.964	OF-335, 2B-11, SS-1

Dave Chalk

CHALK, DAVID LEE BR TR 5′10″ 175 lbs.
B. Aug. 30, 1950, Del Rio, Tex.

Year	Team	Games	BA	SA	AB	H	2B	3B	HR	HR%	R	RBI	BB	SO	SB	Pinch Hit AB	Pinch Hit H	PO	A	E	DP	TC/G	FA	G by Pos
1973	CAL A	24	.232	.261	69	16	2	0	0	0.0	14	6	9	13	0	0	0	36	66	4	20	4.8	.962	SS-22
1974		133	.252	.316	465	117	9	3	5	1.1	44	31	30	57	10	0	0	200	350	34	71	4.3	.942	SS-99, 3B-38
1975		149	.273	.345	513	140	24	2	3	0.6	59	56	66	49	6	0	0	108	333	11	30	3.0	.976	3B-149
1976		142	.217	.253	438	95	14	1	0	0.0	39	33	49	62	0	0	0	176	387	17	54	3.8	.971	SS-102, 3B-49
1977		149	.277	.355	519	144	27	2	3	0.6	58	45	52	69	12	2	0	147	287	25	27	3.0	.946	3B-141, 2B-7, SS-4
1978		135	.253	.285	470	119	12	0	1	0.2	42	34	38	34	5	0	0	216	339	23	62	3.9	.960	SS-97, 2B-29, 3B-22, DH-1
1979	2 teams	TEX A (96G –.250) OAK A (66G –.222)																						
"	total	75	.223	.277	220	49	6	0	2	0.9	15	13	29	14	2	8	3	123	154	11	31	3.8	.962	2B-38, SS-19, 3B-16, DH-2
1980	KC A	69	.251	.341	167	42	10	1	1	0.6	19	20	18	27	1	14	2	57	88	6	10	2.6	.960	3B-33, 2B-17, DH-6, SS-1
1981		27	.224	.286	49	11	3	0	0	0.0	2	5	4	2	0	4	2	19	31	1	5	2.0	.980	3B-14, 2B-10, SS-1
9 yrs.		903	.252	.310	2910	733	107	9	15	0.5	292	243	295	327	36	28	7	1082	2035	132	310	3.5	.959	3B-462, SS-345, 2B-101, DH-9
WORLD SERIES																								
1980	KC A	1	—	—	0	0	0	0	0	—	1	0	1	0	1	0	0	0	1	0	0	1.0	1.000	3B-1

Joe Chamberlain

CHAMBERLAIN, JOSEPH JEREMIAH BR TR 6′ 1″ 175 lbs.
B. May 10, 1910, San Francisco, Calif. D. Jan. 28, 1983, San Francisco, Calif.

Year	Team	Games	BA	SA	AB	H	2B	3B	HR	HR%	R	RBI	BB	SO	SB	Pinch Hit AB	Pinch Hit H	PO	A	E	DP	TC/G	FA	G by Pos
1934	CHI A	43	.241	.333	141	34	5	1	2	1.4	13	17	6	38	1	0	0	42	97	20	12	4.0	.874	SS-26, 3B-14

Wes Chamberlain

CHAMBERLAIN, WESLEY POLK
B. Apr. 13, 1966, Chicago, Ill.
BR TR 6′ 2″ 210 lbs.

Year	Team		Games	BA	SA	AB	H	2B	3B	HR	HR%	R	RBI	BB	SO	SB	Pinch Hit AB	Pinch Hit H	PO	A	E	DP	TC/G	FA	G by Pos
1990	PHI	N	18	.283	.478	46	13	3	0	2	4.3	9	4	1	9	4	8	0	23	0	1	0	2.4	.958	OF-10
1991			101	.240	.399	383	92	16	3	13	3.4	51	50	31	73	9	3	0	199	4	3	0	2.1	.985	OF-98
1992			76	.258	.422	275	71	18	0	9	3.3	26	41	10	55	4	4	1	132	3	4	1	1.9	.971	OF-73
1993			96	.282	.493	284	80	20	2	12	4.2	34	45	17	51	2	20	4	131	10	1	3	1.9	.993	OF-76
1994	2 teams		PHI N (24G –.275)	BOS A (51G –.256)																					
″	total		75	.262	.408	233	61	14	1	6	2.6	20	26	15	50	0	15	1	96	8	0	1	1.6	1.000	OF-52, DH-12
1995	BOS	A	19	.119	.214	42	5	1	0	1	2.4	4	1	3	11	1	6	2	20	1	1	0	1.3	.955	OF-12, DH-5
6 yrs.			385	.255	.424	1263	322	72	6	43	3.4	144	167	77	249	20	56	8	601	26	10	5	1.9	.984	OF-321, DH-17
LEAGUE CHAMPIONSHIP SERIES																									
1993	PHI	N	4	.364	.636	11	4	3	0	0	0.0	1	1	1	3	0	1	0	2	2	0	0	1.3	1.000	OF-3
WORLD SERIES																									
1993	PHI	N	2	.000	.000	2	0	0	0	0	0.0	0	0	0	1	0	2	0	0	0	0	0	0.0	—	

Al Chambers

CHAMBERS, ALBERT EUGENE
B. Mar. 24, 1961, Harrisburg, Pa.
BL TL 6′ 4″ 210 lbs.

Year	Team		Games	BA	SA	AB	H	2B	3B	HR	HR%	R	RBI	BB	SO	SB	Pinch Hit AB	Pinch Hit H	PO	A	E	DP	TC/G	FA	G by Pos
1983	SEA	A	31	.209	.299	67	14	3	0	1	1.5	11	7	18	20	0	7	0	3	0	0	0	0.1	1.000	DH-22, OF-3
1984			22	.224	.306	49	11	1	0	1	2.0	4	4	3	12	2	8	2	18	0	1	0	1.4	.947	OF-13, DH-1
1985			4	.000	.000	4	0	0	0	0	0.0	0	0	0	2	0	4	0	0	0	0	0	0.0	—	
3 yrs.			57	.208	.292	120	25	4	0	2	1.7	15	11	21	34	2	19	2	21	0	1	0	0.6	.955	DH-23, OF-16

Chris Chambliss

CHAMBLISS, CARROLL CHRISTOPHER
B. Dec. 26, 1948, Dayton, Ohio.
BL TR 6′ 1″ 195 lbs.

Year	Team		Games	BA	SA	AB	H	2B	3B	HR	HR%	R	RBI	BB	SO	SB	Pinch Hit AB	Pinch Hit H	PO	A	E	DP	TC/G	FA	G by Pos
1971	CLE	A	111	.275	.407	415	114	20	4	9	2.2	49	48	40	83	2	2	0	943	55	8	85	9.3	.992	1B-108
1972			121	.292	.397	466	136	27	2	6	1.3	51	44	26	63	3	2	0	1109	56	8	109	9.9	.993	1B-119
1973			155	.273	.390	572	156	30	2	11	1.9	70	53	58	76	4	1	0	1437	114	14	153	10.2	.991	1B-154
1974	2 teams		CLE A (17G –.328)	NY A (110G –.242)																					
″	total		127	.255	.349	467	119	20	3	6	1.3	46	50	28	48	0	4	0	1035	84	11	107	9.2	.990	1B-123
1975	NY	A	150	.304	.434	562	171	38	4	9	1.6	66	72	29	50	0	3	0	1222	106	12	113	9.1	.991	1B-147
1976			156	.293	.441	641	188	32	6	17	2.7	79	96	27	80	1	0	0	1440	109	9	123	10.0	.994	1B-155, DH-1
1977			157	.287	.445	600	172	32	6	17	2.8	90	90	45	73	4	4	2	1368	98	16	129	9.4	.989	1B-157
1978			162	.274	.382	625	171	26	3	12	1.9	81	90	41	60	2	1	0	1366	111	4	119	9.1	.997	1B-155, DH-7
1979			149	.280	.437	554	155	27	3	18	3.2	61	63	34	53	3	2	1	1299	95	7	135	9.3	.995	1B-134, DH-16
1980	ATL	N	158	.282	.440	602	170	37	2	18	3.0	83	72	49	73	7	0	0	1626	101	12	140	11.0	.993	1B-158
1981			107	.272	.403	404	110	25	2	8	2.0	44	51	44	41	4	0	0	1046	94	4	83	10.7	.997	1B-107
1982			157	.270	.436	534	144	25	2	20	3.7	57	86	57	57	7	11	5	1352	138	10	144	9.9	.993	1B-151
1983			131	.280	.481	447	125	24	3	20	4.5	59	78	63	68	2	8	5	1092	89	5	117	9.4	.996	1B-126
1984			133	.257	.362	389	100	14	0	9	2.3	47	44	58	54	1	24	4	996	70	8	84	9.9	.993	1B-109
1985			101	.235	.329	170	40	7	0	3	1.8	16	21	18	22	0	54	11	299	25	1	31	8.3	.997	1B-39
1986			97	.311	.426	122	38	8	0	2	1.6	13	14	15	24	0	68	**20**	141	6	1	15	7.4	.993	1B-20
1988	NY	A	1	.000	.000	1	0	0	0	0	0.0	0	0	0	1	0	1	0	0	0	0	0	0.0	—	
17 yrs.			2173	.279	.415	7571	2109	392	42	185	2.4	912	972	632	926	40	185	48	17771	1351	130	1687	9.7	.993	1B-1962, DH-24
LEAGUE CHAMPIONSHIP SERIES																									
1976	NY	A	5	.524	.952	21	11	1	1	2	9.5	5	8	0	1	2	0	0	50	3	1	3	10.8	.981	1B-5
1977			5	.059	.059	17	1	0	0	0	0.0	0	0	3	4	0	0	0	35	7	0	2	8.4	1.000	1B-5
1978			4	.400	.400	15	6	0	0	0	0.0	1	2	0	4	0	0	0	28	1	0	1	7.3	1.000	1B-4
1982	ATL	N	3	.000	.000	10	0	0	0	0	0.0	0	0	1	0	0	0	0	30	5	0	0	11.7	1.000	1B-3
4 yrs.			17	.286	.429	63	18	1	1	2	3.2	6	10	4	9	2	0	0	143	16	1	6	9.4	.994	1B-17
WORLD SERIES																									
1976	NY	A	4	.313	.375	16	5	1	0	0	0.0	1	1	0	2	0	0	0	26	3	1	6	7.5	.967	1B-4
1977			6	.292	.500	24	7	2	0	1	4.2	4	4	0	2	0	0	0	55	5	0	2	10.0	1.000	1B-6
1978			3	.182	.182	11	2	0	0	0	0.0	1	0	1	1	0	0	0	18	0	0	4	6.0	1.000	1B-3
3 yrs.			13	.275	.392	51	14	3	0	1	2.0	6	5	1	5	0	0	0	99	8	1	12	8.3	.991	1B-13

Mike Champion

CHAMPION, ROBERT MICHAEL
B. Feb. 10, 1955, Montgomery, Ala.
BR TR 6′ 185 lbs.

Year	Team		Games	BA	SA	AB	H	2B	3B	HR	HR%	R	RBI	BB	SO	SB	Pinch Hit AB	Pinch Hit H	PO	A	E	DP	TC/G	FA	G by Pos
1976	SD	N	11	.237	.368	38	9	2	0	1	2.6	4	2	1	3	0	0	0	23	24	3	2	4.5	.940	2B-11
1977			150	.229	.286	507	116	14	6	1	0.2	35	43	27	85	3	1	1	301	348	17	82	4.5	.974	2B-149
1978			32	.226	.302	53	12	0	2	0	0.0	3	4	5	13	0	6	2	24	45	5	12	3.1	.932	2B-20, 3B-4
3 yrs.			193	.229	.293	598	137	16	8	2	0.3	42	49	33	101	3	7	3	348	417	25	96	4.3	.968	2B-180, 3B-4

Bob Chance

CHANCE, ROBERT
B. Sept. 10, 1940, Statesboro, Ga.
BL TR 6′ 2″ 196 lbs.

Year	Team		Games	BA	SA	AB	H	2B	3B	HR	HR%	R	RBI	BB	SO	SB	Pinch Hit AB	Pinch Hit H	PO	A	E	DP	TC/G	FA	G by Pos
1963	CLE	A	16	.288	.481	52	15	4	0	2	3.8	5	7	1	10	0	2	0	20	0	2	0	1.6	.909	OF-14
1964			120	.279	.433	390	109	16	1	14	3.6	45	75	40	101	3	19	5	606	24	7	47	5.7	.989	1B-81, OF-31
1965	WAS	A	72	.256	.362	199	51	9	0	4	2.0	20	14	18	44	0	19	5	396	25	5	39	8.4	.988	1B-48, OF-3
1966			37	.175	.281	57	10	3	0	1	1.8	1	8	2	23	0	24	4	73	3	2	6	6.0	.974	1B-13
1967			27	.214	.476	42	9	2	0	3	7.1	5	7	7	13	0	13	3	75	5	0	6	8.0	1.000	1B-10
1969	CAL	A	5	.143	.143	7	1	0	0	0	0.0	0	1	0	4	0	4	1	10	0	1	0	11.0	.909	1B-1
6 yrs.			277	.261	.406	747	195	34	1	24	3.2	76	112	68	195	3	81	18	1180	57	17	98	6.2	.986	1B-153, OF-48

Frank Chance

CHANCE, FRANK LEROY (Husk, The Peerless Leader)
B. Sept. 9, 1877, Fresno, Calif. D. Sept. 15, 1924, Los Angeles, Calif.
Manager 1905–14, 1923.
Hall of Fame 1946.
BR TR 6′ 190 lbs.

Year	Team		Games	BA	SA	AB	H	2B	3B	HR	HR%	R	RBI	BB	SO	SB	Pinch Hit AB	Pinch Hit H	PO	A	E	DP	TC/G	FA	G by Pos
1898	CHI	N	53	.279	.367	147	41	4	3	1	0.7	32	14	7		7	2	1	103	19	13	4	2.5	.904	C-33, OF-17, 1B-3
1899			64	.286	.354	192	55	6	2	1	0.5	37	22	15		10	3	0	168	64	12	6	4.1	.951	C-57, 1B-1, OF-1
1900			56	.295	.396	149	44	9	3	0	0.0	26	13	15		8	4	1	160	66	17	2	4.7	.930	C-51, 1B-1
1901			69	.278	.361	241	67	12	4	0	0.0	38	36	29		30	2	1	143	30	10	3	2.7	.945	OF-50, C-13, 1B-6
1902			75	.284	.369	236	67	9	4	1	0.4	40	31	35		28	4	1	508	47	17	23	8.1	.970	1B-38, C-29, OF-4
1903			125	.327	.440	441	144	24	10	2	0.5	83	81	78		**67**	2	1	1212	68	37	49	10.7	.972	1B-121, C-2
1904			124	.310	.430	451	140	16	10	6	1.3	89	49	36		42	0	0	1213	107	13	48	10.8	.990	1B-123, C-1

Frank Chance *continued*

Year	Team	Games	BA	SA	AB	H	2B	3B	HR	HR%	R	RBI	BB	SO	SB	Pinch Hit AB	Pinch Hit H	PO	A	E	DP	TC/G	FA	G by Pos
1905		118	.316	.434	392	124	16	12	2	0.5	92	70	78		38	3	0	1165	75	13	54	10.9	.990	1B-115
1906		136	.319	.430	474	151	24	10	3	0.6	**103**	71	70		**57**	0	0	1376	82	16	71	10.8	.989	1B-136
1907		111	.293	.361	382	112	19	2	1	0.3	58	49	51		35	2	1	1129	80	10	64	11.2	.992	1B-109
1908		129	.272	.363	452	123	27	4	2	0.4	65	55	37		27	4	2	1291	86	15	56	11.0	.989	1B-126
1909		93	.272	.346	324	88	16	4	0	0.0	53	46	30		29	0	0	901	40	6	43	10.3	.994	1B-92
1910		88	.298	.393	295	88	12	8	0	0.0	54	36	37	15	16	1	0	773	38	3	48	9.4	.996	1B-87
1911		31	.239	.409	88	21	6	3	1	1.1	23	17	25	13	9	1	0	289	11	3	12	10.4	.990	1B-29
1912		2	.200	.200	5	1	0	0	0	0.0	2	0	3	0	1	0	0	22	0	0	1	11.0	1.000	1B-2
1913	NY A	11	.208	.208	24	5	0	0	0	0.0	3	6	8	1	1	3	0	86	5	0	2	11.4	1.000	1B-8
1914		1	—	—	0	0	0	0	0	—	0	0	0	0	0	0	0	1	0	0	0	1.0	1.000	1B-1
17 yrs.		1286	.296	.393	4293	1271	200	79	20	0.5	798	596	554	29	405	31	8	10540	818	185	486	9.2	.984	1B-998, C-186, OF-72
WORLD SERIES																								
1906	CHI N	6	.238	.286	21	5	1	0	0	0.0	3	0	2	1	2	0	0	60	2	0	1	10.3	1.000	1B-6
1907		4	.214	.286	14	3	1	0	0	0.0	3	0	3	2	3	0	0	44	1	0	3	11.3	1.000	1B-4
1908		5	.421	.421	19	8	0	0	0	0.0	4	2	3	1	5	0	0	66	0	3	3	13.8	.957	1B-5
1910		5	.353	.529	17	6	1	1	0	0.0	1	4	0	2	0	0	0	51	4	0	2	11.0	1.000	1B-5
4 yrs.		20	.310	.380	71	22	3	1	0	0.0	11	6	8	6	10 3rd	0	0	221	7	3	9	11.6	.987	1B-20

Darrel Chaney

CHANEY, DARREL LEE BB TR 6′ 2″ 188 lbs.
B. Mar. 9, 1948, Hammond, Ind.

Year	Team	Games	BA	SA	AB	H	2B	3B	HR	HR%	R	RBI	BB	SO	SB	Pinch Hit AB	Pinch Hit H	PO	A	E	DP	TC/G	FA	G by Pos
1969	CIN N	93	.191	.234	209	40	5	2	0	0.0	21	15	24	75	1	1	1	115	191	17	44	3.5	.947	SS-91
1970		57	.232	.295	95	22	3	0	1	1.1	7	4	3	26	1	9	2	56	90	9	15	3.0	.942	SS-30, 2B-18, 3B-3
1971		10	.125	.125	24	3	0	0	0	0.0	2	1	1	3	0	1	0	16	21	0	1	4.1	1.000	SS-7, 3B-1, 2B-1
1972		83	.250	.337	196	49	7	2	2	1.0	29	19	29	28	1	3	2	100	178	10	30	3.3	.965	SS-64, 2B-12, 3B-10
1973		105	.181	.220	227	41	7	1	0	0.0	27	14	26	50	4	3	2	123	246	14	52	3.8	.963	SS-75, 2B-14, 3B-12
1974		117	.200	.304	135	27	6	1	2	1.5	27	16	26	33	1	0	0	90	135	9	21	1.8	.962	3B-81, 2B-38, SS-12
1975		71	.219	.294	160	35	6	0	2	1.3	18	26	14	38	3	5	1	77	164	7	27	3.5	.972	SS-34, 2B-23, 3B-13
1976	ATL N	153	.252	.331	496	125	20	8	1	0.2	42	50	54	92	5	4	2	243	468	37	88	4.9	.951	SS-151, 3B-1, 2B-1
1977		74	.201	.297	209	42	7	2	3	1.4	22	15	17	44	0	14	3	113	182	8	30	4.7	.974	SS-41, 2B-24
1978		89	.224	.306	245	55	9	1	3	1.2	27	20	25	48	1	15	6	100	199	7	32	3.6	.977	SS-77, 3B-8, 2B-1
1979		63	.162	.205	117	19	5	0	0	0.0	15	10	19	34	2	12	2	45	95	8	16	3.0	.946	SS-39, 2B-5, 3B-4, C-1
11 yrs.		915	.217	.288	2113	458	75	17	14	0.7	237	190	238	471	19	67	21	1078	1969	126	356	3.6	.960	SS-621, 2B-137, 3B-133, C-1
LEAGUE CHAMPIONSHIP SERIES																								
1972	CIN N	5	.188	.188	16	3	0	0	0	0.0	3	1	1	1	1	0	0	8	16	3	2	5.4	.889	SS-5
1973		5	.000	.000	9	0	0	0	0	0.0	0	0	3	4	0	0	0	2	10	0	3	2.4	1.000	SS-5
2 yrs.		10	.120	.120	25	3	0	0	0	0.0	3	1	4	5	1	0	0	10	26	3	5	3.9	.923	SS-10
WORLD SERIES																								
1970	CIN N	3	.000	.000	1	0	0	0	0	0.0	0	0	0	1	0	0	0	1	2	0	0	1.0	1.000	SS-3
1972		4	.000	.000	7	0	0	0	0	0.0	0	0	2	2	0	0	0	5	11	0	2	5.3	1.000	SS-3
1975		2	.000	.000	2	0	0	0	0	0.0	0	0	0	1	0	2	0	0	0	0	0	0.0	—	
3 yrs.		9	.000	.000	10	0	0	0	0	0.0	0	0	2	4	0	2	0	6	13	0	2	3.2	1.000	SS-6

Les Channell

CHANNELL, LESTER CLARK (Dude) BL TL 6′ 180 lbs.
B. Mar. 3, 1886, Crestline, Ohio D. May 7, 1954, Denver, Colo.

Year	Team	Games	BA	SA	AB	H	2B	3B	HR	HR%	R	RBI	BB	SO	SB	Pinch Hit AB	Pinch Hit H	PO	A	E	DP	TC/G	FA	G by Pos
1910	NY A	6	.316	.316	19	6	0	0	0	0.0	3	3	2		2	0	0	9	0	0	0	1.5	1.000	OF-6
1914		1	1.000	2.000	1	1	1	0	0	0.0	0	0	0	0	0	1	1	0	0	0	0	0.0	—	
2 yrs.		7	.350	.400	20	7	1	0	0	0.0	3	3	2	0	2	1	1	9	0	0	0	1.5	1.000	OF-6

Charlie Chant

CHANT, CHARLES JOSEPH BR TR 6′ 190 lbs.
B. Aug. 7, 1951, Bell, Calif.

Year	Team	Games	BA	SA	AB	H	2B	3B	HR	HR%	R	RBI	BB	SO	SB	Pinch Hit AB	Pinch Hit H	PO	A	E	DP	TC/G	FA	G by Pos
1975	OAK A	5	.000	.000	5	0	0	0	0	0.0	1	0	0	0	0	0	0	1	0	0	0	0.2	1.000	OF-5, DH-1
1976	STL N	15	.143	.143	14	2	0	0	0	0.0	0	0	0	4	0	1	0	15	1	0	0	1.1	1.000	OF-14
2 yrs.		20	.105	.105	19	2	0	0	0	0.0	1	0	0	4	0	1	0	16	1	0	0	0.9	1.000	OF-19, DH-1

Ed Chaplin

CHAPLIN, BERT EDGAR (Chappy) BL TR 5′ 7″ 158 lbs.
Born Bert Edgar Chapman.
B. Sept. 25, 1893, Pelzer, S. C. D. Aug. 15, 1978, Sanford, Fla.

Year	Team	Games	BA	SA	AB	H	2B	3B	HR	HR%	R	RBI	BB	SO	SB	Pinch Hit AB	Pinch Hit H	PO	A	E	DP	TC/G	FA	G by Pos
1920	BOS A	4	.200	.400	5	1	1	0	0	0.0	2	1	4	1	0	0	0	8	1	1	1	5.0	.900	C-2
1921		3	.000	.000	2	0	0	0	0	0.0	0	0	0	1	0	2	0	0	1	0	0	1.0	1.000	C-1
1922		28	.188	.232	69	13	1	1	0	0.0	8	6	9	9	2	6	0	56	16	3	2	3.6	.960	C-21
3 yrs.		35	.184	.237	76	14	2	1	0	0.0	10	7	13	11	2	8	0	64	18	4	3	3.6	.953	C-24

Ben Chapman

CHAPMAN, WILLIAM BENJAMIN BR TR 6′ 190 lbs.
B. Dec. 25, 1908, Nashville, Tenn. D. July 7, 1993, Hoover, Ala.
Manager 1945–48.

Year	Team	Games	BA	SA	AB	H	2B	3B	HR	HR%	R	RBI	BB	SO	SB	Pinch Hit AB	Pinch Hit H	PO	A	E	DP	TC/G	FA	G by Pos
1930	NY A	138	.316	.474	513	162	31	10	10	1.9	74	81	43	58	14	2	0	232	295	42	47	4.2	.926	3B-91, 2B-45
1931		149	.315	.483	600	189	28	11	17	2.8	120	122	75	77	**61**	1	0	325	47	14	5	2.6	.964	OF-137, 2B-11
1932		150	.299	.473	581	174	41	15	10	1.7	101	107	71	55	**38**	1	0	303	13	17	2	2.2	.949	OF-149
1933		147	.312	.437	565	176	36	4	9	1.6	112	98	72	45	**27**	0	0	288	24	8	4	2.2	.975	OF-147
1934		149	.308	.413	588	181	21	**13**	5	0.9	82	86	67	68	26	0	0	368	12	13	2	2.6	.967	OF-149
1935		140	.289	.430	553	160	38	8	8	1.4	118	74	61	39	17	2	0	372	25	15	7	3.0	.964	OF-138
1936	2 teams	NY A (36G –.266)	WAS A (97G –.332)																					
″	total	133	.315	.472	540	170	50	10	5	0.9	110	81	84	38	20	0	0	377	13	16	4	3.1	.961	OF-133
1937	2 teams	WAS A (35G –.262)	BOS A (113G –.307)																					
″	total	148	.297	.432	553	164	30	12	7	1.3	99	69	83	42	**35**	2	1	349	11	9	1	2.5	.976	OF-144, SS-1
1938	BOS A	127	.340	.494	480	163	40	8	6	1.3	92	80	65	33	13	1	1	267	16	10	5	2.3	.966	OF-126, 3B-1
1939	CLE A	149	.290	.413	545	158	31	9	6	1.1	101	82	87	30	18	2	1	356	12	11	0	2.6	.971	OF-146
1940		143	.286	.403	548	157	40	6	4	0.7	82	50	78	45	13	3	1	307	10	12	3	2.3	.964	OF-140
1941	2 teams	WAS A (28G –.255)	CHI A (57G –.226)																					
″	total	85	.237	.323	300	71	15	1	3	1.0	35	29	29	20	4	10	2	176	9	1	2	2.5	.995	OF-75

Ben Chapman *continued*

Year	Team	Games	BA	SA	AB	H	2B	3B	HR	HR%	R	RBI	BB	SO	SB	Pinch Hit AB	Pinch Hit H	PO	A	E	DP	TC/G	FA	G by Pos
1944	BKN N	20	.368	.474	38	14	4	0	0	0.0	11	11	5	4	1	9	3	3	6	1	0	0.9	.900	P-11
1945	2 teams BKN N (13G –.136) PHI N (24G –.314)																							
"	total	37	.260	.288	73	19	2	0	0	0.0	6	7	4	2	0	10	4	17	21	4	3	1.6	.905	P-13, OF-10, 3B-4
1946	PHI N	1	.000	.000	1	0	0	0	0	0.0	1	0	0	0	0	0	0	0	0	0	0	0.0	.000	P-1
15 yrs.		1716	.302	.440	6478	1958	407	107	90	1.4	1144	977	824	556	287	43	13	3740	514	173	85	2.6	.961	OF-1494, 3B-96, 2B-56, P-25, SS-1
WORLD SERIES																								
1932	NY A	4	.294	.353	17	5	1	0	0	0.0	1	6	2	4	0	0	0	6	1	0	0	1.8	1.000	OF-4

Calvin Chapman

CHAPMAN, CALVIN LOUIS BL TR 5′ 9″ 160 lbs.
B. Dec. 20, 1910, Courtland, Miss. D. Apr. 1, 1983, Batesville, Miss. BB 1935

Year	Team	Games	BA	SA	AB	H	2B	3B	HR	HR%	R	RBI	BB	SO	SB	Pinch Hit AB	Pinch Hit H	PO	A	E	DP	TC/G	FA	G by Pos
1935	CIN N	15	.340	.358	53	18	1	0	0	0.0	6	3	4	5	2	0	0	27	34	4	9	4.1	.938	SS-12, 2B-4
1936		96	.247	.320	219	54	7	3	1	0.5	35	22	16	19	5	40	15	85	49	4	6	2.5	.971	OF-31, 2B-23, 3B-1
2 yrs.		111	.265	.327	272	72	8	3	1	0.4	41	25	20	24	7	40	15	112	83	8	15	2.9	.961	OF-31, 2B-27, SS-12, 3B-1

Fred Chapman

CHAPMAN, WILLIAM FRED (Chappie) BR TR 6′ 1″ 185 lbs.
B. July 17, 1916, Liberty, S. C.

Year	Team	Games	BA	SA	AB	H	2B	3B	HR	HR%	R	RBI	BB	SO	SB	Pinch Hit AB	Pinch Hit H	PO	A	E	DP	TC/G	FA	G by Pos
1939	PHI A	15	.286	.347	49	14	1	1	0	0.0	5	1	1	3	1	0	0	24	38	7	5	4.6	.899	SS-15
1940		26	.159	.174	69	11	1	0	0	0.0	6	4	6	10	1	0	0	40	54	15	12	4.4	.862	SS-25
1941		35	.159	.174	69	11	1	0	0	0.0	1	4	4	15	1	2	1	22	56	8	7	2.8	.907	SS-28, 3B-2, 2B-1
3 yrs.		76	.193	.219	187	36	3	1	0	0.0	12	9	11	28	3	2	1	86	148	30	24	3.7	.886	SS-68, 3B-2, 2B-1

Glenn Chapman

CHAPMAN, GLENN JUSTICE (Pete) BR TR 5′11½″ 170 lbs.
B. Jan. 21, 1906, Cambridge City, Ind. D. Nov. 5, 1988, Richmond, Ind.

Year	Team	Games	BA	SA	AB	H	2B	3B	HR	HR%	R	RBI	BB	SO	SB	Pinch Hit AB	Pinch Hit H	PO	A	E	DP	TC/G	FA	G by Pos
1934	BKN N	67	.280	.387	93	26	5	1	1	1.1	19	10	7	19	1	2	0	66	28	3	4	1.8	.969	OF-40, 2B-14

Harry Chapman

CHAPMAN, HARRY E. BR TR 5′11″ 160 lbs.
B. Oct. 26, 1887, Severance, Kans. D. Oct. 21, 1918, Nevada, Mo.

Year	Team	Games	BA	SA	AB	H	2B	3B	HR	HR%	R	RBI	BB	SO	SB	Pinch Hit AB	Pinch Hit H	PO	A	E	DP	TC/G	FA	G by Pos
1912	CHI N	1	.250	.750	4	1	0	1	0	0.0	1	1	0	0	1	0	0	7	3	0	0	10.0	1.000	C-1
1913	CIN N	2	.500	.500	2	1	0	0	0	0.0	0	0	0	1	0	2	1	0	0	0	0	0.0	—	
1914	STL F	64	.210	.232	181	38	2	1	0	0.0	16	14	13		2	4	1	248	78	9	8	6.2	.973	C-51, 2B-1, 1B-1, OF-1
1915		62	.199	.280	186	37	6	3	1	0.5	19	29	22		4	8	1	293	79	4	6	7.1	.989	C-53
1916	STL A	18	.097	.097	31	3	0	0	0	0.0	2	0	2	5	0	3	0	37	15	1	2	3.8	.981	C-14
5 yrs.		147	.198	.250	404	80	8	5	1	0.2	38	44	37	6	7	17	3	585	175	14	16	6.3	.982	C-119, 2B-1, 1B-1, OF-1

Jack Chapman

CHAPMAN, JOHN CURTIS TR 5′11″ 170 lbs.
B. May 8, 1843, Brooklyn, N. Y. D. June 10, 1916, Brooklyn, N. Y.
Manager 1876–78, 1882–85, 1889–92.

Year	Team	Games	BA	SA	AB	H	2B	3B	HR	HR%	R	RBI	BB	SO	SB	Pinch Hit AB	Pinch Hit H	PO	A	E	DP	TC/G	FA	G by Pos
1876	LOU N	17	.239	.254	67	16	1	0	0	0.0	4	5	1	3		0	0	17	2	7	1	1.4	.731	OF-17, 3B-1

John Chapman

CHAPMAN, JOHN JOSEPH BR TR 5′10″ 180 lbs.
B. Oct. 15, 1899, Centralia, Pa. D. Nov. 3, 1953, Philadelphia, Pa.

Year	Team	Games	BA	SA	AB	H	2B	3B	HR	HR%	R	RBI	BB	SO	SB	Pinch Hit AB	Pinch Hit H	PO	A	E	DP	TC/G	FA	G by Pos
1924	PHI A	19	.282	.366	71	20	4	1	0	0.0	7	7	4	8	0	0	0	32	37	3	10	3.8	.958	SS-19

Kelvin Chapman

CHAPMAN, KELVIN KEITH BR TR 5′11″ 173 lbs.
B. June 2, 1956, Willits, Calif.

Year	Team	Games	BA	SA	AB	H	2B	3B	HR	HR%	R	RBI	BB	SO	SB	Pinch Hit AB	Pinch Hit H	PO	A	E	DP	TC/G	FA	G by Pos
1979	NY N	35	.150	.212	80	12	1	2	0	0.0	7	4	5	15	0	10	2	51	46	2	15	4.3	.980	2B-22, 3B-1
1984		75	.289	.401	197	57	13	0	3	1.5	27	23	19	30	8	14	5	105	133	6	33	4.1	.975	2B-56, 3B-3, SS-1
1985		62	.174	.194	144	25	3	0	0	0.0	16	7	9	15	5	20	6	70	89	5	17	3.3	.970	2B-48, 3B-1
3 yrs.		172	.223	.295	421	94	17	2	3	0.7	50	34	33	60	13	44	13	226	268	13	65	3.8	.974	2B-126, 3B-5, SS-1

Ray Chapman

CHAPMAN, RAYMOND JOHNSON BR TR 5′10″ 170 lbs.
B. Jan. 15, 1891, Beaver Dam, Ky. D. Aug. 17, 1920, New York, N. Y.

Year	Team	Games	BA	SA	AB	H	2B	3B	HR	HR%	R	RBI	BB	SO	SB	Pinch Hit AB	Pinch Hit H	PO	A	E	DP	TC/G	FA	G by Pos
1912	CLE A	31	.312	.422	109	34	6	3	0	0.0	29	19	10		10	0	0	70	72	15	10	5.1	.904	SS-31
1913		140	.258	.341	508	131	19	7	3	0.6	78	39	46	51	29	1	0	299	408	48	59	5.5	.936	SS-138
1914		106	.275	.387	375	103	16	10	2	0.5	59	42	48	48	24	1	0	223	279	42	25	5.2	.923	SS-72, 2B-33
1915		154	.270	.370	570	154	14	17	3	0.5	101	67	70	82	36	0	0	378	469	50	38	5.8	.944	SS-154
1916		109	.231	.289	346	80	10	5	0	0.0	50	27	50	46	21	5	0	207	310	32	35	5.3	.942	SS-52, 3B-36, 2B-16
1917		156	.302	.410	563	170	28	12	3	0.5	98	36	61	65	52	0	0	360	528	59	71	6.1	.938	SS-156
1918		128	.267	.352	446	119	19	8	1	0.2	**84**	32	**84**	46	30	0	0	323	398	50	42	6.0	.935	SS-128, OF-1
1919		115	.300	.420	433	130	23	10	3	0.7	75	53	31	38	18	0	0	255	347	36	44	5.5	.944	SS-115
1920		111	.303	.423	435	132	27	8	3	0.7	97	49	52	38	13	0	0	243	371	26	43	5.8	.959	SS-111
9 yrs.		1050	.278	.378	3785	1053	162	80	18	0.5	671	364	452	414	233	7	0	2358	3182	358	367	5.7	.939	SS-957, 2B-49, 3B-36, OF-1

Sam Chapman

CHAPMAN, SAMUEL BLAKE BR TR 6′ 180 lbs.
B. Apr. 11, 1916, Tiburon, Calif.

Year	Team	Games	BA	SA	AB	H	2B	3B	HR	HR%	R	RBI	BB	SO	SB	Pinch Hit AB	Pinch Hit H	PO	A	E	DP	TC/G	FA	G by Pos
1938	PHI A	114	.259	.461	406	105	17	7	17	4.2	60	63	55	94	3	3	1	229	8	12	0	2.2	.952	OF-114
1939		140	.269	.432	498	134	24	6	15	3.0	74	64	51	62	11	7	1	497	16	21	8	3.9	.961	OF-117, 1B-19
1940		134	.276	.474	508	140	26	3	23	4.5	88	75	46	**96**	2	5	2	348	13	14	2	2.9	.963	OF-129
1941		143	.322	.543	552	178	29	9	25	4.5	97	106	47	49	6	2	0	416	21	15	5	3.2	.967	OF-141
1945		9	.200	.267	30	6	2	0	0	0.0	3	1	2	4	0	0	0	18	0	0	0	2.3	1.000	OF-8
1946		146	.261	.429	545	142	22	5	20	3.7	77	67	54	66	1	1	0	369	13	12	4	2.7	.970	OF-145
1947		149	.252	.379	551	139	18	5	14	2.5	84	83	65	70	3	4	1	428	16	6	2	3.1	.987	OF-146
1948		123	.258	.413	445	115	18	6	13	2.9	58	70	55	50	5	4	0	368	8	7	2	3.2	.982	OF-118
1949		154	.278	.455	589	164	24	4	24	4.1	89	108	80	68	3	0	0	450	11	10	3	3.1	.979	OF-154
1950		144	.251	.434	553	139	20	6	23	4.2	93	95	68	79	3	3	0	428	11	10	4	3.2	.978	OF-140
1951	2 teams PHI A (18G –.169) CLE A (94G –.228)																							
"	total	112	.215	.312	311	67	10	1	6	1.9	31	41	39	44	3	4	0	176	3	4	2	1.8	.978	OF-101, 1B-1
11 yrs.		1368	.266	.438	4988	1329	210	52	180	3.6	754	773	562	682	40	33	5	3727	120	111	32	3.0	.972	OF-1313, 1B-20

Harry Chappas

CHAPPAS, HARRY PERRY BB TR 5′ 3″ 150 lbs.
B. Oct. 26, 1957, Mount Rainier, Md.

Year	Team	Games	BA	SA	AB	H	2B	3B	HR	HR%	R	RBI	BB	SO	SB	Pinch Hit AB	Pinch Hit H	PO	A	E	DP	TC/G	FA	G by Pos
1978	CHI A	20	.267	.280	75	20	1	0	0	0.0	11	6	6	11	1	0	0	28	64	0	8	4.6	1.000	SS-20
1979		26	.288	.356	59	17	1	0	1	1.7	9	4	5	5	1	1	1	28	63	7	13	4.3	.929	SS-23
1980		26	.160	.200	50	8	2	0	0	0.0	6	2	4	10	0	3	0	18	36	1	10	2.5	.982	SS-19, DH-2, 2B-1
3 yrs.		72	.245	.283	184	45	4	0	1	0.5	26	12	15	26	2	4	1	74	163	8	31	3.8	.967	SS-62, DH-2, 2B-1

Larry Chappell

CHAPPELL, LaVERNE ASHFORD BL TL 6′ 186 lbs.
B. Feb. 19, 1890, McCluskey, Ill. D. Nov. 8, 1918, San Francisco, Calif.

Year	Team	Games	BA	SA	AB	H	2B	3B	HR	HR%	R	RBI	BB	SO	SB	Pinch Hit AB	Pinch Hit H	PO	A	E	DP	TC/G	FA	G by Pos
1913	CHI A	60	.231	.279	208	48	8	1	0	0.0	21	15	18	22	7	1	0	114	5	6	1	2.1	.952	OF-59
1914		21	.231	.231	39	9	0	0	0	0.0	3	1	4	11	0	10	1	13	0	1	0	1.6	.929	OF-9
1915		1	.000	.000	1	0	0	0	0	0.0	0	0	0	0	0	1	0	0	0	0	0	0.0	—	
1916	2 teams	CLE A (3G –.000) BOS N (20G –.226)																						
″	total	23	.218	.273	55	12	1	1	0	0.0	4	9	3	8	2	8	1	22	0	1	0	1.6	.957	OF-14
1917	BOS N	4	.000	.000	2	0	0	0	0	0.0	0	1	0	1	0	2	0	0	0	0	0	0.0	.000	OF-1
5 yrs.		109	.226	.269	305	69	9	2	0	0.0	28	26	25	42	9	22	2	149	5	8	1	2.0	.951	OF-83

Joe Charboneau

CHARBONEAU, JOSEPH BR TR 6′ 2″ 205 lbs.
B. June 17, 1955, Belvidere, Ill.

Year	Team	Games	BA	SA	AB	H	2B	3B	HR	HR%	R	RBI	BB	SO	SB	Pinch Hit AB	Pinch Hit H	PO	A	E	DP	TC/G	FA	G by Pos
1980	CLE A	131	.289	.488	453	131	17	2	23	5.1	76	87	49	70	2	8	5	125	6	5	1	1.1	.963	OF-67, DH-57
1981		48	.210	.362	138	29	7	1	4	2.9	14	18	7	22	1	7	2	51	1	2	0	1.3	.963	OF-27, DH-14
1982		22	.214	.393	56	12	2	1	2	3.6	7	9	5	7	0	6	2	21	0	1	0	1.2	.955	OF-18, DH-1
3 yrs.		201	.266	.453	647	172	26	4	29	4.5	97	114	61	99	3	21	9	197	7	8	1	1.2	.962	OF-112, DH-72

Chappy Charles

CHARLES, RAYMOND BR TR 5′11″ 175 lbs.
Born Charles Shuh Achenbach.
B. Mar. 25, 1881, Phillipsburg, N. J. D. Aug. 4, 1959, Bethlehem, Pa.

Year	Team	Games	BA	SA	AB	H	2B	3B	HR	HR%	R	RBI	BB	SO	SB	Pinch Hit AB	Pinch Hit H	PO	A	E	DP	TC/G	FA	G by Pos
1908	STL N	121	.205	.256	454	93	14	3	1	0.2	39	17	19		15	2	0	215	322	49	25	4.9	.916	2B-65, SS-31, 3B-23
1909	2 teams	STL N (99G –.236) CIN N (13G –.256)																						
″	total	112	.238	.277	382	91	9	3	0	0.0	36	34	35		9	0	0	258	312	49	34	5.4	.921	2B-81, SS-31, 3B-2
1910	CIN N	4	.133	.267	15	2	0	1	0	0.0	1	0	0	1	0	0	0	8	10	4	2	5.5	.818	SS-4
3 yrs.		237	.219	.266	851	186	23	7	1	0.1	76	51	54	1	24	2	0	481	644	102	61	5.2	.917	2B-146, SS-66, 3B-25

Ed Charles

CHARLES, EDWIN DOUGLAS (The Glider) BR TR 5′10″ 170 lbs.
B. Apr. 29, 1933, Daytona Beach, Fla.

Year	Team	Games	BA	SA	AB	H	2B	3B	HR	HR%	R	RBI	BB	SO	SB	Pinch Hit AB	Pinch Hit H	PO	A	E	DP	TC/G	FA	G by Pos
1962	KC A	147	.288	.454	535	154	24	7	17	3.2	81	74	54	70	20	7	0	148	286	16	28	3.2	.964	3B-140, 2B-2
1963		158	.267	.395	603	161	28	2	15	2.5	82	79	58	79	15	0	0	153	310	25	19	3.1	.949	3B-158
1964		150	.241	.379	557	134	25	2	16	2.9	69	63	64	92	12	5	1	138	259	19	25	2.8	.954	3B-147
1965		134	.269	.388	480	129	19	7	8	1.7	55	56	44	72	13	5	1	151	254	12	29	3.2	.971	3B-128, 2B-1, SS-1
1966		118	.286	.444	385	110	18	8	9	2.3	52	42	30	53	12	14	6	86	201	11	21	2.8	.963	3B-104, 1B-1, OF-1
1967	2 teams	KC A (19G –.246) NY N (101G –.238)																						
″	total	120	.240	.310	384	92	14	2	3	0.8	37	36	36	71	5	10	1	102	241	19	17	3.4	.948	3B-107
1968	NY N	117	.276	.434	369	102	11	1	15	4.1	41	53	28	57	5	15	6	79	201	13	19	2.7	.956	3B-106, 1B-2
1969		61	.207	.320	169	35	8	1	3	1.8	21	18	18	31	4	12	4	37	86	7	9	2.5	.946	3B-52
8 yrs.		1005	.263	.397	3482	917	147	30	86	2.5	438	421	332	525	86	68	19	894	1838	122	167	3.0	.957	3B-942, 1B-3, 2B-3, OF-1, SS-1
WORLD SERIES																								
1969	NY N	4	.133	.200	15	2	1	0	0	0.0	1	0	0	2	0	0	0	3	9	0	0	3.0	1.000	3B-4

Mike Chartak

CHARTAK, MICHAEL GEORGE (Shotgun) BL TL 6′ 2″ 180 lbs.
B. Apr. 28, 1916, Brooklyn, N. Y. D. July 25, 1967, Cedar Rapids, Iowa.

Year	Team	Games	BA	SA	AB	H	2B	3B	HR	HR%	R	RBI	BB	SO	SB	Pinch Hit AB	Pinch Hit H	PO	A	E	DP	TC/G	FA	G by Pos
1940	NY A	11	.133	.200	15	2	1	0	0	0.0	2	3	5	5	0	5	1	4	0	0	0	1.3	1.000	OF-3
1942	3 teams	NY A (5G –.000) WAS A (24G –.217) STL A (73G –.249)																						
″	total	102	.237	.395	334	79	15	4	10	3.0	48	51	54	43	3	12	3	190	12	8	4	2.4	.962	OF-88
1943	STL A	108	.256	.401	344	88	16	2	10	2.9	38	37	39	55	1	18	3	321	13	9	10	3.6	.974	OF-77, 1B-18
1944		35	.236	.333	72	17	2	1	1	1.4	8	7	6	9	0	17	3	105	5	0	5	5.8	1.000	1B-12, OF-7
4 yrs.		256	.243	.388	765	186	34	7	21	2.7	96	98	104	112	4	52	10	620	30	17	19	3.3	.975	OF-175, 1B-30
WORLD SERIES																								
1944	STL A	2	.000	.000	2	0	0	0	0	0.0	0	0	0	2	0	2	0	0	0	0	0	0.0	—	

Hal Chase

CHASE, HAROLD HOMER (Prince Hal) BR TL 6′ 175 lbs.
B. Feb. 13, 1883, Los Gatos, Calif. D. May 18, 1947, Colusa, Calif.
Manager 1910–11.

Year	Team	Games	BA	SA	AB	H	2B	3B	HR	HR%	R	RBI	BB	SO	SB	Pinch Hit AB	Pinch Hit H	PO	A	E	DP	TC/G	FA	G by Pos
1905	NY A	126	.249	.329	465	116	16	6	3	0.6	60	49	15		22	1	1	1175	62	32	63	10.2	.975	1B-122, SS-1, 2B-1
1906		151	.323	.395	597	193	23	10	0	0.0	84	76	13		28	0	0	1506	92	33	54	10.8	.980	1B-150, 2B-1
1907		125	.287	.357	498	143	23	3	2	0.4	72	68	19		32	0	0	1152	79	34	50	10.1	.973	1B-121, OF-4
1908		106	.257	.306	405	104	11	3	1	0.2	50	36	15		27	1	1	1026	65	26	36	11.0	.977	1B-96, 2B-3, 3B-2, P-1
1909		118	.283	.357	474	134	17	3	4	0.8	60	63	20		25	0	0	1202	71	28	53	11.0	.978	1B-118
1910		130	.290	.365	524	152	20	5	3	0.6	67	73	16		40	0	0	1373	65	28	68	11.3	.981	1B-130
1911		133	.315	.419	527	166	32	7	3	0.6	82	62	21		36	0	0	1271	85	37	65	10.4	.973	1B-124, OF-7, 2B-2, SS-1
1912		131	.274	.372	522	143	21	9	4	0.8	61	58	17		33	2	0	1173	89	32	50	10.0	.975	1B-121, 2B-8
1913	2 teams	NY A (39G –.212) CHI A (102G –.286)																						
″	total	141	.266	.355	530	141	13	14	2	0.4	64	48	27	54	14	0	0	1340	90	37	69	10.4	.975	1B-131, OF-5, 2B-5
1914	2 teams	CHI A (58G –.267) BUF F (75G –.347)																						
″	total	133	.314	.447	497	156	29	14	3	0.6	70	68	29	19	19	2	1	1322	81	28	60	10.9	.980	1B-131
1915	BUF F	145	.291	.471	567	165	31	10	**17**	**3.0**	85	89	20		23	1	0	1463	83	26	84	10.9	.983	1B-143, OF-1
1916	CIN N	142	**.339**	.459	542	**184**	29	12	4	0.7	66	82	19	48	22	7	2	1023	86	20	73	8.1	.982	1B-98, OF-25, 2B-16
1917		152	.277	.394	**602**	167	28	15	4	0.7	71	86	15	49	21	0	0	1499	80	28	100	10.6	.983	1B-151
1918		74	.301	.417	259	78	12	6	2	0.8	30	38	13	15	5	5	0	610	38	13	59	9.6	.980	1B-67, OF-2
1919	NY N	110	.284	.397	408	116	17	7	5	1.2	58	45	17	40	16	2	1	1205	65	21	62	12.1	.984	1B-107
15 yrs.		1917	.291	.391	7417	2158	322	124	57	0.8	980	941	276	225	363	21	6	18340	1131	423	946	10.5	.979	1B-1810, OF-44, 2B-36, 3B-2, SS-2, P-1

Buster Chatham

CHATHAM, CHARLES L. BR TR 5′ 5″ 150 lbs.
B. Dec. 25, 1901, West, Tex. D. Dec. 15, 1975, Waco, Tex.

Year	Team	Lg	Games	BA	SA	AB	H	2B	3B	HR	HR%	R	RBI	BB	SO	SB	Pinch Hit AB	Pinch Hit H	PO	A	E	DP	TC/G	FA	G by Pos
1930	**BOS**	**N**	112	.267	.408	404	108	20	11	5	1.2	48	56	37	41	8	4	0	116	200	23	38	3.1	.932	3B-92, SS-17
1931			17	.227	.318	44	10	1	0	1	2.3	4	3	6	6	0	3	0	11	20	5	4	3.0	.861	SS-6, 3B-6
2 yrs.			129	.263	.400	448	118	21	11	6	1.3	52	59	43	47	8	7	0	127	220	28	42	3.1	.925	3B-98, SS-23

Jim Chatterton

CHATTERTON, JAMES M.
B. Oct. 14, 1864, Brooklyn, N. Y. D. Dec. 15, 1944, Tewksbury, Mass.

Year	Team	Lg	Games	BA	SA	AB	H	2B	3B	HR	HR%	R	RBI	BB	SO	SB	Pinch Hit AB	Pinch Hit H	PO	A	E	DP	TC/G	FA	G by Pos
1884	**KC**	**U**	4	.133	.200	15	2	1	0	0	0.0	4		2			0	0	25	3	2	2	6.0	.933	1B-2, OF-2, P-1

Ossie Chavarria

CHAVARRIA, OSVALDO BR TR 5′11″ 155 lbs.
Born Osvaldo Chavarria (Quijano).
B. Aug. 5, 1940, Colon, Panama.

Year	Team	Lg	Games	BA	SA	AB	H	2B	3B	HR	HR%	R	RBI	BB	SO	SB	Pinch Hit AB	Pinch Hit H	PO	A	E	DP	TC/G	FA	G by Pos
1966	**KC**	**A**	86	.241	.325	191	46	10	0	2	1.0	26	10	18	43	3	17	4	105	86	7	23	2.6	.965	OF-26, SS-23, 2B-14, 1B-8, 3B-5
1967			38	.102	.136	59	6	2	0	0	0.0	2	4	7	16	1	8	1	30	38	2	9	2.4	.971	2B-17, 3B-7, OF-3, SS-2
2 yrs.			124	.208	.280	250	52	12	0	2	0.8	28	14	25	59	4	25	5	135	124	9	32	2.6	.966	2B-31, OF-29, SS-25, 3B-12, 1B-8

Harry Cheek

CHEEK, HARRY G. TR
B. Mar. 1, 1879, Sedalia, Mo. D. June 25, 1956, Paramus, N. J.

Year	Team	Lg	Games	BA	SA	AB	H	2B	3B	HR	HR%	R	RBI	BB	SO	SB	Pinch Hit AB	Pinch Hit H	PO	A	E	DP	TC/G	FA	G by Pos
1910	**PHI**	**N**	2	.500	.750	4	2	1	0	0	0.0	1	0	0	0	0	0	0	2	0	0	0	1.0	1.000	C-2

Paul Chervinko

CHERVINKO, PAUL BR TR 5′ 8″ 185 lbs.
B. July 23, 1910, Trauger, Pa. D. June 3, 1976, Danville, Ill.

Year	Team	Lg	Games	BA	SA	AB	H	2B	3B	HR	HR%	R	RBI	BB	SO	SB	Pinch Hit AB	Pinch Hit H	PO	A	E	DP	TC/G	FA	G by Pos
1937	**BKN**	**N**	30	.146	.188	48	7	0	1	0	0.0	1	2	3	16	0	3	0	56	8	0	0	2.5	1.000	C-26
1938			12	.148	.148	27	4	0	0	0	0.0	0	3	2	0	0	0	0	33	4	1	0	3.2	.974	C-12
2 yrs.			42	.147	.173	75	11	0	1	0	0.0	1	5	5	16	0	3	0	89	12	1	0	2.7	.990	C-38

Cupid Childs

CHILDS, CLARENCE ALGERNON BL TR 5′ 8″ 185 lbs.
B. Aug. 14, 1867, Calvert County, Md. D. Nov. 8, 1912, Baltimore, Md.

Year	Team	Lg	Games	BA	SA	AB	H	2B	3B	HR	HR%	R	RBI	BB	SO	SB	Pinch Hit AB	Pinch Hit H	PO	A	E	DP	TC/G	FA	G by Pos
1888	**PHI**	**N**	2	.000	.000	4	0	0	0	0	0.0	0	0	0	0	0	0	0	2	4	1	1	3.5	.857	2B-2
1890	**SYR**	**AA**	136	.345	.481	493	170	**33**	14	2	0.4	109		72		56	0	0	375	369	58	59	6.4	.928	2B-125, SS-1
1891	**CLE**	**N**	141	.281	.374	551	155	21	12	2	0.4	120	83	97	32	39	0	0	371	455	82	54	6.4	.910	2B-141
1892			145	.317	.398	558	177	14	11	3	0.5	**136**	53	117	20	26	0	0	357	441	53	51	5.9	.938	2B-145
1893			124	.326	.425	485	158	19	10	3	0.6	145	65	120	12	23	0	0	348	424	62	56	6.8	.926	2B-123
1894			118	.353	.459	479	169	21	12	2	0.4	143	52	107	11	17	0	0	313	374	63	51	6.4	.916	2B-118
1895			119	.288	.359	462	133	15	3	4	0.9	96	90	74	24	20	0	0	337	394	63	42	6.7	.921	2B-119
1896			132	.355	.446	498	177	24	9	1	0.2	106	106	100	18	25	0	0	375	487	53	73	6.9	.942	2B-132
1897			114	.338	.419	444	150	15	9	1	0.2	105	61	74		25	0	0	319	384	42	42	6.5	.944	2B-114
1898			110	.288	.337	413	119	9	4	1	0.2	90	31	69		9	0	0	273	370	48	37	6.3	.931	2B-110
1899	**STL**	**N**	125	.265	.343	464	123	11	11	1	0.2	73	48	74		11	0	0	323	355	48	45	5.8	.934	2B-125
1900	**CHI**	**N**	137	.241	.286	531	128	14	5	0	0.0	67	44	57		15	0	0	323	431	52	57	5.9	.935	2B-137
1901			63	.257	.295	237	61	9	0	0	0.0	24	21	29		3	0	0	146	192	22	34	5.8	.939	2B-62
13 yrs.			1466	.306	.389	5619	1720	205	100	20	0.4	1214	654	990	117	269	0	0	3862	4680	647	602	6.3	.930	2B-1453, SS-1

Pete Childs

CHILDS, GEORGE PETER TR
B. Nov. 15, 1871, Philadelphia, Pa. D. Feb. 15, 1922, Philadelphia, Pa.

Year	Team	Lg	Games	BA	SA	AB	H	2B	3B	HR	HR%	R	RBI	BB	SO	SB	Pinch Hit AB	Pinch Hit H	PO	A	E	DP	TC/G	FA	G by Pos
1901	**2 teams**		**STL N** (29G –.266) **CHI N** (61G –.225)																						
"	**total**		90	.236	.264	292	69	6	1	0	0.0	35	22	41		4	6	1	169	248	25	23	5.3	.943	2B-80, OF-2, SS-1
1902	**PHI**	**N**	123	.194	.206	403	78	5	0	0	0.0	25	25	34		6	0	0	271	349	36	26	5.3	.945	2B-123
2 yrs.			213	.212	.230	695	147	11	1	0	0.0	60	47	75		10	6	1	440	597	61	49	5.3	.944	2B-203, OF-2, SS-1

Pearce Chiles

CHILES, PEARCE NUGET (What's the Use) BR TR 5′11″ 185 lbs.
B. May 28, 1867, Deepwater, Mo. Deceased.

Year	Team	Lg	Games	BA	SA	AB	H	2B	3B	HR	HR%	R	RBI	BB	SO	SB	Pinch Hit AB	Pinch Hit H	PO	A	E	DP	TC/G	FA	G by Pos
1899	**PHI**	**N**	97	.320	.462	338	108	28	7	2	0.6	57	76	16		6	**10**	2	330	44	25	18	4.6	.937	OF-46, 1B-25, 2B-16
1900			33	.216	.333	111	24	6	2	1	0.9	15	23	6		4	2	0	169	42	6	14	7.0	.972	1B-16, 2B-12, OF-3
2 yrs.			130	.294	.430	449	132	34	9	3	0.7	72	99	22		10	12	2	499	86	31	32	5.2	.950	OF-49, 1B-41, 2B-28

Rich Chiles

CHILES, RICHARD FRANCIS BL TL 5′11″ 170 lbs.
B. Nov. 22, 1949, Sacramento, Calif.

Year	Team	Lg	Games	BA	SA	AB	H	2B	3B	HR	HR%	R	RBI	BB	SO	SB	Pinch Hit AB	Pinch Hit H	PO	A	E	DP	TC/G	FA	G by Pos
1971	**HOU**	**N**	67	.227	.336	119	27	5	1	2	1.7	12	15	6	20	0	38	11	35	0	0	0	1.3	1.000	OF-27
1972			9	.273	.364	11	3	1	0	0	0.0	0	2	1	1	0	6	2	4	0	0	0	2.0	1.000	OF-2
1973	**NY**	**N**	8	.120	.200	25	3	2	0	0	0.0	2	1	0	2	0	0	0	22	1	0	1	2.9	1.000	OF-8
1976	**HOU**	**N**	5	.500	.750	4	2	1	0	0	0.0	1	0	0	0	0	4	2	1	0	0	0	1.0	1.000	OF-1
1977	**MIN**	**A**	108	.264	.368	261	69	16	1	3	1.1	31	36	23	17	0	29	8	35	0	2	0	0.4	.946	DH-61, OF-22
1978			87	.268	.343	198	53	12	0	1	0.5	22	22	20	25	1	21	5	108	3	4	0	1.7	.965	OF-61, DH-8
6 yrs.			284	.254	.350	618	157	37	2	6	1.0	68	76	50	65	1	98	28	205	4	6	1	1.1	.972	OF-121, DH-69

Dino Chiozza

CHIOZZA, DINO JOSEPH (Dynamo) BL TR 6′ 170 lbs.
Brother of Lou Chiozza.
B. June 30, 1912, Memphis, Tenn. D. Apr. 23, 1972, Memphis, Tenn.

Year	Team	Lg	Games	BA	SA	AB	H	2B	3B	HR	HR%	R	RBI	BB	SO	SB	Pinch Hit AB	Pinch Hit H	PO	A	E	DP	TC/G	FA	G by Pos
1935	**PHI**	**N**	2	—	—	0	0	0	0	0	—	1	0	0	0	0	0	0	1	0	0	0	0.5	1.000	SS-2

Lou Chiozza

CHIOZZA, LOUIS PEO BL TR 6′ 172 lbs.
Brother of Dino Chiozza.
B. May 17, 1910, Tallulah, La. D. Feb. 28, 1971, Memphis, Tenn.

Year	Team	Lg	Games	BA	SA	AB	H	2B	3B	HR	HR%	R	RBI	BB	SO	SB	Pinch Hit AB	Pinch Hit H	PO	A	E	DP	TC/G	FA	G by Pos
1934	**PHI**	**N**	134	.304	.382	484	147	28	5	0	0.0	66	44	34	35	9	9	1	266	298	41	39	4.7	.932	2B-85, 3B-26, OF-17
1935			124	.284	.383	472	134	26	6	3	0.6	71	47	33	44	5	1	0	297	405	39	54	6.1	.947	2B-120, 3B-2
1936			144	.297	.379	572	170	32	6	1	0.2	83	48	37	39	17	2	1	324	144	26	25	3.3	.947	OF-90, 2B-33, 3B-26
1937	**NY**	**N**	117	.232	.294	439	102	11	2	4	0.9	49	29	20	30	6	9	2	121	172	17	9	2.9	.945	3B-93, OF-12, 2B-2
1938			57	.235	.346	179	42	7	2	3	1.7	15	17	12	7	5	7	2	80	112	11	9	4.0	.946	2B-34, OF-16, 3B-1
1939			40	.268	.366	142	38	3	1	3	2.1	19	12	9	10	3	0	0	39	76	8	11	3.2	.935	3B-30, SS-8
6 yrs.			616	.277	.361	2288	633	107	22	14	0.6	303	197	145	165	45	28	6	1127	1207	142	147	4.2	.943	2B-274, 3B-178, OF-135, SS-8

Lou Chiozza *continued*

WORLD SERIES

Year	Team	Lg	Games	BA	SA	AB	H	2B	3B	HR	HR%	R	RBI	BB	SO	SB	Pinch Hit AB	Pinch Hit H	PO	A	E	DP	TC/G	FA	G by Pos
1937	NY	N	2	.286	.286	7	2	0	0	0	0.0	0	0	1	1	0	0	0	6	0	1	0	3.5	.857	OF-2

Walt Chipple

CHIPPLE, WALTER JOHN BR TR 6′½″ 168 lbs.
Born Walter John Chlipala.
B. Sept. 26, 1918, Utica, N. Y. D. June 8, 1988, Tonawanda, N. Y.

Year	Team	Lg	Games	BA	SA	AB	H	2B	3B	HR	HR%	R	RBI	BB	SO	SB	Pinch Hit AB	Pinch Hit H	PO	A	E	DP	TC/G	FA	G by Pos
1945	WAS	A	18	.136	.136	44	6	0	0	0	0.0	4	5	5	6	0	2	0	42	2	1	1	3.5	.978	OF-13

Tom Chism

CHISM, THOMAS RAYMOND BL TL 6′ 1″ 195 lbs.
B. May 9, 1954, Chester, Pa.

Year	Team	Lg	Games	BA	SA	AB	H	2B	3B	HR	HR%	R	RBI	BB	SO	SB	Pinch Hit AB	Pinch Hit H	PO	A	E	DP	TC/G	FA	G by Pos
1979	BAL	A	6	.000	.000	3	0	0	0	0	0.0	0	0	0	0	0	0	0	6	0	0	0	1.5	1.000	1B-4

Harry Chiti

CHITI, HARRY BR TR 6′ 2½″ 221 lbs.
B. Nov. 16, 1932, Kincaid, Ill.

Year	Team	Lg	Games	BA	SA	AB	H	2B	3B	HR	HR%	R	RBI	BB	SO	SB	Pinch Hit AB	Pinch Hit H	PO	A	E	DP	TC/G	FA	G by Pos
1950	CHI	N	3	.333	.333	6	2	0	0	0	0.0	0	0	0	0	0	2	0	1	1	0	0	2.0	1.000	C-1
1951			9	.355	.419	31	11	2	0	0	0.0	1	5	2	2	0	1	0	34	8	4	1	5.8	.913	C-8
1952			32	.274	.451	113	31	5	0	5	4.4	14	13	5	8	0	0	0	170	13	3	6	5.8	.984	C-32
1955			113	.231	.352	338	78	6	1	11	3.3	24	41	25	68	0	1	0	495	69	9	10	5.1	.984	C-113
1956			72	.212	.340	203	43	6	4	4	2.0	17	18	19	35	0	5	2	327	35	7	2	5.5	.981	C-67
1958	KC	A	103	.268	.417	295	79	11	3	9	3.1	32	44	18	48	3	19	3	425	41	6	9	5.7	.987	C-83
1959			55	.272	.444	162	44	11	1	5	3.1	20	25	17	26	0	8	4	228	25	3	5	5.4	.988	C-47
1960	2 teams	KC A (58G –.221) DET A (37G –.163)																							
″	total		95	.201	.296	294	59	7	0	7	2.4	25	33	27	45	1	8	2	436	41	8	1	5.5	.984	C-88
1961	DET	A	5	.083	.083	12	1	0	0	0	0.0	0	0	1	2	0	0	0	19	3	0	0	4.4	1.000	C-5
1962	NY	N	15	.195	.220	41	8	1	0	0	0.0	2	0	1	8	0	2	0	62	4	2	1	4.9	.971	C-14
10 yrs.			502	.238	.365	1495	356	49	9	41	2.7	135	179	115	242	4	46	11	2197	240	42	35	5.4	.983	C-458

Felix Chouinard

CHOUINARD, FELIX GEORGE BR TR 5′ 7″ 150 lbs.
B. Oct. 5, 1887, Hines, Ill. D. Apr. 28, 1955, Hines, Ill.

Year	Team	Lg	Games	BA	SA	AB	H	2B	3B	HR	HR%	R	RBI	BB	SO	SB	Pinch Hit AB	Pinch Hit H	PO	A	E	DP	TC/G	FA	G by Pos
1910	CHI	A	24	.195	.280	82	16	3	2	0	0.0	6	9	8		4	0	0	46	10	2	2	2.4	.966	OF-23, 2B-1
1911			14	.176	.176	17	3	0	0	0	0.0	3	0	0		0	0	0	11	4	2	1	2.1	.882	OF-4, 2B-4
1914	3 teams	PIT F (9G –.300) BKN F (32G –.253) BAL F (5G –.444)																							
″	total		46	.280	.356	118	33	2	2	1	0.8	12	12	4		4	11	2	54	16	5	4	2.5	.933	OF-25, 2B-4, SS-1
1915	BKN	F	4	.500	.500	4	2	0	0	0	0.0	1	2	0		0	1	0	1	0	0	0	0.5	1.000	OF-2
4 yrs.			88	.244	.317	221	54	5	4	1	0.5	22	23	12		8	12	2	112	30	9	7	2.4	.940	OF-54, 2B-9, SS-1

Harry Chozen

CHOZEN, HARRY (Choz) BR TR 5′ 9″ 195 lbs.
B. Sept. 27, 1915, Winnebago, Minn. D. Sept. 16, 1994, Houston, Tex.

Year	Team	Lg	Games	BA	SA	AB	H	2B	3B	HR	HR%	R	RBI	BB	SO	SB	Pinch Hit AB	Pinch Hit H	PO	A	E	DP	TC/G	FA	G by Pos
1937	CIN	N	1	.250	.250	4	1	0	0	0	0.0	0	0	0	0	0	0	0	4	1	1	0	6.0	.833	C-1

Neil Chrisley

CHRISLEY, BARBRA O'NEIL BL TR 6′ 3″ 187 lbs.
B. Dec. 16, 1931, Calhoun Falls, S. C.

Year	Team	Lg	Games	BA	SA	AB	H	2B	3B	HR	HR%	R	RBI	BB	SO	SB	Pinch Hit AB	Pinch Hit H	PO	A	E	DP	TC/G	FA	G by Pos
1957	WAS	A	26	.157	.235	51	8	2	1	0	0.0	6	3	7	7	0	13	2	16	1	4	0	1.9	.810	OF-11
1958			105	.215	.343	233	50	7	4	5	2.1	19	26	16	18	1	38	10	117	6	1	2	1.8	.992	OF-69, 3B-1
1959	DET	A	65	.132	.330	106	14	3	0	6	5.7	7	11	12	10	0	43	5	28	0	0	0	1.3	1.000	OF-21
1960			96	.255	.395	220	56	10	3	5	2.3	27	24	19	26	2	44	10	109	2	3	0	2.3	.974	OF-47, 1B-2
1961	MIL	N	10	.222	.222	9	2	0	0	0	0.0	1	0	1	1	0	9	2	0	0	0	0	0.0	—	
5 yrs.			302	.210	.349	619	130	22	8	16	2.6	60	64	55	62	3	147	29	270	9	8	2	1.9	.972	OF-148, 1B-2, 3B-1

Lloyd Christenbury

CHRISTENBURY, LLOYD REID (Low) BL TR 5′ 7″ 165 lbs.
B. Oct. 19, 1893, Mecklenburg County, N. C. D. Dec. 13, 1944, Birmingham, Ala.

Year	Team	Lg	Games	BA	SA	AB	H	2B	3B	HR	HR%	R	RBI	BB	SO	SB	Pinch Hit AB	Pinch Hit H	PO	A	E	DP	TC/G	FA	G by Pos
1919	BOS	N	7	.290	.323	31	9	1	0	0	0.0	5	4	2	2	0	0	0	14	2	1	1	2.4	.941	OF-7
1920			65	.208	.264	106	22	2	2	0	0.0	17	14	13	12	0	23	4	41	40	9	7	3.1	.900	OF-14, SS-7, 2B-6, 3B-2
1921			62	.352	.504	125	44	6	2	3	2.4	34	16	21	7	3	17	6	64	80	13	9	4.4	.917	2B-32, SS-2, 3B-2
1922			71	.250	.329	152	38	5	2	1	0.7	22	13	18	11	2	27	9	70	22	6	1	2.5	.939	OF-32, 2B-5, 3B-2
4 yrs.			205	.273	.365	414	113	14	6	4	1.0	78	47	54	32	5	67	19	189	144	29	18	3.3	.920	OF-53, 2B-43, SS-9, 3B-6

Bruce Christensen

CHRISTENSEN, BRUCE RAY BL TR 5′11″ 160 lbs.
B. Feb. 22, 1948, Madison, Wis.

Year	Team	Lg	Games	BA	SA	AB	H	2B	3B	HR	HR%	R	RBI	BB	SO	SB	Pinch Hit AB	Pinch Hit H	PO	A	E	DP	TC/G	FA	G by Pos
1971	CAL	A	29	.270	.286	63	17	1	0	0	0.0	4	3	6	5	0	7	2	25	55	1	13	3.4	.988	SS-24

Cuckoo Christensen

CHRISTENSEN, WALTER NEILS (Seacap) BL TL 5′ 6½″ 156 lbs.
B. Oct. 24, 1899, San Francisco, Calif. D. Dec. 20, 1984, Menlo Park, Calif.

Year	Team	Lg	Games	BA	SA	AB	H	2B	3B	HR	HR%	R	RBI	BB	SO	SB	Pinch Hit AB	Pinch Hit H	PO	A	E	DP	TC/G	FA	G by Pos
1926	CIN	N	114	.350	.438	329	115	15	7	0	0.0	41	41	40	18	8	18	7	170	6	4	2	1.9	.978	OF-93
1927			57	.254	.286	185	47	6	0	0	0.0	25	16	20	16	4	5	0	106	6	5	3	2.3	.957	OF-50
2 yrs.			171	.315	.383	514	162	21	7	0	0.0	66	57	60	34	12	23	7	276	12	9	5	2.1	.970	OF-143

John Christensen

CHRISTENSEN, JOHN LAWRENCE BR TR 6′ 3″ 205 lbs.
B. Sept. 15, 1960, Downey, Calif.

Year	Team	Lg	Games	BA	SA	AB	H	2B	3B	HR	HR%	R	RBI	BB	SO	SB	Pinch Hit AB	Pinch Hit H	PO	A	E	DP	TC/G	FA	G by Pos
1984	NY	N	5	.273	.455	11	3	2	0	0	0.0	2	3	1	2	0	1	1	1	0	1	0	0.4	.500	OF-5
1985			51	.186	.319	113	21	4	1	3	2.7	10	13	19	23	1	15	1	41	2	2	0	1.2	.956	OF-38
1987	SEA	A	53	.242	.348	132	32	6	1	2	1.5	19	12	12	28	2	13	2	60	3	0	1	1.2	1.000	OF-43, DH-8
1988	MIN	A	23	.263	.368	38	10	4	0	0	0.0	5	5	3	5	0	6	2	20	0	0	0	1.2	1.000	OF-17
4 yrs.			132	.224	.344	294	66	16	2	5	1.7	36	33	35	58	3	35	6	122	5	3	1	1.2	.977	OF-103, DH-8

Bob Christian

CHRISTIAN, ROBERT CHARLES BR TR 5′10″ 180 lbs.
B. Oct. 17, 1945, Chicago, Ill. D. Feb. 20, 1974, San Diego, Calif.

Year	Team	Lg	Games	BA	SA	AB	H	2B	3B	HR	HR%	R	RBI	BB	SO	SB	Pinch Hit AB	Pinch Hit H	PO	A	E	DP	TC/G	FA	G by Pos
1968	DET	A	3	.333	.667	3	1	1	0	0	0.0	0	0	0	0	0	1	0	3	0	0	0	1.5	1.000	1B-1, OF-1
1969	CHI	A	39	.217	.318	129	28	4	0	3	2.3	11	16	10	19	3	1	1	66	3	3	0	1.9	.958	OF-38
1970			12	.267	.467	15	4	0	0	1	6.7	3	3	1	4	0	9	3	2	0	0	0	0.5	1.000	OF-4
3 yrs.			54	.224	.340	147	33	5	0	4	2.7	14	19	11	23	3	11	4	71	3	3	0	1.8	.961	OF-43, 1B-1

Mark Christman

CHRISTMAN, MARQUETTE JOSEPH BR TR 5′11″ 175 lbs.
B. Oct. 21, 1913, Maplewood, Mo. D. Oct. 9, 1976, St. Louis, Mo.

Year	Team	Games	BA	SA	AB	H	2B	3B	HR	HR%	R	RBI	BB	SO	SB	Pinch Hit AB	Pinch Hit H	PO	A	E	DP	TC/G	FA	G by Pos
1938	DET A	95	.248	.302	318	79	6	4	1	0.3	35	44	27	21	5	0	0	132	212	10	31	3.9	.972	3B-69, SS-21
1939	2 teams	DET A (6G –.250)	STL A (79G –.216)																					
″	total	85	.218	.277	238	52	8	3	0	0.0	27	20	20	12	2	11	0	155	214	16	46	5.4	.958	SS-64, 3B-6, 2B-1
1943	STL A	98	.271	.351	336	91	11	5	2	0.6	31	35	19	19	0	3	0	279	172	3	41	4.8	.993	3B-37, SS-24, 1B-20, 2B-14
1944		148	.271	.353	547	148	25	1	6	1.1	56	83	47	37	5	0	0	205	317	15	36	3.6	.972	3B-145, 1B-3
1945		78	.277	.370	289	80	7	4	4	1.4	32	34	19	19	1	1	0	79	137	6	12	2.9	.973	3B-77
1946		128	.258	.321	458	118	22	2	1	0.2	40	41	22	29	0	6	1	138	308	13	44	3.7	.972	3B-77, SS-47
1947	WAS A	110	.222	.281	374	83	15	2	1	0.3	27	33	33	16	4	3	1	205	293	11	75	4.8	.978	SS-106, 2B-1
1948		120	.259	.318	409	106	17	2	1	0.2	38	40	25	19	0	8	2	225	277	17	60	4.4	.967	SS-102, 3B-9, 2B-3
1949		49	.214	.313	112	24	2	0	3	2.7	8	18	8	7	0	16	2	69	53	4	10	3.7	.968	3B-23, 1B-6, SS-4, 2B-1
9 yrs.		911	.253	.324	3081	781	113	23	19	0.6	294	348	220	179	17	48	6	1487	1983	95	355	4.1	.973	3B-443, SS-368, 1B-29, 2B-20
WORLD SERIES																								
1944	STL A	6	.091	.091	22	2	0	0	0	0.0	0	1	0	6	0	0	0	3	9	1	0	2.2	.923	3B-6

Steve Christmas

CHRISTMAS, STEPHEN RANDALL BL TR 6′ 190 lbs.
B. Dec. 9, 1957, Orlando, Fla.

Year	Team	Games	BA	SA	AB	H	2B	3B	HR	HR%	R	RBI	BB	SO	SB	Pinch Hit AB	Pinch Hit H	PO	A	E	DP	TC/G	FA	G by Pos
1983	CIN N	9	.059	.059	17	1	0	0	0	0.0	0	1	1	3	0	4	0	28	3	0	0	4.4	1.000	C-7
1984	CHI A	12	.364	.727	11	4	1	0	1	9.1	1	4	0	2	0	11	4	2	0	0	0	2.0	1.000	C-1
1986	CHI N	3	.111	.222	9	1	1	0	0	0.0	0	2	0	1	0	1	1	11	2	0	0	6.5	1.000	1B-1, C-1
3 yrs.		24	.162	.297	37	6	2	0	1	2.7	1	7	1	6	0	16	5	41	5	0	0	4.6	1.000	C-9, 1B-1

Joe Christopher

CHRISTOPHER, JOSEPH O'NEAL BR TR 5′10″ 175 lbs.
B. Dec. 13, 1935, Frederiksted, Virgin Islands.

Year	Team	Games	BA	SA	AB	H	2B	3B	HR	HR%	R	RBI	BB	SO	SB	Pinch Hit AB	Pinch Hit H	PO	A	E	DP	TC/G	FA	G by Pos
1959	PIT N	15	.000	.000	12	0	0	0	0	0.0	6	0	1	4	0	0	0	5	0	0	0	0.6	1.000	OF-9
1960		50	.232	.321	56	13	2	0	1	1.8	21	3	5	8	1	6	0	24	0	0	0	1.4	1.000	OF-17
1961		76	.263	.333	186	49	7	3	0	0.0	25	14	18	24	6	11	3	86	2	2	1	1.6	.978	OF-55
1962	NY N	119	.244	.362	271	66	10	2	6	2.2	36	32	35	42	11	18	3	133	5	4	4	1.5	.972	OF-94
1963		64	.221	.289	149	33	5	1	1	0.7	19	8	13	21	1	21	3	58	1	1	1	1.3	.983	OF-45
1964		154	.300	.466	543	163	26	8	16	2.9	78	76	48	92	6	9	3	251	10	7	2	1.8	.974	OF-145
1965		148	.249	.339	437	109	18	3	5	1.1	38	40	35	82	4	34	10	180	3	2	0	1.7	.989	OF-112
1966	BOS A	12	.077	.077	13	1	0	0	0	0.0	1	0	2	4	0	8	0	1	0	0	0	0.5	1.000	OF-2
8 yrs.		638	.260	.374	1667	434	68	17	29	1.7	224	173	157	277	29	107	22	738	21	16	8	1.6	.979	OF-479
WORLD SERIES																								
1960	PIT N	3	—	—	0	0	0	0	0	—	2	0	0	0	0	0	0	0	0	0	0	0.0	—	

Loyd Christopher

CHRISTOPHER, LOYD EUGENE BR TR 6′2″ 190 lbs.
Brother of Russ Christopher.
B. Dec. 31, 1919, Richmond, Calif. D. Sept. 5, 1991, Richmond, Calif.

Year	Team	Games	BA	SA	AB	H	2B	3B	HR	HR%	R	RBI	BB	SO	SB	Pinch Hit AB	Pinch Hit H	PO	A	E	DP	TC/G	FA	G by Pos
1945	2 teams	BOS A (8G –.286)	CHI N (1G –.000)																					
″	total	9	.286	.286	14	4	0	0	0	0.0	4	4	3	2	0	3	0	5	0	0	0	1.3	1.000	OF-4
1947	CHI A	7	.217	.304	23	5	0	1	0	0.0	1	0	2	4	0	0	0	19	1	0	1	2.9	1.000	OF-7
2 yrs.		16	.243	.297	37	9	0	1	0	0.0	5	4	5	6	0	3	0	24	1	0	1	2.3	1.000	OF-11

Hi Church

CHURCH, HIRAM LINCOLN
B. Nov. 23, 1863, Central Square, N. Y. D. Feb. 23, 1926, Jacksonville, Fla.

Year	Team	Games	BA	SA	AB	H	2B	3B	HR	HR%	R	RBI	BB	SO	SB	Pinch Hit AB	Pinch Hit H	PO	A	E	DP	TC/G	FA	G by Pos
1890	BKN AA	3	.111	.111	9	1	0	0	0	0.0	1		0			0	0	1	0	0	0	0.3	1.000	OF-3

John Churry

CHURRY, JOHN BR TR 5′9″ 172 lbs.
B. Nov. 26, 1900, Johnstown, Pa. D. Feb. 8, 1970, Zanesville, Ohio.

Year	Team	Games	BA	SA	AB	H	2B	3B	HR	HR%	R	RBI	BB	SO	SB	Pinch Hit AB	Pinch Hit H	PO	A	E	DP	TC/G	FA	G by Pos
1924	CHI N	6	.143	.286	7	1	1	0	0	0.0	0	0	2	0	0	2	0	7	1	0	0	2.7	1.000	C-3
1925		3	.500	.500	6	3	0	0	0	0.0	1	1	0	0	0	0	0	1	3	0	0	1.3	1.000	C-3
1926		2	.000	.000	4	0	0	0	0	0.0	0	0	1	2	0	1	0	5	0	0	0	5.0	1.000	C-1
1927		1	1.000	1.000	1	1	0	0	0	0.0	0	0	0	0	0	0	0	2	0	0	0	2.0	1.000	C-1
4 yrs.		12	.278	.333	18	5	1	0	0	0.0	1	1	3	2	0	3	0	15	4	0	0	2.4	1.000	C-8

Larry Ciaffone

CIAFFONE, LAWRENCE THOMAS (Symphony) BR TR 5′9½″ 185 lbs.
B. Aug. 17, 1924, Brooklyn, N. Y. D. Dec. 14, 1991, Brooklyn, N. Y.

Year	Team	Games	BA	SA	AB	H	2B	3B	HR	HR%	R	RBI	BB	SO	SB	Pinch Hit AB	Pinch Hit H	PO	A	E	DP	TC/G	FA	G by Pos
1951	STL N	5	.000	.000	5	0	0	0	0	0.0	0	0	1	2	0	3	0	1	0	0	0	1.0	1.000	OF-1

Archi Cianfrocco

CIANFROCCO, ANGELO DOMINIC BR TR 6′5″ 200 lbs.
B. Oct. 6, 1966, Rome, N. Y.

Year	Team	Games	BA	SA	AB	H	2B	3B	HR	HR%	R	RBI	BB	SO	SB	Pinch Hit AB	Pinch Hit H	PO	A	E	DP	TC/G	FA	G by Pos
1992	MON N	86	.241	.358	232	56	5	2	6	2.6	25	30	11	66	3	10	2	387	66	8	26	5.8	.983	1B-56, 3B-19, OF-5
1993	2 teams	MON N (12G –.235)	SD N (84G –.244)																					
″	total	96	.243	.416	296	72	11	2	12	4.1	30	48	17	69	2	2	2	243	97	10	29	3.3	.971	3B-64, 1B-42
1994	SD N	59	.219	.356	146	32	8	0	4	2.7	9	13	3	39	2	12	2	58	67	7	7	2.4	.947	3B-37, 1B-16, SS-1
1995		51	.263	.449	118	31	7	0	5	4.2	22	31	11	28	0	10	4	112	50	3	15	2.8	.982	1B-30, SS-15, OF-7, 3B-3, 2B-3
4 yrs.		292	.241	.393	792	191	31	4	27	3.4	86	122	42	202	7	34	10	800	280	28	77	3.7	.975	1B-144, 3B-123, SS-16, OF-12, 2B-3

Darryl Cias

CIAS, DARRYL RICHARD BR TR 5′11″ 188 lbs.
B. Apr. 23, 1957, New York, N. Y.

Year	Team	Games	BA	SA	AB	H	2B	3B	HR	HR%	R	RBI	BB	SO	SB	Pinch Hit AB	Pinch Hit H	PO	A	E	DP	TC/G	FA	G by Pos
1983	OAK A	19	.333	.389	18	6	1	0	0	0.0	1	1	2	4	1	0	0	27	2	1	1	1.6	.967	C-19

Joe Cicero

CICERO, JOSEPH FRANCIS (Dode) BR TR 5′8″ 167 lbs.
B. Nov. 18, 1910, Atlantic City, N. J. D. Mar. 30, 1983, Clearwater, Fla.

Year	Team	Games	BA	SA	AB	H	2B	3B	HR	HR%	R	RBI	BB	SO	SB	Pinch Hit AB	Pinch Hit H	PO	A	E	DP	TC/G	FA	G by Pos
1929	BOS A	10	.313	.500	32	10	2	2	0	0.0	6	4	0	2	0	3	2	17	0	0	0	2.4	1.000	OF-7
1930		18	.167	.333	30	5	1	2	0	0.0	5	4	1	5	0	11	1	2	5	2	1	1.3	.778	OF-5, 3B-2
1945	PHI A	12	.158	.158	19	3	0	0	0	0.0	3	0	1	6	0	2	0	7	0	0	0	1.0	1.000	OF-7
3 yrs.		40	.222	.358	81	18	3	4	0	0.0	14	8	2	13	0	16	3	26	5	2	1	1.6	.939	OF-19, 3B-2

Ted Cieslak

CIESLAK, THADDEUS WALTER BR TR 5′10″ 175 lbs.
B. Nov. 22, 1916, Milwaukee, Wis.

Year	Team	Games	BA	SA	AB	H	2B	3B	HR	HR%	R	RBI	BB	SO	SB	Pinch Hit AB	Pinch Hit H	PO	A	E	DP	TC/G	FA	G by Pos
1944	PHI N	85	.245	.318	220	54	10	0	2	0.9	18	11	21	17	1	30	5	46	73	15	1	2.5	.888	3B-48, OF-5

Al Cihocki

CIHOCKI, ALBERT JOSEPH BR TR 5′11″ 185 lbs.
B. May 7, 1924, Nanticoke, Pa.

Year	Team	Games	BA	SA	AB	H	2B	3B	HR	HR%	R	RBI	BB	SO	SB	Pinch Hit AB	Pinch Hit H	PO	A	E	DP	TC/G	FA	G by Pos
1945	CLE A	92	.212	.265	283	60	9	3	0	0.0	21	24	11	48	2	0	0	154	208	15	42	4.1	.960	SS-41, 3B-29, 2B-23

Ed Cihocki

CIHOCKI, EDWARD JOSEPH (Cy) BR TR 5′8″ 163 lbs.
B. May 9, 1907, Wilmington, Del. D. Nov. 9, 1987, Newark, Del.

Year	Team	Games	BA	SA	AB	H	2B	3B	HR	HR%	R	RBI	BB	SO	SB	Pinch Hit AB	Pinch Hit H	PO	A	E	DP	TC/G	FA	G by Pos
1932	PHI A	1	.000	.000	1	0	0	0	0	0.0	0	0	0	0	0	1	0	0	0	0	0	0.0	—	
1933		33	.144	.227	97	14	2	3	0	0.0	6	9	7	16	0	2	0	45	74	13	17	4.4	.902	SS-28, 3B-1, 2B-1
2 yrs.		34	.143	.224	98	14	2	3	0	0.0	6	9	7	16	0	3	0	45	74	13	17	4.4	.902	SS-28, 3B-1, 2B-1

Gino Cimoli

CIMOLI, GINO NICHOLAS BR TR 6′1″ 180 lbs.
B. Dec. 18, 1929, San Francisco, Calif.

Year	Team	Games	BA	SA	AB	H	2B	3B	HR	HR%	R	RBI	BB	SO	SB	Pinch Hit AB	Pinch Hit H	PO	A	E	DP	TC/G	FA	G by Pos
1956	BKN N	73	.111	.139	36	4	1	0	0	0.0	3	4	1	8	1	4	1	35	0	2	0	0.6	.946	OF-62
1957		142	.293	.410	532	156	22	5	10	1.9	88	57	39	86	3	3	2	265	11	6	2	2.0	.979	OF-138
1958	LA N	109	.246	.366	325	80	6	3	9	2.8	35	27	18	49	3	8	0	180	10	5	2	1.9	.974	OF-104
1959	STL N	143	.279	.430	519	145	40	7	8	1.5	61	72	37	83	7	3	1	267	12	6	2	2.0	.979	OF-141
1960	PIT N	101	.267	.339	307	82	14	4	0	0.0	36	28	32	43	1	10	2	181	5	7	1	2.1	.964	OF-91
1961	2 teams	PIT N (21G –.299) MIL N (37G –.197)																						
″	total	58	.234	.337	184	43	8	1	3	1.6	16	10	13	28	1	7	1	99	1	2	2	2.0	.980	OF-50
1962	KC A	152	.275	.420	550	151	20	**15**	10	1.8	67	71	40	89	2	7	2	231	8	8	2	1.7	.968	OF-147
1963		145	.263	.363	529	139	19	11	4	0.8	56	48	39	72	3	9	4	256	14	4	3	2.0	.985	OF-136
1964	2 teams	KC A (4G –.000) BAL A (38G –.138)																						
″	total	42	.119	.224	67	8	3	2	0	0.0	7	3	2	14	0	6	1	31	0	3	0	0.9	.912	OF-39
1965	CAL A	4	.000	.000	5	0	0	0	0	0.0	1	1	0	2	0	3	0	2	0	0	0	2.0	1.000	OF-1
10 yrs.		969	.265	.383	3054	808	133	48	44	1.4	370	321	221	474	21	60	14	1547	61	43	14	1.8	.974	OF-909
WORLD SERIES																								
1956	BKN N	1	—	—	0	0	0	0	0	—	0	0	0	0	0	0	0	1	0	0	0	1.0	1.000	OF-1
1960	PIT N	7	.250	.250	20	5	0	0	0	0.0	4	1	2	4	0	1	1	5	0	0	0	0.8	1.000	OF-6
2 yrs.		8	.250	.250	20	5	0	0	0	0.0	4	1	2	4	0	1	1	6	0	0	0	0.9	1.000	OF-7

Frank Cipriani

CIPRIANI, FRANK DOMINICK BR TR 6′ 180 lbs.
B. Apr. 14, 1941, Buffalo, N. Y.

Year	Team	Games	BA	SA	AB	H	2B	3B	HR	HR%	R	RBI	BB	SO	SB	Pinch Hit AB	Pinch Hit H	PO	A	E	DP	TC/G	FA	G by Pos
1961	KC A	13	.250	.250	36	9	0	0	0	0.0	2	2	2	4	0	2	0	20	0	0	0	1.8	1.000	OF-11

Jeff Cirillo

CIRILLO, JEFFREY HOWARD BR TR 6′2″ 190 lbs.
B. Sept. 23, 1969, Pasadena, Calif.

Year	Team	Games	BA	SA	AB	H	2B	3B	HR	HR%	R	RBI	BB	SO	SB	Pinch Hit AB	Pinch Hit H	PO	A	E	DP	TC/G	FA	G by Pos
1994	MIL A	39	.238	.381	126	30	9	0	3	2.4	17	12	11	16	0	3	1	23	60	3	7	2.3	.965	3B-37, 2B-1
1995		125	.277	.442	328	91	19	4	9	2.7	57	39	47	42	7	4	0	114	230	15	38	2.6	.958	3B-108, 2B-25, 1B-3, SS-2
2 yrs.		164	.267	.425	454	121	28	4	12	2.6	74	51	58	58	7	7	1	137	290	18	45	2.5	.960	3B-145, 2B-26, 1B-3, SS-2

George Cisar

CISAR, GEORGE JOSEPH BR TR 6′ 175 lbs.
B. Aug. 25, 1912, Chicago, Ill.

Year	Team	Games	BA	SA	AB	H	2B	3B	HR	HR%	R	RBI	BB	SO	SB	Pinch Hit AB	Pinch Hit H	PO	A	E	DP	TC/G	FA	G by Pos
1937	BKN N	20	.207	.207	29	6	0	0	0	0.0	8	4	2	6	3	1	0	14	0	0	0	1.1	1.000	OF-13

Bill Cissell

CISSELL, CHALMER WILLIAM BR TR 5′11″ 170 lbs.
B. Jan. 3, 1904, Perryville, Mo. D. Mar. 15, 1949, Chicago, Ill.

Year	Team	Games	BA	SA	AB	H	2B	3B	HR	HR%	R	RBI	BB	SO	SB	Pinch Hit AB	Pinch Hit H	PO	A	E	DP	TC/G	FA	G by Pos
1928	CHI A	125	.260	.330	443	115	22	3	1	0.2	66	60	29	41	18	1	1	255	360	41	77	5.3	.938	SS-123
1929		152	.280	.387	618	173	27	12	5	0.8	83	62	28	53	26	0	0	357	459	55	90	5.7	.937	SS-152
1930		141	.270	.363	562	152	28	9	2	0.4	82	48	28	32	16	1	0	290	422	41	69	5.4	.946	2B-106, 3B-24, SS-10
1931		109	.220	.284	409	90	13	5	1	0.2	42	46	16	26	18	0	0	225	302	29	58	5.2	.948	SS-83, 2B-23, 3B-1
1932	2 teams	CHI A (12G –.256) CLE A (131G –.320)																						
″	total	143	.315	.437	584	184	36	7	7	1.2	85	98	29	25	18	0	0	372	509	36	92	6.2	.961	2B-129, SS-18
1933	CLE A	112	.230	.340	409	94	21	3	6	1.5	53	33	31	29	6	2	1	238	351	28	47	5.7	.955	2B-62, SS-46, 3B-1
1934	BOS A	102	.267	.346	416	111	13	4	4	1.0	71	44	28	23	11	2	1	287	292	27	65	5.8	.955	2B-96, SS-7, 3B-2
1937	PHI A	34	.265	.350	117	31	7	0	1	0.9	15	14	17	10	0	1	0	87	115	8	17	6.4	.962	2B-33
1938	NY N	38	.268	.349	149	40	6	0	2	1.3	19	18	6	11	1	0	0	90	138	7	20	6.0	.970	2B-33, 3B-6
9 yrs.		956	.267	.360	3707	990	173	43	29	0.8	516	423	212	250	114	7	3	2201	2948	272	535	5.7	.950	2B-482, SS-439, 3B-34

Moose Clabaugh

CLABAUGH, JOHN WILLIAM BL TR 6′ 185 lbs.
B. Nov. 13, 1901, Albany, Mo. D. July 11, 1984, Tucson, Ariz.

Year	Team	Games	BA	SA	AB	H	2B	3B	HR	HR%	R	RBI	BB	SO	SB	Pinch Hit AB	Pinch Hit H	PO	A	E	DP	TC/G	FA	G by Pos
1926	BKN N	11	.071	.143	14	1	1	0	0	0.0	2	1	0	1	0	9	1	3	0	2	0	2.5	.600	OF-2

Bobby Clack

CLACK, ROBERT S. (Gentlemanly Bobby) BR TR 5′9″ 153 lbs.
Born Robert S. Clark.
B. June 1850, England D. Oct. 22, 1933, Danvers, Mass.

Year	Team	Games	BA	SA	AB	H	2B	3B	HR	HR%	R	RBI	BB	SO	SB	Pinch Hit AB	Pinch Hit H	PO	A	E	DP	TC/G	FA	G by Pos
1876	CIN N	32	.161	.178	118	19	0	1	0	0.0	10	5	5	12		0	0	105	33	26	1	4.8	.841	OF-17, 2B-8, 1B-5, 3B-3, P-1

Dave Claire

CLAIRE, DAVID MATTHEW BR TR 5′8″ 164 lbs.
B. Nov. 17, 1897, Ludington, Mich. D. Jan. 7, 1956, Las Vegas, Nev.

Year	Team	Games	BA	SA	AB	H	2B	3B	HR	HR%	R	RBI	BB	SO	SB	Pinch Hit AB	Pinch Hit H	PO	A	E	DP	TC/G	FA	G by Pos
1920	DET A	3	.143	.143	7	1	0	0	0	0.0	1	0	0	0	0	0	0	2	6	2	0	3.3	.800	SS-3

Al Clancy

CLANCY, ALBERT HARRISON BR TR 5′10½″ 175 lbs.
B. Aug. 14, 1888, Santa Fe, N. M. D. Oct. 17, 1951, Las Cruces, N. M.

Year	Team	Games	BA	SA	AB	H	2B	3B	HR	HR%	R	RBI	BB	SO	SB	Pinch Hit AB	Pinch Hit H	PO	A	E	DP	TC/G	FA	G by Pos
1911	STL A	3	.000	.000	5	0	0	0	0	0.0	0	0	0		0	1	0	1	3	1	1	2.5	.800	3B-2

Bill Clancy

CLANCY, WILLIAM EDWARD BR TR 6′2″ 180 lbs.
B. Apr. 12, 1879, Redfield, N. Y. D. Feb. 10, 1948, Oriskany, N. Y.

Year	Team	Games	BA	SA	AB	H	2B	3B	HR	HR%	R	RBI	BB	SO	SB	Pinch Hit AB	Pinch Hit H	PO	A	E	DP	TC/G	FA	G by Pos
1905	PIT N	56	.229	.330	227	52	11	3	2	0.9	23	34	4		3	0	0	554	27	10	30	10.6	.983	1B-52, OF-4

Bud Clancy

CLANCY, JOHN WILLIAM BL TL 6′ 170 lbs.
B. Sept. 15, 1900, Odell, Ill. D. Sept. 26, 1968, Ottumwa, Iowa.

Year	Team	Games	BA	SA	AB	H	2B	3B	HR	HR%	R	RBI	BB	SO	SB	Pinch Hit AB	Pinch Hit H	PO	A	E	DP	TC/G	FA	G by Pos
1924	CHI A	13	.257	.286	35	9	1	0	0	0.0	5	6	3	2	3	4	1	69	3	3	4	9.4	.960	1B-8
1925		4	.000	.000	3	0	0	0	0	0.0	0	0	1	0	0	3	0	0	0	0	0	0.0	—	
1926		12	.342	.500	38	13	2	2	0	0.0	3	7	1	1	0	2	0	104	6	1	11	11.1	.991	1B-10
1927		130	.300	.373	464	139	21	2	3	0.6	46	53	24	24	4	5	1	1184	81	11	76	10.4	.991	1B-123
1928		130	.271	.368	487	132	19	11	2	0.4	64	37	42	25	6	2	0	1175	93	12	104	10.0	.991	1B-128

Bud Clancy *continued*

Year	Team	Games	BA	SA	AB	H	2B	3B	HR	HR%	R	RBI	BB	SO	SB	Pinch Hit AB	Pinch Hit H	PO	A	E	DP	TC/G	FA	G by Pos
1929		92	.283	.403	290	82	14	6	3	1.0	36	45	16	19	3	16	4	647	49	6	47	9.5	.991	1B-74
1930		68	.244	.342	234	57	8	3	3	1.3	28	27	12	18	3	7	1	583	24	3	38	9.7	.995	1B-63
1932	BKN N	53	.306	.347	196	60	4	2	0	0.0	14	16	6	13	0	0	0	524	40	2	55	10.7	.996	1B-53
1934	PHI N	20	.245	.306	49	12	0	0	1	2.0	8	7	6	4	0	9	2	99	4	0	11	10.3	1.000	1B-10
9 yrs.		522	.281	.368	1796	504	69	26	12	0.7	204	198	111	106	19	48	9	4385	300	38	346	10.1	.992	1B-469

Uke Clanton

CLANTON, EUCAL (Cat) BL TL 5′ 8″ 165 lbs.
B. Feb. 19, 1898, Powell, Mo. D. Feb. 24, 1960, Antlers, Okla.

Year	Team	Games	BA	SA	AB	H	2B	3B	HR	HR%	R	RBI	BB	SO	SB	Pinch Hit AB	Pinch Hit H	PO	A	E	DP	TC/G	FA	G by Pos
1922	CLE A	1	.000	.000	1	0	0	0	0	0.0	0	0	0	1	0	0	0	1	0	1	1	2.0	.500	1B-1

Aaron Clapp

CLAPP, AARON BRONSON TR 5′ 8″ 175 lbs.
Brother of John Clapp.
B. July 1856, Ithaca, N. Y. D. Jan. 13, 1914, Sayre, Pa.

Year	Team	Games	BA	SA	AB	H	2B	3B	HR	HR%	R	RBI	BB	SO	SB	Pinch Hit AB	Pinch Hit H	PO	A	E	DP	TC/G	FA	G by Pos
1879	TRO N	36	.267	.370	146	39	9	3	0	0.0	24	18	6	10		0	0	279	7	25	10	8.6	.920	1B-25, OF-11

John Clapp

CLAPP, JOHN EDGAR BR TR 5′ 7″ 194 lbs.
Brother of Aaron Clapp.
B. July 17, 1851, Ithaca, N. Y. D. Dec. 18, 1904, Ithaca, N. Y.
Manager 1878–81, 1883.

Year	Team	Games	BA	SA	AB	H	2B	3B	HR	HR%	R	RBI	BB	SO	SB	Pinch Hit AB	Pinch Hit H	PO	A	E	DP	TC/G	FA	G by Pos
1876	STL N	64	.305	.332	298	91	4	2	0	0.0	60	29	8	2		0	0	335	56	58	5	6.8	.871	C-61, OF-4, 2B-1
1877		60	.318	.388	255	81	6	6	0	0.0	47	34	8	6		0	0	285	45	42	2	5.8	.887	C-53, OF-10, 1B-1
1878	IND N	63	.304	.357	263	80	10	2	0	0.0	42	29	13	8		0	0	234	33	21	6	4.2	.927	OF-44, 1B-12, C-9, SS-3, 2B-1
1879	BUF N	70	.264	.349	292	77	12	5	1	0.3	47	36	11	11		0	0	297	60	40	4	5.7	.899	C-63, OF-7
1880	CIN N	80	.282	.365	323	91	16	4	1	0.3	33	20	21	10		0	0	436	121	63	5	7.5	.898	C-73, OF-10
1881	CLE N	68	.253	.314	261	66	12	2	0	0.0	47	25	**35**	6		0	0	248	79	44	10	5.4	.881	C-48, OF-21
1883	NY N	20	.178	.178	73	13	0	0	0	0.0	6		5	4		0	0	87	32	15	1	6.4	.888	C-16, OF-5
7 yrs.		425	.283	.344	1765	499	60	21	2	0.1	282	173	101	47		0	0	1922	426	283	33	6.0	.892	C-323, OF-101, 1B-13, SS-3, 2B-2

Doug Clarey

CLAREY, DOUGLAS WILLIAM BR TR 6′ 180 lbs.
B. Apr. 20, 1954, Los Angeles, Calif.

Year	Team	Games	BA	SA	AB	H	2B	3B	HR	HR%	R	RBI	BB	SO	SB	Pinch Hit AB	Pinch Hit H	PO	A	E	DP	TC/G	FA	G by Pos
1976	STL N	9	.250	1.000	4	1	0	0	1	25.0	2	2	0	1	0	2	1	3	1	0	0	0.6	1.000	2B-7

Allie Clark

CLARK, ALFRED ALOYSIUS BR TR 6′ 195 lbs.
B. June 16, 1923, South Amboy, N. J.

Year	Team	Games	BA	SA	AB	H	2B	3B	HR	HR%	R	RBI	BB	SO	SB	Pinch Hit AB	Pinch Hit H	PO	A	E	DP	TC/G	FA	G by Pos
1947	NY A	24	.373	.493	67	25	5	0	1	1.5	9	14	5	2	0	7	2	36	0	0	0	2.3	1.000	OF-16
1948	CLE A	81	.310	.443	271	84	5	2	9	3.3	43	38	23	13	0	11	3	115	9	3	3	1.8	.976	OF-65, 3B-5, 1B-1
1949		35	.176	.270	74	13	4	0	1	1.4	8	9	4	7	0	19	2	15	1	0	0	0.9	1.000	OF-17, 1B-1
1950		59	.215	.374	163	35	6	1	6	3.7	19	21	11	10	0	15	2	75	2	1	0	1.9	.987	OF-41
1951	2 teams	CLE A (3G –.300) PHI A (56G –.248)																						
″	total	59	.251	.421	171	43	12	1	5	2.9	23	25	16	9	2	13	4	72	22	4	4	2.2	.959	OF-35, 3B-10
1952	PHI A	71	.274	.452	186	51	12	0	7	3.8	23	29	10	19	0	21	7	82	2	1	0	1.7	.988	OF-48, 1B-2
1953	2 teams	PHI A (20G –.203) CHI A (9G –.067)																						
″	total	29	.180	.326	89	16	4	0	3	3.4	6	13	3	10	0	9	1	39	2	0	2	2.0	1.000	OF-20, 1B-1
7 yrs.		358	.262	.410	1021	267	48	4	32	3.1	131	149	72	70	2	95	21	434	38	9	9	1.8	.981	OF-242, 3B-15, 1B-5
WORLD SERIES																								
1947	NY A	3	.500	.500	2	1	0	0	0	0.0	1	1	1	0	0	2	1	2	0	0	0	2.0	1.000	OF-1
1948	CLE A	1	.000	.000	3	0	0	0	0	0.0	0	0	0	1	0	0	0	2	0	0	0	2.0	1.000	OF-1
2 yrs.		4	.200	.200	5	1	0	0	0	0.0	1	1	1	1	0	2	1	4	0	0	0	2.0	1.000	OF-2

Bill Clark

CLARK, WILLIAM WINFIELD (Win) BR TR 5′10″ 175 lbs.
B. Apr. 11, 1875, Circleville, Ohio D. Apr. 15, 1959, Los Angeles, Calif.

Year	Team	Games	BA	SA	AB	H	2B	3B	HR	HR%	R	RBI	BB	SO	SB	Pinch Hit AB	Pinch Hit H	PO	A	E	DP	TC/G	FA	G by Pos
1897	LOU N	7	.231	.231	26	6	0	0	0	0.0	2	2	1		1	0	0	12	16	6	1	4.9	.824	2B-3, P-3, 3B-1

Bob Clark

CLARK, ROBERT H. BR TR 5′10″ 175 lbs.
B. May 18, 1863, Covington, Ky. D. Aug. 21, 1919, Covington, Ky.

Year	Team	Games	BA	SA	AB	H	2B	3B	HR	HR%	R	RBI	BB	SO	SB	Pinch Hit AB	Pinch Hit H	PO	A	E	DP	TC/G	FA	G by Pos
1886	BKN AA	71	.216	.260	269	58	8	2	0	0.0	37		17			0	0	246	106	64	11	5.7	.846	C-44, OF-17, SS-12
1887		48	.266	.294	177	47	3	1	0	0.0	24		7		15	0	0	201	66	43	7	6.5	.861	C-45, OF-3
1888		45	.240	.333	150	36	5	3	1	0.7	23	20	9		11	0	0	211	62	37	6	6.9	.881	C-36, OF-8, 1B-1
1889		53	.275	.324	182	50	5	2	0	0.0	32	22	26	7	18	0	0	275	86	54	4	7.8	.870	C-53
1890	BKN N	43	.219	.278	151	33	3	3	0	0.0	24	15	15	8	10	0	0	165	40	40	5	5.7	.837	C-42, OF-1
1891	CIN N	16	.111	.111	54	6	0	0	0	0.0	2	3	6	9	3	0	0	50	16	10	1	4.8	.868	C-16
1893	LOU N	12	.107	.143	28	3	1	0	0	0.0	3	3	5	5	0	0	0	10	11	1	1	1.8	.955	C-10, SS-1, OF-1
7 yrs.		288	.230	.280	1011	233	25	11	1	0.1	145	63	85	29	57	0	0	1158	387	249	35	6.2	.861	C-246, OF-30, SS-13, 1B-1

Bobby Clark

CLARK, ROBERT CALE BR TR 6′ 190 lbs.
B. June 13, 1955, Sacramento, Calif.

Year	Team	Games	BA	SA	AB	H	2B	3B	HR	HR%	R	RBI	BB	SO	SB	Pinch Hit AB	Pinch Hit H	PO	A	E	DP	TC/G	FA	G by Pos
1979	CAL A	19	.296	.463	54	16	2	2	1	1.9	8	5	5	11	1	0	0	41	4	1	0	2.4	.978	OF-19
1980		78	.230	.333	261	60	10	1	5	1.9	26	23	11	42	0	7	3	213	6	4	2	2.9	.982	OF-77
1981		34	.250	.432	88	22	2	1	4	4.5	12	19	7	18	0	3	0	66	5	0	0	2.1	1.000	OF-34
1982		102	.211	.289	90	19	1	0	2	2.2	11	8	0	29	1	1	0	88	2	0	0	0.9	1.000	OF-102
1983		76	.231	.354	212	49	9	1	5	2.4	17	21	9	45	0	1	0	122	0	0	0	1.6	1.000	OF-72, DH-2, 3B-1
1984	MIL A	58	.260	.361	169	44	7	2	2	1.2	17	16	16	35	1	5	3	106	0	2	0	1.9	.981	OF-56
1985		29	.226	.258	93	21	3	0	0	0.0	6	8	7	19	1	3	0	72	1	0	0	2.7	1.000	OF-27
7 yrs.		396	.239	.347	967	231	34	7	19	2.0	97	100	55	199	4	20	6	708	18	7	2	1.9	.990	OF-387, DH-2, 3B-1
LEAGUE CHAMPIONSHIP SERIES																								
1979	CAL A	1	.000	.000	3	0	0	0	0	0.0	0	0	0	2	0	0	0	3	0	0	0	3.0	1.000	OF-1
1982		2	—	—	0	0	0	0	0	—	0	0	0	0	0	0	0	1	0	0	0	0.5	1.000	OF-2
2 yrs.		3	.000	.000	3	0	0	0	0	0.0	0	0	0	2	0	0	0	4	0	0	0	1.3	1.000	OF-3

Cap Clark

CLARK, JOHN CARROLL BL TR 5'11" 180 lbs.
B. Sept. 19, 1906, Snow Camp, N. C. D. Feb. 16, 1957, Fayetteville, N. C.

Year	Team	Lg	Games	BA	SA	AB	H	2B	3B	HR	HR%	R	RBI	BB	SO	SB	Pinch Hit AB	Pinch Hit H	PO	A	E	DP	TC/G	FA	G by Pos
1938	PHI	N	52	.257	.297	74	19	1	1	0	0.0	11	4	9	10	0	20	5	65	8	5	2	2.7	.936	C-29

Danny Clark

CLARK, DANIEL CURREN BL TR 5' 9" 167 lbs.
B. Jan. 18, 1894, Meridian, Miss. D. May 23, 1937, Meridian, Miss.

Year	Team	Lg	Games	BA	SA	AB	H	2B	3B	HR	HR%	R	RBI	BB	SO	SB	Pinch Hit AB	Pinch Hit H	PO	A	E	DP	TC/G	FA	G by Pos
1922	DET	A	83	.292	.432	185	54	11	3	3	1.6	31	26	15	11	1	**36**	8	78	100	10	16	4.3	.947	2B-38, OF-5, 3B-1
1924	BOS	A	104	.277	.385	325	90	23	3	2	0.6	36	54	50	18	4	10	1	88	173	15	8	3.0	.946	3B-93
1927	STL	N	58	.236	.319	72	17	2	2	0	0.0	8	13	8	7	0	40	**12**	25	1	2	1	3.1	.929	OF-9
3 yrs.			245	.277	.392	582	161	36	8	5	0.9	75	93	73	36	5	86	21	191	274	27	25	3.4	.945	3B-94, 2B-38, OF-14

Dave Clark

CLARK, DAVID EARL BL TR 6' 2" 200 lbs.
B. Sept. 3, 1962, Tupelo, Miss.

Year	Team	Lg	Games	BA	SA	AB	H	2B	3B	HR	HR%	R	RBI	BB	SO	SB	Pinch Hit AB	Pinch Hit H	PO	A	E	DP	TC/G	FA	G by Pos
1986	CLE	A	18	.276	.448	58	16	1	0	3	5.2	10	9	7	11	1	0	0	26	0	0	0	1.5	1.000	OF-10, DH-7
1987			29	.207	.368	87	18	5	0	3	3.4	11	12	2	24	1	6	0	24	1	0	0	1.0	1.000	OF-13, DH-12
1988			63	.263	.359	156	41	4	1	3	1.9	11	18	17	28	0	19	4	36	0	2	0	0.8	.947	DH-27, OF-23
1989			102	.237	.379	253	60	12	0	8	3.2	21	29	30	63	0	29	7	27	0	1	0	0.4	.964	DH-55, OF-21
1990	CHI	N	84	.275	.409	171	47	4	2	5	2.9	22	20	8	40	7	42	11	60	2	0	0	1.6	1.000	OF-39
1991	KC	A	11	.200	.200	10	2	0	0	0	0.0	1	1	1	1	0	10	2	0	0	0	0	0.0		OF-1, DH-1
1992	PIT	N	23	.212	.394	33	7	0	0	2	6.1	3	7	6	8	0	11	2	10	0	0	0	1.3	1.000	OF-8
1993			110	.271	.444	277	75	11	2	11	4.0	43	46	38	58	1	22	3	132	3	6	1	1.5	.957	OF-91
1994			86	.296	.489	223	66	11	1	10	4.5	37	46	22	48	2	24	8	107	5	3	1	2.0	.974	OF-57
1995			77	.281	.372	196	55	6	0	4	2.0	30	24	24	38	3	26	9	98	1	4	0	1.7	.961	OF-61
10 yrs.			603	.264	.410	1464	387	54	6	49	3.3	189	212	155	319	15	189	46	520	12	16	2	1.3	.971	OF-324, DH-102

Earl Clark

CLARK, BAILEY EARL BR TR 5'10" 160 lbs.
B. Nov. 6, 1907, Washington, D. C. D. Jan. 16, 1938, Washington, D. C.

Year	Team	Lg	Games	BA	SA	AB	H	2B	3B	HR	HR%	R	RBI	BB	SO	SB	Pinch Hit AB	Pinch Hit H	PO	A	E	DP	TC/G	FA	G by Pos
1927	BOS	N	13	.273	.295	44	12	1	0	0	0.0	6	3	2	4	0	0	0	30	0	0	0	2.3	1.000	OF-13
1928			27	.304	.402	112	34	9	1	0	0.0	18	10	4	8	0	1	0	77	0	1	0	2.9	.987	OF-27
1929			84	.315	.394	279	88	13	3	1	0.4	43	30	12	30	6	4	1	216	7	5	3	3.1	.978	OF-74
1930			82	.296	.408	233	69	11	3	3	1.3	29	28	7	22	3	17	7	165	3	4	0	2.7	.977	OF-63
1931			16	.220	.260	50	11	2	0	0	0.0	8	4	7	4	1	2	0	30	2	1	0	2.4	.970	OF-14
1932			50	.250	.295	44	11	2	0	0	0.0	11	4	2	7	1	16	5	19	2	0	1	1.3	1.000	OF-16
1933			7	.348	.391	23	8	1	0	0	0.0	3	1	2	1	0	0	0	10	0	0	0	1.4	1.000	OF-7
1934	STL	A	13	.171	.220	41	7	2	0	0	0.0	4	1	1	3	0	4	0	22	0	0	0	2.4	1.000	OF-9
8 yrs.			292	.291	.372	826	240	41	7	4	0.5	122	81	37	79	11	44	13	569	14	11	4	2.7	.981	OF-223

Fred Clark

CLARK, ALFRED ROBERT BL TL 5'11" 170 lbs.
B. July 16, 1873, San Francisco, Calif. D. July 26, 1956, Ogden, Utah.

Year	Team	Lg	Games	BA	SA	AB	H	2B	3B	HR	HR%	R	RBI	BB	SO	SB	Pinch Hit AB	Pinch Hit H	PO	A	E	DP	TC/G	FA	G by Pos
1902	CHI	N	12	.186	.209	43	8	1	0	0	0.0	1	2	4		1	0	0	115	6	8	9	10.8	.938	1B-12

Glen Clark

CLARK, GLEN ESTER BB TR 6' 1" 190 lbs.
B. Mar. 7, 1941, Austin, Tex.

Year	Team	Lg	Games	BA	SA	AB	H	2B	3B	HR	HR%	R	RBI	BB	SO	SB	Pinch Hit AB	Pinch Hit H	PO	A	E	DP	TC/G	FA	G by Pos
1967	ATL	N	4	.000	.000	4	0	0	0	0	0.0	0	0	0	1	0	4	0	0	0	0	0	0.0	—	

Jack Clark

CLARK, JACK ANTHONY (The Ripper) BR TR 6' 2" 205 lbs.
B. Nov. 10, 1955, New Brighton, Pa.

Year	Team	Lg	Games	BA	SA	AB	H	2B	3B	HR	HR%	R	RBI	BB	SO	SB	Pinch Hit AB	Pinch Hit H	PO	A	E	DP	TC/G	FA	G by Pos
1975	SF	N	8	.235	.235	17	4	0	0	0	0.0	3	2	1	2	1	3	0	8	1	0	0	1.8	1.000	OF-3, 3B-2
1976			26	.225	.382	102	23	6	2	2	2.0	14	10	8	18	6	0	0	71	3	1	1	2.9	.987	OF-26
1977			136	.252	.407	413	104	17	4	13	3.1	64	51	49	73	12	29	11	226	11	6	2	2.1	.975	OF-114
1978			156	.306	.537	592	181	46	8	25	4.2	90	98	50	72	15	6	2	320	16	6	5	2.3	.982	OF-152
1979			143	.273	.476	527	144	25	2	26	4.9	84	86	63	95	11	2	0	262	13	5	7	2.0	.982	OF-140, 3B-2
1980			127	.284	.517	437	124	20	8	22	5.0	77	82	74	52	2	5	0	229	7	8	1	2.0	.967	OF-120
1981			99	.268	.460	385	103	19	2	17	4.4	60	53	45	45	1	2	0	193	14	4	4	2.2	.981	OF-98
1982			157	.274	.481	563	154	30	3	27	4.8	90	103	90	91	6	4	1	281	10	6	2	1.9	.980	OF-155
1983			135	.268	.441	492	132	25	0	20	4.1	82	66	74	79	5	1	0	262	20	9	5	2.2	.969	OF-133, 1B-2
1984			57	.320	.537	203	65	9	1	11	5.4	33	44	43	29	1	1	0	120	9	2	3	2.3	.985	OF-54, 1B-4
1985	STL	N	126	.281	.502	442	124	26	3	22	5.0	71	87	83	88	1	1	0	1128	66	14	102	9.1	.988	1B-121, OF-12
1986			65	.237	.422	232	55	12	2	9	3.9	34	23	45	61	1	1	1	623	35	3	66	10.3	.995	1B-64
1987			131	.286	**.597**	419	120	23	1	35	**8.4**	93	106	**136**	139	1	4	0	1152	77	14	116	9.8	.989	1B-126, OF-1
1988	NY	A	150	.242	.433	496	120	14	0	27	5.4	81	93	113	141	3	12	3	129	8	5	8	1.0	.965	DH-112, OF-19, 1B-10
1989	SD	N	142	.242	.459	455	110	19	1	26	5.7	76	94	**132**	145	6	1	1	1157	89	15	99	8.8	.988	1B-131, OF-12
1990			115	.266	.533	334	89	12	1	25	7.5	59	62	**104**	91	4	4	1	855	69	6	72	8.5	.994	1B-109
1991	BOS	A	140	.249	.466	481	120	18	1	28	5.8	75	87	96	133	0	6	0	0	0	0	0	0.0	.000	DH-135
1992			81	.210	.311	257	54	11	0	5	1.9	32	33	56	87	1	6	3	111	8	1	7	1.6	.992	DH-64, 1B-13
18 yrs.			1994	.267	.476	6847	1826	332	39	340	5.0	1118	1180	1262	1441	77	88	23	7127	456	105	500	4.0	.986	OF-1039, 1B-580, DH-311, 3B-4
LEAGUE CHAMPIONSHIP SERIES																									
1985	STL	N	6	.381	.524	21	8	0	0	1	4.8	4	4	5	5	0	0	0	55	0	0	3	9.2	1.000	1B-6
1987			1	.000	.000	1	0	0	0	0	0.0	0	0	0	1	0	1	0	0	0	0	0	0.0	—	
2 yrs.			7	.364	.500	22	8	0	0	1	4.5	4	4	5	6	0	1	0	55	0	0	3	9.2	1.000	1B-6
WORLD SERIES																									
1985	STL	N	7	.240	.320	25	6	2	0	0	0.0	1	4	3	9	0	0	0	49	4	0	6	7.6	1.000	1B-7

Jerald Clark

CLARK, JERALD DWAYNE BR TR 6' 4" 189 lbs.
Brother of Phil Clark.
B. Aug. 10, 1963, Crockett, Tex.

Year	Team	Lg	Games	BA	SA	AB	H	2B	3B	HR	HR%	R	RBI	BB	SO	SB	Pinch Hit AB	Pinch Hit H	PO	A	E	DP	TC/G	FA	G by Pos
1988	SD	N	6	.200	.267	15	3	1	0	0	0.0	0	3	0	4	0	3	1	10	1	0	0	2.8	1.000	OF-4
1989			17	.195	.317	41	8	2	0	1	2.4	5	7	3	9	0	4	1	16	2	1	0	1.4	.947	OF-14
1990			53	.267	.475	101	27	4	1	5	5.0	12	11	5	24	0	28	8	102	6	1	3	3.9	.991	1B-15, OF-13
1991			118	.228	.352	369	84	16	0	10	2.7	26	47	31	90	2	10	2	245	10	2	6	2.3	.992	OF-96, 1B-16
1992			146	.242	.383	496	120	22	6	12	2.4	45	58	22	97	3	9	2	344	10	3	5	2.5	.992	OF-134, 1B-11

Jerald Clark *continued*

Year	Team	Lg	Games	BA	SA	AB	H	2B	3B	HR	HR%	R	RBI	BB	SO	SB	Pinch Hit AB	Pinch Hit H	PO	A	E	DP	TC/G	FA	G by Pos
1993	CLR	N	140	.282	.444	478	135	26	6	13	2.7	65	67	20	60	9	16	4	476	23	12	30	3.8	.977	OF-96, 1B-37
1995	MIN	A	36	.339	.550	109	37	8	3	3	2.8	17	15	2	11	3	4	4	80	4	0	3	2.3	1.000	OF-23, 1B-11, DH-3
7 yrs.			516	.257	.408	1609	414	79	16	44	2.7	170	208	83	295	17	74	22	1273	56	19	47	2.8	.986	OF-380, 1B-90, DH-3

Jim Clark

CLARK, JAMES
Born James Petrosky.
B. Sept. 21, 1927, Bagley, Pa.
BR TR 5′ 9″ 150 lbs.

Year	Team	Lg	Games	BA	SA	AB	H	2B	3B	HR	HR%	R	RBI	BB	SO	SB	Pinch Hit AB	Pinch Hit H	PO	A	E	DP	TC/G	FA	G by Pos
1948	WAS	A	9	.250	.250	12	3	0	0	0	0.0	1	0	0	2	0	6	2	2	4	0	0	3.0	1.000	SS-1, 3B-1

Jim Clark

CLARK, JAMES EDWARD
B. Apr. 30, 1947, Kansas City, Kans.
BR TR 6′ 1″ 190 lbs.

Year	Team	Lg	Games	BA	SA	AB	H	2B	3B	HR	HR%	R	RBI	BB	SO	SB	Pinch Hit AB	Pinch Hit H	PO	A	E	DP	TC/G	FA	G by Pos
1971	CLE	A	13	.167	.278	18	3	0	1	0	0.0	2	0	2	7	0	5	1	13	1	1	2	3.8	.933	OF-3, 1B-1

Jim Clark

CLARK, JAMES FRANCIS
B. Dec. 26, 1887, Brooklyn, N. Y. D. May 20, 1969, Beaumont, Tex.
BR TR 5′11″ 175 lbs.

Year	Team	Lg	Games	BA	SA	AB	H	2B	3B	HR	HR%	R	RBI	BB	SO	SB	Pinch Hit AB	Pinch Hit H	PO	A	E	DP	TC/G	FA	G by Pos
1911	STL	N	14	.167	.278	18	3	0	1	0	0.0	2	3	3	4	2	6	1	6	0	0	0	0.8	1.000	OF-8
1912			2	.000	.000	1	0	0	0	0	0.0	0	0	0	1	0	1	0	0	0	0	0	0.0	—	
2 yrs.			16	.158	.263	19	3	0	1	0	0.0	2	3	3	5	2	7	1	6	0	0	0	0.8	1.000	OF-8

Mel Clark

CLARK, MELVIN EARL
B. July 7, 1926, Letart, W. Va.
BR TR 6′ 180 lbs.

Year	Team	Lg	Games	BA	SA	AB	H	2B	3B	HR	HR%	R	RBI	BB	SO	SB	Pinch Hit AB	Pinch Hit H	PO	A	E	DP	TC/G	FA	G by Pos
1951	PHI	N	10	.323	.452	31	10	1	0	1	3.2	2	3	0	3	0	3	0	13	0	0	0	1.9	1.000	OF-7
1952			47	.335	.445	155	52	6	4	1	0.6	20	15	6	13	2	7	1	81	6	0	1	2.2	1.000	OF-38, 3B-1
1953			60	.298	.389	198	59	10	4	0	0.0	31	19	11	17	1	8	3	104	2	1	0	2.1	.991	OF-51
1954			83	.240	.352	233	56	9	7	1	0.4	26	24	17	21	0	21	2	114	9	5	2	2.0	.961	OF-63
1955			10	.156	.250	32	5	3	0	0	0.0	3	1	3	4	0	2	0	19	3	0	1	2.8	1.000	OF-8
1957	DET	A	5	.000	.000	7	0	0	0	0	0.0	0	1	0	3	0	3	0	4	0	0	0	2.0	1.000	OF-2
6 yrs.			215	.277	.381	656	182	29	15	3	0.5	82	63	37	61	3	44	6	335	20	6	4	2.1	.983	OF-169, 3B-1

Pep Clark

CLARK, HARRY
B. Mar. 20, 1883, Union City, Ohio D. June 8, 1965, Milwaukee, Wis.
BR TR 5′ 7½″ 175 lbs.

Year	Team	Lg	Games	BA	SA	AB	H	2B	3B	HR	HR%	R	RBI	BB	SO	SB	Pinch Hit AB	Pinch Hit H	PO	A	E	DP	TC/G	FA	G by Pos
1903	CHI	A	15	.308	.431	65	20	4	2	0	0.0	7	9	2		5	0	0	14	36	7	1	3.8	.877	3B-15

Phil Clark

CLARK, PHILLIP BENJAMIN
Brother of Jerald Clark.
B. May 6, 1968, Crockett, Tex.
BR TR 6′ 180 lbs.

Year	Team	Lg	Games	BA	SA	AB	H	2B	3B	HR	HR%	R	RBI	BB	SO	SB	Pinch Hit AB	Pinch Hit H	PO	A	E	DP	TC/G	FA	G by Pos
1992	DET	A	23	.407	.537	54	22	4	0	1	1.9	3	5	6	9	1	6	3	27	0	2	0	1.5	.931	OF-13, DH-7
1993	SD	N	102	.313	.496	240	75	17	0	9	3.8	33	33	8	31	2	37	13	243	35	8	14	3.8	.972	OF-36, 1B-24, C-11, 3B-5
1994			61	.215	.356	149	32	6	0	5	3.4	14	20	5	17	1	20	4	148	14	4	14	3.5	.976	1B-24, OF-17, C-5, 3B-1
1995			75	.216	.309	97	21	3	0	2	2.1	12	7	8	18	0	38	8	32	0	0	1	0.9	1.000	OF-34, 1B-2
4 yrs.			261	.278	.428	540	150	30	0	17	3.1	62	65	27	75	4	101	28	450	49	14	29	2.9	.973	OF-100, 1B-50, C-16, DH-7, 3B-6

Ron Clark

CLARK, RONALD BRUCE
B. Jan. 14, 1943, Fort Worth, Tex.
BR TR 5′10″ 175 lbs.

Year	Team	Lg	Games	BA	SA	AB	H	2B	3B	HR	HR%	R	RBI	BB	SO	SB	Pinch Hit AB	Pinch Hit H	PO	A	E	DP	TC/G	FA	G by Pos
1966	MIN	A	5	1.000	1.000	1	1	0	0	0	0.0	1	1	0	0	0	0	0	0	0	0	0	0.0	.000	3B-1
1967			20	.167	.350	60	10	3	1	2	3.3	7	11	4	9	0	3	0	7	34	5	0	2.9	.891	3B-16
1968			104	.185	.229	227	42	5	1	1	0.4	14	13	16	44	3	12	1	83	173	17	19	2.6	.938	3B-52, SS-43, 2B-10
1969	2 teams		MIN A (5G –.125) SEA A (57G –.196)																						
″	total		62	.193	.222	171	33	5	0	0	0.0	9	12	13	29	1	3	1	79	117	9	17	3.4	.956	SS-38, 3B-17, 2B-5, 1B-1
1971	OAK	A	2	.000	.000	1	0	0	0	0	0.0	0	0	1	0	0	1	0	0	0	0	0	0.0	—	
1972	2 teams		OAK A (14G –.267) MIL A (22G –.185)																						
″	total		36	.203	.362	69	14	3	1	2	2.9	9	6	7	15	0	7	1	39	61	7	16	3.1	.935	2B-22, 3B-13
1975	PHI	N	1	.000	.000	1	0	0	0	0	0.0	0	0	0	1	0	1	0	0	0	0	0	0.0	—	
7 yrs.			230	.189	.258	530	100	16	3	5	0.9	40	43	41	98	4	27	3	208	385	38	52	2.9	.940	3B-99, SS-81, 2B-37, 1B-1

Roy Clark

CLARK, ROY ELLIOT (Pepper)
B. May 11, 1874, New Haven, Conn. D. Nov. 1, 1925, Bridgeport, Conn.
BL TR 5′ 8½″ 170 lbs.

Year	Team	Lg	Games	BA	SA	AB	H	2B	3B	HR	HR%	R	RBI	BB	SO	SB	Pinch Hit AB	Pinch Hit H	PO	A	E	DP	TC/G	FA	G by Pos
1902	NY	N	21	.145	.158	76	11	1	0	0	0.0	4	3	1		5	1	0	23	2	1	1	1.3	.962	OF-20

Spider Clark

CLARK, OWEN F.
B. Sept. 16, 1867, Brooklyn, N. Y. D. Feb. 8, 1892, Brooklyn, N. Y.
TR 5′10″ 150 lbs.

Year	Team	Lg	Games	BA	SA	AB	H	2B	3B	HR	HR%	R	RBI	BB	SO	SB	Pinch Hit AB	Pinch Hit H	PO	A	E	DP	TC/G	FA	G by Pos
1889	WAS	N	38	.255	.393	145	37	7	2	3	2.1	19	22	6	18	8	0	0	101	75	26	10	5.1	.871	C-14, SS-13, OF-9, 3B-2, 2B-2
1890	BUF	P	69	.265	.327	260	69	11	1	1	0.4	45	25	20	16	8	0	0	168	63	19	14	3.5	.924	OF-34, C-14, 2B-13, 1B-6, 3B-3, SS-1, P-1
2 yrs.			107	.262	.351	405	106	18	3	4	1.0	64	47	26	34	16	0	0	269	138	45	24	4.0	.900	OF-43, C-28, 2B-15, SS-14, 1B-6, 3B-5, P-1

Tony Clark

CLARK, ANTHONY CHRISTOPHER
B. June 15, 1972, Newton, Kans.
BB TR 6′ 8″ 205 lbs.

Year	Team	Lg	Games	BA	SA	AB	H	2B	3B	HR	HR%	R	RBI	BB	SO	SB	Pinch Hit AB	Pinch Hit H	PO	A	E	DP	TC/G	FA	G by Pos
1995	DET	A	27	.238	.396	101	24	5	1	3	3.0	10	11	8	30	0	0	0	252	18	4	25	10.1	.985	1B-27

Will Clark

CLARK, WILLIAM NUSCHLER (The Thrill)
B. Mar. 13, 1964, New Orleans, La.
BL TL 6′ 2″ 190 lbs.

Year	Team	Lg	Games	BA	SA	AB	H	2B	3B	HR	HR%	R	RBI	BB	SO	SB	Pinch Hit AB	Pinch Hit H	PO	A	E	DP	TC/G	FA	G by Pos
1986	SF	N	111	.287	.444	408	117	27	2	11	2.7	66	41	34	76	4	9	6	942	72	11	76	10.0	.989	1B-102
1987			150	.308	.580	529	163	29	5	35	6.6	89	91	49	98	5	11	3	1253	103	13	130	9.8	.991	1B-139
1988			162	.282	.508	575	162	31	6	29	5.0	102	**109**	**100**	129	9	5	0	1492	104	12	126	10.2	.993	1B-158
1989			159	.333	.546	588	196	38	9	23	3.9	**104**	111	74	103	8	1	0	1445	111	10	117	9.9	.994	1B-158
1990			154	.295	.448	600	177	25	5	19	3.2	91	95	62	97	8	1	0	1456	119	12	118	10.4	.992	1B-153
1991			148	.301	**.536**	565	170	32	7	29	5.1	84	116	51	91	4	3	1	1273	110	4	115	9.6	.997	1B-144
1992			144	.300	.476	513	154	40	1	16	3.1	69	73	73	82	12	2	1	1275	105	10	130	9.9	.993	1B-141
1993			132	.283	.432	491	139	27	2	14	2.9	82	73	63	68	2	2	0	1078	88	14	113	9.1	.988	1B-129

Will Clark *continued*

Year	Team		Games	BA	SA	AB	H	2B	3B	HR	HR%	R	RBI	BB	SO	SB	Pinch Hit AB	Pinch Hit H	PO	A	E	DP	TC/G	FA	G by Pos
1994	TEX	A	110	.329	.501	389	128	24	2	13	3.3	73	80	71	59	5	2	0	968	73	10	85	9.7	.990	1B-107, DH-1
1995			123	.302	.480	454	137	27	3	16	3.5	85	92	68	50	0	0	0	1077	87	7	120	9.5	.994	1B-122, DH-1
10 yrs.			1393	.302	.497	5112	1543	300	42	205	4.0	845	881	645	853	57	36	11	12259	972	103	1130	9.8	.992	1B-1353, DH-2
LEAGUE CHAMPIONSHIP SERIES																									
1987	SF	N	7	.360	.560	25	9	2	0	1	4.0	3	3	3	6	1	0	0	63	7	1	10	10.1	.986	1B-7
1989			5	.650	1.200	20	13	3	1	2	10.0	8	8	2	2	0	0	0	43	6	0	6	9.8	1.000	1B-5
2 yrs.			12	.489 1st	.844 1st	45	22	5	1	3	6.7 7th	11	11	5	8	1	0	0	106	13	1	16	10.0	.992	1B-12
WORLD SERIES																									
1989	SF	N	4	.250	.313	16	4	1	0	0	0.0	2	0	1	3	0	0	0	40	2	0	2	10.5	1.000	1B-4

Willie Clark

CLARK, WILLIAM OTIS (Wee Willie) — BL
B. Aug. 16, 1872, Pittsburgh, Pa. D. Nov. 13, 1932, Pittsburgh, Pa.

Year	Team		Games	BA	SA	AB	H	2B	3B	HR	HR%	R	RBI	BB	SO	SB	Pinch Hit AB	Pinch Hit H	PO	A	E	DP	TC/G	FA	G by Pos
1895	NY	N	23	.261	.341	88	23	3	2	0	0.0	9	16	5	6	1	0	0	0	0	0	0	0.0	.000	1B-23
1896			72	.291	.372	247	72	12	4	0	0.0	38	33	15	12	8	7	3	634	25	17	40	10.4	.975	1B-65
1897			116	.283	.385	431	122	17	12	1	0.2	63	75	37		18	1	0	1047	67	18	69	9.8	.984	1B-107, OF-7, 3B-1
1898	PIT	N	57	.306	.431	209	64	9	7	1	0.5	29	31	22		0	0	0	601	27	10	29	11.2	.984	1B-57
1899			80	.285	.396	298	85	13	10	0	0.0	49	44	35		11	2	0	837	36	10	37	11.3	.989	1B-78
5 yrs.			348	.288	.390	1273	366	54	35	2	0.2	188	199	114	18	38	10	3	3119	155	55	175	9.8	.983	1B-330, OF-7, 3B-1

Archie Clarke

CLARKE, ARTHUR FRANKLIN — BR TR 5′ 8″ 155 lbs.
B. May 6, 1865, Providence, R. I. D. Nov. 14, 1949, Brookline, Mass.

Year	Team		Games	BA	SA	AB	H	2B	3B	HR	HR%	R	RBI	BB	SO	SB	Pinch Hit AB	Pinch Hit H	PO	A	E	DP	TC/G	FA	G by Pos
1890	NY	N	101	.225	.296	395	89	12	8	0	0.0	55	49	32	38	44	0	0	288	138	55	11	4.8	.886	C-36, OF-33, 3B-16, 2B-15, SS-1
1891			48	.190	.224	174	33	2	2	0	0.0	17	21	15	16	5	0	0	195	58	26	7	5.7	.907	C-42, 3B-5, OF-2
2 yrs.			149	.214	.274	569	122	14	10	0	0.0	72	70	47	54	49	0	0	483	196	81	18	5.1	.893	C-78, OF-35, 3B-21, 2B-15, SS-1

Boileryard Clarke

CLARKE, WILLIAM JONES (Old Reliable) — BR TR 5′11½″ 170 lbs.
B. Oct. 18, 1868, New York, N. Y. D. July 29, 1959, Princeton, N. J.

Year	Team		Games	BA	SA	AB	H	2B	3B	HR	HR%	R	RBI	BB	SO	SB	Pinch Hit AB	Pinch Hit H	PO	A	E	DP	TC/G	FA	G by Pos
1893	BAL	N	49	.175	.230	183	32	1	3	1	0.5	23	24	19	14	2	0	0	232	48	20	8	6.1	.933	C-38, 1B-11
1894			28	.240	.350	100	24	8	0	1	1.0	18	19	16	14	2	0	0	120	22	12	6	5.5	.922	C-23, 1B-5
1895			67	.290	.378	241	70	15	3	0	0.0	38	35	13	18	8	2	0	219	69	17	13	4.6	.944	C-60, 1B-6
1896			80	.297	.410	300	89	14	7	2	0.7	48	71	14	12	7	1	0	319	55	19	16	4.9	.952	C-67, 1B-14
1897			64	.270	.320	241	65	7	1	1	0.4	32	38	9		5	1	0	226	40	15	6	4.5	.947	C-59, 1B-4
1898			82	.242	.274	285	69	5	2	0	0.0	26	27	4		2	3	0	376	71	17	10	5.8	.963	C-70, 1B-10
1899	BOS	N	60	.224	.283	223	50	3	2	2	0.9	25	32	10		2	0	0	213	69	18	4	5.0	.940	C-60
1900			81	.315	.359	270	85	5	2	1	0.4	35	30	9		0	5	2	306	108	27	9	5.9	.939	C-67, 1B-8
1901	WAS	A	110	.280	.360	422	118	15	5	3	0.7	58	54	23		7	0	0	382	122	25	12	4.8	.953	C-107, 1B-3
1902			87	.268	.392	291	78	15	0	7	2.4	31	42	23		1	0	0	288	97	11	8	4.6	.972	C-87
1903			126	.239	.308	465	111	14	6	2	0.4	35	38	15		12	1	0	1039	90	28	45	9.3	.976	1B-88, C-37
1904			85	.211	.247	275	58	8	1	0	0.0	23	17	17		5	5	0	517	86	13	24	7.6	.979	C-52, 1B-29
1905	NY	N	31	.180	.240	50	9	0	0	1	2.0	2	4	4		1	4	1	137	6	4	4	5.1	.973	1B-17, C-12
13 yrs.			950	.256	.327	3346	858	110	32	21	0.6	394	431	176	58	54	22	3	4374	883	226	165	5.9	.959	C-739, 1B-195

Fred Clarke

CLARKE, FRED CLIFFORD (Cap) — BL TR 5′10½″ 165 lbs.
Brother of Josh Clarke.
B. Oct. 3, 1872, Winterset, Iowa D. Aug. 14, 1960, Winfield, Kans.
Manager 1897–15.
Hall of Fame 1945.

Year	Team		Games	BA	SA	AB	H	2B	3B	HR	HR%	R	RBI	BB	SO	SB	Pinch Hit AB	Pinch Hit H	PO	A	E	DP	TC/G	FA	G by Pos
1894	LOU	N	76	.268	.416	310	83	11	7	7	2.3	54	48	25	27	25	0	0	162	15	23	2	2.6	.885	OF-76
1895			132	.347	.425	550	191	21	5	4	0.7	96	82	34	24	40	0	0	344	20	49	4	3.1	.881	OF-132
1896			131	.325	.476	517	168	15	18	9	1.7	96	79	43	34	34	0	0	277	18	30	2	2.5	.908	OF-131
1897			128	.390	.533	518	202	30	13	6	1.2	120	67	45		57	1	1	282	18	24	0	2.6	.926	OF-127
1898			149	.307	.401	599	184	23	12	3	0.5	116	47	48		40	0	0	344	19	23	3	2.6	.940	OF-149
1899			148	.342	.435	602	206	23	9	5	0.8	122	70	49		49	1	0	340	29	20	2	2.6	.949	OF-144, SS-3
1900	PIT	N	106	.276	.396	399	110	15	12	3	0.8	85	32	51		21	2	0	263	8	16	2	2.8	.944	OF-104
1901			129	.324	.461	527	171	24	15	6	1.1	118	60	51		23	1	1	283	15	12	1	2.4	.961	OF-127, SS-1, 3B-1
1902			114	.321	.453	461	148	27	14	2	0.4	104	53	51		29	0	0	215	13	10	2	2.1	.958	OF-113
1903			104	.351	**.532**	427	150	**32**	15	5	1.2	88	70	41		21	2	1	171	11	7	3	1.8	.963	OF-101, SS-2
1904			72	.306	.410	278	85	7	11	0	0.0	51	25	22		11	2	1	135	4	3	2	2.0	.979	OF-70
1905			141	.299	.402	525	157	18	15	2	0.4	95	51	55		24	3	1	270	16	7	4	2.1	.976	OF-137
1906			118	.309	.412	417	129	14	**13**	1	0.2	69	39	40		18	7	**5**	209	15	6	3	2.1	.974	OF-110
1907			148	.289	.389	501	145	18	13	2	0.4	97	59	68		37	4	1	298	15	4	2	2.2	.987	OF-144
1908			151	.265	.363	551	146	18	15	2	0.4	83	53	65		24	0	0	350	15	10	2	2.5	.973	OF-151
1909			152	.287	.373	550	158	16	11	3	0.5	97	68	**80**		31	0	0	362	17	5	2	2.5	.987	OF-152
1910			123	.263	.373	429	113	23	9	2	0.5	57	63	53	23	12	4	1	284	10	10	4	2.6	.967	OF-118
1911			110	.324	.492	392	127	25	13	5	1.3	73	49	53	27	10	7	3	216	8	7	3	2.3	.970	OF-101
1913			9	.077	.154	13	1	1	0	0	0.0	0	0	0	0	0	6	1	2	0	0	0	1.0	1.000	OF-2
1914			2	.000	.000	2	0	0	0	0	0.0	0	0	0	0	0	1	0	0	0	0	0	0.0	—	
1915			1	.500	.500	2	1	0	0	0	0.0	0	0	0	0	0	0	0	0	0	0	0	0.0	.000	OF-1
21 yrs.			2244	.312	.429	8570	2675	361	220 7th	67	0.8	1621	1015	874	135	506	41	16	4807	266	266	43	2.4	.950	OF-2190, SS-6, 3B-1
WORLD SERIES																									
1903	PIT	N	8	.265	.382	34	9	2	1	0	0.0	3	2	1	5	1	0	0	17	0	1	0	2.3	.944	OF-8
1909			7	.211	.526	19	4	0	0	2	10.5	7	7	5	3	3	0	0	20	0	1	0	3.0	.952	OF-7
2 yrs.			15	.245	.434	53	13	2	1	2	3.8	10	9	6	8	4	0	0	37	0	2	0	2.6	.949	OF-15

Grey Clarke

CLARKE, RICHARD GREY (Noisy) — BR TR 5′ 9″ 183 lbs.
B. Sept. 26, 1912, Fulton, Ala. D. Nov. 25, 1993, Kannapolis, N. C.

Year	Team		Games	BA	SA	AB	H	2B	3B	HR	HR%	R	RBI	BB	SO	SB	Pinch Hit AB	Pinch Hit H	PO	A	E	DP	TC/G	FA	G by Pos
1944	CHI	A	63	.260	.331	169	44	10	1	0	0.0	14	27	22	6	0	15	1	36	107	9	6	3.4	.941	3B-45

Harry Clarke

CLARKE, HARRY CORSON
B. 1861 D. Mar. 3, 1923, Long Beach, Calif.

Year	Team	Games	BA	SA	AB	H	2B	3B	HR	HR%	R	RBI	BB	SO	SB	Pinch Hit AB	Pinch Hit H	PO	A	E	DP	TC/G	FA	G by Pos
1889	WAS N	1	.000	.000	3	0	0	0	0	0.0	0	0	0	1	0	0	0	1	2	0	0	3.0	1.000	OF-1

Horace Clarke

CLARKE, HORACE MEREDITH
B. June 2, 1940, Frederiksted, Virgin Islands.
BB TR 5′ 9″ 170 lbs.

Year	Team	Games	BA	SA	AB	H	2B	3B	HR	HR%	R	RBI	BB	SO	SB	Pinch Hit AB	Pinch Hit H	PO	A	E	DP	TC/G	FA	G by Pos
1965	NY A	51	.259	.296	108	28	1	0	1	0.9	13	9	6	6	2	26	9	21	56	5	5	3.3	.939	3B-17, 2B-7, SS-1
1966		96	.266	.381	312	83	10	4	6	1.9	37	28	27	24	5	11	0	146	196	12	48	4.3	.966	SS-63, 2B-16, 3B-4
1967		143	.272	.316	588	160	17	0	3	0.5	74	29	42	64	21	2	2	348	410	8	79	5.5	.990	2B-140
1968		148	.230	.254	579	133	6	1	2	0.3	52	26	23	46	20	6	2	357	444	13	80	5.9	.984	2B-139
1969		156	.285	.367	**641**	183	26	7	4	0.6	82	48	53	41	33	0	0	373	429	15	112	5.2	.982	2B-156
1970		158	.251	.309	**686**	172	24	2	4	0.6	81	46	35	35	23	1	0	379	478	18	95	5.6	.979	2B-157
1971		159	.250	.318	625	156	23	7	2	0.3	76	41	64	43	17	4	1	386	455	16	97	5.5	.981	2B-156
1972		147	.241	.302	547	132	20	2	3	0.5	65	37	56	44	18	5	1	347	399	11	104	5.3	.985	2B-143
1973		148	.263	.308	590	155	21	0	2	0.3	60	35	47	48	11	2	1	378	442	18	107	5.7	.979	2B-147
1974	2 teams	NY A (24G –.234)	SD N (42G –.189)																					
″	total	66	.204	.219	137	28	2	0	0	0.0	8	5	12	11	1	34	5	67	74	2	11	3.4	.986	2B-41, DH-1
10 yrs.		1272	.256	.313	4813	1230	150	23	27	0.6	548	304	365	362	151	91	21	2802	3383	118	738	5.3	.981	2B-1102, SS-64, 3B-21, DH-1

Josh Clarke

CLARKE, JOSHUA BALDWIN (Pepper)
Brother of Fred Clarke.
B. Mar. 8, 1879, Winfield, Kans. D. July 2, 1962, Ventura, Calif.
BL TR 5′10″ 180 lbs.

Year	Team	Games	BA	SA	AB	H	2B	3B	HR	HR%	R	RBI	BB	SO	SB	Pinch Hit AB	Pinch Hit H	PO	A	E	DP	TC/G	FA	G by Pos
1898	LOU N	6	.167	.167	18	3	0	0	0	0.0	0	0	1		0	1	0	11	0	1	0	2.4	.917	OF-5
1905	STL N	50	.257	.353	167	43	3	2	3	1.8	31	18	27		8	4	1	81	56	13	3	3.3	.913	OF-26, 2B-16, SS-4
1908	CLE A	131	.242	.280	492	119	8	4	1	0.2	70	21	76		37	0	0	220	13	9	1	1.8	.963	OF-131
1909		4	.000	.000	12	0	0	0	0	0.0	1	0	2		0	0	0	3	0	2	0	1.3	.600	OF-4
1911	BOS N	32	.233	.367	120	28	7	3	1	0.8	16	4	29	22	6	2	0	68	7	5	1	2.7	.938	OF-30
5 yrs.		223	.239	.302	809	193	18	9	5	0.6	118	43	135	22	51	7	1	383	76	30	5	2.3	.939	OF-196, 2B-16, SS-4

Nig Clarke

CLARKE, JAY JUSTIN
B. Dec. 15, 1882, Amherstburg, Ont., Canada D. June 15, 1949, River Rouge, Mich.
BL TR 5′ 8″ 165 lbs.
BB 1907

Year	Team	Games	BA	SA	AB	H	2B	3B	HR	HR%	R	RBI	BB	SO	SB	Pinch Hit AB	Pinch Hit H	PO	A	E	DP	TC/G	FA	G by Pos
1905	3 teams	CLE A (5G –.111)	DET A (3G –.429)	CLE A (37G –.202)																				
″	total	45	.208	.292	130	27	6	1	1	0.8	12	10	11	0	0	2	0	187	42	8	3	5.5	.966	C-43
1906	CLE A	57	.358	.486	179	64	12	4	1	0.6	22	21	13		3	0	0	211	58	5	4	5.1	.982	C-54
1907		120	.269	.372	390	105	19	6	3	0.8	44	33	35		3	5	0	470	119	24	9	5.3	.961	C-115
1908		97	.241	.321	290	70	8	6	1	0.3	34	27	30		6	6	0	327	108	14	6	5.0	.969	C-90
1909		55	.274	.323	164	45	4	2	0	0.0	15	14	9		1	10	0	192	65	13	2	6.1	.952	C-44
1910		21	.155	.190	58	9	2	0	0	0.0	4	2	8		0	3	1	82	32	3	0	6.9	.974	C-17
1911	STL A	82	.215	.262	256	55	10	1	0	0.0	22	18	26		2	4	0	288	112	32	17	5.6	.926	C-73, 1B-4
1919	PHI N	26	.242	.290	62	15	3	0	0	0.0	4	2	4	5	1	4	0	63	30	3	1	4.4	.969	C-22
1920	PIT N	3	.000	.000	7	0	0	0	0	0.0	0	0	2	4	0	1	0	12	4	0	0	8.0	1.000	C-2
9 yrs.		506	.254	.333	1536	390	64	20	6	0.4	157	127	138	9	16	35	1	1832	570	102	42	5.4	.959	C-460, 1B-4

Stu Clarke

CLARKE, WILLIAM STUART
B. Jan. 24, 1906, San Francisco, Calif. D. Aug. 26, 1985, Hayward, Calif.
BR TR 5′ 8½″ 160 lbs.

Year	Team	Games	BA	SA	AB	H	2B	3B	HR	HR%	R	RBI	BB	SO	SB	Pinch Hit AB	Pinch Hit H	PO	A	E	DP	TC/G	FA	G by Pos
1929	PIT N	57	.264	.404	178	47	5	7	2	1.1	20	21	19	21	3	0	0	89	151	19	22	4.5	.927	SS-41, 3B-15, 2B-1
1930		4	.444	.667	9	4	0	1	0	0.0	2	2	1	0	0	2	1	6	4	0	0	5.0	1.000	2B-2
2 yrs.		61	.273	.417	187	51	5	8	2	1.1	22	23	20	21	3	2	1	95	155	19	22	4.6	.929	SS-41, 3B-15, 2B-3

Sumpter Clarke

CLARKE, SUMPTER MILLS
Brother of Rufe Clarke.
B. Oct. 18, 1897, Savannah, Ga. D. Mar. 16, 1962, Knoxville, Tenn.
BR TR 5′11″ 170 lbs.

Year	Team	Games	BA	SA	AB	H	2B	3B	HR	HR%	R	RBI	BB	SO	SB	Pinch Hit AB	Pinch Hit H	PO	A	E	DP	TC/G	FA	G by Pos
1920	CHI N	1	.333	.333	3	1	0	0	0	0.0	0	0	0	1	0	0	0	0	1	0	0	1.0	1.000	3B-1
1923	CLE A	1	.000	.000	3	0	0	0	0	0.0	0	0	0	0	0	0	0	1	0	0	0	1.0	1.000	OF-1
1924		45	.231	.308	104	24	6	1	0	0.0	17	11	6	12	0	2	1	48	2	0	1	1.5	1.000	OF-33
3 yrs.		47	.227	.300	110	25	6	1	0	0.0	17	11	6	13	0	2	1	49	3	0	1	1.5	1.000	OF-34, 3B-1

Buzz Clarkson

CLARKSON, JAMES BUSTER
B. Mar. 13, 1915, Hopkins, S. C. D. Jan. 18, 1989, Jeannette, Pa.
BR TR 5′11″ 210 lbs.

Year	Team	Games	BA	SA	AB	H	2B	3B	HR	HR%	R	RBI	BB	SO	SB	Pinch Hit AB	Pinch Hit H	PO	A	E	DP	TC/G	FA	G by Pos
1952	BOS N	14	.200	.200	25	5	0	0	0	0.0	3	1	3	3	0	5	1	11	11	2	0	3.0	.917	SS-6, 3B-2

John Clarkson

CLARKSON, JOHN GIBSON
Brother of Walter Clarkson. Brother of Dad Clarkson.
B. July 1, 1861, Cambridge, Mass. D. Feb. 4, 1909, Belmont, Mass.
Hall of Fame 1963.
BR TR 5′10″ 155 lbs.

Year	Team	Games	BA	SA	AB	H	2B	3B	HR	HR%	R	RBI	BB	SO	SB	Pinch Hit AB	Pinch Hit H	PO	A	E	DP	TC/G	FA	G by Pos
1882	WOR N	3	.364	.545	11	4	2	0	0	0.0	0	2	0	3		0	0	1	6	1	0	2.0	.875	P-3, 1B-1
1884	CHI N	21	.262	.488	84	22	6	2	3	3.6	16		2	16		0	0	14	45	20	6	3.2	.747	P-14, OF-8, 3B-2, 1B-1
1885		72	.216	.332	283	61	11	5	4	1.4	34	31	3	44		0	0	27	175	20	8	3.0	.910	P-70, OF-3, 3B-1
1886		55	.233	.329	210	49	9	1	3	1.4	21	23	0	38		0	0	20	114	19	3	2.5	.876	P-55, OF-5
1887		63	.242	.395	215	52	5	5	6	2.8	40	25	11	25	6	0	0	39	125	8	5	2.6	.953	P-60, OF-5
1888	BOS N	55	.195	.263	205	40	9	1	1	0.5	20	17	7	48	5	0	0	23	117	21	3	2.9	.870	P-54, OF-1
1889		73	.206	.286	262	54	9	3	2	0.8	36	23	11	59	8	0	0	37	172	27	8	3.1	.886	P-73, OF-2, 3B-1
1890		45	.249	.353	173	43	6	3	2	1.2	18	26	8	31	2	0	0	22	72	17	3	2.5	.847	P-44, OF-1
1891		55	.225	.305	187	42	7	4	0	0.0	28	26	18	51	2	0	0	27	114	13	2	2.8	.916	P-55, OF-1
1892	2 teams	BOS N (16G –.228)	CLE N (29G –.139)																					
″	total	45	.171	.209	158	27	3	0	1	0.6	15	17	11	39	3	0	0	11	87	15	4	2.5	.867	P-45
1893	CLE N	37	.206	.305	131	27	6	2	1	0.8	18	17	4	20	2	0	0	15	82	8	1	2.8	.924	P-36, OF-1
1894		22	.200	.255	55	11	0	0	1	1.8	8	7	6	9	1	0	0	3	42	9	2	2.5	.833	P-22
12 yrs.		546	.219	.319	1974	432	73	26	24	1.2	254	214	81	383	29	0	0	239	1151	178	45	2.8	.886	P-531, OF-27, 3B-4, 1B-2

Ellis Clary

CLARY, ELLIS (Cat)
B. Sept. 11, 1916, Valdosta, Ga.
BR TR 5′ 8″ 160 lbs.

Year	Team	Games	BA	SA	AB	H	2B	3B	HR	HR%	R	RBI	BB	SO	SB	Pinch Hit AB	Pinch Hit H	PO	A	E	DP	TC/G	FA	G by Pos
1942	WAS A	76	.275	.313	240	66	9	0	0	0.0	34	16	45	25	2	5	1	163	181	11	37	5.0	.969	2B-69, 3B-2

Ellis Clary *continued*

Year	Team	Games	BA	SA	AB	H	2B	3B	HR	HR%	R	RBI	BB	SO	SB	Pinch Hit AB	Pinch Hit H	PO	A	E	DP	TC/G	FA	G by Pos
1943	2 teams	WAS A (73G –.256) STL A (23G –.275)																						
″	total	96	.260	.331	323	84	21	1	0	0.0	51	24	55	37	9	4	1	104	156	14	10	3.2	.949	3B-82, 2B-3, SS-1
1944	STL A	25	.265	.327	49	13	1	1	0	0.0	6	4	12	9	1	9	1	16	28	1	4	2.6	.978	3B-11, 2B-6
1945		26	.211	.316	38	8	1	0	1	2.6	6	2	2	3	0	4	0	16	21	5	3	2.2	.881	3B-16, 2B-3
4 yrs.		223	.263	.323	650	171	32	2	1	0.2	97	46	114	74	12	22	3	299	386	31	54	3.7	.957	3B-111, 2B-81, SS-1
WORLD SERIES																								
1944	STL A	1	.000	.000	1	0	0	0	0	0.0	0	0	0	0	0	1	0	0	0	0	0	0.0	—	

Bill Clay

CLAY, FREDERICK C. TR
B. Nov. 23, 1874, Baltimore, Md. D. Oct. 12, 1917, York, Pa.

Year	Team	Games	BA	SA	AB	H	2B	3B	HR	HR%	R	RBI	BB	SO	SB	Pinch Hit AB	Pinch Hit H	PO	A	E	DP	TC/G	FA	G by Pos
1902	PHI N	3	.250	.250	8	2	0	0	0	0.0	1	1	0		0	0	0	3	0	1	0	1.3	.750	OF-3

Dain Clay

CLAY, DAIN ELMER (Ding-a-Ling) BR TR 5′10½″ 160 lbs.
B. July 10, 1919, Hicksville, Ohio D. Aug. 28, 1994, Chula Vista, Calif.

Year	Team	Games	BA	SA	AB	H	2B	3B	HR	HR%	R	RBI	BB	SO	SB	Pinch Hit AB	Pinch Hit H	PO	A	E	DP	TC/G	FA	G by Pos
1943	CIN N	49	.269	.376	93	25	2	4	0	0.0	19	9	8	14	1	10	3	42	2	3	0	1.4	.936	OF-33
1944		110	.250	.292	356	89	15	0	0	0.0	51	17	17	18	8	5	1	272	4	2	0	2.8	.993	OF-98
1945		153	.280	.335	**656**	184	29	2	1	0.2	81	50	37	58	19	0	0	446	10	5	3	3.0	.989	OF-152
1946		121	.228	.280	435	99	17	0	2	0.5	52	22	53	40	11	0	0	312	10	4	3	2.7	.988	OF-120
4 yrs.		433	.258	.312	1540	397	63	6	3	0.2	203	98	115	130	39	15	4	1072	26	14	6	2.8	.987	OF-403

Royce Clayton

CLAYTON, ROYCE SPENCER BR TR 6′ 175 lbs.
B. Jan. 2, 1970, Burbank, Calif.

Year	Team	Games	BA	SA	AB	H	2B	3B	HR	HR%	R	RBI	BB	SO	SB	Pinch Hit AB	Pinch Hit H	PO	A	E	DP	TC/G	FA	G by Pos
1991	SF N	9	.115	.154	26	3	1	0	0	0.0	0	2	1	6	0	0	0	16	6	3	1	3.1	.880	SS-8
1992		98	.224	.308	321	72	7	4	4	1.2	31	24	26	63	8	1	0	142	257	11	51	4.3	.973	SS-94, 3B-1
1993		153	.282	.372	549	155	21	5	6	1.1	54	70	38	91	11	1	0	251	449	27	103	4.8	.963	SS-153
1994		108	.236	.327	385	91	14	6	3	0.8	38	30	30	74	23	1	0	178	331	14	62	4.8	.973	SS-108
1995		138	.244	.342	509	124	29	3	5	1.0	56	58	38	109	24	2	0	223	412	20	91	4.8	.969	SS-136
5 yrs.		506	.249	.339	1790	445	72	18	18	1.0	179	184	133	343	66	5	0	810	1455	75	308	4.7	.968	SS-499, 3B-1

Bob Clemens

CLEMENS, ROBERT BAXTER BR TR 5′9″ 163 lbs.
B. Aug. 9, 1886, Mount Hebron, Mo. D. Apr. 5, 1964, Marshall, Mo.

Year	Team	Games	BA	SA	AB	H	2B	3B	HR	HR%	R	RBI	BB	SO	SB	Pinch Hit AB	Pinch Hit H	PO	A	E	DP	TC/G	FA	G by Pos
1914	STL A	7	.231	.385	13	3	0	1	0	0.0	1	3	2	1	0	2	0	5	1	2	0	1.6	.750	OF-5

Chet Clemens

CLEMENS, CHESTER SPURGEON BR TR 6′ 175 lbs.
B. May 10, 1917, San Fernando, Calif.

Year	Team	Games	BA	SA	AB	H	2B	3B	HR	HR%	R	RBI	BB	SO	SB	Pinch Hit AB	Pinch Hit H	PO	A	E	DP	TC/G	FA	G by Pos
1939	BOS N	9	.217	.217	23	5	0	0	0	0.0	2	1	1	3	1	1	1	13	0	2	0	2.1	.867	OF-7
1944		19	.176	.353	17	3	1	1	0	0.0	7	2	2	2	0	4	1	6	0	0	0	0.9	1.000	OF-7
2 yrs.		28	.200	.275	40	8	1	1	0	0.0	9	3	3	5	1	5	2	19	0	2	0	1.5	.905	OF-14

Clem Clemens

CLEMENS, CLEMENT LAMBERT BR TR 5′11″ 176 lbs.
Born Clement Lambert Ulatowski.
B. Nov. 21, 1886, Chicago, Ill. D. Nov. 2, 1967, St. Petersburg, Fla.

Year	Team	Games	BA	SA	AB	H	2B	3B	HR	HR%	R	RBI	BB	SO	SB	Pinch Hit AB	Pinch Hit H	PO	A	E	DP	TC/G	FA	G by Pos
1914	CHI F	13	.148	.148	27	4	0	0	0	0.0	4	2	3		0	5	0	30	8	2	1	5.0	.950	C-8
1915		11	.136	.182	22	3	1	0	0	0.0	3	3	1		0	0	0	29	5	0	1	3.1	1.000	C-9, 2B-2
1916	CHI N	10	.000	.000	15	0	0	0	0	0.0	0	0	1	6	0	1	0	26	6	2	0	3.8	.941	C-9
3 yrs.		34	.109	.125	64	7	1	0	0	0.0	7	5	5	6	0	6	0	85	19	4	2	3.9	.963	C-26, 2B-2

Doug Clemens

CLEMENS, DOUGLAS HORACE BL TR 6′ 180 lbs.
B. June 9, 1939, Leesport, Pa.

Year	Team	Games	BA	SA	AB	H	2B	3B	HR	HR%	R	RBI	BB	SO	SB	Pinch Hit AB	Pinch Hit H	PO	A	E	DP	TC/G	FA	G by Pos
1960	STL N	1	—	—	0	0	0	0	0	—	0	0	0	0	0	0	0	2	0	0	0	2.0	1.000	OF-1
1961		6	.167	.250	12	2	1	0	0	0.0	1	0	3	1	0	3	1	2	0	1	0	1.0	.667	OF-3
1962		48	.237	.301	93	22	1	1	1	1.1	12	12	17	19	0	15	5	38	0	1	0	1.1	.974	OF-34
1963		5	.167	.667	6	1	0	0	1	16.7	1	2	1	2	0	1	0	3	1	0	0	1.3	1.000	OF-3
1964	2 teams	STL N (33G –.205) CHI N (54G –.279)																						
″	total	87	.252	.404	218	55	14	5	3	1.4	31	21	24	38	0	19	3	97	7	7	1	1.8	.937	OF-62
1965	CHI N	128	.221	.288	340	75	11	0	4	1.2	36	26	38	53	5	25	6	145	7	3	0	1.5	.981	OF-105
1966	PHI N	79	.256	.289	121	31	1	0	1	0.8	10	15	16	25	1	**49**	12	43	2	0	1	1.6	1.000	OF-28, 1B-1
1967		69	.178	.247	73	13	5	0	0	0.0	2	4	8	15	0	**54**	11	5	0	0	0	0.5	1.000	OF-10
1968		29	.211	.368	57	12	1	1	2	3.5	6	8	7	13	0	13	3	25	1	0	0	1.5	1.000	OF-17
9 yrs.		452	.229	.321	920	211	34	7	12	1.3	99	88	114	166	6	179	41	360	18	12	2	1.5	.969	OF-263, 1B-1

Wally Clement

CLEMENT, WALLACE OAKES BL TR 5′11″ 175 lbs.
B. July 21, 1881, Auburn, Me. D. Nov. 1, 1953, Coral Gables, Fla.

Year	Team	Games	BA	SA	AB	H	2B	3B	HR	HR%	R	RBI	BB	SO	SB	Pinch Hit AB	Pinch Hit H	PO	A	E	DP	TC/G	FA	G by Pos
1908	PHI N	16	.222	.306	36	8	3	0	0	0.0	0	1	0		2	8	2	21	1	0	1	2.8	1.000	OF-8
1909	2 teams	PHI N (3G –.000) BKN N (92G –.256)																						
″	total	95	.254	.300	343	87	8	4	0	0.0	35	17	18		11	7	1	179	14	7	4	2.3	.965	OF-88
2 yrs.		111	.251	.301	379	95	11	4	0	0.0	35	18	18		13	15	3	200	15	7	5	2.3	.968	OF-96

Roberto Clemente

CLEMENTE, ROBERTO WALKER (Bob) BR TR 5′11″ 175 lbs.
Born Roberto Clemente (Walker).
B. Aug. 18, 1934, Carolina, Puerto Rico D. Dec. 31, 1972, San Juan, Puerto Rico.
Hall of Fame 1973.

Year	Team	Games	BA	SA	AB	H	2B	3B	HR	HR%	R	RBI	BB	SO	SB	Pinch Hit AB	Pinch Hit H	PO	A	E	DP	TC/G	FA	G by Pos
1955	PIT N	124	.255	.382	474	121	23	11	5	1.1	48	47	18	60	2	8	2	253	18	6	5	2.3	.978	OF-118
1956		147	.311	.431	543	169	30	7	7	1.3	66	60	13	58	6	11	4	275	20	15	2	2.2	.952	OF-139, 2B-2, 3B-1
1957		111	.253	.348	451	114	17	7	4	0.9	42	30	23	45	0	2	1	272	9	6	1	2.6	.979	OF-109
1958		140	.289	.408	519	150	24	10	6	1.2	69	50	31	41	8	5	1	312	22	6	3	2.5	.982	OF-135
1959		105	.296	.396	432	128	17	7	4	0.9	60	50	15	51	2	0	0	229	10	13	1	2.4	.948	OF-104
1960		144	.314	.458	570	179	22	6	16	2.8	89	94	39	72	4	3	0	246	19	8	2	1.9	.971	OF-142
1961		146	**.351**	.559	572	201	30	10	23	4.0	100	89	35	59	4	2	1	256	27	9	5	2.0	.969	OF-144

Roberto Clemente *continued*

Year	Team	Games	BA	SA	AB	H	2B	3B	HR	HR%	R	RBI	BB	SO	SB	Pinch Hit AB	Pinch Hit H	PO	A	E	DP	TC/G	FA	G by Pos
1962		144	.312	.454	538	168	28	9	10	1.9	95	74	35	73	6	2	0	269	19	8	1	2.1	.973	OF-142
1963		152	.320	.470	600	192	23	8	17	2.8	77	76	31	64	12	3	1	239	11	11	2	1.7	.958	OF-151
1964		155	**.339**	.484	622	**211**	40	7	12	1.9	95	87	51	87	5	1	0	289	13	10	2	2.0	.968	OF-154
1965		152	**.329**	.463	589	194	21	14	10	1.7	91	65	43	78	8	8	2	288	16	10	1	2.2	.968	OF-145
1966		154	.317	.536	638	202	31	11	29	4.5	105	119	46	109	7	1	0	318	17	12	3	2.3	.965	OF-154
1967		147	**.357**	.554	585	**209**	26	10	23	3.9	103	110	41	103	9	2	0	273	17	9	4	2.1	.970	OF-145
1968		132	.291	.482	502	146	18	12	18	3.6	74	57	51	77	2	2	0	297	9	5	1	2.4	.984	OF-131
1969		138	.345	.544	507	175	20	**12**	19	3.7	87	91	56	73	4	3	2	226	14	5	1	1.8	.980	OF-135
1970		108	.352	.556	412	145	22	10	14	3.4	65	60	38	66	3	4	1	189	12	7	2	2.0	.966	OF-104
1971		132	.341	.502	522	178	29	8	13	2.5	82	86	26	65	1	9	3	267	11	2	4	2.3	.993	OF-124
1972		102	.312	.479	378	118	19	7	10	2.6	68	60	29	49	0	7	1	199	5	0	2	2.2	1.000	OF-94
18 yrs.		2433	.317	.475	9454	3000	440	166	240	2.5	1416	1305	621	1230	83	73	19	4697	269	142	42	2.2	.972	OF-2370, 2B-2, 3B-1
LEAGUE CHAMPIONSHIP SERIES																								
1970	PIT N	3	.214	.214	14	3	0	0	0	0.0	1	1	0	4	0	0	0	7	0	0	0	2.3	1.000	OF-3
1971		4	.333	.333	18	6	0	0	0	0.0	2	4	1	6	0	0	0	12	0	0	0	3.0	1.000	OF-4
1972		5	.235	.471	17	4	1	0	1	5.9	1	2	3	5	0	0	0	10	0	0	0	2.0	1.000	OF-5
3 yrs.		12	.265	.347	49	13	1	0	1	2.0	4	7	4	15	0	0	0	29	0	0	0	2.4	1.000	OF-12
WORLD SERIES																								
1960	PIT N	7	.310	.310	29	9	0	0	0	0.0	1	3	0	4	0	0	0	19	0	0	0	2.7	1.000	OF-7
1971		7	.414	.759	29	12	2	1	2	6.9	3	4	2	2	0	0	0	15	0	0	0	2.1	1.000	OF-7
2 yrs.		14	.362 **9th**	.534	58	21	2	1	2	3.4	4	7	2	6	0	0	0	34	0	0	0	2.4	1.000	OF-14

Ed Clements

CLEMENTS, EDWARD
B. Philadelphia, Pa. Deceased.

Year	Team	Games	BA	SA	AB	H	2B	3B	HR	HR%	R	RBI	BB	SO	SB	Pinch Hit AB	Pinch Hit H	PO	A	E	DP	TC/G	FA	G by Pos
1890	PIT N	1	.000	.000	1	0	0	0	0	0.0	0	0	0	0	0	0	0	1	1	3	0	5.0	.400	SS-1

Jack Clements

CLEMENTS, JOHN J.
B. June 24, 1864, Philadelphia, Pa. D. May 23, 1941, Philadelphia, Pa.
Manager 1890.
BL TL 5′ 8½″ 204 lbs.

Year	Team	Games	BA	SA	AB	H	2B	3B	HR	HR%	R	RBI	BB	SO	SB	Pinch Hit AB	Pinch Hit H	PO	A	E	DP	TC/G	FA	G by Pos
1884	2 teams	**PHI U** (41G –.282) **PHI N** (9G –.233)																						
″	total	50	.275	.401	207	57	13	2	3	1.4	40		13	8		0	0	193	62	45	3	5.8	.850	C-29, OF-22, SS-1
1885	PHI N	52	.191	.298	188	36	11	3	1	0.5	14		2	30		0	0	196	49	32	3	5.3	.884	C-41, OF-11
1886		54	.205	.243	185	38	5	1	0	0.0	15	11	7	34		0	0	334	54	30	3	7.7	.928	C-47, OF-7
1887		66	.280	.402	246	69	13	7	1	0.4	48	47	9	24	7	0	0	338	91	26	10	6.9	.943	C-59, 3B-4, SS-3
1888		86	.245	.304	326	80	8	4	1	0.3	26	32	10	36	3	0	0	496	104	47	6	7.5	.927	C-85, OF-1
1889		78	.284	.384	310	88	17	1	4	1.3	51	35	29	21	3	0	0	380	77	42	7	6.4	.916	C-78
1890		97	.315	.472	381	120	23	8	7	1.8	64	74	45	30	10	0	0	549	95	35	14	7.1	.948	C-91, 1B-5
1891		107	.310	.426	423	131	29	4	4	0.9	58	75	43	19	3	0	0	415	108	41	10	5.2	.927	C-107, 1B-2
1892		109	.264	.415	402	106	25	6	8	2.0	50	76	43	40	7	0	0	557	107	35	12	6.4	.950	C-109
1893		94	.285	.489	376	107	20	3	17	**4.5**	64	80	39	29	3	2	0	330	76	26	6	4.6	.940	C-92, 1B-1
1894		45	.346	.503	159	55	6	5	3	1.9	26	36	24	7	6	0	0	178	32	12	4	4.9	.946	C-45
1895		88	.394	.612	322	127	27	2	13	**4.0**	64	75	22	7	3	0	0	280	69	11	7	4.1	.969	C-88
1896		57	.359	.543	184	66	5	7	5	2.7	35	45	17	14	2	3	0	149	51	7	3	3.9	.966	C-53
1897		55	.238	.378	185	44	4	2	6	3.2	18	36	12		3	5	1	163	40	8	3	4.3	.962	C-49
1898	STL N	99	.257	.370	335	86	19	5	3	0.9	39	41	21		1	**12**	1	287	81	11	8	4.4	.971	C-86
1899	CLE N	4	.250	.250	12	3	0	0	0	0.0	1	0	0		0	0	0	8	7	1	0	4.0	.938	C-4
1900	BOS N	16	.310	.405	42	13	1	0	1	2.4	6	10	3		0	6	0	45	10	3	2	5.8	.948	C-10
17 yrs.		1157	.286	.421	4283	1226	226	60	77	1.8	619	673	339	299	51	28	2	4898	1113	412	101	5.7	.936	C-1073, OF-41, 1B-8, 3B-4, SS-4

Verne Clemons

CLEMONS, VERNE JAMES (Fats)
B. Sept. 8, 1891, Clemons, Iowa D. May 5, 1959, Bay Pines, Fla.
BR TR 5′ 9½″ 190 lbs.

Year	Team	Games	BA	SA	AB	H	2B	3B	HR	HR%	R	RBI	BB	SO	SB	Pinch Hit AB	Pinch Hit H	PO	A	E	DP	TC/G	FA	G by Pos
1916	STL A	4	.143	.286	7	1	1	0	0	0.0	0	0	0	1	0	2	0	5	3	1	0	4.5	.889	C-2
1919	STL N	88	.264	.360	239	63	13	2	2	0.8	14	22	26	13	4	10	5	289	89	7	8	5.1	.982	C-75
1920		112	.281	.355	338	95	10	6	1	0.3	17	36	30	12	1	7	1	408	111	12	11	5.2	.977	C-103
1921		117	.320	.396	341	109	16	2	2	0.6	29	48	33	17	0	8	2	357	101	7	12	4.3	.985	C-109
1922		71	.256	.281	160	41	4	0	0	0.0	9	15	18	5	1	7	1	172	50	1	2	3.5	.996	C-63
1923		57	.285	.369	130	37	9	1	0	0.0	6	13	10	11	0	13	4	124	34	3	1	3.9	.981	C-41
1924		25	.321	.375	56	18	3	0	0	0.0	3	6	2	3	0	7	2	46	11	1	1	3.4	.983	C-17
7 yrs.		474	.286	.360	1271	364	56	11	5	0.4	78	140	119	62	6	54	15	1401	399	32	35	4.5	.983	C-410

Donn Clendenon

CLENDENON, DONN ALVIN
B. July 15, 1935, Neosho, Mo.
BR TR 6′ 4″ 209 lbs.

Year	Team	Games	BA	SA	AB	H	2B	3B	HR	HR%	R	RBI	BB	SO	SB	Pinch Hit AB	Pinch Hit H	PO	A	E	DP	TC/G	FA	G by Pos
1961	PIT N	9	.314	.400	35	11	1	1	0	0.0	7	2	5	10	0	1	0	15	1	0	0	2.0	1.000	OF-8
1962		80	.302	.477	222	67	8	5	7	3.2	39	28	26	58	16	6	1	414	25	6	44	6.3	.987	1B-52, OF-19
1963		154	.275	.430	563	155	28	7	15	2.7	65	57	39	**136**	22	5	0	1450	118	15	154	10.5	.991	1B-151
1964		133	.282	.446	457	129	23	8	12	2.6	53	64	26	96	12	15	7	1153	75	14	116	10.4	.989	1B-119
1965		162	.301	.467	612	184	32	14	14	2.3	89	96	48	128	9	3	1	1572	121	28	161	10.8	.984	1B-158, 3B-1
1966		155	.299	.520	571	171	22	10	28	4.9	80	98	52	142	8	4	1	1452	96	24	182	10.3	.985	1B-152
1967		131	.249	.370	478	119	15	2	13	2.7	46	56	34	107	4	8	1	1199	89	15	122	10.6	.988	1B-123
1968		158	.257	.399	584	150	20	6	17	2.9	63	87	47	**163**	10	2	1	1587	128	17	134	11.2	.990	1B-155
1969	2 teams	**MON N** (38G –.240) **NY N** (72G –.252)																						
″	total	110	.248	.432	331	82	11	1	16	4.8	45	51	25	94	3	24	2	648	47	12	70	7.5	.983	1B-82, OF-12
1970	NY N	121	.288	.515	396	114	18	3	22	5.6	65	97	39	91	4	22	5	722	62	7	72	7.9	.991	1B-100
1971		88	.247	.411	263	65	10	0	11	4.2	29	37	21	78	1	27	2	505	37	8	49	7.6	.985	1B-72
1972	STL N	61	.191	.309	136	26	4	0	4	2.9	13	9	17	37	1	20	4	259	26	4	34	8.0	.986	1B-36
12 yrs.		1362	.274	.442	4648	1273	192	57	159	3.4	594	682	379	1140	90	137	25	10976	825	150	1138	9.6	.987	1B-1200, OF-39, 3B-1

Don Clendenon *continued*

Year	Team	Games	BA	SA	AB	H	2B	3B	HR	HR%	R	RBI	BB	SO	SB	Pinch Hit AB	Pinch Hit H	PO	A	E	DP	TC/G	FA	G by Pos
WORLD SERIES																								
1969	NY N	4	.357	1.071	14	5	1	0	3	21.4	4	4	2	6	0	0	0	30	4	0	0	8.5	1.000	1B-4

Elmer Cleveland

CLEVELAND, ELMER ELLSWORTH BR TR
B. Sept. 15, 1862, Washington, D. C. D. Oct. 8, 1913, Zimmerman, Pa.

Year	Team	Games	BA	SA	AB	H	2B	3B	HR	HR%	R	RBI	BB	SO	SB	Pinch Hit AB	Pinch Hit H	PO	A	E	DP	TC/G	FA	G by Pos
1884	CIN U	29	.322	.443	115	37	9	1	1	0.9	24		4			0	0	48	54	19	0	4.2	.843	3B-29
1888	2 teams	NY N (9G –.235) PIT N (30G –.222)																						
″	total	39	.225	.366	142	32	2	3	4	2.8	16	16	8	24	4	0	0	27	52	19	3	2.5	.806	3B-39
1891	COL AA	12	.171	.171	41	7	0	0	0	0.0	12	4	12	9	4	0	0	23	36	11	1	5.8	.843	3B-12
3 yrs.		80	.255	.369	298	76	11	4	5	1.7	52	20	24	33	8	0	0	98	142	49	4	3.6	.830	3B-80

Stan Cliburn

CLIBURN, STANLEY GENE BR TR 6′ 195 lbs.
Brother of Stewart Cliburn.
B. Dec. 19, 1956, Jackson, Miss.

Year	Team	Games	BA	SA	AB	H	2B	3B	HR	HR%	R	RBI	BB	SO	SB	Pinch Hit AB	Pinch Hit H	PO	A	E	DP	TC/G	FA	G by Pos
1980	CAL A	54	.179	.321	56	10	2	0	2	3.6	7	6	3	9	0	0	0	127	9	4	0	2.6	.971	C-54

Harlond Clift

CLIFT, HARLOND BENTON (Darkie) BR TR 5′11″ 180 lbs.
B. Aug. 12, 1912, El Reno, Okla. D. Apr. 27, 1992, Yakima, Wash.

Year	Team	Games	BA	SA	AB	H	2B	3B	HR	HR%	R	RBI	BB	SO	SB	Pinch Hit AB	Pinch Hit H	PO	A	E	DP	TC/G	FA	G by Pos
1934	STL A	147	.260	.421	572	149	30	10	14	2.4	104	56	84	**100**	7	5	1	150	245	30	28	3.0	.929	3B-141
1935		137	.295	.436	475	140	26	4	11	2.3	101	69	83	39	0	5	1	144	259	27	14	3.2	.937	3B-127, 2B-6
1936		152	.302	.514	576	174	40	11	20	3.5	145	73	115	68	12	0	0	158	310	24	27	3.2	.951	3B-152
1937		155	.306	.546	571	175	36	7	29	5.1	103	118	98	80	8	0	0	198	405	34	50	4.1	.947	3B-155
1938		149	.290	.554	534	155	25	7	34	6.4	119	118	118	67	10	0	0	176	306	19	31	3.4	.962	3B-149
1939		151	.270	.411	526	142	25	2	15	2.9	90	84	**111**	55	4	0	0	184	324	25	34	3.6	.953	3B-149
1940		150	.273	.463	523	143	29	5	20	3.8	92	87	104	62	9	2	1	161	329	21	32	3.5	.959	3B-147
1941		154	.255	.430	584	149	33	9	17	2.9	108	84	113	93	6	0	0	195	316	22	27	3.5	.959	3B-154
1942		143	.274	.399	541	148	39	4	7	1.3	108	55	106	48	6	1	0	160	287	28	28	3.3	.941	3B-141, SS-1
1943	2 teams	STL A (105G –.232) WAS A (8G –.300)																						
″	total	113	.237	.301	409	97	11	3	3	0.7	47	29	59	40	5	0	0	144	264	21	20	3.8	.951	3B-112
1944	WAS A	12	.159	.227	44	7	3	0	0	0.0	4	3	3	3	0	0	0	10	22	6	2	3.2	.842	3B-12
1945		119	.211	.307	375	79	12	0	8	2.1	49	53	76	58	2	8	0	111	214	23	18	3.1	.934	3B-111
12 yrs.		1582	.272	.441	5730	1558	309	62	178	3.1	1070	829	1070	713	69	21	3	1791	3281	280	311	3.4	.948	3B-1550, 2B-6, SS-1

Flea Clifton

CLIFTON, HERMAN EARL BR TR 5′10″ 160 lbs.
B. Dec. 12, 1909, Cincinnati, Ohio.

Year	Team	Games	BA	SA	AB	H	2B	3B	HR	HR%	R	RBI	BB	SO	SB	Pinch Hit AB	Pinch Hit H	PO	A	E	DP	TC/G	FA	G by Pos
1934	DET A	16	.063	.063	16	1	0	0	0	0.0	3	1	1	2	0	8	1	3	7	1	0	2.2	.909	3B-4, 2B-1
1935		43	.255	.300	110	28	5	0	0	0.0	15	9	5	13	2	7	1	34	59	4	9	3.2	.959	3B-21, 2B-5, SS-4
1936		13	.192	.231	26	5	1	0	0	0.0	5	1	4	3	0	1	1	12	16	3	4	3.4	.903	SS-6, 3B-2, 2B-1
1937		15	.116	.140	43	5	1	0	0	0.0	4	2	7	10	3	0	0	21	29	4	4	3.9	.926	3B-7, SS-4, 2B-3
4 yrs.		87	.200	.236	195	39	7	0	0	0.0	27	13	17	28	5	16	3	70	111	12	17	3.3	.938	3B-34, SS-14, 2B-10
WORLD SERIES																								
1935	DET A	4	.000	.000	16	0	0	0	0	0.0	1	0	2	4	0	0	0	2	9	1	0	3.0	.917	3B-4

Monk Cline

CLINE, JOHN P. BL TL 5′ 4″ 150 lbs.
B. Mar. 3, 1858, Louisville, Ky. D. Sept. 23, 1916, Louisville, Ky.

Year	Team	Games	BA	SA	AB	H	2B	3B	HR	HR%	R	RBI	BB	SO	SB	Pinch Hit AB	Pinch Hit H	PO	A	E	DP	TC/G	FA	G by Pos
1882	BAL AA	44	.221	.279	172	38	6	2	0	0.0	18		3			0	0	85	33	28	4	2.9	.808	OF-39, SS-8, 2B-2, 3B-1
1884	LOU AA	94	.290	.381	396	115	16	7	2	0.5	91		27			0	0	146	37	29	1	2.2	.863	OF-90, SS-6
1885		2	.222	.333	9	2	1	0	0	0.0	0		0			0	0	2	1	0	0	1.5	1.000	OF-1, 3B-1
1888	KC AA	73	.235	.294	293	69	13	2	0	0.0	45	19	20		29	0	0	95	27	16	5	1.9	.884	OF-70, 2B-3, 3B-1
1891	LOU AA	19	.300	.371	70	21	3	1	0	0.0	11	11	16	2	2	0	0	24	2	2	0	1.5	.929	OF-19
5 yrs.		232	.261	.334	940	245	39	12	2	0.2	165	30	66	2	31	0	0	352	100	75	10	2.2	.858	OF-219, SS-14, 2B-5, 3B-3

Ty Cline

CLINE, TYRONE ALEXANDER BL TL 6′½″ 170 lbs.
B. June 15, 1939, Hampton, S. C.

Year	Team	Games	BA	SA	AB	H	2B	3B	HR	HR%	R	RBI	BB	SO	SB	Pinch Hit AB	Pinch Hit H	PO	A	E	DP	TC/G	FA	G by Pos
1960	CLE A	7	.308	.423	26	8	1	1	0	0.0	2	2	0	4	0	1	0	22	0	0	0	3.7	1.000	OF-6
1961		12	.209	.302	43	9	2	1	0	0.0	9	1	6	1	1	0	0	19	0	0	0	1.6	1.000	OF-12
1962		118	.248	.331	375	93	15	5	2	0.5	53	28	28	50	5	10	1	238	3	2	1	2.3	.992	OF-107
1963	MIL N	72	.236	.259	174	41	2	1	0	0.0	17	10	10	31	2	7	3	116	5	1	3	2.0	.992	OF-62
1964		101	.302	.397	116	35	4	2	1	0.9	22	13	8	22	0	40	**14**	83	5	1	1	1.5	.989	OF-54, 1B-6
1965		123	.191	.241	220	42	5	3	0	0.0	27	10	16	50	2	29	6	142	7	4	2	1.7	.974	OF-86, 1B-5
1966	2 teams	CHI N (7G –.353) ATL N (42G –.254)																						
″	total	49	.273	.273	88	24	0	0	0	0.0	15	8	3	13	3	22	6	89	2	1	9	3.1	.989	OF-24, 1B-6
1967	2 teams	ATL N (10G –.000) SF N (64G –.270)																						
″	total	74	.254	.369	130	33	5	5	0	0.0	18	4	9	16	2	24	4	52	0	0	0	1.4	1.000	OF-38
1968	SF N	116	.223	.275	291	65	6	3	1	0.3	37	28	11	26	0	26	5	272	14	4	13	3.1	.986	OF-70, 1B-24
1969	MON N	101	.239	.321	209	50	5	3	2	1.0	26	12	32	22	4	42	9	176	8	2	7	3.2	.989	OF-41, 1B-17
1970	2 teams	MON N (2G –.500) CIN N (48G –.270)																						
″	total	50	.277	.415	65	18	7	1	0	0.0	13	8	12	11	1	26	7	33	1	1	1	1.6	.971	OF-20, 1B-2
1971	CIN N	69	.196	.206	97	19	1	0	0	0.0	12	1	18	16	2	39	5	40	0	0	0	1.3	1.000	OF-28, 1B-2
12 yrs.		892	.238	.304	1834	437	53	25	6	0.3	251	125	153	262	22	266	60	1282	45	16	37	2.2	.988	OF-548, 1B-62
LEAGUE CHAMPIONSHIP SERIES																								
1970	CIN N	2	1.000	3.000	1	1	0	1	0	0.0	2	0	1	0	0	1	1	0	0	0	0	0.0	.000	OF-1
WORLD SERIES																								
1970	CIN N	3	.333	.333	3	1	0	0	0	0.0	0	0	0	0	0	3	1	0	0	0	0	0.0	—	

Gene Clines

CLINES, EUGENE ANTHONY BR TR 5′ 9″ 170 lbs.
B. Oct. 6, 1946, San Pablo, Calif.

Year	Team	Games	BA	SA	AB	H	2B	3B	HR	HR%	R	RBI	BB	SO	SB	Pinch Hit AB	Pinch Hit H	PO	A	E	DP	TC/G	FA	G by Pos
1970	PIT N	31	.405	.459	37	15	2	0	0	0.0	4	3	2	5	2	20	8	4	0	0	0	0.6	1.000	OF-7
1971		97	.308	.392	273	84	12	4	1	0.4	52	24	22	36	15	19	7	146	8	3	2	2.1	.981	OF-74

Gene Clines *continued*

Year	Team	Games	BA	SA	AB	H	2B	3B	HR	HR%	R	RBI	BB	SO	SB	Pinch Hit AB	Pinch Hit H	PO	A	E	DP	TC/G	FA	G by Pos
1972		107	.334	.421	311	104	15	6	0	0.0	52	17	16	47	12	19	2	131	7	6	0	1.7	.958	OF-83
1973		110	.263	.329	304	80	11	3	1	0.3	42	23	26	36	8	35	10	145	6	5	0	2.0	.968	OF-77
1974		107	.225	.250	276	62	5	1	0	0.0	29	14	30	40	14	27	6	177	6	2	1	2.4	.989	OF-78
1975	NY N	82	.227	.286	203	46	6	3	0	0.0	25	10	11	21	4	18	2	98	9	2	2	1.8	.982	OF-60
1976	TEX A	116	.276	.316	446	123	12	3	0	0.0	52	38	16	52	11	5	2	215	9	3	1	2.0	.987	OF-103, DH-10
1977	CHI N	101	.293	.397	239	70	12	2	3	1.3	27	41	25	25	1	39	10	68	3	1	0	1.1	.986	OF-63
1978		109	.258	.319	229	59	10	2	0	0.0	31	17	21	28	4	43	10	84	6	2	0	1.4	.978	OF-66
1979		10	.200	.200	10	2	0	0	0	0.0	0	0	0	1	0	10	2	0	0	0	0	0.0	—	
10 yrs.		870	.277	.341	2328	645	85	24	5	0.2	314	187	169	291	71	235	59	1068	54	24	6	1.8	.979	OF-611, DH-10
LEAGUE CHAMPIONSHIP SERIES																								
1971	PIT N	1	.333	1.333	3	1	0	0	1	33.3	1	1	0	1	0	0	0	1	0	0	0	1.0	1.000	OF-1
1972		2	.000	.000	2	0	0	0	0	0.0	1	0	0	1	0	2	0	0	0	0	0	0.0	—	
1974		2	.000	.000	1	0	0	0	0	0.0	1	0	0	0	0	0	0	0	0	0	0	0.0	.000	OF-2
3 yrs.		5	.167	.667	6	1	0	0	1	16.7	3	1	0	2	0	2	0	1	0	0	0	0.3	1.000	OF-3
WORLD SERIES																								
1971	PIT N	3	.091	.273	11	1	0	1	0	0.0	2	0	1	1	1	0	0	6	0	0	0	2.0	1.000	OF-3

Billy Clingman

CLINGMAN, WILLIAM FREDERICK BB TR 5′11″ 150 lbs.
B. Nov. 21, 1869, Cincinnati, Ohio D. May 14, 1958, Cincinnati, Ohio.

Year	Team	Games	BA	SA	AB	H	2B	3B	HR	HR%	R	RBI	BB	SO	SB	Pinch Hit AB	Pinch Hit H	PO	A	E	DP	TC/G	FA	G by Pos
1890	CIN N	7	.259	.296	27	7	1	0	0	0.0	2	5	1	0	0	0	0	8	26	4	4	5.4	.895	SS-6, 2B-1
1891	CIN AA	1	.200	.400	5	1	1	0	0	0.0	0	0	0	0	0	0	0	0	2	1	0	3.0	.667	2B-1
1895	PIT N	106	.259	.322	382	99	16	4	0	0.0	69	45	41	43	19	0	0	137	256	50	16	4.2	.887	3B-106
1896	LOU N	121	.234	.281	423	99	10	2	2	0.5	57	37	57	51	19	0	0	188	281	38	21	4.2	.925	3B-121
1897		113	.228	.314	395	90	14	7	2	0.5	59	47	37		14	0	0	176	269	25	16	4.2	.947	3B-113
1898		154	.257	.301	538	138	12	6	0	0.0	65	50	51		15	0	0	292	458	70	46	5.3	.915	3B-79, SS-74, 2B-1, OF-1
1899		109	.262	.342	366	96	15	4	2	0.5	67	44	46		13	0	0	195	381	53	43	5.8	.916	SS-109
1900	CHI N	47	.208	.245	159	33	6	0	0	0.0	15	11	17		6	0	0	81	150	34	19	5.6	.872	SS-47
1901	WAS A	137	.242	.304	480	116	10	7	2	0.4	66	55	42		10	0	0	290	462	55	56	5.9	.932	SS-137
1903	CLE A	21	.281	.328	64	18	1	1	0	0.0	10	7	11		2	0	0	39	55	8	7	4.9	.922	2B-11, SS-7, 3B-3
10 yrs.		816	.246	.306	2839	697	86	31	8	0.3	410	301	303	94	98	0	0	1406	2340	338	228	5.0	.917	3B-422, SS-380, 2B-14, OF-1

Jim Clinton

CLINTON, JAMES LAWRENCE (Big Jim) BR TR 5′ 8½″ 174 lbs.
B. Aug. 10, 1850, New York, N. Y. D. Sept. 3, 1921, Brooklyn, N. Y.

Year	Team	Games	BA	SA	AB	H	2B	3B	HR	HR%	R	RBI	BB	SO	SB	Pinch Hit AB	Pinch Hit H	PO	A	E	DP	TC/G	FA	G by Pos
1876	LOU N	16	.338	.369	65	22	2	0	0	0.0	8	0	0	0		0	0	20	7	7	1	2.1	.794	OF-14, 1B-1, P-1
1882	WOR N	26	.163	.184	98	16	2	0	0	0.0	9	3	7	13		0	0	43	4	17	1	2.5	.734	OF-26
1883	BAL AA	94	.313	.393	399	125	16	8	0	0.0	69		27			0	0	167	26	39	3	2.5	.832	OF-92, 2B-2
1884		103	.273	.349	433	118	12	6	3	0.7	82		29			0	0	134	20	36	5	1.8	.811	OF-103, 2B-1
1885	CIN AA	105	.238	.275	408	97	5	5	0	0.0	48		15			0	0	215	14	32	4	2.5	.877	OF-105
1886	BAL AA	23	.181	.193	83	15	1	0	0	0.0	8		4			0	0	41	1	5	1	2.0	.894	OF-23
6 yrs.		367	.264	.322	1486	393	38	19	3	0.2	224	3	82	13		0	0	620	72	136	15	2.3	.836	OF-363, 2B-3, 1B-1, P-1

Lu Clinton

CLINTON, LUCIEAN LOUIS BR TR 6′ 1″ 185 lbs.
B. Oct. 13, 1937, Ponca City, Okla.

Year	Team	Games	BA	SA	AB	H	2B	3B	HR	HR%	R	RBI	BB	SO	SB	Pinch Hit AB	Pinch Hit H	PO	A	E	DP	TC/G	FA	G by Pos
1960	BOS A	96	.228	.379	298	68	17	5	6	2.0	37	37	20	66	4	6	1	165	4	6	2	2.0	.966	OF-89
1961		17	.255	.333	51	13	2	1	0	0.0	4	3	2	10	0	2	0	30	3	0	0	2.5	1.000	OF-13
1962		114	.294	.540	398	117	24	10	18	4.5	63	75	34	79	2	9	2	185	6	4	1	1.9	.979	OF-103
1963		148	.232	.416	560	130	23	7	22	3.9	71	77	49	118	0	2	0	319	7	6	0	2.3	.982	OF-146
1964	2 teams	BOS A (37G –.258) LA A (91G –.248)																						
″	total	128	.251	.401	426	107	22	3	12	2.8	45	44	40	73	4	7	1	182	18	2	4	1.7	.990	OF-121
1965	3 teams	CAL A (89G –.243) KC A (1G –.000) CLE A (12G –.176)																						
″	total	102	.233	.331	257	60	13	3	2	0.8	31	10	26	44	2	16	5	122	7	3	1	1.6	.977	OF-83
1966	NY A	80	.220	.403	159	35	10	2	5	3.1	18	21	16	27	0	14	6	80	2	2	0	1.3	.976	OF-63
1967		6	.500	.750	4	2	1	0	0	0.0	1	2	1	1	0	4	2	0	0	0	0	0.0	.000	OF-1
8 yrs.		691	.247	.418	2153	532	112	31	65	3.0	270	269	188	418	12	60	17	1083	47	23	8	1.9	.980	OF-619

Ed Clough

CLOUGH, EDGAR GEORGE (Spec) BL TL 6′ 188 lbs.
B. Oct. 28, 1906, Wiconisco, Pa. D. Jan. 30, 1944, Harrisburg, Pa.

Year	Team	Games	BA	SA	AB	H	2B	3B	HR	HR%	R	RBI	BB	SO	SB	Pinch Hit AB	Pinch Hit H	PO	A	E	DP	TC/G	FA	G by Pos
1924	STL N	7	.071	.071	14	1	0	0	0	0.0	0	1	0	3	0	1	0	12	1	0	0	2.2	1.000	OF-6
1925		3	.250	.250	4	1	0	0	0	0.0	0	0	0	0	0	0	0	1	1	0	0	0.7	1.000	P-3
1926		1	.000	.000	1	0	0	0	0	0.0	0	0	0	0	0	0	0	0	0	0	0	0.0	.000	P-1
3 yrs.		11	.105	.105	19	2	0	0	0	0.0	0	1	0	3	0	1	0	13	2	0	0	1.5	1.000	OF-6, P-4

Bill Clymer

CLYMER, WILLIAM JOHNSTON (Derby Day)
B. Dec. 18, 1873, Philadelphia, Pa. D. Dec. 26, 1936, Philadelphia, Pa.

Year	Team	Games	BA	SA	AB	H	2B	3B	HR	HR%	R	RBI	BB	SO	SB	Pinch Hit AB	Pinch Hit H	PO	A	E	DP	TC/G	FA	G by Pos
1891	PHI AA	3	.000	.000	11	0	0	0	0	0.0	0	0	1	2	1	0	0	8	5	2	0	5.0	.867	SS-3

Otis Clymer

CLYMER, OTIS EDGAR (Gump) BB TR 5′11″ 180 lbs.
B. Jan. 27, 1876, Pine Grove, Pa. D. Feb. 27, 1926, St. Paul, Minn.

Year	Team	Games	BA	SA	AB	H	2B	3B	HR	HR%	R	RBI	BB	SO	SB	Pinch Hit AB	Pinch Hit H	PO	A	E	DP	TC/G	FA	G by Pos
1905	PIT N	96	.296	.353	365	108	11	5	0	0.0	74	23	19		23	6	2	138	8	2	5	1.6	.986	OF-89, 1B-1
1906		11	.244	.289	45	11	0	1	0	0.0	7	1	3		1	0	0	17	1	2	0	1.8	.900	OF-11
1907	2 teams	PIT N (22G –.227) WAS A (57G –.316)																						
″	total	79	.294	.368	272	80	7	5	1	0.4	38	20	23		22	9	3	116	4	13	1	2.0	.902	OF-66, 1B-2
1908	WAS A	110	.253	.313	368	93	11	4	1	0.3	32	35	20		19	9	3	97	34	10	8	1.5	.929	OF-82, 2B-13, 3B-2
1909		45	.196	.261	138	27	5	2	0	0.0	11	6	17		7	2	0	44	3	4	1	1.2	.922	OF-41
1913	2 teams	CHI N (30G –.229) BOS N (14G –.324)																						
″	total	44	.254	.338	142	36	8	2	0	0.0	20	13	17	21	11	6	2	76	2	7	0	2.3	.918	OF-37
6 yrs.		385	.267	.332	1330	355	42	19	2	0.2	182	98	99	21	83	32	10	488	52	38	15	1.7	.934	OF-326, 2B-13, 1B-3, 3B-2

Bobby Coachman

COACHMAN, BOBBY DEAN BR TR 5′ 9″ 175 lbs.
B. Nov. 11, 1961, Cottonwood, Ala.

Year	Team	Games	BA	SA	AB	H	2B	3B	HR	HR%	R	RBI	BB	SO	SB	Pinch Hit AB	Pinch Hit H	PO	A	E	DP	TC/G	FA	G by Pos
1990	CAL A	16	.311	.378	45	14	3	0	0	0.0	3	5	1	7	0	3	0	6	23	2	4	2.4	.935	3B-9, 2B-2, DH-2

Gil Coan

COAN, GILBERT FITZGERALD
B. May 18, 1922, Monroe, N. C.
BL TR 6′ 180 lbs.

Year	Team	Games	BA	SA	AB	H	2B	3B	HR	HR%	R	RBI	BB	SO	SB	Pinch Hit AB	Pinch Hit H	PO	A	E	DP	TC/G	FA	G by Pos
1946	WAS A	59	.209	.328	134	28	3	2	3	2.2	17	9	7	37	2	24	4	62	0	2	0	2.2	.969	OF-29
1947		11	.500	.667	42	21	3	2	0	0.0	5	3	5	6	2	0	0	22	1	0	1	2.1	1.000	OF-11
1948		138	.232	.333	513	119	13	9	7	1.4	56	60	41	78	23	8	1	341	11	11	3	2.8	.970	OF-131
1949		111	.218	.307	358	78	7	8	3	0.8	36	25	29	58	9	11	2	225	8	6	3	2.5	.975	OF-97
1950		104	.303	.429	366	111	17	4	7	1.9	58	50	28	46	10	5	3	220	4	7	1	2.4	.970	OF-98
1951		135	.303	.426	538	163	25	7	9	1.7	85	62	39	62	8	5	0	374	17	14	2	3.1	.965	OF-132
1952		107	.205	.319	332	68	11	6	5	1.5	50	20	32	35	9	16	3	185	4	3	1	2.2	.984	OF-86
1953		68	.196	.286	168	33	1	4	2	1.2	28	17	22	23	7	22	4	105	2	0	1	2.3	1.000	OF-46
1954	BAL A	94	.279	.351	265	74	11	1	2	0.8	29	20	16	17	9	25	2	148	1	5	0	2.3	.968	OF-67
1955	3 teams	BAL A (61G –.238) CHI A (17G –.176) NY N (9G –.154)																						
″	total	87	.225	.300	160	36	7	1	1	0.6	18	12	13	21	4	29	11	59	5	1	0	1.3	.985	OF-51
1956	NY N	4	.000	.000	1	0	0	0	0	0.0	2	0	0	1	0	1	0	0	0	0	0	0.0	—	
11 yrs.		918	.254	.359	2877	731	98	44	39	1.4	384	278	232	384	83	146	30	1741	53	49	12	2.5	.973	OF-748

Joe Cobb

COBB, JOSEPH STANLEY
Born Joseph Stanley Serafin.
B. Jan. 24, 1895, Hudson, Pa. D. Dec. 24, 1947, Allentown, Pa.
BR TR 5′ 9″ 170 lbs.

Year	Team	Games	BA	SA	AB	H	2B	3B	HR	HR%	R	RBI	BB	SO	SB	Pinch Hit AB	Pinch Hit H	PO	A	E	DP	TC/G	FA	G by Pos
1918	DET A	1	—	—	0	0	0	0	0	—	0	0	1	0	0	0	0	0	0	0	0	0.0	—	

Ty Cobb

COBB, TYRUS RAYMOND (The Georgia Peach)
B. Dec. 18, 1886, Narrows, Ga. D. July 17, 1961, Atlanta, Ga.
Manager 1921–26.
Hall of Fame 1936.
BL TR 6′ 1″ 175 lbs.

Year	Team	Games	BA	SA	AB	H	2B	3B	HR	HR%	R	RBI	BB	SO	SB	Pinch Hit AB	Pinch Hit H	PO	A	E	DP	TC/G	FA	G by Pos
1905	DET A	41	.240	.300	150	36	6	0	1	0.7	19	15	10		2	0	0	85	6	4	1	2.3	.958	OF-41
1906		98	.320	.406	350	112	13	7	1	0.3	45	41	19		23	1	0	208	14	9	4	2.4	.961	OF-96
1907		150	**.350**	**.473**	605	**212**	29	15	5	0.8	97	**116**	24		**49**	0	0	238	30	11	12	1.9	.961	OF-150
1908		150	**.324**	**.475**	581	**188**	**36**	**20**	4	0.7	88	**108**	34		39	0	0	212	23	14	5	1.7	.944	OF-150
1909		156	**.377**	**.517**	573	**216**	33	10	**9**	**1.6**	**116**	**107**	48		**76**	0	0	222	24	14	7	1.7	.946	OF-156
1910		140	**.385**	**.554**	509	196	36	13	8	1.6	**106**	91	64		65	3	1	305	18	14	4	2.5	.958	OF-137
1911		146	**.420**	**.621**	591	**248**	**47**	**24**	8	1.4	**147**	**144**	44		**83**	0	0	376	24	18	10	2.9	.957	OF-146
1912		140	**.410**	**.586**	553	**227**	30	23	7	1.3	119	90	43		61	0	0	324	21	22	5	2.6	.940	OF-140
1913		122	**.390**	.535	428	167	18	16	4	0.9	70	67	58	31	52	2	0	263	22	19	8	2.6	.938	OF-118, 2B-1
1914		97	**.368**	**.513**	345	127	22	11	2	0.6	69	57	57	22	35	0	0	177	8	10	0	2.0	.949	OF-96
1915		156	**.369**	.487	563	**208**	31	13	3	0.5	**144**	99	118	43	**96**	0	0	328	22	18	7	2.4	.951	OF-156
1916		145	.371	.493	542	201	31	10	5	0.9	**113**	68	78	39	**68**	0	0	335	18	17	9	2.6	.954	OF-143, 1B-1
1917		152	**.383**	**.571**	**588**	**225**	**44**	**23**	7	1.2	107	102	61	34	**55**	0	0	373	27	11	9	2.7	.973	OF-152
1918		111	**.382**	.515	421	161	19	**14**	3	0.7	83	64	41	21	34	3	1	360	29	10	7	3.6	.975	OF-95, 1B-13, P-2, 3B-1, 2B-1
1919		124	**.384**	.515	497	**191**	36	13	1	0.2	92	70	38	22	28	0	0	272	19	8	3	2.4	.973	OF-123
1920		112	.334	.451	428	143	28	8	2	0.5	86	63	58	28	14	0	0	246	8	9	2	2.3	.966	OF-112
1921		128	.389	.596	507	197	37	16	12	2.4	124	101	56	19	22	7	1	301	27	10	2	2.8	.970	OF-121
1922		137	.401	.565	526	211	42	16	4	0.8	99	99	55	24	9	3	0	330	14	7	3	2.6	.980	OF-134
1923		145	.340	.469	556	189	40	7	6	1.1	103	88	66	14	9	2	1	362	14	12	2	2.8	.969	OF-141
1924		155	.338	.450	625	211	38	10	4	0.6	115	74	85	18	23	0	0	417	12	6	8	2.8	.986	OF-155
1925		121	.378	.598	415	157	31	12	12	2.9	97	102	65	12	13	12	2	267	10	15	1	2.8	.949	OF-105, P-1
1926		79	.339	.511	233	79	18	5	4	1.7	48	62	26	2	9	18	6	109	4	6	2	2.2	.950	OF-55
1927	PHI A	134	.357	.482	490	175	32	7	5	1.0	104	93	67	12	22	8	2	243	9	8	2	2.1	.969	OF-126
1928		95	.323	.431	353	114	27	4	1	0.3	54	40	34	16	5	10	1	154	7	6	0	2.0	.964	OF-85
24 yrs.		3034 **4th**	.367 **1st**	.513	11429 **4th**	4191 **2nd**	724 **4th**	297 **2nd**	118	1.0	2245 **1st**	1961 **4th**	1249	357	892 **3rd**	69	15	6507	410	278	113	2.4	.961	OF-2933, 1B-14, P-3, 2B-2, 3B-1
WORLD SERIES																								
1907	DET A	5	.200	.300	20	4	0	1	0	0.0	1	1	0	3	0	0	0	9	0	0	0	1.8	1.000	OF-5
1908		5	.368	.421	19	7	1	0	0	0.0	3	4	1	2	2	0	0	3	0	2	0	1.0	.600	OF-5
1909		7	.231	.346	26	6	3	0	0	0.0	3	6	2	2	2	0	0	8	0	1	0	1.3	.889	OF-7
3 yrs.		17	.262	.354	65	17	4	1	0	0.0	7	11	3	7	4	0	0	20	0	3	0	1.4	.870	OF-17

Dave Coble

COBLE, DAVID LAMAR
B. Dec. 24, 1912, Monroe, N. C. D. Oct. 15, 1971, Orlando, Fla.
BR TR 6′ 1″ 183 lbs.

Year	Team	Games	BA	SA	AB	H	2B	3B	HR	HR%	R	RBI	BB	SO	SB	Pinch Hit AB	Pinch Hit H	PO	A	E	DP	TC/G	FA	G by Pos
1939	PHI N	15	.280	.320	25	7	1	0	0	0.0	2	0	0	3	0	2	0	27	3	2	0	2.5	.938	C-13

George Cochran

COCHRAN, GEORGE LESLIE
B. Feb. 12, 1889, Rusk, Tex. D. May 21, 1960, Harbor City, Calif.
TR

Year	Team	Games	BA	SA	AB	H	2B	3B	HR	HR%	R	RBI	BB	SO	SB	Pinch Hit AB	Pinch Hit H	PO	A	E	DP	TC/G	FA	G by Pos
1918	BOS A	25	.127	.127	63	8	0	0	0	0.0	8	3	11	7	3	1	0	13	39	2	4	2.3	.963	3B-23, SS-1

Dave Cochrane

COCHRANE, DAVID CARTER
B. Jan. 31, 1963, Riverside, Calif.
BB TR 6′ 2″ 180 lbs.

Year	Team	Games	BA	SA	AB	H	2B	3B	HR	HR%	R	RBI	BB	SO	SB	Pinch Hit AB	Pinch Hit H	PO	A	E	DP	TC/G	FA	G by Pos
1986	CHI A	19	.194	.274	62	12	2	0	1	1.6	4	2	5	22	0	0	0	10	31	6	1	2.5	.872	3B-18, SS-1
1989	SEA A	54	.235	.382	102	24	4	1	3	2.9	13	7	14	27	0	17	5	78	41	5	14	2.2	.960	SS-30, 3B-9, 1B-9, 2B-4, OF-3, C-2
1990		15	.150	.150	20	3	0	0	0	0.0	0	0	0	8	0	9	2	8	10	0	0	1.5	1.000	SS-5, 3B-3, 1B-3, C-1
1991		65	.247	.354	178	44	13	0	2	1.1	16	22	9	38	0	16	4	105	25	7	3	2.2	.949	OF-26, C-19, 3B-13, 1B-4, DH-1
1992		65	.250	.322	152	38	5	0	2	1.3	10	12	12	34	1	17	4	107	29	6	5	2.2	.958	OF-25, C-21, 3B-10, SS-3, 1B-3, DH-2, 2B-1
5 yrs.		218	.235	.333	514	121	24	1	8	1.6	43	43	40	129	1	59	15	308	136	24	23	2.2	.949	OF-54, 3B-53, C-43, SS-39, 1B-19, 2B-5, DH-3

Mickey Cochrane

COCHRANE, GORDON STANLEY (Black Mike)
B. Apr. 6, 1903, Bridgewater, Mass. D. June 28, 1962, Lake Forest, Ill.
Manager 1934–38.
Hall of Fame 1947.
BL TR 5′10½″ 180 lbs.

Year	Team	Games	BA	SA	AB	H	2B	3B	HR	HR%	R	RBI	BB	SO	SB	Pinch Hit AB	Pinch Hit H	PO	A	E	DP	TC/G	FA	G by Pos
1925	PHI A	134	.331	.448	420	139	21	5	6	1.4	69	55	44	19	7	1	1	419	79	8	9	3.8	.984	C-133
1926		120	.273	.408	370	101	8	9	8	2.2	50	47	56	15	5	1	0	502	90	15	9	5.3	.975	C-115
1927		126	.338	.495	432	146	20	6	12	2.8	80	80	50	7	9	3	1	559	85	9	11	5.3	.986	C-123

Mickey Cochrane *continued*

Year	Team	Games	BA	SA	AB	H	2B	3B	HR	HR%	R	RBI	BB	SO	SB	Pinch Hit AB	Pinch Hit H	PO	A	E	DP	TC/G	FA	G by Pos
1928		131	.293	.464	468	137	26	12	10	2.1	92	57	76	25	7	1	0	645	71	25	8	5.7	.966	C-130
1929		135	.331	.475	514	170	37	8	7	1.4	113	95	69	8	7	0	0	659	77	13	9	5.5	.983	C-135
1930		130	.357	.526	487	174	42	5	10	2.1	110	85	55	18	5	0	0	654	69	5	11	5.6	.993	C-130
1931		122	.349	.553	459	160	31	6	17	3.7	87	89	56	21	2	5	0	560	63	9	9	5.4	.986	C-117
1932		139	.293	.510	518	152	35	4	23	4.4	118	112	100	22	0	2	0	652	94	5	15	5.4	.993	C-137, OF-1
1933		130	.322	.515	429	138	30	4	15	3.5	104	60	106	22	8	2	0	476	67	6	8	4.3	.989	C-128
1934	**DET A**	129	.320	.412	437	140	32	1	2	0.5	74	76	78	26	8	8	1	517	69	7	7	4.8	.988	C-124
1935		115	.319	.450	411	131	33	3	5	1.2	93	47	96	15	5	3	1	504	50	6	6	5.1	.989	C-110
1936		44	.270	.381	126	34	8	0	2	1.6	24	17	46	15	1	1	0	159	13	3	1	4.2	.983	C-42
1937		27	.306	.490	98	30	10	1	2	2.0	27	12	25	4	0	0	0	103	13	0	1	4.3	1.000	C-27
13 yrs.		1482	.320	.478	5169	1652	333	64	119	2.3	1041	832	857	217	64	27	4	6409	840	111	104	5.1	.985	C-1451, OF-1
WORLD SERIES																								
1929	**PHI A**	5	.400	.467	15	6	1	0	0	0.0	5	0	7	0	0	0	0	59	2	0	0	12.2	1.000	C-5
1930		6	.222	.611	18	4	1	0	2	11.1	5	3	5	2	0	0	0	39	1	1	0	6.8	.976	C-6
1931		7	.160	.160	25	4	0	0	0	0.0	2	1	5	2	0	0	0	40	4	1	0	6.4	.978	C-7
1934	**DET A**	7	.214	.250	28	6	1	0	0	0.0	2	1	4	3	0	0	0	36	5	0	1	5.9	1.000	C-7
1935		6	.292	.333	24	7	1	0	0	0.0	3	1	4	1	0	0	0	32	3	1	1	6.0	.972	C-6
5 yrs.		31	.245	.336	110	27	4	0	2	1.8	17	6	25 **6th**	8	0	0	0	206	15	3	2	7.2	.987	C-31

Jim Cockman

COCKMAN, JAMES BR TR 5′ 6″ 145 lbs.
B. Apr. 26, 1873, Guelph, Ont., Canada D. Sept. 28, 1947, Guelph, Ont., Canada.

Year	Team	Games	BA	SA	AB	H	2B	3B	HR	HR%	R	RBI	BB	SO	SB	Pinch Hit AB	Pinch Hit H	PO	A	E	DP	TC/G	FA	G by Pos
1905	**NY A**	13	.105	.105	38	4	0	0	0	0.0	5	2	4		2	0	0	10	18	4	0	2.5	.875	3B-13

Jack Coffey

COFFEY, JOHN FRANCIS BR TR 5′11″ 178 lbs.
B. Jan. 28, 1887, New York, N. Y. D. Feb. 14, 1966, Bronx, N. Y.

Year	Team	Games	BA	SA	AB	H	2B	3B	HR	HR%	R	RBI	BB	SO	SB	Pinch Hit AB	Pinch Hit H	PO	A	E	DP	TC/G	FA	G by Pos
1909	**BOS N**	73	.187	.233	257	48	4	4	0	0.0	21	20	11		2	0	0	133	213	40	18	5.3	.896	SS-73
1918	**2 teams**	**DET A** (22G –.209) **BOS A** (15G –.159)																						
″	**total**	37	.189	.261	111	21	1	2	1	0.9	12	6	11	8	4	0	0	74	106	8	6	5.1	.957	2B-23, 3B-14
2 yrs.		110	.188	.242	368	69	5	6	1	0.3	33	26	22	8	6	0	0	207	319	48	24	5.2	.916	SS-73, 2B-23, 3B-14

Frank Coggins

COGGINS, FRANKLIN (Swish) BB TR 6′ 2″ 187 lbs.
B. May 22, 1944, Griffin, Ga.

Year	Team	Games	BA	SA	AB	H	2B	3B	HR	HR%	R	RBI	BB	SO	SB	Pinch Hit AB	Pinch Hit H	PO	A	E	DP	TC/G	FA	G by Pos
1967	**WAS A**	19	.307	.387	75	23	3	0	1	1.3	9	8	2	17	1	0	0	49	59	4	11	5.9	.964	2B-19
1968		62	.175	.222	171	30	6	1	0	0.0	15	7	9	33	1	8	0	122	122	12	33	4.9	.953	2B-52
1972	**CHI N**	6	.000	.000	1	0	0	0	0	0.0	1	0	1	0	0	1	0	0	0	0	0	0.0	—	
3 yrs.		87	.215	.271	247	53	9	1	1	0.4	25	15	12	50	2	9	0	171	181	16	44	5.2	.957	2B-71

Rich Coggins

COGGINS, RICHARD ALLEN BL TL 5′ 8″ 170 lbs.
B. Dec. 7, 1950, Indianapolis, Ind.

Year	Team	Games	BA	SA	AB	H	2B	3B	HR	HR%	R	RBI	BB	SO	SB	Pinch Hit AB	Pinch Hit H	PO	A	E	DP	TC/G	FA	G by Pos
1972	**BAL A**	16	.333	.436	39	13	4	0	0	0.0	5	1	1	6	0	2	1	39	1	0	1	3.1	1.000	OF-13
1973		110	.319	.468	389	124	19	9	7	1.8	54	41	28	24	17	7	1	220	6	3	3	2.2	.987	OF-101, DH-1
1974		113	.243	.319	411	100	13	3	4	1.0	53	32	29	31	26	12	1	238	3	4	1	2.3	.984	OF-105
1975	**2 teams**	**MON N** (13G –.270) **NY A** (51G –.224)																						
″	**total**	64	.236	.299	144	34	4	1	1	0.7	8	10	8	23	3	5	1	78	2	2	2	1.5	.976	OF-46, DH-9
1976	**2 teams**	**NY A** (7G –.250) **CHI A** (32G –.156)																						
″	**total**	39	.160	.180	100	16	2	0	0	0.0	5	6	6	16	4	5	1	48	1	0	0	1.7	1.000	OF-28, DH-1
5 yrs.		342	.265	.361	1083	287	42	13	12	1.1	125	90	72	100	50	31	5	623	13	9	7	2.1	.986	OF-293, DH-11
LEAGUE CHAMPIONSHIP SERIES																								
1973	**BAL A**	2	.444	.556	9	4	1	0	0	0.0	1	0	0	0	0	0	0	4	0	0	0	2.0	1.000	OF-2
1974		3	.000	.000	11	0	0	0	0	0.0	0	0	0	3	0	0	0	6	0	0	0	2.0	1.000	OF-3
2 yrs.		5	.200	.250	20	4	1	0	0	0.0	1	0	0	3	0	0	0	10	0	0	0	2.0	1.000	OF-5

Ed Cogswell

COGSWELL, EDWARD BR TR 5′ 8″ 150 lbs.
B. Feb. 25, 1854, England D. July 27, 1888, Fitchburg, Mass.

Year	Team	Games	BA	SA	AB	H	2B	3B	HR	HR%	R	RBI	BB	SO	SB	Pinch Hit AB	Pinch Hit H	PO	A	E	DP	TC/G	FA	G by Pos
1879	**BOS N**	49	.322	.377	236	76	8	1	1	0.4	51	18	8	5		0	0	539	10	19	24	11.6	.967	1B-49
1880	**TRO N**	47	.301	.364	209	63	7	3	0	0.0	41	13	11	10		0	0	475	15	20	18	10.9	.961	1B-47
1882	**WOR N**	13	.137	.157	51	7	1	0	0	0.0	10	1	6	6		0	0	145	3	10	11	12.2	.937	1B-13
3 yrs.		109	.294	.349	496	146	16	4	1	0.2	102	32	25	21		0	0	1159	28	49	53	11.3	.960	1B-109

Alta Cohen

COHEN, ALTA ALBERT (Schoolboy) BL TL 5′10½″ 170 lbs.
B. Dec. 25, 1908, New York, N. Y.

Year	Team	Games	BA	SA	AB	H	2B	3B	HR	HR%	R	RBI	BB	SO	SB	Pinch Hit AB	Pinch Hit H	PO	A	E	DP	TC/G	FA	G by Pos
1931	**BKN N**	1	.667	.667	3	2	0	0	0	0.0	1	0	0	0	0	0	0	1	2	0	0	3.0	1.000	OF-1
1932		9	.156	.188	32	5	1	0	0	0.0	1	1	3	7	0	0	0	14	3	3	1	2.5	.850	OF-8
1933	**PHI N**	19	.188	.219	32	6	1	0	0	0.0	6	1	6	4	0	10	0	17	0	0	0	2.4	1.000	OF-7
3 yrs.		29	.194	.224	67	13	2	0	0	0.0	8	2	9	11	0	10	0	32	5	3	1	2.5	.925	OF-16

Andy Cohen

COHEN, ANDREW HOWARD BR TR 5′ 8″ 155 lbs.
Brother of Syd Cohen.
B. Oct. 25, 1904, Baltimore, Md. D. Oct. 29, 1988, El Paso, Tex.
Manager 1960.

Year	Team	Games	BA	SA	AB	H	2B	3B	HR	HR%	R	RBI	BB	SO	SB	Pinch Hit AB	Pinch Hit H	PO	A	E	DP	TC/G	FA	G by Pos
1926	**NY N**	32	.257	.314	35	9	0	1	0	0.0	4	8	1	2	0	7	1	11	29	5	1	2.0	.889	2B-10, SS-10, 3B-2
1928		129	.274	.403	504	138	24	7	9	1.8	64	59	31	17	3	0	0	310	446	25	91	6.0	.968	2B-126, SS-3, 3B-1
1929		101	.294	.383	347	102	12	2	5	1.4	40	47	11	15	3	5	0	227	318	20	52	5.9	.965	2B-94, SS-1, 3B-1
3 yrs.		262	.281	.392	886	249	36	10	14	1.6	108	114	43	34	6	12	1	548	793	50	144	5.6	.964	2B-230, SS-14, 3B-4

Jimmie Coker

COKER, JIMMIE GOODWIN BR TR 5′11″ 195 lbs.
B. Mar. 28, 1936, Holly Hill, S. C. D. Oct. 29, 1991, Throckmorton, Tex.

Year	Team	Games	BA	SA	AB	H	2B	3B	HR	HR%	R	RBI	BB	SO	SB	Pinch Hit AB	Pinch Hit H	PO	A	E	DP	TC/G	FA	G by Pos
1958	**PHI N**	2	.167	.167	6	1	0	0	0	0.0	0	0	0	0	0	0	0	11	0	0	0	5.5	1.000	C-2
1960		81	.214	.329	252	54	5	3	6	2.4	18	34	23	45	0	5	1	394	43	8	5	5.9	.982	C-76
1961		11	.400	.560	25	10	1	0	1	4.0	3	4	7	4	1	1	1	59	1	1	0	5.5	.984	C-11

Jimmie Coker *continued*

Year	Team	Games	BA	SA	AB	H	2B	3B	HR	HR%	R	RBI	BB	SO	SB	Pinch Hit AB	Pinch Hit H	PO	A	E	DP	TC/G	FA	G by Pos
1962		5	.000	.000	3	0	0	0	0	0.0	0	1	1	2	0	3	0	0	0	0	0	0.0	—	
1963	SF N	4	.200	.200	5	1	0	0	0	0.0	0	0	1	2	0	4	1	4	0	0	0	2.0	1.000	C-2
1964	CIN N	11	.313	.469	32	10	2	0	1	3.1	3	4	3	5	0	1	1	63	10	0	0	6.6	1.000	C-11
1965		24	.246	.377	61	15	2	0	2	3.3	3	9	8	16	0	6	1	145	7	1	2	8.1	.993	C-19
1966		50	.252	.387	111	28	3	0	4	3.6	9	14	8	5	0	10	2	205	25	5	2	5.7	.979	C-39, OF-2
1967		45	.186	.289	97	18	2	1	2	2.1	8	4	4	20	0	15	6	146	14	4	4	4.8	.976	C-34
9 yrs.		233	.231	.351	592	137	15	4	16	2.7	44	70	55	99	1	45	13	1027	100	19	13	5.8	.983	C-194, OF-2

Rocky Colavito

COLAVITO, ROCCO DOMENICO
B. Aug. 10, 1933, New York, N. Y.
BR TR 6′ 3″ 190 lbs.

Year	Team	Games	BA	SA	AB	H	2B	3B	HR	HR%	R	RBI	BB	SO	SB	Pinch Hit AB	Pinch Hit H	PO	A	E	DP	TC/G	FA	G by Pos
1955	CLE A	5	.444	.667	9	4	2	0	0	0.0	3	0	0	2	0	2	0	7	1	0	1	4.0	1.000	OF-2
1956		101	.276	.531	322	89	11	4	21	6.5	55	65	49	46	0	5	0	177	6	6	0	1.9	.968	OF-98
1957		134	.252	.471	461	116	26	0	25	5.4	66	84	71	80	1	3	1	268	12	11	2	2.2	.962	OF-130
1958		143	.303	**.620**	489	148	26	3	41	**8.4**	80	113	84	89	0	5	1	327	15	9	11	2.5	.974	OF-129, 1B-11, P-1
1959		154	.257	.512	588	151	24	0	**42**	7.1	90	111	71	86	3	0	0	319	7	5	1	2.1	.985	OF-154
1960	DET A	145	.249	.474	555	138	18	1	35	6.3	67	87	53	80	3	2	0	271	11	7	5	2.0	.976	OF-144
1961		163	.290	.580	583	169	30	2	45	7.7	129	140	113	75	1	2	0	329	16	9	4	2.2	.975	OF-161
1962		161	.273	.514	601	164	30	2	37	6.2	90	112	96	68	2	0	0	359	10	3	1	2.3	.992	OF-161
1963		160	.271	.437	597	162	29	2	22	3.7	91	91	84	78	0	1	0	319	10	4	0	2.1	.988	OF-159
1964	KC A	160	.274	.507	588	161	31	2	34	5.8	89	102	83	56	3	1	1	275	10	8	1	1.8	.973	OF-159
1965	CLE A	162	.287	.468	592	170	25	2	26	4.4	92	**108**	**93**	63	1	0	0	265	9	0	1	1.7	1.000	OF-162
1966		151	.238	.432	533	127	13	0	30	5.6	68	72	76	81	2	5	3	261	10	5	0	1.9	.982	OF-146
1967	2 teams	CLE A (63G –.241)	CHI A (60G –.221)																					
″	total	123	.231	.333	381	88	13	1	8	2.1	30	50	49	41	3	12	3	158	4	5	3	1.5	.970	OF-108
1968	2 teams	LA N (40G –.204)	NY A (39G –.220)																					
″	total	79	.211	.373	204	43	5	2	8	3.9	21	24	29	35	0	17	2	72	3	2	1	1.2	.974	OF-61, P-1
14 yrs.		1841	.266	.489	6503	1730	283	21	374	5.8	971	1159	951	880	19	55	11	3407	124	74	31	2.0	.979	OF-1774, 1B-11, P-2

Mike Colbern

COLBERN, MICHAEL MALLOY
B. Apr. 19, 1955, Santa Monica, Calif.
BR TR 6′ 3″ 205 lbs.

Year	Team	Games	BA	SA	AB	H	2B	3B	HR	HR%	R	RBI	BB	SO	SB	Pinch Hit AB	Pinch Hit H	PO	A	E	DP	TC/G	FA	G by Pos
1978	CHI A	48	.270	.362	141	38	5	1	2	1.4	11	20	1	36	0	0	0	203	19	7	1	4.8	.969	C-47, DH-1
1979		32	.241	.325	83	20	5	1	0	0.0	5	8	4	25	0	1	0	121	12	4	4	4.3	.971	C-32
2 yrs.		80	.259	.348	224	58	10	2	2	0.9	16	28	5	61	0	1	0	324	31	11	5	4.6	.970	C-79, DH-1

Craig Colbert

COLBERT, CRAIG CHARLES
B. Feb. 13, 1965, Iowa City, Iowa.
BR TR 6′ 190 lbs.

Year	Team	Games	BA	SA	AB	H	2B	3B	HR	HR%	R	RBI	BB	SO	SB	Pinch Hit AB	Pinch Hit H	PO	A	E	DP	TC/G	FA	G by Pos
1992	SF N	49	.230	.325	126	29	5	2	1	0.8	10	16	9	22	1	11	0	147	24	1	5	3.7	.994	C-35, 3B-9, 2B-2
1993		23	.162	.297	37	6	2	0	1	2.7	2	5	3	13	0	11	0	52	5	1	1	4.5	.983	C-10, 2B-2, 3B-1
2 yrs.		72	.215	.319	163	35	7	2	2	1.2	12	21	12	35	1	22	0	199	29	2	6	3.9	.991	C-45, 3B-10, 2B-4

Nate Colbert

COLBERT, NATHAN
B. Apr. 9, 1946, St. Louis, Mo.
BR TR 6′ 2″ 190 lbs.

Year	Team	Games	BA	SA	AB	H	2B	3B	HR	HR%	R	RBI	BB	SO	SB	Pinch Hit AB	Pinch Hit H	PO	A	E	DP	TC/G	FA	G by Pos
1966	HOU N	19	.000	.000	7	0	0	0	0	0.0	3	0	0	4	0	7	0	0	0	0	0	0.0	—	
1968		20	.151	.170	53	8	1	0	0	0.0	5	4	1	23	1	2	0	62	1	2	2	4.1	.969	OF-11, 1B-5
1969	SD N	139	.255	.482	483	123	20	9	24	5.0	64	66	45	123	6	4	0	1217	87	13	96	9.8	.990	1B-134
1970		156	.259	.509	572	148	17	6	38	6.6	84	86	56	150	3	4	0	1406	90	14	126	9.8	.991	1B-153, 3B-1
1971		156	.264	.462	565	149	25	3	27	4.8	81	84	63	119	5	3	1	1372	106	10	125	9.7	.993	1B-153
1972		151	.250	.508	563	141	27	2	38	6.7	87	111	70	127	15	2	0	1290	103	6	119	9.3	.996	1B-150
1973		145	.270	.450	529	143	25	2	22	4.2	73	80	54	146	9	1	0	1300	98	11	124	9.8	.992	1B-144
1974		119	.207	.364	368	76	16	0	14	3.8	53	54	62	108	10	12	4	605	52	9	43	5.2	.986	1B-79, OF-48
1975	2 teams	DET A (45G –.147)	MON N (38G –.173)																					
″	total	83	.156	.316	237	37	8	3	8	3.4	26	29	22	83	0	19	3	558	31	10	49	8.9	.983	1B-66, DH-1
1976	2 teams	MON N (14G –.200)	OAK A (2G –.000)																					
″	total	16	.178	.356	45	8	2	0	2	4.4	5	6	10	19	3	3	1	66	6	2	3	4.9	.973	OF-7, 1B-6, DH-2
10 yrs.		1004	.243	.451	3422	833	141	25	173	5.1	481	520	383	902	52	57	9	7876	574	77	687	8.9	.991	1B-890, OF-66, DH-3, 3B-1

Greg Colbrunn

COLBRUNN, GREGORY JOSEPH
B. July 26, 1969, Fontana, Calif.
BR TR 6′ 190 lbs.

Year	Team	Games	BA	SA	AB	H	2B	3B	HR	HR%	R	RBI	BB	SO	SB	Pinch Hit AB	Pinch Hit H	PO	A	E	DP	TC/G	FA	G by Pos
1992	MON N	52	.268	.351	168	45	8	0	2	1.2	12	18	6	34	3	5	0	363	29	3	24	8.4	.992	1B-47
1993		70	.255	.392	153	39	9	0	4	2.6	15	23	6	33	4	10	4	372	27	2	31	6.6	.995	1B-61
1994	FLA N	47	.303	.484	155	47	10	0	6	3.9	17	31	9	27	1	5	2	303	26	4	28	8.1	.988	1B-41
1995		138	.277	.453	528	146	22	1	23	4.4	70	89	22	69	11	4	2	1070	88	5	107	8.7	.996	1B-134
4 yrs.		307	.276	.431	1004	277	49	1	35	3.5	114	161	43	163	19	24	8	2108	170	14	190	8.1	.994	1B-283

Alex Cole

COLE, ALEXANDER, JR.
B. Aug. 17, 1965, Fayetteville, N. C.
BL TL 6′ 2″ 170 lbs.

Year	Team	Games	BA	SA	AB	H	2B	3B	HR	HR%	R	RBI	BB	SO	SB	Pinch Hit AB	Pinch Hit H	PO	A	E	DP	TC/G	FA	G by Pos
1990	CLE A	63	.300	.357	227	68	5	4	0	0.0	43	13	28	38	40	0	0	145	3	6	1	2.6	.961	OF-59, DH-1
1991		122	.295	.354	387	114	17	3	0	0.0	58	21	58	47	27	7	1	256	6	8	1	2.4	.970	OF-107, DH-6
1992	2 teams	CLE A (41G –.206)	PIT N (64G –.278)																					
″	total	105	.255	.315	302	77	4	7	0	0.0	44	15	28	67	16	30	4	118	6	2	1	1.6	.984	OF-77, DH-3
1993	CLR N	126	.256	.305	348	89	9	4	0	0.0	50	24	43	58	30	28	6	219	5	4	1	2.5	.982	OF-93
1994	MIN A	105	.296	.403	345	102	15	5	4	1.2	68	23	44	60	29	9	2	245	4	8	0	2.5	.969	OF-100, DH-1
1995		28	.342	.468	79	27	3	2	1	1.3	10	14	8	15	1	9	3	44	1	3	0	1.9	.938	OF-23, DH-2
6 yrs.		549	.283	.352	1688	477	53	25	5	0.3	273	110	209	285	143	83	16	1027	25	31	4	2.3	.971	OF-459, DH-13
LEAGUE CHAMPIONSHIP SERIES																								
1992	PIT N	4	.200	.200	10	2	0	0	0	0.0	2	1	3	2	0	0	0	7	1	0	1	2.0	1.000	OF-4

Dick Cole

COLE, RICHARD ROY
B. May 6, 1926, Long Beach, Calif.
BR TR 6′ 2″ 175 lbs.

Year	Team	Games	BA	SA	AB	H	2B	3B	HR	HR%	R	RBI	BB	SO	SB	Pinch Hit AB	Pinch Hit H	PO	A	E	DP	TC/G	FA	G by Pos
1951	2 teams	STL N (15G –.194) PIT N (42G –.236)																						
″	total	57	.225	.282	142	32	5	0	1	0.7	13	14	21	14	0	0	0	118	129	5	30	4.5	.980	2B-48, SS-8
1953	PIT N	97	.272	.336	235	64	13	1	0	0.0	29	23	38	26	2	9	6	156	203	12	42	4.4	.968	SS-77, 2B-7, 1B-1
1954		138	.270	.342	486	131	22	5	1	0.2	40	40	41	48	0	7	1	192	336	28	41	4.0	.950	SS-66, 3B-55, 2B-17
1955		77	.226	.285	239	54	8	3	0	0.0	16	21	18	22	0	11	2	103	158	10	25	3.9	.963	3B-33, 2B-24, SS-12
1956		72	.212	.253	99	21	2	1	0	0.0	7	9	11	9	0	40	7	20	38	2	8	1.7	.967	3B-18, 2B-12, SS-6
1957	MIL N	15	.071	.071	14	1	0	0	0	0.0	1	0	3	5	0	2	0	12	9	1	5	1.8	.955	2B-10, 3B-1, 1B-1
6 yrs.		456	.249	.312	1215	303	50	10	2	0.2	106	107	132	124	2	69	16	601	873	58	151	3.9	.962	SS-169, 2B-118, 3B-107, 1B-2

Stu Cole

COLE, STEWART BRYAN
B. Feb. 7, 1966, Charlotte, N. C.
BR TR 6′ 1″ 175 lbs.

Year	Team	Games	BA	SA	AB	H	2B	3B	HR	HR%	R	RBI	BB	SO	SB	Pinch Hit AB	Pinch Hit H	PO	A	E	DP	TC/G	FA	G by Pos
1991	KC A	9	.143	.143	7	1	0	0	0	0.0	1	0	2	2	0	2	0	2	4	0	0	0.8	1.000	2B-5, DH-2, SS-1

Willis Cole

COLE, WILLIS RUSSELL
B. Jan. 6, 1882, Milton Junction, Wis. D. Oct. 11, 1965, Madison, Wis.
BR TR 5′ 8″ 170 lbs.

Year	Team	Games	BA	SA	AB	H	2B	3B	HR	HR%	R	RBI	BB	SO	SB	Pinch Hit AB	Pinch Hit H	PO	A	E	DP	TC/G	FA	G by Pos
1909	CHI A	46	.236	.315	165	39	7	3	0	0.0	17	16	16		3	0	0	83	5	11	1	2.2	.889	OF-46
1910		22	.175	.225	80	14	2	1	0	0.0	6	2	4		0	0	0	31	6	1	0	1.7	.974	OF-22
2 yrs.		68	.216	.286	245	53	9	4	0	0.0	23	18	20		3	0	0	114	11	12	1	2.0	.912	OF-68

Bob Coleman

COLEMAN, ROBERT HUNTER
B. Sept. 26, 1890, Huntingburg, Ind. D. July 16, 1959, Boston, Mass.
Manager 1943–45.
BR TR 6′ 2″ 190 lbs.

Year	Team	Games	BA	SA	AB	H	2B	3B	HR	HR%	R	RBI	BB	SO	SB	Pinch Hit AB	Pinch Hit H	PO	A	E	DP	TC/G	FA	G by Pos
1913	PIT N	24	.180	.220	50	9	2	0	0	0.0	5	9	7	8	0	0	0	68	21	2	2	3.8	.978	C-24
1914		73	.267	.327	150	40	4	1	1	0.7	11	14	15	32	3	1	0	223	68	7	4	4.1	.977	C-72
1916	CLE A	19	.214	.286	28	6	2	0	0	0.0	3	4	7	6	0	5	1	24	11	1	1	3.0	.972	C-12
3 yrs.		116	.241	.298	228	55	8	1	1	0.4	19	27	29	46	3	6	1	315	100	10	7	3.9	.976	C-108

Choo Choo Coleman

COLEMAN, CLARENCE
B. Aug. 25, 1937, Orlando, Fla.
BL TR 5′ 9″ 165 lbs.

Year	Team	Games	BA	SA	AB	H	2B	3B	HR	HR%	R	RBI	BB	SO	SB	Pinch Hit AB	Pinch Hit H	PO	A	E	DP	TC/G	FA	G by Pos
1961	PHI N	34	.128	.149	47	6	1	0	0	0.0	3	4	2	8	0	20	2	38	4	1	1	3.1	.977	C-14
1962	NY N	55	.250	.441	152	38	7	2	6	3.9	24	17	11	24	2	14	2	187	22	1	2	4.8	.995	C-44
1963		106	.178	.215	247	44	0	0	3	1.2	22	9	24	49	5	11	2	418	54	15	9	5.3	.969	C-91, OF-1
1966		6	.188	.188	16	3	0	0	0	0.0	2	0	0	4	0	0	0	24	2	1	0	5.4	.963	C-5
4 yrs.		201	.197	.281	462	91	8	2	9	1.9	51	30	37	85	7	45	6	667	82	18	12	4.9	.977	C-154, OF-1

Curt Coleman

COLEMAN, CURTIS HANCOCK
B. Feb. 18, 1887, Salem, Ore. D. July 1, 1980, Newport, Ore.
BL TR 5′11″ 180 lbs.

Year	Team	Games	BA	SA	AB	H	2B	3B	HR	HR%	R	RBI	BB	SO	SB	Pinch Hit AB	Pinch Hit H	PO	A	E	DP	TC/G	FA	G by Pos
1912	NY A	12	.243	.351	37	9	4	0	0	0.0	8	4	7		0	2	0	9	23	5	1	3.7	.865	3B-10

Dave Coleman

COLEMAN, DAVID LEE
B. Oct. 26, 1950, Dayton, Ohio.
BR TR 6′ 3″ 195 lbs.

Year	Team	Games	BA	SA	AB	H	2B	3B	HR	HR%	R	RBI	BB	SO	SB	Pinch Hit AB	Pinch Hit H	PO	A	E	DP	TC/G	FA	G by Pos
1977	BOS A	11	.000	.000	12	0	0	0	0	0.0	1	0	1	3	0	4	0	5	0	0	0	0.6	1.000	OF-9

Ed Coleman

COLEMAN, PARKE EDWARD
B. Dec. 1, 1901, Canby, Ore. D. Aug. 5, 1964, Oregon City, Ore.
BL TR 6′ 2″ 200 lbs.

Year	Team	Games	BA	SA	AB	H	2B	3B	HR	HR%	R	RBI	BB	SO	SB	Pinch Hit AB	Pinch Hit H	PO	A	E	DP	TC/G	FA	G by Pos
1932	PHI A	26	.342	.507	73	25	7	1	1	1.4	13	13	1	6	1	10	2	24	3	0	1	1.7	1.000	OF-16
1933		102	.281	.410	388	109	26	3	6	1.5	48	68	19	51	0	12	2	178	5	10	2	2.2	.948	OF-89
1934		101	.280	.486	329	92	14	6	14	4.3	53	60	29	34	0	15	8	140	8	3	2	1.8	.980	OF-86
1935	2 teams	PHI A (10G –.077) STL A (108G –.287)																						
″	total	118	.280	.485	410	115	15	9	17	4.1	66	71	53	44	0	14	1	173	11	5	1	1.8	.974	OF-103
1936	STL A	92	.292	.431	137	40	5	4	2	1.5	13	34	15	17	0	**62**	**20**	31	0	2	0	1.8	.939	OF-18
5 yrs.		439	.285	.459	1337	381	67	23	40	3.0	193	246	117	152	1	113	33	546	27	20	6	1.9	.966	OF-312

Gordy Coleman

COLEMAN, GORDON CALVIN
B. July 5, 1934, Rockville, Md. D. Mar. 12, 1994, Cincinnati, Ohio.
BL TR 6′ 3″ 208 lbs.

Year	Team	Games	BA	SA	AB	H	2B	3B	HR	HR%	R	RBI	BB	SO	SB	Pinch Hit AB	Pinch Hit H	PO	A	E	DP	TC/G	FA	G by Pos
1959	CLE A	6	.533	.667	15	8	0	1	0	0.0	5	2	1	2	0	2	2	18	3	1	1	7.3	.955	1B-3
1960	CIN N	66	.271	.390	251	68	10	1	6	2.4	26	32	12	32	1	0	0	559	63	1	69	9.4	.998	1B-66
1961		150	.287	.504	520	149	27	4	26	5.0	63	87	45	67	1	6	3	1162	121	11	93	8.6	.991	1B-150
1962		136	.277	.485	476	132	13	1	28	5.9	73	86	36	68	2	15	3	1021	83	12	100	8.7	.989	1B-128
1963		123	.247	.427	365	90	20	2	14	3.8	38	59	29	51	1	19	8	752	65	11	66	7.7	.987	1B-107
1964		89	.242	.369	198	48	6	2	5	2.5	18	27	13	30	2	35	9	352	35	4	28	8.0	.990	1B-49
1965		108	.302	.489	325	98	19	0	14	4.3	39	57	24	38	0	16	6	621	48	6	52	7.6	.991	1B-89
1966		91	.251	.348	227	57	7	0	5	2.2	20	37	16	45	2	25	9	399	29	6	33	6.7	.986	1B-65
1967		4	.000	.000	7	0	0	0	0	0.0	0	0	1	0	0	2	0	9	1	0	0	5.0	1.000	1B-2
9 yrs.		773	.273	.448	2384	650	102	11	98	4.1	282	387	177	333	9	120	40	4893	448	52	442	8.2	.990	1B-659
WORLD SERIES																								
1961	CIN N	5	.250	.400	20	5	0	0	1	5.0	2	2	0	1	0	0	0	30	4	1	6	7.0	.971	1B-5

Jerry Coleman

COLEMAN, GERALD FRANCIS
B. Sept. 14, 1924, San Jose, Calif.
Manager 1980.
BR TR 6′ 165 lbs.

Year	Team	Games	BA	SA	AB	H	2B	3B	HR	HR%	R	RBI	BB	SO	SB	Pinch Hit AB	Pinch Hit H	PO	A	E	DP	TC/G	FA	G by Pos
1949	NY A	128	.275	.358	447	123	21	5	2	0.4	54	42	63	44	8	1	1	304	331	13	106	5.1	.980	2B-122, SS-4
1950		153	.287	.381	522	150	19	6	6	1.1	69	69	67	38	3	1	0	388	390	19	138	5.0	.976	2B-152, SS-6
1951		121	.249	.315	362	90	11	2	3	0.8	48	43	31	36	6	1	0	272	295	18	92	4.9	.969	2B-102, SS-18
1952		11	.405	.500	42	17	2	1	0	0.0	6	4	5	4	0	0	0	33	34	2	17	6.3	.971	2B-11
1953		8	.200	.200	10	2	0	0	0	0.0	1	0	0	2	0	0	0	11	9	1	4	2.6	.952	2B-7, SS-1
1954		107	.217	.277	300	65	7	1	3	1.0	39	21	26	29	3	0	0	209	252	14	71	4.3	.971	2B-79, SS-30, 3B-1
1955		43	.229	.281	96	22	5	0	0	0.0	12	8	11	11	0	1	0	66	74	4	24	3.3	.972	SS-29, 2B-13, 3B-1
1956		80	.257	.295	183	47	5	1	0	0.0	15	18	12	33	1	2	0	138	152	9	46	3.6	.970	2B-41, SS-24, 3B-18
1957		72	.268	.376	157	42	7	2	2	1.3	23	12	20	21	1	4	1	90	120	9	34	3.1	.959	2B-45, 3B-21, SS-4
9 yrs.		723	.263	.339	2119	558	77	18	16	0.8	267	217	235	218	22	10	2	1511	1657	89	532	4.5	.973	2B-572, SS-116, 3B-41

Jerry Coleman *continued*

Year	Team	Games	BA	SA	AB	H	2B	3B	HR	HR%	R	RBI	BB	SO	SB	Pinch Hit AB	Pinch Hit H	PO	A	E	DP	TC/G	FA	G by Pos
WORLD SERIES																								
1949	NY A	5	.250	.400	20	5	3	0	0	0.0	0	4	0	4	0	0	0	10	9	1	3	4.0	.950	2B-5
1950		4	.286	.357	14	4	1	0	0	0.0	2	3	2	0	0	0	0	11	12	0	3	5.8	1.000	2B-4
1951		5	.250	.250	8	2	0	0	0	0.0	2	0	1	2	0	0	0	7	5	0	2	2.4	1.000	2B-5
1955		3	.000	.000	3	0	0	0	0	0.0	0	0	0	1	0	0	0	2	3	0	3	1.7	1.000	SS-3
1956		2	.000	.000	2	0	0	0	0	0.0	0	0	0	0	0	0	0	2	2	0	0	2.0	1.000	2B-2
1957		7	.364	.455	22	8	2	0	0	0.0	2	2	3	1	0	0	0	16	17	0	3	4.7	1.000	2B-7
6 yrs.		26	.275	.362	69	19	6	0	0	0.0	6	9	6	8	0	0	0	48	48	1	14	3.7	.990	2B-23, SS-3

John Coleman

COLEMAN, JOHN FRANCIS BL TR 5′ 9½″ 170 lbs.
B. Mar. 6, 1863, Saratoga Springs, N. Y. D. May 31, 1922, Detroit, Mich. BB 1887

Year	Team	Games	BA	SA	AB	H	2B	3B	HR	HR%	R	RBI	BB	SO	SB	Pinch Hit AB	Pinch Hit H	PO	A	E	DP	TC/G	FA	G by Pos
1883	PHI N	90	.234	.314	354	83	12	8	0	0.0	33		15	39		0	0	91	132	31	6	2.6	.878	P-65, OF-31, 2B-1
1884	2 teams	PHI N (43G –.246) PHI AA (28G –.206)																						
″	total	71	.230	.320	278	64	9	5	2	0.7	32		13	20		0	0	106	55	24	3	2.3	.870	OF-51, P-24, 1B-4
1885	PHI AA	96	.299	.412	398	119	15	12	2	0.5	71		25			0	0	130	32	28	5	1.9	.853	OF-93, P-8
1886	2 teams	PHI AA (121G –.246) PIT AA (11G –.349)																						
″	total	132	.254	.355	535	136	20	17	0	0.0	70		35			0	0	235	32	36	9	2.2	.881	OF-126, 1B-6, P-3, 2B-1
1887	PIT N	115	.293	.396	475	139	21	11	2	0.4	75	54	31	40	25	0	0	226	17	28	3	2.3	.897	OF-115, 1B-2
1888		116	.231	.274	438	101	11	4	0	0.0	49	26	29	52	15	0	0	395	24	20	14	3.8	.954	OF-91, 1B-25
1889	PHI AA	6	.053	.053	19	1	0	0	0	0.0	1	1	1	3	1	0	0	3	10	2	0	2.5	.867	P-5, OF-1
1890	PIT N	3	.182	.182	11	2	0	0	0	0.0	1	0	3	0	1	0	0	2	1	0	0	0.8	1.000	OF-2, P-2
8 yrs.		629	.257	.345	2508	645	88	57	6	0.2	332	81	152	154	42	0	0	1188	303	169	40	2.5	.898	OF-510, P-107, 1B-37, 2B-2

Ray Coleman

COLEMAN, RAYMOND LeROY BL TR 5′11″ 170 lbs.
B. June 4, 1922, Dunsmuir, Calif.

Year	Team	Games	BA	SA	AB	H	2B	3B	HR	HR%	R	RBI	BB	SO	SB	Pinch Hit AB	Pinch Hit H	PO	A	E	DP	TC/G	FA	G by Pos
1947	STL A	110	.259	.344	343	89	9	7	2	0.6	34	30	26	32	2	18	3	174	7	3	4	2.0	.984	OF-93
1948	2 teams	STL A (17G –.172) PHI A (68G –.243)																						
″	total	85	.234	.318	239	56	6	7	0	0.0	34	23	33	22	5	24	2	134	7	4	3	2.5	.972	OF-58
1950	STL A	117	.271	.430	384	104	25	6	8	2.1	54	55	32	37	7	17	6	253	7	4	1	2.7	.985	OF-98
1951	2 teams	STL A (91G –.282) CHI A (51G –.276)																						
″	total	142	.280	.418	522	146	24	12	8	1.5	62	76	39	46	5	6	2	326	12	8	2	2.5	.977	OF-138
1952	2 teams	CHI A (85G –.215) STL A (20G –.196)																						
″	total	105	.212	.286	241	51	10	1	2	0.8	24	15	18	21	0	16	1	158	5	3	0	1.9	.982	OF-89
5 yrs.		559	.258	.374	1729	446	74	33	20	1.2	208	199	148	158	19	81	14	1045	38	22	10	2.3	.980	OF-476

Vince Coleman

COLEMAN, VINCENT MAURICE BB TR 6′ 170 lbs.
B. Sept. 22, 1961, Jacksonville, Fla.

Year	Team	Games	BA	SA	AB	H	2B	3B	HR	HR%	R	RBI	BB	SO	SB	Pinch Hit AB	Pinch Hit H	PO	A	E	DP	TC/G	FA	G by Pos
1985	STL N	151	.267	.335	636	170	20	10	1	0.2	107	40	50	115	**110**	1	0	305	16	7	1	2.2	.979	OF-150
1986		154	.232	.280	600	139	13	8	0	0.0	94	29	60	98	**107**	2	1	300	12	9	2	2.2	.972	OF-149
1987		151	.289	.358	623	180	14	10	3	0.5	121	43	70	126	**109**	1	0	274	16	9	3	2.0	.970	OF-150
1988		153	.260	.339	616	160	20	10	3	0.5	77	38	49	111	**81**	2	0	290	14	9	1	2.1	.971	OF-150
1989		145	.254	.334	563	143	21	9	2	0.4	94	28	50	90	**65**	5	2	247	5	10	1	1.8	.962	OF-142
1990		124	.292	.400	497	145	18	9	6	1.2	73	39	35	88	**77**	5	0	244	12	5	2	2.2	.981	OF-120
1991	NY N	72	.255	.327	278	71	7	5	1	0.4	45	17	39	47	37	2	0	132	5	3	0	2.0	.979	OF-70
1992		71	.275	.358	229	63	11	1	2	0.9	37	21	27	41	24	8	3	112	2	1	2	1.9	.991	OF-61
1993		92	.279	.375	373	104	14	8	2	0.5	64	25	21	58	38	3	1	162	5	3	0	1.9	.982	OF-90
1994	KC A	104	.240	.340	438	105	14	12	2	0.5	61	33	29	72	50	0	0	163	11	7	1	1.8	.961	OF-99, DH-4
1995	2 teams	KC A (75G –.287) SEA A (40G –.290)																						
″	total	115	.288	.398	455	131	23	6	5	1.1	66	29	37	80	42	2	1	190	9	4	1	1.8	.980	OF-107, DH-4
11 yrs.		1332	.266	.347	5308	1411	175	88	27	0.5	839	342	467	926	740 **6th**	31	8	2419	107	67	14	2.0	.974	OF-1288, DH-8
DIVISIONAL PLAYOFF SERIES																								
1995	SEA A	5	.217	.435	23	5	0	1	1	4.3	6	1	2	4	1	0	0	14	0	0	0	2.8	1.000	OF-5
LEAGUE CHAMPIONSHIP SERIES																								
1985	STL N	3	.286	.286	14	4	0	0	0	0.0	2	1	0	2	1	0	0	8	0	0	0	2.7	1.000	OF-3
1987		7	.269	.308	26	7	1	0	0	0.0	3	4	4	6	1	0	0	9	1	0	0	1.4	1.000	OF-7
1995	SEA A	6	.100	.100	20	2	0	0	0	0.0	0	0	2	6	4	0	0	12	0	0	0	2.4	1.000	OF-5
3 yrs.		16	.217	.233	60	13	1	0	0	0.0	5	5	6	14	6 **8th**	0	0	29	1	0	0	2.0	1.000	OF-15
WORLD SERIES																								
1987	STL N	7	.143	.214	28	4	2	0	0	0.0	5	2	2	10	6	0	0	10	2	0	0	1.7	1.000	OF-7

Cad Coles

COLES, CADWALLADER BL TR 6′½″ 174 lbs.
B. Jan. 17, 1886, Rock Hill, S. C. D. June 30, 1942, Miami, Fla.

Year	Team	Games	BA	SA	AB	H	2B	3B	HR	HR%	R	RBI	BB	SO	SB	Pinch Hit AB	Pinch Hit H	PO	A	E	DP	TC/G	FA	G by Pos
1914	KC F	78	.253	.335	194	49	7	3	1	0.5	17	25	5		6	34	7	83	5	8	2	2.3	.917	OF-39, 1B-3

Chuck Coles

COLES, CHARLES EDWARD BL TL 5′ 9″ 180 lbs.
B. June 27, 1931, Fredericktown, Pa.

Year	Team	Games	BA	SA	AB	H	2B	3B	HR	HR%	R	RBI	BB	SO	SB	Pinch Hit AB	Pinch Hit H	PO	A	E	DP	TC/G	FA	G by Pos
1958	CIN N	5	.182	.273	11	2	1	0	0	0.0	0	2	2	6	0	1	0	12	0	0	0	3.0	1.000	OF-4

Darnell Coles

COLES, DARNELL BR TR 6′ 1″ 185 lbs.
B. June 2, 1962, San Bernardino, Calif.

Year	Team	Games	BA	SA	AB	H	2B	3B	HR	HR%	R	RBI	BB	SO	SB	Pinch Hit AB	Pinch Hit H	PO	A	E	DP	TC/G	FA	G by Pos
1983	SEA A	27	.283	.391	92	26	7	0	1	1.1	9	6	7	12	0	1	0	17	47	4	8	2.6	.941	3B-26
1984		48	.161	.196	143	23	3	1	0	0.0	15	6	17	26	2	0	0	31	63	8	10	2.1	.922	3B-42, OF-3, DH-3
1985		27	.237	.356	59	14	4	0	1	1.7	8	5	9	17	0	3	0	25	44	6	10	2.9	.920	SS-15, 3B-7, DH-2, OF-2
1986	DET A	142	.273	.453	521	142	30	2	20	3.8	67	86	45	84	6	1	0	111	242	23	23	2.6	.939	3B-133, DH-7, SS-2, OF-2
1987	2 teams	DET A (53G –.181) PIT N (40G –.227)																						
″	total	93	.201	.369	268	54	13	1	10	3.7	34	39	34	43	1	9	2	123	87	20	6	2.4	.913	3B-46, OF-34, 1B-10, DH-3, SS-1
1988	2 teams	PIT N (68G –.232) SEA A (55G –.292)																						
″	total	123	.261	.438	406	106	23	2	15	3.7	52	70	37	67	4	11	0	166	3	3	0	1.5	.983	OF-102, DH-7, 1B-2, 3B-1
1989	SEA A	146	.252	.359	535	135	21	3	10	1.9	54	59	27	61	5	8	1	317	76	12	20	2.8	.970	OF-89, 3B-26, 1B-18, DH-12

Darnell Coles *continued*

Year	Team	Games	BA	SA	AB	H	2B	3B	HR	HR%	R	RBI	BB	SO	SB	Pinch Hit AB	Pinch Hit H	PO	A	E	DP	TC/G	FA	G by Pos
1990	2 teams	SEA A (37G –.215) DET A (52G –.204)																						
"	total	89	.209	.293	215	45	7	1	3	1.4	22	20	16	38	0	27	8	69	42	9	3	1.5	.925	OF-31, DH-31, 3B-14, 1B-4
1991	SF N	11	.214	.214	14	3	0	0	0	0.0	1	0	0	2	0	7	2	4	0	0	0	1.0	1.000	OF-3, 1B-1
1992	CIN N	55	.312	.482	141	44	11	2	3	2.1	16	18	3	15	1	10	3	161	42	0	8	4.2	1.000	3B-23, 1B-20, OF-5
1993	TOR A	64	.253	.371	194	49	9	1	4	2.1	26	26	16	29	1	4	1	77	20	7	0	1.7	.933	OF-44, 3B-16, 1B-1, DH-1
1994		48	.210	.350	143	30	6	1	4	2.8	15	15	10	25	0	4	0	103	9	4	7	2.5	.966	OF-29, 1B-10, 3B-7, DH-1
1995	STL N	63	.225	.341	138	31	7	0	3	2.2	13	16	16	20	0	17	2	136	33	3	8	4.2	.983	3B-22, 1B-18, OF-1
13 yrs.		936	.245	.381	2869	702	141	14	74	2.6	332	366	237	439	20	102	19	1340	708	99	103	2.4	.954	3B-363, OF-345, 1B-84, DH-67, SS-18

Chris Coletta

COLETTA, CHRISTOPHER MICHAEL BL TL 5′11″ 190 lbs.
B. Aug. 2, 1944, Brooklyn, N. Y.

Year	Team	Games	BA	SA	AB	H	2B	3B	HR	HR%	R	RBI	BB	SO	SB	Pinch Hit AB	Pinch Hit H	PO	A	E	DP	TC/G	FA	G by Pos
1972	CAL A	14	.300	.433	30	9	1	0	1	3.3	5	7	1	4	0	8	3	3	0	0	0	0.4	1.000	OF-7

Bill Colgan

COLGAN, WILLIAM H. (Ed) 180 lbs.
B. East St. Louis, Ill. D. Aug. 13, 1895, Great Falls, Mont.

Year	Team	Games	BA	SA	AB	H	2B	3B	HR	HR%	R	RBI	BB	SO	SB	Pinch Hit AB	Pinch Hit H	PO	A	E	DP	TC/G	FA	G by Pos
1884	PIT AA	48	.155	.193	161	25	4	1	0	0.0	10		3			0	0	234	71	32	5	7.0	.905	C-44, OF-4

Bill Coliver

COLIVER, WILLIAM J.
B. Mar. 21, 1867, Clyde, Ohio D. Mar. 24, 1888, Detroit, Mich.

Year	Team	Games	BA	SA	AB	H	2B	3B	HR	HR%	R	RBI	BB	SO	SB	Pinch Hit AB	Pinch Hit H	PO	A	E	DP	TC/G	FA	G by Pos
1885	BOS N	1	.000	.000	4	0	0	0	0	0.0	0	0	0	1		0	0	0	0	0	0	0.0	.000	OF-1

Collins

COLLINS
Deceased.

Year	Team	Games	BA	SA	AB	H	2B	3B	HR	HR%	R	RBI	BB	SO	SB	Pinch Hit AB	Pinch Hit H	PO	A	E	DP	TC/G	FA	G by Pos
1892	STL N	1	.000	.000	2	0	0	0	0	0.0	0	0	1	2	1	0	0	1	0	0	0	1.0	1.000	OF-1

Bill Collins

COLLINS, WILLIAM J. BR
B. 1863, Dublin, Ireland D. June 8, 1893, New York, N. Y.

Year	Team	Games	BA	SA	AB	H	2B	3B	HR	HR%	R	RBI	BB	SO	SB	Pinch Hit AB	Pinch Hit H	PO	A	E	DP	TC/G	FA	G by Pos
1889	PHI AA	1	.250	.250	4	1	0	0	0	0.0	0	1	1	0	1	0	0	2	2	1	0	5.0	.800	C-1
1890		1	.000	.000	1	0	0	0	0	0.0	0		0		0	0	0	1	1	2	0	4.0	.500	SS-1
1891	CLE N	2	.000	.000	3	0	0	0	0	0.0	0	0	0	0	0	0	0	5	4	1	1	5.0	.900	C-1, OF-1
3 yrs.		4	.125	.125	8	1	0	0	0	0.0	0	1	1	0	1	0	0	8	7	4	1	4.8	.789	C-2, OF-1, SS-1

Bill Collins

COLLINS, WILLIAM SHIRLEY BB TR 6′ 170 lbs.
B. Mar. 27, 1882, Chesterton, Ind. D. June 26, 1961, San Bernardino, Calif.

Year	Team	Games	BA	SA	AB	H	2B	3B	HR	HR%	R	RBI	BB	SO	SB	Pinch Hit AB	Pinch Hit H	PO	A	E	DP	TC/G	FA	G by Pos
1910	BOS N	151	.241	.291	584	141	6	7	3	0.5	67	40	43	48	36	0	0	355	23	9	2	2.6	.977	OF-151
1911	2 teams	BOS N (17G –.136) CHI N (7G –.200)																						
"	total	24	.143	.224	49	7	2	1	0	0.0	10	8	2	11	4	1	1	32	1	0	0	1.8	1.000	OF-17, 3B-1
1913	BKN N	32	.189	.200	95	18	1	0	0	0.0	8	4	8	11	2	4	0	57	1	5	0	2.3	.921	OF-27
1914	BUF F	21	.149	.277	47	7	2	2	0	0.0	6	2	1		0	4	0	14	5	3	0	1.5	.864	OF-15
4 yrs.		228	.223	.275	775	173	11	10	3	0.4	91	54	54	70	42	9	1	458	30	17	2	2.4	.966	OF-210, 3B-1

Bob Collins

COLLINS, ROBERT JOSEPH BR TR 5′11″ 176 lbs.
B. Sept. 18, 1909, Pittsburgh, Pa. D. Apr. 19, 1969, Pittsburgh, Pa.

Year	Team	Games	BA	SA	AB	H	2B	3B	HR	HR%	R	RBI	BB	SO	SB	Pinch Hit AB	Pinch Hit H	PO	A	E	DP	TC/G	FA	G by Pos
1940	CHI N	47	.208	.258	120	25	3	0	1	0.8	11	14	14	18	4	4	1	133	23	8	3	3.9	.951	C-42
1944	NY A	3	.333	.333	3	1	0	0	0	0.0	0	0	1	0	0	0	0	5	1	0	0	2.0	1.000	C-3
2 yrs.		50	.211	.260	123	26	3	0	1	0.8	11	14	15	18	4	4	1	138	24	8	3	3.8	.953	C-45

Chub Collins

COLLINS, CHARLES AUGUSTINE BB 5′11½″ 165 lbs.
B. Oct. 12, 1857, Dundas, Ont., Canada D. May 20, 1914, Dundas, Ont., Canada.

Year	Team	Games	BA	SA	AB	H	2B	3B	HR	HR%	R	RBI	BB	SO	SB	Pinch Hit AB	Pinch Hit H	PO	A	E	DP	TC/G	FA	G by Pos
1884	2 teams	BUF N (45G –.178) IND AA (38G –.225)																						
"	total	83	.199	.235	307	61	9	1	0	0.0	42		23	36		0	0	205	248	53	26	6.1	.895	2B-80, SS-3
1885	DET N	14	.182	.255	55	10	0	2	0	0.0	8	6	0	11		0	0	7	35	11	3	3.8	.792	SS-14
2 yrs.		97	.196	.238	362	71	9	3	0	0.0	50	6	23	47		0	0	212	283	64	29	5.8	.886	2B-80, SS-17

Cyril Collins

COLLINS, CYRIL WILSON BR TR 5′ 9½″ 165 lbs.
B. May 7, 1889, Pulaski, Tenn. D. Feb. 28, 1941, Knoxville, Tenn.

Year	Team	Games	BA	SA	AB	H	2B	3B	HR	HR%	R	RBI	BB	SO	SB	Pinch Hit AB	Pinch Hit H	PO	A	E	DP	TC/G	FA	G by Pos
1913	BOS N	16	.333	.333	3	1	0	0	0	0.0	3	0	0	1	0	0	0	3	0	0	0	0.3	1.000	OF-9
1914		27	.257	.257	35	9	0	0	0	0.0	5	1	2	8	0	1	0	22	0	2	1	1.3	.917	OF-19
2 yrs.		43	.263	.263	38	10	0	0	0	0.0	8	1	2	9	0	1	0	25	0	2	1	1.0	.926	OF-28

Dan Collins

COLLINS, DANIEL THOMAS
B. July 12, 1854, St. Louis, Mo. D. Sept. 21, 1883, New Orleans, La.

Year	Team	Games	BA	SA	AB	H	2B	3B	HR	HR%	R	RBI	BB	SO	SB	Pinch Hit AB	Pinch Hit H	PO	A	E	DP	TC/G	FA	G by Pos
1876	LOU N	7	.143	.179	28	4	1	0	0	0.0	3	9	0	2		0	0	8	2	1	1	1.6	.909	OF-7

Dave Collins

COLLINS, DAVID SCOTT BB TL 5′10″ 175 lbs.
B. Oct. 20, 1952, Rapid City, S. D.

Year	Team	Games	BA	SA	AB	H	2B	3B	HR	HR%	R	RBI	BB	SO	SB	Pinch Hit AB	Pinch Hit H	PO	A	E	DP	TC/G	FA	G by Pos
1975	CAL A	93	.266	.361	319	85	13	4	3	0.9	41	29	36	55	24	5	4	159	3	2	2	1.9	.988	OF-75, DH-12
1976		99	.263	.334	365	96	12	1	4	1.1	45	28	40	55	32	2	0	160	3	1	0	1.8	.994	OF-71, DH-22
1977	SEA A	120	.239	.313	402	96	9	3	5	1.2	46	28	33	66	25	7	4	124	6	2	2	1.2	.985	OF-73, DH-40
1978	CIN N	102	.216	.225	102	22	1	0	0	0.0	13	7	15	18	7	**64**	14	30	1	1	0	1.3	.969	OF-24
1979		122	.318	.402	396	126	16	4	3	0.8	59	35	27	48	16	28	9	223	3	4	8	2.3	.983	OF-91, 1B-10
1980		144	.303	.370	551	167	20	4	3	0.5	94	35	53	68	79	3	1	337	5	5	1	2.5	.986	OF-141
1981		95	.272	.381	360	98	18	6	3	0.8	63	23	41	41	26	1	0	167	4	4	2	1.9	.977	OF-94
1982	NY A	111	.253	.330	348	88	12	3	3	0.9	41	25	28	49	13	7	1	498	28	7	30	4.7	.987	OF-60, 1B-52, DH-1
1983	TOR A	118	.271	.328	402	109	12	4	1	0.2	55	34	43	67	31	18	5	270	9	3	3	2.4	.989	OF-112, 1B-5, DH-1
1984		128	.308	.444	441	136	24	**15**	2	0.5	59	44	33	41	60	14	6	237	11	2	7	2.1	.992	OF-108, 1B-6, DH-4
1985	OAK A	112	.251	.346	379	95	16	4	4	1.1	52	29	29	37	29	17	4	221	1	5	0	2.5	.978	OF-91
1986	DET A	124	.270	.329	419	113	18	2	1	0.2	44	27	44	49	27	11	1	211	2	1	1	1.8	.995	OF-94, DH-24
1987	CIN N	57	.294	.353	85	25	5	0	0	0.0	19	5	11	12	9	35	8	36	0	0	0	1.7	1.000	OF-21

Dave Collins *continued*

Year	Team		Games	BA	SA	AB	H	2B	3B	HR	HR%	R	RBI	BB	SO	SB	Pinch Hit AB	Pinch Hit H	PO	A	E	DP	TC/G	FA	G by Pos
1988			99	.236	.293	174	41	6	2	0	0.0	12	14	11	27	7	58	12	66	2	4	2	1.9	.944	OF-35, 1B-3
1989			78	.236	.274	106	25	4	0	0	0.0	12	7	10	17	3	55	10	41	0	0	0	2.6	1.000	OF-16
1990	**STL**	**N**	99	.224	.241	58	13	1	0	0	0.0	12	3	13	10	7	25	6	89	0	1	5	1.5	.989	1B-49, OF-12
16 yrs.			1701	.272	.351	4907	1335	187	52	32	0.7	667	373	467	660	395	350	85	2869	78	42	63	2.2	.986	OF-1118, 1B-125, DH-104
LEAGUE CHAMPIONSHIP SERIES																									
1979	**CIN**	**N**	3	.357	.429	14	5	1	0	0	0.0	0	1	0	2	2	0	0	5	0	0	0	1.7	1.000	OF-3

Eddie Collins

COLLINS, EDWARD TROWBRIDGE, JR.
Son of Eddie Collins.
B. Nov. 23, 1916, Lansdowne, Pa.

BL TR 5′10″ 175 lbs.

Year	Team		Games	BA	SA	AB	H	2B	3B	HR	HR%	R	RBI	BB	SO	SB	Pinch Hit AB	Pinch Hit H	PO	A	E	DP	TC/G	FA	G by Pos
1939	**PHI**	**A**	32	.238	.286	21	5	1	0	0	0.0	6	0	0	3	1	10	3	11	1	1	0	1.9	.923	OF-6, 2B-1
1941			80	.242	.297	219	53	6	3	0	0.0	29	12	20	24	2	28	6	119	3	4	1	2.5	.968	OF-50
1942			20	.235	.294	34	8	2	0	0	0.0	6	4	4	2	1	5	1	8	0	2	0	1.1	.800	OF-9
3 yrs.			132	.241	.296	274	66	9	3	0	0.0	41	16	24	29	4	43	10	138	4	7	1	2.3	.953	OF-65, 2B-1

Eddie Collins

COLLINS, EDWARD TROWBRIDGE, SR. (Cocky)
Played as Eddie Sullivan in 1906.
Father of Eddie Collins.
B. May 2, 1887, Millerton, N. Y. D. Mar. 25, 1951, Boston, Mass.
Manager 1924–26.
Hall of Fame 1939.

BL TR 5′ 9″ 175 lbs.

Year	Team		Games	BA	SA	AB	H	2B	3B	HR	HR%	R	RBI	BB	SO	SB	Pinch Hit AB	Pinch Hit H	PO	A	E	DP	TC/G	FA	G by Pos
1906	**PHI**	**A**	6	.235	.235	17	4	0	0	0	0.0	1	0	0		1	1	0	9	11	2	0	4.4	.909	SS-3, 3B-1, 2B-1
1907			14	.250	.350	20	5	0	1	0	0.0	0	2	0		0	6	1	11	9	4	1	4.0	.833	SS-6
1908			102	.273	.379	330	90	18	7	1	0.3	39	40	16		8	11	4	184	188	25	12	4.7	.937	2B-47, SS-28, OF-10
1909			153	.346	.449	572	198	30	10	3	0.5	104	56	62		67	0	0	375	410	27	55	5.3	.967	2B-152, SS-1
1910			153	.322	.417	583	188	16	15	3	0.5	81	81	49		**81**	0	0	402	451	25	67	5.7	.972	2B-153
1911			132	.365	.481	493	180	22	13	3	0.6	92	73	62		38	0	0	348	349	24	49	5.5	.967	2B-132
1912			153	.348	.435	543	189	25	11	0	0.0	**137**	64	101		63	0	0	387	426	38	63	5.6	.955	2B-153
1913			148	.345	.453	534	184	23	13	3	0.6	**125**	73	85	37	55	0	0	314	449	28	54	5.3	.965	2B-148
1914			152	.344	.452	526	181	23	14	2	0.4	**122**	85	97	31	58	0	0	354	387	23	55	5.0	.970	2B-152
1915	**CHI**	**A**	155	.332	.436	521	173	22	10	4	0.8	118	77	**119**	27	46	0	0	344	487	22	54	5.5	.974	2B-155
1916			155	.308	.396	545	168	14	17	0	0.0	87	52	86	36	40	0	0	346	415	19	75	5.0	.976	2B-155
1917			156	.289	.363	564	163	18	12	0	0.0	91	67	89	16	53	0	0	353	388	24	68	4.9	.969	2B-156
1918			97	.276	.330	330	91	8	2	2	0.6	51	30	73	13	22	1	1	231	285	14	53	5.5	.974	2B-96
1919			140	.319	.405	518	165	19	7	4	0.8	87	80	68	27	**33**	0	0	347	401	20	66	5.5	.974	2B-140
1920			153	.372	.493	602	224	38	13	3	0.5	117	76	69	19	19	0	0	449	471	23	76	6.2	.976	2B-153
1921			139	.337	.424	526	177	20	10	2	0.4	79	58	66	11	12	3	0	376	458	28	84	6.3	.968	2B-136
1922			154	.324	.403	598	194	20	12	1	0.2	92	69	73	16	20	0	0	406	451	21	73	5.7	.976	2B-154
1923			145	.360	.453	505	182	22	5	5	1.0	89	67	84	8	**47**	3	0	347	430	20	77	5.6	.975	2B-142
1924			152	.349	.455	556	194	27	7	6	1.1	108	86	89	16	**42**	2	0	396	446	20	83	5.7	.977	2B-150
1925			118	.346	.442	425	147	26	3	3	0.7	80	80	87	8	19	2	0	290	346	20	74	5.7	.970	2B-116
1926			106	.344	.459	375	129	32	4	1	0.3	66	62	62	8	13	3	0	228	307	15	53	5.4	.973	2B-101
1927	**PHI**	**A**	95	.338	.413	225	76	12	1	1	0.4	50	15	60	9	6	**34**	**12**	124	150	10	31	5.0	.965	2B-56, SS-1
1928			36	.303	.394	33	10	3	0	0	0.0	3	7	4	4	0	29	8	0	1	0	0	0.3	1.000	2B-2, SS-1
1929			9	.000	.000	7	0	0	0	0	0.0	0	0	2	0	0	7	0	0	0	0	0	0.0	—	
1930			3	.333	.333	3	1	0	0	0	0.0	1	0	0	0	0	3	1	0	0	0	0	0.0	—	
25 yrs.			2826	.333	.429	9951	3313 **8th**	438	187	47	0.5	1820	1300	1503	286	743 **5th**	105	27	6621	7716	452	1223	5.5	.969	2B-2650, SS-40, OF-10, 3B-1
WORLD SERIES																									
1910	**PHI**	**A**	5	.429	.619	21	9	4	0	0	0.0	5	3	2	0	4	0	0	17	17	1	4	7.0	.971	2B-5
1911			6	.286	.333	21	6	1	0	0	0.0	4	1	2	2	2	0	0	12	22	4	1	6.3	.895	2B-6
1913			5	.421	.632	19	8	0	2	0	0.0	5	3	1	2	3	0	0	16	18	1	5	7.0	.971	2B-5
1914			4	.214	.214	14	3	0	0	0	0.0	0	1	2	1	1	0	0	9	12	0	1	5.3	1.000	2B-4
1917	**CHI**	**A**	6	.409	.455	22	9	1	0	0	0.0	4	2	2	3	3	0	0	11	23	0	3	5.7	1.000	2B-6
1919			8	.226	.258	31	7	1	0	0	0.0	2	1	1	2	1	0	0	21	31	2	7	6.8	.963	2B-8
6 yrs.			34	.328	.414	128	42 **10th**	7	2	0	0.0	20	11	10	10	14 **1st**	0	0	86	123	8	21	6.4	.963	2B-34

Hub Collins

COLLINS, HUBERT B.
B. Apr. 15, 1864, Louisville, Ky. D. May 21, 1892, Brooklyn, N. Y.

BR TR 5′ 8″ 160 lbs.

Year	Team		Games	BA	SA	AB	H	2B	3B	HR	HR%	R	RBI	BB	SO	SB	Pinch Hit AB	Pinch Hit H	PO	A	E	DP	TC/G	FA	G by Pos
1886	**LOU**	**AA**	27	.287	.356	101	29	3	2	0	0.0	12		5			0	0	49	4	7	0	2.1	.883	OF-24, 3B-2, SS-1, 2B-1, 1B-1
1887			130	.290	.363	559	162	22	8	1	0.2	122		39		71	0	0	305	47	43	6	3.0	.891	OF-109, 2B-10, 1B-8, SS-4, 3B-1
1888	**2 teams**		**LOU AA** (116G –.307)	**BKN AA** (12G –.310)																					
″	**total**		128	.307	.423	527	162	**31**	12	2	0.4	133	53	50		71	0	0	298	134	56	18	3.8	.885	OF-82, 2B-31, SS-15
1889	**BKN**	**AA**	138	.266	.320	560	149	18	3	2	0.4	139	73	80	41	65	0	0	385	410	61	56	6.2	.929	2B-138
1890	**BKN**	**N**	129	.278	.386	510	142	32	7	3	0.6	**148**	69	85	47	85	0	0	298	420	42	56	5.9	.945	2B-129
1891			107	.276	.356	435	120	16	5	3	0.7	82	31	59	63	32	0	0	226	223	48	19	4.6	.903	2B-72, OF-35
1892			21	.299	.379	87	26	5	1	0	0.0	17	17	14	13	4	0	0	37	0	3	0	1.9	.925	OF-21
7 yrs.			680	.284	.369	2779	790	127	38	11	0.4	653	243	332	164	328	0	0	1598	1238	260	155	4.5	.916	2B-381, OF-271, SS-20, 1B-9, 3B-3

Hugh Collins

COLLINS, HUGH
Deceased.

150 lbs.

Year	Team		Games	BA	SA	AB	H	2B	3B	HR	HR%	R	RBI	BB	SO	SB	Pinch Hit AB	Pinch Hit H	PO	A	E	DP	TC/G	FA	G by Pos
1887	**NY**	**AA**	1	.250	.250	4	1	0	0	0	0.0	0		0		0	0	0	0	0	0	0	0.0	.000	C-1

Jimmy Collins

COLLINS, JAMES JOSEPH
B. Jan. 16, 1870, Buffalo, N. Y. D. Mar. 6, 1943, Buffalo, N. Y.
Manager 1901–06.
Hall of Fame 1945.

BR TR 5′ 9″ 178 lbs.

Year	Team	Games	BA	SA	AB	H	2B	3B	HR	HR%	R	RBI	BB	SO	SB	Pinch Hit AB	Pinch Hit H	PO	A	E	DP	TC/G	FA	G by Pos
1895	2 teams	BOS N (11G –.211)		LOU N (96G –.279)																				
″	total	107	.273	.397	411	112	20	5	7	1.7	75	57	37	20	12	0	0	185	200	32	14	3.9	.923	3B-77, OF-28, 2B-2, SS-1
1896	BOS N	84	.296	.398	304	90	10	9	1	0.3	48	46	30	12	10	0	0	141	218	40	18	4.8	.900	3B-80, SS-4
1897		134	.346	.482	529	183	28	13	6	1.1	103	132	41		14	0	0	214	303	47	20	4.2	.917	3B-134
1898		152	.328	.479	597	196	35	5	**15**	**2.5**	107	111	40		12	0	0	243	332	42	20	4.1	.932	3B-152
1899		151	.277	.386	599	166	28	11	5	0.8	98	92	40		12	0	0	217	376	36	23	4.2	.943	3B-151
1900		142	.304	.394	**586**	178	25	5	6	1.0	104	95	34		23	0	0	252	331	40	21	4.4	.936	3B-141, SS-1
1901	BOS A	138	.332	.495	564	187	42	16	6	1.1	109	94	34		19	0	0	203	328	50	24	4.2	.914	3B-138
1902		108	.322	.459	429	138	21	10	6	1.4	71	61	24		18	0	0	143	255	19	14	3.9	.954	3B-107
1903		130	.296	.448	540	160	33	17	5	0.9	87	72	24		23	0	0	178	260	22	19	3.5	.952	3B-130
1904		156	.266	.374	631	168	33	13	3	0.5	85	67	27		19	0	0	191	320	30	15	3.5	.945	3B-156
1905		131	.276	.368	508	140	25	5	4	0.8	66	65	37		18	0	0	164	268	36	12	3.6	.923	3B-131
1906		37	.275	.408	142	39	8	4	1	0.7	17	16	4		1	5	1	43	70	11	2	3.9	.911	3B-32
1907	2 teams	BOS A (41G –.291)		PHI A (102G –.274)																				
″	total	143	.279	.337	523	146	30	0	0	0.0	51	45	34		8	2	0	143	257	47	13	3.2	.895	3B-141
1908	PHI A	115	.217	.263	433	94	14	3	0	0.0	34	30	20		5	0	0	117	216	26	14	3.1	.928	3B-115
14 yrs.		1728	.294	.408	6796	1997	352	116	65	1.0	1055	983	426	32	194	7	1	2434	3734	478	229	3.9	.928	3B-1685, OF-28, SS-6, 2B-2
WORLD SERIES																								
1903	BOS A	8	.250	.389	36	9	1	2	0	0.0	5	1	1	1	3	0	0	7	22	2	1	3.9	.935	3B-8

Joe Collins

COLLINS, JOSEPH EDWARD
Born Joseph Edward Kollonige.
B. Dec. 3, 1922, Scranton, Pa. D. Aug. 30, 1989, Union, N. J.

BL TL 6′ 185 lbs.

Year	Team	Games	BA	SA	AB	H	2B	3B	HR	HR%	R	RBI	BB	SO	SB	Pinch Hit AB	Pinch Hit H	PO	A	E	DP	TC/G	FA	G by Pos
1948	NY A	5	.200	.400	5	1	1	0	0	0.0	0	2	0	1	0	5	1	0	0	0	0	0.0	—	
1949		7	.100	.100	10	1	0	0	0	0.0	2	4	6	2	0	0	0	23	0	2	2	5.0	.920	1B-5
1950		108	.234	.420	205	48	8	3	8	3.9	47	28	31	34	5	4	0	481	36	7	62	5.2	.987	1B-99, OF-2
1951		125	.286	.458	262	75	8	5	9	3.4	52	48	34	23	9	5	1	575	57	9	65	5.0	.986	1B-114, OF-15
1952		122	.280	.481	428	120	16	8	18	4.2	69	59	55	47	4	1	0	1047	73	11	123	9.5	.990	1B-119
1953		127	.269	.439	387	104	11	2	17	4.4	72	44	59	36	2	11	0	837	65	11	100	7.8	.988	1B-113, OF-4
1954		130	.271	.446	343	93	20	2	12	3.5	67	46	51	37	2	23	4	759	60	7	105	7.1	.992	1B-117
1955		105	.234	.414	278	65	9	1	13	4.7	40	45	44	32	0	13	5	445	45	2	63	4.9	.996	1B-73, OF-27
1956		100	.225	.347	262	59	5	3	7	2.7	38	43	34	33	3	16	4	346	32	1	37	4.0	.997	OF-51, 1B-43
1957		79	.201	.248	149	30	1	0	2	1.3	17	10	24	18	2	32	6	234	15	3	23	5.4	.988	1B-32, OF-15
10 yrs.		908	.256	.421	2329	596	79	24	86	3.7	404	329	338	263	27	110	21	4747	383	53	580	6.3	.990	1B-715, OF-114
WORLD SERIES																								
1950	NY A	1	—	—	0	0	0	0	0	—	0	0	0	0	0	0	0	1	1	0	0	2.0	1.000	1B-1
1951		6	.222	.389	18	4	0	0	1	5.6	2	3	2	1	0	0	0	39	2	0	6	5.9	1.000	1B-6, OF-1
1952		6	.000	.000	12	0	0	0	0	0.0	1	0	1	3	0	0	0	27	1	0	2	4.7	1.000	1B-6
1953		6	.167	.333	24	4	1	0	1	4.2	4	2	3	8	0	0	0	49	4	0	4	8.8	1.000	1B-6
1955		5	.167	.667	12	2	0	0	2	16.7	6	3	6	4	1	0	0	27	3	0	3	5.0	1.000	1B-5, OF-1
1956		6	.238	.333	21	5	2	0	0	0.0	2	2	2	3	0	1	0	30	3	2	4	7.0	.943	1B-5
1957		6	.000	.000	5	0	0	0	0	0.0	0	0	0	3	0	1	0	12	2	0	1	2.8	1.000	1B-5
7 yrs.		36	.163	.326	92	15	3	0	4	4.3	15	10	14	22	1	2	0	185	16	2	20	5.6	.990	1B-34, OF-2

Kevin Collins

COLLINS, KEVIN MICHAEL (Casey)
B. Aug. 4, 1946, Springfield, Mass.

BL TR 6′ 1″ 180 lbs.

Year	Team	Games	BA	SA	AB	H	2B	3B	HR	HR%	R	RBI	BB	SO	SB	Pinch Hit AB	Pinch Hit H	PO	A	E	DP	TC/G	FA	G by Pos
1965	NY N	11	.174	.217	23	4	1	0	0	0.0	3	0	1	9	0	3	1	1	11	0	1	1.2	1.000	3B-7, SS-3
1967		4	.100	.100	10	1	0	0	0	0.0	1	0	0	3	1	2	0	2	7	0	0	4.5	1.000	2B-2
1968		58	.201	.279	154	31	5	2	1	0.6	12	13	7	37	0	14	0	37	64	5	9	2.3	.953	3B-40, 2B-6, SS-1
1969	2 teams	NY N (16G –.150)		MON N (52G –.240)																				
″	total	68	.213	.353	136	29	8	1	3	2.2	6	14	11	26	0	30	9	34	60	6	6	2.0	.940	3B-30, 2B-20
1970	DET A	25	.208	.375	24	5	1	0	1	4.2	2	3	1	10	0	21	4	5	1	0	0	6.0	1.000	1B-1
1971		35	.268	.439	41	11	2	1	1	2.4	6	4	0	12	0	31	9	5	6	0	0	1.6	1.000	3B-4, OF-2, 2B-1
6 yrs.		201	.209	.320	388	81	17	4	6	1.5	30	34	20	97	1	101	23	84	149	11	16	2.1	.955	3B-81, 2B-29, SS-4, OF-2, 1B-1

Orth Collins

COLLINS, ORTH STEIN (Buck)
B. Apr. 27, 1880, Lafayette, Ind. D. Dec. 13, 1949, Fort Lauderdale, Fla.

BL TR 6′ 150 lbs.

Year	Team	Games	BA	SA	AB	H	2B	3B	HR	HR%	R	RBI	BB	SO	SB	Pinch Hit AB	Pinch Hit H	PO	A	E	DP	TC/G	FA	G by Pos
1904	NY A	5	.353	.529	17	6	1	1	0	0.0	3	1	1		0	0	0	4	5	0	0	1.8	1.000	OF-5
1909	WAS A	8	.000	.000	7	0	0	0	0	0.0	0	0	0		0	5	0	1	0	0	0	0.3	1.000	OF-2, P-1
2 yrs.		13	.250	.375	24	6	1	1	0	0.0	3	1	1		0	5	0	5	5	0	0	1.3	1.000	OF-7, P-1

Pat Collins

COLLINS, THARON PATRICK
B. Sept. 13, 1896, Sweet Springs, Mo. D. May 20, 1960, Kansas City, Kans.

BR TR 5′11½″ 178 lbs.

Year	Team	Games	BA	SA	AB	H	2B	3B	HR	HR%	R	RBI	BB	SO	SB	Pinch Hit AB	Pinch Hit H	PO	A	E	DP	TC/G	FA	G by Pos
1919	STL A	10	.150	.200	20	3	1	0	0	0.0	2	1	4	2	0	4	0	20	6	2	0	5.6	.929	C-5
1920		23	.214	.250	28	6	1	0	0	0.0	5	6	3	5	0	13	0	8	2	0	0	1.4	1.000	C-7
1921		58	.243	.297	111	27	3	0	1	0.9	9	10	16	17	1	22	7	105	19	5	3	4.2	.961	C-31
1922		63	.307	.543	127	39	6	0	8	6.3	14	23	21	21	0	22	5	182	22	4	8	6.5	.981	C-27, 1B-5
1923		85	.177	.271	181	32	8	0	3	1.7	9	30	15	45	0	32	6	161	31	4	4	4.2	.980	C-47
1924		31	.302	.396	53	16	2	0	1	1.9	9	11	11	14	0	8	0	52	10	2	0	3.2	.969	C-20
1926	NY A	102	.286	.417	290	83	11	3	7	2.4	41	35	73	55	3	1	0	394	76	14	14	4.8	.971	C-100
1927		92	.275	.418	251	69	9	3	7	2.8	38	36	54	24	0	1	1	267	56	8	1	3.7	.976	C-89
1928		70	.221	.390	136	30	5	0	6	4.4	18	14	35	16	0	0	0	182	30	5	1	3.1	.977	C-70
1929	BOS N	7	.000	.000	5	0	0	0	0	0.0	1	2	3	1	0	1	0	14	2	0	0	2.7	1.000	C-6
10 yrs.		541	.254	.384	1202	305	46	6	33	2.7	146	168	235	200	4	104	19	1385	254	44	31	4.1	.974	C-402, 1B-5
WORLD SERIES																								
1926	NY A	3	.000	.000	2	0	0	0	0	0.0	0	0	0	1	0	0	0	1	0	0	0	0.3	1.000	C-3
1927		2	.600	.800	5	3	1	0	0	0.0	0	0	3	0	0	0	0	5	1	0	0	3.0	1.000	C-2
1928		1	1.000	2.000	1	1	1	0	0	0.0	0	0	0	0	0	0	0	2	0	0	0	2.0	1.000	C-1
3 yrs.		6	.500	.750	8	4	2	0	0	0.0	0	0	3	1	0	0	0	8	1	0	0	1.5	1.000	C-6

Ripper Collins

COLLINS, JAMES ANTHONY
B. Mar. 30, 1904, Altoona, Pa. D. Apr. 15, 1970, New Haven, N. Y.
BB TL 5′ 9″ 165 lbs.

Year	Team	Lg	Games	BA	SA	AB	H	2B	3B	HR	HR%	R	RBI	BB	SO	SB	Pinch Hit AB	Pinch Hit H	PO	A	E	DP	TC/G	FA	G by Pos
1931	STL	N	89	.301	.487	279	84	20	10	4	1.4	34	59	18	24	1	16	2	572	42	4	54	8.7	.994	1B-68, OF-3
1932			149	.279	.474	549	153	28	8	21	3.8	82	91	38	67	4	8	2	797	53	6	74	6.1	.993	1B-81, OF-60
1933			132	.310	.452	493	153	26	7	10	2.0	66	68	38	49	7	8	3	1054	79	7	82	9.3	.994	1B-123
1934			154	.333	**.615**	600	200	40	12	**35**	5.8	116	128	57	50	2	0	0	1289	110	13	115	9.2	.991	1B-154
1935			150	.313	.529	578	181	36	10	23	4.0	109	122	65	45	0	0	0	1269	95	18	107	9.2	.987	1B-150
1936			103	.292	.509	277	81	15	3	13	4.7	48	48	48	30	1	26	8	488	38	6	48	7.6	.989	1B-61, OF-9
1937	CHI	N	115	.274	.436	456	125	16	5	16	3.5	77	71	32	46	2	4	0	1068	80	11	94	10.4	.991	1B-111
1938			143	.267	.424	490	131	22	8	13	2.7	78	61	54	48	1	7	0	1264	111	6	118	10.2	.996	1B-135
1941	PIT	N	49	.210	.306	62	13	2	2	0	0.0	5	11	6	14	0	32	4	66	8	4	5	5.6	.949	1B-11, OF-3
9 yrs.			1084	.296	.492	3784	1121	205	65	135	3.6	615	659	356	373	18	101	19	7867	616	75	697	8.8	.991	1B-894, OF-75
WORLD SERIES																									
1931	STL	N	2	.000	.000	2	0	0	0	0	0.0	0	0	0	1	0	2	0	0	0	0	0	0.0	—	
1934			7	.367	.400	30	11	1	0	0	0.0	4	4	1	2	0	0	0	57	7	1	1	9.3	.985	1B-7
1938	CHI	N	4	.133	.133	15	2	0	0	0	0.0	1	0	0	3	0	0	0	38	1	0	3	9.8	1.000	1B-4
3 yrs.			13	.277	.298	47	13	1	0	0	0.0	5	4	1	6	0	2	0	95	8	1	4	9.5	.990	1B-11

Shano Collins

COLLINS, JOHN FRANCIS
B. Dec. 4, 1885, Charlestown, Mass. D. Sept. 10, 1955, Newton, Mass.
Manager 1931–32.
BR TR 6′ 185 lbs.

Year	Team	Lg	Games	BA	SA	AB	H	2B	3B	HR	HR%	R	RBI	BB	SO	SB	Pinch Hit AB	Pinch Hit H	PO	A	E	DP	TC/G	FA	G by Pos
1910	CHI	A	97	.197	.289	315	62	10	8	1	0.3	29	24	25		10	4	1	356	30	19	17	4.4	.953	OF-65, 1B-27
1911			106	.262	.403	370	97	16	12	4	1.1	48	48	20		14	3	0	884	73	21	46	9.5	.979	1B-97, OF-3, 2B-3
1912			153	.292	.397	575	168	34	10	2	0.3	75	81	29		26	2	0	632	46	10	24	4.6	.985	OF-105, 1B-46
1913			148	.239	.327	535	128	26	9	1	0.2	53	47	32	60	22	1	1	244	19	14	3	1.9	.949	OF-147
1914			154	.274	.376	598	164	34	9	3	0.5	61	65	27	49	30	0	0	268	21	19	5	2.0	.938	OF-154
1915			153	.257	.368	576	148	24	17	2	0.3	73	85	28	50	38	2	0	713	41	20	28	5.1	.974	OF-104, 1B-47
1916			143	.243	.342	527	128	28	12	0	0.0	74	42	59	51	16	3	0	272	24	11	8	2.2	.964	OF-136, 1B-4
1917			82	.234	.321	252	59	13	3	1	0.4	38	14	10	27	14	8	2	125	6	1	4	1.8	.992	OF-73
1918			103	.274	.392	365	100	18	11	1	0.3	30	56	17	19	7	5	1	262	22	9	2	3.0	.969	OF-92, 1B-5, 2B-1
1919			63	.279	.363	179	50	6	3	1	0.6	21	16	7	11	3	9	2	158	11	4	6	3.2	.977	OF-46, 1B-8
1920			133	.303	.392	495	150	21	10	1	0.2	70	63	23	24	12	4	0	1163	63	16	69	9.6	.987	1B-117, OF-12
1921	BOS	A	141	.286	.406	542	155	29	12	4	0.7	63	65	18	38	15	0	0	285	24	10	10	2.3	.969	OF-138, 1B-3
1922			135	.271	.358	472	128	24	7	1	0.2	33	52	7	16	7	16	5	248	6	13	2	2.3	.951	OF-117, 1B-1
1923			97	.231	.289	342	79	10	5	0	0.0	41	18	11	29	7	6	1	164	17	9	2	2.1	.953	OF-89
1924			88	.292	.400	240	70	16	5	0	0.0	36	28	18	17	4	20	7	183	10	9	6	3.0	.955	OF-55, 1B-12
1925			2	.333	.333	3	1	0	0	0	0.0	1	1	0	0	0	1	0	0	0	0	0	0.0	.000	OF-1
16 yrs.			1798	.264	.365	6386	1687	309	133	22	0.3	746	705	331	391	225	84	20	5957	413	185	232	3.8	.972	OF-1337, 1B-367, 2B-4
WORLD SERIES																									
1917	CHI	A	6	.286	.333	21	6	1	0	0	0.0	2	0	0	2	0	0	0	4	1	3	0	1.3	.625	OF-6
1919			4	.250	.313	16	4	1	0	0	0.0	2	0	0	0	0	0	0	5	0	0	0	1.3	1.000	OF-4
2 yrs.			10	.270	.324	37	10	2	0	0	0.0	4	0	0	2	0	0	0	9	1	3	0	1.3	.769	OF-10

Zip Collins

COLLINS, JOHN EDGAR
B. May 2, 1892, Brooklyn, N. Y. D. Dec. 19, 1983, Manassas, Va.
BL TL 5′11″ 152 lbs.

Year	Team	Lg	Games	BA	SA	AB	H	2B	3B	HR	HR%	R	RBI	BB	SO	SB	Pinch Hit AB	Pinch Hit H	PO	A	E	DP	TC/G	FA	G by Pos
1914	PIT	N	49	.242	.253	182	44	2	0	0	0.0	14	15	8	10	3	0	0	92	8	4	2	2.1	.962	OF-49
1915	2 teams	PIT N (106G –.294) BOS N (5G –.286)																							
″	total		111	.293	.359	368	108	9	6	1	0.3	54	23	26	39	7	11	2	223	12	14	3	2.3	.944	OF-106
1916	BOS	N	93	.209	.269	268	56	1	6	1	0.4	39	18	18	42	4	11	1	114	10	7	3	1.7	.947	OF-78
1917			9	.148	.222	27	4	0	1	0	0.0	3	2	0	4	0	4	2	13	0	0	0	2.6	1.000	OF-5
1921	PHI	A	24	.282	.380	71	20	5	1	0	0.0	14	5	6	5	1	3	1	51	3	5	0	3.0	.915	OF-20
5 yrs.			286	.253	.309	916	232	17	14	2	0.2	124	63	58	100	15	29	6	493	33	30	8	2.2	.946	OF-258

Frank Colman

COLMAN, FRANK LLOYD
B. Mar. 2, 1918, London, Ont., Canada D. Feb. 19, 1983, London, Ont., Canada.
BL TL 5′11″ 186 lbs.

Year	Team	Lg	Games	BA	SA	AB	H	2B	3B	HR	HR%	R	RBI	BB	SO	SB	Pinch Hit AB	Pinch Hit H	PO	A	E	DP	TC/G	FA	G by Pos
1942	PIT	N	10	.135	.216	37	5	0	0	1	2.7	2	2	2	2	0	2	0	14	2	0	0	2.0	1.000	OF-8
1943			32	.271	.373	59	16	2	2	0	0.0	9	4	8	7	0	17	4	27	0	0	0	2.5	1.000	OF-11
1944			99	.270	.434	226	61	9	5	6	2.7	30	53	25	27	0	39	11	109	4	4	0	2.0	.966	OF-53, 1B-6
1945			77	.209	.373	153	32	11	1	4	2.6	18	30	9	16	0	42	5	143	14	1	10	4.6	.994	1B-22, OF-12
1946	2 teams	PIT N (26G –.170) NY A (5G –.267)																							
″	total		31	.191	.324	68	13	3	0	2	2.9	5	11	3	8	0	13	2	40	3	1	2	2.9	.977	OF-13, 1B-2
1947	NY	A	22	.107	.321	28	3	0	0	2	7.1	2	6	2	6	0	14	3	7	1	0	0	1.3	1.000	OF-6
6 yrs.			271	.228	.378	571	130	25	8	15	2.6	66	106	49	66	0	127	25	340	24	6	12	2.8	.984	OF-103, 1B-30

Cris Colon

COLON, CRISTOBAL
Born Cristobal Colon (Martinez).
B. Jan. 3, 1969, La Guaira, Venezuela.
BB TR 6′ 2″ 180 lbs.

Year	Team	Lg	Games	BA	SA	AB	H	2B	3B	HR	HR%	R	RBI	BB	SO	SB	Pinch Hit AB	Pinch Hit H	PO	A	E	DP	TC/G	FA	G by Pos
1992	TEX	A	14	.167	.167	36	6	0	0	0	0.0	5	1	1	8	0	1	0	17	36	3	5	4.0	.946	SS-14

Bob Coluccio

COLUCCIO, ROBERT PASQUALI
B. Oct. 2, 1951, Centralia, Wash.
BR TR 5′11″ 183 lbs.

Year	Team	Lg	Games	BA	SA	AB	H	2B	3B	HR	HR%	R	RBI	BB	SO	SB	Pinch Hit AB	Pinch Hit H	PO	A	E	DP	TC/G	FA	G by Pos
1973	MIL	A	124	.224	.411	438	98	21	8	15	3.4	65	58	54	92	13	5	0	236	12	2	3	2.1	.992	OF-108, DH-11
1974			138	.223	.322	394	88	13	4	6	1.5	42	31	43	61	15	2	0	346	10	4	2	2.7	.989	OF-131, DH-2
1975	2 teams	MIL A (22G –.194) CHI A (61G –.205)																							
″	total		83	.202	.314	223	45	4	3	5	2.2	30	18	24	45	5	4	0	149	5	2	0	1.9	.987	OF-81, DH-1
1977	CHI	A	20	.270	.270	37	10	0	0	0	0.0	4	7	6	2	0	0	0	28	1	0	1	1.5	1.000	OF-19
1978	STL	N	5	.000	.000	3	0	0	0	0	0.0	0	0	1	2	0	3	0	1	0	0	0	0.5	1.000	OF-2
5 yrs.			370	.220	.353	1095	241	38	15	26	2.4	141	114	128	202	33	14	0	760	28	8	6	2.2	.990	OF-341, DH-14

Earle Combs

COMBS, EARLE BRYAN (The Kentucky Colonel)
B. May 14, 1899, Pebworth, Ky. D. July 21, 1976, Richmond, Ky.
Hall of Fame 1970.
BL TR 6′ 185 lbs.

Year	Team	Lg	Games	BA	SA	AB	H	2B	3B	HR	HR%	R	RBI	BB	SO	SB	Pinch Hit AB	Pinch Hit H	PO	A	E	DP	TC/G	FA	G by Pos
1924	NY	A	24	.400	.543	35	14	5	0	0	0.0	10	2	4	2	0	8	5	12	0	0	0	1.1	1.000	OF-11
1925			150	.342	.462	593	203	36	13	3	0.5	117	61	65	43	12	0	0	401	12	9	2	2.8	.979	OF-150

Earle Combs *continued*

Year	Team	Games	BA	SA	AB	H	2B	3B	HR	HR%	R	RBI	BB	SO	SB	Pinch Hit AB	Pinch Hit H	PO	A	E	DP	TC/G	FA	G by Pos
1926		145	.299	.429	606	181	31	12	8	1.3	113	56	47	23	8	0	0	375	8	12	2	2.7	.970	OF-145
1927		152	.356	.511	**648**	**231**	36	**23**	6	0.9	137	64	62	31	15	0	0	411	6	14	0	2.8	.968	OF-152
1928		149	.310	.463	626	194	33	**21**	7	1.1	118	56	77	33	10	0	0	424	11	9	7	3.0	.980	OF-149
1929		142	.345	.468	586	202	33	15	3	0.5	119	65	69	32	11	1	0	358	10	13	5	2.7	.966	OF-141
1930		137	.344	.523	532	183	30	**22**	7	1.3	129	82	74	26	16	2	0	275	5	9	1	2.1	.969	OF-135
1931		138	.318	.446	563	179	31	13	5	0.9	120	58	68	34	11	7	3	335	5	9	2	2.7	.974	OF-129
1932		143	.321	.455	591	190	32	10	9	1.5	143	65	81	16	3	3	0	343	6	12	3	2.6	.967	OF-138
1933		122	.298	.463	419	125	22	16	5	1.2	86	60	47	19	6	18	4	227	3	6	1	2.3	.975	OF-104
1934		63	.319	.434	251	80	13	5	2	0.8	47	25	40	9	3	2	1	145	1	1	0	2.4	.993	OF-62
1935		89	.282	.362	298	84	7	4	3	1.0	47	35	36	10	1	15	4	143	2	1	0	2.1	.993	OF-70
12 yrs.		1454	.325	.462	5748	1866	309	154	58	1.0	1186	629	670	278	96	56	17	3449	69	95	23	2.6	.974	OF-1386
WORLD SERIES																								
1926	NY A	7	.357	.429	28	10	2	0	0	0.0	3	2	5	2	0	0	0	17	0	0	0	2.4	1.000	OF-7
1927		4	.313	.313	16	5	0	0	0	0.0	6	2	1	2	0	0	0	16	0	0	0	4.0	1.000	OF-4
1928		1	—	—	0	0	0	0	0	—	0	1	0	0	0	0	0	0	0	0	0	0.0	—	
1932		4	.375	.625	16	6	1	0	1	6.3	8	4	4	3	0	0	0	10	0	0	0	2.5	1.000	OF-4
4 yrs.		16	.350	.450	60	21	3	0	1	1.7	17	9	10	7	0	0	0	43	0	0	0	2.9	1.000	OF-15

Merrill Combs

COMBS, MERRILL RUSSELL BL TR 6′ 172 lbs.
B. Dec. 11, 1919, Los Angeles, Calif. D. July 8, 1981, Riverside, Calif.

Year	Team	Games	BA	SA	AB	H	2B	3B	HR	HR%	R	RBI	BB	SO	SB	Pinch Hit AB	Pinch Hit H	PO	A	E	DP	TC/G	FA	G by Pos
1947	BOS A	17	.221	.279	68	15	1	0	1	1.5	8	6	9	9	0	0	0	17	42	0	6	3.5	1.000	3B-17
1949		14	.208	.250	24	5	1	0	0	0.0	5	1	9	0	0	1	0	13	12	2	2	2.7	.926	3B-9, SS-1
1950	2 teams	BOS A (1G –.000) WAS A (37G –.245)																						
″	total	38	.245	.255	102	25	1	0	0	0.0	19	6	23	16	0	5	1	48	93	5	20	4.9	.966	SS-30
1951	CLE A	19	.179	.250	28	5	2	0	0	0.0	2	2	2	3	0	2	0	16	32	2	5	3.1	.960	SS-16
1952		52	.165	.209	139	23	1	1	1	0.7	11	10	14	15	0	0	0	79	134	6	28	4.2	.973	SS-49, 2B-3
5 yrs.		140	.202	.241	361	73	6	1	2	0.6	45	25	57	43	0	8	1	173	313	15	61	4.0	.970	SS-96, 3B-26, 2B-3

Wayne Comer

COMER, HARRY WAYNE BR TR 5′10″ 175 lbs.
B. Feb. 3, 1944, Shenandoah, Va.

Year	Team	Games	BA	SA	AB	H	2B	3B	HR	HR%	R	RBI	BB	SO	SB	Pinch Hit AB	Pinch Hit H	PO	A	E	DP	TC/G	FA	G by Pos
1967	DET A	4	.333	.333	3	1	0	0	0	0.0	0	0	0	0	0	1	1	0	0	0	0	0.0	.000	OF-1
1968		48	.125	.229	48	6	0	1	1	2.1	8	3	2	7	0	18	2	22	0	0	0	0.8	1.000	OF-27, C-1
1969	SEA A	147	.245	.380	481	118	18	1	15	3.1	88	54	82	79	18	12	1	287	14	6	6	2.2	.980	OF-139, 3B-1, C-1
1970	2 teams	MIL A (13G –.059) WAS A (77G –.233)																						
″	total	90	.212	.240	146	31	4	0	0	0.0	22	9	22	19	4	26	3	75	2	4	0	1.3	.951	OF-63, 3B-1
1972	DET A	27	.111	.111	9	1	0	0	0	0.0	1	1	0	1	0	6	1	5	0	0	0	0.3	1.000	OF-17
5 yrs.		316	.229	.336	687	157	22	2	16	2.3	119	67	106	106	22	63	8	389	16	10	6	1.7	.976	OF-247, 3B-2, C-2
WORLD SERIES																								
1968	DET A	1	1.000	1.000	1	1	0	0	0	0.0	0	0	0	0	0	1	1	0	0	0	0	0.0	—	

Charlie Comiskey

COMISKEY, CHARLES ALBERT (Commy, The Old Roman) BR TR 6′ 180 lbs.
B. Aug. 15, 1859, Chicago, Ill. D. Oct. 26, 1931, Eagle River, Wis.
Manager 1883–94.
Hall of Fame 1939.

Year	Team	Games	BA	SA	AB	H	2B	3B	HR	HR%	R	RBI	BB	SO	SB	Pinch Hit AB	Pinch Hit H	PO	A	E	DP	TC/G	FA	G by Pos
1882	STL AA	78	.243	.310	329	80	9	5	1	0.3	58		4			0	0	861	16	30	25	11.5	.967	1B-77, P-2
1883		96	.294	.397	401	118	17	9	2	0.5	87		11			0	0	1085	20	43	49	11.8	.963	1B-96, OF-1
1884		108	.239	.315	460	110	17	6	2	0.4	76		5			0	0	1193	38	40	56	11.6	.969	1B-108, 2B-1, P-1
1885		83	.256	.359	340	87	15	7	2	0.6	68		14			0	0	879	24	29	34	11.2	.969	1B-83
1886		131	.254	.327	578	147	15	9	3	0.5	95		10			0	0	1186	72	36	71	9.7	.972	1B-122, 2B-9, OF-2
1887		125	.335	.416	538	180	22	5	4	0.7	139		27		117	0	0	1162	75	36	62	9.9	.972	1B-116, 2B-9, OF-3
1888		137	.273	.359	**576**	157	22	5	6	1.0	102	83	12		72	0	0	1298	50	44	52	9.9	.968	1B-133, OF-5, 2B-3
1889		137	.286	.383	587	168	28	10	3	0.5	105	102	19	19	65	0	0	1227	52	39	71	9.3	.970	1B-134, 2B-3, OF-3, P-1
1890	CHI P	88	.244	.289	377	92	11	3	0	0.0	53	59	14	17	34	0	0	882	41	33	52	10.9	.965	1B-88
1891	STL AA	139	.259	.304	572	148	16	2	2	0.3	84	88	33	25	38	0	0	1421	62	31	78	10.7	.980	1B-139, OF-2
1892	CIN N	141	.227	.290	551	125	14	6	3	0.5	61	71	32	16	30	0	0	1469	73	25	103	11.1	.984	1B-141
1893		64	.220	.274	259	57	12	1	0	0.0	38	26	11	2	9	0	0	675	21	15	57	11.1	.979	1B-64
1894		61	.264	.300	220	58	8	0	0	0.0	26	33	5	5	10	0	0	536	24	16	36	9.4	.972	1B-60, OF-1
13 yrs.		1388	.264	.337	5788	1527	206	68	28	0.5	992	462	197	84	375	0	0	13874	568	417	746	10.6	.972	1B-1361, 2B-25, OF-17, P-4

Jim Command

COMMAND, JAMES DALTON (Igor) BL TR 6′ 2″ 200 lbs.
B. Oct. 15, 1928, Grand Rapids, Mich.

Year	Team	Games	BA	SA	AB	H	2B	3B	HR	HR%	R	RBI	BB	SO	SB	Pinch Hit AB	Pinch Hit H	PO	A	E	DP	TC/G	FA	G by Pos
1954	PHI N	9	.222	.444	18	4	1	0	1	5.6	1	6	2	4	0	3	0	5	8	1	0	2.3	.929	3B-6
1955		5	.000	.000	5	0	0	0	0	0.0	0	0	0	0	0	5	0	0	0	0	0	0.0	—	
2 yrs.		14	.174	.348	23	4	1	0	1	4.3	1	6	2	4	0	8	0	5	8	1	0	2.3	.929	3B-6

Adam Comorosky

COMOROSKY, ADAM ANTHONY BR TR 5′10″ 167 lbs.
B. Dec. 9, 1905, Swoyersville, Pa. D. Mar. 2, 1951, Swoyersville, Pa.

Year	Team	Games	BA	SA	AB	H	2B	3B	HR	HR%	R	RBI	BB	SO	SB	Pinch Hit AB	Pinch Hit H	PO	A	E	DP	TC/G	FA	G by Pos
1926	PIT N	8	.267	.467	15	4	1	1	0	0.0	2	0	1	2	1	1	0	7	0	0	0	1.2	1.000	OF-6
1927		18	.230	.246	61	14	1	0	0	0.0	5	4	3	1	0	1	0	43	1	1	0	2.8	.978	OF-16
1928		51	.295	.398	176	52	6	3	2	1.1	22	34	15	6	1	1	1	118	2	4	1	2.5	.968	OF-49
1929		127	.321	.461	473	152	26	11	6	1.3	86	97	40	22	19	3	0	256	6	10	3	2.2	.963	OF-121
1930		152	.313	.529	597	187	47	**23**	12	2.0	112	119	51	33	14	0	0	337	12	11	2	2.4	.969	OF-152
1931		99	.243	.291	350	85	12	1	1	0.3	37	48	34	28	11	7	1	214	4	5	2	2.5	.978	OF-90
1932		108	.286	.389	370	106	18	4	4	1.1	54	46	25	20	7	11	3	255	4	5	2	2.9	.981	OF-92
1933		64	.284	.364	162	46	8	1	1	0.6	18	15	4	9	2	32	9	66	1	0	0	2.2	1.000	OF-30
1934	CIN N	127	.258	.312	446	115	12	6	0	0.0	46	40	34	23	1	4	0	285	5	9	1	2.5	.970	OF-122
1935		59	.248	.328	137	34	3	1	2	1.5	22	14	7	14	1	7	2	79	3	4	0	2.2	.953	OF-40
10 yrs.		813	.285	.400	2787	795	134	51	28	1.0	404	417	214	158	57	67	16	1660	38	49	11	2.4	.972	OF-718

Mike Compton

COMPTON, MICHAEL LYNN BR TR 5′10″ 180 lbs.
B. Aug. 15, 1944, Stamford, Conn.

Year	Team	Games	BA	SA	AB	H	2B	3B	HR	HR%	R	RBI	BB	SO	SB	Pinch Hit AB	Pinch Hit H	PO	A	E	DP	TC/G	FA	G by Pos
1970	PHI N	47	.164	.209	110	18	0	1	1	0.9	8	7	9	22	0	1	0	265	13	4	1	7.1	.986	C-40

Pete Compton

COMPTON, ANNA SEBASTIAN (Bash)
B. Sept. 28, 1889, San Marcos, Tex. D. Feb. 3, 1978, Kansas City, Mo.
BL TL 5′11″ 170 lbs.

Year	Team	Games	BA	SA	AB	H	2B	3B	HR	HR%	R	RBI	BB	SO	SB	Pinch Hit AB	Pinch Hit H	PO	A	E	DP	TC/G	FA	G by Pos
1911	STL A	28	.271	.308	107	29	4	0	0	0.0	9	5	8		2	0	0	37	7	4	3	1.7	.917	OF-28
1912		100	.280	.354	268	75	6	4	2	0.7	26	30	21		11	27	9	139	9	12	1	2.2	.925	OF-72
1913		61	.180	.330	100	18	5	2	2	2.0	14	17	13	13	2	34	7	23	2	4	1	1.4	.862	OF-21
1915	2 teams	STL F (2G –.250) BOS N (35G –.241)																						
"	total	37	.242	.339	124	30	7	1	1	0.8	10	15	8	11	4	3	0	68	2	2	1	1.9	.972	OF-37
1916	2 teams	BOS N (34G –.204) PIT N (5G –.063)																						
"	total	39	.184	.202	114	21	2	0	0	0.0	14	8	9	12	5	3	0	71	2	5	1	2.2	.936	OF-35
1918	NY N	21	.217	.250	60	13	0	1	0	0.0	5	5	5	4	2	2	0	30	3	1	0	1.8	.971	OF-19
6 yrs.		286	.241	.312	773	186	24	8	5	0.6	78	80	64	40	26	69	16	368	25	28	7	2.0	.933	OF-212

Clint Conatser

CONATSER, CLINTON ASTOR (Connie)
B. July 24, 1921, Los Angeles, Calif.
BR TR 5′11″ 182 lbs.

Year	Team	Games	BA	SA	AB	H	2B	3B	HR	HR%	R	RBI	BB	SO	SB	Pinch Hit AB	Pinch Hit H	PO	A	E	DP	TC/G	FA	G by Pos
1948	BOS N	90	.277	.384	224	62	9	3	3	1.3	30	23	32	27	0	11	1	146	3	4	1	2.0	.974	OF-76
1949		53	.263	.362	152	40	6	0	3	2.0	10	16	14	19	0	10	3	93	5	5	0	2.3	.951	OF-44
2 yrs.		143	.271	.375	376	102	15	3	6	1.6	40	39	46	46	0	21	4	239	8	9	1	2.1	.965	OF-120
WORLD SERIES																								
1948	BOS N	2	.000	.000	4	0	0	0	0	0.0	0	1	0	0	0	1	0	1	0	0	0	0.5	1.000	OF-2

Dave Concepcion

CONCEPCION, DAVID ISMAEL
Born David Ismael Concepcion (Benitez).
B. June 17, 1948, Aragua, Venezuela.
BR TR 6′ 2″ 155 lbs.

Year	Team	Games	BA	SA	AB	H	2B	3B	HR	HR%	R	RBI	BB	SO	SB	Pinch Hit AB	Pinch Hit H	PO	A	E	DP	TC/G	FA	G by Pos
1970	CIN N	101	.260	.317	265	69	6	3	1	0.4	38	19	23	45	10	5	1	144	247	22	51	4.3	.947	SS-93, 2B-3
1971		130	.205	.251	327	67	4	4	1	0.3	24	20	18	51	9	1	0	182	310	13	65	3.8	.974	SS-112, 2B-10, 3B-7, OF-5
1972		119	.209	.270	378	79	13	2	2	0.5	40	29	32	65	13	0	0	197	372	19	76	4.7	.968	SS-114, 3B-9, 2B-1
1973		89	.287	.433	328	94	18	3	8	2.4	39	46	21	55	22	2	0	167	292	12	56	5.2	.975	SS-88, OF-2
1974		160	.281	.397	594	167	25	1	14	2.4	70	82	44	79	41	1	0	239	536	30	99	5.0	.963	SS-160
1975		140	.274	.353	507	139	23	1	5	1.0	62	49	39	51	33	8	2	241	446	16	102	5.2	.977	SS-130, 3B-6
1976		152	.281	.401	576	162	28	7	9	1.6	74	69	49	68	21	3	1	304	506	27	93	5.6	.968	SS-150
1977		156	.271	.369	572	155	26	3	8	1.4	59	64	46	77	29	0	0	280	490	11	101	5.0	.986	SS-156
1978		153	.301	.405	565	170	33	4	6	1.1	75	67	51	83	23	3	1	255	459	23	72	4.8	.969	SS-152
1979		149	.281	.415	590	166	25	3	16	2.7	91	84	64	73	19	1	0	284	495	27	102	5.4	.967	SS-148
1980		156	.260	.360	622	162	31	8	5	0.8	72	77	37	107	12	2	0	265	451	16	98	4.7	.978	SS-155, 2B-1
1981		106	.306	.409	421	129	28	0	5	1.2	57	67	37	61	4	0	0	208	322	22	71	5.2	.960	SS-106
1982		147	.287	.371	572	164	25	4	5	0.9	48	53	45	61	13	3	1	271	459	17	95	5.1	.977	SS-145, 1B-1, 3B-1
1983		143	.233	.280	528	123	22	0	1	0.2	54	47	56	81	14	3	1	227	387	13	67	4.3	.979	SS-139, 3B-6, 1B-1
1984		154	.245	.320	531	130	26	1	4	0.8	46	58	52	72	22	13	1	213	324	17	46	3.4	.969	SS-104, 3B-54, 1B-6
1985		155	.252	.330	560	141	19	2	7	1.3	59	48	50	67	16	6	0	214	405	24	64	4.1	.963	SS-151, 3B-5
1986		90	.260	.344	311	81	13	2	3	1.0	42	30	26	43	13	8	1	153	223	10	53	4.2	.974	SS-60, 1B-12, 3B-10, 2B-10
1987		104	.319	.384	279	89	15	0	1	0.4	32	33	28	24	4	24	8	250	169	5	43	4.2	.988	2B-59, 1B-26, 3B-13, SS-2
1988		84	.198	.244	197	39	9	0	0	0.0	11	8	18	23	3	17	4	151	131	2	36	3.3	.993	2B-46, 1B-16, SS-13, 3B-9, P-1
19 yrs.		2488	.267	.357	8723	2326	389	48	101	1.2	993	950	736	1186	321	100	21	4245	7024	326	1390	4.6	.972	SS-2178, 2B-130, 3B-120, 1B-62, OF-7, P-1
LEAGUE CHAMPIONSHIP SERIES																								
1970	CIN N	3	—	—	0	0	0	0	0	—	0	0	0	0	0	0	0	1	1	0	0	0.7	1.000	SS-3
1972		3	.000	.000	2	0	0	0	0	0.0	0	0	0	0	0	1	0	0	0	0	0	0.0	.000	SS-1
1975		3	.455	.727	11	5	0	0	1	9.1	2	1	1	2	2	0	0	6	8	1	2	5.0	.933	SS-3
1976		3	.200	.300	10	2	1	0	0	0.0	4	0	2	1	0	0	0	2	12	0	1	4.7	1.000	SS-3
1979		3	.429	.500	14	6	1	0	0	0.0	1	0	0	3	0	0	0	3	14	0	2	5.7	1.000	SS-3
5 yrs.		15	.351	.486	37	13	2	0	1	2.7	7	1	3	6	2	1	0	12	35	1	5	3.7	.979	SS-13
WORLD SERIES																								
1970	CIN N	3	.333	.556	9	3	0	1	0	0.0	0	3	0	0	0	0	0	2	2	0	0	1.3	1.000	SS-3
1972		6	.308	.462	13	4	0	1	0	0.0	2	2	2	2	1	1	0	4	11	1	1	3.2	.938	SS-5
1975		7	.179	.321	28	5	1	0	1	3.6	3	4	0	1	3	0	0	12	23	1	3	5.1	.972	SS-7
1976		4	.357	.571	14	5	1	1	0	0.0	1	3	1	3	1	0	0	6	11	1	3	4.5	.944	SS-4
4 yrs.		20	.266	.438	64	17	2	3 **4th**	1	1.6	6	12	3	6	5	1	0	24	47	3	7	3.9	.959	SS-19

Onix Concepcion

CONCEPCION, ONIX
Born Onix Cardona Concepcion (Cardona).
B. Oct. 5, 1957, Dorado, Puerto Rico.
BR TR 5′ 6″ 160 lbs.

Year	Team	Games	BA	SA	AB	H	2B	3B	HR	HR%	R	RBI	BB	SO	SB	Pinch Hit AB	Pinch Hit H	PO	A	E	DP	TC/G	FA	G by Pos
1980	KC A	12	.133	.133	15	2	0	0	0	0.0	1	2	0	1	0	2	1	5	10	3	1	3.0	.833	SS-6
1981		2	—	—	0	0	0	0	0	—	0	0	0	0	0	0	0	0	0	0	0	0.0	.000	SS-1
1982		74	.234	.288	205	48	9	1	0	0.0	17	15	5	18	2	3	0	92	168	11	28	3.8	.959	SS-46, 2B-24, DH-1
1983		80	.242	.320	219	53	11	3	0	0.0	22	20	12	12	10	3	1	92	175	15	35	3.5	.947	3B-31, 2B-28, SS-21, DH-1
1984		90	.282	.338	287	81	9	2	1	0.3	36	23	14	33	9	1	0	116	295	11	59	4.6	.974	SS-85, 2B-6, 3B-1
1985		131	.204	.245	314	64	5	1	2	0.6	32	20	16	29	4	1	0	127	370	21	63	4.0	.959	SS-128, 2B-2
1987	PIT N	1	1.000	1.000	1	1	0	0	0	0.0	0	0	0	0	0	1	1	0	0	0	0	0.0	.000	SS-1
7 yrs.		390	.239	.294	1041	249	34	7	3	0.3	108	80	47	93	25	11	3	432	1018	61	186	4.0	.960	SS-288, 2B-60, 3B-32, DH-2
LEAGUE CHAMPIONSHIP SERIES																								
1984	KC A	3	.000	.000	7	0	0	0	0	0.0	0	0	0	0	0	0	0	0	6	1	0	2.3	.857	SS-3
1985		4	.000	.000	1	0	0	0	0	0.0	0	0	0	0	0	0	0	2	4	0	0	1.5	1.000	SS-4
2 yrs.		7	.000	.000	8	0	0	0	0	0.0	0	0	0	0	0	0	0	2	10	1	0	1.9	.923	SS-7
WORLD SERIES																								
1980	KC A	3	—	—	0	0	0	0	0	—	0	0	0	0	0	0	0	0	0	0	0	0.0	—	
1985		3	—	—	0	0	0	0	0	—	1	0	0	0	0	0	0	0	2	0	0	1.0	1.000	SS-2
2 yrs.		6			0	0	0	0	0		1	0	0	0	0	0	0	0	2	0	0	1.0	1.000	SS-2

Ramon Conde

CONDE, RAMON LUIS (Wito)
Born Ramon Luis Conde (Ramon).
B. Dec. 29, 1934, Juana Diaz, Puerto Rico.
BR TR 5′ 8″ 172 lbs.

Year	Team	Games	BA	SA	AB	H	2B	3B	HR	HR%	R	RBI	BB	SO	SB	Pinch Hit AB	Pinch Hit H	PO	A	E	DP	TC/G	FA	G by Pos
1962	CHI A	14	.000	.000	16	0	0	0	0	0.0	0	1	3	3	0	5	0	4	4	1	0	1.3	.889	3B-7

Bunk Congalton

CONGALTON, WILLIAM MILLAR BL TL 5′11″ 190 lbs.
B. Jan. 24, 1875, Guelph, Ont., Canada D. Aug. 16, 1937, Cleveland, Ohio.

Year	Team	Games	BA	SA	AB	H	2B	3B	HR	HR%	R	RBI	BB	SO	SB	Pinch Hit AB	Pinch Hit H	PO	A	E	DP	TC/G	FA	G by Pos
1902	CHI N	45	.223	.257	179	40	3	0	1	0.6	14	24	7		3	0	0	71	6	1	1	1.7	.987	OF-45
1905	CLE A	12	.362	.362	47	17	0	0	0	0.0	4	5	2		3	0	0	10	2	1	0	1.1	.923	OF-12
1906		117	.320	.389	419	134	13	5	2	0.5	51	50	24		12	3	0	174	6	8	0	1.6	.957	OF-114
1907	2 teams	CLE A (9G –.182) BOS A (127G –.286)																						
″	total	136	.282	.346	518	146	11	8	2	0.4	46	49	24		13	4	0	179	19	6	4	1.5	.971	OF-132
4 yrs.		310	.290	.348	1163	337	27	13	5	0.4	115	128	57		31	7	0	434	33	16	5	1.6	.967	OF-303

Billy Conigliaro

CONIGLIARO, WILLIAM MICHAEL BR TR 6′ 180 lbs.
Brother of Tony Conigliaro.
B. Aug. 15, 1947, Revere, Mass.

Year	Team	Games	BA	SA	AB	H	2B	3B	HR	HR%	R	RBI	BB	SO	SB	Pinch Hit AB	Pinch Hit H	PO	A	E	DP	TC/G	FA	G by Pos
1969	BOS A	32	.287	.563	80	23	6	2	4	5.0	14	7	9	23	1	6	3	25	0	2	0	1.1	.926	OF-24
1970		114	.271	.462	398	108	16	3	18	4.5	59	58	35	73	3	6	1	201	8	7	0	2.0	.968	OF-108
1971		101	.262	.436	351	92	26	1	11	3.1	42	33	25	68	3	4	1	232	5	4	2	2.4	.983	OF-100
1972	MIL A	52	.230	.393	191	44	6	2	7	3.7	22	16	8	54	1	3	1	120	5	1	2	2.5	.992	OF-50
1973	OAK A	48	.200	.255	110	22	2	2	0	0.0	5	14	9	26	1	6	2	70	5	0	0	1.8	1.000	OF-40, 2B-1
5 yrs.		347	.256	.429	1130	289	56	10	40	3.5	142	128	86	244	9	25	8	648	23	14	4	2.1	.980	OF-322, 2B-1
LEAGUE CHAMPIONSHIP SERIES																								
1973	OAK A	1	.000	.000	4	0	0	0	0	0.0	0	0	0	2	0	0	0	5	0	0	0	5.0	1.000	OF-1
WORLD SERIES																								
1973	OAK A	3	.000	.000	3	0	0	0	0	0.0	0	0	0	1	0	3	0	0	0	0	0	0.0	—	

Tony Conigliaro

CONIGLIARO, ANTHONY RICHARD BR TR 6′ 3″ 185 lbs.
Brother of Billy Conigliaro.
B. Jan. 7, 1945, Revere, Mass. D. Feb. 24, 1990, Salem, Mass.

Year	Team	Games	BA	SA	AB	H	2B	3B	HR	HR%	R	RBI	BB	SO	SB	Pinch Hit AB	Pinch Hit H	PO	A	E	DP	TC/G	FA	G by Pos
1964	BOS A	111	.290	.530	404	117	21	2	24	5.9	69	52	35	78	2	5	1	176	7	5	0	1.8	.973	OF-106
1965		138	.269	.512	521	140	21	5	**32**	6.1	82	82	51	116	4	0	0	277	11	7	1	2.2	.976	OF-137
1966		150	.265	.487	558	148	26	7	28	5.0	77	93	52	112	0	4	3	244	8	7	1	1.8	.973	OF-146
1967		95	.287	.519	349	100	11	5	20	5.7	59	67	27	58	4	0	0	172	5	3	1	1.9	.983	OF-95
1969		141	.255	.427	506	129	21	3	20	4.0	57	82	48	111	2	4	0	207	4	4	2	1.6	.981	OF-137
1970		146	.266	.498	560	149	20	1	36	6.4	89	116	43	93	4	0	0	252	7	6	1	1.8	.977	OF-146
1971	CAL A	74	.222	.335	266	59	18	0	4	1.5	23	15	23	52	3	2	1	155	6	1	1	2.3	.994	OF-72
1975	BOS A	21	.123	.246	57	7	1	0	2	3.5	8	9	8	9	1	5	0	0	0	0	0	0.0	.000	DH-15
8 yrs.		876	.264	.476	3221	849	139	23	166	5.2	464	516	287	629	20	20	5	1483	48	33	7	1.8	.979	OF-839, DH-15

Jeff Conine

CONINE, JEFFREY GUY BR TR 6′ 1″ 205 lbs.
B. June 27, 1966, Tacoma, Wash.

Year	Team	Games	BA	SA	AB	H	2B	3B	HR	HR%	R	RBI	BB	SO	SB	Pinch Hit AB	Pinch Hit H	PO	A	E	DP	TC/G	FA	G by Pos
1990	KC A	9	.250	.350	20	5	2	0	0	0.0	3	2	2	5	0	0	0	39	4	1	7	4.9	.977	1B-9
1992		28	.253	.352	91	23	5	2	0	0.0	10	9	8	23	0	0	0	75	3	0	1	2.8	1.000	OF-23, 1B-4, DH-1
1993	FLA N	162	.292	.403	595	174	24	3	12	2.0	75	79	52	135	2	4	1	403	25	2	11	2.3	.995	OF-147, 1B-43
1994		115	.319	.525	451	144	27	6	18	4.0	60	82	40	92	1	1	0	409	24	6	19	3.1	.986	OF-97, 1B-46
1995		133	.302	.520	483	146	26	2	25	5.2	72	105	66	94	2	7	1	292	18	6	11	2.4	.981	OF-118, 1B-14
5 yrs.		447	.300	.468	1640	492	84	13	55	3.4	220	277	168	349	5	12	2	1218	74	15	49	2.6	.989	OF-385, 1B-116, DH-1

Jocko Conlan

CONLAN, JOHN BERTRAND BL TL 5′ 7½″ 165 lbs.
B. Dec. 6, 1899, Chicago, Ill. D. Apr. 16, 1989, Scottsdale, Ariz.
Hall of Fame 1974.

Year	Team	Games	BA	SA	AB	H	2B	3B	HR	HR%	R	RBI	BB	SO	SB	Pinch Hit AB	Pinch Hit H	PO	A	E	DP	TC/G	FA	G by Pos
1934	CHI A	63	.249	.324	225	56	11	3	0	0.0	35	16	19	7	2	8	3	122	5	6	1	2.5	.955	OF-54
1935		65	.286	.350	140	40	7	1	0	0.0	20	15	14	6	3	24	5	71	3	3	1	2.1	.961	OF-37
2 yrs.		128	.263	.334	365	96	18	4	0	0.0	55	31	33	13	5	32	8	193	8	9	2	2.3	.957	OF-91

Art Conlon

CONLON, ARTHUR JOSEPH BR TR 5′ 7″ 145 lbs.
B. Dec. 10, 1897, Woburn, Mass. D. Aug. 5, 1987, Falmouth, Mass.

Year	Team	Games	BA	SA	AB	H	2B	3B	HR	HR%	R	RBI	BB	SO	SB	Pinch Hit AB	Pinch Hit H	PO	A	E	DP	TC/G	FA	G by Pos
1923	BOS N	59	.218	.238	147	32	3	0	0	0.0	23	17	11	11	0	9	3	96	136	12	19	5.3	.951	2B-36, SS-6, 3B-4

Bert Conn

CONN, ALBERT THOMAS TR
B. Sept. 22, 1879, Philadelphia, Pa. D. Nov. 2, 1944, Philadelphia, Pa.

Year	Team	Games	BA	SA	AB	H	2B	3B	HR	HR%	R	RBI	BB	SO	SB	Pinch Hit AB	Pinch Hit H	PO	A	E	DP	TC/G	FA	G by Pos
1898	PHI N	1	.333	1.000	3	1	0	1	0	0.0	1	1	0		0	0	0	0	1	0	0	1.0	1.000	P-1
1900		6	.333	.444	9	3	1	0	0	0.0	4	1	0		0	2	0	3	1	2	0	1.5	.667	P-4
1901		5	.222	.278	18	4	1	0	0	0.0	2	0	0		0	0	0	9	13	3	0	5.0	.880	2B-5
3 yrs.		12	.267	.400	30	8	2	1	0	0.0	7	2	0		0	2	0	12	15	5	0	3.2	.844	2B-5, P-5

Fritz Connally

CONNALLY, FRITZIE LEE BR TR 6′ 3″ 210 lbs.
B. May 19, 1958, Bryan, Tex.

Year	Team	Games	BA	SA	AB	H	2B	3B	HR	HR%	R	RBI	BB	SO	SB	Pinch Hit AB	Pinch Hit H	PO	A	E	DP	TC/G	FA	G by Pos
1983	CHI N	8	.100	.100	10	1	0	0	0	0.0	0	0	0	5	0	7	1	1	3	0	0	1.3	1.000	3B-3
1985	BAL A	50	.232	.348	112	26	4	0	3	2.7	16	15	19	21	0	16	5	39	57	2	4	2.0	.980	3B-46, 1B-2, DH-1
2 yrs.		58	.221	.328	122	27	4	0	3	2.5	16	15	19	26	0	23	6	40	60	2	4	2.0	.980	3B-49, 1B-2, DH-1

Red Connally

CONNALLY, JOHN M.
B. 1863, New York, N. Y. D. Mar. 2, 1896, New York, N. Y.

Year	Team	Games	BA	SA	AB	H	2B	3B	HR	HR%	R	RBI	BB	SO	SB	Pinch Hit AB	Pinch Hit H	PO	A	E	DP	TC/G	FA	G by Pos
1886	STL N	2	.000	.000	7	0	0	0	0	0.0	0	0	0	3		0	0	0	0	0	0	0.0	.000	OF-2

Bruce Connatser

CONNATSER, BROADUS MILBURN BR TR 5′11½″ 170 lbs.
B. Sept. 19, 1902, Sevierville, Tenn. D. Jan. 27, 1971, Terre Haute, Ind.

Year	Team	Games	BA	SA	AB	H	2B	3B	HR	HR%	R	RBI	BB	SO	SB	Pinch Hit AB	Pinch Hit H	PO	A	E	DP	TC/G	FA	G by Pos
1931	CLE A	12	.286	.347	49	14	3	0	0	0.0	5	4	2	3	0	0	0	116	9	0	4	10.4	1.000	1B-12
1932		23	.233	.317	60	14	3	1	0	0.0	8	4	4	8	1	8	1	109	8	0	7	8.4	1.000	1B-14
2 yrs.		35	.257	.330	109	28	6	1	0	0.0	13	8	6	11	1	8	1	225	17	0	11	9.3	1.000	1B-26

Frank Connaughton

CONNAUGHTON, FRANK H BR TR 5′ 9″ 165 lbs.
B. Jan. 1, 1869, Clinton, Mass. D. Dec. 1, 1942, Boston, Mass.

Year	Team	Games	BA	SA	AB	H	2B	3B	HR	HR%	R	RBI	BB	SO	SB	Pinch Hit AB	Pinch Hit H	PO	A	E	DP	TC/G	FA	G by Pos
1894	BOS N	46	.345	.456	171	59	9	2	2	1.2	42	33	16	8	3	2	**2**	87	118	22	11	5.2	.903	SS-33, C-7, OF-4
1896	NY N	88	.260	.302	315	82	3	2	2	0.6	53	43	25	7	22	3	0	133	204	43	20	4.5	.887	SS-54, OF-30
1906	BOS N	12	.205	.205	44	9	0	0	0	0.0	3	1	3		1	0	0	27	30	5	2	5.2	.919	SS-11, 2B-1
3 yrs.		146	.283	.343	530	150	12	4	4	0.8	98	77	44	15	26	5	2	247	352	70	33	4.8	.895	SS-98, OF-34, C-7, 2B-1

Gene Connell

CONNELL, EUGENE JOSEPH BR TR 6′½″ 180 lbs.
Brother of Joe Connell.
B. May 10, 1906, Hazleton, Pa. D. Aug. 31, 1937, Waverly, N. Y.

Year	Team	Games	BA	SA	AB	H	2B	3B	HR	HR%	R	RBI	BB	SO	SB	Pinch Hit AB	Pinch Hit H	PO	A	E	DP	TC/G	FA	G by Pos
1931	PHI N	6	.250	.250	12	3	0	0	0	0.0	1	0	0	3	0	0	0	13	1	0	0	2.3	1.000	C-6

Joe Connell

CONNELL, JOSEPH BERNARD BL TL 5′ 8″ 165 lbs.
Brother of Gene Connell.
B. Jan. 16, 1902, Bethlehem, Pa. D. Sept. 21, 1977, Trexlertown, Pa.

Year	Team	Games	BA	SA	AB	H	2B	3B	HR	HR%	R	RBI	BB	SO	SB	Pinch Hit AB	Pinch Hit H	PO	A	E	DP	TC/G	FA	G by Pos
1926	NY N	2	.000	.000	1	0	0	0	0	0.0	1	0	0	0	0	1	0	0	0	0	0	0.0	—	

Pete Connell

CONNELL, PETER J.
B. Brooklyn, N. Y. Deceased.

Year	Team	Games	BA	SA	AB	H	2B	3B	HR	HR%	R	RBI	BB	SO	SB	Pinch Hit AB	Pinch Hit H	PO	A	E	DP	TC/G	FA	G by Pos
1886	NY AA	1	.000	.000	5	0	0	0	0	0.0	0		0			0	0	1	1	1	0	3.0	.667	3B-1

Tom Connelly

CONNELLY, THOMAS MARTIN BL TR 5′11½″ 165 lbs.
B. Oct. 20, 1897, Chicago, Ill. D. Feb. 18, 1941, Hines, Ill.

Year	Team	Games	BA	SA	AB	H	2B	3B	HR	HR%	R	RBI	BB	SO	SB	Pinch Hit AB	Pinch Hit H	PO	A	E	DP	TC/G	FA	G by Pos
1920	NY A	1	.000	.000	1	0	0	0	0	0.0	0	0	0	0	0	1	0	0	0	0	0	0.0	—	
1921		4	.200	.200	5	1	0	0	0	0.0	0	0	1	0	0	1	1	7	0	0	0	2.3	1.000	OF-3
2 yrs.		5	.167	.167	6	1	0	0	0	0.0	0	0	1	0	0	2	1	7	0	0	0	2.3	1.000	OF-3

Bud Connolly

CONNOLLY, MERVIN THOMAS (Mike) BR TR 5′ 8″ 154 lbs.
B. May 25, 1901, San Francisco, Calif. D. June 12, 1964, Berkeley, Calif.

Year	Team	Games	BA	SA	AB	H	2B	3B	HR	HR%	R	RBI	BB	SO	SB	Pinch Hit AB	Pinch Hit H	PO	A	E	DP	TC/G	FA	G by Pos
1925	BOS A	43	.262	.346	107	28	7	1	0	0.0	12	21	23	9	0	8	4	61	75	7	14	4.0	.951	SS-34, 3B-2

Ed Connolly

CONNOLLY, EDWARD JOSEPH, SR. BR TR 5′ 8½″ 180 lbs.
Father of Ed Connolly.
B. July 17, 1908, Brooklyn, N. Y. D. Nov. 12, 1963, Pittsfield, Mass.

Year	Team	Games	BA	SA	AB	H	2B	3B	HR	HR%	R	RBI	BB	SO	SB	Pinch Hit AB	Pinch Hit H	PO	A	E	DP	TC/G	FA	G by Pos
1929	BOS A	5	.000	.000	8	0	0	0	0	0.0	0	0	0	2	0	0	0	7	1	1	0	1.8	.889	C-5
1930		27	.188	.229	48	9	2	0	0	0.0	1	7	4	3	0	0	0	39	12	0	1	2.0	1.000	C-26
1931		42	.075	.086	93	7	1	0	0	0.0	3	3	5	18	0	1	0	87	18	2	1	2.6	.981	C-41
1932		75	.225	.297	222	50	8	4	0	0.0	9	21	20	27	0	0	0	233	55	13	0	4.0	.957	C-75
4 yrs.		149	.178	.229	371	66	11	4	0	0.0	13	31	29	50	0	1	0	366	86	16	2	3.2	.966	C-147

Joe Connolly

CONNOLLY, JOSEPH ALOYSIUS BL TR 5′ 7½″ 165 lbs.
B. Feb. 12, 1888, N. Smithfield, R. I. D. Sept. 1, 1943, Springfield, R. I.

Year	Team	Games	BA	SA	AB	H	2B	3B	HR	HR%	R	RBI	BB	SO	SB	Pinch Hit AB	Pinch Hit H	PO	A	E	DP	TC/G	FA	G by Pos
1913	BOS N	126	.281	.410	427	120	18	11	5	1.2	79	57	66	47	18	1	0	214	16	11	2	1.9	.954	OF-124
1914		120	.306	.494	399	122	28	10	9	2.3	64	65	49	36	12	1	0	168	19	5	1	1.6	.974	OF-118
1915		104	.298	.397	305	91	14	8	0	0.0	48	23	39	35	13	9	1	158	10	5	2	1.9	.971	OF-93
1916		62	.227	.309	110	25	5	2	0	0.0	11	12	14	13	5	25	6	46	4	1	1	1.6	.980	OF-31
4 yrs.		412	.288	.425	1241	358	65	31	14	1.1	202	157	168	131	48	36	7	586	49	22	6	1.8	.967	OF-366
WORLD SERIES																								
1914	BOS N	3	.111	.111	9	1	0	0	0	0.0	1	1	1	1	0	0	0	2	2	1	0	1.7	.800	OF-3

Joe Connolly

CONNOLLY, JOSEPH GEORGE (Coaster Joe) BR TR 6′ 170 lbs.
B. June 4, 1896, San Francisco, Calif. D. Mar. 30, 1960, San Francisco, Calif.

Year	Team	Games	BA	SA	AB	H	2B	3B	HR	HR%	R	RBI	BB	SO	SB	Pinch Hit AB	Pinch Hit H	PO	A	E	DP	TC/G	FA	G by Pos
1921	NY N	2	.000	.000	4	0	0	0	0	0.0	0	0	1	1	0	1	0	2	0	0	0	2.0	1.000	OF-1
1922	CLE A	12	.244	.333	45	11	2	1	0	0.0	6	6	5	8	1	0	0	33	2	1	0	3.0	.972	OF-12
1923		52	.303	.495	109	33	10	1	3	2.8	25	25	13	7	1	9	1	42	2	2	0	1.2	.957	OF-39
1924	BOS A	14	.100	.100	10	1	0	0	0	0.0	1	1	2	2	0	10	1	3	0	0	0	1.0	1.000	OF-3
4 yrs.		80	.268	.417	168	45	12	2	3	1.8	32	32	21	18	2	20	2	80	4	3	0	1.6	.966	OF-55

Tom Connolly

CONNOLLY, THOMAS FRANCIS (Blackie) BL TR 5′11″ 180 lbs.
B. Dec. 30, 1892, Boston, Mass. D. May 14, 1966, Boston, Mass.

Year	Team	Games	BA	SA	AB	H	2B	3B	HR	HR%	R	RBI	BB	SO	SB	Pinch Hit AB	Pinch Hit H	PO	A	E	DP	TC/G	FA	G by Pos
1915	WAS A	50	.184	.234	141	26	3	2	0	0.0	14	7	14	19	5	3	0	57	43	7	4	2.3	.935	3B-24, OF-19, SS-4

Jim Connor

CONNOR, JAMES MATTHEW BR TR
Born James Matthew O'Connor.
B. May 11, 1863, Port Jervis, N. Y. D. Sept. 3, 1950, Providence, R. I.

Year	Team	Games	BA	SA	AB	H	2B	3B	HR	HR%	R	RBI	BB	SO	SB	Pinch Hit AB	Pinch Hit H	PO	A	E	DP	TC/G	FA	G by Pos
1892	CHI N	9	.059	.059	34	2	0	0	0	0.0	0	0	1	7	0	0	0	14	19	3	0	4.0	.917	2B-9
1897		77	.291	.393	285	83	10	5	3	1.1	40	38	24		10	2	1	176	293	32	40	6.6	.936	2B-76
1898		138	.226	.279	505	114	9	9	0	0.0	51	67	42		11	0	0	330	437	44	75	5.9	.946	2B-138
1899		69	.205	.244	234	48	7	1	0	0.0	26	24	18		6	0	0	101	211	26	25	4.9	.923	2B-44, 3B-25
4 yrs.		293	.233	.295	1058	247	26	15	3	0.3	117	129	85	7	27	2	1	621	960	105	140	5.8	.938	2B-267, 3B-25

Joe Connor

CONNOR, JOSEPH FRANCIS BR TR 6′ 2″ 185 lbs.
Brother of Roger Connor.
B. Dec. 8, 1874, Waterbury, Conn. D. Nov. 8, 1957, Waterbury, Conn.

Year	Team	Games	BA	SA	AB	H	2B	3B	HR	HR%	R	RBI	BB	SO	SB	Pinch Hit AB	Pinch Hit H	PO	A	E	DP	TC/G	FA	G by Pos
1895	STL N	2	.000	.000	7	0	0	0	0	0.0	0	1	0	2	0	0	0	2	5	0	0	3.5	1.000	3B-2
1900	BOS N	7	.211	.211	19	4	0	0	0	0.0	2	4	2		1	0	0	23	11	1	2	5.0	.971	C-7
1901	2 teams	MIL A (38G –.275) CLE A (37G –.140)																						
"	total	75	.202	.260	223	45	6	2	1	0.4	23	15	13		6	5	1	216	79	18	3	4.5	.942	C-62, OF-5, SS-1, 2B-1, 3B-1
1905	NY A	8	.227	.273	22	5	1	0	0	0.0	4	2	3		1	0	0	43	13	1	1	7.1	.982	C-6, 1B-2
4 yrs.		92	.199	.251	271	54	7	2	1	0.4	29	22	18	2	8	5	1	284	108	20	6	4.7	.951	C-75, OF-5, 3B-3, 1B-2, SS-1, 2B-1

Roger Connor

CONNOR, ROGER BL TL 6′ 3″ 220 lbs.
Brother of Joe Connor.
B. July 1, 1857, Waterbury, Conn. D. Jan. 4, 1931, Waterbury, Conn.
Manager 1896.
Hall of Fame 1976.

Year	Team	Games	BA	SA	AB	H	2B	3B	HR	HR%	R	RBI	BB	SO	SB	Pinch Hit AB	Pinch Hit H	PO	A	E	DP	TC/G	FA	G by Pos
1880	TRO N	83	.332	.459	340	113	18	8	3	0.9	53	47	13	21		0	0	116	159	60	10	4.0	.821	3B-83
1881		85	.292	.387	367	107	17	6	2	0.5	55	31	15	20		0	0	836	40	46	51	10.8	.950	1B-85
1882		81	.330	.530	349	115	22	**18**	4	1.1	65	42	13	20		0	0	518	57	44	31	7.6	.929	1B-43, OF-24, 3B-14
1883	NY N	98	.357	.506	409	146	28	15	1	0.2	80		25	16		0	0	958	40	44	37	10.6	.958	1B-98
1884		116	.317	.417	477	151	28	4	4	0.8	98		38	32		0	0	299	234	96	32	5.4	.847	2B-67, OF-37, 3B-12

Roger Connor *continued*

Year	Team	Games	BA	SA	AB	H	2B	3B	HR	HR%	R	RBI	BB	SO	SB	Pinch Hit AB	Pinch Hit H	PO	A	E	DP	TC/G	FA	G by Pos
1885		110	**.371**	.495	455	**169**	23	15	1	0.2	102		51	8		0	0	1178	42	31	66	11.4	.975	1B-110
1886		118	.355	.540	485	172	29	**20**	7	1.4	105	71	41	15		0	0	1164	65	34	55	10.7	.973	1B-118
1887		127	.285	.541	471	134	26	22	17	3.6	113	104	75	50	43	0	0	1325	44	10	67	10.9	.993	1B-127
1888		134	.291	.480	481	140	15	17	14	2.9	98	71	**73**	44	27	0	0	1346	45	26	59	10.6	.982	1B-133, 2B-1
1889		131	.317	**.528**	496	157	32	17	13	2.6	117	**130**	93	46	21	0	0	1266	33	30	68	10.1	.977	1B-131, 3B-1
1890	**NY P**	123	.349	**.548**	484	169	24	15	**14**	**2.9**	133	103	88	32	22	0	0	1335	80	21	79	11.7	.985	1B-123
1891	**NY N**	129	.290	.443	479	139	29	13	6	1.3	112	94	83	39	27	0	0	1362	56	25	77	11.2	.983	1B-129
1892	**PHI N**	155	.294	.463	564	166	**37**	11	12	2.1	123	73	116	39	22	0	0	1483	59	23	99	10.1	.985	1B-155
1893	**NY N**	135	.305	.450	511	156	25	8	11	2.2	111	105	91	26	24	0	0	1423	83	40	70	11.4	.974	1B-135, 3B-1
1894	**2 teams**	**NY N** (22G –.293)	**STL N** (99G –.321)																					
″	**total**	121	.316	.552	462	146	35	25	8	1.7	93	93	59	17	19	0	0	1092	83	32	84	10.0	.973	1B-120, OF-1
1895	**STL N**	104	.329	.508	398	131	29	9	8	2.0	78	77	63	10	9	0	0	953	62	14	60	10.0	.986	1B-103
1896		126	.284	.433	483	137	21	9	11	2.3	71	72	52	14	10	0	0	1217	94	16	48	10.5	.988	1B-126
1897		22	.229	.325	83	19	3	1	1	1.2	13	12	13		3	0	0	237	12	4	6	11.5	.984	1B-22
18 yrs.		1998	.317	.486	7794	2467	441	233	137	1.8	1620	1125	1002	449	227	0	0	18108	1288	596	999	10.0	.970	1B-1758, 3B-111, 2B-68, OF-62
								5th																

Chuck Connors

CONNORS, KEVIN JOSEPH ALOYSIUS BL TL 6′ 5″ 190 lbs.
B. Apr. 10, 1921, Brooklyn, N. Y. D. Nov. 10, 1992, Los Angeles, Calif.

Year	Team	Games	BA	SA	AB	H	2B	3B	HR	HR%	R	RBI	BB	SO	SB	Pinch Hit AB	Pinch Hit H	PO	A	E	DP	TC/G	FA	G by Pos
1949	**BKN N**	1	.000	.000	1	0	0	0	0	0.0	0	0	0	0	0	1	0	0	0	0	0	0.0	—	
1951	**CHI N**	66	.239	.303	201	48	5	1	2	1.0	16	18	12	25	4	10	1	452	33	8	41	8.6	.984	1B-57
2 yrs.		67	.238	.302	202	48	5	1	2	1.0	16	18	12	25	4	11	1	452	33	8	41	8.6	.984	1B-57

Jerry Connors

CONNORS, JEREMIAH
B. Cleveland, Ohio Deceased.

Year	Team	Games	BA	SA	AB	H	2B	3B	HR	HR%	R	RBI	BB	SO	SB	Pinch Hit AB	Pinch Hit H	PO	A	E	DP	TC/G	FA	G by Pos
1892	**PHI N**	1	.000	.000	3	0	0	0	0	0.0	0	0	0	1	0	0	0	0	0	0	0	0.0	.000	OF-1

Joe Connors

CONNORS, JOSEPH P.
B. Paterson, N. J. Deceased.

Year	Team	Games	BA	SA	AB	H	2B	3B	HR	HR%	R	RBI	BB	SO	SB	Pinch Hit AB	Pinch Hit H	PO	A	E	DP	TC/G	FA	G by Pos
1884	**2 teams**	**ALT U** (3G –.091)	**KC U** (3G –.091)																					
″	**total**	6	.091	.091	22	2	0	0	0	0.0	2		1			0	0	8	7	3	0	2.6	.833	OF-3, P-3, 3B-1

Merv Connors

CONNORS, MERVYN JAMES BR TR 6′ 2″ 192 lbs.
B. Jan. 23, 1914, Berkeley, Calif.

Year	Team	Games	BA	SA	AB	H	2B	3B	HR	HR%	R	RBI	BB	SO	SB	Pinch Hit AB	Pinch Hit H	PO	A	E	DP	TC/G	FA	G by Pos
1937	**CHI A**	28	.233	.350	103	24	4	1	2	1.9	12	12	14	19	2	0	0	22	53	6	8	2.9	.926	3B-28
1938		24	.355	.710	62	22	4	0	6	9.7	14	13	9	17	0	7	2	129	11	3	17	8.9	.979	1B-16
2 yrs.		52	.279	.485	165	46	8	1	8	4.8	26	25	23	36	2	7	2	151	64	9	25	5.1	.960	3B-28, 1B-16

Ben Conroy

CONROY, BERNARD PATRICK 160 lbs.
B. Mar. 14, 1871, Philadelphia, Pa. D. Nov. 25, 1937, Philadelphia, Pa.

Year	Team	Games	BA	SA	AB	H	2B	3B	HR	HR%	R	RBI	BB	SO	SB	Pinch Hit AB	Pinch Hit H	PO	A	E	DP	TC/G	FA	G by Pos
1890	**PHI AA**	117	.171	.208	404	69	13	1	0	0.0	45		45		17	0	0	221	352	56	39	5.4	.911	SS-74, 2B-42, OF-1

Bill Conroy

CONROY, WILLIAM GORDON BR TR 6′ 185 lbs.
B. Feb. 26, 1915, Bloomington, Ill.

Year	Team	Games	BA	SA	AB	H	2B	3B	HR	HR%	R	RBI	BB	SO	SB	Pinch Hit AB	Pinch Hit H	PO	A	E	DP	TC/G	FA	G by Pos
1935	**PHI A**	1	.250	.500	4	1	1	0	0	0.0	0	0	1	0	0	0	0	11	0	0	0	11.0	1.000	C-1
1936		1	.500	.500	2	1	0	0	0	0.0	0	0	0	1	0	0	0	3	0	0	0	3.0	1.000	C-1
1937		26	.200	.250	60	12	1	1	0	0.0	4	3	7	9	1	5	1	58	6	0	2	3.4	1.000	C-18, 1B-1
1942	**BOS A**	83	.200	.280	250	50	4	2	4	1.6	22	20	40	47	2	0	0	324	40	11	6	4.5	.971	C-83
1943		39	.180	.270	89	16	5	0	1	1.1	13	6	18	19	0	3	1	135	19	5	3	4.2	.969	C-38
1944		19	.213	.255	47	10	2	0	0	0.0	6	4	11	9	0	0	0	60	9	2	2	3.7	.972	C-19
6 yrs.		169	.199	.274	452	90	13	3	5	1.1	45	33	77	85	3	8	2	591	74	18	13	4.2	.974	C-160, 1B-1

Pep Conroy

CONROY, WILLIAM FREDERICK BR TR 5′ 8½″ 160 lbs.
B. Jan. 9, 1899, Chicago, Ill. D. Jan. 23, 1970, Chicago, Ill.

Year	Team	Games	BA	SA	AB	H	2B	3B	HR	HR%	R	RBI	BB	SO	SB	Pinch Hit AB	Pinch Hit H	PO	A	E	DP	TC/G	FA	G by Pos
1923	**WAS A**	18	.133	.233	60	8	2	2	0	0.0	6	2	4	9	0	1	0	56	21	5	7	4.8	.939	3B-10, 1B-6, OF-1

Wid Conroy

CONROY, WILLIAM EDWARD BR TR 5′ 9″ 158 lbs.
B. Apr. 5, 1877, Camden, N. J. D. Dec. 6, 1959, Mt. Holly, N. J.

Year	Team	Games	BA	SA	AB	H	2B	3B	HR	HR%	R	RBI	BB	SO	SB	Pinch Hit AB	Pinch Hit H	PO	A	E	DP	TC/G	FA	G by Pos
1901	**MIL A**	131	.256	.350	503	129	20	6	5	1.0	74	64	36		21	1	0	299	427	64	48	6.1	.919	SS-118, 3B-12
1902	**PIT N**	99	.244	.312	365	89	10	6	1	0.3	55	47	24		10	0	0	194	327	42	39	5.7	.925	SS-95, OF-3
1903	**NY A**	126	.272	.372	503	137	23	12	1	0.2	74	45	32		33	0	0	167	247	36	11	3.5	.920	3B-123, SS-4
1904		140	.243	.335	489	119	18	12	1	0.2	58	52	43		30	0	0	204	295	29	13	3.8	.945	3B-110, SS-27, OF-3
1905		102	.273	.395	385	105	19	11	2	0.5	55	25	32		25	1	0	287	142	24	14	4.6	.947	3B-48, OF-21, SS-18, 1B-9, 2B-3
1906		148	.245	.332	567	139	17	10	4	0.7	67	54	47		32	0	0	295	154	21	15	3.2	.955	OF-97, SS-49, 3B-2
1907		140	.234	.315	530	124	12	11	3	0.6	58	51	30		41	2	0	299	104	24	17	3.1	.944	OF-100, SS-38
1908		141	.237	.296	531	126	22	3	1	0.2	44	39	14		23	0	0	236	285	32	15	3.9	.942	3B-119, 2B-12, OF-10
1909	**WAS A**	139	.244	.293	488	119	13	4	1	0.2	44	20	37		24	0	0	170	276	29	18	3.4	.939	3B-120, 2B-13, OF-5, SS-1
1910		105	.254	.311	351	89	11	3	1	0.3	36	27	30		11	6	1	163	99	13	6	2.8	.953	3B-48, OF-46, 2B-5
1911		104	.231	.298	346	80	11	3	2	0.6	40	28	20		12	4	2	118	178	24	11	3.2	.925	3B-85, OF-13, 2B-1
11 yrs.		1375	.248	.328	5058	1256	176	81	22	0.4	605	452	345		262	14	3	2432	2534	338	207	3.9	.936	3B-667, SS-350, OF-298, 2B-34, 1B-9

Billy Consolo

CONSOLO, WILLIAM ANGELO BR TR 5′11″ 180 lbs.
B. Aug. 18, 1934, Cleveland, Ohio.

Year	Team	Games	BA	SA	AB	H	2B	3B	HR	HR%	R	RBI	BB	SO	SB	Pinch Hit AB	Pinch Hit H	PO	A	E	DP	TC/G	FA	G by Pos
1953	**BOS A**	47	.215	.323	65	14	2	1	1	1.5	9	6	2	23	1	9	1	26	47	6	13	2.9	.924	3B-16, 2B-11
1954		91	.227	.277	242	55	7	1	1	0.4	23	11	33	69	2	4	1	113	184	15	30	3.9	.952	SS-50, 3B-18, 2B-12
1955		8	.222	.222	18	4	0	0	0	0.0	4	0	5	4	0	1	1	11	5	2	1	4.5	.889	2B-4
1956		48	.182	.182	11	2	0	0	0	0.0	13	1	3	5	0	0	0	9	14	2	4	1.0	.920	2B-25
1957		68	.270	.372	196	53	6	1	4	2.0	26	19	23	48	1	0	0	92	189	16	41	4.9	.946	SS-42, 2B-16, 3B-2

Billy Consolo *continued*

Year	Team	Games	BA	SA	AB	H	2B	3B	HR	HR%	R	RBI	BB	SO	SB	Pinch Hit AB	Pinch Hit H	PO	A	E	DP	TC/G	FA	G by Pos
1958		46	.125	.181	72	9	2	1	0	0.0	13	5	6	14	0	1	0	37	55	5	16	3.9	.948	2B-13, SS-11, 3B-1
1959	2 teams	BOS A (10G –.214) WAS A (79G –.213)																						
"	total	89	.213	.269	216	46	6	3	0	0.0	28	10	38	59	1	8	1	126	242	19	48	4.8	.951	SS-77, 2B-4
1960	WAS A	100	.207	.305	174	36	4	2	3	1.7	23	15	25	29	1	7	2	97	183	18	39	3.1	.940	SS-82, 2B-12, 3B-2
1961	MIN A	11	.000	.000	5	0	0	0	0	0.0	1	0	0	1	0	1	0	5	1	0	0	0.9	1.000	SS-3, 2B-3, 3B-1
1962	3 teams	PHI N (13G –.400) LA A (28G –.100) KC A (54G –.240)																						
"	total	95	.229	.274	179	41	4	2	0	0.0	18	16	26	45	3	13	4	78	140	13	28	3.1	.944	SS-52, 3B-21, 2B-1
10 yrs.		603	.221	.289	1178	260	31	11	9	0.8	158	83	161	297	9	44	10	594	1060	96	220	3.7	.945	SS-317, 2B-101, 3B-61

Bill Conway

CONWAY, WILLIAM F.
Brother of Dick Conway.
B. Nov. 28, 1861, Lowell, Mass. D. Dec. 28, 1943, Somerville, Mass.
BR TR 5′ 8½″ 170 lbs.

Year	Team	Games	BA	SA	AB	H	2B	3B	HR	HR%	R	RBI	BB	SO	SB	Pinch Hit AB	Pinch Hit H	PO	A	E	DP	TC/G	FA	G by Pos
1884	PHI N	1	.000	.000	4	0	0	0	0	0.0	0		0	1		0	0	5	2	0	1	7.0	1.000	C-1
1886	BAL AA	7	.143	.143	14	2	0	0	0	0.0	4		7			0	0	33	4	6	0	6.1	.860	C-7
2 yrs.		8	.111	.111	18	2	0	0	0	0.0	4		7	1		0	0	38	6	6	1	6.3	.880	C-8

Charlie Conway

CONWAY, CHARLES CONNELL
B. Apr. 28, 1886, Youngstown, Ohio D. Sept. 12, 1968, Youngstown, Ohio.
BR TR 5′11″ 155 lbs.

Year	Team	Games	BA	SA	AB	H	2B	3B	HR	HR%	R	RBI	BB	SO	SB	Pinch Hit AB	Pinch Hit H	PO	A	E	DP	TC/G	FA	G by Pos
1911	WAS A	2	.333	1.000	3	1	0	1	0	0.0	0	0	0		0	0	0	0	0	1	0	0.5	.000	OF-2

Jack Conway

CONWAY, JACK CLEMENTS
B. July 30, 1919, Bryan, Tex.
BR TR 5′11½″ 175 lbs.

Year	Team	Games	BA	SA	AB	H	2B	3B	HR	HR%	R	RBI	BB	SO	SB	Pinch Hit AB	Pinch Hit H	PO	A	E	DP	TC/G	FA	G by Pos
1941	CLE A	2	.500	.500	2	1	0	0	0	0.0	0	1	0	0	0	0	0	2	3	0	0	2.5	1.000	SS-2
1946		68	.225	.264	258	58	6	2	0	0.0	24	18	20	36	2	2	0	146	163	17	34	4.9	.948	2B-50, SS-14, 3B-3
1947		34	.180	.220	50	9	2	0	0	0.0	3	5	3	8	0	2	0	22	42	8	10	2.4	.889	SS-24, 2B-5, 3B-1
1948	NY N	24	.245	.388	49	12	2	1	1	2.0	8	3	5	10	0	2	0	33	45	2	11	3.6	.975	2B-13, SS-6, 3B-3
4 yrs.		128	.223	.276	359	80	10	3	1	0.3	35	27	28	54	2	6	0	203	253	27	55	4.0	.944	2B-68, SS-46, 3B-7

Owen Conway

CONWAY, OWEN SYLVESTER
B. Oct. 23, 1890, New York, N. Y. D. Mar. 12, 1942, Philadelphia, Pa.
TR

Year	Team	Games	BA	SA	AB	H	2B	3B	HR	HR%	R	RBI	BB	SO	SB	Pinch Hit AB	Pinch Hit H	PO	A	E	DP	TC/G	FA	G by Pos
1915	PHI A	4	.067	.067	15	1	0	0	0	0.0	2	0	0	3	0	0	0	7	11	6	2	6.0	.750	3B-4

Pete Conway

CONWAY, PETER J.
Brother of Jim Conway.
B. Oct. 30, 1866, Burmont, Pa. D. Jan. 13, 1903, Clifton Heights, Pa.
BR TR 5′10½″ 162 lbs.

Year	Team	Games	BA	SA	AB	H	2B	3B	HR	HR%	R	RBI	BB	SO	SB	Pinch Hit AB	Pinch Hit H	PO	A	E	DP	TC/G	FA	G by Pos
1885	BUF N	29	.111	.200	90	10	5	0	1	1.1	7	7	5	28		0	0	7	54	10	0	2.3	.859	P-27, OF-2, SS-1, 1B-1
1886	2 teams	KC N (51G –.242) DET N (12G –.186)																						
"	total	63	.232	.325	237	55	9	2	3	1.3	32	21	6	42		0	0	60	58	22	3	2.1	.843	P-34, OF-32
1887	DET N	24	.232	.337	95	22	5	1	1	1.1	16	7	2	9	0	0	0	26	37	5	0	2.7	.926	P-17, OF-8
1888		45	.275	.377	167	46	4	2	3	1.8	28	23	8	25	1	0	0	10	96	7	4	2.5	.938	P-45, OF-1
1889	PIT N	3	.100	.400	10	1	0	0	1	10.0	2	2	1	3	1	0	0	1	6	1	0	2.0	.875	P-3, OF-1
5 yrs.		164	.224	.324	599	134	23	5	9	1.5	85	60	22	107	2	0	0	104	251	45	7	2.3	.887	P-126, OF-44, SS-1, 1B-1

Rip Conway

CONWAY, RICHARD DANIEL
B. Apr. 18, 1896, White Bear Lake, Minn. D. Dec. 3, 1971, St. Paul, Minn.
BL TR 5′ 6″ 160 lbs.

Year	Team	Games	BA	SA	AB	H	2B	3B	HR	HR%	R	RBI	BB	SO	SB	Pinch Hit AB	Pinch Hit H	PO	A	E	DP	TC/G	FA	G by Pos
1918	BOS N	14	.167	.167	24	4	0	0	0	0.0	4	2	2	4	1	5	2	10	8	4	0	3.7	.818	2B-5, 3B-1

Ed Conwell

CONWELL, EDWARD JAMES (Irish)
B. Jan. 29, 1890, Chicago, Ill. D. May 1, 1926, Chicago, Ill.
BR TR 5′11″ 155 lbs.

Year	Team	Games	BA	SA	AB	H	2B	3B	HR	HR%	R	RBI	BB	SO	SB	Pinch Hit AB	Pinch Hit H	PO	A	E	DP	TC/G	FA	G by Pos
1911	STL N	1	.000	.000	1	0	0	0	0	0.0	0	0	0	1	0	0	0	0	0	1	0	1.0	.000	3B-1

Herb Conyers

CONYERS, HERBERT LEROY
B. Jan. 8, 1921, Cowgill, Mo. D. Sept. 16, 1964, Cleveland, Ohio.
BL TR 6′ 5″ 210 lbs.

Year	Team	Games	BA	SA	AB	H	2B	3B	HR	HR%	R	RBI	BB	SO	SB	Pinch Hit AB	Pinch Hit H	PO	A	E	DP	TC/G	FA	G by Pos
1950	CLE A	7	.333	.667	9	3	0	0	1	11.1	2	1	1	2	1	4	2	6	0	0	0	6.0	1.000	1B-1

Dale Coogan

COOGAN, DALE ROGER
B. Aug. 14, 1930, Los Angeles, Calif. D. Mar. 8, 1989, Mission/viejo, Calif.
BL TL 6′ 1″ 190 lbs.

Year	Team	Games	BA	SA	AB	H	2B	3B	HR	HR%	R	RBI	BB	SO	SB	Pinch Hit AB	Pinch Hit H	PO	A	E	DP	TC/G	FA	G by Pos
1950	PIT N	53	.240	.326	129	31	6	1	1	0.8	19	13	17	24	0	16	2	263	27	6	28	9.3	.980	1B-32

Dan Coogan

COOGAN, DANIEL GEORGE
B. Feb. 16, 1875, Philadelphia, Pa. D. Oct. 28, 1942, Philadelphia, Pa.
128 lbs.

Year	Team	Games	BA	SA	AB	H	2B	3B	HR	HR%	R	RBI	BB	SO	SB	Pinch Hit AB	Pinch Hit H	PO	A	E	DP	TC/G	FA	G by Pos
1895	WAS N	26	.221	.273	77	17	2	1	0	0.0	9	7	13	6	1	1	0	45	53	32	6	5.0	.754	SS-18, C-5, OF-2, 3B-1

Cliff Cook

COOK, RAYMOND CLIFFORD
B. Aug. 20, 1936, Dallas, Tex.
BR TR 6′ 185 lbs.

Year	Team	Games	BA	SA	AB	H	2B	3B	HR	HR%	R	RBI	BB	SO	SB	Pinch Hit AB	Pinch Hit H	PO	A	E	DP	TC/G	FA	G by Pos
1959	CIN N	9	.381	.571	21	8	2	1	0	0.0	3	5	2	8	1	0	0	7	13	2	2	2.4	.909	3B-9
1960		54	.208	.315	149	31	7	0	3	2.0	9	13	8	51	0	0	0	50	77	6	8	2.6	.955	3B-47, OF-4
1961		4	.000	.000	5	0	0	0	0	0.0	0	0	0	4	0	3	0	0	2	0	0	2.0	1.000	3B-1
1962	2 teams	CIN N (6G –.000) NY N (40G –.232)																						
"	total	46	.222	.342	117	26	6	1	2	1.7	12	9	4	36	1	14	4	26	21	6	2	1.8	.887	3B-20, OF-10
1963	NY N	50	.142	.236	106	15	2	1	2	1.9	9	8	12	37	0	19	4	50	27	4	5	2.3	.951	OF-21, 3B-9, 1B-5
5 yrs.		163	.201	.312	398	80	17	3	7	1.8	33	35	26	136	2	36	8	133	140	18	17	2.3	.938	3B-86, OF-35, 1B-5

Doc Cook

COOK, LUTHER ALMUS
B. June 24, 1886, Witt, Tex. D. June 30, 1973, Lawrenceburg, Tenn.
BL TR 6′ 170 lbs.

Year	Team	Games	BA	SA	AB	H	2B	3B	HR	HR%	R	RBI	BB	SO	SB	Pinch Hit AB	Pinch Hit H	PO	A	E	DP	TC/G	FA	G by Pos
1913	NY A	20	.264	.319	72	19	2	1	0	0.0	9	1	10	4	1	0	0	43	3	3	1	2.5	.939	OF-20
1914		131	.283	.326	470	133	11	3	1	0.2	59	40	44	60	26	5	1	171	15	10	2	1.6	.949	OF-126
1915		132	.271	.338	476	129	16	5	2	0.4	70	33	62	43	29	0	0	188	20	9	4	1.7	.959	OF-131
1916		3	.100	.100	10	1	0	0	0	0.0	0	1	0	2	0	0	0	3	0	0	0	1.0	1.000	OF-3
4 yrs.		286	.274	.329	1028	282	29	9	3	0.3	138	75	116	109	56	5	1	405	38	22	7	1.7	.953	OF-280

Jim Cook

COOK, JAMES FITCHIE
B. Nov. 10, 1879, Dundee, Ill. D. June 17, 1949, St. Louis, Mo.
BR TR 5′ 9″ 163 lbs.

Year	Team	Games	BA	SA	AB	H	2B	3B	HR	HR%	R	RBI	BB	SO	SB	Pinch Hit AB	Pinch Hit H	PO	A	E	DP	TC/G	FA	G by Pos
1903	CHI N	8	.154	.192	26	4	1	0	0	0.0	3	2	2		1	0	0	17	3	2	0	2.8	.909	OF-5, 2B-2, 1B-1

Paul Cook

COOK, PAUL BR TR
B. May 5, 1863, Caledonia, N. Y. D. May 25, 1905, Rochester, N. Y.

Year	Team	Games	BA	SA	AB	H	2B	3B	HR	HR%	R	RBI	BB	SO	SB	Pinch Hit AB	Pinch Hit H	PO	A	E	DP	TC/G	FA	G by Pos
1884	PHI N	3	.083	.083	12	1	0	0	0	0.0	0		0	2		0	0	16	2	4	1	7.3	.818	C-3
1886	LOU AA	66	.206	.240	262	54	5	2	0	0.0	28		10			0	0	532	49	47	22	9.5	.925	1B-43, C-21, OF-2
1887		61	.247	.283	223	55	4	2	0	0.0	34		11		15	0	0	270	95	34	5	6.5	.915	C-55, 1B-6
1888		57	.184	.195	185	34	2	0	0	0.0	20	13	5		9	0	0	224	81	37	7	5.9	.892	C-53, OF-4, SS-1
1889		81	.227	.269	286	65	10	1	0	0.0	34	15	15	48	11	0	0	323	142	37	8	6.0	.926	C-74, OF-7, 1B-1, SS-1
1890	BKN P	58	.252	.294	218	55	3	3	0	0.0	32	31	14	18	7	0	0	320	57	30	20	7.0	.926	C-36, 1B-21, OF-1
1891	2 teams	LOU AA (45G –.229)	STL AA (7G –.200)																					
"	total	52	.225	.253	178	40	3	1	0	0.0	24	24	12	19	4	0	0	259	51	24	6	6.4	.928	C-42, 1B-10
7 yrs.		378	.223	.256	1364	304	27	9	0	0.0	172	83	67	87	46	0	0	1944	477	213	69	6.9	.919	C-284, 1B-81, OF-14, SS-2

Dusty Cooke

COOKE, ALLEN LINDSEY BL TR 6′ 1″ 205 lbs.
B. June 23, 1907, Swepsonville, N. C. D. Nov. 21, 1987, Raleigh, N. C.
Manager 1948.

Year	Team	Games	BA	SA	AB	H	2B	3B	HR	HR%	R	RBI	BB	SO	SB	Pinch Hit AB	Pinch Hit H	PO	A	E	DP	TC/G	FA	G by Pos
1930	NY A	92	.255	.421	216	55	12	3	6	2.8	43	29	32	61	4	10	1	133	2	3	1	1.9	.978	OF-73
1931		27	.333	.436	39	13	1	0	1	2.6	10	6	8	11	4	2	0	23	0	0	0	2.1	1.000	OF-11
1932		3	—	—	0	0	0	0	0	—	1	0	1	0	0	0	0	0	0	0	0	0.0	—	
1933	BOS A	119	.291	.445	454	132	35	10	5	1.1	86	54	67	71	7	2	0	257	6	12	5	2.3	.956	OF-118
1934		74	.244	.369	168	41	8	5	1	0.6	34	26	36	25	7	21	4	79	1	2	0	1.9	.976	OF-44
1935		100	.306	.439	294	90	18	6	3	1.0	51	34	46	24	6	11	2	172	4	5	1	2.2	.972	OF-82
1936		111	.273	.402	341	93	20	3	6	1.8	58	47	72	48	4	13	4	207	3	6	2	2.4	.972	OF-91
1938	CIN N	82	.275	.373	233	64	15	1	2	0.9	41	33	28	36	0	27	5	126	4	5	1	2.6	.963	OF-51
8 yrs.		608	.280	.415	1745	488	109	28	24	1.4	324	229	290	276	32	86	16	997	20	33	10	2.2	.969	OF-470

Fred Cooke

COOKE, FREDERICK B.
B. Oct. 1873, Ill. Deceased.

Year	Team	Games	BA	SA	AB	H	2B	3B	HR	HR%	R	RBI	BB	SO	SB	Pinch Hit AB	Pinch Hit H	PO	A	E	DP	TC/G	FA	G by Pos
1897	CLE N	5	.294	.412	17	5	2	0	0	0.0	2	3	3		0	0	0	3	3	1	0	1.4	.857	OF-5

Brent Cookson

COOKSON, BRENT ADAM BR TR 5′11″ 200 lbs.
B. Sept. 7, 1969, Van Nuys, Calif.

Year	Team	Games	BA	SA	AB	H	2B	3B	HR	HR%	R	RBI	BB	SO	SB	Pinch Hit AB	Pinch Hit H	PO	A	E	DP	TC/G	FA	G by Pos
1995	KC A	22	.143	.171	35	5	1	0	0	0.0	2	5	2	7	1	11	1	14	0	0	0	1.0	1.000	OF-12, DH-2

Scott Coolbaugh

COOLBAUGH, SCOTT ROBERT BR TR 5′10″ 185 lbs.
B. June 13, 1966, Binghamton, N. Y.

Year	Team	Games	BA	SA	AB	H	2B	3B	HR	HR%	R	RBI	BB	SO	SB	Pinch Hit AB	Pinch Hit H	PO	A	E	DP	TC/G	FA	G by Pos
1989	TEX A	25	.275	.412	51	14	1	0	2	3.9	7	7	4	12	0	0	0	7	39	2	3	1.9	.958	3B-23, DH-2
1990		67	.200	.267	180	36	6	0	2	1.1	21	13	15	47	1	2	1	42	118	10	12	2.6	.941	3B-66
1991	SD N	60	.217	.306	180	39	8	1	2	1.1	12	15	19	45	0	6	0	32	108	7	8	2.7	.952	3B-54
1994	STL N	15	.190	.476	21	4	0	0	2	9.5	4	6	1	4	0	7	2	24	6	0	3	3.8	1.000	3B-4, 1B-4
4 yrs.		167	.215	.310	432	93	15	1	8	1.9	44	41	39	108	1	15	3	105	271	19	26	2.6	.952	3B-147, 1B-4, DH-2

Duff Cooley

COOLEY, DUFF GORDON (Sir Richard) BL TR 5′11″ 158 lbs.
B. Mar. 29, 1873, Leavenworth, Kans. D. Aug. 9, 1937, Dallas, Tex.

Year	Team	Games	BA	SA	AB	H	2B	3B	HR	HR%	R	RBI	BB	SO	SB	Pinch Hit AB	Pinch Hit H	PO	A	E	DP	TC/G	FA	G by Pos
1893	STL N	29	.346	.421	107	37	2	3	0	0.0	20	21	8	9	8	1	0	46	12	4	2	2.1	.935	OF-15, C-10, SS-5
1894		54	.296	.335	206	61	3	1	1	0.5	35	21	12	16	7	0	0	91	22	27	3	2.6	.807	OF-39, 3B-13, SS-1, 1B-1
1895		132	.339	.462	563	191	9	21	6	1.1	106	75	36	29	27	1	0	336	38	29	3	3.0	.928	OF-124, 3B-5, SS-3, C-1
1896	2 teams	STL N (40G –.307)	PHI N (64G –.307)																					
"	total	104	.307	.375	453	139	11	7	2	0.4	92	35	25	19	30	0	0	221	8	19	2	2.4	.923	OF-104
1897	PHI N	133	.329	.420	**566**	186	14	13	4	0.7	124	40	51		31	0	0	341	16	14	7	2.8	.962	OF-131, 1B-2
1898		149	.312	.407	629	196	24	12	4	0.6	123	55	48		17	0	0	352	15	22	2	2.6	.943	OF-149
1899		94	.276	.360	406	112	15	8	1	0.2	75	31	29		15	1	0	791	34	28	56	9.1	.967	1B-79, OF-14, 2B-1
1900	PIT N	66	.201	.241	249	50	8	1	0	0.0	30	22	14		9	0	0	683	20	8	39	10.8	.989	1B-66
1901	BOS N	63	.258	.338	240	62	13	3	0	0.0	27	27	14		5	0	0	218	9	9	4	3.7	.962	OF-53, 1B-10
1902		135	.296	.372	548	162	26	8	0	0.0	73	58	34		27	1	0	310	13	14	3	2.5	.958	OF-127, 1B-7
1903		138	.289	.378	553	160	26	10	1	0.2	76	70	44		27	0	0	351	14	19	6	2.8	.951	OF-126, 1B-13
1904		122	.272	.373	467	127	18	7	5	1.1	41	70	24		14	0	0	240	3	6	4	2.0	.976	OF-116, 1B-6
1905	DET A	99	.247	.332	377	93	11	9	1	0.3	25	32	26		7	1	1	223	12	10	5	2.5	.959	OF-97
13 yrs.		1318	.294	.380	5364	1576	180	103	25	0.5	847	557	365	73	224	5	1	4203	216	209	136	3.5	.955	OF-1095, 1B-184, 3B-18, C-11, SS-9, 2B-1

Cecil Coombs

COOMBS, CECIL LYSANDER BR TR 5′ 9″ 160 lbs.
B. Mar. 18, 1888, Moweaqua, Ill. D. Nov. 25, 1975, Fort Worth, Tex.

Year	Team	Games	BA	SA	AB	H	2B	3B	HR	HR%	R	RBI	BB	SO	SB	Pinch Hit AB	Pinch Hit H	PO	A	E	DP	TC/G	FA	G by Pos
1914	CHI A	7	.174	.217	23	4	1	0	0	0.0	1	1	1	7	0	0	0	13	2	0	0	2.1	1.000	OF-7

Jack Coombs

COOMBS, JOHN WESLEY (Cy) BB TR 6′ 185 lbs.
B. Nov. 18, 1882, LeGrand, Iowa D. Apr. 15, 1957, Palestine, Tex.
Manager 1919.

Year	Team	Games	BA	SA	AB	H	2B	3B	HR	HR%	R	RBI	BB	SO	SB	Pinch Hit AB	Pinch Hit H	PO	A	E	DP	TC/G	FA	G by Pos
1906	PHI A	24	.239	.269	67	16	2	0	0	0.0	9	3	1		2	1	0	16	44	2	4	2.7	.968	P-23
1907		24	.167	.229	48	8	0	0	1	2.1	4	4	0		1	1	0	9	37	1	2	2.0	.979	P-23
1908		78	.255	.355	220	56	9	5	1	0.5	24	23	9		6	5	4	102	48	4	4	2.1	.974	OF-47, P-26
1909		37	.169	.217	83	14	4	0	0	0.0	4	10	4		1	6	1	12	60	2	2	2.4	.973	P-31
1910		46	.220	.242	132	29	3	0	0	0.0	20	9	7		3	1	0	19	77	1	2	2.2	.990	P-45
1911		52	.319	.418	141	45	6	1	2	1.4	31	23	8		5	4	1	24	71	9	3	2.2	.913	P-47
1912		55	.255	.273	110	28	2	0	0	0.0	10	13	14		1	14	4	16	66	0	4	2.0	1.000	P-40
1913		2	.333	.667	3	1	1	0	0	0.0	1	0	0	2	0	0	0	1	0	1	0	1.0	.500	P-2
1914		5	.273	.364	11	3	1	0	0	0.0	0	2	1	1	0	1	0	4	1	0	0	1.3	1.000	OF-2, P-2
1915	BKN N	29	.280	.320	75	21	1	1	0	0.0	8	5	2	17	0	0	0	17	31	1	2	1.7	.980	P-29
		27	.180	.213	61	11	2	0	0	0.0	2	3	2	10	0	0	0	7	15	0	1	0.8	1.000	P-27
		32	.227	.273	44	10	0	1	0	0.0	4	2	4	9	1	0	0	8	26	1	1	1.1	.971	P-31
		46	.168	.230	113	19	3	2	0	0.0	6	3	7	5	1	3	1	20	41	3	0	1.6	.953	P-27, OF-13
	DET A	2	.000	.000	2	0	0	0	0	0.0	0	0	0	0	0	0	0	0	1	0	0	0.5	1.000	P-2
		459	.235	.295	1110	261	34	10	4	0.4	123	100	59	44	21	36	11	255	518	25	25	1.9	.969	P-355, OF-62

Jack Coombs *continued*

Year	Team	Lg	Games	BA	SA	AB	H	2B	3B	HR	HR%	R	RBI	BB	SO	SB	Pinch Hit AB	Pinch Hit H	PO	A	E	DP	TC/G	FA	G by Pos
WORLD SERIES																									
1910	PHI	A	3	.385	.462	13	5	1	0	0	0.0	0	3	0	3	0	0	0	1	4	2	0	2.3	.714	P-3
1911			2	.250	.250	8	2	0	0	0	0.0	1	0	0	0	0	0	0	1	2	0	0	1.5	1.000	P-2
1916	BKN	N	1	.333	.333	3	1	0	0	0	0.0	0	1	0	0	0	0	0	0	2	0	0	2.0	1.000	P-1
3 yrs.			6	.333	.375	24	8	1	0	0	0.0	1	4	0	3	0	0	0	2	8	2	0	2.0	.833	P-6

Ron Coomer

COOMER, RONALD BRYAN BR TR 5′11″ 195 lbs.
B. Nov. 18, 1966, Crest Hill, Ill.

Year	Team	Lg	Games	BA	SA	AB	H	2B	3B	HR	HR%	R	RBI	BB	SO	SB	Pinch Hit AB	Pinch Hit H	PO	A	E	DP	TC/G	FA	G by Pos
1995	MIN	A	37	.257	.455	101	26	3	1	5	5.0	15	19	9	11	0	5	0	138	33	2	14	4.3	.988	1B-22, 3B-13, DH-4, OF-1

William Coon

COON, WILLIAM K.
B. Mar. 21, 1855, Philadelphia, Pa. D. Aug. 30, 1915, Burlington, N. J.

Year	Team	Lg	Games	BA	SA	AB	H	2B	3B	HR	HR%	R	RBI	BB	SO	SB	Pinch Hit AB	Pinch Hit H	PO	A	E	DP	TC/G	FA	G by Pos
1876	PHI	N	54	.227	.259	220	50	5	1	0	0.0	30	22	2	4		0	0	106	31	60	2	3.5	.695	OF-29, C-18, 2B-4, 3B-4, P-2

Bill Cooney

COONEY, WILLIAM A. TR
B. Apr. 7, 1883, Boston, Mass. D. Nov. 6, 1928, Roxbury, Mass.

Year	Team	Lg	Games	BA	SA	AB	H	2B	3B	HR	HR%	R	RBI	BB	SO	SB	Pinch Hit AB	Pinch Hit H	PO	A	E	DP	TC/G	FA	G by Pos
1909	BOS	N	5	.300	.300	10	3	0	0	0	0.0	0	0	0		0	0	0	2	6	1	0	1.8	.889	P-3, SS-1, 2B-1
1910			8	.250	.250	12	3	0	0	0	0.0	2	1	2	0	0	5	2	0	0	0	0	0.0	.000	OF-2
2 yrs.			13	.273	.273	22	6	0	0	0	0.0	2	1	2	0	0	5	2	2	6	1	0	1.3	.889	P-3, OF-2, SS-1, 2B-1

Jimmy Cooney

COONEY, JAMES EDWARD (Scoops) BR TR 5′11″ 160 lbs.
Brother of Johnny Cooney. Son of Jimmy Cooney.
B. Aug. 24, 1894, Cranston, R. I. D. Aug. 7, 1991, Warwick, R. I.

Year	Team	Lg	Games	BA	SA	AB	H	2B	3B	HR	HR%	R	RBI	BB	SO	SB	Pinch Hit AB	Pinch Hit H	PO	A	E	DP	TC/G	FA	G by Pos
1917	BOS	A	11	.222	.250	36	8	1	0	0	0.0	4	3	6	2	0	0	0	30	39	0	7	6.3	1.000	2B-10, SS-1
1919	NY	N	5	.214	.214	14	3	0	0	0	0.0	3	1	0	0	0	0	0	7	11	0	2	3.6	1.000	SS-4, 2B-1
1924	STL	N	110	.295	.397	383	113	20	8	1	0.3	44	57	20	20	12	0	0	246	331	18	68	5.6	.970	SS-99, 3B-7, 2B-1
1925			54	.273	.353	187	51	11	2	0	0.0	27	18	4	5	1	1	0	97	137	6	31	4.5	.975	SS-37, 2B-15, OF-1
1926	CHI	N	141	.251	.312	513	129	18	5	1	0.2	52	47	23	10	11	0	0	344	492	24	107	6.1	.972	SS-141
1927	2 teams		CHI N (33G –.242)	PHI N (76G –.270)																					
″	total		109	.261	.302	391	102	14	1	0	0.0	49	21	21	16	5	1	0	230	340	13	64	5.4	.978	SS-107
1928	BOS	N	18	.137	.137	51	7	0	0	0	0.0	2	3	2	5	1	4	0	27	43	2	11	4.8	.972	SS-11, 2B-4
7 yrs.			448	.262	.327	1575	413	64	16	2	0.1	181	150	76	58	30	6	0	981	1393	63	290	5.6	.974	SS-400, 2B-31, 3B-7, OF-1

Jimmy Cooney

COONEY, JAMES JOSEPH BB TR 5′9″ 155 lbs.
Father of Johnny Cooney. Father of Jimmy Cooney.
B. July 9, 1865, Cranston, R. I. D. July 1, 1903, Cranston, R. I.

Year	Team	Lg	Games	BA	SA	AB	H	2B	3B	HR	HR%	R	RBI	BB	SO	SB	Pinch Hit AB	Pinch Hit H	PO	A	E	DP	TC/G	FA	G by Pos
1890	CHI	N	135	.272	.361	574	156	19	10	4	0.7	114	52	73	23	45	0	0	238	452	47	50	5.4	.936	SS-135, C-1
1891			118	.245	.290	465	114	15	3	0	0.0	84	42	48	17	21	0	0	145	433	52	39	5.3	.917	SS-118
1892	2 teams		CHI N (65G –.172)	WAS N (6G –.160)																					
″	total		71	.171	.183	263	45	1	1	0	0.0	23	24	27	8	11	0	0	113	224	34	16	5.2	.908	SS-71
3 yrs.			324	.242	.300	1302	315	35	14	4	0.3	221	118	148	48	77	0	0	496	1109	133	105	5.3	.923	SS-324, C-1

Johnny Cooney

COONEY, JOHN WALTER BR TL 5′10″ 165 lbs.
Son of Jimmy Cooney. Brother of Jimmy Cooney.
B. Mar. 18, 1901, Cranston, R. I. D. July 8, 1986, Sarasota, Fla.
Manager 1949.

Year	Team	Lg	Games	BA	SA	AB	H	2B	3B	HR	HR%	R	RBI	BB	SO	SB	Pinch Hit AB	Pinch Hit H	PO	A	E	DP	TC/G	FA	G by Pos
1921	BOS	N	8	.200	.200	5	1	0	0	0	0.0	0	0	0	1	0	0	0	2	5	0	0	0.9	1.000	P-8
1922			4	.000	.000	8	0	0	0	0	0.0	0	0	0	1	0	0	0	1	6	0	1	1.8	1.000	P-4
1923			42	.379	.394	66	25	1	0	0	0.0	7	3	4	2	0	1	1	34	17	0	1	1.5	1.000	P-23, OF-11, 1B-1
1924			55	.254	.285	130	33	2	1	0	0.0	10	4	9	5	0	1	1	70	33	5	3	2.2	.954	P-34, OF-14, 1B-1
1925			54	.320	.388	103	33	7	0	0	0.0	17	13	3	6	1	1	0	32	61	5	10	2.8	.949	P-31, 1B-3, OF-1
1926			64	.302	.357	126	38	3	2	0	0.0	17	18	13	7	6	5	3	251	45	3	28	5.8	.990	1B-32, P-19, OF-1
1927			10	.000	.000	1	0	0	0	0	0.0	3	0	0	0	0	1	0	0	0	0	0	0.0	—	
1928			33	.171	.171	41	7	0	0	0	0.0	2	2	4	3	0	3	0	29	32	1	5	2.1	.984	P-24, 1B-3, OF-2
1929			41	.319	.403	72	23	4	1	0	0.0	10	6	3	3	1	5	3	49	16	1	2	2.2	.985	OF-16, P-14
1930			4	.000	.000	3	0	0	0	0	0.0	0	0	0	0	0	1	0	0	4	0	0	2.0	1.000	P-2
1935	BKN	N	10	.310	.379	29	9	0	1	0	0.0	3	1	3	2	0	0	0	23	0	0	0	2.3	1.000	OF-10
1936			130	.282	.335	507	143	17	5	0	0.0	71	30	24	15	3	0	0	336	11	2	3	2.7	.994	OF-130
1937			120	.293	.358	430	126	18	5	0	0.0	61	37	22	10	5	5	1	281	9	7	2	2.6	.976	OF-111, 1B-2
1938	BOS	N	120	.271	.352	432	117	25	5	0	0.0	45	17	22	12	2	0	0	296	10	4	9	2.5	.987	OF-110, 1B-13
1939			118	.274	.318	368	101	8	1	2	0.5	39	27	21	8	2	0	0	241	10	2	2	2.1	.992	OF-116, 1B-2
1940			108	.318	.373	365	116	14	3	0	0.0	40	21	25	9	4	1	0	294	9	2	5	2.9	.993	OF-99, 1B-7
1941			123	.319	.385	442	141	25	2	0	0.0	52	29	27	15	3	6	1	315	11	1	7	2.8	.997	OF-111, 1B-4
1942			74	.207	.237	198	41	6	0	0	0.0	23	7	23	5	2	0	0	254	12	2	10	3.5	.993	OF-54, 1B-23
1943	BKN	N	37	.206	.206	34	7	0	0	0	0.0	7	2	4	3	1	22	4	20	0	0	1	4.0	1.000	1B-3, OF-2
1944	2 teams		BKN N (7G –.750)	NY A (10G –.125)																					
″	total		17	.333	.333	12	4	0	0	0	0.0	1	2	1	0	0	7	3	6	0	0	1	1.5	1.000	OF-4
20 yrs.			1172	.286	.342	3372	965	130	26	2	0.1	408	219	208	107	30	59	17	2534	291	35	90	2.7	.988	OF-792, P-159, 1B-94

Phil Cooney

COONEY, PHILIP CLARENCE BR TR 5′8″ 155 lbs.
Born Philip Clarence Cohen.
B. Sept. 14, 1882, New York, N. Y. D. Oct. 6, 1957, New York, N. Y.

Year	Team	Lg	Games	BA	SA	AB	H	2B	3B	HR	HR%	R	RBI	BB	SO	SB	Pinch Hit AB	Pinch Hit H	PO	A	E	DP	TC/G	FA	G by Pos
1905	NY	A	1	.000	.000	3	0	0	0	0	0.0	0	0	0		0	0	0	1	1	0	0	2.0	1.000	3B-1

Cecil Cooper

COOPER, CECIL CELESTER BL TL 6′2″ 165 lbs.
B. Dec. 20, 1949, Brenham, Tex.

Year	Team	Lg	Games	BA	SA	AB	H	2B	3B	HR	HR%	R	RBI	BB	SO	SB	Pinch Hit AB	Pinch Hit H	PO	A	E	DP	TC/G	FA	G by Pos
1971	BOS	A	14	.310	.452	42	13	4	1	0	0.0	9	3	5	4	1	3	2	82	3	1	6	7.8	.988	1B-11
1972			12	.235	.294	17	4	1	0	0	0.0	0	2	2	5	0	9	1	19	0	0	2	6.3	1.000	1B-3
1973			30	.238	.347	101	24	2	0	3	3.0	12	11	7	12	1	1	0	227	17	4	25	8.6	.984	1B-29
1974			121	.275	.396	414	114	24	1	8	1.9	55	43	32	74	2	7	1	637	40	12	66	6.0	.983	1B-74, DH-41
1975			106	.311	.544	305	95	17	6	14	4.6	49	44	19	33	1	18	6	197	20	1	20	2.4	.995	DH-54, 1B-35

Cecil Cooper *continued*

Year	Team	Lg	Games	BA	SA	AB	H	2B	3B	HR	HR%	R	RBI	BB	SO	SB	Pinch Hit AB	Pinch Hit H	PO	A	E	DP	TC/G	FA	G by Pos
1976			123	.282	.457	451	127	22	6	15	3.3	66	78	16	62	7	9	0	600	42	4	49	5.4	.994	1B-66, DH-53
1977	MIL	A	160	.300	.463	643	193	31	7	20	3.1	86	78	28	110	13	1	0	1386	118	12	134	9.6	.992	1B-148, DH-10
1978			107	.312	.474	407	127	23	2	13	3.2	60	54	32	72	3	4	1	842	66	11	71	8.9	.988	1B-84, DH-19
1979			150	.308	.508	590	182	**44**	1	24	4.1	83	106	56	77	15	2	1	1323	78	10	119	9.4	.993	1B-135, DH-15
1980			153	.352	.539	622	219	33	4	25	4.0	96	**122**	39	42	17	1	1	1336	106	5	160	9.5	.997	1B-142, DH-11
1981			106	.320	.495	416	133	**35**	1	12	2.9	70	60	28	30	5	2	0	987	72	9	111	10.1	.992	1B-101, DH-5
1982			155	.313	.528	654	205	38	3	32	4.9	104	121	32	53	2	0	0	1428	98	5	156	9.9	.997	1B-154, DH-1
1983			160	.307	.508	661	203	37	3	30	4.5	106	**126**	37	63	2	1	1	1452	87	11	144	9.7	.993	1B-158, DH-2
1984			148	.275	.386	603	166	28	3	11	1.8	63	67	27	59	8	0	0	1061	98	10	106	7.9	.991	1B-122, DH-26
1985			154	.293	.456	631	185	39	8	16	2.5	82	99	30	77	10	1	0	1087	94	17	101	7.8	.986	1B-123, DH-30
1986			134	.258	.373	542	140	24	1	12	2.2	46	75	41	87	1	2	1	697	61	9	78	5.7	.988	1B-90, DH-44
1987			63	.248	.372	250	62	13	0	6	2.4	25	36	17	51	1	1	0	0	0	0	0	0.0	.000	DH-62
17 yrs.			1896	.298	.466	7349	2192	415	47	241	3.3	1012	1125	448	911	89	62	15	13361	1000	121	1348	7.8	.992	1B-1475, DH-373
DIVISIONAL PLAYOFF SERIES																									
1981	MIL	A	5	.222	.222	18	4	0	0	0	0.0	1	3	1	3	0	0	0	47	4	1	0	10.4	.981	1B-5
LEAGUE CHAMPIONSHIP SERIES																									
1975	BOS	A	3	.400	.600	10	4	2	0	0	0.0	0	1	0	2	0	0	0	24	1	1	3	8.7	.962	1B-3
1982	MIL	A	5	.150	.250	20	3	2	0	0	0.0	1	4	0	6	0	0	0	37	3	2	5	8.4	.952	1B-5
2 yrs.			8	.233	.367	30	7	4	0	0	0.0	1	5	0	8	0	0	0	61	4	3	8	8.5	.956	1B-8
WORLD SERIES																									
1975	BOS	A	5	.053	.105	19	1	1	0	0	0.0	0	1	0	3	0	1	0	40	1	0	1	8.2	1.000	1B-5
1982	MIL	A	7	.286	.429	28	8	1	0	1	3.6	3	6	1	1	0	0	0	71	10	1	3	11.7	.988	1B-7
2 yrs.			12	.191	.298	47	9	2	0	1	2.1	3	7	1	4	0	1	0	111	11	1	4	10.3	.992	1B-12

Claude Cooper

COOPER, CLAUDE WILLIAM BL TL 5′ 9″ 158 lbs.
B. Apr. 1, 1892, Troup, Tex. D. Jan. 21, 1974, Plainview, Tex.

Year	Team	Lg	Games	BA	SA	AB	H	2B	3B	HR	HR%	R	RBI	BB	SO	SB	Pinch Hit AB	Pinch Hit H	PO	A	E	DP	TC/G	FA	G by Pos
1913	NY	N	27	.300	.433	30	9	4	0	0	0.0	11	4	4	6	3	2	0	16	1	2	0	1.3	.895	OF-15
1914	BKN	F	113	.241	.346	399	96	14	11	2	0.5	56	25	26		25	8	3	188	12	16	4	2.1	.926	OF-101
1915			153	.294	.400	527	155	26	12	2	0.4	75	63	77		31	0	0	536	44	19	14	3.9	.968	OF-121, 1B-32
1916	PHI	N	56	.192	.212	104	20	2	0	0	0.0	9	11	7	15	1	22	6	52	2	3	0	1.9	.947	OF-29, 1B-1
1917			24	.103	.138	29	3	1	0	0	0.0	5	1	5	4	0	8	0	12	0	1	0	1.1	.923	OF-12
5 yrs.			373	.260	.356	1089	283	47	23	4	0.4	156	104	119	25	60	40	9	804	59	41	18	2.9	.955	OF-278, 1B-33
WORLD SERIES																									
1913	NY	N	2	—	—	0	0	0	0	0	—	0	0	0	0	1	0	0	0	0	0	0	0.0	—	

Gary Cooper

COOPER, GARY CLIFTON BR TR 6′ 1″ 200 lbs.
B. Aug. 13, 1964, Lynwood, Calif.

Year	Team	Lg	Games	BA	SA	AB	H	2B	3B	HR	HR%	R	RBI	BB	SO	SB	Pinch Hit AB	Pinch Hit H	PO	A	E	DP	TC/G	FA	G by Pos
1991	HOU	N	9	.250	.313	16	4	1	0	0	0.0	1	2	3	6	0	4	0	3	2	1	0	1.5	.833	3B-4

Gary Cooper

COOPER, GARY NATHANIEL BB TR 6′ 3″ 175 lbs.
B. Dec. 22, 1956, Savannah, Ga.

Year	Team	Lg	Games	BA	SA	AB	H	2B	3B	HR	HR%	R	RBI	BB	SO	SB	Pinch Hit AB	Pinch Hit H	PO	A	E	DP	TC/G	FA	G by Pos
1980	ATL	N	21	.000	.000	2	0	0	0	0	0.0	3	0	0	1	2	1	0	5	1	0	0	0.5	1.000	OF-13

Pat Cooper

COOPER, ORGE PATTERSON BR TR 6′ 3″ 180 lbs.
B. Nov. 26, 1917, Albermarle, N. C. D. Mar. 15, 1993, Charlotte, N. C.

Year	Team	Lg	Games	BA	SA	AB	H	2B	3B	HR	HR%	R	RBI	BB	SO	SB	Pinch Hit AB	Pinch Hit H	PO	A	E	DP	TC/G	FA	G by Pos
1946	PHI	A	1	—	—	0	0	0	0	0	—	0	0	0	0	0	0	0	0	1	0	0	1.0	1.000	P-1
1947			13	.250	.375	16	4	2	0	0	0.0	0	3	0	5	0	12	3	8	0	0	1	8.0	1.000	1B-1
2 yrs.			14	.250	.375	16	4	2	0	0	0.0	0	3	0	5	0	12	3	8	1	0	1	4.5	1.000	1B-1, P-1

Scott Cooper

COOPER, SCOTT KENDRICK BL TR 6′ 3″ 200 lbs.
B. Oct. 13, 1967, St. Louis, Mo.

Year	Team	Lg	Games	BA	SA	AB	H	2B	3B	HR	HR%	R	RBI	BB	SO	SB	Pinch Hit AB	Pinch Hit H	PO	A	E	DP	TC/G	FA	G by Pos
1990	BOS	A	2	.000	.000	1	0	0	0	0	0.0	0	0	0	1	0	1	0	0	0	0	0	0.0	—	
1991			14	.457	.686	35	16	4	2	0	0.0	6	7	2	2	0	2	1	6	22	2	1	2.3	.933	3B-13
1992			123	.276	.383	337	93	21	0	5	1.5	34	33	37	33	1	15	5	472	136	9	49	5.5	.985	1B-62, 3B-47, DH-2, SS-1, 2B-1
1993			156	.279	.397	526	147	29	3	9	1.7	67	63	58	81	5	4	2	112	244	24	23	2.4	.937	3B-154, 1B-2, SS-1
1994			104	.282	.453	369	104	16	4	13	3.5	49	53	30	65	0	2	0	51	219	16	20	2.8	.944	3B-104
1995	STL	N	118	.230	.313	374	86	18	2	3	0.8	29	40	49	85	0	8	2	65	242	18	22	3.0	.945	3B-110
6 yrs.			517	.272	.393	1642	446	88	11	30	1.8	185	196	176	267	6	32	10	706	863	69	115	3.3	.958	3B-428, 1B-64, DH-2, SS-2, 2B-1

Walker Cooper

COOPER, WILLIAM WALKER BR TR 6′ 3″ 210 lbs.
Brother of Mort Cooper.
B. Jan. 8, 1915, Atherton, Mo. D. Apr. 11, 1991, Scottsdale, Ariz.

Year	Team	Lg	Games	BA	SA	AB	H	2B	3B	HR	HR%	R	RBI	BB	SO	SB	Pinch Hit AB	Pinch Hit H	PO	A	E	DP	TC/G	FA	G by Pos
1940	STL	N	6	.316	.368	19	6	1	0	0	0.0	3	2	2	2	1	0	0	19	4	0	0	3.8	1.000	C-6
1941			68	.245	.315	200	49	9	1	1	0.5	19	20	13	14	1	5	2	247	39	10	11	4.7	.966	C-63
1942			125	.281	.434	438	123	32	7	7	1.6	58	65	29	29	4	10	5	519	62	17	6	5.2	.972	C-115
1943			122	.318	.463	449	143	30	4	9	2.0	52	81	19	19	1	10	1	504	49	14	5	5.1	.975	C-112
1944			112	.317	.504	397	126	25	5	13	3.3	56	72	20	19	4	15	5	442	40	10	7	5.1	.980	C-97
1945			4	.389	.389	18	7	0	0	0	0.0	3	1	0	1	0	0	0	27	1	1	0	7.3	.966	C-4
1946	NY	N	87	.268	.396	280	75	10	1	8	2.9	29	46	17	12	0	13	3	277	38	9	3	4.4	.972	C-73
1947			140	.305	.586	515	157	24	8	35	6.8	79	122	24	43	2	6	1	560	51	13	8	4.7	.979	C-132
1948			91	.266	.472	290	77	12	0	16	5.5	40	54	28	29	1	12	2	307	21	7	3	4.2	.979	C-79
1949	2 teams		NY N (42G –.211) CIN N (82G –.280)																						
″	total		124	.258	.436	454	117	13	4	20	4.4	48	83	28	32	0	5	1	464	61	11	5	4.6	.979	C-117
1950	2 teams		CIN N (15G –.191) BOS N (102G –.329)																						
″	total		117	.313	.495	384	120	22	3	14	3.6	55	64	30	31	1	12	6	448	54	14	9	5.1	.973	C-101
1951	BOS	N	109	.313	.518	342	107	14	1	18	5.3	42	59	28	18	1	18	2	367	57	8	9	4.8	.981	C-90
1952			102	.235	.361	349	82	12	1	10	2.9	33	55	22	32	1	13	4	417	55	8	8	5.4	.983	C-89
1953	MIL	N	53	.219	.328	137	30	6	0	3	2.2	12	16	12	15	1	17	3	165	6	3	1	5.0	.983	C-35
1954	2 teams		PIT N (14G –.200) CHI N (57G –.310)																						
″	total		71	.301	.514	173	52	12	2	7	4.0	21	33	23	24	0	23	5	196	31	5	4	4.6	.978	C-50

Walker Cooper *continued*

Year	Team		Games	BA	SA	AB	H	2B	3B	HR	HR%	R	RBI	BB	SO	SB	Pinch Hit AB	Pinch Hit H	PO	A	E	DP	TC/G	FA	G by Pos
1955	CHI	N	54	.279	.559	111	31	8	1	7	6.3	11	15	6	19	0	28	6	88	11	4	1	3.3	.961	C-31
1956	STL	N	40	.265	.456	68	18	5	1	2	2.9	5	14	3	8	0	22	3	56	4	1	0	3.8	.984	C-16
1957			48	.269	.474	78	21	5	1	3	3.8	7	10	5	10	0	30	7	62	5	3	0	5.4	.957	C-13
18 yrs.			1473	.285	.464	4702	1341	240	40	173	3.7	573	812	309	357	18	239	56	5165	589	138	80	4.8	.977	C-1223
WORLD SERIES																									
1942	STL	N	5	.286	.333	21	6	1	0	0	0.0	3	4	0	1	0	0	0	24	2	1	0	5.4	.963	C-5
1943			5	.294	.294	17	5	0	0	0	0.0	1	0	0	1	0	0	0	28	3	2	0	6.6	.939	C-5
1944			6	.318	.500	22	7	2	1	0	0.0	1	2	3	2	0	0	0	54	0	0	0	9.0	1.000	C-6
3 yrs.			16	.300	.383	60	18	3	1	0	0.0	5	6	3	4	0	0	0	106	5	3	0	7.1	.974	C-16

Joey Cora

CORA, JOSE MANUEL BB TR 5′ 7″ 150 lbs.
Born Jose Manuel Cora (Amaro).
B. May 14, 1965, Caguas, Puerto Rico.

Year	Team		Games	BA	SA	AB	H	2B	3B	HR	HR%	R	RBI	BB	SO	SB	Pinch Hit AB	Pinch Hit H	PO	A	E	DP	TC/G	FA	G by Pos
1987	SD	N	77	.237	.282	241	57	7	2	0	0.0	23	13	28	26	15	8	2	123	200	10	32	4.6	.970	2B-66, SS-6
1989			12	.316	.368	19	6	1	0	0	0.0	5	1	1	0	1	0	0	11	15	2	3	2.8	.929	SS-7, 3B-2, 2B-1
1990			51	.270	.300	100	27	3	0	0	0.0	12	2	6	9	8	8	0	59	49	11	15	3.2	.908	SS-21, 2B-15, C-1
1991	CHI	A	100	.241	.276	228	55	2	3	0	0.0	37	18	20	21	11	7	1	107	192	10	36	3.6	.968	2B-80, SS-5, DH-2
1992			68	.246	.320	122	30	7	1	0	0.0	27	9	22	13	10	9	2	60	84	3	22	2.7	.980	2B-28, DH-16, SS-6, 3B-5
1993			153	.268	.349	579	155	15	13	2	0.3	95	51	67	63	20	3	0	296	413	19	85	4.7	.974	2B-151, 3B-3
1994			90	.276	.362	312	86	13	4	2	0.6	55	30	38	32	8	6	2	161	195	8	47	4.3	.978	2B-84
1995	SEA	A	120	.297	.372	427	127	19	2	3	0.7	64	39	37	31	18	9	2	206	261	23	51	4.3	.953	2B-112, SS-1
8 yrs.			671	.268	.336	2028	543	67	25	7	0.3	318	163	219	195	91	50	9	1023	1409	86	291	4.1	.966	2B-537, SS-46, DH-18, 3B-10, C-1
DIVISIONAL PLAYOFF SERIES																									
1995	SEA	A	5	.316	.526	19	6	1	0	1	5.3	7	1	3	0	1	0	0	10	12	1	2	4.6	.957	2B-5
LEAGUE CHAMPIONSHIP SERIES																									
1993	CHI	A	6	.136	.136	22	3	0	0	0	0.0	1	1	3	6	0	0	0	18	20	3	2	6.8	.927	2B-6
1995	SEA	A	6	.174	.217	23	4	1	0	0	0.0	3	0	1	0	2	0	0	15	12	1	3	4.7	.964	2B-6
2 yrs.			12	.156	.178	45	7	1	0	0	0.0	4	1	4	6	2	0	0	33	32	4	5	5.8	.942	2B-12

Gene Corbett

CORBETT, EUGENE LOUIS BL TR 6′ 1½″ 190 lbs.
B. Oct. 25, 1913, Winona, Minn.

Year	Team		Games	BA	SA	AB	H	2B	3B	HR	HR%	R	RBI	BB	SO	SB	Pinch Hit AB	Pinch Hit H	PO	A	E	DP	TC/G	FA	G by Pos
1936	PHI	N	6	.143	.143	21	3	0	0	0	0.0	1	2	2	3	0	0	0	55	2	0	7	9.5	1.000	1B-6
1937			7	.333	.500	12	4	2	0	0	0.0	4	1	0	0	0	3	1	2	3	1	0	1.5	.833	3B-3, 2B-1
1938			24	.080	.173	75	6	1	0	2	2.7	7	7	6	11	0	1	0	180	11	1	16	8.7	.995	1B-22
3 yrs.			37	.120	.204	108	13	3	0	2	1.9	12	10	8	14	0	4	1	237	16	2	23	8.0	.992	1B-28, 3B-3, 2B-1

Claude Corbitt

CORBITT, CLAUDE ELLIOTT BR TR 5′10″ 170 lbs.
B. July 21, 1915, Sunbury, N. C. D. May 1, 1978, Cincinnati, Ohio.

Year	Team		Games	BA	SA	AB	H	2B	3B	HR	HR%	R	RBI	BB	SO	SB	Pinch Hit AB	Pinch Hit H	PO	A	E	DP	TC/G	FA	G by Pos
1945	BKN	N	2	.500	.500	4	2	0	0	0	0.0	1	0	1	0	0	0	0	1	3	0	1	2.0	1.000	3B-2
1946	CIN	N	82	.248	.303	274	68	10	1	1	0.4	25	16	23	13	3	2	1	126	229	20	45	4.9	.947	SS-77
1948			87	.256	.298	258	66	11	0	0	0.0	24	18	14	16	4	9	3	138	160	7	24	3.9	.977	2B-52, 3B-16, SS-11
1949			44	.181	.191	94	17	1	0	0	0.0	10	3	9	1	1	3	0	66	55	5	17	3.5	.960	SS-18, 2B-17, 3B-1
4 yrs.			215	.243	.286	630	153	22	1	1	0.2	60	37	47	30	8	14	4	331	447	32	87	4.2	.960	SS-106, 2B-69, 3B-19

Art Corcoran

CORCORAN, ARTHUR ANDREW (Bunny) TR
B. Oct. 23, 1894, Roxbury, Mass. D. July 27, 1958, Chelsea, Mass.

Year	Team		Games	BA	SA	AB	H	2B	3B	HR	HR%	R	RBI	BB	SO	SB	Pinch Hit AB	Pinch Hit H	PO	A	E	DP	TC/G	FA	G by Pos
1915	PHI	A	1	.000	.000	4	0	0	0	0	0.0	0	0	0	2	0	0	0	2	1	0	0	3.0	1.000	3B-1

John Corcoran

CORCORAN, JOHN A. TL
B. 1873, Cincinnati, Ohio D. Nov. 1, 1901, Cincinnati, Ohio.

Year	Team		Games	BA	SA	AB	H	2B	3B	HR	HR%	R	RBI	BB	SO	SB	Pinch Hit AB	Pinch Hit H	PO	A	E	DP	TC/G	FA	G by Pos
1895	PIT	N	6	.150	.150	20	3	0	0	0	0.0	0	1	0	2	0	0	0	8	13	2	0	3.8	.913	SS-4, 3B-2

John Corcoran

CORCORAN, JOHN H.
B. 1860, Lowell, Mass. Deceased.

Year	Team		Games	BA	SA	AB	H	2B	3B	HR	HR%	R	RBI	BB	SO	SB	Pinch Hit AB	Pinch Hit H	PO	A	E	DP	TC/G	FA	G by Pos
1884	BKN	AA	52	.211	.265	185	39	4	3	0	0.0	17		8			0	0	205	77	42	5	6.0	.870	C-38, OF-9, 2B-4, SS-2, P-1

Larry Corcoran

CORCORAN, LAWRENCE J. BL TR 120 lbs.
Brother of Mike Corcoran.
B. Aug. 10, 1859, Brooklyn, N. Y. D. Oct. 14, 1891, Newark, N. J.

Year	Team		Games	BA	SA	AB	H	2B	3B	HR	HR%	R	RBI	BB	SO	SB	Pinch Hit AB	Pinch Hit H	PO	A	E	DP	TC/G	FA	G by Pos
1880	CHI	N	72	.231	.276	286	66	11	1	0	0.0	41	25	10	33		0	0	42	146	13	4	2.5	.935	P-63, SS-8, OF-8
1881			47	.222	.265	189	42	8	0	0	0.0	25	9	5	22		0	0	31	70	11	0	2.3	.902	P-45, SS-2, OF-1
1882			40	.207	.308	169	35	10	2	1	0.6	23	24	6	18		0	0	22	64	8	1	2.3	.915	P-40, 3B-1
1883			68	.209	.308	263	55	12	7	0	0.0	40		6	62		0	0	56	94	21	4	2.3	.877	P-56, OF-13, SS-3, 2B-1
1884			64	.243	.299	251	61	3	4	1	0.4	43		10	33		0	0	51	142	25	5	3.3	.885	P-60, OF-4, SS-2
1885	2 teams		CHI N (7G –.273) NY N (3G –.357)																						
″	total		10	.306	.333	36	11	1	0	0	0.0	9	4	6	2		0	0	6	24	2	2	2.9	.938	P-10, SS-1
1886	2 teams		NY N (1G –.000) WAS N (21G –.185)																						
″	total		22	.176	.224	85	15	2	1	0	0.0	9	3	7	16		0	0	21	33	22	4	3.3	.711	OF-12, SS-9, P-2
1887	IND	N	3	.200	.200	10	2	0	0	0	0.0	2	0	2	1	2	0	0	3	4	0	0	1.8	1.000	OF-2, P-2
8 yrs.			326	.223	.287	1289	287	47	15	2	0.2	192	65	52	187	2	0	0	232	577	102	20	2.6	.888	P-278, OF-40, SS-25, 2B-1, 3B-1

Mickey Corcoran

CORCORAN, MICHAEL JOSEPH BR TR 5′ 8″ 165 lbs.
B. Aug. 26, 1882, Buffalo, N. Y. D. Dec. 9, 1950, Buffalo, N. Y.

Year	Team		Games	BA	SA	AB	H	2B	3B	HR	HR%	R	RBI	BB	SO	SB	Pinch Hit AB	Pinch Hit H	PO	A	E	DP	TC/G	FA	G by Pos
1910	CIN	N	14	.217	.283	46	10	3	0	0	0.0	3	7	5	9	0	0	0	26	46	7	6	5.6	.911	2B-14

Tim Corcoran

CORCORAN, TIMOTHY MICHAEL BL TL 5′11″ 175 lbs.
B. Mar. 19, 1953, Glendale, Calif.

Year	Team		Games	BA	SA	AB	H	2B	3B	HR	HR%	R	RBI	BB	SO	SB	Pinch Hit AB	Pinch Hit H	PO	A	E	DP	TC/G	FA	G by Pos
1977	DET	A	55	.282	.398	103	29	3	0	3	2.9	13	15	6	9	0	32	**10**	38	0	0	0	1.8	1.000	OF-18, DH-3
1978			116	.265	.321	324	86	13	1	1	0.3	37	27	24	27	3	12	2	186	6	3	4	1.8	.985	OF-109, DH-1
1979			18	.227	.273	22	5	1	0	0	0.0	4	6	4	2	1	2	1	45	2	0	2	2.9	1.000	OF-9, 1B-5, DH-2
1980			84	.288	.405	153	44	7	1	3	2.0	20	18	22	10	0	16	3	274	19	5	32	4.2	.983	1B-48, OF-18, DH-5
1981	MIN	A	22	.176	.235	51	9	3	0	0	0.0	4	4	6	7	0	4	0	108	9	0	10	6.2	1.000	1B-16, DH-3

Tim Corcoran *continued*

Year	Team	Games	BA	SA	AB	H	2B	3B	HR	HR%	R	RBI	BB	SO	SB	Pinch Hit AB	Pinch Hit H	PO	A	E	DP	TC/G	FA	G by Pos
1983	PHI N	3	—	—	0	0	0	0	0	—	0	0	0	0	0	0	0	4	0	0	0	1.3	1.000	1B-3
1984		102	.341	.486	208	71	13	1	5	2.4	30	36	37	27	0	37	10	338	21	1	20	5.3	.997	1B-51, OF-17
1985		103	.214	.258	182	39	6	1	0	0.0	11	22	29	20	0	32	4	389	25	3	27	6.7	.993	1B-59, OF-3
1986	NY N	6	.000	.000	7	0	0	0	0	0.0	1	0	2	0	0	3	0	8	1	0	1	9.0	1.000	1B-1
9 yrs.		509	.270	.355	1050	283	46	4	12	1.1	120	128	130	102	4	138	30	1390	83	12	96	4.0	.992	1B-183, OF-174, DH-14

Tommy Corcoran

CORCORAN, THOMAS WILLIAM BR TR 5′ 9″ 164 lbs.
B. Jan. 4, 1869, New Haven, Conn. D. June 25, 1960, Plainfield, Conn.

Year	Team	Games	BA	SA	AB	H	2B	3B	HR	HR%	R	RBI	BB	SO	SB	Pinch Hit AB	Pinch Hit H	PO	A	E	DP	TC/G	FA	G by Pos
1890	PIT P	123	.233	.318	503	117	14	13	1	0.2	80	61	38	45	43	0	0	210	431	84	36	5.9	.884	SS-123
1891	PHI AA	133	.254	.376	511	130	11	15	7	1.4	84	71	29	56	30	0	0	300	434	72	5	6.1	.911	SS-133
1892	BKN N	151	.237	.279	613	145	11	6	1	0.2	77	74	34	51	39	0	0	291	495	64	49	5.6	.925	SS-151
1893		115	.275	.355	459	126	11	10	2	0.4	61	58	27	12	14	0	0	218	444	68	44	6.3	.907	SS-115
1894		129	.300	.432	576	173	21	20	5	0.9	123	92	25	17	33	0	0	280	439	76	45	6.2	.904	SS-129
1895		127	.265	.346	535	142	17	10	2	0.4	81	69	23	11	17	0	0	293	488	64	49	6.7	.924	SS-127
1896		132	.289	.361	532	154	15	7	3	0.6	63	73	15	13	16	0	0	323	477	64	69	6.5	.926	SS-132
1897	CIN N	109	.288	.398	445	128	30	5	3	0.7	76	57	13		15	0	0	286	360	48	51	6.3	.931	SS-63, 2B-47
1898		153	.250	.354	619	155	28	15	2	0.3	80	87	26		19	0	0	353	561	67	76	6.4	.932	SS-153
1899		137	.277	.328	537	149	11	8	0	0.0	91	81	28		32	1	1	302	468	54	55	6.0	.934	SS-123, 2B-14
1900		127	.245	.325	523	128	21	9	1	0.2	64	54	22		27	0	0	273	448	61	59	6.1	.922	SS-124, 2B-5
1901		31	.209	.296	115	24	4	3	0	0.0	14	15	11		6	1	1	69	112	16	20	6.6	.919	SS-30
1902		138	.251	.304	537	135	20	4	0	0.0	54	54	11		20	0	0	294	417	56	49	5.6	.927	SS-137, 2B-1
1903		115	.246	.329	459	113	18	7	2	0.4	61	73	12		12	0	0	263	367	38	42	5.8	.943	SS-115
1904		150	.230	.301	578	133	17	9	2	0.3	55	74	19		19	0	0	353	471	56	54	5.9	.936	SS-150
1905		151	.248	.329	605	150	21	11	2	0.3	70	85	23		28	0	0	344	531	44	67	6.1	.952	SS-151
1906		117	.207	.249	430	89	13	1	1	0.2	29	33	19		8	0	0	263	379	40	51	5.8	.941	SS-117
1907	NY N	62	.265	.323	226	60	9	2	0	0.0	21	24	7		9	0	0	108	183	19	15	5.0	.939	2B-62
18 yrs.		2200	.256	.336	8803	2251	292	155	34	0.4	1184	1135	382	205	387	2	2	4823	7505	991	836	6.0	.926	SS-2073, 2B-129

Wil Cordero

CORDERO, WILFREDO BR TR 6′ 2″ 185 lbs.
Born Wilfredo Cordero (Nieva).
B. Oct. 3, 1971, Mayaguez, Puerto Rico.

Year	Team	Games	BA	SA	AB	H	2B	3B	HR	HR%	R	RBI	BB	SO	SB	Pinch Hit AB	Pinch Hit H	PO	A	E	DP	TC/G	FA	G by Pos
1992	MON N	45	.302	.397	126	38	4	1	2	1.6	17	8	9	31	0	2	2	51	92	8	12	3.4	.947	SS-35, 2B-9
1993		138	.248	.387	475	118	32	2	10	2.1	56	58	34	60	12	4	1	163	373	36	61	4.2	.937	SS-134, 3B-2
1994		110	.294	.489	415	122	30	3	15	3.6	65	63	41	62	16	1	1	124	316	22	55	4.2	.952	SS-109
1995		131	.286	.420	514	147	35	2	10	1.9	64	49	36	88	9	0	0	167	282	22	44	3.6	.953	SS-105, OF-26
4 yrs.		424	.278	.427	1530	425	101	8	37	2.4	202	178	120	241	37	7	4	505	1063	88	172	3.9	.947	SS-383, OF-26, 2B-9, 3B-2

Marty Cordova

CORDOVA, MARTIN KEEVIN BR TR 6′ 200 lbs.
B. July 10, 1969, Las Vegas, Nev.

Year	Team	Games	BA	SA	AB	H	2B	3B	HR	HR%	R	RBI	BB	SO	SB	Pinch Hit AB	Pinch Hit H	PO	A	E	DP	TC/G	FA	G by Pos
1995	MIN A	137	.277	.486	512	142	27	4	24	4.7	81	84	52	111	20	0	0	345	12	5	1	2.6	.986	OF-137

Fred Corey

COREY, FREDERICK HARRISON BR TR
B. 1857, S. Kingston, R. I. D. Nov. 27, 1912, Providence, R. I.

Year	Team	Games	BA	SA	AB	H	2B	3B	HR	HR%	R	RBI	BB	SO	SB	Pinch Hit AB	Pinch Hit H	PO	A	E	DP	TC/G	FA	G by Pos
1878	PRO N	7	.143	.143	21	3	0	0	0	0.0	3	1	0	2		0	0	11	11	1	1	2.9	.957	P-5, 2B-2, 1B-1
1880	WOR N	41	.174	.246	138	24	8	1	0	0.0	11	6	4	27		0	0	29	24	15	2	1.2	.779	OF-29, P-25, SS-3, 3B-1, 1B-1
1881		51	.222	.300	203	45	8	4	0	0.0	22	10	5	10		0	0	55	71	15	3	2.6	.894	OF-25, P-23, SS-7
1882		64	.247	.369	255	63	7	12	0	0.0	33	29	5	31		0	0	98	117	35	6	3.4	.860	SS-26, P-21, OF-15, 3B-6, 1B-5
1883	PHI AA	71	.258	.336	298	77	16	2	1	0.3	45		12			0	0	86	150	57	7	3.8	.805	3B-34, P-18, OF-14, 2B-9, SS-1, C-1
1884		104	.276	.421	439	121	17	16	5	1.1	64		17			0	0	121	209	42	10	3.6	.887	3B-104
1885		94	.245	.331	384	94	14	8	1	0.3	61		17			0	0	105	189	43	15	3.6	.872	3B-92, SS-1, P-1
7 yrs.		432	.246	.348	1738	427	70	43	7	0.4	239	46	60	70		0	0	505	771	208	44	3.2	.860	3B-237, P-93, OF-83, SS-38, 2B-11, 1B-7, C-1

Mark Corey

COREY, MARK MUNDELL BR TR 6′ 2″ 200 lbs.
B. Nov. 3, 1955, Tucumcari, N. M.

Year	Team	Games	BA	SA	AB	H	2B	3B	HR	HR%	R	RBI	BB	SO	SB	Pinch Hit AB	Pinch Hit H	PO	A	E	DP	TC/G	FA	G by Pos
1979	BAL A	13	.154	.154	13	2	0	0	0	0.0	1	1	0	4	1	3	0	10	0	0	0	0.8	1.000	OF-11, DH-1
1980		36	.278	.417	36	10	2	0	1	2.8	7	2	5	7	0	4	1	20	0	0	0	0.6	1.000	OF-34
1981		10	.000	.000	8	0	0	0	0	0.0	2	0	2	2	0	1	0	6	1	0	0	0.8	1.000	OF-9
3 yrs.		59	.211	.298	57	12	2	0	1	1.8	10	3	7	13	1	8	1	36	1	0	0	0.7	1.000	OF-54, DH-1

Chuck Corgan

CORGAN, CHARLES HOWARD BB TR 5′11″ 180 lbs.
B. Dec. 4, 1902, Wagoner, Okla. D. June 13, 1928, Wagoner, Okla.

Year	Team	Games	BA	SA	AB	H	2B	3B	HR	HR%	R	RBI	BB	SO	SB	Pinch Hit AB	Pinch Hit H	PO	A	E	DP	TC/G	FA	G by Pos
1925	BKN N	14	.170	.234	47	8	1	1	0	0.0	4	0	3	9	0	0	0	27	52	8	5	6.2	.908	SS-14
1927		19	.263	.281	57	15	1	0	0	0.0	3	1	4	4	0	2	0	24	50	4	5	4.9	.949	2B-13, SS-3
2 yrs.		33	.221	.260	104	23	2	1	0	0.0	7	1	7	13	0	2	0	51	102	12	10	5.5	.927	SS-17, 2B-13

Roy Corhan

CORHAN, ROY GEORGE (Irish) BR TR 5′ 9½″ 165 lbs.
B. Oct. 21, 1887, Indianapolis, Ind. D. Nov. 24, 1958, San Francisco, Calif.

Year	Team	Games	BA	SA	AB	H	2B	3B	HR	HR%	R	RBI	BB	SO	SB	Pinch Hit AB	Pinch Hit H	PO	A	E	DP	TC/G	FA	G by Pos
1911	CHI A	43	.214	.290	131	28	6	2	0	0.0	14	8	15		2	0	0	98	146	20	18	6.1	.924	SS-43
1916	STL N	92	.210	.251	295	62	6	3	0	0.0	30	18	20	31	15	7	3	153	278	39	35	5.6	.917	SS-84
2 yrs.		135	.211	.263	426	90	12	5	0	0.0	44	26	35	31	17	7	3	251	424	59	53	5.8	.920	SS-127

Pop Corkhill

CORKHILL, JOHN STEWART BL TR 5′10″ 180 lbs.
B. Apr. 11, 1858, Parkesburg, Pa. D. Apr. 4, 1921, Pennsauken, N. J.

Year	Team	Games	BA	SA	AB	H	2B	3B	HR	HR%	R	RBI	BB	SO	SB	Pinch Hit AB	Pinch Hit H	PO	A	E	DP	TC/G	FA	G by Pos
1883	CIN AA	88	.216	.301	375	81	10	8	2	0.5	53		3			0	0	172	21	14	0	2.3	.932	OF-85, SS-2, 1B-2, 2B-2
1884		110	.274	.378	452	124	13	11	4	0.9	85		6			0	0	253	66	22	9	3.0	.935	OF-92, SS-11, 1B-6, 3B-3, P-1
1885		112	.252	.318	440	111	10	8	1	0.2	64		7			0	0	234	44	17	6	2.4	.942	OF-110, P-8, 1B-3
1886		129	.265	.333	540	143	9	8	4	0.7	81		23			0	0	228	62	29	8	2.4	.909	OF-112, 3B-12, 1B-7, SS-3, P-1
1887		128	.311	.414	541	168	19	11	5	0.9	79		14		30	0	0	310	31	17	7	2.7	.953	OF-128, P-5
1888	2 teams	CIN AA (118G –.271)	BKN AA (19G –.380)																					
″	total	137	.285	.365	561	160	15	12	2	0.4	85	93	19		30	0	0	316	26	13	5	2.6	.963	OF-135, P-2, 1B-1, 2B-1
9	BKN AA	138	.250	.367	537	134	21	9	8	1.5	91	78	42	24	22	0	0	318	36	19	9	2.7	.949	OF-138, SS-1, 1B-1

Pop Corkhill *continued*

Year	Team	Games	BA	SA	AB	H	2B	3B	HR	HR%	R	RBI	BB	SO	SB	Pinch Hit AB	Pinch Hit H	PO	A	E	DP	TC/G	FA	G by Pos
1890	BKN N	51	.225	.279	204	46	4	2	1	0.5	23	21	15	11	6	0	0	157	6	3	1	3.1	.982	OF-48, 1B-6
1891	3 teams	PHI AA (83G –.209) CIN N (1G –.000) PIT N (41G –.228)																						
"	total	125	.213	.279	498	106	8	8	3	0.6	66	51	33	26	19	0	0	266	23	15	6	2.4	.951	OF-125
1892	PIT N	68	.184	.219	256	47	1	4	0	0.0	23	25	12	19	6	0	0	148	13	8	4	2.5	.953	OF-68
10 yrs.		1086	.254	.337	4404	1120	110	81	30	0.7	650	268	174	80	113	0	0	2402	328	157	55	2.6	.946	OF-1041, 1B-26, SS-17, P-17, 3B-15, 2B-3

Pat Corrales

CORRALES, PATRICK (Ike) BR TR 6′ 180 lbs.
B. Mar. 20, 1941, Los Angeles, Calif.
Manager 1978–80, 1982–87.

Year	Team	Games	BA	SA	AB	H	2B	3B	HR	HR%	R	RBI	BB	SO	SB	Pinch Hit AB	Pinch Hit H	PO	A	E	DP	TC/G	FA	G by Pos
1964	PHI N	2	.000	.000	1	0	0	0	0	0.0	1	0	1	0	0	1	0	0	0	0	0	0.0	—	
1965		63	.224	.316	174	39	8	1	2	1.1	16	15	25	42	0	2	0	358	24	7	2	6.3	.982	C-62
1966	STL N	28	.181	.208	72	13	2	0	0	0.0	5	3	2	17	1	1	0	133	23	4	2	5.9	.975	C-27
1968	CIN N	20	.268	.339	56	15	4	0	0	0.0	3	6	6	16	0	0	0	101	8	1	0	5.5	.991	C-20
1969		29	.264	.375	72	19	5	0	1	1.4	10	5	8	17	0	0	0	133	7	2	3	4.9	.986	C-29
1970		43	.236	.330	106	25	5	1	1	0.9	9	10	8	22	0	3	0	167	11	3	3	4.3	.983	C-42
1971		40	.181	.202	94	17	2	0	0	0.0	6	6	6	17	0	1	0	145	4	3	3	3.9	.980	C-39
1972	2 teams	CIN N (2G –.000) SD N (44G –.193)																						
"	total	46	.192	.192	120	23	0	0	0	0.0	6	6	13	26	0	1	0	251	23	2	3	6.1	.993	C-45
1973	SD N	29	.208	.264	72	15	2	1	0	0.0	7	3	6	10	0	1	0	130	6	2	1	4.9	.986	C-28
9 yrs.		300	.216	.276	767	166	28	3	4	0.5	63	54	75	167	1	10	0	1418	106	24	17	5.3	.984	C-292
WORLD SERIES																								
1970	CIN N	1	.000	.000	1	0	0	0	0	0.0	0	0	0	0	0	1	0	0	0	0	0	0.0	—	

Rod Correia

CORREIA, RONALD DOUGLAS BR TR 5′11″ 185 lbs.
B. Sept. 13, 1967, Providence, R. I.

Year	Team	Games	BA	SA	AB	H	2B	3B	HR	HR%	R	RBI	BB	SO	SB	Pinch Hit AB	Pinch Hit H	PO	A	E	DP	TC/G	FA	G by Pos
1993	CAL A	64	.266	.305	128	34	5	0	0	0.0	12	9	6	20	2	0	0	87	121	3	22	3.7	.986	SS-40, 2B-11, 3B-3, DH-3
1994		6	.235	.294	17	4	1	0	0	0.0	4	0	0	0	0	0	0	12	9	0	3	3.5	1.000	2B-5, SS-1
1995		14	.238	.381	21	5	1	1	0	0.0	3	3	0	5	0	1	0	6	21	5	5	2.5	.844	SS-7, 2B-3, 3B-2, DH-1
3 yrs.		84	.259	.313	166	43	7	1	0	0.0	19	12	6	25	2	1	0	105	151	8	30	3.5	.970	SS-48, 2B-19, 3B-5, DH-4

Vic Correll

CORRELL, VICTOR CROSBY BR TR 5′10″ 185 lbs.
B. Feb. 5, 1946, Washington, D. C.

Year	Team	Games	BA	SA	AB	H	2B	3B	HR	HR%	R	RBI	BB	SO	SB	Pinch Hit AB	Pinch Hit H	PO	A	E	DP	TC/G	FA	G by Pos
1972	BOS A	1	.500	.500	4	2	0	0	0	0.0	1	1	0	1	0	0	0	9	1	0	0	10.0	1.000	C-1
1974	ATL N	73	.238	.381	202	48	15	1	4	2.0	20	29	21	38	0	14	2	282	40	4	4	5.5	.988	C-59
1975		103	.215	.360	325	70	12	1	11	3.4	37	39	42	66	0	6	2	413	63	13	2	5.0	.973	C-97
1976		69	.225	.350	200	45	6	2	5	2.5	26	16	21	37	0	8	3	319	36	7	1	5.6	.981	C-65
1977		54	.208	.403	144	30	7	0	7	4.9	16	16	22	33	2	4	1	247	38	8	2	6.0	.973	C-49
1978	CIN N	52	.238	.333	105	25	7	0	1	1.0	9	6	8	17	0	2	0	180	18	4	0	3.9	.980	C-52
1979		48	.233	.346	133	31	12	0	1	0.8	14	15	14	26	0	1	1	221	19	2	1	5.1	.992	C-47
1980		10	.421	.474	19	8	1	0	0	0.0	1	3	0	2	0	1	0	33	1	3	0	3.7	.919	C-10
8 yrs.		410	.229	.366	1132	259	60	4	29	2.6	124	125	128	220	2	36	9	1704	216	41	10	5.2	.979	C-380

Phillip Corridan

CORRIDAN, PHILIP
B. Ft. Wayne, Ind. Deceased.

Year	Team	Games	BA	SA	AB	H	2B	3B	HR	HR%	R	RBI	BB	SO	SB	Pinch Hit AB	Pinch Hit H	PO	A	E	DP	TC/G	FA	G by Pos
1884	CHI U	2	.143	.143	7	1	0	0	0	0.0	1		0			0	0	4	4	2	0	3.3	.800	2B-2, OF-1

John Corriden

CORRIDEN, JOHN MICHAEL, JR. BB TR 5′ 6″ 160 lbs.
Son of Red Corriden.
B. Oct. 6, 1918, Logansport, Ind.

Year	Team	Games	BA	SA	AB	H	2B	3B	HR	HR%	R	RBI	BB	SO	SB	Pinch Hit AB	Pinch Hit H	PO	A	E	DP	TC/G	FA	G by Pos
1946	BKN N	1	—	—	0	0	0	0	0	—	1	0	0	0	0	0	0	0	0	0	0	0.0	—	

Red Corriden

CORRIDEN, JOHN MICHAEL, SR. BR TR 5′ 9″ 165 lbs.
Father of John Corriden.
B. Sept. 4, 1887, Logansport, Ind. D. Sept. 28, 1959, Indianapolis, Ind.
Manager 1950.

Year	Team	Games	BA	SA	AB	H	2B	3B	HR	HR%	R	RBI	BB	SO	SB	Pinch Hit AB	Pinch Hit H	PO	A	E	DP	TC/G	FA	G by Pos
1910	STL A	26	.155	.226	84	13	3	0	1	1.2	19	4	13		5	0	0	61	81	13	3	6.0	.916	SS-14, 3B-12
1912	DET A	38	.203	.246	138	28	6	0	0	0.0	22	5	15		4	3	0	50	81	14	5	4.1	.903	3B-25, 2B-7, SS-3
1913	CHI N	45	.175	.268	97	17	3	0	2	2.1	13	9	9	14	4	4	1	51	83	14	12	3.8	.905	SS-36, 2B-2, 3B-1
1914		107	.230	.318	318	73	9	5	3	0.9	42	29	35	33	13	6	2	179	223	48	30	4.2	.893	SS-96, 3B-8, 2B-3
1915		6	.000	.000	3	0	0	0	0	0.0	1	0	2	1	0	2	0	1	1	1	0	1.5	.667	3B-1, OF-1
5 yrs.		222	.205	.281	640	131	21	5	6	0.9	97	47	74	48	26	15	3	342	469	90	50	4.3	.900	SS-149, 3B-47, 2B-12, OF-1

Shine Cortazzo

CORTAZZO, JOHN FRANCIS BR TR 5′ 3½″ 142 lbs.
B. Sept. 26, 1904, Wilmerding, Pa. D. Mar. 4, 1963, Pittsburgh, Pa.

Year	Team	Games	BA	SA	AB	H	2B	3B	HR	HR%	R	RBI	BB	SO	SB	Pinch Hit AB	Pinch Hit H	PO	A	E	DP	TC/G	FA	G by Pos
1923	CHI A	1	.000	.000	1	0	0	0	0	0.0	0	0	0	0	0	1	0	0	0	0	0	0.0	—	

Joe Coscarart

COSCARART, JOSEPH MARVIN BR TR 6′ 185 lbs.
Brother of Pete Coscarart.
B. Nov. 18, 1909, Escondido, Calif. D. Apr. 5, 1993, Sequim, Wash.

Year	Team	Games	BA	SA	AB	H	2B	3B	HR	HR%	R	RBI	BB	SO	SB	Pinch Hit AB	Pinch Hit H	PO	A	E	DP	TC/G	FA	G by Pos
1935	BOS N	86	.236	.299	284	67	11	2	1	0.4	30	29	16	28	2	2	0	115	177	14	20	3.7	.954	3B-41, SS-27, 2B-15
1936		104	.245	.302	367	90	11	2	2	0.5	28	44	19	37	0	1	1	103	181	21	18	2.9	.931	3B-97, SS-6, 2B-1
2 yrs.		190	.241	.301	651	157	22	4	3	0.5	58	73	35	65	2	3	1	218	358	35	38	3.3	.943	3B-138, SS-33, 2B-16

Pete Coscarart

COSCARART, PETER JOSEPH BR TR 5′11½″ 175 lbs.
Brother of Joe Coscarart.
B. June 16, 1913, Escondido, Calif.

Year	Team	Games	BA	SA	AB	H	2B	3B	HR	HR%	R	RBI	BB	SO	SB	Pinch Hit AB	Pinch Hit H	PO	A	E	DP	TC/G	FA	G by Pos
1938	BKN N	32	.152	.190	79	12	3	0	0	0.0	10	6	9	18	0	2	0	58	69	6	16	4.9	.955	2B-27
1939		115	.277	.368	419	116	22	2	4	1.0	59	43	46	56	10	0	0	259	348	25	69	5.6	.960	2B-107, 3B-4, SS-2
1940		143	.237	.354	506	120	24	4	9	1.8	55	58	53	59	5	2	1	326	379	31	58	5.3	.958	2B-140
1941		43	.129	.145	62	8	1	0	0	0.0	13	5	7	12	1	15	2	30	45	4	5	4.0	.949	2B-19, SS-1
1942	PIT N	133	.228	.287	487	111	12	4	3	0.6	57	29	38	56	2	1	1	245	367	32	60	4.8	.950	SS-108, 2B-25

Pete Coscarart *continued*

Year	Team	Games	BA	SA	AB	H	2B	3B	HR	HR%	R	RBI	BB	SO	SB	Pinch Hit AB	Pinch Hit H	PO	A	E	DP	TC/G	FA	G by Pos
1943		133	.242	.305	491	119	19	6	0	0.0	57	48	46	48	4	1	1	282	415	28	84	5.5	.961	2B-85, SS-47, 3B-1
1944		139	.264	.354	554	146	30	4	4	0.7	89	42	41	57	10	1	0	377	391	26	71	5.6	.967	2B-136, SS-4, OF-1
1945		123	.242	.357	392	95	17	2	8	2.0	59	38	55	55	2	1	0	257	362	14	74	5.1	.978	2B-122, SS-1
1946		3	.500	1.000	2	1	1	0	0	0.0	0	0	0	0	0	2	1	0	0	0	0	0.0	.000	SS-1
9 yrs.		864	.243	.329	2992	728	129	22	28	0.9	399	269	295	361	34	25	6	1834	2376	166	437	5.3	.962	2B-661, SS-164, 3B-5, OF-1
WORLD SERIES																								
1941	BKN N	3	.000	.000	7	0	0	0	0	0.0	1	0	1	2	0	0	0	7	8	0	1	5.0	1.000	2B-3

Ray Cosey

COSEY, DONALD RAY BL TL 5′10″ 185 lbs.
B. Feb. 15, 1956, San Rafael, Calif.

Year	Team	Games	BA	SA	AB	H	2B	3B	HR	HR%	R	RBI	BB	SO	SB	Pinch Hit AB	Pinch Hit H	PO	A	E	DP	TC/G	FA	G by Pos
1980	OAK A	9	.111	.111	9	1	0	0	0	0.0	0	0	0	0	0	9	1	0	0	0	0	0.0	—	

Dan Costello

COSTELLO, DANIEL FRANCIS (Dashing Dan) BL TR 6′½″ 185 lbs.
B. Sept. 9, 1891, Jessup, Pa. D. Mar. 26, 1936, Pittsburgh, Pa.

Year	Team	Games	BA	SA	AB	H	2B	3B	HR	HR%	R	RBI	BB	SO	SB	Pinch Hit AB	Pinch Hit H	PO	A	E	DP	TC/G	FA	G by Pos
1913	NY A	2	.500	.500	2	1	0	0	0	0.0	1	0	0	0	0	2	1	0	0	0	0	0.0	—	
1914	PIT N	21	.297	.313	64	19	1	0	0	0.0	7	5	8	16	2	1	0	29	3	1	1	1.6	.970	OF-20
1915		71	.216	.264	125	27	4	1	0	0.0	16	11	7	23	7	**46**	**14**	27	1	3	0	1.8	.903	OF-17
1916		60	.239	.283	159	38	1	3	0	0.0	11	8	6	23	3	18	5	82	0	2	0	2.0	.976	OF-41
4 yrs.		154	.243	.283	350	85	6	4	0	0.0	35	24	21	62	12	67	20	138	4	6	1	1.9	.959	OF-78

J.A. Costello

Playing record listed under Ken Nash.

Tim Costo

COSTO, TIMOTHY ROGER BR TR 6′ 5″ 220 lbs.
B. Feb. 16, 1969, Melrose Park, Ill.

Year	Team	Games	BA	SA	AB	H	2B	3B	HR	HR%	R	RBI	BB	SO	SB	Pinch Hit AB	Pinch Hit H	PO	A	E	DP	TC/G	FA	G by Pos
1992	CIN N	12	.222	.278	36	8	2	0	0	0.0	3	2	5	6	0	0	0	84	8	0	15	7.7	1.000	1B-12
1993		31	.224	.367	98	22	5	0	3	3.1	13	12	4	17	0	3	1	51	3	1	0	1.8	.982	OF-26, 3B-2, 1B-2
2 yrs.		43	.224	.343	134	30	7	0	3	2.2	16	14	9	23	0	3	1	135	11	1	15	3.5	.993	OF-26, 1B-14, 3B-2

Henry Cote

COTE, HENRY JOSEPH TR 5′ 9½″ 165 lbs.
B. Dec. 19, 1864, Troy, N. Y. D. Apr. 28, 1940, Troy, N. Y.

Year	Team	Games	BA	SA	AB	H	2B	3B	HR	HR%	R	RBI	BB	SO	SB	Pinch Hit AB	Pinch Hit H	PO	A	E	DP	TC/G	FA	G by Pos
1894	LOU N	10	.290	.484	31	9	2	2	0	0.0	7	3	5	6	2	0	0	40	16	5	3	6.1	.918	C-10
1895		10	.303	.303	33	10	0	0	0	0.0	10	5	3	3	2	0	0	29	5	5	0	3.9	.872	C-10
2 yrs.		20	.297	.391	64	19	2	2	0	0.0	17	8	8	9	4	0	0	69	21	10	3	5.0	.900	C-20

Pete Cote

COTE, WARREN PETER BR TR 5′ 6″ 148 lbs.
B. Aug. 30, 1902, Middleton, Mass. D. Oct. 17, 1987, Middleton, Mass.

Year	Team	Games	BA	SA	AB	H	2B	3B	HR	HR%	R	RBI	BB	SO	SB	Pinch Hit AB	Pinch Hit H	PO	A	E	DP	TC/G	FA	G by Pos
1926	NY N	2	.000	.000	1	0	0	0	0	0.0	0	0	0	0	0	1	0	0	0	0	0	0.0	—	

Dick Cotter

COTTER, RICHARD RAPHAEL BR TR 5′11″ 172 lbs.
B. Oct. 12, 1889, Manchester, N. H. D. Apr. 4, 1945, Brooklyn, N. Y.

Year	Team	Games	BA	SA	AB	H	2B	3B	HR	HR%	R	RBI	BB	SO	SB	Pinch Hit AB	Pinch Hit H	PO	A	E	DP	TC/G	FA	G by Pos
1911	PHI N	20	.283	.283	46	13	0	0	0	0.0	2	5	5	7	1	2	0	56	23	2	2	4.8	.975	C-17
1912	CHI N	26	.278	.352	54	15	0	2	0	0.0	6	10	6	13	1	1	0	64	19	4	0	3.6	.954	C-24
2 yrs.		46	.280	.320	100	28	0	2	0	0.0	8	15	11	20	2	3	0	120	42	6	2	4.1	.964	C-41

Ed Cotter

COTTER, EDWARD CHRISTOPHER BR TR 6′ 185 lbs.
B. July 4, 1904, Hartford, Conn. D. June 14, 1959, Hartford, Conn.

Year	Team	Games	BA	SA	AB	H	2B	3B	HR	HR%	R	RBI	BB	SO	SB	Pinch Hit AB	Pinch Hit H	PO	A	E	DP	TC/G	FA	G by Pos
1926	PHI N	17	.308	.385	26	8	0	1	0	0.0	3	1	1	4	1	4	1	7	18	6	0	2.4	.806	3B-8, SS-5

Harvey Cotter

COTTER, HARVEY LOUIS (Hooks) BL TL 5′10″ 160 lbs.
B. May 22, 1900, Holden, Mo. D. Aug. 6, 1955, Los Angeles, Calif.

Year	Team	Games	BA	SA	AB	H	2B	3B	HR	HR%	R	RBI	BB	SO	SB	Pinch Hit AB	Pinch Hit H	PO	A	E	DP	TC/G	FA	G by Pos
1922	CHI N	1	1.000	2.000	1	1	1	0	0	0.0	0	0	0	0	0	1	1	0	0	0	0	0.0	—	
1924		98	.261	.377	310	81	16	4	4	1.3	39	33	36	31	3	7	2	873	59	10	72	10.5	.989	1B-90
2 yrs.		99	.264	.383	311	82	17	4	4	1.3	39	33	36	31	3	8	3	873	59	10	72	10.5	.989	1B-90

Tom Cotter

COTTER, THOMAS B. BR TR 5′10½″ 149 lbs.
B. Sept. 30, 1866, Waltham, Mass. D. Nov. 22, 1906, Brookline, Mass.

Year	Team	Games	BA	SA	AB	H	2B	3B	HR	HR%	R	RBI	BB	SO	SB	Pinch Hit AB	Pinch Hit H	PO	A	E	DP	TC/G	FA	G by Pos
1891	BOS AA	6	.250	.250	12	3	0	0	0	0.0	1	4	1	2	0	1	0	11	4	1	0	2.7	.938	C-5, OF-1

Chuck Cottier

COTTIER, CHARLES KEITH BR TR 5′10½″ 175 lbs.
B. Jan. 8, 1936, Delta, Colo.
Manager 1984–86.

Year	Team	Games	BA	SA	AB	H	2B	3B	HR	HR%	R	RBI	BB	SO	SB	Pinch Hit AB	Pinch Hit H	PO	A	E	DP	TC/G	FA	G by Pos
1959	MIL N	10	.125	.167	24	3	1	0	0	0.0	1	1	3	7	0	0	0	18	22	1	2	4.1	.976	2B-10
1960		95	.227	.301	229	52	8	0	3	1.3	29	19	14	21	1	1	1	180	214	13	40	4.4	.968	2B-92
1961	2 teams	DET A (10G –.286) WAS A (101G –.234)																						
″	total	111	.235	.317	344	81	14	4	2	0.6	39	35	31	52	9	1	0	242	323	11	76	5.2	.981	2B-102, SS-8
1962	WAS A	136	.242	.341	443	107	14	6	6	1.4	50	40	44	57	14	0	0	368	354	14	100	5.5	.981	2B-134
1963		113	.205	.320	337	69	16	4	5	1.5	30	21	24	63	2	2	0	233	286	25	65	4.9	.954	2B-85, SS-24, 3B-1
1964		73	.168	.307	137	23	6	2	3	2.2	16	10	19	33	2	5	1	110	115	5	31	4.0	.978	2B-53, 3B-3, SS-2
1965		7	.000	.000	1	0	0	0	0	0.0	1	0	0	0	0	1	0	0	0	0	0	0.0	—	
1968	CAL A	33	.194	.284	67	13	4	1	0	0.0	2	1	2	15	0	2	0	15	45	2	2	2.0	.968	3B-27, 2B-4
1969		2	.000	.000	2	0	0	0	0	0.0	0	0	0	0	0	0	0	1	1	0	0	1.0	1.000	2B-2
9 yrs.		580	.220	.317	1584	348	63	17	19	1.2	168	127	137	248	28	12	2	1167	1360	71	316	4.7	.973	2B-482, SS-34, 3B-31

Henry Cotto

COTTO, HENRY BR TR 6′ 2″ 180 lbs.
B. Jan. 5, 1961, Bronx, N. Y.

Year	Team	Games	BA	SA	AB	H	2B	3B	HR	HR%	R	RBI	BB	SO	SB	Pinch Hit AB	Pinch Hit H	PO	A	E	DP	TC/G	FA	G by Pos
1984	CHI N	105	.274	.308	146	40	5	0	0	0.0	24	8	10	23	9	13	3	117	3	2	1	1.4	.984	OF-88
1985	NY A	34	.304	.375	56	17	1	0	1	1.8	4	6	3	12	1	4	1	41	2	1	0	1.5	.977	OF-30
1986		35	.212	.287	80	17	3	0	1	1.3	11	6	2	17	3	2	0	59	1	0	0	2.0	1.000	OF-29, DH-1
1987		68	.235	.403	149	35	10	0	5	3.4	21	20	6	35	4	11	0	89	2	1	0	1.6	.989	OF-57
1988	SEA A	133	.259	.373	386	100	18	1	8	2.1	50	33	23	53	27	7	1	253	6	2	0	2.1	.992	OF-120, DH-2

Henry Cotto *continued*

Year	Team	Games	BA	SA	AB	H	2B	3B	HR	HR%	R	RBI	BB	SO	SB	Pinch Hit AB	Pinch Hit H	PO	A	E	DP	TC/G	FA	G by Pos
1989		100	.264	.407	295	78	11	2	9	3.1	44	33	12	44	10	19	7	153	9	2	3	1.8	.988	OF-90, DH-2
1990		127	.259	.349	355	92	14	3	4	1.1	40	33	22	52	21	29	8	194	4	2	1	1.7	.990	OF-118, DH-3
1991		66	.305	.463	177	54	6	2	6	3.4	35	23	10	27	16	15	10	104	2	2	1	1.7	.981	OF-56, DH-6
1992		108	.259	.354	294	76	11	1	5	1.7	42	27	14	49	23	18	9	170	2	0	0	1.8	1.000	OF-92, DH-3
1993	**2 teams**	**SEA A** (54G –.190)	**FLA N** (54G –.296)																					
"	**total**	108	.250	.346	240	60	8	0	5	2.1	25	21	5	40	16	22	4	144	1	3	0	1.6	.980	OF-80, DH-14
10 yrs.		884	.261	.370	2178	569	87	9	44	2.0	296	210	107	352	130	140	43	1324	32	15	6	1.7	.989	OF-760, DH-31
LEAGUE CHAMPIONSHIP SERIES																								
1984	**CHI N**	3	1.000	1.000	1	1	0	0	0	0.0	1	0	0	0	0	0	0	2	0	0	0	0.7	1.000	OF-3

Bill Coughlin

COUGHLIN, WILLIAM PAUL (Charles Equine) BR TR 5′ 9″ 140 lbs.
B. July 12, 1878, Scranton, Pa. D. May 7, 1943, Scranton, Pa.

Year	Team	Games	BA	SA	AB	H	2B	3B	HR	HR%	R	RBI	BB	SO	SB	Pinch Hit AB	Pinch Hit H	PO	A	E	DP	TC/G	FA	G by Pos
1899	**WAS N**	6	.125	.208	24	3	0	1	0	0.0	2	3	1		1	0	0	7	11	4	0	3.7	.818	3B-6
1901	**WAS A**	137	.278	.398	508	141	17	13	6	1.2	77	68	25		16	0	0	232	275	43	16	4.0	.922	3B-137
1902		123	.301	.414	469	141	27	4	6	1.3	84	71	26		29	0	0	246	344	43	21	5.1	.932	3B-66, SS-31, 2B-26
1903		125	.251	.309	470	118	18	3	1	0.2	56	31	9		30	0	0	187	238	22	14	3.6	.951	3B-119, SS-4, 2B-2
1904	**2 teams**	**WAS A** (65G –.275)	**DET A** (56G –.228)																					
"	**total**	121	.255	.316	471	120	21	4	0	0.0	50	34	14		11	1	1	148	225	26	9	3.3	.935	3B-120
1905	**DET A**	138	.252	.317	489	123	20	6	0	0.0	48	44	34		16	1	0	137	255	37	12	3.1	.914	3B-137
1906		147	.235	.297	498	117	15	5	2	0.4	54	60	36		31	0	0	188	265	29	16	3.3	.940	3B-147
1907		134	.243	.270	519	126	10	2	0	0.0	80	46	35		15	0	0	163	236	30	9	3.2	.930	3B-133
1908		119	.215	.232	405	87	5	1	0	0.0	32	23	23		10	0	0	129	214	21	12	3.1	.942	3B-119
9 yrs.		1050	.253	.320	3853	976	133	39	15	0.4	483	380	203		159	2	1	1437	2063	255	109	3.6	.932	3B-984, SS-35, 2B-28
WORLD SERIES																								
1907	**DET A**	5	.250	.250	20	5	0	0	0	0.0	0	0	1	4	1	0	0	9	5	2	0	3.2	.875	3B-5
1908		3	.125	.125	8	1	0	0	0	0.0	0	1	0	1	0	0	0	3	6	1	1	3.3	.900	3B-3
2 yrs.		8	.214	.214	28	6	0	0	0	0.0	0	1	1	5	1	0	0	12	11	3	1	3.3	.885	3B-8

Ed Coughlin

COUGHLIN, EDWARD E.
B. Aug. 5, 1861, Hartford, Conn. D. Dec. 25, 1952, Hartford, Conn.

Year	Team	Games	BA	SA	AB	H	2B	3B	HR	HR%	R	RBI	BB	SO	SB	Pinch Hit AB	Pinch Hit H	PO	A	E	DP	TC/G	FA	G by Pos
1884	**BUF N**	1	.250	.250	4	1	0	0	0	0.0	0		0	2		0	0	3	0	1	0	2.0	.750	OF-1, P-1

Marlan Coughtry

COUGHTRY, JAMES MARION BL TR 6′ 1″ 170 lbs.
B. Sept. 11, 1934, Hollywood, Calif.

Year	Team	Games	BA	SA	AB	H	2B	3B	HR	HR%	R	RBI	BB	SO	SB	Pinch Hit AB	Pinch Hit H	PO	A	E	DP	TC/G	FA	G by Pos
1960	**BOS A**	15	.158	.158	19	3	0	0	0	0.0	3	0	5	8	0	2	0	17	18	6	1	2.9	.854	2B-13, 3B-1
1962	**3 teams**	**LA A** (11G –.182)	**KC A** (6G –.182)	**CLE A** (3G –.500)																				
"	**total**	20	.200	.200	35	7	0	0	0	0.0	2	4	5	10	0	8	1	11	26	4	5	4.6	.902	3B-7, 2B-2
2 yrs.		35	.185	.185	54	10	0	0	0	0.0	5	4	10	18	0	10	1	28	44	10	6	3.6	.878	2B-15, 3B-8

Bob Coulson

COULSON, ROBERT JACKSON BR TR 5′10½″ 175 lbs.
B. June 17, 1887, Courtney, Pa. D. Sept. 11, 1953, Washington, Pa.

Year	Team	Games	BA	SA	AB	H	2B	3B	HR	HR%	R	RBI	BB	SO	SB	Pinch Hit AB	Pinch Hit H	PO	A	E	DP	TC/G	FA	G by Pos
1908	**CIN N**	8	.333	.500	18	6	1	1	0	0.0	3	1	3		0	1	0	15	1	0	0	2.7	1.000	OF-6
1910	**BKN N**	25	.247	.404	89	22	3	4	1	1.1	14	13	6	14	9	0	0	43	4	4	2	2.0	.922	OF-25
1911		146	.234	.305	521	122	23	7	0	0.0	52	50	42	**78**	32	1	1	253	21	9	5	2.0	.968	OF-145
1914	**PIT F**	18	.203	.219	64	13	1	0	0	0.0	7	3	7		2	0	0	26	1	2	1	1.6	.931	OF-18
4 yrs.		197	.236	.315	692	163	28	12	1	0.1	76	67	58	92	43	2	1	337	27	15	8	2.0	.960	OF-194

Tom Coulter

COULTER, THOMAS LEE (Chip) BB TR 5′10″ 172 lbs.
B. June 5, 1945, Steubenville, Ohio.

Year	Team	Games	BA	SA	AB	H	2B	3B	HR	HR%	R	RBI	BB	SO	SB	Pinch Hit AB	Pinch Hit H	PO	A	E	DP	TC/G	FA	G by Pos
1969	**STL N**	6	.316	.474	19	6	1	1	0	0.0	3	4	2	6	0	0	0	8	16	1	5	4.2	.960	2B-6

Craig Counsell

COUNSELL, CRAIG JOHN BL TR 6′ 177 lbs.
B. Aug. 21, 1970, South Bend, Ind.

Year	Team	Games	BA	SA	AB	H	2B	3B	HR	HR%	R	RBI	BB	SO	SB	Pinch Hit AB	Pinch Hit H	PO	A	E	DP	TC/G	FA	G by Pos
1995	**CLR N**	3	.000	.000	1	0	0	0	0	0.0	0	0	1	0	0	0	0	1	1	0	1	0.7	1.000	SS-3

Clint Courtney

COURTNEY, CLINTON DAWSON (Scrap Iron) BL TR 5′ 8″ 180 lbs.
B. Mar. 16, 1927, Hall Summit, La. D. June 16, 1975, Rochester, N. Y.

Year	Team	Games	BA	SA	AB	H	2B	3B	HR	HR%	R	RBI	BB	SO	SB	Pinch Hit AB	Pinch Hit H	PO	A	E	DP	TC/G	FA	G by Pos
1951	**NY A**	1	.000	.000	2	0	0	0	0	0.0	0	0	1	1	0	0	0	3	1	1	0	5.0	.800	C-1
1952	**STL A**	119	.286	.395	413	118	24	3	5	1.2	38	50	39	26	0	6	0	487	60	2	7	4.9	.996	C-113
1953		106	.251	.330	355	89	12	2	4	1.1	28	19	25	20	0	7	2	436	47	10	7	4.8	.980	C-103
1954	**BAL A**	122	.270	.360	397	107	18	3	4	1.0	25	37	30	7	2	14	5	539	53	6	8	5.4	.990	C-111
1955	**2 teams**	**CHI A** (19G –.378)	**WAS A** (75G –.298)																					
"	**total**	94	.309	.415	275	85	12	4	3	1.1	33	40	26	9	0	11	6	301	31	5	6	4.0	.985	C-84
1956	**WAS A**	101	.300	.445	283	85	20	3	5	1.8	31	44	20	10	0	31	8	290	35	7	7	4.4	.979	C-76
1957		91	.267	.414	232	62	14	1	6	2.6	23	27	16	11	0	27	11	288	35	2	6	5.5	.994	C-59
1958		134	.251	.344	450	113	18	0	8	1.8	46	62	48	23	1	7	2	682	64	7	17	5.9	.991	C-128
1959		72	.233	.296	189	44	4	1	2	1.1	19	18	20	19	0	19	3	213	11	3	2	4.3	.987	C-53
1960	**BAL A**	83	.227	.266	154	35	3	0	1	0.6	14	12	30	14	0	18	7	246	23	7	2	4.8	.975	C-58
1961	**2 teams**	**KC A** (1G –.000)	**BAL A** (22G –.267)																					
"	**total**	23	.261	.304	46	12	2	0	0	0.0	3	4	10	3	0	7	2	71	8	0	1	4.9	1.000	C-16
11 yrs.		946	.268	.367	2796	750	127	17	38	1.4	260	313	265	143	3	147	46	3556	368	50	63	5.0	.987	C-802

Ernie Courtney

COURTNEY, EDWARD ERNEST BL TR 5′10″
B. Jan. 20, 1875, Des Moines, Iowa D. Feb. 29, 1920, Buffalo, N. Y.

Year	Team	Games	BA	SA	AB	H	2B	3B	HR	HR%	R	RBI	BB	SO	SB	Pinch Hit AB	Pinch Hit H	PO	A	E	DP	TC/G	FA	G by Pos
1902	**2 teams**	**BOS N** (48G –.218)	**BAL A** (1G –.500)																					
"	**total**	49	.225	.254	169	38	3	1	0	0.0	26	18	14		3	6	2	81	13	3	1	2.3	.969	OF-39, SS-3, 3B-1
1903	**2 teams**	**NY A** (25G –.266)	**DET A** (23G –.230)																					
"	**total**	48	.248	.327	153	38	3	3	1	0.7	14	14	12		2	2	0	67	114	14	9	4.2	.928	SS-28, 3B-13, 2B-4, 1B-1
1905	**PHI N**	155	.275	.331	601	165	14	7	2	0.3	77	77	47		17	0	0	229	249	40	13	3.3	.923	3B-155

Ernie Courtney *continued*

Year	Team	Games	BA	SA	AB	H	2B	3B	HR	HR%	R	RBI	BB	SO	SB	Pinch Hit AB	Pinch Hit H	PO	A	E	DP	TC/G	FA	G by Pos
1906		116	.236	.276	398	94	12	2	0	0.0	53	42	45		6	4	0	240	172	26	14	3.9	.941	3B-96, 1B-13, OF-3, SS-1
1907		130	.243	.314	440	107	17	4	2	0.5	42	43	55		6	0	0	529	181	35	34	5.7	.953	3B-75, 1B-48, OF-4, 2B-2, SS-2
1908		60	.181	.200	160	29	3	0	0	0.0	14	6	15		1	**17**	3	157	61	6	7	5.3	.973	3B-22, 1B-13, 2B-5, SS-2
6 yrs.		558	.245	.298	1921	471	52	17	5	0.3	226	200	188		35	29	5	1303	790	124	78	4.2	.944	3B-362, 1B-75, OF-46, SS-36, 2B-11

Dee Cousineau

COUSINEAU, EDWARD THOMAS BR TR 6′ 170 lbs.
B. Dec. 16, 1898, Watertown, Mass. D. July 14, 1951, Watertown, Mass.

Year	Team	Games	BA	SA	AB	H	2B	3B	HR	HR%	R	RBI	BB	SO	SB	Pinch Hit AB	Pinch Hit H	PO	A	E	DP	TC/G	FA	G by Pos
1923	BOS N	1	1.000	1.000	2	2	0	0	0	0.0	1	2	0	0	0	0	0	0	0	0	0	0.0	.000	C-1
1924		3	.000	.000	2	0	0	0	0	0.0	0	0	0	0	0	0	0	1	0	1	0	0.7	.500	C-3
1925		1	—	—	0	0	0	0	0	—	0	0	0	0	0	0	0	0	0	0	0	0.0	.000	C-1
3 yrs.		5	.500	.500	4	2	0	0	0	0.0	1	2	0	0	0	0	0	1	0	1	0	0.4	.500	C-5

John Coveney

COVENEY, JOHN PATRICK BR TR 5′ 9″ 175 lbs.
B. June 10, 1880, S. Natick, Mass. D. Mar. 28, 1961, Wayland, Mass.

Year	Team	Games	BA	SA	AB	H	2B	3B	HR	HR%	R	RBI	BB	SO	SB	Pinch Hit AB	Pinch Hit H	PO	A	E	DP	TC/G	FA	G by Pos
1903	STL N	4	.143	.143	14	2	0	0	0	0.0	0	0	0		0	0	0	13	11	2	0	6.5	.923	C-4

Sam Covington

COVINGTON, CLARENCE OTTO BL TR 6′ 1″ 190 lbs.
Brother of Tex Covington.
B. Dec. 17, 1892, Henryville, Tenn. D. Jan. 4, 1963, Denison, Tex.

Year	Team	Games	BA	SA	AB	H	2B	3B	HR	HR%	R	RBI	BB	SO	SB	Pinch Hit AB	Pinch Hit H	PO	A	E	DP	TC/G	FA	G by Pos
1913	STL A	20	.150	.183	60	9	0	1	0	0.0	3	4	4	6	3	4	0	148	17	1	7	10.4	.994	1B-16
1917	BOS N	17	.197	.273	66	13	2	0	1	1.5	8	10	5	5	1	0	0	168	9	1	17	10.5	.994	1B-17
1918		3	.333	.333	3	1	0	0	0	0.0	0	0	0	0	0	3	1	0	0	0	0	0.0	—	
3 yrs.		40	.178	.233	129	23	2	1	1	0.8	11	14	9	11	4	7	1	316	26	2	24	10.4	.994	1B-33

Wes Covington

COVINGTON, JOHN WESLEY BL TR 6′ 1″ 205 lbs.
B. Mar. 27, 1932, Laurinburg, N. C.

Year	Team	Games	BA	SA	AB	H	2B	3B	HR	HR%	R	RBI	BB	SO	SB	Pinch Hit AB	Pinch Hit H	PO	A	E	DP	TC/G	FA	G by Pos
1956	MIL N	75	.283	.355	138	39	4	0	2	1.4	17	16	16	20	1	31	10	44	2	1	1	1.3	.979	OF-35
1957		96	.284	.537	328	93	4	8	21	6.4	51	65	29	44	4	8	1	150	9	3	1	1.8	.981	OF-89
1958		90	.330	.622	294	97	12	1	24	8.2	43	74	20	35	0	7	0	118	3	6	2	1.5	.953	OF-82
1959		103	.279	.397	373	104	17	3	7	1.9	38	45	26	41	0	9	2	148	6	6	2	1.7	.963	OF-94
1960		95	.249	.420	281	70	16	1	10	3.6	25	35	15	37	1	22	5	106	2	4	1	1.6	.964	OF-72
1961	4 teams	MIL N (9G –.190) CHI A (22G –.288) KC A (17G –.159) PHI N (57G –.303)																						
″	total	105	.270	.433	289	78	11	0	12	4.2	34	47	25	33	0	28	6	86	6	5	1	1.3	.948	OF-76
1962	PHI N	116	.283	.418	304	86	12	1	9	3.0	36	44	19	44	0	30	9	98	3	6	2	1.2	.944	OF-88
1963		119	.303	.521	353	107	24	1	17	4.8	46	64	26	56	1	25	8	114	4	8	0	1.2	.937	OF-101
1964		129	.280	.448	339	95	18	0	13	3.8	37	58	38	50	0	31	5	99	4	3	0	1.0	.972	OF-108
1965		101	.247	.489	235	58	10	1	15	6.4	27	45	26	47	0	35	7	88	2	3	0	1.5	.968	OF-64
1966	2 teams	CHI N (9G –.091) LA N (37G –.121)																						
″	total	46	.114	.227	44	5	0	1	1	2.3	1	6	7	7	0	34	4	3	0	0	0	1.0	1.000	OF-3
11 yrs.		1075	.279	.466	2978	832	128	17	131	4.4	355	499	247	414	7	260	57	1054	41	45	10	1.4	.961	OF-812
WORLD SERIES																								
1957	MIL N	7	.208	.250	24	5	1	0	0	0.0	1	1	2	6	1	0	0	13	1	0	1	2.0	1.000	OF-7
1958		7	.269	.269	26	7	0	0	0	0.0	2	4	2	4	0	0	0	11	1	0	0	1.7	1.000	OF-7
1966	LA N	1	.000	.000	1	0	0	0	0	0.0	0	0	0	1	0	1	0	0	0	0	0	0.0	—	
3 yrs.		15	.235	.255	51	12	1	0	0	0.0	3	5	4	11	1	1	0	24	2	0	1	1.9	1.000	OF-14

Billy Cowan

COWAN, BILLY ROLAND BR TR 6′ 170 lbs.
B. Aug. 28, 1938, Calhoun City, Miss.

Year	Team	Games	BA	SA	AB	H	2B	3B	HR	HR%	R	RBI	BB	SO	SB	Pinch Hit AB	Pinch Hit H	PO	A	E	DP	TC/G	FA	G by Pos
1963	CHI N	14	.250	.417	36	9	1	1	1	2.8	1	2	0	11	0	4	1	10	1	1	0	1.2	.917	OF-10
1964		139	.241	.404	497	120	16	4	19	3.8	52	50	18	128	12	4	2	297	2	10	0	2.3	.968	OF-134
1965	2 teams	NY N (82G –.179) MIL N (19G –.185)																						
″	total	101	.180	.301	183	33	9	2	3	1.6	20	9	4	54	3	20	2	91	3	0	2	1.3	1.000	OF-71, 2B-2, SS-1
1967	PHI N	34	.153	.305	59	9	0	0	3	5.1	11	6	4	14	1	5	0	19	0	0	0	0.9	1.000	OF-20, 3B-1, 2B-1
1969	2 teams	NY A (32G –.167) CAL A (28G –.304)																						
″	total	60	.240	.394	104	25	1	0	5	4.8	15	13	6	18	0	33	9	63	5	0	3	2.1	1.000	OF-27, 1B-6
1970	CAL A	68	.276	.470	134	37	9	1	5	3.7	20	25	11	29	0	39	11	96	6	2	7	2.4	.981	OF-27, 1B-14, 3B-2
1971		74	.276	.391	174	48	8	0	4	2.3	12	20	7	41	1	34	8	101	2	1	8	2.3	.990	OF-40, 1B-5
1972		3	.000	.000	3	0	0	0	0	0.0	0	0	0	2	0	3	0	0	0	0	0	0.0	—	
8 yrs.		493	.236	.387	1190	281	44	8	40	3.4	131	125	50	297	17	142	33	677	19	14	20	2.0	.980	OF-329, 1B-25, 3B-3, 2B-3, SS-1

Al Cowens

COWENS, ALFRED EDWARD BR TR 6′ 1″ 197 lbs.
B. Oct. 25, 1951, Los Angeles, Calif.

Year	Team	Games	BA	SA	AB	H	2B	3B	HR	HR%	R	RBI	BB	SO	SB	Pinch Hit AB	Pinch Hit H	PO	A	E	DP	TC/G	FA	G by Pos
1974	KC A	110	.242	.286	269	65	7	1	1	0.4	28	25	23	38	5	8	4	151	14	3	2	1.6	.982	OF-102, DH-4, 3B-2
1975		120	.277	.402	328	91	13	8	4	1.2	44	42	28	36	12	7	2	214	4	5	2	1.9	.978	OF-113, DH-2
1976		152	.265	.341	581	154	23	6	3	0.5	71	59	26	50	23	5	2	329	13	5	3	2.3	.986	OF-148, DH-1
1977		162	.312	.525	606	189	32	14	23	3.8	98	112	41	64	16	6	2	307	14	6	1	2.0	.982	OF-159, DH-1
1978		132	.274	.388	485	133	24	8	5	1.0	63	63	31	54	14	2	0	280	20	4	6	2.3	.987	OF-127, 3B-5, DH-2
1979		136	.295	.409	516	152	18	7	9	1.7	69	73	40	44	10	3	2	288	3	4	0	2.2	.986	OF-134, DH-1
1980	2 teams	CAL A (34G –.227) DET A (108G –.280)																						
″	total	142	.268	.352	522	140	20	3	6	1.1	69	59	49	61	6	5	1	263	11	3	2	2.0	.989	OF-137, DH-2
1981	DET A	85	.261	.348	253	66	11	4	1	0.4	27	18	22	36	3	12	3	166	3	1	0	2.0	.994	OF-83
1982	SEA A	146	.270	.475	560	151	39	8	20	3.6	72	78	46	81	11	0	0	280	14	4	1	2.0	.987	OF-145, DH-1
1983		110	.205	.329	356	73	19	2	7	2.0	39	35	23	38	10	6	1	124	7	2	1	1.3	.985	OF-70, DH-34
1984		139	.277	.435	524	145	34	2	15	2.9	60	78	27	83	9	8	1	228	8	3	0	1.7	.987	OF-130, DH-7
1985		122	.265	.451	452	120	32	5	14	3.1	59	69	30	56	0	8	2	198	10	7	2	1.9	.967	OF-110, DH-5
1986		28	.183	.232	82	15	4	0	0	0.0	5	6	3	18	1	7	1	31	2	1	0	1.7	.971	OF-19, DH-1
13 yrs.		1584	.270	.403	5534	1494	276	68	108	2.0	704	717	389	659	120	77	21	2859	123	48	20	2.0	.984	OF-1477, DH-61, 3B-7

Al Cowens *continued*

LEAGUE CHAMPIONSHIP SERIES

Year	Team	Lg	Games	BA	SA	AB	H	2B	3B	HR	HR%	R	RBI	BB	SO	SB	Pinch Hit AB	Pinch Hit H	PO	A	E	DP	TC/G	FA	G by Pos
1976	KC	A	5	.190	.286	21	4	0	1	0	0.0	3	0	1	1	2	0	0	15	0	0	0	3.0	1.000	OF-5
1977			5	.263	.421	19	5	0	0	1	5.3	2	5	1	3	0	0	0	14	0	0	0	2.8	1.000	OF-5
1978			4	.133	.133	15	2	0	0	0	0.0	2	1	0	2	0	0	0	5	0	0	0	1.3	1.000	OF-4
3 yrs.			14	.200	.291	55	11	0	1	1	1.8	7	6	2	6	2	0	0	34	0	0	0	2.4	1.000	OF-14

Billy Cox

COX, WILLIAM RICHARD
B. Aug. 29, 1919, Newport, Pa. D. Mar. 30, 1978, Harrisburg, Pa.
BR TR 5′10″ 150 lbs.

Year	Team	Lg	Games	BA	SA	AB	H	2B	3B	HR	HR%	R	RBI	BB	SO	SB	Pinch Hit AB	Pinch Hit H	PO	A	E	DP	TC/G	FA	G by Pos
1941	PIT	N	10	.270	.405	37	10	3	1	0	0.0	4	2	3	2	1	0	0	15	35	3	8	5.3	.943	SS-10
1946			121	.290	.387	411	119	22	6	2	0.5	32	36	26	15	4	3	1	235	323	39	59	5.2	.935	SS-114
1947			132	.274	.442	529	145	30	7	15	2.8	75	54	29	28	5	2	1	220	388	20	63	4.9	.968	SS-129
1948	BKN	N	88	.249	.359	237	59	13	2	3	1.3	36	15	38	19	3	6	1	59	120	8	11	2.4	.957	3B-70, SS-6, 2B-1
1949			100	.233	.351	390	91	18	2	8	2.1	48	40	30	18	5	0	0	104	213	12	28	3.3	.964	3B-100
1950			119	.257	.357	451	116	17	2	8	1.8	62	44	35	24	6	1	0	143	274	16	43	3.4	.963	3B-107, 2B-13, SS-9
1951			142	.279	.411	455	127	25	4	9	2.0	62	51	37	30	5	3	1	141	264	14	26	3.0	.967	3B-139, SS-1
1952			116	.259	.338	455	118	12	3	6	1.3	56	34	25	32	10	4	1	140	188	9	34	2.8	.973	3B-100, SS-10, 2B-9
1953			100	.291	.443	327	95	18	1	10	3.1	44	44	37	21	2	5	1	92	147	7	21	2.6	.972	3B-89, SS-6, 2B-1
1954			77	.235	.319	226	53	9	2	2	0.9	26	17	21	13	0	4	1	93	130	7	15	3.0	.970	3B-58, 2B-11, SS-8
1955	BAL	A	53	.211	.314	194	41	7	2	3	1.5	25	14	17	16	1	3	1	55	104	4	10	2.7	.975	3B-37, 2B-18, SS-6
11 yrs.			1058	.262	.380	3712	974	174	32	66	1.8	470	351	298	218	42	31	8	1297	2186	139	318	3.4	.962	3B-700, SS-299, 2B-53

WORLD SERIES

Year	Team	Lg	Games	BA	SA	AB	H	2B	3B	HR	HR%	R	RBI	BB	SO	SB	Pinch Hit AB	Pinch Hit H	PO	A	E	DP	TC/G	FA	G by Pos
1949	BKN	N	2	.333	.333	3	1	0	0	0	0.0	0	0	0	1	0	2	1	1	0	0	0	1.0	1.000	3B-1
1952			7	.296	.370	27	8	2	0	0	0.0	4	0	3	4	0	0	0	9	14	1	1	3.4	.958	3B-7
1953			6	.304	.565	23	7	3	0	1	4.3	3	6	1	4	0	0	0	1	10	1	1	2.0	.917	3B-6
3 yrs.			15	.302	.453	53	16	5	0	1	1.9	7	6	4	9	0	2	1	11	24	2	2	2.6	.946	3B-14

Bobby Cox

COX, ROBERT JOE
B. May 21, 1941, Tulsa, Okla.
Manager 1978–85, 1990–95.
BR TR 5′11″ 180 lbs.

Year	Team	Lg	Games	BA	SA	AB	H	2B	3B	HR	HR%	R	RBI	BB	SO	SB	Pinch Hit AB	Pinch Hit H	PO	A	E	DP	TC/G	FA	G by Pos
1968	NY	A	135	.229	.316	437	100	15	1	7	1.6	33	41	41	85	3	3	0	98	279	17	22	3.0	.957	3B-132
1969			85	.215	.293	191	41	7	1	2	1.0	17	17	34	41	0	20	4	50	145	11	17	3.3	.947	3B-56, 2B-6
2 yrs.			220	.225	.309	628	141	22	2	9	1.4	50	58	75	126	3	23	4	148	424	28	39	3.1	.953	3B-188, 2B-6

Dick Cox

COX, ELMER JOSEPH
B. Sept. 30, 1897, Pasadena, Calif. D. June 1, 1966, Morro Bay, Calif.
BR TR 5′ 7½″ 158 lbs.

Year	Team	Lg	Games	BA	SA	AB	H	2B	3B	HR	HR%	R	RBI	BB	SO	SB	Pinch Hit AB	Pinch Hit H	PO	A	E	DP	TC/G	FA	G by Pos
1925	BKN	N	122	.329	.477	434	143	23	10	7	1.6	68	64	37	29	4	8	3	197	14	7	4	2.0	.968	OF-111
1926			124	.296	.367	398	118	17	4	1	0.3	53	45	46	20	6	6	3	201	12	8	2	1.9	.964	OF-117
2 yrs.			246	.314	.424	832	261	40	14	8	1.0	121	109	83	49	10	14	6	398	26	15	6	1.9	.966	OF-228

Frank Cox

COX, FRANCIS BERNARD (Runt)
B. Aug. 29, 1857, Waltham, Mass. D. June 24, 1928, Hartford, Conn.
5′ 6″

Year	Team	Lg	Games	BA	SA	AB	H	2B	3B	HR	HR%	R	RBI	BB	SO	SB	Pinch Hit AB	Pinch Hit H	PO	A	E	DP	TC/G	FA	G by Pos
1884	DET	N	27	.127	.176	102	13	3	1	0	0.0	6		2	36		0	0	28	80	25	7	4.9	.812	SS-27

Jeff Cox

COX, JEFFREY LINDON
B. Nov. 9, 1955, Los Angeles, Calif.
BR TR 5′11″ 170 lbs.

Year	Team	Lg	Games	BA	SA	AB	H	2B	3B	HR	HR%	R	RBI	BB	SO	SB	Pinch Hit AB	Pinch Hit H	PO	A	E	DP	TC/G	FA	G by Pos
1980	OAK	A	59	.213	.231	169	36	3	0	0	0.0	20	9	14	23	8	0	0	107	167	6	28	4.8	.979	2B-58
1981			2	—	—	0	0	0	0	0	—	0	0	0	0	0	0	0	0	1	0	0	1.0	1.000	2B-1
2 yrs.			61	.213	.231	169	36	3	0	0	0.0	20	9	14	23	8	0	0	107	168	6	28	4.8	.979	2B-59

Jim Cox

COX, JAMES CHARLES
B. May 28, 1950, Bloomington, Ill.
BR TR 5′11″ 175 lbs.

Year	Team	Lg	Games	BA	SA	AB	H	2B	3B	HR	HR%	R	RBI	BB	SO	SB	Pinch Hit AB	Pinch Hit H	PO	A	E	DP	TC/G	FA	G by Pos
1973	MON	N	9	.133	.200	15	2	1	0	0	0.0	1	0	1	4	0	2	0	9	10	1	1	2.9	.950	2B-7
1974			77	.220	.292	236	52	9	1	2	0.8	29	26	23	36	2	1	1	148	220	12	45	5.3	.968	2B-72
1975			11	.259	.407	27	7	1	0	1	3.7	1	5	1	2	1	3	0	10	21	0	7	3.9	1.000	2B-8
1976			13	.172	.241	29	5	0	1	0	0.0	2	2	2	2	0	1	0	24	22	2	6	4.4	.958	2B-11
4 yrs.			110	.215	.293	307	66	11	2	3	1.0	33	33	27	44	3	7	1	191	273	15	59	4.9	.969	2B-98

Larry Cox

COX, LARRY EUGENE
B. Sept. 11, 1947, Bluffton, Ohio D. Feb. 17, 1990, Bellefontaine, Ohio.
BR TR 5′10″ 178 lbs.

Year	Team	Lg	Games	BA	SA	AB	H	2B	3B	HR	HR%	R	RBI	BB	SO	SB	Pinch Hit AB	Pinch Hit H	PO	A	E	DP	TC/G	FA	G by Pos
1973	PHI	N	1	—	—	0	0	0	0	0	—	0	0	0	0	0	0	0							
1974			30	.170	.208	53	9	2	0	0	0.0	5	4	4	9	0	2	1	1	0	0	0	1.0	1.000	C-1
1975			11	.200	.200	5	1	0	0	0	0.0	0	1	1	0	1	1	0	90	9	1	0	3.4	.990	C-29
1977	SEA	A	35	.247	.376	93	23	6	0	2	2.2	6	6	10	12	1	0	0	10	0	0	0	1.0	1.000	C-10
1978	CHI	N	59	.281	.372	121	34	5	0	2	1.7	10	18	12	16	0	0	0	138	26	5	2	4.8	.970	C-35
1979	SEA	A	100	.215	.314	293	63	11	3	4	1.4	32	36	22	39	2	8	0	178	26	7	3	3.6	.967	C-58
1980			105	.202	.292	243	49	6	2	4	1.6	18	20	19	36	1	2	0	408	49	9	6	4.7	.981	C-99
1981	TEX	A	5	.231	.308	13	3	1	0	0	0.0	0	0	0	4	0	0	0	412	45	3	5	4.4	.993	C-104
1982	CHI	N	2	.000	.000	4	0	0	0	0	0.0	1	0	2	1	0	0	0	33	2	0	0	7.0	1.000	C-5
																			9	2	0	1	5.5	1.000	C-2
9 yrs.			348	.221	.314	825	182	31	5	12	1.5	72	85	70	117	5	13	1	1279	159	25	17	4.3	.983	C-343

Ted Cox

COX, WILLIAM TED
B. Jan. 24, 1955, Oklahoma City, Okla.
BR TR 6′ 3″ 195 lbs.

Year	Team	Lg	Games	BA	SA	AB	H	2B	3B	HR	HR%	R	RBI	BB	SO	SB	Pinch Hit AB	Pinch Hit H	PO	A	E	DP	TC/G	FA	G by Pos
1977	BOS	A	13	.362	.500	58	21	3	1	1	1.7	11	6	3	6	0	0	0	0	0	0	0	0.0	.000	DH-13
1978	CLE	A	82	.233	.278	227	53	7	0	1	0.4	14	19	16	30	0	12	1	100	42	4	6	1.9	.973	OF-38, 3B-20, DH-12, 1B-7, SS-1
1979			78	.212	.307	189	40	6	0	4	2.1	17	22	14	27	3	8	2	57	81	6	11	2.0	.958	3B-52, OF-16, 2B-4, DH-1
1980	SEA	A	83	.243	.304	247	60	9	0	2	0.8	17	23	19	25	0	4	3	47	142	11	20	2.5	.945	3B-80
1981	TOR	A	16	.300	.500	50	15	4	0	2	4.0	6	9	5	10	0	0	0	17	19	3	2	2.4	.923	3B-14, 1B-1, DH-1
5 yrs.			272	.245	.324	771	189	29	1	10	1.3	65	79	57	98	3	24	6	221	284	24	39	2.0	.955	3B-166, OF-54, DH-27, 1B-8, 2B-4, SS-1

Toots Coyne

COYNE, MARTIN ALBERT TR
B. Oct. 20, 1894, St. Louis, Mo. D. Sept. 18, 1939, St. Louis, Mo.

Year	Team	Games	BA	SA	AB	H	2B	3B	HR	HR%	R	RBI	BB	SO	SB	Pinch Hit AB	Pinch Hit H	PO	A	E	DP	TC/G	FA	G by Pos
1914	PHI A	1	.000	.000	2	0	0	0	0	0.0	0	0	0	2	0	0	0	0	1	0	0	1.0	1.000	3B-1

Estel Crabtree

CRABTREE, ESTEL CRAYTON (Crabby) BL TR 6′ 168 lbs.
B. Aug. 19, 1903, Crabtree, Ohio D. Jan. 4, 1967, Logan, Ohio.

Year	Team	Games	BA	SA	AB	H	2B	3B	HR	HR%	R	RBI	BB	SO	SB	Pinch Hit AB	Pinch Hit H	PO	A	E	DP	TC/G	FA	G by Pos
1929	CIN N	1	.000	.000	1	0	0	0	0	0.0	0	0	0	0	0	1	0	0	0	0	0	0.0	—	
1931		117	.269	.377	443	119	12	12	4	0.9	70	37	23	33	3	10	3	265	30	11	9	2.9	.964	OF-101, 3B-4, 1B-2
1932		108	.274	.368	402	110	14	9	2	0.5	38	35	23	26	2	7	3	288	9	3	3	3.2	.990	OF-95
1933	STL N	23	.265	.353	34	9	3	0	0	0.0	6	3	2	3	1	12	2	18	0	1	0	2.7	.947	OF-7
1941		77	.341	.503	167	57	6	3	5	3.0	27	28	26	24	1	21	7	71	4	0	0	1.5	1.000	OF-50, 3B-1
1942		10	.333	.556	9	3	2	0	0	0.0	1	2	1	3	0	9	3	0	0	0	0	0.0	—	
1943	CIN N	95	.276	.346	254	70	12	0	2	0.8	25	26	25	17	1	24	10	135	4	9	2	2.3	.939	OF-64
1944		58	.286	.347	98	28	4	1	0	0.0	7	11	13	3	0	32	9	29	1	0	1	1.4	1.000	OF-19, 1B-2
8 yrs.		489	.281	.382	1408	396	53	25	13	0.9	174	142	113	109	8	116	37	806	48	24	15	2.5	.973	OF-336, 3B-5, 1B-4

Harry Craft

CRAFT, HARRY FRANCIS BR TR 6′ 1″ 185 lbs.
B. Apr. 19, 1915, Ellisville, Miss. D. Aug. 3, 1995, Conroe, Tex.
Manager 1957–59, 1961–64.

Year	Team	Games	BA	SA	AB	H	2B	3B	HR	HR%	R	RBI	BB	SO	SB	Pinch Hit AB	Pinch Hit H	PO	A	E	DP	TC/G	FA	G by Pos
1937	CIN N	10	.310	.405	42	13	2	1	0	0.0	7	4	1	3	0	0	0	22	1	0	0	2.3	1.000	OF-10
1938		151	.270	.418	612	165	28	9	15	2.5	70	83	29	46	3	0	0	436	15	8	3	3.0	.983	OF-151
1939		134	.257	.402	502	129	20	7	13	2.6	58	67	27	54	5	0	0	300	13	6	4	2.4	.981	OF-134
1940		115	.244	.353	422	103	18	5	6	1.4	47	48	17	46	2	3	0	300	8	1	3	2.8	.997	OF-109, 1B-2
1941		119	.249	.368	413	103	15	2	10	2.4	48	59	33	43	4	4	1	280	6	5	1	2.5	.983	OF-115
1942		37	.177	.212	113	20	2	1	0	0.0	7	6	3	11	0	1	0	72	4	1	3	2.3	.987	OF-33
6 yrs.		566	.253	.380	2104	533	85	25	44	2.1	237	267	110	203	14	8	1	1410	47	21	14	2.7	.986	OF-552, 1B-2
WORLD SERIES																								
1939	CIN N	4	.091	.091	11	1	0	0	0	0.0	0	0	0	6	0	0	0	7	1	0	0	2.0	1.000	OF-4
1940		1	.000	.000	1	0	0	0	0	0.0	0	0	0	0	0	1	0	0	0	0	0	0.0	—	
2 yrs.		5	.083	.083	12	1	0	0	0	0.0	0	0	0	6	0	1	0	7	1	0	0	2.0	1.000	OF-4

Rodney Craig

CRAIG, RODNEY PAUL BB TR 6′ 1″ 195 lbs.
B. Jan. 12, 1958, Los Angeles, Calif.

Year	Team	Games	BA	SA	AB	H	2B	3B	HR	HR%	R	RBI	BB	SO	SB	Pinch Hit AB	Pinch Hit H	PO	A	E	DP	TC/G	FA	G by Pos
1979	SEA A	16	.385	.577	52	20	8	1	0	0.0	9	6	1	5	1	1	0	24	0	2	0	1.7	.923	OF-15
1980		70	.237	.346	240	57	15	1	3	1.3	30	20	17	35	3	2	1	155	2	2	1	2.5	.987	OF-63
1982	CLE A	49	.231	.262	65	15	2	0	0	0.0	7	1	4	6	3	19	2	28	0	1	0	1.1	.966	OF-22, DH-4
1986	CHI A	10	.200	.200	10	2	0	0	0	0.0	3	0	2	2	0	8	2	0	0	0	0	0.0	.000	OF-2
4 yrs.		145	.256	.360	367	94	25	2	3	0.8	49	27	24	48	7	30	5	207	2	5	1	2.0	.977	OF-102, DH-4

Dick Cramer

CRAMER, WILLIAM B.
B. Brooklyn, N. Y. D. Aug. 12, 1885, Camden, N. J.

Year	Team	Games	BA	SA	AB	H	2B	3B	HR	HR%	R	RBI	BB	SO	SB	Pinch Hit AB	Pinch Hit H	PO	A	E	DP	TC/G	FA	G by Pos
1883	NY N	2	.000	.000	6	0	0	0	0	0.0	0		1	5		0	0	0	0	0	0	0.0	.000	OF-2

Doc Cramer

CRAMER, ROGER MAXWELL (Flit) BL TR 6′ 2″ 185 lbs.
B. July 22, 1905, Beach Haven, N. J. D. Sept. 9, 1990, Manahawkin, N. J.

Year	Team	Games	BA	SA	AB	H	2B	3B	HR	HR%	R	RBI	BB	SO	SB	Pinch Hit AB	Pinch Hit H	PO	A	E	DP	TC/G	FA	G by Pos
1929	PHI A	2	.000	.000	6	0	0	0	0	0.0	0	0	0	2	0	1	0	6	0	0	0	6.0	1.000	OF-1
1930		30	.232	.268	82	19	1	1	0	0.0	12	6	2	8	0	8	0	38	2	3	1	2.0	.930	OF-21, SS-1
1931		65	.260	.341	223	58	8	2	2	0.9	37	20	11	15	2	10	3	133	5	3	1	2.6	.979	OF-55
1932		92	.336	.461	384	129	27	6	3	0.8	73	46	17	27	3	4	2	233	7	6	2	2.9	.976	OF-86
1933		152	.295	.396	**661**	195	27	8	8	1.2	109	75	36	24	5	0	0	387	13	12	2	2.7	.971	OF-152
1934		153	.311	.411	**649**	202	29	9	6	0.9	99	46	40	35	1	0	0	385	12	6	0	2.7	.985	OF-152
1935		149	.332	.416	**644**	214	37	4	3	0.5	96	70	37	34	6	0	0	429	6	11	1	3.0	.975	OF-149
1936	BOS A	154	.292	.362	643	188	31	7	0	0.0	99	41	49	20	4	0	0	443	20	12	6	3.1	.975	OF-154
1937		133	.305	.384	560	171	22	11	0	0.0	90	51	35	14	8	0	0	365	12	12	4	2.9	.969	OF-133
1938		148	.301	.380	**658**	198	36	8	0	0.0	116	71	51	19	4	0	0	417	16	6	3	2.9	.986	OF-148, P-1
1939		137	.311	.382	589	183	30	6	0	0.0	110	56	36	17	3	2	1	356	12	6	0	2.8	.984	OF-135
1940		150	.303	.384	**661**	**200**	27	12	1	0.2	94	51	36	29	3	0	0	333	11	11	2	2.4	.969	OF-149
1941	WAS A	154	.273	.338	**660**	180	25	6	2	0.3	93	66	37	15	4	2	0	369	9	6	1	2.5	.984	OF-152
1942	DET A	151	.263	.317	**630**	166	26	4	0	0.0	71	43	43	18	4	1	1	352	15	7	6	2.5	.981	OF-150
1943		140	.300	.348	606	182	18	4	1	0.2	79	43	31	13	4	2	1	346	9	4	3	2.6	.989	OF-138
1944		143	.292	.369	578	169	20	9	2	0.3	69	42	37	21	6	2	0	337	13	7	2	2.5	.980	OF-141
1945		141	.275	.379	541	149	22	8	6	1.1	62	58	35	21	2	1	0	314	7	3	4	2.3	.991	OF-140
1946		68	.294	.368	204	60	8	2	1	0.5	26	26	15	8	3	16	4	89	2	0	0	1.8	1.000	OF-50
1947		73	.268	.344	157	42	2	2	2	1.3	21	30	20	5	0	33	**9**	79	3	3	0	2.4	.965	OF-35
1948		4	.000	.000	4	0	0	0	0	0.0	1	1	3	0	0	2	0	2	0	0	0	2.0	1.000	OF-1
20 yrs.		2239	.296	.375	9140	2705	396	109	37	0.4	1357	842	571	345	62	84	21	5413	174	118	38	2.7	.979	OF-2142, P-1, SS-1
WORLD SERIES																								
1931	PHI A	2	.500	.500	2	1	0	0	0	0.0	0	2	0	0	0	2	1	0	0	0	0	0.0	—	
1945	DET A	7	.379	.379	29	11	0	0	0	0.0	7	4	1	0	1	0	0	21	0	0	0	3.0	1.000	OF-7
2 yrs.		9	.387	.387	31	12	0	0	0	0.0	7	6	1	0	1	2	1	21	0	0	0	3.0	1.000	OF-7

Del Crandall

CRANDALL, DELMAR WESLEY BR TR 6′ 1½″ 180 lbs.
B. Mar. 5, 1930, Ontario, Calif.
Manager 1972–75, 1983–84.

Year	Team	Games	BA	SA	AB	H	2B	3B	HR	HR%	R	RBI	BB	SO	SB	Pinch Hit AB	Pinch Hit H	PO	A	E	DP	TC/G	FA	G by Pos
1949	BOS N	67	.263	.368	228	60	10	1	4	1.8	21	34	9	18	2	2	1	287	39	6	5	5.3	.982	C-63
1950		79	.220	.310	255	56	11	0	4	1.6	21	37	13	24	0	1	0	319	41	12	7	4.9	.968	C-75, 1B-1
1953	MIL N	116	.272	.429	382	104	13	1	15	3.9	55	51	33	47	2	8	1	566	62	9	13	5.9	.986	C-108
1954		138	.242	.425	463	112	18	2	21	4.5	60	64	40	56	0	3	1	665	79	8	11	5.5	.989	C-136
1955		133	.236	.457	440	104	15	2	26	5.9	61	62	40	56	2	4	1	611	67	10	8	5.3	.985	C-131
1956		112	.238	.450	311	74	14	2	16	5.1	37	48	35	30	1	5	2	448	44	2	9	4.5	.996	C-109
[illegible]57		118	.253	.410	383	97	11	2	15	3.9	45	46	30	38	1	12	4	429	60	7	11	4.4	.986	C-102, OF-9, 1B-1
[illegible]58		131	.272	.457	427	116	23	1	18	4.2	50	63	48	38	4	8	3	659	64	7	6	5.9	.990	C-124
[illegible]		150	.257	.423	518	133	19	2	21	4.1	65	72	46	48	5	4	0	783	71	5	15	5.9	.994	C-146
[illegible]		142	.294	.430	537	158	14	1	19	3.5	81	77	34	36	4	2	0	764	70	10	9	6.0	.988	C-141

Del Crandall *continued*

Year	Team	Lg	Games	BA	SA	AB	H	2B	3B	HR	HR%	R	RBI	BB	SO	SB	Pinch Hit AB	Pinch Hit H	PO	A	E	DP	TC/G	FA	G by Pos
1961			15	.200	.300	30	6	3	0	0	0.0	3	1	1	0	0	8	0	17	3	0	0	4.0	1.000	C-5
1962			107	.297	.417	350	104	12	3	8	2.3	35	45	27	24	3	14	6	488	55	3	9	5.7	.995	C-90, 1B-5
1963			86	.201	.251	259	52	4	0	3	1.2	18	28	18	22	1	6	0	459	43	4	9	6.2	.992	C-75, 1B-7
1964	**SF**	**N**	69	.231	.328	195	45	8	1	3	1.5	12	11	22	21	0	6	2	402	30	3	7	6.7	.993	C-65
1965	**PIT**	**N**	60	.214	.271	140	30	2	0	2	1.4	11	10	14	10	1	0	0	248	23	1	4	4.5	.996	C-60
1966	**CLE**	**A**	50	.231	.361	108	25	2	0	4	3.7	10	8	14	9	0	2	0	304	15	3	2	6.6	.991	C-49
16 yrs.			1573	.254	.404	5026	1276	179	18	179	3.6	585	657	424	477	26	85	21	7449	766	90	125	5.5	.989	C-1479, 1B-14, OF-9
WORLD SERIES																									
1957	**MIL**	**N**	6	.211	.368	19	4	0	0	1	5.3	1	1	1	1	0	0	0	21	4	0	2	4.2	1.000	C-6
1958			7	.240	.360	25	6	0	0	1	4.0	4	3	3	10	0	0	0	43	5	0	2	6.9	1.000	C-7
2 yrs.			13	.227	.364	44	10	0	0	2	4.5	5	4	4	11	0	0	0	64	9	0	4	5.6	1.000	C-13

Doc Crandall

CRANDALL, JAMES OTIS
B. Oct. 8, 1887, Wadena, Ind. D. Aug. 17, 1951, Bell, Calif.
BR TR 5′10½″ 180 lbs.

Year	Team	Lg	Games	BA	SA	AB	H	2B	3B	HR	HR%	R	RBI	BB	SO	SB	Pinch Hit AB	Pinch Hit H	PO	A	E	DP	TC/G	FA	G by Pos
1908	**NY**	**N**	34	.222	.361	72	16	4	0	2	2.8	8	6	4		0	2	0	15	52	1	2	2.1	.985	P-32, 2B-1
1909			30	.244	.366	41	10	0	1	1	2.4	4	1	1		0	0	0	9	39	3	4	1.7	.941	P-30
1910			45	.342	.521	73	25	2	4	1	1.4	10	13	5	7	0	1	0	12	49	1	3	1.4	.984	P-42, SS-1
1911			61	.239	.372	113	27	1	4	2	1.8	12	21	8	16	2	11	2	17	76	6	3	2.0	.939	P-41, SS-6, 2B-3
1912			50	.313	.438	80	25	6	2	0	0.0	9	19	6	7	0	10	4	9	44	2	0	1.4	.964	P-37, 2B-1, 1B-1
1913	**2 teams**		**NY N** (46G –.319) **STL N** (2G –.000)																						
″	**total**		48	.306	.429	49	15	4	1	0	0.0	7	4	3	10	0	10	2	4	34	0	1	1.1	1.000	P-35, 2B-1
1914	**STL**	**F**	118	.309	.424	278	86	16	5	2	0.7	40	41	58		3	17	6	106	204	25	12	3.6	.925	2B-63, P-27, SS-1, OF-1
1915			84	.284	.348	141	40	2	2	1	0.7	18	19	27		4	28	5	15	99	5	3	2.3	.958	P-51
1916	**STL**	**A**	16	.083	.083	12	1	0	0	0	0.0	0	0	2	4	0	12	1	0	0	1	0	0.5	.000	P-2
1918	**BOS**	**N**	14	.286	.286	28	8	0	0	0	0.0	1	2	4	3	0	5	2	7	10	0	1	2.1	1.000	P-5, OF-3
10 yrs.			500	.285	.398	887	253	35	19	9	1.0	109	126	118	47	9	96	22	194	607	44	29	2.2	.948	P-302, 2B-69, SS-8, OF-4, 1B-1
WORLD SERIES																									
1911	**NY**	**N**	3	.500	1.000	2	1	1	0	0	0.0	1	1	2	0	0	0	0	0	2	0	0	1.0	1.000	P-2
1912			1	.000	.000	1	0	0	0	0	0.0	0	0	0	1	0	0	0	0	1	0	0	1.0	1.000	P-1
1913			4	.000	.000	4	0	0	0	0	0.0	0	0	0	0	0	2	0	0	2	0	0	1.0	1.000	P-2
3 yrs.			8	.143	.286	7	1	1	0	0	0.0	1	1	2	1	0	2	0	0	5	0	0	1.0	1.000	P-5

Cannonball Crane

CRANE, EDWARD NICHOLAS
B. May 27, 1862, Boston, Mass. D. Sept. 19, 1896, Rochester, N. Y.
BR TR 5′10½″ 204 lbs.

Year	Team	Lg	Games	BA	SA	AB	H	2B	3B	HR	HR%	R	RBI	BB	SO	SB	Pinch Hit AB	Pinch Hit H	PO	A	E	DP	TC/G	FA	G by Pos
1884	**BOS**	**U**	101	.285	.451	428	122	23	6	12	2.8	83		14			0	0	364	102	88	6	5.1	.841	OF-57, C-42, 1B-5, P-4
1885	**2 teams**		**PRO N** (1G –.000) **BUF N** (13G –.275)																						
″	**total**		14	.264	.415	53	14	0	1	2	3.8	5	10	4	9		0	0	20	1	7	0	2.0	.750	OF-14
1886	**WAS**	**N**	80	.171	.229	292	50	11	3	0	0.0	20	20	13	54		0	0	116	35	20	5	2.1	.883	OF-68, P-10, C-4
1888	**NY**	**N**	12	.162	.297	37	6	2	0	1	2.7	3	2	3	11	1	0	0	3	23	4	0	2.5	.867	P-12
1889			29	.204	.272	103	21	1	0	2	1.9	16	11	13	21	6	0	0	12	24	11	1	1.6	.766	P-29, 1B-1
1890	**NY**	**P**	43	.315	.404	146	46	5	4	0	0.0	27	16	10	26	5	0	0	17	71	16	0	2.4	.846	P-43
1891	**2 teams**		**CIN AA** (34G –.155) **CIN N** (15G –.109)																						
″	**total**		49	.141	.160	156	22	0	0	1	0.6	16	9	11	40	7	0	0	13	81	17	2	2.2	.847	P-47, OF-3
1892	**NY**	**N**	48	.245	.264	163	40	1	1	0	0.0	20	14	11	30	2	0	0	28	69	23	4	2.5	.808	P-47, OF-1
1893	**2 teams**		**NY N** (12G –.462) **BKN N** (3G –.400)																						
″	**total**		15	.452	.516	31	14	2	0	0	0.0	9	3	7	0	0	0	0	3	14	3	0	1.3	.850	P-12, OF-2, 1B-1
9 yrs.			391	.238	.329	1409	335	45	15	18	1.3	199	85	86	191	21	0	0	576	420	189	18	2.9	.841	P-204, OF-145, C-46, 1B-7

Sam Crane

CRANE, SAMUEL BYREN (Red)
B. Sept. 13, 1894, Harrisburg, Pa. D. Nov. 12, 1955, Philadelphia, Pa.
BR TR 5′11½″ 154 lbs.

Year	Team	Lg	Games	BA	SA	AB	H	2B	3B	HR	HR%	R	RBI	BB	SO	SB	Pinch Hit AB	Pinch Hit H	PO	A	E	DP	TC/G	FA	G by Pos
1914	**PHI**	**A**	2	.000	.000	6	0	0	0	0	0.0	0	0	2	3	0	0	0	5	8	1	0	7.0	.929	SS-2
1915			8	.087	.174	23	2	2	0	0	0.0	3	1	0	4	0	1	0	16	21	4	2	5.9	.902	SS-6, 2B-1
1916			2	.250	.250	4	1	0	0	0	0.0	1	0	2	1	0	0	0	1	5	0	0	3.0	1.000	SS-2
1917	**WAS**	**A**	32	.179	.200	95	17	2	0	0	0.0	6	4	4	14	0	0	0	53	75	16	13	4.5	.889	SS-32
1920	**CIN**	**N**	54	.215	.243	144	31	4	0	0	0.0	20	9	7	9	5	7	0	65	91	11	14	4.0	.934	SS-25, 3B-10, 2B-4, OF-3
1921			73	.233	.298	215	50	10	2	0	0.0	20	16	14	14	2	3	0	130	177	16	32	4.9	.950	SS-63, 3B-2, OF-1
1922	**BKN**	**N**	3	.250	.375	8	2	1	0	0	0.0	1	0	0	1	0	0	0	8	13	3	2	8.0	.875	SS-3
7 yrs.			174	.208	.255	495	103	19	2	0	0.0	51	30	29	46	7	11	0	278	390	51	63	4.7	.929	SS-133, 3B-12, 2B-5, OF-4

Sam Crane

CRANE, SAMUEL NEWHALL
B. Jan. 2, 1854, Springfield, Mass. D. June 26, 1925, New York, N. Y.
Manager 1880, 1884.
BR TR

Year	Team	Lg	Games	BA	SA	AB	H	2B	3B	HR	HR%	R	RBI	BB	SO	SB	Pinch Hit AB	Pinch Hit H	PO	A	E	DP	TC/G	FA	G by Pos
1880	**BUF**	**N**	10	.129	.129	31	4	0	0	0	0.0	4	2	1	8		0	0	31	27	9	5	6.1	.866	2B-10, OF-1
1883	**NY**	**AA**	96	.235	.287	349	82	8	5	0	0.0	57		13			0	0	283	249	87	26	6.4	.859	2B-96, OF-1
1884	**CIN**	**U**	80	.233	.291	309	72	9	3	1	0.3	56		11			0	0	224	217	73	27	6.4	.858	2B-80
1885	**DET**	**N**	68	.192	.273	245	47	4	5	2	0.8	23	20	13	45		0	0	179	197	38	21	6.1	.908	2B-68
1886	**2 teams**		**DET N** (47G –.141) **STL N** (39G –.172)																						
″	**total**		86	.153	.199	301	46	5	3	1	0.3	34	19	21	61		0	0	204	231	48	34	5.4	.901	2B-77, SS-8, OF-4
1887	**WAS**	**N**	7	.300	.400	30	9	1	1	0	0.0	6	1	1	6	5	0	0	10	22	5	2	5.3	.865	SS-7
1890	**3 teams**		**NY N** (2G –.000) **PIT N** (22G –.195) **NY N** (2G –.000)																						
″	**total**		26	.170	.202	94	16	3	0	0	0.0	3	3	0	7	6	0	0	57	77	16	7	5.8	.893	2B-17, SS-7, 1B-1, OF-1
7 yrs.			373	.203	.259	1359	276	30	17	4	0.3	183	45	60	127	11	0	0	988	1020	276	122	6.0	.879	2B-348, SS-22, OF-7, 1B-1

Gavvy Cravath

CRAVATH, CLIFFORD CARLTON (Cactus)
B. Mar. 23, 1881, Escondido, Calif. D. May 23, 1963, Laguna Beach, Calif.
Manager 1919–20.
BR TR 5′10½″ 186 lbs.

Year	Team	Lg	Games	BA	SA	AB	H	2B	3B	HR	HR%	R	RBI	BB	SO	SB	Pinch Hit AB	Pinch Hit H	PO	A	E	DP	TC/G	FA	G by Pos
1908	**BOS**	**A**	*94*	.256	.383	277	71	10	11	1	0.4	43	34	38		6	14	5	134	7	13	3	1.9	.916	OF-77, 1B-5
1909	**2 teams**		**CHI A** (19G –*.180*) **WAS A** (3G –.000)																						
″	**total**		22	.164	.218	55	9	0	0	1	1.8	7	9	20		3	2	0	35	1	2	0	2.0	.947	OF-19
1912	**PHI**	**N**	130	.284	.470	436	124	*30*	9	11	**2.5**	63	70	47	77	15	16	4	200	26	8	5	2.1	.966	OF-113
1913			147	.341	**.568**	525	**179**	34	14	**19**	**3.6**	78	**128**	55	63	10	5	4	208	20	10	1	1.7	.958	OF-141
1914			149	.299	.499	499	149	*27*	8	**19**	**3.8**	*76*	100	83	72	14	6	0	205	34	18	7	1.8	.930	OF-143

Gavvy Cravath *continued*

Year	Team	Games	BA	SA	AB	H	2B	3B	HR	HR%	R	RBI	BB	SO	SB	Pinch Hit AB	Pinch Hit H	PO	A	E	DP	TC/G	FA	G by Pos
1915		150	.285	**.510**	522	149	31	7	**24**	**4.6**	**89**	**115**	**86**	77	11	0	0	233	28	15	2	1.8	.946	OF-150
1916		137	.283	.440	448	127	21	8	11	2.5	70	70	64	**89**	9	7	1	182	17	7	2	1.6	.966	OF-130
1917		140	.280	.473	503	141	29	16	**12**	**2.4**	70	83	70	57	6	1	0	209	17	13	3	1.7	.946	OF-139
1918		121	.232	.376	426	99	27	5	**8**	**1.9**	43	54	54	46	7	2	0	184	19	15	3	1.8	.931	OF-118
1919		83	.341	.640	214	73	18	5	**12**	5.6	34	45	35	21	8	19	6	89	7	9	2	1.9	.914	OF-56
1920		46	.289	.467	45	13	5	0	1	2.2	2	11	9	12	0	34	**12**	2	0	1	0	0.6	.667	OF-5
11 yrs.		1219	.287	.478	3950	1134	232	83	119	3.0	575	719	561	514	89	106	32	1681	176	111	28	1.8	.944	OF-1091, 1B-5
WORLD SERIES																								
1915	PHI N	5	.125	.313	16	2	1	1	0	0.0	2	1	2	6	0	0	0	5	0	0	0	1.0	1.000	OF-5

Bill Craver

CRAVER, WILLIAM H.
B. June 1844, Troy, N. Y. D. June 17, 1901, Troy, N. Y.
Manager 1876.
BR TR 5′ 9″ 160 lbs.

Year	Team	Games	BA	SA	AB	H	2B	3B	HR	HR%	R	RBI	BB	SO	SB	Pinch Hit AB	Pinch Hit H	PO	A	E	DP	TC/G	FA	G by Pos
1876	NY N	56	.224	.240	246	55	4	0	0	0.0	24	22	2	7		0	0	158	122	72	10	6.0	.795	2B-42, C-11, SS-6
1877	LOU N	57	.265	.303	238	63	5	2	0	0.0	33	29	5	11		0	0	71	175	26	15	4.8	.904	SS-57
2 yrs.		113	.244	.271	484	118	9	2	0	0.0	57	51	7	18		0	0	229	297	98	25	5.4	.843	SS-63, 2B-42, C-11

Forrest Crawford

CRAWFORD, FORREST A.
B. May 10, 1881, Rockdale, Tex. D. Mar. 29, 1908, Austin, Tex.
BL TR

Year	Team	Games	BA	SA	AB	H	2B	3B	HR	HR%	R	RBI	BB	SO	SB	Pinch Hit AB	Pinch Hit H	PO	A	E	DP	TC/G	FA	G by Pos
1906	STL N	45	.207	.241	145	30	3	1	0	0.0	8	11	7		1	0	0	62	121	14	8	4.4	.929	SS-39, 3B-6
1907		7	.227	.227	22	5	0	0	0	0.0	0	3	2		0	0	0	13	18	3	2	4.9	.912	SS-7
2 yrs.		52	.210	.240	167	35	3	1	0	0.0	8	14	9		1	0	0	75	139	17	10	4.4	.926	SS-46, 3B-6

George Crawford

CRAWFORD, GEORGE
Deceased.

Year	Team	Games	BA	SA	AB	H	2B	3B	HR	HR%	R	RBI	BB	SO	SB	Pinch Hit AB	Pinch Hit H	PO	A	E	DP	TC/G	FA	G by Pos
1890	PHI AA	5	.118	.118	17	2	0	0	0	0.0	1		0		1	0	0	12	3	0	0	3.0	1.000	OF-4, SS-1

Glenn Crawford

CRAWFORD, GLENN MARTIN (Shorty)
B. Dec. 2, 1913, North Branch, Mich. D. Jan. 2, 1972, Saginaw, Mich.
BL TR 5′ 9″ 165 lbs.

Year	Team	Games	BA	SA	AB	H	2B	3B	HR	HR%	R	RBI	BB	SO	SB	Pinch Hit AB	Pinch Hit H	PO	A	E	DP	TC/G	FA	G by Pos
1945	2 teams	STL N (4G –.000) PHI N (82G –.295)																						
″	total	86	.292	.367	305	89	13	2	2	0.7	41	24	37	15	5	4	0	152	148	17	18	3.6	.946	OF-39, SS-34, 2B-14
1946	PHI N	1	.000	.000	1	0	0	0	0	0.0	0	0	0	0	0	1	0	0	0	0	0	0.0	—	
2 yrs.		87	.291	.366	306	89	13	2	2	0.7	41	24	37	15	5	5	0	152	148	17	18	3.6	.946	OF-39, SS-34, 2B-14

Ken Crawford

CRAWFORD, KENNETH DANIEL
B. Oct. 31, 1894, South Bend, Ind. D. Nov. 11, 1976, Pittsburgh, Pa.
BL TR 5′ 9″ 145 lbs.

Year	Team	Games	BA	SA	AB	H	2B	3B	HR	HR%	R	RBI	BB	SO	SB	Pinch Hit AB	Pinch Hit H	PO	A	E	DP	TC/G	FA	G by Pos
1915	BAL F	23	.244	.293	82	20	2	1	0	0.0	4	7	1		0	5	0	133	6	4	3	7.9	.972	1B-14, OF-4

Pat Crawford

CRAWFORD, CLIFFORD RANKIN
B. Jan. 28, 1902, Society Hill, S. C. D. Jan. 25, 1994, Morehead City, N. C.
BL TR 5′11″ 170 lbs.

Year	Team	Games	BA	SA	AB	H	2B	3B	HR	HR%	R	RBI	BB	SO	SB	Pinch Hit AB	Pinch Hit H	PO	A	E	DP	TC/G	FA	G by Pos
1929	NY N	65	.298	.509	57	17	3	0	3	5.3	13	24	11	5	1	**44**	10	42	2	0	1	5.5	1.000	1B-7, 3B-1
1930	2 teams	NY N (25G –.276) CIN N (76G –.290)																						
″	total	101	.287	.400	300	86	10	3	6	2.0	35	43	30	12	2	14	3	249	212	11	43	5.5	.977	2B-72, 1B-14
1933	STL N	91	.268	.321	224	60	8	2	0	0.0	24	21	14	9	1	38	9	287	62	6	25	7.0	.983	1B-29, 2B-15, 3B-7
1934		61	.271	.300	70	19	2	0	0	0.0	3	16	5	3	0	**43**	**11**	11	21	3	4	2.7	.914	3B-9, 2B-4
4 yrs.		318	.280	.372	651	182	23	5	9	1.4	75	104	60	29	4	139	33	589	297	20	73	5.7	.978	2B-91, 1B-50, 3B-17
WORLD SERIES																								
1934	STL N	2	.000	.000	2	0	0	0	0	0.0	0	0	0	0	0	2	0	0	0	0	0	0.0	—	

Rufus Crawford

CRAWFORD, RUFUS (Jake)
B. Mar. 20, 1928, Campbell, Mo.
BR TR 6′ 1½″ 185 lbs.

Year	Team	Games	BA	SA	AB	H	2B	3B	HR	HR%	R	RBI	BB	SO	SB	Pinch Hit AB	Pinch Hit H	PO	A	E	DP	TC/G	FA	G by Pos
1952	STL A	7	.182	.273	11	2	1	0	0	0.0	1	0	1	5	1	4	1	6	0	0	0	2.0	1.000	OF-3

Sam Crawford

CRAWFORD, SAMUEL EARL (Wahoo Sam)
B. Apr. 18, 1880, Wahoo, Neb. D. June 15, 1968, Hollywood, Calif.
Hall of Fame 1957.
BL TL 6′ 190 lbs.

Year	Team	Games	BA	SA	AB	H	2B	3B	HR	HR%	R	RBI	BB	SO	SB	Pinch Hit AB	Pinch Hit H	PO	A	E	DP	TC/G	FA	G by Pos
1899	CIN N	31	.307	.465	127	39	3	7	1	0.8	25	20	2		6	0	0	56	9	2	2	2.2	.970	OF-31
1900		101	.267	.434	389	104	14	15	7	1.8	68	59	28		14	6	1	237	18	14	2	2.9	.948	OF-94
1901		131	.330	.528	515	170	22	16	**16**	**3.1**	91	104	37		13	4	2	209	20	19	6	2.0	.923	OF-126
1902		140	.333	.461	555	185	16	**23**	3	0.5	94	78	47		16	0	0	208	24	17	5	1.8	.932	OF-140
1903	DET A	137	.335	.489	550	184	23	**25**	4	0.7	88	89	25		18	0	0	225	16	10	3	1.8	.960	OF-137
1904		150	.250	.357	571	143	21	17	2	0.4	49	73	44		20	0	0	230	18	7	8	1.7	.973	OF-150
1905		154	.297	.433	575	171	40	10	6	1.0	73	75	50		22	0	0	630	59	13	25	4.6	.981	OF-103, 1B-51
1906		145	.295	.407	563	166	25	16	2	0.4	65	72	38		24	0	0	458	36	5	12	3.4	.990	OF-116, 1B-32
1907		144	.323	.460	582	188	34	17	4	0.7	**102**	81	37		18	0	0	313	22	12	2	2.4	.965	OF-144, 1B-2
1908		152	.311	.457	**591**	184	33	16	**7**	1.2	102	80	37		15	1	0	428	22	14	14	3.1	.970	OF-134, 1B-17
1909		156	.314	.452	589	185	**35**	14	6	1.0	83	97	47		30	0	0	486	17	17	4	3.3	.967	OF-139, 1B-17
1910		154	.289	.423	588	170	26	**19**	5	0.9	83	**120**	37		20	0	0	234	11	9	2	1.6	.965	OF-153, 1B-1
1911		146	.378	.526	574	217	36	14	7	1.2	109	115	61		37	0	0	181	16	5	3	1.4	.975	OF-146
1912		149	.325	.470	581	189	30	21	4	0.7	81	109	42		41	0	0	169	16	3	5	1.3	.984	OF-149
1913		153	.316	.489	**610**	193	32	**23**	9	1.5	78	83	52	28	13	0	0	357	21	14	11	2.6	.964	OF-140, 1B-13
1914		157	.314	.483	582	183	22	**26**	8	1.4	74	**104**	69	31	25	0	0	193	18	5	4	1.4	.977	OF-157
1915		156	.299	.431	612	183	31	**19**	4	0.7	81	**112**	66	29	24	0	0	219	8	6	1	1.5	.974	OF-156
1916		100	.286	.401	322	92	11	13	0	0.0	41	42	37	10	10	15	**8**	104	6	2	3	1.4	.982	OF-79, 1B-2
1917		61	.173	.269	104	18	4	0	2	1.9	6	12	4	6	0	38	7	165	2	2	5	9.4	.988	1B-15, OF-3
19 yrs.		2517	.309	.453	9580	2964	458	311 **1st**	97	1.0	1393	1525	760	104	366	64	18	5102	359	176	117	2.3	.969	OF-2297, 1B-150
WORLD SERIES																								
1907	DET A	5	.238	.286	21	5	1	0	0	0.0	1	2	0	3	0	0	0	7	2	0	1	1.8	1.000	OF-5
1908		5	.238	.286	21	5	1	0	0	0.0	2	1	1	2	0	0	0	16	0	0	0	3.2	1.000	OF-5
1909		7	.250	.464	28	7	3	0	1	3.6	4	3	1	1	1	0	0	17	1	2	0	2.5	.900	OF-7, 1B-1
3 yrs.		17	.243	.357	70	17	5	0	1	1.4	7	6	2	6	1	0	0	40	3	2	1	2.5	.956	OF-17, 1B-1

Willie Crawford

CRAWFORD, WILLIE MURPHY
B. Sept. 7, 1946, Los Angeles, Calif.
BL TL 6′ 1″ 197 lbs.

Year	Team	Lg	G	BA	SA	AB	H	2B	3B	HR	HR%	R	RBI	BB	SO	SB	Pinch Hit AB	Pinch Hit H	PO	A	E	DP	TC/G	FA	G by Pos
1964	LA	N	10	.313	.375	16	5	1	0	0	0.0	3	0	1	7	1	3	1	7	0	0	0	1.8	1.000	OF-4
1965			52	.148	.148	27	4	0	0	0	0.0	10	0	2	8	2	13	0	7	0	0	0	0.9	1.000	OF-8
1966			6	—	—	0	0	0	0	0	—	1	0	0	0	0	0	0	0	0	0	0	0.0	—	
1967			4	.250	.250	4	1	0	0	0	0.0	0	0	1	3	0	3	1	0	0	1	0	1.0	.000	OF-1
1968			61	.251	.400	175	44	12	1	4	2.3	25	14	20	64	1	12	2	78	6	3	1	1.8	.966	OF-48
1969			129	.247	.401	389	96	17	5	11	2.8	64	41	49	85	4	21	6	177	5	5	0	1.7	.973	OF-113
1970			109	.234	.381	299	70	8	6	8	2.7	48	40	33	88	4	15	3	160	9	7	1	1.9	.960	OF-94
1971			114	.281	.442	342	96	16	6	9	2.6	64	40	28	49	5	19	8	146	5	3	1	1.6	.981	OF-97
1972			96	.251	.403	243	61	7	3	8	3.3	28	27	35	55	4	18	4	111	2	2	0	1.6	.983	OF-74
1973			145	.295	.453	457	135	26	2	14	3.1	75	66	78	91	12	7	2	250	13	6	4	1.9	.978	OF-138
1974			139	.295	.432	468	138	23	4	11	2.4	73	61	64	88	7	8	1	225	3	8	1	1.8	.966	OF-133
1975			124	.263	.386	373	98	15	2	9	2.4	46	46	49	43	5	16	3	201	2	2	0	1.8	.990	OF-113
1976	STL	N	120	.304	.441	392	119	17	5	9	2.3	49	50	37	53	2	16	5	209	6	4	1	2.0	.982	OF-107
1977	2 teams	HOU N (42G –.254) OAK A (59G –.184)																							
″	total		101	.216	.300	250	54	10	1	3	1.2	21	34	34	30	0	22	3	88	3	3	2	1.3	.968	OF-52, DH-18
14 yrs.			1210	.268	.408	3435	921	152	35	86	2.5	507	419	431	664	47	173	39	1659	54	44	11	1.8	.975	OF-982, DH-18
LEAGUE CHAMPIONSHIP SERIES																									
1974	LA	N	2	.250	.250	4	1	0	0	0	0.0	1	1	1	1	0	1	1	0	0	0	0	0.0	.000	OF-2
WORLD SERIES																									
1965	LA	N	2	.500	.500	2	1	0	0	0	0.0	0	0	0	1	0	2	1	0	0	0	0	0.0	—	
1974			3	.333	.833	6	2	0	0	1	16.7	1	0	1	0	0	2	1	1	0	0	0	0.5	1.000	OF-2
2 yrs.			5	.375	.750	8	3	0	0	1	12.5	1	0	1	1	0	4	2	1	0	0	0	0.5	1.000	OF-2

George Creamer

CREAMER, GEORGE W.
Born George W. Triebel.
B. 1855, Philadelphia, Pa. D. June 27, 1886, Philadelphia, Pa.
Manager 1884.
BR TR 6′ 2″

Year	Team	Lg	G	BA	SA	AB	H	2B	3B	HR	HR%	R	RBI	BB	SO	SB	Pinch Hit AB	Pinch Hit H	PO	A	E	DP	TC/G	FA	G by Pos
1878	MIL	N	50	.212	.280	193	41	7	3	0	0.0	30	15	5	15		0	0	82	117	37	7	4.6	.843	2B-28, OF-17, 3B-6
1879	SYR	N	15	.217	.250	60	13	2	0	0	0.0	3	3	1	2		0	0	28	41	16	2	5.7	.812	2B-10, SS-3, OF-2
1880	WOR	N	85	.199	.239	306	61	6	3	0	0.0	40	27	4	21		0	0	238	274	68	34	6.8	.883	2B-85
1881			80	.207	.249	309	64	9	2	0	0.0	42	25	11	27		0	0	230	248	51	39	6.6	.904	2B-80
1882			81	.227	.336	286	65	16	6	1	0.3	27	29	14	24		0	0	241	283	54	50	7.1	.907	2B-81
1883	PIT	AA	91	.255	.322	369	94	7	9	0	0.0	54		20			0	0	310	274	67	42	7.2	.897	2B-91
1884			98	.183	.236	339	62	8	5	0	0.0	38		16			0	0	308	336	43	47	7.0	.937	2B-98
7 yrs.			500	.215	.276	1862	400	55	28	1	0.1	234	99	71	89		0	0	1437	1573	336	221	6.7	.900	2B-473, OF-19, 3B-6, SS-3

Birdie Cree

CREE, WILLIAM FRANKLIN
B. Oct. 22, 1882, Khedive, Pa. D. Nov. 8, 1942, Sunbury, Pa.
BR TR 5′ 6″ 150 lbs.

Year	Team	Lg	G	BA	SA	AB	H	2B	3B	HR	HR%	R	RBI	BB	SO	SB	Pinch Hit AB	Pinch Hit H	PO	A	E	DP	TC/G	FA	G by Pos
1908	NY	A	21	.269	.321	78	21	0	2	0	0.0	5	4	7		1	0	0	35	4	0	2	1.9	1.000	OF-21
1909			104	.262	.315	343	90	6	3	2	0.6	48	27	30		10	12	1	134	37	9	4	2.0	.950	OF-77, SS-6, 2B-4, 3B-1
1910			134	.287	.422	467	134	19	16	4	0.9	58	73	40		28	0	0	202	11	10	3	1.7	.955	OF-134
1911			137	.348	.513	520	181	30	22	4	0.8	90	88	56		48	1	1	252	33	15	3	2.1	.950	OF-137, SS-4, 2B-1
1912			50	.332	.453	190	63	11	6	0	0.0	25	22	20		12	0	0	123	5	7	1	2.7	.948	OF-50
1913			145	.272	.346	534	145	25	6	1	0.2	51	63	50	51	22	1	0	239	17	3	5	1.8	.988	OF-144
1914			77	.309	.411	275	85	18	5	0	0.0	45	40	30	24	4	1	0	190	10	5	4	2.7	.976	OF-76
1915			74	.214	.276	196	42	8	2	0	0.0	23	15	36	22	7	18	7	97	6	6	1	2.1	.945	OF-53
8 yrs.			742	.292	.398	2603	761	117	62	11	0.4	345	332	269	97	132	33	9	1272	123	55	23	2.0	.962	OF-692, SS-10, 2B-5, 3B-1

Connie Creeden

CREEDEN, CORNELIUS STEPHEN
B. July 21, 1915, Danvers, Mass. D. Nov. 30, 1969, Santa Ana, Calif.
BL TL 6′ 1″ 200 lbs.

Year	Team	Lg	G	BA	SA	AB	H	2B	3B	HR	HR%	R	RBI	BB	SO	SB	Pinch Hit AB	Pinch Hit H	PO	A	E	DP	TC/G	FA	G by Pos
1943	BOS	N	5	.250	.250	4	1	0	0	0	0.0	0	1	1	0	0	4	1	0	0	0	0	0.0	—	

Pat Creeden

CREEDEN, PATRICK FRANCIS (Whoops)
B. May 23, 1906, Newburyport, Mass. D. Apr. 20, 1992, Brockton, Mass.
BL TR 5′ 8″ 175 lbs.

Year	Team	Lg	G	BA	SA	AB	H	2B	3B	HR	HR%	R	RBI	BB	SO	SB	Pinch Hit AB	Pinch Hit H	PO	A	E	DP	TC/G	FA	G by Pos
1931	BOS	A	5	.000	.000	8	0	0	0	0	0.0	0	0	1	3	0	3	0	6	5	2	1	6.5	.846	2B-2

Marty Creegan

CREEGAN, MARTIN
Deceased.
161 lbs.

Year	Team	Lg	G	BA	SA	AB	H	2B	3B	HR	HR%	R	RBI	BB	SO	SB	Pinch Hit AB	Pinch Hit H	PO	A	E	DP	TC/G	FA	G by Pos
1884	WAS	U	9	.152	.152	33	5	0	0	0	0.0	4		1			0	0	24	9	11	2	3.7	.750	OF-6, C-3, 3B-2, 1B-1

Gus Creely

CREELY, AUGUST L.
B. June 6, 1870, St. Louis, Mo. D. Apr. 22, 1934, St. Louis, Mo.
5′ 6″ 150 lbs.

Year	Team	Lg	G	BA	SA	AB	H	2B	3B	HR	HR%	R	RBI	BB	SO	SB	Pinch Hit AB	Pinch Hit H	PO	A	E	DP	TC/G	FA	G by Pos
1890	STL	AA	4	.000	.000	15	0	0	0	0	0.0	0		0		1	0	0	2	8	3	0	3.3	.769	SS-4

Pete Cregan

CREGAN, PETER JAMES (Peekskill Pete)
B. Apr. 13, 1875, Kingston, N. Y. D. May 18, 1945, New York, N. Y.
BR TR 5′ 7½″ 150 lbs.

Year	Team	Lg	G	BA	SA	AB	H	2B	3B	HR	HR%	R	RBI	BB	SO	SB	Pinch Hit AB	Pinch Hit H	PO	A	E	DP	TC/G	FA	G by Pos
1899	NY	N	1	.000	.000	2	0	0	0	0	0.0	0	0	0		0	0	0	1	0	0	0	1.0	1.000	OF-1
1903	CIN	N	6	.105	.105	19	2	0	0	0	0.0	0	0	1		0	0	0	10	0	3	0	2.2	.769	OF-6
2 yrs.			7	.095	.095	21	2	0	0	0	0.0	0	0	1		0	0	0	11	0	3	0	2.0	.786	OF-7

Bernie Creger

CREGER, BERNARD ODELL
B. Mar. 21, 1927, Wytheville, Va.
BR TR 6′ 175 lbs.

Year	Team	Lg	G	BA	SA	AB	H	2B	3B	HR	HR%	R	RBI	BB	SO	SB	Pinch Hit AB	Pinch Hit H	PO	A	E	DP	TC/G	FA	G by Pos
1947	STL	N	15	.188	.250	16	3	1	0	0	0.0	3	0	1	3	1	0	0	6	18	5	2	2.2	.828	SS-13

Creepy Crespi

CRESPI, FRANK ANGELO JOSEPH
B. Feb. 16, 1918, St. Louis, Mo. D. Mar. 1, 1990, Florissant, Mo.
BR TR 5′ 8½″ 175 lbs.

Year	Team	Lg	G	BA	SA	AB	H	2B	3B	HR	HR%	R	RBI	BB	SO	SB	Pinch Hit AB	Pinch Hit H	PO	A	E	DP	TC/G	FA	G by Pos
1938	STL	N	7	.263	.368	19	5	2	0	0	0.0	2	1	2	7	0	0	0	14	12	6	4	4.6	.813	SS-7
1939			15	.172	.207	29	5	1	0	0	0.0	3	6	3	6	0	3	0	9	25	2	1	3.6	.944	2B-6, SS-4
1940			3	.273	.364	11	3	1	0	0	0.0	2	0	1	2	1	0	0	6	4	1	1	3.7	.909	3B-2, SS-1
1941			146	.279	.350	560	156	24	2	4	0.7	85	46	57	58	3	0	0	382	421	32	94	5.8	.962	2B-145
1942			93	.243	.271	292	71	4	2	0	0.0	33	35	27	29	4	4	1	227	201	16	43	5.0	.964	2B-83, SS-5
5 yrs.			264	.263	.321	911	240	32	4	4	0.4	125	88	90	102	8	7	1	638	663	57	143	5.4	.958	2B-234, SS-17, 3B-2

Creepy Crespi *continued*

Year	Team		Games	BA	SA	AB	H	2B	3B	HR	HR%	R	RBI	BB	SO	SB	Pinch Hit AB	Pinch Hit H	PO	A	E	DP	TC/G	FA	G by Pos
WORLD SERIES																									
1942	STL	N	1	—	—	0	0	0	0	0	—	1	0	0	0	0	0	0	0	0	0	0	0.0	—	

Lou Criger

CRIGER, LOUIS BR TR 5′10″ 165 lbs.
B. Feb. 3, 1872, Elkhart, Ind. D. May 14, 1934, Tucson, Ariz.

Year	Team		Games	BA	SA	AB	H	2B	3B	HR	HR%	R	RBI	BB	SO	SB	Pinch Hit AB	Pinch Hit H	PO	A	E	DP	TC/G	FA	G by Pos
1896	CLE	N	2	.000	.000	5	0	0	0	0	0.0	0	0	1	0	1	1	0	5	2	0	0	7.0	1.000	C-1
1897			39	.225	.268	138	31	4	1	0	0.0	15	22	23		5	0	0	149	37	16	4	5.2	.921	C-37, 1B-2
1898			84	.279	.362	287	80	13	4	1	0.3	43	32	40		2	1	0	322	105	19	9	5.4	.957	C-82
1899	STL	N	77	.256	.333	258	66	4	5	2	0.8	39	44	28		14	2	1	228	91	17	6	4.5	.949	C-75
1900			80	.271	.361	288	78	8	6	2	0.7	30	38	4		5	4	1	283	108	20	8	5.4	.951	C-75, 3B-1
1901	BOS	A	76	.231	.276	268	62	6	3	0	0.0	26	24	11		7	0	0	380	110	16	16	6.7	.968	C-68, 1B-8
1902			83	.256	.361	266	68	16	6	0	0.0	32	28	27		7	1	0	331	117	17	6	5.7	.963	C-80, OF-1
1903			96	.192	.306	317	61	7	10	3	0.9	41	31	26		5	0	0	491	156	14	10	6.9	.979	C-96
1904			98	.211	.298	299	63	10	5	2	0.7	34	34	27		1	3	1	502	112	12	7	6.6	.981	C-95
1905			109	.198	.272	313	62	6	7	1	0.3	33	36	54		5	0	0	539	147	20	5	6.5	.972	C-109
1906			7	.176	.235	17	3	1	0	0	0.0	0	1	1		1	1	0	46	7	1	0	9.0	.981	C-6
1907			75	.181	.199	226	41	4	0	0	0.0	12	14	19		2	1	0	288	109	9	12	5.4	.978	C-75
1908			84	.190	.224	237	45	4	2	0	0.0	12	25	13		1	0	0	380	120	10	11	6.1	.980	C-84
1909	STL	A	74	.170	.184	212	36	1	1	0	0.0	15	9	25		2	1	0	387	98	7	16	6.7	.986	C-73
1910	NY	A	27	.188	.217	69	13	2	0	0	0.0	3	4	10		0	0	0	120	28	1	0	5.5	.993	C-27
1912	STL	A	1	.000	.000	2	0	0	0	0	0.0	1	0	0		0	0	0	5	1	0	0	6.0	1.000	C-1
16 yrs.			1012	.221	.290	3202	709	86	50	11	0.3	336	342	309	0	58	15	3	4456	1348	179	110	6.0	.970	C-984, 1B-10, OF-1, 3B-1
WORLD SERIES																									
1903	BOS	A	8	.231	.231	26	6	0	0	0	0.0	1	4	2	3	0	0	0	54	8	3	2	8.1	.954	C-8

Dave Cripe

CRIPE, DAVID GORDON BR TR 6′ 180 lbs.
B. Apr. 7, 1951, Ramona, Calif.

Year	Team		Games	BA	SA	AB	H	2B	3B	HR	HR%	R	RBI	BB	SO	SB	Pinch Hit AB	Pinch Hit H	PO	A	E	DP	TC/G	FA	G by Pos
1978	KC	A	7	.154	.154	13	2	0	0	0	0.0	1	1	0	2	0	2	0	1	1	0	0	0.4	1.000	3B-5

Dave Criscione

CRISCIONE, DAVID GERALD BR TR 5′ 8″ 185 lbs.
B. Sept. 2, 1951, Dunkirk, N. Y.

Year	Team		Games	BA	SA	AB	H	2B	3B	HR	HR%	R	RBI	BB	SO	SB	Pinch Hit AB	Pinch Hit H	PO	A	E	DP	TC/G	FA	G by Pos
1977	BAL	A	7	.333	.667	9	3	0	0	1	11.1	1	1	0	1	0	0	0	13	0	0	0	1.9	1.000	C-7

Tony Criscola

CRISCOLA, ANTHONY PAUL BL TR 5′11½″ 180 lbs.
B. July 9, 1915, Walla Walla, Wash.

Year	Team		Games	BA	SA	AB	H	2B	3B	HR	HR%	R	RBI	BB	SO	SB	Pinch Hit AB	Pinch Hit H	PO	A	E	DP	TC/G	FA	G by Pos
1942	STL	A	91	.297	.399	158	47	9	2	1	0.6	17	13	8	13	2	32	7	0	0	0	0	0.0	.000	OF-52
1943			29	.154	.154	52	8	0	0	0	0.0	4	1	8	7	0	15	1	24	0	1	0	1.9	.960	OF-13
1944	CIN	N	64	.229	.274	157	36	3	2	0	0.0	14	14	14	12	0	24	4	80	4	2	0	2.5	.977	OF-35
3 yrs.			184	.248	.311	367	91	12	4	1	0.3	35	28	30	32	2	71	12	104	4	3	0	1.1	.973	OF-100

Pat Crisham

CRISHAM, PATRICK J. 6′ 168 lbs.
B. June 4, 1877, Amesbury, Mass. D. June 12, 1915, Syracuse, N. Y.

Year	Team		Games	BA	SA	AB	H	2B	3B	HR	HR%	R	RBI	BB	SO	SB	Pinch Hit AB	Pinch Hit H	PO	A	E	DP	TC/G	FA	G by Pos
1899	BAL	N	53	.291	.355	172	50	5	3	0	0.0	23	20	4		4	4	0	282	23	8	7	6.5	.974	1B-26, C-22

Joe Crisp

CRISP, JOSEPH SHELBY BR TR 6′ 4″ 200 lbs.
B. July 8, 1889, Higginsville, Mo. D. Feb. 5, 1939, Kansas City, Mo.

Year	Team		Games	BA	SA	AB	H	2B	3B	HR	HR%	R	RBI	BB	SO	SB	Pinch Hit AB	Pinch Hit H	PO	A	E	DP	TC/G	FA	G by Pos
1910	STL	A	1	.000	.000	1	0	0	0	0	0.0	0	0	0		0	0	0	2	0	0	0	2.0	1.000	C-1
1911			1	1.000	1.000	1	1	0	0	0	0.0	0	0	0		0	1	1	0	0	0	0	0.0	—	
2 yrs.			2	.500	.500	2	1	0	0	0	0.0	0	0	0		0	1	1	2	0	0	0	2.0	1.000	C-1

Dode Criss

CRISS, DODE BL TR 6′ 2″ 200 lbs.
B. Mar. 12, 1885, Sherman, Miss. D. Sept. 8, 1955, Sherman, Miss.

Year	Team		Games	BA	SA	AB	H	2B	3B	HR	HR%	R	RBI	BB	SO	SB	Pinch Hit AB	Pinch Hit H	PO	A	E	DP	TC/G	FA	G by Pos
1908	STL	A	64	.341	.415	82	28	6	0	0	0.0	15	14	9		1	**41**	**12**	21	4	2	0	1.3	.926	OF-11, P-9, 1B-1
1909			35	.292	.458	48	14	6	1	0	0.0	2	7	0		0	**24**	**7**	2	10	0	0	1.1	1.000	P-11
1910			70	.231	.352	91	21	4	2	1	1.1	11	11	11		2	**44**	**7**	114	10	2	5	7.0	.984	1B-12, P-6
1911			58	.253	.386	83	21	3	1	2	2.4	10	15	11		0	**38**	**9**	124	12	6	5	7.9	.958	1B-14, P-4
4 yrs.			227	.276	.395	304	84	19	4	3	1.0	38	47	31		3	147	35	261	36	10	10	4.5	.967	P-30, 1B-27, OF-11

Ches Crist

CRIST, CHESTER ARTHUR (Squack) BR TR 5′11″ 165 lbs.
B. Feb. 10, 1882, Cozaddale, Ohio D. Jan. 7, 1957, Cincinnati, Ohio.

Year	Team		Games	BA	SA	AB	H	2B	3B	HR	HR%	R	RBI	BB	SO	SB	Pinch Hit AB	Pinch Hit H	PO	A	E	DP	TC/G	FA	G by Pos
1906	PHI	N	6	.000	.000	11	0	0	0	0	0.0	1	0	0		0	0	0	7	1	2	1	1.7	.800	C-6

Hughie Critz

CRITZ, HUGH MELVILLE BR TR 5′ 8″ 147 lbs.
B. Sept. 17, 1900, Starkville, Miss. D. Jan. 10, 1980, Greenwood, Miss.

Year	Team		Games	BA	SA	AB	H	2B	3B	HR	HR%	R	RBI	BB	SO	SB	Pinch Hit AB	Pinch Hit H	PO	A	E	DP	TC/G	FA	G by Pos
1924	CIN	N	102	.322	.448	413	133	15	14	3	0.7	67	35	19	18	19	0	0	233	358	28	58	6.4	.955	2B-96, SS-1
1925			144	.277	.344	541	150	14	8	2	0.4	74	51	34	17	13	0	0	340	542	27	96	6.3	.970	2B-144
1926			155	.270	.371	607	164	24	14	3	0.5	96	79	39	25	7	0	0	357	588	18	107	6.2	.981	2B-155
1927			113	.278	.374	396	110	10	8	4	1.0	50	49	16	18	7	0	0	239	388	20	69	5.7	.969	2B-113
1928			153	.296	.387	641	190	21	11	5	0.8	95	52	37	24	18	0	0	333	497	25	124	5.6	.971	2B-153
1929			107	.247	.336	425	105	17	9	1	0.2	55	50	27	21	9	0	0	211	401	17	72	5.9	.973	2B-106, SS-1
1930	2 teams		CIN N (28G –.231) NY N (124G –.265)																						
″	total		152	.260	.347	662	172	20	13	4	0.6	108	61	30	32	8	0	0	398	510	24	110	6.1	.974	2B-152
1931	NY	N	66	.290	.387	238	69	7	2	4	1.7	33	17	8	17	4	1	1	139	164	5	27	5.7	.984	2B-54
1932			151	.276	.355	**659**	182	32	7	2	0.3	90	50	34	27	3	0	0	392	471	23	94	5.9	.974	2B-151
1933			133	.246	.306	558	137	18	5	2	0.4	68	33	23	24	4	0	0	316	541	16	87	6.6	.982	2B-133
1934			137	.242	.306	571	138	17	1	6	1.1	77	40	19	24	3	0	0	353	510	19	90	6.4	.978	2B-137
1935			65	.187	.242	219	41	0	3	2	0.9	19	14	3	11	2	1	0	140	175	11	31	5.5	.966	2B-59
12 yrs.			1478	.268	.352	5930	1591	195	95	38	0.6	832	531	289	258	97	2	1	3451	5145	233	965	6.1	.974	2B-1453, SS-2
WORLD SERIES																									
1933	NY	N	5	.136	.136	22	3	0	0	0	0.0	2	0	1	0	0	0	0	16	18	1	2	7.0	.971	2B-5

Davey Crockett

CROCKETT, DANIEL SOLOMON BL TR 6′ 1″ 175 lbs.
B. Oct. 5, 1875, Roanoke, Va. D. Feb. 23, 1961, Charlottesville, Va.

Year	Team	Games	BA	SA	AB	H	2B	3B	HR	HR%	R	RBI	BB	SO	SB	Pinch Hit AB	Pinch Hit H	PO	A	E	DP	TC/G	FA	G by Pos
1901	DET A	28	.284	.343	102	29	2	2	0	0.0	10	14	6		1	1	0	317	15	11	20	12.7	.968	1B-27

Art Croft

CROFT, ARTHUR F.
B. Jan. 23, 1855, St. Louis, Mo. D. Mar. 16, 1884, St. Louis, Mo.

Year	Team	Games	BA	SA	AB	H	2B	3B	HR	HR%	R	RBI	BB	SO	SB	Pinch Hit AB	Pinch Hit H	PO	A	E	DP	TC/G	FA	G by Pos
1877	STL N	54	.232	.273	220	51	5	2	0	0.0	23	27	1	15		0	0	340	12	23	10	6.9	.939	1B-28, OF-25, 2B-1
1878	IND N	60	.158	.185	222	35	6	0	0	0.0	22	16	5	23		0	0	552	9	25	19	9.8	.957	1B-51, OF-9
2 yrs.		114	.195	.229	442	86	11	2	0	0.0	45	43	6	38		0	0	892	21	48	29	8.4	.950	1B-79, OF-34, 2B-1

Harry Croft

CROFT, HENRY T.
B. Aug. 1, 1875, Chicago, Ill. D. Dec. 11, 1933, Oak Park, Ill.

Year	Team	Games	BA	SA	AB	H	2B	3B	HR	HR%	R	RBI	BB	SO	SB	Pinch Hit AB	Pinch Hit H	PO	A	E	DP	TC/G	FA	G by Pos
1899	2 teams	LOU N (2G –.000) PHI N (2G –.143)																						
″	total	4	.111	.111	9	1	0	0	0	0.0	0	0	1		0	2	0	2	6	0	0	4.0	1.000	2B-2
1901	CHI N	3	.333	.333	12	4	0	0	0	0.0	1	4	0		0	0	0	5	3	0	0	2.7	1.000	OF-3
2 yrs.		7	.238	.238	21	5	0	0	0	0.0	1	4	1		0	2	0	7	9	0	0	3.2	1.000	OF-3, 2B-2

Fred Crolius

CROLIUS, FRED JOSEPH
B. Dec. 16, 1876, Jersey City, N. J. D. Aug. 25, 1960, Ormond Beach, Fla.

Year	Team	Games	BA	SA	AB	H	2B	3B	HR	HR%	R	RBI	BB	SO	SB	Pinch Hit AB	Pinch Hit H	PO	A	E	DP	TC/G	FA	G by Pos
1901	BOS N	49	.240	.285	200	48	4	1	1	0.5	22	13	9		6	0	0	65	3	12	1	1.6	.850	OF-49
1902	PIT N	9	.263	.368	38	10	2	1	0	0.0	4	7	0		0	0	0	10	1	0	0	1.2	1.000	OF-9
2 yrs.		58	.244	.298	238	58	6	2	1	0.4	26	20	9		6	0	0	75	4	12	1	1.6	.868	OF-58

Warren Cromartie

CROMARTIE, WARREN LIVINGSTON BL TL 6′ 180 lbs.
B. Sept. 29, 1953, Miami Beach, Fla.

Year	Team	Games	BA	SA	AB	H	2B	3B	HR	HR%	R	RBI	BB	SO	SB	Pinch Hit AB	Pinch Hit H	PO	A	E	DP	TC/G	FA	G by Pos
1974	MON N	8	.176	.176	17	3	0	0	0	0.0	2	0	3	3	1	1	1	8	0	0	0	1.3	1.000	OF-6
1976		33	.210	.222	81	17	1	0	0	0.0	8	2	1	5	1	14	1	32	1	2	0	1.8	.943	OF-20
1977		155	.282	.395	620	175	41	7	5	0.8	64	50	33	40	10	0	0	319	10	8	1	2.2	.976	OF-155
1978		159	.297	.418	607	180	32	6	10	1.6	77	56	33	60	8	1	0	351	24	9	5	2.4	.977	OF-158, 1B-4
1979		158	.275	.396	659	181	46	5	8	1.2	84	46	38	78	8	0	0	343	16	9	4	2.3	.976	OF-158
1980		162	.288	.430	597	172	33	5	14	2.3	74	70	51	64	8	2	1	1459	93	14	104	9.8	.991	1B-158, OF-2
1981		99	.304	.419	358	109	19	2	6	1.7	41	42	39	27	2	1	1	570	33	4	38	6.1	.993	1B-62, OF-38
1982		144	.254	.398	497	126	24	3	14	2.8	59	62	69	60	3	6	2	308	13	6	3	2.3	.982	OF-136, 1B-9
1983		120	.278	.386	360	100	26	2	3	0.8	37	43	43	48	8	22	8	209	12	6	2	2.2	.974	OF-101, 1B-1
1991	KC A	69	.313	.420	131	41	7	2	1	0.8	13	20	15	18	1	35	8	221	9	1	20	6.4	.996	1B-29, OF-6, DH-1
10 yrs.		1107	.281	.402	3927	1104	229	32	61	1.6	459	391	325	403	50	82	22	3820	211	59	177	3.9	.986	OF-780, 1B-263, DH-1
DIVISIONAL PLAYOFF SERIES																								
1981	MON N	5	.227	.318	22	5	2	0	0	0.0	1	1	0	9	0	0	0	37	3	1	0	8.2	.976	1B-5
LEAGUE CHAMPIONSHIP SERIES																								
1981	MON N	5	.167	.222	18	3	1	0	0	0.0	0	2	0	2	0	0	0	48	2	0	6	10.0	1.000	1B-5

Tripp Cromer

CROMER, ROY BUNYON III BR TR 6′ 2″ 165 lbs.
B. Nov. 21, 1967, Lake City, S. C.

Year	Team	Games	BA	SA	AB	H	2B	3B	HR	HR%	R	RBI	BB	SO	SB	Pinch Hit AB	Pinch Hit H	PO	A	E	DP	TC/G	FA	G by Pos
1993	STL N	10	.087	.087	23	2	0	0	0	0.0	1	0	1	6	0	1	0	13	18	3	3	3.8	.912	SS-9
1994		2	—	—	0	0	0	0	0	—	1	0	0	0	0	0	0	0	0	1	0	0.5	.000	SS-2
1995		105	.226	.325	345	78	19	0	5	1.4	36	18	14	66	0	2	0	126	293	17	61	4.1	.961	SS-95, 2B-11
3 yrs.		117	.217	.310	368	80	19	0	5	1.4	38	18	15	72	0	3	0	139	311	21	64	4.0	.955	SS-106, 2B-11

Herb Crompton

CROMPTON, HERBERT BRYAN (Workhorse) BR TR 6′ 185 lbs.
B. Nov. 7, 1911, Taylor Ridge, Ill. D. Aug. 5, 1963, Moline, Ill.

Year	Team	Games	BA	SA	AB	H	2B	3B	HR	HR%	R	RBI	BB	SO	SB	Pinch Hit AB	Pinch Hit H	PO	A	E	DP	TC/G	FA	G by Pos
1937	WAS A	2	.333	.333	3	1	0	0	0	0.0	0	0	0	0	0	0	0	3	1	0	0	2.0	1.000	C-2
1945	NY A	36	.192	.222	99	19	3	0	0	0.0	6	12	2	7	0	3	1	105	18	2	1	3.8	.984	C-33
2 yrs.		38	.196	.225	102	20	3	0	0	0.0	6	12	2	7	0	3	1	108	19	2	1	3.7	.984	C-35

Ned Crompton

CROMPTON, EDWARD BL TR 5′10½″ 175 lbs.
B. Feb. 12, 1889, Liverpool, England D. Sept. 28, 1950, Aspinwall, Pa.

Year	Team	Games	BA	SA	AB	H	2B	3B	HR	HR%	R	RBI	BB	SO	SB	Pinch Hit AB	Pinch Hit H	PO	A	E	DP	TC/G	FA	G by Pos
1909	STL A	17	.159	.222	63	10	2	1	0	0.0	7	2	7		1	0	0	26	4	3	1	1.9	.909	OF-17
1910	CIN N	1	.000	.000	2	0	0	0	0	0.0	0	0	0	2	0	0	0	0	0	0	0	0.0	.000	OF-1
2 yrs.		18	.154	.215	65	10	2	1	0	0.0	7	2	7	2	1	0	0	26	4	3	1	1.8	.909	OF-18

Chris Cron

CRON, CHRISTOPHER JOHN BR TR 6′ 2″ 200 lbs.
B. Mar. 31, 1964, Albuquerque, N. M.

Year	Team	Games	BA	SA	AB	H	2B	3B	HR	HR%	R	RBI	BB	SO	SB	Pinch Hit AB	Pinch Hit H	PO	A	E	DP	TC/G	FA	G by Pos
1991	CAL A	6	.133	.133	15	2	0	0	0	0.0	0	0	2	5	0	1	0	32	6	0	1	6.3	1.000	1B-5, DH-1
1992	CHI A	6	.000	.000	10	0	0	0	0	0.0	0	0	0	4	0	4	0	10	2	1	1	2.2	.923	1B-5, OF-1
2 yrs.		12	.080	.080	25	2	0	0	0	0.0	0	0	2	9	0	5	0	42	8	1	2	4.3	.980	1B-10, OF-1, DH-1

Bill Cronin

CRONIN, WILLIAM PATRICK (Crungy) BR TR 5′ 8½″ 167 lbs.
B. Dec. 26, 1902, West Newton, Mass. D. Oct. 26, 1966, Newton, Mass.

Year	Team	Games	BA	SA	AB	H	2B	3B	HR	HR%	R	RBI	BB	SO	SB	Pinch Hit AB	Pinch Hit H	PO	A	E	DP	TC/G	FA	G by Pos
1928	BOS N	3	.000	.000	2	0	0	0	0	0.0	1	0	1	0	0	0	0	2	0	0	0	0.7	1.000	C-3
1929		6	.111	.111	9	1	0	0	0	0.0	0	0	0	0	0	0	0	11	2	0	0	2.2	1.000	C-6
1930		66	.253	.315	178	45	9	1	0	0.0	19	17	4	8	0	2	1	203	31	4	5	3.7	.983	C-64
1931		51	.206	.280	107	22	6	1	0	0.0	8	10	7	5	0	1	0	122	21	9	5	3.0	.941	C-50
4 yrs.		126	.230	.294	296	68	15	2	0	0.0	28	27	12	13	0	3	1	338	54	13	10	3.3	.968	C-123

Dan Cronin

CRONIN, DANIEL T. 5′ 8″ 170 lbs.
B. Apr. 1, 1857, Boston, Mass. D. Nov. 30, 1885, Boston, Mass.

Year	Team	Games	BA	SA	AB	H	2B	3B	HR	HR%	R	RBI	BB	SO	SB	Pinch Hit AB	Pinch Hit H	PO	A	E	DP	TC/G	FA	G by Pos
1884	2 teams	CHI U (1G –.250) STL U (1G –.000)																						
″	total	2	.111	.111	9	1	0	0	0	0.0	1		0			0	0	1	0	6	1	3.5	.143	OF-1, 2B-1

Jim Cronin

CRONIN, JAMES JOHN BB TR 5′10½″ 150 lbs.
B. Aug. 7, 1905, Richmond, Calif. D. June 10, 1983, Concord, Calif.

Year	Team	Games	BA	SA	AB	H	2B	3B	HR	HR%	R	RBI	BB	SO	SB	Pinch Hit AB	Pinch Hit H	PO	A	E	DP	TC/G	FA	G by Pos
1929	PHI A	25	.232	.304	56	13	2	1	0	0.0	7	4	5	7	0	0	0	29	53	4	11	3.7	.953	2B-10, SS-9, 3B-4

Joe Cronin

CRONIN, JOSEPH EDWARD
B. Oct. 12, 1906, San Francisco, Calif. D. Sept. 7, 1984, Osterville, Mass.
Manager 1933–47.
Hall of Fame 1956.
BR TR 5′11½″ 180 lbs.

Year	Team	Games	BA	SA	AB	H	2B	3B	HR	HR%	R	RBI	BB	SO	SB	Pinch Hit AB	Pinch Hit H	PO	A	E	DP	TC/G	FA	G by Pos
1926	**PIT N**	38	.265	.337	83	22	2	2	0	0.0	9	11	6	15	0	0	0	55	82	3	19	4.1	.979	2B-27, SS-7
1927		12	.227	.273	22	5	1	0	0	0.0	2	3	2	3	0	2	0	12	10	4	0	2.2	.846	2B-7, SS-4, 1B-1
1928	**WAS A**	63	.242	.322	227	55	10	4	0	0.0	23	25	22	27	4	0	0	133	190	16	42	5.4	.953	SS-63
1929		145	.281	.421	494	139	29	8	8	1.6	72	61	85	37	5	1	0	286	459	62	92	5.6	.923	SS-143, 2B-1
1930		154	.346	.513	587	203	41	9	13	2.2	127	126	72	36	17	0	0	336	509	35	95	5.7	.960	SS-154
1931		156	.306	.480	611	187	44	13	12	2.0	103	126	81	52	10	0	0	323	488	43	94	5.5	.950	SS-155
1932		143	.318	.492	557	177	43	**18**	6	1.1	95	116	66	45	7	1	1	306	448	32	95	5.6	.959	SS-141
1933		152	.309	.445	602	186	**45**	11	5	0.8	89	118	87	49	5	0	0	297	528	34	95	5.7	.960	SS-152
1934		127	.284	.421	504	143	30	9	7	1.4	68	101	53	28	8	0	0	246	486	38	86	6.1	.951	SS-127
1935	**BOS A**	144	.295	.460	556	164	37	14	9	1.6	70	95	63	40	3	3	0	264	431	37	86	5.3	.949	SS-139
1936		81	.281	.403	295	83	22	4	2	0.7	36	43	32	21	1	1	0	133	229	26	37	4.8	.933	SS-60, 3B-21
1937		148	.307	.486	570	175	40	4	18	3.2	102	110	84	73	5	0	0	300	414	31	89	5.0	.958	SS-148
1938		143	.325	.536	530	172	**51**	5	17	3.2	98	94	91	60	7	1	0	304	449	36	110	5.6	.954	SS-142
1939		143	.308	.492	520	160	33	3	19	3.7	97	107	87	48	6	0	0	306	437	32	93	5.5	.959	SS-142
1940		149	.285	.502	548	156	35	6	24	4.4	104	111	83	65	7	1	0	253	445	38	89	5.0	.948	SS-146, 3B-2
1941		143	.311	.508	518	161	38	8	16	3.1	98	95	82	55	1	3	1	247	362	27	67	4.5	.958	SS-119, 3B-22, OF-1
1942		45	.304	.494	79	24	3	0	4	5.1	7	24	15	21	0	25	6	47	28	6	7	4.8	.926	3B-11, 1B-5, SS-1
1943		59	.312	.558	77	24	4	0	5	6.5	8	29	11	4	0	42	**18**	12	18	1	1	3.1	.968	3B-10
1944		76	.241	.356	191	46	7	0	5	2.6	24	28	34	19	1	24	4	428	27	9	39	9.5	.981	1B-49
1945		3	.375	.375	8	3	0	0	0	0.0	1	1	3	2	0	0	0	2	8	0	2	3.3	1.000	3B-3
20 yrs.		2124	.301	.468	7579	2285	515	118	170	2.2	1233	1424	1059	700	87	104	30	4290	6048	510	1238	5.4	.953	SS-1843, 3B-69, 1B-55, 2B-35, OF-1
WORLD SERIES																								
1933	**WAS A**	5	.318	.318	22	7	0	0	0	0.0	1	2	0	2	0	0	0	7	15	1	3	4.6	.957	SS-5

Tom Crooke

CROOKE, THOMAS ALOYSIUS
B. July 26, 1884, Washington, D. C. D. Apr. 5, 1929, Quantico, Va.
BR TR 6′ 180 lbs.

Year	Team	Games	BA	SA	AB	H	2B	3B	HR	HR%	R	RBI	BB	SO	SB	Pinch Hit AB	Pinch Hit H	PO	A	E	DP	TC/G	FA	G by Pos
1909	**WAS A**	3	.286	.429	7	2	1	0	0	0.0	2	2	2		1	0	0	31	0	1	3	10.7	.969	1B-3
1910		8	.190	.238	21	4	1	0	0	0.0	1	1	1		0	2	1	49	2	0	2	10.2	1.000	1B-5
2 yrs.		11	.214	.286	28	6	2	0	0	0.0	3	3	3		1	2	1	80	2	1	5	10.4	.988	1B-8

Jack Crooks

CROOKS, JOHN CHARLES
B. Nov. 9, 1866, St. Paul, Minn. D. Jan. 29, 1918, St. Louis, Mo.
Manager 1892.
BR TR 5′10″ 170 lbs.

Year	Team	Games	BA	SA	AB	H	2B	3B	HR	HR%	R	RBI	BB	SO	SB	Pinch Hit AB	Pinch Hit H	PO	A	E	DP	TC/G	FA	G by Pos
1889	**COL AA**	12	.326	.512	43	14	2	3	0	0.0	13	7	10	4	10	0	0	31	44	1	4	6.3	.987	2B-12
1890		135	.221	.254	485	107	5	4	1	0.2	86		96		57	0	0	354	350	49	57	5.5	.935	2B-133, 3B-2, OF-1
1891		138	.245	.331	519	127	19	13	0	0.0	110	46	103	47	50	0	0	399	404	36	72	6.1	.957	2B-138
1892	**STL N**	128	.213	.294	445	95	7	4	7	1.6	82	38	**136**	52	23	0	0	316	348	55	44	5.6	.924	2B-102, 3B-24, OF-2
1893		128	.237	.306	448	106	10	9	1	0.2	93	48	**121**	37	31	0	0	223	300	53	21	4.5	.908	3B-123, SS-4, C-1
1895	**WAS N**	117	.279	.408	409	114	19	8	6	1.5	80	57	68	39	36	0	0	327	364	32	43	6.2	.956	2B-117
1896	**2 teams**	**WAS N** (25G –.286) **LOU N** (39G –.238)																						
″	**total**	64	.257	.379	206	53	8	1	5	2.4	39	35	36	16	10	1	0	169	170	29	30	5.8	.921	2B-59, 3B-4
1898	**STL N**	72	.231	.280	225	52	4	2	1	0.4	33	20	40		3	0	0	203	224	19	24	6.2	.957	2B-66, 3B-3, SS-2, OF-1
8 yrs.		794	.240	.321	2780	668	74	44	21	0.8	536	251	610	195	220	1	0	2022	2204	274	295	5.7	.939	2B-627, 3B-156, SS-6, OF-4, C-1

Ed Crosby

CROSBY, EDWARD CARLTON
B. May 26, 1949, Long Beach, Calif.
BL TR 6′ 2″ 175 lbs.

Year	Team	Games	BA	SA	AB	H	2B	3B	HR	HR%	R	RBI	BB	SO	SB	Pinch Hit AB	Pinch Hit H	PO	A	E	DP	TC/G	FA	G by Pos
1970	**STL N**	38	.253	.316	95	24	4	1	0	0.0	9	6	7	5	0	2	1	44	91	7	17	3.5	.951	SS-35, 3B-3, 2B-2
1972		101	.217	.257	276	60	9	1	0	0.0	27	19	18	27	1	15	0	130	197	10	42	3.5	.970	SS-43, 2B-38, 3B-14
1973	**2 teams**	**STL N** (22G –.128) **CIN N** (36G –.216)																						
″	**total**	58	.178	.256	90	16	3	2	0	0.0	8	6	11	16	0	13	4	36	90	9	14	2.7	.933	SS-36, 2B-10, 3B-4
1974	**CLE A**	37	.209	.244	86	18	3	0	0	0.0	11	6	6	12	0	9	3	14	53	5	5	2.1	.931	3B-18, SS-13, 2B-3
1975		61	.234	.258	128	30	3	0	0	0.0	12	7	13	14	0	0	0	69	126	7	18	3.3	.965	SS-30, 2B-19, 3B-13
1976		2	.500	.500	2	1	0	0	0	0.0	0	0	0	0	0	0	0	0	2	0	0	1.0	1.000	3B-1, DH-1
6 yrs.		297	.220	.264	677	149	22	4	0	0.0	67	44	55	74	1	39	8	293	559	38	96	3.1	.957	SS-157, 2B-72, 3B-53, DH-1
LEAGUE CHAMPIONSHIP SERIES																								
1973	**CIN N**	3	.500	.500	2	1	0	0	0	0.0	0	0	0	1	0	1	0	1	2	0	0	1.5	1.000	SS-2

Frankie Crosetti

CROSETTI, FRANK PETER JOSEPH (The Crow)
B. Oct. 4, 1910, San Francisco, Calif.
BR TR 5′10″ 165 lbs.

Year	Team	Games	BA	SA	AB	H	2B	3B	HR	HR%	R	RBI	BB	SO	SB	Pinch Hit AB	Pinch Hit H	PO	A	E	DP	TC/G	FA	G by Pos
1932	**NY A**	115	.241	.374	398	96	20	9	5	1.3	47	57	51	51	3	2	0	187	260	29	51	4.1	.939	SS-83, 3B-33, 2B-1
1933		136	.253	.379	451	114	20	5	9	2.0	71	60	55	40	4	2	1	245	384	43	58	5.1	.936	SS-133
1934		138	.265	.401	554	147	22	10	11	2.0	85	67	61	58	5	2	1	263	389	39	79	4.8	.944	SS-119, 3B-23, 2B-1
1935		87	.256	.430	305	78	17	6	8	2.6	49	50	41	27	3	0	0	153	261	16	42	4.9	.963	SS-87
1936		151	.288	.437	632	182	35	7	15	2.4	137	78	90	83	18	0	0	320	463	43	95	5.5	.948	SS-151
1937		149	.234	.352	611	143	29	5	11	1.8	127	49	86	**105**	13	2	1	313	467	43	86	5.6	.948	SS-147
1938		157	.263	.371	631	166	35	3	9	1.4	113	55	106	**99**	**27**	0	0	352	506	47	120	5.8	.948	SS-157
1939		152	.233	.332	**656**	153	25	5	10	1.5	109	56	65	81	11	0	0	323	460	26	118	5.3	.968	SS-152
1940		145	.194	.273	546	106	23	4	4	0.7	84	31	72	77	14	0	0	246	396	31	73	4.6	.954	SS-145
1941		50	.223	.284	148	33	2	2	1	0.7	13	22	18	14	0	6	1	94	113	12	25	4.9	.945	SS-32, 3B-13
1942		74	.242	.337	285	69	5	5	4	1.4	50	23	31	31	1	1	0	95	139	12	25	3.4	.951	3B-62, SS-8, 2B-2
1943		95	.233	.279	348	81	8	1	2	0.6	36	20	36	47	4	4	1	194	260	26	58	5.3	.946	SS-90
1944		55	.239	.355	197	47	4	2	5	2.5	20	30	11	21	3	1	0	115	150	11	33	5.0	.960	SS-55
1945		130	.238	.293	441	105	12	0	4	0.9	57	48	59	65	7	3	1	264	380	37	86	5.4	.946	SS-126
1946		28	.288	.339	59	17	3	0	0	0.0	4	3	8	2	0	2	0	32	62	6	15	4.2	.940	SS-24
1947		3	.000	.000	1	0	0	0	0	0.0	0	0	0	0	0	1	0	0	0	0	0	0.0		SS-1, 2B-1
1948		17	.286	.429	14	4	0	1	0	0.0	4	0	2	0	0	5	1	6	6	0	4	1.1	1.000	2B-6, SS-5
17 yrs.		1682	.245	.354	6277	1541	260	65	98	1.6	1006	649	792	801	113	31	7	3202	4696	421	968	5.0	.949	SS-1515, 3B-131, 2B-11

Frankie Crosetti *continued*

WORLD SERIES

Year	Team	Games	BA	SA	AB	H	2B	3B	HR	HR%	R	RBI	BB	SO	SB	Pinch Hit AB	Pinch Hit H	PO	A	E	DP	TC/G	FA	G by Pos
1932	NY A	4	.133	.200	15	2	1	0	0	0.0	2	0	2	3	0	0	0	9	12	4	0	6.3	.840	SS-4
1936		6	.269	.346	26	7	2	0	0	0.0	5	3	3	5	0	0	0	11	14	2	2	4.5	.926	SS-6
1937		5	.048	.048	21	1	0	0	0	0.0	2	0	3	2	0	0	0	6	17	0	1	4.6	1.000	SS-5
1938		4	.250	.688	16	4	2	1	1	6.3	1	6	2	4	0	0	0	16	10	1	4	6.8	.963	SS-4
1939		4	.063	.063	16	1	0	0	0	0.0	2	1	2	2	0	0	0	6	14	0	3	5.0	1.000	SS-4
1942		1	.000	.000	3	0	0	0	0	0.0	0	0	0	1	0	0	0	1	1	0	0	2.0	1.000	3B-1
1943		5	.278	.278	18	5	0	0	0	0.0	4	1	2	3	1	0	0	9	16	3	3	5.6	.893	SS-5
7 yrs.		29	.174	.261	115	20	5	1	1	0.9	16	11	14	20	1	0	0	58	84	10	13	5.2	.934	SS-28, 3B-1

Amos Cross

CROSS, AMOS C.
Brother of Lave Cross. Brother of Frank Cross.
B. 1861, Austria-Hungary D. July 16, 1888, Cleveland, Ohio.

Year	Team	Games	BA	SA	AB	H	2B	3B	HR	HR%	R	RBI	BB	SO	SB	Pinch Hit AB	Pinch Hit H	PO	A	E	DP	TC/G	FA	G by Pos
1885	LOU AA	35	.285	.315	130	37	2	1	0	0.0	11		0			0	0	173	48	18	1	6.8	.925	C-35
1886		74	.276	.378	283	78	14	6	1	0.4	51		44			0	0	436	91	46	12	7.7	.920	C-51, 1B-20, SS-2, OF-1
1887		8	.107	.107	28	3	0	0	0	0.0	0		1		0	0	0	23	8	5	2	4.5	.861	C-5, 1B-2, OF-1
3 yrs.		117	.268	.342	441	118	16	7	1	0.2	62		45		0	0	0	632	147	69	15	7.2	.919	C-91, 1B-22, OF-2, SS-2

Clarence Cross

CROSS, CLARENCE (Cleary Daddy)
Born Clarence Crause.
B. Mar. 4, 1856, St. Louis, Mo. D. June 23, 1931, Seattle, Wash.

Year	Team	Games	BA	SA	AB	H	2B	3B	HR	HR%	R	RBI	BB	SO	SB	Pinch Hit AB	Pinch Hit H	PO	A	E	DP	TC/G	FA	G by Pos
1884	3 teams ALT U (2G –.571) PHI U (2G –.222) KC U (25G –.215)																							
"	total	29	.239	.257	109	26	2	0	0	0.0	14		8			0	0	21	100	37	3	5.4	.766	SS-26, 3B-3
1887	NY AA	16	.200	.273	55	11	2	1	0	0.0	9		2		0	0	0	14	36	10	2	3.5	.833	SS-13, 3B-4
2 yrs.		45	.226	.262	164	37	4	1	0	0.0	23		10		0	0	0	35	136	47	5	4.7	.784	SS-39, 3B-7

Frank Cross

CROSS, FRANK ATWELL (Mickey) TR
Brother of Lave Cross. Brother of Amos Cross.
B. Jan. 20, 1873, Cleveland, Ohio D. Nov. 2, 1932, Geauga Lake, Ohio.

Year	Team	Games	BA	SA	AB	H	2B	3B	HR	HR%	R	RBI	BB	SO	SB	Pinch Hit AB	Pinch Hit H	PO	A	E	DP	TC/G	FA	G by Pos
1901	CLE A	1	.600	.600	5	3	0	0	0	0.0	0	0	0		0	0	0	0	0	0	0	0.0	.000	OF-1

Jeff Cross

CROSS, JOFFRE JAMES BR TR 5′11″ 160 lbs.
B. Aug. 28, 1918, Tulsa, Okla.

Year	Team	Games	BA	SA	AB	H	2B	3B	HR	HR%	R	RBI	BB	SO	SB	Pinch Hit AB	Pinch Hit H	PO	A	E	DP	TC/G	FA	G by Pos
1942	STL N	1	.250	.250	4	1	0	0	0	0.0	0	1	0	0	0	0	0	0	3	0	0	3.0	1.000	SS-1
1946		49	.217	.261	69	15	3	0	0	0.0	17	6	10	8	4	3	0	41	50	4	10	3.7	.958	SS-17, 2B-8, 3B-1
1947		51	.102	.122	49	5	1	0	0	0.0	4	3	10	6	0	1	0	24	47	5	10	2.5	.934	3B-15, SS-14, 2B-2
1948	2 teams STL N (2G –.000) CHI N (16G –.100)																							
"	total	18	.100	.100	20	2	0	0	0	0.0	1	0	0	4	0	4	0	3	8	3	0	1.4	.786	SS-9, 2B-1
4 yrs.		119	.162	.190	142	23	4	0	0	0.0	22	10	20	18	4	8	0	68	108	12	20	2.8	.936	SS-41, 3B-16, 2B-11

Lave Cross

CROSS, LAFAYETTE NAPOLEON BR TR 5′ 8½″ 155 lbs.
Brother of Frank Cross. Brother of Amos Cross.
B. May 12, 1866, Milwaukee, Wis. D. Sept. 6, 1927, Toledo, Ohio.
Manager 1899.

Year	Team	Games	BA	SA	AB	H	2B	3B	HR	HR%	R	RBI	BB	SO	SB	Pinch Hit AB	Pinch Hit H	PO	A	E	DP	TC/G	FA	G by Pos
1887	LOU AA	54	.266	.335	203	54	8	3	0	0.0	32		15		15	0	0	267	67	34	8	6.8	.908	C-44, OF-10
1888		47	.227	.243	181	41	3	0	0	0.0	20	15	2		10	0	0	219	67	23	4	6.1	.926	C-37, OF-12, SS-2
1889	PHI AA	55	.221	.281	199	44	8	2	0	0.0	22	23	14	9	11	0	0	278	102	27	7	7.4	.934	C-55
1890	PHI P	63	.298	.429	245	73	7	8	3	1.2	42	47	12	6	5	0	0	216	70	38	7	5.1	.883	C-49, OF-15
1891	PHI AA	110	.301	.458	402	121	20	14	5	1.2	66	52	38	23	14	0	0	297	103	28	12	3.8	.935	OF-43, C-43, 3B-24, SS-1, 2B-1
1892	PHI N	140	.275	.362	541	149	15	10	4	0.7	84	69	39	16	18	0	0	327	236	35	17	4.0	.941	3B-65, C-39, OF-25, 2B-14, SS-5
1893		96	.299	.398	415	124	17	6	4	1.0	81	78	26	7	18	1	1	291	182	27	27	5.2	.946	C-40, 3B-30, OF-10, SS-10, 1B-6
1894		119	.386	.524	529	204	34	9	7	1.3	123	125	29	7	21	0	0	226	259	39	29	4.2	.926	3B-100, C-16, SS-7, 2B-1
1895		125	.271	.364	535	145	26	9	2	0.4	95	101	35	8	21	0	0	191	308	32	23	4.2	.940	3B-125
1896		106	.256	.345	406	104	23	5	1	0.2	63	73	32	14	8	0	0	183	287	29	30	4.7	.942	3B-61, SS-37, 2B-6, OF-2, C-1
1897		88	.259	.363	344	89	17	5	3	0.9	37	51	10		10	0	0	143	217	23	15	4.4	.940	3B-47, 2B-38, OF-2, SS-1
1898	STL N	151	.317	.405	602	191	28	8	3	0.5	71	79	28		14	0	0	218	358	35	22	4.0	.943	3B-149, SS-2
1899	2 teams CLE N (38G –.286) STL N (103G –.303)																							
"	total	141	.298	.377	557	166	19	5	5	0.9	76	84	25		13	0	0	223	358	25	32	4.3	.959	3B-141
1900	2 teams STL N (16G –.295) BKN N (117G –.293)																							
"	total	133	.293	.368	522	153	15	6	4	0.8	79	73	26		21	0	0	173	321	29	11	3.9	.945	3B-133
1901	PHI A	100	.331	.469	420	139	28	12	2	0.5	82	73	19		23	0	0	140	236	33	7	4.1	.919	3B-100
1902		137	.342	.440	559	191	39	8	0	0.0	90	108	27		25	0	0	185	306	30	18	3.8	.942	3B-137
1903		137	.292	.356	559	163	22	4	2	0.4	61	90	10		14	0	0	159	228	20	14	3.0	.951	3B-136, 1B-1
1904		155	.290	.379	607	176	31	10	1	0.2	73	71	13		10	0	0	164	247	28	15	2.8	.936	3B-155
1905		147	.266	.333	583	155	29	5	0	0.0	68	77	26		8	0	0	161	249	32	6	3.0	.928	3B-147
1906	WAS A	130	.263	.322	494	130	14	6	1	0.2	55	46	28		19	0	0	157	242	20	9	3.2	.952	3B-130
1907		41	.199	.248	161	32	8	0	0	0.0	13	10	10		3	0	0	38	98	3	2	3.4	.978	3B-41
21 yrs.		2275	.292	.382	9064	2644	411	135	47	0.5	1333	1345	464	90	301	1	1	4256	4541	590	315	4.1	.937	3B-1721, C-324, OF-119, SS-65, 2B-60, 1B-7

WORLD SERIES

Year	Team	Games	BA	SA	AB	H	2B	3B	HR	HR%	R	RBI	BB	SO	SB	Pinch Hit AB	Pinch Hit H	PO	A	E	DP	TC/G	FA	G by Pos
1905	PHI A	5	.105	.105	19	2	0	0	0	0.0	0	0	1	1	0	0	0	6	7	2	0	3.0	.867	3B-5

Monte Cross

CROSS, MONTFORD MONTGOMERY BR TR 5′ 8½″ 148 lbs.
B. Aug. 31, 1869, Philadelphia, Pa. D. June 21, 1934, Philadelphia, Pa.

Year	Team	Games	BA	SA	AB	H	2B	3B	HR	HR%	R	RBI	BB	SO	SB	Pinch Hit AB	Pinch Hit H	PO	A	E	DP	TC/G	FA	G by Pos
1892	BAL N	15	.160	.160	50	8	0	0	0	0.0	5	2	4	10	2	0	0	18	39	9	2	4.4	.864	SS-15
1894	PIT N	13	.442	.837	43	19	1	5	2	4.7	14	13	5	4	6	0	0	34	39	6	7	6.1	.924	SS-13
1895		108	.257	.382	393	101	14	13	3	0.8	67	54	38	38	39	0	0	256	327	77	42	6.1	.883	SS-107, 2B-1
1896	STL N	125	.244	.337	427	104	10	6	6	1.4	66	52	58	48	40	0	0	298	394	84	31	6.2	.892	SS-125
1897		131	.286	.396	462	132	17	11	4	0.9	59	55	62		38	0	0	327	513	73	47	7.0	.920	SS-131

Monte Cross *continued*

Year	Team	Lg	Games	BA	SA	AB	H	2B	3B	HR	HR%	R	RBI	BB	SO	SB	Pinch Hit AB	Pinch Hit H	PO	A	E	DP	TC/G	FA	G by Pos
1898	PHI	N	149	.257	.330	525	135	25	5	1	0.2	68	50	55		20	0	0	404	506	93	65	6.7	.907	SS-149
1899			154	.257	.339	557	143	25	6	3	0.5	85	65	56		26	0	0	370	529	90	55	6.4	.909	SS-154
1900			131	.202	.258	466	94	11	3	3	0.6	59	62	51		19	0	0	339	459	62	68	6.6	.928	SS-131
1901			139	.197	.236	483	95	14	1	1	0.2	49	44	52		24	0	0	343	445	65	31	6.1	.924	SS-139
1902	PHI	A	137	.231	.302	497	115	22	2	3	0.6	72	59	32		17	0	0	373	466	66	37	6.6	.927	SS-137
1903			137	.247	.319	470	116	21	2	3	0.6	44	45	49		31	0	0	306	396	45	36	5.4	.940	SS-137, 2B-1
1904			153	.189	.256	503	95	23	4	1	0.2	33	38	46		19	0	0	276	424	47	26	4.9	.937	SS-153
1905			78	.270	.355	248	67	17	2	0	0.0	28	24	19		8	0	0	162	198	28	22	5.0	.928	SS-76, 2B-2
1906			134	.200	.272	445	89	23	3	1	0.2	32	40	50		22	0	0	305	411	47	48	5.7	.938	SS-134
1907			77	.206	.282	248	51	9	5	0	0.0	37	18	39		17	1	0	169	226	19	17	5.6	.954	SS-74
15 yrs.			1681	.234	.314	5817	1364	232	68	31	0.5	718	621	616	100	328	1	0	3980	5372	811	534	6.1	.920	SS-1675, 2B-4
WORLD SERIES																									
1905	PHI	A	5	.176	.176	17	3	0	0	0	0.0	0	0	0	7	0	0	0	12	13	2	0	5.4	.926	SS-5

Frank Crossin

CROSSIN, FRANK PATRICK
B. June 15, 1891, Avondale, Pa. D. Dec. 6, 1965, Kingston, Pa.
BR TR 5'10" 160 lbs.

Year	Team	Lg	Games	BA	SA	AB	H	2B	3B	HR	HR%	R	RBI	BB	SO	SB	Pinch Hit AB	Pinch Hit H	PO	A	E	DP	TC/G	FA	G by Pos
1912	STL	A	8	.227	.227	22	5	0	0	0	0.0	2	2	1		1	0	0	17	6	2	0	3.1	.920	C-8
1913			4	.250	.250	4	1	0	0	0	0.0	1	0	1	1	0	2	1	5	1	1	0	3.5	.857	C-2
1914			43	.122	.156	90	11	1	1	0	0.0	5	5	10	10	3	2	0	141	42	13	6	4.8	.934	C-41
3 yrs.			55	.147	.172	116	17	1	1	0	0.0	8	7	12	11	4	4	1	163	49	16	6	4.5	.930	C-51

Joe Crotty

CROTTY, JOSEPH P.
B. Dec. 24, 1860, Cincinnati, Ohio D. June 22, 1926, Minneapolis, Minn.
BR TR

Year	Team	Lg	Games	BA	SA	AB	H	2B	3B	HR	HR%	R	RBI	BB	SO	SB	Pinch Hit AB	Pinch Hit H	PO	A	E	DP	TC/G	FA	G by Pos
1882	2 teams		LOU AA (5G –.100)	STL AA (8G –.143)																					
"	total		13	.125	.146	48	6	1	0	0	0.0	3		3			0	0	59	17	10	4	6.6	.884	C-12, OF-1
1884	CIN	U	21	.262	.393	84	22	4	2	1	1.2	11		1			0	0	90	31	14	0	6.4	.896	C-21
1885	LOU	AA	39	.155	.171	129	20	2	0	0	0.0	14		3			0	0	199	51	22	3	7.0	.919	C-38, 1B-1
1886	NY	AA	14	.170	.213	47	8	0	1	0	0.0	6		4			0	0	60	23	6	1	6.4	.933	C-14
4 yrs.			87	.182	.234	308	56	7	3	1	0.3	34		11			0	0	408	122	52	8	6.7	.911	C-85, 1B-1, OF-1

Jack Crouch

CROUCH, JACK ALBERT (Roxy)
B. June 12, 1903, Salisbury, N. C. D. Aug. 25, 1972, Leesburg, Fla.
BR TR 5'9" 165 lbs.

Year	Team	Lg	Games	BA	SA	AB	H	2B	3B	HR	HR%	R	RBI	BB	SO	SB	Pinch Hit AB	Pinch Hit H	PO	A	E	DP	TC/G	FA	G by Pos
1930	STL	A	6	.143	.214	14	2	1	0	0	0.0	1	1	1	3	0	0	0	19	3	0	0	4.4	1.000	C-5
1931			8	.000	.000	12	0	0	0	0	0.0	0	1	0	4	0	1	0	15	2	2	0	2.7	.895	C-7
1933	2 teams		STL A (19G –.167)	CIN N (10G –.125)																					
"	total		29	.152	.217	46	7	0	0	1	2.2	6	6	2	6	1	10	1	32	9	0	1	2.7	1.000	C-15
3 yrs.			43	.125	.181	72	9	1	0	1	1.4	7	8	3	13	1	11	1	66	14	2	1	3.0	.976	C-27

Frank Croucher

CROUCHER, FRANK DONALD (Dingle)
B. July 23, 1914, San Antonio, Tex. D. May 21, 1980, Houston, Tex.
BR TR 5'11" 165 lbs.

Year	Team	Lg	Games	BA	SA	AB	H	2B	3B	HR	HR%	R	RBI	BB	SO	SB	Pinch Hit AB	Pinch Hit H	PO	A	E	DP	TC/G	FA	G by Pos
1939	DET	A	97	.269	.361	324	87	15	0	5	1.5	38	40	16	42	2	2	2	144	264	29	50	4.6	.934	SS-93, 2B-3
1940			37	.105	.105	57	6	0	0	0	0.0	3	2	4	5	0	5	0	23	30	5	3	1.7	.914	SS-26, 2B-7, 3B-1
1941			136	.254	.325	489	124	21	4	2	0.4	51	39	33	72	2	0	0	270	361	44	85	5.0	.935	SS-136
1942	WAS	A	26	.277	.323	65	18	1	1	0	0.0	2	5	3	9	0	7	2	35	60	5	9	5.6	.950	2B-18
4 yrs.			296	.251	.324	935	235	37	5	7	0.7	94	86	56	128	4	14	4	472	715	83	147	4.5	.935	SS-255, 2B-28, 3B-1
WORLD SERIES																									
1940	DET	A	1	—	—	0	0	0	0	0	—	0	0	0	0	0	0	0	0	0	0	0	0.0	.000	SS-1

Buck Crouse

CROUSE, CLYDE ELSWORTH
B. Jan. 6, 1897, Anderson, Ind. D. Oct. 23, 1983, Muncie, Ind.
BL TR 5'8" 158 lbs.

Year	Team	Lg	Games	BA	SA	AB	H	2B	3B	HR	HR%	R	RBI	BB	SO	SB	Pinch Hit AB	Pinch Hit H	PO	A	E	DP	TC/G	FA	G by Pos
1923	CHI	A	23	.257	.357	70	18	2	1	1	1.4	6	7	3	4	0	0	0	66	18	4	1	4.0	.955	C-22
1924			94	.259	.308	305	79	10	1	1	0.3	30	44	23	12	3	4	0	298	97	23	9	4.6	.945	C-90
1925			54	.351	.450	131	46	7	0	2	1.5	18	25	12	4	1	6	2	104	36	7	5	3.1	.952	C-48
1926			49	.237	.281	135	32	4	1	0	0.0	10	17	14	7	0	3	0	164	34	3	1	4.5	.985	C-45
1927			85	.239	.288	222	53	11	0	0	0.0	22	20	21	10	4	4	2	202	79	8	10	3.6	.972	C-81
1928			78	.252	.321	218	55	5	2	2	0.9	17	20	19	14	3	2	0	196	61	11	3	3.5	.959	C-76
1929			45	.271	.393	107	29	7	0	2	1.9	11	12	5	7	2	4	0	111	29	3	5	3.6	.979	C-40
1930			42	.254	.339	118	30	8	1	0	0.0	14	15	17	10	1	3	0	155	31	4	3	5.0	.979	C-38
8 yrs.			470	.262	.331	1306	342	54	6	8	0.6	128	160	114	68	14	26	4	1296	385	63	37	4.0	.964	C-440

Don Crow

CROW, DONALD LEROY
B. Aug. 18, 1958, Yakima, Wash.
BR TR 6'4" 185 lbs.

Year	Team	Lg	Games	BA	SA	AB	H	2B	3B	HR	HR%	R	RBI	BB	SO	SB	Pinch Hit AB	Pinch Hit H	PO	A	E	DP	TC/G	FA	G by Pos
1982	LA	N	4	.000	.000	4	0	0	0	0	0.0	0	0	0	3	0	0	0	9	1	0	0	2.5	1.000	C-4

George Crowe

CROWE, GEORGE DANIEL
B. Mar. 22, 1921, Whiteland, Ind.
BL TL 6'2" 210 lbs.

Year	Team	Lg	Games	BA	SA	AB	H	2B	3B	HR	HR%	R	RBI	BB	SO	SB	Pinch Hit AB	Pinch Hit H	PO	A	E	DP	TC/G	FA	G by Pos
1952	BOS	N	73	.258	.382	217	56	13	1	4	1.8	25	20	18	25	0	17	5	476	42	8	40	9.6	.985	1B-55
1953	MIL	N	47	.286	.476	42	12	2	0	2	4.8	6	6	2	7	0	37	9	17	2	0	1	2.1	1.000	1B-9
1955			104	.281	.495	303	85	12	4	15	5.0	41	55	45	44	1	21	5	677	61	8	62	9.4	.989	1B-79
1956	CIN	N	77	.250	.486	144	36	2	1	10	6.9	22	23	11	28	0	43	11	225	25	3	15	7.9	.988	1B-32
1957			133	.271	.504	494	134	20	1	31	6.3	71	92	32	62	1	13	5	932	86	11	86	8.6	.989	1B-120
1958			111	.275	.400	345	95	12	5	7	2.0	31	61	41	51	1	20	8	714	53	6	66	8.2	.992	1B-93, 2B-1
1959	STL	N	77	.301	.592	103	31	6	0	8	7.8	14	29	5	12	0	**63**	**17**	82	12	0	9	6.7	1.000	1B-14
1960			73	.236	.444	72	17	3	0	4	5.6	5	13	5	16	0	61	15	21	2	0	1	4.6	1.000	1B-5
1961			7	.143	.143	7	1	0	0	0	0.0	0	0	0	1	0	7	1	0	0	0	0	0.0	—	
9 yrs.			702	.270	.466	1727	467	70	12	81	4.7	215	299	159	246	3	282	76	3144	283	36	280	8.5	.990	1B-407, 2B-1

Bill Crowley

CROWLEY, WILLIAM MICHAEL
B. Apr. 8, 1857, Philadelphia, Pa. D. July 14, 1891, Gloucester, N. J.
BR TR 5'7½" 159 lbs.

Year	Team	Lg	Games	BA	SA	AB	H	2B	3B	HR	HR%	R	RBI	BB	SO	SB	Pinch Hit AB	Pinch Hit H	PO	A	E	DP	TC/G	FA	G by Pos
1877	LOU	N	61	.282	.357	238	67	9	3	1	0.4	30	23	4	13		0	0	123	27	25	2	2.7	.857	OF-58, SS-2, C-2, 3B-1, 2B-1
1879	BUF	N	60	.287	.360	261	75	9	5	0	0.0	41	30	6	14		0	0	182	37	33	12	4.0	.869	OF-43, C-10, 1B-7, 2B-3
1880			85	.268	.336	354	95	16	4	0	0.0	57	20	19	23		0	0	204	46	50	3	3.1	.833	OF-74, C-22
1881	BOS	N	72	.254	.297	279	71	12	0	0	0.0	33	31	14	15		0	0	130	17	20	5	2.3	.880	OF-72
1883	2 teams		PHI AA (23G –.250)	CLE N (11G –.293)																					
"	total		34	.263	.372	137	36	9	3	0	0.0	19		4	7		0	0	59	3	11	0	2.1	.849	OF-33, 1B-1

Bill Crowley *continued*

Year	Team	Games	BA	SA	AB	H	2B	3B	HR	HR%	R	RBI	BB	SO	SB	Pinch Hit AB	Pinch Hit H	PO	A	E	DP	TC/G	FA	G by Pos
1884	BOS N	108	.270	.378	407	110	14	6	6	1.5	50		33	74		0	0	125	22	22	5	1.6	.870	OF-108
1885	BUF N	92	.241	.297	344	83	14	1	1	0.3	29	36	21	32		0	0	152	8	23	1	2.0	.874	OF-92
7 yrs.		512	.266	.341	2020	537	83	22	8	0.4	259	140	101	178		0	0	975	160	184	28	2.5	.861	OF-480, C-34, 1B-8, 2B-4, SS-2, 3B-1

Ed Crowley

CROWLEY, EDGAR JEWEL BR TR 6′ 1″ 180 lbs.
B. Aug. 6, 1906, Watkinsville, Ga. D. Apr. 14, 1970, Birmingham, Ala.

Year	Team	Games	BA	SA	AB	H	2B	3B	HR	HR%	R	RBI	BB	SO	SB	Pinch Hit AB	Pinch Hit H	PO	A	E	DP	TC/G	FA	G by Pos
1928	WAS A	2	.000	.000	1	0	0	0	0	0.0	0	0	0	0	0	0	0	0	0	1	0	1.0	.000	3B-1

John Crowley

CROWLEY, JOHN A. 5′10″ 164 lbs.
B. Jan. 12, 1862, Lawrence, Mass. D. Sept. 23, 1896, Lawrence, Mass.

Year	Team	Games	BA	SA	AB	H	2B	3B	HR	HR%	R	RBI	BB	SO	SB	Pinch Hit AB	Pinch Hit H	PO	A	E	DP	TC/G	FA	G by Pos
1884	PHI N	48	.244	.321	168	41	7	3	0	0.0	26		15	21		0	0	198	49	50	2	6.2	.832	C-48

Terry Crowley

CROWLEY, TERRENCE MICHAEL BL TL 6′ 180 lbs.
B. Feb. 16, 1947, Staten Island, N. Y.

Year	Team	Games	BA	SA	AB	H	2B	3B	HR	HR%	R	RBI	BB	SO	SB	Pinch Hit AB	Pinch Hit H	PO	A	E	DP	TC/G	FA	G by Pos
1969	BAL A	7	.333	.333	18	6	0	0	0	0.0	2	3	1	4	0	2	0	23	2	0	3	5.0	1.000	1B-3, OF-2
1970		83	.257	.388	152	39	5	0	5	3.3	25	20	35	26	2	31	9	138	6	2	9	2.9	.986	OF-27, 1B-23
1971		18	.174	.174	23	4	0	0	0	0.0	2	1	3	4	0	9	4	7	0	0	0	0.9	1.000	OF-6, 1B-2
1972		97	.231	.405	247	57	10	0	11	4.5	30	29	32	26	0	19	4	170	8	1	7	2.2	.994	OF-68, 1B-15
1973		54	.206	.305	131	27	4	0	3	2.3	16	15	16	14	0	14	3	33	5	3	3	1.0	.927	DH-23, OF-10, 1B-7
1974	CIN N	84	.240	.360	125	30	12	0	1	0.8	11	20	10	16	1	52	10	56	5	2	0	2.2	.968	OF-22, 1B-7
1975		66	.268	.394	71	19	6	0	1	1.4	8	11	7	6	0	49	13	43	4	0	4	5.9	1.000	OF-4, 1B-4
1976	2 teams	ATL N (7G –.000) BAL A (33G –.246)																						
″	total	40	.224	.239	67	15	1	0	0	0.0	5	6	7	11	0	23	4	13	2	0	1	0.8	1.000	DH-17, 1B-1
1977	BAL A	18	.364	.545	22	8	1	0	1	4.5	3	9	1	3	0	15	7	3	0	0	0	1.0	1.000	DH-2, 1B-1
1978		62	.253	.274	95	24	2	0	0	0.0	9	12	8	12	0	38	13	1	1	0	0	0.1	1.000	DH-17, OF-2, 1B-1
1979		61	.317	.476	63	20	5	1	1	1.6	8	8	14	13	0	39	11	5	0	0	1	0.3	1.000	DH-15, 1B-2
1980		92	.288	.476	233	67	8	0	12	5.2	33	50	29	21	0	**37**	11	19	5	0	1	0.4	1.000	DH-65, 1B-3
1981		68	.246	.381	134	33	6	0	4	3.0	12	25	29	12	0	21	6	30	2	0	2	0.7	1.000	DH-42, 1B-4
1982		65	.237	.355	93	22	2	0	3	3.2	8	17	21	9	0	35	7	74	6	1	12	3.4	.988	DH-14, 1B-10
1983	MON N	50	.182	.182	44	8	0	0	0	0.0	2	3	9	4	0	35	6	19	0	0	2	4.8	1.000	1B-4
15 yrs.		865	.250	.375	1518	379	62	1	42	2.8	174	229	222	181	3	419	108 **8th**	634	46	9	45	1.6	.987	DH-195, OF-141, 1B-87
LEAGUE CHAMPIONSHIP SERIES																								
1973	BAL A	2	.000	.000	2	0	0	0	0	0.0	0	0	0	0	0	2	0	1	0	0	0	1.0	1.000	OF-1
1975	CIN N	1	—	—	0	0	0	0	0	—	0	0	0	0	0	0	0	0	0	0	0	0.0	—	
1979	BAL A	2	.500	.500	2	1	0	0	0	0.0	0	1	0	0	0	2	1	0	0	0	0	0.0	—	
3 yrs.		5	.250	.250	4	1	0	0	0	0.0	0	1	0	0	0	4	1	1	0	0	0	1.0	1.000	OF-1
WORLD SERIES																								
1970	BAL A	1	.000	.000	1	0	0	0	0	0.0	0	0	0	0	0	1	0	0	0	0	0	0.0	—	
1975	CIN N	2	.500	.500	2	1	0	0	0	0.0	0	0	0	1	0	2	1	0	0	0	0	0.0	—	
1979	BAL A	5	.250	.500	4	1	1	0	0	0.0	0	2	1	0	0	4	1	0	0	0	0	0.0	—	
3 yrs.		8	.286	.429	7	2	1	0	0	0.0	0	2	1	1	0	7	2							

Walt Cruise

CRUISE, WALTON EDWIN BL TR 6′ 175 lbs.
B. May 6, 1890, Childersburg, Ala. D. Jan. 9, 1975, Sylacauga, Ala.

Year	Team	Games	BA	SA	AB	H	2B	3B	HR	HR%	R	RBI	BB	SO	SB	Pinch Hit AB	Pinch Hit H	PO	A	E	DP	TC/G	FA	G by Pos
1914	STL N	95	.227	.332	256	58	9	3	4	1.6	20	28	25	42	3	11	3	158	6	4	1	2.1	.976	OF-81
1916		3	.667	.667	3	2	0	0	0	0.0	0	0	1	0	0	1	1	2	0	0	0	1.0	1.000	OF-2
1917		153	.295	.399	529	156	20	10	5	0.9	70	59	38	73	16	1	1	285	15	11	6	2.0	.965	OF-152
1918		70	.271	.400	240	65	5	4	6	2.5	34	39	30	26	2	5	0	103	4	4	0	1.7	.964	OF-65
1919	2 teams	STL N (9G –.095) BOS N (73G –.216)																						
″	total	82	.206	.248	262	54	8	0	1	0.4	23	21	18	35	8	9	2	135	8	4	1	2.0	.973	OF-71, 1B-2
1920	BOS N	91	.278	.347	288	80	7	5	1	0.3	40	21	31	26	5	6	1	122	10	7	3	1.7	.950	OF-82
1921		108	.346	.503	344	119	16	7	8	2.3	47	55	48	24	10	3	2	252	4	9	3	2.5	.966	OF-102, 1B-2
1922		104	.278	.412	352	98	15	10	4	1.1	51	46	44	20	4	2	0	237	11	12	4	2.5	.954	OF-100, 1B-2
1923		21	.211	.263	38	8	2	0	0	0.0	4	0	3	2	1	9	2	20	0	1	0	2.3	.952	OF-9
1924		9	.444	.889	9	4	1	0	1	11.1	4	3	0	2	0	9	4	0	0	0	0	0.0	—	
10 yrs.		736	.277	.386	2321	644	83	39	30	1.3	293	272	238	250	49	56	16	1314	58	52	18	2.1	.963	OF-664, 1B-6

Gene Crumling

CRUMLING, EUGENE LEON BR TR 6′ 180 lbs.
B. Apr. 5, 1922, Wrightsville, Pa.

Year	Team	Games	BA	SA	AB	H	2B	3B	HR	HR%	R	RBI	BB	SO	SB	Pinch Hit AB	Pinch Hit H	PO	A	E	DP	TC/G	FA	G by Pos
1945	STL N	6	.083	.083	12	1	0	0	0	0.0	0	1	0	1	0	0	0	16	4	0	0	3.3	1.000	C-6

Buddy Crump

CRUMP, ARTHUR ELLIOTT BL TL 5′10″ 156 lbs.
B. Nov. 29, 1901, Norfolk, Va. D. Sept. 7, 1976, Raleigh, N. C.

Year	Team	Games	BA	SA	AB	H	2B	3B	HR	HR%	R	RBI	BB	SO	SB	Pinch Hit AB	Pinch Hit H	PO	A	E	DP	TC/G	FA	G by Pos
1924	NY N	1	.000	.000	4	0	0	0	0	0.0	0	1	0	1	0	0	0	2	0	2	0	4.0	.500	OF-1

Press Cruthers

CRUTHERS, CHARLES PRESTON BR TR 5′ 9″ 152 lbs.
B. Sept. 8, 1890, Marshallton, Del. D. Dec. 27, 1976, Kenosha, Wis.

Year	Team	Games	BA	SA	AB	H	2B	3B	HR	HR%	R	RBI	BB	SO	SB	Pinch Hit AB	Pinch Hit H	PO	A	E	DP	TC/G	FA	G by Pos
1913	PHI A	3	.250	.333	12	3	1	0	0	0.0	0	0	0	0	0	0	0	7	5	1	1	4.3	.923	2B-3
1914		4	.200	.333	15	3	0	1	0	0.0	1	0	0	4	0	0	0	13	11	0	1	6.0	1.000	2B-4
2 yrs.		7	.222	.333	27	6	1	1	0	0.0	1	0	0	4	0	0	0	20	16	1	2	5.3	.973	2B-7

Fausto Cruz

CRUZ, FAUSTO SANTIAGO BR TR 5′10″ 165 lbs.
B. May 1, 1972, Monte Cristi, Dominican Republic.

Year	Team	Games	BA	SA	AB	H	2B	3B	HR	HR%	R	RBI	BB	SO	SB	Pinch Hit AB	Pinch Hit H	PO	A	E	DP	TC/G	FA	G by Pos
1994	OAK A	17	.107	.107	28	3	0	0	0	0.0	2	0	4	6	0	4	0	17	23	2	3	2.8	.952	SS-10, 3B-4, 2B-1
1995		8	.217	.217	23	5	0	0	0	0.0	0	5	3	5	1	0	0	9	24	1	2	4.3	.971	SS-8
2 yrs.		25	.157	.157	51	8	0	0	0	0.0	2	5	7	11	1	4	0	26	47	3	5	3.3	.961	SS-18, 3B-4, 2B-1

Hector Cruz

CRUZ, HECTOR LOUIS (Heity)
Born Hector Louis Cruz (Dilan).
Brother of Tommy Cruz. Brother of Jose Cruz.
B. Apr. 2, 1953, Arroyo, Puerto Rico.

BR TR 5′11″ 170 lbs.

Year	Team	Games	BA	SA	AB	H	2B	3B	HR	HR%	R	RBI	BB	SO	SB	Pinch Hit AB	Pinch Hit H	PO	A	E	DP	TC/G	FA	G by Pos
1973	STL N	11	.000	.000	11	0	0	0	0	0.0	1	0	1	3	0	4	0	7	0	0	0	1.4	1.000	OF-5
1975		23	.146	.271	48	7	2	2	0	0.0	7	6	2	4	0	6	1	20	4	3	0	1.5	.889	3B-12, OF-6
1976		151	.228	.338	526	120	17	1	13	2.5	54	71	42	119	1	3	0	100	270	26	19	2.7	.934	3B-148
1977		118	.236	.357	339	80	19	2	6	1.8	50	42	46	56	2	15	2	154	10	7	2	1.6	.959	OF-106, 3B-2
1978	2 teams	CHI N (30G –.237) SF N (79G –.223)																						
″	total	109	.227	.370	273	62	13	1	8	2.9	27	33	24	45	0	30	7	117	32	2	3	1.7	.987	OF-67, 3B-21
1979	2 teams	SF N (16G –.120) CIN N (74G –.242)																						
″	total	90	.227	.353	207	47	10	2	4	1.9	26	28	34	46	0	16	2	127	10	3	4	1.8	.979	OF-75, 3B-2
1980	CIN N	52	.213	.333	75	16	4	1	1	1.3	5	5	8	16	0	22	1	42	0	2	0	1.5	.955	OF-29
1981	CHI N	53	.229	.468	109	25	5	0	7	6.4	15	15	17	24	2	17	3	33	26	3	0	1.8	.952	3B-18, OF-16
1982		17	.211	.263	19	4	1	0	0	0.0	1	0	2	4	0	15	3	1	0	0	0	0.3	1.000	OF-4
9 yrs.		624	.225	.353	1607	361	71	9	39	2.4	186	200	176	317	5	128	19	601	352	46	28	2.0	.954	OF-308, 3B-203
LEAGUE CHAMPIONSHIP SERIES																								
1979	CIN N	2	.200	.400	5	1	1	0	0	0.0	1	0	0	1	0	1	1	3	0	0	0	3.0	1.000	OF-1

Henry Cruz

CRUZ, HENRY ACOSTA
B. Feb. 27, 1952, Christiansted, Virgin Islands.

BL TL 6′ 175 lbs.

Year	Team	Games	BA	SA	AB	H	2B	3B	HR	HR%	R	RBI	BB	SO	SB	Pinch Hit AB	Pinch Hit H	PO	A	E	DP	TC/G	FA	G by Pos
1975	LA N	53	.266	.319	94	25	3	1	0	0.0	8	5	7	6	1	14	2	48	0	2	0	1.2	.960	OF-41
1976		49	.182	.364	88	16	2	1	4	4.5	8	14	9	11	0	20	3	39	1	1	1	1.8	.976	OF-23
1977	CHI A	16	.286	.571	21	6	0	0	2	9.5	3	5	1	3	0	1	0	5	0	1	0	0.7	.833	OF-9
1978		53	.221	.351	77	17	2	1	2	2.6	13	10	8	11	0	11	1	55	4	0	2	1.4	1.000	OF-40, DH-1
4 yrs.		171	.229	.361	280	64	7	3	8	2.9	32	34	25	31	1	46	6	147	5	4	3	1.4	.974	OF-113, DH-1

Jose Cruz

CRUZ, JOSE (Cheo)
Born Jose Cruz (Dilan).
Brother of Hector Cruz. Brother of Tommy Cruz.
B. Aug. 8, 1947, Arroyo, Puerto Rico.

BL TL 6′ 170 lbs.

Year	Team	Games	BA	SA	AB	H	2B	3B	HR	HR%	R	RBI	BB	SO	SB	Pinch Hit AB	Pinch Hit H	PO	A	E	DP	TC/G	FA	G by Pos
1970	STL N	6	.353	.412	17	6	1	0	0	0.0	2	1	4	0	0	1	1	16	0	0	0	4.0	1.000	OF-4
1971		83	.274	.425	292	80	13	2	9	3.1	46	27	49	35	6	2	1	197	2	5	1	2.5	.975	OF-83
1972		117	.235	.319	332	78	14	4	2	0.6	33	23	36	54	9	13	5	220	9	5	5	2.3	.979	OF-102
1973		132	.227	.379	406	92	22	5	10	2.5	51	57	51	66	10	14	3	276	2	6	1	2.4	.979	OF-118
1974		107	.261	.416	161	42	4	3	5	3.1	24	20	20	27	4	47	11	81	2	2	3	1.6	.976	OF-53, 1B-1
1975	HOU N	120	.257	.403	315	81	15	2	9	2.9	44	49	52	44	6	28	6	187	6	4	0	2.1	.980	OF-94
1976		133	.303	.401	439	133	21	5	4	0.9	49	61	53	46	28	10	3	265	10	8	4	2.3	.972	OF-125
1977		157	.299	.475	579	173	31	10	17	2.9	87	87	69	67	44	4	1	311	11	9	1	2.1	.973	OF-155
1978		153	.315	.460	565	178	34	9	10	1.8	79	83	57	57	37	1	0	328	5	8	1	2.2	.977	OF-152, 1B-2
1979		157	.289	.421	558	161	33	7	9	1.6	73	72	72	66	36	1	0	320	7	14	0	2.2	.959	OF-156
1980		160	.302	.426	612	185	29	7	11	1.8	79	91	60	66	36	2	0	323	16	11	1	2.2	.969	OF-158
1981		107	.267	.425	409	109	16	5	13	3.2	53	55	35	49	5	2	1	237	5	4	2	2.3	.984	OF-105
1982		155	.275	.377	570	157	27	2	9	1.6	62	68	60	67	21	2	1	340	9	13	3	2.3	.964	OF-155
1983		160	.318	.463	594	**189**	28	8	14	2.4	85	92	65	86	30	2	1	322	9	7	1	2.1	.979	OF-160
1984		160	.312	.462	600	187	28	13	12	2.0	96	95	73	68	22	1	0	310	11	8	1	2.1	.976	OF-160
1985		141	.300	.426	544	163	34	4	9	1.7	69	79	43	74	16	3	0	257	12	8	3	2.0	.971	OF-137
1986		141	.278	.403	479	133	22	4	10	2.1	48	72	55	86	3	8	1	237	5	4	1	1.8	.984	OF-134
1987		126	.241	.400	365	88	17	4	11	3.0	47	38	36	65	4	29	5	178	5	3	3	1.9	.984	OF-97
1988	NY A	38	.200	.263	80	16	2	0	1	1.3	9	7	8	8	0	19	3	8	0	1	0	0.4	.889	DH-12, OF-8
19 yrs.		2353	.284	.420	7917	2251	391	94	165	2.1	1036	1077	898	1031	317	189	43	4413	126	120	31	2.1	.974	OF-2156, DH-12, 1B-3
DIVISIONAL PLAYOFF SERIES																								
1981	HOU N	5	.300	.350	20	6	1	0	0	0.0	0	0	1	3	1	0	0	15	0	1	0	3.2	.938	OF-5
LEAGUE CHAMPIONSHIP SERIES																								
1980	HOU N	5	.400	.600	15	6	1	1	0	0.0	3	4	8	1	0	0	0	19	0	0	0	3.8	1.000	OF-5
1986		6	.192	.192	26	5	0	0	0	0.0	0	2	1	8	0	0	0	11	0	0	0	1.8	1.000	OF-6
2 yrs.		11	.268	.341	41	11	1	1	0	0.0	3	6	9	9	0	0	0	30	0	0	0	2.7	1.000	OF-11

Julio Cruz

CRUZ, JULIO LOUIS
B. Dec. 2, 1954, Brooklyn, N. Y.

BB TR 5′ 9″ 165 lbs.

Year	Team	Games	BA	SA	AB	H	2B	3B	HR	HR%	R	RBI	BB	SO	SB	Pinch Hit AB	Pinch Hit H	PO	A	E	DP	TC/G	FA	G by Pos
1977	SEA A	60	.256	.296	199	51	3	1	1	0.5	25	7	24	29	15	2	0	114	171	5	29	5.3	.983	2B-54, DH-1
1978		147	.235	.269	550	129	14	1	1	0.2	77	25	69	66	59	0	0	295	482	11	104	5.4	.986	2B-141, SS-5, DH-1
1979		107	.271	.326	414	112	16	2	1	0.2	70	29	62	61	49	0	0	258	361	13	87	5.9	.979	2B-107
1980		119	.209	.258	422	88	9	3	2	0.5	66	16	59	49	45	0	0	269	355	11	85	5.4	.983	2B-115, DH-3
1981		94	.256	.324	352	90	12	3	2	0.6	57	24	39	40	43	1	0	240	297	11	72	5.9	.980	2B-92, SS-1
1982		154	.242	.344	549	133	22	5	8	1.5	83	49	57	71	46	0	0	322	438	10	98	4.9	.987	2B-151, SS-2, DH-2, 3B-1
1983	2 teams	SEA A (61G –.254) CHI A (99G –.251)																						
″	total	160	.252	.326	515	130	19	5	3	0.6	71	52	49	66	57	1	1	344	471	14	112	5.2	.983	2B-157, DH-1
1984	CHI A	143	.222	.311	415	92	14	4	5	1.2	42	43	45	58	14	0	0	273	452	18	92	5.3	.976	2B-141
1985		91	.197	.231	234	46	2	3	0	0.0	28	15	32	40	8	6	3	158	220	7	59	4.3	.982	2B-87, DH-2
1986		81	.215	.225	209	45	2	0	0	0.0	38	19	42	28	7	0	0	132	205	5	45	4.2	.985	2B-78, DH-3
10 yrs.		1156	.237	.299	3859	916	113	27	23	0.6	557	279	478	508	343	10	4	2405	3452	105	783	5.2	.982	2B-1123, DH-13, SS-8, 3B-1
LEAGUE CHAMPIONSHIP SERIES																								
1983	CHI A	4	.333	.333	12	4	0	0	0	0.0	0	0	3	4	2	0	0	10	14	0	2	6.0	1.000	2B-4

Todd Cruz

CRUZ, TODD RUBEN
B. Nov. 23, 1955, Highland Park, Mich.

BR TR 6′ 175 lbs.

Year	Team	Games	BA	SA	AB	H	2B	3B	HR	HR%	R	RBI	BB	SO	SB	Pinch Hit AB	Pinch Hit H	PO	A	E	DP	TC/G	FA	G by Pos
1978	PHI N	3	.500	.500	4	2	0	0	0	0.0	0	2	0	0	0	0	0	1	6	0	0	3.5	1.000	SS-2
1979	KC A	55	.203	.314	118	24	7	0	2	1.7	9	15	3	19	0	0	0	54	118	7	16	3.1	.961	SS-48, 3B-9
1980	2 teams	CAL A (18G –.275) CHI A (90G –.232)																						
″	total	108	.237	.312	333	79	14	1	3	0.9	28	23	14	62	2	2	1	156	323	28	68	4.7	.945	SS-102, 3B-4, OF-1, 2B-1

Todd Cruz *continued*

Year	Team	Games	BA	SA	AB	H	2B	3B	HR	HR%	R	RBI	BB	SO	SB	Pinch Hit AB	Pinch Hit H	PO	A	E	DP	TC/G	FA	G by Pos
1982	SEA A	136	.230	.376	492	113	20	2	16	3.3	44	57	12	95	2	0	0	215	439	25	98	5.0	.963	SS-136
1983	2 teams	SEA A (65G –.190) BAL A (81G –.208)																						
"	total	146	.199	.311	437	87	13	3	10	2.3	37	48	22	108	4	5	2	146	386	25	61	3.9	.955	3B-79, SS-63, 2B-2
1984	BAL A	96	.218	.310	142	31	4	0	3	2.1	15	9	8	33	1	14	5	23	104	6	10	1.5	.955	3B-89, DH-1, P-1
6 yrs.		544	.220	.333	1526	336	58	6	34	2.2	133	154	59	317	9	21	8	595	1376	91	253	3.8	.956	SS-351, 3B-181, 2B-3, P-1, DH-1, OF-1
LEAGUE CHAMPIONSHIP SERIES																								
1983	BAL A	4	.133	.133	15	2	0	0	0	0.0	0	1	0	5	0	0	0	6	11	0	1	4.3	1.000	3B-4
WORLD SERIES																								
1983	BAL A	5	.125	.125	16	2	0	0	0	0.0	1	0	1	3	0	0	0	0	17	2	1	3.8	.895	3B-5

Tommy Cruz

CRUZ, CIRILO BL TL 5′ 9″ 165 lbs.
Born Cirilo Cruz (Dilan).
Brother of Hector Cruz. Brother of Jose Cruz.
B. Feb. 15, 1951, Arroyo, Puerto Rico.

Year	Team	Games	BA	SA	AB	H	2B	3B	HR	HR%	R	RBI	BB	SO	SB	Pinch Hit AB	Pinch Hit H	PO	A	E	DP	TC/G	FA	G by Pos
1973	STL N	3	—	—	0	0	0	0	0	—	1	0	0	0	0	0	0	0	0	0	0	0.0	.000	OF-1
1977	CHI A	4	.000	.000	2	0	0	0	0	0.0	1	0	0	0	0	1	0	1	0	0	0	0.5	1.000	OF-2
2 yrs.		7	.000	.000	2	0	0	0	0	0.0	2	0	0	0	0	1	0	1	0	0	0	0.3	1.000	OF-3

Mike Cubbage

CUBBAGE, MICHAEL LEE BL TR 6′ 180 lbs.
B. July 21, 1950, Charlottesville, Va.
Manager 1991.

Year	Team	Games	BA	SA	AB	H	2B	3B	HR	HR%	R	RBI	BB	SO	SB	Pinch Hit AB	Pinch Hit H	PO	A	E	DP	TC/G	FA	G by Pos
1974	TEX A	9	.000	.000	15	0	0	0	0	0.0	0	0	0	4	0	4	0	7	9	1	4	3.4	.941	3B-3, 2B-2
1975		58	.224	.350	143	32	6	0	4	2.8	12	21	18	14	0	16	1	68	115	8	24	4.5	.958	2B-37, 3B-3, DH-2
1976	2 teams	TEX A (14G –.219) MIN A (104G –.260)																						
"	total	118	.257	.358	374	96	19	5	3	0.8	42	49	49	44	1	8	3	80	218	19	25	2.8	.940	3B-100, DH-8, 2B-7
1977	MIN A	129	.264	.391	417	110	16	5	9	2.2	60	55	37	49	1	13	2	90	266	18	29	2.9	.952	3B-126, DH-1
1978		125	.282	.401	394	111	12	7	7	1.8	40	57	40	44	3	22	8	69	237	9	25	2.6	.971	3B-115, 2B-5
1979		94	.276	.350	243	67	10	1	2	0.8	26	23	39	26	1	17	3	38	94	10	9	1.7	.930	3B-63, DH-21, 1B-1, 2B-1
1980		103	.246	.361	285	70	9	0	8	2.8	29	42	23	37	0	9	4	545	100	4	64	6.1	.994	1B-72, 3B-32, DH-1, 2B-1
1981	NY N	67	.212	.325	80	17	2	2	1	1.3	9	4	9	15	0	**44**	**12**	5	21	1	0	2.3	.963	3B-12
8 yrs.		703	.258	.369	1951	503	74	20	34	1.7	218	251	215	233	6	133	33	902	1060	70	180	3.3	.966	3B-454, 1B-73, 2B-53, DH-33

Al Cuccinello

CUCCINELLO, ALFRED EDWARD BR TR 5′10″ 165 lbs.
Brother of Tony Cuccinello.
B. Nov. 26, 1914, Long Island City, N. Y.

Year	Team	Games	BA	SA	AB	H	2B	3B	HR	HR%	R	RBI	BB	SO	SB	Pinch Hit AB	Pinch Hit H	PO	A	E	DP	TC/G	FA	G by Pos
1935	NY N	54	.248	.376	165	41	7	1	4	2.4	27	20	1	20	0	3	2	114	140	13	26	5.3	.951	2B-48, 3B-2

Tony Cuccinello

CUCCINELLO, ANTHONY FRANCIS (Chick) BR TR 5′ 7″ 160 lbs.
Brother of Al Cuccinello.
B. Nov. 8, 1907, Long Island City, N. Y. D. Sept. 19, 1995, Tampa, Fla.

Year	Team	Games	BA	SA	AB	H	2B	3B	HR	HR%	R	RBI	BB	SO	SB	Pinch Hit AB	Pinch Hit H	PO	A	E	DP	TC/G	FA	G by Pos
1930	CIN N	125	.312	.451	443	138	22	5	10	2.3	64	78	47	44	5	3	1	111	211	26	23	2.7	.925	3B-109, 2B-15, SS-4
1931		154	.315	.431	575	181	39	11	2	0.3	67	93	54	28	1	0	0	376	499	28	128	5.9	.969	2B-154
1932	BKN N	154	.281	.415	597	168	32	6	12	2.0	76	77	46	47	5	0	0	385	525	25	113	6.1	.973	2B-154
1933		134	.252	.388	485	122	31	4	9	1.9	58	65	44	40	4	0	0	329	359	17	67	5.3	.976	2B-120, 3B-14
1934		140	.261	.409	528	138	32	2	14	2.7	59	94	49	45	0	1	1	300	417	21	60	5.1	.972	2B-101, 3B-43
1935		102	.292	.431	360	105	20	3	8	2.2	49	53	40	35	3	4	1	192	250	13	57	4.6	.971	2B-64, 3B-36
1936	BOS N	150	.308	.402	565	174	26	3	7	1.2	68	86	58	49	1	0	0	383	559	28	128	6.5	.971	2B-150
1937		152	.271	.405	575	156	36	4	11	1.9	77	80	61	40	2	1	0	330	524	29	92	5.8	.967	2B-151
1938		147	.265	.366	555	147	25	2	9	1.6	62	76	52	32	4	0	0	323	458	21	84	5.5	.974	2B-147
1939		81	.306	.387	310	95	17	1	2	0.6	42	40	26	26	5	1	0	208	246	14	66	5.8	.970	2B-80
1940	2 teams	BOS N (34G –.270) NY N (88G –.208)																						
"	total	122	.226	.312	433	98	18	2	5	1.2	40	55	24	51	2	6	1	166	268	9	28	3.8	.980	3B-70, 2B-47
1942	BOS N	40	.202	.260	104	21	3	0	1	1.0	8	8	9	11	1	5	2	34	67	4	13	3.1	.962	3B-20, 2B-14
1943	2 teams	BOS N (13G –.000) CHI A (34G –.272)																						
"	total	47	.230	.320	122	28	5	0	2	1.6	5	13	16	14	3	7	0	40	60	4	7	2.8	.962	3B-34, 2B-2, SS-1
1944	CHI A	38	.262	.285	130	34	3	0	0	0.0	5	17	8	16	0	2	0	42	73	5	7	3.3	.958	3B-30, 2B-6
1945		118	.308	.400	402	124	25	3	2	0.5	50	49	45	19	6	6	1	73	221	20	22	2.8	.936	3B-112
15 yrs.		1704	.280	.394	6184	1729	334	46	94	1.5	730	884	579	497	42	36	7	3292	4737	264	895	4.9	.968	2B-1205, 3B-468, SS-5

Jim Cudworth

CUDWORTH, JAMES ALARIC BR TR 6′ 165 lbs.
B. Aug. 22, 1858, Fairhaven, Mass. D. Dec. 21, 1943, Middleboro, Mass.

Year	Team	Games	BA	SA	AB	H	2B	3B	HR	HR%	R	RBI	BB	SO	SB	Pinch Hit AB	Pinch Hit H	PO	A	E	DP	TC/G	FA	G by Pos
1884	KC U	32	.147	.190	116	17	3	1	0	0.0	7		2			0	0	202	9	8	10	6.6	.963	1B-19, OF-12, P-2

Manuel Cueto

CUETO, MANUEL BR TR 5′ 5″ 157 lbs.
Born Manuel Melo Cueto (Melo).
B. Feb. 8, 1892, Guanajay, Cuba D. June 29, 1942, Regla, Cuba.

Year	Team	Games	BA	SA	AB	H	2B	3B	HR	HR%	R	RBI	BB	SO	SB	Pinch Hit AB	Pinch Hit H	PO	A	E	DP	TC/G	FA	G by Pos
1914	STL F	19	.093	.093	43	4	0	0	0	0.0	2	2	5		0	1	0	23	22	6	3	3.0	.882	3B-10, SS-5, 2B-2
1917	CIN N	56	.200	.243	140	28	3	0	1	0.7	10	11	16	17	4	5	0	89	26	5	1	2.4	.958	OF-38, 2B-6, C-5
1918		46	.296	.361	108	32	5	1	0	0.0	14	14	19	5	4	2	0	60	43	6	2	2.5	.945	OF-20, SS-9, 2B-9, C-6
1919		29	.250	.273	88	22	2	0	0	0.0	10	4	10	4	5	3	0	49	8	2	3	2.3	.966	OF-25, 3B-1
4 yrs.		150	.227	.266	379	86	10	1	1	0.3	36	31	50	26	13	11	0	221	99	19	9	2.5	.944	OF-83, 2B-17, SS-14, C-11, 3B-11

John Cuff

CUFF, JOHN J.
B. June 1864, Jersey City, N. J. Deceased.

Year	Team	Games	BA	SA	AB	H	2B	3B	HR	HR%	R	RBI	BB	SO	SB	Pinch Hit AB	Pinch Hit H	PO	A	E	DP	TC/G	FA	G by Pos
1884	BAL U	3	.091	.182	11	1	1	0	0	0.0	1		1			0	0	12	11	2	1	8.3	.920	C-3

Leon Culberson

CULBERSON, DELBERT LEON BR TR 5′11″ 180 lbs.
B. Aug. 6, 1919, Hall's Station, Ga. D. Sept. 17, 1989, Rome, Ga.

Year	Team	Games	BA	SA	AB	H	2B	3B	HR	HR%	R	RBI	BB	SO	SB	Pinch Hit AB	Pinch Hit H	PO	A	E	DP	TC/G	FA	G by Pos
1943	BOS A	81	.272	.391	312	85	16	6	3	1.0	36	34	31	35	14	1	0	211	10	5	2	2.9	.978	OF-79
1944		75	.238	.333	282	67	11	5	2	0.7	41	21	20	20	6	1	0	182	6	4	2	2.7	.979	OF-72

Leon Culberson *continued*

Year	Team	Games	BA	SA	AB	H	2B	3B	HR	HR%	R	RBI	BB	SO	SB	Pinch Hit AB	Pinch Hit H	PO	A	E	DP	TC/G	FA	G by Pos
1945		97	.275	.429	331	91	21	6	6	1.8	26	45	20	37	4	6	1	219	14	8	6	2.6	.967	OF-91
1946		59	.313	.430	179	56	10	1	3	1.7	34	18	16	19	3	4	0	89	10	5	2	2.0	.952	OF-49, 3B-4
1947		47	.238	.250	84	20	1	0	0	0.0	10	11	12	10	1	20	3	36	6	2	1	1.5	.955	OF-25, 3B-4
1948	WAS A	12	.172	.172	29	5	0	0	0	0.0	1	2	8	5	0	1	0	16	1	0	0	1.5	1.000	OF-11
6 yrs.		371	.266	.379	1217	324	59	18	14	1.2	148	131	107	126	28	33	4	753	47	24	13	2.5	.971	OF-327, 3B-8
WORLD SERIES																								
1946	BOS A	5	.222	.556	9	2	0	0	1	11.1	1	1	1	2	1	2	0	7	0	0	0	2.3	1.000	OF-3

John Cullen

CULLEN, JOHN J.
Deceased.

Year	Team	Games	BA	SA	AB	H	2B	3B	HR	HR%	R	RBI	BB	SO	SB	Pinch Hit AB	Pinch Hit H	PO	A	E	DP	TC/G	FA	G by Pos
1884	WIL U	9	.194	.194	31	6	0	0	0	0.0	2		1			0	0	9	8	9	0	2.9	.654	OF-6, SS-3

Tim Cullen

CULLEN, TIMOTHY LEO
B. Feb. 16, 1942, San Francisco, Calif.
BR TR 6′ 1″ 185 lbs.

Year	Team	Games	BA	SA	AB	H	2B	3B	HR	HR%	R	RBI	BB	SO	SB	Pinch Hit AB	Pinch Hit H	PO	A	E	DP	TC/G	FA	G by Pos
1966	WAS A	18	.235	.265	34	8	1	0	0	0.0	8	0	2	8	0	6	1	14	19	2	4	2.7	.943	3B-8, 2B-5
1967		124	.236	.269	402	95	7	0	2	0.5	35	31	40	47	4	2	0	219	361	27	67	4.6	.956	SS-69, 2B-46, 3B-15, OF-1
1968	2 teams	CHI A (72G –.200)	WAS A (47G –.272)																					
″	total	119	.230	.320	269	62	11	2	3	1.1	24	29	22	35	0	4	2	173	247	16	51	3.5	.963	2B-87, SS-33, 3B-3
1969	WAS A	119	.209	.249	249	52	7	0	1	0.4	22	15	14	27	1	10	2	173	211	10	47	3.4	.975	2B-105, SS-9, 3B-1
1970		123	.214	.279	262	56	10	2	1	0.4	22	18	31	38	3	12	1	212	265	3	65	4.1	.994	2B-112, SS-6
1971		125	.191	.258	403	77	13	4	2	0.5	34	26	33	47	2	1	0	262	379	11	86	4.7	.983	2B-78, SS-62
1972	OAK A	72	.261	.331	142	37	8	1	0	0.0	10	15	5	17	0	3	1	107	121	11	24	3.4	.954	2B-65, 3B-4, SS-1
7 yrs.		700	.220	.278	1761	387	57	9	9	0.5	155	134	147	219	10	38	7	1160	1603	80	344	4.0	.972	2B-498, SS-180, 3B-31, OF-1
LEAGUE CHAMPIONSHIP SERIES																								
1972	OAK A	2	.000	.000	1	0	0	0	0	0.0	0	0	0	0	0	0	0	0	2	0	1	1.0	1.000	SS-2

Roy Cullenbine

CULLENBINE, ROY JOSEPH
B. Oct. 18, 1913, Nashville, Tenn. D. May 28, 1991, Mt. Clemens, Mich.
BB TR 6′ 1″ 195 lbs.

Year	Team	Games	BA	SA	AB	H	2B	3B	HR	HR%	R	RBI	BB	SO	SB	Pinch Hit AB	Pinch Hit H	PO	A	E	DP	TC/G	FA	G by Pos
1938	DET A	25	.284	.388	67	19	1	3	0	0.0	12	9	12	9	2	7	2	34	1	0	0	2.1	1.000	OF-17
1939		75	.240	.413	179	43	9	2	6	3.4	31	23	34	29	0	25	7	104	4	9	5	2.4	.923	OF-46, 1B-2
1940	2 teams	BKN N (22G –.180)	STL A (86G –.230)																					
″	total	108	.220	.346	318	70	12	2	8	2.5	49	40	73	45	2	21	3	191	10	3	6	2.5	.985	OF-76, 1B-6
1941	STL A	149	.317	.465	501	159	29	9	9	1.8	82	98	121	43	6	9	3	451	32	14	24	3.5	.972	OF-120, 1B-22
1942	3 teams	STL A (38G –.193)	WAS A (64G –.286)	NY A (21G –.364)																				
″	total	123	.276	.400	427	118	33	1	6	1.4	61	66	92	40	1	6	1	273	82	17	10	3.4	.954	OF-77, 3B-28, 1B-6
1943	CLE A	138	.289	.404	488	141	24	4	8	1.6	66	56	96	58	3	5	0	376	23	7	15	3.0	.983	OF-121, 1B-13
1944		154	.284	.445	571	162	34	5	16	2.8	98	80	87	49	4	2	0	275	15	10	6	2.0	.967	OF-151
1945	2 teams	CLE A (8G –.077)	DET A (146G –.277)																					
″	total	154	.272	.444	536	146	28	5	18	3.4	83	93	**112**	36	2	1	0	329	26	8	3	2.4	.978	OF-150, 3B-3
1946	DET A	113	.335	.537	328	110	21	0	15	4.6	63	56	88	39	3	9	2	293	30	8	15	3.2	.976	OF-81, 1B-21
1947		142	.224	.422	464	104	18	1	24	5.2	82	78	137	51	3	4	0	1184	139	15	111	9.7	.989	1B-138
10 yrs.		1181	.276	.432	3879	1072	209	32	110	2.8	627	599	852	399	26	89	18	3510	362	91	195	3.7	.977	OF-839, 1B-208, 3B-31
WORLD SERIES																								
1942	NY A	5	.263	.316	19	5	1	0	0	0.0	3	2	1	2	1	0	0	6	0	0	0	1.2	1.000	OF-5
1945	DET A	7	.227	.318	22	5	2	0	0	0.0	5	4	8	2	1	0	0	8	0	0	0	1.1	1.000	OF-7
2 yrs.		12	.244	.317	41	10	3	0	0	0.0	8	6	9	4	2	0	0	14	0	0	0	1.2	1.000	OF-12

Dick Culler

CULLER, RICHARD BROADUS
B. Jan. 15, 1915, High Point, N. C. D. June 16, 1964, Chapel Hill, N. C.
BR TR 5′ 9½″ 155 lbs.

Year	Team	Games	BA	SA	AB	H	2B	3B	HR	HR%	R	RBI	BB	SO	SB	Pinch Hit AB	Pinch Hit H	PO	A	E	DP	TC/G	FA	G by Pos
1936	PHI A	9	.237	.237	38	9	0	0	0	0.0	3	1	1	3	0	0	0	20	19	2	4	4.6	.951	2B-7, SS-2
1943	CHI A	53	.216	.264	148	32	5	1	0	0.0	9	11	16	11	4	0	0	71	121	8	24	4.2	.960	3B-26, 2B-19, SS-3
1944	BOS N	8	.071	.071	28	2	0	0	0	0.0	2	0	4	2	0	0	0	14	33	5	6	6.5	.904	SS-8
1945		136	.262	.300	527	138	12	1	2	0.4	87	30	50	35	7	1	0	261	400	34	81	5.3	.951	SS-126, 3B-6
1946		134	.255	.299	482	123	15	3	0	0.0	70	33	62	18	7	2	1	279	380	36	68	5.3	.948	SS-132
1947		77	.248	.280	214	53	5	1	0	0.0	20	19	19	15	1	1	1	106	212	11	31	4.4	.967	SS-75
1948	CHI N	48	.169	.191	89	15	2	0	0	0.0	4	5	13	3	0	1	0	68	115	6	18	4.2	.968	SS-43, 2B-2
1949	NY N	7	.000	.000	1	0	0	0	0	0.0	0	0	1	0	0	0	0	3	5	1	2	1.3	.889	SS-7
8 yrs.		472	.244	.281	1527	372	39	6	2	0.1	195	99	166	87	19	5	2	822	1285	103	234	4.8	.953	SS-396, 3B-32, 2B-28

Nick Cullop

CULLOP, HENRY NICHOLAS (Tomato Face)
Born Heinrich Nicholas Kolop.
B. Oct. 16, 1900, St. Louis, Mo. D. Dec. 8, 1978, Gahanna, Ohio.
BR TR 6′ 200 lbs.

Year	Team	Games	BA	SA	AB	H	2B	3B	HR	HR%	R	RBI	BB	SO	SB	Pinch Hit AB	Pinch Hit H	PO	A	E	DP	TC/G	FA	G by Pos
1926	NY A	2	.500	.500	2	1	0	0	0	0.0	0	0	0	1	0	2	1	0	0	0	0	0.0	—	
1927	2 teams	WAS A (15G –.217)	CLE A (32G –.235)																					
″	total	47	.231	.374	91	21	4	3	1	1.1	11	9	10	25	0	19	5	59	4	1	0	2.4	.984	OF-25, P-1, 1B-1
1929	BKN N	13	.195	.415	41	8	2	2	1	2.4	7	5	8	7	0	1	0	26	2	0	0	2.3	1.000	OF-11, 1B-1
1930	CIN N	7	.182	.318	22	4	0	0	1	4.5	2	5	1	9	0	2	0	7	2	0	0	1.8	1.000	OF-5
1931		104	.263	.446	334	88	23	7	8	2.4	29	48	21	**86**	1	19	3	177	5	6	3	2.3	.968	OF-83
5 yrs.		173	.249	.424	490	122	29	12	11	2.2	49	67	40	128	1	43	9	269	13	7	3	2.3	.976	OF-124, 1B-2, P-1

Wil Culmer

CULMER, WILFRED HILLARD
B. Nov. 11, 1958, Nassau, Bahamas.
BR TR 6′ 4″ 210 lbs.

Year	Team	Games	BA	SA	AB	H	2B	3B	HR	HR%	R	RBI	BB	SO	SB	Pinch Hit AB	Pinch Hit H	PO	A	E	DP	TC/G	FA	G by Pos
1983	CLE A	7	.105	.105	19	2	0	0	0	0.0	0	1	0	4	0	0	0	2	0	0	0	0.3	1.000	OF-4, DH-2

Benny Culp

CULP, BENJAMIN BALDY
B. Jan. 19, 1914, Philadelphia, Pa.
BR TR 5′ 9″ 175 lbs.

Year	Team	Games	BA	SA	AB	H	2B	3B	HR	HR%	R	RBI	BB	SO	SB	Pinch Hit AB	Pinch Hit H	PO	A	E	DP	TC/G	FA	G by Pos
1942	PHI N	1	—	—	0	0	0	0	0	—	0	0	0	0	0	0	0	1	0	1	0	2.0	.500	C-1
1943		10	.208	.250	24	5	1	0	0	0.0	4	2	3	3	0	0	0	21	2	1	0	2.4	.958	C-10
1944		4	.000	.000	2	0	0	0	0	0.0	1	0	0	0	0	1	0	0	1	0	0	1.0	1.000	C-1
3 yrs.		15	.192	.231	26	5	1	0	0	0.0	5	2	3	3	0	1	0	22	3	2	0	2.3	.926	C-12

Jack Cummings

CUMMINGS, JOHN WILLIAM BR TR 6′ 195 lbs.
B. Apr. 1, 1904, Pittsburgh, Pa. D. Oct. 5, 1962, West Mifflin, Pa.

Year	Team	Games	BA	SA	AB	H	2B	3B	HR	HR%	R	RBI	BB	SO	SB	Pinch Hit AB	Pinch Hit H	PO	A	E	DP	TC/G	FA	G by Pos
1926	NY N	7	.313	.500	16	5	3	0	0	0.0	3	4	4	2	0	1	0	16	7	1	1	4.0	.958	C-6
1927		43	.362	.537	80	29	6	1	2	2.5	8	14	5	10	0	8	3	64	10	2	1	2.2	.974	C-34
1928		33	.333	.630	27	9	2	0	2	7.4	4	9	3	4	0	25	8	5	0	1	0	1.5	.833	C-4
1929	2 teams	NY N (3G –.333) BOS N (3G –.167)																						
″	total	6	.222	.222	9	2	0	0	0	0.0	0	1	0	2	0	2	1	5	0	2	0	1.8	.714	C-4
4 yrs.		89	.341	.530	132	45	11	1	4	3.0	15	28	12	18	0	36	12	90	17	6	2	2.4	.947	C-48

Midre Cummings

CUMMINGS, MIDRE ALMERIC BB TR 6′ 1″ 190 lbs.
B. Oct. 14, 1971, St. Croix, Virgin Islands.

Year	Team	Games	BA	SA	AB	H	2B	3B	HR	HR%	R	RBI	BB	SO	SB	Pinch Hit AB	Pinch Hit H	PO	A	E	DP	TC/G	FA	G by Pos
1993	PIT N	13	.111	.139	36	4	1	0	0	0.0	5	3	4	9	0	2	0	21	0	0	0	1.9	1.000	OF-11
1994		24	.244	.326	86	21	4	0	1	1.2	11	12	4	18	0	0	0	48	1	2	1	2.1	.961	OF-24
1995		59	.243	.342	152	37	7	1	2	1.3	13	15	13	30	1	23	8	79	2	1	0	2.0	.988	OF-41
3 yrs.		96	.226	.310	274	62	12	1	3	1.1	29	30	21	57	1	25	8	148	3	3	1	2.0	.981	OF-76

Bill Cunningham

CUNNINGHAM, WILLIAM ALOYSIUS BR TR 5′ 8″ 155 lbs.
B. July 30, 1895, San Francisco, Calif. D. Sept. 26, 1953, Colusa, Calif.

Year	Team	Games	BA	SA	AB	H	2B	3B	HR	HR%	R	RBI	BB	SO	SB	Pinch Hit AB	Pinch Hit H	PO	A	E	DP	TC/G	FA	G by Pos
1921	NY N	40	.276	.368	76	21	2	1	1	1.3	10	12	3	3	0	18	5	35	1	0	0	1.8	1.000	OF-20
1922		85	.328	.437	229	75	15	2	2	0.9	37	33	7	9	4	13	3	155	7	2	3	2.3	.988	OF-70, 3B-1
1923		79	.271	.389	203	55	7	1	5	2.5	22	27	10	9	5	6	0	127	16	1	2	2.0	.993	OF-68, 2B-4
1924	BOS N	114	.272	.350	437	119	15	8	1	0.2	44	40	32	27	8	5	0	243	16	8	3	2.4	.970	OF-109
4 yrs.		318	.286	.381	945	270	39	12	9	1.0	113	112	52	48	17	42	8	560	40	11	8	2.2	.982	OF-267, 2B-4, 3B-1
WORLD SERIES																								
1922	NY N	4	.200	.200	10	2	0	0	0	0.0	0	2	2	1	0	0	0	10	2	0	0	3.0	1.000	OF-4
1923		4	.143	.143	7	1	0	0	0	0.0	0	1	0	1	0	1	0	2	0	1	0	1.0	.667	OF-3
2 yrs.		8	.176	.176	17	3	0	0	0	0.0	0	3	2	2	0	1	0	12	2	1	0	2.1	.933	OF-7

Bill Cunningham

CUNNINGHAM, WILLIAM JOHN BR TR 5′ 9″ 170 lbs.
B. June 9, 1888, Schenectady, N. Y. D. Feb. 21, 1946, Schenectady, N. Y.

Year	Team	Games	BA	SA	AB	H	2B	3B	HR	HR%	R	RBI	BB	SO	SB	Pinch Hit AB	Pinch Hit H	PO	A	E	DP	TC/G	FA	G by Pos
1910	WAS A	22	.297	.392	74	22	5	1	0	0.0	3	14	12		4	0	0	36	52	4	7	4.2	.957	2B-22
1911		94	.190	.278	331	63	10	5	3	0.9	34	37	19		10	1	0	168	244	30	18	4.8	.932	2B-93
1912		7	.185	.333	27	5	1	0	1	3.7	5	8	3		2	0	0	8	17	1	1	3.7	.962	2B-7
3 yrs.		123	.208	.301	432	90	16	6	4	0.9	42	59	34		16	1	0	212	313	35	26	4.6	.938	2B-122

George Cunningham

CUNNINGHAM, GEORGE HAROLD BR TR 5′11″ 185 lbs.
B. July 13, 1894, Sturgeon Lake, Minn. D. Mar. 10, 1972, Chattanooga, Tenn.

Year	Team	Games	BA	SA	AB	H	2B	3B	HR	HR%	R	RBI	BB	SO	SB	Pinch Hit AB	Pinch Hit H	PO	A	E	DP	TC/G	FA	G by Pos
1916	DET A	35	.268	.415	41	11	2	2	0	0.0	7	3	8	12	0	0	0	6	46	2	2	1.5	.963	P-35
1917		44	.176	.265	34	6	0	0	1	2.9	5	3	3	13	0	0	0	4	43	4	3	1.2	.922	P-44
1918		56	.223	.277	112	25	4	1	0	0.0	11	2	16	34	2	8	3	21	35	5	1	1.3	.918	P-27, OF-20
1919		26	.217	.217	23	5	0	0	0	0.0	4	5	9	8	0	6	1	2	16	3	1	1.2	.857	P-17
1921		1	—	—	0	0	0	0	0	—	0	0	0	0	0	0	0	1	0	0	0	1.0	1.000	OF-1
5 yrs.		162	.224	.295	210	47	6	3	1	0.5	27	13	36	67	2	14	4	34	140	14	7	1.3	.926	P-123, OF-21

Joe Cunningham

CUNNINGHAM, JOSEPH ROBERT BL TL 6′ 180 lbs.
B. Aug. 27, 1931, Paterson, N. J.

Year	Team	Games	BA	SA	AB	H	2B	3B	HR	HR%	R	RBI	BB	SO	SB	Pinch Hit AB	Pinch Hit H	PO	A	E	DP	TC/G	FA	G by Pos
1954	STL N	85	.284	.445	310	88	11	3	11	3.5	40	50	43	40	1	0	0	814	68	10	96	10.5	.989	1B-85
1956		4	.000	.000	3	0	0	0	0	0.0	1	0	1	1	0	2	0	2	0	0	0	2.0	1.000	1B-1
1957		122	.318	.479	261	83	15	0	9	3.4	50	52	56	29	3	29	11	360	18	3	17	3.7	.992	1B-57, OF-46
1958		131	.312	.496	337	105	20	3	12	3.6	61	57	82	23	4	19	5	418	26	3	21	3.4	.993	1B-67, OF-66
1959		144	.345	.478	458	158	28	6	7	1.5	65	60	88	47	2	8	2	359	14	7	23	2.4	.982	OF-121, 1B-35
1960		139	.280	.386	492	138	28	3	6	1.2	68	39	59	59	1	9	2	298	16	10	8	2.5	.969	OF-116, 1B-15
1961		113	.286	.398	322	92	11	2	7	2.2	60	40	53	32	1	20	5	200	3	5	9	2.2	.976	OF-86, 1B-10
1962	CHI A	149	.295	.428	526	155	32	7	8	1.5	91	70	101	59	3	3	1	1287	90	8	118	9.4	.994	1B-143, OF-5
1963		67	.286	.367	210	60	12	1	1	0.5	32	31	33	23	1	6	4	535	24	6	39	9.7	.989	1B-58
1964	2 teams	CHI A (40G –.250) WAS A (49G –.214)																						
″	total	89	.231	.278	234	54	11	0	0	0.0	28	17	37	28	0	14	1	580	29	2	53	8.3	.997	1B-74
1965	WAS A	95	.229	.328	201	46	9	1	3	1.5	29	20	46	27	0	27	5	393	24	6	44	7.2	.986	1B-59
1966		3	.125	.125	8	1	0	0	0	0.0	0	0	0	1	0	0	0	10	4	0	1	4.7	1.000	1B-3
12 yrs.		1141	.291	.417	3362	980	177	26	64	1.9	525	436	599	369	16	137	36	5256	316	60	429	5.4	.989	1B-607, OF-440

Ray Cunningham

CUNNINGHAM, RAYMOND LEE BR TR 5′ 7½″ 150 lbs.
B. Jan. 17, 1905, Mesquite, Tex.

Year	Team	Games	BA	SA	AB	H	2B	3B	HR	HR%	R	RBI	BB	SO	SB	Pinch Hit AB	Pinch Hit H	PO	A	E	DP	TC/G	FA	G by Pos
1931	STL N	3	.000	.000	4	0	0	0	0	0.0	0	1	0	0	0	0	0	0	5	0	0	1.7	1.000	3B-3
1932		11	.182	.227	22	4	1	0	0	0.0	4	0	3	4	0	1	0	11	15	0	1	2.6	1.000	3B-8, 2B-2
2 yrs.		14	.154	.192	26	4	1	0	0	0.0	4	1	3	4	0	1	0	11	20	0	1	2.4	1.000	3B-11, 2B-2

Doc Curley

CURLEY, WALTER JAMES BR TR
B. Mar. 12, 1874, Upton, Mass. D. Sept. 23, 1920, Framingham, Mass.

Year	Team	Games	BA	SA	AB	H	2B	3B	HR	HR%	R	RBI	BB	SO	SB	Pinch Hit AB	Pinch Hit H	PO	A	E	DP	TC/G	FA	G by Pos
1899	CHI N	10	.108	.162	37	4	0	1	0	0.0	7	2	3		0	0	0	12	27	4	2	4.3	.907	2B-10

Pete Curren

CURREN, PETER 175 lbs.
B. Baltimore, Md. Deceased.

Year	Team	Games	BA	SA	AB	H	2B	3B	HR	HR%	R	RBI	BB	SO	SB	Pinch Hit AB	Pinch Hit H	PO	A	E	DP	TC/G	FA	G by Pos
1876	PHI N	3	.333	.417	12	4	1	0	0	0.0	5	2	0	0		0	0	10	2	10	0	7.3	.545	C-2, OF-1

Perry Currin

CURRIN, PERRY GILMORE BL TR 6′ 175 lbs.
B. Sept. 27, 1928, Washington, D. C.

Year	Team	Games	BA	SA	AB	H	2B	3B	HR	HR%	R	RBI	BB	SO	SB	Pinch Hit AB	Pinch Hit H	PO	A	E	DP	TC/G	FA	G by Pos
1947	STL A	3	.000	.000	2	0	0	0	0	0.0	0	0	1	0	0	1	0	2	2	0	2	4.0	1.000	SS-1

Jim Curry

CURRY, JAMES E. BR TR 5′11″ 160 lbs.
B. Mar. 10, 1893, Camden, N. J. D. Sept. 2, 1938, Lakeland, N. J.

Year	Team	Games	BA	SA	AB	H	2B	3B	HR	HR%	R	RBI	BB	SO	SB	Pinch Hit AB	Pinch Hit H	PO	A	E	DP	TC/G	FA	G by Pos
1909	PHI A	1	.250	.250	4	1	0	0	0	0.0	1	0	0		0	0	0	0	2	0	0	2.0	1.000	2B-1
1911	NY A	4	.182	.182	11	2	0	0	0	0.0	3	0	1		0	0	0	11	6	5	1	5.5	.773	2B-4
1918	DET A	5	.250	.300	20	5	1	0	0	0.0	1	0	0	0	0	0	0	0	0	0	0	0.0	.000	2B-5
3 yrs.		10	.229	.257	35	8	1	0	0	0.0	5	0	1	0	0	0	0	11	8	5	1	2.4	.792	2B-10

Tony Curry

CURRY, GEORGE ANTHONY BL TL 5′11″ 185 lbs.
B. Dec. 22, 1938, Nassau, Bahamas.

Year	Team		Games	BA	SA	AB	H	2B	3B	HR	HR%	R	RBI	BB	SO	SB	Pinch Hit AB	Pinch Hit H	PO	A	E	DP	TC/G	FA	G by Pos
1960	PHI	N	95	.261	.408	245	64	14	2	6	2.4	26	34	16	53	0	31	7	96	2	8	0	1.7	.925	OF-64
1961			15	.194	.250	36	7	2	0	0	0.0	3	3	1	8	0	7	3	8	2	2	0	1.5	.833	OF-8
1966	CLE	A	19	.125	.125	16	2	0	0	0	0.0	4	3	3	8	0	16	2	0	0	0	0	0.0	—	
3 yrs.			129	.246	.374	297	73	16	2	6	2.0	33	40	20	69	0	54	12	104	4	10	0	1.6	.915	OF-72

Chad Curtis

CURTIS, CHAD DAVID BR TR 5′10″ 175 lbs.
B. Nov. 6, 1968, Marion, Ind.

Year	Team		Games	BA	SA	AB	H	2B	3B	HR	HR%	R	RBI	BB	SO	SB	Pinch Hit AB	Pinch Hit H	PO	A	E	DP	TC/G	FA	G by Pos
1992	CAL	A	139	.259	.372	441	114	16	2	10	2.3	59	46	51	71	43	5	0	250	16	6	3	2.0	.978	OF-135, DH-1
1993			152	.285	.369	583	166	25	3	6	1.0	94	59	70	89	48	2	1	428	14	9	6	2.9	.980	OF-151, 2B-3
1994			114	.256	.397	453	116	23	4	11	2.4	67	50	37	69	25	0	0	331	9	4	0	3.0	.988	OF-114
1995	DET	A	144	.268	.435	586	157	29	3	21	3.6	96	67	70	93	27	0	0	361	5	3	0	2.6	.992	OF-144
4 yrs.			549	.268	.395	2063	553	93	12	48	2.3	316	222	228	322	143	7	1	1370	44	22	9	2.6	.985	OF-544, 2B-3, DH-1

Fred Curtis

CURTIS, FREDERICK MARION BR TR 6′ 1″
B. Oct. 30, 1880, Beaver Lake, Mich. D. Apr. 5, 1939, Minneapolis, Minn.

Year	Team		Games	BA	SA	AB	H	2B	3B	HR	HR%	R	RBI	BB	SO	SB	Pinch Hit AB	Pinch Hit H	PO	A	E	DP	TC/G	FA	G by Pos
1905	NY	A	2	.222	.333	9	2	1	0	0	0.0	0	2	1		1	0	0	17	1	0	0	9.0	1.000	1B-2

Gene Curtis

CURTIS, EUGENE HOLMES (Eude) BR TR 6′ 3″ 220 lbs.
B. May 5, 1883, Bethany, W. Va. D. Jan. 1, 1919, Steubenville, Ohio.

Year	Team		Games	BA	SA	AB	H	2B	3B	HR	HR%	R	RBI	BB	SO	SB	Pinch Hit AB	Pinch Hit H	PO	A	E	DP	TC/G	FA	G by Pos
1903	PIT	N	5	.421	.474	19	8	1	0	0	0.0	2	3	1		0	0	0	9	1	2	0	2.4	.833	OF-5

Harry Curtis

CURTIS, HARRY ALBERT TR 5′10½″ 170 lbs.
B. Feb. 19, 1883, Portland, Me. D. Aug. 1, 1951, Evanston, Ill.

Year	Team		Games	BA	SA	AB	H	2B	3B	HR	HR%	R	RBI	BB	SO	SB	Pinch Hit AB	Pinch Hit H	PO	A	E	DP	TC/G	FA	G by Pos
1907	NY	N	6	.222	.222	9	2	0	0	0	0.0	2	1	2		2	0	0	16	4	2	1	3.7	.909	C-6

Jim Curtiss

CURTISS, ERWIN DUANE BL TL 5′ 8½″ 157 lbs.
B. Dec. 27, 1861, Coldwater, Mich. D. Feb. 14, 1945, North Adams, Mass.

Year	Team		Games	BA	SA	AB	H	2B	3B	HR	HR%	R	RBI	BB	SO	SB	Pinch Hit AB	Pinch Hit H	PO	A	E	DP	TC/G	FA	G by Pos
1891	2 teams		CIN N (27G –.269) WAS AA (29G –.252)																						
″	total		56	.261	.351	211	55	6	5	1	0.5	28	25	22	35	5	0	0	94	13	22	1	2.3	.829	OF-56

Guy Curtright

CURTRIGHT, GUY PAXTON BR TR 5′11″ 200 lbs.
B. Oct. 18, 1912, Holliday, Mo.

Year	Team		Games	BA	SA	AB	H	2B	3B	HR	HR%	R	RBI	BB	SO	SB	Pinch Hit AB	Pinch Hit H	PO	A	E	DP	TC/G	FA	G by Pos
1943	CHI	A	138	.291	.379	488	142	20	7	3	0.6	67	48	69	60	13	9	2	301	7	9	1	2.5	.972	OF-128
1944			72	.253	.343	198	50	8	2	2	1.0	22	23	23	21	4	22	6	101	8	6	3	2.3	.948	OF-51
1945			98	.281	.407	324	91	15	7	4	1.2	51	32	39	29	3	13	5	196	8	3	0	2.5	.986	OF-84
1946			23	.200	.236	55	11	2	0	0	0.0	7	5	11	14	0	4	2	30	2	0	1	2.1	1.000	OF-15
4 yrs.			331	.276	.374	1065	294	45	16	9	0.8	147	108	142	124	20	48	15	628	25	18	5	2.4	.973	OF-278

Jack Cusick

CUSICK, JOHN PETER BR TR 6′ 170 lbs.
B. June 12, 1928, Weehawken, N. J. D. Nov. 17, 1989, Edgewood, N. J.

Year	Team		Games	BA	SA	AB	H	2B	3B	HR	HR%	R	RBI	BB	SO	SB	Pinch Hit AB	Pinch Hit H	PO	A	E	DP	TC/G	FA	G by Pos
1951	CHI	N	65	.177	.256	164	29	3	2	2	1.2	16	16	17	29	2	3	1	78	147	11	25	4.2	.953	SS-56
1952	BOS	N	49	.167	.179	78	13	1	0	0	0.0	5	6	6	9	0	9	1	45	52	3	4	3.2	.970	SS-28, 3B-3
2 yrs.			114	.174	.231	242	42	4	2	2	0.8	21	22	23	38	2	12	2	123	199	14	29	3.9	.958	SS-84, 3B-3

Tony Cusick

CUSICK, ANDREW DANIEL BR TR 5′ 9½″ 190 lbs.
B. Dec. 1857, Limerick, Ireland D. Aug. 6, 1929, Chicago, Ill.

Year	Team		Games	BA	SA	AB	H	2B	3B	HR	HR%	R	RBI	BB	SO	SB	Pinch Hit AB	Pinch Hit H	PO	A	E	DP	TC/G	FA	G by Pos
1884	2 teams		WIL U (11G –.147) PHI N (9G –.138)																						
″	total		20	.143	.143	63	9	0	0	0	0.0	2		1	3		0	0	99	40	19	5	6.9	.880	C-15, SS-3, OF-3, 2B-1, 3B-1
1885	PHI	N	39	.177	.184	141	25	1	0	0	0.0	12		1	24		0	0	181	60	57	2	7.6	.809	C-38, OF-1
1886			29	.221	.288	104	23	5	1	0	0.0	10	4	3	14		0	0	133	35	19	2	6.4	.898	C-25, OF-3, 1B-1
1887			7	.292	.333	24	7	1	0	0	0.0	3	5	3	1	0	0	0	44	8	12	1	8.0	.813	C-4, 1B-3, 2B-1
4 yrs.			95	.193	.220	332	64	7	1	0	0.0	27	9	8	42	0	0	0	457	143	107	10	7.1	.849	C-82, OF-7, 1B-4, SS-3, 2B-2, 3B-1

Ned Cuthbert

CUTHBERT, EDGAR EDWARD BR TR 5′ 6″ 140 lbs.
B. June 20, 1845, Philadelphia, Pa. D. Feb. 6, 1905, St. Louis, Mo.
Manager 1882.

Year	Team		Games	BA	SA	AB	H	2B	3B	HR	HR%	R	RBI	BB	SO	SB	Pinch Hit AB	Pinch Hit H	PO	A	E	DP	TC/G	FA	G by Pos
1876	STL	N	63	.247	.290	283	70	10	1	0	0.0	46	25	7	4		0	0	95	7	19	2	1.9	.843	OF-63
1877	CIN	N	12	.179	.268	56	10	5	0	0	0.0	6	2	1	2		0	0	34	5	8	2	3.9	.830	OF-12
1882	STL	AA	60	.223	.335	233	52	16	5	0	0.0	28		17			0	0	74	12	10	0	1.6	.896	OF-60
1883			21	.169	.183	71	12	1	0	0	0.0	3		4			0	0	37	5	7	0	2.3	.857	OF-20, 1B-1
1884	BAL	U	44	.202	.232	168	34	5	0	0	0.0	29		10			0	0	41	10	17	0	1.5	.750	OF-44
5 yrs.			200	.219	.280	811	178	37	6	0	0.0	112	27	39	6		0	0	281	39	61	4	1.9	.840	OF-199, 1B-1

George Cutshaw

CUTSHAW, GEORGE WILLIAM (Clancy) BR TR 5′ 9″ 160 lbs.
B. July 27, 1887, Wilmington, Ill. D. Aug. 22, 1973, San Diego, Calif.

Year	Team		Games	BA	SA	AB	H	2B	3B	HR	HR%	R	RBI	BB	SO	SB	Pinch Hit AB	Pinch Hit H	PO	A	E	DP	TC/G	FA	G by Pos
1912	BKN	N	102	.280	.342	357	100	14	4	0	0.0	41	28	31	16	16	5	1	196	294	22	31	5.3	.957	2B-91, 3B-5, SS-1
1913			147	.267	.385	592	158	23	13	7	1.2	72	80	39	22	39	0	0	402	448	38	79	6.0	.957	2B-147
1914			153	.257	.346	583	150	22	12	2	0.3	69	78	30	32	34	0	0	455	444	38	74	6.1	.959	2B-153
1915			154	.246	.309	566	139	18	9	0	0.0	68	62	34	35	28	0	0	397	473	26	53	5.8	.971	2B-154
1916			154	.260	.320	581	151	21	4	2	0.3	58	63	25	32	27	0	0	361	467	36	51	5.6	.958	2B-154
1917			135	.259	.347	487	126	17	7	4	0.8	42	49	21	26	22	1	0	319	377	27	43	5.4	.963	2B-134
1918	PIT	N	126	.285	.395	463	132	16	10	5	1.1	56	68	27	18	25	0	0	323	366	26	60	5.7	.964	2B-126
1919			139	.242	.320	512	124	15	8	3	0.6	49	51	30	22	36	0	0	344	392	15	56	5.4	.980	2B-139
1920			131	.252	.318	488	123	16	8	0	0.0	56	47	23	10	17	2	0	336	423	25	62	6.1	.968	2B-129
1921			98	.340	.414	350	119	18	4	0	0.0	46	53	11	11	14	14	2	196	253	23	36	5.6	.951	2B-84
1922	DET	A	132	.267	.339	499	133	14	8	2	0.4	57	61	20	13	11	0	0	334	390	21	69	5.6	.972	2B-132
1923			45	.224	.259	143	32	1	2	0	0.0	15	13	9	5	2	0	0	104	151	3	2	5.7	.988	2B-43, 3B-2
12 yrs.			1516	.265	.344	5621	1487	195	89	25	0.4	629	653	300	242	271	22	3	3767	4478	300	616	5.7	.965	2B-1486, 3B-7, SS-1
WORLD SERIES																									
1916	BKN	N	5	.105	.158	19	2	1	0	0	0.0	2	2	1	1	0	0	0	19	13	2	1	6.8	.941	2B-5

Kiki Cuyler

CUYLER, HAZEN SHIRLEY BR TR 5′10½″ 180 lbs.
B. Aug. 30, 1898, Harrisville, Mich. D. Feb. 11, 1950, Ann Arbor, Mich.
Hall of Fame 1968.

Year	Team		Games	BA	SA	AB	H	2B	3B	HR	HR%	R	RBI	BB	SO	SB	Pinch Hit AB	Pinch Hit H	PO	A	E	DP	TC/G	FA	G by Pos
1921	PIT	N	1	.000	.000	3	0	0	0	0	0.0	0	0	0	1	0	0	0	1	0	0	0	1.0	1.000	OF-1
1922			1	—	—	0	0	0	0	0	—	0	0	0	0	0	0	0	0	0	0	0	0.0	—	
1923			11	.250	.325	40	10	1	1	0	0.0	4	2	5	3	2	0	0	26	1	2	0	2.6	.931	OF-11
1924			117	.354	.539	466	165	27	16	9	1.9	94	85	30	62	32	3	1	246	19	16	4	2.5	.943	OF-114
1925			153	.357	.593	617	220	43	**26**	17	2.8	**144**	102	58	56	41	0	0	362	21	13	4	2.6	.967	OF-153
1926			157	.321	.459	614	197	31	15	8	1.3	**113**	92	50	66	**35**	0	0	405	19	14	4	2.8	.968	OF-157
1927			85	.309	.435	285	88	13	7	3	1.1	60	31	37	36	20	11	2	195	6	4	0	2.8	.980	OF-73
1928	CHI	N	133	.285	.473	499	142	25	9	17	3.4	92	79	51	61	**37**	5	0	257	18	5	3	2.2	.982	OF-127
1929			139	.360	.532	509	183	29	7	15	2.9	111	102	66	56	**43**	9	4	288	15	8	6	2.4	.974	OF-129
1930			156	.355	.547	642	228	50	17	13	2.0	155	134	72	49	**37**	0	0	377	21	8	7	2.6	.980	OF-156
1931			154	.330	.473	613	202	37	12	9	1.5	110	88	72	54	13	1	0	347	11	11	4	2.4	.970	OF-153
1932			110	.291	.442	446	130	19	9	10	2.2	58	77	29	43	9	1	0	239	7	8	1	2.3	.969	OF-109
1933			70	.317	.447	262	83	13	3	5	1.9	37	35	21	29	4	1	0	130	2	3	0	2.0	.978	OF-69
1934			142	.338	.474	559	189	**42**	8	6	1.1	80	69	31	62	15	0	0	319	15	10	1	2.4	.971	OF-142
1935	2 teams		CHI N (45G –.268) CIN N (62G –.251)																						
″	total		107	.258	.361	380	98	13	4	6	1.6	58	40	37	34	8	6	2	221	10	4	3	2.4	.983	OF-99
1936	CIN	N	144	.326	.453	567	185	29	11	7	1.2	96	74	47	67	16	4	2	322	9	9	3	2.4	.974	OF-140
1937			117	.271	.320	406	110	12	4	0	0.0	48	32	36	50	10	10	2	174	8	5	1	1.8	.973	OF-106
1938	BKN	N	82	.273	.399	253	69	10	8	2	0.8	45	23	34	23	6	11	1	125	9	1	1	2.0	.993	OF-68
18 yrs.			1879	.321	.473	7161	2299	394	157	127	1.8	1305	1065	676	752	328	62	14	4034	191	121	42	2.4	.972	OF-1807
WORLD SERIES																									
1925	PIT	N	7	.269	.500	26	7	3	0	1	3.8	3	6	1	4	0	0	0	12	0	1	0	1.9	.923	OF-7
1929	CHI	N	5	.300	.350	20	6	1	0	0	0.0	4	4	1	7	0	0	0	8	0	1	0	1.8	.889	OF-5
1932			4	.278	.611	18	5	1	1	1	5.6	2	2	0	3	1	0	0	5	0	0	0	1.3	1.000	OF-4
3 yrs.			16	.281	.484	64	18	5	1	2	3.1	9	12	2	14	1	0	0	25	0	2	0	1.7	.926	OF-16

Milt Cuyler

CUYLER, MILTON BB TR 5′10″ 175 lbs.
B. Oct. 7, 1968, Macon, Ga.

Year	Team		Games	BA	SA	AB	H	2B	3B	HR	HR%	R	RBI	BB	SO	SB	Pinch Hit AB	Pinch Hit H	PO	A	E	DP	TC/G	FA	G by Pos
1990	DET	A	19	.255	.353	51	13	3	1	0	0.0	8	8	5	10	1	0	0	38	2	1	0	2.4	.976	OF-17
1991			154	.257	.337	475	122	15	7	3	0.6	77	33	52	92	41	1	0	411	7	6	3	2.8	.986	OF-151
1992			89	.241	.316	291	70	11	1	3	1.0	39	28	10	62	8	0	0	232	4	4	1	2.7	.983	OF-89
1993			82	.213	.313	249	53	11	7	0	0.0	46	19	19	53	13	2	0	211	2	7	1	2.8	.968	OF-80
1994			48	.241	.310	116	28	3	1	1	0.9	20	11	13	21	5	0	0	78	1	2	0	1.8	.975	OF-46
1995			41	.205	.307	88	18	1	4	0	0.0	15	5	8	16	2	2	0	51	2	4	0	1.5	.930	OF-36, DH-2
6 yrs.			433	.239	.324	1270	304	44	21	7	0.6	205	104	107	254	70	5	0	1021	18	24	5	2.5	.977	OF-419, DH-2

Al Cypert

CYPERT, ALFRED BOYD BR TR 5′10½″ 150 lbs.
B. Aug. 8, 1889, Little Rock, Ark. D. Jan. 9, 1973, Washington, D. C.

Year	Team		Games	BA	SA	AB	H	2B	3B	HR	HR%	R	RBI	BB	SO	SB	Pinch Hit AB	Pinch Hit H	PO	A	E	DP	TC/G	FA	G by Pos
1914	CLE	A	1	.000	.000	1	0	0	0	0	0.0	0	0	0	1	0	0	0	0	0	0	0	0.0	.000	3B-1

Paul Dade

DADE, LONNIE PAUL BR TR 6′ 1″ 185 lbs.
B. Dec. 7, 1951, Seattle, Wash.

Year	Team		Games	BA	SA	AB	H	2B	3B	HR	HR%	R	RBI	BB	SO	SB	Pinch Hit AB	Pinch Hit H	PO	A	E	DP	TC/G	FA	G by Pos
1975	CAL	A	11	.200	.333	30	6	4	0	0	0.0	5	1	6	7	0	1	1	8	1	0	0	0.8	1.000	DH-7, OF-3, 3B-1
1976			13	.111	.111	9	1	0	0	0	0.0	2	1	3	3	0	5	1	5	4	1	0	1.3	.900	OF-4, 2B-2, DH-1, 3B-1
1977	CLE	A	134	.291	.356	461	134	15	3	3	0.7	65	45	32	58	16	10	2	192	51	7	3	1.9	.972	OF-99, 3B-26, DH-7, 2B-1
1978			93	.254	.329	307	78	12	1	3	1.0	37	20	34	45	12	8	1	171	6	7	2	2.0	.962	OF-81, DH-9
1979	2 teams		CLE A (44G –.282) SD N (76G –.276)																						
″	total		120	.278	.369	453	126	23	3	4	0.9	60	37	26	70	25	6	2	120	167	14	13	2.6	.953	3B-72, OF-41, DH-4
1980	SD	N	68	.189	.189	53	10	0	0	0	0.0	17	3	12	10	4	11	1	14	19	5	1	1.3	.868	3B-21, OF-8, 2B-1
6 yrs.			439	.270	.345	1313	355	54	7	10	0.8	186	107	113	193	57	41	8	510	248	34	19	2.0	.957	OF-236, 3B-121, DH-28, 2B-4

Angie Dagres

DAGRES, ANGELO GEORGE (Junior) BL TL 5′11″ 175 lbs.
B. Aug. 22, 1934, Newburyport, Mass.

Year	Team		Games	BA	SA	AB	H	2B	3B	HR	HR%	R	RBI	BB	SO	SB	Pinch Hit AB	Pinch Hit H	PO	A	E	DP	TC/G	FA	G by Pos
1955	BAL	A	8	.267	.267	15	4	0	0	0	0.0	5	3	1	2	0	3	1	9	0	2	0	2.2	.818	OF-5

Bill Dahlen

DAHLEN, WILLIAM FREDERICK (Bad Bill) BR TR 5′ 9″ 180 lbs.
B. Jan. 5, 1870, Nelliston, N. Y. D. Dec. 5, 1950, Brooklyn, N. Y.
Manager 1910–13.

Year	Team		Games	BA	SA	AB	H	2B	3B	HR	HR%	R	RBI	BB	SO	SB	Pinch Hit AB	Pinch Hit H	PO	A	E	DP	TC/G	FA	G by Pos
1891	CHI	N	135	.260	.390	549	143	18	13	9	1.6	114	76	67	60	21	0	0	217	264	64	21	4.0	.883	3B-84, OF-37, SS-15
1892			143	.291	.422	581	169	23	19	5	0.9	114	58	45	56	60	0	0	297	423	61	43	5.5	.922	SS-72, 3B-68, OF-2, 2B-1
1893			116	.301	.452	485	146	28	15	5	1.0	113	64	58	30	31	0	0	286	337	72	35	5.9	.896	SS-88, OF-17, 2B-10, 3B-3
1894			121	.357	.566	502	179	32	14	15	3.0	149	107	76	33	42	0	0	282	382	75	53	6.1	.899	SS-66, 3B-55
1895			129	.254	.370	516	131	19	10	7	1.4	106	62	61	51	38	0	0	282	527	86	70	6.9	.904	SS-129, OF-1
1896			125	.352	.553	474	167	30	19	9	1.9	137	74	64	36	51	0	0	310	456	71	66	6.7	.915	SS-125
1897			75	.290	.478	276	80	18	8	6	2.2	67	40	43		15	0	0	215	291	38	48	7.3	.930	SS-75
1898			142	.290	.393	521	151	35	8	1	0.2	96	79	58		27	0	0	369	511	76	77	6.7	.921	SS-142
1899	BKN	N	121	.283	.395	428	121	22	7	4	0.9	87	76	67		29	0	0	275	418	42	53	6.1	.943	SS-110, 3B-11
1900			133	.259	.344	483	125	16	11	1	0.2	87	69	73		31	0	0	321	517	55	59	6.7	.938	SS-133
1901			131	.261	.357	513	134	17	10	4	0.8	69	82	30		23	0	0	304	457	57	49	6.2	.930	SS-129, 2B-2
1902			138	.264	.351	527	139	26	7	2	0.4	67	74	43		20	0	0	278	440	66	34	5.7	.916	SS-138
1903			138	.262	.342	474	124	17	9	1	0.2	71	64	82		34	0	0	296	477	42	48	5.9	.948	SS-138
1904	NY	N	145	.268	.337	523	140	26	2	2	0.4	70	**80**	44		47	0	0	316	494	61	61	6.0	.930	SS-145
1905			148	.242	.337	520	126	20	4	7	1.3	67	81	62		37	0	0	314	501	45	58	5.8	.948	SS-147, OF-1
1906			143	.240	.297	471	113	18	3	1	0.2	63	49	76		16	0	0	287	454	49	36	5.5	.938	SS-143
1907			143	.207	.254	464	96	20	1	0	0.0	40	34	51		11	0	0	292	426	45	39	5.3	.941	SS-143
1908	BOS	N	144	.239	.307	524	125	23	2	3	0.6	50	48	35		10	0	0	291	553	43	58	6.2	.952	SS-144

Bill Dahlen *continued*

Year	Team	Games	BA	SA	AB	H	2B	3B	HR	HR%	R	RBI	BB	SO	SB	Pinch Hit AB	Pinch Hit H	PO	A	E	DP	TC/G	FA	G by Pos
1909		69	.234	.305	197	46	6	1	2	1.0	22	16	29		4	8	2	119	200	32	21	6.2	.909	SS-49, 2B-6, 3B-2
1910	BKN N	3	.000	.000	2	0	0	0	0	0.0	0	0	0	0	0	2	0	0	0	0	0	0.0	—	
1911		1	.000	.000	3	0	0	0	0	0.0	0	0	0	3	0	0	0	2	5	0	1	7.0	1.000	SS-1
21 yrs.		2443	.272	.382	9033	2455	414	163	84	0.9	1589	1233	1064	269	547	10	2	5353	8133	1080	930	6.0	.926	SS-2132, 3B-223, OF-58, 2B-19
WORLD SERIES																								
1905	NY N	5	.000	.000	15	0	0	0	0	0.0	1	1	3	2	2	0	0	10	19	0	1	5.8	1.000	SS-5

Babe Dahlgren

DAHLGREN, ELLSWORTH TENNEY
B. June 15, 1912, San Francisco, Calif.
BR TR 6′ 190 lbs.

Year	Team	Games	BA	SA	AB	H	2B	3B	HR	HR%	R	RBI	BB	SO	SB	Pinch Hit AB	Pinch Hit H	PO	A	E	DP	TC/G	FA	G by Pos
1935	BOS A	149	.263	.392	525	138	27	7	9	1.7	77	63	56	67	6	0	0	1433	69	18	109	10.2	.988	1B-149
1936		16	.281	.421	57	16	3	1	1	1.8	6	7	7	1	2	0	0	136	8	3	10	9.2	.980	1B-16
1937	NY A	1	.000	.000	1	0	0	0	0	0.0	0	0	0	0	0	1	0	0	0	0	0	0.0	—	
1938		29	.186	.209	43	8	1	0	0	0.0	8	1	1	7	0	6	0	37	10	4	2	3.6	.922	3B-8, 1B-6
1939		144	.235	.377	531	125	18	6	15	2.8	71	89	57	54	2	0	0	1303	68	13	140	9.6	.991	1B-144
1940		155	.264	.384	568	150	24	4	12	2.1	51	73	46	54	1	0	0	1488	75	15	143	10.2	.990	1B-155
1941	2 teams	BOS N (44G –.235) CHI N (99G –.281)																						
″	total	143	.267	.459	525	140	28	2	23	4.4	70	89	59	52	2	1	0	1341	78	13	129	10.1	.991	1B-137, 3B-5
1942	3 teams	CHI N (17G –.214) STL A (2G –.000) BKN N (17G –.053)																						
″	total	36	.169	.182	77	13	1	0	0	0.0	6	6	8	7	0	8	0	183	14	2	13	8.3	.990	1B-24
1943	PHI N	136	.287	.362	508	146	19	2	5	1.0	55	56	50	39	2	3	2	800	151	24	81	7.3	.975	1B-73, 3B-35, SS-25, C-1
1944	PIT N	158	.289	.419	599	173	28	7	12	2.0	67	101	47	56	2	0	0	1440	128	20	105	10.1	.987	1B-158
1945		144	.250	.354	531	133	24	8	5	0.9	57	75	51	51	1	2	0	1373	93	6	115	10.4	.996	1B-142
1946	STL A	28	.175	.188	80	14	1	0	0	0.0	2	9	8	13	0	4	1	187	18	4	16	8.7	.981	1B-24
12 yrs.		1139	.261	.383	4045	1056	174	37	82	2.0	470	569	390	401	18	25	3	9721	712	122	863	9.6	.988	1B-1028, 3B-48, SS-25, C-1
WORLD SERIES																								
1939	NY A	4	.214	.571	14	3	2	0	1	7.1	2	2	0	4	0	0	0	41	2	0	4	10.8	1.000	1B-4

Vince Dailey

DAILEY, VINCENT PERRY
B. Dec. 25, 1864, Osceola, Pa. D. Nov. 14, 1919, Hornell, N. Y.
6′ 200 lbs.

Year	Team	Games	BA	SA	AB	H	2B	3B	HR	HR%	R	RBI	BB	SO	SB	Pinch Hit AB	Pinch Hit H	PO	A	E	DP	TC/G	FA	G by Pos
1890	CLE N	64	.289	.366	246	71	5	7	0	0.0	41	32	33	23	17	0	0	103	13	19	2	2.0	.859	OF-64, P-2

Con Daily

DAILY, CORNELIUS F.
Brother of Ed Daily.
B. Sept. 11, 1864, Blackstone, Mass. D. June 14, 1928, Brooklyn, N. Y.
BL 6′ 192 lbs.

Year	Team	Games	BA	SA	AB	H	2B	3B	HR	HR%	R	RBI	BB	SO	SB	Pinch Hit AB	Pinch Hit H	PO	A	E	DP	TC/G	FA	G by Pos
1884	PHI U	2	.000	.000	8	0	0	0	0	0.0	0		0			0	0	15	3	3	0	10.5	.857	C-2
1885	PRO N	60	.260	.296	223	58	6	1	0	0.0	20	19	12	20		0	0	296	74	44	14	6.8	.894	C-48, 1B-7, OF-6
1886	BOS N	50	.239	.283	180	43	4	2	0	0.0	25	21	19	29		0	0	264	55	31	5	7.1	.911	C-49
1887		36	.158	.200	120	19	5	0	0	0.0	12	13	9	8	7	0	0	125	44	21	3	5.3	.889	C-36
1888	IND N	57	.218	.257	202	44	6	1	0	0.0	14	14	10	28	15	0	0	279	77	40	10	6.8	.899	C-42, 1B-5, 3B-5, OF-5, 2B-1
1889		62	.251	.297	219	55	6	2	0	0.0	35	26	28	21	14	0	0	294	57	42	9	6.1	.893	C-51, OF-6, 1B-6, 3B-1
1890	BKN P	46	.250	.321	168	42	6	3	0	0.0	20	35	15	14	6	0	0	197	36	25	10	5.5	.903	C-40, 1B-6, OF-1
1891	BKN N	60	.320	.379	206	66	10	1	0	0.0	25	30	15	13	7	0	0	241	68	26	2	5.5	.922	C-55, OF-3, SS-2, 1B-1
1892		80	.234	.277	278	65	10	1	0	0.0	38	28	38	21	18	0	0	356	88	27	9	5.8	.943	C-68, OF-13
1893		61	.265	.316	215	57	4	2	1	0.5	33	32	20	12	13	1	1	226	47	21	2	4.9	.929	C-51, OF-9
1894		67	.256	.376	234	60	14	7	0	0.0	40	32	31	22	8	0	0	271	63	24	12	5.3	.933	C-60, 1B-7
1895		40	.211	.282	142	30	3	2	1	0.7	17	11	10	18	3	0	0	130	25	7	7	4.1	.957	C-39, OF-1
1896	CHI N	9	.074	.074	27	2	0	0	0	0.0	1	1	1	2	1	0	0	24	7	1	0	3.6	.969	C-9
13 yrs.		630	.243	.299	2222	541	74	22	2	0.1	280	262	208	208	92	1	1	2718	644	312	83	5.8	.915	C-550, OF-44, 1B-32, 3B-6, SS-2, 2B-1

Ed Daily

DAILY, EDWARD M.
Brother of Con Daily.
B. Sept. 7, 1862, Providence, R. I. D. Oct. 21, 1891, Washington, D. C.
BR TR 5′10½″ 174 lbs.

Year	Team	Games	BA	SA	AB	H	2B	3B	HR	HR%	R	RBI	BB	SO	SB	Pinch Hit AB	Pinch Hit H	PO	A	E	DP	TC/G	FA	G by Pos
1885	PHI N	50	.207	.288	184	38	8	2	1	0.5	22		0	25		0	0	11	87	12	2	2.2	.891	P-50
1886		79	.227	.327	309	70	17	1	4	1.3	40	50	7	34		0	0	98	70	27	3	2.3	.862	OF-56, P-27
1887	2 teams	PHI N (26G –.283) WAS N (78G –.251)																						
″	total	104	.259	.374	417	108	17	11	3	0.7	57	53	17	36	34	0	0	144	25	35	1	1.9	.828	OF-99, P-7
1888	WAS N	110	.225	.313	453	102	8	4	8	1.8	56	39	7	42	44	0	0	196	37	22	5	2.3	.914	OF-100, P-9, 1B-1
1889	COL AA	136	.256	.337	578	148	22	8	3	0.5	105	70	38	65	60	0	0	212	27	41	4	2.0	.854	OF-136, P-2
1890	3 teams	BKN AA (91G –.239) NY N (4G –.133) LOU AA (23G –.250)																						
″	total	118	.237	.313	489	116	16	9	1	0.2	93	1	37	4	62	0	0	147	106	26	6	2.3	.907	OF-78, P-41
1891	2 teams	LOU AA (22G –.250) WAS AA (21G –.228)																						
″	total	43	.238	.266	143	34	4	0	0	0.0	23	14	19	16	12	0	0	43	31	17	2	2.1	.813	OF-28, P-15
7 yrs.		640	.239	.326	2573	616	92	35	20	0.8	396	227	125	222	212	0	0	851	383	180	23	2.2	.873	OF-497, P-151, 1B-1

George Daisey

DAISEY, GEORGE K.
B. Altoona, Pa. Deceased.
5′11″ 190 lbs.

Year	Team	Games	BA	SA	AB	H	2B	3B	HR	HR%	R	RBI	BB	SO	SB	Pinch Hit AB	Pinch Hit H	PO	A	E	DP	TC/G	FA	G by Pos
1884	ALT U	1	.000	.000	4	0	0	0	0	0.0	0		0			0	0	0	0	1	0	1.0	.000	OF-1

Pete Dalena

DALENA, PETER MARTIN
B. June 26, 1960, Fresno, Calif.
BL TR 5′11″ 200 lbs.

Year	Team	Games	BA	SA	AB	H	2B	3B	HR	HR%	R	RBI	BB	SO	SB	Pinch Hit AB	Pinch Hit H	PO	A	E	DP	TC/G	FA	G by Pos
1989	CLE A	5	.143	.286	7	1	1	0	0	0.0	0	0	0	3	0	4	1	0	0	0	0	0.0	.000	DH-1

Mark Dalesandro

DALESANDRO, MARK ANTHONY
B. May 14, 1968, Chicago, Ill.
BR TR 6′ 185 lbs.

Year	Team	Games	BA	SA	AB	H	2B	3B	HR	HR%	R	RBI	BB	SO	SB	Pinch Hit AB	Pinch Hit H	PO	A	E	DP	TC/G	FA	G by Pos
1994	CAL A	19	.200	.360	25	5	1	0	1	4.0	5	2	2	4	0	5	1	19	5	1	1	1.4	.960	C-11, 3B-5, OF-2
1995		11	.100	.200	10	1	1	0	0	0.0	1	0	0	2	0	5	0	11	0	0	0	1.1	1.000	C-8, OF-1, DH-1
2 yrs.		30	.171	.314	35	6	2	0	1	2.9	6	2	2	6	0	10	1	30	5	1	1	1.3	.972	C-19, 3B-5, OF-3, DH-1

John Daley

DALEY, JOHN FRANCIS (Daley) BR TR 5′ 7½″ 155 lbs.
B. May 25, 1887, Pittsburgh, Pa. D. Aug. 31, 1988, Mansfield, Ohio.

Year	Team		Games	BA	SA	AB	H	2B	3B	HR	HR%	R	RBI	BB	SO	SB	Pinch Hit AB	Pinch Hit H	PO	A	E	DP	TC/G	FA	G by Pos
1912	STL	A	17	.173	.231	52	9	0	0	1	1.9	7	3	9		4	0	0	27	48	15	7	5.3	.833	SS-17

Jud Daley

DALEY, JUDSON LAWRENCE BL TR 5′ 8″ 172 lbs.
B. Mar. 14, 1884, S. Coventry, Conn. D. Jan. 26, 1967, Gadsden, Ala.

Year	Team		Games	BA	SA	AB	H	2B	3B	HR	HR%	R	RBI	BB	SO	SB	Pinch Hit AB	Pinch Hit H	PO	A	E	DP	TC/G	FA	G by Pos
1911	BKN	N	19	.231	.292	65	15	2	1	0	0.0	8	7	2	8	2	2	0	37	3	2	0	2.6	.952	OF-16
1912			61	.256	.342	199	51	9	1	2	1.0	22	13	24	17	2	6	3	116	10	7	3	2.4	.947	OF-55
2 yrs.			80	.250	.330	264	66	11	2	2	0.8	30	20	26	25	4	8	3	153	13	9	3	2.5	.949	OF-71

Pete Daley

DALEY, PETER HARVEY BR TR 6′ 195 lbs.
B. Jan. 14, 1930, Grass Valley, Calif.

Year	Team		Games	BA	SA	AB	H	2B	3B	HR	HR%	R	RBI	BB	SO	SB	Pinch Hit AB	Pinch Hit H	PO	A	E	DP	TC/G	FA	G by Pos
1955	BOS	A	17	.220	.300	50	11	2	1	0	0.0	4	5	3	6	0	4	0	75	4	0	0	5.6	1.000	C-14
1956			59	.267	.439	187	50	11	3	5	2.7	22	29	18	30	1	3	1	228	14	2	1	4.3	.992	C-57
1957			78	.225	.325	191	43	10	0	3	1.6	17	25	16	31	0	1	1	289	20	0	5	4.0	1.000	C-77
1958			27	.321	.500	56	18	2	1	2	3.6	10	8	7	11	0	0	0	88	10	1	1	3.7	.990	C-27
1959			65	.225	.284	169	38	7	0	1	0.6	9	11	13	31	1	9	2	245	28	1	5	4.7	.996	C-58
1960	KC	A	73	.263	.390	228	60	10	2	5	2.2	19	25	16	41	0	14	5	263	33	3	3	4.8	.990	C-61, OF-1
1961	WAS	A	72	.192	.266	203	39	7	1	2	1.0	12	17	14	37	0	0	0	285	35	4	6	4.5	.988	C-72
7 yrs.			391	.239	.349	1084	259	49	8	18	1.7	93	120	87	187	2	31	9	1473	144	11	21	4.4	.993	C-366, OF-1

Tom Daley

DALEY, THOMAS FRANCIS (Pete) BL TR 5′ 5″ 168 lbs.
B. Nov. 13, 1884, Du Bois, Pa. D. Dec. 2, 1934, Los Angeles, Calif.

Year	Team		Games	BA	SA	AB	H	2B	3B	HR	HR%	R	RBI	BB	SO	SB	Pinch Hit AB	Pinch Hit H	PO	A	E	DP	TC/G	FA	G by Pos
1908	CIN	N	14	.109	.109	46	5	0	0	0	0.0	5	1	3		1	0	0	17	2	0	1	1.5	1.000	OF-13
1913	PHI	A	59	.255	.284	141	36	2	1	0	0.0	13	11	13	28	4	19	2	73	5	3	2	2.1	.963	OF-38
1914	2 teams		PHI A (29G –.256) NY A (67G –.251)																						
″	total		96	.253	.329	277	70	7	7	0	0.0	53	16	50	27	12	12	3	74	16	6	2	1.2	.938	OF-81
1915	NY	A	10	.250	.250	8	2	0	0	0	0.0	2	1	2	2	1	4	1	2	0	0	1	1.0	1.000	OF-2
4 yrs.			179	.239	.292	472	113	9	8	0	0.0	73	29	68	57	18	35	6	166	23	9	6	1.5	.955	OF-134

Dom Dallessandro

DALLESSANDRO, NICHOLAS DOMINIC (Dim Dom) BL TL 5′ 6″ 168 lbs.
B. Oct. 3, 1913, Reading, Pa. D. Apr. 29, 1988, Indianapolis, Ind.

Year	Team		Games	BA	SA	AB	H	2B	3B	HR	HR%	R	RBI	BB	SO	SB	Pinch Hit AB	Pinch Hit H	PO	A	E	DP	TC/G	FA	G by Pos
1937	BOS	A	68	.231	.293	147	34	7	1	0	0.0	18	11	27	16	2	26	7	54	1	2	0	1.6	.965	OF-35
1940	CHI	N	107	.268	.387	287	77	19	6	1	0.3	33	36	34	13	4	29	10	156	1	5	0	2.2	.969	OF-74
1941			140	.272	.391	486	132	36	2	6	1.2	73	85	68	37	3	7	1	292	4	4	0	2.3	.987	OF-131
1942			96	.261	.383	264	69	12	4	4	1.5	30	43	36	18	4	26	**9**	134	6	2	1	2.2	.986	OF-66
1943			87	.222	.318	176	39	8	3	1	0.6	13	31	40	14	1	32	8	87	2	3	0	2.0	.967	OF-45
1944			117	.304	.438	381	116	19	4	8	2.1	53	74	61	29	1	11	3	212	9	4	2	2.1	.982	OF-106
1946			65	.225	.326	89	20	2	2	1	1.1	4	9	23	12	1	29	6	33	0	1	0	1.7	.971	OF-20
1947			66	.287	.391	115	33	7	1	1	0.9	18	14	21	11	0	32	8	50	1	0	1	1.8	1.000	OF-28
8 yrs.			746	.267	.381	1945	520	110	23	22	1.1	242	303	310	150	16	192	52	1018	24	21	4	2.1	.980	OF-505

Abner Dalrymple

DALRYMPLE, ABNER FRANK BL TR 5′10½″ 175 lbs.
B. Sept. 9, 1857, Warren, Ill. D. Jan. 25, 1939, Warren, Ill.

Year	Team		Games	BA	SA	AB	H	2B	3B	HR	HR%	R	RBI	BB	SO	SB	Pinch Hit AB	Pinch Hit H	PO	A	E	DP	TC/G	FA	G by Pos
1878	MIL	N	61	.354	.421	271	96	10	4	0	0.0	52	15	6	29		0	0	128	11	28	3	2.7	.832	OF-61
1879	CHI	N	71	.291	.372	333	97	25	1	0	0.0	47	23	4	29		0	0	103	4	40	1	2.1	.728	OF-71
1880			86	.330	.458	**382**	**126**	25	12	0	0.0	**91**	36	3	18		0	0	157	19	29	4	2.4	.859	OF-86
1881			82	.323	.414	362	117	22	4	1	0.3	72	37	15	22		0	0	143	14	31	1	2.3	.835	OF-82
1882			84	.295	.421	**397**	117	25	11	1	0.3	96	36	14	18		0	0	185	8	27	4	2.6	.877	OF-84
1883			80	.298	.402	363	108	24	4	2	0.6	78		11	29		0	0	149	12	34	3	2.4	.826	OF-80
1884			111	.309	.505	**521**	161	18	9	22	4.2	111		14	39		0	0	176	18	26	5	2.0	.882	OF-111
1885			113	.274	.445	**492**	135	27	12	**11**	**2.2**	109	58	46	42		0	0	180	16	27	2	2.0	.879	OF-113
1886			82	.233	.353	331	77	7	12	3	0.9	62	26	33	44		0	0	126	15	7	1	1.8	.953	OF-82
1887	PIT	N	92	.212	.307	358	76	18	5	2	0.6	45	31	45	43	29	0	0	184	14	22	1	2.4	.900	OF-92
1888			57	.220	.278	227	50	9	2	0	0.0	19	14	6	28	7	0	0	81	9	9	0	1.7	.909	OF-57
1891	MIL	AA	32	.311	.459	135	42	7	5	1	0.7	31	22	7	18	6	0	0	44	6	5	1	1.7	.909	OF-32
12 yrs.			951	.288	.410	4172	1202	217	81	43	1.0	813	298	204	359	42	0	0	1656	146	285	26	2.2	.863	OF-951

Bill Dalrymple

DALRYMPLE, WILLIAM DUNN TR
B. Feb. 7, 1891, Baltimore, Md. D. July 14, 1967, San Diego, Calif.

Year	Team		Games	BA	SA	AB	H	2B	3B	HR	HR%	R	RBI	BB	SO	SB	Pinch Hit AB	Pinch Hit H	PO	A	E	DP	TC/G	FA	G by Pos
1915	STL	A	2	.000	.000	2	0	0	0	0	0.0	0	0	0	0	0	1	0	0	1	0	0	1.0	1.000	3B-1

Clay Dalrymple

DALRYMPLE, CLAYTON ERROL BL TR 6′ 190 lbs.
B. Dec. 3, 1936, Chico, Calif.

Year	Team		Games	BA	SA	AB	H	2B	3B	HR	HR%	R	RBI	BB	SO	SB	Pinch Hit AB	Pinch Hit H	PO	A	E	DP	TC/G	FA	G by Pos
1960	PHI	N	82	.272	.411	158	43	6	2	4	2.5	11	21	15	21	0	42	12	172	25	7	3	4.3	.966	C-48
1961			129	.220	.294	378	83	11	1	5	1.3	23	42	30	30	0	9	1	551	86	14	10	5.3	.978	C-122
1962			123	.276	.416	370	102	13	3	11	3.0	40	54	70	32	1	9	1	635	61	9	11	5.9	.987	C-119
1963			142	.252	.365	452	114	15	3	10	2.2	40	40	45	55	0	3	1	881	90	19	16	7.0	.981	C-142
1964			127	.238	.343	382	91	16	3	6	1.6	36	46	39	40	0	4	1	737	61	7	11	6.5	.991	C-124
1965			103	.213	.302	301	64	5	5	4	1.3	14	23	34	37	0	5	0	657	70	5	10	7.2	.993	C-102
1966			114	.245	.338	331	81	13	3	4	1.2	30	39	60	57	0	6	0	615	48	5	5	6.1	.993	C-110
1967			101	.172	.239	268	46	7	1	3	1.1	12	21	36	49	1	8	3	558	59	4	7	6.4	.994	C-97
1968			85	.207	.290	241	50	9	1	3	1.2	19	26	22	57	1	6	0	463	34	5	3	6.3	.990	C-80
1969	BAL	A	37	.237	.388	80	19	1	1	3	3.8	8	6	13	8	0	8	1	116	17	0	2	4.4	1.000	C-30
1970			13	.219	.344	32	7	1	0	1	3.1	4	3	7	4	0	2	0	78	8	0	0	7.8	1.000	C-11
1971			23	.204	.286	49	10	1	0	1	2.0	6	6	16	13	0	3	0	94	7	3	1	5.8	.971	C-18
12 yrs.			1079	.233	.335	3042	710	98	23	55	1.8	243	327	387	403	3	105	20	5557	566	78	79	6.2	.987	C-1003
WORLD SERIES																									
1969	BAL	A	2	1.000	1.000	2	2	0	0	0	0.0	0	0	0	0	0	2	2	0	0	0	0	0.0	—	

Jack Dalton

DALTON, TALBOT PERCY BR TR 5′10½″ 187 lbs.
B. July 3, 1885, Henderson, Tenn. Deceased.

Year	Team		Games	BA	SA	AB	H	2B	3B	HR	HR%	R	RBI	BB	SO	SB	Pinch Hit AB	Pinch Hit H	PO	A	E	DP	TC/G	FA	G by Pos
1910	BKN	N	77	.227	.300	273	62	9	4	1	0.4	33	21	26	30	5	4	1	129	12	5	3	2.0	.966	OF-72
1914			128	.319	.391	442	141	13	8	1	0.2	65	45	53	39	19	10	4	240	7	9	2	2.2	.965	OF-116

Jack Dalton *continued*

Year	Team	Lg	Games	BA	SA	AB	H	2B	3B	HR	HR%	R	RBI	BB	SO	SB	Pinch Hit AB	Pinch Hit H	PO	A	E	DP	TC/G	FA	G by Pos
1915	BUF	F	132	.293	.359	437	128	17	3	2	0.5	68	46	50		28	12	4	218	11	8	4	2.0	.966	OF-119
1916	DET	A	8	.182	.182	11	2	0	0	0	0.0	1	0	0	5	0	2	1	3	0	0	0	0.8	1.000	OF-4
4 yrs.			345	.286	.356	1163	333	39	15	4	0.3	167	112	129	74	52	28	10	590	30	22	9	2.1	.966	OF-311

Bert Daly

DALY, ALBERT JOSEPH BR TR 5′ 9″ 170 lbs.
B. Apr. 8, 1881, Bayonne, N. J. D. Sept. 3, 1952, Bayonne, N. J.

Year	Team	Lg	Games	BA	SA	AB	H	2B	3B	HR	HR%	R	RBI	BB	SO	SB	Pinch Hit AB	Pinch Hit H	PO	A	E	DP	TC/G	FA	G by Pos
1903	PHI	A	10	.190	.381	21	4	0	2	0	0.0	2	4	1		0	2	0	4	8	3	1	1.9	.800	2B-4, 3B-3, SS-1

Joe Daly

DALY, JOSEPH JOHN TR 5′ 8″ 157 lbs.
Brother of Tom Daly.
B. Sept. 21, 1868, Conshohocken, Pa. D. Mar. 21, 1943, Philadelphia, Pa.

Year	Team	Lg	Games	BA	SA	AB	H	2B	3B	HR	HR%	R	RBI	BB	SO	SB	Pinch Hit AB	Pinch Hit H	PO	A	E	DP	TC/G	FA	G by Pos
1890	PHI	AA	21	.280	.360	75	21	4	1	0	0.0	8		3		1	0	0	39	19	13	0	3.1	.817	OF-14, C-9
1891	CLE	N	1	.000	.000	3	0	0	0	0	0.0	0	0	0	2	0	0	0	2	0	0	0	2.0	1.000	OF-1
1892	BOS	N	1	—	—	0	0	0	0	0	—	0	0	0	0	0	0	0	2	0	0	0	2.0	1.000	C-1
3 yrs.			23	.269	.346	78	21	4	1	0	0.0	8	0	3	2	1	0	0	43	19	13	0	3.0	.827	OF-15, C-10

Sun Daly

DALY, JAMES J.
B. Jan. 6, 1865, Rutland, Vt. D. Apr. 30, 1938, Albany, N. Y.

Year	Team	Lg	Games	BA	SA	AB	H	2B	3B	HR	HR%	R	RBI	BB	SO	SB	Pinch Hit AB	Pinch Hit H	PO	A	E	DP	TC/G	FA	G by Pos
1892	BAL	N	13	.250	.333	48	12	0	2	0	0.0	5	7	1	4	0	0	0	22	2	2	1	2.0	.923	OF-13

Tom Daly

DALY, THOMAS DANIEL BR TR 5′11½″ 171 lbs.
B. Dec. 12, 1891, St. John, N. B., Canada D. Nov. 7, 1946, Bedford, Mass.

Year	Team	Lg	Games	BA	SA	AB	H	2B	3B	HR	HR%	R	RBI	BB	SO	SB	Pinch Hit AB	Pinch Hit H	PO	A	E	DP	TC/G	FA	G by Pos
1913	CHI	A	1	.000	.000	3	0	0	0	0	0.0	0	0	0	0	0	0	0	6	1	0	1	7.0	1.000	C-1
1914			61	.233	.248	133	31	2	0	0	0.0	13	8	7	13	3	24	6	60	6	4	3	2.1	.943	OF-23, 3B-5, C-4, 1B-2
1915			29	.191	.213	47	9	1	0	0	0.0	5	3	5	9	0	9	1	61	9	3	0	3.7	.959	C-19, 1B-1
1916	CLE	A	31	.219	.260	73	16	1	1	0	0.0	3	8	1	2	0	5	1	86	24	2	3	4.3	.982	C-25, OF-1
1918	CHI	N	1	.000	.000	1	0	0	0	0	0.0	0	0	0	0	0	0	0	2	0	1	0	3.0	.667	C-1
1919			25	.220	.260	50	11	0	1	0	0.0	4	1	2	5	0	6	0	55	10	3	2	3.8	.956	C-18
1920			44	.311	.378	90	28	6	0	0	0.0	12	13	2	6	1	14	4	88	18	2	0	3.7	.981	C-29
1921			51	.238	.301	143	34	7	1	0	0.0	12	22	8	8	1	4	1	171	48	6	10	4.8	.973	C-47
8 yrs.			243	.239	.281	540	129	17	3	0	0.0	49	55	25	43	5	62	13	529	116	21	19	3.8	.968	C-144, OF-24, 3B-5, 1B-3

Tom Daly

DALY, THOMAS PETER (Tido) BB TR 5′ 7″ 170 lbs.
Brother of Joe Daly.
B. Feb. 7, 1866, Philadelphia, Pa. D. Oct. 29, 1938, Brooklyn, N. Y.

Year	Team	Lg	Games	BA	SA	AB	H	2B	3B	HR	HR%	R	RBI	BB	SO	SB	Pinch Hit AB	Pinch Hit H	PO	A	E	DP	TC/G	FA	G by Pos
1887	CHI	N	74	.207	.301	256	53	10	4	2	0.8	45	17	22	25	29	0	0	390	161	39	17	7.6	.934	C-64, OF-8, SS-2, 2B-2, 1B-2
1888			65	.192	.256	219	42	2	6	0	0.0	34	29	10	26	10	0	0	411	107	34	10	8.4	.938	C-62, OF-4
1889	WAS	N	71	.300	.404	250	75	13	5	1	0.4	39	40	38	28	18	0	0	354	102	43	8	6.8	.914	C-57, 1B-8, 2B-4, OF-3, SS-1
1890	BKN	N	82	.243	.353	292	71	9	4	5	1.7	55	43	32	43	20	0	0	491	78	21	14	7.2	.964	C-69, 1B-12, OF-1
1891			58	.250	.385	200	50	11	5	2	1.0	29	27	21	34	7	0	0	289	58	38	8	6.5	.901	C-26, 1B-15, SS-11, OF-7
1892			124	.256	.343	446	114	15	6	4	0.9	76	51	64	61	34	0	0	260	170	33	16	3.7	.929	3B-57, OF-30, C-27, 2B-10
1893			126	.289	.445	470	136	21	14	8	1.7	94	70	76	**65**	32	0	0	287	348	77	27	5.6	.892	2B-82, 3B-45
1894			123	.341	.476	492	168	22	10	8	1.6	135	82	77	42	51	0	0	317	354	68	52	6.0	.908	2B-123
1895			120	.281	.367	455	128	17	8	2	0.4	89	68	52	52	28	0	0	318	346	50	42	5.9	.930	2B-120
1896			67	.281	.433	224	63	13	6	3	1.3	43	29	33	25	19	0	0	170	192	37	31	6.0	.907	2B-66, C-1
1898			23	.329	.397	73	24	3	1	0	0.0	11	11	14		6	0	0	56	77	1	12	5.8	.993	2B-23
1899			141	.313	.428	498	156	24	9	5	1.0	95	88	69		43	0	0	377	453	63	69	6.3	.929	2B-141
1900			97	.312	.414	343	107	17	3	4	1.2	70	55	46		27	0	0	261	238	40	41	5.5	.926	2B-93, 1B-3, OF-2
1901			133	.315	.444	520	164	38	10	3	0.6	88	90	42		31	0	0	370	357	43	46	5.8	.944	2B-133
1902	CHI	A	137	.225	.288	489	110	22	3	1	0.2	57	54	55		19	0	0	312	370	31	70	5.2	.957	2B-137
1903	2 teams		CHI A (43G –.207)			CIN N (80G –.293)																			
″	total		123	.265	.365	457	121	25	9	1	0.2	62	57	36		11	1	0	247	324	36	34	5.0	.941	2B-122
16 yrs.			1564	.278	.387	5684	1582	262	103	49	0.9	1022	811	687	401	385	1	0	4910	3735	654	497	5.9	.930	2B-1056, C-306, 3B-102, OF-55, 1B-40, SS-14

Bill Dam

DAM, ELBRIDGE RUST
B. Apr. 4, 1885, Cambridge, Mass. D. June 22, 1930, Quincy, Mass.

Year	Team	Lg	Games	BA	SA	AB	H	2B	3B	HR	HR%	R	RBI	BB	SO	SB	Pinch Hit AB	Pinch Hit H	PO	A	E	DP	TC/G	FA	G by Pos
1909	BOS	N	1	.500	1.000	2	1	1	0	0	0.0	1	0	1		0	0	0	1	0	0	0	1.0	1.000	OF-1

Jack Damaska

DAMASKA, JACK LLOYD BR TR 5′11″ 168 lbs.
B. Aug. 21, 1937, Beaver Falls, Pa.

Year	Team	Lg	Games	BA	SA	AB	H	2B	3B	HR	HR%	R	RBI	BB	SO	SB	Pinch Hit AB	Pinch Hit H	PO	A	E	DP	TC/G	FA	G by Pos
1963	STL	N	5	.200	.200	5	1	0	0	0	0.0	1	1	0	4	0	4	1	0	0	0	0	0.0		OF-1, 2B-1

Johnny Damon

DAMON, JOHNNY DAVID BL TL 6′ 175 lbs.
B. Nov. 5, 1973, Fort Riley, Kans.

Year	Team	Lg	Games	BA	SA	AB	H	2B	3B	HR	HR%	R	RBI	BB	SO	SB	Pinch Hit AB	Pinch Hit H	PO	A	E	DP	TC/G	FA	G by Pos
1995	KC	A	47	.282	.441	188	53	11	5	3	1.6	32	23	12	22	7	1	0	110	0	1	0	2.4	.991	OF-47

Harry Damrau

DAMRAU, HARRY ROBERT BR TR 5′10″ 178 lbs.
B. Sept. 11, 1890, Newburgh, N. Y. D. Aug. 21, 1957, Staten Island, N. Y.

Year	Team	Lg	Games	BA	SA	AB	H	2B	3B	HR	HR%	R	RBI	BB	SO	SB	Pinch Hit AB	Pinch Hit H	PO	A	E	DP	TC/G	FA	G by Pos
1915	PHI	A	16	.196	.214	56	11	1	0	0	0.0	4	3	5	17	1	0	0	16	24	6	1	2.9	.870	3B-16

Jake Daniel

DANIEL, HANDLEY JACOB BL TL 5′11″ 175 lbs.
B. Apr. 22, 1912, Roanoke, Ala.

Year	Team	Lg	Games	BA	SA	AB	H	2B	3B	HR	HR%	R	RBI	BB	SO	SB	Pinch Hit AB	Pinch Hit H	PO	A	E	DP	TC/G	FA	G by Pos
1937	BKN	N	12	.185	.222	27	5	1	0	0	0.0	3	3	3	4	0	2	0	51	3	0	3	7.7	1.000	1B-7

Bert Daniels

DANIELS, BERNARD ELMER BR TR 5′ 9½″ 180 lbs.
B. Oct. 31, 1882, Danville, Ill. D. June 6, 1958, Cedar Grove, N. J.

Year	Team	Lg	Games	BA	SA	AB	H	2B	3B	HR	HR%	R	RBI	BB	SO	SB	Pinch Hit AB	Pinch Hit H	PO	A	E	DP	TC/G	FA	G by Pos
1910	NY	A	95	.253	.343	356	90	13	8	1	0.3	68	17	41		41	0	0	208	21	12	4	2.5	.950	OF-85, 3B-6, 1B-4
1911			131	.286	.372	462	132	16	9	2	0.4	74	31	48		40	6	1	256	15	17	6	2.4	.941	OF-120
1912			133	.274	.381	496	136	25	11	2	0.4	72	41	51		37	2	1	277	13	17	1	2.3	.945	OF-131
1913			93	.216	.287	320	69	13	5	0	0.0	52	22	44	36	27	4	1	128	15	5	3	1.7	.966	OF-87
1914	CIN	N	71	.219	.305	269	59	9	7	0	0.0	29	19	19	40	14	0	0	144	7	4	2	2.2	.974	OF-71
5 yrs.			523	.255	.345	1903	486	76	40	5	0.3	295	130	203	76	159	12	3	1013	71	55	16	2.3	.952	OF-494, 3B-6, 1B-4

Fred Daniels

DANIELS, FREDERICK CLINTON (Tony) BR TR 5′ 9½″ 185 lbs.
B. Dec. 28, 1924, Gastonia, N. C.

Year	Team		Games	BA	SA	AB	H	2B	3B	HR	HR%	R	RBI	BB	SO	SB	Pinch Hit AB	Pinch Hit H	PO	A	E	DP	TC/G	FA	G by Pos
1945	PHI	N	76	.200	.230	230	46	3	2	0	0.0	15	10	12	22	1	0	0	171	215	20	41	5.3	.951	2B-75, 3B-1

Jack Daniels

DANIELS, HAROLD JACK (Sour Mash) BL TL 5′10″ 165 lbs.
B. Dec. 21, 1927, Chester, Pa.

Year	Team		Games	BA	SA	AB	H	2B	3B	HR	HR%	R	RBI	BB	SO	SB	Pinch Hit AB	Pinch Hit H	PO	A	E	DP	TC/G	FA	G by Pos
1952	BOS	N	106	.187	.247	219	41	5	1	2	0.9	31	14	28	30	3	17	2	119	6	3	2	1.5	.977	OF-87

Kal Daniels

DANIELS, KALVOSKI BL TR 5′11″ 195 lbs.
B. Aug. 20, 1963, Vienna, Ga.

Year	Team		Games	BA	SA	AB	H	2B	3B	HR	HR%	R	RBI	BB	SO	SB	Pinch Hit AB	Pinch Hit H	PO	A	E	DP	TC/G	FA	G by Pos
1986	CIN	N	74	.320	.519	181	58	10	4	6	3.3	34	23	22	30	15	23	11	88	0	3	0	1.9	.967	OF-47
1987			108	.334	.617	368	123	24	1	26	7.1	73	64	60	62	26	12	2	178	5	6	0	2.0	.968	OF-94
1988			140	.291	.463	495	144	29	1	18	3.6	95	64	87	94	27	1	0	256	10	5	2	2.0	.982	OF-137
1989	2 teams		CIN N (44G –.218) LA N (11G –.342)																						
″	total		55	.246	.392	171	42	13	0	4	2.3	33	17	43	33	9	5	0	88	4	0	1	1.9	1.000	OF-49
1990	LA	N	130	.296	.531	450	133	23	1	27	6.0	81	94	68	104	4	3	2	207	13	3	2	1.8	.987	OF-127
1991			137	.249	.397	461	115	15	1	17	3.7	54	73	63	116	6	5	1	220	9	5	0	1.8	.979	OF-132
1992	2 teams		LA N (35G –.231) CHI N (48G –.250)																						
″	total		83	.241	.377	212	51	11	0	6	2.8	21	25	22	54	0	24	7	119	9	2	4	2.3	.985	OF-49, 1B-8
7 yrs.			727	.285	.479	2338	666	125	8	104	4.4	391	360	365	493	87	73	23	1156	50	24	9	1.9	.980	OF-635, 1B-8

Law Daniels

DANIELS, LAWRENCE LONG BR TR 5′10″ 170 lbs.
B. July 14, 1862, Newton, Mass. D. Jan. 7, 1929, Waltham, Mass.

Year	Team		Games	BA	SA	AB	H	2B	3B	HR	HR%	R	RBI	BB	SO	SB	Pinch Hit AB	Pinch Hit H	PO	A	E	DP	TC/G	FA	G by Pos
1887	BAL	AA	48	.248	.291	165	41	5	1	0	0.0	23		8		7	0	0	188	44	45	5	5.7	.838	C-26, OF-15, 1B-4, 2B-2, 3B-1, SS-1
1888	KC	AA	61	.202	.225	218	44	2	0	1	0.5	32	28	14		20	0	0	163	71	39	7	4.4	.857	OF-30, C-29, 3B-2, SS-1
2 yrs.			109	.222	.253	383	85	7	1	1	0.3	55	28	22		27	0	0	351	115	84	12	5.0	.847	C-55, OF-45, 1B-4, 3B-3, 2B-2, SS-2

Buck Danner

DANNER, HENRY FREDERICK BR TR 5′ 6½″ 135 lbs.
B. June 8, 1891, Dedham, Mass. D. Sept. 21, 1949, Boston, Mass.

Year	Team		Games	BA	SA	AB	H	2B	3B	HR	HR%	R	RBI	BB	SO	SB	Pinch Hit AB	Pinch Hit H	PO	A	E	DP	TC/G	FA	G by Pos
1915	PHI	A	3	.250	.250	12	3	0	0	0	0.0	1	0	0	1	1	0	0	5	4	3	0	4.0	.750	SS-3

Harry Danning

DANNING, HARRY (Harry The Horse) BR TR 6′ 1″ 190 lbs.
Brother of Ike Danning.
B. Sept. 6, 1911, Los Angeles, Calif.

Year	Team		Games	BA	SA	AB	H	2B	3B	HR	HR%	R	RBI	BB	SO	SB	Pinch Hit AB	Pinch Hit H	PO	A	E	DP	TC/G	FA	G by Pos
1933	NY	N	3	.000	.000	2	0	0	0	0	0.0	0	0	1	0	0	2	0	2	0	0	0	2.0	1.000	C-1
1934			53	.330	.433	97	32	7	0	1	1.0	8	7	1	9	1	16	8	78	13	1	1	2.5	.989	C-37
1935			65	.243	.368	152	37	11	1	2	1.3	16	20	9	15	0	19	2	153	22	4	6	4.1	.978	C-44
1936			32	.159	.246	69	11	2	2	0	0.0	3	4	1	5	0	6	1	70	10	1	2	3.4	.988	C-24
1937			93	.288	.438	292	84	12	4	8	2.7	30	51	18	20	0	11	2	332	57	7	7	4.6	.982	C-86
1938			120	.306	.438	448	137	26	3	9	2.0	59	60	23	40	1	6	2	449	50	8	7	4.4	.984	C-114
1939			135	.313	.479	520	163	28	5	16	3.1	79	74	35	42	4	3	0	550	80	6	13	4.8	.991	C-132
1940			140	.300	.454	524	157	34	4	13	2.5	65	91	35	31	3	9	0	634	91	15	13	5.6	.980	C-131
1941			130	.244	.355	459	112	22	4	7	1.5	58	56	30	25	1	11	3	532	77	4	8	5.2	.993	C-116, 1B-1
1942			119	.279	.350	408	114	20	3	1	0.2	45	34	34	29	3	2	1	459	55	11	7	4.5	.979	C-116
10 yrs.			890	.285	.415	2971	847	162	26	57	1.9	363	397	187	216	13	85	19	3259	455	57	64	4.7	.985	C-801, 1B-1
WORLD SERIES																									
1936	NY	N	2	.000	.000	2	0	0	0	0	0.0	0	0	0	1	0	1	0	3	0	1	0	4.0	.750	C-1
1937			3	.250	.333	12	3	1	0	0	0.0	0	2	0	2	0	0	0	20	1	0	0	7.0	1.000	C-3
2 yrs.			5	.214	.286	14	3	1	0	0	0.0	0	2	0	3	0	1	0	23	1	1	0	6.3	.960	C-4

Ike Danning

DANNING, IKE BR TR 5′10″ 160 lbs.
Brother of Harry Danning.
B. Jan. 20, 1905, Los Angeles, Calif. D. Mar. 30, 1983, Santa Monica, Calif.

Year	Team		Games	BA	SA	AB	H	2B	3B	HR	HR%	R	RBI	BB	SO	SB	Pinch Hit AB	Pinch Hit H	PO	A	E	DP	TC/G	FA	G by Pos
1928	STL	A	2	.500	.500	6	3	0	0	0	0.0	0	1	1	2	0	0	0	8	3	1	0	6.0	.917	C-2

Fats Dantonio

DANTONIO, JOHN JAMES BR TR 5′ 8″ 165 lbs.
B. Dec. 31, 1918, New Orleans, La. D. May 28, 1993, New Orleans, La.

Year	Team		Games	BA	SA	AB	H	2B	3B	HR	HR%	R	RBI	BB	SO	SB	Pinch Hit AB	Pinch Hit H	PO	A	E	DP	TC/G	FA	G by Pos
1944	BKN	N	3	.143	.143	7	1	0	0	0	0.0	0	0	0	1	0	0	0	11	0	2	0	4.3	.846	C-3
1945			47	.250	.313	128	32	6	1	0	0.0	12	12	11	6	3	1	1	141	16	12	0	3.8	.929	C-45
2 yrs.			50	.244	.304	135	33	6	1	0	0.0	12	12	11	7	3	1	1	152	16	14	0	3.8	.923	C-48

Babe Danzig

DANZIG, HAROLD P. BR TR 6′ 2″ 205 lbs.
B. Apr. 30, 1887, Binghamton, N. Y. D. July 14, 1931, San Francisco, Calif.

Year	Team		Games	BA	SA	AB	H	2B	3B	HR	HR%	R	RBI	BB	SO	SB	Pinch Hit AB	Pinch Hit H	PO	A	E	DP	TC/G	FA	G by Pos
1909	BOS	A	6	.154	.154	13	2	0	0	0	0.0	0	0	2		0	2	0	24	0	1	3	8.3	.960	1B-3

Cliff Dapper

DAPPER, CLIFFORD ROLAND BR TR 6′ 2″ 190 lbs.
B. Jan. 2, 1920, Los Angeles, Calif.

Year	Team		Games	BA	SA	AB	H	2B	3B	HR	HR%	R	RBI	BB	SO	SB	Pinch Hit AB	Pinch Hit H	PO	A	E	DP	TC/G	FA	G by Pos
1942	BKN	N	8	.471	.706	17	8	1	0	1	5.9	2	9	2	2	0	0	0	20	3	0	1	2.9	1.000	C-8

Cliff Daringer

DARINGER, CLIFFORD CLARENCE (Shanty) BL TR 5′ 7½″ 155 lbs.
Brother of Rolla Daringer.
B. Apr. 10, 1885, Hayden, Ind. D. Dec. 26, 1971, Sacramento, Calif.

Year	Team		Games	BA	SA	AB	H	2B	3B	HR	HR%	R	RBI	BB	SO	SB	Pinch Hit AB	Pinch Hit H	PO	A	E	DP	TC/G	FA	G by Pos
1914	KC	F	64	.263	.287	160	42	2	1	0	0.0	12	16	11		9	4	1	70	142	19	16	4.1	.918	SS-24, 3B-19, 2B-14

Rolla Daringer

DARINGER, ROLLA HARRISON BL TR 5′10″ 155 lbs.
Brother of Cliff Daringer.
B. Nov. 15, 1888, North Vernon, Ind. D. May 23, 1974, Seymour, Ind.

Year	Team		Games	BA	SA	AB	H	2B	3B	HR	HR%	R	RBI	BB	SO	SB	Pinch Hit AB	Pinch Hit H	PO	A	E	DP	TC/G	FA	G by Pos
1914	STL	N	2	.500	.750	4	2	1	0	0	0.0	1	0	1	2	0	1	0	0	2	1	1	3.0	.667	SS-1
1915			10	.087	.087	23	2	0	0	0	0.0	3	0	9	5	0	0	0	13	23	2	5	3.8	.947	SS-10
2 yrs.			12	.148	.185	27	4	1	0	0	0.0	4	0	10	7	0	1	0	13	25	3	6	3.7	.927	SS-11

Alvin Dark

DARK, ALVIN RALPH (Blackie)
B. Jan. 7, 1922, Comanche, Okla.
Manager 1961–64, 1966–71, 1974–75, 1977.
BR TR 5′11″ 185 lbs.

Year	Team	Games	BA	SA	AB	H	2B	3B	HR	HR%	R	RBI	BB	SO	SB	Pinch Hit AB	Pinch Hit H	PO	A	E	DP	TC/G	FA	G by Pos
1946	BOS N	15	.231	.462	13	3	3	0	0	0.0	0	1	0	3	0	0	0	6	14	2	2	1.7	.909	SS-12, OF-1
1948		137	.322	.433	543	175	39	6	3	0.6	85	48	24	36	4	4	3	253	393	25	66	5.0	.963	SS-133
1949		130	.276	.355	529	146	23	5	3	0.6	74	53	31	43	5	0	0	233	395	26	76	5.1	.960	SS-125, 3B-4
1950	NY N	154	.279	.440	587	164	36	5	16	2.7	79	67	39	60	9	0	0	288	465	30	101	5.1	.962	SS-154
1951		156	.303	.454	646	196	**41**	7	14	2.2	114	69	42	39	12	0	0	295	465	45	114	5.2	.944	SS-156
1952		151	.301	.431	589	177	29	3	14	2.4	92	73	47	39	6	1	0	324	423	27	116	5.2	.965	SS-150
1953		155	.300	.488	**647**	194	41	6	23	3.6	126	88	28	34	7	1	0	325	433	24	102	4.8	.969	SS-110, 2B-26, OF-17, 3B-8, P-1
1954		154	.293	.446	**644**	189	26	6	20	3.1	98	70	27	40	5	0	0	289	487	36	105	5.3	.956	SS-154
1955		115	.282	.394	475	134	20	3	9	1.9	77	45	22	32	2	1	0	213	324	21	70	4.9	.962	SS-115
1956	2 teams	NY N (48G –.252)	STL N (100G –.286)																					
″	total	148	.275	.368	619	170	26	7	6	1.0	73	54	29	46	3	1	0	267	424	29	93	4.9	.960	SS-147
1957	STL N	140	.290	.381	583	169	25	8	4	0.7	80	64	29	56	3	1	0	276	421	25	105	5.2	.965	SS-139, 3B-1
1958	2 teams	STL N (18G –.297)	CHI N (114G –.295)																					
″	total	132	.295	.364	528	156	16	4	4	0.8	61	48	31	29	1	8	5	121	260	21	30	3.2	.948	3B-119, SS-8
1959	CHI N	136	.264	.386	477	126	22	9	6	1.3	60	45	55	50	1	1	0	138	260	21	21	3.1	.950	3B-131, 1B-4, SS-1
1960	2 teams	PHI N (55G –.242)	MIL N (50G –.298)																					
″	total	105	.265	.351	339	90	11	3	4	1.2	45	32	26	27	1	17	3	146	90	10	11	2.6	.959	3B-57, OF-25, 1B-11, 2B-3
14 yrs.		1828	.289	.411	7219	2089	358	72	126	1.7	1064	757	430	534	59	35	11	3174	4854	342	1012	4.6	.959	SS-1404, 3B-320, OF-43, 2B-29, 1B-15, P-1
WORLD SERIES																								
1948	BOS N	6	.167	.208	24	4	1	0	0	0.0	2	0	0	2	0	0	0	7	12	3	1	3.7	.864	SS-6
1951	NY N	6	.417	.667	24	10	3	0	1	4.2	5	4	2	3	0	0	0	10	15	0	4	4.2	1.000	SS-6
1954		4	.412	.412	17	7	0	0	0	0.0	2	0	1	1	0	0	0	7	12	1	1	5.0	.950	SS-4
3 yrs.		16	.323	.431	65	21	4	0	1	1.5	9	4	3	6	0	0	0	24	39	4	6	4.2	.940	SS-16

Dell Darling

DARLING, CONRAD
B. Dec. 21, 1861, Erie, Pa. D. Nov. 20, 1904, Erie, Pa.
BR TR 5′ 8″ 170 lbs.

Year	Team	Games	BA	SA	AB	H	2B	3B	HR	HR%	R	RBI	BB	SO	SB	Pinch Hit AB	Pinch Hit H	PO	A	E	DP	TC/G	FA	G by Pos
1883	BUF N	6	.167	.167	18	3	0	0	0	0.0	1		2	5		0	0	16	5	3	1	4.0	.875	C-6
1887	CHI N	38	.319	.489	141	45	7	4	3	2.1	28	20	22	18	19	0	0	132	45	23	3	5.0	.885	OF-20, C-20
1888		20	.213	.360	75	16	3	1	2	2.7	12	7	3	12	0	0	0	139	26	12	5	8.9	.932	C-20
1889		36	.192	.217	120	23	1	1	0	0.0	14	7	25	22	5	0	0	172	45	9	2	6.3	.960	C-36
1890	CHI P	58	.258	.376	221	57	12	4	2	0.9	45	39	29	28	5	0	0	296	72	37	24	6.2	.909	1B-29, SS-15, C-9, OF-7, 2B-3, 3B-2
1891	STL AA	17	.132	.264	53	7	1	3	0	0.0	9	9	10	11	0	0	0	87	28	15	1	6.5	.885	C-17, 2B-2, SS-1
6 yrs.		175	.240	.354	628	151	24	13	7	1.1	109	82	91	96	29	0	0	842	221	99	36	6.2	.915	C-108, 1B-29, OF-27, SS-16, 2B-5, 3B-2

Jack Darragh

DARRAGH, JAMES S.
B. July 17, 1866, Ebensburg, Pa. D. Aug. 12, 1939, Rochester, N. Y.

Year	Team	Games	BA	SA	AB	H	2B	3B	HR	HR%	R	RBI	BB	SO	SB	Pinch Hit AB	Pinch Hit H	PO	A	E	DP	TC/G	FA	G by Pos
1891	LOU AA	1	.500	.500	2	1	0	0	0	0.0	0	0	0	0	0	0	0	8	1	0	0	9.0	1.000	1B-1

Bobby Darwin

DARWIN, ARTHUR BOBBY LEE
B. Feb. 16, 1943, Los Angeles, Calif.
BR TR 6′ 2″ 190 lbs.

Year	Team	Games	BA	SA	AB	H	2B	3B	HR	HR%	R	RBI	BB	SO	SB	Pinch Hit AB	Pinch Hit H	PO	A	E	DP	TC/G	FA	G by Pos
1962	LA A	1	.000	.000	1	0	0	0	0	0.0	0	0	0	1	0	0	0	0	0	1	0	1.0	.000	P-1
1969	LA N	6	—	—	0	0	0	0	0	—	1	0	0	0	0	0	0	0	0	0	0	0.0	.000	P-3
1971		11	.250	.450	20	5	1	0	1	5.0	2	4	2	9	0	7	2	9	0	0	0	2.3	1.000	OF-4
1972	MIN A	145	.267	.442	513	137	20	2	22	4.3	48	80	38	**145**	2	5	1	289	8	6	1	2.1	.980	OF-142
1973		145	.252	.391	560	141	20	2	18	3.2	69	90	46	**137**	5	6	0	233	13	5	1	1.8	.980	OF-140, DH-1
1974		152	.264	.442	575	152	13	7	25	4.3	67	94	37	**127**	1	9	4	254	8	8	1	1.9	.970	OF-142
1975	2 teams	MIN A (48G –.219)	MIL A (55G –.247)																					
″	total	103	.234	.389	355	83	12	2	13	3.7	45	41	29	98	6	6	2	110	8	3	1	1.2	.975	OF-70, DH-28
1976	2 teams	MIL A (25G –.247)	BOS A (43G –.179)																					
″	total	68	.207	.352	179	37	8	3	4	2.2	15	18	8	51	1	18	3	68	2	2	0	1.3	.972	OF-38, DH-17
1977	2 teams	BOS A (4G –.222)	CHI N (11G –.167)																					
″	total	15	.190	.286	21	4	2	0	0	0.0	3	1	0	9	0	10	2	1	0	1	0	0.5	.500	OF-2, DH-2
9 yrs.		646	.251	.412	2224	559	76	16	83	3.7	250	328	160	577	15	61	14	964	39	26	4	1.7	.975	OF-538, DH-48, P-4

Doug Dascenzo

DASCENZO, DOUGLAS CRAIG
B. June 30, 1964, Cleveland, Ohio.
BB TL 5′ 7″ 150 lbs.

Year	Team	Games	BA	SA	AB	H	2B	3B	HR	HR%	R	RBI	BB	SO	SB	Pinch Hit AB	Pinch Hit H	PO	A	E	DP	TC/G	FA	G by Pos
1988	CHI N	26	.213	.253	75	16	3	0	0	0.0	9	4	9	4	6	5	0	55	1	0	0	2.8	1.000	OF-20
1989		47	.165	.194	139	23	1	0	1	0.7	20	12	13	13	6	0	0	96	0	0	0	2.1	1.000	OF-45
1990		113	.253	.344	241	61	9	5	1	0.4	27	26	21	18	15	6	0	174	2	0	1	1.6	1.000	OF-107, P-1
1991		118	.255	.314	239	61	11	0	1	0.4	40	18	24	26	14	28	3	134	0	2	0	1.5	.985	OF-86, P-3
1992		139	.255	.311	376	96	13	4	0	0.0	37	20	27	32	6	21	9	221	2	5	0	1.9	.978	OF-122
1993	TEX A	76	.199	.288	146	29	5	1	2	1.4	20	10	8	22	2	11	6	91	5	1	2	1.4	.990	OF-68, DH-2
6 yrs.		519	.235	.299	1216	286	42	10	5	0.4	153	90	102	115	49	71	18	771	10	8	3	1.7	.990	OF-448, P-4, DH-2

Wally Dashiell

DASHIELL, JOHN WALLACE
B. May 9, 1902, Jewett, Tex. D. May 20, 1972, Pensacola, Fla.
BR TR 5′ 9½″ 170 lbs.

Year	Team	Games	BA	SA	AB	H	2B	3B	HR	HR%	R	RBI	BB	SO	SB	Pinch Hit AB	Pinch Hit H	PO	A	E	DP	TC/G	FA	G by Pos
1924	CHI A	1	.000	.000	2	0	0	0	0	0.0	0	0	0	0	0	0	0	1	1	1	0	3.0	.667	SS-1

Jeff Datz

DATZ, JEFFREY WILLIAM
B. Nov. 28, 1959, Camden, N. J.
BR TR 6′ 4″ 220 lbs.

Year	Team	Games	BA	SA	AB	H	2B	3B	HR	HR%	R	RBI	BB	SO	SB	Pinch Hit AB	Pinch Hit H	PO	A	E	DP	TC/G	FA	G by Pos
1989	DET A	7	.200	.200	10	2	0	0	0	0.0	0	0	1	1	0	0	0	17	1	0	0	2.6	1.000	C-6, DH-1

Harry Daubert

DAUBERT, HARRY J.
B. June 19, 1892, Columbus, Ohio D. Jan. 8, 1944, Detroit, Mich.
BR TR 6′ 165 lbs.

Year	Team	Games	BA	SA	AB	H	2B	3B	HR	HR%	R	RBI	BB	SO	SB	Pinch Hit AB	Pinch Hit H	PO	A	E	DP	TC/G	FA	G by Pos
1915	PIT N	1	.000	.000	1	0	0	0	0	0.0	0	0	0	1	0	1	0	0	0	0	0	0.0	—	

BL TL 5′10½″ 160 lbs.

DAUBERT, JACOB ELLSWORTH
B. Apr. 17, 1884, Shamokin, Pa. D. Oct. 9, 1924, Cincinnati, Ohio.

Jake Daubert

Year	Team	Games	BA	SA	AB	H	2B	3B	HR	HR%	R	RBI	BB	SO	SB	Pinch Hit AB	Pinch Hit H	PO	A	E	DP	TC/G	FA	G by Pos
1910	BKN N	144	.264	.389	552	146	15	15	8	1.4	67	50	47	53	23	0	0	1418	72	16	81	10.5	.989	1B-144
1911		149	.307	.391	573	176	17	8	5	0.9	89	45	51	56	32	0	0	1485	88	18	91	10.7	.989	1B-149
1912		145	.308	.415	559	172	19	16	3	0.5	81	66	48	45	29	1	0	1373	76	10	68	10.2	.993	1B-143
1913		139	**.350**	.423	508	178	17	7	2	0.4	76	52	44	40	25	1	0	1279	80	13	91	9.9	.991	1B-138
1914		126	**.329**	.432	474	156	17	7	6	1.3	89	45	30	34	25	0	0	1097	48	8	68	9.2	.993	1B-126
1915		150	.301	.381	544	164	21	8	2	0.4	62	47	57	48	11	0	0	1441	102	11	73	10.4	.993	1B-150
1916		127	.316	.397	478	151	16	7	3	0.6	75	33	38	39	21	1	0	1195	66	9	56	10.1	.993	1B-126
1917		125	.261	.299	468	122	4	4	2	0.4	59	30	51	30	11	0	0	1188	82	12	59	10.3	.991	1B-125
1918		108	.308	.429	396	122	12	**15**	2	0.5	50	47	27	18	10	2	0	1069	63	10	43	10.9	.991	1B-105
1919	CIN N	140	.276	.350	537	148	10	12	2	0.4	79	44	35	23	11	0	0	1437	80	17	75	11.0	.989	1B-140
1920		142	.304	.423	553	168	28	13	4	0.7	97	48	47	29	11	2	0	1358	63	15	90	10.3	.990	1B-140
1921		136	.306	.399	516	158	18	12	2	0.4	69	64	24	16	12	0	0	1290	78	10	98	10.1	.993	1B-136
1922		156	.336	.492	610	205	15	**22**	12	2.0	114	66	56	21	14	0	0	1652	79	11	127	11.2	.994	1B-156
1923		125	.292	.398	500	146	27	10	2	0.4	63	54	40	20	11	4	1	1224	77	9	95	10.8	.993	1B-121
1924		102	.281	.368	405	114	14	9	1	0.2	47	31	28	17	5	0	0	1128	74	12	84	11.9	.990	1B-102
15 yrs.		2014	.303	.401	7673	2326	250	165	56	0.7	1117	722	623	489	251	11	1	19634	1128	181	1199	10.5	.991	1B-2001
WORLD SERIES																								
1916	BKN N	4	.176	.294	17	3	0	1	0	0.0	1	0	2	3	0	0	0	40	3	0	1	10.8	1.000	1B-4
1919	CIN N	8	.241	.310	29	7	0	1	0	0.0	4	1	1	2	1	0	0	81	5	2	5	11.0	.977	1B-8
2 yrs.		12	.217	.304	46	10	0	2	0	0.0	5	1	3	5	1	0	0	121	8	2	6	10.9	.985	1B-12

BR TR 6′ 180 lbs.

DAUER, RICHARD FREMONT
B. July 27, 1952, San Bernardino, Calif.

Rich Dauer

Year	Team	Games	BA	SA	AB	H	2B	3B	HR	HR%	R	RBI	BB	SO	SB	Pinch Hit AB	Pinch Hit H	PO	A	E	DP	TC/G	FA	G by Pos
1976	BAL A	11	.103	.103	39	4	0	0	0	0.0	0	3	1	3	0	1	0	22	22	0	7	4.4	1.000	2B-10
1977		96	.243	.349	304	74	15	1	5	1.6	38	25	20	28	1	12	1	182	233	7	56	4.5	.983	2B-83, 3B-9, DH-2
1978		133	.264	.353	459	121	23	0	6	1.3	57	46	26	22	0	3	1	222	321	7	69	3.9	.987	2B-87, 3B-52, DH-1
1979		142	.257	.355	479	123	20	0	9	1.9	63	61	36	36	0	0	0	234	355	17	72	4.1	.972	2B-103, 3B-44
1980		152	.284	.352	557	158	32	0	2	0.4	71	63	46	19	3	1	0	334	418	8	115	4.4	.989	2B-137, 3B-35
1981		96	.263	.369	369	97	27	0	4	1.1	41	38	27	18	0	1	0	201	256	5	71	4.7	.989	2B-94, 3B-4
1982		158	.280	.373	558	156	24	2	8	1.4	75	57	50	34	0	1	0	289	354	8	75	3.5	.988	2B-123, 3B-61
1983		140	.235	.309	459	108	19	0	5	1.1	49	41	47	29	1	0	0	280	333	8	79	4.2	.987	2B-131, 3B-17
1984		127	.254	.335	397	101	26	0	2	0.5	29	24	24	23	1	2	0	225	329	11	76	4.5	.981	2B-123, 3B-3
1985		85	.202	.264	208	42	7	0	2	1.0	25	14	20	7	0	0	0	126	202	4	44	3.6	.988	2B-73, 3B-17, 1B-1
10 yrs.		1140	.257	.343	3829	984	193	3	43	1.1	448	372	297	219	6	21	2	2115	2823	75	664	4.1	.985	2B-964, 3B-242, DH-3, 1B-1
LEAGUE CHAMPIONSHIP SERIES																								
1979	BAL A	4	.182	.182	11	2	0	0	0	0.0	0	0	0	1	0	0	0	10	12	0	2	5.5	1.000	2B-4
1983		4	.000	.000	14	0	0	0	0	0.0	0	1	0	0	0	0	0	8	12	0	1	5.0	1.000	2B-4
2 yrs.		8	.080	.080	25	2	0	0	0	0.0	0	1	0	1	0	0	0	18	24	0	3	5.3	1.000	2B-8
WORLD SERIES																								
1979	BAL A	6	.294	.529	17	5	1	0	1	5.9	2	1	0	1	0	1	1	10	10	0	1	4.0	1.000	2B-5
1983		5	.211	.263	19	4	1	0	0	0.0	2	3	0	3	0	0	0	13	7	0	4	3.3	1.000	2B-5, 3B-1
2 yrs.		11	.250	.389	36	9	2	0	1	2.8	4	4	0	4	0	1	1	23	17	0	5	3.6	1.000	2B-10, 3B-1

BR TR 6′ 180 lbs.

DAUGHERTY, HAROLD RAY
B. Oct. 12, 1927, Paris, Pa.

Doc Daugherty

Year	Team	Games	BA	SA	AB	H	2B	3B	HR	HR%	R	RBI	BB	SO	SB	Pinch Hit AB	Pinch Hit H	PO	A	E	DP	TC/G	FA	G by Pos
1951	DET A	1	.000	.000	1	0	0	0	0	0.0	0	0	0	1	0	1	0	0	0	0	0	0.0	—	

BB TL 6′ 188 lbs.

DAUGHERTY, JOHN MICHAEL
B. July 3, 1960, Hialeah, Fla.

Jack Daugherty

Year	Team	Games	BA	SA	AB	H	2B	3B	HR	HR%	R	RBI	BB	SO	SB	Pinch Hit AB	Pinch Hit H	PO	A	E	DP	TC/G	FA	G by Pos
1987	MON N	11	.100	.200	10	1	1	0	0	0.0	1	1	0	3	0	9	1	1	1	0	0	2.0	1.000	1B-1
1989	TEX A	52	.302	.406	106	32	4	2	1	0.9	15	10	11	21	2	18	7	132	14	0	12	4.1	1.000	1B-23, DH-8, OF-5
1990		125	.300	.435	310	93	20	2	6	1.9	36	47	22	49	0	**45**	10	225	22	3	21	2.7	.988	OF-42, 1B-30, DH-21
1991		58	.194	.264	144	28	3	2	1	0.7	8	11	16	23	1	15	2	120	4	1	4	2.6	.992	OF-37, 1B-11, DH-1
1992		59	.205	.276	127	26	9	0	0	0.0	13	9	16	21	2	23	4	70	7	2	2	1.7	.975	OF-26, DH-13, 1B-8
1993	2 teams	HOU N (4G –.333) CIN N (46G –.220)																						
"	total	50	.226	.355	62	14	2	0	2	3.2	7	9	11	15	0	27	5	32	2	1	1	1.8	.971	OF-17, 1B-3
6 yrs.		355	.256	.362	759	194	39	6	10	1.3	80	87	76	132	5	137	29	580	50	7	40	2.6	.989	OF-127, 1B-76, DH-43

BR TR 6′2″ 185 lbs.

DAUGHTERS, ROBERT FRANCIS (Red)
B. Aug. 5, 1914, Cincinnati, Ohio D. Aug. 22, 1988, Southbury, Conn.

Bob Daughters

Year	Team	Games	BA	SA	AB	H	2B	3B	HR	HR%	R	RBI	BB	SO	SB	Pinch Hit AB	Pinch Hit H	PO	A	E	DP	TC/G	FA	G by Pos
1937	BOS A	1	—	—	0	0	0	0	0	—	1	0	0	0	0	0	0	0	0	0	0	0.0	—	

BL TR 6′2″ 195 lbs.

DAULTON, DARREN ARTHUR
B. Jan. 3, 1962, Arkansas City, Kans.

Darren Daulton

Year	Team	Games	BA	SA	AB	H	2B	3B	HR	HR%	R	RBI	BB	SO	SB	Pinch Hit AB	Pinch Hit H	PO	A	E	DP	TC/G	FA	G by Pos
1983	PHI N	2	.333	.333	3	1	0	0	0	0.0	1	0	1	1	0	0	0	8	0	0	0	4.0	1.000	C-2
1985		36	.204	.369	103	21	3	1	4	3.9	14	11	16	37	3	5	0	160	15	1	1	6.3	.994	C-28
1986		49	.225	.428	138	31	4	0	8	5.8	18	21	38	41	2	1	0	244	21	4	6	5.6	.985	C-48
1987		53	.194	.310	129	25	6	0	3	2.3	10	13	16	37	0	12	3	210	13	2	6	5.5	.991	C-40, 1B-1
1988		58	.208	.271	144	30	6	0	1	0.7	13	12	17	26	2	15	4	205	15	6	1	5.0	.973	C-44, 1B-1
1989		131	.201	.310	368	74	12	2	8	2.2	29	44	52	58	2	11	2	627	56	11	8	5.5	.984	C-126
1990		143	.268	.416	459	123	30	1	12	2.6	62	57	72	72	7	10	2	683	70	8	10	5.5	.989	C-139
1991		89	.196	.365	285	56	12	0	12	4.2	36	42	41	66	5	4	1	493	33	8	5	6.1	.985	C-88
1992		145	.270	.524	485	131	32	5	27	5.6	80	**109**	88	103	11	5	1	760	69	11	8	6.0	.987	C-141
1993		147	.257	.482	510	131	35	4	24	4.7	90	105	117	111	5	2	1	981	67	9	19	7.2	.991	C-146
1994		69	.300	.549	257	77	17	1	15	5.8	43	56	33	43	4	1	0	435	41	3	2	7.0	.994	C-68
1995		98	.249	.401	342	85	19	3	9	2.6	44	55	55	52	3	4	0	632	45	4	5	7.2	.994	C-95
12 yrs.		1020	.244	.423	3223	785	176	17	123	3.8	440	525	546	647	44	70	14	5438	445	67	71	6.2	.989	C-965, 1B-2
LEAGUE CHAMPIONSHIP SERIES																								
1993	PHI N	6	.263	.474	19	5	1	0	1	5.3	2	3	6	3	0	0	0	54	3	0	0	9.5	1.000	C-6
WORLD SERIES																								
1993	PHI N	6	.217	.435	23	5	2	0	1	4.3	4	4	4	5	0	0	0	31	4	0	1	5.8	1.000	C-6

Vic Davalillo

DAVALILLO, VICTOR JOSE
Born Victor Jose Davalillo (Romero).
Brother of Yo-Yo Davalillo.
B. July 31, 1936, Cabimas, Venezuela.

BL TL 5′ 7″ 150 lbs.

Year	Team	Games	BA	SA	AB	H	2B	3B	HR	HR%	R	RBI	BB	SO	SB	Pinch Hit AB	Pinch Hit H	PO	A	E	DP	TC/G	FA	G by Pos
1963	CLE A	90	.292	.424	370	108	18	5	7	1.9	44	36	16	41	3	2	2	247	10	3	0	2.9	.988	OF-89
1964		150	.270	.354	577	156	26	2	6	1.0	64	51	34	77	21	5	0	346	11	5	5	2.5	.986	OF-143
1965		142	.301	.372	505	152	19	1	5	1.0	67	40	35	50	26	8	1	320	5	4	0	2.5	.988	OF-134
1966		121	.250	.317	344	86	6	4	3	0.9	42	19	24	37	8	18	3	208	6	3	1	2.0	.986	OF-108
1967		139	.287	.379	359	103	17	5	2	0.6	47	22	10	30	6	20	4	202	5	3	1	1.7	.986	OF-125
1968	2 teams	CLE A (51G –.239)	CAL A (93G –.298)																					
″	total	144	.277	.355	519	144	17	7	3	0.6	49	31	18	53	25	7	3	296	8	4	3	2.3	.987	OF-135
1969	2 teams	CAL A (33G –.155)	STL N (63G –.265)																					
″	total	96	.219	.290	169	37	4	1	2	1.2	25	11	13	13	4	43	10	73	1	0	1	1.5	1.000	OF-45, 1B-3, P-2
1970	STL N	111	.311	.437	183	57	14	3	1	0.5	29	33	13	19	4	**73**	**24**	67	3	2	1	1.3	.972	OF-54
1971	PIT N	99	.285	.383	295	84	14	6	1	0.3	48	33	11	31	10	27	9	256	15	5	18	3.6	.982	OF-61, 1B-16
1972		117	.318	.413	368	117	19	2	4	1.1	59	28	26	44	14	12	5	200	6	4	2	2.0	.981	OF-97, 1B-8
1973	2 teams	PIT N (59G –.181)	OAK A (38G –.188)																					
″	total	97	.184	.218	147	27	2	0	1	0.7	14	7	5	11	0	49	10	133	11	3	11	3.0	.980	OF-29, 1B-18, DH-2
1974	OAK A	17	.174	.174	23	4	0	0	0	0.0	0	1	2	2	0	6	1	3	0	0	0	0.3	1.000	OF-6, DH-4
1977	LA N	24	.313	.354	48	15	2	0	0	0.0	3	4	0	6	0	14	4	13	0	0	0	1.1	1.000	OF-12
1978		75	.312	.390	77	24	1	1	1	1.3	15	11	3	7	2	47	12	21	1	0	1	0.8	1.000	OF-25, 1B-2
1979		29	.259	.296	27	7	1	0	0	0.0	2	2	2	0	2	24	6	2	0	0	0	0.7	1.000	OF-3
1980		7	.167	.167	6	1	0	0	0	0.0	1	0	0	1	0	5	1	2	0	0	1	2.0	1.000	1B-1
16 yrs.		1458	.279	.364	4017	1122	160	37	36	0.9	509	329	212	422	125	360	95	2389	82	36	45	2.2	.986	OF-1066, 1B-48, DH-6, P-2
LEAGUE CHAMPIONSHIP SERIES																								
1971	PIT N	2	.000	.000	2	0	0	0	0	0.0	0	0	0	1	0	2	0	0	0	0	0	0.0	—	
1972		1	—	—	0	0	0	0	0	—	0	0	1	0	0	0	0	0	0	0	0	0.0	—	
1973	OAK A	4	.625	1.000	8	5	1	1	0	0.0	2	1	1	0	0	1	1	7	0	1	0	2.0	.875	OF-2, 1B-2
1977	LA N	1	1.000	1.000	1	1	0	0	0	0.0	1	0	0	0	0	1	1	0	0	0	0	0.0	—	
4 yrs.		8	.545	.818	11	6	1	1	0	0.0	3	1	2	1	0	4	2	7	0	1	0	2.0	.875	OF-2, 1B-2
WORLD SERIES																								
1971	PIT N	3	.333	.333	3	1	0	0	0	0.0	1	0	0	0	0	3	1	2	0	0	0	1.0	1.000	OF-2
1973	OAK A	6	.091	.091	11	1	0	0	0	0.0	0	0	2	1	0	2	0	15	0	0	0	3.0	1.000	OF-4, 1B-1
1977	LA N	3	.333	.333	3	1	0	0	0	0.0	0	1	0	0	0	3	1	0	0	0	0	0.0	—	
1978		2	.333	.333	3	1	0	0	0	0.0	0	0	0	0	0	1	0	0	0	0	0	0.0	.000	DH-1
4 yrs.		14	.200	.200	20	4	0	0	0	0.0	1	1	2	1	0	9	2	17	0	0	0	2.1	1.000	OF-6, DH-1, 1B-1

Yo-Yo Davalillo

DAVALILLO, POMPEYO ANTONIO
Born Pompeyo Antonio Davalillo (Romero).
Brother of Vic Davalillo.
B. June 30, 1931, Caracas, Venezuela.

BR TR 5′ 3″ 140 lbs.

Year	Team	Games	BA	SA	AB	H	2B	3B	HR	HR%	R	RBI	BB	SO	SB	Pinch Hit AB	Pinch Hit H	PO	A	E	DP	TC/G	FA	G by Pos
1953	WAS A	19	.293	.310	58	17	1	0	0	0.0	10	2	1	7	1	0	0	39	47	6	10	5.4	.935	SS-17

Jerry DaVanon

DaVANON, FRANK GERALD
B. Aug. 21, 1945, Oceanside, Calif.

BR TR 5′11″ 175 lbs.

Year	Team	Games	BA	SA	AB	H	2B	3B	HR	HR%	R	RBI	BB	SO	SB	Pinch Hit AB	Pinch Hit H	PO	A	E	DP	TC/G	FA	G by Pos
1969	2 teams	SD N (24G –.136)	STL N (16G –.300)																					
″	total	40	.202	.273	99	20	4	0	1	1.0	11	10	9	20	0	2	0	63	86	8	13	4.1	.949	SS-23, 2B-15
1970	STL N	11	.111	.167	18	2	1	0	0	0.0	2	0	2	5	0	3	0	8	14	0	3	2.8	1.000	3B-5, 2B-3
1971	BAL A	38	.235	.296	81	19	5	0	0	0.0	14	4	12	20	0	0	0	45	59	4	12	3.1	.963	2B-20, SS-11, 3B-3, 1B-1
1973	CAL A	41	.245	.306	49	12	3	0	0	0.0	6	2	3	9	1	0	0	29	45	6	6	2.4	.925	SS-14, 2B-12, 3B-7
1974	STL N	30	.150	.175	40	6	1	0	0	0.0	4	4	4	5	0	1	0	19	35	5	8	2.0	.915	SS-14, 3B-8, 2B-7, OF-1
1975	HOU N	32	.278	.392	97	27	4	2	1	1.0	15	10	16	7	2	3	0	54	94	7	16	4.7	.955	SS-21, 2B-9, 3B-3
1976		61	.290	.402	107	31	3	3	1	0.9	19	20	21	12	0	15	2	53	94	7	16	3.6	.955	2B-17, SS-17, 3B-9
1977	STL N	9	.000	.000	8	0	0	0	0	0.0	2	0	1	2	0	1	0	4	8	1	0	2.6	.923	2B-5
8 yrs.		262	.234	.315	499	117	21	5	3	0.6	73	50	68	80	3	25	2	275	435	38	74	3.3	.949	SS-100, 2B-88, 3B-35, OF-1, 1B-1

Jim Davenport

DAVENPORT, JAMES HOUSTON
B. Aug. 17, 1933, Siluria, Ala.
Manager 1985.

BR TR 5′11″ 170 lbs.

Year	Team	Games	BA	SA	AB	H	2B	3B	HR	HR%	R	RBI	BB	SO	SB	Pinch Hit AB	Pinch Hit H	PO	A	E	DP	TC/G	FA	G by Pos
1958	SF N	134	.256	.403	434	111	22	3	12	2.8	70	41	33	64	1	1	0	96	232	14	19	2.5	.959	3B-130, SS-5
1959		123	.258	.343	469	121	16	3	6	1.3	65	38	28	65	0	3	0	91	222	7	15	2.6	.978	3B-121, SS-1
1960		112	.251	.358	363	91	15	3	6	1.7	43	38	26	58	0	9	1	83	178	10	14	2.5	.963	3B-103, SS-7
1961		137	.278	.443	436	121	28	4	12	2.8	64	65	45	65	4	5	1	119	235	13	25	2.8	.965	3B-132
1962		144	.297	.456	485	144	25	5	14	2.9	83	58	45	76	2	3	1	125	256	19	28	2.8	.953	3B-141
1963		147	.252	.333	460	116	19	3	4	0.9	40	36	32	87	5	13	2	152	230	13	16	2.6	.967	3B-127, 2B-22, SS-1
1964		116	.236	.330	297	70	10	6	2	0.7	24	26	29	46	2	7	0	138	237	11	29	2.9	.972	SS-64, 3B-41, 2B-30
1965		106	.251	.369	271	68	14	3	4	1.5	29	31	21	47	0	14	4	97	147	14	21	2.5	.946	3B-39, SS-37, 2B-26
1966		111	.249	.370	305	76	6	2	9	3.0	42	30	22	40	1	20	5	107	201	14	27	2.8	.957	SS-58, 3B-36, 2B-21, 1B-2
1967		124	.275	.380	295	81	10	3	5	1.7	42	30	39	50	1	27	10	83	192	4	24	2.7	.986	3B-64, SS-28, 2B-12
1968		113	.224	.246	272	61	1	1	1	0.4	27	17	26	32	0	23	5	58	137	8	17	2.0	.961	3B-82, SS-17, 2B-1
1969		112	.241	.300	303	73	10	1	2	0.7	20	42	29	37	0	14	4	84	159	8	16	2.3	.968	3B-104, OF-1, 1B-1, SS-1
1970		22	.243	.270	37	9	1	0	0	0.0	3	4	7	6	0	11	3	7	7	0	0	1.4	1.000	3B-10
13 yrs.		1501	.258	.367	4427	1142	177	37	77	1.7	552	456	382	673	16	150	36	1240	2433	135	251	2.6	.965	3B-1130, SS-219, 2B-112, 1B-3, OF-1
WORLD SERIES																								
1962	SF N	7	.136	.182	22	3	1	0	0	0.0	1	1	4	7	0	0	0	6	12	3	4	3.0	.857	3B-7

Andre David

DAVID, ANDRE ANTER
B. May 18, 1958, Hollywood, Calif.

BL TL 6′ 170 lbs.

Year	Team	Games	BA	SA	AB	H	2B	3B	HR	HR%	R	RBI	BB	SO	SB	Pinch Hit AB	Pinch Hit H	PO	A	E	DP	TC/G	FA	G by Pos
1984	MIN A	33	.250	.354	48	12	2	0	1	2.1	5	5	7	11	0	15	2	14	0	0	0	0.9	1.000	OF-14, DH-2
1986		5	.200	.200	5	1	0	0	0	0.0	0	0	0	2	0	4	0	0	0	0	0	0.0	—	
2 yrs.		38	.245	.340	53	13	2	0	1	1.9	5	5	7	13	0	19	2	14	0	0	0	0.9	1.000	OF-14, DH-2

Bill Davidson

DAVIDSON, WILLIAM SIMPSON
B. May 10, 1887, Lafayette, Ind. D. May 23, 1954, Lincoln, Neb.
BR TR 5′10″ 170 lbs.

Year	Team	Games	BA	SA	AB	H	2B	3B	HR	HR%	R	RBI	BB	SO	SB	Pinch Hit AB	Pinch Hit H	PO	A	E	DP	TC/G	FA	G by Pos
1909	CHI N	2	.143	.143	7	1	0	0	0	0.0	2	0	1		1	0	0	3	0	0	0	1.5	1.000	OF-2
1910	BKN N	136	.238	.291	509	121	13	7	0	0.0	48	34	24	54	27	4	0	283	11	12	3	2.3	.961	OF-131
1911		87	.233	.281	292	68	3	4	1	0.3	33	26	16	21	18	8	2	168	4	8	1	2.4	.956	OF-74
3 yrs.		225	.235	.286	808	190	16	11	1	0.1	83	60	41	75	46	12	2	454	15	20	4	2.4	.959	OF-207

Claude Davidson

DAVIDSON, CLAUDE BOUCHER (Davey)
B. Oct. 13, 1896, Boston, Mass. D. Apr. 18, 1956, Weymouth, Mass.
BL TR 5′11″ 155 lbs.

Year	Team	Games	BA	SA	AB	H	2B	3B	HR	HR%	R	RBI	BB	SO	SB	Pinch Hit AB	Pinch Hit H	PO	A	E	DP	TC/G	FA	G by Pos
1918	PHI A	31	.185	.198	81	15	1	0	0	0.0	4	4	5	9	0	7	2	39	39	4	8	3.4	.951	2B-15, OF-8, 3B-1
1919	WAS A	2	.429	.429	7	3	0	0	0	0.0	1	0	1	1	0	0	0	3	4	0	0	3.5	1.000	3B-2
2 yrs.		33	.205	.216	88	18	1	0	0	0.0	5	4	6	10	0	7	2	42	43	4	8	3.4	.955	2B-15, OF-8, 3B-3

Homer Davidson

DAVIDSON, HOMER HURD (Divvy)
B. Oct. 14, 1884, Cleveland, Ohio D. July 26, 1948, Detroit, Mich.
BR TR 5′10½″ 155 lbs.

Year	Team	Games	BA	SA	AB	H	2B	3B	HR	HR%	R	RBI	BB	SO	SB	Pinch Hit AB	Pinch Hit H	PO	A	E	DP	TC/G	FA	G by Pos
1908	CLE A	9	.000	.000	4	0	0	0	0	0.0	0	0	0		1	0	0	9	1	0	0	1.7	1.000	C-5, OF-1

Mark Davidson

DAVIDSON, JOHN MARK
B. Feb. 15, 1961, Knoxville, Tenn.
BR TR 6′2″ 180 lbs.

Year	Team	Games	BA	SA	AB	H	2B	3B	HR	HR%	R	RBI	BB	SO	SB	Pinch Hit AB	Pinch Hit H	PO	A	E	DP	TC/G	FA	G by Pos
1986	MIN A	36	.118	.162	68	8	3	0	0	0.0	5	2	6	22	2	2	1	48	0	1	0	1.4	.980	OF-31, DH-3
1987		102	.267	.327	150	40	4	1	1	0.7	32	14	13	26	9	6	3	102	3	0	0	1.1	1.000	OF-86, DH-9
1988		100	.217	.311	106	23	7	0	1	0.9	22	10	10	20	3	9	4	103	3	5	1	1.2	.955	OF-91, 3B-1
1989	HOU N	33	.200	.308	65	13	2	1	1	1.5	7	5	7	14	1	12	2	36	0	0	0	1.6	1.000	OF-23
1990		57	.292	.369	130	38	5	1	1	0.8	12	11	10	18	0	9	1	103	1	2	0	2.1	.981	OF-51
1991		85	.190	.275	142	27	6	0	2	1.4	10	15	12	28	0	29	4	71	1	0	0	1.1	1.000	OF-63
6 yrs.		413	.225	.303	661	149	27	3	6	0.9	88	57	58	128	15	67	15	463	8	8	1	1.3	.983	OF-345, DH-12, 3B-1
LEAGUE CHAMPIONSHIP SERIES																								
1987	MIN A	1	—	—	0	0	0	0	0	—	0	0	0	0	0	0	0	0	0	0	0	0.0	—	
WORLD SERIES																								
1987	MIN A	2	.000	.000	1	0	0	0	0	0.0	0	0	0	0	0	1	0	0	0	0	0	0.0	.000	OF-1

Chick Davies

DAVIES, LLOYD GARRISON
B. Mar. 6, 1892, Peabody, Mass. D. Sept. 5, 1973, Middletown, Conn.
BL TL 5′8″ 145 lbs.

Year	Team	Games	BA	SA	AB	H	2B	3B	HR	HR%	R	RBI	BB	SO	SB	Pinch Hit AB	Pinch Hit H	PO	A	E	DP	TC/G	FA	G by Pos
1914	PHI A	19	.239	.348	46	11	3	1	0	0.0	6	5	5	13	1	6	2	25	3	3	2	2.8	.903	OF-10, P-1
1915		56	.182	.265	132	24	5	3	0	0.0	13	11	14	31	2	16	2	67	14	2	1	2.3	.976	OF-32, P-4
1925	NY N	4	.000	.000	6	0	0	0	0	0.0	1	0	0	1	0	1	0	3	3	0	0	2.0	1.000	P-2, OF-1
1926		38	.222	.222	18	4	0	0	0	0.0	4	1	3	5	0	0	0	4	26	2	2	0.8	.938	P-38
4 yrs.		117	.193	.272	202	39	8	4	0	0.0	24	17	22	50	3	23	4	99	46	7	5	1.7	.954	P-45, OF-43

Alvin Davis

DAVIS, ALVIN GLENN
B. Sept. 9, 1960, Riverside, Calif.
BL TR 6′1″ 190 lbs.

Year	Team	Games	BA	SA	AB	H	2B	3B	HR	HR%	R	RBI	BB	SO	SB	Pinch Hit AB	Pinch Hit H	PO	A	E	DP	TC/G	FA	G by Pos
1984	SEA A	152	.284	.497	567	161	34	3	27	4.8	80	116	97	78	5	0	0	1271	94	11	108	8.9	.992	1B-147, DH-7
1985		155	.287	.441	578	166	33	1	18	3.1	78	78	90	71	1	1	1	1438	103	13	131	10.1	.992	1B-154
1986		135	.271	.426	479	130	18	1	18	3.8	66	72	76	68	0	4	0	880	82	14	112	7.3	.986	1B-101, DH-32
1987		157	.295	.516	580	171	37	2	29	5.0	86	100	72	84	0	0	0	1386	96	9	133	9.5	.994	1B-157
1988		140	.295	.462	478	141	24	1	18	3.8	67	69	95	53	1	1	1	980	65	6	111	7.5	.994	1B-115, DH-25
1989		142	.305	.496	498	152	30	1	21	4.2	84	95	101	49	0	3	1	1106	81	10	119	8.6	.992	1B-125, DH-14
1990		140	.283	.429	494	140	21	0	17	3.4	63	68	85	68	0	1	1	435	31	3	41	3.4	.994	DH-87, 1B-52
1991		145	.221	.335	462	102	15	1	12	2.6	39	69	56	78	0	16	3	116	7	0	14	0.9	1.000	DH-126, 1B-14
1992	CAL A	40	.250	.327	104	26	8	0	0	0.0	5	16	13	9	0	11	6	191	13	1	20	6.6	.995	1B-22, DH-9
9 yrs.		1206	.280	.450	4240	1189	220	10	160	3.8	568	683	685	558	7	37	13	7803	572	67	789	7.1	.992	1B-887, DH-300

Bill Davis

DAVIS, ARTHUR WILLARD
B. June 6, 1942, Graceville, Minn.
BL TL 6′7″ 215 lbs.

Year	Team	Games	BA	SA	AB	H	2B	3B	HR	HR%	R	RBI	BB	SO	SB	Pinch Hit AB	Pinch Hit H	PO	A	E	DP	TC/G	FA	G by Pos
1965	CLE A	10	.300	.400	10	3	1	0	0	0.0	0	0	0	1	0	10	3	0	0	0	0	0.0	—	
1966		23	.158	.263	38	6	1	0	1	2.6	2	4	6	9	0	12	3	47	5	1	6	5.9	.981	1B-9
1969	SD N	31	.175	.193	57	10	1	0	0	0.0	1	1	8	18	0	14	2	114	5	1	11	8.6	.992	1B-14
3 yrs.		64	.181	.238	105	19	3	0	1	1.0	3	5	14	28	0	36	8	161	10	2	17	7.5	.988	1B-23

Bob Davis

DAVIS, ROBERT JOHN EUGENE
B. Mar. 1, 1952, Pryor, Okla.
BR TR 6′ 180 lbs.

Year	Team	Games	BA	SA	AB	H	2B	3B	HR	HR%	R	RBI	BB	SO	SB	Pinch Hit AB	Pinch Hit H	PO	A	E	DP	TC/G	FA	G by Pos
1973	SD N	5	.091	.091	11	1	0	0	0	0.0	1	0	0	5	0	0	0	32	0	2	1	6.8	.941	C-5
1975		43	.234	.289	128	30	3	2	0	0.0	6	7	11	31	0	2	0	195	18	3	4	5.0	.986	C-43
1976		51	.205	.229	83	17	0	1	0	0.0	7	5	5	13	0	0	0	120	19	5	1	3.1	.965	C-47
1977		48	.181	.234	94	17	2	0	1	1.1	9	10	5	24	0	2	1	136	19	4	2	3.5	.975	C-46
1978		19	.200	.225	40	8	1	0	0	0.0	3	2	1	5	0	3	0	43	5	2	0	3.1	.960	C-16
1979	TOR A	32	.124	.180	89	11	2	0	1	1.1	6	8	6	15	0	0	0	114	11	2	1	4.0	.984	C-32
1980		91	.216	.321	218	47	11	0	4	1.8	18	19	12	25	0	4	1	317	28	6	6	3.9	.983	C-89
1981	CAL A	1	.000	.000	2	0	0	0	0	0.0	0	0	0	0	0	0	0	2	0	0	0	2.0	1.000	C-1
8 yrs.		290	.197	.262	665	131	19	3	6	0.9	50	51	40	118	0	11	2	959	100	24	15	3.9	.978	C-279

Brandy Davis

DAVIS, ROBERT BRANDON
B. Sept. 10, 1928, Newark, Del.
BR TR 6′ 170 lbs.

Year	Team	Games	BA	SA	AB	H	2B	3B	HR	HR%	R	RBI	BB	SO	SB	Pinch Hit AB	Pinch Hit H	PO	A	E	DP	TC/G	FA	G by Pos
1952	PIT N	55	.179	.211	95	17	1	1	0	0.0	14	1	11	28	9	11	2	53	2	4	0	2.0	.932	OF-29
1953		12	.205	.256	39	8	2	0	0	0.0	5	2	0	3	0	0	0	21	0	1	0	2.4	.955	OF-9
2 yrs.		67	.187	.224	134	25	3	1	0	0.0	19	3	11	31	9	11	2	74	2	5	0	2.1	.938	OF-38

Brock Davis

DAVIS, BRYSHEAR BENNETT
B. Oct. 19, 1943, Oakland, Calif.
BL TL 5′10″ 160 lbs.

Year	Team	Games	BA	SA	AB	H	2B	3B	HR	HR%	R	RBI	BB	SO	SB	Pinch Hit AB	Pinch Hit H	PO	A	E	DP	TC/G	FA	G by Pos
1963	HOU N	34	.200	.291	55	11	2	0	1	1.8	7	2	4	10	0	17	3	18	1	3	0	1.6	.864	OF-14
1964		1	.000	.000	3	0	0	0	0	0.0	0	0	1	1	0	0	0	2	0	0	0	2.0	1.000	OF-1
1966		10	.148	.185	27	4	1	0	0	0.0	2	1	5	4	1	3	1	15	0	0	0	2.1	1.000	OF-7

Brock Davis *continued*

Year	Team	Games	BA	SA	AB	H	2B	3B	HR	HR%	R	RBI	BB	SO	SB	Pinch Hit AB	Pinch Hit H	PO	A	E	DP	TC/G	FA	G by Pos
1970	CHI N	6	.000	.000	3	0	0	0	0	0.0	0	0	0	1	0	3	0	0	0	0	0	0.0	.000	OF-1
1971		106	.256	.312	301	77	7	5	0	0.0	22	28	35	34	0	10	1	213	5	4	1	2.4	.982	OF-93
1972	MIL A	85	.318	.331	154	49	2	0	0	0.0	17	12	12	23	6	36	8	63	2	2	0	1.6	.970	OF-43
6 yrs.		242	.260	.306	543	141	12	5	1	0.2	48	43	57	73	7	69	13	311	8	9	1	2.1	.973	OF-159

Butch Davis

DAVIS, WALLACE McARTHUR
B. June 19, 1958, Williamston, N. C.
BR TR 6′ 185 lbs.

Year	Team	Games	BA	SA	AB	H	2B	3B	HR	HR%	R	RBI	BB	SO	SB	Pinch Hit AB	Pinch Hit H	PO	A	E	DP	TC/G	FA	G by Pos
1983	KC A	33	.344	.508	122	42	2	6	2	1.6	13	18	4	19	4	0	0	83	1	2	0	2.6	.977	OF-33
1984		41	.147	.224	116	17	3	0	2	1.7	11	12	10	19	4	4	0	69	2	3	1	2.0	.959	OF-35, DH-2
1987	PIT N	7	.143	.286	7	1	1	0	0	0.0	3	0	1	3	0	5	0	3	0	0	0	3.0	1.000	OF-1
1988	BAL A	13	.240	.280	25	6	1	0	0	0.0	2	0	0	8	1	1	0	16	1	0	1	1.5	1.000	OF-10, DH-1
1989		5	.167	.333	6	1	1	0	0	0.0	1	0	0	3	0	1	0	3	0	0	0	0.8	1.000	OF-3, DH-1
1991	LA N	1	.000	.000	1	0	0	0	0	0.0	0	0	0	0	0	1	0	0	0	0	0	0.0	—	
1993	TEX A	62	.245	.415	159	39	10	4	3	1.9	24	20	5	28	3	9	3	94	2	4	1	1.8	.960	OF-44, DH-11
1994		4	.235	.412	17	4	3	0	0	0.0	2	0	0	3	1	0	0	6	1	0	0	1.8	1.000	OF-4
8 yrs.		166	.243	.380	453	110	21	10	7	1.5	56	50	20	83	13	21	3	274	7	9	3	2.0	.969	OF-130, DH-15

Chili Davis

DAVIS, CHARLES THEODORE
B. Jan. 17, 1960, Kingston, Jamaica.
BB TR 6′ 3″ 195 lbs.

Year	Team	Games	BA	SA	AB	H	2B	3B	HR	HR%	R	RBI	BB	SO	SB	Pinch Hit AB	Pinch Hit H	PO	A	E	DP	TC/G	FA	G by Pos
1981	SF N	8	.133	.133	15	2	0	0	0	0.0	1	0	1	2	2	3	1	7	0	0	0	1.2	1.000	OF-6
1982		154	.261	.410	641	167	27	6	19	3.0	86	76	45	115	24	1	1	404	16	12	4	2.8	.972	OF-153
1983		137	.233	.352	486	113	21	2	11	2.3	54	59	55	108	10	4	1	357	7	9	1	2.8	.976	OF-133
1984		137	.315	.507	499	157	21	6	21	4.2	87	81	42	74	12	15	6	292	9	9	2	2.5	.971	OF-123
1985		136	.270	.412	481	130	25	2	13	2.7	53	56	62	74	15	9	2	279	10	6	2	2.3	.980	OF-126
1986		153	.278	.416	526	146	28	3	13	2.5	71	70	84	96	16	7	1	303	9	9	2	2.2	.972	OF-148
1987		149	.250	.442	500	125	22	1	24	4.8	80	76	72	109	16	20	3	265	6	7	2	2.1	.975	OF-135
1988	CAL A	158	.268	.432	600	161	29	3	21	3.5	81	93	56	118	9	1	0	299	10	19	1	2.1	.942	OF-153, DH-3
1989		154	.271	.436	560	152	24	1	22	3.9	81	90	61	109	3	2	0	270	5	6	0	1.8	.979	OF-147, DH-6
1990		113	.265	.398	412	109	17	1	12	2.9	58	58	61	89	1	2	0	77	5	3	1	0.8	.965	DH-60, OF-52
1991	MIN A	153	.277	.507	534	148	34	1	29	5.4	84	93	95	117	5	2	0	2	0	0	0	0.0	1.000	DH-150, OF-2
1992		138	.288	.439	444	128	27	2	12	2.7	63	66	73	76	4	16	5	6	0	0	0	0.0	1.000	DH-125, OF-4, 1B-1
1993	CAL A	152	.243	.440	573	139	32	0	27	4.7	74	112	71	135	4	1	0	0	0	0	0	0.0		DH-150, P-1
1994		108	.311	.561	392	122	18	1	26	6.6	72	84	69	84	3	0	0	5	0	0	0	0.0	1.000	DH-106, OF-2
1995		119	.318	.514	424	135	23	0	20	4.7	81	86	89	79	3	0	0	0	0	0	0	0.0	.000	DH-119
15 yrs.		1969	.273	.444	7087	1934	348	29	270	3.8	1026	1100	936	1385	127	83	20	2566	77	80	15	1.4	.971	OF-1184, DH-719, P-1, 1B-1
LEAGUE CHAMPIONSHIP SERIES																								
1987	SF N	6	.150	.200	20	3	1	0	0	0.0	2	0	1	4	0	0	0	11	1	1	1	2.2	.923	OF-6
1991	MIN A	5	.294	.412	17	5	2	0	0	0.0	3	2	5	8	1	0	0	0	0	0	0	0.0	.000	DH-5
2 yrs.		11	.216	.297	37	8	3	0	0	0.0	5	2	6	12	1	0	0	11	1	1	1	1.2	.923	OF-6, DH-5
WORLD SERIES																								
1991	MIN A	6	.222	.556	18	4	0	0	2	11.1	4	4	2	3	0	1	1	1	0	0	0	0.2	1.000	DH-4, OF-1

Crash Davis

DAVIS, LAWRENCE COLUMBUS
B. July 14, 1919, Canon, Ga.
BR TR 6′ 173 lbs.

Year	Team	Games	BA	SA	AB	H	2B	3B	HR	HR%	R	RBI	BB	SO	SB	Pinch Hit AB	Pinch Hit H	PO	A	E	DP	TC/G	FA	G by Pos
1940	PHI A	23	.269	.313	67	18	1	1	0	0.0	4	9	3	10	1	3	0	53	53	4	11	5.5	.964	2B-19, SS-1
1941		39	.219	.248	105	23	3	0	0	0.0	8	8	11	16	0	7	2	135	68	7	21	6.6	.967	2B-20, 1B-12
1942		86	.224	.283	272	61	8	1	2	0.7	31	26	21	30	1	4	1	179	211	19	31	4.8	.954	2B-57, SS-26, 1B-3
3 yrs.		148	.230	.279	444	102	12	2	2	0.5	43	43	35	56	2	14	3	367	332	30	63	5.3	.959	2B-96, SS-27, 1B-15

Dick Davis

DAVIS, RICHARD EARL
B. Sept. 25, 1953, Long Beach, Calif.
BR TR 6′ 3″ 190 lbs.

Year	Team	Games	BA	SA	AB	H	2B	3B	HR	HR%	R	RBI	BB	SO	SB	Pinch Hit AB	Pinch Hit H	PO	A	E	DP	TC/G	FA	G by Pos
1977	MIL A	22	.275	.314	51	14	2	0	0	0.0	7	6	1	8	0	2	1	13	0	0	0	0.7	1.000	OF-12, DH-6
1978		69	.248	.372	218	54	10	1	5	2.3	28	26	7	23	2	13	3	54	2	0	0	0.9	1.000	DH-34, OF-28
1979		91	.266	.418	335	89	13	1	12	3.6	51	41	16	46	3	6	2	72	1	2	0	0.9	.973	DH-53, OF-35
1980		106	.271	.386	365	99	26	2	4	1.1	50	30	11	43	5	5	2	63	3	2	2	0.7	.971	DH-63, OF-38
1981	PHI N	45	.333	.479	96	32	6	1	2	2.1	12	19	8	13	1	14	5	37	1	1	0	1.2	.974	OF-32
1982	3 teams	PHI N (28G –.279) TOR A (3G –.286) PIT N (39G –.182)																						
″	total	70	.230	.368	152	35	5	2	4	2.6	12	19	7	19	2	26	5	64	0	1	0	1.4	.985	OF-45, DH-1
6 yrs.		403	.265	.394	1217	323	62	7	27	2.2	160	141	50	152	13	66	18	303	7	6	2	0.9	.981	OF-190, DH-157
DIVISIONAL PLAYOFF SERIES																								
1981	PHI N	1	.000	.000	2	0	0	0	0	0.0	0	0	0	1	0	1	0	2	0	0	0	2.0	1.000	OF-1

Doug Davis

DAVIS, DOUGLAS RAYMOND
B. Sept. 24, 1962, Bloomsburg, Pa.
BR TR 6′ 180 lbs.

Year	Team	Games	BA	SA	AB	H	2B	3B	HR	HR%	R	RBI	BB	SO	SB	Pinch Hit AB	Pinch Hit H	PO	A	E	DP	TC/G	FA	G by Pos
1988	CAL A	6	.000	.000	12	0	0	0	0	0.0	1	0	0	3	0	0	0	6	1	1	0	1.3	.875	3B-3, C-3
1992	TEX A	1	1.000	1.000	1	1	0	0	0	0.0	0	0	0	0	0	0	0	0	0	0	0	0.0	—	
2 yrs.		7	.077	.077	13	1	0	0	0	0.0	1	0	0	3	0	0	0	6	1	1	0	1.3	.875	3B-3, C-3

Eric Davis

DAVIS, ERIC KEITH
B. May 29, 1962, Los Angeles, Calif.
BR TR 6′ 3″ 175 lbs.

Year	Team	Games	BA	SA	AB	H	2B	3B	HR	HR%	R	RBI	BB	SO	SB	Pinch Hit AB	Pinch Hit H	PO	A	E	DP	TC/G	FA	G by Pos
1984	CIN N	57	.224	.466	174	39	10	1	10	5.7	33	30	24	48	10	6	1	125	4	1	2	2.5	.992	OF-51
1985		56	.246	.516	122	30	3	3	8	6.6	26	18	7	39	16	8	1	75	3	1	1	1.7	.987	OF-47
1986		132	.277	.523	415	115	15	3	27	6.5	97	71	68	100	80	4	0	274	2	7	0	2.3	.975	OF-121
1987		129	.293	.593	474	139	23	4	37	7.8	120	100	84	134	50	1	0	380	10	4	4	3.1	.990	OF-128
1988		135	.273	.489	472	129	18	3	26	5.5	81	93	65	124	35	3	1	300	2	6	0	2.4	.981	OF-130
1989		131	.281	.541	462	130	14	2	34	7.4	74	101	68	116	21	3	1	298	2	5	1	2.4	.984	OF-125
1990		127	.260	.486	453	118	26	2	24	5.3	84	86	60	100	21	6	1	257	11	2	1	2.2	.993	OF-122
1991		89	.235	.386	285	67	10	0	11	3.9	39	33	48	92	14	8	2	190	5	3	2	2.4	.985	OF-82

Eric Davis *continued*

Year	Team	Games	BA	SA	AB	H	2B	3B	HR	HR%	R	RBI	BB	SO	SB	Pinch Hit AB	Pinch Hit H	PO	A	E	DP	TC/G	FA	G by Pos
1992	LA N	76	.228	.322	267	61	8	1	5	1.9	21	32	36	71	19	0	0	123	0	5	0	1.7	.961	OF-74
1993	2 teams	LA N (108G –.234) DET A (23G –.253)																						
"	total	131	.237	.415	451	107	18	1	20	4.4	71	68	55	106	35	4	0	273	7	3	2	2.2	.989	OF-121, DH-5
1994	DET A	37	.183	.292	120	22	4	0	3	2.5	19	13	18	45	5	2	0	85	1	1	1	2.5	.989	OF-35
11 yrs.		1100	.259	.477	3695	957	149	20	205	5.5	665	645	533	975	306	45	7	2380	47	38	14	2.4	.985	OF-1036, DH-5
LEAGUE CHAMPIONSHIP SERIES																								
1990	CIN N	6	.174	.217	23	4	1	0	0	0.0	2	2	1	9	0	0	0	12	1	0	0	2.2	1.000	OF-6
WORLD SERIES																								
1990	CIN N	4	.286	.500	14	4	0	0	1	7.1	3	5	0	0	0	0	0	4	0	0	0	1.0	1.000	OF-4

George Davis

DAVIS, GEORGE STACEY
B. Aug. 23, 1870, Cohoes, N. Y. D. Oct. 17, 1940, Philadelphia, Pa.
Manager 1895, 1900–01.

BB TR 5′ 9″ 180 lbs.

Year	Team	Games	BA	SA	AB	H	2B	3B	HR	HR%	R	RBI	BB	SO	SB	Pinch Hit AB	Pinch Hit H	PO	A	E	DP	TC/G	FA	G by Pos
1890	CLE N	136	.264	.375	526	139	22	9	6	1.1	98	73	53	34	22	0	0	288	38	18	10	2.5	.948	OF-133, 2B-2, SS-1
1891		136	.289	.409	570	165	35	12	3	0.5	115	89	53	29	42	0	0	292	76	33	6	2.8	.918	OF-116, 3B-22, P-3
1892		144	.241	.352	597	144	27	12	5	0.8	95	82	58	51	36	0	0	198	241	43	17	3.3	.911	3B-79, OF-44, SS-20, 2B-3
1893	NY N	133	.355	.554	549	195	22	27	11	2.0	112	119	42	20	37	0	0	181	307	64	27	4.1	.884	3B-133, SS-1
1894		124	.352	.537	477	168	26	19	8	1.7	120	91	66	10	40	0	0	150	247	40	18	3.5	.908	3B-124
1895		110	.340	.500	430	146	36	9	5	1.2	108	101	55	12	48	0	0	296	220	46	27	5.0	.918	3B-81, 1B-14, 2B-10, OF-7
1896		124	.320	.455	494	158	25	12	6	1.2	98	99	50	24	48	0	0	257	314	47	22	4.9	.924	3B-74, SS-45, OF-3, 1B-3
1897		130	.353	.509	519	183	31	10	10	1.9	112	**134**	41		65	0	0	337	434	62	67	6.4	.926	SS-130
1898		121	.307	.381	486	149	20	5	2	0.4	80	86	32		26	0	0	349	421	55	61	6.8	.933	SS-121
1899		108	.337	.418	416	140	21	5	1	0.2	68	57	37		34	0	0	311	412	42	57	7.1	.945	SS-108
1900		114	.319	.406	426	136	20	4	3	0.7	70	61	35		29	0	0	279	450	43	94	6.8	.944	SS-114
1901		130	.309	.428	495	153	26	6	7	1.4	69	65	40		26	0	0	321	443	48	44	6.2	.941	SS-113, 3B-17
1902	CHI A	132	.299	.402	485	145	27	7	3	0.6	76	93	65		31	1	1	302	428	37	74	5.8	.952	SS-129, 1B-3
1903	NY N	4	.267	.267	15	4	0	0	0	0.0	2	1	1		0	0	0	11	9	3	0	5.8	.870	SS-4
1904	CHI A	152	.252	.359	563	142	27	15	1	0.2	75	69	43		32	0	0	347	514	58	62	6.0	.937	SS-152
1905		157	.278	.340	550	153	29	1	1	0.2	74	55	60		31	0	0	330	501	46	56	5.6	.948	SS-157
1906		133	.277	.355	484	134	26	6	0	0.0	63	80	41		27	3	1	266	475	42	45	6.0	.946	SS-129, 2B-1
1907		132	.238	.292	466	111	18	2	1	0.2	59	52	47		15	0	0	223	485	38	53	5.7	.949	SS-131
1908		128	.217	.255	419	91	14	1	0	0.0	41	26	41		22	5	1	291	384	32	31	5.8	.955	2B-95, SS-23, 1B-4
1909		28	.132	.147	68	9	1	0	0	0.0	5	2	10		4	14	1	190	18	5	7	11.2	.977	1B-17, 2B-2
20 yrs.		2376	.295	.405	9035	2665	453	162	73	0.8	1540	1435	870	180	615	23	4	5219	6417	802	778	5.3	.936	SS-1378, 3B-530, OF-303, 2B-113, 1B-41, P-3
WORLD SERIES																								
1906	CHI A	3	.308	.538	13	4	3	0	0	0.0	4	6	0	1	1	0	0	7	14	2	1	7.7	.913	SS-3

Glenn Davis

DAVIS, GLENN EARLE
B. Mar. 28, 1961, Jacksonville, Fla.

BR TR 6′ 3″ 205 lbs.

Year	Team	Games	BA	SA	AB	H	2B	3B	HR	HR%	R	RBI	BB	SO	SB	Pinch Hit AB	Pinch Hit H	PO	A	E	DP	TC/G	FA	G by Pos
1984	HOU N	18	.213	.393	61	13	5	0	2	3.3	6	8	4	12	0	2	0	151	15	2	13	10.5	.988	1B-16
1985		100	.271	.474	350	95	11	0	20	5.7	51	64	27	68	0	4	1	766	57	12	76	8.5	.986	1B-89, OF-9
1986		158	.265	.493	574	152	32	3	31	5.4	91	101	64	72	3	2	0	1253	111	11	90	8.8	.992	1B-156
1987		151	.251	.458	578	145	35	2	27	4.7	70	93	47	84	4	1	0	1283	112	12	89	9.3	.991	1B-151
1988		152	.271	.478	561	152	26	0	30	5.3	78	99	53	77	4	2	0	1355	103	6	104	9.7	.996	1B-151
1989		158	.269	.492	581	156	26	1	34	5.9	87	89	69	123	4	3	1	1347	113	12	101	9.4	.992	1B-156
1990		93	.251	.523	327	82	15	4	22	6.7	44	64	46	54	8	4	2	796	55	4	56	9.4	.995	1B-91
1991	BAL A	49	.227	.460	176	40	9	1	10	5.7	29	28	16	29	4	3	1	288	38	8	35	7.0	.976	1B-36, DH-12
1992		106	.276	.422	398	110	15	2	13	3.3	46	48	37	65	1	5	2	19	1	0	1	0.2	1.000	DH-103, 1B-2
1993		30	.177	.230	113	20	3	0	1	0.9	8	9	7	29	0	1	0	190	12	2	19	7.0	.990	1B-22, DH-7
10 yrs.		1015	.259	.467	3719	965	177	13	190	5.1	510	603	370	613	28	27	7	7448	617	69	584	8.1	.992	1B-870, DH-122, OF-9
LEAGUE CHAMPIONSHIP SERIES																								
1986	HOU N	6	.269	.423	26	7	1	0	1	3.8	3	3	1	3	0	0	0	62	3	1	2	11.0	.985	1B-6

Harry Davis

DAVIS, HARRY ALBERT (Stinky)
B. May 7, 1908, Shreveport, La.

BL TL 5′10½″ 175 lbs.

Year	Team	Games	BA	SA	AB	H	2B	3B	HR	HR%	R	RBI	BB	SO	SB	Pinch Hit AB	Pinch Hit H	PO	A	E	DP	TC/G	FA	G by Pos
1932	DET A	140	.269	.388	590	159	32	13	4	0.7	92	74	60	53	12	0	0	1327	75	16	123	10.1	.989	1B-140
1933		66	.214	.283	173	37	8	2	0	0.0	24	14	22	8	2	19	3	433	13	10	33	10.4	.978	1B-44
1937	STL A	120	.276	.364	450	124	25	3	3	0.7	89	35	71	26	7	7	2	1065	54	10	108	10.0	.991	1B-112, OF-1
3 yrs.		326	.264	.364	1213	320	65	18	7	0.6	205	123	153	87	21	26	5	2825	142	36	264	10.1	.988	1B-296, OF-1

Harry Davis

DAVIS, HARRY H. (Jasper)
B. July 19, 1873, Philadelphia, Pa. D. Aug. 11, 1947, Philadelphia, Pa.
Manager 1912.

BR TR 5′10″ 180 lbs.

Year	Team	Games	BA	SA	AB	H	2B	3B	HR	HR%	R	RBI	BB	SO	SB	Pinch Hit AB	Pinch Hit H	PO	A	E	DP	TC/G	FA	G by Pos
1895	NY N	7	.292	.375	24	7	0	1	0	0.0	1	6	2	0	1	0	0	62	4	3	4	9.9	.957	1B-7
1896	2 teams	NY N (64G –.275) PIT N (44G –.190)																						
"	total	108	.239	.374	401	96	16	16	2	0.5	67	73	44	41	25	1	0	653	37	29	33	6.6	.960	1B-58, OF-50, SS-1
1897	PIT N	111	.305	.473	429	131	10	**28**	2	0.5	70	63	26		21	2	0	644	85	48	28	7.0	.938	1B-64, 3B-32, OF-14, SS-1
1898	3 teams	PIT N (58G –.293) LOU N (37G –.217) WAS N (1G –.000)																						
"	total	96	.262	.399	363	95	14	15	2	0.6	49	40	19		13	0	0	913	48	27	53	10.2	.973	1B-88, OF-7, 2B-2
1899	WAS N	18	.188	.313	64	12	2	3	0	0.0	3	8	8		2	0	0	161	4	2	6	9.3	.988	1B-18
1901	PHI A	117	.306	.452	496	152	28	10	8	1.6	92	76	23		21	0	0	1265	83	33	67	11.8	.976	1B-117
1902		133	.307	.444	561	172	**43**	8	6	1.1	89	92	30		28	0	0	1255	87	22	58	10.3	.984	1B-128, OF-5
1903		106	.298	.436	420	125	29	7	5	1.2	75	55	24		24	0	0	944	63	30	38	9.8	.971	1B-104, OF-2
1904		102	.309	.490	404	125	21	11	**10**	**2.5**	54	62	23		12	0	0	1011	57	19	33	10.7	.983	1B-102
1905		149	.284	.422	602	171	**47**	6	**8**	**1.3**	**92**	**83**	43		36	0	0	1621	91	24	43	11.7	.986	1B-149
1906		145	.292	.459	551	161	42	7	**12**	**2.2**	94	**96**	49		23	0	0	1352	91	37	66	10.2	.975	1B-145
1907		149	.266	.397	582	155	**36**	8	**8**	**1.4**	84	87	42		20	0	0	1475	103	38	50	10.8	.976	1B-149
1908		147	.248	.357	513	127	23	9	5	1.0	65	62	61		20	0	0	1410	86	22	44	10.3	.986	1B-147
1909		149	.268	.374	530	142	22	11	4	0.8	73	75	51		20	0	0	1432	74	19	65	10.2	.988	1B-149
1910		139	.248	.309	492	122	19	4	1	0.2	61	41	53		17	0	0	1353	64	20	74	10.3	.986	1B-139

Harry Davis *continued*

Year	Team	Lg	Games	BA	SA	AB	H	2B	3B	HR	HR%	R	RBI	BB	SO	SB	Pinch Hit AB	Pinch Hit H	PO	A	E	DP	TC/G	FA	G by Pos
1911			57	.197	.273	183	36	9	1	1	0.5	27	22	24		2	1	0	427	36	11	21	8.9	.977	1B-53
1912	CLE	A	2	.000	.000	5	0	0	0	0	0.0	0	0	0		0	0	0	14	2	1	1	8.5	.941	1B-2
1913	PHI	A	7	.353	.471	17	6	2	0	0	0.0	2	4	1	4	0	1	1	33	4	0	2	6.2	1.000	1B-6
1914			5	.429	.429	7	3	0	0	0	0.0	0	2	1	0	0	3	1	12	0	0	0	12.0	1.000	1B-1
1915			5	.333	.333	3	1	0	0	0	0.0	0	4	0	0	0	3	1	0	0	0	0	0.0	.000	1B-1
1916			1	—	—	0	0	0	0	0	—	0	0	1	0	0	0	0	0	0	0	0	0.0	—	
1917			1	.000	.000	1	0	0	0	0	0.0	0	0	0	0	0	1	0	0	0	0	0	0.0	—	
22 yrs.			1754	.277	.408	6648	1839	363	145	74	1.1	998	951	525	45	285	12	3	16037	1019	385	686	10.0	.978	1B-1627, OF-78, 3B-32, 2B-2, SS-2
WORLD SERIES																									
1905	PHI	A	5	.200	.250	20	4	1	0	0	0.0	0	0	0	1	0	0	0	50	1	0	2	10.2	1.000	1B-5
1910			5	.353	.529	17	6	3	0	0	0.0	5	2	3	4	0	0	0	44	1	3	6	9.6	.938	1B-5
1911			6	.208	.250	24	5	1	0	0	0.0	3	5	0	3	0	0	0	54	3	0	1	9.5	1.000	1B-6
3 yrs.			16	.246	.328	61	15	5	0	0	0.0	8	7	3	8	0	0	0	148	5	3	9	9.8	.981	1B-16

Ike Davis

DAVIS, ISAAC MARION
B. June 14, 1895, Pueblo, Colo. D. Apr. 2, 1984, Tucson, Ariz.
BR TR 5′ 7″ 155 lbs.

Year	Team	Lg	Games	BA	SA	AB	H	2B	3B	HR	HR%	R	RBI	BB	SO	SB	Pinch Hit AB	Pinch Hit H	PO	A	E	DP	TC/G	FA	G by Pos
1919	WAS	A	8	.000	.000	14	0	0	0	0	0.0	0	0	0	6	0	0	0	10	2	2	1	3.5	.857	SS-4
1924	CHI	A	10	.242	.333	33	8	1	1	0	0.0	5	4	2	5	0	5	0	14	33	3	3	5.0	.940	SS-10
1925			146	.240	.327	562	135	31	9	0	0.0	105	61	71	58	19	2	1	313	472	53	97	5.8	.937	SS-144
3 yrs.			164	.235	.320	609	143	32	10	0	0.0	110	65	73	69	19	7	1	337	507	58	101	5.7	.936	SS-158

Ira Davis

DAVIS, J. IRA (Slats)
B. July 8, 1870, Philadelphia, Pa. D. Dec. 21, 1942, Brooklyn, N. Y.
162 lbs.

Year	Team	Lg	Games	BA	SA	AB	H	2B	3B	HR	HR%	R	RBI	BB	SO	SB	Pinch Hit AB	Pinch Hit H	PO	A	E	DP	TC/G	FA	G by Pos
1899	NY	N	6	.235	.412	17	4	1	1	0	0.0	3	2	0		1	1	0	22	9	5	5	7.2	.861	SS-3, 1B-2

Jacke Davis

DAVIS, JACKE SYLVESTER
B. Mar. 5, 1936, Carthage, Tex.
BR TR 5′11″ 190 lbs.

Year	Team	Lg	Games	BA	SA	AB	H	2B	3B	HR	HR%	R	RBI	BB	SO	SB	Pinch Hit AB	Pinch Hit H	PO	A	E	DP	TC/G	FA	G by Pos
1962	PHI	N	48	.213	.280	75	16	0	1	1	1.3	9	6	4	20	1	16	4	25	0	2	0	1.0	.926	OF-26

Jerry Davis

DAVIS, GERALD EDWARD
B. Dec. 25, 1958, Trenton, N. J.
BR TR 6′ 185 lbs.

Year	Team	Lg	Games	BA	SA	AB	H	2B	3B	HR	HR%	R	RBI	BB	SO	SB	Pinch Hit AB	Pinch Hit H	PO	A	E	DP	TC/G	FA	G by Pos
1983	SD	N	5	.333	.467	15	5	2	0	0	0.0	3	1	3	4	1	0	0	8	1	0	0	1.8	1.000	OF-5
1985			44	.293	.379	58	17	3	1	0	0.0	10	2	5	7	0	19	4	18	2	1	0	0.9	.952	OF-23
2 yrs.			49	.301	.397	73	22	5	1	0	0.0	13	3	8	11	1	19	4	26	3	1	0	1.1	.967	OF-28

Jody Davis

DAVIS, JODY RICHARD
B. Nov. 12, 1956, Gainesville, Ga.
BR TR 6′ 4″ 192 lbs.

Year	Team	Lg	Games	BA	SA	AB	H	2B	3B	HR	HR%	R	RBI	BB	SO	SB	Pinch Hit AB	Pinch Hit H	PO	A	E	DP	TC/G	FA	G by Pos
1981	CHI	N	56	.256	.361	180	46	5	1	4	2.2	14	21	21	28	0	0	0	274	44	9	4	5.8	.972	C-56
1982			130	.261	.404	418	109	20	2	12	2.9	41	52	36	92	0	1	0	598	89	11	11	5.4	.984	C-129
1983			151	.271	.480	510	138	31	2	24	4.7	56	84	33	93	0	2	0	730	75	13	7	5.5	.984	C-150
1984			150	.256	.419	523	134	24	2	19	3.6	55	94	47	99	5	4	1	811	89	15	9	6.3	.984	C-146
1985			142	.232	.400	482	112	30	0	17	3.5	47	58	48	83	1	11	2	694	84	8	7	5.7	.990	C-138
1986			148	.250	.428	528	132	27	2	21	4.0	61	74	41	110	0	4	0	885	105	8	14	6.8	.992	C-145, 1B-1
1987			125	.248	.418	428	106	12	2	19	4.4	57	51	52	91	1	3	0	749	79	9	11	6.8	.989	C-123
1988	2 teams	CHI N (88G –.229) ATL N (2G –.250)																							
″	total		90	.230	.346	257	59	9	0	7	2.7	21	36	29	52	0	13	1	396	34	2	1	5.7	.995	C-76
1989	ATL	N	78	.169	.242	231	39	5	0	4	1.7	12	19	23	61	0	8	1	376	40	6	4	5.7	.986	C-72, 1B-2
1990			12	.071	.071	28	2	0	0	0	0.0	0	1	3	3	0	4	0	64	6	0	4	7.0	1.000	1B-6, C-4
10 yrs.			1082	.245	.403	3585	877	163	11	127	3.5	364	490	333	712	7	50	5	5577	645	81	72	6.0	.987	C-1039, 1B-9
LEAGUE CHAMPIONSHIP SERIES																									
1984	CHI	N	5	.389	.833	18	7	2	0	2	11.1	3	6	0	3	0	0	0	23	4	0	0	5.4	1.000	C-5

John Davis

DAVIS, JOHN HUMPHREY (Red)
B. July 15, 1915, Laurel Run, Pa.
BR TR 5′11″ 172 lbs.

Year	Team	Lg	Games	BA	SA	AB	H	2B	3B	HR	HR%	R	RBI	BB	SO	SB	Pinch Hit AB	Pinch Hit H	PO	A	E	DP	TC/G	FA	G by Pos
1941	NY	N	21	.214	.257	70	15	3	0	0	0.0	8	5	8	12	0	0	0	19	45	2	4	3.1	.970	3B-21

Jumbo Davis

DAVIS, JAMES J.
B. Sept. 5, 1861, New York, N. Y. D. Feb. 14, 1921, St. Louis, Mo.
BL TR 5′11″ 190 lbs.

Year	Team	Lg	Games	BA	SA	AB	H	2B	3B	HR	HR%	R	RBI	BB	SO	SB	Pinch Hit AB	Pinch Hit H	PO	A	E	DP	TC/G	FA	G by Pos
1884	KC	U	7	.207	.207	29	6	0	0	0	0.0	3		0			0	0	5	14	11	0	4.3	.633	3B-7
1886	BAL	AA	60	.194	.250	216	42	5	2	1	0.5	23		11			0	0	82	114	35	6	3.8	.848	3B-60
1887			130	.309	.485	485	150	23	**19**	8	1.6	81		28		49	0	0	148	331	98	12	4.4	.830	3B-87, SS-43
1888	KC	AA	121	.267	.363	491	131	22	8	3	0.6	70	61	20		42	0	0	167	361	100	27	5.2	.841	3B-113, SS-8
1889	2 teams	KC AA (62G –.266) STL AA (2G –.000)																							
″	total		64	.261	.302	245	64	4	3	0	0.0	41	30	18	36	25	0	0	95	140	57	14	4.6	.805	3B-62, SS-1, OF-1
1890	2 teams	STL AA (21G –.254) BKN AA (38G –.303)																							
″	total		59	.286	.399	213	61	12	3	2	0.9	41		24		15	0	0	72	140	53	11	4.5	.800	3B-59
1891	WAS	AA	12	.318	.477	44	14	3	2	0	0.0	7	9	7	5	8	0	0	19	22	9	2	4.2	.820	3B-12
7 yrs.			453	.272	.379	1723	468	69	37	14	0.8	266	100	108	41	139	0	0	588	1122	363	72	4.6	.825	3B-400, SS-52, OF-1

Kiddo Davis

DAVIS, GEORGE WILLIS
B. Feb. 12, 1902, Bridgeport, Conn. D. Mar. 4, 1983, Bridgeport, Conn.
BR TR 5′11″ 178 lbs.

Year	Team	Lg	Games	BA	SA	AB	H	2B	3B	HR	HR%	R	RBI	BB	SO	SB	Pinch Hit AB	Pinch Hit H	PO	A	E	DP	TC/G	FA	G by Pos
1926	NY	A	1	—	—	0	0	0	0	0	—	0	0	0	0	0	0	0	0	0	0	0	0.0	.000	OF-1
1932	PHI	N	137	.309	.424	576	178	39	6	5	0.9	100	57	44	56	16	0	0	411	15	11	6	3.3	.975	OF-133
1933	NY	N	126	.258	.371	434	112	20	4	7	1.6	61	37	25	30	10	5	1	248	7	3	3	2.2	.988	OF-120
1934	2 teams	STL N (16G –.303) PHI N (100G –.293)																							
″	total		116	.293	.411	426	125	28	5	4	0.9	56	52	30	29	2	5	2	327	14	4	3	3.2	.988	OF-109
1935	NY	N	47	.264	.429	91	24	7	1	2	2.2	16	6	10	4	2	21	5	42	1	1	0	2.1	.977	OF-21

Kiddo Davis *continued*

Year	Team	Games	BA	SA	AB	H	2B	3B	HR	HR%	R	RBI	BB	SO	SB	Pinch Hit AB	Pinch Hit H	PO	A	E	DP	TC/G	FA	G by Pos
1936		47	.239	.254	67	16	1	0	0	0.0	6	5	6	5	0	9	1	40	3	0	0	2.0	1.000	OF-22
1937	**2 teams**	**NY N** (56G –.263)		**CIN N** (40G –.257)																				
"	**total**	96	.259	.349	212	55	16	0	1	0.5	39	14	26	13	2	13	4	134	1	7	0	2.0	.951	OF-72
1938	**CIN N**	5	.278	.333	18	5	1	0	0	0.0	3	0	1	4	0	0	0	8	1	0	0	1.8	1.000	OF-5
8 yrs.		575	.282	.393	1824	515	112	16	19	1.0	281	171	142	141	32	53	13	1210	42	26	12	2.6	.980	OF-483
WORLD SERIES																								
1933	**NY N**	5	.368	.421	19	7	1	0	0	0.0	1	0	0	3	0	0	0	6	0	0	0	1.2	1.000	OF-5
1936		4	.500	.500	2	1	0	0	0	0.0	2	0	0	0	0	2	1	0	0	0	0	0.0	—	
2 yrs.		9	.381	.429	21	8	1	0	0	0.0	3	0	0	3	0	2	1	6	0	0	0	1.2	1.000	OF-5

Lefty Davis

DAVIS, ALFONZO DeFORD BL TL 5′10″ 170 lbs.
B. Feb. 4, 1875, Nashville, Tenn. D. Feb. 7, 1919, Collins, N. Y.

Year	Team	Games	BA	SA	AB	H	2B	3B	HR	HR%	R	RBI	BB	SO	SB	Pinch Hit AB	Pinch Hit H	PO	A	E	DP	TC/G	FA	G by Pos
1901	**2 teams**	**BKN N** (25G –.209)		**PIT N** (87G –.313)																				
"	**total**	112	.291	.380	426	124	10	11	2	0.5	98	40	66		26	1	0	180	18	12	7	1.9	.943	OF-110, 2B-1
1902	**PIT N**	59	.280	.336	232	65	7	3	0	0.0	52	20	35		19	0	0	80	6	5	1	1.5	.945	OF-59
1903	**NY A**	104	.237	.263	372	88	10	0	0	0.0	54	25	43		11	2	0	176	7	19	1	2.0	.906	OF-102, SS-1
1907	**CIN N**	73	.229	.297	266	61	5	5	1	0.4	28	25	23		9	2	0	160	11	5	3	2.5	.972	OF-70
4 yrs.		348	.261	.322	1296	338	32	19	3	0.2	232	110	167		65	5	0	596	42	41	12	2.0	.940	OF-341, SS-1, 2B-1

Mark Davis

DAVIS, MARK ANTHONY BR TR 6′ 180 lbs.
Brother of Mike Davis.
B. Nov. 25, 1964, San Diego, Calif.

Year	Team	Games	BA	SA	AB	H	2B	3B	HR	HR%	R	RBI	BB	SO	SB	Pinch Hit AB	Pinch Hit H	PO	A	E	DP	TC/G	FA	G by Pos
1991	**CAL A**	3	.000	.000	2	0	0	0	0	0.0	0	0	0	0	0	0	0	1	0	1	0	0.7	.500	OF-3

Mike Davis

DAVIS, MICHAEL DWAYNE BL TL 6′ 2″ 175 lbs.
Brother of Mark Davis.
B. June 11, 1959, San Diego, Calif.

Year	Team	Games	BA	SA	AB	H	2B	3B	HR	HR%	R	RBI	BB	SO	SB	Pinch Hit AB	Pinch Hit H	PO	A	E	DP	TC/G	FA	G by Pos
1980	**OAK A**	51	.211	.284	95	20	2	1	1	1.1	11	8	7	14	2	22	4	76	7	1	6	2.7	.988	OF-18, 1B-7, DH-6
1981		17	.050	.100	20	1	1	0	0	0.0	0	0	2	4	0	10	0	3	0	0	0	0.5	1.000	DH-3, OF-2, 1B-1
1982		23	.400	.493	75	30	4	0	1	1.3	12	10	2	8	3	4	1	65	4	5	5	3.7	.932	OF-13, 1B-7
1983		128	.275	.402	443	122	24	4	8	1.8	61	62	27	74	32	6	3	278	16	8	4	2.4	.974	OF-121, DH-3
1984		134	.230	.364	382	88	18	3	9	2.4	47	46	31	66	14	6	2	287	6	12	4	2.3	.961	OF-127, DH-4
1985		154	.287	.484	547	157	34	1	24	4.4	92	82	50	99	24	3	0	370	6	8	1	2.5	.979	OF-151
1986		142	.268	.454	489	131	28	3	19	3.9	77	55	34	91	27	7	2	310	9	9	2	2.4	.973	OF-139
1987		139	.265	.468	494	131	32	1	22	4.5	69	72	42	94	19	11	2	210	3	13	1	1.6	.942	OF-124, DH-14
1988	**LA N**	108	.196	.270	281	55	11	2	2	0.7	29	17	25	59	7	30	5	121	3	5	2	1.7	.961	OF-76
1989		67	.249	.387	173	43	7	1	5	2.9	21	19	16	28	6	16	3	74	1	1	1	1.6	.987	OF-48
10 yrs.		963	.259	.415	2999	778	161	16	91	3.0	419	371	236	537	134	115	22	1794	55	62	26	2.2	.968	OF-819, DH-30, 1B-15
LEAGUE CHAMPIONSHIP SERIES																								
1981	**OAK A**	1	1.000	1.000	1	1	0	0	0	0.0	0	0	0	0	0	1	1	0	0	0	0	0.0	—	
1988	**LA N**	4	.000	.000	2	0	0	0	0	0.0	0	0	1	0	0	2	0	0	0	0	0	0.0	—	
2 yrs.		5	.333	.333	3	1	0	0	0	0.0	0	0	1	0	0	3	1							
WORLD SERIES																								
1988	**LA N**	4	.143	.571	7	1	0	0	1	14.3	3	2	4	0	2	0	0	0	0	0	0	0.0		DH-2, OF-1

Odie Davis

DAVIS, ODIE ERNEST BR TR 6′ 1″ 178 lbs.
B. Aug. 13, 1955, San Antonio, Tex.

Year	Team	Games	BA	SA	AB	H	2B	3B	HR	HR%	R	RBI	BB	SO	SB	Pinch Hit AB	Pinch Hit H	PO	A	E	DP	TC/G	FA	G by Pos
1980	**TEX A**	17	.125	.125	8	1	0	0	0	0.0	0	0	0	2	0	1	1	7	15	3	3	1.8	.880	SS-13, 3B-1

Otis Davis

DAVIS, OTIS ALLEN (Scat) BL TL 6′ 160 lbs.
B. Sept. 24, 1920, Charleston, Ark.

Year	Team	Games	BA	SA	AB	H	2B	3B	HR	HR%	R	RBI	BB	SO	SB	Pinch Hit AB	Pinch Hit H	PO	A	E	DP	TC/G	FA	G by Pos
1946	**BKN N**	1	—	—	0	0	0	0	0	—	1	0	0	0	0	0	0	0	0	0	0	0.0	—	

Ron Davis

DAVIS, RONALD EVERETTE BR TR 6′ 175 lbs.
B. Oct. 21, 1941, Roanoke Rapids, N. C. D. Sept. 5, 1992, Houston, Tex.

Year	Team	Games	BA	SA	AB	H	2B	3B	HR	HR%	R	RBI	BB	SO	SB	Pinch Hit AB	Pinch Hit H	PO	A	E	DP	TC/G	FA	G by Pos
1962	**HOU N**	6	.214	.214	14	3	0	0	0	0.0	1	1	1	7	1	0	0	9	0	0	0	1.8	1.000	OF-5
1966		48	.247	.340	194	48	10	1	2	1.0	21	19	13	26	2	0	0	98	9	2	1	2.3	.982	OF-48
1967		94	.256	.404	285	73	19	1	7	2.5	31	38	17	48	5	15	3	114	7	3	2	1.5	.976	OF-80
1968	**2 teams**	**HOU N** (52G –.212)		**STL N** (33G –.177)																				
"	**total**	85	.203	.280	296	60	14	3	1	0.3	33	17	18	65	1	0	0	175	7	5	1	2.4	.973	OF-77
1969	**PIT N**	62	.234	.281	64	15	1	1	0	0.0	10	4	7	14	0	8	3	27	1	2	0	0.6	.933	OF-51
5 yrs.		295	.233	.334	853	199	44	6	10	1.2	96	79	56	160	9	23	6	423	24	12	4	1.8	.974	OF-261
WORLD SERIES																								
1968	**STL N**	2	.000	.000	7	0	0	0	0	0.0	0	0	0	2	0	0	0	5	0	0	0	2.5	1.000	OF-2

Russ Davis

DAVIS, RUSSELL STUART BR TR 6′ 170 lbs.
B. Sept. 13, 1969, Birmingham, Ala.

Year	Team	Games	BA	SA	AB	H	2B	3B	HR	HR%	R	RBI	BB	SO	SB	Pinch Hit AB	Pinch Hit H	PO	A	E	DP	TC/G	FA	G by Pos
1994	**NY A**	4	.143	.143	14	2	0	0	0	0.0	0	1	0	4	0	0	0	2	6	0	0	2.0	1.000	3B-4
1995		40	.276	.429	98	27	5	2	2	2.0	14	12	10	26	0	3	2	16	45	2	1	1.6	.968	3B-34, DH-4, 1B-2
2 yrs.		44	.259	.393	112	29	5	2	2	1.8	14	13	10	30	0	3	2	18	51	2	1	1.6	.972	3B-38, DH-4, 1B-2
DIVISIONAL PLAYOFF SERIES																								
1995	**NY A**	2	.200	.200	5	1	0	0	0	0.0	0	0	0	2	0	0	0	0	1	0	0	0.5	1.000	3B-2

Spud Davis

DAVIS, VIRGIL LAWRENCE BR TR 6′ 1″ 197 lbs.
B. Dec. 20, 1904, Birmingham, Ala. D. Aug. 14, 1984, Birmingham, Ala.
Manager 1946.

Year	Team	Games	BA	SA	AB	H	2B	3B	HR	HR%	R	RBI	BB	SO	SB	Pinch Hit AB	Pinch Hit H	PO	A	E	DP	TC/G	FA	G by Pos
1928	**2 teams**	**STL N** (2G –.200)		**PHI N** (67G –.282)																				
"	**total**	69	.280	.345	168	47	2	0	3	1.8	17	19	16	11	0	17	4	155	46	6	7	4.1	.971	C-51
1929	**PHI N**	98	.342	.490	263	90	18	0	7	2.7	31	48	19	17	1	7	3	198	47	10	7	2.6	.961	C-98
1930		106	.313	.495	329	103	16	1	14	4.3	41	65	17	20	1	9	2	307	50	5	5	3.8	.986	C-96
1931		120	.326	.443	393	128	32	1	4	1.0	30	51	36	28	0	5	0	420	78	3	10	4.4	.994	C-114
1932		125	.336	.522	402	135	23	5	14	3.5	44	70	40	39	1	5	3	408	54	6	15	3.9	.987	C-120

Spud Davis *continued*

Year	Team	Games	BA	SA	AB	H	2B	3B	HR	HR%	R	RBI	BB	SO	SB	Pinch Hit AB	Pinch Hit H	PO	A	E	DP	TC/G	FA	G by Pos
1933		141	.349	.473	495	173	28	3	9	1.8	51	65	32	24	2	6	2	395	69	8	9	3.6	.983	C-132
1934	STL N	107	.300	.464	347	104	22	4	9	2.6	45	65	34	27	0	11	3	459	42	6	7	5.4	.988	C-94
1935		102	.317	.416	315	100	24	2	1	0.3	28	60	33	30	0	13	4	383	34	3	6	4.9	.993	C-81, 1B-5
1936		112	.273	.388	363	99	26	2	4	1.1	24	59	35	34	0	7	2	391	63	7	7	4.4	.985	C-103, 3B-2
1937	CIN N	76	.268	.368	209	56	10	1	3	1.4	19	33	23	15	0	13	5	300	40	7	3	5.9	.980	C-59
1938	2 teams	CIN N (12G –.167) PHI N (70G –.247)																						
"	total	82	.235	.291	251	59	8	0	2	0.8	14	24	19	20	1	8	1	260	34	7	6	4.1	.977	C-74
1939	PHI N	87	.307	.356	202	62	8	1	0	0.0	10	23	24	20	0	2	1	260	40	0	1	3.5	1.000	C-85
1940	PIT N	99	.326	.435	285	93	14	1	5	1.8	23	39	35	20	0	10	3	288	61	12	11	4.1	.967	C-87
1941		57	.252	.308	107	27	4	1	0	0.0	3	6	11	11	0	7	2	97	16	0	3	2.3	1.000	C-49
1944		54	.301	.441	93	28	7	0	2	2.2	6	14	10	8	0	17	8	76	10	3	3	2.5	.966	C-35
1945		23	.242	.303	33	8	2	0	0	0.0	2	6	2	2	0	9	2	26	4	1	0	2.4	.968	C-13
16 yrs.		1458	.308	.430	4255	1312	244	22	77	1.8	388	647	386	326	6	146	45	4423	688	84	100	4.0	.984	C-1291, 1B-5, 3B-2
WORLD SERIES																								
1934	STL N	2	1.000	1.000	2	2	0	0	0	0.0	0	1	0	0	0	2	2	0	0	0	0	0.0	—	

Steve Davis

DAVIS, STEVEN MICHAEL
B. Dec. 30, 1953, Oakland, Calif.

BR TR 6′ 1″ 200 lbs.

Year	Team	Games	BA	SA	AB	H	2B	3B	HR	HR%	R	RBI	BB	SO	SB	Pinch Hit AB	Pinch Hit H	PO	A	E	DP	TC/G	FA	G by Pos
1979	CHI N	3	.000	.000	4	0	0	0	0	0.0	0	1	0	0	0	0	0	0	3	0	0	1.0	1.000	2B-2, 3B-1

Tod Davis

DAVIS, THOMAS OSCAR
B. July 24, 1924, Los Angeles, Calif. D. Dec. 31, 1978, West Covina, Calif.

BR TR 6′ 2″ 190 lbs.

Year	Team	Games	BA	SA	AB	H	2B	3B	HR	HR%	R	RBI	BB	SO	SB	Pinch Hit AB	Pinch Hit H	PO	A	E	DP	TC/G	FA	G by Pos
1949	PHI A	31	.267	.333	75	20	0	1	1	1.3	7	6	9	16	0	7	2	31	46	6	15	3.1	.928	SS-14, 3B-12, 2B-1
1951		11	.067	.067	15	1	0	0	0	0.0	0	0	1	3	0	7	1	2	2	0	0	1.3	1.000	2B-2, 3B-1
2 yrs.		42	.233	.289	90	21	0	1	1	1.1	7	6	10	19	0	14	3	33	48	6	15	2.9	.931	SS-14, 3B-13, 2B-3

Tommy Davis

DAVIS, HERMAN THOMAS
B. Mar. 21, 1939, Brooklyn, N. Y.

BR TR 6′ 2″ 195 lbs.

Year	Team	Games	BA	SA	AB	H	2B	3B	HR	HR%	R	RBI	BB	SO	SB	Pinch Hit AB	Pinch Hit H	PO	A	E	DP	TC/G	FA	G by Pos
1959	LA N	1	.000	.000	1	0	0	0	0	0.0	0	0	0	1	0	1	0	0	0	0	0	0.0	—	
1960		110	.276	.426	352	97	18	1	11	3.1	43	44	13	35	6	21	7	153	17	4	2	1.9	.977	OF-87, 3B-5
1961		132	.278	.413	460	128	13	2	15	3.3	60	58	32	53	10	10	3	173	91	17	8	1.9	.940	OF-86, 3B-59
1962		163	**.346**	.535	665	**230**	27	9	27	4.1	120	**153**	33	65	18	2	0	269	60	20	7	1.9	.943	OF-146, 3B-39
1963		146	**.326**	.457	556	181	19	3	16	2.9	69	88	29	59	15	3	0	204	67	15	10	1.7	.948	OF-129, 3B-40
1964		152	.275	.397	592	163	20	5	14	2.4	70	86	29	68	11	4	2	264	9	5	1	1.9	.982	OF-148
1965		17	.250	.300	60	15	1	1	0	0.0	3	9	2	4	2	1	0	21	1	0	1	1.4	1.000	OF-16
1966		100	.313	.383	313	98	11	1	3	1.0	27	27	16	36	3	22	5	99	9	3	1	1.4	.973	OF-79, 3B-2
1967	NY N	154	.302	.440	577	174	32	0	16	2.8	72	73	31	71	9	4	0	236	7	7	0	1.7	.972	OF-149, 1B-1
1968	CHI A	132	.268	.344	456	122	5	3	8	1.8	30	50	16	48	4	12	4	211	9	8	5	1.9	.965	OF-116, 1B-6
1969	2 teams	SEA A (123G –.271) HOU N (24G –.241)																						
"	total	147	.266	.370	533	142	32	1	7	1.3	54	89	38	55	20	16	7	210	4	7	0	1.6	.968	OF-133, 1B-1
1970	3 teams	HOU N (57G –.282) OAK A (66G –.290) CHI N (11G –.262)																						
"	total	134	.284	.387	455	129	23	3	6	1.3	45	65	16	44	10	23	5	196	8	9	10	1.8	.958	OF-108, 1B-8
1971	OAK A	79	.324	.411	219	71	8	1	3	1.4	26	42	15	19	7	28	13	275	37	5	24	5.7	.984	1B-35, OF-16, 2B-3, 3B-2
1972	2 teams	CHI N (15G –.269) BAL A (26G –.256)																						
"	total	41	.259	.296	108	28	4	0	0	0.0	12	12	8	21	2	15	3	82	5	1	0	3.4	.989	OF-20, 1B-6
1973	BAL A	137	.306	.391	552	169	20	3	7	1.3	53	89	30	56	11	6	4	32	2	1	3	0.3	.971	DH-127, 1B-4
1974		158	.289	.377	626	181	20	1	11	1.8	67	84	34	49	6	4	1	0	0	0	0	0.0	.000	DH-155
1975		116	.283	.357	460	130	14	1	6	1.3	43	57	23	52	2	4	1	0	0	0	0	0.0	.000	DH-111
1976	2 teams	CAL A (72G –.265) KC A (8G –.263)																						
"	total	80	.265	.324	238	63	5	0	3	1.3	17	26	16	18	0	21	8	4	0	0	0	0.1	1.000	DH-56, 1B-1
18 yrs.		1999	.294	.405	7223	2121	272	35	153	2.1	811	1052	381	754	136	197	63	2429	326	102	72	1.5	.964	OF-1233, DH-449, 3B-147, 1B-62, 2B-3
LEAGUE CHAMPIONSHIP SERIES																								
1971	OAK A	3	.375	.500	8	3	1	0	0	0.0	1	0	0	0	0	1	0	8	0	0	1	4.0	1.000	1B-2
1973	BAL A	5	.286	.333	21	6	1	0	0	0.0	1	2	1	0	0	0	0	0	0	0	0	0.0	.000	DH-5
1974		4	.267	.267	15	4	0	0	0	0.0	0	1	0	1	0	0	0	0	0	0	0	0.0	.000	DH-4
3 yrs.		12	.295	.341	44	13	2	0	0	0.0	2	3	1	1	0	1	0	8	0	0	1	0.7	1.000	DH-9, 1B-2
WORLD SERIES																								
1963	LA N	4	.400	.667	15	6	0	2	0	0.0	0	2	0	2	1	0	0	6	0	0	0	1.5	1.000	OF-4
1966		4	.250	.250	8	2	0	0	0	0.0	0	0	1	1	0	2	2	3	0	0	0	1.0	1.000	OF-3
2 yrs.		8	.348	.522	23	8	0	2	0	0.0	0	2	1	3	1	2	2	9	0	0	0	1.3	1.000	OF-7

Trench Davis

DAVIS, TRENCH NEAL
B. Sept. 12, 1960, Baltimore, Md.

BL TL 6′ 3″ 171 lbs.

Year	Team	Games	BA	SA	AB	H	2B	3B	HR	HR%	R	RBI	BB	SO	SB	Pinch Hit AB	Pinch Hit H	PO	A	E	DP	TC/G	FA	G by Pos
1985	PIT N	2	.143	.143	7	1	0	0	0	0.0	1	0	0	0	1	0	0	2	0	1	0	1.5	.667	OF-2
1986		15	.130	.130	23	3	0	0	0	0.0	2	1	0	4	0	7	1	10	1	1	0	1.7	.917	OF-7
1987	ATL N	6	.000	.000	3	0	0	0	0	0.0	0	0	0	1	0	3	0	0	0	0	0	0.0	.000	OF-6
3 yrs.		23	.121	.121	33	4	0	0	0	0.0	3	1	0	5	1	10	1	12	1	2	0	1.0	.867	OF-15

Willie Davis

DAVIS, WILLIAM HENRY
B. Apr. 15, 1940, Mineral Springs, Ark.

BL TL 5′11″ 180 lbs.

Year	Team	Games	BA	SA	AB	H	2B	3B	HR	HR%	R	RBI	BB	SO	SB	Pinch Hit AB	Pinch Hit H	PO	A	E	DP	TC/G	FA	G by Pos
1960	LA N	22	.318	.477	88	28	6	1	2	2.3	12	10	4	12	3	0	0	52	1	1	0	2.5	.981	OF-22
1961		128	.254	.451	339	86	19	6	12	3.5	56	45	27	46	12	9	1	224	4	4	1	2.0	.983	OF-114
1962		157	.285	.453	600	171	18	**10**	21	3.5	103	85	42	72	32	0	0	379	13	15	0	2.6	.963	OF-156
1963		156	.245	.365	515	126	19	8	9	1.7	60	60	25	61	25	4	2	337	16	8	3	2.4	.978	OF-153
1964		157	.294	.413	613	180	23	7	12	2.0	91	77	22	59	42	1	0	400	16	7	2	2.7	.983	OF-155
1965		142	.238	.346	558	133	24	3	10	1.8	52	57	14	81	25	2	1	318	6	11	1	2.4	.967	OF-141
1966		153	.284	.405	624	177	31	6	11	1.8	74	61	15	68	21	0	0	347	9	11	0	2.4	.970	OF-152
1967		143	.257	.367	569	146	27	9	6	1.1	65	41	29	65	20	6	1	300	6	9	2	2.3	.971	OF-138
1968		160	.250	.351	643	161	24	10	7	1.1	86	31	31	88	36	2	1	345	9	10	2	2.3	.973	OF-158
1969		129	.311	.456	498	155	23	8	11	2.2	66	59	33	39	24	4	0	271	8	6	1	2.3	.979	OF-125

Willie Davis *continued*

Year	Team	Lg	Games	BA	SA	AB	H	2B	3B	HR	HR%	R	RBI	BB	SO	SB	Pinch Hit AB	Pinch Hit H	PO	A	E	DP	TC/G	FA	G by Pos
1970			146	.305	.438	593	181	23	**16**	8	1.3	92	93	29	54	38	4	0	342	12	3	4	2.5	.992	OF-143
1971			158	.309	.438	641	198	33	10	10	1.6	84	74	23	47	20	3	1	404	7	8	0	2.7	.981	OF-157
1972			149	.289	.441	615	178	22	7	19	3.1	81	79	27	61	20	2	1	373	10	5	1	2.7	.987	OF-146
1973			152	.285	.444	599	171	29	9	16	2.7	82	77	29	62	17	7	3	344	6	7	0	2.4	.980	OF-146
1974	MON	N	153	.295	.427	611	180	27	9	12	2.0	86	89	27	69	25	5	2	369	8	12	1	2.6	.969	OF-151
1975	2 teams		TEX A (42G –.249) STL N (98G –.291)																						
"	total		140	.277	.424	519	144	27	8	11	2.1	57	67	18	52	23	12	3	287	6	7	3	2.3	.977	OF-131
1976	SD	N	141	.268	.375	493	132	18	10	5	1.0	61	46	19	34	14	12	2	349	6	3	2	2.8	.992	OF-128
1979	CAL	A	43	.250	.321	56	14	2	1	0	0.0	9	2	4	7	1	24	5	8	0	0	0	0.6	1.000	OF-7, DH-6
18 yrs.			2429	.279	.412	9174	2561	395	138	182	2.0	1217	1053	418	977	398	97	23	5449	143	127	23	2.5	.978	OF-2323, DH-6
LEAGUE CHAMPIONSHIP SERIES																									
1979	CAL	A	2	.500	1.000	2	1	1	0	0	0.0	1	0	0	0	0	2	1	0	0	0	0	0.0	—	
WORLD SERIES																									
1963	LA	N	4	.167	.333	12	2	2	0	0	0.0	2	3	0	6	0	0	0	6	0	0	0	1.5	1.000	OF-4
1965			7	.231	.231	26	6	0	0	0	0.0	3	0	0	2	3	0	0	11	0	0	0	1.6	1.000	OF-7
1966			4	.063	.063	16	1	0	0	0	0.0	0	0	0	4	0	0	0	6	0	3	0	2.3	.667	OF-4
3 yrs.			15	.167	.204	54	9	2	0	0	0.0	5	3	0	12	3	0	0	23	0	3	0	1.7	.885	OF-15

Andre Dawson

DAWSON, ANDRE NOLAN (The Hawk)
B. July 10, 1954, Miami, Fla.
BR TR 6′ 3″ 180 lbs.

Year	Team	Lg	Games	BA	SA	AB	H	2B	3B	HR	HR%	R	RBI	BB	SO	SB	Pinch Hit AB	Pinch Hit H	PO	A	E	DP	TC/G	FA	G by Pos
1976	MON	N	24	.235	.306	85	20	4	1	0	0.0	9	7	5	13	1	0	0	61	1	2	1	2.7	.969	OF-24
1977			139	.282	.474	525	148	26	9	19	3.6	64	65	34	93	21	5	0	352	9	4	1	2.7	.989	OF-136
1978			157	.253	.442	609	154	24	8	25	4.1	84	72	30	128	28	5	2	411	17	5	2	2.8	.988	OF-153
1979			155	.275	.468	639	176	24	12	25	3.9	90	92	27	115	35	0	0	394	7	5	1	2.7	.988	OF-153
1980			151	.308	.492	577	178	41	7	17	2.9	96	87	44	69	34	3	1	410	14	6	3	2.9	.986	OF-147
1981			103	.302	.553	394	119	21	3	24	6.1	71	64	35	50	26	0	0	327	10	7	1	3.3	.980	OF-103
1982			148	.301	.498	608	183	37	7	23	3.8	107	83	34	96	39	0	0	419	8	8	2	3.0	.982	OF-147
1983			159	.299	.539	633	**189**	36	10	32	5.1	104	113	38	81	25	1	1	435	6	9	2	2.9	.980	OF-157
1984			138	.248	.409	533	132	23	6	17	3.2	73	86	41	80	13	4	0	297	11	8	2	2.4	.975	OF-134
1985			139	.255	.444	529	135	27	2	23	4.3	65	91	29	92	13	9	3	248	9	7	1	2.0	.973	OF-131
1986			130	.284	.478	496	141	32	2	20	4.0	65	78	37	79	18	3	1	200	11	3	2	1.7	.986	OF-127
1987	CHI	N	153	.287	.568	621	178	24	2	**49**	7.9	90	**137**	32	103	11	2	1	271	12	4	0	1.9	.986	OF-152
1988			157	.303	.504	591	179	31	8	24	4.1	78	79	37	73	12	8	2	267	7	3	1	1.9	.989	OF-147
1989			118	.252	.476	416	105	18	6	21	5.0	62	77	35	62	8	5	2	227	4	3	0	2.1	.987	OF-112
1990			147	.310	.535	529	164	28	5	27	5.1	72	100	42	65	16	7	2	250	10	5	4	1.9	.981	OF-139
1991			149	.272	.488	563	153	21	4	31	5.5	69	104	22	80	4	12	2	243	7	3	2	1.8	.988	OF-137
1992			143	.277	.456	542	150	27	2	22	4.1	60	90	30	70	6	6	1	223	11	2	3	1.7	.992	OF-139
1993	BOS	A	121	.273	.425	461	126	29	1	13	2.8	44	67	17	49	2	4	2	42	0	0	0	0.4	1.000	DH-97, OF-20
1994			75	.240	.466	292	70	18	0	16	5.5	34	48	9	53	2	2	1	0	0	0	0	0.0	.000	DH-74
1995	FLA	N	79	.257	.434	226	58	10	3	8	3.5	30	37	9	45	0	19	4	75	3	8	2	1.5	.907	OF-59
20 yrs.			2585	.279	.483	9869	2758	501	98	436	4.4	1367	1577	587	1496	314	95	25	5152	157	92	30	2.2	.983	OF-2317, DH-171
DIVISIONAL PLAYOFF SERIES																									
1981	MON	N	5	.300	.400	20	6	0	1	0	0.0	1	0	1	6	2	0	0	12	1	1	0	2.8	.929	OF-5
LEAGUE CHAMPIONSHIP SERIES																									
1981	MON	N	5	.150	.150	20	3	0	0	0	0.0	2	0	0	4	0	0	0	12	0	0	0	2.4	1.000	OF-5
1989	CHI	N	5	.105	.158	19	2	1	0	0	0.0	0	3	2	6	0	0	0	4	0	0	0	0.8	1.000	OF-5
2 yrs.			10	.128	.154	39	5	1	0	0	0.0	2	3	2	10	0	0	0	16	0	0	0	1.6	1.000	OF-10

Boots Day

DAY, CHARLES FREDERICK
B. Aug. 31, 1947, Ilion, N. Y.
BL TL 5′ 9″ 160 lbs.

Year	Team	Lg	Games	BA	SA	AB	H	2B	3B	HR	HR%	R	RBI	BB	SO	SB	Pinch Hit AB	Pinch Hit H	PO	A	E	DP	TC/G	FA	G by Pos
1969	STL	N	11	.000	.000	6	0	0	0	0	0.0	1	0	1	1	0	5	0	0	0	0	0	0.0	.000	OF-1
1970	2 teams		CHI N (11G –.250) MON N (41G –.269)																						
"	total		52	.267	.302	116	31	4	0	0	0.0	16	5	6	21	3	13	4	81	2	2	0	2.0	.976	OF-42
1971	MON	N	127	.283	.353	371	105	10	2	4	1.1	53	33	33	39	9	15	5	262	10	5	1	2.3	.982	OF-120
1972			128	.233	.272	386	90	7	4	0	0.0	32	30	29	44	3	17	5	225	7	5	3	2.0	.979	OF-117
1973			101	.275	.367	207	57	7	0	4	1.9	36	28	21	28	0	48	13	86	2	0	0	1.7	1.000	OF-51
1974			52	.185	.185	65	12	0	0	0	0.0	8	2	5	8	0	31	3	18	0	0	0	1.1	1.000	OF-16
6 yrs.			471	.256	.312	1151	295	28	6	8	0.7	146	98	95	141	15	129	30	672	21	12	4	2.0	.983	OF-347

Brian Dayett

DAYETT, BRIAN KELLY
B. Jan. 22, 1957, New London, Conn.
BR TR 5′10″ 180 lbs.

Year	Team	Lg	Games	BA	SA	AB	H	2B	3B	HR	HR%	R	RBI	BB	SO	SB	Pinch Hit AB	Pinch Hit H	PO	A	E	DP	TC/G	FA	G by Pos
1983	NY	A	11	.207	.276	29	6	0	1	0	0.0	3	5	2	4	0	3	1	22	1	0	0	2.6	1.000	OF-9
1984			64	.244	.409	127	31	9	0	4	3.1	14	23	9	14	0	7	3	80	3	1	0	1.3	.988	OF-62, DH-1
1985	CHI	N	22	.231	.346	26	6	0	0	1	3.8	1	4	0	6	0	14	4	8	0	0	0	0.8	1.000	OF-10
1986			24	.269	.507	67	18	4	0	4	6.0	7	11	6	10	0	1	0	31	1	0	0	1.3	1.000	OF-24
1987			97	.277	.452	177	49	14	1	5	2.8	20	25	20	37	0	32	7	72	2	0	0	0.9	1.000	OF-78
5 yrs.			218	.258	.430	426	110	27	2	14	3.3	45	68	37	71	0	57	15	213	7	1	0	1.2	.995	OF-183, DH-1

Charlie Deal

DEAL, CHARLES ALBERT
B. Oct. 30, 1891, Wilkinsburg, Pa. D. Sept. 16, 1979, Covina, Calif.
BR TR 6′ 160 lbs.

Year	Team	Lg	Games	BA	SA	AB	H	2B	3B	HR	HR%	R	RBI	BB	SO	SB	Pinch Hit AB	Pinch Hit H	PO	A	E	DP	TC/G	FA	G by Pos
1912	DET	A	41	.225	.282	142	32	4	2	0	0.0	13	11	9		4	0	0	48	113	10	3	4.2	.942	3B-41
1913	2 teams		DET A (16G –.220) BOS N (10G –.306)																						
"	total		26	.256	.314	86	22	1	2	0	0.0	9	6	3	8	3	1	0	25	53	11	4	3.6	.876	3B-15, 2B-10
1914	BOS	N	79	.210	.276	257	54	13	2	0	0.0	17	23	20	23	4	4	0	86	135	13	8	3.1	.944	3B-74, SS-1
1915	STL	F	65	.323	.426	223	72	12	4	1	0.4	21	27	12		10	0	0	76	136	11	9	3.4	.951	3B-65
1916	2 teams		STL A (23G –.135) CHI N (2G –.250)																						
"	total		25	.146	.171	82	12	2	0	0	0.0	9	13	6	8	4	0	0	28	47	2	6	3.1	.974	3B-24, 2B-1
1917	CHI	N	135	.254	.292	449	114	11	3	0	0.0	46	47	19	18	10	5	1	151	254	18	31	3.3	.957	3B-130
1918			119	.239	.290	414	99	9	3	2	0.5	43	34	21	13	11	1	0	144	247	24	21	3.5	.942	3B-118
1919			116	.289	.385	405	117	23	5	2	0.5	37	52	12	12	11	0	0	157	233	11	14	3.5	.973	3B-116

Charlie Deal *continued*

Year	Team	Games	BA	SA	AB	H	2B	3B	HR	HR%	R	RBI	BB	SO	SB	Pinch Hit AB	Pinch Hit H	PO	A	E	DP	TC/G	FA	G by Pos
1920		129	.240	.304	450	108	10	5	3	0.7	48	39	20	14	5	1	1	129	268	11	22	3.2	.973	3B-128
1921		115	.289	.393	422	122	19	8	3	0.7	52	66	13	9	3	2	0	122	239	10	19	3.3	.973	3B-113
10 yrs.		850	.257	.327	2930	752	104	34	11	0.4	295	318	135	105	65	14	2	966	1725	121	137	3.4	.957	3B-824, 2B-11, SS-1
WORLD SERIES																								
1914	BOS N	4	.125	.250	16	2	2	0	0	0.0	1	0	0	0	2	0	0	6	11	0	1	4.3	1.000	3B-4
1918	CHI N	6	.176	.176	17	3	0	0	0	0.0	0	0	0	1	0	0	0	6	9	1	0	2.7	.938	3B-6
2 yrs.		10	.152	.212	33	5	2	0	0	0.0	1	0	0	1	2	0	0	12	20	1	1	3.3	.970	3B-10

Lindsay Deal

DEAL, FRED LINDSAY
B. Sept. 3, 1911, Lenoir, N. C. D. Apr. 18, 1979, Little Rock, Ark.
BL TR 6′ 175 lbs.

Year	Team	Games	BA	SA	AB	H	2B	3B	HR	HR%	R	RBI	BB	SO	SB	Pinch Hit AB	Pinch Hit H	PO	A	E	DP	TC/G	FA	G by Pos
1939	BKN N	4	.000	.000	7	0	0	0	0	0.0	0	0	0	2	0	3	0	3	0	0	0	3.0	1.000	OF-1

Snake Deal

DEAL, JOHN WESLEY
B. Jan. 21, 1879, Lancaster, Pa. D. May 9, 1944, Harrisburg, Pa.
BR TR 6′ 164 lbs.

Year	Team	Games	BA	SA	AB	H	2B	3B	HR	HR%	R	RBI	BB	SO	SB	Pinch Hit AB	Pinch Hit H	PO	A	E	DP	TC/G	FA	G by Pos
1906	CIN N	65	.208	.251	231	48	4	3	0	0.0	13	21	6		15	0	0	624	46	10	25	10.5	.985	1B-65

Pat Dealey

DEALEY, PATRICK J.
B. Burlington, Vt. D. Dec. 17, 1924, Buffalo, N. Y.
BR TR 5′ 8″ 145 lbs.

Year	Team	Games	BA	SA	AB	H	2B	3B	HR	HR%	R	RBI	BB	SO	SB	Pinch Hit AB	Pinch Hit H	PO	A	E	DP	TC/G	FA	G by Pos
1884	STP U	5	.133	.133	15	2	0	0	0	0.0	2		0			0	0	22	9	4	1	7.0	.886	C-4, OF-1
1885	BOS N	35	.223	.292	130	29	4	1	1	0.8	18	9	2	14		0	0	168	53	29	11	6.8	.884	C-29, 3B-3, SS-2, OF-2, 1B-1
1886		15	.326	.391	46	15	1	1	0	0.0	9	3	4	4		0	0	76	16	8	1	6.7	.920	C-14, OF-1
1887	WAS N	58	.272	.321	312	85	8	2	1	0.3	33	18	8	8	36	0	0	171	105	34	9	5.1	.890	C-28, SS-23, OF-5, 3B-5
1890	SYR AA	18	.182	.197	66	12	1	0	0	0.0	9		5		4	0	0	39	26	12	1	4.3	.844	C-10, 3B-6, OF-2
5 yrs.		131	.251	.301	569	143	14	4	2	0.4	71	30	19	26	40	0	0	476	209	87	23	5.7	.887	C-85, SS-25, 3B-14, OF-11, 1B-1

Chubby Dean

DEAN, ALFRED LOVELL
B. Aug. 24, 1916, Mt. Airy, N. C. D. Dec. 21, 1970, Riverside, Calif.
BL TL 5′11″ 181 lbs.

Year	Team	Games	BA	SA	AB	H	2B	3B	HR	HR%	R	RBI	BB	SO	SB	Pinch Hit AB	Pinch Hit H	PO	A	E	DP	TC/G	FA	G by Pos
1936	PHI A	111	.287	.374	342	98	21	3	1	0.3	41	48	24	24	3	34	13	680	37	8	62	9.4	.989	1B-77
1937		104	.262	.353	309	81	14	4	2	0.6	36	31	42	10	2	23	6	706	40	7	55	9.4	.991	1B-78, P-2
1938		16	.300	.400	20	6	2	0	0	0.0	3	1	1	4	0	9	2	0	8	0	0	1.3	1.000	P-6
1939		80	.351	.403	77	27	4	0	0	0.0	12	19	8	4	0	26	10	3	36	2	4	0.8	.951	P-54
1940		67	.289	.311	90	26	2	0	0	0.0	6	6	16	9	0	28	9	12	36	1	2	1.6	.980	P-30, 1B-1
1941	2 teams	PHI A (27G –.237) CLE A (17G –.167)																						
″	total	44	.210	.258	62	13	3	0	0	0.0	2	11	7	5	0	14	2	7	28	0	1	1.3	1.000	P-26, 1B-1
1942	CLE A	70	.267	.277	101	27	1	0	0	0.0	4	7	11	7	0	37	5	7	24	2	0	1.2	.939	P-27
1943		41	.196	.196	46	9	0	0	0	0.0	2	5	6	2	0	20	2	2	11	1	1	0.8	.929	P-17
8 yrs.		533	.274	.341	1047	287	47	7	3	0.3	106	128	115	65	5	191	49	1417	220	21	125	5.2	.987	P-162, 1B-157

Tommy Dean

DEAN, TOMMY DOUGLAS
B. Aug. 30, 1945, Iuka, Miss.
BR TR 6′ 165 lbs.

Year	Team	Games	BA	SA	AB	H	2B	3B	HR	HR%	R	RBI	BB	SO	SB	Pinch Hit AB	Pinch Hit H	PO	A	E	DP	TC/G	FA	G by Pos
1967	LA N	12	.143	.179	28	4	1	0	0	0.0	1	2	0	9	0	0	0	19	33	1	10	4.4	.981	SS-12
1969	SD N	101	.176	.245	273	48	9	2	2	0.7	14	9	27	54	0	0	0	141	255	9	41	4.1	.978	SS-97, 2B-2
1970		61	.222	.304	158	35	5	1	2	1.3	18	13	11	29	2	1	1	84	143	6	30	4.2	.974	SS-55
1971		41	.114	.114	70	8	0	0	0	0.0	2	1	4	13	1	2	1	38	71	5	13	2.8	.956	SS-28, 3B-11, 2B-1
4 yrs.		215	.180	.242	529	95	15	3	4	0.8	35	25	42	105	3	3	2	282	502	21	94	3.9	.974	SS-192, 3B-11, 2B-3

Wayland Dean

DEAN, WAYLAND OGDEN
B. June 20, 1902, Richwood, W. Va. D. Apr. 10, 1930, Huntington, W. Va.
BB TR 6′ 2″ 178 lbs.

Year	Team	Games	BA	SA	AB	H	2B	3B	HR	HR%	R	RBI	BB	SO	SB	Pinch Hit AB	Pinch Hit H	PO	A	E	DP	TC/G	FA	G by Pos
1924	NY N	26	.200	.350	40	8	0	0	2	5.0	5	4	1	9	0	0	0	12	41	3	2	2.2	.946	P-26
1925		33	.235	.373	51	12	2	1	1	2.0	7	7	3	12	0	0	0	10	36	6	1	1.6	.885	P-33
1926	PHI N	63	.265	.392	102	27	4	0	3	2.9	11	19	5	26	0	26	6	6	44	3	3	1.6	.943	P-33
1927	2 teams	PHI N (3G –.667) CHI N (2G –.000)																						
″	total	5	.667	1.333	3	2	0	1	0	0.0	1	1	0	0	0	1	0	0	2	0	1	0.5	1.000	P-4
4 yrs.		127	.250	.393	196	49	6	2	6	3.1	24	31	9	47	0	27	6	28	123	12	7	1.7	.926	P-96
WORLD SERIES																								
1924	NY N	1	—	—	0	0	0	0	0	—	0	0	0	0	0	0	0	0	0	0	0	0.0	.000	P-1

Buddy Dear

DEAR, PAUL STANFORD
B. Dec. 1, 1905, Norfolk, Va. D. Aug. 29, 1989, Radford, Va.
BR TR 5′ 8″ 143 lbs.

Year	Team	Games	BA	SA	AB	H	2B	3B	HR	HR%	R	RBI	BB	SO	SB	Pinch Hit AB	Pinch Hit H	PO	A	E	DP	TC/G	FA	G by Pos
1927	WAS A	2	.000	.000	1	0	0	0	0	0.0	1	0	0	0	0	0	0	0	0	0	0	0.0	.000	2B-1

Charlie DeArmond

DeARMOND, CHARLES HOMMER (Hummer)
B. Feb. 13, 1877, Okeana, Ohio D. Dec. 17, 1933, Morning Sun, Ohio.
BR TR 5′10″ 165 lbs.

Year	Team	Games	BA	SA	AB	H	2B	3B	HR	HR%	R	RBI	BB	SO	SB	Pinch Hit AB	Pinch Hit H	PO	A	E	DP	TC/G	FA	G by Pos
1903	CIN N	11	.282	.385	39	11	2	1	0	0.0	10	7	3		1	0	0	20	16	5	1	3.7	.878	3B-11

John Deasley

DEASLEY, JOHN
Brother of Pat Deasley.
B. Jan. 1861, Philadelphia, Pa. D. Dec. 25, 1910, Philadelphia, Pa.

Year	Team	Games	BA	SA	AB	H	2B	3B	HR	HR%	R	RBI	BB	SO	SB	Pinch Hit AB	Pinch Hit H	PO	A	E	DP	TC/G	FA	G by Pos
1884	2 teams	WAS U (31G –.216) KC U (13G –.175)																						
″	total	44	.207	.236	174	36	3	1	0	0.0	23		5			0	0	39	118	31	11	4.3	.835	SS-44

Pat Deasley

DEASLEY, THOMAS H.
Brother of John Deasley.
B. Nov. 17, 1857, Philadelphia, Pa. D. Apr. 1, 1943, Philadelphia, Pa.
BR TR 5′ 8½″ 154 lbs.

Year	Team	Games	BA	SA	AB	H	2B	3B	HR	HR%	R	RBI	BB	SO	SB	Pinch Hit AB	Pinch Hit H	PO	A	E	DP	TC/G	FA	G by Pos
1881	BOS N	43	.238	.299	147	35	5	2	0	0.0	13	8	5	10		0	0	159	48	21	6	5.2	.908	C-28, SS-7, OF-7, 1B-2
1882		67	.265	.295	264	70	8	0	0	0.0	36	29	7	22		0	0	372	56	25	1	6.4	.945	C-56, OF-14, SS-1
1883	STL AA	58	.257	.277	206	53	2	1	0	0.0	27		6			0	0	302	59	27	6	6.7	.930	C-56, OF-2
1884		75	.205	.256	254	52	5	4	0	0.0	27		7			0	0	429	120	48	3	7.7	.920	C-75, OF-2, 1B-1
1885	NY N	54	.256	.290	207	53	5	1	0	0.0	22		9	20		0	0	283	81	25	4	6.8	.936	C-54, OF-2, SS-1

Pat Deasley *continued*

Year	Team	Games	BA	SA	AB	H	2B	3B	HR	HR%	R	RBI	BB	SO	SB	Pinch Hit AB	Pinch Hit H	PO	A	E	DP	TC/G	FA	G by Pos
1886		41	.266	.322	143	38	6	1	0	0.0	18	17	4	12		0	0	167	42	21	4	5.1	.909	C-30, OF-15
1887		30	.314	.356	118	37	5	0	0	0.0	12	23	9	7	3	0	0	98	37	24	0	5.0	.849	C-24, 3B-7, SS-1
1888	WAS N	34	.157	.165	127	20	1	0	0	0.0	6	4	2	18	2	0	0	180	65	21	3	7.8	.921	C-31, SS-1, OF-1, 2B-1
8 yrs.		402	.244	.282	1466	358	37	9	0	0.0	161	81	49	89	5	0	0	1990	508	212	27	6.5	.922	C-354, OF-43, SS-11, 3B-7, 1B-3, 2B-1

Hank DeBerry

DeBERRY, JOHN HERMAN BR TR 5′11″ 195 lbs.
B. Dec. 29, 1894, Savannah, Tenn. D. Sept. 10, 1951, Savannah, Tenn.

Year	Team	Games	BA	SA	AB	H	2B	3B	HR	HR%	R	RBI	BB	SO	SB	Pinch Hit AB	Pinch Hit H	PO	A	E	DP	TC/G	FA	G by Pos
1916	CLE A	15	.273	.394	33	9	4	0	0	0.0	7	4	6	9	0	1	0	34	13	0	1	3.4	1.000	C-14
1917		25	.273	.333	33	9	2	0	0	0.0	3	1	2	7	0	14	3	22	8	1	1	3.4	.968	C-9
1922	BKN N	85	.301	.382	259	78	10	1	3	1.2	29	35	20	9	4	3	1	309	64	11	5	4.7	.971	C-81
1923		78	.285	.396	235	67	11	6	1	0.4	21	48	20	12	2	13	3	273	65	10	8	5.8	.971	C-60
1924		77	.243	.358	218	53	10	3	3	1.4	20	26	20	21	0	12	2	394	57	3	8	7.2	.993	C-63
1925		67	.259	.342	193	50	8	1	2	1.0	26	24	16	8	2	11	1	309	50	7	4	6.7	.981	C-55
1926		48	.287	.383	115	33	11	0	0	0.0	6	13	8	5	0	10	2	180	22	5	3	5.6	.976	C-37
1927		68	.234	.284	201	47	3	2	1	0.5	15	21	17	8	1	1	1	339	59	5	8	6.0	.988	C-67
1928		82	.252	.298	258	65	8	2	0	0.0	19	23	18	15	3	2	0	377	56	10	5	5.5	.977	C-80
1929		68	.262	.338	210	55	11	1	1	0.5	13	25	17	15	1	0	0	304	36	3	3	5.0	.991	C-68
1930		35	.295	.326	95	28	3	0	0	0.0	11	14	4	10	0	0	0	160	14	4	2	5.1	.978	C-35
11 yrs.		648	.267	.346	1850	494	81	16	11	0.6	170	234	148	119	13	67	13	2701	444	59	48	5.6	.982	C-569

Adam DeBus

DeBUS, ADAM JOSEPH BR TR 5′10½″ 150 lbs.
B. Oct. 7, 1892, Chicago, Ill. D. May 13, 1977, Chicago, Ill.

Year	Team	Games	BA	SA	AB	H	2B	3B	HR	HR%	R	RBI	BB	SO	SB	Pinch Hit AB	Pinch Hit H	PO	A	E	DP	TC/G	FA	G by Pos
1917	PIT N	38	.229	.328	131	30	5	4	0	0.0	9	7	7	14	2	0	0	61	92	19	10	4.4	.890	SS-21, 3B-18

Doug DeCinces

DeCINCES, DOUGLAS VERNON BR TR 6′2″ 190 lbs.
B. Aug. 29, 1950, Burbank, Calif.

Year	Team	Games	BA	SA	AB	H	2B	3B	HR	HR%	R	RBI	BB	SO	SB	Pinch Hit AB	Pinch Hit H	PO	A	E	DP	TC/G	FA	G by Pos
1973	BAL A	10	.111	.111	18	2	0	0	0	0.0	2	3	1	5	0	0	0	4	19	2	2	2.3	.920	3B-8, 2B-2, SS-1
1974		1	.000	.000	1	0	0	0	0	0.0	0	0	1	0	0	0	0	0	2	0	0	2.0	1.000	3B-1
1975		61	.251	.395	167	42	6	3	4	2.4	20	23	13	32	0	7	1	92	115	7	20	3.6	.967	3B-34, SS-13, 2B-11, 1B-2
1976		129	.234	.357	440	103	17	2	11	2.5	36	42	29	68	8	2	0	191	257	20	21	3.3	.957	3B-109, 2B-17, 1B-11, SS-2, DH-1
1977		150	.259	.433	522	135	28	3	19	3.6	63	69	64	86	8	1	0	125	331	20	34	3.2	.958	3B-148, 2B-1, DH-1, 1B-1
1978		142	.286	.526	511	146	37	1	28	5.5	72	80	46	81	7	0	0	138	308	14	38	3.2	.970	3B-130, 2B-12
1979		120	.230	.412	422	97	27	1	16	3.8	67	61	54	68	5	0	0	99	247	13	21	3.0	.964	3B-120
1980		145	.249	.403	489	122	23	2	16	3.3	64	64	49	83	11	3	0	122	340	19	41	3.4	.960	3B-142, 1B-1
1981		100	.263	.454	346	91	23	2	13	3.8	49	55	41	32	0	1	0	91	191	17	31	2.9	.943	3B-100, OF-1, 1B-1
1982	CAL A	153	.301	.548	575	173	42	5	30	5.2	94	97	66	80	7	0	0	113	400	22	41	3.5	.959	3B-153, SS-2
1983		95	.281	.495	370	104	19	3	18	4.9	49	65	32	56	2	1	0	79	216	14	26	3.3	.955	3B-84, DH-10
1984		146	.269	.431	547	147	23	3	20	3.7	77	82	53	79	4	1	0	107	266	14	22	2.7	.964	3B-140, DH-5
1985		120	.244	.440	427	104	22	1	20	4.7	50	78	47	71	1	4	1	95	202	13	27	2.7	.958	3B-111, DH-3
1986		140	.256	.459	512	131	20	3	26	5.1	69	96	52	74	2	6	1	119	216	12	19	2.6	.965	3B-132, DH-3, SS-1
1987	2 teams	CAL A (133G –.234)	STL N (4G –.222)																					
"	total	137	.234	.392	462	108	25	0	16	3.5	66	64	70	89	3	10	1	108	234	19	27	2.7	.947	3B-131, 1B-4, SS-1
15 yrs.		1649	.259	.445	5809	1505	312	29	237	4.1	778	879	618	904	58	36	4	1483	3344	206	370	3.1	.959	3B-1543, 2B-43, DH-23, 1B-20, SS-20, OF-1
LEAGUE CHAMPIONSHIP SERIES																								
1979	BAL A	4	.308	.385	13	4	1	0	0	0.0	4	3	1	1	0	0	0	5	8	0	1	3.3	1.000	3B-4
1982	CAL A	5	.316	.421	19	6	2	0	0	0.0	5	0	1	5	0	0	0	9	12	3	3	4.8	.875	3B-5
1986		7	.281	.469	32	9	3	0	1	3.1	2	3	0	2	0	0	0	6	18	2	3	3.7	.923	3B-7
3 yrs.		16	.297	.438	64	19	6 7th	0	1	1.6	11	6	2	8	0	0	0	20	38	5	7	3.9	.921	3B-16
WORLD SERIES																								
1979	BAL A	7	.200	.320	25	5	0	0	1	4.0	2	3	5	5	1	0	0	7	21	3	0	4.4	.903	3B-7

Frank Decker

DECKER, FRANK BR TR
B. Feb. 26, 1856, St. Louis, Mo. D. Feb. 5, 1940, St. Louis, Mo.

Year	Team	Games	BA	SA	AB	H	2B	3B	HR	HR%	R	RBI	BB	SO	SB	Pinch Hit AB	Pinch Hit H	PO	A	E	DP	TC/G	FA	G by Pos
1879	SYR N	3	.100	.100	10	1	0	0	0	0.0	0	0	0	3		0	0	14	0	4	0	4.5	.778	C-2, 1B-1, OF-1
1882	STL AA	2	.250	.250	8	2	0	0	0	0.0	0		0			0	0	6	7	3	1	8.0	.813	2B-2
2 yrs.		5	.167	.167	18	3	0	0	0	0.0	0	0	0	3		0	0	20	7	7	1	5.7	.794	C-2, 2B-2, 1B-1, OF-1

George Decker

DECKER, GEORGE A. BL TL 6′1″ 180 lbs.
B. June 1, 1869, York, Pa. D. June 7, 1909, Patton, Calif.

Year	Team	Games	BA	SA	AB	H	2B	3B	HR	HR%	R	RBI	BB	SO	SB	Pinch Hit AB	Pinch Hit H	PO	A	E	DP	TC/G	FA	G by Pos
1892	CHI N	78	.227	.306	291	66	6	7	1	0.3	32	28	20	49	9	0	0	95	49	22	6	2.1	.867	OF-62, 2B-16
1893		81	.271	.366	328	89	9	8	2	0.6	57	48	24	22	22	0	0	333	79	33	25	5.4	.926	OF-33, 1B-27, 2B-20, SS-2
1894		91	.313	.451	384	120	17	6	8	2.1	74	92	24	17	23	4	1	497	39	32	32	6.5	.944	1B-48, OF-29, 3B-7, 2B-2, SS-1
1895		73	.276	.374	297	82	9	7	2	0.7	51	41	17	22	11	0	0	212	16	12	10	3.3	.950	OF-57, 1B-11, 3B-3, SS-1, 2B-1
1896		107	.280	.423	421	118	23	11	5	1.2	68	61	23	14	20	0	0	482	29	17	25	4.9	.968	OF-71, 1B-36
1897		111	.290	.386	428	124	12	7	5	1.2	72	63	24		11	1	0	507	35	16	23	4.9	.971	OF-75, 1B-38, 2B-1
1898	2 teams	STL N (76G –.259)	LOU N (42G –.297)																					
"	total	118	.272	.325	434	118	14	3	1	0.2	53	64	29		13	5	2	1055	30	19	49	9.8	.983	1B-107, OF-6
1899	2 teams	LOU N (38G –.267)	WAS N (4G –.000)																					
"	total	42	.250	.326	144	36	8	0	1	0.7	13	18	12		3	1	0	426	16	15	22	11.1	.967	1B-40, OF-1
8 yrs.		701	.276	.376	2727	753	98	49	25	0.9	420	415	173	124	112	11	3	3607	293	166	192	5.9	.959	OF-334, 1B-307, 2B-40, 3B-10, SS-4

Harry Decker

DECKER, EARLE HARRY BR TR 5′11″ 183 lbs.
B. June 1865, Lockport, Ill. Deceased.

Year	Team	Games	BA	SA	AB	H	2B	3B	HR	HR%	R	RBI	BB	SO	SB	Pinch Hit AB	Pinch Hit H	PO	A	E	DP	TC/G	FA	G by Pos
1884	2 teams	IND AA (4G –.267)	KC U (23G –.133)																					
"	total	27	.156	.189	90	14	3	0	0	0.0	9		6			0	0	90	21	13	4	4.0	.895	OF-16, C-15
1886	2 teams	DET N (14G –.222)	WAS N (7G –.217)																					
"	total	21	.221	.273	77	17	2	1	0	0.0	2	7	3	14		0	0	118	46	23	1	8.5	.877	C-18, 3B-2, SS-1, OF-1

Harry Decker *continued*

Year	Team		Games	BA	SA	AB	H	2B	3B	HR	HR%	R	RBI	BB	SO	SB	Pinch Hit AB	Pinch Hit H	PO	A	E	DP	TC/G	FA	G by Pos
1889	PHI	N	11	.100	.100	30	3	0	0	0	0.0	4	2	2	5	1	0	0	26	20	8	4	4.9	.852	2B-7, C-3, OF-1
1890	2 teams	PHI N (5G –.368) PIT N (92G –.274)																							
"	total		97	.279	.375	373	104	15	3	5	1.3	57	40	30	37	12	0	0	459	87	49	22	6.1	.918	C-71, 1B-18, OF-6, SS-1, 2B-1
4 yrs.			156	.242	.318	570	138	20	4	5	0.9	72	49	41	56	13	0	0	693	174	93	31	6.0	.903	C-107, OF-24, 1B-18, 2B-8, 3B-2, SS-2

Steve Decker

DECKER, STEVEN MICHAEL
B. Oct. 25, 1965, Rock Island, Ill.
BR TR 6′3″ 205 lbs.

Year	Team		Games	BA	SA	AB	H	2B	3B	HR	HR%	R	RBI	BB	SO	SB	Pinch Hit AB	Pinch Hit H	PO	A	E	DP	TC/G	FA	G by Pos
1990	SF	N	15	.296	.500	54	16	2	0	3	5.6	5	8	1	10	0	0	0	75	11	1	2	5.8	.989	C-15
1991			79	.206	.309	233	48	7	1	5	2.1	11	24	16	44	0	4	1	385	41	7	5	5.6	.984	C-78
1992			15	.163	.186	43	7	1	0	0	0.0	3	1	6	7	0	0	0	94	4	0	1	6.5	1.000	C-15
1993	FLA	N	8	.000	.000	15	0	0	0	0	0.0	0	1	3	3	0	2	0	28	2	1	0	6.2	.968	C-5
1995			51	.226	.323	133	30	2	1	3	2.3	12	13	19	22	1	5	1	298	25	5	2	6.8	.985	C-46, 1B-2
5 yrs.			168	.211	.314	478	101	12	2	11	2.3	31	47	45	86	1	11	2	880	83	14	10	6.1	.986	C-159, 1B-2

Artie Dede

DEDE, ARTHUR RICHARD
B. July 12, 1895, Brooklyn, N. Y. D. Sept. 6, 1971, Keene, N. H.
BR TR 5′9″ 155 lbs.

Year	Team		Games	BA	SA	AB	H	2B	3B	HR	HR%	R	RBI	BB	SO	SB	Pinch Hit AB	Pinch Hit H	PO	A	E	DP	TC/G	FA	G by Pos
1916	BKN	N	1	.000	.000	1	0	0	0	0	0.0	0	0	0	0	0	0	0	1	0	0	0	1.0	1.000	C-1

Raoul Dedeaux

DEDEAUX, RAOUL MARTIAL (Rod)
B. Feb. 17, 1915, New Orleans, La.
BR TR 5′11″ 160 lbs.

Year	Team		Games	BA	SA	AB	H	2B	3B	HR	HR%	R	RBI	BB	SO	SB	Pinch Hit AB	Pinch Hit H	PO	A	E	DP	TC/G	FA	G by Pos
1935	BKN	N	2	.250	.250	4	1	0	0	0	0.0	0	1	0	0	0	0	0	2	4	1	1	3.5	.857	SS-2

Jim Dee

DEE, JAMES D.
B. Buffalo, N. Y. Deceased.

Year	Team		Games	BA	SA	AB	H	2B	3B	HR	HR%	R	RBI	BB	SO	SB	Pinch Hit AB	Pinch Hit H	PO	A	E	DP	TC/G	FA	G by Pos
1884	PIT	AA	12	.125	.125	40	5	0	0	0	0.0	0		1			0	0	13	36	8	6	4.8	.860	SS-12

Shorty Dee

DEE, MAURICE LEO
B. Oct. 4, 1889, Halifax, Nova Scotia, Canada D. Aug. 12, 1971, Jamaica Plain, Mass.
BR TR 5′6″ 155 lbs.

Year	Team		Games	BA	SA	AB	H	2B	3B	HR	HR%	R	RBI	BB	SO	SB	Pinch Hit AB	Pinch Hit H	PO	A	E	DP	TC/G	FA	G by Pos
1915	STL	A	1	.000	.000	3	0	0	0	0	0.0	1	0	1	0	0	0	0	1	1	2	0	4.0	.500	SS-1

Rob Deer

DEER, ROBERT GEORGE
B. Sept. 29, 1960, Orange, Calif.
BR TR 6′3″ 215 lbs.

Year	Team		Games	BA	SA	AB	H	2B	3B	HR	HR%	R	RBI	BB	SO	SB	Pinch Hit AB	Pinch Hit H	PO	A	E	DP	TC/G	FA	G by Pos
1984	SF	N	13	.167	.542	24	4	0	0	3	12.5	5	3	7	10	1	3	0	19	0	2	0	2.3	.905	OF-9
1985			78	.185	.377	162	30	5	1	8	4.9	22	20	23	71	0	30	5	127	2	2	4	2.8	.985	OF-37, 1B-10
1986	MIL	A	134	.232	.494	466	108	17	3	33	**7.1**	75	86	72	179	5	1	1	312	8	8	3	2.4	.976	OF-131, 1B-4
1987			134	.238	.456	474	113	15	2	28	5.9	71	80	86	**186**	12	2	0	304	16	8	7	2.4	.976	OF-123, 1B-12, DH-4
1988			135	.252	.441	492	124	24	0	23	4.7	71	85	51	**153**	9	1	0	284	10	3	3	2.2	.990	OF-133, DH-1
1989			130	.210	.425	466	98	18	2	26	5.6	72	65	60	158	4	1	1	267	10	8	1	2.2	.972	OF-125, DH-5
1990			134	.209	.432	440	92	15	1	27	6.1	57	69	64	147	2	6	1	373	25	10	19	2.9	.975	OF-117, 1B-21, DH-1
1991	DET	A	134	.179	.386	448	80	14	2	25	5.6	64	64	89	**175**	1	1	0	310	8	7	4	2.4	.978	OF-132, DH-2
1992			110	.247	.547	393	97	20	1	32	8.1	66	64	51	131	4	3	0	229	8	4	1	2.2	.983	OF-106, DH-2
1993	2 teams	DET A (90G –.217) BOS A (38G –.196)																							
"	total		128	.210	.386	466	98	17	1	21	4.5	66	55	58	**169**	5	8	2	286	7	8	3	2.4	.973	OF-122, DH-6
10 yrs.			1130	.220	.442	3831	844	145	13	226	5.9	569	591	561	1379	43	56	10	2511	94	60	45	2.4	.977	OF-1035, 1B-47, DH-21

Charlie Dees

DEES, CHARLES HENRY
B. June 24, 1935, Birmingham, Ala.
BL TL 6′1″ 173 lbs.

Year	Team		Games	BA	SA	AB	H	2B	3B	HR	HR%	R	RBI	BB	SO	SB	Pinch Hit AB	Pinch Hit H	PO	A	E	DP	TC/G	FA	G by Pos
1963	LA	A	60	.307	.416	202	62	11	1	3	1.5	23	27	11	31	3	4	1	474	32	7	41	9.2	.986	1B-56
1964			26	.077	.115	26	2	1	0	0	0.0	3	1	1	4	1	6	1	48	3	1	7	4.3	.981	1B-12
1965	CAL	A	12	.156	.156	32	5	0	0	0	0.0	1	1	1	8	1	4	0	69	2	1	5	9.0	.986	1B-8
3 yrs.			98	.265	.354	260	69	12	1	3	1.2	27	29	13	43	5	14	2	591	37	9	53	8.4	.986	1B-76

Tony DeFate

DeFATE, CLYDE HERBERT
B. Feb. 22, 1895, Kansas City, Mo. D. Sept. 3, 1963, New Orleans, La.
BR TR 5′8½″ 158 lbs.

Year	Team		Games	BA	SA	AB	H	2B	3B	HR	HR%	R	RBI	BB	SO	SB	Pinch Hit AB	Pinch Hit H	PO	A	E	DP	TC/G	FA	G by Pos
1917	2 teams	STL N (14G –.143) DET A (3G –.000)																							
"	total		17	.125	.125	16	2	0	0	0	0.0	1	1	4	6	0	6	1	1	6	0	1	1.0	1.000	3B-5, 2B-2

Art DeFreitas

DeFREITAS, ARTURO MARCELINO
Born Arturo Marcelino DeFreitas (Simon).
B. Apr. 26, 1953, San Pedro de Macoris, Dominican Republic.
BR TR 6′2″ 195 lbs.

Year	Team		Games	BA	SA	AB	H	2B	3B	HR	HR%	R	RBI	BB	SO	SB	Pinch Hit AB	Pinch Hit H	PO	A	E	DP	TC/G	FA	G by Pos
1978	CIN	N	9	.211	.421	19	4	1	0	1	5.3	1	2	1	4	0	2	1	40	3	0	5	7.2	1.000	1B-6
1979			23	.206	.265	34	7	2	0	0	0.0	2	4	0	16	0	17	3	38	0	1	5	5.6	.974	1B-6, OF-1
2 yrs.			32	.208	.321	53	11	3	0	1	1.9	3	6	1	20	0	19	4	78	3	1	10	6.3	.988	1B-12, OF-1

Rube DeGroff

DeGROFF, EDWARD ARTHUR
B. Sept. 2, 1879, Hyde Park, N. Y. D. Dec. 17, 1955, Poughkeepsie, N. Y.
BL 5′11″

Year	Team		Games	BA	SA	AB	H	2B	3B	HR	HR%	R	RBI	BB	SO	SB	Pinch Hit AB	Pinch Hit H	PO	A	E	DP	TC/G	FA	G by Pos
1905	STL	N	15	.250	.321	56	14	2	1	0	0.0	3	5	5		1	0	0	27	3	3	1	2.2	.909	OF-15
1906			1	.000	.000	4	0	0	0	0	0.0	1	0	0		0	0	0	0	0	0	0	0.0	.000	OF-1
2 yrs.			16	.233	.300	60	14	2	1	0	0.0	4	5	5		1	0	0	27	3	3	1	2.1	.909	OF-16

Dutch Dehlman

DEHLMAN, HERMAN J.
B. 1850, Catasauqua, Pa. D. Mar. 13, 1885, Wilkes-Barre, Pa.

Year	Team		Games	BA	SA	AB	H	2B	3B	HR	HR%	R	RBI	BB	SO	SB	Pinch Hit AB	Pinch Hit H	PO	A	E	DP	TC/G	FA	G by Pos
1876	STL	N	64	.184	.208	245	45	6	0	0	0.0	40	9	9	10		0	0	750	8	33	21	12.4	.958	1B-64
1877			32	.185	.218	119	22	4	0	0	0.0	24	11	7	21		0	0	309	4	23	14	10.5	.932	1B-31, OF-1
2 yrs.			96	.184	.212	364	67	10	0	0	0.0	64	20	16	31		0	0	1059	12	56	35	11.7	.950	1B-95, OF-1

Jim Deidel

DEIDEL, JAMES LAWRENCE
B. June 6, 1949, Denver, Colo.
BR TR 6′2″ 195 lbs.

Year	Team		Games	BA	SA	AB	H	2B	3B	HR	HR%	R	RBI	BB	SO	SB	Pinch Hit AB	Pinch Hit H	PO	A	E	DP	TC/G	FA	G by Pos
1974	NY	A	2	.000	.000	2	0	0	0	0	0.0	0	0	0	0	0	0	0	7	1	0	0	4.0	1.000	C-2

Pep Deininger

DEININGER, OTTO CHARLES BL TL 5′ 8½″ 180 lbs.
B. Oct. 10, 1877, Wasseralfingen, Germany D. Sept. 25, 1950, Boston, Mass.

Year	Team	Lg	Games	BA	SA	AB	H	2B	3B	HR	HR%	R	RBI	BB	SO	SB	Pinch Hit AB	Pinch Hit H	PO	A	E	DP	TC/G	FA	G by Pos
1902	BOS	A	2	.333	.833	6	2	1	1	0	0.0	0	0	0		0	0	0	0	1	0	1	0.5	1.000	P-2
1908	PHI	N	1	—	—	0	0	0	0	0	—	0	0	0	0	0	0	0	0	0	0	0	0.0	.000	OF-1
1909			55	.260	.314	169	44	9	0	0	0.0	22	16	11		5	6	0	83	5	2	0	2.0	.978	OF-45, 2B-1
3 yrs.			58	.263	.331	175	46	10	1	0	0.0	22	16	11	0	5	6	0	83	6	2	1	1.9	.978	OF-46, P-2, 2B-1

Pat Deisel

DEISEL, EDWARD BR TR 5′ 5″ 145 lbs.
B. Apr. 29, 1876, Ripley, Ohio D. Apr. 17, 1948, Cincinnati, Ohio.

Year	Team	Lg	Games	BA	SA	AB	H	2B	3B	HR	HR%	R	RBI	BB	SO	SB	Pinch Hit AB	Pinch Hit H	PO	A	E	DP	TC/G	FA	G by Pos
1902	BKN	N	1	.667	.667	3	2	0	0	0	0.0	0	1	1		0	0	0	8	0	0	0	8.0	1.000	C-1
1903	CIN	N	2	—	—	0	0	0	0	0	—	0	0	1		0	0	0	0	0	0	0	0.0	.000	C-1
2 yrs.			3	.667	.667	3	2	0	0	0	0.0	0	1	2		0	0	0	8	0	0	0	4.0	1.000	C-2

Mike Dejan

DEJAN, MICHAEL DAN BL TL 6′ 1″ 185 lbs.
B. Jan. 13, 1915, Cleveland, Ohio D. Feb. 2, 1953, West Los Angeles, Calif.

Year	Team	Lg	Games	BA	SA	AB	H	2B	3B	HR	HR%	R	RBI	BB	SO	SB	Pinch Hit AB	Pinch Hit H	PO	A	E	DP	TC/G	FA	G by Pos
1940	CIN	N	12	.188	.313	16	3	0	1	0	0.0	1	2	3	3	0	8	1	4	0	0	0	2.0	1.000	OF-2

Ivan DeJesus

DeJESUS, IVAN BR TR 5′11″ 175 lbs.
Born Ivan (Alvarez).
B. Jan. 9, 1953, Santurce, Puerto Rico.

Year	Team	Lg	Games	BA	SA	AB	H	2B	3B	HR	HR%	R	RBI	BB	SO	SB	Pinch Hit AB	Pinch Hit H	PO	A	E	DP	TC/G	FA	G by Pos
1974	LA	N	3	.333	.333	3	1	0	0	0	0.0	1	0	0	2	0	1	0	1	0	0	0	0.5	1.000	SS-2
1975			63	.184	.230	87	16	2	1	0	0.0	10	2	11	15	1	2	0	45	107	4	18	2.5	.974	SS-63
1976			22	.171	.268	41	7	2	1	0	0.0	4	2	4	9	0	1	0	20	47	3	7	3.5	.957	SS-13, 3B-7
1977	CHI	N	155	.266	.353	624	166	31	7	3	0.5	91	40	56	90	24	0	0	234	595	33	94	5.6	.962	SS-154
1978			160	.278	.354	619	172	24	7	3	0.5	**104**	35	74	78	41	0	0	232	558	27	96	5.1	.967	SS-160
1979			160	.283	.379	636	180	26	10	5	0.8	92	52	59	82	24	0	0	235	507	32	97	4.8	.959	SS-160
1980			157	.259	.325	618	160	26	3	3	0.5	78	33	60	81	44	0	0	229	529	24	99	5.0	.969	SS-156
1981			106	.194	.233	403	78	8	4	0	0.0	49	13	46	61	21	0	0	221	343	24	81	5.5	.959	SS-106
1982	PHI	N	161	.239	.313	536	128	21	5	3	0.6	53	59	54	70	14	0	0	222	488	21	81	4.5	.971	SS-154, 3B-7
1983			158	.254	.336	497	126	15	7	4	0.8	60	45	53	77	11	0	0	214	438	23	64	4.3	.966	SS-158
1984			144	.257	.306	435	112	15	3	0	0.0	40	35	43	76	12	2	0	166	400	29	57	4.2	.951	SS-141
1985	STL	N	59	.222	.292	72	16	5	0	0	0.0	11	7	4	16	2	24	6	15	40	2	3	1.7	.965	3B-20, SS-13
1986	NY	A	7	.000	.000	4	0	0	0	0	0.0	1	0	1	1	0	0	0	5	4	1	0	1.4	.900	SS-7
1987	SF	N	9	.200	.200	10	2	0	0	0	0.0	0	1	0	2	0	1	0	7	14	4	2	2.8	.840	SS-9
1988	DET	A	7	.176	.176	17	3	0	0	0	0.0	1	0	1	4	0	0	0	8	17	3	4	4.0	.893	SS-7
15 yrs.			1371	.254	.326	4602	1167	175	48	21	0.5	595	324	466	664	194	31	6	1854	4087	230	703	4.6	.963	SS-1303, 3B-34
LEAGUE CHAMPIONSHIP SERIES																									
1983	PHI	N	4	.250	.250	12	3	0	0	0	0.0	0	1	3	3	0	0	0	4	10	2	0	4.0	.875	SS-4
WORLD SERIES																									
1983	PHI	N	5	.125	.125	16	2	0	0	0	0.0	0	0	1	2	0	0	0	5	14	1	2	4.0	.950	SS-5
1985	STL	N	1	.000	.000	1	0	0	0	0	0.0	0	0	0	0	0	1	0	0	0	0	0	0.0	—	
2 yrs.			6	.118	.118	17	2	0	0	0	0.0	0	0	1	2	0	1	0	5	14	1	2	4.0	.950	SS-5

Mark DeJohn

DeJOHN, MARK STEPHEN BB TR 5′11″ 170 lbs.
B. Sept. 18, 1953, Middletown, Conn.

Year	Team	Lg	Games	BA	SA	AB	H	2B	3B	HR	HR%	R	RBI	BB	SO	SB	Pinch Hit AB	Pinch Hit H	PO	A	E	DP	TC/G	FA	G by Pos
1982	DET	A	24	.190	.286	21	4	2	0	0	0.0	1	1	4	4	1	0	0	20	31	2	10	2.1	.962	SS-20, 3B-4, 2B-1

Bill DeKoning

DeKONING, WILLIAM CALLAHAN, JR. BR TR 5′11″ 185 lbs.
B. Dec. 19, 1918, Brooklyn, N. Y. D. July 26, 1979, Palm Harbor, Fla.

Year	Team	Lg	Games	BA	SA	AB	H	2B	3B	HR	HR%	R	RBI	BB	SO	SB	Pinch Hit AB	Pinch Hit H	PO	A	E	DP	TC/G	FA	G by Pos
1945	NY	N	3	.000	.000	1	0	0	0	0	0.0	0	0	0	1	0	1	0	1	0	0	0	0.5	1.000	C-2

Ed Delahanty

DELAHANTY, EDWARD JAMES (Big Ed) BR TR 6′ 1″ 170 lbs.
Brother of Tom Delahanty. Brother of Joe Delahanty. Brother of Jim Delahanty.
Brother of Frank Delahanty.
B. Oct. 30, 1867, Cleveland, Ohio D. July 2, 1903, Niagara Falls, Ont., Canada.
Hall of Fame 1945.

Year	Team	Lg	Games	BA	SA	AB	H	2B	3B	HR	HR%	R	RBI	BB	SO	SB	Pinch Hit AB	Pinch Hit H	PO	A	E	DP	TC/G	FA	G by Pos
1888	PHI	N	74	.228	.293	290	66	12	2	1	0.3	40	31	12	26	38	0	0	157	173	47	20	5.2	.875	2B-56, OF-17
1889			56	.293	.370	246	72	13	3	0	0.0	37	27	14	17	19	0	0	116	61	18	11	3.5	.908	OF-31, 2B-24, SS-1
1890	CLE	P	115	.298	.416	517	154	26	13	3	0.6	107	64	24	30	25	0	0	243	305	94	44	5.4	.854	SS-76, 2B-20, OF-18, 3B-3, 1B-1
1891	PHI	N	128	.243	.333	543	132	19	9	4	0.7	92	86	33	50	25	0	0	466	43	38	20	4.2	.931	OF-99, 1B-27, 2B-3
1892			123	.306	**.495**	477	146	30	**21**	6	1.3	79	91	31	32	29	0	0	263	28	18	6	2.5	.942	OF-121, 3B-4
1893			132	.368	**.583**	595	219	35	18	**19**	3.2	145	**146**	47	20	37	0	0	391	78	26	23	3.6	.947	OF-117, 2B-15, 1B-6
1894			114	.407	.585	489	199	39	18	4	0.8	147	131	60	16	21	0	0	325	96	42	19	3.8	.909	OF-88, 1B-12, 3B-9, SS-8, 2B-6
1895			116	.404	.617	480	194	**49**	10	11	2.3	149	106	86	31	46	0	0	282	55	31	8	3.1	.916	OF-103, SS-9, 2B-6, 3B-1
1896			123	.397	**.631**	499	198	**44**	17	13	2.6	131	**126**	62	22	37	1	1	482	29	21	15	4.4	.961	OF-99, 1B-22, 2B-1
1897			129	.377	.538	530	200	40	15	5	0.9	109	96	60		26	0	0	276	23	9	4	2.4	.971	OF-129, 1B-1
1898			144	.334	.454	548	183	36	9	4	0.7	115	92	77		**58**	0	0	302	20	12	5	2.3	.964	OF-144
1899			146	**.410**	**.582**	581	**238**	**55**	9	9	1.5	135	**137**	55		30	3	2	284	26	10	4	2.2	.969	OF-143
1900			131	.323	.430	539	174	32	10	2	0.4	82	109	41		16	1	0	1299	66	27	86	10.7	.981	1B-130
1901			139	.357	.533	538	192	**39**	16	8	1.5	106	108	65		29	0	0	732	31	22	22	5.5	.972	OF-84, 1B-58
1902	WAS	A	123	**.376**	**.590**	473	178	**43**	14	10	2.1	103	93	62		16	0	0	379	18	16	5	3.3	.961	OF-111, 1B-13
1903			42	.333	.436	156	52	11	1	1	0.6	22	21	12		3	1	0	74	6	3	1	2.0	.964	OF-40, 1B-1
16 yrs.			1835	.346 4th	.505	7501	2597	523	185	100	1.3	1599	1464	741	244	455	6	3	6071	1058	434	293	4.1	.943	OF-1344, 1B-271, 2B-131, SS-94, 3B-17

Frank Delahanty

DELAHANTY, FRANK GEORGE (Pudgie) BR TR 5′ 9″ 160 lbs.
Brother of Tom Delahanty. Brother of Joe Delahanty. Brother of Jim Delahanty.
Brother of Ed Delahanty.
B. Jan. 29, 1883, Cleveland, Ohio D. July 22, 1966, Cleveland, Ohio.

Year	Team	Lg	Games	BA	SA	AB	H	2B	3B	HR	HR%	R	RBI	BB	SO	SB	Pinch Hit AB	Pinch Hit H	PO	A	E	DP	TC/G	FA	G by Pos
1905	NY	A	9	.222	.259	27	6	1	0	0	0.0	0	2	1		0	1	0	43	2	3	0	6.0	.938	1B-5, OF-3
1906			92	.238	.345	307	73	11	8	2	0.7	37	41	16		11	5	2	180	7	9	1	2.1	.954	OF-92
1907	CLE	A	15	.173	.212	52	9	0	1	0	0.0	3	4	4		2	0	0	19	3	2	0	1.6	.917	OF-15

Frank Delahanty *continued*

Year	Team	Games	BA	SA	AB	H	2B	3B	HR	HR%	R	RBI	BB	SO	SB	Pinch Hit AB	Pinch Hit H	PO	A	E	DP	TC/G	FA	G by Pos
1908	NY A	37	.256	.296	125	32	1	2	0	0.0	12	10	10		9	1	0	64	2	3	0	1.9	.957	OF-36
1914	2 teams	BUF F (79G –.201)	PIT F (41G –.239)																					
"	total	120	.215	.305	433	93	8	11	3	0.7	54	34	34		28	1	0	179	24	8	2	1.8	.962	OF-114, 2B-4
1915	PIT F	14	.238	.262	42	10	1	0	0	0.0	3	3	1		0	2	0	20	2	0	0	2.0	1.000	OF-11
6 yrs.		287	.226	.308	986	223	22	22	5	0.5	109	94	66		50	10	2	505	40	25	3	2.0	.956	OF-271, 1B-5, 2B-4

Jim Delahanty

DELAHANTY, JAMES CHRISTOPHER BR TR 5′10½″ 170 lbs.
Brother of Tom Delahanty. Brother of Joe Delahanty. Brother of Frank Delahanty.
Brother of Ed Delahanty.
B. June 20, 1879, Cleveland, Ohio D. Oct. 17, 1953, Cleveland, Ohio.

Year	Team	Games	BA	SA	AB	H	2B	3B	HR	HR%	R	RBI	BB	SO	SB	Pinch Hit AB	Pinch Hit H	PO	A	E	DP	TC/G	FA	G by Pos
1901	CHI N	17	.190	.222	63	12	2	0	0	0.0	4	4	3		5	0	0	21	29	7	2	3.2	.877	3B-17, 2B-1
1902	NY N	7	.231	.269	26	6	1	0	0	0.0	3	3	1		0	0	0	11	0	1	0	1.7	.917	OF-7
1904	BOS N	142	.285	.389	499	142	27	8	3	0.6	56	60	27		16	0	0	214	267	57	13	3.8	.894	3B-113, 2B-18, OF-9, P-1
1905		125	.258	.349	461	119	11	8	5	1.1	50	55	28		12	1	0	186	17	8	1	1.7	.962	OF-124, P-1
1906	CIN N	115	.280	.364	379	106	21	4	1	0.3	63	39	45		21	3	1	146	179	35	4	3.2	.903	3B-105, SS-5, OF-2
1907	2 teams	STL A (33G –.221)	WAS A (109G –.292)																					
"	total	142	.279	.361	499	139	21	7	2	0.4	52	60	41		24	8	0	307	263	41	24	4.5	.933	2B-70, 3B-48, OF-13, 1B-4
1908	WAS A	83	.317	.394	287	91	11	4	1	0.3	33	30	24		16	2	0	181	232	16	25	5.4	.963	2B-79
1909	2 teams	WAS A (90G –.222)	DET A (46G –.253)																					
"	total	136	.232	.316	452	105	23	6	1	0.2	47	41	40		13	5	0	265	338	31	39	4.8	.951	2B-131
1910	DET A	106	.294	.368	378	111	16	3	2	0.5	67	45	43		15	0	0	246	267	33	36	5.2	.940	2B-106
1911		144	.339	.463	542	184	30	14	3	0.6	83	94	56		15	1	0	917	225	48	41	8.3	.960	1B-72, 2B-59, 3B-12
1912		78	.286	.346	266	76	14	1	0	0.0	34	41	42		9	1	0	148	120	23	19	3.8	.921	2B-44, OF-33
1914	BKN F	74	.290	.397	214	62	13	5	0	0.0	28	15	25		4	13	2	137	119	12	18	4.5	.955	2B-55, 1B-5
1915		17	.240	.280	25	6	1	0	0	0.0	0	2	3		1	11	1	7	11	3	0	5.3	.857	2B-4
13 yrs.		1186	.283	.373	4091	1159	191	60	18	0.4	520	489	378		151	45	4	2786	2067	315	222	4.5	.939	2B-567, 3B-295, OF-188, 1B-81, SS-5, P-2
WORLD SERIES																								
1909	DET A	7	.346	.500	26	9	4	0	0	0.0	2	4	2	5	0	0	0	11	16	2	0	4.1	.931	2B-7

Joe Delahanty

DELAHANTY, JOSEPH NICHOLAS BR TR 5′9″ 168 lbs.
Brother of Tom Delahanty. Brother of Jim Delahanty. Brother of Frank Delahanty.
Brother of Ed Delahanty.
B. Oct. 18, 1875, Cleveland, Ohio D. Jan. 9, 1936, Cleveland, Ohio.

Year	Team	Games	BA	SA	AB	H	2B	3B	HR	HR%	R	RBI	BB	SO	SB	Pinch Hit AB	Pinch Hit H	PO	A	E	DP	TC/G	FA	G by Pos
1907	STL N	6	.333	.476	21	7	0	0	1	4.8	3	2	0		3	0	0	14	0	1	0	2.5	.933	OF-6
1908		140	.255	.333	499	127	14	11	1	0.2	37	44	32		11	1	0	243	11	6	1	1.9	.977	OF-138
1909		123	.214	.287	411	88	16	4	2	0.5	28	54	42		10	10	3	203	121	22	11	3.1	.936	OF-63, 2B-48
3 yrs.		269	.238	.316	931	222	30	15	4	0.4	68	100	74		24	11	3	460	132	29	12	2.4	.953	OF-207, 2B-48

Tom Delahanty

DELAHANTY, THOMAS JAMES BL TR 5′8″ 175 lbs.
Brother of Joe Delahanty. Brother of Jim Delahanty. Brother of Frank Delahanty.
Brother of Ed Delahanty.
B. Mar. 9, 1872, Cleveland, Ohio D. Jan. 10, 1951, Sanford, Fla.

Year	Team	Games	BA	SA	AB	H	2B	3B	HR	HR%	R	RBI	BB	SO	SB	Pinch Hit AB	Pinch Hit H	PO	A	E	DP	TC/G	FA	G by Pos
1894	PHI N	1	.250	.250	4	1	0	0	0	0.0	0	0	0	1	0	0	0	5	2	1	0	8.0	.875	2B-1
1896	2 teams	CLE N (16G –.232)	PIT N (1G –.333)																					
"	total	17	.237	.305	59	14	4	0	0	0.0	12	4	8	4	4	0	0	18	36	12	2	3.9	.818	3B-16, SS-1
1897	LOU N	1	.250	.500	4	1	1	0	0	0.0	1	2	0		0	0	0	1	0	2	0	3.0	.333	2B-1
3 yrs.		19	.239	.313	67	16	5	0	0	0.0	13	6	8	5	4	0	0	24	38	15	2	4.1	.805	3B-16, 2B-2, SS-1

Mike de la Hoz

de la HOZ, MIGUEL ANGEL BR TR 5′11″ 170 lbs.
Born Miguel Angel de la Hoz (Piloto).
B. Oct. 2, 1938, Havana, Cuba.

Year	Team	Games	BA	SA	AB	H	2B	3B	HR	HR%	R	RBI	BB	SO	SB	Pinch Hit AB	Pinch Hit H	PO	A	E	DP	TC/G	FA	G by Pos
1960	CLE A	49	.256	.431	160	41	6	2	6	3.8	20	23	9	12	0	2	1	65	104	10	14	3.9	.944	SS-38, 3B-8
1961		61	.260	.370	173	45	10	0	3	1.7	20	23	7	10	0	16	2	77	116	9	10	4.0	.955	2B-17, SS-17, 3B-16
1962		12	.083	.083	12	1	0	0	0	0.0	0	0	0	3	0	12	1	0	2	0	0	1.0	1.000	2B-2
1963		67	.267	.433	150	40	10	0	5	3.3	15	25	9	29	0	26	1	69	102	9	20	4.1	.950	2B-34, 3B-6, OF-2, SS-2
1964	MIL N	78	.291	.402	189	55	7	1	4	2.1	25	12	14	22	1	32	11	65	109	10	17	3.2	.946	2B-25, 3B-25, SS-8
1965		81	.256	.330	176	45	3	2	2	1.1	15	11	8	21	0	38	4	61	99	8	20	2.3	.952	SS-41, 3B-22, 2B-10, 1B-1
1966	ATL N	71	.218	.300	110	24	3	0	2	1.8	11	7	5	18	0	37	8	25	35	3	3	1.6	.952	3B-30, 2B-8, SS-1
1967		74	.203	.287	143	29	3	0	3	2.1	10	14	4	14	1	34	8	48	59	2	10	2.4	.982	2B-23, 3B-22, SS-1
1969	CIN N	1	.000	.000	1	0	0	0	0	0.0	0	0	0	1	0	1	0	0	0	0	0	0.0	—	
9 yrs.		494	.251	.365	1114	280	42	5	25	2.2	116	115	56	130	2	198	36	410	626	51	94	3.0	.953	3B-129, 2B-119, SS-108, OF-2, 1B-1

Bill DeLancey

DeLANCEY, WILLIAM PINKNEY BL TR 5′11½″ 185 lbs.
B. Nov. 28, 1911, Greensboro, N. C. D. Nov. 28, 1946, Phoenix, Ariz.

Year	Team	Games	BA	SA	AB	H	2B	3B	HR	HR%	R	RBI	BB	SO	SB	Pinch Hit AB	Pinch Hit H	PO	A	E	DP	TC/G	FA	G by Pos
1932	STL N	8	.192	.346	26	5	0	2	0	0.0	1	2	2	1	0	0	0	32	8	3	3	5.4	.930	C-8
1934		93	.316	.565	253	80	18	3	13	5.1	41	40	41	37	1	15	3	363	35	8	5	5.3	.980	C-77
1935		103	.279	.419	301	84	14	5	6	2.0	37	41	42	34	0	17	4	372	29	12	6	5.0	.971	C-83
1940		15	.222	.222	18	4	0	0	0	0.0	0	2	0	2	0	1	0	24	2	2	0	2.3	.929	C-12
4 yrs.		219	.289	.472	598	173	32	10	19	3.2	79	85	85	74	1	33	7	791	74	25	14	4.9	.972	C-180
WORLD SERIES																								
1934	STL N	7	.172	.379	29	5	3	0	1	3.4	3	4	2	8	0	0	0	50	6	1	1	8.1	.982	C-7

Bill Delaney

DELANEY, WILLIAM L. BR TR
B. Mar. 5, 1863, Cincinnati, Ohio D. Mar. 1, 1942, Canton, Ohio.

Year	Team	Games	BA	SA	AB	H	2B	3B	HR	HR%	R	RBI	BB	SO	SB	Pinch Hit AB	Pinch Hit H	PO	A	E	DP	TC/G	FA	G by Pos
1890	CLE N	36	.190	.241	116	22	1	1	1	0.9	16	7	21	19	5	0	0	82	93	14	18	5.3	.926	2B-36

Jesus de la Rosa

de la ROSA, JESUS
Born Jesus de los Santos (de la Rosa).
B. Aug. 5, 1953, Santo Domingo, Dominican Republic.

BR TR 6′ 1″ 185 lbs.

Year	Team	Games	BA	SA	AB	H	2B	3B	HR	HR%	R	RBI	BB	SO	SB	Pinch Hit AB	Pinch Hit H	PO	A	E	DP	TC/G	FA	G by Pos
1975	HOU N	3	.333	.667	3	1	1	0	0	0.0	1	0	0	0	0	3	1	0	0	0	0	0.0	—	

Carlos Delgado

DELGADO, CARLOS JUAN
Born Carlos Juan Delgado (Hernandez).
B. June 25, 1972, Mayaguez, Puerto Rico.

BL TR 6′ 3″ 215 lbs.

Year	Team	Games	BA	SA	AB	H	2B	3B	HR	HR%	R	RBI	BB	SO	SB	Pinch Hit AB	Pinch Hit H	PO	A	E	DP	TC/G	FA	G by Pos
1993	TOR A	2	.000	.000	1	0	0	0	0	0.0	0	0	1	0	0	1	0	2	0	0	0	1.0	1.000	C-1, DH-1
1994		43	.215	.438	130	28	2	0	9	6.9	17	24	25	46	1	3	0	56	2	2	0	1.4	.967	OF-41, C-1
1995		37	.165	.297	91	15	3	0	3	3.3	7	11	6	26	0	13	1	54	2	0	3	2.0	1.000	OF-17, DH-7, 1B-4
3 yrs.		82	.194	.378	222	43	5	0	12	5.4	24	35	32	72	1	17	1	112	4	2	3	1.6	.983	OF-58, DH-8, 1B-4, C-2

Luis Delgado

DELGADO, LUIS FELIPE
Born Luis Felipe Delgado (Robles).
B. Feb. 2, 1954, Hatillo, Puerto Rico.

BB TL 5′11″ 170 lbs.

Year	Team	Games	BA	SA	AB	H	2B	3B	HR	HR%	R	RBI	BB	SO	SB	Pinch Hit AB	Pinch Hit H	PO	A	E	DP	TC/G	FA	G by Pos
1977	SEA A	13	.182	.182	22	4	0	0	0	0.0	4	2	1	8	0	0	0	14	1	0	0	1.2	1.000	OF-13

Bobby Del Greco

DEL GRECO, ROBERT GEORGE
B. Apr. 7, 1933, Pittsburgh, Pa.

BR TR 5′10½″ 185 lbs.

Year	Team	Games	BA	SA	AB	H	2B	3B	HR	HR%	R	RBI	BB	SO	SB	Pinch Hit AB	Pinch Hit H	PO	A	E	DP	TC/G	FA	G by Pos
1952	PIT N	99	.217	.279	341	74	14	2	1	0.3	34	20	38	70	6	4	1	246	11	6	3	2.8	.977	OF-93
1956	2 teams	PIT N (14G –.200) STL N (102G –.215)																						
″	total	116	.214	.355	290	62	16	2	7	2.4	33	21	35	53	1	7	0	228	6	3	0	2.2	.987	OF-107, 3B-3
1957	2 teams	CHI N (20G –.200) NY A (8G –.429)																						
″	total	28	.234	.277	47	11	2	0	0	0.0	5	3	12	19	2	6	1	32	2	1	0	1.6	.971	OF-22
1958	NY A	12	.200	.200	5	1	0	0	0	0.0	1	0	1	1	0	0	0	5	0	0	0	0.4	1.000	OF-12
1960	PHI N	100	.237	.417	300	71	16	4	10	3.3	48	26	54	64	1	11	3	247	10	8	1	3.0	.970	OF-89
1961	2 teams	PHI N (41G –.259) KC A (74G –.230)																						
″	total	115	.239	.359	351	84	19	1	7	2.0	48	32	42	48	1	9	1	248	9	3	2	2.4	.988	OF-105, 3B-1, 2B-1
1962	KC A	132	.254	.402	338	86	21	1	9	2.7	61	38	49	62	4	6	1	245	9	4	0	2.1	.984	OF-124
1963		121	.212	.320	306	65	7	1	8	2.6	40	29	40	52	1	8	2	209	5	4	0	1.9	.982	OF-110, 3B-2
1965	PHI N	8	.000	.000	4	0	0	0	0	0.0	1	0	0	3	0	2	0	0	0	0	0	0.0	.000	OF-4
9 yrs.		731	.229	.352	1982	454	95	11	42	2.1	271	169	271	372	16	53	9	1460	52	29	6	2.3	.981	OF-666, 3B-6, 2B-1

Juan Delis

DELIS, JUAN FRANCISCO
B. Feb. 27, 1928, Santiago, Cuba.

BR TR 5′11″ 170 lbs.

Year	Team	Games	BA	SA	AB	H	2B	3B	HR	HR%	R	RBI	BB	SO	SB	Pinch Hit AB	Pinch Hit H	PO	A	E	DP	TC/G	FA	G by Pos
1955	WAS A	54	.189	.227	132	25	3	1	0	0.0	12	11	3	15	1	16	2	25	45	6	6	2.3	.921	3B-24, OF-8, 2B-1

Eddie Delker

DELKER, EDWARD ALBERTS
B. Apr. 17, 1907, DeAlto, Pa.

BR TR 5′10½″ 170 lbs.

Year	Team	Games	BA	SA	AB	H	2B	3B	HR	HR%	R	RBI	BB	SO	SB	Pinch Hit AB	Pinch Hit H	PO	A	E	DP	TC/G	FA	G by Pos
1929	STL N	22	.150	.200	40	6	0	1	0	0.0	5	3	2	12	0	2	0	16	20	5	2	2.2	.878	SS-9, 2B-7, 3B-3
1931		1	.500	1.000	2	1	1	0	0	0.0	0	2	0	0	0	0	0	1	0	0	0	1.0	1.000	3B-1
1932	2 teams	STL N (20G –.119) PHI N (30G –.161)																						
″	total	50	.144	.240	104	15	5	1	1	1.0	8	9	14	21	0	1	0	76	85	10	19	3.7	.942	2B-37, 3B-5, SS-4
1933	PHI N	25	.171	.293	41	7	3	1	0	0.0	6	1	0	12	0	3	0	26	47	3	5	3.6	.961	2B-17, 3B-4
4 yrs.		98	.155	.251	187	29	9	3	1	0.5	19	15	16	45	0	6	0	119	152	18	26	3.3	.938	2B-61, SS-13, 3B-13

Bert Delmas

DELMAS, ALBERT CHARLES
B. May 20, 1911, San Francisco, Calif. D. Dec. 4, 1979, Huntington Beach, Calif.

BL TR 5′11″ 165 lbs.

Year	Team	Games	BA	SA	AB	H	2B	3B	HR	HR%	R	RBI	BB	SO	SB	Pinch Hit AB	Pinch Hit H	PO	A	E	DP	TC/G	FA	G by Pos
1933	BKN N	12	.250	.250	28	7	0	0	0	0.0	4	0	1	7	0	1	0	14	17	3	3	3.4	.912	2B-10

Luis de los Santos

de los SANTOS, LUIS MANUEL
Born Luis Manuel de Los Santos (Martinez).
B. Dec. 29, 1966, San Cristobal, Dominican Republic.

BR TR 6′ 5″ 190 lbs.

Year	Team	Games	BA	SA	AB	H	2B	3B	HR	HR%	R	RBI	BB	SO	SB	Pinch Hit AB	Pinch Hit H	PO	A	E	DP	TC/G	FA	G by Pos
1988	KC A	11	.091	.227	22	2	1	1	0	0.0	1	1	4	4	0	2	0	31	1	0	3	4.0	1.000	1B-5, DH-3
1989		28	.253	.310	87	22	3	1	0	0.0	6	6	5	14	0	2	0	203	16	3	23	8.2	.986	1B-27
1991	DET A	16	.167	.233	30	5	2	0	0	0.0	1	0	2	4	0	5	1	8	1	1	0	0.6	.900	DH-9, OF-3, 3B-2, 1B-2
3 yrs.		55	.209	.281	139	29	6	2	0	0.0	8	7	11	22	0	9	1	242	18	4	26	5.2	.985	1B-34, DH-12, OF-3, 3B-2

Garton Del Savio

DEL SAVIO, GARTON ORVILLE
B. Nov. 26, 1913, New York, N. Y.

BR TR 5′ 9½″ 165 lbs.

Year	Team	Games	BA	SA	AB	H	2B	3B	HR	HR%	R	RBI	BB	SO	SB	Pinch Hit AB	Pinch Hit H	PO	A	E	DP	TC/G	FA	G by Pos
1943	PHI N	4	.091	.091	11	1	0	0	0	0.0	0	0	1	0	0	0	0	6	12	3	1	5.3	.857	SS-4

Jim Delsing

DELSING, JAMES HENRY
B. Nov. 13, 1925, Rudolph, Wis.

BL TR 5′10″ 175 lbs.

Year	Team	Games	BA	SA	AB	H	2B	3B	HR	HR%	R	RBI	BB	SO	SB	Pinch Hit AB	Pinch Hit H	PO	A	E	DP	TC/G	FA	G by Pos
1948	CHI A	20	.190	.190	63	12	0	0	0	0.0	5	5	5	12	0	4	0	36	1	0	0	2.5	1.000	OF-15
1949	NY A	9	.350	.550	20	7	1	0	1	5.0	5	3	1	2	0	4	2	6	0	0	0	1.2	1.000	OF-5
1950	2 teams	NY A (12G –.400) STL A (69G –.263)																						
″	total	81	.269	.311	219	59	5	2	0	0.0	27	17	22	23	1	24	8	150	4	1	3	2.4	.994	OF-53
1951	STL A	131	.249	.356	449	112	20	2	8	1.8	59	45	56	39	2	4	1	340	15	6	5	2.9	.983	OF-124
1952	2 teams	STL A (93G –.255) DET A (33G –.274)																						
″	total	126	.260	.360	411	107	15	7	4	1.0	48	49	36	37	4	11	4	273	5	6	2	2.4	.979	OF-117
1953	DET A	138	.288	.436	479	138	26	6	11	2.3	77	62	66	39	1	6	1	354	7	3	2	2.7	.992	OF-133
1954		122	.248	.372	371	92	24	2	6	1.6	39	38	49	38	4	13	5	221	5	1	0	2.1	.996	OF-108
1955		114	.239	.374	356	85	14	2	10	2.8	49	60	48	40	2	14	3	178	3	1	1	1.8	.995	OF-101
1956	2 teams	DET A (10G –.000) CHI A (55G –.122)																						
″	total	65	.094	.151	53	5	3	0	0	0.0	11	2	13	16	1	21	3	24	1	1	0	0.8	.962	OF-32
1960	KC A	16	.250	.325	40	10	3	0	0	0.0	2	5	3	5	0	6	1	24	0	0	0	2.4	1.000	OF-10
10 yrs.		822	.255	.366	2461	627	111	21	40	1.6	322	286	299	251	15	107	28	1606	41	19	13	2.3	.989	OF-698

Joe De Maestri

DE MAESTRI, JOSEPH PAUL (Oats)
B. Dec. 9, 1928, San Francisco, Calif.
BR TR 6′ 170 lbs.

Year	Team	Games	BA	SA	AB	H	2B	3B	HR	HR%	R	RBI	BB	SO	SB	Pinch Hit AB	Pinch Hit H	PO	A	E	DP	TC/G	FA	G by Pos
1951	CHI A	56	.203	.297	74	15	0	2	1	1.4	8	3	5	11	0	6	1	43	61	5	14	2.4	.954	SS-27, 2B-11, 3B-8
1952	STL A	81	.226	.301	186	42	9	1	1	0.5	13	18	8	25	0	1	0	106	159	17	31	3.6	.940	SS-77, 3B-1, 2B-1
1953	PHI A	111	.255	.352	420	107	17	3	6	1.4	53	35	24	39	0	0	0	191	297	18	53	4.7	.964	SS-108
1954		146	.230	.315	539	124	16	3	8	1.5	49	40	20	63	1	3	0	285	408	25	90	5.0	.965	SS-142, 3B-1, 2B-1
1955	KC A	123	.249	.324	457	114	14	1	6	1.3	42	37	20	47	3	1	1	206	358	21	78	4.8	.964	SS-122
1956		133	.233	.316	434	101	16	1	6	1.4	41	39	25	73	3	1	0	210	407	23	95	4.8	.964	SS-132, 2B-2
1957		135	.245	.360	461	113	14	6	9	2.0	44	33	22	82	6	1	0	248	387	13	87	4.8	.980	SS-134
1958		139	.219	.290	442	97	11	1	6	1.4	32	38	16	84	1	2	1	226	417	13	95	4.8	.980	SS-137
1959		118	.244	.369	352	86	16	5	6	1.7	31	34	28	65	1	2	0	167	320	22	63	4.4	.957	SS-115
1960	NY A	49	.229	.257	35	8	1	0	0	0.0	8	2	0	9	0	7	1	22	29	1	4	1.4	.981	2B-19, SS-17
1961		30	.146	.146	41	6	0	0	0	0.0	1	2	0	13	0	0	0	24	44	1	11	2.6	.986	SS-18, 2B-5, 3B-4
11 yrs.		1121	.236	.325	3441	813	114	23	49	1.4	322	281	168	511	15	24	4	1728	2887	159	621	4.4	.967	SS-1029, 2B-39, 3B-14
WORLD SERIES																								
1960	NY A	4	.500	.500	2	1	0	0	0	0.0	1	0	0	1	0	0	0	0	2	0	0	0.7	1.000	SS-3

Frank Demaree

DEMAREE, JOSEPH FRANKLIN
Born Joseph Franklin Dimaria.
B. June 10, 1910, Winters, Calif. D. Aug. 30, 1958, Los Angeles, Calif.
BR TR 5′11½″ 185 lbs.

Year	Team	Games	BA	SA	AB	H	2B	3B	HR	HR%	R	RBI	BB	SO	SB	Pinch Hit AB	Pinch Hit H	PO	A	E	DP	TC/G	FA	G by Pos
1932	CHI N	23	.250	.304	56	14	3	0	0	0.0	4	6	2	7	0	5	1	31	2	0	1	1.9	1.000	OF-17
1933		134	.272	.377	515	140	24	6	6	1.2	68	51	22	42	4	0	0	321	12	12	1	2.6	.965	OF-133
1935		107	.325	.410	385	125	19	4	2	0.5	60	66	26	23	6	8	2	204	13	6	3	2.3	.973	OF-98
1936		154	.350	.496	605	212	34	3	16	2.6	93	96	49	30	4	0	0	285	16	10	1	2.0	.968	OF-154
1937		154	.324	.485	615	199	36	6	17	2.8	104	115	57	31	6	0	0	283	17	6	6	2.0	.980	OF-154
1938		129	.273	.384	476	130	15	7	8	1.7	63	62	45	34	1	4	1	199	12	6	1	1.7	.972	OF-125
1939	NY N	150	.304	.418	560	170	27	2	11	2.0	68	79	66	40	2	0	0	329	11	5	2	2.3	.986	OF-150
1940		121	.302	.413	460	139	18	6	7	1.5	68	61	45	39	5	2	1	233	6	5	5	2.1	.980	OF-119
1941	2 teams	NY N (16G –.171) BOS N (48G –.230)																						
″	total	64	.216	.318	148	32	5	2	2	1.4	23	16	16	6	2	22	3	60	2	0	0	1.6	1.000	OF-38
1942	BOS N	64	.225	.299	187	42	5	0	3	1.6	18	24	17	10	2	13	1	114	4	0	1	2.4	1.000	OF-49
1943	STL N	39	.291	.314	86	25	2	0	0	0.0	5	9	8	4	1	13	1	35	1	0	0	1.6	1.000	OF-23
1944	STL A	16	.255	.294	51	13	2	0	0	0.0	4	6	6	3	0	0	0	30	1	1	0	2.0	.969	OF-16
12 yrs.		1155	.299	.415	4144	1241	190	36	72	1.7	578	591	359	269	33	67	10	2124	97	51	21	2.1	.978	OF-1076
WORLD SERIES																								
1932	CHI N	2	.286	.714	7	2	0	0	1	14.3	1	4	1	0	0	0	0	4	0	1	0	2.5	.800	OF-2
1935		6	.250	.542	24	6	1	0	2	8.3	2	2	1	4	0	0	0	8	1	0	0	1.5	1.000	OF-6
1938		3	.100	.100	10	1	0	0	0	0.0	1	0	1	2	0	0	0	6	0	0	0	2.0	1.000	OF-3
1943	STL N	1	.000	.000	1	0	0	0	0	0.0	0	0	0	0	0	1	0	0	0	0	0	0.0	—	
4 yrs.		12	.214	.452	42	9	1	0	3	7.1	4	6	3	6	0	1	0	18	1	1	0	1.8	.950	OF-11

Billy DeMars

DeMARS, WILLIAM LESTER (Kid)
B. Aug. 26, 1925, Brooklyn, N. Y.
BR TR 5′10″ 160 lbs.

Year	Team	Games	BA	SA	AB	H	2B	3B	HR	HR%	R	RBI	BB	SO	SB	Pinch Hit AB	Pinch Hit H	PO	A	E	DP	TC/G	FA	G by Pos
1948	PHI A	18	.172	.172	29	5	0	0	0	0.0	3	1	5	3	0	2	0	18	25	3	8	4.2	.935	SS-9, 3B-1, 2B-1
1950	STL A	61	.247	.287	178	44	5	1	0	0.0	25	13	22	13	0	2	0	118	129	19	32	4.5	.929	SS-54, 3B-5
1951		1	.250	.250	4	1	0	0	0	0.0	1	0	1	0	0	0	0	1	4	0	1	5.0	1.000	SS-1
3 yrs.		80	.237	.270	211	50	5	1	0	0.0	29	14	28	16	0	4	0	137	158	22	41	4.5	.931	SS-64, 3B-6, 2B-1

John DeMerit

DeMERIT, JOHN STEPHEN (Thumper)
B. Jan. 8, 1936, West Bend, Wis.
BR TR 6′ 1½″ 195 lbs.

Year	Team	Games	BA	SA	AB	H	2B	3B	HR	HR%	R	RBI	BB	SO	SB	Pinch Hit AB	Pinch Hit H	PO	A	E	DP	TC/G	FA	G by Pos
1957	MIL N	33	.147	.147	34	5	0	0	0	0.0	8	1	0	8	1	6	1	21	0	0	0	1.6	1.000	OF-13
1958		3	.667	.667	3	2	0	0	0	0.0	1	0	0	0	0	0	0	2	0	0	0	1.0	1.000	OF-2
1959		11	.200	.200	5	1	0	0	0	0.0	4	0	1	2	0	0	0	7	0	0	0	1.8	1.000	OF-4
1961		32	.162	.284	74	12	3	0	2	2.7	5	5	5	19	0	6	1	40	2	0	0	2.0	1.000	OF-21
1962	NY N	14	.188	.375	16	3	0	0	1	6.3	3	1	2	4	0	1	0	4	0	0	0	0.4	1.000	OF-9
5 yrs.		93	.174	.265	132	23	3	0	3	2.3	21	7	8	33	1	13	2	74	2	0	0	1.6	1.000	OF-49
WORLD SERIES																								
1957	MIL N	1	—	—	0	0	0	0	0	—	0	0	0	0	0	0	0	0	0	0	0	0.0	—	

Don Demeter

DEMETER, DONALD LEE
B. June 25, 1935, Oklahoma City, Okla.
BR TR 6′ 4″ 190 lbs.

Year	Team	Games	BA	SA	AB	H	2B	3B	HR	HR%	R	RBI	BB	SO	SB	Pinch Hit AB	Pinch Hit H	PO	A	E	DP	TC/G	FA	G by Pos
1956	BKN N	3	.333	1.333	3	1	0	0	1	33.3	1	1	0	1	0	2	0	1	0	0	0	1.0	1.000	OF-1
1958	LA N	43	.189	.349	106	20	2	0	5	4.7	11	8	5	32	2	4	0	70	0	0	0	1.8	1.000	OF-39
1959		139	.256	.437	371	95	11	1	18	4.9	55	70	16	87	5	22	3	223	5	4	1	1.9	.983	OF-124
1960		64	.274	.488	168	46	7	1	9	5.4	23	29	8	34	0	8	2	92	2	1	1	1.5	.989	OF-62
1961	2 teams	LA N (15G –.172) PHI N (106G –.257)																						
″	total	121	.251	.467	411	103	18	4	21	5.1	57	70	22	80	2	13	2	339	25	4	25	3.2	.989	OF-93, 1B-22
1962	PHI N	153	.307	.520	550	169	24	3	29	5.3	85	107	41	93	2	6	2	200	177	20	19	2.3	.950	3B-105, OF-63, 1B-1
1963		154	.258	.433	515	133	20	2	22	4.3	63	83	31	93	1	11	2	375	86	14	15	2.5	.971	OF-119, 3B-43, 1B-26
1964	DET A	134	.256	.460	441	113	22	1	22	5.0	57	80	17	85	4	27	5	366	15	2	13	3.5	.995	OF-88, 1B-23
1965		122	.278	.463	389	108	16	4	16	4.1	50	58	23	65	4	15	6	377	11	4	20	3.4	.990	OF-81, 1B-34
1966	2 teams	DET A (32G –.212) BOS A (73G –.292)																						
″	total	105	.268	.458	325	87	18	1	14	4.3	43	41	8	61	2	21	2	203	10	3	4	2.4	.986	OF-84, 1B-6
1967	2 teams	BOS A (20G –.279) CLE A (51G –.207)																						
″	total	71	.226	.390	164	37	9	0	6	3.7	22	16	9	27	0	26	7	80	5	1	2	1.8	.988	OF-47, 3B-2
11 yrs.		1109	.265	.459	3443	912	147	17	163	4.7	467	563	180	658	22	155	31	2326	336	53	100	2.6	.980	OF-801, 3B-150, 1B-112
WORLD SERIES																								
1959	LA N	6	.250	.250	12	3	0	0	0	0.0	2	0	1	3	0	0	0	9	0	0	0	1.5	1.000	OF-6

Steve Demeter

DEMETER, STEPHEN BR TR 5′ 9½″ 185 lbs.
B. Jan. 27, 1935, Homer City, Pa.

Year	Team	Games	BA	SA	AB	H	2B	3B	HR	HR%	R	RBI	BB	SO	SB	Pinch Hit AB	Pinch Hit H	PO	A	E	DP	TC/G	FA	G by Pos
1959	DET A	11	.111	.167	18	2	1	0	0	0.0	1	1	0	1	0	9	1	4	6	1	1	2.8	.909	3B-4
1960	CLE A	4	.000	.000	5	0	0	0	0	0.0	0	0	0	1	0	2	0	3	1	0	1	1.3	1.000	3B-3
2 yrs.		15	.087	.130	23	2	1	0	0	0.0	1	1	0	2	0	11	1	7	7	1	2	2.1	.933	3B-7

Ray Demmitt

DEMMITT, CHARLES RAYMOND BL TR 5′ 8½″ 170 lbs.
B. Feb. 2, 1884, Illiopolis, Ill. D. Feb. 19, 1956, Glen Ellyn, Ill.

Year	Team	Games	BA	SA	AB	H	2B	3B	HR	HR%	R	RBI	BB	SO	SB	Pinch Hit AB	Pinch Hit H	PO	A	E	DP	TC/G	FA	G by Pos
1909	NY A	123	.246	.358	427	105	12	12	4	0.9	68	30	55		16	0	0	185	22	21	7	2.1	.908	OF-109
1910	STL A	10	.174	.217	23	4	1	0	0	0.0	4	2	3		0	2	0	11	2	0	0	1.6	1.000	OF-8
1914	2 teams	DET A (1G –.000) CHI A (146G –.258)																						
″	total	147	.258	.342	515	133	13	12	2	0.4	63	46	61	48	12	3	1	217	24	12	3	1.8	.953	OF-142
1915	CHI A	9	.000	.000	6	0	0	0	0	0.0	0	0	1	2	0	6	0	1	0	0	0	0.3	1.000	OF-3
1917	STL A	14	.283	.377	53	15	1	2	0	0.0	6	7	0	8	1	0	0	15	0	0	0	1.1	1.000	OF-14
1918		116	.281	.370	405	114	23	5	1	0.2	45	61	38	35	10	1	0	206	25	12	8	2.1	.951	OF-114
1919		79	.238	.327	202	48	11	2	1	0.5	19	19	14	27	3	**27**	6	60	6	10	0	1.6	.868	OF-49
7 yrs.		498	.257	.349	1631	419	61	33	8	0.5	205	165	172	120	42	39	7	695	79	55	18	1.9	.934	OF-439

Gene DeMontreville

DeMONTREVILLE, EUGENE NAPOLEON BR TR 5′ 8″ 165 lbs.
Brother of Lee DeMontreville.
B. Mar. 26, 1874, St. Paul, Minn. D. Feb. 18, 1935, Memphis, Tenn.

Year	Team	Games	BA	SA	AB	H	2B	3B	HR	HR%	R	RBI	BB	SO	SB	Pinch Hit AB	Pinch Hit H	PO	A	E	DP	TC/G	FA	G by Pos
1894	PIT N	2	.250	.250	8	2	0	0	0	0.0	0	0	1	4	0	0	0	1	7	1	0	4.5	.889	SS-2
1895	WAS N	12	.217	.370	46	10	1	3	0	0.0	7	9	3	4	5	0	0	33	45	6	8	7.0	.929	SS-12
1896		133	.343	.452	533	183	24	5	8	1.5	94	77	29	27	28	0	0	305	479	97	53	6.6	.890	SS-133
1897		133	.341	.433	**566**	193	27	8	3	0.5	92	93	21		30	1	1	340	455	91	53	6.7	.897	SS-99, 2B-33
1898	BAL N	151	.328	.369	567	186	19	2	0	0.0	93	86	52		49	0	0	369	486	60	46	6.1	.934	2B-123, SS-28
1899	2 teams	CHI N (82G –.281) BAL N (60G –.279)																						
″	total	142	.280	.345	550	154	19	7	1	0.2	83	76	27		47	0	0	366	503	69	54	6.6	.926	SS-82, 2B-60
1900	BKN N	69	.244	.286	234	57	8	1	0	0.0	32	28	10		21	1	0	159	176	25	19	5.2	.931	2B-48, SS-12, 3B-7, OF-1, 1B-1
1901	BOS N	140	.304	.368	570	173	14	4	5	0.9	83	72	17		25	0	0	294	403	43	37	5.3	.942	2B-120, 3B-20
1902		124	.268	.322	481	129	16	5	0	0.0	51	53	12		23	2	0	293	333	43	28	5.5	.936	2B-112, SS-10
1903	WAS A	12	.273	.318	44	12	2	0	0	0.0	0	3	0		0	0	0	30	26	4	1	5.0	.933	2B-11, SS-1
1904	STL A	4	.111	.111	9	1	0	0	0	0.0	0	0	2		0	1	0	5	7	0	0	4.0	1.000	2B-3
11 yrs.		922	.305	.374	3608	1100	130	35	17	0.5	535	497	174	35	228	5	1	2195	2920	439	299	6.1	.921	2B-510, SS-379, 3B-27, OF-1, 1B-1

Lee DeMontreville

DeMONTREVILLE, LEON BR TR 5′ 7″ 140 lbs.
Brother of Gene DeMontreville.
B. Sept. 23, 1875, Washington County, Minn. D. Mar. 22, 1962, Pelham Manor, N. Y.

Year	Team	Games	BA	SA	AB	H	2B	3B	HR	HR%	R	RBI	BB	SO	SB	Pinch Hit AB	Pinch Hit H	PO	A	E	DP	TC/G	FA	G by Pos
1903	STL N	26	.243	.314	70	17	3	1	0	0.0	8	7	8		3	5	1	37	52	13	8	5.1	.873	SS-15, 2B-4, OF-1

Rick Dempsey

DEMPSEY, JOHN RIKARD BR TR 6′ 180 lbs.
B. Sept. 13, 1949, Fayetteville, Tenn.

Year	Team	Games	BA	SA	AB	H	2B	3B	HR	HR%	R	RBI	BB	SO	SB	Pinch Hit AB	Pinch Hit H	PO	A	E	DP	TC/G	FA	G by Pos
1969	MIN A	5	.500	.667	6	3	1	0	0	0.0	1	0	1	0	0	1	0	5	0	1	0	2.0	.833	C-3
1970		5	.000	.000	7	0	0	0	0	0.0	1	0	1	1	0	1	0	12	0	1	0	4.3	.923	C-3
1971		6	.308	.385	13	4	1	0	0	0.0	2	0	1	1	0	0	0	30	4	2	0	6.0	.944	C-6
1972		25	.200	.225	40	8	1	0	0	0.0	0	0	6	8	0	2	1	67	5	1	0	3.2	.986	C-23
1973	NY A	6	.182	.182	11	2	0	0	0	0.0	0	0	1	3	0	0	0	9	0	2	0	2.2	.818	C-5
1974		43	.239	.321	109	26	3	0	2	1.8	12	12	8	7	1	12	2	152	22	4	0	5.2	.978	C-31, OF-2, DH-1
1975		71	.262	.338	145	38	8	0	1	0.7	18	11	21	15	0	23	5	92	9	3	1	2.3	.971	C-19, DH-18, OF-8, 3B-1
1976	2 teams	NY A (21G –.119) BAL A (59G –.213)																						
″	total	80	.194	.204	216	42	2	0	0	0.0	12	12	18	21	1	6	1	308	40	4	8	4.8	.989	C-67, OF-7
1977	BAL A	91	.226	.315	270	61	7	4	3	1.1	27	34	34	34	2	1	1	416	52	11	10	5.3	.977	C-91
1978		136	.259	.356	441	114	25	0	6	1.4	41	32	48	54	7	4	1	636	79	11	14	5.4	.985	C-135
1979		124	.239	.351	368	88	23	0	6	1.6	48	41	38	37	0	39	11	615	81	7	13	5.7	.990	C-124
1980		119	.262	.425	362	95	26	3	9	2.5	51	40	36	45	3	9	1	544	55	8	10	5.0	.987	C-112, OF-6, 1B-2, DH-1
1981		92	.215	.335	251	54	10	1	6	2.4	24	15	32	36	0	7	0	384	35	1	6	4.6	.998	C-90, DH-1
1982		125	.256	.349	344	88	15	1	5	1.5	35	36	46	37	0	8	3	491	46	5	8	4.3	.991	C-124, DH-1
1983		128	.231	.323	347	80	16	2	4	1.2	33	32	40	54	1	7	0	591	65	2	7	5.1	.997	C-128
1984		109	.230	.364	330	76	11	0	11	3.3	37	34	40	58	1	0	0	453	43	4	5	4.6	.992	C-108
1985		132	.254	.406	362	92	19	0	12	3.3	54	52	50	87	0	6	1	575	49	8	5	4.8	.987	C-131
1986		122	.208	.379	327	68	15	1	13	4.0	42	29	45	78	1	9	1	659	53	7	9	5.9	.990	C-121
1987	CLE A	60	.177	.270	141	25	10	0	1	0.7	16	9	23	29	0	2	1	293	18	5	3	5.4	.984	C-59
1988	LA N	77	.251	.455	167	42	13	0	7	4.2	25	30	25	44	1	8	1	333	29	4	4	4.9	.989	C-74
1989		79	.179	.305	151	27	7	0	4	2.6	16	16	30	37	1	24	5	265	35	5	4	4.9	.984	C-62
1990		62	.195	.281	128	25	5	0	2	1.6	13	15	23	29	1	16	1	213	27	2	3	4.6	.992	C-53
1991	MIL A	61	.231	.347	147	34	5	0	4	2.7	15	21	23	20	0	4	2	246	23	2	4	4.6	.993	C-56, P-2, 1B-1
1992	BAL A	8	.111	.111	9	1	0	0	0	0.0	2	0	2	1	0	0	0	13	1	0	0	1.8	1.000	C-8
24 yrs.		1766	.233	.347	4692	1093	223	12	96	2.0	525	471	592	736	20	189	38	7402	771	100	114	4.9	.988	C-1633, OF-23, DH-22, 1B-3, P-2, 3B-1
LEAGUE CHAMPIONSHIP SERIES																								
1979	BAL A	3	.400	.600	10	4	2	0	0	0.0	3	2	1	0	1	0	0	10	1	0	0	3.7	1.000	C-3
1983		4	.167	.167	12	2	0	0	0	0.0	1	0	1	1	0	0	0	29	5	1	1	8.8	.971	C-4
1988	LA N	4	.400	.800	5	2	2	0	0	0.0	1	2	1	0	0	1	0	7	0	0	0	2.3	1.000	C-3
3 yrs.		11	.296	.444	27	8	4	0	0	0.0	5	4	3	1	1	1	0	46	6	1	1	5.3	.981	C-10
WORLD SERIES																								
1979	BAL A	7	.286	.381	21	6	2	0	0	0.0	3	0	1	3	0	0	0	38	2	0	0	6.7	1.000	C-6
1983		5	.385	.923	13	5	4	0	1	7.7	3	2	2	2	0	0	0	27	4	0	0	6.2	1.000	C-5
1988	LA N	2	.200	.400	5	1	1	0	0	0.0	0	1	1	2	0	0	0	13	1	0	0	7.0	1.000	C-2
3 yrs.		14	.308	.564	39	12	7	0	1	2.6	6	3	4	7	0	0	0	78	7	0	0	6.5	1.000	C-13

Tod Dennehey

DENNEHEY, THOMAS FRANCIS BL TL 5′10″ 180 lbs.
B. May 12, 1899, Philadelphia, Pa. D. Aug. 8, 1977, Philadelphia, Pa.

Year	Team	Games	BA	SA	AB	H	2B	3B	HR	HR%	R	RBI	BB	SO	SB	Pinch Hit AB	Pinch Hit H	PO	A	E	DP	TC/G	FA	G by Pos
1923	PHI N	9	.292	.375	24	7	2	0	0	0.0	4	2	1	3	0	0	0	16	0	0	0	1.8	1.000	OF-9

Otto Denning

DENNING, OTTO GEORGE (Dutch)
B. Dec. 28, 1912, Hays, Kans. D. May 25, 1992, Chicago, Ill.

BR TR 6′ 180 lbs.

Year	Team	Games	BA	SA	AB	H	2B	3B	HR	HR%	R	RBI	BB	SO	SB	Pinch Hit AB	Pinch Hit H	PO	A	E	DP	TC/G	FA	G by Pos
1942	CLE A	92	.210	.290	214	45	14	0	1	0.5	15	19	18	14	0	20	3	217	36	2	6	3.2	.992	C-78, OF-2
1943		37	.240	.287	129	31	6	0	0	0.0	8	13	5	1	3	3	0	326	18	12	39	10.5	.966	1B-34
2 yrs.		129	.222	.289	343	76	20	0	1	0.3	23	32	23	15	3	23	3	543	54	14	45	5.4	.977	C-78, 1B-34, OF-2

Jerry Denny

DENNY, JEREMIAH DENNIS
Born Jeremiah Dennis Eldridge.
B. Mar. 16, 1859, New York, N. Y. D. Aug. 16, 1927, Houston, Tex.

BR TR 5′11½″ 180 lbs.

Year	Team	Games	BA	SA	AB	H	2B	3B	HR	HR%	R	RBI	BB	SO	SB	Pinch Hit AB	Pinch Hit H	PO	A	E	DP	TC/G	FA	G by Pos
1881	PRO N	85	.241	.313	320	77	16	2	1	0.3	38	24	5	44		0	0	144	181	62	12	4.6	.840	3B-85
1882		84	.246	.350	329	81	10	9	2	0.6	54		4	46		0	0	136	206	55	7	4.7	.861	3B-84
1883		98	.275	.443	393	108	26	8	8	2.0	73		9	48		0	0	178	188	52	13	4.3	.876	3B-98
1884		110	.248	.380	439	109	22	9	6	1.4	57		14	58		0	0	237	185	48	11	4.2	.898	3B-99, 1B-9, 2B-3, C-1
1885		83	.223	.321	318	71	14	4	3	0.9	40	25	12	53		0	0	128	157	43	10	4.0	.869	3B-83
1886	STL N	119	.257	.389	475	122	24	6	9	1.9	58	62	14	68		0	0	186	282	55	24	4.4	.895	3B-117, SS-3
1887	IND N	122	.324	.502	510	165	34	12	11	2.2	86	97	13	22	29	0	0	219	288	59	24	4.6	.896	3B-116, SS-4, OF-1, 2B-1
1888		126	.261	.408	524	137	27	7	12	2.3	92	63	9	**79**	32	0	0	236	312	64	23	4.8	.895	3B-96, SS-25, 2B-5, OF-1, P-1
1889		133	.282	.417	578	163	24	0	18	3.1	96	112	27	63	22	0	0	237	309	49	17	4.4	.918	3B-123, 2B-7, SS-5
1890	NY N	114	.213	.307	437	93	18	7	3	0.7	50	42	28	62	11	0	0	184	237	49	19	4.1	.896	3B-106, SS-7, 2B-1
1891	3 teams	NY N (4G –.250) CLE N (36G –.225) PHI N (19G –.288)																						
″	total	59	.247	.286	227	56	7	1	0	0.0	22	33	16	32	6	0	0	184	79	23	8	4.8	.920	3B-40, 1B-12, OF-8
1893	LOU N	44	.246	.337	175	43	5	4	1	0.6	22	22	9	15	4	0	0	97	145	20	16	6.0	.924	SS-42, 3B-2
1894		60	.276	.389	221	61	11	7	0	0.0	26	32	13	12	10	0	0	85	124	30	12	4.0	.874	3B-60
13 yrs.		1237	.260	.384	4946	1286	238	76	74	1.5	714	512	173	602	114	0	0	2251	2693	609	196	4.5	.890	3B-1109, SS-86, 1B-21, 2B-17, OF-10, P-1, C-1

Drew Denson

DENSON, ANDREW
B. Nov. 16, 1965, Cincinnati, Ohio

BB TR 6′ 5″ 210 lbs.

Year	Team	Games	BA	SA	AB	H	2B	3B	HR	HR%	R	RBI	BB	SO	SB	Pinch Hit AB	Pinch Hit H	PO	A	E	DP	TC/G	FA	G by Pos
1989	ATL N	12	.250	.278	36	9	1	0	0	0.0	1	5	3	9	1	0	0	71	11	1	3	6.9	.988	1B-12
1993	CHI A	4	.200	.200	5	1	0	0	0	0.0	0	0	0	2	0	4	1	4	0	1	1	1.7	.800	1B-3
2 yrs.		16	.244	.268	41	10	1	0	0	0.0	1	5	3	11	1	4	1	75	11	2	4	5.9	.977	1B-15

Bucky Dent

DENT, RUSSELL EARL
Born Russell Earl O'Dey.
B. Nov. 25, 1951, Savannah, Ga.
Manager 1989–90.

BR TR 5′ 9″ 170 lbs.

Year	Team	Games	BA	SA	AB	H	2B	3B	HR	HR%	R	RBI	BB	SO	SB	Pinch Hit AB	Pinch Hit H	PO	A	E	DP	TC/G	FA	G by Pos
1973	CHI A	40	.248	.265	117	29	2	0	0	0.0	17	10	10	18	2	1	0	55	134	7	23	4.9	.964	SS-36, 2B-3, 3B-1
1974		154	.274	.347	496	136	15	3	5	1.0	55	45	28	48	3	0	0	251	499	22	108	5.0	.972	SS-154
1975		157	.264	.341	602	159	29	4	3	0.5	52	58	36	48	2	0	0	279	543	16	105	5.3	.981	SS-157
1976		158	.246	.302	562	138	18	4	2	0.4	44	52	43	45	3	1	0	279	468	18	96	4.8	.976	SS-158
1977	NY A	158	.247	.352	477	118	18	4	8	1.7	54	49	39	28	1	0	0	250	434	18	90	4.5	.974	SS-157
1978		123	.243	.317	379	92	11	1	5	1.3	40	40	23	24	3	0	0	178	341	10	56	4.3	.981	SS-123
1979		141	.230	.285	431	99	14	2	2	0.5	47	32	37	30	0	0	0	219	512	17	107	5.3	.977	SS-141
1980		141	.262	.354	489	128	26	2	5	1.0	57	52	48	37	0	0	0	224	489	13	77	5.1	.982	SS-141
1981		73	.238	.379	227	54	11	0	7	3.1	20	27	19	17	0	0	0	104	217	10	49	4.5	.970	SS-73
1982	2 teams	NY A (59G –.169) TEX A (46G –.219)																						
″	total	105	.193	.242	306	59	10	1	1	0.3	27	23	21	21	0	2	0	129	323	14	57	4.5	.970	SS-103
1983	TEX A	131	.237	.297	417	99	15	2	2	0.5	36	34	23	31	3	0	0	150	369	11	71	4.1	.979	SS-129, DH-1
1984	KC A	11	.333	.333	9	3	0	0	0	0.0	2	1	1	2	0	0	0	4	6	0	0	0.9	1.000	SS-9, 3B-2
12 yrs.		1392	.247	.321	4512	1114	169	23	40	0.9	451	423	328	349	17	4	0	2122	4335	156	839	4.8	.976	SS-1381, 2B-3, 3B-3, DH-1
LEAGUE CHAMPIONSHIP SERIES																								
1977	NY A	5	.214	.286	14	3	1	0	0	0.0	1	2	1	0	0	0	0	10	14	1	0	5.0	.960	SS-5
1978		4	.200	.200	15	3	0	0	0	0.0	0	4	0	0	0	0	0	2	8	1	0	2.8	.909	SS-4
1980		3	.182	.182	11	2	0	0	0	0.0	0	0	0	1	0	0	0	9	12	0	2	7.0	1.000	SS-3
3 yrs.		12	.200	.225	40	8	1	0	0	0.0	1	6	1	1	0	0	0	21	34	2	2	4.8	.965	SS-12
WORLD SERIES																								
1977	NY A	6	.263	.263	19	5	0	0	0	0.0	0	2	2	1	0	0	0	2	15	1	2	3.0	.944	SS-6
1978		6	.417	.458	24	10	1	0	0	0.0	3	7	1	2	0	0	0	8	16	2	4	4.3	.923	SS-6
2 yrs.		12	.349	.372	43	15	1	0	0	0.0	3	9	3	3	0	0	0	10	31	3	6	3.7	.932	SS-12

Sam Dente

DENTE, SAMUEL JOSEPH (Blackie)
B. Apr. 26, 1922, Harrison, N. J.

BR TR 5′11″ 175 lbs.

Year	Team	Games	BA	SA	AB	H	2B	3B	HR	HR%	R	RBI	BB	SO	SB	Pinch Hit AB	Pinch Hit H	PO	A	E	DP	TC/G	FA	G by Pos
1947	BOS A	46	.232	.280	168	39	4	2	0	0.0	14	11	19	15	0	0	0	40	83	8	11	2.8	.939	3B-46
1948	STL A	98	.270	.326	267	72	11	2	0	0.0	26	22	22	8	1	17	5	141	216	16	47	4.5	.957	SS-76, 3B-6
1949	WAS A	153	.273	.332	590	161	24	4	1	0.2	48	53	31	24	4	0	0	314	462	35	106	5.3	.957	SS-153
1950		155	.239	.299	603	144	20	5	2	0.3	56	59	39	19	1	0	0	316	497	34	111	5.4	.960	SS-128, 2B-29
1951		88	.238	.275	273	65	8	1	0	0.0	21	29	25	10	3	14	2	161	210	14	52	4.8	.964	SS-65, 2B-10, 3B-5
1952	CHI A	62	.221	.234	145	32	0	1	0	0.0	12	11	5	8	0	12	1	85	95	6	23	3.2	.968	SS-27, 3B-18, OF-6, 2B-6, 1B-2
1953		2	—	—	0	0	0	0	0	—	0	0	0	0	0	0	0	0	0	0	0	0.0	.000	SS-1
1954	CLE A	68	.266	.337	169	45	7	1	1	0.6	18	19	14	4	0	1	1	76	147	8	36	3.4	.965	SS-60, 2B-7
1955		73	.257	.295	105	27	4	0	0	0.0	10	10	12	8	0	3	1	42	105	3	17	2.1	.980	SS-53, 3B-13, 2B-4
9 yrs.		745	.252	.305	2320	585	78	16	4	0.2	205	214	167	96	9	47	10	1175	1815	124	403	4.4	.960	SS-563, 3B-88, 2B-56, OF-6, 1B-2
WORLD SERIES																								
1954	CLE A	3	.000	.000	3	0	0	0	0	0.0	1	0	1	0	0	0	0	1	1	0	1	0.7	1.000	SS-3

Mike DePangher

DePANGHER, MICHAEL ANTHONY
B. Sept. 11, 1858, Marysville, Calif. D. July 7, 1915, San Francisco, Calif.

BL 5′ 8″ 190 lbs.

Year	Team	Games	BA	SA	AB	H	2B	3B	HR	HR%	R	RBI	BB	SO	SB	Pinch Hit AB	Pinch Hit H	PO	A	E	DP	TC/G	FA	G by Pos
1884	PHI N	4	.200	.200	10	2	0	0	0	0.0	0		1	3		0	0	16	7	2	0	6.3	.920	C-4

Tony DePhillips

DePHILLIPS, ANTHONY ANDREW BR TR 6′ 2″ 185 lbs.
B. Sept. 20, 1912, New York, N. Y. D. May 5, 1994, Port Jefferson, N. Y.

Year	Team	Lg	Games	BA	SA	AB	H	2B	3B	HR	HR%	R	RBI	BB	SO	SB	Pinch Hit AB	Pinch Hit H	PO	A	E	DP	TC/G	FA	G by Pos
1943	CIN	N	35	.100	.150	20	2	1	0	0	0.0	0	2	1	5	0	0	0	47	5	1	0	1.5	.981	C-35

Gene Derby

DERBY, EUGENE A. 5′ 7″ 160 lbs.
B. Feb. 3, 1860, Fitchburg, Mass. Deceased.

Year	Team	Lg	Games	BA	SA	AB	H	2B	3B	HR	HR%	R	RBI	BB	SO	SB	Pinch Hit AB	Pinch Hit H	PO	A	E	DP	TC/G	FA	G by Pos
1885	BAL	AA	10	.129	.129	31	4	0	0	0	0.0	4		1			0	0	51	9	4	1	6.4	.938	C-9, OF-1

Bob Dernier

DERNIER, ROBERT EUGENE BR TR 6′ 160 lbs.
B. Jan. 5, 1957, Kansas City, Mo.

Year	Team	Lg	Games	BA	SA	AB	H	2B	3B	HR	HR%	R	RBI	BB	SO	SB	Pinch Hit AB	Pinch Hit H	PO	A	E	DP	TC/G	FA	G by Pos
1980	PHI	N	10	.571	.571	7	4	0	0	0	0.0	5	1	1	0	3	0	0	9	0	0	0	3.0	1.000	OF-3
1981			10	.750	.750	4	3	0	0	0	0.0	0	0	0	0	2	0	0	2	0	0	0	0.4	1.000	OF-5
1982			122	.249	.319	370	92	10	2	4	1.1	56	21	36	69	42	1	0	255	5	5	0	2.2	.981	OF-119
1983			122	.231	.290	221	51	10	0	1	0.5	41	15	18	21	35	3	0	164	3	2	1	1.6	.988	OF-107
1984	CHI	N	143	.278	.362	536	149	26	5	3	0.6	94	32	63	60	45	2	0	355	5	5	1	2.6	.986	OF-140
1985			121	.254	.316	469	119	20	3	1	0.2	63	21	40	44	31	4	0	310	4	9	1	2.8	.972	OF-116
1986			108	.225	.312	324	73	14	1	4	1.2	32	18	22	41	27	2	2	222	3	3	2	2.2	.987	OF-105
1987			93	.317	.497	199	63	4	4	8	4.0	38	21	19	19	16	31	7	86	2	1	1	1.3	.989	OF-71
1988	PHI	N	68	.289	.337	166	48	3	1	1	0.6	19	10	9	19	13	12	5	98	2	2	0	1.9	.980	OF-54
1989			107	.171	.214	187	32	5	0	1	0.5	26	13	14	28	4	41	4	95	1	3	0	1.3	.970	OF-74
10 yrs.			904	.255	.333	2483	634	92	16	23	0.9	374	152	222	301	218	96	18	1596	25	30	6	2.1	.982	OF-794
LEAGUE CHAMPIONSHIP SERIES																									
1983	PHI	N	1	—	—	0	0	0	0	0	—	0	0	0	0	0	0	0	0	0	0	0	0.0	.000	OF-1
1984	CHI	N	5	.235	.529	17	4	2	0	1	5.9	5	1	5	4	2	0	0	12	1	0	0	2.6	1.000	OF-5
2 yrs.			6	.235	.529	17	4	2	0	1	5.9	5	1	5	4	2	0	0	12	1	0	0	2.2	1.000	OF-6
WORLD SERIES																									
1983	PHI	N	1	—	—	0	0	0	0	0	—	1	0	0	0	0	0	0	0	0	0	0	0.0	—	

Claud Derrick

DERRICK, CLAUD LESTER (Deek) BR TR 6′ 175 lbs.
B. June 11, 1886, Burton, Ga. D. July 15, 1974, Clayton, Ga.

Year	Team	Lg	Games	BA	SA	AB	H	2B	3B	HR	HR%	R	RBI	BB	SO	SB	Pinch Hit AB	Pinch Hit H	PO	A	E	DP	TC/G	FA	G by Pos
1910	PHI	A	1	.000	.000	1	0	0	0	0	0.0	0	0	0		0	0	0	1	0	1	0	2.0	.500	SS-1
1911			36	.230	.280	100	23	1	2	0	0.0	14	5	7		7	1	0	69	71	4	7	4.5	.972	2B-21, SS-5, 1B-4, 3B-2
1912			21	.241	.276	58	14	0	1	0	0.0	7	7	5		1	3	0	27	57	11	5	5.3	.884	SS-18
1913	NY	A	22	.292	.354	65	19	1	0	1	1.5	7	7	5	8	2	2	0	36	59	14	9	5.7	.872	SS-13, 3B-4, 2B-2
1914	2 teams	CIN N (2G –.333) CHI N (28G –.219)																							
″	total		30	.225	.284	102	23	4	1	0	0.0	7	14	5	13	3	1	0	69	92	19	10	6.0	.894	SS-30
5 yrs.			110	.242	.294	326	79	6	4	1	0.3	35	33	22	21	13	7	0	202	279	49	31	5.3	.908	SS-67, 2B-23, 3B-6, 1B-4

Jim Derrick

DERRICK, JAMES MICHAEL BL TR 6′ 190 lbs.
B. Sept. 19, 1943, Columbia, S. C.

Year	Team	Lg	Games	BA	SA	AB	H	2B	3B	HR	HR%	R	RBI	BB	SO	SB	Pinch Hit AB	Pinch Hit H	PO	A	E	DP	TC/G	FA	G by Pos
1970	BOS	A	24	.212	.242	33	7	1	0	0	0.0	3	5	0	11	0	21	2	11	0	0	0	3.7	1.000	OF-2, 1B-1

Russ Derry

DERRY, ALVA RUSSELL BL TR 6′ 1″ 180 lbs.
B. Oct. 7, 1916, Princeton, Mo.

Year	Team	Lg	Games	BA	SA	AB	H	2B	3B	HR	HR%	R	RBI	BB	SO	SB	Pinch Hit AB	Pinch Hit H	PO	A	E	DP	TC/G	FA	G by Pos
1944	NY	A	38	.254	.386	114	29	3	0	4	3.5	14	14	20	19	1	7	5	54	2	3	0	2.1	.949	OF-28
1945			78	.225	.419	253	57	6	2	13	5.1	37	45	31	49	1	9	3	170	4	4	2	2.6	.978	OF-68
1946	PHI	A	69	.207	.304	184	38	8	5	0	0.0	17	14	27	54	0	16	3	127	3	2	2	2.6	.985	OF-50
1949	STL	N	2	.000	.000	2	0	0	0	0	0.0	0	0	0	2	0	2	0	0	0	0	0	0.0	—	
4 yrs.			187	.224	.373	553	124	17	7	17	3.1	68	73	78	124	2	34	11	351	9	9	4	2.5	.976	OF-146

Joe DeSa

DeSA, JOSEPH BL TL 5′11″ 170 lbs.
B. July 27, 1959, Honolulu, Hawaii D. Dec. 20, 1986, San Juan, Puerto Rico.

Year	Team	Lg	Games	BA	SA	AB	H	2B	3B	HR	HR%	R	RBI	BB	SO	SB	Pinch Hit AB	Pinch Hit H	PO	A	E	DP	TC/G	FA	G by Pos
1980	STL	N	7	.273	.273	11	3	0	0	0	0.0	0	0	0	2	0	5	2	3	0	0	0	1.5	1.000	OF-1, 1B-1
1985	CHI	A	28	.182	.364	44	8	2	0	2	4.5	5	7	3	6	0	14	2	70	7	0	4	5.5	1.000	1B-9, DH-4, OF-1
2 yrs.			35	.200	.345	55	11	2	0	2	3.6	5	7	3	8	0	19	4	73	7	0	4	5.0	1.000	1B-10, DH-4, OF-2

Gene Desautels

DESAUTELS, EUGENE ABRAHAM (Red) BR TR 5′11″ 170 lbs.
B. June 13, 1907, Worcester, Mass. D. Nov. 5, 1994, Flint, Mich.

Year	Team	Lg	Games	BA	SA	AB	H	2B	3B	HR	HR%	R	RBI	BB	SO	SB	Pinch Hit AB	Pinch Hit H	PO	A	E	DP	TC/G	FA	G by Pos
1930	DET	A	42	.190	.254	126	24	4	2	0	0.0	13	9	7	9	2	0	0	209	23	1	3	5.5	.996	C-42
1931			3	.091	.091	11	1	0	0	0	0.0	1	0	1	1	0	0	0	7	3	0	0	3.3	1.000	C-3
1932			28	.236	.264	72	17	2	0	0	0.0	8	2	13	11	0	3	0	109	13	2	0	5.2	.984	C-24
1933			30	.143	.167	42	6	1	0	0	0.0	5	4	4	6	0	0	0	75	5	2	0	2.7	.976	C-30
1937	BOS	A	96	.243	.295	305	74	10	3	0	0.0	33	27	36	26	1	1	1	491	44	4	4	5.7	.993	C-94
1938			108	.291	.369	333	97	16	2	2	0.6	47	48	57	31	1	0	0	423	52	7	7	4.5	.985	C-108
1939			76	.243	.305	226	55	14	0	0	0.0	26	21	33	13	3	2	1	310	48	2	5	4.9	.994	C-73
1940			71	.225	.266	222	50	7	1	0	0.0	19	17	32	13	0	0	0	325	27	3	8	5.1	.992	C-70
1941	CLE	A	66	.201	.254	189	38	5	1	1	0.5	20	17	14	12	1	0	0	300	32	1	5	5.0	.997	C-66
1942			62	.247	.278	162	40	5	0	0	0.0	14	9	12	13	1	1	0	180	16	5	0	3.3	.975	C-61
1943			68	.205	.249	185	38	6	1	0	0.0	14	19	11	16	2	2	0	251	28	5	4	4.3	.982	C-66
1945			10	.111	.111	9	1	0	0	0	0.0	1	0	1	1	0	0	0	8	3	0	1	1.1	1.000	C-10
1946	PHI	A	52	.215	.254	130	28	3	1	0	0.0	10	13	12	16	1	0	0	151	31	2	4	3.5	.989	C-52
13 yrs.			712	.233	.285	2012	469	73	11	3	0.1	211	186	233	168	12	9	2	2839	325	34	41	4.6	.989	C-699

Delino DeShields

DeSHIELDS, DELINO LAMONT BL TR 6′ 1″ 170 lbs.
B. Jan. 15, 1969, Seaford, Del.

Year	Team	Lg	Games	BA	SA	AB	H	2B	3B	HR	HR%	R	RBI	BB	SO	SB	Pinch Hit AB	Pinch Hit H	PO	A	E	DP	TC/G	FA	G by Pos
1990	MON	N	129	.289	.393	499	144	28	6	4	0.8	69	45	66	96	42	4	0	236	371	12	65	4.8	.981	2B-128
1991			151	.238	.332	563	134	15	4	10	1.8	83	51	95	**151**	56	5	0	285	405	27	72	4.8	.962	2B-148
1992			135	.292	.398	530	155	19	8	7	1.3	82	56	54	108	46	0	0	251	360	15	71	4.7	.976	2B-134
1993			123	.295	.372	481	142	17	7	2	0.4	75	29	72	64	43	0	0	243	381	11	74	5.2	.983	2B-123
1994	LA	N	89	.250	.322	320	80	11	3	2	0.6	51	33	54	53	27	2	1	156	282	7	48	4.5	.984	2B-88, SS-10
1995			127	.256	.369	425	109	18	3	8	1.9	66	37	63	83	39	10	3	203	330	11	54	4.8	.980	2B-114
6 yrs.			754	.271	.367	2818	764	108	31	33	1.2	426	251	404	555	253	21	4	1374	2129	83	384	4.8	.977	2B-735, SS-10

Delino DeShields *continued*

Year	Team		Games	BA	SA	AB	H	2B	3B	HR	HR%	R	RBI	BB	SO	SB	Pinch Hit AB	Pinch Hit H	PO	A	E	DP	TC/G	FA	G by Pos
DIVISIONAL PLAYOFF SERIES																									
1995	LA	N	3	.250	.250	12	3	0	0	0	0.0	1	0	1	3	0	0	0	8	7	0	2	5.0	1.000	2B-3

Orestes Destrade

DESTRADE, ORESTES BB TR 6′ 4″ 210 lbs.
Born Orestes Destrade (Cucuas).
B. May 8, 1962, Santiago, Cuba.

Year	Team		Games	BA	SA	AB	H	2B	3B	HR	HR%	R	RBI	BB	SO	SB	Pinch Hit AB	Pinch Hit H	PO	A	E	DP	TC/G	FA	G by Pos
1987	NY	A	9	.263	.263	19	5	0	0	0	0.0	5	1	5	5	0	4	0	20	1	0	2	4.2	1.000	1B-3, DH-2
1988	PIT	N	36	.149	.234	47	7	1	0	1	2.1	2	3	5	17	0	24	4	61	2	0	3	7.9	1.000	1B-8
1993	FLA	N	153	.255	.406	569	145	20	3	20	3.5	61	87	58	130	0	1	0	1313	90	19	109	9.4	.987	1B-152
1994			39	.208	.354	130	27	4	0	5	3.8	12	15	19	32	1	1	1	273	19	5	29	8.0	.983	1B-37
4 yrs.			237	.241	.383	765	184	25	3	26	3.4	80	106	87	184	1	30	5	1667	112	24	143	8.9	.987	1B-200, DH-2

Bob Detherage

DETHERAGE, ROBERT WAYNE BR TR 6′ 180 lbs.
B. Sept. 20, 1954, Springfield, Mo.

Year	Team		Games	BA	SA	AB	H	2B	3B	HR	HR%	R	RBI	BB	SO	SB	Pinch Hit AB	Pinch Hit H	PO	A	E	DP	TC/G	FA	G by Pos
1980	KC	A	26	.308	.500	26	8	2	0	1	3.8	2	7	1	4	1	0	0	16	0	0	0	0.8	1.000	OF-20

George Detore

DETORE, GEORGE FRANCIS BR TR 5′ 8″ 170 lbs.
Born George Francis DeTore.
B. Nov. 11, 1906, Utica, N. Y. D. Feb. 7, 1991, Utica, N. Y.

Year	Team		Games	BA	SA	AB	H	2B	3B	HR	HR%	R	RBI	BB	SO	SB	Pinch Hit AB	Pinch Hit H	PO	A	E	DP	TC/G	FA	G by Pos
1930	CLE	A	3	.167	.250	12	2	1	0	0	0.0	0	2	0	2	0	0	0	1	2	1	1	1.3	.750	3B-3
1931			30	.268	.375	56	15	6	0	0	0.0	3	7	8	0	2	4	0	28	44	8	9	3.1	.900	3B-13, SS-10, 2B-3
2 yrs.			33	.250	.353	68	17	7	0	0	0.0	3	9	8	2	2	4	0	29	46	9	10	2.9	.893	3B-16, SS-10, 2B-3

Ducky Detweiler

DETWEILER, ROBERT STERLING BR TR 5′11″ 178 lbs.
B. Feb. 15, 1919, Trumbauersville, Pa.

Year	Team		Games	BA	SA	AB	H	2B	3B	HR	HR%	R	RBI	BB	SO	SB	Pinch Hit AB	Pinch Hit H	PO	A	E	DP	TC/G	FA	G by Pos
1942	BOS	N	12	.318	.409	44	14	2	1	0	0.0	3	5	2	7	0	0	0	10	16	2	2	2.3	.929	3B-12
1946			1	.000	.000	1	0	0	0	0	0.0	0	0	0	0	0	1	0	0	0	0	0	0.0	—	
2 yrs.			13	.311	.400	45	14	2	1	0	0.0	3	5	2	7	0	1	0	10	16	2	2	2.3	.929	3B-12

Cesar Devarez

DEVAREZ, CESAR SALVATORE BR TR 5′10″ 175 lbs.
Born Cesar Salvatore Devarez (Santana).
B. Sept. 22, 1969, San Francisco de Macoris, Dominican Republic.

Year	Team		Games	BA	SA	AB	H	2B	3B	HR	HR%	R	RBI	BB	SO	SB	Pinch Hit AB	Pinch Hit H	PO	A	E	DP	TC/G	FA	G by Pos
1995	BAL	A	6	.000	.000	4	0	0	0	0	0.0	0	0	0	0	0	1	0	14	0	0	0	2.3	1.000	C-6

Mike Devereaux

DEVEREAUX, MICHAEL BR TR 6′ 195 lbs.
B. Apr. 10, 1963, Casper, Wyo.

Year	Team		Games	BA	SA	AB	H	2B	3B	HR	HR%	R	RBI	BB	SO	SB	Pinch Hit AB	Pinch Hit H	PO	A	E	DP	TC/G	FA	G by Pos
1987	LA	N	19	.222	.278	54	12	3	0	0	0.0	7	4	3	10	3	5	0	21	1	0	0	1.2	1.000	OF-18
1988			30	.116	.140	43	5	1	0	0	0.0	4	2	2	10	0	7	1	29	0	0	0	1.1	1.000	OF-26
1989	BAL	A	122	.266	.379	391	104	14	3	8	2.0	55	46	36	60	22	14	0	288	1	5	0	2.5	.983	OF-112, DH-5
1990			108	.240	.392	367	88	18	1	12	3.3	48	49	28	48	13	6	3	281	4	5	1	2.7	.983	OF-104, DH-3
1991			149	.260	.431	608	158	27	10	19	3.1	82	59	47	115	16	8	2	399	10	3	1	2.8	.993	OF-149
1992			156	.276	.464	653	180	29	11	24	3.7	76	107	44	94	10	1	1	431	5	5	3	2.8	.989	OF-155
1993			131	.250	.400	527	132	31	3	14	2.7	72	75	43	99	3	0	0	311	8	4	3	2.5	.988	OF-130
1994			85	.203	.332	301	61	8	2	9	3.0	35	33	22	72	1	2	1	203	3	1	1	2.4	.995	OF-84, DH-1
1995	2 teams		CHI A (92G –.306) ATL N (29G –.255)																						
″	total		121	.299	.451	388	116	24	1	11	2.8	55	63	27	62	8	13	3	229	4	3	1	2.0	.987	OF-117
9 yrs.			921	.257	.409	3332	856	155	31	97	2.9	434	438	252	570	76	56	11	2192	36	26	10	2.5	.988	OF-895, DH-9
DIVISIONAL PLAYOFF SERIES																									
1995	ATL	N	4	.200	.200	5	1	0	0	0	0.0	1	0	0	0	0	3	0	2	0	0	0	0.7	1.000	OF-3
LEAGUE CHAMPIONSHIP SERIES																									
1995	ATL	N	4	.308	.615	13	4	1	0	1	7.7	2	5	1	2	0	0	0	2	0	0	0	0.5	1.000	OF-4
WORLD SERIES																									
1995	ATL	N	5	.250	.250	4	1	0	0	0	0.0	0	1	2	1	0	1	1	0	0	1	0	0.2	.000	OF-4, DH-1

Jim Devine

DEVINE, WALTER JAMES TL
B. Oct. 5, 1858, Brooklyn, N. Y. D. Jan. 11, 1905, Syracuse, N. Y.

Year	Team		Games	BA	SA	AB	H	2B	3B	HR	HR%	R	RBI	BB	SO	SB	Pinch Hit AB	Pinch Hit H	PO	A	E	DP	TC/G	FA	G by Pos
1883	BAL	AA	2	.222	.222	9	2	0	0	0	0.0	4		0			0	0	1	0	1	0	0.7	.500	P-2, OF-1
1886	NY	N	1	.000	.000	3	0	0	0	0	0.0	0	0	0	1		0	0	0	0	0	0	0.0	.000	OF-1
2 yrs.			3	.167	.167	12	2	0	0	0	0.0	4	0	0	1		0	0	1	0	1	0	0.5	.500	P-2, OF-2

Mickey Devine

DEVINE, WILLIAM PATRICK BR TR 5′10″ 165 lbs.
B. May 9, 1892, Albany, N. Y. D. Oct. 1, 1937, Albany, N. Y.

Year	Team		Games	BA	SA	AB	H	2B	3B	HR	HR%	R	RBI	BB	SO	SB	Pinch Hit AB	Pinch Hit H	PO	A	E	DP	TC/G	FA	G by Pos
1918	PHI	N	4	.125	.250	8	1	1	0	0	0.0	0	0	0	1	0	1	0	8	2	1	1	3.7	.909	C-3
1920	BOS	A	8	.167	.167	12	2	0	0	0	0.0	1	0	1	2	1	3	0	19	2	1	0	4.4	.955	C-5
1925	NY	N	21	.273	.364	33	9	3	0	0	0.0	6	4	2	3	0	4	1	35	7	3	0	3.8	.933	C-11, 3B-1
3 yrs.			33	.226	.302	53	12	4	0	0	0.0	7	4	3	6	1	8	1	62	11	5	1	3.9	.936	C-19, 3B-1

Bernie DeViveiros

DeVIVEIROS, BERNARD JOHN BR TR 5′ 7″ 160 lbs.
B. Apr. 19, 1901, Oakland, Calif. D. July 5, 1994, Oakland, Calif.

Year	Team		Games	BA	SA	AB	H	2B	3B	HR	HR%	R	RBI	BB	SO	SB	Pinch Hit AB	Pinch Hit H	PO	A	E	DP	TC/G	FA	G by Pos
1924	CHI	A	1	.000	.000	1	0	0	0	0	0.0	0	0	0	0	0	0	0	1	0	2	0	3.0	.333	SS-1
1927	DET	A	24	.227	.273	22	5	1	0	0	0.0	4	2	2	8	1	2	0	7	14	2	4	1.5	.913	SS-14, 3B-1
2 yrs.			25	.217	.261	23	5	1	0	0	0.0	4	2	2	8	1	2	0	8	14	4	4	1.6	.846	SS-15, 3B-1

Art Devlin

DEVLIN, ARTHUR McARTHUR BR TR 6′ 175 lbs.
B. Oct. 16, 1879, Washington, D. C. D. Sept. 18, 1948, Jersey City, N. J.

Year	Team		Games	BA	SA	AB	H	2B	3B	HR	HR%	R	RBI	BB	SO	SB	Pinch Hit AB	Pinch Hit H	PO	A	E	DP	TC/G	FA	G by Pos
1904	NY	N	130	.281	.354	474	133	16	8	1	0.2	81	66	62		33	0	0	126	285	42	10	3.5	.907	3B-130
1905			153	.246	.310	525	129	14	7	2	0.4	74	61	66		**59**	0	0	156	299	33	14	3.2	.932	3B-153
1906			148	.299	.390	498	149	23	8	2	0.4	76	65	74		54	0	0	171	355	31	22	3.8	.944	3B-148

Art Devlin *continued*

Year	Team	Games	BA	SA	AB	H	2B	3B	HR	HR%	R	RBI	BB	SO	SB	Pinch Hit AB	Pinch Hit H	PO	A	E	DP	TC/G	FA	G by Pos
1907		143	.277	.324	491	136	16	2	1	0.2	61	54	63		38	0	0	181	292	31	12	3.5	.938	3B-140, SS-3
1908		157	.253	.313	534	135	18	4	2	0.4	59	45	62		19	0	0	203	331	30	19	3.6	.947	3B-157
1909		143	.265	.336	491	130	19	8	0	0.0	61	55	65		24	0	0	191	317	36	21	3.8	.934	3B-142
1910		147	.260	.327	493	128	17	5	2	0.4	71	67	62	32	28	0	0	179	284	33	20	3.4	.933	3B-147
1911		83	.273	.350	260	71	16	2	0	0.0	42	25	42	19	9	0	0	128	154	16	5	3.1	.946	3B-79, SS-6, 1B-6, 2B-6
1912	BOS N	124	.289	.367	436	126	18	8	0	0.0	59	54	51	37	11	4	1	768	140	15	52	7.6	.984	1B-69, SS-26, 3B-26, OF-1
1913		73	.229	.310	210	48	7	5	0	0.0	19	12	29	17	8	3	2	83	134	6	4	3.2	.973	3B-69
10 yrs.		1301	.269	.338	4412	1185	164	57	10	0.2	603	504	576	105	283	7	3	2186	2591	273	179	3.9	.946	3B-1191, 1B-75, SS-35, 2B-6, OF-1
WORLD SERIES																								
1905	NY N	5	.250	.313	16	4	1	0	0	0.0	0	1	1	3	3	0	0	7	17	2	0	5.2	.923	3B-5

Jim Devlin

DEVLIN, JAMES RAYMOND
B. Aug. 25, 1922, Plains, Pa.
BL TR 5′11½″ 165 lbs.

Year	Team	Games	BA	SA	AB	H	2B	3B	HR	HR%	R	RBI	BB	SO	SB	Pinch Hit AB	Pinch Hit H	PO	A	E	DP	TC/G	FA	G by Pos
1944	CLE A	1	.000	.000	1	0	0	0	0	0.0	0	0	0	0	0	0	0	1	1	0	0	2.0	1.000	C-1

Rex DeVogt

DeVOGT, REX EUGENE
B. Jan. 4, 1888, Clare, Mich. D. Nov. 9, 1935, Alma, Mich.
BR TR 5′ 9″ 170 lbs.

Year	Team	Games	BA	SA	AB	H	2B	3B	HR	HR%	R	RBI	BB	SO	SB	Pinch Hit AB	Pinch Hit H	PO	A	E	DP	TC/G	FA	G by Pos
1913	BOS N	3	.000	.000	6	0	0	0	0	0.0	0	0	0	3	0	0	0	12	4	1	0	5.7	.941	C-3

Josh Devore

DEVORE, JOSHUA D.
B. Nov. 13, 1887, Murray City, Ohio D. Oct. 6, 1954, Chillicothe, Ohio.
BL TL 5′ 6″ 160 lbs.

Year	Team	Games	BA	SA	AB	H	2B	3B	HR	HR%	R	RBI	BB	SO	SB	Pinch Hit AB	Pinch Hit H	PO	A	E	DP	TC/G	FA	G by Pos
1908	NY N	5	.167	.167	6	1	0	0	0	0.0	1	2	1		1	2	0	1	0	0	0	0.5	1.000	OF-2
1909		22	.143	.179	28	4	1	0	0	0.0	6	1	2		3	5	0	13	1	3	0	1.4	.824	OF-12
1910		133	.304	.380	490	149	11	10	2	0.4	92	27	46	67	43	1	0	191	18	16	3	1.7	.929	OF-130
1911		149	.280	.365	565	158	19	10	3	0.5	96	50	81	69	61	0	0	241	29	19	5	1.9	.934	OF-149
1912		106	.275	.373	327	90	14	6	2	0.6	66	37	51	43	27	4	0	155	14	15	3	1.9	.918	OF-96
1913	3 teams	NY N (16G –.190) CIN N (66G –.267) PHI N (23G –.282)																						
″	total	105	.264	.357	277	73	7	5	3	1.1	43	20	19	32	23	12	3	125	12	12	3	1.9	.919	OF-79
1914	2 teams	PHI N (30G –.302) BOS N (51G –.227)																						
″	total	81	.249	.298	181	45	6	0	1	0.6	27	12	22	19	2	25	11	65	7	6	3	1.5	.923	OF-51
7 yrs.		601	.277	.359	1874	520	58	31	11	0.6	331	149	222	230	160	49	14	791	81	71	17	1.8	.925	OF-519
WORLD SERIES																								
1911	NY N	6	.167	.208	24	4	1	0	0	0.0	1	3	1	8	0	0	0	16	0	1	0	2.8	.941	OF-6
1912		7	.250	.250	24	6	0	0	0	0.0	4	0	7	5	4	0	0	10	2	2	1	2.0	.857	OF-7
1914	BOS N	1	.000	.000	1	0	0	0	0	0.0	0	0	0	1	0	1	0	0	0	0	0	0.0	—	
3 yrs.		14	.204	.224	49	10	1	0	0	0.0	5	3	8	14	4	1	0	26	2	3	1	2.4	.903	OF-13

Al DeVormer

DeVORMER, ALBERT E.
B. Aug. 19, 1891, Grand Rapids, Mich. D. Aug. 29, 1966, Grand Rapids, Mich.
BR TR 6′½″ 175 lbs.

Year	Team	Games	BA	SA	AB	H	2B	3B	HR	HR%	R	RBI	BB	SO	SB	Pinch Hit AB	Pinch Hit H	PO	A	E	DP	TC/G	FA	G by Pos
1918	CHI A	8	.263	.368	19	5	2	0	0	0.0	2	0	0	4	1	1	0	12	4	0	0	2.3	1.000	C-6, OF-1
1921	NY A	22	.347	.429	49	17	4	0	0	0.0	6	7	2	4	2	5	1	48	9	3	1	3.5	.950	C-17
1922		24	.203	.305	59	12	4	1	0	0.0	8	11	1	6	0	4	1	66	11	2	0	4.4	.975	C-17, 1B-1
1923	BOS A	74	.258	.321	209	54	7	3	0	0.0	20	18	6	21	3	12	3	183	48	5	3	4.1	.979	C-55, 1B-2
1927	NY N	68	.248	.326	141	35	3	1	2	1.4	14	21	11	11	1	8	4	151	29	7	4	3.3	.963	C-54, 1B-3
5 yrs.		196	.258	.333	477	123	20	5	2	0.4	50	57	20	46	7	30	9	460	101	17	8	3.7	.971	C-149, 1B-6, OF-1
WORLD SERIES																								
1921	NY A	2	.000	.000	1	0	0	0	0	0.0	0	0	0	0	0	0	0	1	0	0	0	1.0	1.000	C-1

Walt Devoy

DEVOY, WALTER JOSEPH
B. Mar. 14, 1885, St. Louis, Mo. D. Dec. 17, 1953, St. Louis, Mo.
5′11″ 165 lbs.

Year	Team	Games	BA	SA	AB	H	2B	3B	HR	HR%	R	RBI	BB	SO	SB	Pinch Hit AB	Pinch Hit H	PO	A	E	DP	TC/G	FA	G by Pos
1909	STL A	19	.246	.319	69	17	3	1	0	0.0	7	8	3		4	0	0	46	3	1	0	2.6	.980	OF-16, 1B-3

Jeff DeWillis

DeWILLIS, JEFFREY ALLEN
B. Apr. 13, 1965, Houston, Tex.
BR TR 6′ 2″ 170 lbs.

Year	Team	Games	BA	SA	AB	H	2B	3B	HR	HR%	R	RBI	BB	SO	SB	Pinch Hit AB	Pinch Hit H	PO	A	E	DP	TC/G	FA	G by Pos
1987	TOR A	13	.120	.280	25	3	1	0	1	4.0	2	2	2	12	0	0	0	49	5	2	1	4.3	.964	C-13

Charlie Dexter

DEXTER, CHARLES DANA
B. June 15, 1876, Evansville, Ind. D. June 9, 1934, Cedar Rapids, Iowa.
BR TR 5′ 7″ 190 lbs.

Year	Team	Games	BA	SA	AB	H	2B	3B	HR	HR%	R	RBI	BB	SO	SB	Pinch Hit AB	Pinch Hit H	PO	A	E	DP	TC/G	FA	G by Pos
1896	LOU N	107	.279	.381	402	112	18	7	3	0.7	65	37	17	34	21	5	1	266	71	37	12	3.7	.901	C-55, OF-47
1897		76	.280	.389	257	72	12	5	2	0.8	43	46	21		12	5	0	132	68	27	8	3.2	.881	OF-32, C-23, 3B-14, SS-2
1898		112	.314	.375	421	132	13	5	1	0.2	76	66	26		44	3	1	207	41	12	5	2.4	.954	OF-95, 2B-8, C-7
1899		80	.258	.298	295	76	7	1	1	0.3	47	33	21		21	3	0	137	35	16	3	2.4	.915	OF-71, SS-6
1900	CHI N	40	.200	.288	125	25	5	0	2	1.6	7	20	1		2	4	1	98	37	6	4	3.9	.957	C-22, OF-13, 2B-1
1901		116	.267	.315	460	123	9	5	1	0.2	46	66	16		22	2	0	618	125	27	32	6.6	.965	1B-54, 3B-25, OF-21, 2B-13, C-3
1902	2 teams	CHI N (69G –.226) BOS N (48G –.257)																						
″	total	117	.238	.292	449	107	15	0	3	0.7	63	44	35		29	0	0	414	184	46	32	5.4	.929	3B-40, SS-22, 1B-22, 2B-19, OF-17
1903	BOS N	123	.223	.280	457	102	15	1	3	0.7	82	34	61		32	2	0	231	34	21	10	2.4	.927	OF-106, SS-9, C-6
8 yrs.		771	.261	.328	2866	749	94	24	16	0.6	429	346	198	34	183	24	3	2103	595	192	106	3.8	.934	OF-402, C-116, 3B-79, 1B-76, 2B-41, SS-39

Alex Diaz

DIAZ, ALEXIS
B. Oct. 5, 1968, Brooklyn, N. Y.
BB TR 5′11″ 175 lbs.

Year	Team	Games	BA	SA	AB	H	2B	3B	HR	HR%	R	RBI	BB	SO	SB	Pinch Hit AB	Pinch Hit H	PO	A	E	DP	TC/G	FA	G by Pos
1992	MIL A	22	.111	.111	9	1	0	0	0	0.0	5	1	0	0	3	0	0	10	0	0	0	0.8	1.000	OF-11, DH-2
1993		32	.319	.348	69	22	2	0	0	0.0	9	1	0	12	5	4	1	46	1	1	0	1.7	.979	OF-28, DH-1
1994		79	.251	.369	187	47	5	7	1	0.5	17	17	10	19	5	1	1	138	11	2	0	2.0	.987	OF-73, 2B-2, DH-1
1995	SEA A	103	.248	.333	270	67	14	0	3	1.1	44	27	13	27	18	20	6	146	4	2	1	1.7	.987	OF-88
4 yrs.		236	.256	.344	535	137	21	7	4	0.7	75	46	23	58	31	25	8	340	16	5	1	1.8	.986	OF-200, DH-4, 2B-2

Alex Diaz *continued*

Year	Team		Games	BA	SA	AB	H	2B	3B	HR	HR%	R	RBI	BB	SO	SB	Pinch Hit AB	Pinch Hit H	PO	A	E	DP	TC/G	FA	G by Pos
DIVISIONAL PLAYOFF SERIES																									
1995	SEA	A	2	.333	.333	3	1	0	0	0	0.0	0	0	1	1	0	1	1	1	1	0	0	2.0	1.000	OF-1
LEAGUE CHAMPIONSHIP SERIES																									
1995	SEA	A	4	.429	.571	7	3	1	0	0	0.0	0	0	1	1	0	3	1	1	0	0	0	0.3	1.000	OF-3

Bo Diaz

DIAZ, BAUDILIO JOSE
Born Baudilio Jose Diaz (Seijas).
B. Mar. 23, 1953, Cua, Venezuela D. Nov. 23, 1990, Caracas, Venezuela.
BR TR 5′11″ 185 lbs.

Year	Team		Games	BA	SA	AB	H	2B	3B	HR	HR%	R	RBI	BB	SO	SB	Pinch Hit AB	Pinch Hit H	PO	A	E	DP	TC/G	FA	G by Pos
1977	BOS	A	2	.000	.000	1	0	0	0	0	0.0	0	0	0	1	0	1	0	5	0	0	0	2.5	1.000	C-2
1978	CLE	A	44	.236	.315	127	30	4	0	2	1.6	12	11	4	17	0	0	0	183	18	6	4	4.7	.971	C-44
1979			15	.156	.219	32	5	2	0	0	0.0	0	1	2	6	0	0	0	63	6	3	1	4.8	.958	C-15
1980			76	.227	.343	207	47	11	2	3	1.4	15	32	7	27	1	9	2	317	35	4	4	4.7	.989	C-75
1981			63	.313	.533	182	57	19	0	7	3.8	25	38	13	23	2	12	3	247	27	7	0	5.2	.975	C-51, DH-3
1982	PHI	N	144	.288	.450	525	151	29	1	18	3.4	69	85	36	87	3	2	1	850	80	10	7	6.5	.989	C-144
1983			136	.236	.367	471	111	17	0	15	3.2	49	64	38	57	1	4	2	903	97	14	7	7.6	.986	C-134
1984			27	.213	.307	75	16	4	0	1	1.3	5	9	5	13	0	4	0	114	9	1	1	5.4	.992	C-23
1985	2 teams		PHI N (26G –.211)	CIN N (51G –.261)																					
″	total		77	.245	.371	237	58	13	1	5	2.1	21	31	21	25	0	3	0	428	42	8	10	6.4	.983	C-75
1986	CIN	N	134	.272	.380	474	129	21	0	10	2.1	50	56	40	52	1	0	0	732	83	13	10	6.2	.984	C-134
1987			140	.270	.421	496	134	28	1	15	3.0	49	82	19	73	1	2	0	747	70	7	6	6.0	.992	C-137
1988			92	.219	.343	315	69	9	0	10	3.2	26	35	7	41	0	7	0	468	44	5	9	5.9	.990	C-88
1989			43	.205	.265	132	27	5	0	1	0.8	6	8	6	7	0	5	0	237	14	4	1	5.9	.984	C-43
13 yrs.			993	.255	.387	3274	834	162	5	87	2.7	327	452	198	429	9	49	8	5294	525	82	60	6.1	.986	C-965, DH-3
LEAGUE CHAMPIONSHIP SERIES																									
1983	PHI	N	4	.154	.231	13	2	1	0	0	0.0	0	0	2	1	0	0	0	32	2	0	0	8.5	1.000	C-4
WORLD SERIES																									
1983	PHI	N	5	.333	.400	15	5	1	0	0	0.0	1	0	1	2	0	0	0	37	1	1	0	7.8	.974	C-5

Carlos Diaz

DIAZ, CARLOS FRANCISCO
B. Dec. 24, 1964, Jersey City, N. J.
BR TR 6′ 3″ 190 lbs.

Year	Team		Games	BA	SA	AB	H	2B	3B	HR	HR%	R	RBI	BB	SO	SB	Pinch Hit AB	Pinch Hit H	PO	A	E	DP	TC/G	FA	G by Pos
1990	TOR	A	9	.333	.333	3	1	0	0	0	0.0	1	0	0	2	0	0	0	13	3	0	0	1.8	1.000	C-9

Edgar Diaz

DIAZ, EDGAR
Born Edgar Diaz (Serrano).
B. Feb. 8, 1964, Santurce, Puerto Rico.
BR TR 6′ 165 lbs.

Year	Team		Games	BA	SA	AB	H	2B	3B	HR	HR%	R	RBI	BB	SO	SB	Pinch Hit AB	Pinch Hit H	PO	A	E	DP	TC/G	FA	G by Pos
1986	MIL	A	5	.231	.231	13	3	0	0	0	0.0	0	0	1	3	0	0	0	6	8	2	2	3.2	.875	SS-5
1990			86	.271	.298	218	59	2	2	0	0.0	27	14	21	32	3	2	2	125	197	17	43	3.9	.950	SS-65, 2B-15, 3B-7, DH-1
2 yrs.			91	.268	.294	231	62	2	2	0	0.0	27	14	22	35	3	2	2	131	205	19	45	3.8	.946	SS-70, 2B-15, 3B-7, DH-1

Mario Diaz

DIAZ, MARIO RAFAEL
Born Mario Rafael Diaz (Torres).
B. Jan. 10, 1962, Humacao, Puerto Rico.
BR TR 5′10″ 145 lbs.

Year	Team		Games	BA	SA	AB	H	2B	3B	HR	HR%	R	RBI	BB	SO	SB	Pinch Hit AB	Pinch Hit H	PO	A	E	DP	TC/G	FA	G by Pos
1987	SEA	A	11	.304	.391	23	7	0	1	0	0.0	4	3	0	4	0	1	0	10	25	1	6	3.6	.972	SS-10
1988			28	.306	.375	72	22	5	0	0	0.0	6	9	3	5	0	3	1	31	47	1	11	2.9	.987	SS-21, 2B-4, 3B-1, 1B-1
1989			52	.135	.176	74	10	0	0	1	1.4	9	7	7	7	0	3	1	35	54	5	10	1.7	.947	SS-37, 2B-14, 3B-3
1990	NY	N	16	.136	.182	22	3	1	0	0	0.0	0	1	0	3	0	7	2	5	18	1	1	2.2	.958	SS-10, 2B-1
1991	TEX	A	96	.264	.319	182	48	7	0	1	0.5	24	22	15	18	0	14	3	93	143	7	32	2.6	.971	SS-65, 2B-20, 3B-8, DH-1
1992			19	.226	.258	31	7	1	0	0	0.0	2	1	1	2	0	1	0	16	26	1	2	2.2	.977	SS-16, 2B-3, 3B-1
1993			71	.273	.361	205	56	10	1	2	1.0	24	24	8	13	1	3	1	90	153	3	30	3.5	.988	SS-57, 3B-12, 1B-1
1994	FLA	N	32	.325	.429	77	25	4	2	0	0.0	10	11	6	6	0	13	5	19	40	1	11	2.4	.983	3B-11, SS-7, 2B-7
1995			49	.230	.299	87	20	3	0	1	1.1	5	6	1	12	0	32	6	23	30	2	12	3.2	.964	2B-9, SS-5, 3B-3
9 yrs.			374	.256	.326	773	198	31	4	5	0.6	84	84	41	70	1	77	19	322	536	22	115	2.7	.975	SS-228, 2B-58, 3B-39, 1B-2, DH-1

Mike Diaz

DIAZ, MICHAEL ANTHONY
B. Apr. 15, 1960, San Francisco, Calif.
BR TR 6′ 2″ 205 lbs.

Year	Team		Games	BA	SA	AB	H	2B	3B	HR	HR%	R	RBI	BB	SO	SB	Pinch Hit AB	Pinch Hit H	PO	A	E	DP	TC/G	FA	G by Pos
1983	CHI	N	6	.286	.429	7	2	1	0	0	0.0	2	1	0	0	0	3	1	5	0	0	0	1.7	1.000	C-3
1986	PIT	N	97	.268	.483	209	56	9	0	12	5.7	22	36	19	43	0	33	11	202	8	3	9	3.3	.986	OF-38, 1B-20, 3B-5, C-1
1987			103	.241	.490	241	58	8	2	16	6.6	28	48	31	42	1	32	7	303	23	6	14	4.3	.982	OF-37, 1B-32, C-8
1988	2 teams		PIT N (47G –.230)	CHI A (40G –.237)																					
″	total		87	.235	.314	226	53	9	0	3	1.3	18	17	21	43	0	18	2	415	29	5	35	6.8	.989	1B-45, OF-19, DH-1, C-1
4 yrs.			293	.247	.429	683	169	27	2	31	4.5	70	102	71	128	1	86	21	925	60	14	58	4.8	.986	1B-97, OF-94, C-13, 3B-5, DH-1

Paul Dicken

DICKEN, PAUL FRANKLIN
B. Oct. 2, 1943, Deland, Fla.
BR TR 6′ 5″ 195 lbs.

Year	Team		Games	BA	SA	AB	H	2B	3B	HR	HR%	R	RBI	BB	SO	SB	Pinch Hit AB	Pinch Hit H	PO	A	E	DP	TC/G	FA	G by Pos
1964	CLE	A	11	.000	.000	11	0	0	0	0	0.0	0	0	0	5	0	11	0	0	0	0	0	0.0	—	
1966			2	.000	.000	2	0	0	0	0	0.0	0	0	0	1	0	2	0	0	0	0	0	0.0	—	
2 yrs.			13	.000	.000	13	0	0	0	0	0.0	0	0	0	6	0	13	0							

Buttercup Dickerson

DICKERSON, LOUIS PESSANO
B. Oct. 11, 1858, Tyaskin, Md. D. July 23, 1920, Baltimore, Md.
BL TR 5′ 6″ 140 lbs.

Year	Team		Games	BA	SA	AB	H	2B	3B	HR	HR%	R	RBI	BB	SO	SB	Pinch Hit AB	Pinch Hit H	PO	A	E	DP	TC/G	FA	G by Pos
1878	CIN	N	29	.309	.366	123	38	5	1	0	0.0	17	9	0	7		0	0	56	1	8	0	2.2	.877	OF-29
1879			81	.291	.440	350	102	18	**14**	2	0.6	73	57	3	27		0	0	144	9	38	1	2.4	.801	OF-81
1880	2 teams		TRO N (30G –.193)	WOR N (31G –.293)																					
″	total		61	.246	.349	252	62	10	8	0	0.0	37	30	3	5		0	0	126	12	18	5	2.5	.885	OF-61, SS-1
1881	WOR	N	80	.316	.406	367	116	18	6	1	0.3	48	31	8	8		0	0	153	28	22	6	2.5	.892	OF-80
1883	PIT	AA	85	.248	.296	355	88	15	1	0	0.0	62		17			0	0	118	45	46	3	2.4	.780	OF-78, SS-8, 2B-2

Buttercup Dickerson *continued*

Year	Team	Games	BA	SA	AB	H	2B	3B	HR	HR%	R	RBI	BB	SO	SB	Pinch Hit AB	Pinch Hit H	PO	A	E	DP	TC/G	FA	G by Pos
1884	3 teams	STL U (46G –.365)	BAL AA (13G –.214)	LOU AA (8G –.143)																				
″	total	67	.315	.410	295	93	17	4	1	0.3	64		15			0	0	99	21	17	2	2.0	.876	OF-62, 3B-5
1885	BUF N	5	.048	.095	21	1	1	0	0	0.0	1	0	1	4		0	0	6	2	0	0	1.6	1.000	OF-5
7 yrs.		408	.284	.377	1763	500	84	34	4	0.2	302	127	47	51		0	0	702	118	149	17	2.4	.846	OF-396, SS-9, 3B-5, 2B-2

Bill Dickey

DICKEY, WILLIAM MALCOLM BL TR 6′ 1½″ 185 lbs.
Brother of George Dickey.
B. June 6, 1907, Bastrop, La. D. Nov. 12, 1993, Little Rock, Ark.
Manager 1946.
Hall of Fame 1954.

Year	Team	Games	BA	SA	AB	H	2B	3B	HR	HR%	R	RBI	BB	SO	SB	Pinch Hit AB	Pinch Hit H	PO	A	E	DP	TC/G	FA	G by Pos
1928	NY A	10	.200	.400	15	3	1	1	0	0.0	1	2	0	2	0	0	0	6	2	0	0	0.8	1.000	C-10
1929		130	.324	.485	447	145	30	6	10	2.2	60	65	14	16	4	3	1	476	95	12	13	4.6	.979	C-127
1930		109	.339	.486	366	124	25	7	5	1.4	55	65	21	14	7	5	3	418	51	11	5	4.8	.977	C-101
1931		130	.327	.442	477	156	17	10	6	1.3	65	78	39	20	2	4	0	670	78	3	6	6.0	.996	C-125
1932		108	.310	.482	423	131	20	4	15	3.5	66	84	34	13	2	0	0	639	53	9	6	6.5	.987	C-108
1933		130	.318	.490	478	152	24	8	14	2.9	58	97	47	14	3	3	1	721	82	6	15	6.4	.993	C-127
1934		104	.322	.494	395	127	24	4	12	3.0	56	72	38	18	0	0	0	527	49	8	13	5.6	.986	C-104
1935		120	.279	.458	448	125	26	6	14	3.1	54	81	35	11	1	2	1	536	62	3	7	5.1	.995	C-118
1936		112	.362	.617	423	153	26	8	22	5.2	99	107	46	16	0	6	2	499	61	14	10	5.4	.976	C-107
1937		140	.332	.570	530	176	35	2	29	5.5	87	133	73	22	3	3	1	692	80	7	11	5.7	.991	C-137
1938		132	.313	.568	454	142	27	4	27	5.9	84	115	75	22	3	6	1	518	94	8	7	4.9	.987	C-126
1939		128	.302	.512	480	145	23	3	24	5.0	98	105	77	37	5	2	0	571	57	7	8	5.0	.989	C-126
1940		106	.247	.355	372	92	11	1	9	2.4	45	54	48	32	0	4	0	425	55	3	9	4.7	.994	C-102
1941		109	.284	.417	348	99	15	5	7	2.0	35	71	45	17	2	6	1	422	45	3	11	4.5	.994	C-104
1942		82	.295	.373	268	79	13	1	2	0.7	28	37	26	11	2	2	0	322	44	9	7	4.7	.976	C-80
1943		85	.351	.492	242	85	18	2	4	1.7	29	33	41	12	2	10	4	322	37	2	5	5.1	.994	C-71
1946		54	.261	.366	134	35	8	0	2	1.5	10	10	19	12	0	11	3	201	29	3	4	6.0	.987	C-39
17 yrs.		1789	.313	.486	6300	1969	343	72	202	3.2	930	1209	678	289	36	67	18	7965	974	108	137	5.3	.988	C-1712
WORLD SERIES																								
1932	NY A	4	.438	.438	16	7	0	0	0	0.0	2	4	2	1	0	0	0	25	1	0	0	6.5	1.000	C-4
1936		6	.120	.240	25	3	0	0	1	4.0	5	5	3	4	0	0	0	38	4	1	0	7.2	.977	C-6
1937		5	.211	.316	19	4	0	1	0	0.0	3	3	2	2	0	0	0	26	1	0	0	5.4	1.000	C-5
1938		4	.400	.600	15	6	0	0	1	6.7	2	2	1	0	1	0	0	31	5	0	0	9.0	1.000	C-4
1939		4	.267	.667	15	4	0	0	2	13.3	2	5	1	2	0	0	0	27	2	0	1	7.3	1.000	C-4
1941		5	.167	.222	18	3	1	0	0	0.0	3	1	3	1	0	0	0	24	2	0	1	5.2	1.000	C-5
1942		5	.263	.263	19	5	0	0	0	0.0	1	0	1	0	0	0	0	25	1	1	1	5.4	.963	C-5
1943		5	.278	.444	18	5	0	0	1	5.6	1	4	2	2	0	0	0	28	3	0	0	6.2	1.000	C-5
8 yrs.		38	.255	.379	145	37	1	1	5	3.4	19	24 8th	15	12	1	0	0	224	19	2	3	6.4	.992	C-38

George Dickey

DICKEY, GEORGE WILLARD (Skeets) BB TR 6′ 2″ 180 lbs.
Brother of Bill Dickey.
B. July 10, 1915, Kensett, Ark. D. June 16, 1976, DeWitt, Ark.

Year	Team	Games	BA	SA	AB	H	2B	3B	HR	HR%	R	RBI	BB	SO	SB	Pinch Hit AB	Pinch Hit H	PO	A	E	DP	TC/G	FA	G by Pos
1935	BOS A	5	.000	.000	11	0	0	0	0	0.0	1	1	1	3	0	1	0	7	0	0	0	1.8	1.000	C-4
1936		10	.043	.087	23	1	1	0	0	0.0	0	0	2	3	0	0	0	25	6	3	1	3.4	.912	C-10
1941	CHI A	32	.200	.327	55	11	1	0	2	3.6	6	8	5	7	0	14	3	56	5	0	1	3.6	1.000	C-17
1942		59	.233	.284	116	27	3	0	1	0.9	6	17	9	11	0	31	9	90	11	9	5	3.8	.918	C-29
1946		37	.192	.205	78	15	1	0	0	0.0	8	1	12	13	0	8	3	97	14	0	3	3.7	1.000	C-30
1947		83	.223	.265	211	47	6	0	1	0.5	15	27	34	25	4	4	2	285	35	5	5	4.1	.985	C-80
6 yrs.		226	.204	.253	494	101	12	0	4	0.8	36	54	63	62	4	58	17	560	71	17	15	3.8	.974	C-170

Johnny Dickshot

DICKSHOT, JOHN OSCAR BR TR 6′ 195 lbs.
Born John Oscar Dicksus.
B. Jan. 24, 1910, Waukegan, Ill.

Year	Team	Games	BA	SA	AB	H	2B	3B	HR	HR%	R	RBI	BB	SO	SB	Pinch Hit AB	Pinch Hit H	PO	A	E	DP	TC/G	FA	G by Pos
1936	PIT N	9	.222	.222	9	2	0	0	0	0.0	2	1	1	2	0	7	1	0	0	0	0	0.0	.000	OF-1
1937		82	.254	.348	264	67	8	4	3	1.1	42	33	26	36	0	15	3	109	5	6	2	1.9	.950	OF-64
1938		29	.229	.229	35	8	0	0	0	0.0	3	4	8	5	3	9	3	16	0	0	0	1.6	1.000	OF-10
1939	NY N	10	.235	.235	34	8	0	0	0	0.0	3	5	5	3	0	0	0	13	1	0	1	1.4	1.000	OF-10
1944	CHI A	62	.253	.364	162	41	8	5	0	0.0	18	15	13	10	2	20	5	72	3	2	1	1.9	.974	OF-40
1945		130	.302	.407	486	147	19	10	4	0.8	74	58	48	41	18	5	1	253	13	8	3	2.2	.971	OF-124
6 yrs.		322	.276	.371	990	273	35	19	7	0.7	142	116	101	97	23	56	13	463	22	16	7	2.0	.968	OF-249

Bob Didier

DIDIER, ROBERT DANIEL BB TR 6′ 190 lbs.
B. Feb. 16, 1949, Hattiesburg, Miss.

Year	Team	Games	BA	SA	AB	H	2B	3B	HR	HR%	R	RBI	BB	SO	SB	Pinch Hit AB	Pinch Hit H	PO	A	E	DP	TC/G	FA	G by Pos
1969	ATL N	114	.256	.307	352	90	16	1	0	0.0	30	32	34	39	1	0	0	633	52	4	3	6.0	.994	C-114
1970		57	.149	.173	168	25	2	1	0	0.0	9	7	12	11	1	0	0	297	25	4	3	5.7	.988	C-57
1971		51	.219	.258	155	34	4	1	0	0.0	9	5	6	17	0	2	1	230	24	0	2	5.1	1.000	C-50
1972		13	.300	.400	40	12	2	1	0	0.0	5	5	2	4	0	2	0	50	11	0	1	5.5	1.000	C-11
1973	DET A	7	.455	.500	22	10	1	0	0	0.0	3	1	3	0	0	0	0	38	5	0	2	6.1	1.000	C-7
1974	BOS A	5	.071	.071	14	1	0	0	0	0.0	0	1	2	1	0	0	0	28	2	1	0	6.2	.968	C-5
6 yrs.		247	.229	.273	751	172	25	4	0	0.0	56	51	59	72	2	4	1	1276	119	9	11	5.8	.994	C-244
LEAGUE CHAMPIONSHIP SERIES																								
1969	ATL N	3	.000	.000	11	0	0	0	0	0.0	0	0	0	2	0	0	0	24	1	0	1	8.3	1.000	C-3

Ernie Diehl

DIEHL, ERNEST GUY BR TR 6′ 1″ 190 lbs.
B. Oct. 2, 1877, Cincinnati, Ohio D. Nov. 6, 1958, Miami, Fla.

Year	Team	Games	BA	SA	AB	H	2B	3B	HR	HR%	R	RBI	BB	SO	SB	Pinch Hit AB	Pinch Hit H	PO	A	E	DP	TC/G	FA	G by Pos
1903	PIT N	1	.333	.333	3	1	0	0	0	0.0	0	0	0		0	0	0	0	0	0	0	0.0	.000	OF-1
1904		12	.162	.162	37	6	0	0	0	0.0	6	4	6		3	1	1	15	20	3	1	3.5	.921	OF-7, SS-4

Ernie Diehl *continued*

Year	Team	Games	BA	SA	AB	H	2B	3B	HR	HR%	R	RBI	BB	SO	SB	Pinch Hit AB	Pinch Hit H	PO	A	E	DP	TC/G	FA	G by Pos
1906	BOS N	3	.455	.636	11	5	0	1	0	0.0	1	0	0		0	0	0	5	1	0	0	2.0	1.000	OF-2, SS-1
1909		1	.500	.750	4	2	1	0	0	0.0	1	0	0		0	0	0	3	1	1	0	5.0	.800	OF-1
4 yrs.		17	.255	.309	55	14	1	1	0	0.0	8	4	6		3	1	1	23	22	4	1	3.1	.918	OF-11, SS-5

Chuck Diering

DIERING, CHARLES EDWARD ALLEN BR TR 5′10″ 165 lbs.
B. Feb. 5, 1923, St. Louis, Mo.

Year	Team	Games	BA	SA	AB	H	2B	3B	HR	HR%	R	RBI	BB	SO	SB	Pinch Hit AB	Pinch Hit H	PO	A	E	DP	TC/G	FA	G by Pos
1947	STL N	105	.216	.365	74	16	3	1	2	2.7	22	11	19	22	3	8	1	55	3	0	1	0.8	1.000	OF-75
1948		7	.000	.000	7	0	0	0	0	0.0	2	0	2	2	1	0	0	4	1	0	0	1.0	1.000	OF-5
1949		131	.263	.388	369	97	21	8	3	0.8	60	38	35	49	1	1	0	300	7	4	1	2.5	.987	OF-124
1950		89	.250	.353	204	51	12	0	3	1.5	34	18	35	38	1	0	0	178	8	2	2	2.3	.989	OF-81
1951		64	.259	.341	85	22	5	1	0	0.0	9	8	6	15	0	8	3	67	3	0	0	1.6	1.000	OF-44
1952	NY N	41	.174	.304	23	4	1	1	0	0.0	2	2	4	3	0	0	0	25	1	0	0	0.7	1.000	OF-36
1954	BAL A	128	.258	.311	418	108	14	1	2	0.5	35	29	56	57	3	6	2	330	17	6	6	3.0	.983	OF-119
1955		137	.256	.334	371	95	16	2	3	0.8	38	31	57	45	5	4	1	282	74	9	8	2.4	.975	OF-107, 3B-34, SS-12
1956		50	.186	.258	97	18	4	0	1	1.0	15	4	23	19	2	4	0	74	5	2	0	1.9	.975	OF-40, 3B-2
9 yrs.		752	.249	.338	1648	411	76	14	14	0.8	217	141	237	250	16	31	7	1315	119	23	18	2.1	.984	OF-631, 3B-36, SS-12

Bill Dietrick

DIETRICK, WILLIAM ALEXANDER BR TR 5′10″ 160 lbs.
B. Apr. 20, 1902, Hanover County, Va. D. May 6, 1946, Bethesda, Md.

Year	Team	Games	BA	SA	AB	H	2B	3B	HR	HR%	R	RBI	BB	SO	SB	Pinch Hit AB	Pinch Hit H	PO	A	E	DP	TC/G	FA	G by Pos
1927	PHI N	5	.167	.167	6	1	0	0	0	0.0	1	0	0	0	0	0	0	4	2	2	2	1.6	.750	SS-5
1928		52	.200	.260	100	20	6	0	0	0.0	13	7	17	10	1	15	5	50	19	2	2	2.4	.972	OF-21, SS-8
2 yrs.		57	.198	.255	106	21	6	0	0	0.0	14	7	17	10	1	15	5	54	21	4	4	2.3	.949	OF-21, SS-13

Dick Dietz

DIETZ, RICHARD ALLEN BR TR 6′ 1″ 195 lbs.
B. Sept. 18, 1941, Crawfordsville, Ind.

Year	Team	Games	BA	SA	AB	H	2B	3B	HR	HR%	R	RBI	BB	SO	SB	Pinch Hit AB	Pinch Hit H	PO	A	E	DP	TC/G	FA	G by Pos
1966	SF N	13	.043	.043	23	1	0	0	0	0.0	1	0	0	9	0	7	0	22	3	0	0	4.2	1.000	C-6
1967		56	.225	.350	120	27	3	0	4	3.3	10	19	25	44	0	15	4	206	19	4	1	5.3	.983	C-43
1968		98	.272	.392	301	82	14	2	6	2.0	21	38	34	68	1	12	6	497	37	13	10	6.1	.976	C-90
1969		79	.230	.406	244	56	8	1	11	4.5	28	35	53	53	0	2	2	432	31	13	5	6.5	.973	C-73
1970		148	.300	.515	493	148	36	2	22	4.5	82	107	109	106	0	9	1	820	58	14	9	6.4	.984	C-139
1971		142	.252	.419	453	114	19	0	19	4.2	58	72	97	86	1	9	4	712	37	14	4	5.7	.982	C-135
1972	LA N	27	.161	.232	56	9	1	0	1	1.8	4	6	14	11	2	7	0	104	12	0	1	5.3	1.000	C-22
1973	ATL N	83	.295	.432	139	41	8	1	3	2.2	22	24	49	25	0	18	6	325	29	6	19	6.4	.983	1B-36, C-20
8 yrs.		646	.261	.425	1829	478	89	6	66	3.6	226	301	381	402	4	79	23	3118	226	64	49	6.0	.981	C-528, 1B-36
LEAGUE CHAMPIONSHIP SERIES																								
1971	SF N	4	.067	.067	15	1	0	0	0	0.0	0	0	2	5	0	0	0	34	2	0	1	9.0	1.000	C-4

Roy Dietzel

DIETZEL, LEROY LOUIS BR TR 6′ 190 lbs.
B. Jan. 9, 1931, Baltimore, Md.

Year	Team	Games	BA	SA	AB	H	2B	3B	HR	HR%	R	RBI	BB	SO	SB	Pinch Hit AB	Pinch Hit H	PO	A	E	DP	TC/G	FA	G by Pos
1954	WAS A	9	.238	.238	21	5	0	0	0	0.0	1	1	5	4	0	0	0	10	16	1	4	3.0	.963	2B-7, 3B-2

Jay Difani

DIFANI, CLARENCE JOSEPH BR TR 6′ 170 lbs.
B. Dec. 21, 1923, Crystal City, Mo.

Year	Team	Games	BA	SA	AB	H	2B	3B	HR	HR%	R	RBI	BB	SO	SB	Pinch Hit AB	Pinch Hit H	PO	A	E	DP	TC/G	FA	G by Pos
1948	WAS A	2	.000	.000	2	0	0	0	0	0.0	0	0	0	2	0	2	0	0	0	0	0	0.0	—	
1949		2	1.000	2.000	1	1	1	0	0	0.0	0	0	0	0	0	1	1	0	1	0	0	1.0	1.000	2B-1
2 yrs.		4	.333	.667	3	1	1	0	0	0.0	0	0	0	2	0	3	1	0	1	0	0	1.0	1.000	2B-1

Steve Dignan

DIGNAN, STEPHEN E.
B. May 16, 1859, Boston, Mass. D. July 11, 1881, Boston, Mass.

Year	Team	Games	BA	SA	AB	H	2B	3B	HR	HR%	R	RBI	BB	SO	SB	Pinch Hit AB	Pinch Hit H	PO	A	E	DP	TC/G	FA	G by Pos
1880	2 teams BOS N (8G –.324) WOR N (3G –.300)																							
″	total	11	.318	.386	44	14	1	1	0	0.0	5	6	0	4		0	0	13	3	7	2	2.1	.696	OF-11

Don Dillard

DILLARD, DAVID DONALD BL TR 6′ 1″ 200 lbs.
B. Jan. 8, 1937, Greenville, S. C.

Year	Team	Games	BA	SA	AB	H	2B	3B	HR	HR%	R	RBI	BB	SO	SB	Pinch Hit AB	Pinch Hit H	PO	A	E	DP	TC/G	FA	G by Pos
1959	CLE A	10	.400	.400	10	4	0	0	0	0.0	0	1	0	2	0	10	4	0	0	0	0	0.0	—	
1960		6	.143	.143	7	1	0	0	0	0.0	0	0	1	3	0	5	1	0	0	0	0	0.0	.000	OF-1
1961		74	.272	.449	147	40	5	0	7	4.8	27	17	15	28	0	35	15	68	0	0	0	1.7	1.000	OF-39
1962		95	.230	.356	174	40	5	1	5	2.9	22	14	11	25	0	45	11	54	1	2	0	1.1	.965	OF-50
1963	MIL N	67	.235	.378	119	28	6	4	1	0.8	9	12	5	21	0	35	6	34	5	2	0	1.4	.951	OF-30
1965		20	.158	.316	19	3	0	0	1	5.3	1	3	0	6	0	19	3	0	0	0	0	0.0	.000	OF-1
6 yrs.		272	.244	.387	476	116	16	5	14	2.9	59	47	32	85	0	149	40	156	6	4	0	1.4	.976	OF-121

Pat Dillard

DILLARD, ROBERT LEE BL TR 6′ 180 lbs.
B. June 12, 1873, Chattanooga, Tenn. D. July 22, 1907, Denver, Colo.

Year	Team	Games	BA	SA	AB	H	2B	3B	HR	HR%	R	RBI	BB	SO	SB	Pinch Hit AB	Pinch Hit H	PO	A	E	DP	TC/G	FA	G by Pos
1900	STL N	57	.230	.279	183	42	5	2	0	0.0	24	12	13		7	8	1	76	51	16	2	2.9	.888	OF-26, 3B-21, SS-3

Steve Dillard

DILLARD, STEPHEN BRADLEY BR TR 6′ 1″ 171 lbs.
B. Feb. 8, 1951, Memphis, Tenn.

Year	Team	Games	BA	SA	AB	H	2B	3B	HR	HR%	R	RBI	BB	SO	SB	Pinch Hit AB	Pinch Hit H	PO	A	E	DP	TC/G	FA	G by Pos
1975	BOS A	1	.400	.400	5	2	0	0	0	0.0	2	0	0	0	1	0	0	5	4	0	1	9.0	1.000	2B-1
1976		57	.275	.377	167	46	14	0	1	0.6	22	15	17	20	6	3	1	58	102	11	21	3.2	.936	3B-18, 2B-17, SS-12, DH-7
1977		66	.241	.312	141	34	7	0	1	0.7	22	13	7	13	4	7	1	90	122	6	23	3.6	.972	2B-45, SS-9, DH-6
1978	DET A	56	.223	.292	130	29	5	2	0	0.0	21	7	6	11	1	1	0	88	118	9	31	4.8	.958	2B-41, DH-4
1979	CHI N	89	.283	.422	166	47	6	1	5	3.0	31	24	17	24	1	17	6	114	138	4	32	3.7	.984	2B-60, 3B-9
1980		100	.225	.316	244	55	8	1	4	1.6	31	27	20	54	2	13	3	92	171	14	19	3.0	.949	3B-51, 2B-38, SS-2
1981		53	.218	.345	119	26	7	1	2	1.7	18	11	8	20	0	11	3	59	96	6	22	3.9	.963	2B-32, 3B-7, SS-2
1982	CHI A	16	.171	.293	41	7	3	1	0	0.0	1	5	1	5	0	0	0	29	42	3	5	4.6	.959	2B-16
8 yrs.		438	.243	.343	1013	246	50	6	13	1.3	148	102	76	147	15	52	14	535	793	53	154	3.7	.962	2B-250, 3B-85, SS-25, DH-17

Pickles Dillhoefer

DILLHOEFER, WILLIAM MARTIN BR TR 5′ 7″ 154 lbs.
B. Oct. 13, 1894, Cleveland, Ohio D. Feb. 23, 1922, St. Louis, Mo.

Year	Team	Games	BA	SA	AB	H	2B	3B	HR	HR%	R	RBI	BB	SO	SB	Pinch Hit AB	Pinch Hit H	PO	A	E	DP	TC/G	FA	G by Pos
1917	CHI N	42	.126	.158	95	12	1	1	0	0.0	3	8	2	9	1	4	0	146	49	3	2	5.4	.985	C-37
1918	PHI N	8	.091	.091	11	1	0	0	0	0.0	0	0	1	1	2	2	0	9	3	1	0	2.2	.923	C-6
1919	STL N	45	.213	.278	108	23	3	2	0	0.0	11	12	8	6	5	1	1	122	35	5	6	4.2	.969	C-39
1920		76	.263	.326	224	59	8	3	0	0.0	26	13	13	7	2	2	0	291	72	18	6	5.2	.953	C-73
1921		76	.241	.315	162	39	4	4	0	0.0	19	15	11	7	2	4	0	170	52	11	0	3.4	.953	C-69
5 yrs.		247	.223	.283	600	134	16	10	0	0.0	59	48	35	30	12	13	1	738	211	38	14	4.4	.961	C-224

Bob Dillinger

DILLINGER, ROBERT BERNARD BR TR 5′11½″ 170 lbs.
B. Sept. 17, 1918, Glendale, Calif.

Year	Team	Games	BA	SA	AB	H	2B	3B	HR	HR%	R	RBI	BB	SO	SB	Pinch Hit AB	Pinch Hit H	PO	A	E	DP	TC/G	FA	G by Pos
1946	STL A	83	.280	.333	225	63	6	3	0	0.0	33	11	19	32	8	18	8	57	103	13	11	3.1	.925	3B-54, SS-1
1947		137	.294	.371	571	168	23	6	3	0.5	70	37	56	38	**34**	0	0	169	265	19	21	3.3	.958	3B-137
1948		153	.321	.415	644	**207**	34	10	2	0.3	110	44	65	34	**28**	1	0	187	242	20	30	2.9	.955	3B-153
1949		137	.324	.417	544	176	22	13	1	0.2	68	51	51	40	**20**	4	1	166	209	25	22	3.0	.938	3B-133
1950	2 teams	PHI A (84G –.309) PIT N (58G –.288)																						
″	total	142	.301	.410	578	174	29	11	4	0.7	78	50	44	42	9	5	0	152	289	20	31	3.4	.957	3B-135
1951	2 teams	PIT N (12G –.233) CHI A (89G –.301)																						
″	total	101	.292	.342	342	100	9	4	0	0.0	42	20	16	19	5	15	4	81	131	15	10	2.8	.934	3B-80
6 yrs.		753	.306	.391	2904	888	123	47	10	0.3	401	213	251	205	104	43	13	812	1239	112	125	3.1	.948	3B-692, SS-1

Pop Dillon

DILLON, FRANK EDWARD BL TR 6′ 1″ 185 lbs.
B. Oct. 17, 1873, Normal, Ill. D. Sept. 12, 1931, Pasadena, Calif.

Year	Team	Games	BA	SA	AB	H	2B	3B	HR	HR%	R	RBI	BB	SO	SB	Pinch Hit AB	Pinch Hit H	PO	A	E	DP	TC/G	FA	G by Pos
1899	PIT N	30	.256	.298	121	31	5	0	0	0.0	21	20	5		5	0	0	301	17	4	16	10.7	.988	1B-30
1900		5	.111	.167	18	2	1	0	0	0.0	3	1	0		0	0	0	47	5	1	2	10.6	.981	1B-5
1901	DET A	74	.288	.391	281	81	14	6	1	0.4	40	42	15		14	0	0	777	44	18	57	11.3	.979	1B-74
1902	2 teams	DET A (66G –.206) BAL A (2G –.286)																						
″	total	68	.208	.264	250	52	6	4	0	0.0	22	22	18		2	0	0	731	54	20	45	11.8	.975	1B-68
1904	BKN N	135	.258	.317	511	132	18	6	0	0.0	60	31	40		13	0	0	1304	99	25	56	10.7	.982	1B-134
5 yrs.		312	.252	.319	1181	298	44	16	1	0.1	146	116	78		34	0	0	3160	219	68	176	11.1	.980	1B-311

Miguel Dilone

DILONE, MIGUEL ANGEL BB TR 6′ 160 lbs.
Born Miguel Angel Dilone (Reyes).
B. Nov. 1, 1954, Santiago, Dominican Republic.

Year	Team	Games	BA	SA	AB	H	2B	3B	HR	HR%	R	RBI	BB	SO	SB	Pinch Hit AB	Pinch Hit H	PO	A	E	DP	TC/G	FA	G by Pos
1974	PIT N	12	.000	.000	2	0	0	0	0	0.0	3	0	1	0	2	2	0	1	0	0	0	0.5	1.000	OF-2
1975		18	.000	.000	6	0	0	0	0	0.0	8	0	0	1	2	1	0	3	0	0	0	1.5	1.000	OF-2
1976		16	.235	.235	17	4	0	0	0	0.0	7	0	0	0	5	4	0	11	0	0	0	3.7	1.000	OF-3
1977		29	.136	.136	44	6	0	0	0	0.0	5	0	2	3	12	10	1	21	1	0	0	1.3	1.000	OF-17
1978	OAK A	135	.229	.271	258	59	8	0	1	0.4	34	14	23	30	50	1	0	196	4	5	1	2.0	.976	OF-99, 3B-3, DH-1
1979	2 teams	OAK A (30G –.187) CHI N (43G –.306)																						
″	total	73	.220	.283	127	28	1	2	1	0.8	29	7	8	12	21	2	1	74	0	2	0	1.6	.974	OF-47
1980	CLE A	132	.341	.432	528	180	30	9	0	0.0	82	40	28	45	61	3	0	249	7	7	2	2.0	.973	OF-118, DH-11
1981		72	.290	.346	269	78	5	5	0	0.0	33	19	18	28	29	4	2	126	7	4	1	2.0	.971	OF-56, DH-11
1982		104	.235	.306	379	89	12	3	3	0.8	50	25	25	36	33	12	1	187	3	7	1	2.0	.964	OF-97, DH-1
1983	3 teams	CLE A (32G –.191) CHI A (4G –.000) PIT N (7G –.000)																						
″	total	43	.183	.254	71	13	3	1	0	0.0	17	7	10	5	8	4	0	47	0	0	0	2.0	1.000	OF-21, DH-2
1984	MON N	88	.278	.367	169	47	8	2	1	0.6	28	10	17	18	27	37	9	76	1	1	0	1.9	.987	OF-41
1985	2 teams	MON N (51G –.190) SD N (27G –.217)																						
″	total	78	.200	.246	130	26	0	3	0	0.0	18	7	10	19	17	29	4	57	2	3	0	1.7	.952	OF-36
12 yrs.		800	.265	.333	2000	530	67	25	6	0.3	314	129	142	197	267	109	18	1048	25	29	5	1.9	.974	OF-539, DH-26, 3B-3

Dom DiMaggio

DiMAGGIO, DOMINIC PAUL (The Little Professor) BR TR 5′ 9″ 168 lbs.
Brother of Vince DiMaggio. Brother of Joe DiMaggio.
B. Feb. 12, 1917, San Francisco, Calif.

Year	Team	Games	BA	SA	AB	H	2B	3B	HR	HR%	R	RBI	BB	SO	SB	Pinch Hit AB	Pinch Hit H	PO	A	E	DP	TC/G	FA	G by Pos
1940	BOS A	108	.301	.464	418	126	32	6	8	1.9	81	46	41	46	7	10	4	239	16	6	5	2.8	.977	OF-94
1941		144	.283	.408	584	165	37	6	8	1.4	117	58	90	57	13	0	0	386	16	15	2	2.9	.964	OF-144
1942		151	.286	.437	622	178	36	8	14	2.3	110	48	70	52	16	0	0	439	19	6	7	3.1	.987	OF-151
1946		142	.316	.427	534	169	24	7	7	1.3	85	73	66	58	10	0	0	390	9	6	2	2.9	.985	OF-142
1947		136	.283	.390	513	145	21	5	8	1.6	75	71	74	62	10	1	0	413	19	10	4	3.3	.977	OF-134
1948		155	.285	.401	**648**	185	40	4	9	1.4	127	87	101	58	10	0	0	503	13	10	4	3.4	.981	OF-155
1949		145	.307	.420	605	186	34	5	8	1.3	126	60	96	55	9	1	0	420	13	10	1	3.1	.977	OF-144
1950		141	.328	.452	588	193	30	**11**	7	1.2	**131**	70	82	68	**15**	1	1	390	15	7	2	2.9	.983	OF-140
1951		146	.296	.418	**639**	189	34	4	12	1.9	**113**	72	73	53	4	0	0	376	15	11	1	2.8	.973	OF-146
1952		128	.294	.377	486	143	20	1	6	1.2	81	33	57	61	6	5	2	303	12	8	4	2.6	.975	OF-123
1953		3	.333	.333	3	1	0	0	0	0.0	0	0	0	1	0	3	1	0	0	0	0	0.0	—	
11 yrs.		1399	.298	.419	5640	1680	308	57	87	1.5	1046	618	750	571	100	21	8	3859	147	89	32	3.0	.978	OF-1373
WORLD SERIES																								
1946	BOS A	7	.259	.370	27	7	3	0	0	0.0	2	3	2	2	0	0	0	19	3	0	1	3.1	1.000	OF-7

Joe DiMaggio

DiMAGGIO, JOSEPH PAUL (Joltin' Joe, The Yankee Clipper) BR TR 6′ 2″ 193 lbs.
Brother of Vince DiMaggio. Brother of Dom DiMaggio.
B. Nov. 25, 1914, Martinez, Calif.
Hall of Fame 1955.

Year	Team	Games	BA	SA	AB	H	2B	3B	HR	HR%	R	RBI	BB	SO	SB	Pinch Hit AB	Pinch Hit H	PO	A	E	DP	TC/G	FA	G by Pos
1936	NY A	138	.323	.576	637	206	44	**15**	29	4.6	132	125	24	39	4	0	0	339	22	8	2	2.7	.978	OF-138
1937		151	.346	**.673**	621	215	35	15	**46**	7.4	**151**	167	64	37	3	1	1	413	21	17	4	3.0	.962	OF-150
1938		145	.324	.581	599	194	32	13	32	5.3	129	140	59	21	6	0	0	366	20	15	4	2.8	.963	OF-145
1939		120	**.381**	.671	462	176	32	6	30	6.5	108	126	52	20	3	1	1	328	13	5	2	3.0	.986	OF-117
1940		132	**.352**	.626	508	179	28	9	31	6.1	93	133	61	30	1	2	1	359	5	8	2	2.9	.978	OF-130
1941		139	.357	.643	541	193	43	11	30	5.5	122	**125**	76	13	4	0	0	385	16	9	5	2.9	.978	OF-139
1942		154	.305	.498	610	186	29	13	21	3.4	123	114	68	36	4	0	0	409	10	8	3	2.8	.981	OF-154
1946		132	.290	.511	503	146	20	8	25	5.0	81	95	59	24	1	1	0	314	15	6	3	2.6	.982	OF-131

Joe DiMaggio *continued*

Year	Team	Games	BA	SA	AB	H	2B	3B	HR	HR%	R	RBI	BB	SO	SB	Pinch Hit AB	Pinch Hit H	PO	A	E	DP	TC/G	FA	G by Pos
1947		141	.315	.522	534	168	31	10	20	3.7	97	97	64	32	3	2	0	316	2	1	0	2.3	.997	OF-139
1948		153	.320	.598	594	190	26	11	**39**	**6.6**	110	**155**	67	30	1	1	1	441	8	13	1	3.0	.972	OF-152
1949		76	.346	.596	272	94	14	6	14	5.1	58	67	55	18	0	0	0	195	1	3	0	2.6	.985	OF-76
1950		139	.301	**.585**	525	158	33	10	32	6.1	114	122	80	33	0	1	0	376	9	9	1	2.9	.977	OF-137, 1B-1
1951		116	.263	.422	415	109	22	4	12	2.9	72	71	61	36	0	3	2	288	11	3	3	2.7	.990	OF-113
13 yrs.		1736	.325	.579	6821	2214	389	131	361	5.3	1390	1537	790	369	30	12	6	4529	153	105	30	2.8	.978	OF-1721, 1B-1
				6th																				
WORLD SERIES																								
1936	**NY A**	6	.346	.462	26	9	3	0	0	0.0	3	3	1	3	0	0	0	18	0	1	0	3.2	.947	OF-6
1937		5	.273	.409	22	6	0	0	1	4.5	2	4	0	3	0	0	0	18	0	0	0	3.6	1.000	OF-5
1938		4	.267	.467	15	4	0	0	1	6.7	4	2	1	1	0	0	0	10	0	0	0	2.5	1.000	OF-4
1939		4	.313	.500	16	5	0	0	1	6.3	3	3	1	1	0	0	0	11	0	0	0	2.8	1.000	OF-4
1941		5	.263	.263	19	5	0	0	0	0.0	1	1	2	2	0	0	0	19	0	0	0	3.8	1.000	OF-5
1942		5	.333	.333	21	7	0	0	0	0.0	3	3	0	1	0	0	0	20	0	0	0	4.0	1.000	OF-5
1947		7	.231	.462	26	6	0	0	2	7.7	4	5	6	2	0	0	0	22	0	0	0	3.1	1.000	OF-7
1949		5	.111	.278	18	2	0	0	1	5.6	2	2	3	5	0	0	0	7	0	0	0	1.4	1.000	OF-5
1950		4	.308	.615	13	4	1	0	1	7.7	2	2	3	1	0	0	0	8	0	0	0	2.0	1.000	OF-4
1951		6	.261	.478	23	6	2	0	1	4.3	3	5	2	4	0	0	0	17	0	0	0	2.8	1.000	OF-6
10 yrs.		51	.271	.422	199	54	6	0	8	4.0	27	30	19	23	0	0	0	150	0	1	0	3.0	.993	OF-51
		7th			**3rd**	**4th**			**7th**		**5th**	**5th**	**10th**	**10th**										

Vince DiMaggio

DiMAGGIO, VINCENT PAUL
Brother of Joe DiMaggio. Brother of Dom DiMaggio.
B. Sept. 6, 1912, Martinez, Calif. D. Oct. 3, 1986, North Hollywood, Calif.
BR TR 5′11″ 183 lbs.

Year	Team	Games	BA	SA	AB	H	2B	3B	HR	HR%	R	RBI	BB	SO	SB	Pinch Hit AB	Pinch Hit H	PO	A	E	DP	TC/G	FA	G by Pos
1937	**BOS N**	132	.256	.387	493	126	18	4	13	2.6	56	69	39	**111**	8	2	0	351	21	7	2	2.9	.982	OF-130
1938		150	.228	.369	540	123	28	3	14	2.6	71	61	65	**134**	11	0	0	419	19	12	10	3.0	.973	OF-149, 2B-1
1939	**CIN N**	8	.071	.143	14	1	1	0	0	0.0	1	2	2	10	0	1	0	11	1	0	1	1.7	1.000	OF-7
1940	**2 teams**	**CIN N** (2G –.250)	**PIT N** (110G –.289)																					
″	**total**	112	.289	.519	360	104	26	0	19	5.3	61	54	38	83	11	0	0	222	13	5	3	2.2	.979	OF-109
1941	**PIT N**	151	.267	.456	528	141	27	5	21	4.0	73	100	68	100	10	0	0	391	11	10	3	2.7	.976	OF-151
1942		143	.238	.385	496	118	22	3	15	3.0	57	75	52	**87**	10	4	1	383	20	9	5	3.0	.978	OF-138
1943		157	.248	.403	580	144	41	2	15	2.6	64	88	70	**126**	11	0	0	458	20	8	3	3.1	.984	OF-156, SS-1
1944		109	.240	.401	342	82	20	4	9	2.6	41	50	33	**83**	6	9	2	235	10	4	4	2.4	.984	OF-101, 3B-1
1945	**PHI N**	127	.257	.451	452	116	25	3	19	4.2	64	84	43	**91**	12	5	1	337	16	2	4	2.9	.994	OF-121
1946	**2 teams**	**PHI N** (6G –.211)	**NY N** (15G –.000)																					
″	**total**	21	.091	.114	44	4	1	0	0	0.0	3	1	2	12	0	1	0	39	0	1	0	2.1	.975	OF-19
10 yrs.		1110	.249	.413	3849	959	209	24	125	3.2	491	584	412	837	79	22	4	2846	131	58	35	2.8	.981	OF-1081, SS-1, 3B-1, 2B-1

Mike Dimmel

DIMMEL, MICHAEL WAYNE
B. Oct. 16, 1954, Albert Lea, Minn.
BR TR 6′ 180 lbs.

Year	Team	Games	BA	SA	AB	H	2B	3B	HR	HR%	R	RBI	BB	SO	SB	Pinch Hit AB	Pinch Hit H	PO	A	E	DP	TC/G	FA	G by Pos
1977	**BAL A**	25	.000	.000	5	0	0	0	0	0.0	8	0	0	1	1	0	0	14	1	0	0	0.7	1.000	OF-23
1978		8	—	—	0	0	0	0	0	—	2	0	0	0	0	0	0	2	0	1	0	0.4	.667	OF-7
1979	**STL N**	6	.333	.333	3	1	0	0	0	0.0	1	0	0	0	0	0	0	3	0	0	0	0.6	1.000	OF-5
3 yrs.		39	.125	.125	8	1	0	0	0	0.0	11	0	0	1	1	0	0	19	1	1	0	0.6	.952	OF-35

Kerry Dineen

DINEEN, KERRY MICHAEL
B. July 1, 1952, Englewood, N. J.
BL TL 5′11″ 165 lbs.

Year	Team	Games	BA	SA	AB	H	2B	3B	HR	HR%	R	RBI	BB	SO	SB	Pinch Hit AB	Pinch Hit H	PO	A	E	DP	TC/G	FA	G by Pos
1975	**NY A**	7	.364	.409	22	8	1	0	0	0.0	3	1	2	1	0	0	0	19	0	0	0	2.7	1.000	OF-7
1976		4	.286	.286	7	2	0	0	0	0.0	0	1	1	2	1	0	0	9	0	1	0	2.5	.900	OF-4
1978	**PHI N**	5	.250	.375	8	2	1	0	0	0.0	0	0	1	0	0	3	0	1	0	0	0	1.0	1.000	OF-1
3 yrs.		16	.324	.378	37	12	2	0	0	0.0	3	2	4	3	1	3	0	29	0	1	0	2.5	.967	OF-12

Vance Dinges

DINGES, VANCE GEORGE (George)
B. May 29, 1915, Elizabeth, N. J.
BL TL 6′2″ 175 lbs.

Year	Team	Games	BA	SA	AB	H	2B	3B	HR	HR%	R	RBI	BB	SO	SB	Pinch Hit AB	Pinch Hit H	PO	A	E	DP	TC/G	FA	G by Pos
1945	**PHI N**	109	.287	.353	397	114	15	4	1	0.3	46	36	35	17	5	2	1	527	34	8	41	5.3	.986	OF-65, 1B-42
1946		50	.308	.404	104	32	5	1	1	1.0	7	10	9	12	2	22	3	184	17	3	16	7.6	.985	1B-26, OF-1
2 yrs.		159	.291	.363	501	146	20	5	2	0.4	53	46	44	29	7	24	4	711	51	11	57	5.8	.986	1B-68, OF-66

Bill Dinneen

DINNEEN, WILLIAM HENRY (Big Bill)
B. Apr. 5, 1876, Syracuse, N. Y. D. Jan. 13, 1955, Syracuse, N. Y.
BR TR 6′1″ 190 lbs.

Year	Team	Games	BA	SA	AB	H	2B	3B	HR	HR%	R	RBI	BB	SO	SB	Pinch Hit AB	Pinch Hit H	PO	A	E	DP	TC/G	FA	G by Pos
1898	**WAS N**	32	.100	.125	80	8	0	1	0	0.0	10	3	9		1	1	0	6	50	5	1	2.0	.918	P-29, OF-2
1899		37	.303	.319	119	36	2	0	0	0.0	9	4	8		0	0	0	16	85	10	1	2.9	.910	P-37, OF-1
1900	**BOS N**	44	.280	.288	125	35	1	0	0	0.0	14	9	9		6	3	0	25	80	6	0	2.8	.946	P-40
1901		54	.211	.265	147	31	5	0	1	0.7	13	6	8		8	**11**	2	39	72	9	2	2.9	.925	P-37, OF-3, 1B-2
1902	**BOS A**	44	.128	.149	141	18	3	0	0	0.0	13	9	9		2	0	0	9	77	6	1	2.1	.935	P-42, OF-2
1903		37	.160	.198	106	17	2	1	0	0.0	6	8	11		1	0	0	11	79	2	4	2.5	.978	P-37
1904		37	.208	.225	120	25	0	1	0	0.0	9	9	3		5	0	0	19	98	4	3	3.3	.967	P-37
1905		31	.148	.170	88	13	2	0	0	0.0	6	4	2		4	0	0	11	77	6	3	3.0	.936	P-31
1906		28	.111	.143	63	7	0	1	0	0.0	5	2	8		2	0	0	10	58	7	1	2.7	.907	P-28
1907	**2 teams**	**BOS A** (5G –.000)	**STL A** (24G –.204)																					
″	**total**	29	.169	.220	59	10	1	1	0	0.0	5	3	6		0	0	0	5	46	3	1	1.9	.944	P-29
1908	**STL A**	27	.203	.220	59	12	1	0	0	0.0	4	1	2		0	0	0	3	44	1	1	1.8	.979	P-27
1909		17	.194	.222	36	7	1	0	0	0.0	6	2	5		0	0	0	6	34	1	1	2.4	.976	P-17
12 yrs.		417	.192	.219	1143	219	18	5	1	0.1	100	60	80		29	15	2	160	800	60	19	2.5	.941	P-391, OF-8, 1B-2
WORLD SERIES																								
1903	**BOS A**	4	.250	.250	12	3	0	0	0	0.0	1	0	1	2	0	0	0	1	9	0	0	2.5	1.000	P-4

Bob DiPietro

DiPIETRO, ROBERT LOUIS PAUL BR TR 5′11″ 185 lbs.
B. Sept. 1, 1927, San Francisco, Calif.

Year	Team	Games	BA	SA	AB	H	2B	3B	HR	HR%	R	RBI	BB	SO	SB	Pinch Hit AB	Pinch Hit H	PO	A	E	DP	TC/G	FA	G by Pos
1951	BOS A	4	.091	.091	11	1	0	0	0	0.0	0	0	1	1	0	0	0	4	1	1	1	2.0	.833	OF-3

Gary DiSarcina

DiSARCINA, GARY THOMAS BR TR 6′ 1″ 170 lbs.
B. Nov. 19, 1967, Malden, Mass.

Year	Team	Games	BA	SA	AB	H	2B	3B	HR	HR%	R	RBI	BB	SO	SB	Pinch Hit AB	Pinch Hit H	PO	A	E	DP	TC/G	FA	G by Pos
1989	CAL A	2	—	—	0	0	0	0	0	—	0	0	0	0	0	0	0	0	0	0	0	0.0	.000	SS-1
1990		18	.140	.193	57	8	1	1	0	0.0	8	0	3	10	1	1	0	17	57	4	9	4.6	.949	SS-14, 2B-3
1991		18	.211	.246	57	12	2	0	0	0.0	5	3	3	4	0	0	0	29	45	4	5	4.1	.949	SS-10, 2B-7, 3B-2
1992		157	.247	.301	518	128	19	0	3	0.6	48	42	20	50	9	1	0	250	486	25	109	4.8	.967	SS-157
1993		126	.238	.313	416	99	20	1	3	0.7	44	45	15	38	5	1	0	193	362	14	77	4.5	.975	SS-126
1994		112	.260	.329	389	101	14	2	3	0.8	53	33	18	28	3	2	1	160	359	9	66	4.8	.983	SS-110
1995		99	.307	.459	362	111	28	6	5	1.4	61	41	20	25	7	0	0	146	275	6	46	4.4	.986	SS-98
7 yrs.		532	.255	.336	1799	459	84	10	14	0.8	219	164	79	155	25	5	1	795	1584	62	312	4.6	.975	SS-516, 2B-10, 3B-2

Benny Distefano

DISTEFANO, BENITO JAMES BL TL 6′ 1″ 195 lbs.
B. Jan. 23, 1962, Brooklyn, N. Y.

Year	Team	Games	BA	SA	AB	H	2B	3B	HR	HR%	R	RBI	BB	SO	SB	Pinch Hit AB	Pinch Hit H	PO	A	E	DP	TC/G	FA	G by Pos
1984	PIT N	45	.167	.346	78	13	1	2	3	3.8	10	9	5	13	0	14	2	88	9	3	6	2.7	.970	OF-20, 1B-17
1986		31	.179	.282	39	7	1	0	1	2.6	3	5	1	5	0	20	3	13	0	0	0	1.3	1.000	OF-9, 1B-1
1988		16	.345	.621	29	10	3	1	1	3.4	6	6	3	4	0	8	3	41	3	0	1	6.3	1.000	1B-5, OF-2
1989		96	.247	.338	154	38	8	0	2	1.3	12	15	17	30	1	48	13	305	16	6	21	6.3	.982	1B-48, C-3, OF-1
1992	HOU N	52	.233	.300	60	14	0	2	0	0.0	4	7	5	14	0	32	6	39	3	0	4	2.3	1.000	OF-12, 1B-6
5 yrs.		240	.228	.350	360	82	13	5	7	1.9	35	42	31	66	1	122	27	486	31	9	32	4.2	.983	1B-77, OF-44, C-3

Dutch Distel

DISTEL, GEORGE ADAM BR TR 5′ 9″ 165 lbs.
B. Apr. 15, 1896, Madison, Ind. D. Feb. 12, 1967, Madison, Ind.

Year	Team	Games	BA	SA	AB	H	2B	3B	HR	HR%	R	RBI	BB	SO	SB	Pinch Hit AB	Pinch Hit H	PO	A	E	DP	TC/G	FA	G by Pos
1918	STL N	8	.176	.353	17	3	1	1	0	0.0	3	1	2	3	0	1	0	6	14	4	1	3.0	.833	2B-5, SS-2, OF-1

Jack Dittmer

DITTMER, JOHN DOUGLAS BL TR 6′ 1″ 175 lbs.
B. Jan. 10, 1928, Elkader, Iowa.

Year	Team	Games	BA	SA	AB	H	2B	3B	HR	HR%	R	RBI	BB	SO	SB	Pinch Hit AB	Pinch Hit H	PO	A	E	DP	TC/G	FA	G by Pos
1952	BOS N	93	.193	.291	326	63	7	2	7	2.1	26	41	26	26	1	3	0	228	267	9	60	5.6	.982	2B-90
1953	MIL N	138	.266	.367	504	134	22	1	9	1.8	54	63	18	35	1	0	0	290	343	23	95	4.8	.965	2B-138
1954		66	.245	.380	192	47	8	0	6	3.1	22	20	19	17	0	11	2	119	141	6	31	4.8	.977	2B-55
1955		38	.125	.208	72	9	1	1	1	1.4	4	4	4	15	0	11	1	44	42	2	9	3.1	.977	2B-28
1956		44	.245	.314	102	25	4	0	1	1.0	8	6	8	8	0	4	2	64	78	3	15	3.5	.979	2B-42
1957	DET A	16	.227	.273	22	5	1	0	0	0.0	3	2	2	1	0	12	4	4	4	0	0	2.0	1.000	3B-3, 2B-1
6 yrs.		395	.232	.333	1218	283	43	4	24	2.0	117	136	77	102	2	41	9	749	875	43	210	4.7	.974	2B-354, 3B-3

Moxie Divis

DIVIS, EDWARD GEORGE
B. 1894, Cleveland, Ohio D. Dec. 19, 1955, Lakewood, Ohio.

Year	Team	Games	BA	SA	AB	H	2B	3B	HR	HR%	R	RBI	BB	SO	SB	Pinch Hit AB	Pinch Hit H	PO	A	E	DP	TC/G	FA	G by Pos
1916	PHI A	3	.167	.167	6	1	0	0	0	0.0	0	0	0	2	0	2	0	1	0	0	0	1.0	1.000	OF-1

Leo Dixon

DIXON, LEO MOSES BR TR 5′11″ 170 lbs.
B. Sept. 4, 1894, Chicago, Ill. D. Apr. 11, 1984, Chicago, Ill.

Year	Team	Games	BA	SA	AB	H	2B	3B	HR	HR%	R	RBI	BB	SO	SB	Pinch Hit AB	Pinch Hit H	PO	A	E	DP	TC/G	FA	G by Pos
1925	STL A	76	.224	.302	205	46	11	1	1	0.5	27	19	24	42	3	0	0	233	70	6	8	4.1	.981	C-75
1926		33	.191	.247	89	17	3	1	0	0.0	7	8	11	14	1	0	0	101	29	3	3	4.0	.977	C-33
1927		36	.194	.243	103	20	3	1	0	0.0	6	12	7	6	0	1	0	116	32	10	1	4.5	.937	C-35
1929	CIN N	14	.167	.233	30	5	2	0	0	0.0	0	2	3	7	0	0	0	42	8	0	0	3.6	1.000	C-14
4 yrs.		159	.206	.272	427	88	19	3	1	0.2	40	41	45	69	4	1	0	492	139	19	12	4.1	.971	C-157

Dan Dobbek

DOBBEK, DANIEL JOHN BL TR 6′ 195 lbs.
B. Dec. 6, 1934, Ontonagon, Mich.

Year	Team	Games	BA	SA	AB	H	2B	3B	HR	HR%	R	RBI	BB	SO	SB	Pinch Hit AB	Pinch Hit H	PO	A	E	DP	TC/G	FA	G by Pos
1959	WAS A	16	.250	.383	60	15	1	2	1	1.7	8	5	5	13	0	0	0	29	1	0	0	1.9	1.000	OF-16
1960		110	.218	.387	248	54	8	2	10	4.0	32	30	35	41	4	32	5	141	5	4	1	1.9	.973	OF-78
1961	MIN A	72	.168	.304	125	21	3	1	4	3.2	12	14	13	18	1	23	3	64	1	1	0	1.4	.985	OF-48
3 yrs.		198	.208	.363	433	90	12	5	15	3.5	52	49	53	72	5	55	8	234	7	5	1	1.7	.980	OF-142

John Dobbs

DOBBS, JOHN GORDON BL TR 5′ 9½″ 170 lbs.
B. June 3, 1875, Chattanooga, Tenn. D. Sept. 9, 1934, Charlotte, N. C.

Year	Team	Games	BA	SA	AB	H	2B	3B	HR	HR%	R	RBI	BB	SO	SB	Pinch Hit AB	Pinch Hit H	PO	A	E	DP	TC/G	FA	G by Pos
1901	CIN N	109	.274	.345	435	119	17	4	2	0.5	71	27	36		19	1	0	196	22	17	5	2.2	.928	OF-100, 3B-8
1902	2 teams	CIN N (63G –.297) CHI N (59G –.302)																						
″	total	122	.299	.358	491	147	16	5	1	0.2	70	51	37		10	0	0	268	19	9	7	2.4	.970	OF-122
1903	2 teams	CHI N (16G –.230) BKN N (111G –.237)																						
″	total	127	.236	.316	475	112	16	8	2	0.4	69	63	55		23	1	1	278	12	9	4	2.4	.970	OF-126
1904	BKN N	101	.248	.303	363	90	16	2	0	0.0	36	30	28		11	3	0	207	19	16	1	2.5	.934	OF-92, SS-2, 2B-2
1905		123	.254	.330	460	117	21	4	2	0.4	59	36	31		15	0	0	246	11	17	1	2.2	.938	OF-123
5 yrs.		582	.263	.332	2224	585	86	23	7	0.3	305	207	187		78	5	1	1195	83	68	18	2.3	.949	OF-563, 3B-8, SS-2, 2B-2

Larry Doby

DOBY, LAWRENCE EUGENE BL TR 6′ 1″ 180 lbs.
B. Dec. 13, 1924, Camden, S. C.
Manager 1978.

Year	Team	Games	BA	SA	AB	H	2B	3B	HR	HR%	R	RBI	BB	SO	SB	Pinch Hit AB	Pinch Hit H	PO	A	E	DP	TC/G	FA	G by Pos
1947	CLE A	29	.156	.188	32	5	1	0	0	0.0	3	2	1	11	0	21	4	11	4	0	1	2.5	1.000	2B-4, SS-1, 1B-1
1948		121	.301	.490	439	132	23	9	14	3.2	83	66	54	77	9	6	2	287	12	14	3	2.7	.955	OF-114
1949		147	.280	.468	547	153	25	3	24	4.4	106	85	91	90	10	0	0	355	7	9	2	2.5	.976	OF-147
1950		142	.326	.545	503	164	25	5	25	5.0	110	102	98	71	8	2	1	367	2	5	1	2.7	.987	OF-140
1951		134	.295	.512	447	132	27	5	20	4.5	84	69	101	81	4	2	0	321	12	8	3	2.6	.977	OF-132
1952		140	.276	**.541**	519	143	26	8	**32**	6.2	**104**	104	90	**111**	5	3	1	398	11	6	3	3.1	.986	OF-136
1953		149	.263	.487	513	135	18	5	29	5.7	92	102	96	**121**	3	3	1	354	10	6	3	2.5	.984	OF-146
1954		153	.272	.484	577	157	18	4	**32**	5.5	94	**126**	85	94	3	0	0	411	14	2	6	2.8	.995	OF-153
1955		131	.291	.505	491	143	17	5	26	5.3	91	75	61	100	2	2	0	313	6	2	1	2.5	.994	OF-129
1956	CHI A	140	.268	.466	504	135	22	3	24	4.8	89	102	102	105	0	3	1	371	4	5	2	2.8	.987	OF-137

Larry Doby *continued*

Year	Team	Games	BA	SA	AB	H	2B	3B	HR	HR%	R	RBI	BB	SO	SB	Pinch Hit AB	Pinch Hit H	PO	A	E	DP	TC/G	FA	G by Pos
1957		119	.288	.464	416	120	27	2	14	3.4	57	79	56	79	2	9	1	255	3	4	0	2.4	.985	OF-110
1958	CLE A	89	.283	.490	247	70	10	1	13	5.3	41	45	26	49	0	18	5	141	5	0	0	2.1	1.000	OF-68
1959	2 teams	DET A (18G –.218) CHI A (21G –.241)																						
"	total	39	.230	.301	113	26	4	2	0	0.0	6	12	10	22	1	9	2	56	3	3	5	2.1	.952	OF-28, 1B-2
13 yrs.		1533	.283	.490	5348	1515	243	52	253	4.7	960	969	871	1011	47	78	18	3640	93	64	30	2.6	.983	OF-1440, 2B-4, 1B-3, SS-1
WORLD SERIES																								
1948	CLE A	6	.318	.500	22	7	1	0	1	4.5	1	2	2	4	0	0	0	11	0	1	0	2.0	.917	OF-6
1954		4	.125	.125	16	2	0	0	0	0.0	0	0	2	4	0	0	0	7	0	0	0	1.8	1.000	OF-4
2 yrs.		10	.237	.342	38	9	1	0	1	2.6	1	2	4	8	0	0	0	18	0	1	0	1.9	.947	OF-10

Ona Dodd

DODD, ORAN A.
B. Sept. 14, 1889, Bagwell, Tex. D. Mar. 31, 1929, Newport, Ark.
BR TR 5′8″ 150 lbs.

Year	Team	Games	BA	SA	AB	H	2B	3B	HR	HR%	R	RBI	BB	SO	SB	Pinch Hit AB	Pinch Hit H	PO	A	E	DP	TC/G	FA	G by Pos
1912	PIT N	5	.000	.000	9	0	0	0	0	0.0	0	1	1	3	0	0	0	1	5	0	1	1.5	1.000	2B-4

Tom Dodd

DODD, THOMAS MARION
B. Aug. 15, 1958, Portland, Ore.
BR TR 6′ 190 lbs.

Year	Team	Games	BA	SA	AB	H	2B	3B	HR	HR%	R	RBI	BB	SO	SB	Pinch Hit AB	Pinch Hit H	PO	A	E	DP	TC/G	FA	G by Pos
1986	BAL A	8	.231	.462	13	3	0	0	1	7.7	1	2	2	2	0	5	1	0	0	0	0	0.0		DH-6, 3B-1

John Dodge

DODGE, JOHN LEWIS
B. Apr. 27, 1889, Bolivar, Tenn. D. June 19, 1916, Mobile, Ala.
BR TR 5′11½″ 165 lbs.

Year	Team	Games	BA	SA	AB	H	2B	3B	HR	HR%	R	RBI	BB	SO	SB	Pinch Hit AB	Pinch Hit H	PO	A	E	DP	TC/G	FA	G by Pos
1912	PHI N	30	.120	.130	92	11	1	0	0	0.0	3	3	4	11	2	0	0	48	63	3	5	3.9	.974	3B-23, 2B-5, SS-1
1913	2 teams	PHI N (3G –.333) CIN N (94G –.241)																						
"	total	97	.242	.353	326	79	8	8	4	1.2	35	45	12	34	11	2	0	98	173	27	10	3.2	.909	3B-91, SS-3
2 yrs.		127	.215	.304	418	90	9	8	4	1.0	38	48	16	45	13	2	0	146	236	30	15	3.3	.927	3B-114, 2B-5, SS-4

Pat Dodson

DODSON, PATRICK NEAL
B. Oct. 11, 1959, Santa Monica, Calif.
BL TL 6′4″ 210 lbs.

Year	Team	Games	BA	SA	AB	H	2B	3B	HR	HR%	R	RBI	BB	SO	SB	Pinch Hit AB	Pinch Hit H	PO	A	E	DP	TC/G	FA	G by Pos
1986	BOS A	9	.417	.833	12	5	2	0	1	8.3	3	3	3	3	0	2	1	25	1	0	6	3.7	1.000	1B-7
1987		26	.167	.381	42	7	3	0	2	4.8	4	6	8	13	0	3	1	99	4	0	12	4.7	1.000	1B-21, DH-1
1988		17	.178	.356	45	8	3	1	1	2.2	5	1	6	17	0	2	0	87	12	0	7	5.8	1.000	1B-17
3 yrs.		52	.202	.424	99	20	8	1	4	4.0	12	10	17	33	0	7	2	211	17	0	25	5.0	1.000	1B-45, DH-1

Bobby Doerr

DOERR, ROBERT PERSHING
B. Apr. 7, 1918, Los Angeles, Calif.
Hall of Fame 1986.
BR TR 5′11″ 175 lbs.

Year	Team	Games	BA	SA	AB	H	2B	3B	HR	HR%	R	RBI	BB	SO	SB	Pinch Hit AB	Pinch Hit H	PO	A	E	DP	TC/G	FA	G by Pos
1937	BOS A	55	.224	.313	147	33	5	1	2	1.4	22	14	18	25	2	0	0	94	124	6	29	4.8	.973	2B-47
1938		145	.289	.397	509	147	26	7	5	1.0	70	80	59	39	5	0	0	372	420	26	118	5.6	.968	2B-145
1939		127	.318	.448	525	167	28	2	12	2.3	75	73	38	32	1	1	0	336	431	19	95	6.2	.976	2B-126
1940		151	.291	.497	595	173	37	10	22	3.7	87	105	57	53	10	0	0	401	480	21	118	6.0	.977	2B-151
1941		132	.282	.450	500	141	28	4	16	3.2	74	93	43	43	1	0	0	290	389	20	85	5.3	.971	2B-132
1942		144	.290	.455	545	158	35	5	15	2.8	71	102	67	55	4	2	0	376	453	21	105	6.0	.975	2B-142
1943		155	.270	.412	604	163	32	3	16	2.6	78	75	62	59	8	0	0	415	490	9	132	5.9	.990	2B-155
1944		125	.325	**.528**	468	152	30	10	15	3.2	95	81	58	31	5	0	0	341	363	17	96	5.8	.976	2B-125
1946		151	.271	.453	583	158	34	9	18	3.1	95	116	66	67	5	0	0	420	483	13	129	6.1	.986	2B-151
1947		146	.258	.426	561	145	23	10	17	3.0	79	95	59	47	3	0	0	376	466	16	118	5.9	.981	2B-146
1948		140	.285	.505	527	150	23	6	27	5.1	94	111	83	49	3	1	0	366	430	6	119	5.8	.993	2B-138
1949		139	.309	.497	541	167	30	9	18	3.3	91	109	75	33	2	0	0	395	439	17	134	6.1	.980	2B-139
1950		149	.294	.519	586	172	29	**11**	27	4.6	103	120	67	42	3	0	0	443	431	11	130	5.9	.988	2B-149
1951		106	.289	.448	402	116	21	2	13	3.2	60	73	57	33	2	0	0	303	311	12	99	5.9	.981	2B-106
14 yrs.		1865	.288	.461	7093	2042	381	89	223	3.1	1094	1247	809	608	54	4	0	4928	5710	214	1507	5.9	.980	2B-1852
WORLD SERIES																								
1946	BOS A	6	.409	.591	22	9	1	0	1	4.5	1	3	2	2	0	0	0	18	31	0	3	8.2	1.000	2B-6

John Doherty

DOHERTY, JOHN MICHAEL
B. Aug. 22, 1951, Woburn, Mass.
BL TL 5′11″ 185 lbs.

Year	Team	Games	BA	SA	AB	H	2B	3B	HR	HR%	R	RBI	BB	SO	SB	Pinch Hit AB	Pinch Hit H	PO	A	E	DP	TC/G	FA	G by Pos
1974	CAL A	74	.256	.368	223	57	14	1	3	1.3	20	15	8	13	2	9	1	538	30	5	55	8.0	.991	1B-70, DH-2
1975		30	.202	.266	94	19	3	0	1	1.1	7	12	8	12	1	2	1	216	14	4	20	8.7	.983	1B-26, DH-1
2 yrs.		104	.240	.338	317	76	17	1	4	1.3	27	27	16	25	3	11	2	754	44	9	75	8.2	.989	1B-96, DH-3

Biddy Dolan

DOLAN, LEON MARK
B. July 9, 1881, Onalaska, Wis. D. July 15, 1950, Indianapolis, Ind.
BR TR 6′

Year	Team	Games	BA	SA	AB	H	2B	3B	HR	HR%	R	RBI	BB	SO	SB	Pinch Hit AB	Pinch Hit H	PO	A	E	DP	TC/G	FA	G by Pos
1914	IND F	32	.223	.330	103	23	4	2	1	1.0	13	15	12		5	0	0	310	19	7	14	10.8	.979	1B-31

Cozy Dolan

DOLAN, ALBERT J.
Born James Alberts.
B. Dec. 23, 1889, Chicago, Ill. D. Dec. 10, 1958, Chicago, Ill.
BR TR 5′10″ 160 lbs.

Year	Team	Games	BA	SA	AB	H	2B	3B	HR	HR%	R	RBI	BB	SO	SB	Pinch Hit AB	Pinch Hit H	PO	A	E	DP	TC/G	FA	G by Pos
1909	CIN N	3	.167	.167	6	1	0	0	0	0.0	2	0	2		0	0	0	2	4	2	1	2.7	.750	3B-3
1911	NY A	19	.304	.420	69	21	1	2	1	1.4	19	6	8		12	0	0	21	33	3	4	3.0	.947	3B-19
1912	2 teams	NY A (17G –.200) PHI N (11G –.280)																						
"	total	28	.236	.355	110	26	3	5	0	0.0	23	18	6	10	8	0	0	28	49	18	2	3.4	.811	3B-24, SS-4
1913	2 teams	PHI N (55G –.262) PIT N (35G –.203)																						
"	total	90	.232	.282	259	60	9	2	0	0.0	37	17	16	35	23	13	3	88	111	22	12	3.1	.900	3B-39, OF-12, SS-10, 2B-9, 1B-1
1914	STL N	126	.240	.321	421	101	16	3	4	1.0	76	32	55	74	42	1	1	205	59	23	3	2.3	.920	OF-97, 3B-29
1915		111	.280	.398	322	90	14	9	2	0.6	53	38	34	37	17	3	1	179	4	14	0	2.0	.929	OF-98
1922	NY N	1	—	—	0	0	0	0	0	—	0	0	0	0	0	0	0	0	0	0	0	0.0	—	
7 yrs.		378	.252	.341	1187	299	43	21	7	0.6	210	111	121	156	102	17	5	523	260	82	22	2.5	.905	OF-207, 3B-114, SS-14, 2B-9, 1B-1

Cozy Dolan

DOLAN, PATRICK HENRY BL TL 5′10″ 160 lbs.
B. Dec. 3, 1872, Cambridge, Mass. D. Mar. 29, 1907, Louisville, Ky.

Year	Team	Games	BA	SA	AB	H	2B	3B	HR	HR%	R	RBI	BB	SO	SB	Pinch Hit AB	Pinch Hit H	PO	A	E	DP	TC/G	FA	G by Pos
1895	BOS N	26	.241	.313	83	20	4	1	0	0.0	12	7	6	7	3	0	0	14	62	5	2	3.1	.938	P-25, OF-1
1896		6	.143	.143	14	2	0	0	0	0.0	4	0	0	1	0	0	0	5	8	4	0	2.8	.765	P-6
1900	CHI N	13	.271	.292	48	13	1	0	0	0.0	5	2	2		2	0	0	18	1	4	0	1.8	.826	OF-13
1901	2 teams	CHI N (43G –.263) BKN N (66G –.261)																						
″	total	109	.262	.304	424	111	12	3	0	0.0	62	45	24		10	4	1	171	18	14	5	1.9	.931	OF-105
1902	BKN N	141	.280	.336	**592**	166	16	7	1	0.2	72	54	33		24	0	0	283	10	20	2	2.2	.936	OF-141
1903	2 teams	CHI A (27G –.260) CIN N (93G –.288)																						
″	total	120	.282	.350	489	138	25	4	0	0.0	80	65	34		16	4	0	341	27	16	9	3.3	.958	OF-97, 1B-19
1904	CIN N	129	.284	.383	465	132	8	10	6	1.3	88	51	39		19	3	0	356	29	16	10	3.2	.960	OF-102, 1B-24
1905	2 teams	CIN N (22G –.234) BOS N (112G –.275)																						
″	total	134	.269	.343	510	137	13	8	3	0.6	51	52	34		23	0	0	325	28	21	9	2.7	.944	OF-120, 1B-15, P-2
1906	BOS N	152	.248	.299	549	136	20	4	0	0.0	54	39	55		17	0	0	221	43	22	5	1.9	.923	OF-144, 2B-7, P-2, 1B-1
9 yrs.		830	.269	.333	3174	855	99	37	10	0.3	428	315	227	8	114	11	1	1734	226	122	42	2.5	.941	OF-723, 1B-59, P-35, 2B-7

Joe Dolan

DOLAN, JOSEPH TR 5′10½″ 155 lbs.
B. Feb. 24, 1873, Baltimore, Md. D. Mar. 24, 1938, Omaha, Neb.

Year	Team	Games	BA	SA	AB	H	2B	3B	HR	HR%	R	RBI	BB	SO	SB	Pinch Hit AB	Pinch Hit H	PO	A	E	DP	TC/G	FA	G by Pos
1896	LOU N	44	.212	.291	165	35	2	1	3	1.8	14	18	9	12	6	0	0	92	159	16	25	6.1	.940	SS-44
1897		36	.211	.256	133	28	2	2	0	0.0	10	7	8		6	0	0	84	113	26	14	6.2	.883	SS-18, 2B-18
1899	PHI N	61	.257	.324	222	57	6	3	1	0.5	27	30	11		3	0	0	113	190	28	10	5.4	.915	2B-61
1900		74	.198	.261	257	51	7	3	1	0.4	39	27	16		10	0	0	136	198	26	17	5.0	.928	3B-31, 2B-29, SS-12
1901	2 teams	PHI N (10G –.081) PHI A (98G –.216)																						
″	total	108	.203	.277	375	76	21	2	1	0.3	50	40	28		3	0	0	144	350	57	40	5.1	.897	SS-61, 3B-35, 2B-11, OF-1
5 yrs.		323	.214	.282	1152	247	38	11	6	0.5	140	122	72	12	28	0	0	569	1010	153	106	5.4	.912	SS-135, 2B-119, 3B-66, OF-1

Tom Dolan

DOLAN, THOMAS J. BR TR
B. Jan. 10, 1859, New York, N. Y. D. Jan. 16, 1913, St. Louis, Mo.

Year	Team	Games	BA	SA	AB	H	2B	3B	HR	HR%	R	RBI	BB	SO	SB	Pinch Hit AB	Pinch Hit H	PO	A	E	DP	TC/G	FA	G by Pos
1879	CHI N	1	.000	.000	4	0	0	0	0	0.0	0	0	0	2		0	0	6	2	0	0	8.0	1.000	C-1
1882	BUF N	22	.157	.180	89	14	0	1	0	0.0	12		2	11		0	0	72	28	8	1	4.5	.926	C-18, OF-4, 3B-2
1883	STL AA	81	.214	.268	295	63	9	2	1	0.3	32		9			0	0	269	63	23	6	4.3	.935	C-42, OF-40, P-1
1884	2 teams	STL AA (35G –.263) STL U (19G –.188)																						
″	total	54	.238	.301	206	49	9	2	0	0.0	28		10			0	0	298	81	54	4	7.9	.875	C-48, OF-4, 3B-3
1885	STL N	3	.222	.222	9	2	0	0	0	0.0	1	0	2	1		0	0	10	7	4	0	7.0	.810	C-3
1886	2 teams	STL N (15G –.250) BAL AA (38G –.152)																						
″	total	53	.178	.237	169	30	6	2	0	0.0	21	1	15	9		0	0	267	106	38	2	7.8	.908	C-50, OF-3
1888	STL AA	11	.194	.222	36	7	1	0	0	0.0	1	1	1		1	0	0	50	14	6	0	6.4	.914	C-11
7 yrs.		225	.204	.256	808	165	25	7	1	0.1	95	2	39	23	1	0	0	972	301	133	13	6.1	.905	C-173, OF-51, 3B-5, P-1

Frank Doljack

DOLJACK, FRANK JOSEPH BR TR 5′11″ 175 lbs.
B. Oct. 5, 1907, Cleveland, Ohio D. Jan. 23, 1948, Cleveland, Ohio.

Year	Team	Games	BA	SA	AB	H	2B	3B	HR	HR%	R	RBI	BB	SO	SB	Pinch Hit AB	Pinch Hit H	PO	A	E	DP	TC/G	FA	G by Pos
1930	DET A	20	.257	.473	74	19	5	1	3	4.1	10	17	2	11	0	0	0	38	2	3	1	2.2	.930	OF-20
1931		63	.278	.444	187	52	13	3	4	2.1	20	20	15	17	3	7	0	140	8	12	1	3.0	.925	OF-54
1932		8	.385	.538	26	10	1	0	1	3.8	5	7	2	2	1	1	0	6	0	0	0	1.0	1.000	OF-6
1933		42	.286	.347	147	42	5	2	0	0.0	18	22	14	13	2	5	1	74	6	5	3	2.3	.941	OF-37
1934		56	.233	.333	120	28	7	1	1	0.8	15	19	13	15	2	22	4	67	4	4	0	2.3	.947	OF-30, 1B-3
1943	CLE A	3	.000	.000	7	0	0	0	0	0.0	0	0	1	2	0	1	0	2	0	0	0	0.7	1.000	OF-3
6 yrs.		192	.269	.398	561	151	31	7	9	1.6	68	85	47	60	8	36	5	327	20	24	5	2.4	.935	OF-150, 1B-3
WORLD SERIES																								
1934	DET A	2	.000	.000	2	0	0	0	0	0.0	0	0	0	0	0	1	0	1	0	0	0	1.0	1.000	OF-1

Jiggs Donahue

DONAHUE, JOHN AUGUSTUS BL TL 6′ 1″ 178 lbs.
Brother of Pat Donahue.
B. July 13, 1879, Springfield, Ohio D. July 19, 1913, Columbus, Ohio.

Year	Team	Games	BA	SA	AB	H	2B	3B	HR	HR%	R	RBI	BB	SO	SB	Pinch Hit AB	Pinch Hit H	PO	A	E	DP	TC/G	FA	G by Pos
1900	PIT N	3	.200	.400	10	2	0	1	0	0.0	1	3	0		1	0	0	8	1	1	0	3.3	.900	C-2, OF-1
1901	2 teams	PIT N (2G –.000) MIL A (37G –.306)																						
″	total	39	.306	.426	108	33	5	4	0	0.0	10	16	10		4	5	0	186	30	17	8	6.9	.927	C-20, 1B-13, OF-1
1902	STL A	30	.236	.303	89	21	1	1	1	1.1	11	7	12		2	2	0	118	29	8	6	5.5	.948	C-23, 1B-5
1904	CHI A	102	.248	.319	367	91	9	7	1	0.3	46	48	25		18	1	1	1067	85	25	49	11.7	.979	1B-101
1905		149	.287	.349	533	153	22	4	1	0.2	71	76	44		32	0	0	1645	114	21	77	11.9	.988	1B-149
1906		154	.257	.318	556	143	17	7	1	0.2	70	57	48		36	0	0	1697	118	22	62	11.9	.988	1B-154
1907		157	.259	.307	**609**	158	16	5	1	0.2	75	68	28		27	0	0	1846	140	12	78	12.7	.994	1B-157
1908		93	.204	.243	304	62	8	2	0	0.0	22	22	25		14	10	1	968	57	6	30	12.4	.994	1B-83
1909	2 teams	CHI A (2G –.000) WAS A (84G –.237)																						
″	total	86	.233	.282	287	67	12	1	0	0.0	13	30	23		9	3	2	777	36	13	28	10.0	.984	1B-83
9 yrs.		813	.255	.314	2863	730	90	32	5	0.2	319	327	215		143	21	4	8312	610	125	338	11.4	.986	1B-745, C-45, OF-2
WORLD SERIES																								
1906	CHI A	6	.333	.556	18	6	2	1	0	0.0	0	4	3	4	0	0	0	79	8	1	3	14.7	.989	1B-6

Jim Donahue

DONAHUE, JAMES AUGUSTUS BR TR 6′ 175 lbs.
B. Jan. 8, 1862, Lockport, Ill. D. Apr. 19, 1935, Lockport, Ill.

Year	Team	Games	BA	SA	AB	H	2B	3B	HR	HR%	R	RBI	BB	SO	SB	Pinch Hit AB	Pinch Hit H	PO	A	E	DP	TC/G	FA	G by Pos
1886	NY AA	49	.199	.199	186	37	0	0	0	0.0	14		10			0	0	141	37	22	1	3.9	.890	OF-32, C-19
1887		60	.282	.323	220	62	4	1	1	0.5	33		21		6	0	0	258	95	51	3	6.5	.874	C-51, OF-5, 1B-4, 3B-1, 2B-1
1888	KC AA	88	.234	.294	337	79	11	3	1	0.3	29	28	21		12	0	0	320	122	51	10	5.4	.897	C-67, OF-18, 3B-5, 2B-1
1889		67	.234	.286	252	59	5	4	0	0.0	30	32	21	20	12	0	0	187	100	46	7	4.8	.862	C-46, OF-14, 3B-10
1891	COL AA	77	.218	.254	280	61	4	3	0	0.0	27	35	31	18	2	0	0	352	108	28	11	6.3	.943	C-75, OF-1, 1B-1
5 yrs.		341	.234	.275	1275	298	24	11	2	0.2	133	95	104	38	32	0	0	1258	462	198	32	5.5	.897	C-258, OF-70, 3B-16, 1B-5, 2B-2

John Donahue

DONAHUE, JOHN FREDERICK (Jiggs) BB TR 5′ 8″ 170 lbs.
B. Apr. 19, 1894, Roxbury, Mass. D. Oct. 3, 1949, Boston, Mass.

Year	Team	Games	BA	SA	AB	H	2B	3B	HR	HR%	R	RBI	BB	SO	SB	Pinch Hit AB	Pinch Hit H	PO	A	E	DP	TC/G	FA	G by Pos
1923	BOS A	10	.278	.389	36	10	4	0	0	0.0	5	1	4	5	0	1	1	21	4	0	1	2.8	1.000	OF-9

Pat Donahue

DONAHUE, PATRICK WILLIAM
Brother of Jiggs Donahue.
B. Nov. 3, 1884, Springfield, Ohio D. Jan. 31, 1966, Springfield, Ohio.
BR TR 6′ 175 lbs.

Year	Team	Games	BA	SA	AB	H	2B	3B	HR	HR%	R	RBI	BB	SO	SB	Pinch Hit AB	Pinch Hit H	PO	A	E	DP	TC/G	FA	G by Pos
1908	BOS A	35	.198	.256	86	17	2	0	1	1.2	8	6	9		0	0	0	143	37	7	2	5.3	.963	C-32, 1B-3
1909		64	.239	.307	176	42	4	1	2	1.1	14	25	17		2	6	2	249	71	6	3	5.6	.982	C-58
1910	3 teams	BOS A (2G –.000)	PHI A (15G –.162)	CLE A (2G –.000)																				
″	total	19	.133	.133	45	6	0	0	0	0.0	2	4	3		1	2	0	80	26	0	3	6.2	1.000	C-17
3 yrs.		118	.212	.267	307	65	6	1	3	1.0	24	35	29		3	8	2	472	134	13	8	5.6	.979	C-107, 1B-3

She Donahue

DONAHUE, CHARLES MICHAEL
B. June 29, 1877, Oswego, N. Y. D. Aug. 28, 1947, New York, N. Y.
BR TR 5′ 9″

Year	Team	Games	BA	SA	AB	H	2B	3B	HR	HR%	R	RBI	BB	SO	SB	Pinch Hit AB	Pinch Hit H	PO	A	E	DP	TC/G	FA	G by Pos
1904	2 teams	STL N (4G –.267)	PHI N (58G –.215)																					
″	total	62	.219	.237	215	47	4	0	0	0.0	22	16	3		10	0	0	114	116	38	11	4.3	.858	SS-30, 3B-24, 2B-5, 1B-3

Tim Donahue

DONAHUE, TIMOTHY CORNELIUS
B. June 8, 1870, Raynham, Mass. D. June 12, 1902, Taunton, Mass.
BL TR 5′11″ 180 lbs.

Year	Team	Games	BA	SA	AB	H	2B	3B	HR	HR%	R	RBI	BB	SO	SB	Pinch Hit AB	Pinch Hit H	PO	A	E	DP	TC/G	FA	G by Pos
1891	BOS AA	4	.000	.000	7	0	0	0	0	0.0	0	0	0	5	0	0	0	4	1	1	0	1.5	.833	C-4
1895	CHI N	63	.269	.347	219	59	9	1	2	0.9	29	36	20	25	5	0	0	234	45	26	8	4.8	.915	C-63
1896		57	.218	.282	188	41	10	1	0	0.0	27	20	11	15	11	0	0	235	60	20	7	5.5	.937	C-57
1897		58	.239	.309	188	45	7	3	0	0.0	28	21	9		3	1	1	222	68	17	2	5.3	.945	C-55, SS-2, 1B-1
1898		122	.220	.265	396	87	12	3	0	0.0	52	39	49		17	0	0	450	107	22	16	4.7	.962	C-122
1899		92	.248	.302	278	69	9	3	0	0.0	39	29	34		10	0	0	305	100	21	13	4.6	.951	C-91, 1B-1
1900		67	.236	.292	216	51	10	1	0	0.0	21	17	19		8	0	0	234	64	24	6	4.8	.925	C-66, 2B-1
1902	WAS A	3	.250	.250	8	2	0	0	0	0.0	0	1	0		0	0	0	8	3	0	0	3.7	1.000	C-3
8 yrs.		466	.236	.294	1500	354	57	12	2	0.1	196	163	142	45	54	1	1	1692	448	131	52	4.9	.942	C-461, SS-2, 1B-2, 2B-1

John Donaldson

DONALDSON, JOHN DAVID
B. May 5, 1943, Charlotte, N. C.
BL TR 5′11″ 160 lbs.

Year	Team	Games	BA	SA	AB	H	2B	3B	HR	HR%	R	RBI	BB	SO	SB	Pinch Hit AB	Pinch Hit H	PO	A	E	DP	TC/G	FA	G by Pos
1966	KC A	15	.133	.133	30	4	0	0	0	0.0	4	1	3	4	1	5	0	22	12	0	2	3.8	1.000	2B-9
1967		105	.276	.345	377	104	16	5	0	0.0	27	28	37	39	6	4	2	210	230	8	40	4.4	.982	2B-101, SS-1
1968	OAK A	127	.220	.273	363	80	9	2	2	0.6	37	27	45	44	5	26	6	178	271	13	49	4.4	.972	2B-98, 3B-5, SS-1
1969	2 teams	OAK A (12G –.077)	SEA A (95G –.234)																					
″	total	107	.228	.276	351	80	8	3	1	0.3	23	19	38	40	6	10	0	212	247	13	57	5.0	.972	2B-91, 3B-2, SS-1
1970	OAK A	41	.247	.326	89	22	2	1	1	1.1	4	11	9	6	1	13	6	31	66	1	9	3.5	.990	2B-21, SS-6, 3B-1
1974		10	.133	.133	15	2	0	0	0	0.0	1	0	0	0	0	1	0	11	14	1	5	2.6	.962	2B-7, 3B-3
6 yrs.		405	.238	.295	1225	292	35	11	4	0.3	96	86	132	133	19	59	14	664	840	36	162	4.4	.977	2B-327, 3B-11, SS-9

Len Dondero

DONDERO, LEONARD PETER (Mike)
B. Sept. 12, 1903, Newark, Calif.
BR TR 5′11″ 178 lbs.

Year	Team	Games	BA	SA	AB	H	2B	3B	HR	HR%	R	RBI	BB	SO	SB	Pinch Hit AB	Pinch Hit H	PO	A	E	DP	TC/G	FA	G by Pos
1929	STL A	19	.194	.290	31	6	0	0	1	3.2	2	8	0	4	0	4	0	8	10	2	1	1.3	.900	3B-10, 2B-5

Mike Donlin

DONLIN, MICHAEL JOSEPH (Highlonesome)
B. May 30, 1878, Peoria, Ill. D. Sept. 24, 1933, Hollywood, Calif.
BL TL 5′9″ 170 lbs.

Year	Team	Games	BA	SA	AB	H	2B	3B	HR	HR%	R	RBI	BB	SO	SB	Pinch Hit AB	Pinch Hit H	PO	A	E	DP	TC/G	FA	G by Pos
1899	STL N	66	.323	.470	266	86	9	6	6	2.3	49	27	17		20	0	0	215	25	29	7	3.8	.892	OF-51, 1B-13, SS-3, P-3
1900		78	.326	.507	276	90	8	6	10	3.6	40	48	14		14	10	**4**	308	11	21	14	5.0	.938	OF-47, 1B-21
1901	BAL A	121	.347	.481	476	165	23	13	5	1.1	107	67	53		33	1	1	614	36	26	21	5.6	.962	OF-74, 1B-47
1902	CIN N	34	.294	.392	143	42	4	5	0	0.0	30	9	9		9	1	0	60	6	9	1	2.2	.880	OF-32, SS-1, P-1
1903		126	.351	.516	496	174	25	18	7	1.4	110	67	56		26	2	1	275	20	28	7	2.6	.913	OF-118, 1B-7
1904	2 teams	CIN N (60G –.356)	NY N (42G –.280)																					
″	total	102	.329	.457	368	121	18	10	3	0.8	59	52	28		22	6	0	186	12	21	2	2.3	.904	OF-90, 1B-6
1905	NY N	150	.356	.495	606	216	31	16	7	1.2	**124**	80	56		33	0	0	250	17	19	4	1.9	.934	OF-150
1906		37	.314	.397	121	38	5	1	1	0.8	15	14	11		9	6	0	49	1	3	0	1.8	.943	OF-29, 1B-1
1908		155	.334	.452	593	198	26	13	6	1.0	71	106	23		30	0	0	239	21	6	1	1.7	.977	OF-155
1911	2 teams	NY N (12G –.333)	BOS N (56G –.315)																					
″	total	68	.316	.432	234	74	16	1	3	1.3	36	35	22	18	9	9	2	118	8	12	2	2.3	.913	OF-59
1912	PIT N	77	.316	.443	244	77	9	8	2	0.8	27	35	20	16	8	13	2	102	8	2	1	1.8	.982	OF-62
1914	NY N	35	.161	.355	31	5	1	1	1	3.2	1	3	3	5	0	31	5	0	0	0	0	0.0	—	
12 yrs.		1049	.334	.470	3854	1286	175	98	51	1.3	669	543	312	39	213	79	15	2416	165	176	60	2.8	.936	OF-867, 1B-95, SS-4, P-4
WORLD SERIES																								
1905	NY N	5	.316	.368	19	6	1	0	0	0.0	4	1	2	1	2	0	0	18	1	2	0	4.2	.905	OF-5

Jim Donnelly

DONNELLY, JAMES B.
B. July 19, 1865, New Haven, Conn. D. Mar. 15, 1915, New Haven, Conn.
BR TR

Year	Team	Games	BA	SA	AB	H	2B	3B	HR	HR%	R	RBI	BB	SO	SB	Pinch Hit AB	Pinch Hit H	PO	A	E	DP	TC/G	FA	G by Pos
1884	2 teams	KC U (6G –.130)	IND AA (40G –.254)																					
″	total	46	.236	.280	157	37	3	2	0	0.0	24		6			0	0	46	70	36	2	3.3	.763	3B-29, SS-8, OF-6, 2B-2, C-1
1885	DET N	56	.232	.294	211	49	4	3	1	0.5	24	22	10	29		0	0	86	103	32	4	3.9	.855	3B-55, 1B-1
1886	KC N	113	.201	.240	438	88	11	3	0	0.0	51	38	36	57		0	0	153	245	73	13	4.2	.845	3B-113
1887	WAS N	117	.200	.256	425	85	9	6	1	0.2	51	46	16	26	42	0	0	139	282	64	21	4.1	.868	3B-115, SS-2
1888		122	.201	.241	428	86	9	4	0	0.0	43	23	20	16	44	0	0	133	243	56	16	3.5	.870	3B-117, SS-5
1889		4	.154	.154	13	2	0	0	0	0.0	3	0	2	0	1	0	0	2	6	4	1	3.0	.667	3B-4
1890	STL AA	11	.333	.333	42	14	0	0	0	0.0	11		8		5	0	0	15	16	8	4	3.5	.795	3B-11
1891	COL AA	17	.241	.241	54	13	0	0	0	0.0	6	9	13	5	7	0	0	19	46	11	5	4.5	.855	3B-17
1896	BAL N	106	.328	.414	396	130	14	10	0	0.0	70	71	34	11	38	0	0	140	217	47	15	3.8	.884	3B-106
1897	2 teams	PIT N (44G –.193)	NY N (23G –.188)																					
″	total	67	.191	.220	246	47	7	0	0	0.0	41	25	25		20	0	0	69	122	20	3	3.1	.905	3B-67
1898	STL N	1	1.000	1.000	1	1	0	0	0	0.0	0	0	0		0	0	0	0	1	1	0	2.0	.500	3B-1
11 yrs.		660	.229	.278	2411	552	57	28	2	0.1	324	234	170	144	157	0	0	802	1351	352	84	3.8	.859	3B-635, SS-15, OF-6, 2B-2, 1B-1, C-1

Chris Donnels

DONNELS, CHRIS BARTON
B. Apr. 21, 1966, Los Angeles, Calif.
BL TR 6′ 185 lbs.

Year	Team	Games	BA	SA	AB	H	2B	3B	HR	HR%	R	RBI	BB	SO	SB	Pinch Hit AB	Pinch Hit H	PO	A	E	DP	TC/G	FA	G by Pos
1991	NY N	37	.225	.247	89	20	2	0	0	0.0	7	5	14	19	1	13	1	131	34	2	13	6.4	.988	1B-15, 3B-11
1992		45	.174	.207	121	21	4	0	0	0.0	8	6	17	25	1	4	0	34	77	5	6	2.8	.957	3B-29, 2B-12

Chris Donnels *continued*

Year	Team		Games	BA	SA	AB	H	2B	3B	HR	HR%	R	RBI	BB	SO	SB	Pinch Hit AB	Pinch Hit H	PO	A	E	DP	TC/G	FA	G by Pos
1993	HOU	N	88	.257	.391	179	46	14	2	2	1.1	18	24	19	33	2	34	7	169	54	8	21	4.2	.965	3B-31, 1B-23, 2B-1
1994			54	.267	.430	86	23	5	0	3	3.5	12	5	13	18	1	30	8	42	27	0	5	3.1	1.000	3B-14, 2B-4, 1B-4
1995	2 teams		HOU N (19G –.300) BOS A (40G –.253)																						
"	total		59	.264	.364	121	32	2	2	2	1.7	17	13	12	24	0	13	6	57	47	6	12	2.3	.945	3B-36, 1B-8, 2B-4
5 yrs.			283	.238	.332	596	142	27	4	7	1.2	62	53	75	119	5	94	22	433	239	21	57	3.6	.970	3B-121, 1B-50, 2B-21

Joe Donohue

DONOHUE, JOSEPH F.
B. 1869, Syracuse, N. Y. Deceased.

Year	Team		Games	BA	SA	AB	H	2B	3B	HR	HR%	R	RBI	BB	SO	SB	Pinch Hit AB	Pinch Hit H	PO	A	E	DP	TC/G	FA	G by Pos
1891	PHI	N	6	.318	.364	22	7	1	0	0	0.0	2	2	1	3	0	0	0	14	2	2	0	3.0	.889	OF-4, SS-2

Tom Donohue

DONOHUE, THOMAS JAMES BR TR 6′ 185 lbs.
B. Nov. 15, 1952, Mineola, N. Y.

Year	Team		Games	BA	SA	AB	H	2B	3B	HR	HR%	R	RBI	BB	SO	SB	Pinch Hit AB	Pinch Hit H	PO	A	E	DP	TC/G	FA	G by Pos
1979	CAL	A	38	.224	.355	107	24	3	1	3	2.8	13	14	3	29	2	0	0	136	16	3	4	4.1	.981	C-38
1980			84	.188	.243	218	41	4	1	2	0.9	18	14	7	63	5	0	0	330	29	5	5	4.3	.986	C-84
2 yrs.			122	.200	.280	325	65	7	2	5	1.5	31	28	10	92	7	0	0	466	45	8	9	4.3	.985	C-122

Fred Donovan

DONOVAN, FREDERICK MAURICE BR TR
B. July 4, 1864, Auburn, N. H. D. Mar. 7, 1916, Springfield, Ill.

Year	Team		Games	BA	SA	AB	H	2B	3B	HR	HR%	R	RBI	BB	SO	SB	Pinch Hit AB	Pinch Hit H	PO	A	E	DP	TC/G	FA	G by Pos
1895	CLE	N	3	.083	.083	12	1	0	0	0	0.0	1	1	1	2	0	0	0	13	2	1	1	5.3	.938	C-3

Jerry Donovan

DONOVAN, JEREMIAH FRANCIS BR TR
B. Sept. 3, 1876, Lock Haven, Pa. D. June 27, 1938, St. Petersburg, Fla.

Year	Team		Games	BA	SA	AB	H	2B	3B	HR	HR%	R	RBI	BB	SO	SB	Pinch Hit AB	Pinch Hit H	PO	A	E	DP	TC/G	FA	G by Pos
1906	PHI	N	61	.199	.223	166	33	4	0	0	0.0	11	15	6		2	7	1	222	52	13	4	5.3	.955	C-52, SS-1, OF-1

Mike Donovan

DONOVAN, MICHAEL BERCHMAN BR TR 5′ 8″ 155 lbs.
B. Oct. 18, 1881, Brooklyn, N. Y. D. Feb. 3, 1938, New York, N. Y.

Year	Team		Games	BA	SA	AB	H	2B	3B	HR	HR%	R	RBI	BB	SO	SB	Pinch Hit AB	Pinch Hit H	PO	A	E	DP	TC/G	FA	G by Pos
1904	CLE	A	2	.000	.000	2	0	0	0	0	0.0	0	0	0		0	1	0	0	0	0	0	0.0	.000	SS-1
1908	NY	A	5	.263	.316	19	5	1	0	0	0.0	2	2	0		0	0	0	13	9	0	0	4.4	1.000	3B-5
2 yrs.			7	.238	.286	21	5	1	0	0	0.0	2	2	0		0	1	0	13	9	0	0	3.7	1.000	3B-5, SS-1

Patsy Donovan

DONOVAN, PATRICK JOSEPH BL TL 5′11½″ 175 lbs.
B. Mar. 16, 1865, Queenstown, Ireland D. Dec. 25, 1953, Lawrence, Mass.
Manager 1897, 1899, 1901–04, 1906–08, 1910–11.

Year	Team		Games	BA	SA	AB	H	2B	3B	HR	HR%	R	RBI	BB	SO	SB	Pinch Hit AB	Pinch Hit H	PO	A	E	DP	TC/G	FA	G by Pos
1890	2 teams		BOS N (32G –.257) BKN N (28G –.219)																						
"	total		60	.241	.269	245	59	5	1	0	0.0	34	17	13	22	13	0	0	111	7	6	2	2.1	.952	OF-60
1891	2 teams		LOU AA (105G –.321) WAS AA (17G –.200)																						
"	total		122	.305	.350	509	155	11	3	2	0.4	82	56	34	23	28	0	0	236	17	26	1	2.3	.907	OF-122
1892	2 teams		WAS N (40G –.239) PIT N (90G –.294)																						
"	total		130	.278	.343	551	153	18	6	2	0.4	106	38	31	29	56	0	0	167	27	31	7	1.7	.862	OF-130
1893	PIT	N	113	.317	.371	499	158	5	8	2	0.4	114	56	42	8	46	1	0	178	16	13	5	1.8	.937	OF-112
1894			132	.302	.394	576	174	21	10	4	0.7	145	76	33	12	41	0	0	267	22	21	5	2.3	.932	OF-132
1895			125	.308	.370	519	160	17	6	1	0.2	114	58	47	19	36	0	0	187	11	8	2	1.6	.961	OF-125
1896			131	.319	.387	573	183	20	5	3	0.5	113	59	35	18	48	0	0	224	24	12	8	2.0	.954	OF-131
1897			120	.322	.384	479	154	16	7	0	0.0	82	57	25		34	0	0	186	17	11	5	1.8	.949	OF-120
1898			147	.302	.357	610	184	16	9	0	0.0	112	37	34		41	0	0	238	21	20	4	1.9	.928	OF-147
1899			121	.294	.347	531	156	11	7	1	0.2	82	55	17		26	0	0	184	9	12	3	1.7	.941	OF-121
1900	STL	N	126	.316	.342	503	159	11	1	0	0.0	78	61	38		**45**	2	1	180	13	10	4	1.6	.951	OF-124
1901			130	.292	.361	527	154	23	5	1	0.2	92	73	27		28	0	0	215	19	5	8	1.9	.979	OF-129
1902			126	.315	.355	502	158	12	4	0	0.0	70	35	28		34	0	0	179	30	9	6	1.7	.959	OF-126
1903			105	.327	.378	410	134	15	3	0	0.0	63	39	25		25	0	0	142	16	8	5	1.6	.952	OF-105
1904	WAS	A	125	.229	.243	436	100	6	0	0	0.0	30	19	24		17	3	0	217	15	9	4	2.0	.963	OF-122
1906	BKN	N	7	.238	.238	21	5	0	0	0	0.0	1	0	0		0	1	0	9	0	0	0	1.5	1.000	OF-6
1907			1	.000	.000	1	0	0	0	0	0.0	0	0	0		0	0	0	4	0	0	0	4.0	1.000	OF-1
17 yrs.			1821	.300	.354	7492	2246	207	75	16	0.2	1318	736	453	131	518	7	1	2924	264	201	69	1.9	.941	OF-1813

Tom Donovan

DONOVAN, THOMAS JOSEPH BR TR 6′ 2″ 168 lbs.
B. Jan. 1, 1873, West Troy, N. Y. D. Mar. 25, 1933, Watervliet, N. Y.

Year	Team		Games	BA	SA	AB	H	2B	3B	HR	HR%	R	RBI	BB	SO	SB	Pinch Hit AB	Pinch Hit H	PO	A	E	DP	TC/G	FA	G by Pos
1901	CLE	A	18	.254	.324	71	18	3	1	0	0.0	9	5	0		1	0	0	21	6	4	0	1.6	.871	OF-18, P-1

Wild Bill Donovan

DONOVAN, WILLIAM EDWARD BB TR 5′11″ 190 lbs.
B. Oct. 13, 1876, Lawrence, Mass. D. Dec. 9, 1923, Forsyth, N. Y.
Manager 1915–17, 1921.

Year	Team		Games	BA	SA	AB	H	2B	3B	HR	HR%	R	RBI	BB	SO	SB	Pinch Hit AB	Pinch Hit H	PO	A	E	DP	TC/G	FA	G by Pos
1898	WAS	N	39	.165	.272	103	17	2	3	1	1.0	11	8	4		2	2	1	45	22	8	6	1.9	.893	OF-20, P-17, SS-1, 2B-1
1899	BKN	N	5	.231	.308	13	3	1	0	0	0.0	2	0	0		0	0	0	1	5	1	0	1.4	.857	P-5
1900			5	.000	.000	13	0	0	0	0	0.0	0	2	0		0	0	0	0	12	0	0	2.4	1.000	P-5
1901			46	.170	.237	135	23	3	0	2	1.5	16	13	8		1	0	0	14	75	7	5	2.1	.927	P-45
1902			48	.168	.230	161	27	3	2	1	0.6	16	16	9		7	0	0	117	81	7	5	4.3	.966	P-35, 1B-8, OF-4, 2B-1
1903	DET	A	40	.242	.298	124	30	3	2	0	0.0	11	12	4		3	2	0	26	71	8	3	2.7	.924	P-35, SS-2, 2B-1, OF-1
1904			46	.271	.321	140	38	2	1	1	0.7	12	6	3		2	2	1	80	89	7	3	4.1	.960	P-34, 1B-8, OF-1
1905			46	.192	.223	130	25	4	0	0	0.0	16	5	12		8	0	0	28	73	7	3	2.5	.935	P-34, OF-8, 2B-2
1906			28	.121	.143	91	11	0	1	0	0.0	5	0	1		6	0	0	17	65	5	1	3.0	.943	P-25, 2B-3, OF-1
1907			37	.266	.367	109	29	7	2	0	0.0	20	19	6		4	4	0	13	56	4	0	2.3	.945	P-32
1908			30	.159	.171	82	13	1	0	0	0.0	5	2	10		2	0	0	16	39	5	0	2.1	.917	P-29
1909			22	.200	.200	45	9	0	0	0	0.0	6	1	2		0	0	0	9	29	1	1	1.9	.974	P-21
1910			26	.145	.159	69	10	1	0	0	0.0	6	2	5		0	0	0	9	33	2	2	1.7	.955	P-26
1911			24	.200	.333	60	12	3	1	1	1.7	11	6	11		1	1	1	4	25	2	0	1.5	.935	P-20
1912			6	.077	.077	13	1	0	0	0	0.0	3	0	1		0	0	0	5	1	1	0	1.0	.857	P-3, 1B-2, OF-2

Wild Bill Donovan *continued*

Year	Team	Games	BA	SA	AB	H	2B	3B	HR	HR%	R	RBI	BB	SO	SB	Pinch Hit AB	Pinch Hit H	PO	A	E	DP	TC/G	FA	G by Pos
1915	NY A	10	.083	.083	12	1	0	0	0	0.0	1	0	1	6	0	0	0	1	7	0	0	0.9	1.000	P-9
1916		1	—	—	0	0	0	0	0	—	0	0	0	0	0	0	0	0	0	0	0	0.0	.000	P-1
1918	DET A	2	.500	.500	2	1	0	0	0	0.0	1	1	0	0	0	0	0	0	1	0	0	0.5	1.000	P-2
18 yrs.		461	.192	.247	1302	250	30	12	6	0.5	142	93	77	6	36	11	3	385	684	65	29	2.6	.943	P-378, OF-37, 1B-18, 2B-8, SS-3
WORLD SERIES																								
1907	DET A	2	.000	.000	8	0	0	0	0	0.0	0	0	0	3	0	0	0	3	3	0	0	3.0	1.000	P-2
1908		2	.000	.000	4	0	0	0	0	0.0	0	0	1	1	1	0	0	1	2	1	0	2.0	.750	P-2
1909		2	.000	.000	4	0	0	0	0	0.0	0	0	0	1	0	0	0	0	5	1	0	3.0	.833	P-2
3 yrs.		6	.000	.000	16	0	0	0	0	0.0	0	0	1	5	1	0	0	4	10	2	0	2.7	.875	P-6

Red Dooin

DOOIN, CHARLES SEBASTIAN
B. June 12, 1879, Cincinnati, Ohio D. May 12, 1952, Rochester, N. Y.
Manager 1910–14.
BR TR 5′ 9½″ 165 lbs.

Year	Team	Games	BA	SA	AB	H	2B	3B	HR	HR%	R	RBI	BB	SO	SB	Pinch Hit AB	Pinch Hit H	PO	A	E	DP	TC/G	FA	G by Pos
1902	PHI N	94	.231	.270	333	77	7	3	0	0.0	20	35	10		8	4	1	443	117	30	10	6.6	.949	C-84, OF-6
1903		62	.218	.255	188	41	5	1	0	0.0	18	14	8		9	**9**	3	190	82	17	2	5.5	.941	C-51, OF-1, 1B-1
1904		108	.242	.346	355	86	11	4	6	**1.7**	41	36	8		15	5	0	447	154	41	12	6.2	.936	C-96, 1B-4, OF-3, 3B-1
1905		113	.250	.311	380	95	13	5	0	0.0	45	36	10		12	5	3	505	152	24	9	6.3	.965	C-107, 3B-1
1906		113	.245	.305	351	86	19	1	0	0.0	25	32	13		15	6	1	475	111	32	9	5.8	.948	C-107
1907		101	.211	.262	313	66	8	4	0	0.0	18	14	15		10	5	1	439	125	24	14	6.1	.959	C-94, 2B-1, OF-1
1908		133	.248	.306	435	108	17	4	0	0.0	28	41	17		20	1	0	554	191	26	17	5.8	.966	C-132
1909		141	.224	.271	468	105	14	1	2	0.4	42	38	21		14	1	0	517	199	40	14	5.4	.947	C-140
1910		103	.242	.305	331	80	13	4	0	0.0	30	30	22	17	10	8	3	473	131	28	14	6.7	.956	C-91, OF-3
1911		74	.328	.409	247	81	15	1	1	0.4	18	16	14	12	6	0	0	436	97	18	5	7.4	.967	C-74
1912		69	.234	.283	184	43	9	0	0	0.0	20	22	5	12	8	8	1	254	69	14	2	5.8	.958	C-58
1913		55	.256	.302	129	33	4	1	0	0.0	6	13	3	9	1	5	2	194	57	10	7	5.2	.962	C-50
1914		53	.178	.220	118	21	2	0	1	0.8	10	8	4	14	4	8	2	151	52	7	4	5.3	.967	C-40
1915	2 teams	CIN N (10G –.323) NY N (46G –.218)																						
"	total	56	.239	.277	155	37	2	2	0	0.0	11	9	5	20	1	0	0	227	55	13	4	5.3	.956	C-56
1916	NY N	15	.118	.118	17	2	0	0	0	0.0	1	0	0	3	0	0	0	30	5	1	0	2.4	.972	C-15
15 yrs.		1290	.240	.298	4004	961	139	31	10	0.2	333	344	155	87	133	65	17	5335	1597	325	123	6.0	.955	C-1195, OF-14, 1B-5, 3B-2, 2B-1

Mickey Doolan

DOOLAN, MICHAEL JOSEPH
Born Michael Joseph Doolittle.
B. May 7, 1880, Ashland, Pa. D. Nov. 1, 1951, Orlando, Fla.
BR TR 5′10½″ 170 lbs.

Year	Team	Games	BA	SA	AB	H	2B	3B	HR	HR%	R	RBI	BB	SO	SB	Pinch Hit AB	Pinch Hit H	PO	A	E	DP	TC/G	FA	G by Pos
1905	PHI N	136	.254	.360	492	125	27	11	1	0.2	53	48	24		17	1	0	299	432	51	45	5.8	.935	SS-135
1906		154	.230	.297	535	123	19	7	1	0.2	41	55	27		16	0	0	395	480	66	51	6.1	.930	SS-154
1907		145	.204	.275	509	104	19	7	1	0.2	33	47	25		18	0	0	327	463	60	59	5.9	.929	SS-145
1908		129	.234	.321	445	104	25	4	2	0.4	29	49	17		5	0	0	269	419	45	32	5.7	.939	SS-129
1909		147	.219	.290	493	108	12	10	1	0.2	39	35	37		10	0	0	352	484	54	58	6.1	.939	SS-147
1910		148	.263	.354	536	141	31	6	2	0.4	58	57	35	56	16	0	0	283	500	43	71	5.6	.948	SS-148
1911		146	.238	.313	512	122	23	6	1	0.2	51	49	44	65	14	1	0	295	474	53	68	5.7	.936	SS-145
1912		146	.258	.335	532	137	26	6	1	0.2	47	62	34	59	6	0	0	289	476	40	49	5.5	.950	SS-146
1913		151	.218	.270	518	113	12	6	1	0.2	32	43	29	68	17	0	0	347	494	52	63	5.9	.942	SS-148, 2B-3
1914	BAL F	145	.245	.323	486	119	23	6	1	0.2	58	53	40		30	0	0	305	476	42	55	5.7	.949	SS-145
1915	2 teams	BAL F (119G –.186) CHI F (24G –.267)																						
"	total	143	.200	.273	490	98	14	8	2	0.4	50	30	26		15	0	0	349	481	52	72	6.2	.941	SS-143
1916	2 teams	CHI N (28G –.214) NY N (18G –.235)																						
"	total	46	.223	.322	121	27	5	2	1	0.8	8	8	10	11	1	3	0	78	123	14	14	5.1	.935	SS-40, 2B-2
1918	BKN N	92	.179	.218	308	55	8	2	0	0.0	14	18	22	24	8	0	0	230	283	17	37	5.8	.968	2B-91
13 yrs.		1728	.230	.306	5977	1376	244	81	15	0.3	513	554	370	283	173	5	0	3818	5585	589	674	5.8	.941	SS-1625, 2B-96

Jack Dooms

DOOMS, HENRY E. (Harry)
B. Jan. 30, 1867, St. Louis, Mo. D. Dec. 14, 1899, St. Louis, Mo.

Year	Team	Games	BA	SA	AB	H	2B	3B	HR	HR%	R	RBI	BB	SO	SB	Pinch Hit AB	Pinch Hit H	PO	A	E	DP	TC/G	FA	G by Pos
1892	LOU N	1	.000	.000	4	0	0	0	0	0.0	0	0	1	3	0	0	0	0	0	1	0	1.0	.000	OF-1

Bill Doran

DORAN, WILLIAM DONALD
B. May 28, 1958, Cincinnati, Ohio.
BB TR 5′11″ 175 lbs.

Year	Team	Games	BA	SA	AB	H	2B	3B	HR	HR%	R	RBI	BB	SO	SB	Pinch Hit AB	Pinch Hit H	PO	A	E	DP	TC/G	FA	G by Pos
1982	HOU N	26	.278	.309	97	27	3	0	0	0.0	11	6	4	11	5	0	0	41	78	3	17	4.7	.975	2B-26
1983		154	.271	.364	535	145	12	7	8	1.5	70	39	86	67	12	3	1	347	461	17	109	5.4	.979	2B-153
1984		147	.261	.356	548	143	18	11	4	0.7	92	41	66	69	21	2	0	274	440	12	90	4.8	.983	2B-139, SS-13
1985		148	.287	.434	578	166	31	6	14	2.4	84	59	71	69	23	2	1	345	440	16	108	5.4	.980	2B-147
1986		145	.276	.373	550	152	29	3	6	1.1	92	37	81	57	42	1	0	262	329	16	62	4.2	.974	2B-144
1987		162	.283	.406	625	177	23	3	16	2.6	82	79	82	64	31	0	0	300	432	7	70	4.5	.991	2B-162, SS-3
1988		132	.248	.333	480	119	18	1	7	1.5	66	53	65	60	17	2	1	260	371	8	73	4.9	.987	2B-130
1989		142	.219	.323	507	111	25	2	8	1.6	65	58	59	63	22	8	0	254	345	12	64	4.4	.980	2B-138
1990	2 teams	HOU N (109G –.288) CIN N (17G –.373)																						
"	total	126	.300	.434	403	121	29	2	7	1.7	59	37	79	58	23	9	2	198	306	8	49	4.5	.984	2B-111, 3B-4
1991	CIN N	111	.280	.374	361	101	12	2	6	1.7	51	35	46	39	5	15	4	183	208	7	50	4.1	.982	2B-88, OF-6, 1B-4
1992		132	.235	.349	387	91	16	2	8	2.1	48	47	64	40	7	14	1	306	249	5	60	4.3	.991	2B-104, 1B-25
1993	MIL A	28	.217	.283	60	13	4	0	0	0.0	7	6	6	3	1	10	2	44	28	2	7	3.5	.973	2B-17, 1B-4
12 yrs.		1453	.266	.373	5131	1366	220	39	84	1.6	727	497	709	600	209	66	12	2814	3687	113	759	4.7	.983	2B-1359, 1B-33, SS-16, OF-6, 3B-4
LEAGUE CHAMPIONSHIP SERIES																								
1986	HOU N	6	.222	.333	27	6	0	0	1	3.7	3	3	2	2	2	0	0	10	17	0	1	4.5	1.000	2B-6

Bill Doran

DORAN, WILLIAM JAMES
B. June 14, 1900, San Francisco, Calif. D. Mar. 9, 1978, Santa Monica, Calif.
BL TR 5′11½″ 175 lbs.

Year	Team	Games	BA	SA	AB	H	2B	3B	HR	HR%	R	RBI	BB	SO	SB	Pinch Hit AB	Pinch Hit H	PO	A	E	DP	TC/G	FA	G by Pos
1922	CLE A	3	.500	.500	2	1	0	0	0	0.0	0	0	1	0	0	0	0	0	0	0	0	0.0	.000	3B-2

Tom Doran

DORAN, THOMAS J. BL TR 5′11″ 152 lbs.
B. Dec. 2, 1880, Westchester County, N. Y. D. June 22, 1910, New York, N. Y.

Year	Team	Games	BA	SA	AB	H	2B	3B	HR	HR%	R	RBI	BB	SO	SB	Pinch Hit AB	Pinch Hit H	PO	A	E	DP	TC/G	FA	G by Pos
1904	BOS A	12	.125	.188	32	4	0	1	0	0.0	1	0	4		1	1	0	39	5	5	1	4.5	.898	C-11
1905	2 teams	BOS A (2G –.000) DET A (34G –.160)																						
″	total	36	.156	.188	96	15	3	0	0	0.0	8	4	8		2	3	1	125	34	6	0	5.0	.964	C-33
1906	BOS A	2	.000	.000	3	0	0	0	0	0.0	1	0	0		0	0	0	3	1	0	0	2.0	1.000	C-2
3 yrs.		50	.145	.183	131	19	3	1	0	0.0	10	4	12		3	4	1	167	40	11	1	4.7	.950	C-46

Jerry Dorgan

DORGAN, JEREMIAH F. BL TR 165 lbs.
Brother of Mike Dorgan.
B. 1856, Meriden, Conn. D. June 10, 1891, New Haven, Conn.

Year	Team	Games	BA	SA	AB	H	2B	3B	HR	HR%	R	RBI	BB	SO	SB	Pinch Hit AB	Pinch Hit H	PO	A	E	DP	TC/G	FA	G by Pos
1880	WOR N	10	.200	.229	35	7	1	0	0	0.0	2	1	0	1		0	0	16	2	4	0	2.2	.818	OF-9, C-1
1882	PHI AA	44	.282	.343	181	51	9	1	0	0.0	25		4			0	0	159	30	30	1	4.6	.863	C-25, OF-22, 3B-1
1884	2 teams	IND AA (34G –.298) BKN AA (4G –.308)																						
″	total	38	.299	.351	154	46	6	1	0	0.0	24		2			0	0	82	23	16	1	3.2	.868	OF-29, C-9
1885	DET N	39	.286	.348	161	46	6	2	0	0.0	23	24	8	10		0	0	55	5	10	2	1.8	.857	OF-39
4 yrs.		131	.282	.339	531	150	22	4	0	0.0	74	25	14	11		0	0	312	60	60	4	3.2	.861	OF-99, C-35, 3B-1

Mike Dorgan

DORGAN, MICHAEL CORNELIUS BR TR 5′ 9″ 180 lbs.
Brother of Jerry Dorgan.
B. Oct. 2, 1853, Middletown, Conn. D. Apr. 26, 1909, Hartford, Conn.
Manager 1879–81.

Year	Team	Games	BA	SA	AB	H	2B	3B	HR	HR%	R	RBI	BB	SO	SB	Pinch Hit AB	Pinch Hit H	PO	A	E	DP	TC/G	FA	G by Pos
1877	STL N	60	.308	.395	266	82	9	7	0	0.0	45	23	9	13		0	0	118	21	29	3	2.5	.827	OF-50, C-12, 3B-2, SS-1, 2B-1
1879	SYR N	59	.267	.356	270	72	11	5	1	0.4	38	17	4	13		0	0	275	60	46	10	6.2	.879	1B-21, OF-16, 3B-11, SS-6, C-4, P-2, 2B-1
1880	PRO N	79	.246	.283	321	79	10	1	0	0.0	45	31	10	18		0	0	98	28	24	4	1.9	.840	OF-77, 3B-2, P-1
1881	2 teams	WOR N (51G –.277) DET N (8G –.235)																						
″	total	59	.272	.295	254	69	6	0	0	0.0	41	23	9	4		0	0	367	25	26	13	7.1	.938	OF-28, 1B-27, 3B-2, SS-2
1883	NY N	64	.234	.299	261	61	11	3	0	0.0	32		2	23		0	0	108	11	22	1	2.1	.844	OF-59, C-6, P-1
1884		83	.276	.352	341	94	11	6	1	0.3	61		13	27		0	0	153	52	49	4	2.9	.807	OF-64, P-14, C-6, 2B-3
1885		89	.326	.421	347	113	17	8	0	0.0	60		11	24		0	0	153	11	16	6	2.0	.911	OF-88, 1B-1
1886		118	.292	.369	442	129	19	3	3	0.7	61	79	29	37		0	0	174	14	22	5	1.8	.895	OF-116, 1B-3
1887		71	.258	.293	283	73	10	0	0	0.0	41	34	15	20	22	0	0	140	6	20	1	2.3	.880	OF-69, 1B-2
1890	SYR AA	33	.216	.273	139	30	8	0	0	0.0	19		16		8	0	0	40	5	5	1	1.5	.900	OF-33
10 yrs.		715	.274	.340	2924	802	112	33	5	0.2	443	207	118	179	30	0	0	1626	233	259	48	2.9	.878	OF-600, 1B-54, C-28, P-18, 3B-17, SS-9, 2B-5

Charlie Dorman

DORMAN, CHARLES WILLIAM BR TR 6′ 2″ 185 lbs.
B. Apr. 23, 1898, San Francisco, Calif. D. Nov. 15, 1928, San Francisco, Calif.

Year	Team	Games	BA	SA	AB	H	2B	3B	HR	HR%	R	RBI	BB	SO	SB	Pinch Hit AB	Pinch Hit H	PO	A	E	DP	TC/G	FA	G by Pos
1923	CHI A	1	.500	.500	2	1	0	0	0	0.0	0	0	0	0	0	0	0	1	1	0	0	2.0	1.000	C-1

Red Dorman

DORMAN, DWIGHT DEXTER BR TR 5′10½″ 180 lbs.
B. Oct. 3, 1905, Jacksonville, Ill. D. July 7, 1974, Anaheim, Calif.

Year	Team	Games	BA	SA	AB	H	2B	3B	HR	HR%	R	RBI	BB	SO	SB	Pinch Hit AB	Pinch Hit H	PO	A	E	DP	TC/G	FA	G by Pos
1928	CLE A	25	.364	.442	77	28	6	0	0	0.0	12	11	9	6	1	1	1	53	1	5	1	2.5	.915	OF-24

Brian Dorsett

DORSETT, BRIAN RICHARD BR TR 6′ 3″ 215 lbs.
B. Apr. 9, 1961, Terre Haute, Ind.

Year	Team	Games	BA	SA	AB	H	2B	3B	HR	HR%	R	RBI	BB	SO	SB	Pinch Hit AB	Pinch Hit H	PO	A	E	DP	TC/G	FA	G by Pos
1987	CLE A	5	.273	.545	11	3	0	0	1	9.1	2	3	0	3	0	2	1	12	0	0	0	3.0	1.000	C-4
1988	CAL A	7	.091	.091	11	1	0	0	0	0.0	0	2	1	5	0	0	0	19	3	0	1	3.1	1.000	C-7
1989	NY A	8	.364	.409	22	8	1	0	0	0.0	3	4	1	3	0	0	0	29	3	0	1	4.0	1.000	C-8
1990		14	.143	.200	35	5	2	0	0	0.0	2	0	2	4	0	2	0	31	0	0	1	2.2	1.000	C-9, DH-5
1991	SD N	11	.083	.083	12	1	0	0	0	0.0	0	1	0	3	0	10	1	4	1	0	0	2.5	1.000	1B-2
1993	CIN N	25	.254	.413	63	16	4	0	2	3.2	7	12	3	14	0	8	2	119	5	0	0	5.9	1.000	C-18, 1B-3
1994		76	.245	.352	216	53	8	0	5	2.3	21	26	21	33	0	8	3	413	34	4	2	6.1	.991	C-73, 1B-1
7 yrs.		146	.235	.341	370	87	15	0	8	2.2	35	48	28	65	0	30	7	627	46	4	5	5.2	.994	C-119, 1B-6, DH-5

Jerry Dorsey

DORSEY, JEREMIAH BL TL 5′11″ 175 lbs.
B. 1885, Oakland, Calif. Deceased.

Year	Team	Games	BA	SA	AB	H	2B	3B	HR	HR%	R	RBI	BB	SO	SB	Pinch Hit AB	Pinch Hit H	PO	A	E	DP	TC/G	FA	G by Pos
1911	PIT N	2	.000	.000	6	0	0	0	0	0.0	0	0	0	1	0	1	0	4	0	0	0	4.0	1.000	OF-1

Jerry Dorsey

DORSEY, MICHAEL JEREMIAH
B. 1854 D. Nov. 3, 1938, Auburn, N. Y.

Year	Team	Games	BA	SA	AB	H	2B	3B	HR	HR%	R	RBI	BB	SO	SB	Pinch Hit AB	Pinch Hit H	PO	A	E	DP	TC/G	FA	G by Pos
1884	BAL U	1	.000	.000	3	0	0	0	0	0.0	0		0			0	0	0	1	0	0	0.5	1.000	P-1, OF-1

Herm Doscher

DOSCHER, JOHN HENRY, SR. BR TR 5′10″ 182 lbs.
Father of Jack Doscher.
B. Dec. 20, 1852, New York, N. Y. D. Mar. 20, 1934, Buffalo, N. Y.

Year	Team	Games	BA	SA	AB	H	2B	3B	HR	HR%	R	RBI	BB	SO	SB	Pinch Hit AB	Pinch Hit H	PO	A	E	DP	TC/G	FA	G by Pos
1879	2 teams	TRO N (47G –.220) CHI N (3G –.182)																						
″	total	50	.218	.257	202	44	8	0	0	0.0	17	19	2	13		0	0	51	101	38	7	3.8	.800	3B-50
1881	CLE N	5	.211	.211	19	4	0	0	0	0.0	2	0	0	2		0	0	7	10	2	1	3.8	.895	3B-5
1882		25	.240	.260	104	25	2	0	0	0.0	7	10	0	11		0	0	38	45	13	3	3.8	.865	3B-22, OF-2, SS-1
3 yrs.		80	.225	.255	325	73	10	0	0	0.0	26	29	2	26		0	0	96	156	53	11	3.8	.826	3B-77, OF-2, SS-1

Dutch Dotterer

DOTTERER, HENRY JOHN BR TR 6′ 209 lbs.
B. Nov. 11, 1931, Syracuse, N. Y.

Year	Team	Games	BA	SA	AB	H	2B	3B	HR	HR%	R	RBI	BB	SO	SB	Pinch Hit AB	Pinch Hit H	PO	A	E	DP	TC/G	FA	G by Pos
1957	CIN N	4	.083	.083	12	1	0	0	0	0.0	0	2	1	2	0	1	0	17	0	0	0	4.3	1.000	C-4
1958		11	.250	.393	28	7	1	0	1	3.6	1	2	2	4	0	3	0	48	4	1	2	6.6	.981	C-8
1959		52	.267	.348	161	43	7	0	2	1.2	21	17	16	23	0	1	0	230	20	2	3	4.9	.992	C-51
1960		33	.228	.367	79	18	5	0	2	2.5	4	11	13	10	0	3	1	122	15	3	1	4.5	.979	C-31
1961	WAS A	7	.263	.368	19	5	2	0	0	0.0	1	1	3	5	0	0	0	26	8	0	0	4.9	1.000	C-7
5 yrs.		107	.247	.348	299	74	15	0	5	1.7	27	33	35	44	0	8	1	443	47	6	6	4.9	.988	C-101

Charlie Dougherty

DOUGHERTY, CHARLES WILLIAM
B. Feb. 7, 1862, Darlington, Wis. D. Feb. 18, 1925, Milwaukee, Wis.

Year	Team	Games	BA	SA	AB	H	2B	3B	HR	HR%	R	RBI	BB	SO	SB	Pinch Hit AB	Pinch Hit H	PO	A	E	DP	TC/G	FA	G by Pos
1884	ALT U	23	.259	.318	85	22	5	0	0	0.0	6		2			0	0	61	47	17	2	5.0	.864	2B-16, OF-8, SS-1

Patsy Dougherty

DOUGHERTY, PATRICK HENRY
B. Oct. 27, 1876, Andover, N. Y. D. Apr. 30, 1940, Bolivar, N. Y.
BL TR 6′ 2″ 190 lbs.

Year	Team	Games	BA	SA	AB	H	2B	3B	HR	HR%	R	RBI	BB	SO	SB	Pinch Hit AB	Pinch Hit H	PO	A	E	DP	TC/G	FA	G by Pos
1902	BOS A	108	.342	.397	438	150	12	6	0	0.0	77	34	42		20	3	2	175	9	21	1	2.0	.898	OF-102, 3B-1
1903		139	.331	.424	**590**	**195**	19	12	4	0.7	**108**	59	33		35	0	0	259	16	14	3	2.1	.952	OF-139
1904	2 teams	BOS A (49G –.272) NY A (106G –.283)																						
"	total	155	.280	.379	**647**	181	18	14	6	0.9	**113**	26	44		21	0	0	230	18	20	4	1.7	.925	OF-155
1905	NY A	116	.263	.335	418	110	9	6	3	0.7	56	29	28		17	5	1	173	11	21	2	1.9	.898	OF-108, 3B-1
1906	2 teams	NY A (12G –.192) CHI A (75G –.233)																						
"	total	87	.226	.298	305	69	11	4	1	0.3	33	31	19		11	0	0	141	13	2	2	1.8	.987	OF-86
1907	CHI A	148	.270	.315	533	144	17	2	1	0.2	69	59	36		33	0	0	209	19	13	4	1.6	.946	OF-148
1908		138	.278	.326	482	134	11	6	0	0.0	68	45	58		**47**	9	2	173	7	10	1	1.4	.947	OF-138
1909		139	.285	.391	491	140	23	13	1	0.2	71	55	51		36	1	0	184	10	12	0	1.5	.942	OF-138
1910		127	.248	.300	443	110	8	6	1	0.2	45	43	41		22	3	1	158	9	14	2	1.5	.923	OF-121
1911		76	.289	.422	211	61	10	9	0	0.0	39	32	26		19	19	3	78	6	6	1	1.6	.933	OF-56
10 yrs.		1233	.284	.360	4558	1294	138	78	17	0.4	679	413	378		261	40	9	1780	118	133	20	1.7	.935	OF-1191, 3B-2
WORLD SERIES																								
1903	BOS A	8	.235	.529	34	8	0	2	2	5.9	3	5	2	5	0	0	0	15	3	1	1	2.4	.947	OF-8
1906	CHI A	6	.100	.100	20	2	0	0	0	0.0	1	1	3	3	2	0	0	4	0	1	0	0.8	.800	OF-6
2 yrs.		14	.185	.370	54	10	0	2	2	3.7	4	6	5	8	2	0	0	19	3	2	1	1.7	.917	OF-14

John Douglas

DOUGLAS, JOHN FRANKLIN
B. Sept. 14, 1917, Thayer, W. Va. D. Feb. 11, 1984, Miami, Fla.
BL TL 6′ 2½″ 195 lbs.

Year	Team	Games	BA	SA	AB	H	2B	3B	HR	HR%	R	RBI	BB	SO	SB	Pinch Hit AB	Pinch Hit H	PO	A	E	DP	TC/G	FA	G by Pos
1945	BKN N	5	.000	.000	9	0	0	0	0	0.0	0	0	2	4	0	1	0	33	0	1	1	8.5	.971	1B-4

Astyanax Douglass

DOUGLASS, ASTYANAX SAUNDERS
B. Sept. 19, 1899, Covington, Tex. D. Jan. 26, 1975, El Paso, Tex.
BL TR 6′ 1″ 190 lbs.

Year	Team	Games	BA	SA	AB	H	2B	3B	HR	HR%	R	RBI	BB	SO	SB	Pinch Hit AB	Pinch Hit H	PO	A	E	DP	TC/G	FA	G by Pos
1921	CIN N	4	.143	.143	7	1	0	0	0	0.0	1	0	0	1	0	0	0	6	3	0	0	2.3	1.000	C-4
1925		7	.176	.176	17	3	0	0	0	0.0	1	1	1	3	0	0	0	10	6	2	0	2.6	.889	C-7
2 yrs.		11	.167	.167	24	4	0	0	0	0.0	2	1	1	4	0	0	0	16	9	2	0	2.5	.926	C-11

Klondike Douglass

DOUGLASS, WILLIAM BINGHAM
B. May 10, 1872, Boston, Pa. D. Dec. 13, 1953, Bend, Ore.
BL TR 6′ 200 lbs.

Year	Team	Games	BA	SA	AB	H	2B	3B	HR	HR%	R	RBI	BB	SO	SB	Pinch Hit AB	Pinch Hit H	PO	A	E	DP	TC/G	FA	G by Pos
1896	STL N	81	.264	.321	296	78	6	4	1	0.3	42	28	35	15	18	1	0	123	22	15	5	2.0	.906	OF-74, C-6, SS-2
1897		125	.329	.405	516	170	15	3	6	1.2	77	50	52		12	1	1	393	80	21	10	3.8	.957	C-61, OF-43, 1B-17, 3B-7, SS-1
1898	PHI N	146	.258	.326	582	150	26	4	2	0.3	105	48	55		18	0	0	1236	73	32	74	9.2	.976	1B-146
1899		77	.255	.320	275	70	6	6	0	0.0	26	27	10		7	1	0	207	83	9	8	4.0	.970	C-66, 3B-4, 1B-4, OF-1
1900		50	.300	.406	160	48	9	4	0	0.0	23	25	13		7	2	1	138	59	14	4	4.3	.934	C-47, 3B-2
1901		51	.324	.370	173	56	6	1	0	0.0	14	23	11		10	3	0	252	30	5	4	5.9	.983	C-41, 1B-6, OF-2
1902		109	.233	.277	408	95	12	3	0	0.0	37	37	23		6	1	0	802	65	19	28	8.2	.979	1B-69, C-29, OF-10
1903		105	.255	.297	377	96	5	4	1	0.3	43	36	28		6	5	1	902	51	15	41	10.0	.985	1B-97
1904		3	.300	.300	10	3	0	0	0	0.0	1	1	0		0	0	0	31	1	1	1	11.0	.970	1B-3
9 yrs.		747	.274	.336	2797	766	85	29	10	0.4	368	275	227	15	84	14	3	4084	464	131	175	6.3	.972	1B-342, C-250, OF-130, 3B-13, SS-3

Taylor Douthit

DOUTHIT, TAYLOR LEE
B. Apr. 22, 1901, Little Rock, Ark. D. May 28, 1986, Fremont, Calif.
BR TR 5′11½″ 175 lbs.

Year	Team	Games	BA	SA	AB	H	2B	3B	HR	HR%	R	RBI	BB	SO	SB	Pinch Hit AB	Pinch Hit H	PO	A	E	DP	TC/G	FA	G by Pos
1923	STL N	9	.185	.333	27	5	0	2	0	0.0	3	0	0	4	1	2	0	12	1	0	0	1.9	1.000	OF-7
1924		53	.277	.364	173	48	13	1	0	0.0	24	13	16	19	4	1	0	118	5	3	2	2.5	.976	OF-50
1925		30	.274	.384	73	20	3	1	1	1.4	13	8	2	6	0	9	5	50	1	1	0	2.5	.981	OF-21
1926		139	.308	.377	530	163	20	4	3	0.6	96	52	55	46	23	1	0	440	14	20	2	3.4	.958	OF-138
1927		130	.262	.377	488	128	29	6	5	1.0	81	50	52	45	6	4	2	396	8	15	4	3.4	.964	OF-125
1928		154	.295	.372	648	191	35	3	3	0.5	111	43	84	36	11	0	0	547	10	9	4	3.7	.984	OF-154
1929		150	.336	.471	613	206	42	7	9	1.5	128	62	79	49	8	0	0	442	8	12	1	3.1	.974	OF-150
1930		154	.303	.426	**664**	201	41	10	7	1.1	109	93	60	38	4	0	0	425	8	16	3	2.9	.964	OF-154
1931	2 teams	STL N (36G –.331) CIN N (95G –.262)																						
"	total	131	.280	.337	507	142	20	3	1	0.2	63	45	53	33	5	0	0	391	6	8	3	3.1	.980	OF-131
1932	CIN N	96	.243	.285	333	81	12	1	0	0.0	28	25	31	29	3	2	0	251	6	4	2	3.0	.985	OF-88
1933	2 teams	CIN N (1G –.000) CHI N (27G –.225)																						
"	total	28	.225	.296	71	16	5	0	0	0.0	9	5	11	7	2	1	0	37	3	3	0	2.4	.930	OF-18
11 yrs.		1074	.291	.384	4127	1201	220	38	29	0.7	665	396	443	312	67	20	7	3109	70	91	21	3.2	.972	OF-1036
WORLD SERIES																								
1926	STL N	4	.267	.400	15	4	2	0	0	0.0	3	1	3	2	0	0	0	4	2	0	0	1.5	1.000	OF-4
1928		3	.091	.091	11	1	0	0	0	0.0	1	0	1	1	0	0	0	6	1	0	0	2.3	1.000	OF-3
1930		6	.083	.208	24	2	0	0	1	4.2	1	2	0	2	0	0	0	14	0	0	0	2.3	1.000	OF-6
3 yrs.		13	.140	.240	50	7	2	0	1	2.0	5	3	4	5	0	0	0	24	3	0	0	2.1	1.000	OF-13

Clarence Dow

DOW, CLARENCE G.
B. Oct. 11, 1854, Charlestown, Mass. D. Mar. 11, 1893, Somerville, Mass.

Year	Team	Games	BA	SA	AB	H	2B	3B	HR	HR%	R	RBI	BB	SO	SB	Pinch Hit AB	Pinch Hit H	PO	A	E	DP	TC/G	FA	G by Pos
1884	BOS U	1	.333	.333	6	2	0	0	0	0.0	1		0			0	0	1	2	0	0	3.0	1.000	OF-1

John Dowd

DOWD, JOHN LEO
Born John Leo O'Dowd.
B. Jan. 3, 1891, Weymouth, Mass. D. Jan. 31, 1981, Fort Lauderdale, Fla.
BR TR 5′ 8″ 170 lbs.

Year	Team	Games	BA	SA	AB	H	2B	3B	HR	HR%	R	RBI	BB	SO	SB	Pinch Hit AB	Pinch Hit H	PO	A	E	DP	TC/G	FA	G by Pos
1912	NY A	10	.194	.226	31	6	1	0	0	0.0	1	0	6		0	0	0	14	28	8	1	5.0	.840	SS-10

Year	Team	Games	BA	SA	AB	H	2B	3B	HR	HR%	R	RBI	BB	SO	SB	Pinch Hit AB	Pinch Hit H	PO	A	E	DP	TC/G	FA	G by Pos

Snooks Dowd

DOWD, RAYMOND BERNARD BR TR 5′ 8″ 163 lbs.
B. Dec. 20, 1897, Springfield, Mass. D. Apr. 4, 1962, Northampton, Mass.

Year	Team	Games	BA	SA	AB	H	2B	3B	HR	HR%	R	RBI	BB	SO	SB	Pinch Hit AB	Pinch Hit H	PO	A	E	DP	TC/G	FA	G by Pos
1919	2 teams	DET A (1G –.000) PHI A (13G –.167)																						
″	total	14	.167	.167	18	3	0	0	0	0.0	4	6	0	5	2	1	0	4	11	2	2	2.4	.882	2B-3, SS-2, OF-1, 3B-1
1926	BKN N	2	.000	.000	8	0	0	0	0	0.0	0	0	0	0	0	0	0	4	2	0	0	3.0	1.000	2B-2
2 yrs.		16	.115	.115	26	3	0	0	0	0.0	4	6	0	5	2	1	0	8	13	2	2	2.6	.913	2B-5, SS-2, OF-1, 3B-1

Tommy Dowd

DOWD, THOMAS JEFFERSON (Buttermilk Tommy) BR TR 5′ 8″ 173 lbs.
B. Apr. 20, 1869, Holyoke, Mass. D. July 2, 1933, Holyoke, Mass.
Manager 1896–97.

Year	Team	Games	BA	SA	AB	H	2B	3B	HR	HR%	R	RBI	BB	SO	SB	Pinch Hit AB	Pinch Hit H	PO	A	E	DP	TC/G	FA	G by Pos
1891	2 teams	BOS AA (4G –.091) WAS AA (112G –.259)																						
″	total	116	.255	.322	475	121	9	10	1	0.2	67	44	19	45	39	0	0	240	287	68	38	5.1	.886	2B-107, OF-9
1892	WAS N	144	.243	.298	584	142	9	10	1	0.2	94	50	34	49	49	0	0	283	315	84	39	4.7	.877	2B-98, OF-23, 3B-18, SS-6
1893	STL N	132	.282	.343	581	164	18	7	1	0.2	114	54	49	23	59	0	0	225	27	16	9	2.0	.940	OF-132, 2B-1
1894		123	.271	.355	524	142	16	8	4	0.8	92	62	54	33	31	0	0	219	33	20	6	2.2	.926	OF-117, 2B-7, 3B-1
1895		129	.323	.463	505	163	19	17	6	1.2	95	74	30	31	30	2	0	238	40	27	3	2.3	.911	OF-115, 3B-17, 2B-2
1896		126	.265	.369	521	138	17	11	5	1.0	93	46	42	19	40	0	0	293	224	43	24	4.4	.923	2B-78, OF-48
1897	2 teams	STL N (35G –.262) PHI N (91G –.292)																						
″	total	126	.284	.345	536	152	23	5	0	0.0	93	52	25		41	0	0	237	80	32	8	2.7	.908	OF-103, 2B-24
1898	STL N	139	.244	.297	586	143	17	7	0	0.0	70	32	30		16	0	0	231	39	25	6	2.1	.915	OF-129, 2B-11
1899	CLE N	147	.278	.336	605	168	17	6	2	0.3	81	35	48		28	0	0	341	10	17	2	2.5	.954	OF-147
1901	BOS A	138	.268	.337	594	159	18	7	3	0.5	104	52	38		33	0	0	302	12	20	3	2.4	.940	OF-137, 1B-2, 3B-1
10 yrs.		1320	.271	.345	5511	1492	163	88	23	0.4	903	501	369	200	366	2	0	2609	1067	352	138	3.0	.913	OF-960, 2B-328, 3B-37, SS-6, 1B-2

Ken Dowell

DOWELL, KENNETH ALLEN BR TR 5′ 9″ 160 lbs.
B. Jan. 19, 1961, Sacramento, Calif.

Year	Team	Games	BA	SA	AB	H	2B	3B	HR	HR%	R	RBI	BB	SO	SB	Pinch Hit AB	Pinch Hit H	PO	A	E	DP	TC/G	FA	G by Pos
1987	PHI N	15	.128	.128	39	5	0	0	0	0.0	4	1	2	5	0	0	0	17	36	0	7	3.5	1.000	SS-15

Joe Dowie

DOWIE, JOSEPH E. 5′ 8″ 150 lbs.
B. July 15, 1865, New Orleans, La.

Year	Team	Games	BA	SA	AB	H	2B	3B	HR	HR%	R	RBI	BB	SO	SB	Pinch Hit AB	Pinch Hit H	PO	A	E	DP	TC/G	FA	G by Pos
1889	BAL AA	20	.227	.293	75	17	5	0	0	0.0	12	8	2	10	5	0	0	34	2	2	0	1.9	.947	OF-20

Red Downey

DOWNEY, ALEXANDER CUMMINGS BL TL 5′11″ 174 lbs.
B. Feb. 6, 1889, Aurora, Ind. D. July 10, 1949, Detroit, Mich.

Year	Team	Games	BA	SA	AB	H	2B	3B	HR	HR%	R	RBI	BB	SO	SB	Pinch Hit AB	Pinch Hit H	PO	A	E	DP	TC/G	FA	G by Pos
1909	BKN N	19	.256	.269	78	20	1	0	0	0.0	7	8	2		4	0	0	25	2	0	0	1.4	1.000	OF-19

Tom Downey

DOWNEY, THOMAS EDWARD BR TR 6′ 170 lbs.
B. Jan. 1, 1884, Lewiston, Me. D. Aug. 3, 1961, Passaic, N. J.

Year	Team	Games	BA	SA	AB	H	2B	3B	HR	HR%	R	RBI	BB	SO	SB	Pinch Hit AB	Pinch Hit H	PO	A	E	DP	TC/G	FA	G by Pos
1909	CIN N	119	.231	.288	416	96	9	6	1	0.2	39	32	32		16	0	0	260	363	62	54	5.7	.909	SS-119, C-1
1910		111	.270	.325	378	102	9	3	2	0.5	43	32	34	28	12	0	0	201	281	60	26	5.0	.889	SS-68, 3B-41
1911		111	.261	.344	360	94	16	7	0	0.0	50	36	44	38	10	4	0	218	299	53	28	5.3	.907	SS-93, 2B-6, 3B-5, 1B-2, OF-1
1912	2 teams	PHI N (54G –.292) CHI N (13G –.182)																						
″	total	67	.280	.378	193	54	6	5	1	0.5	31	27	22	25	3	7	2	78	106	26	5	3.6	.876	3B-49, SS-8, 2B-1
1914	BUF F	151	.218	.277	541	118	20	3	2	0.4	69	42	40		35	1	0	304	438	29	54	5.1	.962	2B-129, SS-16, 3B-5
1915		92	.199	.248	282	56	9	1	1	0.4	24	19	26		11	5	1	175	200	24	26	4.6	.940	2B-48, 3B-35, SS-2, 1B-1
6 yrs.		651	.240	.304	2170	520	69	25	7	0.3	256	188	198	91	87	17	3	1236	1687	254	193	5.0	.920	SS-306, 2B-184, 3B-135, 1B-3, OF-1, C-1

Brian Downing

DOWNING, BRIAN JAY BR TR 5′10″ 170 lbs.
B. Oct. 9, 1950, Los Angeles, Calif.

Year	Team	Games	BA	SA	AB	H	2B	3B	HR	HR%	R	RBI	BB	SO	SB	Pinch Hit AB	Pinch Hit H	PO	A	E	DP	TC/G	FA	G by Pos
1973	CHI A	34	.178	.274	73	13	1	0	2	2.7	5	4	10	17	0	8	2	72	17	5	0	2.9	.947	OF-13, C-11, 3B-8
1974		108	.225	.375	293	66	12	1	10	3.4	41	39	51	72	0	5	0	337	30	2	5	3.3	.995	C-63, OF-39, DH-9
1975		138	.240	.324	420	101	12	1	7	1.7	58	41	76	75	13	0	0	730	84	8	5	6.0	.990	C-137, DH-1
1976		104	.256	.328	317	81	14	0	3	0.9	38	30	40	55	7	3	1	450	38	6	4	4.8	.988	C-93, DH-11
1977		69	.284	.402	169	48	4	2	4	2.4	28	25	34	21	1	3	1	325	28	6	5	5.4	.983	C-61, OF-3, DH-2
1978	CAL A	133	.255	.342	412	105	15	0	7	1.7	42	46	52	47	3	3	1	681	82	5	6	5.9	.993	C-128, DH-2
1979		148	.326	.462	509	166	27	3	12	2.4	87	75	77	57	3	3	1	669	35	11	5	4.9	.985	C-129, DH-18
1980		30	.290	.419	93	27	6	0	2	2.2	5	25	12	12	0	2	0	69	6	0	0	2.6	1.000	C-16, DH-13
1981		93	.249	.379	317	79	14	0	9	2.8	47	41	46	35	1	2	0	237	18	2	2	2.6	.992	OF-56, C-37, DH-5
1982		158	.281	.482	623	175	37	2	28	4.5	109	84	86	58	2	1	0	321	9	0	0	2.1	1.000	OF-158
1983		113	.246	.429	403	99	15	1	19	4.7	68	53	62	59	1	3	1	160	9	1	0	1.5	.994	OF-84, DH-26
1984		156	.275	.462	539	148	28	2	23	4.3	65	91	70	66	0	3	1	272	5	0	0	1.8	1.000	OF-131, DH-21
1985		150	.263	.427	520	137	23	1	20	3.8	80	85	78	60	5	7	0	244	5	2	0	1.7	.992	OF-121, DH-25
1986		152	.267	.452	513	137	27	4	20	3.9	90	95	90	84	4	8	0	267	5	3	0	1.9	.989	OF-138, DH-10
1987		155	.272	.487	567	154	29	3	29	5.1	110	77	**106**	85	5	4	0	47	2	0	0	0.3	1.000	DH-118, OF-34
1988		135	.242	.442	484	117	18	2	25	5.2	80	64	81	63	3	3	1	0	0	0	0	0.0	.000	DH-132
1989		142	.283	.414	544	154	25	2	14	2.6	59	59	56	87	0	1	0	0	0	0	0	0.0	.000	DH-141
1990		96	.273	.467	330	90	18	2	14	4.2	47	51	50	45	0	8	0	0	0	0	0	0.0	.000	DH-87
1991	TEX A	123	.278	.455	407	113	17	2	17	4.2	76	49	58	70	1	24	9	0	0	0	0	0.0	.000	DH-109
1992		107	.278	.428	320	89	18	0	10	3.1	53	39	62	58	1	12	0	0	0	0	0	0.0	.000	DH-93
20 yrs.		2344	.267	.425	7853	2099	360	28	275	3.5	1188	1073	1197	1126	50	103	18	4881	373	51	32	2.3	.990	DH-823, OF-777, C-675, 3B-8
LEAGUE CHAMPIONSHIP SERIES																								
1979	CAL A	4	.200	.200	15	3	0	0	0	0.0	1	1	1	1	0	0	0	27	0	0	2	6.8	1.000	C-4
1982		5	.158	.211	19	3	1	0	0	0.0	4	0	3	2	0	0	0	5	0	0	0	1.0	1.000	OF-5
1986		7	.222	.333	27	6	0	0	1	3.7	2	7	4	5	0	0	0	18	0	0	0	2.6	1.000	OF-7
3 yrs.		16	.197	.262	61	12	1	0	1	1.6	7	8	8	8	0	0	0	50	0	0	2	3.1	1.000	OF-12, C-4

Red Downs

DOWNS, JEROME WILLIS
B. Aug. 22, 1883, Neola, Iowa D. Oct. 19, 1939, Council Bluffs, Iowa.
BR TR 5′11″ 155 lbs.

Year	Team	Games	BA	SA	AB	H	2B	3B	HR	HR%	R	RBI	BB	SO	SB	Pinch Hit AB	Pinch Hit H	PO	A	E	DP	TC/G	FA	G by Pos
1907	DET A	105	.219	.289	374	82	13	5	1	0.3	28	42	13		3	4	1	188	210	30	11	4.2	.930	2B-80, OF-20, SS-1, 3B-1
1908		84	.221	.287	289	64	10	3	1	0.3	29	35	5		2	1	0	181	266	36	25	5.8	.925	2B-82, 3B-1
1912	2 teams BKN N (9G –.250) CHI N (43G –.263)																							
″	total	52	.260	.386	127	33	7	3	1	0.8	11	17	10	22	8	11	2	49	96	15	12	4.1	.906	2B-25, SS-9, 3B-5
3 yrs.		241	.227	.304	790	179	30	11	3	0.4	68	94	28	22	13	16	3	418	572	81	48	4.8	.924	2B-187, OF-20, SS-10, 3B-7
WORLD SERIES																								
1908	DET A	2	.167	.333	6	1	1	0	0	0.0	1	1	1	2	0	0	0	2	8	1	1	5.5	.909	2B-2

Tom Dowse

DOWSE, THOMAS JOSEPH
B. Aug. 12, 1866, Ireland D. Dec. 14, 1946, Riverside, Calif.
BR TR 5′11″ 175 lbs.

Year	Team	Games	BA	SA	AB	H	2B	3B	HR	HR%	R	RBI	BB	SO	SB	Pinch Hit AB	Pinch Hit H	PO	A	E	DP	TC/G	FA	G by Pos
1890	CLE N	40	.208	.233	159	33	2	1	0	0.0	20	9	12	22	3	0	0	151	14	11	10	4.4	.938	OF-26, 1B-10, C-3, P-1
1891	COL AA	55	.224	.259	201	45	7	0	0	0.0	24	22	13	22	2	0	0	258	52	29	6	6.1	.914	C-51, OF-5
1892	4 teams LOU N (41G –.145) CIN N (1G –.000) PHI N (16G –.185) WAS N (7G –.259)																							
″	total	65	.165	.178	230	38	3	0	0	0.0	18	15	4	22	2	1	0	301	68	21	13	5.8	.946	C-48, 1B-11, OF-7, 2B-1
3 yrs.		160	.197	.220	590	116	12	1	0	0.0	62	46	29	66	7	1	0	710	134	61	29	5.6	.933	C-102, OF-38, 1B-21, 2B-1, P-1

Brian Doyle

DOYLE, BRIAN REED
Brother of Denny Doyle.
B. Jan. 26, 1955, Glasgow, Ky.
BL TR 5′10″ 160 lbs.

Year	Team	Games	BA	SA	AB	H	2B	3B	HR	HR%	R	RBI	BB	SO	SB	Pinch Hit AB	Pinch Hit H	PO	A	E	DP	TC/G	FA	G by Pos
1978	NY A	39	.192	.192	52	10	0	0	0	0.0	6	0	0	3	0	0	0	39	65	1	14	2.6	.990	2B-29, SS-7, 3B-5
1979		20	.125	.188	32	4	2	0	0	0.0	2	5	3	1	0	0	0	12	27	2	5	2.2	.951	2B-13, 3B-6
1980		34	.173	.227	75	13	1	0	1	1.3	8	5	6	7	1	1	0	40	77	5	14	3.6	.959	2B-20, SS-12, 3B-2
1981	OAK A	17	.125	.125	40	5	0	0	0	0.0	2	3	1	2	0	0	0	29	39	0	6	4.0	1.000	2B-17
4 yrs.		110	.161	.191	199	32	3	0	1	0.5	18	13	10	13	1	1	0	120	208	8	39	3.0	.976	2B-79, SS-19, 3B-13
LEAGUE CHAMPIONSHIP SERIES																								
1978	NY A	3	.286	.286	7	2	0	0	0	0.0	0	1	1	1	0	0	0	3	6	0	0	3.0	1.000	2B-3
WORLD SERIES																								
1978	NY A	6	.438	.500	16	7	1	0	0	0.0	4	2	0	0	0	0	0	16	7	0	6	3.8	1.000	2B-6

Conny Doyle

DOYLE, CORNELIUS J.
B. Sept. 26, 1857, Holyoke, Mass. D. Oct. 6, 1938, West Springfield, Mass.
5′10″ 185 lbs.

Year	Team	Games	BA	SA	AB	H	2B	3B	HR	HR%	R	RBI	BB	SO	SB	Pinch Hit AB	Pinch Hit H	PO	A	E	DP	TC/G	FA	G by Pos
1883	PHI N	16	.221	.324	68	15	3	2	0	0.0	3		0	15		0	0	23	3	7	0	2.1	.788	OF-16
1884	PIT AA	15	.293	.414	58	17	3	2	0	0.0	8		2			0	0	17	5	4	0	1.7	.846	OF-14, SS-1
2 yrs.		31	.254	.365	126	32	6	4	0	0.0	11		2	15		0	0	40	8	11	0	1.9	.814	OF-30, SS-1

Danny Doyle

DOYLE, HOWARD JAMES
B. Jan. 24, 1917, McLoud, Okla.
BB TR 6′1″ 195 lbs.

Year	Team	Games	BA	SA	AB	H	2B	3B	HR	HR%	R	RBI	BB	SO	SB	Pinch Hit AB	Pinch Hit H	PO	A	E	DP	TC/G	FA	G by Pos
1943	BOS A	13	.209	.233	43	9	1	0	0	0.0	2	6	7	9	0	0	0	46	8	2	0	4.3	.964	C-13

Denny Doyle

DOYLE, ROBERT DENNIS
Brother of Brian Doyle.
B. Jan. 17, 1944, Glasgow, Ky.
BL TR 5′9″ 175 lbs.

Year	Team	Games	BA	SA	AB	H	2B	3B	HR	HR%	R	RBI	BB	SO	SB	Pinch Hit AB	Pinch Hit H	PO	A	E	DP	TC/G	FA	G by Pos
1970	PHI N	112	.208	.281	413	86	10	7	2	0.5	43	16	33	64	6	7	0	251	228	11	55	4.8	.978	2B-103
1971		95	.231	.298	342	79	12	1	3	0.9	34	24	19	31	4	3	0	241	264	17	62	5.7	.967	2B-91
1972		123	.249	.296	442	110	14	2	1	0.2	33	26	31	33	6	1	0	265	288	10	66	4.7	.982	2B-119
1973		116	.273	.338	370	101	9	3	3	0.8	45	26	31	32	1	6	1	231	296	14	71	4.7	.974	2B-114
1974	CAL A	147	.260	.311	511	133	19	2	1	0.2	47	34	25	49	6	1	1	311	405	12	99	4.9	.984	2B-146, SS-2
1975	2 teams CAL A (8G –.067) BOS A (89G –.310)																							
″	total	97	.298	.412	325	97	21	2	4	1.2	50	36	15	12	5	5	1	155	220	12	37	3.9	.969	2B-90, 3B-7, SS-2
1976	BOS A	117	.250	.308	432	108	15	5	0	0.0	51	26	22	39	8	8	2	209	311	12	67	4.7	.977	2B-113
1977		137	.240	.308	455	109	13	6	2	0.4	54	49	29	50	2	5	0	230	412	14	90	4.8	.979	2B-137
8 yrs.		944	.250	.316	3290	823	113	28	16	0.5	357	237	205	310	38	36	5	1893	2424	102	547	4.8	.977	2B-913, 3B-7, SS-4
LEAGUE CHAMPIONSHIP SERIES																								
1975	BOS A	3	.273	.273	11	3	0	0	0	0.0	3	1	0	1	0	0	0	5	8	1	2	4.7	.929	2B-3
WORLD SERIES																								
1975	BOS A	7	.267	.367	30	8	1	1	0	0.0	3	0	2	1	0	0	0	13	23	3	2	5.6	.923	2B-7

Jack Doyle

DOYLE, JOHN JOSEPH (Dirty Jack)
B. Oct. 25, 1869, Killorglin, Ireland D. Dec. 31, 1958, Holyoke, Mass.
Manager 1895, 1898.
BR TR 5′9″ 155 lbs.

Year	Team	Games	BA	SA	AB	H	2B	3B	HR	HR%	R	RBI	BB	SO	SB	Pinch Hit AB	Pinch Hit H	PO	A	E	DP	TC/G	FA	G by Pos
1889	COL AA	11	.278	.361	36	10	1	1	0	0.0	6	3	6	6	9	0	0	34	12	5	1	4.3	.902	C-7, OF-3, 2B-2
1890		77	.268	.393	298	80	17	7	2	0.7	47		13		27	0	0	231	153	54	14	5.4	.877	C-38, SS-25, OF-9, 2B-6, 3B-3
1891	CLE N	69	.276	.364	250	69	14	4	0	0.0	43	43	26	44	24	0	0	178	73	38	5	4.1	.869	C-29, OF-21, 3B-20, SS-1
1892	2 teams CLE N (24G –.295) NY N (90G –.298)																							
″	total	114	.297	.403	454	135	26	2	6	1.3	78	69	24	40	47	1	1	297	169	72	16	4.6	.866	C-35, 2B-31, OF-29, 3B-13, SS-8, 1B-1
1893	NY N	82	.321	.415	318	102	17	5	1	0.3	56	51	27	12	40	0	0	266	89	34	13	4.6	.913	C-48, OF-29, SS-4, 3B-3, 1B-1
1894		105	.367	.498	422	155	30	8	3	0.7	90	100	35	3	42	0	0	1004	66	42	51	10.6	.962	1B-99, C-6
1895		82	.313	.408	319	100	21	3	1	0.3	52	66	24	12	35	2	1	654	96	39	31	9.7	.951	1B-58, 2B-13, 3B-6, C-4
1896	BAL N	118	.339	.421	487	165	29	4	1	0.2	116	101	42	15	73	0	0	1173	42	33	85	10.5	.974	1B-118, 2B-1
1897		114	.354	.441	460	163	29	4	1	0.2	91	87	29		62	0	0	1105	75	25	72	10.6	.979	1B-114
1898	2 teams WAS N (43G –.305) NY N (82G –.283)																							
″	total	125	.291	.367	474	138	17	5	3	0.6	68	69	19		23	1	1	642	105	35	40	6.2	.955	1B-62, OF-38, SS-15, 3B-5, 2B-5, C-2
1899	NY N	118	.299	.384	448	134	15	7	3	0.7	55	76	33		35	1	0	1129	73	30	77	10.4	.976	1B-113, C-5
1900		133	.267	.325	505	135	24	1	1	0.2	69	66	34		34	0	0	1269	96	41	92	10.6	.971	1B-133
1901	CHI N	75	.232	.277	285	66	9	2	0	0.0	21	39	7		8	0	0	698	60	21	32	10.4	.973	1B-75
1902	2 teams NY N (49G –.301) WAS A (78G –.247)																							
″	total	127	.267	.341	498	133	27	2	2	0.4	73	39	39		18	0	0	707	235	31	47	7.5	.968	2B-68, 1B-56, OF-4, C-1
1903	BKN N	139	.313	.387	524	164	27	6	0	0.0	84	91	54		34	0	0	1418	83	29	74	11.0	.981	1B-139

Jack Doyle *continued*

Year	Team	Games	BA	SA	AB	H	2B	3B	HR	HR%	R	RBI	BB	SO	SB	Pinch Hit AB	Pinch Hit H	PO	A	E	DP	TC/G	FA	G by Pos
1904	2 teams	BKN N (8G –.227)	PHI N (66G –.220)																					
"	total	74	.221	.298	258	57	11	3	1	0.4	22	24	25		5	0	0	668	62	15	28	10.1	.980	1B-73, 2B-1
1905	NY A	1	.000	.000	3	0	0	0	0	0.0	0	0	0		0	0	0	10	0	2	0	12.0	.833	1B-1
17 yrs.		1564	.299	.385	6039	1806	314	64	25	0.4	971	924	437	132	516	5	3	11483	1489	546	678	8.6	.960	1B-1043, C-175, OF-133, 2B-127, SS-53, 3B-50

Jeff Doyle

DOYLE, JEFFREY DONALD BB TR 5′ 8″ 160 lbs.
B. Oct. 2, 1956, Havre, Mont.

Year	Team	Games	BA	SA	AB	H	2B	3B	HR	HR%	R	RBI	BB	SO	SB	Pinch Hit AB	Pinch Hit H	PO	A	E	DP	TC/G	FA	G by Pos
1983	STL N	13	.297	.432	37	11	1	2	0	0.0	4	2	1	3	0	1	0	29	28	2	11	4.9	.966	2B-12

Jim Doyle

DOYLE, JAMES FRANCIS BR TR 5′10″ 168 lbs.
B. Dec. 25, 1881, Detroit, Mich. D. Feb. 1, 1912, Syracuse, N. Y.

Year	Team	Games	BA	SA	AB	H	2B	3B	HR	HR%	R	RBI	BB	SO	SB	Pinch Hit AB	Pinch Hit H	PO	A	E	DP	TC/G	FA	G by Pos
1910	CIN N	7	.154	.308	13	2	2	0	0	0.0	1	1	0	2	0	1	0	5	2	1	0	1.3	.875	3B-5, OF-1
1911	CHI N	130	.282	.413	472	133	23	12	5	1.1	69	62	40	54	19	3	1	134	278	35	25	3.5	.922	3B-127
2 yrs.		137	.278	.410	485	135	25	12	5	1.0	70	63	40	56	19	4	1	139	280	36	25	3.4	.921	3B-132, OF-1

Larry Doyle

DOYLE, LAWRENCE JOSEPH (Laughing Larry) BL TR 5′10″ 165 lbs.
B. July 31, 1886, Caseyville, Ill. D. Mar. 1, 1974, Saranac Lake, N. Y.

Year	Team	Games	BA	SA	AB	H	2B	3B	HR	HR%	R	RBI	BB	SO	SB	Pinch Hit AB	Pinch Hit H	PO	A	E	DP	TC/G	FA	G by Pos
1907	NY N	69	.260	.273	227	59	3	0	0	0.0	16	16	20		3	0	0	128	158	26	7	4.5	.917	2B-69
1908		104	.308	.398	377	116	16	9	0	0.0	65	33	22		17	3	1	180	291	33	28	4.9	.935	2B-102
1909		146	.302	.419	570	**172**	27	11	6	1.1	86	49	45		30	3	2	292	322	39	51	4.6	.940	2B-143
1910		151	.285	.412	575	164	21	14	8	1.4	97	69	71	26	39	0	0	313	388	53	62	5.0	.930	2B-151
1911		143	.310	.527	526	163	25	**25**	13	2.5	102	77	71	39	41	2	1	272	340	36	46	4.6	.944	2B-141
1912		143	.330	.471	558	184	33	8	10	1.8	98	90	56	20	36	0	0	313	379	38	68	5.1	.948	2B-143
1913		132	.280	.388	482	135	25	6	5	1.0	67	73	59	29	38	2	1	315	345	31	55	5.3	.955	2B-130
1914		145	.260	.353	539	140	19	8	5	0.9	87	63	58	25	17	0	0	307	379	29	61	4.9	.959	2B-145
1915		150	**.320**	.442	591	**189**	**40**	10	4	0.7	86	70	32	28	22	3	0	313	396	40	66	5.0	.947	2B-150
1916	2 teams	NY N (113G –.268)	CHI N (9G –.395)																					
"	total	122	.278	.403	479	133	29	11	3	0.6	61	54	28	24	19	0	0	289	387	27	63	5.8	.962	2B-122
1917	CHI N	135	.254	.353	476	121	19	5	6	1.3	48	61	48	28	5	7	3	300	348	33	54	5.3	.952	2B-128
1918	NY N	75	.261	.354	257	67	7	4	3	1.2	38	36	37	10	10	2	0	121	221	11	24	4.8	.969	2B-73
1919		113	.289	.433	381	110	14	10	7	1.8	61	52	31	17	12	11	1	214	311	24	48	5.5	.956	2B-100
1920		137	.285	.363	471	134	21	2	4	0.8	48	50	47	28	11	4	0	278	389	23	61	5.2	.967	2B-133
14 yrs.		1765	.290	.408	6509	1887	299	123	74	1.1	960	793	625	274	300	37	9	3635	4654	443	694	5.0	.949	2B-1730
WORLD SERIES																								
1911	NY N	6	.304	.522	23	7	3	1	0	0.0	3	1	2	1	2	0	0	13	15	1	2	4.8	.966	2B-6
1912		8	.242	.364	33	8	1	0	1	3.0	5	2	3	2	2	0	0	15	26	4	1	5.6	.911	2B-8
1913		5	.150	.150	20	3	0	0	0	0.0	1	2	0	1	0	0	0	13	19	3	1	7.0	.914	2B-5
3 yrs.		19	.237	.355	76	18	4	1	1	1.3	9	5	5	4	4	0	0	41	60	8	4	5.7	.927	2B-19

D. J. Dozier

DOZIER, WILLIAM HENRY BR TR 6′ 202 lbs.
B. Sept. 21, 1965, Norfolk, Va.

Year	Team	Games	BA	SA	AB	H	2B	3B	HR	HR%	R	RBI	BB	SO	SB	Pinch Hit AB	Pinch Hit H	PO	A	E	DP	TC/G	FA	G by Pos
1992	NY N	25	.191	.234	47	9	2	0	0	0.0	4	2	4	19	4	5	0	33	0	1	0	2.0	.971	OF-17

Delos Drake

DRAKE, DELOS DANIEL BL TL 5′11½″ 170 lbs.
B. Dec. 3, 1886, Girard, Ohio D. Oct. 3, 1965, Findlay, Ohio.

Year	Team	Games	BA	SA	AB	H	2B	3B	HR	HR%	R	RBI	BB	SO	SB	Pinch Hit AB	Pinch Hit H	PO	A	E	DP	TC/G	FA	G by Pos
1911	DET A	91	.279	.375	315	88	9	9	1	0.3	37	36	17		20	9	3	155	5	11	1	2.0	.936	OF-83, 1B-2
1914	STL F	138	.251	.335	514	129	18	8	3	0.6	51	42	31		17	4	0	353	21	13	14	2.9	.966	OF-116, 1B-18
1915		102	.265	.364	343	91	23	4	1	0.3	32	41	23		6	4	0	181	10	5	2	2.0	.974	OF-99, 1B-1
3 yrs.		331	.263	.354	1172	308	50	21	5	0.4	120	119	71		43	17	3	689	36	29	17	2.4	.962	OF-298, 1B-21

Larry Drake

DRAKE, LARRY FRANCIS BL TR 6′ 1½″ 195 lbs.
B. May 4, 1921, McKinney, Tex. D. July 14, 1985, Houston, Tex.

Year	Team	Games	BA	SA	AB	H	2B	3B	HR	HR%	R	RBI	BB	SO	SB	Pinch Hit AB	Pinch Hit H	PO	A	E	DP	TC/G	FA	G by Pos
1945	PHI A	1	.000	.000	2	0	0	0	0	0.0	0	0	0	2	0	0	0	2	0	0	0	2.0	1.000	OF-1
1948	WAS A	4	.286	.286	7	2	0	0	0	0.0	0	1	1	3	0	2	0	3	0	0	0	1.5	1.000	OF-2
2 yrs.		5	.222	.222	9	2	0	0	0	0.0	0	1	1	5	0	2	0	5	0	0	0	1.7	1.000	OF-3

Lyman Drake

DRAKE, LYMAN DANIEL
B. Feb. 9, 1852, Berea, Ohio D. Feb. 6, 1932, Muskegon, Mich.

Year	Team	Games	BA	SA	AB	H	2B	3B	HR	HR%	R	RBI	BB	SO	SB	Pinch Hit AB	Pinch Hit H	PO	A	E	DP	TC/G	FA	G by Pos
1884	WAS AA	2	.286	.429	7	2	1	0	0	0.0	0		0			0	0	0	0	1	0	0.5	.000	OF-2

Sammy Drake

DRAKE, SAMUEL HARRISON BB TR 5′11″ 175 lbs.
Brother of Solly Drake.
B. Oct. 7, 1934, Little Rock, Ark.

Year	Team	Games	BA	SA	AB	H	2B	3B	HR	HR%	R	RBI	BB	SO	SB	Pinch Hit AB	Pinch Hit H	PO	A	E	DP	TC/G	FA	G by Pos
1960	CHI N	15	.067	.067	15	1	0	0	0	0.0	5	0	1	4	0	4	1	3	3	0	0	0.8	1.000	3B-6, 2B-2
1961		13	.000	.000	5	0	0	0	0	0.0	1	0	1	1	0	2	0	1	0	0	0	1.0	1.000	OF-1
1962	NY N	25	.192	.192	52	10	0	0	0	0.0	2	7	6	12	0	6	3	24	26	2	6	3.3	.962	2B-10, 3B-6
3 yrs.		53	.153	.153	72	11	0	0	0	0.0	8	7	8	17	0	12	4	28	29	2	6	2.4	.966	3B-12, 2B-12, OF-1

Solly Drake

DRAKE, SOLOMON LOUIS BB TR 6′ 170 lbs.
Brother of Sammy Drake.
B. Oct. 23, 1930, Little Rock, Ark.

Year	Team	Games	BA	SA	AB	H	2B	3B	HR	HR%	R	RBI	BB	SO	SB	Pinch Hit AB	Pinch Hit H	PO	A	E	DP	TC/G	FA	G by Pos
1956	CHI N	65	.256	.335	215	55	9	1	2	0.9	29	15	23	35	9	8	3	142	3	1	1	2.8	.993	OF-53
1959	2 teams	LA N (9G –.250)	PHI N (67G –.145)																					
"	total	76	.157	.171	70	11	1	0	0	0.0	12	3	9	18	6	22	0	37	0	1	0	0.9	.974	OF-41
2 yrs.		141	.232	.295	285	66	10	1	2	0.7	41	18	32	53	15	30	3	179	3	2	1	2.0	.989	OF-94

Jake Drauby

DRAUBY, JACOB C. 5′10″ 163 lbs.
B. 1865, Harrisburg, Pa. Deceased.

Year	Team	Games	BA	SA	AB	H	2B	3B	HR	HR%	R	RBI	BB	SO	SB	Pinch Hit AB	Pinch Hit H	PO	A	E	DP	TC/G	FA	G by Pos
1892	WAS N	10	.206	.265	34	7	0	1	0	0.0	3	3	2	12	0	0	0	11	18	9	2	3.8	.763	3B-10

Bill Dreesen

DREESEN, WILLIAM RICHARD BL TR 5′ 7½″ 160 lbs.
B. July 26, 1904, New York, N. Y. D. Nov. 9, 1971, Mount Vernon, N. Y.

Year	Team	Games	BA	S	AB	H	2B	3B	HR	HR%	R	RBI	BB	SO	SB	Pinch Hit AB	Pinch Hit H	PO	A	E	DP	TC/G	FA	G by Pos
1931	BOS N				180	40	10	4	1	0.6	38	10	23	23	1	1	1	28	83	11	1	2.6	.910	3B-47

Bill D

DRESCHER, WILLIAM CLAYTON (Dutch, Moose) BL TR 6′ 2″ 190 lbs.
B. May 23, 1921, Congers, N. Y. D. May 15, 1968, Haverstraw, N. Y.

Year	Team	Games	BA	S	AB	H	2B	3B	HR	HR%	R	RBI	BB	SO	SB	Pinch Hit AB	Pinch Hit H	PO	A	E	DP	TC/G	FA	G by Pos
1944	N			.143	7	1	0	0	0	0.0	0	0	0	0	0	3	0	7	0	1	0	8.0	.875	C-1
1945				.310	126	34	3	1	0	0.0	10	15	8	5	0	14	2	101	13	1	1	3.5	.991	C-33
194				.500	6	2	1	0	0	0.0	0	1	0	0	0	2	0	6	1	0	1	2.3	1.000	C-3
		6		.309	139	37	4	1	0	0.0	10	16	8	5	0	19	2	114	14	2	2	3.5	.985	C-37

…en

DRESSEN, CHARLES WALTER BR TR 5′ 5½″ 146 lbs.
B. Sept. 20, 1898, Decatur, Ill. D. Aug. 10, 1966, Detroit, Mich.
Manager 1934–37, 1951–53, 1955–57, 1960–61, 1963–66.

Year	Team	Games	BA	S	AB	H	2B	3B	HR	HR%	R	RBI	BB	SO	SB	Pinch Hit AB	Pinch Hit H	PO	A	E	DP	TC/G	FA	G by Pos
			.274	.372	215	59	8	2	3	1.4	35	19	12	4	5	10	0	54	109	8	9	3.1	.953	3B-47, 2B-5, OF-4
			.266	.395	474	126	27	11	4	0.8	76	48	49	31	0	0	0	111	284	15	19	3.3	.963	3B-123, SS-1, OF-1
		44	.292	.405	548	160	36	10	2	0.4	78	55	71	32	7	1	0	132	319	19	20	3.3	.960	3B-142, SS-2
		135	.291	.361	498	145	26	3	1	0.2	72	59	43	22	10	0	0	122	283	27	27	3.2	.938	3B-135
		110	.244	.322	401	98	22	3	1	0.2	49	36	41	21	8	5	0	86	191	17	11	2.8	.942	3B-98, 2B-8
		33	.211	.211	19	4	0	0	0	0.0	0	1	1	3	0	13	2	3	7	0	0	0.8	1.000	3B-10, 2B-3
		5	.067	.067	15	1	0	0	0	0.0	0	0	1	1	0	0	0	4	7	2	1	3.3	.846	3B-4
	N	16	.222	.311	45	10	4	0	0	0.0	3	3	1	4	0	0	0	14	21	1	2	2.3	.972	3B-16
		646	.272	.369	2215	603	123	29	11	0.5	313	221	219	118	30	29	2	526	1221	89	89	3.1	.952	3B-575, 2B-16, OF-5, SS-3

Lee Dressen

DRESSEN, LEE AUGUST BL TL 6′ 165 lbs.
B. July 23, 1889, Ellinwood, Kans. D. June 30, 1931, Diller, Neb.

Year	Team	Games	BA	S	AB	H	2B	3B	HR	HR%	R	RBI	BB	SO	SB	Pinch Hit AB	Pinch Hit H	PO	A	E	DP	TC/G	FA	G by Pos
1914	STL N	46	.233	.272	103	24	2	1	0	0.0	16	7	11	20	2	7	1	258	13	5	15	7.3	.982	1B-38
1918	DET A	31	.178	.224	107	19	1	2	0	0.0	10	3	21	10	2	1	0	322	11	4	12	11.2	.988	1B-30
2 yrs.		77	.205	.248	210	43	3	3	0	0.0	26	10	32	30	4	8	1	580	24	9	27	9.0	.985	1B-68

Cameron Drew

DREW, CAMERON STEWARD BL TR 6′ 5″ 230 lbs.
B. Feb. 12, 1964, Boston, Mass.

Year	Team	Games	BA	S	AB	H	2B	3B	HR	HR%	R	RBI	BB	SO	SB	Pinch Hit AB	Pinch Hit H	PO	A	E	DP	TC/G	FA	G by Pos
1988	HOU N	7	.188	.313	16	3	0	1	0	0.0	1	1	0	1	0	2	0	10	0	0	0	2.0	1.000	OF-5

Dave Drew

DREW, DAVID
Deceased.

Year	Team	Games	BA	S	AB	H	2B	3B	HR	HR%	R	RBI	BB	SO	SB	Pinch Hit AB	Pinch Hit H	PO	A	E	DP	TC/G	FA	G by Pos
1884	2 teams	PHI U (2G –.444) WAS U (13G –.302)																						
″	total	15	.323	.403	62	20	1	2	0	0.0	9		1			0	0	62	30	12	4	6.1	.885	SS-9, 1B-5, OF-1, 2B-1, P-1

Frank Drews

DREWS, FRANK JOHN BR TR 5′10″ 175 lbs.
B. May 25, 1916, Buffalo, N. Y. D. Apr. 22, 1972, Buffalo, N. Y.

Year	Team	Games	BA	S	AB	H	2B	3B	HR	HR%	R	RBI	BB	SO	SB	Pinch Hit AB	Pinch Hit H	PO	A	E	DP	TC/G	FA	G by Pos
1944	BOS N	46	.206	.284	141	29	9	1	0	0.0	14	10	25	14	0	0	0	123	132	11	27	5.8	.959	2B-46
1945		49	.204	.245	147	30	4	1	0	0.0	13	19	16	18	0	0	0	98	141	6	27	5.1	.976	2B-48
2 yrs.		95	.205	.264	288	59	13	2	0	0.0	27	29	41	32	0	0	0	221	273	17	54	5.4	.967	2B-94

Dan Driessen

DRIESSEN, DANIEL BL TR 5′11″ 187 lbs.
B. July 29, 1951, Hilton Head, S. C.

Year	Team	Games	BA	S	AB	H	2B	3B	HR	HR%	R	RBI	BB	SO	SB	Pinch Hit AB	Pinch Hit H	PO	A	E	DP	TC/G	FA	G by Pos
1973	CIN N	102	.301	.385	366	110	15	2	4	1.1	49	47	24	37	8	7	3	160	157	12	30	2.7	.964	3B-87, 1B-35, OF-1
1974		150	.281	.400	470	132	23	6	7	1.5	63	56	48	62	10	14	5	186	206	26	37	2.4	.938	3B-126, 1B-47, OF-3
1975		88	.281	.429	210	59	8	1	7	3.3	38	38	35	30	10	21	5	309	20	5	34	4.8	.985	1B-41, OF-29
1976		98	.247	.402	219	54	11	1	7	3.2	32	44	43	32	14	34	6	314	23	2	33	5.7	.994	1B-40, OF-20
1977		151	.300	.468	536	161	31	4	17	3.2	75	91	64	85	31	6	1	1182	75	7	116	8.5	.994	1B-148
1978		153	.250	.397	524	131	23	3	16	3.1	68	70	75	79	28	5	0	1264	93	6	92	9.0	.996	1B-151
1979		150	.250	.414	515	129	24	3	18	3.5	72	75	62	77	11	7	1	1289	79	9	112	9.6	.993	1B-143
1980		154	.265	.418	524	139	36	1	14	2.7	81	74	**93**	68	19	1	0	1349	85	7	115	9.5	.995	1B-151
1981		82	.236	.386	233	55	14	0	7	3.0	35	33	40	31	2	5	1	558	30	3	54	8.0	.995	1B-74
1982		149	.269	.421	516	139	25	1	17	3.3	64	57	82	62	11	3	0	1239	78	3	123	9.2	.998	1B-144
1983		122	.277	.420	386	107	17	1	12	3.1	57	57	75	51	6	8	2	917	71	4	73	8.9	.996	1B-112
1984	2 teams	CIN N (81G –.280) MON N (51G –.254)																						
″	total	132	.269	.455	387	104	24	0	16	4.1	47	60	54	40	2	17	1	870	52	7	69	8.1	.992	1B-115
1985	2 teams	MON N (91G –.250) SF N (54G –.232)																						
″	total	145	.243	.351	493	120	26	0	9	1.8	53	47	50	51	2	7	0	1203	91	4	111	9.5	.997	1B-137
1986	2 teams	SF N (15G –.188) HOU N (17G –.292)																						
″	total	32	.250	.400	40	10	3	0	1	2.5	7	3	9	6	0	12	3	77	6	0	5	5.2	1.000	1B-16
1987	STL N	24	.233	.317	60	14	2	0	1	1.7	5	11	7	8	0	2	0	141	10	1	13	7.2	.993	1B-21
15 yrs.		1732	.267	.411	5479	1464	282	23	153	2.8	746	763	761	719	154	149	28	11058	1076	96	1017	7.5	.992	1B-1375, 3B-213, OF-53
LEAGUE CHAMPIONSHIP SERIES																								
1973	CIN N	4	.167	.250	12	2	1	0	0	0.0	0	1	0	2	0	0	0	3	2	1	0	1.5	.833	3B-4
1976		1	.000	.000	1	0	0	0	0	0.0	0	0	0	0	0	1	0	0	0	0	0	0.0	—	
1979		3	.083	.083	12	1	0	0	0	0.0	1	0	1	3	0	0	0	32	0	0	2	10.7	1.000	1B-3
1987	STL N	5	.250	.417	12	3	2	0	0	0.0	1	1	1	1	0	2	1	26	3	1	2	7.5	.967	1B-4
4 yrs.		13	.162	.243	37	6	3	0	0	0.0	2	2	2	6	0	3	1	61	5	2	4	6.2	.971	1B-7, 3B-4
WORLD SERIES																								
1975	CIN N	2	.000	.000	2	0	0	0	0	0.0	0	0	0	0	0	2	0	0	0	0	0	0.0	—	
1976		4	.357	.714	14	5	2	0	1	7.1	4	1	2	0	1	0	0	0	0	0	0	0.0	.000	DH-4
1987	STL N	4	.231	.385	13	3	2	0	0	0.0	3	1	1	1	0	0	0	27	1	0	0	7.0	1.000	1B-4
3 yrs.		10	.276	.517	29	8	4	0	1	3.4	7	2	3	1	1	2	0	27	1	0	0	3.5	1.000	1B-4, DH-4

Lew Drill

DRILL, LEWIS L BR TR 5′ 6″ 186 lbs.
B. May 9, 1877, Browerville, Minn. D. July 4, 1969, St. Paul, Minn.

Year	Team	Games	BA	S	AB	H	2B	3B	HR	HR%	R	RBI	BB	SO	SB	Pinch Hit AB	Pinch Hit H	PO	A	E	DP	TC/G	FA	G by Pos
1902	2 teams	BAL A (2G –.250) WAS A (71G –.262)																						
″	total	73	.262	.354	229	60	10	4	1	0.4	35	29	26		5	4	0	204	66	26	5	4.3	.912	C-54, OF-8, 2B-5, 1B-1, 3B-1

Lew Drill *continued*

Year	Team	Games	BA	SA	AB	H	2B	3B	HR	HR%	R	RBI	BB	SO	SB	Pinch Hit AB	Pinch Hit H	PO	A	E	DP			G by Pos
1903	WAS A	51	.253	.351	154	39	9	3	0	0.0	11	23	15		4	1	0	226	48	9	9	5.7		
1904	2 teams	WAS A (46G –.268) DET A (51G –.244)																						
″	total	97	.255	.328	302	77	13	3	1	0.3	24	24	41		5	2	1	344	84	26	12	4.8	.94	
1905	DET A	71	.261	.303	211	55	9	0	0	0.0	17	24	32		7	1	0	345	73	13	10	6.2	.970	
4 yrs.		292	.258	.333	896	231	41	10	2	0.2	87	100	114		21	8	1	1119	271	74	36	5.2	.949	

Denny Driscoll

DRISCOLL, JOHN F. BL TL
B. Nov. 19, 1855, Lowell, Mass. D. July 11, 1886, Lowell, Mass.

Year	Team	Games	BA	SA	AB	H	2B	3B	HR	HR%	R	RBI	BB	SO	SB	Pinch Hit AB	Pinch Hit H	PO	A	E	DP			G by Pos
1880	BUF N	18	.154	.169	65	10	1	0	0	0.0	1	4	1	7		0	0	18	10	4	2	1.6	.875	OF-14, P-6
1882	PIT AA	23	.138	.200	80	11	2	0	1	1.3	12		3			0	0	4	50	7	1	2.7	.885	P-23
1883		41	.182	.209	148	27	2	1	0	0.0	19		4			0	0	14	99	14	2	2.8	.890	P-41, OF-4, 3B-
1884	LOU AA	13	.188	.208	48	9	1	0	0	0.0	5		2			0	0	3	37	9	2	3.3	.816	P-13, OF-2
1885	BUF N	7	.158	.158	19	3	0	0	0	0.0	2	0	2	5		0	0	12	11	9	1	4.6	.719	2B-7
5 yrs.		102	.167	.197	360	60	6	1	1	0.3	39	4	12	12		0	0	51	207	43	8	2.7	.857	P-83, OF-20, 2B-7, 3B

Jim Driscoll

DRISCOLL, JAMES BERNARD BL TR 5′11″ 175 l
B. May 14, 1944, Medford, Mass.

Year	Team	Games	BA	SA	AB	H	2B	3B	HR	HR%	R	RBI	BB	SO	SB	Pinch Hit AB	Pinch Hit H	PO	A	E	DP			G by Pos
1970	OAK A	21	.192	.250	52	10	0	0	1	1.9	2	2	2	15	0	5	2	30	29	6	8	4.6	.908	SS-7, 2B-7
1972	TEX A	15	.000	.000	18	0	0	0	0	0.0	0	0	2	3	0	11	0	6	8	1	2	2.5	.933	2B-4, 3B-2
2 yrs.		36	.143	.186	70	10	0	0	1	1.4	2	2	4	18	0	16	2	36	37	7	10	4.0	.913	2B-11, SS-7, 3B-2

Paddy Driscoll

DRISCOLL, JOHN LEO BR TR 5′ 8½″ 155 lbs.
B. Jan. 11, 1895, Evanston, Ill. D. June 28, 1968, Chicago, Ill.

Year	Team	Games	BA	SA	AB	H	2B	3B	HR	HR%	R	RBI	BB	SO	SB	Pinch Hit AB	Pinch Hit H	PO	A	E	DP			G by Pos
1917	CHI N	13	.107	.143	28	3	1	0	0	0.0	2	3	2	6	2	0	0	15	24	7	4	4.2	.848	2B-8, 3B-2, SS-1

Mike Drissel

DRISSEL, MICHAEL F. BR TR 5′11″
B. Dec. 19, 1864, St. Louis, Mo. D. Feb. 26, 1913, St. Louis, Mo.

Year	Team	Games	BA	SA	AB	H	2B	3B	HR	HR%	R	RBI	BB	SO	SB	Pinch Hit AB	Pinch Hit H	PO	A	E	DP			G by Pos
1885	STL AA	6	.050	.050	20	1	0	0	0	0.0	0		0			0	0	23	10	1	1	5.7	.971	C-6

Walt Dropo

DROPO, WALTER (Moose) BR TR 6′ 5″ 220 lbs.
B. Jan. 30, 1923, Moosup, Conn.

Year	Team	Games	BA	SA	AB	H	2B	3B	HR	HR%	R	RBI	BB	SO	SB	Pinch Hit AB	Pinch Hit H	PO	A	E	DP			G by Pos
1949	BOS A	11	.146	.195	41	6	2	0	0	0.0	3	1	3	7	0	0	0	103	4	0	13	9.7	1.000	1B-11
1950		136	.322	.583	559	180	28	8	34	6.1	101	**144**	45	75	0	2	0	1142	77	15	147	9.2	.988	1B-134
1951		99	.239	.369	360	86	14	0	11	3.1	37	57	38	52	0	7	2	878	63	12	91	10.2	.987	1B-93
1952	2 teams	BOS A (37G –.265) DET A (115G –.279)																						
″	total	152	.276	.477	591	163	24	4	29	4.9	69	97	37	85	2	2	0	1324	99	14	135	9.6	.990	1B-150
1953	DET A	152	.248	.371	606	150	30	3	13	2.1	61	96	29	69	2	2	1	1260	127	14	121	9.3	.990	1B-150
1954		107	.281	.375	320	90	14	2	4	1.3	27	44	24	41	0	18	5	681	54	3	60	7.8	.996	1B-95
1955	CHI A	141	.280	.448	453	127	15	2	19	4.2	55	79	42	71	0	2	1	1101	62	6	104	8.4	.995	1B-140
1956		125	.266	.374	361	96	13	1	8	2.2	42	52	37	51	1	10	2	855	50	6	95	7.8	.993	1B-117
1957		93	.256	.439	223	57	2	0	13	5.8	24	49	16	40	0	31	11	483	39	7	49	7.7	.987	1B-69
1958	2 teams	CHI A (28G –.192) CIN N (63G –.290)																						
″	total	91	.266	.449	214	57	8	2	9	4.2	21	39	17	42	0	31	7	398	35	0	39	7.3	1.000	1B-59
1959	2 teams	CIN N (26G –.103) BAL A (62G –.278)																						
″	total	88	.242	.405	190	46	10	0	7	3.7	21	23	16	27	0	11	1	489	31	4	54	6.6	.992	1B-77, 3B-2
1960	BAL A	79	.268	.380	179	48	8	0	4	2.2	16	21	20	19	0	14	2	397	27	3	50	6.3	.993	1B-67, 3B-1
1961		14	.259	.370	27	7	0	0	1	3.7	1	2	4	3	0	2	1	62	6	0	11	5.7	1.000	1B-12
13 yrs.		1288	.270	.432	4124	1113	168	22	152	3.7	478	704	328	582	5	132	33	9173	674	84	969	8.4	.992	1B-1174, 3B-3

Keith Drumright

DRUMRIGHT, KEITH ALAN BL TR 5′10″ 170 lbs.
B. Oct. 21, 1954, Springfield, Mo.

Year	Team	Games	BA	SA	AB	H	2B	3B	HR	HR%	R	RBI	BB	SO	SB	Pinch Hit AB	Pinch Hit H	PO	A	E	DP			G by Pos
1978	HOU N	17	.164	.164	55	9	0	0	0	0.0	5	2	3	4	0	0	0	27	41	4	9	4.2	.944	2B-17
1981	OAK A	31	.291	.326	86	25	1	1	0	0.0	8	11	4	4	0	7	2	38	50	1	7	3.7	.989	2B-19, DH-5
2 yrs.		48	.241	.262	141	34	1	1	0	0.0	13	13	7	8	0	7	2	65	91	5	16	3.9	.969	2B-36, DH-5
DIVISIONAL PLAYOFF SERIES																								
1981	OAK A	1	.250	.250	4	1	0	0	0	0.0	0	0	0	0	0	0	0	0	0	0	0	0.0	.000	DH-1
LEAGUE CHAMPIONSHIP SERIES																								
1981	OAK A	3	.000	.000	4	0	0	0	0	0.0	0	0	1	0	0	3	0	0	0	0	0	0.0	.000	DH-1

Jean Dubuc

DUBUC, JEAN JOSEPH OCTAVE (Chauncey) BR TR 5′10½″ 185 lbs.
Born Jean Baptiste Arthur Dubuc.
B. Sept. 15, 1888, St. Johnsbury, Vt. D. Aug. 28, 1958, Ft. Myers, Fla.

Year	Team	Games	BA	SA	AB	H	2B	3B	HR	HR%	R	RBI	BB	SO	SB	Pinch Hit AB	Pinch Hit H	PO	A	E	DP			G by Pos
1908	CIN N	15	.138	.172	29	4	1	0	0	0.0	2	2	0		0	0	0	6	26	2	0	2.3	.941	P-15
1909		19	.167	.167	18	3	0	0	0	0.0	1	0	2		0	0	0	4	23	5	0	1.7	.844	P-19
1912	DET A	40	.269	.389	108	29	6	2	1	0.9	16	9	3		0	1	0	12	94	4	5	2.8	.964	P-37, OF-2
1913		68	.267	.393	135	36	5	3	2	1.5	17	11	2	17	1	28	3	16	110	6	7	3.4	.955	P-36, OF-3
1914		70	.226	.331	124	28	8	1	1	0.8	9	11	7	11	1	32	6	14	83	6	3	2.9	.942	P-36
1915		60	.205	.241	112	23	2	1	0	0.0	7	14	8	15	0	17	5	9	86	3	2	2.5	.969	P-39
1916		52	.256	.308	78	20	0	2	0	0.0	3	7	7	12	0	12	2	7	73	4	5	2.3	.952	P-36
1918	BOS A	5	.167	.167	6	1	0	0	0	0.0	0	0	1	2	0	2	0	2	2	0	0	2.0	1.000	P-2
1919	NY N	36	.143	.214	42	6	1	1	0	0.0	2	2	0	6	0	1	0	8	46	2	1	1.6	.964	P-36
9 yrs.		365	.230	.314	652	150	23	10	4	0.6	57	56	30	63	2	93	16	78	543	32	23	2.5	.951	P-256, OF-5
WORLD SERIES																								
1918	BOS A	1	.000	.000	1	0	0	0	0	0.0	0	0	0	1	0	1	0	0	0	0	0	0.0	—	

Rob Ducey

DUCEY, ROBERT THOMAS BL TR 6′ 2″ 175 lbs.
B. May 24, 1965, Toronto, Ont., Canada.

Year	Team	Games	BA	SA	AB	H	2B	3B	HR	HR%	R	RBI	BB	SO	SB	Pinch Hit AB	Pinch Hit H	PO	A	E	DP			G by Pos
1987	TOR A	34	.188	.271	48	9	1	0	1	2.1	12	6	8	10	2	3	1	31	0	0	0	1.1	1.000	OF-28
1988		27	.315	.426	54	17	4	1	0	0.0	15	6	5	7	1	0	0	35	1	0	0	1.4	1.000	OF-26
1989		41	.211	.263	76	16	4	0	0	0.0	5	7	9	25	2	6	0	56	3	0	2	1.6	1.000	OF-35, DH-1
1990		19	.302	.396	53	16	5	0	0	0.0	7	7	7	15	1	0	0	37	0	0	0	1.9	1.000	OF-19
1991		39	.235	.368	68	16	2	2	1	1.5	8	4	6	26	2	14	3	32	1	4	0	1.4	.892	OF-24, DH-2

Rob Ducey *continued*

Year	Team	Games	BA	SA	AB	H	2B	3B	HR	HR%	R	RBI	BB	SO	SB	Pinch Hit AB	Pinch Hit H	PO	A	E	DP	TC/G	FA	G by Pos
1992	2 teams	TOR A (23G –.048)	CAL A (31G –.237)																					
"	total	54	.188	.237	80	15	4	0	0	0.0	7	2	5	22	2	10	3	43	2	2	0	1.2	.957	OF-33, DH-5
1993	TEX A	27	.282	.494	85	24	6	3	2	2.4	15	9	10	17	2	1	1	51	1	0	0	2.0	1.000	OF-26
1994		11	.172	.207	29	5	1	0	0	0.0	1	1	2	1	0	1	0	15	0	2	0	1.7	.882	OF-10
8 yrs.		252	.239	.343	493	118	27	6	4	0.8	70	42	52	123	12	35	8	300	8	8	2	1.5	.975	OF-201, DH-8
LEAGUE CHAMPIONSHIP SERIES																								
1991	TOR A	1	.000	.000	1	0	0	0	0	0.0	0	0	0	0	0	0	0	0	0	0	0	0.0	.000	OF-1

Dud Dudley

Playing record listed under Dud Lee.

John Dudra

DUDRA, JOHN JOSEPH
B. May 27, 1916, Assumption, Ill. D. Oct. 24, 1965, Pana, Ill.
BR TR 5′11½″ 175 lbs.

Year	Team	Games	BA	SA	AB	H	2B	3B	HR	HR%	R	RBI	BB	SO	SB	Pinch Hit AB	Pinch Hit H	PO	A	E	DP	TC/G	FA	G by Pos
1941	BOS N	14	.360	.560	25	9	3	1	0	0.0	3	3	3	4	0	1	0	20	13	1	5	2.8	.971	2B-5, 3B-5, 1B-1, SS-1

Pat Duff

DUFF, PATRICK HENRY
B. May 6, 1875, Providence, R. I. D. Sept. 11, 1925, Providence, R. I.
TR

Year	Team	Games	BA	SA	AB	H	2B	3B	HR	HR%	R	RBI	BB	SO	SB	Pinch Hit AB	Pinch Hit H	PO	A	E	DP	TC/G	FA	G by Pos
1906	WAS A	1	.000	.000	1	0	0	0	0	0.0	0	0	0		0	1	0	0	0	0	0	0.0	—	

Charlie Duffee

DUFFEE, CHARLES EDWARD (Home Run)
B. Jan. 27, 1866, Mobile, Ala. D. Dec. 24, 1894, Mobile, Ala.
BR TR

Year	Team	Games	BA	SA	AB	H	2B	3B	HR	HR%	R	RBI	BB	SO	SB	Pinch Hit AB	Pinch Hit H	PO	A	E	DP	TC/G	FA	G by Pos
1889	STL AA	137	.244	.409	509	124	15	12	15	2.9	93	86	60	**81**	21	0	0	307	56	31	8	2.8	.921	OF-132, 3B-5, 2B-2
1890		98	.275	.365	378	104	11	7	3	0.8	68		37		20	0	0	163	78	21	11	2.6	.920	OF-66, 3B-33, SS-1
1891	COL AA	137	.301	.420	552	166	28	4	10	1.8	86	90	42	36	41	0	0	250	53	25	10	2.4	.924	OF-128, 3B-7, SS-2
1892	WAS N	132	.248	.354	492	122	12	11	6	1.2	64	51	36	33	28	0	0	278	46	30	11	2.6	.915	OF-125, 3B-6, 1B-4
1893	CIN N	4	.167	.250	12	2	1	0	0	0.0	3	0	5	0	0	0	0	2	0	3	0	1.3	.400	OF-4
5 yrs.		508	.267	.389	1943	518	67	34	34	1.7	314	227	180	150	110	0	0	1000	233	110	40	2.6	.918	OF-455, 3B-51, 1B-4, SS-3, 2B-2

Frank Duffy

DUFFY, FRANK THOMAS
B. Oct. 14, 1946, Oakland, Calif.
BR TR 6′ 1″ 180 lbs.

Year	Team	Games	BA	SA	AB	H	2B	3B	HR	HR%	R	RBI	BB	SO	SB	Pinch Hit AB	Pinch Hit H	PO	A	E	DP	TC/G	FA	G by Pos
1970	CIN N	6	.182	.364	11	2	2	0	0	0.0	1	0	1	2	1	2	0	4	12	0	4	3.2	1.000	SS-5
1971	2 teams	CIN N (13G –.188)	SF N (21G –.179)																					
"	total	34	.182	.205	44	8	1	0	0	0.0	4	3	1	12	0	9	2	24	43	3	10	3.9	.957	SS-16, 3B-1, 2B-1
1972	CLE A	130	.239	.325	385	92	16	4	3	0.8	23	27	31	54	6	4	1	197	360	13	75	4.5	.977	SS-126
1973		116	.263	.396	361	95	16	4	8	2.2	34	50	25	41	6	0	0	198	377	8	82	5.1	.986	SS-115
1974		158	.233	.310	549	128	18	0	8	1.5	62	48	30	64	7	0	0	242	491	15	83	4.7	.980	SS-158
1975		146	.243	.303	482	117	22	2	1	0.2	44	47	27	60	10	2	0	225	464	16	85	4.9	.977	SS-145
1976		133	.212	.265	392	83	11	2	2	0.5	38	30	29	50	10	1	0	222	344	10	83	4.4	.983	SS-132
1977		122	.201	.287	334	67	13	2	4	1.2	30	31	21	47	8	1	0	145	301	15	62	3.8	.967	SS-121
1978	BOS A	64	.260	.308	104	27	5	0	0	0.0	12	4	6	11	1	2	1	63	98	8	19	2.8	.953	3B-22, SS-21, 2B-12, DH-6
1979		6	.000	.000	3	0	0	0	0	0.0	0	0	0	1	0	0	0	3	2	0	0	1.3	1.000	2B-3, 1B-1
10 yrs.		915	.232	.311	2665	619	104	14	26	1.0	248	240	171	342	49	21	4	1323	2492	88	503	4.4	.977	SS-839, 3B-23, 2B-16, DH-6, 1B-1
LEAGUE CHAMPIONSHIP SERIES																								
1971	SF N	1	.000	.000	1	0	0	0	0	0.0	0	0	0	1	0	1	0	0	0	0	0	0.0	—	

Hugh Duffy

DUFFY, HUGH
B. Nov. 26, 1866, Cranston, R. I. D. Oct. 19, 1954, Boston, Mass.
Manager 1901, 1904–06, 1910–11, 1921–22.
Hall of Fame 1945.
BR TR 5′ 7″ 168 lbs.

Year	Team	Games	BA	SA	AB	H	2B	3B	HR	HR%	R	RBI	BB	SO	SB	Pinch Hit AB	Pinch Hit H	PO	A	E	DP	TC/G	FA	G by Pos
1888	CHI N	71	.282	.413	298	84	10	4	7	2.3	60	41	9	32	13	0	0	107	30	17	5	2.2	.890	OF-67, SS-3, 3B-1
1889		136	.295	.416	**584**	172	21	7	12	2.1	144	89	46	30	52	0	0	187	46	32	4	1.9	.879	OF-126, SS-10
1890	CHI P	137	.320	.470	**596**	**191**	36	16	7	1.2	**161**	82	59	20	78	0	0	255	34	26	5	2.3	.917	OF-137
1891	BOS AA	127	.336	.448	536	180	20	8	8	1.5	134	108	61	29	85	0	0	176	28	17	3	1.7	.923	OF-124, 3B-3, SS-1
1892	BOS N	147	.301	.410	612	184	28	12	5	0.8	125	81	60	37	51	0	0	259	19	20	4	2.0	.933	OF-146, 3B-2
1893		131	.362	.461	560	203	23	7	6	1.1	147	118	50	13	44	0	0	313	15	16	6	2.6	.953	OF-131
1894		125	**.440**[1]	**.690**	539	**237**	**51**	15	**18**	3.3	160	**145**	66	15	48	0	0	319	33	31	5	3.0	.919	OF-124, SS-2
1895		131	.352	.482	531	187	30	6	9	1.7	110	100	63	16	42	0	0	322	20	20	7	2.8	.945	OF-130
1896		131	.300	.389	527	158	16	8	5	0.9	97	112	52	19	39	0	0	267	53	18	5	2.5	.947	OF-126, 2B-9, SS-2
1897		134	.340	.482	550	187	25	10	**11**	2.0	131	129	52		41	0	0	277	26	8	3	2.3	.974	OF-129, 2B-6, SS-2
1898		152	.298	.373	568	169	13	3	8	1.4	97	108	59		29	0	0	334	18	16	2	2.4	.957	OF-152, 3B-1, 1B-1, C-1
1899		147	.279	.378	588	164	29	7	5	0.9	103	102	39		26	0	0	344	9	11	1	2.5	.970	OF-147
1900		55	.304	.409	181	55	5	4	2	1.1	28	31	16		12	4	1	109	7	5	2	2.4	.959	OF-49, 2B-1
1901	MIL A	79	.308	.444	286	88	15	9	2	0.7	41	45	16		13	2	0	141	5	5	0	2.0	.967	OF-77
1904	PHI N	18	.283	.348	46	13	1	1	0	0.0	10	5	13		3	4	1	16	1	3	0	1.4	.850	OF-14
1905		15	.300	.400	40	12	2	1	0	0.0	7	3	1		0	7	3	19	1	2	0	2.8	.909	OF-8
1906		1	.000	.000	1	0	0	0	0	0.0	0	0	0		0	1	0	0	0	0	0	0.0	—	
17 yrs.		1737	.324	.449	7043	2284	325	118	105	1.5	1555	1299	662	211	576	18	5	3445	345	247	52	2.3	.939	OF-1687, SS-20, 2B-16, 3B-7, 1B-1, C-1

Bill Dugan

DUGAN, WILLIAM H.
Brother of Ed Dugan.
B. 1864, Kingston, N. Y. D. July 24, 1921, New York, N. Y.

Year	Team	Games	BA	SA	AB	H	2B	3B	HR	HR%	R	RBI	BB	SO	SB	Pinch Hit AB	Pinch Hit H	PO	A	E	DP	TC/G	FA	G by Pos
1884	2 teams	RIC AA (9G –.071)	KC U (3G –.000)																					
"	total	12	.059	.088	34	2	1	0	0	0.0	4	0	0	0	0	0	0	46	12	10	1	5.7	.853	C-9, OF-3

Joe Dugan

DUGAN, JOSEPH ANTHONY (Jumping Joe)
B. May 12, 1897, Mahanoy City, Pa. D. July 7, 1982, Norwood, Mass.
BR TR 5'11" 160 lbs.

Year	Team	Games	BA	SA	AB	H	2B	3B	HR	HR%	R	RBI	BB	SO	SB	Pinch Hit AB	Pinch Hit H	PO	A	E	DP	TC/G	FA	G by Pos
1917	PHI A	43	.194	.254	134	26	8	0	0	0.0	9	16	3	16	0	0	0	61	111	16	13	4.6	.915	SS-39, 2B-2
1918		120	.195	.259	406	79	11	3	3	0.7	25	34	16	55	4	0	0	304	397	48	69	6.2	.936	SS-85, 2B-35
1919		104	.271	.333	387	105	17	2	1	0.3	25	30	11	30	9	0	0	243	319	44	43	5.8	.927	SS-98, 2B-4, 3B-2
1920		123	.322	.442	491	158	40	5	3	0.6	65	60	19	51	5	0	0	225	328	35	48	4.8	.940	3B-59, SS-32, 2B-32
1921		119	.295	.434	461	136	22	6	10	2.2	54	58	28	45	5	0	0	118	208	16	19	2.9	.953	3B-119
1922	2 teams	BOS A (84G –.287) NY A (60G –.286)																						
"	total	144	.287	.383	593	170	31	4	6	1.0	89	63	22	49	3	1	0	176	306	25	34	3.5	.951	3B-123, SS-20
1923	NY A	146	.283	.384	**644**	182	30	7	7	1.1	111	67	25	41	4	0	0	155	300	12	28	3.2	.974	3B-146
1924		148	.302	.390	610	184	31	7	3	0.5	105	56	31	32	1	0	0	178	251	17	22	3.0	.962	3B-148, 2B-2
1925		102	.292	.359	404	118	19	4	0	0.0	50	31	19	20	2	5	1	118	202	10	19	3.4	.970	3B-96
1926		123	.288	.362	434	125	19	5	1	0.2	39	64	25	16	2	1	0	122	221	16	10	2.9	.955	3B-122
1927		112	.269	.362	387	104	24	3	2	0.5	44	43	27	37	1	1	1	93	196	19	15	2.8	.938	3B-111
1928		94	.276	.381	312	86	15	0	6	1.9	33	34	16	15	1	2	0	87	129	11	13	2.5	.952	3B-91
1929	BOS N	60	.304	.384	125	38	10	0	0	0.0	14	15	8	8	0	26	9	21	43	7	5	2.2	.901	3B-24, SS-5, OF-2, 2B-2
1931	DET A	8	.235	.235	17	4	0	0	0	0.0	1	0	0	3	0	3	1	4	5	1	0	2.0	.900	3B-5
14 yrs.		1446	.280	.372	5405	1515	277	46	42	0.8	664	571	250	418	37	39	12	1905	3016	277	338	3.7	.947	3B-1046, SS-279, 2B-77, OF-2
WORLD SERIES																								
1922	NY A	5	.250	.300	20	5	1	0	0	0.0	4	0	0	1	0	0	0	5	8	0	0	2.6	1.000	3B-5
1923		6	.280	.560	25	7	2	1	1	4.0	5	5	3	0	0	0	0	7	13	0	2	3.3	1.000	3B-6
1926		7	.333	.375	24	8	1	0	0	0.0	2	2	1	1	0	0	0	8	14	1	0	3.3	.957	3B-7
1927		4	.200	.200	15	3	0	0	0	0.0	2	0	0	0	0	0	0	3	6	0	1	2.3	1.000	3B-4
1928		3	.167	.167	6	1	0	0	0	0.0	0	1	0	0	0	0	0	4	0	0	0	1.3	1.000	3B-3
5 yrs.		25	.267	.367	90	24	4	1	1	1.1	13	8	4	2	0	0	0	27	41	1	3	2.8	.986	3B-25

Gus Dugas

DUGAS, AUGUSTIN JOSEPH
B. Mar. 24, 1907, St.-Jean-de-Matha, Que., Canada.
BL TL 5'9" 165 lbs.

Year	Team	Games	BA	SA	AB	H	2B	3B	HR	HR%	R	RBI	BB	SO	SB	Pinch Hit AB	Pinch Hit H	PO	A	E	DP	TC/G	FA	G by Pos
1930	PIT N	9	.290	.355	31	9	2	0	0	0.0	8	1	7	4	0	0	0	18	1	3	0	2.4	.864	OF-9
1932		55	.237	.423	97	23	3	3	3	3.1	13	12	7	11	0	33	5	40	0	2	0	2.1	.952	OF-20
1933	PHI N	37	.169	.211	71	12	3	0	0	0.0	4	9	1	9	0	24	5	113	8	2	7	10.3	.984	1B-11, OF-1
1934	WAS A	24	.053	.105	19	1	1	0	0	0.0	2	1	3	3	0	18	0	3	0	0	0	1.5	1.000	OF-2
4 yrs.		125	.206	.317	218	45	9	3	3	1.4	27	23	18	27	0	75	10	174	9	7	7	4.4	.963	OF-32, 1B-11

Dan Dugdale

DUGDALE, DANIEL EDWARD (Dug)
B. Oct. 28, 1864, Peoria, Ill. D. Mar. 9, 1934, Seattle, Wash.
5'8" 180 lbs.

Year	Team	Games	BA	SA	AB	H	2B	3B	HR	HR%	R	RBI	BB	SO	SB	Pinch Hit AB	Pinch Hit H	PO	A	E	DP	TC/G	FA	G by Pos
1886	KC N	12	.175	.175	40	7	0	0	0	0.0	4	2	2	13		0	0	33	13	8	0	4.2	.852	C-7, OF-6
1894	WAS N	38	.239	.299	134	32	4	2	0	0.0	19	16	13	14	7	0	0	74	36	18	0	3.4	.859	C-33, 3B-3, OF-2
2 yrs.		50	.224	.270	174	39	4	2	0	0.0	23	18	15	27	7	0	0	107	49	26	0	3.6	.857	C-40, OF-8, 3B-3

Oscar Dugey

DUGEY, OSCAR JOSEPH
B. Oct. 25, 1887, Palestine, Tex. D. Jan. 1, 1966, Dallas, Tex.
BR TR 5'8" 160 lbs.

Year	Team	Games	BA	SA	AB	H	2B	3B	HR	HR%	R	RBI	BB	SO	SB	Pinch Hit AB	Pinch Hit H	PO	A	E	DP	TC/G	FA	G by Pos
1913	BOS N	5	.250	.250	8	2	0	0	0	0.0	1	0	1	1	0	1	0	4	4	2	0	2.5	.800	3B-2, SS-1, 2B-1
1914		58	.193	.239	109	21	2	0	1	0.9	17	10	10	15	10	21	4	52	26	8	3	2.5	.907	OF-17, 2B-16, 3B-1
1915	PHI N	42	.154	.179	39	6	1	0	0	0.0	4	0	7	5	2	16	1	10	22	2	1	2.4	.941	2B-14
1916		41	.220	.280	50	11	3	0	0	0.0	9	1	9	8	3	9	1	22	36	2	3	5.0	.967	2B-12
1917		44	.194	.278	72	14	4	1	0	0.0	12	9	4	9	2	19	4	32	30	8	3	3.7	.886	2B-15, OF-4
1920	BOS N	5	—	—	0	0	0	0	0	—	2	0	0	0	0	0	0	0	0	0	0	0.0	—	
6 yrs.		195	.194	.248	278	54	10	1	1	0.4	45	20	31	38	17	66	10	120	118	22	10	3.1	.915	2B-58, OF-21, 3B-3, SS-1
WORLD SERIES																								
1915	PHI N	2	—	—	0	0	0	0	0	—	0	0	0	0	1	0	0	0	0	0	0	0.0	—	

Jim Duggan

DUGGAN, JAMES ELMER
B. June 3, 1884, Whiteland, Ind. D. Dec. 5, 1951, Indianapolis, Ind.
BL TL 5'10" 165 lbs.

Year	Team	Games	BA	SA	AB	H	2B	3B	HR	HR%	R	RBI	BB	SO	SB	Pinch Hit AB	Pinch Hit H	PO	A	E	DP	TC/G	FA	G by Pos
1911	STL A	1	.000	.000	4	0	0	0	0	0.0	1	1	1		0	0	0	11	1	0	2	12.0	1.000	1B-1

Tommy Dunbar

DUNBAR, THOMAS JEROME
B. Nov. 24, 1959, Graniteville, S. C.
BL TL 6'2" 185 lbs.

Year	Team	Games	BA	SA	AB	H	2B	3B	HR	HR%	R	RBI	BB	SO	SB	Pinch Hit AB	Pinch Hit H	PO	A	E	DP	TC/G	FA	G by Pos
1983	TEX A	12	.250	.250	24	6	0	0	0	0.0	3	3	5	7	3	0	0	7	0	1	0	0.8	.875	OF-9, DH-1
1984		34	.258	.340	97	25	2	0	2	2.1	9	10	6	16	1	10	2	31	0	2	0	1.3	.939	OF-20, DH-5
1985		45	.202	.269	104	21	4	0	1	1.0	7	5	12	9	0	14	1	14	0	1	0	0.5	.933	DH-18, OF-14
3 yrs.		91	.231	.298	225	52	6	0	3	1.3	19	18	23	32	4	24	3	52	0	4	0	0.8	.929	OF-43, DH-24

Dave Duncan

DUNCAN, DAVID EDWIN
B. Sept. 26, 1945, Dallas, Tex.
BR TR 6'2" 190 lbs.

Year	Team	Games	BA	SA	AB	H	2B	3B	HR	HR%	R	RBI	BB	SO	SB	Pinch Hit AB	Pinch Hit H	PO	A	E	DP	TC/G	FA	G by Pos
1964	KC A	25	.170	.264	53	9	0	1	1	1.9	2	5	2	20	0	2	1	99	7	2	6	4.9	.981	C-22
1967		34	.188	.376	101	19	4	0	5	5.0	9	11	4	50	0	2	0	176	13	4	2	6.0	.979	C-32
1968	OAK A	82	.191	.293	246	47	4	0	7	2.8	15	28	25	68	1	3	2	474	41	7	5	6.6	.987	C-79
1969		58	.126	.220	127	16	3	0	3	2.4	11	22	19	41	0	4	0	209	15	4	1	4.1	.982	C-56
1970		86	.259	.418	232	60	7	0	10	4.3	21	29	22	38	0	10	4	373	28	9	9	5.6	.978	C-73
1971		103	.253	.419	363	92	13	1	15	4.1	39	40	28	77	1	1	1	678	41	12	3	7.2	.984	C-102
1972		121	.218	.392	403	88	13	0	19	4.7	39	59	34	68	0	8	1	661	43	5	9	6.3	.993	C-113
1973	CLE A	95	.233	.419	344	80	11	1	17	4.9	43	43	35	86	3	0	0	533	41	7	8	6.1	.988	C-86, DH-9
1974		136	.200	.341	425	85	10	1	16	3.8	45	46	42	91	0	1	0	564	48	15	10	4.5	.976	C-134, 1B-3, DH-1
1975	BAL A	96	.205	.345	307	63	7	0	12	3.9	30	41	16	82	0	7	0	397	41	8	5	4.7	.982	C-95
1976		93	.204	.271	284	58	7	0	4	1.4	20	17	25	56	0	1	0	371	35	6	9	4.4	.985	C-93
11 yrs.		929	.214	.357	2885	617	79	4	109	3.8	274	341	252	677	5	39	9	4535	353	79	67	5.5	.984	C-885, DH-10, 1B-3
LEAGUE CHAMPIONSHIP SERIES																								
1971	OAK A	2	.500	.667	6	3	1	0	0	0.0	0	2	0	0	0	0	0	15	0	0	0	7.5	1.000	C-2
1972		2	.000	.000	2	0	0	0	0	0.0	0	0	1	1	0	1	0	5	1	0	0	3.0	1.000	C-2
2 yrs.		4	.375	.500	8	3	1	0	0	0.0	0	2	1	1	0	1	0	20	1	0	0	5.3	1.000	C-4
WORLD SERIES																								
1972	OAK A	3	.200	.200	5	1	0	0	0	0.0	0	0	1	3	0	2	1	5	1	0	0	6.0	1.000	C-1

Jim Duncan

DUNCAN, JAMES WILLIAM BR TR 5′ 8″ 140 lbs.
B. July 1, 1871, Saltsburg, Pa. D. Oct. 16, 1901, Foxburg, Pa.

Year	Team	Games	BA	SA	AB	H	2B	3B	HR	HR%	R	RBI	BB	SO	SB	Pinch Hit AB	Pinch Hit H	PO	A	E	DP	TC/G	FA	G by Pos
1899	**2 teams**	**WAS N** (15G –.234)	**CLE N** (31G –.229)																					
″	**total**	46	.230	.336	152	35	4	3	2	1.3	14	14	8		1	2	0	233	41	16	13	6.4	.945	C-28, 1B-17

Mariano Duncan

DUNCAN, MARIANO BR TR 6′ 165 lbs.
Born Mariano Duncan (Nolasco). BB 1985–1987
B. Mar. 13, 1963, San Pedro de Macoris, Dominican Republic.

Year	Team	Games	BA	SA	AB	H	2B	3B	HR	HR%	R	RBI	BB	SO	SB	Pinch Hit AB	Pinch Hit H	PO	A	E	DP	TC/G	FA	G by Pos
1985	**LA N**	142	.244	.340	562	137	24	6	6	1.1	74	39	38	113	38	2	1	224	430	30	64	4.8	.956	SS-123, 2B-19
1986		109	.229	.305	407	93	7	0	8	2.0	47	30	30	78	48	2	0	172	317	25	46	4.8	.951	SS-106
1987		76	.215	.322	261	56	8	1	6	2.3	31	18	17	62	11	1	0	101	213	21	40	4.4	.937	SS-67, 2B-7, OF-2
1989	**2 teams**	**LA N** (49G –.250)	**CIN N** (45G –.247)																					
″	**total**	94	.248	.357	258	64	15	2	3	1.2	32	21	8	51	9	18	7	101	155	14	30	3.4	.948	SS-60, 2B-13, OF-7
1990	**CIN N**	125	.306	.476	435	133	22	**11**	10	2.3	67	55	24	67	13	5	0	265	303	18	55	4.6	.969	2B-115, SS-12, OF-1
1991		100	.258	.411	333	86	7	4	12	3.6	46	40	12	57	5	8	2	169	212	9	41	3.9	.977	2B-62, SS-32, OF-7
1992	**PHI N**	142	.267	.389	574	153	40	3	8	1.4	71	50	17	108	23	3	1	256	210	16	43	3.0	.967	OF-65, 2B-52, SS-42, 3B-4
1993		124	.282	.417	496	140	26	4	11	2.2	68	73	12	88	6	10	4	180	304	21	50	4.1	.958	2B-65, SS-59
1994		88	.268	.406	347	93	22	1	8	2.3	49	48	17	72	10	3	2	148	188	12	38	3.9	.966	2B-37, 3B-28, SS-19, 1B-6
1995	**2 teams**	**PHI N** (52G –.286)	**CIN N** (29G –.290)																					
″	**total**	81	.287	.423	265	76	14	2	6	2.3	36	36	5	62	1	18	7	215	145	11	42	5.1	.970	2B-31, SS-20, 1B-18, OF-3, 3B-1
10 yrs.		1081	.262	.385	3938	1031	185	34	78	2.0	521	410	180	758	164	70	24	1831	2477	177	449	4.1	.961	SS-540, 2B-401, OF-85, 3B-33, 1B-24
DIVISIONAL PLAYOFF SERIES																								
1995	**CIN N**	2	.667	.667	3	2	0	0	0	0.0	1	1	0	0	1	1	0	0	1	0	0	1.0	1.000	2B-1
LEAGUE CHAMPIONSHIP SERIES																								
1985	**LA N**	5	.222	.444	18	4	2	1	0	0.0	2	1	1	3	1	0	0	7	16	1	3	4.8	.958	SS-5
1990	**CIN N**	6	.300	.450	20	6	0	0	1	5.0	1	4	0	8	0	0	0	6	11	1	0	3.0	.944	2B-6
1993	**PHI N**	3	.267	.533	15	4	0	2	0	0.0	3	0	0	5	0	0	0	5	6	1	0	4.0	.917	2B-3
1995	**CIN N**	3	.000	.000	3	0	0	0	0	0.0	0	0	1	1	0	1	0	9	0	0	1	9.0	1.000	1B-1
4 yrs.		17	.250	.446	56	14	2	3 **2nd**	1	1.8	6	5	2	17 **10th**	1	1	0	27	33	3	4	4.2	.952	2B-9, SS-5, 1B-1
WORLD SERIES																								
1990	**CIN N**	4	.143	.143	14	2	0	0	0	0.0	1	1	2	2	1	0	0	9	9	0	2	4.5	1.000	2B-4
1993	**PHI N**	6	.345	.414	29	10	0	1	0	0.0	5	2	1	7	3	0	0	11	17	1	5	4.8	.966	2B-5, DH-1
2 yrs.		10	.279	.326	43	12	0	1	0	0.0	6	3	3	9	4	0	0	20	26	1	7	4.7	.979	2B-9, DH-1

Pat Duncan

DUNCAN, LOUIS BAIRD BR TR 5′ 9″ 170 lbs.
B. Oct. 6, 1893, Coalton, Ohio D. July 17, 1960, Jackson, Ohio.

Year	Team	Games	BA	SA	AB	H	2B	3B	HR	HR%	R	RBI	BB	SO	SB	Pinch Hit AB	Pinch Hit H	PO	A	E	DP	TC/G	FA	G by Pos
1915	**PIT N**	3	.200	.200	5	1	0	0	0	0.0	0	0	0	1	0	2	1	1	0	0	0	1.0	1.000	OF-1
1919	**CIN N**	31	.244	.411	90	22	3	3	2	2.2	9	17	8	7	2	3	0	51	3	1	1	2.0	.982	OF-27
1920		154	.295	.372	576	170	16	11	2	0.3	75	83	42	42	18	0	0	334	15	13	4	2.4	.964	OF-154
1921		145	.308	.408	532	164	27	10	2	0.4	57	60	44	33	7	0	0	349	19	11	2	2.6	.971	OF-145
1922		151	.328	.479	607	199	44	12	8	1.3	94	94	40	31	12	0	0	316	19	10	4	2.3	.971	OF-151
1923		147	.327	.438	566	185	26	8	7	1.2	92	83	30	27	15	1	0	291	11	2	2	2.1	.993	OF-146
1924		96	.270	.392	319	86	21	6	2	0.6	34	37	20	23	1	13	4	124	3	10	0	1.7	.927	OF-83
7 yrs.		727	.307	.420	2695	827	137	50	23	0.9	361	374	184	164	55	19	5	1466	70	47	13	2.2	.970	OF-707
WORLD SERIES																								
1919	**CIN N**	8	.269	.346	26	7	2	0	0	0.0	3	8	2	2	0	0	0	9	1	0	0	1.3	1.000	OF-8

Taylor Duncan

DUNCAN, TAYLOR McDOWELL BR TR 6′ 170 lbs.
B. May 12, 1953, Memphis, Tenn.

Year	Team	Games	BA	SA	AB	H	2B	3B	HR	HR%	R	RBI	BB	SO	SB	Pinch Hit AB	Pinch Hit H	PO	A	E	DP	TC/G	FA	G by Pos
1977	**STL N**	8	.333	.583	12	4	0	0	1	8.3	2	2	2	1	0	2	0	0	2	0	0	0.4	1.000	3B-5
1978	**OAK A**	104	.257	.335	319	82	15	2	2	0.6	25	37	19	38	1	13	1	73	128	9	6	2.0	.957	3B-84, 2B-11, DH-7, SS-1
2 yrs.		112	.260	.344	331	86	15	2	3	0.9	27	39	21	39	1	15	1	73	130	9	6	2.0	.958	3B-89, 2B-11, DH-7, SS-1

Vern Duncan

DUNCAN, VERNON VAN DUKE BL TR 5′ 9″ 155 lbs.
B. Jan. 6, 1890, Clayton, N. C. D. June 1, 1954, Daytona Beach, Fla.

Year	Team	Games	BA	SA	AB	H	2B	3B	HR	HR%	R	RBI	BB	SO	SB	Pinch Hit AB	Pinch Hit H	PO	A	E	DP	TC/G	FA	G by Pos
1913	**PHI N**	8	.417	.500	12	5	1	0	0	0.0	3	1	0	3	0	4	2	2	1	0	0	1.0	1.000	OF-3
1914	**BAL F**	157	.287	.363	557	160	20	8	2	0.4	99	53	67		13	2	0	266	32	27	8	2.1	.917	OF-148, 3B-8, 2B-1
1915		146	.267	.328	531	142	18	4	2	0.4	68	43	54		19	4	0	285	51	27	12	2.5	.926	OF-124, 3B-21, 2B-1
3 yrs.		311	.279	.347	1100	307	39	12	4	0.4	170	97	121	3	32	10	2	553	84	54	20	2.3	.922	OF-275, 3B-29, 2B-2

Ed Dundon

DUNDON, EDWARD JOSEPH (Dummy) TR
B. July 10, 1859, Columbus, Ohio D. Aug. 18, 1893, Columbus, Ohio.

Year	Team	Games	BA	SA	AB	H	2B	3B	HR	HR%	R	RBI	BB	SO	SB	Pinch Hit AB	Pinch Hit H	PO	A	E	DP	TC/G	FA	G by Pos
1883	**COL AA**	26	.161	.172	93	15	1	0	0	0.0	8		3			0	0	24	37	12	3	2.4	.836	P-20, OF-9, 2B-1
1884		26	.140	.209	86	12	2	2	0	0.0	6		5			0	0	60	22	5	3	2.9	.943	OF-16, P-11, 1B-3
2 yrs.		52	.151	.190	179	27	3	2	0	0.0	14		8			0	0	84	59	17	6	2.7	.894	P-31, OF-25, 1B-3, 2B-1

Gus Dundon

DUNDON, AUGUSTUS JOSEPH BR TR 5′10″ 165 lbs.
B. July 10, 1874, Columbus, Ohio D. Sept. 1, 1940, Pittsburgh, Pa.

Year	Team	Games	BA	SA	AB	H	2B	3B	HR	HR%	R	RBI	BB	SO	SB	Pinch Hit AB	Pinch Hit H	PO	A	E	DP	TC/G	FA	G by Pos
1904	**CHI A**	108	.228	.268	373	85	9	3	0	0.0	40	36	30		19	0	0	194	289	13	26	4.6	.974	2B-103, 3B-3, SS-2
1905		106	.192	.228	364	70	7	3	0	0.0	30	22	23		14	0	0	223	328	12	25	5.3	.979	2B-104, SS-2
1906		33	.135	.146	96	13	1	0	0	0.0	7	4	11		4	1	0	81	91	14	8	5.8	.925	2B-18, SS-14
3 yrs.		247	.202	.236	833	168	17	6	0	0.0	77	62	64		37	1	0	498	708	39	59	5.1	.969	2B-225, SS-18, 3B-3

Sam Dungan

DUNGAN, SAMUEL MORRISON (Terrible Sammy) BR 5′11″ 180 lbs.
B. July 29, 1866, Ferndale, Calif. D. Mar. 16, 1939, Santa Ana, Calif.

Year	Team	Games	BA	SA	AB	H	2B	3B	HR	HR%	R	RBI	BB	SO	SB	Pinch Hit AB	Pinch Hit H	PO	A	E	DP	TC/G	FA	G by Pos
1892	**CHI N**	113	.284	.360	433	123	19	7	0	0.0	46	53	35	19	15	0	0	183	8	20	2	1.9	.905	OF-113
1893		107	.297	.389	465	138	23	7	2	0.4	86	64	29	8	11	0	0	175	20	17	3	2.0	.920	OF-107
1894	**2 teams**	**CHI N** (10G –.231)	**LOU N** (8G –.344)																					
″	**total**	18	.282	.324	71	20	3	0	0	0.0	11	6	11	2	3	0	0	30	3	1	2	1.9	.971	OF-18

Sam Dungan *continued*

Year	Team	Games	BA	SA	AB	H	2B	3B	HR	HR%	R	RBI	BB	SO	SB	Pinch Hit AB	Pinch Hit H	PO	A	E	DP	TC/G	FA	G by Pos
1900	**CHI N**	6	.267	.267	15	4	0	0	0	0.0	1	1	1		0	3	1	4	0	1	0	1.7	.800	OF-3
1901	**WAS A**	138	.320	.415	559	179	26	12	1	0.2	70	73	40		9	0	0	494	26	16	19	3.9	.970	OF-104, 1B-35
5 yrs.		382	.301	.386	1543	464	71	26	3	0.2	214	197	116	29	38	3	1	886	57	55	26	2.6	.945	OF-345, 1B-35

Lee Dunham

DUNHAM, LELAND HUFFIELD BL TL 5′11″ 185 lbs.
B. June 9, 1902, Atlanta, Ill. D. May 11, 1961, Atlanta, Ill.

Year	Team	Games	BA	SA	AB	H	2B	3B	HR	HR%	R	RBI	BB	SO	SB	Pinch Hit AB	Pinch Hit H	PO	A	E	DP	TC/G	FA	G by Pos
1926	**PHI N**	5	.250	.250	4	1	0	0	0	0.0	0	1	0	1	0	3	0	2	0	0	0	1.0	1.000	1B-2

Bill Dunlap

DUNLAP, WILLIAM JAMES BR TR 5′11″ 170 lbs.
B. May 1, 1909, Palmer, Mass. D. Nov. 29, 1980, Reading, Pa.

Year	Team	Games	BA	SA	AB	H	2B	3B	HR	HR%	R	RBI	BB	SO	SB	Pinch Hit AB	Pinch Hit H	PO	A	E	DP	TC/G	FA	G by Pos
1929	**BOS N**	10	.414	.586	29	12	0	1	1	3.4	6	4	4	4	0	1	0	16	0	2	0	2.0	.889	OF-9
1930		16	.069	.103	29	2	1	0	0	0.0	3	0	0	6	0	9	0	15	0	0	0	2.1	1.000	OF-7
2 yrs.		26	.241	.345	58	14	1	1	1	1.7	9	4	4	10	0	10	0	31	0	2	0	2.1	.939	OF-16

Fred Dunlap

DUNLAP, FREDERICK C. (Sure Shot) BR TR 5′ 8″ 165 lbs.
B. May 21, 1859, Philadelphia, Pa. D. Dec. 1, 1902, Philadelphia, Pa.
Manager 1882, 1884–85, 1889.

Year	Team	Games	BA	SA	AB	H	2B	3B	HR	HR%	R	RBI	BB	SO	SB	Pinch Hit AB	Pinch Hit H	PO	A	E	DP	TC/G	FA	G by Pos
1880	**CLE N**	85	.276	.429	373	103	**27**	9	4	1.1	61	30	7	32		0	0	252	290	53	44	7.0	.911	2B-85
1881		80	.325	.444	351	114	25	4	3	0.9	60	24	18	24		0	0	258	255	52	41	7.1	.908	2B-79, 3B-1
1882		84	.280	.354	364	102	19	4	0	0.0	68	28	23	26		0	0	268	297	63	62	7.5	.900	2B-84
1883		93	.326	.452	396	129	34	2	4	1.0	81		22	21		0	0	305	290	58	49	6.9	.911	2B-93, OF-1
1884	**STL U**	101	**.412**	**.621**	449	**185**	39	8	**13**	**2.9**	**160**		29			0	0	343	302	51	54	6.8	.927	2B-100, OF-1, P-1
1885	**STL N**	106	.270	.333	423	114	11	5	2	0.5	70	25	41	24		0	0	314	374	49	53	7.0	.934	2B-106
1886	**2 teams**	**STL N** (71G –.267) **DET N** (51G –.286)																						
″	**total**	122	.274	.387	481	132	23	5	7	1.5	85	69	44	51		0	0	333	393	58	64	6.4	.926	2B-122, OF-1
1887	**DET N**	65	.265	.441	272	72	13	10	5	1.8	60	45	25	12	15	0	0	212	225	24	44	7.0	.948	2B-65, P-1
1888	**PIT N**	82	.262	.333	321	84	12	4	1	0.3	41	36	16	30	24	0	0	240	279	33	44	6.7	.940	2B-82
1889		121	.235	.290	451	106	19	0	2	0.4	59	65	46	33	21	0	0	342	393	39	51	6.4	.950	2B-121
1890	**2 teams**	**PIT N** (17G –.172) **NY P** (1G –.500)																						
″	**total**	18	.191	.235	68	13	1	1	0	0.0	10	3	7	6	2	0	0	37	54	13	4	5.8	.875	2B-18
1891	**WAS AA**	8	.200	.320	25	5	1	1	0	0.0	4	4	5	4	3	0	0	8	19	6	3	4.1	.818	2B-8
12 yrs.		965	.292	.406	3974	1159	224	53	41	1.0	759	329	283	263	65	0	0	2912	3171	499	513	6.8	.924	2B-963, OF-3, P-2, 3B-1

Grant Dunlap

DUNLAP, GRANT LESTER (Snap) BR TR 6′ 2″ 180 lbs.
B. Dec. 20, 1923, Stockton, Calif.

Year	Team	Games	BA	SA	AB	H	2B	3B	HR	HR%	R	RBI	BB	SO	SB	Pinch Hit AB	Pinch Hit H	PO	A	E	DP	TC/G	FA	G by Pos
1953	**STL N**	16	.353	.647	17	6	0	1	1	5.9	2	3	0	2	0	15	5	0	0	0	0	0.0	.000	OF-1

Jack Dunleavy

DUNLEAVY, JOHN FRANCIS TL 5′ 6″ 167 lbs.
B. Sept. 14, 1879, Harrison, N. J. D. Apr. 11, 1944, South Norwalk, Conn.

Year	Team	Games	BA	SA	AB	H	2B	3B	HR	HR%	R	RBI	BB	SO	SB	Pinch Hit AB	Pinch Hit H	PO	A	E	DP	TC/G	FA	G by Pos
1903	**STL N**	61	.249	.295	193	48	3	3	0	0.0	23	10	13		10	**9**	**4**	58	43	3	5	2.0	.971	OF-38, P-14
1904		51	.233	.326	172	40	7	3	1	0.6	23	14	16		8	0	0	77	20	2	2	1.9	.980	OF-44, P-7
1905		119	.241	.303	435	105	8	8	1	0.2	52	25	55		15	0	0	177	28	8	7	1.8	.962	OF-118, 2B-1
3 yrs.		231	.241	.306	800	193	18	14	2	0.3	98	49	84		33	9	4	312	91	13	14	1.9	.969	OF-200, P-21, 2B-1

George Dunlop

DUNLOP, GEORGE HENRY BR TR 5′10″ 170 lbs.
B. July 19, 1888, Meriden, Conn. D. Dec. 12, 1972, Meriden, Conn.

Year	Team	Games	BA	SA	AB	H	2B	3B	HR	HR%	R	RBI	BB	SO	SB	Pinch Hit AB	Pinch Hit H	PO	A	E	DP	TC/G	FA	G by Pos
1913	**CLE A**	7	.235	.294	17	4	1	0	0	0.0	3	0	0	5	0	0	0	9	13	1	0	3.3	.957	SS-4, 3B-3
1914		1	.000	.000	3	0	0	0	0	0.0	0	0	1	1	0	0	0	0	1	0	0	1.0	1.000	SS-1
2 yrs.		8	.200	.250	20	4	1	0	0	0.0	3	0	1	6	0	0	0	9	14	1	0	3.0	.958	SS-5, 3B-3

Jack Dunn

DUNN, JOHN JOSEPH (Handyman) BR TR 5′ 9″
B. Oct. 6, 1872, Meadville, Pa. D. Oct. 22, 1928, Towson, Md.

Year	Team	Games	BA	SA	AB	H	2B	3B	HR	HR%	R	RBI	BB	SO	SB	Pinch Hit AB	Pinch Hit H	PO	A	E	DP	TC/G	FA	G by Pos
1897	**BKN N**	36	.221	.252	131	29	4	0	0	0.0	20	17	4		2	0	0	31	74	14	3	3.3	.882	P-25, 2B-4, OF-3, 3B-3, SS-1
1898		51	.246	.257	167	41	0	1	0	0.0	21	19	7		3	0	0	42	91	12	6	2.8	.917	P-41, SS-4, OF-4, 3B-2
1899		43	.246	.279	122	30	2	1	0	0.0	21	16	3		3	1	0	21	83	4	1	2.6	.963	P-41, SS-1
1900	**2 teams**	**BKN N** (10G –.231) **PHI N** (10G –.303)																						
″	**total**	20	.271	.288	59	16	1	0	0	0.0	5	6	1		1	0	0	7	40	3	0	2.5	.940	P-20
1901	**2 teams**	**PHI N** (2G –1.000) **BAL A** (96G –.249)																						
″	**total**	98	.251	.298	363	91	9	4	0	0.0	42	36	22		10	0	0	157	207	53	14	4.2	.873	3B-67, SS-19, P-11, OF-1, 2B-1
1902	**NY N**	100	.211	.249	342	72	11	1	0	0.0	26	14	20		13	1	1	154	153	23	17	3.2	.930	OF-43, SS-36, 3B-18, P-3, 2B-2
1903		78	.241	.307	257	62	15	1	0	0.0	35	37	15		12	6	1	101	173	26	24	4.2	.913	SS-27, 3B-25, 2B-19, OF-1
1904		64	.309	.414	181	56	12	2	1	0.6	27	19	11		11	6	1	61	89	15	7	3.0	.909	3B-28, SS-10, 2B-9, OF-7, P-1
8 yrs.		490	.245	.292	1622	397	54	10	1	0.1	197	164	83		55	14	3	574	910	150	72	3.4	.908	3B-143, P-142, SS-98, OF-59, 2B-35

Joe Dunn

DUNN, JOSEPH EDWARD BR TR 5′ 9″ 160 lbs.
B. Mar. 11, 1885, Springfield, Ohio D. Mar. 19, 1944, Springfield, Ohio.

Year	Team	Games	BA	SA	AB	H	2B	3B	HR	HR%	R	RBI	BB	SO	SB	Pinch Hit AB	Pinch Hit H	PO	A	E	DP	TC/G	FA	G by Pos
1908	**BKN N**	20	.172	.219	64	11	3	0	0	0.0	3	5	0		0	0	0	93	42	6	3	7.1	.957	C-20
1909		10	.160	.200	25	4	1	0	0	0.0	1	2	0		0	3	0	33	7	2	2	6.0	.952	C-7
2 yrs.		30	.169	.213	89	15	4	0	0	0.0	4	7	0		0	3	0	126	49	8	5	6.8	.956	C-27

Ron Dunn

DUNN, RONALD RAY BR TR 5′11″ 180 lbs.
B. Jan. 24, 1950, Oklahoma City, Okla.

Year	Team	Games	BA	SA	AB	H	2B	3B	HR	HR%	R	RBI	BB	SO	SB	Pinch Hit AB	Pinch Hit H	PO	A	E	DP	TC/G	FA	G by Pos
1974	**CHI N**	23	.294	.485	68	20	7	0	2	2.9	6	15	12	8	0	1	0	31	46	7	6	3.1	.917	2B-21, 3B-6
1975		32	.159	.295	44	7	3	0	1	2.3	2	6	6	17	0	17	3	6	17	1	0	1.7	.958	3B-11, OF-2, 2B-1
2 yrs.		55	.241	.411	112	27	10	0	3	2.7	8	21	18	25	0	18	3	37	63	8	6	2.6	.926	2B-22, 3B-17, OF-2

Steve Dunn

DUNN, STEPHEN B. 5′ 9½″ 173 lbs.
B. Dec. 21, 1858, London, Ont., Canada D. May 5, 1933, London, Ont., Canada.

Year	Team	Games	BA	SA	AB	H	2B	3B	HR	HR%	R	RBI	BB	SO	SB	Pinch Hit AB	Pinch Hit H	PO	A	E	DP	TC/G	FA	G by Pos
1884	**STP U**	9	.250	.313	32	8	2	0	0	0.0	2		0			0	0	67	5	4	3	7.6	.947	1B-9, 3B-1

Steve Dunn

DUNN, STEVEN ROBERT — BL TL 6′ 4″ 225 lbs.
B. Apr. 18, 1970, Champaign, Ill.

Year	Team	Games	BA	SA	AB	H	2B	3B	HR	HR%	R	RBI	BB	SO	SB	Pinch Hit AB	Pinch Hit H	PO	A	E	DP	TC/G	FA	G by Pos
1994	MIN A	14	.229	.371	35	8	5	0	0	0.0	2	4	1	12	0	2	1	91	8	1	11	8.3	.990	1B-12
1995		5	.000	.000	6	0	0	0	0	0.0	0	0	1	3	0	3	0	5	0	0	2	1.7	1.000	1B-3
2 yrs.		19	.195	.317	41	8	5	0	0	0.0	2	4	2	15	0	5	1	96	8	1	13	7.0	.990	1B-15

Shawon Dunston

DUNSTON, SHAWON DONNELL — BR TR 6′ 1″ 175 lbs.
B. Mar. 21, 1963, Brooklyn, N. Y.

Year	Team	Games	BA	SA	AB	H	2B	3B	HR	HR%	R	RBI	BB	SO	SB	Pinch Hit AB	Pinch Hit H	PO	A	E	DP	TC/G	FA	G by Pos
1985	CHI N	74	.260	.388	250	65	12	4	4	1.6	40	18	19	42	11	0	0	144	248	17	39	5.6	.958	SS-73
1986		150	.250	.410	581	145	36	3	17	2.9	66	68	21	114	13	2	1	320	465	32	96	5.5	.961	SS-149
1987		95	.246	.358	346	85	18	3	5	1.4	40	22	10	68	12	1	0	160	271	14	54	4.7	.969	SS-94
1988		155	.249	.357	575	143	23	6	9	1.6	69	56	16	108	30	3	0	257	455	20	76	4.8	.973	SS-151
1989		138	.278	.403	471	131	20	6	9	1.9	52	60	30	86	19	1	0	213	379	17	76	4.4	.972	SS-138
1990		146	.262	.426	545	143	22	8	17	3.1	73	66	15	87	25	0	0	255	392	20	77	4.6	.970	SS-144
1991		142	.260	.407	492	128	22	7	12	2.4	59	50	23	64	21	2	1	261	383	21	69	4.7	.968	SS-142
1992		18	.315	.384	73	23	3	1	0	0.0	8	2	3	13	2	0	0	28	42	1	9	3.9	.986	SS-18
1993		7	.400	.600	10	4	2	0	0	0.0	3	2	0	1	0	5	2	5	0	0	0	2.5	1.000	SS-2
1994		88	.278	.435	331	92	19	0	11	3.3	38	35	16	48	3	3	2	121	219	12	47	4.2	.966	SS-84
1995		127	.296	.472	477	141	30	6	14	2.9	58	69	10	75	10	1	0	188	336	17	50	4.3	.969	SS-125
11 yrs.		1140	.265	.407	4151	1100	207	44	98	2.4	506	448	163	706	146	18	6	1952	3190	171	593	4.7	.968	SS-1120
LEAGUE CHAMPIONSHIP SERIES																								
1989	CHI N	5	.316	.316	19	6	0	0	0	0.0	2	0	1	1	1	0	0	10	14	1	1	5.0	.960	SS-5

Dan Duran

DURAN, DANIEL JAMES — BL TL 5′11″ 190 lbs.
B. Mar. 16, 1954, Palo Alto, Calif.

Year	Team	Games	BA	SA	AB	H	2B	3B	HR	HR%	R	RBI	BB	SO	SB	Pinch Hit AB	Pinch Hit H	PO	A	E	DP	TC/G	FA	G by Pos
1981	TEX A	13	.250	.250	16	4	0	0	0	0.0	1	0	1	1	0	5	2	7	1	0	0	1.0	1.000	OF-7, 1B-1

Kid Durbin

DURBIN, BLAINE ALPHONSUS — BL TL 5′ 8″ 155 lbs.
B. Sept. 10, 1886, Lamar, Mo. D. Sept. 11, 1943, Kirkwood, Mo.

Year	Team	Games	BA	SA	AB	H	2B	3B	HR	HR%	R	RBI	BB	SO	SB	Pinch Hit AB	Pinch Hit H	PO	A	E	DP	TC/G	FA	G by Pos
1907	CHI N	11	.333	.333	18	6	0	0	0	0.0	2	0	1		0	1	0	4	7	0	0	1.1	1.000	OF-5, P-5
1908		14	.250	.286	28	7	1	0	0	0.0	3	0	2		0	2	0	15	0	0	0	1.4	1.000	OF-11
1909	2 teams	CIN N (6G –.200) PIT N (1G –.000)																						
″	total	7	.200	.200	5	1	0	0	0	0.0	1	0	1		0	5	1	0	0	0	0	0.0	—	
3 yrs.		32	.275	.294	51	14	1	0	0	0.0	6	0	4		0	8	1	19	7	0	0	1.2	1.000	OF-16, P-5

Joe Durham

DURHAM, JOSEPH VANN (Pop) — BR TR 6′ 1″ 186 lbs.
B. July 31, 1931, Newport News, Va.

Year	Team	Games	BA	SA	AB	H	2B	3B	HR	HR%	R	RBI	BB	SO	SB	Pinch Hit AB	Pinch Hit H	PO	A	E	DP	TC/G	FA	G by Pos
1954	BAL A	10	.225	.300	40	9	0	0	1	2.5	4	3	4	7	0	0	0	22	0	2	0	2.4	.917	OF-10
1957		77	.185	.274	157	29	2	0	4	2.5	19	17	16	42	1	15	1	70	1	0	0	1.2	1.000	OF-59
1959	STL N	6	.000	.000	5	0	0	0	0	0.0	2	0	0	1	0	2	0	2	0	0	0	2.0	1.000	OF-1
3 yrs.		93	.188	.272	202	38	2	0	5	2.5	25	20	20	50	1	17	1	94	1	2	0	1.4	.979	OF-70

Leon Durham

DURHAM, LEON (Bull) — BL TL 6′ 1″ 185 lbs.
B. July 31, 1957, Cincinnati, Ohio.

Year	Team	Games	BA	SA	AB	H	2B	3B	HR	HR%	R	RBI	BB	SO	SB	Pinch Hit AB	Pinch Hit H	PO	A	E	DP	TC/G	FA	G by Pos
1980	STL N	96	.271	.426	303	82	15	4	8	2.6	42	42	18	55	8	16	5	180	22	3	8	2.4	.985	OF-78, 1B-8
1981	CHI N	87	.290	.460	328	95	14	6	10	3.0	42	35	27	53	25	3	1	175	4	5	2	2.1	.973	OF-83, 1B-3
1982		148	.312	.521	539	168	33	7	22	4.1	84	90	66	77	28	5	2	311	12	12	1	2.3	.964	OF-143, 1B-1
1983		100	.258	.466	337	87	18	8	12	3.6	58	55	66	83	12	1	0	203	4	6	2	2.1	.972	OF-95, 1B-6
1984		137	.279	.505	473	132	30	4	23	4.9	86	96	69	86	16	8	2	1162	96	7	96	9.7	.994	1B-130
1985		153	.282	.465	542	153	32	2	21	3.9	58	75	64	99	7	2	0	1421	107	7	121	10.2	.995	1B-151
1986		141	.262	.452	484	127	18	7	20	4.1	66	65	67	98	8	2	0	1231	80	7	101	9.3	.995	1B-141
1987		131	.273	.513	439	120	22	1	27	6.2	70	63	51	92	2	8	2	1049	57	11	90	9.1	.990	1B-123
1988	2 teams	CHI N (24G –.219) CIN N (21G –.216)																						
″	total	45	.218	.403	124	27	9	1	4	3.2	14	8	14	32	0	8	0	296	21	2	24	8.6	.994	1B-37
1989	STL N	29	.056	.111	18	1	1	0	0	0.0	2	1	2	4	0	11	1	44	5	2	7	2.8	.961	1B-18
10 yrs.		1067	.277	.475	3587	992	192	40	147	4.1	522	530	444	679	106	64	13	6072	408	62	452	6.4	.991	1B-618, OF-399
LEAGUE CHAMPIONSHIP SERIES																								
1984	CHI N	5	.150	.450	20	3	0	0	2	10.0	2	4	1	4	0	0	0	48	3	1	6	10.4	.981	1B-5

Ray Durham

DURHAM, RAY — BB TR 5′ 8″ 170 lbs.
B. Nov. 30, 1971, Charlotte, N. C.

Year	Team	Games	BA	SA	AB	H	2B	3B	HR	HR%	R	RBI	BB	SO	SB	Pinch Hit AB	Pinch Hit H	PO	A	E	DP	TC/G	FA	G by Pos
1995	CHI A	125	.257	.384	471	121	27	6	7	1.5	68	51	31	83	18	4	1	245	299	15	66	4.5	.973	2B-122, DH-1

Bobby Durnbaugh

DURNBAUGH, ROBERT EUGENE (Scroggy) — BR TR 5′ 8″ 170 lbs.
B. Jan. 15, 1933, Dayton, Ohio.

Year	Team	Games	BA	SA	AB	H	2B	3B	HR	HR%	R	RBI	BB	SO	SB	Pinch Hit AB	Pinch Hit H	PO	A	E	DP	TC/G	FA	G by Pos
1957	CIN N	2	.000	.000	1	0	0	0	0	0.0	0	0	0	0	0	0	0	0	1	1	0	1.0	.500	SS-2

George Durning

DURNING, GEORGE DEWEY — BR TR 5′11″ 175 lbs.
B. May 9, 1898, Philadelphia, Pa. D. Apr. 18, 1986, Tampa, Fla.

Year	Team	Games	BA	SA	AB	H	2B	3B	HR	HR%	R	RBI	BB	SO	SB	Pinch Hit AB	Pinch Hit H	PO	A	E	DP	TC/G	FA	G by Pos
1925	PHI N	5	.357	.357	14	5	0	0	0	0.0	3	1	2	1	0	1	0	11	2	0	1	3.3	1.000	OF-4

Leo Durocher

DUROCHER, LEO ERNEST (The Lip) — BR TR 5′10″ 160 lbs. BB 1928
B. July 27, 1905, W. Springfield, Mass. D. Oct. 7, 1991, Palm Springs, Calif.
Manager 1939–46, 1948–55, 1966–73.
Hall of Fame 1994.

Year	Team	Games	BA	SA	AB	H	2B	3B	HR	HR%	R	RBI	BB	SO	SB	Pinch Hit AB	Pinch Hit H	PO	A	E	DP	TC/G	FA	G by Pos
1925	NY A	2	.000	.000	1	0	0	0	0	0.0	1	0	0	0	0	1	0	0	0	0	0	0.0	—	
1928		102	.270	.338	296	80	8	6	0	0.0	46	31	22	52	1	3	1	158	274	18	42	4.7	.960	2B-66, SS-29
1929		106	.246	.287	341	84	4	5	0	0.0	53	32	34	33	3	1	0	218	318	23	66	5.3	.959	SS-93, 2B-12
1930	CIN N	119	.243	.328	354	86	15	3	3	0.8	31	32	20	45	0	0	0	240	380	24	82	5.6	.963	SS-103, 2B-13
1931		121	.227	.294	361	82	11	5	1	0.3	26	29	18	32	0	0	0	212	344	20	86	4.8	.965	SS-120

Leo Durocher *continued*

Year	Team	Games	BA	SA	AB	H	2B	3B	HR	HR%	R	RBI	BB	SO	SB	Pinch Hit AB	Pinch Hit H	PO	A	E	DP	TC/G	FA	G by Pos
1932		143	.217	.293	457	99	22	5	1	0.2	43	33	36	40	3	0	0	283	429	30	76	5.2	.960	SS-142
1933	2 teams	CIN N (16G –.216) STL N (123G –.258)																						
"	total	139	.253	.334	446	113	19	4	3	0.7	51	44	30	37	3	0	0	275	422	29	74	5.2	.960	SS-139
1934	STL N	146	.260	.350	500	130	26	5	3	0.6	62	70	33	40	2	0	0	320	407	33	86	5.2	.957	SS-146
1935		143	.265	.376	513	136	23	5	8	1.6	62	78	29	46	4	0	0	313	420	28	81	5.4	.963	SS-142
1936		136	.286	.347	510	146	22	3	1	0.2	57	58	29	47	3	0	0	300	392	21	80	5.2	.971	SS-136
1937		135	.203	.245	477	97	11	3	1	0.2	46	47	38	36	6	0	0	279	381	28	72	5.1	.959	SS-134
1938	BKN N	141	.219	.284	479	105	18	5	1	0.2	41	56	47	30	3	0	0	287	399	24	90	5.0	.966	SS-141
1939		116	.277	.369	390	108	21	6	1	0.3	42	34	27	24	2	2	0	228	324	25	73	5.1	.957	SS-113, 3B-1
1940		62	.231	.319	160	37	9	1	1	0.6	10	14	12	13	1	1	0	108	138	11	24	4.5	.957	SS-53, 2B-4
1941		18	.286	.310	42	12	1	0	0	0.0	2	6	1	3	0	5	1	17	28	4	3	3.8	.918	SS-12, 2B-1
1943		6	.222	.222	18	4	0	0	0	0.0	1	1	1	2	0	0	0	23	11	0	5	5.7	1.000	SS-6
1945		2	.200	.200	5	1	0	0	0	0.0	1	2	0	0	0	0	0	3	4	0	0	3.5	1.000	2B-2
17 yrs.		1637	.247	.320	5350	1320	210	56	24	0.4	575	567	377	480	31	13	2	3264	4671	318	940	5.1	.961	SS-1509, 2B-98, 3B-1
WORLD SERIES																								
1928	NY A	4	.000	.000	2	0	0	0	0	0.0	0	0	0	1	0	0	0	1	1	0	1	0.5	1.000	2B-4
1934	STL N	7	.259	.370	27	7	1	1	0	0.0	4	0	0	0	0	0	0	13	17	0	1	4.3	1.000	SS-7
2 yrs.		11	.241	.345	29	7	1	1	0	0.0	4	0	0	1	0	0	0	14	18	0	2	2.9	1.000	SS-7, 2B-4

Red Durrett

DURRETT, ELMER CABLE BL TL 5′10″ 170 lbs.
B. Feb. 3, 1921, Sherman, Tex. D. Jan. 17, 1992, Waxahachie, Tex.

Year	Team	Games	BA	SA	AB	H	2B	3B	HR	HR%	R	RBI	BB	SO	SB	Pinch Hit AB	Pinch Hit H	PO	A	E	DP	TC/G	FA	G by Pos
1944	BKN N	11	.156	.281	32	5	1	0	1	3.1	3	1	7	10	0	1	0	27	1	2	1	3.3	.933	OF-9
1945		8	.125	.125	16	2	0	0	0	0.0	2	0	3	3	0	2	0	8	0	0	0	2.0	1.000	OF-4
2 yrs.		19	.146	.229	48	7	1	0	1	2.1	5	1	10	13	0	3	0	35	1	2	1	2.9	.947	OF-13

Cedric Durst

DURST, CEDRIC MONTGOMERY BL TL 5′11″ 160 lbs.
B. Aug. 23, 1896, Austin, Tex. D. Feb. 16, 1971, San Diego, Calif.

Year	Team	Games	BA	SA	AB	H	2B	3B	HR	HR%	R	RBI	BB	SO	SB	Pinch Hit AB	Pinch Hit H	PO	A	E	DP	TC/G	FA	G by Pos
1922	STL A	15	.333	.417	12	4	1	0	0	0.0	5	0	0	1	0	3	1	6	0	1	0	1.2	.857	OF-6
1923		45	.212	.412	85	18	2	0	5	5.9	11	11	8	14	0	20	3	84	2	3	6	4.9	.966	OF-10, 1B-8
1926		80	.237	.356	219	52	7	5	3	1.4	32	16	22	19	0	15	3	167	8	4	0	2.9	.978	OF-57, 1B-4
1927	NY A	65	.248	.326	129	32	4	3	0	0.0	18	25	6	7	0	21	4	48	2	1	0	1.3	.980	OF-36, 1B-2
1928		74	.252	.326	135	34	2	1	2	1.5	18	10	7	9	1	33	3	75	4	1	1	2.2	.988	OF-33, 1B-3
1929		92	.257	.361	202	52	3	3	4	2.0	32	31	15	25	3	16	5	153	5	2	1	2.2	.988	OF-72, 1B-1
1930	2 teams	NY A (8G –.158) BOS A (102G –.245)																						
"	total	110	.240	.343	321	77	20	5	1	0.3	29	29	17	25	3	25	7	156	4	5	1	2.0	.970	OF-83
7 yrs.		481	.244	.351	1103	269	39	17	15	1.4	145	122	75	100	7	133	26	689	25	17	9	2.3	.977	OF-297, 1B-18
WORLD SERIES																								
1927	NY A	1	.000	.000	1	0	0	0	0	0.0	0	0	0	0	0	1	0	0	0	0	0	0.0	—	
1928		4	.375	.750	8	3	0	0	1	12.5	3	2	0	1	0	0	0	3	0	0	0	0.8	1.000	OF-4
2 yrs.		5	.333	.667	9	3	0	0	1	11.1	3	2	0	1	0	1	0	3	0	0	0	0.8	1.000	OF-4

Erv Dusak

DUSAK, ERVIN FRANK (Four Sack) BR TR 6′ 2″ 185 lbs.
B. July 29, 1920, Chicago, Ill. D. Nov. 6, 1994, Glendale Heights, Ill.

Year	Team	Games	BA	SA	AB	H	2B	3B	HR	HR%	R	RBI	BB	SO	SB	Pinch Hit AB	Pinch Hit H	PO	A	E	DP	TC/G	FA	G by Pos
1941	STL N	6	.143	.143	14	2	0	0	0	0.0	1	3	2	6	1	2	0	10	0	0	0	2.5	1.000	OF-4
1942		12	.185	.296	27	5	3	0	0	0.0	4	3	3	7	0	1	0	14	5	0	1	2.1	1.000	OF-8, 3B-1
1946		100	.240	.378	275	66	9	1	9	3.3	38	42	33	63	7	7	2	146	32	2	5	2.0	.989	OF-77, 3B-11, 2B-2
1947		111	.284	.378	328	93	7	3	6	1.8	56	28	50	34	1	13	1	181	24	6	3	2.2	.972	OF-89, 3B-7
1948		114	.209	.309	311	65	9	2	6	1.9	60	19	49	55	3	9	3	191	80	5	14	2.6	.982	OF-68, 2B-29, 3B-9, SS-1, P-1
1949		1	—	—	0	0	0	0	0	—	1	0	0	0	0	0	0	0	0	0	0	0.0	—	
1950		23	.083	.167	12	1	1	0	0	0.0	0	0	0	3	0	0	0	6	7	0	1	0.8	1.000	P-14, OF-2
1951	2 teams	STL N (5G –.500) PIT N (21G –.308)																						
"	total	26	.317	.537	41	13	3	0	2	4.9	7	8	3	12	0	1	0	13	4	1	1	0.8	.944	OF-12, P-8, 2B-2, 3B-2
1952	PIT N	20	.222	.333	27	6	0	0	1	3.7	1	3	2	8	0	11	2	7	2	2	1	1.0	.818	OF-11
9 yrs.		413	.243	.355	1035	251	32	6	24	2.3	168	106	142	188	12	44	8	568	154	16	26	2.1	.978	OF-271, 2B-33, 3B-30, P-23, SS-1
WORLD SERIES																								
1946	STL N	4	.250	.500	4	1	1	0	0	0.0	0	0	2	2	0	1	0	1	1	0	0	0.5	1.000	OF-4

Ward Dwight

DWIGHT, ALBERT WARD
B. Jan. 4, 1856, New York, N. Y. D. Feb. 20, 1903, San Francisco, Calif.

Year	Team	Games	BA	SA	AB	H	2B	3B	HR	HR%	R	RBI	BB	SO	SB	Pinch Hit AB	Pinch Hit H	PO	A	E	DP	TC/G	FA	G by Pos
1884	KC U	12	.233	.279	43	10	2	0	0	0.0	8		2			0	0	48	22	6	2	6.3	.921	C-10, OF-1, 2B-1

Double Joe Dwyer

DWYER, JOSEPH MICHAEL BL TL 5′ 9″ 186 lbs.
B. Mar. 27, 1903, Orange, N. J. D. Oct. 21, 1992, Glen Ridge, N. J.

Year	Team	Games	BA	SA	AB	H	2B	3B	HR	HR%	R	RBI	BB	SO	SB	Pinch Hit AB	Pinch Hit H	PO	A	E	DP	TC/G	FA	G by Pos
1937	CIN N	12	.273	.273	11	3	0	0	0	0.0	2	1	1	0	0	11	3	0	0	0	0	0.0	—	

Frank Dwyer

DWYER, JOHN FRANCIS BR TR 5′ 8″ 145 lbs.
B. Mar. 25, 1868, Lee, Mass. D. Feb. 4, 1943, Pittsfield, Mass.
Manager 1902.

Year	Team	Games	BA	SA	AB	H	2B	3B	HR	HR%	R	RBI	BB	SO	SB	Pinch Hit AB	Pinch Hit H	PO	A	E	DP	TC/G	FA	G by Pos
1888	CHI N	5	.190	.238	21	4	1	0	0	0.0	2	2	0	5	0	0	0	2	10	2	0	2.8	.857	P-5
1889		36	.200	.244	135	27	1	1	1	0.7	14	6	4	8	0	0	0	32	49	8	5	2.4	.910	P-32, OF-3, SS-2
1890	CHI P	16	.264	.302	53	14	2	0	0	0.0	10	11	0	2	1	0	0	6	24	4	0	2.1	.882	P-12, OF-4
1891	2 teams	CIN AA (37G –.284) MIL AA (11G –.225)																						
"	total	48	.271	.331	181	49	5	3	0	0.0	25	20	6	16	5	0	0	31	97	11	1	2.7	.921	P-45, OF-4, 2B-2
1892	2 teams	STL N (10G –.080) CIN N (40G –.163)																						
"	total	50	.149	.175	154	23	0	2	0	0.0	19	6	8	11	2	1	0	23	70	5	3	2.0	.949	P-43, OF-6

Frank Dwyer *continued*

Year	Team	Games	BA	SA	AB	H	2B	3B	HR	HR%	R	RBI	BB	SO	SB	Pinch Hit AB	Pinch Hit H	PO	A	E	DP	TC/G	FA	G by Pos
1893	CIN N	38	.200	.267	120	24	1	2	1	0.8	22	17	9	5	2	0	0	47	66	2	7	2.9	.983	P-37, OF-1, 1B-1
1894		54	.267	.378	172	46	9	2	2	1.2	31	28	15	13	0	1	0	37	67	7	2	1.9	.937	P-45, OF-10, SS-2
1895		37	.265	.407	113	30	3	5	1	0.9	14	16	5	5	2	0	0	26	54	4	6	2.3	.952	P-37
1896		36	.264	.373	110	29	4	4	0	0.0	17	15	11	15	3	0	0	24	52	6	5	2.3	.927	P-36
1897		37	.266	.298	94	25	1	1	0	0.0	13	10	5		0	0	0	11	42	4	0	1.5	.930	P-37
1898		31	.141	.176	85	12	1	1	0	0.0	11	5	7		1	0	0	11	52	6	3	2.2	.913	P-31
1899		5	.364	.364	11	4	0	0	0	0.0	0	0	0		0	0	0	1	8	0	1	1.8	1.000	P-5
12 yrs.		393	.230	.298	1249	287	28	21	5	0.4	178	136	70	80	16	2	0	251	591	59	33	2.3	.935	P-365, OF-28, SS-4, 2B-2, 1B-1

Jim Dwyer

DWYER, JAMES EDWARD
B. Jan. 3, 1950, Evergreen Park, Ill.

BL TL 5′10″ 165 lbs.

Year	Team	Games	BA	SA	AB	H	2B	3B	HR	HR%	R	RBI	BB	SO	SB	Pinch Hit AB	Pinch Hit H	PO	A	E	DP	TC/G	FA	G by Pos
1973	STL N	28	.193	.246	57	11	1	1	0	0.0	7	0	1	5	0	8	1	32	0	0	0	1.6	1.000	OF-20
1974		74	.279	.360	86	24	1	0	2	2.3	13	11	11	16	0	41	10	31	3	0	2	1.2	1.000	OF-25, 1B-3
1975	2 teams STL N (21G –.194) MON N (60G –.286)																							
″	total	81	.272	.364	206	56	8	1	3	1.5	26	21	27	36	4	21	6	104	8	4	1	1.9	.966	OF-61
1976	2 teams MON N (50G –.185) NY N (11G –.154)																							
″	total	61	.181	.229	105	19	3	1	0	0.0	9	5	13	11	0	38	6	35	0	1	0	1.7	.972	OF-21
1977	STL N	13	.226	.258	31	7	1	0	0	0.0	3	2	4	5	0	2	1	16	0	0	0	1.3	1.000	OF-12
1978	2 teams STL N (34G –.215) SF N (73G –.225)																							
″	total	107	.223	.366	238	53	12	2	6	2.5	30	26	37	32	7	24	5	216	15	3	14	2.7	.987	OF-58, 1B-29
1979	BOS A	76	.265	.381	113	30	7	0	2	1.8	19	14	17	9	3	22	7	167	16	4	15	3.9	.979	1B-25, OF-19, DH-4
1980		93	.285	.438	260	74	11	1	9	3.5	41	38	28	23	3	11	2	143	15	4	9	1.9	.975	OF-65, DH-12, 1B-9
1981	BAL A	68	.224	.306	134	30	0	1	3	2.2	16	10	20	19	0	6	0	97	2	2	2	1.6	.980	OF-59, 1B-3, DH-1
1982		71	.304	.493	148	45	4	3	6	4.1	28	15	27	24	2	23	6	87	0	2	0	1.7	.978	OF-49, 1B-1, DH-1
1983		100	.286	.505	196	56	17	1	8	4.1	37	38	31	29	1	33	8	123	2	4	4	2.2	.969	OF-56, 1B-4
1984		76	.255	.360	161	41	9	1	2	1.2	22	21	23	24	0	27	7	83	3	3	1	1.6	.966	OF-52, DH-3
1985		101	.249	.399	233	58	8	3	7	3.0	35	36	37	31	0	26	5	131	4	1	0	1.7	.993	OF-78, DH-3
1986		93	.244	.487	160	39	13	1	8	5.0	18	31	22	31	0	42	9	33	4	0	1	0.8	1.000	OF-24, DH-24, 1B-1
1987		92	.274	.498	241	66	7	1	15	6.2	54	33	37	57	4	24	7	57	1	0	0	0.8	1.000	DH-41, OF-30
1988	2 teams BAL A (35G –.226) MIN A (20G –.293)																							
″	total	55	.255	.330	94	24	1	0	2	2.1	9	18	25	19	0	24	6	3	0	0	0	0.1	1.000	DH-30, OF-2
1989	2 teams MIN A (88G –.316) MON N (13G –.300)																							
″	total	101	.315	.404	235	74	12	0	3	1.3	35	25	29	24	2	29	8	0	0	0	0	0.0		DH-74, OF-1
1990	MIN A	37	.190	.238	63	12	0	0	1	1.6	7	5	12	7	0	15	6	2	0	0	0	0.1	1.000	DH-23, OF-2
18 yrs.		1327	.260	.398	2761	719	115	17	77	2.8	409	349	401	402	26	416	100	1360	73	28	49	1.6	.981	OF-634, DH-216, 1B-75
LEAGUE CHAMPIONSHIP SERIES																								
1983	BAL A	2	.250	.500	4	1	1	0	0	0.0	1	0	1	0	0	1	0	4	0	0	0	4.0	1.000	OF-1
WORLD SERIES																								
1983	BAL A	2	.375	.875	8	3	1	0	1	12.5	3	1	0	0	0	0	0	2	0	0	0	1.0	1.000	OF-2

John Dwyer

DWYER, JOHN E.
B. Lisbon, Ill. Deceased.

Year	Team	Games	BA	SA	AB	H	2B	3B	HR	HR%	R	RBI	BB	SO	SB	Pinch Hit AB	Pinch Hit H	PO	A	E	DP	TC/G	FA	G by Pos
1882	CLE N	1	.000	.000	3	0	0	0	0	0.0	0	1	0	0		0	0	1	1	0	0	1.0	1.000	C-1, OF-1

Jerry Dybzinski

DYBZINSKI, JEROME MATHEW
B. July 7, 1955, Cleveland, Ohio.

BR TR 6′ 2″ 180 lbs.

Year	Team	Games	BA	SA	AB	H	2B	3B	HR	HR%	R	RBI	BB	SO	SB	Pinch Hit AB	Pinch Hit H	PO	A	E	DP	TC/G	FA	G by Pos
1980	CLE A	114	.230	.294	248	57	11	1	1	0.4	32	23	13	35	4	3	0	146	263	13	47	3.9	.969	SS-73, 2B-29, 3B-4, DH-2
1981		48	.298	.298	57	17	0	0	0	0.0	10	6	5	8	7	1	0	35	70	5	11	2.7	.955	SS-34, 3B-3, 2B-3, DH-1
1982		80	.231	.278	212	49	6	2	0	0.0	19	22	21	25	3	2	0	120	244	17	40	4.8	.955	SS-77, 3B-3
1983	CHI A	127	.230	.289	256	59	10	1	1	0.4	30	32	18	29	11	1	0	141	258	14	47	3.3	.966	SS-118, 3B-9
1984		94	.235	.311	132	31	5	1	1	0.8	17	10	13	12	7	0	0	69	160	7	32	2.6	.970	SS-76, 3B-14, DH-1, 2B-1
1985	PIT N	5	.000	.000	4	0	0	0	0	0.0	0	0	0	0	0	0	0	4	5	1	0	2.0	.900	3B-5
6 yrs.		468	.234	.290	909	213	32	5	3	0.3	108	93	70	109	32	7	0	515	1000	57	177	3.5	.964	SS-378, 3B-38, 2B-33, DH-4
LEAGUE CHAMPIONSHIP SERIES																								
1983	CHI A	2	.250	.250	4	1	0	0	0	0.0	0	0	0	0	0	0	0	3	9	0	2	6.0	1.000	SS-2

Jim Dyck

DYCK, JAMES ROBERT
B. Feb. 3, 1922, Omaha, Neb.

BR TR 6′ 2″ 200 lbs.

Year	Team	Games	BA	SA	AB	H	2B	3B	HR	HR%	R	RBI	BB	SO	SB	Pinch Hit AB	Pinch Hit H	PO	A	E	DP	TC/G	FA	G by Pos
1951	STL A	4	.067	.067	15	1	0	0	0	0.0	1	0	1	1	0	0	0	7	6	0	1	3.3	1.000	3B-4
1952		122	.269	.450	402	108	22	3	15	3.7	60	64	50	68	0	9	3	197	154	11	14	3.0	.970	3B-74, OF-48
1953		112	.213	.344	334	71	15	1	9	2.7	38	27	38	40	3	9	0	162	106	15	13	2.7	.947	OF-55, 3B-51
1954	CLE A	2	1.000	1.000	1	1	0	0	0	0.0	0	1	1	0	0	1	1	0	0	0	0	0.0	—	
1955	BAL A	61	.279	.386	197	55	13	1	2	1.0	32	22	28	21	1	9	3	104	37	5	2	2.4	.966	OF-45, 3B-17
1956	2 teams BAL A (11G –.217) CIN N (18G –.091)																							
″	total	29	.176	.235	34	6	2	0	0	0.0	8	0	13	10	0	9	0	14	3	1	0	1.6	.944	OF-9, 3B-1, 1B-1
6 yrs.		330	.246	.389	983	242	52	5	26	2.6	139	114	131	140	4	37	7	484	306	32	30	2.7	.961	OF-157, 3B-147, 1B-1

Ben Dyer

DYER, BENJAMIN FRANKLIN
B. Feb. 13, 1893, Chicago, Ill. D. Aug. 7, 1959, Kenosha, Wis.

BR TR 5′10″ 170 lbs.

Year	Team	Games	BA	SA	AB	H	2B	3B	HR	HR%	R	RBI	BB	SO	SB	Pinch Hit AB	Pinch Hit H	PO	A	E	DP	TC/G	FA	G by Pos
1914	NY N	7	.250	.250	4	1	0	0	0	0.0	1	0	0	1	1	0	0	2	5	1	1	1.1	.875	SS-6, 2B-1
1915		7	.211	.316	19	4	0	1	0	0.0	4	0	4	3	0	0	0	9	12	2	0	3.3	.913	3B-6, SS-1
1916	DET A	4	.286	.357	14	4	1	0	0	0.0	4	1	1	1	0	0	0	4	7	0	0	2.8	1.000	SS-4
1917		30	.209	.284	67	14	5	0	0	0.0	6	0	2	17	3	8	0	25	46	10	4	3.7	.877	SS-14, 3B-8
1918		13	.278	.278	18	5	0	0	0	0.0	1	2	0	6	0	6	2	14	5	0	1	2.7	1.000	1B-2, OF-2, P-2, 2B-1
1919		44	.247	.294	85	21	4	0	0	0.0	11	15	8	19	0	8	3	36	62	6	3	3.0	.942	3B-23, SS-11, OF-1
6 yrs.		105	.237	.295	207	49	10	1	0	0.0	27	18	15	47	4	22	5	90	137	19	9	3.0	.923	3B-37, SS-36, OF-3, 1B-2, P-2, 2B-2

Duffy Dyer

DYER, DON ROBERT
B. Aug. 15, 1945, Dayton, Ohio.

BR TR 6′ 187 lbs.

Year	Team		Games	BA	SA	AB	H	2B	3B	HR	HR%	R	RBI	BB	SO	SB	Pinch Hit AB	Pinch Hit H	PO	A	E	DP	TC/G	FA	G by Pos
1968	NY	N	1	.333	.333	3	1	0	0	0	0.0	0	0	1	1	0	0	0	8	0	0	0	8.0	1.000	C-1
1969			29	.257	.446	74	19	3	1	3	4.1	5	12	4	22	0	8	3	105	10	1	0	6.1	.991	C-19
1970			59	.209	.257	148	31	1	0	2	1.4	8	12	21	32	1	1	1	294	20	3	6	5.6	.991	C-57
1971			59	.231	.320	169	39	7	1	2	1.2	13	18	14	45	1	9	4	336	21	3	3	6.8	.992	C-53
1972			94	.231	.375	325	75	17	3	8	2.5	33	36	28	71	0	3	2	690	61	6	12	8.2	.992	C-91, OF-1
1973			70	.185	.243	189	35	6	1	1	0.5	9	9	13	40	0	10	2	308	26	2	7	5.6	.994	C-60
1974			63	.211	.232	142	30	1	1	0	0.0	14	10	18	15	0	17	8	196	19	4	4	4.9	.982	C-45
1975	PIT	N	48	.227	.364	132	30	5	2	3	2.3	8	16	6	22	0	11	3	187	14	2	0	5.6	.990	C-36
1976			69	.223	.315	184	41	8	0	3	1.6	12	9	29	35	0	12	5	279	37	2	4	5.5	.994	C-58
1977			94	.241	.322	270	65	11	1	3	1.1	27	19	54	49	6	3	0	502	41	2	10	5.9	.996	C-93
1978			58	.211	.269	175	37	8	1	0	0.0	7	13	18	32	2	3	2	326	22	3	2	6.4	.991	C-55
1979	MON	N	28	.243	.365	74	18	6	0	1	1.4	4	8	9	17	0	1	0	141	10	1	1	5.6	.993	C-27
1980	DET	A	48	.185	.306	108	20	1	0	4	3.7	11	11	13	34	0	3	0	129	10	2	2	3.0	.986	C-37, DH-10
1981			2	—	—	0	0	0	0	0	—	0	0	0	0	0	0	0	0	0	0	0	0.0	.000	C-2
14 yrs.			722	.221	.315	1993	441	74	11	30	1.5	151	173	228	415	10	81	30	3501	291	31	51	5.9	.992	C-634, DH-10, OF-1
LEAGUE CHAMPIONSHIP SERIES																									
1975	PIT	N	1	—	—	0	0	0	0	0	—	0	1	1	0	0	0	0	0	0	0	0	0.0	—	
WORLD SERIES																									
1969	NY	N	1	.000	.000	1	0	0	0	0	0.0	0	0	0	0	0	1	0	0	0	0	0	0.0	—	

Eddie Dyer

DYER, EDWIN HAWLEY
B. Oct. 11, 1900, Morgan City, La. D. Apr. 20, 1964, Houston, Tex.
Manager 1946–50.

BL TL 5′11½″ 168 lbs.

Year	Team		Games	BA	SA	AB	H	2B	3B	HR	HR%	R	RBI	BB	SO	SB	Pinch Hit AB	Pinch Hit H	PO	A	E	DP	TC/G	FA	G by Pos
1922	STL	N	6	.333	.667	3	1	1	0	0	0.0	1	0	0	0	0	1	1	3	0	0	0	1.5	1.000	P-2
1923			35	.267	.467	45	12	3	0	2	4.4	17	5	3	5	1	14	3	18	4	0	0	1.8	1.000	OF-8, P-4
1924			50	.237	.342	76	18	2	3	0	0.0	8	8	3	8	1	16	4	10	40	5	1	1.8	.909	P-29, OF-1
1925			31	.097	.129	31	3	1	0	0	0.0	4	0	3	1	1	1	0	0	22	2	1	0.9	.917	P-27
1926			6	.500	.500	2	1	0	0	0	0.0	1	0	0	0	0	0	0	0	3	0	0	0.5	1.000	P-6
1927			1	—	—	0	0	0	0	0	—	0	0	1	0	0	0	0	0	0	0	0	0.0	.000	P-1
6 yrs.			129	.223	.344	157	35	7	3	2	1.3	31	13	10	14	3	32	8	31	69	7	2	1.4	.935	P-69, OF-9

Jimmy Dykes

DYKES, JAMES JOSEPH
B. Nov. 10, 1896, Philadelphia, Pa. D. June 15, 1976, Philadelphia, Pa.
Manager 1934–46, 1951–54, 1958–61.

BR TR 5′9″ 185 lbs.

Year	Team		Games	BA	SA	AB	H	2B	3B	HR	HR%	R	RBI	BB	SO	SB	Pinch Hit AB	Pinch Hit H	PO	A	E	DP	TC/G	FA	G by Pos
1918	PHI	A	59	.188	.237	186	35	3	3	0	0.0	13	13	19	32	3	2	0	139	190	21	33	6.1	.940	2B-56, 3B-1
1919			17	.184	.204	49	9	1	0	0	0.0	4	1	7	11	0	0	0	28	58	5	5	5.7	.945	2B-16
1920			142	.256	.361	546	140	25	4	8	1.5	81	35	52	73	6	0	0	363	457	45	53	6.0	.948	2B-108, 3B-36
1921			155	.274	.447	613	168	32	13	16	2.6	88	77	60	75	6	0	0	434	522	46	88	6.5	.954	2B-155
1922			145	.275	.421	501	138	23	7	12	2.4	66	68	55	**98**	6	0	0	193	307	30	21	3.7	.943	3B-140, 2B-5
1923			124	.252	.353	416	105	28	1	4	1.0	50	43	35	40	6	0	0	285	366	25	64	5.5	.963	2B-102, SS-20, 3B-2
1924			110	.312	.427	410	128	26	6	3	0.7	68	50	38	59	1	2	1	257	326	26	52	5.6	.957	2B-78, 3B-27, SS-4
1925			122	.323	.471	465	150	32	11	5	1.1	93	55	46	49	3	3	2	225	302	21	45	4.4	.962	3B-64, 2B-58, SS-2
1926			124	.287	.392	429	123	32	5	1	0.2	54	44	49	34	6	1	0	198	322	20	43	4.4	.963	3B-77, 2B-44, SS-1
1927			121	.324	.453	417	135	33	6	3	0.7	61	60	44	23	2	5	3	864	112	16	63	8.0	.984	1B-82, 3B-25, 2B-5, SS-5, OF-5, P-2
1928			85	.277	.384	242	67	11	0	5	2.1	39	30	27	21	2	3	0	166	164	9	21	4.0	.973	2B-32, SS-23, 3B-20, 1B-8, OF-1
1929			119	.327	.539	401	131	34	6	13	3.2	76	79	51	25	8	2	0	203	273	33	41	4.2	.935	SS-60, 3B-48, 2B-13
1930			125	.301	.425	435	131	28	4	6	1.4	69	73	74	53	3	1	0	125	191	13	18	2.7	.960	3B-123, OF-1
1931			101	.273	.389	355	97	28	2	3	0.8	48	46	48	47	1	0	0	136	188	15	27	3.3	.956	3B-87, SS-15
1932			153	.265	.373	558	148	29	5	7	1.3	71	90	77	65	8	1	0	158	282	11	26	3.0	.976	3B-141, SS-10, 2B-1
1933	CHI	A	151	.260	.327	554	144	22	6	1	0.2	49	68	69	37	3	0	0	132	296	21	22	3.0	.953	3B-151
1934			127	.268	.368	456	122	17	4	7	1.5	52	82	64	28	1	1	1	383	252	27	40	5.2	.959	3B-74, 2B-27, 1B-27
1935			117	.288	.387	403	116	24	2	4	1.0	45	61	59	28	4	1	0	290	185	15	29	4.2	.969	3B-98, 1B-16, 2B-3
1936			127	.267	.366	435	116	16	3	7	1.6	62	60	61	36	1	1	0	108	240	18	14	2.9	.951	3B-125
1937			30	.306	.400	85	26	5	0	1	1.2	10	23	9	7	0	4	2	152	27	1	15	6.9	.994	1B-15, 3B-11
1938			26	.303	.461	89	27	4	2	2	2.2	9	13	10	8	0	1	0	75	72	9	13	6.5	.942	2B-23, 3B-1
1939			2	.000	.000	1	0	0	0	0	0.0	0	0	0	0	0	0	0	2	0	1	0	1.5	.667	3B-2
22 yrs.			2282	.280	.399	8046	2256	453	90	108	1.3	1108	1071	954	849	70	28	9	4916	5132	428	733	4.6	.959	3B-1253, 2B-726, 1B-148, SS-140, OF-7, P-2
WORLD SERIES																									
1929	PHI	A	5	.421	.474	19	8	1	0	0	0.0	2	4	1	1	0	0	0	3	4	2	1	1.8	.778	3B-5
1930			6	.222	.556	18	4	3	0	1	5.6	2	5	5	3	0	0	0	8	6	1	1	2.5	.933	3B-6
1931			7	.227	.227	22	5	0	0	0	0.0	2	2	5	1	0	0	0	4	12	0	1	2.3	1.000	3B-7
3 yrs.			18	.288	.407	59	17	4	0	1	1.7	6	11	11	5	0	0	0	15	22	3	3	2.2	.925	3B-18

Len Dykstra

DYKSTRA, LEONARD KYLE (Nails)
B. Feb. 10, 1963, Santa Ana, Calif.

BL TL 5′10″ 160 lbs.

Year	Team		Games	BA	SA	AB	H	2B	3B	HR	HR%	R	RBI	BB	SO	SB	Pinch Hit AB	Pinch Hit H	PO	A	E	DP	TC/G	FA	G by Pos
1985	NY	N	83	.254	.331	236	60	9	3	1	0.4	40	19	30	24	15	9	3	165	6	1	2	2.3	.994	OF-74
1986			147	.295	.445	431	127	27	7	8	1.9	77	45	58	55	31	14	4	283	8	3	2	2.1	.990	OF-139
1987			132	.285	.455	431	123	37	3	10	2.3	86	43	40	67	27	18	5	239	4	3	1	2.1	.988	OF-118
1988			126	.270	.385	429	116	19	3	8	1.9	57	33	30	43	30	12	5	270	3	1	0	2.4	.996	OF-112
1989	2 teams		NY N (56G –.270) PHI N (90G –.222)																						
″	total		146	.237	.356	511	121	32	4	7	1.4	66	32	60	53	30	9	3	332	10	4	0	2.5	.988	OF-139
1990	PHI	N	149	.325	.441	590	**192**	35	3	9	1.5	106	60	89	48	33	1	0	439	7	6	5	3.0	.987	OF-149
1991			63	.297	.427	246	73	13	5	3	1.2	48	12	37	20	24	1	1	167	3	4	2	2.8	.977	OF-63
1992			85	.301	.406	345	104	18	0	6	1.7	53	39	40	32	30	0	0	253	6	3	4	3.1	.989	OF-85
1993			161	.305	.482	**637**	**194**	44	6	19	3.0	**143**	66	**129**	64	37	1	0	469	2	10	0	3.0	.979	OF-160
1994			84	.273	.435	315	86	26	5	5	1.6	68	24	68	44	15	1	1	235	4	4	0	2.9	.984	OF-83
1995			62	.264	.354	254	67	15	1	2	0.8	37	18	33	28	10	1	0	152	2	2	1	2.6	.987	OF-61
11 yrs.			1238	.285	.419	4425	1263	275	40	78	1.8	781	391	614	478	282	67	22	3004	55	41	17	2.6	.987	OF-1183

Len Dykstra *continued*

LEAGUE CHAMPIONSHIP SERIES

Year	Team	Games	BA	SA	AB	H	2B	3B	HR	HR%	R	RBI	BB	SO	SB	Pinch Hit AB	Pinch Hit H	PO	A	E	DP	TC/G	FA	G by Pos
1986	NY N	6	.304	.565	23	7	1	1	1	4.3	3	3	2	4	1	2	1	10	0	0	0	1.7	1.000	OF-6
1988		7	.429	.857	14	6	3	0	1	7.1	6	3	4	0	0	0	0	9	0	0	0	1.3	1.000	OF-7
1993	PHI N	6	.280	.560	25	7	1	0	2	8.0	5	2	5	8	0	0	0	13	0	0	0	2.2	1.000	OF-6
3 yrs.		19	.323	.629	62	20	5	1	4	6.5	14	8	11	12	1	2	1	32	0	0	0	1.7	1.000	OF-19
				4th						**9th**	**7th**		**9th**											

WORLD SERIES

Year	Team	Games	BA	SA	AB	H	2B	3B	HR	HR%	R	RBI	BB	SO	SB	Pinch Hit AB	Pinch Hit H	PO	A	E	DP	TC/G	FA	G by Pos
1986	NY N	7	.296	.519	27	8	0	0	2	7.4	4	3	2	7	0	1	1	14	0	0	0	2.0	1.000	OF-7
1993	PHI N	6	.348	.913	23	8	1	0	4	17.4	9	8	7	4	4	0	0	18	1	0	0	3.2	1.000	OF-6
2 yrs.		13	.320	.700	50	16	1	0	6	12.0	13	11	9	11	4	1	1	32	1	0	0	2.5	1.000	OF-13
				4th						**1st**														

John Dyler

DYLER, JOHN F.
B. June 1852, Louisville, Ky. Deceased.

Year	Team	Games	BA	SA	AB	H	2B	3B	HR	HR%	R	RBI	BB	SO	SB	Pinch Hit AB	Pinch Hit H	PO	A	E	DP	TC/G	FA	G by Pos
1882	LOU AA	1	.000	.000	4	0	0	0	0	0.0	0		0			0	0	0	0	0	0	0.0	.000	OF-1

Don Eaddy

EADDY, DONALD JOHNSON BR TR 5′11″ 165 lbs.
B. Feb. 16, 1934, Grand Rapids, Mich.

Year	Team	Games	BA	SA	AB	H	2B	3B	HR	HR%	R	RBI	BB	SO	SB	Pinch Hit AB	Pinch Hit H	PO	A	E	DP	TC/G	FA	G by Pos
1959	CHI N	15	.000	.000	1	0	0	0	0	0.0	3	0	0	1	0	0	0	0	1	1	0	2.0	.500	3B-1

Bad Bill Eagan

EAGAN, WILLIAM
B. June 1, 1869, Camden, N. J. D. Feb. 13, 1905, Denver, Colo.

Year	Team	Games	BA	SA	AB	H	2B	3B	HR	HR%	R	RBI	BB	SO	SB	Pinch Hit AB	Pinch Hit H	PO	A	E	DP	TC/G	FA	G by Pos
1891	STL AA	82	.219	.323	297	65	11	4	4	1.3	49	43	44	53	21	0	0	174	274	34	29	5.9	.929	2B-82
1893	CHI N	6	.263	.263	19	5	0	0	0	0.0	3	2	5	5	4	0	0	12	19	3	4	5.7	.912	2B-6
1898	PIT N	19	.328	.459	61	20	2	3	0	0.0	14	5	8		1	0	0	46	60	10	10	6.8	.914	2B-17
3 yrs.		107	.239	.342	377	90	13	7	4	1.1	66	50	57	58	26	0	0	232	353	47	43	6.0	.926	2B-105

Truck Eagan

EAGAN, CHARLES EUGENE BR TR 5′11″ 190 lbs.
B. Aug. 10, 1877, San Francisco, Calif. D. Mar. 19, 1949, San Francisco, Calif.

Year	Team	Games	BA	SA	AB	H	2B	3B	HR	HR%	R	RBI	BB	SO	SB	Pinch Hit AB	Pinch Hit H	PO	A	E	DP	TC/G	FA	G by Pos
1901	2 teams	PIT N (4G –.083) CLE A (5G –.167)																						
″	total	9	.133	.200	30	4	0	1	0	0.0	2	4	1		1	1	0	7	27	1	0	3.9	.971	2B-5, SS-3, 3B-1

Bill Eagle

EAGLE, WILLIAM LYCURGUS
B. July 25, 1877, Rockville, Md. D. Apr. 27, 1951, Churchton, Md.

Year	Team	Games	BA	SA	AB	H	2B	3B	HR	HR%	R	RBI	BB	SO	SB	Pinch Hit AB	Pinch Hit H	PO	A	E	DP	TC/G	FA	G by Pos
1898	WAS N	4	.308	.385	13	4	1	0	0	0.0	0	2	0		0	0	0	2	1	1	0	1.0	.750	OF-4

Charlie Eakle

EAKLE, CHARLES EMORY
B. Sept. 27, 1887, Baltimore, Md. D. June 15, 1959, Baltimore, Md.

Year	Team	Games	BA	SA	AB	H	2B	3B	HR	HR%	R	RBI	BB	SO	SB	Pinch Hit AB	Pinch Hit H	PO	A	E	DP	TC/G	FA	G by Pos
1915	BAL F	2	.286	.429	7	2	1	0	0	0.0	0	0	0		1	0	0	1	2	2	0	2.5	.600	2B-2

Howard Earl

EARL, HOWARD J. (Slim Jim) 6′ 2″ 180 lbs.
B. Feb. 25, 1867, Palmyra, N. Y. D. Dec. 23, 1916, North Bay, N. Y.

Year	Team	Games	BA	SA	AB	H	2B	3B	HR	HR%	R	RBI	BB	SO	SB	Pinch Hit AB	Pinch Hit H	PO	A	E	DP	TC/G	FA	G by Pos
1890	CHI N	92	.247	.336	384	95	10	3	6	1.6	57	51	18	47	17	0	0	178	158	46	12	4.0	.880	OF-49, 2B-39, SS-4, 1B-3
1891	MIL AA	31	.248	.341	129	32	5	2	1	0.8	21	17	5	13	3	0	0	61	3	3	1	2.1	.955	OF-30, 1B-2
2 yrs.		123	.248	.337	513	127	15	5	7	1.4	78	68	23	60	20	0	0	239	161	49	13	3.5	.891	OF-79, 2B-39, 1B-5, SS-4

Scott Earl

EARL, WILLIAM SCOTT BR TR 5′11″ 165 lbs.
B. Sept. 18, 1960, Seymour, Ind.

Year	Team	Games	BA	SA	AB	H	2B	3B	HR	HR%	R	RBI	BB	SO	SB	Pinch Hit AB	Pinch Hit H	PO	A	E	DP	TC/G	FA	G by Pos
1984	DET A	14	.114	.171	35	4	0	1	0	0.0	3	1	0	9	1	0	0	23	24	2	9	3.5	.959	2B-14

Billy Earle

EARLE, WILLIAM MOFFAT (The Little Globetrotter) BR TR 5′10½″ 170 lbs.
B. Nov. 10, 1867, Philadelphia, Pa. D. May 30, 1946, Omaha, Neb.

Year	Team	Games	BA	SA	AB	H	2B	3B	HR	HR%	R	RBI	BB	SO	SB	Pinch Hit AB	Pinch Hit H	PO	A	E	DP	TC/G	FA	G by Pos
1889	CIN AA	53	.266	.444	169	45	4	7	4	2.4	37	31	30	24	26	0	0	200	34	36	6	5.0	.867	OF-26, C-23, 1B-5
1890	STL AA	22	.233	.301	73	17	3	1	0	0.0	16		7		6	0	0	124	33	9	1	6.9	.946	C-18, OF-3, 3B-1, SS-1, 2B-1
1892	PIT N	5	.538	.692	13	7	2	0	0	0.0	5	3	4	1	2	0	0	15	5	2	0	4.4	.909	C-5
1893		27	.253	.442	95	24	4	4	2	2.1	21	15	7	6	1	0	0	99	19	5	2	4.6	.959	C-27
1894	2 teams	LOU N (21G –.354) BKN N (14G –.340)																						
″	total	35	.348	.409	115	40	7	0	0	0.0	23	13	15	5	6	1	0	94	52	11	1	4.5	.930	C-30, 2B-2, 1B-1, 3B-1, OF-1
5 yrs.		142	.286	.419	465	133	20	12	6	1.3	102	62	63	36	41	1	0	532	143	63	10	5.1	.915	C-103, OF-30, 1B-6, 2B-3, 3B-2, SS-1

Jake Early

EARLY, JACOB WILLARD BL TR 5′11″ 168 lbs.
B. May 19, 1915, King's Mountain, N. C. D. May 31, 1985, Melbourne, Fla.

Year	Team	Games	BA	SA	AB	H	2B	3B	HR	HR%	R	RBI	BB	SO	SB	Pinch Hit AB	Pinch Hit H	PO	A	E	DP	TC/G	FA	G by Pos
1939	WAS A	32	.262	.393	84	22	7	2	0	0.0	8	14	5	14	0	6	2	95	9	4	1	4.5	.963	C-24
1940		80	.257	.408	206	53	8	4	5	2.4	26	14	23	22	0	21	4	276	41	10	5	5.8	.969	C-56
1941		104	.287	.468	355	102	20	7	10	2.8	42	54	24	38	0	6	3	385	52	16	13	4.5	.965	C-100
1942		104	.204	.280	353	72	14	2	3	0.8	31	46	37	37	0	7	0	392	71	9	11	4.8	.981	C-98
1943		126	.258	.362	423	109	23	3	5	1.2	37	60	52	43	5	4	0	443	83	11	10	4.4	.980	C-122
1946		64	.201	.296	189	38	6	0	4	2.1	13	18	23	27	0	0	0	246	45	12	7	4.7	.960	C-64
1947	STL A	87	.224	.336	214	48	9	3	3	1.4	25	19	54	34	0	3	1	301	43	4	5	4.1	.989	C-85
1948	WAS A	97	.220	.276	246	54	7	2	1	0.4	22	28	36	33	2	5	2	268	51	3	7	3.5	.991	C-92
1949		53	.246	.297	138	34	4	0	1	0.7	12	11	26	11	0	3	0	160	22	5	6	3.5	.973	C-53
9 yrs.		747	.241	.350	2208	532	98	23	32	1.4	216	264	280	259	7	55	12	2566	417	74	65	4.4	.976	C-694

Mike Easler

EASLER, MICHAEL ANTHONY BL TR 6′ 190 lbs.
B. Nov. 29, 1950, Cleveland, Ohio.

Year	Team	Games	BA	SA	AB	H	2B	3B	HR	HR%	R	RBI	BB	SO	SB	Pinch Hit AB	Pinch Hit H	PO	A	E	DP	TC/G	FA	G by Pos
1973	HOU N	6	.000	.000	7	0	0	0	0	0.0	1	0	2	4	0	2	0	1	0	1	0	1.0	.500	OF-2
1974		15	.067	.067	15	1	0	0	0	0.0	0	0	0	5	0	15	1	0	0	0	0	0.0	—	
1975		5	.000	.000	5	0	0	0	0	0.0	0	0	0	1	0	5	0	0	0	0	0	0.0	—	

Mike Easler *continued*

Year	Team	Lg	Games	BA	SA	AB	H	2B	3B	HR	HR%	R	RBI	BB	SO	SB	Pinch Hit AB	Pinch Hit H	PO	A	E	DP	TC/G	FA	G by Pos
1976	**CAL**	**A**	21	.241	.296	54	13	1	1	0	0.0	6	4	2	11	1	5	2	0	0	0	0	0.0	.000	DH-16
1977	**PIT**	**N**	10	.444	.722	18	8	2	0	1	5.6	3	5	0	1	0	6	2	7	0	0	0	1.8	1.000	OF-4
1979			55	.278	.444	54	15	1	1	2	3.7	8	11	8	13	0	44	10	0	0	0	0	0.0	.000	OF-4
1980			132	.338	.583	393	133	27	3	21	5.3	66	74	43	65	5	12	4	201	6	3	1	1.8	.986	OF-119
1981			95	.286	.431	339	97	18	5	7	2.1	43	42	24	45	4	6	2	188	13	4	2	2.3	.980	OF-90
1982			142	.276	.436	475	131	27	2	15	3.2	52	58	40	85	1	10	5	243	8	7	2	1.9	.973	OF-138
1983			115	.307	.441	381	117	17	2	10	2.6	44	54	22	64	4	17	8	158	6	6	1	1.6	.965	OF-105
1984	**BOS**	**A**	156	.313	.516	601	188	31	5	27	4.5	87	91	58	134	1	1	0	256	29	7	21	1.9	.976	DH-126, 1B-29
1985			155	.262	.412	568	149	29	4	16	2.8	71	74	53	129	0	5	2	32	0	3	0	0.2	.914	DH-130, OF-20
1986	**NY**	**A**	146	.302	.449	490	148	26	2	14	2.9	64	78	49	87	3	19	4	23	0	1	0	0.2	.958	DH-129, OF-11
1987	**2 teams**		**PHI N** (33G –.282)	**NY A** (65G –.281)																					
″	**total**		98	.282	.372	277	78	10	0	5	1.8	20	31	20	52	1	22	5	73	5	1	2	1.0	.987	OF-45, DH-32
14 yrs.			1151	.293	.454	3677	1078	189	25	118	3.2	465	522	321	696	20	169	45	1182	67	33	29	1.3	.974	OF-538, DH-433, 1B-29
LEAGUE CHAMPIONSHIP SERIES																									
1979	**PIT**	**N**	1	.000	.000	1	0	0	0	0	0.0	0	0	0	0	0	1	0	0	0	0	0	0.0	—	
WORLD SERIES																									
1979	**PIT**	**N**	2	.000	.000	1	0	0	0	0	0.0	0	0	1	0	0	1	0	0	0	0	0	0.0	—	

Damion Easley

EASLEY, JACINTO DAMION BR TR 5′11″ 155 lbs.
B. Nov. 11, 1969, New York, N. Y.

Year	Team	Lg	Games	BA	SA	AB	H	2B	3B	HR	HR%	R	RBI	BB	SO	SB	Pinch Hit AB	Pinch Hit H	PO	A	E	DP	TC/G	FA	G by Pos
1992	**CAL**	**A**	47	.258	.311	151	39	5	0	1	0.7	14	12	8	26	9	4	1	30	102	5	13	2.9	.964	3B-45, SS-3
1993			73	.313	.413	230	72	13	2	2	0.9	33	22	28	35	6	3	1	111	157	6	29	4.0	.978	2B-54, 3B-14, DH-1
1994			88	.215	.329	316	68	16	1	6	1.9	41	30	29	48	4	3	1	122	178	7	34	3.5	.977	3B-47, 2B-40
1995			114	.216	.300	357	77	14	2	4	1.1	35	35	32	47	5	0	0	186	276	10	60	4.2	.979	2B-88, SS-25
4 yrs.			322	.243	.335	1054	256	48	5	13	1.2	123	99	97	156	24	10	3	449	713	28	136	3.8	.976	2B-182, 3B-106, SS-28, DH-1

Carl East

EAST, CARLTON WILLIAM BL TR 6′2″ 178 lbs.
B. Aug. 27, 1894, Marietta, Ga. D. Jan. 15, 1953, Whitesburg, Ga.

Year	Team	Lg	Games	BA	SA	AB	H	2B	3B	HR	HR%	R	RBI	BB	SO	SB	Pinch Hit AB	Pinch Hit H	PO	A	E	DP	TC/G	FA	G by Pos
1915	**STL**	**A**	1	.000	.000	1	0	0	0	0	0.0	0	0	0	0	0	0	0	0	0	0	0	0.0	.000	P-1
1924	**WAS**	**A**	2	.333	.500	6	2	1	0	0	0.0	1	2	2	1	0	0	0	4	0	1	0	2.5	.800	OF-2
2 yrs.			3	.286	.429	7	2	1	0	0	0.0	1	2	2	1	0	0	0	4	0	1	0	1.7	.800	OF-2, P-1

Harry East

EAST, HARRY H.
B. Apr. 1863, St. Louis, Mo. Deceased.

Year	Team	Lg	Games	BA	SA	AB	H	2B	3B	HR	HR%	R	RBI	BB	SO	SB	Pinch Hit AB	Pinch Hit H	PO	A	E	DP	TC/G	FA	G by Pos
1882	**BAL**	**AA**	1	.000	.000	4	0	0	0	0	0.0	0		0			0	0	1	2	2	0	5.0	.600	3B-1

Luke Easter

EASTER, LUSCIOUS LUKE BL TR 6′4½″ 240 lbs.
B. Aug. 4, 1915, Jonestown, Miss. D. Mar. 29, 1979, Euclid, Ohio.

Year	Team	Lg	Games	BA	SA	AB	H	2B	3B	HR	HR%	R	RBI	BB	SO	SB	Pinch Hit AB	Pinch Hit H	PO	A	E	DP	TC/G	FA	G by Pos
1949	**CLE**	**A**	21	.222	.289	45	10	3	0	0	0.0	6	2	8	6	0	6	1	9	0	0	0	0.8	1.000	OF-12
1950			141	.280	.487	540	151	20	4	28	5.2	96	107	70	95	0	1	1	1114	82	11	114	8.6	.991	1B-128, OF-13
1951			128	.270	.481	486	131	12	5	27	5.6	65	103	37	71	0	3	0	1043	68	14	108	9.0	.988	1B-125
1952			127	.263	.513	437	115	10	3	31	**7.1**	63	97	44	84	1	9	2	940	90	18	87	8.9	.983	1B-118
1953			68	.303	.445	211	64	9	0	7	3.3	26	31	15	35	0	11	4	442	30	9	54	8.6	.981	1B-56
1954			6	.167	.167	6	1	0	0	0	0.0	0	0	0	2	0	6	1	0	0	0	0	0.0	—	
6 yrs.			491	.274	.481	1725	472	54	12	93	5.4	256	340	174	293	1	36	9	3548	270	52	363	8.6	.987	1B-427, OF-25

Henry Easterday

EASTERDAY, HENRY P. BR TR 5′6″ 145 lbs.
B. Sept. 16, 1864, Philadelphia, Pa. D. Mar. 30, 1895, Philadelphia, Pa.

Year	Team	Lg	Games	BA	SA	AB	H	2B	3B	HR	HR%	R	RBI	BB	SO	SB	Pinch Hit AB	Pinch Hit H	PO	A	E	DP	TC/G	FA	G by Pos
1884	**PHI**	**U**	28	.243	.287	115	28	5	0	0	0.0	12		5			0	0	35	98	19	6	5.4	.875	SS-28
1888	**KC**	**AA**	115	.190	.259	401	76	7	6	3	0.7	42	37	31		23	0	0	120	459	73	30	5.7	.888	SS-115
1889	**COL**	**AA**	95	.173	.275	324	56	5	8	4	1.2	43	34	41	57	10	0	0	140	340	60	30	5.7	.889	SS-89, 2B-5, 3B-1
1890	**3 teams**		**COL AA** (58G –.157)	**PHI AA** (19G –.147)	**LOU AA** (7G –.083)																				
″	**total**		84	.149	.194	289	43	6	2	1	0.3	44		35		10	0	0	122	287	58	28	5.6	.876	SS-83, 3B-1
4 yrs.			322	.180	.250	1129	203	23	16	8	0.7	141	71	112	57	43	0	0	417	1184	210	94	5.6	.884	SS-315, 2B-5, 3B-2

Paul Easterling

EASTERLING, PAUL BR TR 5′11″ 180 lbs.
B. Sept. 28, 1905, Reidsville, Ga. D. Mar. 15, 1993, Reidsville, Ga.

Year	Team	Lg	Games	BA	SA	AB	H	2B	3B	HR	HR%	R	RBI	BB	SO	SB	Pinch Hit AB	Pinch Hit H	PO	A	E	DP	TC/G	FA	G by Pos
1928	**DET**	**A**	43	.325	.482	114	37	7	1	3	2.6	17	12	8	24	2	8	3	68	2	6	0	2.2	.921	OF-34
1930			29	.203	.316	79	16	6	0	1	1.3	7	14	6	18	0	2	0	29	3	0	2	1.3	1.000	OF-25
1938	**PHI**	**A**	4	.286	.286	7	2	0	0	0	0.0	1	0	1	2	0	3	0	3	0	1	0	4.0	.750	OF-1
3 yrs.			76	.275	.410	200	55	13	1	4	2.0	25	26	15	44	2	13	3	100	5	7	2	1.9	.938	OF-60

Ted Easterly

EASTERLY, THEODORE HARRISON BL TR 5′8″ 165 lbs.
B. Apr. 20, 1885, Lincoln, Neb. D. July 6, 1951, Clear Lake Highlands, Calif.

Year	Team	Lg	Games	BA	SA	AB	H	2B	3B	HR	HR%	R	RBI	BB	SO	SB	Pinch Hit AB	Pinch Hit H	PO	A	E	DP	TC/G	FA	G by Pos
1909	**CLE**	**A**	98	.261	.390	287	75	14	10	1	0.3	32	27	13		8	22	4	335	110	16	9	6.1	.965	C-76
1910			110	.306	.383	363	111	16	6	0	0.0	34	55	21		10	14	4	239	109	15	8	3.8	.959	C-66, OF-30
1911			99	.324	.436	287	93	19	5	1	0.3	34	37	8		6	23	8	168	32	15	3	2.8	.930	OF-54, C-23
1912	**2 teams**		**CLE A** (63G –.296)	**CHI A** (30G –.364)																					
″	**total**		93	.311	.349	241	75	6	0	1	0.4	22	35	9		4	**30**	**13**	266	82	15	14	5.9	.959	C-61, OF-1
1913	**CHI**	**A**	60	.237	.247	97	23	1	0	0	0.0	3	8	4	9	2	**37**	8	96	24	3	0	6.5	.976	C-19
1914	**KC**	**F**	134	.335	.443	436	146	20	12	1	0.2	58	67	31		10	6	0	570	173	24	16	6.0	.969	C-128
1915			110	.272	.372	309	84	12	5	3	1.0	32	32	21		2	20	8	398	132	17	11	6.2	.969	C-88
7 yrs.			704	.300	.392	2020	607	88	38	7	0.3	215	261	107	9	42	152	45	2072	662	105	61	5.2	.963	C-461, OF-85

Roy Easterwood

EASTERWOOD, ROY CHARLES (Shag) BR TR 6′½″ 196 lbs.
B. Jan. 12, 1915, Waxahachie, Tex. D. Aug. 24, 1984, Graham, Tex.

Year	Team	Lg	Games	BA	SA	AB	H	2B	3B	HR	HR%	R	RBI	BB	SO	SB	Pinch Hit AB	Pinch Hit H	PO	A	E	DP	TC/G	FA	G by Pos
1944	**CHI**	**N**	17	.212	.364	33	7	2	0	1	3.0	1	2	1	11	0	5	1	29	4	0	1	2.8	1.000	C-12

John Easton

EASTON, JOHN DAVID (Goose) B. Mar. 4, 1933, Trenton, N. J. — BR TR 6′ 2″ 185 lbs.

Year	Team	Games	BA	SA	AB	H	2B	3B	HR	HR%	R	RBI	BB	SO	SB	Pinch Hit AB	Pinch Hit H	PO	A	E	DP	TC/G	FA	G by Pos
1955	PHI N	1	—	—	0	0	0	0	0	—	0	0	0	0	0	0	0	0	0	0	0	0.0	—	
1959		3	.000	.000	3	0	0	0	0	0.0	0	0	0	3	0	3	0	0	0	0	0	0.0	—	
2 yrs.		4	.000	.000	3	0	0	0	0	0.0	0	0	0	3	0	3	0	0	0	0	0	0.0	—	

Eddie Eayrs

EAYRS, EDWIN B. Nov. 10, 1890, Blackstone, Mass. D. Nov. 30, 1969, Warwick, R. I. — BL TL 5′ 7″ 160 lbs.

Year	Team	Games	BA	SA	AB	H	2B	3B	HR	HR%	R	RBI	BB	SO	SB	Pinch Hit AB	Pinch Hit H	PO	A	E	DP	TC/G	FA	G by Pos
1913	PIT N	4	.167	.167	6	1	0	0	0	0.0	0	0	0	1	0	2	0	0	2	1	0	1.5	.667	P-2
1920	BOS N	87	.328	.377	244	80	5	2	1	0.4	31	24	30	18	4	16	5	109	18	6	2	1.9	.955	OF-63, P-7
1921	2 teams	BOS N (15G –.067) BKN N (8G –.167)																						
″	total	23	.095	.095	21	2	0	0	0	0.0	1	2	2	4	0	18	1	0	0	0	0	0.0		P-2, OF-1
3 yrs.		114	.306	.351	271	83	5	2	1	0.4	32	26	32	23	4	36	6	109	20	7	2	1.8	.949	OF-64, P-11

Hi Ebright

EBRIGHT, HIRAM C. (Buck) B. June 12, 1859, Lancaster County, Pa. D. Oct. 24, 1916, Milwaukee, Wis. — BR TR

Year	Team	Games	BA	SA	AB	H	2B	3B	HR	HR%	R	RBI	BB	SO	SB	Pinch Hit AB	Pinch Hit H	PO	A	E	DP	TC/G	FA	G by Pos
1889	WAS N	16	.254	.407	59	15	2	2	1	1.7	7	6	3	8	1	0	0	51	33	11	0	5.9	.884	C-9, OF-4, SS-3

Johnny Echols

ECHOLS, JOHN GRESHAM B. Jan. 9, 1917, Atlanta, Ga. D. Nov. 13, 1972, Atlanta, Ga. — BR TR 5′10½″ 175 lbs.

Year	Team	Games	BA	SA	AB	H	2B	3B	HR	HR%	R	RBI	BB	SO	SB	Pinch Hit AB	Pinch Hit H	PO	A	E	DP	TC/G	FA	G by Pos
1939	STL N	2	—	—	0	0	0	0	0	—	0	0	0	0	0	0	0	0	0	0	0	0.0	—	

Ox Eckhardt

ECKHARDT, OSCAR GEORGE B. Dec. 23, 1901, Yorktown, Tex. D. Apr. 22, 1951, Yorktown, Tex. — BL TR 6′ 1″ 185 lbs.

Year	Team	Games	BA	SA	AB	H	2B	3B	HR	HR%	R	RBI	BB	SO	SB	Pinch Hit AB	Pinch Hit H	PO	A	E	DP	TC/G	FA	G by Pos
1932	BOS N	8	.250	.250	8	2	0	0	0	0.0	1	1	0	1	0	8	2	0	0	0	0	0.0	—	
1936	BKN N	16	.182	.273	44	8	1	0	1	2.3	5	6	5	2	0	3	0	23	1	0	0	2.4	1.000	OF-10
2 yrs.		24	.192	.269	52	10	1	0	1	1.9	6	7	5	3	0	11	2	23	1	0	0	2.4	1.000	OF-10

Charlie Eden

EDEN, CHARLES M. B. Jan. 18, 1855, Lexington, Ky. D. Sept. 17, 1920, Cincinnati, Ohio. — BL TL 168 lbs.

Year	Team	Games	BA	SA	AB	H	2B	3B	HR	HR%	R	RBI	BB	SO	SB	Pinch Hit AB	Pinch Hit H	PO	A	E	DP	TC/G	FA	G by Pos
1877	CHI N	15	.218	.255	55	12	0	1	0	0.0	9	5	3	6		0	0	17	2	9	1	1.9	.679	OF-15
1879	CLE N	81	.272	.425	353	96	**31**	7	3	0.8	40	34	6	20		0	0	114	22	32	3	2.0	.810	OF-80, 1B-3, C-1
1884	PIT AA	32	.270	.418	122	33	7	4	1	0.8	12		7			0	0	40	4	14	0	1.8	.759	OF-31, P-2
1885		98	.254	.328	405	103	18	6	0	0.0	57		17			0	0	113	10	32	2	1.5	.794	OF-96, P-4, 3B-2
4 yrs.		226	.261	.372	935	244	56	18	4	0.4	118	39	33	26		0	0	284	38	87	6	1.7	.787	OF-222, P-6, 1B-3, 3B-2, C-1

Mike Eden

EDEN, EDWARD MICHAEL B. May 22, 1949, Fort Clayton, Canal Zone. — BB TR 5′10″ 170 lbs.

Year	Team	Games	BA	SA	AB	H	2B	3B	HR	HR%	R	RBI	BB	SO	SB	Pinch Hit AB	Pinch Hit H	PO	A	E	DP	TC/G	FA	G by Pos
1976	ATL N	5	.000	.000	8	0	0	0	0	0.0	0	1	0	0	0	2	0	2	5	0	1	3.5	1.000	2B-2
1978	CHI A	10	.118	.118	17	2	0	0	0	0.0	1	0	4	0	0	0	0	14	13	2	5	3.2	.931	SS-5, 2B-4
2 yrs.		15	.080	.080	25	2	0	0	0	0.0	1	1	4	0	0	2	0	16	18	2	6	3.3	.944	2B-6, SS-5

Stump Edington

EDINGTON, JACOB FRANK B. July 4, 1891, Roleen, Ind. D. Nov. 11, 1969, Bastrop, La. — BL TL 5′ 8″ 170 lbs.

Year	Team	Games	BA	SA	AB	H	2B	3B	HR	HR%	R	RBI	BB	SO	SB	Pinch Hit AB	Pinch Hit H	PO	A	E	DP	TC/G	FA	G by Pos
1912	PIT N	15	.302	.377	53	16	0	2	0	0.0	4	12	3	1	0	2	0	22	3	0	0	1.8	1.000	OF-14

Dave Edler

EDLER, DAVID DELMAR B. Aug. 5, 1956, Sioux City, Iowa. — BR TR 6′ 195 lbs.

Year	Team	Games	BA	SA	AB	H	2B	3B	HR	HR%	R	RBI	BB	SO	SB	Pinch Hit AB	Pinch Hit H	PO	A	E	DP	TC/G	FA	G by Pos
1980	SEA A	28	.225	.337	89	20	1	0	3	3.4	11	9	8	16	2	0	0	18	64	3	6	3.0	.965	3B-28
1981		29	.141	.179	78	11	3	0	0	0.0	7	5	11	13	3	3	1	18	43	8	4	2.6	.884	3B-26, SS-1
1982		40	.279	.394	104	29	2	2	2	1.9	14	18	11	13	4	5	2	24	53	6	4	2.4	.928	3B-31, OF-2, DH-2
1983		29	.190	.286	63	12	1	1	1	1.6	2	4	5	11	3	4	0	29	22	4	6	2.2	.927	3B-13, DH-6, 1B-5, OF-1
4 yrs.		126	.216	.308	334	72	7	3	6	1.8	34	36	35	53	12	12	3	89	182	21	20	2.5	.928	3B-98, DH-8, 1B-5, OF-3, SS-1

Jim Edmonds

EDMONDS, JAMES PATRICK B. June 27, 1970, Fullerton, Calif. — BL TL 6′ 1″ 190 lbs.

Year	Team	Games	BA	SA	AB	H	2B	3B	HR	HR%	R	RBI	BB	SO	SB	Pinch Hit AB	Pinch Hit H	PO	A	E	DP	TC/G	FA	G by Pos
1993	CAL A	18	.246	.344	61	15	4	1	0	0.0	5	4	2	16	0	1	1	47	4	1	2	3.1	.981	OF-17
1994		94	.273	.377	289	79	13	1	5	1.7	35	37	30	72	4	4	0	301	20	3	10	3.3	.991	OF-77, 1B-22
1995		141	.290	.536	558	162	30	4	33	5.9	120	107	51	130	1	3	0	402	8	1	2	3.0	.998	OF-139
3 yrs.		253	.282	.472	908	256	47	6	38	4.2	160	148	83	218	5	8	1	750	32	5	14	3.1	.994	OF-233, 1B-22

Eddie Edmonson

EDMONSON, EARL EDWARD (Axel) B. Nov. 20, 1889, Hopewell, Pa. D. May 10, 1971, Leesberg, Fla. — BL TR 6′ 175 lbs.

Year	Team	Games	BA	SA	AB	H	2B	3B	HR	HR%	R	RBI	BB	SO	SB	Pinch Hit AB	Pinch Hit H	PO	A	E	DP	TC/G	FA	G by Pos
1913	CLE A	2	.000	.000	5	0	0	0	0	0.0	0	0	0	0	0	0	0	5	0	1	0	3.0	.833	OF-1, 1B-1

Bob Edmundson

EDMUNDSON, ROBERT E. B. Apr. 30, 1879, Paris, Ky. D. Aug. 14, 1931, Lawrence, Kans. — BR TR 5′11″ 185 lbs.

Year	Team	Games	BA	SA	AB	H	2B	3B	HR	HR%	R	RBI	BB	SO	SB	Pinch Hit AB	Pinch Hit H	PO	A	E	DP	TC/G	FA	G by Pos
1908	WAS A	26	.188	.263	80	15	4	1	0	0.0	5	2	7		0	2	1	34	2	5	1	1.7	.878	OF-24

Bruce Edwards

EDWARDS, CHARLES BRUCE (Bull) B. July 15, 1923, Quincy, Ill. D. Apr. 25, 1975, Sacramento, Calif. — BR TR 5′ 8″ 180 lbs.

Year	Team	Games	BA	SA	AB	H	2B	3B	HR	HR%	R	RBI	BB	SO	SB	Pinch Hit AB	Pinch Hit H	PO	A	E	DP	TC/G	FA	G by Pos
1946	BKN N	92	.267	.356	292	78	13	5	1	0.3	24	25	34	20	1	0	0	431	53	9	9	5.4	.982	C-91
1947		130	.295	.418	471	139	15	8	9	1.9	53	80	49	55	2	2	0	592	58	11	11	5.2	.983	C-128
1948		96	.276	.434	286	79	17	2	8	2.8	36	54	26	28	4	9	2	264	43	12	2	3.8	.962	C-48, OF-21, 3B-14, 1B-1
1949		64	.209	.392	148	31	3	0	8	5.4	24	25	25	15	0	17	3	190	13	3	0	4.5	.985	C-41, OF-4, 3B-1
1950		50	.183	.394	142	26	4	1	8	5.6	16	16	13	22	1	8	1	194	19	4	6	5.4	.982	C-38, 1B-2
1951	2 teams	BKN N (17G –.250) CHI N (51G –.234)																						
″	total	68	.237	.390	177	42	11	2	4	2.3	25	25	17	17	1	22	8	219	25	9	9	5.0	.964	C-42, 1B-9
1952	CHI N	50	.245	.340	94	23	2	2	1	1.1	7	12	8	12	0	24	7	82	8	1	2	4.0	.989	C-22, 2B-1
1954		4	.000	.000	3	0	0	0	0	0.0	1	1	2	2	0	3	0	0	0	0	0	0.0	—	
1955	WAS A	30	.175	.211	57	10	2	0	0	0.0	5	3	16	6	0	1	0	93	19	3	5	4.3	.974	C-22, 3B-5
1956	CIN N	7	.200	.200	5	1	0	0	0	0.0	0	0	0	2	0	5	1	0	1	1	0	0.5	.500	C-2, 2B-1, 3B-1
10 yrs.		591	.256	.390	1675	429	67	20	39	2.3	191	241	190	179	9	91	22	2065	239	53	44	4.8	.978	C-434, OF-25, 3B-21, 1B-12, 2B-2

Bruce Edwards *continued*

Year	Team	Games	BA	SA	AB	H	2B	3B	HR	HR%	R	RBI	BB	SO	SB	Pinch Hit AB	Pinch Hit H	PO	A	E	DP	TC/G	FA	G by Pos
WORLD SERIES																								
1947	**BKN N**	7	.222	.259	27	6	1	0	0	0.0	3	2	2	7	0	0	0	44	4	1	1	7.0	.980	C-7
1949		2	.500	.500	2	1	0	0	0	0.0	0	0	0	1	0	2	1	0	0	0	0	0.0	—	
2 yrs.		9	.241	.276	29	7	1	0	0	0.0	3	2	2	8	0	2	1	44	4	1	1	7.0	.980	C-7

Dave Edwards

EDWARDS, DAVID LEONARD BR TR 6′ 170 lbs.
Brother of Marshall Edwards. Brother of Mike Edwards.
B. Feb. 24, 1954, Los Angeles, Calif.

Year	Team	Games	BA	SA	AB	H	2B	3B	HR	HR%	R	RBI	BB	SO	SB	Pinch Hit AB	Pinch Hit H	PO	A	E	DP	TC/G	FA	G by Pos
1978	**MIN A**	15	.250	.386	44	11	3	0	1	2.3	7	3	7	13	1	1	0	35	3	2	1	2.7	.950	OF-15
1979		96	.249	.389	229	57	8	0	8	3.5	42	35	24	45	6	6	0	165	7	3	0	2.0	.983	OF-86, DH-3
1980		81	.250	.335	200	50	9	1	2	1.0	26	20	12	51	2	5	2	144	7	11	1	2.2	.932	OF-72, DH-3
1981	**SD N**	58	.214	.321	112	24	4	1	2	1.8	13	13	11	24	3	17	4	59	6	2	2	1.4	.970	OF-49
1982		71	.182	.273	55	10	2	0	1	1.8	7	2	1	14	0	20	3	34	0	2	0	0.8	.944	OF-45, 1B-1
5 yrs.		321	.237	.350	640	152	26	2	14	2.2	95	73	55	147	12	49	9	437	23	20	4	1.8	.958	OF-267, DH-6, 1B-1

Doc Edwards

EDWARDS, HOWARD RODNEY BR TR 6′ 2″ 215 lbs.
B. Dec. 10, 1936, Red Jacket, W. Va.
Manager 1987–89.

Year	Team	Games	BA	SA	AB	H	2B	3B	HR	HR%	R	RBI	BB	SO	SB	Pinch Hit AB	Pinch Hit H	PO	A	E	DP	TC/G	FA	G by Pos
1962	**CLE A**	53	.273	.378	143	39	6	0	3	2.1	13	9	9	14	0	11	2	223	16	2	2	6.2	.992	C-39
1963	**2 teams**	**CLE A** (10G –.258) **KC A** (71G –.250)																						
″	**total**	81	.251	.369	271	68	14	0	6	2.2	22	35	13	29	0	11	1	421	33	6	5	6.3	.987	C-73
1964	**KC A**	97	.224	.310	294	66	10	0	5	1.7	25	28	13	40	0	12	4	522	37	8	7	6.6	.986	C-79, 1B-7
1965	**2 teams**	**KC A** (6G –.150) **NY A** (45G –.190)																						
″	**total**	51	.183	.233	120	22	3	0	1	0.8	4	9	14	16	1	2	0	230	18	3	6	5.1	.988	C-49
1970	**PHI N**	35	.269	.269	78	21	0	0	0	0.0	5	6	4	10	0	1	0	177	19	6	6	5.9	.970	C-34
5 yrs.		317	.238	.325	906	216	33	0	15	1.7	69	87	53	109	1	37	7	1573	123	25	26	6.1	.985	C-274, 1B-7

Hank Edwards

EDWARDS, HENRY ALBERT BL TL 6′ 190 lbs.
B. Jan. 29, 1919, Elmwood Place, Ohio D. June 22, 1988, Santa Ana, Calif.

Year	Team	Games	BA	SA	AB	H	2B	3B	HR	HR%	R	RBI	BB	SO	SB	Pinch Hit AB	Pinch Hit H	PO	A	E	DP	TC/G	FA	G by Pos
1941	**CLE A**	16	.221	.309	68	15	1	1	1	1.5	10	6	2	4	0	0	0	23	3	2	0	1.8	.929	OF-16
1942		13	.250	.333	48	12	2	1	0	0.0	6	7	5	8	2	1	0	30	0	1	0	2.6	.968	OF-12
1943		92	.276	.407	297	82	18	6	3	1.0	38	28	30	34	4	15	4	173	4	3	0	2.4	.983	OF-74
1946		124	.301	.509	458	138	33	**16**	10	2.2	62	54	43	48	1	2	1	226	13	8	1	2.0	.968	OF-123
1947		108	.260	.420	393	102	12	3	15	3.8	54	59	31	55	1	8	3	199	3	2	0	2.0	.990	OF-100
1948		55	.269	.406	160	43	9	2	3	1.9	27	18	18	18	1	12	2	76	1	1	0	1.9	.987	OF-41
1949	**2 teams**	**CLE A** (5G –.267) **CHI N** (58G –.290)																						
″	**total**	63	.288	.497	191	55	8	4	8	4.2	28	22	20	24	0	6	1	86	4	1	2	1.6	.989	OF-56
1950	**CHI N**	41	.364	.536	110	40	11	1	2	1.8	13	21	10	13	0	10	0	38	2	1	0	1.4	.976	OF-29
1951	**2 teams**	**BKN N** (35G –.226) **CIN N** (41G –.315)																						
″	**total**	76	.297	.443	158	47	12	1	3	1.9	15	23	17	26	0	**37**	8	64	0	1	0	1.9	.985	OF-34
1952	**2 teams**	**CIN N** (74G –.283) **CHI A** (8G –.333)																						
″	**total**	82	.287	.470	202	58	7	6	6	3.0	26	29	19	24	0	26	4	88	2	1	0	1.7	.989	OF-54
1953	**STL A**	65	.198	.226	106	21	3	0	0	0.0	6	9	13	10	0	40	12	36	2	0	0	1.8	1.000	OF-21
11 yrs.		735	.280	.440	2191	613	116	41	51	2.3	285	276	208	264	9	157	35	1039	34	21	3	2.0	.981	OF-560

Johnny Edwards

EDWARDS, JOHN ALBAN BL TR 6′ 4″ 220 lbs.
B. June 10, 1938, Columbus, Ohio.

Year	Team	Games	BA	SA	AB	H	2B	3B	HR	HR%	R	RBI	BB	SO	SB	Pinch Hit AB	Pinch Hit H	PO	A	E	DP	TC/G	FA	G by Pos
1961	**CIN N**	52	.186	.262	145	27	5	0	2	1.4	14	14	18	28	1	2	0	257	15	5	2	5.3	.982	C-52
1962		133	.254	.392	452	115	28	5	8	1.8	47	50	45	70	1	7	4	807	92	12	11	7.0	.987	C-130
1963		148	.259	.380	495	128	19	4	11	2.2	46	67	45	93	1	2	2	1008	87	6	16	7.4	.995	C-148
1964		126	.281	.390	423	119	23	1	7	1.7	47	55	34	65	1	8	0	890	73	8	17	8.1	.992	C-120
1965		114	.267	.474	371	99	22	2	17	4.6	47	51	50	45	0	11	5	761	61	8	9	7.5	.990	C-110
1966		98	.191	.284	282	54	8	0	6	2.1	24	39	31	42	1	1	0	617	40	5	3	6.8	.992	C-98
1967		80	.206	.263	209	43	6	0	2	1.0	10	20	16	28	1	7	1	454	30	5	4	6.7	.990	C-73
1968	**STL N**	85	.239	.326	230	55	9	1	3	1.3	14	29	16	20	1	26	7	350	25	3	2	7.0	.992	C-54
1969	**HOU N**	151	.232	.333	496	115	20	6	6	1.2	52	50	53	69	2	1	0	1135	79	7	9	8.1	.994	C-151
1970		140	.221	.319	458	101	16	4	7	1.5	46	49	51	63	1	2	2	854	74	5	11	6.7	.995	C-139
1971		106	.233	.309	317	74	13	4	1	0.3	18	23	26	38	1	7	2	555	48	3	7	5.8	.995	C-104
1972		108	.268	.373	332	89	16	2	5	1.5	33	40	50	39	2	6	0	645	41	8	8	6.6	.988	C-105
1973		79	.244	.360	250	61	10	2	5	2.0	24	27	19	23	1	7	1	435	22	5	3	6.1	.989	C-76
1974		50	.222	.325	117	26	7	1	1	0.9	8	10	11	12	1	17	5	157	16	2	3	5.5	.989	C-32
14 yrs.		1470	.242	.353	4577	1106	202	32	81	1.8	430	524	465	635	15	104	29	8925	703	82	105	7.0	.992	C-1392
WORLD SERIES																								
1961	**CIN N**	3	.364	.545	11	4	2	0	0	0.0	1	2	0	0	0	0	0	17	1	0	0	6.0	1.000	C-3
1968	**STL N**	1	.000	.000	1	0	0	0	0	0.0	0	0	0	1	0	1	0	0	0	0	0	0.0	—	
2 yrs.		4	.333	.500	12	4	2	0	0	0.0	1	2	0	1	0	1	0	17	1	0	0	6.0	1.000	C-3

Marshall Edwards

EDWARDS, MARSHALL LYNN BL TL 5′ 9″ 157 lbs.
Brother of Dave Edwards. Brother of Mike Edwards.
B. Aug. 27, 1952, Fort Lewis, Wash.

Year	Team	Games	BA	SA	AB	H	2B	3B	HR	HR%	R	RBI	BB	SO	SB	Pinch Hit AB	Pinch Hit H	PO	A	E	DP	TC/G	FA	G by Pos
1981	**MIL A**	40	.241	.293	58	14	1	1	0	0.0	10	4	0	2	6	0	0	46	1	1	0	1.3	.979	OF-36, DH-1
1982		69	.247	.315	178	44	4	1	2	1.1	24	14	4	8	10	9	3	119	2	2	1	2.0	.984	OF-54, DH-6
1983		51	.297	.338	74	22	1	1	0	0.0	14	5	1	9	5	3	1	57	4	0	1	1.6	1.000	OF-35, DH-4
3 yrs.		160	.258	.316	310	80	6	3	2	0.6	48	23	5	19	21	12	4	222	7	3	2	1.7	.987	OF-125, DH-11
DIVISIONAL PLAYOFF SERIES																								
1981	**MIL A**	2	.000	.000	1	0	0	0	0	0.0	0	0	0	1	0	0	0	0	0	0	0	0.0	.000	OF-2
LEAGUE CHAMPIONSHIP SERIES																								
1982	**MIL A**	3	.000	.000	1	0	0	0	0	0.0	2	0	0	0	1	0	0	2	0	0	0	0.7	1.000	DH-2, OF-1
WORLD SERIES																								
1982	**MIL A**	1	—	—	0	0	0	0	0	—	0	0	0	0	0	0	0	0	0	0	0	0.0	.000	OF-1

Year	Team	Games	BA	SA	AB	H	2B	3B	HR	HR%	R	RBI	BB	SO	SB	Pinch Hit AB	Pinch Hit H	PO	A	E	DP	TC/G	FA	G by Pos

Mike Edwards

EDWARDS, MICHAEL LEWIS
Brother of Marshall Edwards. Brother of Dave Edwards.
B. Aug. 27, 1952, Fort Lewis, Wash.
BR TR 5′10″ 154 lbs.

Year	Team	Games	BA	SA	AB	H	2B	3B	HR	HR%	R	RBI	BB	SO	SB	Pinch Hit AB	Pinch Hit H	PO	A	E	DP	TC/G	FA	G by Pos
1977	PIT N	7	.000	.000	6	0	0	0	0	0.0	1	0	0	3	0	0	0	7	8	0	2	3.8	1.000	2B-4
1978	OAK A	142	.273	.329	414	113	16	2	1	0.2	48	23	16	32	27	0	0	233	318	22	72	3.9	.962	2B-133, SS-9, DH-4
1979		122	.233	.280	400	93	12	2	1	0.3	35	23	15	37	10	3	1	246	318	22	54	5.0	.962	2B-113, SS-3, DH-2
1980		46	.237	.237	59	14	0	0	0	0.0	10	3	1	5	1	2	1	19	48	2	7	2.4	.971	2B-23, DH-5, OF-1
4 yrs.		317	.250	.298	879	220	28	4	2	0.2	94	49	32	77	38	5	2	505	692	46	135	4.2	.963	2B-273, SS-12, DH-11, OF-1

Ralph Edwards

EDWARDS, RALPH STRUNK
B. Dec. 14, 1882, Brewster, N. Y. D. Jan. 5, 1949, White Plains, N. Y.
BR TR 5′9″ 165 lbs.

Year	Team	Games	BA	SA	AB	H	2B	3B	HR	HR%	R	RBI	BB	SO	SB	Pinch Hit AB	Pinch Hit H	PO	A	E	DP	TC/G	FA	G by Pos
1915	PHI A	2	.000	.000	5	0	0	0	0	0.0	0	0	0	3	0	1	0	0	1	0	0	1.0	1.000	2B-1

Robert Eenhoorn

EENHOORN, ROBERT
B. Feb. 9, 1968, Rotterdam, Netherlands.
BR TR 6′3″ 170 lbs.

Year	Team	Games	BA	SA	AB	H	2B	3B	HR	HR%	R	RBI	BB	SO	SB	Pinch Hit AB	Pinch Hit H	PO	A	E	DP	TC/G	FA	G by Pos
1994	NY A	3	.500	.750	4	2	1	0	0	0.0	1	0	0	0	0	2	0	0	1	0	1	0.3	1.000	SS-3
1995		5	.143	.214	14	2	1	0	0	0.0	1	2	1	3	0	1	0	12	8	1	2	4.2	.952	2B-3, SS-2
2 yrs.		8	.222	.333	18	4	2	0	0	0.0	2	2	1	3	0	3	0	12	9	1	3	2.8	.955	SS-5, 2B-3

Ben Egan

EGAN, ARTHUR AUGUSTUS
B. Nov. 20, 1883, Augusta, N. Y. D. Feb. 18, 1968, Sherrill, N. Y.
BR TR 6′ 195 lbs.

Year	Team	Games	BA	SA	AB	H	2B	3B	HR	HR%	R	RBI	BB	SO	SB	Pinch Hit AB	Pinch Hit H	PO	A	E	DP	TC/G	FA	G by Pos
1908	PHI A	2	.167	.333	6	1	1	0	0	0.0	1	0	1		0	0	0	11	3	1	0	7.5	.933	C-2
1912		48	.174	.254	138	24	3	4	0	0.0	9	13	6		3	2	1	175	75	11	5	5.7	.958	C-46
1914	CLE A	29	.227	.273	88	20	2	1	0	0.0	7	11	3	20	0	2	1	146	48	5	3	7.4	.975	C-27
1915		42	.108	.133	120	13	3	0	0	0.0	4	6	8	14	0	2	0	199	59	8	5	6.7	.970	C-40
4 yrs.		121	.165	.219	352	58	9	5	0	0.0	21	30	18	34	3	6	2	531	185	25	13	6.4	.966	C-115

Dick Egan

EGAN, RICHARD JOSEPH
B. June 23, 1884, Portland, Ore. D. July 7, 1947, Oakland, Calif.
BR TR 5′11″ 162 lbs.

Year	Team	Games	BA	SA	AB	H	2B	3B	HR	HR%	R	RBI	BB	SO	SB	Pinch Hit AB	Pinch Hit H	PO	A	E	DP	TC/G	FA	G by Pos
1908	CIN N	18	.206	.279	68	14	3	1	0	0.0	8	5	2		7	0	0	35	47	10	10	5.1	.891	2B-18
1909		127	.275	.329	480	132	14	3	2	0.4	59	53	37		39	1	0	294	402	39	49	5.8	.947	2B-116, SS-10
1910		135	.245	.289	474	116	11	5	0	0.0	70	46	53	38	41	0	0	268	388	27	50	5.1	.960	2B-131, SS-3
1911		153	.249	.292	558	139	11	5	1	0.2	80	56	59	50	37	1	1	341	480	44	67	5.7	.949	2B-152
1912		149	.247	.294	507	125	14	5	0	0.0	69	52	56	26	24	0	0	345	452	22	55	5.5	.973	2B-149
1913		60	.282	.349	195	55	7	3	0	0.0	15	22	15	13	6	4	0	115	151	15	20	4.9	.947	2B-38, SS-17, 3B-2
1914	BKN N	106	.226	.282	337	76	10	3	1	0.3	30	21	22	25	8	6	5	177	256	39	25	4.8	.917	SS-83, 3B-10, OF-3, 2B-2, 1B-1
1915	2 teams	BKN N (3G –.000) BOS N (83G –.259)																						
″	total	86	.256	.305	223	57	9	1	0	0.0	20	21	28	18	3	15	3	179	92	16	20	4.2	.944	OF-24, 2B-22, SS-10, 1B-9, 3B-4
1916	BOS N	83	.223	.282	238	53	8	3	0	0.0	23	16	19	21	2	11	5	94	149	16	13	3.5	.938	2B-53, SS-12, 3B-8
9 yrs.		917	.249	.300	3080	767	87	29	4	0.1	374	292	291	191	167	38	14	1848	2417	228	309	5.1	.949	2B-681, SS-135, OF-27, 3B-24, 1B-10

Jim Egan

EGAN, JAMES K. (Troy Terrier)
B. 1858, Derby, Conn. D. Sept. 26, 1884, New Haven, Conn.
TL

Year	Team	Games	BA	SA	AB	H	2B	3B	HR	HR%	R	RBI	BB	SO	SB	Pinch Hit AB	Pinch Hit H	PO	A	E	DP	TC/G	FA	G by Pos
1882	TRO N	30	.200	.261	115	23	3	2	0	0.0	15	10	1	21		0	0	36	15	20	3	2.2	.718	OF-18, P-12, C-2

Tom Egan

EGAN, THOMAS PATRICK
B. June 9, 1946, Los Angeles, Calif.
BR TR 6′4″ 218 lbs.
BB 1974–1975

Year	Team	Games	BA	SA	AB	H	2B	3B	HR	HR%	R	RBI	BB	SO	SB	Pinch Hit AB	Pinch Hit H	PO	A	E	DP	TC/G	FA	G by Pos
1965	CAL A	18	.263	.316	38	10	0	1	0	0.0	3	1	3	12	0	2	1	61	3	0	0	4.0	1.000	C-16
1966		7	.000	.000	11	0	0	0	0	0.0	0	0	1	5	0	0	0	24	2	0	0	4.3	1.000	C-6
1967		1	.000	.000	1	0	0	0	0	0.0	0	0	0	0	0	0	0	3	0	0	0	3.0	1.000	C-1
1968		16	.116	.209	43	5	1	0	1	2.3	2	4	2	15	0	3	0	72	7	0	2	5.6	1.000	C-14
1969		46	.142	.275	120	17	1	0	5	4.2	7	16	17	41	0	1	0	240	28	4	4	5.9	.985	C-46
1970		79	.238	.324	210	50	6	0	4	1.9	14	20	14	67	0	1	0	367	31	5	4	5.1	.988	C-79
1971	CHI A	85	.239	.410	251	60	11	1	10	4.0	29	34	26	94	1	10	5	445	41	7	3	6.3	.986	C-77, 1B-1
1972		50	.191	.255	141	27	3	0	2	1.4	8	9	4	48	0	11	3	257	19	4	2	6.1	.986	C-46
1974	CAL A	43	.117	.117	94	11	0	0	0	0.0	4	4	8	40	1	2	0	249	21	1	5	6.6	.996	C-41
1975		28	.229	.300	70	16	3	1	0	0.0	7	3	5	14	0	0	0	145	19	6	4	6.1	.965	C-28
10 yrs.		373	.200	.299	979	196	25	3	22	2.2	74	91	80	336	2	30	9	1863	171	27	24	5.8	.987	C-354, 1B-1

Elmer Eggert

EGGERT, ELMER ALBERT (Mose)
B. Jan. 29, 1902, Rochester, N. Y. D. Apr. 9, 1971, Rochester, N. Y.
BR TR 5′9″ 160 lbs.

Year	Team	Games	BA	SA	AB	H	2B	3B	HR	HR%	R	RBI	BB	SO	SB	Pinch Hit AB	Pinch Hit H	PO	A	E	DP	TC/G	FA	G by Pos
1927	BOS A	5	.000	.000	3	0	0	0	0	0.0	0	0	1	1	0	2	0	0	0	0	0	0.0	.000	2B-1

Dave Eggler

EGGLER, DAVID DANIEL
B. Apr. 30, 1851, Brooklyn, N. Y. D. Apr. 5, 1902, Buffalo, N. Y.
BR TR 5′9″ 165 lbs.

Year	Team	Games	BA	SA	AB	H	2B	3B	HR	HR%	R	RBI	BB	SO	SB	Pinch Hit AB	Pinch Hit H	PO	A	E	DP	TC/G	FA	G by Pos
1876	PHI N	39	.299	.322	174	52	4	0	0	0.0	28	19	2	4		0	0	109	6	11	1	3.2	.913	OF-39
1877	CHI N	33	.265	.287	136	36	3	0	0	0.0	20	20	1	5		0	0	60	8	11	3	2.4	.861	OF-33
1879	BUF N	78	.208	.268	317	66	5	7	0	0.0	41	27	11	41		0	0	114	11	11	2	1.7	.919	OF-78
1883	2 teams	BAL AA (53G –.188) BUF N (38G –.248)																						
″	total	91	.214	.231	355	76	4	1	0	0.0	28		3	29		0	0	175	10	25	2	2.3	.881	OF-91
1884	BUF N	63	.195	.216	241	47	3	1	0	0.0	25		6	54		0	0	104	14	15	1	2.1	.887	OF-63
1885		6	.083	.083	24	2	0	0	0	0.0	0	0	2	4		0	0	14	1	1	0	2.7	.938	OF-6
6 yrs.		310	.224	.253	1247	279	19	9	0	0.0	142	66	25	137		0	0	576	50	74	9	2.3	.894	OF-310

Red Ehret

EHRET, PHILIP SYDNEY
B. Aug. 31, 1868, Louisville, Ky. D. July 28, 1940, Cincinnati, Ohio.
BR TR 6′ 175 lbs.

Year	Team	Games	BA	SA	AB	H	2B	3B	HR	HR%	R	RBI	BB	SO	SB	Pinch Hit AB	Pinch Hit H	PO	A	E	DP	TC/G	FA	G by Pos
1888	KC AA	17	.190	.254	63	12	4	0	0	0.0	4	4	1		1	0	0	24	18	6	0	2.5	.875	OF-10, P-7, 1B-1, 2B-1
1889	LOU AA	67	.252	.333	258	65	6	6	1	0.4	27	31	4	23	4	0	0	43	109	29	4	2.6	.840	P-45, OF-22, 2B-1, 3B-1, SS-1
1890		43	.212	.240	146	31	2	1	0	0.0	11		1		1	0	0	9	64	12	2	2.0	.859	P-43
1891		26	.242	.286	91	22	2	1	0	0.0	9	9	5	15	3	0	0	4	57	9	4	2.7	.871	P-26
1892	PIT N	40	.258	.273	132	34	2	0	0	0.0	12	19	7	22	1	1	0	14	57	12	1	2.1	.855	P-39
1893		40	.176	.221	136	24	3	0	1	0.7	16	17	10	18	1	0	0	12	80	11	0	2.6	.893	P-39
1894		46	.170	.215	135	23	4	1	0	0.0	6	11	8	22	0	0	0	12	61	12	2	1.8	.859	P-46

Red Ehret *continued*

Year	Team	Lg	Games	BA	SA	AB	H	2B	3B	HR	HR%	R	RBI	BB	SO	SB	Pinch Hit AB	Pinch Hit H	PO	A	E	DP	TC/G	FA	G by Pos
1895	STL	N	37	.219	.292	96	21	2	1	1	1.0	13	9	6	12	0	0	0	11	56	12	0	2.1	.848	P-37
1896	CIN	N	34	.196	.245	102	20	2	0	1	1.0	10	20	10	12	2	0	0	15	69	7	3	2.6	.923	P-34, 1B-1
1897			34	.197	.227	66	13	2	0	0	0.0	6	6	4		2	0	0	12	33	2	4	1.4	.957	P-34
1898	LOU	N	13	.225	.350	40	9	3	1	0	0.0	3	4	1		0	1	0	3	17	5	0	2.1	.800	P-12
11 yrs.			397	.217	.269	1265	274	32	11	4	0.3	117	130	57	124	15	2	0	159	621	117	20	2.2	.870	P-362, OF-32, 1B-2, 2B-2, 3B-1, SS-1

Hack Eibel

EIBEL, HENRY HACK BL TL 5′11″ 220 lbs.
B. Dec. 6, 1893, Brooklyn, N. Y. D. Oct. 16, 1945, Macon, Ga.

Year	Team	Lg	Games	BA	SA	AB	H	2B	3B	HR	HR%	R	RBI	BB	SO	SB	Pinch Hit AB	Pinch Hit H	PO	A	E	DP	TC/G	FA	G by Pos
1912	CLE	A	1	.000	.000	3	0	0	0	0	0.0	0	0	0		0	0	0	0	0	0	0	0.0	.000	OF-1
1920	BOS	A	29	.186	.233	43	8	2	0	0	0.0	4	6	3	6	1	17	3	5	4	1	0	1.1	.900	OF-5, P-3, 1B-1
2 yrs.			30	.174	.217	46	8	2	0	0	0.0	4	6	3	6	1	17	3	5	4	1	0	1.0	.900	OF-6, P-3, 1B-1

Fred Eichrodt

EICHRODT, FREDERICK GEORGE (Ike) BR TR 5′11½″ 167 lbs.
B. Jan. 6, 1903, Chicago, Ill. D. July 14, 1965, Indianapolis, Ind.

Year	Team	Lg	Games	BA	SA	AB	H	2B	3B	HR	HR%	R	RBI	BB	SO	SB	Pinch Hit AB	Pinch Hit H	PO	A	E	DP	TC/G	FA	G by Pos
1925	CLE	A	15	.231	.327	52	12	3	1	0	0.0	4	4	2	7	0	2	0	30	0	2	0	2.5	.938	OF-13
1926			37	.313	.425	80	25	7	1	0	0.0	14	7	2	11	1	10	2	38	3	1	1	1.6	.976	OF-27
1927			85	.221	.307	267	59	19	2	0	0.0	24	25	16	25	2	4	0	170	13	4	6	2.3	.979	OF-81
1931	CHI	A	34	.214	.274	117	25	5	1	0	0.0	9	15	1	8	0	2	1	70	0	0	0	2.2	1.000	OF-32
4 yrs.			171	.234	.320	516	121	34	5	0	0.0	51	51	21	51	3	18	3	308	16	7	7	2.2	.979	OF-153

Jim Eisenreich

EISENREICH, JAMES MICHAEL BL TL 5′11″ 175 lbs.
B. Apr. 18, 1959, St. Cloud, Minn.

Year	Team	Lg	Games	BA	SA	AB	H	2B	3B	HR	HR%	R	RBI	BB	SO	SB	Pinch Hit AB	Pinch Hit H	PO	A	E	DP	TC/G	FA	G by Pos
1982	MIN	A	34	.303	.424	99	30	6	0	2	2.0	10	9	11	13	0	3	1	72	0	2	0	2.5	.973	OF-30
1983			2	.286	.429	7	2	1	0	0	0.0	1	0	1	1	0	0	0	6	1	0	0	3.5	1.000	OF-2
1984			12	.219	.250	32	7	1	0	0	0.0	1	3	2	4	2	3	1	5	0	0	0	0.6	1.000	DH-6, OF-3
1987	KC	A	44	.238	.467	105	25	8	2	4	3.8	10	21	7	13	1	15	5	0	0	0	0	0.0	.000	DH-26
1988			82	.218	.282	202	44	8	1	1	0.5	26	19	6	31	9	9	1	109	0	4	0	1.5	.965	OF-64, DH-13
1989			134	.293	.448	475	139	33	7	9	1.9	64	59	37	44	27	6	2	273	4	3	0	2.1	.989	OF-123, DH-10
1990			142	.280	.397	496	139	29	7	5	1.0	61	51	42	51	12	8	4	261	6	1	3	1.9	.996	OF-138, DH-2
1991			135	.301	.392	375	113	22	3	2	0.5	47	47	20	35	5	32	7	243	12	5	12	2.1	.981	OF-105, 1B-15, DH-1
1992			113	.269	.340	353	95	13	3	2	0.6	31	28	24	36	11	27	10	180	1	1	0	1.9	.995	OF-88, DH-8
1993	PHI	N	153	.318	.445	362	115	17	4	7	1.9	51	54	26	36	5	21	3	223	6	1	0	1.7	.996	OF-137, 1B-1
1994			104	.300	.421	290	87	15	4	4	1.4	42	43	33	31	6	17	4	178	4	2	2	2.0	.989	OF-93
1995			129	.316	.464	377	119	22	2	10	2.7	46	55	38	44	10	20	4	205	2	0	1	1.9	1.000	OF-111
12 yrs.			1084	.288	.408	3173	915	175	33	46	1.4	390	389	247	339	88	161	42	1755	36	19	18	1.9	.990	OF-894, DH-66, 1B-16
LEAGUE CHAMPIONSHIP SERIES																									
1993	PHI	N	6	.133	.200	15	2	1	0	0	0.0	0	1	0	2	0	1	1	6	0	0	0	1.2	1.000	OF-5
WORLD SERIES																									
1993	PHI	N	6	.231	.346	26	6	0	0	1	3.8	3	7	2	4	0	0	0	18	0	0	0	3.0	1.000	OF-6

Kid Elberfeld

ELBERFELD, NORMAN ARTHUR (The Tabasco Kid) BR TR 5′7″ 158 lbs.
B. Apr. 13, 1875, Pomeroy, Ohio D. Jan. 13, 1944, Chattanooga, Tenn.
Manager 1908.

Year	Team	Lg	Games	BA	SA	AB	H	2B	3B	HR	HR%	R	RBI	BB	SO	SB	Pinch Hit AB	Pinch Hit H	PO	A	E	DP	TC/G	FA	G by Pos
1898	PHI	N	14	.237	.342	38	9	4	0	0	0.0	1	7	5		0	0	0	13	18	8	1	2.8	.795	3B-14
1899	CIN	N	41	.261	.319	138	36	4	2	0	0.0	23	22	15		5	0	0	74	108	25	9	4.9	.879	SS-24, 3B-18
1901	DET	A	122	.310	.429	436	135	21	11	3	0.7	76	76	57		24	0	0	332	411	76	62	6.8	.907	SS-121
1902			130	.260	.326	488	127	17	6	1	0.2	70	64	55		19	0	0	326	459	67	63	6.6	.921	SS-130
1903	2 teams		DET A (35G –.341) NY A (90G –.287)																						
″	total		125	.301	.383	481	145	23	8	0	0.0	78	64	33		22	0	0	295	410	62	51	6.1	.919	SS-124, 3B-1
1904	NY	A	122	.263	.328	445	117	13	5	2	0.4	55	46	37		18	0	0	237	432	48	44	5.9	.933	SS-122
1905			111	.262	.318	390	102	18	2	0	0.0	48	53	23		18	2	0	244	317	57	35	5.7	.908	SS-108
1906			99	.306	.384	346	106	11	5	2	0.6	59	31	30		19	0	0	200	317	42	18	5.7	.925	SS-98
1907			120	.271	.336	447	121	17	6	0	0.0	61	51	36		22	2	2	295	400	52	31	6.3	.930	SS-118
1908			19	.196	.250	56	11	3	0	0	0.0	11	5	6		1	2	0	36	51	8	2	5.6	.916	SS-17
1909			106	.237	.288	379	90	9	5	0	0.0	47	26	28		23	2	0	196	269	26	30	4.7	.947	SS-61, 3B-43
1910	WAS	A	127	.251	.292	455	114	9	2	2	0.4	53	42	35		19	3	0	166	245	29	17	3.5	.934	3B-113, 2B-10, SS-3
1911			127	.272	.339	404	110	19	4	0	0.0	58	47	65		24	7	1	233	297	31	34	4.7	.945	2B-66, 3B-54
1914	BKN	N	30	.226	.242	62	14	1	0	0	0.0	7	1	2	4	0	6	1	33	35	7	6	3.9	.907	SS-18, 2B-1
14 yrs.			1293	.271	.339	4565	1237	169	56	10	0.2	647	535	427	4	214	24	4	2680	3769	538	403	5.5	.923	SS-944, 3B-243, 2B-77

George Elder

ELDER, GEORGE REZIN BL TR 5′11″ 180 lbs.
B. Mar. 10, 1921, Lebanon, Ky.

Year	Team	Lg	Games	BA	SA	AB	H	2B	3B	HR	HR%	R	RBI	BB	SO	SB	Pinch Hit AB	Pinch Hit H	PO	A	E	DP	TC/G	FA	G by Pos
1949	STL	A	41	.250	.318	44	11	3	0	0	0.0	9	2	4	11	0	17	5	19	0	0	0	1.9	1.000	OF-10

Lee Elia

ELIA, LEE CONSTANTINE BR TR 5′11″ 175 lbs.
B. July 16, 1937, Philadelphia, Pa.
Manager 1982–83, 1987–88.

Year	Team	Lg	Games	BA	SA	AB	H	2B	3B	HR	HR%	R	RBI	BB	SO	SB	Pinch Hit AB	Pinch Hit H	PO	A	E	DP	TC/G	FA	G by Pos
1966	CHI	A	80	.205	.297	195	40	5	2	3	1.5	16	22	15	39	0	1	0	103	186	14	39	4.0	.954	SS-75
1968	CHI	N	15	.176	.176	17	3	0	0	0	0.0	1	3	0	6	0	10	2	3	2	0	0	1.3	1.000	SS-2, 3B-1, 2B-1
2 yrs.			95	.203	.288	212	43	5	2	3	1.4	17	25	15	45	0	11	2	106	188	14	39	3.9	.955	SS-77, 3B-1, 2B-1

Pete Elko

ELKO, PETER (Piccolo Pete) BR TR 5′11″ 185 lbs.
B. June 17, 1918, Wilkes-Barre, Pa. D. Sept. 17, 1993, Wilkes-Barre, Pa.

Year	Team	Lg	Games	BA	SA	AB	H	2B	3B	HR	HR%	R	RBI	BB	SO	SB	Pinch Hit AB	Pinch Hit H	PO	A	E	DP	TC/G	FA	G by Pos
1943	CHI	N	9	.133	.133	30	4	0	0	0	0.0	1	0	4	5	0	0	0	8	15	4	1	3.0	.852	3B-9
1944			7	.227	.273	22	5	1	0	0	0.0	2	0	0	1	0	1	1	6	8	0	1	2.3	1.000	3B-6
2 yrs.			16	.173	.192	52	9	1	0	0	0.0	3	0	4	6	0	1	1	14	23	4	2	2.7	.902	3B-15

Roy Ellam

ELLAM, ROY (Slippery, Whitey)
B. Feb. 8, 1886, Conshohocken, Pa. D. Oct. 28, 1948, Conshohocken, Pa.
BR TR 5′10½″ 203 lbs.

Year	Team	Games	BA	SA	AB	H	2B	3B	HR	HR%	R	RBI	BB	SO	SB	Pinch Hit AB	Pinch Hit H	PO	A	E	DP	TC/G	FA	G by Pos
1909	CIN N	10	.190	.429	21	4	0	1	1	4.8	4	4	7		1	0	0	14	20	4	4	4.2	.895	SS-9
1918	PIT N	26	.130	.169	77	10	1	1	0	0.0	9	2	17	17	2	0	0	42	67	9	6	4.5	.924	SS-26
2 yrs.		36	.143	.224	98	14	1	2	1	1.0	13	6	24	17	3	0	0	56	87	13	10	4.5	.917	SS-35

Frank Ellerbe

ELLERBE, FRANCIS ROGERS (Governor)
B. Dec. 25, 1895, Marion County, S. C. D. July 8, 1988, Latta, S. C.
BR TR 5′10½″ 165 lbs.

Year	Team	Games	BA	SA	AB	H	2B	3B	HR	HR%	R	RBI	BB	SO	SB	Pinch Hit AB	Pinch Hit H	PO	A	E	DP	TC/G	FA	G by Pos
1919	WAS A	28	.276	.333	105	29	4	1	0	0.0	13	17	2	15	5	0	0	63	74	8	5	5.2	.945	SS-28
1920		101	.292	.345	336	98	14	2	0	0.0	38	36	19	23	5	6	1	127	210	28	10	3.8	.923	3B-75, SS-19, OF-1
1921	2 teams	WAS A (10G –.200) STL A (105G –.288)																						
″	total	115	.286	.405	440	126	20	13	2	0.5	66	50	22	44	1	9	2	158	226	19	9	3.8	.953	3B-106
1922	STL A	91	.246	.319	342	84	16	3	1	0.3	42	33	25	37	1	0	0	137	224	17	20	4.2	.955	3B-91
1923		18	.184	.184	49	9	0	0	0	0.0	6	1	1	5	0	4	0	11	18	1	2	2.1	.967	3B-14
1924	2 teams	STL A (21G –.197) CLE A (46G –.258)																						
″	total	67	.238	.309	181	43	4	3	1	0.6	14	16	3	12	0	4	0	71	110	7	9	3.0	.963	3B-60, 2B-2
6 yrs.		420	.268	.346	1453	389	58	22	4	0.3	179	153	72	136	12	23	3	567	862	80	55	3.8	.947	3B-346, SS-47, 2B-2, OF-1

Joe Ellick

ELLICK, JOSEPH J.
B. Apr. 3, 1854, Cincinnati, Ohio D. Apr. 21, 1923, Kansas City, Mo.
Manager 1884.
5′10″ 162 lbs.

Year	Team	Games	BA	SA	AB	H	2B	3B	HR	HR%	R	RBI	BB	SO	SB	Pinch Hit AB	Pinch Hit H	PO	A	E	DP	TC/G	FA	G by Pos
1878	MIL N	3	.154	.154	13	2	0	0	0	0.0	2	1	0	1		0	0	8	3	3	1	3.5	.786	C-2, 3B-1, P-1
1880	WOR N	5	.056	.056	18	1	0	0	0	0.0	1	0	1	2		0	0	4	11	2	0	3.4	.882	3B-5
1884	4 teams	CHI U (74G –.255) PIT U (18G –.163) KC U (2G –.000) BAL U (7G –.148)																						
″	total	101	.226	.252	429	97	11	0	0	0.0	73		18			0	0	89	118	30	6	2.3	.873	OF-59, SS-39, 2B-5
3 yrs.		109	.217	.241	460	100	11	0	0	0.0	76	1	19	3		0	0	101	132	35	7	2.4	.869	OF-59, SS-39, 3B-6, 2B-5, C-2, P-1

Larry Elliot

ELLIOT, LAWRENCE LEE
B. Mar. 5, 1938, San Diego, Calif.
BL TL 6′ 2″ 200 lbs.

Year	Team	Games	BA	SA	AB	H	2B	3B	HR	HR%	R	RBI	BB	SO	SB	Pinch Hit AB	Pinch Hit H	PO	A	E	DP	TC/G	FA	G by Pos
1962	PIT N	8	.300	.600	10	3	0	0	1	10.0	2	2	0	1	0	5	2	3	0	0	0	1.0	1.000	OF-3
1963		4	.000	.000	4	0	0	0	0	0.0	0	0	0	3	0	4	0	0	0	0	0	0.0	—	
1964	NY N	80	.228	.384	224	51	8	0	9	4.0	27	22	28	55	1	15	3	130	2	2	1	2.1	.985	OF-63
1966		65	.246	.412	199	49	14	2	5	2.5	24	32	17	46	0	10	2	73	10	8	0	1.7	.912	OF-54
4 yrs.		157	.236	.398	437	103	22	2	15	3.4	53	56	45	105	1	34	7	206	12	10	1	1.9	.956	OF-120

Allen Elliott

ELLIOTT, ALLEN CLIFFORD (Ace)
B. Dec. 25, 1897, St. Louis, Mo. D. May 6, 1979, St. Louis, Mo.
BL TR 6′ 170 lbs.

Year	Team	Games	BA	SA	AB	H	2B	3B	HR	HR%	R	RBI	BB	SO	SB	Pinch Hit AB	Pinch Hit H	PO	A	E	DP	TC/G	FA	G by Pos
1923	CHI N	53	.250	.357	168	42	8	2	2	1.2	21	29	2	12	3	0	0	450	19	4	36	9.1	.992	1B-52
1924		10	.143	.143	14	2	0	0	0	0.0	0	0	0	1	0	0	0	46	1	0	3	4.7	1.000	1B-10
2 yrs.		63	.242	.341	182	44	8	2	2	1.1	21	29	2	13	3	0	0	496	20	4	39	8.4	.992	1B-62

Bob Elliott

ELLIOTT, ROBERT IRVING
B. Nov. 26, 1916, San Francisco, Calif. D. May 4, 1966, San Diego, Calif.
Manager 1960.
BR TR 6′ 185 lbs.

Year	Team	Games	BA	SA	AB	H	2B	3B	HR	HR%	R	RBI	BB	SO	SB	Pinch Hit AB	Pinch Hit H	PO	A	E	DP	TC/G	FA	G by Pos
1939	PIT N	32	.333	.527	129	43	10	3	3	2.3	18	19	9	4	0	2	0	88	1	2	0	3.0	.978	OF-30
1940		148	.292	.421	551	161	34	11	5	0.9	88	64	45	28	13	1	0	302	12	7	0	2.2	.978	OF-147
1941		141	.273	.374	527	144	24	10	3	0.6	74	76	64	52	6	2	0	281	9	9	2	2.2	.970	OF-139
1942		143	.296	.416	560	166	26	7	9	1.6	75	89	52	35	2	1	0	176	286	36	22	3.5	.928	3B-142, OF-1
1943		156	.315	.444	581	183	30	12	7	1.2	82	101	56	24	4	4	0	150	296	25	34	3.1	.947	3B-151, 2B-2, SS-1
1944		143	.297	.465	538	160	28	16	10	1.9	85	108	75	42	9	3	0	169	285	27	22	3.4	.944	3B-140, SS-1
1945		144	.290	.423	541	157	36	6	8	1.5	80	108	64	38	5	3	0	219	185	23	18	3.0	.946	3B-81, OF-61
1946		140	.263	.358	486	128	25	3	5	1.0	50	68	64	44	6	4	2	232	90	7	10	2.4	.979	OF-92, 3B-43
1947	BOS N	150	.317	.517	555	176	35	5	22	4.0	93	113	87	60	3	2	0	129	302	20	25	3.0	.956	3B-148
1948		151	.283	.474	540	153	24	5	23	4.3	99	100	**131**	57	6	1	0	146	298	26	18	3.1	.945	3B-150
1949		139	.280	.467	482	135	29	5	17	3.5	77	76	90	38	0	10	5	141	300	17	27	3.5	.963	3B-130
1950		142	.305	.512	531	162	28	5	24	4.5	94	107	68	67	2	5	1	141	256	20	26	3.0	.952	3B-137
1951		136	.285	.448	480	137	29	2	15	3.1	73	70	65	56	2	7	1	138	242	24	31	3.2	.941	3B-127
1952	NY N	98	.228	.375	272	62	6	2	10	3.7	33	35	36	20	1	18	3	102	31	4	3	1.8	.971	OF-65, 3B-13
1953	2 teams	STL A (48G –.250) CHI A (67G –.260)																						
″	total	115	.255	.391	368	94	19	2	9	2.4	43	61	61	39	1	8	2	105	197	14	21	3.0	.956	3B-103, OF-2
15 yrs.		1978	.289	.440	7141	2061	383	94	170	2.4	1064	1195	967	604	60	71	14	2519	2790	261	259	2.9	.953	3B-1365, OF-537, SS-2, 2B-2
WORLD SERIES																								
1948	BOS N	6	.333	.619	21	7	0	0	2	9.5	4	5	2	2	0	0	0	11	14	3	1	4.7	.893	3B-6

Carter Elliott

ELLIOTT, CARTER WARD
B. Nov. 29, 1893, Atchison, Kans. D. May 21, 1959, Palm Springs, Calif.
BL TR 5′11″ 165 lbs.

Year	Team	Games	BA	SA	AB	H	2B	3B	HR	HR%	R	RBI	BB	SO	SB	Pinch Hit AB	Pinch Hit H	PO	A	E	DP	TC/G	FA	G by Pos
1921	CHI N	12	.250	.321	28	7	2	0	0	0.0	5	0	5	3	0	0	0	24	30	2	4	5.6	.964	SS-10

Gene Elliott

ELLIOTT, EUGENE BIRMINGHOUSE
B. Feb. 8, 1889, Fayette City, Pa. D. Jan. 5, 1976, Huntingdon, Pa.
BL TR 5′ 7″ 150 lbs.

Year	Team	Games	BA	SA	AB	H	2B	3B	HR	HR%	R	RBI	BB	SO	SB	Pinch Hit AB	Pinch Hit H	PO	A	E	DP	TC/G	FA	G by Pos
1911	NY A	5	.077	.154	13	1	1	0	0	0.0	1	1	2		0	2	0	1	1	1	0	1.0	.667	OF-2, 3B-1

Harry Elliott

ELLIOTT, HARRY LEWIS
B. Oct. 30, 1923, San Francisco, Calif.
BR TR 5′ 9″ 175 lbs.

Year	Team	Games	BA	SA	AB	H	2B	3B	HR	HR%	R	RBI	BB	SO	SB	Pinch Hit AB	Pinch Hit H	PO	A	E	DP	TC/G	FA	G by Pos
1953	STL N	24	.254	.441	59	15	6	1	1	1.7	6	6	3	8	0	6	0	34	1	0	0	2.1	1.000	OF-17
1955		68	.256	.316	117	30	4	0	1	0.9	9	12	11	9	0	38	7	44	1	1	0	1.6	.978	OF-28
2 yrs.		92	.256	.358	176	45	10	1	2	1.1	15	18	14	17	0	44	7	78	2	1	0	1.8	.988	OF-45

Randy Elliott

ELLIOTT, RANDY LEE
B. June 5, 1951, Oxnard, Calif.
BR TR 6′ 2″ 190 lbs.

Year	Team	Games	BA	SA	AB	H	2B	3B	HR	HR%	R	RBI	BB	SO	SB	Pinch Hit AB	Pinch Hit H	PO	A	E	DP	TC/G	FA	G by Pos
1972	SD N	14	.204	.306	49	10	3	1	0	0.0	5	6	2	11	0	2	1	29	0	0	0	2.2	1.000	OF-13
1974		13	.212	.333	33	7	1	0	1	3.0	5	2	7	9	0	2	0	10	0	0	0	0.8	1.000	OF-11, 1B-1

Randy Elliott *continued*

Year	Team	Lg	Games	BA	SA	AB	H	2B	3B	HR	HR%	R	RBI	BB	SO	SB	Pinch Hit AB	Pinch Hit H	PO	A	E	DP	TC/G	FA	G by Pos
1977	SF	N	73	.240	.407	167	40	5	1	7	4.2	17	26	8	24	0	31	11	68	5	2	1	1.6	.973	OF-46
1980	OAK	A	14	.128	.205	39	5	3	0	0	0.0	4	1	1	13	0	4	0	0	0	0	0	0.0	.000	DH-11
4 yrs.			114	.215	.354	288	62	12	2	8	2.8	31	35	18	57	0	39	12	107	5	2	1	1.4	.982	OF-70, DH-11, 1B-1

Rowdy Elliott

ELLIOTT, HAROLD B. BR TR 5′ 9½″ 160 lbs.
B. July 8, 1890, Kokomo, Ind. D. Feb. 12, 1934, San Francisco, Calif.

Year	Team	Lg	Games	BA	SA	AB	H	2B	3B	HR	HR%	R	RBI	BB	SO	SB	Pinch Hit AB	Pinch Hit H	PO	A	E	DP	TC/G	FA	G by Pos
1910	BOS	N	3	.000	.000	2	0	0	0	0	0.0	0	0	0	0	0	2	0	1	0	0	0	1.0	1.000	C-1
1916	CHI	N	23	.255	.309	55	14	3	0	0	0.0	5	3	3	5	1	4	0	77	17	3	1	5.4	.969	C-18
1917			85	.251	.332	223	56	8	5	0	0.0	18	28	11	11	4	12	2	307	93	13	9	5.7	.969	C-73
1918			5	.000	.000	10	0	0	0	0	0.0	0	0	2	1	0	0	0	15	5	1	0	4.2	.952	C-5
1920	BKN	N	41	.241	.304	112	27	4	0	1	0.9	13	13	3	6	0	2	0	144	44	7	1	5.0	.964	C-39
5 yrs.			157	.241	.311	402	97	15	5	1	0.2	36	44	19	23	5	20	2	544	159	24	11	5.3	.967	C-136

Ben Ellis

ELLIS, BENJAMIN FRANKLIN 5′10″
B. July 1870, New York, N. Y. Deceased.

Year	Team	Lg	Games	BA	SA	AB	H	2B	3B	HR	HR%	R	RBI	BB	SO	SB	Pinch Hit AB	Pinch Hit H	PO	A	E	DP	TC/G	FA	G by Pos
1896	PHI	N	4	.063	.063	16	1	0	0	0	0.0	0	0	3	6	0	0	0	5	10	4	1	4.8	.789	SS-2, 3B-2

John Ellis

ELLIS, JOHN CHARLES BR TR 6′ 2½″ 225 lbs.
B. Aug. 21, 1948, New London, Conn.

Year	Team	Lg	Games	BA	SA	AB	H	2B	3B	HR	HR%	R	RBI	BB	SO	SB	Pinch Hit AB	Pinch Hit H	PO	A	E	DP	TC/G	FA	G by Pos
1969	NY	A	22	.290	.403	62	18	4	0	1	1.6	2	8	1	11	0	7	2	83	7	2	1	6.1	.978	C-15
1970			78	.248	.403	226	56	12	1	7	3.1	24	29	18	47	0	20	2	461	41	5	35	8.4	.990	1B-53, 3B-5, C-2
1971			83	.244	.340	238	58	12	1	3	1.3	16	34	23	42	0	15	4	625	35	7	66	10.0	.990	1B-65, C-2
1972			52	.294	.456	136	40	5	1	5	3.7	13	25	8	22	0	17	4	190	12	6	5	6.3	.971	C-25, 1B-8
1973	CLE	A	127	.270	.403	437	118	12	2	14	3.2	59	68	46	57	0	5	1	487	31	10	11	4.3	.981	C-72, DH-38, 1B-12
1974			128	.285	.421	477	136	23	6	10	2.1	58	64	32	53	1	3	1	823	55	9	61	6.7	.990	1B-69, C-42, DH-21
1975			92	.230	.345	296	68	11	1	7	2.4	22	32	14	33	0	10	5	413	45	13	4	5.3	.972	C-84, DH-3, 1B-2
1976	TEX	A	11	.419	.581	31	13	2	0	1	3.2	4	8	0	4	0	4	1	21	2	0	0	2.3	1.000	C-7, DH-3
1977			49	.235	.395	119	28	7	0	4	3.4	7	15	8	26	0	16	2	89	5	0	1	2.4	1.000	C-16, DH-15, 1B-8
1978			34	.245	.383	94	23	4	0	3	3.2	7	17	6	20	0	5	2	81	10	4	1	3.3	.958	C-22, DH-7
1979			111	.285	.437	316	90	12	0	12	3.8	33	61	15	55	2	26	7	232	12	5	18	2.5	.980	DH-62, 1B-30, C-7
1980			73	.236	.313	182	43	9	1	1	0.5	12	23	14	23	3	15	4	244	12	2	22	4.2	.992	1B-39, DH-20, C-3
1981			23	.138	.241	58	8	3	0	1	1.7	2	7	5	10	0	8	1	140	8	1	16	7.8	.993	1B-18, DH-1
13 yrs.			883	.262	.392	2672	699	116	13	69	2.6	259	391	190	403	6	151	36	3889	275	64	241	5.4	.985	1B-304, C-297, DH-170, 3B-5

Rob Ellis

ELLIS, ROBERT WALTER BR TR 5′11″ 180 lbs.
B. July 3, 1950, Grand Rapids, Mich.

Year	Team	Lg	Games	BA	SA	AB	H	2B	3B	HR	HR%	R	RBI	BB	SO	SB	Pinch Hit AB	Pinch Hit H	PO	A	E	DP	TC/G	FA	G by Pos
1971	MIL	A	36	.198	.216	111	22	2	0	0	0.0	9	6	12	24	0	4	2	37	23	4	5	1.9	.938	3B-19, OF-15
1974			22	.292	.333	48	14	2	0	0	0.0	4	4	4	11	0	1	0	13	3	0	0	0.8	1.000	OF-11, DH-9, 3B-1
1975			6	.286	.286	7	2	0	0	0	0.0	3	0	0	0	0	0	0	1	0	0	0	0.2	1.000	OF-5, DH-1
3 yrs.			64	.229	.253	166	38	4	0	0	0.0	16	10	16	35	0	5	2	51	26	4	5	1.3	.951	OF-31, 3B-20, DH-10

Rube Ellis

ELLIS, GEORGE WILLIAM BL TL 6′ 160 lbs.
B. Nov. 17, 1885, Downey, Calif. D. Mar. 13, 1938, Rivera, Calif.

Year	Team	Lg	Games	BA	SA	AB	H	2B	3B	HR	HR%	R	RBI	BB	SO	SB	Pinch Hit AB	Pinch Hit H	PO	A	E	DP	TC/G	FA	G by Pos
1909	STL	N	149	.268	.332	575	154	10	9	3	0.5	76	46	54		16	4	1	332	28	17	9	2.6	.955	OF-145
1910			142	.258	.342	550	142	18	8	4	0.7	87	54	62	70	25	0	0	268	25	18	4	2.2	.942	OF-141
1911			155	.250	.339	555	139	20	10	3	0.5	69	66	66	64	9	6	1	297	21	21	3	2.3	.938	OF-148
1912			109	.269	.380	305	82	18	2	4	1.3	47	33	34	36	6	27	8	173	10	14	5	2.6	.929	OF-76
4 yrs.			555	.260	.344	1985	517	66	29	14	0.7	279	199	216	170	56	37	10	1070	84	70	21	2.4	.943	OF-510

Babe Ellison

ELLISON, HERBERT SPENCER BR TR 5′11″ 170 lbs.
B. Nov. 15, 1895, Rutland, Ark. D. Aug. 11, 1955, San Francisco, Calif.

Year	Team	Lg	Games	BA	SA	AB	H	2B	3B	HR	HR%	R	RBI	BB	SO	SB	Pinch Hit AB	Pinch Hit H	PO	A	E	DP	TC/G	FA	G by Pos
1916	DET	A	2	.143	.143	7	1	0	0	0	0.0	0	1	0	1	0	0	0	4	1	0	0	2.5	1.000	3B-2
1917			9	.172	.448	29	5	1	2	1	3.4	2	4	6	3	0	0	0	98	1	2	5	11.2	.980	1B-9
1918			7	.261	.304	23	6	1	0	0	0.0	1	2	3	1	1	0	0	8	14	0	1	3.1	1.000	OF-4, 2B-3
1919			56	.216	.246	134	29	4	0	0	0.0	18	11	13	24	4	15	3	59	65	4	7	3.6	.969	2B-25, OF-10, SS-1
1920			61	.219	.290	155	34	7	2	0	0.0	11	21	8	26	4	17	3	365	29	2	14	9.2	.995	1B-38, OF-4, 3B-1
5 yrs.			135	.216	.284	348	75	13	4	1	0.3	32	39	30	55	9	32	6	534	110	8	27	6.7	.988	1B-47, 2B-28, OF-18, 3B-3, SS-1

Verdo Elmore

ELMORE, VERDO WILSON BL TR 5′11″ 185 lbs.
B. Dec. 10, 1899, Gordo, Ala. D. Aug. 5, 1969, Birmingham, Ala.

Year	Team	Lg	Games	BA	SA	AB	H	2B	3B	HR	HR%	R	RBI	BB	SO	SB	Pinch Hit AB	Pinch Hit H	PO	A	E	DP	TC/G	FA	G by Pos
1924	STL	A	7	.176	.353	17	3	3	0	0	0.0	2	0	1	3	0	4	1	0	0	1	0	0.3	.000	OF-3

Roy Elsh

ELSH, EUGENE ROY (Dory) BR TR 5′ 9″ 165 lbs.
B. Mar. 1, 1892, Pennsgrove, N. J. D. Nov. 12, 1978, Philadelphia, Pa.

Year	Team	Lg	Games	BA	SA	AB	H	2B	3B	HR	HR%	R	RBI	BB	SO	SB	Pinch Hit AB	Pinch Hit H	PO	A	E	DP	TC/G	FA	G by Pos
1923	CHI	A	81	.249	.301	209	52	7	2	0	0.0	28	24	16	23	15	15	4	127	7	6	1	2.5	.957	OF-57
1924			60	.306	.381	147	45	9	1	0	0.0	21	11	10	14	6	16	3	65	3	5	0	1.8	.932	OF-38, 1B-2
1925			32	.188	.208	48	9	1	0	0	0.0	6	4	5	7	2	13	3	25	2	1	2	1.5	.964	OF-16, 1B-3
3 yrs.			173	.262	.319	404	106	17	3	0	0.0	55	39	31	44	23	44	10	217	12	12	3	2.1	.950	OF-111, 1B-5

Kevin Elster

ELSTER, KEVIN DANIEL BR TR 6′ 2″ 180 lbs.
B. Aug. 3, 1964, San Pedro, Calif.

Year	Team	Lg	Games	BA	SA	AB	H	2B	3B	HR	HR%	R	RBI	BB	SO	SB	Pinch Hit AB	Pinch Hit H	PO	A	E	DP	TC/G	FA	G by Pos
1986	NY	N	19	.167	.200	30	5	1	0	0	0.0	3	0	3	8	0	0	0	16	35	2	6	2.8	.962	SS-19
1987			5	.400	.600	10	4	2	0	0	0.0	1	1	0	1	0	2	2	4	6	1	0	3.7	.909	SS-3
1988			149	.214	.313	406	87	11	1	9	2.2	41	37	35	47	2	1	0	196	345	13	61	3.7	.977	SS-148
1989			151	.231	.360	458	106	25	2	10	2.2	52	55	34	77	4	0	0	235	374	15	63	4.2	.976	SS-150
1990			92	.207	.363	314	65	20	1	9	2.9	36	45	30	54	2	0	0	159	251	17	42	4.6	.960	SS-92
1991			115	.241	.351	348	84	16	2	6	1.7	33	36	40	53	2	9	2	149	299	14	39	4.3	.970	SS-107
1992			6	.222	.222	18	4	0	0	0	0.0	0	0	0	2	0	1	0	8	10	0	3	3.6	1.000	SS-5
1994	NY	A	7	.000	.000	20	0	0	0	0	0.0	0	0	1	6	0	0	0	5	27	0	7	4.6	1.000	SS-7
1995	2 teams		NY A (10G –.118) PHI N (26G –.208)																						
″	total		36	.186	.329	70	13	5	1	1	1.4	11	9	8	19	0	3	1	47	52	1	14	2.8	.990	SS-29, 1B-4, 3B-2, 2B-1
9 yrs.			580	.220	.339	1674	368	80	7	35	2.1	177	183	151	267	10	16	5	819	1399	63	235	4.0	.972	SS-560, 1B-4, 3B-2, 2B-1

Kevin Elster *continued*

Year	Team	Games	BA	SA	AB	H	2B	3B	HR	HR%	R	RBI	BB	SO	SB	Pinch Hit AB	Pinch Hit H	PO	A	E	DP	TC/G	FA	G by Pos
LEAGUE CHAMPIONSHIP SERIES																								
1986	NY N	4	.000	.000	3	0	0	0	0	0.0	0	0	0	1	0	0	0	2	3	0	0	1.3	1.000	SS-4
1988		5	.250	.375	8	2	1	0	0	0.0	1	1	3	0	0	0	0	7	7	2	2	3.2	.875	SS-5
2 yrs.		9	.182	.273	11	2	1	0	0	0.0	1	1	3	1	0	0	0	9	10	2	2	2.3	.905	SS-9
WORLD SERIES																								
1986	NY N	1	.000	.000	1	0	0	0	0	0.0	0	0	0	0	0	0	0	3	3	1	1	7.0	.857	SS-1

Bones Ely

ELY, WILLIAM FREDERICK BR TR 6′ 1″ 155 lbs.
B. June 7, 1863, North Girard, Pa. D. Jan. 10, 1952, Imola, Calif.

Year	Team	Games	BA	SA	AB	H	2B	3B	HR	HR%	R	RBI	BB	SO	SB	Pinch Hit AB	Pinch Hit H	PO	A	E	DP	TC/G	FA	G by Pos
1884	BUF N	1	.000	.000	4	0	0	0	0	0.0	0		0	2		0	0	0	1	1	0	1.0	.500	OF-1, P-1
1886	LOU AA	10	.156	.156	32	5	0	0	0	0.0	5		2			0	0	9	8	1	0	1.6	.944	P-6, OF-5
1890	SYR AA	119	.262	.319	496	130	16	6	0	0.0	72		31		44	0	0	298	143	33	20	3.9	.930	OF-78, SS-36, 1B-4, 2B-2, 3B-1, P-1
1891	BKN N	31	.153	.171	111	17	0	1	0	0.0	9	11	7	9	4	0	0	58	117	26	9	6.5	.871	SS-28, 3B-2, 2B-1
1893	STL N	44	.253	.326	178	45	1	6	0	0.0	25	16	17	13	2	0	0	98	139	25	16	6.0	.905	SS-44
1894		127	.306	.463	510	156	20	12	12	2.4	85	89	30	34	23	0	0	276	446	81	51	6.3	.899	SS-126, 2B-1, P-1
1895		117	.259	.308	467	121	16	2	1	0.2	68	46	19	17	28	0	0	247	407	53	52	6.0	.925	SS-117
1896	PIT N	128	.285	.363	537	153	15	9	3	0.6	85	77	33	33	18	0	0	258	432	62	52	5.9	.918	SS-128
1897		133	.283	.364	516	146	20	8	2	0.4	63	74	25		10	0	0	308	451	60	41	6.2	.927	SS-133
1898		148	.212	.270	519	110	14	5	2	0.4	49	44	24		6	0	0	311	527	51	58	6.0	.943	SS-148
1899		138	.278	.352	522	145	18	6	3	0.6	66	72	22		8	0	0	289	500	59	47	6.1	.930	SS-132, 2B-6
1900		130	.244	.282	475	116	6	6	0	0.0	60	51	17		6	0	0	242	503	52	62	6.1	.935	SS-130
1901	2 teams	PIT N (65G –.208) PHI A (45G –.216)																						
″	total	110	.212	.265	411	87	12	5	0	0.0	29	44	9		11	1	0	197	372	53	42	5.7	.915	SS-109, 3B-1
1902	WAS A	105	.262	.310	381	100	11	2	1	0.3	39	62	21		3	0	0	238	350	49	31	6.1	.923	SS-105
14 yrs.		1341	.258	.327	5159	1331	149	68	24	0.5	655	586	257	108	163	1	0	2829	4396	606	481	5.8	.923	SS-1236, OF-84, 2B-10, P-9, 1B-4, 3B-4

Chester Emerson

EMERSON, CHESTER ARTHUR (Chuck) BL TR 5′ 8″ 165 lbs.
B. Oct. 27, 1889, Stow, Me. D. July 2, 1971, Augusta, Me.

Year	Team	Games	BA	SA	AB	H	2B	3B	HR	HR%	R	RBI	BB	SO	SB	Pinch Hit AB	Pinch Hit H	PO	A	E	DP	TC/G	FA	G by Pos
1911	PHI A	7	.222	.222	18	4	0	0	0	0.0	2	0	6		1	0	0	17	0	0	0	2.4	1.000	OF-7
1912		1	.000	.000	1	0	0	0	0	0.0	0	0	0		0	1	0	0	0	0	0	0.0	—	
2 yrs.		8	.211	.211	19	4	0	0	0	0.0	2	0	6		1	1	0	17	0	0	0	2.4	1.000	OF-7

Cal Emery

EMERY, CALVIN WAYNE BL TL 6′ 2″ 205 lbs.
B. June 28, 1937, Centre Hall, Pa.

Year	Team	Games	BA	SA	AB	H	2B	3B	HR	HR%	R	RBI	BB	SO	SB	Pinch Hit AB	Pinch Hit H	PO	A	E	DP	TC/G	FA	G by Pos
1963	PHI N	16	.158	.211	19	3	1	0	0	0.0	0	0	0	2	0	14	1	16	0	0	0	8.0	1.000	1B-2

Spoke Emery

EMERY, HERRICK SMITH BR TR 5′ 9″ 165 lbs.
B. Dec. 10, 1898, Bay City, Mich. D. June 2, 1975, Cape Canaveral, Fla.

Year	Team	Games	BA	SA	AB	H	2B	3B	HR	HR%	R	RBI	BB	SO	SB	Pinch Hit AB	Pinch Hit H	PO	A	E	DP	TC/G	FA	G by Pos
1924	PHI N	5	.667	.667	3	2	0	0	0	0.0	3	0	0	0	0	1	0	2	0	0	0	2.0	1.000	OF-1

Frank Emmer

EMMER, FRANK WILLIAM BR TR 5′ 8″ 150 lbs.
B. Feb. 17, 1896, Crestline, Ohio D. Oct. 18, 1963, Homestead, Fla.

Year	Team	Games	BA	SA	AB	H	2B	3B	HR	HR%	R	RBI	BB	SO	SB	Pinch Hit AB	Pinch Hit H	PO	A	E	DP	TC/G	FA	G by Pos
1916	CIN N	42	.146	.202	89	13	3	1	0	0.0	8	2	7	27	1	0	0	56	88	17	7	4.9	.894	SS-29, OF-2, 2B-1, 3B-1
1926		80	.196	.281	224	44	7	6	0	0.0	22	18	13	30	1	0	0	141	242	34	40	5.3	.918	SS-79
2 yrs.		122	.182	.259	313	57	10	7	0	0.0	30	20	20	57	2	0	0	197	330	51	47	5.2	.912	SS-108, OF-2, 2B-1, 3B-1

Bob Emmerich

EMMERICH, ROBERT GEORGE BR TR 5′ 3″ 155 lbs.
B. Aug. 1, 1897, New York, N. Y. D. Nov. 22, 1948, Bridgeport, Conn.

Year	Team	Games	BA	SA	AB	H	2B	3B	HR	HR%	R	RBI	BB	SO	SB	Pinch Hit AB	Pinch Hit H	PO	A	E	DP	TC/G	FA	G by Pos
1923	BOS N	13	.083	.083	24	2	0	0	0	0.0	3	0	2	3	1	0	0	14	1	0	0	1.9	1.000	OF-8

Angelo Encarnacion

ENCARNACION, ANGELO BENJAMIN BR TR 5′ 8″ 180 lbs.
B. Apr. 18, 1973, Santo Domingo, Dominican Republic.

Year	Team	Games	BA	SA	AB	H	2B	3B	HR	HR%	R	RBI	BB	SO	SB	Pinch Hit AB	Pinch Hit H	PO	A	E	DP	TC/G	FA	G by Pos
1995	PIT N	58	.226	.333	159	36	7	2	2	1.3	18	10	13	28	1	5	1	278	42	7	2	5.9	.979	C-55

Bill Endicott

ENDICOTT, WILLIAM FRANKLIN BL TL 5′11½″ 175 lbs.
B. Sept. 4, 1918, Acorn, Mo.

Year	Team	Games	BA	SA	AB	H	2B	3B	HR	HR%	R	RBI	BB	SO	SB	Pinch Hit AB	Pinch Hit H	PO	A	E	DP	TC/G	FA	G by Pos
1946	STL N	20	.200	.350	20	4	3	0	0	0.0	2	3	4	4	0	14	3	4	0	0	0	2.0	1.000	OF-2

Charlie Engle

ENGLE, CHARLIE AUGUST (Cholly) BR TR 5′ 8″ 145 lbs.
B. Aug. 27, 1903, New York, N. Y. D. Oct. 12, 1983, San Antonio, Tex.

Year	Team	Games	BA	SA	AB	H	2B	3B	HR	HR%	R	RBI	BB	SO	SB	Pinch Hit AB	Pinch Hit H	PO	A	E	DP	TC/G	FA	G by Pos
1925	PHI A	1	—	—	0	0	0	0	0	—	0	0	0	0	0	0	0	0	0	0	0	0.0	.000	SS-1
1926		19	.105	.105	19	2	0	0	0	0.0	7	0	10	6	0	0	0	13	27	3	6	2.7	.930	SS-16
1930	PIT N	67	.264	.319	216	57	10	1	0	0.0	34	15	22	20	1	7	2	113	161	15	18	5.1	.948	3B-24, SS-23, 2B-10
3 yrs.		87	.251	.302	235	59	10	1	0	0.0	41	15	32	26	1	7	2	126	188	18	24	4.5	.946	SS-40, 3B-24, 2B-10

Clyde Engle

ENGLE, ARTHUR CLYDE (Hack) BR TR 5′10″ 190 lbs.
B. Mar. 19, 1884, Dayton, Ohio D. Dec. 26, 1939, Boston, Mass.

Year	Team	Games	BA	SA	AB	H	2B	3B	HR	HR%	R	RBI	BB	SO	SB	Pinch Hit AB	Pinch Hit H	PO	A	E	DP	TC/G	FA	G by Pos
1909	NY A	135	.278	.358	492	137	20	5	3	0.6	66	71	47		18	1	1	299	17	18	5	2.5	.946	OF-134
1910	2 teams	NY A (5G –.231) BOS A (106G –.264)																						
″	total	111	.263	.364	376	99	18	7	2	0.5	59	38	33		13	7	0	135	223	30	17	3.8	.923	3B-51, 2B-27, OF-18, SS-7
1911	BOS A	146	.270	.319	514	139	13	3	2	0.4	58	48	51		24	5	1	636	187	48	34	6.3	.945	1B-65, 3B-51, 2B-13, OF-10
1912		57	.234	.298	171	40	5	3	0	0.0	32	18	28		12	3	0	248	60	13	15	5.9	.960	1B-25, 2B-15, 3B-11, SS-2, OF-1
1913		143	.289	.384	498	144	17	12	2	0.4	75	50	53	41	28	7	0	1241	59	17	56	9.8	.987	1B-133, OF-2
1914	2 teams	BOS A (55G –.194) BUF F (32G –.255)																						
″	total	87	.221	.254	244	54	6	1	0	0.0	26	21	25	11	9	18	5	330	46	14	16	5.7	.964	1B-29, 3B-25, OF-9, 2B-5
1915	BUF F	141	.261	.355	501	131	22	8	3	0.6	56	71	34		24	5	2	261	71	12	11	2.5	.965	OF-100, 2B-21, 3B-17, 1B-1
1916	CLE A	11	.154	.154	26	4	0	0	0	0.0	1	1	0	6	0	1	0	10	12	4	0	2.6	.846	3B-7, 1B-2, OF-1
8 yrs.		831	.265	.341	2822	748	101	39	12	0.4	373	318	271	58	128	47	9	3160	675	156	154	5.1	.961	OF-275, 1B-255, 3B-162, 2B-81, SS-9

Clyde Engle *continued*

Year	Team	Games	BA	SA	AB	H	2B	3B	HR	HR%	R	RBI	BB	SO	SB	Pinch Hit AB	Pinch Hit H	PO	A	E	DP	TC/G	FA	G by Pos
WORLD SERIES																								
1912	BOS A	3	.333	.667	3	1	1	0	0	0.0	1	2	0	0	0	3	1	0	0	0	0	0.0	—	

Dave Engle

ENGLE, RALPH DAVID
B. Nov. 30, 1956, San Diego, Calif.
BR TR 6′ 3″ 210 lbs.

Year	Team	Games	BA	SA	AB	H	2B	3B	HR	HR%	R	RBI	BB	SO	SB	Pinch Hit AB	Pinch Hit H	PO	A	E	DP	TC/G	FA	G by Pos
1981	MIN A	82	.258	.407	248	64	14	4	5	2.0	29	32	13	37	0	1	0	144	4	3	0	1.9	.980	OF-76, DH-1, 3B-1
1982		58	.226	.349	186	42	7	2	4	2.2	20	16	10	22	0	13	3	63	3	1	1	1.2	.985	OF-34, DH-20
1983		120	.305	.449	374	114	22	4	8	2.1	46	43	28	39	2	20	6	306	26	9	3	3.2	.974	C-73, DH-29, OF-4
1984		109	.266	.353	391	104	20	1	4	1.0	56	38	26	22	0	6	0	376	34	8	3	3.9	.981	C-86, DH-22
1985		70	.256	.448	172	44	8	2	7	4.1	28	25	21	28	2	18	4	66	4	1	1	1.2	.986	DH-38, C-17, OF-3
1986	DET A	35	.256	.337	86	22	7	0	0	0.0	6	4	7	13	0	5	1	185	14	0	20	5.7	1.000	1B-23, DH-5, OF-4, C-3
1987	MON N	59	.226	.310	84	19	4	0	1	1.2	7	14	6	11	1	41	11	33	3	0	0	1.8	1.000	OF-11, C-6, 1B-2, 3B-1
1988		34	.216	.297	37	8	3	0	0	0.0	4	1	5	5	0	23	2	25	1	0	0	1.9	1.000	C-9, OF-4, 3B-1
1989	MIL A	27	.215	.354	65	14	3	0	2	3.1	5	8	4	13	0	6	1	134	12	4	11	6.3	.973	1B-18, C-3, DH-3
9 yrs.		594	.262	.388	1643	431	88	13	31	1.9	201	181	120	190	5	133	28	1332	101	26	39	2.9	.982	C-197, OF-136, DH-118, 1B-43, 3B-3

Charlie English

ENGLISH, CHARLES DEWIE
B. Apr. 8, 1910, Darlington, S. C.
BR TR 5′ 9½″ 160 lbs.

Year	Team	Games	BA	SA	AB	H	2B	3B	HR	HR%	R	RBI	BB	SO	SB	Pinch Hit AB	Pinch Hit H	PO	A	E	DP	TC/G	FA	G by Pos
1932	CHI A	24	.317	.444	63	20	3	1	1	1.6	7	8	3	7	0	9	2	10	25	8	2	3.1	.814	3B-13, SS-1
1933		3	.444	.667	9	4	2	0	0	0.0	2	1	1	1	0	0	0	6	6	1	2	4.3	.923	2B-3
1936	NY N	6	.000	.000	1	0	0	0	0	0.0	0	0	0	0	0	1	0	0	0	0	0	0.0	.000	2B-1
1937	CIN N	17	.238	.317	63	15	3	1	0	0.0	1	4	0	2	0	0	0	20	34	3	3	3.4	.947	3B-15, 2B-2
4 yrs.		50	.287	.397	136	39	8	2	1	0.7	10	13	4	10	0	10	2	36	65	12	7	3.2	.894	3B-28, 2B-6, SS-1

Gil English

ENGLISH, GILBERT RAYMOND
B. July 2, 1909, Glenola, N. C.
BR TR 5′11″ 180 lbs.

Year	Team	Games	BA	SA	AB	H	2B	3B	HR	HR%	R	RBI	BB	SO	SB	Pinch Hit AB	Pinch Hit H	PO	A	E	DP	TC/G	FA	G by Pos
1931	NY N	3	.000	.000	8	0	0	0	0	0.0	0	0	1	3	0	0	0	1	3	0	0	1.3	1.000	3B-3
1932		59	.225	.338	204	46	7	5	2	1.0	22	19	5	20	0	1	0	77	133	14	18	3.6	.938	3B-39, SS-23
1936	DET A	1	.000	.000	1	0	0	0	0	0.0	0	0	0	1	0	0	0	1	1	0	0	2.0	1.000	3B-1
1937	2 teams	DET A (18G –.262) BOS N (79G –.290)																						
″	total	97	.284	.341	334	95	6	2	3	0.9	31	43	29	31	4	6	4	87	155	10	14	2.8	.960	3B-77, 2B-12
1938	BOS N	53	.248	.321	165	41	6	0	2	1.2	17	21	15	16	1	4	2	39	77	6	3	2.4	.951	3B-43, OF-3, SS-2, 2B-2
1944	BKN N	27	.152	.228	79	12	3	0	1	1.3	4	7	6	7	0	1	0	28	51	6	8	3.3	.929	SS-13, 3B-11, 2B-2
6 yrs.		240	.245	.321	791	194	22	7	8	1.0	74	90	56	78	5	12	6	233	420	36	43	3.0	.948	3B-174, SS-38, 2B-16, OF-3

Woody English

ENGLISH, ELWOOD GEORGE
B. Mar. 2, 1907, Fredonia, Ohio.
BR TR 5′10″ 155 lbs.

Year	Team	Games	BA	SA	AB	H	2B	3B	HR	HR%	R	RBI	BB	SO	SB	Pinch Hit AB	Pinch Hit H	PO	A	E	DP	TC/G	FA	G by Pos
1927	CHI N	87	.290	.365	334	97	14	4	1	0.3	46	28	16	26	1	0	0	179	285	29	47	5.8	.941	SS-84, 3B-1
1928		116	.299	.375	475	142	22	4	2	0.4	68	34	30	28	4	0	0	245	382	36	85	5.7	.946	SS-114, 3B-2
1929		144	.276	.339	608	168	29	3	1	0.2	131	52	68	50	13	0	0	332	497	39	107	6.0	.955	SS-144
1930		156	.335	.511	638	214	36	17	14	2.2	152	59	100	72	3	0	0	256	386	22	76	4.1	.967	3B-83, SS-78
1931		156	.319	.413	634	202	38	8	2	0.3	117	53	68	80	12	0	0	340	482	29	78	5.5	.966	SS-138, 3B-18
1932		127	.272	.360	522	142	23	7	3	0.6	70	47	55	73	5	1	0	162	275	20	30	3.5	.956	3B-93, SS-38
1933		105	.261	.342	398	104	19	2	3	0.8	54	41	53	44	5	0	0	80	174	7	9	2.5	.973	3B-103, SS-1
1934		109	.278	.385	421	117	26	5	3	0.7	65	31	48	65	6	0	0	145	260	14	31	3.8	.967	SS-56, 3B-46, 2B-7
1935		34	.202	.298	84	17	2	0	2	2.4	11	8	20	4	1	4	2	29	54	6	6	3.2	.933	3B-16, SS-12
1936		64	.247	.297	182	45	9	0	0	0.0	33	20	40	28	1	5	0	92	152	5	30	4.2	.980	SS-42, 3B-17, 2B-1
1937	BKN N	129	.238	.299	378	90	16	2	1	0.3	45	42	65	55	4	2	0	239	324	26	64	4.6	.956	SS-116, 2B-11
1938		34	.250	.278	72	18	2	0	0	0.0	9	7	8	11	2	7	1	24	37	2	5	2.3	.968	3B-21, SS-3, 2B-3
12 yrs.		1261	.286	.378	4746	1356	236	52	32	0.7	801	422	571	536	57	19	3	2123	3308	235	568	4.5	.959	SS-826, 3B-400, 2B-22
WORLD SERIES																								
1929	CHI N	5	.190	.286	21	4	2	0	0	0.0	1	0	1	6	0	0	0	8	12	4	3	4.8	.833	SS-5
1932		4	.176	.176	17	3	0	0	0	0.0	2	1	2	2	0	0	0	3	4	1	0	2.0	.875	3B-4
2 yrs.		9	.184	.237	38	7	2	0	0	0.0	3	1	3	8	0	0	0	11	16	5	3	3.6	.844	SS-5, 3B-4

Del Ennis

ENNIS, DELMER
B. June 8, 1925, Philadelphia, Pa. D. Feb. 8, 1996, Huntingdon Valley, Pa.
BR TR 6′ 195 lbs.

Year	Team	Games	BA	SA	AB	H	2B	3B	HR	HR%	R	RBI	BB	SO	SB	Pinch Hit AB	Pinch Hit H	PO	A	E	DP	TC/G	FA	G by Pos
1946	PHI N	141	.313	.485	540	169	30	6	17	3.1	70	73	39	65	5	3	0	332	16	9	4	2.6	.975	OF-138
1947		139	.275	.410	541	149	25	6	12	2.2	71	81	37	51	9	4	1	320	12	7	2	2.5	.979	OF-135
1948		152	.290	.525	589	171	40	4	30	5.1	86	95	47	58	2	2	1	297	15	14	4	2.2	.957	OF-151
1949		154	.302	.525	610	184	39	11	25	4.1	92	110	59	61	2	0	0	359	16	13	1	2.5	.966	OF-154
1950		153	.311	.551	595	185	34	8	31	5.2	92	**126**	56	59	2	4	0	279	10	9	3	2.0	.970	OF-149
1951		144	.267	.408	532	142	20	5	15	2.8	76	73	68	42	4	8	2	268	14	9	3	2.0	.969	OF-144
1952		151	.289	.475	592	171	30	10	20	3.4	90	107	47	65	6	2	0	277	11	9	1	2.0	.970	OF-149
1953		152	.285	.484	578	165	22	3	29	5.0	79	125	57	53	1	2	0	284	14	6	4	2.0	.980	OF-150
1954		145	.261	.444	556	145	23	2	25	4.5	73	119	50	60	2	1	0	311	9	15	1	2.3	.955	OF-142, 1B-1
1955		146	.296	.518	564	167	24	7	29	5.1	82	120	46	46	4	1	0	298	9	4	2	2.1	.987	OF-145
1956		153	.260	.430	630	164	23	3	26	4.1	80	95	33	62	7	0	0	269	8	11	0	1.9	.962	OF-153
1957	STL N	136	.286	.494	490	140	24	3	24	4.9	61	105	37	50	1	8	3	180	3	11	0	1.5	.943	OF-127
1958		106	.261	.350	329	86	18	1	3	0.9	22	47	15	35	0	22	2	122	11	1	2	1.6	.993	OF-84
1959	2 teams	CIN N (5G –.333) CHI A (26G –.219)																						
″	total	31	.231	.343	108	25	6	0	2	1.9	11	8	6	12	0	3	1	33	2	3	0	1.4	.921	OF-28
14 yrs.		1903	.284	.472	7254	2063	358	69	288	4.0	985	1284	597	719	45	60	10	3629	150	121	27	2.1	.969	OF-1849, 1B-1
WORLD SERIES																								
1950	PHI N	4	.143	.214	14	2	1	0	0	0.0	1	0	0	1	0	0	0	9	0	0	0	2.3	1.000	OF-4

Russ Ennis

ENNIS, RUSSELL ELWOOD (Hack)
B. Mar. 10, 1897, Superior, Wis. D. Jan. 21, 1949, Superior, Wis.
BR TR 5′11½″ 160 lbs.

Year	Team	Games	BA	SA	AB	H	2B	3B	HR	HR%	R	RBI	BB	SO	SB	Pinch Hit AB	Pinch Hit H	PO	A	E	DP	TC/G	FA	G by Pos
1926	WAS A	1	—	—	0	0	0	0	0	—	0	0	0	0	0	0	0	0	0	0	0	0.0	.000	C-1

George Enright

ENRIGHT, GEORGE ALBERT BR TR 5′11″ 175 lbs.
B. May 9, 1954, New Britain, Conn.

Year	Team	Games	BA	SA	AB	H	2B	3B	HR	HR%	R	RBI	BB	SO	SB	Pinch Hit AB	Pinch Hit H	PO	A	E	DP	TC/G	FA	G by Pos
1976	CHI A	2	.000	.000	1	0	0	0	0	0.0	0	0	0	0	0	0	0	4	0	0	0	2.0	1.000	C-2

Jewel Ens

ENS, JEWEL WINKLEMEYER BR TR 5′10½″ 165 lbs.
Brother of Mutz Ens.
B. Aug. 24, 1889, St. Louis, Mo. D. Jan. 17, 1950, Syracuse, N. Y.
Manager 1929–31.

Year	Team	Games	BA	SA	AB	H	2B	3B	HR	HR%	R	RBI	BB	SO	SB	Pinch Hit AB	Pinch Hit H	PO	A	E	DP	TC/G	FA	G by Pos
1922	PIT N	47	.296	.387	142	42	7	3	0	0.0	18	17	7	9	3	13	3	69	77	7	7	4.4	.954	2B-29, 3B-3, 1B-2, SS-1
1923		12	.276	.379	29	8	1	1	0	0.0	3	5	0	3	2	5	2	39	7	2	5	6.9	.958	1B-4, 3B-2, SS-1
1924		5	.300	.300	10	3	0	0	0	0.0	2	0	0	3	0	0	0	25	1	0	1	5.2	1.000	1B-5
1925		3	.200	.800	5	1	0	0	1	20.0	2	2	0	1	0	0	0	16	0	0	0	5.3	1.000	1B-3
4 yrs.		67	.290	.392	186	54	8	4	1	0.5	25	24	7	16	5	18	5	149	85	9	13	4.9	.963	2B-29, 1B-14, 3B-5, SS-2

Mutz Ens

ENS, ANTON BL TL 6′1″ 180 lbs.
Brother of Jewel Ens.
B. Nov. 8, 1884, St. Louis, Mo. D. June 28, 1950, St. Louis, Mo.

Year	Team	Games	BA	SA	AB	H	2B	3B	HR	HR%	R	RBI	BB	SO	SB	Pinch Hit AB	Pinch Hit H	PO	A	E	DP	TC/G	FA	G by Pos
1912	CHI A	3	.000	.000	6	0	0	0	0	0.0	0	0	0		0	0	0	12	0	2	1	4.7	.857	1B-3

Charlie Enwright

ENWRIGHT, CHARLES MASSEY BL TR 5′10″
B. Oct. 6, 1887, Sacramento, Calif. D. Jan. 19, 1917, Sacramento, Calif.

Year	Team	Games	BA	SA	AB	H	2B	3B	HR	HR%	R	RBI	BB	SO	SB	Pinch Hit AB	Pinch Hit H	PO	A	E	DP	TC/G	FA	G by Pos
1909	STL N	3	.143	.143	7	1	0	0	0	0.0	1	1	2		0	1	0	2	2	5	0	4.5	.444	SS-2

Jack Enzenroth

ENZENROTH, CLARENCE HERMAN BR TR 5′10″ 164 lbs.
B. Nov. 4, 1885, Mineral Point, Wis. D. Feb. 21, 1944, Detroit, Mich.

Year	Team	Games	BA	SA	AB	H	2B	3B	HR	HR%	R	RBI	BB	SO	SB	Pinch Hit AB	Pinch Hit H	PO	A	E	DP	TC/G	FA	G by Pos
1914	2 teams	STL A (3G –.167) KC F (26G –.179)																						
″	total	29	.178	.260	73	13	4	1	0	0.0	7	5	7	3	0	2	1	91	31	5	6	4.7	.961	C-27
1915	KC F	14	.158	.158	19	3	0	0	0	0.0	3	3	6		0	1	1	25	11	1	2	4.6	.973	C-8
2 yrs.		43	.174	.239	92	16	4	1	0	0.0	10	8	13	3	0	3	2	116	42	6	8	4.7	.963	C-35

Jim Eppard

EPPARD, JAMES GERHARD BL TL 6′2″ 180 lbs.
B. Apr. 27, 1960, South Bend, Ind.

Year	Team	Games	BA	SA	AB	H	2B	3B	HR	HR%	R	RBI	BB	SO	SB	Pinch Hit AB	Pinch Hit H	PO	A	E	DP	TC/G	FA	G by Pos
1987	CAL A	8	.333	.333	9	3	0	0	0	0.0	2	0	2	0	0	5	3	1	0	0	0	1.0	1.000	OF-1
1988		56	.283	.327	113	32	3	1	0	0.0	7	14	11	15	0	26	**8**	63	4	2	2	2.1	.971	OF-17, DH-10, 1B-6
1989		12	.250	.250	12	3	0	0	0	0.0	0	2	1	4	0	9	2	12	0	0	2	3.0	1.000	1B-4
1990	TOR A	6	.200	.200	5	1	0	0	0	0.0	0	0	0	2	0	5	1	0	0	0	0	0.0	—	
4 yrs.		82	.281	.317	139	39	3	1	0	0.0	9	16	14	21	0	45	14	76	4	2	4	2.2	.976	OF-18, 1B-10, DH-10

Aubrey Epps

EPPS, AUBREY LEE (Yo-Yo) BR TR 5′10″ 170 lbs.
B. Mar. 3, 1912, Memphis, Tenn. D. Nov. 13, 1984, Ackerman, Miss.

Year	Team	Games	BA	SA	AB	H	2B	3B	HR	HR%	R	RBI	BB	SO	SB	Pinch Hit AB	Pinch Hit H	PO	A	E	DP	TC/G	FA	G by Pos
1935	PIT N	1	.750	1.250	4	3	0	1	0	0.0	1	3	0	0	0	0	0	6	0	2	0	8.0	.750	C-1

Hal Epps

EPPS, HAROLD FRANKLIN BL TL 6′ 175 lbs.
B. Mar. 26, 1914, Athens, Ga.

Year	Team	Games	BA	SA	AB	H	2B	3B	HR	HR%	R	RBI	BB	SO	SB	Pinch Hit AB	Pinch Hit H	PO	A	E	DP	TC/G	FA	G by Pos
1938	STL N	17	.300	.360	50	15	0	0	1	2.0	8	3	2	4	2	7	0	26	0	1	0	2.7	.963	OF-10
1940		11	.200	.200	15	3	0	0	0	0.0	6	1	0	3	0	2	0	4	0	1	0	1.7	.800	OF-3
1943	STL A	8	.286	.400	35	10	4	0	0	0.0	2	1	3	4	1	0	0	18	0	0	0	2.3	1.000	OF-8
1944	2 teams	STL A (22G –.177) PHI A (67G –.262)																						
″	total	89	.244	.337	291	71	9	9	0	0.0	42	16	32	32	2	10	3	188	7	6	3	2.6	.970	OF-78
4 yrs.		125	.253	.340	391	99	13	9	1	0.3	58	21	37	43	5	19	3	236	7	8	3	2.5	.968	OF-99

Mike Epstein

EPSTEIN, MICHAEL PETER (Superjew) BL TL 6′3½″ 230 lbs.
B. Apr. 4, 1943, Bronx, N. Y.

Year	Team	Games	BA	SA	AB	H	2B	3B	HR	HR%	R	RBI	BB	SO	SB	Pinch Hit AB	Pinch Hit H	PO	A	E	DP	TC/G	FA	G by Pos
1966	BAL A	6	.182	.364	11	2	0	1	0	0.0	1	3	1	3	0	1	0	36	2	0	3	9.5	1.000	1B-4
1967	2 teams	BAL A (9G –.154) WAS A (96G –.229)																						
″	total	105	.226	.367	297	67	7	4	9	3.0	32	29	41	79	1	19	3	743	55	10	74	9.7	.988	1B-83
1968	WAS A	123	.234	.366	385	90	8	2	13	3.4	40	33	48	91	1	13	2	947	70	13	83	9.4	.987	1B-110
1969		131	.278	.551	403	112	18	1	30	7.4	73	85	85	99	2	12	3	1035	69	11	99	9.4	.990	1B-118
1970		140	.256	.444	430	110	15	3	20	4.7	55	56	73	117	2	18	2	1100	70	10	104	9.7	.992	1B-122
1971	2 teams	WAS A (24G –.247) OAK A (104G –.234)																						
″	total	128	.237	.413	414	98	14	1	19	4.6	49	60	74	102	1	9	1	938	64	6	123	8.4	.994	1B-120
1972	OAK A	138	.270	.490	455	123	18	2	26	5.7	63	70	68	68	0	1	0	1111	73	12	101	8.7	.990	1B-137
1973	2 teams	TEX A (27G –.188) CAL A (91G –.215)																						
″	total	118	.209	.315	397	83	11	2	9	2.3	39	38	48	73	0	4	1	910	62	7	80	8.8	.993	1B-111
1974	CAL A	18	.161	.387	62	10	2	0	4	6.5	10	6	10	13	0	0	0	137	12	1	14	8.3	.993	1B-18
9 yrs.		907	.244	.424	2854	695	93	16	130	4.6	362	380	448	645	7	77	12	6957	477	70	681	9.1	.991	1B-823
LEAGUE CHAMPIONSHIP SERIES																								
1971	OAK A	2	.200	.200	5	1	0	0	0	0.0	0	0	0	3	0	1	0	4	0	0	2	4.0	1.000	1B-1
1972		5	.188	.375	16	3	0	0	1	6.3	1	1	4	5	0	0	0	55	2	0	5	11.4	1.000	1B-5
2 yrs.		7	.190	.333	21	4	0	0	1	4.8	1	1	4	8	0	1	0	59	2	0	7	10.2	1.000	1B-6
WORLD SERIES																								
1972	OAK A	6	.000	.000	16	0	0	0	0	0.0	1	0	5	3	0	0	0	35	2	2	1	6.5	.949	1B-6

Joe Erautt

ERAUTT, JOSEPH MICHAEL (Stubby) BR TR 5′9″ 175 lbs.
Brother of Eddie Erautt.
B. Sept. 1, 1921, Vibank, Sask., Canada D. Oct. 6, 1976, Portland, Ore.

Year	Team	Games	BA	SA	AB	H	2B	3B	HR	HR%	R	RBI	BB	SO	SB	Pinch Hit AB	Pinch Hit H	PO	A	E	DP	TC/G	FA	G by Pos
1950	CHI A	16	.222	.222	18	4	0	0	0	0.0	0	1	1	3	0	10	2	12	2	0	0	2.8	1.000	C-5
1951		16	.160	.200	25	4	1	0	0	0.0	3	0	3	2	0	4	1	37	6	1	1	3.7	.977	C-12
2 yrs.		32	.186	.209	43	8	1	0	0	0.0	3	1	4	5	0	14	3	49	8	1	1	3.4	.983	C-17

Hank Erickson

ERICKSON, HENRY NELS (Popeye) BR TR 6′1″ 185 lbs.
B. Nov. 11, 1907, Chicago, Ill. D. Dec. 13, 1964, Louisville, Ky.

Year	Team	Games	BA	SA	AB	H	2B	3B	HR	HR%	R	RBI	BB	SO	SB	Pinch Hit AB	Pinch Hit H	PO	A	E	DP	TC/G	FA	G by Pos
1935	CIN N	37	.261	.375	88	23	3	2	1	1.1	9	4	6	4	0	12	2	84	19	3	7	4.2	.972	C-25

Cal Ermer

ERMER, CALVIN COOLIDGE BR TR 6′½″ 175 lbs.
B. Nov. 10, 1923, Baltimore, Md.
Manager 1967–68.

Year	Team	Games	BA	SA	AB	H	2B	3B	HR	HR%	R	RBI	BB	SO	SB	Pinch Hit AB	Pinch Hit H	PO	A	E	DP	TC/G	FA	G by Pos
1947	WAS A	1	.000	.000	3	0	0	0	0	0.0	0	0	0	0	0	0	0	4	3	0	0	7.0	1.000	2B-1

Frank Ernaga

ERNAGA, FRANK JOHN BR TR 6′ 1″ 195 lbs.
B. Aug. 22, 1930, Susanville, Calif.

Year	Team	Games	BA	SA	AB	H	2B	3B	HR	HR%	R	RBI	BB	SO	SB	Pinch Hit AB	Pinch Hit H	PO	A	E	DP	TC/G	FA	G by Pos
1957	CHI N	20	.314	.686	35	11	3	2	2	5.7	9	7	9	14	0	7	1	19	0	1	0	2.0	.950	OF-10
1958		9	.125	.125	8	1	0	0	0	0.0	0	0	0	2	0	8	1	0	0	0	0	0.0	—	
2 yrs.		29	.279	.581	43	12	3	2	2	4.7	9	7	9	16	0	15	2	19	0	1	0	2.0	.950	OF-10

Tex Erwin

ERWIN, ROSS EMIL BL TR 6′ 185 lbs.
B. Dec. 22, 1885, Forney, Tex. D. Apr. 5, 1953, Rochester, N. Y.

Year	Team	Games	BA	SA	AB	H	2B	3B	HR	HR%	R	RBI	BB	SO	SB	Pinch Hit AB	Pinch Hit H	PO	A	E	DP	TC/G	FA	G by Pos
1907	DET A	4	.200	.200	5	1	0	0	0	0.0	0	1	1		0	0	0	7	3	1	0	2.8	.909	C-4
1910	BKN N	81	.188	.228	202	38	3	1	1	0.5	15	10	24	12	3	12	1	259	114	20	10	5.8	.949	C-68
1911		91	.271	.445	218	59	13	2	7	3.2	30	34	31	23	5	15	4	273	98	11	6	5.2	.971	C-74
1912		59	.211	.278	133	28	3	0	2	1.5	14	14	18	16	1	12	2	176	46	12	3	5.7	.949	C-41
1913		20	.258	.290	31	8	1	0	0	0.0	6	3	4	5	0	7	1	32	6	2	0	3.1	.950	C-13
1914	2 teams	BKN N (9G –.455) CIN N (12G –.314)																						
″	total	21	.348	.478	46	16	3	0	1	2.2	5	8	4	4	1	6	3	69	15	3	0	5.4	.966	C-16
6 yrs.		276	.236	.334	635	150	23	3	11	1.7	70	70	82	60	10	52	11	816	282	49	19	5.3	.957	C-216

Nick Esasky

ESASKY, NICHOLAS ANDREW BR TR 6′ 3″ 190 lbs.
B. Feb. 24, 1960, Hialeah, Fla.

Year	Team	Games	BA	SA	AB	H	2B	3B	HR	HR%	R	RBI	BB	SO	SB	Pinch Hit AB	Pinch Hit H	PO	A	E	DP	TC/G	FA	G by Pos
1983	CIN N	85	.265	.450	302	80	10	5	12	4.0	41	46	27	99	6	1	0	53	133	13	11	2.4	.935	3B-84
1984		113	.193	.348	322	62	10	5	10	3.1	30	45	52	103	1	12	0	220	137	18	19	3.5	.952	3B-82, 1B-25
1985		125	.262	.465	413	108	21	0	21	5.1	61	66	41	102	3	10	4	169	106	8	16	2.2	.972	3B-62, OF-54, 1B-12
1986		102	.230	.403	330	76	17	2	12	3.6	35	41	47	97	0	5	1	585	33	5	14	5.5	.992	1B-70, OF-42, 3B-1
1987		100	.272	.529	346	94	19	2	22	6.4	48	59	29	76	0	6	1	773	41	6	72	8.6	.993	1B-93, OF-1, 3B-1
1988		122	.243	.412	391	95	17	2	15	3.8	40	62	48	104	7	11	0	982	52	6	70	9.0	.994	1B-116
1989	BOS A	154	.277	.500	564	156	26	5	30	5.3	79	108	66	117	1	4	0	1319	107	6	129	9.3	.996	1B-153, OF-1
1990	ATL N	9	.171	.171	35	6	0	0	0	0.0	2	0	4	14	0	0	0	79	5	5	7	9.9	.944	1B-9
8 yrs.		810	.250	.446	2703	677	120	21	122	4.5	336	427	314	712	18	49	6	4180	614	67	338	6.0	.986	1B-478, 3B-230, OF-98

Nino Escalera

ESCALERA, SATURNINO BL TR 5′10″ 165 lbs.
Born Saturnino Escalera (Cuadrado).
B. Dec. 1, 1929, Santurce, Puerto Rico.

Year	Team	Games	BA	SA	AB	H	2B	3B	HR	HR%	R	RBI	BB	SO	SB	Pinch Hit AB	Pinch Hit H	PO	A	E	DP	TC/G	FA	G by Pos
1954	CIN N	73	.159	.203	69	11	1	1	0	0.0	15	3	7	11	1	29	6	44	4	1	1	2.1	.980	OF-14, 1B-8, SS-1

Jim Eschen

ESCHEN, JAMES GODRICH BR TR 5′10½″ 160 lbs.
Father of Larry Eschen.
B. Aug. 21, 1891, Brooklyn, N. Y. D. Sept. 27, 1960, Sloatsburg, N. Y.

Year	Team	Games	BA	SA	AB	H	2B	3B	HR	HR%	R	RBI	BB	SO	SB	Pinch Hit AB	Pinch Hit H	PO	A	E	DP	TC/G	FA	G by Pos
1915	CLE A	15	.238	.262	42	10	1	0	0	0.0	11	2	5	9	0	5	2	29	1	1	0	3.1	.968	OF-10

Larry Eschen

ESCHEN, LAWRENCE EDWARD BR TR 6′ 180 lbs.
Son of Jim Eschen.
B. Sept. 22, 1920, Suffern, N. Y.

Year	Team	Games	BA	SA	AB	H	2B	3B	HR	HR%	R	RBI	BB	SO	SB	Pinch Hit AB	Pinch Hit H	PO	A	E	DP	TC/G	FA	G by Pos
1942	PHI A	12	.000	.000	11	0	0	0	0	0.0	0	0	4	6	0	2	0	11	4	3	0	2.3	.833	SS-7, 2B-1

Angel Escobar

ESCOBAR, ANGEL RUBENQUE BB TR 6′ 160 lbs.
Born Angel Rubenque Escobar (Rivas).
B. May 12, 1965, LaSabana, Venezuela.

Year	Team	Games	BA	SA	AB	H	2B	3B	HR	HR%	R	RBI	BB	SO	SB	Pinch Hit AB	Pinch Hit H	PO	A	E	DP	TC/G	FA	G by Pos
1988	SF N	3	.333	.333	3	1	0	0	0	0.0	1	0	0	0	0	1	0	2	1	0	0	1.5	1.000	SS-1, 3B-1

Jose Escobar

ESCOBAR, JOSE ELIAS BR TR 5′10″ 140 lbs.
Born Jose Elias Escobar (Sanchez).
B. Oct. 30, 1960, Las Flores, Venezuela.

Year	Team	Games	BA	SA	AB	H	2B	3B	HR	HR%	R	RBI	BB	SO	SB	Pinch Hit AB	Pinch Hit H	PO	A	E	DP	TC/G	FA	G by Pos
1991	CLE A	10	.200	.200	15	3	0	0	0	0.0	0	1	1	4	0	0	0	15	13	0	4	2.8	1.000	SS-5, 2B-4, 3B-1

Jimmy Esmond

ESMOND, JAMES JOSEPH BR TR 5′11″ 167 lbs.
B. Oct. 8, 1889, Albany, N. Y. D. June 26, 1948, Troy, N. Y.

Year	Team	Games	BA	SA	AB	H	2B	3B	HR	HR%	R	RBI	BB	SO	SB	Pinch Hit AB	Pinch Hit H	PO	A	E	DP	TC/G	FA	G by Pos
1911	CIN N	73	.273	.369	198	54	4	6	1	0.5	27	11	17	30	7	5	2	138	126	22	21	4.8	.923	SS-44, 3B-14, 2B-2
1912		82	.195	.255	231	45	5	3	1	0.4	24	40	20	31	11	1	0	154	180	25	22	4.9	.930	SS-74
1914	IND F	151	.295	.404	542	160	23	**15**	2	0.4	74	49	40		25	0	0	317	448	67	54	5.5	.919	SS-151
1915	NWK F	155	.258	.355	569	147	20	10	5	0.9	79	62	59		18	0	0	353	482	54	67	5.7	.939	SS-155
4 yrs.		461	.264	.359	1540	406	52	34	9	0.6	204	162	136	61	61	6	2	962	1236	168	164	5.4	.929	SS-424, 3B-14, 2B-2

Juan Espino

ESPINO, JUAN BR TR 6′ 1″ 190 lbs.
Born Juan Espino (Reyes).
B. Mar. 16, 1956, Bonao, Dominican Republic.

Year	Team	Games	BA	SA	AB	H	2B	3B	HR	HR%	R	RBI	BB	SO	SB	Pinch Hit AB	Pinch Hit H	PO	A	E	DP	TC/G	FA	G by Pos
1982	NY A	3	.000	.000	2	0	0	0	0	0.0	0	0	0	1	0	0	0	4	0	0	0	1.3	1.000	C-3
1983		10	.261	.391	23	6	0	0	1	4.3	1	3	1	5	0	0	0	38	1	0	0	3.9	1.000	C-10
1985		9	.364	.364	11	4	0	0	0	0.0	0	0	0	0	0	0	0	16	4	0	0	2.2	1.000	C-9
1986		27	.162	.216	37	6	2	0	0	0.0	1	5	2	9	0	1	0	72	6	1	0	2.9	.987	C-27
4 yrs.		49	.219	.288	73	16	2	0	1	1.4	2	8	3	15	0	1	0	130	11	1	0	2.9	.993	C-49

Alvaro Espinoza

ESPINOZA, ALVARO ALBERTO BR TR 6′ 160 lbs.
Born Alvaro Alberto Espinoza (Ramirez).
B. Feb. 19, 1962, Valencia, Venezuela.

Year	Team	Games	BA	SA	AB	H	2B	3B	HR	HR%	R	RBI	BB	SO	SB	Pinch Hit AB	Pinch Hit H	PO	A	E	DP	TC/G	FA	G by Pos
1984	MIN A	1	—	—	0	0	0	0	0	—	0	0	0	0	0	0	0	0	0	0	0	0.0	.000	SS-1
1985		32	.263	.298	57	15	2	0	0	0.0	5	9	1	9	0	0	0	25	69	5	15	3.2	.949	SS-31
1986		37	.214	.238	42	9	1	0	0	0.0	4	1	1	10	0	1	0	23	52	4	11	2.1	.949	2B-19, SS-18
1988	NY A	3	.000	.000	3	0	0	0	0	0.0	0	0	0	0	0	0	0	5	2	0	1	2.3	1.000	2B-2, SS-1
1989		146	.282	.332	503	142	23	1	0	0.0	51	41	14	60	3	0	0	237	471	22	114	5.0	.970	SS-146

Alvaro Espinoza *continued*

Year	Team	Games	BA	SA	AB	H	2B	3B	HR	HR%	R	RBI	BB	SO	SB	Pinch Hit AB	Pinch Hit H	PO	A	E	DP	TC/G	FA	G by Pos
1990		150	.224	.274	438	98	12	2	2	0.5	31	20	16	54	1	0	0	268	447	17	100	4.9	.977	SS-150
1991		148	.256	.344	480	123	23	2	5	1.0	51	33	16	57	4	1	0	225	441	21	113	4.6	.969	SS-147, 3B-2, P-1
1993	CLE A	129	.278	.380	263	73	15	0	4	1.5	34	27	8	36	2	9	3	66	157	12	24	1.7	.949	3B-99, SS-35, 2B-2
1994		90	.238	.307	231	55	13	0	1	0.4	27	19	6	33	1	1	0	93	209	10	42	3.3	.968	3B-37, SS-36, 2B-20, 1B-3
1995		66	.252	.322	143	36	4	0	2	1.4	15	17	2	16	0	2	0	50	99	5	17	2.3	.968	2B-22, 3B-22, SS-19, 2B-2, DH-1
10 yrs.		802	.255	.322	2160	551	93	5	14	0.6	218	167	64	275	11	14	3	992	1947	96	437	3.7	.968	SS-584, 3B-160, 2B-65, 1B-5, DH-1, P-1
DIVISIONAL PLAYOFF SERIES																								
1995	CLE A	1	.000	.000	1	0	0	0	0	0.0	0	0	0	0	0	0	0	0	0	0	0	0.0	.000	3B-1
LEAGUE CHAMPIONSHIP SERIES																								
1995	CLE A	4	.125	.125	8	1	0	0	0	0.0	1	0	0	3	0	0	0	0	3	1	0	1.0	.750	3B-4
WORLD SERIES																								
1995	CLE A	2	.500	.500	2	1	0	0	0	0.0	1	0	0	0	0	0	0	1	1	0	0	2.0	1.000	3B-1

Sammy Esposito

ESPOSITO, SAMUEL
B. Dec. 15, 1931, Chicago, Ill.
BR TR 5′ 9″ 165 lbs.

Year	Team	Games	BA	SA	AB	H	2B	3B	HR	HR%	R	RBI	BB	SO	SB	Pinch Hit AB	Pinch Hit H	PO	A	E	DP	TC/G	FA	G by Pos
1952	CHI A	1	.250	.250	4	1	0	0	0	0.0	0	0	0	2	0	0	0	1	1	2	0	4.0	.500	SS-1
1955		3	.000	.000	4	0	0	0	0	0.0	3	0	1	0	0	0	0	1	0	0	0	0.5	1.000	3B-2
1956		81	.228	.342	184	42	8	2	3	1.6	30	25	41	19	1	8	1	52	132	6	19	2.3	.968	3B-61, SS-19, 2B-3
1957		94	.205	.256	176	36	3	0	2	1.1	26	15	38	27	5	11	3	84	168	10	23	3.3	.962	3B-53, SS-22, 2B-4, OF-1
1958		98	.247	.284	81	20	3	0	0	0.0	16	3	12	6	1	7	1	36	78	5	9	1.4	.958	3B-63, SS-22, 2B-2, OF-1
1959		69	.167	.227	66	11	1	0	1	1.5	12	5	11	16	0	5	1	39	57	2	6	1.6	.980	3B-45, SS-14, 2B-2
1960		57	.182	.286	77	14	5	0	1	1.3	14	11	10	20	0	4	1	17	51	5	5	1.4	.932	3B-37, SS-11, 2B-5
1961		63	.170	.255	94	16	5	0	1	1.1	12	8	12	21	0	2	0	51	85	3	11	2.4	.978	3B-28, SS-20, 2B-11
1962		75	.235	.247	81	19	1	0	0	0.0	14	4	17	13	0	3	1	29	72	7	7	1.6	.935	3B-41, SS-20, 2B-7
1963	**2 teams**	**CHI A** (1G –.000)	**KC A** (18G –.200)																					
″	**total**	19	.200	.240	25	5	1	0	0	0.0	3	2	3	3	0	1	1	7	15	2	2	1.7	.917	2B-7, SS-4, 3B-3
10 yrs.		560	.207	.277	792	164	27	2	8	1.0	130	73	145	127	7	41	9	317	659	42	82	2.0	.959	3B-333, SS-133, 2B-41, OF-2
WORLD SERIES																								
1959	CHI A	2	.000	.000	2	0	0	0	0	0.0	0	0	0	1	0	0	0	1	0	0	0	0.5	1.000	3B-2

Cecil Espy

ESPY, CECIL EDWARD
B. Jan. 20, 1963, San Diego, Calif.
BB TR 6′ 3″ 190 lbs.

Year	Team	Games	BA	SA	AB	H	2B	3B	HR	HR%	R	RBI	BB	SO	SB	Pinch Hit AB	Pinch Hit H	PO	A	E	DP	TC/G	FA	G by Pos
1983	LA N	20	.273	.364	11	3	1	0	0	0.0	4	1	1	2	0	2	1	11	0	0	0	0.7	1.000	OF-15
1987	TEX A	14	.000	.000	8	0	0	0	0	0.0	1	0	1	3	2	1	0	8	1	0	1	1.1	1.000	OF-8
1988		123	.248	.349	347	86	17	6	2	0.6	46	39	20	83	33	13	5	200	11	7	0	1.9	.968	OF-98, DH-12, SS-3, C-2, 1B-1, 2B-1
1989		142	.257	.331	475	122	12	7	3	0.6	65	31	38	99	45	13	6	281	5	3	2	2.1	.990	OF-133, DH-3
1990		52	.127	.127	71	9	0	0	0	0.0	10	1	10	20	11	6	0	56	1	0	0	1.3	1.000	OF-39, DH-4, 2B-1
1991	PIT N	43	.244	.329	82	20	4	0	1	1.2	7	11	5	17	4	6	2	54	3	2	2	1.7	.966	OF-35
1992		112	.258	.340	194	50	7	3	1	0.5	21	20	15	40	6	54	13	83	1	4	0	1.1	.955	OF-82
1993	CIN N	40	.233	.267	60	14	2	0	0	0.0	6	5	14	13	2	22	4	25	2	2	0	1.6	.931	OF-18
8 yrs.		546	.244	.321	1248	304	43	16	7	0.6	160	108	104	277	103	117	31	718	24	18	5	1.7	.976	OF-428, DH-19, SS-3, 2B-2, C-2, 1B-1
LEAGUE CHAMPIONSHIP SERIES																								
1991	PIT N	2	.000	.000	2	0	0	0	0	0.0	0	0	0	2	0	2	0	0	0	0	0	0.0	—	
1992		4	.667	.667	3	2	0	0	0	0.0	0	0	0	1	0	3	2	0	0	0	0	0.0	.000	OF-2
2 yrs.		6	.400	.400	5	2	0	0	0	0.0	0	0	0	3	0	5	2	0	0	0	0	0.0		OF-2

Chuck Essegian

ESSEGIAN, CHARLES ABRAHAM
B. Aug. 9, 1931, Boston, Mass.
BR TR 5′11″ 200 lbs.

Year	Team	Games	BA	SA	AB	H	2B	3B	HR	HR%	R	RBI	BB	SO	SB	Pinch Hit AB	Pinch Hit H	PO	A	E	DP	TC/G	FA	G by Pos
1958	PHI N	39	.246	.456	114	28	5	2	5	4.4	15	16	12	34	0	9	2	59	1	3	0	2.1	.952	OF-30
1959	**2 teams**	**STL N** (17G –.179)	**LA N** (24G –.304)																					
″	**total**	41	.247	.400	85	21	8	1	1	1.2	8	10	5	24	0	22	5	19	1	0	0	1.1	1.000	OF-19
1960	LA N	52	.215	.367	79	17	3	0	3	3.8	8	11	8	24	0	37	8	29	1	1	0	1.7	.968	OF-18
1961	**3 teams**	**BAL A** (1G –.000)	**KC A** (4G –.333)	**CLE A** (60G –.289)																				
″	**total**	65	.289	.555	173	50	8	1	12	6.9	26	36	11	35	0	20	7	89	5	3	1	1.9	.969	OF-50
1962	CLE A	106	.274	.497	336	92	12	0	21	6.3	59	50	42	68	0	14	2	154	1	1	0	1.7	.994	OF-90
1963	KC A	101	.225	.329	231	52	9	0	5	2.2	23	27	19	48	0	40	9	95	2	1	0	1.8	.990	OF-53
6 yrs.		404	.255	.446	1018	260	45	4	47	4.6	139	150	97	233	0	142	33	445	11	9	1	1.8	.981	OF-260
WORLD SERIES																								
1959	LA N	4	.667	2.667	3	2	0	0	2	66.7	2	2	1	1	0	3	2	0	0	0	0	0.0	—	

Jim Essian

ESSIAN, JAMES SARKIS
B. Jan. 2, 1951, Detroit, Mich.
Manager 1991.
BR TR 6′ 2″ 195 lbs.

Year	Team	Games	BA	SA	AB	H	2B	3B	HR	HR%	R	RBI	BB	SO	SB	Pinch Hit AB	Pinch Hit H	PO	A	E	DP	TC/G	FA	G by Pos
1973	PHI N	2	.000	.000	3	0	0	0	0	0.0	0	0	0	1	0	2	0	0	0	0	0	0.0	.000	C-1
1974		17	.100	.100	20	2	0	0	0	0.0	1	0	2	1	0	1	0	38	4	1	1	2.5	.977	C-15, 3B-1, 1B-1
1975		2	1.000	1.000	1	1	0	0	0	0.0	1	1	1	0	0	1	1	1	1	0	0	1.0	1.000	C-2
1976	CHI A	78	.246	.281	199	49	7	0	0	0.0	20	21	23	28	2	0	0	320	53	10	10	4.8	.974	C-77, 1B-2, 3B-1
1977		114	.273	.435	322	88	18	2	10	3.1	50	44	52	35	1	0	0	593	62	9	8	5.9	.986	C-111, 3B-2
1978	OAK A	126	.223	.295	278	62	9	1	3	1.1	21	26	44	22	2	4	0	452	79	10	14	4.3	.982	C-119, 1B-3, DH-3, 2B-1
1979		98	.243	.371	313	76	16	0	8	2.6	34	40	25	29	0	8	2	400	79	9	11	5.4	.982	C-70, 3B-10, OF-4, 1B-4, DH-3
1980		87	.232	.323	285	66	11	0	5	1.8	19	29	30	18	1	8	1	339	46	5	5	4.9	.987	C-68, DH-11, 1B-1
1981	CHI A	27	.308	.365	52	16	3	0	0	0.0	6	5	4	5	0	2	0	92	9	2	0	3.8	.981	C-25, 3B-2
1982	SEA A	48	.275	.386	153	42	8	0	3	2.0	14	20	11	7	2	1	1	282	26	2	1	6.5	.994	C-48
1983	CLE A	48	.204	.312	93	19	4	0	2	2.2	11	11	16	8	0	0	0	170	14	2	3	3.9	.989	C-47, 3B-1
1984	OAK A	62	.228	.338	136	31	9	0	2	1.5	17	10	23	17	1	3	0	229	30	5	6	4.3	.981	C-59, 3B-1, DH-1
12 yrs.		709	.244	.346	1855	452	85	3	33	1.8	194	207	231	171	9	30	5	2916	403	55	59	4.9	.984	C-642, 3B-18, DH-18, 1B-11, OF-4, 2B-1

Bobby Estalella

ESTALELLA, ROBERTO
Born Roberto Estalella (Ventoza).
B. Apr. 25, 1911, Cardenas, Cuba D. Jan. 6, 1991, Hialeah, Fla.

BR TR 5′ 8″ 180 lbs.

Year	Team	Games	BA	SA	AB	H	2B	3B	HR	HR%	R	RBI	BB	SO	SB	Pinch Hit AB	Pinch Hit H	PO	A	E	DP	TC/G	FA	G by Pos
1935	WAS A	15	.314	.471	51	16	2	0	2	3.9	7	10	17	7	1	0	0	14	37	6	1	3.8	.895	3B-15
1936		13	.222	.667	9	2	0	2	0	0.0	2	0	4	5	0	9	2	0	0	0	0	0.0	—	
1939		82	.275	.468	280	77	18	6	8	2.9	51	41	40	27	2	8	2	157	3	6	1	2.2	.964	OF-74
1941	STL A	46	.241	.337	83	20	6	1	0	0.0	7	14	18	13	0	22	6	23	0	0	0	1.4	1.000	OF-17
1942	WAS A	133	.277	.413	429	119	24	5	8	1.9	68	65	85	42	5	18	4	158	136	15	5	2.7	.951	3B-78, OF-36
1943	PHI A	117	.259	.409	367	95	14	4	11	3.0	43	63	52	44	1	20	7	225	5	6	1	2.4	.975	OF-97
1944		140	.298	.409	506	151	17	9	7	1.4	54	60	59	60	3	11	4	346	16	4	5	2.7	.989	OF-128, 1B-6
1945		126	.299	.435	451	135	25	6	8	1.8	45	52	74	46	1	2	1	314	10	4	3	2.6	.988	OF-124
1949		8	.250	.250	20	5	0	0	0	0.0	2	3	1	2	0	1	0	9	1	0	1	1.7	1.000	OF-6
9 yrs.		680	.282	.421	2196	620	106	33	44	2.0	279	308	350	246	13	91	26	1246	208	41	17	2.6	.973	OF-482, 3B-93, 1B-6

Dude Esterbrook

ESTERBROOK, THOMAS JOHN
B. June 9, 1857, Staten Island, N. Y. D. Apr. 30, 1901, Middletown, N. Y.
Manager 1889.

BR TR 5′11″ 167 lbs.

Year	Team	Games	BA	SA	AB	H	2B	3B	HR	HR%	R	RBI	BB	SO	SB	Pinch Hit AB	Pinch Hit H	PO	A	E	DP	TC/G	FA	G by Pos
1880	BUF N	64	.241	.296	253	61	12	1	0	0.0	20	35	0	15		0	0	494	37	45	21	8.2	.922	1B-47, OF-15, 2B-6, SS-1, C-1
1882	CLE N	45	.246	.302	179	44	4	3	0	0.0	13	19	5	12		0	0	107	15	14	7	3.0	.897	OF-45, 1B-1
1883	NY AA	97	.253	.310	407	103	9	7	0	0.0	55		15			0	0	110	173	42	8	3.4	.871	3B-97
1884		112	.314	.428	477	150	29	11	1	0.2	110		12			0	0	126	208	43	11	3.4	.886	3B-112
1885	NY N	88	.256	.340	359	92	14	5	2	0.6	48		4	28		0	0	116	161	36	14	3.6	.885	3B-84, OF-4
1886		123	.264	.351	473	125	20	6	3	0.6	62	43	8	43		0	0	148	219	43	9	3.3	.895	3B-123
1887	NY AA	26	.168	.178	101	17	1	0	0	0.0	11		6		8	0	0	105	27	22	6	5.9	.857	1B-9, OF-7, 2B-5, SS-5
1888	2 teams	IND N (64G –.220) LOU AA (23G –.226)																						
″	total	87	.221	.263	339	75	14	0	0	0.0	30	24	5	20	16	0	0	851	32	27	40	10.5	.970	1B-84, 3B-3
1889	LOU AA	11	.318	.386	44	14	3	0	0	0.0	8	9	5	2	6	0	0	79	6	7	3	8.4	.924	1B-8, OF-2, SS-1
1890	NY N	45	.289	.371	197	57	14	1	0	0.0	29	29	10	8	12	0	0	430	13	7	24	10.0	.984	1B-45
1891	BKN N	3	.375	.375	8	3	0	0	0	0.0	1	0	0	1	0	0	0	4	0	1	0	1.7	.800	OF-2, 2B-1
11 yrs.		701	.261	.334	2837	741	120	34	6	0.2	387	159	70	129	42	0	0	2570	891	287	143	5.3	.923	3B-419, 1B-194, OF-75, 2B-12, SS-7, C-1

Francisco Estrada

ESTRADA, FRANCISCO
Born Francisco Estrada (Soto).
B. Feb. 12, 1948, Navojoa, Mexico.

BR TR 5′ 8″ 182 lbs.

Year	Team	Games	BA	SA	AB	H	2B	3B	HR	HR%	R	RBI	BB	SO	SB	Pinch Hit AB	Pinch Hit H	PO	A	E	DP	TC/G	FA	G by Pos
1971	NY N	1	.500	.500	2	1	0	0	0	0.0	0	0	0	0	0	0	0	1	0	0	0	1.0	1.000	C-1

Andy Etchebarren

ETCHEBARREN, ANDREW AUGUSTE
B. June 20, 1943, Whittier, Calif.

BR TR 6′ 1″ 190 lbs.

Year	Team	Games	BA	SA	AB	H	2B	3B	HR	HR%	R	RBI	BB	SO	SB	Pinch Hit AB	Pinch Hit H	PO	A	E	DP	TC/G	FA	G by Pos
1962	BAL A	2	.333	.333	6	2	0	0	0	0.0	0	1	0	2	0	0	0	7	0	1	0	4.0	.875	C-2
1965		5	.167	.667	6	1	0	0	1	16.7	1	4	0	2	0	0	0	21	2	0	0	4.6	1.000	C-5
1966		121	.221	.364	412	91	14	6	11	2.7	49	50	38	106	0	0	0	799	65	10	7	7.2	.989	C-121
1967		112	.215	.318	330	71	13	0	7	2.1	29	35	38	80	1	6	1	673	57	8	10	6.7	.989	C-110
1968		74	.233	.392	189	44	11	2	5	2.6	20	20	19	46	0	6	2	414	29	1	3	6.3	.998	C-70
1969		73	.249	.350	217	54	9	2	3	1.4	29	26	28	42	1	10	1	380	27	4	1	5.7	.990	C-72
1970		78	.243	.348	230	56	10	1	4	1.7	19	28	21	41	4	8	4	392	29	7	3	5.6	.984	C-76
1971		70	.270	.428	222	60	8	0	9	4.1	21	29	16	40	1	4	1	337	24	5	2	5.2	.986	C-70
1972		71	.202	.277	188	38	6	1	2	1.1	11	21	17	43	0	10	3	334	22	3	2	5.1	.992	C-70
1973		54	.257	.368	152	39	9	1	2	1.3	16	23	12	21	1	4	0	201	14	2	5	4.3	.991	C-51
1974		62	.222	.300	180	40	8	0	2	1.1	13	15	6	26	1	3	1	269	19	7	3	4.9	.976	C-60
1975	2 teams	BAL A (8G –.200) CAL A (31G –.280)																						
″	total	39	.267	.367	120	32	1	1	3	2.5	10	20	14	22	1	1	1	216	17	4	2	6.2	.983	C-38
1976	CAL A	103	.227	.271	247	56	9	1	0	0.0	15	21	24	37	0	3	1	539	46	12	7	5.9	.980	C-102
1977		80	.254	.307	114	29	2	2	0	0.0	11	14	12	19	3	0	0	289	12	4	0	3.8	.987	C-80
1978	MIL A	4	.400	.600	5	2	1	0	0	0.0	1	2	1	2	0	0	0	13	2	0	0	3.8	1.000	C-4
15 yrs.		948	.235	.343	2618	615	101	17	49	1.9	245	309	246	529	13	55	15	4884	365	68	45	5.7	.987	C-931
LEAGUE CHAMPIONSHIP SERIES																								
1969	BAL A	2	.000	.000	4	0	0	0	0	0.0	0	0	0	0	0	0	0	12	0	0	0	6.0	1.000	C-2
1970		2	.111	.111	9	1	0	0	0	0.0	1	0	0	3	0	0	0	12	0	0	0	6.0	1.000	C-2
1971		2	.000	.000	5	0	0	0	0	0.0	0	0	0	0	0	1	0	11	0	0	0	5.5	1.000	C-2
1973		4	.357	.643	14	5	1	0	1	7.1	1	4	0	1	0	0	0	30	2	0	0	8.0	1.000	C-4
1974		2	.333	.333	6	2	0	0	0	0.0	0	0	0	0	0	0	0	7	1	0	0	4.0	1.000	C-2
5 yrs.		12	.211	.316	38	8	1	0	1	2.6	2	4	0	4	0	1	0	72	3	0	0	6.3	1.000	C-12
WORLD SERIES																								
1966	BAL A	4	.083	.083	12	1	0	0	0	0.0	2	0	2	4	0	0	0	32	1	0	1	8.3	1.000	C-4
1969		2	.000	.000	6	0	0	0	0	0.0	0	0	0	1	0	0	0	16	0	0	0	8.0	1.000	C-2
1970		2	.143	.143	7	1	0	0	0	0.0	1	0	2	3	0	0	0	10	0	1	0	5.5	.909	C-2
1971		1	.000	.000	2	0	0	0	0	0.0	0	0	0	0	0	0	0	6	0	0	0	6.0	1.000	C-1
4 yrs.		9	.074	.074	27	2	0	0	0	0.0	3	0	4	8	0	0	0	64	1	1	1	7.3	.985	C-9

Buck Etchison

ETCHISON, CLARENCE HAMPTON
B. Jan. 27, 1915, Baltimore, Md. D. Jan. 24, 1980, East New Market, Md.

BL TL 6′ 1″ 190 lbs.

Year	Team	Games	BA	SA	AB	H	2B	3B	HR	HR%	R	RBI	BB	SO	SB	Pinch Hit AB	Pinch Hit H	PO	A	E	DP	TC/G	FA	G by Pos
1943	BOS N	10	.316	.474	19	6	3	0	0	0.0	2	2	2	2	0	4	2	41	2	2	7	7.5	.956	1B-6
1944		109	.214	.344	308	66	16	0	8	2.6	30	33	33	50	1	21	3	757	48	6	64	9.5	.993	1B-85
2 yrs.		119	.220	.352	327	72	19	0	8	2.4	32	35	35	52	1	25	5	798	50	8	71	9.4	.991	1B-91

Bobby Etheridge

ETHERIDGE, BOBBY LAMAR (Luke)
B. Nov. 25, 1942, Greenville, Miss.

BR TR 5′ 9″ 170 lbs.

Year	Team	Games	BA	SA	AB	H	2B	3B	HR	HR%	R	RBI	BB	SO	SB	Pinch Hit AB	Pinch Hit H	PO	A	E	DP	TC/G	FA	G by Pos
1967	SF N	40	.226	.348	115	26	7	2	1	0.9	13	15	7	12	0	4	1	21	53	6	7	2.2	.925	3B-37
1969		56	.260	.351	131	34	9	0	1	0.8	13	10	19	26	0	15	2	23	67	10	5	2.5	.900	3B-39, SS-1
2 yrs.		96	.244	.350	246	60	16	2	2	0.8	26	25	26	38	0	19	3	44	120	16	12	2.3	.911	3B-76, SS-1

Nick Etten

ETTEN, NICHOLAS RAYMOND THOMAS
B. Sept. 19, 1913, Spring Grove, Ill. D. Oct. 18, 1990, Hinsdale, Ill.
BL TL 6′ 2″ 198 lbs.

Year	Team	Games	BA	SA	AB	H	2B	3B	HR	HR%	R	RBI	BB	SO	SB	Pinch Hit AB	Pinch Hit H	PO	A	E	DP	TC/G	FA	G by Pos
1938	PHI A	22	.259	.383	81	21	6	2	0	0.0	6	11	9	7	1	0	0	212	10	3	20	10.2	.987	1B-22
1939		43	.252	.406	155	39	11	2	3	1.9	20	29	16	11	0	2	0	376	19	4	29	9.7	.990	1B-41
1941	PHI N	151	.311	.454	540	168	27	4	14	2.6	78	79	82	33	9	1	0	1286	89	23	124	9.3	.984	1B-150
1942		139	.264	.375	459	121	21	3	8	1.7	37	41	67	26	3	3	2	1152	83	19	99	9.3	.985	1B-135
1943	NY A	154	.271	.420	583	158	35	5	14	2.4	78	107	76	31	3	0	0	1410	79	17	148	9.8	.989	1B-154
1944		154	.293	.466	573	168	25	4	**22**	3.8	88	91	**97**	29	4	0	0	1382	106	16	144	9.8	.989	1B-154
1945		152	.285	.437	565	161	24	4	18	3.2	77	**111**	90	23	2	0	0	1401	94	17	149	9.9	.989	1B-152
1946		108	.232	.365	323	75	14	1	9	2.8	37	49	38	35	0	22	4	717	55	7	80	9.3	.991	1B-84
1947	PHI N	14	.244	.415	41	10	4	0	1	2.4	5	8	5	4	0	3	0	94	10	1	4	9.5	.990	1B-11
9 yrs.		937	.277	.423	3320	921	167	25	89	2.7	426	526	480	199	22	31	6	8030	545	107	797	9.6	.988	1B-903
WORLD SERIES																								
1943	NY A	5	.105	.105	19	2	0	0	0	0.0	0	2	1	2	0	0	0	46	2	1	3	9.8	.980	1B-5

Ferd Eunick

EUNICK, FERNANDES BOWEN
B. Apr. 22, 1892, Baltimore, Md. D. Dec. 9, 1959, Baltimore, Md.
BR TR 5′ 6″ 148 lbs.

Year	Team	Games	BA	SA	AB	H	2B	3B	HR	HR%	R	RBI	BB	SO	SB	Pinch Hit AB	Pinch Hit H	PO	A	E	DP	TC/G	FA	G by Pos
1917	CLE A	1	.000	.000	2	0	0	0	0	0.0	0	0	0	0	0	0	0	0	1	0	0	1.0	1.000	3B-1

Tony Eusebio

EUSEBIO, RAUL ANTONIO
Born Raul Antonio Bare (Eusebio).
B. Apr. 27, 1967, San Jose de Los Llamos, Dominican Republic.
BR TR 6′ 2″ 180 lbs.

Year	Team	Games	BA	SA	AB	H	2B	3B	HR	HR%	R	RBI	BB	SO	SB	Pinch Hit AB	Pinch Hit H	PO	A	E	DP	TC/G	FA	G by Pos
1991	HOU N	10	.105	.158	19	2	1	0	0	0.0	4	0	6	8	0	1	0	49	4	1	0	6.0	.981	C-9
1994		55	.296	.459	159	47	9	1	5	3.1	18	30	8	33	0	3	1	263	24	2	1	5.6	.993	C-52
1995		113	.299	.410	368	110	21	1	6	1.6	46	58	31	59	0	18	7	644	50	5	6	6.8	.993	C-103
3 yrs.		178	.291	.416	546	159	31	2	11	2.0	68	88	45	100	0	22	8	956	78	8	7	6.4	.992	C-164

Frank Eustace

EUSTACE, FRANK JOHN
B. Nov. 7, 1873, New York, N. Y. D. Oct. 20, 1932, Pottsville, Pa.
5′ 9″ 160 lbs.

Year	Team	Games	BA	SA	AB	H	2B	3B	HR	HR%	R	RBI	BB	SO	SB	Pinch Hit AB	Pinch Hit H	PO	A	E	DP	TC/G	FA	G by Pos
1896	LOU N	25	.170	.260	100	17	2	2	1	1.0	18	11	6	14	4	0	0	52	77	23	8	6.1	.849	SS-22, 2B-3

Al Evans

EVANS, ALFRED HUBERT
B. Sept. 28, 1916, Kenly, N. C. D. Apr. 6, 1979, Wilson, N. C.
BR TR 5′11″ 190 lbs.

Year	Team	Games	BA	SA	AB	H	2B	3B	HR	HR%	R	RBI	BB	SO	SB	Pinch Hit AB	Pinch Hit H	PO	A	E	DP	TC/G	FA	G by Pos
1939	WAS A	7	.333	.333	21	7	0	0	0	0.0	2	1	5	2	0	1	0	21	6	1	0	4.7	.964	C-6
1940		14	.320	.400	25	8	2	0	0	0.0	1	7	6	7	1	4	1	34	2	0	0	4.0	1.000	C-9
1941		53	.277	.396	159	44	8	4	1	0.6	16	19	9	18	0	3	0	195	24	7	6	4.4	.969	C-51
1942		74	.229	.256	223	51	4	1	0	0.0	22	10	25	36	3	10	1	254	42	12	5	4.6	.961	C-67
1944		14	.091	.091	22	2	0	0	0	0.0	5	0	2	6	0	1	0	19	4	1	1	3.0	.958	C-8
1945		51	.260	.400	150	39	11	2	2	1.3	19	19	17	22	2	7	0	160	19	5	4	4.5	.973	C-41
1946		88	.254	.342	272	69	10	4	2	0.7	30	30	30	28	1	7	0	336	30	13	5	4.7	.966	C-81
1947		99	.241	.304	319	77	8	3	2	0.6	17	23	28	25	2	5	1	389	48	5	14	4.7	.989	C-94
1948		93	.259	.338	228	59	6	3	2	0.9	19	28	38	20	0	11	2	245	38	5	6	3.4	.983	C-85
1949		109	.271	.346	321	87	12	3	2	0.6	32	42	50	19	4	3	1	322	47	3	2	3.5	.992	C-107
1950		90	.235	.304	289	68	8	3	2	0.7	24	30	29	21	0	1	0	289	23	4	8	3.6	.987	C-88
1951	BOS A	12	.125	.167	24	3	1	0	0	0.0	1	2	4	2	0	1	0	40	1	0	0	4.1	1.000	C-10
12 yrs.		704	.250	.326	2053	514	70	23	13	0.6	188	211	243	206	13	54	6	2304	284	56	51	4.1	.979	C-647

Barry Evans

EVANS, BARRY STEVEN
B. Nov. 30, 1955, Atlanta, Ga.
BR TR 6′ 1″ 185 lbs.

Year	Team	Games	BA	SA	AB	H	2B	3B	HR	HR%	R	RBI	BB	SO	SB	Pinch Hit AB	Pinch Hit H	PO	A	E	DP	TC/G	FA	G by Pos
1978	SD N	24	.267	.300	90	24	1	1	0	0.0	7	4	4	10	0	0	0	13	59	4	4	3.2	.947	3B-24
1979		56	.216	.265	162	35	5	0	1	0.6	9	14	5	16	0	1	1	30	110	7	12	2.6	.952	3B-53, SS-2, 2B-1
1980		73	.232	.312	125	29	3	2	1	0.8	11	14	17	21	1	1	1	52	87	2	13	2.1	.986	3B-43, 2B-19, SS-4, 1B-1
1981		54	.323	.376	93	30	5	0	0	0.0	11	7	9	9	2	16	1	98	33	2	10	3.2	.985	3B-24, 1B-10, 2B-6, SS-2
1982	NY A	17	.258	.355	31	8	3	0	0	0.0	2	2	6	6	0	1	0	14	26	0	3	2.2	1.000	2B-8, 3B-6, SS-4
5 yrs.		224	.251	.309	501	126	17	3	2	0.4	40	41	41	62	3	19	3	207	315	15	42	2.6	.972	3B-150, 2B-34, SS-12, 1B-11

Darrell Evans

EVANS, DARRELL WAYNE
B. May 26, 1947, Pasadena, Calif.
BL TR 6′ 2″ 200 lbs.

Year	Team	Games	BA	SA	AB	H	2B	3B	HR	HR%	R	RBI	BB	SO	SB	Pinch Hit AB	Pinch Hit H	PO	A	E	DP	TC/G	FA	G by Pos
1969	ATL N	12	.231	.231	26	6	0	0	0	0.0	3	1	1	8	0	4	0	4	7	1	0	2.0	.917	3B-6
1970		12	.318	.386	44	14	1	1	0	0.0	4	9	7	5	0	0	0	6	26	2	0	2.8	.941	3B-12
1971		89	.242	.431	260	63	11	1	12	4.6	42	38	39	54	2	10	1	77	138	14	13	3.1	.939	3B-72, OF-3
1972		125	.254	.419	418	106	12	0	19	4.5	67	71	90	58	4	1	0	126	273	25	20	3.4	.941	3B-123
1973		161	.281	.556	595	167	25	8	41	6.9	114	104	**124**	104	6	2	0	266	335	24	44	3.8	.962	3B-146, 1B-20
1974		160	.240	.419	571	137	21	3	25	4.4	99	79	**126**	88	4	0	0	185	367	26	45	3.6	.955	3B-160
1975		156	.243	.406	567	138	22	2	22	3.9	82	73	105	106	12	3	1	164	382	36	41	3.7	.938	3B-156, 1B-3
1976	2 teams	ATL N (44G –.173)	SF N (92G –.222)																					
″	total	136	.205	.316	396	81	9	1	11	2.8	53	46	72	71	9	7	0	978	110	10	80	8.4	.991	1B-119, 3B-12
1977	SF N	144	.254	.416	461	117	18	3	17	3.7	64	72	69	50	9	16	4	324	83	13	15	2.7	.969	OF-81, 1B-41, 3B-35
1978		159	.243	.404	547	133	24	2	20	3.7	82	78	105	64	4	5	1	147	348	25	25	3.4	.952	3B-155
1979		160	.253	.391	562	142	23	2	17	3.0	68	70	91	80	6	2	1	129	369	30	28	3.3	.943	3B-159
1980		154	.264	.414	556	147	23	0	20	3.6	69	78	83	65	17	4	1	232	340	27	35	3.9	.955	3B-140, 1B-14
1981		102	.258	.417	357	92	13	4	12	3.4	51	48	54	33	2	2	0	188	202	14	22	4.1	.965	3B-87, 1B-12
1982		141	.256	.419	465	119	20	4	16	3.4	64	61	77	64	5	12	2	471	233	21	45	5.0	.971	3B-84, 1B-49, SS-13
1983		142	.277	.516	523	145	29	3	30	5.7	94	82	84	81	6	2	1	1001	164	19	67	7.7	.984	1B-113, 3B-32, SS-9
1984	DET A	131	.232	.384	401	93	11	1	16	4.0	60	63	77	70	2	18	3	331	62	2	34	3.1	.995	DH-62, 1B-47, 3B-19
1985		151	.248	.519	505	125	17	0	**40**	**7.9**	81	94	85	85	0	10	2	831	125	20	81	6.4	.980	1B-113, DH-33, 3B-7
1986		151	.241	.442	507	122	15	0	29	5.7	78	85	91	105	3	8	3	809	109	2	85	6.2	.998	1B-105, DH-42, 3B-2
1987		150	.257	.501	499	128	20	0	34	6.8	90	99	100	84	6	10	6	815	108	4	86	5.9	.996	1B-105, DH-44, 3B-7
1988		144	.208	.380	437	91	9	0	22	5.0	48	64	84	89	1	23	3	509	58	4	43	4.2	.993	DH-72, 1B-65
1989	ATL N	107	.207	.355	276	57	6	1	11	4.0	31	39	41	46	0	31	5	371	90	10	37	6.0	.979	1B-50, 3B-28
21 yrs.		2687	.248	.431	8973	2223	329	36	414	4.6	1344	1354	1605 **8th**	1410	98	170	34	7964	3929	329	846	4.6	.973	3B-1442, 1B-856, DH-253, OF-84, SS-22

Darrell Evans *continued*

Year	Team		Games	BA	SA	AB	H	2B	3B	HR	HR%	R	RBI	BB	SO	SB	Pinch Hit AB	Pinch Hit H	PO	A	E	DP	TC/G	FA	G by Pos
LEAGUE CHAMPIONSHIP SERIES																									
1984	DET	A	3	.300	.400	10	3	1	0	0	0.0	1	1	1	0	1	0	0	22	3	0	0	6.3	1.000	1B-3, 3B-1
1987			5	.294	.294	17	5	0	0	0	0.0	0	0	4	2	0	0	0	42	4	3	1	8.2	.939	1B-5, 3B-1
2 yrs.			8	.296	.333	27	8	1	0	0	0.0	1	1	5	2	1	0	0	64	7	3	1	7.4	.959	1B-8, 3B-2
WORLD SERIES																									
1984	DET	A	5	.067	.067	15	1	0	0	0	0.0	1	1	4	4	0	0	0	17	3	0	1	3.3	1.000	1B-4, 3B-2

Dwight Evans

EVANS, DWIGHT MICHAEL (Dewey)
B. Nov. 3, 1951, Santa Monica, Calif.
BR TR 6′ 2″ 180 lbs.

Year	Team		Games	BA	SA	AB	H	2B	3B	HR	HR%	R	RBI	BB	SO	SB	Pinch Hit AB	Pinch Hit H	PO	A	E	DP	TC/G	FA	G by Pos
1972	BOS	A	18	.263	.404	57	15	3	1	1	1.8	2	6	7	13	0	1	1	25	3	0	0	1.6	1.000	OF-17
1973			119	.223	.383	282	63	13	1	10	3.5	46	32	40	52	5	3	0	178	4	1	0	1.6	.995	OF-113
1974			133	.281	.421	463	130	19	8	10	2.2	60	70	38	77	4	12	2	294	8	3	2	2.4	.990	OF-122, DH-7
1975			128	.274	.456	412	113	24	6	13	3.2	61	56	47	60	3	6	0	281	15	4	8	2.5	.987	OF-115, DH-7
1976			146	.242	.431	501	121	34	5	17	3.4	61	62	57	92	6	2	1	324	15	2	4	2.3	.994	OF-145, DH-1
1977			73	.287	.526	230	66	9	2	14	6.1	39	36	28	58	4	7	1	126	2	1	0	1.6	.992	OF-63, DH-17
1978			147	.247	.449	497	123	24	2	24	4.8	75	63	65	119	8	4	1	305	14	6	2	2.2	.982	OF-142, DH-4
1979			152	.274	.456	489	134	24	1	21	4.3	69	58	69	76	6	5	1	307	15	4	5	2.2	.988	OF-149
1980			148	.266	.484	463	123	37	5	18	3.9	72	60	64	98	3	5	0	268	11	5	7	1.9	.982	OF-144, DH-2
1981			108	.296	.522	412	122	19	4	**22**	5.3	84	71	**85**	85	3	0	0	259	9	2	1	2.5	.993	OF-108
1982			162	.292	.534	609	178	37	7	32	5.3	122	98	112	125	3	0	0	346	9	10	3	2.3	.973	OF-161, DH-1
1983			126	.238	.436	470	112	19	4	22	4.7	74	58	70	97	3	5	2	222	6	3	1	1.9	.987	OF-99, DH-21
1984			162	.295	.532	630	186	37	8	32	5.1	**121**	104	96	115	3	0	0	311	7	2	2	2.0	.994	OF-161, DH-1
1985			159	.263	.454	617	162	29	1	29	4.7	110	78	**114**	105	7	0	0	291	9	3	1	1.9	.990	OF-152, DH-7
1986			152	.259	.476	529	137	33	2	26	4.9	86	97	97	117	3	1	0	280	10	5	3	2.0	.983	OF-149, DH-1
1987			154	.305	.569	541	165	37	2	34	6.3	109	123	**106**	98	4	2	0	753	46	13	72	5.1	.984	1B-79, OF-77, DH-4
1988			149	.293	.487	559	164	31	7	21	3.8	96	111	76	99	5	2	1	611	34	9	39	4.2	.986	OF-85, 1B-64, DH-6
1989			146	.285	.463	520	148	27	3	20	3.8	82	100	99	84	3	0	0	153	5	3	1	1.1	.981	OF-77, DH-69
1990			123	.249	.391	445	111	18	3	13	2.9	66	63	67	73	3	0	0	0	0	0	0	0.0	.000	DH-122
1991	BAL	A	101	.270	.378	270	73	9	1	6	2.2	35	38	54	54	2	25	10	116	6	2	2	1.4	.984	OF-67, DH-21
20 yrs.			2606	.272	.470	8996	2446	483	73	385	4.3	1470	1384	1391	1697	78	80	20	5450	228	78	153	2.2	.986	OF-2146, DH-291, 1B-143
LEAGUE CHAMPIONSHIP SERIES																									
1975	BOS	A	3	.100	.200	10	1	1	0	0	0.0	1	1	1	2	0	0	0	7	0	0	0	2.3	1.000	OF-3
1986			7	.214	.357	28	6	1	0	1	3.6	2	4	3	3	0	0	0	11	0	0	0	1.6	1.000	OF-7
1988			4	.167	.250	12	2	1	0	0	0.0	1	1	3	5	0	0	0	11	0	0	0	2.8	1.000	OF-4
1990			4	.231	.308	13	3	1	0	0	0.0	0	0	1	3	0	0	0	0	0	0	0	0.0	.000	DH-4
4 yrs.			18	.190	.302	63	12	4	0	1	1.6	4	6	8	13	0	0	0	29	0	0	0	1.6	1.000	OF-14, DH-4
WORLD SERIES																									
1975	BOS	A	7	.292	.542	24	7	1	1	1	4.2	3	5	3	4	0	0	0	23	1	0	1	3.4	1.000	OF-7
1986			7	.308	.615	26	8	2	0	2	7.7	4	9	4	3	0	0	0	16	1	1	0	2.6	.944	OF-7
2 yrs.			14	.300	.580	50	15	3	1	3	6.0	7	14	7	7	0	0	0	39	2	1	1	3.0	.976	OF-14

Jake Evans

EVANS, URIAH L.P. (Bloody Jake)
B. Sept. 1856, Baltimore, Md. D. Jan. 16, 1907, Baltimore, Md.
TR 5′ 8″ 154 lbs.

Year	Team		Games	BA	SA	AB	H	2B	3B	HR	HR%	R	RBI	BB	SO	SB	Pinch Hit AB	Pinch Hit H	PO	A	E	DP	TC/G	FA	G by Pos
1879	TRO	N	72	.232	.300	280	65	9	5	0	0.0	30	17	5	18		0	0	153	30	24	4	2.9	.884	OF-72
1880			47	.256	.311	180	46	8	1	0	0.0	31	22	7	15		0	0	69	11	8	4	1.8	.909	OF-47, P-1
1881			83	.241	.308	315	76	11	5	0	0.0	35	28	14	30		0	0	145	31	14	5	2.3	.926	OF-83
1882	WOR	N	80	.213	.266	334	71	10	4	0	0.0	33	25	7	22		0	0	142	78	26	8	3.0	.894	OF-68, SS-11, P-1, 3B-1, 2B-1
1883	CLE	N	90	.238	.289	332	79	13	2	0	0.0	36		8	38		0	0	133	43	20	2	2.1	.898	OF-86, SS-3, 3B-3, 2B-1, P-1
1884			80	.259	.345	313	81	18	3	1	0.3	32	39	15	49		0	0	150	35	17	6	2.5	.916	OF-76, 2B-4, SS-2
1885	BAL	AA	20	.221	.260	77	17	1	1	0	0.0	18		7			0	0	37	5	5	2	2.3	.894	OF-20
7 yrs.			472	.238	.300	1831	435	70	21	1	0.1	215	131	63	172		0	0	829	233	114	31	2.4	.903	OF-452, SS-16, 2B-6, 3B-4, P-3

Joe Evans

EVANS, JOSEPH PATTON (Doc)
B. May 15, 1895, Meridian, Miss. D. Aug. 8, 1953, Gulfport, Miss.
BR TR 5′ 9″ 160 lbs.

Year	Team		Games	BA	SA	AB	H	2B	3B	HR	HR%	R	RBI	BB	SO	SB	Pinch Hit AB	Pinch Hit H	PO	A	E	DP	TC/G	FA	G by Pos
1915	CLE	A	42	.257	.330	109	28	4	2	0	0.0	17	11	22	18	6	10	3	26	71	13	2	3.4	.882	3B-30, 2B-2
1916			33	.146	.159	82	12	1	0	0	0.0	4	1	7	12	4	3	0	27	59	8	3	3.4	.915	3B-28
1917			132	.190	.242	385	73	4	5	2	0.5	36	33	42	44	12	1	0	138	279	27	20	3.5	.939	3B-127
1918			79	.263	.358	243	64	6	7	1	0.4	38	22	30	29	7	2	1	91	155	18	17	3.6	.932	3B-74
1919			21	.071	.071	14	1	0	0	0	0.0	9	0	2	1	1	0	0	3	9	1	0	2.2	.923	SS-6
1920			55	.349	.506	172	60	9	9	0	0.0	32	23	15	3	6	2	0	93	25	8	0	2.6	.937	OF-43, SS-6
1921			57	.333	.405	153	51	11	0	0	0.0	36	21	19	5	4	1	0	90	8	7	2	2.2	.933	OF-47
1922			75	.269	.338	145	39	6	2	0	0.0	35	22	8	4	11	0	0	92	1	3	0	2.0	.969	OF-49
1923	WAS	A	106	.263	.320	372	98	15	3	0	0.0	42	38	27	18	6	6	2	235	48	8	11	3.0	.973	OF-72, 3B-21, 1B-5
1924	STL	A	77	.254	.297	209	53	3	3	0	0.0	30	18	23	12	1	24	9	118	3	4	1	2.6	.968	OF-48
1925			55	.314	.390	159	50	12	0	0	0.0	27	20	16	6	6	6	2	96	3	0	2	2.1	1.000	OF-47
11 yrs.			732	.259	.328	2043	529	71	31	3	0.1	306	209	211	152	64	55	17	1009	661	97	58	2.9	.945	OF-306, 3B-280, SS-12, 1B-5, 2B-2
WORLD SERIES																									
1920	CLE	A	4	.308	.308	13	4	0	0	0	0.0	0	0	1	0	0	1	0	7	0	0	0	1.8	1.000	OF-4

Steve Evans

EVANS, LOUIS RICHARD
B. Feb. 17, 1885, Cleveland, Ohio D. Dec. 28, 1943, Cleveland, Ohio.
BL TL 5′10½″ 175 lbs.

Year	Team		Games	BA	SA	AB	H	2B	3B	HR	HR%	R	RBI	BB	SO	SB	Pinch Hit AB	Pinch Hit H	PO	A	E	DP	TC/G	FA	G by Pos
1908	NY	N	2	.500	.500	2	1	0	0	0	0.0	0	0	0		0	1	0	0	0	0	0	0.0	.000	OF-1
1909	STL	N	143	.259	.329	498	129	17	6	2	0.4	67	56	66		14	0	0	235	19	14	11	1.9	.948	OF-141, 1B-2
1910			151	.241	.326	506	122	21	8	2	0.4	73	73	78	63	10	0	0	330	18	11	7	2.4	.969	OF-141, 1B-10
1911			154	.294	.413	547	161	24	13	5	0.9	74	71	46	52	13	3	1	258	17	8	5	1.9	.972	OF-150
1912			135	.283	.403	491	139	23	9	6	1.2	59	72	36	51	11	1	0	219	24	15	2	1.9	.942	OF-134

Steve Evans *continued*

Year	Team	Games	BA	SA	AB	H	2B	3B	HR	HR%	R	RBI	BB	SO	SB	Pinch Hit AB	Pinch Hit H	PO	A	E	DP	TC/G	FA	G by Pos
1913		97	.249	.371	245	61	15	6	1	0.4	18	31	20	28	5	20	4	113	5	4	0	1.6	.967	OF-74, 1B-1
1914	**BKN F**	145	.348	**.556**	514	179	41	**15**	12	2.3	93	96	50		18	7	1	442	35	21	19	3.6	.958	OF-112, 1B-27
1915	**2 teams**	**BKN F** (63G –.296) **BAL F** (88G –.315)																						
"	**total**	151	.308	.426	556	171	**34**	10	4	0.7	94	67	63		15	1	0	206	21	15	6	1.6	.938	OF-149, 1B-5
8 yrs.		978	.287	.407	3359	963	175	67	32	1.0	478	466	359	194	86	33	6	1803	139	88	50	2.1	.957	OF-902, 1B-45

Carl Everett

EVERETT, CARL EDWARD
B. June 3, 1970, Tampa, Fla.

BB TR 6′ 180 lbs.

Year	Team	Games	BA	SA	AB	H	2B	3B	HR	HR%	R	RBI	BB	SO	SB	Pinch Hit AB	Pinch Hit H	PO	A	E	DP	TC/G	FA	G by Pos
1993	**FLA N**	11	.105	.105	19	2	0	0	0	0.0	0	0	1	9	1	3	0	6	0	1	0	0.9	.857	OF-8
1994		16	.216	.353	51	11	1	0	2	3.9	7	6	3	15	4	1	0	28	2	0	0	1.9	1.000	OF-16
1995	**NY N**	79	.260	.436	289	75	13	1	12	4.2	48	54	39	67	2	2	0	147	10	3	1	2.1	.981	OF-77
3 yrs.		106	.245	.407	359	88	14	1	14	3.9	55	60	43	91	7	6	0	181	12	4	1	2.0	.980	OF-101

Bill Everitt

EVERITT, WILLIAM LEE (Bad Bill)
B. Dec. 13, 1868, Fort Wayne, Ind. D. Jan. 19, 1938, Denver, Colo.

BL TR 6′½″ 185 lbs.

Year	Team	Games	BA	SA	AB	H	2B	3B	HR	HR%	R	RBI	BB	SO	SB	Pinch Hit AB	Pinch Hit H	PO	A	E	DP	TC/G	FA	G by Pos
1895	**CHI N**	133	.358	.440	550	197	16	10	3	0.5	129	88	33	42	47	0	0	178	272	76	12	4.0	.856	3B-130, 2B-3
1896		132	.320	.403	575	184	16	13	2	0.3	130	46	41	43	46	0	0	213	184	53	10	3.4	.882	3B-97, OF-35
1897		92	.314	.427	379	119	14	7	5	1.3	63	39	36		26	1	0	137	147	43	9	3.6	.869	3B-83, OF-8
1898		149	.319	.364	596	190	15	6	0	0.0	102	69	53		28	0	0	1519	70	42	123	10.9	.974	1B-149
1899		136	.310	.366	536	166	17	5	1	0.2	87	74	31		30	0	0	1491	95	47	103	12.0	.971	1B-136
1900		23	.264	.308	91	24	4	0	0	0.0	10	17	3		2	0	0	264	10	6	14	12.2	.979	1B-23
1901	**WAS A**	33	.191	.252	115	22	3	2	0	0.0	14	8	15		7	0	0	319	8	11	12	10.2	.967	1B-33
7 yrs.		698	.317	.389	2842	902	85	43	11	0.4	535	341	212	85	186	1	0	4121	786	278	283	7.4	.946	1B-341, 3B-310, OF-43, 2B-3

Hoot Evers

EVERS, WALTER ARTHUR
B. Feb. 8, 1921, St. Louis, Mo. D. Jan. 25, 1991, Houston, Tex.

BR TR 6′ 2″ 180 lbs.

Year	Team	Games	BA	SA	AB	H	2B	3B	HR	HR%	R	RBI	BB	SO	SB	Pinch Hit AB	Pinch Hit H	PO	A	E	DP	TC/G	FA	G by Pos
1941	**DET A**	1	.000	.000	4	0	0	0	0	0.0	0	0	0	2	0	0	0	0	0	0	0	0.0	.000	OF-1
1946		81	.266	.359	304	81	8	4	4	1.3	42	33	34	43	7	2	0	196	2	5	0	2.7	.975	OF-76
1947		126	.296	.435	460	136	24	5	10	2.2	67	67	45	49	8	2	1	354	10	8	2	3.0	.978	OF-123
1948		139	.314	.454	538	169	33	6	10	1.9	81	103	51	31	3	1	0	392	8	11	0	3.0	.973	OF-138
1949		132	.303	.428	432	131	21	6	7	1.6	68	72	70	38	6	10	2	319	12	2	2	2.7	.994	OF-123
1950		143	.323	.551	526	170	35	**11**	21	4.0	100	103	71	40	5	1	0	325	15	1	3	2.5	.997	OF-139
1951		116	.224	.356	393	88	15	2	11	2.8	47	46	40	47	5	8	2	234	9	6	1	2.3	.976	OF-108
1952	**2 teams**	**DET A** (1G –1.000) **BOS A** (106G –.262)																						
"	**total**	107	.264	.430	402	106	17	4	14	3.5	53	59	29	55	5	2	1	219	8	6	3	2.2	.974	OF-105
1953	**BOS A**	99	.240	.390	300	72	10	1	11	3.7	39	31	23	41	2	7	1	161	3	2	0	1.8	.988	OF-93
1954	**3 teams**	**BOS A** (6G –.000) **NY N** (12G –.091) **DET A** (30G –.183)																						
"	**total**	48	.152	.241	79	12	4	0	1	1.3	7	8	5	16	1	17	1	38	1	0	0	1.3	1.000	OF-29
1955	**2 teams**	**BAL A** (60G –.238) **CLE A** (39G –.288)																						
"	**total**	99	.251	.430	251	63	17	2	8	3.2	31	39	22	40	2	16	6	139	2	1	1	1.8	.993	OF-80
1956	**2 teams**	**CLE A** (3G –.000) **BAL A** (48G –.241)																						
"	**total**	51	.241	.295	112	27	3	0	1	0.9	21	4	25	18	1	10	2	63	1	1	1	1.8	.985	OF-36
12 yrs.		1142	.278	.426	3801	1055	187	41	98	2.6	556	565	415	420	45	76	16	2440	71	43	13	2.4	.983	OF-1051

Joe Evers

EVERS, JOSEPH FRANCIS
Brother of Johnny Evers.
B. Sept. 10, 1891, Troy, N. Y. D. Jan. 4, 1949, Albany, N. Y.

BR TR 5′ 9″ 135 lbs.

Year	Team	Games	BA	SA	AB	H	2B	3B	HR	HR%	R	RBI	BB	SO	SB	Pinch Hit AB	Pinch Hit H	PO	A	E	DP	TC/G	FA	G by Pos
1913	**NY N**	1	—	—	0	0	0	0	0	—	0	0	0	0	0	0	0	0	0	0	0	0.0	—	

Johnny Evers

EVERS, JOHN JOSEPH (The Crab, The Trojan)
Brother of Joe Evers.
B. July 21, 1881, Troy, N. Y. D. Mar. 28, 1947, Albany, N. Y.
Manager 1913, 1921, 1924.
Hall of Fame 1946.

BL TR 5′ 9″ 125 lbs.

Year	Team	Games	BA	SA	AB	H	2B	3B	HR	HR%	R	RBI	BB	SO	SB	Pinch Hit AB	Pinch Hit H	PO	A	E	DP	TC/G	FA	G by Pos
1902	**CHI N**	26	.225	.225	89	20	0	0	0	0.0	7	2	3		1	0	0	48	87	5	6	5.4	.964	2B-18, SS-8
1903		124	.293	.381	464	136	27	7	0	0.0	70	52	19		25	0	0	268	336	51	40	5.3	.922	2B-110, SS-11, 3B-2
1904		152	.265	.318	532	141	14	7	0	0.0	49	47	28		26	0	0	381	518	54	53	6.3	.943	2B-152
1905		99	.276	.329	340	94	11	2	1	0.3	44	37	27		19	0	0	249	290	36	38	5.8	.937	2B-99
1906		154	.255	.315	533	136	17	6	1	0.2	65	51	36		49	0	0	344	441	44	51	5.4	.947	2B-153, 3B-1
1907		151	.250	.313	508	127	18	4	2	0.4	66	51	38		46	0	0	346	500	32	58	5.8	.964	2B-151
1908		126	.300	.375	416	125	19	6	0	0.0	83	37	66		36	2	1	237	361	25	39	5.1	.960	2B-123
1909		127	.263	.337	463	122	19	6	1	0.2	88	24	73		28	0	0	262	354	38	29	5.2	.942	2B-126
1910		125	.263	.321	433	114	11	7	0	0.0	87	28	108	18	28	0	0	282	347	33	55	5.3	.950	2B-125
1911		46	.226	.290	155	35	4	3	0	0.0	29	7	34	10	6	2	0	79	105	7	19	4.3	.963	2B-33, 3B-11
1912		143	.341	.441	478	163	23	11	1	0.2	73	63	74	18	16	0	0	319	439	32	71	5.5	.959	2B-143
1913		135	.284	.372	444	126	20	5	3	0.7	81	49	50	14	11	0	0	303	426	30	70	5.6	.960	2B-135
1914	**BOS N**	139	.279	.338	491	137	20	3	1	0.2	81	40	87	26	12	0	0	301	397	17	73	5.1	.976	2B-139
1915		83	.263	.295	278	73	4	1	1	0.4	38	22	50	16	7	0	0	170	209	16	33	4.8	.959	2B-83
1916		71	.216	.241	241	52	4	1	0	0.0	33	15	40	19	5	0	0	98	175	14	29	4.0	.951	2B-71
1917	**2 teams**	**BOS N** (24G –.193) **PHI N** (56G –.224)																						
"	**total**	80	.214	.252	266	57	5	1	1	0.4	25	12	43	21	9	0	0	116	227	12	28	4.4	.966	2B-73, 3B-7
1922	**CHI A**	1	.000	.000	3	0	0	0	0	0.0	0	1	2	0	0	0	0	3	3	0	1	6.0	1.000	2B-1
1929	**BOS N**	1	—	—	0	0	0	0	0	—	0	0	0	0	0	0	0	0	0	1	0	1.0	.000	2B-1
18 yrs.		1783	.270	.334	6134	1658	216	70	12	0.2	919	538	778	142	324	4	1	3806	5215	447	693	5.3	.953	2B-1736, 3B-21, SS-19
WORLD SERIES																								
1906	**CHI N**	6	.150	.200	20	3	1	0	0	0.0	2	1	1	3	2	0	0	12	20	1	3	5.5	.970	2B-6
1907		5	.350	.450	20	7	2	0	0	0.0	2	1	0	1	3	0	0	9	12	3	2	4.0	.875	2B-5, SS-1
1908		5	.350	.400	20	7	1	0	0	0.0	5	2	1	2	2	0	0	5	21	1	1	5.4	.963	2B-5
1914	**BOS N**	4	.438	.438	16	7	0	0	0	0.0	2	2	2	2	1	0	0	8	16	1	2	6.3	.960	2B-4
4 yrs.		20	.316	.368	76	24	4	0	0	0.0	11	6	4	8	8 **8th**	0	0	34	69	6	8	5.2	.945	2B-20, SS-1

Year	Team		Games	BA	SA	AB	H	2B	3B	HR	HR%	R	RBI	BB	SO	SB	Pinch Hit AB	Pinch Hit H	PO	A	E	DP	TC/G	FA	G by Pos

Tom Evers

EVERS, THOMAS FRANCIS TL 5′ 9″ 135 lbs.
B. Mar. 31, 1852, Troy, N. Y. D. Mar. 23, 1925, Washington, D. C.

Year	Team		Games	BA	SA	AB	H	2B	3B	HR	HR%	R	RBI	BB	SO	SB	PH AB	PH H	PO	A	E	DP	TC/G	FA	G by Pos
1882	BAL	AA	1	.000	.000	4	0	0	0	0	0.0	0		0			0	0	3	0	3	0	6.0	.500	2B-1
1884	WAS	U	109	.232	.251	427	99	6	1	0	0.0	54		7			0	0	326	296	94	28	6.6	.869	2B-109
2 yrs.			110	.230	.248	431	99	6	1	0	0.0	54		7			0	0	329	296	97	28	6.6	.866	2B-110

Buck Ewing

EWING, WILLIAM BR TR 5′10″ 188 lbs.
Brother of John Ewing.
B. Oct. 17, 1859, Hoagland, Ohio D. Oct. 20, 1906, Cincinnati, Ohio.
Manager 1890, 1895–1900.
Hall of Fame 1939.

Year	Team		Games	BA	SA	AB	H	2B	3B	HR	HR%	R	RBI	BB	SO	SB	PH AB	PH H	PO	A	E	DP	TC/G	FA	G by Pos
1880	TRO	N	13	.178	.200	45	8	1	0	0	0.0	1	5	1	3		0	0	48	7	11	0	4.7	.833	C-10, OF-4
1881			67	.250	.353	272	68	14	7	0	0.0	40	25	7	8		0	0	254	185	43	18	7.0	.911	C-44, SS-22, OF-2, 3B-1
1882			74	.271	.405	328	89	16	11	2	0.6	67	29	10	15		0	0	204	172	47	19	5.6	.889	3B-44, C-25, 2B-4, 1B-1, OF-1, P-1
1883	NY	N	88	.303	.481	376	114	11	13	**10**	**2.7**	90		20	14		0	0	310	145	50	12	5.4	.901	C-63, OF-14, 2B-11, SS-4, 3B-1
1884			94	.277	.445	382	106	15	**20**	3	0.8	90		28	22		0	0	458	139	46	11	6.6	.928	C-80, OF-12, SS-3, P-1, 3B-1
1885			81	.304	.471	342	104	15	12	6	1.8	81		13	17		0	0	377	119	47	9	6.2	.913	C-63, OF-14, 3B-8, SS-1, P-1, 1B-1
1886			73	.309	.444	275	85	11	7	4	1.5	59	31	16	17		0	0	311	97	36	4	5.9	.919	C-50, OF-23, 1B-2
1887			77	.305	.497	318	97	17	13	6	1.9	83	44	30	33	26	0	0	153	173	48	17	4.8	.872	3B-51, 2B-19, C-8
1888			103	.306	.465	415	127	18	15	6	1.4	83	58	24	28	53	0	0	515	185	53	16	7.2	.930	C-78, 3B-21, SS-4, P-2
1889			99	.327	.477	407	133	23	13	4	1.0	91	87	37	32	34	0	0	525	152	47	10	7.2	.935	C-97, P-3, OF-1
1890	NY	P	83	.338	.545	352	119	19	15	8	2.3	98	72	39	12	36	0	0	374	113	28	8	6.2	.946	C-81, 2B-1, P-1
1891	NY	N	14	.347	.429	49	17	2	1	0	0.0	8	18	5	5	5	0	0	35	33	10	4	5.6	.872	2B-8, C-6
1892			105	.310	.466	393	122	10	15	7	1.8	58	76	38	26	42	0	0	855	97	33	38	9.4	.966	1B-73, C-30, 2B-2
1893	CLE	N	116	.344	.496	500	172	28	15	6	1.2	117	122	41	18	47	0	0	217	29	21	4	2.2	.921	OF-112, 2B-5, C-1, 1B-1
1894			53	.251	.374	211	53	12	4	2	0.9	32	39	24	9	18	0	0	87	8	10	2	2.0	.905	OF-52, 2B-1
1895	CIN	N	105	.318	.468	434	138	24	13	5	1.2	90	94	30	22	34	0	0	957	79	26	69	10.1	.976	1B-105
1896			69	.278	.373	263	73	14	4	1	0.4	41	38	29	13	41	0	0	669	49	15	41	10.6	.980	1B-69
1897			1	.000	.000	1	0	0	0	0	0.0	0	0	0		0	0	0	4	0	1	0	5.0	.800	1B-1
18 yrs.			1315	.303	.455	5363	1625	250	178	70	1.3	1129	738	392	294	336	0	0	6353	1782	572	282	6.5	.934	C-636, 1B-253, OF-235, 3B-127, 2B-51, SS-34, P-9

Reuben Ewing

EWING, REUBEN BR TR 5′ 4½″ 150 lbs.
Born Reuben Cohen.
B. Nov. 30, 1899, Odessa, Russia D. Oct. 5, 1970, W. Hartford, Conn.

Year	Team		Games	BA	SA	AB	H	2B	3B	HR	HR%	R	RBI	BB	SO	SB	PH AB	PH H	PO	A	E	DP	TC/G	FA	G by Pos
1921	STL	N	3	.000	.000	1	0	0	0	0	0.0	0	0	0	1	0	1	0	0	1	0	0	1.0	1.000	SS-1

Sam Ewing

EWING, SAMUEL JAMES BL TR 6′ 3″ 200 lbs.
B. Apr. 9, 1949, Lewisburg, Tenn.

Year	Team		Games	BA	SA	AB	H	2B	3B	HR	HR%	R	RBI	BB	SO	SB	PH AB	PH H	PO	A	E	DP	TC/G	FA	G by Pos
1973	CHI	A	11	.150	.200	20	3	1	0	0	0.0	1	2	2	6	0	5	1	34	4	0	7	9.5	1.000	1B-4
1976			19	.220	.317	41	9	2	1	0	0.0	3	2	2	8	0	8	3	4	0	0	0	0.3	1.000	DH-12, 1B-1
1977	TOR	A	97	.287	.385	244	70	8	2	4	1.6	24	34	19	42	1	27	9	68	1	3	0	1.0	.958	OF-46, DH-27, 1B-2
1978			40	.179	.286	56	10	0	0	2	3.6	3	9	5	9	0	29	5	4	0	0	0	0.3	1.000	DH-9, OF-3
4 yrs.			167	.255	.352	361	92	11	3	6	1.7	31	47	28	65	1	69	18	110	5	3	7	1.1	.975	OF-49, DH-48, 1B-7

Art Ewoldt

EWOLDT, ARTHUR LEE (Sheriff) BR TR 5′10″ 165 lbs.
B. Jan. 8, 1894, Paullina, Iowa D. Dec. 8, 1977, Des Moines, Iowa.

Year	Team		Games	BA	SA	AB	H	2B	3B	HR	HR%	R	RBI	BB	SO	SB	PH AB	PH H	PO	A	E	DP	TC/G	FA	G by Pos
1919	PHI	A	9	.219	.250	32	7	1	0	0	0.0	2	2	1	5	0	0	0	11	16	0	0	3.0	1.000	3B-9

Homer Ezzell

EZZELL, HOMER ESTELL BR TR 5′10″ 158 lbs.
B. Feb. 28, 1896, Victoria, Tex. D. Aug. 3, 1976, San Antonio, Tex.

Year	Team		Games	BA	SA	AB	H	2B	3B	HR	HR%	R	RBI	BB	SO	SB	PH AB	PH H	PO	A	E	DP	TC/G	FA	G by Pos
1923	STL	A	89	.244	.265	279	68	6	0	0	0.0	32	14	15	20	4	2	0	96	175	10	16	3.5	.964	3B-73, 2B-8
1924	BOS	A	89	.275	.333	273	75	8	4	0	0.0	33	32	13	20	12	4	0	95	188	14	15	3.5	.953	3B-62, SS-21, C-1
1925			58	.285	.360	186	53	6	4	0	0.0	40	15	19	18	9	0	0	63	97	20	7	3.2	.889	3B-47, 2B-9
3 yrs.			236	.266	.314	738	196	20	8	0	0.0	105	61	47	58	25	6	0	254	460	44	38	3.4	.942	3B-182, SS-21, 2B-17, C-1

Jay Faatz

FAATZ, JAYSON S. BR TR 6′ 4″
B. Oct. 24, 1860, Weedsport, N. Y. D. Apr. 10, 1923, Syracuse, N. Y.
Manager 1890.

Year	Team		Games	BA	SA	AB	H	2B	3B	HR	HR%	R	RBI	BB	SO	SB	PH AB	PH H	PO	A	E	DP	TC/G	FA	G by Pos
1884	PIT	AA	29	.241	.313	112	27	2	3	0	0.0	18		1			0	0	283	6	11	16	10.3	.963	1B-29
1888	CLE	AA	120	.264	.294	470	124	10	2	0	0.0	73	51	12		64	0	0	1171	39	13	50	10.2	.989	1B-120
1889	CLE	N	117	.231	.294	442	102	12	5	2	0.5	50	38	17	28	27	0	0	1145	62	24	67	10.5	.981	1B-117
1890	BUF	P	32	.189	.252	111	21	0	2	1	0.9	18	16	9	5	2	0	0	312	7	6	18	10.2	.982	1B-32
4 yrs.			298	.241	.292	1135	274	24	12	3	0.3	159	105	39	33	93	0	0	2911	114	54	151	10.3	.982	1B-298

Jorge Fabregas

FABREGAS, JORGE BL TR 6′ 3″ 205 lbs.
B. Mar. 13, 1970, Miami, Fla.

Year	Team		Games	BA	SA	AB	H	2B	3B	HR	HR%	R	RBI	BB	SO	SB	PH AB	PH H	PO	A	E	DP	TC/G	FA	G by Pos
1994	CAL	A	43	.283	.307	127	36	3	0	0	0.0	12	16	7	18	2	7	3	217	16	3	1	5.8	.987	C-41
1995			73	.247	.304	227	56	10	0	1	0.4	24	22	17	28	0	3	1	391	36	6	1	5.9	.986	C-73
2 yrs.			116	.260	.305	354	92	13	0	1	0.3	36	38	24	46	2	10	4	608	52	9	2	5.9	.987	C-114

Bunny Fabrique

FABRIQUE, ALBERT LaVERNE BB TR 5′ 8½″ 150 lbs.
B. Dec. 23, 1887, Clinton, Mich. D. Jan. 10, 1960, Ann Arbor, Mich.

Year	Team		Games	BA	SA	AB	H	2B	3B	HR	HR%	R	RBI	BB	SO	SB	PH AB	PH H	PO	A	E	DP	TC/G	FA	G by Pos
1916	BKN	N	2	.000	.000	2	0	0	0	0	0.0	0	0	0	1	0	0	0	2	2	0	1	2.0	1.000	SS-2
1917			25	.205	.273	88	18	3	0	1	1.1	8	3	8	9	0	4	0	55	63	17	8	6.4	.874	SS-21
2 yrs.			27	.200	.267	90	18	3	0	1	1.1	8	3	8	10	0	4	0	57	65	17	9	6.0	.878	SS-23

Len Faedo

FAEDO, LEONARDO LAGO, JR. BR TR 6′ 170 lbs.
B. May 13, 1960, Tampa, Fla.

Year	Team		Games	BA	SA	AB	H	2B	3B	HR	HR%	R	RBI	BB	SO	SB	PH AB	PH H	PO	A	E	DP	TC/G	FA	G by Pos
1980	MIN	A	5	.250	.375	8	2	1	0	0	0.0	1	0	0	0	0	0	0	4	5	2	0	2.2	.818	SS-5
1981			12	.195	.244	41	8	0	1	0	0.0	3	6	1	5	0	0	0	24	42	2	10	5.7	.971	SS-12
1982			90	.243	.310	255	62	8	0	3	1.2	16	22	16	22	1	1	0	129	218	12	52	4.0	.967	SS-88, DH-1

Len Faedo *continued*

Year	Team	Games	BA	SA	AB	H	2B	3B	HR	HR%	R	RBI	BB	SO	SB	Pinch Hit AB	Pinch Hit H	PO	A	E	DP	TC/G	FA	G by Pos
1983		51	.277	.335	173	48	7	0	1	0.6	16	18	4	19	0	0	0	53	133	9	22	3.8	.954	SS-51
1984		16	.250	.327	52	13	1	0	1	1.9	6	6	4	3	0	1	0	22	39	2	4	3.9	.968	SS-15, DH-1
5 yrs.		174	.251	.316	529	133	17	1	5	0.9	42	52	25	49	1	2	0	232	437	27	88	4.0	.961	SS-171, DH-2

Fred Fagin

FAGIN, FREDERICK H.
B. Cincinnati, Ohio Deceased.

Year	Team	Games	BA	SA	AB	H	2B	3B	HR	HR%	R	RBI	BB	SO	SB	Pinch Hit AB	Pinch Hit H	PO	A	E	DP	TC/G	FA	G by Pos
1895	STL N	1	.333	.333	3	1	0	0	0	0.0	0	2	0	0	0	0	0	4	3	4	0	11.0	.636	C-1

Bill Fahey

FAHEY, WILLIAM ROGER
B. June 14, 1950, Detroit, Mich.
BL TR 6′ 200 lbs.

Year	Team	Games	BA	SA	AB	H	2B	3B	HR	HR%	R	RBI	BB	SO	SB	Pinch Hit AB	Pinch Hit H	PO	A	E	DP	TC/G	FA	G by Pos
1971	WAS A	2	.000	.000	8	0	0	0	0	0.0	0	0	0	0	0	0	0	8	2	1	0	5.5	.909	C-2
1972	TEX A	39	.168	.210	119	20	2	0	1	0.8	8	10	12	23	4	1	1	236	26	2	4	6.8	.992	C-39
1974		6	.250	.250	16	4	0	0	0	0.0	1	0	0	1	0	0	0	21	2	0	0	3.8	1.000	C-6
1975		21	.297	.378	37	11	1	1	0	0.0	3	3	1	10	0	2	0	54	5	1	1	2.9	.983	C-21
1976		38	.250	.313	80	20	2	0	1	1.3	12	9	11	6	1	1	0	126	19	1	3	3.8	.993	C-38
1977		37	.221	.279	68	15	4	0	0	0.0	3	5	1	8	0	1	0	104	5	0	0	3.2	1.000	C-34
1979	SD N	73	.287	.378	209	60	8	1	3	1.4	14	19	21	17	1	6	1	277	33	2	5	4.6	.994	C-68
1980		93	.257	.286	241	62	4	0	1	0.4	18	22	21	16	2	11	2	309	34	8	6	4.1	.977	C-85
1981	DET A	27	.254	.328	67	17	2	0	1	1.5	5	9	2	4	0	0	0	96	9	2	3	4.0	.981	C-27
1982		28	.149	.179	67	10	2	0	0	0.0	7	4	0	5	1	2	0	85	16	0	2	3.6	1.000	C-28
1983		19	.273	.318	22	6	1	0	0	0.0	4	2	5	3	0	1	0	39	2	0	0	2.3	1.000	C-18
11 yrs.		383	.241	.296	934	225	26	2	7	0.7	75	83	74	93	9	25	4	1355	153	17	24	4.2	.989	C-366

Frank Fahey

FAHEY, FRANCIS RAYMOND
B. Jan. 22, 1896, Milford, Mass. D. Mar. 19, 1954, Boston, Mass.
BB TR 6′ 1″ 190 lbs.

Year	Team	Games	BA	SA	AB	H	2B	3B	HR	HR%	R	RBI	BB	SO	SB	Pinch Hit AB	Pinch Hit H	PO	A	E	DP	TC/G	FA	G by Pos
1918	PHI A	10	.176	.235	17	3	1	0	0	0.0	2	1	0	3	0	1	0	4	0	0	0	0.5	1.000	OF-5, P-3

Howard Fahey

FAHEY, HOWARD SIMPSON (Cap, Kid)
B. June 24, 1892, Medford, Mass. D. Oct. 24, 1971, Clearwater, Fla.
BR TR 5′ 7½″ 145 lbs.

Year	Team	Games	BA	SA	AB	H	2B	3B	HR	HR%	R	RBI	BB	SO	SB	Pinch Hit AB	Pinch Hit H	PO	A	E	DP	TC/G	FA	G by Pos
1912	PHI A	5	.000	.000	8	0	0	0	0	0.0	0	0	0		0	1	0	4	0	1	1	1.3	.800	3B-2, SS-1, 2B-1

Ferris Fain

FAIN, FERRIS ROY (Burrhead)
B. May 29, 1921, San Antonio, Tex.
BL TL 5′11″ 180 lbs.

Year	Team	Games	BA	SA	AB	H	2B	3B	HR	HR%	R	RBI	BB	SO	SB	Pinch Hit AB	Pinch Hit H	PO	A	E	DP	TC/G	FA	G by Pos
1947	PHI A	136	.291	.423	461	134	28	6	7	1.5	70	71	95	34	4	4	0	1141	101	19	118	9.6	.985	1B-132
1948		145	.281	.396	520	146	27	6	7	1.3	81	88	113	37	10	0	0	1284	120	16	148	9.8	.989	1B-145
1949		150	.263	.339	525	138	21	5	3	0.6	81	78	136	51	8	0	0	1275	122	22	194	9.5	.984	1B-150
1950		151	.282	.402	522	147	25	4	10	1.9	83	83	133	26	8	0	0	1286	124	19	192	9.5	.987	1B-151
1951		117	**.344**	.471	425	146	30	3	6	1.4	63	57	80	20	0	0	0	942	115	14	125	9.0	.987	1B-108, OF-11
1952		145	**.327**	.429	538	176	**43**	3	2	0.4	82	59	105	26	3	1	0	1245	150	22	124	9.8	.984	1B-144
1953	CHI A	128	.256	.345	446	114	18	2	6	1.3	73	52	108	28	3	1	1	1108	106	13	98	9.7	.989	1B-127
1954		65	.302	.417	235	71	10	1	5	2.1	30	51	40	14	5	0	0	565	31	8	54	9.4	.987	1B-64
1955	2 teams	DET A (58G –.264)	CLE A (56G –.254)																					
″	total	114	.260	.326	258	67	11	0	2	0.8	32	31	94	25	5	13	4	695	60	8	72	8.0	.990	1B-95
9 yrs.		1151	.290	.396	3930	1139	213	30	48	1.2	595	570	904	261	46	19	5	9541	929	141	1125	9.4	.987	1B-1116, OF-11

George Fair

FAIR, GEORGE T.
B. Jan. 14, 1856, Boston, Mass. D. Feb. 12, 1939, Roslindale, Mass.
5′ 7½″ 140 lbs.

Year	Team	Games	BA	SA	AB	H	2B	3B	HR	HR%	R	RBI	BB	SO	SB	Pinch Hit AB	Pinch Hit H	PO	A	E	DP	TC/G	FA	G by Pos
1876	NY N	1	.000	.000	4	0	0	0	0	0.0	0	0	0	0		0	0	2	4	2	1	8.0	.750	2B-1

Jim Fairey

FAIREY, JAMES BURKE
B. Sept. 22, 1944, Orangeburg, S. C.
BL TL 5′10″ 190 lbs.

Year	Team	Games	BA	SA	AB	H	2B	3B	HR	HR%	R	RBI	BB	SO	SB	Pinch Hit AB	Pinch Hit H	PO	A	E	DP	TC/G	FA	G by Pos
1968	LA N	99	.199	.276	156	31	3	3	1	0.6	17	10	9	32	1	37	8	65	3	4	1	1.1	.944	OF-63
1969	MON N	20	.286	.367	49	14	1	0	1	2.0	6	6	1	7	0	11	2	20	1	2	0	1.8	.913	OF-13
1970		92	.242	.355	211	51	9	3	3	1.4	35	25	14	38	1	37	14	86	1	2	0	1.5	.978	OF-59
1971		92	.245	.310	200	49	8	1	1	0.5	19	19	12	23	3	36	11	85	7	3	1	1.6	.968	OF-58
1972		86	.234	.305	141	33	7	0	1	0.7	9	15	10	21	1	**55**	10	40	1	3	0	1.2	.932	OF-37
1973	LA N	10	.222	.222	9	2	0	0	0	0.0	0	0	1	1	0	9	2	0	0	0	0	0.0	—	
6 yrs.		399	.235	.317	766	180	28	7	7	0.9	86	75	47	122	6	185	47	296	13	14	2	1.4	.957	OF-230

Ron Fairly

FAIRLY, RONALD RAY
B. July 12, 1938, Macon, Ga.
BL TL 5′10″ 175 lbs.

Year	Team	Games	BA	SA	AB	H	2B	3B	HR	HR%	R	RBI	BB	SO	SB	Pinch Hit AB	Pinch Hit H	PO	A	E	DP	TC/G	FA	G by Pos
1958	LA N	15	.283	.415	53	15	1	0	2	3.8	6	8	6	7	0	0	0	33	0	1	0	2.3	.971	OF-15
1959		118	.238	.344	244	58	12	1	4	1.6	27	23	31	29	0	31	7	97	8	4	1	1.2	.963	OF-88
1960		14	.108	.351	37	4	0	3	1	2.7	6	3	7	12	0	1	0	15	1	0	0	1.2	1.000	OF-13
1961		111	.322	.522	245	79	15	2	10	4.1	42	48	48	22	0	20	6	242	18	3	17	2.8	.989	OF-71, 1B-23
1962		147	.278	.433	460	128	15	7	14	3.0	80	71	75	59	1	7	0	1007	45	11	76	6.3	.990	1B-120, OF-48
1963		152	.271	.388	490	133	21	0	12	2.4	62	77	58	69	5	5	2	946	48	7	74	6.1	.993	1B-119, OF-45
1964		150	.256	.385	454	116	19	5	10	2.2	62	74	65	59	4	9	2	1081	82	15	89	8.4	.987	1B-141
1965		158	.274	.377	555	152	28	1	9	1.6	73	70	76	72	2	3	0	361	13	6	7	2.4	.984	OF-148, 1B-13
1966		117	.288	.464	351	101	20	0	14	4.0	53	61	52	38	3	6	2	264	14	4	20	2.3	.986	OF-98, 1B-25
1967		153	.220	.321	486	107	19	0	10	2.1	45	55	54	51	1	9	1	727	55	11	55	4.8	.986	OF-97, 1B-68
1968		141	.234	.299	441	103	15	1	4	0.9	32	43	41	61	0	12	4	406	26	3	27	3.1	.993	OF-105, 1B-36
1969	2 teams	LA N (30G –.219)	MON N (70G –.289)																					
″	total	100	.274	.476	317	87	16	6	12	3.8	38	47	37	28	1	10	3	543	46	7	58	6.3	.988	1B-64, OF-31
1970	MON N	119	.288	.455	385	111	19	0	15	3.9	54	61	72	64	10	7	2	945	90	5	112	8.5	.995	1B-118, OF-4
1971		146	.257	.396	447	115	23	0	13	2.9	58	71	81	65	1	17	5	1116	104	10	110	8.5	.992	1B-135, OF-10
1972		140	.278	.430	446	124	15	1	17	3.8	51	68	46	45	3	13	4	646	46	6	39	5.1	.991	OF-70, 1B-68
1973		142	.298	.458	413	123	13	1	17	4.1	70	49	86	33	2	25	3	202	5	5	4	1.7	.976	OF-121, 1B-5
1974		101	.245	.411	282	69	9	1	12	4.3	35	43	57	28	2	15	1	603	43	7	41	7.5	.989	1B-67, OF-20
1975	STL N	107	.301	.467	229	69	13	2	7	3.1	32	37	45	22	0	35	12	383	33	8	33	5.6	.981	1B-56, OF-20

Ron Fairly *continued*

Year	Team	Games	BA	SA	AB	H	2B	3B	HR	HR%	R	RBI	BB	SO	SB	Pinch Hit AB	Pinch Hit H	PO	A	E	DP	TC/G	FA	G by Pos
1976	2 teams STL N (73G –.264) OAK A (15G –.239)																							
"	total	88	.256	.346	156	40	5	0	3	1.9	22	31	32	24	0	47	11	295	31	1	29	7.8	.997	1B-42
1977	TOR A	132	.279	.465	458	128	24	2	19	4.1	60	64	58	58	0	4	2	375	34	7	28	3.2	.983	DH-58, 1B-40, OF-33
1978	CAL A	91	.217	.366	235	51	5	0	10	4.3	23	40	25	31	0	13	1	482	31	1	47	6.2	.998	1B-78, DH-5
21 yrs.		2442	.266	.408	7184	1913	307	33	215	3.0	931	1044	1052	877	35	289	68	10769	773	122	867	5.0	.990	1B-1218, OF-1037, DH-63
WORLD SERIES																								
1959	LA N	6	.000	.000	3	0	0	0	0	0.0	0	0	0	1	0	2	0	0	0	0	0	0.0	.000	OF-4
1963		4	.000	.000	1	0	0	0	0	0.0	0	0	3	0	0	0	0	3	0	0	0	0.8	1.000	OF-4
1965		7	.379	.690	29	11	3	0	2	6.9	7	6	0	1	0	0	0	8	0	0	0	1.1	1.000	OF-7
1966		3	.143	.143	7	1	0	0	0	0.0	0	0	2	4	0	1	0	3	0	1	0	1.3	.750	OF-2, 1B-1
4 yrs.		20	.300	.525	40	12	3	0	2	5.0	7	6	5	6	0	3	0	14	0	1	0	0.8	.933	OF-17, 1B-1

Anton Falch

FALCH, ANTON C. 6′ 6″ 220 lbs.
B. Dec. 4, 1860, Milwaukee, Wis. D. Mar. 31, 1936, Wauwatosa, Wis.

Year	Team	Games	BA	SA	AB	H	2B	3B	HR	HR%	R	RBI	BB	SO	SB	Pinch Hit AB	Pinch Hit H	PO	A	E	DP	TC/G	FA	G by Pos
1884	MIL U	5	.111	.111	18	2	0	0	0	0.0	0		0			0	0	16	8	3	0	5.4	.889	OF-3, C-2

Bibb Falk

FALK, BIBB AUGUST (Jockey) BL TL 6′ 175 lbs.
Brother of Chet Falk.
B. Jan. 27, 1899, Austin, Tex. D. June 8, 1989, Austin, Tex.
Manager 1933.

Year	Team	Games	BA	SA	AB	H	2B	3B	HR	HR%	R	RBI	BB	SO	SB	Pinch Hit AB	Pinch Hit H	PO	A	E	DP	TC/G	FA	G by Pos
1920	CHI A	7	.294	.471	17	5	1	1	0	0.0	1	2	0	5	0	3	1	5	0	0	0	1.3	1.000	OF-4
1921		152	.285	.402	585	167	31	11	5	0.9	62	82	37	69	4	3	1	288	9	13	5	2.1	.958	OF-149
1922		131	.298	.433	483	144	27	1	12	2.5	58	79	27	55	2	1	0	253	10	10	2	2.1	.963	OF-131
1923		87	.307	.471	274	84	18	6	5	1.8	44	38	25	12	4	7	2	148	6	8	3	2.0	.951	OF-80
1924		138	.352	.487	526	185	37	8	6	1.1	77	99	47	21	6	3	1	292	26	10	4	2.4	.970	OF-134
1925		154	.301	.409	602	181	35	9	4	0.7	80	99	51	25	4	0	0	306	18	14	4	2.2	.959	OF-154
1926		155	.345	.477	566	195	43	4	8	1.4	86	108	66	22	9	0	0	338	16	3	4	2.3	.992	OF-155
1927		145	.327	.465	535	175	35	6	9	1.7	76	83	52	19	5	0	0	372	22	9	9	2.8	.978	OF-145
1928		98	.290	.392	286	83	18	4	1	0.3	42	37	25	16	5	16	3	164	9	5	0	2.3	.972	OF-78
1929	CLE A	126	.309	.502	430	133	30	7	13	3.0	66	94	42	14	4	4	1	219	15	14	4	2.0	.944	OF-121
1930		82	.325	.461	191	62	12	1	4	2.1	34	36	23	8	2	**34**	**13**	84	4	3	3	2.2	.967	OF-42
1931		79	.304	.435	161	49	13	1	2	1.2	30	28	17	13	1	43	**14**	55	1	3	0	1.8	.949	OF-33
12 yrs.		1354	.314	.448	4656	1463	300	59	69	1.5	656	785	412	279	46	114	36	2524	136	92	38	2.2	.967	OF-1226

Charlie Fallon

FALLON, CHARLES AUGUSTUS BR TR 5′ 6″
B. Mar. 7, 1881, New York, N. Y. D. June 10, 1960, King's Park, N. Y.

Year	Team	Games	BA	SA	AB	H	2B	3B	HR	HR%	R	RBI	BB	SO	SB	Pinch Hit AB	Pinch Hit H	PO	A	E	DP	TC/G	FA	G by Pos
1905	NY A	1	—	—	0	0	0	0	0	—	0	0	0	0	0	0	0	0	0	0	0	0.0	—	

George Fallon

FALLON, GEORGE DECATUR (Flash) BR TR 5′ 9″ 155 lbs.
B. July 8, 1914, Jersey City, N. J. D. Oct. 25, 1994, Lake Worth, Fla.

Year	Team	Games	BA	SA	AB	H	2B	3B	HR	HR%	R	RBI	BB	SO	SB	Pinch Hit AB	Pinch Hit H	PO	A	E	DP	TC/G	FA	G by Pos
1937	BKN N	4	.250	.375	8	2	1	0	0	0.0	0	0	1	0	0	0	0	9	8	2	1	4.8	.895	2B-4
1943	STL N	36	.231	.244	78	18	1	0	0	0.0	6	5	2	9	0	0	0	65	86	5	18	4.3	.968	2B-36
1944		69	.199	.262	141	28	6	0	1	0.7	16	9	16	11	1	0	0	100	120	6	28	3.3	.973	2B-38, SS-24, 3B-6
1945		24	.236	.309	55	13	2	1	0	0.0	4	7	6	6	1	0	0	39	41	4	8	3.5	.952	SS-20, 2B-4
4 yrs.		133	.216	.270	282	61	10	1	1	0.4	26	21	25	26	2	0	0	213	255	17	55	3.7	.965	2B-82, SS-44, 3B-6
WORLD SERIES																								
1944	STL N	2	.000	.000	2	0	0	0	0	0.0	0	0	0	1	0	0	0	0	0	0	0	0.0	.000	2B-2

Pete Falsey

FALSEY, PETER JAMES BL TL 5′ 6½″ 132 lbs.
B. Apr. 24, 1891, New Haven, Conn. D. May 23, 1976, Los Angeles, Calif.

Year	Team	Games	BA	SA	AB	H	2B	3B	HR	HR%	R	RBI	BB	SO	SB	Pinch Hit AB	Pinch Hit H	PO	A	E	DP	TC/G	FA	G by Pos
1914	PIT N	3	.000	.000	1	0	0	0	0	0.0	0	0	0	1	0	1	0	0	0	0	0	0.0	—	

Rikkert Faneyte

FANEYTE, RIKKERT BR TR 6′ 170 lbs.
B. May 31, 1969, Amsterdam, Netherlands.

Year	Team	Games	BA	SA	AB	H	2B	3B	HR	HR%	R	RBI	BB	SO	SB	Pinch Hit AB	Pinch Hit H	PO	A	E	DP	TC/G	FA	G by Pos
1993	SF N	7	.133	.133	15	2	0	0	0	0.0	2	0	2	4	0	1	0	10	0	0	0	1.7	1.000	OF-6
1994		19	.115	.231	26	3	3	0	0	0.0	1	4	3	11	0	12	1	9	0	1	0	1.7	.900	OF-6
1995		46	.198	.267	86	17	4	1	0	0.0	7	4	11	27	1	10	2	49	3	1	0	1.6	.981	OF-34
3 yrs.		72	.173	.244	127	22	7	1	0	0.0	10	8	16	42	1	23	3	68	3	2	0	1.6	.973	OF-46

Jim Fanning

FANNING, WILLIAM JAMES BR TR 5′11″ 180 lbs.
B. Sept. 14, 1927, Chicago, Ill.
Manager 1981–82, 1984.

Year	Team	Games	BA	SA	AB	H	2B	3B	HR	HR%	R	RBI	BB	SO	SB	Pinch Hit AB	Pinch Hit H	PO	A	E	DP	TC/G	FA	G by Pos
1954	CHI N	11	.184	.184	38	7	0	0	0	0.0	2	1	1	7	0	0	0	40	6	0	0	4.2	1.000	C-11
1955		5	.000	.000	10	0	0	0	0	0.0	0	0	1	2	0	0	0	30	2	0	0	6.4	1.000	C-5
1956		1	.250	.250	4	1	0	0	0	0.0	0	0	0	0	0	0	0	5	3	2	1	10.0	.800	C-1
1957		47	.180	.202	89	16	2	0	0	0.0	3	4	4	17	0	12	1	138	14	3	4	4.4	.981	C-35
4 yrs.		64	.170	.184	141	24	2	0	0	0.0	5	5	6	26	0	12	1	213	25	5	5	4.7	.979	C-52

Carmen Fanzone

FANZONE, CARMEN RONALD BR TR 6′ 200 lbs.
B. Aug. 30, 1941, Detroit, Mich.

Year	Team	Games	BA	SA	AB	H	2B	3B	HR	HR%	R	RBI	BB	SO	SB	Pinch Hit AB	Pinch Hit H	PO	A	E	DP	TC/G	FA	G by Pos
1970	BOS A	10	.200	.267	15	3	1	0	0	0.0	0	3	2	2	0	4	0	4	8	4	1	3.2	.750	3B-5
1971	CHI N	12	.186	.372	43	8	2	0	2	4.7	5	5	2	7	0	2	1	22	9	2	2	3.0	.939	OF-6, 3B-3, 1B-2
1972		86	.225	.383	222	50	11	0	8	3.6	26	42	35	45	2	15	4	243	115	9	21	5.1	.975	3B-36, 1B-21, 2B-13, OF-1, SS-1
1973		64	.273	.440	150	41	7	0	6	4.0	22	22	20	38	1	15	5	193	41	8	13	4.4	.967	3B-25, 1B-24, OF-6
1974		65	.190	.304	158	30	6	0	4	2.5	13	22	15	27	0	15	4	87	82	15	14	3.5	.918	3B-35, 2B-10, 1B-7, OF-1
5 yrs.		237	.224	.372	588	132	27	0	20	3.4	66	94	74	119	3	51	14	549	255	38	51	4.3	.955	3B-104, 1B-54, 2B-23, OF-14, SS-1

Paul Faries

FARIES, PAUL TYRRELL BR TR 5′10″ 165 lbs.
B. Feb. 20, 1965, Berkeley, Calif.

Year	Team	Games	BA	SA	AB	H	2B	3B	HR	HR%	R	RBI	BB	SO	SB	Pinch Hit AB	Pinch Hit H	PO	A	E	DP	TC/G	FA	G by Pos
1990	SD N	14	.189	.216	37	7	1	0	0	0.0	4	2	4	7	0	1	0	21	34	2	8	4.8	.965	2B-7, SS-4, 3B-1
1991		57	.177	.215	130	23	3	1	0	0.0	13	7	14	21	3	2	0	80	117	2	20	3.6	.990	2B-36, 3B-12, SS-8

Paul Faries *continued*

Year	Team	Games	BA	SA	AB	H	2B	3B	HR	HR%	R	RBI	BB	SO	SB	Pinch Hit AB	Pinch Hit H	PO	A	E	DP	TC/G	FA	G by Pos
1992		10	.455	.545	11	5	1	0	0	0.0	3	1	1	2	0	4	3	4	4	0	1	1.1	1.000	2B-4, 3B-2, SS-1
1993	SF N	15	.222	.333	36	8	2	1	0	0.0	6	4	1	4	2	1	0	15	23	1	3	3.3	.974	2B-7, SS-4, 3B-1
4 yrs.		96	.201	.252	214	43	7	2	0	0.0	26	14	20	34	5	8	3	120	178	5	32	3.5	.983	2B-54, SS-17, 3B-16

Monty Fariss

FARISS, MONTY TED
B. Oct. 13, 1967, Cordell, Okla. BR TR 6′4″ 180 lbs.

Year	Team	Games	BA	SA	AB	H	2B	3B	HR	HR%	R	RBI	BB	SO	SB	Pinch Hit AB	Pinch Hit H	PO	A	E	DP	TC/G	FA	G by Pos
1991	TEX A	19	.258	.387	31	8	1	0	1	3.2	6	6	7	11	0	6	1	25	9	0	3	2.1	1.000	OF-8, 2B-4, DH-4
1992		67	.217	.325	166	36	7	1	3	1.8	13	21	17	51	0	14	1	73	13	0	5	1.2	1.000	OF-49, 2B-17, DH-4, 1B-1
1993	FLA N	18	.172	.310	29	5	2	1	0	0.0	3	2	5	13	0	10	1	13	0	0	0	1.6	1.000	OF-8
3 yrs.		104	.217	.332	226	49	10	2	4	1.8	22	29	29	75	0	30	3	111	22	0	8	1.4	1.000	OF-65, 2B-21, DH-8, 1B-1

Bob Farley

FARLEY, ROBERT JACOB
B. Nov. 15, 1937, Watsontown, Pa. BL TL 6′2″ 200 lbs.

Year	Team	Games	BA	SA	AB	H	2B	3B	HR	HR%	R	RBI	BB	SO	SB	Pinch Hit AB	Pinch Hit H	PO	A	E	DP	TC/G	FA	G by Pos
1961	SF N	13	.100	.100	20	2	0	0	0	0.0	3	1	3	5	0	8	1	7	0	0	1	1.8	1.000	OF-3, 1B-1
1962	2 teams CHI A (35G –.189) DET A (36G –.160)																							
″	total	71	.175	.282	103	18	3	1	2	1.9	16	8	27	23	0	33	4	111	7	4	11	4.7	.967	1B-20, OF-6
2 yrs.		84	.163	.252	123	20	3	1	2	1.6	19	9	30	28	0	41	5	118	7	4	12	4.3	.969	1B-21, OF-9

Tom Farley

FARLEY, THOMAS T.
B. Chicago, Ill. D. Feb. 26, 1903, Chicago, Ill.

Year	Team	Games	BA	SA	AB	H	2B	3B	HR	HR%	R	RBI	BB	SO	SB	Pinch Hit AB	Pinch Hit H	PO	A	E	DP	TC/G	FA	G by Pos
1884	WAS AA	14	.212	.288	52	11	4	0	0	0.0	5		1			0	0	24	2	4	1	2.1	.867	OF-14

Alex Farmer

FARMER, ALEXANDER JOHNSON
B. May 9, 1880, New York, N. Y. D. Mar. 5, 1920, New York, N. Y. BR TR 6′ 175 lbs.

Year	Team	Games	BA	SA	AB	H	2B	3B	HR	HR%	R	RBI	BB	SO	SB	Pinch Hit AB	Pinch Hit H	PO	A	E	DP	TC/G	FA	G by Pos
1908	BKN N	12	.167	.200	30	5	1	0	0	0.0	1	2	1		0	1	0	50	7	3	2	5.5	.950	C-11

Bill Farmer

FARMER, WILLIAM
B. Dec. 27, 1870, Philadelphia, Pa. Deceased. BR TR 5′11½″ 187 lbs.

Year	Team	Games	BA	SA	AB	H	2B	3B	HR	HR%	R	RBI	BB	SO	SB	Pinch Hit AB	Pinch Hit H	PO	A	E	DP	TC/G	FA	G by Pos
1888	2 teams PIT N (2G –.000) PHI AA (3G –.167)																							
″	total	5	.125	.125	16	2	0	0	0	0.0	0	1	0	1	0	0	0	28	4	3	0	7.0	.914	C-4, OF-1

Jack Farmer

FARMER, FLOYD HASKELL
B. July 14, 1892, Granville, Tenn. D. May 21, 1970, Columbia, La. BR TR 6′ 180 lbs.

Year	Team	Games	BA	SA	AB	H	2B	3B	HR	HR%	R	RBI	BB	SO	SB	Pinch Hit AB	Pinch Hit H	PO	A	E	DP	TC/G	FA	G by Pos
1916	PIT N	55	.271	.355	166	45	6	4	0	0.0	10	14	7	24	1	7	0	81	91	15	7	3.6	.920	2B-31, OF-15, SS-5, 3B-1
1918	CLE A	7	.222	.222	9	2	0	0	0	0.0	1	1	0	3	2	4	2	6	10	1	0	3.4	.941	3B-5
2 yrs.		62	.269	.349	175	47	6	4	0	0.0	11	15	7	27	3	11	2	87	101	16	7	3.6	.922	2B-31, OF-15, 3B-6, SS-5

Sid Farrar

FARRAR, SIDNEY DOUGLAS
B. Aug. 10, 1859, Paris Hill, Me. D. May 7, 1935, New York, N. Y. TR 5′10″ 185 lbs.

Year	Team	Games	BA	SA	AB	H	2B	3B	HR	HR%	R	RBI	BB	SO	SB	Pinch Hit AB	Pinch Hit H	PO	A	E	DP	TC/G	FA	G by Pos
1883	PHI N	99	.233	.329	377	88	19	7	1	0.3	41		4	37		0	0	1038	31	39	45	11.2	.965	1B-99
1884		111	.245	.318	428	105	16	6	1	0.2	62		9	25		0	0	1142	42	42	41	11.0	.966	1B-111
1885		111	.245	.329	420	103	20	3	3	0.7	49		28	34		0	0	1153	41	31	50	11.0	.975	1B-111
1886		118	.248	.358	439	109	19	7	5	1.1	55	50	16	47		0	0	1220	45	26	38	10.9	.980	1B-118
1887		116	.282	.395	443	125	20	9	4	0.9	83	72	42	29	24	0	0	1149	46	28	55	10.5	.977	1B-116
1888		131	.244	.325	508	124	24	7	1	0.2	53	53	31	38	21	0	0	1345	53	30	57	10.9	.979	1B-131
1889		130	.268	.342	477	128	22	2	3	0.6	70	58	52	36	28	0	0	1265	42	30	66	10.3	.978	1B-130
1890	PHI P	127	.254	.341	481	122	17	11	1	0.2	84	69	51	23	9	0	0	1238	58	36	79	10.5	.973	1B-127
8 yrs.		943	.253	.342	3573	904	157	52	19	0.5	497	302	233	269	82	0	0	9550	358	262	431	10.8	.974	1B-943

Bill Farrell

FARRELL, WILLIAM
B. Bridgeport, Conn. Deceased.

Year	Team	Games	BA	SA	AB	H	2B	3B	HR	HR%	R	RBI	BB	SO	SB	Pinch Hit AB	Pinch Hit H	PO	A	E	DP	TC/G	FA	G by Pos
1882	PHI AA	2	.286	.429	7	2	1	0	0	0.0	2		1			0	0	0	0	0	0	0.0		OF-2, C-1
1883	BAL AA	2	.000	.000	7	0	0	0	0	0.0	0		1			0	0	1	5	2	1	4.0	.750	SS-2
2 yrs.		4	.143	.214	14	2	1	0	0	0.0	2		2			0	0	1	5	2	1	1.6	.750	OF-2, SS-2, C-1

Doc Farrell

FARRELL, EDWARD STEPHEN
B. Dec. 26, 1901, Johnson City, N. Y. D. Dec. 20, 1966, Livingston, N. J. BR TR 5′8″ 160 lbs.

Year	Team	Games	BA	SA	AB	H	2B	3B	HR	HR%	R	RBI	BB	SO	SB	Pinch Hit AB	Pinch Hit H	PO	A	E	DP	TC/G	FA	G by Pos
1925	NY N	27	.214	.232	56	12	1	0	0	0.0	6	4	4	6	0	3	0	14	46	4	4	3.0	.938	SS-13, 3B-7, 2B-1
1926		67	.287	.392	171	49	10	1	2	1.2	19	23	12	17	4	8	2	111	130	12	23	4.5	.953	SS-53, 2B-3
1927	2 teams NY N (42G –.387) BOS N (110G –.292)																							
″	total	152	.316	.389	566	179	23	3	4	0.7	57	92	26	32	4	4	2	331	454	58	67	5.5	.931	SS-93, 2B-40, 3B-20
1928	BOS N	134	.215	.271	483	104	14	2	3	0.6	36	43	26	26	3	1	0	289	419	51	73	5.7	.933	SS-132, 2B-1
1929	2 teams BOS N (5G –.125) NY N (63G –.213)																							
″	total	68	.210	.242	186	39	6	0	0	0.0	18	18	9	18	2	8	1	95	131	15	21	4.1	.938	3B-28, 2B-26, SS-5
1930	2 teams STL N (23G –.213) CHI N (46G –.292)																							
″	total	69	.264	.333	174	46	7	1	1	0.6	24	22	13	7	1	2	0	114	160	16	32	4.8	.945	SS-53, 2B-7, 1B-1
1932	NY A	26	.175	.222	63	11	1	1	0	0.0	4	4	2	8	0	0	0	39	39	3	9	3.4	.963	2B-16, SS-5, 1B-2, 3B-1
1933		44	.269	.269	93	25	0	0	0	0.0	16	6	16	6	0	0	0	67	77	9	12	3.6	.941	SS-22, 2B-20
1935	BOS A	4	.286	.429	7	2	1	0	0	0.0	1	1	1	0	0	0	0	6	5	1	1	3.0	.917	2B-4
9 yrs.		591	.260	.320	1799	467	63	8	10	0.6	181	213	109	120	14	26	5	1066	1461	169	242	4.9	.937	SS-376, 2B-118, 3B-56, 1B-3

Duke Farrell

FARRELL, CHARLES ANDREW
B. Aug. 31, 1866, Oakdale, Mass. D. Feb. 15, 1925, Boston, Mass. BB TR 6′2″ 180 lbs.

Year	Team	Games	BA	SA	AB	H	2B	3B	HR	HR%	R	RBI	BB	SO	SB	Pinch Hit AB	Pinch Hit H	PO	A	E	DP	TC/G	FA	G by Pos
1888	CHI N	64	.232	.320	241	56	6	3	3	1.2	34	19	4	41	8	0	0	231	53	39	4	5.0	.879	C-33, OF-31, 1B-1
1889		101	.248	.410	407	101	19	7	11	2.7	66	75	41	21	13	0	0	398	123	53	3	5.7	.908	C-76, OF-25
1890	CHI P	117	.290	.404	451	131	21	12	2	0.4	79	84	42	28	8	0	0	587	147	49	21	6.4	.937	C-90, 1B-22, OF-10
1891	BOS AA	122	.302	.474	473	143	19	13	**12**	**2.5**	108	**110**	59	48	21	0	0	305	235	45	15	4.5	.923	3B-66, C-37, OF-23, 1B-4
1892	PIT N	152	.215	.314	605	130	10	13	8	1.3	96	77	46	53	20	0	0	221	291	72	20	3.8	.877	3B-133, OF-20
1893	WAS N	124	.280	.380	511	143	13	13	4	0.8	84	75	47	12	11	0	0	411	232	57	12	5.6	.919	C-81, 3B-41, 1B-3
1894	NY N	114	.284	.424	401	114	20	12	4	1.0	47	66	35	15	9	1	0	510	148	52	14	6.3	.927	C-104, 3B-5, 1B-4
1895		90	.288	.407	312	90	16	9	1	0.3	38	58	38	18	11	2	1	315	115	33	15	5.3	.929	C-62, 3B-24, 1B-2
1896	2 teams NY N (58G –.283) WAS N (37G –.300)																							
″	total	95	.290	.389	321	93	14	6	2	0.6	41	67	26	10	4	**10**	4	219	130	31	14	4.4	.918	C-52, 3B-21, SS-13
1897	WAS N	78	.322	.402	261	84	9	6	0	0.0	41	53	17		8	**14**	**8**	226	92	19	11	5.3	.944	C-63, 1B-1

Duke Farrell *continued*

Year	Team	Games	BA	SA	AB	H	2B	3B	HR	HR%	R	RBI	BB	SO	SB	Pinch Hit AB	Pinch Hit H	PO	A	E	DP	TC/G	FA	G by Pos
1898		99	.314	.393	338	106	12	6	1	0.3	47	53	34		12	10	**5**	434	96	27	22	6.3	.952	C-61, 1B-28
1899	**2 teams**	**WAS N** (5G –.333) **BKN N** (80G –.299)																						
"	**total**	85	.301	.417	266	80	11	7	2	0.8	42	56	37		7	3	1	260	116	20	9	4.8	.949	C-82
1900	**BKN N**	76	.275	.352	273	75	11	5	0	0.0	33	39	11		3	2	0	252	88	20	8	4.9	.944	C-74
1901		80	.296	.384	284	84	10	6	1	0.4	38	31	7		7	4	**3**	443	98	15	16	7.3	.973	C-59, 1B-17
1902		74	.242	.277	264	64	5	2	0	0.0	14	24	12		6	2	0	469	90	12	8	7.8	.979	C-49, 1B-24
1903	**BOS A**	17	.404	.538	52	21	5	1	0	0.0	5	8	5		1	0	0	71	25	4	1	5.9	.960	C-17
1904		68	.212	.278	198	42	9	2	0	0.0	11	15	15		1	**11**	1	234	62	13	6	5.5	.958	C-56
1905		7	.286	.333	21	6	1	0	0	0.0	2	2	1		0	0	0	37	10	0	0	6.7	1.000	C-7
18 yrs.		1563	.275	.383	5679	1563	211	123	51	0.9	826	912	477	246	150	59	23	5623	2151	561	199	5.5	.933	C-1003, 3B-290, OF-109, 1B-106, SS-13
WORLD SERIES																								
1903	**BOS A**	2	.000	.000	2	0	0	0	0	0.0	0	1	0	0	0	2	0	0	0	0	0	0.0	—	

Jack Farrell

FARRELL, JOHN A. (Moose) BR TR 5′ 9″ 165 lbs.
B. July 5, 1857, Newark, N. J. D. Feb. 10, 1914, Overbrook, N. J.
Manager 1881.

Year	Team	Games	BA	SA	AB	H	2B	3B	HR	HR%	R	RBI	BB	SO	SB	Pinch Hit AB	Pinch Hit H	PO	A	E	DP	TC/G	FA	G by Pos
1879	**2 teams**	**SYR N** (54G –.303) **PRO N** (12G –.255)																						
"	**total**	66	.295	.346	292	86	8	2	1	0.3	45	26	3	13		0	0	204	241	61	24	7.7	.879	2B-66
1880	**PRO N**	80	.271	.363	339	92	12	5	3	0.9	46	36	10	6		0	0	207	274	61	26	6.8	.887	2B-80
1881		84	.238	.357	345	82	16	5	5	1.4	69	36	29	23		0	0	216	273	68	40	6.6	.878	2B-82, OF-3
1882		84	.254	.361	366	93	21	6	2	0.5	67		16	23		0	0	212	283	71	41	6.7	.875	2B-84
1883		95	.305	.436	420	128	24	11	3	0.7	92		15	21		0	0	258	365	51	51	7.1	.924	2B-95
1884		111	.217	.277	469	102	13	6	1	0.2	70		35	44		0	0	251	353	54	36	5.9	.918	2B-109, 3B-3
1885		68	.206	.253	257	53	7	1	1	0.4	27	19	10	25		0	0	158	194	39	16	5.8	.900	2B-68
1886	**2 teams**	**PHI N** (17G –.183) **WAS N** (47G –.240)																						
"	**total**	64	.225	.342	231	52	11	5	2	0.9	31	21	18	23		0	0	121	189	39	14	5.5	.888	2B-64
1887	**WAS N**	87	.221	.316	339	75	14	9	0	0.0	40	41	20	12	31	0	0	161	287	55	19	5.7	.891	SS-48, 2B-40
1888	**BAL AA**	103	.204	.299	398	81	19	5	3	0.8	72	36	26		29	0	0	170	354	47	36	5.4	.918	SS-54, 2B-52
1889		42	.210	.248	157	33	3	0	1	0.6	25	26	15	15	14	0	0	65	131	24	13	5.2	.891	SS-42
11 yrs.		884	.243	.332	3613	877	148	55	22	0.6	584	241	197	205	74	0	0	2023	2944	570	316	6.2	.897	2B-740, SS-144, 3B-3, OF-3

Jack Farrell

FARRELL, JOHN J BB TR 5′ 8″ 145 lbs.
B. June 16, 1889, Chicago, Ill. D. Dec. 2, 1918, Chicago, Ill.

Year	Team	Games	BA	SA	AB	H	2B	3B	HR	HR%	R	RBI	BB	SO	SB	Pinch Hit AB	Pinch Hit H	PO	A	E	DP	TC/G	FA	G by Pos
1914	**CHI F**	156	.235	.294	524	123	23	4	0	0.0	58	35	52		12	0	0	361	463	40	54	5.5	.954	2B-155, SS-3
1915		70	.216	.270	222	48	10	1	0	0.0	27	14	25		8	0	0	138	182	20	26	4.8	.941	2B-70, SS-1
2 yrs.		226	.229	.287	746	171	33	5	0	0.0	85	49	77		20	0	0	499	645	60	80	5.3	.950	2B-225, SS-4

Joe Farrell

FARRELL, JOSEPH F. BR 5′ 6″ 160 lbs.
B. 1857, Brooklyn, N. Y. D. Apr. 18, 1893, Brooklyn, N. Y.

Year	Team	Games	BA	SA	AB	H	2B	3B	HR	HR%	R	RBI	BB	SO	SB	Pinch Hit AB	Pinch Hit H	PO	A	E	DP	TC/G	FA	G by Pos
1882	**DET N**	69	.247	.314	283	70	12	2	1	0.4	34	24	4	20		0	0	129	150	49	11	4.8	.851	3B-42, 2B-18, SS-9
1883		101	.243	.295	444	108	13	5	0	0.0	58		5	29		0	0	111	248	66	13	4.2	.845	3B-101
1884		110	.226	.289	461	104	10	5	3	0.7	59		14	66		0	0	126	198	61	12	3.5	.842	3B-110, OF-1
1886	**BAL AA**	73	.209	.266	301	63	8	3	1	0.3	36		12			0	0	111	180	46	9	4.6	.864	2B-45, 3B-27, OF-1
4 yrs.		353	.232	.291	1489	345	43	15	5	0.3	187	24	35	115		0	0	477	776	222	45	4.2	.849	3B-280, 2B-63, SS-9, OF-2

John Farrell

FARRELL, JOHN SEBASTIAN (Little Johnny) BR TR 5′10″ 160 lbs.
B. Dec. 4, 1876, Covington, Ky. D. May 14, 1921, Kansas City, Mo.

Year	Team	Games	BA	SA	AB	H	2B	3B	HR	HR%	R	RBI	BB	SO	SB	Pinch Hit AB	Pinch Hit H	PO	A	E	DP	TC/G	FA	G by Pos
1901	**WAS A**	135	.272	.386	555	151	32	11	3	0.5	100	63	52		25	0	0	332	262	54	46	4.8	.917	2B-72, OF-62, 3B-1
1902	**STL N**	138	.250	.290	565	141	13	5	0	0.0	68	25	43		9	0	0	337	501	49	76	6.4	.945	2B-118, SS-21
1903		130	.272	.356	519	141	25	8	1	0.2	83	32	48		17	0	0	320	399	54	52	5.9	.930	2B-118, OF-12
1904		131	.255	.312	509	130	23	3	0	0.0	72	20	46		16	1	0	297	450	53	55	6.2	.934	2B-130
1905		7	.167	.250	24	4	0	1	0	0.0	6	1	4		1	0	0	19	14	4	0	5.3	.892	2B-7
5 yrs.		541	.261	.335	2172	567	93	28	4	0.2	329	141	193		68	1	0	1305	1626	214	229	5.8	.932	2B-445, OF-74, SS-21, 3B-1

Kerby Farrell

FARRELL, MAJOR KERBY BL TL 5′11″ 172 lbs.
B. Sept. 3, 1913, Leapwood, Tenn. D. Dec. 17, 1975, Nashville, Tenn.
Manager 1957.

Year	Team	Games	BA	SA	AB	H	2B	3B	HR	HR%	R	RBI	BB	SO	SB	Pinch Hit AB	Pinch Hit H	PO	A	E	DP	TC/G	FA	G by Pos
1943	**BOS N**	85	.268	.325	280	75	14	1	0	0.0	11	21	16	15	1	11	2	740	55	4	62	10.8	.995	1B-69, P-5
1945	**CHI A**	103	.258	.301	396	102	11	3	0	0.0	44	34	24	18	4	6	3	913	74	11	76	10.3	.989	1B-97
2 yrs.		188	.262	.311	676	177	25	4	0	0.0	55	55	40	33	5	17	5	1653	129	15	138	10.5	.992	1B-166, P-5

John Farrow

FARROW, JOHN JACOB BL TR
B. Nov. 8, 1853, Verplanc Point, N. Y. D. Dec. 31, 1914, Perth Amboy, N. J.

Year	Team	Games	BA	SA	AB	H	2B	3B	HR	HR%	R	RBI	BB	SO	SB	Pinch Hit AB	Pinch Hit H	PO	A	E	DP	TC/G	FA	G by Pos
1884	**BKN AA**	16	.190	.224	58	11	2	0	0	0.0	7		3			0	0	82	25	10	1	7.3	.915	C-16

Buck Fausett

FAUSETT, ROBERT SHAW (Leaky) BL TR 5′10″ 170 lbs.
B. Apr. 8, 1908, Sheridan, Ark. D. May 2, 1994, College Station, Tex.

Year	Team	Games	BA	SA	AB	H	2B	3B	HR	HR%	R	RBI	BB	SO	SB	Pinch Hit AB	Pinch Hit H	PO	A	E	DP	TC/G	FA	G by Pos
1944	**CIN N**	13	.097	.161	31	3	0	1	0	0.0	2	1	1	2	0	5	0	6	23	1	1	3.8	.967	3B-6, P-2

Joe Fautsch

FAUTSCH, JOSEPH ROAMAN BR TR 5′10″ 162 lbs.
B. Feb. 28, 1887, Minneapolis, Minn. D. Mar. 16, 1971, New Hope, Minn.

Year	Team	Games	BA	SA	AB	H	2B	3B	HR	HR%	R	RBI	BB	SO	SB	Pinch Hit AB	Pinch Hit H	PO	A	E	DP	TC/G	FA	G by Pos
1916	**CHI A**	1	.000	.000	1	0	0	0	0	0.0	0	0	0	0	0	1	0	0	0	0	0	0.0	—	

Ernie Fazio

FAZIO, ERNEST JOSEPH BR TR 5′ 7″ 165 lbs.
B. Jan. 25, 1942, Oakland, Calif.

Year	Team	Games	BA	SA	AB	H	2B	3B	HR	HR%	R	RBI	BB	SO	SB	Pinch Hit AB	Pinch Hit H	PO	A	E	DP	TC/G	FA	G by Pos
1962	**HOU N**	12	.083	.083	12	1	0	0	0	0.0	3	1	2	5	0	1	0	5	13	5	1	2.3	.783	SS-10
1963		102	.184	.281	228	42	10	3	2	0.9	31	5	27	70	4	9	2	132	145	8	18	3.3	.972	2B-84, SS-1, 3B-1
1966	**KC A**	27	.206	.265	34	7	0	1	0	0.0	3	2	4	10	1	12	1	8	24	0	4	2.3	1.000	2B-10, SS-4
3 yrs.		141	.182	.270	274	50	10	4	2	0.7	37	8	33	85	5	22	3	145	182	13	23	3.1	.962	2B-94, SS-15, 3B-1

Al Federoff

FEDEROFF, ALFRED (Whitey)
B. July 11, 1924, Bairdford, Pa.

BR TR 5′10½″ 165 lbs.

Year	Team	Games	BA	SA	AB	H	2B	3B	HR	HR%	R	RBI	BB	SO	SB	Pinch Hit AB	Pinch Hit H	PO	A	E	DP	TC/G	FA	G by Pos
1951	DET A	2	.000	.000	4	0	0	0	0	0.0	0	0	0	0	0	0	0	3	5	1	0	9.0	.889	2B-1
1952		74	.242	.277	231	56	4	2	0	0.0	14	14	16	13	1	0	0	148	203	9	45	4.7	.975	2B-70, SS-7
2 yrs.		76	.238	.272	235	56	4	2	0	0.0	14	14	16	13	1	0	0	151	208	10	45	4.7	.973	2B-71, SS-7

Bill Fehring

FEHRING, WILLIAM PAUL (Dutch)
B. May 31, 1912, Columbus, Ind.

BB TR 6′ 195 lbs.

Year	Team	Games	BA	SA	AB	H	2B	3B	HR	HR%	R	RBI	BB	SO	SB	Pinch Hit AB	Pinch Hit H	PO	A	E	DP	TC/G	FA	G by Pos
1934	CHI A	1	.000	.000	1	0	0	0	0	0.0	0	0	0	1	0	0	0	2	0	0	0	2.0	1.000	C-1

Eddie Feinberg

FEINBERG, EDWARD ISADORE (Itzy)
B. Sept. 20, 1918, Philadelphia, Pa. D. Apr. 20, 1986, Hollywood, Fla.

BB TR 5′ 9″ 165 lbs.

Year	Team	Games	BA	SA	AB	H	2B	3B	HR	HR%	R	RBI	BB	SO	SB	Pinch Hit AB	Pinch Hit H	PO	A	E	DP	TC/G	FA	G by Pos
1938	PHI N	10	.150	.150	20	3	0	0	0	0.0	0	0	0	1	0	0	0	15	13	1	3	4.8	.966	SS-4, OF-2
1939		6	.222	.278	18	4	1	0	0	0.0	2	0	2	0	0	0	0	4	6	1	2	2.2	.909	2B-4, SS-1
2 yrs.		16	.184	.211	38	7	1	0	0	0.0	2	0	2	1	0	0	0	19	19	2	5	3.6	.950	SS-5, 2B-4, OF-2

Mike Felder

FELDER, MICHAEL OTIS
B. Nov. 18, 1961, Vallejo, Calif.

BB TR 5′ 8″ 160 lbs.

Year	Team	Games	BA	SA	AB	H	2B	3B	HR	HR%	R	RBI	BB	SO	SB	Pinch Hit AB	Pinch Hit H	PO	A	E	DP	TC/G	FA	G by Pos
1985	MIL A	15	.196	.214	56	11	1	0	0	0.0	8	0	5	6	4	1	1	32	1	0	0	2.4	1.000	OF-14
1986		44	.239	.323	155	37	2	4	1	0.6	24	13	13	16	16	0	0	98	0	0	0	2.3	1.000	OF-42, DH-1
1987		108	.266	.353	289	77	5	7	2	0.7	48	31	28	23	34	7	1	190	10	5	3	2.0	.976	OF-99, DH-3, 2B-1
1988		50	.173	.185	81	14	1	0	0	0.0	14	5	0	11	8	2	0	40	1	1	0	0.9	.976	OF-28, DH-16, 2B-1
1989		117	.241	.324	315	76	11	3	3	1.0	50	23	23	38	26	7	3	203	24	4	7	2.0	.983	OF-93, DH-11, 2B-10
1990		121	.274	.359	237	65	7	2	3	1.3	38	27	22	17	20	8	1	167	9	5	6	1.6	.972	OF-109, 3B-1, 2B-1, DH-1
1991	SF N	132	.264	.328	348	92	10	6	0	0.0	51	18	30	31	21	36	10	193	10	4	3	1.9	.981	OF-107, 3B-3, 2B-1
1992		145	.286	.382	322	92	13	3	4	1.2	44	23	21	29	14	49	11	159	3	1	0	1.5	.994	OF-105, 2B-3
1993	SEA A	109	.211	.269	342	72	7	5	1	0.3	31	20	22	34	15	23	3	143	12	2	1	1.5	.987	OF-95, DH-6, 3B-2
1994	HOU N	58	.239	.291	117	28	2	2	0	0.0	10	13	4	12	3	27	5	36	2	1	0	1.2	.974	OF-32
10 yrs.		899	.249	.322	2262	564	59	32	14	0.6	318	173	168	217	161	160	35	1261	72	23	20	1.7	.983	OF-724, DH-38, 2B-17, 3B-6

Marv Felderman

FELDERMAN, MARVIN WILFRED (Coonie)
B. Dec. 20, 1915, Bellevue, Iowa.

BR TR 6′ 1″ 187 lbs.

Year	Team	Games	BA	SA	AB	H	2B	3B	HR	HR%	R	RBI	BB	SO	SB	Pinch Hit AB	Pinch Hit H	PO	A	E	DP	TC/G	FA	G by Pos
1942	CHI N	3	.167	.167	6	1	0	0	0	0.0	0	0	1	4	0	0	0	8	2	0	0	5.0	1.000	C-2

Gus Felix

FELIX, AUGUST GUENTHER
B. May 24, 1895, Cincinnati, Ohio D. May 12, 1960, Montgomery, Ala.

BR TR 6′ 180 lbs.

Year	Team	Games	BA	SA	AB	H	2B	3B	HR	HR%	R	RBI	BB	SO	SB	Pinch Hit AB	Pinch Hit H	PO	A	E	DP	TC/G	FA	G by Pos
1923	BOS N	139	.273	.350	506	138	17	2	6	1.2	64	44	51	65	8	3	1	293	28	17	4	2.6	.950	OF-123, 2B-5, 3B-4
1924		59	.211	.270	204	43	7	1	1	0.5	25	10	18	16	0	3	2	147	6	8	1	3.2	.950	OF-51
1925		121	.307	.405	459	141	25	7	2	0.4	60	66	30	34	5	7	1	328	15	10	3	3.1	.972	OF-114
1926	BKN N	134	.280	.382	432	121	21	7	3	0.7	64	53	51	32	9	8	1	270	11	13	2	2.4	.956	OF-125
1927		130	.265	.348	445	118	21	8	0	0.0	43	57	39	47	6	11	4	221	13	13	1	2.1	.947	OF-119
5 yrs.		583	.274	.361	2046	561	91	25	12	0.6	256	230	189	194	28	32	9	1259	73	61	11	2.6	.956	OF-532, 2B-5, 3B-4

Junior Felix

FELIX, JUNIOR FRANCISCO
Born Junior Francisco Felix (Sanchez).
B. Oct. 3, 1967, Laguna Salada, Dominican Republic.

BB TR 6′ 170 lbs.

Year	Team	Games	BA	SA	AB	H	2B	3B	HR	HR%	R	RBI	BB	SO	SB	Pinch Hit AB	Pinch Hit H	PO	A	E	DP	TC/G	FA	G by Pos
1989	TOR A	110	.258	.395	415	107	14	8	9	2.2	62	46	33	101	18	2	0	243	9	9	0	2.4	.966	OF-107, DH-2
1990		127	.263	.441	463	122	23	7	15	3.2	73	65	45	99	13	2	0	244	11	9	3	2.1	.966	OF-125, DH-1
1991	CAL A	66	.283	.370	230	65	10	2	2	0.9	32	26	11	55	7	1	0	126	1	3	0	2.0	.977	OF-65
1992		139	.246	.361	509	125	22	5	9	1.8	63	72	33	128	8	7	1	340	9	6	3	2.6	.983	OF-128, DH-8
1993	FLA N	57	.238	.397	214	51	11	1	7	3.3	25	22	10	50	2	5	1	91	3	6	0	1.9	.940	OF-52
1994	DET A	86	.306	.525	301	92	25	1	13	4.3	54	49	26	76	1	4	0	188	4	4	0	2.4	.980	OF-81, DH-2
6 yrs.		585	.264	.413	2132	562	105	24	55	2.6	309	280	158	509	49	21	2	1232	37	37	6	2.3	.972	OF-558, DH-13
LEAGUE CHAMPIONSHIP SERIES																								
1989	TOR A	3	.273	.364	11	3	1	0	0	0.0	0	3	0	2	0	0	0	8	0	0	0	2.7	1.000	OF-3

Jack Feller

FELLER, JACK LELAND
B. Dec. 10, 1936, Adrian, Mich.

BR TR 5′10½″ 185 lbs.

Year	Team	Games	BA	SA	AB	H	2B	3B	HR	HR%	R	RBI	BB	SO	SB	Pinch Hit AB	Pinch Hit H	PO	A	E	DP	TC/G	FA	G by Pos
1958	DET A	1	—	—	0	0	0	0	0	—	0	0	0	0	0	0	0	1	0	0	0	1.0	1.000	C-1

Happy Felsch

FELSCH, OSCAR EMIL
B. Aug. 22, 1891, Milwaukee, Wis. D. Aug. 17, 1964, Milwaukee, Wis.

BR TR 5′11″ 175 lbs.

Year	Team	Games	BA	SA	AB	H	2B	3B	HR	HR%	R	RBI	BB	SO	SB	Pinch Hit AB	Pinch Hit H	PO	A	E	DP	TC/G	FA	G by Pos
1915	CHI A	121	.248	.363	427	106	18	11	3	0.7	65	53	51	59	16	3	0	247	9	11	1	2.3	.959	OF-118
1916		146	.300	.427	546	164	24	12	7	1.3	73	70	31	67	13	4	2	340	19	7	5	2.6	.981	OF-141
1917		152	.308	.403	575	177	17	10	6	1.0	75	102	33	52	26	0	0	440	24	7	5	3.1	.985	OF-152
1918		53	.252	.325	206	52	2	5	1	0.5	16	20	15	13	6	0	0	149	7	7	5	3.1	.957	OF-53
1919		135	.275	.428	502	138	34	11	7	1.4	68	86	40	35	19	0	0	360	32	13	15	3.0	.968	OF-135
1920		142	.338	.540	556	188	40	15	14	2.5	88	115	37	25	8	0	0	385	25	8	10	2.9	.981	OF-142
6 yrs.		749	.293	.427	2812	825	135	64	38	1.4	385	446	207	251	88	7	2	1921	116	53	41	2.8	.975	OF-741
WORLD SERIES																								
1917	CHI A	6	.273	.455	22	6	1	0	1	4.5	4	3	1	5	0	0	0	16	2	0	1	3.0	1.000	OF-6
1919		8	.192	.231	26	5	1	0	0	0.0	2	3	1	4	0	0	0	23	1	2	1	3.3	.923	OF-8
2 yrs.		14	.229	.333	48	11	2	0	1	2.1	6	6	2	9	0	0	0	39	3	2	2	3.1	.955	OF-14

John Felske

FELSKE, JOHN FREDERICK
B. May 30, 1942, Chicago, Ill.
Manager 1985–87.

BR TR 6′ 3″ 195 lbs.

Year	Team	Games	BA	SA	AB	H	2B	3B	HR	HR%	R	RBI	BB	SO	SB	Pinch Hit AB	Pinch Hit H	PO	A	E	DP	TC/G	FA	G by Pos
1968	CHI N	4	.000	.000	2	0	0	0	0	0.0	0	0	0	1	0	1	0	5	0	1	0	2.0	.833	C-3
1972	MIL A	37	.138	.212	80	11	3	0	1	1.3	6	5	8	23	0	8	2	124	9	3	5	4.4	.978	C-23, 1B-8
1973		13	.136	.227	22	3	0	1	0	0.0	1	4	1	11	0	1	0	41	4	0	1	3.5	1.000	C-7, 1B-6
3 yrs.		54	.135	.212	104	14	3	1	1	1.0	7	9	9	35	0	10	2	170	13	4	6	4.0	.979	C-33, 1B-14

Frank Fennelly

FENNELLY, FRANCIS JOHN
B. Feb. 18, 1860, Fall River, Mass. D. Aug. 4, 1920, Fall River, Mass.
BR TR 5′ 8″ 168 lbs.

Year	Team	Games	BA	SA	AB	H	2B	3B	HR	HR%	R	RBI	BB	SO	SB	Pinch Hit AB	Pinch Hit H	PO	A	E	DP	TC/G	FA	G by Pos
1884	2 teams WAS AA (62G –.292) CIN AA (28G –.352)																							
"	total	90	.311	.480	379	118	22	15	4	1.1	94		31			0	0	124	310	75	27	5.5	.853	SS-88, 2B-4
1885	CIN AA	112	.273	.445	454	124	14	17	10	2.2	82		38			0	0	151	359	74	46	5.2	.873	SS-112
1886		132	.249	.380	497	124	13	17	6	1.2	113		60			0	0	169	485	117	54	5.8	.848	SS-132
1887		134	.266	.401	526	140	15	16	8	1.5	133		82		74	0	0	161	421	99	31	5.1	.855	SS-134
1888	2 teams CIN AA (120G –.196) PHI AA (15G –.234)																							
"	total	135	.200	.275	495	99	10	9	3	0.6	77	68	72		48	0	0	184	476	106	41	5.7	.862	SS-127, OF-4, 2B-4
1889	PHI AA	138	.257	.322	513	132	20	5	1	0.2	70	64	65	78	15	0	0	181	453	93	53	5.3	.872	SS-138
1890	BKN AA	45	.247	.360	178	44	8	3	2	1.1	40		30		6	0	0	80	156	38	12	6.1	.861	SS-38, 3B-7
7 yrs.		786	.257	.378	3042	781	102	82	34	1.1	609	132	378	78	143	0	0	1050	2660	602	264	5.5	.860	SS-769, 2B-8, 3B-7, OF-4

Bobby Fenwick

FENWICK, ROBERT RICHARD (Bloop)
B. Dec. 10, 1946, Naha, Okinawa.
BR TR 5′ 9″ 165 lbs.

Year	Team	Games	BA	SA	AB	H	2B	3B	HR	HR%	R	RBI	BB	SO	SB	Pinch Hit AB	Pinch Hit H	PO	A	E	DP	TC/G	FA	G by Pos
1972	HOU N	36	.180	.240	50	9	3	0	0	0.0	7	4	3	13	0	5	0	22	37	3	12	2.7	.952	2B-17, SS-4, 3B-2
1973	STL N	5	.167	.167	6	1	0	0	0	0.0	0	1	0	2	0	2	0	2	1	1	2	1.3	.750	2B-3
2 yrs.		41	.179	.232	56	10	3	0	0	0.0	7	5	3	15	0	7	0	24	38	4	14	2.5	.939	2B-20, SS-4, 3B-2

Bob Ferguson

FERGUSON, ROBERT VAVASOUR (Death to Flying Things)
B. Jan. 31, 1845, Brooklyn, N. Y. D. May 3, 1894, Brooklyn, N. Y.
Manager 1876–84, 1886–87.
BB TR 5′ 9½″ 149 lbs.

Year	Team	Games	BA	SA	AB	H	2B	3B	HR	HR%	R	RBI	BB	SO	SB	Pinch Hit AB	Pinch Hit H	PO	A	E	DP	TC/G	FA	G by Pos
1876	HAR N	69	.265	.323	310	82	8	5	0	0.0	48	32	2	11		0	0	124	133	54	5	4.5	.826	3B-69
1877		58	.256	.299	254	65	7	2	0	0.0	40	35	3	10		0	0	113	159	51	6	5.5	.842	3B-56, P-3
1878	CHI N	61	.351	.405	259	91	10	2	0	0.0	44	39	10	12		0	0	91	238	46	17	6.0	.877	SS-57, 2B-4, C-1
1879	TRO N	30	.252	.325	123	31	5	2	0	0.0	18	4	4	3		0	0	53	81	25	9	5.3	.843	3B-24, 2B-6
1880		82	.262	.289	332	87	9	0	0	0.0	55	22	**24**	24		0	0	294	255	58	38	7.4	.904	2B-82
1881		85	.283	.360	339	96	13	5	1	0.3	56	35	29	12		0	0	263	254	55	47	6.7	.904	2B-85
1882		81	.257	.317	319	82	15	2	0	0.0	44	33	23	21		0	0	248	227	50	38	6.5	.905	2B-79, SS-2
1883	PHI N	86	.258	.298	329	85	9	2	0	0.0	39		18	21		0	0	261	288	88	38	7.3	.862	2B-86, P-1
1884	PIT AA	10	.146	.146	41	6	0	0	0	0.0	2		0			0	0	41	0	6	0	4.7	.872	OF-6, 1B-3, 3B-1
9 yrs.		562	.271	.323	2306	625	76	20	1	0.0	346	200	113	114		0	0	1488	1635	433	198	6.3	.878	2B-342, 3B-150, SS-59, OF-6, P-4, 1B-3, C-1

Charlie Ferguson

FERGUSON, CHARLES J.
B. Apr. 17, 1863, Charlottesville, Va. D. Apr. 29, 1888, Philadelphia, Pa.
BB TR 6′ 165 lbs.

Year	Team	Games	BA	SA	AB	H	2B	3B	HR	HR%	R	RBI	BB	SO	SB	Pinch Hit AB	Pinch Hit H	PO	A	E	DP	TC/G	FA	G by Pos
1884	PHI N	52	.246	.305	203	50	6	3	0	0.0	26		19	54		0	0	35	73	13	4	2.2	.893	P-50, OF-5
1885		61	.306	.379	235	72	8	3	1	0.4	42		23	18		0	0	56	89	15	3	2.5	.906	P-48, OF-15
1886		72	.253	.318	261	66	9	1	2	0.8	56	25	37	28		0	0	72	101	14	1	2.5	.925	P-48, OF-27
1887		72	.337	.470	264	89	14	6	3	1.1	67	85	34	19	13	0	0	93	130	22	11	3.3	.910	P-37, 2B-27, OF-6, 3B-5
4 yrs.		257	.288	.372	963	277	37	13	6	0.6	191	110	113	119	13	0	0	256	393	64	19	2.7	.910	P-183, OF-53, 2B-27, 3B-5

Joe Ferguson

FERGUSON, JOSEPH VANCE
B. Sept. 19, 1946, San Francisco, Calif.
BR TR 6′ 2″ 200 lbs.

Year	Team	Games	BA	SA	AB	H	2B	3B	HR	HR%	R	RBI	BB	SO	SB	Pinch Hit AB	Pinch Hit H	PO	A	E	DP	TC/G	FA	G by Pos
1970	LA N	5	.250	.250	4	1	0	0	0	0.0	0	1	2	2	0	0	0	9	0	0	0	3.0	1.000	C-3
1971		36	.216	.304	102	22	3	0	2	2.0	13	7	12	15	1	2	1	167	9	3	0	5.1	.983	C-35
1972		8	.292	.542	24	7	3	0	1	4.2	2	5	2	4	0	0	0	42	1	0	1	4.8	1.000	C-7, OF-2
1973		136	.263	.470	487	128	26	0	25	5.1	84	88	87	81	1	1	1	786	57	5	17	6.0	.994	C-122, OF-20
1974		111	.252	.436	349	88	14	1	16	4.6	54	57	75	73	2	6	0	486	40	7	2	4.7	.987	C-82, OF-32
1975		66	.208	.302	202	42	2	1	5	2.5	15	23	35	47	2	8	4	215	20	2	4	3.4	.992	C-35, OF-34
1976	2 teams LA N (54G –.222) STL N (71G –.201)																							
"	total	125	.211	.353	374	79	15	4	10	2.7	46	39	57	81	6	14	2	409	44	14	8	4.0	.970	C-65, OF-53
1977	HOU N	132	.257	.435	421	108	21	3	16	3.8	59	61	85	79	6	12	2	644	80	11	10	6.0	.985	C-122, 1B-1
1978	2 teams HOU N (51G –.207) LA N (67G –.237)																							
"	total	118	.224	.391	348	78	16	0	14	4.0	40	50	71	71	1	5	1	573	52	7	2	5.4	.989	C-113, OF-3
1979	LA N	122	.262	.466	363	95	14	0	20	5.5	54	69	70	68	1	9	1	414	37	9	8	3.9	.980	C-67, OF-52
1980		77	.238	.436	172	41	3	2	9	5.2	20	29	38	46	2	14	2	297	23	7	4	4.9	.979	C-66, OF-1
1981	2 teams LA N (17G –.143) CAL A (12G –.233)																							
"	total	29	.205	.318	44	9	2	0	1	2.3	7	6	11	13	0	13	0	41	5	1	1	3.6	.979	C-8, OF-5
1982	CAL A	36	.226	.357	84	19	2	0	3	3.6	10	8	12	19	0	0	0	139	13	1	2	4.5	.993	C-32, OF-2
1983		12	.074	.074	27	2	0	0	0	0.0	3	2	5	8	0	0	0	31	3	1	0	2.9	.971	C-9, OF-3
14 yrs.		1013	.240	.409	3001	719	121	11	122	4.1	407	445	562	607	22	84	14	4253	384	68	59	4.8	.986	C-766, OF-207, 1B-1
LEAGUE CHAMPIONSHIP SERIES																								
1974	LA N	4	.231	.231	13	3	0	0	0	0.0	3	2	5	1	0	0	0	9	0	1	0	2.0	.900	OF-3, C-2
1978		2	.000	.000	2	0	0	0	0	0.0	0	0	0	1	0	2	0	0	0	0	0	0.0	—	
2 yrs.		6	.200	.200	15	3	0	0	0	0.0	3	2	5	2	0	2	0	9	0	1	0	2.0	.900	OF-3, C-2
WORLD SERIES																								
1974	LA N	5	.125	.313	16	2	0	0	1	6.3	2	2	4	6	1	0	0	10	0	2	0	2.0	.833	OF-4, C-2
1978		2	.500	1.000	4	2	2	0	0	0.0	1	0	0	1	0	0	0	11	0	1	0	6.0	.917	C-2
2 yrs.		7	.200	.450	20	4	2	0	1	5.0	3	2	4	7	1	0	0	21	0	3	0	3.0	.875	C-4, OF-4

Felix Fermin

FERMIN, FELIX JOSE
Born Felix Jose Fermin (Minaya).
B. Oct. 9, 1963, Mao Valverde, Dominican Republic.
BR TR 5′11″ 160 lbs.

Year	Team	Games	BA	SA	AB	H	2B	3B	HR	HR%	R	RBI	BB	SO	SB	Pinch Hit AB	Pinch Hit H	PO	A	E	DP	TC/G	FA	G by Pos
1987	PIT N	23	.250	.250	68	17	0	0	0	0.0	6	4	4	9	0	0	0	36	62	2	13	4.3	.980	SS-23
1988		43	.276	.322	87	24	0	2	0	0.0	9	2	8	10	3	1	0	51	76	6	14	3.1	.955	SS-43
1989	CLE A	156	.238	.260	484	115	9	1	0	0.0	50	21	41	27	6	0	0	253	517	26	84	5.1	.967	SS-153, 2B-2
1990		148	.256	.304	414	106	13	2	1	0.2	47	40	26	22	3	0	0	214	423	16	81	4.4	.975	SS-147, 2B-1
1991		129	.262	.302	424	111	13	2	0	0.0	30	31	26	27	5	0	0	214	372	12	74	4.6	.980	SS-129
1992		79	.270	.321	215	58	7	2	0	0.0	27	13	18	10	0	2	1	79	168	8	42	3.1	.969	SS-55, 3B-17, 2B-7, 1B-2
1993		140	.263	.317	480	126	16	2	2	0.4	48	45	24	14	4	0	0	211	346	23	87	4.1	.960	SS-140
1994	SEA A	101	.317	.380	379	120	21	0	1	0.3	52	35	11	22	4	0	0	168	251	10	57	4.2	.977	SS-77, 2B-25
1995		73	.195	.225	200	39	6	0	0	0.0	21	15	6	6	2	0	0	107	168	6	41	3.7	.979	SS-46, 2B-29
9 yrs.		892	.260	.304	2751	716	85	11	4	0.1	290	206	164	147	27	3	1	1333	2383	109	493	4.3	.972	SS-813, 2B-64, 3B-17, 1B-2

Felix Fermin *continued*

DIVISIONAL PLAYOFF SERIES

Year	Team	Games	BA	SA	AB	H	2B	3B	HR	HR%	R	RBI	BB	SO	SB	Pinch Hit AB	Pinch Hit H	PO	A	E	DP	TC/G	FA	G by Pos
1995	SEA A	3	.000	.000	1	0	0	0	0	0.0	0	0	0	1	0	0	0	3	3	0	1	2.0	1.000	SS-2, 2B-1

LEAGUE CHAMPIONSHIP SERIES

Year	Team	Games	BA	SA	AB	H	2B	3B	HR	HR%	R	RBI	BB	SO	SB	Pinch Hit AB	Pinch Hit H	PO	A	E	DP	TC/G	FA	G by Pos
1995	SEA A	2	—	—	0	0	0	0	0	—	0	0	0	0	0	0	0	0	0	0	0	0.0		SS-1, 2B-1

Ed Fernandes

FERNANDES, EDWARD PAUL
B. Mar. 11, 1918, Oakland, Calif. D. Nov. 27, 1968, Hayward, Calif.
BB TR 5′ 9″ 185 lbs.

Year	Team	Games	BA	SA	AB	H	2B	3B	HR	HR%	R	RBI	BB	SO	SB	Pinch Hit AB	Pinch Hit H	PO	A	E	DP	TC/G	FA	G by Pos
1940	PIT N	28	.121	.152	33	4	1	0	0	0.0	1	2	7	6	0	1	0	47	5	1	1	2.0	.981	C-27
1946	CHI A	14	.250	.313	32	8	2	0	0	0.0	4	4	8	7	0	2	0	41	6	4	1	4.3	.922	C-12
2 yrs.		42	.185	.231	65	12	3	0	0	0.0	5	6	15	13	0	3	0	88	11	5	2	2.7	.952	C-39

Chico Fernandez

FERNANDEZ, HUMBERTO
Born Humberto Fernandez (Perez).
B. Mar. 2, 1932, Havana, Cuba.
BR TR 6′ 165 lbs.

Year	Team	Games	BA	SA	AB	H	2B	3B	HR	HR%	R	RBI	BB	SO	SB	Pinch Hit AB	Pinch Hit H	PO	A	E	DP	TC/G	FA	G by Pos
1956	BKN N	34	.227	.303	66	15	2	0	1	1.5	11	9	3	10	2	1	0	34	56	2	11	3.7	.978	SS-25
1957	PHI N	149	.262	.336	500	131	14	4	5	1.0	42	51	31	64	18	0	0	241	377	26	69	4.3	.960	SS-149
1958		148	.230	.318	522	120	18	5	6	1.1	38	51	37	48	12	0	0	296	415	18	88	4.9	.975	SS-148
1959		45	.211	.268	123	26	5	1	0	0.0	15	3	10	11	2	0	0	77	86	7	23	4.0	.959	SS-40, 2B-2
1960	DET A	133	.241	.313	435	105	13	3	4	0.9	44	35	39	50	13	2	0	226	381	34	67	4.9	.947	SS-130
1961		133	.248	.322	435	108	15	4	3	0.7	41	40	36	45	8	4	2	217	322	23	59	4.4	.959	SS-121, 3B-8
1962		141	.249	.410	503	125	17	2	20	4.0	64	59	42	69	10	1	0	239	338	24	53	4.3	.960	SS-138, 3B-2, 1B-1
1963	2 teams	DET A (15G –.143)	NY N (58G –.200)																					
″	total	73	.186	.237	194	36	7	0	1	0.5	15	11	15	41	3	15	1	99	131	15	25	3.7	.939	SS-59, 3B-5, 2B-3
8 yrs.		856	.240	.329	2778	666	91	19	40	1.4	270	259	213	338	68	23	3	1429	2106	149	395	4.4	.960	SS-810, 3B-15, 2B-5, 1B-1

Chico Fernandez

FERNANDEZ, LORENZO MARTO
Born Lorenzo Marto Fernandez (Mosquera).
B. Apr. 23, 1939, Havana, Cuba.
BR TR 5′10″ 160 lbs.

Year	Team	Games	BA	SA	AB	H	2B	3B	HR	HR%	R	RBI	BB	SO	SB	Pinch Hit AB	Pinch Hit H	PO	A	E	DP	TC/G	FA	G by Pos
1968	BAL A	24	.111	.111	18	2	0	0	0	0.0	0	0	1	2	0	9	2	6	9	1	2	1.5	.938	SS-7, 2B-4

Frank Fernandez

FERNANDEZ, FRANK
B. Apr. 16, 1943, Staten Island, N. Y.
BR TR 6′ 185 lbs.

Year	Team	Games	BA	SA	AB	H	2B	3B	HR	HR%	R	RBI	BB	SO	SB	Pinch Hit AB	Pinch Hit H	PO	A	E	DP	TC/G	FA	G by Pos
1967	NY A	9	.214	.393	28	6	2	0	1	3.6	1	4	2	7	1	0	0	43	4	0	0	5.2	1.000	C-7, OF-2
1968		51	.170	.385	135	23	6	1	7	5.2	15	30	35	50	1	1	0	245	28	3	2	5.6	.989	C-45, OF-4
1969		89	.223	.415	229	51	6	1	12	5.2	34	29	65	68	1	11	1	336	30	3	2	4.7	.992	C-65, OF-14
1970	OAK A	94	.214	.413	252	54	5	0	15	6.0	30	44	40	76	1	14	5	407	25	3	6	5.6	.993	C-76, OF-1
1971	3 teams	OAK A (4G –.111)	WAS A (18G –.100)	CHI N (17G –.171)																				
″	total	39	.138	.313	80	11	2	0	4	5.0	12	9	22	28	0	14	1	114	8	2	0	4.8	.984	C-20, OF-6
1972	CHI N	3	.000	.000	3	0	0	0	0	0.0	0	0	0	2	0	2	0	1	0	0	0	1.0	1.000	C-1
6 yrs.		285	.199	.395	727	145	21	2	39	5.4	92	116	164	231	4	42	7	1146	95	11	10	5.2	.991	C-214, OF-27

Nanny Fernandez

FERNANDEZ, FROILAN
B. Oct. 25, 1918, Wilmington, Calif.
BR TR 5′ 9″ 170 lbs.

Year	Team	Games	BA	SA	AB	H	2B	3B	HR	HR%	R	RBI	BB	SO	SB	Pinch Hit AB	Pinch Hit H	PO	A	E	DP	TC/G	FA	G by Pos
1942	BOS N	145	.255	.347	577	147	29	3	6	1.0	63	55	38	61	15	3	1	240	210	32	16	3.4	.934	3B-98, OF-44
1946		115	.255	.323	372	95	15	2	2	0.5	37	42	30	44	1	8	1	133	186	21	19	3.0	.938	3B-81, SS-18, OF-14
1947		83	.206	.254	209	43	4	0	2	1.0	16	21	22	20	2	2	0	105	152	18	22	3.6	.935	SS-62, OF-8, 3B-6
1950	PIT N	65	.258	.404	198	51	11	0	6	3.0	23	27	19	17	2	12	6	48	101	12	6	3.1	.925	3B-52
4 yrs.		408	.248	.334	1356	336	59	5	16	1.2	139	145	109	142	20	25	8	526	649	83	63	3.3	.934	3B-237, SS-80, OF-66

Tony Fernandez

FERNANDEZ, OCTAVIO ANTONIO
Born Octavio Antonio Fernando (Castro).
B. June 30, 1962, San Pedro de Macoris, Dominican Republic.
BB TR 6′ 1″ 160 lbs.

Year	Team	Games	BA	SA	AB	H	2B	3B	HR	HR%	R	RBI	BB	SO	SB	Pinch Hit AB	Pinch Hit H	PO	A	E	DP	TC/G	FA	G by Pos
1983	TOR A	15	.265	.353	34	9	1	1	0	0.0	5	2	2	2	0	2	1	16	17	0	6	2.4	1.000	SS-13, DH-1
1984		88	.270	.356	233	63	5	3	3	1.3	29	19	17	15	5	6	1	119	195	9	41	3.8	.972	SS-73, 3B-10, DH-1
1985		161	.289	.390	564	163	31	10	2	0.4	71	51	43	41	13	3	1	283	478	30	109	4.9	.962	SS-160
1986		163	.310	.428	**687**	213	33	9	10	1.5	91	65	27	52	25	1	1	294	445	13	103	4.6	.983	SS-163
1987		146	.322	.426	578	186	29	8	5	0.9	90	67	51	48	32	1	0	270	396	14	88	4.7	.979	SS-146
1988		154	.287	.386	648	186	41	4	5	0.8	76	70	45	65	15	0	0	247	470	14	106	4.7	.981	SS-154
1989		140	.257	.389	573	147	25	9	11	1.9	64	64	29	51	22	0	0	260	475	6	93	5.3	.992	SS-140
1990		161	.276	.391	635	175	27	**17**	4	0.6	84	66	71	70	26	0	0	297	480	9	93	4.9	.989	SS-161
1991	SD N	145	.272	.360	558	152	27	5	4	0.7	81	38	55	74	23	2	0	247	440	20	78	4.9	.972	SS-145
1992		155	.275	.359	622	171	32	4	4	0.6	84	37	56	62	20	0	0	240	405	11	65	4.3	.983	SS-154
1993	2 teams	NY N (48G –.225)	TOR A (94G –.306)																					
″	total	142	.279	.394	526	147	23	11	5	1.0	65	64	56	45	21	0	0	279	410	13	90	4.9	.981	SS-142
1994	CIN N	104	.279	.426	366	102	18	6	8	2.2	50	50	44	40	12	5	1	67	194	4	13	2.5	.985	3B-93, SS-9, 2B-5
1995	NY A	108	.245	.346	384	94	20	2	5	1.3	57	45	42	40	6	0	0	147	283	10	63	4.1	.977	SS-103, 2B-4
13 yrs.		1682	.282	.390	6408	1808	312	89	66	1.0	847	638	538	605	220	20	5	2766	4688	153	948	4.5	.980	SS-1563, 3B-103, 2B-9, DH-2

DIVISIONAL PLAYOFF SERIES

Year	Team	Games	BA	SA	AB	H	2B	3B	HR	HR%	R	RBI	BB	SO	SB	Pinch Hit AB	Pinch Hit H	PO	A	E	DP	TC/G	FA	G by Pos
1995	NY A	5	.238	.333	21	5	2	0	0	0.0	0	0	2	2	0	0	0	9	15	0	2	4.8	1.000	SS-5

LEAGUE CHAMPIONSHIP SERIES

Year	Team	Games	BA	SA	AB	H	2B	3B	HR	HR%	R	RBI	BB	SO	SB	Pinch Hit AB	Pinch Hit H	PO	A	E	DP	TC/G	FA	G by Pos
1985	TOR A	7	.333	.417	24	8	2	0	0	0.0	2	2	1	2	0	0	0	11	14	2	2	3.9	.926	SS-7
1989		5	.350	.500	20	7	3	0	0	0.0	6	1	1	2	5	0	0	9	15	0	3	4.8	1.000	SS-5
1993		6	.318	.318	22	7	0	0	0	0.0	1	1	2	4	0	0	0	12	8	0	5	3.3	1.000	SS-6
3 yrs.		18	.333	.409	66	22	5	0	0	0.0	9	4	4	8	5	0	0	32	37	2	10	3.9	.972	SS-18

WORLD SERIES

Year	Team	Games	BA	SA	AB	H	2B	3B	HR	HR%	R	RBI	BB	SO	SB	Pinch Hit AB	Pinch Hit H	PO	A	E	DP	TC/G	FA	G by Pos
1993	TOR A	6	.333	.381	21	7	1	0	0	0.0	2	9	3	3	0	0	0	11	8	0	4	3.2	1.000	SS-6

Al Ferrara

FERRARA, ALFRED JOHN (The Bull)
B. Dec. 22, 1939, Brooklyn, N. Y.
BR TR 6′ 1″ 200 lbs.

Year	Team	Games	BA	SA	AB	H	2B	3B	HR	HR%	R	RBI	BB	SO	SB	Pinch Hit AB	Pinch Hit H	PO	A	E	DP	TC/G	FA	G by Pos
1963	LA N	21	.159	.227	44	7	0	0	1	2.3	2	1	6	9	0	8	1	18	1	1	0	1.8	.950	OF-11
1965		41	.210	.296	81	17	2	1	1	1.2	5	10	9	20	0	12	3	38	0	3	0	1.5	.927	OF-27
1966		63	.270	.435	115	31	4	0	5	4.3	15	23	9	35	0	31	5	43	0	2	0	1.4	.956	OF-32

Al Ferrara *continued*

Year	Team	Games	BA	SA	AB	H	2B	3B	HR	HR%	R	RBI	BB	SO	SB	Pinch Hit AB	Pinch Hit H	PO	A	E	DP	TC/G	FA	G by Pos
1967		122	.277	.467	347	96	16	1	16	4.6	41	50	33	73	0	28	5	135	1	3	0	1.5	.978	OF-94
1968		2	.143	.143	7	1	0	0	0	0.0	0	0	0	2	0	0	0	1	0	1	0	1.0	.500	OF-2
1969	SD N	138	.260	.440	366	95	22	1	14	3.8	39	56	45	69	0	38	7	131	5	6	2	1.5	.958	OF-96
1970		138	.277	.444	372	103	15	4	13	3.5	44	51	46	63	0	36	9	119	2	4	0	1.3	.968	OF-96
1971	2 teams	SD N (17G –.118)	CIN N (32G –.182)																					
"	total	49	.160	.240	50	8	1	0	1	2.0	2	7	8	15	0	37	6	8	0	0	0	1.1	1.000	OF-7
8 yrs.		574	.259	.423	1382	358	60	7	51	3.7	148	198	156	286	0	190	36	493	9	20	2	1.4	.962	OF-365
WORLD SERIES																								
1966	LA N	1	1.000	1.000	1	1	0	0	0	0.0	0	0	0	0	0	1	1	0	0	0	0	0.0	—	

Mike Ferraro

FERRARO, MICHAEL DENNIS BR TR 5′11″ 175 lbs.
B. Aug. 14, 1944, Kingston, N. Y.
Manager 1983, 1986.

Year	Team	Games	BA	SA	AB	H	2B	3B	HR	HR%	R	RBI	BB	SO	SB	Pinch Hit AB	Pinch Hit H	PO	A	E	DP	TC/G	FA	G by Pos
1966	NY A	10	.179	.179	28	5	0	0	0	0.0	4	0	3	3	0	0	0	4	21	2	3	2.7	.926	3B-10
1968		23	.161	.184	87	14	0	1	0	0.0	5	1	2	17	0	1	0	16	61	2	3	3.6	.975	3B-22
1969	SEA A	5	.000	.000	4	0	0	0	0	0.0	0	0	1	0	0	4	0	0	0	0	0	0.0	—	
1972	MIL A	124	.255	.323	381	97	18	1	2	0.5	19	29	17	41	0	9	2	94	174	14	16	2.4	.950	3B-115, SS-1
4 yrs.		162	.232	.288	500	116	18	2	2	0.4	28	30	23	61	0	14	2	114	256	18	22	2.6	.954	3B-147, SS-1

Rick Ferrell

FERRELL, RICHARD BENJAMIN BR TR 5′10″ 160 lbs.
Brother of Wes Ferrell.
B. Oct. 12, 1905, Durham, N. C. D. July 27, 1995, Bloomfield Hills, Mich.
Hall of Fame 1984.

Year	Team	Games	BA	SA	AB	H	2B	3B	HR	HR%	R	RBI	BB	SO	SB	Pinch Hit AB	Pinch Hit H	PO	A	E	DP	TC/G	FA	G by Pos
1929	STL A	64	.229	.285	144	33	6	1	0	0.0	21	20	32	10	1	16	2	140	35	7	3	4.0	.962	C-45
1930		101	.268	.360	314	84	18	4	1	0.3	43	41	46	10	1	0	0	336	66	7	5	4.0	.983	C-101
1931		117	.306	.427	386	118	30	4	3	0.8	47	57	56	12	2	7	3	412	86	14	11	4.7	.973	C-108
1932		126	.315	.420	438	138	30	5	2	0.5	67	65	66	18	5	6	1	486	78	8	9	4.8	.986	C-120
1933	2 teams	STL A (22G –.250)	BOS A (118G –.297)																					
"	total	140	.290	.373	493	143	21	4	4	0.8	58	77	70	23	4	3	1	591	92	7	10	5.0	.990	C-137
1934	BOS A	132	.297	.389	437	130	29	4	1	0.2	50	48	66	20	0	5	1	531	72	6	7	4.8	.990	C-128
1935		133	.301	.413	458	138	34	4	3	0.7	54	61	65	15	5	4	0	520	79	13	12	4.7	.979	C-131
1936		121	.312	.461	410	128	27	5	8	2.0	59	55	65	17	0	1	0	556	55	8	5	5.1	.987	C-121
1937	2 teams	BOS A (18G –.308)	WAS A (86G –.229)																					
"	total	104	.244	.285	344	84	8	0	2	0.6	39	36	65	22	1	1	0	434	52	6	6	4.8	.988	C-102
1938	WAS A	135	.292	.382	411	120	24	5	1	0.2	55	58	75	17	1	4	0	512	69	11	15	4.5	.981	C-131
1939		87	.281	.336	274	77	13	1	0	0.0	32	31	41	12	1	4	0	327	46	9	9	4.6	.976	C-83
1940		103	.273	.340	326	89	18	2	0	0.0	35	28	47	15	1	4	0	427	67	10	5	5.1	.980	C-99
1941	2 teams	WAS A (21G –.273)	STL A (100G –.252)																					
"	total	121	.256	.336	387	99	19	3	2	0.5	38	36	67	26	3	3	0	425	64	4	12	4.1	.992	C-119
1942	STL A	99	.223	.253	273	61	6	1	0	0.0	20	26	33	13	0	3	0	356	57	6	7	4.4	.986	C-95
1943		74	.239	.273	209	50	7	0	0	0.0	12	20	34	14	0	3	1	327	52	5	7	5.5	.987	C-70
1944	WAS A	99	.277	.316	339	94	11	1	0	0.0	14	25	46	13	2	1	0	403	71	9	8	5.0	.981	C-96
1945		91	.266	.325	286	76	12	1	1	0.3	33	38	43	13	2	8	2	331	64	4	3	4.8	.990	C-83
1947		37	.303	.414	99	30	11	0	0	0.0	10	12	14	7	0	0	0	134	22	1	5	4.2	.994	C-37
18 yrs.		1884	.281	.363	6028	1692	324	45	28	0.5	687	734	931	277	29	73	11	7248	1127	135	139	4.7	.984	C-1806

Wes Ferrell

FERRELL, WESLEY CHEEK BR TR 6′ 2″ 195 lbs.
Brother of Rick Ferrell.
B. Feb. 2, 1908, Greensboro, N. C. D. Dec. 9, 1976, Sarasota, Fla.

Year	Team	Games	BA	SA	AB	H	2B	3B	HR	HR%	R	RBI	BB	SO	SB	Pinch Hit AB	Pinch Hit H	PO	A	E	DP	TC/G	FA	G by Pos
1927	CLE A	1	—	—	0	0	0	0	0	—	0	0	0	0	0	0	0	0	0	0	0	0.0	.000	P-1
1928		2	.250	.750	4	1	0	1	0	0.0	0	0	0	0	0	0	0	1	4	0	0	2.5	1.000	P-2
1929		47	.237	.387	93	22	5	3	1	1.1	12	12	6	28	1	4	2	10	63	2	3	1.7	.973	P-43
1930		53	.297	.415	118	35	8	3	0	0.0	19	14	12	15	0	7	3	19	39	2	0	1.4	.967	P-43
1931		48	.319	.621	116	37	6	1	9	7.8	24	30	10	21	0	7	0	19	74	3	3	2.4	.969	P-40
1932		55	.242	.359	128	31	5	2	2	1.6	14	18	6	21	0	17	4	14	59	1	5	1.9	.986	P-38
1933		61	.271	.471	140	38	7	0	7	5.0	26	26	20	22	0	14	2	43	49	0	5	2.2	1.000	P-28, OF-13
1934	BOS A	34	.282	.487	78	22	4	0	4	5.1	12	17	7	15	1	8	3	8	23	1	2	1.2	.969	P-26
1935		75	.347	.533	150	52	5	1	7	4.7	25	32	21	16	0	32	9	9	76	2	1	2.1	.977	P-41
1936		61	.267	.437	135	36	6	1	5	3.7	20	24	14	10	0	19	0	9	42	2	2	1.4	.962	P-39
1937	2 teams	BOS A (18G –.364)	WAS A (53G –.255)																					
"	total	71	.281	.353	139	39	7	0	1	0.7	14	25	16	21	0	28	8	11	55	2	4	1.8	.971	P-37
1938	2 teams	WAS A (26G –.224)	NY A (5G –.167)																					
"	total	31	.213	.311	61	13	3	0	1	1.6	7	7	16	11	0	2	0	10	41	2	6	1.9	.962	P-28
1939	NY A	3	.125	.250	8	1	1	0	0	0.0	0	1	0	2	0	0	0	0	4	0	0	1.3	1.000	P-3
1940	BKN N	2	.000	.000	2	0	0	0	0	0.0	0	0	0	2	0	1	0	0	3	0	0	3.0	1.000	P-1
1941	BOS N	4	.500	1.250	4	2	0	0	1	25.0	2	2	1	1	0	0	0	0	1	0	0	0.3	1.000	P-4
15 yrs.		548	.280	.446	1176	329	57	12	38	3.2	175	208	129	185	2	139	31	153	533	17	31	1.8	.976	P-374, OF-13

Sergio Ferrer

FERRER, SERGIO BB TR 5′ 7″ 145 lbs.
Born Sergio Ferrer (Marrero).
B. Jan. 29, 1951, Santurce, Puerto Rico.

Year	Team	Games	BA	SA	AB	H	2B	3B	HR	HR%	R	RBI	BB	SO	SB	Pinch Hit AB	Pinch Hit H	PO	A	E	DP	TC/G	FA	G by Pos
1974	MIN A	24	.281	.351	57	16	0	2	0	0.0	12	0	8	6	3	1	0	18	37	9	7	3.0	.859	SS-20, 2B-1
1975		32	.247	.309	81	20	3	1	0	0.0	14	2	3	11	3	1	0	32	62	6	12	3.3	.940	SS-18, 2B-10, DH-2
1978	NY N	37	.212	.273	33	7	0	1	0	0.0	8	1	4	7	1	0	0	27	48	2	9	2.3	.974	SS-29, 2B-3, 3B-2
1979		32	.000	.000	7	0	0	0	0	0.0	7	0	2	3	0	0	0	8	10	1	3	0.9	.947	3B-12, SS-5, 2B-4
4 yrs.		125	.242	.303	178	43	3	4	0	0.0	41	3	17	27	7	2	0	85	157	18	31	2.5	.931	SS-72, 2B-18, 3B-14, DH-2

Hobe Ferris

FERRIS, ALBERT SAYLES BR TR 5′ 8″ 162 lbs.
B. Dec. 7, 1877, Providence, R. I. D. Mar. 18, 1938, Detroit, Mich.

Year	Team	Games	BA	SA	AB	H	2B	3B	HR	HR%	R	RBI	BB	SO	SB	Pinch Hit AB	Pinch Hit H	PO	A	E	DP	TC/G	FA	G by Pos
1901	BOS A	138	.250	.350	523	131	16	15	2	0.4	68	63	23		13	0	0	359	450	61	68	6.3	.930	2B-138, SS-1
1902		134	.244	.381	499	122	16	14	8	1.6	57	63	21		11	0	0	312	461	39	59	6.1	.952	2B-134
1903		141	.251	.366	525	132	19	7	9	1.7	69	66	25		11	0	0	319	441	40	51	5.7	.950	2B-139, SS-2

Hobe Ferris *continued*

Year	Team	Games	BA	SA	AB	H	2B	3B	HR	HR%	R	RBI	BB	SO	SB	Pinch Hit AB	Pinch Hit H	PO	A	E	DP	TC/G	FA	G by Pos
1904		156	.213	.306	563	120	23	10	3	0.5	50	63	23		7	0	0	366	460	33	42	5.5	.962	2B-156
1905		141	.220	.361	523	115	24	16	6	1.1	51	59	23		11	0	0	321	425	31	38	5.5	.960	2B-140, OF-1
1906		130	.244	.360	495	121	25	13	2	0.4	47	44	10		8	0	0	323	386	31	42	5.7	.958	2B-126, 3B-4
1907		150	.241	.314	561	135	25	2	4	0.7	41	60	10		11	0	0	424	459	30	43	6.1	.967	2B-150
1908	STL A	148	.270	.353	555	150	26	7	2	0.4	54	74	14		6	0	0	222	316	27	27	3.8	.952	3B-148
1909		148	.216	.282	556	120	18	5	3	0.5	36	58	12		11	0	0	249	330	36	28	4.2	.941	3B-114, 2B-34
9 yrs.		1286	.239	.340	4800	1146	192	89	39	0.8	473	550	161		89	0	0	2895	3728	328	398	5.4	.953	2B-1017, 3B-266, SS-3, OF-1
WORLD SERIES																								
1903	BOS A	8	.290	.355	31	9	0	1	0	0.0	3	7	0	5	0	0	0	17	19	2	2	4.8	.947	2B-8

Boo Ferriss

FERRISS, DAVID MEADOW
B. Dec. 5, 1921, Shaw, Miss.
BL TR 6′ 2″ 208 lbs.

Year	Team	Games	BA	SA	AB	H	2B	3B	HR	HR%	R	RBI	BB	SO	SB	Pinch Hit AB	Pinch Hit H	PO	A	E	DP	TC/G	FA	G by Pos
1945	BOS A	61	.267	.367	120	32	7	1	1	0.8	16	19	19	11	0	20	5	22	67	2	10	2.6	.978	P-35
1946		45	.209	.261	115	24	6	0	0	0.0	12	7	7	19	0	4	1	25	43	1	5	1.7	.986	P-40
1947		52	.273	.384	99	27	5	3	0	0.0	11	19	7	10	0	17	4	13	33	2	2	1.5	.958	P-33
1948		31	.243	.270	37	9	1	0	0	0.0	4	6	6	6	0	0	0	10	21	0	1	1.0	1.000	P-31
1949		4	1.000	2.000	1	1	1	0	0	0.0	1	1	0	0	0	0	0	1	0	0	0	0.3	1.000	P-4
1950		1	—	—	0	0	0	0	0	—	0	0	0	0	0	0	0	0	0	0	0	0.0	.000	P-1
6 yrs.		194	.250	.333	372	93	20	4	1	0.3	44	52	39	46	0	41	10	71	164	5	18	1.7	.979	P-144
WORLD SERIES																								
1946	BOS A	2	.000	.000	6	0	0	0	0	0.0	0	0	0	1	0	0	0	0	3	0	0	1.5	1.000	P-2

Willy Fetzer

FETZER, WILLIAM McKINNON
B. June 24, 1884, Concord, N. C. D. May 3, 1959, Butner, N. C.
BL TR 5′10½″ 180 lbs.

Year	Team	Games	BA	SA	AB	H	2B	3B	HR	HR%	R	RBI	BB	SO	SB	Pinch Hit AB	Pinch Hit H	PO	A	E	DP	TC/G	FA	G by Pos
1906	PHI A	1	.000	.000	1	0	0	0	0	0.0	0	0	0		0	1	0	0	0	0	0	0.0	—	

Chick Fewster

FEWSTER, WILSON LLOYD
B. Nov. 10, 1895, Baltimore, Md. D. Apr. 16, 1945, Baltimore, Md.
BR TR 5′11″ 160 lbs.

Year	Team	Games	BA	SA	AB	H	2B	3B	HR	HR%	R	RBI	BB	SO	SB	Pinch Hit AB	Pinch Hit H	PO	A	E	DP	TC/G	FA	G by Pos
1917	NY A	11	.222	.222	36	8	0	0	0	0.0	2	1	5	5	1	0	0	26	31	5	5	5.6	.919	2B-11
1918		5	.500	.500	2	1	0	0	0	0.0	1	0	0	0	0	1	0	0	0	0	0	0.0	.000	2B-2
1919		81	.283	.357	244	69	9	3	1	0.4	38	15	34	36	8	7	3	126	86	18	10	3.3	.922	OF-41, SS-23, 2B-4, 3B-2
1920		21	.286	.333	21	6	1	0	0	0.0	8	1	7	2	0	4	1	9	13	4	1	3.7	.846	SS-5, 2B-2
1921		66	.280	.386	207	58	19	0	1	0.5	44	19	28	43	4	4	0	105	59	12	11	3.0	.932	OF-43, 2B-15
1922	2 teams NY A (44G –.242) BOS A (23G –.289)																							
″	total	67	.260	.330	215	56	8	2	1	0.5	28	18	22	33	10	1	0	100	74	6	6	2.9	.967	OF-38, 3B-23, 2B-2
1923	BOS A	90	.236	.278	284	67	10	1	0	0.0	32	15	39	35	7	1	0	179	240	33	31	5.4	.927	2B-48, SS-36
1924	CLE A	101	.267	.317	322	86	12	2	0	0.0	36	36	24	36	12	0	0	200	233	17	36	4.5	.962	2B-94, 3B-5
1925		93	.248	.320	294	73	16	1	1	0.3	39	38	36	25	6	2	1	227	250	30	43	5.2	.941	2B-86, 3B-10, OF-1
1926	BKN N	105	.243	.326	337	82	16	3	2	0.6	53	24	45	49	9	1	0	225	297	26	38	5.3	.953	2B-103
1927		4	.000	.000	1	0	0	0	0	0.0	1	0	0	0	0	1	0	0	0	0	0	0.0	—	
11 yrs.		644	.258	.326	1963	506	91	12	6	0.3	282	167	240	264	57	22	5	1197	1283	151	181	4.4	.943	2B-367, OF-123, SS-64, 3B-40
WORLD SERIES																								
1921	NY A	4	.200	.500	10	2	0	0	1	10.0	3	2	3	3	0	0	0	7	0	0	0	1.8	1.000	OF-4

Neil Fiala

FIALA, NEIL STEPHEN
B. Aug. 24, 1956, St. Louis, Mo.
BL TR 6′ 1″ 185 lbs.

Year	Team	Games	BA	SA	AB	H	2B	3B	HR	HR%	R	RBI	BB	SO	SB	Pinch Hit AB	Pinch Hit H	PO	A	E	DP	TC/G	FA	G by Pos
1981	2 teams STL N (3G –.000) CIN N (2G –.500)																							
″	total	5	.200	.200	5	1	0	0	0	0.0	1	1	0	2	0	5	1	0	0	0	0	0.0	—	

Jim Field

FIELD, JAMES C.
B. Apr. 24, 1863, Philadelphia, Pa. D. May 13, 1953, Atlantic City, N. J.
6′ 1″ 170 lbs.

Year	Team	Games	BA	SA	AB	H	2B	3B	HR	HR%	R	RBI	BB	SO	SB	Pinch Hit AB	Pinch Hit H	PO	A	E	DP	TC/G	FA	G by Pos
1883	COL AA	76	.254	.339	295	75	10	6	1	0.3	31		7			0	0	781	10	52	44	11.1	.938	1B-76
1884		105	.233	.317	417	97	9	7	4	1.0	74		23			0	0	1150	27	52	58	11.7	.958	1B-105
1885	2 teams PIT AA (56G –.239) BAL AA (38G –.208)																							
″	total	94	.227	.286	353	80	12	3	1	0.3	44		26			0	0	995	28	38	48	11.3	.964	1B-94
1890	ROC AA	52	.202	.356	188	38	7	5	4	2.1	30		21		8	0	0	486	13	18	24	9.8	.965	1B-51, P-2
1898	WAS N	5	.095	.095	21	2	0	0	0	0.0	1	0	0		1	0	0	45	2	1	0	9.6	.979	1B-5
5 yrs.		332	.229	.316	1274	292	38	21	10	0.8	180	0	77		9	0	0	3457	80	161	174	11.1	.956	1B-331, P-2

Sam Field

FIELD, SAMUEL JAY
B. Oct. 12, 1848, Philadelphia, Pa. D. Oct. 28, 1904, Sinking Spring, Pa.
BR TR 5′ 9½″ 182 lbs.

Year	Team	Games	BA	SA	AB	H	2B	3B	HR	HR%	R	RBI	BB	SO	SB	Pinch Hit AB	Pinch Hit H	PO	A	E	DP	TC/G	FA	G by Pos
1876	CIN N	4	.000	.000	14	0	0	0	0	0.0	2	0	1	3		0	0	10	1	5	0	3.2	.688	C-3, 2B-2

Cecil Fielder

FIELDER, CECIL GRANT
B. Sept. 21, 1963, Los Angeles, Calif.
BR TR 6′ 3″ 230 lbs.

Year	Team	Games	BA	SA	AB	H	2B	3B	HR	HR%	R	RBI	BB	SO	SB	Pinch Hit AB	Pinch Hit H	PO	A	E	DP	TC/G	FA	G by Pos
1985	TOR A	30	.311	.527	74	23	4	0	4	5.4	6	16	6	16	0	4	1	171	17	4	21	7.7	.979	1B-25
1986		34	.157	.325	83	13	2	0	4	4.8	7	13	6	27	0	9	1	37	4	1	3	1.3	.976	DH-22, 1B-7, 3B-2, OF-1
1987		82	.269	.560	175	47	7	1	14	8.0	30	32	20	48	0	19	4	98	6	0	12	1.4	1.000	DH-55, 1B-16, 3B-2
1988		74	.230	.431	174	40	6	1	9	5.2	24	23	14	53	0	21	5	101	12	1	10	1.6	.991	DH-50, 1B-17, 3B-3, 2B-2
1990	DET A	159	.277	**.592**	573	159	25	1	**51**	**8.9**	104	**132**	90	**182**	0	3	0	1190	111	14	137	8.3	.989	1B-143, DH-15
1991		162	.261	.513	624	163	25	0	**44**	7.1	102	**133**	78	151	0	0	0	1055	83	8	110	7.0	.993	1B-122, DH-42
1992		155	.244	.458	594	145	22	0	35	5.9	80	**124**	73	151	0	0	0	957	92	10	98	6.7	.991	1B-114, DH-43
1993		154	.267	.464	573	153	23	0	30	5.2	80	117	90	125	0	1	0	971	78	10	84	6.8	.991	1B-119, DH-36
1994		109	.259	.504	425	110	16	2	28	6.6	67	90	50	110	0	0	0	887	108	7	72	9.2	.993	1B-102, DH-7
1995		136	.243	.472	494	120	18	1	31	6.3	70	82	75	116	0	1	0	631	73	5	65	5.3	.993	1B-77, DH-58
10 yrs.		1095	.257	.497	3789	973	148	6	250	6.6	570	762	502	979	0	58	11	6098	584	60	612	6.2	.991	1B-742, DH-328, 3B-7, 2B-2, OF-1
LEAGUE CHAMPIONSHIP SERIES																								
1985	TOR A	3	.333	.667	3	1	1	0	0	0.0	0	0	0	1	0	3	1	0	0	0	0	0.0	—	

Bruce Fields

FIELDS, BRUCE ALAN BL TR 6′ 185 lbs.
B. Oct. 6, 1960, Cleveland, Ohio.

Year	Team	Games	BA	SA	AB	H	2B	3B	HR	HR%	R	RBI	BB	SO	SB	Pinch Hit AB	Pinch Hit H	PO	A	E	DP	TC/G	FA	G by Pos
1986	DET A	16	.279	.349	43	12	1	1	0	0.0	4	6	1	6	1	2	1	25	0	1	0	1.7	.962	OF-14, DH-1
1988	SEA A	39	.269	.388	67	18	5	0	1	1.5	8	5	4	11	0	12	3	23	0	0	0	0.8	1.000	OF-23, DH-6
1989		3	.333	.667	3	1	1	0	0	0.0	2	0	0	1	0	2	1	0	0	0	0	0.0	.000	OF-1
3 yrs.		58	.274	.381	113	31	7	1	1	0.9	14	11	5	18	1	16	5	48	0	1	0	1.1	.980	OF-38, DH-7

Jocko Fields

FIELDS, JOHN JOSEPH BR TR 5′10″ 160 lbs.
B. Oct. 20, 1864, Cork, Ireland D. Oct. 14, 1950, Jersey City, N. J.

Year	Team	Games	BA	SA	AB	H	2B	3B	HR	HR%	R	RBI	BB	SO	SB	Pinch Hit AB	Pinch Hit H	PO	A	E	DP	TC/G	FA	G by Pos
1887	PIT N	43	.268	.348	164	44	9	2	0	0.0	26	17	7	13	7	0	0	141	29	18	2	4.1	.904	OF-27, C-14, 1B-3, P-1, 3B-1
1888		45	.195	.278	169	33	7	2	1	0.6	22	15	8	19	9	0	0	103	25	24	2	3.3	.842	OF-29, C-14, 3B-3
1889		75	.311	.443	289	90	22	5	2	0.7	41	43	29	30	7	0	0	159	30	28	3	2.9	.871	OF-60, C-16
1890	PIT P	126	.283	.445	526	149	18	20	9	1.7	101	86	57	52	24	0	0	286	107	60	13	3.5	.868	OF-80, 2B-30, C-15, SS-4
1891	2 teams	PIT N (23G –.240) PHI N (8G –.233)																						
″	total	31	.238	.305	105	25	5	1	0	0.0	14	10	14	15	1	0	0	96	41	24	0	5.2	.851	C-23, SS-8
1892	NY N	21	.273	.394	66	18	4	2	0	0.0	8	5	9	10	2	0	0	61	19	13	2	4.4	.860	OF-11, C-10
6 yrs.		341	.272	.397	1319	359	65	32	12	0.9	212	176	124	139	50	0	0	846	251	167	22	3.6	.868	OF-207, C-92, 2B-30, SS-12, 3B-4, 1B-3, P-1

Bien Figueroa

FIGUEROA, BIENVENIDO BR TR 5′10″ 170 lbs.
Born Bienvenido Figueroa (DeLeon).
B. Feb. 7, 1964, Santo Domingo, Dominican Republic.

Year	Team	Games	BA	SA	AB	H	2B	3B	HR	HR%	R	RBI	BB	SO	SB	Pinch Hit AB	Pinch Hit H	PO	A	E	DP	TC/G	FA	G by Pos
1992	STL N	12	.182	.273	11	2	1	0	0	0.0	1	4	1	2	0	1	1	7	11	1	0	1.6	.947	SS-9, 2B-3

Jesus Figueroa

FIGUEROA, JESUS MARIA BL TL 5′10″ 160 lbs.
Born Jesus Maria Figueroa (Figueroa).
B. Feb. 20, 1957, Santo Domingo, Dominican Republic.

Year	Team	Games	BA	SA	AB	H	2B	3B	HR	HR%	R	RBI	BB	SO	SB	Pinch Hit AB	Pinch Hit H	PO	A	E	DP	TC/G	FA	G by Pos
1980	CHI N	115	.253	.293	198	50	5	0	1	0.5	20	11	14	16	2	53	15	89	6	2	2	1.7	.979	OF-57

Sam File

FILE, LAWRENCE SAMUEL BR TR 5′11″ 160 lbs.
B. May 18, 1922, Chester, Pa.

Year	Team	Games	BA	SA	AB	H	2B	3B	HR	HR%	R	RBI	BB	SO	SB	Pinch Hit AB	Pinch Hit H	PO	A	E	DP	TC/G	FA	G by Pos
1940	PHI N	7	.077	.077	13	1	0	0	0	0.0	0	1	0	2	0	0	0	5	14	3	2	3.1	.864	SS-6, 3B-1

Steve Filipowicz

FILIPOWICZ, STEPHEN CHARLES (Flip) BR TR 5′8″ 195 lbs.
B. June 28, 1921, Donora, Pa. D. Feb. 21, 1975, Wilkes-Barre, Pa.

Year	Team	Games	BA	SA	AB	H	2B	3B	HR	HR%	R	RBI	BB	SO	SB	Pinch Hit AB	Pinch Hit H	PO	A	E	DP	TC/G	FA	G by Pos
1944	NY N	15	.195	.293	41	8	2	1	0	0.0	10	7	3	7	0	1	0	20	0	0	0	1.8	1.000	OF-10, C-1
1945		35	.205	.304	112	23	5	0	2	1.8	14	16	4	13	0	3	0	42	1	3	0	1.5	.935	OF-31
1948	CIN N	7	.346	.423	26	9	0	1	0	0.0	0	3	2	1	0	0	0	10	1	0	0	1.6	1.000	OF-7
3 yrs.		57	.223	.318	179	40	7	2	2	1.1	24	26	9	21	0	4	0	72	2	3	0	1.6	.961	OF-48, C-1

Jack Fimple

FIMPLE, JOHN JOSEPH BR TR 6′2″ 185 lbs.
B. Feb. 10, 1959, Darby, Pa.

Year	Team	Games	BA	SA	AB	H	2B	3B	HR	HR%	R	RBI	BB	SO	SB	Pinch Hit AB	Pinch Hit H	PO	A	E	DP	TC/G	FA	G by Pos
1983	LA N	54	.250	.358	148	37	8	1	2	1.4	16	22	11	39	1	0	0	336	32	4	2	6.9	.989	C-54
1984		12	.192	.231	26	5	1	0	0	0.0	2	3	1	6	0	0	0	54	4	1	0	4.9	.983	C-12
1986		13	.077	.077	13	1	0	0	0	0.0	2	2	6	6	0	3	0	30	4	0	0	3.8	1.000	C-7, 1B-1, 2B-1
1987	CAL A	13	.200	.200	10	2	0	0	0	0.0	1	1	1	2	0	0	0	18	3	2	0	1.8	.913	C-13
4 yrs.		92	.228	.315	197	45	9	1	2	1.0	21	28	19	53	1	3	0	438	43	7	2	5.5	.986	C-86, 1B-1, 2B-1
LEAGUE CHAMPIONSHIP SERIES																								
1983	LA N	3	.143	.143	7	1	0	0	0	0.0	0	1	0	3	0	0	0	14	2	0	0	5.3	1.000	C-3

Jim Finigan

FINIGAN, JAMES LEROY BR TR 5′11″ 175 lbs.
B. Aug. 19, 1928, Quincy, Ill. D. May 16, 1981, Quincy, Ill.

Year	Team	Games	BA	SA	AB	H	2B	3B	HR	HR%	R	RBI	BB	SO	SB	Pinch Hit AB	Pinch Hit H	PO	A	E	DP	TC/G	FA	G by Pos
1954	PHI A	136	.302	.421	487	147	25	6	7	1.4	57	51	64	66	2	1	0	151	305	25	34	3.5	.948	3B-136
1955	KC A	150	.255	.385	545	139	30	7	9	1.7	72	68	61	49	1	2	1	291	363	20	85	4.5	.970	2B-90, 3B-59
1956		91	.216	.284	250	54	7	2	2	0.8	29	21	30	28	3	9	0	143	175	16	42	4.0	.952	2B-52, 3B-32
1957	DET A	64	.270	.316	174	47	4	2	0	0.0	20	17	23	18	1	3	0	66	112	9	11	3.0	.952	3B-59, 2B-3
1958	SF N	23	.200	.280	25	5	2	0	0	0.0	3	1	3	5	0	12	2	4	10	2	2	1.3	.875	2B-8, 3B-4
1959	BAL A	48	.252	.328	119	30	6	0	1	0.8	14	10	9	10	1	5	2	36	75	4	6	2.3	.965	3B-42, 2B-6, SS-2
6 yrs.		512	.264	.367	1600	422	74	17	19	1.2	195	168	190	176	8	32	5	691	1040	76	180	3.7	.958	3B-332, 2B-159, SS-2

Bill Finley

FINLEY, WILLIAM JAMES 5′3″ 170 lbs.
B. Oct. 4, 1863, New York, N. Y. D. Oct. 6, 1912, Asbury Park, N. J.

Year	Team	Games	BA	SA	AB	H	2B	3B	HR	HR%	R	RBI	BB	SO	SB	Pinch Hit AB	Pinch Hit H	PO	A	E	DP	TC/G	FA	G by Pos
1886	NY N	13	.182	.182	44	8	0	0	0	0.0	2	5	1	8		0	0	29	10	5	1	2.8	.886	OF-8, C-8

Bob Finley

FINLEY, ROBERT EDWARD BR TR 6′1″ 200 lbs.
B. Nov. 25, 1915, Ennis, Tex. D. Jan. 2, 1986, West Covina, Calif.

Year	Team	Games	BA	SA	AB	H	2B	3B	HR	HR%	R	RBI	BB	SO	SB	Pinch Hit AB	Pinch Hit H	PO	A	E	DP	TC/G	FA	G by Pos
1943	PHI N	28	.259	.321	81	21	2	0	1	1.2	9	7	4	10	0	4	1	78	23	4	0	4.4	.962	C-24
1944		94	.249	.306	281	70	11	1	1	0.4	18	21	12	25	1	20	4	289	34	11	7	4.5	.967	C-74
2 yrs.		122	.251	.309	362	91	13	1	2	0.6	27	28	16	35	1	24	5	367	57	15	7	4.5	.966	C-98

Steve Finley

FINLEY, STEVEN ALLEN BL TL 6′2″ 175 lbs.
B. May 12, 1965, Paducah, Tenn.

Year	Team	Games	BA	SA	AB	H	2B	3B	HR	HR%	R	RBI	BB	SO	SB	Pinch Hit AB	Pinch Hit H	PO	A	E	DP	TC/G	FA	G by Pos
1989	BAL A	81	.249	.318	217	54	5	2	2	0.9	35	25	15	30	17	5	1	144	1	2	0	1.9	.986	OF-76, DH-3
1990		142	.256	.328	464	119	16	4	3	0.6	46	37	32	53	22	12	0	298	4	7	1	2.3	.977	OF-133, DH-2
1991	HOU N	159	.285	.406	596	170	28	10	8	1.3	84	54	42	65	34	9	2	323	13	5	2	2.2	.985	OF-153
1992		162	.292	.407	607	177	29	13	5	0.8	84	55	58	63	44	2	0	417	8	3	3	2.7	.993	OF-160
1993		142	.266	.385	545	145	15	**13**	8	1.5	69	44	28	65	19	3	2	329	12	4	4	2.5	.988	OF-140
1994		94	.276	.434	373	103	16	5	11	2.9	64	33	28	52	13	2	0	214	9	4	0	2.5	.982	OF-92
1995	SD N	139	.297	.420	562	167	23	8	10	1.8	104	44	59	62	36	1	1	289	8	7	0	2.2	.977	OF-138
7 yrs.		919	.278	.392	3364	935	132	55	47	1.4	486	292	262	390	185	34	6	2014	55	32	10	2.3	.985	OF-892, DH-5

Mickey Finn

FINN, CORNELIUS FRANCIS (Neal) BR TR 5′11″ 168 lbs.
B. Jan. 24, 1904, Brooklyn, N. Y. D. July 7, 1933, Allentown, Pa.

Year	Team	Games	BA	SA	AB	H	2B	3B	HR	HR%	R	RBI	BB	SO	SB	Pinch Hit AB	Pinch Hit H	PO	A	E	DP	TC/G	FA	G by Pos
1930	BKN N	87	.278	.359	273	76	13	0	3	1.1	42	30	26	18	3	2	0	182	235	23	63	5.4	.948	2B-81
1931		118	.274	.337	413	113	22	2	0	0.0	46	45	21	42	2	4	1	260	331	15	65	5.4	.975	2B-112

Mickey Finn *continued*

Year	Team	Games	BA	SA	AB	H	2B	3B	HR	HR%	R	RBI	BB	SO	SB	Pinch Hit AB	Pinch Hit H	PO	A	E	DP	TC/G	FA	G by Pos
1932		65	.238	.286	189	45	5	2	0	0.0	22	14	11	15	2	3	2	36	96	9	8	2.7	.936	3B-50, 2B-2, SS-1
1933	PHI N	51	.237	.272	169	40	4	1	0	0.0	15	13	10	14	2	0	0	107	164	10	34	5.5	.964	2B-51
4 yrs.		321	.262	.323	1044	274	44	5	3	0.3	125	102	68	89	9	9	3	585	826	57	170	4.9	.961	2B-246, 3B-50, SS-1

Hal Finney

FINNEY, HAROLD WILSON
Brother of Lou Finney.
B. July 30, 1905, Lafayette, Ala. D. Dec. 20, 1991, Lafayette, Ala.

BR TR 5′11″ 170 lbs.

Year	Team	Games	BA	SA	AB	H	2B	3B	HR	HR%	R	RBI	BB	SO	SB	Pinch Hit AB	Pinch Hit H	PO	A	E	DP	TC/G	FA	G by Pos
1931	PIT N	10	.308	.346	26	8	1	0	0	0.0	2	2	0	1	1	4	0	18	3	0	1	3.5	1.000	C-6
1932		31	.212	.303	33	7	3	0	0	0.0	14	4	3	4	0	0	0	30	3	1	0	3.1	.971	C-11
1933		56	.233	.301	133	31	4	1	1	0.8	17	18	3	19	0	7	3	122	12	1	4	2.9	.993	C-47
1934		5	—	—	0	0	0	0	0	—	3	0	0	0	0	0	0	0	0	0	0	0.0	.000	C-5
1936		21	.000	.000	35	0	0	0	0	0.0	3	3	0	8	0	0	0	38	5	2	1	3.2	.956	C-14
5 yrs.		123	.203	.260	227	46	8	1	1	0.4	39	27	6	32	1	11	3	208	23	4	6	2.8	.983	C-83

Lou Finney

FINNEY, LOUIS KLOPSCHE
Brother of Hal Finney.
B. Aug. 13, 1910, Buffalo, Ala. D. Apr. 22, 1966, Lafayette, Ala.

BL TR 6′ 180 lbs.

Year	Team	Games	BA	SA	AB	H	2B	3B	HR	HR%	R	RBI	BB	SO	SB	Pinch Hit AB	Pinch Hit H	PO	A	E	DP	TC/G	FA	G by Pos
1931	PHI A	9	.375	.458	24	9	0	1	0	0.0	7	3	6	1	0	1	0	19	1	0	1	2.5	1.000	OF-8
1933		74	.267	.371	240	64	12	2	3	1.3	26	32	13	17	1	12	2	136	6	8	1	2.4	.947	OF-63
1934		92	.279	.360	272	76	11	4	1	0.4	32	28	14	17	4	21	4	232	12	9	17	3.7	.964	OF-54, 1B-15
1935		109	.273	.329	410	112	11	6	0	0.0	45	31	18	18	7	14	3	316	15	9	18	3.6	.974	OF-76, 1B-18
1936		151	.302	.377	**653**	197	26	10	1	0.2	100	41	47	22	7	1	0	961	37	13	71	6.7	.987	1B-78, OF-73
1937		92	.251	.343	379	95	14	9	1	0.3	53	20	20	16	2	3	0	519	31	12	39	6.2	.979	1B-50, OF-39, 2B-1
1938		122	.275	.441	454	125	21	12	10	2.2	61	48	39	25	5	14	5	698	28	9	35	6.7	.988	1B-64, OF-46
1939	2 teams	PHI A (9G –.136) BOS A (95G –.325)																						
″	total	104	.310	.410	271	84	18	3	1	0.4	44	47	26	11	2	**40**	**13**	340	12	6	28	6.0	.983	1B-32, OF-28
1940	BOS A	130	.320	.463	534	171	31	15	5	0.9	73	73	33	13	5	9	1	652	33	7	41	5.8	.990	OF-69, 1B-51
1941		127	.288	.400	497	143	24	10	4	0.8	83	53	38	17	2	10	5	395	22	14	10	3.7	.968	OF-92, 1B-24
1942		113	.285	.383	397	113	16	7	3	0.8	58	61	29	11	3	15	3	221	8	5	3	2.4	.979	OF-95, 1B-2
1944		68	.287	.347	251	72	11	2	0	0.0	37	32	23	7	1	6	1	528	24	7	53	9.2	.987	1B-59, OF-2
1945	2 teams	BOS A (2G –.000) STL A (57G –.277)																						
″	total	59	.274	.377	215	59	8	4	2	0.9	24	22	21	7	0	3	0	234	18	3	14	4.3	.988	OF-36, 1B-22, 3B-1
1946	STL A	16	.300	.300	30	9	0	0	0	0.0	0	3	2	4	0	6	4	14	1	1	0	2.3	.938	OF-7
1947	PHI N	4	.000	.000	4	0	0	0	0	0.0	0	0	0	0	0	4	0	0	0	0	0	0.0	—	
15 yrs.		1270	.287	.388	4631	1329	203	85	31	0.7	643	494	329	186	39	159	41	5265	248	103	331	5.1	.982	OF-688, 1B-415, 3B-1, 2B-1

Mike Fiore

FIORE, MICHAEL GARY JOSEPH (Lefty)
B. Oct. 11, 1944, Brooklyn, N. Y.

BL TL 6′ 175 lbs.

Year	Team	Games	BA	SA	AB	H	2B	3B	HR	HR%	R	RBI	BB	SO	SB	Pinch Hit AB	Pinch Hit H	PO	A	E	DP	TC/G	FA	G by Pos
1968	BAL A	6	.059	.059	17	1	0	0	0	0.0	2	0	4	4	0	0	0	31	3	2	7	6.0	.944	1B-5, OF-1
1969	KC A	107	.274	.428	339	93	14	1	12	3.5	53	35	84	63	4	5	4	709	94	11	54	7.8	.986	1B-91, OF-13
1970	2 teams	KC A (25G –.181) BOS A (41G –.140)																						
″	total	66	.164	.180	122	20	2	0	0	0.0	11	8	21	28	1	26	5	191	22	3	14	5.5	.986	1B-37, OF-2
1971	BOS A	51	.177	.258	62	11	2	0	1	1.6	9	6	12	14	0	33	8	74	5	0	8	6.6	1.000	1B-12
1972	2 teams	STL N (17G –.100) SD N (7G –.000)																						
″	total	24	.063	.063	16	1	0	0	0	0.0	0	1	3	6	0	16	1	7	0	0	2	1.0	1.000	1B-6, OF-1
5 yrs.		254	.227	.333	556	126	18	1	13	2.3	75	50	124	115	5	80	18	1012	124	16	85	6.9	.986	1B-151, OF-17

Dan Firova

FIROVA, DANIEL MICHAEL
B. Oct. 16, 1956, Refugio, Tex.

BR TR 6′ 185 lbs.

Year	Team	Games	BA	SA	AB	H	2B	3B	HR	HR%	R	RBI	BB	SO	SB	Pinch Hit AB	Pinch Hit H	PO	A	E	DP	TC/G	FA	G by Pos
1981	SEA A	13	.000	.000	2	0	0	0	0	0.0	0	0	0	1	0	0	0	8	0	0	0	0.6	1.000	C-13
1982		3	.000	.000	5	0	0	0	0	0.0	0	0	0	0	0	0	0	8	1	1	0	3.3	.900	C-3
1988	CLE A	1	—	—	0	0	0	0	0	—	0	0	0	0	0	0	0	0	0	0	0	0.0	.000	C-1
3 yrs.		17	.000	.000	7	0	0	0	0	0.0	0	0	0	1	0	0	0	16	1	1	0	1.1	.944	C-17

Bill Fischer

FISCHER, WILLIAM CHARLES
B. Mar. 2, 1891, New York, N. Y. D. Sept. 4, 1945, Richmond, Va.

BL TR 6′ 174 lbs.

Year	Team	Games	BA	SA	AB	H	2B	3B	HR	HR%	R	RBI	BB	SO	SB	Pinch Hit AB	Pinch Hit H	PO	A	E	DP	TC/G	FA	G by Pos
1913	BKN N	62	.267	.388	165	44	9	4	1	0.6	16	12	10	5	0	1	0	193	65	7	2	5.2	.974	C-51
1914		43	.257	.305	105	27	1	2	0	0.0	12	8	8	12	1	12	5	136	45	8	6	6.3	.958	C-30
1915	CHI F	105	.329	.449	292	96	15	4	4	1.4	30	50	24		5	21	7	324	100	12	9	5.4	.972	C-80
1916	2 teams	CHI N (65G –.196) PIT N (42G –.257)																						
″	total	107	.219	.315	292	64	16	3	2	0.7	26	20	21	11	3	12	0	429	119	15	8	6.2	.973	C-91
1917	PIT N	95	.286	.376	245	70	9	2	3	1.2	25	25	27	19	11	16	3	279	77	14	8	5.2	.962	C-69, 1B-2
5 yrs.		412	.274	.374	1099	301	50	15	10	0.9	109	115	90	47	20	62	15	1361	406	56	33	5.6	.969	C-321, 1B-2

Mike Fischlin

FISCHLIN, MICHAEL THOMAS
B. Sept. 13, 1955, Sacramento, Calif.

BR TR 6′ 1″ 165 lbs.

Year	Team	Games	BA	SA	AB	H	2B	3B	HR	HR%	R	RBI	BB	SO	SB	Pinch Hit AB	Pinch Hit H	PO	A	E	DP	TC/G	FA	G by Pos
1977	HOU N	13	.200	.200	15	3	0	0	0	0.0	0	0	0	2	0	0	0	3	17	0	1	1.7	1.000	SS-12
1978		44	.116	.128	86	10	1	0	0	0.0	3	0	4	9	1	3	0	49	67	9	11	3.0	.928	SS-41
1980		1	.000	.000	1	0	0	0	0	0.0	0	0	0	1	0	0	0	1	0	0	0	1.0	1.000	SS-1
1981	CLE A	22	.233	.256	43	10	1	0	0	0.0	3	5	3	6	3	0	0	33	39	4	8	3.8	.947	SS-19, 2B-1
1982		112	.268	.319	276	74	12	1	0	0.0	34	21	34	36	9	2	2	142	257	13	43	3.6	.968	SS-101, 3B-8, 2B-6, C-1
1983		95	.209	.276	225	47	5	2	2	0.9	31	23	26	32	9	1	0	169	226	14	59	4.5	.966	2B-71, SS-15, 3B-4, DH-1
1984		85	.226	.308	133	30	4	2	1	0.8	17	14	12	20	2	1	1	104	146	8	30	3.0	.969	2B-55, 3B-17, SS-15
1985		73	.200	.300	60	12	4	1	0	0.0	12	2	5	7	0	0	0	73	89	4	20	2.5	.976	2B-31, SS-22, 1B-6, DH-5, 3B-3
1986	NY A	71	.206	.225	102	21	2	0	0	0.0	9	3	8	29	0	0	0	63	107	7	18	2.6	.960	SS-42, 2B-27
1987	ATL N	1	—	—	0	0	0	0	0	—	0	0	0	0	0	0	0	0	0	0	0	0.0	.000	SS-1
10 yrs.		517	.220	.273	941	207	29	6	3	0.3	109	68	92	142	24	7	3	637	948	59	190	3.3	.964	SS-269, 2B-191, 3B-32, DH-6, 1B-6, C-1

Sam Fishburn

FISHBURN, SAMUEL E.
B. May 15, 1893, Haverhill, Mass. D. Apr. 11, 1965, Bethlehem, Pa.

BR TR 5′ 9″ 157 lbs.

Year	Team	Games	BA	SA	AB	H	2B	3B	HR	HR%	R	RBI	BB	SO	SB	Pinch Hit AB	Pinch Hit H	PO	A	E	DP	TC/G	FA	G by Pos
1919	STL N	9	.333	.500	6	2	1	0	0	0.0	0	2	0	0	0	1	1	11	0	0	1	5.5	1.000	2B-1, 1B-1

John Fishel

FISHEL, JOHN ALAN — BR TR 5′11″ 185 lbs.
B. Nov. 8, 1962, Fullerton, Calif.

Year	Team	Games	BA	SA	AB	H	2B	3B	HR	HR%	R	RBI	BB	SO	SB	Pinch Hit AB	Pinch Hit H	PO	A	E	DP	TC/G	FA	G by Pos
1988	HOU N	19	.231	.346	26	6	0	0	1	3.8	1	2	3	6	0	16	3	2	0	0	0	0.3	1.000	OF-6

Bob Fisher

FISHER, ROBERT TAYLOR — BR TR 5′ 9½″ 170 lbs.
Brother of Ike Fisher.
B. Nov. 3, 1886, Nashville, Tenn. D. Aug. 4, 1963, Jacksonville, Fla.

Year	Team	Games	BA	SA	AB	H	2B	3B	HR	HR%	R	RBI	BB	SO	SB	Pinch Hit AB	Pinch Hit H	PO	A	E	DP	TC/G	FA	G by Pos
1912	BKN N	82	.233	.296	257	60	10	3	0	0.0	27	26	14	32	7	4	0	123	200	30	23	4.6	.915	SS-74, 2B-1, 3B-1
1913		132	.262	.352	474	124	11	10	4	0.8	42	54	10	43	16	11	2	263	364	52	60	5.2	.923	SS-131
1914	CHI N	15	.300	.420	50	15	2	2	0	0.0	5	5	3	4	2	0	0	20	46	4	3	4.7	.943	SS-15
1915		147	.287	.370	568	163	22	5	5	0.9	70	53	30	51	9	2	0	277	434	51	35	5.2	.933	SS-147
1916	CIN N	61	.272	.346	136	37	4	3	0	0.0	9	11	8	14	7	25	6	59	84	15	9	4.4	.905	SS-29, 2B-6, OF-1
1918	STL N	63	.317	.411	246	78	11	3	2	0.8	36	20	15	11	7	0	0	147	232	8	34	6.1	.979	2B-63
1919		3	.273	.364	11	3	1	0	0	0.0	0	1	0	2	0	0	0	9	9	2	2	6.7	.900	2B-3
7 yrs.		503	.276	.359	1742	480	61	26	11	0.6	189	170	80	157	48	42	8	898	1369	162	166	5.2	.933	SS-396, 2B-73, OF-1, 3B-1

Charlie Fisher

FISHER, CHARLES
B. Baltimore, Md. Deceased.

Year	Team	Games	BA	SA	AB	H	2B	3B	HR	HR%	R	RBI	BB	SO	SB	Pinch Hit AB	Pinch Hit H	PO	A	E	DP	TC/G	FA	G by Pos
1889	LOU AA	1	.500	.500	2	1	0	0	0	0.0	0	0	0	0	0	0	0	0	0	0	0	0.0	.000	OF-1

Charlie Fisher

FISHER, CHARLES G. — BL TR 5′ 8″ 143 lbs.
Born Charles G. Fish.
B. Mar. 10, 1852, Boxford, Mass. D. Feb. 18, 1917, Eagle, Alaska.

Year	Team	Games	BA	SA	AB	H	2B	3B	HR	HR%	R	RBI	BB	SO	SB	Pinch Hit AB	Pinch Hit H	PO	A	E	DP	TC/G	FA	G by Pos
1884	2 teams	KC U (10G –.200) CHI U (1G –.667)																						
″	total	11	.233	.279	43	10	2	0	0	0.0	4		1			0	0	11	24	15	0	4.5	.700	3B-10, SS-1

George Fisher

FISHER, GEORGE C. — BL
B. Wilmington, Del. Deceased.

Year	Team	Games	BA	SA	AB	H	2B	3B	HR	HR%	R	RBI	BB	SO	SB	Pinch Hit AB	Pinch Hit H	PO	A	E	DP	TC/G	FA	G by Pos
1884	2 teams	WIL U (8G –.069) CLE N (6G –.125)																						
″	total	14	.094	.094	53	5	0	0	0	0.0	2	0	0	3		0	0	26	17	7	3	3.3	.860	OF-6, 2B-6, SS-2, C-1

Gus Fisher

FISHER, AUGUST HARRIS — BL TR 5′10″ 175 lbs.
B. Oct. 21, 1885, Pottsborough, Tex. D. Apr. 8, 1972, Portland, Ore.

Year	Team	Games	BA	SA	AB	H	2B	3B	HR	HR%	R	RBI	BB	SO	SB	Pinch Hit AB	Pinch Hit H	PO	A	E	DP	TC/G	FA	G by Pos
1911	CLE A	70	.261	.320	203	53	6	3	0	0.0	20	12	7		6	10	2	307	96	18	11	7.1	.957	C-58, 1B-1
1912	NY A	4	.100	.100	10	1	0	0	0	0.0	1	0	0		0	0	0	17	4	0	0	5.3	1.000	C-4
2 yrs.		74	.254	.310	213	54	6	3	0	0.0	21	12	7		6	10	2	324	100	18	11	7.0	.959	C-62, 1B-1

Harry Fisher

FISHER, HARRY DEVERAUX — BL TR 6′ 180 lbs.
B. Jan. 3, 1926, Newbury, Ont., Canada D. Sept. 20, 1981, Waterloo, Ont., Canada.

Year	Team	Games	BA	SA	AB	H	2B	3B	HR	HR%	R	RBI	BB	SO	SB	Pinch Hit AB	Pinch Hit H	PO	A	E	DP	TC/G	FA	G by Pos
1951	PIT N	3	.000	.000	3	0	0	0	0	0.0	0	0	0	0	0	3	0	0	0	0	0	0.0	—	
1952		15	.333	.400	15	5	1	0	0	0.0	0	1	0	3	0	7	3	1	1	0	0	0.3	1.000	P-8
2 yrs.		18	.278	.333	18	5	1	0	0	0.0	0	1	0	3	0	10	3	1	1	0	0	0.3	1.000	P-8

Ike Fisher

FISHER, NEWTON — BR TR 5′ 9½″ 171 lbs.
Brother of Bob Fisher.
B. June 28, 1871, Nashville, Tenn. D. Feb. 28, 1947, Chicago, Ill.

Year	Team	Games	BA	SA	AB	H	2B	3B	HR	HR%	R	RBI	BB	SO	SB	Pinch Hit AB	Pinch Hit H	PO	A	E	DP	TC/G	FA	G by Pos
1898	PHI N	9	.115	.154	26	3	1	0	0	0.0	0	0	0		1	0	0	24	6	5	1	3.9	.857	C-8, 3B-1

Red Fisher

FISHER, JOHN GUS — BL TR
B. June 22, 1887, Pittsburgh, Pa. D. Jan. 31, 1940, Louisville, Ky.

Year	Team	Games	BA	SA	AB	H	2B	3B	HR	HR%	R	RBI	BB	SO	SB	Pinch Hit AB	Pinch Hit H	PO	A	E	DP	TC/G	FA	G by Pos
1910	STL A	23	.125	.181	72	9	2	1	0	0.0	5	3	8		5	3	0	27	2	2	0	1.6	.935	OF-19

Showboat Fisher

FISHER, GEORGE ALOYS — BL TR 5′10″ 170 lbs.
B. Jan. 16, 1899, Wesley, Iowa D. May 15, 1994, St. Cloud, Minn.

Year	Team	Games	BA	SA	AB	H	2B	3B	HR	HR%	R	RBI	BB	SO	SB	Pinch Hit AB	Pinch Hit H	PO	A	E	DP	TC/G	FA	G by Pos
1923	WAS A	13	.261	.348	23	6	2	0	0	0.0	4	2	4	3	0	4	1	7	2	3	1	2.4	.750	OF-5
1924		15	.220	.244	41	9	1	0	0	0.0	7	6	6	6	2	4	2	14	0	1	0	1.4	.933	OF-11
1930	STL N	92	.374	.587	254	95	18	6	8	3.1	49	61	25	21	4	20	8	122	6	5	0	2.0	.962	OF-67
1932	STL A	18	.182	.182	22	4	0	0	0	0.0	2	2	2	5	0	11	2	6	0	0	0	1.2	1.000	OF-5
4 yrs.		138	.335	.503	340	114	21	6	8	2.4	62	71	37	35	6	39	13	149	8	9	1	1.9	.946	OF-88
WORLD SERIES																								
1930	STL N	2	.500	1.000	2	1	1	0	0	0.0	0	0	0	1	0	2	1	0	0	0	0	0.0	—	

Wilbur Fisher

FISHER, WILBUR McCULLOUGH (Levy, Hod) — BL TL 5′11½″ 200 lbs.
B. July 18, 1894, Green Bottom, W. Va. D. Oct. 24, 1960, Welch, W. Va.

Year	Team	Games	BA	SA	AB	H	2B	3B	HR	HR%	R	RBI	BB	SO	SB	Pinch Hit AB	Pinch Hit H	PO	A	E	DP	TC/G	FA	G by Pos
1916	PIT N	1	.000	.000	1	0	0	0	0	0.0	0	0	0	0	0	1	0	0	0	0	0	0.0	—	

Carlton Fisk

FISK, CARLTON ERNEST (Pudge) — BR TR 6′ 3″ 200 lbs.
B. Dec. 26, 1947, Bellows Falls, Vt.

Year	Team	Games	BA	SA	AB	H	2B	3B	HR	HR%	R	RBI	BB	SO	SB	Pinch Hit AB	Pinch Hit H	PO	A	E	DP	TC/G	FA	G by Pos
1969	BOS A	2	.000	.000	5	0	0	0	0	0.0	0	0	0	2	0	1	0	2	0	0	1	2.0	1.000	C-1
1971		14	.313	.521	48	15	2	1	2	4.2	7	6	1	10	0	0	0	72	6	2	1	5.7	.975	C-14
1972		131	.293	.538	457	134	28	**9**	22	4.8	74	61	52	83	5	0	0	846	72	15	10	7.1	.984	C-131
1973		135	.246	.441	508	125	21	0	26	5.1	65	71	37	99	7	1	1	739	50	14	8	6.0	.983	C-131, DH-3
1974		52	.299	.551	187	56	12	1	11	5.9	36	26	24	23	5	0	0	267	26	6	2	5.8	.980	C-50, DH-2
1975		79	.331	.529	263	87	14	4	10	3.8	47	52	27	32	4	2	0	347	30	8	2	5.0	.979	C-71, DH-6
1976		134	.255	.415	487	124	17	5	17	3.5	76	58	56	71	12	1	0	649	73	12	9	5.5	.984	C-133, DH-1
1977		152	.315	.521	536	169	26	3	26	4.9	106	102	75	85	7	2	0	779	69	11	7	5.7	.987	C-151
1978		157	.284	.475	571	162	39	5	20	3.5	94	88	71	83	7	2	1	734	90	17	13	5.4	.980	C-154, OF-1, DH-1
1979		91	.272	.450	320	87	23	2	10	3.1	49	42	10	38	3	13	3	155	8	3	1	2.0	.982	DH-42, C-39, OF-1
1980		131	.289	.467	478	138	25	3	18	3.8	73	62	36	62	11	0	0	543	56	11	8	4.7	.982	C-115, OF-5, DH-5, 3B-3, 1B-3
1981	CHI A	96	.263	.361	338	89	12	0	7	2.1	44	45	38	37	3	0	0	479	46	6	14	5.6	.989	C-92, OF-1, 3B-1, 1B-1
1982		135	.267	.403	476	127	17	3	14	2.9	66	65	46	60	17	3	1	648	63	5	8	5.3	.993	C-133, 1B-2
1983		138	.289	.518	488	141	26	4	26	5.3	85	86	46	88	9	6	1	709	46	7	5	5.6	.991	C-133, DH-2
1984		102	.231	.468	359	83	20	1	21	5.8	54	43	26	60	6	11	1	421	38	6	4	4.9	.987	C-90, DH-5

Carlton Fisk *continued*

Year	Team	Games	BA	SA	AB	H	2B	3B	HR	HR%	R	RBI	BB	SO	SB	Pinch Hit AB	Pinch Hit H	PO	A	E	DP	TC/G	FA	G by Pos
1985		153	.238	.488	543	129	23	1	37	6.8	85	107	52	81	17	1	0	801	60	10	13	5.5	.989	C-130, DH-28
1986		125	.221	.337	457	101	11	0	14	3.1	42	63	22	92	2	8	1	455	44	8	3	4.1	.984	C-71, OF-31, DH-22
1987		135	.256	.460	454	116	22	1	23	5.1	68	71	39	72	1	12	3	597	66	7	22	5.0	.990	C-122, 1B-9, OF-2
1988		76	.277	.542	253	70	8	1	19	7.5	37	50	37	40	0	6	0	338	36	2	7	5.1	.995	C-74
1989		103	.293	.475	375	110	25	2	13	3.5	47	68	36	60	1	3	0	419	37	3	1	4.5	.993	C-90, DH-13
1990		137	.285	.451	452	129	21	0	18	4.0	65	65	61	73	7	9	2	660	63	4	14	5.6	.994	C-116, DH-14
1991		134	.241	.413	460	111	25	0	18	3.9	42	74	32	86	1	14	2	625	65	6	13	5.3	.991	C-106, DH-13, 1B-12
1992		62	.229	.309	188	43	4	1	3	1.6	12	21	23	38	3	6	2	252	26	2	2	5.0	.993	C-54, DH-2
1993		25	.189	.245	53	10	0	0	1	1.9	2	4	2	11	0	3	0	75	5	0	0	3.2	1.000	C-25
24 yrs.		2499	.269	.457	8756	2356	421	47	376	4.3	1276	1330	849	1386	128	104	18	11612	1075	165	168	5.2	.987	C-2226, DH-159, OF-41, 1B-27, 3B-4
LEAGUE CHAMPIONSHIP SERIES																								
1975	BOS A	3	.417	.500	12	5	1	0	0	0.0	4	2	0	2	1	0	0	15	0	0	0	5.0	1.000	C-3
1983	CHI A	4	.176	.235	17	3	1	0	0	0.0	0	0	1	3	0	0	0	27	3	0	0	7.5	1.000	C-4
2 yrs.		7	.276	.345	29	8	2	0	0	0.0	4	2	1	5	1	0	0	42	3	0	0	6.4	1.000	C-7
WORLD SERIES																								
1975	BOS A	7	.240	.480	25	6	0	0	2	8.0	5	4	7	7	0	0	0	37	3	2	1	6.0	.952	C-7

Wes Fisler

FISLER, WESTON DICKSON
B. July 5, 1841, Camden, N. J. D. Dec. 25, 1922, Philadelphia, Pa.
BR 5′ 6″ 137 lbs.

Year	Team	Games	BA	SA	AB	H	2B	3B	HR	HR%	R	RBI	BB	SO	SB	Pinch Hit AB	Pinch Hit H	PO	A	E	DP	TC/G	FA	G by Pos
1876	PHI N	59	.288	.360	278	80	15	1	1	0.4	42	30	2	4		0	0	234	75	30	11	5.7	.912	OF-24, 2B-21, 1B-14, SS-1

Charlie Fitzberger

FITZBERGER, CHARLES CASPAR (Hon)
B. Feb. 13, 1904, Baltimore, Md. D. Jan. 25, 1965, Baltimore, Md.
BL TL 6′ 1½″ 170 lbs.

Year	Team	Games	BA	SA	AB	H	2B	3B	HR	HR%	R	RBI	BB	SO	SB	Pinch Hit AB	Pinch Hit H	PO	A	E	DP	TC/G	FA	G by Pos
1928	BOS N	7	.286	.286	7	2	0	0	0	0.0	0	0	0	3	0	7	2	0	0	0	0	0.0	—	

Dennis Fitzgerald

FITZGERALD, DENNIS S.
B. Mar. 1865, England D. Oct. 16, 1936, New Haven, Conn.
5′10″ 160 lbs.

Year	Team	Games	BA	SA	AB	H	2B	3B	HR	HR%	R	RBI	BB	SO	SB	Pinch Hit AB	Pinch Hit H	PO	A	E	DP	TC/G	FA	G by Pos
1890	PHI AA	2	.250	.250	8	2	0	0	0	0.0	0		0		0	0	0	2	4	3	0	4.5	.667	SS-2

Ed Fitz Gerald

FITZ GERALD, EDWARD RAYMOND
B. May 21, 1924, Santa Ynez, Calif.
BR TR 6′ 170 lbs.

Year	Team	Games	BA	SA	AB	H	2B	3B	HR	HR%	R	RBI	BB	SO	SB	Pinch Hit AB	Pinch Hit H	PO	A	E	DP	TC/G	FA	G by Pos
1948	PIT N	102	.267	.336	262	70	9	3	1	0.4	31	35	32	37	3	6	2	338	36	15	4	4.1	.961	C-96
1949		75	.263	.344	160	42	7	0	2	1.3	16	18	8	27	1	16	1	163	22	5	5	3.4	.974	C-56
1950		6	.067	.133	15	1	1	0	0	0.0	1	0	0	3	0	0	0	16	3	1	0	4.0	.950	C-5
1951		55	.227	.289	97	22	6	0	0	0.0	8	13	7	10	1	14	2	98	13	4	2	3.0	.965	C-38
1952		51	.233	.288	73	17	1	0	1	1.4	4	7	7	15	0	29	6	55	5	1	0	3.0	.984	C-18, 3B-2
1953	2 teams	PIT N (6G –.118) WAS A (88G –.250)																						
″	total	94	.243	.318	305	74	14	0	3	1.0	25	40	19	36	2	6	2	332	36	4	3	4.1	.989	C-90
1954	WAS A	115	.289	.386	360	104	13	5	4	1.1	33	40	33	22	0	9	2	396	38	12	5	4.2	.973	C-107
1955		74	.237	.309	236	56	3	1	4	1.7	28	19	25	23	0	4	0	304	30	6	5	4.7	.982	C-72
1956		64	.304	.399	148	45	8	0	2	1.4	15	12	20	16	0	16	3	206	19	6	5	4.6	.974	C-50
1957		45	.272	.360	125	34	8	0	1	0.8	14	13	10	9	2	10	4	142	16	6	3	4.4	.963	C-37
1958		58	.263	.289	114	30	3	0	0	0.0	7	11	8	15	0	33	12	125	5	3	5	5.1	.977	C-21, 1B-5
1959	2 teams	WAS A (19G –.194) CLE A (49G –.271)																						
″	total	68	.246	.319	191	47	9	1	1	0.5	17	9	16	22	0	5	1	260	39	5	5	5.0	.984	C-61
12 yrs.		807	.260	.336	2086	542	82	10	19	0.9	199	217	185	235	9	148	35	2435	262	68	42	4.2	.975	C-651, 1B-5, 3B-2

Howie Fitzgerald

FITZGERALD, HOWARD CHUMNEY (Lefty)
B. May 16, 1902, Eagle Lake, Tex. D. Feb. 27, 1959, Matthews, Tex.
BL TL 5′11½″ 163 lbs.

Year	Team	Games	BA	SA	AB	H	2B	3B	HR	HR%	R	RBI	BB	SO	SB	Pinch Hit AB	Pinch Hit H	PO	A	E	DP	TC/G	FA	G by Pos
1922	CHI N	10	.333	.375	24	8	1	0	0	0.0	3	4	3	2	1	3	2	9	0	2	0	1.1	.818	OF-10
1924		7	.158	.158	19	3	0	0	0	0.0	1	2	0	2	0	2	0	4	0	0	0	0.8	1.000	OF-5
1926	BOS A	31	.258	.278	97	25	2	0	0	0.0	11	8	5	7	1	8	2	28	2	4	0	1.5	.882	OF-23
3 yrs.		48	.257	.279	140	36	3	0	0	0.0	15	14	8	11	2	13	4	41	2	6	0	1.3	.878	OF-38

Matty Fitzgerald

FITZGERALD, MATTHEW WILLIAM
B. Aug. 31, 1880, Albany, N. Y. D. Sept. 22, 1949, Albany, N. Y.
BR TR 6′ 185 lbs.

Year	Team	Games	BA	SA	AB	H	2B	3B	HR	HR%	R	RBI	BB	SO	SB	Pinch Hit AB	Pinch Hit H	PO	A	E	DP	TC/G	FA	G by Pos
1906	NY N	4	.667	.667	6	4	0	0	0	0.0	2	2	0		1	1	0	9	0	0	1	3.0	1.000	C-3
1907		7	.133	.200	15	2	1	0	0	0.0	1	1	0		0	1	0	16	4	1	1	3.5	.952	C-6
2 yrs.		11	.286	.333	21	6	1	0	0	0.0	3	3	0		1	2	0	25	4	1	2	3.3	.967	C-9

Mike Fitzgerald

FITZGERALD, JUSTIN HOWARD
B. June 22, 1890, San Mateo, Calif. D. Jan. 17, 1945, San Mateo, Calif.
BL TR 5′ 8″ 160 lbs.

Year	Team	Games	BA	SA	AB	H	2B	3B	HR	HR%	R	RBI	BB	SO	SB	Pinch Hit AB	Pinch Hit H	PO	A	E	DP	TC/G	FA	G by Pos
1911	NY A	16	.270	.297	37	10	1	0	0	0.0	6	6	4		4	7	1	9	1	0	0	1.1	1.000	OF-9
1918	PHI N	66	.293	.353	133	39	8	0	0	0.0	21	6	13	6	3	**30**	**8**	54	2	2	1	1.0	.966	OF-57
2 yrs.		82	.288	.341	170	49	9	0	0	0.0	27	12	17	6	7	37	9	63	3	2	1	1.0	.971	OF-66

Mike Fitzgerald

FITZGERALD, MICHAEL PATRICK
B. Mar. 28, 1964, Savannah, Ga.
BR TR 6′ 1″ 200 lbs.

Year	Team	Games	BA	SA	AB	H	2B	3B	HR	HR%	R	RBI	BB	SO	SB	Pinch Hit AB	Pinch Hit H	PO	A	E	DP	TC/G	FA	G by Pos
1988	STL N	13	.196	.217	46	9	1	0	0	0.0	4	1	0	9	0	1	0	96	4	1	10	8.4	.990	1B-12

Mike Fitzgerald

FITZGERALD, MICHAEL ROY (Fitz)
B. July 13, 1960, Long Beach, Calif.
BR TR 6′ 185 lbs.

Year	Team	Games	BA	SA	AB	H	2B	3B	HR	HR%	R	RBI	BB	SO	SB	Pinch Hit AB	Pinch Hit H	PO	A	E	DP	TC/G	FA	G by Pos
1983	NY N	8	.100	.250	20	2	0	0	1	5.0	1	2	3	6	0	0	0	37	8	2	2	5.9	.957	C-8
1984		112	.242	.306	360	87	15	1	2	0.6	20	33	24	71	1	7	1	715	47	4	6	7.2	.995	C-107
1985	MON N	108	.207	.288	295	61	7	1	5	1.7	25	34	38	55	5	3	1	542	46	8	7	5.5	.987	C-108
1986		73	.282	.440	209	59	13	1	6	2.9	20	37	27	34	3	3	0	415	35	3	5	6.4	.993	C-71
1987		107	.240	.310	287	69	11	0	3	1.0	32	36	42	54	3	5	2	603	27	12	2	6.1	.981	C-104, 1B-1, 2B-1
1988		63	.271	.419	155	42	6	1	5	3.2	17	23	19	22	2	15	4	262	21	6	2	5.7	.979	C-47, OF-4
1989		100	.238	.386	290	69	18	2	7	2.4	33	42	35	61	3	10	3	465	44	8	5	5.7	.985	C-77, 3B-8, OF-6
1990		111	.243	.393	313	76	18	1	9	2.9	36	41	60	60	8	11	4	565	42	6	10	5.9	.990	C-98, OF-6

Mike Fitzgerald *continued*

Year	Team	Games	BA	SA	AB	H	2B	3B	HR	HR%	R	RBI	BB	SO	SB	Pinch Hit AB	Pinch Hit H	PO	A	E	DP	TC/G	FA	G by Pos
1991		71	.202	.308	198	40	5	2	4	2.0	17	28	22	35	4	8	2	331	27	2	4	6.0	.994	C-54, OF-3, 1B-3
1992	CAL A	95	.212	.317	189	40	2	0	6	3.2	19	17	22	34	2	10	1	296	21	3	4	3.5	.991	C-74, OF-11, 3B-3, 1B-2, DH-1, 2B-1
10 yrs.		848	.235	.346	2316	545	95	9	48	2.1	220	293	292	432	31	72	18	4231	318	54	47	5.8	.988	C-748, OF-30, 3B-11, 1B-6, 2B-2, DH-1

Ray Fitzgerald

FITZGERALD, RAYMOND FRANCIS
B. Dec. 5, 1904, Chicopee, Mass. D. Sept. 6, 1977, Westfield, Mass.
BR TR 5′ 9″ 168 lbs.

Year	Team	Games	BA	SA	AB	H	2B	3B	HR	HR%	R	RBI	BB	SO	SB	Pinch Hit AB	Pinch Hit H	PO	A	E	DP	TC/G	FA	G by Pos
1931	CIN N	1	.000	.000	1	0	0	0	0	0.0	0	0	0	0	0	1	0	0	0	0	0	0.0	—	

Shaun Fitzmaurice

FITZMAURICE, SHAUN EARLE
B. Aug. 25, 1942, Worcester, Mass.
BR TR 6′ 180 lbs.

Year	Team	Games	BA	SA	AB	H	2B	3B	HR	HR%	R	RBI	BB	SO	SB	Pinch Hit AB	Pinch Hit H	PO	A	E	DP	TC/G	FA	G by Pos
1966	NY N	9	.154	.154	13	2	0	0	0	0.0	2	0	2	6	1	1	0	9	1	0	0	2.0	1.000	OF-5

Ed Fitzpatrick

FITZPATRICK, EDWARD HENRY
B. Dec. 9, 1889, Lewiston, Pa. D. Oct. 23, 1965, Bethlehem, Pa.
BR TR 5′ 8″ 165 lbs.

Year	Team	Games	BA	SA	AB	H	2B	3B	HR	HR%	R	RBI	BB	SO	SB	Pinch Hit AB	Pinch Hit H	PO	A	E	DP	TC/G	FA	G by Pos
1915	BOS N	105	.221	.304	303	67	19	3	0	0.0	54	24	43	36	13	2	0	178	161	10	23	3.5	.971	2B-71, OF-29
1916		83	.213	.264	216	46	8	0	1	0.5	17	18	15	26	5	8	2	114	96	9	14	3.0	.959	2B-46, OF-28
1917		63	.253	.343	178	45	8	4	0	0.0	20	17	12	22	4	3	0	71	67	15	5	2.7	.902	2B-22, OF-19, 3B-15
3 yrs.		251	.227	.301	697	158	35	7	1	0.1	91	59	70	84	22	13	2	363	324	34	42	3.1	.953	2B-139, OF-76, 3B-15

Tom Fitzsimmons

FITZSIMMONS, THOMAS WILLIAM
B. Apr. 6, 1890, Oakland, Calif. D. Dec. 20, 1971, Oakland, Calif.
BR TR 6′ 1″ 190 lbs.

Year	Team	Games	BA	SA	AB	H	2B	3B	HR	HR%	R	RBI	BB	SO	SB	Pinch Hit AB	Pinch Hit H	PO	A	E	DP	TC/G	FA	G by Pos
1919	BKN N	4	.000	.000	4	0	0	0	0	0.0	1	0	1	2	0	0	0	1	1	2	0	1.0	.500	3B-4

Max Flack

FLACK, MAX JOHN
B. Feb. 5, 1890, Belleville, Ill. D. July 31, 1975, Belleville, Ill.
BL TL 5′ 7″ 148 lbs.

Year	Team	Games	BA	SA	AB	H	2B	3B	HR	HR%	R	RBI	BB	SO	SB	Pinch Hit AB	Pinch Hit H	PO	A	E	DP	TC/G	FA	G by Pos
1914	CHI F	134	.247	.301	502	124	15	3	2	0.4	66	39	51		37	1	0	232	18	7	2	1.9	.973	OF-133
1915		141	.314	.423	523	164	20	14	3	0.6	88	45	40		37	3	2	226	24	8	5	1.9	.969	OF-138
1916	CHI N	141	.258	.320	465	120	14	3	3	0.6	65	20	42	43	24	3	0	193	22	2	4	1.6	.991	OF-136
1917		131	.248	.320	447	111	18	7	0	0.0	65	21	51	34	17	10	3	199	14	12	3	1.9	.947	OF-117
1918		123	.257	.360	478	123	17	10	4	0.8	74	41	56	19	17	0	0	199	20	5	5	1.9	.978	OF-121
1919		116	.294	.392	469	138	20	4	6	1.3	71	35	34	13	18	0	0	194	18	3	1	1.9	.986	OF-116
1920		135	.302	.406	520	157	30	6	4	0.8	85	49	52	15	13	2	0	216	16	8	2	1.8	.967	OF-132
1921		133	.301	.400	572	172	31	4	6	1.0	80	37	32	15	17	3	1	244	19	3	2	2.0	.989	OF-130
1922	2 teams	CHI N (17G –.222) STL N (66G –.292)																						
″	total	83	.280	.346	321	90	13	1	2	0.6	53	27	33	15	5	1	0	144	5	6	3	1.9	.961	OF-83
1923	STL N	128	.291	.376	505	147	16	9	3	0.6	82	28	41	16	7	6	3	242	8	13	4	2.2	.951	OF-121
1924		67	.263	.373	209	55	11	3	2	1.0	31	21	21	5	3	13	3	90	9	3	0	2.0	.971	OF-52
1925		79	.249	.344	241	60	7	8	0	0.0	23	28	21	9	5	19	3	103	8	1	1	1.9	.991	OF-59
12 yrs.		1411	.278	.366	5252	1461	212	72	35	0.7	783	391	474	184	200	61	15	2282	181	71	32	1.9	.972	OF-1338
WORLD SERIES																								
1918	CHI N	6	.263	.263	19	5	0	0	0	0.0	2	1	4	1	1	0	0	14	2	1	0	2.8	.941	OF-6

Wally Flager

FLAGER, WALTER LEONARD
B. Nov. 3, 1921, Chicago Heights, Ill. D. Dec. 16, 1990, Keizer, Ore.
BL TR 5′11″ 160 lbs.

Year	Team	Games	BA	SA	AB	H	2B	3B	HR	HR%	R	RBI	BB	SO	SB	Pinch Hit AB	Pinch Hit H	PO	A	E	DP	TC/G	FA	G by Pos
1945	2 teams	CIN N (21G –.212) PHI N (49G –.250)																						
″	total	70	.241	.300	220	53	5	1	2	0.9	26	21	25	20	1	5	1	121	179	18	29	5.0	.943	SS-63, 2B-1

Ira Flagstead

FLAGSTEAD, IRA JAMES (Pete)
B. Sept. 22, 1893, Montague, Mich. D. Mar. 13, 1940, Olympia, Wash.
BR TR 5′ 9″ 165 lbs.

Year	Team	Games	BA	SA	AB	H	2B	3B	HR	HR%	R	RBI	BB	SO	SB	Pinch Hit AB	Pinch Hit H	PO	A	E	DP	TC/G	FA	G by Pos
1917	DET A	4	.000	.000	4	0	0	0	0	0.0	0	0	0	1	0	2	0	0	0	0	0	0.0	.000	OF-2
1919		97	.331	.481	287	95	22	3	5	1.7	43	41	35	39	6	11	3	140	15	8	4	2.0	.951	OF-83
1920		110	.235	.338	311	73	13	5	3	1.0	40	35	37	27	3	26	6	164	13	6	4	2.2	.967	OF-82
1921		85	.305	.371	259	79	15	1	0	0.0	40	31	21	21	7	7	2	150	165	28	22	4.5	.918	SS-55, OF-12, 2B-8, 3B-1
1922		44	.308	.527	91	28	5	3	3	3.3	21	8	14	16	0	8	2	54	4	2	1	1.9	.967	OF-31
1923	2 teams	DET A (1G –.000) BOS A (109G –.312)																						
″	total	110	.311	.454	383	119	23	4	8	2.1	55	53	37	26	8	6	0	218	33	10	8	2.6	.962	OF-102
1924	BOS A	149	.305	.420	560	171	35	7	5	0.9	106	43	75	41	10	5	2	370	9	10	2	2.7	.974	OF-143
1925		148	.280	.385	572	160	38	2	6	1.0	84	61	63	30	5	3	1	429	24	11	6	3.2	.976	OF-144
1926		98	.299	.429	415	124	31	7	3	0.7	65	31	36	22	4	0	0	264	14	5	4	2.9	.982	OF-98
1927		131	.285	.401	466	133	26	8	4	0.9	63	69	57	25	12	2	0	326	19	5	4	2.7	.986	OF-129
1928		140	.290	.392	510	148	41	4	1	0.2	84	39	60	23	12	4	0	346	18	10	4	2.8	.973	OF-135
1929	3 teams	BOS A (14G –.306) WAS A (18G –.179) PIT N (26G –.280)																						
″	total	58	.256	.312	125	32	5	1	0	0.0	22	18	13	8	3	23	9	75	4	2	1	2.5	.975	OF-33
1930	PIT N	44	.250	.385	156	39	7	4	2	1.3	21	21	17	9	1	3	0	70	4	3	1	1.9	.961	OF-40
13 yrs.		1218	.290	.406	4139	1201	261	49	40	1.0	644	450	465	288	71	100	25	2606	322	100	61	2.8	.967	OF-1034, SS-55, 2B-8, 3B-1

John Flaherty

FLAHERTY, JOHN TIMOTHY
B. Oct. 21, 1967, New York, N. Y.
BR TR 6′ 1″ 195 lbs.

Year	Team	Games	BA	SA	AB	H	2B	3B	HR	HR%	R	RBI	BB	SO	SB	Pinch Hit AB	Pinch Hit H	PO	A	E	DP	TC/G	FA	G by Pos
1992	BOS A	35	.197	.227	66	13	2	0	0	0.0	3	2	3	7	0	1	0	102	7	2	2	3.3	.982	C-34
1993		13	.120	.200	25	3	2	0	0	0.0	3	2	2	6	0	0	0	35	9	0	0	3.4	1.000	C-13
1994	DET A	34	.150	.175	40	6	1	0	0	0.0	2	4	1	11	0	1	0	78	9	0	0	2.6	1.000	C-33, DH-1
1995		112	.243	.404	354	86	22	1	11	3.1	39	40	18	47	0	2	0	570	33	11	4	5.5	.982	C-112
4 yrs.		194	.223	.351	485	108	27	1	11	2.3	47	48	24	71	0	4	0	785	58	13	6	4.4	.985	C-192, DH-1

Marty Flaherty

FLAHERTY, MARTIN J.
B. Sept. 24, 1853, Worcester, Mass. D. June 10, 1920, Providence, R. I.
BL TL

Year	Team	Games	BA	SA	AB	H	2B	3B	HR	HR%	R	RBI	BB	SO	SB	Pinch Hit AB	Pinch Hit H	PO	A	E	DP	TC/G	FA	G by Pos
1881	WOR N	1	.000	.000	2	0	0	0	0	0.0	0	0	0	2		0	0	0	0	1	0	1.0	.000	OF-1

Pat Flaherty

FLAHERTY, PATRICK HENRY
B. Jan. 31, 1866, St Louis, Mo. D. Jan. 28, 1946, Chicago, Ill.
5′ 9″ 166 lbs.

Year	Team	Games	BA	SA	AB	H	2B	3B	HR	HR%	R	RBI	BB	SO	SB	Pinch Hit AB	Pinch Hit H	PO	A	E	DP	TC/G	FA	G by Pos
1894	LOU N	38	.297	.372	145	43	5	3	0	0.0	15	15	9	6	2	0	0	42	70	19	7	3.4	.855	3B-38

Patsy Flaherty

FLAHERTY, PATRICK JOSEPH — BL TL 5′ 8″ 165 lbs.
B. June 29, 1876, Mansfield, Pa. D. Jan. 23, 1968, Alexandria, La.

Year	Team		Games	BA	SA	AB	H	2B	3B	HR	HR%	R	RBI	BB	SO	SB	Pinch Hit AB	Pinch Hit H	PO	A	E	DP	TC/G	FA	G by Pos
1899	LOU	N	7	.208	.333	24	5	1	1	0	0.0	3	6	3		0	0	0	4	8	5	0	2.4	.706	P-5, OF-2
1900	PIT	N	4	.111	.111	9	1	0	0	0	0.0	0	0	1		0	0	0	0	10	0	0	2.5	1.000	P-4
1903	CHI	A	40	.137	.176	102	14	4	0	0	0.0	7	5	5		4	0	0	21	107	12	5	3.5	.914	P-40
1904	2 teams		CHI A (5G –.333) PIT N (36G –.212)																						
″	total		41	.224	.379	116	26	4	4	2	1.7	10	19	12		0	5	1	34	105	7	3	4.1	.952	P-34, OF-2
1905	PIT	N	30	.197	.303	76	15	4	2	0	0.0	7	4	3		0	1	0	9	70	9	1	3.0	.898	P-27, OF-2
1907	BOS	N	41	.191	.304	115	22	3	2	2	1.7	9	11	2		1	4	1	26	78	9	8	3.2	.920	P-27, OF-8
1908			32	.140	.186	86	12	0	2	0	0.0	8	5	6		2	1	0	20	79	4	3	3.3	.961	P-31
1910	PHI	N	2	.500	.500	2	1	0	0	0	0.0	0	0	0	0	0	0	0	1	0	0	0	0.5	1.000	OF-1, P-1
1911	BOS	N	38	.287	.426	94	27	3	2	2	2.1	9	20	8	11	2	17	**6**	26	6	4	0	1.6	.889	OF-19, P-4
9 yrs.			235	.197	.298	624	123	19	13	6	1.0	53	70	40	11	9	28	8	141	463	50	20	3.2	.924	P-173, OF-34

Al Flair

FLAIR, ALBERT DELL (Broadway) — BL TL 6′ 4″ 195 lbs.
B. July 24, 1916, New Orleans, La. D. July 25, 1988, New Orleans, La.

Year	Team		Games	BA	SA	AB	H	2B	3B	HR	HR%	R	RBI	BB	SO	SB	Pinch Hit AB	Pinch Hit H	PO	A	E	DP	TC/G	FA	G by Pos
1941	BOS	A	10	.200	.333	30	6	2	1	0	0.0	3	2	1	1	1	2	0	63	4	0	5	8.4	1.000	1B-8

Charlie Flanagan

FLANAGAN, CHARLES JAMES — BR TR 6′ 175 lbs.
B. Dec. 31, 1891, Oakland, Calif. D. Jan. 8, 1930, San Francisco, Calif.

Year	Team		Games	BA	SA	AB	H	2B	3B	HR	HR%	R	RBI	BB	SO	SB	Pinch Hit AB	Pinch Hit H	PO	A	E	DP	TC/G	FA	G by Pos
1913	STL	A	4	.000	.000	3	0	0	0	0	0.0	0	0	1	0	0	1	0	1	0	0	0	0.5	1.000	OF-1, 3B-1

Ed Flanagan

FLANAGAN, EDWARD J. — TR 6′ 1″ 190 lbs.
B. Sept. 15, 1861, Lowell, Mass. D. Nov. 10, 1926, Lowell, Mass.

Year	Team		Games	BA	SA	AB	H	2B	3B	HR	HR%	R	RBI	BB	SO	SB	Pinch Hit AB	Pinch Hit H	PO	A	E	DP	TC/G	FA	G by Pos
1887	PHI	AA	19	.250	.350	80	20	5	0	1	1.3	12		3		3	0	0	158	5	9	9	9.1	.948	1B-19
1889	LOU	AA	23	.250	.398	88	22	7	3	0	0.0	11	8	7	11	1	0	0	254	10	13	11	12.0	.953	1B-23
2 yrs.			42	.250	.375	168	42	12	3	1	0.6	23	8	10	11	4	0	0	412	15	22	20	10.7	.951	1B-42

Steamer Flanagan

FLANAGAN, JAMES PAUL — BL TL 6′ 1″ 185 lbs.
B. Apr. 20, 1881, Kingston, Pa. D. Apr. 21, 1947, Wilkes-Barre, Pa.

Year	Team		Games	BA	SA	AB	H	2B	3B	HR	HR%	R	RBI	BB	SO	SB	Pinch Hit AB	Pinch Hit H	PO	A	E	DP	TC/G	FA	G by Pos
1905	PIT	N	7	.280	.400	25	7	1	1	0	0.0	7	3	1		3	2	0	19	0	0	0	3.8	1.000	OF-5

John Flannery

FLANNERY, JOHN MICHAEL — BR TR 6′ 3″ 173 lbs.
B. Jan. 25, 1957, Long Beach, Calif.

Year	Team		Games	BA	SA	AB	H	2B	3B	HR	HR%	R	RBI	BB	SO	SB	Pinch Hit AB	Pinch Hit H	PO	A	E	DP	TC/G	FA	G by Pos
1977	CHI	A	7	.000	.000	2	0	0	0	0	0.0	1	0	1	1	0	0	0	1	4	0	1	0.8	1.000	SS-4, DH-1, 3B-1

Tim Flannery

FLANNERY, TIMOTHY EARL — BL TR 5′11″ 175 lbs.
B. Sept. 29, 1957, Tulsa, Okla.

Year	Team		Games	BA	SA	AB	H	2B	3B	HR	HR%	R	RBI	BB	SO	SB	Pinch Hit AB	Pinch Hit H	PO	A	E	DP	TC/G	FA	G by Pos
1979	SD	N	22	.154	.185	65	10	0	1	0	0.0	2	4	4	5	0	0	0	45	60	1	16	5.0	.991	2B-21
1980			95	.240	.281	292	70	12	0	0	0.0	15	25	18	30	2	12	5	140	204	8	34	3.7	.977	2B-53, 3B-41
1981			37	.254	.343	67	17	4	1	0	0.0	4	6	2	4	1	16	6	16	32	2	5	2.3	.960	3B-15, 2B-7
1982			122	.264	.330	379	100	11	7	0	0.0	40	30	30	32	1	16	3	226	278	14	47	4.7	.973	2B-104, 3B-5, SS-2
1983			92	.234	.336	214	50	7	3	3	1.4	24	19	20	23	2	19	4	63	156	4	19	2.8	.982	3B-52, 2B-21, SS-7
1984			86	.273	.391	128	35	3	3	2	1.6	24	10	12	17	4	40	7	36	69	5	12	2.2	.955	2B-22, SS-14, 3B-14
1985			126	.281	.341	384	108	14	3	1	0.3	50	40	58	39	2	13	3	261	287	13	72	4.6	.977	2B-121, 3B-1
1986			134	.280	.345	368	103	11	2	3	0.8	48	28	54	61	3	16	3	226	275	5	56	3.6	.990	2B-108, 3B-23, SS-8
1987			106	.228	.254	276	63	5	1	0	0.0	23	20	42	30	2	23	2	142	226	7	42	4.0	.981	2B-84, 3B-8, SS-2
1988			79	.265	.341	170	45	5	4	0	0.0	16	19	24	32	3	26	8	28	76	3	8	2.0	.972	3B-51, 2B-2, SS-1
1989			73	.231	.269	130	30	5	0	0	0.0	9	8	13	20	2	35	9	14	56	6	3	2.2	.921	3B-33, 2B-1
11 yrs.			972	.255	.317	2473	631	77	25	9	0.4	255	209	277	293	22	216	50	1197	1719	68	314	3.6	.977	2B-544, 3B-243, SS-34
LEAGUE CHAMPIONSHIP SERIES																									
1984	SD	N	3	.500	.500	2	1	0	0	0	0.0	2	0	0	0	0	2	1	0	0	0	0	0.0	—	
WORLD SERIES																									
1984	SD	N	1	1.000	1.000	1	1	0	0	0	0.0	0	0	0	0	0	1	1	1	0	0	0	1.0	1.000	2B-1

Ray Flaskamper

FLASKAMPER, RAYMOND HAROLD (Flash) — BB TR 5′ 7″ 140 lbs.
B. Oct. 31, 1901, St. Louis, Mo. D. Feb. 3, 1978, San Antonio, Tex.

Year	Team		Games	BA	SA	AB	H	2B	3B	HR	HR%	R	RBI	BB	SO	SB	Pinch Hit AB	Pinch Hit H	PO	A	E	DP	TC/G	FA	G by Pos
1927	CHI	A	26	.221	.274	95	21	5	0	0	0.0	12	6	3	8	0	1	0	55	70	5	10	5.2	.962	SS-25

Angel Fleitas

FLEITAS, ANGEL FELIX — BR TR 5′ 9″ 160 lbs.
Born Angel Felix Fleitas (Husta).
B. Nov. 10, 1914, Los Abreus, Cuba.

Year	Team		Games	BA	SA	AB	H	2B	3B	HR	HR%	R	RBI	BB	SO	SB	Pinch Hit AB	Pinch Hit H	PO	A	E	DP	TC/G	FA	G by Pos
1948	WAS	A	15	.077	.077	13	1	0	0	0	0.0	1	1	3	5	0	3	1	7	13	1	0	3.0	.952	SS-7

Les Fleming

FLEMING, LESLIE HARVEY (Moe) — BL TL 5′10″ 185 lbs.
B. Aug. 7, 1915, Singleton, Tex. D. Mar. 5, 1980, Cleveland, Tex.

Year	Team		Games	BA	SA	AB	H	2B	3B	HR	HR%	R	RBI	BB	SO	SB	Pinch Hit AB	Pinch Hit H	PO	A	E	DP	TC/G	FA	G by Pos
1939	DET	A	8	.000	.000	16	0	0	0	0	0.0	0	1	0	4	0	5	0	6	0	0	0	2.0	1.000	OF-3
1941	CLE	A	2	.250	.375	8	2	1	0	0	0.0	0	2	0	0	0	0	0	20	1	0	3	10.5	1.000	1B-2
1942			156	.292	.432	548	160	27	4	14	2.6	71	82	106	57	6	0	0	1503	90	12	152	10.3	.993	1B-156
1945			42	.329	.493	140	46	10	2	3	2.1	18	22	11	5	0	3	1	91	6	5	4	2.7	.951	OF-33, 1B-5
1946			99	.278	.444	306	85	17	5	8	2.6	40	42	50	42	1	17	5	608	62	12	60	8.4	.982	1B-80, OF-1
1947			103	.242	.349	281	68	14	2	4	1.4	39	43	53	42	0	20	6	662	63	8	78	9.5	.989	1B-77
1949	PIT	N	24	.258	.387	31	8	0	2	0	0.0	0	7	6	2	0	16	4	43	0	0	4	8.6	1.000	1B-5
7 yrs.			434	.277	.417	1330	369	69	15	29	2.2	168	199	226	152	7	61	16	2933	222	37	301	8.8	.988	1B-325, OF-37

Tom Fleming

FLEMING, THOMAS VINCENT (Sleuth) — BL TL 5′11″ 155 lbs.
B. Nov. 20, 1873, Philadelphia, Pa. D. Dec. 26, 1957, Boston, Mass.

Year	Team		Games	BA	SA	AB	H	2B	3B	HR	HR%	R	RBI	BB	SO	SB	Pinch Hit AB	Pinch Hit H	PO	A	E	DP	TC/G	FA	G by Pos
1899	NY	N	22	.208	.247	77	16	1	1	0	0.0	9	4	1		1	0	0	35	5	4	0	2.0	.909	OF-22
1902	PHI	N	5	.375	.375	16	6	0	0	0	0.0	2	2	1		0	0	0	3	2	0	0	1.0	1.000	OF-5
1904			3	.000	.000	6	0	0	0	0	0.0	0	0	0		0	2	0	0	1	0	0	1.0	1.000	OF-1
3 yrs.			30	.222	.253	99	22	1	1	0	0.0	11	6	2		1	2	0	38	8	4	0	1.8	.920	OF-28

Art Fletcher

FLETCHER, ARTHUR BR TR 5′10½″ 170 lbs.
B. Jan. 5, 1885, Collinsville, Ill. D. Feb. 6, 1950, Los Angeles, Calif.
Manager 1923–26, 1929.

Year	Team	Games	BA	SA	AB	H	2B	3B	HR	HR%	R	RBI	BB	SO	SB	Pinch Hit AB	Pinch Hit H	PO	A	E	DP	TC/G	FA	G by Pos
1909	NY N	29	.214	.235	98	21	0	1	0	0.0	7	6	1		0	0	0	52	80	17	10	5.1	.886	SS-19, 3B-5, 2B-5
1910		51	.224	.256	125	28	2	1	0	0.0	12	13	4	9	9	4	0	59	67	12	8	3.1	.913	SS-22, 3B-11, 2B-11
1911		112	.319	.429	326	104	17	8	1	0.3	73	37	30	27	20	2	1	153	285	32	27	4.4	.932	SS-74, 3B-21, 2B-13
1912		129	.282	.372	419	118	17	9	1	0.2	64	57	16	29	16	0	0	241	429	53	60	5.6	.927	SS-126, 2B-2, 3B-1
1913		136	.297	.390	538	160	20	9	4	0.7	76	71	24	35	32	0	0	245	435	50	42	5.4	.932	SS-136
1914		135	.286	.379	514	147	26	8	2	0.4	62	79	22	37	15	0	0	299	446	63	46	6.0	.922	SS-135
1915		149	.254	.326	562	143	17	7	3	0.5	59	74	6	36	12	0	0	302	544	58	76	6.1	.936	SS-149
1916		133	.286	.382	500	143	23	8	3	0.6	53	66	13	36	15	0	0	253	497	48	56	6.0	.940	SS-133
1917		151	.260	.343	557	145	24	5	4	0.7	70	56	23	28	12	0	0	276	565	39	71	5.8	.956	SS-151
1918		124	.263	.314	468	123	20	2	0	0.0	51	47	18	26	12	0	0	268	484	32	54	6.3	.959	SS-124
1919		127	.277	.357	488	135	20	5	3	0.6	54	54	9	28	6	0	0	265	521	47	49	6.6	.944	SS-127
1920	2 teams	NY N (41G –.257) PHI N (102G –.296)																						
″	total	143	.284	.396	550	156	32	9	4	0.7	57	62	16	43	7	1	0	302	522	48	63	6.1	.945	SS-142
1922	PHI N	110	.280	.409	396	111	20	5	7	1.8	46	53	21	14	3	4	1	202	379	38	63	5.8	.939	SS-106
13 yrs.		1529	.277	.365	5541	1534	238	77	32	0.6	684	675	203	348	159	11	2	2917	5254	537	625	5.8	.938	SS-1444, 3B-38, 2B-31
WORLD SERIES																								
1911	NY N	6	.130	.174	23	3	1	0	0	0.0	1	1	0	4	0	0	0	11	17	4	1	5.3	.875	SS-6
1912		8	.179	.214	28	5	1	0	0	0.0	1	3	1	4	1	0	0	16	23	4	1	5.4	.907	SS-8
1913		5	.278	.278	18	5	0	0	0	0.0	1	4	1	1	1	0	0	8	10	1	0	3.8	.947	SS-5
1917		6	.200	.240	25	5	1	0	0	0.0	2	0	0	2	0	0	0	9	17	3	1	4.8	.897	SS-6
4 yrs.		25	.191	.223	94	18	3	0	0	0.0	5	8	2	11	2	0	0	44	67	12	3	4.9	.902	SS-25

Darrin Fletcher

FLETCHER, DARRIN GLEN BL TR 6′ 2″ 195 lbs.
Son of Tom Fletcher.
B. Oct. 3, 1966, Elmhurst, Ill.

Year	Team	Games	BA	SA	AB	H	2B	3B	HR	HR%	R	RBI	BB	SO	SB	Pinch Hit AB	Pinch Hit H	PO	A	E	DP	TC/G	FA	G by Pos
1989	LA N	5	.500	.875	8	4	0	0	1	12.5	1	2	1	0	0	2	1	16	1	0	0	3.4	1.000	C-5
1990	2 teams	LA N (2G –.000) PHI N (9G –.136)																						
″	total	11	.130	.174	23	3	1	0	0	0.0	3	1	1	6	0	4	0	30	3	0	0	4.7	1.000	C-7
1991	PHI N	46	.228	.309	136	31	8	0	1	0.7	5	12	5	15	0	1	0	242	22	2	1	5.9	.992	C-45
1992	MON N	83	.243	.333	222	54	10	2	2	0.9	13	26	14	28	0	16	4	360	33	2	3	5.7	.995	C-69
1993		133	.255	.379	396	101	20	1	9	2.3	33	60	34	40	0	16	7	620	41	8	3	5.3	.988	C-127
1994		94	.260	.435	285	74	18	1	10	3.5	28	57	25	23	0	12	2	479	20	2	2	6.2	.996	C-81
1995		110	.286	.446	350	100	21	1	11	3.1	42	45	32	23	0	11	4	612	45	4	5	6.7	.994	C-98
7 yrs.		482	.258	.392	1420	367	78	5	34	2.4	125	203	112	135	0	62	18	2359	165	18	14	5.9	.993	C-432

Elbie Fletcher

FLETCHER, ELBURT PRESTON BL TL 6′ 180 lbs.
B. Mar. 18, 1916, Milton, Mass. D. Mar. 9, 1994, Milton, Mass.

Year	Team	Games	BA	SA	AB	H	2B	3B	HR	HR%	R	RBI	BB	SO	SB	Pinch Hit AB	Pinch Hit H	PO	A	E	DP	TC/G	FA	G by Pos
1934	BOS N	8	.500	.500	4	2	0	0	0	0.0	4	0	0	2	1	0	0	7	0	1	1	8.0	.875	1B-1
1935		39	.236	.318	148	35	7	1	1	0.7	12	9	7	13	1	0	0	353	27	1	22	9.8	.997	1B-39
1937		148	.247	.308	539	133	22	4	1	0.2	56	38	56	64	3	0	0	1587	108	12	117	11.5	.993	1B-148
1938		147	.272	.378	529	144	24	7	6	1.1	71	48	60	40	5	1	0	1424	126	15	108	10.7	.990	1B-146
1939	2 teams	BOS N (35G –.245) PIT N (102G –.303)																						
″	total	137	.290	.435	476	138	25	4	12	2.5	63	77	67	33	4	4	1	1345	64	13	97	10.8	.991	1B-132
1940	PIT N	147	.273	.437	510	139	22	7	16	3.1	94	104	**119**	54	5	0	0	1512	104	11	128	11.1	.993	1B-147
1941		151	.288	.457	521	150	29	13	11	2.1	95	74	**118**	54	5	0	0	1444	118	14	113	10.4	.991	1B-151
1942		145	.289	.393	506	146	22	5	7	1.4	86	57	105	60	0	1	1	1379	118	12	104	10.5	.992	1B-144
1943		154	.283	.395	544	154	24	5	9	1.7	91	70	95	49	1	0	0	1541	108	6	141	10.7	.996	1B-154
1946		148	.256	.355	532	136	25	8	4	0.8	72	66	111	37	4	1	0	1356	106	8	97	10.0	.995	1B-147
1947		69	.242	.331	157	38	9	1	1	0.6	22	22	29	24	2	18	2	324	25	5	28	7.1	.986	1B-50
1949	BOS N	122	.262	.402	413	108	19	3	11	2.7	57	51	84	65	1	0	0	965	71	9	96	8.6	.991	1B-121
12 yrs.		1415	.271	.390	4879	1323	228	58	79	1.6	723	616	851	495	32	25	4	13237	975	107	1052	10.4	.993	1B-1380

Frank Fletcher

FLETCHER, OLIVER FRANK (Fletch) BR TR 5′10″ 165 lbs.
B. Mar. 6, 1891, Hindreth, Ill. D. Oct. 7, 1974, St. Petersburg, Fla.

Year	Team	Games	BA	SA	AB	H	2B	3B	HR	HR%	R	RBI	BB	SO	SB	Pinch Hit AB	Pinch Hit H	PO	A	E	DP	TC/G	FA	G by Pos
1914	PHI N	1	.000	.000	1	0	0	0	0	0.0	0	0	0	1	0	1	0	0	0	0	0	0.0	—	

Scott Fletcher

FLETCHER, SCOTT BRIAN BR TR 5′11″ 168 lbs.
B. July 30, 1958, Fort Walton Beach, Fla.

Year	Team	Games	BA	SA	AB	H	2B	3B	HR	HR%	R	RBI	BB	SO	SB	Pinch Hit AB	Pinch Hit H	PO	A	E	DP	TC/G	FA	G by Pos
1981	CHI N	19	.217	.304	46	10	4	0	0	0.0	6	1	2	4	0	0	0	34	44	3	10	4.5	.963	2B-13, SS-4, 3B-1
1982		11	.167	.167	24	4	0	0	0	0.0	4	1	4	5	1	0	0	11	23	0	3	3.1	1.000	SS-11
1983	CHI A	114	.237	.370	262	62	16	5	3	1.1	42	31	29	22	5	0	0	126	308	16	64	3.8	.964	SS-100, 2B-12, 3B-7, DH-1
1984		149	.250	.311	456	114	13	3	3	0.7	46	35	46	46	10	0	0	234	439	19	89	4.2	.973	SS-134, 2B-28, 3B-3
1985		119	.256	.309	301	77	8	1	2	0.7	38	31	35	47	5	12	3	123	208	8	36	2.5	.976	3B-55, SS-44, 2B-37, DH-2
1986	TEX A	147	.300	.400	530	159	34	5	3	0.6	82	50	47	59	12	0	0	216	388	16	93	3.9	.974	SS-136, 3B-12, 2B-11, DH-1
1987		156	.287	.374	588	169	28	4	5	0.9	82	63	61	66	13	3	1	249	413	23	98	4.4	.966	SS-155
1988		140	.276	.328	515	142	19	4	0	0.0	59	47	62	34	8	2	0	215	414	11	90	4.6	.983	SS-139
1989	2 teams	TEX A (83G –.239) CHI A (59G –.272)																						
″	total	142	.253	.311	546	138	25	2	1	0.2	77	43	64	60	2	1	0	241	362	15	88	4.3	.976	SS-89, 2B-53, DH-1
1990	CHI A	151	.242	.312	509	123	18	3	4	0.8	54	56	45	63	1	0	0	305	436	9	115	5.0	.988	2B-151
1991		90	.206	.266	248	51	10	1	1	0.4	14	28	17	26	0	6	2	178	192	3	49	4.1	.992	2B-86, 3B-4
1992	MIL A	123	.275	.360	386	106	18	3	3	0.8	53	51	30	33	17	4	0	236	382	9	84	4.9	.986	2B-106, SS-22, 3B-1
1993	BOS A	121	.285	.402	480	137	31	5	5	1.0	81	45	37	35	16	4	0	217	371	11	68	5.0	.982	2B-116, SS-2, DH-1, 3B-1
1994		63	.227	.335	185	42	9	1	3	1.6	31	11	16	14	8	2	0	118	163	1	40	4.9	.996	2B-54, DH-4
1995	DET A	67	.231	.313	182	42	10	1	1	0.5	19	17	19	27	1	1	0	111	162	0	48	4.1	1.000	2B-63, SS-3, 1B-1
15 yrs.		1612	.262	.342	5258	1376	243	38	34	0.6	688	510	514	541	99	35	6	2614	4305	144	975	4.2	.980	SS-839, 2B-730, 3B-84, DH-10, 1B-1
LEAGUE CHAMPIONSHIP SERIES																								
1983	CHI A	3	.000	.000	7	0	0	0	0	0.0	0	0	1	0	0	0	0	3	8	0	1	3.7	1.000	SS-3

Elmer Flick

FLICK, ELMER HARRISON BL TR 5′ 9″ 168 lbs.
B. Jan. 11, 1876, Bedford, Ohio D. Jan. 9, 1971, Bedford, Ohio.
Hall of Fame 1963.

Year	Team	Games	BA	SA	AB	H	2B	3B	HR	HR%	R	RBI	BB	SO	SB	Pinch Hit AB	Pinch Hit H	PO	A	E	DP	TC/G	FA	G by Pos
1898	PHI N	134	.302	.448	453	137	16	13	8	1.8	84	81	86		23	1	0	237	21	19	4	2.1	.931	OF-133
1899		127	.342	.445	485	166	22	11	2	0.4	98	98	42		31	2	1	234	24	19	7	2.2	.931	OF-125
1900		138	.367	.545	545	200	32	16	11	2.0	106	**110**	56		35	0	0	232	23	24	6	2.0	.914	OF-138
1901		138	.336	.500	542	182	31	17	8	1.5	112	88	52		30	0	0	278	23	12	7	2.3	.962	OF-138
1902	2 teams	PHI A (11G –.297) CLE A (110G –.297)																						
″	total	121	.297	.410	461	137	22	12	2	0.4	85	64	53		24	0	0	173	14	14	2	1.7	.930	OF-121
1903	CLE A	142	.299	.414	529	158	23	16	2	0.4	84	51	51		24	0	0	219	15	11	3	1.8	.955	OF-140
1904		150	.306	.453	579	177	31	18	6	1.0	97	56	51		**42**	0	0	248	42	12	6	2.0	.960	OF-144, 2B-6
1905		131	**.306**	**.466**	496	152	29	**19**	4	0.8	71	64	53		35	0	0	181	20	14	3	1.6	.935	OF-130, 2B-1
1906		157	.311	.439	**624**	194	33	**22**	1	0.2	**98**	62	54		**39**	0	0	263	38	7	7	1.9	.977	OF-150, 2B-8
1907		147	.302	.412	549	166	15	**18**	3	0.5	78	58	64		41	0	0	219	22	11	7	1.7	.956	OF-147
1908		9	.229	.314	35	8	1	1	0	0.0	4	2	3		0	0	0	10	1	0	1	1.2	1.000	OF-9
1909		66	.255	.315	235	60	10	2	0	0.0	28	15	22		9	5	2	87	4	4	1	1.6	.958	OF-61
1910		24	.265	.368	68	18	2	1	1	1.5	5	7	10		1	4	0	21	0	1	0	1.2	.955	OF-18
13 yrs.		1484	.313	.446	5601	1755	267	166	48	0.9	950	756	597		334	12	3	2402	247	148	54	1.9	.947	OF-1454, 2B-15

Lew Flick

FLICK, LEWIS MILLER BL TL 5′ 9″ 155 lbs.
B. Feb. 18, 1915, Bristol, Tenn. D. Dec. 7, 1990, Weber City, Va.

Year	Team	Games	BA	SA	AB	H	2B	3B	HR	HR%	R	RBI	BB	SO	SB	Pinch Hit AB	Pinch Hit H	PO	A	E	DP	TC/G	FA	G by Pos
1943	PHI A	1	.600	.600	5	3	0	0	0	0.0	2	0	0	0	0	0	0	3	0	0	0	3.0	1.000	OF-1
1944		19	.114	.114	35	4	0	0	0	0.0	1	2	1	2	1	13	0	9	0	0	0	1.5	1.000	OF-6
2 yrs.		20	.175	.175	40	7	0	0	0	0.0	3	2	1	2	1	13	0	12	0	0	0	1.7	1.000	OF-7

Don Flinn

FLINN, DON RAPHAEL BR TR 6′ 1″ 185 lbs.
B. Nov. 17, 1892, Bluffdale, Tex. D. Mar. 9, 1959, Waco, Tex.

Year	Team	Games	BA	SA	AB	H	2B	3B	HR	HR%	R	RBI	BB	SO	SB	Pinch Hit AB	Pinch Hit H	PO	A	E	DP	TC/G	FA	G by Pos
1917	PIT N	14	.297	.378	37	11	1	1	0	0.0	1	1	1	6	1	2	1	24	1	0	0	2.1	1.000	OF-12

Silver Flint

FLINT, FRANK SYLVESTER BR TR 6′ 180 lbs.
B. Aug. 3, 1855, Philadelphia, Pa. D. Jan. 14, 1892, Chicago, Ill.
Manager 1879.

Year	Team	Games	BA	SA	AB	H	2B	3B	HR	HR%	R	RBI	BB	SO	SB	Pinch Hit AB	Pinch Hit H	PO	A	E	DP	TC/G	FA	G by Pos
1878	IND N	63	.224	.252	254	57	7	0	0	0.0	23	18	2	15		0	0	296	102	44	7	6.5	.900	C-59, OF-9
1879	CHI N	79	.284	.398	324	92	22	6	1	0.3	46	41	6	44		0	0	343	109	42	6	6.3	.915	C-78, OF-1
1880		74	.162	.225	284	46	10	4	0	0.0	30	17	5	32		0	0	394	119	39	5	6.9	.929	C-67, OF-13
1881		80	.310	.379	306	95	18	0	1	0.3	46	34	6	39		0	0	326	92	27	6	5.0	.939	C-80, OF-8, 1B-1
1882		81	.251	.390	331	83	18	8	4	1.2	48	44	2	**50**		0	0	446	91	38	3	6.3	.934	C-81, OF-10
1883		85	.265	.358	332	88	23	4	0	0.0	57		3	69		0	0	311	106	61	4	4.5	.872	C-83, OF-23
1884		73	.204	.333	279	57	5	2	9	3.2	35		7	57		0	0	354	110	61	9	7.2	.884	C-73
1885		68	.209	.269	249	52	8	2	1	0.4	27	19	2	52		0	0	356	100	36	2	7.1	.927	C-68, OF-1
1886		54	.202	.277	173	35	6	2	1	0.6	30	13	12	36		0	0	313	94	47	3	8.0	.896	C-54, 1B-3
1887		49	.267	.422	187	50	8	6	3	1.6	22	21	4	28	7	0	0	280	74	34	4	7.9	.912	C-47, 1B-2
1888		22	.182	.221	77	14	3	0	0	0.0	6	3	1	21	1	0	0	96	42	11	7	6.8	.926	C-22
1889		15	.232	.304	56	13	1	0	1	1.8	6	9	3	18	1	0	0	65	19	9	0	6.2	.903	C-15
12 yrs.		743	.239	.330	2852	682	129	34	21	0.7	376	219	53	461	9	0	0	3580	1058	449	56	6.4	.912	C-727, OF-65, 1B-6

Curt Flood

FLOOD, CURTIS CHARLES BR TR 5′ 9″ 165 lbs.
B. Jan. 18, 1938, Houston, Tex.

Year	Team	Games	BA	SA	AB	H	2B	3B	HR	HR%	R	RBI	BB	SO	SB	Pinch Hit AB	Pinch Hit H	PO	A	E	DP	TC/G	FA	G by Pos
1956	CIN N	5	.000	.000	1	0	0	0	0	0.0	0	0	0	1	0	1	0	0	0	0	0	0.0	—	
1957		3	.333	1.333	3	1	0	0	1	33.3	2	1	0	0	0	1	0	1	0	0	0	0.3	1.000	3B-2, 2B-1
1958	STL N	121	.261	.382	422	110	17	2	10	2.4	50	41	31	56	2	0	0	346	18	8	3	3.1	.978	OF-120, 3B-1
1959		121	.255	.418	208	53	7	3	7	3.4	24	26	16	35	2	10	5	147	1	5	1	1.4	.967	OF-106, 2B-1
1960		140	.237	.354	396	94	20	1	8	2.0	37	38	35	54	0	2	0	291	7	2	0	2.2	.993	OF-134, 3B-1
1961		132	.322	.415	335	108	15	5	2	0.6	53	21	35	33	6	12	4	241	13	4	4	2.2	.984	OF-119
1962		151	.296	.416	635	188	30	5	12	1.9	99	70	42	57	8	0	0	387	12	4	5	2.7	.990	OF-151
1963		158	.302	.403	**662**	200	34	9	5	0.8	112	63	42	57	17	1	0	401	12	5	2	2.6	.988	OF-158
1964		162	.311	.378	**679**	**211**	25	3	5	0.7	97	46	43	53	8	1	0	391	10	5	2	2.5	.988	OF-162
1965		156	.310	.421	617	191	30	3	11	1.8	90	83	51	50	9	5	0	349	7	5	3	2.4	.986	OF-151
1966		160	.267	.364	626	167	21	5	10	1.6	64	78	26	50	14	0	0	391	5	0	1	2.5	1.000	OF-159
1967		134	.335	.414	514	172	24	1	5	1.0	68	50	37	46	2	8	4	314	4	4	1	2.6	.988	OF-126
1968		150	.301	.366	618	186	17	4	5	0.8	71	60	33	58	11	2	0	386	11	7	4	2.7	.983	OF-149
1969		153	.285	.366	606	173	31	3	4	0.7	80	57	48	57	9	2	1	362	14	4	2	2.5	.989	OF-152
1971	WAS A	13	.200	.200	35	7	0	0	0	0.0	4	2	5	2	0	1	0	16	0	1	0	1.7	.941	OF-10
15 yrs.		1759	.293	.389	6357	1861	271	44	85	1.3	851	636	444	609	88	46	14	4023	114	54	28	2.5	.987	OF-1697, 3B-4, 2B-2
WORLD SERIES																								
1964	STL N	7	.200	.267	30	6	0	1	0	0.0	5	3	3	1	0	0	0	13	0	0	0	1.9	1.000	OF-7
1967		7	.179	.214	28	5	1	0	0	0.0	2	3	3	3	0	0	0	15	0	0	0	2.1	1.000	OF-7
1968		7	.286	.321	28	8	1	0	0	0.0	4	2	2	2	3	0	0	13	0	0	0	1.9	1.000	OF-7
3 yrs.		21	.221	.267	86	19	2	1	0	0.0	11	8	8	6	3	0	0	41	0	0	0	2.0	1.000	OF-21

Tim Flood

FLOOD, TIMOTHY A. BR TR 5′ 9″ 160 lbs.
B. Mar. 13, 1877, Montgomery City, Mo. D. June 15, 1929, St. Louis, Mo.

Year	Team	Games	BA	SA	AB	H	2B	3B	HR	HR%	R	RBI	BB	SO	SB	Pinch Hit AB	Pinch Hit H	PO	A	E	DP	TC/G	FA	G by Pos
1899	STL N	10	.290	.290	31	9	0	0	0	0.0	0	3	4		1	0	0	15	28	6	3	4.9	.878	2B-10
1902	BKN N	132	.218	.277	476	104	11	4	3	0.6	43	50	23		8	0	0	298	374	41	33	5.4	.942	2B-132, OF-1
1903		89	.249	.311	309	77	15	2	0	0.0	27	32	15		14	2	0	200	227	36	37	5.3	.922	2B-84, SS-2, OF-1
3 yrs.		231	.233	.290	816	190	26	6	3	0.4	70	85	42		23	2	0	513	629	83	73	5.3	.932	2B-226, SS-2, OF-2

Kevin Flora

FLORA, KEVIN SCOT BR TR 6′ 180 lbs.
B. June 10, 1969, Fontana, Calif.

Year	Team	Games	BA	SA	AB	H	2B	3B	HR	HR%	R	RBI	BB	SO	SB	Pinch Hit AB	Pinch Hit H	PO	A	E	DP	TC/G	FA	G by Pos
1991	CAL A	3	.125	.125	8	1	0	0	0	0.0	1	0	1	5	1	0	0	8	3	2	1	4.3	.846	2B-3
1995	2 teams	CAL A (2G –.000) PHI N (24G –.213)																						
″	total	26	.211	.329	76	16	3	0	2	2.6	13	7	4	23	1	5	0	33	1	0	0	1.6	1.000	OF-20, DH-1
2 yrs.		29	.202	.310	84	17	3	0	2	2.4	14	7	5	28	2	5	0	41	4	2	1	2.0	.957	OF-20, 2B-3, DH-1

Year	Team	Games	BA	SA	AB	H	2B	3B	HR	HR%	R	RBI	BB	SO	SB	Pinch Hit AB	Pinch Hit H	PO	A	E	DP	TC/G	FA	G by Pos

Paul Florence

FLORENCE, PAUL ROBERT (Pep) BB TR 6′ 1″ 185 lbs.
B. Apr. 22, 1900, Chicago, Ill. D. May 28, 1986, Gainesville, Fla.

Year	Team	Games	BA	SA	AB	H	2B	3B	HR	HR%	R	RBI	BB	SO	SB	Pinch Hit AB	Pinch Hit H	PO	A	E	DP	TC/G	FA	G by Pos
1926	NY N	76	.229	.314	188	43	4	3	2	1.1	19	14	23	12	2	0	0	212	41	17	7	3.6	.937	C-76

Gil Flores

FLORES, GILBERTO BR TR 6′ 185 lbs.
Born Gilberto Flores (Garcia).
B. Oct. 27, 1952, Ponce, Puerto Rico.

Year	Team	Games	BA	SA	AB	H	2B	3B	HR	HR%	R	RBI	BB	SO	SB	Pinch Hit AB	Pinch Hit H	PO	A	E	DP	TC/G	FA	G by Pos
1977	CAL A	104	.278	.365	342	95	19	4	1	0.3	41	26	23	39	12	10	2	177	5	4	2	2.0	.978	OF-85, DH-8
1978	NY N	11	.276	.345	29	8	0	1	0	0.0	8	1	3	5	1	1	0	17	0	1	0	2.3	.944	OF-8
1979		70	.194	.258	93	18	1	1	1	1.1	9	10	8	17	2	39	7	39	1	1	0	1.3	.976	OF-32
3 yrs.		185	.261	.343	464	121	20	6	2	0.4	58	37	34	61	15	50	9	233	6	6	2	1.8	.976	OF-125, DH-8

Jake Flowers

FLOWERS, D'ARCY RAYMOND BR TR 5′11½″ 170 lbs.
B. Mar. 16, 1902, Cambridge, Md. D. Dec. 27, 1962, Clearwater, Fla.

Year	Team	Games	BA	SA	AB	H	2B	3B	HR	HR%	R	RBI	BB	SO	SB	Pinch Hit AB	Pinch Hit H	PO	A	E	DP	TC/G	FA	G by Pos
1923	STL N	13	.094	.125	32	3	1	0	0	0.0	0	2	2	7	1	1	0	15	28	2	1	4.1	.956	SS-7, 3B-2, 2B-2
1926		40	.270	.405	74	20	1	0	3	4.1	13	9	5	9	1	23	6	38	45	3	5	5.7	.965	2B-11, 1B-3, SS-1
1927	BKN N	67	.234	.325	231	54	5	5	2	0.9	26	20	21	25	3	1	0	139	189	19	29	5.3	.945	SS-65, 2B-1
1928		103	.274	.360	339	93	11	6	2	0.6	51	44	47	30	10	3	1	263	273	16	46	5.5	.971	2B-94, SS-6
1929		46	.200	.269	130	26	6	0	1	0.8	16	16	22	6	9	5	2	96	109	8	17	5.5	.962	2B-39
1930		89	.320	.439	253	81	18	3	2	0.8	37	50	21	18	5	16	6	154	200	19	42	5.7	.949	2B-65, OF-1
1931	2 teams BKN N (22G –.226) STL N (45G –.248)																							
″	total	67	.244	.357	168	41	11	1	2	1.2	22	20	16	10	8	12	3	89	135	4	29	4.6	.982	2B-26, SS-23, 3B-1
1932	STL N	67	.255	.332	247	63	11	1	2	0.8	35	18	31	18	7	4	2	75	106	4	14	2.9	.978	3B-54, SS-7, 2B-2
1933	BKN N	78	.233	.333	210	49	11	2	2	1.0	28	22	24	15	13	7	2	130	158	11	21	4.7	.963	SS-36, 2B-19, 3B-8, OF-1
1934	CIN N	13	.333	.333	9	3	0	0	0	0.0	1	0	1	1	1	9	3	0	0	0	0	0.0	—	
10 yrs.		583	.256	.350	1693	433	75	18	16	0.9	229	201	190	139	58	81	25	999	1243	86	204	4.9	.963	2B-259, SS-145, 3B-65, 1B-3, OF-2

WORLD SERIES

Year	Team	Games	BA	SA	AB	H	2B	3B	HR	HR%	R	RBI	BB	SO	SB	Pinch Hit AB	Pinch Hit H	PO	A	E	DP	TC/G	FA	G by Pos
1926	STL N	3	.000	.000	3	0	0	0	0	0.0	0	0	0	1	0	3	0	0	0	0	0	0.0	—	
1931		5	.091	.182	11	1	1	0	0	0.0	1	0	1	0	0	1	0	3	4	1	0	2.0	.875	3B-4
2 yrs.		8	.071	.143	14	1	1	0	0	0.0	1	0	1	1	0	4	0	3	4	1	0	2.0	.875	3B-4

Bobby Floyd

FLOYD, ROBERT NATHAN BR TR 6′ 1″ 180 lbs.
B. Oct. 20, 1943, Hawthorne, Calif.

Year	Team	Games	BA	SA	AB	H	2B	3B	HR	HR%	R	RBI	BB	SO	SB	Pinch Hit AB	Pinch Hit H	PO	A	E	DP	TC/G	FA	G by Pos
1968	BAL A	5	.111	.222	9	1	1	0	0	0.0	0	1	0	3	0	0	0	6	10	0	3	4.0	1.000	SS-4
1969		39	.202	.250	84	17	4	0	0	0.0	7	1	6	17	0	1	0	64	84	6	15	3.9	.961	2B-15, SS-15, 3B-9
1970	2 teams BAL A (3G –.000) KC A (14G –.326)																							
″	total	17	.311	.400	45	14	4	0	0	0.0	5	9	4	11	0	0	0	27	36	6	5	4.1	.913	SS-10, 3B-6, 2B-1
1971	KC A	31	.152	.197	66	10	3	0	0	0.0	8	2	7	21	0	3	1	34	56	2	14	3.8	.978	SS-15, 2B-8, 3B-1
1972		61	.179	.201	134	24	3	0	0	0.0	9	5	5	29	1	0	0	54	84	5	15	2.3	.965	3B-30, SS-29, 2B-2
1973		51	.333	.397	78	26	3	1	0	0.0	10	8	4	14	1	0	0	52	76	6	14	2.7	.955	2B-25, SS-24
1974		10	.111	.111	9	1	0	0	0	0.0	1	0	2	4	0	0	0	4	13	0	0	2.1	1.000	2B-5, 3B-2, SS-1
7 yrs.		214	.219	.266	425	93	18	1	0	0.0	40	26	28	99	2	4	1	241	359	25	66	3.1	.960	SS-98, 2B-56, 3B-48

Bubba Floyd

FLOYD, LESLIE ROE BR TR 5′11″ 160 lbs.
B. June 23, 1917, Dallas, Tex.

Year	Team	Games	BA	SA	AB	H	2B	3B	HR	HR%	R	RBI	BB	SO	SB	Pinch Hit AB	Pinch Hit H	PO	A	E	DP	TC/G	FA	G by Pos
1944	DET A	3	.444	.556	9	4	1	0	0	0.0	1	0	1	0	0	0	0	1	8	0	0	3.0	1.000	SS-3

Cliff Floyd

FLOYD, CORNELIUS CLIFFORD BL TL 6′ 5″ 220 lbs.
B. Dec. 5, 1972, Chicago, Ill.

Year	Team	Games	BA	SA	AB	H	2B	3B	HR	HR%	R	RBI	BB	SO	SB	Pinch Hit AB	Pinch Hit H	PO	A	E	DP	TC/G	FA	G by Pos
1993	MON N	10	.226	.323	31	7	0	0	1	3.2	3	2	0	9	0	2	0	79	4	0	5	8.3	1.000	1B-10
1994		100	.281	.398	334	94	19	4	4	1.2	43	41	24	63	10	6	3	565	41	6	43	5.9	.990	1B-77, OF-26
1995		29	.130	.188	69	9	1	0	1	1.4	6	8	7	22	3	8	0	146	12	3	13	7.3	.981	1B-18, OF-4
3 yrs.		139	.253	.359	434	110	20	4	6	1.4	52	51	31	94	13	16	3	790	57	9	61	6.3	.989	1B-105, OF-30

John Fluhrer

FLUHRER, JOHN L. BR TR 5′ 9″ 165 lbs.
Played as William Morris in 1915.
B. Jan. 3, 1894, Adrian, Mich. D. July 17, 1946, Columbus, Ohio.

Year	Team	Games	BA	SA	AB	H	2B	3B	HR	HR%	R	RBI	BB	SO	SB	Pinch Hit AB	Pinch Hit H	PO	A	E	DP	TC/G	FA	G by Pos
1915	CHI N	6	.333	.333	6	2	0	0	0	0.0	0	0	1	0	1	3	0	1	0	1	0	1.0	.500	OF-2

Doug Flynn

FLYNN, ROBERT DOUGLAS BR TR 5′11″ 165 lbs.
B. Apr. 18, 1951, Lexington, Ky.

Year	Team	Games	BA	SA	AB	H	2B	3B	HR	HR%	R	RBI	BB	SO	SB	Pinch Hit AB	Pinch Hit H	PO	A	E	DP	TC/G	FA	G by Pos
1975	CIN N	89	.268	.346	127	34	7	0	1	0.8	17	20	11	13	3	7	1	57	118	2	20	2.0	.989	3B-40, 2B-30, SS-17
1976		93	.283	.338	219	62	5	2	1	0.5	20	20	10	24	2	1	0	107	152	4	33	2.7	.985	2B-55, 3B-23, SS-20
1977	2 teams CIN N (36G –.250) NY N (90G –.191)																							
″	total	126	.197	.232	314	62	7	2	0	0.0	14	19	2	21	1	4	0	171	235	14	42	3.1	.967	SS-69, 2B-38, 3B-27
1978	NY N	156	.237	.289	532	126	12	8	0	0.0	37	36	30	50	3	0	0	332	426	15	91	4.1	.981	2B-128, SS-60
1979		157	.243	.317	555	135	19	5	4	0.7	35	61	17	46	0	1	1	402	421	16	107	5.0	.981	2B-148, SS-20
1980		128	.255	.312	443	113	9	8	0	0.0	46	24	22	20	2	0	0	284	374	6	70	5.1	.991	2B-128, SS-3
1981		105	.222	.292	325	72	12	4	1	0.3	24	20	11	19	1	0	0	229	319	7	61	5.3	.987	2B-100, SS-5
1982	2 teams TEX A (88G –.211) MON N (58G –.244)																							
″	total	146	.225	.268	463	104	12	4	0	0.0	26	39	8	37	6	0	0	296	411	14	88	4.9	.981	2B-113, SS-35
1983	MON N	143	.237	.294	452	107	18	4	0	0.0	44	26	19	38	2	0	0	249	375	11	77	4.4	.983	2B-107, SS-37
1984		124	.243	.281	366	89	12	1	0	0.0	23	17	12	41	0	3	2	189	291	13	66	4.0	.974	2B-88, SS-34
1985	2 teams MON N (9G –.167) DET A (32G –.255)																							
″	total	41	.246	.316	57	14	2	1	0	0.0	2	2	0	3	0	5	1	42	46	1	17	2.3	.989	2B-26, SS-9, 3B-4
11 yrs.		1308	.238	.294	3853	918	115	39	7	0.2	288	284	142	312	20	21	5	2358	3168	103	672	4.1	.982	2B-961, SS-309, 3B-94

LEAGUE CHAMPIONSHIP SERIES

Year	Team	Games	BA	SA	AB	H	2B	3B	HR	HR%	R	RBI	BB	SO	SB	Pinch Hit AB	Pinch Hit H	PO	A	E	DP	TC/G	FA	G by Pos
1976	CIN N	1	—	—	0	0	0	0	0	—	0	0	0	0	0	0	0	0	0	0	0	0.0	.000	2B-1

Ed Flynn

FLYNN, EDWARD J. BL 5′ 9″ 165 lbs.
B. June 25, 1864, Chicago, Ill. Deceased.

Year	Team	Games	BA	SA	AB	H	2B	3B	HR	HR%	R	RBI	BB	SO	SB	Pinch Hit AB	Pinch Hit H	PO	A	E	DP	TC/G	FA	G by Pos
1887	CLE AA	7	.185	.222	27	5	1	0	0	0.0	0		1		3	0	0	16	9	6	0	4.4	.806	3B-6, OF-1

George Flynn

FLYNN, GEORGE A. (Dibby)
B. May 24, 1871, Chicago, Ill. D. Dec. 28, 1901, Chicago, Ill.

Year	Team	Games	BA	SA	AB	H	2B	3B	HR	HR%	R	RBI	BB	SO	SB	Pinch Hit AB	Pinch Hit H	PO	A	E	DP	TC/G	FA	G by Pos
1896	CHI N	29	.255	.302	106	27	1	2	0	0.0	15	4	11	9	12	0	0	66	6	10	3	2.8	.878	OF-29

Jocko Flynn

FLYNN, JOHN A.
B. June 30, 1864, Lawrence, Mass. D. Dec. 30, 1907, Lawrence, Mass.
TR 5′ 6½″ 143 lbs.

Year	Team	Games	BA	SA	AB	H	2B	3B	HR	HR%	R	RBI	BB	SO	SB	Pinch Hit AB	Pinch Hit H	PO	A	E	DP	TC/G	FA	G by Pos
1886	CHI N	57	.200	.307	205	41	6	2	4	2.0	40	19	18	45		0	0	34	59	9	2	1.7	.912	P-32, OF-28
1887		1	—	—	0	0	0	0	0	—	0	0	0	0	0	0	0	0	0	1	0	1.0	.000	OF-1
2 yrs.		58	.200	.307	205	41	6	2	4	2.0	40	19	18	45	0	0	0	34	59	10	2	1.7	.903	P-32, OF-29

Joe Flynn

FLYNN, JOSEPH
B. Philadelphia, Pa. Deceased.

Year	Team	Games	BA	SA	AB	H	2B	3B	HR	HR%	R	RBI	BB	SO	SB	Pinch Hit AB	Pinch Hit H	PO	A	E	DP	TC/G	FA	G by Pos
1884	2 teams	PHI U (52G –.249) BOS U (9G –.226)																						
″	total	61	.246	.375	240	59	11	4	4	1.7	42		13			0	0	136	40	46	4	3.3	.793	OF-47, C-17, 1B-2, SS-1

John Flynn

FLYNN, JOHN ANTHONY
B. Sept. 7, 1883, Providence, R. I. D. Mar. 23, 1935, Providence, R. I.
BR TR 6′½″ 175 lbs.

Year	Team	Games	BA	SA	AB	H	2B	3B	HR	HR%	R	RBI	BB	SO	SB	Pinch Hit AB	Pinch Hit H	PO	A	E	DP	TC/G	FA	G by Pos
1910	PIT N	96	.274	.370	332	91	10	2	6	**1.8**	32	52	30	47	6	3	2	869	49	22	54	10.1	.977	1B-93
1911		33	.203	.237	59	12	0	1	0	0.0	5	3	9	8	0	15	3	101	8	1	7	7.9	.991	1B-13, OF-1
1912	WAS A	20	.169	.254	71	12	4	1	0	0.0	9	5	7		2	0	0	176	15	5	9	9.8	.974	1B-20
3 yrs.		149	.249	.335	462	115	14	4	6	1.3	46	60	46	55	8	18	5	1146	72	28	70	9.8	.978	1B-126, OF-1

Mike Flynn

FLYNN, MICHAEL J.
B. Mar. 15, 1872, County Kildare, Ireland D. June 16, 1941, Los Angeles, Calif.

Year	Team	Games	BA	SA	AB	H	2B	3B	HR	HR%	R	RBI	BB	SO	SB	Pinch Hit AB	Pinch Hit H	PO	A	E	DP	TC/G	FA	G by Pos
1891	BOS AA	1	.000	.000	2	0	0	0	0	0.0	0	0	0	1	0	0	0	4	2	0	0	6.0	1.000	C-1

Jim Fogarty

FOGARTY, JAMES G.
Brother of Joe Fogarty.
B. Feb. 12, 1864, San Francisco, Calif. D. May 20, 1891, Philadelphia, Pa.
Manager 1890.
BR TR 5′10½″ 180 lbs.

Year	Team	Games	BA	SA	AB	H	2B	3B	HR	HR%	R	RBI	BB	SO	SB	Pinch Hit AB	Pinch Hit H	PO	A	E	DP	TC/G	FA	G by Pos
1884	PHI N	97	.212	.283	378	80	12	6	1	0.3	42		20	54		0	0	229	43	34	5	3.1	.889	OF-78, 3B-14, 2B-4, SS-3, P-1
1885		111	.232	.276	427	99	13	3	0	0.0	49		30	37		0	0	273	92	29	12	3.5	.926	OF-88, 2B-10, SS-8, 3B-5
1886		77	.293	.407	280	82	13	5	3	1.1	54	47	42	16		0	0	152	51	22	10	2.8	.902	OF-60, 2B-13, 3B-3, SS-3, P-1
1887		126	.261	.410	495	129	26	12	8	1.6	113	50	**82**	44	102	0	0	274	47	29	10	2.7	.917	OF-123, 3B-2, SS-2, 2B-1, P-1
1888		121	.236	.300	454	107	14	6	1	0.2	72	35	53	66	58	0	0	251	35	25	11	2.5	.920	OF-117, 3B-5, SS-1
1889		128	.259	.375	499	129	15	17	3	0.6	107	54	65	60	**99**	0	0	302	43	15	6	2.7	.958	OF-128, P-4
1890	PHI P	91	.239	.357	347	83	17	6	4	1.2	71	58	59	50	36	0	0	192	17	8	3	2.4	.963	OF-91, 3B-1
7 yrs.		751	.246	.343	2880	709	110	55	20	0.7	508	244	351	327	295	0	0	1673	328	162	57	2.8	.925	OF-685, 3B-30, 2B-28, SS-17, P-7

Joe Fogarty

FOGARTY, JOSEPH J.
Brother of Jim Fogarty.
B. Nov. 8, 1868, San Francisco, Calif. D. Mar. 28, 1918, San Francisco, Calif.

Year	Team	Games	BA	SA	AB	H	2B	3B	HR	HR%	R	RBI	BB	SO	SB	Pinch Hit AB	Pinch Hit H	PO	A	E	DP	TC/G	FA	G by Pos
1885	STL N	2	.125	.125	8	1	0	0	0	0.0	1	0	0	1		0	0	2	0	0	0	1.0	1.000	OF-2

Lee Fohl

FOHL, LEO ALEXANDER
B. Nov. 28, 1870, Pittsburgh, Pa. D. Oct. 30, 1965, Cleveland, Ohio.
Manager 1915–19, 1921–26.
BL TR 5′10″ 175 lbs.

Year	Team	Games	BA	SA	AB	H	2B	3B	HR	HR%	R	RBI	BB	SO	SB	Pinch Hit AB	Pinch Hit H	PO	A	E	DP	TC/G	FA	G by Pos
1902	PIT N	1	.000	.000	3	0	0	0	0	0.0	0	1	0		0	0	0	5	2	1	0	8.0	.875	C-1
1903	CIN N	4	.357	.571	14	5	1	1	0	0.0	3	2	0		0	0	0	15	6	1	0	5.5	.955	C-4
2 yrs.		5	.294	.471	17	5	1	1	0	0.0	3	3	0		0	0	0	20	8	2	0	6.0	.933	C-5

Hank Foiles

FOILES, HENRY LEE
B. June 10, 1929, Richmond, Va.
BR TR 6′ 195 lbs.

Year	Team	Games	BA	SA	AB	H	2B	3B	HR	HR%	R	RBI	BB	SO	SB	Pinch Hit AB	Pinch Hit H	PO	A	E	DP	TC/G	FA	G by Pos
1953	2 teams	CIN N (5G –.154) CLE A (7G –.143)																						
″	total	12	.150	.150	20	3	0	0	0	0.0	3	0	2	3	0	2	0	17	7	2	1	2.6	.923	C-10
1955	CLE A	62	.261	.369	111	29	9	0	1	0.9	13	7	17	18	0	20	6	222	23	3	7	6.0	.988	C-41
1956	2 teams	CLE A (1G –.000) PIT N (79G –.212)																						
″	total	80	.212	.369	222	47	10	2	7	3.2	24	25	17	56	0	5	1	291	30	4	8	4.4	.988	C-74
1957	PIT N	109	.270	.431	281	76	10	4	9	3.2	32	36	37	53	1	4	0	436	32	9	2	4.4	.981	C-109
1958		104	.205	.348	264	54	10	2	8	3.0	31	30	45	53	0	0	0	456	41	5	5	4.9	.990	C-103
1959		53	.225	.375	80	18	3	0	3	3.8	10	4	7	16	0	1	0	153	8	0	3	3.2	1.000	C-51
1960	3 teams	KC A (6G –.571) CLE A (24G –.279) DET A (26G –.250)																						
″	total	56	.282	.336	131	37	4	0	1	0.8	15	10	11	15	1	6	1	204	23	3	5	5.0	.987	C-46
1961	BAL A	43	.274	.468	124	34	6	0	6	4.8	18	19	12	27	0	4	0	194	17	1	4	5.6	.995	C-38
1962	CIN N	43	.275	.496	131	36	6	1	7	5.3	17	25	13	39	0	5	2	249	14	5	1	6.5	.981	C-41
1963	2 teams	CIN N (1G –.000) LA A (41G –.214)																						
″	total	42	.207	.379	87	18	1	1	4	4.6	8	10	9	13	1	11	2	140	14	4	4	5.1	.975	C-31
1964	LA A	4	.250	.250	4	1	0	0	0	0.0	0	0	0	2	0	4	1	0	0	0	0	0.0	—	
11 yrs.		608	.243	.392	1455	353	59	10	46	3.2	171	166	170	295	3	62	13	2362	209	36	40	4.8	.986	C-544

Curry Foley

FOLEY, CHARLES JOSEPH
B. Jan. 14, 1856, Milltown, Ireland D. Oct. 20, 1898, New York, N. Y.
TL 5′10″ 160 lbs.

Year	Team	Games	BA	SA	AB	H	2B	3B	HR	HR%	R	RBI	BB	SO	SB	Pinch Hit AB	Pinch Hit H	PO	A	E	DP	TC/G	FA	G by Pos
1879	BOS N	35	.315	.349	146	46	3	1	0	0.0	16	17	3	4		0	0	29	29	13	0	1.8	.817	P-21, OF-17, 1B-2
1880		80	.292	.361	332	97	13	2	2	0.6	44	31	8	14		0	0	276	63	25	10	3.8	.931	P-36, OF-35, 1B-25
1881	BUF N	83	.256	.328	**375**	96	20	2	1	0.3	58	25	7	27		0	0	372	32	38	14	4.8	.914	OF-55, 1B-27, P-10
1882		84	.305	.402	341	104	16	4	3	0.9	51		12	26		0	0	118	22	28	7	2.0	.833	OF-84, P-1
1883		23	.270	.369	111	30	5	3	0	0.0	23		4	12		0	0	44	2	6	0	2.2	.885	OF-23, P-1
5 yrs.		305	.286	.362	1305	373	57	12	6	0.5	192	73	34	83		0	0	839	148	110	31	3.3	.900	OF-214, P-69, 1B-54

Marv Foley

FOLEY, MARVIS EDWIN
B. Aug. 29, 1953, Stanford, Ky.
BL TR 6′ 195 lbs.

Year	Team	Games	BA	SA	AB	H	2B	3B	HR	HR%	R	RBI	BB	SO	SB	Pinch Hit AB	Pinch Hit H	PO	A	E	DP	TC/G	FA	G by Pos
1978	CHI A	11	.353	.353	34	12	0	0	0	0.0	3	6	4	6	0	1	0	41	4	3	0	4.8	.938	C-10
1979		34	.247	.340	97	24	3	0	2	2.1	6	10	7	5	0	2	1	128	11	1	1	4.2	.993	C-33
1980		68	.212	.336	137	29	5	0	4	2.9	14	15	9	22	0	8	3	220	17	2	3	3.6	.992	C-64, 1B-3

Marv Foley *continued*

Year	Team	Games	BA	SA	AB	H	2B	3B	HR	HR%	R	RBI	BB	SO	SB	Pinch Hit AB	Pinch Hit H	PO	A	E	DP	TC/G	FA	G by Pos
1982		27	.111	.111	36	4	0	0	0	0.0	1	1	6	4	0	11	1	47	4	1	0	2.7	.981	C-15, 3B-2, DH-1, 1B-1
1984	TEX A	63	.217	.391	115	25	2	0	6	5.2	13	19	15	24	0	28	7	148	14	2	3	3.9	.988	C-36, DH-4, 3B-1, 1B-1
5 yrs.		203	.224	.334	419	94	10	0	12	2.9	37	51	41	61	0	50	12	584	50	9	7	3.8	.986	C-158, DH-5, 1B-5, 3B-3

Pat Foley

Playing record listed under Willie Greene.

Ray Foley

FOLEY, RAYMOND KIRWIN BL TR 5′11″ 173 lbs.
B. June 23, 1906, Naugatuck, Conn. D. Mar. 22, 1980, Vero Beach, Fla.

Year	Team	Games	BA	SA	AB	H	2B	3B	HR	HR%	R	RBI	BB	SO	SB	Pinch Hit AB	Pinch Hit H	PO	A	E	DP	TC/G	FA	G by Pos
1928	NY N	2	.000	.000	1	0	0	0	0	0.0	1	0	1	1	0	1	0	0	0	0	0	0.0	—	

Tom Foley

FOLEY, THOMAS MICHAEL BL TR 6′ 1″ 160 lbs.
B. Sept. 9, 1959, Fort Benning, Ga.

Year	Team	Games	BA	SA	AB	H	2B	3B	HR	HR%	R	RBI	BB	SO	SB	Pinch Hit AB	Pinch Hit H	PO	A	E	DP	TC/G	FA	G by Pos
1983	CIN N	68	.204	.265	98	20	4	1	0	0.0	7	9	13	17	1	20	4	54	76	2	16	3.1	.985	SS-37, 2B-5
1984		106	.253	.357	277	70	8	3	5	1.8	26	27	24	36	3	13	5	119	228	11	36	3.8	.969	SS-83, 2B-10, 3B-1
1985	2 teams CIN N (43G –.196) PHI N (46G –.266)																							
″	total	89	.240	.336	250	60	13	1	3	1.2	24	23	19	34	2	12	1	127	202	7	47	4.3	.979	SS-60, 2B-18, 3B-1
1986	2 teams PHI N (39G –.295) MON N (64G –.257)																							
″	total	103	.266	.357	263	70	15	3	1	0.4	26	23	30	37	10	22	5	117	190	6	29	3.3	.981	SS-53, 2B-26, 3B-16
1987	MON N	106	.293	.432	280	82	18	3	5	1.8	35	28	11	40	6	24	5	134	190	9	43	3.4	.973	SS-49, 2B-39, 3B-9
1988		127	.265	.377	377	100	21	3	5	1.3	33	43	30	49	2	14	1	204	324	15	61	4.2	.972	2B-89, SS-32, 3B-9
1989		122	.229	.347	375	86	19	2	7	1.9	34	39	45	53	2	12	2	203	317	8	58	3.8	.985	2B-108, 3B-16, SS-14, P-1
1990		73	.213	.238	164	35	2	1	0	0.0	11	12	12	22	0	10	1	80	123	5	26	2.8	.976	SS-45, 2B-20, 3B-7, 1B-1
1991		86	.208	.286	168	35	11	1	0	0.0	12	15	14	30	2	14	3	200	93	6	23	3.6	.980	SS-43, 1B-31, 3B-6, 2B-2
1992		72	.174	.217	115	20	3	1	0	0.0	7	5	8	21	3	11	3	74	97	5	20	2.8	.972	SS-33, 2B-13, 1B-12, 3B-4, OF-1
1993	PIT N	86	.253	.366	194	49	11	1	3	1.5	18	22	11	26	0	32	9	116	105	5	29	3.8	.978	2B-35, 1B-12, 3B-7, SS-6
1994		59	.236	.366	123	29	7	0	3	2.4	13	15	13	18	0	17	2	51	94	3	25	3.5	.980	2B-17, 3B-14, SS-8, 1B-3
1995	MON N	11	.208	.292	24	5	2	0	0	0.0	2	2	2	4	1	4	0	23	7	0	3	4.3	1.000	1B-4, 2B-3
13 yrs.		1108	.244	.344	2708	661	134	20	32	1.2	248	263	232	387	32	205	41	1502	2046	82	416	3.6	.977	SS-463, 2B-385, 3B-90, 1B-63, OF-1, P-1

Will Foley

FOLEY, WILLIAM BROWN BR TR 5′ 9½″ 150 lbs.
B. Nov. 15, 1855, Chicago, Ill. D. Nov. 12, 1916, Chicago, Ill.

Year	Team	Games	BA	SA	AB	H	2B	3B	HR	HR%	R	RBI	BB	SO	SB	Pinch Hit AB	Pinch Hit H	PO	A	E	DP	TC/G	FA	G by Pos
1876	CIN N	58	.226	.258	221	50	3	2	0	0.0	19	9	0	14		0	0	137	111	63	5	4.7	.797	3B-46, C-20
1877		56	.190	.222	216	41	5	1	0	0.0	23	18	4	13		0	0	94	130	44	9	4.8	.836	3B-56
1878	MIL N	56	.271	.349	229	62	8	5	0	0.0	33	22	7	14		0	0	101	103	39	8	4.1	.840	3B-53, C-7
1879	CIN N	56	.211	.243	218	46	5	1	0	0.0	22	25	2	16		0	0	90	72	34	8	3.4	.827	3B-29, OF-25, 2B-3
1881	DET N	5	.133	.133	15	2	0	0	0	0.0	0	1	2	3		0	0	5	5	3	3	2.6	.769	3B-5
1884	CHI U	19	.282	.324	71	20	1	1	0	0.0	15		5			0	0	18	23	10	2	2.7	.804	3B-19
6 yrs.		250	.228	.271	970	221	22	10	0	0.0	112	75	20	60		0	0	445	444	193	35	4.1	.822	3B-208, C-27, OF-25, 2B-3

Tim Foli

FOLI, TIMOTHY JOHN (Crazy Horse) BR TR 6′ 179 lbs.
B. Dec. 8, 1950, Culver City, Calif.

Year	Team	Games	BA	SA	AB	H	2B	3B	HR	HR%	R	RBI	BB	SO	SB	Pinch Hit AB	Pinch Hit H	PO	A	E	DP	TC/G	FA	G by Pos
1970	NY N	5	.364	.364	11	4	0	0	0	0.0	0	1	0	2	0	1	1	4	10	0	1	3.5	1.000	SS-2, 3B-2
1971		97	.226	.281	288	65	12	2	0	0.0	32	24	18	50	5	2	0	150	199	12	43	3.4	.967	2B-58, 3B-36, SS-12, OF-1
1972	MON N	149	.241	.281	540	130	12	2	2	0.4	45	35	25	43	11	1	0	281	487	27	94	5.3	.966	SS-148, 2B-1
1973		126	.240	.277	458	110	11	0	2	0.4	37	36	28	40	6	0	0	248	399	27	85	5.3	.960	SS-123, 2B-2, OF-1
1974		121	.254	.290	441	112	10	3	0	0.0	41	39	28	27	8	1	1	220	412	19	85	5.4	.971	SS-120, OF-1
1975		152	.238	.294	572	136	25	2	1	0.2	64	29	36	49	13	3	0	261	497	21	104	5.1	.973	SS-151, 2B-1
1976		149	.264	.366	546	144	36	1	6	1.1	41	54	16	33	6	5	1	249	470	18	102	5.0	.976	SS-146, 3B-1
1977	2 teams MON N (13G –.175) SF N (104G –.228)																							
″	total	117	.221	.320	425	94	22	4	4	0.9	32	30	11	20	2	4	2	217	345	13	78	4.9	.977	SS-115, 2B-1, 3B-1, OF-1
1978	NY N	113	.257	.320	413	106	21	1	1	0.2	37	27	14	30	2	1	0	190	314	18	78	4.7	.966	SS-112
1979	2 teams NY N (3G –.000) PIT N (133G –.291)																							
″	total	136	.288	.340	532	153	23	1	1	0.2	70	65	28	14	6	1	0	259	410	15	98	5.1	.978	SS-135
1980	PIT N	127	.265	.327	495	131	22	0	3	0.6	61	38	19	23	11	1	0	212	402	12	87	5.0	.981	SS-125
1981		86	.247	.297	316	78	12	2	0	0.0	32	20	17	10	7	4	0	140	247	14	52	5.0	.965	SS-81
1982	CAL A	150	.252	.308	480	121	14	2	3	0.6	46	56	14	22	2	1	0	247	462	12	93	4.8	.983	SS-139, 2B-8, 3B-2
1983		88	.252	.300	330	83	10	0	2	0.6	29	29	5	18	2	0	0	131	298	13	54	5.1	.971	SS-74, 3B-13
1984	NY A	61	.252	.319	163	41	11	0	0	0.0	8	16	2	16	0	4	0	88	122	6	32	3.5	.972	SS-28, 2B-21, 3B-10, 1B-2
1985	PIT N	19	.189	.189	37	7	0	0	0	0.0	1	2	4	2	0	6	2	16	34	1	6	3.9	.980	SS-13
16 yrs.		1696	.251	.309	6047	1515	241	20	25	0.4	576	501	265	399	81	35	7	2913	5108	228	1092	4.9	.972	SS-1524, 2B-92, 3B-65, OF-4, 1B-2
LEAGUE CHAMPIONSHIP SERIES																								
1979	PIT N	3	.333	.417	12	4	1	0	0	0.0	1	3	0	0	0	0	0	3	9	0	1	4.0	1.000	SS-3
1982	CAL A	5	.125	.125	16	2	0	0	0	0.0	0	1	0	3	0	0	0	6	7	0	1	2.6	1.000	SS-5
2 yrs.		8	.214	.250	28	6	1	0	0	0.0	1	4	0	3	0	0	0	9	16	0	2	3.1	1.000	SS-8
WORLD SERIES																								
1979	PIT N	7	.333	.433	30	10	1	1	0	0.0	6	3	2	0	0	0	0	8	32	3	7	6.1	.930	SS-7

Dee Fondy

FONDY, DEE VIRGIL BL TL 6′ 3″ 195 lbs.
B. Oct. 31, 1924, Slaton, Tex.

Year	Team	Games	BA	SA	AB	H	2B	3B	HR	HR%	R	RBI	BB	SO	SB	Pinch Hit AB	Pinch Hit H	PO	A	E	DP	TC/G	FA	G by Pos
1951	CHI N	49	.271	.388	170	46	7	2	3	1.8	23	20	11	20	5	5	1	387	27	10	40	9.6	.976	1B-44
1952		145	.300	.424	554	166	21	9	10	1.8	69	67	28	60	13	2	0	1257	103	14	92	9.6	.990	1B-143
1953		150	.309	.477	595	184	24	11	18	3.0	79	78	44	106	10	1	0	1274	115	18	105	9.4	.987	1B-149
1954		141	.285	.400	568	162	30	4	9	1.6	77	49	35	84	20	2	1	1228	119	9	129	9.8	.993	1B-138
1955		150	.265	.422	574	152	23	8	17	3.0	69	65	35	87	8	0	0	1304	107	13	135	9.7	.991	1B-147

Dee Fondy *continued*

Year	Team	Games	BA	SA	AB	H	2B	3B	HR	HR%	R	RBI	BB	SO	SB	Pinch Hit AB	Pinch Hit H	PO	A	E	DP	TC/G	FA	G by Pos
1956		137	.269	.392	543	146	22	9	9	1.7	52	46	20	74	9	4	1	1048	94	17	101	8.7	.985	1B-133
1957	2 teams	CHI N (11G –.314) PIT N (95G –.313)																						
"	total	106	.313	.388	374	117	16	3	2	0.5	45	37	25	68	12	23	6	801	60	15	73	10.4	.983	1B-84
1958	CIN N	89	.218	.266	124	27	1	1	1	0.8	23	11	5	27	7	23	4	160	16	2	15	3.1	.989	1B-36, OF-22
8 yrs.		967	.286	.413	3502	1000	144	47	69	2.0	437	373	203	526	84	60	13	7459	641	98	690	9.1	.988	1B-874, OF-22

Lew Fonseca

FONSECA, LEWIS ALBERT
B. Jan. 21, 1899, Oakland, Calif. D. Nov. 26, 1989, Ely, Iowa.
Manager 1932–34.
BR TR 5'10½" 180 lbs.

Year	Team	Games	BA	SA	AB	H	2B	3B	HR	HR%	R	RBI	BB	SO	SB	Pinch Hit AB	Pinch Hit H	PO	A	E	DP	TC/G	FA	G by Pos
1921	CIN N	82	.276	.340	297	82	10	3	1	0.3	38	41	8	13	2	2	0	307	155	14	30	5.8	.971	2B-50, OF-16, 1B-16
1922		91	.361	.491	291	105	20	3	4	1.4	55	45	14	18	7	18	8	197	251	14	40	6.5	.970	2B-71
1923		65	.278	.397	237	66	11	4	3	1.3	33	28	9	16	4	6	2	252	176	15	37	7.5	.966	2B-45, 1B-14
1924		20	.228	.298	57	13	2	1	0	0.0	5	9	4	4	1	4	0	62	30	1	4	5.8	.989	2B-10, 1B-6
1925	PHI N	126	.319	.450	467	149	30	5	7	1.5	78	60	21	42	6	5	1	648	245	20	68	7.4	.978	2B-69, 1B-55
1927	CLE A	112	.311	.404	428	133	20	7	2	0.5	60	40	12	17	12	6	1	347	305	16	60	6.1	.976	2B-96, 1B-13
1928		75	.327	.464	263	86	19	4	3	1.1	38	36	13	17	4	0	0	553	78	3	67	8.3	.995	1B-56, 3B-15, SS-4, 2B-1
1929		148	**.369**	.532	566	209	44	15	6	1.1	97	103	50	23	19	1	0	1486	107	8	141	10.9	.995	1B-147
1930		40	.279	.380	129	36	9	2	0	0.0	20	17	7	7	1	5	0	277	29	9	15	9.3	.971	1B-28, 3B-6
1931	2 teams	CLE A (26G –.370) CHI A (121G –.299)																						
"	total	147	.312	.410	573	179	35	6	3	0.5	86	85	40	29	7	4	1	518	68	9	28	4.1	.985	OF-95, 1B-28, 2B-21, 3B-1
1932	CHI A	18	.135	.162	37	5	1	0	0	0.0	0	6	1	7	0	7	3	14	2	0	1	1.8	1.000	OF-8, P-1
1933		23	.203	.339	59	12	2	0	2	3.4	8	15	7	6	1	10	1	138	12	0	15	12.5	1.000	1B-12
12 yrs.		947	.316	.432	3404	1075	203	50	31	0.9	518	485	186	199	64	68	17	4799	1458	109	506	7.2	.983	1B-375, 2B-363, OF-119, 3B-22, SS-4, P-1

Chad Fonville

FONVILLE, CHAD EVERETTE
B. Mar. 5, 1971, Jacksonville, N. C.
BB TR 5' 6" 155 lbs.

Year	Team	Games	BA	SA	AB	H	2B	3B	HR	HR%	R	RBI	BB	SO	SB	Pinch Hit AB	Pinch Hit H	PO	A	E	DP	TC/G	FA	G by Pos
1995	2 teams	MON N (14G –.333) LA N (88G –.276)																						
"	total	102	.278	.303	320	89	6	1	0	0.0	43	16	23	42	20	16	4	125	195	11	28	3.8	.967	SS-38, 2B-38, OF-11
DIVISIONAL PLAYOFF SERIES																								
1995	LA N	3	.500	.500	12	6	0	0	0	0.0	1	0	0	1	0	0	0	1	7	1	2	3.0	.889	SS-3

Barry Foote

FOOTE, BARRY CLIFTON
B. Feb. 16, 1952, Smithfield, N. C.
BR TR 6' 3" 205 lbs.

Year	Team	Games	BA	SA	AB	H	2B	3B	HR	HR%	R	RBI	BB	SO	SB	Pinch Hit AB	Pinch Hit H	PO	A	E	DP	TC/G	FA	G by Pos
1973	MON N	6	.667	1.000	6	4	0	1	0	0.0	0	1	0	0	0	6	4	0	0	0	0	0.0	—	
1974		125	.262	.414	420	110	23	4	11	2.6	44	60	35	74	2	3	2	640	83	12	12	6.0	.984	C-122
1975		118	.194	.295	387	75	16	1	7	1.8	25	30	17	48	0	6	3	590	50	10	10	5.7	.985	C-115
1976		105	.234	.340	350	82	12	2	7	2.0	32	27	17	32	2	8	2	487	61	6	13	5.6	.989	C-96, 3B-2, 1B-1
1977	2 teams	MON N (15G –.245) PHI N (18G –.219)																						
"	total	33	.235	.420	81	19	4	1	3	3.7	7	11	7	16	0	4	0	121	11	2	2	4.5	.985	C-30
1978	PHI N	39	.158	.211	57	9	0	0	1	1.8	4	4	1	11	0	13	1	78	5	0	0	2.7	1.000	C-31
1979	CHI N	132	.254	.427	429	109	26	0	16	3.7	47	56	34	49	5	5	0	713	63	17	9	6.1	.979	C-129
1980		63	.238	.401	202	48	13	1	6	3.0	16	28	13	18	1	9	2	317	36	3	5	6.5	.992	C-55
1981	2 teams	CHI N (9G –.000) NY A (40G –.208)																						
"	total	49	.177	.327	147	26	4	0	6	4.1	12	11	11	28	0	4	0	261	17	1	6	5.9	.996	C-42, DH-4, 1B-1
1982	NY A	17	.146	.250	48	7	5	0	0	0.0	4	2	1	11	0	0	0	71	2	2	0	4.4	.973	C-17
10 yrs.		687	.230	.368	2127	489	103	10	57	2.7	191	230	136	287	10	58	14	3278	328	53	57	5.7	.986	C-637, DH-4, 3B-2, 1B-2
DIVISIONAL PLAYOFF SERIES																								
1981	NY A	1	—	—	0	0	0	0	0	—	0	0	0	0	0	0	0	0	0	0	0	0.0	—	
LEAGUE CHAMPIONSHIP SERIES																								
1978	PHI N	1	.000	.000	1	0	0	0	0	0.0	0	0	0	1	0	1	0	0	0	0	0	0.0	—	
1981	NY A	2	1.000	1.000	1	1	0	0	0	0.0	0	0	0	0	0	1	1	0	0	0	0	0.0	.000	C-1
2 yrs.		3	.500	.500	2	1	0	0	0	0.0	0	0	0	1	0	2	1	0	0	0	0	0.0		C-1
WORLD SERIES																								
1981	NY A	1	.000	.000	1	0	0	0	0	0.0	0	0	0	1	0	1	0	0	0	0	0	0.0	—	

Davy Force

FORCE, DAVID W. (Tom Thumb)
B. July 27, 1849, New York, N. Y. D. June 21, 1918, Englewood, N. J.
BR TR 5' 4" 130 lbs.

Year	Team	Games	BA	SA	AB	H	2B	3B	HR	HR%	R	RBI	BB	SO	SB	Pinch Hit AB	Pinch Hit H	PO	A	E	DP	TC/G	FA	G by Pos
1876	2 teams	PHI N (60G –.232) NY N (1G –.000)																						
"	total	61	.230	.251	287	66	6	0	0	0.0	48	17	5	3		0	0	112	243	42	11	6.3	.894	SS-61, 3B-2
1877	STL N	58	.262	.311	225	59	5	3	0	0.0	24	22	11	15		0	0	86	175	24	9	4.9	.916	SS-50, 3B-8
1879	BUF N	79	.209	.237	316	66	5	2	0	0.0	36	8	13	37		0	0	75	265	26	26	4.6	.929	SS-78, 3B-1
1880		81	.169	.203	290	49	10	0	0	0.0	22	17	10	35		0	0	222	324	38	37	7.0	.935	2B-53, SS-30
1881		75	.180	.219	278	50	9	1	0	0.0	21	15	11	29		0	0	195	299	32	25	6.9	.939	2B-51, SS-21, OF-3, 3B-1
1882		73	.241	.295	278	67	10	1	1	0.4	39		12	17		0	0	85	230	32	13	4.8	.908	SS-61, 3B-11, 2B-1
1883		96	.217	.262	378	82	11	3	0	0.0	40		12	39		0	0	117	280	53	28	4.6	.882	SS-78, 3B-13, 2B-7
1884		106	.206	.253	403	83	13	3	0	0.0	47		27	41		0	0	113	315	49	21	4.5	.897	SS-105, 2B-1
1885		71	.225	.257	253	57	6	1	0	0.0	20	17	13	19		0	0	148	213	47	29	5.7	.885	2B-42, SS-24, 3B-6
1886	WAS N	68	.182	.211	242	44	5	1	0	0.0	26	16	17	26		0	0	77	246	34	25	5.3	.905	SS-56, 2B-8, 3B-4
10 yrs.		768	.211	.249	2950	623	80	15	1	0.0	323	112	131	261		0	0	1230	2590	377	224	5.4	.910	SS-564, 2B-163, 3B-46, OF-3

Curt Ford

FORD, CURTIS GLENN
B. Oct. 11, 1960, Jackson, Miss.
BL TR 5'10" 150 lbs.

Year	Team	Games	BA	SA	AB	H	2B	3B	HR	HR%	R	RBI	BB	SO	SB	Pinch Hit AB	Pinch Hit H	PO	A	E	DP	TC/G	FA	G by Pos
1985	STL N	11	.500	.667	12	6	2	0	0	0.0	2	3	4	1	1	4	2	3	0	1	0	1.0	.750	OF-4
1986		85	.248	.364	214	53	15	2	2	0.9	30	29	23	29	13	25	5	109	7	3	5	1.9	.975	OF-64
1987		89	.285	.408	228	65	9	5	3	1.3	32	26	14	32	11	18	7	157	2	3	0	2.2	.981	OF-75
1988		91	.195	.266	128	25	6	0	1	0.8	11	18	8	26	6	40	9	95	6	2	5	2.2	.981	OF-40, 1B-7
1989	PHI N	108	.218	.289	142	31	5	1	1	0.7	13	13	16	33	5	62	11	46	5	0	0	0.9	1.000	OF-52, 2B-1, 1B-1
1990		22	.111	.111	18	2	0	0	0	0.0	0	0	1	5	0	17	2	2	0	0	0	0.7	1.000	OF-3
6 yrs.		406	.245	.345	742	182	37	8	7	0.9	88	89	66	126	36	166	36	412	20	9	10	1.8	.980	OF-238, 1B-8, 2B-1

Curt Ford *continued*

Year	Team	Games	BA	SA	AB	H	2B	3B	HR	HR%	R	RBI	BB	SO	SB	Pinch Hit AB	Pinch Hit H	PO	A	E	DP	TC/G	FA	G by Pos
LEAGUE CHAMPIONSHIP SERIES																								
1987	STL N	4	.333	.333	9	3	0	0	0	0.0	2	0	1	1	0	1	1	6	0	0	0	1.5	1.000	OF-4
WORLD SERIES																								
1987	STL N	5	.308	.308	13	4	0	0	0	0.0	1	2	1	1	0	1	0	5	0	0	0	1.3	1.000	OF-4

Dan Ford

FORD, DARNELL GLENN (Disco Danny)
B. May 19, 1952, Los Angeles, Calif.
BR TR 6′ 1″ 185 lbs.

Year	Team	Games	BA	SA	AB	H	2B	3B	HR	HR%	R	RBI	BB	SO	SB	Pinch Hit AB	Pinch Hit H	PO	A	E	DP	TC/G	FA	G by Pos
1975	MIN A	130	.280	.434	440	123	21	1	15	3.4	72	59	30	79	6	6	2	246	3	3	2	2.0	.988	OF-120, DH-3
1976		145	.267	.457	514	137	24	7	20	3.9	87	86	36	118	17	6	2	267	6	9	1	2.0	.968	OF-139, DH-3
1977		144	.267	.426	453	121	25	7	11	2.4	66	60	41	79	6	20	7	205	9	8	2	1.6	.964	OF-137, DH-3
1978		151	.274	.424	592	162	36	10	11	1.9	78	82	48	88	7	2	0	376	6	9	2	2.6	.977	OF-149, DH-1
1979	CAL A	142	.290	.464	569	165	26	5	21	3.7	100	101	40	86	8	1	0	332	10	8	2	2.5	.977	OF-141
1980		65	.279	.420	226	63	11	0	7	3.1	22	26	19	45	0	7	3	75	3	5	0	1.4	.940	OF-45, DH-15
1981		97	.277	.440	375	104	14	1	15	4.0	53	48	23	71	2	0	0	188	3	8	0	2.1	.960	OF-97
1982	BAL A	123	.235	.371	421	99	21	3	10	2.4	46	43	23	71	5	18	4	263	6	7	2	2.3	.975	OF-119, DH-1
1983		103	.280	.440	407	114	30	4	9	2.2	63	55	29	55	9	2	1	218	2	3	0	2.2	.987	OF-103
1984		25	.231	.308	91	21	4	0	1	1.1	7	5	7	13	1	1	0	36	1	0	0	1.6	1.000	OF-15, DH-8
1985		28	.187	.253	75	14	2	0	1	1.3	4	1	7	17	0	9	1	0	0	0	0	0.0	.000	DH-28
11 yrs.		1153	.270	.427	4163	1123	214	38	121	2.9	598	566	303	722	61	72	20	2206	49	60	11	2.1	.974	OF-1065, DH-62
LEAGUE CHAMPIONSHIP SERIES																								
1979	CAL A	4	.294	.706	17	5	1	0	2	11.8	2	4	0	0	0	0	0	6	0	1	0	1.8	.857	OF-4
1983	BAL A	2	.200	.400	5	1	1	0	0	0.0	0	0	0	1	0	1	0	1	0	0	0	0.5	1.000	OF-1, DH-1
2 yrs.		6	.273	.636	22	6	2	0	2	9.1	2	4	0	1	0	1	0	7	0	1	0	1.3	.875	OF-5, DH-1
WORLD SERIES																								
1983	BAL A	5	.167	.417	12	2	0	0	1	8.3	1	1	1	5	0	2	0	5	1	0	0	1.5	1.000	OF-4

Ed Ford

FORD, EDWARD L.
B. 1862, Richmond, Va. Deceased.
5′ 9½″ 160 lbs.

Year	Team	Games	BA	SA	AB	H	2B	3B	HR	HR%	R	RBI	BB	SO	SB	Pinch Hit AB	Pinch Hit H	PO	A	E	DP	TC/G	FA	G by Pos
1884	RIC AA	2	.000	.000	5	0	0	0	0	0.0	0		0			0	0	13	8	4	0	12.5	.840	SS-1, 1B-1

Hod Ford

FORD, HORACE HILLS
B. July 23, 1897, New Haven, Conn. D. Jan. 29, 1977, Winchester, Mass.
BR TR 5′10″ 165 lbs.

Year	Team	Games	BA	SA	AB	H	2B	3B	HR	HR%	R	RBI	BB	SO	SB	Pinch Hit AB	Pinch Hit H	PO	A	E	DP	TC/G	FA	G by Pos
1919	BOS N	10	.214	.286	28	6	0	1	0	0.0	4	3	2	6	0	0	0	13	31	2	3	4.6	.957	SS-8, 3B-2
1920		88	.241	.339	257	62	12	5	1	0.4	16	30	18	25	3	6	0	174	285	19	26	5.9	.960	2B-59, SS-18, 1B-4
1921		152	.279	.360	555	155	29	5	2	0.4	50	61	36	49	2	0	0	393	526	26	64	6.2	.972	2B-119, SS-33
1922		143	.272	.363	515	140	23	9	2	0.4	58	60	30	36	2	0	0	335	481	35	71	6.0	.959	SS-115, 2B-28
1923		111	.271	.366	380	103	16	7	2	0.5	27	50	31	30	1	0	0	252	352	22	67	5.5	.965	2B-95, SS-19
1924	PHI N	145	.272	.358	530	144	27	5	3	0.6	58	53	27	40	1	0	0	337	543	27	96	6.3	.970	2B-145
1925	BKN N	66	.273	.338	216	59	11	0	1	0.5	32	15	26	15	0	0	0	126	185	11	33	4.9	.966	SS-66
1926	CIN N	57	.279	.320	197	55	6	1	0	0.0	14	18	14	12	1	0	0	152	190	13	57	6.2	.963	SS-57
1927		115	.274	.330	409	112	16	2	1	0.2	45	46	33	34	0	0	0	239	354	27	80	5.3	.956	SS-104, 2B-12
1928		149	.241	.291	506	122	17	4	0	0.0	49	54	47	31	1	0	0	355	508	25	128	6.0	.972	SS-149
1929		148	.276	.342	529	146	14	6	3	0.6	68	50	41	25	8	0	0	333	520	35	116	5.9	.961	SS-108, 2B-42
1930		132	.231	.309	424	98	16	7	1	0.2	36	34	24	28	2	1	0	291	415	15	90	5.2	.979	SS-74, 2B-66
1931		84	.229	.286	175	40	8	1	0	0.0	18	13	13	13	0	7	1	111	169	13	43	3.8	.956	SS-73, 2B-3, 3B-1
1932	2 teams	STL N (1G –.000) BOS N (40G –.274)																						
"	total	41	.268	.361	97	26	5	2	0	0.0	9	6	6	9	0	2	0	59	82	3	17	3.7	.979	2B-20, SS-17, 3B-2
1933	BOS N	5	.067	.067	15	1	0	0	0	0.0	0	1	3	1	0	0	0	17	23	0	4	8.0	1.000	SS-5
15 yrs.		1446	.263	.337	4833	1269	200	55	16	0.3	484	494	351	354	21	16	1	3187	4664	273	895	5.6	.966	SS-846, 2B-589, 3B-5, 1B-4

Ted Ford

FORD, THEODORE HENRY
B. Feb. 7, 1947, Vineland, N. J.
BR TR 5′10″ 180 lbs.

Year	Team	Games	BA	SA	AB	H	2B	3B	HR	HR%	R	RBI	BB	SO	SB	Pinch Hit AB	Pinch Hit H	PO	A	E	DP	TC/G	FA	G by Pos
1970	CLE A	26	.174	.261	46	8	1	0	1	2.2	5	1	3	13	0	12	1	24	1	0	0	2.1	1.000	OF-12
1971		74	.194	.255	196	38	6	0	2	1.0	15	14	9	34	2	19	3	107	4	0	0	2.0	1.000	OF-55
1972	TEX A	129	.235	.382	429	101	19	1	14	3.3	43	50	37	80	4	10	2	242	11	6	2	2.2	.977	OF-119
1973	CLE A	11	.225	.275	40	9	0	1	0	0.0	3	3	2	7	1	1	0	6	0	0	0	0.6	1.000	OF-10
4 yrs.		240	.219	.333	711	156	26	2	17	2.4	66	68	51	134	7	42	6	379	16	6	2	2.0	.985	OF-196

Brook Fordyce

FORDYCE, BROOK ALEXANDER
B. May 7, 1970, New London, Conn.
BR TR 6′ 1″ 185 lbs.

Year	Team	Games	BA	SA	AB	H	2B	3B	HR	HR%	R	RBI	BB	SO	SB	Pinch Hit AB	Pinch Hit H	PO	A	E	DP	TC/G	FA	G by Pos
1995	NY N	4	.500	1.000	2	1	1	0	0	0.0	1	0	1	0	0	2	1	0	0	0	0	0.0	—	

Tom Forster

FORSTER, THOMAS W.
B. May 1, 1859, New York, N. Y. D. July 17, 1946, New York, N. Y.
BR 5′ 9″ 153 lbs.

Year	Team	Games	BA	SA	AB	H	2B	3B	HR	HR%	R	RBI	BB	SO	SB	Pinch Hit AB	Pinch Hit H	PO	A	E	DP	TC/G	FA	G by Pos
1882	DET N	21	.092	.092	76	7	0	0	0	0.0	5	2	5	12		0	0	58	54	23	5	6.4	.830	2B-21
1884	PIT AA	35	.222	.262	126	28	5	0	0	0.0	10		7			0	0	56	116	22	8	5.5	.887	SS-28, 3B-6, 2B-1
1885	NY AA	57	.221	.272	213	47	7	2	0	0.0	28		17			0	0	135	143	35	21	5.5	.888	2B-52, OF-5
1886		67	.195	.235	251	49	3	2	1	0.4	33		20			0	0	157	202	47	29	6.1	.884	2B-62, OF-4, SS-1
4 yrs.		180	.197	.236	666	131	15	4	1	0.2	76	2	49	12		0	0	406	515	127	63	5.8	.879	2B-136, SS-29, OF-9, 3B-6

Edward Forsyth

FORSYTH, EDWARD JAMES
B. Apr. 30, 1887, Kingston, N. Y. D. June 22, 1956, Hoboken, N. J.
BR TR 5′10″ 155 lbs.

Year	Team	Games	BA	SA	AB	H	2B	3B	HR	HR%	R	RBI	BB	SO	SB	Pinch Hit AB	Pinch Hit H	PO	A	E	DP	TC/G	FA	G by Pos
1915	BAL F	1	.000	.000	3	0	0	0	0	0.0	0	0	1		0	0	0	0	2	1	0	3.0	.667	3B-1

George Foss

FOSS, GEORGE DUEWARD (Deeby)
B. June 13, 1897, Register, Ga. D. Nov. 10, 1969, Brandon, Fla.
BR TR 5′10½″ 170 lbs.

Year	Team	Games	BA	SA	AB	H	2B	3B	HR	HR%	R	RBI	BB	SO	SB	Pinch Hit AB	Pinch Hit H	PO	A	E	DP	TC/G	FA	G by Pos
1921	WAS A	4	.000	.000	7	0	0	0	0	0.0	0	0	0	1	0	2	0	1	2	1	1	2.0	.750	3B-2

Ray Fosse

FOSSE, RAYMOND EARL
B. Apr. 4, 1947, Marion, Ill.
BR TR 6′ 2″ 215 lbs.

Year	Team	Games	BA	SA	AB	H	2B	3B	HR	HR%	R	RBI	BB	SO	SB	Pinch Hit AB	Pinch Hit H	PO	A	E	DP	TC/G	FA	G by Pos
1967	CLE A	7	.063	.063	16	1	0	0	0	0.0	0	0	0	5	0	0	0	46	7	0	0	7.6	1.000	C-7
1968		1	—	—	0	0	0	0	0	—	0	0	0	0	0	0	0	1	0	0	0	1.0	1.000	C-1
1969		37	.172	.250	116	20	3	0	2	1.7	11	9	8	29	1	1	0	237	18	6	2	7.1	.977	C-37
1970		120	.307	.469	450	138	17	1	18	4.0	62	61	39	55	1	0	0	854	70	10	7	7.8	.989	C-120
1971		133	.276	.397	486	134	21	1	12	2.5	53	62	36	62	4	6	0	767	73	10	22	6.5	.988	C-126, 1B-4
1972		134	.241	.354	457	110	20	1	10	2.2	42	41	45	46	5	8	3	740	71	12	12	6.5	.985	C-124, 1B-3
1973	OAK A	143	.256	.354	492	126	23	2	7	1.4	37	52	25	62	2	0	0	712	63	10	5	5.5	.987	C-141, DH-2
1974		69	.196	.324	204	40	8	3	4	2.0	20	23	11	31	1	0	0	299	28	9	6	4.9	.973	C-68, DH-1
1975		82	.140	.191	136	19	3	2	0	0.0	14	12	8	19	0	2	0	253	15	5	1	3.3	.982	C-82, 1B-1, 2B-1
1976	CLE A	90	.301	.362	276	83	9	1	2	0.7	26	30	20	20	1	4	0	493	43	7	10	6.1	.987	C-85, 1B-3, DH-1
1977	2 teams	CLE A (78G –.265)	SEA A (11G –.353)																					
″	total	89	.276	.386	272	75	10	1	6	2.2	28	32	9	28	0	1	0	456	49	9	5	5.8	.982	C-85, DH-3, 1B-1
1979	MIL A	19	.231	.327	52	12	3	1	0	0.0	6	2	2	6	0	3	1	41	3	0	1	2.3	1.000	C-13, DH-5, 1B-1
12 yrs.		924	.256	.367	2957	758	117	13	61	2.1	299	324	203	363	15	25	4	4899	440	78	71	5.9	.986	C-889, 1B-13, DH-12, 2B-1
LEAGUE CHAMPIONSHIP SERIES																								
1973	OAK A	5	.091	.182	11	1	1	0	0	0.0	2	3	2	2	0	0	0	25	4	0	2	5.8	1.000	C-5
1974		4	.333	.667	12	4	1	0	1	8.3	1	3	1	2	0	0	0	21	3	0	1	6.0	1.000	C-4
1975		1	.000	.000	2	0	0	0	0	0.0	0	0	0	1	0	0	0	3	0	0	1	3.0	1.000	C-1
3 yrs.		10	.200	.400	25	5	2	0	1	4.0	3	6	3	5	0	0	0	49	7	0	4	5.6	1.000	C-10
WORLD SERIES																								
1973	OAK A	7	.158	.211	19	3	1	0	0	0.0	0	0	1	4	0	0	0	32	3	0	2	5.0	1.000	C-7
1974		5	.143	.357	14	2	0	0	1	7.1	1	1	1	5	0	0	0	27	1	0	0	5.6	1.000	C-5
2 yrs.		12	.152	.273	33	5	1	0	1	3.0	1	1	2	9	0	0	0	59	4	0	2	5.3	1.000	C-12

Eddie Foster

FOSTER, EDWARD CUNNINGHAM (Kid)
B. Feb. 13, 1887, Chicago, Ill. D. Jan. 15, 1937, Washington, D. C.
BR TR 5′ 6½″ 145 lbs.

Year	Team	Games	BA	SA	AB	H	2B	3B	HR	HR%	R	RBI	BB	SO	SB	Pinch Hit AB	Pinch Hit H	PO	A	E	DP	TC/G	FA	G by Pos
1910	NY A	30	.133	.157	83	11	2	0	0	0.0	5	1	8		2	7	1	37	63	10	6	5.0	.909	SS-22
1912	WAS A	154	.285	.379	**618**	176	34	9	2	0.3	98	70	53		27	0	0	168	348	45	22	3.6	.920	3B-154
1913		106	.247	.306	409	101	11	5	1	0.2	56	41	36	31	22	1	0	112	217	36	20	3.5	.901	3B-105
1914		156	.282	.351	**616**	174	16	10	2	0.3	82	50	60	47	31	0	0	200	247	34	25	3.1	.929	3B-156
1915		154	.275	.348	**618**	170	25	10	0	0.0	75	52	48	30	20	0	0	253	353	39	45	4.2	.940	3B-79, 2B-75
1916		158	.252	.317	606	153	18	9	1	0.2	75	44	68	26	23	2	0	230	356	33	41	4.0	.947	3B-84, 2B-72
1917		143	.235	.292	554	130	16	8	0	0.0	66	43	46	23	11	0	0	217	331	33	34	4.1	.943	3B-86, 2B-57
1918		129	.283	.320	**519**	147	13	3	0	0.0	70	29	41	20	12	0	0	159	287	32	31	3.7	.933	3B-127, 2B-2
1919		120	.264	.310	478	126	12	5	0	0.0	57	26	33	21	20	4	1	120	267	22	16	3.6	.946	3B-115
1920	BOS A	117	.259	.334	386	100	17	6	0	0.0	48	41	42	17	10	6	1	127	280	19	29	3.9	.955	3B-88, 2B-21
1921		119	.284	.357	412	117	18	6	0	0.0	51	30	57	15	13	3	2	116	250	21	28	3.4	.946	3B-94, 2B-21
1922	2 teams	BOS A (48G –.211)	STL A (37G –.306)																					
″	total	85	.265	.292	253	67	7	0	0	0.0	40	15	29	18	4	15	5	64	123	19	14	3.0	.908	3B-65, SS-2, C-2
1923	STL A	27	.180	.200	100	18	2	0	0	0.0	9	4	7	7	0	0	0	42	52	5	8	3.7	.949	2B-20, 3B-7
13 yrs.		1498	.264	.326	5652	1490	191	71	6	0.1	732	446	528	255	195	38	10	1845	3174	348	319	3.7	.935	3B-1160, 2B-268, SS-24, C-2

Elmer Foster

FOSTER, ELMER ELLSWORTH
B. Aug. 15, 1861, Minneapolis, Minn. D. July 22, 1946, Deep Haven, Minn.
BR TL 5′10″ 178 lbs.

Year	Team	Games	BA	SA	AB	H	2B	3B	HR	HR%	R	RBI	BB	SO	SB	Pinch Hit AB	Pinch Hit H	PO	A	E	DP	TC/G	FA	G by Pos
1884	2 teams	PHI AA (4G –.182)	PHI U (1G –.333)																					
″	total	5	.214	.357	14	3	0	1	0	0.0	4		3			0	0	19	9	6	0	5.7	.824	C-5, OF-1
1886	NY AA	35	.184	.200	125	23	0	1	0	0.0	16		7			0	0	77	77	32	4	5.3	.828	2B-21, OF-14
1888	NY N	37	.147	.199	136	20	3	2	0	0.0	15	10	9	20	13	0	0	64	5	14	0	2.2	.831	OF-37, 3B-1
1889		2	.000	.000	4	0	0	0	0	0.0	2	0	3	1	2	0	0	5	0	0	0	2.5	1.000	OF-2
1890	CHI N	27	.248	.467	105	26	4	2	5	4.8	20	23	9	21	18	0	0	69	2	1	0	2.7	.986	OF-27
1891		4	.188	.375	16	3	0	0	1	6.3	3	1	1	2	1	0	0	6	1	1	0	2.0	.875	OF-4
6 yrs.		110	.188	.280	400	75	7	6	6	1.5	60	34	32	44	34	0	0	240	94	54	4	3.5	.861	OF-85, 2B-21, C-5, 3B-1

George Foster

FOSTER, GEORGE ARTHUR
B. Dec. 1, 1948, Tuscaloosa, Ala.
BR TR 6′ 1½″ 180 lbs.

Year	Team	Games	BA	SA	AB	H	2B	3B	HR	HR%	R	RBI	BB	SO	SB	Pinch Hit AB	Pinch Hit H	PO	A	E	DP	TC/G	FA	G by Pos
1969	SF N	9	.400	.400	5	2	0	0	0	0.0	1	1	0	1	0	0	0	3	0	0	0	0.4	1.000	OF-8
1970		9	.316	.632	19	6	1	1	1	5.3	2	4	2	5	0	2	1	10	0	0	0	1.4	1.000	OF-7
1971	2 teams	SF N (36G –.267)	CIN N (104G –.234)																					
″	total	140	.241	.389	473	114	23	4	13	2.7	50	58	29	120	7	10	2	315	9	5	3	2.5	.985	OF-132
1972	CIN N	59	.200	.283	145	29	4	1	2	1.4	15	12	5	44	2	12	4	71	1	2	1	1.6	.973	OF-47
1973		17	.282	.667	39	11	3	0	4	10.3	6	9	4	7	0	4	0	19	1	0	1	1.5	1.000	OF-13
1974		106	.264	.406	276	73	18	0	7	2.5	31	41	30	52	3	17	3	172	2	2	1	1.8	.989	OF-98
1975		134	.300	.518	463	139	24	4	23	5.0	71	78	40	73	2	9	4	299	11	3	3	2.5	.990	OF-125, 1B-1
1976		144	.306	.530	562	172	21	9	29	5.2	86	**121**	52	89	17	6	0	322	9	2	3	2.3	.994	OF-142, 1B-1
1977		158	.320	**.631**	615	197	31	2	**52**	**8.5**	**124**	**149**	61	107	6	0	0	352	12	3	1	2.3	.992	OF-158
1978		158	.281	.546	604	170	26	7	**40**	**6.6**	97	**120**	70	138	4	1	0	319	10	10	1	2.2	.971	OF-157
1979		121	.302	.561	440	133	18	3	30	6.8	68	98	59	105	0	4	1	214	7	4	1	1.9	.982	OF-116
1980		144	.273	.473	528	144	21	5	25	4.7	79	93	75	99	1	3	0	295	6	1	1	2.1	.997	OF-141
1981		108	.295	.519	414	122	23	2	22	5.3	64	90	51	75	4	0	0	224	8	2	1	2.2	.991	OF-108
1982	NY N	151	.247	.367	550	136	23	2	13	2.4	64	70	50	123	1	11	2	289	12	8	4	2.2	.974	OF-138
1983		157	.241	.419	601	145	19	2	28	4.7	74	90	38	111	1	5	1	314	12	4	3	2.2	.988	OF-153
1984		146	.269	.443	553	149	22	1	24	4.3	67	86	30	122	2	5	1	278	6	7	1	2.1	.976	OF-141
1985		129	.263	.460	452	119	24	1	21	4.6	57	77	46	87	0	6	1	198	7	5	2	1.7	.976	OF-123
1986	2 teams	NY N (72G –.227)	CHI A (15G –.216)																					
″	total	87	.225	.415	284	64	6	3	14	4.9	30	42	24	61	1	9	0	115	6	4	1	1.6	.968	OF-73, DH-3
18 yrs.		1977	.274	.480	7023	1925	307	47	348	5.0	986	1239	666	1419	51	104	20	3809	119	62	28	2.1	.984	OF-1880, DH-3, 1B-2
LEAGUE CHAMPIONSHIP SERIES																								
1972	CIN N	1	—	—	0	0	0	0	0	—	1	0	0	0	0	0	0	0	0	0	0	0.0	—	
1975		3	.364	.364	11	4	0	0	0	0.0	3	0	1	2	1	0	0	7	0	0	0	2.3	1.000	OF-3

George Foster *continued*

Year	Team	Games	BA	SA	AB	H	2B	3B	HR	HR%	R	RBI	BB	SO	SB	Pinch Hit AB	Pinch Hit H	PO	A	E	DP	TC/G	FA	G by Pos
1976		3	.167	.667	12	2	0	0	2	16.7	2	4	0	4	0	0	0	7	0	0	0	2.3	1.000	OF-3
1979		3	.200	.500	10	2	0	0	1	10.0	1	2	4	3	0	0	0	6	2	0	0	2.7	1.000	OF-3
4 yrs.		10	.242	.515	33	8	0	0	3	9.1	7	6	5	9	1	0	0	20	2	0	0	2.4	1.000	OF-9
WORLD SERIES																								
1972	CIN N	2	—	—	0	0	0	0	0	—	0	0	0	0	0	0	0	0	0	0	0	0.0	.000	OF-1
1975		7	.276	.310	29	8	1	0	0	0.0	1	2	1	1	1	0	0	13	1	0	1	2.0	1.000	OF-7
1976		4	.429	.500	14	6	1	0	0	0.0	3	4	2	3	0	0	0	14	0	0	0	3.5	1.000	OF-4
3 yrs.		13	.326	.372	43	14	2	0	0	0.0	4	6	3	4	1	0	0	27	1	0	1	2.3	1.000	OF-12

Leo Foster

FOSTER, LEONARD NORRIS BR TR 5'11" 165 lbs.
B. Feb. 2, 1951, Covington, Ky.

Year	Team	Games	BA	SA	AB	H	2B	3B	HR	HR%	R	RBI	BB	SO	SB	Pinch Hit AB	Pinch Hit H	PO	A	E	DP	TC/G	FA	G by Pos
1971	ATL N	9	.000	.000	10	0	0	0	0	0.0	1	0	0	1	0	2	0	1	8	1	2	3.3	.900	SS-3
1973		3	.167	.333	6	1	1	0	0	0.0	1	0	0	2	0	1	0	5	1	0	1	6.0	1.000	SS-1
1974		72	.196	.241	112	22	2	0	1	0.9	16	5	9	22	1	10	2	49	92	6	14	2.6	.959	SS-43, 2B-10, 3B-3, OF-1
1976	NY N	24	.203	.288	59	12	2	0	1	1.7	11	15	8	5	3	2	0	18	42	2	2	3.3	.968	3B-9, SS-7, 2B-3
1977		36	.227	.267	75	17	3	0	0	0.0	6	6	5	14	3	5	1	36	47	5	10	2.9	.943	2B-20, SS-8, 3B-2
5 yrs.		144	.198	.252	262	52	8	0	2	0.8	35	26	22	44	7	20	3	109	190	14	29	2.8	.955	SS-62, 2B-33, 3B-14, OF-1

Pop Foster

FOSTER, CLARENCE FRANCIS BR TR 5'8½"
B. Apr. 8, 1878, New Haven, Conn. D. Apr. 16, 1944, Princeton, N. J.

Year	Team	Games	BA	SA	AB	H	2B	3B	HR	HR%	R	RBI	BB	SO	SB	Pinch Hit AB	Pinch Hit H	PO	A	E	DP	TC/G	FA	G by Pos
1898	NY N	32	.268	.339	112	30	6	1	0	0.0	10	9	0		0	0	0	37	25	11	1	2.2	.849	OF-21, 3B-10, SS-2
1899		84	.296	.402	301	89	9	7	3	1.0	48	57	20		7	0	0	106	9	7	3	1.4	.943	OF-84, SS-1, 3B-1
1900		31	.262	.321	84	22	3	1	0	0.0	19	11	11		0	5	0	33	47	9	4	3.7	.899	OF-12, SS-7, 2B-5
1901	2 teams	WAS A (103G –.278) CHI A (12G –.286)																						
"	total	115	.279	.422	427	119	18	11	7	1.6	69	59	45		10	3	1	209	18	18	1	2.2	.927	OF-111, SS-2
4 yrs.		262	.281	.396	924	260	36	20	10	1.1	146	136	76		17	8	1	385	99	45	9	2.1	.915	OF-228, SS-12, 3B-11, 2B-5

Reddy Foster

FOSTER, OSCAR E.
B. Aug. 1864, Richmond, Va. D. Dec. 19, 1908, Richmond, Va.

Year	Team	Games	BA	SA	AB	H	2B	3B	HR	HR%	R	RBI	BB	SO	SB	Pinch Hit AB	Pinch Hit H	PO	A	E	DP	TC/G	FA	G by Pos
1896	NY N	1	.000	.000	1	0	0	0	0	0.0	0	0	0	0	0	1	0	0	0	0	0	0.0	—	

Roy Foster

FOSTER, ROY BR TR 6' 185 lbs.
B. July 29, 1945, Bixby, Okla.

Year	Team	Games	BA	SA	AB	H	2B	3B	HR	HR%	R	RBI	BB	SO	SB	Pinch Hit AB	Pinch Hit H	PO	A	E	DP	TC/G	FA	G by Pos
1970	CLE A	139	.268	.468	477	128	26	0	23	4.8	66	60	54	75	3	8	2	188	6	7	0	1.5	.965	OF-131
1971		125	.245	.439	396	97	21	1	18	4.5	51	45	35	48	6	20	5	174	9	6	2	1.8	.968	OF-107
1972		73	.224	.336	143	32	4	0	4	2.8	19	13	21	23	0	26	4	54	2	2	0	1.3	.966	OF-45
3 yrs.		337	.253	.438	1016	257	51	1	45	4.4	136	118	110	146	9	54	11	416	17	15	2	1.6	.967	OF-283

Bob Fothergill

FOTHERGILL, ROBERT ROY (Fats) BR TR 5'10½" 230 lbs.
B. Aug. 16, 1897, Massillon, Ohio D. Mar. 20, 1938, Detroit, Mich.

Year	Team	Games	BA	SA	AB	H	2B	3B	HR	HR%	R	RBI	BB	SO	SB	Pinch Hit AB	Pinch Hit H	PO	A	E	DP	TC/G	FA	G by Pos
1922	DET A	42	.322	.454	152	49	12	4	0	0.0	20	29	8	9	1	3	1	50	2	3	1	1.4	.945	OF-39
1923		101	.315	.419	241	76	18	2	1	0.4	34	49	12	19	4	30	9	121	4	3	0	1.9	.977	OF-68
1924		54	.301	.386	166	50	8	3	0	0.0	28	15	5	13	2	9	3	89	2	3	1	2.1	.968	OF-45
1925		71	.353	.451	204	72	14	0	2	1.0	38	28	6	3	2	11	5	120	6	3	2	2.2	.977	OF-59
1926		110	.367	.506	387	142	31	7	3	0.8	63	73	33	23	4	6	4	245	3	10	0	2.5	.961	OF-103
1927		143	.359	.516	527	189	38	9	9	1.7	93	114	47	31	9	5	2	315	3	13	1	2.4	.961	OF-137
1928		111	.317	.481	347	110	28	10	3	0.9	49	63	24	19	8	19	4	179	6	8	0	2.1	.959	OF-90
1929		115	.354	.570	277	98	24	9	6	2.2	42	62	11	11	3	**53**	**19**	116	2	4	1	2.1	.967	OF-59
1930	2 teams	DET A (55G –.259) CHI A (52G –.296)																						
"	total	107	.277	.385	278	77	18	3	2	0.7	24	38	10	18	1	**34**	6	102	3	10	0	1.7	.913	OF-68
1931	CHI A	108	.282	.365	312	88	9	4	3	1.0	25	56	17	17	2	31	8	169	2	5	0	2.4	.972	OF-74
1932		116	.295	.431	346	102	24	1	7	2.0	36	50	27	10	4	29	8	136	4	7	0	1.7	.952	OF-86
1933	BOS A	28	.344	.375	32	11	1	0	0	0.0	1	5	2	4	0	23	7	4	0	0	0	1.0	1.000	OF-4
12 yrs.		1106	.325	.459	3269	1064	225	52	36	1.1	453	582	202	177	40	253	76	1646	37	69	6	2.1	.961	OF-832

Jack Fournier

FOURNIER, JOHN FRANK BL TR 6' 195 lbs.
B. Sept. 28, 1889, Au Sable, Mich. D. Sept. 5, 1973, Tacoma, Wash.

Year	Team	Games	BA	SA	AB	H	2B	3B	HR	HR%	R	RBI	BB	SO	SB	Pinch Hit AB	Pinch Hit H	PO	A	E	DP	TC/G	FA	G by Pos
1912	CHI A	35	.192	.315	73	14	5	2	0	0.0	5	2	4		1	18	5	154	16	2	4	10.1	.988	1B-17
1913		68	.233	.355	172	40	8	5	1	0.6	20	23	21	23	9	13	1	306	23	5	10	6.4	.985	1B-29, OF-23
1914		109	.311	.443	379	118	14	9	6	**1.6**	44	44	31	44	10	6	0	1034	79	27	31	11.1	.976	1B-97, OF-6
1915		126	.322	**.491**	422	136	20	18	5	1.2	86	77	64	37	21	4	2	784	51	17	34	7.0	.980	1B-65, OF-57
1916		105	.240	.367	313	75	13	9	3	1.0	36	44	36	40	19	14	2	857	49	20	47	10.8	.978	1B-85, OF-1
1917		1	.000	.000	1	0	0	0	0	0.0	0	0	0	1	0	1	0	0	0	0	0	0.0	—	
1918	NY A	27	.350	.430	100	35	6	1	0	0.0	9	12	7	7	7	0	0	274	13	7	23	10.9	.976	1B-27
1920	STL N	141	.306	.438	530	162	33	14	3	0.6	77	61	42	42	26	3	2	1373	88	25	100	10.8	.983	1B-138
1921		149	.343	.505	574	197	27	9	16	2.8	103	86	56	48	20	0	0	1416	73	19	91	10.1	.987	1B-149
1922		128	.295	.470	404	119	23	9	10	2.5	64	61	40	21	6	12	5	902	61	18	63	8.9	.982	1B-109, P-1
1923	BKN N	133	.351	.588	515	181	30	13	22	4.3	91	102	43	28	11	0	0	1281	82	21	90	10.4	.985	1B-133
1924		154	.334	.536	563	188	25	4	**27**	**4.8**	93	116	83	46	7	1	0	1388	99	22	102	9.9	.985	1B-153
1925		145	.350	.569	545	191	21	16	22	4.0	99	130	**86**	39	4	0	0	1317	82	15	105	9.8	.989	1B-145
1926		87	.284	.473	243	69	9	2	11	4.5	39	48	30	16	0	18	4	548	28	8	19	9.1	.986	1B-64
1927	BOS N	122	.283	.422	374	106	18	2	10	2.7	55	53	44	16	4	19	8	901	63	11	63	9.6	.989	1B-102
15 yrs.		1530	.313	.483	5208	1631	252	113	136	2.6	821	859	587	408	145	109	29	12535	807	217	782	9.7	.984	1B-1313, OF-87, P-1

Bill Fouser

FOUSER, WILLIAM C.
B. Oct. 1855, Philadelphia, Pa. D. Mar. 1, 1919, Philadelphia, Pa.

Year	Team	Games	BA	SA	AB	H	2B	3B	HR	HR%	R	RBI	BB	SO	SB	Pinch Hit AB	Pinch Hit H	PO	A	E	DP	TC/G	FA	G by Pos
1876	PHI N	21	.135	.157	89	12	0	1	0	0.0	11	2	0	0		0	0	52	56	24	3	6.0	.818	2B-14, OF-7, 1B-1

Dave Foutz

FOUTZ, DAVID LUTHER (Scissors)
Brother of Frank Foutz.
B. Sept. 7, 1856, Carroll County, Md. D. Mar. 5, 1897, Waverly, Md.
Manager 1893–96.

BR TR 6′ 2″ 161 lbs.

Year	Team	Games	BA	SA	AB	H	2B	3B	HR	HR%	R	RBI	BB	SO	SB	Pinch Hit AB	Pinch Hit H	PO	A	E	DP	TC/G	FA	G by Pos
1884	STL AA	33	.227	.261	119	27	4	0	0	0.0	17		8			0	0	26	45	6	6	2.0	.922	P-25, OF-14
1885		65	.248	.307	238	59	6	4	0	0.0	42		11			0	0	189	109	23	15	4.9	.928	P-47, 1B-15, OF-4
1886		102	.280	.389	414	116	18	9	3	0.7	66		9			0	0	211	86	19	7	3.0	.940	P-59, OF-34, 1B-11
1887		102	.357	.508	423	151	26	13	4	0.9	79		23		22	0	0	282	65	23	11	3.5	.938	OF-50, P-40, 1B-15
1888	BKN AA	140	.277	.375	563	156	20	13	3	0.5	91	99	28		35	0	0	588	71	28	28	4.8	.959	OF-78, 1B-42, P-23
1889		138	.277	.378	553	153	19	8	7	1.3	118	113	64	23	43	0	0	1376	48	31	66	10.0	.979	1B-134, P-12
1890	BKN N	129	.303	.432	509	154	25	13	5	1.0	106	98	52	25	42	0	0	1222	44	30	64	9.9	.977	1B-113, OF-13, P-5
1891		130	.257	.349	521	134	26	8	2	0.4	87	73	40	25	48	0	0	1246	60	31	52	10.2	.977	1B-124, P-6, SS-1
1892		61	.186	.250	220	41	5	3	1	0.5	33	26	14	14	19	1	0	109	62	16	5	3.0	.914	OF-29, P-27, 1B-6
1893		130	.246	.355	557	137	20	10	7	1.3	91	67	32	34	39	0	0	735	36	27	22	5.8	.966	OF-77, 1B-54, P-6
1894		72	.307	.410	293	90	12	9	0	0.0	40	51	14	13	14	0	0	658	33	17	37	9.7	.976	1B-72, P-1
1895		31	.296	.348	115	34	4	1	0	0.0	14	21	4	2	1	3	0	109	3	9	4	4.3	.926	OF-20, 1B-8
1896		2	.250	.375	8	2	1	0	0	0.0	0	0	1	0	0	0	0	7	2	1	0	5.0	.900	OF-1, 1B-1
13 yrs.		1135	.277	.379	4533	1254	186	91	32	0.7	784	548	300	136	263	4	0	6758	664	261	317	6.6	.966	1B-595, OF-320, P-251, SS-1

Frank Foutz

FOUTZ, FRANK HAYES
Brother of Dave Foutz.
B. Apr. 8, 1877, Baltimore, Md. D. Dec. 25, 1961, Lima, Ohio.

BR TR 5′11″ 165 lbs.

Year	Team	Games	BA	SA	AB	H	2B	3B	HR	HR%	R	RBI	BB	SO	SB	Pinch Hit AB	Pinch Hit H	PO	A	E	DP	TC/G	FA	G by Pos
1901	BAL A	20	.236	.403	72	17	4	1	2	2.8	13	14	8		0	0	0	176	11	8	8	9.8	.959	1B-20

Boob Fowler

FOWLER, JOSEPH CHESTER
B. Nov. 11, 1900, Waco, Tex. D. Oct. 8, 1988, Dallas, Tex.

BL TR 5′11½″ 180 lbs.

Year	Team	Games	BA	SA	AB	H	2B	3B	HR	HR%	R	RBI	BB	SO	SB	Pinch Hit AB	Pinch Hit H	PO	A	E	DP	TC/G	FA	G by Pos
1923	CIN N	11	.333	.485	33	11	0	1	1	3.0	9	6	1	3	1	0	0	22	28	9	6	5.9	.847	SS-10
1924		59	.333	.395	129	43	6	1	0	0.0	20	9	5	15	2	3	0	51	92	10	14	4.0	.935	SS-32, 2B-4, 3B-2
1925		6	.400	.600	5	2	1	0	0	0.0	0	2	0	1	0	5	2	0	0	0	0	0.0	—	
1926	BOS A	2	.125	.125	8	1	0	0	0	0.0	1	1	0	0	0	0	0	2	6	2	0	5.0	.800	3B-2
4 yrs.		78	.326	.406	175	57	7	2	1	0.6	30	18	6	19	3	8	2	75	126	21	20	4.4	.905	SS-42, 2B-4, 3B-4

Bill Fox

FOX, WILLIAM HENRY
B. Jan. 15, 1872, Sturbridge, Mass. D. May 7, 1946, Minneapolis, Minn.

BB TR 5′10″ 160 lbs.

Year	Team	Games	BA	SA	AB	H	2B	3B	HR	HR%	R	RBI	BB	SO	SB	Pinch Hit AB	Pinch Hit H	PO	A	E	DP	TC/G	FA	G by Pos
1897	WAS N	4	.286	.286	14	4	0	0	0	0.0	4	0	1		0	0	0	12	11	5	3	7.0	.821	SS-2, 2B-2
1901	CIN N	43	.176	.201	159	28	2	1	0	0.0	9	7	4		9	0	0	103	134	11	19	5.8	.956	2B-43
2 yrs.		47	.185	.208	173	32	2	1	0	0.0	13	7	5		9	0	0	115	145	16	22	5.9	.942	2B-45, SS-2

Charlie Fox

FOX, CHARLES FRANCIS (Irish)
B. Oct. 7, 1921, New York, N. Y.
Manager 1970–74, 1976, 1983.

BR TR 5′11″ 180 lbs.

Year	Team	Games	BA	SA	AB	H	2B	3B	HR	HR%	R	RBI	BB	SO	SB	Pinch Hit AB	Pinch Hit H	PO	A	E	DP	TC/G	FA	G by Pos
1942	NY N	3	.429	.429	7	3	0	0	0	0.0	1	1	1	2	0	0	0	7	0	0	0	2.3	1.000	C-3

Eric Fox

FOX, ERIC HOLLIS
B. Aug. 15, 1963, Lemoore, Calif.

BB TL 5′10″ 180 lbs.

Year	Team	Games	BA	SA	AB	H	2B	3B	HR	HR%	R	RBI	BB	SO	SB	Pinch Hit AB	Pinch Hit H	PO	A	E	DP	TC/G	FA	G by Pos
1992	OAK A	51	.238	.364	143	34	5	2	3	2.1	24	13	13	29	3	4	0	92	3	1	1	2.1	.990	OF-43, DH-3
1993		29	.143	.214	56	8	1	0	1	1.8	5	5	2	7	0	3	0	47	0	0	1	1.7	1.000	OF-26, DH-1
1994		26	.205	.318	44	9	2	0	1	2.3	7	1	3	8	2	4	1	32	1	0	0	1.4	1.000	OF-24
1995	TEX A	10	.000	.000	15	0	0	0	0	0.0	2	0	3	4	0	0	0	13	0	0	0	1.4	1.000	OF-8, DH-1
4 yrs.		116	.198	.302	258	51	8	2	5	1.9	38	19	21	48	5	11	1	184	4	1	2	1.8	.995	OF-101, DH-5
LEAGUE CHAMPIONSHIP SERIES																								
1992	OAK A	4	.000	.000	1	0	0	0	0	0.0	0	0	1	0	2	0	0	1	0	0	0	0.5	1.000	OF-1, DH-1

Jack Fox

FOX, JOHN PAUL
B. May 21, 1885, Reading, Pa. D. June 28, 1963, Reading, Pa.

BR TR 5′10″ 185 lbs.

Year	Team	Games	BA	SA	AB	H	2B	3B	HR	HR%	R	RBI	BB	SO	SB	Pinch Hit AB	Pinch Hit H	PO	A	E	DP	TC/G	FA	G by Pos
1908	PHI A	9	.200	.200	30	6	0	0	0	0.0	2	0	0		2	0	0	12	0	1	0	1.6	.923	OF-8

Nellie Fox

FOX, JACOB NELSON
B. Dec. 25, 1927, St. Thomas, Pa. D. Dec. 1, 1975, Baltimore, Md.

BL TR 5′10″ 160 lbs.

Year	Team	Games	BA	SA	AB	H	2B	3B	HR	HR%	R	RBI	BB	SO	SB	Pinch Hit AB	Pinch Hit H	PO	A	E	DP	TC/G	FA	G by Pos
1947	PHI A	7	.000	.000	3	0	0	0	0	0.0	2	0	1	0	0	2	0	1	0	0	0	1.0	1.000	2B-1
1948		3	.154	.154	13	2	0	0	0	0.0	0	0	1	0	1	0	0	13	6	1	1	6.7	.950	2B-3
1949		88	.255	.296	247	63	6	2	0	0.0	42	21	32	9	2	2	0	191	196	7	68	5.1	.982	2B-77
1950	CHI A	130	.247	.304	457	113	12	7	0	0.0	45	30	35	17	4	8	2	340	344	18	100	5.8	.974	2B-121
1951		147	.313	.425	604	189	32	12	4	0.7	93	55	43	11	9	0	0	413	449	17	112	6.0	.981	2B-147
1952		152	.296	.366	**648**	**192**	25	10	0	0.0	76	39	34	14	5	1	0	406	433	13	111	5.6	.985	2B-151
1953		154	.285	.375	624	178	31	8	3	0.5	92	72	49	18	4	0	0	451	426	15	101	5.8	.983	2B-154
1954		155	.319	.391	631	**201**	24	8	2	0.3	111	47	51	12	16	0	0	400	392	9	103	5.2	.989	2B-155
1955		154	.311	.406	**636**	198	28	7	6	0.9	100	59	38	15	7	0	0	399	483	24	110	5.9	.974	2B-154
1956		154	.296	.376	**649**	192	20	10	4	0.6	109	52	44	14	8	0	0	478	396	12	124	5.8	.986	2B-154
1957		155	.317	.415	619	**196**	27	8	6	1.0	110	61	75	13	5	0	0	453	453	13	141	5.9	.986	2B-155
1958		155	.300	.353	623	**187**	21	6	0	0.0	82	49	47	11	5	0	0	444	399	13	117	5.5	.985	2B-155
1959		156	.306	.389	**624**	191	34	6	2	0.3	84	70	71	13	5	0	0	364	453	10	93	5.3	.988	2B-156
1960		150	.289	.372	**605**	175	24	**10**	2	0.3	85	59	50	13	2	1	0	412	447	13	126	5.9	.985	2B-149
1961		159	.251	.295	606	152	11	5	2	0.3	67	51	59	12	2	2	1	413	407	15	97	5.3	.982	2B-159
1962		157	.267	.343	621	166	27	7	2	0.3	79	54	38	12	1	3	0	376	428	8	93	5.3	.990	2B-154
1963		137	.260	.306	539	140	19	0	2	0.4	54	42	24	17	0	6	2	305	342	8	71	4.9	.988	2B-134
1964	HOU N	133	.265	.319	442	117	12	6	0	0.0	45	28	27	13	0	13	1	231	317	13	51	4.9	.977	2B-115
1965		21	.268	.317	41	11	2	0	0	0.0	3	1	0	2	0	12	4	12	14	0	2	2.9	1.000	3B-6, 1B-2, 2B-1
19 yrs.		2367	.288	.363	9232	2663	355	112	35	0.4	1279	790	719	216	76	50	10	6102	6385	209	1621	5.5	.984	2B-2295, 3B-6, 1B-2
WORLD SERIES																								
1959	CHI A	6	.375	.500	24	9	3	0	0	0.0	4	0	4	1	0	0	1	14	23	0	2	6.2	1.000	2B-6

Paddy Fox

FOX, GEORGE B.
B. Dec. 1, 1868, Pottstown, Pa. D. May 8, 1914, Philadelphia, Pa.

Year	Team	Games	BA	SA	AB	H	2B	3B	HR	HR%	R	RBI	BB	SO	SB	Pinch Hit AB	Pinch Hit H	PO	A	E	DP	TC/G	FA	G by Pos
1891	LOU AA	6	.105	.211	19	2	0	1	0	0.0	1	2	2	3	0	0	0	0	0	0	0	0.0	.000	3B-6
1899	PIT N	13	.244	.366	41	10	0	1	1	2.4	4	3	3		2	1	0	104	10	3	11	9.8	.974	1B-9, C-3
2 yrs.		19	.200	.317	60	12	0	2	1	1.7	5	5	5	3	2	1	0	104	10	3	11	6.5	.974	1B-9, 3B-6, C-3

Pete Fox

FOX, ERVIN BR TR 5′11″ 165 lbs.
B. Mar. 8, 1909, Evansville, Ind. D. July 5, 1966, Detroit, Mich.

Year	Team	Games	BA	SA	AB	H	2B	3B	HR	HR%	R	RBI	BB	SO	SB	Pinch Hit AB	Pinch Hit H	PO	A	E	DP	TC/G	FA	G by Pos
1933	DET A	128	.288	.424	535	154	26	13	7	1.3	82	57	23	38	9	3	0	313	5	7	0	2.6	.978	OF-124
1934		128	.285	.364	516	147	31	2	2	0.4	101	45	49	53	25	6	1	245	13	7	4	2.2	.974	OF-121
1935		131	.321	.513	517	166	38	8	15	2.9	116	73	45	52	14	6	3	244	9	3	1	2.0	.988	OF-125
1936		73	.305	.423	220	67	12	1	4	1.8	46	26	34	23	1	15	2	118	3	4	0	2.3	.968	OF-55
1937		148	.331	.476	628	208	39	8	12	1.9	116	82	41	43	12	3	2	321	6	8	0	2.3	.976	OF-143
1938		155	.293	.413	634	186	35	10	7	1.1	91	96	31	39	16	0	0	301	13	2	2	2.1	.994	OF-154
1939		141	.295	.405	519	153	24	6	7	1.3	69	66	35	41	23	14	2	275	12	9	3	2.3	.970	OF-126
1940		93	.289	.403	350	101	17	4	5	1.4	49	48	21	30	7	9	1	169	6	6	0	2.1	.967	OF-85
1941	BOS A	73	.302	.399	268	81	12	7	0	0.0	38	31	21	32	9	7	0	123	5	3	2	2.1	.977	OF-62
1942		77	.262	.395	256	67	15	5	3	1.2	42	42	20	28	8	3	1	111	2	4	0	1.6	.966	OF-71
1943		127	.288	.366	489	141	24	4	2	0.4	54	44	34	40	22	1	0	261	10	11	2	2.3	.961	OF-125
1944		121	.315	.421	496	156	38	6	1	0.2	70	64	27	34	10	2	0	228	7	3	1	2.0	.987	OF-119
1945		66	.245	.274	208	51	4	1	0	0.0	21	20	11	18	2	5	0	84	5	1	1	1.6	.989	OF-57
13 yrs.		1461	.298	.415	5636	1678	315	75	65	1.2	895	694	392	471	158	74	12	2793	96	68	16	2.2	.977	OF-1367
WORLD SERIES																								
1934	DET A	7	.286	.500	28	8	6	0	0	0.0	1	2	1	4	0	0	0	15	0	0	0	2.1	1.000	OF-7
1935		6	.385	.577	26	10	3	1	0	0.0	1	4	0	1	0	0	0	8	2	1	0	1.8	.909	OF-6
1940		1	.000	.000	1	0	0	0	0	0.0	0	0	0	0	0	1	0	0	0	0	0	0.0	—	
3 yrs.		14	.327	.527	55	18	9	1	0	0.0	2	6	1	5	0	1	0	23	2	1	0	2.0	.962	OF-13
							3rd																	

Jimmie Foxx

FOXX, JAMES EMORY (Double X, The Beast) BR TR 6′ 195 lbs.
B. Oct. 22, 1907, Sudlersville, Md. D. July 21, 1967, Miami, Fla.
Hall of Fame 1951.

Year	Team	Games	BA	SA	AB	H	2B	3B	HR	HR%	R	RBI	BB	SO	SB	Pinch Hit AB	Pinch Hit H	PO	A	E	DP	TC/G	FA	G by Pos
1925	PHI A	10	.667	.778	9	6	1	0	0	0.0	2	0	0	1	0	9	6	0	0	0	0	0.0	.000	C-1
1926		26	.313	.438	32	10	2	1	0	0.0	8	5	1	6	1	8	0	19	5	0	0	1.6	1.000	C-12, OF-3
1927		61	.323	.515	130	42	6	5	3	2.3	23	20	14	11	2	20	7	272	16	7	10	8.0	.976	1B-32, C-5
1928		118	.328	.547	400	131	29	10	13	3.3	85	79	60	43	3	8	2	412	154	17	32	5.3	.971	3B-61, 1B-30, C-20
1929		149	.354	.625	517	183	23	9	33	6.4	123	117	103	**70**	10	0	0	1233	91	7	100	8.9	.995	1B-142, 3B-7
1930		153	.335	.637	562	188	33	13	37	6.6	127	156	93	**66**	7	0	0	1362	79	14	101	9.5	.990	1B-153
1931		139	.291	.567	515	150	32	10	30	5.8	93	120	73	**84**	4	2	1	990	104	15	93	8.3	.986	1B-112, 3B-20, OF-1
1932		154	.364	**.749**	585	213	33	9	**58**	**9.9**	**151**	**169**	116	96	3	0	0	1338	97	11	116	9.4	.992	1B-141, 3B-13
1933		149	**.356**	**.703**	573	204	37	9	**48**	**8.4**	125	**163**	96	**93**	2	0	0	1402	94	15	98	10.1	.990	1B-149, SS-1
1934		150	.334	.653	539	180	28	6	44	8.2	120	130	**111**	75	11	1	0	1388	102	10	134	10.1	.993	1B-140, 3B-9
1935		147	.346	**.636**	535	185	33	7	**36**	**6.7**	118	115	114	**99**	6	0	0	1226	93	4	108	8.9	.997	1B-121, C-26, 3B-2
1936	BOS A	155	.338	.631	585	198	32	8	41	7.0	130	143	105	**119**	13	0	0	1254	77	13	108	8.6	.990	1B-139, OF-16, 3B-1
1937		150	.285	.538	569	162	24	6	36	6.3	111	127	99	96	10	0	0	1287	106	8	122	9.3	.994	1B-150, C-1
1938		149	**.349**	**.704**	565	197	33	9	50	8.8	139	**175**	**119**	76	5	0	0	1282	116	19	153	9.5	.987	1B-149
1939		124	.360	**.694**	467	168	31	10	**35**	**7.5**	130	105	89	72	4	1	0	1101	91	10	104	9.7	.992	1B-123, P-1
1940		144	.297	.581	515	153	30	4	36	7.0	106	119	101	87	4	4	1	1023	100	10	89	8.2	.991	1B-95, C-42, 3B-1
1941		135	.300	.505	487	146	27	8	19	3.9	87	105	93	**103**	2	4	2	1162	118	14	106	10.0	.989	1B-124, 3B-5, OF-1
1942	2 teams	BOS A (30G –.270) CHI N (70G –.205)																						
"	total	100	.226	.344	305	69	12	0	8	2.6	43	33	40	70	1	18	3	722	58	10	60	9.9	.987	1B-79, C-1
1944	CHI N	15	.050	.100	20	1	1	0	0	0.0	0	2	2	5	0	11	0	9	6	0	0	5.0	1.000	3B-2, C-1
1945	PHI N	89	.268	.420	224	60	11	1	7	3.1	30	38	23	39	0	26	8	304	54	8	19	5.8	.978	1B-40, 3B-14, P-9
20 yrs.		2317	.325	.609	8134	2646	458	125	534	6.6	1751	1921	1452	1311	88	112	30	17786	1561	192	1553	8.9	.990	1B-1919, 3B-135, C-109, OF-21, P-10, SS-1
				4th					9th	7th		6th												
WORLD SERIES																								
1929	PHI A	5	.350	.700	20	7	1	0	2	10.0	5	5	1	1	0	0	0	38	1	0	2	7.8	1.000	1B-5
1930		6	.333	.667	21	7	2	1	1	4.8	3	3	2	4	0	0	0	53	3	0	2	9.3	1.000	1B-6
1931		7	.348	.478	23	8	0	0	1	4.3	3	3	6	5	0	0	0	69	2	1	4	10.3	.986	1B-7
3 yrs.		18	.344	.609	64	22	3	1	4	6.3	11	11	9	10	0	0	0	160	6	1	8	9.3	.994	1B-18

Joe Foy

FOY, JOSEPH ANTHONY BR TR 6′ 215 lbs.
B. Feb. 21, 1943, New York, N. Y. D. Oct. 12, 1989, Bronx, N. Y.

Year	Team	Games	BA	SA	AB	H	2B	3B	HR	HR%	R	RBI	BB	SO	SB	Pinch Hit AB	Pinch Hit H	PO	A	E	DP	TC/G	FA	G by Pos
1966	BOS A	151	.262	.413	554	145	23	8	15	2.7	97	63	91	80	2	1	0	169	310	27	35	3.3	.947	3B-139, SS-13
1967		130	.251	.426	446	112	22	4	16	3.6	70	49	46	87	8	13	2	110	204	27	13	2.9	.921	3B-118, OF-1
1968		150	.225	.326	515	116	18	2	10	1.9	65	60	84	91	26	1	0	118	313	30	36	3.1	.935	3B-147, OF-3
1969	KC A	145	.262	.370	519	136	19	2	11	2.1	72	71	74	75	37	1	0	285	230	18	29	3.5	.966	3B-113, OF-16, 1B-16, SS-5, 2B-3
1970	NY N	99	.236	.329	322	76	12	0	6	1.9	39	37	68	58	22	2	0	90	179	18	20	3.0	.937	3B-97
1971	WAS A	41	.234	.297	128	30	8	0	0	0.0	12	11	27	14	4	4	0	44	80	5	12	3.1	.961	3B-37, 2B-3, SS-1
6 yrs.		716	.248	.372	2484	615	102	16	58	2.3	355	291	390	405	99	22	2	816	1316	125	145	3.2	.945	3B-651, OF-20, SS-19, 1B-16, 2B-6
WORLD SERIES																								
1967	BOS A	6	.133	.200	15	2	1	0	0	0.0	2	1	1	5	0	3	0	7	10	1	0	6.0	.944	3B-3

Julio Franco

FRANCO, JULIO CESAR BR TR 6′ 160 lbs.
Born Julio Cesar Robles (Franco).
B. Aug. 23, 1958, Hato Mayor, Dominican Republic.

Year	Team	Games	BA	SA	AB	H	2B	3B	HR	HR%	R	RBI	BB	SO	SB	Pinch Hit AB	Pinch Hit H	PO	A	E	DP	TC/G	FA	G by Pos
1982	PHI N	16	.276	.310	29	8	1	0	0	0.0	3	3	2	4	0	0	0	8	25	0	2	2.5	1.000	SS-11, 3B-2
1983	CLE A	149	.273	.388	560	153	24	8	8	1.4	68	80	27	50	32	0	0	247	438	28	92	4.8	.961	SS-149
1984		160	.286	.348	**658**	188	22	5	3	0.5	82	79	43	68	19	0	0	280	481	36	116	5.0	.955	SS-159, DH-1
1985		160	.288	.381	636	183	33	4	6	0.9	97	90	54	74	13	2	0	252	437	36	99	4.5	.950	SS-151, 2B-8, DH-1
1986		149	.306	.422	599	183	30	5	10	1.7	80	74	32	66	10	1	0	248	413	19	90	4.5	.972	SS-134, 2B-13, DH-3

Julio Franco *continued*

Year	Team	Games	BA	SA	AB	H	2B	3B	HR	HR%	R	RBI	BB	SO	SB	Pinch Hit AB	Pinch Hit H	PO	A	E	DP	TC/G	FA	G by Pos
1987		128	.319	.428	495	158	24	3	8	1.6	86	52	57	56	32	1	1	175	313	18	56	4.0	.964	SS-111, 2B-9, DH-8
1988		152	.303	.409	613	186	23	6	10	1.6	88	54	56	72	25	0	0	310	434	14	87	5.0	.982	2B-151, DH-1
1989	TEX A	150	.316	.462	548	173	31	5	13	2.4	80	92	66	69	21	1	1	256	386	13	70	4.4	.980	2B-140, DH-10
1990		157	.296	.402	582	172	27	1	11	1.9	96	69	82	83	31	1	1	310	444	19	101	5.0	.975	2B-152, DH-3
1991		146	**.341**	.474	589	201	27	3	15	2.5	108	78	65	78	36	2	1	294	372	14	80	4.7	.979	2B-146
1992		35	.234	.355	107	25	7	0	2	1.9	19	8	15	17	1	7	3	21	17	3	2	1.5	.927	DH-15, 2B-9, OF-4
1993		144	.289	.438	532	154	31	3	14	2.6	85	84	62	95	9	3	1	0	0	0	0	0.0	.000	DH-140
1994	CHI A	112	.319	.510	433	138	19	2	20	4.6	72	98	62	75	8	0	0	88	7	3	9	0.9	.969	DH-99, 1B-14
13 yrs.		1658	.301	.419	6381	1922	299	45	120	1.9	964	861	623	807	237	18	8	2489	3767	203	804	3.9	.969	SS-715, 2B-628, DH-281, 1B-14, OF-4, 3B-2

Matt Franco

FRANCO, MATTHEW NEIL
B. Aug. 19, 1969, Santa Monica, Calif.
BL TR 6′ 2″ 200 lbs.

Year	Team	Games	BA	SA	AB	H	2B	3B	HR	HR%	R	RBI	BB	SO	SB	Pinch Hit AB	Pinch Hit H	PO	A	E	DP	TC/G	FA	G by Pos
1995	CHI N	16	.294	.353	17	5	1	0	0	0.0	3	1	0	4	0	11	3	2	2	0	0	0.8	1.000	2B-3, 1B-1, 3B-1

Terry Francona

FRANCONA, TERRY JON
Son of Tito Francona.
B. Apr. 22, 1959, Aberdeen, S. D.
BL TL 6′ 1″ 190 lbs.

Year	Team	Games	BA	SA	AB	H	2B	3B	HR	HR%	R	RBI	BB	SO	SB	Pinch Hit AB	Pinch Hit H	PO	A	E	DP	TC/G	FA	G by Pos
1981	MON N	34	.274	.326	95	26	0	1	1	1.1	11	8	5	6	1	10	5	41	5	0	0	1.7	1.000	OF-26, 1B-1
1982		46	.321	.344	131	42	3	0	0	0.0	14	9	8	11	2	7	2	65	0	3	2	1.4	.956	OF-33, 1B-16
1983		120	.257	.352	230	59	11	1	3	1.3	21	22	6	20	0	38	8	172	10	3	10	1.9	.984	OF-51, 1B-47
1984		58	.346	.467	214	74	19	2	1	0.5	18	18	5	12	0	3	0	431	50	3	43	8.6	.994	1B-50, OF-6
1985		107	.267	.349	281	75	15	1	2	0.7	19	31	12	12	5	31	6	431	40	6	32	5.5	.987	1B-57, OF-28, 3B-1
1986	CHI N	86	.250	.323	124	31	3	0	2	1.6	13	8	6	8	0	42	8	123	7	0	9	2.5	1.000	OF-30, 1B-23
1987	CIN N	102	.227	.295	207	47	5	0	3	1.4	16	12	10	12	2	43	11	377	45	2	38	6.5	.995	1B-57, OF-8
1988	CLE A	62	.311	.363	212	66	8	0	1	0.5	24	12	5	18	0	15	5	47	5	1	3	1.1	.981	DH-38, OF-5, 1B-5
1989	MIL A	90	.232	.322	233	54	10	1	3	1.3	26	23	8	20	2	8	1	339	26	4	32	4.3	.989	1B-46, DH-23, OF-16, P-1
1990		3	.000	.000	4	0	0	0	0	0.0	1	0	0	0	0	0	0	6	0	0	1	2.0	1.000	1B-2, DH-1
10 yrs.		708	.274	.351	1731	474	74	6	16	0.9	163	143	65	119	12	197	46	2032	188	22	170	3.9	.990	1B-304, OF-203, DH-62, P-1, 3B-1
DIVISIONAL PLAYOFF SERIES																								
1981	MON N	5	.333	.333	12	4	0	0	0	0.0	0	0	2	2	2	0	0	8	0	0	0	1.6	1.000	OF-5
LEAGUE CHAMPIONSHIP SERIES																								
1981	MON N	2	.000	.000	1	0	0	0	0	0.0	0	0	0	1	0	1	0	0	0	0	0	0.0	.000	OF-1

Tito Francona

FRANCONA, JOHN PATSY
Father of Terry Francona.
B. Nov. 4, 1933, Aliquippa, Pa.
BL TL 5′11″ 190 lbs.

Year	Team	Games	BA	SA	AB	H	2B	3B	HR	HR%	R	RBI	BB	SO	SB	Pinch Hit AB	Pinch Hit H	PO	A	E	DP	TC/G	FA	G by Pos
1956	BAL A	139	.258	.373	445	115	16	4	9	2.0	62	57	51	60	11	18	4	326	13	7	8	2.4	.980	OF-122, 1B-21
1957		97	.233	.358	279	65	8	3	7	2.5	35	38	29	48	7	23	3	130	1	1	2	1.7	.992	OF-73, 1B-4
1958	2 teams	CHI A (41G –.258) DET A (45G –.246)																						
″	total	86	.254	.330	197	50	8	2	1	0.5	21	20	29	40	2	29	11	73	3	0	1	1.4	1.000	OF-53, 1B-1
1959	CLE A	122	.363	.566	399	145	17	2	20	5.0	68	79	35	42	2	20	5	432	21	5	21	4.6	.989	OF-64, 1B-35
1960		147	.292	.460	544	159	**36**	2	17	3.1	84	79	67	67	4	3	0	346	12	4	6	2.4	.989	OF-138, 1B-13
1961		155	.301	.459	592	178	30	8	16	2.7	87	85	56	52	2	7	1	395	11	8	10	2.7	.981	OF-138, 1B-14
1962		158	.272	.401	621	169	28	5	14	2.3	82	70	47	74	3	0	0	1402	127	22	5	9.8	.986	1B-158
1963		142	.228	.346	500	114	29	0	10	2.0	57	41	47	77	9	13	4	292	8	3	3	2.3	.990	OF-122, 1B-11
1964		111	.248	.400	270	67	13	2	8	3.0	35	24	44	46	1	29	6	157	7	2	10	1.9	.988	OF-69, 1B-17
1965	STL N	81	.259	.402	174	45	6	2	5	2.9	15	19	17	30	0	35	9	137	3	2	8	3.0	.986	OF-34, 1B-13
1966		83	.212	.327	156	33	4	1	4	2.6	14	17	7	27	0	41	7	224	18	3	20	6.3	.988	1B-30, OF-9
1967	2 teams	PHI N (27G –.205) ATL N (82G –.248)																						
″	total	109	.239	.318	327	78	6	1	6	1.8	35	28	27	44	1	27	3	675	48	5	51	8.4	.993	1B-80, OF-7
1968	ATL N	122	.286	.347	346	99	13	1	2	0.6	32	47	51	45	3	24	5	382	12	4	18	4.1	.990	OF-65, 1B-33
1969	2 teams	ATL N (51G –.295) OAK A (32G –.341)																						
″	total	83	.318	.457	173	55	7	1	5	2.9	17	42	25	21	0	32	8	222	11	4	15	5.6	.983	1B-26, OF-16
1970	2 teams	OAK A (32G –.242) MIL A (52G –.231)																						
″	total	84	.235	.296	98	23	3	0	1	1.0	6	10	12	21	1	**64**	**15**	123	10	0	13	6.7	1.000	1B-19, OF-1
15 yrs.		1719	.272	.403	5121	1395	224	34	125	2.4	650	656	544	694	46	365	81	5316	305	70	191	4.1	.988	OF-911, 1B-475

Charlie Frank

FRANK, CHARLES
B. May 30, 1870, Mobile, Ala. D. May 24, 1922, Memphis, Tenn.
5′10″ 170 lbs.

Year	Team	Games	BA	SA	AB	H	2B	3B	HR	HR%	R	RBI	BB	SO	SB	Pinch Hit AB	Pinch Hit H	PO	A	E	DP	TC/G	FA	G by Pos
1893	STL N	40	.335	.427	164	55	6	3	1	0.6	29	17	18	8	8	0	0	84	9	7	1	2.5	.930	OF-40
1894		80	.279	.398	319	89	12	7	4	1.3	52	42	44	13	14	0	0	191	12	26	4	2.8	.886	OF-77, 1B-3, P-2
2 yrs.		120	.298	.408	483	144	18	10	5	1.0	81	59	62	21	22	0	0	275	21	33	5	2.7	.900	OF-117, 1B-3, P-2

Fred Frank

FRANK, FREDERICK
B. Mar. 11, 1874, Louisa, Ky. D. Mar. 27, 1950, Ashland, Ky.

Year	Team	Games	BA	SA	AB	H	2B	3B	HR	HR%	R	RBI	BB	SO	SB	Pinch Hit AB	Pinch Hit H	PO	A	E	DP	TC/G	FA	G by Pos
1898	CLE N	17	.208	.264	53	11	1	1	0	0.0	3	3	4		1	0	0	40	3	4	2	2.8	.915	OF-17

Franklin

FRANKLIN,
Deceased.

Year	Team	Games	BA	SA	AB	H	2B	3B	HR	HR%	R	RBI	BB	SO	SB	Pinch Hit AB	Pinch Hit H	PO	A	E	DP	TC/G	FA	G by Pos
1884	WAS U	1	.000	.000	3	0	0	0	0	0.0	0		0			0	0	2	0	0	0	2.0	1.000	OF-1

Murray Franklin

FRANKLIN, MURRAY ASHER (Moe)
B. Apr. 1, 1914, Chicago, Ill. D. Mar. 16, 1978, Harbor City, Calif.
BR TR 6′ 175 lbs.

Year	Team	Games	BA	SA	AB	H	2B	3B	HR	HR%	R	RBI	BB	SO	SB	Pinch Hit AB	Pinch Hit H	PO	A	E	DP	TC/G	FA	G by Pos
1941	DET A	13	.300	.400	10	3	1	0	0	0.0	1	0	2	2	0	7	2	1	2	1	1	0.8	.750	SS-4, 3B-1
1942		48	.260	.344	154	40	7	0	2	1.3	24	16	7	5	0	5	0	82	92	6	17	4.6	.967	SS-32, 2B-7
2 yrs.		61	.262	.348	164	43	8	0	2	1.2	25	16	9	7	0	12	2	83	94	7	18	4.2	.962	SS-36, 2B-7, 3B-1

Herman Franks

FRANKS, HERMAN LOUIS BL TR 5′10½″ 187 lbs.
B. Jan. 4, 1914, Price, Utah.
Manager 1965–68, 1977–79.

Year	Team	Games	BA	SA	AB	H	2B	3B	HR	HR%	R	RBI	BB	SO	SB	Pinch Hit AB	Pinch Hit H	PO	A	E	DP	TC/G	FA	G by Pos
1939	STL N	17	.059	.059	17	1	0	0	0	0.0	1	3	3	3	0	2	0	34	2	1	0	2.8	.973	C-13
1940	BKN N	65	.183	.237	131	24	4	0	1	0.8	11	14	20	6	2	19	3	183	22	2	3	4.8	.990	C-43
1941		59	.201	.273	139	28	7	0	1	0.7	10	11	14	13	0	2	1	191	21	3	6	3.9	.986	C-54, OF-1
1947	PHI A	8	.200	.333	15	3	0	1	0	0.0	2	1	4	4	0	2	0	12	1	0	0	3.3	1.000	C-4
1948		40	.224	.347	98	22	7	1	1	1.0	10	14	16	11	0	9	1	113	17	3	2	4.9	.977	C-27
1949	NY N	1	.667	.667	3	2	0	0	0	0.0	1	0	0	0	0	0	0	4	1	0	0	5.0	1.000	C-1
6 yrs.		190	.199	.275	403	80	18	2	3	0.7	35	43	57	37	2	34	5	537	64	9	11	4.3	.985	C-142, OF-1
WORLD SERIES																								
1941	BKN N	1	.000	.000	1	0	0	0	0	0.0	0	0	0	0	0	0	0	0	1	0	0	1.0	1.000	C-1

Joe Frazier

FRAZIER, JOSEPH FILMORE (Cobra Joe) BL TR 6′ 180 lbs.
B. Oct. 6, 1922, Liberty, N. C.
Manager 1976–77.

Year	Team	Games	BA	SA	AB	H	2B	3B	HR	HR%	R	RBI	BB	SO	SB	Pinch Hit AB	Pinch Hit H	PO	A	E	DP	TC/G	FA	G by Pos
1947	CLE A	9	.071	.143	14	1	1	0	0	0.0	1	0	1	1	0	2	0	6	0	1	0	1.4	.857	OF-5
1954	STL N	81	.295	.500	88	26	5	2	3	3.4	8	18	13	17	0	**62**	**20**	16	1	1	0	1.5	.944	OF-11, 1B-1
1955		58	.200	.386	70	14	1	0	4	5.7	12	9	6	12	0	45	4	16	0	0	0	1.1	1.000	OF-14
1956	3 teams	STL N (14G –.211)	CIN N (10G –.235)	BAL A (45G –.257)																				
″	total	69	.245	.400	110	27	8	0	3	2.7	10	18	15	16	0	40	9	35	2	1	0	1.5	.974	OF-26
4 yrs.		217	.241	.415	282	68	15	2	10	3.5	31	45	35	46	0	149	33	73	3	3	0	1.4	.962	OF-56, 1B-1

Lou Frazier

FRAZIER, ARTHUR LOUIS BB TR 6′ 2″ 175 lbs.
B. Jan. 26, 1965, St. Louis, Mo.

Year	Team	Games	BA	SA	AB	H	2B	3B	HR	HR%	R	RBI	BB	SO	SB	Pinch Hit AB	Pinch Hit H	PO	A	E	DP	TC/G	FA	G by Pos
1993	MON N	112	.286	.349	189	54	7	1	1	0.5	27	16	16	24	17	48	12	98	9	2	1	1.6	.982	OF-60, 1B-8, 2B-1
1994		76	.271	.307	140	38	3	1	0	0.0	25	14	18	23	20	24	5	61	4	1	1	1.5	.985	OF-36, 2B-6, 1B-1
1995	2 teams	MON N (35G –.190)	TEX A (49G –.212)																					
″	total	84	.204	.228	162	33	4	0	0	0.0	25	11	15	32	13	10	0	105	3	3	0	1.5	.973	OF-72, DH-2, 2B-1
3 yrs.		272	.255	.297	491	125	14	2	1	0.2	77	41	49	79	50	82	17	264	16	6	2	1.5	.979	OF-168, 1B-9, 2B-8, DH-2

Johnny Frederick

FREDERICK, JOHN HENRY BL TL 5′11″ 165 lbs.
B. Jan. 26, 1902, Denver, Colo. D. June 18, 1977, Tigard, Ore.

Year	Team	Games	BA	SA	AB	H	2B	3B	HR	HR%	R	RBI	BB	SO	SB	Pinch Hit AB	Pinch Hit H	PO	A	E	DP	TC/G	FA	G by Pos
1929	BKN N	148	.328	.545	628	206	**52**	6	24	3.8	127	75	39	34	6	5	2	410	13	11	1	3.0	.975	OF-143
1930		142	.334	.524	616	206	44	11	17	2.8	120	76	46	34	1	0	0	394	12	4	3	2.9	.990	OF-142
1931		146	.270	.435	611	165	34	8	17	2.8	81	71	31	46	2	1	0	398	10	15	2	2.9	.965	OF-145
1932		118	.299	.508	384	115	28	2	16	4.2	54	56	25	35	1	29	9	201	6	5	2	2.4	.976	OF-88
1933		147	.308	.410	556	171	22	7	7	1.3	65	64	36	14	9	9	2	289	8	9	1	2.2	.971	OF-138
1934		104	.296	.407	307	91	20	1	4	1.3	51	35	33	13	4	18	6	123	13	6	3	1.8	.958	OF-77, 1B-1
6 yrs.		805	.308	.477	3102	954	200	35	85	2.7	498	377	210	176	23	62	19	1815	62	50	12	2.6	.974	OF-733, 1B-1

Ed Freed

FREED, EDWIN CHARLES BR TR 5′ 6″ 165 lbs.
B. Aug. 22, 1919, Centre Valley, Pa.

Year	Team	Games	BA	SA	AB	H	2B	3B	HR	HR%	R	RBI	BB	SO	SB	Pinch Hit AB	Pinch Hit H	PO	A	E	DP	TC/G	FA	G by Pos
1942	PHI N	13	.303	.455	33	10	3	1	0	0.0	3	1	4	3	1	2	0	13	2	0	0	1.4	1.000	OF-11

Roger Freed

FREED, ROGER VERNON BR TR 6′ 190 lbs.
B. June 2, 1946, Los Angeles, Calif. D. Jan. 9, 1996, Chino, Calif.

Year	Team	Games	BA	SA	AB	H	2B	3B	HR	HR%	R	RBI	BB	SO	SB	Pinch Hit AB	Pinch Hit H	PO	A	E	DP	TC/G	FA	G by Pos
1970	BAL A	4	.154	.154	13	2	0	0	0	0.0	0	1	3	4	0	0	0	25	1	0	6	6.5	1.000	1B-3, OF-1
1971	PHI N	118	.221	.313	348	77	12	1	6	1.7	23	37	44	86	0	14	2	185	4	2	1	1.8	.990	OF-106, C-1
1972		73	.225	.395	129	29	4	0	6	4.7	10	18	23	39	0	27	4	64	4	2	2	1.5	.971	OF-46
1974	CIN N	6	.333	.833	6	2	0	0	1	16.7	1	3	1	1	0	6	2	2	0	0	0	2.0	1.000	1B-1
1976	MON N	8	.200	.267	15	3	1	0	0	0.0	0	1	0	3	0	5	1	25	1	0	1	6.5	1.000	1B-3, OF-1
1977	STL N	49	.398	.627	83	33	2	1	5	6.0	10	21	11	9	0	23	9	107	7	1	13	4.8	.991	1B-18, OF-6
1978		52	.239	.370	92	22	6	0	2	2.2	3	20	8	17	1	29	11	113	10	1	13	5.9	.992	1B-15, OF-6
1979		34	.258	.516	31	8	2	0	2	6.5	2	8	5	7	0	27	6	7	1	1	0	9.0	.889	1B-1
8 yrs.		344	.245	.381	717	176	27	2	22	3.1	49	109	95	166	1	131	35	528	28	7	36	2.7	.988	OF-166, 1B-41, C-1

Bill Freehan

FREEHAN, WILLIAM ASHLEY BR TR 6′ 3″ 203 lbs.
B. Nov. 29, 1941, Detroit, Mich.

Year	Team	Games	BA	SA	AB	H	2B	3B	HR	HR%	R	RBI	BB	SO	SB	Pinch Hit AB	Pinch Hit H	PO	A	E	DP	TC/G	FA	G by Pos
1961	DET A	4	.400	.400	10	4	0	0	0	0.0	1	4	1	0	0	0	0	14	4	0	0	6.0	1.000	C-3
1963		100	.243	.387	300	73	12	2	9	3.0	37	36	39	56	2	9	3	554	38	3	19	6.5	.995	C-73, 1B-19
1964		144	.300	.462	520	156	14	8	18	3.5	69	80	36	68	5	6	1	930	61	7	7	7.0	.993	C-141, 1B-1
1965		130	.234	.339	431	101	15	0	10	2.3	45	43	39	63	4	3	1	865	57	4	4	7.2	.996	C-129
1966		136	.234	.352	492	115	22	0	12	2.4	47	46	40	72	5	1	1	942	60	4	14	7.3	.996	C-132, 1B-5
1967		155	.282	.447	517	146	23	1	20	3.9	66	74	73	71	1	2	2	1027	68	8	15	7.0	.993	C-147, 1B-11
1968		155	.263	.454	540	142	24	2	25	4.6	73	84	65	64	0	3	1	1133	83	7	26	7.6	.994	C-138, 1B-21, OF-1
1969		143	.262	.405	489	128	16	3	16	3.3	61	49	53	55	1	8	1	959	56	10	14	7.3	.990	C-120, 1B-20
1970		117	.241	.420	395	95	17	3	16	4.1	44	52	52	48	0	3	1	742	42	2	6	6.9	.997	C-114
1971		148	.277	.465	516	143	26	4	21	4.1	57	71	54	48	2	4	1	912	50	4	6	6.7	.996	C-144, OF-1
1972		111	.262	.401	374	98	18	2	10	2.7	51	56	48	51	0	8	3	654	60	8	9	6.8	.989	C-105, 1B-1
1973		110	.234	.313	380	89	10	1	6	1.6	33	29	40	30	0	3	0	638	53	3	5	6.6	.996	C-98, 1B-7
1974		130	.297	.479	445	132	17	5	18	4.0	58	60	42	44	2	1	0	902	81	9	55	7.7	.991	1B-65, C-63, DH-1
1975		120	.246	.398	427	105	17	3	14	3.3	42	47	32	56	2	2	1	635	66	6	12	6.0	.992	C-113, 1B-5
1976		71	.270	.384	237	64	10	1	5	2.1	22	27	12	27	0	6	0	328	34	6	4	5.6	.984	C-61, DH-3, 1B-2
15 yrs.		1774	.262	.412	6073	1591	241	35	200	3.3	706	758	626	753	24	59	16	11235	813	81	196	7.0	.993	C-1581, 1B-157, DH-4, OF-2
LEAGUE CHAMPIONSHIP SERIES																								
1972	DET A	3	.250	.583	12	3	1	0	1	8.3	2	3	0	1	0	0	0	24	3	0	1	9.0	1.000	C-3
WORLD SERIES																								
1968	DET A	7	.083	.125	24	2	1	0	0	0.0	0	2	4	8	0	0	0	45	6	2	1	7.6	.962	C-7

Buck Freeman

FREEMAN, JOHN FRANK BL TL 5′ 9″ 169 lbs.
B. Oct. 30, 1871, Catasauqua, Pa. D. June 25, 1949, Wilkes-Barre, Pa.

Year	Team	Games	BA	SA	AB	H	2B	3B	HR	HR%	R	RBI	BB	SO	SB	Pinch Hit AB	Pinch Hit H	PO	A	E	DP	TC/G	FA	G by Pos
1891	WAS AA	5	.222	.278	18	4	1	0	0	0.0	1	1	2	2	0	0	0	0	10	3	0	2.6	.769	P-5
1898	WAS N	29	.364	.523	107	39	2	3	3	2.8	19	21	7		2	0	0	39	5	1	2	1.6	.978	OF-29

Buck Freeman *continued*

Year	Team	Games	BA	SA	AB	H	2B	3B	HR	HR%	R	RBI	BB	SO	SB	Pinch Hit AB	Pinch Hit H	PO	A	E	DP	TC/G	FA	G by Pos
1899		155	.318	.563	588	187	19	25	**25**	**4.3**	107	122	23		21	0	0	220	17	15	3	1.6	.940	OF-155, P-2
1900	BOS N	117	.301	.452	418	126	19	13	6	1.4	58	65	25		10	8	1	278	16	12	6	2.8	.961	OF-91, 1B-19
1901	BOS A	129	.345	.527	490	169	23	15	12	2.4	86	114	44		17	0	0	1279	55	36	71	10.5	.974	1B-128, OF-1, 2B-1
1902		138	.309	.502	564	174	38	19	11	2.0	75	**121**	32		17	0	0	222	15	14	3	1.8	.944	OF-138
1903		141	.287	.496	567	163	39	20	**13**	2.3	74	**104**	30		5	0	0	195	13	15	2	1.6	.933	OF-141
1904		157	.280	.412	597	167	20	**19**	7	1.2	64	84	32		7	0	0	216	14	11	4	1.5	.954	OF-157
1905		130	.240	.338	455	109	20	8	3	0.7	59	49	46		8	5	3	649	29	21	20	5.6	.970	1B-72, OF-51, 3B-2
1906		121	.250	.349	392	98	18	9	1	0.3	42	30	28		5	8	3	472	50	9	23	4.7	.983	OF-65, 1B-43, 3B-4
1907		4	.182	.455	11	2	0	0	1	9.1	1	2	3		0	1	0	6	0	0	0	2.0	1.000	OF-3
11 yrs.		1126	.294	.462	4207	1238	199	131	82	1.9	586	713	272	2	92	22	7	3576	224	137	134	3.6	.965	OF-831, 1B-262, P-7, 3B-6, 2B-1
WORLD SERIES																								
1903	BOS A	8	.281	.469	32	9	0	3 4th	0	0.0	6	4	2	2	0	0	0	8	0	0	0	1.0	1.000	OF-8

Jerry Freeman

FREEMAN, FRANK ELLSWORTH (Buck)
B. Dec. 26, 1879, Placerville, Calif. D. Sept. 30, 1952, Los Angeles, Calif.
BL TR 6′ 2″ 220 lbs.

Year	Team	Games	BA	SA	AB	H	2B	3B	HR	HR%	R	RBI	BB	SO	SB	Pinch Hit AB	Pinch Hit H	PO	A	E	DP	TC/G	FA	G by Pos
1908	WAS A	154	.252	.305	531	134	15	5	1	0.2	45	45	36		6	0	0	1548	66	41	69	10.7	.975	1B-154
1909		19	.167	.208	48	8	0	1	0	0.0	2	3	4		3	4	0	146	7	8	11	10.7	.950	1B-14, OF-1
2 yrs.		173	.245	.297	579	142	15	6	1	0.2	47	48	40		9	4	0	1694	73	49	80	10.7	.973	1B-168, OF-1

John Freeman

FREEMAN, JOHN EDWARD (Buck)
B. Jan. 24, 1901, Boston, Mass. D. Apr. 14, 1958, Washington, D. C.
BR TR 5′ 8″ 160 lbs.

Year	Team	Games	BA	SA	AB	H	2B	3B	HR	HR%	R	RBI	BB	SO	SB	Pinch Hit AB	Pinch Hit H	PO	A	E	DP	TC/G	FA	G by Pos
1927	BOS A	4	.000	.000	2	0	0	0	0	0.0	0	0	0	0	0	0	0	0	0	0	0	0.0	.000	OF-3

LaVel Freeman

FREEMAN, LaVEL MAURICE
B. Feb. 18, 1963, Oakland, Calif.
BL TL 5′ 9″ 170 lbs.

Year	Team	Games	BA	SA	AB	H	2B	3B	HR	HR%	R	RBI	BB	SO	SB	Pinch Hit AB	Pinch Hit H	PO	A	E	DP	TC/G	FA	G by Pos
1989	MIL A	2	.000	.000	3	0	0	0	0	0.0	1	0	0	2	0	0	0	0	0	0	0	0.0	.000	DH-2

Gene Freese

FREESE, EUGENE LEWIS (Augie)
Brother of George Freese.
B. Jan. 8, 1934, Wheeling, W. Va.
BR TR 5′11″ 175 lbs.

Year	Team	Games	BA	SA	AB	H	2B	3B	HR	HR%	R	RBI	BB	SO	SB	Pinch Hit AB	Pinch Hit H	PO	A	E	DP	TC/G	FA	G by Pos
1955	PIT N	134	.253	.426	455	115	21	8	14	3.1	69	44	34	57	5	12	3	183	300	22	57	4.1	.956	3B-65, 2B-57
1956		65	.208	.295	207	43	9	0	3	1.4	17	14	16	45	2	10	0	69	115	4	9	2.6	.979	3B-47, 2B-26
1957		114	.283	.399	346	98	18	2	6	1.7	44	31	17	42	9	30	9	94	149	18	20	2.8	.931	3B-74, OF-10, 2B-10
1958	2 teams	PIT N (17G –.167) STL N (62G –.257)																						
″	total	79	.249	.411	209	52	11	1	7	3.3	29	18	11	34	1	29	6	82	87	13	14	4.0	.929	SS-28, 2B-14, 3B-4
1959	PHI N	132	.268	.500	400	107	14	5	23	5.8	60	70	43	61	8	20	7	91	160	23	16	2.4	.916	3B-109, 2B-6
1960	CHI A	127	.273	.481	455	124	32	6	17	3.7	60	79	29	65	10	6	1	88	263	20	29	3.0	.946	3B-122
1961	CIN N	152	.277	.466	575	159	27	2	26	4.5	78	87	27	78	8	1	0	125	254	20	23	2.6	.950	3B-151, 2B-1
1962		18	.143	.167	42	6	1	0	0	0.0	2	1	6	8	0	5	0	11	10	0	1	2.1	1.000	3B-10
1963		66	.244	.378	217	53	9	1	6	2.8	20	26	17	42	4	3	0	44	103	11	8	2.5	.930	3B-62, OF-1
1964	PIT N	99	.225	.377	289	65	13	2	9	3.1	33	40	19	45	1	30	5	48	112	14	12	2.4	.920	3B-72
1965	2 teams	PIT N (43G –.263) CHI A (17G –.281)																						
″	total	60	.268	.348	112	30	4	1	1	0.9	8	12	11	27	0	31	12	16	37	5	2	2.1	.914	3B-27
1966	2 teams	CHI A (48G –.208) HOU N (21G –.091)																						
″	total	69	.180	.259	139	25	2	0	3	2.2	9	10	13	31	3	29	2	20	79	12	5	2.6	.892	3B-38, 2B-3, OF-1
12 yrs.		1115	.254	.418	3446	877	161	28	115	3.3	429	432	243	535	51	206	45	871	1669	162	196	2.9	.940	3B-781, 2B-117, SS-28, OF-12
WORLD SERIES																								
1961	CIN N	5	.063	.125	16	1	1	0	0	0.0	0	0	3	4	0	0	0	6	4	0	1	2.0	1.000	3B-5

George Freese

FREESE, GEORGE WALTER (Bud)
Brother of Gene Freese.
B. Sept. 12, 1926, Wheeling, W. Va.
BR TR 6′ 190 lbs.

Year	Team	Games	BA	SA	AB	H	2B	3B	HR	HR%	R	RBI	BB	SO	SB	Pinch Hit AB	Pinch Hit H	PO	A	E	DP	TC/G	FA	G by Pos
1953	DET A	1	.000	.000	1	0	0	0	0	0.0	0	0	0	0	0	1	0	0	0	0	0	0.0	—	
1955	PIT N	51	.257	.374	179	46	8	2	3	1.7	17	22	17	18	1	1	0	50	82	9	3	2.8	.936	3B-50
1961	CHI N	9	.286	.286	7	2	0	0	0	0.0	0	1	1	4	0	7	2	0	0	0	0	0.0	—	
3 yrs.		61	.257	.369	187	48	8	2	3	1.6	17	23	18	22	1	9	2	50	82	9	3	2.8	.936	3B-50

Jim Fregosi

FREGOSI, JAMES LOUIS
B. Apr. 4, 1942, San Francisco, Calif.
Manager 1978–81, 1986–88, 1991–95.
BR TR 6′ 1″ 190 lbs.

Year	Team	Games	BA	SA	AB	H	2B	3B	HR	HR%	R	RBI	BB	SO	SB	Pinch Hit AB	Pinch Hit H	PO	A	E	DP	TC/G	FA	G by Pos
1961	LA A	11	.222	.222	27	6	0	0	0	0.0	7	3	1	4	0	0	0	12	22	2	3	3.3	.944	SS-11
1962		58	.291	.406	175	51	3	4	3	1.7	15	23	18	27	2	0	0	96	150	15	35	5.0	.943	SS-52
1963		154	.287	.422	592	170	29	12	9	1.5	83	50	36	104	2	1	0	271	446	27	90	4.9	.964	SS-151
1964		147	.277	.463	505	140	22	9	18	3.6	86	72	72	87	8	9	3	225	421	23	89	4.9	.966	SS-137
1965	CAL A	161	.277	.407	602	167	19	7	15	2.5	66	64	54	107	13	2	0	312	481	26	93	5.1	.968	SS-160
1966		162	.252	.391	611	154	32	7	13	2.1	78	67	67	89	17	1	0	299	531	35	125	5.3	.960	SS-162, 1B-1
1967		151	.290	.395	590	171	23	6	9	1.5	75	56	49	77	9	0	0	258	435	25	73	4.8	.965	SS-151
1968		159	.244	.365	614	150	21	**13**	9	1.5	77	49	60	101	9	0	0	273	454	29	92	4.8	.962	SS-159
1969		161	.260	.381	580	151	22	6	12	2.1	78	47	93	86	9	1	0	255	465	21	88	4.6	.972	SS-160
1970		158	.278	.459	601	167	33	5	22	3.7	95	82	69	92	0	2	1	313	475	20	103	5.2	.975	SS-150, 1B-6
1971		107	.233	.326	347	81	15	1	5	1.4	31	33	39	61	2	10	3	241	251	22	44	5.2	.957	SS-74, 1B-18, OF-7
1972	NY N	101	.232	.344	340	79	15	4	5	1.5	31	32	38	71	0	7	1	91	162	15	15	2.9	.944	3B-85, SS-6, 1B-3
1973	2 teams	NY N (45G –.234) TEX A (45G –.268)																						
″	total	90	.253	.374	281	71	10	3	6	2.1	32	27	32	56	1	5	0	145	123	14	23	3.2	.950	3B-51, SS-23, 1B-13, OF-1
1974	TEX A	78	.261	.439	230	60	5	0	12	5.2	31	34	22	41	0	7	2	331	73	5	35	5.2	.988	1B-47, 3B-32
1975		77	.262	.398	191	50	5	0	7	3.7	25	33	20	39	0	20	1	356	35	6	31	5.6	.985	1B-54, DH-13, 3B-4

Jim Fregosi *continued*

Year	Team	Games	BA	SA	AB	H	2B	3B	HR	HR%	R	RBI	BB	SO	SB	Pinch Hit AB	Pinch Hit H	PO	A	E	DP	TC/G	FA	G by Pos
1976		58	.233	.331	133	31	7	0	2	1.5	17	12	23	33	2	15	3	183	18	2	20	4.1	.990	1B-26, DH-18, 3B-5
1977	2 teams	TEX A (13G –.250) PIT N (36G –.286)																						
"	total	49	.274	.464	84	23	2	1	4	4.8	14	21	16	14	2	20	3	130	9	2	11	5.9	.986	1B-20, DH-3, 3B-1
1978	PIT N	20	.200	.250	20	4	1	0	0	0.0	3	1	6	8	0	12	4	14	4	2	1	2.9	.900	3B-5, 1B-2
18 yrs.		1902	.265	.398	6523	1726	264	78	151	2.3	844	706	715	1097	76	112	21	3805	4555	291	971	4.8	.966	SS-1396, 1B-190, 3B-183, DH-34, OF-8

Vern Freiburger

FREIBURGER, VERN DONALD BR TL 6′ 1″ 170 lbs.
B. Dec. 19, 1923, Detroit, Mich.

Year	Team	Games	BA	SA	AB	H	2B	3B	HR	HR%	R	RBI	BB	SO	SB	Pinch Hit AB	Pinch Hit H	PO	A	E	DP	TC/G	FA	G by Pos
1941	CLE A	2	.125	.125	8	1	0	0	0	0.0	0	1	0	2	0	0	0	15	3	1	2	9.5	.947	1B-2

Howard Freigau

FREIGAU, HOWARD EARL (Ty) BR TR 5′10½″ 160 lbs.
B. Aug. 1, 1902, Dayton, Ohio D. July 18, 1932, Chattanooga, Tenn.

Year	Team	Games	BA	SA	AB	H	2B	3B	HR	HR%	R	RBI	BB	SO	SB	Pinch Hit AB	Pinch Hit H	PO	A	E	DP	TC/G	FA	G by Pos
1922	STL N	3	.000	.000	1	0	0	0	0	0.0	0	0	0	0	0	0	0	2	3	0	1	1.7	1.000	SS-2, 3B-1
1923		113	.263	.327	358	94	18	1	1	0.3	30	35	25	36	5	0	0	273	340	46	57	5.8	.930	SS-87, 2B-16, 1B-9, 3B-1, OF-1
1924		98	.269	.362	376	101	17	6	2	0.5	35	39	19	24	10	0	0	128	172	13	24	3.1	.958	3B-98, SS-2
1925	2 teams	STL N (9G –.154) CHI N (117G –.307)																						
"	total	126	.299	.430	502	150	22	10	8	1.6	79	71	32	32	10	0	0	195	270	39	42	3.9	.923	3B-96, SS-24, 1B-7, 2B-1
1926	CHI N	140	.270	.368	508	137	27	7	3	0.6	51	51	43	42	6	4	2	136	244	13	22	2.8	.967	3B-135, SS-2, OF-1
1927		30	.233	.291	86	20	5	0	0	0.0	12	10	9	10	0	0	0	22	46	9	3	2.6	.883	3B-30
1928	2 teams	BKN N (17G –.206) BOS N (52G –.257)																						
"	total	69	.245	.350	143	35	10	1	1	0.7	17	20	10	17	1	26	8	56	69	12	9	3.8	.912	SS-15, 2B-11, 3B-10
7 yrs.		579	.272	.370	1974	537	99	25	15	0.8	224	226	138	161	32	30	10	812	1144	132	158	3.8	.937	3B-371, SS-132, 2B-28, 1B-16, OF-2

Charlie French

FRENCH, CHARLES CALVIN BL TR 5′ 6″ 140 lbs.
B. Oct. 12, 1883, Indianapolis, Ind. D. Mar. 30, 1962, Indianapolis, Ind.

Year	Team	Games	BA	SA	AB	H	2B	3B	HR	HR%	R	RBI	BB	SO	SB	Pinch Hit AB	Pinch Hit H	PO	A	E	DP	TC/G	FA	G by Pos
1909	BOS A	51	.251	.281	167	42	3	1	0	0.0	13	13	15		8	0	0	86	140	24	14	4.9	.904	2B-28, SS-23
1910	2 teams	BOS A (9G –.200) CHI A (45G –.165)																						
"	total	54	.171	.190	210	36	2	1	0	0.0	21	7	11		5	0	0	82	81	15	9	3.4	.916	2B-36, OF-16
2 yrs.		105	.207	.231	377	78	5	2	0	0.0	34	20	26		13	0	0	168	221	39	23	4.2	.909	2B-64, SS-23, OF-16

Jim French

FRENCH, RICHARD JAMES BL TR 5′ 8″ 180 lbs.
B. Aug. 13, 1941, Warren, Ohio.

Year	Team	Games	BA	SA	AB	H	2B	3B	HR	HR%	R	RBI	BB	SO	SB	Pinch Hit AB	Pinch Hit H	PO	A	E	DP	TC/G	FA	G by Pos
1965	WAS A	13	.297	.378	37	11	0	0	1	2.7	4	7	9	5	1	0	0	68	8	2	0	6.0	.974	C-13
1966		10	.208	.250	24	5	1	0	0	0.0	0	3	4	5	0	0	0	45	2	1	0	4.8	.979	C-10
1967		6	.063	.063	16	1	0	0	0	0.0	0	1	3	4	0	0	0	28	2	1	0	5.2	.968	C-6
1968		59	.194	.242	165	32	5	0	1	0.6	9	10	19	19	1	8	1	268	42	5	2	5.9	.984	C-53
1969		63	.184	.297	158	29	6	3	2	1.3	14	13	41	15	1	0	0	316	44	4	8	5.8	.989	C-63
1970		69	.211	.259	166	35	3	1	1	0.6	20	13	38	23	0	7	1	267	23	8	4	4.7	.973	C-62, OF-1
1971		14	.146	.195	41	6	2	0	0	0.0	6	4	7	7	0	0	0	60	7	1	2	4.9	.985	C-14
7 yrs.		234	.196	.262	607	119	17	4	5	0.8	53	51	121	78	3	15	2	1052	128	22	16	5.4	.982	C-221, OF-1

Pat French

FRENCH, FRANK ALEXANDER BR TR 6′ 1″ 180 lbs.
B. Sept. 22, 1893, Dover, N. H. D. July 13, 1969, Bath, Me.

Year	Team	Games	BA	SA	AB	H	2B	3B	HR	HR%	R	RBI	BB	SO	SB	Pinch Hit AB	Pinch Hit H	PO	A	E	DP	TC/G	FA	G by Pos
1917	PHI A	3	.000	.000	2	0	0	0	0	0.0	0	0	0	0	0	0	0	1	0	0	0	1.0	1.000	OF-1

Ray French

FRENCH, RAYMOND EDWARD BR TR 5′ 9½″ 158 lbs.
B. Jan. 9, 1895, Alameda, Calif. D. Apr. 3, 1978, Alameda, Calif.

Year	Team	Games	BA	SA	AB	H	2B	3B	HR	HR%	R	RBI	BB	SO	SB	Pinch Hit AB	Pinch Hit H	PO	A	E	DP	TC/G	FA	G by Pos
1920	NY A	2	.000	.000	2	0	0	0	0	0.0	2	1	0	1	0	0	0	1	0	1	0	2.0	.500	SS-1
1923	BKN N	43	.219	.274	73	16	2	1	0	0.0	14	7	4	7	0	1	0	43	82	18	17	4.8	.874	SS-30
1924	CHI A	37	.179	.214	112	20	4	0	0	0.0	13	11	10	13	3	5	0	38	90	10	9	4.5	.928	SS-28, 2B-3
3 yrs.		82	.193	.235	187	36	6	1	0	0.0	29	19	14	21	3	6	0	82	172	29	26	4.6	.898	SS-59, 2B-3

Walter French

FRENCH, WALTER EDWARD (Fitz) BL TR 5′ 7½″ 155 lbs.
B. July 12, 1899, Moorestown, N. J. D. May 13, 1984, Mountain Home, Ark.

Year	Team	Games	BA	SA	AB	H	2B	3B	HR	HR%	R	RBI	BB	SO	SB	Pinch Hit AB	Pinch Hit H	PO	A	E	DP	TC/G	FA	G by Pos
1923	PHI A	16	.231	.308	39	9	3	0	0	0.0	7	2	5	7	0	3	0	17	1	0	0	1.8	1.000	OF-10
1925		67	.370	.460	100	37	9	0	0	0.0	20	14	1	9	1	37	**13**	31	3	1	0	1.8	.971	OF-19
1926		112	.305	.393	397	121	18	7	1	0.3	51	36	18	24	2	11	4	186	12	6	7	2.1	.971	OF-99
1927		109	.304	.365	326	99	10	5	0	0.0	48	41	16	14	9	7	0	190	6	9	2	2.2	.956	OF-94
1928		49	.257	.311	74	19	4	0	0	0.0	9	7	2	5	1	27	5	33	1	0	0	1.7	1.000	OF-20
1929		45	.267	.400	45	12	1	1	1	2.2	7	9	2	3	0	28	6	8	0	0	0	0.8	1.000	OF-10
6 yrs.		398	.303	.381	981	297	45	13	2	0.2	142	109	44	62	13	113	28	465	23	16	9	2.0	.968	OF-252
WORLD SERIES																								
1929	PHI A	1	.000	.000	1	0	0	0	0	0.0	0	0	0	1	0	1	0	0	0	0	0	0.0	—	

Larry Freund

FREUND, LAWRENCE L. TR 5′10″ 180 lbs.
B. July 5, 1875, Jeffersonville, Indiana D. Nov. 5, 1933, Jeffersonville, Ind.

Year	Team	Games	BA	SA	AB	H	2B	3B	HR	HR%	R	RBI	BB	SO	SB	Pinch Hit AB	Pinch Hit H	PO	A	E	DP	TC/G	FA	G by Pos
1896	LOU N	2	.200	.200	5	1	0	0	0	0.0	1	0	1	1	0	0	0	3	2	0	0	2.5	1.000	C-2

Lonny Frey

FREY, LINUS REINHARD (Junior) BL TR 5′10″ 160 lbs.
B. Aug. 23, 1910, St. Louis, Mo. BB 1933–1938

Year	Team	Games	BA	SA	AB	H	2B	3B	HR	HR%	R	RBI	BB	SO	SB	Pinch Hit AB	Pinch Hit H	PO	A	E	DP	TC/G	FA	G by Pos
1933	BKN N	34	.319	.400	135	43	5	3	0	0.0	25	12	13	13	4	0	0	66	89	18	11	5.1	.896	SS-34
1934		125	.284	.402	490	139	24	5	8	1.6	77	57	52	54	11	2	0	245	400	40	82	5.6	.942	SS-109, 3B-13
1935		131	.262	.437	515	135	35	11	11	2.1	88	77	66	68	6	2	0	274	401	44	75	5.5	.939	SS-127, 2B-4
1936		148	.279	.372	524	146	29	4	4	0.8	63	60	71	56	7	3	0	303	405	62	64	5.2	.919	SS-117, 2B-30, OF-1
1937	CHI N	78	.278	.369	198	55	9	3	1	0.5	33	22	33	15	6	14	2	90	101	10	18	3.5	.950	SS-30, 2B-13, 3B-9, OF-5
1938	CIN N	124	.265	.365	501	133	26	6	4	0.8	76	36	49	50	4	0	0	281	401	27	81	5.7	.962	2B-121, SS-3
1939		125	.291	.452	484	141	27	9	11	2.3	95	55	72	46	5	1	1	324	412	18	83	6.1	.976	2B-123
1940		150	.266	.371	563	150	23	6	8	1.4	102	54	80	48	**22**	0	0	366	512	21	111	6.0	.977	2B-150
1941		146	.254	.359	543	138	29	5	6	1.1	78	59	72	37	16	1	1	340	432	24	93	5.5	.970	2B-145
1942		141	.266	.344	523	139	23	6	2	0.4	66	39	87	38	9	1	0	340	424	18	95	5.6	.977	2B-140

Lonny Frey *continued*

Year	Team	Games	BA	SA	AB	H	2B	3B	HR	HR%	R	RBI	BB	SO	SB	Pinch Hit AB	Pinch Hit H	PO	A	E	DP	TC/G	FA	G by Pos
1943		144	.263	.334	586	154	20	8	2	0.3	78	43	76	56	7	0	0	399	461	13	112	6.1	.985	2B-144
1946		111	.246	.321	333	82	10	3	3	0.9	46	24	63	31	5	17	4	210	176	15	33	4.3	.963	2B-65, OF-28
1947	2 teams	CHI N (24G –.209) NY A (24G –.179)																						
"	total	48	.197	.225	71	14	2	0	0	0.0	14	5	14	7	3	14	4	31	42	3	11	2.4	.961	2B-32
1948	2 teams	NY A (1G –.000) NY N (29G –.255)																						
"	total	30	.255	.333	51	13	1	0	1	2.0	7	6	4	6	0	14	2	24	22	4	4	3.8	.920	2B-13
14 yrs.		1535	.269	.374	5517	1482	263	69	61	1.1	848	549	752	525	105	67	14	3293	4278	317	873	5.4	.960	2B-980, SS-420, OF-34, 3B-22
WORLD SERIES																								
1939	CIN N	4	.000	.000	17	0	0	0	0	0.0	0	0	1	4	0	0	0	8	10	0	0	4.5	1.000	2B-4
1940		3	.000	.000	2	0	0	0	0	0.0	0	0	0	0	0	2	0	0	0	0	0	0.0	—	
1947	NY A	1	.000	.000	1	0	0	0	0	0.0	0	1	0	0	0	1	0	0	0	0	0	0.0	—	
3 yrs.		8	.000	.000	20	0	0	0	0	0.0	0	1	1	4	0	3	0	8	10	0	0	4.5	1.000	2B-4

Pepe Frias

FRIAS, JESUS MARIA
Born Jesus Maria Frias (Andujar).
B. July 14, 1948, San Pedro de Macoris, Dominican Republic.

BR TR 5′10″ 159 lbs.
BB 1976–1978

Year	Team	Games	BA	SA	AB	H	2B	3B	HR	HR%	R	RBI	BB	SO	SB	Pinch Hit AB	Pinch Hit H	PO	A	E	DP	TC/G	FA	G by Pos
1973	MON N	100	.231	.284	225	52	10	1	0	0.0	19	22	10	24	1	2	0	122	215	15	47	3.6	.957	SS-46, 2B-44, 3B-6, OF-1
1974		75	.214	.268	112	24	4	1	0	0.0	12	7	7	10	1	4	1	64	115	5	18	2.5	.973	SS-30, 3B-27, 2B-15, OF-3
1975		51	.125	.156	64	8	2	0	0	0.0	4	4	3	13	0	4	0	55	67	7	16	2.7	.946	SS-29, 3B-11, 2B-7
1976		76	.248	.292	113	28	5	0	0	0.0	7	8	4	14	1	1	0	81	116	11	28	2.8	.947	2B-35, SS-35, 3B-4
1977		53	.257	.271	70	18	1	0	0	0.0	10	5	0	10	1	13	2	27	50	1	9	2.2	.987	2B-20, SS-14, 3B-1
1978		73	.267	.533	15	4	2	1	0	0.0	5	5	0	3	0	2	0	17	28	0	6	0.7	1.000	2B-61, SS-3
1979	ATL N	140	.259	.320	475	123	18	4	1	0.2	41	44	20	36	3	3	1	229	432	32	79	5.1	.954	SS-137
1980	2 teams	TEX A (116G –.242) LA N (14G –.222)																						
"	total	130	.242	.275	236	57	6	1	0	0.0	28	10	4	23	5	5	1	129	191	18	42	2.7	.947	SS-117, 3B-7, 2B-2
1981	LA N	25	.250	.278	36	9	1	0	0	0.0	6	3	1	3	0	1	0	15	21	4	3	1.8	.900	SS-15, 2B-6, 3B-1
9 yrs.		723	.240	.290	1346	323	49	8	1	0.1	132	108	49	136	12	35	5	739	1235	93	248	3.1	.955	SS-426, 2B-190, 3B-57, OF-4

Barney Friberg

FRIBERG, GUSTAF BERNHARD
B. Aug. 18, 1899, Manchester, N. H. D. Dec. 8, 1958, Lynn, Mass.

BR TR 5′11″ 178 lbs.

Year	Team	Games	BA	SA	AB	H	2B	3B	HR	HR%	R	RBI	BB	SO	SB	Pinch Hit AB	Pinch Hit H	PO	A	E	DP	TC/G	FA	G by Pos
1919	CHI N	8	.200	.250	20	4	1	0	0	0.0	0	1	0	2	0	1	0	13	0	0	0	1.9	1.000	OF-7
1920		50	.211	.272	114	24	5	1	0	0.0	11	7	6	20	2	2	0	85	76	6	9	3.5	.964	OF-24, 2B-24
1922		97	.311	.351	296	92	8	2	0	0.0	51	23	37	37	8	12	2	175	21	4	11	2.3	.980	OF-74, 1B-6, 3B-5, 2B-3
1923		146	.318	.473	547	174	27	11	12	2.2	91	88	45	49	13	0	0	168	294	22	33	3.3	.955	3B-146
1924		142	.279	.360	495	138	19	3	5	1.0	67	82	66	53	19	0	0	163	268	21	21	3.2	.954	3B-142
1925	2 teams	CHI N (44G –.257) PHI N (91G –.270)																						
"	total	135	.265	.360	456	121	17	4	6	1.3	53	38	53	57	1	2	0	284	318	25	45	4.5	.960	2B-77, 3B-40, OF-12, 1B-6, SS-2, P-1, C-1
1926	PHI N	144	.268	.331	478	128	21	3	1	0.2	38	51	57	**77**	2	0	0	381	512	22	89	6.4	.976	2B-144
1927		111	.233	.278	335	78	8	2	1	0.3	31	28	41	49	3	4	2	134	238	15	24	3.6	.961	3B-103, 2B-5
1928		52	.202	.266	94	19	3	0	1	1.1	11	7	12	16	0	6	1	62	79	11	20	3.5	.928	SS-31, 3B-5, 2B-3, OF-3, 1B-2
1929		128	.301	.437	455	137	21	10	7	1.5	74	55	49	54	1	5	2	252	214	28	35	4.0	.943	SS-73, OF-40, 2B-8, 1B-2
1930		105	.341	.447	331	113	21	1	4	1.2	62	42	47	35	1	7	3	185	175	21	29	3.8	.945	2B-44, OF-35, SS-12, 3B-8
1931		103	.261	.351	353	92	19	5	1	0.3	33	26	33	25	1	3	0	220	268	21	48	5.2	.959	2B-64, 3B-25, 1B-5, SS-3
1932		61	.240	.318	154	37	8	2	0	0.0	17	14	19	23	0	2	0	107	137	11	22	4.6	.957	2B-56
1933	BOS A	17	.317	.390	41	13	3	0	0	0.0	5	9	6	1	0	3	1	17	32	3	6	4.0	.942	2B-6, 3B-5, SS-2
14 yrs.		1299	.281	.373	4169	1170	181	44	38	0.9	544	471	471	498	51	47	11	2246	2632	210	392	4.1	.959	3B-479, 2B-434, OF-195, SS-123, 1B-21, P-1, C-1

Jim Fridley

FRIDLEY, JAMES RILEY (Big Jim)
B. Sept. 6, 1924, Philippi, W. Va.

BR TR 6′ 2″ 205 lbs.

Year	Team	Games	BA	SA	AB	H	2B	3B	HR	HR%	R	RBI	BB	SO	SB	Pinch Hit AB	Pinch Hit H	PO	A	E	DP	TC/G	FA	G by Pos
1952	CLE A	62	.251	.331	175	44	2	0	4	2.3	23	16	14	40	3	6	1	87	3	2	0	1.7	.978	OF-54
1954	BAL A	85	.246	.371	240	59	8	5	4	1.7	25	36	21	41	0	18	6	132	1	2	0	2.0	.985	OF-67
1958	CIN N	5	.222	.444	9	2	2	0	0	0.0	2	1	0	2	0	4	1	1	0	0	0	0.5	1.000	OF-2
3 yrs.		152	.248	.356	424	105	12	5	8	1.9	50	53	35	83	3	28	8	220	4	4	0	1.9	.982	OF-123

Bill Friel

FRIEL, WILLIAM EDWARD
Brother of Pat Friel.
B. Apr. 1, 1876, Renovo, Pa. D. Dec. 24, 1959, St. Louis, Mo.

BL TR 5′10″ 165 lbs.

Year	Team	Games	BA	SA	AB	H	2B	3B	HR	HR%	R	RBI	BB	SO	SB	Pinch Hit AB	Pinch Hit H	PO	A	E	DP	TC/G	FA	G by Pos
1901	MIL A	106	.266	.370	376	100	13	7	4	1.1	51	35	23		15	3	2	142	183	46	16	3.6	.876	3B-61, OF-28, 2B-9, SS-6
1902	STL A	80	.240	.311	267	64	9	2	2	0.7	26	20	14		4	5	2	194	94	15	17	3.7	.950	OF-33, 2B-25, 1B-10, 3B-8, SS-3, P-1, C-1
1903		97	.228	.305	351	80	11	8	0	0.0	46	25	23		4	2	1	142	237	39	16	4.4	.907	2B-63, 3B-24, OF-9
3 yrs.		283	.245	.331	994	244	33	17	6	0.6	123	80	60		23	10	5	478	514	100	49	3.9	.908	2B-97, 3B-93, OF-70, 1B-10, SS-9, P-1, C-1

Pat Friel

FRIEL, PATRICK HENRY
Brother of Bill Friel.
B. June 11, 1860, Lewisburg, W. Va. D. Jan. 15, 1924, Providence, R. I.

BB 5′11″ 170 lbs.

Year	Team	Games	BA	SA	AB	H	2B	3B	HR	HR%	R	RBI	BB	SO	SB	Pinch Hit AB	Pinch Hit H	PO	A	E	DP	TC/G	FA	G by Pos
1890	SYR AA	62	.249	.330	261	65	8	2	3	1.1	51		17		34	0	0	77	7	8	2	1.5	.913	OF-62
1891	PHI AA	2	.250	.375	8	2	1	0	0	0.0	2	0	0	0	0	0	0	1	0	0	0	0.5	1.000	OF-2
2 yrs.		64	.249	.331	269	67	9	2	3	1.1	53	0	17	0	34	0	0	78	7	8	2	1.5	.914	OF-64

Owen Friend

FRIEND, OWEN LACEY (Red)
B. Mar. 21, 1927, Granite City, Ill.

BR TR 6′ 1″ 180 lbs.

Year	Team	Games	BA	SA	AB	H	2B	3B	HR	HR%	R	RBI	BB	SO	SB	Pinch Hit AB	Pinch Hit H	PO	A	E	DP	TC/G	FA	G by Pos
1949	STL A	2	.375	.375	8	3	0	0	0	0.0	1	1	0	0	0	0	0	4	8	0	1	6.0	1.000	2B-2
1950		119	.237	.352	372	88	15	2	8	2.2	48	50	40	68	2	1	1	271	340	30	68	5.3	.953	2B-93, 3B-24, SS-3
1953	2 teams	DET A (31G –.177) CLE A (34G –.235)																						
"	total	65	.201	.329	164	33	6	0	5	3.0	17	23	11	25	0	2	1	112	126	8	38	4.6	.967	2B-45, SS-8, 3B-1
1955	2 teams	BOS A (14G –.262) CHI N (6G –.100)																						
"	total	20	.231	.288	52	12	3	0	0	0.0	3	2	4	14	0	3	0	23	40	3	5	3.7	.955	SS-15, 3B-2, 2B-1
1956	CHI N	2	.000	.000	2	0	0	0	0	0.0	0	0	0	2	0	2	0	0	0	0	0	0.0	—	
5 yrs.		208	.227	.339	598	136	24	2	13	2.2	69	76	55	109	2	8	2	410	514	41	112	5.0	.958	2B-141, 3B-27, SS-26

Buck Frierson

FRIERSON, ROBERT LAWRENCE BR TR 6′ 3″ 195 lbs.
B. July 29, 1917, Chicota, Tex.

Year	Team	Games	BA	SA	AB	H	2B	3B	HR	HR%	R	RBI	BB	SO	SB	Pinch Hit AB	Pinch Hit H	PO	A	E	DP	TC/G	FA	G by Pos
1941	CLE A	5	.273	.364	11	3	1	0	0	0.0	2	2	1	1	0	2	1	2	0	0	0	0.7	1.000	OF-3

Fred Frink

FRINK, FRED FERDINAND BR TR 6′ 1″ 180 lbs.
B. Aug. 25, 1911, Macon, Ga.

Year	Team	Games	BA	SA	AB	H	2B	3B	HR	HR%	R	RBI	BB	SO	SB	Pinch Hit AB	Pinch Hit H	PO	A	E	DP	TC/G	FA	G by Pos
1934	PHI N	2	—	—	0	0	0	0	0	—	0	0	0	0	0	0	0	0	0	0	0	0.0	.000	OF-1

Charlie Frisbee

FRISBEE, CHARLES AUGUSTUS (Bunt) BB TR 5′ 9″ 175 lbs.
B. Feb. 2, 1874, Dows, Iowa D. Nov. 7, 1954, Alden, Iowa.

Year	Team	Games	BA	SA	AB	H	2B	3B	HR	HR%	R	RBI	BB	SO	SB	Pinch Hit AB	Pinch Hit H	PO	A	E	DP	TC/G	FA	G by Pos
1899	BOS N	42	.329	.382	152	50	4	2	0	0.0	22	20	9		10	1	0	68	9	11	1	2.2	.875	OF-40
1900	NY N	4	.154	.231	13	2	1	0	0	0.0	2	3	2		0	0	0	2	0	3	0	1.3	.400	OF-4
2 yrs.		46	.315	.370	165	52	5	2	0	0.0	24	23	11		10	1	0	70	9	14	1	2.1	.849	OF-44

Frankie Frisch

FRISCH, FRANK FRANCIS (The Fordham Flash) BB TR 5′11″ 165 lbs.
B. Sept. 9, 1898, Bronx, N. Y. D. Mar. 12, 1973, Wilmington, Del.
Manager 1933–38, 1940–46, 1949–51.
Hall of Fame 1947.

Year	Team	Games	BA	SA	AB	H	2B	3B	HR	HR%	R	RBI	BB	SO	SB	Pinch Hit AB	Pinch Hit H	PO	A	E	DP	TC/G	FA	G by Pos
1919	NY N	54	.226	.295	190	43	3	2	2	1.1	21	24	4	14	15	3	0	102	134	7	7	4.2	.971	2B-29, 3B-28, SS-1
1920		110	.280	.375	440	123	10	10	4	0.9	57	77	20	18	34	1	0	106	256	12	23	3.3	.968	3B-110, SS-2
1921		153	.341	.485	618	211	31	17	8	1.3	121	100	42	28	**49**	0	0	226	418	33	52	4.4	.951	3B-93, 2B-61
1922		132	.327	.438	514	168	16	13	5	1.0	101	51	47	13	31	0	0	228	406	22	53	4.7	.966	2B-85, 3B-53, SS-1
1923		151	.348	.485	641	**223**	32	10	12	1.9	116	111	46	12	29	0	0	327	493	22	83	5.5	.974	2B-135, 3B-17
1924		145	.328	.468	603	198	33	15	7	1.2	**121**	69	56	24	22	0	0	408	557	27	104	6.4	.973	2B-143, SS-10, 3B-2
1925		120	.331	.472	502	166	26	6	11	2.2	89	48	32	14	21	0	0	215	393	37	45	5.1	.943	3B-46, 2B-42, SS-39
1926		135	.314	.409	545	171	29	4	5	0.9	75	44	33	16	23	1	1	270	486	21	71	5.8	.973	2B-127, 3B-7
1927	STL N	153	.337	.472	617	208	31	11	10	1.6	112	78	43	10	**48**	0	0	396	643	22	104	6.9	.979	2B-153, SS-1
1928		141	.300	.441	547	164	29	9	10	1.8	107	86	64	17	29	2	1	383	474	21	80	6.3	.976	2B-139
1929		138	.334	.484	527	176	40	12	5	0.9	93	74	53	12	24	3	2	305	407	22	67	5.4	.970	2B-121, 3B-13, SS-1
1930		133	.346	.520	540	187	46	9	10	1.9	121	114	55	16	15	0	0	315	493	27	96	6.3	.968	2B-123, 3B-10
1931		131	.311	.396	518	161	24	4	4	0.8	96	82	45	13	**28**	2	0	290	424	19	93	5.7	.974	2B-129
1932		115	.292	.372	486	142	26	2	3	0.6	59	60	25	13	18	0	0	257	319	16	60	5.1	.973	2B-75, 3B-37, SS-4
1933		147	.303	.398	585	177	32	6	4	0.7	74	66	48	16	18	4	2	395	413	18	80	5.6	.978	2B-132, SS-15
1934		140	.305	.398	550	168	30	6	3	0.5	74	75	45	10	11	2	0	325	388	20	80	5.2	.973	2B-115, 3B-25
1935		103	.294	.359	354	104	16	2	1	0.3	52	55	33	16	2	9	1	199	258	10	48	5.0	.979	2B-88, 3B-5
1936		93	.274	.317	303	83	10	0	1	0.3	40	26	36	10	2	8	3	159	194	15	32	4.4	.959	2B-61, 3B-22, SS-1
1937		17	.219	.281	32	7	2	0	0	0.0	3	4	1	0	0	12	2	12	14	0	0	1.5	1.000	2B-17
19 yrs.		2311	.316	.432	9112	2880	466	138	105	1.2	1532	1244	728	272	419	47	12	4918	7170	371	1178	5.4	.970	2B-1775, 3B-468, SS-75
WORLD SERIES																								
1921	NY N	8	.300	.367	30	9	0	1	0	0.0	5	1	4	3	3	0	0	12	25	2	3	4.9	.949	3B-8
1922		5	.471	.529	17	8	1	0	0	0.0	3	2	1	0	1	0	0	10	20	1	3	6.2	.968	2B-5
1923		6	.400	.480	25	10	0	1	0	0.0	2	1	0	0	0	0	0	17	18	1	7	6.0	.972	2B-6
1924		7	.333	.533	30	10	4	1	0	0.0	1	0	4	1	1	0	0	17	26	0	3	5.4	1.000	2B-7, 3B-1
1928	STL N	4	.231	.231	13	3	0	0	0	0.0	1	1	2	2	2	0	0	8	13	0	2	5.3	1.000	2B-4
1930		6	.208	.292	24	5	2	0	0	0.0	0	0	0	0	1	0	0	13	14	3	2	5.0	.900	2B-6
1931		7	.259	.333	27	7	2	0	0	0.0	2	1	1	2	1	0	0	23	19	0	5	6.0	1.000	2B-7
1934		7	.194	.226	31	6	1	0	0	0.0	2	4	0	1	0	0	0	16	26	2	1	6.3	.955	2B-7
8 yrs.		50	.294	.376	197	58	10	3	0	0.0	16	10	12	9	9	0	0	116	161	9	26	5.6	.969	2B-42, 3B-9
		8th			**4th**	**3rd**	**1st**	**4th**							**6th**									

Emil Frisk

FRISK, JOHN EMIL BL TR 6′ 1″ 190 lbs.
B. Oct. 15, 1874, Kalkaska, Mich. D. Jan. 27, 1922, Seattle, Wash.

Year	Team	Games	BA	SA	AB	H	2B	3B	HR	HR%	R	RBI	BB	SO	SB	Pinch Hit AB	Pinch Hit H	PO	A	E	DP	TC/G	FA	G by Pos
1899	CIN N	9	.280	.320	25	7	1	0	0	0.0	5	2	2		0	0	0	4	15	1	0	2.2	.950	P-9
1901	DET A	20	.313	.438	48	15	3	0	1	2.1	10	7	3		0	6	2	7	36	8	0	3.9	.843	P-11, OF-2
1905	STL A	127	.261	.336	429	112	11	6	3	0.7	58	36	42		7	7	1	117	15	11	2	1.2	.923	OF-116
1907		4	.250	.250	4	1	0	0	0	0.0	0	0	1		0	4	1	0	0	0	0	0.0	—	
4 yrs.		160	.267	.344	506	135	15	6	4	0.8	73	45	48		7	17	4	128	66	20	2	1.6	.907	OF-118, P-20

Harry Fritz

FRITZ, HARRY KOCH (Dutchman) BR TR 5′ 8″ 170 lbs.
B. Sept. 30, 1890, Philadelphia, Pa. D. Nov. 4, 1974, Columbus, Ohio.

Year	Team	Games	BA	SA	AB	H	2B	3B	HR	HR%	R	RBI	BB	SO	SB	Pinch Hit AB	Pinch Hit H	PO	A	E	DP	TC/G	FA	G by Pos
1913	PHI A	5	.000	.000	13	0	0	0	0	0.0	1	0	2	4	0	0	0	6	5	2	0	2.6	.846	3B-5
1914	CHI F	65	.213	.253	174	37	5	1	0	0.0	16	13	18		2	5	1	48	76	10	11	2.4	.925	3B-46, SS-9, 2B-1
1915		79	.250	.356	236	59	8	4	3	1.3	27	26	13		4	3	2	85	109	7	8	2.6	.965	3B-70, 2B-6, SS-1
3 yrs.		149	.227	.303	423	96	13	5	3	0.7	44	39	33	4	6	8	3	139	190	19	19	2.5	.945	3B-121, SS-10, 2B-7

Larry Fritz

FRITZ, LAWRENCE JOSEPH BL TL 6′ 2″ 225 lbs.
B. Feb. 14, 1949, East Chicago, Ind.

Year	Team	Games	BA	SA	AB	H	2B	3B	HR	HR%	R	RBI	BB	SO	SB	Pinch Hit AB	Pinch Hit H	PO	A	E	DP	TC/G	FA	G by Pos
1975	PHI N	1	.000	.000	1	0	0	0	0	0.0	0	0	0	0	0	1	0	0	0	0	0	0.0	—	

Doug Frobel

FROBEL, DOUGLAS STEVEN BL TR 6′ 4″ 196 lbs.
B. June 6, 1959, Ottawa, Ont., Canada.

Year	Team	Games	BA	SA	AB	H	2B	3B	HR	HR%	R	RBI	BB	SO	SB	Pinch Hit AB	Pinch Hit H	PO	A	E	DP	TC/G	FA	G by Pos
1982	PIT N	16	.206	.441	34	7	2	0	2	5.9	5	3	1	11	1	4	1	18	0	0	0	1.5	1.000	OF-12
1983		32	.283	.533	60	17	4	1	3	5.0	10	11	4	17	1	5	1	27	0	1	0	1.2	.964	OF-24
1984		126	.203	.388	276	56	9	3	12	4.3	33	28	24	84	7	17	3	188	9	9	3	1.8	.956	OF-112
1985	2 teams	PIT N (53G –.202) MON N (12G –.130)																						
"	total	65	.189	.258	132	25	6	0	1	0.8	17	11	21	30	4	20	6	58	2	4	1	1.5	.938	OF-42
1987	CLE A	29	.100	.250	40	4	0	0	2	5.0	5	5	5	13	0	15	2	6	0	0	0	0.4	1.000	OF-12, DH-5
5 yrs.		268	.201	.365	542	109	21	4	20	3.7	70	58	55	155	13	61	13	297	11	14	4	1.6	.957	OF-202, DH-5

Ben Froelich

FROELICH, WILLIAM PALMER BR TR
B. Nov. 12, 1887, Pittsburgh, Pa. D. Sept. 1, 1916, Pittsburgh, Pa.

Year	Team	Games	BA	SA	AB	H	2B	3B	HR	HR%	R	RBI	BB	SO	SB	Pinch Hit AB	Pinch Hit H	PO	A	E	DP	TC/G	FA	G by Pos
1909	PHI N	1	.000	.000	1	0	0	0	0	0.0	0	0	0		0	0	0	0	0	0	0	0.0	.000	C-1

Year	Team	Games	BA	SA	AB	H	2B	3B	HR	HR%	R	RBI	BB	SO	SB	Pinch Hit AB	Pinch Hit H	PO	A	E	DP	TC/G	FA	G by Pos
Jerry Fry					FRY, JERRY RAY — B. Feb. 29, 1956, Salinas, Calif.																			BR TR 6′ 185 lbs.
1978	MON N	4	.000	.000	9	0	0	0	0	0.0	0	0	1	5	0	0	0	16	1	0	0	4.3	1.000	C-4
Jeff Frye					FRYE, JEFFREY DUSTIN — B. Aug. 31, 1966, Oakland, Calif.																			BR TR 5′ 9″ 180 lbs.
1992	TEX A	67	.256	.327	199	51	9	1	1	0.5	24	12	16	27	1	0	0	120	196	7	43	4.8	.978	2B-67
1994		57	.327	.454	205	67	20	3	0	0.0	37	18	29	23	6	2	1	89	135	4	28	4.1	.982	2B-54, DH-1, 3B-1
1995		90	.278	.377	313	87	15	2	4	1.3	38	29	24	45	3	6	0	172	246	11	51	5.2	.974	2B-83
3 yrs.		214	.286	.385	717	205	44	6	5	0.7	99	59	69	95	10	8	1	381	577	22	122	4.8	.978	2B-204, DH-1, 3B-1
Travis Fryman					FRYMAN, DAVID TRAVIS — B. Mar. 25, 1969, Lexington, Ky.																			BR TR 6′ 1″ 180 lbs.
1990	DET A	66	.297	.470	232	69	11	1	9	3.9	32	27	17	51	3	1	0	47	145	14	21	3.1	.932	3B-48, SS-17, DH-1
1991		149	.259	.447	557	144	36	3	21	3.8	65	91	40	149	12	1	1	153	354	23	61	3.4	.957	3B-86, SS-71
1992		161	.266	.416	**659**	175	31	4	20	3.0	87	96	45	144	8	0	0	220	489	22	95	4.5	.970	SS-137, 3B-26
1993		151	.300	.486	607	182	37	5	22	3.6	98	97	77	128	9	0	0	169	382	23	70	3.8	.960	SS-81, 3B-69, DH-1
1994		114	.263	.474	**464**	122	34	5	18	3.9	66	85	45	**128**	2	0	0	78	222	14	12	2.8	.955	3B-114
1995		144	.275	.409	567	156	21	5	15	2.6	79	81	63	100	4	0	0	106	335	14	38	3.2	.969	3B-144
6 yrs.		785	.275	.447	3086	848	170	23	105	3.4	427	477	287	700	38	2	1	773	1927	110	297	3.5	.961	3B-487, SS-306, DH-2
Mike Fuentes					FUENTES, MICHAEL JAY — B. July 11, 1958, Miami, Fla.																			BR TR 6′ 3″ 190 lbs.
1983	MON N	6	.250	.250	4	1	0	0	0	0.0	1	0	0	2	0	4	1	0	0	0	0	0.0	—	
1984		3	.250	.250	4	1	0	0	0	0.0	0	0	1	2	0	2	1	4	0	0	0	4.0	1.000	OF-1
2 yrs.		9	.250	.250	8	2	0	0	0	0.0	1	0	1	4	0	6	2	4	0	0	0	4.0	1.000	OF-1
Tito Fuentes					FUENTES, RIGOBERTO — Born Rigoberto Fuentes (Peat). B. Jan. 4, 1944, Havana, Cuba.																			BB TR 5′11″ 175 lbs. BR 1965–1967
1965	SF N	26	.208	.222	72	15	1	0	0	0.0	12	1	5	14	0	0	0	27	49	5	8	3.1	.938	SS-18, 2B-7, 3B-1
1966		133	.261	.360	541	141	21	3	9	1.7	63	40	9	57	6	1	0	283	403	30	68	5.3	.958	SS-76, 2B-60
1967		133	.209	.294	344	72	12	1	5	1.5	27	29	27	61	4	0	0	276	315	12	79	4.5	.980	2B-130, SS-5
1969		67	.295	.366	183	54	4	3	1	0.5	28	14	15	25	2	1	0	50	117	13	18	2.7	.928	3B-36, SS-30
1970		123	.267	.343	435	116	13	7	2	0.5	49	32	36	52	4	7	0	202	324	19	57	3.9	.965	2B-78, SS-36, 3B-24
1971		152	.273	.356	630	172	28	6	4	0.6	63	52	18	46	12	1	0	373	465	23	109	5.7	.973	2B-152
1972		152	.264	.379	572	151	33	6	7	1.2	64	53	39	56	16	1	0	361	417	29	89	5.3	.964	2B-152
1973		160	.277	.358	656	182	25	5	6	0.9	78	63	45	62	12	0	0	386	479	6	102	5.4	.993	2B-160, 3B-1
1974		108	.249	.297	390	97	15	2	0	0.0	33	22	22	32	7	7	2	238	287	11	70	5.2	.979	2B-103
1975	SD N	146	.280	.349	565	158	21	3	4	0.7	57	43	25	51	8	2	0	389	448	26	105	6.1	.970	2B-142
1976		135	.263	.310	520	137	18	0	2	0.4	48	36	18	38	5	8	2	339	387	22	91	5.9	.971	2B-127
1977	DET A	151	.309	.397	615	190	19	10	5	0.8	83	51	38	61	4	1	0	379	459	26	115	5.7	.970	2B-151, DH-1
1978	OAK A	13	.140	.163	43	6	1	0	0	0.0	5	2	1	6	0	2	0	17	17	2	4	2.8	.944	2B-13
13 yrs.		1499	.268	.347	5566	1491	211	46	45	0.8	610	438	298	561	80	31	4	3320	4167	224	915	5.1	.971	2B-1275, SS-165, 3B-62, DH-1
LEAGUE CHAMPIONSHIP SERIES																								
1971	SF N	4	.313	.563	16	5	1	0	1	6.3	4	2	1	3	0	0	0	9	5	1	1	3.8	.933	2B-4
Ollie Fuhrman					FUHRMAN, ALFRED GEORGE — B. July 20, 1896, Jordan, Minn. D. Jan. 11, 1969, Peoria, Ill.																			BB TR 5′11″ 185 lbs.
1922	PHI A	6	.333	.500	6	2	1	0	0	0.0	1	0	0	0	0	2	0	5	0	0	0	1.3	1.000	C-4
Dot Fulghum					FULGHUM, JAMES LAVOISIER — B. July 4, 1900, Valdosta, Ga. D. Nov. 11, 1967, Miami, Fla.																			BR TR 5′ 8½″ 165 lbs.
1921	PHI A	2	.000	.000	2	0	0	0	0	0.0	0	0	1	1	0	0	0	0	0	0	0	0.0	.000	SS-1
Frank Fuller					FULLER, FRANK EDWARD (Rabbit) — B. Jan. 1, 1893, Detroit, Mich. D. Oct. 29, 1965, Warren, Mich.																			BB TR 5′ 7″ 150 lbs.
1915	DET A	14	.156	.156	32	5	0	0	0	0.0	6	2	9	7	2	2	1	8	20	2	1	3.0	.933	2B-9, SS-1
1916		20	.100	.100	10	1	0	0	0	0.0	2	1	1	4	3	1	0	4	7	2	2	1.4	.846	2B-8, SS-1
1923	BOS A	6	.238	.238	21	5	0	0	0	0.0	3	0	1	1	1	0	0	20	20	2	1	7.0	.952	2B-6
3 yrs.		40	.175	.175	63	11	0	0	0	0.0	11	3	11	12	6	3	1	32	47	6	4	3.4	.929	2B-23, SS-2
Harry Fuller					FULLER, HENRY W. — Brother of Shorty Fuller. B. Dec. 5, 1862, Cincinnati, Ohio D. Dec. 12, 1895, Cincinnati, Ohio.																			
1891	STL AA	1	.000	.000	2	0	0	0	0	0.0	0	0	0	1	0	0	0	0	0	2	0	2.0	.000	3B-1
Jim Fuller					FULLER, JAMES HARDY — B. Nov. 28, 1950, Bethesda, Md.																			BR TR 6′ 3″ 215 lbs.
1973	BAL A	9	.115	.346	26	3	0	0	2	7.7	2	4	1	17	0	3	1	20	2	0	1	2.8	1.000	OF-5, 1B-2, DH-1
1974		64	.222	.392	189	42	11	0	7	3.7	17	28	8	68	1	5	1	131	4	6	2	2.2	.957	OF-59, 1B-4, DH-2
1977	HOU N	34	.160	.280	100	16	6	0	2	2.0	5	9	10	45	0	5	0	56	5	1	1	2.2	.984	OF-27, 1B-1
3 yrs.		107	.194	.352	315	61	17	0	11	3.5	24	41	19	130	1	13	2	207	11	7	4	2.2	.969	OF-91, 1B-7, DH-3
John Fuller					FULLER, JOHN EDWARD — B. Jan. 29, 1950, Lynwood, Calif.																			BL TL 6′ 2″ 180 lbs.
1974	ATL N	3	.333	.333	3	1	0	0	0	0.0	1	0	0	0	0	2	0	1	0	0	0	1.0	1.000	OF-1
Nig Fuller					FULLER, CHARLES F. — B. Mar. 30, 1879, Toledo, Ohio D. Nov. 12, 1947, Toledo, Ohio.																			BR TR 5′11″ 165 lbs.
1902	BKN N	3	.000	.000	9	0	0	0	0	0.0	0	1	0		0	0	0	11	1	0	0	4.0	1.000	C-3

Shorty Fuller

FULLER, WILLIAM BENJAMIN — BR TR 5′ 6″ 157 lbs.
Brother of Harry Fuller.
B. Oct. 10, 1867, Cincinnati, Ohio D. Apr. 11, 1904, Cincinnati, Ohio.

Year	Team	Games	BA	SA	AB	H	2B	3B	HR	HR%	R	RBI	BB	SO	SB	Pinch Hit AB	Pinch Hit H	PO	A	E	DP	TC/G	FA	G by Pos
1888	WAS N	49	.182	.235	170	31	5	2	0	0.0	11	12	10	14	6	0	0	69	143	38	14	5.1	.848	SS-47, 2B-2
1889	STL AA	140	.226	.284	517	117	18	6	0	0.0	91	51	52	56	38	0	0	240	459	67	46	5.5	.913	SS-140
1890		130	.278	.335	526	146	9	9	1	0.2	118		73		60	0	0	222	389	91	39	5.4	.870	SS-130
1891		135	.212	.271	576	122	14	7	2	0.3	105	61	67	28	42	0	0	246	417	95	57	5.4	.875	SS-102, 2B-38
1892	NY N	141	.226	.270	508	115	11	4	1	0.2	74	48	52	22	37	0	0	294	434	92	44	5.8	.888	SS-141
1893		130	.236	.300	474	112	14	8	0	0.0	78	51	60	21	26	0	0	260	464	71	48	6.1	.911	SS-130
1894		93	.283	.359	368	104	14	4	2	0.5	81	46	52	16	32	0	0	213	300	69	40	6.2	.881	SS-89, OF-2, 3B-2, 2B-1
1895		126	.225	.262	458	103	11	3	0	0.0	82	32	64	34	15	0	0	270	499	73	59	6.7	.913	SS-126
1896		18	.167	.167	72	12	0	0	0	0.0	10	7	14	5	4	0	0	42	62	15	8	6.6	.874	SS-18
9 yrs.		962	.235	.289	3669	862	96	43	6	0.2	650	308	444	196	260	0	0	1856	3167	611	355	5.8	.892	SS-923, 2B-41, OF-2, 3B-2

Vern Fuller

FULLER, VERNON GORDON — BR TR 6′ 1″ 170 lbs.
B. Mar. 1, 1944, Menomonie, Wis.

Year	Team	Games	BA	SA	AB	H	2B	3B	HR	HR%	R	RBI	BB	SO	SB	Pinch Hit AB	Pinch Hit H	PO	A	E	DP	TC/G	FA	G by Pos
1964	CLE A	2	.000	.000	1	0	0	0	0	0.0	0	0	0	0	0	1	0	0	0	0	0	0.0	—	
1966		16	.234	.447	47	11	2	1	2	4.3	7	2	7	6	0	0	0	29	27	0	12	3.5	1.000	2B-16
1967		73	.223	.374	206	46	10	0	7	3.4	18	21	19	55	2	6	1	133	144	4	39	4.3	.986	2B-64, SS-2
1968		97	.242	.291	244	59	8	2	0	0.0	14	18	24	49	2	4	0	133	150	7	25	2.9	.976	2B-73, 3B-23, SS-4
1969		108	.236	.335	254	60	11	1	4	1.6	25	22	20	53	2	5	2	222	196	9	55	3.9	.979	2B-102, 3B-7
1970		29	.182	.333	33	6	2	0	1	3.0	3	2	3	9	0	8	1	18	23	3	4	2.1	.932	2B-16, 3B-4, 1B-1
6 yrs.		325	.232	.338	785	182	33	4	14	1.8	67	65	73	172	6	24	4	535	540	23	135	3.5	.979	2B-271, 3B-34, SS-6, 1B-1

Chick Fullis

FULLIS, CHARLES PHILIP — BR TR 5′ 9″ 170 lbs.
B. Feb. 27, 1904, Girardville, Pa. D. Mar. 28, 1946, Ashland, Pa.

Year	Team	Games	BA	SA	AB	H	2B	3B	HR	HR%	R	RBI	BB	SO	SB	Pinch Hit AB	Pinch Hit H	PO	A	E	DP	TC/G	FA	G by Pos
1928	NY N	11	.000	.000	1	0	0	0	0	0.0	5	0	1	1	0	1	0	0	0	0	0	0.0	—	
1929		86	.288	.412	274	79	11	1	7	2.6	67	29	30	26	7	2	0	151	3	6	0	2.1	.963	OF-78
1930		13	.000	.000	6	0	0	0	0	0.0	2	0	0	1	1	5	0	0	0	0	0	0.0	.000	OF-2
1931		89	.328	.421	302	99	15	2	3	1.0	61	28	23	13	13	6	3	166	29	4	6	2.6	.980	OF-68, 2B-9
1932		96	.298	.396	235	70	14	3	1	0.4	35	21	11	12	1	32	7	97	2	1	0	1.8	.990	OF-55, 2B-1
1933	PHI N	151	.309	.380	**647**	200	31	6	1	0.2	91	45	36	34	18	0	0	410	15	10	3	2.9	.977	OF-151, 3B-1
1934	2 teams	PHI N (28G –.225) STL N (69G –.261)																						
″	total	97	.249	.306	301	75	15	1	0	0.0	29	38	24	15	6	15	6	166	3	6	1	2.1	.966	OF-83
1936	STL N	47	.281	.371	89	25	6	1	0	0.0	15	6	7	11	0	12	2	53	2	0	2	2.1	1.000	OF-26
8 yrs.		590	.295	.380	1855	548	92	14	12	0.6	305	167	132	113	46	73	18	1043	54	27	12	2.4	.976	OF-463, 2B-10, 3B-1
WORLD SERIES																								
1934	STL N	3	.400	.400	5	2	0	0	0	0.0	0	0	0	0	0	0	0	6	0	1	0	2.3	.857	OF-3

Chick Fulmer

FULMER, CHARLES JOHN — BR TR 6′ 158 lbs.
Brother of Washington Fulmer.
B. Feb. 12, 1851, Philadelphia, Pa. D. Feb. 15, 1940, Philadelphia, Pa.

Year	Team	Games	BA	SA	AB	H	2B	3B	HR	HR%	R	RBI	BB	SO	SB	Pinch Hit AB	Pinch Hit H	PO	A	E	DP	TC/G	FA	G by Pos
1876	LOU N	66	.273	.356	267	73	9	5	1	0.4	28	29	1	10		0	0	83	209	47	12	5.1	.861	SS-66
1879	BUF N	76	.268	.337	306	82	11	5	0	0.0	30	28	5	34		0	0	273	301	60	46	8.3	.905	2B-76
1880		11	.159	.159	44	7	0	0	0	0.0	3	1	2	4		0	0	34	33	9	2	6.9	.882	2B-11
1882	CIN AA	79	.281	.346	324	91	13	4	0	0.0	54		10			0	0	130	243	43	14	5.3	.897	SS-79
1883		92	.258	.363	361	93	13	5	5	1.4	52		13			0	0	134	243	60	26	4.8	.863	SS-92
1884	2 teams	CIN AA (31G –.175) STL AA (1G –.000)																						
″	total	32	.168	.202	119	20	2	1	0	0.0	13		1			0	0	27	73	27	7	3.8	.787	SS-29, OF-2, 2B-1, 3B-1
6 yrs.		356	.258	.332	1421	366	48	20	6	0.4	180	58	32	48		0	0	681	1102	246	107	5.7	.879	SS-266, 2B-88, OF-2, 3B-1

Chris Fulmer

FULMER, CHRISTOPHER — BR TR 5′ 8″ 165 lbs.
B. July 4, 1858, Tamaqua, Pa. D. Nov. 9, 1931, Tamaqua, Pa.

Year	Team	Games	BA	SA	AB	H	2B	3B	HR	HR%	R	RBI	BB	SO	SB	Pinch Hit AB	Pinch Hit H	PO	A	E	DP	TC/G	FA	G by Pos
1884	WAS U	48	.276	.326	181	50	9	0	0	0.0	39		11			0	0	267	45	18	4	6.0	.945	C-34, OF-16, 1B-5
1886	BAL AA	80	.244	.311	270	66	9	3	1	0.4	54		48			0	0	480	117	37	5	7.8	.942	C-68, OF-12, P-1
1887		56	.269	.363	201	54	11	4	0	0.0	52		36		35	0	0	216	73	31	5	5.7	.903	C-48, OF-8
1888		52	.187	.229	166	31	5	1	0	0.0	20	10	21		10	0	0	244	44	32	5	6.2	.900	C-45, OF-7
1889		16	.259	.345	58	15	3	1	0	0.0	11	13	6	12	2	0	0	25	2	3	0	1.9	.900	OF-14, C-2
5 yrs.		252	.247	.313	876	216	37	9	1	0.1	176	23	122	12	47	0	0	1232	281	121	19	6.3	.926	C-197, OF-57, 1B-5, P-1

Dave Fultz

FULTZ, DAVID LEWIS (Swarthy Dave) — BR TR 5′11″ 170 lbs.
B. May 29, 1875, Staunton, Va. D. Oct. 29, 1959, Deland, Fla.

Year	Team	Games	BA	SA	AB	H	2B	3B	HR	HR%	R	RBI	BB	SO	SB	Pinch Hit AB	Pinch Hit H	PO	A	E	DP	TC/G	FA	G by Pos
1898	PHI N	19	.182	.291	55	10	2	2	0	0.0	7	5	6		1	1	0	35	8	6	1	2.7	.878	OF-14, 2B-3, SS-1
1899	2 teams	PHI N (2G –.400) BAL N (57G –.295)																						
″	total	59	.298	.330	215	64	3	2	0	0.0	31	18	13		18	2	0	104	45	19	3	3.0	.887	OF-31, 3B-20, 2B-3, SS-1, 1B-1
1901	PHI A	132	.292	.355	561	164	17	9	0	0.0	95	52	32		36	0	0	264	100	33	2	3.0	.917	OF-106, 2B-18, SS-9
1902		129	.302	.368	506	153	20	5	1	0.2	**109**	49	62		44	0	0	263	43	14	6	2.5	.956	OF-114, 2B-16
1903	NY A	79	.224	.271	295	66	12	1	0	0.0	39	25	25		29	1	0	159	16	15	2	2.4	.921	OF-77, 3B-2
1904		97	.274	.366	339	93	17	4	2	0.6	39	32	24		17	6	**2**	194	8	5	2	2.3	.976	OF-90
1905		130	.232	.277	422	98	13	3	0	0.0	49	42	39		44	5	1	252	14	9	2	2.3	.967	OF-122
7 yrs.		645	.271	.331	2393	648	84	26	3	0.1	369	223	201		189	15	3	1271	234	101	18	2.6	.937	OF-554, 2B-40, 3B-22, SS-11, 1B-1

Mark Funderburk

FUNDERBURK, MARK CLIFFORD — BR TR 6′ 4″ 226 lbs.
B. May 16, 1957, Charlotte, N. C.

Year	Team	Games	BA	SA	AB	H	2B	3B	HR	HR%	R	RBI	BB	SO	SB	Pinch Hit AB	Pinch Hit H	PO	A	E	DP	TC/G	FA	G by Pos
1981	MIN A	8	.200	.267	15	3	1	0	0	0.0	2	2	2	1	0	2	0	4	1	0	0	0.7	1.000	OF-6, DH-1
1985		23	.314	.529	70	22	7	1	2	2.9	7	13	5	12	0	4	1	15	0	0	0	0.7	1.000	DH-15, OF-5, 1B-1
2 yrs.		31	.294	.482	85	25	8	1	2	2.4	9	15	7	13	0	6	1	19	1	0	0	0.7	1.000	DH-16, OF-11, 1B-1

Liz Funk

FUNK, ELIAS CALVIN — BL TL 5′ 8½″ 160 lbs.
B. Oct. 28, 1904, La Cygne, Kans. D. Jan. 16, 1968, Norman, Okla.

Year	Team	Games	BA	SA	AB	H	2B	3B	HR	HR%	R	RBI	BB	SO	SB	Pinch Hit AB	Pinch Hit H	PO	A	E	DP	TC/G	FA	G by Pos
1929	NY A	1	—	—	0	0	0	0	0	—	0	0	0	0	0	0	0	0	0	0	0	0.0	—	
1930	DET A	140	.275	.389	527	145	26	11	4	0.8	74	65	29	39	12	10	0	354	8	13	4	2.9	.965	OF-129

Liz Funk *continued*

Year	Team	Games	BA	SA	AB	H	2B	3B	HR	HR%	R	RBI	BB	SO	SB	Pinch Hit AB	Pinch Hit H	PO	A	E	DP	TC/G	FA	G by Pos
1932	CHI A	122	.259	.343	440	114	21	5	2	0.5	59	40	43	19	17	1	0	318	15	7	4	2.8	.979	OF-120
1933		10	.222	.222	9	2	0	0	0	0.0	1	0	1	0	0	8	2	0	0	0	0	0.0	.000	OF-2
4 yrs.		273	.267	.367	976	261	47	16	6	0.6	134	105	73	58	29	19	2	672	23	20	8	2.8	.972	OF-251

Carl Furillo

FURILLO, CARL ANTHONY (Skoonj, The Reading Rifle)
B. Mar. 8, 1922, Stony Creek Mills, Pa. D. Jan. 21, 1989, Stony Creek Mills, Pa.
BR TR 6′ 190 lbs.

Year	Team	Games	BA	SA	AB	H	2B	3B	HR	HR%	R	RBI	BB	SO	SB	Pinch Hit AB	Pinch Hit H	PO	A	E	DP	TC/G	FA	G by Pos
1946	BKN N	117	.284	.400	335	95	18	6	3	0.9	29	35	31	20	6	4	1	292	9	5	4	2.7	.984	OF-112
1947		124	.295	.437	437	129	24	7	8	1.8	61	88	34	24	7	2	1	287	9	7	3	2.5	.977	OF-121
1948		108	.297	.407	364	108	20	4	4	1.1	55	44	43	32	6	4	0	274	13	5	2	2.8	.983	OF-104
1949		142	.322	.506	549	177	27	10	18	3.3	95	106	37	29	4	0	0	286	13	11	2	2.2	.965	OF-142
1950		153	.305	.460	620	189	30	6	18	2.9	99	106	41	40	8	0	0	246	18	8	2	1.8	.971	OF-153
1951		158	.295	.427	**667**	197	32	4	16	2.4	93	91	43	33	8	1	0	330	24	5	6	2.3	.986	OF-157
1952		134	.247	.351	425	105	18	1	8	1.9	52	59	31	33	1	2	0	225	12	3	2	1.8	.988	OF-131
1953		132	**.344**	.580	479	165	38	6	21	4.4	82	92	34	32	1	2	0	232	11	3	3	1.9	.988	OF-131
1954		150	.294	.444	547	161	23	1	19	3.5	56	96	49	35	2	1	0	306	10	9	3	2.2	.972	OF-149
1955		140	.314	.520	523	164	24	3	26	5.0	83	95	43	43	4	1	0	249	10	5	4	1.9	.981	OF-140
1956		149	.289	.467	523	151	30	0	21	4.0	66	83	57	41	1	3	0	230	10	4	2	1.7	.984	OF-146
1957		119	.306	.461	395	121	17	4	12	3.0	61	66	29	33	0	10	1	153	7	2	1	1.5	.988	OF-107
1958	LA N	122	.290	.482	411	119	19	3	18	4.4	54	83	35	28	0	5	3	187	5	5	0	1.7	.975	OF-119
1959		50	.290	.333	93	27	4	0	0	0.0	8	13	7	11	0	25	7	23	0	2	0	1.0	.920	OF-25
1960		8	.200	.400	10	2	0	1	0	0.0	1	1	0	2	0	5	1	2	0	0	0	1.0	1.000	OF-2
15 yrs.		1806	.299	.458	6378	1910	324	56	192	3.0	895	1058	514	436	48	65	14	3322	151	74	34	2.0	.979	OF-1739
WORLD SERIES																								
1947	BKN N	6	.353	.471	17	6	2	0	0	0.0	2	3	3	0	0	2	2	14	1	1	0	2.7	.938	OF-6
1949		3	.125	.125	8	1	0	0	0	0.0	0	0	1	0	0	1	0	2	0	0	0	1.0	1.000	OF-2
1952		7	.174	.261	23	4	2	0	0	0.0	1	0	3	3	0	0	0	13	0	0	0	1.9	1.000	OF-7
1953		6	.333	.542	24	8	2	0	1	4.2	4	4	1	3	0	0	0	10	0	2	0	2.0	.833	OF-6
1955		7	.296	.444	27	8	1	0	1	3.7	4	3	3	5	0	0	0	8	0	0	0	1.1	1.000	OF-7
1956		7	.240	.320	25	6	2	0	0	0.0	2	1	2	3	0	0	0	7	0	0	0	1.0	1.000	OF-7
1959	LA N	4	.250	.250	4	1	0	0	0	0.0	0	2	0	1	0	4	1	0	0	0	0	0.0	.000	OF-1
7 yrs.		40	.266	.383	128	34	9 **3rd**	0	2	1.6	13	13	13	15	0	7	3	54	1	3	0	1.6	.948	OF-36

Ed Fusselbach

FUSSELBACH, EDWARD L.
B. July 4, 1858, Philadelphia, Pa. D. Apr. 14, 1926, Philadelphia, Pa.
BR 5′ 6″ 156 lbs.

Year	Team	Games	BA	SA	AB	H	2B	3B	HR	HR%	R	RBI	BB	SO	SB	Pinch Hit AB	Pinch Hit H	PO	A	E	DP	TC/G	FA	G by Pos
1882	STL AA	35	.228	.243	136	31	2	0	0	0.0	13		5			0	0	92	54	25	4	4.5	.854	C-19, OF-15, P-4
1884	BAL U	68	.284	.366	303	86	16	3	1	0.3	60		3			0	0	395	163	61	6	9.0	.901	C-54, 3B-6, SS-5, OF-4
1885	PHI AA	5	.316	.368	19	6	1	0	0	0.0	2		0			0	0	30	11	4	0	9.0	.911	C-5
1888	LOU AA	1	.250	.250	4	1	0	0	0	0.0	0	1	0		0	0	0	0	1	0	0	1.0	1.000	OF-1
4 yrs.		109	.268	.329	462	124	19	3	1	0.2	75	1	8		0	0	0	517	229	90	10	7.4	.892	C-78, OF-20, 3B-6, SS-5, P-4

Les Fusselman

FUSSELMAN, LESTER LeROY
B. Mar. 7, 1921, Pryor, Okla. D. May 21, 1970, Cleveland, Ohio.
BR TR 6′ 1″ 195 lbs.

Year	Team	Games	BA	SA	AB	H	2B	3B	HR	HR%	R	RBI	BB	SO	SB	Pinch Hit AB	Pinch Hit H	PO	A	E	DP	TC/G	FA	G by Pos
1952	STL N	32	.159	.254	63	10	3	0	1	1.6	5	3	0	9	0	1	0	97	11	1	1	3.4	.991	C-32
1953		11	.250	.375	8	2	1	0	0	0.0	1	0	0	0	0	0	0	20	2	0	0	2.0	1.000	C-11
2 yrs.		43	.169	.268	71	12	4	0	1	1.4	6	3	0	9	0	1	0	117	13	1	1	3.0	.992	C-43

Bill Gabler

GABLER, WILLIAM LOUIS (Gabe)
B. Aug. 4, 1930, St. Louis, Mo.
BL TR 6′ 1″ 190 lbs.

Year	Team	Games	BA	SA	AB	H	2B	3B	HR	HR%	R	RBI	BB	SO	SB	Pinch Hit AB	Pinch Hit H	PO	A	E	DP	TC/G	FA	G by Pos
1958	CHI N	3	.000	.000	3	0	0	0	0	0.0	0	0	0	3	0	3	0	0	0	0	0	0.0	—	

Len Gabrielson

GABRIELSON, LEONARD GARY
Son of Len Gabrielson.
B. Feb. 14, 1940, Oakland, Calif.
BL TR 6′ 4″ 210 lbs.

Year	Team	Games	BA	SA	AB	H	2B	3B	HR	HR%	R	RBI	BB	SO	SB	Pinch Hit AB	Pinch Hit H	PO	A	E	DP	TC/G	FA	G by Pos
1960	MIL N	4	.000	.000	3	0	0	0	0	0.0	1	0	1	0	0	3	0	0	0	0	0	0.0	.000	OF-1
1963		46	.217	.333	120	26	5	0	3	2.5	14	15	8	23	1	12	4	143	9	4	5	3.8	.974	OF-22, 1B-16, 3B-3
1964	2 teams	MIL N (24G –.184) CHI N (89G –.246)																						
″	total	113	.239	.342	310	74	13	2	5	1.6	22	24	20	45	10	25	8	240	12	2	16	2.8	.992	OF-70, 1B-20
1965	2 teams	CHI N (28G –.250) SF N (88G –.301)																						
″	total	116	.293	.410	317	93	6	5	7	2.2	40	31	33	64	4	22	4	157	9	3	5	1.7	.982	OF-91, 1B-6
1966	SF N	94	.217	.296	240	52	7	0	4	1.7	27	16	21	51	0	25	5	116	5	4	5	1.7	.968	OF-67, 1B-6
1967	2 teams	CAL A (11G –.083) LA N (90G –.261)																						
″	total	101	.252	.400	250	63	10	3	7	2.8	22	31	17	45	3	34	6	92	7	2	0	1.5	.980	OF-69
1968	LA N	108	.270	.428	304	82	16	1	10	3.3	38	35	32	47	1	27	7	114	6	3	1	1.4	.976	OF-86
1969		83	.270	.326	178	48	5	1	1	0.6	13	18	12	25	1	36	13	61	1	1	0	1.3	.984	OF-47, 1B-2
1970		43	.190	.238	42	8	2	0	0	0.0	1	6	1	15	0	38	8	3	1	0	1	1.3	1.000	OF-2, 1B-1
9 yrs.		708	.253	.366	1764	446	64	12	37	2.1	178	176	145	315	20	222	55	926	50	19	33	2.0	.981	OF-455, 1B-51, 3B-3

Len Gabrielson

GABRIELSON, LEONARD HILBOURNE
Father of Len Gabrielson.
B. Sept. 8, 1915, Oakland, Calif.
BL TL 6′ 3″ 210 lbs.

Year	Team	Games	BA	SA	AB	H	2B	3B	HR	HR%	R	RBI	BB	SO	SB	Pinch Hit AB	Pinch Hit H	PO	A	E	DP	TC/G	FA	G by Pos
1939	PHI N	5	.222	.222	18	4	0	0	0	0.0	3	1	2	3	0	0	0	34	9	1	3	8.8	.977	1B-5

Eddie Gaedel

GAEDEL, EDWARD CARL
B. June 8, 1925, Chicago, Ill. D. June 18, 1961, Chicago, Ill.
BR TL 3′ 7″ 65 lbs.

Year	Team	Games	BA	SA	AB	H	2B	3B	HR	HR%	R	RBI	BB	SO	SB	Pinch Hit AB	Pinch Hit H	PO	A	E	DP	TC/G	FA	G by Pos
1951	STL A	1	—	—	0	0	0	0	0	—	0	0	1	0	0	0	0	0	0	0	0	0.0	—	

Gary Gaetti

GAETTI, GARY JOSEPH
B. Aug. 19, 1958, Centralia, Ill.
BR TR 6′ 180 lbs.

Year	Team	Games	BA	SA	AB	H	2B	3B	HR	HR%	R	RBI	BB	SO	SB	Pinch Hit AB	Pinch Hit H	PO	A	E	DP	TC/G	FA	G by Pos
1981	MIN A	9	.192	.423	26	5	0	0	2	7.7	4	3	0	6	0	0	0	5	17	0	1	2.4	1.000	3B-8, DH-1
1982		145	.230	.443	508	117	25	4	25	4.9	59	84	37	107	0	1	0	106	291	17	36	2.9	.959	3B-142, SS-2
1983		157	.245	.414	584	143	30	3	21	3.6	81	78	54	121	7	2	1	131	361	17	46	3.2	.967	3B-154, SS-3, DH-1
1984		162	.262	.350	588	154	29	4	5	0.9	55	65	44	81	11	0	0	163	335	21	27	3.2	.960	3B-154, OF-8, SS-2
1985		160	.246	.409	560	138	31	0	20	3.6	71	63	37	89	13	1	0	162	316	18	31	3.1	.964	3B-156, OF-4, DH-1, 1B-1

Gary Gaetti *continued*

Year	Team	Lg	Games	BA	SA	AB	H	2B	3B	HR	HR%	R	RBI	BB	SO	SB	Pinch Hit AB	Pinch Hit H	PO	A	E	DP	TC/G	FA	G by Pos
1986			157	.287	.518	596	171	34	1	34	5.7	91	108	52	108	14	1	0	120	335	21	36	3.0	.956	3B-156, SS-2, OF-1, 2B-1
1987			154	.257	.485	584	150	36	2	31	5.3	95	109	37	92	10	3	2	134	261	11	28	2.7	.973	3B-150, DH-2
1988			133	.301	.551	468	141	29	2	28	6.0	66	88	36	85	7	14	4	105	191	7	24	2.5	.977	3B-115, DH-5, SS-2
1989			130	.251	.404	498	125	11	4	19	3.8	63	75	25	87	6	3	1	115	253	10	24	2.9	.974	3B-125, DH-3, 1B-2
1990			154	.229	.376	577	132	27	5	16	2.8	61	85	36	101	6	2	0	125	319	18	36	3.0	.961	3B-151, SS-2, 1B-2
1991	CAL	A	152	.246	.379	586	144	22	1	18	3.1	58	66	33	104	5	1	1	111	353	17	39	3.2	.965	3B-152
1992			130	.226	.342	456	103	13	2	12	2.6	41	48	21	79	3	7	2	423	196	22	53	5.0	.966	3B-67, 1B-44, DH-17
1993	2 teams		CAL A (20G –.180) KC A (82G –.256)																						
"	total		102	.245	.438	331	81	20	1	14	4.2	40	50	21	87	1	8	1	185	153	7	29	3.2	.980	3B-79, 1B-24, DH-6
1994	KC	A	90	.287	.462	327	94	15	3	12	3.7	53	57	19	63	0	2	1	99	166	4	20	2.9	.985	3B-85, 1B-9
1995			137	.261	.518	514	134	27	0	35	6.8	76	96	47	91	3	5	1	182	230	16	30	3.1	.963	3B-123, 1B-11, DH-6
15 yrs.			1972	.254	.433	7203	1832	349	32	292	4.1	914	1075	499	1301	86	50	14	2166	3777	206	460	3.1	.966	3B-1817, 1B-93, DH-42, OF-13, SS-13, 2B-1
LEAGUE CHAMPIONSHIP SERIES																									
1987	MIN	A	5	.300	.650	20	6	1	0	2	10.0	5	5	1	3	0	0	0	8	7	0	1	3.0	1.000	3B-5
WORLD SERIES																									
1987	MIN	A	7	.259	.519	27	7	2	1	1	3.7	4	4	2	5	2	0	0	6	15	0	2	3.0	1.000	3B-7

Fabian Gaffke

GAFFKE, FABIAN SEBASTIAN
B. Aug. 5, 1913, Milwaukee, Wis. D. Feb. 8, 1992, Milwaukee, Wis.
BR TR 5′10″ 185 lbs.

Year	Team	Lg	Games	BA	SA	AB	H	2B	3B	HR	HR%	R	RBI	BB	SO	SB	Pinch Hit AB	Pinch Hit H	PO	A	E	DP	TC/G	FA	G by Pos
1936	BOS	A	15	.127	.218	55	7	2	0	1	1.8	5	3	4	5	0	0	0	24	1	0	0	1.7	1.000	OF-15
1937			54	.288	.484	184	53	10	4	6	3.3	32	34	15	25	1	4	1	80	3	3	0	1.7	.965	OF-50
1938			15	.100	.100	10	1	0	0	0	0.0	2	1	3	2	0	8	1	1	1	0	0	0.7	1.000	OF-2, C-1
1939			1	.000	.000	1	0	0	0	0	0.0	0	1	0	0	0	1	0	0	0	0	0	0.0	—	
1941	CLE	A	4	.250	.250	4	1	0	0	0	0.0	0	0	2	2	0	2	1	2	0	0	0	1.0	1.000	OF-2
1942			40	.164	.194	67	11	2	0	0	0.0	4	3	6	13	1	24	4	29	0	0	0	1.8	1.000	OF-16
6 yrs.			129	.227	.361	321	73	14	4	7	2.2	43	42	30	47	2	39	7	136	5	3	0	1.7	.979	OF-85, C-1

Phil Gagliano

GAGLIANO, PHILIP JOSEPH
Brother of Ralph Gagliano.
B. Dec. 27, 1941, Memphis, Tenn.
BR TR 6′ 1″ 180 lbs.

Year	Team	Lg	Games	BA	SA	AB	H	2B	3B	HR	HR%	R	RBI	BB	SO	SB	Pinch Hit AB	Pinch Hit H	PO	A	E	DP	TC/G	FA	G by Pos
1963	STL	N	10	.400	.400	5	2	0	0	0	0.0	1	1	1	1	0	2	0	5	3	0	0	2.0	1.000	2B-3, 3B-1
1964			40	.259	.379	58	15	4	0	1	1.7	5	9	3	10	0	19	3	26	28	4	6	3.6	.931	2B-12, OF-2, 1B-1, 3B-1
1965			122	.240	.355	363	87	14	2	8	2.2	46	53	40	45	2	26	5	201	169	16	34	3.8	.959	2B-57, OF-25, 3B-19
1966			90	.254	.338	213	54	8	2	2	0.9	23	15	24	29	2	36	4	95	86	2	16	3.3	.989	3B-41, 1B-8, OF-5, 2B-1
1967			73	.221	.281	217	48	7	0	2	0.9	20	21	19	26	0	17	0	115	99	8	16	3.8	.964	2B-27, 3B-25, 1B-4, SS-2
1968			53	.229	.305	105	24	4	2	0	0.0	13	13	7	12	0	17	4	31	52	1	8	2.6	.988	2B-17, 3B-10, OF-5
1969			62	.227	.266	128	29	2	0	1	0.8	7	10	14	12	0	21	2	108	55	2	16	4.1	.988	2B-20, 3B-9, 1B-9, OF-2
1970	2 teams		STL N (18G –.188) CHI N (26G –.150)																						
"	total		44	.167	.167	72	12	0	0	0	0.0	5	7	6	8	0	16	3	49	33	2	6	2.9	.976	2B-18, 3B-7, 1B-4
1971	BOS	A	47	.324	.397	68	22	5	0	0	0.0	11	13	11	5	0	22	8	22	14	0	2	1.6	1.000	OF-11, 2B-7, 3B-4
1972			52	.256	.329	82	21	4	1	0	0.0	9	10	10	13	1	26	9	31	15	2	0	2.1	.958	OF-12, 3B-5, 2B-4, 1B-2
1973	CIN	N	63	.290	.319	69	20	2	0	0	0.0	8	7	13	16	0	41	15	9	14	3	1	3.3	.885	2B-4, 3B-2, OF-1, 1B-1
1974			46	.065	.065	31	2	0	0	0	0.0	2	0	15	7	0	29	2	5	2	0	0	1.8	1.000	2B-2, 3B-1, 1B-1
12 yrs.			702	.238	.313	1411	336	50	7	14	1.0	150	159	163	184	5	272	55	697	570	40	105	3.3	.969	2B-172, 3B-125, OF-63, 1B-30, SS-2
LEAGUE CHAMPIONSHIP SERIES																									
1973	CIN	N	3	.000	.000	3	0	0	0	0	0.0	0	0	0	2	0	3	0	0	0	0	0	0.0	—	
WORLD SERIES																									
1967	STL	N	1	.000	.000	1	0	0	0	0	0.0	0	0	0	0	0	1	0	0	0	0	0	0.0	—	
1968			3	.000	.000	3	0	0	0	0	0.0	0	0	0	0	0	3	0	0	0	0	0	0.0	—	
2 yrs.			4	.000	.000	4	0	0	0	0	0.0	0	0	0	0	0	4	0							

Ralph Gagliano

GAGLIANO, RALPH MICHAEL
Brother of Phil Gagliano.
B. Oct. 8, 1946, Memphis, Tenn.
BL TR 5′11″ 170 lbs.

Year	Team	Lg	Games	BA	SA	AB	H	2B	3B	HR	HR%	R	RBI	BB	SO	SB	Pinch Hit AB	Pinch Hit H	PO	A	E	DP	TC/G	FA	G by Pos
1965	CLE	A	1	—	—	0	0	0	0	0	—	0	0	0	0	0	0	0	0	0	0	0	0.0	—	

Greg Gagne

GAGNE, GREGORY CHRISTOPHER
B. Nov. 12, 1961, Fall River, Mass.
BR TR 5′11″ 175 lbs.

Year	Team	Lg	Games	BA	SA	AB	H	2B	3B	HR	HR%	R	RBI	BB	SO	SB	Pinch Hit AB	Pinch Hit H	PO	A	E	DP	TC/G	FA	G by Pos
1983	MIN	A	10	.111	.148	27	3	1	0	0	0.0	2	3	0	6	0	0	0	10	14	2	2	2.6	.923	SS-10
1984			2	.000	.000	1	0	0	0	0	0.0	0	0	0	0	0	1	0	0	0	0	0	0.0	—	
1985			114	.225	.317	293	66	15	3	2	0.7	37	23	20	57	10	4	1	149	269	14	48	3.9	.968	SS-106, DH-5
1986			156	.250	.398	472	118	22	6	12	2.5	63	54	30	108	12	0	0	228	381	26	96	4.0	.959	SS-155, 2B-4
1987			137	.265	.430	437	116	28	7	10	2.3	68	40	25	84	6	0	0	196	391	18	75	4.3	.970	SS-136, OF-4, 2B-1
1988			149	.236	.397	461	109	20	6	14	3.0	70	48	27	110	15	1	0	202	373	18	79	4.0	.970	SS-146, OF-2, 3B-1, 2B-1
1989			149	.272	.424	460	125	29	7	9	2.0	69	48	17	80	11	5	0	218	389	18	66	4.3	.971	SS-146, OF-1
1990			138	.235	.361	388	91	22	3	7	1.8	38	38	24	76	8	2	0	184	377	14	62	4.2	.976	SS-135, DH-2, OF-1
1991			139	.265	.395	408	108	23	3	8	2.0	52	42	26	72	11	2	1	181	377	9	69	4.1	.984	SS-137, DH-1
1992			146	.246	.346	439	108	23	0	7	1.6	53	39	19	83	6	1	0	208	438	18	83	4.7	.973	SS-141
1993	KC	A	159	.280	.406	540	151	32	3	10	1.9	66	57	33	93	10	1	0	266	451	10	93	4.6	.986	SS-159
1994			107	.259	.392	375	97	23	3	7	1.9	39	51	27	79	10	0	0	189	323	12	63	4.9	.977	SS-106
1995			120	.256	.374	430	110	25	4	6	1.4	58	49	38	60	3	6	3	175	387	18	87	4.8	.969	SS-118, DH-2
13 yrs.			1526	.254	.387	4731	1202	263	45	92	1.9	615	492	286	908	102	23	5	2206	4170	177	823	4.3	.973	SS-1495, DH-10, OF-8, 2B-6, 3B-1
LEAGUE CHAMPIONSHIP SERIES																									
1987	MIN	A	5	.278	.778	18	5	3	0	2	11.1	5	3	3	4	0	0	0	9	13	2	2	4.8	.917	SS-5
1991			5	.235	.235	17	4	0	0	0	0.0	1	1	1	5	0	0	0	9	9	2	1	4.0	.900	SS-5
2 yrs.			10	.257	.514	35	9	3	0	2	5.7	6	4	4	9	0	0	0	18	22	4	3	4.4	.909	SS-10

Greg Gagne *continued*

WORLD SERIES

Year	Team	Games	BA	SA	AB	H	2B	3B	HR	HR%	R	RBI	BB	SO	SB	Pinch Hit AB	Pinch Hit H	PO	A	E	DP	TC/G	FA	G by Pos
1987	MIN A	7	.200	.333	30	6	1	0	1	3.3	5	3	1	6	0	0	0	6	20	2	2	4.0	.929	SS-7
1991		7	.167	.333	24	4	1	0	1	4.2	1	3	0	7	0	0	0	13	24	0	5	5.3	1.000	SS-7
2 yrs.		14	.185	.333	54	10	2	0	2	3.7	6	6	1	13	0	0	0	19	44	2	7	4.6	.969	SS-14

Ed Gagnier

GAGNIER, EDWARD JAMES
B. Apr. 16, 1883, Paris, France D. Sept. 13, 1946, Detroit, Mich.
BR TR 5′ 9″ 170 lbs.

Year	Team	Games	BA	SA	AB	H	2B	3B	HR	HR%	R	RBI	BB	SO	SB	Pinch Hit AB	Pinch Hit H	PO	A	E	DP	TC/G	FA	G by Pos
1914	BKN F	94	.187	.234	337	63	12	2	0	0.0	22	25	13		8	0	0	230	254	35	39	5.5	.933	SS-88, 3B-6
1915	2 teams	BKN F (20G –.260) BUF F (1G –.000)																						
″	total	21	.250	.269	52	13	1	0	0	0.0	8	4	10		2	0	0	36	56	6	7	4.9	.939	SS-13, 2B-7
2 yrs.		115	.195	.239	389	76	13	2	0	0.0	30	29	23		10	0	0	266	310	41	46	5.4	.934	SS-101, 2B-7, 3B-6

Chick Gagnon

GAGNON, HAROLD DENNIS
B. Sept. 27, 1897, Millbury, Mass. D. Apr. 30, 1970, Wilmington, Del.
BR TR 5′ 7½″ 158 lbs.

Year	Team	Games	BA	SA	AB	H	2B	3B	HR	HR%	R	RBI	BB	SO	SB	Pinch Hit AB	Pinch Hit H	PO	A	E	DP	TC/G	FA	G by Pos
1922	DET A	10	.250	.250	4	1	0	0	0	0.0	2	0	0	2	0	2	1	0	0	1	0	0.5	.000	3B-1, SS-1
1924	WAS A	4	.200	.200	5	1	0	0	0	0.0	1	1	0	0	0	2	1	3	4	0	0	3.5	1.000	SS-2
2 yrs.		14	.222	.222	9	2	0	0	0	0.0	3	1	0	2	0	4	2	3	4	1	0	2.0	.875	SS-3, 3B-1

Del Gainer

GAINER, DELLOS CLINTON (Sheriff)
B. Nov. 10, 1886, Montrose, W. Va. D. Jan. 29, 1947, Elkins, W. Va.
BR TR 6′ 180 lbs.

Year	Team	Games	BA	SA	AB	H	2B	3B	HR	HR%	R	RBI	BB	SO	SB	Pinch Hit AB	Pinch Hit H	PO	A	E	DP	TC/G	FA	G by Pos
1909	DET A	2	.200	.200	5	1	0	0	0	0.0	0	0	0		0	0	0	12	1	1	0	7.0	.929	1B-2
1911		70	.302	.403	248	75	11	4	2	0.8	32	25	20		10	0	0	671	38	18	36	10.5	.975	1B-69
1912		51	.240	.335	179	43	5	6	0	0.0	28	20	18		14	0	0	547	22	8	25	11.5	.986	1B-50
1913		104	.267	.372	363	97	16	8	2	0.6	47	25	30	45	10	2	1	1118	50	14	55	11.6	.988	1B-102
1914	2 teams	DET A (1G –.000) BOS A (38G –.238)																						
″	total	39	.238	.464	84	20	9	2	2	2.4	11	13	8	14	2	8	1	127	33	4	6	5.5	.976	1B-19, 2B-11
1915	BOS A	82	.295	.415	200	59	5	8	1	0.5	30	29	21	31	7	14	4	462	34	6	22	8.1	.988	1B-56, OF-6
1916		56	.254	.359	142	36	6	0	3	2.1	14	18	10	24	5	4	0	362	24	1	18	7.7	.997	1B-48, 2B-2
1917		52	.308	.424	172	53	10	2	2	1.2	28	19	15	21	1	1	0	490	27	6	29	10.5	.989	1B-50
1919		47	.237	.322	118	28	6	2	0	0.0	9	13	13	15	5	6	1	190	12	5	6	5.3	.976	1B-21, OF-18
1922	STL N	43	.268	.485	97	26	7	4	2	2.1	19	23	14	6	0	9	1	189	11	5	8	5.7	.976	1B-26, OF-10
10 yrs.		546	.272	.390	1608	438	75	36	14	0.9	218	185	149	156	54	44	8	4168	252	68	205	9.2	.985	1B-443, OF-34, 2B-13

WORLD SERIES

Year	Team	Games	BA	SA	AB	H	2B	3B	HR	HR%	R	RBI	BB	SO	SB	Pinch Hit AB	Pinch Hit H	PO	A	E	DP	TC/G	FA	G by Pos
1915	BOS A	1	.333	.333	3	1	0	0	0	0.0	1	0	0	0	0	1	0	9	0	0	0	9.0	1.000	1B-1
1916		1	1.000	1.000	1	1	0	0	0	0.0	0	1	0	0	0	1	1	0	0	0	0	0.0	—	
2 yrs.		2	.500	.500	4	2	0	0	0	0.0	1	1	0	0	0	2	1	9	0	0	0	9.0	1.000	1B-1

Jay Gainer

GAINER, JOHNATHAN KEITH
B. Oct. 8, 1966, Panama City, Fla.
BL TL 6′ 190 lbs.

Year	Team	Games	BA	SA	AB	H	2B	3B	HR	HR%	R	RBI	BB	SO	SB	Pinch Hit AB	Pinch Hit H	PO	A	E	DP	TC/G	FA	G by Pos
1993	CLR N	23	.171	.390	41	7	0	0	3	7.3	4	6	4	12	1	16	3	52	2	1	3	7.9	.982	1B-7

Joe Gaines

GAINES, ARNESTA JOE
B. Nov. 22, 1936, Bryan, Tex.
BR TR 6′ 1″ 190 lbs.

Year	Team	Games	BA	SA	AB	H	2B	3B	HR	HR%	R	RBI	BB	SO	SB	Pinch Hit AB	Pinch Hit H	PO	A	E	DP	TC/G	FA	G by Pos
1960	CIN N	11	.200	.200	15	3	0	0	0	0.0	2	1	0	1	0	2	1	6	0	0	0	2.0	1.000	OF-3
1961		5	.000	.000	3	0	0	0	0	0.0	2	0	2	1	0	1	0	1	0	1	0	0.7	.500	OF-3
1962		64	.231	.346	52	12	3	0	1	1.9	12	7	8	16	0	40	12	8	0	0	0	0.6	1.000	OF-13
1963	BAL A	66	.286	.476	126	36	4	1	6	4.8	24	20	20	39	2	25	5	52	0	3	0	1.4	.945	OF-39
1964	2 teams	BAL A (16G –.154) HOU N (89G –.254)																						
″	total	105	.246	.387	333	82	9	7	8	2.4	39	36	30	76	8	17	2	141	4	8	1	1.8	.948	OF-86
1965	HOU N	100	.227	.349	229	52	8	1	6	2.6	21	31	18	59	4	32	8	83	1	8	0	1.4	.913	OF-65
1966		11	.077	.154	13	1	1	0	0	0.0	4	0	3	5	0	6	0	1	0	1	0	0.7	.500	OF-3
7 yrs.		362	.241	.379	771	186	25	9	21	2.7	104	95	81	197	14	123	28	292	5	21	1	1.5	.934	OF-212

Ty Gainey

GAINEY, TELMANCH
B. Dec. 25, 1960, Cheraw, S. C.
BL TR 6′ 1″ 190 lbs.

Year	Team	Games	BA	SA	AB	H	2B	3B	HR	HR%	R	RBI	BB	SO	SB	Pinch Hit AB	Pinch Hit H	PO	A	E	DP	TC/G	FA	G by Pos
1985	HOU N	13	.162	.162	37	6	0	0	0	0.0	5	0	2	9	0	2	0	21	0	2	0	2.6	.913	OF-9
1986		26	.300	.460	50	15	3	1	1	2.0	6	6	6	19	3	6	2	30	0	0	0	1.6	1.000	OF-19
1987		18	.125	.125	24	3	0	0	0	0.0	1	1	2	9	1	11	0	10	0	0	0	1.7	1.000	OF-6
3 yrs.		57	.216	.288	111	24	3	1	1	0.9	12	7	10	37	4	19	2	61	0	2	0	1.9	.968	OF-34

Augie Galan

GALAN, AUGUST JOHN
B. May 25, 1912, Berkeley, Calif. D. Dec. 28, 1993, Fairfield, Calif.
BB TR 6′ 175 lbs.
BL 1944–1949

Year	Team	Games	BA	SA	AB	H	2B	3B	HR	HR%	R	RBI	BB	SO	SB	Pinch Hit AB	Pinch Hit H	PO	A	E	DP	TC/G	FA	G by Pos
1934	CHI N	66	.260	.391	192	50	6	2	5	2.6	31	22	16	15	4	12	5	92	115	8	18	4.6	.963	2B-43, 3B-3, SS-1
1935		154	.314	.467	646	203	41	11	12	1.9	**133**	79	87	53	**22**	0	0	351	12	8	4	2.4	.978	OF-154
1936		145	.264	.365	575	152	26	4	8	1.4	74	81	67	50	16	2	0	381	9	5	3	2.7	.987	OF-145
1937		147	.252	.412	611	154	24	10	18	2.9	104	78	79	48	**23**	0	0	338	44	9	7	2.6	.977	OF-140, 2B-8, SS-2
1938		110	.286	.418	395	113	16	9	6	1.5	52	69	49	17	8	6	0	211	10	3	3	2.2	.987	OF-103
1939		148	.304	.432	549	167	36	8	6	1.1	104	71	75	26	8	3	0	290	6	9	0	2.1	.970	OF-145
1940		68	.230	.359	209	48	14	2	3	1.4	33	22	37	23	9	9	2	119	11	4	2	2.4	.970	OF-54, 2B-2
1941	2 teams	CHI N (65G –.208) BKN N (17G –.259)																						
″	total	82	.218	.279	147	32	6	0	1	0.7	21	17	25	11	0	40	7	56	3	2	0	1.6	.967	OF-37
1942	BKN N	69	.263	.340	209	55	16	0	0	0.0	24	22	24	12	2	9	3	136	8	1	2	2.3	.993	OF-55, 1B-4, 2B-3
1943		139	.287	.406	495	142	26	3	9	1.8	83	67	**103**	39	6	1	0	478	29	7	9	3.8	.986	OF-124, 1B-13
1944		151	.318	.495	547	174	43	9	12	2.2	96	93	**101**	23	4	4	2	323	10	4	3	2.3	.988	OF-147, 2B-2
1945		152	.307	.441	576	177	36	7	9	1.6	114	92	114	27	13	1	1	693	116	17	59	5.3	.979	1B-66, OF-49, 3B-40
1946		99	.310	.460	274	85	22	5	3	1.1	53	38	68	21	8	7	1	211	44	16	3	3.0	.941	OF-60, 3B-19, 1B-12
1947	CIN N	124	.314	.416	392	123	18	2	6	1.5	60	61	94	19	0	5	2	246	2	3	0	2.1	.988	OF-118
1948		54	.286	.455	77	22	3	2	2	2.6	18	16	26	4	0	26	3	29	0	1	0	1.7	.967	OF-18
1949	2 teams	NY N (22G –.059) PHI A (12G –.308)																						
″	total	34	.209	.279	43	9	3	0	0	0.0	4	2	14	5	0	18	2	23	0	0	1	1.8	1.000	OF-10, 1B-3
16 yrs.		1742	.287	.419	5937	1706	336	74	100	1.7	1004	830	979	393	123	143	28	3977	419	97	114	2.8	.978	OF-1359, 1B-98, 3B-62, 2B-58, SS-3

Augie Galan *continued*

Year	Team	Games	BA	SA	AB	H	2B	3B	HR	HR%	R	RBI	BB	SO	SB	Pinch Hit AB	Pinch Hit H	PO	A	E	DP	TC/G	FA	G by Pos
WORLD SERIES																								
1935	CHI N	6	.160	.200	25	4	1	0	0	0.0	2	2	2	2	0	0	0	12	1	1	0	2.3	.929	OF-6
1938		2	.000	.000	2	0	0	0	0	0.0	0	0	0	1	0	2	0	0	0	0	0	0.0	—	
1941	BKN N	2	.000	.000	2	0	0	0	0	0.0	0	0	0	1	0	2	0	0	0	0	0	0.0	—	
3 yrs.		10	.138	.172	29	4	1	0	0	0.0	2	2	2	4	0	4	0	12	1	1	0	2.3	.929	OF-6

Andres Galarraga

GALARRAGA, ANDRES JOSE (Big Cat)
Born Andres Jose Padovani (Galarraga).
B. June 18, 1961, Caracas, Venezuela.
BR TR 6′ 3″ 235 lbs.

Year	Team	Games	BA	SA	AB	H	2B	3B	HR	HR%	R	RBI	BB	SO	SB	Pinch Hit AB	Pinch Hit H	PO	A	E	DP	TC/G	FA	G by Pos
1985	MON N	24	.187	.280	75	14	1	0	2	2.7	9	4	3	18	1	2	1	173	22	1	14	8.5	.995	1B-23
1986		105	.271	.405	321	87	13	0	10	3.1	39	42	30	79	6	7	1	805	40	4	59	8.3	.995	1B-102
1987		147	.305	.459	551	168	40	3	13	2.4	72	90	41	127	7	1	0	1300	103	10	96	9.7	.993	1B-146
1988		157	.302	.540	609	**184**	**42**	8	29	4.8	99	92	39	**153**	13	2	1	1464	103	15	124	10.1	.991	1B-156
1989		152	.257	.434	572	147	30	1	23	4.0	76	85	48	**158**	12	6	1	1335	91	11	97	9.8	.992	1B-147
1990		155	.256	.409	579	148	29	0	20	3.5	65	87	40	**169**	10	7	0	1300	94	10	93	9.1	.993	1B-154
1991		107	.219	.336	375	82	13	2	9	2.4	34	33	23	86	5	2	0	887	80	9	68	9.3	.991	1B-105
1992	STL N	95	.243	.391	325	79	14	2	10	3.1	38	39	11	69	5	6	0	777	62	8	71	9.4	.991	1B-90
1993	CLR N	120	**.370**	.602	470	174	35	4	22	4.7	71	98	24	73	2	1	0	1018	103	11	88	9.5	.990	1B-119
1994		103	.319	.592	417	133	21	0	31	7.4	77	85	19	93	8	0	0	954	64	8	89	10.0	.992	1B-103
1995		143	.280	.511	554	155	29	3	31	5.6	89	106	32	**146**	12	1	0	1300	119	13	128	10.1	.991	1B-142
11 yrs.		1308	.283	.471	4848	1371	267	23	200	4.1	669	761	310	1171	81	35	4	11313	881	100	927	9.6	.992	1B-1287
DIVISIONAL PLAYOFF SERIES																								
1995	CLR N	4	.278	.333	18	5	1	0	0	0.0	1	2	0	6	0	0	0	41	2	0	4	10.8	1.000	1B-4

Milt Galatzer

GALATZER, MILTON
B. May 4, 1907, Chicago, Ill. D. Jan. 29, 1976, San Francisco, Calif.
BL TL 5′10″ 168 lbs.

Year	Team	Games	BA	SA	AB	H	2B	3B	HR	HR%	R	RBI	BB	SO	SB	Pinch Hit AB	Pinch Hit H	PO	A	E	DP	TC/G	FA	G by Pos
1933	CLE A	57	.237	.281	160	38	2	1	1	0.6	19	17	23	21	2	12	2	104	7	2	2	2.5	.982	OF-40, 1B-5
1934		49	.270	.342	196	53	10	2	0	0.0	29	15	21	8	3	0	0	91	7	2	0	2.0	.980	OF-49
1935		93	.301	.359	259	78	9	3	0	0.0	45	19	35	8	4	11	1	134	7	10	0	1.9	.934	OF-81
1936		49	.237	.299	97	23	4	1	0	0.0	12	6	13	8	1	3	0	52	3	2	2	1.3	.965	OF-42, 1B-1, P-1
1939	CIN N	3	.000	.000	5	0	0	0	0	0.0	0	0	0	1	0	0	0	11	0	0	0	5.5	1.000	1B-2
5 yrs.		251	.268	.326	717	192	25	7	1	0.1	105	57	92	46	10	26	3	392	24	16	4	2.0	.963	OF-212, 1B-8, P-1

Alan Gallagher

GALLAGHER, ALAN MITCHELL EDWARD GEORGE PATRICK HENRY (Dirty Al)
B. Oct. 19, 1945, San Francisco, Calif.
BR TR 6′ 180 lbs.

Year	Team	Games	BA	SA	AB	H	2B	3B	HR	HR%	R	RBI	BB	SO	SB	Pinch Hit AB	Pinch Hit H	PO	A	E	DP	TC/G	FA	G by Pos
1970	SF N	109	.266	.376	282	75	15	2	4	1.4	31	28	30	37	2	18	7	70	128	6	12	2.2	.971	3B-91
1971		136	.277	.378	429	119	18	5	5	1.2	47	57	40	57	2	9	3	88	204	15	18	2.4	.951	3B-128
1972		82	.223	.270	233	52	3	1	2	0.9	19	18	33	39	2	12	3	64	120	5	7	2.7	.974	3B-69
1973	2 teams	SF N (5G –.222) CAL A (110G –.273)																						
″	total	115	.272	.297	320	87	6	1	0	0.0	17	27	35	31	1	9	0	64	187	11	13	2.5	.958	3B-103, SS-1, 2B-1
4 yrs.		442	.263	.337	1264	333	42	9	11	0.9	114	130	138	164	7	48	13	286	639	37	50	2.4	.962	3B-391, SS-1, 2B-1
LEAGUE CHAMPIONSHIP SERIES																								
1971	SF N	4	.100	.100	10	1	0	0	0	0.0	0	0	0	2	0	0	0	0	4	0	0	1.0	1.000	3B-4

Bill Gallagher

GALLAGHER, WILLIAM HOWARD
B. Feb. 4, 1874, Boston, Mass. D. Mar. 11, 1950, Worcester, Mass.

Year	Team	Games	BA	SA	AB	H	2B	3B	HR	HR%	R	RBI	BB	SO	SB	Pinch Hit AB	Pinch Hit H	PO	A	E	DP	TC/G	FA	G by Pos
1896	PHI N	14	.306	.347	49	15	2	0	0	0.0	9	6	10	0	0	0	0	17	42	7	5	4.7	.894	SS-14

Bill Gallagher

GALLAGHER, WILLIAM JOHN
B. Philadelphia, Pa. Deceased.
TL

Year	Team	Games	BA	SA	AB	H	2B	3B	HR	HR%	R	RBI	BB	SO	SB	Pinch Hit AB	Pinch Hit H	PO	A	E	DP	TC/G	FA	G by Pos
1883	2 teams	BAL AA (16G –.164) PHI N (2G –.000)																						
″	total	18	.145	.217	69	10	3	1	0	0.0	10		3	4		0	0	21	13	9	1	2.0	.791	OF-11, P-7, SS-4
1884	PHI U	3	.091	.091	11	1	0	0	0	0.0	1		0			0	0	2	6	2	0	3.3	.800	P-3
2 yrs.		21	.138	.200	80	11	3	1	0	0.0	11		3	4		0	0	23	19	11	1	2.1	.792	OF-11, P-10, SS-4

Bob Gallagher

GALLAGHER, ROBERT COLLINS
B. July 7, 1948, Newton, Mass.
BL TL 6′ 3″ 185 lbs.

Year	Team	Games	BA	SA	AB	H	2B	3B	HR	HR%	R	RBI	BB	SO	SB	Pinch Hit AB	Pinch Hit H	PO	A	E	DP	TC/G	FA	G by Pos
1972	BOS A	7	.000	.000	5	0	0	0	0	0.0	0	0	0	3	0	5	0	0	0	0	0	0.0	—	
1973	HOU N	71	.264	.338	148	39	3	1	2	1.4	16	10	3	27	0	29	7	78	1	0	0	1.8	1.000	OF-42, 1B-1
1974		102	.172	.195	87	15	2	0	0	0.0	13	3	12	23	1	40	6	51	1	1	0	0.8	.981	OF-62, 1B-4
1975	NY N	33	.133	.200	15	2	1	0	0	0.0	5	0	1	3	0	10	1	9	0	1	0	0.6	.900	OF-16
4 yrs.		213	.220	.275	255	56	6	1	2	0.8	34	13	16	56	1	84	14	138	2	2	0	1.1	.986	OF-120, 1B-5

Dave Gallagher

GALLAGHER, DAVID THOMAS
B. Sept. 20, 1960, Trenton, N. J.
BR TR 6′ 180 lbs.

Year	Team	Games	BA	SA	AB	H	2B	3B	HR	HR%	R	RBI	BB	SO	SB	Pinch Hit AB	Pinch Hit H	PO	A	E	DP	TC/G	FA	G by Pos
1987	CLE A	15	.111	.194	36	4	1	1	0	0.0	2	1	2	5	2	0	0	34	1	1	1	2.6	.972	OF-14
1988	CHI A	101	.303	.406	347	105	15	3	5	1.4	59	31	29	40	5	11	2	228	5	0	2	2.4	1.000	OF-95, DH-2
1989		161	.266	.314	601	160	22	2	1	0.2	74	46	46	79	5	2	0	390	8	3	4	2.5	.993	OF-160, DH-1
1990	2 teams	CHI A (45G –.280) BAL A (23G –.216)																						
″	total	68	.254	.302	126	32	4	1	0	0.0	12	7	7	12	1	10	2	96	3	2	2	1.6	.980	OF-57, DH-6
1991	CAL A	90	.293	.367	270	79	17	0	1	0.4	32	30	24	43	2	11	4	180	8	0	1	2.1	1.000	OF-87, DH-2
1992	NY N	98	.240	.331	175	42	11	1	1	0.6	20	21	19	16	4	30	5	105	4	2	3	1.5	.982	OF-76
1993		99	.274	.443	201	55	12	2	6	3.0	34	28	20	18	1	27	10	139	7	0	1	1.8	1.000	OF-72, 1B-9
1994	ATL N	89	.224	.296	152	34	5	0	2	1.3	27	14	22	17	0	21	4	93	4	1	1	1.3	.990	OF-77, 1B-1
1995	2 teams	PHI N (62G –.318) CAL A (11G –.188)																						
″	total	73	.306	.399	173	53	13	0	1	0.6	13	12	18	21	0	14	7	98	2	0	0	1.6	1.000	OF-61, DH-1
9 yrs.		794	.271	.353	2081	564	100	10	17	0.8	273	190	187	251	20	126	34	1363	42	9	15	2.0	.994	OF-699, DH-12, 1B-10

Gil Gallagher

GALLAGHER, LAWRENCE KIRBY
B. Sept. 5, 1896, Washington, D. C. D. Jan. 6, 1957, Washington, D. C.
BB TR 5′ 8″ 155 lbs.

Year	Team	Games	BA	SA	AB	H	2B	3B	HR	HR%	R	RBI	BB	SO	SB	Pinch Hit AB	Pinch Hit H	PO	A	E	DP	TC/G	FA	G by Pos
1922	BOS N	7	.045	.091	22	1	1	0	0	0.0	1	2	1	7	0	1	0	4	21	3	0	4.7	.893	SS-6

Jackie Gallagher

GALLAGHER, JOHN LAURENCE
B. Jan. 28, 1902, Providence, R. I. D. Sept. 10, 1984, Gladwyn, Pa.
BL TR 5′10″ 175 lbs.

Year	Team	Games	BA	SA	AB	H	2B	3B	HR	HR%	R	RBI	BB	SO	SB	Pinch Hit AB	Pinch Hit H	PO	A	E	DP	TC/G	FA	G by Pos
1923	CLE A	1	1.000	1.000	1	1	0	0	0	0.0	0	1	0	0	0	0	0	0	0	0	0	0.0	.000	OF-1

Jim Gallagher

GALLAGHER, JAMES E.
B. Findlay, Ohio D. Mar. 29, 1894, Scranton, Pa.

Year	Team	Games	BA	SA	AB	H	2B	3B	HR	HR%	R	RBI	BB	SO	SB	Pinch Hit AB	Pinch Hit H	PO	A	E	DP	TC/G	FA	G by Pos
1886	WAS N	1	.200	.200	5	1	0	0	0	0.0	1	0	0	2		0	0	1	6	1	0	8.0	.875	SS-1

Joe Gallagher

GALLAGHER, JOSEPH EMMETT (Muscles)
B. Mar. 7, 1914, Buffalo, N. Y.
BR TR 6′2″ 210 lbs.

Year	Team	Games	BA	SA	AB	H	2B	3B	HR	HR%	R	RBI	BB	SO	SB	Pinch Hit AB	Pinch Hit H	PO	A	E	DP	TC/G	FA	G by Pos
1939	2 teams	NY A (14G –.244) STL A (71G –.282)																						
″	total	85	.277	.459	307	85	17	3	11	3.6	49	49	20	50	1	5	2	161	9	9	1	2.3	.950	OF-79
1940	2 teams	STL A (23G –.271) BKN N (57G –.264)																						
″	total	80	.267	.422	180	48	9	2	5	2.8	24	24	6	26	3	42	12	58	2	3	1	1.4	.952	OF-46
2 yrs.		165	.273	.446	487	133	26	5	16	3.3	73	73	26	76	4	47	14	219	11	12	2	1.9	.950	OF-125

John Gallagher

GALLAGHER, JOHN CARROLL
B. Feb. 18, 1892, Pittsburgh, Pa. D. Mar. 30, 1952, Norfolk, Va.
BR TR 5′10½″ 156 lbs.

Year	Team	Games	BA	SA	AB	H	2B	3B	HR	HR%	R	RBI	BB	SO	SB	Pinch Hit AB	Pinch Hit H	PO	A	E	DP	TC/G	FA	G by Pos
1915	BAL F	40	.198	.230	126	25	4	0	0	0.0	11	4	5		1	0	0	51	100	11	10	3.8	.932	2B-37, SS-5, 3B-1

Shorty Gallagher

GALLAGHER, CHARLES WILLIAM (Charlie)
B. Apr. 30, 1872, Detroit, Mich. D. June 23, 1924, Detroit, Mich.

Year	Team	Games	BA	SA	AB	H	2B	3B	HR	HR%	R	RBI	BB	SO	SB	Pinch Hit AB	Pinch Hit H	PO	A	E	DP	TC/G	FA	G by Pos
1901	CLE A	2	.000	.000	4	0	0	0	0	0.0	0	0	0		0	0	0	2	0	1	0	1.5	.667	OF-2

Stan Galle

GALLE, STANLEY JOSEPH
Born Stanley Joseph Galazewski.
B. Feb. 7, 1919, Milwaukee, Wis.
BR TR 5′7″ 165 lbs.

Year	Team	Games	BA	SA	AB	H	2B	3B	HR	HR%	R	RBI	BB	SO	SB	Pinch Hit AB	Pinch Hit H	PO	A	E	DP	TC/G	FA	G by Pos
1942	WAS A	13	.111	.111	18	2	0	0	0	0.0	3	1	1	0	0	10	2	3	3	1	0	2.3	.857	3B-3

Mike Gallego

GALLEGO, MICHAEL ANTHONY
B. Oct. 31, 1960, Whittier, Calif.
BR TR 5′8″ 160 lbs.

Year	Team	Games	BA	SA	AB	H	2B	3B	HR	HR%	R	RBI	BB	SO	SB	Pinch Hit AB	Pinch Hit H	PO	A	E	DP	TC/G	FA	G by Pos
1985	OAK A	76	.208	.338	77	16	5	1	1	1.3	13	9	12	14	1	2	0	57	94	1	25	2.0	.993	2B-42, SS-21, 3B-12
1986		20	.270	.324	37	10	2	0	0	0.0	2	4	1	6	0	0	0	24	51	1	6	3.5	.987	2B-19, 3B-2, SS-1
1987		72	.250	.347	124	31	6	0	2	1.6	18	14	12	21	0	4	1	75	122	8	29	2.8	.961	2B-31, 3B-24, SS-17
1988		129	.209	.260	277	58	8	0	2	0.7	38	20	34	53	2	3	0	155	254	8	49	3.0	.981	2B-83, SS-42, 3B-16
1989		133	.252	.328	357	90	14	2	3	0.8	45	30	35	43	7	2	0	211	363	19	86	4.3	.968	SS-94, 2B-41, 3B-3, DH-1
1990		140	.206	.272	389	80	13	2	3	0.8	36	34	35	50	5	2	1	207	379	13	78	4.0	.978	2B-83, SS-38, 3B-27, OF-1, DH-1
1991		159	.247	.369	482	119	15	4	12	2.5	67	49	67	84	6	0	0	283	446	12	90	3.9	.984	2B-135, SS-55
1992	NY A	53	.254	.358	173	44	7	1	3	1.7	24	14	20	22	0	0	0	112	153	6	41	5.0	.978	2B-40, SS-14
1993		119	.283	.412	403	114	20	1	10	2.5	63	54	50	65	3	1	0	169	368	13	76	4.1	.976	SS-55, 2B-52, 3B-27, DH-1
1994		89	.239	.359	306	73	17	1	6	2.0	39	41	38	46	0	0	0	141	311	11	69	4.7	.976	SS-72, 2B-26
1995	OAK A	43	.233	.233	120	28	0	0	0	0.0	11	8	9	24	0	1	1	46	90	5	15	3.2	.965	2B-18, SS-14, 3B-12
11 yrs.		1033	.242	.335	2745	663	107	12	42	1.5	356	277	313	428	24	15	3	1480	2631	97	564	3.8	.977	2B-570, SS-423, 3B-123, DH-3, OF-1
LEAGUE CHAMPIONSHIP SERIES																								
1988	OAK A	4	.083	.083	12	1	0	0	0	0.0	1	0	0	3	0	0	0	7	6	0	4	3.3	1.000	2B-4
1989		4	.273	.364	11	3	1	0	0	0.0	3	1	0	2	0	0	0	6	14	0	2	5.0	1.000	SS-2, 2B-2
1990		4	.400	.500	10	4	1	0	0	0.0	1	2	1	1	0	0	0	8	9	0	2	3.4	1.000	SS-3, 2B-2
3 yrs.		12	.242	.303	33	8	2	0	0	0.0	5	3	1	6	0	0	0	21	29	0	8	3.8	1.000	2B-8, SS-5
WORLD SERIES																								
1988	OAK A	1	—	—	0	0	0	0	0	—	0	0	0	0	0	0	0	0	0	0	0	0.0	.000	2B-1
1989		2	.000	.000	1	0	0	0	0	0.0	0	0	0	0	0	1	0	0	0	0	0	0.0		3B-1, 2B-1
1990		4	.091	.091	11	1	0	0	0	0.0	0	1	1	3	1	0	0	7	10	1	3	4.5	.944	SS-4
3 yrs.		7	.083	.083	12	1	0	0	0	0.0	0	1	1	3	1	1	0	7	10	1	3	2.6	.944	SS-4, 2B-2, 3B-1

John Galligan

GALLIGAN, JOHN T.
B. 1868, Easton, Pa. D. July 17, 1906, New York, N. Y.
5′10″ 160 lbs.

Year	Team	Games	BA	SA	AB	H	2B	3B	HR	HR%	R	RBI	BB	SO	SB	Pinch Hit AB	Pinch Hit H	PO	A	E	DP	TC/G	FA	G by Pos
1889	LOU AA	31	.167	.200	120	20	0	2	0	0.0	6	7	6	17	1	0	0	58	7	6	1	2.3	.915	OF-31

Bad News Galloway

GALLOWAY, JAMES CATO
B. Sept. 16, 1887, Iredell, Tex. D. May 3, 1950, Fort Worth, Tex.
BB TR 6′3″ 187 lbs.

Year	Team	Games	BA	SA	AB	H	2B	3B	HR	HR%	R	RBI	BB	SO	SB	Pinch Hit AB	Pinch Hit H	PO	A	E	DP	TC/G	FA	G by Pos
1912	STL N	21	.185	.222	54	10	2	0	0	0.0	4	4	5	8	2	3	0	27	46	2	5	4.4	.973	2B-16, SS-1

Chick Galloway

GALLOWAY, CLARENCE EDWARD
B. Aug. 4, 1896, Clinton, S. C. D. Nov. 7, 1969, Clinton, S. C.
BR TR 5′8″ 160 lbs.

Year	Team	Games	BA	SA	AB	H	2B	3B	HR	HR%	R	RBI	BB	SO	SB	Pinch Hit AB	Pinch Hit H	PO	A	E	DP	TC/G	FA	G by Pos
1919	PHI A	17	.143	.143	63	9	0	0	0	0.0	2	4	1	8	0	0	0	45	49	3	11	5.7	.969	SS-17
1920		98	.201	.252	298	60	9	3	0	0.0	28	18	22	22	2	6	0	200	265	35	29	5.5	.930	SS-84, 2B-4, 3B-3
1921		131	.265	.366	465	123	28	5	3	0.6	42	47	29	43	12	0	0	226	355	48	52	4.8	.924	SS-110, 3B-20, 2B-1
1922		155	.324	.433	571	185	26	9	6	1.1	83	69	39	38	10	0	0	321	493	41	76	5.5	.952	SS-155
1923		134	.278	.361	504	140	18	9	2	0.4	64	62	37	30	12	0	0	285	408	41	73	5.5	.944	SS-134
1924		129	.276	.341	464	128	16	4	2	0.4	41	48	23	23	11	0	0	285	389	34	71	5.5	.952	SS-129
1925		149	.241	.299	481	116	11	4	3	0.6	52	71	59	28	16	1	0	296	431	35	89	5.1	.954	SS-148
1926		133	.240	.301	408	98	13	6	0	0.0	37	49	31	20	8	0	0	274	315	41	49	4.7	.935	SS-133
1927		77	.265	.365	181	48	10	4	0	0.0	15	22	18	9	1	9	6	119	157	15	20	4.3	.948	SS-61, 3B-7
1928	DET A	53	.264	.345	148	39	5	2	1	0.7	17	17	15	3	7	4	2	76	92	11	14	4.0	.939	SS-22, 3B-21, OF-1, 1B-1
10 yrs.		1076	.264	.342	3583	946	136	46	17	0.5	381	407	274	224	79	20	8	2127	2954	304	484	5.1	.944	SS-993, 3B-51, 2B-5, OF-1, 1B-1

Jim Galvin

GALVIN, JAMES JOSEPH
B. Aug. 11, 1907, Somerville, Mass. D. Sept. 30, 1969, Marietta, Ga.
BR TR 5′11½″ 198 lbs.

Year	Team	Games	BA	SA	AB	H	2B	3B	HR	HR%	R	RBI	BB	SO	SB	Pinch Hit AB	Pinch Hit H	PO	A	E	DP	TC/G	FA	G by Pos
1930	BOS A	2	.000	.000	2	0	0	0	0	0.0	0	0	0	0	0	2	0	0	0	0	0	0.0	—	

Pud Galvin

GALVIN, JAMES FRANCIS (Gentle Jeems, The Little Steam Engine) BR TR 5′ 8″ 190 lbs.
B. Dec. 25, 1856, St. Louis, Mo. D. Mar. 7, 1902, Pittsburgh, Pa.
Manager 1885.
Hall of Fame 1965.

Year	Team		Games	BA	SA	AB	H	2B	3B	HR	HR%	R	RBI	BB	SO	SB	Pinch Hit AB	Pinch Hit H	PO	A	E	DP	TC/G	FA	G by Pos
1879	BUF	N	67	.249	.336	265	66	11	6	0	0.0	34	27	1	**56**		0	0	36	143	27	8	3.1	.869	P-66, SS-1
1880			66	.212	.266	241	51	9	2	0	0.0	25	12	5	**57**		0	0	44	100	21	1	2.1	.873	P-58, OF-19
1881			62	.212	.297	236	50	12	4	0	0.0	19	21	3	**70**		0	0	52	126	22	7	2.8	.890	P-56, OF-14, SS-1
1882			54	.214	.286	206	44	7	4	0	0.0	21		2	49		0	0	22	87	9	1	2.0	.924	P-52, OF-6
1883			80	.220	.276	322	71	11	2	1	0.3	41		3	**79**		0	0	45	130	13	4	2.2	.931	P-76, OF-8
1884			72	.179	.208	274	49	6	1	0	0.0	34		2	80		0	0	32	154	7	3	2.6	.964	P-72, OF-1
1885	2 teams		BUF N (33G –.189) PIT AA (11G –.105)																						
″	total		44	.169	.237	160	27	4	2	1	0.6	16	10	1	27		0	0	21	98	17	3	3.0	.875	P-44, OF-1
1886	PIT	AA	50	.253	.309	194	49	7	2	0	0.0	24		3			0	0	22	101	8	3	2.6	.939	P-50
1887	PIT	N	49	.212	.311	193	41	7	3	2	1.0	10	22	2	47	5	0	0	22	123	11	2	3.1	.929	P-49, OF-1
1888			50	.143	.177	175	25	1	1	1	0.6	6	3	1	51	4	0	0	23	113	10	2	2.9	.932	P-50, OF-1
1889			41	.187	.260	150	28	7	2	0	0.0	15	16	3	46	2	0	0	20	72	11	6	2.5	.893	P-41
1890	PIT	P	26	.206	.247	97	20	2	1	0	0.0	8	12	6	20	1	0	0	22	71	7	1	3.8	.930	P-26
1891	PIT	N	33	.165	.165	109	18	0	0	0	0.0	11	7	3	29	0	0	0	20	52	8	1	2.4	.900	P-33
1892	2 teams		PIT N (12G –.122) STL N (12G –.051)																						
″	total		24	.087	.100	80	7	1	0	0	0.0	6	5	3	19	0	0	0	7	35	7	1	2.0	.857	P-24
14 yrs.			718	.202	.261	2702	546	85	30	5	0.2	270	135	38	630	12	0	0	388	1405	178	43	2.6	.910	P-697, OF-51, SS-2

John Gamble

GAMBLE, JOHN ROBERT, JR. BR TR 5′10″ 165 lbs.
B. Feb. 10, 1948, Reno, Nev.

Year	Team		Games	BA	SA	AB	H	2B	3B	HR	HR%	R	RBI	BB	SO	SB	Pinch Hit AB	Pinch Hit H	PO	A	E	DP	TC/G	FA	G by Pos
1972	DET	A	6	.000	.000	3	0	0	0	0	0.0	0	0	0	0	0	1	0	3	2	0	0	5.0	1.000	SS-1
1973			7	—	—	0	0	0	0	0	—	1	0	0	0	0	0	0	0	0	0	0	0.0	—	
2 yrs.			13	.000	.000	3	0	0	0	0	0.0	1	0	0	0	0	1	0	3	2	0	0	5.0	1.000	SS-1

Lee Gamble

GAMBLE, LEE JESSE BL TR 6′ 1″ 170 lbs.
B. June 28, 1910, Renovo, Pa. D. Oct. 5, 1994, Punxsutawney, Pa.

Year	Team		Games	BA	SA	AB	H	2B	3B	HR	HR%	R	RBI	BB	SO	SB	Pinch Hit AB	Pinch Hit H	PO	A	E	DP	TC/G	FA	G by Pos
1935	CIN	N	2	.500	.750	4	2	1	0	0	0.0	2	2	1	0	1	0	0	3	0	0	0	1.5	1.000	OF-2
1938			53	.320	.387	75	24	3	1	0	0.0	13	5	0	6	0	37	11	20	0	0	0	2.2	1.000	OF-9
1939			72	.267	.317	221	59	7	2	0	0.0	24	14	9	14	5	11	1	87	5	1	0	1.7	.989	OF-56
1940			38	.143	.167	42	6	1	0	0	0.0	12	0	0	1	0	9	2	18	1	0	0	1.9	1.000	OF-10
4 yrs.			165	.266	.319	342	91	12	3	0	0.0	51	21	10	21	6	57	14	128	6	1	0	1.8	.993	OF-77
WORLD SERIES																									
1939	CIN	N	1	.000	.000	1	0	0	0	0	0.0	0	0	0	1	0	1	0	0	0	0	0	0.0	—	

Oscar Gamble

GAMBLE, OSCAR CHARLES BL TR 5′11″ 160 lbs.
B. Dec. 20, 1949, Ramer, Ala.

Year	Team		Games	BA	SA	AB	H	2B	3B	HR	HR%	R	RBI	BB	SO	SB	Pinch Hit AB	Pinch Hit H	PO	A	E	DP	TC/G	FA	G by Pos
1969	CHI	N	24	.225	.310	71	16	1	1	1	1.4	6	5	10	12	0	0	0	41	1	4	0	1.9	.913	OF-24
1970	PHI	N	88	.262	.345	275	72	12	4	1	0.4	31	19	27	37	5	14	4	148	4	7	0	2.1	.956	OF-74
1971			92	.221	.332	280	62	11	1	6	2.1	24	23	21	35	5	13	4	125	4	4	1	1.7	.970	OF-80
1972			74	.237	.326	135	32	5	2	1	0.7	17	13	19	16	0	30	9	54	2	0	1	1.6	1.000	OF-35, 1B-1
1973	CLE	A	113	.267	.464	390	104	11	3	20	5.1	56	44	34	37	3	8	2	67	1	2	0	0.7	.971	DH-70, OF-37
1974			135	.291	.469	454	132	16	4	19	4.2	74	59	48	51	5	7	0	19	1	0	0	0.2	1.000	DH-115, OF-13
1975			121	.261	.454	348	91	16	3	15	4.3	60	45	53	39	11	11	2	146	8	2	2	1.4	.987	OF-82, DH-29
1976	NY	A	110	.232	.426	340	79	13	1	17	5.0	43	57	38	38	5	16	6	199	10	4	3	2.0	.981	OF-104, DH-1
1977	CHI	A	137	.297	.588	408	121	22	2	31	**7.6**	75	83	54	54	1	18	8	73	1	1	0	0.6	.987	DH-79, OF-49
1978	SD	N	126	.275	.387	375	103	15	3	7	1.9	46	47	51	45	1	13	6	172	12	4	3	1.8	.979	OF-107
1979	2 teams		TEX A (64G –.335) NY A (36G –.389)																						
″	total		100	.358	.609	274	98	10	1	19	6.9	48	64	50	28	2	18	5	88	5	3	4	1.1	.969	OF-48, DH-43
1980	NY	A	78	.278	.567	194	54	10	2	14	7.2	40	50	28	21	2	17	4	65	2	0	1	1.0	1.000	OF-49, DH-20
1981			80	.238	.439	189	45	8	0	10	5.3	24	27	35	23	0	15	5	77	0	0	0	1.0	1.000	OF-43, DH-33
1982			108	.272	.522	316	86	21	2	18	5.7	49	57	58	47	6	18	2	59	6	0	1	0.6	1.000	DH-74, OF-29
1983			74	.261	.456	180	47	10	2	7	3.9	26	26	25	23	0	20	6	64	1	4	1	1.3	.942	OF-32, DH-21
1984			54	.184	.440	125	23	2	0	10	8.0	17	27	25	18	1	13	1	15	1	0	0	0.4	1.000	DH-26, OF-12
1985	CHI	A	70	.203	.318	148	30	5	0	4	2.7	20	20	34	22	0	24	3	0	0	0	0	0.0	.000	DH-48
17 yrs.			1584	.265	.454	4502	1195	188	31	200	4.4	656	666	610	546	47	255	67	1412	59	35	17	1.1	.977	OF-818, DH-559, 1B-1
DIVISIONAL PLAYOFF SERIES																									
1981	NY	A	4	.556	1.333	9	5	1	0	2	22.2	2	3	1	2	0	1	1	0	0	0	0	0.0	.000	DH-4
LEAGUE CHAMPIONSHIP SERIES																									
1976	NY	A	3	.250	.375	8	2	1	0	0	0.0	1	1	1	1	0	1	1	4	0	2	0	2.0	.667	OF-3
1980			2	.200	.200	5	1	0	0	0	0.0	1	0	1	1	0	1	1	1	0	0	0	0.5	1.000	OF-1, DH-1
1981			3	.167	.167	6	1	0	0	0	0.0	2	1	5	3	0	0	0	4	0	0	0	1.3	1.000	DH-2, OF-1
3 yrs.			8	.211	.263	19	4	1	0	0	0.0	4	2	7	5	0	2	2	9	0	2	0	1.4	.818	OF-5, DH-3
WORLD SERIES																									
1976	NY	A	3	.125	.125	8	1	0	0	0	0.0	0	1	0	0	0	1	0	3	0	0	0	1.5	1.000	OF-2
1981			3	.333	.333	6	2	0	0	0	0.0	1	1	1	0	0	0	0	4	0	0	0	2.0	1.000	OF-2
2 yrs.			6	.214	.214	14	3	0	0	0	0.0	1	2	1	0	0	1	0	7	0	0	0	1.8	1.000	OF-4

Daff Gammons

GAMMONS, JOHN ASHLEY BR TR 5′11″ 170 lbs.
B. Mar. 17, 1876, New Bedford, Mass. D. Sept. 24, 1963, East Greenwich, R. I.

Year	Team		Games	BA	SA	AB	H	2B	3B	HR	HR%	R	RBI	BB	SO	SB	Pinch Hit AB	Pinch Hit H	PO	A	E	DP	TC/G	FA	G by Pos
1901	BOS	N	28	.194	.215	93	18	0	1	0	0.0	10	10	3		5	1	0	44	8	11	1	2.4	.825	OF-23, 2B-2, 3B-1

Chick Gandil

GANDIL, ARNOLD BR TR 6′ 1½″ 190 lbs.
B. Jan. 19, 1887, St. Paul, Minn. D. Dec. 13, 1970, Calistoga, Calif.

Year	Team		Games	BA	SA	AB	H	2B	3B	HR	HR%	R	RBI	BB	SO	SB	Pinch Hit AB	Pinch Hit H	PO	A	E	DP	TC/G	FA	G by Pos
1910	CHI	A	77	.193	.262	275	53	7	3	2	0.7	21	21	24		12	0	0	857	57	10	34	12.2	.989	1B-74, OF-2
1912	WAS	A	117	.305	.431	443	135	20	15	2	0.5	59	81	27		21	0	0	1106	68	12	49	10.1	.990	1B-117
1913			148	.318	.398	550	175	25	8	1	0.2	61	72	36	33	22	3	0	1436	103	15	89	10.7	.990	1B-145
1914			145	.259	.359	526	136	24	10	3	0.6	48	75	44	44	30	0	0	1284	143	13	84	9.9	.991	1B-145
1915			136	.291	.406	485	141	20	15	2	0.4	53	64	29	33	20	2	1	1237	77	19	65	9.9	.986	1B-134
1916	CLE	A	146	.259	.341	533	138	26	9	0	0.0	51	72	36	48	13	1	1	1557	105	9	84	11.5	.995	1B-145
1917	CHI	A	149	.273	.315	553	151	9	7	0	0.0	53	57	30	36	16	0	0	1405	77	8	84	10.0	.995	1B-149

Chick Gandil *continued*

Year	Team	Games	BA	SA	AB	H	2B	3B	HR	HR%	R	RBI	BB	SO	SB	Pinch Hit AB	Pinch Hit H	PO	A	E	DP	TC/G	FA	G by Pos
1918		114	.271	.330	439	119	18	4	0	0.0	49	55	27	19	9	0	0	1123	64	10	70	10.5	.992	1B-114
1919		115	.290	.383	441	128	24	7	1	0.2	54	60	20	20	10	0	0	1116	60	3	71	10.3	.997	1B-115
9 yrs.		1147	.277	.362	4245	1176	173	78	11	0.3	449	557	273	233	153	6	2	11121	754	99	630	10.5	.992	1B-1138, OF-2
WORLD SERIES																								
1917	CHI A	6	.261	.304	23	6	1	0	0	0.0	1	5	0	2	1	0	0	67	4	1	6	12.0	.986	1B-6
1919		8	.233	.300	30	7	0	1	0	0.0	1	5	1	3	1	0	0	79	2	1	6	10.3	.988	1B-8
2 yrs.		14	.245	.302	53	13	1	1	0	0.0	2	10	1	5	2	0	0	146	6	2	12	11.0	.987	1B-14

Bob Gandy

GANDY, ROBERT BRINKLEY (String)
B. Aug. 25, 1893, Jacksonville, Fla. D. June 19, 1945, Jacksonville, Fla.
BL TR 6′ 3″ 180 lbs.

Year	Team	Games	BA	SA	AB	H	2B	3B	HR	HR%	R	RBI	BB	SO	SB	Pinch Hit AB	Pinch Hit H	PO	A	E	DP	TC/G	FA	G by Pos
1916	PHI N	1	.000	.000	2	0	0	0	0	0.0	0	0	0	1	0	0	0	3	0	0	0	3.0	1.000	OF-1

Bob Ganley

GANLEY, ROBERT STEPHEN
B. Apr. 23, 1875, Lowell, Mass. D. Oct. 9, 1945, Lowell, Mass.
BL TL 5′ 7″ 156 lbs.

Year	Team	Games	BA	SA	AB	H	2B	3B	HR	HR%	R	RBI	BB	SO	SB	Pinch Hit AB	Pinch Hit H	PO	A	E	DP	TC/G	FA	G by Pos
1905	PIT N	32	.315	.354	127	40	1	2	0	0.0	12	7	8		3	0	0	46	3	0	0	1.5	1.000	OF-32
1906		137	.258	.295	511	132	7	6	0	0.0	63	31	41		19	3	1	207	16	8	5	1.7	.965	OF-134
1907	WAS A	154	.276	.314	605	167	10	5	1	0.2	73	35	54		40	0	0	276	23	19	5	2.1	.940	OF-154
1908		150	.239	.311	549	131	19	9	1	0.2	61	36	45		30	0	0	280	13	11	1	2.0	.964	OF-150
1909	2 teams	WAS A (19G –.254)	PHI A (80G –.197)																					
″	total	99	.208	.240	337	70	7	2	0	0.0	37	14	29		20	4	0	214	9	4	2	2.4	.982	OF-94
5 yrs.		572	.254	.300	2129	540	44	24	2	0.1	246	123	177		112	7	1	1023	64	42	13	2.0	.963	OF-564

Bill Gannon

GANNON, WILLIAM G.
B. 1876, New Haven, Conn. D. Apr. 26, 1927, Ft. Worth, Tex.
5′ 9″ 170 lbs.

Year	Team	Games	BA	SA	AB	H	2B	3B	HR	HR%	R	RBI	BB	SO	SB	Pinch Hit AB	Pinch Hit H	PO	A	E	DP	TC/G	FA	G by Pos
1901	CHI N	15	.148	.148	61	9	0	0	0	0.0	2	0	1		5	0	0	16	2	0	0	1.2	1.000	OF-15

Ron Gant

GANT, RONALD EDWIN
B. Mar. 2, 1965, Victoria, Tex.
BR TR 6′ 200 lbs.

Year	Team	Games	BA	SA	AB	H	2B	3B	HR	HR%	R	RBI	BB	SO	SB	Pinch Hit AB	Pinch Hit H	PO	A	E	DP	TC/G	FA	G by Pos
1987	ATL N	21	.265	.386	83	22	4	0	2	2.4	9	9	1	11	4	1	0	45	59	3	17	5.3	.972	2B-20
1988		146	.259	.439	563	146	28	8	19	3.4	85	60	46	118	19	2	0	316	417	31	88	5.3	.959	2B-122, 3B-22
1989		75	.177	.335	260	46	8	3	9	3.5	26	25	20	63	9	8	1	70	103	17	8	2.8	.911	3B-53, OF-14
1990		152	.303	.539	575	174	34	3	32	5.6	107	84	50	86	33	10	2	357	7	8	2	2.5	.978	OF-146
1991		154	.251	.496	561	141	35	3	32	5.7	101	105	71	104	34	6	0	338	7	6	1	2.4	.983	OF-148
1992		153	.259	.415	544	141	22	6	17	3.1	74	80	45	101	32	9	2	277	5	4	1	1.9	.986	OF-147
1993		157	.274	.510	606	166	27	4	36	5.9	113	117	67	117	26	1	0	271	5	11	1	1.9	.962	OF-155
1995	CIN N	119	.276	.554	410	113	19	4	29	7.1	79	88	74	108	23	1	0	191	7	3	0	1.7	.985	OF-117
8 yrs.		977	.263	.476	3602	949	177	31	176	4.9	594	568	374	708	180	38	5	1865	610	83	118	2.7	.968	OF-727, 2B-142, 3B-75
DIVISIONAL PLAYOFF SERIES																								
1995	CIN N	3	.231	.462	13	3	0	0	1	7.7	3	2	0	3	0	0	0	8	1	0	0	3.0	1.000	OF-3
LEAGUE CHAMPIONSHIP SERIES																								
1991	ATL N	7	.259	.407	27	7	1	0	1	3.7	4	3	2	4	7	0	0	15	2	0	0	2.4	1.000	OF-7
1992		7	.182	.455	22	4	0	0	2	9.1	5	6	4	4	1	0	0	16	0	0	0	2.3	1.000	OF-7
1993		6	.185	.296	27	5	3	0	0	0.0	4	3	2	9	0	0	0	10	1	1	0	2.0	.917	OF-6
1995	CIN N	4	.188	.188	16	3	0	0	0	0.0	1	1	0	3	0	0	0	9	0	0	0	2.3	1.000	OF-4
4 yrs.		24	.207	.348	92 **7th**	19	4	0	3	3.3	14 **7th**	13 **9th**	8	20 **4th**	8 **4th**	0	0	50	3	1	0	2.3	.981	OF-24
WORLD SERIES																								
1991	ATL N	7	.267	.333	30	8	0	1	0	0.0	3	4	2	3	1	0	0	19	0	0	0	2.7	1.000	OF-7
1992		4	.125	.250	8	1	1	0	0	0.0	2	0	1	2	2	0	0	3	1	0	0	1.3	1.000	OF-3
2 yrs.		11	.237	.316	38	9	1	1	0	0.0	5	4	3	5	3	0	0	22	1	0	0	2.3	1.000	OF-10

Joe Gantenbein

GANTENBEIN, JOSEPH STEPHEN (Sep)
B. Aug. 25, 1916, San Francisco, Calif.
BL TR 5′ 9″ 168 lbs.

Year	Team	Games	BA	SA	AB	H	2B	3B	HR	HR%	R	RBI	BB	SO	SB	Pinch Hit AB	Pinch Hit H	PO	A	E	DP	TC/G	FA	G by Pos
1939	PHI A	111	.290	.388	348	101	14	4	4	1.1	47	36	32	22	1	16	6	178	203	23	30	4.3	.943	2B-76, 3B-14, SS-5
1940		75	.239	.350	197	47	6	2	4	2.0	21	23	11	21	1	18	4	57	78	8	11	2.6	.944	3B-45, 1B-6, SS-3, OF-1
2 yrs.		186	.272	.374	545	148	20	6	8	1.5	68	59	43	43	2	34	10	235	281	31	41	3.6	.943	2B-76, 3B-59, SS-8, 1B-6, OF-1

Jim Gantner

GANTNER, JAMES ELMER
B. Jan. 5, 1953, Fond du Lac, Wis.
BL TR 6′ 180 lbs.

Year	Team	Games	BA	SA	AB	H	2B	3B	HR	HR%	R	RBI	BB	SO	SB	Pinch Hit AB	Pinch Hit H	PO	A	E	DP	TC/G	FA	G by Pos
1976	MIL A	26	.246	.261	69	17	1	0	0	0.0	6	7	6	11	1	1	0	17	37	1	3	2.1	.982	3B-24, DH-2
1977		14	.298	.383	47	14	1	0	1	2.1	4	2	2	5	2	1	1	8	29	4	3	2.9	.902	3B-14
1978		43	.216	.258	97	21	1	0	1	1.0	14	8	5	10	2	4	1	46	82	5	13	3.5	.962	2B-21, 3B-15, SS-1, 1B-1
1979		70	.284	.389	208	59	10	3	2	1.0	29	22	16	17	3	0	0	80	161	7	26	3.6	.972	3B-42, 2B-22, SS-3, P-1
1980		132	.282	.376	415	117	21	3	4	1.0	47	40	30	29	11	2	0	159	335	15	70	3.7	.971	3B-69, 2B-66, SS-1
1981		107	.267	.330	352	94	14	1	2	0.6	35	33	29	29	3	3	0	251	352	10	95	5.7	.984	2B-107
1982		132	.295	.369	447	132	17	2	4	0.9	48	43	26	36	6	4	1	307	398	13	104	5.5	.982	2B-131
1983		161	.282	.401	603	170	23	8	11	1.8	85	74	38	46	5	3	0	374	512	14	128	5.7	.984	2B-158
1984		153	.282	.344	613	173	27	1	3	0.5	61	56	30	51	6	2	1	362	469	13	111	5.5	.985	2B-153
1985		143	.254	.327	523	133	15	4	5	1.0	63	44	33	42	11	1	1	278	436	11	94	4.9	.985	2B-124, 3B-24, SS-1
1986		139	.274	.370	497	136	25	1	7	1.4	58	38	26	50	13	2	0	309	353	10	87	4.8	.985	2B-135, 3B-3, DH-1, SS-1
1987		81	.272	.370	265	72	14	0	4	1.5	37	30	19	22	6	3	1	119	193	6	44	3.3	.981	2B-57, 3B-38, DH-1
1988		155	.276	.336	539	149	28	2	0	0.0	67	47	34	50	20	2	1	325	430	11	92	4.9	.986	2B-154, 3B-1
1989		116	.274	.333	409	112	18	3	0	0.0	51	34	21	33	20	1	0	241	362	8	88	5.3	.987	2B-114, DH-2
1990		88	.263	.319	323	85	8	5	0	0.0	36	25	29	19	18	0	0	167	240	9	56	4.7	.978	2B-80, 3B-9
1991		140	.283	.361	526	149	27	4	2	0.4	63	47	27	34	4	4	1	160	345	12	46	3.5	.977	3B-90, 2B-59
1992		101	.246	.313	256	63	12	1	1	0.4	22	18	12	17	6	6	1	155	208	3	45	3.6	.992	2B-68, 3B-31, 1B-2, DH-2
17 yrs.		1801	.274	.351	6189	1696	262	38	47	0.8	726	568	383	501	137	39	9	3358	4942	152	1105	4.6	.982	2B-1449, 3B-360, DH-8, SS-7, 1B-3, P-1
DIVISIONAL PLAYOFF SERIES																								
1981	MIL A	4	.143	.214	14	2	1	0	0	0.0	1	0	0	2	0	0	0	3	15	2	0	5.0	.900	2B-4
LEAGUE CHAMPIONSHIP SERIES																								
1982	MIL A	5	.188	.188	16	3	0	0	0	0.0	1	2	1	1	0	0	0	12	8	0	4	4.0	1.000	2B-5

Jim Gantner *continued*

Year	Team		Games	BA	SA	AB	H	2B	3B	HR	HR%	R	RBI	BB	SO	SB	Pinch Hit AB	Pinch Hit H	PO	A	E	DP	TC/G	FA	G by Pos
WORLD SERIES																									
1982	MIL	A	7	.333	.583	24	8	4	1	0	0.0	5	4	1	1	0	0	0	9	33	5	2	6.7	.894	2B-7

Babe Ganzel

GANZEL, FOSTER PIRIE BR TR 5′10½″ 172 lbs.
Son of Charlie Ganzel.
B. May 22, 1901, Malden, Mass. D. Feb. 6, 1978, Jacksonville, Fla.

Year	Team		Games	BA	SA	AB	H	2B	3B	HR	HR%	R	RBI	BB	SO	SB	Pinch Hit AB	Pinch Hit H	PO	A	E	DP	TC/G	FA	G by Pos
1927	WAS	A	13	.438	.667	48	21	4	2	1	2.1	7	13	7	3	0	0	0	33	1	2	0	2.8	.944	OF-13
1928			10	.077	.115	26	2	1	0	0	0.0	2	4	1	4	0	3	0	10	1	0	0	1.6	1.000	OF-7
2 yrs.			23	.311	.473	74	23	5	2	1	1.4	9	17	8	7	0	3	0	43	2	2	0	2.3	.957	OF-20

Charlie Ganzel

GANZEL, CHARLES WILLIAM BR TR 6′ 1″ 188 lbs.
Brother of John Ganzel. Father of Babe Ganzel.
B. June 18, 1862, Waterford, Wis. D. Apr. 7, 1914, Quincy, Mass.

Year	Team		Games	BA	SA	AB	H	2B	3B	HR	HR%	R	RBI	BB	SO	SB	Pinch Hit AB	Pinch Hit H	PO	A	E	DP	TC/G	FA	G by Pos
1884	STP	U	7	.217	.217	23	5	0	0	0	0.0	2		0			0	0	36	7	2	0	6.4	.956	C-6, OF-1
1885	PHI	N	34	.168	.208	125	21	3	1	0	0.0	15		4	13		0	0	176	39	27	3	7.1	.888	C-33, OF-1
1886	2 teams		PHI N (1G –.000) DET N (57G –.272)																						
″	total		58	.269	.333	216	58	7	2	1	0.5	28	31	7	23		0	0	333	67	39	12	7.6	.911	C-46, OF-7, 1B-5
1887	DET	N	57	.260	.330	227	59	6	5	0	0.0	40	20	8	2	3	0	0	301	76	35	8	7.1	.915	C-51, OF-4, 1B-2, 3B-1
1888			95	.249	.316	386	96	13	5	1	0.3	45	46	14	15	12	0	0	288	241	52	24	6.1	.910	2B-49, C-28, 3B-9, OF-5, SS-3, 1B-1
1889	BOS	N	73	.265	.324	275	73	3	5	1	0.4	30	43	15	11	13	0	0	292	87	30	19	5.2	.927	C-39, OF-26, 1B-7, SS-6, 3B-1
1890			38	.270	.350	163	44	7	3	0	0.0	21	24	5	6	1	0	0	151	42	8	11	4.9	.960	C-22, OF-15, SS-3, 2B-1
1891			70	.259	.376	263	68	18	5	1	0.4	33	29	12	13	7	0	0	304	61	16	3	5.3	.958	C-59, OF-13
1892			54	.268	.343	198	53	9	3	0	0.0	25	25	18	12	7	0	0	218	50	18	1	5.3	.937	C-51, OF-2, 1B-1
1893			73	.267	.327	281	75	10	2	1	0.4	50	48	22	9	6	1	0	278	49	15	14	4.7	.956	C-40, OF-23, 1B-10
1894			70	.278	.383	266	74	7	6	3	1.1	51	56	19	6	1	1	0	257	58	29	11	4.8	.916	C-59, 1B-7, OF-3, SS-2, 2B-1
1895			80	.264	.318	277	73	2	5	1	0.4	38	52	24	6	1	1	0	358	74	17	10	5.6	.962	C-76, SS-2, 1B-2
1896			47	.263	.291	179	47	2	0	1	0.6	28	18	9	5	2	1	1	170	50	8	6	5.0	.965	C-41, 1B-3, SS-2
1897			30	.267	.362	105	28	4	3	0	0.0	15	14	4		2	2	0	113	27	9	2	5.1	.940	C-27, 1B-2
14 yrs.			786	.259	.330	2984	774	91	45	10	0.3	421	406	161	121	55	6	1	3275	928	305	124	5.6	.932	C-578, OF-100, 2B-51, 1B-40, SS-18, 3B-11

John Ganzel

GANZEL, JOHN HENRY BR TR 6′½″ 195 lbs.
Brother of Charlie Ganzel.
B. Apr. 7, 1874, Kalamazoo, Mich. D. Jan. 14, 1959, Orlando, Fla.
Manager 1908, 1915.

Year	Team		Games	BA	SA	AB	H	2B	3B	HR	HR%	R	RBI	BB	SO	SB	Pinch Hit AB	Pinch Hit H	PO	A	E	DP	TC/G	FA	G by Pos
1898	PIT	N	15	.133	.133	45	6	0	0	0	0.0	5	2	4		0	2	0	102	3	4	5	8.4	.963	1B-12, P-1
1900	CHI	N	78	.275	.394	284	78	14	4	4	1.4	29	32	10		5	0	0	817	34	17	40	11.1	.980	1B-78
1901	NY	N	138	.215	.262	526	113	13	3	2	0.4	42	66	20		6	0	0	1421	77	21	59	11.0	.986	1B-138
1903	NY	A	129	.277	.378	476	132	25	7	3	0.6	62	71	30		9	0	0	1385	94	18	68	11.6	.988	1B-129
1904			130	.260	.376	465	121	16	10	6	1.3	50	48	24		13	4	**2**	1254	96	18	53	10.7	.987	1B-118, 2B-9, SS-1
1907	CIN	N	145	.254	.363	531	135	20	**16**	2	0.4	61	64	29		9	2	0	1346	84	14	89	10.1	.990	1B-143
1908			112	.250	.351	388	97	16	10	1	0.3	32	53	19		6	5	1	1116	61	12	52	11.0	.990	1B-108
7 yrs.			747	.251	.346	2715	682	104	50	18	0.7	281	336	136		48	13	3	7441	449	104	366	10.8	.987	1B-726, 2B-9, SS-1, P-1

Joe Garagiola

GARAGIOLA, JOSEPH HENRY BL TR 6′ 190 lbs.
B. Feb. 12, 1926, St. Louis, Mo.

Year	Team		Games	BA	SA	AB	H	2B	3B	HR	HR%	R	RBI	BB	SO	SB	Pinch Hit AB	Pinch Hit H	PO	A	E	DP	TC/G	FA	G by Pos
1946	STL	N	74	.237	.308	211	50	4	1	3	1.4	21	22	23	25	0	4	2	260	25	3	6	4.1	.990	C-70
1947			77	.257	.415	183	47	10	2	5	2.7	20	25	40	14	0	4	1	281	23	4	2	4.2	.987	C-74
1948			24	.107	.232	56	6	1	0	2	3.6	9	7	12	9	0	1	0	83	14	1	1	4.3	.990	C-23
1949			81	.261	.357	241	63	14	0	3	1.2	25	26	31	19	0	2	1	332	35	6	1	4.7	.984	C-80
1950			34	.318	.477	88	28	6	1	2	2.3	8	20	10	7	0	4	0	99	8	0	2	3.6	1.000	C-30
1951	2 teams		STL N (27G –.194) PIT N (72G –.255)																						
″	total		99	.239	.423	284	68	11	4	11	3.9	33	44	41	27	4	12	0	336	36	4	6	4.5	.989	C-84
1952	PIT	N	118	.273	.410	344	94	15	4	8	2.3	35	54	50	24	0	12	4	418	63	11	9	4.7	.978	C-105
1953	2 teams		PIT N (27G –.233) CHI N (74G –.272)																						
″	total		101	.262	.365	301	79	14	4	3	1.0	30	35	31	34	1	13	3	378	44	5	2	4.7	.988	C-90
1954	2 teams		CHI N (63G –.281) NY N (5G –.273)																						
″	total		68	.280	.415	164	46	7	0	5	3.0	17	22	29	14	0	11	2	208	23	4	0	4.1	.983	C-58
9 yrs.			676	.257	.385	1872	481	82	16	42	2.2	198	255	267	173	5	63	13	2395	271	38	29	4.4	.986	C-614
WORLD SERIES																									
1946	STL	N	5	.316	.421	19	6	2	0	0	0.0	2	4	0	3	0	0	0	22	2	0	1	4.8	1.000	C-5

Bob Garbark

GARBARK, ROBERT MICHAEL BR TR 5′11″ 178 lbs.
Born Robert Michael Garbach.
Brother of Mike Garbark.
B. Nov. 13, 1909, Houston, Tex. D. Aug. 15, 1990, Meadville, Pa.

Year	Team		Games	BA	SA	AB	H	2B	3B	HR	HR%	R	RBI	BB	SO	SB	Pinch Hit AB	Pinch Hit H	PO	A	E	DP	TC/G	FA	G by Pos
1934	CLE	A	5	.000	.000	11	0	0	0	0	0.0	1	0	1	3	0	0	0	8	0	0	0	1.6	1.000	C-5
1935			6	.333	.389	18	6	1	0	0	0.0	4	4	5	1	0	0	0	33	3	0	0	6.0	1.000	C-6
1937	CHI	N	1	.000	.000	1	0	0	0	0	0.0	0	0	0	0	0	1	0	0	0	0	0	0.0	—	
1938			23	.259	.259	54	14	0	0	0	0.0	2	5	1	0	0	1	0	66	7	0	0	3.5	1.000	C-20, 1B-1
1939			24	.143	.143	21	3	0	0	0	0.0	1	0	0	3	0	2	0	22	3	0	0	1.2	1.000	C-21
1944	PHI	A	18	.261	.348	23	6	2	0	0	0.0	2	2	1	0	0	3	0	23	1	0	0	1.6	1.000	C-15
1945	BOS	A	68	.261	.291	199	52	6	0	0	0.0	21	17	18	10	0	1	0	249	31	2	9	4.2	.993	C-67
7 yrs.			145	.248	.275	327	81	9	0	0	0.0	31	28	26	17	0	8	0	401	45	2	9	3.3	.996	C-134, 1B-1

Mike Garbark

GARBARK, MICHAEL NATHANIEL BR TR 6′ 200 lbs.
Born Michael Nathaniel Garbach.
Brother of Bob Garbark.
B. Feb. 2, 1916, Houston, Tex. D. Aug. 31, 1994, Charlotte, N. C.

Year	Team	Games	BA	SA	AB	H	2B	3B	HR	HR%	R	RBI	BB	SO	SB	Pinch Hit AB	Pinch Hit H	PO	A	E	DP	TC/G	FA	G by Pos
1944	NY A	89	.261	.328	299	78	9	4	1	0.3	23	33	25	27	0	4	1	372	47	5	9	5.0	.988	C-85
1945		60	.216	.295	176	38	5	3	1	0.6	23	26	23	12	0	1	0	202	41	7	10	4.2	.972	C-59
2 yrs.		149	.244	.316	475	116	14	7	2	0.4	46	59	48	39	0	5	1	574	88	12	19	4.7	.982	C-144

Barbaro Garbey

GARBEY, BARBARO BR TR 5′10″ 170 lbs.
Born Barbaro Garbey (Garbey).
B. Dec. 4, 1956, Santiago, Cuba.

Year	Team	Games	BA	SA	AB	H	2B	3B	HR	HR%	R	RBI	BB	SO	SB	Pinch Hit AB	Pinch Hit H	PO	A	E	DP	TC/G	FA	G by Pos
1984	DET A	110	.287	.391	327	94	17	1	5	1.5	45	52	17	35	6	25	8	411	58	12	53	4.1	.975	1B-65, 3B-20, DH-18, OF-10, 2B-3
1985		86	.257	.380	237	61	9	1	6	2.5	27	29	15	37	3	20	3	228	20	3	24	3.0	.988	1B-37, OF-24, DH-21, 3B-1
1988	TEX A	30	.194	.226	62	12	2	0	0	0.0	4	5	4	11	0	10	3	45	8	1	3	3.0	.981	OF-8, 1B-7, 3B-3
3 yrs.		226	.267	.371	626	167	28	2	11	1.8	76	86	36	83	9	55	14	684	86	16	80	3.6	.980	1B-109, OF-42, DH-39, 3B-24, 2B-3
LEAGUE CHAMPIONSHIP SERIES																								
1984	DET A	3	.333	.333	9	3	0	0	0	0.0	1	0	0	1	0	1	0	0	0	0	0	0.0	.000	DH-2
WORLD SERIES																								
1984	DET A	4	.000	.000	12	0	0	0	0	0.0	0	0	0	2	0	1	0	0	0	0	0	0.0	.000	DH-3

Alex Garbowski

GARBOWSKI, ALEXANDER BR TR 6′ 1″ 185 lbs.
B. June 25, 1925, Yonkers, N. Y.

Year	Team	Games	BA	SA	AB	H	2B	3B	HR	HR%	R	RBI	BB	SO	SB	Pinch Hit AB	Pinch Hit H	PO	A	E	DP	TC/G	FA	G by Pos
1952	DET A	2	—	—	0	0	0	0	0	—	0	0	0	0	0	0	0	0	0	0	0	0.0	—	

Carlos Garcia

GARCIA, CARLOS JESUS BR TR 6′ 1″ 185 lbs.
Born Carlos Jesus Garcia (Guerrero).
B. Oct. 15, 1967, Tachira, Venezuela.

Year	Team	Games	BA	SA	AB	H	2B	3B	HR	HR%	R	RBI	BB	SO	SB	Pinch Hit AB	Pinch Hit H	PO	A	E	DP	TC/G	FA	G by Pos
1990	PIT N	4	.500	.500	4	2	0	0	0	0.0	1	0	0	2	0	1	1	0	4	0	1	1.3	1.000	SS-3
1991		12	.250	.417	24	6	0	2	0	0.0	2	1	1	8	0	1	0	11	18	1	3	2.5	.967	SS-9, 3B-2, 2B-1
1992		22	.205	.231	39	8	1	0	0	0.0	4	4	0	9	0	3	1	25	35	2	11	2.8	.968	2B-14, SS-8
1993		141	.269	.399	546	147	25	5	12	2.2	77	47	31	67	18	2	1	299	347	11	87	4.6	.983	2B-140, SS-3
1994		98	.277	.367	412	114	15	2	6	1.5	49	28	16	67	18	0	0	226	316	12	78	5.7	.978	2B-98
1995		104	.294	.420	367	108	24	2	6	1.6	41	50	25	55	8	0	0	235	298	15	75	5.1	.973	2B-92, SS-15
6 yrs.		381	.277	.391	1392	385	65	11	24	1.7	174	130	73	208	44	7	3	796	1018	41	255	4.8	.978	2B-345, SS-38, 3B-2
LEAGUE CHAMPIONSHIP SERIES																								
1992	PIT N	1	.000	.000	1	0	0	0	0	0.0	0	0	0	0	0	0	0	0	0	0	0	0.0	.000	2B-1

Chico Garcia

GARCIA, VINCIO BR TR 5′ 8″ 170 lbs.
Born Vincio Garcia (Uzcanga).
B. Dec. 24, 1924, Veracruz, Mexico.

Year	Team	Games	BA	SA	AB	H	2B	3B	HR	HR%	R	RBI	BB	SO	SB	Pinch Hit AB	Pinch Hit H	PO	A	E	DP	TC/G	FA	G by Pos
1954	BAL A	39	.113	.177	62	7	0	2	0	0.0	6	5	8	3	0	5	1	57	44	4	15	4.4	.962	2B-24

Damaso Garcia

GARCIA, DAMASO DOMINGO BR TR 6′ 1″ 165 lbs.
Born Damaso Domingo Garcia (Sanchez).
B. Feb. 7, 1957, Moca, Dominican Republic.

Year	Team	Games	BA	SA	AB	H	2B	3B	HR	HR%	R	RBI	BB	SO	SB	Pinch Hit AB	Pinch Hit H	PO	A	E	DP	TC/G	FA	G by Pos
1978	NY A	18	.195	.195	41	8	0	0	0	0.0	5	1	2	6	1	0	0	36	35	4	10	3.9	.947	2B-16, SS-3
1979		11	.263	.289	38	10	1	0	0	0.0	3	4	0	2	2	0	0	9	28	4	4	3.7	.902	SS-10, 3B-1
1980	TOR A	140	.278	.381	543	151	30	7	4	0.7	50	46	12	55	13	2	0	316	471	16	112	5.8	.980	2B-138, DH-1
1981		64	.252	.304	250	63	8	1	1	0.4	24	13	9	32	13	1	0	132	181	9	32	5.1	.972	2B-62, DH-1
1982		147	.310	.399	597	185	32	3	5	0.8	89	42	21	44	54	0	0	273	461	15	94	5.2	.980	2B-141, DH-4
1983		131	.307	.390	525	161	23	6	3	0.6	84	38	24	34	31	2	0	266	360	12	75	4.9	.981	2B-130
1984		152	.284	.374	633	180	32	5	5	0.8	79	46	16	46	46	2	2	267	427	14	95	4.7	.980	2B-149, DH-1
1985		146	.282	.377	600	169	25	4	8	1.3	70	65	15	41	28	4	1	302	371	13	88	4.8	.981	2B-143
1986		122	.281	.375	424	119	22	0	6	1.4	57	46	13	32	9	5	3	225	286	8	66	4.4	.985	2B-106, DH-11, 1B-1
1988	ATL N	21	.117	.183	60	7	1	0	1	1.7	3	4	3	10	1	8	1	26	35	1	5	4.8	.984	2B-13
1989	MON N	80	.271	.369	203	55	9	1	3	1.5	26	18	15	20	5	26	4	86	157	7	25	4.0	.972	2B-62, 3B-1
11 yrs.		1032	.283	.371	3914	1108	183	27	36	0.9	490	323	130	322	203	50	11	1938	2812	103	606	4.9	.979	2B-960, DH-18, SS-13, 3B-2, 1B-1
LEAGUE CHAMPIONSHIP SERIES																								
1985	TOR A	7	.233	.367	30	7	4	0	0	0.0	4	1	3	3	0	0	0	10	10	0	3	2.9	1.000	2B-7

Danny Garcia

GARCIA, DANIEL RAPHAEL BL TL 6′ 1″ 182 lbs.
B. Apr. 29, 1954, Brooklyn, N. Y.

Year	Team	Games	BA	SA	AB	H	2B	3B	HR	HR%	R	RBI	BB	SO	SB	Pinch Hit AB	Pinch Hit H	PO	A	E	DP	TC/G	FA	G by Pos
1981	KC A	12	.143	.143	14	2	0	0	0	0.0	4	0	0	2	0	1	0	7	0	0	0	0.9	1.000	OF-6, 1B-2

Freddy Garcia

GARCIA, FREDDY ADRIAN BR TR 6′ 2″ 190 lbs.
Born Freddy Adrian Garcia (Felix).
B. Aug. 1, 1972, La Romana, Dominican Republic.

Year	Team	Games	BA	SA	AB	H	2B	3B	HR	HR%	R	RBI	BB	SO	SB	Pinch Hit AB	Pinch Hit H	PO	A	E	DP	TC/G	FA	G by Pos
1995	PIT N	42	.140	.193	57	8	1	1	0	0.0	5	1	8	17	0	20	2	19	15	1	4	1.9	.971	OF-10, 3B-8

Karim Garcia

GARCIA, GUSTAVO KARIM BL TL 6′ 200 lbs.
B. Oct. 29, 1975, Ciudad Obregon, Mexico.

Year	Team	Games	BA	SA	AB	H	2B	3B	HR	HR%	R	RBI	BB	SO	SB	Pinch Hit AB	Pinch Hit H	PO	A	E	DP	TC/G	FA	G by Pos
1995	LA N	13	.200	.200	20	4	0	0	0	0.0	1	0	0	4	0	8	2	5	2	0	1	1.4	1.000	OF-5

Kiko Garcia

GARCIA, ALFONSO RAFAEL BR TR 5′11″ 180 lbs.
B. Oct. 14, 1953, Martinez, Calif.

Year	Team	Games	BA	SA	AB	H	2B	3B	HR	HR%	R	RBI	BB	SO	SB	Pinch Hit AB	Pinch Hit H	PO	A	E	DP	TC/G	FA	G by Pos
1976	BAL A	11	.219	.406	32	7	1	1	1	3.1	2	4	0	4	2	0	0	15	27	0	7	3.8	1.000	SS-11
1977		65	.221	.313	131	29	6	0	2	1.5	20	10	6	31	2	0	0	78	152	8	43	3.9	.966	SS-61
1978		79	.263	.339	186	49	6	4	0	0.0	17	13	7	43	7	3	1	87	175	16	35	3.6	.942	SS-74, 2B-3
1979		126	.247	.362	417	103	15	9	5	1.2	54	24	32	87	11	4	0	209	321	27	78	3.9	.952	SS-113, 2B-25, OF-2, 3B-2
1980		111	.199	.235	311	62	8	0	1	0.3	27	27	24	57	8	0	0	177	292	11	65	3.9	.977	SS-96, 2B-27, OF-1

Kiko Garcia *continued*

Year	Team	Games	BA	SA	AB	H	2B	3B	HR	HR%	R	RBI	BB	SO	SB	Pinch Hit AB	Pinch Hit H	PO	A	E	DP	TC/G	FA	G by Pos
1981	HOU N	48	.272	.331	136	37	6	1	0	0.0	9	15	10	16	2	2	1	58	119	11	14	3.8	.941	SS-28, 3B-13, 2B-9
1982		34	.211	.316	76	16	5	0	1	1.3	5	5	3	15	1	9	1	29	62	5	13	4.0	.948	SS-21, 3B-2, 2B-1
1983	PHI N	84	.288	.415	118	34	7	1	2	1.7	22	9	9	20	1	2	0	94	115	6	18	2.6	.972	2B-52, SS-22, 3B-10
1984		57	.233	.267	60	14	2	0	0	0.0	6	5	4	11	0	3	0	25	54	2	6	1.5	.975	SS-30, 3B-23, 2B-1
1985		4	.000	.000	3	0	0	0	0	0.0	0	0	0	1	0	0	0	0	2	0	0	0.5	1.000	SS-3, 3B-1
10 yrs.		619	.239	.323	1470	351	56	16	12	0.8	162	112	95	285	34	23	3	772	1319	86	279	3.5	.960	SS-459, 2B-118, 3B-51, OF-3
DIVISIONAL PLAYOFF SERIES																								
1981	HOU N	2	.000	.000	4	0	0	0	0	0.0	0	0	0	1	0	1	0	2	4	0	0	6.0	1.000	SS-1
LEAGUE CHAMPIONSHIP SERIES																								
1979	BAL A	3	.273	.273	11	3	0	0	0	0.0	1	2	2	4	0	0	0	6	16	2	3	8.0	.917	SS-3
WORLD SERIES																								
1979	BAL A	6	.400	.600	20	8	2	1	0	0.0	4	6	1	3	0	0	0	10	17	1	2	4.7	.964	SS-6

Leo Garcia

GARCIA, LEONARDO ANTONIO BL TL 5′8″ 160 lbs.
Born Leonardo Antonio Garcia (Peralta).
B. Nov. 6, 1962, Santiago, Dominican Republic.

Year	Team	Games	BA	SA	AB	H	2B	3B	HR	HR%	R	RBI	BB	SO	SB	Pinch Hit AB	Pinch Hit H	PO	A	E	DP	TC/G	FA	G by Pos
1987	CIN N	31	.200	.300	30	6	0	0	1	3.3	8	2	4	8	3	9	2	19	0	0	0	1.4	1.000	OF-14
1988		23	.143	.179	28	4	1	0	0	0.0	2	0	4	5	0	12	3	12	0	0	0	1.3	1.000	OF-9
2 yrs.		54	.172	.241	58	10	1	0	1	1.7	10	2	8	13	3	21	5	31	0	0	0	1.3	1.000	OF-23

Pedro Garcia

GARCIA, PEDRO MODESTO BR TR 5′10″ 175 lbs.
Born Pedro Modesto Garcia (Delfi).
B. Apr. 17, 1950, Guayama, Puerto Rico.

Year	Team	Games	BA	SA	AB	H	2B	3B	HR	HR%	R	RBI	BB	SO	SB	Pinch Hit AB	Pinch Hit H	PO	A	E	DP	TC/G	FA	G by Pos
1973	MIL A	160	.245	.395	580	142	**32**	5	15	2.6	67	54	40	119	11	0	0	405	470	27	111	5.6	.970	2B-160
1974		141	.199	.330	452	90	15	4	12	2.7	46	54	26	67	8	0	0	382	365	23	102	5.5	.970	2B-140
1975		98	.225	.348	302	68	15	2	6	2.0	40	38	18	59	12	1	0	230	293	8	67	5.6	.985	2B-94, DH-1
1976	2 teams	MIL A (41G –.217)	DET A (77G –.198)																					
″	total	118	.204	.309	333	68	17	3	4	1.2	33	29	13	63	4	3	0	242	314	22	79	5.0	.962	2B-116
1977	TOR A	41	.208	.300	130	27	10	1	0	0.0	10	9	5	21	0	2	0	73	97	5	22	4.6	.971	2B-34, DH-4
5 yrs.		558	.220	.348	1797	395	89	15	37	2.1	196	184	102	329	35	6	0	1332	1539	85	381	5.4	.971	2B-544, DH-5

Al Gardella

GARDELLA, ALFRED STEPHEN BL TL 5′10″ 172 lbs.
Brother of Danny Gardella.
B. Jan. 11, 1918, New York, N. Y.

Year	Team	Games	BA	SA	AB	H	2B	3B	HR	HR%	R	RBI	BB	SO	SB	Pinch Hit AB	Pinch Hit H	PO	A	E	DP	TC/G	FA	G by Pos
1945	NY N	16	.077	.077	26	2	0	0	0	0.0	2	1	4	3	0	6	0	70	4	3	2	8.6	.961	1B-8, OF-1

Danny Gardella

GARDELLA, DANIEL LEWIS BL TL 5′7½″ 160 lbs.
Brother of Al Gardella.
B. Feb. 26, 1920, New York, N. Y.

Year	Team	Games	BA	SA	AB	H	2B	3B	HR	HR%	R	RBI	BB	SO	SB	Pinch Hit AB	Pinch Hit H	PO	A	E	DP	TC/G	FA	G by Pos
1944	NY N	47	.250	.464	112	28	2	2	6	5.4	20	14	11	13	0	16	4	58	4	6	1	2.7	.912	OF-25
1945		121	.272	.426	430	117	10	1	18	4.2	54	71	46	55	2	11	4	319	22	12	9	3.2	.966	OF-94, 1B-15
1950	STL N	1	.000	.000	1	0	0	0	0	0.0	0	0	0	0	0	1	0	0	0	0	0	0.0	—	
3 yrs.		169	.267	.433	543	145	12	3	24	4.4	74	85	57	68	2	28	8	377	26	18	10	3.1	.957	OF-119, 1B-15

Ron Gardenhire

GARDENHIRE, RONALD CLYDE BR TR 6′ 175 lbs.
B. Oct. 24, 1957, Butzbach, West Germany.

Year	Team	Games	BA	SA	AB	H	2B	3B	HR	HR%	R	RBI	BB	SO	SB	Pinch Hit AB	Pinch Hit H	PO	A	E	DP	TC/G	FA	G by Pos
1981	NY N	27	.271	.292	48	13	1	0	0	0.0	2	3	5	9	2	0	0	28	50	2	7	3.2	.975	SS-18, 2B-6, 3B-1
1982		141	.240	.313	384	92	17	1	3	0.8	29	33	23	55	5	2	1	235	399	29	68	4.8	.956	SS-135, 2B-1, 3B-1
1983		17	.063	.063	32	2	0	0	0	0.0	1	1	1	4	0	1	0	13	30	0	4	2.9	1.000	SS-15
1984		74	.246	.304	207	51	7	1	1	0.5	20	10	9	43	6	5	2	98	154	12	20	3.6	.955	SS-49, 2B-18, 3B-7
1985		26	.179	.282	39	7	2	1	0	0.0	5	2	8	11	0	6	0	21	32	4	3	2.8	.930	SS-13, 2B-5, 3B-2
5 yrs.		285	.232	.296	710	165	27	3	4	0.6	57	49	46	122	13	14	3	395	665	47	102	4.1	.958	SS-230, 2B-30, 3B-11

Alex Gardner

GARDNER, ALEXANDER
B. Apr. 28, 1861, Toronto, Ont., Canada D. June 18, 1926, Danvers, Mass.

Year	Team	Games	BA	SA	AB	H	2B	3B	HR	HR%	R	RBI	BB	SO	SB	Pinch Hit AB	Pinch Hit H	PO	A	E	DP	TC/G	FA	G by Pos
1884	WAS AA	1	.000	.000	3	0	0	0	0	0.0	0		0			0	0	6	3	6	0	15.0	.600	C-1

Art Gardner

GARDNER, ARTHUR JUNIOR BL TL 5′11″ 175 lbs.
B. Sept. 21, 1952, Madden, Miss.

Year	Team	Games	BA	SA	AB	H	2B	3B	HR	HR%	R	RBI	BB	SO	SB	Pinch Hit AB	Pinch Hit H	PO	A	E	DP	TC/G	FA	G by Pos
1975	HOU N	13	.194	.194	31	6	0	0	0	0.0	3	2	1	8	1	9	0	14	0	0	0	1.8	1.000	OF-8
1977		66	.154	.154	65	10	0	0	0	0.0	7	3	3	15	0	26	5	31	1	0	1	1.2	1.000	OF-26
1978	SF N	7	.000	.000	3	0	0	0	0	0.0	2	0	0	2	0	3	0	0	0	0	0	0.0	—	
3 yrs.		86	.162	.162	99	16	0	0	0	0.0	12	5	4	25	1	38	5	45	1	0	1	1.4	1.000	OF-34

Billy Gardner

GARDNER, WILLIAM FREDERICK (Shotgun) BR TR 6′ 170 lbs.
B. July 19, 1927, Waterford, Conn.
Manager 1981–85, 1987.

Year	Team	Games	BA	SA	AB	H	2B	3B	HR	HR%	R	RBI	BB	SO	SB	Pinch Hit AB	Pinch Hit H	PO	A	E	DP	TC/G	FA	G by Pos
1954	NY N	62	.213	.287	108	23	5	0	1	0.9	10	7	6	19	0	3	1	42	82	2	4	2.6	.984	3B-30, 2B-13, SS-5
1955		59	.203	.316	187	38	10	1	3	1.6	26	17	13	19	0	8	0	76	139	13	29	4.4	.943	SS-38, 3B-10, 2B-4
1956	BAL A	144	.231	.334	515	119	16	2	11	2.1	53	50	29	53	5	1	0	301	386	18	77	4.3	.974	2B-132, SS-25, 3B-6
1957		154	.262	.356	**644**	169	**36**	3	6	0.9	79	55	53	67	10	0	0	406	450	12	103	5.5	.986	2B-148, SS-9
1958		151	.225	.298	560	126	28	2	3	0.5	32	33	34	53	2	0	0	354	356	11	113	4.4	.985	2B-151, SS-13
1959		140	.217	.304	401	87	13	2	6	1.5	34	27	38	61	2	0	0	334	393	18	104	5.3	.976	2B-139, SS-1, 3B-1
1960	WAS A	145	.257	.363	592	152	26	5	9	1.5	71	56	43	76	0	0	0	360	418	21	103	5.1	.974	2B-145, SS-13
1961	2 teams	MIN A (45G –.234)	NY A (41G –.212)																					
″	total	86	.225	.304	253	57	14	0	2	0.8	24	13	16	32	0	3	1	121	160	11	40	3.6	.962	2B-47, 3B-35
1962	2 teams	NY A (4G –.000)	BOS A (53G –.271)																					
″	total	57	.270	.335	200	54	9	2	0	0.0	23	12	10	40	0	3	1	81	123	10	23	4.2	.953	2B-39, 3B-8, SS-4
1963	BOS A	36	.190	.238	84	16	2	1	0	0.0	4	1	4	19	0	12	2	37	59	1	13	4.2	.990	2B-21, 3B-2
10 yrs.		1034	.237	.327	3544	841	159	18	41	1.2	356	271	246	439	19	30	5	2112	2566	117	609	4.6	.976	2B-839, SS-108, 3B-92
WORLD SERIES																								
1961	NY A	1	.000	.000	1	0	0	0	0	0.0	0	0	0	0	0	1	0	0	0	0	0	0.0	—	

Earl Gardner

GARDNER, EARLE McCLURKIN
B. Jan. 24, 1884, Sparta, Ill. D. Mar. 2, 1943, Sparta, Ill.
BR TR 5′11″ 160 lbs.

Year	Team	Games	BA	SA	AB	H	2B	3B	HR	HR%	R	RBI	BB	SO	SB	Pinch Hit AB	Pinch Hit H	PO	A	E	DP	TC/G	FA	G by Pos
1908	NY A	20	.213	.240	75	16	2	0	0	0.0	7	4	1		0	0	0	49	59	6	13	5.7	.947	2B-20
1909		22	.329	.376	85	28	4	0	0	0.0	12	15	3		4	0	0	35	51	5	3	4.1	.945	2B-22
1910		86	.244	.284	271	66	4	2	1	0.4	36	24	21		9	14	4	169	199	25	36	5.6	.936	2B-70
1911		102	.263	.311	357	94	13	2	0	0.0	36	39	20		14	1	0	181	290	20	44	4.9	.959	2B-101
1912		43	.281	.313	160	45	3	1	0	0.0	14	26	5		11	0	0	93	107	17	11	5.0	.922	2B-43
5 yrs.		273	.263	.304	948	249	26	5	1	0.1	105	108	50		38	15	4	527	706	73	107	5.1	.944	2B-256

Gid Gardner

GARDNER, FRANKLIN WASHINGTON
B. June 9, 1859, Attleboro, Mass. D. Aug. 1, 1914, Cambridge, Mass.
165 lbs.

Year	Team	Games	BA	SA	AB	H	2B	3B	HR	HR%	R	RBI	BB	SO	SB	Pinch Hit AB	Pinch Hit H	PO	A	E	DP	TC/G	FA	G by Pos
1879	TRO N	2	.167	.167	6	1	0	0	0	0.0	1	0	0	0		0	0	1	2	4	0	3.5	.429	P-2
1880	CLE N	10	.188	.281	32	6	1	1	0	0.0	0	4	2	4		0	0	0	17	3	0	2.0	.850	P-9, OF-1
1883	BAL AA	42	.273	.391	161	44	10	3	1	0.6	28		18			0	0	74	25	22	0	2.8	.818	OF-35, 2B-4, 3B-3, P-2
1884	4 teams	BAL AA (41G –.214)	CHI U (22G –.247)	PIT U (16G –.266)	BAL U (1G –.250)																			
″	total	80	.233	.362	326	76	16	10	2	0.6	54	0	24	0	0	0	0	125	34	21	6	2.2	.883	OF-69, 3B-8, 1B-2, 2B-1, SS-1, P-1
1885	BAL AA	44	.218	.294	170	37	5	4	0	0.0	22		12			0	0	129	135	35	17	6.5	.883	2B-39, OF-5, P-1, 1B-1
1887	IND N	18	.175	.238	63	11	1	0	1	1.6	8	8	12	11	7	0	0	26	23	5	1	3.0	.907	OF-11, 2B-7
1888	2 teams	WAS N (2G –.250)	PHI N (1G –.667)																					
″	total	3	.429	.429	7	3	0	0	0	0.0	0	1	1	1	0	0	0	6	5	2	0	4.3	.846	2B-2, SS-1
7 yrs.		199	.233	.339	765	178	33	18	4	0.5	113	13	69	16	7	0	0	361	241	92	24	3.4	.867	OF-121, 2B-53, P-15, 3B-11, 1B-3, SS-2

Jeff Gardner

GARDNER, JEFFREY SCOTT
B. Feb. 4, 1964, Newport Beach, Calif.
BL TR 5′11″ 165 lbs.

Year	Team	Games	BA	SA	AB	H	2B	3B	HR	HR%	R	RBI	BB	SO	SB	Pinch Hit AB	Pinch Hit H	PO	A	E	DP	TC/G	FA	G by Pos
1991	NY N	13	.162	.162	37	6	0	0	0	0.0	3	1	4	6	0	2	1	11	29	6	2	4.2	.870	SS-8, 2B-3
1992	SD N	15	.105	.105	19	2	0	0	0	0.0	0	0	1	8	0	4	0	11	20	0	3	2.8	1.000	2B-11
1993		140	.262	.356	404	106	21	7	1	0.2	53	24	45	69	2	17	2	214	294	10	48	3.8	.981	2B-133, SS-1, 3B-1
1994	MON N	18	.219	.281	32	7	0	1	0	0.0	4	1	3	5	0	8	2	6	4	2	1	0.9	.833	3B-9, 2B-4
4 yrs.		186	.246	.327	492	121	21	8	1	0.2	60	26	53	88	2	31	5	242	347	18	54	3.6	.970	2B-151, 3B-10, SS-9

Larry Gardner

GARDNER, WILLIAM LAWRENCE
B. May 13, 1886, Enosburg Falls, Vt. D. Mar. 11, 1976, St. George, Vt.
BL TR 5′8″ 165 lbs.

Year	Team	Games	BA	SA	AB	H	2B	3B	HR	HR%	R	RBI	BB	SO	SB	Pinch Hit AB	Pinch Hit H	PO	A	E	DP	TC/G	FA	G by Pos
1908	BOS A	2	.500	.500	6	3	0	0	0	0.0	0	1	0		0	0	0	1	0	2	0	1.5	.333	3B-2
1909		19	.297	.432	37	11	1	2	0	0.0	8	5	4		1	5	1	10	16	5	1	2.4	.839	3B-8, SS-5
1910		113	.283	.375	413	117	12	10	2	0.5	55	36	41		8	0	0	222	320	32	28	5.1	.944	2B-113
1911		138	.285	.376	492	140	17	8	4	0.8	80	44	64		27	4	3	244	356	23	34	4.6	.963	3B-72, 2B-62
1912		143	.315	.449	517	163	24	18	3	0.6	88	86	56		25	0	0	167	296	35	16	3.5	.930	3B-143
1913		131	.281	.359	473	133	17	10	0	0.0	64	63	47	34	18	1	0	126	220	21	13	2.8	.943	3B-130
1914		155	.259	.385	553	143	23	19	3	0.5	50	68	35	39	16	2	0	187	312	31	18	3.5	.942	3B-153
1915		127	.258	.326	430	111	14	6	1	0.2	51	55	39	24	11	0	0	134	227	26	16	3.0	.933	3B-127
1916		148	.308	.387	493	152	19	7	2	0.4	47	62	48	27	12	1	0	149	278	21	24	3.0	.953	3B-147
1917		146	.265	.345	501	133	23	7	1	0.2	53	61	54	37	16	0	0	148	315	31	18	3.4	.937	3B-146
1918	PHI A	127	.285	.365	463	132	22	6	1	0.2	50	52	43	22	9	0	0	158	291	17	33	3.7	.964	3B-127
1919	CLE A	139	.300	.393	524	157	29	7	2	0.4	67	79	39	29	7	0	0	143	291	25	23	3.3	.946	3B-139
1920		154	.310	.414	597	185	31	11	3	0.5	72	118	53	25	3	0	0	156	362	13	32	3.4	.976	3B-154
1921		153	.319	.437	586	187	32	14	3	0.5	101	115	65	16	3	1	0	179	335	27	23	3.6	.950	3B-152
1922		137	.285	.377	470	134	31	3	2	0.4	74	68	49	21	9	9	4	133	259	20	24	3.2	.951	3B-128
1923		52	.253	.342	79	20	5	1	0	0.0	4	12	12	7	0	30	9	10	41	2	2	2.8	.962	3B-19
1924		38	.200	.200	50	10	0	0	0	0.0	3	4	5	1	0	22	5	9	18	3	2	2.1	.900	3B-8, 2B-6
17 yrs.		1922	.289	.385	6684	1931	300	129	27	0.4	867	929	654	282	165	75	22	2176	3937	334	307	3.5	.948	3B-1655, 2B-181, SS-5
WORLD SERIES																								
1912	BOS A	8	.179	.429	28	5	2	1	1	3.6	4	4	2	5	0	0	0	9	12	4	0	3.1	.840	3B-8
1915		5	.235	.353	17	4	0	1	0	0.0	2	0	1	0	0	0	0	5	14	0	0	3.8	1.000	3B-5
1916		5	.176	.529	17	3	0	0	2	11.8	2	6	0	2	0	0	0	7	18	2	1	5.4	.926	3B-5
1920	CLE A	7	.208	.250	24	5	1	0	0	0.0	1	1	1	1	0	0	0	9	15	2	3	3.7	.923	3B-7
4 yrs.		25	.198	.384	86	17	3	2	3	3.5	9	11	4	8	0	0	0	30	59	8	4	3.9	.918	3B-25

Ray Gardner

GARDNER, RAYMOND VINCENT
B. Oct. 25, 1901, Frederick, Md. D. May 3, 1968, Frederick, Md.
BR TR 5′8″ 145 lbs.

Year	Team	Games	BA	SA	AB	H	2B	3B	HR	HR%	R	RBI	BB	SO	SB	Pinch Hit AB	Pinch Hit H	PO	A	E	DP	TC/G	FA	G by Pos
1929	CLE A	82	.262	.301	256	67	3	2	1	0.4	28	24	29	16	10	0	0	175	240	21	50	5.3	.952	SS-82
1930		33	.077	.077	13	1	0	0	0	0.0	7	1	0	1	0	1	0	12	19	5	1	1.6	.861	SS-22
2 yrs.		115	.253	.290	269	68	3	2	1	0.4	35	25	29	17	10	1	0	187	259	26	51	4.5	.945	SS-104

Art Garibaldi

GARIBALDI, ARTHUR EDWARD
B. Aug. 20, 1907, San Francisco, Calif. D. Oct. 19, 1967, Sacramento, Calif.
BR TR 5′8″ 175 lbs.

Year	Team	Games	BA	SA	AB	H	2B	3B	HR	HR%	R	RBI	BB	SO	SB	Pinch Hit AB	Pinch Hit H	PO	A	E	DP	TC/G	FA	G by Pos
1936	STL N	71	.276	.341	232	64	12	0	1	0.4	30	20	16	30	3	1	0	97	119	11	7	3.2	.952	3B-46, 2B-24

Debs Garms

GARMS, DEBS C.
B. June 26, 1908, Bangs, Tex. D. Dec. 16, 1984, Glen Rose, Tex.
BL TR 5′8½″ 165 lbs.

Year	Team	Games	BA	SA	AB	H	2B	3B	HR	HR%	R	RBI	BB	SO	SB	Pinch Hit AB	Pinch Hit H	PO	A	E	DP	TC/G	FA	G by Pos
1932	STL A	34	.284	.373	134	38	7	1	1	0.7	20	8	17	7	4	1	0	79	3	4	1	2.6	.953	OF-33
1933		78	.317	.455	189	60	10	2	4	2.1	35	24	30	21	2	23	5	91	5	4	1	2.1	.960	OF-47
1934		91	.293	.388	232	68	14	4	0	0.0	25	31	27	19	0	27	7	111	2	7	0	2.1	.942	OF-56
1935		10	.267	.267	15	4	0	0	0	0.0	1	0	2	2	0	6	1	4	0	1	0	2.5	.800	OF-2
1937	BOS N	125	.259	.337	478	124	15	8	2	0.4	60	37	37	33	2	10	3	200	69	7	2	2.4	.975	OF-81, 3B-36
1938		117	.315	.364	428	135	19	1	0	0.0	62	47	34	22	4	4	1	174	104	11	8	2.4	.962	OF-63, 3B-54, 2B-1
1939		132	.298	.392	513	153	24	9	2	0.4	68	37	39	20	2	2	0	214	89	12	7	2.4	.962	OF-96, 3B-37
1940	PIT N	103	**.355**	.500	358	127	23	7	5	1.4	76	57	23	6	3	18	5	97	126	9	15	2.8	.961	3B-64, OF-19
1941		83	.264	.373	220	58	9	3	3	1.4	25	42	22	12	0	31	**10**	73	44	9	1	2.4	.929	3B-29, OF-24
1943	STL N	90	.257	.313	249	64	10	2	0	0.0	26	22	13	8	1	20	6	112	25	9	5	2.1	.938	OF-47, 3B-23, SS-1
1944		73	.201	.221	149	30	3	0	0	0.0	17	5	13	8	0	30	6	48	16	1	1	1.5	.985	OF-23, 3B-21
1945		74	.336	.411	146	49	7	2	0	0.0	23	18	31	3	0	26	10	30	43	3	4	1.8	.961	3B-32, OF-10
12 yrs.		1010	.293	.379	3111	910	141	39	17	0.5	438	328	288	161	18	198	54	1233	526	77	45	2.3	.958	OF-501, 3B-296, SS-1, 2B-1

Debs Garms *continued*

Year	Team	Games	BA	SA	AB	H	2B	3B	HR	HR%	R	RBI	BB	SO	SB	Pinch Hit AB	Pinch Hit H	PO	A	E	DP	TC/G	FA	G by Pos
WORLD SERIES																								
1943	STL N	2	.000	.000	5	0	0	0	0	0.0	0	0	0	2	0	1	0	1	0	0	0	1.0	1.000	OF-1
1944		2	.000	.000	2	0	0	0	0	0.0	0	0	0	0	0	2	0	0	0	0	0	0.0	—	
2 yrs.		4	.000	.000	7	0	0	0	0	0.0	0	0	0	2	0	3	0	1	0	0	0	1.0	1.000	OF-1

Phil Garner

GARNER, PHILIP MASON (Scrap Iron)
B. Apr. 30, 1949, Jefferson City, Tenn.
Manager 1992–95.

BR TR 5′10″ 175 lbs.

Year	Team	Games	BA	SA	AB	H	2B	3B	HR	HR%	R	RBI	BB	SO	SB	Pinch Hit AB	Pinch Hit H	PO	A	E	DP	TC/G	FA	G by Pos
1973	OAK A	9	.000	.000	5	0	0	0	0	0.0	0	0	0	3	0	0	0	2	3	0	1	0.6	1.000	3B-9
1974		30	.179	.214	28	5	1	0	0	0.0	4	1	1	5	1	0	0	11	24	1	1	2.8	.972	SS-8, 2B-3, DH-2
1975		160	.246	.346	488	120	21	5	6	1.2	46	54	30	65	4	0	0	355	427	26	94	5.0	.968	2B-160, SS-1
1976		159	.261	.400	555	145	29	12	8	1.4	54	74	36	71	35	0	0	378	465	22	91	5.4	.975	2B-159
1977	PIT N	153	.260	.441	585	152	35	10	17	2.9	99	77	55	65	32	2	0	223	351	17	49	3.5	.971	3B-107, 2B-50, SS-12
1978		154	.261	.400	528	138	25	9	10	1.9	66	66	66	71	27	1	0	258	389	28	63	4.1	.959	2B-81, 3B-81, SS-4
1979		150	.293	.441	549	161	32	8	11	2.0	76	59	55	74	17	0	0	234	396	22	82	3.7	.966	2B-83, 3B-78, SS-14
1980		151	.259	.358	548	142	27	6	5	0.9	62	58	46	53	32	0	0	349	500	21	116	5.7	.976	2B-151, SS-1
1981	2 teams	PIT N (56G –.254)	HOU N (31G –.239)																					
″	total	87	.248	.310	294	73	9	3	1	0.3	35	26	36	32	10	3	2	183	250	12	48	5.5	.973	2B-81
1982	HOU N	155	.274	.423	588	161	33	8	13	2.2	65	83	40	92	24	1	0	285	464	17	94	5.0	.978	2B-136, 3B-18
1983		154	.238	.362	567	135	24	2	14	2.5	76	79	63	84	18	0	0	100	311	24	22	2.8	.945	3B-154
1984		128	.278	.388	374	104	17	6	4	1.1	60	45	43	63	3	24	6	136	251	12	42	3.4	.970	3B-82, 2B-35
1985		135	.268	.400	463	124	23	10	6	1.3	65	51	34	72	4	15	7	101	229	21	24	2.5	.940	3B-123, 2B-15
1986		107	.265	.415	313	83	14	3	9	2.9	43	41	30	45	12	16	3	66	152	23	15	2.6	.905	3B-84, 2B-7
1987	2 teams	HOU N (43G –.223)	LA N (70G –.190)																					
″	total	113	.206	.307	238	49	9	0	5	2.1	29	23	28	44	6	24	4	65	144	13	10	2.3	.941	3B-82, 2B-14, SS-2
1988	SF N	15	.154	.154	13	2	0	0	0	0.0	0	1	1	3	0	13	2	0	0	0	0	0.0	.000	3B-2
16 yrs.		1860	.260	.389	6136	1594	299	82	109	1.8	780	738	564	842	225	99	24	2746	4356	259	752	4.0	.965	2B-975, 3B-820, SS-42, DH-2
DIVISIONAL PLAYOFF SERIES																								
1981	HOU N	5	.111	.111	18	2	0	0	0	0.0	1	0	3	3	0	0	0	6	8	1	0	3.0	.933	2B-5
LEAGUE CHAMPIONSHIP SERIES																								
1975	OAK A	3	.000	.000	5	0	0	0	0	0.0	0	0	0	1	0	0	0	7	4	1	2	4.0	.917	2B-3
1979	PIT N	3	.417	.833	12	5	0	1	1	8.3	4	1	1	0	0	0	0	8	9	0	2	4.3	1.000	2B-3, SS-1
1986	HOU N	3	.222	.333	9	2	1	0	0	0.0	1	2	1	2	0	0	0	1	9	0	0	3.3	1.000	3B-3
3 yrs.		9	.269	.500	26	7	1	1	1	3.8	5	3	2	3	0	0	0	16	22	1	4	3.9	.974	2B-6, 3B-3, SS-1
WORLD SERIES																								
1979	PIT N	7	.500	.667	24	12	4	0	0	0.0	4	5	3	1	0	0	0	21	23	2	10	6.6	.957	2B-7

Ralph Garr

GARR, RALPH ALLEN (Roadrunner)
B. Dec. 12, 1945, Monroe, La.

BL TR 5′11″ 185 lbs.

Year	Team	Games	BA	SA	AB	H	2B	3B	HR	HR%	R	RBI	BB	SO	SB	Pinch Hit AB	Pinch Hit H	PO	A	E	DP	TC/G	FA	G by Pos
1968	ATL N	11	.286	.286	7	2	0	0	0	0.0	3	0	1	0	1	7	2	0	0	0	0	0.0	—	
1969		22	.222	.259	27	6	1	0	0	0.0	6	2	2	4	1	5	2	6	0	1	0	1.0	.857	OF-7
1970		37	.281	.313	96	27	3	0	0	0.0	18	8	5	12	5	10	1	43	0	0	0	2.0	1.000	OF-21
1971		154	.343	.441	639	219	24	6	9	1.4	101	44	30	68	30	1	1	315	15	11	3	2.2	.968	OF-153
1972		134	.325	.430	554	180	22	0	12	2.2	87	53	25	41	25	3	0	246	8	10	1	2.0	.962	OF-131
1973		148	.299	.415	668	200	32	6	11	1.6	94	55	22	64	35	0	0	293	9	10	2	2.1	.968	OF-148
1974		143	**.353**	.503	606	**214**	24	**17**	11	1.8	87	54	28	52	26	1	1	255	8	9	2	2.0	.967	OF-139
1975		151	.278	.384	625	174	26	**11**	6	1.0	74	31	44	50	14	3	2	298	12	11	2	2.2	.966	OF-148
1976	CHI A	136	.300	.387	527	158	22	6	4	0.8	63	36	17	41	14	5	2	254	7	6	2	2.1	.978	OF-125
1977		134	.300	.435	543	163	29	7	10	1.8	78	54	27	44	12	7	1	225	10	3	2	1.9	.987	OF-126, DH-2
1978		118	.275	.377	443	122	18	9	3	0.7	67	29	24	41	7	2	0	205	5	9	2	1.9	.959	OF-109, DH-9
1979	2 teams	CHI A (102G –.280)	CAL A (6G –.125)																					
″	total	108	.269	.393	331	89	10	2	9	2.7	34	39	17	22	2	23	6	94	3	5	1	1.1	.951	OF-67, DH-23
1980	CAL A	21	.190	.214	42	8	1	0	0	0.0	5	3	4	6	0	9	1	3	0	1	0	0.4	.750	DH-8, OF-2
13 yrs.		1317	.306	.416	5108	1562	212	64	75	1.5	717	408	246	445	172	76	19	2237	77	76	17	2.0	.968	OF-1176, DH-42

Adrian Garrett

GARRETT, HENRY ADRIAN
Brother of Wayne Garrett.
B. Jan. 3, 1943, Brooksville, Fla.

BL TR 6′3″ 185 lbs.

Year	Team	Games	BA	SA	AB	H	2B	3B	HR	HR%	R	RBI	BB	SO	SB	Pinch Hit AB	Pinch Hit H	PO	A	E	DP	TC/G	FA	G by Pos
1966	ATL N	4	.000	.000	3	0	0	0	0	0.0	0	0	0	2	0	3	0	0	0	0	0	0.0	.000	OF-1
1970	CHI N	3	.000	.000	3	0	0	0	0	0.0	0	0	0	3	0	3	0	0	0	0	0	0.0	—	
1971	OAK A	14	.143	.286	21	3	0	0	1	4.8	1	2	5	7	0	7	0	9	0	0	0	1.8	1.000	OF-5
1972		14	.000	.000	11	0	0	0	0	0.0	0	0	1	4	0	11	0	1	0	0	0	0.5	1.000	OF-2
1973	CHI N	36	.222	.389	54	12	0	0	3	5.6	7	8	4	18	1	21	6	35	6	2	0	3.3	.953	OF-7, C-6
1974		10	.000	.000	8	0	0	0	0	0.0	0	0	1	1	0	6	0	3	1	0	0	0.8	1.000	C-3, OF-1, 1B-1
1975	2 teams	CHI N (16G –.095)	CAL A (37G –.262)																					
″	total	53	.234	.438	128	30	5	0	7	5.5	18	24	15	36	3	9	0	100	12	1	14	2.8	.991	DH-23, 1B-14, OF-2, C-1
1976	CAL A	29	.125	.188	48	6	3	0	0	0.0	4	3	5	16	0	12	2	43	1	1	2	2.3	.978	C-15, DH-4, 1B-1
8 yrs.		163	.185	.333	276	51	8	0	11	4.0	30	37	31	87	4	72	8	191	20	4	16	2.5	.981	DH-27, C-25, OF-18, 1B-16

Wayne Garrett

GARRETT, RONALD WAYNE (Red)
Brother of Adrian Garrett.
B. Dec. 3, 1947, Brooksville, Fla.

BL TR 5′11″ 175 lbs.

Year	Team	Games	BA	SA	AB	H	2B	3B	HR	HR%	R	RBI	BB	SO	SB	Pinch Hit AB	Pinch Hit H	PO	A	E	DP	TC/G	FA	G by Pos
1969	NY N	124	.218	.268	400	87	11	3	1	0.3	38	39	40	75	4	14	1	147	218	11	37	2.9	.971	3B-72, 2B-47, SS-9
1970		114	.254	.421	366	93	17	4	12	3.3	74	45	81	60	5	5	0	152	205	12	34	3.2	.967	3B-70, 2B-45, SS-1
1971		56	.213	.238	202	43	2	0	1	0.5	20	11	28	31	1	2	0	48	100	4	11	2.5	.974	3B-53, 2B-9
1972		111	.232	.315	298	69	13	3	2	0.7	41	29	70	58	3	8	0	114	188	14	19	3.0	.956	3B-82, 2B-22
1973		140	.256	.403	504	129	20	3	16	3.2	76	58	72	74	6	4	4	102	313	26	46	3.0	.941	3B-130, SS-9, 2B-6
1974		151	.224	.337	522	117	14	3	13	2.5	55	53	89	96	4	3	2	123	349	20	33	3.2	.959	3B-144, SS-9
1975		107	.266	.383	274	73	8	3	6	2.2	49	34	50	45	3	12	6	65	161	8	24	2.4	.966	3B-94, SS-3

Wayne Garrett *continued*

Year	Team	Games	BA	SA	AB	H	2B	3B	HR	HR%	R	RBI	BB	SO	SB	Pinch Hit AB	Pinch Hit H	PO	A	E	DP	TC/G	FA	G by Pos
1976	**2 teams**	**NY N** (80G –.223) **MON N** (59G –.243)																						
"	**total**	139	.231	.311	428	99	12	2	6	1.4	51	37	82	46	9	17	3	195	314	15	48	4.0	.971	3B-66, 2B-64, SS-1
1977	**MON N**	68	.270	.358	159	43	6	1	2	1.3	17	22	30	18	2	18	1	34	101	0	2	2.7	1.000	3B-49, 2B-1
1978	**2 teams**	**MON N** (49G –.174) **STL N** (33G –.333)																						
"	**total**	82	.250	.326	132	33	4	0	2	1.5	17	12	19	26	1	43	9	18	51	4	7	2.3	.945	3B-32
10 yrs.		1092	.239	.341	3285	786	107	22	61	1.9	438	340	561	529	38	126	26	998	2000	114	261	3.1	.963	3B-792, 2B-194, SS-32
LEAGUE CHAMPIONSHIP SERIES																								
1969	**NY N**	3	.385	.769	13	5	2	0	1	7.7	3	3	2	2	1	0	0	1	6	0	0	2.3	1.000	3B-3
1973		5	.087	.130	23	2	1	0	0	0.0	1	1	0	5	0	0	0	4	6	1	0	2.2	.909	3B-5
2 yrs.		8	.194	.361	36	7	3	0	1	2.8	4	4	2	7	1	0	0	5	12	1	0	2.3	.944	3B-8
WORLD SERIES																								
1969	**NY N**	2	.000	.000	1	0	0	0	0	0.0	0	0	2	1	0	0	0	1	0	1	0	1.0	.500	3B-2
1973		7	.167	.367	30	5	0	0	2	6.7	4	2	5	11	0	0	0	4	19	3	1	3.7	.885	3B-7
2 yrs.		9	.161	.355	31	5	0	0	2	6.5	4	2	7	12	0	0	0	5	19	4	1	3.1	.857	3B-9

Gil Garrido

GARRIDO, GIL GONZALO
B. June 26, 1941, Panama City, Panama.
BR TR 5′9″ 150 lbs.

Year	Team	Games	BA	SA	AB	H	2B	3B	HR	HR%	R	RBI	BB	SO	SB	Pinch Hit AB	Pinch Hit H	PO	A	E	DP	TC/G	FA	G by Pos
1964	**SF N**	14	.080	.080	25	2	0	0	0	0.0	1	1	2	7	1	0	0	5	26	1	3	2.3	.969	SS-14
1968	**ATL N**	18	.208	.208	53	11	0	0	0	0.0	5	2	2	2	0	1	0	26	51	1	12	4.6	.987	SS-17
1969		82	.220	.251	227	50	5	1	0	0.0	18	10	16	11	0	0	0	99	192	8	32	3.7	.973	SS-81
1970		101	.264	.308	367	97	5	4	1	0.3	38	19	15	16	0	1	1	162	292	10	46	4.4	.978	SS-80, 2B-26
1971		79	.216	.240	125	27	3	0	0	0.0	8	12	15	12	0	8	3	61	128	6	29	2.5	.969	SS-32, 3B-28, 2B-18
1972		40	.267	.280	75	20	1	0	0	0.0	11	7	11	6	1	3	1	43	62	1	11	3.1	.991	2B-21, SS-10, 3B-3
6 yrs.		334	.237	.268	872	207	14	5	1	0.1	81	51	61	54	2	13	5	396	751	27	133	3.6	.977	SS-234, 2B-65, 3B-31
LEAGUE CHAMPIONSHIP SERIES																								
1969	**ATL N**	3	.200	.200	10	2	0	0	0	0.0	0	0	1	1	0	0	0	4	8	0	3	4.0	1.000	SS-3

Rabbit Garriott

GARRIOTT, VIRGIL CECIL
B. Aug. 15, 1916, Harristown, Ill. D. Feb. 20, 1990, Lake Elsinore, Calif.
BL TR 5′8″ 165 lbs.

Year	Team	Games	BA	SA	AB	H	2B	3B	HR	HR%	R	RBI	BB	SO	SB	Pinch Hit AB	Pinch Hit H	PO	A	E	DP	TC/G	FA	G by Pos
1946	**CHI N**	6	.000	.000	5	0	0	0	0	0.0	1	0	0	2	0	5	0	0	0	0	0	0.0	—	

Ford Garrison

GARRISON, ROBERT FORD (Rocky, Snapper)
B. Aug. 29, 1915, Greenville, S. C.
BR TR 5′10½″ 180 lbs.

Year	Team	Games	BA	SA	AB	H	2B	3B	HR	HR%	R	RBI	BB	SO	SB	Pinch Hit AB	Pinch Hit H	PO	A	E	DP	TC/G	FA	G by Pos
1943	**BOS A**	36	.279	.357	129	36	5	1	1	0.8	13	11	5	14	0	2	0	77	2	1	0	2.5	.988	OF-32
1944	**2 teams**	**BOS A** (13G –.245) **PHI A** (121G –.269)																						
"	**total**	134	.267	.331	498	133	16	2	4	0.8	63	39	28	44	10	2	0	320	6	5	0	2.5	.985	OF-131
1945	**PHI A**	6	.304	.478	23	7	1	0	1	4.3	3	6	4	3	1	1	0	11	1	0	0	2.4	1.000	OF-5
1946		9	.108	.108	37	4	0	0	0	0.0	1	0	0	6	0	1	1	8	0	0	0	1.0	1.000	OF-8
4 yrs.		185	.262	.329	687	180	22	3	6	0.9	80	56	37	67	11	6	1	416	9	6	0	2.4	.986	OF-176

Hank Garrity

GARRITY, FRANCIS JOSEPH
B. Feb. 4, 1908, Boston, Mass. D. Sept. 1, 1962, Boston, Mass.
BR TR 6′1″ 185 lbs.

Year	Team	Games	BA	SA	AB	H	2B	3B	HR	HR%	R	RBI	BB	SO	SB	Pinch Hit AB	Pinch Hit H	PO	A	E	DP	TC/G	FA	G by Pos
1931	**CHI A**	8	.214	.286	14	3	1	0	0	0.0	0	2	1	2	0	0	0	11	5	1	0	2.4	.941	C-7

Steve Garvey

GARVEY, STEVEN PATRICK
B. Dec. 22, 1948, Tampa, Fla.
BR TR 5′10″ 192 lbs.

Year	Team	Games	BA	SA	AB	H	2B	3B	HR	HR%	R	RBI	BB	SO	SB	Pinch Hit AB	Pinch Hit H	PO	A	E	DP	TC/G	FA	G by Pos
1969	**LA N**	3	.333	.333	3	1	0	0	0	0.0	0	0	0	1	0	3	1	0	0	0	0	0.0	—	
1970		34	.269	.355	93	25	5	0	1	1.1	8	6	6	17	1	10	3	23	59	5	4	3.1	.943	3B-27, 2B-1
1971		81	.227	.382	225	51	12	1	7	3.1	27	26	21	33	1	2	0	53	161	14	11	2.9	.939	3B-79
1972		96	.269	.422	294	79	14	2	9	3.1	36	30	19	36	4	11	3	104	189	28	21	3.6	.913	3B-85, 1B-3
1973		114	.304	.438	349	106	17	3	8	2.3	37	50	11	42	0	30	12	731	27	7	58	8.9	.991	1B-76, OF-10
1974		156	.312	.469	642	200	32	3	21	3.3	95	111	31	66	5	0	0	1536	62	8	108	10.3	.995	1B-156
1975		160	.319	.476	659	210	38	6	18	2.7	85	95	33	66	11	0	0	1500	77	8	96	9.9	.995	1B-160
1976		162	.317	.450	631	200	37	4	13	2.1	85	80	50	69	19	0	0	1583	67	3	138	10.2	.998	1B-162
1977		162	.297	.498	646	192	25	3	33	5.1	91	115	38	90	9	1	0	1606	55	8	137	10.4	.995	1B-160
1978		162	.316	.499	639	**202**	36	9	21	3.3	89	113	40	70	10	0	0	1546	74	9	121	10.1	.994	1B-162
1979		162	.315	.497	648	204	32	1	28	4.3	92	110	37	59	3	0	0	1402	93	7	101	9.3	.995	1B-162
1980		163	.304	.467	658	**200**	27	1	26	4.0	78	106	36	67	6	1	0	1502	112	6	122	10.0	.996	1B-162
1981		110	.283	.411	431	122	23	1	10	2.3	63	64	25	49	3	1	0	1019	55	1	84	9.8	.999	1B-110
1982		162	.282	.418	625	176	35	1	16	2.6	66	86	20	86	5	5	0	1539	111	8	132	10.5	.995	1B-158
1983	**SD N**	100	.294	.459	388	114	22	0	14	3.6	76	59	29	39	4	0	0	888	49	6	69	9.4	.994	1B-100
1984		161	.284	.373	617	175	27	2	8	1.3	72	86	24	64	1	1	1	1232	87	0	117	8.2	1.000	1B-160
1985		162	.281	.430	654	184	34	6	17	2.6	80	81	35	67	0	0	0	1442	92	5	138	9.5	.997	1B-162
1986		155	.255	.408	557	142	22	0	21	3.8	58	81	23	72	1	11	2	1160	53	7	94	8.2	.994	1B-148
1987		27	.211	.276	76	16	2	0	1	1.3	5	9	1	10	0	7	4	138	11	0	10	7.4	1.000	1B-20
19 yrs.		2332	.294	.446	8835	2599	440	43	272	3.1	1143	1308	479	1003	83	82	26	19004	1434	130	1561	9.1	.994	1B-2061, 3B-191, OF-10, 2B-1
DIVISIONAL PLAYOFF SERIES																								
1981	**LA N**	5	.368	.789	19	7	0	1	2	10.5	4	4	0	2	0	0	0	49	5	0	0	10.8	1.000	1B-5
LEAGUE CHAMPIONSHIP SERIES																								
1974	**LA N**	4	.389	.778	18	7	1	0	2	11.1	4	5	1	1	0	0	0	40	2	1	6	10.8	.977	1B-4
1977		4	.308	.308	13	4	0	0	0	0.0	2	0	2	1	1	0	0	40	1	0	3	10.3	1.000	1B-4
1978		4	.389	1.222	18	7	1	1	4	22.2	6	7	0	1	0	0	0	44	5	0	4	12.3	1.000	1B-4
1981		5	.286	.429	21	6	0	0	1	4.8	2	2	0	4	0	0	0	49	2	0	4	10.2	1.000	1B-5
1984	**SD N**	5	.400	.600	20	8	1	0	1	5.0	1	7	1	2	0	0	0	35	3	0	3	7.6	1.000	1B-5
5 yrs.		22	.356	.678	90	32	3	1	8	8.9	15	21	4	9	1	0	0	208	13	1	20	10.1	.995	1B-22
			7th	**3rd**	**9th**	**4th**			**2nd**	**1st**	**5th**	**1st**												
WORLD SERIES																								
1974	**LA N**	5	.381	.381	21	8	0	0	0	0.0	2	1	0	3	0	0	0	34	3	0	4	7.4	1.000	1B-5
1977		6	.375	.625	24	9	1	1	1	4.2	5	3	1	4	0	0	0	59	6	0	4	10.8	1.000	1B-6
1978		6	.208	.250	24	5	1	0	0	0.0	1	0	1	7	1	0	0	58	3	1	4	10.3	.984	1B-6

Steve Garvey *continued*

Year	Team	Games	BA	SA	AB	H	2B	3B	HR	HR%	R	RBI	BB	SO	SB	Pinch Hit AB	Pinch Hit H	PO	A	E	DP	TC/G	FA	G by Pos
1981		6	.417	.458	24	10	1	0	0	0.0	3	0	2	5	0	0	0	44	3	0	5	7.8	1.000	1B-6
1984	SD N	5	.200	.300	20	4	2	0	0	0.0	2	2	0	2	0	0	0	34	3	0	4	7.4	1.000	1B-5
5 yrs.		28	.319	.407	113	36	5	1	1	0.9	13	6	4	21	1	0	0	229	18	1	21	8.9	.996	1B-28

Rod Gaspar

GASPAR, RODNEY EARL BB TL 5′11″ 165 lbs.
B. Apr. 3, 1946, Long Beach, Calif.

Year	Team	Games	BA	SA	AB	H	2B	3B	HR	HR%	R	RBI	BB	SO	SB	Pinch Hit AB	Pinch Hit H	PO	A	E	DP	TC/G	FA	G by Pos
1969	NY N	118	.228	.279	215	49	6	1	1	0.5	26	14	25	19	7	25	4	104	12	2	6	1.3	.983	OF-91
1970		11	.000	.000	14	0	0	0	0	0.0	4	0	1	4	1	1	0	13	0	0	0	1.6	1.000	OF-8
1971	SD N	16	.118	.118	17	2	0	0	0	0.0	1	2	3	3	0	11	1	4	0	0	0	2.0	1.000	OF-2
1974		33	.214	.214	14	3	0	0	0	0.0	4	1	4	3	0	12	3	6	1	0	0	0.7	1.000	OF-8, 1B-2
4 yrs.		178	.208	.250	260	54	6	1	1	0.4	35	17	33	29	8	49	8	127	13	2	6	1.3	.986	OF-109, 1B-2
LEAGUE CHAMPIONSHIP SERIES																								
1969	NY N	3	—	—	0	0	0	0	0	—	0	0	0	0	0	0	0	2	0	0	0	0.7	1.000	OF-3
WORLD SERIES																								
1969	NY N	3	.000	.000	2	0	0	0	0	0.0	1	0	0	0	0	1	0	2	0	0	0	2.0	1.000	OF-1

Tommy Gastall

GASTALL, THOMAS EVERETT BR TR 6′2″ 187 lbs.
B. June 13, 1932, Fall River, Mass. D. Sept. 20, 1956, Riviera Beach, Md.

Year	Team	Games	BA	SA	AB	H	2B	3B	HR	HR%	R	RBI	BB	SO	SB	Pinch Hit AB	Pinch Hit H	PO	A	E	DP	TC/G	FA	G by Pos
1955	BAL A	20	.148	.185	27	4	1	0	0	0.0	4	0	3	5	0	5	1	28	1	1	1	2.0	.967	C-15
1956		32	.196	.232	56	11	2	0	0	0.0	3	4	3	8	0	12	0	67	6	0	1	3.7	1.000	C-20
2 yrs.		52	.181	.217	83	15	3	0	0	0.0	7	4	6	13	0	17	1	95	7	1	2	2.9	.990	C-35

Ed Gastfield

GASTFIELD, EDWARD BR 5′9½″ 155 lbs.
B. Aug. 1, 1865, Chicago, Ill. D. Dec. 1, 1899, Chicago, Ill.

Year	Team	Games	BA	SA	AB	H	2B	3B	HR	HR%	R	RBI	BB	SO	SB	Pinch Hit AB	Pinch Hit H	PO	A	E	DP	TC/G	FA	G by Pos
1884	DET N	23	.073	.085	82	6	1	0	0	0.0	6		2	34		0	0	142	53	36	4	10.0	.844	C-19, OF-2, 1B-2
1885	2 teams DET N (1G –.000) CHI N (1G –.000)																							
″	total	2	.000	.000	6	0	0	0	0	0.0	0	0	0	3		0	0	14	2	2	1	9.0	.889	C-2
2 yrs.		25	.068	.080	88	6	1	0	0	0.0	6	0	2	37		0	0	156	55	38	5	10.0	.847	C-21, OF-2, 1B-2

Alex Gaston

GASTON, ALEXANDER NATHANIEL BR TR 5′9″ 170 lbs.
Brother of Milt Gaston.
B. Mar. 12, 1893, New York, N. Y. D. Feb. 8, 1976, Santa Monica, Calif.

Year	Team	Games	BA	SA	AB	H	2B	3B	HR	HR%	R	RBI	BB	SO	SB	Pinch Hit AB	Pinch Hit H	PO	A	E	DP	TC/G	FA	G by Pos
1920	NY N	4	.100	.100	10	1	0	0	0	0.0	2	1	1	2	0	1	0	10	1	1	0	4.0	.917	C-3
1921		20	.227	.364	22	5	1	1	0	0.0	1	3	1	9	0	9	2	19	0	1	0	1.8	.950	C-11
1922		16	.192	.192	26	5	0	0	0	0.0	1	1	0	3	1	3	1	24	3	0	0	1.9	1.000	C-14
1923		22	.205	.333	39	8	2	0	1	2.6	3	5	0	6	0	1	0	34	11	2	0	2.2	.957	C-21
1926	BOS A	98	.223	.259	301	67	5	3	0	0.0	37	21	21	28	3	0	0	284	69	7	5	3.7	.981	C-98
1929		55	.224	.353	116	26	5	2	2	1.7	14	9	6	8	1	4	1	116	25	2	6	2.9	.986	C-49
6 yrs.		215	.218	.284	514	112	13	6	3	0.6	58	40	29	56	5	18	4	487	109	13	11	3.1	.979	C-196

Cito Gaston

GASTON, CLARENCE EDWIN BR TR 6′3″ 190 lbs.
B. Mar. 17, 1944, San Antonio, Tex.
Manager 1989–95.

Year	Team	Games	BA	SA	AB	H	2B	3B	HR	HR%	R	RBI	BB	SO	SB	Pinch Hit AB	Pinch Hit H	PO	A	E	DP	TC/G	FA	G by Pos
1967	ATL N	9	.120	.200	25	3	0	1	0	0.0	1	1	0	5	1	1	0	7	1	2	0	1.4	.800	OF-7
1969	SD N	129	.230	.309	391	90	11	7	2	0.5	20	28	24	117	4	17	1	243	12	11	4	2.4	.959	OF-113
1970		146	.318	.543	584	186	26	9	29	5.0	92	93	41	142	4	4	1	310	7	8	0	2.3	.975	OF-142
1971		141	.228	.386	518	118	13	9	17	3.3	57	61	24	121	1	11	1	271	8	5	1	2.1	.982	OF-133
1972		111	.269	.361	379	102	14	0	7	1.8	30	44	22	76	0	18	4	158	10	4	3	1.8	.977	OF-94
1973		133	.250	.405	476	119	18	4	16	3.4	51	57	20	88	0	13	3	198	16	12	4	1.9	.947	OF-119
1974		106	.213	.322	267	57	11	0	6	2.2	19	33	16	51	0	39	9	119	7	1	1	2.0	.992	OF-63
1975	ATL N	64	.241	.397	141	34	4	0	6	4.3	17	15	17	33	1	25	7	80	2	3	1	2.4	.965	OF-35, 1B-1
1976		69	.291	.410	134	39	4	0	4	3.0	15	25	13	21	1	40	12	58	2	1	2	2.0	.984	OF-28, 1B-2
1977		56	.271	.424	85	23	4	0	3	3.5	6	21	5	19	1	37	12	44	4	1	2	3.5	.980	OF-9, 1B-5
1978	2 teams ATL N (61G –.229) PIT N (1G –.500)																							
″	total	62	.233	.267	120	28	1	0	1	0.8	6	9	3	20	0	29	9	66	2	3	1	2.1	.958	OF-30, 1B-4
11 yrs.		1026	.256	.397	3120	799	106	30	91	2.9	314	387	185	693	13	234	59	1554	71	51	19	2.1	.970	OF-773, 1B-12

Brent Gates

GATES, BRENT ROBERT BB TR 6′1″ 180 lbs.
B. Mar. 14, 1970, Grand Rapids, Mich.

Year	Team	Games	BA	SA	AB	H	2B	3B	HR	HR%	R	RBI	BB	SO	SB	Pinch Hit AB	Pinch Hit H	PO	A	E	DP	TC/G	FA	G by Pos
1993	OAK A	139	.290	.391	535	155	29	2	7	1.3	64	69	56	75	7	3	1	281	431	14	88	5.2	.981	2B-139
1994		64	.283	.365	233	66	11	1	2	0.9	29	24	21	32	3	2	1	112	160	8	28	4.4	.971	2B-63, 1B-1
1995		136	.254	.344	524	133	24	4	5	1.0	60	56	46	84	3	1	0	240	427	12	80	5.0	.982	2B-132, DH-3, 1B-1
3 yrs.		339	.274	.367	1292	354	64	7	14	1.1	153	149	123	191	13	6	2	633	1018	34	196	5.0	.980	2B-334, DH-3, 1B-2

Joe Gates

GATES, JOSEPH DANIEL BL TR 5′7″ 175 lbs.
B. Oct. 3, 1954, Gary, Ind.

Year	Team	Games	BA	SA	AB	H	2B	3B	HR	HR%	R	RBI	BB	SO	SB	Pinch Hit AB	Pinch Hit H	PO	A	E	DP	TC/G	FA	G by Pos
1978	CHI A	8	.250	.250	24	6	0	0	0	0.0	6	1	4	6	1	0	0	9	26	1	4	4.5	.972	2B-8
1979		16	.063	.188	16	1	0	1	0	0.0	5	1	2	3	1	3	0	12	17	1	3	3.0	.967	2B-8, 3B-1, DH-1
2 yrs.		24	.175	.225	40	7	0	1	0	0.0	11	2	6	9	2	3	0	21	43	2	7	3.7	.970	2B-16, 3B-1, DH-1

Mike Gates

GATES, MICHAEL GRANT BL TR 6′ 165 lbs.
B. Sept. 20, 1956, Culver City, Calif.

Year	Team	Games	BA	SA	AB	H	2B	3B	HR	HR%	R	RBI	BB	SO	SB	Pinch Hit AB	Pinch Hit H	PO	A	E	DP	TC/G	FA	G by Pos
1981	MON N	1	.500	1.500	2	1	0	1	0	0.0	1	1	0	1	0	1	0	0	1	0	0	1.0	1.000	2B-1
1982		36	.231	.298	121	28	2	3	0	0.0	16	8	9	19	0	2	0	53	91	0	18	4.0	1.000	2B-36
2 yrs.		37	.236	.317	123	29	2	4	0	0.0	17	9	9	20	0	3	0	53	92	0	18	3.9	1.000	2B-37

Frank Gatins

GATINS, FRANK ANTHONY
B. Mar. 6, 1871, Johnstown, Pa. D. Nov. 8, 1911, Johnstown, Pa.

Year	Team	Games	BA	SA	AB	H	2B	3B	HR	HR%	R	RBI	BB	SO	SB	Pinch Hit AB	Pinch Hit H	PO	A	E	DP	TC/G	FA	G by Pos
1898	WAS N	17	.224	.259	58	13	2	0	0	0.0	6	5	3		2	0	0	22	42	17	6	4.8	.790	SS-17
1901	BKN N	50	.228	.299	197	45	7	2	1	0.5	21	21	5		6	0	0	73	72	11	7	3.1	.929	3B-46, SS-5
2 yrs.		67	.227	.290	255	58	9	2	1	0.4	27	26	8		8	0	0	95	114	28	13	3.5	.882	3B-46, SS-22

Jim Gaudet

GAUDET, JAMES JENNINGS
B. June 3, 1955, New Orleans, La.
BR TR 6' 185 lbs.

Year	Team	Games	BA	SA	AB	H	2B	3B	HR	HR%	R	RBI	BB	SO	SB	Pinch Hit AB	Pinch Hit H	PO	A	E	DP	TC/G	FA	G by Pos
1978	KC A	3	.000	.000	8	0	0	0	0	0.0	0	0	0	3	0	0	0	14	1	1	0	5.3	.938	C-3
1979		3	.167	.167	6	1	0	0	0	0.0	0	0	0	0	0	0	0	13	0	0	0	4.3	1.000	C-3
2 yrs.		6	.071	.071	14	1	0	0	0	0.0	0	0	0	3	0	0	0	27	1	1	0	4.8	.966	C-6

Mike Gaule

GAULE, MICHAEL JOHN
B. Aug. 4, 1869, Baltimore, Md. D. Jan. 24, 1918, Baltimore, Md.
BL TL 6' 2"

Year	Team	Games	BA	SA	AB	H	2B	3B	HR	HR%	R	RBI	BB	SO	SB	Pinch Hit AB	Pinch Hit H	PO	A	E	DP	TC/G	FA	G by Pos
1889	LOU AA	1	.000	.000	2	0	0	0	0	0.0	0	0	0	1	0	0	0	0	0	1	0	1.0	.000	OF-1

Doc Gautreau

GAUTREAU, WALTER PAUL
B. July 26, 1901, Cambridge, Mass. D. Aug. 23, 1970, Salt Lake City, Utah.
BR TR 5' 4" 129 lbs.

Year	Team	Games	BA	SA	AB	H	2B	3B	HR	HR%	R	RBI	BB	SO	SB	Pinch Hit AB	Pinch Hit H	PO	A	E	DP	TC/G	FA	G by Pos
1925	2 teams	PHI A (4G –.000)	BOS N (68G –.262)																					
"	total	72	.255	.322	286	73	13	3	0	0.0	45	23	35	16	11	0	0	178	238	11	40	5.9	.974	2B-72
1926	BOS N	79	.267	.331	266	71	9	4	0	0.0	36	8	35	24	17	3	0	170	205	23	42	5.4	.942	2B-74
1927		87	.246	.314	236	58	12	2	0	0.0	38	20	25	20	11	17	0	136	196	12	22	6.0	.965	2B-57
1928		23	.278	.389	18	5	0	1	0	0.0	3	1	4	3	1	15	4	2	2	1	1	1.0	.800	2B-4, SS-1
4 yrs.		261	.257	.324	806	207	34	10	0	0.0	122	52	99	63	40	35	4	486	641	47	105	5.6	.960	2B-207, SS-1

Sid Gautreaux

GAUTREAUX, SIDNEY ALLEN (Pudge)
B. May 4, 1912, Schriever, La. D. Apr. 19, 1980, Morgan City, La.
BB TR 5' 8" 190 lbs.

Year	Team	Games	BA	SA	AB	H	2B	3B	HR	HR%	R	RBI	BB	SO	SB	Pinch Hit AB	Pinch Hit H	PO	A	E	DP	TC/G	FA	G by Pos
1936	BKN N	75	.268	.310	71	19	3	0	0	0.0	8	16	9	7	0	**55**	**16**	23	3	1	2	1.8	.963	C-15
1937		11	.100	.200	10	1	1	0	0	0.0	0	2	1	1	0	10	1	0	0	0	0	0.0	—	
2 yrs.		86	.247	.296	81	20	4	0	0	0.0	8	18	10	8	0	65	17	23	3	1	2	1.8	.963	C-15

Mike Gazella

GAZELLA, MICHAEL
B. Oct. 13, 1896, Olyphant, Pa. D. Sept. 11, 1978, Odessa, Tex.
BR TR 5' 7½" 165 lbs.

Year	Team	Games	BA	SA	AB	H	2B	3B	HR	HR%	R	RBI	BB	SO	SB	Pinch Hit AB	Pinch Hit H	PO	A	E	DP	TC/G	FA	G by Pos
1923	NY A	8	.077	.077	13	1	0	0	0	0.0	2	1	2	3	0	0	0	4	9	0	0	1.6	1.000	SS-4, 3B-2, 2B-2
1926		66	.232	.268	168	39	6	0	0	0.0	21	21	25	24	2	9	4	59	103	16	9	3.2	.910	3B-45, SS-11
1927		54	.278	.417	115	32	8	4	0	0.0	17	9	23	16	4	0	0	41	61	5	6	2.1	.953	3B-44, SS-6
1928		32	.232	.232	56	13	0	0	0	0.0	11	2	6	7	2	6	0	10	31	3	1	2.1	.932	3B-14, 2B-4, SS-3
4 yrs.		160	.241	.304	352	85	14	4	0	0.0	51	33	56	50	8	15	4	114	204	24	16	2.5	.930	3B-105, SS-24, 2B-6
WORLD SERIES																								
1926	NY A	1	—	—	0	0	0	0	0	—	0	0	0	0	0	0	0	1	2	0	0	3.0	1.000	3B-1

Dale Gear

GEAR, DALE DUDLEY
B. Feb. 2, 1872, Lone Elm, Kans. D. Sept. 23, 1951, Topeka, Kans.
BR TR 5'11" 165 lbs.

Year	Team	Games	BA	SA	AB	H	2B	3B	HR	HR%	R	RBI	BB	SO	SB	Pinch Hit AB	Pinch Hit H	PO	A	E	DP	TC/G	FA	G by Pos
1896	CLE N	4	.400	.600	15	6	1	1	0	0.0	5	3	1	1	0	0	0	9	4	2	1	3.8	.867	P-3, 1B-1
1897		7	.167	.208	24	4	1	0	0	0.0	3	2	3		2	0	0	9	3	4	0	2.7	.750	OF-6
1901	WAS A	58	.236	.302	199	47	9	2	0	0.0	17	20	4		2	2	0	56	59	6	3	2.1	.950	OF-34, P-24
3 yrs.		69	.239	.311	238	57	11	3	0	0.0	25	25	8	1	4	2	0	74	66	12	4	2.2	.921	OF-40, P-27, 1B-1

Lloyd Gearhart

GEARHART, LLOYD WILLIAM (Gary)
B. Aug. 10, 1923, New Lebanon, Ohio.
BR TL 5'11" 180 lbs.

Year	Team	Games	BA	SA	AB	H	2B	3B	HR	HR%	R	RBI	BB	SO	SB	Pinch Hit AB	Pinch Hit H	PO	A	E	DP	TC/G	FA	G by Pos
1947	NY N	73	.246	.397	179	44	9	0	6	3.4	26	17	17	30	1	20	5	94	4	4	1	2.3	.961	OF-44

Huck Geary

GEARY, EUGENE FRANCIS JOSEPH
B. Jan. 22, 1917, Buffalo, N. Y. D. Jan. 27, 1981, Cuba, N. Y.
BL TR 5'10½" 170 lbs.

Year	Team	Games	BA	SA	AB	H	2B	3B	HR	HR%	R	RBI	BB	SO	SB	Pinch Hit AB	Pinch Hit H	PO	A	E	DP	TC/G	FA	G by Pos
1942	PIT N	9	.227	.227	22	5	0	0	0	0.0	3	2	2	3	0	1	1	17	14	2	5	4.1	.939	SS-8
1943		46	.151	.193	166	25	4	0	1	0.6	17	13	18	6	3	0	0	92	127	10	25	5.0	.956	SS-46
2 yrs.		55	.160	.197	188	30	4	0	1	0.5	20	15	20	9	3	1	1	109	141	12	30	4.9	.954	SS-54

Elmer Gedeon

GEDEON, ELMER JOHN
B. Apr. 15, 1917, Cleveland, Ohio D. Apr. 20, 1944, St. Pol, France.
BR TR 6' 4" 196 lbs.

Year	Team	Games	BA	SA	AB	H	2B	3B	HR	HR%	R	RBI	BB	SO	SB	Pinch Hit AB	Pinch Hit H	PO	A	E	DP	TC/G	FA	G by Pos
1939	WAS A	5	.200	.200	15	3	0	0	0	0.0	1	1	2	5	0	0	0	17	0	0	0	3.4	1.000	OF-5

Joe Gedeon

GEDEON, ELMER JOSEPH
B. Dec. 5, 1893, Sacramento, Calif. D. May 19, 1941, San Francisco, Calif.
BR TR 6' 167 lbs.

Year	Team	Games	BA	SA	AB	H	2B	3B	HR	HR%	R	RBI	BB	SO	SB	Pinch Hit AB	Pinch Hit H	PO	A	E	DP	TC/G	FA	G by Pos
1913	WAS A	27	.183	.296	71	13	1	2	1	1.4	3	6	1	6	3	2	0	32	16	3	2	2.0	.941	OF-14, 3B-8, 2B-2, P-1, SS-1
1914		3	.000	.000	2	0	0	0	0	0.0	0	1	0	1	0	0	0	2	0	1	0	1.0	.667	OF-3
1916	NY A	122	.211	.262	435	92	14	4	0	0.0	50	27	40	61	14	0	0	235	341	27	55	4.9	.955	2B-122
1917		33	.239	.299	117	28	7	0	0	0.0	15	8	7	13	4	2	0	83	86	3	12	5.5	.983	2B-31
1918	STL A	123	.213	.265	441	94	14	3	1	0.2	39	41	27	29	7	0	0	309	409	17	45	6.0	.977	2B-123
1919		120	.254	.302	437	111	13	4	0	0.0	57	27	50	35	4	1	0	290	345	16	44	5.5	.975	2B-118
1920		153	.292	.366	606	177	33	6	0	0.0	95	61	55	36	1	0	0	365	421	29	75	5.3	.964	2B-153
7 yrs.		581	.244	.304	2109	515	82	19	2	0.1	259	171	180	181	33	5	0	1316	1618	96	233	5.3	.968	2B-549, OF-17, 3B-8, P-1, SS-1

Rich Gedman

GEDMAN, RICHARD LEO
B. Sept. 26, 1959, Worcester, Mass.
BL TR 6' 210 lbs.

Year	Team	Games	BA	SA	AB	H	2B	3B	HR	HR%	R	RBI	BB	SO	SB	Pinch Hit AB	Pinch Hit H	PO	A	E	DP	TC/G	FA	G by Pos
1980	BOS A	9	.208	.208	24	5	0	0	0	0.0	2	1	0	5	0	5	0	13	0	2	0	2.5	.867	DH-4, C-2
1981		62	.288	.434	205	59	15	0	5	2.4	22	26	9	31	0	3	1	275	30	3	1	5.2	.990	C-59
1982		92	.249	.363	289	72	17	2	4	1.4	30	26	10	37	0	9	2	397	29	10	5	5.1	.977	C-86
1983		81	.294	.412	204	60	16	1	2	1.0	21	18	15	37	0	19	5	274	26	6	5	4.4	.980	C-69
1984		133	.269	.506	449	121	26	4	24	5.3	54	72	29	72	0	15	5	693	58	18	5	6.2	.977	C-125
1985		144	.295	.484	498	147	30	5	18	3.6	66	80	50	79	2	9	4	768	78	15	13	6.2	.983	C-139
1986		135	.258	.424	462	119	29	0	16	3.5	49	65	37	61	1	9	4	866	65	6	10	7.0	.994	C-134
1987		52	.205	.278	151	31	8	0	1	0.7	11	13	10	24	0	4	1	306	14	8	1	6.4	.976	C-51
1988		95	.231	.368	299	69	14	0	9	3.0	33	39	18	49	0	2	0	570	40	5	4	6.5	.992	C-93, DH-1
1989		93	.212	.292	260	55	9	0	4	1.5	24	16	23	47	0	5	1	486	36	10	6	5.8	.981	C-91
1990	2 teams	BOS A (10G –.200)	HOU N (40G –.202)																					
"	total	50	.202	.286	119	24	7	0	1	0.8	7	10	20	30	0	4	1	207	30	1	6	5.0	.996	C-48
1991	STL N	46	.106	.213	94	10	1	0	3	3.2	7	8	4	15	0	6	0	192	13	5	4	4.9	.976	C-43
1992		41	.219	.286	105	23	4	0	1	1.0	5	8	11	22	0	2	0	227	12	3	2	6.1	.988	C-40
13 yrs.		1033	.252	.399	3159	795	176	12	88	2.8	331	382	236	509	3	92	24	5274	431	92	62	5.9	.984	C-980, DH-5

Rich Gedman *continued*

Year	Team	Games	BA	SA	AB	H	2B	3B	HR	HR%	R	RBI	BB	SO	SB	Pinch Hit AB	Pinch Hit H	PO	A	E	DP	TC/G	FA	G by Pos
LEAGUE CHAMPIONSHIP SERIES																								
1986	BOS A	7	.357	.500	28	10	1	0	1	3.6	4	6	0	4	0	0	0	45	4	0	0	7.0	1.000	C-7
1988		4	.357	.571	14	5	0	0	1	7.1	1	1	2	1	0	0	0	34	5	0	1	9.8	1.000	C-4
2 yrs.		11	.357	.524	42	15	1	0	2	4.8	5	7	2	5	0	0	0	79	9	0	1	8.0	1.000	C-11
WORLD SERIES																								
1986	BOS A	7	.200	.333	30	6	1	0	1	3.3	1	1	0	10	0	0	0	46	3	2	2	7.3	.961	C-7

Billy Geer

GEER, WILLIAM HENRY HARRISON TR 5′ 8″ 160 lbs.
Born George Harrison Geer.
B. Aug. 13, 1849, Syracuse, N. Y. D. Jan. 5, 1922, Syracuse, N. Y.

Year	Team	Games	BA	SA	AB	H	2B	3B	HR	HR%	R	RBI	BB	SO	SB	Pinch Hit AB	Pinch Hit H	PO	A	E	DP	TC/G	FA	G by Pos
1878	CIN N	61	.219	.291	237	52	13	2	0	0.0	31	20	10	18		0	0	62	181	38	15	4.5	.865	SS-60, 2B-2
1880	WOR N	2	.000	.000	6	0	0	0	0	0.0	0	0	0	0		0	0	1	4	1	0	3.0	.833	SS-1, OF-1
1884	2 teams	PHI U (9G –.250) BKN AA (107G –.210)																						
″	total	116	.213	.290	427	91	17	8	0	0.0	75		42			0	0	187	398	94	35	5.7	.862	SS-115, P-2, 2B-2, 1B-1
1885	LOU AA	14	.118	.157	51	6	2	0	0	0.0	2		2			0	0	26	49	11	2	6.1	.872	SS-14
4 yrs.		193	.207	.279	721	149	32	10	0	0.0	108	20	54	18		0	0	276	632	144	52	5.3	.863	SS-190, 2B-4, P-2, 1B-1, OF-1

Charlie Geggus

GEGGUS, CHARLES FREDERICK
B. Mar. 25, 1862, San Francisco, Calif. D. Jan. 16, 1917, San Francisco, Calif.

Year	Team	Games	BA	SA	AB	H	2B	3B	HR	HR%	R	RBI	BB	SO	SB	Pinch Hit AB	Pinch Hit H	PO	A	E	DP	TC/G	FA	G by Pos
1884	WAS U	44	.247	.305	154	38	7	1	0	0.0	14		4			0	0	50	49	23	1	2.5	.811	P-23, OF-21, SS-3, 2B-1

Lou Gehrig

GEHRIG, HENRY LOUIS (Columbia Lou, The Iron Horse) BL TL 6′ 200 lbs.
Born Ludwig Heinrich Gehrig.
B. June 19, 1903, New York, N. Y. D. June 2, 1941, New York, N. Y.
Hall of Fame 1939.

Year	Team	Games	BA	SA	AB	H	2B	3B	HR	HR%	R	RBI	BB	SO	SB	Pinch Hit AB	Pinch Hit H	PO	A	E	DP	TC/G	FA	G by Pos
1923	NY A	13	.423	.769	26	11	4	1	1	3.8	6	9	2	5	0	4	1	53	3	4	4	6.7	.933	1B-9
1924		10	.500	.583	12	6	1	0	0	0.0	2	5	1	3	0	6	2	10	1	0	0	3.7	1.000	1B-2, OF-1
1925		126	.295	.531	437	129	23	10	20	4.6	73	68	46	49	6	6	1	1135	53	15	72	10.0	.988	1B-114, OF-6
1926		155	.313	.549	572	179	47	**20**	16	2.8	135	107	105	72	6	0	0	1566	73	15	87	10.7	.991	1B-155
1927		155	.373	.765	584	218	**52**	18	47	8.0	149	**175**	109	84	10	0	0	1662	88	15	108	11.4	.992	1B-155
1928		154	.374	.648	562	210	**47**	13	27	4.8	139	**142**	95	69	4	0	0	1488	79	18	112	10.3	.989	1B-154
1929		154	.300	.582	553	166	33	9	35	6.3	127	126	122	68	4	0	0	1458	82	9	134	10.1	.994	1B-154
1930		154	.379	.721	581	220	42	17	41	7.1	143	**174**	101	63	12	0	0	1300	89	15	109	9.1	.989	1B-153, OF-1
1931		155	.341	.662	619	**211**	31	15	**46**	7.4	**163**	**184**	117	56	17	0	0	1355	58	14	120	9.2	.990	1B-154, OF-1
1932		156	.349	.621	596	208	42	9	34	5.7	138	151	108	38	4	0	0	1293	75	18	101	8.9	.987	1B-155
1933		152	.334	.605	593	198	41	12	32	5.4	**138**	139	92	42	9	0	0	1290	64	9	102	9.0	.993	1B-152
1934		154	**.363**	**.706**	579	210	40	6	**49**	**8.5**	128	**165**	109	31	9	0	0	1284	80	8	126	8.9	.994	1B-153, SS-1
1935		149	.329	.583	535	176	26	10	30	5.6	**125**	119	**132**	38	8	0	0	1337	82	15	96	9.6	.990	1B-149
1936		155	.354	**.696**	579	205	37	7	**49**	**8.5**	**167**	152	**130**	46	3	0	0	1377	82	9	128	9.5	.994	1B-155
1937		157	.351	.643	569	200	37	9	37	6.5	138	159	**127**	49	4	0	0	1370	74	16	113	9.3	.989	1B-157
1938		157	.295	.523	576	170	32	6	29	5.0	115	114	107	75	6	0	0	1483	100	14	157	10.2	.991	1B-157
1939		8	.143	.143	28	4	0	0	0	0.0	2	1	5	1	0	0	0	64	4	2	5	8.8	.971	1B-8
17 yrs.		2164	.340	.632 **3rd**	8001	2721	535	162	493	6.2	1888 **7th**	1990 **3rd**	1508	789	102	16	4	19525	1087	196	1574	9.7	.991	1B-2136, OF-9, SS-1
WORLD SERIES																								
1926	NY A	7	.348	.435	23	8	2	0	0	0.0	1	3	5	4	0	0	0	78	1	0	3	11.3	1.000	1B-7
1927		4	.308	.769	13	4	2	2	0	0.0	2	5	3	3	0	0	0	41	3	0	3	11.0	1.000	1B-4
1928		4	.545	1.727	11	6	1	0	4	36.4	5	9	6	0	0	0	0	33	0	0	3	8.3	1.000	1B-4
1932		4	.529	1.118	17	9	1	0	3	17.6	9	8	2	1	0	0	0	37	2	1	1	10.0	.975	1B-4
1936		6	.292	.583	24	7	1	0	2	8.3	5	7	3	2	0	0	0	45	2	0	2	7.8	1.000	1B-6
1937		5	.294	.647	17	5	1	1	1	5.9	4	3	5	4	0	0	0	50	1	0	2	10.2	1.000	1B-5
1938		4	.286	.286	14	4	0	0	0	0.0	4	0	2	3	0	0	0	25	3	0	4	7.0	1.000	1B-4
7 yrs.		34	.361 **10th**	.731 **3rd**	119	43 **9th**	8 **6th**	3 **4th**	10 **5th**	8.4 **6th**	30 **4th**	35 **3rd**	26 **5th**	17	0	0	0	309	12	1	18	9.5	.997	1B-34

Charlie Gehringer

GEHRINGER, CHARLES LEONARD (The Mechanical Man) BL TR 5′11″ 180 lbs.
B. May 11, 1903, Fowlerville, Mich. D. Jan. 21, 1993, Bloomfield Hills, Mich.
Hall of Fame 1949.

Year	Team	Games	BA	SA	AB	H	2B	3B	HR	HR%	R	RBI	BB	SO	SB	Pinch Hit AB	Pinch Hit H	PO	A	E	DP	TC/G	FA	G by Pos
1924	DET A	5	.462	.462	13	6	0	0	0	0.0	2	1	0	2	1	0	0	12	17	1	2	6.0	.967	2B-5
1925		8	.167	.167	18	3	0	0	0	0.0	3	0	2	0	0	2	0	8	20	0	5	4.7	1.000	2B-6
1926		123	.277	.399	459	127	19	17	1	0.2	62	48	30	42	9	6	0	264	340	16	56	5.3	.974	2B-112, 3B-6
1927		133	.317	.441	508	161	29	11	4	0.8	110	61	52	31	17	9	3	304	438	27	84	6.4	.965	2B-121
1928		154	.320	.451	603	193	29	16	6	1.0	108	74	69	22	15	0	0	377	507	35	101	6.0	.962	2B-154
1929		155	.339	.532	634	**215**	**45**	**19**	13	2.1	**131**	106	64	19	**28**	1	0	404	501	23	93	6.0	.975	2B-154
1930		154	.330	.534	610	201	47	15	16	2.6	144	98	69	17	19	0	0	399	501	19	97	6.0	.979	2B-154
1931		101	.311	.431	383	119	24	5	4	1.0	67	53	29	15	13	12	1	292	242	11	57	6.3	.980	2B-78, 1B-9
1932		152	.298	.497	618	184	44	11	19	3.1	112	107	68	34	9	0	0	396	495	30	110	6.1	.967	2B-152
1933		155	.325	.468	628	204	42	6	12	1.9	103	105	68	27	5	0	0	358	542	17	111	5.9	.981	2B-155
1934		154	.356	.517	601	**214**	50	7	11	1.8	**134**	127	99	25	11	0	0	355	516	17	100	5.8	.981	2B-154
1935		150	.330	.502	610	201	32	8	19	3.1	123	108	79	16	11	2	1	349	489	13	99	5.7	.985	2B-149
1936		154	.354	.555	641	227	**60**	12	15	2.3	144	116	83	13	4	0	0	397	524	25	116	6.1	.974	2B-154
1937		144	**.371**	.520	564	209	40	1	14	2.5	133	96	90	25	11	1	0	331	485	12	102	5.8	.986	2B-142
1938		152	.306	.486	568	174	32	5	20	3.5	133	107	112	21	14	0	0	393	455	21	115	5.7	.976	2B-152
1939		118	.325	.544	406	132	29	6	16	3.9	86	86	68	16	4	9	4	245	312	13	67	5.3	.977	2B-107
1940		139	.313	.447	515	161	33	3	10	1.9	108	81	101	17	10	1	0	276	374	19	72	4.8	.972	2B-138
1941		127	.220	.303	436	96	19	4	3	0.7	65	46	95	26	1	10	3	279	324	11	59	5.3	.982	2B-116
1942		45	.267	.333	45	12	0	0	1	2.2	6	7	7	4	0	**38**	**11**	7	9	0	1	5.3	1.000	2B-3
19 yrs.		2323	.320	.480	8860	2839	574	146	184	2.1	1774	1427	1185	372	182	91	23	5446	7091	310	1447	5.8	.976	2B-2206, 1B-9, 3B-6

Charlie Gehringer *continued*

Year	Team	Games	BA	SA	AB	H	2B	3B	HR	HR%	R	RBI	BB	SO	SB	Pinch Hit AB	Pinch Hit H	PO	A	E	DP	TC/G	FA	G by Pos
WORLD SERIES																								
1934	DET A	7	.379	.517	29	11	1	0	1	3.4	5	2	3	0	1	0	0	19	26	3	3	6.9	.938	2B-7
1935		6	.375	.500	24	9	3	0	0	0.0	4	4	2	1	1	0	0	14	25	0	6	6.5	1.000	2B-6
1940		7	.214	.214	28	6	0	0	0	0.0	3	1	2	0	0	0	0	18	20	0	3	5.4	1.000	2B-7
3 yrs.		20	.321	.407	81	26	4	0	1	1.2	12	7	7	1	2	0	0	51	71	3	12	6.3	.976	2B-20

Phil Geier

GEIER, PHILIP LOUIS (Little Phil)
B. Nov. 3, 1876, Washington, D. C. D. Sept. 20, 1967, Spokane, Wash.
BL TR 5′ 7″ 145 lbs.

Year	Team	Games	BA	SA	AB	H	2B	3B	HR	HR%	R	RBI	BB	SO	SB	Pinch Hit AB	Pinch Hit H	PO	A	E	DP	TC/G	FA	G by Pos
1896	PHI N	17	.232	.268	56	13	0	1	0	0.0	12	6	6	7	3	0	0	18	11	4	3	1.9	.879	OF-12, 2B-3, C-2
1897		92	.278	.320	316	88	6	2	1	0.3	51	35	56		19	2	0	174	147	22	8	3.8	.936	OF-45, 2B-37, SS-6, 3B-2
1900	CIN N	30	.257	.336	113	29	1	4	0	0.0	18	10	7		3	1	0	61	7	8	1	2.6	.895	OF-27, 3B-2
1901	2 teams	PHI A (50G –.232)	MIL A (11G –.179)																					
″	total	61	.224	.272	250	56	6	3	0	0.0	46	24	29		11	0	0	91	15	10	2	1.8	.914	OF-58, 3B-4, SS-2
1904	BOS N	149	.243	.284	580	141	17	2	1	0.2	70	27	56		18	1	0	256	44	28	11	2.2	.915	OF-137, 3B-7, 2B-5, SS-1
5 yrs.		349	.249	.294	1315	327	30	12	2	0.2	197	102	154	7	54	4	0	600	224	72	25	2.6	.920	OF-279, 2B-45, 3B-15, SS-9, C-2

Gary Geiger

GEIGER, GARY MERLE
B. Apr. 4, 1937, Sand Ridge, Ill.
BL TR 6′ 168 lbs.

Year	Team	Games	BA	SA	AB	H	2B	3B	HR	HR%	R	RBI	BB	SO	SB	Pinch Hit AB	Pinch Hit H	PO	A	E	DP	TC/G	FA	G by Pos
1958	CLE A	91	.231	.272	195	45	3	1	1	0.5	28	6	27	43	2	32	6	133	7	4	2	2.6	.972	OF-53, 3B-2, P-1
1959	BOS A	120	.245	.397	335	82	10	4	11	3.3	45	48	21	55	9	24	9	173	5	2	1	1.9	.989	OF-95
1960		77	.302	.490	245	74	13	3	9	3.7	32	33	23	38	2	12	5	121	9	0	1	2.0	1.000	OF-66
1961		140	.232	.407	499	116	21	6	18	3.6	82	64	87	91	16	5	2	324	12	4	1	2.5	.988	OF-137
1962		131	.249	.408	466	116	18	4	16	3.4	67	54	67	66	18	8	2	287	8	4	1	2.3	.987	OF-129
1963		121	.263	.441	399	105	13	5	16	4.0	67	44	36	63	9	23	3	246	13	5	2	2.6	.981	OF-95, 1B-6
1964		5	.385	.538	13	5	0	1	0	0.0	3	1	2	2	0	1	1	6	0	0	0	1.5	1.000	OF-4
1965		24	.200	.333	45	9	3	0	1	2.2	5	2	13	10	3	7	0	32	0	1	0	2.1	.970	OF-16
1966	ATL N	78	.262	.444	126	33	5	3	4	3.2	23	10	21	29	0	27	4	49	5	1	1	1.1	.982	OF-49
1967		69	.162	.214	117	19	1	1	1	0.9	17	5	20	35	1	24	1	47	2	1	0	1.3	.980	OF-38
1969	HOU N	93	.224	.272	125	28	4	1	0	0.0	19	16	24	34	2	26	7	57	3	2	0	1.0	.968	OF-65
1970		5	.250	.250	4	1	0	0	0	0.0	0	0	0	0	0	2	0	1	0	0	0	0.5	1.000	OF-2
12 yrs.		954	.246	.394	2569	633	91	29	77	3.0	388	283	341	466	62	191	40	1476	64	24	9	2.1	.985	OF-749, 1B-6, 3B-2, P-1

Bill Geiss

GEISS, WILLIAM J.
Brother of Emil Geiss.
B. July 15, 1858, Chicago, Ill. D. Sept. 18, 1924, Chicago, Ill.
5′10″ 164 lbs.

Year	Team	Games	BA	SA	AB	H	2B	3B	HR	HR%	R	RBI	BB	SO	SB	Pinch Hit AB	Pinch Hit H	PO	A	E	DP	TC/G	FA	G by Pos
1884	DET N	75	.177	.265	283	50	11	4	2	0.7	23		6	60		0	0	203	218	65	28	6.4	.866	2B-73, OF-1, P-1, 1B-1

Emil Geiss

GEISS, EMIL AUGUST
Brother of Bill Geiss.
B. Mar. 20, 1867, Chicago, Ill. D. Oct. 4, 1911, Chicago, Ill.
BR TR 5′11″ 170 lbs.

Year	Team	Games	BA	SA	AB	H	2B	3B	HR	HR%	R	RBI	BB	SO	SB	Pinch Hit AB	Pinch Hit H	PO	A	E	DP	TC/G	FA	G by Pos
1887	CHI N	3	.083	.083	12	1	0	0	0	0.0	0	0	0	7	0	0	0	13	4	3	0	6.7	.850	1B-1, 2B-1, P-1

Charley Gelbert

GELBERT, CHARLES MAGNUS
B. Jan. 26, 1906, Scranton, Pa. D. Jan. 13, 1967, Easton, Pa.
BR TR 5′11″ 170 lbs.

Year	Team	Games	BA	SA	AB	H	2B	3B	HR	HR%	R	RBI	BB	SO	SB	Pinch Hit AB	Pinch Hit H	PO	A	E	DP	TC/G	FA	G by Pos
1929	STL N	146	.262	.367	512	134	29	8	3	0.6	60	65	51	46	8	0	0	338	499	46	95	6.0	.948	SS-146
1930		139	.304	.441	513	156	39	11	3	0.6	92	72	43	41	6	0	0	322	472	44	104	6.0	.947	SS-139
1931		131	.289	.383	447	129	29	5	1	0.2	61	62	54	31	7	0	0	281	435	31	91	5.7	.959	SS-131
1932		122	.268	.376	455	122	28	9	1	0.2	60	45	39	30	8	0	0	246	389	37	69	5.5	.945	SS-122
1935		62	.292	.393	168	49	7	2	2	1.2	24	21	17	18	0	5	1	65	98	5	16	2.8	.970	3B-37, SS-21, 2B-3
1936		93	.229	.329	280	64	15	2	3	1.1	33	27	25	26	2	2	0	107	162	10	31	2.9	.964	3B-60, SS-28, 2B-8
1937	2 teams	CIN N (43G –.193)	DET A (20G –.085)																					
″	total	63	.161	.217	161	26	6	0	1	0.6	16	14	19	23	1	6	0	110	135	9	27	4.0	.965	SS-53, 2B-9, 3B-1
1939	WAS A	68	.255	.394	188	48	7	5	3	1.6	36	29	30	11	2	16	2	61	123	7	21	3.9	.963	SS-28, 3B-20, 2B-1
1940	2 teams	WAS A (22G –.370)	BOS A (30G –.198)																					
″	total	52	.262	.338	145	38	9	1	0	0.0	16	15	12	19	0	4	0	47	94	12	8	3.4	.922	3B-29, SS-13, P-2, 2B-1
9 yrs.		876	.267	.374	2869	766	169	43	17	0.6	398	350	290	245	34	33	3	1577	2407	201	462	4.9	.952	SS-681, 3B-147, 2B-22, P-2
WORLD SERIES																								
1930	STL N	6	.353	.471	17	6	0	1	0	0.0	2	2	3	3	0	0	0	5	23	0	3	4.7	1.000	SS-6
1931		7	.261	.304	23	6	1	0	0	0.0	0	3	0	4	0	0	0	13	29	0	6	6.0	1.000	SS-7
2 yrs.		13	.300	.375	40	12	1	1	0	0.0	2	5	3	7	0	0	0	18	52	0	9	5.4	1.000	SS-13

Frank Genins

GENINS, C. FRANK (Frenchy)
B. Nov. 2, 1866, St. Louis, Mo. D. Sept. 30, 1922, St. Louis, Mo.
TR

Year	Team	Games	BA	SA	AB	H	2B	3B	HR	HR%	R	RBI	BB	SO	SB	Pinch Hit AB	Pinch Hit H	PO	A	E	DP	TC/G	FA	G by Pos
1892	2 teams	CIN N (35G –.182)	STL N (15G –.196)																					
″	total	50	.186	.217	161	30	5	0	0	0.0	17	11	13	23	10	0	0	92	113	31	14	4.7	.869	SS-31, OF-15, 3B-4
1895	PIT N	73	.250	.306	252	63	8	0	2	0.8	43	24	22	14	19	3	0	127	99	29	7	3.6	.886	OF-29, 2B-16, 3B-16, SS-8, 1B-2
1901	CLE A	26	.228	.277	101	23	5	0	0	0.0	15	9	8		3	0	0	60	3	4	1	2.6	.940	OF-26
3 yrs.		149	.226	.272	514	116	18	0	2	0.4	75	44	43	37	32	3	0	279	215	64	22	3.8	.885	OF-70, SS-39, 3B-20, 2B-16, 1B-2

George Genovese

GENOVESE, GEORGE MICHAEL
B. Feb. 22, 1922, Staten Island, N. Y.
BL TR 5′ 6½″ 160 lbs.

Year	Team	Games	BA	SA	AB	H	2B	3B	HR	HR%	R	RBI	BB	SO	SB	Pinch Hit AB	Pinch Hit H	PO	A	E	DP	TC/G	FA	G by Pos
1950	WAS A	3	.000	.000	1	0	0	0	0	0.0	1	0	1	0	0	1	0	0	0	0	0	0.0	—	

Jim Gentile

GENTILE, JAMES EDWARD (Diamond Jim)
B. June 3, 1934, San Francisco, Calif.
BL TL 6′ 3½″ 210 lbs.

Year	Team	Games	BA	SA	AB	H	2B	3B	HR	HR%	R	RBI	BB	SO	SB	Pinch Hit AB	Pinch Hit H	PO	A	E	DP	TC/G	FA	G by Pos
1957	BKN N	4	.167	.667	6	1	0	0	1	16.7	1	1	1	1	0	1	0	14	0	0	3	7.0	1.000	1B-2
1958	LA N	12	.133	.167	30	4	1	0	0	0.0	0	4	4	6	0	4	1	50	2	1	9	6.6	.981	1B-8
1960	BAL A	138	.292	.500	384	112	17	0	21	5.5	67	98	68	72	0	28	8	885	52	7	98	7.6	.993	1B-124
1961		148	.302	.646	486	147	25	2	46	9.5	96	**141**	96	106	1	11	3	1209	100	14	129	9.2	.989	1B-144
1962		152	.251	.475	545	137	21	1	33	6.1	80	87	77	100	1	2	0	1214	121	16	121	9.0	.988	1B-150

Jim Gentile *continued*

Year	Team	Games	BA	SA	AB	H	2B	3B	HR	HR%	R	RBI	BB	SO	SB	Pinch Hit AB	Pinch Hit H	PO	A	E	DP	TC/G	FA	G by Pos
1963		145	.248	.429	496	123	16	1	24	4.8	65	72	76	101	1	3	1	1185	110	6	122	9.1	.995	1B-143
1964	**KC A**	136	.251	.465	439	110	10	0	28	6.4	71	71	84	122	0	6	1	1018	84	13	92	8.7	.988	1B-128
1965	**2 teams**	**KC A** (38G –.246) **HOU N** (81G –.242)																						
″	**total**	119	.243	.443	345	84	16	1	17	4.9	36	53	43	98	0	14	3	783	60	9	65	8.3	.989	1B-103
1966	**2 teams**	**HOU N** (49G –.243) **CLE A** (33G –.128)																						
″	**total**	82	.215	.403	191	41	7	1	9	4.7	18	22	26	57	0	30	6	367	35	7	32	7.9	.983	1B-52
9 yrs.		936	.260	.486	2922	759	113	6	179	6.1	434	549	475	663	3	99	23	6725	564	73	671	8.6	.990	1B-854

Sam Gentile

GENTILE, SAMUEL CHRISTOPHER BL TR 5′11″ 180 lbs.
B. Oct. 12, 1916, Charlestown, Mass.

Year	Team	Games	BA	SA	AB	H	2B	3B	HR	HR%	R	RBI	BB	SO	SB	Pinch Hit AB	Pinch Hit H	PO	A	E	DP	TC/G	FA	G by Pos
1943	**BOS N**	8	.250	.500	4	1	1	0	0	0.0	1	0	1	0	0	4	1	0	0	0	0	0.0	—	

Harvey Gentry

GENTRY, HARVEY WILLIAM BL TR 6′ 170 lbs.
B. May 27, 1926, Winston-Salem, N. C.

Year	Team	Games	BA	SA	AB	H	2B	3B	HR	HR%	R	RBI	BB	SO	SB	Pinch Hit AB	Pinch Hit H	PO	A	E	DP	TC/G	FA	G by Pos
1954	**NY N**	5	.250	.250	4	1	0	0	0	0.0	0	1	1	0	0	4	1	0	0	0	0	0.0	—	

Alex George

GEORGE, ALEX THOMAS M. BL TR 5′11½″ 170 lbs.
B. Sept. 27, 1938, Kansas City, Mo.

Year	Team	Games	BA	SA	AB	H	2B	3B	HR	HR%	R	RBI	BB	SO	SB	Pinch Hit AB	Pinch Hit H	PO	A	E	DP	TC/G	FA	G by Pos
1955	**KC A**	5	.100	.100	10	1	0	0	0	0.0	0	0	1	7	0	2	0	6	5	1	1	2.4	.917	SS-5

Greek George

GEORGE, CHARLES PETER BR TR 6′ 2″ 200 lbs.
B. Dec. 25, 1912, Waycross, Ga.

Year	Team	Games	BA	SA	AB	H	2B	3B	HR	HR%	R	RBI	BB	SO	SB	Pinch Hit AB	Pinch Hit H	PO	A	E	DP	TC/G	FA	G by Pos
1935	**CLE A**	2	—	—	0	0	0	0	0	—	0	0	0	0	0	0	0	2	0	0	0	2.0	1.000	C-1
1936		23	.195	.234	77	15	3	0	0	0.0	3	5	9	16	0	1	0	164	16	1	1	8.2	.994	C-22
1938	**BKN N**	7	.200	.300	20	4	0	1	0	0.0	0	2	0	4	0	0	0	23	5	0	1	4.0	1.000	C-7
1941	**CHI N**	35	.156	.188	64	10	2	0	0	0.0	4	6	2	10	0	17	0	63	9	2	2	4.1	.973	C-18
1945	**PHI A**	51	.174	.217	138	24	4	1	0	0.0	8	11	17	29	0	5	0	161	14	5	3	3.9	.972	C-46
5 yrs.		118	.177	.221	299	53	9	2	0	0.0	15	24	28	59	0	23	0	413	44	8	7	4.9	.983	C-94

Ben Geraghty

GERAGHTY, BENJAMIN RAYMOND BR TR 5′11″ 175 lbs.
B. July 19, 1912, Jersey City, N. J. D. June 18, 1963, Jacksonville, Fla.

Year	Team	Games	BA	SA	AB	H	2B	3B	HR	HR%	R	RBI	BB	SO	SB	Pinch Hit AB	Pinch Hit H	PO	A	E	DP	TC/G	FA	G by Pos
1936	**BKN N**	51	.194	.225	129	25	4	0	0	0.0	11	9	8	16	4	1	0	78	89	12	11	4.0	.933	SS-31, 2B-9, 3B-5
1943	**BOS N**	8	.000	.000	1	0	0	0	0	0.0	2	0	0	0	0	0	0	2	2	0	0	1.3	1.000	2B-1, 3B-1, SS-1
1944		11	.250	.250	16	4	0	0	0	0.0	3	0	1	2	0	0	0	10	7	2	0	2.7	.895	2B-4, 3B-3
3 yrs.		70	.199	.226	146	29	4	0	0	0.0	16	9	9	18	4	1	0	90	98	14	11	3.7	.931	SS-32, 2B-14, 3B-9

Craig Gerber

GERBER, CRAIG STUART BL TR 6′ 175 lbs.
B. Jan. 8, 1959, Chicago, Ill.

Year	Team	Games	BA	SA	AB	H	2B	3B	HR	HR%	R	RBI	BB	SO	SB	Pinch Hit AB	Pinch Hit H	PO	A	E	DP	TC/G	FA	G by Pos
1985	**CAL A**	65	.264	.319	91	24	1	2	0	0.0	8	6	2	3	0	0	0	56	112	5	7	2.7	.971	SS-53, 3B-9, DH-1, 2B-1

Wally Gerber

GERBER, WALTER (Spooks) BR TR 5′10″ 152 lbs.
B. Aug. 18, 1891, Columbus, Ohio D. June 19, 1951, Columbus, Ohio.

Year	Team	Games	BA	SA	AB	H	2B	3B	HR	HR%	R	RBI	BB	SO	SB	Pinch Hit AB	Pinch Hit H	PO	A	E	DP	TC/G	FA	G by Pos
1914	**PIT N**	17	.241	.296	54	13	1	1	0	0.0	5	5	2	8	0	0	0	31	62	8	7	5.9	.921	SS-17
1915		56	.194	.208	144	28	2	0	0	0.0	8	7	9	16	6	7	0	83	104	13	11	4.2	.935	3B-23, SS-23, 2B-2
1917	**STL A**	14	.308	.385	39	12	1	1	0	0.0	2	2	3	2	1	0	0	16	38	4	4	4.1	.931	SS-12, 2B-2
1918		56	.240	.263	171	41	4	0	0	0.0	10	10	19	11	2	0	0	109	174	24	20	5.5	.922	SS-56
1919		140	.227	.290	462	105	14	6	1	0.2	43	37	49	36	1	0	0	287	422	45	42	5.4	.940	SS-140
1920		154	.279	.341	584	163	26	2	2	0.3	70	60	58	32	4	0	0	288	513	52	65	5.5	.939	SS-154
1921		114	.278	.360	436	121	12	9	2	0.5	55	48	34	19	3	1	0	269	331	36	60	5.6	.943	SS-113
1922		153	.267	.334	604	161	22	8	1	0.2	81	51	52	34	6	0	0	322	470	47	93	5.5	.944	SS-153
1923		154	.281	.339	605	170	26	3	1	0.2	85	62	54	50	4	0	0	334	461	42	86	5.4	.950	SS-154
1924		148	.272	.329	496	135	20	4	0	0.0	61	55	43	34	4	1	0	317	422	42	77	5.3	.946	SS-146
1925		72	.272	.333	246	67	13	1	0	0.0	29	19	26	15	1	1	0	144	206	19	39	5.2	.949	SS-71
1926		131	.270	.290	411	111	8	0	0	0.0	37	42	40	29	0	1	0	261	358	37	92	5.1	.944	SS-129
1927		142	.224	.295	438	98	13	9	0	0.0	44	45	35	25	2	0	0	290	427	41	91	5.3	.946	SS-141, 3B-1
1928	**2 teams**	**STL A** (6G –.278) **BOS A** (104G –.213)																						
″	**total**	110	.217	.245	318	69	7	1	0	0.0	22	28	33	34	6	0	0	207	340	30	54	5.3	.948	SS-109
1929	**BOS A**	61	.165	.220	91	15	3	1	0	0.0	6	5	8	12	1	0	0	70	115	10	14	3.8	.949	SS-30, 2B-22
15 yrs.		1522	.257	.313	5099	1309	172	46	7	0.1	558	476	465	357	41	11	0	3028	4443	450	755	5.3	.943	SS-1448, 2B-26, 3B-24

Bob Geren

GEREN, ROBERT PETER BR TR 6′ 3″ 205 lbs.
B. Sept. 22, 1961, San Diego, Calif.

Year	Team	Games	BA	SA	AB	H	2B	3B	HR	HR%	R	RBI	BB	SO	SB	Pinch Hit AB	Pinch Hit H	PO	A	E	DP	TC/G	FA	G by Pos
1988	**NY A**	10	.100	.100	10	1	0	0	0	0.0	0	0	2	3	0	0	0	18	3	0	0	2.1	1.000	C-10
1989		65	.288	.454	205	59	5	1	9	4.4	26	27	12	44	0	7	1	308	24	3	4	5.4	.991	C-60, DH-2
1990		110	.213	.325	277	59	7	0	8	2.9	21	31	13	73	0	7	1	487	55	4	5	5.1	.993	C-107, DH-1
1991		64	.219	.289	128	28	3	0	2	1.6	7	12	9	31	0	1	0	255	18	3	2	4.4	.989	C-63
1993	**SD N**	58	.214	.317	145	31	6	0	3	2.1	8	6	13	28	0	8	2	252	29	2	6	5.5	.993	C-49, 3B-1, 1B-1
5 yrs.		307	.233	.349	765	178	21	1	22	2.9	62	76	49	179	0	23	4	1320	129	12	17	5.0	.992	C-289, DH-3, 3B-1, 1B-1

Joe Gerhardt

GERHARDT, JOHN JOSEPH (Move Up Joe) BR TR 6′ 160 lbs.
B. Feb. 14, 1855, Washington, D. C. D. Mar. 11, 1922, Middletown, N. Y.
Manager 1883, 1890.

Year	Team	Games	BA	SA	AB	H	2B	3B	HR	HR%	R	RBI	BB	SO	SB	Pinch Hit AB	Pinch Hit H	PO	A	E	DP	TC/G	FA	G by Pos
1876	**LOU N**	65	.260	.336	292	76	10	3	2	0.7	33	18	3	5		0	0	695	44	47	15	11.9	.940	1B-54, 2B-5, SS-3, OF-2, 3B-2
1877		59	.304	.380	250	76	6	5	1	0.4	41	35	5	8		0	0	183	248	52	30	8.1	.892	2B-57, SS-1, 1B-1, OF-1
1878	**CIN N**	60	.297	.340	259	77	7	2	0	0.0	46	28	7	14		0	0	159	206	38	26	6.7	.906	2B-60
1879		79	.198	.265	313	62	12	3	1	0.3	22	39	3	19		0	0	307	232	55	31	7.4	.907	2B-55, 3B-16, 1B-8, SS-1
1881	**DET N**	80	.242	.327	297	72	13	6	0	0.0	35	36	7	31		0	0	261	242	51	62	6.9	.908	2B-79, 3B-1
1883	**LOU AA**	78	.263	.354	319	84	11	9	0	0.0	56		14			0	0	278	263	56	42	7.7	.906	2B-78
1884		106	.220	.277	404	89	7	8	0	0.0	39		13			0	0	341	391	64	64	7.5	.920	2B-105, SS-1
1885	**NY N**	112	.155	.195	399	62	12	2	0	0.0	43		24	47		0	0	314	352	65	59	6.5	.911	2B-112
1886		123	.190	.249	426	81	11	7	0	0.0	44	40	22	63		0	0	340	355	57	50	6.1	.924	2B-123
1887	**2 teams**	**NY N** (1G –.000) **NY AA** (85G –.221)																						
″	**total**	86	.219	.273	311	68	13	2	0	0.0	40	0	24	0	15	0	0	289	275	65	48	7.3	.897	2B-84, 3B-2

Joe Gerhardt *continued*

Year	Team	Games	BA	SA	AB	H	2B	3B	HR	HR%	R	RBI	BB	SO	SB	Pinch Hit AB	Pinch Hit H	PO	A	E	DP	TC/G	FA	G by Pos
1890	2 teams	BKN AA (99G –.203)		STL AA (37G –.256)																				
"	total	136	.217	.273	494	107	10	3	4	0.8	49		39		14	0	0	427	440	56	75	6.8	.939	2B-119, 3B-17
1891	LOU AA	2	.000	.000	6	0	0	0	0	0.0	0	0	1	0	0	0	0	4	6	2	0	6.0	.833	2B-2
12 yrs.		986	.227	.289	3770	854	112	50	8	0.2	448	196	162	187	29	0	0	3598	3054	608	502	7.3	.916	2B-879, 1B-63, 3B-38, SS-6, OF-3

Ken Gerhart

GERHART, HAROLD KENNETH
B. May 19, 1961, Charleston, S. C.
BR TR 6′ 190 lbs.

Year	Team	Games	BA	SA	AB	H	2B	3B	HR	HR%	R	RBI	BB	SO	SB	Pinch Hit AB	Pinch Hit H	PO	A	E	DP	TC/G	FA	G by Pos
1986	BAL A	20	.232	.304	69	16	2	0	1	1.4	4	7	4	18	0	1	0	34	0	1	0	1.8	.971	OF-20
1987		92	.243	.440	284	69	10	2	14	4.9	41	34	17	53	9	3	1	174	3	5	0	2.0	.973	OF-91
1988		103	.195	.344	262	51	10	1	9	3.4	27	23	21	57	7	8	2	192	3	5	1	2.1	.975	OF-93, DH-3
3 yrs.		215	.221	.384	615	136	22	3	24	3.9	72	64	42	128	16	12	3	400	6	11	1	2.0	.974	OF-204, DH-3

George Gerken

GERKEN, GEORGE HERBERT (Pickles)
B. July 28, 1903, Chicago, Ill. D. Oct. 23, 1977, Arcadia, Calif.
BR TR 5′11½″ 175 lbs.

Year	Team	Games	BA	SA	AB	H	2B	3B	HR	HR%	R	RBI	BB	SO	SB	Pinch Hit AB	Pinch Hit H	PO	A	E	DP	TC/G	FA	G by Pos
1927	CLE A	6	.214	.214	14	3	0	0	0	0.0	1	2	1	3	0	0	0	10	1	1	0	2.4	.917	OF-5
1928		38	.226	.322	115	26	7	2	0	0.0	16	9	12	22	3	0	0	75	3	5	0	2.4	.940	OF-34
2 yrs.		44	.225	.310	129	29	7	2	0	0.0	17	11	13	25	3	0	0	85	4	6	0	2.4	.937	OF-39

Johnny Gerlach

GERLACH, JOHN GLENN
B. May 11, 1917, Shullsburg, Wis.
BR TR 5′ 9″ 165 lbs.

Year	Team	Games	BA	SA	AB	H	2B	3B	HR	HR%	R	RBI	BB	SO	SB	Pinch Hit AB	Pinch Hit H	PO	A	E	DP	TC/G	FA	G by Pos
1938	CHI A	9	.280	.280	25	7	0	0	0	0.0	2	1	4	2	0	0	0	17	20	2	9	4.9	.949	SS-8
1939		3	1.000	1.000	2	2	0	0	0	0.0	0	0	0	0	0	1	1	0	1	0	0	1.0	1.000	3B-1
2 yrs.		12	.333	.333	27	9	0	0	0	0.0	2	1	4	2	0	1	1	17	21	2	9	4.4	.950	SS-8, 3B-1

Dick Gernert

GERNERT, RICHARD EDWARD
B. Sept. 28, 1928, Reading, Pa.
BR TR 6′ 3″ 209 lbs.

Year	Team	Games	BA	SA	AB	H	2B	3B	HR	HR%	R	RBI	BB	SO	SB	Pinch Hit AB	Pinch Hit H	PO	A	E	DP	TC/G	FA	G by Pos
1952	BOS A	102	.243	.463	367	89	20	2	19	5.2	58	67	35	83	4	4	1	877	67	12	104	9.7	.987	1B-99
1953		139	.253	.415	494	125	15	1	21	4.3	73	71	88	82	0	3	0	1223	84	19	139	9.8	.986	1B-136
1954		14	.261	.348	23	6	2	0	0	0.0	2	1	6	4	0	7	1	47	1	0	5	8.0	1.000	1B-6
1955		7	.200	.300	20	4	2	0	0	0.0	6	1	1	5	0	1	0	35	3	1	2	7.8	.974	1B-5
1956		106	.291	.484	306	89	11	0	16	5.2	53	68	56	57	1	22	4	367	41	4	38	4.7	.990	OF-50, 1B-37
1957		99	.237	.430	316	75	13	3	14	4.4	45	58	39	62	1	18	6	697	50	10	82	8.7	.987	1B-71, OF-16
1958		122	.237	.425	431	102	19	1	20	4.6	59	69	59	78	2	7	3	1101	93	11	118	10.6	.991	1B-114
1959		117	.262	.426	298	78	14	1	11	3.7	41	42	52	49	1	21	4	588	51	4	54	6.4	.994	1B-75, OF-25
1960	2 teams	CHI N (52G –.250)		DET A (21G –.300)																				
"	total	73	.267	.336	146	39	7	0	1	0.7	14	16	14	24	1	31	8	242	21	3	26	6.3	.989	1B-31, OF-11
1961	2 teams	DET A (6G –.200)		CIN N (40G –.302)																				
"	total	46	.294	.353	68	20	1	0	1	1.5	5	8	8	11	0	25	6	125	17	1	9	6.8	.993	1B-21
1962	HOU N	10	.208	.208	24	5	0	0	0	0.0	1	1	5	7	0	1	0	62	2	0	9	7.1	1.000	1B-9
11 yrs.		835	.254	.426	2493	632	104	8	103	4.1	357	402	363	462	10	140	33	5364	430	65	586	8.3	.989	1B-604, OF-102
WORLD SERIES																								
1961	CIN N	4	.000	.000	4	0	0	0	0	0.0	0	0	0	1	0	4	0	0	0	0	0	0.0	—	

Cesar Geronimo

GERONIMO, CESAR FRANCISCO
Born Cesar Francisco Geronimo (Zorrilla).
B. Mar. 11, 1948, El Seibo, Dominican Republic.
BL TL 6′ 165 lbs.

Year	Team	Games	BA	SA	AB	H	2B	3B	HR	HR%	R	RBI	BB	SO	SB	Pinch Hit AB	Pinch Hit H	PO	A	E	DP	TC/G	FA	G by Pos
1969	HOU N	28	.250	.375	8	2	1	0	0	0.0	8	0	0	3	0	5	1	1	0	0	0	0.1	1.000	OF-9
1970		47	.243	.243	37	9	0	0	0	0.0	5	2	2	5	0	11	4	23	0	2	0	1.0	.920	OF-26
1971		94	.220	.329	82	18	2	2	1	1.2	13	6	5	31	2	11	2	42	1	1	0	0.7	.977	OF-64
1972	CIN N	120	.275	.412	255	70	9	7	4	1.6	32	29	24	64	2	12	1	150	10	3	1	1.5	.982	OF-106
1973		139	.210	.309	324	68	14	3	4	1.2	35	33	23	74	5	7	1	243	9	2	2	2.0	.992	OF-130
1974		150	.281	.395	474	133	17	8	7	1.5	73	54	46	96	9	7	0	355	13	5	2	2.6	.987	OF-145
1975		148	.257	.363	501	129	25	5	6	1.2	69	53	48	97	13	3	1	408	12	3	5	2.9	.993	OF-148
1976		149	.307	.414	486	149	24	11	2	0.4	59	49	56	95	22	4	2	386	4	6	2	2.7	.985	OF-146
1977		149	.266	.388	492	131	22	4	10	2.0	54	52	35	89	10	7	3	375	9	3	2	2.6	.992	OF-147
1978		122	.226	.334	296	67	15	1	5	1.7	28	27	43	67	8	11	5	259	4	5	1	2.3	.981	OF-115
1979		123	.239	.343	356	85	17	4	4	1.1	38	38	37	56	1	9	2	291	11	2	2	2.6	.993	OF-118
1980		103	.255	.331	145	37	5	0	2	1.4	16	9	14	24	2	21	5	110	2	0	1	1.3	1.000	OF-86
1981	KC A	59	.246	.331	118	29	0	2	2	1.7	14	13	11	16	6	2	2	96	1	2	0	1.7	.980	OF-57
1982		53	.269	.471	119	32	6	3	4	3.4	14	23	8	16	2	10	2	93	3	0	0	2.1	1.000	OF-44, DH-1
1983		38	.207	.253	87	18	4	0	0	0.0	2	4	2	13	0	6	1	69	2	1	0	2.1	.986	OF-35
15 yrs.		1522	.258	.368	3780	977	161	50	51	1.3	460	392	354	746	82	126	32	2901	81	35	18	2.2	.988	OF-1376, DH-1
DIVISIONAL PLAYOFF SERIES																								
1981	KC A	1	—	—	0	0	0	0	0	—	0	0	0	0	0	0	0	0	0	0	0	0.0	—	
LEAGUE CHAMPIONSHIP SERIES																								
1972	CIN N	5	.100	.250	20	2	0	0	1	5.0	2	1	0	2	0	0	0	11	1	0	0	2.4	1.000	OF-5
1973		4	.067	.067	15	1	0	0	0	0.0	0	0	0	7	0	0	0	11	1	0	0	3.0	1.000	OF-4
1975		3	.000	.000	10	0	0	0	0	0.0	0	1	1	7	0	0	0	13	0	0	0	4.3	1.000	OF-3
1976		3	.182	.364	11	2	0	1	0	0.0	0	2	1	3	0	0	0	10	0	0	0	3.3	1.000	OF-3
1979		2	.143	.143	7	1	0	0	0	0.0	0	0	0	5	0	0	0	8	0	1	0	4.5	.889	OF-2
5 yrs.		17	.095	.175	63	6	0	1	1	1.6	2	4	2	24 **2nd**	0	0	0	53	2	1	0	3.3	.982	OF-17
WORLD SERIES																								
1972	CIN N	7	.158	.158	19	3	0	0	0	0.0	1	3	1	4	1	0	0	9	0	0	0	1.3	1.000	OF-7
1975		7	.280	.600	25	7	0	1	2	8.0	3	3	3	5	0	0	0	23	1	0	1	3.4	1.000	OF-7
1976		4	.308	.462	13	4	2	0	0	0.0	3	1	2	2	2	0	0	12	0	1	0	3.3	.923	OF-4
3 yrs.		18	.246	.421	57	14	2	1	2	3.5	7	7	6	11	3	0	0	44	1	1	1	2.6	.978	OF-18

Lou Gertenrich

GERTENRICH, LOUIS WILHELM BR TR 5′ 8″ 175 lbs.
B. May 4, 1875, Chicago, Ill. D. Oct. 23, 1933, Chicago, Ill.

Year	Team	Games	BA	SA	AB	H	2B	3B	HR	HR%	R	RBI	BB	SO	SB	Pinch Hit AB	Pinch Hit H	PO	A	E	DP	TC/G	FA	G by Pos
1901	MIL A	2	.333	.333	3	1	0	0	0	0.0	1	0	0		0	1	0	0	0	0	0	0.0	.000	OF-1
1903	PIT N	1	.000	.000	3	0	0	0	0	0.0	0	0	0		0	0	0	2	0	0	0	2.0	1.000	OF-1
2 yrs.		3	.167	.167	6	1	0	0	0	0.0	1	0	0		0	1	0	2	0	0	0	1.0	1.000	OF-2

Doc Gessler

GESSLER, HARRY HOMER (Brownie) BL TR 5′10″ 185 lbs.
B. Dec. 23, 1880, Greensburg, Pa. D. Dec. 25, 1924, Pittsburgh, Pa.
Manager 1914.

Year	Team	Games	BA	SA	AB	H	2B	3B	HR	HR%	R	RBI	BB	SO	SB	Pinch Hit AB	Pinch Hit H	PO	A	E	DP	TC/G	FA	G by Pos
1903	2 teams	DET A (29G –.238) BKN N (49G –.247)																						
″	total	78	.243	.347	259	63	13	7	0	0.0	29	30	20		10	4	1	92	5	2	2	1.4	.980	OF-71
1904	BKN N	104	.290	.384	341	99	18	4	2	0.6	41	28	30		13	12	2	181	17	17	2	2.4	.921	OF-88, 2B-1, 1B-1
1905		126	.290	.369	431	125	17	4	3	0.7	44	46	38		26	7	2	1036	81	36	54	9.7	.969	1B-107, OF-12
1906	2 teams	BKN N (9G –.242) CHI N (34G –.253)																						
″	total	43	.250	.319	116	29	4	2	0	0.0	11	14	15		7	11	2	110	13	5	4	4.1	.961	OF-21, 1B-10
1908	BOS A	128	.308	.423	435	134	13	14	3	0.7	55	63	51		19	2	2	162	8	9	4	1.4	.950	OF-126
1909	2 teams	BOS A (111G –.298) WAS A (17G –.241)																						
″	total	128	.291	.359	440	128	26	2	0	0.0	66	54	43		20	1	0	176	21	11	2	1.6	.947	OF-127, 1B-2
1910	WAS A	145	.259	.351	487	126	17	11	2	0.4	58	50	62		18	1	0	161	23	9	3	1.3	.953	OF-144
1911		128	.282	.373	450	127	19	5	4	0.9	65	78	74		29	1	0	135	20	9	2	1.3	.945	OF-126, 1B-1
8 yrs.		880	.281	.371	2959	831	127	49	14	0.5	369	363	333		142	39	9	2053	188	98	73	2.8	.958	OF-715, 1B-121, 2B-1
WORLD SERIES																								
1906	CHI N	2	.000	.000	1	0	0	0	0	0.0	0	0	1	0	0	1	0	0	0	0	0	0.0	—	

Charlie Gettig

GETTIG, CHARLES HENRY BR 5′10″ 172 lbs.
B. Dec. 1870, Baltimore, Md. D. Apr. 11, 1935, Baltimore, Md.

Year	Team	Games	BA	SA	AB	H	2B	3B	HR	HR%	R	RBI	BB	SO	SB	Pinch Hit AB	Pinch Hit H	PO	A	E	DP	TC/G	FA	G by Pos
1896	NY N	6	.333	.444	9	3	1	0	0	0.0	3	0	0	0	0	2	0	0	5	0	0	1.3	1.000	P-4
1897		22	.200	.280	75	15	6	0	0	0.0	8	12	6		3	1	0	19	26	16	1	2.8	.738	3B-7, 2B-6, SS-3, OF-3, P-3
1898		64	.250	.301	196	49	6	2	0	0.0	30	26	15		5	0	0	70	103	21	6	2.9	.892	OF-21, P-17, 2B-12, SS-9, 3B-4, 1B-2, C-1
1899		34	.247	.278	97	24	3	0	0	0.0	7	9	7		4	1	0	27	59	16	0	3.1	.843	P-18, 3B-8, 2B-3, 1B-3, OF-1
4 yrs.		126	.241	.294	377	91	16	2	0	0.0	48	47	28	0	12	4	0	116	193	53	7	2.9	.854	P-42, OF-25, 2B-21, 3B-19, SS-12, 1B-5, C-1

Tom Gettinger

GETTINGER, LEWIS THOMAS LEYTON BL TL 5′10″ 180 lbs.
Born Lewis Thomas Leyton Gittinger.
B. Dec. 11, 1868, Frederick, Md. D. July 26, 1943, Pensacola, Fla.

Year	Team	Games	BA	SA	AB	H	2B	3B	HR	HR%	R	RBI	BB	SO	SB	Pinch Hit AB	Pinch Hit H	PO	A	E	DP	TC/G	FA	G by Pos
1889	STL AA	4	.438	.625	16	7	0	0	1	6.3	2	2	2	1	0	0	0	6	0	2	0	2.0	.750	OF-4
1890		58	.238	.352	227	54	7	5	3	1.3	31		20		8	0	0	62	8	9	1	1.4	.886	OF-58
1895	LOU N	63	.269	.373	260	70	11	5	2	0.8	28	32	8	15	6	0	0	127	7	14	1	2.3	.905	OF-63, P-2
3 yrs.		125	.260	.372	503	131	18	10	6	1.2	61	34	30	16	14	0	0	195	15	25	2	1.9	.894	OF-125, P-2

Jake Gettman

GETTMAN, JACOB JOHN BB TL 5′11″ 185 lbs.
B. Oct. 25, 1876, Frank, Russia D. Oct. 4, 1956, Denver, Colo.

Year	Team	Games	BA	SA	AB	H	2B	3B	HR	HR%	R	RBI	BB	SO	SB	Pinch Hit AB	Pinch Hit H	PO	A	E	DP	TC/G	FA	G by Pos
1897	WAS N	36	.315	.469	143	45	7	3	3	2.1	28	29	7		8	0	0	49	3	1	0	1.5	.981	OF-36
1898		142	.277	.349	567	157	16	5	5	0.9	75	47	29		32	0	0	261	22	21	7	2.1	.931	OF-139, 1B-3
1899		19	.210	.226	62	13	1	0	0	0.0	5	2	4		4	1	1	50	1	0	0	2.8	1.000	OF-16, 1B-2
3 yrs.		197	.278	.361	772	215	24	8	8	1.0	108	78	40		44	1	1	360	26	22	7	2.1	.946	OF-191, 1B-5

Gus Getz

GETZ, GUSTAVE (Gee-Gee) BR TR 5′11″ 165 lbs.
B. Aug. 3, 1889, Pittsburgh, Pa. D. May 28, 1969, Keansburg, N. J.

Year	Team	Games	BA	SA	AB	H	2B	3B	HR	HR%	R	RBI	BB	SO	SB	Pinch Hit AB	Pinch Hit H	PO	A	E	DP	TC/G	FA	G by Pos
1909	BOS N	40	.223	.236	148	33	2	0	0	0.0	6	9	1		2	0	0	36	92	10	3	3.5	.928	3B-36, SS-2, 2B-2
1910		54	.194	.208	144	28	0	1	0	0.0	14	7	6	10	2	6	1	57	83	9	6	3.2	.940	3B-22, 2B-13, OF-8, SS-4
1914	BKN N	55	.248	.295	210	52	8	1	0	0.0	13	20	2	15	9	0	0	69	134	11	12	3.9	.949	3B-55
1915		130	.258	.312	477	123	10	5	2	0.4	39	46	8	14	19	0	0	143	290	24	14	3.5	.947	3B-128, SS-2
1916		40	.219	.271	96	21	1	2	0	0.0	9	8	0	5	9	7	0	53	45	6	4	3.5	.942	3B-20, SS-7, 1B-3
1917	CIN N	7	.286	.286	14	4	0	0	0	0.0	2	3	3	0	0	0	0	8	4	2	1	2.0	.857	2B-4, 3B-3
1918	2 teams	CLE A (6G –.133) PIT N (7G –.200)																						
″	total	13	.160	.200	25	4	1	0	0	0.0	2	0	4	2	0	4	0	6	4	5	1	3.0	.667	OF-3, 3B-2
7 yrs.		339	.238	.279	1114	265	22	9	2	0.2	85	93	24	46	41	17	1	372	652	67	41	3.5	.939	3B-266, 2B-19, SS-15, OF-11, 1B-3
WORLD SERIES																								
1916	BKN N	1	.000	.000	1	0	0	0	0	0.0	0	0	0	0	0	1	0	0	0	0	0	0.0	—	

Chappie Geygan

GEYGAN, JAMES EDWARD BR TR 5′11″ 170 lbs.
B. June 3, 1903, Ironton, Ohio D. Mar. 15, 1966, Columbus, Ohio.

Year	Team	Games	BA	SA	AB	H	2B	3B	HR	HR%	R	RBI	BB	SO	SB	Pinch Hit AB	Pinch Hit H	PO	A	E	DP	TC/G	FA	G by Pos
1924	BOS A	33	.256	.366	82	21	5	2	0	0.0	7	4	4	16	0	1	1	63	76	7	12	4.6	.952	SS-32
1925		3	.182	.182	11	2	0	0	0	0.0	0	0	0	2	0	0	0	7	6	3	1	5.3	.813	SS-3
1926		4	.300	.300	10	3	0	0	0	0.0	0	0	1	1	0	1	0	3	5	2	0	3.3	.800	3B-3
3 yrs.		40	.252	.340	103	26	5	2	0	0.0	7	4	5	19	0	2	1	73	87	12	13	4.5	.930	SS-35, 3B-3

Patsy Gharrity

GHARRITY, EDWARD PATRICK BR TR 5′10″ 170 lbs.
B. Mar. 13, 1892, Parnell, Iowa D. Oct. 10, 1966, Beloit, Wis.

Year	Team	Games	BA	SA	AB	H	2B	3B	HR	HR%	R	RBI	BB	SO	SB	Pinch Hit AB	Pinch Hit H	PO	A	E	DP	TC/G	FA	G by Pos
1916	WAS A	39	.228	.304	92	21	5	1	0	0.0	8	9	8	18	2	6	0	191	16	3	5	6.4	.986	C-18, 1B-15
1917		76	.284	.313	176	50	5	0	0	0.0	15	18	14	18	7	20	3	374	30	9	19	7.9	.978	1B-46, C-5, OF-1
1918		4	.250	.500	4	1	1	0	0	0.0	0	2	0	1	0	4	1	0	0	0	0	0.0	—	
1919		111	.271	.366	347	94	19	4	2	0.6	35	43	25	39	4	10	1	394	73	17	9	4.8	.965	C-60, OF-33, 1B-7
1920		131	.245	.322	428	105	18	3	3	0.7	51	44	37	52	6	4	0	476	150	23	14	5.1	.965	C-120, 1B-7, OF-1
1921		121	.310	.455	387	120	19	8	7	1.8	62	55	45	44	4	5	2	408	110	12	14	4.6	.977	C-115
1922		96	.256	.414	273	70	16	6	5	1.8	40	45	36	30	3	8	1	282	85	7	9	4.3	.981	C-87
1923		96	.207	.311	251	52	9	4	3	1.2	26	33	22	27	6	20	5	417	47	8	27	6.9	.983	C-35, 1B-33
1929		3	.000	.000	2	0	0	0	0	0.0	0	0	1	2	0	2	0	0	0	0	0	0.0	—	
1930		2	.000	.000	1	0	0	0	0	0.0	0	0	0	0	0	1	0	2	0	0	0	2.0	1.000	1B-1
10 yrs.		679	.262	.366	1961	513	92	26	20	1.0	237	249	188	231	32	80	13	2544	511	79	97	5.4	.975	C-440, 1B-109, OF-35

Jason Giambi

GIAMBI, JASON GILBERT
B. Jan. 8, 1971, West Covina, Calif.
BL TR 6′ 2″ 200 lbs.

Year	Team	Games	BA	SA	AB	H	2B	3B	HR	HR%	R	RBI	BB	SO	SB	Pinch Hit AB	Pinch Hit H	PO	A	E	DP	TC/G	FA	G by Pos
1995	OAK A	54	.256	.398	176	45	7	0	6	3.4	27	25	28	31	2	3	0	195	55	4	24	4.4	.984	3B-30, 1B-26, DH-2

Ray Giannelli

GIANNELLI, RAYMOND JOHN
B. Feb. 5, 1966, Brooklyn, N. Y.
BL TR 6′ 195 lbs.

Year	Team	Games	BA	SA	AB	H	2B	3B	HR	HR%	R	RBI	BB	SO	SB	Pinch Hit AB	Pinch Hit H	PO	A	E	DP	TC/G	FA	G by Pos
1991	TOR A	9	.167	.208	24	4	1	0	0	0.0	2	0	5	9	1	1	1	0	12	1	2	1.4	.923	3B-9
1995	STL N	9	.091	.091	11	1	0	0	0	0.0	0	0	3	4	0	4	1	10	0	0	1	2.5	1.000	OF-2, 1B-2
2 yrs.		18	.143	.171	35	5	1	0	0	0.0	2	0	8	13	1	5	2	10	12	1	3	1.8	.957	3B-9, OF-2, 1B-2

Joe Giannini

GIANNINI, JOSEPH FRANCIS
B. Sept. 8, 1888, San Francisco, Calif. D. Sept. 26, 1942, San Francisco, Calif.
BL TR 5′ 8″ 155 lbs.

Year	Team	Games	BA	SA	AB	H	2B	3B	HR	HR%	R	RBI	BB	SO	SB	Pinch Hit AB	Pinch Hit H	PO	A	E	DP	TC/G	FA	G by Pos
1911	BOS A	1	.500	1.000	2	1	1	0	0	0.0	0	0	0		0	0	0	0	2	2	0	4.0	.500	SS-1

John Gibbons

GIBBONS, JOHN MICHAEL
B. June 8, 1962, Great Falls, Mont.
BR TR 5′11″ 185 lbs.

Year	Team	Games	BA	SA	AB	H	2B	3B	HR	HR%	R	RBI	BB	SO	SB	Pinch Hit AB	Pinch Hit H	PO	A	E	DP	TC/G	FA	G by Pos
1984	NY N	10	.065	.065	31	2	0	0	0	0.0	1	1	3	11	0	1	0	54	5	1	0	6.7	.983	C-9
1986		8	.474	.842	19	9	4	0	1	5.3	4	1	3	5	0	0	0	33	5	0	1	4.8	1.000	C-8
2 yrs.		18	.220	.360	50	11	4	0	1	2.0	5	2	6	16	0	1	0	87	10	1	1	5.8	.990	C-17

Jake Gibbs

GIBBS, JERRY DEAN
B. Nov. 7, 1938, Grenada, Miss.
BL TR 6′ 180 lbs.

Year	Team	Games	BA	SA	AB	H	2B	3B	HR	HR%	R	RBI	BB	SO	SB	Pinch Hit AB	Pinch Hit H	PO	A	E	DP	TC/G	FA	G by Pos
1962	NY A	2	—	—	0	0	0	0	0	—	2	0	0	0	0	0	0	0	0	0	0	0.0	.000	3B-1
1963		4	.250	.250	8	2	0	0	0	0.0	1	0	0	1	0	3	2	5	0	0	0	5.0	1.000	C-1
1964		3	.167	.167	6	1	0	0	0	0.0	1	0	0	2	0	1	1	10	0	0	0	5.0	1.000	C-2
1965		37	.221	.324	68	15	1	0	2	2.9	6	7	4	20	0	16	3	106	10	1	1	5.6	.991	C-21
1966		62	.258	.341	182	47	6	0	3	1.6	19	20	19	16	5	5	1	295	27	4	4	6.0	.988	C-54
1967		116	.233	.289	374	87	7	1	4	1.1	33	25	28	57	7	17	3	582	55	16	7	6.6	.975	C-99
1968		124	.213	.277	423	90	12	3	3	0.7	31	29	27	68	9	4	1	642	55	6	7	5.8	.991	C-121
1969		71	.224	.283	219	49	9	2	0	0.0	18	18	23	30	3	2	0	364	31	4	6	6.0	.990	C-66
1970		49	.301	.542	153	46	9	2	8	5.2	23	26	7	14	2	5	1	208	19	3	1	5.2	.987	C-44
1971		70	.218	.335	206	45	9	0	5	2.4	23	21	12	23	2	16	1	229	12	3	1	4.8	.988	C-51
10 yrs.		538	.233	.321	1639	382	53	8	25	1.5	157	146	120	231	28	69	13	2441	209	37	27	5.8	.986	C-459, 3B-1

Steve Gibralter

GIBRALTER, STEPHAN BENSON
B. Oct. 9, 1972, Dallas, Tex.
BR TR 6′ 185 lbs.

Year	Team	Games	BA	SA	AB	H	2B	3B	HR	HR%	R	RBI	BB	SO	SB	Pinch Hit AB	Pinch Hit H	PO	A	E	DP	TC/G	FA	G by Pos
1995	CIN N	4	.333	.333	3	1	0	0	0	0.0	0	0	0	0	0	2	1	1	0	0	0	0.5	1.000	OF-2

Charlie Gibson

GIBSON, CHARLES ELLSWORTH
B. Nov. 17, 1879, Sharon, Pa. D. Nov. 22, 1954, Sharon, Pa.
BR TR 6′ 160 lbs.

Year	Team	Games	BA	SA	AB	H	2B	3B	HR	HR%	R	RBI	BB	SO	SB	Pinch Hit AB	Pinch Hit H	PO	A	E	DP	TC/G	FA	G by Pos
1905	STL A	1	.000	.000	3	0	0	0	0	0.0	0	0	0		0	0	0	2	1	0	0	3.0	1.000	C-1

Charlie Gibson

GIBSON, CHARLES GRIFFIN
B. Nov. 21, 1899, LaGrange, Ga. D. Dec. 18, 1990, LaGrange, Ga.
BR TR 5′ 8″ 160 lbs.

Year	Team	Games	BA	SA	AB	H	2B	3B	HR	HR%	R	RBI	BB	SO	SB	Pinch Hit AB	Pinch Hit H	PO	A	E	DP	TC/G	FA	G by Pos
1924	PHI A	12	.133	.133	15	2	0	0	0	0.0	1	1	2	0	0	0	0	14	6	3	0	1.9	.870	C-12

Frank Gibson

GIBSON, FRANK GILBERT
B. Sept. 27, 1890, Omaha, Neb. D. Apr. 27, 1961, Austin, Tex.
BB TR 6′½″ 172 lbs.
BL 1913

Year	Team	Games	BA	SA	AB	H	2B	3B	HR	HR%	R	RBI	BB	SO	SB	Pinch Hit AB	Pinch Hit H	PO	A	E	DP	TC/G	FA	G by Pos
1913	DET A	20	.140	.158	57	8	1	0	0	0.0	8	2	3	9	2	0	0	57	17	8	1	4.1	.902	C-19, OF-1
1921	BOS N	63	.264	.416	125	33	5	4	2	1.6	14	13	3	17	0	17	4	111	31	3	4	3.5	.979	C-41
1922		66	.299	.421	164	49	7	2	3	1.8	15	20	10	27	4	15	2	245	28	5	14	5.7	.982	C-29, 1B-20
1923		41	.300	.320	50	15	1	0	0	0.0	13	5	7	7	0	15	6	31	5	3	1	2.0	.923	C-20
1924		90	.310	.441	229	71	15	6	1	0.4	25	30	10	23	1	31	0	268	58	11	13	5.8	.967	C-46, 1B-10, 3B-2
1925		104	.278	.402	316	88	23	5	2	0.6	36	50	15	28	3	15	7	276	61	11	7	3.9	.968	C-88, 1B-2
1926		24	.340	.426	47	16	4	0	0	0.0	3	7	4	6	0	12	6	37	12	0	2	4.1	1.000	C-12
1927		60	.222	.251	167	37	1	2	0	0.0	7	19	3	10	2	12	4	130	35	6	3	3.6	.965	C-47
8 yrs.		468	.274	.377	1155	317	57	19	8	0.7	121	146	55	127	12	117	29	1155	247	47	45	4.3	.968	C-302, 1B-32, 3B-2, OF-1

George Gibson

GIBSON, GEORGE C. (Moon)
B. July 22, 1880, London, Ont., Canada D. Jan. 25, 1967, London, Ont., Canada.
Manager 1920–22, 1925, 1932–34.
BR TR 5′11½″ 190 lbs.

Year	Team	Games	BA	SA	AB	H	2B	3B	HR	HR%	R	RBI	BB	SO	SB	Pinch Hit AB	Pinch Hit H	PO	A	E	DP	TC/G	FA	G by Pos
1905	PIT N	46	.178	.267	135	24	2	2	2	1.5	14	14	15		2	1	0	200	54	9	4	6.0	.966	C-44
1906		81	.178	.208	259	46	6	1	0	0.0	8	20	16		1	0	0	336	97	13	10	5.5	.971	C-81
1907		113	.220	.301	382	84	8	7	3	0.8	28	35	18		2	3	1	501	125	18	12	5.9	.972	C-109, 1B-1
1908		143	.228	.296	486	111	19	4	2	0.4	37	45	19		4	3	1	607	136	21	10	5.5	.973	C-140
1909		150	.265	.361	510	135	25	9	2	0.4	42	52	44		9	0	0	655	192	15	9	5.7	.983	C-150
1910		143	.259	.349	482	125	22	6	3	0.6	53	44	47	31	7	0	0	633	203	14	8	5.9	.984	C-143
1911		100	.209	.260	311	65	12	2	0	0.0	32	19	29	16	3	1	1	452	117	12	16	5.9	.979	C-98
1912		95	.240	.327	300	72	14	3	2	0.7	23	35	20	16	0	1	1	484	101	6	11	6.3	.990	C-94
1913		48	.280	.347	118	33	4	2	0	0.0	6	12	10	8	2	0	0	182	34	3	4	4.6	.986	C-48
1914		102	.285	.354	274	78	9	5	0	0.0	19	30	27	27	4	1	0	358	126	13	8	4.9	.974	C-101
1915		120	.251	.336	351	88	15	6	1	0.3	28	30	31	25	5	2	0	551	134	25	14	5.9	.965	C-120
1916		33	.202	.274	84	17	2	2	0	0.0	4	4	3	7	0	2	0	140	39	2	2	6.2	.989	C-29
1917	NY N	35	.171	.207	82	14	3	0	0	0.0	1	5	7	2	1	0	0	116	27	2	4	4.1	.986	C-35
1918		4	.500	1.000	2	1	1	0	0	0.0	0	0	0	0	0	0	0	1	1	0	0	0.5	1.000	C-4
14 yrs.		1213	.236	.312	3776	893	142	49	15	0.4	295	345	286	132	40	14	4	5216	1386	153	112	5.6	.977	C-1196, 1B-1
WORLD SERIES																								
1909	PIT N	7	.240	.320	25	6	2	0	0	0.0	2	2	1	1	2	0	0	28	8	0	0	5.1	1.000	C-7

Kirk Gibson

GIBSON, KIRK HAROLD
B. May 28, 1957, Pontiac, Mich.
BL TL 6′ 3″ 215 lbs.

Year	Team	Games	BA	SA	AB	H	2B	3B	HR	HR%	R	RBI	BB	SO	SB	Pinch Hit AB	Pinch Hit H	PO	A	E	DP	TC/G	FA	G by Pos
1979	DET A	12	.237	.395	38	9	3	0	1	2.6	3	4	1	3	3	2	0	15	0	0	0	1.5	1.000	OF-10
1980		51	.263	.440	175	46	2	1	9	5.1	23	16	10	45	4	5	1	122	1	1	0	2.5	.992	OF-49, DH-1
1981		83	.328	.479	290	95	11	3	9	3.1	41	40	18	64	17	8	1	142	1	4	0	1.9	.973	OF-67, DH-9

Kirk Gibson *continued*

Year	Team		Games	BA	SA	AB	H	2B	3B	HR	HR%	R	RBI	BB	SO	SB	Pinch Hit AB	Pinch Hit H	PO	A	E	DP	TC/G	FA	G by Pos
1982			69	.278	.444	266	74	16	2	8	3.0	34	35	25	41	9	1	0	167	4	1	3	2.5	.994	OF-64, DH-4
1983			128	.227	.414	401	91	12	9	15	3.7	60	51	53	96	14	20	5	116	2	3	0	1.0	.975	DH-66, OF-54
1984			149	.282	.516	531	150	23	10	27	5.1	92	91	63	103	29	11	1	245	4	12	2	1.8	.954	OF-139, DH-6
1985			154	.287	.518	581	167	37	5	29	5.0	96	97	71	137	30	3	2	286	1	11	0	2.0	.963	OF-144, DH-8
1986			119	.268	.492	441	118	11	2	28	6.3	84	86	68	107	34	2	1	190	2	2	1	1.6	.990	OF-114, DH-4
1987			128	.277	.489	487	135	25	3	24	4.9	95	79	71	117	26	3	0	253	6	7	0	2.1	.974	OF-121, DH-4
1988	LA	N	150	.290	.483	542	157	28	1	25	4.6	106	76	73	120	31	3	0	311	6	12	3	2.2	.964	OF-148
1989			71	.213	.368	253	54	8	2	9	3.6	35	28	35	55	12	2	1	146	3	3	2	2.2	.980	OF-70
1990			89	.260	.400	315	82	20	0	8	2.5	59	38	39	65	26	6	1	191	4	1	1	2.4	.995	OF-81
1991	KC	A	132	.236	.403	462	109	17	6	16	3.5	81	55	69	103	18	9	2	162	3	4	0	1.4	.976	OF-94, DH-30
1992	PIT	N	16	.196	.304	56	11	0	0	2	3.6	6	5	3	12	3	3	0	25	1	0	0	2.0	1.000	OF-13
1993	DET	A	116	.261	.432	403	105	18	6	13	3.2	62	62	44	87	15	11	2	76	0	1	0	0.7	.987	DH-76, OF-32
1994			98	.276	.548	330	91	17	2	23	7.0	71	72	42	69	4	8	2	76	3	1	0	0.9	.988	DH-56, OF-38
1995			70	.260	.449	227	59	12	2	9	4.0	37	35	33	61	9	6	3	0	0	0	0	0.0		DH-63, OF-1
17 yrs.			1635	.268	.463	5798	1553	260	54	255	4.4	985	870	718	1285	284	103	22	2523	41	63	12	1.7	.976	OF-1239, DH-327
LEAGUE CHAMPIONSHIP SERIES																									
1984	DET	A	3	.417	.750	12	5	1	0	1	8.3	2	2	2	1	1	0	0	7	0	0	0	2.3	1.000	OF-3
1987			5	.286	.476	21	6	1	0	1	4.8	4	4	3	8	3	0	0	10	1	0	0	2.2	1.000	OF-5
1988	LA	N	7	.154	.385	26	4	0	0	2	7.7	2	6	3	6	2	0	0	17	1	1	0	2.7	.947	OF-7
3 yrs.			15	.254	.492	59	15	2	0	4	6.8 **5th**	8	12	8	15	6 **8th**	0	0	34	2	1	0	2.5	.973	OF-15
WORLD SERIES																									
1984	DET	A	5	.333	.667	18	6	0	0	2	11.1	4	7	4	4	3	0	0	5	1	2	0	1.6	.750	OF-5
1988	LA	N	1	1.000	4.000	1	1	0	0	1	100.0	1	2	0	0	0	1	1	0	0	0	0	0.0	—	
2 yrs.			6	.368	.842	19	7	0	0	3	15.8	5	9	4	4	3	1	1	5	1	2	0	1.6	.750	OF-5

Russ Gibson

GIBSON, JOHN RUSSELL BR TR 6′ 1″ 195 lbs.
B. May 6, 1939, Fall River, Mass.

Year	Team		Games	BA	SA	AB	H	2B	3B	HR	HR%	R	RBI	BB	SO	SB	Pinch Hit AB	Pinch Hit H	PO	A	E	DP	TC/G	FA	G by Pos
1967	BOS	A	49	.203	.275	138	28	7	0	1	0.7	8	15	12	31	0	4	0	254	16	0	3	5.6	1.000	C-48
1968			76	.225	.320	231	52	11	1	3	1.3	15	20	8	38	1	3	1	431	36	8	7	6.3	.983	C-74, 1B-1
1969			85	.251	.321	287	72	9	1	3	1.0	21	27	15	25	1	4	1	466	41	11	2	6.2	.979	C-83
1970	SF	N	24	.232	.319	69	16	6	0	0	0.0	3	6	7	12	0	1	0	126	7	4	1	6.0	.971	C-23
1971			25	.193	.298	57	11	1	1	1	1.8	2	7	2	13	0	2	0	79	4	3	0	3.9	.965	C-22
1972			5	.167	.333	12	2	0	1	0	0.0	0	3	0	4	0	1	0	16	1	0	1	3.4	1.000	C-5
6 yrs.			264	.228	.311	794	181	34	4	8	1.0	49	78	44	123	2	15	2	1372	105	26	14	5.9	.983	C-255, 1B-1
WORLD SERIES																									
1967	BOS	A	2	.000	.000	2	0	0	0	0	0.0	0	0	0	2	0	0	0	9	0	0	0	4.5	1.000	C-2

Whitey Gibson

GIBSON, LEIGHTON P. TR 5′ 9″ 178 lbs.
B. Oct. 6, 1868, Lancaster, Pa. D. Oct. 11, 1907, Talmadge, Pa.

Year	Team		Games	BA	SA	AB	H	2B	3B	HR	HR%	R	RBI	BB	SO	SB	Pinch Hit AB	Pinch Hit H	PO	A	E	DP	TC/G	FA	G by Pos
1888	PHI	AA	1	.000	.000	3	0	0	0	0	0.0	0	0	0		0	0	0	2	4	0	0	6.0	1.000	C-1

Joe Giebel

GIEBEL, JOSEPH HENRY BR TR 5′10½″ 175 lbs.
B. Nov. 30, 1891, Washington, D. C. D. Mar. 17, 1981, Silver Spring, Md.

Year	Team		Games	BA	SA	AB	H	2B	3B	HR	HR%	R	RBI	BB	SO	SB	Pinch Hit AB	Pinch Hit H	PO	A	E	DP	TC/G	FA	G by Pos
1913	PHI	A	1	.333	.333	3	1	0	0	0	0.0	0	0	0	1	0	0	0	5	0	0	0	5.0	1.000	C-1

Norm Gigon

GIGON, NORMAN PHILLIP BR TR 6′ 195 lbs.
B. May 12, 1938, Teaneck, N. J.

Year	Team		Games	BA	SA	AB	H	2B	3B	HR	HR%	R	RBI	BB	SO	SB	Pinch Hit AB	Pinch Hit H	PO	A	E	DP	TC/G	FA	G by Pos
1967	CHI	N	34	.171	.286	70	12	3	1	1	1.4	8	6	4	14	0	15	2	21	36	1	6	3.4	.983	2B-12, OF-4, 3B-1

Benji Gil

GIL, ROMAR BENJAMIN BR TR 6′ 2″ 180 lbs.
Born Romar Benjamin Gil (Aguilar).
B. Oct. 6, 1972, Tijuana, Mexico.

Year	Team		Games	BA	SA	AB	H	2B	3B	HR	HR%	R	RBI	BB	SO	SB	Pinch Hit AB	Pinch Hit H	PO	A	E	DP	TC/G	FA	G by Pos
1993	TEX	A	22	.123	.123	57	7	0	0	0	0.0	3	2	5	22	1	0	0	27	76	5	10	4.9	.954	SS-22
1995			130	.219	.347	415	91	20	3	9	2.2	36	46	26	147	2	0	0	228	409	17	92	5.0	.974	SS-130
2 yrs.			152	.208	.320	472	98	20	3	9	1.9	39	48	31	169	3	0	0	255	485	22	102	5.0	.971	SS-152

Gus Gil

GIL, TOMAS GUSTAVO BR TR 5′10″ 180 lbs.
Born Tomas Gustavo Gil (Guillen).
B. Apr. 19, 1939, Caracas, Venezuela.

Year	Team		Games	BA	SA	AB	H	2B	3B	HR	HR%	R	RBI	BB	SO	SB	Pinch Hit AB	Pinch Hit H	PO	A	E	DP	TC/G	FA	G by Pos
1967	CLE	A	51	.115	.156	96	11	4	0	0	0.0	11	5	9	18	0	1	0	79	67	0	13	2.9	1.000	2B-49, 1B-1
1969	SEA	A	92	.222	.253	221	49	7	0	0	0.0	20	17	16	28	2	36	10	65	130	9	16	3.0	.956	3B-38, 2B-18, SS-12
1970	MIL	A	64	.185	.244	119	22	4	0	1	0.8	12	12	21	12	2	11	3	79	74	3	14	3.0	.981	2B-38, 3B-14
1971			14	.156	.188	32	5	1	0	0	0.0	3	3	10	5	1	4	0	20	27	1	3	3.4	.979	2B-8, 3B-6
4 yrs.			221	.186	.226	468	87	16	0	1	0.2	46	37	56	63	5	52	13	243	298	13	46	3.0	.977	2B-113, 3B-58, SS-12, 1B-1

Andy Gilbert

GILBERT, ANDREW BR TR 6′ 1″ 203 lbs.
B. July 18, 1914, Bradenville, Pa. D. Aug. 29, 1992, Davis, Calif.

Year	Team		Games	BA	SA	AB	H	2B	3B	HR	HR%	R	RBI	BB	SO	SB	Pinch Hit AB	Pinch Hit H	PO	A	E	DP	TC/G	FA	G by Pos
1942	BOS	A	6	.091	.091	11	1	0	0	0	0.0	0	1	1	3	0	1	0	6	0	0	0	1.2	1.000	OF-5
1946			2	.000	.000	1	0	0	0	0	0.0	1	0	0	0	0	1	0	0	0	0	0	0.0	.000	OF-1
2 yrs.			8	.083	.083	12	1	0	0	0	0.0	1	1	1	3	0	2	0	6	0	0	0	1.0	1.000	OF-6

Billy Gilbert

GILBERT, WILLIAM OLIVER BR TR 5′ 4″ 153 lbs.
B. June 21, 1876, Tullytown, Pa. D. Aug. 8, 1927, New York, N. Y.

Year	Team		Games	BA	SA	AB	H	2B	3B	HR	HR%	R	RBI	BB	SO	SB	Pinch Hit AB	Pinch Hit H	PO	A	E	DP	TC/G	FA	G by Pos
1901	MIL	A	127	.270	.327	492	133	14	7	0	0.0	77	43	31		19	0	0	319	395	49	66	6.0	.936	2B-127
1902	BAL	A	129	.245	.299	445	109	12	3	2	0.4	74	38	45		38	0	0	349	410	78	72	6.5	.907	SS-129
1903	NY	N	128	.252	.281	413	104	9	0	1	0.2	62	40	41		37	0	0	314	366	47	42	5.7	.935	2B-128
1904			146	.253	.299	478	121	13	3	1	0.2	57	54	46		33	0	0	305	466	44	48	5.6	.946	2B-146
1905			115	.247	.293	376	93	11	3	0	0.0	45	24	41		11	0	0	245	367	34	41	5.6	.947	2B-115

Billy Gilbert *continued*

Year	Team	Games	BA	SA	AB	H	2B	3B	HR	HR%	R	RBI	BB	SO	SB	Pinch Hit AB	Pinch Hit H	PO	A	E	DP	TC/G	FA	G by Pos
1906		104	.231	.267	307	71	6	1	1	0.3	44	27	42		22	4	1	223	324	35	32	5.9	.940	2B-98
1908	STL N	89	.214	.239	276	59	7	0	0	0.0	12	10	20		6	0	0	222	254	24	23	5.6	.952	2B-89
1909		12	.172	.172	29	5	0	0	0	0.0	4	1	4		1	0	0	19	28	4	1	4.3	.922	2B-12
8 yrs.		850	.247	.290	2816	695	72	17	5	0.2	375	237	270		167	4	1	1996	2610	315	325	5.8	.936	2B-715, SS-129
WORLD SERIES																								
1905	NY N	5	.235	.235	17	4	0	0	0	0.0	1	1	0	2	1	0	0	10	16	0	0	5.2	1.000	2B-5

Buddy Gilbert

GILBERT, DREW EDWARD BL TR 6′ 3″ 195 lbs.
B. July 26, 1935, Knoxville, Tenn.

Year	Team	Games	BA	SA	AB	H	2B	3B	HR	HR%	R	RBI	BB	SO	SB	Pinch Hit AB	Pinch Hit H	PO	A	E	DP	TC/G	FA	G by Pos
1959	CIN N	7	.150	.450	20	3	0	0	2	10.0	4	2	3	4	0	1	0	15	0	0	0	2.5	1.000	OF-6

Charlie Gilbert

GILBERT, CHARLES MADER BL TL 5′ 9″ 165 lbs.
Son of Larry Gilbert. Brother of Tookie Gilbert.
B. July 8, 1919, New Orleans, La. D. Aug. 13, 1983, New Orleans, La.

Year	Team	Games	BA	SA	AB	H	2B	3B	HR	HR%	R	RBI	BB	SO	SB	Pinch Hit AB	Pinch Hit H	PO	A	E	DP	TC/G	FA	G by Pos
1940	BKN N	57	.246	.366	142	35	9	1	2	1.4	23	8	8	13	0	8	1	91	4	4	1	2.3	.960	OF-43
1941	CHI N	39	.279	.326	86	24	2	1	0	0.0	11	12	11	6	1	14	2	51	0	0	0	2.3	1.000	OF-22
1942		74	.184	.251	179	33	6	3	0	0.0	18	7	25	24	1	23	2	99	6	2	2	2.3	.981	OF-47
1943		8	.150	.150	20	3	0	0	0	0.0	1	0	3	3	1	2	0	9	1	0	0	1.7	1.000	OF-6
1946	2 teams	CHI N (15G –.077) PHI N (88G –.242)																						
″	total	103	.234	.278	273	64	5	2	1	0.4	36	18	26	22	3	28	0	155	10	0	4	2.3	1.000	OF-71
1947	PHI N	83	.237	.336	152	36	5	2	2	1.3	20	10	13	14	1	**40**	9	70	4	3	2	2.1	.961	OF-37
6 yrs.		364	.229	.299	852	195	27	9	5	0.6	109	55	86	82	7	115	14	475	25	9	9	2.3	.982	OF-226

Harry Gilbert

GILBERT, HARRY H.
Brother of John Gilbert.
B. July 8, 1868, Pottstown, Pa. D. Dec. 23, 1909, Pottstown, Pa.

Year	Team	Games	BA	SA	AB	H	2B	3B	HR	HR%	R	RBI	BB	SO	SB	Pinch Hit AB	Pinch Hit H	PO	A	E	DP	TC/G	FA	G by Pos
1890	PIT N	2	.250	.250	8	2	0	0	0	0.0	1	0	0	3	0	0	0	1	5	0	1	3.0	1.000	2B-2

Jack Gilbert

GILBERT, JOHN ROBERT (Jackrabbit)
B. Sept. 7, 1875, Rhinecliff, N. Y. D. July 7, 1941, Albany, N. Y.

Year	Team	Games	BA	SA	AB	H	2B	3B	HR	HR%	R	RBI	BB	SO	SB	Pinch Hit AB	Pinch Hit H	PO	A	E	DP	TC/G	FA	G by Pos
1898	2 teams	WAS N (2G –.200) NY N (1G –.250)																						
″	total	3	.222	.222	9	2	0	0	0	0.0	0	1	1		2	0	0	1	1	2	0	1.3	.500	OF-3
1904	PIT N	25	.241	.241	87	21	0	0	0	0.0	13	3	12		3	0	0	30	0	5	0	1.4	.857	OF-25
2 yrs.		28	.240	.240	96	23	0	0	0	0.0	13	4	13		5	0	0	31	1	7	0	1.4	.821	OF-28

John Gilbert

GILBERT, JOHN G.
Brother of Harry Gilbert.
B. Jan. 8, 1864, Pottstown, Pa. D. Nov. 12, 1903, Pottstown, Pa.

Year	Team	Games	BA	SA	AB	H	2B	3B	HR	HR%	R	RBI	BB	SO	SB	Pinch Hit AB	Pinch Hit H	PO	A	E	DP	TC/G	FA	G by Pos
1890	PIT N	2	.000	.000	8	0	0	0	0	0.0	0	0	0	2	0	0	0	4	5	0	1	4.5	1.000	SS-2

Larry Gilbert

GILBERT, LAWRENCE WILLIAM BL TL 5′ 9″ 158 lbs.
Father of Tookie Gilbert. Father of Charlie Gilbert.
B. Dec. 3, 1891, New Orleans, La. D. Feb. 17, 1965, New Orleans, La.

Year	Team	Games	BA	SA	AB	H	2B	3B	HR	HR%	R	RBI	BB	SO	SB	Pinch Hit AB	Pinch Hit H	PO	A	E	DP	TC/G	FA	G by Pos
1914	BOS N	72	.268	.371	224	60	6	1	5	2.2	32	25	26	34	3	10	1	79	14	2	2	1.6	.979	OF-60
1915		45	.151	.189	106	16	4	0	0	0.0	11	4	11	13	4	14	3	28	4	2	1	1.3	.941	OF-27
2 yrs.		117	.230	.312	330	76	10	1	5	1.5	43	29	37	47	7	24	4	107	18	4	3	1.5	.969	OF-87
WORLD SERIES																								
1914	BOS N	1	—	—	0	0	0	0	0	—	0	0	1	0	0	0	0	0	0	0	0	0.0	—	

Mark Gilbert

GILBERT, MARK DAVID BB TR 6′ 175 lbs.
B. Aug. 2, 1956, Atlanta, Ga.

Year	Team	Games	BA	SA	AB	H	2B	3B	HR	HR%	R	RBI	BB	SO	SB	Pinch Hit AB	Pinch Hit H	PO	A	E	DP	TC/G	FA	G by Pos
1985	CHI A	7	.273	.318	22	6	1	0	0	0.0	3	3	4	5	0	1	0	14	0	0	0	2.0	1.000	OF-7

Pete Gilbert

GILBERT, PETER TR 5′ 8″ 180 lbs.
B. Sept. 6, 1867, Baltic, Conn. D. Jan. 1, 1912, Springfield, Mass.

Year	Team	Games	BA	SA	AB	H	2B	3B	HR	HR%	R	RBI	BB	SO	SB	Pinch Hit AB	Pinch Hit H	PO	A	E	DP	TC/G	FA	G by Pos
1890	BAL AA	29	.280	.350	100	28	2	1	1	1.0	25		10		12	0	0	34	55	10	5	3.4	.899	3B-29
1891		139	.230	.304	513	118	15	7	3	0.6	81	72	37	77	31	0	0	201	324	84	34	4.4	.862	3B-139
1892	BAL N	4	.200	.200	15	3	0	0	0	0.0	0	0	1	3	1	0	0	4	12	2	0	4.5	.889	3B-4
1894	2 teams	BKN N (6G –.080) LOU N (28G –.306)																						
″	total	34	.263	.323	133	35	3	1	1	0.8	14	15	6	7	4	0	0	57	69	35	7	4.7	.783	3B-31, 2B-3
4 yrs.		206	.242	.311	761	184	20	9	5	0.7	120	87	54	87	48	0	0	296	460	131	46	4.3	.852	3B-203, 2B-3

Tookie Gilbert

GILBERT, HAROLD JOSEPH BL TR 6′ 2½″ 185 lbs.
Son of Larry Gilbert. Brother of Charlie Gilbert.
B. Apr. 4, 1929, New Orleans, La. D. June 23, 1967, New Orleans, La.

Year	Team	Games	BA	SA	AB	H	2B	3B	HR	HR%	R	RBI	BB	SO	SB	Pinch Hit AB	Pinch Hit H	PO	A	E	DP	TC/G	FA	G by Pos
1950	NY N	113	.220	.307	322	71	12	2	4	1.2	40	32	43	36	3	2	0	784	65	10	80	7.7	.988	1B-111
1953		70	.169	.244	160	27	3	0	3	1.9	12	16	22	21	1	23	4	381	26	2	34	9.3	.995	1B-44
2 yrs.		183	.203	.286	482	98	15	2	7	1.5	52	48	65	57	4	25	4	1165	91	12	114	8.2	.991	1B-155

Wally Gilbert

GILBERT, WALTER JOHN BR TR 6′ 180 lbs.
B. Dec. 19, 1900, Oscoda, Mich. D. Sept. 7, 1958, Duluth, Minn.

Year	Team	Games	BA	SA	AB	H	2B	3B	HR	HR%	R	RBI	BB	SO	SB	Pinch Hit AB	Pinch Hit H	PO	A	E	DP	TC/G	FA	G by Pos
1928	BKN N	39	.203	.229	153	31	4	0	0	0.0	26	3	14	8	2	0	0	30	81	4	7	2.9	.965	3B-39
1929		143	.304	.388	569	173	31	4	3	0.5	88	58	42	29	7	1	0	137	271	19	16	3.0	.956	3B-142
1930		150	.294	.379	623	183	34	5	3	0.5	92	67	47	33	7	0	0	130	312	26	27	3.1	.944	3B-150
1931		145	.266	.333	552	147	25	6	0	0.0	60	46	39	38	3	0	0	125	295	23	14	3.1	.948	3B-145
1932	CIN N	114	.214	.274	420	90	18	2	1	0.2	35	40	20	23	2	2	1	90	198	22	16	2.8	.929	3B-111
5 yrs.		591	.269	.341	2317	624	112	17	7	0.3	301	214	162	131	21	3	1	512	1157	94	80	3.0	.947	3B-587

Rod Gilbreath

GILBREATH, RODNEY JOE BR TR 6′ 2″ 180 lbs.
BB 1975
B. Sept. 24, 1952, Laurel, Miss.

Year	Team	Games	BA	SA	AB	H	2B	3B	HR	HR%	R	RBI	BB	SO	SB	Pinch Hit AB	Pinch Hit H	PO	A	E	DP	TC/G	FA	G by Pos
1972	ATL N	18	.237	.263	38	9	1	0	0	0.0	2	1	2	10	1	4	0	16	26	1	4	3.9	.977	2B-7, 3B-4
1973		29	.284	.338	74	21	2	1	0	0.0	10	2	6	10	2	10	3	16	32	2	4	2.3	.960	3B-22
1974		3	.333	.333	6	2	0	0	0	0.0	2	0	2	0	0	0	0	5	6	0	1	5.5	1.000	2B-2

Rod Gilbreath *continued*

Year	Team	Lg	Games	BA	SA	AB	H	2B	3B	HR	HR%	R	RBI	BB	SO	SB	Pinch Hit AB	Pinch Hit H	PO	A	E	DP	TC/G	FA	G by Pos
1975			90	.243	.297	202	49	3	1	2	1.0	24	16	24	26	5	25	10	127	141	6	29	4.3	.978	2B-52, 3B-10, SS-1
1976			116	.251	.329	383	96	11	8	1	0.3	57	32	42	36	7	5	1	245	314	17	77	5.1	.970	2B-104, 3B-7, SS-1
1977			128	.243	.349	407	99	15	2	8	2.0	47	43	45	79	3	5	0	277	308	13	61	4.9	.978	2B-122, 3B-1
1978			116	.245	.331	326	80	13	3	3	0.9	22	31	26	51	7	11	1	108	204	9	22	3.2	.972	3B-62, 2B-39
7 yrs.			500	.248	.329	1436	356	45	15	14	1.0	164	125	147	212	25	60	15	794	1031	48	198	4.3	.974	2B-326, 3B-106, SS-2

Don Gile

GILE, DONALD LOREN (Bear) BR TR 6′ 6″ 220 lbs.
B. Apr. 19, 1935, Modesto, Calif.

Year	Team	Lg	Games	BA	SA	AB	H	2B	3B	HR	HR%	R	RBI	BB	SO	SB	Pinch Hit AB	Pinch Hit H	PO	A	E	DP	TC/G	FA	G by Pos
1959	BOS	A	3	.200	.300	10	2	1	0	0	0.0	1	1	0	2	0	0	0	17	1	0	0	6.0	1.000	C-3
1960			29	.176	.294	51	9	1	1	1	2.0	6	4	1	13	0	5	0	92	7	1	8	3.8	.990	C-15, 1B-11
1961			8	.278	.444	18	5	0	0	1	5.6	2	1	1	5	0	1	0	45	2	2	3	7.0	.959	1B-6, C-1
1962			18	.049	.122	41	2	0	0	1	2.4	3	3	3	15	0	2	0	90	5	1	11	6.9	.990	1B-14
4 yrs.			58	.150	.258	120	18	2	1	3	2.5	12	9	5	35	0	8	0	244	15	4	22	5.3	.985	1B-31, C-19

Brian Giles

GILES, BRIAN JEFFREY BR TR 6′ 1″ 165 lbs.
B. Apr. 27, 1960, Manhattan, Kans.

Year	Team	Lg	Games	BA	SA	AB	H	2B	3B	HR	HR%	R	RBI	BB	SO	SB	Pinch Hit AB	Pinch Hit H	PO	A	E	DP	TC/G	FA	G by Pos
1981	NY	N	9	.000	.000	7	0	0	0	0	0.0	0	0	0	3	0	2	0	5	8	0	2	3.3	1.000	SS-2, 2B-2
1982			45	.210	.312	138	29	5	0	3	2.2	14	10	12	29	6	0	0	122	133	2	28	5.5	.992	2B-45, SS-2
1983			145	.245	.297	400	98	15	0	2	0.5	39	27	36	77	17	5	0	309	390	14	90	4.7	.980	2B-140, SS-12
1985	MIL	A	34	.172	.241	58	10	1	0	1	1.7	6	1	7	16	2	0	0	48	58	2	10	3.1	.981	SS-20, 2B-13, DH-2
1986	CHI	A	9	.273	.273	11	3	0	0	0	0.0	0	1	0	2	0	1	0	15	11	0	6	3.3	1.000	2B-7, SS-1
1990	SEA	A	45	.232	.421	95	22	6	0	4	4.2	15	11	15	24	2	5	1	57	88	3	28	3.6	.980	SS-37, 2B-2, 3B-1, DH-1
6 yrs.			287	.228	.309	709	162	27	0	10	1.4	74	50	70	151	27	13	1	556	688	21	164	4.4	.983	2B-209, SS-74, DH-3, 3B-1

Brian Giles

GILES, BRIAN STEPHEN BL TL 5′11″ 195 lbs.
B. Jan. 21, 1971, El Cajon, Calif.

Year	Team	Lg	Games	BA	SA	AB	H	2B	3B	HR	HR%	R	RBI	BB	SO	SB	Pinch Hit AB	Pinch Hit H	PO	A	E	DP	TC/G	FA	G by Pos
1995	CLE	A	6	.556	.889	9	5	0	0	1	11.1	6	3	0	1	0	2	2	2	1	0	0	0.8	1.000	OF-3, DH-1

George Gilham

GILHAM, GEORGE LOUIS BR TR 5′11″ 164 lbs.
B. Sept. 8, 1899, Shamokin, Pa. D. Apr. 25, 1937, Lansdowne, Pa.

Year	Team	Lg	Games	BA	SA	AB	H	2B	3B	HR	HR%	R	RBI	BB	SO	SB	Pinch Hit AB	Pinch Hit H	PO	A	E	DP	TC/G	FA	G by Pos
1920	STL	N	1	.000	.000	3	0	0	0	0	0.0	0	0	0	1	0	0	0	2	1	1	0	4.0	.750	C-1
1921			1	.000	.000	1	0	0	0	0	0.0	0	0	0	0	0	1	0	0	0	0	0	0.0	—	
2 yrs.			2	.000	.000	4	0	0	0	0	0.0	0	0	0	1	0	1	0	2	1	1	0	4.0	.750	C-1

Frank Gilhooley

GILHOOLEY, FRANK PATRICK (Flash) BL TR 5′ 8″ 155 lbs.
B. June 10, 1892, Toledo, Ohio D. July 11, 1959, Toledo, Ohio.

Year	Team	Lg	Games	BA	SA	AB	H	2B	3B	HR	HR%	R	RBI	BB	SO	SB	Pinch Hit AB	Pinch Hit H	PO	A	E	DP	TC/G	FA	G by Pos
1911	STL	N	1	—	—	0	0	0	0	0	—	0	0	0	0	0	0	0	0	0	0	0	0.0	.000	OF-1
1912			13	.224	.224	49	11	0	0	0	0.0	5	2	3	8	0	1	0	16	1	0	0	1.5	1.000	OF-11
1913	NY	A	24	.341	.388	85	29	2	1	0	0.0	10	14	4	9	6	0	0	40	2	1	0	1.8	.977	OF-24
1914			1	.667	.667	3	2	0	0	0	0.0	0	0	1	0	0	0	0	0	0	0	0	0.0	.000	OF-1
1915			1	.000	.000	4	0	0	0	0	0.0	0	0	0	1	0	0	0	1	0	0	0	1.0	1.000	OF-1
1916			58	.278	.341	223	62	5	3	1	0.4	40	10	37	17	16	1	1	93	9	3	3	1.8	.971	OF-57
1917			54	.242	.291	165	40	6	1	0	0.0	14	8	30	13	6	2	1	78	5	6	1	1.9	.933	OF-46
1918			112	.276	.337	427	118	13	5	1	0.2	59	23	53	24	7	1	0	206	15	9	8	2.1	.961	OF-111
1919	BOS	A	48	.241	.277	112	27	4	0	0	0.0	14	1	12	8	2	10	2	44	3	4	0	1.5	.922	OF-33
9 yrs.			312	.271	.323	1068	289	30	10	2	0.2	142	58	140	80	37	15	4	478	35	23	12	1.9	.957	OF-285

Bernard Gilkey

GILKEY, OTIS BERNARD BR TR 6′ 170 lbs.
B. Sept. 24, 1966, St. Louis, Mo.

Year	Team	Lg	Games	BA	SA	AB	H	2B	3B	HR	HR%	R	RBI	BB	SO	SB	Pinch Hit AB	Pinch Hit H	PO	A	E	DP	TC/G	FA	G by Pos
1990	STL	N	18	.297	.484	64	19	5	2	1	1.6	11	3	8	5	6	0	0	47	2	2	0	2.8	.961	OF-18
1991			81	.216	.313	268	58	7	2	5	1.9	28	20	39	33	14	7	1	164	6	1	1	2.3	.994	OF-74
1992			131	.302	.427	384	116	19	4	7	1.8	56	43	39	52	18	20	4	217	9	5	3	2.1	.978	OF-111
1993			137	.305	.481	557	170	40	5	16	2.9	99	70	56	66	15	1	1	251	20	8	4	2.0	.971	OF-134, 1B-3
1994			105	.253	.363	380	96	22	1	6	1.6	52	45	39	65	15	4	2	168	9	3	3	1.8	.983	OF-102
1995			121	.298	.490	480	143	33	4	17	3.5	73	69	42	70	12	3	1	206	10	3	4	1.9	.986	OF-118
6 yrs.			593	.282	.431	2133	602	126	18	52	2.4	319	250	223	291	80	35	9	1053	56	22	15	2.0	.981	OF-557, 1B-3

Bob Gilks

GILKS, ROBERT JAMES BR TR 5′ 8″ 178 lbs.
B. July 2, 1864, Cincinnati, Ohio D. Aug. 21, 1944, Brunswick, Ga.

Year	Team	Lg	Games	BA	SA	AB	H	2B	3B	HR	HR%	R	RBI	BB	SO	SB	Pinch Hit AB	Pinch Hit H	PO	A	E	DP	TC/G	FA	G by Pos
1887	CLE	AA	22	.313	.337	83	26	2	0	0	0.0	12		3		5	0	0	65	33	7	6	4.6	.933	P-13, 1B-6, OF-3, 2B-1
1888			119	.229	.281	484	111	14	4	1	0.2	59	63	7		16	0	0	172	94	38	12	2.5	.875	OF-87, 3B-28, SS-4, P-4, 2B-1
1889	CLE	N	53	.238	.281	210	50	5	2	0	0.0	17	18	7	20	6	0	0	172	54	9	9	4.4	.962	OF-29, SS-13, 1B-10, 2B-1
1890			130	.213	.243	544	116	10	3	0	0.0	65	41	32	38	17	0	0	249	39	20	5	2.3	.935	OF-123, P-4, SS-3, 2B-2
1893	BAL	N	15	.266	.297	64	17	2	0	0	0.0	10	7	0	3	3	0	0	26	5	1	1	2.1	.969	OF-15
5 yrs.			339	.231	.270	1385	320	33	9	1	0.1	163	129	49	61	47	0	0	684	225	75	33	2.8	.924	OF-257, 3B-28, P-21, SS-20, 1B-16, 2B-5

Jim Gill

GILL, JAMES C.
B. St. Louis, Mo. Deceased.

Year	Team	Lg	Games	BA	SA	AB	H	2B	3B	HR	HR%	R	RBI	BB	SO	SB	Pinch Hit AB	Pinch Hit H	PO	A	E	DP	TC/G	FA	G by Pos
1889	STL	AA	2	.250	.375	8	2	1	0	0	0.0	2	1	1	2	1	0	0	7	1	1	0	4.5	.889	OF-1, 2B-1

Johnny Gill

GILL, JOHN WESLEY (Patcheye) BL TR 6′ 2″ 190 lbs.
B. Mar. 27, 1905, Nashville, Tenn. D. Dec. 26, 1984, Nashville, Tenn.

Year	Team	Lg	Games	BA	SA	AB	H	2B	3B	HR	HR%	R	RBI	BB	SO	SB	Pinch Hit AB	Pinch Hit H	PO	A	E	DP	TC/G	FA	G by Pos
1927	CLE	A	21	.217	.317	60	13	3	0	1	1.7	8	4	7	13	1	2	2	24	2	0	1	1.5	1.000	OF-17
1928			2	.000	.000	2	0	0	0	0	0.0	0	0	0	1	0	2	0	0	0	0	0	0.0	—	
1931	WAS	A	8	.267	.400	30	8	2	1	0	0.0	2	5	1	6	0	0	0	24	2	0	2	3.3	1.000	OF-8
1934			13	.245	.415	53	13	3	0	2	3.8	7	7	2	3	0	0	0	25	0	0	0	1.9	1.000	OF-13
1935	CHI	N	3	.333	.667	3	1	1	0	0	0.0	2	1	0	1	0	3	1	0	0	0	0	0.0	—	
1936			71	.253	.420	174	44	8	0	7	4.0	20	28	13	19	0	25	6	72	3	5	1	2.0	.938	OF-41
6 yrs.			118	.245	.398	322	79	17	1	10	3.1	39	45	23	43	1	32	9	145	7	5	4	2.0	.968	OF-79

Warren Gill

GILL, WARREN DARST (Doc)
B. Dec. 21, 1878, Ladoga, Ind. D. Nov. 26, 1952, Laguna Beach, Calif.
BR TR 6′ 1″ 175 lbs.

Year	Team	Lg	Games	BA	SA	AB	H	2B	3B	HR	HR%	R	RBI	BB	SO	SB	Pinch Hit AB	Pinch Hit H	PO	A	E	DP	TC/G	FA	G by Pos
1908	PIT	N	27	.224	.250	76	17	0	1	0	0.0	10	14	11		3	1	1	237	7	0	10	9.8	1.000	1B-25

Sam Gillen

GILLEN, SAMUEL
Born Samuel Gilleland.
B. Jan. 1871, Pittsburgh, Pa. D. May 13, 1905, Pittsburgh, Pa.
5′ 8″

Year	Team	Lg	Games	BA	SA	AB	H	2B	3B	HR	HR%	R	RBI	BB	SO	SB	Pinch Hit AB	Pinch Hit H	PO	A	E	DP	TC/G	FA	G by Pos
1893	PIT	N	3	.000	.000	6	0	0	0	0	0.0	0	0	0	1	0	0	0	1	5	2	1	2.7	.750	SS-3
1897	PHI	N	75	.259	.319	270	70	10	3	0	0.0	32	27	35		2	0	0	136	203	39	6	5.0	.897	SS-69, 3B-6
2 yrs.			78	.254	.312	276	70	10	3	0	0.0	32	27	35	1	2	0	0	137	208	41	7	4.9	.894	SS-72, 3B-6

Tom Gillen

GILLEN, THOMAS J.
B. May 18, 1862, Philadelphia, Pa. D. Jan. 26, 1889, Philadelphia, Pa.
5′ 8″ 160 lbs.

Year	Team	Lg	Games	BA	SA	AB	H	2B	3B	HR	HR%	R	RBI	BB	SO	SB	Pinch Hit AB	Pinch Hit H	PO	A	E	DP	TC/G	FA	G by Pos
1884	PHI	U	29	.155	.172	116	18	2	0	0	0.0	5		1			0	0	154	61	25	1	8.0	.896	C-27, OF-3
1886	DET	N	2	.400	.400	10	4	0	0	0	0.0	2	4	0	1		0	0	5	3	1	0	4.5	.889	C-2
2 yrs.			31	.175	.190	126	22	2	0	0	0.0	7	4	1	1		0	0	159	64	26	1	7.8	.896	C-29, OF-3

Carden Gillenwater

GILLENWATER, CARDEN EDISON
B. May 13, 1918, Riceville, Tenn.
BR TR 6′ 1″ 175 lbs.

Year	Team	Lg	Games	BA	SA	AB	H	2B	3B	HR	HR%	R	RBI	BB	SO	SB	Pinch Hit AB	Pinch Hit H	PO	A	E	DP	TC/G	FA	G by Pos
1940	STL	N	7	.160	.200	25	4	1	0	0	0.0	1	5	0	2	0	0	0	12	0	0	0	1.7	1.000	OF-7
1943	BKN	N	8	.176	.176	17	3	0	0	0	0.0	1	2	2	3	0	3	0	5	1	0	0	1.2	1.000	OF-5
1945	BOS	N	144	.288	.375	517	149	20	2	7	1.4	74	72	73	70	13	3	1	451	24	10	5	3.5	.979	OF-140
1946			99	.228	.295	224	51	10	1	1	0.4	30	14	39	27	3	14	2	180	6	4	2	2.4	.979	OF-78
1948	WAS	A	77	.244	.367	221	54	10	4	3	1.4	23	21	39	36	4	11	0	186	4	5	0	2.9	.974	OF-67
5 yrs.			335	.260	.348	1004	261	41	7	11	1.1	129	114	153	138	20	31	3	834	35	19	7	3.0	.979	OF-297

Jim Gillespie

GILLESPIE, JAMES WHEATFIELD
B. Sept. 1858 D. Sept. 5, 1921, North Tonawanda, N. Y.
BL TR

Year	Team	Lg	Games	BA	SA	AB	H	2B	3B	HR	HR%	R	RBI	BB	SO	SB	Pinch Hit AB	Pinch Hit H	PO	A	E	DP	TC/G	FA	G by Pos
1890	BUF	P	1	.000	.000	3	0	0	0	0	0.0	0	0	0	2	0	0	0	0	1	3	0	4.0	.250	OF-1

Paul Gillespie

GILLESPIE, PAUL ALLEN
B. Sept. 18, 1920, Cartersville, Ga. D. Aug. 11, 1970, Anniston, Ala.
BL TR 6′ 3″ 195 lbs.

Year	Team	Lg	Games	BA	SA	AB	H	2B	3B	HR	HR%	R	RBI	BB	SO	SB	Pinch Hit AB	Pinch Hit H	PO	A	E	DP	TC/G	FA	G by Pos
1942	CHI	N	5	.250	.625	16	4	0	0	2	12.5	3	4	1	2	0	1	0	13	2	0	0	3.8	1.000	C-4
1944			9	.269	.423	26	7	1	0	1	3.8	2	2	3	3	0	2	0	22	6	3	0	4.4	.903	C-7
1945			75	.288	.380	163	47	6	0	3	1.8	12	25	18	9	2	24	7	162	20	2	1	4.0	.989	C-45, OF-1
3 yrs.			89	.283	.405	205	58	7	0	6	2.9	17	31	22	14	2	27	7	197	28	5	1	4.0	.978	C-56, OF-1
WORLD SERIES																									
1945	CHI	N	3	.000	.000	6	0	0	0	0	0.0	0	0	0	0	0	2	0	3	0	0	0	3.0	1.000	C-1

Pete Gillespie

GILLESPIE, PETER PATRICK
B. Nov. 30, 1851, Carbondale, Pa. D. May 5, 1910, Carbondale, Pa.
BL TR 6′ 1½″ 178 lbs.

Year	Team	Lg	Games	BA	SA	AB	H	2B	3B	HR	HR%	R	RBI	BB	SO	SB	Pinch Hit AB	Pinch Hit H	PO	A	E	DP	TC/G	FA	G by Pos
1880	TRO	N	82	.243	.347	346	84	20	5	2	0.6	50	24	17	35		0	0	185	14	21	5	2.7	.905	OF-82
1881			84	.276	.333	348	96	14	3	0	0.0	43	41	9	24		0	0	180	16	14	5	2.5	.933	OF-84
1882			74	.275	.339	298	82	5	4	2	0.7	46	32	9	14		0	0	144	9	32	1	2.5	.827	OF-74
1883	NY	N	98	.314	.436	411	129	23	12	1	0.2	64		9	27		0	0	216	11	26	6	2.6	.897	OF-98
1884			101	.264	.315	413	109	7	4	2	0.5	75		19	35		0	0	159	8	20	1	1.9	.893	OF-101
1885			102	.293	.362	420	123	17	6	0	0.0	67		15	32		0	0	133	12	9	2	1.5	.942	OF-102
1886			97	.273	.346	396	108	13	8	0	0.0	65	58	16	30		0	0	121	6	14	0	1.5	.901	OF-97
1887			76	.264	.346	295	78	9	3	3	1.0	40	37	12	21	37	0	0	91	14	6	1	1.4	.946	OF-76, 3B-1
8 yrs.			714	.276	.354	2927	809	108	45	10	0.3	450	192	106	218	37	0	0	1229	90	142	21	2.0	.903	OF-714, 3B-1

Jim Gilliam

GILLIAM, JAMES WILLIAM (Junior)
B. Oct. 17, 1928, Nashville, Tenn. D. Oct. 8, 1978, Inglewood, Calif.
BB TR 5′10½″ 175 lbs.

Year	Team	Lg	Games	BA	SA	AB	H	2B	3B	HR	HR%	R	RBI	BB	SO	SB	Pinch Hit AB	Pinch Hit H	PO	A	E	DP	TC/G	FA	G by Pos
1953	BKN	N	151	.278	.415	605	168	31	**17**	6	1.0	125	63	100	38	21	2	1	332	426	19	102	5.2	.976	2B-149
1954			146	.282	.418	607	171	28	8	13	2.1	107	52	76	30	8	2	0	349	388	17	99	5.1	.977	2B-143, OF-5
1955			147	.249	.355	538	134	20	8	7	1.3	110	40	70	37	15	6	3	309	271	19	64	4.1	.968	2B-99, OF-46
1956			153	.300	.396	594	178	23	8	6	1.0	102	43	95	39	21	1	0	340	332	12	65	4.3	.982	2B-102, OF-56
1957			149	.250	.314	617	154	26	4	2	0.3	89	37	64	31	26	0	0	416	390	11	90	5.4	.987	2B-148, OF-2
1958	LA	N	147	.261	.335	555	145	25	5	2	0.4	81	43	78	22	18	5	1	245	176	12	37	2.9	.972	OF-75, 3B-44, 2B-32
1959			145	.282	.345	553	156	18	4	3	0.5	91	34	**96**	25	23	7	1	143	258	17	20	2.9	.959	3B-132, 2B-8, OF-4
1960			151	.248	.318	557	138	20	2	5	0.9	96	40	96	28	12	2	1	152	331	16	33	3.1	.968	3B-130, 2B-30
1961			144	.244	.344	439	107	26	3	4	0.9	74	32	79	34	8	11	3	195	283	13	54	3.1	.974	3B-74, 2B-71, OF-11
1962			160	.270	.335	588	159	24	1	4	0.7	83	43	93	35	17	2	0	243	388	20	72	3.2	.969	2B-113, 3B-90, OF-1
1963			148	.282	.383	525	148	27	4	6	1.1	77	49	60	28	19	9	1	267	343	13	67	3.6	.979	2B-119, 3B-55
1964			116	.228	.287	334	76	8	3	2	0.6	44	27	42	21	4	13	3	101	171	18	15	2.6	.938	3B-86, 2B-25, OF-2
1965			111	.280	.384	372	104	19	4	4	1.1	54	39	53	31	9	7	1	85	142	10	15	2.2	.958	3B-80, OF-22, 2B-5
1966			88	.217	.268	235	51	9	0	1	0.4	30	16	34	17	2	22	3	43	103	7	8	2.1	.954	3B-70, 2B-2, 1B-2
14 yrs.			1956	.265	.355	7119	1889	304	71	65	0.9	1163	558	1036	416	203	89	18	3220	4002	204	741	3.7	.973	2B-1046, 3B-761, OF-224, 1B-2
WORLD SERIES																									
1953	BKN	N	6	.296	.630	27	8	3	0	2	7.4	4	4	0	2	0	0	0	15	16	1	3	5.3	.969	2B-6
1955			7	.292	.333	24	7	1	0	0	0.0	2	3	8	1	1	0	0	8	13	0	4	2.3	1.000	2B-5, OF-4
1956			7	.083	.083	24	2	0	0	0	0.0	2	2	7	3	1	0	0	19	17	0	4	5.1	1.000	2B-6, OF-1
1959	LA	N	6	.240	.240	25	6	0	0	0	0.0	2	0	2	2	2	0	0	4	10	0	1	2.3	1.000	3B-6
1963			4	.154	.154	13	2	0	0	0	0.0	3	0	3	1	0	0	0	2	2	0	0	1.0	1.000	3B-4
1965			7	.214	.250	28	6	1	0	0	0.0	2	2	1	0	0	0	0	4	7	2	0	1.9	.846	3B-7
1966			2	.000	.000	6	0	0	0	0	0.0	0	1	2	0	0	0	0	3	4	1	1	4.0	.875	3B-2
7 yrs.			39	.211	.286	147	31	5	0	2	1.4	15	12	23 **7th**	9	4	0	0	55	69	4	13	3.1	.969	3B-19, 2B-17, OF-5

Barney Gilligan

GILLIGAN, ANDREW BERNARD
B. Jan. 3, 1856, Cambridge, Mass. D. Apr. 1, 1934, Lynn, Mass.
BR TR 5′ 6½″ 130 lbs.

Year	Team	Lg	Games	BA	SA	AB	H	2B	3B	HR	HR%	R	RBI	BB	SO	SB	Pinch Hit AB	Pinch Hit H	PO	A	E	DP	TC/G	FA	G by Pos
1879	CLE	N	52	.171	.220	205	35	6	2	0	0.0	20	11	0	13		0	0	182	54	37	0	5.3	.864	C-27, OF-23, SS-2
1880			30	.172	.303	99	17	4	3	1	1.0	9	13	6	12		0	0	134	48	6	7	6.1	.968	C-23, SS-4, OF-4
1881	PRO	N	46	.219	.279	183	40	7	2	0	0.0	19	20	9	24		0	0	194	73	25	9	6.2	.914	C-36, SS-10, OF-1
1882			56	.224	.318	201	45	7	6	0	0.0	32		4	26		0	0	287	87	29	9	7.2	.928	C-54, SS-2
1883			74	.198	.270	263	52	13	3	0	0.0	34		26	32		0	0	379	108	54	10	7.3	.900	C-74

Barney Gilligan *continued*

Year	Team	Games	BA	SA	AB	H	2B	3B	HR	HR%	R	RBI	BB	SO	SB	Pinch Hit AB	Pinch Hit H	PO	A	E	DP	TC/G	FA	G by Pos
1884		82	.245	.313	294	72	13	2	1	0.3	47		35	41		0	0	613	94	55	7	9.2	.928	C-81, 1B-1, 3B-1
1885		71	.214	.266	252	54	7	3	0	0.0	23	12	23	33		0	0	315	102	63	13	6.7	.869	C-65, SS-5, OF-1, 2B-1
1886	WAS N	81	.190	.238	273	52	9	2	0	0.0	23	17	39	35		0	0	379	108	45	9	6.1	.915	C-71, OF-14, 3B-1, SS-1
1887		28	.200	.256	90	18	2	0	1	1.1	7	6	5	18	2	0	0	99	47	22	4	5.6	.869	C-26, SS-3, OF-1
1888	DET N	1	.200	.200	5	1	0	0	0	0.0	1	0	0	1	0	0	0	5	2	1	1	8.0	.875	C-1
10 yrs.		521	.207	.273	1865	386	68	23	3	0.2	215	79	147	235	2	0	0	2587	723	337	69	6.8	.908	C-458, OF-44, SS-27, 3B-2, 2B-1, 1B-1

Grant Gillis

GILLIS, GRANT BR TR 5′10″ 165 lbs.
B. Jan. 24, 1901, Grove Hill, Ala. D. Feb. 4, 1981, Thomasville, Ala.

Year	Team	Games	BA	SA	AB	H	2B	3B	HR	HR%	R	RBI	BB	SO	SB	Pinch Hit AB	Pinch Hit H	PO	A	E	DP	TC/G	FA	G by Pos
1927	WAS A	10	.222	.361	36	8	3	1	0	0.0	8	2	2	0	0	0	0	19	22	0	6	4.1	1.000	SS-10
1928		24	.253	.333	87	22	5	1	0	0.0	13	10	4	5	0	0	0	39	47	8	6	3.9	.915	SS-16, 2B-5, 3B-3
1929	BOS A	28	.247	.301	73	18	4	0	0	0.0	5	11	6	8	0	1	0	40	69	5	11	4.6	.956	2B-25
3 yrs.		62	.245	.327	196	48	12	2	0	0.0	26	23	12	13	0	1	0	98	138	13	23	4.2	.948	2B-30, SS-26, 3B-3

Jim Gilman

GILMAN, JAMES J.
B. Cleveland, Ohio Deceased.

Year	Team	Games	BA	SA	AB	H	2B	3B	HR	HR%	R	RBI	BB	SO	SB	Pinch Hit AB	Pinch Hit H	PO	A	E	DP	TC/G	FA	G by Pos
1893	CLE N	2	.286	.286	7	2	0	0	0	0.0	1	1	0	2	0	0	0	1	3	2	0	3.0	.667	2B-2

Pit Gilman

GILMAN, PITKIN CLARK BL TL 170 lbs.
B. Mar. 14, 1864, Laporte, Ohio D. Aug. 17, 1950, Elyria, Ohio.

Year	Team	Games	BA	SA	AB	H	2B	3B	HR	HR%	R	RBI	BB	SO	SB	Pinch Hit AB	Pinch Hit H	PO	A	E	DP	TC/G	FA	G by Pos
1884	CLE N	2	.100	.100	10	1	0	0	0	0.0	0	0	0	3		0	0	5	0	0	0	2.5	1.000	OF-2

Ernie Gilmore

GILMORE, ERNEST GROVER BL TL 5′ 9½″ 170 lbs.
B. Nov. 1, 1888, Chicago, Ill. D. Nov. 25, 1919, Sioux City, Iowa.

Year	Team	Games	BA	SA	AB	H	2B	3B	HR	HR%	R	RBI	BB	SO	SB	Pinch Hit AB	Pinch Hit H	PO	A	E	DP	TC/G	FA	G by Pos
1914	KC F	139	.287	.358	530	152	25	5	1	0.2	91	32	37		23	7	2	196	24	6	7	1.7	.973	OF-132
1915		119	.285	.418	411	117	22	15	1	0.2	53	47	26		19	0	0	215	17	5	4	2.0	.979	OF-119
2 yrs.		258	.286	.385	941	269	47	20	2	0.2	144	79	63		42	7	2	411	41	11	11	1.8	.976	OF-251

Tinsley Ginn

GINN, TINSLEY RUCKER BL TR 5′ 9″ 180 lbs.
B. Sept. 26, 1891, Royston, Ga. D. Aug. 30, 1931, Atlanta, Ga.

Year	Team	Games	BA	SA	AB	H	2B	3B	HR	HR%	R	RBI	BB	SO	SB	Pinch Hit AB	Pinch Hit H	PO	A	E	DP	TC/G	FA	G by Pos
1914	CLE A	2	.000	.000	1	0	0	0	0	0.0	0	0	0	0	0	0	0	0	0	0	0	0.0	.000	OF-2

Joe Ginsberg

GINSBERG, MYRON NATHAN BL TR 5′11″ 180 lbs.
B. Oct. 11, 1926, New York, N. Y.

Year	Team	Games	BA	SA	AB	H	2B	3B	HR	HR%	R	RBI	BB	SO	SB	Pinch Hit AB	Pinch Hit H	PO	A	E	DP	TC/G	FA	G by Pos
1948	DET A	11	.361	.361	36	13	0	0	0	0.0	7	1	3	1	0	0	0	46	4	3	3	4.8	.943	C-11
1950		36	.232	.295	95	22	6	0	0	0.0	12	12	11	6	1	4	1	97	8	2	3	3.5	.981	C-31
1951		102	.260	.385	304	79	10	2	8	2.6	44	37	43	21	0	8	2	388	56	10	7	4.8	.978	C-95
1952		113	.221	.336	307	68	13	2	6	2.0	29	36	51	21	1	16	2	442	41	8	7	4.9	.984	C-101
1953	2 teams	DET A (18G –.302)	CLE A (46G –.284)																					
″	total	64	.290	.327	162	47	6	0	0	0.0	16	13	24	5	0	12	2	201	22	6	4	4.2	.974	C-54
1954	CLE A	3	.500	1.500	2	1	0	1	0	0.0	0	1	0	0	0	2	1	1	0	0	0	1.0	1.000	C-1
1956	2 teams	KC A (71G –.246)	BAL A (15G –.071)																					
″	total	86	.224	.283	223	50	8	1	1	0.4	15	14	25	21	1	18	3	269	31	3	3	4.7	.990	C-65
1957	BAL A	85	.274	.360	175	48	8	2	1	0.6	15	18	18	19	2	18	3	252	20	4	6	4.2	.986	C-66
1958		61	.211	.303	109	23	1	0	3	2.8	4	16	13	14	0	20	4	156	8	1	2	4.2	.994	C-39
1959		65	.181	.211	166	30	2	0	1	0.6	14	14	21	3	1	5	1	241	29	2	4	4.4	.993	C-62
1960	2 teams	BAL A (14G –.267)	CHI A (28G –.253)																					
″	total	42	.257	.305	105	27	5	0	0	0.0	11	15	16	9	1	2	0	188	12	5	0	5.3	.976	C-39
1961	2 teams	CHI A (6G –.000)	BOS A (19G –.250)																					
″	total	25	.222	.222	27	6	0	0	0	0.0	1	5	1	4	0	16	3	14	1	0	0	1.9	1.000	C-8
1962	NY N	2	.000	.000	5	0	0	0	0	0.0	0	0	0	1	0	0	0	9	2	0	1	5.5	1.000	C-2
13 yrs.		695	.241	.320	1716	414	59	8	20	1.2	168	182	226	125	7	121	22	2304	234	44	40	4.5	.983	C-574

Al Gionfriddo

GIONFRIDDO, ALBERT FRANCIS BL TL 5′ 6″ 165 lbs.
B. Mar. 8, 1922, Dysart, Pa.

Year	Team	Games	BA	SA	AB	H	2B	3B	HR	HR%	R	RBI	BB	SO	SB	Pinch Hit AB	Pinch Hit H	PO	A	E	DP	TC/G	FA	G by Pos
1944	PIT N	4	.167	.167	6	1	0	0	0	0.0	0	0	1	1	0	3	1	3	0	0	0	3.0	1.000	OF-1
1945		122	.284	.386	409	116	18	9	2	0.5	74	42	60	22	12	14	2	235	6	9	2	2.4	.964	OF-106
1946		64	.255	.314	102	26	2	2	0	0.0	11	10	14	5	1	24	5	49	2	3	0	1.6	.944	OF-33
1947	2 teams	PIT N (1G –.000)	BKN N (37G –.177)																					
″	total	38	.175	.238	63	11	2	1	0	0.0	10	6	16	11	2	13	2	29	1	2	0	1.9	.938	OF-17
4 yrs.		228	.266	.355	580	154	22	12	2	0.3	95	58	91	39	15	54	10	316	9	14	2	2.2	.959	OF-157
WORLD SERIES																								
1947	BKN N	4	.000	.000	3	0	0	0	0	0.0	2	0	1	0	1	1	0	1	0	0	0	1.0	1.000	OF-1

Tommy Giordano

GIORDANO, THOMAS ARTHUR (T-Bone) BR TR 6′ 175 lbs.
B. Oct. 9, 1925, Newark, N. J.

Year	Team	Games	BA	SA	AB	H	2B	3B	HR	HR%	R	RBI	BB	SO	SB	Pinch Hit AB	Pinch Hit H	PO	A	E	DP	TC/G	FA	G by Pos
1953	PHI A	11	.175	.375	40	7	2	0	2	5.0	6	5	5	6	0	0	0	31	32	1	11	5.8	.984	2B-11

Ed Giovanola

GIOVANOLA, EDWARD THOMAS BL TR 5′10″ 170 lbs.
B. Mar. 4, 1969, Los Gatos, Calif.

Year	Team	Games	BA	SA	AB	H	2B	3B	HR	HR%	R	RBI	BB	SO	SB	Pinch Hit AB	Pinch Hit H	PO	A	E	DP	TC/G	FA	G by Pos
1995	ATL N	13	.071	.071	14	1	0	0	0	0.0	2	0	3	5	0	2	0	9	7	0	1	1.5	1.000	2B-7, 3B-3, SS-1

Joe Girardi

GIRARDI, JOSEPH ELLIOTT BR TR 5′11″ 195 lbs.
B. Oct. 14, 1964, Peoria, Ill.

Year	Team	Games	BA	SA	AB	H	2B	3B	HR	HR%	R	RBI	BB	SO	SB	Pinch Hit AB	Pinch Hit H	PO	A	E	DP	TC/G	FA	G by Pos
1989	CHI N	59	.248	.331	157	39	10	0	1	0.6	15	14	11	26	2	0	0	332	28	7	1	6.2	.981	C-59
1990		133	.270	.344	419	113	24	2	1	0.2	36	38	17	50	8	0	0	653	61	11	5	5.5	.985	C-133
1991		21	.191	.234	47	9	2	0	0	0.0	3	6	6	6	0	1	1	95	11	3	1	5.2	.972	C-21
1992		91	.270	.300	270	73	3	1	1	0.4	19	12	19	38	0	10	5	369	51	4	6	4.9	.991	C-86
1993	CLR N	86	.290	.397	310	90	14	5	3	1.0	35	31	24	41	6	2	0	478	46	6	7	6.3	.989	C-84
1994		93	.276	.364	330	91	9	4	4	1.2	47	34	21	48	3	0	0	548	55	5	5	6.5	.992	C-93
1995		125	.262	.359	462	121	17	2	8	1.7	63	55	29	76	3	4	2	729	61	10	3	6.6	.988	C-122
7 yrs.		608	.269	.349	1995	536	79	14	18	0.9	218	190	127	285	22	17	8	3204	313	46	28	6.0	.987	C-598

Joe Girardi *continued*

Year	Team	Games	BA	SA	AB	H	2B	3B	HR	HR%	R	RBI	BB	SO	SB	Pinch Hit AB	Pinch Hit H	PO	A	E	DP	TC/G	FA	G by Pos
DIVISIONAL PLAYOFF SERIES																								
1995	**CLR N**	4	.125	.125	16	2	0	0	0	0.0	0	0	0	2	0	0	0	25	3	1	2	7.3	.966	C-4
LEAGUE CHAMPIONSHIP SERIES																								
1989	**CHI N**	4	.100	.100	10	1	0	0	0	0.0	1	0	1	2	0	0	0	20	0	0	0	5.0	1.000	C-4

Tony Giuliani

GIULIANI, ANGELO JOHN
B. Nov. 24, 1912, St. Paul, Minn.
BR TR 5′11″ 175 lbs.

Year	Team	Games	BA	SA	AB	H	2B	3B	HR	HR%	R	RBI	BB	SO	SB	Pinch Hit AB	Pinch Hit H	PO	A	E	DP	TC/G	FA	G by Pos
1936	**STL A**	71	.217	.232	198	43	3	0	0	0.0	17	13	11	13	0	8	1	226	29	9	7	4.0	.966	C-66
1937		19	.302	.321	53	16	1	0	0	0.0	6	3	3	3	0	0	0	61	10	1	1	3.8	.986	C-19
1938	**WAS A**	46	.217	.252	115	25	4	0	0	0.0	10	15	8	3	1	0	0	138	17	0	4	3.4	1.000	C-46
1939		54	.250	.308	172	43	6	2	0	0.0	20	18	4	7	0	3	1	201	28	5	3	4.7	.979	C-50
1940	**BKN N**	1	.000	.000	1	0	0	0	0	0.0	0	0	0	0	0	3	0	1	0	0	0	1.0	1.000	C-1
1941		3	.000	.000	2	0	0	0	0	0.0	0	0	0	0	0	0	0	5	1	0	0	2.0	1.000	C-3
1943	**WAS A**	49	.226	.271	133	30	4	1	0	0.0	5	20	12	14	0	0	0	154	24	7	1	3.8	.962	C-49
7 yrs.		243	.233	.269	674	157	18	3	0	0.0	58	69	38	40	1	11	2	786	109	22	16	3.9	.976	C-234

Jim Gladd

GLADD, JAMES WALTER
B. Oct. 2, 1922, Fort Gibson, Okla. D. Nov. 8, 1977, Long Beach, Calif.
BR TR 6′2″ 190 lbs.

Year	Team	Games	BA	SA	AB	H	2B	3B	HR	HR%	R	RBI	BB	SO	SB	Pinch Hit AB	Pinch Hit H	PO	A	E	DP	TC/G	FA	G by Pos
1946	**NY N**	4	.091	.091	11	1	0	0	0	0.0	0	0	1	4	0	0	0	31	2	0	0	8.3	1.000	C-4

Dan Gladden

GLADDEN, CLINTON DANIEL III
B. July 7, 1957, San Jose, Calif.
BR TR 5′11″ 175 lbs.

Year	Team	Games	BA	SA	AB	H	2B	3B	HR	HR%	R	RBI	BB	SO	SB	Pinch Hit AB	Pinch Hit H	PO	A	E	DP	TC/G	FA	G by Pos
1983	**SF N**	18	.222	.302	63	14	2	0	1	1.6	6	9	5	11	4	1	0	53	0	0	0	2.9	1.000	OF-18
1984		86	.351	.447	342	120	17	2	4	1.2	71	31	33	37	31	2	0	232	8	3	1	2.9	.988	OF-85
1985		142	.243	.347	502	122	15	8	7	1.4	64	41	40	78	32	19	8	273	3	7	0	2.3	.975	OF-124
1986		102	.276	.362	351	97	16	1	4	1.1	55	29	39	59	27	9	1	226	7	3	2	2.7	.987	OF-89
1987	**MIN A**	121	.249	.361	438	109	21	2	8	1.8	69	38	38	72	25	9	2	223	9	3	2	2.0	.987	OF-111, DH-4
1988		141	.269	.403	576	155	32	6	11	1.9	91	62	46	74	28	4	1	319	12	3	5	2.3	.991	OF-140, 3B-1, P-1, 2B-1
1989		121	.295	.410	461	136	23	3	8	1.7	69	46	23	53	23	1	1	245	8	9	3	2.2	.966	OF-117, DH-2, P-1
1990		136	.275	.376	534	147	27	6	5	0.9	64	40	26	67	25	5	1	286	12	6	3	2.3	.980	OF-133, DH-2
1991		126	.247	.356	461	114	14	9	6	1.3	65	52	36	60	15	3	1	240	4	3	1	2.0	.988	OF-126
1992	**DET A**	113	.254	.357	417	106	20	1	7	1.7	57	42	30	64	4	6	2	227	9	3	2	2.2	.987	OF-108, DH-2
1993		91	.267	.433	356	95	16	2	13	3.7	52	56	21	50	8	4	1	196	9	3	1	2.3	.986	OF-86, DH-5
11 yrs.		1197	.270	.382	4501	1215	203	40	74	1.6	663	446	337	625	222	63	18	2520	81	43	20	2.3	.984	OF-1137, DH-15, P-2, 3B-1, 2B-1
LEAGUE CHAMPIONSHIP SERIES																								
1987	**MIN A**	5	.350	.450	20	7	2	0	0	0.0	5	5	2	1	0	0	0	12	0	0	0	2.4	1.000	OF-5
1991		5	.261	.261	23	6	0	0	0	0.0	4	3	1	3	3	0	0	20	0	0	0	4.0	1.000	OF-5
2 yrs.		10	.302	.349	43	13	2	0	0	0.0	9	8	3	4	3	0	0	32	0	0	0	3.2	1.000	OF-10
WORLD SERIES																								
1987	**MIN A**	7	.290	.516	31	9	2	1	1	3.2	3	7	3	4	2	0	0	12	0	0	0	1.7	1.000	OF-7
1991		7	.233	.433	30	7	2	2	0	0.0	5	0	3	4	2	0	0	25	1	1	0	3.9	.963	OF-7
2 yrs.		14	.262	.475	61	16	4	3 **4th**	1	1.6	8	7	6	8	4	0	0	37	1	1	0	2.8	.974	OF-14

Buck Gladman

GLADMAN, JOHN H.
B. 1864, Washington, D. C. Deceased.

Year	Team	Games	BA	SA	AB	H	2B	3B	HR	HR%	R	RBI	BB	SO	SB	Pinch Hit AB	Pinch Hit H	PO	A	E	DP	TC/G	FA	G by Pos
1883	**PHI N**	1	.000	.000	4	0	0	0	0	0.0	1		0	2		0	0	0	1	0	0	1.0	1.000	3B-1
1884	**WAS AA**	56	.156	.219	224	35	5	3	1	0.4	17		3			0	0	70	94	40	6	3.6	.804	3B-53, OF-2, SS-1
1886	**WAS N**	44	.138	.230	152	21	5	3	1	0.7	17	15	12	30		0	0	53	74	26	8	3.5	.830	3B-44
3 yrs.		101	.147	.221	380	56	10	6	2	0.5	35	15	15	32		0	0	123	169	66	14	3.5	.816	3B-98, OF-2, SS-1

Roland Gladu

GLADU, ROLAND EDOUARD
B. May 10, 1911, Montreal, Que., Canada D. July 26, 1994, Montreal, Que., Canada.
BL TR 5′8½″ 185 lbs.

Year	Team	Games	BA	SA	AB	H	2B	3B	HR	HR%	R	RBI	BB	SO	SB	Pinch Hit AB	Pinch Hit H	PO	A	E	DP	TC/G	FA	G by Pos
1944	**BOS N**	21	.242	.348	66	16	2	1	1	1.5	5	7	3	8	0	2	0	21	21	5	6	2.6	.894	3B-15, OF-3

Jack Glasscock

GLASSCOCK, JOHN WESLEY (Old Battle Ax)
B. July 22, 1859, Wheeling, W. Va. D. Feb. 24, 1947, Wheeling, W. Va.
Manager 1889, 1892.
BR TR 5′8″ 160 lbs.

Year	Team	Games	BA	SA	AB	H	2B	3B	HR	HR%	R	RBI	BB	SO	SB	Pinch Hit AB	Pinch Hit H	PO	A	E	DP	TC/G	FA	G by Pos
1879	**CLE N**	80	.209	.255	325	68	9	3	0	0.0	31	29	6	24		0	0	233	238	43	18	6.4	.916	2B-66, 3B-14
1880		77	.243	.307	296	72	13	3	0	0.0	37	27	2	21		0	0	107	252	44	21	5.2	.891	SS-77
1881		85	.257	.313	335	86	9	5	0	0.0	49	33	15	8		0	0	128	296	46	32	5.5	.902	SS-79, 2B-6
1882		84	.291	.450	358	104	27	9	4	1.1	66	46	13	9		0	0	112	313	47	41	5.6	.900	SS-83, 3B-1
1883		96	.287	.368	383	110	19	6	0	0.0	67		13	23		0	0	145	325	40	31	5.3	.922	SS-93, 2B-3
1884	**2 teams**	**CLE N** (72G –.249) **CIN U** (38G –.419)																						
″	**total**	110	.313	.402	453	142	13	9	3	0.7	93	22	33	16		0	0	182	389	69	24	5.7	.892	SS-105, 2B-5, P-2
1885	**STL N**	111	.280	.341	446	125	18	3	1	0.2	66	40	29	10		0	0	158	404	50	33	5.5	.918	SS-110, 2B-1
1886		121	.325	.432	486	158	29	7	3	0.6	96	40	38	13		0	0	157	392	57	43	5.0	.906	SS-120, OF-1
1887	**IND N**	122	.294	.360	483	142	18	7	0	0.0	91	40	41	8	62	0	0	211	493	73	58	6.3	.906	SS-122, P-1
1888		113	.269	.328	442	119	17	3	1	0.2	63	45	14	17	48	0	0	209	347	61	39	5.4	.901	SS-110, 2B-3, P-1
1889		134	.352	.467	582	**205**	40	3	7	1.2	128	85	31	10	57	0	0	249	485	68	61	5.9	.915	SS-132, 2B-2, P-1
1890	**NY N**	124	**.336**	.439	512	**172**	32	9	1	0.2	91	66	41	8	54	0	0	275	421	69	46	6.2	.910	SS-124
1891		97	.241	.306	369	89	12	6	0	0.0	46	55	36	11	29	0	0	164	274	42	39	4.9	.912	SS-97
1892	**STL N**	139	.267	.348	566	151	27	5	3	0.5	83	72	44	19	26	0	0	280	472	69	46	5.9	.916	SS-139
1893	**2 teams**	**STL N** (48G –.287) **PIT N** (66G –.341)																						
″	**total**	114	.320	.412	488	156	15	12	2	0.4	81	100	42	7	36	0	0	240	398	53	59	6.1	.923	SS-114
1894	**PIT N**	86	.280	.361	332	93	10	7	1	0.3	46	63	31	4	18	1	0	189	295	35	46	6.1	.933	SS-85
1895	**2 teams**	**LOU N** (18G –.338) **WAS N** (25G –.230)																						
″	**total**	43	.276	.333	174	48	5	1	1	0.6	29	16	10	4	4	0	0	124	155	29	19	7.2	.906	SS-38, 1B-5
17 yrs.		1736	.290	.374	7030	2040	313	98	27	0.4	1163	779	439	212	334	1	0	3163	5949	895	656	5.8	.911	SS-1628, 2B-86, 3B-15, 1B-5, P-5, OF-1

Tommy Glaviano

GLAVIANO, THOMAS GIATANO (Rabbit) BR TR 5′ 9″ 175 lbs.
B. Oct. 26, 1923, Sacramento, Calif.

Year	Team	Games	BA	SA	AB	H	2B	3B	HR	HR%	R	RBI	BB	SO	SB	Pinch Hit AB	Pinch Hit H	PO	A	E	DP	TC/G	FA	G by Pos
1949	STL N	87	.267	.407	258	69	16	1	6	2.3	32	36	41	35	0	7	3	81	190	20	18	3.6	.931	3B-73, 2B-7
1950		115	.285	.446	410	117	29	2	11	2.7	92	44	90	74	6	4	0	119	269	25	21	3.7	.939	3B-106, 2B-5, SS-1
1951		54	.183	.250	104	19	4	0	1	1.0	20	4	26	18	3	23	4	53	25	2	6	1.8	.975	OF-35, 2B-9
1952		80	.241	.340	162	39	5	1	3	1.9	30	19	27	26	0	10	2	47	95	10	5	2.9	.934	3B-52, 2B-1
1953	PHI N	53	.203	.392	74	15	1	2	3	4.1	17	5	24	20	2	20	2	31	39	6	5	2.8	.921	3B-14, 2B-12, SS-1
5 yrs.		389	.257	.395	1008	259	55	6	24	2.4	191	108	208	173	11	64	11	331	618	63	55	3.2	.938	3B-245, OF-35, 2B-34, SS-2

Bill Gleason

GLEASON, WILLIAM G. (Will) BR TR 5′ 8″ 170 lbs.
Brother of Jack Gleason.
B. Nov. 12, 1858, St. Louis, Mo. D. July 21, 1932, St. Louis, Mo.

Year	Team	Games	BA	SA	AB	H	2B	3B	HR	HR%	R	RBI	BB	SO	SB	Pinch Hit AB	Pinch Hit H	PO	A	E	DP	TC/G	FA	G by Pos
1882	STL AA	79	.288	.363	347	100	11	6	1	0.3	63		6			0	0	131	294	85	23	6.5	.833	SS-79
1883		98	.287	.393	425	122	21	9	2	0.5	81		16			0	0	120	257	56	22	4.4	.871	SS-98
1884		110	.269	.350	472	127	21	7	1	0.2	97		28			0	0	119	316	67	23	4.5	.867	SS-110, 3B-1
1885		112	.252	.311	472	119	9	5	3	0.6	79		29			0	0	115	303	63	18	4.3	.869	SS-112
1886		125	.269	.323	524	141	18	5	0	0.0	97		43			0	0	128	352	83	37	4.5	.853	SS-125
1887		135	.288	.323	598	172	19	1	0	0.0	135		41		23	0	0	169	411	83	27	4.9	.875	SS-135
1888	PHI AA	123	.224	.253	499	112	10	2	0	0.0	55	61	12		27	0	0	118	371	82	32	4.6	.856	SS-121, 3B-1, 1B-1
1889	LOU AA	16	.241	.276	58	14	2	0	0	0.0	6	5	4	1	1	0	0	26	57	18	4	6.3	.822	SS-16
8 yrs.		798	.267	.327	3395	907	111	35	7	0.2	613	66	179	1	51	0	0	926	2361	537	186	4.8	.860	SS-796, 3B-2, 1B-1

Bill Gleason

GLEASON, WILLIAM PATRICK BR TR 5′ 6½″ 157 lbs.
B. Sept. 6, 1894, Chicago, Ill. D. Jan. 9, 1957, Holyoke, Mass.

Year	Team	Games	BA	SA	AB	H	2B	3B	HR	HR%	R	RBI	BB	SO	SB	Pinch Hit AB	Pinch Hit H	PO	A	E	DP	TC/G	FA	G by Pos
1916	PIT N	1	.000	.000	2	0	0	0	0	0.0	0	0	0	0	0	0	0	1	1	0	0	2.0	1.000	2B-1
1917		13	.167	.190	42	7	1	0	0	0.0	3	0	5	5	1	0	0	18	27	1	3	3.5	.978	2B-13
1921	STL A	26	.257	.284	74	19	0	1	0	0.0	6	8	6	6	0	0	0	38	57	4	10	4.0	.960	2B-25
3 yrs.		40	.220	.246	118	26	1	1	0	0.0	9	8	11	11	1	0	0	57	85	5	13	3.8	.966	2B-39

Harry Gleason

GLEASON, HARRY GILBERT BR TR 5′ 6″ 160 lbs.
Brother of Kid Gleason.
B. Mar. 28, 1875, Camden, N. J. D. Oct. 21, 1961, Camden, N. J.

Year	Team	Games	BA	SA	AB	H	2B	3B	HR	HR%	R	RBI	BB	SO	SB	Pinch Hit AB	Pinch Hit H	PO	A	E	DP	TC/G	FA	G by Pos
1901	BOS A	1	1.000	1.000	1	1	0	0	0	0.0	0	0	0		1	0	0	0	2	1	1	3.0	.667	3B-1
1902		71	.225	.313	240	54	5	5	2	0.8	30	25	10		6	8	**3**	95	75	15	8	3.0	.919	3B-35, OF-23, 2B-4
1903		6	.154	.231	13	2	1	0	0	0.0	3	2	0		0	4	0	0	3	1	0	2.0	.750	3B-2
1904	STL A	46	.213	.271	155	33	7	1	0	0.0	10	6	4		1	1	0	66	108	15	11	4.1	.921	3B-20, SS-20, 2B-5, OF-1
1905		150	.217	.262	535	116	11	5	1	0.2	45	57	34		23	0	0	144	292	39	9	3.2	.918	3B-144, 2B-6
5 yrs.		274	.218	.276	944	206	24	11	3	0.3	88	90	48		31	13	3	305	480	71	29	3.3	.917	3B-202, OF-24, SS-20, 2B-15

Jack Gleason

GLEASON, JOHN DAY BR TR 170 lbs.
Brother of Bill Gleason.
B. July 14, 1854, St. Louis, Mo. D. Sept. 4, 1944, St. Louis, Mo.

Year	Team	Games	BA	SA	AB	H	2B	3B	HR	HR%	R	RBI	BB	SO	SB	Pinch Hit AB	Pinch Hit H	PO	A	E	DP	TC/G	FA	G by Pos
1877	STL N	1	.250	.250	4	1	0	0	0	0.0	0	0	0	1		0	0	0	0	0	0	0.0	.000	OF-1
1882	STL AA	78	.254	.308	331	84	10	1	2	0.6	53		**27**			0	0	112	171	84	11	4.6	.771	3B-73, OF-6, 2B-1
1883	2 teams	STL AA (9G –.235)	LOU AA (84G –.296)																					
″	total	93	.290	.355	389	113	11	4	2	0.5	71		29			0	0	92	116	52	6	2.8	.800	3B-84, OF-9, SS-1
1884	STL U	92	.324	.433	395	128	30	2	3	0.8	90		23			0	0	95	170	80	11	3.8	.768	3B-92
1885	STL N	2	.143	.143	7	1	0	0	0	0.0	0	0	0	1		0	0	3	3	1	0	3.5	.857	3B-2
1886	PHI AA	77	.187	.271	299	56	8	7	1	0.3	39		16			0	0	85	150	60	19	3.8	.797	3B-77
6 yrs.		343	.269	.347	1425	383	59	14	8	0.6	253	0	95	2		0	0	387	610	277	47	3.7	.783	3B-328, OF-16, SS-1, 2B-1

Kid Gleason

GLEASON, WILLIAM J. (Youngster) BB TR 5′ 7″ 158 lbs.
Brother of Harry Gleason.
B. Oct. 26, 1866, Camden, N. J. D. Jan. 2, 1933, Philadelphia, Pa.
Manager 1919–23.

Year	Team	Games	BA	SA	AB	H	2B	3B	HR	HR%	R	RBI	BB	SO	SB	Pinch Hit AB	Pinch Hit H	PO	A	E	DP	TC/G	FA	G by Pos
1888	PHI N	24	.205	.229	83	17	2	0	0	0.0	4	5	3	16	3	0	0	6	31	7	1	1.8	.841	P-24, OF-1
1889		30	.253	.303	99	25	5	0	0	0.0	11	8	8	12	4	0	0	19	52	10	1	2.5	.877	P-29, 2B-2, OF-1
1890		63	.210	.223	224	47	3	0	0	0.0	22	17	12	21	10	0	0	26	102	11	4	2.2	.921	P-60, 2B-2
1891		65	.248	.290	214	53	5	2	0	0.0	31	17	20	17	6	0	0	47	78	15	3	2.1	.893	P-53, OF-9, SS-4
1892	STL N	66	.215	.288	233	50	4	2	3	1.3	35	25	34	23	7	0	0	0	0	0	0	0.0		P-47, OF-11, 2B-10, 1B-1, C-1
1893		59	.256	.327	199	51	6	4	0	0.0	25	20	19	8	2	2	1	53	91	16	3	2.7	.900	P-48, OF-11, SS-1
1894	2 teams	STL N (9G –.250)	BAL N (26G –.349)																					
″	total	35	.325	.404	114	37	5	2	0	0.0	25	18	9	3	1	4	**2**	41	38	7	2	2.8	.919	P-29, 1B-2
1895	BAL N	112	.309	.399	421	130	14	12	0	0.0	90	74	33	18	19	3	0	234	277	61	33	5.2	.893	2B-85, 3B-12, P-9, OF-4
1896	NY N	133	.299	.372	541	162	17	5	4	0.7	79	89	42	13	46	0	0	334	404	50	38	5.9	.937	2B-130, 3B-3, OF-1
1897		131	.319	.369	540	172	16	4	1	0.2	85	106	26		43	0	0	314	403	56	44	5.9	.928	2B-129, SS-3
1898		150	.221	.253	570	126	8	5	0	0.0	78	62	39		21	0	0	383	488	60	58	6.2	.936	2B-144, SS-6
1899		146	.264	.302	576	152	14	4	0	0.0	72	59	24		29	0	0	403	465	50	60	6.3	.946	2B-146
1900		111	.248	.295	420	104	11	3	1	0.2	60	29	17		23	0	0	323	327	51	51	6.3	.927	2B-111, SS-1
1901	DET A	135	.274	.364	547	150	16	12	3	0.5	82	75	41		32	0	0	334	457	64	67	6.3	.925	2B-135
1902		118	.247	.297	441	109	11	4	1	0.2	42	38	25		17	0	0	320	349	42	66	6.0	.941	2B-118
1903	PHI N	106	.284	.367	412	117	19	6	1	0.2	65	49	23		12	0	0	242	280	23	30	5.1	.958	2B-102, OF-4
1904		153	.274	.334	587	161	23	6	0	0.0	61	42	37		17	0	0	380	464	52	44	5.9	.942	2B-152, 3B-1
1905		155	.247	.303	608	150	17	7	1	0.2	95	50	45		16	0	0	365	457	46	49	5.6	.947	2B-155
1906		135	.227	.269	494	112	17	2	0	0.0	47	34	36		17	0	0	215	358	32	39	4.5	.947	2B-135
1907		36	.143	.167	126	18	3	0	0	0.0	11	6	7		3	1	0	112	72	5	11	5.4	.974	2B-26, SS-4, 1B-4, OF-1
1908		2	.000	.000	1	0	0	0	0	0.0	0	0	0		0	0	0	3	1	0	0	2.0	1.000	OF-1, 2B-1
1912	CHI A	1	.500	.500	2	1	0	0	0	0.0	0	0	0		0	0	0	1	1	1	0	3.0	.667	2B-1
22 yrs.		1966	.261	.317	7452	1944	216	80	15	0.2	1020	823	500	131	328	10	3	4155	5195	659	604	5.1	.934	2B-1584, P-299, OF-44, SS-19, 3B-16, 1B-7, C-1

Roy Gleason

GLEASON, ROY WILLIAM BB TR 6′ 5½″ 220 lbs.
B. Apr. 9, 1943, Melrose Park, Ill.

Year	Team	Games	BA	SA	AB	H	2B	3B	HR	HR%	R	RBI	BB	SO	SB	Pinch Hit AB	Pinch Hit H	PO	A	E	DP	TC/G	FA	G by Pos
1963	LA N	8	1.000	2.000	1	1	1	0	0	0.0	3	0	0	0	0	1	1	0	0	0	0	0.0	—	

Jim Gleeson

GLEESON, JAMES JOSEPH (Gee Gee)
B. Mar. 5, 1912, Kansas City, Mo.
BB TR 6′ 1″ 191 lbs.

Year	Team	Lg	Games	BA	SA	AB	H	2B	3B	HR	HR%	R	RBI	BB	SO	SB	Pinch Hit AB	Pinch Hit H	PO	A	E	DP	TC/G	FA	G by Pos
1936	CLE	A	41	.259	.439	139	36	9	2	4	2.9	26	12	18	17	2	7	0	67	1	3	0	2.2	.958	OF-33
1939	CHI	N	111	.223	.352	332	74	19	6	4	1.2	43	45	39	46	7	17	4	175	5	8	1	2.1	.957	OF-91
1940			129	.313	.470	485	152	39	11	5	1.0	76	61	54	52	4	5	1	273	14	5	3	2.4	.983	OF-123
1941	CIN	N	102	.233	.296	301	70	10	0	3	1.0	47	34	45	30	7	14	3	153	1	3	0	1.9	.981	OF-84
1942			9	.200	.200	20	4	0	0	0	0.0	3	2	2	2	0	3	0	7	1	1	0	1.8	.889	OF-5
5 yrs.			392	.263	.391	1277	336	77	19	16	1.3	195	154	158	147	20	46	8	675	22	20	4	2.1	.972	OF-336

Frank Gleich

GLEICH, FRANK ELMER (Inch)
B. Mar. 7, 1894, Columbus, Ohio D. Mar. 27, 1949, Columbus, Ohio.
BL TR 5′11″ 175 lbs.

Year	Team	Lg	Games	BA	SA	AB	H	2B	3B	HR	HR%	R	RBI	BB	SO	SB	Pinch Hit AB	Pinch Hit H	PO	A	E	DP	TC/G	FA	G by Pos
1919	NY	A	5	.250	.250	4	1	0	0	0	0.0	0	1	1	0	0	0	0	0	0	1	0	0.3	.000	OF-4
1920			24	.122	.122	41	5	0	0	0	0.0	6	3	6	10	0	9	1	19	0	3	0	1.5	.864	OF-15
2 yrs.			29	.133	.133	45	6	0	0	0	0.0	6	4	7	10	0	9	1	19	0	4	0	1.2	.826	OF-19

Bob Glenalvin

GLENALVIN, ROBERT J.
Born Robert J. Dowling.
B. Jan. 17, 1867, Indianapolis, Ind. D. Mar. 24, 1944, Detroit, Mich.
TR 5′ 9″ 160 lbs.

Year	Team	Lg	Games	BA	SA	AB	H	2B	3B	HR	HR%	R	RBI	BB	SO	SB	Pinch Hit AB	Pinch Hit H	PO	A	E	DP	TC/G	FA	G by Pos
1890	CHI	N	66	.268	.380	250	67	10	3	4	1.6	43	26	19	31	30	0	0	128	194	25	20	5.3	.928	2B-66
1893			16	.344	.426	61	21	3	1	0	0.0	11	12	7	3	7	0	0	35	42	6	4	5.2	.928	2B-16
2 yrs.			82	.283	.389	311	88	13	4	4	1.3	54	38	26	34	37	0	0	163	236	31	24	5.2	.928	2B-82

Ed Glenn

GLENN, EDWARD C.
B. Sept. 19, 1860, Richmond, Va. D. Feb. 10, 1892, Richmond, Va.
BR TR 5′10″ 160 lbs.

Year	Team	Lg	Games	BA	SA	AB	H	2B	3B	HR	HR%	R	RBI	BB	SO	SB	Pinch Hit AB	Pinch Hit H	PO	A	E	DP	TC/G	FA	G by Pos
1884	RIC	AA	43	.246	.320	175	43	2	4	1	0.6	26		5			0	0	85	5	18	2	2.5	.833	OF-43
1886	PIT	AA	71	.191	.249	277	53	6	5	0	0.0	32		17			0	0	124	10	21	2	2.2	.865	OF-71
1888	2 teams		KC AA (3G –.000) BOS N (20G –.154)																						
″	total		23	.137	.192	73	10	0	2	0	0.0	8	3	2	8	1	0	0	49	2	3	2	2.3	.944	OF-22, 3B-1
3 yrs.			137	.202	.265	525	106	8	11	1	0.2	66	3	24	8	1	0	0	258	17	42	6	2.3	.868	OF-136, 3B-1

Ed Glenn

GLENN, EDWARD D.
B. Oct. 1875, Ohio D. Dec. 6, 1911, Ludlow, Ky.
BR TR

Year	Team	Lg	Games	BA	SA	AB	H	2B	3B	HR	HR%	R	RBI	BB	SO	SB	Pinch Hit AB	Pinch Hit H	PO	A	E	DP	TC/G	FA	G by Pos
1898	2 teams		WAS N (1G –.000) NY N (2G –.250)																						
″	total		3	.125	.125	8	1	0	0	0	0.0	1	0	3		1	0	0	2	4	1	0	2.3	.857	SS-3
1902	CHI	N	2	.000	.000	7	0	0	0	0	0.0	0	0	1		0	0	0	0	6	0	0	3.0	1.000	SS-2
2 yrs.			5	.067	.067	15	1	0	0	0	0.0	1	0	4		1	0	0	2	10	1	0	2.6	.923	SS-5

Harry Glenn

GLENN, HARRY MELVILLE
B. June 9, 1890, Shelburn, Ind. D. Oct. 12, 1918, St. Paul, Minn.
BL TR 6′ 1″ 200 lbs.

Year	Team	Lg	Games	BA	SA	AB	H	2B	3B	HR	HR%	R	RBI	BB	SO	SB	Pinch Hit AB	Pinch Hit H	PO	A	E	DP	TC/G	FA	G by Pos
1915	STL	N	6	.313	.313	16	5	0	0	0	0.0	1	1	3	0	0	1	0	22	4	2	0	5.6	.929	C-5

Joe Glenn

GLENN, JOSEPH CHARLES (Gabber)
Born Joseph Charles Gurzensky.
B. Nov. 19, 1908, Dickson City, Pa. D. May 6, 1985, Tunkhannock, Pa.
BR TR 5′11″ 175 lbs.

Year	Team	Lg	Games	BA	SA	AB	H	2B	3B	HR	HR%	R	RBI	BB	SO	SB	Pinch Hit AB	Pinch Hit H	PO	A	E	DP	TC/G	FA	G by Pos
1932	NY	A	6	.125	.125	16	2	0	0	0	0.0	0	0	1	5	0	1	0	17	1	0	0	3.6	1.000	C-5
1933			5	.143	.143	21	3	0	0	0	0.0	1	1	0	3	0	0	0	24	0	0	1	4.8	1.000	C-5
1935			17	.233	.326	43	10	4	0	0	0.0	7	6	4	1	0	1	0	54	7	1	0	3.9	.984	C-16
1936			44	.271	.349	129	35	7	0	1	0.8	21	20	20	10	1	0	0	167	24	6	2	4.5	.970	C-44
1937			25	.283	.396	53	15	2	2	0	0.0	6	4	10	11	0	1	0	79	12	2	1	3.9	.978	C-24
1938			41	.260	.350	123	32	7	2	0	0.0	9	25	10	14	1	1	0	134	15	4	3	3.8	.974	C-40
1939	STL	A	88	.273	.367	286	78	13	1	4	1.4	29	29	31	40	4	4	3	280	48	11	4	4.1	.968	C-82
1940	BOS	A	22	.128	.149	47	6	1	0	0	0.0	3	4	5	7	0	4	1	67	6	3	0	4.0	.961	C-19
8 yrs.			248	.252	.334	718	181	34	5	5	0.7	76	89	81	91	6	12	4	822	113	27	11	4.1	.972	C-235

John Glenn

GLENN, JOHN
B. July 10, 1928, Moultrie, Ga.
BR TR 6′ 3″ 180 lbs.

Year	Team	Lg	Games	BA	SA	AB	H	2B	3B	HR	HR%	R	RBI	BB	SO	SB	Pinch Hit AB	Pinch Hit H	PO	A	E	DP	TC/G	FA	G by Pos
1960	STL	N	32	.258	.323	31	8	0	1	0	0.0	4	5	0	9	0	3	0	19	0	0	0	0.7	1.000	OF-28

John Glenn

GLENN, JOHN W.
B. 1849, Rochester, N. Y. D. Nov. 10, 1888, Sandy Hill, N. Y.
BR TR 5′ 8½″ 169 lbs.

Year	Team	Lg	Games	BA	SA	AB	H	2B	3B	HR	HR%	R	RBI	BB	SO	SB	Pinch Hit AB	Pinch Hit H	PO	A	E	DP	TC/G	FA	G by Pos
1876	CHI	N	66	.304	.351	276	84	9	2	0	0.0	55	32	12	6		0	0	240	5	26	5	3.8	.904	OF-56, 1B-15
1877			50	.228	.267	202	46	6	1	0	0.0	31	20	8	16		0	0	226	11	17	10	5.1	.933	OF-36, 1B-14
2 yrs.			116	.272	.316	478	130	15	3	0	0.0	86	52	20	22		0	0	466	16	43	15	4.3	.918	OF-92, 1B-29

Norm Glockson

GLOCKSON, NORMAN STANLEY
B. June 15, 1894, Blue Island, Ill. D. Aug. 5, 1955, Maywood, Ill.
BR TR 6′ 2″ 200 lbs.

Year	Team	Lg	Games	BA	SA	AB	H	2B	3B	HR	HR%	R	RBI	BB	SO	SB	Pinch Hit AB	Pinch Hit H	PO	A	E	DP	TC/G	FA	G by Pos
1914	CIN	N	7	.000	.000	12	0	0	0	0	0.0	0	0	1	6	0	0	0	19	5	2	0	3.7	.923	C-7

Al Glossop

GLOSSOP, ALBAN
B. July 23, 1915, Christopher, Ill. D. July 2, 1991, Walnut Creek, Calif.
BB TR 6′ 170 lbs.

Year	Team	Lg	Games	BA	SA	AB	H	2B	3B	HR	HR%	R	RBI	BB	SO	SB	Pinch Hit AB	Pinch Hit H	PO	A	E	DP	TC/G	FA	G by Pos
1939	NY	N	10	.188	.281	32	6	0	0	1	3.1	3	3	4	2	0	0	0	15	34	1	7	5.0	.980	2B-10
1940	2 teams		NY N (27G –.209) BOS N (60G –.236)																						
″	total		87	.226	.343	239	54	5	1	7	2.9	33	22	27	38	2	25	5	104	188	16	24	4.4	.948	2B-42, 3B-18, SS-10
1942	PHI	N	121	.225	.289	454	102	15	1	4	0.9	33	40	29	35	3	3	1	322	351	27	79	5.9	.961	2B-118, 3B-1
1943	BKN	N	87	.171	.253	217	37	9	0	3	1.4	28	21	28	27	0	11	0	102	161	24	24	3.9	.916	SS-33, 2B-24, 3B-17
1946	CHI	N	4	.000	.000	10	0	0	0	0	0.0	2	0	1	3	0	0	0	9	7	1	0	4.3	.941	SS-2, 2B-2
5 yrs.			309	.209	.291	952	199	29	2	15	1.6	99	86	89	105	5	39	6	552	741	69	134	4.9	.949	2B-196, SS-45, 3B-36

Bill Glynn

GLYNN, WILLIAM VINCENT
B. July 30, 1925, Sussex, N. J.
BL TL 6′ 190 lbs.

Year	Team	Lg	Games	BA	SA	AB	H	2B	3B	HR	HR%	R	RBI	BB	SO	SB	Pinch Hit AB	Pinch Hit H	PO	A	E	DP	TC/G	FA	G by Pos
1949	PHI	N	8	.200	.200	10	2	0	0	0	0.0	0	1	0	3	0	6	2	10	1	0	0	11.0	1.000	1B-1
1952	CLE	A	44	.272	.391	92	25	5	0	2	2.2	15	7	5	16	1	14	3	167	16	5	18	5.9	.973	1B-32
1953			147	.243	.309	411	100	14	2	3	0.7	60	30	44	65	1	10	3	1042	81	8	133	8.3	.993	1B-135, OF-2
1954			111	.251	.380	171	43	3	2	5	2.9	19	18	12	21	3	17	2	424	35	6	38	4.8	.987	1B-96, OF-1
4 yrs.			310	.249	.336	684	170	22	4	10	1.5	94	56	61	105	5	47	10	1643	133	19	189	6.7	.989	1B-264, OF-3

Bill Glynn *continued*

Year	Team	Lg	Games	BA	SA	AB	H	2B	3B	HR	HR%	R	RBI	BB	SO	SB	Pinch Hit AB	Pinch Hit H	PO	A	E	DP	TC/G	FA	G by Pos
WORLD SERIES																									
1954	CLE	A	2	.500	1.000	2	1	1	0	0	0.0	1	0	0	1	0	2	1	0	0	0	0	0.0	.000	1B-1

John Gochnaur

GOCHNAUR, JOHN PETER BR TR 5′9″ 160 lbs.
B. Sept. 12, 1875, Altoona, Pa. D. Sept. 27, 1929, Altoona, Pa.

Year	Team	Lg	Games	BA	SA	AB	H	2B	3B	HR	HR%	R	RBI	BB	SO	SB	Pinch Hit AB	Pinch Hit H	PO	A	E	DP	TC/G	FA	G by Pos
1901	BKN	N	3	.364	.364	11	4	0	0	0	0.0	1	2	1		1	0	0	4	9	0	0	4.3	1.000	SS-3
1902	CLE	A	127	.185	.237	459	85	16	4	0	0.0	45	37	38		7	0	0	223	447	48	59	5.7	.933	SS-127
1903			134	.185	.240	438	81	16	4	0	0.0	48	48	48		10	0	0	236	414	98	45	5.6	.869	SS-134
3 yrs.			264	.187	.240	908	170	32	8	0	0.0	94	87	87		18	0	0	463	870	146	104	5.6	.901	SS-264

John Godar

GODAR, JOHN MICHAEL BR TR 5′9″ 170 lbs.
B. Oct. 25, 1864, Cincinnati, Ohio D. June 23, 1949, Park Ridge, Ill.

Year	Team	Lg	Games	BA	SA	AB	H	2B	3B	HR	HR%	R	RBI	BB	SO	SB	Pinch Hit AB	Pinch Hit H	PO	A	E	DP	TC/G	FA	G by Pos
1892	BAL	N	5	.214	.214	14	3	0	0	0	0.0	2	1	2	1	1	0	0	4	1	0	0	1.0	1.000	OF-5

Danny Godby

GODBY, DANNY RAY BR TR 6′ 185 lbs.
B. Nov. 4, 1946, Logan, W. Va.

Year	Team	Lg	Games	BA	SA	AB	H	2B	3B	HR	HR%	R	RBI	BB	SO	SB	Pinch Hit AB	Pinch Hit H	PO	A	E	DP	TC/G	FA	G by Pos
1974	STL	N	13	.154	.154	13	2	0	0	0	0.0	2	1	3	4	0	6	1	8	1	0	0	2.3	1.000	OF-4

Joe Goddard

GODDARD, JOSEPH HAROLD BR TR 5′11″ 181 lbs.
B. July 23, 1950, Beckley, W. Va.

Year	Team	Lg	Games	BA	SA	AB	H	2B	3B	HR	HR%	R	RBI	BB	SO	SB	Pinch Hit AB	Pinch Hit H	PO	A	E	DP	TC/G	FA	G by Pos
1972	SD	N	12	.200	.257	35	7	2	0	0	0.0	0	2	5	9	0	0	0	67	5	2	1	6.2	.973	C-12

John Godwin

GODWIN, JOHN HENRY BR TR 6′ 190 lbs.
B. Mar. 10, 1877, East Liverpool, Ohio D. May 5, 1956, East Liverpool, Ohio.

Year	Team	Lg	Games	BA	SA	AB	H	2B	3B	HR	HR%	R	RBI	BB	SO	SB	Pinch Hit AB	Pinch Hit H	PO	A	E	DP	TC/G	FA	G by Pos
1905	BOS	A	13	.351	.378	37	13	1	0	0	0.0	4	10	3		3	3	0	25	10	4	1	3.5	.897	OF-6, 2B-5
1906			66	.187	.207	193	36	2	1	0	0.0	11	15	6		6	9	2	79	115	26	11	4.0	.882	3B-27, SS-14, OF-10, 2B-3, 1B-1
2 yrs.			79	.213	.235	230	49	3	1	0	0.0	15	25	9		9	12	2	104	125	30	12	3.9	.884	3B-27, OF-16, SS-14, 2B-8, 1B-1

Ed Goebel

GOEBEL, EDWIN BR TR 5′11″ 170 lbs.
B. Sept. 1, 1899, Brooklyn, N. Y. D. Aug. 12, 1959, Brooklyn, N. Y.

Year	Team	Lg	Games	BA	SA	AB	H	2B	3B	HR	HR%	R	RBI	BB	SO	SB	Pinch Hit AB	Pinch Hit H	PO	A	E	DP	TC/G	FA	G by Pos
1922	WAS	A	37	.271	.339	59	16	1	0	1	1.7	13	3	8	16	1	13	1	29	1	0	0	1.8	1.000	OF-17

Bill Goeckel

GOECKEL, WILLIAM JOHN BR TL
B. Sept. 3, 1871, Wilkes-Barre, Pa. D. Nov. 1, 1922, Philadelphia, Pa.

Year	Team	Lg	Games	BA	SA	AB	H	2B	3B	HR	HR%	R	RBI	BB	SO	SB	Pinch Hit AB	Pinch Hit H	PO	A	E	DP	TC/G	FA	G by Pos
1899	PHI	N	37	.262	.298	141	37	3	1	0	0.0	17	16	1		6	1	0	384	11	9	12	11.2	.978	1B-36

Jerry Goff

GOFF, JERRY LEROY BL TR 6′3″ 205 lbs.
B. Apr. 12, 1964, San Rafael, Calif.

Year	Team	Lg	Games	BA	SA	AB	H	2B	3B	HR	HR%	R	RBI	BB	SO	SB	Pinch Hit AB	Pinch Hit H	PO	A	E	DP	TC/G	FA	G by Pos
1990	MON	N	52	.227	.311	119	27	1	0	3	2.5	14	7	21	36	0	6	3	216	17	9	3	5.5	.963	C-38, 3B-3, 1B-3
1992			3	.000	.000	3	0	0	0	0	0.0	0	0	0	3	0	3	0	0	0	0	0	0.0	—	
1993	PIT	N	14	.297	.514	37	11	2	0	2	5.4	5	6	8	9	0	2	1	54	7	1	0	4.4	.984	C-14
1994			8	.080	.080	25	2	0	0	0	0.0	0	1	0	11	0	1	0	34	4	2	0	5.7	.950	C-7
1995	HOU	N	12	.154	.346	26	4	2	0	1	3.8	2	3	4	13	0	1	0	80	5	0	1	7.7	1.000	C-11
5 yrs.			89	.210	.319	210	44	5	0	6	2.9	21	17	33	72	0	13	4	384	33	12	4	5.6	.972	C-70, 3B-3, 1B-3

Chuck Goggin

GOGGIN, CHARLES FRANCIS III BB TR 5′11″ 175 lbs.
B. July 7, 1945, Pompano Beach, Fla.

Year	Team	Lg	Games	BA	SA	AB	H	2B	3B	HR	HR%	R	RBI	BB	SO	SB	Pinch Hit AB	Pinch Hit H	PO	A	E	DP	TC/G	FA	G by Pos
1972	PIT	N	5	.286	.286	7	2	0	0	0	0.0	0	0	1	1	0	3	0	0	4	0	0	4.0	1.000	2B-1
1973	2 teams		PIT N (1G –1.000) ATL N (64G –.289)																						
″	total		65	.297	.352	91	27	5	0	0	0.0	19	7	9	19	0	29	8	23	37	5	7	2.0	.923	2B-19, OF-6, SS-5, C-2
1974	BOS	A	2	.000	.000	1	0	0	0	0	0.0	0	0	0	1	0	0	0	0	2	1	2	1.5	.667	2B-2
3 yrs.			72	.293	.343	99	29	5	0	0	0.0	19	7	10	21	0	32	8	23	43	6	9	2.1	.917	2B-22, OF-6, SS-5, C-2

Mike Golden

GOLDEN, MICHAEL HENRY BR TR 5′7″ 166 lbs.
B. Sept. 11, 1851, Shirley, Mass. D. Jan. 11, 1929, Rockford, Ill.

Year	Team	Lg	Games	BA	SA	AB	H	2B	3B	HR	HR%	R	RBI	BB	SO	SB	Pinch Hit AB	Pinch Hit H	PO	A	E	DP	TC/G	FA	G by Pos
1878	MIL	N	55	.206	.262	214	44	6	3	0	0.0	16	20	3	35		0	0	75	45	22	2	2.3	.845	OF-39, P-22, 1B-1

Jonah Goldman

GOLDMAN, JONAH JOHN BR TR 5′7″ 170 lbs.
B. Aug. 29, 1906, New York, N. Y. D. Aug. 17, 1980, Palm Beach, Fla.

Year	Team	Lg	Games	BA	SA	AB	H	2B	3B	HR	HR%	R	RBI	BB	SO	SB	Pinch Hit AB	Pinch Hit H	PO	A	E	DP	TC/G	FA	G by Pos
1928	CLE	A	7	.238	.286	21	5	1	0	0	0.0	1	2	3	0	0	0	0	13	23	5	2	5.9	.878	SS-7
1930			111	.242	.310	306	74	18	0	1	0.3	32	44	28	25	3	0	0	222	275	27	58	4.6	.948	SS-93, 3B-20
1931			30	.129	.145	62	8	1	0	0	0.0	0	3	4	6	1	0	0	42	82	7	12	4.4	.947	SS-30
3 yrs.			148	.224	.283	389	87	20	0	1	0.3	33	49	35	31	4	0	0	277	380	39	72	4.6	.944	SS-130, 3B-20

Gordon Goldsberry

GOLDSBERRY, GORDON FREDERICK BL TL 6′ 170 lbs.
B. Aug. 30, 1927, Sacramento, Calif. D. Feb. 23, 1996, Lake Forest, Calif.

Year	Team	Lg	Games	BA	SA	AB	H	2B	3B	HR	HR%	R	RBI	BB	SO	SB	Pinch Hit AB	Pinch Hit H	PO	A	E	DP	TC/G	FA	G by Pos
1949	CHI	A	39	.248	.317	145	36	3	2	1	0.7	25	13	18	9	2	1	0	359	24	4	37	10.2	.990	1B-38
1950			82	.268	.409	127	34	8	2	2	1.6	19	25	26	18	0	**39**	**12**	236	29	3	37	6.2	.989	1B-40, OF-3
1951			10	.091	.091	11	1	0	0	0	0.0	4	1	2	2	0	2	0	28	5	0	4	4.1	1.000	1B-8
1952	STL	A	86	.229	.335	227	52	9	3	3	1.3	30	17	34	37	0	10	2	528	40	10	56	7.8	.983	1B-72, OF-2
4 yrs.			217	.241	.343	510	123	20	7	6	1.2	78	56	80	66	2	52	14	1151	98	17	134	7.8	.987	1B-158, OF-5

Walt Goldsby

GOLDSBY, WALTON HUGH BL
B. Dec. 31, 1861, Louisiana D. Jan. 11, 1924, Dallas, Tex.

Year	Team	Lg	Games	BA	SA	AB	H	2B	3B	HR	HR%	R	RBI	BB	SO	SB	Pinch Hit AB	Pinch Hit H	PO	A	E	DP	TC/G	FA	G by Pos
1884	3 teams		STL AA (5G –.200) WAS AA (6G –.375) RIC AA (11G –.225)																						
″	total		22	.262	.274	84	22	1	0	0	0.0	10		2			0	0	28	4	8	2	1.8	.800	OF-22
1886	WAS	N	6	.222	.278	18	4	1	0	0	0.0	0	1	2	3		0	0	9	0	2	0	1.8	.818	OF-6
1888	BAL	AA	45	.236	.255	165	39	1	1	0	0.0	13	14	8		17	0	0	53	3	6	0	1.4	.903	OF-45
3 yrs.			73	.243	.262	267	65	3	1	0	0.0	23	15	12	3	17	0	0	90	7	16	2	1.5	.858	OF-73

Fred Goldsmith

GOLDSMITH, FRED ERNEST BR TR 6′ 1″ 195 lbs.
B. May 15, 1852, New Haven, Conn. D. Mar. 28, 1939, Berkley, Mich.

Year	Team	Games	BA	SA	AB	H	2B	3B	HR	HR%	R	RBI	BB	SO	SB	Pinch Hit AB	Pinch Hit H	PO	A	E	DP	TC/G	FA	G by Pos
1879	TRO N	9	.237	.263	38	9	1	0	0	0.0	6	2	1	3		0	0	9	14	5	1	2.5	.821	P-8, OF-2, 1B-1
1880	CHI N	35	.261	.317	142	37	4	2	0	0.0	24	15	2	15		0	0	55	53	11	0	3.0	.908	P-26, OF-10, 1B-4
1881		42	.241	.310	158	38	3	4	0	0.0	24	16	6	17		0	0	21	97	21	2	3.3	.849	P-39, OF-3
1882		45	.230	.301	183	42	11	1	0	0.0	23	19	4	29		0	0	33	67	7	0	2.4	.935	P-44, 1B-1
1883		60	.221	.311	235	52	12	3	1	0.4	38		4	35		0	0	55	89	24	3	2.6	.857	P-46, OF-16, 1B-2
1884	2 teams	CHI N (22G –.136)	BAL AA (4G –.143)																					
″	total	26	.137	.221	95	13	2	0	2	2.1	13		9	26		0	0	17	42	14	0	2.6	.808	P-25, OF-2, 1B-1
6 yrs.		217	.224	.297	851	191	33	10	3	0.4	128	52	26	125		0	0	190	362	82	6	2.8	.871	P-188, OF-33, 1B-9

Lonnie Goldstein

GOLDSTEIN, LESLIE ELMER BL TL 6′ 2½″ 190 lbs.
B. May 13, 1918, Austin, Tex.

Year	Team	Games	BA	SA	AB	H	2B	3B	HR	HR%	R	RBI	BB	SO	SB	Pinch Hit AB	Pinch Hit H	PO	A	E	DP	TC/G	FA	G by Pos
1943	CIN N	5	.200	.200	5	1	0	0	0	0.0	1	0	2	1	0	3	1	7	0	0	1	3.5	1.000	1B-2
1946		6	.000	.000	5	0	0	0	0	0.0	1	0	1	1	0	5	0	0	0	0	0	0.0	—	
2 yrs.		11	.100	.100	10	1	0	0	0	0.0	2	0	3	2	0	8	1	7	0	0	1	3.5	1.000	1B-2

Purnal Goldy

GOLDY, PURNAL WILLIAM BR TR 6′ 5″ 200 lbs.
B. Nov. 28, 1937, Camden, N. J.

Year	Team	Games	BA	SA	AB	H	2B	3B	HR	HR%	R	RBI	BB	SO	SB	Pinch Hit AB	Pinch Hit H	PO	A	E	DP	TC/G	FA	G by Pos
1962	DET A	20	.229	.400	70	16	1	1	3	4.3	8	12	0	12	0	3	1	26	1	1	0	1.9	.964	OF-15
1963		9	.250	.250	8	2	0	0	0	0.0	1	0	0	4	0	8	2	0	0	0	0	0.0	—	
2 yrs.		29	.231	.385	78	18	1	1	3	3.8	9	12	0	16	0	11	3	26	1	1	0	1.9	.964	OF-15

Stan Goletz

GOLETZ, STANLEY (Stash) BL TL 6′ 3″ 200 lbs.
B. May 21, 1918, Crescent, Ohio.

Year	Team	Games	BA	SA	AB	H	2B	3B	HR	HR%	R	RBI	BB	SO	SB	Pinch Hit AB	Pinch Hit H	PO	A	E	DP	TC/G	FA	G by Pos
1941	CHI A	5	.600	.600	5	3	0	0	0	0.0	0	0	0	2	0	5	3	0	0	0	0	0.0	—	

Mike Goliat

GOLIAT, MIKE MITCHELL BR TR 6′ 180 lbs.
B. Nov. 5, 1925, Yatesboro, Pa.

Year	Team	Games	BA	SA	AB	H	2B	3B	HR	HR%	R	RBI	BB	SO	SB	Pinch Hit AB	Pinch Hit H	PO	A	E	DP	TC/G	FA	G by Pos
1949	PHI N	55	.212	.323	189	40	6	3	3	1.6	24	19	20	32	0	0	0	187	145	9	36	6.2	.974	2B-50, 1B-5
1950		145	.234	.366	483	113	13	6	13	2.7	49	64	53	75	3	5	0	345	393	21	89	5.5	.972	2B-139
1951	2 teams	PHI N (41G –.225)	STL A (5G –.182)																					
″	total	46	.221	.329	149	33	2	1	4	2.7	14	16	9	19	0	4	0	97	109	7	26	5.2	.967	2B-39, 3B-2
1952	STL A	3	.000	.000	4	0	0	0	0	0.0	0	0	1	1	0	1	0	4	4	0	3	2.7	1.000	2B-3
4 yrs.		249	.225	.348	825	186	21	10	20	2.4	87	99	83	127	3	10	0	633	651	37	154	5.6	.972	2B-231, 1B-5, 3B-2
WORLD SERIES																								
1950	PHI N	4	.214	.214	14	3	0	0	0	0.0	1	1	1	2	0	0	0	13	9	1	0	5.8	.957	2B-4

Walt Golvin

GOLVIN, WALTER GEORGE BL TL 6′ 165 lbs.
B. Feb. 1, 1894, Hershey, Neb. D. June 11, 1973, Gardinia, Calif.

Year	Team	Games	BA	SA	AB	H	2B	3B	HR	HR%	R	RBI	BB	SO	SB	Pinch Hit AB	Pinch Hit H	PO	A	E	DP	TC/G	FA	G by Pos
1922	CHI N	2	.000	.000	2	0	0	0	0	0.0	0	1	0	0	0	0	0	4	0	0	0	2.0	1.000	1B-2

Chile Gomez

GOMEZ, JOSE LUIS BR TR 5′10″ 165 lbs.
Born Jose Luis Gomez (Gonzales).
B. Mar. 23, 1909, Villa Union, Mexico D. Dec. 1, 1992, Nuevo Laredo, Mexico.

Year	Team	Games	BA	SA	AB	H	2B	3B	HR	HR%	R	RBI	BB	SO	SB	Pinch Hit AB	Pinch Hit H	PO	A	E	DP	TC/G	FA	G by Pos
1935	PHI N	67	.230	.243	222	51	3	0	0	0.0	24	16	17	34	2	0	0	150	216	19	36	5.7	.951	SS-36, 2B-32
1936		108	.232	.250	332	77	4	1	0	0.0	24	28	14	32	0	0	0	217	347	37	56	5.4	.938	2B-71, SS-40
1942	WAS A	25	.192	.274	73	14	2	2	0	0.0	8	6	9	7	1	1	0	46	61	3	13	4.6	.973	2B-23, 3B-1
3 yrs.		200	.226	.250	627	142	9	3	0	0.0	56	50	40	73	3	1	0	413	624	59	105	5.4	.946	2B-126, SS-76, 3B-1

Chris Gomez

GOMEZ, CHRISTOPHER CORY BR TR 6′ 1″ 183 lbs.
B. June 16, 1971, Los Angeles, Calif.

Year	Team	Games	BA	SA	AB	H	2B	3B	HR	HR%	R	RBI	BB	SO	SB	Pinch Hit AB	Pinch Hit H	PO	A	E	DP	TC/G	FA	G by Pos
1993	DET A	46	.250	.320	128	32	7	1	0	0.0	11	11	9	17	2	0	0	69	118	5	23	4.1	.974	SS-29, 2B-17, DH-1
1994		84	.257	.402	296	76	19	0	8	2.7	32	53	33	64	5	0	0	141	210	8	39	4.1	.978	SS-57, 2B-30
1995		123	.223	.355	431	96	20	2	11	2.6	49	50	41	96	4	3	1	210	362	15	78	4.6	.974	SS-97, 2B-31, DH-1
3 yrs.		253	.239	.366	855	204	46	3	19	2.2	92	114	83	177	11	3	1	420	690	28	140	4.3	.975	SS-183, 2B-78, DH-2

Leo Gomez

GOMEZ, LEONARDO BR TR 6′ 180 lbs.
Born Leonardo Gomez (Velez).
B. Mar. 2, 1966, Canovanas, Puerto Rico.

Year	Team	Games	BA	SA	AB	H	2B	3B	HR	HR%	R	RBI	BB	SO	SB	Pinch Hit AB	Pinch Hit H	PO	A	E	DP	TC/G	FA	G by Pos
1990	BAL A	12	.231	.231	39	9	0	0	0	0.0	3	1	8	7	0	0	0	11	20	4	2	2.9	.886	3B-12
1991		118	.233	.409	391	91	17	2	16	4.1	40	45	40	82	1	5	0	78	184	7	20	2.3	.974	3B-105, DH-10, 1B-3
1992		137	.265	.425	468	124	24	0	17	3.6	62	64	63	78	2	0	0	106	246	18	19	2.7	.951	3B-137
1993		71	.197	.348	244	48	7	0	10	4.1	30	25	32	60	0	0	0	48	145	10	16	2.9	.951	3B-70, DH-1
1994		84	.274	.502	285	78	20	0	15	5.3	46	56	41	55	0	2	0	56	141	5	12	2.4	.975	3B-78, DH-5, 1B-1
1995		53	.236	.370	127	30	5	0	4	3.1	16	12	18	23	0	9	3	28	68	2	3	1.9	.980	3B-44, DH-5, 1B-3
6 yrs.		475	.245	.414	1554	380	73	2	62	4.0	197	203	202	305	3	16	3	327	804	46	72	2.5	.961	3B-446, DH-21, 1B-7

Luis Gomez

GOMEZ, LUIS BR TR 5′ 9″ 150 lbs.
Born Luis Gomez (Sanchez).
B. Aug. 19, 1951, Guadalajara, Mexico.

Year	Team	Games	BA	SA	AB	H	2B	3B	HR	HR%	R	RBI	BB	SO	SB	Pinch Hit AB	Pinch Hit H	PO	A	E	DP	TC/G	FA	G by Pos
1974	MIN A	82	.208	.214	168	35	1	0	0	0.0	18	3	12	16	2	0	0	97	194	12	37	3.9	.960	SS-74, 2B-2, DH-1
1975		89	.139	.139	72	10	0	0	0	0.0	7	5	4	12	0	0	0	55	80	3	20	1.7	.978	SS-70, DH-7, 2B-6
1976		38	.193	.211	57	11	1	0	0	0.0	5	3	3	3	1	0	0	36	58	1	17	2.5	.989	SS-24, 2B-8, 3B-4, OF-1, DH-1
1977		32	.246	.369	65	16	4	2	0	0.0	6	11	4	9	0	4	0	46	55	2	15	3.1	.981	2B-19, SS-7, 3B-4, DH-2, OF-1
1978	TOR A	153	.223	.254	413	92	7	3	0	0.0	39	32	34	41	2	0	0	247	400	16	97	4.3	.976	SS-153
1979		59	.239	.282	163	39	7	0	0	0.0	11	11	6	17	1	0	0	70	116	3	25	3.3	.984	3B-22, 2B-20, SS-15
1980	ATL N	121	.191	.212	278	53	6	0	0	0.0	18	24	17	27	0	0	0	135	319	15	55	3.9	.968	SS-119
1981		35	.200	.200	35	7	0	0	0	0.0	4	1	6	4	0	2	0	23	25	4	2	1.5	.923	SS-21, 3B-9, 2B-3, P-1
8 yrs.		609	.210	.239	1251	263	26	5	0	0.0	108	90	86	129	6	6	0	709	1247	56	268	3.4	.972	SS-483, 2B-58, 3B-39, DH-11, OF-2, P-1

Preston Gomez

GOMEZ, PEDRO BR TR 5′11″ 170 lbs.
Born Pedro Gomez (Martinez).
B. Apr. 20, 1923, Central Preston, Cuba.
Manager 1969–72, 1974–75, 1980.

Year	Team	Games	BA	SA	AB	H	2B	3B	HR	HR%	R	RBI	BB	SO	SB	Pinch Hit AB	Pinch Hit H	PO	A	E	DP	TC/G	FA	G by Pos
1944	WAS A	8	.286	.429	7	2	1	0	0	0.0	2	2	0	4	0	0	0	4	1	1	0	1.5	.833	SS-2, 2B-2

Randy Gomez

GOMEZ, RANDALL SCOTT BR TR 5′10″ 185 lbs.
B. Feb. 4, 1957, San Mateo, Calif.

Year	Team	Games	BA	SA	AB	H	2B	3B	HR	HR%	R	RBI	BB	SO	SB	Pinch Hit AB	Pinch Hit H	PO	A	E	DP	TC/G	FA	G by Pos
1984	SF N	14	.167	.200	30	5	1	0	0	0.0	0	0	8	3	0	0	0	69	8	4	1	5.8	.951	C-14

Jesse Gonder

GONDER, JESSE LEMAR BL TR 5′10″ 180 lbs.
B. Jan. 20, 1936, Monticello, Ark.

Year	Team	Games	BA	SA	AB	H	2B	3B	HR	HR%	R	RBI	BB	SO	SB	Pinch Hit AB	Pinch Hit H	PO	A	E	DP	TC/G	FA	G by Pos
1960	NY A	7	.286	.714	7	2	0	0	1	14.3	1	3	1	1	0	5	1	7	0	0	0	7.0	1.000	C-1
1961		15	.333	.417	12	4	1	0	0	0.0	2	3	3	1	0	12	4	0	0	0	0	0.0	—	
1962	CIN N	4	.000	.000	4	0	0	0	0	0.0	0	0	0	3	0	4	0	0	0	0	0	0.0	—	
1963	2 teams	CIN N (31G –.313) NY N (42G –.302)																						
″	total	73	.304	.456	158	48	6	0	6	3.8	17	20	7	37	1	34	10	141	18	3	3	4.3	.981	C-38
1964	NY N	131	.270	.370	341	92	11	1	7	2.1	28	35	29	65	0	43	8	397	70	10	7	4.9	.979	C-97
1965	2 teams	NY N (53G –.238) MIL N (31G –.151)																						
″	total	84	.209	.342	158	33	6	0	5	3.2	8	14	15	29	0	**52**	13	181	28	2	6	4.8	.991	C-44
1966	PIT N	59	.225	.388	160	36	3	1	7	4.4	13	16	12	39	0	12	2	238	27	6	4	5.2	.978	C-52
1967		22	.139	.167	36	5	1	0	0	0.0	4	3	5	9	0	5	1	56	10	2	0	3.8	.971	C-18
8 yrs.		395	.251	.377	876	220	28	2	26	3.0	73	94	72	184	1	167	39	1020	153	23	20	4.8	.981	C-250

Larry Gonzales

GONZALES, LAWRENCE CHRISTOPHER BR TR 6′ 3″ 200 lbs.
B. Mar. 28, 1967, West Covina, Calif.

Year	Team	Games	BA	SA	AB	H	2B	3B	HR	HR%	R	RBI	BB	SO	SB	Pinch Hit AB	Pinch Hit H	PO	A	E	DP	TC/G	FA	G by Pos
1993	CAL A	2	.500	.500	2	1	0	0	0	0.0	0	1	1	0	0	0	0	4	0	0	0	2.0	1.000	C-2

Rene Gonzales

GONZALES, RENE ADRIAN BR TR 6′ 3″ 180 lbs.
B. Sept. 23, 1960, Austin, Tex.

Year	Team	Games	BA	SA	AB	H	2B	3B	HR	HR%	R	RBI	BB	SO	SB	Pinch Hit AB	Pinch Hit H	PO	A	E	DP	TC/G	FA	G by Pos
1984	MON N	29	.233	.267	30	7	1	0	0	0.0	5	2	2	5	0	0	0	17	28	2	5	1.7	.957	SS-27
1986		11	.115	.115	26	3	0	0	0	0.0	1	0	2	7	0	0	0	7	19	0	3	2.4	1.000	SS-6, 3B-5
1987	BAL A	37	.267	.383	60	16	2	1	1	1.7	14	7	3	11	1	0	0	22	43	2	5	1.9	.970	3B-29, 2B-6, SS-1
1988		92	.215	.266	237	51	6	0	2	0.8	13	15	13	32	2	0	0	66	185	8	26	2.6	.969	3B-80, 2B-14, SS-2, OF-1, 1B-1
1989		71	.217	.259	166	36	4	0	1	0.6	16	11	12	30	5	2	0	103	146	7	37	3.6	.973	2B-54, 3B-17, SS-1
1990		67	.214	.291	103	22	3	1	1	1.0	13	12	12	14	1	0	0	68	114	2	23	2.7	.989	2B-43, 3B-16, SS-9, OF-1
1991	TOR A	71	.195	.246	118	23	3	0	1	0.8	16	6	12	22	0	2	1	61	118	7	17	2.5	.962	SS-36, 3B-26, 2B-11, 1B-2
1992	CAL A	104	.277	.398	329	91	17	1	7	2.1	47	38	41	46	7	2	1	191	229	9	49	3.7	.979	3B-53, 2B-42, 1B-13, SS-8
1993		117	.251	.319	335	84	17	0	2	0.6	34	31	49	45	5	5	2	234	170	12	46	3.5	.971	3B-79, 1B-31, SS-5, 2B-4, P-1
1994	CLE A	22	.348	.609	23	8	1	1	1	4.3	6	5	5	3	2	3	1	17	21	1	2	1.8	.974	3B-13, SS-4, 1B-4, 2B-1
1995	CAL A	30	.333	.556	18	6	1	0	1	5.6	1	3	0	4	0	5	2	6	12	0	0	0.7	1.000	3B-18, 2B-6, SS-1
11 yrs.		651	.240	.319	1445	347	55	4	17	1.2	166	130	151	219	23	19	7	792	1085	50	213	2.9	.974	3B-336, 2B-181, SS-100, 1B-51, OF-2, P-1
LEAGUE CHAMPIONSHIP SERIES																								
1991	TOR A	2	—	—	0	0	0	0	0	—	0	0	0	0	0	0	0	2	0	0	0	1.0	1.000	1B-1, SS-1

Alex Gonzalez

GONZALEZ, ALEXANDER SCOTT BR TR 6′ 180 lbs.
B. Apr. 8, 1973, Miami, Fla.

Year	Team	Games	BA	SA	AB	H	2B	3B	HR	HR%	R	RBI	BB	SO	SB	Pinch Hit AB	Pinch Hit H	PO	A	E	DP	TC/G	FA	G by Pos
1994	TOR A	15	.151	.245	53	8	3	1	0	0.0	7	1	4	17	3	0	0	18	49	6	5	4.9	.918	SS-15
1995		111	.243	.398	367	89	19	4	10	2.7	51	42	44	114	4	3	0	164	227	19	45	3.8	.954	SS-97, 3B-9, DH-3
2 yrs.		126	.231	.379	420	97	22	5	10	2.4	58	43	48	131	7	3	0	182	276	25	50	3.9	.948	SS-112, 3B-9, DH-3

Dan Gonzalez

GONZALEZ, DANIEL DAVID BL TR 6′ 1″ 195 lbs.
B. Sept. 30, 1953, Whittier, Calif.

Year	Team	Games	BA	SA	AB	H	2B	3B	HR	HR%	R	RBI	BB	SO	SB	Pinch Hit AB	Pinch Hit H	PO	A	E	DP	TC/G	FA	G by Pos
1979	DET A	7	.222	.278	18	4	1	0	0	0.0	1	2	0	2	1	3	0	3	0	0	0	0.8	1.000	OF-3, DH-1
1980		2	.143	.143	7	1	0	0	0	0.0	1	0	0	1	0	1	0	3	0	1	0	2.0	.750	OF-1, DH-1
2 yrs.		9	.200	.240	25	5	1	0	0	0.0	2	2	0	3	1	4	0	6	0	1	0	1.2	.857	OF-4, DH-2

Denny Gonzalez

GONZALEZ, DENIO MARIANO BR TR 5′11″ 165 lbs.
Born Denio Mariano Gonzalez (Manzueta).
B. July 22, 1963, Sabana Grande Boya, Dominican Republic.

Year	Team	Games	BA	SA	AB	H	2B	3B	HR	HR%	R	RBI	BB	SO	SB	Pinch Hit AB	Pinch Hit H	PO	A	E	DP	TC/G	FA	G by Pos
1984	PIT N	26	.183	.244	82	15	3	1	0	0.0	9	4	7	21	1	0	0	26	53	3	10	3.4	.963	3B-11, SS-10, OF-3
1985		35	.226	.355	124	28	4	0	4	3.2	11	12	13	27	2	1	0	44	42	8	5	2.3	.915	3B-21, OF-13, 2B-6
1987		5	.000	.000	7	0	0	0	0	0.0	1	0	1	2	0	4	0	2	1	0	0	3.0	1.000	SS-1
1988		24	.188	.219	32	6	1	0	0	0.0	5	1	6	10	0	10	3	20	22	2	5	2.2	.955	SS-14, 2B-4, 3B-2
1989	CLE A	8	.294	.353	17	5	1	0	0	0.0	3	1	0	4	0	3	1	0	0	1	0	0.1	.000	DH-6, 3B-1
5 yrs.		98	.206	.294	262	54	9	1	4	1.5	29	18	27	64	3	18	4	92	118	14	20	2.4	.938	3B-35, SS-25, OF-16, 2B-10, DH-6

Eusebio Gonzalez

GONZALEZ, EUSEBIO MIGUEL BR TR 5′10″ 165 lbs.
Born Eusebio Miguel Gonzalez (Lopez).
B. July 13, 1892, Havana, Cuba D. Feb. 14, 1976, Havana, Cuba.

Year	Team	Games	BA	SA	AB	H	2B	3B	HR	HR%	R	RBI	BB	SO	SB	Pinch Hit AB	Pinch Hit H	PO	A	E	DP	TC/G	FA	G by Pos
1918	BOS A	2	.500	1.500	2	1	0	1	0	0.0	1	0	0	0	0	0	0	1	2	0	0	1.5	1.000	SS-2

Fernando Gonzalez

GONZALEZ, JOSE FERNANDO BR TR 5′10″ 165 lbs.
Born Jose Fernando Gonzalez (Quinones).
B. June 19, 1950, Arecibo, Puerto Rico.

Year	Team	Games	BA	SA	AB	H	2B	3B	HR	HR%	R	RBI	BB	SO	SB	Pinch Hit AB	Pinch Hit H	PO	A	E	DP	TC/G	FA	G by Pos
1972	PIT N	3	.000	.000	2	0	0	0	0	0.0	0	0	0	2	0	2	0	0	1	1	0	2.0	.500	3B-1
1973		37	.224	.327	49	11	0	1	1	2.0	5	5	1	11	0	29	8	5	7	1	0	2.6	.923	3B-5
1974	2 teams	KC A (9G –.143) NY A (51G –.215)																						
″	total	60	.204	.282	142	29	6	1	1	0.7	12	9	7	11	1	3	0	104	105	5	24	3.5	.977	2B-42, 3B-15, SS-3, DH-1

Fernando Gonzalez *continued*

Year	Team	Games	BA	SA	AB	H	2B	3B	HR	HR%	R	RBI	BB	SO	SB	Pinch Hit AB	Pinch Hit H	PO	A	E	DP	TC/G	FA	G by Pos
1977	PIT N	80	.276	.398	181	50	10	0	4	2.2	17	27	13	21	3	27	10	43	66	2	6	1.8	.982	3B-37, OF-16, 2B-6, SS-2
1978	2 teams	PIT N (10G –.190) SD N (100G –.250)																						
"	total	110	.246	.308	341	84	11	2	2	0.6	29	29	19	35	4	9	4	197	262	10	68	4.6	.979	2B-98, 3B-3
1979	SD N	114	.217	.359	323	70	13	3	9	2.8	22	34	18	34	0	16	4	218	226	11	52	4.3	.976	2B-103, 3B-3
6 yrs.		404	.235	.336	1038	244	40	7	17	1.6	85	104	58	114	8	86	26	567	667	30	150	3.8	.976	2B-249, 3B-64, OF-16, SS-5, DH-1

Jose Gonzalez

Playing record listed under Jose Uribe.

Jose Gonzalez

GONZALEZ, JOSE RAFAEL BR TR 6′ 3″ 197 lbs.
Born Jose Rafael Gonzalez (Gutierrez).
B. Nov. 23, 1964, Puerto Plata, Dominican Republic.

Year	Team	Games	BA	SA	AB	H	2B	3B	HR	HR%	R	RBI	BB	SO	SB	Pinch Hit AB	Pinch Hit H	PO	A	E	DP	TC/G	FA	G by Pos
1985	LA N	23	.273	.455	11	3	2	0	0	0.0	6	0	1	3	1	1	0	10	0	0	0	0.6	1.000	OF-18
1986		57	.215	.355	93	20	5	1	2	2.2	15	6	7	29	4	5	1	73	0	6	0	1.4	.924	OF-57
1987		19	.188	.313	16	3	2	0	0	0.0	2	1	1	2	5	2	0	19	1	0	0	1.3	1.000	OF-16
1988		37	.083	.125	24	2	1	0	0	0.0	7	0	2	10	3	9	2	15	0	1	0	0.7	.938	OF-24
1989		95	.268	.360	261	70	11	2	3	1.1	31	18	23	53	9	14	5	171	8	6	2	2.1	.968	OF-87
1990		106	.232	.404	99	23	5	3	2	2.0	15	8	6	27	3	21	3	62	1	0	0	0.8	1.000	OF-81
1991	3 teams	LA N (42G –.000) PIT N (16G –.100) CLE A (33G –.159)																						
"	total	91	.111	.197	117	13	2	1	2	1.7	15	7	13	42	8	18	0	90	2	1	0	1.3	.989	OF-73
1992	CAL A	33	.182	.218	55	10	2	0	0	0.0	4	2	7	20	0	8	1	30	1	0	1	1.3	1.000	OF-22, DH-1
8 yrs.		461	.213	.318	676	144	30	7	9	1.3	95	42	60	186	33	78	12	470	13	14	3	1.3	.972	OF-378, DH-1
LEAGUE CHAMPIONSHIP SERIES																								
1988	LA N	5	—	—	0	0	0	0	0	—	2	0	0	0	0	0	0	3	0	0	0	0.8	1.000	OF-4
WORLD SERIES																								
1988	LA N	4	.000	.000	2	0	0	0	0	0.0	0	0	0	2	0	2	0	2	0	0	0	0.7	1.000	OF-3

Juan Gonzalez

GONZALEZ, JUAN ALBERTO BR TR 6′ 3″ 175 lbs.
Born Juan Alberto Gonzalez (Vasquez).
B. Oct. 16, 1969, Vega Baja, Puerto Rico.

Year	Team	Games	BA	SA	AB	H	2B	3B	HR	HR%	R	RBI	BB	SO	SB	Pinch Hit AB	Pinch Hit H	PO	A	E	DP	TC/G	FA	G by Pos
1989	TEX A	24	.150	.250	60	9	3	0	1	1.7	6	7	6	17	0	1	0	53	0	2	0	2.3	.964	OF-24
1990		25	.289	.522	90	26	7	1	4	4.4	11	12	2	18	0	3	1	33	0	0	0	1.3	1.000	OF-16, DH-9
1991		142	.264	.479	545	144	34	1	27	5.0	78	102	42	118	4	3	0	310	6	6	1	2.3	.981	OF-136, DH-4
1992		155	.260	.529	584	152	24	2	**43**	7.4	77	109	35	143	0	6	1	379	9	10	2	2.6	.975	OF-148, DH-4
1993		140	.310	**.632**	536	166	33	1	**46**	**8.6**	105	118	37	99	4	1	1	265	5	4	0	2.0	.985	OF-129, DH-10
1994		107	.275	.472	422	116	18	4	19	4.5	57	85	30	66	6	0	0	223	9	2	1	2.2	.991	OF-107
1995		90	.295	.594	352	104	20	2	27	7.7	57	82	17	66	0	3	0	6	1	0	0	0.1	1.000	DH-83, OF-5
7 yrs.		683	.277	.533	2589	717	139	11	167	6.5	391	515	169	527	14	17	3	1269	30	24	4	2.0	.982	OF-565, DH-110

Julio Gonzalez

GONZALEZ, JULIO CESAR BR TR 5′11″ 162 lbs.
Born Julio Cesar Gonzalez (Hernandez).
B. Dec. 25, 1952, Caguas, Puerto Rico.

Year	Team	Games	BA	SA	AB	H	2B	3B	HR	HR%	R	RBI	BB	SO	SB	Pinch Hit AB	Pinch Hit H	PO	A	E	DP	TC/G	FA	G by Pos
1977	HOU N	110	.245	.316	383	94	18	3	1	0.3	34	27	19	45	3	7	1	154	293	27	56	4.4	.943	SS-63, 2B-45
1978		78	.233	.269	223	52	3	1	1	0.4	24	16	8	31	6	12	1	83	139	7	28	3.1	.969	2B-54, SS-17, 3B-4
1979		68	.249	.298	181	45	5	2	0	0.0	16	10	5	14	2	7	3	92	146	5	27	3.9	.979	2B-32, SS-21, 3B-9
1980		40	.115	.135	52	6	1	0	0	0.0	5	1	1	8	1	10	0	22	31	1	8	1.9	.981	SS-16, 3B-11, 2B-2
1981	STL N	20	.318	.500	22	7	1	0	1	4.5	2	3	1	3	0	10	2	7	13	1	1	1.9	.952	SS-5, 2B-4, 3B-2
1982		42	.241	.356	87	21	3	2	1	1.1	9	7	1	24	1	12	1	21	44	4	5	2.2	.942	3B-21, 2B-9, SS-1
1983	DET A	12	.143	.190	21	3	1	0	0	0.0	0	2	1	7	0	0	0	10	26	4	3	3.3	.900	SS-6, 2B-5, 3B-1
7 yrs.		370	.235	.297	969	228	32	8	4	0.4	90	66	36	132	13	58	8	389	692	49	128	3.4	.957	2B-151, SS-129, 3B-48

Luis Gonzalez

GONZALEZ, LUIS EMILIO BL TR 6′ 180 lbs.
B. Sept. 3, 1967, Tampa, Fla.

Year	Team	Games	BA	SA	AB	H	2B	3B	HR	HR%	R	RBI	BB	SO	SB	Pinch Hit AB	Pinch Hit H	PO	A	E	DP	TC/G	FA	G by Pos
1990	HOU N	12	.190	.286	21	4	2	0	0	0.0	1	0	2	5	0	5	1	22	10	0	1	5.3	1.000	3B-4, 1B-2
1991		137	.254	.433	473	120	28	9	13	2.7	51	69	40	101	10	5	1	294	6	5	1	2.3	.984	OF-133
1992		122	.243	.385	387	94	19	3	10	2.6	40	55	24	52	7	17	5	261	5	2	1	2.4	.993	OF-111
1993		154	.300	.457	540	162	34	3	15	2.8	82	72	47	83	20	6	3	347	10	8	2	2.4	.978	OF-149
1994		112	.273	.429	392	107	29	4	8	2.0	57	67	49	57	15	2	1	228	5	2	1	2.1	.991	OF-111
1995	2 teams	HOU N (56G –.258) CHI N (77G –.290)																						
"	total	133	.276	.454	471	130	29	8	13	2.8	69	69	57	63	6	4	3	266	7	6	0	2.1	.978	OF-131
6 yrs.		670	.270	.433	2284	617	141	27	59	2.6	300	332	219	361	58	39	14	1418	43	23	6	2.3	.985	OF-635, 3B-4, 1B-2

Mike Gonzalez

GONZALEZ, MIGUEL ANGEL BR TR 6′ 1″ 200 lbs.
Born Miguel Angel Gonzalez (Cordero).
B. Sept. 24, 1890, Havana, Cuba D. Feb. 19, 1977, Havana, Cuba.
Manager 1938, 1940.

Year	Team	Games	BA	SA	AB	H	2B	3B	HR	HR%	R	RBI	BB	SO	SB	Pinch Hit AB	Pinch Hit H	PO	A	E	DP	TC/G	FA	G by Pos
1912	BOS N	1	.000	.000	2	0	0	0	0	0.0	0	0	1	1	0	0	0	3	4	1	0	8.0	.875	C-1
1914	CIN N	95	.233	.267	176	41	6	0	0	0.0	19	10	13	16	2	9	2	252	101	17	5	4.5	.954	C-83
1915	STL N	51	.227	.289	97	22	2	2	0	0.0	12	10	8	9	4	6	1	175	31	2	9	5.3	.990	C-31, 1B-8
1916		118	.239	.308	331	79	15	4	0	0.0	33	29	28	18	5	10	0	483	138	10	15	6.0	.984	C-93, 1B-13
1917		106	.262	.307	290	76	8	1	1	0.3	28	28	22	24	12	17	2	444	110	12	19	6.5	.979	C-68, 1B-18, OF-1
1918		117	.252	.338	349	88	13	4	3	0.9	33	20	39	30	14	8	1	370	124	11	18	4.7	.978	C-100, OF-5, 1B-2
1919	NY N	58	.190	.228	158	30	6	0	0	0.0	18	8	20	9	3	3	0	205	52	10	5	4.8	.963	C-52, 1B-4
1920		11	.231	.231	13	3	0	0	0	0.0	1	0	3	1	1	2	0	9	4	0	0	1.6	1.000	C-8
1921		13	.375	.417	24	9	1	0	0	0.0	3	0	1	0	0	4	1	55	2	1	5	7.3	.983	1B-6, C-2
1924	STL N	120	.296	.391	402	119	27	1	3	0.7	34	53	24	22	1	1	1	413	96	7	15	4.3	.986	C-119
1925	2 teams	STL N (22G –.310) CHI N (70G –.264)																						
"	total	92	.276	.377	268	74	16	1	3	1.1	35	22	19	17	3	9	2	338	53	4	16	4.9	.990	C-72, 1B-9
1926	CHI N	80	.249	.336	253	63	13	3	1	0.4	24	23	13	17	3	2	0	306	53	4	5	4.7	.989	C-78

Mike Gonzalez *continued*

Year	Team	Games	BA	SA	AB	H	2B	3B	HR	HR%	R	RBI	BB	SO	SB	Pinch Hit AB	Pinch Hit H	PO	A	E	DP	TC/G	FA	G by Pos
1927		39	.241	.324	108	26	4	1	1	0.9	15	15	10	8	1	3	1	136	29	1	6	4.6	.994	C-36
1928		49	.272	.373	158	43	9	2	1	0.6	12	21	12	7	2	4	0	198	35	4	8	5.3	.983	C-45
1929		60	.240	.257	167	40	3	0	0	0.0	15	18	18	14	1	0	0	212	34	2	7	4.1	.992	C-60
1931	STL N	15	.105	.105	19	2	0	0	0	0.0	1	3	0	3	0	3	0	15	4	0	0	1.6	1.000	C-12
1932		17	.143	.143	14	2	0	0	0	0.0	0	3	0	2	0	10	2	12	1	0	0	1.9	1.000	C-7
17 yrs.		1042	.253	.324	2829	717	123	19	13	0.5	283	263	231	198	52	91	13	3626	871	86	133	4.9	.981	C-867, 1B-60, OF-6
WORLD SERIES																								
1929	CHI N	2	.000	.000	1	0	0	0	0	0.0	0	0	0	1	0	1	0	2	0	0	0	2.0	1.000	C-1

Orlando Gonzalez

GONZALEZ, ORLANDO EUGENE BR TR 6′ 2″ 180 lbs.
B. Nov. 15, 1951, Havana, Cuba.

Year	Team	Games	BA	SA	AB	H	2B	3B	HR	HR%	R	RBI	BB	SO	SB	Pinch Hit AB	Pinch Hit H	PO	A	E	DP	TC/G	FA	G by Pos
1976	CLE A	28	.250	.279	68	17	2	0	0	0.0	5	4	5	7	1	6	2	123	8	1	7	5.5	.992	1B-15, OF-7, DH-2
1978	PHI N	26	.192	.192	26	5	0	0	0	0.0	1	0	1	1	0	14	3	16	0	0	0	1.1	1.000	OF-11, 1B-3
1980	OAK A	25	.243	.243	70	17	0	0	0	0.0	10	1	9	8	0	4	0	95	8	1	7	5.0	.990	1B-11, DH-8, OF-2
3 yrs.		79	.238	.250	164	39	2	0	0	0.0	16	5	15	16	1	24	5	234	16	2	14	4.3	.992	1B-29, OF-20, DH-10
LEAGUE CHAMPIONSHIP SERIES																								
1978	PHI N	1	.000	.000	1	0	0	0	0	0.0	0	0	0	1	0	1	0	0	0	0	0	0.0	—	

Pedro Gonzalez

GONZALEZ, PEDRO BR TR 6′ 176 lbs.
Born Pedro Gonzales (Olivares).
B. Dec. 12, 1937, San Pedro de Macoris, Dominican Republic.

Year	Team	Games	BA	SA	AB	H	2B	3B	HR	HR%	R	RBI	BB	SO	SB	Pinch Hit AB	Pinch Hit H	PO	A	E	DP	TC/G	FA	G by Pos
1963	NY A	14	.192	.231	26	5	1	0	0	0.0	3	1	0	5	0	5	1	17	9	1	2	3.9	.963	2B-7
1964		80	.277	.366	112	31	8	1	0	0.0	18	5	7	22	3	8	1	161	37	3	13	3.0	.985	1B-31, OF-20, 3B-9, 2B-6
1965	2 teams NY A (7G –.400) CLE A (116G –.253)																							
″	total	123	.254	.343	405	103	15	3	5	1.2	38	39	18	59	7	8	3	266	287	11	59	4.8	.980	2B-112, OF-3, 3B-2
1966	CLE A	110	.233	.287	352	82	9	2	2	0.6	21	17	15	54	8	3	0	237	260	8	62	4.8	.984	2B-104, 3B-1, OF-1
1967		80	.228	.275	189	43	6	0	1	0.5	19	8	12	36	4	7	3	124	122	8	29	3.4	.969	2B-64, 3B-4, 1B-4, SS-3
5 yrs.		407	.244	.313	1084	264	39	6	8	0.7	99	70	52	176	22	31	8	805	715	31	165	4.2	.980	2B-293, 1B-35, OF-24, 3B-16, SS-3
WORLD SERIES																								
1964	NY A	1	.000	.000	1	0	0	0	0	0.0	0	0	0	0	0	0	0	1	3	0	0	4.0	1.000	3B-1

Tony Gonzalez

GONZALEZ, ANDRES ANTONIO BL TR 5′ 9″ 170 lbs.
Born Andres Antonio Gonzalez (Gonzalez).
B. Aug. 28, 1936, Central Cunagua, Cuba.

Year	Team	Games	BA	SA	AB	H	2B	3B	HR	HR%	R	RBI	BB	SO	SB	Pinch Hit AB	Pinch Hit H	PO	A	E	DP	TC/G	FA	G by Pos
1960	2 teams CIN N (39G –.212) PHI N (78G –.299)																							
″	total	117	.274	.453	340	93	22	6	9	2.6	37	47	15	74	3	29	5	189	8	5	0	2.1	.975	OF-98
1961	PHI N	126	.277	.437	426	118	16	8	12	2.8	58	58	49	66	15	16	6	246	7	4	4	2.2	.984	OF-118
1962		118	.302	.494	437	132	16	4	20	4.6	76	63	40	82	17	4	1	268	8	0	2	2.4	1.000	OF-114
1963		155	.306	.436	555	170	36	12	4	0.7	78	66	53	68	13	7	0	263	11	4	2	1.8	.986	OF-151
1964		131	.278	.380	421	117	25	3	4	1.0	55	40	44	74	0	16	3	243	5	1	2	2.1	.996	OF-119
1965		108	.295	.457	370	109	19	1	13	3.5	48	41	31	52	3	11	2	167	3	3	1	1.7	.983	OF-104
1966		132	.286	.406	384	110	20	4	6	1.6	53	40	26	60	2	19	5	206	7	3	1	1.8	.986	OF-121
1967		149	.339	.472	508	172	23	9	9	1.8	74	59	47	58	10	17	7	260	10	2	1	1.9	.993	OF-143
1968		121	.264	.337	416	110	13	4	3	0.7	45	38	40	42	6	8	3	227	4	5	1	2.0	.979	OF-117
1969	2 teams SD N (53G –.225) ATL N (89G –.294)																							
″	total	142	.269	.386	502	135	19	2	12	2.4	68	58	46	46	4	13	2	287	3	5	0	2.3	.983	OF-131
1970	2 teams ATL N (123G –.265) CAL A (26G –.304)																							
″	total	149	.272	.364	522	142	20	2	8	1.5	66	67	48	56	6	9	2	281	3	5	0	2.0	.983	OF-143
1971	CAL A	111	.245	.315	314	77	9	2	3	1.0	32	38	28	28	0	29	10	146	4	2	1	1.7	.987	OF-88
12 yrs.		1559	.286	.413	5195	1485	238	57	103	2.0	690	615	467	706	79	178	46	2783	73	39	15	2.0	.987	OF-1447
LEAGUE CHAMPIONSHIP SERIES																								
1969	ATL N	3	.357	.643	14	5	1	0	1	7.1	4	2	1	4	0	0	0	3	1	1	0	1.7	.800	OF-3

Charlie Gooch

GOOCH, CHARLES FURMAN BR TR 5′ 9″ 170 lbs.
B. June 5, 1902, Smyrna, Tenn. D. May 30, 1982, Lanham, Md.

Year	Team	Games	BA	SA	AB	H	2B	3B	HR	HR%	R	RBI	BB	SO	SB	Pinch Hit AB	Pinch Hit H	PO	A	E	DP	TC/G	FA	G by Pos
1929	WAS A	39	.281	.351	57	16	2	1	0	0.0	6	5	7	8	0	22	7	31	11	2	2	2.9	.955	1B-7, 3B-7, SS-1

Johnny Gooch

GOOCH, JOHN BEVERLEY BB TR 5′11″ 175 lbs.
B. Nov. 9, 1897, Smyrna, Tenn. D. May 15, 1975, Nashville, Tenn.

Year	Team	Games	BA	SA	AB	H	2B	3B	HR	HR%	R	RBI	BB	SO	SB	Pinch Hit AB	Pinch Hit H	PO	A	E	DP	TC/G	FA	G by Pos
1921	PIT N	13	.237	.237	38	9	0	0	0	0.0	2	3	3	3	1	0	0	49	15	1	2	5.0	.985	C-13
1922		105	.329	.397	353	116	15	3	1	0.3	45	42	39	15	1	2	1	382	102	15	10	4.8	.970	C-103
1923		66	.277	.361	202	56	10	2	1	0.5	16	20	17	13	2	0	0	217	56	7	7	4.2	.975	C-66
1924		70	.290	.362	224	65	6	5	0	0.0	26	25	16	12	1	1	0	198	47	3	12	3.6	.988	C-69
1925		79	.298	.372	215	64	8	4	0	0.0	24	30	20	16	1	3	0	172	39	7	8	2.9	.968	C-76
1926		86	.271	.362	218	59	15	1	1	0.5	19	42	20	14	1	3	0	202	38	5	6	3.1	.980	C-80
1927		101	.258	.351	291	75	17	2	2	0.7	22	48	19	21	0	9	1	285	57	9	7	3.9	.974	C-91
1928	2 teams PIT N (31G –.237) BKN N (42G –.317)																							
″	total	73	.282	.331	181	51	3	3	0	0.0	16	17	10	15	0	4	1	204	35	9	6	3.6	.964	C-69
1929	2 teams BKN N (1G –.000) CIN N (92G –.300)																							
″	total	93	.299	.378	288	86	13	5	0	0.0	22	34	24	10	4	7	1	251	61	8	7	3.7	.975	C-86
1930	CIN N	92	.243	.322	276	67	10	3	2	0.7	29	30	27	15	0	2	0	233	42	13	4	3.6	.955	C-79
1933	BOS A	37	.182	.221	77	14	1	1	0	0.0	6	2	11	7	0	8	1	86	19	1	2	4.1	.991	C-26
11 yrs.		815	.280	.355	2363	662	98	29	7	0.3	227	293	206	141	11	39	5	2279	511	78	71	3.8	.973	C-758
WORLD SERIES																								
1925	PIT N	3	.000	.000	3	0	0	0	0	0.0	0	0	0	0	0	0	0	9	3	0	0	4.0	1.000	C-3
1927		3	.000	.000	5	0	0	0	0	0.0	0	0	1	1	0	0	0	19	1	0	0	6.7	1.000	C-3
2 yrs.		6	.000	.000	8	0	0	0	0	0.0	0	0	1	1	0	0	0	28	4	0	0	5.3	1.000	C-6

				A	SA	AB	H	2B	3B	HR	HR%	R	RBI	BB	SO	SB	Pinch Hit AB	Pinch Hit H	PO	A	E	DP	TC/G	FA	G by Pos

…och

GOOCH, LEE CURRIN BR TR 6′ 190 lbs.
B. Feb. 23, 1890, Oxford, N. C. D. May 18, 1966, Raleigh, N. C.

	…LE	A	2	.500	.500	2	1	0	0	0	0.0	0	0	0	0	0	2	1	0	0	0	0	0.0	—	
	PHI	A	17	.288	.373	59	17	2	0	1	1.7	4	8	4	10	0	1	0	24	1	3	0	1.8	.893	OF-16
2 yrs.			19	.295	.377	61	18	2	0	1	1.6	4	8	4	10	0	3	1	24	1	3	0	1.8	.893	OF-16

Gene Good

GOOD, EUGENE J. BL TL 5′ 6″ 130 lbs.
B. Dec. 13, 1882, Roxbury, Mass. D. Aug. 6, 1947, Boston, Mass.

1906	BOS	N	34	.151	.151	119	18	0	0	0	0.0	4	0	13		2	0	0	50	5	8	1	1.9	.873	OF-34

Wilbur Good

GOOD, WILBUR DAVID (Lefty) BL TL 5′ 6″ 165 lbs.
B. Sept. 28, 1885, Punxsutawney, Pa. D. Dec. 30, 1963, Brooksville, Fla.

1905	NY	A	6	.375	.375	8	3	0	0	0	0.0	0	0	0		0	0	0	1	7	1	0	1.8	.889	P-5
1908	CLE	A	46	.279	.344	154	43	1	3	1	0.6	23	14	13		7	2	1	62	0	11	0	1.7	.849	OF-42
1909			94	.214	.264	318	68	6	5	0	0.0	33	17	28		13	10	1	110	12	6	2	1.6	.953	OF-80
1910	BOS	N	23	.337	.488	86	29	5	4	0	0.0	15	11	6	13	5	0	0	56	7	2	1	2.8	.969	OF-23
1911	2 teams		BOS N (43G –.267)		CHI N (58G –.269)																				
″	total		101	.268	.377	310	83	14	7	2	0.6	48	36	23	39	13	12	1	182	16	13	2	2.5	.938	OF-83
1912	CHI	N	39	.143	.143	35	5	0	0	0	0.0	7	1	3	7	3	21	3	7	1	0	0	0.8	1.000	OF-10
1913			49	.253	.363	91	23	3	2	1	1.1	11	12	11	16	5	16	4	37	1	1	0	1.5	.974	OF-26
1914			154	.272	.348	580	158	24	7	2	0.3	70	43	53	74	31	0	0	242	25	20	10	1.9	.930	OF-154
1915			128	.253	.337	498	126	18	9	2	0.4	66	27	34	65	19	2	1	192	13	14	4	1.8	.936	OF-125
1916	PHI	N	75	.250	.346	136	34	4	3	1	0.7	25	15	8	13	7	22	3	55	4	1	1	1.3	.983	OF-46
1918	CHI	A	35	.250	.365	148	37	9	4	0	0.0	24	11	11	16	1	0	0	103	4	2	1	3.1	.982	OF-35
11 yrs.			750	.258	.342	2364	609	84	44	9	0.4	322	187	190	243	104	85	14	1047	90	71	21	1.9	.941	OF-624, P-5

Bill Goodenough

GOODENOUGH, WILLIAM B. 6′ 1″ 170 lbs.
B. 1863, St. Louis, Mo. D. May 24, 1905, St. Louis, Mo.

1893	STL	N	10	.161	.194	31	5	1	0	0	0.0	4	2	3	4	2	0	0	21	1	3	0	2.5	.880	OF-10

Mike Goodfellow

GOODFELLOW, MICHAEL J. BR TR 6′ 180 lbs.
B. Oct. 3, 1866, Port Jervis, N. Y. D. Feb. 12, 1920, Newark, N. J.

1887	STL	AA	1	.000	.000	4	0	0	0	0	0.0	0		0		0	0	0	2	2	1	0	5.0	.800	C-1
1888	CLE	AA	68	.245	.271	269	66	7	0	0	0.0	24	29	11		7	0	0	138	12	18	2	2.4	.893	OF-62, C-4, 1B-3, SS-1
2 yrs.			69	.242	.267	273	66	7	0	0	0.0	24	29	11		7	0	0	140	14	19	2	2.4	.890	OF-62, C-5, 1B-3, SS-1

Billy Goodman

GOODMAN, WILLIAM DALE BL TR 5′11″ 165 lbs.
B. Mar. 22, 1926, Concord, N. C. D. Oct. 1, 1984, Sarasota, Fla.

1947	BOS	A	12	.182	.182	11	2	0	0	0	0.0	1	1	1	2	0	9	1	2	0	0	0	2.0	1.000	OF-1
1948			127	.310	.387	445	138	27	2	1	0.2	65	66	74	44	5	4	2	1101	73	9	120	9.8	.992	1B-117, 3B-2, 2B-2
1949			122	.298	.363	443	132	23	3	0	0.0	54	56	58	21	2	3	2	1069	79	9	148	9.9	.992	1B-117
1950			110	**.354**	.455	424	150	25	3	4	0.9	91	68	52	25	2	11	2	344	89	9	28	4.5	.980	OF-45, 3B-27, 1B-21, 2B-5, SS-1
1951			141	.297	.374	546	162	34	4	0	0.0	92	50	79	37	7	1	0	742	170	14	96	6.4	.985	1B-62, 2B-44, OF-38, 3B-1
1952			138	.306	.394	513	157	27	3	4	0.8	79	56	48	23	8	6	1	473	367	20	112	6.4	.977	2B-103, 1B-23, 3B-5, OF-4
1953			128	.313	.409	514	161	33	5	2	0.4	73	41	57	11	1	2	2	418	319	21	106	5.7	.972	2B-112, 1B-20
1954			127	.303	.376	489	148	25	4	1	0.2	71	36	51	15	3	10	3	393	248	14	90	5.3	.979	2B-72, 1B-27, OF-13, 3B-12
1955			149	.294	.352	599	176	31	2	0	0.0	100	52	99	44	5	0	0	395	378	24	96	5.3	.970	2B-143, 1B-5, OF-1
1956			105	.293	.404	399	117	22	8	2	0.5	61	38	40	22	0	9	2	215	266	17	69	5.2	.966	2B-95
1957	2 teams		BOS A (18G –.063)		BAL A (73G –.308)																				
″	total		91	.294	.387	279	82	11	3	3	1.1	37	33	23	19	0	22	2	134	110	11	20	3.1	.957	3B-54, OF-9, 1B-8, SS-5, 2B-5
1958	CHI	A	116	.299	.358	425	127	15	5	0	0.0	41	40	37	21	1	4	2	89	210	14	18	2.7	.955	3B-111, 1B-3, SS-1, 2B-1
1959			104	.250	.321	268	67	14	1	1	0.4	21	28	19	20	3	31	7	61	140	10	11	2.7	.953	3B-74, 2B-3
1960			30	.234	.286	77	18	4	0	0	0.0	5	6	12	8	0	6	0	26	52	1	7	2.9	.987	3B-20, 2B-7
1961			41	.255	.392	51	13	4	0	1	2.0	4	10	7	6	0	27	9	11	14	1	1	2.6	.962	3B-7, 1B-2, 2B-1
1962	HOU	N	82	.255	.292	161	41	4	1	0	0.0	12	10	12	11	0	53	14	36	67	9	8	2.3	.920	2B-31, 3B-17, 1B-1
16 yrs.			1623	.300	.378	5644	1691	299	44	19	0.3	807	591	669	329	37	198	49	5509	2582	183	930	5.6	.978	2B-624, 1B-406, 3B-330, OF-111, SS-7
WORLD SERIES																									
1959	CHI	A	5	.231	.231	13	3	0	0	0	0.0	1	1	0	5	0	2	0	1	2	0	0	0.6	1.000	3B-5

Ival Goodman

GOODMAN, IVAL RICHARD (Goodie) BL TR 5′11″ 170 lbs.
B. July 23, 1908, Northview, Mo. D. Nov. 25, 1984, Cincinnati, Ohio.

1935	CIN	N	148	.269	.429	592	159	23	**18**	12	2.0	86	72	35	50	14	2	0	322	17	14	4	2.4	.960	OF-146
1936			136	.284	.476	489	139	15	**14**	17	3.5	81	71	38	53	6	15	5	274	6	8	2	2.4	.972	OF-120
1937			147	.273	.428	549	150	25	12	12	2.2	86	55	55	58	10	3	1	291	13	8	0	2.2	.974	OF-141
1938			145	.292	.533	568	166	27	10	30	5.3	103	92	53	51	3	3	1	306	10	4	1	2.3	.988	OF-142
1939			124	.323	.515	470	152	37	16	7	1.5	85	84	54	32	2	1	1	246	16	5	4	2.2	.981	OF-123
1940			136	.258	.389	519	134	20	6	12	2.3	78	63	60	54	9	0	0	252	6	8	0	2.0	.970	OF-135
1941			42	.268	.349	149	40	5	2	1	0.7	14	12	16	15	1	1	0	84	1	3	0	2.2	.966	OF-40
1942			87	.243	.332	226	55	18	1	0	0.0	21	15	24	32	0	23	6	101	7	1	2	1.9	.991	OF-57
1943	CHI	N	80	.320	.449	225	72	10	5	3	1.3	31	45	24	20	4	17	5	120	2	4	1	2.1	.968	OF-61
1944			62	.262	.355	141	37	8	1	1	0.7	24	16	23	15	0	23	6	65	0	0	0	1.9	1.000	OF-35
10 yrs.			1107	.281	.445	3928	1104	188	85	95	2.4	609	525	382	380	49	88	25	2061	78	55	14	2.2	.975	OF-1000
WORLD SERIES																									
1939	CIN	N	4	.333	.400	15	5	1	0	0	0.0	3	1	1	2	1	0	0	10	1	1	0	3.0	.917	OF-4
1940			7	.276	.345	29	8	2	0	0	0.0	5	5	0	3	0	0	0	10	0	0	0	1.4	1.000	OF-7
2 yrs.			11	.295	.364	44	13	3	0	0	0.0	8	6	1	5	1	0	0	20	1	1	0	2.0	.955	OF-11

Jake Goodman

GOODMAN, JACOB 6′ 1½″
B. Sept. 14, 1853, Lancaster, Pa. D. Mar. 9, 1890, Reading, Pa.

1878	MIL	N	60	.246	.298	252	62	4	3	1	0.4	28	27	7	33		0	0	693	12	42	15	12.4	.944	1B-60
1882	PIT	AA	10	.317	.463	41	13	2	2	0	0.0	5		2			0	0	73	4	3	0	8.0	.963	1B-10
2 yrs.			70	.256	.321	293	75	6	5	1	0.3	33	27	9	33		0	0	766	16	45	15	11.8	.946	1B-70

Ed Goodson

GOODSON, JAMES EDWARD
B. Jan. 25, 1948, Pulaski, Va.
BL TR 6′ 3″ 180 lbs.
BB 1975

Year	Team		Games	BA	SA	AB	H	2B	3B	HR	HR%	R	RBI	BB	SO	SB	Pinch Hit AB	Pinch Hit H	PO	A	E	DP	TC/G	FA	G by Pos
1970	SF	N	7	.273	.273	11	3	0	0	0	0.0	1	0	0	2	0	5	2	14	2	1	1	8.5	.941	1B-2
1971			20	.190	.214	42	8	1	0	0	0.0	4	1	2	4	0	7	1	81	7	0	3	6.3	1.000	1B-14
1972			58	.280	.420	150	42	1	1	6	4.0	15	30	8	12	0	15	4	299	27	3	28	7.8	.991	1B-42
1973			102	.302	.453	384	116	20	1	12	3.1	37	53	15	44	0	8	3	64	171	23	13	2.8	.911	3B-93
1974			98	.272	.383	298	81	15	0	6	2.0	25	48	18	22	1	20	6	600	46	2	53	8.0	.997	1B-73, 3B-8
1975	2 teams	SF N (39G –.207) ATL N (47G –.211)																							
″	total		86	.208	.284	197	41	9	0	2	1.0	15	16	9	22	0	40	9	240	52	6	23	6.9	.980	1B-29, 3B-14
1976	LA	N	83	.229	.339	118	27	4	0	3	2.5	8	17	8	19	0	56	15	17	27	7	2	2.3	.863	3B-16, 1B-3, OF-2, 2B-1
1977			61	.167	.227	66	11	1	0	1	1.5	3	5	3	10	0	45	8	38	9	0	5	2.8	1.000	1B-13, 3B-4
8 yrs.			515	.260	.374	1266	329	51	2	30	2.4	108	170	63	135	1	196	48	1353	341	42	128	5.5	.976	1B-176, 3B-135, OF-2, 2B-1
LEAGUE CHAMPIONSHIP SERIES																									
1977	LA	N	1	.000	.000	1	0	0	0	0	0.0	0	0	0	0	0	1	0	0	0	0	0	0.0	—	
WORLD SERIES																									
1977	LA	N	1	.000	.000	1	0	0	0	0	0.0	0	0	0	1	0	1	0	0	0	0	0	0.0	—	

Curtis Goodwin

GOODWIN, CURTIS LaMAR
B. Sept. 30, 1972, Oakland, Calif.
BL TL 5′11″ 180 lbs.

Year	Team		Games	BA	SA	AB	H	2B	3B	HR	HR%	R	RBI	BB	SO	SB	Pinch Hit AB	Pinch Hit H	PO	A	E	DP	TC/G	FA	G by Pos
1995	BAL	A	87	.263	.332	289	76	11	3	1	0.3	40	24	15	53	22	2	1	202	1	2	1	2.4	.990	OF-84, DH-2

Danny Goodwin

GOODWIN, DANNY KAY
B. Sept. 2, 1953, St. Louis, Mo.
BL TR 6′ 1″ 195 lbs.

Year	Team		Games	BA	SA	AB	H	2B	3B	HR	HR%	R	RBI	BB	SO	SB	Pinch Hit AB	Pinch Hit H	PO	A	E	DP	TC/G	FA	G by Pos
1975	CAL	A	4	.100	.100	10	1	0	0	0	0.0	0	0	0	5	0	1	0	0	0	0	0	0.0	.000	DH-3
1977			35	.209	.330	91	19	6	1	1	1.1	5	8	5	19	0	12	1	0	0	0	0	0.0	.000	DH-23
1978			24	.276	.466	58	16	5	0	2	3.4	9	10	10	13	0	8	2	0	0	0	0	0.0	.000	DH-15
1979	MIN	A	58	.289	.497	159	46	8	5	5	3.1	22	27	11	23	0	11	4	40	2	0	5	0.7	1.000	DH-51, 1B-8
1980			55	.200	.270	115	23	5	0	1	0.9	12	11	17	32	0	22	6	87	6	0	6	1.8	1.000	DH-38, 1B-13
1981			59	.225	.318	151	34	6	1	2	1.3	18	17	16	32	3	10	3	342	20	3	27	7.9	.992	1B-40, DH-5, OF-1
1982	OAK	A	17	.212	.404	52	11	2	1	2	3.8	6	8	2	13	0	2	1	0	0	0	0	0.0	.000	DH-15
7 yrs.			252	.236	.373	636	150	32	8	13	2.0	72	81	61	137	3	66	17	469	28	3	38	2.4	.994	DH-150, 1B-61, OF-1

Pep Goodwin

GOODWIN, CLAIRE VERNON
B. Dec. 19, 1891, Pocatello, Ida. D. Feb. 15, 1972, Oakland, Calif.
BL TR 5′10½″ 160 lbs.

Year	Team		Games	BA	SA	AB	H	2B	3B	HR	HR%	R	RBI	BB	SO	SB	Pinch Hit AB	Pinch Hit H	PO	A	E	DP	TC/G	FA	G by Pos
1914	KC	F	112	.235	.316	374	88	15	6	1	0.3	38	32	27		4	6	2	136	275	43	25	4.2	.905	SS-67, 3B-40, 1B-1
1915			81	.236	.266	229	54	5	1	0	0.0	22	16	15		6	14	2	106	180	24	17	4.8	.923	SS-42, 2B-23
2 yrs.			193	.235	.297	603	142	20	7	1	0.2	60	48	42		10	20	4	242	455	67	42	4.4	.912	SS-109, 3B-40, 2B-23, 1B-1

Tom Goodwin

GOODWIN, THOMAS JONES
B. July 27, 1968, Fresno, Calif.
BL TR 6′ 1″ 165 lbs.

Year	Team		Games	BA	SA	AB	H	2B	3B	HR	HR%	R	RBI	BB	SO	SB	Pinch Hit AB	Pinch Hit H	PO	A	E	DP	TC/G	FA	G by Pos
1991	LA	N	16	.143	.143	7	1	0	0	0	0.0	3	0	0	0	1	1	0	8	0	0	0	1.6	1.000	OF-5
1992			57	.233	.274	73	17	1	1	0	0.0	15	3	6	10	7	5	2	43	0	0	0	1.0	1.000	OF-45
1993			30	.294	.353	17	5	1	0	0	0.0	6	1	1	4	1	5	1	8	0	0	0	0.7	1.000	OF-12
1994	KC	A	2	.000	.000	2	0	0	0	0	0.0	0	0	0	1	0	0	0	1	0	0	0	0.5	1.000	OF-1, DH-1
1995			133	.287	.358	480	138	16	3	4	0.8	72	28	38	72	50	0	0	290	6	3	1	2.3	.990	OF-130, DH-2
5 yrs.			238	.278	.344	579	161	18	4	4	0.7	96	32	45	87	59	11	3	350	6	3	1	1.8	.992	OF-193, DH-3

Ray Goolsby

GOOLSBY, RAYMOND DANIEL (Ox)
B. Sept. 5, 1919, Florala, Ala.
BR TR 6′ 1″ 185 lbs.

Year	Team		Games	BA	SA	AB	H	2B	3B	HR	HR%	R	RBI	BB	SO	SB	Pinch Hit AB	Pinch Hit H	PO	A	E	DP	TC/G	FA	G by Pos
1946	WAS	A	3	.000	.000	4	0	0	0	0	0.0	0	0	1	1	0	2	0	1	0	0	0	1.0	1.000	OF-1

Greg Goossen

GOOSSEN, GREGORY BRYANT
B. Dec. 14, 1945, Los Angeles, Calif.
BR TR 6′ 1½″ 210 lbs.

Year	Team		Games	BA	SA	AB	H	2B	3B	HR	HR%	R	RBI	BB	SO	SB	Pinch Hit AB	Pinch Hit H	PO	A	E	DP	TC/G	FA	G by Pos
1965	NY	N	11	.290	.387	31	9	0	0	1	3.2	2	2	1	5	0	2	0	45	1	1	0	5.9	.979	C-8
1966			13	.188	.344	32	6	2	0	1	3.1	1	5	1	11	0	2	0	29	3	0	0	2.9	1.000	C-11
1967			37	.159	.174	69	11	1	0	0	0.0	2	3	4	26	0	20	4	101	7	3	2	4.8	.973	C-23
1968			38	.208	.274	106	22	7	0	0	0.0	4	6	10	21	0	6	0	237	24	3	18	8.3	.989	1B-31, C-1
1969	SEA	A	52	.309	.597	139	43	8	1	10	7.2	19	24	14	29	1	19	2	268	24	2	15	8.9	.993	1B-31, OF-2
1970	2 teams	MIL A (21G –.255) WAS A (21G –.222)																							
″	total		42	.241	.349	83	20	6	0	1	1.2	5	4	12	20	0	19	5	113	8	1	12	5.5	.992	1B-17, OF-5
6 yrs.			193	.241	.383	460	111	24	1	13	2.8	33	44	42	112	1	68	11	793	67	10	47	6.7	.989	1B-79, C-43, OF-7

Glen Gorbous

GORBOUS, GLEN EDWARD
B. July 8, 1930, Drumheller, Alta., Canada D. June 12, 1990, Calgary, Alta., Canada.
BL TR 6′ 2″ 175 lbs.

Year	Team		Games	BA	SA	AB	H	2B	3B	HR	HR%	R	RBI	BB	SO	SB	Pinch Hit AB	Pinch Hit H	PO	A	E	DP	TC/G	FA	G by Pos
1955	2 teams	CIN N (6G –.333) PHI N (91G –.237)																							
″	total		97	.244	.351	242	59	12	1	4	1.7	27	27	24	18	0	37	10	125	10	4	2	2.2	.971	OF-62
1956	PHI	N	15	.182	.182	33	6	0	0	0	0.0	1	1	0	1	0	6	0	8	0	0	0	1.0	1.000	OF-8
1957			3	.500	1.000	2	1	1	0	0	0.0	1	1	1	0	0	2	1	0	0	0	0	0.0	—	
3 yrs.			115	.238	.336	277	66	13	1	4	1.4	29	29	25	19	0	45	11	133	10	4	2	2.1	.973	OF-70

Joe Gordon

GORDON, JOSEPH LOWELL (Flash)
B. Feb. 18, 1915, Los Angeles, Calif. D. Apr. 14, 1978, Sacramento, Calif.
Manager 1958–61, 1969.
BR TR 5′10″ 180 lbs.

Year	Team		Games	BA	SA	AB	H	2B	3B	HR	HR%	R	RBI	BB	SO	SB	Pinch Hit AB	Pinch Hit H	PO	A	E	DP	TC/G	FA	G by Pos
1938	NY	A	127	.255	.502	458	117	24	7	25	5.5	83	97	56	72	11	1	1	290	450	31	98	6.1	.960	2B-126
1939			151	.284	.506	567	161	32	5	28	4.9	92	111	75	57	11	0	0	370	461	28	116	5.7	.967	2B-151
1940			155	.281	.511	616	173	32	10	30	4.9	112	103	52	57	18	0	0	374	505	23	116	5.8	.975	2B-155
1941			156	.276	.466	588	162	26	7	24	4.1	104	87	72	80	10	0	0	556	414	36	144	6.2	.964	2B-131, 1B-30
1942			147	.322	.491	538	173	29	4	18	3.3	88	103	79	**95**	12	0	0	354	442	28	121	5.6	.966	2B-147
1943			152	.249	.413	543	135	28	5	17	3.1	82	69	98	75	4	0	0	407	490	29	114	6.1	.969	2B-152
1946			112	.210	.338	376	79	15	0	11	2.9	35	47	49	72	2	4	0	281	346	17	87	6.0	.974	2B-108
1947	CLE	A	155	.272	.496	562	153	27	6	29	5.2	89	93	62	49	7	0	0	341	466	18	110	5.3	.978	2B-155
1948			144	.280	.507	550	154	21	4	32	5.8	96	124	77	68	5	1	0	332	439	23	98	5.4	.971	2B-144, SS-2
1949			148	.251	.407	541	136	18	3	20	3.7	74	84	83	33	5	3	0	297	430	15	123	5.1	.980	2B-145
1950			119	.236	.429	368	87	12	1	19	5.2	59	57	56	44	4	12	1	224	283	16	69	5.0	.969	2B-105
11 yrs.			1566	.268	.466	5707	1530	264	52	253	4.4	914	975	759	702	89	21	2	3826	4726	264	1196	5.7	.970	2B-1519, 1B-30, SS-2

Joe Gordon *continued*

WORLD SERIES

Year	Team	Games	BA	SA	AB	H	2B	3B	HR	HR%	R	RBI	BB	SO	SB	Pinch Hit AB	Pinch Hit H	PO	A	E	DP	TC/G	FA	G by Pos
1938	NY A	4	.400	.733	15	6	2	0	1	6.7	3	6	1	3	1	0	0	12	12	2	3	6.5	.923	2B-4
1939		4	.143	.143	14	2	0	0	0	0.0	1	1	0	2	0	0	0	7	12	0	4	4.8	1.000	2B-4
1941		5	.500	.929	14	7	1	1	1	7.1	2	5	7	0	0	0	0	6	19	1	5	5.2	.962	2B-5
1942		5	.095	.143	21	2	1	0	0	0.0	1	0	0	7	0	0	0	11	12	0	1	4.6	1.000	2B-5
1943		5	.235	.471	17	4	1	0	1	5.9	2	2	3	3	0	0	0	20	23	0	3	8.6	1.000	2B-5
1948	CLE A	6	.182	.318	22	4	0	0	1	4.5	3	2	1	2	1	0	0	15	13	1	7	4.8	.966	2B-6
6 yrs.		29	.243	.427	103	25	5	1	4	3.9	12	16	12	17	2	0	0	71	91	4	23	5.7	.976	2B-29

Keith Gordon

GORDON, KEITH BRADLEY
B. Jan. 22, 1969, Bethesda, Md.

BR TR 6′ 1″ 200 lbs.

Year	Team	Games	BA	SA	AB	H	2B	3B	HR	HR%	R	RBI	BB	SO	SB	Pinch Hit AB	Pinch Hit H	PO	A	E	DP	TC/G	FA	G by Pos
1993	CIN N	3	.167	.167	6	1	0	0	0	0.0	0	0	0	2	0	1	0	2	0	0	0	1.0	1.000	OF-2

Mike Gordon

GORDON, MICHAEL WILLIAM
B. Sept. 11, 1953, Leominster, Mass.

BB TR 6′ 3″ 215 lbs.

Year	Team	Games	BA	SA	AB	H	2B	3B	HR	HR%	R	RBI	BB	SO	SB	Pinch Hit AB	Pinch Hit H	PO	A	E	DP	TC/G	FA	G by Pos
1977	CHI N	8	.043	.043	23	1	0	0	0	0.0	0	2	2	8	0	0	0	31	1	1	1	4.1	.970	C-8
1978		4	.200	.200	5	1	0	0	0	0.0	0	0	3	2	0	0	0	14	0	0	0	3.5	1.000	C-4
2 yrs.		12	.071	.071	28	2	0	0	0	0.0	0	2	5	10	0	0	0	45	1	1	1	3.9	.979	C-12

Sid Gordon

GORDON, SIDNEY
B. Aug. 13, 1917, Brooklyn, N. Y. D. June 17, 1975, New York, N. Y.

BR TR 5′10″ 185 lbs.

Year	Team	Games	BA	SA	AB	H	2B	3B	HR	HR%	R	RBI	BB	SO	SB	Pinch Hit AB	Pinch Hit H	PO	A	E	DP	TC/G	FA	G by Pos
1941	NY N	9	.258	.355	31	8	1	1	0	0.0	4	4	6	1	0	0	0	18	0	0	0	2.0	1.000	OF-9
1942		6	.316	.421	19	6	0	1	0	0.0	4	2	3	2	0	0	0	9	12	2	0	3.8	.913	3B-6
1943		131	.251	.373	474	119	9	11	9	1.9	50	63	43	32	2	6	1	551	148	17	59	5.7	.976	3B-53, 1B-41, OF-28, 2B-3
1946		135	.293	.378	450	132	15	4	5	1.1	64	45	60	27	1	5	2	215	62	5	3	2.2	.982	OF-101, 3B-30
1947		130	.272	.442	437	119	19	8	13	3.0	57	57	50	21	2	4	1	254	12	12	0	2.2	.957	OF-124, 3B-2
1948		142	.299	.537	521	156	26	4	30	5.8	100	107	74	39	8	5	0	166	223	19	19	3.0	.953	3B-115, OF-23
1949		141	.284	.505	489	139	26	2	26	5.3	87	90	95	37	1	5	0	151	206	14	18	2.7	.962	3B-123, OF-15, 1B-1
1950	BOS N	134	.304	.557	481	146	33	4	27	5.6	78	103	78	31	2	1	0	283	32	4	1	2.4	.987	OF-123, 3B-10
1951		150	.287	.500	550	158	28	1	29	5.3	96	109	80	32	2	0	0	300	75	9	9	2.5	.977	OF-122, 3B-34
1952		144	.289	.483	522	151	22	2	25	4.8	69	75	77	49	0	0	0	266	13	1	0	1.9	.996	OF-142, 3B-2
1953	MIL N	140	.274	.461	464	127	22	4	19	4.1	67	75	71	40	1	3	1	245	10	6	2	1.9	.977	OF-137
1954	PIT N	131	.306	.438	363	111	12	0	12	3.3	38	49	67	24	0	17	3	149	80	11	6	2.1	.954	OF-73, 3B-40
1955	2 teams	PIT N (16G –.170) NY N (66G –.243)																						
″	total	82	.225	.382	191	43	7	1	7	3.7	21	26	27	21	0	21	1	69	82	1	10	2.5	.993	3B-39, OF-21
13 yrs.		1475	.283	.466	4992	1415	220	43	202	4.0	735	805	731	356	19	67	9	2676	955	101	127	2.6	.973	OF-918, 3B-454, 1B-42, 2B-3

George Gore

GORE, GEORGE F.
B. May 3, 1857, Saccarappa, Me. D. Sept. 16, 1933, Utica, N. Y.
Manager 1892.

BL TR 5′11″ 195 lbs.

Year	Team	Games	BA	SA	AB	H	2B	3B	HR	HR%	R	RBI	BB	SO	SB	Pinch Hit AB	Pinch Hit H	PO	A	E	DP	TC/G	FA	G by Pos
1879	CHI N	63	.263	.357	266	70	17	4	0	0.0	43	32	8	30		0	0	201	11	20	3	3.7	.914	OF-54, 1B-9
1880		77	**.360**	**.463**	322	116	23	2	2	0.6	70	47	21	10		0	0	180	18	23	6	2.7	.896	OF-74, 1B-7
1881		73	.298	.424	309	92	18	9	1	0.3	**86**	44	27	23		0	0	154	22	25	4	2.7	.876	OF-72, 3B-1, 1B-1
1882		84	.319	.422	367	117	15	7	3	0.8	**99**	51	**29**	19		0	0	153	23	33	5	2.5	.842	OF-84
1883		92	.334	.472	392	131	30	9	2	0.5	105		27	13		0	0	195	27	34	4	2.8	.867	OF-92
1884		103	.318	.415	422	134	18	4	5	1.2	104		**61**	26		0	0	185	25	32	5	2.3	.868	OF-103
1885		109	.313	.454	441	138	21	13	5	1.1	115	51	68	25		0	0	204	17	29	2	2.3	.884	OF-109
1886		118	.304	.444	444	135	20	12	6	1.4	150	63	**102**	30		0	0	184	20	29	4	2.0	.876	OF-118
1887	NY N	111	.290	.353	459	133	16	5	1	0.2	95	49	42	18	39	0	0	221	20	30	7	2.4	.889	OF-111
1888		64	.220	.291	254	56	4	4	2	0.8	37	17	30	31	11	0	0	88	4	18	0	1.7	.836	OF-64
1889		120	.305	.420	488	149	21	7	7	1.4	132	54	84	28	28	0	0	239	21	41	5	2.5	.864	OF-120
1890	NY P	93	.318	.499	399	127	26	8	10	2.5	132	55	77	23	28	0	0	146	11	22	3	1.9	.877	OF-93
1891	NY N	130	.284	.364	528	150	22	7	2	0.4	103	48	74	34	19	0	0	234	16	25	3	2.1	.909	OF-130
1892	2 teams	NY N (53G –.254) STL N (20G –.205)																						
″	total	73	.241	.305	266	64	11	3	0	0.0	56	15	67	22	22	0	0	137	11	15	2	2.2	.908	OF-73
14 yrs.		1310	.301	.411	5357	1612	262	94	46	0.9	1327	526	717	332	147	0	0	2521	246	376	53	2.4	.880	OF-1297, 1B-17, 3B-1

Bob Gorinski

GORINSKI, ROBERT JOHN
B. Jan. 7, 1952, Latrobe, Pa.

BR TR 6′ 3″ 215 lbs.

Year	Team	Games	BA	SA	AB	H	2B	3B	HR	HR%	R	RBI	BB	SO	SB	Pinch Hit AB	Pinch Hit H	PO	A	E	DP	TC/G	FA	G by Pos
1977	MIN A	54	.195	.322	118	23	4	1	3	2.5	14	22	5	29	1	16	1	44	0	3	0	1.0	.936	OF-37, DH-9

Herb Gorman

GORMAN, HERBERT ALLEN
B. Dec. 18, 1924, San Francisco, Calif. D. Apr. 5, 1953, San Diego, Calif.

BL TL 5′11″ 180 lbs.

Year	Team	Games	BA	SA	AB	H	2B	3B	HR	HR%	R	RBI	BB	SO	SB	Pinch Hit AB	Pinch Hit H	PO	A	E	DP	TC/G	FA	G by Pos
1952	STL N	1	.000	.000	1	0	0	0	0	0.0	0	0	0	0	0	1	0	0	0	0	0	0.0	—	

Howie Gorman

GORMAN, HOWARD PAUL (Lefty)
B. May 14, 1913, Pittsburgh, Pa. D. Apr. 29, 1984, Harrisburg, Pa.

BL TL 6′ 2″ 160 lbs.

Year	Team	Games	BA	SA	AB	H	2B	3B	HR	HR%	R	RBI	BB	SO	SB	Pinch Hit AB	Pinch Hit H	PO	A	E	DP	TC/G	FA	G by Pos
1937	PHI N	13	.211	.263	19	4	1	0	0	0.0	3	1	1	1	1	4	0	1	0	1	0	0.3	.500	OF-7
1938		1	.000	.000	1	0	0	0	0	0.0	0	0	0	0	0	1	0	0	0	0	0	0.0	—	
2 yrs.		14	.200	.250	20	4	1	0	0	0.0	3	1	1	1	1	5	0	1	0	1	0	0.3	.500	OF-7

Jack Gorman

GORMAN, JOHN F. (Stooping Jack)
B. 1859, St. Louis, Mo. D. Sept. 9, 1889, St. Louis, Mo.

Year	Team	Games	BA	SA	AB	H	2B	3B	HR	HR%	R	RBI	BB	SO	SB	Pinch Hit AB	Pinch Hit H	PO	A	E	DP	TC/G	FA	G by Pos
1883	STL AA	1	.000	.000	4	0	0	0	0	0.0	0		0			0	0	1	1	1	0	3.0	.667	OF-1
1884	2 teams	KC U (33G –.277) PIT AA (8G –.148)																						
″	total	41	.256	.323	164	42	5	3	0	0.0	28		5			0	0	286	15	25	8	8.0	.923	1B-24, OF-8, 3B-6, P-3
2 yrs.		42	.250	.315	168	42	5	3	0	0.0	28		5			0	0	287	16	26	8	7.8	.921	1B-24, OF-9, 3B-6, P-3

John Goryl

GORYL, JOHN ALBERT BR TR 5'10" 175 lbs.
B. Oct. 21, 1933, Cumberland, R. I.
Manager 1980–81.

Year	Team	Games	BA	SA	AB	H	2B	3B	HR	HR%	R	RBI	BB	SO	SB	Pinch Hit AB	Pinch Hit H	PO	A	E	DP	TC/G	FA	G by Pos
1957	CHI N	9	.211	.263	38	8	2	0	0	0.0	7	1	5	9	0	0	0	6	14	1	4	2.3	.952	3B-9
1958		83	.242	.365	219	53	9	3	4	1.8	27	14	27	34	0	10	3	91	153	16	26	3.3	.938	3B-44, 2B-35
1959		25	.188	.354	48	9	3	1	1	2.1	1	6	5	3	1	8	1	11	31	1	2	2.9	.977	2B-11, 3B-4
1962	MIN A	37	.192	.500	26	5	0	1	2	7.7	6	2	2	6	0	19	3	2	10	1	1	2.6	.923	2B-4, SS-1
1963		64	.287	.540	150	43	5	3	9	6.0	29	24	15	29	0	12	2	75	92	7	18	3.3	.960	2B-34, 3B-11, SS-7
1964		58	.140	.175	114	16	0	2	0	0.0	9	1	10	25	1	22	4	73	70	3	9	3.6	.979	2B-28, 3B-13
6 yrs.		276	.225	.371	595	134	19	10	16	2.7	79	48	64	106	2	71	13	258	370	29	60	3.3	.956	2B-112, 3B-81, SS-8

Jim Gosger

GOSGER, JAMES CHARLES BL TL 5'11" 185 lbs.
B. Nov. 6, 1942, Port Huron, Mich.

Year	Team	Games	BA	SA	AB	H	2B	3B	HR	HR%	R	RBI	BB	SO	SB	Pinch Hit AB	Pinch Hit H	PO	A	E	DP	TC/G	FA	G by Pos
1963	BOS A	19	.063	.063	16	1	0	0	0	0.0	3	0	3	5	0	6	1	9	0	2	0	2.8	.818	OF-4
1965		81	.256	.410	324	83	15	4	9	2.8	45	35	29	61	3	0	0	195	4	5	2	2.5	.975	OF-81
1966	2 teams	BOS A (40G –.254) KC A (88G –.224)																224	3	2	0	2.1	.991	OF-109
"	total	128	.234	.359	398	93	18	1	10	2.5	50	44	52	73	5	23	6	201	6	4	1	1.9	.981	OF-113
1967	KC A	134	.242	.351	356	86	14	5	5	1.4	31	36	53	69	5	26	7	99	5	0	3	1.6	1.000	OF-64
1968	OAK A	88	.180	.200	150	27	1	1	0	0.0	7	5	17	21	4	18	3							
1969	2 teams	SEA A (39G –.109) NY N (10G –.133)																41	1	0	0	1.4	1.000	OF-31
"	total	49	.114	.243	70	8	4	1	1	1.4	4	2	7	17	2	15	1	252	12	3	15	3.0	.989	OF-71, 1B-19
1970	MON N	91	.263	.372	274	72	11	2	5	1.8	38	37	35	35	5	10	1	79	5	2	2	3.0	.977	OF-23, 1B-6
1971		51	.157	.216	102	16	2	2	0	0.0	7	8	9	17	1	23	3	45	0	0	0	1.3	1.000	OF-35
1973	NY N	38	.239	.261	92	22	2	0	0	0.0	9	10	9	16	0	4	0	17	0	0	0	0.7	1.000	OF-24
1974		26	.091	.091	33	3	0	0	0	0.0	3	0	3	2	0	2	0							
10 yrs.		705	.226	.331	1815	411	67	16	30	1.7	197	177	217	316	25	127	22	1162	36	18	23	2.1	.985	OF-555, 1B-25

Goose Goslin

GOSLIN, LEON ALLEN BL TR 5'11½" 185 lbs.
B. Oct. 16, 1900, Salem, N. J. D. May 15, 1971, Bridgeton, N. J.
Hall of Fame 1968.

Year	Team	Games	BA	SA	AB	H	2B	3B	HR	HR%	R	RBI	BB	SO	SB	Pinch Hit AB	Pinch Hit H	PO	A	E	DP	TC/G	FA	G by Pos
1921	WAS A	14	.260	.380	50	13	1	1	1	2.0	8	6	6	5	0	0	0	30	1	0	0	2.2	1.000	OF-14
1922		101	.324	.441	358	116	19	7	3	0.8	44	53	25	26	4	5	0	197	8	15	1	2.4	.932	OF-93
1923		150	.300	.453	600	180	29	**18**	9	1.5	86	99	40	53	7	1	1	310	26	15	5	2.4	.957	OF-149
1924		154	.344	.516	579	199	30	17	12	2.1	100	**129**	68	29	16	0	0	369	12	16	4	2.6	.960	OF-154
1925		150	.334	.547	601	201	34	**20**	18	3.0	116	113	53	50	26	0	0	385	24	12	1	2.8	.971	OF-150
1926		147	.354	.543	567	201	26	15	17	3.0	105	108	63	38	8	0	0	373	25	15	8	2.8	.964	OF-147
1927		148	.334	.516	581	194	37	15	13	2.2	96	120	50	28	21	0	0	356	8	17	3	2.6	.955	OF-148
1928		135	**.379**	.614	456	173	36	10	17	3.7	80	102	48	19	16	7	2	266	14	11	4	2.3	.962	OF-125
1929		145	.288	.461	553	159	28	7	18	3.3	82	91	66	33	10	3	3	299	7	10	1	2.2	.968	OF-142
1930	2 teams	WAS A (47G –.271) STL A (101G –.326)																						
"	total	148	.308	.601	584	180	36	12	37	6.3	115	138	67	54	17	0	0	309	15	12	1	2.3	.964	OF-148
1931	STL A	151	.328	.555	591	194	42	10	24	4.1	114	105	80	41	9	0	0	319	14	14	1	2.3	.960	OF-151
1932		150	.299	.469	572	171	28	9	17	3.0	88	104	92	35	12	0	0	331	19	18	5	2.5	.951	OF-149, 3B-1
1933	WAS A	132	.297	.452	549	163	35	10	10	1.8	97	64	42	32	5	4	2	261	17	10	7	2.3	.965	OF-128
1934	DET A	151	.305	.453	614	187	38	7	13	2.1	106	100	65	38	5	2	0	290	15	15	2	2.1	.953	OF-149
1935		147	.292	.415	590	172	34	6	9	1.5	88	109	56	31	5	3	1	326	6	12	2	2.4	.965	OF-144
1936		147	.315	.526	572	180	33	8	24	4.2	122	125	85	50	14	3	0	266	11	13	1	2.0	.955	OF-144
1937		79	.238	.376	181	43	11	1	4	2.2	30	35	35	18	0	29	**9**	93	3	5	1	2.5	.950	OF-40, 1B-1
1938	WAS A	38	.158	.316	57	9	3	0	2	3.5	6	8	8	5	0	18	4	25	0	0	0	1.9	1.000	OF-13
18 yrs.		2287	.316	.500	8655	2735	500	173	248	2.9	1483	1609	949	585	175	75	22	4805	225	210	47	2.4	.960	OF-2188, 1B-1, 3B-1
WORLD SERIES																								
1924	WAS A	7	.344	.656	32	11	1	0	3	9.4	4	7	0	7	0	0	0	15	1	0	0	2.3	1.000	OF-7
1925		7	.308	.692	26	8	1	0	3	11.5	6	5	3	3	1	0	0	15	0	0	0	2.1	1.000	OF-7
1933		5	.250	.450	20	5	1	0	1	5.0	2	1	1	3	0	0	0	8	1	0	0	1.8	1.000	OF-5
1934	DET A	7	.241	.276	29	7	1	0	0	0.0	2	2	3	1	0	0	0	20	1	2	0	3.3	.913	OF-7
1935		6	.273	.318	22	6	1	0	0	0.0	2	3	5	0	0	0	0	12	0	1	0	2.2	.923	OF-6
5 yrs.		32	.287	.488	129	37	5	0	7 **10th**	5.4	16	18	12	14	1	0	0	70	3	3	0	2.4	.961	OF-32

Howie Goss

GOSS, HOWARD WAYNE BR TR 6'4" 204 lbs.
B. Nov. 1, 1934, Wewoka, Okla.

Year	Team	Games	BA	SA	AB	H	2B	3B	HR	HR%	R	RBI	BB	SO	SB	Pinch Hit AB	Pinch Hit H	PO	A	E	DP	TC/G	FA	G by Pos
1962	PIT N	89	.243	.351	111	27	6	0	2	1.8	19	10	9	36	5	8	2	62	2	1	1	1.0	.985	OF-66
1963	HOU N	133	.209	.328	411	86	18	2	9	2.2	37	44	31	128	4	15	2	276	7	2	2	2.3	.993	OF-123
2 yrs.		222	.216	.333	522	113	24	2	11	2.1	56	54	40	164	9	23	4	338	9	3	3	1.9	.991	OF-189

Dick Gossett

GOSSETT, JOHN STAR BR TR 5'11" 185 lbs.
B. Aug. 21, 1891, Denison, Ohio D. Oct. 6, 1962, Massillon, Ohio.

Year	Team	Games	BA	SA	AB	H	2B	3B	HR	HR%	R	RBI	BB	SO	SB	Pinch Hit AB	Pinch Hit H	PO	A	E	DP	TC/G	FA	G by Pos
1913	NY A	39	.162	.181	105	17	2	0	0	0.0	9	9	10	22	1	1	1	123	50	6	2	4.7	.966	C-38
1914		9	.143	.143	21	3	0	0	0	0.0	3	1	5	5	0	0	0	37	6	1	0	4.9	.977	C-9
2 yrs.		48	.159	.175	126	20	2	0	0	0.0	12	10	15	27	1	1	1	160	56	7	2	4.7	.969	C-47

Julio Gotay

GOTAY, JULIO ENRIQUE BR TR 6' 180 lbs.
Born Julio Enrique Gotay (Sanchez).
B. June 9, 1939, Fajardo, Puerto Rico.

Year	Team	Games	BA	SA	AB	H	2B	3B	HR	HR%	R	RBI	BB	SO	SB	Pinch Hit AB	Pinch Hit H	PO	A	E	DP	TC/G	FA	G by Pos
1960	STL N	3	.375	.375	8	3	0	0	0	0.0	1	0	0	2	1	1	1	1	3	1	0	1.7	.800	SS-2, 3B-1
1961		10	.244	.333	45	11	4	0	0	0.0	5	5	3	5	0	0	0	16	25	10	6	5.1	.804	SS-10
1962		127	.255	.309	369	94	12	1	2	0.5	47	27	27	47	7	1	0	190	360	25	70	4.4	.957	SS-120, 2B-8, OF-2, 3B-1
1963	PIT N	4	.500	.500	2	1	0	0	0	0.0	0	0	0	0	0	1	1	2	0	1	0	3.0	.667	2B-1
1964		3	.500	.500	2	1	0	0	0	0.0	1	0	1	0	0	2	1	0	0	0	0	0.0	—	
1965	CAL A	40	.247	.338	77	19	4	0	1	1.3	6	3	4	9	0	8	2	34	63	3	9	3.0	.970	2B-23, 3B-9, SS-1
1966	HOU N	4	.000	.000	5	0	0	0	0	0.0	0	0	0	0	0	3	0	1	1	0	0	2.0	1.000	3B-1
1967		77	.282	.368	234	66	10	2	2	0.9	30	15	15	30	1	19	6	93	143	8	27	4.6	.967	2B-30, SS-20, 3B-3
1968		75	.248	.285	165	41	3	0	1	0.6	9	11	4	21	1	25	8	116	103	4	28	4.6	.982	2B-48, 3B-1
1969		46	.259	.321	81	21	5	0	0	0.0	7	9	7	13	2	30	6	34	41	1	12	4.5	.987	2B-16, 3B-1
10 yrs.		389	.260	.323	988	257	38	3	6	0.6	106	70	61	127	12	90	25	487	739	53	152	4.3	.959	SS-153, 2B-126, 3B-17, OF-2

Charlie Gould

GOULD, CHARLES HARVEY
B. Aug. 21, 1847, Cincinnati, Ohio D. Apr. 10, 1917, Flushing, N. Y.
Manager 1876.
BR TR 6' 172 lbs.

Year	Team	Games	BA	SA	AB	H	2B	3B	HR	HR%	R	RBI	BB	SO	SB	Pinch Hit AB	Pinch Hit H	PO	A	E	DP	TC/G	FA	G by Pos
1876	CIN N	61	.252	.279	258	65	7	0	0	0.0	27	11	6	11		0	0	584	14	40	28	10.1	.937	1B-61, P-2
1877		24	.275	.319	91	25	2	1	0	0.0	5	13	5	5		0	0	231	9	20	13	10.4	.923	1B-24, OF-1
2 yrs.		85	.258	.289	349	90	9	1	0	0.0	32	24	11	16		0	0	815	23	60	41	10.2	.933	1B-85, P-2, OF-1

Nick Goulish

GOULISH, NICHOLAS EDWARD
B. Nov. 13, 1917, Punxsutawney, Pa. D. May 15, 1984, Youngstown, Ohio.
BL TL 6' 1" 179 lbs.

Year	Team	Games	BA	SA	AB	H	2B	3B	HR	HR%	R	RBI	BB	SO	SB	Pinch Hit AB	Pinch Hit H	PO	A	E	DP	TC/G	FA	G by Pos
1944	PHI N	1	.000	.000	1	0	0	0	0	0.0	0	0	0	0	0	1	0	0	0	0	0	0.0	—	
1945		13	.273	.273	11	3	0	0	0	0.0	4	2	1	3	0	9	2	1	0	0	0	0.5	1.000	OF-2
2 yrs.		14	.250	.250	12	3	0	0	0	0.0	4	2	1	3	0	10	2	1	0	0	0	0.5	1.000	OF-2

Claude Gouzzie

GOUZZIE, CLAUDE
B. 1873, France D. Sept. 21, 1907, Denver, Colo.
BR TR 5' 9" 170 lbs.

Year	Team	Games	BA	SA	AB	H	2B	3B	HR	HR%	R	RBI	BB	SO	SB	Pinch Hit AB	Pinch Hit H	PO	A	E	DP	TC/G	FA	G by Pos
1903	STL A	1	.000	.000	1	0	0	0	0	0.0	0	0	0		0	0	0	0	1	0	0	1.0	1.000	2B-1

Hank Gowdy

GOWDY, HENRY MORGAN
B. Aug. 24, 1889, Columbus, Ohio D. Aug. 1, 1966, Columbus, Ohio.
Manager 1946.
BR TR 6' 2" 182 lbs.

Year	Team	Games	BA	SA	AB	H	2B	3B	HR	HR%	R	RBI	BB	SO	SB	Pinch Hit AB	Pinch Hit H	PO	A	E	DP	TC/G	FA	G by Pos
1910	NY N	7	.214	.286	14	3	1	0	0	0.0	1	2	2	3	1	2	0	30	3	2	1	7.0	.943	1B-5
1911	2 teams	NY N (4G –.250)	BOS N (29G –.289)																					
"	total	33	.287	.376	101	29	5	2	0	0.0	10	16	6	19	2	3	0	273	15	9	9	10.2	.970	1B-28, C-1
1912	BOS N	44	.271	.448	96	26	6	1	3	3.1	16	10	16	13	3	14	3	138	34	9	7	6.2	.950	C-22, 1B-7
1913		3	.600	.800	5	3	1	0	0	0.0	0	2	3	2	0	0	0	9	0	0	0	4.5	1.000	C-2
1914		128	.243	.347	366	89	17	6	3	0.8	42	46	48	40	14	3	1	534	156	22	16	5.7	.969	C-115, 1B-9
1915		118	.247	.332	316	78	15	3	2	0.6	27	30	41	34	10	1	1	460	148	16	11	5.3	.974	C-118
1916		118	.252	.301	349	88	12	1	1	0.3	32	34	24	33	8	2	0	533	158	14	19	6.1	.980	C-116
1917		49	.214	.260	154	33	7	0	0	0.0	12	14	15	13	2	0	0	204	75	9	3	5.9	.969	C-49
1919		78	.279	.338	219	61	8	1	1	0.5	18	22	19	16	5	2	0	240	105	8	11	4.7	.977	C-74, 1B-1
1920		80	.243	.313	214	52	11	2	0	0.0	14	18	20	15	6	5	2	231	104	7	12	4.6	.980	C-74
1921		64	.299	.402	164	49	7	2	2	1.2	17	17	16	11	2	8	3	162	50	4	3	4.1	.981	C-53
1922		92	.317	.389	221	70	11	1	1	0.5	23	27	24	13	2	17	5	210	63	8	7	3.8	.972	C-72, 1B-1
1923	2 teams	BOS N (23G –.125)	NY N (53G –.328)																					
"	total	76	.271	.376	170	46	7	4	1	0.6	18	23	36	14	3	12	3	164	30	3	1	3.4	.985	C-58
1924	NY N	87	.325	.445	191	62	9	1	4	2.1	25	37	26	11	1	9	4	223	51	5	8	3.6	.982	C-78
1925		47	.325	.491	114	37	4	3	3	2.6	14	19	12	7	0	6	3	124	26	0	1	3.7	1.000	C-41
1929	BOS N	10	.438	.438	16	7	0	0	0	0.0	1	3	0	2	0	1	0	11	2	0	1	1.4	1.000	C-9
1930		16	.200	.240	25	5	1	0	0	0.0	0	2	3	1	0	0	0	31	4	1	0	2.4	.972	C-15
17 yrs.		1050	.270	.357	2735	738	122	27	21	0.8	270	322	311	247	59	85	25	3577	1024	117	110	5.0	.975	C-897, 1B-51
WORLD SERIES																								
1914	BOS N	4	.545	1.273	11	6	3	1	1	9.1	3	3	5	1	1	0	0	31	4	0	1	8.8	1.000	C-4
1923	NY N	3	.000	.000	4	0	0	0	0	0.0	0	0	1	0	0	1	0	7	0	0	0	3.5	1.000	C-2
1924		7	.259	.259	27	7	0	0	0	0.0	4	1	2	2	0	0	0	37	5	1	0	6.1	.977	C-7
3 yrs.		14	.310	.500	42	13	3	1	1	2.4	7	4	8	3	1	1	0	75	9	1	1	6.5	.988	C-13

Billy Grabarkewitz

GRABARKEWITZ, BILLY CORDELL
B. Jan. 18, 1946, Lockhart, Tex.
BR TR 5'10" 165 lbs.

Year	Team	Games	BA	SA	AB	H	2B	3B	HR	HR%	R	RBI	BB	SO	SB	Pinch Hit AB	Pinch Hit H	PO	A	E	DP	TC/G	FA	G by Pos
1969	LA N	34	.092	.138	65	6	1	1	0	0.0	4	5	4	19	1	3	0	20	51	3	4	2.7	.959	SS-18, 3B-6, 2B-3
1970		156	.289	.454	529	153	20	8	17	3.2	92	84	95	149	19	2	1	178	367	21	45	3.4	.963	3B-97, SS-50, 2B-20
1971		44	.225	.296	71	16	5	0	0	0.0	9	6	19	16	1	11	3	33	52	0	10	3.5	1.000	2B-13, 3B-10, SS-1
1972		53	.167	.278	144	24	4	0	4	2.8	17	16	18	53	3	5	1	61	84	11	14	3.5	.929	3B-24, 2B-19, SS-2
1973	2 teams	CAL A (61G –.163)	PHI N (25G –.288)																					
"	total	86	.205	.333	195	40	8	1	5	2.6	39	16	40	45	5	16	6	93	110	9	30	3.9	.958	2B-38, 3B-14, OF-2, SS-1
1974	2 teams	PHI N (34G –.133)	CHI N (53G –.248)																					
"	total	87	.226	.310	155	35	3	2	2	1.3	28	14	26	38	4	14	2	83	122	8	10	3.3	.962	2B-45, SS-7, 3B-7, OF-5
1975	OAK A	6	.000	.000	2	0	0	0	0	0.0	0	0	0	1	0	2	0	4	1	1	0	1.2	.833	2B-4, DH-1
7 yrs.		466	.236	.364	1161	274	41	12	28	2.4	189	141	202	321	33	53	13	472	787	53	113	3.4	.960	3B-158, 2B-142, SS-79, OF-7, DH-1

Rod Graber

GRABER, RODNEY BLAINE
B. June 20, 1931, Massillon, Ohio.
BL TL 5'11" 175 lbs.

Year	Team	Games	BA	SA	AB	H	2B	3B	HR	HR%	R	RBI	BB	SO	SB	Pinch Hit AB	Pinch Hit H	PO	A	E	DP	TC/G	FA	G by Pos
1958	CLE A	4	.125	.125	8	1	0	0	0	0.0	0	0	1	2	0	2	0	4	0	0	0	2.0	1.000	OF-2

Johnny Grabowski

GRABOWSKI, JOHN PATRICK (Nig)
B. Jan. 7, 1900, Ware, Mass. D. May 23, 1946, Albany, N. Y.
BR TR 5'10" 185 lbs.

Year	Team	Games	BA	SA	AB	H	2B	3B	HR	HR%	R	RBI	BB	SO	SB	Pinch Hit AB	Pinch Hit H	PO	A	E	DP	TC/G	FA	G by Pos
1924	CHI A	20	.250	.304	56	14	3	0	0	0.0	10	3	2	4	0	0	0	48	22	2	0	3.8	.972	C-19
1925		21	.304	.435	46	14	4	1	0	0.0	5	10	2	4	0	0	0	48	9	1	0	2.8	.983	C-21
1926		48	.262	.311	122	32	1	1	1	0.8	6	11	4	15	0	8	4	128	22	4	0	3.9	.974	C-38, 1B-1
1927	NY A	70	.277	.328	195	54	2	4	0	0.0	29	25	20	15	0	2	0	197	47	4	3	3.6	.984	C-68
1928		75	.238	.297	202	48	7	1	1	0.5	21	21	10	21	0	0	0	265	32	4	8	4.0	.987	C-75
1929		22	.203	.220	59	12	1	0	0	0.0	4	2	3	6	1	0	0	70	12	5	1	4.0	.943	C-22
1931	DET A	40	.235	.324	136	32	7	1	1	0.7	9	14	6	19	0	1	1	160	28	3	5	4.9	.984	C-39
7 yrs.		296	.252	.314	816	206	25	8	3	0.4	84	86	47	84	1	11	5	916	172	23	17	3.9	.979	C-282, 1B-1
WORLD SERIES																								
1927	NY A	1	.000	.000	2	0	0	0	0	0.0	0	0	0	0	0	0	0	3	0	0	0	3.0	1.000	C-1

Earl Grace

GRACE, ROBERT EARL
B. Feb. 24, 1907, Barlow, Ky. D. Dec. 22, 1980, Phoenix, Ariz.
BL TR 6' 175 lbs.

Year	Team	Games	BA	SA	AB	H	2B	3B	HR	HR%	R	RBI	BB	SO	SB	Pinch Hit AB	Pinch Hit H	PO	A	E	DP	TC/G	FA	G by Pos
1929	CHI N	27	.250	.338	80	20	1	0	2	2.5	7	17	9	7	0	0	0	106	18	0	1	4.6	1.000	C-27
1931	2 teams	CHI N (7G –.111)	PIT N (47G –.280)																					
"	total	54	.270	.340	159	43	6	1	1	0.6	10	21	17	6	0	6	0	137	24	4	5	3.5	.976	C-47
1932	PIT N	115	.274	.397	390	107	17	5	7	1.8	41	55	14	23	0	1	0	364	48	1	10	3.6	.998	C-114
1933		93	.289	.371	291	84	13	1	3	1.0	22	44	26	23	0	4	0	305	37	7	7	4.0	.980	C-88
1934		95	.270	.377	289	78	17	1	4	1.4	27	24	20	19	0	10	5	312	27	6	5	4.1	.983	C-83, 1B-1

Earl Grace *continued*

Year	Team	Games	BA	SA	AB	H	2B	3B	HR	HR%	R	RBI	BB	SO	SB	Pinch Hit AB	Pinch Hit H	PO	A	E	DP	TC/G	FA	G by Pos
1935		77	.263	.348	224	59	8	1	3	1.3	19	29	32	17	1	8	3	269	35	3	9	4.4	.990	C-69
1936	PHI N	86	.249	.353	221	55	11	0	4	1.8	24	32	34	20	0	19	2	217	29	6	3	3.9	.976	C-65
1937		80	.211	.345	223	47	10	1	6	2.7	19	29	33	15	0	13	0	275	30	3	10	4.8	.990	C-64
8 yrs.		627	.263	.365	1877	493	83	10	30	1.6	169	251	185	130	1	61	10	1985	248	30	50	4.1	.987	C-557, 1B-1

Joe Grace

GRACE, JOSEPH LaVERNE BL TR 6′ 1″ 180 lbs.
B. Jan. 5, 1914, Gorham, Ill. D. Sept. 18, 1969, Murphysboro, Ill.

Year	Team	Games	BA	SA	AB	H	2B	3B	HR	HR%	R	RBI	BB	SO	SB	Pinch Hit AB	Pinch Hit H	PO	A	E	DP	TC/G	FA	G by Pos
1938	STL A	12	.340	.362	47	16	1	0	0	0.0	7	4	2	3	0	0	0	13	1	1	0	1.3	.933	OF-12
1939		74	.304	.420	207	63	11	2	3	1.4	35	22	19	24	3	15	5	83	9	3	0	1.8	.968	OF-53
1940		80	.258	.402	229	59	14	2	5	2.2	45	25	26	23	2	17	4	102	7	4	1	1.8	.965	OF-51, C-12
1941		115	.309	.428	362	112	17	4	6	1.7	53	60	57	31	1	15	6	184	15	5	1	2.1	.975	OF-88, C-9
1946	2 teams	STL A (48G –.230) WAS A (77G –.302)																						
″	total	125	.278	.371	482	134	24	6	3	0.6	60	44	40	39	2	7	2	267	10	11	3	2.5	.962	OF-117
1947	WAS A	78	.248	.359	234	58	9	4	3	1.3	25	17	35	15	1	10	2	162	4	4	0	2.5	.976	OF-67
6 yrs.		484	.283	.393	1561	442	76	18	20	1.3	225	172	179	135	9	64	19	811	46	28	5	2.2	.968	OF-388, C-21

Mark Grace

GRACE, MARK EUGENE BL TL 6′ 2″ 190 lbs.
B. June 28, 1964, Winston-Salem, N. C.

Year	Team	Games	BA	SA	AB	H	2B	3B	HR	HR%	R	RBI	BB	SO	SB	Pinch Hit AB	Pinch Hit H	PO	A	E	DP	TC/G	FA	G by Pos
1988	CHI N	134	.296	.403	486	144	23	4	7	1.4	65	57	60	43	3	7	3	1182	87	17	91	9.7	.987	1B-133
1989		142	.314	.457	510	160	28	3	13	2.5	74	79	80	42	14	1	1	1230	126	6	93	9.6	.996	1B-142
1990		157	.309	.413	589	182	32	1	9	1.5	72	82	59	54	15	7	2	1324	180	12	116	9.9	.992	1B-153
1991		160	.273	.373	**619**	169	28	5	8	1.3	87	58	70	53	3	4	0	1520	167	8	106	10.6	.995	1B-160
1992		158	.307	.430	603	185	37	5	9	1.5	72	79	72	36	6	1	0	1580	141	4	119	11.0	.998	1B-157
1993		155	.325	.475	594	193	39	4	14	2.4	86	98	71	32	8	1	0	1456	112	5	134	10.2	.997	1B-154
1994		106	.298	.414	403	120	23	3	6	1.5	55	44	48	41	0	5	2	925	76	7	90	9.8	.993	1B-103
1995		143	.326	.516	552	180	**51**	3	16	2.9	97	92	65	46	6	0	0	1211	115	7	91	9.3	.995	1B-143
8 yrs.		1155	.306	.435	4356	1333	261	28	82	1.9	608	589	525	347	55	26	8	10428	1004	66	840	10.0	.994	1B-1145
LEAGUE CHAMPIONSHIP SERIES																								
1989	CHI N	5	.647	1.118	17	11	3	1	1	5.9	3	8	4	1	1	0	0	44	3	0	1	9.4	1.000	1B-5

Mike Grace

GRACE, MICHAEL LEE BR TR 6′ 175 lbs.
B. June 14, 1956, Pontiac, Mich.

Year	Team	Games	BA	SA	AB	H	2B	3B	HR	HR%	R	RBI	BB	SO	SB	Pinch Hit AB	Pinch Hit H	PO	A	E	DP	TC/G	FA	G by Pos
1978	CIN N	5	.000	.000	3	0	0	0	0	0.0	0	0	0	2	0	3	0	0	2	0	0	1.0	1.000	3B-2

John Grady

GRADY, JOHN J. 5′ 7″ 150 lbs.
B. June 18, 1860, Lowell, Mass. D. July 15, 1893, Lowell, Mass.

Year	Team	Games	BA	SA	AB	H	2B	3B	HR	HR%	R	RBI	BB	SO	SB	Pinch Hit AB	Pinch Hit H	PO	A	E	DP	TC/G	FA	G by Pos
1884	ALT U	9	.306	.389	36	11	3	0	0	0.0	5		2			0	0	87	3	10	1	11.1	.900	1B-8, OF-1

Mike Grady

GRADY, MICHAEL WILLIAM (Michaelangelo) BR TR 5′11″ 190 lbs.
B. Dec. 23, 1869, Kennett Square, Pa. D. Dec. 3, 1943, Kennett Square, Pa.

Year	Team	Games	BA	SA	AB	H	2B	3B	HR	HR%	R	RBI	BB	SO	SB	Pinch Hit AB	Pinch Hit H	PO	A	E	DP	TC/G	FA	G by Pos
1894	PHI N	60	.363	.516	190	69	13	8	0	0.0	45	40	14	13	3	3	**2**	175	33	23	11	4.1	.900	C-44, 1B-11, OF-2
1895		46	.325	.390	123	40	3	1	1	0.8	21	23	14	8	5	2	1	109	11	12	2	2.9	.909	C-38, OF-5, 3B-1, 1B-1
1896		72	.318	.471	242	77	20	7	1	0.4	49	44	16	19	10	4	0	173	68	20	12	3.8	.923	C-61, 3B-7
1897	2 teams	PHI N (4G –.154) STL N (83G –.280)																						
″	total	87	.275	.388	335	92	11	3	7	**2.1**	49	55	27		7	1	0	809	52	23	54	10.2	.974	1B-83, C-3, OF-1
1898	NY N	93	.296	.429	287	85	19	5	3	1.0	64	49	38		20	2	0	321	74	34	7	4.4	.921	C-57, OF-30, 1B-7, SS-3
1899		86	.334	.463	311	104	18	8	2	0.6	47	54	29		20	1	1	183	140	29	15	4.1	.918	C-43, 3B-35, OF-4, 1B-4
1900		83	.219	.283	251	55	8	4	0	0.0	36	27	34		9	6	2	247	106	37	18	5.0	.905	C-41, 1B-12, SS-11, 3B-7, OF-5, 2B-2
1901	WAS A	94	.285	.470	347	99	17	10	9	**2.6**	57	56	27		14	2	0	688	83	26	38	8.7	.967	1B-59, C-30, OF-3
1904	STL N	101	.313	.474	323	101	15	11	5	1.5	44	43	31		6	7	1	421	93	20	11	5.8	.963	C-77, 1B-11, 2B-3, 3B-1
1905		100	.286	.434	311	89	20	7	4	1.3	41	41	33		15	9	2	468	96	26	12	6.5	.956	C-71, 1B-20
1906		97	.250	.343	280	70	11	3	3	1.1	33	27	48		5	5	1	414	85	11	16	5.2	.978	C-60, 1B-38
11 yrs.		919	.294	.425	3000	881	155	67	35	1.2	486	459	311	40	114	42	10	4008	841	261	196	5.7	.949	C-525, 1B-246, 3B-51, OF-50, SS-14, 2B-5

Fred Graff

GRAFF, FREDERICK GOTTLIEB BR TR 5′10½″ 164 lbs.
B. Aug. 25, 1889, Canton, Ohio D. Oct. 4, 1979, Chattanooga, Tenn.

Year	Team	Games	BA	SA	AB	H	2B	3B	HR	HR%	R	RBI	BB	SO	SB	Pinch Hit AB	Pinch Hit H	PO	A	E	DP	TC/G	FA	G by Pos
1913	STL A	4	.400	.600	5	2	1	0	0	0.0	1	2	3	3	0	0	0	0	4	0	1	1.0	1.000	3B-4

Louis Graff

GRAFF, LOUIS GEORGE (Chappie) TR
B. July 25, 1866, Philadelphia, Pa. D. Apr. 16, 1955, Bryn Mawr, Pa.

Year	Team	Games	BA	SA	AB	H	2B	3B	HR	HR%	R	RBI	BB	SO	SB	Pinch Hit AB	Pinch Hit H	PO	A	E	DP	TC/G	FA	G by Pos
1890	SYR AA	1	.400	.600	5	2	1	0	0	0.0	0		0		0	0	0	1	0	2	0	3.0	.333	C-1

Milt Graff

GRAFF, MILTON EDWARD BL TR 5′ 7½″ 158 lbs.
B. Dec. 30, 1930, Jefferson Center, Pa.

Year	Team	Games	BA	SA	AB	H	2B	3B	HR	HR%	R	RBI	BB	SO	SB	Pinch Hit AB	Pinch Hit H	PO	A	E	DP	TC/G	FA	G by Pos
1957	KC A	56	.181	.245	155	28	4	3	0	0.0	16	10	15	10	2	1	1	110	127	3	36	4.5	.988	2B-53
1958		5	.000	.000	1	0	0	0	0	0.0	0	0	0	0	0	1	0	1	0	0	0	1.0	1.000	2B-1
2 yrs.		61	.179	.244	156	28	4	3	0	0.0	16	10	15	10	2	2	1	111	127	3	36	4.5	.988	2B-54

Barney Graham

GRAHAM, BARNEY
B. Philadelphia, Pa. D. Dec. 31, 1896, Mobile, Ala.

Year	Team	Games	BA	SA	AB	H	2B	3B	HR	HR%	R	RBI	BB	SO	SB	Pinch Hit AB	Pinch Hit H	PO	A	E	DP	TC/G	FA	G by Pos
1889	PHI AA	4	.167	.167	18	3	0	0	0	0.0	0	0	0	0	0	0	0	2	12	1	1	3.8	.933	3B-4

Bernie Graham

GRAHAM, BERNARD W. BL
B. 1860, Beloit, Wis. D. Oct. 31, 1886, Mobile, Ala.

Year	Team	Games	BA	SA	AB	H	2B	3B	HR	HR%	R	RBI	BB	SO	SB	Pinch Hit AB	Pinch Hit H	PO	A	E	DP	TC/G	FA	G by Pos
1884	2 teams	CHI U (1G –.200) BAL U (41G –.269)																						
″	total	42	.267	.331	172	46	11	0	0	0.0	23		2			0	0	75	10	17	3	2.4	.833	OF-41, 1B-1

Bert Graham

GRAHAM, BERT BB TR 5′11½″ 187 lbs.
B. Apr. 3, 1886, Tilton, Ill. D. June 19, 1971, Cottonwood, Ariz.

Year	Team	Games	BA	SA	AB	H	2B	3B	HR	HR%	R	RBI	BB	SO	SB	Pinch Hit AB	Pinch Hit H	PO	A	E	DP	TC/G	FA	G by Pos
1910	STL A	8	.115	.269	26	3	2	1	0	0.0	1	5	1		0	1	0	51	11	4	3	9.4	.939	1B-5, 2B-2

Charlie Graham

GRAHAM, CHARLES HENRY BR TR 5′11″ 180 lbs.
B. Apr. 25, 1878, Santa Clara, Calif. D. Aug. 29, 1948, San Francisco, Calif.

Year	Team	Games	BA	SA	AB	H	2B	3B	HR	HR%	R	RBI	BB	SO	SB	Pinch Hit AB	Pinch Hit H	PO	A	E	DP	TC/G	FA	G by Pos
1906	BOS A	30	.233	.278	90	21	1	0	1	1.1	10	12	10		1	3	0	130	54	7	2	7.1	.963	C-27

Dan Graham

GRAHAM, DANIEL JAY BL TR 6′ 1″ 205 lbs.
B. July 19, 1954, Ray, Ariz.

Year	Team	Games	BA	SA	AB	H	2B	3B	HR	HR%	R	RBI	BB	SO	SB	Pinch Hit AB	Pinch Hit H	PO	A	E	DP	TC/G	FA	G by Pos
1979	MIN A	2	.000	.000	4	0	0	0	0	0.0	0	0	0	0	0	1	0	0	0	0	0	0.0	.000	DH-1
1980	BAL A	86	.278	.481	266	74	7	1	15	5.6	32	54	14	40	0	1	0	333	42	7	5	4.5	.982	C-73, 3B-9, DH-2
1981		55	.176	.239	142	25	3	0	2	1.4	7	11	13	32	0	8	0	141	24	5	2	3.4	.971	C-40, DH-6, 3B-4
3 yrs.		143	.240	.393	412	99	10	1	17	4.1	39	65	27	72	0	10	0	474	66	12	7	4.1	.978	C-113, 3B-13, DH-9

Jack Graham

GRAHAM, JOHN BERNARD BL TL 6′ 2″ 200 lbs.
Son of Peaches Graham.
B. Dec. 24, 1916, Minneapolis, Minn.

Year	Team	Games	BA	SA	AB	H	2B	3B	HR	HR%	R	RBI	BB	SO	SB	Pinch Hit AB	Pinch Hit H	PO	A	E	DP	TC/G	FA	G by Pos
1946	2 teams BKN N (2G –.200) NY N (100G –.219)																							
″	total	102	.218	.422	275	60	6	4	14	5.1	34	47	23	37	1	25	4	181	12	6	0	2.8	.970	OF-62, 1B-9
1949	STL A	137	.238	.430	500	119	22	1	24	4.8	71	79	61	62	0	1	1	1118	87	19	120	9.0	.984	1B-136
2 yrs.		239	.231	.427	775	179	28	5	38	4.9	105	126	84	99	1	26	5	1299	99	25	120	6.9	.982	1B-145, OF-62

Lee Graham

GRAHAM, LEE WILLARD BL TL 5′10″ 170 lbs.
B. Sept. 22, 1959, Summerfield, Fla.

Year	Team	Games	BA	SA	AB	H	2B	3B	HR	HR%	R	RBI	BB	SO	SB	Pinch Hit AB	Pinch Hit H	PO	A	E	DP	TC/G	FA	G by Pos
1983	BOS A	5	.000	.000	6	0	0	0	0	0.0	2	1	0	0	0	0	0	6	1	0	0	2.3	1.000	OF-3

Moonlight Graham

GRAHAM, ARCHIBALD WRIGHT BL TR 5′10½″ 170 lbs.
B. Nov. 9, 1876, Fayetteville, N. C. D. Aug. 25, 1965, Chisholm, Minn.

Year	Team	Games	BA	SA	AB	H	2B	3B	HR	HR%	R	RBI	BB	SO	SB	Pinch Hit AB	Pinch Hit H	PO	A	E	DP	TC/G	FA	G by Pos
1905	NY N	1	—	—	0	0	0	0	0	—	0	0	0		0	0	0	0	0	0	0	0.0	.000	OF-1

Peaches Graham

GRAHAM, GEORGE FREDERICK BR TR 5′ 9″ 180 lbs.
Father of Jack Graham.
B. Mar. 23, 1877, Aledo, Ill. D. July 25, 1939, Long Beach, Calif.

Year	Team	Games	BA	SA	AB	H	2B	3B	HR	HR%	R	RBI	BB	SO	SB	Pinch Hit AB	Pinch Hit H	PO	A	E	DP	TC/G	FA	G by Pos
1902	CLE A	2	.333	.333	6	2	0	0	0	0.0	0	1	1		0	1	0	2	5	0	0	7.0	1.000	2B-1
1903	CHI N	1	.000	.000	2	0	0	0	0	0.0	0	0	0		0	0	0	0	3	0	0	3.0	1.000	P-1
1908	BOS N	75	.274	.298	215	59	5	0	0	0.0	22	22	23		4	8	2	249	86	17	6	5.3	.952	C-62, 2B-5
1909		92	.240	.285	267	64	6	3	0	0.0	27	17	24		7	10	1	200	119	23	15	4.1	.933	C-76, OF-6, 3B-1, SS-1
1910		110	.282	.340	291	82	13	2	0	0.0	31	21	33	15	5	20	7	322	135	17	11	5.2	.964	C-87, 3B-2, 1B-1, OF-1
1911	2 teams BOS N (33G –.273) CHI N (36G –.239)																							
″	total	69	.258	.327	159	41	9	1	0	0.0	13	20	25	13	4	13	3	182	56	16	7	4.7	.937	C-54
1912	PHI N	24	.288	.356	59	17	1	0	1	1.7	6	4	8	5	1	2	2	77	25	6	0	5.7	.944	C-19
7 yrs.		373	.265	.314	999	265	34	6	1	0.1	99	85	114	33	21	54	15	1032	429	79	39	4.9	.949	C-298, OF-7, 2B-6, 3B-3, SS-1, 1B-1, P-1

Roy Graham

GRAHAM, ROY VINCENT BR TR 5′10½″ 175 lbs.
B. Feb. 22, 1895, San Francisco, Calif. D. Apr. 26, 1933, Manila, Philippines.

Year	Team	Games	BA	SA	AB	H	2B	3B	HR	HR%	R	RBI	BB	SO	SB	Pinch Hit AB	Pinch Hit H	PO	A	E	DP	TC/G	FA	G by Pos
1922	CHI A	5	.000	.000	3	0	0	0	0	0.0	0	0	0	0	0	1	0	3	0	0	0	1.0	1.000	C-3
1923		36	.195	.220	82	16	2	0	0	0.0	3	6	9	6	0	2	0	78	15	5	1	3.0	.949	C-33
2 yrs.		41	.188	.212	85	16	2	0	0	0.0	3	6	9	6	0	3	0	81	15	5	1	2.8	.950	C-36

Skinny Graham

GRAHAM, ARTHUR WILLIAM BL TR 5′ 7″ 181 lbs.
B. Aug. 12, 1909, Somerville, Mass. D. July 10, 1967, Cambridge, Mass.

Year	Team	Games	BA	SA	AB	H	2B	3B	HR	HR%	R	RBI	BB	SO	SB	Pinch Hit AB	Pinch Hit H	PO	A	E	DP	TC/G	FA	G by Pos
1934	BOS A	13	.234	.319	47	11	2	1	0	0.0	7	3	6	13	2	0	0	20	1	0	0	1.6	1.000	OF-13
1935		8	.300	.300	10	3	0	0	0	0.0	1	1	1	3	1	3	1	2	0	0	0	1.0	1.000	OF-2
2 yrs.		21	.246	.316	57	14	2	1	0	0.0	8	4	7	16	3	3	1	22	1	0	0	1.5	1.000	OF-15

Tiny Graham

GRAHAM, DAWSON FRANCIS BR TR 6′ 2″ 185 lbs.
B. Sept. 9, 1892, Nashville, Tenn. D. Dec. 29, 1962, Nashville, Tenn.

Year	Team	Games	BA	SA	AB	H	2B	3B	HR	HR%	R	RBI	BB	SO	SB	Pinch Hit AB	Pinch Hit H	PO	A	E	DP	TC/G	FA	G by Pos
1914	CIN N	25	.230	.246	61	14	1	0	0	0.0	5	3	3	10	1	0	0	187	9	8	14	8.2	.961	1B-25

Wayne Graham

GRAHAM, WAYNE LEON BR TR 6′ 200 lbs.
B. Apr. 6, 1937, Yoakum, Tex.

Year	Team	Games	BA	SA	AB	H	2B	3B	HR	HR%	R	RBI	BB	SO	SB	Pinch Hit AB	Pinch Hit H	PO	A	E	DP	TC/G	FA	G by Pos
1963	PHI N	10	.182	.182	22	4	0	0	0	0.0	1	0	3	1	0	3	0	6	0	1	0	1.2	.857	OF-6
1964	NY N	20	.091	.121	33	3	1	0	0	0.0	1	0	0	5	0	12	1	4	7	0	0	1.0	1.000	3B-11
2 yrs.		30	.127	.145	55	7	1	0	0	0.0	2	0	3	6	0	15	1	10	7	1	0	1.1	.944	3B-11, OF-6

Alex Grammas

GRAMMAS, ALEXANDER PETER BR TR 6′ 175 lbs.
B. Apr. 3, 1926, Birmingham, Ala.
Manager 1969, 1976–77.

Year	Team	Games	BA	SA	AB	H	2B	3B	HR	HR%	R	RBI	BB	SO	SB	Pinch Hit AB	Pinch Hit H	PO	A	E	DP	TC/G	FA	G by Pos
1954	STL N	142	.264	.342	401	106	17	4	2	0.5	57	29	40	29	6	0	0	253	432	24	100	5.0	.966	SS-142, 3B-1
1955		128	.240	.328	366	88	19	2	3	0.8	32	25	33	36	4	1	0	235	340	19	76	4.7	.968	SS-126
1956	2 teams STL N (6G –.250) CIN N (77G –.243)																							
″	total	83	.243	.316	152	37	11	0	0	0.0	18	17	17	20	0	2	1	60	105	5	12	2.1	.971	3B-58, SS-17, 2B-5
1957	CIN N	73	.303	.343	99	30	4	0	0	0.0	14	8	10	6	1	2	0	60	75	3	10	1.9	.978	SS-42, 2B-20, 3B-9
1958		105	.218	.255	216	47	8	0	0	0.0	25	12	34	24	2	1	0	126	174	6	32	2.7	.980	SS-61, 3B-38, 2B-14
1959	STL N	131	.269	.342	368	99	14	2	3	0.8	43	30	38	26	3	1	1	216	373	22	80	4.7	.964	SS-130
1960		102	.245	.337	196	48	4	1	4	2.0	20	17	12	15	0	7	2	102	171	9	33	3.1	.968	SS-40, 2B-38, 3B-13
1961		89	.212	.282	170	36	10	1	0	0.0	23	21	19	21	0	5	1	112	182	10	40	3.5	.967	SS-65, 2B-18, 3B-3
1962	2 teams STL N (21G –.111) CHI N (23G –.233)																							
″	total	44	.205	.244	78	16	3	0	0	0.0	3	4	3	13	1	4	0	34	66	2	14	2.9	.980	SS-29, 2B-5, 3B-1
1963	CHI N	16	.185	.185	27	5	0	0	0	0.0	1	0	0	3	0	3	0	8	13	1	1	1.7	.955	SS-13
10 yrs.		913	.247	.317	2073	512	90	10	12	0.6	236	163	206	193	17	26	5	1206	1931	101	398	3.6	.969	SS-665, 3B-123, 2B-100

Jack Graney

GRANEY, JOHN GLADSTONE BL TL 5′ 9″ 180 lbs.
B. June 10, 1886, St. Thomas, Ont., Canada D. Apr. 20, 1978, Louisiana, Mo.

Year	Team	Games	BA	SA	AB	H	2B	3B	HR	HR%	R	RBI	BB	SO	SB	Pinch Hit AB	Pinch Hit H	PO	A	E	DP	TC/G	FA	G by Pos
1908	CLE A	2	—	—	0	0	0	0	0	—	0	0	0		0	0	0	0	0	0	0	0.0	.000	P-2
1910		116	.236	.311	454	107	13	9	1	0.2	62	31	37		18	2	1	209	14	12	5	2.1	.949	OF-114
1911		146	.269	.342	527	142	25	5	1	0.2	84	45	66		21	4	2	258	22	22	5	2.1	.927	OF-142
1912		78	.242	.307	264	64	13	2	0	0.0	44	20	50		9	3	0	148	11	7	5	2.2	.958	OF-75
1913		148	.267	.366	517	138	18	12	3	0.6	56	68	48	55	27	0	0	275	16	9	5	2.0	.970	OF-148

Jack Graney *continued*

Year	Team	Games	BA	SA	AB	H	2B	3B	HR	HR%	R	RBI	BB	SO	SB	Pinch Hit AB	Pinch Hit H	PO	A	E	DP	TC/G	FA	G by Pos
1914		130	.265	.352	460	122	17	10	1	0.2	63	39	67	46	20	3	2	274	15	20	0	2.4	.935	OF-127
1915		116	.260	.351	404	105	20	7	1	0.2	42	56	59	29	12	1	0	227	17	7	1	2.2	.972	OF-115
1916		155	.241	.384	589	142	**41**	14	5	0.8	106	54	102	72	10	1	1	309	22	14	5	2.2	.959	OF-154
1917		146	.228	.325	535	122	29	7	3	0.6	87	35	**94**	49	16	1	0	288	14	13	6	2.2	.959	OF-145
1918		72	.237	.322	177	42	7	4	0	0.0	27	9	29	13	3	18	**7**	77	2	2	0	1.8	.975	OF-45
1919		128	.234	.323	461	108	22	8	1	0.2	79	30	**105**	39	7	1	1	281	13	12	2	2.4	.961	OF-125
1920		62	.296	.382	152	45	11	1	0	0.0	31	13	27	21	4	12	6	76	4	5	0	1.8	.941	OF-47
1921		68	.299	.383	107	32	3	0	2	1.9	19	18	20	9	1	27	8	42	0	3	0	1.4	.933	OF-32
1922		37	.155	.155	58	9	0	0	0	0.0	6	2	9	12	0	19	1	24	1	4	0	2.2	.862	OF-13
14 yrs.		1404	.250	.342	4705	1178	219	79	18	0.4	706	420	713	345	148	92	29	2488	151	130	34	2.2	.953	OF-1282, P-2
WORLD SERIES																								
1920	CLE A	3	.000	.000	3	0	0	0	0	0.0	0	0	0	2	0	3	0	0	0	0	0	0.0	.000	OF-2

Eddie Grant

GRANT, EDWARD LESLIE (Harvard Eddie) BL TR 5′11½″ 168 lbs.
B. May 21, 1883, Franklin, Mass. D. Oct. 5, 1918, Argonne, France.

Year	Team	Games	BA	SA	AB	H	2B	3B	HR	HR%	R	RBI	BB	SO	SB	Pinch Hit AB	Pinch Hit H	PO	A	E	DP	TC/G	FA	G by Pos
1905	CLE A	2	.375	.375	8	3	0	0	0	0.0	1	0	0		0	0	0	1	4	1	0	3.0	.833	2B-2
1907	PHI N	74	.243	.280	268	65	4	3	0	0.0	26	19	10		10	0	0	106	145	23	6	3.7	.916	3B-74
1908		147	.244	.293	**598**	146	13	8	0	0.0	69	32	35		27	0	0	228	310	42	24	3.9	.928	3B-134, SS-13
1909		154	.269	.315	**631**	170	18	4	1	0.2	75	37	35		28	0	0	184	310	22	18	3.4	.957	3B-154
1910		152	.268	.316	579	155	15	5	1	0.2	70	67	39	54	25	0	0	193	256	31	22	3.2	.935	3B-152
1911	CIN N	136	.223	.286	458	102	12	7	1	0.2	49	53	51	47	28	0	0	178	234	27	23	3.3	.938	3B-122, SS-11
1912		96	.239	.294	255	61	6	1	2	0.8	37	20	18	27	11	5	1	119	192	18	22	4.6	.945	SS-56, 3B-15
1913	2 teams	CIN N (27G –.213) NY N (27G –.200)																						
"	total	54	.211	.228	114	24	2	0	0	0.0	20	10	13	12	8	5	1	27	59	6	5	2.6	.935	3B-31, 2B-3, SS-1
1914	NY N	88	.277	.309	282	78	7	1	0	0.0	34	29	23	21	11	2	0	97	191	23	16	3.5	.926	3B-52, SS-21, 2B-16
1915		57	.208	.229	192	40	2	1	0	0.0	18	10	9	20	5	32	7	54	79	4	3	2.1	.971	3B-55, 2B-9, SS-1, 1B-1
10 yrs.		960	.249	.295	3385	844	79	30	5	0.1	399	277	233	181	153	44	9	1187	1780	197	139	3.4	.938	3B-789, SS-103, 2B-30, 1B-1
WORLD SERIES																								
1913	NY N	2	.000	.000	1	0	0	0	0	0.0	1	0	0	0	0	1	0	0	0	0	0	0.0	—	

Jimmy Grant

GRANT, JAMES CHARLES BL TR 5′ 8″ 166 lbs.
B. Oct. 6, 1918, Racine, Wis. D. July 8, 1970, Rochester, Minn.

Year	Team	Games	BA	SA	AB	H	2B	3B	HR	HR%	R	RBI	BB	SO	SB	Pinch Hit AB	Pinch Hit H	PO	A	E	DP	TC/G	FA	G by Pos
1942	CHI A	12	.167	.250	36	6	1	1	0	0.0	0	1	5	6	0	1	0	15	19	2	3	3.6	.944	3B-10
1943	2 teams	CHI A (58G –.259) CLE A (15G –.136)																						
"	total	73	.247	.370	219	54	11	2	4	1.8	26	23	22	41	4	19	2	46	128	20	11	3.5	.897	3B-56
1944	CLE A	61	.273	.404	99	27	4	3	1	1.0	12	12	11	20	1	**32**	5	44	51	7	6	4.3	.931	2B-20, 3B-4
3 yrs.		146	.246	.367	354	87	16	6	5	1.4	38	36	38	67	5	52	7	105	198	29	20	3.7	.913	3B-70, 2B-20

Tom Grant

GRANT, THOMAS RAYMOND BL TR 6′ 2″ 185 lbs.
B. May 28, 1957, Worcester, Mass.

Year	Team	Games	BA	SA	AB	H	2B	3B	HR	HR%	R	RBI	BB	SO	SB	Pinch Hit AB	Pinch Hit H	PO	A	E	DP	TC/G	FA	G by Pos
1983	CHI N	16	.150	.200	20	3	1	0	0	0.0	2	2	3	4	0	5	0	6	1	0	0	0.7	1.000	OF-10

George Grantham

GRANTHAM, GEORGE FARLEY (Boots) BL TR 5′10″ 170 lbs.
B. May 20, 1900, Galena, Kans. D. Mar. 16, 1954, Kingman, Ariz.

Year	Team	Games	BA	SA	AB	H	2B	3B	HR	HR%	R	RBI	BB	SO	SB	Pinch Hit AB	Pinch Hit H	PO	A	E	DP	TC/G	FA	G by Pos
1922	CHI N	7	.174	.304	23	4	1	1	0	0.0	3	3	1	3	2	1	0	5	4	0	1	1.8	1.000	3B-5
1923		152	.281	.414	570	160	36	8	8	1.4	81	70	71	**92**	43	2	0	374	518	55	90	6.3	.942	2B-150
1924		127	.316	.458	469	148	19	6	12	2.6	85	60	55	**63**	21	2	0	277	442	48	78	6.2	.937	2B-118, 3B-6
1925	PIT N	114	.326	.493	359	117	24	6	8	2.2	74	52	50	29	14	9	1	925	44	11	96	9.6	.989	1B-102
1926		141	.318	.490	449	143	27	13	8	1.8	66	70	60	42	6	6	2	1203	66	13	106	9.7	.990	1B-132
1927		151	.305	.454	531	162	33	11	8	1.5	96	66	74	39	9	0	0	526	375	35	87	6.1	.963	2B-124, 1B-29
1928		124	.323	.486	440	142	24	9	10	2.3	93	85	59	37	9	4	0	1118	73	17	84	10.0	.986	1B-119, 3B-1, 2B-1
1929		110	.307	.533	349	107	23	10	12	3.4	85	90	93	38	10	5	0	301	244	17	60	5.3	.970	2B-76, OF-19, 1B-12
1930		146	.324	.534	552	179	34	14	18	3.3	120	99	81	66	5	1	0	357	492	36	88	6.1	.959	2B-141, 1B-4
1931		127	.305	.452	465	142	26	6	10	2.2	91	46	71	50	5	4	0	856	169	35	101	8.2	.967	1B-78, 2B-51
1932	CIN N	126	.292	.412	493	144	29	6	6	1.2	81	39	56	40	4	0	0	373	352	28	52	6.0	.963	2B-115, 1B-10
1933		87	.204	.327	260	53	14	3	4	1.5	32	28	38	21	4	7	2	274	196	19	42	5.5	.961	2B-72, 1B-17
1934	NY N	32	.241	.414	29	7	2	0	1	3.4	5	4	8	6	0	21	6	22	2	0	1	4.0	1.000	1B-4, 3B-2
13 yrs.		1444	.302	.461	4989	1508	292	93	105	2.1	912	712	717	526	132	62	11	6611	2977	314	886	7.1	.968	2B-848, 1B-507, OF-19, 3B-14
WORLD SERIES																								
1925	PIT N	5	.133	.133	15	2	0	0	0	0.0	0	0	0	3	1	1	0	42	6	0	3	12.0	1.000	1B-4
1927		3	.364	.455	11	4	1	0	0	0.0	0	0	1	1	0	0	0	6	7	1	1	4.7	.929	2B-3
2 yrs.		8	.231	.269	26	6	1	0	0	0.0	0	0	1	4	1	1	0	48	13	1	4	8.9	.984	1B-4, 2B-3

Mickey Grasso

GRASSO, NEWTON MICHAEL BR TR 6′ 195 lbs.
B. May 10, 1920, Newark, N. J. D. Oct. 15, 1975, Miami, Fla.

Year	Team	Games	BA	SA	AB	H	2B	3B	HR	HR%	R	RBI	BB	SO	SB	Pinch Hit AB	Pinch Hit H	PO	A	E	DP	TC/G	FA	G by Pos
1946	NY N	7	.136	.136	22	3	0	0	0	0.0	1	1	0	3	0	0	0	24	5	1	0	4.3	.967	C-7
1950	WAS A	75	.287	.333	195	56	4	1	1	0.5	25	22	25	31	1	6	1	238	38	17	6	4.2	.942	C-69
1951		52	.206	.240	175	36	3	0	1	0.6	16	14	14	17	0	4	0	182	26	7	6	4.4	.967	C-49
1952		115	.216	.241	361	78	9	0	0	0.0	22	27	29	36	1	1	0	485	64	17	4	5.0	.970	C-114
1953		61	.209	.276	196	41	7	0	2	1.0	13	22	9	20	0	2	0	219	24	4	4	4.2	.984	C-59
1954	CLE A	4	.333	.833	6	2	0	0	1	16.7	1	1	1	1	0	0	0	9	1	2	0	3.0	.833	C-4
1955	NY N	8	.000	.000	2	0	0	0	0	0.0	0	0	3	0	0	0	0	9	0	1	0	1.3	.900	C-8
7 yrs.		322	.226	.268	957	216	23	1	5	0.5	78	87	81	108	2	13	1	1166	158	49	20	4.4	.964	C-310
WORLD SERIES																								
1954	CLE A	1	—	—	0	0	0	0	0	—	0	0	0	0	0	0	0	1	0	0	0	1.0	1.000	C-1

Lew Graulich

GRAULICH, LEWIS
B. Camden, N. J. Deceased.

Year	Team	Games	BA	SA	AB	H	2B	3B	HR	HR%	R	RBI	BB	SO	SB	Pinch Hit AB	Pinch Hit H	PO	A	E	DP	TC/G	FA	G by Pos
1891	PHI N	7	.308	.308	26	8	0	0	0	0.0	2	3	1	2	0	0	0	47	3	9	1	8.4	.847	C-4, 1B-3

Frank Graves

GRAVES, FRANK M.
B. Nov. 2, 1860, Cincinnati, Ohio Deceased.
6′ 163 lbs.

Year	Team	Lg	Games	BA	SA	AB	H	2B	3B	HR	HR%	R	RBI	BB	SO	SB	Pinch Hit AB	Pinch Hit H	PO	A	E	DP	TC/G	FA	G by Pos
1886	STL	N	43	.152	.167	138	21	2	0	0	0.0	7	9	7	48		0	0	227	77	41	3	7.7	.881	C-41, OF-3, P-1

Joe Graves

GRAVES, JOSEPH EBENEZER
Brother of Sid Graves.
B. Feb. 26, 1906, Marblehead, Mass. D. Dec. 22, 1980, Salem, Mass.
BL TR 5′10″ 160 lbs.

Year	Team	Lg	Games	BA	SA	AB	H	2B	3B	HR	HR%	R	RBI	BB	SO	SB	Pinch Hit AB	Pinch Hit H	PO	A	E	DP	TC/G	FA	G by Pos
1926	CHI	N	2	.000	.000	5	0	0	0	0	0.0	0	0	0	1	0	0	0	0	1	3	1	2.0	.250	3B-2

Sid Graves

GRAVES, SAMUEL SIDNEY (Whitey)
Brother of Joe Graves.
B. Nov. 30, 1901, Marblehead, Mass. D. Dec. 26, 1983, Biddeford, Me.
BR TR 6′ 170 lbs.

Year	Team	Lg	Games	BA	SA	AB	H	2B	3B	HR	HR%	R	RBI	BB	SO	SB	Pinch Hit AB	Pinch Hit H	PO	A	E	DP	TC/G	FA	G by Pos
1927	BOS	N	7	.250	.400	20	5	1	1	0	0.0	5	2	0	1	1	1	0	10	2	2	0	2.8	.857	OF-5

Dick Gray

GRAY, RICHARD BENJAMIN
B. July 11, 1931, Jefferson, Pa.
BR TR 5′11″ 165 lbs.

Year	Team	Lg	Games	BA	SA	AB	H	2B	3B	HR	HR%	R	RBI	BB	SO	SB	Pinch Hit AB	Pinch Hit H	PO	A	E	DP	TC/G	FA	G by Pos
1958	LA	N	58	.249	.472	197	49	5	6	9	4.6	25	30	19	30	1	4	2	56	139	15	18	3.8	.929	3B-55
1959	2 teams		LA N (21G –.154) STL N (36G –.314)																						
″	total		57	.233	.340	103	24	2	0	3	2.9	17	10	12	20	3	25	5	16	37	3	5	1.7	.946	3B-17, SS-13, 2B-2, OF-1
1960	STL	N	9	.000	.000	5	0	0	0	0	0.0	1	1	2	2	0	3	0	2	5	0	2	1.4	1.000	2B-4, 3B-1
3 yrs.			124	.239	.420	305	73	7	6	12	3.9	43	41	33	52	4	32	7	74	181	18	25	2.9	.934	3B-73, SS-13, 2B-6, OF-1

Gary Gray

GRAY, GARY GEORGE
B. Sept. 21, 1952, New Orleans, La.
BR TR 6′ 187 lbs.

Year	Team	Lg	Games	BA	SA	AB	H	2B	3B	HR	HR%	R	RBI	BB	SO	SB	Pinch Hit AB	Pinch Hit H	PO	A	E	DP	TC/G	FA	G by Pos
1977	TEX	A	1	.000	.000	2	0	0	0	0	0.0	0	0	0	1	0	0	0	0	0	0	0	0.0	.000	OF-1
1978			17	.240	.380	50	12	1	0	2	4.0	4	6	1	12	1	5	1	0	0	0	0	0.0	.000	DH-11
1979			16	.238	.238	42	10	0	0	0	0.0	4	1	2	8	1	5	2	0	0	0	0	0.0	.000	DH-13
1980	CLE	A	28	.148	.278	54	8	1	0	2	3.7	4	4	3	13	0	12	1	16	2	0	1	0.9	1.000	DH-9, OF-6, 1B-6
1981	SEA	A	69	.245	.476	208	51	7	1	13	6.3	27	31	4	44	2	19	5	281	16	2	34	5.6	.993	1B-34, DH-15, OF-4
1982			80	.257	.401	269	69	14	2	7	2.6	26	29	24	59	1	7	2	476	31	8	36	7.0	.984	1B-60, DH-14
6 yrs.			211	.240	.402	625	150	23	3	24	3.8	65	71	34	137	5	48	11	773	49	10	71	4.8	.988	1B-100, DH-62, OF-11

Jim Gray

GRAY, JAMES W.
B. Aug. 7, 1862, Pittsburgh, Pa. D. Jan. 31, 1938, Pittsburgh, Pa.
TR

Year	Team	Lg	Games	BA	SA	AB	H	2B	3B	HR	HR%	R	RBI	BB	SO	SB	Pinch Hit AB	Pinch Hit H	PO	A	E	DP	TC/G	FA	G by Pos
1884	PIT	AA	1	.500	.500	2	1	0	0	0	0.0	0		0			0	0	0	2	2	0	4.0	.500	3B-1

Lorenzo Gray

GRAY, LORENZO
B. Mar. 4, 1958, Mound Bayou, Miss.
BR TR 6′ 1″ 180 lbs.

Year	Team	Lg	Games	BA	SA	AB	H	2B	3B	HR	HR%	R	RBI	BB	SO	SB	Pinch Hit AB	Pinch Hit H	PO	A	E	DP	TC/G	FA	G by Pos
1982	CHI	A	17	.286	.321	28	8	1	0	0	0.0	4	0	2	4	1	1	0	9	10	3	2	1.4	.864	3B-16
1983			41	.179	.256	78	14	3	0	1	1.3	18	4	8	16	1	3	1	17	46	4	3	1.8	.940	3B-31, DH-7
2 yrs.			58	.208	.274	106	22	4	0	1	0.9	22	4	10	20	2	4	1	26	56	7	5	1.6	.921	3B-47, DH-7

Milt Gray

GRAY, MILTON MARSHALL
B. Feb. 21, 1914, Louisville, Ky. D. June 30, 1969, Quincy, Fla.
BR TR 6′ 1″ 170 lbs.

Year	Team	Lg	Games	BA	SA	AB	H	2B	3B	HR	HR%	R	RBI	BB	SO	SB	Pinch Hit AB	Pinch Hit H	PO	A	E	DP	TC/G	FA	G by Pos
1937	WAS	A	2	.000	.000	6	0	0	0	0	0.0	0	0	0	1	0	0	0	10	0	0	0	5.0	1.000	C-2

Pete Gray

GRAY, PETER
Born Peter J. Wyshner.
B. Mar. 6, 1915, Nanticoke, Pa.
BL TL 6′ 1″ 169 lbs.

Year	Team	Lg	Games	BA	SA	AB	H	2B	3B	HR	HR%	R	RBI	BB	SO	SB	Pinch Hit AB	Pinch Hit H	PO	A	E	DP	TC/G	FA	G by Pos
1945	STL	A	77	.218	.261	234	51	6	2	0	0.0	26	13	13	11	5	12	1	162	3	7	1	2.8	.959	OF-61

Reddy Gray

GRAY, JAMES D.
Deceased.
TR

Year	Team	Lg	Games	BA	SA	AB	H	2B	3B	HR	HR%	R	RBI	BB	SO	SB	Pinch Hit AB	Pinch Hit H	PO	A	E	DP	TC/G	FA	G by Pos
1890	2 teams		PIT P (2G –.222) PIT N (1G –.000)																						
″	total		3	.167	.417	12	2	0	0	1	8.3	3	3	0	3	0	0	0	10	7	6	1	7.7	.739	2B-2, SS-1
1893	PIT	N	2	.444	.556	9	4	1	0	0	0.0	0	2	0	1	0	0	0	3	1	1	0	2.5	.800	SS-2
2 yrs.			5	.286	.476	21	6	1	0	1	4.8	3	5	0	4	0	0	0	13	8	7	1	5.6	.750	SS-3, 2B-2

Stan Gray

GRAY, STANLEY OSCAR (Dolly)
B. Dec. 10, 1888, Ladonia, Tex. D. Oct. 11, 1964, Snyder, Tex.
BR TR 6′ 1½″ 184 lbs.

Year	Team	Lg	Games	BA	SA	AB	H	2B	3B	HR	HR%	R	RBI	BB	SO	SB	Pinch Hit AB	Pinch Hit H	PO	A	E	DP	TC/G	FA	G by Pos
1912	PIT	N	6	.250	.350	20	5	0	1	0	0.0	4	2	0	3	0	1	0	39	0	0	2	9.8	1.000	1B-4

Craig Grebeck

GREBECK, CRAIG ALLEN
B. Dec. 29, 1964, Johnstown, Pa.
BR TR 5′ 8″ 160 lbs.

Year	Team	Lg	Games	BA	SA	AB	H	2B	3B	HR	HR%	R	RBI	BB	SO	SB	Pinch Hit AB	Pinch Hit H	PO	A	E	DP	TC/G	FA	G by Pos
1990	CHI	A	59	.168	.235	119	20	3	1	1	0.8	7	9	8	24	0	4	1	36	98	3	10	2.4	.978	3B-35, SS-16, 2B-6, DH-1
1991			107	.281	.460	224	63	16	3	6	2.7	37	31	38	40	1	14	3	104	183	10	34	2.7	.966	3B-49, 2B-36, SS-26
1992			88	.268	.387	287	77	21	2	3	1.0	24	35	30	34	0	0	0	112	283	8	47	4.3	.980	SS-85, 3B-7, OF-2
1993			72	.226	.268	190	43	5	0	1	0.5	25	12	26	26	1	3	0	91	185	5	40	3.7	.982	SS-46, 2B-16, 3B-14
1994			35	.309	.361	97	30	5	0	0	0.0	17	5	12	5	0	1	0	44	65	2	13	3.2	.982	2B-14, SS-14, 3B-7
1995			53	.260	.357	154	40	12	0	1	0.6	19	18	21	23	0	2	2	77	127	7	25	3.7	.967	SS-31, 3B-18, 2B-8
6 yrs.			414	.255	.358	1071	273	62	6	12	1.1	129	110	135	152	2	24	6	464	941	35	169	3.3	.976	SS-218, 3B-130, 2B-80, OF-2, DH-1
LEAGUE CHAMPIONSHIP SERIES																									
1993	CHI	A	1	1.000	1.000	1	1	0	0	0	0.0	0	0	0	0	0	1	1	0	0	0	0	0.0	.000	3B-1

Danny Green

GREEN, EDWARD
B. Nov. 6, 1876, Burlington, N. J. D. Nov. 9, 1914, Camden, N. J.
BL TR

Year	Team	Lg	Games	BA	SA	AB	H	2B	3B	HR	HR%	R	RBI	BB	SO	SB	Pinch Hit AB	Pinch Hit H	PO	A	E	DP	TC/G	FA	G by Pos
1898	CHI	N	47	.314	.431	188	59	4	3	4	2.1	26	27	7		12	0	0	87	10	3	5	2.1	.970	OF-47
1899			117	.295	.404	475	140	12	11	6	1.3	90	56	35		18	2	0	175	22	11	11	1.8	.947	OF-115
1900			103	.298	.416	389	116	21	5	5	1.3	63	49	17		28	2	1	218	10	15	2	2.4	.938	OF-101
1901			133	.313	.421	537	168	16	12	6	1.1	82	60	40		31	0	0	312	17	24	7	2.7	.932	OF-133
1902	CHI	A	129	.312	.391	481	150	16	11	0	0.0	77	62	53		35	0	0	217	11	14	4	1.9	.942	OF-129

Danny Green *continued*

Year	Team	Lg	Games	BA	SA	AB	H	2B	3B	HR	HR%	R	RBI	BB	SO	SB	Pinch Hit AB	Pinch Hit H	PO	A	E	DP	TC/G	FA	G by Pos
1903			135	.309	.425	499	154	26	7	6	1.2	75	62	47		29	2	1	219	16	17	8	1.9	.933	OF-133
1904			147	.265	.343	536	142	16	10	2	0.4	83	62	63		28	1	0	231	13	9	5	1.7	.964	OF-146
1905			112	.243	.309	379	92	13	6	0	0.0	56	44	53		11	5	0	119	9	12	3	1.3	.914	OF-107
8 yrs.			923	.293	.391	3484	1021	124	65	29	0.8	552	422	315		192	12	2	1578	108	105	45	2.0	.941	OF-911

David Green

GREEN, DAVID ALEJANDRO — BR TR 6′ 3″ 170 lbs.
Born David Alejandro Green (Casaya).
B. Dec. 4, 1960, Managua, Nicaragua.

Year	Team	Lg	Games	BA	SA	AB	H	2B	3B	HR	HR%	R	RBI	BB	SO	SB	Pinch Hit AB	Pinch Hit H	PO	A	E	DP	TC/G	FA	G by Pos
1981	STL	N	21	.147	.176	34	5	1	0	0	0.0	6	2	6	5	0	2	0	31	1	1	0	1.8	.970	OF-18
1982			76	.283	.373	166	47	7	1	2	1.2	21	23	8	29	11	12	4	111	4	1	1	1.7	.991	OF-68
1983			146	.284	.422	422	120	14	10	8	1.9	52	69	26	76	34	20	6	214	10	7	2	1.7	.970	OF-136
1984			126	.268	.416	452	121	14	4	15	3.3	49	65	20	105	17	5	1	1103	70	10	99	9.0	.992	1B-117, OF-14
1985	SF	N	106	.248	.347	294	73	10	2	5	1.7	36	20	22	58	6	11	1	645	42	10	54	7.7	.986	1B-78, OF-12
1987	STL	N	14	.267	.500	30	8	2	1	1	3.3	4	1	2	5	0	5	0	18	1	2	1	1.6	.905	OF-10, 1B-3
6 yrs.			489	.268	.394	1398	374	48	18	31	2.2	168	180	84	278	68	55	12	2122	128	31	157	5.0	.986	OF-258, 1B-198
LEAGUE CHAMPIONSHIP SERIES																									
1982	STL	N	2	1.000	1.000	1	1	0	0	0	0.0	1	0	0	0	0	0	0	0	0	0	0	0.0	.000	OF-2
WORLD SERIES																									
1982	STL	N	7	.200	.500	10	2	1	1	0	0.0	3	0	1	3	0	1	0	4	0	0	0	0.6	1.000	OF-4, DH-3

Dick Green

GREEN, RICHARD LARRY — BR TR 5′10″ 180 lbs.
B. Apr. 21, 1941, Sioux City, Iowa.

Year	Team	Lg	Games	BA	SA	AB	H	2B	3B	HR	HR%	R	RBI	BB	SO	SB	Pinch Hit AB	Pinch Hit H	PO	A	E	DP	TC/G	FA	G by Pos
1963	KC	A	13	.270	.405	37	10	2	0	1	2.7	5	4	2	10	0	2	0	14	37	3	5	5.4	.944	SS-6, 2B-4
1964			130	.264	.395	435	115	14	5	11	2.5	48	37	27	87	3	3	2	262	361	6	69	5.2	.990	2B-120
1965			133	.232	.363	474	110	15	1	15	3.2	64	55	50	110	0	7	2	252	341	12	73	4.8	.980	2B-126
1966			140	.250	.363	507	127	24	3	9	1.8	58	62	27	101	6	1	0	302	390	16	86	5.1	.977	2B-137, 3B-2
1967			122	.198	.298	349	69	12	4	5	1.4	26	37	30	68	6	14	4	177	198	10	34	3.5	.974	3B-59, 2B-50, SS-1, 1B-1
1968	OAK	A	76	.233	.351	202	47	6	0	6	3.0	19	18	21	41	3	9	3	125	170	8	35	4.8	.974	2B-61, 3B-1, C-1
1969			136	.275	.427	483	133	25	6	12	2.5	61	64	53	94	2	4	1	302	379	10	93	5.3	.986	2B-131
1970			135	.190	.240	384	73	7	0	4	1.0	34	29	38	73	3	7	2	261	336	13	67	4.6	.979	2B-127, 3B-5, C-1
1971			144	.244	.354	475	116	14	1	12	2.5	58	49	51	83	1	1	0	366	384	11	98	5.3	.986	2B-143, SS-1
1972			26	.286	.357	42	12	1	1	0	0.0	1	3	3	5	0	0	0	35	45	3	9	3.2	.964	2B-26
1973			133	.262	.340	332	87	17	0	3	0.9	33	42	21	63	0	0	0	265	298	7	86	4.2	.988	2B-133, SS-1, 3B-1
1974			100	.213	.275	287	61	8	2	2	0.7	20	22	22	50	2	0	0	233	243	8	67	4.8	.983	2B-100
12 yrs.			1288	.240	.347	4007	960	145	23	80	2.0	427	422	345	785	26	48	14	2594	3182	107	722	4.8	.982	2B-1158, 3B-68, SS-9, C-2, 1B-1
LEAGUE CHAMPIONSHIP SERIES																									
1971	OAK	A	3	.286	.286	7	2	0	0	0	0.0	0	0	1	1	0	0	0	8	4	0	3	4.0	1.000	2B-3
1972			5	.125	.250	8	1	1	0	0	0.0	0	0	0	0	0	0	0	5	7	0	1	2.4	1.000	2B-5
1973			5	.077	.154	13	1	1	0	0	0.0	0	1	1	4	0	0	0	12	11	2	4	5.0	.920	2B-5
1974			4	.222	.222	9	2	0	0	0	0.0	0	0	2	1	0	0	0	10	8	2	3	5.0	.900	2B-4
4 yrs.			17	.162	.216	37	6	2	0	0	0.0	0	1	4	6	0	0	0	35	30	4	11	4.1	.942	2B-17
WORLD SERIES																									
1972	OAK	A	7	.333	.444	18	6	2	0	0	0.0	0	1	0	4	0	0	0	12	13	0	2	3.6	1.000	2B-7
1973			7	.063	.063	16	1	0	0	0	0.0	0	0	1	6	0	0	0	14	11	1	4	3.7	.962	2B-7
1974			5	.000	.000	13	0	0	0	0	0.0	1	1	1	4	0	0	0	15	14	1	6	6.0	.967	2B-5
3 yrs.			19	.149	.191	47	7	2	0	0	0.0	1	2	2	14	0	0	0	41	38	2	12	4.3	.975	2B-19

Gary Green

GREEN, GARY ALLAN — BR TR 6′ 3″ 175 lbs.
Son of Freddie Green.
B. Jan. 14, 1962, Pittsburgh, Pa.

Year	Team	Lg	Games	BA	SA	AB	H	2B	3B	HR	HR%	R	RBI	BB	SO	SB	Pinch Hit AB	Pinch Hit H	PO	A	E	DP	TC/G	FA	G by Pos
1986	SD	N	13	.212	.242	33	7	1	0	0	0.0	2	2	1	11	0	0	0	16	35	0	9	3.9	1.000	SS-13
1989			15	.259	.370	27	7	3	0	0	0.0	4	0	1	1	0	0	0	6	29	3	7	3.2	.921	SS-11, 3B-1
1990	TEX	A	62	.216	.250	88	19	3	0	0	0.0	10	8	6	18	1	0	0	61	112	5	27	3.1	.972	SS-58
1991			8	.150	.200	20	3	1	0	0	0.0	0	1	1	6	0	0	0	10	20	1	5	3.9	.968	SS-8
1992	CIN	N	8	.333	.417	12	4	1	0	0	0.0	3	0	0	2	0	1	0	1	5	0	0	0.9	1.000	SS-6, 3B-1
5 yrs.			106	.222	.272	180	40	9	0	0	0.0	19	11	9	38	1	1	0	94	201	9	48	3.1	.970	SS-96, 3B-2

Gene Green

GREEN, GENE LEROY — BR TR 6′ 2½″ 200 lbs.
B. June 26, 1933, Los Angeles, Calif. D. May 23, 1981, St. Louis, Mo.

Year	Team	Lg	Games	BA	SA	AB	H	2B	3B	HR	HR%	R	RBI	BB	SO	SB	Pinch Hit AB	Pinch Hit H	PO	A	E	DP	TC/G	FA	G by Pos
1957	STL	N	6	.200	.267	15	3	1	0	0	0.0	0	2	0	3	0	3	0	2	0	0	0	0.7	1.000	OF-3
1958			137	.281	.423	442	124	18	3	13	2.9	47	55	37	48	2	13	1	428	35	9	5	3.8	.981	OF-75, C-48
1959			30	.189	.311	74	14	6	0	1	1.4	8	3	5	18	0	2	0	62	9	2	2	2.4	.973	OF-19, C-11
1960	BAL	A	1	.250	.250	4	1	0	0	0	0.0	0	0	0	0	0	0	0	0	1	0	0	1.0	1.000	OF-1
1961	WAS	A	110	.280	.489	364	102	16	3	18	4.9	52	62	35	65	0	11	2	354	22	5	3	3.8	.987	C-79, OF-21
1962	CLE	A	66	.280	.552	143	40	4	1	11	7.7	16	28	8	21	0	30	10	56	2	2	1	1.7	.967	OF-33, 1B-2
1963	2 teams		CLE A (43G –.205) CIN N (15G –.226)																						
"	total		58	.211	.330	109	23	4	0	3	2.8	7	10	4	30	0	31	5	53	5	3	0	2.3	.951	OF-18, C-8
7 yrs.			408	.267	.441	1151	307	49	7	46	4.0	130	160	89	185	2	90	18	955	74	21	11	3.3	.980	OF-170, C-146, 1B-2

Jim Green

GREEN, JAMES R.
B. Cleveland, Ohio Deceased.

Year	Team	Lg	Games	BA	SA	AB	H	2B	3B	HR	HR%	R	RBI	BB	SO	SB	Pinch Hit AB	Pinch Hit H	PO	A	E	DP	TC/G	FA	G by Pos
1884	WAS	U	10	.139	.167	36	5	1	0	0	0.0	4		0			0	0	5	15	4	0	2.4	.833	3B-9, OF-1

Joe Green

GREEN, JOSEPH HENRY (Tilly) — BR TR 6′ 2″ 170 lbs.
B. Sept. 17, 1897, Philadelphia, Pa. D. Feb. 4, 1972, Bryn Mawr, Pa.

Year	Team	Lg	Games	BA	SA	AB	H	2B	3B	HR	HR%	R	RBI	BB	SO	SB	Pinch Hit AB	Pinch Hit H	PO	A	E	DP	TC/G	FA	G by Pos
1924	PHI	A	1	.000	.000	1	0	0	0	0	0.0	0	0	0	0	0	1	0	0	0	0	0	0.0	—	

Lenny Green

GREEN, LEONARD CHARLES — BL TL 5′11″ 170 lbs.
B. Jan. 6, 1933, Detroit, Mich.

Year	Team	Lg	Games	BA	SA	AB	H	2B	3B	HR	HR%	R	RBI	BB	SO	SB	Pinch Hit AB	Pinch Hit H	PO	A	E	DP	TC/G	FA	G by Pos
1957	BAL	A	19	.182	.364	33	6	1	1	1	3.0	2	5	1	4	0	2	0	19	0	1	0	1.3	.950	OF-15
1958			69	.231	.275	91	21	4	0	0	0.0	10	4	9	10	0	9	1	81	1	3	0	1.6	.965	OF-53

Lenny Green *continued*

Year	Team	Games	BA	SA	AB	H	2B	3B	HR	HR%	R	RBI	BB	SO	SB	Pinch Hit AB	Pinch Hit H	PO	A	E	DP	TC/G	FA	G by Pos
1959	**2 teams**	**BAL A** (27G –.292) **WAS A** (88G –.242)																						
″	**total**	115	.248	.327	214	53	6	1	3	1.4	32	17	21	18	9	35	11	98	6	2	0	1.3	.981	OF-81
1960	**WAS A**	127	.294	.430	330	97	16	7	5	1.5	62	33	43	25	21	29	8	219	4	2	0	2.3	.991	OF-100
1961	**MIN A**	156	.285	.400	600	171	28	7	9	1.5	92	50	81	50	17	2	1	356	3	8	0	2.4	.978	OF-153
1962		158	.271	.402	619	168	33	3	14	2.3	97	63	88	36	8	3	1	361	8	2	2	2.4	.995	OF-156
1963		145	.239	.325	280	67	10	1	4	1.4	41	27	31	21	11	23	4	165	1	2	0	1.4	.988	OF-119
1964	**3 teams**	**MIN A** (26G –.000) **LA A** (39G –.250) **BAL A** (14G –.190)																						
″	**total**	79	.211	.273	128	27	2	0	2	1.6	16	5	21	17	3	33	4	65	1	1	0	1.8	.985	OF-38
1965	**BOS A**	119	.276	.429	373	103	24	6	7	1.9	69	24	48	43	8	24	7	198	2	4	1	2.1	.980	OF-95
1966		85	.241	.308	133	32	6	0	1	0.8	18	12	15	19	0	52	14	41	3	1	0	1.7	.978	OF-27
1967	**DET A**	58	.278	.364	151	42	8	1	1	0.7	22	13	9	17	1	11	1	57	0	1	0	1.3	.983	OF-44
1968		6	.250	.250	4	1	0	0	0	0.0	0	0	1	0	0	3	1	0	0	0	0	0.0	.000	OF-2
12 yrs.		1136	.267	.379	2956	788	138	27	47	1.6	461	253	368	260	78	226	53	1660	29	27	3	1.9	.984	OF-883

Pumpsie Green

GREEN, ELIJAH JERRY BB TR 6′ 175 lbs.
B. Oct. 27, 1933, Oakland, Calif.

Year	Team	Games	BA	SA	AB	H	2B	3B	HR	HR%	R	RBI	BB	SO	SB	Pinch Hit AB	Pinch Hit H	PO	A	E	DP	TC/G	FA	G by Pos
1959	**BOS A**	50	.233	.320	172	40	6	3	1	0.6	30	10	29	22	4	4	0	109	132	7	38	5.4	.972	2B-45, SS-1
1960		133	.242	.338	260	63	10	3	3	1.2	36	21	44	47	3	24	8	151	169	11	33	3.0	.967	2B-69, SS-41
1961		88	.260	.425	219	57	12	3	6	2.7	33	27	42	32	4	25	7	91	172	16	36	4.4	.943	SS-57, 2B-7
1962		56	.231	.341	91	21	2	1	2	2.2	12	11	11	18	1	35	8	22	35	5	8	2.7	.919	2B-18, SS-5
1963	**NY N**	17	.278	.426	54	15	1	2	1	1.9	8	5	12	13	0	0	0	12	36	8	2	3.5	.857	3B-16
5 yrs.		344	.246	.364	796	196	31	12	13	1.6	119	74	138	132	12	88	23	385	544	47	117	3.8	.952	2B-139, SS-104, 3B-16

Shawn Green

GREEN, SHAWN DAVID BL TL 6′ 4″ 190 lbs.
B. Nov. 10, 1972, Des Plaines, Ill.

Year	Team	Games	BA	SA	AB	H	2B	3B	HR	HR%	R	RBI	BB	SO	SB	Pinch Hit AB	Pinch Hit H	PO	A	E	DP	TC/G	FA	G by Pos
1993	**TOR A**	3	.000	.000	6	0	0	0	0	0.0	0	0	0	1	0	0	0	1	0	0	0	0.3	1.000	OF-2, DH-1
1994		14	.091	.121	33	3	1	0	0	0.0	1	1	1	8	1	0	0	12	2	0	0	1.0	1.000	OF-14
1995		121	.288	.509	379	109	31	4	15	4.0	52	54	20	68	1	15	3	207	9	6	2	2.0	.973	OF-109
3 yrs.		138	.268	.471	418	112	32	4	15	3.6	53	55	21	77	2	15	3	220	11	6	2	1.9	.975	OF-125, DH-1

Hank Greenberg

GREENBERG, HENRY BENJAMIN (Hammerin' Hank) BR TR 6′ 3½″ 210 lbs.
B. Jan. 1, 1911, New York, N. Y. D. Sept. 4, 1986, Beverly Hills, Calif.
Hall of Fame 1956.

Year	Team	Games	BA	SA	AB	H	2B	3B	HR	HR%	R	RBI	BB	SO	SB	Pinch Hit AB	Pinch Hit H	PO	A	E	DP	TC/G	FA	G by Pos
1930	**DET A**	1	.000	.000	1	0	0	0	0	0.0	0	0	0	0	0	1	0	0	0	0	0	0.0	—	
1933		117	.301	.468	449	135	33	3	12	2.7	59	87	46	78	6	1	0	1133	63	14	111	10.3	.988	1B-117
1934		153	.339	.600	593	201	**63**	7	26	4.4	118	139	63	93	9	0	0	1454	84	16	124	10.2	.990	1B-153
1935		152	.328	.628	619	203	46	16	**36**	5.8	121	**170**	87	91	4	0	0	1437	99	13	142	10.2	.992	1B-152
1936		12	.348	.630	46	16	6	2	1	2.2	10	16	9	6	1	0	0	119	9	1	14	10.8	.992	1B-12
1937		154	.337	.668	594	200	49	14	40	6.7	137	**183**	102	101	8	0	0	1477	102	13	133	10.3	.992	1B-154
1938		155	.315	.683	556	175	23	4	**58**	**10.4**	**144**	146	**119**	92	7	0	0	1484	120	14	146	10.4	.991	1B-155
1939		138	.312	.622	500	156	42	7	33	6.6	112	112	91	**95**	8	1	0	1205	75	9	108	9.5	.993	1B-136
1940		148	.340	**.670**	573	195	**50**	8	**41**	**7.2**	129	**150**	93	75	6	0	0	298	14	15	1	2.2	.954	OF-148
1941		19	.269	.463	67	18	5	1	2	3.0	12	12	16	12	1	0	0	32	0	3	0	1.8	.914	OF-19
1945		78	.311	.544	270	84	20	2	13	4.8	47	60	42	40	3	5	2	129	3	0	0	1.8	1.000	OF-72
1946		142	.277	.604	523	145	29	5	**44**	**8.4**	91	**127**	80	88	5	2	0	1272	93	15	110	9.9	.989	1B-140
1947	**PIT N**	125	.249	.478	402	100	13	2	25	6.2	71	74	**104**	73	0	6	1	983	79	9	85	9.0	.992	1B-119
13 yrs.		1394	.313	.605	5193	1628	379	71	331	6.4	1051	1276	852	844	58	16	3	11023	741	122	974	8.6	.990	1B-1138, OF-239
				5th						**10th**														
WORLD SERIES																								
1934	**DET A**	7	.321	.571	28	9	2	1	1	3.6	4	7	4	9	1	0	0	60	4	1	5	9.3	.985	1B-7
1935		2	.167	.667	6	1	0	0	1	16.7	1	2	1	0	0	0	0	17	2	3	2	11.0	.864	1B-2
1940		7	.357	.607	28	10	2	1	1	3.6	5	6	2	5	0	0	0	12	0	0	0	1.7	1.000	OF-7
1945		7	.304	.696	23	7	3	0	2	8.7	7	7	6	5	0	0	0	8	1	0	0	1.3	1.000	OF-7
4 yrs.		23	.318	.624	85	27	7	2	5	5.9	17	22	13	19	1	0	0	97	7	4	7	4.7	.963	OF-14, 1B-9
				9th																				

Al Greene

GREENE, ALTAR ALPHONSE BL TR 5′11″ 190 lbs.
B. Nov. 9, 1954, Detroit, Mich.

Year	Team	Games	BA	SA	AB	H	2B	3B	HR	HR%	R	RBI	BB	SO	SB	Pinch Hit AB	Pinch Hit H	PO	A	E	DP	TC/G	FA	G by Pos
1979	**DET A**	29	.136	.305	59	8	1	0	3	5.1	9	6	10	15	0	6	2	14	0	0	0	0.7	1.000	DH-15, OF-6

June Greene

GREENE, JULIUS FOUST BL TR 6′ 2½″ 185 lbs.
B. June 25, 1899, Ramseur, N. C. D. Mar. 19, 1974, Glendora, Calif.

Year	Team	Games	BA	SA	AB	H	2B	3B	HR	HR%	R	RBI	BB	SO	SB	Pinch Hit AB	Pinch Hit H	PO	A	E	DP	TC/G	FA	G by Pos
1928	**PHI N**	11	.500	.500	6	3	0	0	0	0.0	0	0	3	1	0	6	3	0	2	0	0	2.0	1.000	P-1
1929		21	.211	.263	19	4	1	0	0	0.0	1	0	2	4	0	14	2	1	4	0	0	1.0	1.000	P-5
2 yrs.		32	.280	.320	25	7	1	0	0	0.0	1	0	5	5	0	20	5	1	6	0	0	1.2	1.000	P-6

Willie Greene

GREENE, PATRICK JOSEPH BR TR 5′ 8″ 150 lbs.
Played as Pat Foley in 1902.
B. Mar. 20, 1875, Providence, R. I. D. Oct. 20, 1934, Providence, R. I.

Year	Team	Games	BA	SA	AB	H	2B	3B	HR	HR%	R	RBI	BB	SO	SB	Pinch Hit AB	Pinch Hit H	PO	A	E	DP	TC/G	FA	G by Pos
1902	**PHI N**	19	.169	.185	65	11	1	0	0	0.0	6	1	2		2	0	0	22	40	6	2	3.6	.912	3B-19
1903	**2 teams**	**NY A** (4G –.308) **DET A** (1G –.000)																						
″	**total**	5	.250	.313	16	4	1	0	0	0.0	1	0	0		0	1	0	5	11	2	0	4.5	.889	3B-3, SS-1
2 yrs.		24	.185	.210	81	15	2	0	0	0.0	7	1	2		2	1	0	27	51	8	2	3.7	.907	3B-22, SS-1

Willie Greene

GREENE, WILLIE LOUIS BL TR 5′11″ 180 lbs.
B. Sept. 23, 1971, Milledgeville, Ga.

Year	Team	Games	BA	SA	AB	H	2B	3B	HR	HR%	R	RBI	BB	SO	SB	Pinch Hit AB	Pinch Hit H	PO	A	E	DP	TC/G	FA	G by Pos
1992	**CIN N**	29	.269	.430	93	25	5	2	2	2.2	10	13	10	23	0	4	0	15	40	3	6	2.3	.948	3B-25
1993		15	.160	.340	50	8	1	1	2	4.0	7	5	2	19	0	1	0	19	37	1	8	3.8	.982	SS-10, 3B-5
1994		16	.216	.270	37	8	2	0	0	0.0	5	3	6	14	0	4	1	2	21	1	1	1.7	.958	3B-13, OF-1
1995		8	.105	.105	19	2	0	0	0	0.0	1	0	3	7	0	1	0	1	13	0	1	2.0	1.000	3B-7
4 yrs.		68	.216	.347	199	43	8	3	4	2.0	23	21	21	63	0	10	1	37	111	5	16	2.5	.967	3B-50, SS-10, OF-1

Jim Greengrass

GREENGRASS, JAMES RAYMOND BR TR 6′ 1″ 200 lbs.
B. Oct. 24, 1927, Addison, N. Y.

Year	Team	Games	BA	SA	AB	H	2B	3B	HR	HR%	R	RBI	BB	SO	SB	Pinch Hit AB	Pinch Hit H	PO	A	E	DP	TC/G	FA	G by Pos
1952	CIN N	18	.309	.588	68	21	2	1	5	7.4	10	24	7	12	0	1	0	55	0	2	0	3.4	.965	OF-17
1953		154	.285	.444	606	173	22	7	20	3.3	86	100	47	83	6	1	0	341	11	6	0	2.3	.983	OF-153
1954		139	.280	.494	542	152	27	4	27	5.0	79	95	41	81	0	2	0	298	9	10	0	2.3	.968	OF-137
1955	2 teams	CIN N (13G –.103)	PHI N (94G –.272)																					
″	total	107	.254	.425	362	92	22	2	12	3.3	44	38	42	52	0	8	2	191	12	5	0	2.2	.976	OF-94, 3B-2
1956	PHI N	86	.205	.335	215	44	9	2	5	2.3	24	25	28	43	0	22	6	104	3	1	1	1.7	.991	OF-62
5 yrs.		504	.269	.448	1793	482	82	16	69	3.8	243	282	165	271	6	34	8	989	35	24	1	2.3	.977	OF-463, 3B-2

Mike Greenwell

GREENWELL, MICHAEL LEWIS BL TR 6′ 170 lbs.
B. July 18, 1963, Louisville, Ky.

Year	Team	Games	BA	SA	AB	H	2B	3B	HR	HR%	R	RBI	BB	SO	SB	Pinch Hit AB	Pinch Hit H	PO	A	E	DP	TC/G	FA	G by Pos
1985	BOS A	17	.323	.742	31	10	1	0	4	12.9	7	8	3	4	1	1	0	14	0	0	0	0.8	1.000	OF-17
1986		31	.314	.371	35	11	2	0	0	0.0	4	4	5	7	0	12	2	18	1	0	1	1.1	1.000	OF-15, DH-3
1987		125	.328	.570	412	135	31	6	19	4.6	71	89	35	40	5	17	5	165	8	6	0	1.7	.966	OF-91, DH-15, C-1
1988		158	.325	.531	590	192	39	8	22	3.7	86	119	87	38	16	0	0	302	6	6	2	2.0	.981	OF-147, DH-11
1989		145	.308	.443	578	178	36	0	14	2.4	87	95	56	44	13	1	1	220	11	8	1	1.7	.967	OF-139, DH-5
1990		159	.297	.434	610	181	30	6	14	2.3	71	73	65	43	8	1	0	287	13	7	1	1.9	.977	OF-159
1991		147	.300	.419	544	163	26	6	9	1.7	76	83	43	35	15	4	1	263	9	3	3	1.9	.989	OF-143, DH-1
1992		49	.233	.278	180	42	2	0	2	1.1	16	18	18	19	2	2	2	85	1	0	0	1.8	1.000	OF-41, DH-6
1993		146	.315	.480	540	170	38	6	13	2.4	77	72	54	46	5	3	0	261	6	2	1	1.9	.993	OF-134, DH-10
1994		95	.269	.453	327	88	25	1	11	3.4	60	45	38	26	2	7	2	141	10	1	1	1.7	.993	OF-84, DH-6
1995		120	.297	.459	481	143	25	4	15	3.1	67	76	38	35	9	0	0	202	10	6	1	1.8	.972	OF-118, DH-2
11 yrs.		1192	.303	.465	4328	1313	255	37	123	2.8	622	682	442	337	76	48	13	1958	75	39	11	1.8	.981	OF-1088, DH-59, C-1
DIVISIONAL PLAYOFF SERIES																								
1995	BOS A	3	.200	.200	15	3	0	0	0	0.0	0	0	0	1	0	0	0	8	0	0	0	2.7	1.000	OF-3
LEAGUE CHAMPIONSHIP SERIES																								
1986	BOS A	2	.500	.500	2	1	0	0	0	0.0	0	0	0	0	0	2	1	0	0	0	0	0.0	—	
1988		4	.214	.500	14	3	1	0	1	7.1	2	3	3	0	0	0	0	4	0	0	0	1.0	1.000	OF-4
1990		4	.000	.000	14	0	0	0	0	0.0	1	0	2	2	0	0	0	3	0	1	0	1.0	.750	OF-4
3 yrs.		10	.133	.267	30	4	1	0	1	3.3	3	3	5	2	0	2	1	7	0	1	0	1.0	.875	OF-8
WORLD SERIES																								
1986	BOS A	4	.000	.000	3	0	0	0	0	0.0	0	0	1	2	0	3	0	0	0	0	0	0.0	—	

Bill Greenwood

GREENWOOD, WILLIAM F. BB TL 5′ 7½″ 180 lbs.
B. 1857, Philadelphia, Pa. D. May 2, 1902, Philadelphia, Pa.

Year	Team	Games	BA	SA	AB	H	2B	3B	HR	HR%	R	RBI	BB	SO	SB	Pinch Hit AB	Pinch Hit H	PO	A	E	DP	TC/G	FA	G by Pos
1882	PHI AA	7	.300	.333	30	9	1	0	0	0.0	8		1			0	0	10	2	2	0	1.6	.857	OF-7, 2B-2
1884	BKN AA	92	.216	.275	385	83	8	3	3	0.8	52		10			0	0	230	300	59	40	6.3	.900	2B-92, SS-1
1887	BAL AA	118	.263	.319	495	130	16	6	0	0.0	114		54		71	0	0	357	360	56	33	6.6	.928	2B-117, OF-1
1888		115	.191	.227	409	78	13	1	0	0.0	69	29	30		46	0	0	203	299	59	25	4.9	.895	2B-86, SS-28, OF-1
1889	COL AA	118	.225	.312	414	93	7	10	3	0.7	62	49	58	71	37	0	0	313	322	60	50	5.9	.914	2B-118
1890	ROC AA	124	.222	.288	437	97	11	6	2	0.5	76		48		40	0	0	333	346	60	60	6.0	.919	2B-123, SS-1
6 yrs.		574	.226	.287	2170	490	56	26	8	0.4	381	78	201	71	194	0	0	1446	1629	296	208	5.8	.912	2B-538, SS-30, OF-9

Brian Greer

GREER, BRIAN KEITH BR TR 6′ 3″ 210 lbs.
B. May 14, 1959, Lynwood, Calif.

Year	Team	Games	BA	SA	AB	H	2B	3B	HR	HR%	R	RBI	BB	SO	SB	Pinch Hit AB	Pinch Hit H	PO	A	E	DP	TC/G	FA	G by Pos
1977	SD N	1	.000	.000	1	0	0	0	0	0.0	0	0	0	1	0	1	0	0	0	0	0	0.0	—	
1979		4	.000	.000	3	0	0	0	0	0.0	0	0	0	1	0	0	0	4	0	0	0	1.0	1.000	OF-4
2 yrs.		5	.000	.000	4	0	0	0	0	0.0	0	0	0	2	0	1	0	4	0	0	0	1.0	1.000	OF-4

Ed Greer

GREER, EDWARD C. BR
B. 1865, Philadelphia, Pa. D. Feb. 4, 1890, Philadelphia, Pa.

Year	Team	Games	BA	SA	AB	H	2B	3B	HR	HR%	R	RBI	BB	SO	SB	Pinch Hit AB	Pinch Hit H	PO	A	E	DP	TC/G	FA	G by Pos
1885	BAL AA	56	.199	.232	211	42	7	0	0	0.0	32		8			0	0	127	19	16	1	2.7	.901	OF-47, C-12
1886	2 teams	BAL AA (11G –.132)	PHI AA (71G –.193)																					
″	total	82	.185	.235	302	56	6	3	1	0.3	35		10			0	0	157	19	17	5	2.4	.912	OF-79, C-3
1887	2 teams	PHI AA (3G –.182)	BKN AA (91G –.254)																					
″	total	94	.251	.320	338	85	13	2	2	0.6	50		25		35	0	0	230	31	22	4	3.0	.922	OF-79, C-16
3 yrs.		232	.215	.268	851	183	26	5	3	0.4	117		43		35	0	0	514	69	55	10	2.7	.914	OF-205, C-31

Rusty Greer

GREER, THURMAN CLYDE III BL TL 6′ 190 lbs.
B. Jan. 21, 1969, Fort Rucker, Ala.

Year	Team	Games	BA	SA	AB	H	2B	3B	HR	HR%	R	RBI	BB	SO	SB	Pinch Hit AB	Pinch Hit H	PO	A	E	DP	TC/G	FA	G by Pos
1994	TEX A	80	.314	.487	277	87	16	1	10	3.6	36	46	46	46	0	2	0	216	4	6	10	2.8	.973	OF-73, 1B-9
1995		131	.271	.424	417	113	21	2	13	3.1	58	61	55	66	3	15	6	241	9	6	3	2.0	.977	OF-125, 1B-3
2 yrs.		211	.288	.450	694	200	37	3	23	3.3	94	107	101	112	3	17	6	457	13	12	13	2.3	.975	OF-198, 1B-12

Tommy Gregg

GREGG, WILLIAM THOMAS BL TL 6′ 1″ 190 lbs.
B. July 29, 1963, Boone, N. C.

Year	Team	Games	BA	SA	AB	H	2B	3B	HR	HR%	R	RBI	BB	SO	SB	Pinch Hit AB	Pinch Hit H	PO	A	E	DP	TC/G	FA	G by Pos
1987	PIT N	10	.250	.375	8	2	1	0	0	0.0	3	0	0	2	0	7	2	1	0	0	0	0.3	1.000	OF-4
1988	2 teams	PIT N (14G –.200)	ATL N (11G –.345)																					
″	total	25	.295	.455	44	13	4	0	1	2.3	5	7	3	6	0	12	2	26	1	0	1	2.1	1.000	OF-13
1989	ATL N	102	.243	.337	276	67	8	0	6	2.2	24	23	18	45	3	28	6	321	17	2	18	4.0	.994	OF-48, 1B-37
1990		124	.264	.389	239	63	13	1	5	2.1	18	32	20	39	4	51	**18**	356	34	6	31	5.7	.985	1B-50, OF-20
1991		72	.187	.308	107	20	8	1	1	0.9	13	4	12	24	2	39	9	121	9	0	6	4.8	1.000	OF-14, 1B-13
1992		18	.263	.421	19	5	0	0	1	5.3	1	1	1	7	1	8	2	15	0	0	0	1.7	1.000	OF-9
1993	CIN N	10	.167	.167	12	2	0	0	0	0.0	1	1	0	0	0	5	0	2	0	0	0	0.5	1.000	OF-4
1995	FLA N	72	.237	.385	156	37	5	0	6	3.8	20	20	16	33	3	28	4	80	1	1	2	2.0	.988	OF-38, 1B-2
8 yrs.		433	.243	.362	861	209	39	2	20	2.3	85	88	70	156	13	178	43	922	62	9	58	3.9	.991	OF-150, 1B-102
LEAGUE CHAMPIONSHIP SERIES																								
1991	ATL N	4	.250	.250	4	1	0	0	0	0.0	0	0	0	2	0	4	1	0	0	0	0	0.0	—	
WORLD SERIES																								
1991	ATL N	4	.000	.000	3	0	0	0	0	0.0	0	0	0	2	0	3	0	0	0	0	0	0.0	—	

Ed Gremminger

GREMMINGER, LORENZO EDWARD (Battleship)
B. Mar. 30, 1874, Canton, Ohio D. May 26, 1942, Canton, Ohio.
BR TR 6′ 1″ 200 lbs.

Year	Team	Games	BA	SA	AB	H	2B	3B	HR	HR%	R	RBI	BB	SO	SB	Pinch Hit AB	Pinch Hit H	PO	A	E	DP	TC/G	FA	G by Pos
1895	CLE N	20	.269	.282	78	21	1	0	0	0.0	10	15	5	13	0	0	0	24	38	9	3	3.5	.873	3B-20
1902	BOS N	140	.257	.347	522	134	20	12	1	0.2	55	66	39		7	0	0	222	282	26	15	3.8	.951	3B-140
1903		140	.264	.376	511	135	24	9	5	1.0	57	56	31		12	0	0	217	300	36	20	4.0	.935	3B-140
1904	DET A	83	.214	.285	309	66	13	3	1	0.3	18	28	14		3	0	0	103	123	12	3	2.9	.950	3B-83
4 yrs.		383	.251	.340	1420	356	58	24	7	0.5	140	165	89	13	22	0	0	566	743	83	41	3.6	.940	3B-383

Buddy Gremp

GREMP, LOUIS EDWARD
B. Aug. 5, 1919, Denver, Colo.
BR TR 6′ 1″ 175 lbs.

Year	Team	Games	BA	SA	AB	H	2B	3B	HR	HR%	R	RBI	BB	SO	SB	Pinch Hit AB	Pinch Hit H	PO	A	E	DP	TC/G	FA	G by Pos
1940	BOS N	4	.222	.222	9	2	0	0	0	0.0	0	2	0	0	0	1	0	18	1	0	2	6.3	1.000	1B-3
1941		37	.240	.280	75	18	3	0	0	0.0	7	10	5	3	0	8	1	171	10	5	16	6.2	.973	1B-21, 2B-6, C-3
1942		72	.217	.314	207	45	11	0	3	1.4	12	19	13	21	1	8	3	506	35	5	45	8.7	.991	1B-62, 3B-1
3 yrs.		113	.223	.302	291	65	14	0	3	1.0	19	31	18	24	1	17	4	695	46	10	63	7.8	.987	1B-86, 2B-6, C-3, 3B-1

Bill Grey

GREY, WILLIAM TOBIN
B. Apr. 15, 1871, Philadelphia, Pa. D. Dec. 8, 1932, Philadelphia, Pa.
5′11″ 175 lbs.

Year	Team	Games	BA	SA	AB	H	2B	3B	HR	HR%	R	RBI	BB	SO	SB	Pinch Hit AB	Pinch Hit H	PO	A	E	DP	TC/G	FA	G by Pos
1890	PHI N	34	.242	.367	128	31	8	4	0	0.0	20	21	6	3	5	0	0	69	42	18	4	3.8	.860	OF-10, 2B-8, 3B-8, C-7, 1B-1
1891		23	.240	.240	75	18	0	0	0	0.0	11	7	3	10	3	0	0	47	13	14	1	3.0	.811	C-11, OF-10, SS-3, 3B-1
1895	CIN N	52	.304	.459	181	55	17	4	1	0.6	24	29	15	8	4	0	0	89	108	24	13	4.1	.891	3B-27, 2B-16, C-5, SS-5, OF-1
1896		46	.207	.240	121	25	2	1	0	0.0	15	17	19	11	6	5	0	81	83	16	9	4.9	.911	2B-12, C-11, SS-8, OF-3, 1B-2, 3B-1
1898	PIT N	137	.229	.280	528	121	17	5	0	0.0	56	67	28		5	0	0	172	258	59	16	3.6	.879	3B-137
5 yrs.		292	.242	.315	1033	250	44	14	1	0.1	126	141	71	32	23	5	0	458	504	131	43	3.8	.880	3B-174, 2B-36, C-34, OF-24, SS-16, 1B-3

Reddy Grey

GREY, ROMER CARL
Born Romer Carl Gray.
B. Jan. 4, 1875, Zanesville, Ohio D. Nov. 9, 1934, Altadena, Calif.
BL TL 5′11″ 175 lbs.

Year	Team	Games	BA	SA	AB	H	2B	3B	HR	HR%	R	RBI	BB	SO	SB	Pinch Hit AB	Pinch Hit H	PO	A	E	DP	TC/G	FA	G by Pos
1903	PIT N	2	.333	.333	6	2	0	0	0	0.0	1	1	1		0	0	0	1	0	0	0	0.5	1.000	OF-2

Bobby Grich

GRICH, ROBERT ANTHONY
B. Jan. 15, 1949, Muskegon, Mich.
BR TR 6′ 2″ 180 lbs.

Year	Team	Games	BA	SA	AB	H	2B	3B	HR	HR%	R	RBI	BB	SO	SB	Pinch Hit AB	Pinch Hit H	PO	A	E	DP	TC/G	FA	G by Pos
1970	BAL A	30	.211	.284	95	20	1	3	0	0.0	11	8	9	21	1	1	0	56	79	7	9	4.7	.951	SS-20, 2B-9, 3B-1
1971		7	.300	.400	30	9	0	0	1	3.3	7	6	5	8	1	0	0	11	31	0	4	6.0	1.000	SS-5, 2B-2
1972		133	.278	.415	460	128	21	3	12	2.6	66	50	53	96	13	3	1	299	338	20	81	4.4	.970	SS-81, 2B-45, 1B-16, 3B-8
1973		162	.251	.387	581	146	29	7	12	2.1	82	50	107	91	17	0	0	431	509	5	130	5.8	.995	2B-162
1974		160	.263	.431	582	153	29	6	19	3.3	92	82	90	117	17	0	0	484	453	20	132	6.0	.979	2B-160
1975		150	.260	.399	524	136	26	4	13	2.5	81	57	107	88	14	1	0	423	484	21	122	6.2	.977	2B-150
1976		144	.266	.417	518	138	31	4	13	2.5	93	54	86	99	14	3	1	389	400	12	91	5.6	.985	2B-140, 3B-2
1977	CAL A	52	.243	.392	181	44	6	0	7	3.9	24	23	37	40	6	0	0	88	141	4	23	4.5	.983	SS-52
1978		144	.251	.329	487	122	16	2	6	1.2	68	42	75	83	4	0	0	325	419	13	77	5.3	.983	2B-144
1979		153	.294	.537	534	157	30	5	30	5.6	78	101	59	84	1	1	0	340	438	13	111	5.2	.984	2B-153
1980		150	.271	.408	498	135	22	2	14	2.8	60	62	84	108	3	4	2	353	464	9	102	5.4	.989	2B-146, 1B-3, DH-3
1981		100	.304	**.543**	352	107	14	2	**22**	**6.3**	56	61	40	71	2	0	0	230	349	10	85	5.9	.983	2B-100
1982		145	.261	.449	506	132	28	5	19	3.8	74	65	82	109	3	2	1	338	450	11	112	5.6	.986	2B-142, DH-1
1983		120	.292	.460	387	113	17	0	16	4.1	65	62	76	62	2	3	2	271	415	22	94	5.9	.969	2B-118, SS-1
1984		116	.256	.452	363	93	15	1	18	5.0	60	58	57	70	2	5	1	311	282	12	84	4.4	.980	2B-91, 1B-25, 3B-21
1985		144	.242	.372	479	116	17	3	13	2.7	74	53	81	77	3	2	0	331	408	3	115	4.8	.996	2B-116, 1B-16, 3B-15, DH-6
1986		98	.268	.412	313	84	18	0	9	2.9	42	30	39	54	1	14	5	202	231	7	54	4.4	.984	2B-87, 1B-11, 3B-2
17 yrs.		2008	.266	.424	6890	1833	320	47	224	3.3	1033	864	1087	1278	104	39	13	4882	5891	189	1426	5.3	.983	2B-1765, SS-159, 1B-71, 3B-49, DH-10

LEAGUE CHAMPIONSHIP SERIES

Year	Team	Games	BA	SA	AB	H	2B	3B	HR	HR%	R	RBI	BB	SO	SB	Pinch Hit AB	Pinch Hit H	PO	A	E	DP	TC/G	FA	G by Pos
1973	BAL A	5	.100	.250	20	2	0	0	1	5.0	1	1	2	5	0	0	0	6	9	0	1	3.0	1.000	2B-5
1974		4	.250	.500	16	4	1	0	1	6.3	2	2	0	1	0	0	0	13	12	1	3	6.5	.962	2B-4
1979	CAL A	4	.154	.231	13	2	1	0	0	0.0	0	2	1	1	0	0	0	4	12	1	4	4.3	.941	2B-4
1982		5	.200	.267	15	3	1	0	0	0.0	1	1	2	7	0	0	0	10	17	0	3	5.4	1.000	2B-5
1986		6	.208	.333	24	5	0	0	1	4.2	1	3	0	8	0	0	0	29	9	3	3	6.8	.927	2B-3, 1B-3
5 yrs.		24	.182	.318	88	16	3	0	3	3.4	5	9	5	22 **3rd**	0	0	0	62	59	5	14	5.3	.960	2B-21, 1B-3

Tim Griesenbeck

GRIESENBECK, CARLOS PHILLIPE
B. Dec. 10, 1897, San Antonio, Tex. D. Mar. 25, 1953, San Antonio, Tex.
BR TR 5′10½″ 190 lbs.

Year	Team	Games	BA	SA	AB	H	2B	3B	HR	HR%	R	RBI	BB	SO	SB	Pinch Hit AB	Pinch Hit H	PO	A	E	DP	TC/G	FA	G by Pos
1920	STL N	5	.333	.333	3	1	0	0	0	0.0	1	0	0	0	0	1	0	2	0	0	0	0.7	1.000	C-3

Tom Grieve

GRIEVE, THOMAS ALAN
B. Mar. 4, 1948, Pittsfield, Mass.
BR TR 6′ 2″ 190 lbs.

Year	Team	Games	BA	SA	AB	H	2B	3B	HR	HR%	R	RBI	BB	SO	SB	Pinch Hit AB	Pinch Hit H	PO	A	E	DP	TC/G	FA	G by Pos
1970	WAS A	47	.198	.336	116	23	5	1	3	2.6	12	10	14	38	0	12	2	46	0	3	0	1.3	.939	OF-39
1972	TEX A	64	.204	.296	142	29	2	1	3	2.1	12	11	11	39	1	17	4	60	6	1	0	1.4	.985	OF-49
1973		66	.309	.528	123	38	6	0	7	5.7	22	21	7	25	1	5	2	68	0	0	0	1.1	1.000	OF-59, DH-1
1974		84	.255	.429	259	66	10	4	9	3.5	30	32	20	48	0	7	2	64	5	0	2	0.9	1.000	DH-40, OF-38, 1B-1
1975		118	.276	.442	369	102	17	1	14	3.8	46	61	22	74	0	14	1	93	3	1	0	0.9	.990	OF-63, DH-45
1976		149	.255	.418	546	139	23	3	20	3.7	57	81	35	119	4	3	1	112	4	2	2	0.8	.983	DH-96, OF-52
1977		79	.225	.352	236	53	9	0	7	3.0	24	30	13	57	1	12	4	77	5	2	1	1.2	.976	OF-60, DH-13
1978	NY N	54	.208	.297	101	21	3	0	2	2.0	5	8	9	23	0	25	2	43	3	1	0	1.8	.979	OF-26
1979	STL N	9	.200	.267	15	3	1	0	0	0.0	1	0	4	1	0	1	0	7	0	1	0	1.6	.875	OF-5
9 yrs.		670	.249	.401	1907	474	76	10	65	3.4	209	254	135	424	7	96	18	570	26	11	5	1.0	.982	OF-391, DH-195, 1B-1

Ken Griffey

GRIFFEY, GEORGE KENNETH, JR.
Son of Ken Griffey.
B. Nov. 21, 1969, Donora, Pa.
BL TL 6′ 3″ 195 lbs.

Year	Team	Games	BA	SA	AB	H	2B	3B	HR	HR%	R	RBI	BB	SO	SB	Pinch Hit AB	Pinch Hit H	PO	A	E	DP	TC/G	FA	G by Pos
1989	SEA A	127	.264	.420	455	120	23	0	16	3.5	61	61	44	83	16	3	1	302	12	10	6	2.6	.969	OF-127
1990		155	.300	.481	597	179	28	7	22	3.7	91	80	63	81	16	3	1	330	8	7	1	2.3	.980	OF-151, DH-2
1991		154	.327	.527	548	179	42	1	22	4.0	76	100	71	82	18	4	1	360	15	4	4	2.5	.989	OF-152, DH-1
1992		142	.308	.535	565	174	39	4	27	4.8	83	103	44	67	10	3	1	359	8	1	4	2.6	.997	OF-137, DH-3
1993		156	.309	.617	582	180	38	3	45	7.7	113	109	96	91	17	0	0	317	8	3	3	2.1	.991	OF-139, DH-19, 1B-1

Ken Griffey *continued*

Year	Team	Games	BA	SA	AB	H	2B	3B	HR	HR%	R	RBI	BB	SO	SB	Pinch Hit AB	Pinch Hit H	PO	A	E	DP	TC/G	FA	G by Pos
1994		111	.323	.674	433	140	24	4	**40**	9.2	94	90	56	73	11	0	0	225	12	4	1	2.2	.983	OF-103, DH-9
1995		72	.258	.481	260	67	7	0	17	6.5	52	42	52	53	4	0	0	190	5	2	1	2.7	.990	OF-70, DH-2
7 yrs.		917	.302	.536	3440	1039	201	19	189	5.5	570	585	426	530	92	13	4	2083	68	31	20	2.4	.986	OF-879, DH-36, 1B-1
DIVISIONAL PLAYOFF SERIES																								
1995	**SEA A**	5	.391	1.043	23	9	0	0	5	21.7	9	7	2	4	1	0	0	15	1	0	0	3.2	1.000	OF-5
LEAGUE CHAMPIONSHIP SERIES																								
1995	**SEA A**	6	.333	.571	21	7	2	0	1	4.8	2	2	4	4	2	0	0	13	0	1	0	2.3	.929	OF-6

Ken Griffey

GRIFFEY, GEORGE KENNETH, SR. BL TL 5′11″ 190 lbs.
Father of Ken Griffey.
B. Apr. 10, 1950, Donora, Pa.

Year	Team	Games	BA	SA	AB	H	2B	3B	HR	HR%	R	RBI	BB	SO	SB	Pinch Hit AB	Pinch Hit H	PO	A	E	DP	TC/G	FA	G by Pos
1973	**CIN N**	25	.384	.570	86	33	5	1	3	3.5	19	14	6	10	4	3	2	25	1	0	0	1.2	1.000	OF-21
1974		88	.251	.361	227	57	9	5	2	0.9	24	19	27	43	9	15	4	115	5	0	1	1.7	1.000	OF-70
1975		132	.305	.402	463	141	15	9	4	0.9	95	46	67	67	16	10	2	202	6	7	0	1.8	.967	OF-119
1976		148	.336	.450	562	189	28	9	6	1.1	111	74	62	65	34	10	3	270	10	6	2	2.0	.979	OF-144
1977		154	.318	.467	585	186	35	8	12	2.1	117	57	69	84	17	4	1	298	10	3	3	2.1	.990	OF-147
1978		158	.288	.417	614	177	33	8	10	1.6	90	63	54	70	23	6	3	296	13	10	2	2.1	.969	OF-154
1979		95	.316	.471	380	120	27	4	8	2.1	62	32	36	39	12	1	1	175	8	3	1	2.0	.984	OF-93
1980		146	.294	.454	544	160	28	10	13	2.4	89	85	62	77	23	7	4	266	5	6	3	2.0	.978	OF-138
1981		101	.311	.409	396	123	21	6	2	0.5	65	34	39	42	12	1	0	268	8	3	1	2.8	.989	OF-99
1982	**NY A**	127	.277	.407	484	134	23	2	12	2.5	70	54	39	58	10	7	1	282	8	5	2	2.4	.983	OF-125
1983		118	.306	.437	458	140	21	3	11	2.4	60	46	34	45	6	5	1	870	57	8	82	8.0	.991	1B-101, OF-14, DH-2
1984		120	.273	.381	399	109	20	1	7	1.8	44	56	29	32	2	18	5	422	22	16	23	4.1	.965	OF-82, 1B-27, DH-2
1985		127	.274	.425	438	120	28	4	10	2.3	68	69	41	51	7	18	2	227	8	7	3	2.1	.971	OF-110, DH-7, 1B-1
1986	**2 teams**	**NY A** (59G –.303) **ATL N** (80G –.308)																						
″	**total**	139	.306	.492	490	150	22	3	21	4.3	69	58	35	67	14	19	8	232	7	5	2	1.9	.980	OF-128, DH-2, 1B-1
1987	**ATL N**	122	.286	.456	399	114	24	1	14	3.5	65	64	46	54	4	18	11	205	8	2	3	2.0	.991	OF-107, 1B-3
1988	**2 teams**	**ATL N** (69G –.249) **CIN N** (25G –.280)																						
″	**total**	94	.255	.329	243	62	6	0	4	1.6	26	23	19	31	1	31	5	193	16	4	9	3.4	.981	OF-42, 1B-21
1989	**CIN N**	106	.263	.424	236	62	8	3	8	3.4	26	30	29	42	4	42	8	122	2	2	4	1.9	.984	OF-58, 1B-9
1990	**2 teams**	**CIN N** (46G –.206) **SEA A** (21G –.377)																						
″	**total**	67	.300	.414	140	42	4	0	4	2.9	19	26	12	8	2	32	6	79	5	2	2	2.5	.977	OF-26, 1B-9
1991	**SEA A**	30	.282	.400	85	24	7	0	1	1.2	10	9	13	13	0	5	4	31	0	0	0	1.1	1.000	OF-26, DH-1
19 yrs.		2097	.296	.431	7229	2143	364	77	152	2.1	1129	859	719	898	200	252	71	4578	199	89	143	2.6	.982	OF-1703, 1B-172, DH-14
LEAGUE CHAMPIONSHIP SERIES																								
1973	**CIN N**	3	.143	.286	7	1	1	0	0	0.0	0	0	0	1	0	1	0	2	0	0	0	1.0	1.000	OF-2
1975		3	.333	.417	12	4	1	0	0	0.0	4	4	0	3	3	0	0	4	1	0	0	1.7	1.000	OF-3
1976		3	.385	.538	13	5	0	1	0	0.0	2	2	2	1	2	0	0	11	0	0	0	3.7	1.000	OF-3
3 yrs.		9	.313	.438	32	10	2	1	0	0.0	6	6	2	5	5	1	0	17	1	0	0	2.3	1.000	OF-8
WORLD SERIES																								
1975	**CIN N**	7	.269	.462	26	7	3	1	0	0.0	4	4	4	2	2	0	0	10	1	0	0	1.6	1.000	OF-7
1976		4	.059	.059	17	1	0	0	0	0.0	2	1	0	1	1	0	0	5	0	0	0	1.3	1.000	OF-4
2 yrs.		11	.186	.302	43	8	3	1	0	0.0	6	5	4	3	3	0	0	15	1	0	0	1.5	1.000	OF-11

Alfredo Griffin

GRIFFIN, ALFREDO CLAUDINO BB TR 5′11″ 160 lbs.
Born Alfredo Claudino Baptist (Griffin).
B. Oct. 6, 1957, Santo Domingo, Dominican Republic.

Year	Team	Games	BA	SA	AB	H	2B	3B	HR	HR%	R	RBI	BB	SO	SB	Pinch Hit AB	Pinch Hit H	PO	A	E	DP	TC/G	FA	G by Pos
1976	**CLE A**	12	.250	.250	4	1	0	0	0	0.0	0	0	0	2	0	0	0	1	2	1	0	0.4	.750	SS-6, DH-4
1977		14	.146	.171	41	6	1	0	0	0.0	5	3	3	5	2	0	0	17	30	3	6	3.6	.940	SS-13, DH-1
1978		5	.500	.750	4	2	1	0	0	0.0	1	0	2	1	0	0	0	4	7	1	5	6.0	.917	SS-2
1979	**TOR A**	153	.287	.364	624	179	22	10	2	0.3	81	31	40	59	21	0	0	272	501	36	124	5.3	.956	SS-153
1980		155	.254	.349	653	166	26	**15**	2	0.3	63	41	24	58	18	0	0	295	489	37	126	5.3	.955	SS-155
1981		101	.209	.289	388	81	19	6	0	0.0	30	21	17	38	8	1	0	191	279	31	66	4.9	.938	SS-97, 3B-4, 2B-1
1982		162	.241	.314	539	130	20	8	1	0.2	57	48	22	48	10	0	0	319	479	26	92	5.1	.968	SS-162
1983		162	.250	.348	528	132	22	9	4	0.8	62	47	27	44	8	0	0	287	422	25	86	4.5	.966	SS-157, 2B-5, DH-1
1984		140	.241	.298	419	101	8	2	4	1.0	53	30	4	33	11	0	0	230	320	21	72	4.0	.963	SS-115, 2B-21, DH-5
1985	**OAK A**	162	.270	.332	614	166	18	7	2	0.3	75	64	20	50	24	0	0	278	440	30	87	4.6	.960	SS-162
1986		162	.285	.364	594	169	23	6	4	0.7	74	51	35	52	33	0	0	282	421	25	85	4.5	.966	SS-162
1987		144	.263	.348	494	130	23	5	3	0.6	69	60	28	41	26	0	0	250	389	24	73	4.8	.964	SS-137, 2B-1
1988	**LA N**	95	.199	.253	316	63	8	3	1	0.3	39	27	24	30	7	0	0	145	264	15	44	4.6	.965	SS-93
1989		136	.247	.308	506	125	27	2	0	0.0	49	29	29	57	10	5	1	208	333	14	69	4.2	.975	SS-131
1990		141	.210	.254	461	97	11	3	1	0.2	38	35	29	65	6	1	0	221	382	26	63	4.5	.959	SS-139
1991		109	.243	.271	350	85	6	2	0	0.0	27	27	22	49	5	0	0	186	349	22	45	5.1	.961	SS-109
1992	**TOR A**	63	.233	.280	150	35	7	0	0	0.0	21	10	9	19	3	5	0	61	136	7	17	3.2	.966	SS-48, 2B-16
1993		46	.211	.242	95	20	3	0	0	0.0	15	3	3	13	0	2	0	59	66	4	15	3.5	.969	SS-20, 2B-11, 3B-6
18 yrs.		1962	.249	.319	6780	1688	245	78	24	0.4	759	527	338	664	192	14	1	3306	5309	348	1075	4.6	.961	SS-1861, 2B-55, DH-11, 3B-10
LEAGUE CHAMPIONSHIP SERIES																								
1988	**LA N**	7	.160	.200	25	4	1	0	0	0.0	1	3	0	5	0	0	0	17	13	0	7	4.3	1.000	SS-7
1992	**TOR A**	2	.000	.000	2	0	0	0	0	0.0	0	0	0	0	0	0	0	0	3	0	0	3.0	1.000	SS-1
2 yrs.		9	.148	.185	27	4	1	0	0	0.0	1	3	0	5	0	0	0	17	16	0	7	4.1	1.000	SS-8
WORLD SERIES																								
1988	**LA N**	5	.188	.188	16	3	0	0	0	0.0	2	0	2	4	0	0	0	7	13	1	2	4.2	.952	SS-5
1992	**TOR A**	2	—	—	0	0	0	0	0	—	0	0	0	0	0	0	0	0	1	1	0	1.0	.500	SS-2
1993		3	—	—	0	0	0	0	0	—	0	0	0	0	0	0	0	0	0	0	0	0.0	.000	3B-2
3 yrs.		10	.188	.188	16	3	0	0	0	0.0	2	0	2	4	0	0	0	7	14	2	2	2.6	.913	SS-7, 3B-2

Doug Griffin

GRIFFIN, DOUGLAS LEE BR TR 6′ 160 lbs.
B. June 4, 1947, South Gate, Calif.

Year	Team	Games	BA	SA	AB	H	2B	3B	HR	HR%	R	RBI	BB	SO	SB	Pinch Hit AB	Pinch Hit H	PO	A	E	DP	TC/G	FA	G by Pos
1970	**CAL A**	18	.127	.145	55	7	1	0	0	0.0	2	4	6	5	0	0	0	24	42	2	9	3.6	.971	2B-11, 3B-8
1971	**BOS A**	125	.244	.319	483	118	23	2	3	0.6	51	27	31	45	11	1	0	311	344	9	90	5.4	.986	2B-124
1972		129	.260	.302	470	122	12	1	2	0.4	43	35	45	48	9	0	0	321	331	15	81	5.2	.978	2B-129

Doug Griffin *continued*

Year	Team	Games	BA	SA	AB	H	2B	3B	HR	HR%	R	RBI	BB	SO	SB	Pinch Hit AB	Pinch Hit H	PO	A	E	DP	TC/G	FA	G by Pos
1973		113	.255	.323	396	101	14	5	1	0.3	43	33	21	42	7	0	0	294	284	6	77	5.2	.990	2B-113
1974		93	.266	.330	312	83	12	4	0	0.0	35	33	28	21	2	2	1	180	243	9	54	4.7	.979	2B-91, SS-1
1975		100	.240	.272	287	69	6	0	1	0.3	21	29	18	29	2	16	8	195	215	14	45	4.2	.967	2B-99, SS-1
1976		49	.189	.205	127	24	2	0	0	0.0	14	4	9	14	2	3	0	77	98	2	15	3.8	.989	2B-44, DH-2
1977		5	.000	.000	6	0	0	0	0	0.0	0	0	0	0	0	2	0	2	4	0	1	2.0	1.000	2B-3
8 yrs.		632	.245	.299	2136	524	70	12	7	0.3	209	165	158	204	33	24	9	1404	1561	57	372	4.8	.981	2B-614, 3B-8, DH-2, SS-2
WORLD SERIES																								
1975	BOS A	1	.000	.000	1	0	0	0	0	0.0	0	0	0	0	0	0	0	0	0	0	0	0.0	—	

Ivy Griffin

GRIFFIN, IVY MOORE BL TR 5′11″ 180 lbs.
B. Dec. 25, 1896, Thomasville, Ala. D. Aug. 25, 1957, Gainesville, Fla.

Year	Team	Games	BA	SA	AB	H	2B	3B	HR	HR%	R	RBI	BB	SO	SB	Pinch Hit AB	Pinch Hit H	PO	A	E	DP	TC/G	FA	G by Pos
1919	PHI A	17	.294	.382	68	20	2	2	0	0.0	5	6	3	10	0	0	0	162	21	2	11	10.9	.989	1B-17
1920		129	.238	.274	467	111	15	1	0	0.0	46	20	15	49	3	1	0	1259	102	15	77	10.8	.989	1B-126, 2B-2
1921		39	.320	.398	103	33	4	2	0	0.0	14	13	5	6	1	10	2	236	13	7	12	9.1	.973	1B-28
3 yrs.		185	.257	.306	638	164	21	5	0	0.0	65	39	23	65	4	11	2	1657	136	24	100	10.5	.987	1B-171, 2B-2

Mike Griffin

GRIFFIN, MICHAEL JOSEPH BL TR 5′ 7″ 160 lbs.
B. Mar. 20, 1865, Utica, N. Y. D. Apr. 10, 1908, Utica, N. Y.
Manager 1898.

Year	Team	Games	BA	SA	AB	H	2B	3B	HR	HR%	R	RBI	BB	SO	SB	Pinch Hit AB	Pinch Hit H	PO	A	E	DP	TC/G	FA	G by Pos
1887	BAL AA	136	.301	.427	532	160	32	13	3	0.6	142		55		94	0	0	256	13	22	1	2.1	.924	OF-136
1888		137	.256	.336	542	139	21	11	0	0.0	103	46	55		46	0	0	274	27	20	6	2.3	.938	OF-137
1889		137	.279	.394	531	148	21	14	4	0.8	**152**	48	91	29	39	0	0	298	91	52	12	3.2	.882	OF-109, SS-25, 2B-5
1890	PHI P	115	.286	.407	489	140	29	6	6	1.2	127	54	64	19	30	0	0	278	33	15	10	2.8	.954	OF-115
1891	BKN N	134	.267	.388	521	139	**36**	9	3	0.6	106	65	57	31	65	0	0	353	31	16	7	3.0	.960	OF-134
1892		129	.277	.383	452	125	17	11	3	0.7	103	66	68	36	49	0	0	268	34	7	8	2.4	.977	OF-127, SS-2
1893		95	.285	.431	362	103	21	7	6	1.7	85	59	59	23	30	0	0	234	25	10	8	2.8	.963	OF-93, 2B-2
1894		107	.365	.499	405	148	29	5	5	1.2	123	75	78	14	39	1	0	297	14	10	5	3.0	.969	OF-106
1895		131	.333	.457	519	173	38	7	4	0.8	140	65	93	29	27	0	0	349	29	14	12	3.0	.964	OF-131, SS-1
1896		122	.308	.424	493	152	27	9	4	0.8	101	51	48	25	23	0	0	316	8	13	1	2.8	.961	OF-122
1897		134	.316	.416	534	169	25	11	2	0.4	136	56	81		16	0	0	353	13	17	6	2.9	.956	OF-134
1898		134	.300	.367	537	161	18	6	2	0.4	88	40	60		15	0	0	314	20	9	7	2.6	.974	OF-134
12 yrs.		1511	.297	.408	5917	1757	314	109	42	0.7	1406	625	809	206	473	1	0	3590	338	205	83	2.7	.950	OF-1478, SS-28, 2B-7

Pug Griffin

GRIFFIN, FRANCIS ARTHUR BR TR 5′11½″ 187 lbs.
B. Apr. 24, 1896, Lincoln, Neb. D. Oct. 12, 1951, Colorado Springs, Colo.

Year	Team	Games	BA	SA	AB	H	2B	3B	HR	HR%	R	RBI	BB	SO	SB	Pinch Hit AB	Pinch Hit H	PO	A	E	DP	TC/G	FA	G by Pos
1917	PHI A	18	.200	.360	25	5	1	0	1	4.0	4	3	1	9	1	13	2	30	3	0	1	11.0	1.000	1B-3
1920	NY N	5	.250	.250	4	1	0	0	0	0.0	0	0	1	2	0	2	0	1	0	0	0	0.5	1.000	OF-2
2 yrs.		23	.207	.345	29	6	1	0	1	3.4	4	3	2	11	1	15	2	31	3	0	1	6.8	1.000	1B-3, OF-2

Sandy Griffin

GRIFFIN, TOBIAS CHARLES BR TR 5′10″ 160 lbs.
B. July 19, 1858, Fayetteville, N. Y. D. June 5, 1926, Fayetteville, N. Y.
Manager 1891.

Year	Team	Games	BA	SA	AB	H	2B	3B	HR	HR%	R	RBI	BB	SO	SB	Pinch Hit AB	Pinch Hit H	PO	A	E	DP	TC/G	FA	G by Pos
1884	NY N	16	.177	.210	62	11	2	0	0	0.0	7		1	19		0	0	14	2	3	1	1.2	.842	OF-16
1890	ROC AA	107	.307	.432	407	125	28	4	5	1.2	85		50		21	0	0	160	8	29	1	1.8	.853	OF-107, 2B-1
1891	WAS AA	20	.275	.391	69	19	4	2	0	0.0	15	10	10	3	2	0	0	30	1	2	1	1.6	.939	OF-20
1893	STL N	23	.196	.228	92	18	1	1	0	0.0	9	9	16	2	2	0	0	46	2	5	0	2.3	.906	OF-23
4 yrs.		166	.275	.376	630	173	35	7	5	0.8	116	19	77	24	25	0	0	250	13	39	3	1.8	.871	OF-166, 2B-1

Tom Griffin

GRIFFIN, THOMAS WILLIAM
B. Jan. 1857, Titusville, Pa. D. Apr. 17, 1933, Rockford, Ill.

Year	Team	Games	BA	SA	AB	H	2B	3B	HR	HR%	R	RBI	BB	SO	SB	Pinch Hit AB	Pinch Hit H	PO	A	E	DP	TC/G	FA	G by Pos
1884	MIL U	11	.220	.268	41	9	2	0	0	0.0	5		3			0	0	100	1	9	0	10.0	.918	1B-11

Bart Griffith

GRIFFITH, BARTHOLOMEW JOSEPH BR TR 5′11″ 185 lbs.
B. Mar. 30, 1896, St. Louis, Mo. D. May 5, 1973, Bishop, Calif.

Year	Team	Games	BA	SA	AB	H	2B	3B	HR	HR%	R	RBI	BB	SO	SB	Pinch Hit AB	Pinch Hit H	PO	A	E	DP	TC/G	FA	G by Pos
1922	BKN N	106	.308	.443	325	100	22	8	2	0.6	45	35	5	11	5	23	4	192	11	4	5	2.5	.981	OF-77, 1B-6
1923		79	.294	.383	248	73	8	4	2	0.8	23	37	13	16	1	17	3	111	1	6	0	1.9	.949	OF-62
1924	WAS A	6	.125	.125	8	1	0	0	0	0.0	1	0	0	1	0	4	0	7	0	0	0	3.5	1.000	OF-2
3 yrs.		191	.299	.413	581	174	30	12	4	0.7	69	72	18	28	6	44	7	310	12	10	5	2.3	.970	OF-141, 1B-6

Clark Griffith

GRIFFITH, CLARK CALVIN (General, Griff) BR TR 5′ 6½″ 156 lbs.
B. Nov. 20, 1869, Clear Creek, Mo. D. Oct. 27, 1955, Washington, D. C.
Manager 1901–20.
Hall of Fame 1946.

Year	Team	Games	BA	SA	AB	H	2B	3B	HR	HR%	R	RBI	BB	SO	SB	Pinch Hit AB	Pinch Hit H	PO	A	E	DP	TC/G	FA	G by Pos
1891	2 teams	STL AA (27G –.156) BOS AA (10G –.174)																						
"	total	37	.160	.260	100	16	2	1	2	2.0	17	11	14	20	3	1	0	12	51	6	1	1.9	.913	P-34, OF-3
1893	CHI N	4	.182	.182	11	2	0	0	0	0.0	1	2	0	1	0	0	0	2	6	0	0	2.0	1.000	P-4
1894		46	.232	.324	142	33	5	4	0	0.0	27	15	23	9	6	2	1	27	46	10	1	1.9	.880	P-36, OF-7, SS-1
1895		43	.319	.361	144	46	3	0	1	0.7	20	27	16	9	2	0	0	28	81	9	2	2.7	.924	P-42, OF-1
1896		38	.267	.356	135	36	5	2	1	0.7	22	16	9	7	3	2	0	20	79	9	3	3.0	.917	P-36
1897		46	.235	.333	162	38	8	4	0	0.0	27	21	18		2	0	0	31	96	12	4	3.0	.914	P-41, SS-2, OF-2, 1B-1, 3B-1
1898		38	.164	.230	122	20	2	3	0	0.0	15	15	13		1	0	0	18	82	5	2	2.8	.952	P-38
1899		39	.258	.300	120	31	5	0	0	0.0	15	14	14		2	0	0	18	110	11	3	3.6	.921	P-38, SS-1
1900		30	.253	.347	95	24	4	1	1	1.1	16	7	8		2	0	0	9	57	6	0	2.4	.917	P-30
1901	CHI A	35	.303	.427	89	27	3	1	2	2.2	21	14	23		0	0	0	9	78	5	3	2.6	.946	P-35
1902		35	.217	.250	92	20	3	0	0	0.0	11	8	7		0	4	0	13	55	0	1	2.2	1.000	P-28, OF-3
1903	NY A	25	.159	.261	69	11	4	0	1	1.4	5	7	11		1	0	0	8	50	1	1	2.4	.983	P-25
1904		16	.143	.190	42	6	2	0	0	0.0	2	1	4		0	0	0	3	32	2	0	2.3	.946	P-16
1905		26	.219	.313	32	7	1	1	0	0.0	2	5	3		0	0	0	1	23	1	0	1.0	.960	P-25, OF-1
1906		17	.111	.111	18	2	0	0	0	0.0	0	1	3		0	0	0	1	23	0	2	1.4	1.000	P-17
1907		4	.000	.000	2	0	0	0	0	0.0	0	0	0		0	0	0	0	4	1	0	1.3	.800	P-4
1909	CIN N	1	.000	.000	2	0	0	0	0	0.0	0	0	0		0	0	0	1	4	0	0	5.0	1.000	P-1

Clark Griffith *continued*

Year	Team	Games	BA	SA	AB	H	2B	3B	HR	HR%	R	RBI	BB	SO	SB	Pinch Hit AB	Pinch Hit H	PO	A	E	DP	TC/G	FA	G by Pos
1910		1	—	—	0	0	0	0	0	—	1	0	0	0	0	0	0	0	0	0	0	0.0	—	
1912	WAS A	1	.000	.000	1	0	0	0	0	0.0	0	0	0		0	0	0	0	2	0	0	1.0	1.000	2B-1, P-1
1913		1	1.000	2.000	1	1	1	0	0	0.0	0	1	0	0	0	0	0	0	0	0	0	0.0		OF-1, P-1
1914		1	1.000	2.000	1	1	1	0	0	0.0	0	1	0	0	0	0	0	0	0	0	0	0.0	.000	P-1
21 yrs.		484	.233	.310	1380	321	49	17	8	0.6	202	166	166	46	22	9	1	201	879	78	23	2.4	.933	P-453, OF-18, SS-4, 1B-1, 2B-1, 3B-1

Derrell Griffith

GRIFFITH, ROBERT DERRELL
B. Dec. 12, 1943, Anadarko, Okla.
BL TR 6′ 168 lbs.

Year	Team	Games	BA	SA	AB	H	2B	3B	HR	HR%	R	RBI	BB	SO	SB	Pinch Hit AB	Pinch Hit H	PO	A	E	DP	TC/G	FA	G by Pos
1963	LA N	1	.000	.000	2	0	0	0	0	0.0	0	0	0	0	0	1	0	0	0	0	0	0.0	.000	2B-1
1964		78	.290	.424	238	69	16	2	4	1.7	27	23	5	21	5	12	1	57	56	23	3	2.1	.831	3B-35, OF-29
1965		22	.171	.244	41	7	0	0	1	2.4	3	2	0	9	0	8	2	17	0	0	0	1.5	1.000	OF-11
1966		23	.067	.067	15	1	0	0	0	0.0	3	2	2	3	0	9	1	5	0	0	0	0.7	1.000	OF-7
4 yrs.		124	.260	.378	296	77	16	2	5	1.7	33	27	7	33	5	30	4	79	56	23	3	1.9	.854	OF-47, 3B-35, 2B-1

Tommy Griffith

GRIFFITH, THOMAS HERMAN
B. Oct. 26, 1889, Prospect, Ohio D. Apr. 13, 1967, Cincinnati, Ohio.
BL TR 5′10″ 175 lbs.

Year	Team	Games	BA	SA	AB	H	2B	3B	HR	HR%	R	RBI	BB	SO	SB	Pinch Hit AB	Pinch Hit H	PO	A	E	DP	TC/G	FA	G by Pos
1913	BOS N	37	.252	.323	127	32	4	1	1	0.8	16	12	9	8	1	1	0	55	7	8	1	2.0	.886	OF-35
1914		16	.104	.104	48	5	0	0	0	0.0	3	1	2	6	0	2	2	20	7	2	2	2.1	.931	OF-14
1915	CIN N	160	.307	.436	583	179	31	16	4	0.7	59	85	41	34	6	0	0	225	11	12	1	1.5	.952	OF-160
1916		155	.266	.346	595	158	28	7	2	0.3	50	61	36	37	16	0	0	238	28	9	5	1.8	.967	OF-155
1917		115	.270	.366	363	98	18	7	1	0.3	45	45	19	23	5	13	4	165	19	5	3	1.9	.974	OF-100
1918		118	.265	.321	427	113	10	4	2	0.5	47	48	39	30	10	0	0	201	18	7	3	1.9	.969	OF-118
1919	BKN N	125	.281	.372	484	136	18	4	6	1.2	65	57	23	32	8	0	0	210	20	11	3	1.9	.954	OF-125
1920		93	.260	.329	334	87	9	4	2	0.6	41	30	15	18	3	1	1	132	7	4	1	1.6	.972	OF-92
1921		129	.312	.464	455	142	21	6	12	2.6	66	71	36	13	3	4	1	215	27	7	5	2.0	.972	OF-124
1922		99	.316	.453	329	104	17	8	4	1.2	44	49	23	10	7	14	4	167	13	9	4	2.3	.952	OF-82
1923		131	.293	.424	481	141	21	9	8	1.7	70	66	50	19	8	2	0	215	14	18	4	1.9	.927	OF-128
1924		140	.251	.330	482	121	19	5	3	0.6	43	67	34	19	0	0	0	210	9	8	3	1.6	.965	OF-139
1925	2 teams	BKN N (7G –.000)	CHI N (76G –.285)																					
″	total	83	.280	.427	239	67	12	1	7	2.9	40	27	24	13	3	16	3	111	9	8	1	2.1	.938	OF-62
13 yrs.		1401	.280	.382	4947	1383	208	72	52	1.1	589	619	351	262	70	53	15	2164	189	108	36	1.8	.956	OF-1334
WORLD SERIES																								
1920	BKN N	7	.190	.286	21	4	2	0	0	0.0	1	3	0	2	0	0	0	9	0	0	0	1.3	1.000	OF-7

Art Griggs

GRIGGS, ART CARLE
B. Dec. 10, 1883, Topeka, Kans. D. Dec. 19, 1938, Los Angeles, Calif.
BR TR 5′11″ 185 lbs.

Year	Team	Games	BA	SA	AB	H	2B	3B	HR	HR%	R	RBI	BB	SO	SB	Pinch Hit AB	Pinch Hit H	PO	A	E	DP	TC/G	FA	G by Pos
1909	STL A	108	.280	.354	364	102	17	5	0	0.0	38	43	24		11	9	1	517	60	22	23	6.1	.963	1B-49, OF-40, 2B-8, SS-1
1910		123	.236	.327	416	98	22	5	2	0.5	28	30	25		11	10	1	322	120	32	29	4.2	.932	OF-49, 2B-41, 1B-17, SS-3, 3B-3
1911	CLE A	27	.250	.397	68	17	3	2	1	1.5	7	7	5		1	5	1	39	36	3	3	4.1	.962	2B-11, OF-4, 3B-3, 1B-1
1912		89	.304	.414	273	83	16	7	0	0.0	29	39	33		10	18	3	661	43	10	33	10.1	.986	1B-71
1914	BKN F	40	.286	.384	112	32	6	1	1	0.9	10	15	5		1	12	2	238	8	6	10	9.0	.976	1B-27, OF-1
1915		27	.289	.395	38	11	1	0	1	2.6	4	2	3		0	16	5	56	4	0	3	10.0	1.000	1B-5, OF-1
1918	DET A	28	.364	.444	99	36	8	0	0	0.0	11	16	10	5	2	2	2	263	9	4	10	11.0	.986	1B-25
7 yrs.		442	.277	.370	1370	379	73	20	5	0.4	127	152	105	5	36	72	15	2096	280	77	111	6.8	.969	1B-195, OF-95, 2B-60, 3B-6, SS-4

Denver Grigsby

GRIGSBY, DENVER CLARENCE
B. Mar. 24, 1901, Jackson, Ky. D. Nov. 10, 1973, Sapulpa, Okla.
BL TR 5′ 9″ 155 lbs.

Year	Team	Games	BA	SA	AB	H	2B	3B	HR	HR%	R	RBI	BB	SO	SB	Pinch Hit AB	Pinch Hit H	PO	A	E	DP	TC/G	FA	G by Pos
1923	CHI N	24	.292	.417	72	21	5	2	0	0.0	8	5	7	5	1	1	1	41	1	0	0	1.9	1.000	OF-22
1924		124	.299	.375	411	123	18	2	3	0.7	58	48	31	47	10	2	0	244	16	7	4	2.2	.974	OF-121
1925		51	.255	.292	137	35	5	0	0	0.0	20	20	19	12	1	8	0	81	4	3	2	2.3	.966	OF-39
3 yrs.		199	.289	.361	620	179	28	4	3	0.5	86	73	57	64	12	11	1	366	21	10	6	2.2	.975	OF-182

John Grim

GRIM, JOHN HELM
B. Aug. 9, 1867, Lebanon, Ky. D. July 28, 1961, Indianapolis, Ind.
BR TR 6′ 2″ 175 lbs.

Year	Team	Games	BA	SA	AB	H	2B	3B	HR	HR%	R	RBI	BB	SO	SB	Pinch Hit AB	Pinch Hit H	PO	A	E	DP	TC/G	FA	G by Pos
1888	PHI N	2	.143	.143	7	1	0	0	0	0.0	0	0	0	0	0	0	0	1	4	2	0	3.5	.714	2B-1, OF-1
1890	ROC AA	50	.266	.422	192	51	6	9	2	1.0	30		7		14	0	0	151	99	27	15	5.1	.903	SS-21, C-15, 3B-8, 2B-4, OF-3, 1B-2, P-1
1891	MIL AA	29	.235	.319	119	28	5	1	1	0.8	14	14	2	5	1	0	0	111	46	15,	4	5.9	.913	C-16, 3B-10, 2B-3
1892	LOU N	97	.243	.316	370	90	16	4	1	0.3	40	36	13	24	18	0	0	405	120	29	17	5.5	.948	C-69, 1B-11, 2B-10, OF-8, 3B-1, SS-1
1893		99	.267	.373	415	111	19	8	3	0.7	68	54	12	10	15	0	0	313	117	23	18	4.6	.949	C-92, 1B-3, 2B-2, OF-1, SS-1
1894		108	.298	.449	410	122	27	7	7	1.7	66	70	16	15	14	1	0	387	177	41	25	5.6	.932	C-77, 2B-24, 1B-7, 3B-1
1895	BKN N	93	.280	.362	329	92	17	5	0	0.0	54	44	13	9	9	0	0	261	103	20	10	4.1	.948	C-91, 1B-1, OF-1
1896		81	.267	.342	281	75	13	1	2	0.7	32	35	12	14	7	0	0	277	82	22	8	4.6	.942	C-77, 1B-5
1897		80	.248	.290	290	72	10	1	0	0.0	26	25	1		3	3	0	241	98	19	8	4.6	.947	C-77
1898		52	.281	.320	178	50	5	1	0	0.0	17	11	8		1	0	0	155	56	11	6	4.3	.950	C-52
1899		15	.277	.298	47	13	1	0	0	0.0	3	7	1		0	3	0	39	17	2	3	4.8	.966	C-12
11 yrs.		706	.267	.359	2638	705	119	37	16	0.6	350	296	85	77	82	7	0	2341	919	211	114	4.9	.939	C-578, 2B-44, 1B-29, SS-23, 3B-20, OF-14, P-1

Ed Grimes

GRIMES, EDWARD ADELBERT
B. Sept. 8, 1905, Chicago, Ill. D. Oct. 5, 1974, Chicago, Ill.
BR TR 5′10″ 178 lbs.

Year	Team	Games	BA	SA	AB	H	2B	3B	HR	HR%	R	RBI	BB	SO	SB	Pinch Hit AB	Pinch Hit H	PO	A	E	DP	TC/G	FA	G by Pos
1931	STL A	43	.263	.351	57	15	1	2	0	0.0	9	5	9	3	1	5	0	17	24	4	0	1.6	.911	3B-22, 2B-4, SS-3
1932		31	.235	.265	68	16	0	1	0	0.0	7	13	6	12	0	3	0	17	38	6	5	2.9	.902	3B-18, 2B-2, SS-1
2 yrs.		74	.248	.304	125	31	1	3	0	0.0	16	18	15	15	1	8	0	34	62	10	5	2.1	.906	3B-40, 2B-6, SS-4

Oscar Grimes

GRIMES, OSCAR RAY, JR. BR TR 5′11″ 178 lbs.
Son of Ray Grimes.
B. Apr. 13, 1915, Minerva, Ohio D. May 19, 1993, Westlake, Ohio.

Year	Team	Games	BA	SA	AB	H	2B	3B	HR	HR%	R	RBI	BB	SO	SB	Pinch Hit AB	Pinch Hit H	PO	A	E	DP	TC/G	FA	G by Pos
1938	CLE A	4	.200	.400	10	2	0	1	0	0.0	2	2	2	0	0	1	0	10	2	0	2	4.0	1.000	2B-2, 1B-1
1939		119	.269	.385	364	98	20	5	4	1.1	51	56	56	61	8	3	0	501	192	22	75	5.6	.969	2B-48, 1B-43, SS-37
1940		11	.000	.000	13	0	0	0	0	0.0	3	0	0	5	0	1	0	21	6	1	2	5.6	.964	1B-4, 3B-1
1941		77	.238	.348	244	58	9	3	4	1.6	28	24	39	47	4	1	0	572	62	5	60	8.4	.992	1B-62, 2B-13, 3B-1
1942		51	.179	.202	84	15	2	0	0	0.0	10	2	13	17	3	9	1	55	52	8	12	3.4	.930	2B-24, 3B-8, SS-1, 1B-1
1943	NY A	9	.150	.150	20	3	0	0	0	0.0	4	1	3	7	0	4	0	10	8	0	6	4.5	1.000	SS-3, 1B-1
1944		116	.279	.403	387	108	17	8	5	1.3	44	46	59	57	6	1	0	140	246	24	24	3.5	.941	3B-97, SS-20
1945		142	.265	.358	480	127	19	7	4	0.8	64	45	97	73	7	1	0	166	297	31	35	3.5	.937	3B-141, 1B-1
1946	2 teams	NY A (14G –.205)	PHI A (59G –.262)																					
″	total	73	.252	.291	230	58	6	0	1	0.4	29	24	28	36	2	7	2	142	155	20	36	4.9	.937	2B-48, SS-11, 3B-6
9 yrs.		602	.256	.352	1832	469	73	24	18	1.0	235	200	297	303	30	28	3	1617	1020	111	252	4.8	.960	3B-254, 2B-135, 1B-113, SS-72

Ray Grimes

GRIMES, OSCAR RAY, SR. BR TR 5′11″ 168 lbs.
Brother of Roy Grimes. Father of Oscar Grimes.
B. Sept. 11, 1893, Bergholz, Ohio D. May 25, 1953, Minerva, Ohio.

Year	Team	Games	BA	SA	AB	H	2B	3B	HR	HR%	R	RBI	BB	SO	SB	Pinch Hit AB	Pinch Hit H	PO	A	E	DP	TC/G	FA	G by Pos
1920	BOS A	1	.250	.250	4	1	0	0	0	0.0	1	0	1	0	0	0	0	13	0	0	2	13.0	1.000	1B-1
1921	CHI N	147	.321	.449	530	170	38	6	6	1.1	91	79	70	55	5	0	0	1544	68	12	93	11.0	.993	1B-147
1922		138	.354	.572	509	180	45	12	14	2.8	99	99	75	33	7	0	0	1378	68	19	106	10.6	.987	1B-138
1923		64	.329	.407	216	71	7	2	2	0.9	32	36	24	17	5	2	0	629	30	6	46	10.7	.991	1B-62
1924		51	.299	.475	177	53	6	5	5	2.8	33	34	28	15	4	1	0	530	12	10	40	11.0	.982	1B-50
1926	PHI N	32	.297	.347	101	30	5	0	0	0.0	13	15	6	13	0	3	0	241	16	5	28	9.4	.981	1B-28
6 yrs.		433	.329	.480	1537	505	101	25	27	1.8	269	263	204	133	21	6	0	4335	194	52	315	10.8	.989	1B-426

Roy Grimes

GRIMES, AUSTIN ROY BR TR 6′ 1″ 185 lbs.
Brother of Ray Grimes.
B. Sept. 11, 1893, Bergholz, Ohio D. Sept. 13, 1954, Gilford Lake, Ohio.

Year	Team	Games	BA	SA	AB	H	2B	3B	HR	HR%	R	RBI	BB	SO	SB	Pinch Hit AB	Pinch Hit H	PO	A	E	DP	TC/G	FA	G by Pos
1920	NY N	26	.158	.175	57	9	1	0	0	0.0	5	3	3	8	1	5	1	24	49	4	3	3.7	.948	2B-21

Charlie Grimm

GRIMM, CHARLES JOHN (Jolly Cholly) BL TL 5′11½″ 173 lbs.
B. Aug. 28, 1898, St. Louis, Mo. D. Nov. 15, 1983, Scottsdale, Ariz.
Manager 1932–38, 1944–49, 1952–56, 1960.

Year	Team	Games	BA	SA	AB	H	2B	3B	HR	HR%	R	RBI	BB	SO	SB	Pinch Hit AB	Pinch Hit H	PO	A	E	DP	TC/G	FA	G by Pos
1916	PHI A	12	.091	.091	22	2	0	0	0	0.0	0	0	2	4	0	4	0	7	0	1	0	1.1	.875	OF-7
1918	STL N	50	.220	.270	141	31	7	0	0	0.0	11	12	6	15	2	5	0	389	17	12	24	9.3	.971	1B-42, OF-2, 3B-1
1919	PIT N	12	.318	.477	44	14	1	3	0	0.0	6	6	2	4	1	0	0	118	2	4	1	11.3	.968	1B-11
1920		148	.227	.289	533	121	13	7	2	0.4	38	54	30	40	7	0	0	1496	95	8	95	10.8	.995	1B-148
1921		151	.274	.409	562	154	21	17	7	1.2	62	71	31	38	6	1	0	1517	67	9	93	10.6	.994	1B-150
1922		154	.292	.383	593	173	28	13	0	0.0	64	76	43	15	6	0	0	1478	68	10	104	10.1	.994	1B-154
1923		152	.345	.480	563	194	29	13	7	1.2	78	99	41	43	6	0	0	1453	81	8	130	10.1	.995	1B-152
1924		151	.288	.389	542	156	25	12	2	0.4	53	63	37	22	3	0	0	1596	72	8	139	11.1	.995	1B-151
1925	CHI N	141	.306	.439	519	159	29	5	10	1.9	73	76	38	25	4	2	0	1317	73	15	125	10.1	.989	1B-139
1926		147	.277	.403	524	145	30	6	8	1.5	58	82	49	25	3	0	0	1416	68	18	139	10.2	.988	1B-147
1927		147	.311	.398	543	169	29	6	2	0.4	68	74	45	21	3	0	0	1437	99	15	117	10.6	.990	1B-147
1928		147	.294	.386	547	161	25	5	5	0.9	67	62	39	20	7	0	0	1458	70	10	147	10.5	.993	1B-147
1929		120	.298	.436	463	138	28	3	10	2.2	66	91	42	25	3	0	0	1228	74	10	114	10.9	.992	1B-120
1930		114	.289	.403	429	124	27	2	6	1.4	58	66	41	26	1	1	0	1040	68	6	103	9.9	.995	1B-113
1931		146	.331	.458	531	176	33	11	4	0.8	65	66	53	29	1	1	0	1357	79	10	107	10.0	.993	1B-144
1932		149	.307	.425	570	175	42	2	7	1.2	66	80	35	22	2	0	0	1429	123	11	127	10.5	.993	1B-149
1933		107	.247	.320	384	95	15	2	3	0.8	38	37	23	15	1	2	0	979	84	4	94	10.3	.996	1B-104
1934		75	.296	.390	267	79	8	1	5	1.9	24	47	16	12	1	1	0	683	43	4	39	9.9	.995	1B-74
1935		2	.000	.000	8	0	0	0	0	0.0	0	0	0	1	0	0	0	27	1	0	4	14.0	1.000	1B-2
1936		39	.250	.303	132	33	4	0	1	0.8	13	16	5	8	0	4	1	297	33	0	31	9.4	1.000	1B-35
20 yrs.		2164	.290	.397	7917	2299	394	108	79	1.0	908	1078	578	410	57	21	1	20722	1217	163	1733	10.3	.993	1B-2129, OF-9, 3B-1
WORLD SERIES																								
1929	CHI N	5	.389	.556	18	7	0	0	1	5.6	2	4	1	2	0	0	0	40	1	0	4	8.2	1.000	1B-5
1932		4	.333	.467	15	5	2	0	0	0.0	2	1	2	2	0	0	0	28	3	0	5	7.8	1.000	1B-4
2 yrs.		9	.364	.515	33	12	2	0	1	3.0	4	5	3	4	0	0	0	68	4	0	9	8.0	1.000	1B-9

Moose Grimshaw

GRIMSHAW, MYRON FREDERICK BB TR 6′ 1″ 173 lbs.
B. Nov. 30, 1875, St. Johnsville, N. Y. D. Dec. 11, 1936, Canajoharie, N. Y.

Year	Team	Games	BA	SA	AB	H	2B	3B	HR	HR%	R	RBI	BB	SO	SB	Pinch Hit AB	Pinch Hit H	PO	A	E	DP	TC/G	FA	G by Pos
1905	BOS A	85	.239	.323	285	68	8	2	4	1.4	39	35	21		4	11	3	768	35	16	35	11.1	.980	1B-74
1906		110	.290	.383	428	124	16	12	0	0.0	46	48	23		5	0	0	1165	64	16	39	11.3	.987	1B-110
1907		64	.204	.265	181	37	7	2	0	0.0	19	33	16		6	14	2	168	11	6	10	4.6	.968	OF-23, 1B-15, SS-2
3 yrs.		259	.256	.340	894	229	31	16	4	0.4	104	116	60		15	25	5	2101	110	38	84	10.0	.983	1B-199, OF-23, SS-2

Marquis Grissom

GRISSOM, MARQUIS DEON BR TR 5′11″ 190 lbs.
B. Apr. 17, 1967, Atlanta, Ga.

Year	Team	Games	BA	SA	AB	H	2B	3B	HR	HR%	R	RBI	BB	SO	SB	Pinch Hit AB	Pinch Hit H	PO	A	E	DP	TC/G	FA	G by Pos
1989	MON N	26	.257	.324	74	19	2	0	1	1.4	16	2	12	21	1	3	0	32	1	2	0	1.5	.943	OF-23
1990		98	.257	.351	288	74	14	2	3	1.0	42	29	27	40	22	21	6	165	5	2	0	2.0	.988	OF-87
1991		148	.267	.373	558	149	23	9	6	1.1	73	39	34	89	**76**	8	1	350	15	6	2	2.7	.984	OF-138
1992		159	.276	.418	**653**	180	39	6	14	2.1	99	66	42	81	**78**	1	0	401	7	7	2	2.6	.983	OF-157
1993		157	.298	.438	630	188	27	2	19	3.0	104	95	52	76	53	1	0	416	8	7	3	2.7	.984	OF-157
1994		110	.288	.427	475	137	25	4	11	2.3	96	45	41	66	36	1	1	321	7	5	0	3.1	.985	OF-109
1995	ATL N	139	.258	.376	551	142	23	3	12	2.2	80	42	47	61	29	4	0	309	9	2	1	2.4	.994	OF-136
7 yrs.		837	.275	.400	3229	889	153	26	66	2.0	510	318	255	434	295	39	8	1994	52	31	8	2.6	.985	OF-807
DIVISIONAL PLAYOFF SERIES																								
1995	ATL N	4	.524	1.048	21	11	2	0	3	14.3	5	4	0	3	2	0	0	9	0	0	0	2.3	1.000	OF-4
LEAGUE CHAMPIONSHIP SERIES																								
1995	ATL N	4	.263	.368	19	5	0	1	0	0.0	2	0	1	4	0	0	0	8	0	1	0	2.3	.889	OF-4
WORLD SERIES																								
1995	ATL N	6	.360	.400	25	9	1	0	0	0.0	3	1	1	3	3	0	0	13	0	0	0	2.2	1.000	OF-6

Dick Groat

GROAT, RICHARD MORROW — BR TR 5′11½″ 180 lbs.
B. Nov. 4, 1930, Wilkinsburg, Pa.

Year	Team	Games	BA	SA	AB	H	2B	3B	HR	HR%	R	RBI	BB	SO	SB	Pinch Hit AB	Pinch Hit H	PO	A	E	DP	TC/G	FA	G by Pos
1952	PIT N	95	.284	.313	384	109	6	1	1	0.3	38	29	19	27	2	1	0	229	272	25	61	5.6	.952	SS-94
1955		151	.267	.351	521	139	28	2	4	0.8	45	51	38	26	0	1	0	330	450	32	107	5.4	.961	SS-149
1956		142	.273	.321	520	142	19	3	0	0.0	40	37	35	25	0	0	0	288	424	34	75	5.2	.954	SS-141, 3B-2
1957		125	.315	.437	501	158	30	5	7	1.4	58	54	27	28	0	0	0	226	385	21	74	5.1	.967	SS-123, 3B-2
1958		151	.300	.408	584	175	36	9	3	0.5	67	66	23	32	2	1	0	307	461	20	127	5.3	.975	SS-149
1959		147	.275	.361	593	163	22	7	5	0.8	74	51	32	35	0	2	0	301	473	29	97	5.5	.964	SS-145
1960		138	**.325**	.394	573	186	26	4	2	0.3	85	50	39	35	0	1	0	237	443	24	92	5.2	.966	SS-136
1961		148	.275	.367	596	164	25	6	6	1.0	71	55	40	44	0	2	0	237	474	32	117	5.1	.957	SS-144, 3B-1
1962		161	.294	.361	678	199	34	3	2	0.3	76	61	31	61	2	0	0	314	521	38	126	5.4	.956	SS-161
1963	STL N	158	.319	.450	631	201	**43**	11	6	1.0	85	73	56	58	3	1	0	257	448	26	91	4.6	.964	SS-158
1964		161	.292	.371	636	186	35	6	1	0.2	70	70	44	42	2	1	0	249	499	40	91	4.9	.949	SS-160
1965		153	.254	.315	587	149	26	5	0	0.0	55	52	56	50	1	6	3	242	455	27	87	4.8	.963	SS-148, 3B-2
1966	PHI N	155	.260	.320	584	152	21	4	2	0.3	58	53	40	38	2	2	1	278	491	20	81	4.9	.975	SS-139, 3B-20, 1B-1
1967	2 teams	PHI N (10G –.115) SF N (34G –.171)																						
″	total	44	.156	.188	96	15	1	1	0	0.0	7	5	10	11	0	14	1	31	68	8	15	3.5	.925	SS-30, 2B-1
14 yrs.		1929	.286	.366	7484	2138	352	67	39	0.5	829	707	490	512	14	32	5	3526	5864	376	1241	5.1	.961	SS-1877, 3B-27, 2B-1, 1B-1
WORLD SERIES																								
1960	PIT N	7	.214	.286	28	6	2	0	0	0.0	3	2	0	1	0	0	0	12	12	2	2	3.7	.923	SS-7
1964	STL N	7	.192	.308	26	5	1	1	0	0.0	3	1	4	3	0	0	0	11	16	2	6	4.1	.931	SS-7
2 yrs.		14	.204	.296	54	11	3	1	0	0.0	6	3	4	4	0	0	0	23	28	4	8	3.9	.927	SS-14

Heinie Groh

GROH, HENRY KNIGHT — BR TR 5′ 8″ 158 lbs.
Brother of Lew Groh.
B. Sept. 18, 1889, Rochester, N. Y. D. Aug. 22, 1968, Cincinnati, Ohio.
Manager 1918.

Year	Team	Games	BA	SA	AB	H	2B	3B	HR	HR%	R	RBI	BB	SO	SB	Pinch Hit AB	Pinch Hit H	PO	A	E	DP	TC/G	FA	G by Pos
1912	NY N	27	.271	.354	48	13	2	1	0	0.0	8	3	8	7	6	0	0	34	41	8	4	3.3	.904	2B-12, SS-7, 3B-6
1913	2 teams	NY N (4G –.000) CIN N (117G –.282)																						
″	total	121	.281	.376	399	112	19	5	3	0.8	51	48	38	37	24	0	0	256	366	24	44	5.4	.963	2B-113, SS-5, 3B-2
1914	CIN N	139	.288	.358	455	131	18	4	2	0.4	59	32	64	28	24	2	0	257	399	45	57	5.2	.936	2B-134, SS-2
1915		160	.290	.390	587	170	32	9	3	0.5	72	50	50	33	12	0	0	216	360	18	46	3.7	.970	3B-131, 2B-29
1916		149	.269	.374	553	149	24	14	2	0.4	85	28	**84**	34	13	1	0	226	369	23	43	4.2	.963	3B-110, 2B-33, SS-5
1917		156	.304	.411	599	**182**	**39**	11	1	0.2	91	53	71	30	15	1	0	186	340	18	30	3.5	.967	3B-154, 2B-2
1918		126	.320	.396	493	158	**28**	3	1	0.2	**88**	37	54	24	11	0	0	180	253	14	37	3.5	.969	3B-126
1919		122	.310	.431	448	139	17	11	5	1.1	79	63	56	26	21	0	0	171	226	12	22	3.4	.971	3B-121
1920		145	.298	.393	550	164	28	12	0	0.0	86	49	60	29	16	1	0	180	255	14	30	3.1	.969	3B-144, SS-1
1921		97	.331	.417	357	118	19	6	0	0.0	54	48	36	17	22	0	0	97	188	15	27	3.1	.950	3B-97
1922	NY N	115	.265	.350	426	113	21	3	3	0.7	63	51	53	21	5	5	1	100	207	11	25	2.9	.965	3B-110
1923		123	.290	.385	465	135	22	5	4	0.9	91	48	60	22	3	5	1	117	233	9	18	3.0	.975	3B-118
1924		145	.281	.360	559	157	32	3	2	0.4	82	46	52	29	8	0	0	121	286	7	13	2.9	.983	3B-145
1925		25	.231	.292	65	15	4	0	0	0.0	7	4	6	3	0	5	1	16	18	3	1	2.1	.919	3B-16, 2B-2
1926		12	.229	.286	35	8	2	0	0	0.0	2	3	2	3	0	4	1	6	13	1	1	2.9	.950	3B-7
1927	PIT N	14	.286	.314	35	10	1	0	0	0.0	2	3	2	2	0	2	1	9	14	1	0	2.0	.958	3B-12
16 yrs.		1676	.292	.384	6074	1774	308	87	26	0.4	920	566	696	345	180	26	5	2172	3568	223	398	3.6	.963	3B-1299, 2B-325, SS-20
WORLD SERIES																								
1919	CIN N	8	.172	.241	29	5	2	0	0	0.0	6	2	6	4	0	0	0	8	19	2	2	3.6	.931	3B-8
1922	NY N	5	.474	.579	19	9	0	1	0	0.0	4	0	2	1	0	0	0	6	14	0	0	4.0	1.000	3B-5
1923		6	.182	.273	22	4	0	1	0	0.0	3	2	3	1	0	0	0	4	15	0	1	3.2	1.000	3B-6
1924		1	1.000	1.000	1	1	0	0	0	0.0	0	0	0	0	0	1	1	0	0	0	0	0.0	—	
1927	PIT N	1	.000	.000	1	0	0	0	0	0.0	0	0	0	0	0	1	0	0	0	0	0	0.0	—	
5 yrs.		21	.264	.347	72	19	2	2	0	0.0	13	4	11	6	0	2	1	18	48	2	3	3.6	.971	3B-19

Lew Groh

GROH, LEWIS CARL (Silver) — BR TR
Brother of Heinie Groh.
B. Oct. 16, 1883, Rochester, N. Y. D. Oct. 20, 1960, Rochester, N. Y.

Year	Team	Games	BA	SA	AB	H	2B	3B	HR	HR%	R	RBI	BB	SO	SB	Pinch Hit AB	Pinch Hit H	PO	A	E	DP	TC/G	FA	G by Pos
1919	PHI A	2	.000	.000	4	0	0	0	0	0.0	0	0	0	2	0	1	0	0	1	0	0	1.0	1.000	3B-1

Em Gross

GROSS, EMIL MICHAEL — BR TR 6′ 190 lbs.
B. Mar. 4, 1858, Chicago, Ill. D. Aug. 24, 1921, Eagle River, Wis.

Year	Team	Games	BA	SA	AB	H	2B	3B	HR	HR%	R	RBI	BB	SO	SB	Pinch Hit AB	Pinch Hit H	PO	A	E	DP	TC/G	FA	G by Pos
1879	PRO N	30	.348	.492	132	46	9	5	0	0.0	31	24	4	8		0	0	152	39	22	1	7.1	.897	C-30
1880		87	.259	.337	347	90	18	3	1	0.3	43	34	16	15		0	0	429	126	86	5	7.4	.866	C-87
1881		51	.275	.385	182	50	9	4	1	0.5	15	24	13	11		0	0	241	70	38	5	6.8	.891	C-50, OF-1
1883	PHI N	57	.307	.489	231	71	25	7	1	0.4	39		12	18		0	0	210	70	77	1	6.3	.784	C-55, OF-2
1884	CHI U	23	.358	.589	95	34	6	2	4	4.2	13		6			0	0	103	44	28	1	7.3	.840	C-15, OF-9
5 yrs.		248	.295	.427	987	291	67	21	7	0.7	141	82	51	52		0	0	1135	349	251	13	7.0	.855	C-237, OF-12

Greg Gross

GROSS, GREGORY EUGENE — BL TL 5′10″ 160 lbs.
B. Aug. 1, 1952, York, Pa.

Year	Team	Games	BA	SA	AB	H	2B	3B	HR	HR%	R	RBI	BB	SO	SB	Pinch Hit AB	Pinch Hit H	PO	A	E	DP	TC/G	FA	G by Pos
1973	HOU N	14	.231	.333	39	9	2	1	0	0.0	5	1	4	4	2	4	0	13	2	0	0	1.7	1.000	OF-9
1974		156	.314	.377	589	185	21	8	0	0.0	78	36	76	39	12	5	2	296	15	2	4	2.1	.994	OF-151
1975		132	.294	.364	483	142	14	10	0	0.0	67	41	63	37	2	8	1	216	14	10	2	2.0	.958	OF-121
1976		128	.286	.329	426	122	12	3	0	0.0	52	27	64	39	2	13	1	208	13	5	4	2.0	.978	OF-115
1977	CHI N	115	.322	.460	239	77	10	4	5	2.1	43	32	33	19	0	39	10	109	3	1	0	1.6	.991	OF-71
1978		124	.265	.349	347	92	12	7	1	0.3	34	39	33	19	3	20	5	182	6	4	1	1.7	.979	OF-111
1979	PHI N	111	.333	.402	174	58	6	3	0	0.0	21	15	29	5	5	51	14	82	5	2	2	1.2	.978	OF-73
1980		127	.240	.312	154	37	7	2	0	0.0	19	12	24	7	1	39	10	69	5	2	2	0.8	.974	OF-91, 1B-1
1981		83	.225	.304	102	23	6	1	0	0.0	14	7	15	5	2	39	6	48	7	1	2	1.0	.982	OF-55
1982		119	.299	.328	134	40	4	0	0	0.0	14	10	19	8	4	53	**19**	55	3	1	0	0.8	.983	OF-71
1983		136	.302	.376	245	74	12	3	0	0.0	25	29	34	16	3	33	7	105	1	1	0	1.0	.991	OF-110, 1B-1
1984		112	.322	.376	202	65	9	1	0	0.0	19	16	24	11	1	46	13	195	13	2	9	2.8	.990	OF-48, 1B-28
1985		93	.260	.314	169	44	5	2	0	0.0	21	14	32	9	1	41	7	66	8	0	1	1.2	1.000	OF-52, 1B-8
1986		87	.248	.297	101	25	5	0	0	0.0	11	8	21	11	1	52	13	40	3	0	0	1.3	1.000	OF-27, 1B-5, P-1
1987		114	.286	.353	133	38	4	1	1	0.8	14	12	25	12	0	55	15	53	2	0	1	0.9	1.000	OF-50, 1B-11

Greg Gross *continued*

Year	Team	Games	BA	SA	AB	H	2B	3B	HR	HR%	R	RBI	BB	SO	SB	Pinch Hit AB	Pinch Hit H	PO	A	E	DP	TC/G	FA	G by Pos
1988		98	.203	.211	133	27	1	0	0	0.0	10	5	16	3	0	52	13	108	7	1	13	2.3	.991	OF-37, 1B-14
1989	**HOU N**	60	.200	.200	75	15	0	0	0	0.0	2	4	11	6	0	38	7	37	1	1	2	2.1	.974	OF-12, 1B-6, P-1
17 yrs.		1809	.287	.351	3745	1073	130	46	7	0.2	449	308	523	250	39	588	143 3rd	1882	108	33	43	1.6	.984	OF-1204, 1B-74, P-2
DIVISIONAL PLAYOFF SERIES																								
1981	**PHI N**	4	.000	.000	4	0	0	0	0	0.0	0	0	0	0	0	3	0	0	0	0	0	0.0	.000	OF-2
LEAGUE CHAMPIONSHIP SERIES																								
1980	**PHI N**	4	.750	.750	4	3	0	0	0	0.0	2	1	0	0	0	2	2	1	0	0	0	1.0	1.000	OF-1
1983		4	.000	.000	5	0	0	0	0	0.0	1	0	2	2	0	0	0	4	0	0	0	1.3	1.000	OF-3
2 yrs.		8	.333	.333	9	3	0	0	0	0.0	3	1	2	2	0	2	2	5	0	0	0	1.3	1.000	OF-4
WORLD SERIES																								
1980	**PHI N**	4	.000	.000	2	0	0	0	0	0.0	0	0	0	0	0	1	0	1	0	0	0	0.3	1.000	OF-3
1983		2	.000	.000	6	0	0	0	0	0.0	0	0	0	0	0	0	0	8	0	0	0	4.0	1.000	OF-2
2 yrs.		6	.000	.000	8	0	0	0	0	0.0	0	0	0	0	0	1	0	9	0	0	0	1.8	1.000	OF-5

Turkey Gross

GROSS, EWELL BR TR 6′ 165 lbs.
B. Feb. 21, 1896, Mesquite, Tex. D. Jan. 11, 1936, Dallas, Tex.

Year	Team	Games	BA	SA	AB	H	2B	3B	HR	HR%	R	RBI	BB	SO	SB	Pinch Hit AB	Pinch Hit H	PO	A	E	DP	TC/G	FA	G by Pos
1925	**BOS A**	9	.094	.156	32	3	0	1	0	0.0	2	2	2	2	0	0	0	12	29	1	4	4.7	.976	SS-9

Wayne Gross

GROSS, WAYNE DALE BL TR 6′ 2″ 210 lbs.
B. Jan. 14, 1952, Riverside, Calif.

Year	Team	Games	BA	SA	AB	H	2B	3B	HR	HR%	R	RBI	BB	SO	SB	Pinch Hit AB	Pinch Hit H	PO	A	E	DP	TC/G	FA	G by Pos
1976	**OAK A**	10	.222	.222	18	4	0	0	0	0.0	0	1	2	1	0	5	2	30	1	1	2	4.0	.969	1B-3, DH-3, OF-2
1977		146	.233	.416	485	113	21	1	22	4.5	66	63	86	84	5	0	0	127	242	27	26	2.7	.932	3B-145, 1B-1
1978		118	.200	.323	285	57	10	2	7	2.5	18	23	40	63	0	12	2	120	150	22	25	2.4	.925	3B-106, 1B-15
1979		138	.224	.367	442	99	19	1	14	3.2	54	50	72	62	4	5	2	252	225	21	27	3.6	.958	3B-120, 1B-18, OF-2
1980		113	.281	.467	366	103	20	3	14	3.8	45	61	44	39	5	13	3	125	136	11	16	2.5	.960	3B-99, 1B-10, DH-1
1981		82	.206	.366	243	50	7	1	10	4.1	29	31	34	28	2	9	1	68	127	12	7	2.7	.942	3B-73, 1B-2, DH-1
1982		129	.251	.358	386	97	14	0	9	2.3	43	41	53	50	3	20	6	203	189	11	31	3.2	.973	3B-108, 1B-16, DH-1
1983		137	.233	.392	339	79	18	0	12	3.5	34	44	36	52	3	8	3	473	113	9	51	4.2	.985	1B-74, 3B-67, DH-1, P-1
1984	**BAL A**	127	.216	.442	342	74	9	1	22	6.4	53	64	68	69	1	13	4	69	205	18	13	2.4	.938	3B-117, 1B-3, DH-1
1985		103	.235	.424	217	51	8	0	11	5.1	31	18	46	48	1	29	7	81	102	10	15	2.2	.948	3B-67, DH-10, 1B-9
1986	**OAK A**	3	.000	.000	2	0	0	0	0	0.0	0	0	1	0	0	2	0	0	0	1	0	1.0	.000	3B-1
11 yrs.		1106	.233	.395	3125	727	126	9	121	3.9	373	396	482	496	24	116	30	1548	1490	143	213	3.0	.955	3B-903, 1B-151, DH-18, OF-4, P-1
DIVISIONAL PLAYOFF SERIES																								
1981	**OAK A**	2	.400	1.000	5	2	0	0	1	20.0	1	3	0	0	0	1	0	1	4	0	0	5.0	1.000	3B-1
LEAGUE CHAMPIONSHIP SERIES																								
1981	**OAK A**	3	.000	.000	5	0	0	0	0	0.0	0	0	0	0	0	3	0	2	0	0	0	0.7	1.000	3B-3

George Grossart

GROSSART, GEORGE ALBERT
B. Apr. 11, 1880, Pittsburgh, Pa. D. Apr. 18, 1902, Homestead, Pa.

Year	Team	Games	BA	SA	AB	H	2B	3B	HR	HR%	R	RBI	BB	SO	SB	Pinch Hit AB	Pinch Hit H	PO	A	E	DP	TC/G	FA	G by Pos
1901	**BOS N**	7	.115	.115	26	3	0	0	0	0.0	4	1	0		0	0	0	18	0	0	0	2.6	1.000	OF-7

Howdie Grossklos

GROSSKLOS, HOWARD HOFFMAN BR TR 5′ 9″ 176 lbs.
B. Apr. 9, 1907, Pittsburgh, Pa.

Year	Team	Games	BA	SA	AB	H	2B	3B	HR	HR%	R	RBI	BB	SO	SB	Pinch Hit AB	Pinch Hit H	PO	A	E	DP	TC/G	FA	G by Pos
1930	**PIT N**	2	.333	.333	3	1	0	0	0	0.0	0	1	0	0	0	1	0	0	0	1	0	1.0	.000	SS-1
1931		53	.280	.348	161	45	7	2	0	0.0	13	20	11	16	1	12	4	93	117	5	36	5.1	.977	2B-39, SS-3
1932		17	.100	.100	20	2	0	0	0	0.0	1	0	0	3	0	16	2	2	2	1	0	5.0	.800	SS-1
3 yrs.		72	.261	.321	184	48	7	2	0	0.0	14	21	11	19	1	29	6	95	119	7	36	5.0	.968	2B-39, SS-5

Jerry Grote

GROTE, GERALD WAYNE BR TR 5′10″ 185 lbs.
B. Oct. 6, 1942, San Antonio, Tex.

Year	Team	Games	BA	SA	AB	H	2B	3B	HR	HR%	R	RBI	BB	SO	SB	Pinch Hit AB	Pinch Hit H	PO	A	E	DP	TC/G	FA	G by Pos
1963	**HOU N**	3	.200	.200	5	1	0	0	0	0.0	0	1	1	3	0	0	0	10	0	0	0	3.3	1.000	C-3
1964		100	.181	.262	298	54	9	3	3	1.0	26	24	20	75	0	2	0	522	52	9	5	5.9	.985	C-98
1966	**NY N**	120	.237	.315	317	75	12	2	3	0.9	26	31	40	81	4	5	1	519	55	11	8	5.0	.981	C-115, 3B-2
1967		120	.195	.253	344	67	8	0	4	1.2	25	23	14	65	2	2	0	609	62	7	8	5.7	.990	C-119
1968		124	.282	.349	404	114	18	0	3	0.7	29	31	44	81	1	8	2	754	60	5	8	7.1	.994	C-115
1969		113	.252	.351	365	92	12	3	6	1.6	38	40	32	59	2	4	1	718	63	7	11	7.0	.991	C-112
1970		126	.255	.308	415	106	14	1	2	0.5	38	34	36	39	2	0	0	855	46	8	12	7.3	.991	C-125
1971		125	.270	.347	403	109	25	0	2	0.5	35	35	40	47	1	4	0	892	41	9	4	7.7	.990	C-122
1972		64	.210	.288	205	43	5	1	3	1.5	15	21	26	27	1	2	0	407	43	1	5	7.2	.998	C-59, 3B-3, OF-1
1973		84	.256	.316	285	73	10	2	1	0.4	17	32	13	23	0	1	0	546	37	4	1	7.1	.993	C-81, 3B-2
1974		97	.257	.335	319	82	8	1	5	1.6	25	36	33	33	0	3	0	549	36	7	1	6.3	.988	C-94
1975		119	.295	.373	386	114	14	5	2	0.5	28	39	38	23	0	8	2	706	55	4	8	6.9	.995	C-111
1976		101	.272	.365	323	88	14	2	4	1.2	30	28	38	19	1	10	4	622	49	5	6	7.0	.993	C-95, OF-2
1977	**2 teams**	**NY N** (42G –.270) **LA N** (18G –.259)																						
″	**total**	60	.268	.303	142	38	3	1	0	0.0	11	11	11	17	0	11	3	180	40	2	4	3.9	.991	C-44, 3B-13
1978	**LA N**	41	.271	.343	70	19	5	0	0	0.0	5	9	10	5	0	2	1	125	21	3	0	3.8	.980	C-32, 3B-7
1981	**2 teams**	**KC A** (22G –.304) **LA N** (2G –.000)																						
″	**total**	24	.293	.431	58	17	3	1	1	1.7	4	9	3	3	1	0	0	89	6	0	0	4.1	1.000	C-23
16 yrs.		1421	.252	.326	4339	1092	160	22	39	0.9	352	404	399	600	15	62	14	8103	666	82	81	6.4	.991	C-1348, 3B-27, OF-3
LEAGUE CHAMPIONSHIP SERIES																								
1969	**NY N**	3	.167	.250	12	2	1	0	0	0.0	3	1	1	4	0	0	0	22	1	0	0	7.7	1.000	C-3
1973		5	.211	.211	19	4	0	0	0	0.0	2	2	1	3	0	0	0	42	1	1	0	8.8	.977	C-5
1977	**LA N**	2	—	—	0	0	0	0	0	—	0	0	1	0	0	0	0	0	0	0	0	0.0	.000	C-1
1978		1	—	—	0	0	0	0	0	—	0	0	0	0	0	0	0	2	0	0	0	2.0	1.000	C-1
4 yrs.		11	.194	.226	31	6	1	0	0	0.0	5	3	3	7	0	0	0	66	2	1	0	6.9	.986	C-10
WORLD SERIES																								
1969	**NY N**	5	.211	.316	19	4	2	0	0	0.0	1	1	1	3	0	0	0	29	2	0	0	6.2	1.000	C-5
1973		7	.267	.267	30	8	0	0	0	0.0	2	0	0	1	0	0	0	67	5	0	1	10.3	1.000	C-7

Jerry Grote *continued*

Year	Team	Lg	Games	BA	SA	AB	H	2B	3B	HR	HR%	R	RBI	BB	SO	SB	Pinch Hit AB	Pinch Hit H	PO	A	E	DP	TC/G	FA	G by Pos
1977	LA	N	1	.000	.000	1	0	0	0	0	0.0	0	0	0	0	0	0	0	3	3	0	0	6.0	1.000	C-1
1978			2	—	—	0	0	0	0	0	—	0	0	0	0	0	0	0	3	0	0	0	1.5	1.000	C-2
4 yrs.			15	.240	.280	50	12	2	0	0	0.0	3	1	1	4	0	0	0	102	10	0	1	7.5	1.000	C-15

Jeff Grotewold

GROTEWOLD, JEFFREY SCOTT BL TR 6′ 215 lbs.
B. Dec. 8, 1965, Madera, Calif.

Year	Team	Lg	Games	BA	SA	AB	H	2B	3B	HR	HR%	R	RBI	BB	SO	SB	Pinch Hit AB	Pinch Hit H	PO	A	E	DP	TC/G	FA	G by Pos
1992	PHI	N	72	.200	.369	65	13	2	0	3	4.6	7	5	9	16	0	**61**	13	6	0	0	0	1.2	1.000	OF-2, C-2, 1B-1
1995	KC	A	15	.278	.389	36	10	1	0	1	2.8	4	6	9	7	0	2	0	3	0	1	1	0.3	.750	DH-11, 1B-1
2 yrs.			87	.228	.376	101	23	3	0	4	4.0	11	11	18	23	0	63	13	9	0	1	1	0.6	.900	DH-11, OF-2, 1B-2, C-2

Johnny Groth

GROTH, JOHN THOMAS BR TR 6′ 182 lbs.
B. July 23, 1926, Chicago, Ill.

Year	Team	Lg	Games	BA	SA	AB	H	2B	3B	HR	HR%	R	RBI	BB	SO	SB	Pinch Hit AB	Pinch Hit H	PO	A	E	DP	TC/G	FA	G by Pos
1946	DET	A	4	.000	.000	9	0	0	0	0	0.0	1	0	0	3	0	0	0	6	0	0	0	1.5	1.000	OF-4
1947			2	.250	.250	4	1	0	0	0	0.0	1	0	2	1	0	1	0	5	0	0	0	5.0	1.000	OF-1
1948			6	.471	.824	17	8	3	0	1	5.9	3	5	1	1	0	1	0	8	1	1	1	2.5	.900	OF-4
1949			103	.293	.471	348	102	19	5	11	3.2	60	73	65	27	3	3	0	247	8	9	3	2.7	.966	OF-99
1950			157	.306	.451	566	173	30	8	12	2.1	95	85	95	27	1	0	0	374	9	6	0	2.5	.985	OF-157
1951			118	.299	.393	428	128	29	1	3	0.7	41	49	31	32	1	6	2	266	12	2	3	2.5	.993	OF-112
1952			141	.284	.357	524	149	22	2	4	0.8	56	51	51	39	2	3	0	329	14	5	3	2.5	.986	OF-139
1953	STL	A	141	.253	.370	557	141	27	4	10	1.8	65	57	42	53	5	0	0	425	18	4	5	3.2	.991	OF-141
1954	CHI	A	125	.275	.372	422	116	20	0	7	1.7	41	60	42	37	3	1	0	314	7	4	3	2.6	.988	OF-125
1955	2 teams		CHI A (32G –.338) WAS A (63G –.219)																						
″	total		95	.254	.381	260	66	11	5	4	1.5	35	28	24	31	3	14	5	183	3	2	1	2.5	.989	OF-74
1956	KC	A	95	.258	.398	244	63	13	3	5	2.0	22	37	30	31	1	13	4	140	8	0	3	1.8	1.000	OF-84
1957	2 teams		KC A (55G –.254) DET A (38G –.291)																						
″	total		93	.278	.340	162	45	10	0	0	0.0	21	18	13	13	0	4	0	110	0	1	0	1.3	.991	OF-86
1958	DET	A	88	.281	.384	146	41	5	2	2	1.4	24	11	13	19	0	16	6	95	2	1	1	1.2	.990	OF-80
1959			55	.235	.353	102	24	7	1	1	1.0	12	10	7	14	0	13	4	58	0	1	0	1.4	.983	OF-41
1960			25	.368	.421	19	7	1	0	0	0.0	3	2	3	1	0	8	3	6	0	0	0	0.8	1.000	OF-8
15 yrs.			1248	.279	.395	3808	1064	197	31	60	1.6	480	486	419	329	19	83	24	2566	82	36	23	2.3	.987	OF-1155

Roy Grover

GROVER, ROY ARTHUR BR TR 5′ 8″ 150 lbs.
B. Jan. 17, 1892, Snohomish, Wash. D. Feb. 7, 1978, Milwaukie, Ore.

Year	Team	Lg	Games	BA	SA	AB	H	2B	3B	HR	HR%	R	RBI	BB	SO	SB	Pinch Hit AB	Pinch Hit H	PO	A	E	DP	TC/G	FA	G by Pos
1916	PHI	A	20	.273	.338	77	21	1	2	0	0.0	8	7	6	10	5	0	0	40	40	4	7	4.2	.952	2B-20
1917			141	.224	.284	482	108	15	7	0	0.0	45	34	43	53	12	1	0	279	425	29	51	5.3	.960	2B-139
1919	2 teams		PHI A (22G –.232) WAS A (24G –.187)																						
″	total		46	.206	.214	131	27	1	0	0	0.0	14	9	11	16	2	5	0	88	81	14	9	4.7	.923	2B-36, 3B-3
3 yrs.			207	.226	.277	690	156	17	9	0	0.0	67	50	60	79	19	6	0	407	546	47	67	5.1	.953	2B-195, 3B-3

Harvey Grubb

GRUBB, HARVEY HARRISON BR TR 6′ 165 lbs.
B. Sept. 18, 1890, Lexington, N. C. D. Jan. 25, 1970, Corpus Christi, Tex.

Year	Team	Lg	Games	BA	SA	AB	H	2B	3B	HR	HR%	R	RBI	BB	SO	SB	Pinch Hit AB	Pinch Hit H	PO	A	E	DP	TC/G	FA	G by Pos
1912	CLE	A	1	—	—	0	0	0	0	0	—	0	0	0		0	0	0	1	0	0	0	1.0	1.000	OF-1

Johnny Grubb

GRUBB, JOHN RAYMOND, JR. BL TR 6′ 3″ 175 lbs.
B. Aug. 4, 1948, Richmond, Va.

Year	Team	Lg	Games	BA	SA	AB	H	2B	3B	HR	HR%	R	RBI	BB	SO	SB	Pinch Hit AB	Pinch Hit H	PO	A	E	DP	TC/G	FA	G by Pos
1972	SD	N	7	.333	.476	21	7	1	1	0	0.0	4	1	1	3	0	1	0	16	0	0	0	2.7	1.000	OF-6
1973			113	.311	.445	389	121	22	3	8	2.1	52	37	37	50	9	12	7	229	11	3	1	2.3	.988	OF-102, 3B-2
1974			140	.286	.403	444	127	20	4	8	1.8	53	42	46	47	4	17	3	321	8	8	1	2.7	.976	OF-122, 3B-2
1975			144	.269	.363	553	149	36	2	4	0.7	72	38	59	59	2	6	0	334	3	3	0	2.4	.991	OF-139
1976			109	.284	.385	384	109	22	1	5	1.3	54	27	65	53	1	5	0	248	7	6	7	2.4	.977	OF-98, 1B-9, 3B-3
1977	CLE	A	34	.301	.462	93	28	3	3	2	2.2	8	14	19	18	0	1	0	47	2	0	0	1.5	1.000	OF-28, DH-4
1978	2 teams		CLE A (113G –.265) TEX A (21G –.394)																						
″	total		134	.275	.460	411	113	19	6	15	3.6	62	67	70	65	6	11	5	213	16	6	5	1.9	.974	OF-123, DH-3
1979	TEX	A	102	.273	.426	289	79	14	0	10	3.5	42	37	34	44	2	24	6	135	8	2	4	1.6	.986	OF-82, DH-6
1980			110	.277	.427	274	76	12	1	9	3.3	40	32	42	35	2	28	7	112	6	6	1	1.5	.952	OF-77, DH-8
1981			67	.231	.332	199	46	9	1	3	1.5	26	26	23	25	0	9	2	95	2	1	0	1.7	.990	OF-58
1982			103	.279	.370	308	86	13	3	3	1.0	35	26	39	37	0	14	4	135	4	5	1	1.5	.965	OF-77, DH-18
1983	DET	A	57	.254	.410	134	34	5	2	4	3.0	20	22	28	17	0	10	4	34	1	0	0	0.8	1.000	OF-26, DH-18
1984			86	.267	.432	176	47	5	0	8	4.5	25	17	36	36	1	22	8	47	0	0	0	0.7	1.000	OF-36, DH-33
1985			78	.245	.400	155	38	7	1	5	3.2	19	25	24	25	0	24	4	23	0	0	0	0.5	1.000	DH-33, OF-18
1986			81	.333	.590	210	70	13	1	13	6.2	32	51	28	28	0	19	5	26	1	0	0	0.4	1.000	DH-52, OF-19
1987			59	.202	.307	114	23	6	0	2	1.8	9	13	15	16	0	21	4	42	1	0	0	0.9	1.000	OF-31, DH-16, 3B-1
16 yrs.			1424	.278	.413	4154	1153	207	29	99	2.4	553	475	566	558	27	224	59	2057	70	40	20	1.7	.982	OF-1042, DH-191, 1B-9, 3B-8
LEAGUE CHAMPIONSHIP SERIES																									
1984	DET	A	1	.250	.500	4	1	1	0	0	0.0	0	2	0	0	0	0	0	0	0	0	0	0.0	—	
1987			4	.571	.571	7	4	0	0	0	0.0	0	0	0	1	0	3	2	0	0	0	0	0.0	.000	DH-1
2 yrs.			5	.455	.545	11	5	1	0	0	0.0	0	2	0	1	0	3	2	0	0	0	0	0.0		DH-1
WORLD SERIES																									
1984	DET	A	4	.333	.333	3	1	0	0	0	0.0	0	0	0	0	0	0	0	0	0	0	0	0.0	.000	DH-2

Frank Grube

GRUBE, FRANKLIN THOMAS (Hans) BR TR 5′ 9″ 190 lbs.
B. Jan. 7, 1905, Easton, Pa. D. July 2, 1945, New York, N. Y.

Year	Team	Lg	Games	BA	SA	AB	H	2B	3B	HR	HR%	R	RBI	BB	SO	SB	Pinch Hit AB	Pinch Hit H	PO	A	E	DP	TC/G	FA	G by Pos
1931	CHI	A	88	.219	.294	265	58	13	2	1	0.4	29	24	22	22	2	6	1	248	50	7	3	3.8	.977	C-81
1932			93	.282	.354	277	78	16	2	0	0.0	36	31	33	13	6	1	0	303	55	16	5	4.1	.957	C-92
1933			85	.230	.281	256	59	13	0	0	0.0	23	23	38	20	1	1	0	266	44	5	5	3.8	.984	C-83
1934	STL	A	65	.288	.347	170	49	10	0	0	0.0	22	11	24	11	2	9	0	186	21	8	4	3.9	.963	C-55
1935	2 teams		STL A (3G –.333) CHI A (9G –.368)																						
″	total		12	.360	.480	25	9	3	0	0	0.0	4	6	3	3	0	0	0	36	6	2	0	3.7	.955	C-12
1936	CHI	A	33	.161	.204	93	15	2	1	0	0.0	6	11	9	15	1	2	0	89	19	1	2	3.4	.991	C-32
1941	STL	A	18	.154	.205	39	6	2	0	0	0.0	1	1	2	4	0	0	0	45	13	3	1	3.4	.951	C-18
7 yrs.			394	.244	.308	1125	274	59	5	1	0.1	121	107	131	88	12	19	1	1173	208	42	20	3.8	.970	C-373

Kelly Gruber

GRUBER, KELLY WAYNE BR TR 6′ 175 lbs.
B. Feb. 26, 1962, Houston, Tex.

Year	Team	Games	BA	SA	AB	H	2B	3B	HR	HR%	R	RBI	BB	SO	SB	Pinch Hit AB	Pinch Hit H	PO	A	E	DP	TC/G	FA	G by Pos
1984	TOR A	15	.063	.250	16	1	0	0	1	6.3	1	2	0	5	0	4	1	6	12	2	0	1.3	.900	3B-12, OF-2, SS-1
1985		5	.231	.231	13	3	0	0	0	0.0	0	1	0	3	0	1	1	2	6	0	0	1.3	1.000	3B-5, 2B-1
1986		87	.196	.343	143	28	4	1	5	3.5	20	15	5	27	2	9	2	43	77	7	8	1.5	.945	3B-42, 2B-14, DH-14, OF-9, SS-5
1987		138	.235	.399	341	80	14	3	12	3.5	50	36	17	70	12	16	2	76	200	13	19	1.9	.955	3B-119, SS-21, 2B-7, OF-2
1988		158	.278	.438	569	158	33	5	16	2.8	75	81	38	92	23	3	0	121	365	16	35	3.0	.968	3B-156, 2B-7, OF-2, SS-1
1989		135	.290	.448	545	158	24	4	18	3.3	83	73	30	60	10	1	1	121	295	22	16	3.2	.950	3B-119, OF-16, SS-1, DH-1
1990		150	.274	.512	592	162	36	6	31	5.2	92	118	48	94	14	2	1	129	280	19	21	2.8	.956	3B-145, OF-6, DH-1
1991		113	.252	.443	429	108	18	2	20	4.7	58	65	31	70	12	1	0	97	231	13	16	3.0	.962	3B-111, DH-2
1992		120	.229	.352	446	102	16	3	11	2.5	42	43	26	72	7	1	0	104	215	17	10	2.8	.949	3B-120
1993	CAL A	18	.277	.462	65	18	3	0	3	4.6	10	9	2	11	0	0	0	20	42	4	3	3.5	.939	3B-17, OF-1, DH-1
10 yrs.		939	.259	.432	3159	818	148	24	117	3.7	431	443	197	504	80	38	8	719	1723	113	128	2.7	.956	3B-846, OF-38, 2B-29, SS-29, DH-19
LEAGUE CHAMPIONSHIP SERIES																								
1989	TOR A	5	.294	.353	17	5	1	0	0	0.0	2	1	3	2	1	0	0	4	8	0	1	2.4	1.000	3B-5
1991		5	.286	.333	21	6	1	0	0	0.0	1	4	0	4	1	0	0	3	6	3	0	2.4	.750	3B-5
1992		6	.091	.273	22	2	1	0	1	4.5	3	2	2	3	0	0	0	5	16	1	2	3.7	.955	3B-6
3 yrs.		16	.217	.317	60	13	3	0	1	1.7	6	7	5	9	2	0	0	12	30	4	3	2.9	.913	3B-16
WORLD SERIES																								
1992	TOR A	6	.105	.263	19	2	0	0	1	5.3	2	1	2	5	1	0	0	5	5	1	0	1.8	.909	3B-6

Mark Grudzielanek

GRUDZIELANEK, MARK JAMES BR TR 6′ 1″ 185 lbs.
B. June 30, 1970, Milwaukee, Wis.

Year	Team	Games	BA	SA	AB	H	2B	3B	HR	HR%	R	RBI	BB	SO	SB	Pinch Hit AB	Pinch Hit H	PO	A	E	DP	TC/G	FA	G by Pos
1995	MON N	78	.245	.316	269	66	12	2	1	0.4	27	20	14	47	8	3	0	94	197	10	25	3.9	.967	SS-34, 3B-31, 2B-13

Sig Gryska

GRYSKA, SIGMUND STANLEY BR TR 5′11½″ 173 lbs.
B. Nov. 4, 1915, Chicago, Ill.

Year	Team	Games	BA	SA	AB	H	2B	3B	HR	HR%	R	RBI	BB	SO	SB	Pinch Hit AB	Pinch Hit H	PO	A	E	DP	TC/G	FA	G by Pos
1938	STL A	7	.476	.667	21	10	2	1	0	0.0	3	4	3	3	0	0	0	14	17	3	5	4.9	.912	SS-7
1939		18	.265	.306	49	13	2	0	0	0.0	4	8	6	10	3	3	1	20	35	8	4	4.5	.873	SS-14
2 yrs.		25	.329	.414	70	23	4	1	0	0.0	7	12	9	13	3	3	1	34	52	11	9	4.6	.887	SS-21

Marv Gudat

GUDAT, MARVIN JOHN BL TL 5′11″ 162 lbs.
B. Aug. 27, 1905, Goliad, Tex. D. Mar. 1, 1954, Los Angeles, Calif.

Year	Team	Games	BA	SA	AB	H	2B	3B	HR	HR%	R	RBI	BB	SO	SB	Pinch Hit AB	Pinch Hit H	PO	A	E	DP	TC/G	FA	G by Pos
1929	CIN N	9	.200	.200	10	2	0	0	0	0.0	0	0	0	0	0	2	0	0	4	1	0	0.7	.800	P-7
1932	CHI N	60	.255	.351	94	24	4	1	1	1.1	15	15	16	10	0	30	10	77	4	2	4	3.6	.976	OF-14, 1B-8, P-1
2 yrs.		69	.250	.337	104	26	4	1	1	1.0	15	15	16	10	0	32	10	77	8	3	4	2.9	.966	OF-14, 1B-8, P-8
WORLD SERIES																								
1932	CHI N	2	.000	.000	2	0	0	0	0	0.0	0	0	0	1	0	2	0	0	0	0	0	0.0	—	

Mike Guerra

GUERRA, FERMIN BR TR 5′10″ 155 lbs.
Born Fermin Guerra (Romero).
B. Oct. 11, 1912, Havana, Cuba D. Oct. 9, 1992, Miami Beach, Fla.

Year	Team	Games	BA	SA	AB	H	2B	3B	HR	HR%	R	RBI	BB	SO	SB	Pinch Hit AB	Pinch Hit H	PO	A	E	DP	TC/G	FA	G by Pos
1937	WAS A	1	.000	.000	3	0	0	0	0	0.0	0	0	0	2	0	0	0	3	0	1	0	4.0	.750	C-1
1944		75	.281	.348	210	59	7	2	1	0.5	29	29	13	14	8	6	3	211	32	10	8	4.3	.960	C-58, OF-1
1945		56	.210	.254	138	29	1	1	1	0.7	11	15	10	12	4	12	3	163	28	2	3	5.1	.990	C-38
1946		41	.253	.301	83	21	2	1	0	0.0	3	4	5	6	1	10	1	75	16	6	4	3.6	.938	C-27
1947	PHI A	72	.215	.244	209	45	2	2	0	0.0	20	18	10	15	1	7	1	203	36	9	5	4.0	.964	C-62
1948		53	.211	.289	142	30	4	2	1	0.7	18	23	18	13	2	2	0	163	20	5	1	4.0	.973	C-47
1949		98	.265	.349	298	79	14	1	3	1.0	41	31	37	26	3	1	0	328	48	7	3	4.0	.982	C-95
1950		87	.282	.377	252	71	10	4	2	0.8	25	26	16	12	1	9	1	253	33	3	8	3.7	.990	C-78
1951	2 teams	BOS A (10G –.156)	WAS A (72G –.201)																					
″	total	82	.195	.224	246	48	2	1	1	0.4	21	22	22	23	4	4	1	238	29	5	1	3.6	.982	C-76
9 yrs.		565	.242	.303	1581	382	42	14	9	0.6	168	168	131	123	24	51	10	1637	242	48	33	4.0	.975	C-482, OF-1

Juan Guerrero

GUERRERO, JUAN ANTONIO BR TR 5′11″ 160 lbs.
Born Juan Antonio Guerrero (De La Cruz).
B. Feb. 1, 1967, Los Llanos, Dominican Republic.

Year	Team	Games	BA	SA	AB	H	2B	3B	HR	HR%	R	RBI	BB	SO	SB	Pinch Hit AB	Pinch Hit H	PO	A	E	DP	TC/G	FA	G by Pos
1992	HOU N	79	.200	.288	125	25	4	2	1	0.8	8	14	10	32	1	38	5	19	50	2	5	2.0	.972	SS-19, 3B-12, OF-3, 2B-2

Mario Guerrero

GUERRERO, MARIO MIGUEL BR TR 5′10″ 155 lbs.
Born Mario Miguel Guerrero (Abud).
B. Sept. 28, 1949, Santo Domingo, Dominican Republic.

Year	Team	Games	BA	SA	AB	H	2B	3B	HR	HR%	R	RBI	BB	SO	SB	Pinch Hit AB	Pinch Hit H	PO	A	E	DP	TC/G	FA	G by Pos
1973	BOS A	66	.233	.274	219	51	5	2	0	0.0	19	11	10	21	2	0	0	106	183	8	49	4.2	.973	SS-46, 2B-24
1974		93	.246	.282	284	70	6	2	0	0.0	18	23	13	22	3	0	0	136	266	13	50	4.5	.969	SS-93
1975	STL N	64	.239	.288	184	44	9	0	0	0.0	17	11	10	7	0	0	0	76	198	13	29	4.5	.955	SS-64
1976	CAL A	83	.284	.340	268	76	12	0	1	0.4	24	18	7	12	0	1	0	129	172	14	32	3.5	.956	2B-41, SS-41, DH-7
1977		86	.283	.344	244	69	8	2	1	0.4	17	28	4	16	0	27	4	61	105	2	18	2.7	.988	SS-31, DH-19, 2B-12
1978	OAK A	143	.275	.345	505	139	18	4	3	0.6	27	38	15	35	0	2	0	258	330	26	67	4.3	.958	SS-142
1979		46	.229	.259	166	38	5	0	0	0.0	12	18	6	7	0	3	0	68	129	10	33	4.8	.952	SS-43
1980		116	.239	.307	381	91	16	2	2	0.5	32	23	19	32	3	0	0	184	276	18	50	4.1	.962	SS-116
8 yrs.		697	.257	.312	2251	578	79	12	7	0.3	166	170	84	152	8	33	4	1018	1659	104	328	4.1	.963	SS-576, 2B-77, DH-26

Pedro Guerrero

GUERRERO, PEDRO (Pete) BR TR 5′11″ 176 lbs.
B. June 29, 1956, San Pedro de Macoris, Dominican Republic.

Year	Team	Games	BA	SA	AB	H	2B	3B	HR	HR%	R	RBI	BB	SO	SB	Pinch Hit AB	Pinch Hit H	PO	A	E	DP	TC/G	FA	G by Pos
1978	LA N	5	.625	.875	8	5	0	1	0	0.0	3	1	0	0	0	1	1	25	1	0	0	6.5	1.000	1B-4
1979		25	.242	.371	62	15	2	0	2	3.2	7	9	1	14	2	7	3	53	4	1	1	2.5	.983	OF-12, 1B-8, 3B-3
1980		75	.322	.497	183	59	9	1	7	3.8	27	31	12	31	2	17	11	103	37	3	5	2.5	.979	OF-40, 2B-12, 3B-3, 1B-2
1981		98	.300	.464	347	104	17	2	12	3.5	46	48	34	57	5	4	1	165	55	11	5	2.4	.952	OF-75, 3B-21, 1B-1
1982		150	.304	.536	575	175	27	5	32	5.6	87	100	65	89	22	0	0	282	53	12	9	2.2	.965	OF-137, 3B-24
1983		160	.298	.531	584	174	28	6	32	5.5	87	103	72	110	23	1	1	130	308	31	22	2.9	.934	3B-157, 1B-2
1984		144	.303	.462	535	162	29	4	16	3.0	85	72	49	105	9	7	1	271	151	22	24	3.0	.950	3B-76, OF-58, 1B-16
1985		137	.320	**.577**	487	156	22	2	33	**6.8**	99	87	83	68	12	3	0	251	123	13	18	2.8	.966	OF-81, 3B-44, 1B-12
1986		31	.246	.541	61	15	3	0	5	8.2	7	10	2	19	0	17	3	39	1	0	4	2.9	1.000	OF-10, 1B-4
1987		152	.338	.539	545	184	25	2	27	5.0	89	89	74	85	9	4	0	482	44	12	30	3.6	.978	OF-109, 1B-40

Pedro Guerrero *continued*

Year	Team	Games	BA	SA	AB	H	2B	3B	HR	HR%	R	RBI	BB	SO	SB	Pinch Hit AB	Pinch Hit H	PO	A	E	DP	TC/G	FA	G by Pos
1988	**2 teams**	**LA N** (59G –.298)	**STL N** (44G –.268)																					
″	**total**	103	.286	.418	364	104	14	2	10	2.7	40	65	46	59	4	1	0	466	99	12	26	5.4	.979	1B-52, 3B-45, OF-9
1989	**STL N**	162	.311	.477	570	177	**42**	1	17	3.0	60	117	79	84	2	1	1	1445	72	15	99	9.6	.990	1B-160
1990		136	.281	.426	498	140	31	1	13	2.6	42	80	44	70	1	3	1	1083	73	13	74	8.9	.989	1B-132
1991		115	.272	.361	427	116	12	1	8	1.9	41	70	37	46	4	3	2	953	66	16	73	9.2	.985	1B-112
1992		43	.219	.295	146	32	6	1	1	0.7	10	16	11	25	2	3	0	259	6	4	17	7.1	.985	1B-28, OF-10
15 yrs.		1536	.300	.480	5392	1618	267	29	215	4.0	730	898	609	862	97	72	25	6007	1093	165	407	4.8	.977	1B-573, OF-541, 3B-373, 2B-12
DIVISIONAL PLAYOFF SERIES																								
1981	**LA N**	5	.176	.412	17	3	1	0	1	5.9	1	1	2	4	1	0	0	3	15	1	0	3.8	.947	3B-5
LEAGUE CHAMPIONSHIP SERIES																								
1981	**LA N**	5	.105	.263	19	2	0	0	1	5.3	1	2	1	4	0	0	0	9	2	0	1	2.2	1.000	OF-5
1983		4	.250	.500	12	3	1	1	0	0.0	1	2	3	3	0	0	0	0	9	0	1	2.3	1.000	3B-4
1985		6	.250	.300	20	5	1	0	0	0.0	2	4	5	2	2	0	0	11	0	0	0	1.8	1.000	OF-6
3 yrs.		15	.196	.333	51	10	2	1	1	2.0	4	8	9	9	2	0	0	20	11	0	2	2.1	1.000	OF-11, 3B-4
WORLD SERIES																								
1981	**LA N**	6	.333	.762	21	7	1	1	2	9.5	2	7	2	6	0	0	0	17	1	0	0	3.0	1.000	OF-6

Ozzie Guillen

GUILLEN, OSWALDO JOSE BL TR 5′11″ 160 lbs.
Born Oswaldo Jose Guillen (Barrios).
B. Jan. 20, 1964, Oculare del Tuy, Venezuela.

Year	Team	Games	BA	SA	AB	H	2B	3B	HR	HR%	R	RBI	BB	SO	SB	Pinch Hit AB	Pinch Hit H	PO	A	E	DP	TC/G	FA	G by Pos
1985	**CHI A**	150	.273	.358	491	134	21	9	1	0.2	71	33	12	36	7	13	1	220	382	12	80	4.1	.980	SS-150
1986		159	.250	.311	547	137	19	4	2	0.4	58	47	12	52	8	2	0	261	459	22	93	4.7	.970	SS-157, DH-1
1987		149	.279	.354	560	156	22	7	2	0.4	64	51	22	52	25	2	1	266	475	19	105	5.1	.975	SS-149
1988		156	.261	.314	566	148	16	7	0	0.0	58	39	25	40	25	0	0	273	570	20	115	5.5	.977	SS-156
1989		155	.253	.318	597	151	20	8	1	0.2	63	54	15	48	36	0	0	272	512	22	106	5.2	.973	SS-155
1990		160	.279	.341	516	144	21	4	1	0.2	61	58	26	37	13	2	0	252	474	17	100	4.7	.977	SS-159
1991		154	.273	.340	524	143	20	3	3	0.6	52	49	11	38	21	6	1	249	439	21	88	4.8	.970	SS-149
1992		12	.200	.300	40	8	4	0	0	0.0	5	7	1	5	1	0	0	20	39	0	7	4.9	1.000	SS-12
1993		134	.280	.374	457	128	23	4	4	0.9	44	50	10	41	5	3	1	189	361	16	82	4.3	.972	SS-133
1994		100	.288	.348	365	105	9	5	1	0.3	46	39	14	35	5	2	0	141	235	16	44	4.0	.959	SS-99
1995		122	.248	.318	415	103	20	3	1	0.2	50	41	13	25	6	8	3	167	318	12	55	4.1	.976	SS-120, DH-1
11 yrs.		1451	.267	.336	5078	1357	195	54	16	0.3	572	468	161	409	152	38	7	2310	4264	177	875	4.7	.974	SS-1439, DH-2
LEAGUE CHAMPIONSHIP SERIES																								
1993	**CHI A**	6	.273	.318	22	6	1	0	0	0.0	4	2	0	2	1	0	0	12	14	0	4	4.3	1.000	SS-6

Bob Guindon

GUINDON, ROBERT JOSEPH BL TL 6′ 2″ 185 lbs.
B. Sept. 4, 1943, Brookline, Mass.

Year	Team	Games	BA	SA	AB	H	2B	3B	HR	HR%	R	RBI	BB	SO	SB	Pinch Hit AB	Pinch Hit H	PO	A	E	DP	TC/G	FA	G by Pos
1964	**BOS A**	5	.125	.250	8	1	1	0	0	0.0	0	0	1	4	0	0	0	8	0	0	0	4.0	1.000	OF-1, 1B-1

Ben Guiney

GUINEY, BENJAMIN FRANKLIN BB TR 6′ 170 lbs.
B. Nov. 16, 1858, Detroit, Mich. D. Dec. 5, 1930, Detroit, Mich.

Year	Team	Games	BA	SA	AB	H	2B	3B	HR	HR%	R	RBI	BB	SO	SB	Pinch Hit AB	Pinch Hit H	PO	A	E	DP	TC/G	FA	G by Pos
1883	**DET N**	1	.200	.200	5	1	0	0	0	0.0	1		0	1		0	0	0	0	1	0	0.5	.000	2B-1, OF-1
1884		2	.000	.000	7	0	0	0	0	0.0	0		0	3		0	0	3	3	2	0	4.0	.750	C-2
2 yrs.		3	.083	.083	12	1	0	0	0	0.0	1		0	4		0	0	3	3	3	0	2.3	.667	C-2, 2B-1, OF-1

Ben Guintini

GUINTINI, BENJAMIN JOHN BR TR 6′ 1½″ 190 lbs.
B. Jan. 13, 1920, Los Banos, Calif.

Year	Team	Games	BA	SA	AB	H	2B	3B	HR	HR%	R	RBI	BB	SO	SB	Pinch Hit AB	Pinch Hit H	PO	A	E	DP	TC/G	FA	G by Pos
1946	**PIT N**	2	.000	.000	3	0	0	0	0	0.0	0	0	0	0	0	1	0	1	0	0	0	1.0	1.000	OF-1
1950	**PHI A**	3	.000	.000	4	0	0	0	0	0.0	0	0	0	1	0	2	0	0	1	0	0	1.0	1.000	OF-1
2 yrs.		5	.000	.000	7	0	0	0	0	0.0	0	0	0	1	0	3	0	1	1	0	0	1.0	1.000	OF-2

Lou Guisto

GUISTO, LOUIS JOSEPH BR TR 5′11″ 193 lbs.
B. Jan. 16, 1895, Napa, Calif. D. Oct. 15, 1989, Napa, Calif.

Year	Team	Games	BA	SA	AB	H	2B	3B	HR	HR%	R	RBI	BB	SO	SB	Pinch Hit AB	Pinch Hit H	PO	A	E	DP	TC/G	FA	G by Pos
1916	**CLE A**	6	.158	.158	19	3	0	0	0	0.0	2	2	4	3	1	0	0	66	3	0	3	11.5	1.000	1B-6
1917		73	.185	.225	200	37	4	2	0	0.0	9	29	25	18	3	11	2	611	33	7	45	11.0	.989	1B-59
1921		2	.500	.500	2	1	0	0	0	0.0	0	1	0	1	0	1	1	5	1	0	0	6.0	1.000	1B-1
1922		35	.250	.393	84	21	10	1	0	0.0	7	9	2	7	0	10	3	202	14	1	15	9.0	.995	1B-24
1923		40	.181	.215	144	26	5	0	0	0.0	17	18	15	15	1	0	0	389	28	5	30	10.6	.988	1B-40
5 yrs.		156	.196	.252	449	88	19	3	0	0.0	35	59	46	44	5	22	6	1273	79	13	93	10.5	.990	1B-130

Brad Gulden

GULDEN, BRADLEY LEE BL TR 5′10″ 175 lbs.
B. June 10, 1956, New Ulm, Minn.

Year	Team	Games	BA	SA	AB	H	2B	3B	HR	HR%	R	RBI	BB	SO	SB	Pinch Hit AB	Pinch Hit H	PO	A	E	DP	TC/G	FA	G by Pos
1978	**LA N**	3	.000	.000	4	0	0	0	0	0.0	0	0	0	2	0	0	0	8	1	0	1	3.0	1.000	C-3
1979	**NY A**	40	.163	.207	92	15	4	0	0	0.0	10	6	9	16	0	0	0	178	24	1	4	5.1	.995	C-40
1980		2	.333	1.333	3	1	0	0	1	33.3	1	2	0	0	0	0	0	3	0	0	0	1.5	1.000	C-2
1981	**SEA A**	8	.188	.313	16	3	2	0	0	0.0	0	1	0	2	0	4	0	24	3	0	0	3.4	1.000	C-6, DH-2
1982	**MON N**	5	.000	.000	6	0	0	0	0	0.0	1	0	1	1	0	3	0	6	2	0	0	4.0	1.000	C-2
1984	**CIN N**	107	.226	.308	292	66	8	2	4	1.4	31	33	33	35	2	20	3	485	53	14	8	5.5	.975	C-100
1986	**SF N**	17	.091	.091	22	2	0	0	0	0.0	2	1	2	5	0	9	0	26	1	0	0	2.7	1.000	C-10
7 yrs.		182	.200	.276	435	87	14	2	5	1.1	45	43	45	61	2	36	3	730	84	15	13	5.0	.982	C-163, DH-2

Tom Gulley

GULLEY, THOMAS JEFFERSON BL TR 5′11″ 178 lbs.
B. Dec. 25, 1899, Garner, N. C. D. Nov. 24, 1966, St. Charles, Ark.

Year	Team	Games	BA	SA	AB	H	2B	3B	HR	HR%	R	RBI	BB	SO	SB	Pinch Hit AB	Pinch Hit H	PO	A	E	DP	TC/G	FA	G by Pos
1923	**CLE A**	2	.333	.667	3	1	1	0	0	0.0	1	0	0	0	0	1	0	1	0	0	0	1.0	1.000	OF-1
1924		8	.150	.250	20	3	0	1	0	0.0	4	1	3	2	0	3	0	14	0	1	0	3.0	.933	OF-5
1926	**CHI A**	16	.229	.371	35	8	3	1	0	0.0	5	8	5	2	0	4	1	19	0	0	0	1.6	1.000	OF-12
3 yrs.		26	.207	.345	58	12	4	2	0	0.0	10	9	8	4	0	8	1	34	0	1	0	1.9	.971	OF-18

Year	Team	Lg	Games	BA	SA	AB	H	2B	3B	HR	HR%	R	RBI	BB	SO	SB	Pinch Hit AB	Pinch Hit H	PO	A	E	DP	TC/G	FA	G by Pos

Ted Gullic

GULLIC, THEODORE JASPER BR TR 6′ 2″ 175 lbs.
B. Jan. 2, 1907, Koshkonong, Mo.

Year	Team	Lg	Games	BA	SA	AB	H	2B	3B	HR	HR%	R	RBI	BB	SO	SB	PH AB	PH H	PO	A	E	DP	TC/G	FA	G by Pos
1930	STL	A	92	.250	.344	308	77	7	5	4	1.3	39	44	27	43	4	6	0	165	17	5	3	2.2	.973	OF-82, 1B-3
1933			104	.243	.372	304	74	18	3	5	1.6	34	35	15	38	3	24	4	229	74	5	8	3.7	.984	OF-36, 3B-33, 1B-14
2 yrs.			196	.247	.358	612	151	25	8	9	1.5	73	79	42	81	7	30	4	394	91	10	11	2.9	.980	OF-118, 3B-33, 1B-17

Glenn Gulliver

GULLIVER, GLENN JAMES BL TR 5′11″ 175 lbs.
B. Oct. 15, 1954, Detroit, Mich.

Year	Team	Lg	Games	BA	SA	AB	H	2B	3B	HR	HR%	R	RBI	BB	SO	SB	PH AB	PH H	PO	A	E	DP	TC/G	FA	G by Pos
1982	BAL	A	50	.200	.269	145	29	7	0	1	0.7	24	5	37	18	0	1	0	34	97	4	6	2.7	.970	3B-50
1983			23	.213	.277	47	10	3	0	0	0.0	5	2	9	5	0	4	0	14	31	0	3	2.1	1.000	3B-21
2 yrs.			73	.203	.271	192	39	10	0	1	0.5	29	7	46	23	0	5	0	48	128	4	9	2.5	.978	3B-71

Ad Gumbert

GUMBERT, ADDISON COURTNEY BR TR 5′10″ 200 lbs.
Brother of Billy Gumbert.
B. Oct. 10, 1868, Pittsburgh, Pa. D. Apr. 23, 1925, Pittsburgh, Pa.

Year	Team	Lg	Games	BA	SA	AB	H	2B	3B	HR	HR%	R	RBI	BB	SO	SB	PH AB	PH H	PO	A	E	DP	TC/G	FA	G by Pos
1888	CHI	N	7	.333	.417	24	8	0	1	0	0.0	3	2	0	2	0	0	0	4	8	1	0	1.6	.923	P-6, OF-2
1889			41	.288	.471	153	44	3	2	7	4.6	30	29	11	36	2	0	0	48	44	15	1	2.4	.860	P-31, OF-13
1890	BOS	P	44	.241	.366	145	35	7	1	3	2.1	23	20	18	26	5	0	0	24	83	14	0	2.6	.884	P-39, OF-7
1891	CHI	N	34	.305	.448	105	32	7	4	0	0.0	18	16	13	14	4	0	0	19	56	8	4	2.4	.904	P-32, 1B-1, OF-1
1892			52	.236	.281	178	42	1	2	1	0.6	18	8	14	24	5	0	0	20	97	11	1	2.4	.914	P-46, OF-7
1893	PIT	N	29	.221	.316	95	21	3	3	0	0.0	17	10	10	16	0	0	0	19	24	1	3	1.5	.977	P-22, OF-7
1894			38	.292	.442	113	33	4	5	1	0.9	18	19	6	20	1	1	0	18	49	4	3	1.9	.944	P-37
1895	BKN	N	34	.361	.485	97	35	6	0	2	2.1	21	13	7	10	0	0	0	15	48	5	0	2.0	.926	P-33, OF-1
1896	2 teams BKN N (5G –.182) PHI N (11G –.265)																								
″	total		16	.244	.400	45	11	2	1	1	2.2	7	7	1	5	1	0	0	5	28	2	1	2.2	.943	P-16
9 yrs.			295	.273	.395	955	261	33	19	15	1.6	155	124	80	153	18	1	0	172	437	61	13	2.2	.909	P-262, OF-38, 1B-1

Fred Gunkle

GUNKLE, FREDERICK W.
B. Reading, Pa. Deceased.

Year	Team	Lg	Games	BA	SA	AB	H	2B	3B	HR	HR%	R	RBI	BB	SO	SB	PH AB	PH H	PO	A	E	DP	TC/G	FA	G by Pos
1879	CLE	N	1	.000	.000	3	0	0	0	0	0.0	1	0	0	1		0	0	2	0	3	0	2.5	.400	OF-1, C-1

Hy Gunning

GUNNING, HYLAND BL TR 6′ 1½″ 189 lbs.
B. Aug. 6, 1888, Maplewood, N. J. D. Mar. 28, 1975, Togus, Me.

Year	Team	Lg	Games	BA	SA	AB	H	2B	3B	HR	HR%	R	RBI	BB	SO	SB	PH AB	PH H	PO	A	E	DP	TC/G	FA	G by Pos
1911	BOS	A	4	.111	.111	9	1	0	0	0	0.0	0	2	2		0	0	0	25	0	0	0	6.3	1.000	1B-4

Tom Gunning

GUNNING, THOMAS FRANCIS BR TR 5′10″ 160 lbs.
B. Mar. 4, 1862, Newmarket, N. H. D. Mar. 17, 1931, Fall River, Mass.

Year	Team	Lg	Games	BA	SA	AB	H	2B	3B	HR	HR%	R	RBI	BB	SO	SB	PH AB	PH H	PO	A	E	DP	TC/G	FA	G by Pos
1884	BOS	N	12	.111	.178	45	5	1	1	0	0.0	4		1	12		0	0	60	14	7	1	6.8	.914	C-12
1885			48	.184	.201	174	32	3	0	0	0.0	17	15	5	29		0	0	252	68	45	4	7.6	.877	C-48
1886			27	.224	.265	98	22	2	1	0	0.0	15	7	3	19		0	0	162	27	23	4	7.9	.892	C-27
1887	PHI	N	28	.260	.365	104	27	6	1	1	1.0	22	16	5	6	18	0	0	133	55	22	6	7.5	.895	C-28
1888	PHI	AA	23	.196	.196	92	18	0	0	0	0.0	18	5	2		14	0	0	130	38	20	4	8.2	.894	C-23
1889			8	.250	.458	24	6	0	1	1	4.2	3	1	0	4	3	0	0	24	7	6	2	4.6	.838	C-8
6 yrs.			146	.205	.253	537	110	12	4	2	0.4	79	44	16	70	35	0	0	761	209	123	21	7.5	.887	C-146

Joe Gunson

GUNSON, JOSEPH BROOK BR TR 5′ 6″ 160 lbs.
B. Mar. 23, 1863, Philadelphia, Pa. D. Nov. 15, 1942, Philadelphia, Pa.

Year	Team	Lg	Games	BA	SA	AB	H	2B	3B	HR	HR%	R	RBI	BB	SO	SB	PH AB	PH H	PO	A	E	DP	TC/G	FA	G by Pos
1884	WAS	U	45	.139	.151	166	23	2	0	0	0.0	15		3			0	0	237	59	33	0	6.5	.900	C-33, OF-18
1889	KC	AA	34	.197	.238	122	24	3	1	0	0.0	15	12	3	17	2	0	0	118	44	27	2	5.6	.857	C-32, 3B-1, OF-1
1892	BAL	N	89	.213	.277	314	67	10	5	0	0.0	35	32	16	17	2	0	0	324	98	37	6	5.1	.919	C-67, OF-20, 1B-2, 2B-1
1893	2 teams STL N (40G –.272) CLE N (21G –.260)																								
″	total		61	.268	.295	224	60	6	0	0	0.0	31	24	12	6	0	2	1	198	58	18	6	4.6	.934	C-55, OF-5
4 yrs.			229	.211	.251	826	174	21	6	0	0.0	96	68	34	40	4	2	1	877	259	115	14	5.3	.908	C-187, OF-44, 1B-2, 2B-1, 3B-1

Ernie Gust

GUST, ERNEST HERMAN FRANK (Red) BR TR 6′ 170 lbs.
B. Jan. 24, 1888, Bay City, Mich. D. Oct. 26, 1945, Maupin, Ore.

Year	Team	Lg	Games	BA	SA	AB	H	2B	3B	HR	HR%	R	RBI	BB	SO	SB	PH AB	PH H	PO	A	E	DP	TC/G	FA	G by Pos
1911	STL	A	3	.000	.000	12	0	0	0	0	0.0	0	0	0		0	0	0	35	2	1	2	12.7	.974	1B-3

Frankie Gustine

GUSTINE, FRANK WILLIAM BR TR 6′ 175 lbs.
B. Feb. 20, 1920, Hoopeston, Ill. D. Apr. 1, 1991, Davenport, Iowa.

Year	Team	Lg	Games	BA	SA	AB	H	2B	3B	HR	HR%	R	RBI	BB	SO	SB	PH AB	PH H	PO	A	E	DP	TC/G	FA	G by Pos
1939	PIT	N	22	.186	.229	70	13	3	0	0	0.0	5	3	9	4	0	0	0	17	52	8	3	3.5	.896	3B-22
1940			133	.281	.374	524	147	32	7	1	0.2	59	55	35	39	7	3	1	288	402	43	92	5.6	.941	2B-130
1941			121	.270	.359	463	125	24	7	1	0.2	46	46	28	38	5	2	0	293	353	36	47	5.7	.947	2B-104, 3B-15
1942			115	.229	.294	388	89	11	4	2	0.5	34	35	29	27	5	3	0	233	316	27	54	5.1	.953	2B-108, 3B-2, SS-2, C-1
1943			112	.290	.355	414	120	21	3	0	0.0	40	43	32	36	12	5	1	213	345	33	65	5.4	.944	SS-68, 2B-40, 1B-1
1944			127	.230	.304	405	93	18	3	2	0.5	42	42	33	41	8	1	0	206	351	36	55	4.6	.939	SS-116, 2B-11, 3B-1
1945			128	.280	.370	478	134	27	5	2	0.4	67	66	37	33	8	1	0	248	366	41	63	4.9	.937	SS-104, 2B-29, C-1
1946			131	.259	.378	495	128	23	6	8	1.6	60	52	40	52	2	1	0	319	387	24	70	5.5	.967	2B-113, SS-13, 3B-7
1947			156	.297	.409	616	183	30	6	9	1.5	102	67	63	65	5	0	0	198	330	31	35	3.6	.945	3B-156
1948			131	.267	.379	449	120	19	2	9	2.0	68	42	42	62	5	10	2	119	256	21	21	3.3	.947	3B-119
1949	CHI	N	76	.226	.352	261	59	13	4	4	1.5	29	27	18	22	3	5	0	104	157	16	28	3.9	.942	3B-55, 2B-16
1950	STL	A	9	.158	.211	19	3	1	0	0	0.0	1	2	3	8	0	1	0	10	8	3	3	3.5	.857	3B-6
12 yrs.			1261	.265	.359	4582	1214	222	47	38	0.8	553	480	369	427	60	32	4	2248	3323	319	536	4.8	.946	2B-551, 3B-383, SS-303, C-2, 1B-1

Bucky Guth

GUTH, CHARLES HENRY BR TR 6′ 1″ 180 lbs.
B. Aug. 18, 1947, Baltimore, Md.

Year	Team	Lg	Games	BA	SA	AB	H	2B	3B	HR	HR%	R	RBI	BB	SO	SB	PH AB	PH H	PO	A	E	DP	TC/G	FA	G by Pos
1972	MIN	A	3	.000	.000	3	0	0	0	0	0.0	1	0	0	0	0	0	0	0	4	0	0	4.0	1.000	SS-1

Cesar Gutierrez

GUTIERREZ, CESAR DARIO (Coca) BR TR 5′ 9″ 155 lbs.
B. Jan. 26, 1943, Coro, Venezuela.

Year	Team	Lg	Games	BA	SA	AB	H	2B	3B	HR	HR%	R	RBI	BB	SO	SB	PH AB	PH H	PO	A	E	DP	TC/G	FA	G by Pos
1967	SF	N	18	.143	.143	21	3	0	0	0	0.0	4	0	1	4	1	1	1	17	20	2	4	2.4	.949	SS-15, 2B-1
1969	2 teams SF N (15G –.217) DET A (17G –.245)																								
″	total		32	.236	.264	72	17	2	0	0	0.0	9	0	11	5	2	2	1	28	61	7	6	3.6	.927	SS-20, 3B-7

Cesar Gutierrez *continued*

Year	Team	Games	BA	SA	AB	H	2B	3B	HR	HR%	R	RBI	BB	SO	SB	Pinch Hit AB	Pinch Hit H	PO	A	E	DP	TC/G	FA	G by Pos
1970	DET A	135	.243	.299	415	101	11	6	0	0.0	40	22	18	39	4	0	0	183	326	23	60	3.9	.957	SS-135
1971		38	.189	.189	37	7	0	0	0	0.0	8	4	0	3	0	9	3	14	26	1	4	2.0	.976	SS-14, 3B-5, 2B-2
4 yrs.		223	.235	.281	545	128	13	6	0	0.0	61	26	30	51	7	12	5	242	433	33	74	3.6	.953	SS-184, 3B-12, 2B-3

Jackie Gutierrez

GUTIERREZ, JOAQUIN FERNANDO BR TR 5′11″ 168 lbs.
Born Joaquin Fernando Gutierrez (Hernandez).
B. June 27, 1960, Cartagena, Colombia.

Year	Team	Games	BA	SA	AB	H	2B	3B	HR	HR%	R	RBI	BB	SO	SB	Pinch Hit AB	Pinch Hit H	PO	A	E	DP	TC/G	FA	G by Pos
1983	BOS A	5	.300	.300	10	3	0	0	0	0.0	2	0	1	1	0	0	0	9	6	1	1	4.0	.938	SS-4
1984		151	.263	.316	449	118	12	3	2	0.4	55	29	15	49	12	0	0	228	347	31	60	4.0	.949	SS-150
1985		103	.218	.273	275	60	5	2	2	0.7	33	21	12	37	10	1	0	143	238	23	47	4.1	.943	SS-99
1986	BAL A	61	.186	.207	145	27	3	0	0	0.0	8	4	3	27	3	0	0	96	108	4	29	3.5	.981	2B-53, 3B-6, DH-1
1987		3	.000	.000	1	0	0	0	0	0.0	0	0	0	0	0	0	0	0	0	0	0	0.0		3B-1, 2B-1
1988	PHI N	33	.247	.299	77	19	4	0	0	0.0	8	9	2	9	0	1	0	28	59	8	7	2.7	.916	SS-22, 3B-13
6 yrs.		356	.237	.285	957	227	24	5	4	0.4	106	63	33	123	25	2	0	504	758	67	144	3.8	.950	SS-275, 2B-54, 3B-20, DH-1

Ricky Gutierrez

GUTIERREZ, RICARDO BR TR 6′ 1″ 175 lbs.
B. May 23, 1970, Miami, Fla.

Year	Team	Games	BA	SA	AB	H	2B	3B	HR	HR%	R	RBI	BB	SO	SB	Pinch Hit AB	Pinch Hit H	PO	A	E	DP	TC/G	FA	G by Pos
1993	SD N	133	.251	.331	438	110	10	5	5	1.1	76	26	50	97	4	8	2	194	305	14	55	3.9	.973	SS-117, 2B-6, OF-5, 3B-4
1994		90	.240	.305	275	66	11	2	1	0.4	27	28	32	54	2	6	1	93	202	22	34	3.7	.931	SS-78, 2B-7
1995	HOU N	52	.276	.314	156	43	6	0	0	0.0	22	12	10	33	5	4	1	64	107	8	17	3.9	.955	SS-44, 3B-2
3 yrs.		275	.252	.320	869	219	27	7	6	0.7	125	66	92	184	11	18	4	351	614	44	106	3.8	.956	SS-239, 2B-13, 3B-6, OF-5

Don Gutteridge

GUTTERIDGE, DONALD JOSEPH BR TR 5′10½″ 165 lbs.
B. June 19, 1912, Pittsburg, Kans.
Manager 1969–70.

Year	Team	Games	BA	SA	AB	H	2B	3B	HR	HR%	R	RBI	BB	SO	SB	Pinch Hit AB	Pinch Hit H	PO	A	E	DP	TC/G	FA	G by Pos
1936	STL N	23	.319	.538	91	29	3	4	3	3.3	13	16	1	14	3	0	0	25	34	2	3	2.7	.967	3B-23
1937		119	.271	.421	447	121	26	10	7	1.6	66	61	25	66	12	8	1	145	192	9	20	3.1	.974	3B-105, SS-8
1938		142	.255	.397	552	141	21	15	9	1.6	61	64	29	49	14	2	0	244	344	45	56	4.5	.929	3B-73, SS-68
1939		148	.269	.376	524	141	27	4	7	1.3	71	54	27	70	5	2	0	136	204	24	24	2.5	.934	3B-143, SS-2
1940		69	.269	.398	108	29	5	0	3	2.8	19	14	5	15	3	20	2	24	33	8	3	1.7	.877	3B-39
1942	STL A	147	.255	.339	616	157	27	11	1	0.2	90	50	59	54	16	1	1	377	455	23	94	5.8	.973	2B-145, 3B-2
1943		132	.273	.366	538	147	35	6	1	0.2	77	36	50	46	10	1	0	328	331	29	64	5.2	.958	2B-132
1944		148	.245	.342	603	148	27	11	3	0.5	89	36	51	63	20	1	0	368	407	35	95	5.5	.957	2B-146
1945		143	.238	.304	543	129	24	3	2	0.4	72	49	43	46	9	1	0	357	334	22	66	5.0	.969	2B-128, OF-14
1946	BOS A	22	.234	.362	47	11	3	0	1	2.1	8	6	2	7	0	1	0	15	25	4	3	2.6	.909	2B-9, 3B-8
1947		54	.168	.229	131	22	2	0	2	1.5	20	5	17	13	3	5	1	56	73	8	11	3.5	.942	2B-20, 3B-19
1948	PIT N	4	.000	.000	2	0	0	0	0	0.0	0	0	0	1	0	2	0	0	0	0	0	0.0	—	
12 yrs.		1151	.256	.362	4202	1075	200	64	39	0.9	586	391	309	444	95	44	5	2075	2432	209	439	4.4	.956	2B-580, 3B-412, SS-78, OF-14
WORLD SERIES																								
1944	STL A	6	.143	.190	21	3	1	0	0	0.0	1	0	3	5	0	0	0	15	11	3	3	4.8	.897	2B-6
1946	BOS A	3	.400	.400	5	2	0	0	0	0.0	1	1	0	0	0	0	0	0	2	0	0	1.0	1.000	2B-2
2 yrs.		9	.192	.231	26	5	1	0	0	0.0	2	1	3	5	0	0	0	15	13	3	3	3.9	.903	2B-8

Doug Gwosdz

GWOSDZ, DOUGLAS WAYNE (Eyechart) BR TR 5′11″ 180 lbs.
B. June 20, 1960, Houston, Tex.

Year	Team	Games	BA	SA	AB	H	2B	3B	HR	HR%	R	RBI	BB	SO	SB	Pinch Hit AB	Pinch Hit H	PO	A	E	DP	TC/G	FA	G by Pos
1981	SD N	16	.167	.250	24	4	2	0	0	0.0	1	3	3	6	0	4	0	40	5	0	3	3.5	1.000	C-13
1982		7	.176	.176	17	3	0	0	0	0.0	1	0	2	7	0	1	0	34	2	0	0	5.1	1.000	C-7
1983		39	.109	.182	55	6	1	0	1	1.8	7	4	7	19	0	5	1	95	5	3	0	3.2	.971	C-32
1984		7	.250	.250	8	2	0	0	0	0.0	0	1	2	5	0	0	0	25	1	1	0	4.5	.963	C-6
4 yrs.		69	.144	.202	104	15	3	0	1	1.0	9	8	14	37	0	10	1	194	13	4	3	3.6	.981	C-58

Chris Gwynn

GWYNN, CHRISTOPHER KARLTON BL TL 6′ 200 lbs.
Brother of Tony Gwynn.
B. Oct. 13, 1964, Los Angeles, Calif.

Year	Team	Games	BA	SA	AB	H	2B	3B	HR	HR%	R	RBI	BB	SO	SB	Pinch Hit AB	Pinch Hit H	PO	A	E	DP	TC/G	FA	G by Pos
1987	LA N	17	.219	.250	32	7	1	0	0	0.0	2	2	1	7	0	6	0	12	0	0	0	1.2	1.000	OF-10
1988		12	.182	.182	11	2	0	0	0	0.0	1	0	1	2	0	9	2	0	0	0	0	0.0	.000	OF-4
1989		32	.235	.324	68	16	4	1	0	0.0	8	7	2	9	1	14	3	26	1	0	1	1.4	1.000	OF-19
1990		101	.284	.418	141	40	2	1	5	3.5	19	22	7	28	0	**56**	13	39	1	0	0	0.9	1.000	OF-44
1991		94	.252	.410	139	35	5	1	5	3.6	18	22	10	23	1	**56**	13	37	2	0	0	1.0	1.000	OF-41
1992	KC A	34	.286	.405	84	24	3	2	1	1.2	10	7	3	10	0	10	2	33	0	0	0	1.6	1.000	OF-19, DH-2
1993		103	.300	.387	287	86	14	4	1	0.3	36	25	24	34	0	16	6	161	7	1	1	1.9	.994	OF-83, DH-5, 1B-1
1994	LA N	58	.268	.394	71	19	0	0	3	4.2	9	13	7	7	0	35	11	14	0	0	0	0.7	1.000	OF-20
1995		67	.214	.333	84	18	3	2	1	1.2	8	10	6	23	0	43	10	26	1	0	2	1.4	1.000	OF-17, 1B-2
9 yrs.		518	.269	.381	917	247	32	11	16	1.7	111	108	61	143	2	245	60	348	12	1	4	1.4	.997	OF-257, DH-7, 1B-3
DIVISIONAL PLAYOFF SERIES																								
1995	LA N	1	.000	.000	1	0	0	0	0	0.0	0	0	0	1	0	1	0	0	0	0	0	0.0	—	

Tony Gwynn

GWYNN, ANTHONY KEITH BL TL 5′11″ 185 lbs.
Brother of Chris Gwynn.
B. May 9, 1960, Los Angeles, Calif.

Year	Team	Games	BA	SA	AB	H	2B	3B	HR	HR%	R	RBI	BB	SO	SB	Pinch Hit AB	Pinch Hit H	PO	A	E	DP	TC/G	FA	G by Pos
1982	SD N	54	.289	.389	190	55	12	2	1	0.5	33	17	14	16	8	4	1	110	1	1	0	2.2	.991	OF-52
1983		86	.309	.372	304	94	12	2	1	0.3	34	37	23	21	7	6	1	163	9	1	1	2.1	.994	OF-81
1984		158	**.351**	.444	606	**213**	21	10	5	0.8	88	71	59	23	33	2	1	345	11	4	4	2.3	.989	OF-156
1985		154	.317	.408	622	197	29	5	6	1.0	90	46	45	33	14	2	0	337	14	4	2	2.3	.989	OF-152
1986		160	.329	.467	**642**	**211**	33	7	14	2.2	**107**	59	52	35	37	1	0	337	19	4	3	2.3	.989	OF-160
1987		157	**.370**	.511	589	**218**	36	13	7	1.2	119	54	82	35	56	2	1	298	13	6	1	2.0	.981	OF-156
1988		133	**.313**	.415	521	163	22	5	7	1.3	64	70	51	40	26	1	0	264	8	5	1	2.1	.982	OF-133
1989		158	**.336**	.424	604	**203**	27	7	4	0.7	82	62	56	30	40	0	0	353	13	6	1	2.4	.984	OF-157
1990		141	.309	.415	573	177	29	10	4	0.7	79	72	44	23	17	0	0	327	11	5	2	2.4	.985	OF-141
1991		134	.317	.432	530	168	27	11	4	0.8	69	62	34	19	8	1	0	291	8	3	2	2.3	.990	OF-134

Tony Gwynn *continued*

Year	Team	Lg	Games	BA	SA	AB	H	2B	3B	HR	HR%	R	RBI	BB	SO	SB	Pinch Hit AB	Pinch Hit H	PO	A	E	DP	TC/G	FA	G by Pos
1992			128	.317	.415	520	165	27	3	6	1.2	77	41	46	16	3	1	0	270	9	5	2	2.2	.982	OF-127
1993			122	.358	.497	489	175	41	3	7	1.4	70	59	36	19	14	2	0	244	8	5	2	2.1	.981	OF-121
1994			110	**.394**	.568	419	**165**	35	1	12	2.9	79	64	48	19	5	5	1	191	6	3	1	1.9	.985	OF-106
1995			135	**.368**	.484	535	**197**	33	1	9	1.7	82	90	35	15	17	2	1	245	8	2	1	1.9	.992	OF-133
14 yrs.			1830	.336	.449	7144	2401	384	80	87	1.2	1073	804	625	344	285	28	6	3775	138	54	23	2.2	.986	OF-1809
LEAGUE CHAMPIONSHIP SERIES																									
1984	SD	N	5	.368	.526	19	7	3	0	0	0.0	6	3	1	2	0	0	0	9	0	0	0	1.8	1.000	OF-5
WORLD SERIES																									
1984	SD	N	5	.263	.263	19	5	0	0	0	0.0	1	0	3	2	1	0	0	12	1	1	1	2.8	.929	OF-5

Dick Gyselman

GYSELMAN, RICHARD RONALD BR TR 6′ 2″ 170 lbs.
B. Apr. 6, 1908, San Francisco, Calif. D. Sept. 20, 1990, Seattle, Wash.

Year	Team	Lg	Games	BA	SA	AB	H	2B	3B	HR	HR%	R	RBI	BB	SO	SB	Pinch Hit AB	Pinch Hit H	PO	A	E	DP	TC/G	FA	G by Pos
1933	BOS	N	58	.239	.303	155	37	6	2	0	0.0	10	12	7	21	0	3	1	47	97	11	5	3.2	.929	3B-42, 2B-5, SS-1
1934			24	.167	.250	36	6	1	1	0	0.0	7	4	2	11	0	4	1	10	13	7	2	1.8	.767	3B-15, 2B-2
2 yrs.			82	.225	.293	191	43	7	3	0	0.0	17	16	9	32	0	7	2	57	110	18	7	2.8	.903	3B-57, 2B-7, SS-1

Bert Haas

HAAS, BERTHOLD JOHN BR TR 5′11″ 178 lbs.
B. Feb. 8, 1914, Naperville, Ill.

Year	Team	Lg	Games	BA	SA	AB	H	2B	3B	HR	HR%	R	RBI	BB	SO	SB	Pinch Hit AB	Pinch Hit H	PO	A	E	DP	TC/G	FA	G by Pos
1937	BKN	N	16	.400	.520	25	10	3	0	0	0.0	2	2	1	1	0	9	4	18	0	0	1	2.6	1.000	OF-4, 1B-3
1938			1	—	—	0	0	0	0	0	—	0	0	0	0	0	0	0	0	0	0	0	0.0	—	
1942	CIN	N	154	.239	.326	585	140	21	6	6	1.0	59	54	59	54	6	0	0	235	276	36	38	3.6	.934	3B-146, 1B-6, OF-2
1943			101	.262	.386	332	87	17	6	4	1.2	39	44	22	26	6	16	4	432	97	9	52	6.3	.983	1B-44, 3B-23, OF-18
1946			140	.264	.351	535	141	24	7	3	0.6	57	50	33	42	22	2	1	1355	105	9	142	10.7	.994	1B-131, 3B-6
1947			135	.286	.369	482	138	17	7	3	0.6	58	67	42	27	9	11	2	680	25	16	49	5.9	.978	OF-69, 1B-53
1948	PHI	N	95	.282	.357	333	94	9	2	4	1.2	35	34	36	25	8	9	2	366	107	24	26	5.6	.952	3B-54, 1B-35
1949	2 teams	PHI N (2G –.000) NY N (54G –.260)																							
″	total		56	.257	.362	105	27	2	3	1	1.0	12	10	6	9	0	19	4	166	19	6	14	5.6	.969	1B-23, 3B-11
1951	CHI	A	25	.163	.279	43	7	0	1	1	2.3	1	2	5	4	0	11	3	44	5	0	4	4.1	1.000	1B-7, OF-4, 3B-1
9 yrs.			723	.264	.355	2440	644	93	32	22	0.9	263	263	204	188	51	77	20	3296	634	100	326	6.3	.975	1B-302, 3B-241, OF-97

Bruno Haas

HAAS, BRUNO PHILIP (Boon) BB TL 5′10″ 180 lbs.
B. May 5, 1891, Worcester, Mass. D. June 5, 1952, Sarasota, Fla.

Year	Team	Lg	Games	BA	SA	AB	H	2B	3B	HR	HR%	R	RBI	BB	SO	SB	Pinch Hit AB	Pinch Hit H	PO	A	E	DP	TC/G	FA	G by Pos
1915	PHI	A	12	.056	.056	18	1	0	0	0	0.0	1	0	1	7	0	1	0	9	6	1	0	1.8	.938	P-6, OF-3

Eddie Haas

HAAS, GEORGE EDWIN BL TR 5′11″ 178 lbs.
B. May 26, 1935, Paducah, Ky.
Manager 1985.

Year	Team	Lg	Games	BA	SA	AB	H	2B	3B	HR	HR%	R	RBI	BB	SO	SB	Pinch Hit AB	Pinch Hit H	PO	A	E	DP	TC/G	FA	G by Pos
1957	CHI	N	14	.208	.250	24	5	1	0	0	0.0	1	4	1	5	0	8	2	4	0	0	0	1.0	1.000	OF-4
1958	MIL	N	9	.357	.357	14	5	0	0	0	0.0	2	1	2	1	0	4	3	5	0	0	0	1.7	1.000	OF-3
1960			32	.219	.375	32	7	2	0	1	3.1	4	5	5	14	0	25	6	2	0	0	0	1.0	1.000	OF-2
3 yrs.			55	.243	.329	70	17	3	0	1	1.4	7	10	8	20	0	37	11	11	0	0	0	1.2	1.000	OF-9

Mule Haas

HAAS, GEORGE WILLIAM BL TR 6′ 1″ 175 lbs.
B. Oct. 15, 1903, Montclair, N. J. D. June 30, 1974, New Orleans, La.

Year	Team	Lg	Games	BA	SA	AB	H	2B	3B	HR	HR%	R	RBI	BB	SO	SB	Pinch Hit AB	Pinch Hit H	PO	A	E	DP	TC/G	FA	G by Pos
1925	PIT	N	4	.000	.000	3	0	0	0	0	0.0	1	0	0	1	0	1	0	2	0	0	0	1.0	1.000	OF-2
1928	PHI	A	91	.280	.422	332	93	21	4	6	1.8	41	39	23	20	2	8	0	175	9	5	1	2.3	.974	OF-82
1929			139	.313	.498	578	181	41	9	16	2.8	115	82	34	38	0	0	0	373	10	7	2	2.8	.982	OF-139
1930			132	.299	.398	532	159	33	7	2	0.4	91	68	43	33	2	1	0	360	11	9	5	2.9	.976	OF-131
1931			102	.323	.475	440	142	29	7	8	1.8	82	56	30	29	0	0	0	272	6	3	4	2.8	.989	OF-102
1932			143	.305	.405	558	170	28	5	6	1.1	91	65	62	49	1	6	3	372	6	5	2	2.8	.987	OF-137
1933	CHI	A	146	.287	.362	585	168	33	4	1	0.2	97	51	65	41	0	0	0	347	9	6	2	2.5	.983	OF-146
1934			106	.268	.348	351	94	16	3	2	0.6	54	22	47	22	1	13	4	204	5	2	1	2.4	.991	OF-89
1935			92	.291	.382	327	95	22	1	2	0.6	44	40	37	17	4	7	2	183	4	2	1	2.3	.989	OF-84
1936			119	.284	.358	408	116	26	2	0	0.0	75	46	64	29	1	15	3	253	11	5	8	2.6	.981	OF-96, 1B-7
1937			54	.207	.288	111	23	3	3	0	0.0	8	15	16	10	1	16	2	254	19	8	22	8.3	.972	1B-32, OF-2
1938	PHI	A	40	.205	.231	78	16	2	0	0	0.0	7	12	12	10	0	20	1	67	2	0	3	3.8	1.000	OF-12, 1B-6
12 yrs.			1168	.292	.402	4303	1257	254	45	43	1.0	706	496	433	299	12	87	15	2862	92	52	51	2.8	.983	OF-1022, 1B-45
WORLD SERIES																									
1929	PHI	A	5	.238	.524	21	5	0	0	2	9.5	3	6	1	3	0	0	0	5	0	0	0	1.0	1.000	OF-5
1930			6	.111	.222	18	2	0	1	0	0.0	1	1	1	3	0	0	0	14	0	0	0	2.3	1.000	OF-6
1931			7	.130	.174	23	3	1	0	0	0.0	1	2	3	5	0	0	0	17	0	0	0	2.4	1.000	OF-7
3 yrs.			18	.161	.306	62	10	1	1	2	3.2	5	9	5	11	0	0	0	36	0	0	0	2.0	1.000	OF-18

Emil Haberer

HABERER, EMIL KARL BR TR 6′ 1″ 204 lbs.
B. Feb. 2, 1878, Cincinnati, Ohio D. Oct. 19, 1951, Louisville, Ky.

Year	Team	Lg	Games	BA	SA	AB	H	2B	3B	HR	HR%	R	RBI	BB	SO	SB	Pinch Hit AB	Pinch Hit H	PO	A	E	DP	TC/G	FA	G by Pos
1901	CIN	N	6	.167	.278	18	3	0	1	0	0.0	2	1	3		0	1	0	21	6	5	3	6.4	.844	3B-3, 1B-2
1903			5	.077	.077	13	1	0	0	0	0.0	1	0	2		0	1	1	11	3	1	0	3.8	.933	C-4
1909			5	.188	.250	16	3	1	0	0	0.0	1	2	0		0	1	0	15	2	2	1	4.8	.895	C-4
3 yrs.			16	.149	.213	47	7	1	1	0	0.0	4	3	5		0	3	1	47	11	8	4	5.1	.879	C-8, 3B-3, 1B-2

Irv Hach

HACH, IRVIN WILLIAM (Major) BR TR
B. June 6, 1873, Louisville, Ky. D. Aug. 13, 1936, Louisville, Ky.

Year	Team	Lg	Games	BA	SA	AB	H	2B	3B	HR	HR%	R	RBI	BB	SO	SB	Pinch Hit AB	Pinch Hit H	PO	A	E	DP	TC/G	FA	G by Pos
1897	LOU	N	16	.216	.255	51	11	2	0	0	0.0	5	3	5		1	0	0	24	38	9	4	4.4	.873	2B-9, 3B-7

Stan Hack

HACK, STANLEY CAMFIELD (Smiling Stan) BL TR 6′ 170 lbs.
B. Dec. 6, 1909, Sacramento, Calif. D. Dec. 15, 1979, Dixon, Ill.
Manager 1954–56, 1958.

Year	Team	Lg	Games	BA	SA	AB	H	2B	3B	HR	HR%	R	RBI	BB	SO	SB	Pinch Hit AB	Pinch Hit H	PO	A	E	DP	TC/G	FA	G by Pos
1932	CHI	N	72	.236	.365	178	42	5	6	2	1.1	32	19	17	16	5	14	2	36	90	12	5	2.7	.913	3B-51
1933			20	.350	.483	60	21	3	1	1	1.7	10	2	8	3	4	0	0	19	40	1	8	3.5	.983	3B-17
1934			111	.289	.366	402	116	16	6	1	0.2	54	21	45	42	11	2	0	102	198	16	10	2.9	.949	3B-109
1935			124	.311	.436	427	133	23	9	4	0.9	75	64	65	17	14	5	2	153	244	21	26	3.5	.950	3B-111, 1B-7
1936			149	.298	.392	561	167	27	4	6	1.1	102	78	89	39	17	0	0	225	210	17	28	3.0	.962	3B-140, 1B-11

Stan Hack *continued*

Year	Team	Games	BA	SA	AB	H	2B	3B	HR	HR%	R	RBI	BB	SO	SB	Pinch Hit AB	Pinch Hit H	PO	A	E	DP	TC/G	FA	G by Pos
1937		154	.297	.375	582	173	27	6	2	0.3	106	63	83	42	16	1	0	172	251	14	30	2.8	.968	3B-150, 1B-4
1938		152	.320	.432	609	195	34	11	4	0.7	109	67	94	39	**16**	0	0	178	300	23	26	3.3	.954	3B-152
1939		156	.298	.398	641	191	28	6	8	1.2	112	56	65	35	**17**	0	0	177	278	21	15	3.1	.956	3B-156
1940		149	.317	.439	603	**191**	38	6	8	1.3	101	40	75	24	21	0	0	182	304	23	27	3.4	.955	3B-148, 1B-1
1941		151	.317	.427	586	**186**	33	5	7	1.2	111	45	99	40	10	0	0	139	295	21	22	3.0	.954	3B-150, 1B-1
1942		140	.300	.409	553	166	36	3	6	1.1	91	39	94	40	9	0	0	154	261	15	21	3.1	.965	3B-139
1943		144	.289	.366	533	154	24	4	3	0.6	78	35	82	27	5	7	0	149	264	17	11	3.2	.960	3B-136
1944		98	.282	.352	383	108	16	1	3	0.8	65	32	53	21	5	4	1	226	174	19	23	4.5	.955	3B-75, 1B-18
1945		150	.323	.405	597	193	29	7	2	0.3	110	43	99	30	12	0	0	233	314	14	29	3.7	.975	3B-146, 1B-5
1946		92	.285	.350	323	92	13	4	0	0.0	55	26	83	32	3	2	0	102	168	9	6	3.1	.968	3B-90
1947		76	.271	.333	240	65	11	2	0	0.0	28	12	41	19	0	10	2	64	136	8	11	3.2	.962	3B-66
16 yrs.		1938	.301	.397	7278	2193	363	81	57	0.8	1239	642	1092	466	165	45	7	2311	3527	251	298	3.2	.959	3B-1836, 1B-47
WORLD SERIES																								
1932	**CHI N**	1	—	—	0	0	0	0	0	—	0	0	0	0	0	0	0	0	0	0	0	0.0	—	
1935		6	.227	.364	22	5	1	1	0	0.0	2	0	2	2	1	0	0	5	11	0	0	2.3	1.000	3B-6, SS-1
1938		4	.471	.529	17	8	1	0	0	0.0	3	1	1	2	0	0	0	4	4	0	0	2.0	1.000	3B-4
1945		7	.367	.467	30	11	3	0	0	0.0	1	4	4	2	0	0	0	12	13	3	0	4.0	.893	3B-7
4 yrs.		18	.348	.449	69	24	5	1	0	0.0	6	5	7	6	1	0	0	21	28	3	0	2.9	.942	3B-17, SS-1

Rich Hacker

HACKER, RICHARD WARREN BB TR 6′ 160 lbs.
B. Oct. 6, 1947, Belleville, Ill.

Year	Team	Games	BA	SA	AB	H	2B	3B	HR	HR%	R	RBI	BB	SO	SB	Pinch Hit AB	Pinch Hit H	PO	A	E	DP	TC/G	FA	G by Pos
1971	**MON N**	16	.121	.152	33	4	1	0	0	0.0	2	2	3	12	0	0	0	17	44	1	9	3.9	.984	SS-16

Jim Hackett

HACKETT, JAMES JOSEPH (Sunny Jim) BR TR 6′ 2″ 185 lbs.
B. Oct. 1, 1877, Jacksonville, Ill. D. Mar. 28, 1961, Douglas, Mich.

Year	Team	Games	BA	SA	AB	H	2B	3B	HR	HR%	R	RBI	BB	SO	SB	Pinch Hit AB	Pinch Hit H	PO	A	E	DP	TC/G	FA	G by Pos
1902	**STL N**	6	.286	.333	21	6	1	0	0	0.0	2	4	2		1	0	0	6	7	3	0	2.7	.813	P-4, OF-2
1903		99	.228	.311	351	80	13	8	0	0.0	24	36	19		2	3	0	949	53	29	63	10.7	.972	1B-89, P-7
2 yrs.		105	.231	.312	372	86	14	8	0	0.0	26	40	21		3	3	0	955	60	32	63	10.3	.969	1B-89, P-11, OF-2

Mert Hackett

HACKETT, MORTIMER MARTIN BR TR 5′10½″ 175 lbs.
Brother of Walter Hackett.
B. Nov. 11, 1859, Cambridge, Mass. D. Feb. 22, 1938, Cambridge, Mass.

Year	Team	Games	BA	SA	AB	H	2B	3B	HR	HR%	R	RBI	BB	SO	SB	Pinch Hit AB	Pinch Hit H	PO	A	E	DP	TC/G	FA	G by Pos
1883	**BOS N**	46	.235	.380	179	42	8	6	2	1.1	20	24	1	48		0	0	255	58	34	2	7.2	.902	C-44, OF-4
1884		72	.205	.280	268	55	13	2	1	0.4	28		2	66		0	0	513	108	50	2	9.3	.925	C-71, 3B-1
1885		34	.183	.261	115	21	7	1	0	0.0	9	4	2	28		0	0	194	53	27	6	8.1	.901	C-34
1886	**KC N**	62	.217	.317	230	50	8	3	3	1.3	18	25	4	59		0	0	262	63	28	6	5.4	.921	C-52, OF-13
1887	**IND N**	42	.238	.361	147	35	6	3	2	1.4	12	10	7	24	4	0	0	130	52	13	4	4.5	.933	C-40, OF-2, 1B-1
5 yrs.		256	.216	.318	939	203	42	15	8	0.9	87	63	16	225	4	0	0	1354	334	152	20	7.0	.917	C-241, OF-19, 1B-1, 3B-1

Walter Hackett

HACKETT, WALTER HENRY
Brother of Mert Hackett.
B. Aug. 15, 1857, Cambridge, Mass. D. Oct. 2, 1920, Cambridge, Mass.

Year	Team	Games	BA	SA	AB	H	2B	3B	HR	HR%	R	RBI	BB	SO	SB	Pinch Hit AB	Pinch Hit H	PO	A	E	DP	TC/G	FA	G by Pos
1884	**BOS U**	103	.243	.296	415	101	19	0	1	0.2	71		7			0	0	126	294	71	12	4.8	.855	SS-103
1885	**BOS N**	35	.184	.208	125	23	3	0	0	0.0	8	9	3	22		0	0	59	86	22	9	4.8	.868	2B-20, SS-15
2 yrs.		138	.230	.276	540	124	22	0	1	0.2	79	9	10	22		0	0	185	380	93	21	4.8	.859	SS-118, 2B-20

Harvey Haddix

HADDIX, HARVEY (The Kitten) BL TL 5′ 9½″ 170 lbs.
B. Sept. 18, 1925, Medway, Ohio D. Jan. 8, 1994, Springfield, Ohio.

Year	Team	Games	BA	SA	AB	H	2B	3B	HR	HR%	R	RBI	BB	SO	SB	Pinch Hit AB	Pinch Hit H	PO	A	E	DP	TC/G	FA	G by Pos
1952	**STL N**	9	.214	.214	14	3	0	0	0	0.0	3	2	1	5	1	0	0	0	5	1	0	0.8	.833	P-7, OF-1
1953		48	.289	.412	97	28	3	3	1	1.0	21	11	5	19	0	2	1	15	43	2	5	1.7	.967	P-36
1954		61	.194	.280	93	18	4	2	0	0.0	16	4	5	11	2	0	0	14	39	3	3	1.3	.946	P-43
1955		37	.164	.288	73	12	2	2	1	1.4	10	7	4	15	2	0	0	14	38	4	2	1.5	.929	P-37
1956	**2 teams**	**STL N** (5G –.222) **PHI N** (46G –.237)																						
″	**total**	51	.235	.284	102	24	5	0	0	0.0	7	11	7	13	0	15	4	10	31	1	1	1.2	.976	P-35
1957	**PHI N**	41	.309	.382	68	21	3	1	0	0.0	6	6	3	12	1	7	1	10	15	2	0	1.0	.926	P-27
1958	**CIN N**	42	.180	.295	61	11	4	0	1	1.6	11	1	8	18	0	2	0	10	26	1	1	1.3	.973	P-29
1959	**PIT N**	31	.145	.193	83	12	4	0	0	0.0	3	5	3	17	0	0	0	8	35	0	3	1.4	1.000	P-31
1960		29	.254	.313	67	17	4	0	0	0.0	7	7	3	15	0	0	0	9	46	1	2	1.9	.982	P-29
1961		31	.143	.196	56	8	3	0	0	0.0	2	3	6	14	0	0	0	5	29	2	4	1.2	.944	P-29
1962		28	.250	.404	52	13	3	1	1	1.9	9	5	1	11	0	0	0	10	19	2	2	1.1	.935	P-28
1963		50	.182	.364	11	2	2	0	0	0.0	0	2	0	1	0	1	1	5	10	1	0	0.3	.938	P-49
1964	**BAL A**	49	.000	.000	19	0	0	0	0	0.0	0	0	0	10	0	1	0	4	16	0	1	0.4	1.000	P-49
1965		24	.000	.000	2	0	0	0	0	0.0	0	0	0	1	0	0	0	1	6	1	0	0.3	.875	P-24
14 yrs.		531	.212	.296	798	169	37	9	4	0.5	95	64	46	162	4	28	7	115	358	21	24	1.1	.957	P-453, OF-1
WORLD SERIES																								
1960	**PIT N**	2	.333	.333	3	1	0	0	0	0.0	0	0	0	1	0	0	0	1	1	0	0	1.0	1.000	P-2

George Haddock

HADDOCK, GEORGE SILAS (Gentleman George) BR TR 5′11″ 155 lbs.
B. Dec. 25, 1866, Portsmouth, N. H. D. Apr. 18, 1926, Boston, Mass.

Year	Team	Games	BA	SA	AB	H	2B	3B	HR	HR%	R	RBI	BB	SO	SB	Pinch Hit AB	Pinch Hit H	PO	A	E	DP	TC/G	FA	G by Pos
1888	**WAS N**	2	.200	.200	5	1	0	0	0	0.0	0	0	1	2	0	0	0	2	8	1	0	5.5	.909	P-2
1889		34	.223	.304	112	25	3	0	2	1.8	13	14	19	27	3	0	0	14	55	9	3	2.2	.885	P-33, OF-3
1890	**BUF P**	42	.247	.322	146	36	11	0	0	0.0	21	24	24	32	3	0	0	26	88	9	2	2.9	.927	P-35, OF-7
1891	**BOS AA**	58	.243	.324	185	45	4	1	3	1.6	30	23	21	46	3	0	0	27	116	14	2	2.7	.911	P-51, OF-8
1892	**BKN N**	47	.177	.228	158	28	6	1	0	0.0	23	11	12	31	2	0	0	23	81	12	5	2.5	.897	P-46, OF-1
1893		29	.282	.376	85	24	1	2	1	1.2	21	7	8	15	2	0	0	13	19	10	0	1.4	.762	P-23, OF-7
1894	**2 teams**	**PHI N** (10G –.172) **WAS N** (5G –.188)																						
″	**total**	15	.178	.311	45	8	2	2	0	0.0	6	4	4	4	1	0	0	6	20	1	0	1.8	.963	P-14, OF-1
7 yrs.		227	.227	.304	736	167	27	6	6	0.8	114	83	89	157	14	0	0	111	387	56	12	2.4	.899	P-204, OF-27

Kent Hadley

HADLEY, KENT WILLIAM BL TL 6' 3" 190 lbs.
B. Dec. 17, 1934, Pocatello, Ida.

Year	Team	Games	BA	SA	AB	H	2B	3B	HR	HR%	R	RBI	BB	SO	SB	Pinch Hit AB	Pinch Hit H	PO	A	E	DP	TC/G	FA	G by Pos
1958	KC A	3	.182	.182	11	2	0	0	0	0.0	1	0	0	4	0	1	0	21	0	0	1	10.5	1.000	1B-2
1959		113	.253	.403	288	73	11	1	10	3.5	40	39	24	74	1	16	2	656	42	8	66	7.4	.989	1B-95
1960	NY A	55	.203	.422	64	13	2	0	4	6.3	8	11	6	19	0	29	6	99	6	1	10	4.4	.991	1B-24
3 yrs.		171	.242	.399	363	88	13	1	14	3.9	49	50	30	97	1	46	8	776	48	9	77	6.9	.989	1B-121

Bill Haeffner

HAEFFNER, WILLIAM BERNARD BR TR 5' 9" 165 lbs.
B. July 8, 1894, Philadelphia, Pa. D. Jan. 27, 1982, Delaware County, Pa.

Year	Team	Games	BA	SA	AB	H	2B	3B	HR	HR%	R	RBI	BB	SO	SB	Pinch Hit AB	Pinch Hit H	PO	A	E	DP	TC/G	FA	G by Pos
1915	PHI A	3	.250	.250	4	1	0	0	0	0.0	0	0	0	1	0	0	0	0	1	0	0	0.3	1.000	C-3
1920	PIT N	54	.194	.229	175	34	4	1	0	0.0	8	14	8	14	1	2	0	192	48	7	1	4.8	.972	C-52
1928	NY N	2	.000	.000	1	0	0	0	0	0.0	0	0	0	0	0	0	0	3	0	1	0	2.0	.750	C-2
3 yrs.		59	.194	.228	180	35	4	1	0	0.0	8	14	8	15	1	2	0	195	49	8	1	4.4	.968	C-57

Bud Hafey

HAFEY, DANIEL ALBERT BR TR 6' 185 lbs.
Brother of Tom Hafey.
B. Aug. 6, 1912, Berkeley, Calif. D. July 27, 1986, Sacramento, Calif.

Year	Team	Games	BA	SA	AB	H	2B	3B	HR	HR%	R	RBI	BB	SO	SB	Pinch Hit AB	Pinch Hit H	PO	A	E	DP	TC/G	FA	G by Pos
1935	2 teams	CHI A (2G –.000) PIT N (58G –.228)																						
"	total	60	.228	.408	184	42	11	2	6	3.3	30	16	16	48	0	5	1	125	5	4	3	2.9	.970	OF-47
1936	PIT N	39	.212	.381	118	25	6	1	4	3.4	19	13	10	27	0	9	0	66	3	5	0	2.6	.932	OF-29
1939	2 teams	CIN N (6G –.154) PHI N (18G –.176)																						
"	total	24	.172	.203	64	11	2	0	0	0.0	4	4	4	16	2	5	1	37	2	0	0	2.1	1.000	OF-17, P-2
3 yrs.		123	.213	.363	366	78	19	3	10	2.7	53	33	30	91	2	19	2	228	10	9	3	2.6	.964	OF-93, P-2

Chick Hafey

HAFEY, CHARLES JAMES BR TR 6' 185 lbs.
B. Feb. 12, 1903, Berkeley, Calif. D. July 2, 1973, Calistoga, Calif.
Hall of Fame 1971.

Year	Team	Games	BA	SA	AB	H	2B	3B	HR	HR%	R	RBI	BB	SO	SB	Pinch Hit AB	Pinch Hit H	PO	A	E	DP	TC/G	FA	G by Pos
1924	STL N	24	.253	.418	91	23	5	2	2	2.2	10	22	4	8	1	0	0	48	3	4	1	2.3	.927	OF-24
1925		93	.302	.425	358	108	25	2	5	1.4	36	57	10	29	3	5	1	180	9	9	2	2.3	.955	OF-88
1926		78	.271	.427	225	61	19	2	4	1.8	30	38	11	36	2	22	7	106	6	3	1	2.1	.974	OF-54
1927		103	.329	**.590**	346	114	26	5	18	5.2	62	63	36	41	12	9	5	179	19	4	7	2.1	.980	OF-94
1928		138	.337	.604	520	175	46	6	27	5.2	101	111	40	53	8	4	0	287	13	11	3	2.3	.965	OF-133
1929		134	.338	.632	517	175	47	9	29	5.6	101	125	45	42	7	3	0	278	8	10	1	2.3	.966	OF-130
1930		120	.336	.652	446	150	39	12	26	5.8	108	107	46	51	12	1	0	189	11	5	0	1.8	.976	OF-116
1931		122	**.349**	.569	450	157	35	8	16	3.6	94	95	39	43	11	4	1	226	4	4	1	2.0	.983	OF-118
1932	CIN N	83	.344	.466	253	87	19	3	2	0.8	34	36	22	20	4	18	5	131	5	5	0	1.7	.965	OF-83
1933		144	.303	.421	568	172	34	6	7	1.2	77	62	40	44	3	0	0	364	16	5	5	2.7	.987	OF-144
1934		140	.293	.471	535	157	29	6	18	3.4	75	67	52	63	4	0	0	380	7	13	1	2.9	.968	OF-140
1935		15	.339	.525	59	20	6	1	1	1.7	10	9	4	5	1	0	0	31	0	3	0	2.3	.912	OF-15
1937		89	.261	.447	257	67	11	5	9	3.5	39	41	23	42	2	22	3	128	5	4	0	2.1	.971	OF-64
13 yrs.		1283	.317	.526	4625	1466	341	67	164	3.5	777	833	372	477	70	88	22	2527	106	80	22	2.3	.971	OF-1203
WORLD SERIES																								
1926	STL N	7	.185	.259	27	5	2	0	0	0.0	2	0	0	7	0	0	0	21	1	0	0	3.1	1.000	OF-7
1928		4	.200	.200	15	3	0	0	0	0.0	0	0	1	4	0	0	0	8	0	1	0	2.3	.889	OF-4
1930		6	.273	.500	22	6	5	0	0	0.0	2	2	1	3	0	0	0	9	0	0	0	1.5	1.000	OF-6
1931		6	.167	.167	24	4	0	0	0	0.0	1	0	0	5	1	0	0	8	0	1	0	1.5	.889	OF-6
4 yrs.		23	.205	.284	88	18	7	0	0	0.0	5	2	2	19	1	0	0	46	1	2	0	2.1	.959	OF-23

Tom Hafey

HAFEY, THOMAS FRANCIS (The Arm) BR TR 6' 1" 180 lbs.
Brother of Bud Hafey.
B. July 12, 1913, Berkeley, Calif.

Year	Team	Games	BA	SA	AB	H	2B	3B	HR	HR%	R	RBI	BB	SO	SB	Pinch Hit AB	Pinch Hit H	PO	A	E	DP	TC/G	FA	G by Pos
1939	NY N	70	.242	.359	256	62	10	1	6	2.3	37	26	10	44	1	0	0	61	130	8	10	2.8	.960	3B-70
1944	STL A	8	.357	.500	14	5	2	0	0	0.0	1	2	1	4	0	3	1	9	1	0	0	2.0	1.000	OF-4, 1B-1
2 yrs.		78	.248	.367	270	67	12	1	6	2.2	38	28	11	48	1	3	1	70	131	8	10	2.8	.962	3B-70, OF-4, 1B-1

Bill Hague

HAGUE, WILLIAM L. BR TR 5' 9" 164 lbs.
Born William L. Haug.
B. 1852, Philadelphia, Pa. Deceased.

Year	Team	Games	BA	SA	AB	H	2B	3B	HR	HR%	R	RBI	BB	SO	SB	Pinch Hit AB	Pinch Hit H	PO	A	E	DP	TC/G	FA	G by Pos
1876	LOU N	67	.265	.303	294	78	8	0	1	0.3	31	22	2	10		0	0	67	90	52	5	3.1	.751	3B-67, SS-1
1877		59	.266	.312	263	70	7	1	1	0.4	38	24	7	18		0	0	78	78	29	4	3.1	.843	3B-59
1878	PRO N	62	.204	.216	250	51	3	0	0	0.0	21	25	5	34		0	0	81	177	21	5	4.5	.925	3B-62
1879		51	.225	.249	209	47	3	1	0	0.0	20	21	3	19		0	0	54	122	38	2	4.2	.822	3B-51
4 yrs.		239	.242	.273	1016	246	21	2	2	0.2	110	92	17	81		0	0	280	467	140	16	3.7	.842	3B-239, SS-1

Joe Hague

HAGUE, JOE CLARENCE BL TL 6' 195 lbs.
B. Apr. 25, 1944, Huntington, W. Va. D. Nov. 5, 1994, San Antonio, Tex.

Year	Team	Games	BA	SA	AB	H	2B	3B	HR	HR%	R	RBI	BB	SO	SB	Pinch Hit AB	Pinch Hit H	PO	A	E	DP	TC/G	FA	G by Pos
1968	STL N	7	.235	.412	17	4	0	0	1	5.9	2	1	2	2	0	1	0	19	1	1	1	4.2	.952	OF-3, 1B-2
1969		40	.170	.270	100	17	2	1	2	2.0	8	8	12	23	0	14	1	104	5	2	3	4.3	.982	OF-17, 1B-9
1970		139	.271	.417	451	122	16	4	14	3.1	58	68	63	87	2	17	7	749	51	5	66	6.0	.994	1B-82, OF-52
1971		129	.226	.392	380	86	9	3	16	4.2	46	54	58	69	0	17	2	676	50	5	63	5.8	.993	1B-91, OF-36
1972	2 teams	STL N (27G –.237) CIN N (69G –.246)																						
"	total	96	.243	.416	214	52	12	2	7	3.3	25	31	37	36	1	32	11	386	20	0	29	6.2	1.000	1B-44, OF-22
1973	CIN N	19	.152	.212	33	5	2	0	0	0.0	2	1	5	5	1	8	3	26	2	0	3	3.1	1.000	OF-5, 1B-4
6 yrs.		430	.239	.391	1195	286	41	10	40	3.3	141	163	177	222	4	89	24	1960	129	13	165	5.7	.994	1B-232, OF-135
LEAGUE CHAMPIONSHIP SERIES																								
1972	CIN N	3	.000	.000	1	0	0	0	0	0.0	0	0	2	1	0	1	0	0	0	0	0	0.0	—	
WORLD SERIES																								
1972	CIN N	3	.000	.000	3	0	0	0	0	0.0	0	0	0	0	0	3	0	0	0	0	0	0.0	.000	OF-1

Dick Hahn

HAHN, RICHARD FREDERICK BR TR 5'11" 176 lbs.
B. July 24, 1916, Canton, Ohio D. Nov. 5, 1992, Orlando, Fla.

Year	Team	Games	BA	SA	AB	H	2B	3B	HR	HR%	R	RBI	BB	SO	SB	Pinch Hit AB	Pinch Hit H	PO	A	E	DP	TC/G	FA	G by Pos
1940	WAS A	1	.000	.000	3	0	0	0	0	0.0	0	0	0	0	0	0	0	1	1	2	0	4.0	.500	C-1

Don Hahn

HAHN, DONALD ANTONE BR TR 6′ 1″ 180 lbs.
B. Nov. 16, 1948, San Francisco, Calif.

Year	Team	Games	BA	SA	AB	H	2B	3B	HR	HR%	R	RBI	BB	SO	SB	Pinch Hit AB	Pinch Hit H	PO	A	E	DP	TC/G	FA	G by Pos
1969	MON N	4	.111	.111	9	1	0	0	0	0.0	0	2	0	5	0	0	0	3	1	0	0	1.3	1.000	OF-3
1970		82	.255	.309	149	38	8	0	0	0.0	22	8	27	27	4	18	5	65	5	1	1	1.2	.986	OF-61
1971	NY N	98	.236	.292	178	42	5	1	1	0.6	16	11	21	32	2	8	2	140	2	4	1	1.8	.973	OF-80
1972		17	.162	.162	37	6	0	0	0	0.0	0	1	4	12	0	6	0	8	0	0	0	0.8	1.000	OF-10
1973		93	.229	.290	262	60	10	0	2	0.8	22	21	22	43	2	9	2	176	2	2	0	2.1	.989	OF-87
1974		110	.251	.337	323	81	14	1	4	1.2	34	28	37	34	2	8	3	217	8	3	0	2.2	.987	OF-106
1975	3 teams	PHI N (9G –.000) STL N (7G –.125) SD N (34G –.231)																						
″	total	50	.179	.308	39	7	1	2	0	0.0	10	3	11	5	1	5	0	32	2	0	0	0.9	1.000	OF-37
7 yrs.		454	.236	.303	997	235	38	4	7	0.7	104	74	122	158	11	54	12	641	20	10	2	1.7	.985	OF-384
LEAGUE CHAMPIONSHIP SERIES																								
1973	NY N	5	.235	.235	17	4	0	0	0	0.0	2	1	2	4	0	0	0	12	0	0	0	2.4	1.000	OF-5
WORLD SERIES																								
1973	NY N	7	.241	.345	29	7	1	1	0	0.0	2	2	1	6	0	0	0	13	1	1	0	2.1	.933	OF-7

Ed Hahn

HAHN, WILLIAM EDGAR BL TR 160 lbs.
B. Aug. 27, 1875, Nevada, Ohio D. Nov. 29, 1941, Des Moines, Iowa.

Year	Team	Games	BA	SA	AB	H	2B	3B	HR	HR%	R	RBI	BB	SO	SB	Pinch Hit AB	Pinch Hit H	PO	A	E	DP	TC/G	FA	G by Pos
1905	NY A	43	.319	.350	160	51	5	0	0	0.0	32	11	25		1	0	0	83	5	4	1	2.1	.957	OF-43
1906	2 teams	NY A (11G –.091) CHI A (130G –.227)																						
″	total	141	.221	.257	506	112	8	5	0	0.0	82	28	72		21	1	0	177	21	10	3	1.5	.952	OF-137
1907	CHI A	156	.255	.294	592	151	9	7	0	0.0	87	45	84		17	0	0	182	24	2	6	1.3	.990	OF-156
1908		122	.251	.313	447	112	12	8	0	0.0	58	21	39		11	3	1	160	4	6	2	1.4	.965	OF-118
1909		76	.181	.213	287	52	6	0	1	0.3	30	16	31		9	0	0	93	3	1	1	1.3	.990	OF-76
1910		15	.113	.151	53	6	2	0	0	0.0	2	1	7		0	0	0	14	0	1	0	1.0	.933	OF-15
6 yrs.		553	.237	.278	2045	484	42	20	1	0.0	291	122	258		59	4	1	709	57	24	13	1.4	.970	OF-545
WORLD SERIES																								
1906	CHI A	6	.273	.273	22	6	0	0	0	0.0	4	0	1	1	0	0	0	3	0	0	0	0.5	1.000	OF-6

Ed Haigh

HAIGH, EDWARD E.
B. Feb. 7, 1867, Philadelphia, Pa. D. Feb. 13, 1953, Atlantic City, N. J.

Year	Team	Games	BA	SA	AB	H	2B	3B	HR	HR%	R	RBI	BB	SO	SB	Pinch Hit AB	Pinch Hit H	PO	A	E	DP	TC/G	FA	G by Pos
1892	STL N	1	.250	.250	4	1	0	0	0	0.0	0	0	0	2	0	0	0	0	0	0	0	0.0	.000	OF-1

Hinkey Haines

HAINES, HENRY LUTHER BR TR 5′10″ 170 lbs.
B. Dec. 23, 1898, Red Lion, Pa. D. Jan. 9, 1979, Sharon Hill, Pa.

Year	Team	Games	BA	SA	AB	H	2B	3B	HR	HR%	R	RBI	BB	SO	SB	Pinch Hit AB	Pinch Hit H	PO	A	E	DP	TC/G	FA	G by Pos
1923	NY A	28	.160	.240	25	4	2	0	0	0.0	9	3	4	5	3	3	0	17	1	0	0	1.3	1.000	OF-14
WORLD SERIES																								
1923	NY A	2	.000	.000	1	0	0	0	0	0.0	1	0	0	0	0	0	0	0	0	0	0	0.0	.000	OF-2

Jerry Hairston

HAIRSTON, JERRY WAYNE BB TR 5′10″ 170 lbs.
Brother of John Hairston. Son of Sam Hairston.
B. Feb. 16, 1952, Birmingham, Ala.

Year	Team	Games	BA	SA	AB	H	2B	3B	HR	HR%	R	RBI	BB	SO	SB	Pinch Hit AB	Pinch Hit H	PO	A	E	DP	TC/G	FA	G by Pos
1973	CHI A	60	.271	.333	210	57	11	1	0	0.0	25	23	33	30	0	2	0	194	13	5	11	3.5	.976	OF-33, 1B-19, DH-8
1974		45	.229	.294	109	25	7	0	0	0.0	8	8	13	18	0	12	2	24	1	2	0	0.8	.926	OF-22, DH-10
1975		69	.283	.320	219	62	8	0	0	0.0	26	23	46	23	1	3	0	111	6	6	1	1.8	.951	OF-59, DH-8
1976		44	.227	.277	119	27	2	2	0	0.0	20	10	24	19	1	4	1	71	1	2	0	1.9	.973	OF-40
1977	2 teams	CHI A (13G –.308) PIT N (51G –.192)																						
″	total	64	.231	.359	78	18	4	0	2	2.6	8	10	11	17	0	34	7	28	1	1	0	1.2	.967	OF-25, 2B-1
1981	CHI A	9	.280	.440	25	7	1	0	1	4.0	5	6	2	4	0	2	1	14	0	1	0	2.1	.933	OF-7
1982		85	.233	.456	90	21	5	0	5	5.6	11	18	9	15	0	**47**	11	34	2	0	1	0.9	1.000	OF-36, DH-2
1983		101	.294	.500	126	37	9	1	5	4.0	17	22	23	16	0	**62**	**17**	29	1	1	0	0.9	.968	OF-32, DH-4
1984		115	.260	.401	227	59	13	2	5	2.2	41	19	41	29	2	**59**	**18**	57	2	2	0	1.1	.967	OF-37, DH-20
1985		95	.243	.343	140	34	8	0	2	1.4	9	20	29	18	0	**53**	**14**	5	0	0	0	0.1	1.000	DH-29, OF-5
1986		101	.271	.404	225	61	15	0	5	2.2	32	26	26	26	0	46	14	132	9	0	11	2.4	1.000	DH-29, 1B-19, OF-11
1987		66	.230	.413	126	29	8	0	5	4.0	14	20	25	25	0	32	8	82	5	1	7	2.7	.989	OF-13, DH-13, 1B-7
1988		2	.000	.000	2	0	0	0	0	0.0	0	0	0	0	0	2	0	0	0	0	0	0.0	—	
1989		3	.333	.333	3	1	0	0	0	0.0	0	0	0	0	0	3	1	0	0	0	0	0.0	.000	DH-2
14 yrs.		859	.258	.371	1699	438	91	6	30	1.8	216	205	282	240	4	361	94	781	41	21	31	1.7	.975	OF-320, DH-125, 1B-45, 2B-1
LEAGUE CHAMPIONSHIP SERIES																								
1983	CHI A	2	.000	.000	3	0	0	0	0	0.0	0	0	1	1	0	2	0	1	0	1	0	1.0	.500	OF-2

John Hairston

HAIRSTON, JOHN LOUIS BR TR 6′ 2″ 200 lbs.
Brother of Jerry Hairston. Son of Sam Hairston.
B. Aug. 27, 1944, Birmingham, Ala.

Year	Team	Games	BA	SA	AB	H	2B	3B	HR	HR%	R	RBI	BB	SO	SB	Pinch Hit AB	Pinch Hit H	PO	A	E	DP	TC/G	FA	G by Pos
1969	CHI N	3	.250	.250	4	1	0	0	0	0.0	0	0	0	2	0	1	1	3	1	0	0	2.0	1.000	C-1, OF-1

Sam Hairston

HAIRSTON, SAMUEL HARDING BR TR 5′10½″ 187 lbs.
Father of Jerry Hairston. Father of John Hairston.
B. Jan. 20, 1920, Crawford, Miss.

Year	Team	Games	BA	SA	AB	H	2B	3B	HR	HR%	R	RBI	BB	SO	SB	Pinch Hit AB	Pinch Hit H	PO	A	E	DP	TC/G	FA	G by Pos
1951	CHI A	4	.400	.600	5	2	1	0	0	0.0	1	1	2	0	0	1	0	3	0	0	0	1.5	1.000	C-2

Chet Hajduk

HAJDUK, CHESTER BR TR 6′ 195 lbs.
B. July 21, 1918, Chicago, Ill.

Year	Team	Games	BA	SA	AB	H	2B	3B	HR	HR%	R	RBI	BB	SO	SB	Pinch Hit AB	Pinch Hit H	PO	A	E	DP	TC/G	FA	G by Pos
1941	CHI A	1	.000	.000	1	0	0	0	0	0.0	0	0	0	0	0	1	0	0	0	0	0	0.0	—	

David Hajek

HAJEK, DAVID VINCENT BR TR 5′10″ 165 lbs.
B. Oct. 14, 1967, Roseville, Calif.

Year	Team	Games	BA	SA	AB	H	2B	3B	HR	HR%	R	RBI	BB	SO	SB	Pinch Hit AB	Pinch Hit H	PO	A	E	DP	TC/G	FA	G by Pos
1995	HOU N	5	.000	.000	2	0	0	0	0	0.0	0	0	1	1	1	2	0	0	0	0	0	0.0	—	

George Halas

HALAS, GEORGE STANLEY BB TR 6′ 164 lbs.
B. Feb. 2, 1895, Chicago, Ill. D. Oct. 31, 1983, Chicago, Ill.

Year	Team	Games	BA	SA	AB	H	2B	3B	HR	HR%	R	RBI	BB	SO	SB	Pinch Hit AB	Pinch Hit H	PO	A	E	DP	TC/G	FA	G by Pos
1919	NY A	12	.091	.091	22	2	0	0	0	0.0	0	0	0	8	0	4	0	8	0	0	0	1.3	1.000	OF-6

John Haldeman

HALDEMAN, JOHN AVERY BL TR 5′10″ 175 lbs.
B. Dec. 2, 1855, Pewee Valley, Ky. D. Sept. 17, 1899, Louisville, Ky.

Year	Team	Games	BA	SA	AB	H	2B	3B	HR	HR%	R	RBI	BB	SO	SB	Pinch Hit AB	Pinch Hit H	PO	A	E	DP	TC/G	FA	G by Pos
1877	LOU N	1	.000	.000	4	0	0	0	0	0.0	0	0	0	0		0	0	0	4	3	0	7.0	.571	2B-1

Bob Hale

HALE, ROBERT HOUSTON BL TL 5′10″ 195 lbs.
B. Nov. 7, 1933, Sarasota, Fla.

Year	Team	Games	BA	SA	AB	H	2B	3B	HR	HR%	R	RBI	BB	SO	SB	Pinch Hit AB	Pinch Hit H	PO	A	E	DP	TC/G	FA	G by Pos
1955	BAL A	67	.357	.407	182	65	7	1	0	0.0	13	29	5	19	0	26	10	300	33	9	25	7.8	.974	1B-44
1956		85	.237	.309	207	49	10	1	1	0.5	18	24	11	10	0	36	6	366	29	10	33	7.9	.975	1B-51
1957		42	.250	.250	44	11	0	0	0	0.0	2	7	2	2	0	35	9	22	1	0	1	4.6	1.000	1B-5
1958		19	.350	.450	20	7	2	0	0	0.0	2	3	2	1	0	15	5	11	3	0	3	7.0	1.000	1B-2
1959		40	.185	.241	54	10	3	0	0	0.0	2	7	2	6	0	30	7	48	2	0	5	6.3	1.000	1B-8
1960	CLE A	70	.300	.400	70	21	7	0	0	0.0	2	12	3	6	0	**63**	**19**	14	3	1	1	3.6	.944	1B-5
1961	2 teams	CLE A (42G –.167) NY A (11G –.154)																						
″	total	53	.163	.224	49	8	0	0	1	2.0	2	7	1	7	0	44	6	15	1	0	1	3.2	1.000	1B-5
7 yrs.		376	.273	.335	626	171	29	2	2	0.3	41	89	26	51	0	249	62	776	72	20	69	7.2	.977	1B-120

Chip Hale

HALE, WALTER WILLIAM BL TR 5′11″ 180 lbs.
B. Dec. 2, 1964, Santa Clara, Calif.

Year	Team	Games	BA	SA	AB	H	2B	3B	HR	HR%	R	RBI	BB	SO	SB	Pinch Hit AB	Pinch Hit H	PO	A	E	DP	TC/G	FA	G by Pos
1989	MIN A	28	.209	.254	67	14	3	0	0	0.0	6	4	1	6	0	8	0	15	40	1	8	2.1	.982	2B-16, 3B-9, DH-2
1990		1	.000	.000	2	0	0	0	0	0.0	0	2	0	1	0	0	0	2	6	0	2	8.0	1.000	2B-1
1993		69	.333	.425	186	62	6	1	3	1.6	25	27	18	17	2	17	7	39	63	4	11	1.7	.962	2B-21, 3B-19, DH-19, 1B-1, SS-1
1994		67	.263	.364	118	31	9	0	1	0.8	13	11	16	14	0	**31**	**11**	45	51	3	7	2.3	.970	3B-21, DH-10, 1B-7, 2B-5, OF-1
1995		69	.262	.359	103	27	4	0	2	1.9	10	18	11	20	0	**47**	14	16	6	0	2	0.5	1.000	DH-27, 2B-7, 3B-5, 1B-3
5 yrs.		234	.282	.370	476	134	22	1	6	1.3	54	62	46	58	2	103	32	117	166	8	30	1.7	.973	DH-58, 3B-54, 2B-50, 1B-11, OF-1, SS-1

George Hale

HALE, GEORGE WAGNER (Ducky) BR TR 5′10″ 160 lbs.
B. Aug. 3, 1894, Dexter, Kans. D. Nov. 1, 1945, Wichita, Kans.

Year	Team	Games	BA	SA	AB	H	2B	3B	HR	HR%	R	RBI	BB	SO	SB	Pinch Hit AB	Pinch Hit H	PO	A	E	DP	TC/G	FA	G by Pos
1914	STL A	6	.182	.182	11	2	0	0	0	0.0	1	0	0	3	0	0	0	9	8	2	0	3.2	.895	C-6
1916		4	.000	.000	1	0	0	0	0	0.0	0	0	0	1	0	1	0	3	0	0	0	1.0	1.000	C-3
1917		38	.197	.262	61	12	2	1	0	0.0	4	8	10	12	0	7	2	75	26	8	3	3.9	.927	C-28
1918		12	.133	.167	30	4	1	0	0	0.0	0	1	1	5	0	1	0	41	11	1	1	4.8	.981	C-11
4 yrs.		60	.175	.223	103	18	3	1	0	0.0	5	9	11	21	0	9	2	128	45	11	4	3.8	.940	C-48

John Hale

HALE, JOHN STEVEN BL TR 6′2″ 195 lbs.
B. Aug. 5, 1953, Fresno, Calif.

Year	Team	Games	BA	SA	AB	H	2B	3B	HR	HR%	R	RBI	BB	SO	SB	Pinch Hit AB	Pinch Hit H	PO	A	E	DP	TC/G	FA	G by Pos
1974	LA N	4	1.000	1.250	4	4	1	0	0	0.0	2	2	0	0	0	1	1	0	0	0	0	0.0	.000	OF-3
1975		71	.211	.333	204	43	7	0	6	2.9	20	22	26	51	1	7	2	128	2	3	0	2.0	.977	OF-68
1976		44	.154	.198	91	14	2	1	0	0.0	4	8	16	14	4	6	0	55	3	1	0	1.6	.983	OF-37
1977		79	.241	.352	108	26	4	1	2	1.9	10	11	15	28	2	5	1	68	1	1	0	1.0	.986	OF-73
1978	SEA A	107	.171	.265	211	36	8	0	4	1.9	24	22	34	64	3	6	1	160	1	2	0	1.6	.988	OF-98, DH-3
1979		54	.222	.365	63	14	3	0	2	3.2	6	7	12	26	0	8	0	34	0	0	0	0.8	1.000	OF-42, DH-2
6 yrs.		359	.201	.305	681	137	25	2	14	2.1	66	72	103	183	10	33	5	445	7	7	0	1.4	.985	OF-321, DH-5

Odell Hale

HALE, ARVEL ODELL (Bad News) BR TR 5′10″ 175 lbs.
B. Aug. 10, 1908, Hosston, La. D. June 9, 1980, El Dorado, Ark.

Year	Team	Games	BA	SA	AB	H	2B	3B	HR	HR%	R	RBI	BB	SO	SB	Pinch Hit AB	Pinch Hit H	PO	A	E	DP	TC/G	FA	G by Pos
1931	CLE A	25	.283	.424	92	26	2	4	1	1.1	14	5	8	8	2	0	0	34	51	12	4	3.7	.876	3B-15, 2B-10, SS-1
1933		98	.276	.462	351	97	19	8	10	2.8	49	64	30	37	2	3	1	237	287	29	47	5.9	.948	2B-73, 3B-21
1934		143	.302	.471	563	170	44	6	13	2.3	82	101	48	50	8	3	1	412	488	41	108	6.6	.956	2B-137, 3B-5
1935		150	.304	.486	589	179	37	11	16	2.7	80	101	52	55	15	1	0	160	313	31	17	3.4	.938	3B-149, 2B-1
1936		153	.316	.506	620	196	50	13	14	2.3	126	87	64	43	8	2	0	172	338	28	28	3.6	.948	3B-148, 2B-3
1937		154	.267	.371	561	150	32	4	6	1.1	74	82	56	41	9	1	1	276	406	22	61	4.6	.969	3B-90, 2B-64
1938		130	.278	.399	496	138	32	2	8	1.6	69	69	44	39	8	3	1	304	343	25	72	5.3	.963	2B-127
1939		108	.312	.439	253	79	16	2	4	1.6	36	48	25	18	4	35	10	142	147	11	31	4.0	.963	2B-73, 3B-2
1940		48	.220	.320	50	11	3	1	0	0.0	3	6	5	7	0	**40**	8	2	5	3	0	3.3	.700	3B-3
1941	2 teams	BOS A (12G –.208) NY N (41G –.196)																						
″	total	53	.198	.262	126	25	5	0	1	0.8	18	10	21	17	1	12	1	99	76	9	16	5.1	.951	2B-30, 3B-6
10 yrs.		1062	.289	.441	3701	1071	240	51	73	2.0	551	573	353	315	57	100	23	1838	2454	211	384	4.7	.953	2B-518, 3B-439, SS-1

Sammy Hale

HALE, SAMUEL DOUGLAS BR TR 5′8½″ 160 lbs.
B. Sept. 10, 1896, Glen Rose, Tex. D. Sept. 6, 1974, Wheeler, Tex.

Year	Team	Games	BA	SA	AB	H	2B	3B	HR	HR%	R	RBI	BB	SO	SB	Pinch Hit AB	Pinch Hit H	PO	A	E	DP	TC/G	FA	G by Pos
1920	DET A	76	.293	.397	116	34	3	3	1	0.9	13	14	5	15	2	**52**	**17**	14	32	5	2	2.4	.902	3B-16, OF-4, 2B-1
1921		9	.000	.000	2	0	0	0	0	0.0	2	0	0	1	0	2	0	0	0	0	0	0.0	—	
1923	PHI A	115	.288	.396	434	125	22	8	3	0.7	68	51	17	31	8	5	2	85	222	28	17	3.1	.916	3B-107
1924		80	.318	.410	261	83	14	2	2	0.8	41	17	17	19	3	14	2	42	111	9	10	2.6	.944	3B-55, OF-5, SS-1, C-1
1925		110	.345	.540	391	135	30	11	8	2.0	62	63	17	27	7	12	4	98	174	24	19	3.1	.919	3B-96, 2B-1
1926		111	.281	.440	327	92	22	9	4	1.2	49	43	13	36	1	28	6	82	152	13	16	3.2	.947	3B-77, OF-1
1927		131	.313	.423	501	157	24	8	5	1.0	77	81	32	32	11	1	0	152	247	16	46	3.2	.961	3B-128
1928		88	.309	.468	314	97	20	9	4	1.3	38	58	9	21	2	8	3	86	189	20	17	3.7	.932	3B-79
1929		101	.277	.338	379	105	14	3	1	0.3	51	40	12	18	6	0	0	94	172	12	14	2.8	.957	3B-99, 2B-1
1930	STL A	62	.274	.358	190	52	8	1	2	1.1	21	25	8	18	1	12	2	46	80	7	5	2.8	.947	3B-47
10 yrs.		883	.302	.424	2915	880	157	54	30	1.0	422	392	130	218	41	134	36	699	1379	134	146	3.1	.939	3B-704, OF-10, 2B-3, SS-1, C-1

Fred Haley

HALEY, FREDERICK TR
B. June 18, 1853, Wheeling, W. Va. Deceased.

Year	Team	Games	BA	SA	AB	H	2B	3B	HR	HR%	R	RBI	BB	SO	SB	Pinch Hit AB	Pinch Hit H	PO	A	E	DP	TC/G	FA	G by Pos
1880	TRO N	2	.000	.000	7	0	0	0	0	0.0	0	0	1	2		0	0	11	4	5	0	10.0	.750	C-2

Ray Haley

HALEY, RICHARD TIMOTHY BR TR 5′11″ 180 lbs.
B. Jan. 23, 1891, Danbury, Iowa D. Oct. 8, 1973, Bradenton, Fla.

Year	Team	Games	BA	SA	AB	H	2B	3B	HR	HR%	R	RBI	BB	SO	SB	Pinch Hit AB	Pinch Hit H	PO	A	E	DP	TC/G	FA	G by Pos
1915	BOS A	5	.143	.286	7	1	1	0	0	0.0	2	0	1	0	0	0	0	10	4	0	0	3.5	1.000	C-4
1916	2 teams	BOS A (1G –.000) PHI A (34G –.231)																						
″	total	35	.229	.275	109	25	5	0	0	0.0	8	4	6	20	0	2	0	154	65	4	7	6.8	.982	C-33
1917	PHI A	41	.276	.316	98	27	2	1	0	0.0	7	11	4	12	2	7	0	99	27	7	3	3.9	.947	C-34
3 yrs.		81	.248	.294	214	53	8	1	0	0.0	17	15	11	32	2	9	0	263	96	11	10	5.2	.970	C-71

Al Hall

HALL, ARCHIBALD W.
B. Worcester, Mass. D. Feb. 10, 1885, Warren, Pa.

Year	Team	Lg	Games	BA	SA	AB	H	2B	3B	HR	HR%	R	RBI	BB	SO	SB	Pinch Hit AB	Pinch Hit H	PO	A	E	DP	TC/G	FA	G by Pos
1879	**TRO**	**N**	67	.258	.301	306	79	7	3	0	0.0	30	14	3	13		0	0	126	18	27	3	2.6	.842	OF-67
1880	**CLE**	**N**	3	.125	.125	8	1	0	0	0	0.0	1	0	0	0		0	0	1	0	0	0	0.3	1.000	OF-3
2 yrs.			70	.255	.296	314	80	7	3	0	0.0	31	14	3	13		0	0	127	18	27	3	2.5	.843	OF-70

Albert Hall

HALL, ALBERT BB TR 5′11″ 155 lbs.
B. Mar. 7, 1958, Birmingham, Ala.

Year	Team	Lg	Games	BA	SA	AB	H	2B	3B	HR	HR%	R	RBI	BB	SO	SB	Pinch Hit AB	Pinch Hit H	PO	A	E	DP	TC/G	FA	G by Pos
1981	**ATL**	**N**	6	.000	.000	2	0	0	0	0	0.0	1	0	1	1	0	1	0	0	0	0	0	0.0	.000	OF-2
1982			5	—	—	0	0	0	0	0	—	1	0	0	0	0	0	0	0	0	0	0	0.0	—	
1983			10	.000	.000	8	0	0	0	0	0.0	2	0	2	2	1	1	0	3	0	1	0	1.0	.750	OF-4
1984			87	.261	.338	142	37	6	1	1	0.7	25	9	10	18	6	13	5	64	4	5	1	1.1	.932	OF-66
1985			54	.149	.191	47	7	0	1	0	0.0	5	3	9	12	1	32	5	7	2	1	0	0.8	.900	OF-13
1986			16	.240	.280	50	12	2	0	0	0.0	6	1	5	6	8	1	0	26	1	3	0	2.1	.900	OF-14
1987			92	.284	.411	292	83	20	4	3	1.0	54	24	38	36	33	25	7	148	5	3	1	2.3	.981	OF-69
1988			85	.247	.299	231	57	7	1	1	0.4	27	15	21	35	15	16	2	137	7	4	1	2.3	.973	OF-63
1989	**PIT**	**N**	20	.182	.303	33	6	2	1	0	0.0	4	1	3	5	3	7	2	10	0	1	0	0.9	.909	OF-12
9 yrs.			375	.251	.335	805	202	37	8	5	0.6	125	53	89	115	67	96	21	395	19	18	3	1.8	.958	OF-243

Bill Hall

HALL, WILLIAM LEMUEL BL TR 5′11″ 165 lbs.
B. July 30, 1928, Moultrie, Ga. D. Jan. 1, 1986, Moultrie, Ga.

Year	Team	Lg	Games	BA	SA	AB	H	2B	3B	HR	HR%	R	RBI	BB	SO	SB	Pinch Hit AB	Pinch Hit H	PO	A	E	DP	TC/G	FA	G by Pos
1954	**PIT**	**N**	5	.000	.000	7	0	0	0	0	0.0	0	0	0	0	0	3	0	4	0	0	0	4.0	1.000	C-1
1956			1	.000	.000	3	0	0	0	0	0.0	0	0	0	1	0	0	0	7	1	0	1	8.0	1.000	C-1
1958			51	.284	.362	116	33	6	0	1	0.9	15	15	15	13	0	1	0	195	24	4	4	4.4	.982	C-51
3 yrs.			57	.262	.333	126	33	6	0	1	0.8	15	15	15	14	0	4	0	206	25	4	5	4.4	.983	C-53

Bob Hall

HALL, ROBERT PRILL TR 5′10″ 158 lbs.
B. Dec. 20, 1878, Baltimore, Md. D. Dec. 1, 1950, Wellesley, Mass.

Year	Team	Lg	Games	BA	SA	AB	H	2B	3B	HR	HR%	R	RBI	BB	SO	SB	Pinch Hit AB	Pinch Hit H	PO	A	E	DP	TC/G	FA	G by Pos
1904	**PHI**	**N**	46	.160	.184	163	26	4	0	0	0.0	11	17	14		5	0	0	149	80	31	13	5.7	.881	3B-20, SS-15, 1B-11
1905	**2 teams**		**NY N** (1G –.333) **BKN N** (56G –.236)																						
″	**total**		57	.238	.296	206	49	4	1	2	1.0	22	15	11		8	4	0	147	37	19	5	3.8	.906	OF-43, 2B-7, 1B-3
2 yrs.			103	.203	.247	369	75	8	1	2	0.5	33	32	25		13	4	0	296	117	50	18	4.7	.892	OF-43, 3B-20, SS-15, 1B-14, 2B-7

Charley Hall

HALL, CHARLES LOUIS (Sea Lion) BL TR 6′ 1″ 187 lbs.
Born Carlos Clolo.
B. July 27, 1885, Ventura, Calif. D. Dec. 6, 1943, Ventura, Calif.

Year	Team	Lg	Games	BA	SA	AB	H	2B	3B	HR	HR%	R	RBI	BB	SO	SB	Pinch Hit AB	Pinch Hit H	PO	A	E	DP	TC/G	FA	G by Pos
1906	**CIN**	**N**	17	.128	.170	47	6	2	0	0	0.0	7	2	2		0	1	0	17	29	4	3	3.1	.920	P-14, 1B-2
1907			12	.269	.346	26	7	0	1	0	0.0	1	1	0		0	1	0	3	14	1	0	1.6	.944	P-11
1909	**BOS**	**A**	11	.158	.158	19	3	0	0	0	0.0	0	4	0		0	0	0	5	16	1	2	2.0	.955	P-11
1910			47	.207	.329	82	17	2	4	0	0.0	6	8	6		1	8	1	9	62	4	0	2.0	.947	P-35, OF-3
1911			39	.141	.234	64	9	1	1	1	1.6	6	8	4		0	7	1	4	30	2	0	1.1	.944	P-32
1912			34	.267	.413	75	20	4	2	1	1.3	10	14	4		0	0	0	9	59	3	0	2.1	.958	P-34
1913			43	.214	.286	42	9	1	1	0	0.0	2	2	1	10	0	7	0	6	27	2	1	1.0	.943	P-35, 3B-1
1916	**STL**	**N**	10	.143	.143	14	2	0	0	0	0.0	0	1	0	6	0	0	0	1	13	2	2	1.6	.875	P-10
1918	**DET**	**A**	6	.000	.000	2	0	0	0	0	0.0	0	0	0	0	0	0	0	1	1	1	1	0.5	.667	P-6
9 yrs.			219	.197	.288	371	73	10	9	2	0.5	32	40	17	16	1	24	2	55	251	20	9	1.7	.939	P-188, OF-3, 1B-2, 3B-1
WORLD SERIES																									
1912	**BOS**	**A**	2	.750	1.000	4	3	1	0	0	0.0	0	0	1	0	0	0	0	0	5	1	0	3.0	.833	P-2

Charlie Hall

HALL, CHARLES WALTER (Doc)
B. Aug. 24, 1863, Toulon, Ill. D. June 24, 1921, Tacoma, Wash.

Year	Team	Lg	Games	BA	SA	AB	H	2B	3B	HR	HR%	R	RBI	BB	SO	SB	Pinch Hit AB	Pinch Hit H	PO	A	E	DP	TC/G	FA	G by Pos
1887	**NY**	**AA**	3	.083	.083	12	1	0	0	0	0.0	1		2		1	0	0	9	0	0	0	3.0	1.000	OF-3

Dick Hall

HALL, RICHARD WALLACE BR TR 6′ 6″ 200 lbs.
B. Sept. 27, 1930, St. Louis, Mo.

Year	Team	Lg	Games	BA	SA	AB	H	2B	3B	HR	HR%	R	RBI	BB	SO	SB	Pinch Hit AB	Pinch Hit H	PO	A	E	DP	TC/G	FA	G by Pos
1952	**PIT**	**N**	26	.138	.150	80	11	1	0	0	0.0	6	2	2	17	0	5	1	44	11	1	0	2.9	.982	OF-14, 3B-5
1953			7	.167	.167	24	4	0	0	0	0.0	2	1	1	3	1	0	0	21	23	1	6	6.4	.978	2B-7
1954			112	.239	.310	310	74	8	4	2	0.6	38	27	33	46	3	12	1	235	5	11	1	2.5	.956	OF-102
1955			21	.175	.275	40	7	1	0	1	2.5	3	3	6	5	0	3	1	9	6	0	0	0.8	1.000	P-15, OF-3
1956			33	.345	.345	29	10	0	0	0	0.0	5	1	5	7	0	12	6	6	7	0	0	0.6	1.000	P-19, 1B-1
1957			10	.000	.000	1	0	0	0	0	0.0	0	0	0	1	0	0	0	0	0	0	0	0.0	.000	P-8
1959			2	.000	.000	2	0	0	0	0	0.0	0	0	0	0	0	0	0	0	1	0	0	0.5	1.000	P-2
1960	**KC**	**A**	32	.107	.107	56	6	0	0	0	0.0	5	4	4	15	1	0	0	9	28	3	1	1.4	.925	P-29
1961	**BAL**	**A**	30	.139	.139	36	5	0	0	0	0.0	4	1	3	13	0	0	0	9	23	1	1	1.1	.970	P-29
1962			44	.167	.208	24	4	1	0	0	0.0	3	1	4	9	0	0	0	9	17	0	1	0.6	1.000	P-43
1963			48	.464	.607	28	13	1	0	1	3.6	7	4	0	8	0	0	0	7	21	0	1	0.6	1.000	P-47
1964			45	.125	.125	16	2	0	0	0	0.0	1	3	1	3	0	1	0	7	12	0	1	0.4	1.000	P-45
1965			49	.333	.467	15	5	2	0	0	0.0	1	4	1	4	0	0	0	4	8	1	2	0.3	.923	P-48
1966			32	.167	.167	12	2	0	0	0	0.0	0	2	0	5	0	2	0	4	10	0	0	0.4	1.000	P-32
1967	**PHI**	**N**	48	.071	.071	14	1	0	0	0	0.0	1	0	0	5	0	0	0	2	21	0	1	0.5	1.000	P-48
1968			32	.333	.333	3	1	0	0	0	0.0	0	0	0	1	0	0	0	2	6	0	0	0.3	1.000	P-32
1969	**BAL**	**A**	39	.286	.286	7	2	0	0	0	0.0	1	2	1	1	1	0	0	4	6	0	2	0.3	1.000	P-39
1970			32	.083	.083	12	1	0	0	0	0.0	2	1	0	3	0	0	0	3	3	0	0	0.2	1.000	P-32
1971			27	.400	.600	5	2	1	0	0	0.0	0	0	0	1	0	0	0	1	3	1	0	0.2	.800	P-27
19 yrs.			669	.210	.259	714	150	15	4	4	0.6	79	56	61	147	6	35	9	376	211	19	17	1.0	.969	P-495, OF-119, 2B-7, 3B-5, 1B-1
LEAGUE CHAMPIONSHIP SERIES																									
1969	**BAL**	**A**	1	—	—	0	0	0	0	0	—	0	0	0	0	0	0	0	0	0	0	0	0.0	.000	P-1
1970			1	.500	.500	2	1	0	0	0	0.0	0	0	0	1	0	0	0	0	0	0	0	0.0	.000	P-1
2 yrs.			2	.500	.500	2	1	0	0	0	0.0	0	0	0	1	0	0	0	0	0	0	0	0.0		P-2

Dick Hall *continued*

Year	Team	Games	BA	SA	AB	H	2B	3B	HR	HR%	R	RBI	BB	SO	SB	Pinch Hit AB	Pinch Hit H	PO	A	E	DP	TC/G	FA	G by Pos
WORLD SERIES																								
1969	BAL A	1	—	—	0	0	0	0	0	—	0	0	0	0	0	0	0	0	0	0	0	0.0	.000	P-1
1970		1	.000	.000	1	0	0	0	0	0.0	0	0	0	1	0	0	0	0	0	0	0	0.0	.000	P-1
1971		1	—	—	0	0	0	0	0	—	0	0	0	0	0	0	0	1	0	0	0	1.0	1.000	P-1
3 yrs.		3	.000	.000	1	0	0	0	0	0.0	0	0	0	1	0	0	0	1	0	0	0	0.3	1.000	P-3

George Hall

HALL, GEORGE WILLIAM BL 5′ 7″ 142 lbs.
B. Mar. 29, 1849, Stepney, England D. June 11, 1923, Ridgewood, N. Y.

Year	Team	Games	BA	SA	AB	H	2B	3B	HR	HR%	R	RBI	BB	SO	SB	Pinch Hit AB	Pinch Hit H	PO	A	E	DP	TC/G	FA	G by Pos
1876	PHI N	60	.366	.545	268	98	7	13	**5**	**1.9**	51	45	8	4		0	0	150	7	39	3	3.3	.801	OF-60
1877	LOU N	61	.323	.439	269	87	15	8	0	0.0	53	26	12	19		0	0	92	7	11	1	1.8	.900	OF-61
2 yrs.		121	.345	.492	537	185	22	21	5	0.9	104	71	20	23		0	0	242	14	50	4	2.5	.837	OF-121

Irv Hall

HALL, IRVIN GLADSTONE BR TR 5′10½″ 160 lbs.
B. Oct. 7, 1918, Alberton, Md.

Year	Team	Games	BA	SA	AB	H	2B	3B	HR	HR%	R	RBI	BB	SO	SB	Pinch Hit AB	Pinch Hit H	PO	A	E	DP	TC/G	FA	G by Pos
1943	PHI A	151	.256	.298	544	139	15	4	0	0.0	37	54	22	42	10	1	1	300	440	41	93	5.2	.948	SS-148, 3B-1, 2B-1
1944		143	.268	.333	559	150	20	8	0	0.0	60	45	31	46	2	2	0	366	419	26	71	5.8	.968	2B-97, SS-40, 1B-4
1945		151	.261	.305	616	161	17	5	0	0.0	62	50	35	42	3	0	0	422	498	21	108	6.2	.978	2B-151
1946		63	.249	.303	185	46	6	2	0	0.0	19	19	9	18	1	13	2	115	122	7	23	5.2	.971	2B-40, SS-7
4 yrs.		508	.261	.311	1904	496	58	19	0	0.0	178	168	97	148	16	16	3	1203	1479	95	295	5.7	.966	2B-289, SS-195, 1B-4, 3B-1

Jimmie Hall

HALL, JIMMIE RANDOLPH BL TR 6′ 175 lbs.
B. Mar. 17, 1938, Mt. Holly, N. C.

Year	Team	Games	BA	SA	AB	H	2B	3B	HR	HR%	R	RBI	BB	SO	SB	Pinch Hit AB	Pinch Hit H	PO	A	E	DP	TC/G	FA	G by Pos
1963	MIN A	156	.260	.521	497	129	21	5	33	6.6	88	80	63	101	3	13	5	306	13	6	5	2.3	.982	OF-143
1964		149	.282	.480	510	144	20	3	25	4.9	61	75	44	112	5	10	3	323	13	5	0	2.5	.985	OF-137
1965		148	.285	.464	522	149	25	4	20	3.8	81	86	51	79	14	10	2	282	7	7	2	2.1	.976	OF-141
1966		120	.239	.449	356	85	7	4	20	5.6	52	47	33	66	1	21	4	175	6	4	1	1.8	.978	OF-103
1967	CAL A	129	.249	.404	401	100	8	3	16	4.0	54	55	42	65	4	14	8	197	6	2	1	1.7	.990	OF-120
1968	2 teams	CAL A (46G –.214) CLE A (58G –.198)																						
″	total	104	.207	.262	237	49	7	0	2	0.8	19	16	26	38	2	35	6	109	1	2	1	1.6	.982	OF-68
1969	3 teams	CLE A (4G –.000) NY A (80G –.236) CHI N (11G –.208)																						
″	total	95	.224	.337	246	55	9	5	3	1.2	23	27	22	42	9	22	5	144	6	5	4	2.4	.968	OF-58, 1B-7
1970	2 teams	CHI N (28G –.094) ATL N (39G –.213)																						
″	total	67	.165	.278	79	13	3	0	2	2.5	9	5	6	26	0	29	4	27	1	0	0	0.8	1.000	OF-36
8 yrs.		968	.254	.434	2848	724	100	24	121	4.2	387	391	287	529	38	154	37	1563	53	31	14	2.0	.981	OF-806, 1B-7
WORLD SERIES																								
1965	MIN A	2	.143	.143	7	1	0	0	0	0.0	0	0	1	5	0	0	0	2	0	0	0	1.0	1.000	OF-2

Joe Hall

HALL, JOSEPH GEROY BR TR 6′ 180 lbs.
B. Mar. 6, 1966, Paducah, Ky.

Year	Team	Games	BA	SA	AB	H	2B	3B	HR	HR%	R	RBI	BB	SO	SB	Pinch Hit AB	Pinch Hit H	PO	A	E	DP	TC/G	FA	G by Pos
1994	CHI A	17	.393	.607	28	11	3	0	1	3.6	6	5	2	4	0	8	3	11	0	1	0	1.1	.917	OF-9, DH-2
1995	DET A	7	.133	.133	15	2	0	0	0	0.0	2	0	2	3	0	1	0	11	1	0	0	2.0	1.000	OF-5, DH-1
2 yrs.		24	.302	.442	43	13	3	0	1	2.3	8	5	4	7	0	9	3	22	1	1	0	1.4	.958	OF-14, DH-3

Mel Hall

HALL, MELVIN, JR. BL TL 6′ 185 lbs.
B. Sept. 16, 1960, Lyons, N. Y.

Year	Team	Games	BA	SA	AB	H	2B	3B	HR	HR%	R	RBI	BB	SO	SB	Pinch Hit AB	Pinch Hit H	PO	A	E	DP	TC/G	FA	G by Pos
1981	CHI N	10	.091	.364	11	1	0	0	1	9.1	1	2	1	4	0	7	1	0	0	0	0	0.0	.000	OF-3
1982		24	.263	.350	80	21	3	2	0	0.0	6	4	5	17	0	1	0	42	4	3	1	2.2	.939	OF-22
1983		112	.283	.488	410	116	23	5	17	4.1	60	56	42	101	6	2	1	239	8	3	2	2.2	.988	OF-112
1984	2 teams	CHI N (48G –.280) CLE A (83G –.257)																						
″	total	131	.265	.425	407	108	24	4	11	2.7	68	52	47	78	3	14	3	212	8	4	2	1.8	.982	OF-115, DH-9
1985	CLE A	23	.318	.409	66	21	6	0	0	0.0	7	12	8	12	0	6	2	18	0	0	0	0.9	1.000	OF-15, DH-5
1986		140	.296	.493	442	131	29	2	18	4.1	68	77	33	65	6	19	6	233	7	7	1	1.9	.972	OF-126, DH-7
1987		142	.280	.439	485	136	21	1	18	3.7	57	76	20	68	5	17	2	264	3	3	2	2.0	.989	OF-122, DH-14
1988		150	.280	.392	515	144	32	4	6	1.2	69	71	28	50	7	11	4	288	3	10	1	2.0	.967	OF-141, DH-6
1989	NY A	113	.260	.427	361	94	9	0	17	4.7	54	58	21	37	0	16	4	141	3	1	2	1.3	.993	OF-75, DH-34
1990		113	.258	.433	360	93	23	2	12	3.3	41	46	6	46	0	15	3	70	2	2	0	0.7	.973	DH-54, OF-50
1991		141	.285	.455	492	140	23	2	19	3.9	67	80	26	40	0	14	4	221	8	3	2	1.8	.987	OF-120, DH-10
1992		152	.280	.429	583	163	36	3	15	2.6	67	81	29	53	4	12	4	283	10	3	2	2.0	.990	OF-136, DH-11
12 yrs.		1251	.277	.439	4212	1168	229	25	134	3.2	565	615	266	571	31	134	34	2011	56	39	15	1.8	.981	OF-1037, DH-150

Russ Hall

HALL, ROBERT RUSSELL TL 5′10″ 170 lbs.
B. Sept. 29, 1871, Shelbyville, Ky. D. July 1, 1937, Los Angeles, Calif.

Year	Team	Games	BA	SA	AB	H	2B	3B	HR	HR%	R	RBI	BB	SO	SB	Pinch Hit AB	Pinch Hit H	PO	A	E	DP	TC/G	FA	G by Pos
1898	STL N	39	.245	.273	143	35	2	1	0	0.0	13	10	7		1	0	0	53	114	32	14	5.1	.839	SS-35, 3B-3, OF-1
1901	CLE A	1	.500	.500	4	2	0	0	0	0.0	2	0	0		0	0	0	1	2	3	0	6.0	.500	SS-1
2 yrs.		40	.252	.279	147	37	2	1	0	0.0	15	10	7		1	0	0	54	116	35	14	5.1	.829	SS-36, 3B-3, OF-1

Tom Haller

HALLER, THOMAS FRANK BL TR 6′ 4″ 195 lbs.
B. June 23, 1937, Lockport, Ill.

Year	Team	Games	BA	SA	AB	H	2B	3B	HR	HR%	R	RBI	BB	SO	SB	Pinch Hit AB	Pinch Hit H	PO	A	E	DP	TC/G	FA	G by Pos
1961	SF N	30	.145	.258	62	9	1	0	2	3.2	5	8	9	23	0	4	0	117	7	0	4	5.0	1.000	C-25
1962		99	.261	.515	272	71	13	1	18	6.6	53	55	51	59	1	9	0	472	38	4	6	5.6	.992	C-91
1963		98	.255	.430	298	76	8	1	14	4.7	32	44	34	45	4	8	2	506	39	4	7	6.0	.993	C-85, OF-7
1964		117	.253	.428	388	98	14	3	16	4.1	43	48	55	51	4	7	1	739	50	9	12	6.9	.989	C-113, OF-3
1965		134	.251	.389	422	106	4	3	16	3.8	40	49	47	67	0	3	1	864	50	12	9	7.0	.987	C-133
1966		142	.240	.461	471	113	19	2	27	5.7	74	67	53	74	1	10	1	830	59	8	8	6.4	.991	C-136, 1B-4
1967		141	.251	.415	455	114	23	5	14	3.1	54	49	62	61	0	12	5	797	64	3	5	6.3	.997	C-136, OF-1
1968	LA N	144	.285	.388	474	135	27	5	4	0.8	37	53	46	76	1	12	1	863	81	6	23	6.8	.994	C-139
1969		134	.263	.357	445	117	18	3	6	1.3	46	39	48	58	0	7	3	800	48	7	4	6.5	.992	C-132
1970		112	.286	.465	325	93	16	6	10	3.1	47	47	32	35	3	12	5	524	26	4	7	5.2	.993	C-106
1971		84	.267	.366	202	54	5	0	5	2.5	23	32	25	30	0	17	6	320	34	8	3	5.4	.978	C-67
1972	DET A	59	.207	.331	121	25	5	2	2	1.7	7	13	15	14	0	20	2	220	15	0	1	6.5	1.000	C-36
12 yrs.		1294	.257	.414	3935	1011	153	31	134	3.4	461	504	477	593	14	121	27	7052	511	65	89	6.3	.991	C-1199, OF-11, 1B-4

Tom Haller *continued*

Year	Team	Lg	Games	BA	SA	AB	H	2B	3B	HR	HR%	R	RBI	BB	SO	SB	Pinch Hit AB	Pinch Hit H	PO	A	E	DP	TC/G	FA	G by Pos
LEAGUE CHAMPIONSHIP SERIES																									
1972	DET	A	1	.000	.000	1	0	0	0	0	0.0	0	0	0	0	0	1	0	0	0	0	0	0.0	—	
WORLD SERIES																									
1962	SF	N	4	.286	.571	14	4	1	0	1	7.1	1	3	0	2	0	0	0	29	2	0	1	7.8	1.000	C-4

Newt Halliday

HALLIDAY, NEWTON REESE BR TR 6′ 1″ 175 lbs.
B. June 18, 1896, Chicago, Ill. D. Apr. 6, 1918, Great Lakes, Ill.

Year	Team	Lg	Games	BA	SA	AB	H	2B	3B	HR	HR%	R	RBI	BB	SO	SB	Pinch Hit AB	Pinch Hit H	PO	A	E	DP	TC/G	FA	G by Pos
1916	PIT	N	1	.000	.000	1	0	0	0	0	0.0	0	0	0	1	0	0	0	3	1	0	0	4.0	1.000	1B-1

Jocko Halligan

HALLIGAN, WILLIAM E. BL 5′ 9″ 166 lbs.
B. Dec. 8, 1868, Avon, N. Y. D. Feb. 13, 1945, Buffalo, N. Y.

Year	Team	Lg	Games	BA	SA	AB	H	2B	3B	HR	HR%	R	RBI	BB	SO	SB	Pinch Hit AB	Pinch Hit H	PO	A	E	DP	TC/G	FA	G by Pos
1890	BUF	P	57	.251	.355	211	53	9	2	3	1.4	28	33	20	19	7	0	0	104	27	36	3	2.8	.784	OF-43, C-16
1891	CIN	N	61	.312	.449	247	77	13	6	3	1.2	43	44	24	25	5	0	0	89	6	16	1	1.8	.856	OF-61
1892	2 teams		CIN N (26G –.287) BAL N (46G –.270)																						
″	total		72	.276	.398	279	77	8	7	4	1.4	52	55	42	33	11	1	0	258	17	25	11	4.2	.917	OF-48, 1B-19, C-5
3 yrs.			190	.281	.403	737	207	30	15	10	1.4	123	132	86	77	23	1	0	451	50	77	15	3.0	.867	OF-152, C-21, 1B-19

Ed Hallinan

HALLINAN, EDWARD S. BR TR 5′ 9″ 168 lbs.
B. Aug. 23, 1888, San Francisco, Calif. D. Aug. 24, 1940, San Francisco, Calif.

Year	Team	Lg	Games	BA	SA	AB	H	2B	3B	HR	HR%	R	RBI	BB	SO	SB	Pinch Hit AB	Pinch Hit H	PO	A	E	DP	TC/G	FA	G by Pos
1911	STL	A	52	.207	.237	169	35	3	1	0	0.0	13	14	14		4	0	0	120	136	25	24	5.4	.911	SS-34, 2B-15, 3B-3
1912			28	.221	.244	86	19	2	0	0	0.0	11	1	5		3	1	0	48	62	17	13	4.9	.866	SS-26
2 yrs.			80	.212	.239	255	54	5	1	0	0.0	24	15	19		7	1	0	168	198	42	37	5.2	.897	SS-60, 2B-15, 3B-3

Jimmy Hallinan

HALLINAN, JAMES H. BL TL 5′ 9″ 172 lbs.
B. May 27, 1849, Ireland D. Oct. 28, 1879, Chicago, Ill.

Year	Team	Lg	Games	BA	SA	AB	H	2B	3B	HR	HR%	R	RBI	BB	SO	SB	Pinch Hit AB	Pinch Hit H	PO	A	E	DP	TC/G	FA	G by Pos
1876	NY	N	54	.279	.383	240	67	7	6	2	0.8	45	36	2	4		0	0	49	178	73	7	5.4	.757	SS-50, 2B-4, OF-2
1877	2 teams		CIN N (16G –.370) CHI N (19G –.281)																						
″	total		35	.321	.377	162	52	5	2	0	0.0	35	18	5	3		0	0	79	37	22	9	3.9	.841	OF-19, 2B-16
1878	2 teams		CHI N (16G –.284) IND N (3G –.250)																						
″	total		19	.278	.342	79	22	5	0	0	0.0	14	3	5	8		0	0	30	14	14	1	3.1	.759	OF-14, 2B-5
3 yrs.			108	.293	.374	481	141	17	8	2	0.4	94	57	12	15		0	0	158	229	109	17	4.5	.780	SS-50, OF-35, 2B-25

Bill Hallman

HALLMAN, WILLIAM HARRY BL TL
B. Mar. 15, 1876, Philadelphia, Pa. D. Apr. 23, 1950, Philadelphia, Pa.

Year	Team	Lg	Games	BA	SA	AB	H	2B	3B	HR	HR%	R	RBI	BB	SO	SB	Pinch Hit AB	Pinch Hit H	PO	A	E	DP	TC/G	FA	G by Pos
1901	MIL	A	139	.246	.328	549	135	27	6	2	0.4	70	47	41		12	0	0	226	22	26	6	2.0	.905	OF-139
1903	CHI	A	63	.208	.280	207	43	7	4	0	0.0	29	18	31		11	6	0	114	7	6	0	2.2	.953	OF-57
1906	PIT	N	23	.270	.360	89	24	3	1	1	1.1	12	6	15		3	0	0	40	3	3	0	2.0	.935	OF-23
1907			94	.222	.255	302	67	6	2	0	0.0	39	15	33		21	9	2	134	9	5	1	1.8	.966	OF-84
4 yrs.			319	.235	.303	1147	269	43	13	3	0.3	150	86	120		47	15	2	514	41	40	7	2.0	.933	OF-303

Bill Hallman

HALLMAN, WILLIAM WILSON BR TR 5′ 8″
B. Mar. 31, 1867, Pittsburgh, Pa. D. Sept. 11, 1920, Philadelphia, Pa.
Manager 1897.

Year	Team	Lg	Games	BA	SA	AB	H	2B	3B	HR	HR%	R	RBI	BB	SO	SB	Pinch Hit AB	Pinch Hit H	PO	A	E	DP	TC/G	FA	G by Pos
1888	PHI	N	18	.206	.302	63	13	4	1	0	0.0	5	6	1	12	1	0	0	54	24	12	2	4.7	.867	C-10, 2B-4, OF-3, SS-1, 3B-1
1889			119	.253	.346	462	117	21	8	2	0.4	67	60	36	54	20	0	0	278	370	79	46	6.1	.891	SS-106, 2B-13, C-1
1890	PHI	P	84	.267	.360	356	95	16	7	1	0.3	59	37	33	24	6	0	0	194	103	36	15	3.9	.892	OF-34, C-26, 2B-14, 3B-10, SS-2
1891	PHI	AA	141	.283	.394	587	166	21	13	6	1.0	112	69	38	56	18	0	0	327	399	55	53	5.5	.930	2B-141
1892	PHI	N	138	.292	.382	586	171	27	10	2	0.3	106	84	32	52	19	0	0	335	379	49	60	5.5	.936	2B-138
1893			132	.307	.398	596	183	28	7	4	0.7	119	76	51	27	22	0	0	388	375	36	61	6.1	.955	2B-120, 1B-12
1894			119	.309	.374	505	156	19	7	0	0.0	107	66	36	15	36	0	0	318	320	48	62	5.8	.930	2B-119
1895			124	.314	.386	539	169	26	5	1	0.2	94	91	34	20	16	0	0	300	401	45	57	6.0	.940	2B-122, SS-3
1896			120	.320	.390	469	150	21	3	2	0.4	82	83	45	23	16	0	0	304	368	39	62	5.9	.945	2B-120, P-1
1897	2 teams		PHI N (31G –.262) STL N (79G –.221)																						
″	total		110	.233	.264	424	99	9	2	0	0.0	47	41	32		13	0	0	289	327	36	45	5.9	.945	2B-108, 1B-3
1898	BKN	N	134	.244	.303	509	124	10	7	2	0.4	57	63	29		9	0	0	273	432	45	47	5.6	.940	2B-124, 3B-10
1901	2 teams		CLE A (5G –.211) PHI N (123G –.184)																						
″	total		128	.185	.235	464	86	13	5	0	0.0	48	41	28		13	0	0	221	333	22	23	4.5	.962	2B-90, 3B-33, SS-5
1902	PHI	N	73	.248	.311	254	63	8	4	0	0.0	15	35	14		9	1	1	71	147	16	3	3.3	.932	3B-72
1903			63	.212	.288	198	42	11	2	0	0.0	20	17	16		2	6	0	148	101	16	6	4.6	.940	2B-22, 3B-19, 1B-9, OF-4, SS-3
14 yrs.			1503	.272	.348	6012	1634	234	81	20	0.3	938	769	425	283	200	7	1	3500	4079	534	542	5.4	.934	2B-1135, 3B-145, SS-120, OF-41, C-37, 1B-24, P-1

Jim Halpin

HALPIN, JAMES NATHANIEL
B. Oct. 4, 1863, England D. Jan. 4, 1893, Boston, Mass.

Year	Team	Lg	Games	BA	SA	AB	H	2B	3B	HR	HR%	R	RBI	BB	SO	SB	Pinch Hit AB	Pinch Hit H	PO	A	E	DP	TC/G	FA	G by Pos
1882	WOR	N	2	.000	.000	8	0	0	0	0	0.0	0	0	0	0		0	0	3	2	3	0	4.0	.625	3B-2
1884	WAS	U	46	.185	.202	168	31	3	0	0	0.0	24		2			0	0	44	97	36	4	3.8	.797	SS-39, 3B-7
1885	DET	N	15	.130	.167	54	7	2	0	0	0.0	3	1	1	12		0	0	12	54	12	3	5.2	.846	SS-15
3 yrs.			63	.165	.187	230	38	5	0	0	0.0	27	1	3	12		0	0	59	153	51	7	4.2	.806	SS-54, 3B-9

Al Halt

HALT, ALVA WILLIAM BR TR 6′ 180 lbs.
B. Nov. 23, 1890, Sandusky, Ohio D. Jan. 22, 1973, Sandusky, Ohio.

Year	Team	Lg	Games	BA	SA	AB	H	2B	3B	HR	HR%	R	RBI	BB	SO	SB	Pinch Hit AB	Pinch Hit H	PO	A	E	DP	TC/G	FA	G by Pos
1914	BKN	F	80	.234	.307	261	61	6	2	3	1.1	26	25	13		11	4	0	168	186	43	30	5.3	.892	SS-71, 2B-3, OF-1
1915			151	.250	.336	524	131	22	7	3	0.6	41	64	39		20	0	0	240	349	48	33	4.2	.925	3B-111, SS-40
1918	CLE	A	26	.174	.203	69	12	2	0	0	0.0	9	1	9	12	4	1	0	33	43	2	4	3.3	.974	3B-14, 2B-4, SS-4, 1B-2
3 yrs.			257	.239	.316	854	204	30	9	6	0.7	76	90	61	12	35	5	0	441	578	93	67	4.4	.916	3B-125, SS-115, 2B-7, 1B-2, OF-1

Charlie Hamburg

HAMBURG, CHARLES H. 6′ 175 lbs.
Born Charles H. Hambrick.
B. Nov. 22, 1863, Louisville, Ky. D. May 18, 1931, Union, N. J.

Year	Team	Lg	Games	BA	SA	AB	H	2B	3B	HR	HR%	R	RBI	BB	SO	SB	Pinch Hit AB	Pinch Hit H	PO	A	E	DP	TC/G	FA	G by Pos
1890	LOU	AA	133	.272	.344	485	132	22	2	3	0.6	93		69		46	0	0	229	16	14	3	1.9	.946	OF-133

Sam Hamby

HAMBY, JAMES SANFORD (Cracker) BR TR 6′ 170 lbs.
B. July 29, 1897, Wilkesboro, N. C. D. Oct. 21, 1991, Springfield, Ill.

Year	Team	Games	BA	SA	AB	H	2B	3B	HR	HR%	R	RBI	BB	SO	SB	Pinch Hit AB	Pinch Hit H	PO	A	E	DP	TC/G	FA	G by Pos
1926	NY N	1	.000	.000	3	0	0	0	0	0.0	0	0	0	0	0	0	0	3	0	2	0	5.0	.600	C-1
1927		21	.192	.231	52	10	0	1	0	0.0	6	5	7	7	1	1	0	49	17	7	1	3.8	.904	C-19
2 yrs.		22	.182	.218	55	10	0	1	0	0.0	6	5	7	7	1	1	0	52	17	9	1	3.9	.885	C-20

Bob Hamelin

HAMELIN, ROBERT JAMES III (The Hammer) BL TL 6′ 1″ 240 lbs.
B. Nov. 29, 1967, Elizabeth, N. J.

Year	Team	Games	BA	SA	AB	H	2B	3B	HR	HR%	R	RBI	BB	SO	SB	Pinch Hit AB	Pinch Hit H	PO	A	E	DP	TC/G	FA	G by Pos
1993	KC A	16	.224	.408	49	11	3	0	2	4.1	2	5	6	15	0	1	0	129	9	2	10	9.3	.986	1B-15
1994		101	.282	.599	312	88	25	1	24	7.7	64	65	56	62	4	6	2	234	18	2	11	2.7	.992	DH-70, 1B-24
1995		72	.168	.313	208	35	7	1	7	3.4	20	25	26	56	0	9	3	66	9	0	11	1.2	1.000	DH-56, 1B-8
3 yrs.		189	.236	.478	569	134	35	2	33	5.8	86	95	88	133	4	16	5	429	36	4	32	2.7	.991	DH-126, 1B-47

Billy Hamilton

HAMILTON, WILLIAM ROBERT (Sliding Billy) BL TR 5′ 6″ 165 lbs.
B. Feb. 16, 1866, Newark, N. J. D. Dec. 16, 1940, Worcester, Mass.
Hall of Fame 1961.

Year	Team	Games	BA	SA	AB	H	2B	3B	HR	HR%	R	RBI	BB	SO	SB	Pinch Hit AB	Pinch Hit H	PO	A	E	DP	TC/G	FA	G by Pos
1888	KC AA	35	.264	.357	129	34	4	4	0	0.0	21	11	4		19	0	0	45	4	2	0	1.5	.961	OF-35
1889		137	.301	.395	534	161	17	12	3	0.6	144	77	87	41	**111**	0	0	202	20	37	6	1.9	.857	OF-137
1890	PHI N	123	.325	.399	496	161	13	9	2	0.4	133	49	83	37	**102**	0	0	232	23	34	4	2.3	.882	OF-123
1891		133	**.340**	.421	527	**179**	23	7	2	0.4	**141**	60	**102**	28	**111**	0	0	287	17	31	7	2.5	.907	OF-133
1892		139	.330	.410	554	183	21	7	3	0.5	132	53	81	29	57	0	0	291	26	28	7	2.5	.919	OF-139
1893		82	**.380**	.524	355	135	22	7	5	1.4	110	44	63	7	43	0	0	228	8	16	6	3.1	.937	OF-82
1894		131	.404	.528	544	220	25	15	4	0.7	**192**[1]	87	**126**	17	**98**	0	0	361	15	14	4	3.0	.964	OF-129
1895		123	.389	.495	517	201	22	6	7	1.4	**166**	74	**96**	30	**97**	0	0	313	11	31	5	2.9	.913	OF-123
1896	BOS N	131	.365	.463	523	191	24	9	3	0.6	152	52	**110**	29	83	0	0	276	8	20	2	2.3	.934	OF-131
1897		127	.343	.414	507	174	17	5	3	0.6	**152**	61	**105**		66	0	0	296	10	12	0	2.5	.962	OF-126
1898		110	.369	.453	417	154	16	5	3	0.7	110	50	87		54	0	0	189	8	21	2	2.0	.904	OF-110
1899		84	.310	.350	297	92	7	1	1	0.3	63	33	72		19	2	0	166	11	9	2	2.3	.952	OF-81
1900		136	.333	.396	520	173	20	5	1	0.2	102	47	107		29	0	0	326	14	19	6	2.6	.947	OF-136
1901		102	.292	.361	349	102	11	2	3	0.9	70	38	64		19	3	2	232	7	14	4	2.6	.945	OF-99
14 yrs.		1593	.345 **6th**	.432	6269	2160	242	94	40	0.6	1688	736	1187	218	908	5	2	3444	182	288	55	2.5	.926	OF-1584

Darryl Hamilton

HAMILTON, DARRYL QUINN BL TR 6′ 1″ 180 lbs.
B. Dec. 3, 1963, Baton Rouge, La.

Year	Team	Games	BA	SA	AB	H	2B	3B	HR	HR%	R	RBI	BB	SO	SB	Pinch Hit AB	Pinch Hit H	PO	A	E	DP	TC/G	FA	G by Pos
1988	MIL A	44	.184	.252	103	19	4	0	1	1.0	14	11	12	9	7	3	1	75	1	0	0	1.9	1.000	OF-37, DH-3
1990		89	.295	.346	156	46	5	0	1	0.6	27	18	9	12	10	5	1	120	1	1	0	1.5	.992	OF-72, DH-9
1991		122	.311	.385	405	126	15	6	1	0.2	64	57	33	38	16	3	3	234	3	1	0	2.0	.996	OF-117
1992		128	.298	.400	470	140	19	7	5	1.1	67	62	45	42	41	3	1	279	10	0	0	2.3	1.000	OF-124
1993		135	.310	.406	520	161	21	1	9	1.7	74	48	45	62	21	5	0	340	10	3	1	2.7	.992	OF-129
1994		36	.262	.369	141	37	10	1	1	0.7	23	13	15	17	3	0	0	60	2	0	1	1.8	1.000	OF-32, DH-3
1995		112	.271	.389	398	108	20	6	5	1.3	54	44	47	35	11	8	1	262	4	3	0	2.4	.989	OF-109, DH-2
7 yrs.		666	.290	.384	2193	637	94	21	23	1.0	323	253	206	215	109	27	7	1370	31	8	2	2.2	.994	OF-620, DH-17

Jeff Hamilton

HAMILTON, JEFFREY ROBERT BR TR 6′ 3″ 190 lbs.
B. Mar. 19, 1964, Flint, Mich.

Year	Team	Games	BA	SA	AB	H	2B	3B	HR	HR%	R	RBI	BB	SO	SB	Pinch Hit AB	Pinch Hit H	PO	A	E	DP	TC/G	FA	G by Pos
1986	LA N	71	.224	.361	147	33	5	0	5	3.4	22	19	2	43	0	6	2	40	87	4	6	1.9	.969	3B-66, SS-2
1987		35	.217	.253	83	18	3	0	0	0.0	5	1	7	22	0	6	0	27	60	6	5	2.9	.935	3B-31, SS-1
1988		111	.236	.353	309	73	14	2	6	1.9	34	33	10	51	0	9	3	67	160	14	9	2.2	.942	3B-105, SS-2, 1B-1
1989		151	.245	.378	548	134	35	1	12	2.2	45	56	20	71	0	5	1	139	234	19	29	2.6	.952	3B-147, P-1, SS-1, 2B-1
1990		7	.125	.125	24	3	0	0	0	0.0	1	1	0	3	0	1	0	3	12	0	2	2.1	1.000	3B-7
1991		41	.223	.298	94	21	4	0	1	1.1	4	14	4	21	0	11	0	21	43	5	2	2.0	.928	3B-33, SS-1
6 yrs.		416	.234	.349	1205	282	61	3	24	2.0	111	124	43	211	0	38	6	297	596	48	53	2.4	.949	3B-389, SS-7, 2B-1, P-1, 1B-1
LEAGUE CHAMPIONSHIP SERIES																								
1988	LA N	7	.217	.217	23	5	0	0	0	0.0	2	1	3	4	0	0	0	9	10	2	0	3.0	.905	3B-7
WORLD SERIES																								
1988	LA N	5	.105	.105	19	2	0	0	0	0.0	1	0	1	4	0	0	0	2	5	1	0	1.6	.875	3B-5

Tom Hamilton

HAMILTON, THOMAS BAIL (Ham) BL TR 6′ 4″ 213 lbs.
B. Sept. 29, 1925, Altoona, Kans. D. Nov. 29, 1973, Tyler, Tex.

Year	Team	Games	BA	SA	AB	H	2B	3B	HR	HR%	R	RBI	BB	SO	SB	Pinch Hit AB	Pinch Hit H	PO	A	E	DP	TC/G	FA	G by Pos
1952	PHI A	9	.200	.300	10	2	1	0	0	0.0	1	1	1	1	0	4	1	11	0	0	1	2.2	1.000	1B-5
1953		58	.196	.232	56	11	2	0	0	0.0	8	5	7	11	0	43	8	22	2	0	0	2.7	1.000	1B-7, OF-2
2 yrs.		67	.197	.242	66	13	3	0	0	0.0	9	6	8	12	0	47	9	33	2	0	1	2.5	1.000	1B-12, OF-2

Ken Hamlin

HAMLIN, KENNETH LEE BR TR 5′10″ 170 lbs.
B. May 18, 1935, Detroit, Mich.

Year	Team	Games	BA	SA	AB	H	2B	3B	HR	HR%	R	RBI	BB	SO	SB	Pinch Hit AB	Pinch Hit H	PO	A	E	DP	TC/G	FA	G by Pos
1957	PIT N	2	.000	.000	1	0	0	0	0	0.0	0	0	0	0	0	0	0	2	0	0	0	2.0	1.000	SS-1
1959		3	.125	.125	8	1	0	0	0	0.0	1	0	2	1	0	0	0	4	6	0	2	3.3	1.000	SS-3
1960	KC A	140	.224	.271	428	96	10	2	2	0.5	51	24	44	48	1	1	1	195	341	25	61	4.0	.955	SS-139
1961	LA A	42	.209	.275	91	19	3	0	1	1.1	4	5	11	9	0	2	1	63	93	6	25	4.2	.963	SS-39
1962	WAS A	98	.253	.325	292	74	12	0	3	1.0	29	22	22	22	7	6	2	126	210	13	47	3.9	.963	SS-87, 2B-2
1965		117	.273	.370	362	99	21	1	4	1.1	45	22	33	45	8	9	2	185	210	12	45	3.3	.971	2B-77, SS-47, 3B-1
1966		66	.215	.291	158	34	7	1	1	0.6	13	16	13	21	1	18	1	91	120	8	28	4.3	.963	2B-50, 3B-1
7 yrs.		468	.241	.311	1340	323	53	4	11	0.8	143	89	125	146	17	36	7	666	980	64	208	3.8	.963	SS-316, 2B-129, 3B-2

Jack Hammond

HAMMOND, WALTER CHARLES (Wobby) BR TR 5′11″ 170 lbs.
B. Feb. 26, 1891, Amsterdam, N. Y. D. Mar. 4, 1942, Kenosha, Wis.

Year	Team	Games	BA	SA	AB	H	2B	3B	HR	HR%	R	RBI	BB	SO	SB	Pinch Hit AB	Pinch Hit H	PO	A	E	DP	TC/G	FA	G by Pos
1915	CLE A	35	.214	.262	84	18	2	1	0	0.0	9	4	1	19	0	9	1	24	42	3	5	3.6	.957	2B-19
1922	**2 teams** **CLE A** (1G –.250) **PIT N** (9G –.273)																							
″	**total**	10	.267	.267	15	4	0	0	0	0.0	4	0	1	0	0	0	0	9	8	4	2	4.2	.810	2B-5
2 yrs.		45	.222	.263	99	22	2	1	0	0.0	13	4	2	19	0	9	1	33	50	7	7	3.8	.922	2B-24

Steve Hammond

HAMMOND, STEVEN BENJAMIN
B. May 9, 1957, Atlanta, Ga.
BL TR 6′ 2″ 190 lbs.

Year	Team		Games	BA	SA	AB	H	2B	3B	HR	HR%	R	RBI	BB	SO	SB	Pinch Hit AB	Pinch Hit H	PO	A	E	DP	TC/G	FA	G by Pos
1982	KC	A	46	.230	.310	126	29	5	1	1	0.8	14	11	4	18	0	11	2	81	3	0	1	2.2	1.000	OF-37, DH-1

Jeffrey Hammonds

HAMMONDS, JEFFREY BRYAN
B. Mar. 5, 1971, Plainfield, N. J.
BR TR 6′ 195 lbs.

Year	Team		Games	BA	SA	AB	H	2B	3B	HR	HR%	R	RBI	BB	SO	SB	Pinch Hit AB	Pinch Hit H	PO	A	E	DP	TC/G	FA	G by Pos
1993	BAL	A	33	.305	.467	105	32	8	0	3	2.9	10	19	2	16	4	2	2	47	2	2	0	1.7	.961	OF-23, DH-7
1994			68	.296	.480	250	74	18	2	8	3.2	45	31	17	39	5	0	0	147	5	6	0	2.4	.962	OF-67
1995			57	.242	.371	178	43	9	1	4	2.2	18	23	9	30	4	6	1	88	1	1	0	1.8	.989	OF-46, DH-5
3 yrs.			158	.280	.441	533	149	35	3	15	2.8	73	73	28	85	13	8	3	282	8	9	0	2.0	.970	OF-136, DH-12

Garvin Hamner

HAMNER, WESLEY GARVIN (Wes)
Brother of Granny Hamner.
B. Mar. 18, 1924, Richmond, Va.
BR TR 5′11″ 172 lbs.

Year	Team		Games	BA	SA	AB	H	2B	3B	HR	HR%	R	RBI	BB	SO	SB	Pinch Hit AB	Pinch Hit H	PO	A	E	DP	TC/G	FA	G by Pos
1945	PHI	N	32	.198	.228	101	20	3	0	0	0.0	12	5	7	9	2	0	0	66	81	15	13	5.2	.907	2B-21, SS-9, 3B-1

Granny Hamner

HAMNER, GRANVILLE WILBUR
Brother of Garvin Hamner.
B. Apr. 26, 1927, Richmond, Va. D. Sept. 12, 1993, Philadelphia, Pa.
BR TR 5′10″ 163 lbs.

Year	Team		Games	BA	SA	AB	H	2B	3B	HR	HR%	R	RBI	BB	SO	SB	Pinch Hit AB	Pinch Hit H	PO	A	E	DP	TC/G	FA	G by Pos
1944	PHI	N	21	.247	.260	77	19	1	0	0	0.0	6	5	3	7	0	0	0	27	98	9	17	6.4	.933	SS-21
1945			14	.171	.220	41	7	2	0	0	0.0	3	6	1	3	0	0	0	31	37	11	7	6.1	.861	SS-13
1946			2	.143	.143	7	1	0	0	0	0.0	0	0	0	3	0	0	0	1	5	1	1	3.5	.857	SS-2
1947			2	.286	.286	7	2	0	0	0	0.0	1	0	1	0	0	0	0	5	6	0	1	5.5	1.000	SS-2
1948			129	.260	.350	446	116	21	5	3	0.7	42	48	22	39	2	4	1	270	318	27	66	4.8	.956	2B-87, SS-37, 3B-3
1949			154	.263	.353	**662**	174	32	5	6	0.9	83	53	25	47	6	0	0	280	506	32	101	5.3	.961	SS-154
1950			157	.270	.380	637	172	27	5	11	1.7	78	82	39	35	2	0	0	293	513	48	100	5.4	.944	SS-157
1951			150	.255	.363	589	150	23	7	9	1.5	61	72	29	32	10	0	0	255	458	31	93	5.0	.958	SS-150
1952			151	.275	.428	596	164	30	5	17	2.9	74	87	27	51	7	1	0	267	470	38	102	5.1	.951	SS-151
1953			154	.276	.455	609	168	30	8	21	3.4	90	92	32	28	2	1	0	285	459	37	105	4.8	.953	2B-93, SS-71
1954			152	.299	.466	596	178	39	11	13	2.2	83	89	53	44	1	0	0	362	416	18	98	5.2	.977	2B-152, SS-1
1955			104	.257	.343	405	104	12	4	5	1.2	57	43	41	30	0	1	0	201	261	21	51	4.2	.957	2B-82, SS-32
1956			122	.224	.329	401	90	24	3	4	1.0	42	42	30	42	2	5	1	183	307	32	70	4.2	.939	SS-110, 2B-11, P-3
1957			133	.227	.345	502	114	19	5	10	2.0	59	62	34	42	3	8	0	264	291	21	55	4.4	.964	2B-125, SS-5, P-1
1958			35	.301	.444	133	40	7	3	2	1.5	18	18	8	16	0	0	0	44	79	3	11	3.5	.976	3B-22, 2B-11, SS-3
1959	2 teams	PHI N (21G –.297) CLE A (27G –.164)																							
″	total		48	.229	.351	131	30	5	1	3	2.3	14	9	6	13	0	17	2	43	79	5	10	3.3	.961	SS-25, 2B-7, 3B-6
1962	KC	A	3	—	—	0	0	0	0	0	—	0	0	0	0	0	0	0	0	1	0	0	0.3	1.000	P-3
17 yrs.			1531	.262	.383	5839	1529	272	62	104	1.8	711	708	351	432	35	37	4	2811	4304	334	888	4.8	.955	SS-934, 2B-568, 3B-31, P-7
WORLD SERIES																									
1950	PHI	N	4	.429	.714	14	6	2	1	0	0.0	1	0	1	2	1	0	0	6	7	1	1	3.5	.929	SS-4

Ike Hampton

HAMPTON, ISAAC BERNARD
B. Aug. 22, 1951, Camden, S. C.
BB TR 6′ 1″ 185 lbs.
BR 1978–1979

Year	Team		Games	BA	SA	AB	H	2B	3B	HR	HR%	R	RBI	BB	SO	SB	Pinch Hit AB	Pinch Hit H	PO	A	E	DP	TC/G	FA	G by Pos
1974	NY	N	4	.000	.000	4	0	0	0	0	0.0	0	1	0	1	0	3	0	2	0	0	0	2.0	1.000	C-1
1975	CAL	A	31	.152	.197	66	10	3	0	0	0.0	8	4	7	19	0	0	0	113	15	8	1	4.4	.941	C-28, SS-2, 3B-1
1976			3	.000	.000	2	0	0	0	0	0.0	0	0	0	0	0	0	0	2	2	0	1	1.0	1.000	C-2, SS-1, DH-1
1977			52	.295	.523	44	13	1	0	3	6.8	5	9	2	10	0	5	3	87	5	3	0	1.9	.968	C-47, DH-2
1978			19	.214	.571	14	3	0	1	1	7.1	2	4	2	7	1	1	0	20	1	2	0	1.3	.913	C-13, DH-4, 1B-1
1979			4	.400	.400	5	2	0	0	0	0.0	0	0	0	1	0	1	0	10	2	0	0	6.0	1.000	1B-2
6 yrs.			113	.207	.341	135	28	4	1	4	3.0	15	18	11	38	1	10	3	234	25	13	2	2.6	.952	C-91, DH-7, SS-3, 1B-3, 3B-1

Bert Hamric

HAMRIC, ODBERT HERMAN
B. Mar. 1, 1928, Clarksburg, W. Va. D. Aug. 4, 1984, Springboro, Ohio.
BL TR 6′ 165 lbs.

Year	Team		Games	BA	SA	AB	H	2B	3B	HR	HR%	R	RBI	BB	SO	SB	Pinch Hit AB	Pinch Hit H	PO	A	E	DP	TC/G	FA	G by Pos
1955	BKN	N	2	.000	.000	1	0	0	0	0	0.0	0	0	0	1	0	1	0	0	0	0	0	0.0	—	
1958	BAL	A	8	.125	.125	8	1	0	0	0	0.0	0	0	0	6	0	8	1	0	0	0	0	0.0	—	
2 yrs.			10	.111	.111	9	1	0	0	0	0.0	0	0	0	7	0	9	1							

Ray Hamrick

HAMRICK, RAYMOND BERNARD
B. Aug. 1, 1921, Nashville, Tenn.
BR TR 5′11½″ 160 lbs.

Year	Team		Games	BA	SA	AB	H	2B	3B	HR	HR%	R	RBI	BB	SO	SB	Pinch Hit AB	Pinch Hit H	PO	A	E	DP	TC/G	FA	G by Pos
1943	PHI	N	44	.200	.231	160	32	3	1	0	0.0	12	9	8	28	0	0	0	86	114	10	12	4.9	.952	2B-31, SS-12
1944			74	.205	.257	292	60	10	1	1	0.3	22	23	23	34	1	0	0	160	293	25	55	6.5	.948	SS-74
2 yrs.			118	.204	.248	452	92	13	2	1	0.2	34	32	31	62	1	0	0	246	407	35	67	5.9	.949	SS-86, 2B-31

Buddy Hancken

HANCKEN, MORRIS MEDLOCK
B. Aug. 30, 1914, Birmingham, Ala.
BR TR 6′ 1″ 175 lbs.

Year	Team		Games	BA	SA	AB	H	2B	3B	HR	HR%	R	RBI	BB	SO	SB	Pinch Hit AB	Pinch Hit H	PO	A	E	DP	TC/G	FA	G by Pos
1940	PHI	A	1	—	—	0	0	0	0	0	—	0	0	0	C	0	0	0	1	0	0	0	1.0	1.000	C-1

Fred Hancock

HANCOCK, FRED JAMES
B. Mar. 28, 1920, Allenport, Pa. D. Mar. 12, 1986, Clearwater, Fla.
BR TR 5′ 8″ 170 lbs.

Year	Team		Games	BA	SA	AB	H	2B	3B	HR	HR%	R	RBI	BB	SO	SB	Pinch Hit AB	Pinch Hit H	PO	A	E	DP	TC/G	FA	G by Pos
1949	CHI	A	39	.135	.212	52	7	2	1	0	0.0	7	9	8	9	0	5	1	22	28	2	10	1.7	.962	SS-27, 3B-3, OF-1

Garry Hancock

HANCOCK, RONALD GARRY
B. Jan. 23, 1954, Tampa, Fla.
BL TL 6′ 175 lbs.

Year	Team		Games	BA	SA	AB	H	2B	3B	HR	HR%	R	RBI	BB	SO	SB	Pinch Hit AB	Pinch Hit H	PO	A	E	DP	TC/G	FA	G by Pos
1978	BOS	A	38	.225	.263	80	18	3	0	0	0.0	10	4	1	12	0	8	3	29	3	0	1	1.0	1.000	OF-19, DH-13
1980			46	.287	.443	115	33	6	0	4	3.5	9	19	3	11	0	12	2	49	3	2	0	1.4	.963	OF-27, DH-12
1981			26	.156	.222	45	7	3	0	0	0.0	4	3	2	4	0	12	1	11	2	0	0	1.1	1.000	OF-8, DH-4
1982			11	.000	.000	14	0	0	0	0	0.0	3	0	1	1	0	4	0	4	0	0	0	0.6	1.000	OF-7
1983	OAK	A	101	.273	.418	256	70	7	3	8	3.1	29	30	5	13	2	14	7	249	10	4	17	2.6	.985	OF-67, 1B-27, DH-9
1984			51	.217	.250	60	13	2	0	0	0.0	2	8	0	1	0	33	6	24	0	0	1	0.9	1.000	OF-18, DH-5, 1B-4, P-1
6 yrs.			273	.247	.358	570	141	21	3	12	2.1	57	64	12	42	2	83	19	366	18	6	19	1.8	.985	OF-146, DH-43, 1B-31, P-1

Mike Handiboe

HANDIBOE, ALOYSIUS JAMES (Coalyard Mike)
B. July 21, 1887, Washington, D. C. D. Jan. 31, 1953, Savannah, Ga.
BL TL 5′10″ 155 lbs.

Year	Team		Games	BA	SA	AB	H	2B	3B	HR	HR%	R	RBI	BB	SO	SB	Pinch Hit AB	Pinch Hit H	PO	A	E	DP	TC/G	FA	G by Pos
1911	NY	A	5	.067	.067	15	1	0	0	0	0.0	0	0	2		0	0	0	7	0	0	0	1.8	1.000	OF-4

Gene Handley

HANDLEY, EUGENE LOUIS BR TR 5′10½″ 165 lbs.
Brother of Lee Handley.
B. Nov. 25, 1914, Kennett, Mo.

Year	Team	Games	BA	SA	AB	H	2B	3B	HR	HR%	R	RBI	BB	SO	SB	Pinch Hit AB	Pinch Hit H	PO	A	E	DP	TC/G	FA	G by Pos
1946	PHI A	89	.251	.323	251	63	8	5	0	0.0	31	21	22	25	8	8	3	163	152	17	33	4.5	.949	2B-68, 3B-4, SS-1
1947		36	.256	.300	90	23	2	1	0	0.0	10	8	10	2	1	3	0	43	58	7	11	3.9	.935	2B-17, 3B-10, SS-1
2 yrs.		125	.252	.317	341	86	10	6	0	0.0	41	29	32	27	9	11	3	206	210	24	44	4.4	.945	2B-85, 3B-14, SS-2

Lee Handley

HANDLEY, LEE ELMER (Jeep) BR TR 5′ 7″ 160 lbs.
Brother of Gene Handley.
B. June 13, 1913, Clarion, Iowa D. Apr. 8, 1970, Pittsburgh, Pa.

Year	Team	Games	BA	SA	AB	H	2B	3B	HR	HR%	R	RBI	BB	SO	SB	Pinch Hit AB	Pinch Hit H	PO	A	E	DP	TC/G	FA	G by Pos
1936	CIN N	24	.308	.397	78	24	1	0	2	2.6	10	8	7	16	3	1	0	49	58	8	8	5.0	.930	2B-16, 3B-7
1937	PIT N	127	.250	.362	480	120	21	12	3	0.6	59	37	37	40	5	0	0	296	375	35	67	5.6	.950	2B-126, 3B-1
1938		139	.268	.372	570	153	25	8	6	1.1	91	51	53	31	7	0	0	119	304	23	26	3.3	.948	3B-136
1939		101	.285	.356	376	107	14	5	1	0.3	43	42	32	20	**17**	1	0	83	180	18	14	2.8	.936	3B-100
1940		98	.281	.341	302	85	7	4	1	0.3	50	19	27	16	7	4	1	89	143	19	15	2.9	.924	3B-80, 2B-7
1941		124	.288	.344	459	132	18	4	0	0.0	59	33	35	22	16	6	1	125	247	21	19	3.4	.947	3B-114
1944		40	.221	.244	86	19	2	0	0	0.0	7	5	3	5	1	4	1	51	56	4	10	3.4	.964	2B-19, 3B-11, SS-3
1945		98	.298	.372	312	93	16	2	1	0.3	39	32	20	16	7	11	5	85	183	15	13	3.6	.947	3B-79
1946		116	.238	.298	416	99	8	7	1	0.2	43	28	29	20	4	5	0	116	239	17	13	3.5	.954	3B-102, 2B-3
1947	PHI N	101	.253	.310	277	70	10	3	0	0.0	17	42	24	18	1	7	2	93	149	9	8	2.9	.964	3B-83, 2B-3, SS-1
10 yrs.		968	.269	.345	3356	902	122	45	15	0.4	418	297	267	204	68	39	10	1106	1934	169	193	3.6	.947	3B-713, 2B-174, SS-4

Harry Hanebrink

HANEBRINK, HARRY ALOYSIUS BL TR 6′ 165 lbs.
B. Nov. 12, 1927, St. Louis, Mo.

Year	Team	Games	BA	SA	AB	H	2B	3B	HR	HR%	R	RBI	BB	SO	SB	Pinch Hit AB	Pinch Hit H	PO	A	E	DP	TC/G	FA	G by Pos
1953	MIL N	51	.237	.313	80	19	1	1	1	1.3	8	8	6	8	1	25	2	39	55	2	18	4.4	.979	2B-21, 3B-1
1957		6	.286	.286	7	2	0	0	0	0.0	0	0	1	2	0	4	1	0	4	0	0	2.0	1.000	3B-2
1958		63	.188	.301	133	25	3	0	4	3.0	14	10	13	9	0	19	5	58	10	1	1	1.7	.986	OF-33, 3B-7
1959	PHI N	57	.258	.340	97	25	3	1	1	1.0	10	7	2	12	0	41	11	17	28	5	6	2.0	.900	2B-15, 3B-9, OF-1
4 yrs.		177	.224	.315	317	71	7	2	6	1.9	32	25	22	31	1	89	19	114	97	8	25	2.5	.963	2B-36, OF-34, 3B-19
WORLD SERIES																								
1958	MIL N	2	.000	.000	2	0	0	0	0	0.0	0	0	0	0	0	2	0	0	0	0	0	0.0	—	

Fred Haney

HANEY, FRED GIRARD (Pudge) BR TR 5′ 6″ 170 lbs.
B. Apr. 25, 1898, Albuquerque, N. M. D. Nov. 9, 1977, Beverly Hills, Calif.
Manager 1939–41, 1953–59.

Year	Team	Games	BA	SA	AB	H	2B	3B	HR	HR%	R	RBI	BB	SO	SB	Pinch Hit AB	Pinch Hit H	PO	A	E	DP	TC/G	FA	G by Pos
1922	DET A	81	.352	.423	213	75	7	4	0	0.0	41	25	32	14	3	9	3	158	112	12	17	5.1	.957	3B-42, 1B-11, SS-2
1923		142	.282	.348	503	142	13	4	4	0.8	85	67	45	23	12	0	0	261	351	28	47	4.6	.956	2B-69, 3B-55, SS-16
1924		86	.309	.371	256	79	11	1	1	0.4	54	30	39	13	7	13	4	57	163	18	10	3.6	.924	3B-59, SS-4, 2B-3
1925		114	.279	.332	398	111	15	3	0	0.0	84	40	66	29	11	5	1	115	207	16	22	3.2	.953	3B-107
1926	BOS A	138	.221	.284	462	102	15	7	0	0.0	47	52	74	28	13	1	0	149	322	21	30	3.6	.957	3B-137
1927	2 teams	BOS A (47G –.276) CHI N (4G –.000)																						
″	total	51	.269	.395	119	32	4	1	3	2.5	23	12	25	14	4	14	4	61	56	8	5	3.6	.936	3B-34, OF-1
1929	STL N	10	.115	.231	26	3	1	1	0	0.0	4	2	1	2	0	2	1	8	15	1	2	4.0	.958	3B-6
7 yrs.		622	.275	.342	1977	544	66	21	8	0.4	338	228	282	123	50	44	13	809	1226	104	133	3.9	.951	3B-440, 2B-72, SS-22, 1B-11, OF-1

Larry Haney

HANEY, WALLACE LARRY BR TR 6′ 2″ 195 lbs.
Father of Chris Haney.
B. Nov. 19, 1942, Charlottesville, Va.

Year	Team	Games	BA	SA	AB	H	2B	3B	HR	HR%	R	RBI	BB	SO	SB	Pinch Hit AB	Pinch Hit H	PO	A	E	DP	TC/G	FA	G by Pos
1966	BAL A	20	.161	.232	56	9	1	0	1	1.8	3	3	1	15	0	1	0	123	6	2	1	6.6	.985	C-20
1967		58	.268	.390	164	44	11	0	3	1.8	13	20	6	28	1	1	0	311	31	3	3	6.1	.991	C-57
1968		38	.236	.326	89	21	3	1	1	1.1	5	5	0	19	0	6	2	149	18	1	3	5.3	.994	C-32
1969	2 teams	SEA A (22G –.254) OAK A (53G –.151)																						
″	total	75	.193	.324	145	28	7	0	4	2.8	11	19	13	31	1	2	1	255	24	6	5	3.9	.979	C-73
1970	OAK A	2	.000	.000	2	0	0	0	0	0.0	2	0	2	1	0	1	0	6	0	0	0	6.0	1.000	C-1
1972		5	.000	.000	4	0	0	0	0	0.0	0	0	0	1	0	1	0	4	0	1	0	1.0	.800	C-4, 2B-1
1973	2 teams	OAK A (2G –.500) STL N (2G –.000)																						
″	total	4	.333	.333	3	1	0	0	0	0.0	0	0	0	1	0	0	0	4	0	0	0	1.0	1.000	C-4
1974	OAK A	76	.165	.248	121	20	4	0	2	1.7	12	3	3	18	1	1	0	219	21	3	2	3.1	.988	C-73, 3B-3, 1B-2
1975		47	.192	.308	26	5	0	0	1	3.8	3	2	1	4	0	0	0	70	4	0	1	1.6	1.000	C-43, 3B-4
1976		88	.226	.237	177	40	2	0	0	0.0	12	10	13	26	0	1	0	290	45	9	2	4.0	.974	C-87
1977	MIL A	63	.228	.244	127	29	2	0	0	0.0	7	10	5	30	0	0	0	223	32	4	3	4.1	.985	C-63
1978		4	.200	.200	5	1	0	0	0	0.0	0	1	0	1	0	0	0	6	0	0	0	1.5	1.000	C-4
12 yrs.		480	.215	.289	919	198	30	1	12	1.3	68	73	44	175	3	14	3	1660	181	29	20	4.0	.984	C-461, 3B-7, 1B-2, 2B-1
WORLD SERIES																								
1974	OAK A	2	—	—	0	0	0	0	0	—	0	0	0	0	0	0	0	6	0	0	0	3.0	1.000	C-2

Todd Haney

HANEY, TODD MICHAEL BR TR 5′ 9″ 165 lbs.
B. July 30, 1965, Galveston, Tex.

Year	Team	Games	BA	SA	AB	H	2B	3B	HR	HR%	R	RBI	BB	SO	SB	Pinch Hit AB	Pinch Hit H	PO	A	E	DP	TC/G	FA	G by Pos
1992	MON N	7	.300	.400	10	3	1	0	0	0.0	0	1	0	0	0	1	0	2	6	0	1	1.6	1.000	2B-5
1994	CHI N	17	.162	.243	37	6	0	0	1	2.7	6	2	3	3	2	1	0	20	28	1	8	3.5	.980	2B-11, 3B-3
1995		25	.411	.603	73	30	8	0	2	2.7	11	6	7	11	0	3	2	34	61	2	12	4.6	.979	2B-17, 3B-4
3 yrs.		49	.325	.475	120	39	9	0	3	2.5	17	9	10	14	2	5	2	56	95	3	21	3.8	.981	2B-33, 3B-7

Charlie Hanford

HANFORD, CHARLES JOSEPH BR TR 5′ 6½″ 145 lbs.
B. June 3, 1881, Tunstall, England D. July 19, 1963, Trenton, N. J.

Year	Team	Games	BA	SA	AB	H	2B	3B	HR	HR%	R	RBI	BB	SO	SB	Pinch Hit AB	Pinch Hit H	PO	A	E	DP	TC/G	FA	G by Pos
1914	BUF F	155	.291	.447	597	174	28	13	13	2.2	83	90	32		37	0	0	331	24	10	5	2.4	.973	OF-155
1915	CHI F	77	.240	.318	179	43	4	5	0	0.0	27	22	12		10	26	7	66	2	2	0	1.6	.971	OF-43
2 yrs.		232	.280	.418	776	217	32	18	13	1.7	110	112	44		47	26	7	397	26	12	5	2.2	.972	OF-198

Jay Hankins

HANKINS, JAY NELSON BL TR 5′ 7″ 170 lbs.
B. Nov. 7, 1935, St. Louis County, Mo.

Year	Team	Games	BA	SA	AB	H	2B	3B	HR	HR%	R	RBI	BB	SO	SB	Pinch Hit AB	Pinch Hit H	PO	A	E	DP	TC/G	FA	G by Pos
1961	KC A	76	.185	.272	173	32	0	3	3	1.7	23	6	8	17	2	3	1	97	1	3	0	1.6	.970	OF-65
1963		10	.176	.324	34	6	0	1	1	2.9	2	4	0	3	0	1	1	19	1	1	1	2.3	.952	OF-9
2 yrs.		86	.184	.280	207	38	0	4	4	1.9	25	10	8	20	2	4	2	116	2	4	1	1.6	.967	OF-74

Frank Hankinson

HANKINSON, FRANK EDWARD BR TR 5′11″ 168 lbs.
B. Apr. 29, 1856, New York, N. Y. D. Apr. 5, 1911, Palisades Park, N. J.

Year	Team	Games	BA	SA	AB	H	2B	3B	HR	HR%	R	RBI	BB	SO	SB	Pinch Hit AB	Pinch Hit H	PO	A	E	DP	TC/G	FA	G by Pos
1878	CHI N	58	.267	.338	240	64	8	3	1	0.4	38	27	5	36		0	0	95	138	33	9	4.6	.876	3B-57, P-1
1879		44	.181	.205	171	31	4	0	0	0.0	14	8	2	14		0	0	42	87	14	1	3.2	.902	P-26, OF-14, 3B-5
1880	CLE N	69	.209	.278	263	55	7	4	1	0.4	32	19	1	23		0	0	79	101	29	7	2.9	.861	3B-56, OF-12, P-4
1881	TRO N	85	.193	.249	321	62	15	0	1	0.3	34	19	10	41		0	0	152	170	34	22	4.2	.904	3B-84, SS-1
1883	NY N	94	.220	.312	337	74	13	6	2	0.6	40		19	38		0	0	123	166	44	9	3.5	.868	3B-93, OF-1
1884		105	.231	.324	389	90	16	7	2	0.5	44		23	59		0	0	135	182	47	8	3.4	.871	3B-105, OF-1
1885	NY AA	94	.224	.285	362	81	12	2	2	0.6	43		12			0	0	106	212	33	9	3.7	.906	3B-94, P-1
1886		136	.241	.299	522	126	14	5	2	0.4	66		49			0	0	181	316	72	26	4.2	.873	3B-136
1887		127	.268	.373	512	137	29	11	1	0.2	79		38		19	0	0	161	276	69	26	4.0	.864	3B-127
1888	KC AA	37	.174	.232	155	27	4	1	1	0.6	20	20	11		2	0	0	72	84	18	12	4.6	.897	2B-13, SS-9, OF-7, 3B-7, 1B-2
10 yrs.		849	.228	.301	3272	747	122	39	13	0.4	410	93	170	211	21	0	0	1146	1732	393	129	3.8	.880	3B-764, OF-35, P-32, 2B-13, SS-10, 1B-2

Bill Hanlon

HANLON, WILLIAM JOSEPH (Big Bill) 6′
B. June 24, 1876, Los Angeles, Calif. D. Nov. 23, 1905, Los Angeles, Calif.

Year	Team	Games	BA	SA	AB	H	2B	3B	HR	HR%	R	RBI	BB	SO	SB	Pinch Hit AB	Pinch Hit H	PO	A	E	DP	TC/G	FA	G by Pos
1903	CHI N	8	.095	.095	21	2	0	0	0	0.0	4	2	6		1	0	0	92	4	2	2	12.3	.980	1B-8

Ned Hanlon

HANLON, EDWARD HUGH BL TR 5′ 9½″ 170 lbs.
B. Aug. 22, 1857, Montville, Conn. D. Apr. 14, 1937, Baltimore, Md.
Manager 1889–07.
Hall of Fame 1996.

Year	Team	Games	BA	SA	AB	H	2B	3B	HR	HR%	R	RBI	BB	SO	SB	Pinch Hit AB	Pinch Hit H	PO	A	E	DP	TC/G	FA	G by Pos
1880	CLE N	73	.246	.304	280	69	10	3	0	0.0	30	32	11	30		0	0	140	18	35	5	2.6	.819	OF-69, SS-4
1881	DET N	76	.279	.397	305	85	14	8	2	0.7	63	28	22	11		0	0	143	20	24	4	2.5	.872	OF-74, SS-2
1882		82	.231	.360	347	80	18	6	5	1.4	68	38	26	25		0	0	197	20	27	8	2.9	.889	OF-82, 2B-1
1883		100	.242	.291	413	100	13	2	1	0.2	65		34	44		0	0	247	41	44	10	3.3	.867	OF-90, 2B-11
1884		114	.264	.364	450	119	18	6	5	1.1	86		40	52		0	0	241	30	39	5	2.7	.874	OF-114
1885		105	.302	.389	424	128	18	8	1	0.2	93	29	47	18		0	0	220	19	38	2	2.6	.863	OF-105
1886		126	.235	.296	494	116	6	6	4	0.8	105	60	57	39		0	0	205	18	17	4	1.9	.929	OF-126, 2B-1
1887		118	.274	.357	471	129	13	7	4	0.8	79	69	30	24	69	0	0	264	18	30	4	2.6	.904	OF-118
1888		109	.266	.346	459	122	6	8	5	1.1	64	39	15	32	38	0	0	230	7	21	3	2.4	.919	OF-109
1889	PIT N	116	.239	.325	461	110	14	10	2	0.4	81	37	58	25	53	0	0	277	18	26	2	2.8	.919	OF-116
1890	PIT P	118	.278	.343	472	131	16	6	1	0.2	106	44	80	24	65	0	0	291	15	30	4	2.8	.911	OF-118
1891	PIT N	119	.266	.327	455	121	12	8	0	0.0	87	60	48	30	54	0	0	219	25	33	1	2.3	.881	OF-119, SS-1
1892	BAL N	11	.163	.233	43	7	1	1	0	0.0	3	2	3	3	0	0	0	20	2	6	0	2.5	.786	OF-11
13 yrs.		1267	.260	.340	5074	1317	159	79	30	0.6	930	438	471	357	279	0	0	2694	251	370	52	2.6	.888	OF-1251, 2B-13, SS-7

John Hanna

HANNA, JOHN
B. Nov. 3, 1863, Philadelphia, Pa. D. Nov. 7, 1930, Philadelphia, Pa.

Year	Team	Games	BA	SA	AB	H	2B	3B	HR	HR%	R	RBI	BB	SO	SB	Pinch Hit AB	Pinch Hit H	PO	A	E	DP	TC/G	FA	G by Pos
1884	2 teams WAS AA (23G –.066) RIC AA (22G –.194)																							
″	total	45	.126	.154	143	18	2	1	0	0.0	14		6			0	0	210	77	35	5	7.0	.891	C-39, OF-6, SS-1

Truck Hannah

HANNAH, JAMES HARRISON BR TR 6′ 1″ 190 lbs.
B. June 5, 1889, Larimore, N. D. D. Apr. 27, 1982, Fountain Valley, Calif.

Year	Team	Games	BA	SA	AB	H	2B	3B	HR	HR%	R	RBI	BB	SO	SB	Pinch Hit AB	Pinch Hit H	PO	A	E	DP	TC/G	FA	G by Pos
1918	NY A	90	.220	.268	250	55	6	0	2	0.8	24	21	51	25	5	2	0	343	111	12	16	5.3	.974	C-88
1919		75	.238	.313	227	54	8	3	1	0.4	14	21	22	19	0	1	1	299	66	7	12	5.0	.981	C-73, 1B-1
1920		79	.247	.320	259	64	11	1	2	0.8	24	25	24	35	2	1	0	308	64	15	1	5.0	.961	C-78
3 yrs.		244	.235	.300	736	173	25	4	5	0.7	62	67	97	79	7	4	1	950	241	34	29	5.1	.972	C-239, 1B-1

Pat Hannifan

HANNIFAN, PATRICK JAMES TL
B. 1868, Nova Scotia, Canada D. Nov. 5, 1908, Springfield, Mass.

Year	Team	Games	BA	SA	AB	H	2B	3B	HR	HR%	R	RBI	BB	SO	SB	Pinch Hit AB	Pinch Hit H	PO	A	E	DP	TC/G	FA	G by Pos
1897	BKN N	10	.250	.250	20	5	0	0	0	0.0	4	2	1		4	3	1	16	3	3	1	4.4	.864	OF-3, 2B-2

Jack Hannifin

HANNIFIN, JOHN JOSEPH BR TR 5′11″ 167 lbs.
B. Feb. 25, 1883, Holyoke, Mass. D. Oct. 27, 1945, Northampton, Mass.

Year	Team	Games	BA	SA	AB	H	2B	3B	HR	HR%	R	RBI	BB	SO	SB	Pinch Hit AB	Pinch Hit H	PO	A	E	DP	TC/G	FA	G by Pos
1906	2 teams PHI A (1G –1.000) NY N (10G –.200)																							
″	total	11	.226	.290	31	7	0	1	0	0.0	4	3	2		1	0	0	12	22	5	2	3.9	.872	SS-6, 3B-3, 2B-1
1907	NY N	56	.228	.336	149	34	7	3	1	0.7	16	15	15		6	7	1	271	36	4	9	6.2	.987	1B-29, 3B-10, SS-9, OF-2
1908	2 teams NY N (1G –.000) BOS N (74G –.206)																							
″	total	75	.205	.266	259	53	6	2	2	0.8	30	22	28		7	11	2	152	179	19	15	4.3	.946	3B-35, 2B-22, SS-15, OF-9
3 yrs.		142	.214	.292	439	94	13	6	3	0.7	50	40	45		14	18	3	435	237	28	26	5.0	.960	3B-48, SS-30, 1B-29, 2B-23, OF-11

Bob Hansen

HANSEN, ROBERT JOSEPH BL TL 6′ 195 lbs.
B. May 26, 1948, Boston, Mass.

Year	Team	Games	BA	SA	AB	H	2B	3B	HR	HR%	R	RBI	BB	SO	SB	Pinch Hit AB	Pinch Hit H	PO	A	E	DP	TC/G	FA	G by Pos
1974	MIL A	58	.295	.432	88	26	4	1	2	2.3	8	9	3	16	2	34	14	11	0	0	0	0.5	1.000	DH-18, 1B-3
1976		24	.164	.180	61	10	1	0	0	0.0	4	4	6	8	0	7	1	0	0	0	0	0.0		DH-14, 1B-1
2 yrs.		82	.242	.329	149	36	5	1	2	1.3	12	13	9	24	2	41	15	11	0	0	0	0.3	1.000	DH-32, 1B-4

Dave Hansen

HANSEN, DAVID ANDREW BL TR 6′ 180 lbs.
B. Nov. 24, 1968, Long Beach, Calif.

Year	Team	Games	BA	SA	AB	H	2B	3B	HR	HR%	R	RBI	BB	SO	SB	Pinch Hit AB	Pinch Hit H	PO	A	E	DP	TC/G	FA	G by Pos
1990	LA N	5	.143	.143	7	1	0	0	0	0.0	0	1	0	3	0	3	0	0	1	1	0	1.0	.500	3B-2
1991		53	.268	.393	56	15	4	0	1	1.8	3	5	2	12	1	32	10	5	19	0	2	1.1	1.000	3B-21, SS-1
1992		132	.214	.299	341	73	11	0	6	1.8	30	22	34	49	0	25	5	61	183	8	13	2.3	.968	3B-108
1993		84	.362	.505	105	38	3	0	4	3.8	13	30	21	13	0	55	18	11	27	3	1	2.3	.927	3B-18
1994		40	.341	.409	44	15	3	0	0	0.0	3	5	5	5	0	31	8	0	6	1	0	1.0	.857	3B-7
1995		100	.287	.359	181	52	10	0	1	0.6	19	14	28	28	0	35	11	27	70	7	6	1.8	.933	3B-58
6 yrs.		414	.264	.356	734	194	31	0	12	1.6	68	77	90	110	1	181	52	104	306	20	22	2.0	.953	3B-214, SS-1
DIVISIONAL PLAYOFF SERIES																								
1995	LA N	3	.667	.667	3	2	0	0	0	0.0	0	0	0	0	0	3	2	0	0	0	0	0.0	—	

Doug Hansen

HANSEN, DOUGLAS WILLIAM BR TR 6′ 180 lbs.
B. Dec. 16, 1928, Los Angeles, Calif.

Year	Team	Games	BA	SA	AB	H	2B	3B	HR	HR%	R	RBI	BB	SO	SB	Pinch Hit AB	Pinch Hit H	PO	A	E	DP	TC/G	FA	G by Pos
1951	CLE A	3	—	—	0	0	0	0	0	—	2	0	0	0	0	0	0	0	0	0	0	0.0	—	

Ron Hansen

HANSEN, RONALD LAVERN BR TR 6′ 3″ 190 lbs.
B. Apr. 5, 1938, Oxford, Neb.

Year	Team	Games	BA	SA	AB	H	2B	3B	HR	HR%	R	RBI	BB	SO	SB	Pinch Hit AB	Pinch Hit H	PO	A	E	DP	TC/G	FA	G by Pos
1958	BAL A	12	.000	.000	19	0	0	0	0	0.0	1	1	0	7	0	0	0	10	23	2	4	2.9	.943	SS-12
1959		2	.000	.000	4	0	0	0	0	0.0	0	0	1	1	0	0	0	2	6	1	1	4.5	.889	SS-2
1960		153	.255	.440	530	135	22	5	22	4.2	72	86	69	94	3	1	0	325	456	29	110	5.3	.964	SS-153
1961		155	.248	.347	533	132	13	2	12	2.3	51	51	66	96	1	0	0	272	460	31	118	4.9	.959	SS-149, 2B-7
1962		71	.173	.255	196	34	7	0	3	1.5	12	17	30	36	0	6	2	114	159	10	37	4.4	.965	SS-64
1963	CHI A	144	.226	.351	482	109	17	2	13	2.7	55	67	78	74	1	0	0	247	483	13	95	5.2	.983	SS-144
1964		158	.261	.419	575	150	25	3	20	3.5	85	68	73	73	1	0	0	292	514	21	105	5.2	.975	SS-158
1965		162	.235	.344	587	138	23	4	11	1.9	61	66	60	73	1	0	0	287	527	26	97	5.2	.969	SS-161, 2B-1
1966		23	.176	.189	74	13	1	0	0	0.0	3	4	15	10	0	0	0	49	73	7	17	5.6	.946	SS-23
1967		157	.233	.321	498	116	20	0	8	1.6	35	51	64	51	0	0	0	243	482	27	91	4.8	.964	SS-157
1968	2 teams	WAS A (86G –.185)			CHI A (40G –.230)																			
″	total	126	.196	.312	362	71	15	0	9	2.5	35	32	46	61	0	6	2	170	336	21	54	4.3	.960	SS-88, 3B-34, 2B-2
1969	CHI A	85	.259	.335	185	48	6	1	2	1.1	15	22	18	25	2	25	6	216	83	8	28	5.0	.974	2B-26, 1B-21, SS-8, 3B-7
1970	NY A	59	.297	.473	91	27	4	0	4	4.4	13	14	19	9	0	28	4	25	57	1	7	3.1	.988	SS-15, 3B-11, 2B-1
1971		61	.207	.269	145	30	3	0	2	1.4	6	20	9	27	0	22	4	52	72	8	16	3.1	.939	3B-30, 2B-9, SS-3
1972	KC A	16	.133	.133	30	4	0	0	0	0.0	2	2	3	6	0	7	1	5	28	1	3	3.1	.971	SS-6, 3B-4, 2B-1
15 yrs.		1384	.234	.351	4311	1007	156	17	106	2.5	446	501	551	643	9	95	19	2309	3759	206	783	4.8	.967	SS-1143, 3B-86, 2B-47, 1B-21

Don Hanski

HANSKI, DONALD THOMAS BL TL 5′11″ 180 lbs.
Born Donald Thomas Hanyzewski.
B. Feb. 27, 1916, LaPorte, Ind. D. Sept. 2, 1957, Worth, Ill.

Year	Team	Games	BA	SA	AB	H	2B	3B	HR	HR%	R	RBI	BB	SO	SB	Pinch Hit AB	Pinch Hit H	PO	A	E	DP	TC/G	FA	G by Pos
1943	CHI A	9	.238	.286	21	5	1	0	0	0.0	1	2	0	5	0	3	0	37	3	2	5	7.0	.952	1B-5, P-1
1944		2	.000	.000	1	0	0	0	0	0.0	0	0	0	0	0	0	0	0	0	0	0	0.0	.000	P-2
2 yrs.		11	.227	.273	22	5	1	0	0	0.0	1	2	0	5	0	3	0	37	3	2	5	5.3	.952	1B-5, P-3

Joe Hanson

HANSON, HARRY FRANCIS BR TR 5′11″
B. Jan. 17, 1896, Elgin, Ill. D. Oct. 5, 1966, Savannah, Ga.

Year	Team	Games	BA	SA	AB	H	2B	3B	HR	HR%	R	RBI	BB	SO	SB	Pinch Hit AB	Pinch Hit H	PO	A	E	DP	TC/G	FA	G by Pos
1913	NY A	1	.000	.000	2	0	0	0	0	0.0	0	0	0	0	0	0	0	1	1	0	0	2.0	1.000	C-1

John Happenny

HAPPENNY, JOHN CLIFFORD (Cliff) BR TR 5′11″ 165 lbs.
B. May 18, 1901, Waltham, Mass. D. Dec. 29, 1988, Coral Springs, Fla.

Year	Team	Games	BA	SA	AB	H	2B	3B	HR	HR%	R	RBI	BB	SO	SB	Pinch Hit AB	Pinch Hit H	PO	A	E	DP	TC/G	FA	G by Pos
1923	CHI A	32	.221	.279	86	19	5	0	0	0.0	7	10	3	13	0	1	0	39	64	7	13	3.9	.936	2B-20, SS-8

Bill Harbidge

HARBIDGE, WILLIAM ARTHUR BL TL 162 lbs.
B. Mar. 29, 1855, Philadelphia, Pa. D. Mar. 17, 1924, Philadelphia, Pa.

Year	Team	Games	BA	SA	AB	H	2B	3B	HR	HR%	R	RBI	BB	SO	SB	Pinch Hit AB	Pinch Hit H	PO	A	E	DP	TC/G	FA	G by Pos
1876	HAR N	30	.217	.255	106	23	2	1	0	0.0	11	6	3	2		0	0	111	31	36	1	5.6	.798	C-24, OF-6, 1B-2
1877		41	.222	.275	167	37	5	2	0	0.0	18	8	3	6		0	0	163	41	33	2	5.6	.861	C-32, OF-5, 2B-4, 3B-1
1878	CHI N	54	.296	.346	240	71	12	0	0	0.0	32	37	6	13		0	0	265	67	46	1	6.5	.878	C-50, OF-8
1879		4	.111	.111	18	2	0	0	0	0.0	2	1	0	5		0	0	3	1	3	0	1.8	.571	OF-4
1880	TRO N	9	.370	.444	27	10	0	1	0	0.0	3	2	0	3		0	0	38	10	7	2	5.5	.873	C-9, OF-1
1882		32	.187	.211	123	23	1	1	0	0.0	11	13	10	17		0	0	107	5	17	4	4.0	.868	OF-23, 1B-6, C-3
1883	PHI N	73	.221	.286	280	62	12	3	0	0.0	32		24	20		0	0	138	79	62	3	3.7	.778	OF-44, SS-11, 2B-9, C-7, 3B-5
1884	CIN U	82	.279	.361	341	95	12	5	2	0.6	59		25			0	0	121	31	17	3	2.0	.899	OF-80, SS-3, 1B-2
8 yrs.		325	.248	.306	1302	323	44	13	2	0.2	168	67	71	66		0	0	946	265	221	16	4.2	.846	OF-171, C-125, SS-14, 2B-13, 1B-10, 3B-6

Scott Hardesty

HARDESTY, SCOTT DURBIN
B. Jan. 26, 1870, Bellville, Ohio D. Oct. 29, 1944, Fostoria, Ohio.

Year	Team	Games	BA	SA	AB	H	2B	3B	HR	HR%	R	RBI	BB	SO	SB	Pinch Hit AB	Pinch Hit H	PO	A	E	DP	TC/G	FA	G by Pos
1899	NY N	22	.222	.222	72	16	0	0	0	0.0	4	4	1		2	0	0	48	68	12	10	5.8	.906	SS-20, 1B-2

Pat Hardgrove

HARDGROVE, WILLIAM HENRY BR TR 5′10″ 158 lbs.
B. May 10, 1895, Palmyra, Kans. D. Jan. 26, 1973, Jackson, Miss.

Year	Team	Games	BA	SA	AB	H	2B	3B	HR	HR%	R	RBI	BB	SO	SB	Pinch Hit AB	Pinch Hit H	PO	A	E	DP	TC/G	FA	G by Pos
1918	CHI A	2	.000	.000	2	0	0	0	0	0.0	0	0	0	0	0	2	0	0	0	0	0	0.0	—	

Lew Hardie

HARDIE, LOUIS W. 5′11″ 180 lbs.
B. Aug. 24, 1864, New York, N. Y. D. Mar. 5, 1929, Oakland, Calif.

Year	Team	Games	BA	SA	AB	H	2B	3B	HR	HR%	R	RBI	BB	SO	SB	Pinch Hit AB	Pinch Hit H	PO	A	E	DP	TC/G	FA	G by Pos
1884	PHI N	3	.375	.625	8	3	2	0	0	0.0	0		0	2		0	0	5	1	1	0	2.3	.857	C-3
1886	CHI N	16	.176	.176	51	9	0	0	0	0.0	4	3	4	10		0	0	68	16	3	1	5.4	.966	C-13, OF-2, 3B-1
1890	BOS N	47	.227	.319	185	42	8	0	3	1.6	17	17	18	36	4	0	0	171	49	28	5	5.1	.887	C-25, OF-15, 3B-7, SS-1, 1B-1
1891	BAL AA	15	.232	.339	56	13	0	3	0	0.0	7	1	8	8	3	0	0	34	1	0	0	2.3	1.000	OF-15
4 yrs.		81	.223	.307	300	67	10	3	3	1.0	28	21	30	56	7	0	0	278	67	32	6	4.5	.915	C-41, OF-32, 3B-8, SS-1, 1B-1

Bud Hardin

HARDIN, WILLIAM EDGAR BR TR 5′10″ 165 lbs.
B. June 14, 1922, Shelby, N. C.

Year	Team	Games	BA	SA	AB	H	2B	3B	HR	HR%	R	RBI	BB	SO	SB	Pinch Hit AB	Pinch Hit H	PO	A	E	DP	TC/G	FA	G by Pos
1952	CHI N	3	.143	.143	7	1	0	0	0	0.0	1	0	0	0	0	1	0	6	4	0	1	3.3	1.000	SS-2, 2B-1

Lou Harding

HARDING, LOUIS EDWARD (Jumbo) 5′ 9½″ 213 lbs.
B. 1865, San Francisco, Calif. Deceased.

Year	Team	Games	BA	SA	AB	H	2B	3B	HR	HR%	R	RBI	BB	SO	SB	Pinch Hit AB	Pinch Hit H	PO	A	E	DP	TC/G	FA	G by Pos
1886	STL AA	1	.333	.667	3	1	1	0	0	0.0	0		0			0	0	4	4	1	0	9.0	.889	C-1

Carroll Hardy

HARDY, CARROLL WILLIAM BR TR 6′ 185 lbs.
B. May 18, 1933, Sturgis, S. D.

Year	Team	Games	BA	SA	AB	H	2B	3B	HR	HR%	R	RBI	BB	SO	SB	Pinch Hit AB	Pinch Hit H	PO	A	E	DP	TC/G	FA	G by Pos
1958	CLE A	27	.204	.327	49	10	3	0	1	2.0	10	6	6	14	1	6	1	35	2	0	0	2.2	1.000	OF-17
1959		32	.208	.226	53	11	1	0	0	0.0	12	2	3	7	1	12	1	41	0	0	0	2.7	1.000	OF-15
1960	2 teams	CLE A (29G –.111)			BOS A (73G –.234)																			
″	total	102	.221	.319	163	36	6	2	2	1.2	33	16	19	42	3	7	2	105	3	3	1	1.5	.973	OF-76
1961	BOS A	85	.263	.381	281	74	20	2	3	1.1	46	36	26	53	4	14	3	142	7	6	3	2.0	.961	OF-76
1962		115	.215	.345	362	78	13	5	8	2.2	52	36	54	68	3	7	0	205	7	2	1	2.0	.991	OF-105

Carroll Hardy *continued*

Year	Team	Games	BA	SA	AB	H	2B	3B	HR	HR%	R	RBI	BB	SO	SB	Pinch Hit AB	Pinch Hit H	PO	A	E	DP	TC/G	FA	G by Pos
1963	**HOU N**	15	.227	.295	44	10	3	0	0	0.0	5	3	3	7	1	4	0	17	1	1	0	1.9	.947	OF-10
1964		46	.185	.242	157	29	1	1	2	1.3	13	12	8	30	0	5	1	100	3	1	0	2.5	.990	OF-41
1967	**MIN A**	11	.375	.750	8	3	0	0	1	12.5	1	2	1	1	0	7	3	0	0	0	0	0.0	.000	OF-4
8 yrs.		433	.225	.330	1117	251	47	10	17	1.5	172	113	120	222	13	62	11	645	23	13	5	2.0	.981	OF-344

Jack Hardy

HARDY, JOHN D. (Do-Little) BR TR 6′ 185 lbs.
B. June 23, 1877, Cleveland, Ohio D. Oct. 20, 1921, Cleveland, Ohio.

Year	Team	Games	BA	SA	AB	H	2B	3B	HR	HR%	R	RBI	BB	SO	SB	Pinch Hit AB	Pinch Hit H	PO	A	E	DP	TC/G	FA	G by Pos
1903	**CLE A**	5	.158	.211	19	3	1	0	0	0.0	1	1	1		1	0	0	5	0	0	0	1.0	1.000	OF-5
1907	**CHI N**	1	.250	.250	4	1	0	0	0	0.0	0	0	0		0	0	0	9	1	1	0	11.0	.909	C-1
1909	**WAS A**	10	.167	.167	24	4	0	0	0	0.0	3	4	1		0	0	0	35	7	1	1	4.3	.977	C-9, 2B-1
1910		7	.250	.250	8	2	0	0	0	0.0	1	0	0		0	2	0	11	3	2	2	3.2	.875	C-4, OF-1
4 yrs.		23	.182	.200	55	10	1	0	0	0.0	5	5	2		1	2	0	60	11	4	3	3.6	.947	C-14, OF-6, 2B-1

Shawn Hare

HARE, SHAWN ROBERT BL TL 6′ 2″ 190 lbs.
B. Mar. 26, 1967, St. Louis, Mo.

Year	Team	Games	BA	SA	AB	H	2B	3B	HR	HR%	R	RBI	BB	SO	SB	Pinch Hit AB	Pinch Hit H	PO	A	E	DP	TC/G	FA	G by Pos
1991	**DET A**	9	.053	.105	19	1	1	0	0	0.0	0	0	2	1	0	2	0	9	1	0	0	1.3	1.000	OF-6, DH-2
1992		15	.115	.154	26	3	1	0	0	0.0	0	5	2	4	0	4	3	33	2	0	2	2.7	1.000	OF-9, 1B-4
1994	**NY N**	22	.225	.300	40	9	1	1	0	0.0	7	2	4	11	0	7	1	23	0	0	0	1.6	1.000	OF-14
1995	**TEX A**	18	.250	.292	24	6	1	0	0	0.0	2	2	4	6	0	6	2	10	1	0	0	0.9	1.000	OF-9, DH-2, 1B-1
4 yrs.		64	.174	.229	109	19	4	1	0	0.0	9	9	12	22	0	19	6	75	4	0	2	1.7	1.000	OF-38, 1B-5, DH-4

Gary Hargis

HARGIS, GARY LYNN BR TR 5′11″ 165 lbs.
B. Nov. 2, 1956, Minneapolis, Minn.

Year	Team	Games	BA	SA	AB	H	2B	3B	HR	HR%	R	RBI	BB	SO	SB	Pinch Hit AB	Pinch Hit H	PO	A	E	DP	TC/G	FA	G by Pos
1979	**PIT N**	1	—	—	0	0	0	0	0	—	0	0	0	0	0	0	0	0	0	0	0	0.0	—	

Bubbles Hargrave

HARGRAVE, EUGENE FRANKLIN BR TR 5′10½″ 174 lbs.
Brother of Pinky Hargrave.
B. July 15, 1892, New Haven, Ind. D. Feb. 23, 1969, Cincinnati, Ohio.

Year	Team	Games	BA	SA	AB	H	2B	3B	HR	HR%	R	RBI	BB	SO	SB	Pinch Hit AB	Pinch Hit H	PO	A	E	DP	TC/G	FA	G by Pos
1913	**CHI N**	3	.333	.333	3	1	0	0	0	0.0	0	1	0	0	0	1	0	3	1	0	0	2.0	1.000	C-2
1914		23	.222	.278	36	8	2	0	0	0.0	3	2	0	4	2	7	1	34	6	3	0	2.7	.930	C-16
1915		15	.158	.263	19	3	0	1	0	0.0	2	2	1	5	0	6	1	13	7	0	0	2.2	1.000	C-9
1921	**CIN N**	93	.289	.426	263	76	17	8	1	0.4	28	38	12	15	4	19	3	270	50	9	2	4.5	.973	C-73
1922		98	.316	.512	320	101	22	10	7	2.2	49	57	26	18	7	10	0	261	60	6	5	3.8	.982	C-87
1923		118	.333	.521	378	126	23	9	10	2.6	54	78	44	22	4	7	1	404	90	6	12	4.6	.988	C-109
1924		98	.301	.455	312	94	19	10	3	1.0	42	33	30	20	2	6	2	322	80	7	7	4.5	.983	C-91
1925		87	.300	.414	273	82	13	6	2	0.7	28	33	25	23	4	3	0	283	42	7	1	4.0	.979	C-84
1926		105	**.353**	.525	326	115	22	8	6	1.8	42	62	25	17	2	11	3	276	50	4	7	3.5	.988	C-93
1927		102	.308	.387	305	94	18	3	0	0.0	36	35	31	18	0	9	1	261	57	4	10	3.5	.988	C-92
1928		65	.295	.389	190	56	12	3	0	0.0	19	23	13	14	4	6	2	181	37	2	2	3.9	.991	C-57
1930	**NY A**	45	.278	.343	108	30	7	0	0	0.0	11	12	10	9	0	11	0	112	13	1	0	3.7	.992	C-34
12 yrs.		852	.310	.452	2533	786	155	58	29	1.1	314	376	217	165	29	96	14	2420	493	49	46	4.0	.983	C-747

Pinky Hargrave

HARGRAVE, WILLIAM McKINLEY BB TR 5′ 8½″ 180 lbs.
Brother of Bubbles Hargrave. BR 1923–1926
B. Jan. 31, 1896, New Haven, Ind. D. Oct. 3, 1942, Fort Wayne, Ind.

Year	Team	Games	BA	SA	AB	H	2B	3B	HR	HR%	R	RBI	BB	SO	SB	Pinch Hit AB	Pinch Hit H	PO	A	E	DP	TC/G	FA	G by Pos
1923	**WAS A**	33	.288	.322	59	17	2	0	0	0.0	4	8	2	6	0	18	7	19	9	2	2	2.1	.933	3B-8, C-5, OF-1
1924		24	.152	.242	33	5	1	1	0	0.0	3	5	1	4	0	14	1	17	2	0	0	2.4	1.000	C-8
1925	**2 teams**	**WAS A** (5G –.500) **STL A** (67G –.284)																						
″	**total**	72	.290	.476	231	67	15	2	8	3.5	34	43	14	15	2	9	5	217	45	5	4	4.2	.981	C-63
1926	**STL A**	92	.281	.464	235	66	16	3	7	3.0	20	37	10	38	3	33	9	165	50	5	7	3.7	.977	C-59
1928	**DET A**	121	.274	.439	321	88	13	5	10	3.1	38	63	32	28	4	25	9	301	35	8	5	3.9	.977	C-88
1929		76	.330	.443	185	61	12	0	3	1.6	26	26	20	24	2	26	5	175	38	6	7	4.6	.973	C-48
1930	**2 teams**	**DET A** (55G –.285) **WAS A** (10G –.194)																						
″	**total**	65	.268	.458	168	45	10	2	6	3.6	21	25	23	13	3	15	2	214	18	3	6	4.8	.987	C-49
1931	**WAS A**	40	.325	.463	80	26	8	0	1	1.3	6	19	9	12	1	15	4	79	8	2	1	3.6	.978	C-25
1932	**BOS N**	82	.263	.410	217	57	14	3	4	1.8	20	33	24	18	1	7	2	206	39	8	4	3.5	.968	C-73
1933		45	.178	.178	73	13	0	0	0	0.0	5	6	5	7	1	18	1	59	7	3	3	2.8	.957	C-25
10 yrs.		650	.278	.428	1602	445	91	16	39	2.4	177	265	140	165	17	180	45	1452	251	42	39	3.9	.976	C-443, 3B-8, OF-1

Charlie Hargreaves

HARGREAVES, CHARLES RUSSELL BR TR 6′ 170 lbs.
B. Dec. 14, 1896, Trenton, N. J. D. May 9, 1979, Neptune, N. J.

Year	Team	Games	BA	SA	AB	H	2B	3B	HR	HR%	R	RBI	BB	SO	SB	Pinch Hit AB	Pinch Hit H	PO	A	E	DP	TC/G	FA	G by Pos
1923	**BKN N**	20	.281	.281	57	16	0	0	0	0.0	5	4	1	2	0	5	1	48	10	5	0	4.2	.921	C-15
1924		15	.407	.481	27	11	2	0	0	0.0	4	5	1	1	0	5	1	24	4	0	0	3.1	1.000	C-9
1925		45	.277	.337	83	23	3	1	0	0.0	9	13	6	1	1	22	5	69	21	2	2	4.6	.978	C-18, 1B-2
1926		85	.250	.361	208	52	13	2	2	1.0	14	23	19	10	1	13	2	224	65	4	6	4.2	.986	C-70
1927		44	.286	.323	133	38	3	1	0	0.0	9	11	14	7	1	2	0	160	32	3	6	4.4	.985	C-44
1928	**2 teams**	**BKN N** (20G –.197) **PIT N** (79G –.285)																						
″	**total**	99	.268	.321	321	86	10	2	1	0.3	18	37	18	15	2	2	0	311	60	13	8	4.0	.966	C-97
1929	**PIT N**	102	.268	.345	328	88	12	5	1	0.3	33	44	16	12	1	1	0	308	56	7	7	3.6	.981	C-102
1930		11	.226	.258	31	7	1	0	0	0.0	4	2	2	1	0	0	0	50	9	0	1	5.4	1.000	C-11
8 yrs.		421	.270	.336	1188	321	44	11	4	0.3	96	139	77	49	6	50	9	1194	257	34	30	4.0	.977	C-366, 1B-2

Mike Hargrove

HARGROVE, DUDLEY MICHAEL (The Human Rain Delay) BL TL 6′ 195 lbs.
B. Oct. 26, 1949, Perryton, Tex.
Manager 1991–95.

Year	Team	Games	BA	SA	AB	H	2B	3B	HR	HR%	R	RBI	BB	SO	SB	Pinch Hit AB	Pinch Hit H	PO	A	E	DP	TC/G	FA	G by Pos
1974	**TEX A**	131	.323	.424	415	134	18	6	4	1.0	57	66	49	42	0	10	3	638	72	9	57	5.6	.987	1B-91, DH-32, OF-6
1975		145	.303	.416	519	157	22	2	11	2.1	82	62	79	66	4	8	4	513	45	13	24	3.7	.977	OF-96, 1B-48, DH-12
1976		151	.287	.384	541	155	30	1	7	1.3	80	58	**97**	64	2	4	0	1222	110	21	103	9.3	.984	1B-141, DH-5
1977		153	.305	.476	525	160	28	4	18	3.4	98	69	103	59	2	2	0	1393	100	11	134	9.9	.993	1B-152
1978		146	.251	.346	494	124	24	1	7	1.4	63	40	**107**	47	2	2	0	1221	116	17	90	9.4	.987	1B-140, DH-4
1979	**2 teams**	**SD N** (52G –.192) **CLE A** (100G –.325)																						
″	**total**	152	.289	.428	463	134	26	4	10	2.2	75	64	88	55	2	16	3	679	33	7	47	5.2	.990	OF-65, 1B-65, DH-7
1980	**CLE A**	160	.304	.404	589	179	22	2	11	1.9	86	85	111	36	4	0	0	1391	88	10	128	9.3	.993	1B-160

Mike Hargrove *continued*

Year	Team	Games	BA	SA	AB	H	2B	3B	HR	HR%	R	RBI	BB	SO	SB	Pinch Hit AB	Pinch Hit H	PO	A	E	DP	TC/G	FA	G by Pos
1981		94	.317	.401	322	102	21	0	2	0.6	43	49	60	16	5	2	2	766	76	9	67	9.3	.989	1B-88, DH-4
1982		160	.271	.338	591	160	26	1	4	0.7	67	65	101	58	2	0	0	1293	123	5	110	9.0	.996	1B-153, DH-5
1983		134	.286	.367	469	134	21	4	3	0.6	57	57	78	40	0	4	2	1098	115	7	131	9.2	.994	1B-131, DH-1
1984		133	.267	.335	352	94	14	2	2	0.6	44	44	53	38	0	12	1	790	83	8	86	7.1	.991	1B-124
1985		107	.285	.352	284	81	14	1	1	0.4	31	27	39	29	1	20	3	599	66	6	66	7.7	.991	1B-84, DH-2, OF-1
12 yrs.		1666	.290	.391	5564	1614	266	28	80	1.4	783	686	965	550	24	80	18	11603	1027	123	1043	7.9	.990	1B-1377, OF-168, DH-72

John Harkins

HARKINS, JOHN JOSEPH (Pa) BR TR 6′ 1″ 205 lbs.
B. Apr. 12, 1859, New Brunswick, N. J. D. Nov. 18, 1940, New Brunswick, N. J.

Year	Team	Games	BA	SA	AB	H	2B	3B	HR	HR%	R	RBI	BB	SO	SB	Pinch Hit AB	Pinch Hit H	PO	A	E	DP	TC/G	FA	G by Pos
1884	CLE N	61	.205	.240	229	47	4	2	0	0.0	24	20	7	45		0	0	43	85	25	3	2.4	.837	P-46, OF-17, 3B-1, SS-1
1885	BKN AA	43	.264	.333	159	42	4	2	1	0.6	20		9			0	0	45	63	21	0	2.9	.837	P-34, OF-9, 3B-1
1886		41	.225	.303	142	32	4	2	1	0.7	18		17			0	0	29	61	11	2	2.4	.891	P-34, OF-8
1887		27	.235	.286	98	23	5	0	0	0.0	10		7		4	0	0	13	37	6	2	1.9	.893	P-24, OF-4, 2B-1
1888	BAL AA	1	.000	.000	3	0	0	0	0	0.0	1	0	1		0	0	0	0	4	0	0	4.0	1.000	P-1
5 yrs.		173	.228	.284	631	144	17	6	2	0.3	73	20	41	45	4	0	0	130	250	63	7	2.4	.858	P-139, OF-38, 3B-2, 2B-1, SS-1

Tim Harkness

HARKNESS, THOMAS WILLIAM BL TL 6′ 2″ 182 lbs.
B. Dec. 23, 1937, Lachine, Que., Canada.

Year	Team	Games	BA	SA	AB	H	2B	3B	HR	HR%	R	RBI	BB	SO	SB	Pinch Hit AB	Pinch Hit H	PO	A	E	DP	TC/G	FA	G by Pos
1961	LA N	5	.500	.750	8	4	2	0	0	0.0	4	0	3	1	1	2	1	11	1	0	2	6.0	1.000	1B-2
1962		92	.258	.387	62	16	2	0	2	3.2	9	7	10	20	1	30	8	116	8	0	14	2.1	1.000	1B-59
1963	NY N	123	.211	.339	375	79	12	3	10	2.7	35	41	36	79	4	16	1	898	112	14	73	9.7	.986	1B-106
1964		39	.282	.368	117	33	2	1	2	1.7	11	13	9	18	1	9	0	251	28	2	32	8.8	.993	1B-32
4 yrs.		259	.235	.356	562	132	18	4	14	2.5	59	61	58	118	7	57	10	1276	149	16	121	7.2	.989	1B-199

Dick Harley

HARLEY, RICHARD JOSEPH BL TR 5′10½″ 150 lbs.
B. Sept. 25, 1872, Philadelphia, Pa. D. Apr. 3, 1952, Philadelphia, Pa.

Year	Team	Games	BA	SA	AB	H	2B	3B	HR	HR%	R	RBI	BB	SO	SB	Pinch Hit AB	Pinch Hit H	PO	A	E	DP	TC/G	FA	G by Pos
1897	STL N	89	.291	.361	330	96	6	4	3	0.9	43	35	36		23	0	0	186	19	23	3	2.6	.899	OF-89
1898		142	.246	.275	549	135	6	5	0	0.0	74	42	34		13	1	1	311	26	27	3	2.6	.926	OF-141
1899	CLE N	142	.250	.307	567	142	15	7	1	0.2	70	50	40		15	0	0	299	27	27	7	2.5	.924	OF-142
1900	CIN N	5	.429	.476	21	9	1	0	0	0.0	2	5	1		4	0	0	6	0	0	0	1.2	1.000	OF-5
1901		133	.273	.327	535	146	13	2	4	0.7	69	27	31		37	0	0	245	20	30	2	2.2	.898	OF-133
1902	DET A	125	.281	.344	491	138	9	8	2	0.4	59	44	36		20	0	0	238	15	19	1	2.2	.930	OF-125
1903	CHI N	104	.231	.259	386	89	9	1	0	0.0	72	33	45		27	2	2	162	18	15	2	1.9	.923	OF-103
7 yrs.		740	.262	.312	2879	755	59	27	10	0.3	389	236	223		139	3	3	1447	125	141	18	2.3	.918	OF-738

Larry Harlow

HARLOW, LARRY DUANE BL TL 6′ 2″ 185 lbs.
B. Nov. 13, 1951, Colorado Springs, Colo.

Year	Team	Games	BA	SA	AB	H	2B	3B	HR	HR%	R	RBI	BB	SO	SB	Pinch Hit AB	Pinch Hit H	PO	A	E	DP	TC/G	FA	G by Pos
1975	BAL A	4	.333	.333	3	1	0	0	0	0.0	1	0	0	1	0	0	0	2	0	0	0	0.5	1.000	OF-4
1977		46	.208	.250	48	10	0	1	0	0.0	4	0	5	8	6	3	0	47	0	6	0	1.4	.887	OF-38
1978		147	.243	.354	460	112	25	1	8	1.7	67	26	55	72	14	9	0	313	7	7	2	2.4	.979	OF-138, P-1
1979	2 teams	BAL A (38G –.268) CAL A (62G –.233)																						
″	total	100	.240	.305	200	48	9	2	0	0.0	27	15	32	38	2	8	2	147	4	4	1	1.7	.974	OF-89, DH-1
1980	CAL A	109	.276	.385	301	83	13	4	4	1.3	47	27	48	61	3	12	4	235	11	6	5	2.6	.976	OF-94, 1B-1, DH-1
1981		43	.207	.220	82	17	1	0	0	0.0	13	4	16	25	1	7	0	52	1	1	0	1.4	.981	OF-39
6 yrs.		449	.248	.339	1094	271	48	8	12	1.1	159	72	156	205	26	39	6	796	23	24	8	2.1	.972	OF-402, DH-2, 1B-1, P-1
LEAGUE CHAMPIONSHIP SERIES																								
1979	CAL A	3	.125	.250	8	1	1	0	0	0.0	0	1	1	2	0	0	0	6	0	0	0	3.0	1.000	OF-2

Bill Harman

HARMAN, WILLIAM BELL BR TR 6′ 4″ 200 lbs.
B. Jan. 2, 1919, Bridgewater, Va.

Year	Team	Games	BA	SA	AB	H	2B	3B	HR	HR%	R	RBI	BB	SO	SB	Pinch Hit AB	Pinch Hit H	PO	A	E	DP	TC/G	FA	G by Pos
1941	PHI N	15	.071	.071	14	1	0	0	0	0.0	1	0	0	3	0	5	0	4	4	0	0	0.8	1.000	P-5, C-5

Chuck Harmon

HARMON, CHARLES BYRON BR TR 6′ 2″ 175 lbs.
B. Apr. 23, 1924, Washington, Ind.

Year	Team	Games	BA	SA	AB	H	2B	3B	HR	HR%	R	RBI	BB	SO	SB	Pinch Hit AB	Pinch Hit H	PO	A	E	DP	TC/G	FA	G by Pos
1954	CIN N	94	.238	.304	286	68	7	3	2	0.7	39	25	17	27	7	23	3	86	132	8	22	3.2	.965	3B-67, 1B-3
1955		96	.253	.389	198	50	6	3	5	2.5	31	28	26	24	9	15	4	126	50	6	6	2.4	.967	3B-39, OF-32, 1B-4
1956	2 teams	CIN N (13G –.000) STL N (20G –.000)																						
″	total	33	.000	.000	19	0	0	0	0	0.0	4	0	2	2	1	3	0	16	0	0	1	0.7	1.000	OF-17, 1B-4, 3B-1
1957	2 teams	STL N (9G –.333) PHI N (57G –.256)																						
″	total	66	.258	.326	89	23	2	2	0	0.0	16	6	1	4	8	10	3	54	8	1	4	1.6	.984	OF-33, 3B-5, 1B-2
4 yrs.		289	.238	.326	592	141	15	8	7	1.2	90	59	46	57	25	51	10	282	190	15	33	2.4	.969	3B-112, OF-82, 1B-13

Terry Harmon

HARMON, TERRY WALTER BR TR 6′ 2″ 180 lbs.
B. Apr. 12, 1944, Toledo, Ohio.

Year	Team	Games	BA	SA	AB	H	2B	3B	HR	HR%	R	RBI	BB	SO	SB	Pinch Hit AB	Pinch Hit H	PO	A	E	DP	TC/G	FA	G by Pos
1967	PHI N	2	—	—	0	0	0	0	0	—	0	0	0	0	0	0	0	0	0	0	0	0.0	—	
1969		87	.239	.289	201	48	8	1	0	0.0	25	16	22	31	1	18	4	94	169	7	42	4.6	.974	SS-38, 2B-19, 3B-2
1970		71	.248	.326	129	32	2	4	0	0.0	16	7	12	22	6	9	2	64	81	2	16	2.8	.986	SS-37, 2B-14, 3B-2
1971		79	.204	.240	221	45	4	2	0	0.0	27	12	20	45	3	0	0	144	191	7	44	4.8	.980	2B-58, SS-9, 3B-3, 1B-2
1972		73	.284	.367	218	62	8	2	2	0.9	35	13	29	28	3	8	1	116	164	5	32	4.1	.982	2B-50, SS-15, 3B-5
1973		72	.209	.230	148	31	3	0	0	0.0	17	8	13	14	1	15	2	100	103	3	26	3.3	.985	2B-43, SS-19, 3B-1
1974		27	.133	.133	15	2	0	0	0	0.0	5	0	3	3	0	9	2	9	6	0	1	1.3	1.000	SS-7, 2B-5
1975		48	.181	.250	72	13	1	2	0	0.0	14	5	9	13	0	0	0	32	65	1	9	3.0	.990	SS-25, 2B-7, 3B-1
1976		42	.295	.393	61	18	4	1	0	0.0	12	6	3	10	3	7	2	28	49	3	7	2.2	.962	SS-19, 2B-13, 3B-5
1977		46	.183	.300	60	11	1	0	2	3.3	13	5	6	9	0	3	0	37	65	8	14	2.3	.927	2B-28, SS-16, 3B-3
10 yrs.		547	.233	.292	1125	262	31	12	4	0.4	164	72	117	175	17	69	13	624	893	36	191	3.5	.977	2B-237, SS-185, 3B-22, 1B-2
LEAGUE CHAMPIONSHIP SERIES																								
1976	PHI N	1	—	—	0	0	0	0	0	—	1	0	0	0	0	0	0	0	0	0	0	0.0	—	

Brian Harper

HARPER, BRIAN DAVID BR TR 6′ 2″ 195 lbs.
B. Oct. 16, 1959, Los Angeles, Calif.

Year	Team	Games	BA	SA	AB	H	2B	3B	HR	HR%	R	RBI	BB	SO	SB	Pinch Hit AB	Pinch Hit H	PO	A	E	DP	TC/G	FA	G by Pos
1979	CAL A	1	.000	.000	2	0	0	0	0	0.0	0	0	0	1	0	1	0	0	0	0	0	0.0	.000	DH-1
1981		4	.273	.273	11	3	0	0	0	0.0	1	1	0	0	1	1	0	5	0	1	0	2.0	.833	OF-2, DH-1

Brian Harper *continued*

Year	Team	Games	BA	SA	AB	H	2B	3B	HR	HR%	R	RBI	BB	SO	SB	Pinch Hit AB	Pinch Hit H	PO	A	E	DP	TC/G	FA	G by Pos
1982	PIT N	20	.276	.517	29	8	1	0	2	6.9	4	4	1	4	0	12	5	10	0	0	0	1.3	1.000	OF-8
1983		61	.221	.427	131	29	4	1	7	5.3	16	20	2	15	0	27	6	40	0	0	0	1.1	1.000	OF-35, 1B-1
1984		48	.259	.348	112	29	4	0	2	1.8	4	11	5	11	0	11	2	57	3	1	0	1.6	.984	OF-37, C-2
1985	STL N	43	.250	.327	52	13	4	0	0	0.0	5	8	2	3	0	26	7	15	5	0	0	0.9	1.000	OF-13, 3B-6, C-2, 1B-1
1986	DET A	19	.139	.167	36	5	1	0	0	0.0	2	3	3	3	0	4	2	25	2	1	2	1.3	.964	OF-11, DH-6, 1B-2, C-2
1987	OAK A	11	.235	.294	17	4	1	0	0	0.0	1	3	0	4	0	4	1	0	0	0	0	0.0		DH-7, OF-1
1988	MIN A	60	.295	.428	166	49	11	1	3	1.8	15	20	10	12	0	7	1	208	15	2	0	4.1	.991	C-48, DH-5, 3B-2
1989		126	.325	.449	385	125	24	0	8	2.1	43	57	13	16	2	7	1	462	36	11	7	4.0	.978	C-101, DH-19, OF-3, 3B-2, 1B-2
1990		134	.294	.432	479	141	42	3	6	1.3	61	54	19	27	3	1	0	686	58	11	5	5.6	.985	C-120, DH-11, 3B-3, 1B-2
1991		123	.311	.447	441	137	28	1	10	2.3	54	69	14	22	1	2	0	643	33	8	7	5.6	.988	C-119, DH-2, 1B-1, OF-1
1992		140	.307	.410	502	154	25	0	9	1.8	58	73	26	22	0	8	1	744	58	13	8	6.0	.984	C-133, DH-2
1993		147	.304	.425	530	161	26	1	12	2.3	52	73	29	29	1	8	5	736	64	10	6	5.7	.988	C-134, DH-7
1994	MIL A	64	.291	.398	251	73	15	0	4	1.6	23	32	9	18	0	1	0	143	13	3	2	2.5	.981	DH-36, C-25, OF-3
1995	OAK A	2	.000	.000	7	0	0	0	0	0.0	0	0	0	1	0	0	0	6	0	0	0	3.0	1.000	C-2
16 yrs.		1003	.295	.419	3151	931	186	7	63	2.0	339	428	133	188	8	120	31	3780	287	61	37	4.5	.985	C-688, OF-114, DH-97, 3B-13, 1B-9
LEAGUE CHAMPIONSHIP SERIES																								
1985	STL N	1	.000	.000	1	0	0	0	0	0.0	0	0	0	0	0	1	0	0	0	0	0	0.0	—	
1991	MIN A	5	.278	.389	18	5	2	0	0	0.0	1	1	0	2	0	0	0	23	1	1	0	5.0	.960	C-5
2 yrs.		6	.263	.368	19	5	2	0	0	0.0	1	1	0	2	0	1	0	23	1	1	0	5.0	.960	C-5
WORLD SERIES																								
1985	STL N	4	.250	.250	4	1	0	0	0	0.0	0	1	0	1	0	4	1	0	0	0	0	0.0	—	
1991	MIN A	7	.381	.476	21	8	2	0	0	0.0	2	1	2	2	0	2	0	33	5	1	1	5.6	.974	C-7
2 yrs.		11	.360	.440	25	9	2	0	0	0.0	2	2	2	3	0	6	1	33	5	1	1	5.6	.974	C-7

George Harper

HARPER, GEORGE WASHINGTON
B. June 24, 1892, Arlington, Ky. D. Aug. 18, 1978, Magnolia, Ark.
BL TR 5′ 8″ 167 lbs.

Year	Team	Games	BA	SA	AB	H	2B	3B	HR	HR%	R	RBI	BB	SO	SB	Pinch Hit AB	Pinch Hit H	PO	A	E	DP	TC/G	FA	G by Pos
1916	DET A	44	.161	.179	56	9	1	0	0	0.0	4	3	5	8	0	24	4	15	3	2	0	1.4	.900	OF-14
1917		47	.205	.231	117	24	3	0	0	0.0	6	12	11	15	2	16	4	48	2	1	0	1.6	.980	OF-31
1918		69	.242	.282	227	55	5	2	0	0.0	19	16	18	14	3	3	0	125	5	6	2	2.1	.956	OF-64
1922	CIN N	128	.340	.442	430	146	22	8	2	0.5	67	68	35	22	11	14	3	220	15	11	2	2.3	.955	OF-109
1923		61	.256	.392	125	32	4	2	3	2.4	14	16	11	9	0	28	7	56	3	2	2	2.1	.967	OF-29
1924	2 teams	CIN N (28G –.270) PHI N (109G –.294)																						
"	total	137	.291	.474	485	141	29	6	16	3.3	75	58	51	28	11	2	0	270	16	4	4	2.2	.986	OF-131
1925	PHI N	132	.349	.558	495	173	35	7	18	3.6	86	97	28	32	10	6	3	319	16	10	5	2.7	.971	OF-126
1926		56	.314	.505	194	61	6	5	7	3.6	32	38	16	7	6	1	1	111	2	7	1	2.2	.942	OF-55
1927	NY N	145	.331	.495	483	160	19	6	16	3.3	85	87	84	27	7	3	1	299	13	8	5	2.3	.975	OF-142
1928	2 teams	NY N (19G –.228) STL N (99G –.305)																						
"	total	118	.292	.505	329	96	9	2	19	5.8	52	65	61	19	3	13	4	196	17	4	3	2.1	.982	OF-103
1929	BOS N	136	.291	.433	457	133	25	5	10	2.2	65	68	69	27	5	5	0	266	7	8	2	2.2	.972	OF-130
11 yrs.		1073	.303	.455	3398	1030	158	43	91	2.7	505	528	389	208	58	115	27	1925	99	63	26	2.2	.970	OF-934
WORLD SERIES																								
1928	STL N	3	.111	.111	9	1	0	0	0	0.0	1	0	2	2	0	0	0	5	0	0	0	1.7	1.000	OF-3

Terry Harper

HARPER, TERRY JOE
B. Aug. 19, 1955, Douglasville, Ga.
BR TR 6′ 1″ 195 lbs.

Year	Team	Games	BA	SA	AB	H	2B	3B	HR	HR%	R	RBI	BB	SO	SB	Pinch Hit AB	Pinch Hit H	PO	A	E	DP	TC/G	FA	G by Pos
1980	ATL N	21	.185	.259	54	10	2	1	0	0.0	3	3	6	5	2	3	0	30	0	1	0	1.7	.968	OF-18
1981		40	.260	.356	73	19	1	0	2	2.7	9	8	11	17	5	15	3	38	2	1	1	1.5	.976	OF-27
1982		48	.287	.347	150	43	3	0	2	1.3	16	16	14	28	7	8	1	74	4	1	1	1.9	.987	OF-41
1983		80	.264	.383	201	53	13	1	3	1.5	19	26	20	43	6	18	3	95	5	5	1	1.8	.952	OF-60
1984		40	.157	.206	102	16	3	1	0	0.0	4	8	4	21	4	12	2	60	3	0	0	2.2	1.000	OF-29
1985		138	.264	.407	492	130	15	2	17	3.5	58	72	44	76	9	12	3	215	10	5	0	1.8	.978	OF-131
1986		106	.257	.392	265	68	12	0	8	3.0	26	30	29	39	3	32	6	92	5	3	0	1.2	.970	OF-83
1987	2 teams	DET A (31G –.203) PIT N (36G –.288)																						
"	total	67	.246	.385	130	32	6	0	4	3.1	12	17	16	19	1	23	2	45	0	1	0	0.9	.978	OF-34, DH-15
8 yrs.		540	.253	.371	1467	371	55	5	36	2.5	147	180	144	248	37	123	20	649	29	17	2	1.6	.976	OF-423, DH-15
LEAGUE CHAMPIONSHIP SERIES																								
1982	ATL N	1	.000	.000	1	0	0	0	0	0.0	1	0	0	0	0	0	0	0	0	0	0	0.0	.000	OF-1

Tommy Harper

HARPER, TOMMY
B. Oct. 14, 1940, Oak Grove, La.
BR TR 5′ 9″ 165 lbs.

Year	Team	Games	BA	SA	AB	H	2B	3B	HR	HR%	R	RBI	BB	SO	SB	Pinch Hit AB	Pinch Hit H	PO	A	E	DP	TC/G	FA	G by Pos
1962	CIN N	6	.174	.174	23	4	0	0	0	0.0	1	1	2	6	1	0	0	6	7	1	1	2.3	.929	3B-6
1963		129	.260	.377	408	106	12	3	10	2.5	67	37	44	72	12	6	2	224	7	4	1	2.0	.983	OF-118, 3B-1
1964		102	.243	.309	317	77	5	2	4	1.3	42	22	39	56	24	10	3	149	6	1	2	1.7	.994	OF-92, 3B-2
1965		159	.257	.393	646	166	28	3	18	2.8	**126**	64	78	127	35	0	0	279	10	5	0	1.8	.983	OF-159, 3B-2, 2B-1
1966		149	.278	.363	553	154	22	5	5	0.9	85	31	57	85	29	3	1	257	5	1	2	1.8	.996	OF-147
1967		103	.225	.345	365	82	17	3	7	1.9	55	22	43	51	23	1	0	208	6	1	0	2.2	.995	OF-100
1968	CLE A	130	.217	.374	235	51	15	2	6	2.6	26	26	26	56	11	14	2	121	1	2	0	1.1	.984	OF-115, 2B-2
1969	SEA A	148	.235	.311	537	126	10	2	9	1.7	78	41	95	90	**73**	5	1	232	268	22	42	3.6	.958	2B-59, 3B-59, OF-26
1970	MIL A	154	.296	.522	604	179	35	4	31	5.1	104	82	77	107	38	2	1	192	330	28	33	3.4	.949	3B-128, 2B-22, OF-13
1971		152	.258	.385	585	151	26	3	14	2.4	79	52	65	92	25	4	1	227	118	18	11	2.3	.950	OF-90, 3B-70, 2B-1
1972	BOS A	144	.254	.388	556	141	29	2	14	2.5	92	49	67	104	25	0	0	321	4	5	4	2.3	.985	OF-144
1973		147	.281	.422	566	159	23	3	17	3.0	92	71	61	93	**54**	0	0	251	13	4	2	1.9	.985	OF-143, DH-1
1974		118	.237	.318	443	105	15	3	5	1.1	66	24	46	65	28	5	4	105	2	2	0	1.0	.982	OF-61, DH-51
1975	2 teams	CAL A (89G –.239) OAK A (34G –.319)																						
"	total	123	.254	.342	354	90	14	1	5	1.4	51	38	43	60	26	7	3	246	10	6	22	2.3	.977	DH-60, 1B-35, OF-18, 3B-2
1976	BAL A	46	.234	.338	77	18	5	0	1	1.3	8	7	10	16	4	10	4	2	0	0	0	0.1	1.000	DH-27, 1B-1, OF-1
15 yrs.		1810	.257	.379	6269	1609	256	36	146	2.3	972	567	753	1080	408	67	22	2820	787	100	120	2.1	.973	OF-1227, 3B-270, DH-139, 2B-85, 1B-36

Year	Team	Games	BA	SA	AB	H	2B	3B	HR	HR%	R	RBI	BB	SO	SB	Pinch Hit AB	Pinch Hit H	PO	A	E	DP	TC/G	FA	G by Pos

Tommy Harper *continued*

Year	Team	Games	BA	SA	AB	H	2B	3B	HR	HR%	R	RBI	BB	SO	SB	Pinch Hit AB	Pinch Hit H	PO	A	E	DP	TC/G	FA	G by Pos
LEAGUE CHAMPIONSHIP SERIES																								
1975	OAK A	1	—	—	0	0	0	0	0	—	0	0	1	0	0	0	0	0	0	0	0	0.0	—	

Toby Harrah

HARRAH, COLBERT DALE
B. Oct. 26, 1948, Sissonville, W. Va.
Manager 1992.
BR TR 6′ 175 lbs.

Year	Team	Games	BA	SA	AB	H	2B	3B	HR	HR%	R	RBI	BB	SO	SB	Pinch Hit AB	Pinch Hit H	PO	A	E	DP	TC/G	FA	G by Pos
1969	WAS A	8	.000	.000	1	0	0	0	0	0.0	4	0	0	0	0	1	0	0	0	0	0	0.0	.000	SS-1
1971		127	.230	.290	383	88	11	3	2	0.5	45	22	40	48	10	4	1	187	321	24	70	4.3	.955	SS-116, 3B-7
1972	TEX A	116	.259	.321	374	97	14	3	1	0.3	47	31	34	31	16	3	2	166	308	20	64	4.7	.960	SS-106
1973		118	.260	.364	461	120	16	1	10	2.2	64	50	46	49	10	1	0	155	332	27	45	4.0	.947	SS-76, 3B-52
1974		161	.260	.417	573	149	23	2	21	3.7	79	74	50	65	15	0	0	283	474	29	98	4.9	.963	SS-158, 3B-3
1975		151	.293	.458	522	153	24	1	20	3.8	81	93	98	71	23	0	0	253	481	29	82	4.6	.962	SS-118, 3B-28, 2B-21
1976		155	.260	.377	584	152	21	1	15	2.6	64	67	91	59	8	1	1	294	481	37	82	5.2	.954	SS-146, 3B-5, DH-4
1977		159	.263	.479	539	142	25	5	27	5.0	90	87	**109**	73	27	0	0	108	278	15	20	2.5	.963	3B-159, SS-1
1978		139	.229	.360	450	103	17	3	12	2.7	56	59	83	66	31	2	2	129	330	11	40	3.4	.977	3B-91, SS-49
1979	CLE A	149	.279	.444	527	147	25	1	20	3.8	99	77	89	60	20	1	0	113	215	19	30	2.1	.945	3B-127, SS-33, DH-9
1980		160	.267	.380	561	150	22	4	11	2.0	100	72	98	60	17	1	0	121	319	13	28	2.8	.971	3B-156, DH-3, SS-2
1981		103	.291	.388	361	105	12	4	5	1.4	64	44	57	44	12	1	1	64	180	13	12	2.4	.949	3B-101, SS-3, DH-1
1982		162	.304	.490	602	183	29	4	25	4.2	100	78	84	52	17	1	0	126	279	12	25	2.5	.971	3B-159, 2B-3, SS-2
1983		138	.266	.365	526	140	23	1	9	1.7	81	53	75	49	16	0	0	101	273	11	32	2.8	.971	3B-137, DH-1, 2B-1
1984	NY A	88	.217	.296	253	55	9	4	1	0.4	40	27	42	28	3	11	2	52	132	6	17	2.4	.968	3B-74, 2B-4, OF-1
1985	TEX A	126	.270	.389	396	107	18	1	9	2.3	65	44	113	60	11	4	3	212	351	6	71	4.6	.989	2B-122, SS-2, DH-1
1986		95	.218	.367	289	63	18	2	7	2.4	36	41	44	53	2	4	0	166	211	7	49	4.1	.982	2B-93
17 yrs.		2155	.264	.395	7402	1954	307	40	195	2.6	1115	919	1153	868	238	35	12	2530	4965	279	765	3.6	.964	3B-1099, SS-813, 2B-244, DH-19, OF-1

Billy Harrell

HARRELL, WILLIAM
B. July 18, 1928, Norristown, Pa.
BR TR 6′ 1½″ 180 lbs.

Year	Team	Games	BA	SA	AB	H	2B	3B	HR	HR%	R	RBI	BB	SO	SB	Pinch Hit AB	Pinch Hit H	PO	A	E	DP	TC/G	FA	G by Pos
1955	CLE A	13	.421	.421	19	8	0	0	0	0.0	2	1	3	3	1	1	0	7	18	2	1	2.5	.926	SS-11
1957		22	.263	.368	57	15	1	1	1	1.8	6	5	4	7	3	3	1	21	40	6	6	3.2	.910	SS-14, 3B-6, 2B-1
1958		101	.218	.328	229	50	4	0	7	3.1	36	19	15	36	12	9	1	81	159	9	32	2.5	.964	3B-46, SS-45, 2B-7, OF-1
1961	BOS A	37	.162	.216	37	6	2	0	0	0.0	10	1	1	8	1	6	0	26	23	2	6	2.7	.961	3B-10, SS-7, 1B-2
4 yrs.		173	.231	.327	342	79	7	1	8	2.3	54	26	23	54	17	19	2	135	240	19	45	2.6	.952	SS-77, 3B-62, 2B-8, 1B-2, OF-1

John Harrell

HARRELL, JOHN ROBERT
B. Nov. 27, 1947, Long Beach, Calif.
BR TR 6′ 2″ 190 lbs.

Year	Team	Games	BA	SA	AB	H	2B	3B	HR	HR%	R	RBI	BB	SO	SB	Pinch Hit AB	Pinch Hit H	PO	A	E	DP	TC/G	FA	G by Pos
1969	SF N	2	.500	.500	6	3	0	0	0	0.0	0	2	2	1	0	0	0	10	1	0	1	5.5	1.000	C-2

Bud Harrelson

HARRELSON, DERREL McKINLEY
B. June 6, 1944, Niles, Calif.
Manager 1990–91.
BB TR 5′11″ 160 lbs.
BR 1965

Year	Team	Games	BA	SA	AB	H	2B	3B	HR	HR%	R	RBI	BB	SO	SB	Pinch Hit AB	Pinch Hit H	PO	A	E	DP	TC/G	FA	G by Pos
1965	NY N	19	.108	.189	37	4	1	1	0	0.0	3	0	2	11	0	0	0	28	36	3	6	3.7	.955	SS-18
1966		33	.222	.323	99	22	2	4	0	0.0	20	4	13	23	7	2	1	52	91	1	26	5.0	.993	SS-29
1967		151	.254	.304	540	137	16	4	1	0.2	59	28	48	64	12	0	0	254	467	32	88	5.1	.958	SS-149
1968		111	.219	.251	402	88	7	3	0	0.0	38	14	29	68	4	6	0	199	317	15	58	5.0	.972	SS-106
1969		123	.248	.306	395	98	11	6	0	0.0	42	24	54	54	1	0	0	243	347	19	70	5.1	.969	SS-119
1970		157	.243	.309	564	137	18	8	1	0.2	72	42	95	74	23	2	0	305	401	21	84	4.7	.971	SS-156
1971		142	.252	.303	547	138	16	6	0	0.0	55	32	53	59	28	0	0	257	441	16	86	5.1	.978	SS-140
1972		115	.215	.266	418	90	10	4	1	0.2	54	24	58	57	12	0	0	191	334	16	51	4.7	.970	SS-115
1973		106	.258	.309	356	92	12	3	0	0.0	35	20	48	49	5	0	0	153	315	10	49	4.6	.979	SS-103
1974		106	.227	.266	331	75	10	0	1	0.3	48	13	71	39	9	2	0	196	325	17	65	5.5	.968	SS-97
1975		34	.219	.247	73	16	2	0	0	0.0	5	3	12	13	0	2	1	44	67	7	18	3.5	.941	SS-34
1976		118	.234	.298	359	84	12	4	1	0.3	34	26	63	56	9	1	0	183	330	20	44	4.6	.962	SS-117
1977		107	.178	.227	269	48	6	2	1	0.4	25	12	27	28	5	0	0	141	239	6	41	3.9	.984	SS-98
1978	PHI N	71	.214	.223	103	22	1	0	0	0.0	16	9	18	21	5	7	0	72	109	4	31	3.2	.978	2B-43, SS-15
1979		53	.282	.366	71	20	6	0	0	0.0	7	7	13	14	3	0	0	63	71	4	13	2.7	.971	2B-25, SS-17, 3B-9, OF-1
1980	TEX A	87	.272	.322	180	49	6	0	1	0.6	26	9	29	23	4	0	0	121	222	18	58	4.1	.950	SS-87, 2B-2
16 yrs.		1533	.236	.288	4744	1120	136	45	7	0.1	539	267	633	653	127	22	2	2502	4112	209	788	4.6	.969	SS-1400, 2B-70, 3B-9, OF-1
LEAGUE CHAMPIONSHIP SERIES																								
1969	NY N	3	.182	.455	11	2	1	1	0	0.0	2	3	1	2	0	0	0	6	6	1	2	4.3	.923	SS-3
1973		5	.167	.167	18	3	0	0	0	0.0	1	2	1	1	0	0	0	12	14	0	3	5.2	1.000	SS-5
2 yrs.		8	.172	.276	29	5	1	1	0	0.0	3	5	2	3	0	0	0	18	20	1	5	4.9	.974	SS-8
WORLD SERIES																								
1969	NY N	5	.176	.176	17	3	0	0	0	0.0	1	0	3	4	0	0	0	12	17	0	0	5.8	1.000	SS-5
1973		7	.250	.292	24	6	1	0	0	0.0	2	1	5	3	0	0	0	11	24	0	1	5.0	1.000	SS-7
2 yrs.		12	.220	.244	41	9	1	0	0	0.0	3	1	8	7	0	0	0	23	41	0	1	5.3	1.000	SS-12

Ken Harrelson

HARRELSON, KENNETH SMITH (Hawk)
B. Sept. 4, 1941, Woodruff, S. C.
BR TR 6′ 2″ 190 lbs.

Year	Team	Games	BA	SA	AB	H	2B	3B	HR	HR%	R	RBI	BB	SO	SB	Pinch Hit AB	Pinch Hit H	PO	A	E	DP	TC/G	FA	G by Pos
1963	KC A	79	.230	.363	226	52	10	1	6	2.7	16	23	23	58	1	17	5	326	17	7	24	5.6	.980	1B-34, OF-28
1964		49	.194	.381	139	27	5	0	7	5.0	15	12	13	34	0	12	4	145	15	1	14	4.1	.994	OF-24, 1B-15
1965		150	.238	.429	483	115	17	3	23	4.8	61	66	66	112	9	21	5	1049	71	10	93	8.8	.991	1B-125, OF-4
1966	2 teams	KC A (63G –.224) WAS A (71G –.248)																						
″	total	134	.237	.348	460	109	13	1	12	2.6	49	50	53	112	13	4	1	1129	86	14	95	9.4	.989	1B-128, OF-3
1967	3 teams	WAS A (26G –.203) KC A (61G –.305) BOS A (23G –.200)																						
″	total	110	.255	.414	333	85	15	1	12	3.6	42	54	29	44	10	24	5	576	42	6	38	6.8	.990	1B-69, OF-23
1968	BOS A	150	.275	.518	535	147	17	4	35	6.5	79	**109**	69	90	2	2	1	376	17	3	10	2.6	.992	OF-132, 1B-19
1969	2 teams	BOS A (10G –.217) CLE A (149G –.222)																						
″	total	159	.221	.419	565	125	14	4	30	5.3	89	92	99	102	17	2	0	402	22	5	23	2.5	.988	OF-144, 1B-26

Ken Harrelson *continued*

Year	Team	Games	BA	SA	AB	H	2B	3B	HR	HR%	R	RBI	BB	SO	SB	Pinch Hit AB	Pinch Hit H	PO	A	E	DP	TC/G	FA	G by Pos
1970	CLE A	17	.282	.385	39	11	1	0	1	2.6	3	1	6	4	0	4	1	80	7	0	15	6.7	1.000	1B-13
1971		52	.199	.304	161	32	2	0	5	3.1	20	14	24	21	1	5	2	320	23	4	29	7.4	.988	1B-40, OF-7
9 yrs.		900	.239	.414	2941	703	94	14	131	4.5	374	421	382	577	53	91	24	4403	300	50	341	5.7	.989	1B-469, OF-365
WORLD SERIES																								
1967	BOS A	4	.077	.077	13	1	0	0	0	0.0	0	1	1	3	0	0	0	5	0	0	0	1.3	1.000	OF-4

Andy Harrington

HARRINGTON, ANDREW MATTHEW BR TR 5′11″ 170 lbs.
B. Feb. 12, 1903, Mountain View, Calif. D. Jan. 29, 1979, Boise, Ida.

Year	Team	Games	BA	SA	AB	H	2B	3B	HR	HR%	R	RBI	BB	SO	SB	Pinch Hit AB	Pinch Hit H	PO	A	E	DP	TC/G	FA	G by Pos
1925	DET A	1	.000	.000	1	0	0	0	0	0.0	0	0	0	0	0	1	0	0	0	0	0	0.0	—	

Jerry Harrington

HARRINGTON, JEREMIAH PETER BR TR 5′11″ 220 lbs.
B. Aug. 12, 1869, Keokuk, Iowa D. Apr. 16, 1913, Keokuk, Iowa.

Year	Team	Games	BA	SA	AB	H	2B	3B	HR	HR%	R	RBI	BB	SO	SB	Pinch Hit AB	Pinch Hit H	PO	A	E	DP	TC/G	FA	G by Pos
1890	CIN N	65	.246	.297	236	58	7	1	1	0.4	25	23	15	29	4	0	0	345	73	19	3	6.7	.957	C-65
1891		92	.228	.306	333	76	10	5	2	0.6	25	41	19	34	4	0	0	388	106	50	6	5.8	.908	C-92, 3B-1
1892		22	.213	.230	61	13	1	0	0	0.0	6	3	6	1	0	0	0	76	22	2	0	4.3	.980	C-22, 1B-1
1893	LOU N	10	.111	.139	36	4	1	0	0	0.0	4	6	3	9	0	0	0	23	6	5	1	3.4	.853	C-10
4 yrs.		189	.227	.287	666	151	19	6	3	0.5	60	73	43	73	8	0	0	832	207	76	10	5.8	.932	C-189, 1B-1, 3B-1

Joe Harrington

HARRINGTON, JOSEPH C. BR TR 5′8½″ 162 lbs.
B. Dec. 21, 1869, Fall River, Mass. D. Sept. 13, 1933, Fall River, Mass.

Year	Team	Games	BA	SA	AB	H	2B	3B	HR	HR%	R	RBI	BB	SO	SB	Pinch Hit AB	Pinch Hit H	PO	A	E	DP	TC/G	FA	G by Pos
1895	BOS N	18	.277	.431	65	18	0	2	2	3.1	21	13	7	5	3	0	0	47	57	10	7	6.3	.912	2B-18
1896		54	.197	.268	198	39	5	3	1	0.5	25	25	19	17	2	0	0	62	110	42	8	4.0	.804	3B-49, SS-4, 2B-1
2 yrs.		72	.217	.308	263	57	5	5	3	1.1	46	38	26	22	5	0	0	109	167	52	15	4.6	.841	3B-49, 2B-19, SS-4

Mike Harrington

HARRINGTON, CHARLES MICHAEL BR TR 6′4″ 205 lbs.
B. Oct. 8, 1934, Hattiesburg, Miss.

Year	Team	Games	BA	SA	AB	H	2B	3B	HR	HR%	R	RBI	BB	SO	SB	Pinch Hit AB	Pinch Hit H	PO	A	E	DP	TC/G	FA	G by Pos
1963	PHI N	1	—	—	0	0	0	0	0	—	0	0	0	0	0	0	0	0	0	0	0	0.0	—	

Alonzo Harris

HARRIS, ALONZO (Candy) BB TR 6′ 160 lbs.
B. Sept. 17, 1947, Selma, Ala.

Year	Team	Games	BA	SA	AB	H	2B	3B	HR	HR%	R	RBI	BB	SO	SB	Pinch Hit AB	Pinch Hit H	PO	A	E	DP	TC/G	FA	G by Pos
1967	HOU N	6	.000	.000	1	0	0	0	0	0.0	0	0	0	1	0	0	0	0	0	0	0	0.0	—	

Billy Harris

HARRIS, JAMES WILLIAM BL TR 6′ 175 lbs.
B. Nov. 24, 1943, Hamlet, N. C.

Year	Team	Games	BA	SA	AB	H	2B	3B	HR	HR%	R	RBI	BB	SO	SB	Pinch Hit AB	Pinch Hit H	PO	A	E	DP	TC/G	FA	G by Pos
1968	CLE A	38	.213	.287	94	20	5	1	0	0.0	10	3	8	22	2	5	1	40	71	4	11	3.0	.965	2B-27, 3B-10, SS-1
1969	KC A	5	.286	.429	7	2	1	0	0	0.0	1	0	0	1	0	4	1	1	2	0	0	3.0	1.000	2B-1
2 yrs.		43	.218	.297	101	22	6	1	0	0.0	11	3	8	23	2	9	2	41	73	4	11	3.0	.966	2B-28, 3B-10, SS-1

Bob Harris

HARRIS, ROBERT NED BL TL 5′11″ 175 lbs.
B. July 9, 1916, Ames, Iowa D. Dec. 18, 1976, West Palm Beach, Fla.

Year	Team	Games	BA	SA	AB	H	2B	3B	HR	HR%	R	RBI	BB	SO	SB	Pinch Hit AB	Pinch Hit H	PO	A	E	DP	TC/G	FA	G by Pos
1941	DET A	26	.213	.344	61	13	3	1	1	1.6	11	4	6	13	1	11	1	16	0	0	0	1.3	1.000	OF-12
1942		121	.271	.430	398	108	16	10	9	2.3	53	45	49	35	5	15	6	164	5	10	2	1.7	.944	OF-104
1943		114	.254	.362	354	90	14	3	6	1.7	43	32	47	29	6	18	5	192	6	8	2	2.1	.961	OF-96
1946		1	.000	.000	1	0	0	0	0	0.0	0	0	0	0	0	1	0	0	0	0	0	0.0	—	
4 yrs.		262	.259	.393	814	211	33	14	16	2.0	107	81	102	77	12	45	12	372	11	18	4	1.9	.955	OF-212

Bucky Harris

HARRIS, STANLEY RAYMOND BR TR 5′9½″ 156 lbs.
B. Nov. 8, 1896, Port Jervis, N. Y. D. Nov. 8, 1977, Bethesda, Md.
Manager 1924–43, 1947–48, 1950–56.
Hall of Fame 1975.

Year	Team	Games	BA	SA	AB	H	2B	3B	HR	HR%	R	RBI	BB	SO	SB	Pinch Hit AB	Pinch Hit H	PO	A	E	DP	TC/G	FA	G by Pos
1919	WAS A	8	.214	.286	28	6	2	0	0	0.0	0	4	1	3	0	0	0	21	28	4	4	6.6	.925	2B-8
1920		137	.300	.381	506	152	26	6	1	0.2	76	68	41	36	16	1	1	345	401	33	59	5.8	.958	2B-135
1921		154	.289	.354	584	169	22	8	0	0.0	82	54	54	39	29	0	0	407	481	38	91	6.0	.959	2B-154
1922		154	.269	.346	602	162	24	8	2	0.3	95	40	52	38	25	0	0	479	483	30	116	6.4	.970	2B-154
1923		145	.282	.382	532	150	21	13	2	0.4	60	70	50	29	23	0	0	418	451	36	120	6.2	.960	2B-144, SS-1
1924		143	.268	.358	544	146	28	9	1	0.2	88	58	56	41	19	0	0	393	386	26	100	5.6	.968	2B-143
1925		144	.287	.358	551	158	30	3	1	0.2	91	66	64	21	14	0	0	402	429	26	107	6.0	.970	2B-144
1926		141	.283	.395	537	152	39	9	1	0.2	94	63	58	41	16	0	0	356	427	30	74	5.8	.963	2B-141
1927		128	.267	.328	475	127	20	3	1	0.2	98	55	66	33	18	0	0	316	413	21	68	5.9	.972	2B-128
1928		99	.204	.263	358	73	11	5	0	0.0	34	28	27	26	5	0	0	254	326	18	61	6.1	.970	2B-96, 3B-1, OF-1
1929	DET A	7	.091	.091	11	1	0	0	0	0.0	3	0	2	2	1	0	0	5	13	2	0	4.0	.900	2B-4, SS-1
1931		4	.125	.250	8	1	1	0	0	0.0	1	0	1	1	0	0	0	5	6	0	1	3.7	1.000	2B-3
12 yrs.		1264	.274	.354	4736	1297	224	64	9	0.2	722	506	472	310	166	1	1	3401	3844	264	801	6.0	.965	2B-1254, SS-2, 3B-1, OF-1
WORLD SERIES																								
1924	WAS A	7	.333	.515	33	11	0	0	2	6.1	5	7	1	4	0	0	0	26	28	2	8	8.0	.964	2B-7
1925		7	.087	.087	23	2	0	0	0	0.0	2	0	1	3	0	0	0	24	18	0	5	6.0	1.000	2B-7
2 yrs.		14	.232	.339	56	13	0	0	2	3.6	7	7	2	7	0	0	0	50	46	2	13	7.0	.980	2B-14

Charlie Harris

HARRIS, CHARLES JENKINS BR TR 5′8″ 200 lbs.
B. Oct. 21, 1877, Macon, Ga. D. Mar. 14, 1963, Gainesville, Fla.

Year	Team	Games	BA	SA	AB	H	2B	3B	HR	HR%	R	RBI	BB	SO	SB	Pinch Hit AB	Pinch Hit H	PO	A	E	DP	TC/G	FA	G by Pos
1899	BAL N	30	.279	.324	68	19	3	0	0	0.0	16	1	3		4	1	1	20	31	6	2	2.1	.895	3B-21, OF-3, 2B-2, SS-1

Dave Harris

HARRIS, DAVID STANLEY (Sheriff) BR TR 5′11″ 195 lbs.
B. July 14, 1900, Summerfield, N. C. D. Sept. 18, 1973, Atlanta, Ga.

Year	Team	Games	BA	SA	AB	H	2B	3B	HR	HR%	R	RBI	BB	SO	SB	Pinch Hit AB	Pinch Hit H	PO	A	E	DP	TC/G	FA	G by Pos
1925	BOS N	92	.265	.374	340	90	8	7	5	1.5	49	36	27	44	6	1	0	217	12	9	3	2.6	.962	OF-90
1928		7	.118	.176	17	2	1	0	0	0.0	2	0	2	6	0	1	0	10	0	2	0	2.0	.833	OF-6
1930	2 teams	CHI A (33G –.244) WAS A (73G –.317)																						
″	total	106	.296	.522	291	86	21	9	9	3.1	56	57	35	57	6	21	9	152	9	2	3	2.0	.988	OF-82, 2B-1
1931	WAS A	77	.312	.506	231	72	14	8	5	2.2	49	50	49	38	7	13	5	111	4	6	1	2.0	.950	OF-60
1932		81	.327	.538	156	51	7	4	6	3.8	26	29	19	34	4	**43**	**14**	66	3	5	0	2.2	.932	OF-34

Dave Harris *continued*

Year	Team	Games	BA	SA	AB	H	2B	3B	HR	HR%	R	RBI	BB	SO	SB	Pinch Hit AB	Pinch Hit H	PO	A	E	DP	TC/G	FA	G by Pos
1933		82	.260	.418	177	46	9	2	5	2.8	33	38	25	26	3	24	8	101	2	3	1	2.0	.972	OF-45, 1B-6, 3B-2
1934		97	.251	.362	235	59	14	3	2	0.9	28	37	39	40	2	26	4	111	16	4	2	1.9	.969	OF-64, 3B-5
7 yrs.		542	.281	.444	1447	406	74	33	32	2.2	243	247	196	245	28	129	40	768	46	31	10	2.1	.963	OF-381, 3B-7, 1B-6, 2B-1
WORLD SERIES																								
1933	**WAS A**	3	.000	.000	2	0	0	0	0	0.0	0	0	2	0	0	1	0	2	0	0	0	2.0	1.000	OF-1

Donald Harris

HARRIS, DONALD
B. Nov. 12, 1967, Waco, Tex.
BR TR 6′ 1″ 185 lbs.

Year	Team	Games	BA	SA	AB	H	2B	3B	HR	HR%	R	RBI	BB	SO	SB	Pinch Hit AB	Pinch Hit H	PO	A	E	DP	TC/G	FA	G by Pos
1991	**TEX A**	18	.375	.750	8	3	0	0	1	12.5	4	2	1	3	1	0	0	7	0	0	0	0.5	1.000	OF-12, DH-3
1992		24	.182	.212	33	6	1	0	0	0.0	3	1	0	15	1	2	1	36	1	1	1	1.6	.974	OF-24
1993		40	.197	.263	76	15	2	0	1	1.3	10	8	5	18	0	3	1	47	3	3	0	1.3	.943	OF-38, DH-2
3 yrs.		82	.205	.282	117	24	3	0	2	1.7	17	11	6	36	2	5	2	90	4	4	1	1.2	.959	OF-74, DH-5

Frank Harris

HARRIS, FRANK WALTER
B. Nov. 2, 1858, Pittsburgh, Pa. D. Nov. 26, 1939, East Moline, Ill.
BR TR

Year	Team	Games	BA	SA	AB	H	2B	3B	HR	HR%	R	RBI	BB	SO	SB	Pinch Hit AB	Pinch Hit H	PO	A	E	DP	TC/G	FA	G by Pos
1884	**ALT U**	24	.263	.305	95	25	2	1	0	0.0	10		3			0	0	179	8	11	1	7.9	.944	1B-17, OF-8

Gail Harris

HARRIS, BOYD GAIL
B. Oct. 15, 1931, Abingdon, Va.
BL TL 6′ 195 lbs.

Year	Team	Games	BA	SA	AB	H	2B	3B	HR	HR%	R	RBI	BB	SO	SB	Pinch Hit AB	Pinch Hit H	PO	A	E	DP	TC/G	FA	G by Pos
1955	**NY N**	79	.232	.403	263	61	9	0	12	4.6	27	36	20	46	0	4	2	617	50	12	65	9.1	.982	1B-75
1956		12	.132	.263	38	5	0	1	1	2.6	2	1	3	10	0	1	0	108	9	3	12	10.9	.975	1B-11
1957		90	.240	.418	225	54	7	3	9	4.0	28	31	16	28	1	25	2	502	37	8	53	9.0	.985	1B-61
1958	**DET A**	134	.273	.481	451	123	18	8	20	4.4	63	83	36	60	1	14	5	942	79	15	90	8.5	.986	1B-122
1959		114	.221	.327	349	77	4	3	9	2.6	39	39	29	49	0	22	4	728	57	6	59	8.5	.992	1B-93
1960		8	.000	.000	5	0	0	0	0	0.0	0	0	2	1	0	3	0	8	1	0	1	1.8	1.000	1B-5
6 yrs.		437	.240	.406	1331	320	38	15	51	3.8	159	190	106	194	2	69	13	2905	233	44	280	8.7	.986	1B-367

Joe Harris

HARRIS, JOSEPH (Moon)
B. May 20, 1891, Coulters, Pa. D. Dec. 10, 1959, Renton, Pa.
BR TR 5′ 9″ 170 lbs.

Year	Team	Games	BA	SA	AB	H	2B	3B	HR	HR%	R	RBI	BB	SO	SB	Pinch Hit AB	Pinch Hit H	PO	A	E	DP	TC/G	FA	G by Pos
1914	**NY A**	2	.000	.000	1	0	0	0	0	0.0	0	0	3	1	0	0	0	11	0	0	0	5.5	1.000	OF-1, 1B-1
1917	**CLE A**	112	.304	.385	369	112	22	4	0	0.0	40	65	55	32	11	8	0	1029	89	18	58	11.2	.984	1B-95, OF-5, 3B-1
1919		62	.375	.489	184	69	16	1	1	0.5	30	46	33	21	2	12	4	458	44	6	23	10.2	.988	1B-46, SS-4
1922	**BOS A**	119	.316	.478	408	129	30	9	6	1.5	53	54	30	15	2	15	4	359	29	13	14	3.9	.968	OF-83, 1B-21
1923		142	.335	.520	483	162	28	11	13	2.7	82	76	52	27	7	4	1	357	16	12	5	2.7	.969	OF-132, 1B-9
1924		134	.301	.430	491	148	36	9	3	0.6	82	77	81	25	6	2	0	1275	101	10	100	10.7	.993	1B-127, OF-3
1925	**2 teams**	**BOS A** (8G –.158) **WAS A** (100G –.323)																						
″	**total**	108	.313	.564	319	100	21	10	13	4.1	64	61	56	33	5	10	1	506	42	6	42	5.3	.989	1B-63, OF-41
1926	**WAS A**	92	.307	.486	257	79	13	9	5	1.9	43	55	37	9	2	18	4	354	20	3	20	5.3	.992	1B-36, OF-35
1927	**PIT N**	129	.326	.472	411	134	27	9	5	1.2	57	73	48	19	0	10	2	1057	78	11	84	9.6	.990	1B-116, OF-3
1928	**2 teams**	**PIT N** (16G –.391) **BKN N** (55G –.236)																						
″	**total**	71	.268	.402	112	30	8	2	1	0.9	10	10	18	6	0	**42**	**9**	57	7	1	8	3.0	.985	OF-16, 1B-6
10 yrs.		971	.317	.472	3035	963	201	64	47	1.5	461	517	413	188	35	121	25	5463	426	80	354	7.1	.987	1B-520, OF-319, SS-4, 3B-1
WORLD SERIES																								
1925	**WAS A**	7	.440	.880	25	11	2	0	3	12.0	5	6	3	4	0	0	0	9	1	0	0	1.4	1.000	OF-7
1927	**PIT N**	4	.200	.200	15	3	0	0	0	0.0	0	1	0	0	0	0	0	35	2	0	2	9.3	1.000	1B-4
2 yrs.		11	.350	.625	40	14	2	0	3	7.5	5	7	3	4	0	0	0	44	3	0	2	4.3	1.000	OF-7, 1B-4

John Harris

HARRIS, JOHN THOMAS, JR.
B. Sept. 13, 1954, Portland, Ore.
BL TL 6′ 3″ 205 lbs.

Year	Team	Games	BA	SA	AB	H	2B	3B	HR	HR%	R	RBI	BB	SO	SB	Pinch Hit AB	Pinch Hit H	PO	A	E	DP	TC/G	FA	G by Pos
1979	**CAL A**	1	.000	.000	2	0	0	0	0	0.0	0	0	0	0	0	0	0	6	0	0	0	6.0	1.000	1B-1
1980		19	.293	.561	41	12	5	0	2	4.9	8	7	7	4	0	7	1	63	3	0	4	5.1	1.000	1B-10, OF-3
1981		36	.247	.403	77	19	3	0	3	3.9	5	9	3	11	0	19	3	85	5	2	9	4.2	.978	1B-11, OF-10, DH-1
3 yrs.		56	.258	.450	120	31	8	0	5	4.2	13	16	10	15	0	26	4	154	8	2	13	4.6	.988	1B-22, OF-13, DH-1

Lenny Harris

HARRIS, LEONARD ANTHONY
B. Oct. 28, 1964, Miami, Fla.
BL TR 5′10″ 195 lbs.

Year	Team	Games	BA	SA	AB	H	2B	3B	HR	HR%	R	RBI	BB	SO	SB	Pinch Hit AB	Pinch Hit H	PO	A	E	DP	TC/G	FA	G by Pos
1988	**CIN N**	16	.372	.395	43	16	1	0	0	0.0	7	8	5	4	4	0	0	14	33	1	2	3.0	.979	3B-10, 2B-6
1989	**2 teams**	**CIN N** (61G –.223) **LA N** (54G –.252)																						
″	**total**	115	.236	.299	335	79	10	1	3	0.9	36	26	20	33	14	20	8	147	168	15	32	3.0	.955	2B-46, 3B-24, OF-21, SS-18
1990	**LA N**	137	.304	.374	431	131	16	4	2	0.5	61	29	29	31	15	23	3	140	205	11	24	2.5	.969	3B-94, 2B-44, OF-2, SS-1
1991		145	.287	.350	429	123	16	1	3	0.7	59	38	37	32	12	24	3	125	250	20	35	2.5	.949	3B-113, 2B-27, SS-20, OF-1
1992		135	.271	.303	347	94	11	0	0	0.0	28	30	24	24	19	29	6	199	248	27	48	3.4	.943	2B-81, 3B-33, OF-15, SS-10
1993		107	.237	.325	160	38	6	1	2	1.3	20	11	15	15	3	45	8	61	99	3	11	2.9	.982	2B-35, 3B-17, SS-3, OF-2
1994	**CIN N**	66	.310	.360	100	31	3	1	0	0.0	13	14	5	13	7	45	12	27	29	6	2	2.6	.903	3B-15, 1B-4, OF-3, 2B-2
1995		101	.208	.310	197	41	8	3	2	1.0	32	16	14	20	10	50	11	147	68	4	14	3.9	.982	3B-24, 1B-23, OF-8, 2B-1
8 yrs.		822	.271	.334	2042	553	71	11	12	0.6	256	172	149	172	84	236	51	860	1100	87	168	2.9	.957	3B-330, 2B-242, SS-52, OF-52, 1B-27
LEAGUE CHAMPIONSHIP SERIES																								
1995	**CIN N**	3	1.000	1.000	2	2	0	0	0	0.0	0	1	0	0	1	2	2	0	0	0	0	0.0	—	

Spence Harris

HARRIS, ANTHONY SPENCER
B. Aug. 12, 1900, Duluth, Minn. D. July 3, 1982, Minneapolis, Minn.
BL TL 5′ 9″ 145 lbs.

Year	Team	Games	BA	SA	AB	H	2B	3B	HR	HR%	R	RBI	BB	SO	SB	Pinch Hit AB	Pinch Hit H	PO	A	E	DP	TC/G	FA	G by Pos
1925	**CHI A**	56	.283	.337	92	26	2	0	1	1.1	12	13	14	13	1	24	7	42	3	2	0	1.7	.957	OF-27
1926		80	.252	.356	222	56	11	3	2	0.9	36	27	20	15	8	14	2	106	6	6	2	1.9	.949	OF-63
1929	**WAS A**	6	.214	.286	14	3	1	0	0	0.0	1	1	0	3	1	0	0	7	0	0	0	1.8	1.000	OF-4
1930	**PHI A**	22	.184	.204	49	9	1	0	0	0.0	4	5	5	2	0	7	1	21	2	1	1	1.8	.958	OF-13
4 yrs.		164	.249	.329	377	94	15	3	3	0.8	53	46	39	33	10	45	10	176	11	9	3	1.8	.954	OF-107

Vic Harris

HARRIS, VICTOR LANIER
B. Mar. 27, 1950, Los Angeles, Calif.
BB TR 5′11″ 165 lbs.

Year	Team	Games	BA	SA	AB	H	2B	3B	HR	HR%	R	RBI	BB	SO	SB	Pinch Hit AB	Pinch Hit H	PO	A	E	DP	TC/G	FA	G by Pos
1972	**TEX A**	61	.140	.177	186	26	5	1	0	0.0	8	10	12	39	7	4	0	113	135	10	30	4.4	.961	2B-58, SS-1
1973		152	.249	.342	555	138	14	7	8	1.4	71	44	55	81	13	1	0	354	79	21	16	2.9	.954	OF-113, 3B-25, 2B-18

Vic Harris *continued*

Year	Team		Games	BA	SA	AB	H	2B	3B	HR	HR%	R	RBI	BB	SO	SB	Pinch Hit AB	Pinch Hit H	PO	A	E	DP	TC/G	FA	G by Pos
1974	CHI	N	62	.195	.255	200	39	6	3	0	0.0	18	11	29	26	9	4	0	122	144	16	20	5.0	.943	2B-56
1975			51	.179	.179	56	10	0	0	0	0.0	6	5	6	7	0	24	4	15	14	2	2	1.3	.935	OF-11, 3B-7, 2B-5
1976	STL	N	97	.228	.309	259	59	12	3	1	0.4	21	19	16	55	1	23	4	173	103	14	21	3.4	.952	2B-37, OF-35, 3B-12, SS-1
1977	SF	N	69	.261	.370	165	43	12	0	2	1.2	28	14	19	36	2	25	3	69	96	8	21	3.5	.954	2B-27, SS-11, 3B-9, OF-3
1978			53	.150	.220	100	15	4	0	1	1.0	8	11	11	24	0	16	1	40	58	5	8	2.7	.951	SS-22, 2B-10, OF-6
1980	MIL	A	34	.213	.315	89	19	4	1	1	1.1	8	7	12	13	4	1	0	59	4	2	1	1.9	.969	OF-31, 3B-2, 2B-1
8 yrs.			579	.217	.295	1610	349	57	15	13	0.8	168	121	160	281	36	98	12	945	633	78	119	3.3	.953	2B-212, OF-199, 3B-55, SS-35

Ben Harrison

HARRISON, LEO J. BR
Deceased.

Year	Team		Games	BA	SA	AB	H	2B	3B	HR	HR%	R	RBI	BB	SO	SB	Pinch Hit AB	Pinch Hit H	PO	A	E	DP	TC/G	FA	G by Pos
1901	WAS	A	1	.000	.000	2	0	0	0	0	0.0	0	0	1		0	0	0	0	0	0	0	0.0	.000	OF-1

Chuck Harrison

HARRISON, CHARLES WILLIAM BR TR 5′10″ 185 lbs.
B. Apr. 25, 1941, Abilene, Tex.

Year	Team		Games	BA	SA	AB	H	2B	3B	HR	HR%	R	RBI	BB	SO	SB	Pinch Hit AB	Pinch Hit H	PO	A	E	DP	TC/G	FA	G by Pos
1965	HOU	N	15	.200	.356	45	9	4	0	1	2.2	2	9	8	9	0	2	0	107	8	2	9	9.8	.983	1B-12
1966			119	.256	.380	434	111	23	2	9	2.1	52	52	37	69	2	5	0	974	78	8	68	9.3	.992	1B-114
1967			70	.243	.350	177	43	7	3	2	1.1	13	26	13	30	0	11	4	438	27	6	24	8.0	.987	1B-59
1969	KC	A	75	.221	.296	213	47	5	1	3	1.4	18	18	16	20	1	20	4	415	36	3	27	8.3	.993	1B-55
1971			49	.217	.287	143	31	4	0	2	1.4	9	21	11	19	0	11	1	335	24	3	31	9.3	.992	1B-39
5 yrs.			328	.238	.343	1012	241	43	6	17	1.7	94	126	85	147	3	49	9	2269	173	22	159	8.8	.991	1B-279

Tom Harrison

HARRISON, THOMAS JAMES BR TR 6′ 3″ 200 lbs.
B. Jan. 18, 1945, Trail, B. C., Canada.

Year	Team		Games	BA	SA	AB	H	2B	3B	HR	HR%	R	RBI	BB	SO	SB	Pinch Hit AB	Pinch Hit H	PO	A	E	DP	TC/G	FA	G by Pos
1965	KC	A	2	—	—	0	0	0	0	0	—	0	0	0	0	0	0	0	0	0	0	0	0.0	.000	P-1

Sam Harshaney

HARSHANEY, SAMUEL BR TR 6′ 180 lbs.
B. May 1, 1910, Madison, Ill.

Year	Team		Games	BA	SA	AB	H	2B	3B	HR	HR%	R	RBI	BB	SO	SB	Pinch Hit AB	Pinch Hit H	PO	A	E	DP	TC/G	FA	G by Pos
1937	STL	A	5	.091	.182	11	1	1	0	0	0.0	0	0	3	0	0	0	0	15	4	2	0	5.3	.905	C-4
1938			11	.292	.292	24	7	0	0	0	0.0	2	0	3	2	0	1	1	35	4	1	0	4.0	.975	C-10
1939			42	.241	.255	145	35	2	0	0	0.0	15	15	9	8	0	6	3	153	23	1	3	4.9	.994	C-36
1940			3	.000	.000	1	0	0	0	0	0.0	0	0	1	0	0	1	0	0	0	0	0	0.0	.000	C-2
4 yrs.			61	.238	.254	181	43	3	0	0	0.0	17	15	16	10	0	8	4	203	31	4	3	4.6	.983	C-52

Jack Harshman

HARSHMAN, JOHN ELVIN BL TL 6′ 2″ 178 lbs.
B. July 12, 1927, San Diego, Calif.

Year	Team		Games	BA	SA	AB	H	2B	3B	HR	HR%	R	RBI	BB	SO	SB	Pinch Hit AB	Pinch Hit H	PO	A	E	DP	TC/G	FA	G by Pos
1948	NY	N	5	.250	.250	8	2	0	0	0	0.0	0	1	1	3	0	2	0	17	1	0	2	6.0	1.000	1B-3
1950			9	.125	.313	32	4	0	0	2	6.3	3	4	3	6	0	0	0	83	7	1	7	10.1	.989	1B-9
1952			3	.000	.000	2	0	0	0	0	0.0	0	0	0	0	0	1	0	0	2	0	0	1.0	1.000	P-2
1954	CHI	A	36	.143	.268	56	8	1	0	2	3.6	6	5	12	21	0	0	0	5	27	1	1	0.9	.970	P-35, 1B-1
1955			32	.183	.300	60	11	1	0	2	3.3	6	8	9	17	0	0	0	3	29	1	1	1.0	.970	P-32
1956			36	.169	.437	71	12	1	0	6	8.5	8	19	11	21	0	1	0	2	29	4	3	1.0	.886	P-34
1957			30	.222	.400	45	10	2	0	2	4.4	5	5	10	17	0	0	0	3	15	1	1	0.6	.947	P-30
1958	BAL	A	47	.195	.427	82	16	1	0	6	7.3	11	14	17	22	0	9	2	5	43	1	1	1.4	.980	P-34, OF-1
1959	3 teams		BAL A (15G –.200) BOS A (9G –.143) CLE A (21G –.206)																						
"	total		45	.196	.275	51	10	1	0	1	2.0	7	8	9	8	0	9	1	8	25	0	2	0.9	1.000	P-35
1960	CLE	A	15	.176	.235	17	3	1	0	0	0.0	0	1	0	4	0	0	0	2	5	0	1	0.5	1.000	P-15
10 yrs.			258	.179	.347	424	76	8	0	21	5.0	46	65	72	119	0	22	3	128	183	9	19	1.4	.972	P-217, 1B-13, OF-1

Bill Hart

HART, WILLIAM FRANKLIN (Uncle Billy) TR 5′10″ 163 lbs.
B. July 19, 1865, Louisville, Ky. D. Sept. 19, 1936, Cincinnati, Ohio.

Year	Team		Games	BA	SA	AB	H	2B	3B	HR	HR%	R	RBI	BB	SO	SB	Pinch Hit AB	Pinch Hit H	PO	A	E	DP	TC/G	FA	G by Pos
1886	PHI	AA	22	.137	.178	73	10	1	1	0	0.0	3		3			0	0	7	40	5	1	2.4	.904	P-22
1887			3	.077	.077	13	1	0	0	0	0.0	0		0		0	0	0	0	8	5	0	4.3	.615	P-3
1892	BKN	N	37	.192	.328	125	24	3	4	2	1.6	14	17	7	22	4	0	0	31	59	9	1	2.5	.909	P-28, OF-12
1895	PIT	N	36	.236	.321	106	25	5	2	0	0.0	8	11	1	12	1	0	0	12	84	5	4	2.8	.950	P-36
1896	STL	N	49	.186	.273	161	30	4	5	0	0.0	9	15	3	15	7	0	0	38	106	8	3	3.0	.947	P-42, OF-8
1897			46	.250	.321	156	39	1	2	2	1.3	14	14	1		4	0	0	31	76	10	4	2.5	.915	P-39, OF-6, 1B-1
1898	PIT	N	16	.240	.280	50	12	0	1	0	0.0	4	3	1		1	0	0	3	34	6	3	2.7	.860	P-16
1901	CLE	A	20	.219	.219	64	14	0	0	0	0.0	7	6	1		0	0	0	5	55	3	2	3.2	.952	P-20
8 yrs.			229	.207	.282	748	155	14	15	4	0.5	59	66	17	49	17	0	0	127	462	51	18	2.7	.920	P-206, OF-26, 1B-1

Bill Hart

HART, WILLIAM WOODROW BR TR 6′ 175 lbs.
B. Mar. 4, 1913, Wiconisco, Pa. D. July 29, 1968, Lykins, Pa.

Year	Team		Games	BA	SA	AB	H	2B	3B	HR	HR%	R	RBI	BB	SO	SB	Pinch Hit AB	Pinch Hit H	PO	A	E	DP	TC/G	FA	G by Pos
1943	BKN	N	8	.158	.158	19	3	0	0	0	0.0	0	1	1	2	0	1	0	7	17	0	4	3.4	1.000	3B-6, SS-1
1944			29	.178	.267	90	16	4	2	0	0.0	8	4	9	7	1	2	1	37	74	7	7	4.4	.941	SS-25, 3B-2
1945			58	.230	.348	161	37	6	2	3	1.9	27	27	14	21	7	8	1	56	72	11	8	3.0	.921	3B-39, SS-8
3 yrs.			95	.207	.307	270	56	10	4	3	1.1	35	32	24	30	8	11	2	100	163	18	19	3.5	.936	3B-47, SS-34

Burt Hart

HART, JAMES BURTON BB 6′ 3″ 200 lbs.
B. June 28, 1870, Lone Tree Lake, Minn. D. Jan. 29, 1921, Sacramento, Calif.

Year	Team		Games	BA	SA	AB	H	2B	3B	HR	HR%	R	RBI	BB	SO	SB	Pinch Hit AB	Pinch Hit H	PO	A	E	DP	TC/G	FA	G by Pos
1901	BAL	A	58	.311	.374	206	64	3	5	0	0.0	33	23	20		7	0	0	561	9	14	28	10.1	.976	1B-58

Hub Hart

HART, JAMES HENRY BL TR 5′11″ 170 lbs.
B. Feb. 2, 1878, Everett, Mass. D. Oct. 10, 1960, Fort Wayne, Ind.

Year	Team		Games	BA	SA	AB	H	2B	3B	HR	HR%	R	RBI	BB	SO	SB	Pinch Hit AB	Pinch Hit H	PO	A	E	DP	TC/G	FA	G by Pos
1905	CHI	A	10	.118	.118	17	2	0	0	0	0.0	2	4	3		0	4	1	21	2	0	0	3.8	1.000	C-6
1906			17	.162	.162	37	6	0	0	0	0.0	1	0	2		0	2	0	36	7	3	1	3.1	.935	C-15
1907			29	.271	.286	70	19	1	0	0	0.0	6	7	5		1	4	0	85	23	5	2	4.5	.956	C-25
3 yrs.			56	.218	.226	124	27	1	0	0	0.0	9	11	10		1	10	1	142	32	8	3	4.0	.956	C-46

Jim Ray Hart

HART, JAMES RAY BR TR 5′11″ 185 lbs.
B. Oct. 30, 1941, Hookerton, N. C.

Year	Team		Games	BA	SA	AB	H	2B	3B	HR	HR%	R	RBI	BB	SO	SB	Pinch Hit AB	Pinch Hit H	PO	A	E	DP	TC/G	FA	G by Pos
1963	SF	N	7	.200	.250	20	4	1	0	0	0.0	1	2	3	6	0	0	0	10	9	0	1	2.7	1.000	3B-7
1964			153	.286	.498	566	162	15	6	31	5.5	71	81	47	94	5	2	0	143	278	28	25	2.9	.938	3B-149, OF-6
1965			160	.299	.487	591	177	30	6	23	3.9	91	96	47	75	6	3	2	151	231	34	16	2.6	.918	3B-144, OF-15

Jim Ray Hart *continued*

Year	Team	Games	BA	SA	AB	H	2B	3B	HR	HR%	R	RBI	BB	SO	SB	Pinch Hit AB	Pinch Hit H	PO	A	E	DP	TC/G	FA	G by Pos
1966		156	.285	.510	578	165	23	4	33	5.7	88	93	48	75	2	4	1	131	283	26	24	2.8	.941	3B-139, OF-17
1967		158	.289	.509	578	167	26	7	29	5.0	98	99	77	100	1	1	0	141	180	18	11	2.1	.947	3B-89, OF-72
1968		136	.258	.444	480	124	14	3	23	4.8	67	78	46	74	3	3	1	165	112	19	12	2.2	.936	3B-72, OF-65
1969		95	.254	.331	236	60	9	0	3	1.3	27	26	28	49	0	23	7	80	7	6	1	1.3	.935	OF-68, 3B-3
1970		76	.282	.431	255	72	12	1	8	3.1	30	37	30	29	0	4	1	60	71	12	2	1.9	.916	3B-56, OF-18
1971		31	.256	.410	39	10	0	0	2	5.1	5	5	6	8	0	23	6	7	3	1	2	1.8	.909	OF-3, 3B-3
1972		24	.304	.557	79	24	5	0	5	6.3	10	8	6	10	0	3	0	17	22	5	2	2.2	.886	3B-20
1973	2 teams SF N (5G –.000) NY A (114G –.254)																							
"	total	119	.251	.415	342	86	13	2	13	3.8	29	53	39	46	0	9	1	0	3	2	0	0.0	.600	DH-106, 1B-1
1974	NY A	10	.053	.053	19	1	0	0	0	0.0	1	0	3	7	0	5	0	0	0	0	0	0.0	.000	DH-4
12 yrs.		1125	.278	.467	3783	1052	148	29	170	4.5	518	578	380	573	17	80	19	905	1199	151	96	2.1	.933	3B-682, OF-264, DH-110, 1B-1
LEAGUE CHAMPIONSHIP SERIES																								
1971	SF N	3	.000	.000	5	0	0	0	0	0.0	0	0	0	2	0	1	0	0	2	0	0	2.0	1.000	3B-1

Mike Hart

HART, JAMES MICHAEL BB TR 6′3″ 185 lbs.
B. Dec. 20, 1951, Kalamazoo, Mich.

Year	Team	Games	BA	SA	AB	H	2B	3B	HR	HR%	R	RBI	BB	SO	SB	Pinch Hit AB	Pinch Hit H	PO	A	E	DP	TC/G	FA	G by Pos
1980	TEX A	5	.250	.250	4	1	0	0	0	0.0	1	0	1	1	0	0	0	1	0	0	0	0.5	1.000	OF-2

Mike Hart

HART, MICHAEL LAWRENCE BL TL 5′11″ 185 lbs.
B. Feb. 17, 1958, Milwaukee, Wis.

Year	Team	Games	BA	SA	AB	H	2B	3B	HR	HR%	R	RBI	BB	SO	SB	Pinch Hit AB	Pinch Hit H	PO	A	E	DP	TC/G	FA	G by Pos
1984	MIN A	13	.172	.172	29	5	0	0	0	0.0	0	5	1	2	0	3	0	24	1	0	0	2.3	1.000	OF-11
1987	BAL A	34	.158	.342	76	12	2	0	4	5.3	7	12	6	19	1	2	0	74	0	0	0	2.3	1.000	OF-32
2 yrs.		47	.162	.295	105	17	2	0	4	3.8	7	17	7	21	1	5	0	98	1	0	0	2.3	1.000	OF-43

Tom Hart

HART, THOMAS HENRY 5′7″ 160 lbs.
B. June 15, 1869, Canaan, N. Y. D. Sept. 17, 1939, Gardner, Mass.

Year	Team	Games	BA	SA	AB	H	2B	3B	HR	HR%	R	RBI	BB	SO	SB	Pinch Hit AB	Pinch Hit H	PO	A	E	DP	TC/G	FA	G by Pos
1891	WAS AA	8	.125	.125	24	3	0	0	0	0.0	1	2	2	1	1	0	0	19	8	0	0	3.4	1.000	C-5, OF-3

Bruce Hartford

HARTFORD, BRUCE DANIEL BR TR 6′½″ 190 lbs.
B. May 14, 1892, Chicago, Ill. D. May 25, 1975, Los Angeles, Calif.

Year	Team	Games	BA	SA	AB	H	2B	3B	HR	HR%	R	RBI	BB	SO	SB	Pinch Hit AB	Pinch Hit H	PO	A	E	DP	TC/G	FA	G by Pos
1914	CLE A	8	.182	.227	22	4	1	0	0	0.0	5	0	4	9	0	0	0	5	16	2	0	2.9	.913	SS-8

Chris Hartje

HARTJE, CHRISTIAN HENRY BR TR 5′10½″ 165 lbs.
B. Mar. 25, 1915, San Francisco, Calif. D. June 26, 1946, Seattle, Wash.

Year	Team	Games	BA	SA	AB	H	2B	3B	HR	HR%	R	RBI	BB	SO	SB	Pinch Hit AB	Pinch Hit H	PO	A	E	DP	TC/G	FA	G by Pos
1939	BKN N	9	.313	.375	16	5	1	0	0	0.0	2	5	1	0	0	1	1	9	1	1	0	1.4	.909	C-8

Chick Hartley

HARTLEY, WALTER SCOTT BR TR 5′8″ 180 lbs.
B. Aug. 22, 1880, Philadelphia, Pa. D. July 18, 1948, Philadelphia, Pa.

Year	Team	Games	BA	SA	AB	H	2B	3B	HR	HR%	R	RBI	BB	SO	SB	Pinch Hit AB	Pinch Hit H	PO	A	E	DP	TC/G	FA	G by Pos
1902	NY N	1	.000	.000	4	0	0	0	0	0.0	0	0	0		0	0	0	2	0	0	0	2.0	1.000	OF-1

Grover Hartley

HARTLEY, GROVER ALLEN (Slick) BR TR 5′11″ 175 lbs.
B. July 2, 1888, Osgood, Ind. D. Oct. 19, 1964, Daytona Beach, Fla.

Year	Team	Games	BA	SA	AB	H	2B	3B	HR	HR%	R	RBI	BB	SO	SB	Pinch Hit AB	Pinch Hit H	PO	A	E	DP	TC/G	FA	G by Pos
1911	NY N	11	.222	.333	18	4	2	0	0	0.0	1	1	1	1	1	0	0	44	7	2	0	5.3	.962	C-10
1912		25	.235	.353	34	8	2	1	0	0.0	3	7	8	4	2	0	0	63	9	3	1	3.0	.960	C-25
1913		23	.316	.316	19	6	0	0	0	0.0	4	0	1	2	4	1	1	41	7	1	0	2.2	.980	C-21, 1B-1
1914	STL F	86	.288	.382	212	61	13	2	1	0.5	24	25	12		4	24	**8**	249	79	11	12	5.7	.968	C-32, 2B-13, 1B-9, 3B-3, OF-2
1915		120	.274	.365	394	108	21	6	1	0.3	47	50	42		10	6	0	565	151	21	11	6.5	.972	C-113, 1B-1
1916	STL A	89	.225	.261	222	50	8	0	0	0.0	19	12	30	24	4	9	2	263	98	12	10	5.0	.968	C-75
1917		19	.231	.231	13	3	0	0	0	0.0	2		2	1	0	11	2	6	4	1	0	1.8	.909	C-4, 3B-1, SS-1
1924	NY N	4	.286	.429	7	2	1	0	0	0.0	1	1	1	0	1	1	0	6	2	0	0	2.7	1.000	C-3
1925		46	.316	.347	95	30	1	1	0	0.0	9	8	8	3	2	1	0	137	27	4	14	3.7	.976	C-37, 1B-8
1926		13	.048	.048	21	1	0	0	0	0.0	0	0	5	0	0	0	0	31	4	0	1	2.7	1.000	C-13
1927	BOS A	103	.275	.332	244	67	11	0	1	0.4	23	31	22	14	1	15	2	214	51	9	5	3.2	.967	C-86
1929	CLE A	24	.273	.333	33	9	0	1	0	0.0	2	8	2	1	0	10	3	16	0	0	0	1.2	1.000	C-13
1930		1	.750	.750	4	3	0	0	0	0.0	0	1	0	0	0	0	0	2	1	1	0	4.0	.750	C-1
1934	STL A	5	.333	.667	3	1	1	0	0	0.0	0	0	1	0	0	2	1	3	0	0	0	1.5	1.000	C-2
14 yrs.		569	.268	.337	1319	353	60	11	3	0.2	135	144	135	50	29	80	19	1640	440	65	54	4.5	.970	C-435, 1B-19, 2B-13, 3B-4, OF-2, SS-1

Fred Hartman

HARTMAN, FREDERICK ORRIN (Dutch) BR TR 5′8″ 170 lbs.
B. Apr. 25, 1868, Allegheny, Pa. D. Nov. 11, 1938, McKeesport, Pa.

Year	Team	Games	BA	SA	AB	H	2B	3B	HR	HR%	R	RBI	BB	SO	SB	Pinch Hit AB	Pinch Hit H	PO	A	E	DP	TC/G	FA	G by Pos
1894	PIT N	49	.319	.451	182	58	4	7	2	1.1	41	20	16	11	12	0	0	65	97	23	6	3.8	.876	3B-49
1897	STL N	124	.306	.390	516	158	21	8	2	0.4	67	67	26		18	0	0	159	253	63	14	3.8	.867	3B-124
1898	NY N	123	.272	.364	475	129	16	11	2	0.4	57	88	25		11	0	0	146	280	57	16	3.9	.882	3B-123
1899		50	.236	.328	174	41	3	5	1	0.6	25	16	12		2	0	0	56	100	20	11	3.5	.886	3B-50
1901	CHI A	120	.309	.431	473	146	23	13	3	0.6	77	89	25		31	1	1	151	263	49	15	3.9	.894	3B-119
1902	STL N	114	.216	.255	416	90	10	3	0	0.0	30	52	14		14	2	1	168	241	42	11	4.0	.907	3B-105, SS-4, 1B-3
6 yrs.		580	.278	.368	2236	622	77	47	10	0.4	297	332	118	11	88	3	2	745	1234	254	73	3.9	.886	3B-570, SS-4, 1B-3

J. C. Hartman

HARTMAN, J. C. BR TR 6′ 175 lbs.
B. Apr. 15, 1934, Cottonton, Ala.

Year	Team	Games	BA	SA	AB	H	2B	3B	HR	HR%	R	RBI	BB	SO	SB	Pinch Hit AB	Pinch Hit H	PO	A	E	DP	TC/G	FA	G by Pos
1962	HOU N	51	.223	.257	148	33	5	0	0	0.0	11	5	4	16	1	2	0	87	121	6	31	4.5	.972	SS-48
1963		39	.122	.133	90	11	1	0	0	0.0	2	3	2	13	1	7	2	45	69	6	14	3.8	.950	SS-32
2 yrs.		90	.185	.210	238	44	6	0	0	0.0	13	8	6	29	2	9	2	132	190	12	45	4.2	.964	SS-80

Gabby Hartnett

HARTNETT, CHARLES LEO BR TR 6′1″ 195 lbs.
B. Dec. 20, 1900, Woonsocket, R. I. D. Dec. 20, 1972, Park Ridge, Ill.
Manager 1938–40.
Hall of Fame 1955.

Year	Team	Games	BA	SA	AB	H	2B	3B	HR	HR%	R	RBI	BB	SO	SB	Pinch Hit AB	Pinch Hit H	PO	A	E	DP	TC/G	FA	G by Pos
1922	CHI N	31	.194	.236	72	14	1	1	0	0.0	4	4	6	8	1	4	1	79	29	2	0	4.1	.982	C-27
1923		85	.268	.442	231	62	12	2	8	3.5	28	39	25	22	4	15	2	413	39	5	25	6.5	.989	C-39, 1B-31
1924		111	.299	.523	354	106	17	7	16	4.5	56	67	39	37	10	4	0	369	97	18	12	4.6	.963	C-105

Year	Team	Games	BA	SA	AB	H	2B	3B	HR	HR%	R	RBI	BB	SO	SB	Pinch Hit AB	Pinch Hit H	PO	A	E	DP	TC/G	FA	G by Pos

Gabby Hartnett *continued*

Year	Team	Games	BA	SA	AB	H	2B	3B	HR	HR%	R	RBI	BB	SO	SB	Pinch Hit AB	Pinch Hit H	PO	A	E	DP	TC/G	FA	G by Pos
1925		117	.289	.555	398	115	28	3	24	6.0	61	67	36	**77**	1	6	2	409	114	23	15	5.0	.958	C-110
1926		93	.275	.468	284	78	25	3	8	2.8	35	41	32	37	0	3	1	307	86	9	6	4.6	.978	C-88
1927		127	.294	.454	449	132	32	5	10	2.2	56	80	44	42	2	2	1	479	99	16	21	4.8	.973	C-125
1928		120	.302	.523	388	117	26	9	14	3.6	61	57	65	32	3	2	0	455	103	6	14	4.8	.989	C-118
1929		25	.273	.591	22	6	2	1	1	4.5	2	9	5	5	1	20	6	4	0	0	0	4.0	1.000	C-1
1930		141	.339	.630	508	172	31	3	37	7.3	84	122	55	62	0	3	2	646	68	8	11	5.3	.989	C-136
1931		116	.282	.434	380	107	32	1	8	2.1	53	70	52	48	3	10	0	444	68	10	16	5.0	.981	C-105
1932		121	.271	.436	406	110	25	3	12	3.0	52	52	51	59	0	2	1	498	75	10	10	4.9	.983	C-117, 1B-1
1933		140	.276	.433	490	135	21	4	16	3.3	55	88	37	51	1	0	0	550	77	7	17	4.5	.989	C-140
1934		130	.299	.502	438	131	21	1	22	5.0	58	90	37	46	0	1	0	605	86	3	11	5.4	.996	C-129
1935		116	.344	.545	413	142	32	6	13	3.1	67	91	41	46	1	6	1	477	77	9	11	5.1	.984	C-110
1936		121	.307	.443	424	130	25	6	7	1.7	49	64	30	36	0	7	0	504	75	5	8	5.1	.991	C-114
1937		110	.354	.548	356	126	21	6	12	3.4	47	82	43	19	0	8	2	436	65	2	7	5.0	.996	C-101
1938		88	.274	.445	299	82	19	1	10	3.3	40	59	48	17	1	4	2	358	40	2	8	4.8	.995	C-83
1939		97	.278	.467	306	85	18	2	12	3.9	36	59	37	32	0	8	3	336	47	3	3	4.5	.992	C-86
1940		37	.266	.359	64	17	3	0	1	1.6	3	12	8	7	0	13	5	70	10	4	2	3.7	.952	C-22, 1B-1
1941	NY N	64	.300	.433	150	45	5	0	5	3.3	20	26	12	14	0	26	8	138	15	1	1	4.5	.994	C-34
20 yrs.		1990	.297	.489	6432	1912	396	64	236	3.7	867	1179	703	697	28	144	37	7577	1270	143	198	4.9	.984	C-1790, 1B-33
WORLD SERIES																								
1929	CHI N	3	.000	.000	3	0	0	0	0	0.0	0	0	0	3	0	3	0	0	0	0	0	0.0	—	
1932		4	.313	.625	16	5	2	0	1	6.3	2	1	1	3	0	0	0	31	5	1	2	9.3	.973	C-4
1935		6	.292	.417	24	7	0	0	1	4.2	1	2	0	3	0	0	0	33	6	0	0	6.5	1.000	C-6
1938		3	.091	.273	11	1	0	1	0	0.0	0	0	0	2	0	0	0	14	3	0	0	5.7	1.000	C-3
4 yrs.		16	.241	.426	54	13	2	1	2	3.7	3	3	1	11	0	3	0	78	14	1	2	7.2	.989	C-13

Pat Hartnett

HARTNETT, PATRICK J. (Happy) 6′ 1″ 175 lbs.
B. Oct. 20, 1863, Boston, Mass. D. Apr. 10, 1935, Boston, Mass.

Year	Team	Games	BA	SA	AB	H	2B	3B	HR	HR%	R	RBI	BB	SO	SB	Pinch Hit AB	Pinch Hit H	PO	A	E	DP	TC/G	FA	G by Pos
1890	STL AA	14	.189	.264	53	10	2	1	0	0.0	6		6		1	0	0	140	5	7	2	10.9	.954	1B-14

Greg Harts

HARTS, GREGORY RUDOLPH BL TL 6′ 168 lbs.
B. Apr. 21, 1950, Atlanta, Ga.

Year	Team	Games	BA	SA	AB	H	2B	3B	HR	HR%	R	RBI	BB	SO	SB	Pinch Hit AB	Pinch Hit H	PO	A	E	DP	TC/G	FA	G by Pos
1973	NY N	3	.500	.500	2	1	0	0	0	0.0	0	0	0	0	0	2	1	0	0	0	0	0.0	—	

Topsy Hartsel

HARTSEL, TULLY FREDERICK BL TL 5′ 5″ 155 lbs.
B. June 26, 1874, Polk, Ohio D. Oct. 14, 1944, Toledo, Ohio.

Year	Team	Games	BA	SA	AB	H	2B	3B	HR	HR%	R	RBI	BB	SO	SB	Pinch Hit AB	Pinch Hit H	PO	A	E	DP	TC/G	FA	G by Pos
1898	LOU N	22	.324	.324	71	23	0	0	0	0.0	11	9	11		2	0	0	25	2	2	1	1.4	.931	OF-21
1899		30	.240	.320	75	18	1	1	1	1.3	8	7	11		1	6	2	36	2	3	1	1.9	.927	OF-22
1900	CIN N	18	.328	.484	64	21	2	1	2	3.1	10	5	8		7	0	0	22	0	1	0	1.3	.957	OF-18
1901	CHI N	140	.335	.475	558	187	25	16	7	1.3	111	54	74		41	0	0	273	16	15	3	2.2	.951	OF-140
1902	PHI A	137	.283	.391	545	154	20	12	5	0.9	**109**	58	**87**		**47**	0	0	238	18	12	2	2.0	.955	OF-137
1903		98	.311	.477	373	116	19	14	5	1.3	65	26	49		13	1	0	144	6	5	0	1.6	.968	OF-96
1904		147	.253	.341	534	135	17	12	2	0.4	79	25	75		19	0	0	216	15	10	2	1.6	.959	OF-147
1905		148	.276	.347	533	147	22	8	0	0.0	88	28	**121**		36	1	0	253	6	17	1	1.9	.938	OF-147
1906		144	.255	.334	533	136	21	9	1	0.2	96	30	**88**		31	0	0	238	15	8	5	1.8	.969	OF-144
1907		143	.280	.367	507	142	23	6	3	0.6	93	29	**106**		20	0	0	191	11	7	2	1.5	.967	OF-143
1908		129	.243	.330	460	112	16	6	4	0.9	73	29	**93**		15	0	0	211	6	9	2	1.8	.960	OF-129
1909		83	.270	.322	267	72	4	5	0	0.0	30	18	48		3	8	2	140	0	5	0	2.0	.966	OF-74
1910		90	.221	.277	285	63	10	3	0	0.0	45	22	58		11	4	0	113	8	7	2	1.5	.945	OF-83
1911		25	.237	.289	38	9	2	0	0	0.0	8	1	8		0	11	2	13	3	1	0	1.7	.941	OF-10
14 yrs.		1354	.276	.370	4843	1335	182	93	30	0.6	826	341	837		246	31	6	2113	108	102	21	1.8	.956	OF-1311
WORLD SERIES																								
1905	PHI A	5	.294	.353	17	5	1	0	0	0.0	1	0	2	1	2	0	0	9	1	1	0	2.2	.909	OF-5
1910		1	.200	.200	5	1	0	0	0	0.0	2	0	0	1	2	0	0	2	0	0	0	2.0	1.000	OF-1
2 yrs.		6	.273	.318	22	6	1	0	0	0.0	3	0	2	2	4	0	0	11	1	1	0	2.2	.923	OF-6

Roy Hartsfield

HARTSFIELD, ROY THOMAS BR TR 5′ 9″ 165 lbs.
B. Oct. 25, 1925, Chattahoochee, Ga.
Manager 1977–79.

Year	Team	Games	BA	SA	AB	H	2B	3B	HR	HR%	R	RBI	BB	SO	SB	Pinch Hit AB	Pinch Hit H	PO	A	E	DP	TC/G	FA	G by Pos
1950	BOS N	107	.277	.372	419	116	15	2	7	1.7	62	24	27	61	7	8	3	236	247	26	53	5.3	.949	2B-96
1951		120	.271	.344	450	122	11	2	6	1.3	63	31	41	73	7	6	0	336	293	20	87	5.7	.969	2B-114
1952		38	.262	.355	107	28	4	3	0	0.0	13	4	5	12	0	1	0	61	73	7	10	4.9	.950	2B-29
3 yrs.		265	.273	.358	976	266	30	7	13	1.3	138	59	73	146	14	15	3	633	613	53	150	5.4	.959	2B-239

Clint Hartung

HARTUNG, CLINTON CLARENCE (Floppy, The Hondo Hurricane) BR TR 6′ 5″ 210 lbs.
B. Aug. 10, 1922, Hondo, Tex.

Year	Team	Games	BA	SA	AB	H	2B	3B	HR	HR%	R	RBI	BB	SO	SB	Pinch Hit AB	Pinch Hit H	PO	A	E	DP	TC/G	FA	G by Pos
1947	NY N	34	.309	.543	94	29	4	3	4	4.3	13	13	3	21	0	4	1	15	22	2	0	1.3	.949	P-23, OF-7
1948		43	.179	.232	56	10	1	1	0	0.0	5	3	7	24	0	4	2	6	29	0	1	1.0	1.000	P-36
1949		38	.190	.381	63	12	0	0	4	6.3	7	7	4	21	0	4	0	9	36	2	1	1.4	.957	P-33
1950		32	.302	.605	43	13	2	1	3	7.0	7	10	1	13	0	9	3	14	23	2	0	1.7	.949	P-20, OF-2, 1B-1
1951		21	.205	.227	44	9	1	0	0	0.0	4	2	1	9	0	7	3	11	1	0	0	1.0	1.000	OF-12
1952		28	.218	.385	78	17	2	1	3	3.8	6	8	9	24	0	3	1	38	3	3	1	1.8	.932	OF-24
6 yrs.		196	.238	.407	378	90	10	6	14	3.7	42	43	25	112	0	31	10	93	114	9	3	1.4	.958	P-112, OF-45, 1B-1
WORLD SERIES																								
1951	NY N	2	.000	.000	4	0	0	0	0	0.0	0	0	0	0	0	0	0	1	1	1	0	1.5	.667	OF-2

Roy Hartzell

HARTZELL, ROY ALLEN BL TR 5′ 8½″ 155 lbs.
B. July 6, 1881, Golden, Colo. D. Nov. 6, 1961, Golden, Colo.

Year	Team	Games	BA	SA	AB	H	2B	3B	HR	HR%	R	RBI	BB	SO	SB	Pinch Hit AB	Pinch Hit H	PO	A	E	DP	TC/G	FA	G by Pos
1906	STL A	113	.213	.230	404	86	7	0	0	0.0	43	24	19		21	1	0	125	227	44	13	3.6	.889	3B-103, SS-6, 2B-2
1907		60	.236	.295	220	52	3	5	0	0.0	20	13	11		7	3	0	88	120	16	6	3.9	.929	3B-38, 2B-15, OF-2, SS-2
1908		115	.265	.320	422	112	5	6	2	0.5	41	32	19		24	2	0	161	88	24	11	2.5	.912	OF-82, SS-18, 3B-7, 2B-4
1909		152	.271	.308	**595**	161	12	5	0	0.0	64	32	29		14	1	0	257	219	34	20	3.4	.933	OF-85, SS-65, 2B-1
1910		151	.218	.271	542	118	13	5	2	0.4	52	30	49		18	0	0	233	316	42	34	3.9	.929	3B-89, SS-38, OF-23

Roy Hartzell *continued*

Year	Team	Lg	Games	BA	SA	AB	H	2B	3B	HR	HR%	R	RBI	BB	SO	SB	Pinch Hit AB	Pinch Hit H	PO	A	E	DP	TC/G	FA	G by Pos
1911	NY	A	144	.296	.387	527	156	17	11	3	0.6	67	91	63		22	1	0	195	253	29	22	3.3	.939	3B-124, SS-12, OF-8
1912			123	.272	.356	416	113	10	11	1	0.2	50	38	64		20	1	0	220	141	35	6	3.2	.912	3B-56, OF-55, SS-10, 2B-2
1913			141	.259	.300	490	127	18	1	0	0.0	60	38	67	40	26	3	2	286	270	32	36	4.3	.946	2B-81, OF-30, 3B-21, SS-4
1914			137	.233	.308	481	112	15	9	1	0.2	55	32	68	38	22	4	0	249	26	9	2	2.1	.968	OF-128, 2B-5
1915			119	.251	.313	387	97	11	2	3	0.8	39	60	57	37	7	5	3	208	21	9	2	2.1	.962	OF-107, 2B-5, 3B-2
1916			33	.188	.203	64	12	1	0	0	0.0	12	7	9	3	1	5	1	27	1	0	0	1.0	1.000	OF-28
11 yrs.			1288	.252	.309	4548	1146	112	55	12	0.3	503	397	455	118	182	26	6	2049	1682	274	152	3.2	.932	OF-548, 3B-440, SS-155, 2B-115

Luther Harvel

HARVEL, LUTHER RAYMOND (Red) BR TR 5′11″ 180 lbs.
B. Sept. 30, 1905, Cambria, Ill. D. Apr. 10, 1986, Kansas City, Mo.

Year	Team	Lg	Games	BA	SA	AB	H	2B	3B	HR	HR%	R	RBI	BB	SO	SB	Pinch Hit AB	Pinch Hit H	PO	A	E	DP	TC/G	FA	G by Pos
1928	CLE	A	40	.221	.279	136	30	6	1	0	0.0	12	12	4	17	1	1	0	86	6	5	0	2.5	.948	OF-39

Ervin Harvey

HARVEY, ERVIN KING (Zaza) BL TL 6′ 190 lbs.
B. Jan. 5, 1879, Saratoga, Calif. D. June 3, 1954, Santa Monica, Calif.

Year	Team	Lg	Games	BA	SA	AB	H	2B	3B	HR	HR%	R	RBI	BB	SO	SB	Pinch Hit AB	Pinch Hit H	PO	A	E	DP	TC/G	FA	G by Pos
1900	CHI	N	2	.000	.000	3	0	0	0	0	0.0	0	0	0		0	1	0	1	0	0	0	1.0	1.000	P-1
1901	2 teams		CHI A (17G –.250) CLE A (45G –.353)																						
″	total		62	.333	.443	210	70	8	6	1	0.5	32	27	11		16	1	0	87	42	14	6	2.3	.902	OF-45, P-16
1902	CLE	A	12	.348	.391	46	16	2	0	0	0.0	5	5	3		1	0	0	16	2	0	1	1.5	1.000	OF-12
3 yrs.			76	.332	.429	259	86	10	6	1	0.4	37	32	14		17	2	0	104	44	14	7	2.2	.914	OF-57, P-17

Ziggy Hasbrook

HASBROOK, ROBERT LYNDON BR TR 6′ 1″ 180 lbs.
B. Nov. 21, 1893, Grundy Center, Iowa D. Feb. 9, 1976, Garland, Tex.

Year	Team	Lg	Games	BA	SA	AB	H	2B	3B	HR	HR%	R	RBI	BB	SO	SB	Pinch Hit AB	Pinch Hit H	PO	A	E	DP	TC/G	FA	G by Pos
1916	CHI	A	9	.125	.125	8	1	0	0	0	0.0	1	0	1	2	0	1	0	24	3	0	1	3.9	1.000	1B-7
1917			2	.000	.000	1	0	0	0	0	0.0	1	0	0	0	0	0	0	0	2	0	1	2.0	1.000	2B-1
2 yrs.			11	.111	.111	9	1	0	0	0	0.0	2	0	1	2	0	1	0	24	5	0	2	3.6	1.000	1B-7, 2B-1

Bill Haselman

HASELMAN, WILLIAM JOSEPH BR TR 6′ 3″ 205 lbs.
B. May 25, 1966, Long Branch, N. J.

Year	Team	Lg	Games	BA	SA	AB	H	2B	3B	HR	HR%	R	RBI	BB	SO	SB	Pinch Hit AB	Pinch Hit H	PO	A	E	DP	TC/G	FA	G by Pos
1990	TEX	A	7	.154	.154	13	2	0	0	0	0.0	0	3	1	5	0	3	1	8	0	0	0	2.0	1.000	DH-3, C-1
1992	SEA	A	8	.263	.263	19	5	0	0	0	0.0	1	0	0	7	0	1	1	19	2	0	0	3.0	1.000	C-5, OF-2
1993			58	.255	.423	137	35	8	0	5	3.6	21	16	12	19	2	6	1	236	17	2	1	4.6	.992	C-49, DH-4, OF-2
1994			38	.193	.337	83	16	7	1	1	1.2	11	8	3	11	1	3	1	157	5	3	0	4.5	.982	C-33, OF-2, DH-2
1995	BOS	A	64	.243	.395	152	37	6	1	5	3.3	22	23	17	30	0	9	1	259	16	3	0	4.6	.989	C-48, DH-11, 1B-1, 3B-1
5 yrs.			175	.235	.379	404	95	21	2	11	2.7	55	50	33	72	3	22	5	679	40	8	1	4.4	.989	C-136, DH-20, OF-6, 1B-1, 3B-1
DIVISIONAL PLAYOFF SERIES																									
1995	BOS	A	1	.000	.000	2	0	0	0	0	0.0	0	0	0	0	0	0	0	6	0	0	0	6.0	1.000	C-1

Don Hasenmayer

HASENMAYER, DONALD IRVIN BR TR 5′10½″ 180 lbs.
B. Apr. 4, 1927, Roslyn, Pa.

Year	Team	Lg	Games	BA	SA	AB	H	2B	3B	HR	HR%	R	RBI	BB	SO	SB	Pinch Hit AB	Pinch Hit H	PO	A	E	DP	TC/G	FA	G by Pos
1945	PHI	N	5	.111	.111	18	2	0	0	0	0.0	1	1	2	1	0	0	0	10	20	2	1	6.4	.938	2B-4, 3B-1
1946			6	.083	.167	12	1	1	0	0	0.0	0	0	0	2	0	1	0	4	7	0	2	3.7	1.000	3B-3
2 yrs.			11	.100	.133	30	3	1	0	0	0.0	1	1	2	3	0	1	0	14	27	2	3	5.4	.953	2B-4, 3B-4

Mickey Haslin

HASLIN, MICHAEL JOSEPH BR TR 5′ 8″ 165 lbs.
B. Oct. 31, 1910, Wilkes-Barre, Pa.

Year	Team	Lg	Games	BA	SA	AB	H	2B	3B	HR	HR%	R	RBI	BB	SO	SB	Pinch Hit AB	Pinch Hit H	PO	A	E	DP	TC/G	FA	G by Pos
1933	PHI	N	26	.236	.258	89	21	2	0	0	0.0	3	9	3	5	1	0	0	52	79	6	12	5.3	.956	2B-26
1934			72	.265	.355	166	44	8	2	1	0.6	28	11	16	13	1	16	5	67	98	11	11	3.5	.938	3B-26, 2B-21, SS-4
1935			110	.265	.344	407	108	17	3	3	0.7	53	52	19	25	5	3	1	247	299	39	54	5.5	.933	SS-87, 3B-11, 2B-9
1936	2 teams		PHI N (16G –.344) BOS N (36G –.279)																						
″	total		52	.304	.387	168	51	2	3	2	1.2	20	17	8	14	0	10	2	57	86	11	18	3.8	.929	3B-22, 2B-19
1937	NY	N	27	.190	.214	42	8	1	0	0	0.0	8	5	9	3	1	2	0	13	47	4	6	3.8	.938	SS-9, 3B-4, 2B-4
1938			31	.324	.441	102	33	3	0	3	2.9	13	15	4	4	0	1	0	35	66	8	8	3.9	.927	3B-15, 2B-13
6 yrs.			318	.272	.350	974	265	33	8	9	0.9	125	109	59	64	8	32	8	471	675	79	109	4.5	.936	SS-100, 2B-92, 3B-78

Pete Hasney

HASNEY, PETER JAMES
B. May 26, 1865, England D. May 24, 1908, Philadelphia, Pa.

Year	Team	Lg	Games	BA	SA	AB	H	2B	3B	HR	HR%	R	RBI	BB	SO	SB	Pinch Hit AB	Pinch Hit H	PO	A	E	DP	TC/G	FA	G by Pos
1890	PHI	AA	2	.143	.143	7	1	0	0	0	0.0	1		1		0	0	0	0	0	2	0	1.0	.000	OF-2

Bill Hassamaer

HASSAMAER, WILLIAM LOUIS (Roaring Bill) 6′ 180 lbs.
B. July 26, 1864, St. Louis, Mo. D. May 29, 1910, St. Louis, Mo.

Year	Team	Lg	Games	BA	SA	AB	H	2B	3B	HR	HR%	R	RBI	BB	SO	SB	Pinch Hit AB	Pinch Hit H	PO	A	E	DP	TC/G	FA	G by Pos
1894	WAS	N	118	.322	.482	494	159	33	17	4	0.8	106	90	41	20	16	1	0	225	135	45	14	3.5	.889	OF-68, 3B-31, 2B-14, SS-4
1895	2 teams		WAS N (85G –.279) LOU N (23G –.208)																						
″	total		108	.264	.341	454	120	20	6	1	0.2	49	74	29	17	8	0	0	370	40	16	22	3.9	.962	OF-75, 1B-30, SS-2, 2B-1, 3B-1
1896	LOU	N	30	.245	.349	106	26	5	0	2	1.9	8	14	14	7	1	1	0	292	31	8	24	11.4	.976	1B-29
3 yrs.			256	.289	.408	1054	305	58	23	7	0.7	163	178	84	44	25	2	0	887	206	69	60	4.6	.941	OF-143, 1B-59, 3B-32, 2B-15, SS-6

Buddy Hassett

HASSETT, JOHN ALOYSIUS BL TL 5′11″ 180 lbs.
B. Sept. 5, 1911, New York, N. Y.

Year	Team	Lg	Games	BA	SA	AB	H	2B	3B	HR	HR%	R	RBI	BB	SO	SB	Pinch Hit AB	Pinch Hit H	PO	A	E	DP	TC/G	FA	G by Pos
1936	BKN	N	156	.310	.405	635	197	29	11	3	0.5	79	82	35	17	5	0	0	1401	121	26	89	9.9	.983	1B-156
1937			137	.304	.387	556	169	31	6	1	0.2	71	53	20	19	13	0	0	1140	116	21	96	9.3	.984	1B-131, OF-7
1938			115	.293	.361	335	98	11	6	0	0.0	49	40	32	19	3	32	12	215	13	11	6	3.0	.954	OF-71, 1B-8
1939	BOS	N	147	.308	.354	590	182	15	3	2	0.3	72	60	29	14	13	2	1	1184	114	20	127	8.8	.985	1B-127, OF-23
1940			124	.234	.293	458	107	19	4	0	0.0	59	27	25	16	4	12	0	899	91	21	102	9.1	.979	1B-98, OF-13
1941			118	.296	.346	405	120	9	4	1	0.2	59	33	36	15	10	16	5	895	78	9	92	9.9	.991	1B-99
1942	NY	A	132	.284	.364	538	153	16	6	5	0.9	80	48	32	16	5	0	0	1128	118	11	130	9.5	.991	1B-132
7 yrs.			929	.292	.362	3517	1026	130	40	12	0.3	469	343	209	116	53	62	18	6862	651	119	642	8.8	.984	1B-751, OF-114
WORLD SERIES																									
1942	NY	A	3	.333	.444	9	3	1	0	0	0.0	1	2	0	1	0	0	0	15	1	1	0	5.7	.941	1B-3

Ron Hassey

HASSEY, RONALD WILLIAM — B. Feb. 27, 1953, Tucson, Ariz. — BL TR 6′ 2″ 200 lbs.

Year	Team	Games	BA	SA	AB	H	2B	3B	HR	HR%	R	RBI	BB	SO	SB	Pinch Hit AB	Pinch Hit H	PO	A	E	DP	TC/G	FA	G by Pos
1978	CLE A	25	.203	.284	74	15	0	0	2	2.7	5	9	5	7	2	1	0	130	15	1	1	6.1	.993	C-24
1979		75	.287	.404	223	64	14	0	4	1.8	20	32	19	19	1	7	2	368	29	3	5	5.6	.993	C-68, 1B-2, DH-1
1980		130	.318	.446	390	124	18	4	8	2.1	43	65	49	51	0	18	6	564	52	4	9	5.0	.994	C-113, DH-7, 1B-3
1981		61	.232	.268	190	44	4	0	1	0.5	8	25	17	11	0	4	2	327	44	3	7	6.0	.992	C-56, 1B-5, DH-1
1982		113	.251	.353	323	81	18	0	5	1.5	33	34	53	32	3	10	3	566	38	4	6	5.6	.993	C-105, 1B-2, DH-2
1983		117	.270	.384	341	92	21	0	6	1.8	48	42	38	35	2	9	3	514	43	3	4	4.9	.995	C-113, DH-1
1984	2 teams	CLE A (48G –.255) CHI N (19G –.333)																						
″	total	67	.269	.341	182	49	5	1	2	1.1	16	24	19	32	1	9	2	263	18	2	3	5.1	.993	C-50, 1B-5, DH-1
1985	NY A	92	.296	.509	267	79	16	1	13	4.9	31	42	28	21	0	20	5	420	20	7	4	6.1	.984	C-69, 1B-2, DH-2
1986	2 teams	NY A (64G –.298) CHI A (49G –.353)																						
″	total	113	.323	.481	341	110	25	1	9	2.6	45	49	46	27	1	18	10	318	14	4	4	3.4	.988	C-62, DH-37
1987	CHI A	49	.214	.338	145	31	9	0	3	2.1	15	12	17	11	0	6	0	114	12	0	4	3.0	1.000	C-24, DH-18
1988	OAK A	107	.257	.368	323	83	15	0	7	2.2	32	45	30	42	2	14	2	465	31	3	7	5.0	.994	C-91, DH-9
1989		97	.228	.328	268	61	12	0	5	1.9	29	23	24	45	1	16	3	425	25	4	4	5.6	.991	C-78, DH-2, 1B-1
1990		94	.213	.299	254	54	7	0	5	2.0	18	22	27	29	0	20	6	312	18	1	3	4.3	.997	C-59, DH-15, 1B-3
1991	MON N	52	.227	.319	119	27	8	0	1	0.8	5	14	13	16	1	13	2	172	13	2	1	5.5	.989	C-34
14 yrs.		1192	.266	.382	3440	914	172	7	71	2.1	348	438	385	378	14	165	46	4958	372	41	62	5.0	.992	C-946, DH-96, 1B-23
LEAGUE CHAMPIONSHIP SERIES																								
1988	OAK A	4	.500	1.000	8	4	1	0	1	12.5	2	3	1	1	0	0	0	13	0	0	0	3.3	1.000	C-4
1989		2	.167	.167	6	1	0	0	0	0.0	0	1	1	2	0	0	0	10	0	0	0	5.0	1.000	C-2
1990		2	.333	.333	3	1	0	0	0	0.0	0	0	2	0	0	0	0	6	0	0	0	3.0	1.000	C-1, DH-1
3 yrs.		8	.353	.588	17	6	1	0	1	5.9	2	4	4	3	0	0	0	29	0	0	0	3.6	1.000	C-7, DH-1
WORLD SERIES																								
1988	OAK A	5	.250	.250	8	2	0	0	0	0.0	0	1	3	3	0	1	1	28	1	0	0	7.3	1.000	C-4
1990		3	.333	.333	6	2	0	0	0	0.0	0	1	0	0	0	2	0	2	0	1	0	3.0	.667	C-1
2 yrs.		8	.286	.286	14	4	0	0	0	0.0	0	2	3	3	0	3	1	30	1	1	0	6.4	.969	C-5

Joe Hassler

HASSLER, JOSEPH FREDERICK — B. Apr. 7, 1905, Fort Smith, Ark. D. Sept. 4, 1971, Duncan, Okla. — BR TR 6′ 165 lbs.

Year	Team	Games	BA	SA	AB	H	2B	3B	HR	HR%	R	RBI	BB	SO	SB	Pinch Hit AB	Pinch Hit H	PO	A	E	DP	TC/G	FA	G by Pos
1928	PHI A	28	.265	.324	34	9	2	0	0	0.0	5	3	2	4	0	0	0	26	32	8	5	2.4	.879	SS-28
1929		4	.000	.000	4	0	0	0	0	0.0	1	0	0	2	0	2	0	1	2	2	0	2.5	.600	SS-2
1930	STL A	5	.250	.250	8	2	0	0	0	0.0	3	1	0	1	0	0	0	3	6	0	3	3.0	1.000	SS-3
3 yrs.		37	.239	.283	46	11	2	0	0	0.0	9	4	2	7	0	2	0	30	40	10	8	2.4	.875	SS-33

Gene Hasson

HASSON, CHARLES EUGENE — B. July 20, 1915, Connellsville, Pa. — BL TL 6′ 197 lbs.

Year	Team	Games	BA	SA	AB	H	2B	3B	HR	HR%	R	RBI	BB	SO	SB	Pinch Hit AB	Pinch Hit H	PO	A	E	DP	TC/G	FA	G by Pos
1937	PHI A	28	.306	.520	98	30	6	3	3	3.1	12	14	13	14	0	0	0	290	8	0	31	10.6	1.000	1B-28
1938		19	.275	.464	69	19	6	2	1	1.4	10	12	12	7	0	0	0	154	6	7	17	8.8	.958	1B-19
2 yrs.		47	.293	.497	167	49	12	5	4	2.4	22	26	25	21	0	0	0	444	14	7	48	9.9	.985	1B-47

Scott Hastings

HASTINGS, WINFIELD SCOTT — B. Aug. 10, 1846, Hillsboro, Ohio D. Aug. 14, 1907, Sawtelle, Calif. — BR TR 5′ 8″ 161 lbs.

Year	Team	Games	BA	SA	AB	H	2B	3B	HR	HR%	R	RBI	BB	SO	SB	Pinch Hit AB	Pinch Hit H	PO	A	E	DP	TC/G	FA	G by Pos
1876	LOU N	67	.258	.286	283	73	6	1	0	0.0	36	21	5	11		0	0	122	17	27	4	2.4	.837	OF-65, C-5
1877	CIN N	20	.141	.155	71	10	1	0	0	0.0	7	3	3	6		0	0	63	24	23	1	5.2	.791	C-20, OF-1
2 yrs.		87	.234	.260	354	83	7	1	0	0.0	43	24	8	17		0	0	185	41	50	5	3.0	.819	OF-66, C-25

Billy Hatcher

HATCHER, WILLIAM AUGUSTUS — B. Oct. 4, 1960, Williams, Ariz. — BR TR 5′ 9″ 175 lbs.

Year	Team	Games	BA	SA	AB	H	2B	3B	HR	HR%	R	RBI	BB	SO	SB	Pinch Hit AB	Pinch Hit H	PO	A	E	DP	TC/G	FA	G by Pos
1984	CHI N	8	.111	.111	9	1	0	0	0	0.0	1	0	1	0	2	3	0	2	1	0	0	0.8	1.000	OF-4
1985		53	.245	.368	163	40	12	1	2	1.2	24	10	8	12	2	9	1	77	2	1	0	1.8	.988	OF-44
1986	HOU N	127	.258	.356	419	108	15	4	6	1.4	55	36	22	52	38	4	0	226	7	4	0	2.0	.983	OF-121
1987		141	.296	.415	564	167	28	3	11	2.0	96	63	42	70	53	1	1	276	16	4	6	2.1	.986	OF-140
1988		145	.268	.370	530	142	25	4	7	1.3	79	52	37	56	32	5	1	280	7	5	2	2.1	.983	OF-142
1989	2 teams	HOU N (108G –.228) PIT N (27G –.244)																						
″	total	135	.231	.308	481	111	19	3	4	0.8	59	51	30	62	24	15	5	250	1	2	1	2.0	.992	OF-124
1990	CIN N	139	.276	.381	504	139	28	5	5	1.0	68	25	33	42	30	13	3	308	10	1	2	2.4	.997	OF-131
1991		138	.262	.360	442	116	25	3	4	0.9	45	41	26	55	11	19	3	248	4	5	0	2.1	.981	OF-121
1992	2 teams	CIN N (43G –.287) BOS A (75G –.238)																						
″	total	118	.249	.328	409	102	19	2	3	0.7	47	33	22	52	4	21	5	174	5	6	0	1.9	.968	OF-98
1993	BOS A	136	.287	.400	508	146	24	3	9	1.8	71	57	28	46	14	4	1	284	6	2	2	2.2	.993	OF-130, 2B-2
1994	2 teams	BOS A (44G –.244) PHI N (43G –.246)																						
″	total	87	.245	.336	298	73	14	2	3	1.0	39	31	17	28	8	5	3	155	7	3	1	2.0	.982	OF-83, DH-1
1995	TEX A	6	.083	.167	12	1	1	0	0	0.0	2	0	1	1	0	1	0	9	1	0	0	1.7	1.000	OF-5, DH-1
12 yrs.		1233	.264	.364	4339	1146	210	30	54	1.2	586	399	267	476	218	100	23	2289	67	33	14	2.1	.986	OF-1143, DH-2, 2B-2
LEAGUE CHAMPIONSHIP SERIES																								
1986	HOU N	6	.280	.400	25	7	0	0	1	4.0	4	2	3	2	3	0	0	11	0	1	0	2.0	.917	OF-6
1990	CIN N	4	.333	.600	15	5	1	0	1	6.7	2	2	0	2	0	0	0	5	1	0	0	1.5	1.000	OF-4
2 yrs.		10	.300	.475	40	12	1	0	2	5.0	6	4	3	4	3	0	0	16	1	1	0	1.8	.944	OF-10
WORLD SERIES																								
1990	CIN N	4	.750	1.250	12	9	4	1	0	0.0	6	2	2	0	0	0	0	11	0	0	0	2.8	1.000	OF-4

Mickey Hatcher

HATCHER, MICHAEL VAUGHN, JR. — B. Mar. 15, 1955, Cleveland, Ohio. — BR TR 6′ 2″ 200 lbs.

Year	Team	Games	BA	SA	AB	H	2B	3B	HR	HR%	R	RBI	BB	SO	SB	Pinch Hit AB	Pinch Hit H	PO	A	E	DP	TC/G	FA	G by Pos
1979	LA N	33	.269	.366	93	25	4	1	1	1.1	9	5	7	12	1	6	1	47	24	5	0	2.1	.934	OF-19, 3B-17
1980		57	.226	.286	84	19	2	0	1	1.2	4	5	2	12	0	21	4	31	23	3	2	1.3	.947	OF-25, 3B-18
1981	MIN A	99	.255	.350	377	96	23	2	3	0.8	36	37	15	29	3	2	1	296	11	3	5	3.1	.990	OF-91, 1B-7, 3B-2, DH-1
1982		84	.249	.343	277	69	13	2	3	1.1	23	26	8	27	0	9	3	81	17	1	1	1.2	.990	OF-47, DH-29, 3B-5
1983		105	.317	.445	375	119	15	3	9	2.4	50	47	14	19	2	15	6	199	11	3	9	2.1	.986	OF-56, DH-39, 1B-7, 3B-1
1984		152	.302	.406	576	174	35	5	5	0.9	61	69	37	34	0	2	0	364	20	9	10	2.5	.977	OF-100, DH-37, 1B-17, 3B-1
1985		116	.282	.365	444	125	28	0	3	0.7	46	49	16	23	0	6	2	246	7	3	4	2.3	.988	OF-97, DH-11, 1B-4
1986		115	.278	.366	317	88	13	3	3	0.9	40	32	19	26	2	38	6	220	16	4	16	2.4	.983	OF-46, DH-28, 1B-22, 3B-3
1987	LA N	101	.282	.429	287	81	19	1	7	2.4	27	42	20	19	2	16	1	277	105	11	36	4.2	.972	3B-49, 1B-37, OF-7
1988		88	.293	.351	191	56	8	0	1	0.5	22	25	7	7	0	38	12	189	19	3	7	3.7	.986	OF-29, 1B-25, 3B-3

Mickey Hatcher *continued*

Year	Team	Games	BA	SA	AB	H	2B	3B	HR	HR%	R	RBI	BB	SO	SB	Pinch Hit AB	Pinch Hit H	PO	A	E	DP	TC/G	FA	G by Pos
1989		94	.295	.379	224	66	9	2	2	0.9	18	25	13	16	1	34	6	89	21	4	7	1.6	.965	OF-48, 3B-16, 1B-5, P-1
1990		85	.212	.250	132	28	3	1	0	0.0	12	13	6	22	0	47	14	86	17	3	9	2.4	.972	1B-25, OF-10, 3B-10
12 yrs.		1129	.280	.377	3377	946	172	20	38	1.1	348	375	164	246	11	234	56	2125	291	52	106	2.5	.979	OF-575, 1B-149, DH-145, 3B-125, P-1
LEAGUE CHAMPIONSHIP SERIES																								
1988	LA N	6	.238	.333	21	5	2	0	0	0.0	4	3	3	0	0	0	0	34	1	2	6	5.3	.946	1B-6, OF-1
WORLD SERIES																								
1988	LA N	5	.368	.737	19	7	1	0	2	10.5	5	5	1	3	0	0	0	8	0	0	0	1.6	1.000	OF-5

Fred Hatfield

HATFIELD, FRED JAMES
B. Mar. 18, 1925, Lanett, Ala.
BL TR 6′ 1″ 171 lbs.

Year	Team	Games	BA	SA	AB	H	2B	3B	HR	HR%	R	RBI	BB	SO	SB	Pinch Hit AB	Pinch Hit H	PO	A	E	DP	TC/G	FA	G by Pos
1950	BOS A	10	.250	.250	12	3	0	0	0	0.0	3	2	3	1	0	1	0	4	9	0	2	4.3	1.000	3B-3
1951		80	.172	.258	163	28	4	2	2	1.2	23	14	22	27	1	14	2	40	124	7	15	3.5	.959	3B-49
1952	2 teams BOS A (19G –.320) DET A (112G –.236)																							
″	total	131	.240	.300	466	112	13	3	3	0.6	48	28	39	54	2	0	0	132	289	14	35	3.3	.968	3B-124, SS-9
1953	DET A	109	.254	.325	311	79	11	1	3	1.0	41	19	40	34	3	19	7	120	208	9	34	4.1	.973	3B-54, 2B-28, SS-1
1954		81	.294	.376	218	64	12	0	2	0.9	31	25	28	24	4	17	5	129	152	11	33	4.2	.962	2B-54, 3B-15
1955		122	.232	.341	413	96	15	3	8	1.9	51	33	61	49	3	3	0	252	324	21	80	4.9	.965	2B-92, 3B-16, SS-14
1956	2 teams DET A (8G –.250) CHI A (106G –.262)																							
″	total	114	.261	.357	333	87	9	1	7	2.1	48	35	39	37	1	12	2	91	197	11	22	2.8	.963	3B-100, 2B-4, SS-3
1957	CHI A	69	.202	.228	114	23	3	0	0	0.0	14	8	15	20	1	23	4	23	74	5	10	2.3	.951	3B-44
1958	2 teams CLE A (3G –.125) CIN N (3G –.000)																							
″	total	6	.111	.111	9	1	0	0	0	0.0	0	1	1	1	0	2	0	1	6	0	0	3.5	1.000	3B-2
9 yrs.		722	.242	.321	2039	493	67	10	25	1.2	259	165	248	247	15	91	20	792	1383	78	231	3.7	.965	3B-407, 2B-178, SS-27

Gil Hatfield

HATFIELD, GILBERT
Brother of John Hatfield.
B. Jan. 27, 1855, Hoboken, N. J. D. May 27, 1921, Hoboken, N. J.
TR 5′ 9″ 168 lbs.

Year	Team	Games	BA	SA	AB	H	2B	3B	HR	HR%	R	RBI	BB	SO	SB	Pinch Hit AB	Pinch Hit H	PO	A	E	DP	TC/G	FA	G by Pos
1885	BUF N	11	.133	.200	30	4	0	1	0	0.0	1	0	0	11		0	0	10	23	6	0	3.5	.846	3B-8, 2B-3
1887	NY N	2	.429	.571	7	3	1	0	0	0.0	2	3	0	1	0	0	0	5	3	0	0	4.0	1.000	3B-2
1888		28	.181	.190	105	19	1	0	0	0.0	7	9	2	18	8	0	0	30	63	24	5	4.0	.795	3B-14, SS-13, OF-1, 2B-1
1889		32	.184	.224	125	23	2	0	1	0.8	21	12	9	15	9	0	0	55	85	22	7	5.1	.864	SS-24, P-6, 3B-2
1890	NY P	71	.279	.376	287	80	13	6	1	0.3	32	37	17	19	12	0	0	81	156	55	13	4.0	.812	3B-42, SS-27, P-3, OF-1
1891	WAS AA	134	.256	.316	500	128	11	8	1	0.2	83	48	50	39	43	0	0	268	396	98	43	5.5	.871	SS-105, 3B-27, P-4, OF-3
1893	BKN N	34	.292	.417	120	35	3	3	2	1.7	24	19	17	5	9	0	0	47	65	16	2	3.8	.875	3B-34
1895	LOU N	5	.188	.188	16	3	0	0	0	0.0	3	1	1	1	0	0	0	3	6	1	0	2.0	.900	3B-3, SS-2
8 yrs.		317	.248	.317	1190	295	31	18	5	0.4	173	129	96	109	81	0	0	499	797	222	70	4.7	.854	SS-171, 3B-132, P-13, OF-5, 2B-4

John Hatfield

HATFIELD, JOHN VAN BUSKIRK
Brother of Gil Hatfield.
B. July 20, 1847, N. J. D. Feb. 20, 1909, Long Island City, N. Y.
5′10″ 165 lbs.

Year	Team	Games	BA	SA	AB	H	2B	3B	HR	HR%	R	RBI	BB	SO	SB	Pinch Hit AB	Pinch Hit H	PO	A	E	DP	TC/G	FA	G by Pos
1876	NY N	1	.250	.250	4	1	0	0	0	0.0	0	1	0	0		0	0	1	4	1	0	6.0	.833	2B-1

Scott Hatteberg

HATTEBERG, SCOTT ALLEN
B. Dec. 14, 1969, Salem, Ore.
BL TR 6′ 1″ 192 lbs.

Year	Team	Games	BA	SA	AB	H	2B	3B	HR	HR%	R	RBI	BB	SO	SB	Pinch Hit AB	Pinch Hit H	PO	A	E	DP	TC/G	FA	G by Pos
1995	BOS A	2	.500	.500	2	1	0	0	0	0.0	1	0	0	0	0	1	1	4	0	0	0	2.0	1.000	C-2

Grady Hatton

HATTON, GRADY EDGEBERT
B. Oct. 7, 1922, Beaumont, Tex.
Manager 1966–68.
BL TR 5′ 8½″ 170 lbs.

Year	Team	Games	BA	SA	AB	H	2B	3B	HR	HR%	R	RBI	BB	SO	SB	Pinch Hit AB	Pinch Hit H	PO	A	E	DP	TC/G	FA	G by Pos
1946	CIN N	116	.271	.422	436	118	18	3	14	3.2	56	69	66	53	6	0	0	110	194	20	14	2.7	.938	3B-116, OF-2
1947		146	.281	.448	524	147	24	8	16	3.1	91	77	81	50	7	7	2	143	248	26	18	3.1	.938	3B-136
1948		133	.240	.345	458	110	17	2	9	2.0	58	44	72	50	7	3	1	145	248	28	22	3.3	.933	3B-123, 2B-3, SS-2, OF-1
1949		137	.263	.413	537	141	38	5	11	2.0	71	69	62	48	4	1	0	143	290	11	29	3.3	.975	3B-136
1950		130	.260	.379	438	114	17	1	11	2.5	67	54	70	39	6	4	1	146	230	18	19	3.1	.954	3B-126, 2B-1, SS-1
1951		96	.254	.335	331	84	9	3	4	1.2	41	37	33	32	4	7	2	104	178	8	24	3.3	.972	3B-87, OF-2
1952		128	.212	.312	433	92	14	1	9	2.1	48	57	66	60	5	7	1	316	289	6	68	5.1	.990	2B-120
1953		83	.233	.396	159	37	3	1	7	4.4	22	22	29	24	0	38	7	133	56	1	30	3.8	.995	2B-35, 1B-10, 3B-5
1954	3 teams CIN N (1G –.000) CHI A (13G –.167) BOS A (99G –.281)																							
″	total	113	.270	.372	333	90	13	3	5	1.5	43	36	63	28	2	8	0	96	222	10	22	3.0	.970	3B-103, 1B-4, SS-1
1955	BOS A	126	.245	.326	380	93	11	4	4	1.1	48	49	76	28	0	12	1	97	225	8	22	2.9	.976	3B-111, 2B-1
1956	3 teams BOS A (5G –.400) STL N (44G –.247) BAL A (27G –.148)																							
″	total	76	.209	.273	139	29	2	2	1	0.7	14	12	26	13	1	35	9	48	75	4	11	3.1	.969	2B-28, 3B-13
1960	CHI N	28	.342	.342	38	13	0	0	0	0.0	3	7	2	5	0	16	3	11	16	2	2	3.6	.931	2B-8
12 yrs.		1312	.254	.374	4206	1068	166	33	91	2.2	562	533	646	430	42	138	27	1492	2271	142	281	3.3	.964	3B-956, 2B-196, 1B-14, OF-5, SS-4

Art Haugher

HAUGHER, JOHN ARTHUR
B. Nov. 18, 1893, Delhi, Ohio D. Aug. 2, 1944, Redwood City, Calif.
BL TR 5′11″ 168 lbs.

Year	Team	Games	BA	SA	AB	H	2B	3B	HR	HR%	R	RBI	BB	SO	SB	Pinch Hit AB	Pinch Hit H	PO	A	E	DP	TC/G	FA	G by Pos
1912	CLE A	15	.056	.056	18	1	0	0	0	0.0	0	0	1		0	10	0	4	0	0	0	0.8	1.000	OF-5

Arnold Hauser

HAUSER, ARNOLD GEORGE (Pee Wee)
B. Sept. 25, 1888, Chicago, Ill. D. May 22, 1966, Aurora, Ill.
BR TR 5′ 6″ 145 lbs.

Year	Team	Games	BA	SA	AB	H	2B	3B	HR	HR%	R	RBI	BB	SO	SB	Pinch Hit AB	Pinch Hit H	PO	A	E	DP	TC/G	FA	G by Pos
1910	STL N	119	.205	.251	375	77	7	2	2	0.5	37	36	49	39	15	1	0	212	346	41	31	5.1	.932	SS-117, 3B-1
1911		136	.241	.311	515	124	11	8	3	0.6	61	46	26	67	24	0	0	225	402	56	52	5.0	.918	SS-134, 3B-2
1912		133	.259	.324	479	124	14	7	1	0.2	73	42	39	69	26	1	1	262	446	50	54	5.7	.934	SS-132
1913		22	.289	.422	45	13	0	3	0	0.0	3	9	2	2	1	8	4	18	25	5	4	4.0	.896	SS-8, 2B-4
1915	CHI F	23	.204	.222	54	11	1	0	0	0.0	6	4	5		2	0	0	28	43	11	7	3.7	.866	SS-16, 3B-6
5 yrs.		433	.238	.300	1468	349	33	20	6	0.4	180	137	121	177	68	10	5	745	1262	163	148	5.2	.925	SS-407, 3B-9, 2B-4

Joe Hauser

HAUSER, JOSEPH JOHN (Unser Choe) BL TL 5′10½″ 175 lbs.
B. Jan. 12, 1899, Milwaukee, Wis.

Year	Team	Lg	Games	BA	SA	AB	H	2B	3B	HR	HR%	R	RBI	BB	SO	SB	Pinch Hit AB	Pinch Hit H	PO	A	E	DP	TC/G	FA	G by Pos
1922	**PHI**	**A**	111	.323	.481	368	119	21	5	9	2.4	61	43	30	37	1	16	6	936	55	14	61	10.7	.986	1B-94
1923			146	.307	.473	537	165	21	10	16	3.0	93	94	69	52	6	0	0	1475	86	15	109	10.8	.990	1B-146
1924			149	.288	.516	562	162	31	8	27	4.8	97	115	56	52	7	1	0	1513	94	12	131	11.1	.993	1B-146
1926			91	.192	.341	229	44	10	0	8	3.5	31	36	39	34	1	22	5	630	35	3	39	10.3	.996	1B-65
1928			95	.260	.517	300	78	19	5	16	5.3	61	59	52	45	4	7	0	811	41	12	51	9.8	.986	1B-88
1929	**CLE**	**A**	37	.250	.500	48	12	1	1	3	6.3	8	9	4	8	0	25	5	65	5	1	2	8.9	.986	1B-8
6 yrs.			629	.284	.478	2044	580	103	29	79	3.9	351	356	250	228	19	71	16	5430	316	57	393	10.6	.990	1B-547

George Hausmann

HAUSMANN, GEORGE JOHN BR TR 5′ 5″ 145 lbs.
B. Feb. 11, 1916, St. Louis, Mo.

Year	Team	Lg	Games	BA	SA	AB	H	2B	3B	HR	HR%	R	RBI	BB	SO	SB	Pinch Hit AB	Pinch Hit H	PO	A	E	DP	TC/G	FA	G by Pos
1944	**NY**	**N**	131	.266	.333	466	124	20	4	1	0.2	70	30	40	25	3	1	0	301	350	27	66	5.6	.960	2B-122
1945			154	.279	.339	623	174	15	8	2	0.3	98	45	73	46	7	0	0	376	489	29	65	5.8	.968	2B-154
1949			16	.128	.170	47	6	0	1	0	0.0	5	3	7	6	0	1	0	25	37	1	8	4.8	.984	2B-13
3 yrs.			301	.268	.329	1136	304	35	13	3	0.3	173	78	120	77	10	2	0	702	876	57	139	5.7	.965	2B-289

Charlie Hautz

HAUTZ, CHARLES A. BR 5′ 7″ 150 lbs.
B. Feb. 5, 1852, St. Louis, Mo. D. Jan. 24, 1929, St. Louis, Mo.

Year	Team	Lg	Games	BA	SA	AB	H	2B	3B	HR	HR%	R	RBI	BB	SO	SB	Pinch Hit AB	Pinch Hit H	PO	A	E	DP	TC/G	FA	G by Pos
1884	**PIT**	**AA**	7	.208	.208	24	5	0	0	0	0.0	0		3			0	0	50	2	1	3	7.6	.981	1B-5, OF-2

Bill Hawes

HAWES, WILLIAM HILDRETH BR TR 5′10″ 155 lbs.
B. Nov. 17, 1853, Nashua, N. H. D. June 16, 1940, Lowell, Mass.

Year	Team	Lg	Games	BA	SA	AB	H	2B	3B	HR	HR%	R	RBI	BB	SO	SB	Pinch Hit AB	Pinch Hit H	PO	A	E	DP	TC/G	FA	G by Pos
1879	**BOS**	**N**	38	.200	.258	155	31	3	3	0	0.0	19	9	2	13		0	0	60	15	14	2	2.3	.843	OF-34, C-5
1884	**CIN**	**U**	79	.278	.355	349	97	7	4	4	1.1	80		5			0	0	274	10	27	4	3.9	.913	OF-58, 1B-21
2 yrs.			117	.254	.325	504	128	10	7	4	0.8	99	9	7	13		0	0	334	25	41	6	3.4	.897	OF-92, 1B-21, C-5

Roy Hawes

HAWES, ROY LEE BL TL 6′ 2″ 190 lbs.
B. July 5, 1926, Shiloh, Ill.

Year	Team	Lg	Games	BA	SA	AB	H	2B	3B	HR	HR%	R	RBI	BB	SO	SB	Pinch Hit AB	Pinch Hit H	PO	A	E	DP	TC/G	FA	G by Pos
1951	**WAS**	**A**	3	.167	.167	6	1	0	0	0	0.0	0	0	0	1	0	2	1	13	0	0	0	13.0	1.000	1B-1

Thorny Hawkes

HAWKES, THORNDIKE PROCTOR BR TR 5′ 8″ 135 lbs.
B. Oct. 15, 1852, Danvers, Mass. D. Feb. 3, 1929, Danvers, Mass.

Year	Team	Lg	Games	BA	SA	AB	H	2B	3B	HR	HR%	R	RBI	BB	SO	SB	Pinch Hit AB	Pinch Hit H	PO	A	E	DP	TC/G	FA	G by Pos
1879	**TRO**	**N**	64	.208	.240	250	52	6	1	0	0.0	24	20	4	14		0	0	220	264	56	26	8.4	.896	2B-64
1884	**WAS**	**AA**	38	.278	.331	151	42	4	2	0	0.0	16		4			0	0	128	107	22	10	6.4	.914	2B-38, OF-2
2 yrs.			102	.234	.274	401	94	10	3	0	0.0	40	20	8	14		0	0	348	371	78	36	7.7	.902	2B-102, OF-2

Chicken Hawks

HAWKS, NELSON LOUIS BL TL 5′11″ 167 lbs.
B. Feb. 3, 1896, San Francisco, Calif. D. May 26, 1973, San Rafael, Calif.

Year	Team	Lg	Games	BA	SA	AB	H	2B	3B	HR	HR%	R	RBI	BB	SO	SB	Pinch Hit AB	Pinch Hit H	PO	A	E	DP	TC/G	FA	G by Pos
1921	**NY**	**A**	41	.288	.479	73	21	2	3	2	2.7	16	15	5	12	0	23	8	32	0	1	0	2.2	.970	OF-15
1925	**PHI**	**N**	105	.322	.447	320	103	15	5	5	1.6	52	45	32	33	3	13	5	775	45	12	64	9.2	.986	1B-90
2 yrs.			146	.316	.453	393	124	17	8	7	1.8	68	60	37	45	3	36	13	807	45	13	64	8.2	.985	1B-90, OF-15

Howie Haworth

HAWORTH, HOMER HOWARD (Cully) BL TR 5′10½″ 165 lbs.
B. Aug. 27, 1893, Newburg, Ore. D. Jan. 28, 1953, Troutdale, Ore.

Year	Team	Lg	Games	BA	SA	AB	H	2B	3B	HR	HR%	R	RBI	BB	SO	SB	Pinch Hit AB	Pinch Hit H	PO	A	E	DP	TC/G	FA	G by Pos
1915	**CLE**	**A**	7	.143	.143	7	1	0	0	0	0.0	0	1	2	2	0	1	0	10	1	1	0	2.4	.917	C-5

Jack Hayden

HAYDEN, JOHN FRANCIS BL TL 5′ 9″
B. Oct. 21, 1880, Bryn Mawr, Pa. D. Aug. 3, 1942, Haverford, Pa.

Year	Team	Lg	Games	BA	SA	AB	H	2B	3B	HR	HR%	R	RBI	BB	SO	SB	Pinch Hit AB	Pinch Hit H	PO	A	E	DP	TC/G	FA	G by Pos
1901	**PHI**	**A**	51	.265	.332	211	56	6	4	0	0.0	35	17	18		4	1	0	63	11	14	0	1.8	.841	OF-50
1906	**BOS**	**A**	85	.280	.332	322	90	6	4	1	0.3	22	13	17		6	0	0	136	7	4	1	1.7	.973	OF-85
1908	**CHI**	**N**	11	.200	.244	45	9	2	0	0	0.0	3	2	1		1	0	0	19	0	0	0	1.7	1.000	OF-11
3 yrs.			147	.268	.325	578	155	14	8	1	0.2	60	32	36		11	1	0	218	18	18	1	1.7	.929	OF-146

Bill Hayes

HAYES, WILLIAM ERNEST BR TR 6′ 195 lbs.
B. Oct. 24, 1957, Cheverly, Md.

Year	Team	Lg	Games	BA	SA	AB	H	2B	3B	HR	HR%	R	RBI	BB	SO	SB	Pinch Hit AB	Pinch Hit H	PO	A	E	DP	TC/G	FA	G by Pos
1980	**CHI**	**N**	4	.222	.333	9	2	1	0	0	0.0	0	0	0	3	0	1	0	9	2	0	0	3.7	1.000	C-3
1981			1	—	—	0	0	0	0	0	—	0	0	0	0	0	0	0	0	0	0	0	0.0	.000	C-1
2 yrs.			5	.222	.333	9	2	1	0	0	0.0	0	0	0	3	0	1	0	9	2	0	0	2.8	1.000	C-4

Charlie Hayes

HAYES, CHARLES DEWAYNE BR TR 6′ 224 lbs.
B. May 29, 1965, Hattiesburg, Miss.

Year	Team	Lg	Games	BA	SA	AB	H	2B	3B	HR	HR%	R	RBI	BB	SO	SB	Pinch Hit AB	Pinch Hit H	PO	A	E	DP	TC/G	FA	G by Pos
1988	**SF**	**N**	7	.091	.091	11	1	0	0	0	0.0	0	0	0	3	0	2	0	5	0	0	0	0.7	1.000	OF-4, 3B-3
1989	**2 teams**		**SF N** (3G –.200) **PHI N** (84G –.258)																						
″	**total**		87	.257	.391	304	78	15	1	8	2.6	26	43	11	50	3	5	2	51	174	22	15	2.9	.911	3B-85
1990	**PHI**	**N**	152	.258	.348	561	145	20	0	10	1.8	56	57	28	91	4	6	2	151	329	20	31	3.3	.960	3B-146, 1B-4, 2B-1
1991			142	.230	.363	460	106	23	1	12	2.6	34	53	16	75	3	8	4	88	240	15	25	2.5	.956	3B-138, SS-2
1992	**NY**	**A**	142	.257	.409	509	131	19	2	18	3.5	52	66	28	100	3	1	0	125	249	13	32	2.7	.966	3B-139, 1B-4
1993	**CLR**	**N**	157	.305	.522	573	175	**45**	2	25	4.4	89	98	43	82	11	6	1	123	292	20	22	2.8	.954	3B-154, SS-1
1994			113	.288	.433	423	122	23	4	10	2.4	46	50	36	71	3	3	1	72	216	17	19	2.8	.944	3B-110
1995	**PHI**	**N**	141	.276	.406	529	146	30	3	11	2.1	58	85	50	88	5	0	0	104	262	14	25	2.7	.963	3B-141
8 yrs.			941	.268	.412	3370	904	175	13	94	2.8	361	452	212	560	32	31	10	719	1762	121	169	2.8	.953	3B-916, 1B-8, OF-4, SS-3, 2B-1

Frankie Hayes

HAYES, FRANK WHITMAN (Blimp) BR TR 6′ 185 lbs.
B. Oct. 13, 1914, Jamesburg, N. J. D. June 22, 1955, Point Pleasant, N. J.

Year	Team	Lg	Games	BA	SA	AB	H	2B	3B	HR	HR%	R	RBI	BB	SO	SB	Pinch Hit AB	Pinch Hit H	PO	A	E	DP	TC/G	FA	G by Pos
1933	**PHI**	**A**	3	.000	.000	5	0	0	0	0	0.0	0	0	0	2	0	0	0	7	1	1	0	3.0	.889	C-3
1934			92	.226	.339	248	56	10	0	6	2.4	24	30	20	44	2	4	3	279	36	15	4	3.7	.955	C-89
1936			144	.271	.388	505	137	25	2	10	2.0	59	67	46	58	3	1	0	489	69	16	8	4.0	.972	C-143
1937			60	.261	.489	188	49	11	1	10	5.3	24	38	29	34	0	4	1	208	23	7	4	4.3	.971	C-56
1938			99	.291	.475	316	92	19	3	11	3.5	56	55	54	51	2	7	3	319	38	9	2	4.1	.975	C-90
1939			124	.283	.510	431	122	28	5	20	4.6	66	83	40	55	4	10	5	380	60	10	12	3.9	.978	C-114
1940			136	.308	.477	465	143	23	4	16	3.4	73	70	61	59	9	2	1	531	63	18	9	4.5	.971	C-134, 1B-2
1941			126	.280	.442	439	123	27	4	12	2.7	66	63	62	56	2	3	0	403	65	8	11	3.9	.983	C-123
1942	**2 teams**		**PHI A** (21G –.238) **STL A** (56G –.252)																						
″	**total**		77	.248	.320	222	55	10	0	2	0.9	22	22	37	47	1	6	2	241	36	6	2	4.0	.979	C-71
1943	**STL**	**A**	88	.188	.276	250	47	7	0	5	2.0	16	30	37	36	1	9	3	301	41	6	8	4.5	.983	C-76, 1B-1

Frankie Hayes *continued*

Year	Team	Games	BA	SA	AB	H	2B	3B	HR	HR%	R	RBI	BB	SO	SB	Pinch Hit AB	Pinch Hit H	PO	A	E	DP	TC/G	FA	G by Pos
1944	PHI A	155	.248	.367	581	144	18	6	13	2.2	62	78	57	59	2	0	0	637	89	13	11	4.7	.982	C-155, 1B-1
1945	2 teams PHI A (32G –.227) CLE A (119G –.236)																							
"	total	151	.234	.352	495	116	17	7	9	1.8	51	57	71	66	2	0	0	639	91	8	29	4.9	.989	C-151
1946	2 teams CLE A (51G –.256) CHI A (53G –.212)																							
"	total	104	.233	.331	335	78	18	0	5	1.5	26	34	50	59	2	2	1	501	48	11	6	5.6	.980	C-100
1947	BOS A	5	.154	.154	13	2	0	0	0	0.0	0	1	0	1	0	1	0	20	2	2	1	6.0	.917	C-4
14 yrs.		1364	.259	.400	4493	1164	213	32	119	2.6	545	628	564	627	30	49	19	4955	662	130	107	4.4	.977	C-1309, 1B-4

Jack Hayes

HAYES, JOHN J. TR
B. June 27, 1861, Brooklyn, N. Y. Deceased.

Year	Team	Games	BA	SA	AB	H	2B	3B	HR	HR%	R	RBI	BB	SO	SB	Pinch Hit AB	Pinch Hit H	PO	A	E	DP	TC/G	FA	G by Pos
1882	WOR N	78	.270	.399	326	88	22	4	4	1.2	27	54	6	26		0	0	162	40	41	4	3.1	.831	OF-58, C-15, 3B-5, SS-1
1883	PIT AA	85	.262	.382	351	92	23	5	3	0.9	41		15			0	0	354	85	49	2	5.4	.900	C-62, OF-18, SS-5, 1B-5, 2B-1
1884	2 teams PIT AA (33G –.226) BKN AA (16G –.235)																							
"	total	49	.229	.291	175	40	9	1	0	0.0	15		7			0	0	274	59	27	7	7.3	.925	C-38, 1B-5, OF-5, 2B-1
1885	BKN AA	42	.131	.153	137	18	3	0	0	0.0	10		5			0	0	209	53	29	4	6.9	.900	C-42
1886	WAS N	26	.191	.326	89	17	3	0	3	3.4	8	9	4	23		0	0	85	23	8	2	4.3	.931	C-14, OF-12, 2B-1
1887	BAL AA	8	.143	.250	28	4	3	0	0	0.0	2		0		0	0	0	7	5	6	0	2.3	.667	OF-4, 3B-3, C-1
1890	BKN P	12	.190	.190	42	8	0	0	0	0.0	3	5	2	4	0	0	0	23	4	6	1	2.8	.818	OF-6, SS-3, C-2, 2B-1
7 yrs.		300	.233	.331	1148	267	63	10	10	0.9	106	68	39	53	0	0	0	1114	269	166	20	5.0	.893	C-174, OF-103, 1B-10, SS-9, 3B-8, 2B-4

Jackie Hayes

HAYES, MINTER CARNEY BR TR 5′10½″ 165 lbs.
B. July 19, 1906, Clanton, Ala. D. Feb. 9, 1983, Birmingham, Ala.

Year	Team	Games	BA	SA	AB	H	2B	3B	HR	HR%	R	RBI	BB	SO	SB	Pinch Hit AB	Pinch Hit H	PO	A	E	DP	TC/G	FA	G by Pos
1927	WAS A	10	.241	.241	29	7	0	0	0	0.0	2	2	1	2	0	0	0	12	22	1	2	3.9	.971	SS-8, 3B-1
1928		60	.257	.319	210	54	7	3	0	0.0	30	22	5	10	3	2	1	134	177	10	36	5.5	.969	2B-41, SS-15, 3B-2
1929		123	.276	.351	424	117	20	3	2	0.5	52	57	24	29	4	2	0	181	312	18	57	4.2	.965	3B-63, 2B-56, SS-2
1930		51	.283	.367	166	47	7	2	1	0.6	25	20	7	8	2	5	1	149	110	5	33	5.7	.981	2B-29, 3B-9, 1B-8
1931		38	.222	.259	108	24	2	1	0	0.0	11	8	6	4	2	7	1	58	62	4	8	4.1	.968	2B-19, 3B-8, SS-3
1932	CHI A	117	.257	.333	475	122	20	5	2	0.4	53	54	30	28	7	0	0	274	386	30	83	5.9	.957	2B-97, SS-10, 3B-10
1933		138	.258	.331	535	138	23	5	2	0.4	65	47	55	36	2	0	0	344	497	16	89	6.2	.981	2B-138
1934		62	.257	.319	226	58	9	1	1	0.4	19	31	23	20	3	0	0	147	188	7	35	5.6	.980	2B-61
1935		89	.267	.347	329	88	14	0	4	1.2	45	45	29	15	3	5	0	202	275	17	48	5.8	.966	2B-85
1936		108	.312	.444	417	130	34	3	5	1.2	53	84	35	25	4	3	0	253	380	15	82	6.2	.977	2B-89, SS-13, 3B-2
1937		143	.229	.300	573	131	27	4	2	0.3	63	79	41	37	1	0	0	353	490	14	115	6.0	.984	2B-143
1938		62	.328	.445	238	78	21	2	1	0.4	40	20	24	6	3	1	0	146	183	8	51	5.5	.976	2B-61
1939		72	.249	.316	269	67	12	3	0	0.0	34	23	27	10	0	2	0	172	201	10	51	5.6	.974	2B-69
1940		18	.195	.244	41	8	0	1	0	0.0	2	1	2	11	0	2	0	21	32	1	8	3.6	.981	2B-15
14 yrs.		1091	.265	.344	4040	1069	196	33	20	0.5	494	493	309	241	34	29	3	2446	3315	156	698	5.6	.974	2B-903, 3B-95, SS-51, 1B-8

Mike Hayes

HAYES, MICHAEL 5′ 7½″ 170 lbs.
B. 1853, Cleveland, Ohio Deceased.

Year	Team	Games	BA	SA	AB	H	2B	3B	HR	HR%	R	RBI	BB	SO	SB	Pinch Hit AB	Pinch Hit H	PO	A	E	DP	TC/G	FA	G by Pos
1876	NY N	5	.143	.333	21	3	0	2	0	0.0	1	2	0	0		0	0	15	0	2	0	3.4	.882	OF-5

Von Hayes

HAYES, VON FRANCIS BL TR 6′ 5″ 185 lbs.
B. Aug. 31, 1958, Stockton, Calif.

Year	Team	Games	BA	SA	AB	H	2B	3B	HR	HR%	R	RBI	BB	SO	SB	Pinch Hit AB	Pinch Hit H	PO	A	E	DP	TC/G	FA	G by Pos
1981	CLE A	43	.257	.394	109	28	8	2	1	0.9	21	17	14	10	8	9	4	30	4	3	1	0.9	.919	DH-21, OF-13, 3B-5
1982		150	.250	.389	527	132	25	3	14	2.7	65	82	42	63	32	11	2	323	17	6	6	2.3	.983	OF-139, 3B-5, 1B-4
1983	PHI N	124	.265	.370	351	93	9	5	6	1.7	45	32	36	55	20	21	5	165	7	5	0	1.7	.972	OF-103
1984		152	.292	.447	561	164	27	6	16	2.9	85	67	59	84	48	12	2	341	2	4	1	2.3	.988	OF-148
1985		152	.263	.398	570	150	30	4	13	2.3	76	70	61	99	21	6	4	368	9	6	1	2.6	.984	OF-146
1986		158	.305	.480	610	186	**46**	2	19	3.1	**107**	98	74	77	24	2	0	1247	100	13	106	8.2	.990	1B-134, OF-31
1987		158	.277	.473	556	154	36	5	21	3.8	84	84	121	77	16	4	0	1216	80	13	100	7.4	.990	1B-144, OF-32
1988		104	.272	.409	367	100	28	2	6	1.6	43	45	49	59	20	5	1	756	58	9	66	7.9	.989	1B-85, OF-16, 3B-3
1989		154	.259	.461	540	140	27	2	26	4.8	93	78	101	103	28	4	0	426	47	9	24	2.9	.981	OF-128, 1B-30, 3B-10
1990		129	.261	.413	467	122	14	3	17	3.6	70	73	87	81	16	3	1	272	8	6	0	2.3	.979	OF-127
1991		77	.225	.285	284	64	15	1	0	0.0	43	21	31	42	9	4	1	202	3	2	2	2.9	.990	OF-72
1992	CAL A	94	.225	.326	307	69	17	1	4	1.3	35	29	37	54	11	4	2	190	3	3	3	2.1	.985	OF-85, DH-5, 1B-4
12 yrs.		1495	.267	.416	5249	1402	282	36	143	2.7	767	696	712	804	253	85	22	5536	338	79	310	4.0	.987	OF-1040, 1B-401, DH-26, 3B-23
LEAGUE CHAMPIONSHIP SERIES																								
1983	PHI N	2	.000	.000	2	0	0	0	0	0.0	0	0	0	0	0	1	0	0	0	0	0	0.0	.000	OF-1
WORLD SERIES																								
1983	PHI N	4	.000	.000	3	0	0	0	0	0.0	0	0	0	1	0	3	0	1	0	0	0	1.0	1.000	OF-1

Ray Hayworth

HAYWORTH, RAYMOND HALL BR TR 6′ 180 lbs.
Brother of Red Hayworth.
B. Jan. 29, 1904, High Point, N. C.

Year	Team	Games	BA	SA	AB	H	2B	3B	HR	HR%	R	RBI	BB	SO	SB	Pinch Hit AB	Pinch Hit H	PO	A	E	DP	TC/G	FA	G by Pos
1926	DET A	12	.273	.273	11	3	0	0	0	0.0	1	5	1	1	0	3	0	9	0	0	0	1.1	1.000	C-8
1929		14	.256	.256	43	11	0	0	0	0.0	5	4	3	8	0	0	0	46	12	3	1	4.4	.951	C-14
1930		77	.278	.379	227	63	15	4	0	0.0	24	22	20	19	0	0	0	277	27	7	4	4.1	.977	C-76
1931		88	.256	.315	273	70	10	3	0	0.0	28	25	19	27	0	0	0	334	61	11	5	4.6	.973	C-88
1932		108	.293	.382	338	99	20	2	2	0.6	41	44	31	22	1	3	1	399	59	4	8	4.4	.991	C-105
1933		134	.245	.299	425	104	14	3	1	0.2	37	45	35	28	0	1	0	546	79	4	14	4.7	.994	C-133
1934		54	.293	.347	167	49	5	2	0	0.0	20	27	16	22	0	1	0	226	23	4	3	4.7	.984	C-54
1935		51	.309	.411	175	54	14	2	0	0.0	22	22	9	14	0	3	1	211	35	1	4	5.1	.996	C-48
1936		81	.240	.292	250	60	10	0	1	0.4	31	30	39	18	0	1	0	305	28	4	5	4.2	.988	C-81
1937		30	.269	.333	78	21	2	0	1	1.3	9	8	14	15	0	1	0	118	14	1	2	4.8	.992	C-28
1938	2 teams DET A (8G –.211) BKN N (5G –.000)																							
"	total	13	.174	.174	23	4	0	0	0	0.0	1	5	4	5	1	2	1	36	1	1	0	3.8	.974	C-10
1939	2 teams BKN N (21G –.154) NY N (5G –.231)																							
"	total	26	.179	.231	39	7	2	0	0	0.0	1	1	4	8	0	2	0	51	7	0	0	2.5	1.000	C-23

Ray Hayworth *continued*

Year	Team	Games	BA	SA	AB	H	2B	3B	HR	HR%	R	RBI	BB	SO	SB	Pinch Hit AB	Pinch Hit H	PO	A	E	DP	TC/G	FA	G by Pos
1942	STL A	1	1.000	1.000	1	1	0	0	0	0.0	0	0	0	0	0	1	1	0	0	0	0	0.0	—	
1944	BKN N	7	.000	.000	10	0	0	0	0	0.0	1	0	2	1	0	1	0	18	2	0	0	3.3	1.000	C-6
1945		2	.000	.000	2	0	0	0	0	0.0	0	0	1	0	0	0	0	5	0	0	0	2.5	1.000	C-2
15 yrs.		698	.265	.332	2062	546	92	16	5	0.2	221	238	198	188	2	19	4	2581	348	40	46	4.4	.987	C-676
WORLD SERIES																								
1934	DET A	1	—	—	0	0	0	0	0	—	0	0	0	0	0	0	0	1	0	0	0	1.0	1.000	C-1

Red Hayworth

HAYWORTH, MYRON CLAUDE — BR TR 6′ 1½″ 200 lbs.
Brother of Ray Hayworth.
B. May 14, 1915, High Point, N. C.

Year	Team	Games	BA	SA	AB	H	2B	3B	HR	HR%	R	RBI	BB	SO	SB	Pinch Hit AB	Pinch Hit H	PO	A	E	DP	TC/G	FA	G by Pos
1944	STL A	89	.223	.283	269	60	11	1	1	0.4	20	25	10	13	0	4	1	336	39	13	4	4.5	.966	C-86
1945		56	.194	.219	160	31	4	0	0	0.0	7	17	7	6	0	2	0	216	23	2	5	4.4	.992	C-55
2 yrs.		145	.212	.259	429	91	15	1	1	0.2	27	42	17	19	0	6	1	552	62	15	9	4.5	.976	C-141
WORLD SERIES																								
1944	STL A	6	.118	.176	17	2	1	0	0	0.0	1	1	3	1	0	0	0	45	2	1	0	8.0	.979	C-6

Drungo Hazewood

HAZEWOOD, DRUNGO LaRUE — BR TR 6′ 3″ 210 lbs.
B. Sept. 2, 1959, Mobile, Ala.

Year	Team	Games	BA	SA	AB	H	2B	3B	HR	HR%	R	RBI	BB	SO	SB	Pinch Hit AB	Pinch Hit H	PO	A	E	DP	TC/G	FA	G by Pos
1980	BAL A	6	.000	.000	5	0	0	0	0	0.0	1	0	0	4	0	1	0	1	0	0	0	0.3	1.000	OF-3

Bob Hazle

HAZLE, ROBERT SIDNEY (Hurricane) — BL TR 6′ 190 lbs.
B. Dec. 9, 1930, Laurens, S. C. D. Apr. 25, 1992, Columbia

Year	Team	Games	BA	SA	AB	H	2B	3B	HR	HR%	R	RBI	BB	SO	SB	Pinch Hit AB	Pinch Hit H	PO	A	E	DP	TC/G	FA	G by Pos
1955	CIN N	6	.231	.231	13	3	0	0	0	0.0	0	0	0	3	0	3	1	12	1	0	0	3.3	1.000	OF-4
1957	MIL N	41	.403	.649	134	54	12	0	7	5.2	26	27	18	15	1	1	1	57	1	6	0	1.6	.906	OF-40
1958	2 teams	MIL N (20G –.179) DET A (43G –.241)																						
″	total	63	.211	.281	114	24	2	0	2	1.8	11	10	14	17	0	29	6	45	0	0	0	1.4	1.000	OF-32
3 yrs.		110	.310	.467	261	81	14	0	9	3.4	37	37	32	35	1	33	8	114	2	6	0	1.6	.951	OF-76
WORLD SERIES																								
1957	MIL N	4	.154	.154	13	2	0	0	0	0.0	2	0	1	2	0	0	0	6	0	0	0	1.5	1.000	OF-4

Doc Hazleton

HAZLETON, WILLARD CARPENTER
B. Aug. 28, 1876, Strafford, Vt. D. Mar. 10, 1941, Burlington, Vt.

Year	Team	Games	BA	SA	AB	H	2B	3B	HR	HR%	R	RBI	BB	SO	SB	Pinch Hit AB	Pinch Hit H	PO	A	E	DP	TC/G	FA	G by Pos
1902	STL N	7	.130	.130	23	3	0	0	0	0.0	0	0	2		0	0	0	67	4	2	8	10.4	.973	1B-7

Fran Healy

HEALY, FRANCIS XAVIER — BR TR 6′ 5″ 220 lbs.
B. Sept. 6, 1946, Holyoke, Mass.

Year	Team	Games	BA	SA	AB	H	2B	3B	HR	HR%	R	RBI	BB	SO	SB	Pinch Hit AB	Pinch Hit H	PO	A	E	DP	TC/G	FA	G by Pos
1969	KC A	6	.400	.500	10	4	1	0	0	0.0	0	0	0	5	0	2	1	16	1	0	0	3.4	1.000	C-5
1971	SF N	47	.280	.376	93	26	3	0	2	2.2	10	11	15	24	1	22	5	104	8	4	1	5.3	.966	C-22
1972		45	.152	.222	99	15	4	0	1	1.0	12	8	13	24	0	1	0	174	21	1	3	4.6	.995	C-43
1973	KC A	95	.276	.409	279	77	15	2	6	2.2	25	34	31	56	3	1	0	429	43	10	4	5.2	.979	C-92, DH-1
1974		139	.252	.375	445	112	24	2	9	2.0	59	53	62	73	16	5	0	620	64	16	4	5.1	.977	C-138
1975		56	.255	.335	188	48	5	2	2	1.1	16	18	14	19	4	2	2	258	17	5	2	5.1	.982	C-51, DH-4
1976	2 teams	KC A (8G –.125) NY A (46G –.267)																						
″	total	54	.243	.264	144	35	3	0	0	0.0	12	10	13	27	5	7	3	134	20	2	0	4.0	.987	C-37, DH-2
1977	NY A	27	.224	.299	67	15	5	0	0	0.0	10	7	6	13	1	1	0	98	3	3	0	4.0	.971	C-26
1978		1	.000	.000	1	0	0	0	0	0.0	0	0	0	1	0	0	0	0	0	0	0	0.0	.000	C-1
9 yrs.		470	.250	.350	1326	332	60	6	20	1.5	144	141	154	242	30	41	11	1833	177	41	14	4.9	.980	C-415, DH-7

Francis Healy

HEALY, FRANCIS XAVIER PAUL — BR TR 5′ 9½″ 175 lbs.
B. July 29, 1910, Holyoke, Mass.

Year	Team	Games	BA	SA	AB	H	2B	3B	HR	HR%	R	RBI	BB	SO	SB	Pinch Hit AB	Pinch Hit H	PO	A	E	DP	TC/G	FA	G by Pos
1930	NY N	7	.000	.000	2	0	0	0	0	0.0	2	0	0	0	0	2	0	0	0	0	0	0.0	.000	C-1
1931		6	.143	.143	7	1	0	0	0	0.0	1	0	0	0	0	0	0	10	0	0	2	1.7	1.000	C-6
1932		14	.250	.313	32	8	2	0	0	0.0	5	4	2	8	0	2	0	43	5	2	0	4.5	.960	C-11
1934	STL N	15	.308	.385	13	4	1	0	0	0.0	1	1	0	2	0	8	3	4	1	0	1	1.3	1.000	C-2, OF-1, 3B-1
4 yrs.		42	.241	.296	54	13	3	0	0	0.0	9	5	2	10	0	12	3	57	6	2	3	3.0	.969	C-20, OF-1, 3B-1

Tom Healy

HEALY, THOMAS FITZGERALD — BR TR 6′ 172 lbs.
B. Oct. 30, 1895, Altoona, Pa. D. Jan. 10, 1977, Cleveland, Ohio.

Year	Team	Games	BA	SA	AB	H	2B	3B	HR	HR%	R	RBI	BB	SO	SB	Pinch Hit AB	Pinch Hit H	PO	A	E	DP	TC/G	FA	G by Pos
1915	PHI A	23	.221	.234	77	17	1	0	0	0.0	11	5	6	4	0	5	0	29	44	5	4	4.3	.936	3B-17, SS-1
1916		6	.261	.391	23	6	1	1	0	0.0	4	2	1	2	1	0	0	6	12	1	1	3.2	.947	3B-6
2 yrs.		29	.230	.270	100	23	2	1	0	0.0	15	7	7	6	1	5	0	35	56	6	5	4.0	.938	3B-23, SS-1

Charlie Heard

HEARD, CHARLES — BR TR 6′ 2″ 190 lbs.
B. Jan. 30, 1872, Philadelphia, Pa. D. Feb. 20, 1945, Philadelphia, Pa.

Year	Team	Games	BA	SA	AB	H	2B	3B	HR	HR%	R	RBI	BB	SO	SB	Pinch Hit AB	Pinch Hit H	PO	A	E	DP	TC/G	FA	G by Pos
1890	PIT N	12	.186	.233	43	8	2	0	0	0.0	2	0	1	15	0	0	0	7	6	6	1	1.6	.684	OF-6, P-6

Ed Hearn

HEARN, EDMUND — BR TR 5′ 9″ 160 lbs.
B. Sept. 17, 1888, Ventura, Calif. D. Sept. 8, 1952, Sawtelle, Calif.

Year	Team	Games	BA	SA	AB	H	2B	3B	HR	HR%	R	RBI	BB	SO	SB	Pinch Hit AB	Pinch Hit H	PO	A	E	DP	TC/G	FA	G by Pos
1910	BOS A	2	.000	.000	2	0	0	0	0	0.0	0	0	0		0	0	0	3	4	1	0	4.0	.875	SS-2

Ed Hearn

HEARN, EDWARD JOHN — BR TR 6′ 3″ 215 lbs.
B. Aug. 23, 1960, Stuart, Fla.

Year	Team	Games	BA	SA	AB	H	2B	3B	HR	HR%	R	RBI	BB	SO	SB	Pinch Hit AB	Pinch Hit H	PO	A	E	DP	TC/G	FA	G by Pos
1986	NY N	49	.265	.390	136	36	5	0	4	2.9	16	10	12	19	0	6	2	223	11	3	1	5.3	.987	C-45
1987	KC A	6	.294	.412	17	5	2	0	0	0.0	2	3	4	2	0	1	0	25	0	0	0	5.0	1.000	C-5
1988		7	.222	.333	18	4	2	0	0	0.0	1	1	0	1	0	2	1	12	1	0	0	2.2	1.000	C-4, DH-2
3 yrs.		62	.263	.386	171	45	9	0	4	2.3	19	14	16	22	0	9	3	260	12	3	1	4.9	.989	C-54, DH-2

Hugh Hearne

HEARNE, HUGH JOSEPH — BR TR 5′ 8″ 182 lbs.
B. Apr. 18, 1873, Troy, N. Y. D. Sept. 22, 1932, Troy, N. Y.

Year	Team	Games	BA	SA	AB	H	2B	3B	HR	HR%	R	RBI	BB	SO	SB	Pinch Hit AB	Pinch Hit H	PO	A	E	DP	TC/G	FA	G by Pos
1901	BKN N	2	.400	.400	5	2	0	0	0	0.0	1	3	0		0	0	0	4	3	0	0	3.5	1.000	C-2
1902		66	.281	.325	231	65	10	0	0	0.0	22	28	16		3	1	0	298	67	13	7	5.8	.966	C-65
1903		26	.281	.404	57	16	3	2	0	0.0	8	4	3		2	6	1	73	27	4	1	5.5	.962	C-17, 1B-2
3 yrs.		94	.283	.341	293	83	13	2	0	0.0	31	35	19		5	7	1	375	97	17	8	5.7	.965	C-84, 1B-2

Jeff Hearron

HEARRON, JEFFREY VERNON — BR TR 6′ 1″ 195 lbs.
B. Nov. 19, 1961, Long Beach, Calif.

Year	Team	Games	BA	SA	AB	H	2B	3B	HR	HR%	R	RBI	BB	SO	SB	Pinch Hit AB	Pinch Hit H	PO	A	E	DP	TC/G	FA	G by Pos
1985	**TOR A**	4	.143	.143	7	1	0	0	0	0.0	0	0	0	2	0	0	0	16	1	0	0	4.3	1.000	C-4
1986		12	.217	.261	23	5	1	0	0	0.0	2	4	3	7	0	0	0	47	3	1	0	4.3	.980	C-12
2 yrs.		16	.200	.233	30	6	1	0	0	0.0	2	4	3	9	0	0	0	63	4	1	0	4.3	.985	C-16
LEAGUE CHAMPIONSHIP SERIES																								
1985	**TOR A**	2	—	—	0	0	0	0	0	—	0	0	0	0	0	0	0	2	0	0	0	1.0	1.000	C-2

Bill Heath

HEATH, WILLIAM CHRIS — BL TR 5′ 8″ 175 lbs.
B. Mar. 10, 1939, Yuba City, Calif.

Year	Team	Games	BA	SA	AB	H	2B	3B	HR	HR%	R	RBI	BB	SO	SB	Pinch Hit AB	Pinch Hit H	PO	A	E	DP	TC/G	FA	G by Pos
1965	**CHI A**	1	.000	.000	1	0	0	0	0	0.0	0	0	0	0	0	1	0	0	0	0	0	0.0	—	
1966	**HOU N**	55	.301	.350	123	37	6	0	0	0.0	12	8	9	11	1	16	4	167	20	1	1	5.1	.995	C-37
1967	**2 teams**	**HOU N** (9G –.091)	**DET A** (20G –.125)																					
″	**total**	29	.116	.116	43	5	0	0	0	0.0	0	4	5	7	0	19	2	58	6	0	2	5.3	1.000	C-12
1969	**CHI N**	27	.156	.219	32	5	0	1	0	0.0	1	1	12	4	0	12	2	44	3	1	1	5.3	.979	C-9
4 yrs.		112	.236	.276	199	47	6	1	0	0.0	13	13	26	22	1	48	8	269	29	2	4	5.2	.993	C-58

Jeff Heath

HEATH, JOHN GEOFFREY — BL TR 5′11½″ 200 lbs.
B. Apr. 1, 1915, Ft. William, Ont., Canada D. Dec. 9, 1975, Seattle, Wash.

Year	Team	Games	BA	SA	AB	H	2B	3B	HR	HR%	R	RBI	BB	SO	SB	Pinch Hit AB	Pinch Hit H	PO	A	E	DP	TC/G	FA	G by Pos
1936	**CLE A**	12	.341	.634	41	14	3	3	1	2.4	6	8	3	4	1	0	0	10	1	0	0	0.9	1.000	OF-12
1937		20	.230	.377	61	14	1	4	0	0.0	8	8	0	9	0	6	1	27	0	0	0	1.9	1.000	OF-14
1938		126	.343	.602	502	172	31	**18**	21	4.2	104	112	33	55	3	3	1	254	5	7	2	2.2	.974	OF-122
1939		121	.292	.494	431	126	31	7	14	3.2	64	69	41	64	8	13	3	263	7	10	2	2.6	.964	OF-108
1940		100	.219	.399	356	78	16	3	14	3.9	55	50	40	62	5	10	1	197	6	6	1	2.3	.971	OF-90
1941		151	.340	.586	585	199	32	**20**	24	4.1	89	123	50	69	18	0	0	259	20	15	1	1.9	.949	OF-151
1942		147	.278	.442	568	158	37	13	10	1.8	82	76	62	66	9	0	0	326	12	7	3	2.4	.980	OF-146
1943		118	.274	.481	424	116	22	6	18	4.2	58	79	63	58	5	7	1	264	4	9	1	2.5	.968	OF-111
1944		60	.331	.490	151	50	5	2	5	3.3	20	33	18	12	0	22	9	76	4	4	2	2.3	.952	OF-37
1945		102	.305	.508	370	113	16	7	15	4.1	60	61	56	39	3	1	0	214	3	6	1	2.2	.973	OF-101
1946	**2 teams**	**WAS A** (48G –.283)	**STL A** (86G –.275)																					
″	**total**	134	.278	.473	482	134	32	7	16	3.3	69	84	73	73	0	4	1	239	8	9	1	2.0	.965	OF-130
1947	**STL A**	141	.251	.485	491	123	20	7	27	5.5	81	85	88	87	2	1	0	297	7	4	4	2.2	.987	OF-140
1948	**BOS N**	115	.319	.582	364	116	26	5	20	5.5	64	76	51	46	2	9	0	223	6	2	2	2.2	.991	OF-106
1949		36	.306	.613	111	34	7	0	9	8.1	17	23	15	26	0	6	3	56	2	1	1	1.9	.983	OF-31
14 yrs.		1383	.293	.509	4937	1447	279	102	194	3.9	777	887	593	670	56	82	20	2705	85	80	21	2.2	.972	OF-1299

Kelly Heath

HEATH, KELLY MARK — BR TR 5′ 7″ 155 lbs.
B. Sept. 4, 1957, Plattsburg, N. Y.

Year	Team	Games	BA	SA	AB	H	2B	3B	HR	HR%	R	RBI	BB	SO	SB	Pinch Hit AB	Pinch Hit H	PO	A	E	DP	TC/G	FA	G by Pos
1982	**KC A**	1	.000	.000	1	0	0	0	0	0.0	0	0	0	0	0	0	0	1	2	0	1	3.0	1.000	2B-1

Mickey Heath

HEATH, MINOR WILSON — BL TL 6′ 175 lbs.
B. Oct. 30, 1903, Toledo, Ohio D. July 30, 1986, Dallas, Tex.

Year	Team	Games	BA	SA	AB	H	2B	3B	HR	HR%	R	RBI	BB	SO	SB	Pinch Hit AB	Pinch Hit H	PO	A	E	DP	TC/G	FA	G by Pos
1931	**CIN N**	7	.269	.269	26	7	0	0	0	0.0	2	3	2	5	0	0	0	57	3	0	7	8.6	1.000	1B-7
1932		39	.201	.254	134	27	1	3	0	0.0	14	15	20	23	0	0	0	399	31	4	28	11.1	.991	1B-39
2 yrs.		46	.213	.256	160	34	1	3	0	0.0	16	18	22	28	0	0	0	456	34	4	35	10.7	.992	1B-46

Mike Heath

HEATH, MICHAEL THOMAS — BR TR 5′11″ 180 lbs.
B. Feb. 5, 1955, Tampa, Fla.

Year	Team	Games	BA	SA	AB	H	2B	3B	HR	HR%	R	RBI	BB	SO	SB	Pinch Hit AB	Pinch Hit H	PO	A	E	DP	TC/G	FA	G by Pos
1978	**NY A**	33	.228	.283	92	21	3	1	0	0.0	6	8	4	9	0	0	0	151	11	5	1	5.1	.970	C-33
1979	**OAK A**	74	.256	.322	258	66	8	0	3	1.2	19	27	17	18	1	5	3	167	32	5	2	2.6	.975	OF-46, C-22, 3B-7, DH-3
1980		92	.243	.298	305	74	10	2	1	0.3	27	33	16	28	3	6	1	292	20	4	5	3.7	.987	C-47, DH-31, OF-8
1981		84	.236	.346	301	71	7	1	8	2.7	26	30	13	36	3	4	2	399	45	10	6	5.4	.978	C-78, OF-6
1982		101	.242	.352	318	77	18	4	3	0.9	43	39	27	36	8	2	1	368	54	12	8	4.1	.972	C-90, OF-10, 3B-5
1983		96	.281	.383	345	97	17	0	6	1.7	45	33	18	59	3	3	1	362	47	11	6	3.9	.974	C-80, OF-24, DH-2, 3B-2
1984		139	.248	.396	475	118	21	5	13	2.7	49	64	26	72	7	10	1	495	56	8	8	3.6	.986	C-108, OF-45, 3B-2, SS-1
1985		138	.250	.408	436	109	18	6	13	3.0	71	55	41	63	7	6	3	539	67	12	10	3.9	.981	C-112, OF-35, 3B-13
1986	**2 teams**	**STL N** (65G –.205)	**DET A** (30G –.265)																					
″	**total**	95	.226	.354	288	65	11	1	8	2.8	30	36	27	53	6	4	0	405	39	13	5	4.8	.972	C-92, OF-2, 3B-1
1987	**DET A**	93	.281	.430	270	76	16	0	8	3.0	34	33	21	42	1	12	3	384	43	5	8	4.2	.988	C-67, OF-24, 3B-4, 1B-4, SS-2, DH-1, 2B-1
1988		86	.247	.365	219	54	7	2	5	2.3	24	18	18	32	1	6	0	361	24	6	3	4.7	.985	C-75, OF-9
1989		122	.263	.389	396	104	16	2	10	2.5	38	43	24	71	7	11	3	584	68	10	10	5.3	.985	C-117, 3B-4, OF-3, DH-1
1990		122	.270	.386	370	100	18	2	7	1.9	46	38	19	71	7	8	3	588	54	13	7	5.3	.980	C-117, OF-3, DH-2, SS-1
1991	**ATL N**	49	.209	.266	139	29	3	1	1	0.7	4	12	7	26	0	6	1	192	33	2	1	5.0	.991	C-45
14 yrs.		1324	.252	.367	4212	1061	173	27	86	2.0	462	469	278	616	54	83	22	5287	593	116	80	4.3	.981	C-1083, OF-215, DH-40, 3B-38, 1B-4, SS-4, 2B-1
DIVISIONAL PLAYOFF SERIES																								
1981	**OAK A**	2	.000	.000	8	0	0	0	0	0.0	0	0	0	1	0	0	0	9	1	0	0	5.0	1.000	C-2
LEAGUE CHAMPIONSHIP SERIES																								
1981	**OAK A**	3	.333	.333	6	2	0	0	0	0.0	1	0	0	1	0	0	0	3	1	0	0	1.3	1.000	C-2, OF-1
1987	**DET A**	3	.286	.714	7	2	0	0	1	14.3	1	2	0	0	0	0	0	14	0	0	0	4.7	1.000	C-3
2 yrs.		6	.308	.538	13	4	0	0	1	7.7	2	2	0	1	0	0	0	17	1	0	0	3.0	1.000	C-5, OF-1
WORLD SERIES																								
1978	**NY A**	1	—	—	0	0	0	0	0	—	0	0	0	0	0	0	0	0	0	0	0	0.0	.000	C-1

Tommy Heath

HEATH, THOMAS GEORGE — BR TR 5′10½″ 185 lbs.
B. Aug. 18, 1913, Akron, Colo. D. Feb. 26, 1967, Los Gatos, Calif.

Year	Team	Games	BA	SA	AB	H	2B	3B	HR	HR%	R	RBI	BB	SO	SB	Pinch Hit AB	Pinch Hit H	PO	A	E	DP	TC/G	FA	G by Pos
1935	**STL A**	47	.237	.269	93	22	3	0	0	0.0	10	9	20	13	0	10	3	97	10	2	3	2.9	.982	C-37
1937		17	.233	.395	43	10	0	2	1	2.3	4	3	10	3	0	2	1	55	6	0	1	4.4	1.000	C-14
1938		70	.227	.325	194	44	13	0	2	1.0	22	22	35	24	0	3	1	315	42	5	5	5.6	.986	C-65
3 yrs.		134	.230	.318	330	76	16	2	3	0.9	36	34	65	40	0	15	5	467	58	7	9	4.6	.987	C-116

Cliff Heathcote

HEATHCOTE, CLIFTON EARL BL TL 5′10½″ 160 lbs.
B. Jan. 24, 1898, Glen Rock, Pa. D. Jan. 19, 1939, York, Pa.

Year	Team	Games	BA	SA	AB	H	2B	3B	HR	HR%	R	RBI	BB	SO	SB	Pinch Hit AB	Pinch Hit H	PO	A	E	DP	TC/G	FA	G by Pos
1918	STL N	88	.259	.345	348	90	12	3	4	1.1	37	32	20	40	12	0	0	222	6	16	0	2.8	.934	OF-88
1919		114	.279	.339	401	112	13	4	1	0.2	53	29	20	41	26	9	3	249	10	8	3	2.6	.970	OF-101, 1B-2
1920		133	.284	.372	489	139	18	8	3	0.6	55	56	25	31	21	3	0	296	26	12	3	2.6	.964	OF-129
1921		62	.244	.308	156	38	6	2	0	0.0	18	9	10	9	7	7	1	83	5	7	0	1.9	.926	OF-51
1922	2 teams	STL N (34G –.245)	CHI N (76G –.280)																					
″	total	110	.270	.370	341	92	13	9	1	0.3	48	48	27	19	5	12	3	224	7	7	2	2.6	.971	OF-92
1923	CHI N	117	.249	.308	393	98	14	3	1	0.3	48	27	25	22	32	2	0	231	14	5	1	2.2	.980	OF-112
1924		113	.309	.393	392	121	19	7	0	0.0	66	30	28	28	26	1	0	228	7	5	3	2.2	.979	OF-111
1925		109	.263	.366	380	100	14	5	5	1.3	57	39	39	26	15	10	1	241	21	8	8	2.7	.970	OF-99
1926		139	.276	.412	510	141	33	3	10	2.0	98	53	58	30	18	3	1	306	22	5	8	2.5	.985	OF-133
1927		83	.294	.408	228	67	12	4	2	0.9	28	25	20	16	6	17	0	136	13	2	7	2.6	.987	OF-57
1928		67	.285	.409	137	39	8	0	3	2.2	26	18	17	12	6	21	5	67	5	2	0	1.9	.973	OF-39
1929		82	.313	.415	224	70	17	0	2	0.9	45	31	25	17	9	22	7	131	4	2	2	2.6	.985	OF-52
1930		70	.260	.520	150	39	10	1	9	6.0	30	18	18	15	4	31	5	66	4	1	0	2.0	.986	OF-35
1931	CIN N	90	.258	.365	252	65	15	6	0	0.0	24	28	32	16	3	25	6	164	13	2	4	3.0	.989	OF-59
1932	2 teams	CIN N (8G –.000)	PHI N (30G –.282)																					
″	total	38	.262	.381	42	11	2	0	1	2.4	10	5	3	3	0	20	4	47	3	2	7	7.4	.962	1B-7
15 yrs.		1415	.275	.375	4443	1222	206	55	42	0.9	643	448	367	325	190	183	36	2691	160	84	48	2.5	.971	OF-1158, 1B-9
WORLD SERIES																								
1929	CHI N	2	.000	.000	1	0	0	0	0	0.0	0	0	0	0	0	1	0	0	0	0	0	0.0	—	

Richie Hebner

HEBNER, RICHARD JOSEPH BL TR 6′ 1″ 195 lbs.
B. Nov. 26, 1947, Boston, Mass.

Year	Team	Games	BA	SA	AB	H	2B	3B	HR	HR%	R	RBI	BB	SO	SB	Pinch Hit AB	Pinch Hit H	PO	A	E	DP	TC/G	FA	G by Pos
1968	PIT N	2	.000	.000	1	0	0	0	0	0.0	0	0	0	0	0	1	0	0	0	0	0	0.0	—	
1969		129	.301	.420	459	138	23	4	8	1.7	72	47	53	53	4	4	1	81	240	19	32	2.7	.944	3B-124, 1B-1
1970		120	.290	.464	420	122	24	8	11	2.6	60	46	42	48	2	6	2	64	235	19	24	2.7	.940	3B-117
1971		112	.271	.487	388	105	17	8	17	4.4	50	67	32	68	2	7	2	89	172	14	21	2.5	.949	3B-108
1972		124	.300	.508	427	128	24	4	19	4.4	63	72	52	54	0	5	1	76	210	9	17	2.4	.969	3B-121
1973		144	.271	.477	509	138	28	1	25	4.9	73	74	56	60	0	7	1	92	260	23	19	2.7	.939	3B-139
1974		146	.291	.449	550	160	21	6	18	3.3	97	68	60	53	0	7	1	115	304	28	34	3.2	.937	3B-141
1975		128	.246	.392	472	116	16	4	15	3.2	65	57	43	48	0	3	1	86	244	19	17	2.8	.946	3B-126
1976		132	.249	.366	434	108	21	3	8	1.8	60	51	47	39	1	7	0	87	236	16	16	2.7	.953	3B-126
1977	PHI N	118	.285	.484	397	113	17	4	18	4.5	67	62	61	46	7	10	3	933	85	11	93	8.8	.989	1B-103, 3B-13, 2B-1
1978		137	.283	.464	435	123	22	3	17	3.9	61	71	53	58	4	9	5	994	94	8	90	8.0	.993	1B-117, 3B-19, 2B-1
1979	NY N	136	.268	.393	473	127	25	2	10	2.1	54	79	59	59	3	4	1	125	248	23	27	2.8	.942	3B-134, 1B-6
1980	DET A	104	.290	.466	341	99	10	7	12	3.5	48	82	38	45	0	11	6	485	84	4	45	5.8	.993	1B-61, 3B-32, DH-5
1981		78	.226	.345	226	51	8	2	5	2.2	19	28	27	28	1	11	1	531	29	3	36	7.8	.995	1B-61, DH-11
1982	2 teams	DET A (68G –.274)	PIT N (25G –.300)																					
″	total	93	.281	.434	249	70	8	0	10	4.0	31	30	30	24	5	17	3	338	28	4	16	4.3	.989	1B-44, OF-21, DH-20, 3B-1
1983	PIT N	78	.265	.395	162	43	4	1	5	3.1	23	26	17	28	8	27	7	63	45	2	4	2.0	.982	3B-40, OF-7, 1B-7
1984	CHI N	44	.333	.444	81	27	3	0	2	2.5	12	8	10	15	1	26	8	39	26	1	6	3.3	.985	3B-14, OF-3, 1B-3
1985		83	.217	.308	120	26	2	0	3	2.5	10	22	7	15	0	59	12	110	24	4	15	6.9	.971	1B-12, 3B-7, OF-1
18 yrs.		1908	.276	.438	6144	1694	273	57	203	3.3	865	890	687	741	38	221	55	4308	2564	207	512	4.1	.971	3B-1262, 1B-415, DH-36, OF-32, 2B-2
LEAGUE CHAMPIONSHIP SERIES																								
1970	PIT N	2	.667	1.000	6	4	2	0	0	0.0	0	0	2	1	0	0	0	0	4	0	0	2.0	1.000	3B-2
1971		4	.294	.706	17	5	1	0	2	11.8	3	4	0	4	0	1	0	4	3	1	0	2.0	.875	3B-4
1972		5	.188	.250	16	3	1	0	0	0.0	2	1	1	3	0	0	0	5	11	0	1	3.2	1.000	3B-5
1974		4	.231	.462	13	3	0	0	1	7.7	1	4	1	4	0	0	0	5	7	0	1	3.0	1.000	3B-4
1975		3	.333	.417	12	4	1	0	0	0.0	2	2	1	1	0	0	0	0	2	0	0	0.7	1.000	3B-3
1977	PHI N	4	.357	.500	14	5	2	0	0	0.0	2	0	0	1	0	1	0	32	0	0	2	10.7	1.000	1B-3
1978		3	.111	.111	9	1	0	0	0	0.0	0	1	0	0	0	1	0	21	0	0	3	10.5	1.000	1B-2
1984	CHI N	1	.000	.000	1	0	0	0	0	0.0	0	0	0	0	0	1	0	0	0	0	0	0.0	—	
8 yrs.		26 9th	.284	.466	88	25	7 1st	0	3	3.4	10	12	5	14	0	4	0	67	27	1	7	4.1	.989	3B-18, 1B-5
WORLD SERIES																								
1971	PIT N	3	.167	.417	12	2	0	0	1	8.3	2	3	3	3	0	0	0	1	3	1	1	1.7	.800	3B-3

Mike Hechinger

HECHINGER, MICHAEL VINCENT BR TR 6′ 175 lbs.
B. Feb. 14, 1890, Chicago, Ill. D. Aug. 13, 1967, Chicago, Ill.

Year	Team	Games	BA	SA	AB	H	2B	3B	HR	HR%	R	RBI	BB	SO	SB	Pinch Hit AB	Pinch Hit H	PO	A	E	DP	TC/G	FA	G by Pos
1912	CHI N	2	.000	.000	3	0	0	0	0	0.0	0	0	2	0	0	0	0	7	2	0	0	4.5	1.000	C-2
1913	2 teams	CHI N (2G –.000)	BKN N (9G –.182)																					
″	total	11	.154	.231	13	2	1	0	0	0.0	1	0	0	2	0	7	1	4	1	0	0	1.3	1.000	C-4
2 yrs.		13	.125	.188	16	2	1	0	0	0.0	1	0	2	2	0	7	1	11	3	0	0	2.3	1.000	C-6

Guy Hecker

HECKER, GUY JACKSON (Blond Guy) BR TR 6′ 190 lbs.
B. Apr. 3, 1856, Youngsville, Pa. D. Dec. 3, 1938, Wooster, Ohio.
Manager 1890.

Year	Team	Games	BA	SA	AB	H	2B	3B	HR	HR%	R	RBI	BB	SO	SB	Pinch Hit AB	Pinch Hit H	PO	A	E	DP	TC/G	FA	G by Pos
1882	LOU AA	78	.276	.368	340	94	14	4	3	0.9	62		5			0	0	699	68	31	43	9.9	.961	1B-66, P-13, OF-2
1883		79	.273	.339	322	88	6	6	1	0.3	56		10			0	0	144	100	24	7	3.0	.910	P-55, OF-23, 1B-10
1884		78	.297	.430	316	94	14	8	4	1.3	53		10			0	0	55	145	12	3	2.6	.943	P-76, OF-5
1885		72	.273	.337	297	81	9	2	2	0.7	48		5			0	0	174	106	15	16	4.0	.949	P-54, 1B-17, OF-3
1886		84	.341	.446	343	117	14	5	4	1.2	76		32			0	0	243	10	23	12	3.0	.917	P-52, 1B-22, OF-17
1887		91	.319	.441	370	118	21	6	4	1.1	89		31		48	0	0	429	82	29	27	5.9	.946	1B-43, P-33, OF-16
1888		56	.227	.289	211	48	9	2	0	0.0	32	29	11		20	0	0	305	57	25	12	6.6	.935	1B-30, P-28, OF-1
1889		82	.284	.376	327	93	17	5	1	0.3	42	36	18	27	17	0	0	616	55	23	45	8.2	.967	1B-65, P-19, OF-1
1890	PIT N	86	.226	.318	340	77	13	9	0	0.0	43	38	19	17	13	0	0	627	53	28	26	7.9	.960	1B-69, P-14, OF-7
9 yrs.		706	.283	.376	2866	810	117	47	19	0.7	501	103	141	44	98	0	0	3292	676	210	191	5.6	.950	P-344, 1B-322, OF-75

Danny Heep

HEEP, DANIEL WILLIAM
B. July 3, 1957, San Antonio, Tex.
BL TL 5′11″ 185 lbs.

Year	Team	Games	BA	SA	AB	H	2B	3B	HR	HR%	R	RBI	BB	SO	SB	Pinch Hit AB	Pinch Hit H	PO	A	E	DP	TC/G	FA	G by Pos
1979	HOU N	14	.143	.143	14	2	0	0	0	0.0	0	2	1	4	0	10	1	7	0	0	0	3.5	1.000	OF-2
1980		33	.276	.368	87	24	8	0	0	0.0	6	6	8	9	0	8	2	188	8	2	8	9.0	.990	1B-22
1981		33	.250	.281	96	24	3	0	0	0.0	6	11	10	11	0	9	4	198	9	2	12	9.1	.990	1B-22, OF-1
1982		85	.237	.379	198	47	14	1	4	2.0	16	22	21	31	0	23	6	192	6	1	10	3.6	.995	OF-39, 1B-16
1983	NY N	115	.253	.395	253	64	12	0	8	3.2	30	21	29	40	3	40	11	159	11	0	12	2.3	1.000	OF-61, 1B-14
1984		99	.231	.312	199	46	9	2	1	0.5	36	12	27	22	3	38	8	137	7	4	4	2.6	.973	OF-48, 1B-10
1985		95	.280	.421	271	76	17	0	7	2.6	26	42	27	27	2	13	1	154	5	4	3	2.0	.975	OF-78, 1B-4
1986		86	.282	.421	195	55	8	2	5	2.6	24	33	30	31	1	30	9	83	2	1	1	1.5	.988	OF-56
1987	LA N	60	.163	.204	98	16	4	0	0	0.0	7	9	8	10	1	35	5	52	6	1	3	2.1	.983	OF-22, 1B-6
1988		95	.242	.255	149	36	2	0	0	0.0	14	11	22	13	2	44	4	129	10	3	5	3.2	.979	OF-32, 1B-12, P-1
1989	BOS A	113	.300	.400	320	96	17	0	5	1.6	36	49	29	26	0	20	4	216	14	3	18	2.3	.987	OF-75, 1B-19, DH-9
1990		41	.174	.217	69	12	1	1	0	0.0	3	8	7	14	0	18	2	42	4	1	2	1.8	.979	OF-14, DH-6, 1B-5, P-1
1991	ATL N	14	.417	.500	12	5	1	0	0	0.0	4	3	1	4	0	12	5	1	0	0	0	0.5	1.000	1B-1, OF-1
13 yrs.		883	.257	.357	1961	503	96	6	30	1.5	208	229	220	242	12	300	62	1558	82	22	78	2.9	.987	OF-429, 1B-131, DH-15, P-2
LEAGUE CHAMPIONSHIP SERIES																								
1980	HOU N	1	.000	.000	1	0	0	0	0	0.0	0	0	0	0	0	1	0	0	0	0	0	0.0	—	
1986	NY N	5	.250	.250	4	1	0	0	0	0.0	0	1	0	2	0	3	1	0	0	0	0	0.0	.000	OF-1
1988	LA N	3	.000	.000	1	0	0	0	0	0.0	0	0	1	1	0	1	0	0	0	0	0	0.0	—	
1990	BOS A	2	.000	.000	2	0	0	0	0	0.0	0	0	0	0	0	2	0	0	0	0	0	0.0	—	
4 yrs.		11	.125	.125	8	1	0	0	0	0.0	0	1	1	3	0	7	1	0	0	0	0	0.0		OF-1
WORLD SERIES																								
1986	NY N	5	.091	.091	11	1	0	0	0	0.0	0	2	1	1	0	2	0	1	0	0	0	0.3	1.000	DH-2, OF-1
1988	LA N	3	.250	.375	8	2	1	0	0	0.0	0	0	0	2	0	2	0	0	0	0	0	0.0		OF-1, DH-1
2 yrs.		8	.158	.211	19	3	1	0	0	0.0	0	2	1	3	0	4	0	1	0	0	0	0.2	1.000	DH-3, OF-2

Bert Heffernan

HEFFERNAN, BERTRAM ALEXANDER
B. Mar. 3, 1965, Centereach, N. Y.
BL TR 5′10″ 185 lbs.

Year	Team	Games	BA	SA	AB	H	2B	3B	HR	HR%	R	RBI	BB	SO	SB	Pinch Hit AB	Pinch Hit H	PO	A	E	DP	TC/G	FA	G by Pos
1992	SEA A	8	.091	.182	11	1	1	0	0	0.0	0	1	0	1	0	2	0	19	1	0	0	4.0	1.000	C-5

Don Heffner

HEFFNER, DONALD HENRY (Jeep)
B. Feb. 8, 1911, Rouzerville, Pa. D. Aug. 1, 1989, Pasadena, Calif.
Manager 1966.
BR TR 5′10″ 155 lbs.

Year	Team	Games	BA	SA	AB	H	2B	3B	HR	HR%	R	RBI	BB	SO	SB	Pinch Hit AB	Pinch Hit H	PO	A	E	DP	TC/G	FA	G by Pos
1934	NY A	72	.261	.320	241	63	8	3	0	0.0	29	25	25	18	1	2	2	158	179	10	46	5.1	.971	2B-68
1935		10	.306	.444	36	11	3	1	0	0.0	3	8	4	1	0	0	0	20	29	1	5	5.0	.980	2B-10
1936		19	.229	.313	48	11	2	1	0	0.0	7	6	6	5	0	2	1	19	38	2	7	3.7	.966	3B-8, 2B-5, SS-3
1937		60	.249	.328	201	50	6	5	0	0.0	23	21	19	19	1	4	1	127	132	6	30	4.7	.977	2B-38, SS-13, 3B-3, OF-1, 1B-1
1938	STL A	141	.245	.319	473	116	23	3	2	0.4	47	69	65	53	1	0	0	365	363	22	103	5.3	.971	2B-141
1939		110	.267	.312	375	100	10	2	1	0.3	45	35	48	39	1	4	2	222	315	29	54	5.4	.949	SS-73, 2B-32
1940		126	.236	.310	487	115	23	2	3	0.6	52	53	39	37	5	1	0	311	426	17	102	6.0	.977	2B-125
1941		110	.233	.278	399	93	14	2	0	0.0	48	17	38	27	5	6	1	224	307	14	52	5.2	.974	2B-105
1942		19	.167	.222	36	6	2	0	0	0.0	2	3	1	4	1	7	2	34	19	3	5	5.6	.946	2B-6, 1B-4
1943	2 teams	STL A (18G –.121)	PHI A (52G –.208)																					
"	total	70	.194	.227	211	41	7	0	0	0.0	19	10	20	14	3	6	1	126	145	6	31	4.5	.978	2B-60, 1B-2
1944	DET A	6	.211	.263	19	4	1	0	0	0.0	0	1	5	1	0	1	0	12	13	1	4	5.2	.962	2B-5
11 yrs.		743	.241	.303	2526	610	99	19	6	0.2	275	248	270	218	18	33	10	1618	1966	111	439	5.3	.970	2B-595, SS-89, 3B-11, 1B-7, OF-1

Jim Hegan

HEGAN, JAMES EDWARD
Father of Mike Hegan.
B. Aug. 3, 1920, Lynn, Mass. D. June 17, 1984, Swampscott, Mass.
BR TR 6′ 2″ 195 lbs.

Year	Team	Games	BA	SA	AB	H	2B	3B	HR	HR%	R	RBI	BB	SO	SB	Pinch Hit AB	Pinch Hit H	PO	A	E	DP	TC/G	FA	G by Pos
1941	CLE A	16	.319	.426	47	15	2	0	1	2.1	4	5	4	7	0	0	0	63	10	2	2	4.7	.973	C-16
1942		68	.194	.224	170	33	5	0	0	0.0	10	11	11	31	1	2	1	227	32	6	7	4.0	.977	C-66
1946		88	.236	.314	271	64	11	5	0	0.0	29	17	17	44	1	0	0	486	47	5	11	6.2	.991	C-87
1947		135	.249	.344	378	94	14	5	4	1.1	38	42	41	49	3	1	0	566	54	7	14	4.7	.989	C-133
1948		144	.248	.407	472	117	21	6	14	3.0	60	61	48	74	6	3	0	637	76	7	17	5.1	.990	C-142
1949		152	.224	.338	468	105	19	5	8	1.7	54	55	49	89	1	0	0	651	73	7	16	4.8	.990	C-152
1950		131	.219	.383	415	91	16	5	14	3.4	53	58	42	52	1	0	0	656	64	5	14	5.6	.993	C-129
1951		133	.238	.346	416	99	17	5	6	1.4	60	43	38	72	0	2	0	597	66	6	8	5.2	.991	C-129
1952		112	.225	.324	333	75	17	2	4	1.2	39	41	29	47	0	3	0	498	53	7	7	5.2	.987	C-107
1953		112	.217	.348	299	65	10	1	9	3.0	37	37	25	41	1	0	0	399	42	11	3	4.3	.976	C-106
1954		139	.234	.374	423	99	12	7	11	2.6	56	40	34	48	0	2	0	661	49	4	9	5.2	.994	C-137
1955		116	.220	.339	304	67	5	2	9	3.0	30	40	34	33	0	2	0	583	34	2	12	5.6	.997	C-111
1956		122	.222	.340	315	70	15	2	6	1.9	42	34	49	54	1	3	1	648	28	10	2	5.8	.985	C-118
1957		58	.216	.345	148	32	7	0	4	2.7	14	15	16	23	0	0	0	287	14	0	4	5.2	1.000	C-58
1958	2 teams	DET A (45G –.192)	PHI N (25G –.220)																					
"	total	70	.201	.280	189	38	12	0	1	0.5	19	13	14	48	0	0	0	315	27	2	5	4.9	.994	C-70
1959	2 teams	PHI N (25G –.196)	SF N (21G –.133)																					
"	total	46	.173	.198	81	14	2	0	0	0.0	1	8	4	20	0	0	0	156	17	3	3	3.8	.983	C-46
1960	CHI N	24	.209	.372	43	9	2	1	1	2.3	4	5	1	10	0	2	0	76	9	2	2	4.0	.977	C-22
17 yrs.		1666	.228	.344	4772	1087	187	46	92	1.9	550	525	456	742	15	20	2	7506	695	86	136	5.1	.990	C-1629
WORLD SERIES																								
1948	CLE A	6	.211	.368	19	4	0	0	1	5.3	2	5	1	4	1	0	0	25	5	0	1	5.0	1.000	C-6
1954		4	.154	.231	13	2	1	0	0	0.0	1	0	1	1	0	0	0	27	3	0	0	7.5	1.000	C-4
2 yrs.		10	.188	.313	32	6	1	0	1	3.1	3	5	2	5	1	0	0	52	8	0	1	6.0	1.000	C-10

Mike Hegan

HEGAN, JAMES MICHAEL
Son of Jim Hegan.
B. July 21, 1942, Cleveland, Ohio.
BL TL 6′ 1″ 188 lbs.

Year	Team	Games	BA	SA	AB	H	2B	3B	HR	HR%	R	RBI	BB	SO	SB	Pinch Hit AB	Pinch Hit H	PO	A	E	DP	TC/G	FA	G by Pos
1964	NY A	5	.000	.000	5	0	0	0	0	0.0	0	0	1	2	0	1	0	17	4	0	2	10.5	1.000	1B-2
1966		13	.205	.256	39	8	0	1	0	0.0	7	2	7	11	1	0	0	103	8	1	6	8.6	.991	1B-13
1967		68	.136	.212	118	16	4	1	1	0.8	12	3	20	40	7	5	2	326	20	0	29	5.4	1.000	1B-54, OF-10
1969	SEA A	95	.292	.461	267	78	9	6	8	3.0	54	37	62	61	6	8	2	236	20	6	15	3.2	.977	OF-64, 1B-19
1970	MIL A	148	.244	.366	476	116	21	2	11	2.3	70	52	67	116	9	14	5	1104	113	7	104	8.3	.994	1B-139, OF-8

Mike Hegan *continued*

Year	Team	Games	BA	SA	AB	H	2B	3B	HR	HR%	R	RBI	BB	SO	SB	Pinch Hit AB	Pinch Hit H	PO	A	E	DP	TC/G	FA	G by Pos
1971	2 teams	**MIL A** (46G –.221) **OAK A** (65G –.236)																						
"	total	111	.226	.345	177	40	7	1	4	2.3	24	14	31	32	2	22	8	435	45	1	34	5.1	.998	1B-92, OF-2
1972	OAK A	98	.329	.430	79	26	3	1	1	1.3	13	5	7	20	1	31	7	170	11	0	22	2.7	1.000	1B-64, OF-3
1973	2 teams	**OAK A** (75G –.183) **NY A** (37G –.275)																						
"	total	112	.243	.391	202	49	5	2	7	3.5	20	19	12	51	0	20	2	512	31	5	38	5.5	.991	1B-93, OF-3, DH-3
1974	2 teams	**NY A** (18G –.226) **MIL A** (89G –.237)																						
"	total	107	.235	.391	243	57	9	1	9	3.7	24	41	38	43	1	18	4	273	13	1	21	3.3	.997	DH-37, 1B-34, OF-17
1975	MIL A	93	.251	.379	203	51	11	0	5	2.5	19	22	31	42	1	18	4	241	21	2	19	3.6	.992	OF-42, 1B-27, DH-5
1976		80	.248	.362	218	54	4	3	5	2.3	30	31	25	54	0	10	1	88	6	2	8	1.4	.979	DH-40, OF-20, 1B-10
1977		35	.170	.283	53	9	0	0	2	3.8	8	3	10	17	0	16	1	48	4	1	3	2.5	.981	OF-8, DH-7, 1B-6
12 yrs.		965	.242	.371	2080	504	73	18	53	2.5	281	229	311	489	28	163	36	3553	296	26	301	4.7	.993	1B-553, OF-177, DH-92
LEAGUE CHAMPIONSHIP SERIES																								
1971	OAK A	1	.000	.000	1	0	0	0	0	0.0	0	0	0	1	0	1	0	0	0	0	0	0.0	—	
1972		3	.000	.000	1	0	0	0	0	0.0	1	0	0	0	0	1	0	1	0	0	0	1.0	1.000	1B-1
2 yrs.		4	.000	.000	2	0	0	0	0	0.0	1	0	0	1	0	2	0	1	0	0	0	1.0	1.000	1B-1
WORLD SERIES																								
1964	NY A	3	.000	.000	1	0	0	0	0	0.0	1	0	1	1	0	1	0	0	0	0	0	0.0	—	
1972	OAK A	6	.200	.200	5	1	0	0	0	0.0	0	0	0	2	0	1	0	11	1	0	1	2.4	1.000	1B-5
2 yrs.		9	.167	.167	6	1	0	0	0	0.0	1	0	1	3	0	2	0	11	1	0	1	2.4	1.000	1B-5

Bob Hegman

HEGMAN, ROBERT HILMER BR TR 6′ 1″ 180 lbs.
B. Feb. 26, 1958, Springfield, Minn.

Year	Team	Games	BA	SA	AB	H	2B	3B	HR	HR%	R	RBI	BB	SO	SB	Pinch Hit AB	Pinch Hit H	PO	A	E	DP	TC/G	FA	G by Pos
1985	KC A	1	—	—	0	0	0	0	0	—	0	0	0	0	0	0	0	0	0	0	0	0.0	.000	2B-1

Jack Heidemann

HEIDEMANN, JACK SEALE BR TR 6′ 175 lbs.
B. July 11, 1949, Brenham, Tex.

Year	Team	Games	BA	SA	AB	H	2B	3B	HR	HR%	R	RBI	BB	SO	SB	Pinch Hit AB	Pinch Hit H	PO	A	E	DP	TC/G	FA	G by Pos
1969	CLE A	3	.000	.000	3	0	0	0	0	0.0	0	0	0	2	0	0	0	1	5	0	0	2.0	1.000	SS-3
1970		133	.211	.292	445	94	14	2	6	1.3	44	37	34	88	2	1	0	216	354	23	79	4.5	.961	SS-132
1971		81	.208	.237	240	50	7	0	0	0.0	16	9	12	46	1	0	0	113	188	7	34	3.8	.977	SS-81
1972		10	.150	.150	20	3	0	0	0	0.0	0	0	2	3	0	0	0	10	17	1	3	2.8	.964	SS-10
1974	2 teams	**CLE A** (12G –.091) **STL N** (47G –.271)																						
"	total	59	.247	.259	81	20	1	0	0	0.0	10	3	5	12	0	5	0	47	52	3	9	1.8	.971	SS-49, 3B-7, 1B-1, 2B-1
1975	NY N	61	.214	.290	145	31	4	2	1	0.7	12	16	17	28	1	18	1	72	89	10	14	3.5	.942	SS-44, 3B-4, 2B-1
1976	2 teams	**NY N** (5G –.083) **MIL A** (69G –.219)																						
"	total	74	.209	.253	158	33	1	0	2	1.3	11	10	7	24	1	6	0	79	96	3	22	2.6	.983	3B-40, 2B-25, SS-3, DH-1
1977	MIL A	5	.000	.000	1	0	0	0	0	0.0	1	0	1	0	0	1	0	2	1	0	1	0.8	1.000	DH-3, 2B-1
8 yrs.		426	.211	.268	1093	231	27	4	9	0.8	94	75	78	203	5	31	1	540	802	47	162	3.4	.966	SS-322, 3B-51, 2B-28, DH-4, 1B-1

Emmett Heidrick

HEIDRICK, R. EMMETT (Snags) BL TR 6′ 185 lbs.
B. July 29, 1876, Queenstown, Pa. D. Jan. 20, 1916, Clarion, Pa.

Year	Team	Games	BA	SA	AB	H	2B	3B	HR	HR%	R	RBI	BB	SO	SB	Pinch Hit AB	Pinch Hit H	PO	A	E	DP	TC/G	FA	G by Pos
1898	CLE N	19	.303	.382	76	23	2	2	0	0.0	10	8	3		3	0	0	29	5	6	1	2.1	.850	OF-19
1899	STL N	146	.328	.421	591	194	21	14	2	0.3	109	82	34		55	1	1	211	34	20	6	1.8	.925	OF-145
1900		85	.301	.383	339	102	6	8	2	0.6	51	45	18		22	2	0	215	21	10	4	3.0	.959	OF-83
1901		118	.339	.470	502	170	24	12	6	1.2	94	67	21		32	0	0	258	15	16	2	2.4	.945	OF-118
1902	STL A	110	.289	.396	447	129	19	10	3	0.7	75	56	34		17	0	0	268	16	21	4	2.7	.931	OF-109, SS-1, 3B-1, P-1
1903		120	.280	.395	461	129	20	15	1	0.2	55	42	19		19	1	0	252	17	13	5	2.3	.954	OF-119, C-1
1904		133	.273	.342	538	147	14	10	1	0.2	66	36	16		35	3	0	291	22	12	6	2.5	.963	OF-130
1908		26	.215	.312	93	20	2	2	1	1.1	8	6	1		3	1	0	42	3	2	1	1.9	.957	OF-25
8 yrs.		757	.300	.399	3047	914	108	73	16	0.5	468	342	146		186	8	1	1566	133	100	29	2.4	.944	OF-748, SS-1, 3B-1, C-1, P-1

Chink Heileman

HEILEMAN, JOHN GEORGE BR TR 5′ 8″ 155 lbs.
B. Aug. 10, 1872, Cincinnati, Ohio D. July 19, 1940, Cincinnati, Ohio.

Year	Team	Games	BA	SA	AB	H	2B	3B	HR	HR%	R	RBI	BB	SO	SB	Pinch Hit AB	Pinch Hit H	PO	A	E	DP	TC/G	FA	G by Pos
1901	CIN N	5	.133	.200	15	2	1	0	0	0.0	1	1	0		0	0	0	4	5	4	2	2.6	.692	3B-4, 2B-1

Harry Heilmann

HEILMANN, HARRY EDWIN (Slug) BR TR 6′ 1″ 195 lbs.
B. Aug. 3, 1894, San Francisco, Calif. D. July 9, 1951, Southfield, Mich.
Hall of Fame 1952.

Year	Team	Games	BA	SA	AB	H	2B	3B	HR	HR%	R	RBI	BB	SO	SB	Pinch Hit AB	Pinch Hit H	PO	A	E	DP	TC/G	FA	G by Pos
1914	DET A	67	.225	.313	182	41	8	1	2	1.1	25	22	22	29	1	11	3	209	31	11	11	4.9	.956	OF-29, 1B-16, 2B-6
1916		136	.282	.410	451	127	30	11	2	0.4	57	76	42	40	9	16	5	433	47	13	16	4.3	.974	OF-77, 1B-30, 2B-9
1917		150	.281	.387	556	156	22	11	5	0.9	57	86	41	54	11	0	0	466	40	13	13	3.5	.975	OF-123, 1B-27
1918		79	.276	.406	286	79	10	6	5	1.7	34	44	35	10	13	1	1	427	28	8	13	5.9	.983	OF-40, 1B-37, 2B-2
1919		140	.320	.477	537	172	30	15	8	1.5	74	95	37	41	7	0	0	1402	78	31	61	10.8	.979	1B-140
1920		145	.309	.429	543	168	28	5	9	1.7	66	89	39	32	3	1	0	1234	86	19	52	9.4	.986	1B-122, OF-21
1921		149	**.394**	.606	602	**237**	43	14	19	3.2	114	139	53	37	2	1	1	257	13	11	2	1.9	.961	OF-143, 1B-4
1922		118	.356	.598	455	162	27	10	21	4.6	92	92	58	28	8	0	0	200	11	10	3	1.8	.955	OF-115, 1B-5
1923		144	**.403**	.632	524	211	44	11	18	3.4	121	115	74	40	8	1	1	373	21	13	7	2.9	.968	OF-130, 1B-12
1924		153	.346	.533	570	197	**45**	16	10	1.8	107	113	78	41	13	2	0	317	35	10	10	2.4	.972	OF-147, 1B-4
1925		150	**.393**	.569	573	225	40	11	13	2.3	97	133	67	27	6	2	1	278	9	9	1	2.0	.970	OF-148
1926		141	.367	.534	502	184	41	8	9	1.8	90	103	67	19	6	6	1	228	18	7	4	1.9	.972	OF-134
1927		141	**.398**	.616	505	201	50	9	14	2.8	106	120	72	16	11	5	1	218	11	8	5	1.8	.966	OF-135
1928		151	.328	.507	558	183	38	10	14	2.5	83	107	57	45	7	1	0	449	34	9	22	3.3	.982	OF-126, 1B-25
1929		125	.344	.565	453	156	41	7	15	3.3	86	120	50	39	5	7	1	193	8	7	3	1.8	.966	OF-113, 1B-1
1930	CIN N	142	.333	.577	459	153	43	6	19	4.1	79	91	64	50	2	12	5	457	30	19	22	4.0	.962	OF-106, 1B-19
1932		15	.258	.323	31	8	2	0	0	0.0	3	6	0	2	0	9	3	49	3	1	2	8.8	.981	1B-6
17 yrs.		2146	.342	.520	7787	2660	542	151	183	2.4	1291	1551	856	550	112	75	23	7190	503	199	247	3.8	.975	OF-1587, 1B-448, 2B-17

Val Heim

HEIM, VAL RAYMOND BL TR 5′11″ 170 lbs.
B. Nov. 4, 1920, Plymouth, Wis.

Year	Team	Games	BA	SA	AB	H	2B	3B	HR	HR%	R	RBI	BB	SO	SB	Pinch Hit AB	Pinch Hit H	PO	A	E	DP	TC/G	FA	G by Pos
1942	CHI A	13	.200	.267	45	9	1	1	0	0.0	6	7	5	3	1	1	0	23	0	1	0	2.0	.958	OF-12

Fred Heimach

HEIMACH, FREDERICK AMOS (Lefty)
B. Jan. 27, 1901, Camden, N. J. D. June 1, 1973, Fort Myers, Fla.
BL TL 6′ 175 lbs.

Year	Team	Games	BA	SA	AB	H	2B	3B	HR	HR%	R	RBI	BB	SO	SB	Pinch Hit AB	Pinch Hit H	PO	A	E	DP	TC/G	FA	G by Pos
1920	PHI A	1	.000	.000	1	0	0	0	0	0.0	0	0	0	0	0	0	0	1	5	0	0	6.0	1.000	P-1
1921		1	.250	.250	4	1	0	0	0	0.0	0	1	0	1	0	0	0	1	5	0	0	6.0	1.000	P-1
1922		37	.250	.333	60	15	3	1	0	0.0	6	7	5	12	1	0	0	7	46	3	4	1.5	.946	P-37
1923		63	.254	.331	118	30	4	1	1	0.8	14	11	4	18	0	12	4	69	56	6	3	2.8	.954	P-40, 1B-6
1924		58	.322	.400	90	29	3	2	0	0.0	14	12	3	8	1	16	7	11	57	2	1	1.8	.971	P-40
1925		15	.167	.167	6	1	0	0	0	0.0	3	0	0	2	0	1	0	1	6	0	1	0.7	1.000	P-10
1926	2 teams	PHI A (14G –.100) BOS A (26G –.295)																						
″	total	40	.259	.278	54	14	1	0	0	0.0	2	4	3	13	0	6	4	8	58	4	3	2.1	.943	P-33
1928	NY A	18	.167	.167	30	5	0	0	0	0.0	2	2	2	6	0	5	1	0	16	0	2	1.2	1.000	P-13
1929		36	.184	.286	49	9	2	0	1	2.0	5	2	3	12	0	0	0	6	37	0	1	1.2	1.000	P-35
1930	BKN N	13	.250	.250	4	1	0	0	0	0.0	0	0	0	1	0	4	1	0	3	0	1	0.3	1.000	P-9
1931		39	.197	.230	61	12	0	1	0	0.0	3	5	4	7	0	7	3	8	44	0	3	1.7	1.000	P-31
1932		37	.164	.255	55	9	2	0	1	1.8	9	4	4	18	0	1	0	10	41	0	1	1.4	1.000	P-36
1933		10	.200	.200	10	2	0	0	0	0.0	0	1	0	0	0	0	0	0	6	0	1	0.6	1.000	P-10
13 yrs.		368	.236	.299	542	128	15	5	3	0.6	58	49	28	98	2	52	20	122	380	15	21	1.7	.971	P-296, 1B-6

Bud Heine

HEINE, WILLIAM HENRY
B. Sept. 22, 1900, Elmira, N. Y. D. Sept. 2, 1976, Ft. Lauderdale, Fla.
BL TR 5′ 8″ 145 lbs.

Year	Team	Games	BA	SA	AB	H	2B	3B	HR	HR%	R	RBI	BB	SO	SB	Pinch Hit AB	Pinch Hit H	PO	A	E	DP	TC/G	FA	G by Pos
1921	NY N	1	.000	.000	2	0	0	0	0	0.0	0	0	0	0	0	0	0	1	2	0	0	3.0	1.000	2B-1

Tom Heintzelman

HEINTZELMAN, THOMAS KENNETH
Son of Ken Heintzelman.
B. Nov. 3, 1946, St. Charles, Mo.
BR TR 6′ 1″ 180 lbs.

Year	Team	Games	BA	SA	AB	H	2B	3B	HR	HR%	R	RBI	BB	SO	SB	Pinch Hit AB	Pinch Hit H	PO	A	E	DP	TC/G	FA	G by Pos
1973	STL N	23	.310	.310	29	9	0	0	0	0.0	5	0	3	3	0	15	4	8	13	0	3	3.5	1.000	2B-6
1974		38	.230	.324	74	17	4	0	1	1.4	10	6	9	14	0	7	1	41	56	2	12	3.2	.980	2B-28, 3B-2, SS-1
1977	SF N	2	.000	.000	2	0	0	0	0	0.0	0	0	0	0	0	2	0	0	0	0	0	0.0	—	
1978		27	.229	.429	35	8	1	0	2	5.7	2	6	2	5	0	19	4	5	19	0	1	2.4	1.000	2B-5, 3B-3, 1B-2
4 yrs.		90	.243	.343	140	34	5	0	3	2.1	17	12	14	22	0	43	9	54	88	2	16	3.1	.986	2B-39, 3B-5, 1B-2, SS-1

John Heinzman

HEINZMAN, JOHN PETER
B. Sept. 27, 1863, New Albany, Ind. D. Nov. 10, 1914, Louisville, Ky.
BR TR

Year	Team	Games	BA	SA	AB	H	2B	3B	HR	HR%	R	RBI	BB	SO	SB	Pinch Hit AB	Pinch Hit H	PO	A	E	DP	TC/G	FA	G by Pos
1886	LOU AA	1	.000	.000	5	0	0	0	0	0.0	1		0			0	0	7	0	0	0	7.0	1.000	1B-1

Bob Heise

HEISE, ROBERT LOWELL
B. May 12, 1947, San Antonio, Tex.
BR TR 6′ 175 lbs.

Year	Team	Games	BA	SA	AB	H	2B	3B	HR	HR%	R	RBI	BB	SO	SB	Pinch Hit AB	Pinch Hit H	PO	A	E	DP	TC/G	FA	G by Pos
1967	NY N	16	.323	.387	62	20	4	0	0	0.0	7	3	3	1	0	0	0	46	43	3	6	5.4	.967	2B-12, SS-3, 3B-2
1968		6	.217	.217	23	5	0	0	0	0.0	3	1	1	1	0	0	0	6	8	1	5	2.1	.933	SS-6, 2B-1
1969		4	.300	.400	10	3	1	0	0	0.0	1	0	3	2	0	1	1	4	5	0	0	3.0	1.000	SS-3
1970	SF N	67	.234	.299	154	36	5	1	1	0.6	15	22	5	13	0	7	2	78	124	13	24	3.4	.940	SS-33, 2B-28, 3B-2
1971	2 teams	SF N (13G –.000) MIL A (68G –.254)																						
″	total	81	.240	.275	200	48	7	0	0	0.0	12	7	7	16	1	10	1	100	163	11	40	3.8	.960	SS-54, 3B-13, 2B-4, OF-1
1972	MIL A	95	.266	.310	271	72	10	1	0	0.0	23	12	12	14	1	18	5	125	170	6	31	3.7	.980	2B-49, 3B-24, SS-9
1973		49	.204	.224	98	20	2	0	0	0.0	8	4	4	4	1	0	0	50	79	5	9	2.9	.963	SS-29, 3B-9, 1B-4, 2B-4
1974	2 teams	STL N (3G –.143) CAL A (29G –.267)																						
″	total	32	.256	.341	82	21	7	0	0	0.0	7	6	5	10	0	2	0	44	63	0	15	3.7	1.000	2B-20, 3B-6, SS-3
1975	BOS A	63	.214	.238	126	27	3	0	0	0.0	12	21	4	6	0	2	0	52	106	10	12	2.6	.940	3B-45, 2B-14, SS-4, 1B-1
1976		32	.268	.304	56	15	2	0	0	0.0	5	5	1	2	0	0	0	27	43	5	7	2.3	.933	3B-22, SS-9, 2B-1
1977	KC A	54	.258	.323	62	16	2	1	0	0.0	11	5	2	8	0	1	0	42	67	6	19	2.1	.948	2B-21, SS-21, 3B-12, 1B-1
11 yrs.		499	.247	.293	1144	283	43	3	1	0.1	104	86	47	77	3	41	9	574	871	60	168	3.2	.960	SS-174, 2B-154, 3B-135, 1B-6, OF-1

Al Heist

HEIST, ALFRED MICHAEL
B. Oct. 5, 1927, Brooklyn, N. Y.
BR TR 6′ 2″ 185 lbs.

Year	Team	Games	BA	SA	AB	H	2B	3B	HR	HR%	R	RBI	BB	SO	SB	Pinch Hit AB	Pinch Hit H	PO	A	E	DP	TC/G	FA	G by Pos
1960	CHI N	41	.275	.412	102	28	5	3	1	1.0	11	6	10	12	3	10	2	65	2	1	0	2.1	.985	OF-33
1961		109	.255	.383	321	82	14	3	7	2.2	48	37	39	51	3	8	1	211	9	5	0	2.3	.978	OF-99
1962	HOU N	27	.222	.236	72	16	1	0	0	0.0	4	3	3	9	0	4	0	36	1	1	0	1.7	.974	OF-23
3 yrs.		177	.255	.368	495	126	20	6	8	1.6	63	46	52	72	6	22	3	312	12	7	0	2.1	.979	OF-155

Heinie Heitmuller

HEITMULLER, WILLIAM FREDERICK
B. May 23, 1883, San Francisco, Calif. D. Oct. 8, 1912, Los Angeles, Calif.
BR TR 6′ 2″ 215 lbs.

Year	Team	Games	BA	SA	AB	H	2B	3B	HR	HR%	R	RBI	BB	SO	SB	Pinch Hit AB	Pinch Hit H	PO	A	E	DP	TC/G	FA	G by Pos
1909	PHI A	64	.286	.405	210	60	9	8	0	0.0	36	15	18		7	4	2	111	4	9	2	2.1	.927	OF-60
1910		31	.243	.297	111	27	2	2	0	0.0	11	7	7		6	3	1	49	2	1	2	1.9	.981	OF-28
2 yrs.		95	.271	.368	321	87	11	10	0	0.0	47	22	25		13	7	3	160	6	10	4	2.0	.943	OF-88

Woodie Held

HELD, WOODSON GEORGE
B. Mar. 25, 1932, Sacramento, Calif.
BR TR 5′10½″ 167 lbs.

Year	Team	Games	BA	SA	AB	H	2B	3B	HR	HR%	R	RBI	BB	SO	SB	Pinch Hit AB	Pinch Hit H	PO	A	E	DP	TC/G	FA	G by Pos
1954	NY A	4	.000	.000	3	0	0	0	0	0.0	2	0	2	1	0	0	0	2	3	0	1	1.0	1.000	SS-4, 3B-1
1957	2 teams	NY A (1G –.000) KC A (92G –.239)																						
″	total	93	.239	.483	327	78	14	3	20	6.1	48	50	37	81	4	1	0	266	12	1	2	3.0	.996	OF-92
1958	2 teams	KC A (47G –.214) CLE A (67G –.194)																						
″	total	114	.204	.309	275	56	6	1	7	2.5	25	33	25	64	1	11	1	178	55	7	7	2.2	.971	OF-84, SS-15, 3B-8
1959	CLE A	143	.251	.465	525	132	19	3	29	5.5	82	71	47	118	1	1	0	217	365	20	51	4.0	.967	SS-103, 3B-40, OF-6, 2B-3
1960		109	.258	.471	376	97	15	1	21	5.6	45	67	44	73	0	0	0	208	345	19	87	5.2	.967	SS-109
1961		146	.267	.468	509	136	23	5	23	4.5	67	78	69	111	0	2	1	258	393	27	90	4.7	.960	SS-144
1962		139	.249	.406	466	116	12	2	19	4.1	55	58	73	107	5	3	1	227	377	27	102	4.5	.957	SS-133, 3B-5, OF-1
1963		133	.248	.435	416	103	19	4	17	4.1	61	61	61	96	2	9	2	243	260	13	53	3.7	.975	2B-96, OF-35, SS-5, 3B-3
1964		118	.236	.420	364	86	13	0	18	4.9	50	49	43	88	1	8	0	183	182	14	40	3.1	.963	2B-52, OF-41, 3B-30
1965	WAS A	122	.247	.452	332	82	16	2	16	4.8	46	54	49	74	0	15	2	183	15	8	5	1.8	.961	OF-106, 3B-5, 2B-4, SS-2
1966	BAL A	56	.207	.305	82	17	3	1	1	1.2	6	7	12	30	0	34	6	23	18	2	1	2.0	.953	OF-10, 2B-5, SS-3, 3B-3
1967	2 teams	BAL A (26G –.146) CAL A (58G –.220)																						
″	total	84	.203	.319	182	37	6	0	5	2.7	19	23	24	53	0	22	1	66	92	4	17	2.4	.975	3B-24, OF-19, SS-13, 2B-12

Woodie Held *continued*

Year	Team	Games	BA	SA	AB	H	2B	3B	HR	HR%	R	RBI	BB	SO	SB	Pinch Hit AB	Pinch Hit H	PO	A	E	DP	TC/G	FA	G by Pos
1968	**2 teams**	**CAL A** (33G –.111) **CHI A** (40G –.167)																						
″	**total**	73	.141	.162	99	14	2	0	0	0.0	9	2	10	29	0	22	3	46	24	2	3	1.3	.972	OF-36, 3B-10, 2B-6, SS-5
1969	**CHI A**	56	.143	.317	63	9	2	0	3	4.8	9	6	13	19	0	19	2	23	15	0	1	1.5	1.000	OF-18, SS-3, 3B-3, 2B-1
14 yrs.		1390	.240	.421	4019	963	150	22	179	4.5	524	559	509	944	14	147	19	2123	2156	144	460	3.4	.967	SS-539, OF-448, 2B-179, 3B-132

Hank Helf

HELF, HENRY HARTZ BR TR 6′ 1″ 196 lbs.
B. Aug. 26, 1913, Austin, Tex. D. Oct. 27, 1984, Austin, Tex.

Year	Team	Games	BA	SA	AB	H	2B	3B	HR	HR%	R	RBI	BB	SO	SB	Pinch Hit AB	Pinch Hit H	PO	A	E	DP	TC/G	FA	G by Pos
1938	**CLE A**	6	.077	.077	13	1	0	0	0	0.0	1	1	1	1	0	1	0	13	5	1	1	3.8	.947	C-5
1940		1	.000	.000	1	0	0	0	0	0.0	0	0	0	0	0	0	0	1	0	0	0	1.0	1.000	C-1
1946	**STL A**	71	.192	.352	182	35	11	0	6	3.3	17	21	9	40	0	1	0	251	51	11	7	4.5	.965	C-69
3 yrs.		78	.184	.332	196	36	11	0	6	3.1	18	22	10	41	0	2	0	265	56	12	8	4.4	.964	C-75

Eric Helfand

HELFAND, ERIC JAMES BL TR 6′ 195 lbs.
B. Mar. 25, 1969, Erie, Pa.

Year	Team	Games	BA	SA	AB	H	2B	3B	HR	HR%	R	RBI	BB	SO	SB	Pinch Hit AB	Pinch Hit H	PO	A	E	DP	TC/G	FA	G by Pos
1993	**OAK A**	8	.231	.231	13	3	0	0	0	0.0	1	1	0	1	0	3	1	25	5	0	1	6.0	1.000	C-5
1994		7	.167	.167	6	1	0	0	0	0.0	1	1	0	1	0	3	0	12	2	0	0	2.3	1.000	C-6
1995		38	.163	.209	86	14	2	1	0	0.0	9	7	11	25	0	5	0	167	13	1	3	5.0	.994	C-36
3 yrs.		53	.171	.210	105	18	2	1	0	0.0	11	9	11	27	0	11	1	204	20	1	4	4.8	.996	C-47

Ty Helfrich

HELFRICH, EMORY WILBUR BR TR 5′10″ 178 lbs.
B. Oct. 9, 1890, Pleasantville, N. J. D. Mar. 18, 1955, Pleasantville, N. J.

Year	Team	Games	BA	SA	AB	H	2B	3B	HR	HR%	R	RBI	BB	SO	SB	Pinch Hit AB	Pinch Hit H	PO	A	E	DP	TC/G	FA	G by Pos
1915	**BKN F**	43	.240	.298	104	25	6	0	0	0.0	12	5	15		2	5	0	45	81	12	4	3.9	.913	2B-34, OF-1

Tony Hellman

HELLMAN, ANTHONY JOSEPH
B. May 29, 1861, Cincinnati, Ohio D. Mar. 29, 1898, Cincinnati, Ohio.

Year	Team	Games	BA	SA	AB	H	2B	3B	HR	HR%	R	RBI	BB	SO	SB	Pinch Hit AB	Pinch Hit H	PO	A	E	DP	TC/G	FA	G by Pos
1886	**BAL AA**	1	.000	.000	3	0	0	0	0	0.0	0		0			0	0	10	2	0	0	12.0	1.000	C-1

Tommy Helms

HELMS, TOMMY VANN BR TR 5′10″ 165 lbs.
B. May 5, 1941, Charlotte, N. C.
Manager 1988–89.

Year	Team	Games	BA	SA	AB	H	2B	3B	HR	HR%	R	RBI	BB	SO	SB	Pinch Hit AB	Pinch Hit H	PO	A	E	DP	TC/G	FA	G by Pos
1964	**CIN N**	2	.000	.000	1	0	0	0	0	0.0	0	0	0	1	0	0	0	0	0	0	0	0.0	—	
1965		21	.381	.524	42	16	2	2	0	0.0	4	6	3	7	1	10	3	17	22	1	6	3.6	.975	SS-8, 3B-2, 2B-1
1966		138	.284	.380	542	154	23	1	9	1.7	72	49	24	31	3	5	3	155	258	13	25	3.2	.969	3B-113, 2B-20
1967		137	.274	.356	497	136	27	4	2	0.4	40	35	24	41	5	3	1	264	347	21	75	4.7	.967	2B-88, SS-46
1968		127	.288	.363	507	146	28	2	2	0.4	35	47	12	27	5	0	0	322	372	15	82	5.5	.979	2B-127, SS-2, 3B-1
1969		126	.269	.317	480	129	18	1	1	0.2	38	40	18	33	4	1	0	325	347	17	89	5.3	.975	2B-125, SS-4
1970		150	.237	.282	575	136	21	1	1	0.2	42	45	21	33	2	2	0	353	412	13	107	4.9	.983	2B-148, SS-12
1971		150	.258	.325	547	141	26	1	3	0.5	40	52	26	33	3	1	0	395	468	9	130	5.9	.990	2B-149
1972	**HOU N**	139	.259	.346	518	134	20	5	5	1.0	45	60	24	27	4	0	0	353	441	17	115	5.8	.979	2B-139
1973		146	.287	.368	543	156	28	2	4	0.7	44	61	32	21	1	0	0	325	438	9	104	5.3	.988	2B-145
1974		137	.279	.363	452	126	21	1	5	1.1	32	50	23	27	5	6	1	308	360	10	99	5.1	.985	2B-133
1975		64	.207	.222	135	28	2	0	0	0.0	7	14	10	8	0	27	9	58	109	2	19	3.7	.988	2B-42, 3B-3, SS-1
1976	**PIT N**	62	.276	.391	87	24	5	1	1	1.1	10	13	10	5	0	23	8	30	46	3	8	2.3	.962	3B-22, 2B-11, SS-1
1977	**2 teams**	**PIT N** (15G –.000) **BOS A** (21G –.271)																						
″	**total**	36	.225	.296	71	16	2	0	1	1.4	5	5	4	7	0	15	2	4	4	0	0	0.5	1.000	DH-13, 3B-2, 2B-1
14 yrs.		1435	.269	.342	4997	1342	223	21	34	0.7	414	477	231	301	33	93	27	2909	3624	130	859	4.9	.980	2B-1129, 3B-143, SS-74, DH-13
LEAGUE CHAMPIONSHIP SERIES																								
1970	**CIN N**	3	.273	.273	11	3	0	0	0	0.0	0	0	0	1	0	0	0	11	12	0	1	7.7	1.000	2B-3
WORLD SERIES																								
1970	**CIN N**	5	.222	.222	18	4	0	0	0	0.0	1	0	1	1	0	0	0	10	13	0	2	4.6	1.000	2B-5

Heinie Heltzel

HELTZEL, WILLIAM WADE BR TR 5′10″ 150 lbs.
B. Dec. 21, 1913, York, Pa.

Year	Team	Games	BA	SA	AB	H	2B	3B	HR	HR%	R	RBI	BB	SO	SB	Pinch Hit AB	Pinch Hit H	PO	A	E	DP	TC/G	FA	G by Pos
1943	**BOS N**	29	.151	.186	86	13	3	0	0	0.0	6	5	7	13	0	0	0	18	48	9	3	2.6	.880	3B-29
1944	**PHI N**	11	.182	.227	22	4	1	0	0	0.0	1	0	2	3	0	0	0	17	17	3	1	3.7	.919	SS-10
2 yrs.		40	.157	.194	108	17	4	0	0	0.0	7	5	9	16	0	0	0	35	65	12	4	2.9	.893	3B-29, SS-10

Ed Hemingway

HEMINGWAY, EDSON MARSHALL BB TR 5′11½″ 165 lbs.
B. May 8, 1893, Sheridan, Mich. D. July 5, 1969, Grand Rapids, Mich.

Year	Team	Games	BA	SA	AB	H	2B	3B	HR	HR%	R	RBI	BB	SO	SB	Pinch Hit AB	Pinch Hit H	PO	A	E	DP	TC/G	FA	G by Pos
1914	**STL A**	3	.000	.000	5	0	0	0	0	0.0	0	0	1	1	1	0	0	4	2	0	0	2.0	1.000	3B-3
1917	**NY N**	7	.320	.440	25	8	1	1	0	0.0	3	1	2	1	2	0	0	8	15	1	2	3.4	.958	3B-7
1918	**PHI N**	33	.213	.269	108	23	4	1	0	0.0	7	12	7	9	4	0	0	69	95	8	9	5.5	.953	2B-27, 3B-3, 1B-1
3 yrs.		43	.225	.290	138	31	5	2	0	0.0	10	13	10	11	7	0	0	81	112	9	11	4.9	.955	2B-27, 3B-13, 1B-1

Scott Hemond

HEMOND, SCOTT MATHEW BR TR 6′ 205 lbs.
B. Nov. 18, 1965, Taunton, Mass.

Year	Team	Games	BA	SA	AB	H	2B	3B	HR	HR%	R	RBI	BB	SO	SB	Pinch Hit AB	Pinch Hit H	PO	A	E	DP	TC/G	FA	G by Pos
1989	**OAK A**	4	—	—	0	0	0	0	0	—	2	0	0	0	0	0	0	0	0	0	0	0.0	—	
1990		7	.154	.154	13	2	0	0	0	0.0	0	1	0	5	0	0	0	2	5	0	0	0.9	1.000	3B-7, 2B-1
1991		23	.217	.217	23	5	0	0	0	0.0	4	0	1	7	1	0	0	27	14	1	3	1.9	.976	C-8, 2B-7, DH-4, 3B-2, SS-1
1992	**2 teams**	**OAK A** (17G –.222) **CHI A** (8G –.231)																						
″	**total**	25	.225	.275	40	9	2	0	0	0.0	8	2	4	13	1	3	1	34	6	1	0	1.7	.976	C-9, DH-5, OF-4, SS-3, 3B-3
1993	**OAK A**	91	.256	.414	215	55	16	0	6	2.8	31	26	32	55	14	3	1	404	39	4	6	5.2	.991	C-75, OF-6, DH-3, 2B-1, 1B-1
1994		91	.222	.323	198	44	11	0	3	1.5	23	20	16	51	7	4	0	245	93	6	17	4.0	.983	C-39, 2B-25, 3B-12, 1B-7, OF-2, DH-2
1995	**STL N**	57	.144	.229	118	17	1	0	3	2.5	11	9	12	31	0	15	1	189	22	3	1	4.9	.986	C-38, 2B-6
7 yrs.		298	.217	.326	607	132	30	0	12	2.0	79	58	65	162	23	25	3	901	179	15	27	4.0	.986	C-169, 2B-40, 3B-24, DH-14, OF-12, 1B-8, SS-4

Ducky Hemp

HEMP, WILLIAM H.
B. Dec. 27, 1867, St. Louis, Mo. D. Mar. 6, 1923, St. Louis, Mo.

Year	Team	Games	BA	SA	AB	H	2B	3B	HR	HR%	R	RBI	BB	SO	SB	Pinch Hit AB	Pinch Hit H	PO	A	E	DP	TC/G	FA	G by Pos
1887	LOU AA	1	.333	.667	3	1	1	0	0	0.0	1		1		0	0	0	0	0	1	0	1.0	.000	OF-1
1890	2 teams PIT N (21G –.235) SYR AA (9G –.152)																							
"	total	30	.211	.254	114	24	1	2	0	0.0	10	4	8	12	4	0	0	48	9	7	5	2.1	.891	OF-30
2 yrs.		31	.214	.265	117	25	2	2	0	0.0	11	4	9	12	4	0	0	48	9	8	5	2.1	.877	OF-31

Charlie Hemphill

HEMPHILL, CHARLES JUDSON (Eagle Eye) BL TL 5′ 9″ 160 lbs.
Brother of Frank Hemphill.
B. Apr. 20, 1876, Greenville, Mich. D. June 22, 1953, Detroit, Mich.

Year	Team	Games	BA	SA	AB	H	2B	3B	HR	HR%	R	RBI	BB	SO	SB	Pinch Hit AB	Pinch Hit H	PO	A	E	DP	TC/G	FA	G by Pos
1899	2 teams STL N (11G –.243) CLE N (55G –.277)																							
"	total	66	.272	.364	239	65	3	5	3	1.3	27	26	12		3	1	1	74	8	16	2	1.5	.837	OF-64
1901	BOS A	136	.261	.332	545	142	10	10	3	0.6	71	62	39		11	0	0	188	22	17	4	1.7	.925	OF-136
1902	2 teams CLE A (25G –.266) STL A (103G –.317)																							
"	total	128	.308	.418	510	157	16	11	6	1.2	81	69	49		27	6	2	200	23	16	7	2.0	.933	OF-120, 2B-2
1903	STL A	105	.245	.300	383	94	6	3	3	0.8	36	29	23		16	1	0	155	17	7	4	1.7	.961	OF-104
1904		114	.256	.308	438	112	13	2	2	0.5	47	45	35		23	4	1	179	14	15	5	1.9	.928	OF-108, 2B-1
1906		154	.289	.383	585	169	19	12	4	0.7	90	62	43		33	0	0	304	17	13	1	2.2	.961	OF-154
1907		153	.259	.322	603	156	20	9	0	0.0	66	38	51		14	0	0	320	12	15	2	2.3	.957	OF-153
1908	NY A	142	.297	.356	505	150	12	9	0	0.0	62	44	59		42	0	0	285	13	20	2	2.2	.937	OF-142
1909		73	.243	.282	181	44	5	1	0	0.0	23	10	32		10	**24**	6	75	6	2	1	1.8	.976	OF-45
1910		102	.239	.288	351	84	9	4	0	0.0	45	21	55		19	4	1	159	10	5	2	1.9	.971	OF-94
1911		69	.284	.338	201	57	4	2	1	0.5	32	15	37		9	9	0	95	4	5	0	1.9	.952	OF-56
11 yrs.		1242	.271	.341	4541	1230	117	68	22	0.5	580	421	435		207	49	11	2034	146	131	30	2.0	.943	OF-1176, 2B-3

Frank Hemphill

HEMPHILL, FRANK VERNON BR TR 5′11″ 165 lbs.
Brother of Charlie Hemphill.
B. May 13, 1878, Greenville, Mich. D. Nov. 16, 1950, Chicago, Ill.

Year	Team	Games	BA	SA	AB	H	2B	3B	HR	HR%	R	RBI	BB	SO	SB	Pinch Hit AB	Pinch Hit H	PO	A	E	DP	TC/G	FA	G by Pos
1906	CHI A	13	.075	.075	40	3	0	0	0	0.0	0	2	9		1	0	0	31	1	1	0	2.5	.970	OF-13
1909	WAS A	1	.000	.000	3	0	0	0	0	0.0	0	0	0		0	0	0	2	0	0	0	2.0	1.000	OF-1
2 yrs.		14	.070	.070	43	3	0	0	0	0.0	0	2	9		1	0	0	33	1	1	0	2.5	.971	OF-14

Rollie Hemsley

HEMSLEY, RALSTON BURDETT BR TR 5′10″ 170 lbs.
B. June 24, 1907, Syracuse, Ohio D. July 31, 1972, Washington, D. C.

Year	Team	Games	BA	SA	AB	H	2B	3B	HR	HR%	R	RBI	BB	SO	SB	Pinch Hit AB	Pinch Hit H	PO	A	E	DP	TC/G	FA	G by Pos
1928	PIT N	50	.271	.331	133	36	2	3	0	0.0	14	18	4	10	1	1	0	127	24	6	4	3.2	.962	C-49
1929		88	.289	.404	235	68	13	7	0	0.0	31	37	11	22	1	6	0	240	48	14	7	3.8	.954	C-80
1930		104	.253	.367	324	82	19	6	2	0.6	45	45	22	21	3	5	1	325	50	8	11	3.9	.979	C-98
1931	2 teams PIT N (10G –.171) CHI N (66G –.309)																							
"	total	76	.289	.444	239	69	20	4	3	1.3	31	32	20	33	4	9	3	271	45	7	7	4.3	.978	C-75
1932	CHI N	60	.238	.424	151	36	10	3	4	2.6	27	20	10	16	2	8	3	174	18	5	3	4.1	.975	C-47, OF-1
1933	2 teams CIN N (49G –.190) STL A (32G –.242)																							
"	total	81	.213	.284	211	45	10	1	1	0.5	16	22	17	20	0	7	1	207	35	8	3	3.7	.968	C-68
1934	STL A	123	.309	.427	431	133	31	7	2	0.5	47	52	29	37	6	5	2	499	92	16	15	5.1	.974	C-114, OF-6
1935		144	.290	.381	504	146	32	7	0	0.0	57	48	44	41	3	6	1	510	105	13	10	4.5	.979	C-141
1936		116	.263	.353	377	99	24	2	2	0.5	43	39	46	30	2	8	2	340	68	13	16	3.7	.969	C-114
1937		100	.222	.302	334	74	12	3	3	0.9	30	28	25	29	0	3	2	338	71	13	13	4.4	.969	C-94, 1B-2
1938	CLE A	66	.296	.409	203	60	11	3	2	1.0	27	28	23	14	1	6	0	358	38	8	5	7.0	.980	C-58
1939		107	.263	.342	395	104	17	4	2	0.5	58	36	26	26	2	0	0	499	58	9	7	5.3	.984	C-106
1940		119	.267	.368	416	111	20	5	4	1.0	46	42	22	25	1	2	0	591	65	4	8	5.6	.994	C-117
1941		98	.240	.330	288	69	10	5	2	0.7	29	24	18	19	2	2	0	401	42	9	8	4.7	.980	C-96
1942	2 teams CIN N (36G –.113) NY A (31G –.294)																							
"	total	67	.190	.240	200	38	4	3	0	0.0	19	22	9	20	1	2	0	302	26	5	6	5.3	.985	C-63
1943	NY A	62	.239	.339	180	43	6	3	2	1.1	12	24	13	9	0	10	1	234	31	5	3	5.2	.981	C-52
1944		81	.268	.366	284	76	12	5	2	0.7	23	26	9	13	0	6	1	298	41	6	7	4.5	.983	C-76
1946	PHI N	49	.223	.266	139	31	4	1	0	0.0	7	11	9	10	0	3	1	170	42	5	10	4.8	.977	C-45
1947		2	.333	.333	3	1	0	0	0	0.0	0	1	0	0	0	0	0	3	0	0	0	1.5	1.000	C-2
19 yrs.		1593	.262	.360	5047	1321	257	72	31	0.6	562	555	357	395	29	89	18	5887	899	154	143	4.6	.978	C-1495, OF-7, 1B-2
WORLD SERIES																								
1932	CHI N	3	.000	.000	3	0	0	0	0	0.0	0	0	0	3	0	3	0	0	0	0	0	0.0	.000	C-1

Solly Hemus

HEMUS, SOLOMON JOSEPH BL TR 5′ 9″ 165 lbs.
B. Apr. 17, 1923, Phoenix, Ariz.
Manager 1959–61.

Year	Team	Games	BA	SA	AB	H	2B	3B	HR	HR%	R	RBI	BB	SO	SB	Pinch Hit AB	Pinch Hit H	PO	A	E	DP	TC/G	FA	G by Pos
1949	STL N	20	.333	.364	33	11	1	0	0	0.0	8	2	7	3	0	2	0	29	24	1	4	3.4	.981	2B-16
1950		11	.133	.200	15	2	1	0	0	0.0	1	0	2	4	0	5	0	2	8	0	1	2.0	1.000	3B-5
1951		128	.281	.381	420	118	18	9	2	0.5	68	32	75	31	7	4	0	221	376	21	86	5.3	.966	SS-105, 2B-12
1952		151	.268	.425	570	153	28	8	15	2.6	**105**	52	96	55	1	1	0	256	459	30	104	5.0	.960	SS-148, 3B-2
1953		154	.279	.443	585	163	32	11	14	2.4	110	61	86	40	2	2	1	257	477	27	90	5.0	.965	SS-150, 2B-3
1954		124	.304	.430	214	65	15	3	2	0.9	43	27	55	27	5	38	10	85	151	10	29	2.3	.959	SS-66, 3B-27, 2B-12
1955		96	.243	.383	206	50	10	2	5	2.4	36	21	27	22	1	37	4	56	91	5	10	1.8	.967	3B-43, 2B-40, SS-2
1956	2 teams STL N (8G –.200) PHI N (78G –.289)																							
"	total	86	.286	.458	192	55	10	4	5	2.6	25	26	29	21	1	33	9	95	95	5	18	3.9	.974	2B-49, 3B-1
1957	PHI N	70	.185	.259	108	20	6	1	0	0.0	8	5	20	8	1	33	2	51	45	2	10	4.1	.980	2B-24
1958		105	.284	.416	334	95	14	3	8	2.4	53	36	51	34	3	20	3	188	220	13	52	5.0	.969	2B-84, 3B-1
1959	STL N	24	.235	.353	17	4	2	0	0	0.0	2	1	8	2	0	14	2	0	5	0	0	2.5	1.000	3B-1, 2B-1
11 yrs.		969	.273	.411	2694	736	137	41	51	1.9	459	263	456	247	21	189	31	1240	1951	114	404	4.2	.966	SS-471, 2B-241, 3B-80

Dave Henderson

HENDERSON, DAVID LEE (Hendu) BR TR 6′ 2″ 210 lbs.
B. July 21, 1958, Merced, Calif.

Year	Team	Games	BA	SA	AB	H	2B	3B	HR	HR%	R	RBI	BB	SO	SB	Pinch Hit AB	Pinch Hit H	PO	A	E	DP	TC/G	FA	G by Pos
1981	SEA A	59	.167	.333	126	21	3	0	6	4.8	17	13	16	24	2	6	1	105	4	0	1	1.9	1.000	OF-58
1982		104	.253	.441	324	82	17	1	14	4.3	47	48	36	67	2	4	0	249	11	4	4	2.6	.985	OF-101
1983		137	.269	.444	484	130	24	5	17	3.5	50	55	28	93	9	4	1	304	17	6	4	2.4	.982	OF-133, DH-3
1984		112	.280	.466	350	98	23	0	14	4.0	42	43	19	56	5	5	1	242	11	3	5	2.4	.988	OF-97, DH-10
1985		139	.241	.388	502	121	28	2	14	2.8	70	68	48	104	6	2	1	335	8	5	3	2.5	.986	OF-138

Dave Henderson *continued*

Year	Team	Games	BA	SA	AB	H	2B	3B	HR	HR%	R	RBI	BB	SO	SB	Pinch Hit AB	Pinch Hit H	PO	A	E	DP	TC/G	FA	G by Pos
1986	2 teams	SEA A (103G –.276) BOS A (36G –.196)																						
"	total	139	.265	.459	388	103	22	4	15	3.9	59	47	39	110	2	8	2	231	11	5	1	1.8	.980	OF-112, DH-22
1987	2 teams	BOS A (75G –.234) SF N (15G –.238)																						
"	total	90	.234	.410	205	48	12	0	8	3.9	32	26	30	53	3	15	3	124	1	5	0	1.8	.962	OF-73
1988	OAK A	146	.304	.525	507	154	38	1	24	4.7	100	94	47	92	2	6	3	382	5	7	2	2.8	.982	OF-143
1989		152	.250	.380	579	145	24	3	15	2.6	77	80	54	131	8	4	0	385	5	9	1	2.6	.977	OF-149, DH-2
1990		127	.271	.467	450	122	28	0	20	4.4	65	63	40	105	3	7	1	319	5	4	1	2.7	.988	OF-116, DH-6
1991		150	.276	.465	572	158	33	0	25	4.4	86	85	58	113	6	7	0	362	10	1	2	2.5	.997	OF-140, DH-7, 2B-1
1992		20	.143	.159	63	9	1	0	0	0.0	1	2	2	16	0	6	0	19	0	1	0	1.3	.950	OF-12, DH-4
1993		107	.220	.427	382	84	19	0	20	5.2	37	53	32	113	0	8	1	205	7	2	4	2.1	.991	OF-76, DH-28
1994	KC A	56	.247	.404	198	49	14	1	5	2.5	27	31	16	28	2	3	1	72	4	3	0	1.4	.962	OF-40, DH-16
14 yrs.		1538	.258	.436	5130	1324	286	17	197	3.8	710	708	465	1105	50	85	15	3334	99	55	28	2.3	.984	OF-1388, DH-98, 2B-1
LEAGUE CHAMPIONSHIP SERIES																								
1986	BOS A	5	.111	.444	9	1	0	0	1	11.1	3	4	2	2	0	0	0	11	0	0	0	2.2	1.000	OF-5
1988	OAK A	4	.375	.625	16	6	1	0	1	6.3	2	4	1	7	0	0	0	11	0	2	0	3.3	.846	OF-4
1989		5	.263	.579	19	5	3	0	1	5.3	4	1	2	5	0	0	0	22	0	0	0	4.4	1.000	OF-5
1990		2	.167	.167	6	1	0	0	0	0.0	0	1	0	2	1	0	0	7	0	0	0	3.5	1.000	OF-2
4 yrs.		16	.260	.520	50	13	4	0	3	6.0	9	10	5	16	1	0	0	51	0	2	0	3.3	.962	OF-16
WORLD SERIES																								
1986	BOS A	7	.400	.760	25	10	1	1	2	8.0	6	5	2	6	0	0	0	22	0	0	0	3.1	1.000	OF-7
1988	OAK A	5	.300	.400	20	6	2	0	0	0.0	1	1	2	7	0	0	0	12	0	0	0	2.4	1.000	OF-5
1989		4	.308	.923	13	4	2	0	2	15.4	6	4	4	3	0	0	0	13	0	0	0	3.3	1.000	OF-4
1990		4	.231	.308	13	3	1	0	0	0.0	2	0	1	3	0	1	0	7	0	0	0	2.3	1.000	OF-3
4 yrs.		20	.324	.606	71	23	6	1	4	5.6	15	10	9	19	0	1	0	54	0	0	0	2.8	1.000	OF-19

Ken Henderson

HENDERSON, KENNETH JOSEPH
B. June 15, 1946, Carroll, Iowa
BB TR 6′ 2″ 180 lbs.

Year	Team	Games	BA	SA	AB	H	2B	3B	HR	HR%	R	RBI	BB	SO	SB	Pinch Hit AB	Pinch Hit H	PO	A	E	DP	TC/G	FA	G by Pos
1965	SF N	63	.192	.233	73	14	1	1	0	0.0	10	7	9	19	1	7	0	47	2	1	2	1.0	.980	OF-48
1966		11	.310	.517	29	9	1	1	1	3.4	4	1	2	3	0	1	0	11	0	1	0	1.2	.917	OF-10
1967		65	.190	.274	179	34	3	0	4	2.2	15	14	19	52	0	11	3	86	3	5	1	1.8	.947	OF-52
1968		3	.333	.333	3	1	0	0	0	0.0	1	0	2	1	0	0	0	2	0	0	0	1.0	1.000	OF-2
1969		113	.225	.332	374	84	14	4	6	1.6	42	44	42	64	6	1	0	175	12	6	2	1.7	.969	OF-111, 3B-3
1970		148	.294	.460	554	163	35	3	17	3.1	104	88	87	78	20	4	1	272	15	10	2	2.1	.966	OF-140
1971		141	.264	.429	504	133	26	6	15	3.0	80	65	84	76	18	2	0	277	3	10	1	2.1	.966	OF-138, 1B-1
1972		130	.257	.437	439	113	21	2	18	4.1	60	51	38	66	14	7	1	247	14	7	3	2.2	.974	OF-123
1973	CHI A	73	.260	.378	262	68	13	0	6	2.3	32	32	27	49	3	1	1	102	1	3	0	1.5	.972	OF-44, DH-26
1974		162	.292	.467	602	176	35	5	20	3.3	76	95	66	112	12	0	0	462	7	6	3	2.9	.987	OF-162
1975		140	.251	.355	513	129	20	3	9	1.8	65	53	74	65	5	3	1	394	7	4	0	2.9	.990	OF-137, DH-1
1976	ATL N	133	.262	.395	435	114	19	0	13	3.0	52	61	62	68	5	10	2	219	3	3	0	1.8	.987	OF-122
1977	TEX A	75	.258	.377	244	63	14	0	5	2.0	23	23	18	37	2	9	2	113	0	2	0	1.7	.983	OF-65, DH-3
1978	2 teams	NY N (7G –.227) CIN N (64G –.167)																						
"	total	71	.175	.307	166	29	8	1	4	2.4	12	23	27	36	0	28	6	93	0	0	0	2.1	1.000	OF-45
1979	2 teams	CIN N (10G –.231) CHI N (62G –.235)																						
"	total	72	.234	.330	94	22	3	0	2	2.1	12	10	15	18	0	50	9	21	0	1	0	0.9	.955	OF-25
1980	CHI N	44	.195	.305	82	16	3	0	2	2.4	7	9	17	19	0	19	3	31	3	2	1	1.6	.944	OF-22
16 yrs.		1444	.257	.396	4553	1168	216	26	122	2.7	595	576	589	763	86	153	29	2552	70	61	15	2.1	.977	OF-1246, DH-30, 3B-3, 1B-1
LEAGUE CHAMPIONSHIP SERIES																								
1971	SF N	4	.313	.375	16	5	1	0	0	0.0	3	2	2	1	1	0	0	4	0	0	0	1.0	1.000	OF-4

Rickey Henderson

HENDERSON, RICKEY HENLEY
B. Dec. 25, 1957, Chicago, Ill.
BR TL 5′10″ 180 lbs.

Year	Team	Games	BA	SA	AB	H	2B	3B	HR	HR%	R	RBI	BB	SO	SB	Pinch Hit AB	Pinch Hit H	PO	A	E	DP	TC/G	FA	G by Pos
1979	OAK A	89	.274	.336	351	96	13	3	1	0.3	49	26	34	39	33	0	0	215	5	6	0	2.6	.973	OF-88
1980		158	.303	.399	591	179	22	4	9	1.5	111	53	117	54	**100**	0	0	407	15	7	1	2.7	.984	OF-157, DH-1
1981		108	.319	.437	423	**135**	18	7	6	1.4	**89**	35	64	68	**56**	1	0	327	7	7	0	3.2	.979	OF-107
1982		149	.267	.382	536	143	24	4	10	1.9	119	51	**116**	94	**130**[1]	0	0	379	2	9	0	2.6	.977	OF-144, DH-4
1983		145	.292	.421	513	150	25	7	9	1.8	105	48	**103**	80	**108**	6	1	349	9	3	1	2.5	.992	OF-142, DH-1
1984		142	.293	.458	502	147	27	4	16	3.2	113	58	86	81	**66**	2	0	341	7	11	1	2.6	.969	OF-140
1985	NY A	143	.314	.516	547	172	28	5	24	4.4	**146**	72	99	65	**80**	1	0	439	7	9	3	3.2	.980	OF-141, DH-1
1986		153	.263	.469	608	160	31	5	28	4.6	**130**	74	89	81	**87**	3	0	426	4	6	0	2.9	.986	OF-146, DH-5
1987		95	.291	.497	358	104	17	3	17	4.7	78	37	80	52	41	2	0	189	3	4	1	2.1	.980	OF-69, DH-24
1988		140	.305	.399	554	169	30	2	6	1.1	118	50	82	54	**93**	0	0	320	7	12	5	2.4	.965	OF-136, DH-3
1989	2 teams	NY A (65G –.247) OAK A (85G –.294)																						
"	total	150	.274	.399	541	148	26	3	12	2.2	**113**	57	**126**	68	**77**	2	2	335	6	4	1	2.3	.988	OF-147, DH-3
1990	OAK A	136	.325	.577	489	159	33	3	28	5.7	**119**	61	97	60	**65**	1	0	289	5	5	0	2.2	.983	OF-118, DH-15
1991		134	.268	.423	470	126	17	1	18	3.8	105	57	98	73	**58**	6	1	249	10	8	1	2.1	.970	OF-119, DH-10
1992		117	.283	.457	396	112	18	3	15	3.8	77	46	95	56	48	3	1	231	9	4	2	2.1	.984	OF-108, DH-6
1993	2 teams	OAK A (90G –.327) TOR A (44G –.215)																						
"	total	134	.289	.474	481	139	22	2	21	4.4	114	59	120	65	53	2	0	258	6	7	0	2.0	.974	OF-118, DH-16
1994	OAK A	87	.260	.365	296	77	13	0	6	2.0	66	20	72	45	22	3	0	166	4	4	0	2.1	.977	OF-71, DH-13
1995		112	.300	.447	407	122	31	1	9	2.2	67	54	72	66	32	5	2	161	5	2	1	1.5	.988	OF-90, DH-19
17 yrs.		2192	.290	.441	8063	2338	395	57	235	2.9	1719	858	1550	1101	1149 **1st**	37	7	5081	111	108	17	2.5	.980	OF-2041, DH-121
DIVISIONAL PLAYOFF SERIES																								
1981	OAK A	3	.182	.182	11	2	0	0	0	0.0	3	0	2	0	2	0	0	8	0	0	0	2.7	1.000	OF-3
LEAGUE CHAMPIONSHIP SERIES																								
1981	OAK A	3	.364	.727	11	4	2	1	0	0.0	0	1	1	2	2	0	0	6	0	1	0	2.3	.857	OF-3
1989		5	.400	1.000	15	6	1	1	2	13.3	8	5	7	0	8	0	0	13	0	1	0	2.8	.929	OF-5
1990		4	.294	.294	17	5	0	0	0	0.0	1	3	1	2	2	0	0	10	0	0	0	2.5	1.000	OF-4
1992		6	.261	.261	23	6	0	0	0	0.0	5	1	4	4	2	0	0	15	0	3	0	3.0	.833	OF-6
1993	TOR A	6	.120	.200	25	3	2	0	0	0.0	4	0	4	5	2	0	0	9	0	1	0	1.7	.900	OF-6
5 yrs.		24	.264	.429	91 **8th**	24	5	2 **4th**	2	2.2	18 **2nd**	10	17 **2nd**	13	16 **1st**	0	0	53	0	6	0	2.5	.898	OF-24

Rickey Henderson *continued*

WORLD SERIES

Year	Team	Games	BA	SA	AB	H	2B	3B	HR	HR%	R	RBI	BB	SO	SB	Pinch Hit AB	Pinch Hit H	PO	A	E	DP	TC/G	FA	G by Pos
1989	**OAK** **A**	4	.474	.895	19	9	1	2	1	5.3	4	3	2	2	3	0	0	9	0	0	0	2.3	1.000	OF-4
1990		4	.333	.667	15	5	2	0	1	6.7	2	1	3	4	3	0	0	12	1	0	0	3.3	1.000	OF-4
1993	**TOR** **A**	6	.227	.318	22	5	2	0	0	0.0	6	2	5	2	1	0	0	8	0	0	0	1.3	1.000	OF-6
3 yrs.		14	.339	.607	56	19	5	2	2	3.6	12	6	10	8	7 **9th**	0	0	29	1	0	0	2.1	1.000	OF-14

Steve Henderson

HENDERSON, STEPHEN CURTIS (Hendu) BR TR 6′ 2″ 190 lbs.
B. Nov. 18, 1952, Houston, Tex.

Year	Team	Games	BA	SA	AB	H	2B	3B	HR	HR%	R	RBI	BB	SO	SB	Pinch Hit AB	Pinch Hit H	PO	A	E	DP	TC/G	FA	G by Pos
1977	**NY** **N**	99	.297	.480	350	104	16	6	12	3.4	67	65	43	79	6	2	0	189	4	4	1	2.0	.980	OF-97
1978		157	.266	.399	587	156	30	9	10	1.7	83	65	60	109	13	4	4	315	18	11	3	2.2	.968	OF-155
1979		98	.306	.440	350	107	16	8	5	1.4	42	39	38	58	13	3	2	201	6	2	3	2.2	.990	OF-94
1980		143	.290	.402	513	149	17	8	8	1.6	75	58	62	90	23	8	1	299	7	6	1	2.3	.981	OF-136
1981	**CHI** **N**	82	.293	.411	287	84	9	5	5	1.7	32	35	42	61	5	4	0	152	4	8	2	2.1	.951	OF-77
1982		92	.233	.335	257	60	12	4	2	0.8	23	29	22	64	6	25	6	126	5	6	0	2.0	.956	OF-70
1983	**SEA** **A**	121	.294	.450	436	128	32	3	10	2.3	50	54	44	82	10	6	1	182	15	6	2	1.7	.970	OF-112, DH-6
1984		109	.262	.409	325	85	12	3	10	3.1	42	35	38	62	2	15	4	84	4	6	0	0.9	.936	OF-53, DH-51
1985	**OAK** **A**	85	.301	.420	193	58	8	3	3	1.6	25	31	18	34	0	27	8	79	3	4	0	1.5	.953	OF-58, DH-1
1986		11	.077	.115	26	2	1	0	0	0.0	2	3	0	5	0	2	0	8	0	2	0	1.3	.800	OF-7, DH-1
1987		46	.289	.430	114	33	7	0	3	2.6	14	9	12	19	0	11	1	33	0	2	0	0.9	.943	OF-31, DH-9
1988	**HOU** **N**	42	.217	.261	46	10	2	0	0	0.0	4	5	7	14	1	30	6	14	1	0	0	1.7	1.000	OF-8, 1B-1
12 yrs.		1085	.280	.413	3484	976	162	49	68	2.0	459	428	386	677	79	137	33	1682	67	57	12	1.9	.968	OF-898, DH-68, 1B-1

George Hendrick

HENDRICK, GEORGE ANDREW BR TR 6′ 3″ 195 lbs.
B. Oct. 18, 1949, Los Angeles, Calif.

Year	Team	Games	BA	SA	AB	H	2B	3B	HR	HR%	R	RBI	BB	SO	SB	Pinch Hit AB	Pinch Hit H	PO	A	E	DP	TC/G	FA	G by Pos
1971	**OAK** **A**	42	.237	.289	114	27	4	1	0	0.0	8	8	3	20	0	5	2	52	1	1	0	1.5	.981	OF-36
1972		58	.182	.306	121	22	1	1	4	3.3	10	15	3	22	3	19	5	68	0	0	0	1.7	1.000	OF-41
1973	**CLE** **A**	113	.268	.452	440	118	18	0	21	4.8	64	61	25	71	7	3	1	242	7	3	1	2.3	.988	OF-110
1974		139	.279	.444	495	138	23	1	19	3.8	65	67	33	73	6	5	0	355	9	4	2	2.7	.989	OF-133, DH-1
1975		145	.258	.431	561	145	21	2	24	4.3	82	86	40	78	6	2	1	338	4	6	1	2.4	.983	OF-143
1976		149	.265	.448	551	146	20	3	25	4.5	72	81	51	82	4	1	1	288	13	4	6	2.1	.987	OF-146
1977	**SD** **N**	152	.311	.492	541	168	25	2	23	4.3	75	81	61	74	11	9	2	386	11	7	2	2.8	.983	OF-142
1978	**2 teams**	**SD N** (36G –.243) **STL N** (102G –.288)																						
″	**total**	138	.278	.467	493	137	31	1	20	4.1	64	75	40	60	2	5	3	313	6	2	0	2.4	.994	OF-134
1979	**STL** **N**	140	.300	.456	493	148	27	1	16	3.2	67	75	49	62	2	7	2	254	20	2	7	2.0	.993	OF-138
1980		150	.302	.498	572	173	33	2	25	4.4	73	109	32	67	6	3	0	322	10	2	2	2.2	.994	OF-149
1981		101	.284	.485	394	112	19	3	18	4.6	67	61	41	44	4	0	0	227	6	4	0	2.3	.983	OF-101
1982		136	.282	.450	515	145	20	5	19	3.7	65	104	37	80	3	2	1	238	6	5	1	1.9	.980	OF-134
1983		144	.318	.493	529	168	33	3	18	3.4	73	97	51	76	3	5	1	904	79	8	72	6.9	.992	1B-92, OF-51
1984		120	.277	.406	441	122	28	1	9	2.0	57	69	32	75	0	4	0	189	9	2	1	1.7	.990	OF-116, 1B-1
1985	**2 teams**	**PIT N** (69G –.230) **CAL A** (16G –.122)																						
″	**total**	85	.215	.310	297	64	16	0	4	1.3	28	31	22	50	1	6	2	151	3	4	0	2.0	.975	OF-77, DH-1
1986	**CAL** **A**	102	.272	.473	283	77	13	1	14	4.9	45	47	26	41	1	11	3	188	9	5	5	1.9	.975	OF-93, 1B-7, DH-4
1987		65	.241	.395	162	39	10	0	5	3.1	14	25	14	18	0	15	6	114	5	3	7	2.1	.975	OF-45, 1B-9, DH-5
1988		69	.244	.323	127	31	1	0	3	2.4	12	19	7	20	0	**29**	**8**	129	9	3	10	3.6	.979	OF-24, 1B-12, DH-3
18 yrs.		2048	.278	.446	7129	1980	343	27	267	3.7	941	1111	567	1013	59	131	38	4758	207	65	117	2.6	.987	OF-1813, 1B-121, DH-14

LEAGUE CHAMPIONSHIP SERIES

Year	Team	Games	BA	SA	AB	H	2B	3B	HR	HR%	R	RBI	BB	SO	SB	Pinch Hit AB	Pinch Hit H	PO	A	E	DP	TC/G	FA	G by Pos
1972	**OAK** **A**	5	.143	.143	7	1	0	0	0	0.0	2	0	0	1	0	4	1	1	0	0	0	1.0	1.000	OF-1
1982	**STL** **N**	3	.308	.308	13	4	0	0	0	0.0	2	2	1	2	0	0	0	5	0	0	0	1.7	1.000	OF-3
1986	**CAL** **A**	3	.083	.083	12	1	0	0	0	0.0	0	0	0	2	0	0	0	14	2	0	0	5.3	1.000	OF-2, 1B-1
3 yrs.		11	.188	.188	32	6	0	0	0	0.0	4	2	1	5	0	4	1	20	2	0	0	3.1	1.000	OF-6, 1B-1

WORLD SERIES

Year	Team	Games	BA	SA	AB	H	2B	3B	HR	HR%	R	RBI	BB	SO	SB	Pinch Hit AB	Pinch Hit H	PO	A	E	DP	TC/G	FA	G by Pos
1972	**OAK** **A**	5	.133	.133	15	2	0	0	0	0.0	3	0	1	2	0	0	0	12	0	0	0	2.4	1.000	OF-5
1982	**STL** **N**	7	.321	.321	28	9	0	0	0	0.0	5	5	2	1	0	0	0	10	1	0	0	1.6	1.000	OF-7
2 yrs.		12	.256	.256	43	11	0	0	0	0.0	8	5	3	3	0	0	0	22	1	0	0	1.9	1.000	OF-12

Harvey Hendrick

HENDRICK, HARVEY (Gink) BL TR 6′ 2″ 190 lbs.
B. Nov. 9, 1897, Mason, Tenn. D. Oct. 29, 1941, Covington, Tenn.

Year	Team	Games	BA	SA	AB	H	2B	3B	HR	HR%	R	RBI	BB	SO	SB	Pinch Hit AB	Pinch Hit H	PO	A	E	DP	TC/G	FA	G by Pos
1923	**NY** **A**	37	.273	.485	66	18	3	1	3	4.5	9	12	2	8	3	24	6	16	2	1	0	1.6	.947	OF-12
1924		40	.263	.303	76	20	0	0	1	1.3	7	11	2	7	1	21	4	38	1	1	0	2.4	.975	OF-17
1925	**CLE** **A**	25	.286	.464	28	8	1	2	0	0.0	2	9	3	5	0	16	6	26	2	0	1	9.3	1.000	1B-3
1927	**BKN** **N**	128	.310	.424	458	142	18	11	4	0.9	55	50	24	40	29	10	3	560	40	11	38	5.2	.982	OF-64, 1B-53, 2B-1
1928		126	.318	.478	425	135	15	10	11	2.6	83	59	54	34	16	13	5	110	202	26	20	3.1	.923	3B-91, OF-17
1929		110	.354	.560	384	136	25	6	14	3.6	69	82	31	20	14	13	7	467	62	16	29	5.9	.971	OF-42, 1B-39, 3B-7, SS-4
1930		68	.257	.419	167	43	10	1	5	3.0	29	28	20	19	2	16	4	92	5	4	6	2.1	.960	OF-42, 1B-7
1931	**2 teams**	**BKN N** (1G –.000) **CIN N** (137G –.315)																						
″	**total**	138	.315	.414	531	167	32	9	1	0.2	74	75	53	40	3	1	0	1348	67	18	147	10.5	.987	1B-137
1932	**2 teams**	**STL N** (28G –.250) **CIN N** (94G –.302)																						
″	**total**	122	.294	.406	470	138	32	3	5	1.1	64	45	28	38	3	9	3	936	78	18	75	9.3	.983	1B-94, 3B-12, OF-5
1933	**CHI** **N**	69	.291	.455	189	55	13	3	4	2.1	30	23	13	17	4	19	6	344	25	8	39	8.0	.979	1B-38, OF-8, 3B-1
1934	**PHI** **N**	59	.293	.362	116	34	8	0	0	0.0	12	19	9	15	0	31	7	69	9	4	4	3.2	.951	OF-12, 3B-7, 1B-7
11 yrs.		922	.308	.443	2910	896	157	46	48	1.6	434	413	239	243	75	173	51	4006	493	107	359	6.4	.977	1B-378, OF-219, 3B-118, SS-4, 2B-1

WORLD SERIES

Year	Team	Games	BA	SA	AB	H	2B	3B	HR	HR%	R	RBI	BB	SO	SB	Pinch Hit AB	Pinch Hit H	PO	A	E	DP	TC/G	FA	G by Pos
1923	**NY** **A**	1	.000	.000	1	0	0	0	0	0.0	0	0	0	0	0	1	0	0	0	0	0	0.0	—	

Ellie Hendricks

HENDRICKS, ELROD JEROME BL TR 6′ 1″ 175 lbs.
B. Dec. 22, 1940, Charlotte Amalie, Virgin Islands

Year	Team	Games	BA	SA	AB	H	2B	3B	HR	HR%	R	RBI	BB	SO	SB	Pinch Hit AB	Pinch Hit H	PO	A	E	DP	TC/G	FA	G by Pos
1968	**BAL** **A**	79	.202	.372	183	37	8	1	7	3.8	19	23	19	51	0	27	4	303	21	3	3	6.2	.991	C-53
1969		105	.244	.383	295	72	5	0	12	4.1	36	38	39	44	0	16	5	488	41	1	2	5.8	.998	C-87, 1B-4

Ellie Hendricks *continued*

Year	Team	Games	BA	SA	AB	H	2B	3B	HR	HR%	R	RBI	BB	SO	SB	Pinch Hit AB	Pinch Hit H	PO	A	E	DP	TC/G	FA	G by Pos
1970		106	.242	.382	322	78	9	0	12	3.7	32	41	33	44	1	16	3	509	35	8	6	5.8	.986	C-95
1971		101	.250	.386	316	79	14	1	9	2.8	33	42	39	38	0	11	3	453	34	7	8	5.3	.986	C-90, 1B-3
1972	2 teams	BAL A (33G –.155) CHI N (17G –.116)																						
"	total	50	.142	.228	127	18	5	0	2	1.6	13	10	25	27	0	4	0	213	22	4	4	5.4	.983	C-44
1973	BAL A	41	.178	.337	101	18	5	1	3	3.0	9	15	10	22	0	2	0	148	9	1	1	4.2	.994	C-38
1974		66	.208	.340	159	33	8	2	3	1.9	18	8	17	25	0	14	5	194	13	0	4	3.7	1.000	C-54, 1B-1, DH-1
1975		85	.215	.377	223	48	8	2	8	3.6	32	38	34	40	0	8	1	332	36	2	3	4.5	.995	C-83
1976	2 teams	BAL A (28G –.139) NY A (26G –.226)																						
"	total	54	.174	.280	132	23	2	0	4	3.0	8	9	10	23	0	12	2	147	17	3	2	3.7	.982	C-45
1977	NY A	10	.273	.636	11	3	1	0	1	9.1	1	5	0	2	0	3	1	11	0	0	0	1.8	1.000	C-6
1978	BAL A	13	.333	.556	18	6	1	0	1	5.6	4	1	3	3	0	6	1	19	2	1	0	2.8	.955	C-6, DH-1, P-1
1979		1	.000	.000	1	0	0	0	0	0.0	0	0	0	0	0	0	0	1	0	1	0	2.0	.500	C-1
12 yrs.		711	.220	.361	1888	415	66	7	62	3.3	205	230	229	319	1	119	25	2818	230	31	33	5.0	.990	C-602, 1B-8, DH-2, P-1
LEAGUE CHAMPIONSHIP SERIES																								
1969	BAL A	3	.250	.500	8	2	2	0	0	0.0	2	3	1	3	0	0	0	18	0	0	0	6.0	1.000	C-3
1970		1	.400	.400	5	2	0	0	0	0.0	2	0	0	1	0	0	0	5	0	0	0	5.0	1.000	C-1
1971		2	.500	1.250	4	2	0	0	1	25.0	1	2	1	1	0	0	0	6	0	0	0	3.0	1.000	C-2
1974		3	.167	.167	6	1	0	0	0	0.0	1	0	1	3	0	0	0	11	1	0	0	4.0	1.000	C-3
1976	NY A	1	1.000	1.000	1	1	0	0	0	0.0	0	0	0	0	0	1	1	0	0	0	0	0.0	—	
5 yrs.		10	.333	.542	24	8	2	0	1	4.2	6	5	3	8	0	1	1	40	1	0	0	4.6	1.000	C-9
WORLD SERIES																								
1969	BAL A	3	.100	.100	10	1	0	0	0	0.0	1	0	1	0	0	0	0	21	1	0	1	7.3	1.000	C-3
1970		3	.364	.727	11	4	1	0	1	9.1	1	4	1	2	0	0	0	17	2	1	0	6.7	.950	C-3
1971		6	.263	.316	19	5	1	0	0	0.0	3	1	3	3	0	0	0	40	4	1	0	7.5	.978	C-6
1976	NY A	2	.000	.000	2	0	0	0	0	0.0	0	0	0	0	0	2	0	0	0	0	0	0.0	—	
4 yrs.		14	.238	.357	42	10	2	0	1	2.4	5	5	5	5	0	2	0	78	7	2	1	7.3	.977	C-12

Jack Hendricks

HENDRICKS, JOHN CHARLES BL TL 5′11½″ 160 lbs.
B. Apr. 9, 1875, Joliet, Ill. D. May 13, 1943, Chicago, Ill.
Manager 1918, 1924–29.

Year	Team	Games	BA	SA	AB	H	2B	3B	HR	HR%	R	RBI	BB	SO	SB	Pinch Hit AB	Pinch Hit H	PO	A	E	DP	TC/G	FA	G by Pos
1902	2 teams	NY N (8G –.231) CHI N (2G –.571)																						
"	total	10	.303	.424	33	10	2	1	0	0.0	1	0	2		2	1	0	18	1	1	0	2.2	.950	OF-9
1903	WAS A	32	.179	.241	112	20	1	3	0	0.0	10	4	13		3	0	0	40	1	5	1	1.4	.891	OF-32
2 yrs.		42	.207	.283	145	30	3	4	0	0.0	11	4	15		5	1	0	58	2	6	1	1.6	.909	OF-41

Claude Hendrix

HENDRIX, CLAUDE RAYMOND BR TR 6′ 195 lbs.
B. Apr. 13, 1889, Olathe, Kans. D. Mar. 22, 1944, Allentown, Pa.

Year	Team	Games	BA	SA	AB	H	2B	3B	HR	HR%	R	RBI	BB	SO	SB	Pinch Hit AB	Pinch Hit H	PO	A	E	DP	TC/G	FA	G by Pos
1911	PIT N	22	.098	.171	41	4	1	1	0	0.0	2	2	1	15	0	0	0	12	45	1	2	2.6	.983	P-22
1912		39	.322	.529	121	39	10	6	1	0.8	25	15	3	18	1	5	2	7	91	3	2	2.6	.970	P-39
1913		53	.273	.434	99	27	5	4	1	1.0	13	8	3	16	0	8	0	6	67	4	6	1.8	.948	P-42
1914	CHI F	52	.231	.300	130	30	3	0	2	1.5	15	13	7		3	2	1	10	137	5	5	3.1	.967	P-49
1915		50	.265	.469	113	30	7	2	4	3.5	22	18	5		1	9	2	11	69	3	2	2.1	.964	P-40
1916	CHI N	45	.200	.275	80	16	3	0	1	1.3	4	5	6	24	0	7	1	10	65	4	2	2.2	.949	P-36
1917		48	.256	.314	86	22	3	1	0	0.0	7	7	5	20	1	5	1	6	52	4	1	1.5	.935	P-40, OF-2
1918		35	.264	.462	91	24	3	3	3	3.3	14	17	4	11	1	3	1	6	75	2	1	2.6	.976	P-32
1919		36	.192	.244	78	15	1	0	1	1.3	6	6	2	19	0	3	1	5	67	1	0	2.2	.986	P-33
1920		34	.181	.217	83	15	3	0	0	0.0	10	6	3	11	2	7	1	4	56	5	1	2.4	.923	P-27
10 yrs.		414	.241	.362	922	222	39	17	13	1.4	118	97	39	134	9	49	10	77	724	32	22	2.3	.962	P-360, OF-2
WORLD SERIES																								
1918	CHI N	2	1.000	1.000	1	1	0	0	0	0.0	0	0	0	0	0	1	1	0	0	0	0	0.0	.000	P-1

Tim Hendryx

HENDRYX, TIMOTHY GREEN BR TR 5′9″ 170 lbs.
B. Jan. 31, 1891, LeRoy, Ill. D. Aug. 14, 1957, Corpus Christi, Tex.

Year	Team	Games	BA	SA	AB	H	2B	3B	HR	HR%	R	RBI	BB	SO	SB	Pinch Hit AB	Pinch Hit H	PO	A	E	DP	TC/G	FA	G by Pos
1911	CLE A	2	.250	.250	4	1	0	0	0	0.0	0	0	0		0	0	0	2	3	0	0	2.5	1.000	3B-2
1912		23	.243	.429	70	17	2	4	1	1.4	9	14	8		3	1	0	44	1	0	0	2.0	1.000	OF-22
1915	NY A	13	.200	.250	40	8	2	0	0	0.0	4	1	4	2	0	1	0	28	2	1	0	2.6	.968	OF-12
1916		15	.290	.435	62	18	7	1	0	0.0	10	5	8	6	4	0	0	18	1	0	0	1.3	1.000	OF-15
1917		125	.249	.359	393	98	14	7	5	1.3	43	44	62	45	6	16	4	215	17	11	1	2.3	.955	OF-107
1918	STL A	88	.279	.370	219	61	14	3	0	0.0	22	33	37	35	5	18	0	108	4	2	2	1.8	.982	OF-65
1920	BOS A	99	.328	.413	363	119	21	5	0	0.0	54	73	42	27	7	1	0	208	6	8	1	2.3	.964	OF-98
1921		49	.241	.328	137	33	8	2	0	0.0	10	21	24	13	1	6	1	66	2	3	0	1.7	.958	OF-41
8 yrs.		414	.276	.377	1288	355	68	22	6	0.5	152	191	185	128	26	43	5	689	36	25	4	2.1	.967	OF-360, 3B-2

Dave Hengel

HENGEL, DAVID LEE BR TR 6′ 185 lbs.
B. Dec. 18, 1961, Oakland, Calif.

Year	Team	Games	BA	SA	AB	H	2B	3B	HR	HR%	R	RBI	BB	SO	SB	Pinch Hit AB	Pinch Hit H	PO	A	E	DP	TC/G	FA	G by Pos
1986	SEA A	21	.190	.254	63	12	1	0	1	1.6	3	6	1	13	0	4	1	9	1	0	0	0.5	1.000	DH-11, OF-8
1987		10	.316	.474	19	6	0	0	1	5.3	2	4	0	4	0	4	2	7	0	1	0	1.0	.875	OF-7, DH-1
1988		26	.167	.283	60	10	1	0	2	3.3	3	7	1	15	0	8	1	20	0	1	0	0.9	.952	OF-12, DH-12
1989	CLE A	12	.120	.160	25	3	1	0	0	0.0	2	1	2	4	0	3	0	12	1	0	0	1.1	1.000	OF-9, DH-3
4 yrs.		69	.186	.275	167	31	3	0	4	2.4	10	18	4	36	0	19	4	48	2	2	0	0.8	.962	OF-36, DH-27

Moxie Hengle

HENGLE, EMERY J. BR 5′8″ 144 lbs.
Brother of Ed Hengle.
B. Oct. 7, 1857, Chicago, Ill. D. Dec. 11, 1924, River Forest, Ill.

Year	Team	Games	BA	SA	AB	H	2B	3B	HR	HR%	R	RBI	BB	SO	SB	Pinch Hit AB	Pinch Hit H	PO	A	E	DP	TC/G	FA	G by Pos
1884	2 teams	CHI U (19G –.203) STP U (9G –.152)																						
"	total	28	.187	.252	107	20	3	2	0	0.0	11		3			0	0	65	62	19	5	5.2	.870	2B-28
1885	BUF N	7	.154	.154	26	4	0	0	0	0.0	2	0	1	2		0	0	14	8	5	1	3.4	.815	2B-5, OF-3
2 yrs.		35	.180	.233	133	24	3	2	0	0.0	13	0	4	2		0	0	79	70	24	6	4.8	.861	2B-33, OF-3

Gail Henley

HENLEY, GAIL CURTICE BL TR 5′9″ 180 lbs.
B. Oct. 15, 1928, Wichita, Kans.

Year	Team	Games	BA	SA	AB	H	2B	3B	HR	HR%	R	RBI	BB	SO	SB	Pinch Hit AB	Pinch Hit H	PO	A	E	DP	TC/G	FA	G by Pos
1954	PIT N	14	.300	.433	30	9	1	0	1	3.3	7	2	4	4	0	5	1	13	1	0	0	1.6	1.000	OF-9

Year	Team	Games	BA	SA	AB	H	2B	3B	HR	HR%	R	RBI	BB	SO	SB	Pinch Hit AB	Pinch Hit H	PO	A	E	DP	TC/G	FA	G by Pos

Butch Henline

HENLINE, WALTER JOHN BR TR 5′10″ 175 lbs.
B. Dec. 20, 1894, Fort Wayne, Ind. D. Oct. 9, 1957, Sarasota, Fla.

Year	Team	Games	BA	SA	AB	H	2B	3B	HR	HR%	R	RBI	BB	SO	SB	PH AB	PH H	PO	A	E	DP	TC/G	FA	G by Pos
1921	**2 teams**	**NY N** (16 –.000)	**PHI N** (33G –.306)																					
″	**total**	34	.304	.321	112	34	2	0	0	0.0	8	8	2	7	1	2	0	113	44	2	5	5.0	.987	C-32
1922	**PHI N**	125	.316	.479	430	136	20	4	14	3.3	57	64	36	33	2	4	2	400	113	9	13	4.4	.983	C-119
1923		111	.324	.448	330	107	14	3	7	2.1	45	46	37	33	7	12	3	291	71	8	8	3.8	.978	C-96, OF-1
1924		115	.284	.426	289	82	18	4	5	1.7	41	35	27	15	1	28	7	249	76	9	12	3.9	.973	C-83, OF-2
1925		93	.304	.479	263	80	12	5	8	3.0	43	48	24	16	3	18	2	211	53	12	9	4.0	.957	C-68, OF-1
1926		99	.283	.360	283	80	14	1	2	0.7	32	30	21	18	1	17	4	244	48	9	12	3.6	.970	C-77, 1B-4, OF-2
1927	**BKN N**	67	.266	.373	177	47	10	3	1	0.6	12	18	17	10	1	7	1	216	50	15	6	4.7	.947	C-60
1928		55	.212	.295	132	28	3	1	2	1.5	12	8	17	8	2	8	2	141	22	4	1	3.7	.976	C-45
1929		27	.242	.323	62	15	2	0	1	1.6	5	7	9	9	0	5	0	72	15	3	2	4.3	.967	C-21
1930	**CHI A**	3	.125	.125	8	1	0	0	0	0.0	1	2	0	3	0	0	0	10	2	0	0	4.0	1.000	C-3
1931		11	.067	.133	15	1	1	0	0	0.0	2	2	2	4	0	5	1	14	2	2	0	4.5	.889	C-4
11 yrs.		740	.291	.414	2101	611	96	21	40	1.9	258	268	192	156	18	106	22	1961	496	73	68	4.1	.971	C-608, OF-6, 1B-4

Les Hennessy

HENNESSY, LESTER BAKER BR TR 6′ 190 lbs.
B. Dec. 12, 1893, Lynn, Mass. D. Nov. 20, 1976, New York, N. Y.

Year	Team	Games	BA	SA	AB	H	2B	3B	HR	HR%	R	RBI	BB	SO	SB	PH AB	PH H	PO	A	E	DP	TC/G	FA	G by Pos
1913	**DET A**	12	.136	.136	22	3	0	0	0	0.0	2	0	3	6	2	2	0	8	14	3	0	2.8	.880	2B-9

Bobby Henrich

HENRICH, ROBERT EDWARD BR TR 6′ 1″ 185 lbs.
B. Dec. 24, 1938, Lawrence, Kans.

Year	Team	Games	BA	SA	AB	H	2B	3B	HR	HR%	R	RBI	BB	SO	SB	PH AB	PH H	PO	A	E	DP	TC/G	FA	G by Pos
1957	**CIN N**	29	.200	.200	10	2	0	0	0	0.0	8	1	1	4	0	4	1	3	7	1	1	0.7	.909	SS-7, OF-6, 3B-2, 2B-1
1958		5	.000	.000	3	0	0	0	0	0.0	2	0	0	2	0	0	0	2	2	0	0	2.0	1.000	SS-2
1959		14	.000	.000	3	0	0	0	0	0.0	3	0	0	1	0	1	0	2	0	0	0	0.3	1.000	SS-5, 3B-1
3 yrs.		48	.125	.125	16	2	0	0	0	0.0	13	1	1	7	0	5	1	7	9	1	1	0.7	.941	SS-14, OF-6, 3B-3, 2B-1

Fritz Henrich

HENRICH, FRANK WILDE BL TL 5′10″ 160 lbs.
B. May 8, 1899, Cincinnati, Ohio D. May 1, 1959, Philadelphia, Pa.

Year	Team	Games	BA	SA	AB	H	2B	3B	HR	HR%	R	RBI	BB	SO	SB	PH AB	PH H	PO	A	E	DP	TC/G	FA	G by Pos
1924	**PHI N**	36	.211	.256	90	19	4	0	0	0.0	4	4	2	12	0	4	0	42	2	1	0	1.4	.978	OF-32

Tommy Henrich

HENRICH, THOMAS DAVID (Old Reliable) BL TL 6′ 180 lbs.
B. Feb. 20, 1913, Massillon, Ohio.

Year	Team	Games	BA	SA	AB	H	2B	3B	HR	HR%	R	RBI	BB	SO	SB	PH AB	PH H	PO	A	E	DP	TC/G	FA	G by Pos
1937	**NY A**	67	.320	.553	206	66	14	5	8	3.9	39	42	35	17	4	7	1	90	6	3	1	1.7	.970	OF-59
1938		131	.270	.490	471	127	24	7	22	4.7	109	91	92	32	6	1	0	239	14	4	1	2.0	.984	OF-130
1939		99	.277	.429	347	96	18	4	9	2.6	64	57	51	23	7	11	4	207	7	2	1	2.4	.991	OF-88, 1B-1
1940		90	.307	.539	293	90	28	5	10	3.4	57	53	48	30	1	12	4	152	10	5	2	2.1	.970	OF-76, 1B-2
1941		144	.277	.519	538	149	27	5	31	5.8	106	85	81	40	3	4	1	280	13	6	4	2.2	.980	OF-139
1942		127	.267	.431	483	129	30	5	13	2.7	77	67	58	42	4	3	1	278	13	3	14	2.3	.990	OF-119, 1B-7
1946		150	.251	.411	565	142	25	4	19	3.4	92	83	87	63	5	0	0	588	32	7	40	4.1	.989	OF-111, 1B-41
1947		142	.287	.485	550	158	35	**13**	16	2.9	109	98	71	54	3	5	1	337	14	5	8	2.6	.986	OF-132, 1B-6
1948		146	.308	.554	588	181	42	**14**	25	4.3	**138**	100	76	42	2	1	0	568	29	11	45	4.1	.982	OF-102, 1B-46
1949		115	.287	.526	411	118	20	3	24	5.8	90	85	86	34	2	2	0	555	33	7	66	5.3	.988	OF-61, 1B-52
1950		73	.272	.536	151	41	6	8	6	4.0	20	34	27	6	0	33	7	224	7	3	23	6.9	.987	1B-34
11 yrs.		1284	.282	.491	4603	1297	269	73	183	4.0	901	795	712	383	37	79	19	3518	178	56	205	3.1	.985	OF-1017, 1B-189
WORLD SERIES																								
1938	**NY A**	4	.250	.500	16	4	1	0	1	6.3	3	1	0	1	0	0	0	6	0	1	0	1.8	.857	OF-4
1941		5	.167	.389	18	3	1	0	1	5.6	4	1	3	3	0	0	0	6	0	0	0	1.2	1.000	OF-5
1947		7	.323	.484	31	10	2	0	1	3.2	2	5	2	3	0	0	0	12	0	0	0	1.7	1.000	OF-7
1949		5	.263	.421	19	5	0	0	1	5.3	4	1	3	0	0	0	0	48	1	0	4	9.8	1.000	1B-5
4 yrs.		21	.262	.452	84	22	4	0	4	4.8	13	8	8	7	0	0	0	72	1	1	4	3.5	.986	OF-16, 1B-5

Olaf Henriksen

HENRIKSEN, OLAF (Swede) BL TL 5′ 7½″ 158 lbs.
B. Apr. 26, 1888, Kirkerup, Denmark D. Oct. 17, 1962, Norwood, Mass.

Year	Team	Games	BA	SA	AB	H	2B	3B	HR	HR%	R	RBI	BB	SO	SB	PH AB	PH H	PO	A	E	DP	TC/G	FA	G by Pos
1911	**BOS A**	27	.366	.409	93	34	2	1	0	0.0	17	8	14		4	2	0	38	3	2	1	1.7	.953	OF-25
1912		37	.321	.411	56	18	3	1	0	0.0	20	8	14		0	25	6	10	0	1	0	1.1	.909	OF-10
1913		30	.375	.400	40	15	1	0	0	0.0	8	2	7	5	3	17	6	9	0	0	0	1.3	1.000	OF-7
1914		61	.263	.337	95	25	2	1	1	1.1	16	5	22	12	5	26	5	35	1	2	0	1.4	.947	OF-27
1915		73	.196	.261	92	18	2	2	0	0.0	9	13	18	7	1	31	7	27	2	1	2	1.2	.967	OF-25
1916		68	.202	.263	99	20	2	2	0	0.0	13	11	19	15	2	21	4	43	2	0	0	1.5	1.000	OF-31
1917		15	.083	.083	12	1	0	0	0	0.0	1	1	3	4	0	12	1	0	0	0	0	0.0	—	
7 yrs.		311	.269	.329	487	131	12	7	1	0.2	84	48	97	43	15	134	29	162	8	6	3	1.4	.966	OF-125
WORLD SERIES																								
1912	**BOS A**	2	1.000	2.000	1	1	1	0	0	0.0	0	1	0	0	0	1	1	0	0	0	0	0.0	—	
1915		2	.000	.000	2	0	0	0	0	0.0	0	0	0	0	0	2	0	0	0	0	0	0.0	—	
1916		1	—	—	0	0	0	0	0	—	1	0	1	0	0	0	0	0	0	0	0	0.0	—	
3 yrs.		5	.333	.667	3	1	1	0	0	0.0	1	1	1	0	0	3	1							

George Henry

HENRY, GEORGE WASHINGTON BR TR 5′ 9″ 180 lbs.
B. Aug. 10, 1863, Philadelphia, Pa. D. Dec. 30, 1934, Lynn, Mass.

Year	Team	Games	BA	SA	AB	H	2B	3B	HR	HR%	R	RBI	BB	SO	SB	PH AB	PH H	PO	A	E	DP	TC/G	FA	G by Pos
1893	**CIN N**	21	.277	.313	83	23	3	0	0	0.0	11	13	11	12	2	0	0	49	6	2	1	2.7	.965	OF-21

John Henry

HENRY, JOHN MICHAEL TL
B. Sept. 2, 1863, Springfield, Mass. D. June 11, 1939, Hartford, Conn.

Year	Team	Games	BA	SA	AB	H	2B	3B	HR	HR%	R	RBI	BB	SO	SB	PH AB	PH H	PO	A	E	DP	TC/G	FA	G by Pos
1884	**CLE N**	9	.154	.154	26	4	0	0	0	0.0	2	0	0	12		0	0	7	12	1	0	2.2	.950	P-5, OF-4
1885	**BAL AA**	10	.265	.353	34	9	3	0	0	0.0	4		1			0	0	10	18	2	1	3.0	.933	P-9, OF-1
1886	**WAS N**	4	.357	.357	14	5	0	0	0	0.0	3	0	0	3		0	0	2	3	1	0	1.5	.833	P-4
1890	**NY N**	37	.243	.285	144	35	6	0	0	0.0	19	16	7	12	12	0	0	56	4	9	1	1.9	.870	OF-37
4 yrs.		60	.243	.284	218	53	9	0	0	0.0	28	16	8	27	12	0	0	75	37	13	2	2.1	.896	OF-42, P-18

John Henry

HENRY, JOHN PARK (Bull) BR TR 6′ 190 lbs.
B. Dec. 26, 1889, Amherst, Mass. D. Nov. 24, 1941, Fort Huachuca, Ariz.

Year	Team	Games	BA	SA	AB	H	2B	3B	HR	HR%	R	RBI	BB	SO	SB	PH AB	PH H	PO	A	E	DP	TC/G	FA	G by Pos
1910	**WAS A**	28	.149	.184	87	13	1	1	0	0.0	2	5	2		2	0	0	165	35	1	10	7.2	.995	C-18, 1B-10
1911		85	.203	.222	261	53	5	0	0	0.0	24	21	25		8	3	0	549	123	21	15	8.6	.970	C-51, 1B-30

John Henry *continued*

Year	Team	Games	BA	SA	AB	H	2B	3B	HR	HR%	R	RBI	BB	SO	SB	Pinch Hit AB	Pinch Hit H	PO	A	E	DP	TC/G	FA	G by Pos
1912		63	.194	.225	191	37	4	1	0	0.0	23	9	31		10	0	0	347	113	11	7	7.5	.977	C-63
1913		96	.223	.293	273	61	8	4	1	0.4	26	26	30	43	5	0	0	476	127	11	9	6.4	.982	C-96
1914		91	.169	.226	261	44	7	4	0	0.0	22	20	37	47	7	0	0	513	124	13	9	7.1	.980	C-91
1915		95	.220	.278	277	61	9	2	1	0.4	20	22	36	28	10	1	0	478	122	17	4	6.6	.972	C-94
1916		117	.249	.308	305	76	12	3	0	0.0	28	46	49	40	12	1	0	538	124	13	17	5.8	.981	C-116
1917		65	.190	.227	163	31	6	0	0	0.0	10	18	24	16	1	4	0	274	54	4	6	5.6	.988	C-59
1918	**BOS N**	43	.206	.225	102	21	2	0	0	0.0	6	4	10	15	0	3	1	121	38	6	5	4.3	.964	C-38
9 yrs.		683	.207	.254	1920	397	54	15	2	0.1	161	171	244	189	55	12	1	3461	860	97	82	6.6	.978	C-626, 1B-40

Ron Henry

HENRY, RONALD BAXTER BR TR 6′ 1″ 180 lbs.
B. Aug. 7, 1936, Chester, Pa.

Year	Team	Games	BA	SA	AB	H	2B	3B	HR	HR%	R	RBI	BB	SO	SB	Pinch Hit AB	Pinch Hit H	PO	A	E	DP	TC/G	FA	G by Pos
1961	**MIN A**	20	.143	.143	28	4	0	0	0	0.0	1	3	2	7	0	14	3	22	2	0	0	4.0	1.000	C-5, 1B-1
1964		22	.122	.341	41	5	1	1	2	4.9	4	5	2	17	0	11	1	54	6	1	2	4.7	.984	C-13
2 yrs.		42	.130	.261	69	9	1	1	2	2.9	5	8	4	24	0	25	4	76	8	1	2	4.5	.988	C-18, 1B-1

Snake Henry

HENRY, FREDERICK MARSHALL BL TL 6′ 170 lbs.
B. July 19, 1895, Waynesville, N. C. D. Oct. 12, 1987, Wendell, N. C.

Year	Team	Games	BA	SA	AB	H	2B	3B	HR	HR%	R	RBI	BB	SO	SB	Pinch Hit AB	Pinch Hit H	PO	A	E	DP	TC/G	FA	G by Pos
1922	**BOS N**	18	.197	.288	66	13	4	1	0	0.0	5	5	2	8	2	0	0	170	12	1	7	10.2	.995	1B-18
1923		11	.111	.111	9	1	0	0	0	0.0	1	2	1	1	0	9	1	0	0	0	0	0.0	—	
2 yrs.		29	.187	.267	75	14	4	1	0	0.0	6	7	3	9	2	9	1	170	12	1	7	10.2	.995	1B-18

Babe Herman

HERMAN, FLOYD CAVES BL TL 6′ 4″ 190 lbs.
B. June 26, 1903, Buffalo, N. Y. D. Nov. 27, 1987, Glendale, Calif.

Year	Team	Games	BA	SA	AB	H	2B	3B	HR	HR%	R	RBI	BB	SO	SB	Pinch Hit AB	Pinch Hit H	PO	A	E	DP	TC/G	FA	G by Pos
1926	**BKN N**	137	.319	.500	496	158	35	11	11	2.2	64	81	44	53	8	6	2	974	64	17	55	7.8	.984	1B-101, OF-35
1927		130	.272	.481	412	112	26	9	14	3.4	65	73	39	41	4	20	7	969	68	21	64	10.0	.980	1B-105, OF-1
1928		134	.340	.514	486	165	37	6	12	2.5	64	91	38	36	1	6	1	225	12	16	2	2.0	.937	OF-127
1929		146	.381	.612	569	217	42	13	21	3.7	105	113	55	45	21	3	2	260	11	17	3	2.0	.941	OF-141, 1B-2
1930		153	.393	.678	614	241	48	11	35	5.7	143	130	66	56	18	0	0	260	10	6	1	1.8	.978	OF-153
1931		151	.313	.525	610	191	43	16	18	3.0	93	97	50	65	17	0	0	287	24	13	7	2.2	.960	OF-150
1932	**CIN N**	148	.326	.541	577	188	38	**19**	16	2.8	87	87	60	45	7	2	1	392	18	13	6	2.9	.969	OF-146
1933	**CHI N**	137	.289	.502	508	147	36	12	16	3.1	77	93	50	57	6	5	4	252	12	12	1	2.1	.957	OF-131
1934		125	.304	.488	467	142	34	5	14	3.0	65	84	35	71	1	6	2	251	10	7	7	2.2	.974	OF-113, 1B-7
1935	**2 teams**	**PIT N** (26G –.235)	**CIN N** (92G –.335)																					
"	**total**	118	.316	.486	430	136	31	6	10	2.3	52	65	38	35	5	10	0	319	15	9	12	3.2	.974	OF-91, 1B-17
1936	**CIN N**	119	.279	.458	380	106	25	2	13	3.4	59	71	39	36	4	19	4	184	4	6	1	2.0	.969	OF-92, 1B-4
1937	**DET A**	17	.300	.450	20	6	3	0	0	0.0	2	3	1	6	2	14	3	3	0	0	0	1.5	1.000	OF-2
1945	**BKN N**	37	.265	.382	34	9	1	0	1	2.9	6	9	5	7	0	29	6	0	0	0	0	0.0	.000	OF-3
13 yrs.		1552	.324	.532	5603	1818	399	110	181	3.2	882	997	520	553	94	120	32	4376	248	137	159	3.4	.971	OF-1185, 1B-236

Billy Herman

HERMAN, WILLIAM JENNINGS BRYAN BR TR 5′11″ 180 lbs.
B. July 7, 1909, New Albany, Ind. D. Sept. 5, 1992, West Palm Beach, Fla.
Manager 1947, 1964–66.
Hall of Fame 1975.

Year	Team	Games	BA	SA	AB	H	2B	3B	HR	HR%	R	RBI	BB	SO	SB	Pinch Hit AB	Pinch Hit H	PO	A	E	DP	TC/G	FA	G by Pos
1931	**CHI N**	25	.327	.398	98	32	7	0	0	0.0	14	16	13	6	2	0	0	76	79	10	17	6.6	.939	2B-25
1932		154	.314	.404	656	206	42	7	1	0.2	102	51	40	33	14	0	0	401	527	38	102	6.3	.961	2B-154
1933		153	.279	.342	619	173	35	2	0	0.0	82	44	45	34	5	0	0	466	512	45	114	6.7	.956	2B-153
1934		113	.303	.395	456	138	21	6	3	0.7	79	42	34	31	6	1	0	278	385	17	64	6.1	.975	2B-111
1935		154	.341	.476	666	**227**	**57**	6	7	1.1	113	83	42	29	6	0	0	416	520	35	109	6.3	.964	2B-154
1936		153	.334	.470	632	211	57	7	5	0.8	101	93	59	30	5	0	0	457	492	24	110	6.4	.975	2B-153
1937		138	.335	.479	564	189	35	11	8	1.4	106	65	56	22	2	1	0	384	468	41	97	6.5	.954	2B-137
1938		152	.277	.359	624	173	34	7	1	0.2	86	56	59	31	3	1	0	404	517	18	111	6.2	.981	2B-151
1939		156	.307	.453	623	191	34	**18**	7	1.1	111	70	66	31	9	0	0	377	485	29	95	5.7	.967	2B-156
1940		135	.292	.376	558	163	24	4	5	0.9	77	57	47	30	1	0	0	366	448	22	94	6.2	.974	2B-135
1941	**2 teams**	**CHI N** (11G –.194)	**BKN N** (133G –.291)																					
"	**total**	144	.285	.371	572	163	30	5	3	0.5	81	41	67	43	1	0	0	330	374	26	69	5.1	.964	2B-144
1942	**BKN N**	155	.256	.333	571	146	34	2	2	0.4	76	65	72	52	6	0	0	412	404	23	99	5.4	.973	2B-153, 1B-3
1943		153	.330	.417	585	193	41	2	2	0.3	76	100	66	26	4	0	0	345	390	21	71	4.9	.972	2B-117, 3B-37
1946	**2 teams**	**BKN N** (47G –.288)	**BOS N** (75G –.306)																					
"	**total**	122	.298	.413	436	130	31	5	3	0.7	56	50	69	23	3	4	1	352	207	16	61	3.6	.972	2B-76, 3B-63, 1B-22
1947	**PIT N**	15	.213	.298	47	10	4	0	0	0.0	3	6	2	7	0	1	0	20	15	0	2	2.9	1.000	2B-10, 1B-2
15 yrs.		1922	.304	.407	7707	2345	486	82	47	0.6	1163	839	737	428	67	8	1	5084	5823	365	1215	5.8	.968	2B-1829, 3B-100, 1B-27
WORLD SERIES																								
1932	**CHI N**	4	.222	.278	18	4	1	0	0	0.0	5	1	1	3	0	0	0	5	12	1	6	4.5	.944	2B-4
1935		6	.333	.625	24	8	2	1	1	4.2	3	6	0	2	0	0	0	15	19	1	4	5.8	.971	2B-6
1938		4	.188	.188	16	3	0	0	0	0.0	1	0	1	4	0	0	0	5	14	2	2	5.3	.905	2B-4
1941	**BKN N**	4	.125	.125	8	1	0	0	0	0.0	0	0	2	0	0	0	0	4	13	0	2	4.3	1.000	2B-4
4 yrs.		18	.242	.364	66	16	3	1	1	1.5	9	7	4	9	0	0	0	29	58	4	14	5.1	.956	2B-18

Al Hermann

HERMANN, ALBERT BARTEL BR TR 6′ 180 lbs.
B. Mar. 28, 1899, Milltown, N. J. D. Aug. 20, 1980, Lewes, Del.

Year	Team	Games	BA	SA	AB	H	2B	3B	HR	HR%	R	RBI	BB	SO	SB	Pinch Hit AB	Pinch Hit H	PO	A	E	DP	TC/G	FA	G by Pos
1923	**BOS N**	31	.237	.280	93	22	4	0	0	0.0	2	11	0	7	3	7	0	62	52	6	5	5.0	.950	2B-15, 3B-5, 1B-4
1924		1	.000	.000	1	0	0	0	0	0.0	0	0	0	1	0	1	0	0	0	0	0	0.0	—	
2 yrs.		32	.234	.277	94	22	4	0	0	0.0	2	11	0	8	3	8	0	62	52	6	5	5.0	.950	2B-15, 3B-5, 1B-4

Gene Hermanski

HERMANSKI, EUGENE VICTOR BL TR 5′11½″ 185 lbs.
B. May 11, 1920, Pittsfield, Mass.

Year	Team	Games	BA	SA	AB	H	2B	3B	HR	HR%	R	RBI	BB	SO	SB	Pinch Hit AB	Pinch Hit H	PO	A	E	DP	TC/G	FA	G by Pos
1943	**BKN N**	18	.300	.367	60	18	2	1	0	0.0	6	12	11	7	1	0	0	36	4	1	1	2.3	.976	OF-18
1946		64	.200	.255	110	22	2	2	0	0.0	15	8	17	10	2	24	2	45	0	3	0	1.4	.938	OF-34
1947		79	.275	.434	189	52	7	1	7	3.7	36	39	28	7	5	12	4	105	5	2	0	1.7	.982	OF-66
1948		133	.290	.492	400	116	22	7	15	3.8	63	60	64	46	15	12	3	225	13	7	1	2.1	.971	OF-119
1949		87	.299	.487	224	67	12	3	8	3.6	48	42	47	21	12	13	5	140	7	3	1	1.9	.980	OF-77

Gene Hermanski *continued*

Year	Team	Games	BA	SA	AB	H	2B	3B	HR	HR%	R	RBI	BB	SO	SB	Pinch Hit AB	Pinch Hit H	PO	A	E	DP	TC/G	FA	G by Pos
1950		94	.298	.450	289	86	17	3	7	2.4	36	34	36	26	2	12	3	172	5	2	0	2.3	.989	OF-78
1951	2 teams	BKN N (31G –.250) CHI N (75G –.281)																						
"	total	106	.273	.370	311	85	16	1	4	1.3	36	25	45	42	3	20	7	175	11	6	2	2.0	.969	OF-94
1952	CHI N	99	.255	.320	275	70	6	0	4	1.5	28	34	29	32	2	21	10	146	7	3	3	2.1	.981	OF-76
1953	2 teams	CHI N (18G –.150) PIT N (41G –.177)																						
"	total	59	.167	.206	102	17	1	0	1	1.0	8	5	12	21	1	29	4	44	0	0	0	1.7	1.000	OF-26
9 yrs.		739	.272	.404	1960	533	85	18	46	2.3	276	259	289	212	43	143	38	1088	52	27	8	2.0	.977	OF-588
WORLD SERIES																								
1947	BKN N	7	.158	.263	19	3	0	1	0	0.0	4	1	3	3	0	0	0	15	0	0	0	2.1	1.000	OF-7
1949		4	.308	.462	13	4	0	1	0	0.0	1	2	3	3	0	0	0	7	0	0	0	1.8	1.000	OF-4
2 yrs.		11	.219	.344	32	7	0	2	0	0.0	5	3	6	6	0	0	0	22	0	0	0	2.0	1.000	OF-11

Angel Hermoso

HERMOSO, ANGEL REMIGIO (Remy) BR TR 5′ 8″ 155 lbs.
B. Oct. 1, 1947, Carabobo, Venezuela.

Year	Team	Games	BA	SA	AB	H	2B	3B	HR	HR%	R	RBI	BB	SO	SB	Pinch Hit AB	Pinch Hit H	PO	A	E	DP	TC/G	FA	G by Pos
1967	ATL N	11	.308	.308	26	8	0	0	0	0.0	3	0	2	4	1	0	0	16	24	2	4	3.8	.952	SS-9, 2B-2
1969	MON N	28	.162	.162	74	12	0	0	0	0.0	6	3	5	10	3	3	0	35	60	4	18	4.1	.960	2B-18, SS-6
1970		4	.000	.000	1	0	0	0	0	0.0	1	0	0	0	0	1	0	1	1	0	0	1.0	1.000	3B-1, 2B-1
1974	CLE A	48	.221	.262	122	27	3	1	0	0.0	15	5	7	7	2	1	0	86	121	7	27	4.8	.967	2B-45
4 yrs.		91	.211	.233	223	47	3	1	0	0.0	25	8	14	21	6	5	0	138	206	13	49	4.4	.964	2B-66, SS-15, 3B-1

Carlos Hernandez

HERNANDEZ, CARLOS ALBERTO BR TR 5′11″ 185 lbs.
Born Carlos Alberto Hernandez (Almeida).
B. May 24, 1967, San Felix, Venezuela.

Year	Team	Games	BA	SA	AB	H	2B	3B	HR	HR%	R	RBI	BB	SO	SB	Pinch Hit AB	Pinch Hit H	PO	A	E	DP	TC/G	FA	G by Pos
1990	LA N	10	.200	.250	20	4	1	0	0	0.0	2	1	0	2	0	0	0	37	2	0	0	3.9	1.000	C-10
1991		15	.214	.286	14	3	1	0	0	0.0	1	1	0	5	1	2	0	24	4	1	0	2.1	.966	C-13, 3B-1
1992		69	.260	.335	173	45	4	0	3	1.7	11	17	11	21	0	10	0	295	37	7	4	5.4	.979	C-63
1993		50	.253	.364	99	25	5	0	2	2.0	6	7	2	11	0	11	2	181	15	7	0	4.7	.966	C-43
1994		32	.219	.344	64	14	2	0	2	3.1	6	6	1	14	0	6	0	104	12	0	0	4.3	1.000	C-27
1995		45	.149	.223	94	14	1	0	2	2.1	3	8	7	25	0	5	2	210	24	4	2	5.8	.983	C-41
6 yrs.		221	.226	.315	464	105	14	0	9	1.9	29	40	21	78	1	34	4	851	94	19	6	4.9	.980	C-197, 3B-1

Cesar Hernandez

HERNANDEZ, CESAR DARIO BR TR 6′ 160 lbs.
Born Cesar Dario Hernandez (Perez).
B. Sept. 28, 1966, Yamasa, Dominican Republic.

Year	Team	Games	BA	SA	AB	H	2B	3B	HR	HR%	R	RBI	BB	SO	SB	Pinch Hit AB	Pinch Hit H	PO	A	E	DP	TC/G	FA	G by Pos
1992	CIN N	34	.275	.353	51	14	4	0	0	0.0	6	4	0	10	3	18	6	18	2	1	1	1.2	.952	OF-18
1993		27	.083	.083	24	2	0	0	0	0.0	3	1	1	8	1	2	0	30	2	1	0	1.4	.970	OF-23
2 yrs.		61	.213	.267	75	16	4	0	0	0.0	9	5	1	18	4	20	6	48	4	2	1	1.3	.963	OF-41

Enzo Hernandez

HERNANDEZ, ENZO OCTAVIO BR TR 5′ 8″ 155 lbs.
B. Feb. 12, 1949, Valle de Guanape, Venezuela.

Year	Team	Games	BA	SA	AB	H	2B	3B	HR	HR%	R	RBI	BB	SO	SB	Pinch Hit AB	Pinch Hit H	PO	A	E	DP	TC/G	FA	G by Pos
1971	SD N	143	.222	.250	549	122	9	3	0	0.0	58	12	54	34	21	0	0	260	445	33	82	5.2	.955	SS-143
1972		114	.195	.249	329	64	11	2	1	0.3	33	15	22	25	24	1	0	169	319	19	59	4.6	.963	SS-107, OF-3
1973		70	.223	.239	247	55	2	1	0	0.0	26	9	17	14	15	2	0	106	190	7	42	4.5	.977	SS-67
1974		147	.232	.277	512	119	19	2	0	0.0	55	34	38	36	37	1	1	229	449	24	64	4.8	.966	SS-145
1975		116	.218	.265	344	75	12	2	0	0.0	37	19	26	25	20	0	0	168	327	18	70	4.6	.965	SS-111
1976		113	.256	.321	340	87	13	3	1	0.3	31	24	32	16	12	3	2	132	344	18	64	4.9	.964	SS-101
1977		7	.000	.000	3	0	0	0	0	0.0	1	0	0	0	0	0	0	4	6	0	0	1.4	1.000	SS-7
1978	LA N	4	.000	.000	3	0	0	0	0	0.0	0	0	0	1	0	0	0	0	0	0	0	0.0	.000	SS-2
8 yrs.		714	.224	.266	2327	522	66	13	2	0.1	241	113	189	151	129	7	3	1068	2080	119	381	4.8	.964	SS-683, OF-3

Jackie Hernandez

HERNANDEZ, JACINTO BR TR 5′11″ 165 lbs.
Born Jacinto Hernandez (Zulueta).
B. Sept. 11, 1940, Central Tinguaro, Cuba.

Year	Team	Games	BA	SA	AB	H	2B	3B	HR	HR%	R	RBI	BB	SO	SB	Pinch Hit AB	Pinch Hit H	PO	A	E	DP	TC/G	FA	G by Pos
1965	CAL A	6	.333	.500	6	2	1	0	0	0.0	2	1	0	1	1	0	0	1	3	2	0	2.0	.667	SS-2, 3B-1
1966		58	.043	.043	23	1	0	0	0	0.0	19	2	1	4	1	2	0	22	24	4	7	1.7	.920	3B-11, SS-8, 2B-8, OF-3
1967	MIN A	29	.143	.143	28	4	0	0	0	0.0	1	3	0	6	0	2	0	27	24	2	4	1.9	.962	SS-15, 3B-13
1968		83	.176	.221	199	35	3	0	2	1.0	13	17	9	52	5	0	0	122	197	25	44	4.3	.927	SS-79, 1B-1
1969	KC A	145	.222	.282	504	112	14	2	4	0.8	54	40	38	111	17	0	0	306	375	33	60	5.0	.954	SS-144
1970		83	.231	.282	238	55	4	1	2	0.8	14	10	15	50	1	3	1	142	187	17	38	4.5	.951	SS-77
1971	PIT N	88	.206	.300	233	48	7	3	3	1.3	30	26	17	45	0	1	0	109	252	18	42	4.5	.953	SS-75, 3B-9
1972		72	.188	.256	176	33	7	1	1	0.6	12	14	9	43	0	0	0	110	182	22	34	4.4	.930	SS-68, 3B-4
1973		54	.247	.315	73	18	1	2	0	0.0	8	8	4	12	0	2	1	45	81	8	19	2.7	.940	SS-49
9 yrs.		618	.208	.270	1480	308	37	9	12	0.8	153	121	93	324	25	10	2	884	1325	131	248	4.1	.944	SS-517, 3B-38, 2B-8, OF-3, 1B-1
LEAGUE CHAMPIONSHIP SERIES																								
1971	PIT N	4	.231	.231	13	3	0	0	0	0.0	2	1	0	4	0	0	0	7	9	1	2	4.3	.941	SS-4
WORLD SERIES																								
1971	PIT N	7	.222	.222	18	4	0	0	0	0.0	2	1	2	5	1	0	0	9	16	0	3	3.6	1.000	SS-7

Jose Hernandez

HERNANDEZ, JOSE ANTONIO BR TR 6′ 1″ 180 lbs.
Born Jose Antonio Hernandez (Figueroa).
B. July 14, 1969, Rio Piedras, Puerto Rico.

Year	Team	Games	BA	SA	AB	H	2B	3B	HR	HR%	R	RBI	BB	SO	SB	Pinch Hit AB	Pinch Hit H	PO	A	E	DP	TC/G	FA	G by Pos
1991	TEX A	45	.184	.224	98	18	2	1	0	0.0	8	4	3	31	0	0	0	49	111	4	18	3.6	.976	SS-44, 3B-1
1992	CLE A	3	.000	.000	4	0	0	0	0	0.0	0	0	0	2	0	0	0	3	3	1	0	2.3	.857	SS-3
1994	CHI N	56	.242	.326	132	32	2	3	1	0.8	18	9	8	29	2	8	2	46	85	4	15	2.3	.970	3B-28, SS-21, 2B-8, OF-1
1995		93	.245	.482	245	60	11	4	13	5.3	37	40	13	69	1	10	3	112	189	9	35	3.4	.971	SS-43, 2B-29, 3B-20
4 yrs.		197	.230	.382	479	110	15	8	14	2.9	63	53	24	131	3	18	5	210	388	18	68	3.1	.971	SS-111, 3B-49, 2B-37, OF-1

Keith Hernandez

HERNANDEZ, KEITH (Mex) BL TL 6′ 180 lbs.
B. Oct. 20, 1953, San Francisco, Calif.

Year	Team	Games	BA	SA	AB	H	2B	3B	HR	HR%	R	RBI	BB	SO	SB	Pinch Hit AB	Pinch Hit H	PO	A	E	DP	TC/G	FA	G by Pos
1974	STL N	14	.294	.441	34	10	1	2	0	0.0	3	2	7	8	0	3	1	70	1	2	8	8.1	.973	1B-9
1975		64	.250	.362	188	47	8	2	3	1.6	20	20	17	26	0	9	3	469	36	2	34	9.1	.996	1B-56

Keith Hernandez *continued*

Year	Team		Games	BA	SA	AB	H	2B	3B	HR	HR%	R	RBI	BB	SO	SB	Pinch Hit AB	Pinch Hit H	PO	A	E	DP	TC/G	FA	G by Pos
1976			129	.289	.428	374	108	21	5	7	1.9	54	46	49	53	4	17	4	862	107	10	87	8.9	.990	1B-110
1977			161	.291	.459	560	163	41	4	15	2.7	90	91	79	88	7	6	1	1453	106	12	146	9.9	.992	1B-158
1978			159	.255	.389	542	138	32	4	11	2.0	90	64	82	68	13	5	1	1436	96	10	124	9.8	.994	1B-158
1979			161	**.344**	.513	610	210	**48**	11	11	1.8	**116**	105	80	78	11	2	2	1489	146	8	145	10.3	.995	1B-160
1980			159	.321	.494	595	191	39	8	16	2.7	**111**	99	86	73	14	2	0	1572	115	9	146	10.8	.995	1B-157
1981			103	.306	.463	376	115	27	4	8	2.1	65	48	61	45	12	2	0	1056	86	3	99	11.3	.997	1B-98, OF-3
1982			160	.299	.413	579	173	33	6	7	1.2	79	94	100	67	19	1	1	1591	135	11	140	10.7	.994	1B-158, OF-4
1983	**2 teams**		**STL N** (55G –.284) **NY N** (95G –.306)																						
"	**total**		150	.297	.433	538	160	23	7	12	2.2	77	63	88	72	9	5	1	1418	147	13	147	11.0	.992	1B-144
1984	**NY**	**N**	154	.311	.449	550	171	31	0	15	2.7	83	94	97	89	2	1	0	1214	142	8	127	8.9	.994	1B-153
1985			158	.309	.430	593	183	34	4	10	1.7	87	91	77	59	3	3	1	1310	139	4	113	9.3	.997	1B-157
1986			149	.310	.446	551	171	34	1	13	2.4	94	83	**94**	69	2	0	0	1199	149	5	115	9.1	.996	1B-149
1987			154	.290	.436	587	170	28	2	18	3.1	87	89	81	104	0	1	0	1298	149	10	110	9.5	.993	1B-154
1988			95	.276	.417	348	96	16	0	11	3.2	43	55	31	57	2	1	0	734	77	2	63	8.7	.998	1B-93
1989			75	.233	.326	215	50	8	0	4	1.9	18	19	27	39	0	17	2	405	31	4	22	7.6	.991	1B-58
1990	**CLE**	**A**	43	.200	.238	130	26	2	0	1	0.8	7	8	14	17	0	1	0	340	20	2	28	8.6	.994	1B-42
17 yrs.			2088	.296	.436	7370	2182	426	60	162	2.2	1124	1071	1070	1012	98	76	17	17916	1682	115	1654	9.8	.994	1B-2014, OF-7
LEAGUE CHAMPIONSHIP SERIES																									
1982	**STL**	**N**	3	.333	.333	12	4	0	0	0	0.0	3	1	2	3	0	0	0	35	1	0	3	12.0	1.000	1B-3
1986	**NY**	**N**	6	.269	.385	26	7	1	1	0	0.0	3	3	3	6	0	0	0	66	11	0	5	12.8	1.000	1B-6
1988			7	.269	.385	26	7	0	0	1	3.8	2	5	6	7	1	0	0	57	4	1	2	8.9	.984	1B-7
3 yrs.			16	.281	.375	64	18	1	1	1	1.6	8	9	11	16	1	0	0	158	16	1	10	10.9	.994	1B-16
														9th											
WORLD SERIES																									
1982	**STL**	**N**	7	.259	.444	27	7	2	0	1	3.7	4	8	4	2	0	0	0	62	7	2	10	10.1	.972	1B-7
1986	**NY**	**N**	7	.231	.231	26	6	0	0	0	0.0	1	4	5	1	0	0	0	48	4	1	4	7.6	.981	1B-7
2 yrs.			14	.245	.340	53	13	2	0	1	1.9	5	12	9	3	0	0	0	110	11	3	14	8.9	.976	1B-14

Leo Hernandez

HERNANDEZ, LEONARDO JESUS BR TR 5′11″ 170 lbs.
Born Leonardo Jesus Antiah (Hernandez).
B. Nov. 6, 1959, Santa Lucia, Venezuela.

Year	Team		Games	BA	SA	AB	H	2B	3B	HR	HR%	R	RBI	BB	SO	SB	Pinch Hit AB	Pinch Hit H	PO	A	E	DP	TC/G	FA	G by Pos
1982	**BAL**	**A**	2	.000	.000	2	0	0	0	0	0.0	0	0	0	2	0	2	0	0	0	0	0	0.0	—	
1983			64	.246	.374	203	50	6	1	6	3.0	21	26	12	19	1	0	0	44	109	13	3	2.6	.922	3B-64
1985			12	.045	.045	22	1	0	0	0	0.0	0	0	0	4	0	6	0	2	0	0	0	0.2	1.000	DH-8, 1B-1, OF-1
1986	**NY**	**A**	7	.227	.455	22	5	2	0	1	4.5	2	4	1	8	0	0	0	5	10	0	0	1.7	1.000	3B-7, SS-1, 2B-1
4 yrs.			85	.225	.349	249	56	8	1	7	2.8	23	30	13	33	1	8	0	51	119	13	3	2.2	.929	3B-71, DH-8, 1B-1, 2B-1, SS-1, OF-1

Pedro Hernandez

HERNANDEZ, PEDRO JULIO BR TR 6′ 1″ 160 lbs.
Born Pedro Julio Montas (Hernandez).
B. Apr. 4, 1959, La Romana, Dominican Republic.

Year	Team		Games	BA	SA	AB	H	2B	3B	HR	HR%	R	RBI	BB	SO	SB	Pinch Hit AB	Pinch Hit H	PO	A	E	DP	TC/G	FA	G by Pos
1979	**TOR**	**A**	3	—	—	0	0	0	0	0	—	1	0	0	0	0	0	0	0	0	0	0	0.0	.000	DH-2
1982			8	.000	.000	9	0	0	0	0	0.0	1	0	0	3	0	3	0	0	0	0	0	0.0		DH-3, 3B-2, OF-1
2 yrs.			11	.000	.000	9	0	0	0	0	0.0	2	0	0	3	0	3	0	0	0	0	0	0.0		DH-5, 3B-2, OF-1

Rudy Hernandez

HERNANDEZ, RODOLFO BR TR 5′ 9″ 150 lbs.
Born Rodolfo Hernandez (Acosta).
B. Oct. 18, 1951, Empalme, Mexico.

Year	Team		Games	BA	SA	AB	H	2B	3B	HR	HR%	R	RBI	BB	SO	SB	Pinch Hit AB	Pinch Hit H	PO	A	E	DP	TC/G	FA	G by Pos
1972	**CHI**	**A**	8	.190	.190	21	4	0	0	0	0.0	0	1	0	3	0	2	1	10	16	0	3	4.3	1.000	SS-6

Sal Hernandez

HERNANDEZ, SALVADOR JOSE (Chico) BR TR 6′ 1″ 195 lbs.
Born Salvador Jose Hernandez (Ramos).
B. Jan. 3, 1916, Havana, Cuba D. Jan. 3, 1986, Havana, Cuba.

Year	Team		Games	BA	SA	AB	H	2B	3B	HR	HR%	R	RBI	BB	SO	SB	Pinch Hit AB	Pinch Hit H	PO	A	E	DP	TC/G	FA	G by Pos
1942	**CHI**	**N**	47	.229	.271	118	27	5	0	0	0.0	6	7	11	13	0	3	1	140	17	4	0	3.7	.975	C-43
1943			43	.270	.302	126	34	4	0	0	0.0	10	9	9	9	0	2	0	132	21	3	1	3.8	.981	C-41
2 yrs.			90	.250	.287	244	61	9	0	0	0.0	16	16	20	22	0	5	1	272	38	7	1	3.8	.978	C-84

Toby Hernandez

HERNANDEZ, RAFAEL TOBIAS BR TR 6′ 1″ 160 lbs.
Born Rafael Tobias Hernandez (Alvarado).
B. Nov. 30, 1958, Calabozo, Venezuela.

Year	Team		Games	BA	SA	AB	H	2B	3B	HR	HR%	R	RBI	BB	SO	SB	Pinch Hit AB	Pinch Hit H	PO	A	E	DP	TC/G	FA	G by Pos
1984	**TOR**	**A**	3	.500	.500	2	1	0	0	0	0.0	1	0	0	0	0	0	0	1	0	0	0	0.3	1.000	C-3

Larry Herndon

HERNDON, LARRY DARNELL BR TR 6′ 3″ 190 lbs.
B. Nov. 3, 1953, Sunflower, Tex.

Year	Team		Games	BA	SA	AB	H	2B	3B	HR	HR%	R	RBI	BB	SO	SB	Pinch Hit AB	Pinch Hit H	PO	A	E	DP	TC/G	FA	G by Pos
1974	**STL**	**N**	12	1.000	1.000	1	1	0	0	0	0.0	3	0	0	0	0	0	0	1	0	0	0	1.0	1.000	OF-1
1976	**SF**	**N**	115	.288	.356	337	97	11	3	2	0.6	42	23	23	45	12	6	2	226	8	8	4	2.2	.967	OF-110
1977			49	.239	.358	109	26	4	3	1	0.9	13	5	5	20	4	5	1	87	2	4	0	2.1	.957	OF-44
1978			151	.259	.335	471	122	15	9	1	0.2	52	32	35	71	13	4	2	369	3	10	0	2.6	.974	OF-149
1979			132	.257	.384	354	91	14	5	7	2.0	35	36	29	70	8	19	7	196	10	8	2	1.8	.963	OF-122
1980			139	.258	.385	493	127	17	11	8	1.6	54	49	19	91	8	21	6	247	8	11	1	2.2	.959	OF-122
1981			96	.288	.415	364	105	15	8	5	1.4	48	41	20	55	15	4	0	207	8	5	1	2.4	.977	OF-93
1982	**DET**	**A**	157	.292	.480	614	179	21	13	23	3.7	92	88	38	92	12	3	0	328	11	6	3	2.2	.983	OF-155, DH-3
1983			153	.302	.478	603	182	28	9	20	3.3	88	92	46	95	9	5	1	283	6	15	1	2.0	.951	OF-133, DH-19
1984			125	.280	.400	407	114	18	5	7	1.7	52	43	32	63	6	24	7	199	7	3	0	1.7	.986	OF-117, DH-4
1985			137	.244	.384	443	108	12	7	12	2.7	45	37	33	79	2	5	3	273	7	7	4	2.1	.976	OF-136
1986			106	.247	.385	283	70	13	1	8	2.8	33	37	27	40	2	26	6	156	2	2	0	1.6	.988	OF-83, DH-18
1987			89	.324	.520	225	73	13	2	9	4.0	32	47	23	35	1	21	8	82	4	1	1	1.1	.989	OF-57, DH-23
1988			76	.224	.322	174	39	5	0	4	2.3	16	20	23	37	0	17	4	21	0	0	0	0.3	1.000	DH-53, OF-15
14 yrs.			1537	.273	.409	4878	1334	186	76	107	2.2	605	550	353	793	92	160	47	2675	76	80	17	1.9	.972	OF-1337, DH-120

Larry Herndon *continued*

Year	Team	Games	BA	SA	AB	H	2B	3B	HR	HR%	R	RBI	BB	SO	SB	Pinch Hit AB	Pinch Hit H	PO	A	E	DP	TC/G	FA	G by Pos
LEAGUE CHAMPIONSHIP SERIES																								
1984	DET A	2	.200	.800	5	1	0	0	1	20.0	1	1	1	2	0	0	0	6	0	0	0	3.0	1.000	OF-2
1987		3	.333	.444	9	3	1	0	0	0.0	1	2	1	1	0	1	1	2	0	1	0	1.0	.667	OF-2, DH-1
2 yrs.		5	.286	.571	14	4	1	0	1	7.1	2	3	2	3	0	1	1	8	0	1	0	1.8	.889	OF-4, DH-1
WORLD SERIES																								
1984	DET A	5	.333	.533	15	5	0	0	1	6.7	1	3	3	2	0	2	0	6	0	0	0	1.2	1.000	OF-5

Tom Hernon

HERNON, THOMAS H. BR TR
B. Nov. 4, 1866, E. Bridgewater, Mass. D. Feb. 4, 1902, New Bedford, Mass.

Year	Team	Games	BA	SA	AB	H	2B	3B	HR	HR%	R	RBI	BB	SO	SB	Pinch Hit AB	Pinch Hit H	PO	A	E	DP	TC/G	FA	G by Pos
1897	CHI N	4	.063	.063	16	1	0	0	0	0.0	2	2	0		1	0	0	10	0	0	0	2.5	1.000	OF-4

Ed Herr

HERR, EDWARD JOSEPH BR TR 5′ 9½″ 179 lbs.
B. May 18, 1862, St. Louis, Mo. D. July 18, 1943, St. Louis, Mo.

Year	Team	Games	BA	SA	AB	H	2B	3B	HR	HR%	R	RBI	BB	SO	SB	Pinch Hit AB	Pinch Hit H	PO	A	E	DP	TC/G	FA	G by Pos
1887	CLE AA	11	.273	.318	44	12	2	0	0	0.0	6		6		2	0	0	18	17	13	1	4.4	.729	3B-11
1888	STL AA	43	.267	.372	172	46	7	1	3	1.7	21	43	11		9	0	0	66	77	20	4	3.8	.877	SS-28, OF-11, 3B-4
1890		12	.220	.317	41	9	2	1	0	0.0	5		5		2	0	0	19	12	7	1	3.2	.816	2B-7, OF-4, 3B-1
3 yrs.		66	.261	.354	257	67	11	2	3	1.2	32	43	22		13	0	0	103	106	40	6	3.8	.839	SS-28, 3B-16, OF-15, 2B-7

Tommy Herr

HERR, THOMAS MITCHELL BB TR 6′ 175 lbs.
B. Apr. 4, 1956, Lancaster, Pa.

Year	Team	Games	BA	SA	AB	H	2B	3B	HR	HR%	R	RBI	BB	SO	SB	Pinch Hit AB	Pinch Hit H	PO	A	E	DP	TC/G	FA	G by Pos
1979	STL N	14	.200	.200	10	2	0	0	0	0.0	4	1	2	2	1	1	0	12	11	0	3	3.8	1.000	2B-6
1980		76	.248	.347	222	55	12	5	0	0.0	29	15	16	21	9	9	2	124	184	7	47	4.4	.978	2B-58, SS-14
1981		103	.268	.345	411	110	14	9	0	0.0	50	46	39	30	23	0	0	211	374	5	74	5.7	.992	2B-103
1982		135	.266	.320	493	131	19	4	0	0.0	83	36	57	56	25	5	2	263	427	9	97	5.5	.987	2B-128
1983		89	.323	.412	313	101	14	4	2	0.6	43	31	43	27	6	5	2	178	245	6	60	5.0	.986	2B-86
1984		145	.276	.346	558	154	23	2	4	0.7	67	49	49	56	13	1	1	328	452	6	106	5.5	.992	2B-144
1985		159	.302	.416	596	180	38	3	8	1.3	97	110	80	55	31	1	1	337	448	12	120	5.0	.985	2B-158
1986		152	.252	.331	559	141	30	4	2	0.4	48	61	73	75	22	0	0	352	414	9	121	5.1	.988	2B-152
1987		141	.263	.331	510	134	29	0	2	0.4	73	83	68	62	19	2	1	306	350	7	103	4.8	.989	2B-137
1988	2 teams	STL N (15G –.260) MIN A (86G –.263)																						
″	total	101	.263	.325	354	93	16	0	2	0.6	46	24	51	51	13	10	3	168	230	5	63	4.3	.988	2B-88, DH-3, SS-2
1989	PHI N	151	.287	.364	561	161	25	6	2	0.4	65	37	54	63	10	8	3	281	415	7	80	4.9	.990	2B-144
1990	2 teams	PHI N (119G –.264) NY N (27G –.250)																						
″	total	146	.261	.347	547	143	26	3	5	0.9	48	60	50	58	7	7	2	275	349	7	94	4.5	.989	2B-140
1991	2 teams	NY N (70G –.194) SF N (32G –.250)																						
″	total	102	.209	.270	215	45	8	1	1	0.5	23	21	45	28	9	28	5	116	151	0	33	3.5	1.000	2B-72, 3B-3, OF-1
13 yrs.		1514	.271	.350	5349	1450	254	41	28	0.5	676	574	627	584	188	77	22	2951	4050	80	1001	4.9	.989	2B-1416, SS-16, 3B-3, DH-3, OF-1
LEAGUE CHAMPIONSHIP SERIES																								
1982	STL N	3	.231	.308	13	3	1	0	0	0.0	1	0	1	2	0	0	0	2	0	0	3	0.7	1.000	2B-3
1985		6	.333	.667	21	7	4	0	1	4.8	2	6	5	2	1	0	0	13	10	0	3	3.8	1.000	2B-6
1987		7	.222	.222	27	6	0	0	0	0.0	0	3	0	1	1	0	0	12	11	1	3	3.4	.958	2B-7
3 yrs.		16	.262	.393	61	16	5	0	1	1.6	3	9	6	5	2	0	0	27	21	1	9	3.1	.980	2B-16
WORLD SERIES																								
1982	STL N	7	.160	.240	25	4	2	0	0	0.0	2	5	3	3	0	0	0	11	19	1	6	4.4	.968	2B-7
1985		7	.154	.231	26	4	2	0	0	0.0	2	0	2	2	0	0	0	11	13	0	8	3.4	1.000	2B-7
1987		7	.250	.357	28	7	0	0	1	3.6	2	1	2	2	0	0	0	23	17	0	1	5.7	1.000	2B-7
3 yrs.		21	.190	.278	79	15	4	0	1	1.3	6	6	7	7	0	0	0	45	49	1	15	4.5	.989	2B-21

Jose Herrera

HERRERA, JOSE CONCEPCION (Loco) BR TR 5′ 8″ 165 lbs.
Born Jose Concepcion Herrera (Ontiveros).
B. Apr. 8, 1942, San Lorenzo, Venezuela.

Year	Team	Games	BA	SA	AB	H	2B	3B	HR	HR%	R	RBI	BB	SO	SB	Pinch Hit AB	Pinch Hit H	PO	A	E	DP	TC/G	FA	G by Pos
1967	HOU N	5	.250	.250	4	1	0	0	0	0.0	0	1	0	1	0	4	1	0	0	0	0	0.0	—	
1968		27	.240	.290	100	24	5	0	0	0.0	9	7	4	12	0	4	1	37	20	4	4	2.5	.934	OF-17, 2B-7
1969	MON N	47	.286	.373	126	36	5	0	2	1.6	7	12	3	14	1	13	3	48	2	1	0	1.5	.980	OF-31, 2B-2, 3B-1
1970		1	.000	.000	1	0	0	0	0	0.0	0	0	0	1	0	1	0	0	0	0	0	0.0	—	
4 yrs.		80	.264	.333	231	61	10	0	2	0.9	16	20	7	28	1	22	5	85	22	5	4	1.9	.955	OF-48, 2B-9, 3B-1

Jose Herrera

HERRERA, JOSE RAMON BL TL 6′ 165 lbs.
Born Jose Ramon Herrera (Catalino).
B. Aug. 30, 1972, Santo Domingo, Dominican Republic.

Year	Team	Games	BA	SA	AB	H	2B	3B	HR	HR%	R	RBI	BB	SO	SB	Pinch Hit AB	Pinch Hit H	PO	A	E	DP	TC/G	FA	G by Pos
1995	OAK A	33	.243	.314	70	17	1	2	0	0.0	9	2	6	11	1	7	2	41	2	2	1	1.5	.956	OF-25, DH-5

Mike Herrera

HERRERA, RAMON BR TR 5′ 6″ 147 lbs.
B. Dec. 19, 1897, Havana, Cuba D. Feb. 3, 1978, Havana, Cuba.

Year	Team	Games	BA	SA	AB	H	2B	3B	HR	HR%	R	RBI	BB	SO	SB	Pinch Hit AB	Pinch Hit H	PO	A	E	DP	TC/G	FA	G by Pos
1925	BOS A	10	.385	.385	39	15	0	0	0	0.0	2	8	2	2	1	0	0	25	43	3	3	7.1	.958	2B-10
1926		74	.257	.325	237	61	14	1	0	0.0	20	19	15	13	0	4	0	135	212	14	34	5.3	.961	2B-48, 3B-16, SS-4
2 yrs.		84	.275	.333	276	76	14	1	0	0.0	22	27	17	15	1	4	0	160	255	17	37	5.5	.961	2B-58, 3B-16, SS-4

Pancho Herrera

HERRERA, JUAN FRANCISCO BR TR 6′ 3″ 220 lbs.
Born Juan Francisco Herrera (Willavicencio).
B. June 16, 1934, Santiago, Cuba.

Year	Team	Games	BA	SA	AB	H	2B	3B	HR	HR%	R	RBI	BB	SO	SB	Pinch Hit AB	Pinch Hit H	PO	A	E	DP	TC/G	FA	G by Pos
1958	PHI N	29	.270	.365	63	17	3	0	1	1.6	5	6	7	15	1	2	0	52	31	1	6	3.1	.988	3B-16, 1B-11
1960		145	.281	.455	512	144	26	6	17	3.3	61	71	51	**136**	2	3	1	1053	155	15	99	8.1	.988	1B-134, 2B-17
1961		126	.258	.407	400	103	17	2	13	3.3	56	51	55	120	5	10	3	1003	96	8	104	9.6	.993	1B-115
3 yrs.		300	.271	.430	975	264	46	8	31	3.2	122	128	113	271	8	15	4	2108	282	24	209	8.2	.990	1B-260, 2B-17, 3B-16

Lefty Herring

HERRING, SILAS CLARKE BL TL 5′11″ 160 lbs.
B. Mar. 4, 1880, Philadelphia, Pa. D. Feb. 11, 1965, Massapequa, N. Y.

Year	Team	Games	BA	SA	AB	H	2B	3B	HR	HR%	R	RBI	BB	SO	SB	Pinch Hit AB	Pinch Hit H	PO	A	E	DP	TC/G	FA	G by Pos
1899	WAS N	2	1.000	1.000	1	1	0	0	0	0.0	1	0	1		0	0	0	0	1	0	0	0.5	1.000	P-2
1904	WAS A	15	.174	.196	46	8	1	0	0	0.0	3	2	7		0	0	0	105	10	2	6	7.8	.983	1B-10, OF-5
2 yrs.		17	.191	.213	47	9	1	0	0	0.0	4	2	8		0	0	0	105	11	2	6	6.9	.983	1B-10, OF-5, P-2

Ed Herrmann

HERRMANN, EDWARD MARTIN BL TR 6′ 1″ 195 lbs.
B. Aug. 27, 1946, San Diego, Calif.

Year	Team	Games	BA	SA	AB	H	2B	3B	HR	HR%	R	RBI	BB	SO	SB	Pinch Hit AB	Pinch Hit H	PO	A	E	DP	TC/G	FA	G by Pos
1967	CHI A	2	.667	1.000	3	2	1	0	0	0.0	1	1	1	0	0	0	0	12	1	0	0	6.5	1.000	C-2
1969		102	.231	.341	290	67	8	0	8	2.8	31	31	30	35	0	11	1	420	41	8	7	5.1	.983	C-92
1970		96	.283	.505	297	84	9	0	19	6.4	42	52	31	41	0	7	1	433	51	6	10	5.6	.988	C-88
1971		101	.214	.347	294	63	6	0	11	3.7	32	35	44	48	2	7	0	556	56	3	5	6.3	.995	C-97
1972		116	.249	.359	354	88	9	0	10	2.8	23	40	43	37	0	5	2	641	69	8	10	6.4	.989	C-112
1973		119	.224	.354	379	85	17	1	10	2.6	42	39	31	55	2	2	0	617	70	11	11	6.0	.984	C-114, DH-2
1974		107	.259	.381	367	95	13	1	10	2.7	32	39	16	49	1	0	0	561	55	8	8	5.8	.987	C-107
1975	NY A	80	.255	.410	200	51	9	2	6	3.0	16	30	16	23	0	19	3	121	18	3	5	2.4	.979	DH-35, C-24
1976	2 teams	CAL A (29G –.174) HOU N (79G –.204)																						
″	total	108	.199	.283	311	62	11	0	5	1.6	19	33	29	48	0	4	0	486	46	10	6	5.1	.982	C-106
1977	HOU N	56	.291	.354	158	46	7	0	1	0.6	7	17	15	18	1	7	2	280	29	3	2	6.4	.990	C-49
1978	2 teams	HOU N (16G –.111) MON N (19G –.175)																						
″	total	35	.145	.171	76	11	2	0	0	0.0	2	3	4	7	0	10	3	104	6	1	1	4.3	.991	C-26
11 yrs.		922	.240	.364	2729	654	92	4	80	2.9	247	320	260	361	6	72	12	4231	442	61	65	5.5	.987	C-817, DH-37

John Herrnstein

HERRNSTEIN, JOHN ELLETT BL TL 6′ 3″ 215 lbs.
B. Mar. 31, 1938, Hampton, Va.

Year	Team	Games	BA	SA	AB	H	2B	3B	HR	HR%	R	RBI	BB	SO	SB	Pinch Hit AB	Pinch Hit H	PO	A	E	DP	TC/G	FA	G by Pos
1962	PHI N	6	.200	.200	5	1	0	0	0	0.0	0	1	1	3	0	5	1	0	0	0	0	0.0	.000	OF-1
1963		15	.167	.417	12	2	0	0	1	8.3	1	1	1	5	0	10	1	7	0	0	0	2.3	1.000	OF-2, 1B-1
1964		125	.234	.360	303	71	12	4	6	2.0	38	25	22	67	1	21	7	531	22	6	33	4.1	.989	OF-69, 1B-68
1965		63	.200	.259	85	17	2	0	1	1.2	8	5	2	18	0	30	5	123	9	2	13	4.2	.985	1B-18, OF-14
1966	3 teams	PHI N (4G –.100) CHI N (9G –.176) ATL N (17G –.222)																						
″	total	30	.178	.178	45	8	0	0	0	0.0	5	2	3	22	0	20	4	46	0	1	3	3.9	.979	OF-8, 1B-4
5 yrs.		239	.220	.322	450	99	14	4	8	1.8	52	34	29	115	1	86	18	707	31	9	49	4.0	.988	OF-94, 1B-91

Rick Herrscher

HERRSCHER, RICHARD FRANKLIN BR TR 6′ 2½″ 187 lbs.
B. Nov. 3, 1936, St. Louis, Mo.

Year	Team	Games	BA	SA	AB	H	2B	3B	HR	HR%	R	RBI	BB	SO	SB	Pinch Hit AB	Pinch Hit H	PO	A	E	DP	TC/G	FA	G by Pos
1962	NY N	35	.220	.340	50	11	3	0	1	2.0	5	6	5	11	0	8	2	83	19	2	11	4.5	.981	1B-10, 3B-6, OF-4, SS-3

Earl Hersh

HERSH, EARL WALTER BL TL 6′ 205 lbs.
B. May 21, 1932, Ebbvale, Md.

Year	Team	Games	BA	SA	AB	H	2B	3B	HR	HR%	R	RBI	BB	SO	SB	Pinch Hit AB	Pinch Hit H	PO	A	E	DP	TC/G	FA	G by Pos
1956	MIL N	7	.231	.462	13	3	3	0	0	0.0	0	0	0	5	0	5	0	0	0	1	0	0.5	.000	OF-2

Mike Hershberger

HERSHBERGER, NORMAN MICHAEL BR TR 5′10″ 175 lbs.
B. Oct. 9, 1939, Massillon, Ohio.

Year	Team	Games	BA	SA	AB	H	2B	3B	HR	HR%	R	RBI	BB	SO	SB	Pinch Hit AB	Pinch Hit H	PO	A	E	DP	TC/G	FA	G by Pos
1961	CHI A	15	.309	.364	55	17	3	0	0	0.0	9	5	2	2	1	1	0	29	2	0	0	2.4	1.000	OF-13
1962		148	.262	.333	427	112	14	2	4	0.9	54	46	37	36	10	13	3	236	7	4	0	1.8	.984	OF-135
1963		135	.279	.361	476	133	26	2	3	0.6	64	45	39	39	9	14	2	230	13	6	3	2.1	.976	OF-119
1964		141	.230	.290	452	104	15	3	2	0.4	55	31	48	47	8	10	1	231	10	4	2	1.8	.984	OF-134
1965	KC A	150	.231	.312	494	114	15	5	5	1.0	43	48	37	42	7	9	5	238	14	3	7	1.8	.988	OF-144
1966		146	.253	.340	538	136	27	7	2	0.4	55	57	47	37	13	5	0	285	14	7	3	2.1	.977	OF-143
1967		142	.254	.317	480	122	25	1	1	0.2	55	49	38	40	10	12	5	206	17	4	2	1.7	.982	OF-130
1968	OAK A	99	.272	.386	246	67	9	2	5	2.0	23	32	21	22	8	12	5	128	5	3	0	1.5	.978	OF-90
1969		51	.202	.240	129	26	2	0	1	0.8	11	10	10	15	1	15	3	50	0	1	0	1.5	.980	OF-35
1970	MIL A	49	.235	.316	98	23	5	0	1	1.0	7	6	10	8	1	16	3	34	1	2	0	1.1	.946	OF-35
1971	CHI A	74	.260	.345	177	46	9	0	2	1.1	22	15	30	23	6	20	5	96	1	4	0	1.7	.960	OF-59
11 yrs.		1150	.252	.328	3572	900	150	22	26	0.7	398	344	319	311	74	127	32	1763	84	38	17	1.8	.980	OF-1037

Willard Hershberger

HERSHBERGER, WILLARD McKEE BR TR 5′10½″ 167 lbs.
B. May 28, 1910, Lemon Cove, Calif. D. Aug. 3, 1940, Boston, Mass.

Year	Team	Games	BA	SA	AB	H	2B	3B	HR	HR%	R	RBI	BB	SO	SB	Pinch Hit AB	Pinch Hit H	PO	A	E	DP	TC/G	FA	G by Pos
1938	CIN N	49	.276	.324	105	29	3	1	0	0.0	12	12	5	6	1	7	1	108	13	6	2	3.2	.953	C-39, 2B-1
1939		63	.345	.420	174	60	9	2	0	0.0	23	32	9	4	1	3	0	204	21	3	2	3.8	.987	C-60
1940		48	.309	.374	123	38	4	2	0	0.0	6	26	6	6	0	9	4	121	11	2	0	3.6	.985	C-37
3 yrs.		160	.316	.381	402	127	16	5	0	0.0	41	70	20	16	2	19	5	433	45	11	4	3.6	.978	C-136, 2B-1
WORLD SERIES																								
1939	CIN N	3	.500	.500	2	1	0	0	0	0.0	0	1	0	0	0	1	1	1	0	0	0	0.5	1.000	C-2

Neal Hertweck

HERTWECK, NEAL CHARLES BL TL 6′ 1½″ 175 lbs.
B. Nov. 22, 1931, St. Louis, Mo.

Year	Team	Games	BA	SA	AB	H	2B	3B	HR	HR%	R	RBI	BB	SO	SB	Pinch Hit AB	Pinch Hit H	PO	A	E	DP	TC/G	FA	G by Pos
1952	STL N	2	.000	.000	6	0	0	0	0	0.0	0	0	1	1	0	0	0	20	1	0	4	10.5	1.000	1B-2

Steve Hertz

HERTZ, STEPHEN ALLAN BR TR 6′ 1″ 195 lbs.
B. Feb. 26, 1945, Fairfield, Ohio.

Year	Team	Games	BA	SA	AB	H	2B	3B	HR	HR%	R	RBI	BB	SO	SB	Pinch Hit AB	Pinch Hit H	PO	A	E	DP	TC/G	FA	G by Pos
1964	HOU N	5	.000	.000	4	0	0	0	0	0.0	2	0	0	3	0	2	0	1	0	0	0	0.5	1.000	3B-2

Buck Herzog

HERZOG, CHARLES LINCOLN BR TR 5′11″ 160 lbs.
B. July 9, 1885, Baltimore, Md. D. Sept. 4, 1953, Baltimore, Md.
Manager 1914–16.

Year	Team	Games	BA	SA	AB	H	2B	3B	HR	HR%	R	RBI	BB	SO	SB	Pinch Hit AB	Pinch Hit H	PO	A	E	DP	TC/G	FA	G by Pos
1908	NY N	64	.300	.362	160	48	6	2	0	0.0	38	11	36		16	3	0	83	159	22	21	4.6	.917	2B-42, SS-11, 3B-3, OF-1
1909		42	.185	.200	130	24	2	0	0	0.0	16	8	13		2	1	0	53	9	6	3	1.8	.912	OF-29, 3B-4, 2B-4, SS-1
1910	BOS N	106	.250	.342	380	95	20	3	3	0.8	51	32	30	34	13	1	0	110	223	31	17	3.5	.915	3B-105
1911	2 teams	BOS N (79G –.310) NY N (69G –.267)																						
″	total	148	.290	.418	541	157	33	9	6	1.1	90	67	47	40	48	1	0	249	404	46	40	4.8	.934	SS-75, 3B-69, 2B-3
1912	NY N	140	.263	.355	482	127	20	9	2	0.4	72	47	57	34	37	0	0	159	308	29	21	3.5	.942	3B-140
1913		96	.286	.390	290	83	15	3	3	1.0	46	31	22	12	23	2	1	97	142	13	18	2.9	.948	3B-84, 2B-2
1914	CIN N	138	.281	.347	498	140	14	8	1	0.2	54	40	42	27	46	0	0	344	475	53	60	6.3	.939	SS-137, 1B-2
1915		155	.264	.328	579	153	14	10	1	0.2	61	42	34	21	35	0	0	400	515	53	90	6.2	.945	SS-153, 1B-2
1916	2 teams	CIN N (79G –.267) NY N (77G –.261)																						
″	total	156	.264	.333	561	148	24	6	1	0.2	70	49	43	36	34	1	1	317	462	44	59	5.2	.947	SS-74, 2B-44, 3B-39, OF-1
1917	NY N	114	.235	.312	417	98	10	8	2	0.5	69	31	31	36	12	0	0	251	327	32	60	5.4	.948	2B-113

Buck Herzog *continued*

Year	Team	Games	BA	SA	AB	H	2B	3B	HR	HR%	R	RBI	BB	SO	SB	Pinch Hit AB	Pinch Hit H	PO	A	E	DP	TC/G	FA	G by Pos
1918	BOS N	118	.228	.279	473	108	12	6	0	0.0	57	26	29	28	10	0	0	374	342	30	50	6.3	.960	2B-99, 1B-12, SS-7
1919	2 teams	BOS N (73G –.280) CHI N (52G –.275)																						
″	total	125	.278	.348	468	130	12	9	1	0.2	42	42	23	18	28	2	1	213	342	19	37	4.7	.967	2B-122, 1B-1
1920	CHI N	91	.193	.236	305	59	9	2	0	0.0	39	19	20	21	8	2	0	154	241	29	32	4.8	.932	2B-59, 3B-28, 1B-1
13 yrs.		1493	.259	.335	5284	1370	191	75	20	0.4	705	445	427	307	312	13	3	2804	3949	407	508	4.9	.943	2B-488, 3B-472, SS-458, OF-31, 1B-18
WORLD SERIES																								
1911	NY N	6	.190	.286	21	4	2	0	0	0.0	3	0	2	3	2	0	0	7	14	3	0	4.0	.875	3B-6
1912		8	.400	.600	30	12	4	1	0	0.0	6	4	1	3	2	0	0	11	16	0	1	3.4	1.000	3B-8
1913		5	.053	.053	19	1	0	0	0	0.0	1	0	0	1	0	0	0	6	8	0	0	2.8	1.000	3B-5
1917		6	.250	.333	24	6	0	1	0	0.0	1	2	0	4	0	0	0	12	12	2	3	4.3	.923	2B-6
4 yrs.		25	.245	.351	94	23	6	2	0	0.0	11	6	3	11	4	0	0	36	50	5	4	3.6	.945	3B-19, 2B-6

Whitey Herzog

HERZOG, DORREL NORMAN ELVERT (The White Rat) BL TL 5′11″ 182 lbs.
B. Nov. 9, 1931, New Athens, Ill.
Manager 1973–90.

Year	Team	Games	BA	SA	AB	H	2B	3B	HR	HR%	R	RBI	BB	SO	SB	Pinch Hit AB	Pinch Hit H	PO	A	E	DP	TC/G	FA	G by Pos
1956	WAS A	117	.245	.337	421	103	13	7	4	1.0	49	35	35	74	8	11	5	274	10	7	3	2.7	.976	OF-103, 1B-5
1957		36	.167	.205	78	13	3	0	0	0.0	7	4	13	12	1	10	0	53	0	1	0	1.9	.981	OF-28
1958	2 teams	WAS A (8G –.000) KC A (88G –.240)																						
″	total	96	.228	.277	101	23	1	2	0	0.0	11	9	17	26	0	32	7	146	6	3	9	2.3	.981	OF-44, 1B-22
1959	KC A	38	.293	.390	123	36	7	1	1	0.8	25	9	34	23	1	2	1	87	2	3	1	2.6	.967	OF-34, 1B-1
1960		83	.266	.417	252	67	10	2	8	3.2	43	38	40	32	0	12	5	137	6	4	3	2.1	.973	OF-69, 1B-2
1961	BAL A	113	.291	.409	323	94	11	6	5	1.5	39	35	50	41	1	18	6	143	2	0	0	1.5	1.000	OF-98
1962		99	.266	.403	263	70	13	1	7	2.7	34	35	41	36	2	26	5	132	4	3	0	2.0	.978	OF-70
1963	DET A	52	.151	.226	53	8	2	1	0	0.0	5	7	11	17	0	35	4	44	1	1	2	4.2	.978	1B-7, OF-4
8 yrs.		634	.257	.365	1614	414	60	20	25	1.5	213	172	241	261	13	146	33	1016	31	22	18	2.2	.979	OF-450, 1B-37

Otto Hess

HESS, OTTO C. BL TL 6′ 1″ 170 lbs.
B. Oct. 10, 1878, Berne, Switzerland D. Feb. 25, 1926, Tucson, Ariz.

Year	Team	Games	BA	SA	AB	H	2B	3B	HR	HR%	R	RBI	BB	SO	SB	Pinch Hit AB	Pinch Hit H	PO	A	E	DP	TC/G	FA	G by Pos
1902	CLE A	7	.071	.071	14	1	0	0	0	0.0	2	1	2		0	0	0	4	16	3	0	3.3	.870	P-7
1904		34	.120	.160	100	12	2	1	0	0.0	4	5	3		0	1	0	25	49	5	0	2.4	.937	P-21, OF-12
1905		54	.251	.343	175	44	8	1	2	1.1	15	13	7		2	0	0	74	67	9	2	2.8	.940	OF-27, P-26
1906		53	.201	.260	154	31	5	2	0	0.0	13	11	2		1	5	0	29	87	6	4	2.5	.951	P-43, OF-5
1907		19	.133	.133	30	4	0	0	0	0.0	4	0	4		1	1	0	6	26	2	0	1.8	.941	P-17, OF-2
1908		8	.000	.000	14	0	0	0	0	0.0	0	0	1		0	0	0	4	3	0	0	0.9	1.000	OF-4, P-4
1912	BOS N	33	.245	.372	94	23	4	4	0	0.0	10	10	0	26	0	0	0	11	47	3	3	1.8	.951	P-33
1913		35	.313	.410	83	26	0	1	2	2.4	9	11	7	15	0	5	0	11	58	4	2	2.5	.945	P-29
1914		31	.234	.319	47	11	1	0	1	2.1	5	6	1	11	0	12	2	22	33	2	3	3.0	.965	P-14, 1B-5
1915		5	.400	.600	5	2	1	0	0	0.0	1	1	0	2	0	0	0	1	4	1	0	1.2	.833	P-4, 1B-1
10 yrs.		279	.215	.291	716	154	21	9	5	0.7	63	58	27	54	4	24	2	187	390	35	14	2.4	.943	P-198, OF-50, 1B-6

Tom Hess

HESS, THOMAS
Born Thomas Heslin.
B. Aug. 15, 1875, Brooklyn, N. Y. D. Dec. 15, 1945, Albany, N. Y.

Year	Team	Games	BA	SA	AB	H	2B	3B	HR	HR%	R	RBI	BB	SO	SB	Pinch Hit AB	Pinch Hit H	PO	A	E	DP	TC/G	FA	G by Pos
1892	BAL N	1	.000	.000	2	0	0	0	0	0.0	0	0	0	0	0	0	0	0	0	0	0	0.0	.000	C-1

Gus Hetling

HETLING, AUGUST JULIUS BR TR 5′10″ 165 lbs.
B. Nov. 21, 1885, St. Louis, Mo. D. Oct. 13, 1962, Wichita, Kans.

Year	Team	Games	BA	SA	AB	H	2B	3B	HR	HR%	R	RBI	BB	SO	SB	Pinch Hit AB	Pinch Hit H	PO	A	E	DP	TC/G	FA	G by Pos
1906	DET A	2	.143	.143	7	1	0	0	0	0.0	0	0	0		0	0	0	3	2	0	0	2.5	1.000	3B-2

George Heubel

HEUBEL, GEORGE A. 5′11½″ 178 lbs.
B. 1849, Paterson, N. J. D. Jan. 22, 1896, Philadelphia, Pa.

Year	Team	Games	BA	SA	AB	H	2B	3B	HR	HR%	R	RBI	BB	SO	SB	Pinch Hit AB	Pinch Hit H	PO	A	E	DP	TC/G	FA	G by Pos
1876	NY N	1	.000	.000	4	0	0	0	0	0.0	0	0	0	0		0	0	6	0	2	0	8.0	.750	1B-1

Johnnie Heving

HEVING, JOHN ALOYSIUS BR TR 6′ 175 lbs.
Brother of Joe Heving.
B. Apr. 29, 1896, Covington, Ky. D. Dec. 24, 1968, Salisbury, N. C.

Year	Team	Games	BA	SA	AB	H	2B	3B	HR	HR%	R	RBI	BB	SO	SB	Pinch Hit AB	Pinch Hit H	PO	A	E	DP	TC/G	FA	G by Pos
1920	STL A	1	.000	.000	1	0	0	0	0	0.0	0	0	0	0	0	1	0	0	0	0	0	0.0	—	
1924	BOS A	44	.287	.352	108	31	5	1	0	0.0	15	10	10	7	0	15	3	93	33	4	1	4.5	.969	C-29
1925		45	.168	.227	119	20	7	0	0	0.0	14	6	12	7	0	10	3	103	35	6	1	4.2	.958	C-34
1928		82	.259	.329	158	41	7	2	0	0.0	11	11	11	10	1	18	7	153	25	6	2	3.0	.967	C-62
1929		76	.319	.372	188	60	4	3	0	0.0	26	23	8	7	1	19	4	207	40	3	4	4.5	.988	C-55
1930		75	.277	.327	220	61	5	3	0	0.0	15	17	11	14	2	3	1	195	37	3	7	3.3	.987	C-71
1931	PHI A	42	.239	.327	113	27	3	2	1	0.9	8	12	6	8	0	2	1	139	11	1	0	3.8	.993	C-40
1932		33	.273	.377	77	21	6	1	0	0.0	14	10	7	6	0	5	1	85	5	0	2	3.2	1.000	C-28
8 yrs.		398	.265	.330	984	261	37	12	1	0.1	103	89	65	59	4	73	20	975	186	23	17	3.7	.981	C-319
WORLD SERIES																								
1931	PHI A	1	.000	.000	1	0	0	0	0	0.0	0	0	0	0	0	1	0	0	0	0	0	0.0	—	

Mike Heydon

HEYDON, MICHAEL EDWARD BL TR 6′
B. July 15, 1874, Missouri D. Oct. 13, 1913, Indianapolis, Ind.

Year	Team	Games	BA	SA	AB	H	2B	3B	HR	HR%	R	RBI	BB	SO	SB	Pinch Hit AB	Pinch Hit H	PO	A	E	DP	TC/G	FA	G by Pos
1898	BAL N	3	.111	.111	9	1	0	0	0	0.0	2	1	2		0	0	0	8	3	1	1	4.0	.917	C-3
1899	WAS N	3	.000	.000	3	0	0	0	0	0.0	0	0	2		0	1	0	3	2	1	0	3.0	.833	C-2
1901	STL N	16	.209	.349	43	9	1	1	1	2.3	2	6	5		2	1	0	54	10	4	2	4.9	.941	C-13, OF-1
1904	CHI A	4	.100	.200	10	1	1	0	0	0.0	0	1	1		0	0	0	16	5	0	1	5.3	1.000	C-4
1905	WAS A	77	.192	.265	245	47	7	4	1	0.4	20	26	21		5	0	0	368	125	23	7	6.7	.955	C-77
1906		49	.159	.221	145	23	7	1	0	0.0	14	10	14		2	0	0	200	68	18	4	5.8	.937	C-49
1907		62	.183	.201	164	30	3	0	0	0.0	14	9	25		3	4	0	247	52	12	4	5.5	.961	C-57
7 yrs.		214	.179	.239	619	111	19	6	2	0.3	52	53	70		12	6	0	896	265	59	19	5.9	.952	C-205, OF-1

Jack Hiatt

HIATT, JACK E. BR TR 6′ 2″ 190 lbs.
B. July 27, 1942, Bakersfield, Calif.

Year	Team	Games	BA	SA	AB	H	2B	3B	HR	HR%	R	RBI	BB	SO	SB	Pinch Hit AB	Pinch Hit H	PO	A	E	DP	TC/G	FA	G by Pos
1964	LA A	9	.375	.375	16	6	0	0	0	0.0	2	2	2	3	0	4	3	17	2	1	2	4.0	.950	C-3, 1B-2
1965	SF N	40	.284	.388	67	19	4	0	1	1.5	5	7	12	14	0	16	6	119	10	3	4	4.7	.977	C-21, 1B-7
1966		18	.304	.391	23	7	2	0	0	0.0	2	1	4	5	0	9	3	49	6	1	4	8.0	.982	1B-7
1967		73	.275	.431	153	42	6	0	6	3.9	24	26	27	37	0	31	8	303	18	4	25	7.9	.988	1B-36, C-3, OF-2
1968		90	.232	.348	224	52	10	2	4	1.8	14	34	41	61	0	21	6	387	37	2	6	6.3	.995	C-58, 1B-10
1969		69	.196	.325	194	38	4	0	7	3.6	18	34	48	58	0	2	0	359	30	3	10	6.2	.992	C-60, 1B-3
1970	2 teams	MON N (17G –.326) CHI N (66G –.242)																						
″	total	83	.258	.357	221	57	14	1	2	0.9	23	29	45	62	0	7	0	466	24	7	1	6.3	.986	C-75, 1B-4
1971	HOU N	69	.276	.351	174	48	8	1	1	0.6	16	16	35	39	0	4	2	329	20	3	6	5.3	.991	C-65, 1B-1
1972	2 teams	HOU N (10G –.200) CAL A (22G –.289)																						
″	total	32	.257	.371	70	18	3	1	1	1.4	6	5	10	16	0	7	2	84	8	0	1	3.4	1.000	C-27
9 yrs.		483	.251	.363	1142	287	51	5	22	1.9	110	154	224	295	0	101	30	2113	155	24	59	6.0	.990	C-312, 1B-70, OF-2

Phil Hiatt

HIATT, PHILIP FARRELL BR TR 6′ 3″ 200 lbs.
B. May 1, 1969, Pensacola, Fla.

Year	Team	Games	BA	SA	AB	H	2B	3B	HR	HR%	R	RBI	BB	SO	SB	Pinch Hit AB	Pinch Hit H	PO	A	E	DP	TC/G	FA	G by Pos
1993	KC A	81	.218	.366	238	52	12	1	7	2.9	30	36	16	82	6	2	0	45	114	16	6	2.2	.909	3B-70, DH-9
1995		52	.204	.363	113	23	6	0	4	3.5	11	12	9	37	1	16	4	62	4	3	1	1.4	.957	OF-47, DH-2
2 yrs.		133	.214	.365	351	75	18	1	11	3.1	41	48	25	119	7	18	4	107	118	19	7	1.9	.922	3B-70, OF-47, DH-11

Jim Hibbs

HIBBS, JAMES KERR BR TR 6′ 190 lbs.
B. Sept. 10, 1944, Klamath Falls, Ore.

Year	Team	Games	BA	SA	AB	H	2B	3B	HR	HR%	R	RBI	BB	SO	SB	Pinch Hit AB	Pinch Hit H	PO	A	E	DP	TC/G	FA	G by Pos
1967	CAL A	3	.000	.000	3	0	0	0	0	0.0	0	0	0	2	0	3	0	0	0	0	0	0.0	—	

Ed Hickey

HICKEY, EDWARD A.
B. Aug. 18, 1872, Cleveland, Ohio D. Mar. 25, 1941, Tacoma, Wash.

Year	Team	Games	BA	SA	AB	H	2B	3B	HR	HR%	R	RBI	BB	SO	SB	Pinch Hit AB	Pinch Hit H	PO	A	E	DP	TC/G	FA	G by Pos
1901	CHI N	10	.162	.162	37	6	0	0	0	0.0	4	3	2		1	0	0	8	18	9	2	3.5	.743	3B-10

Mike Hickey

HICKEY, MICHAEL FRANCIS BR TR 5′10½″ 150 lbs.
B. Dec. 25, 1871, Chicopee, Mass. D. June 11, 1918, Springfield, Mass.

Year	Team	Games	BA	SA	AB	H	2B	3B	HR	HR%	R	RBI	BB	SO	SB	Pinch Hit AB	Pinch Hit H	PO	A	E	DP	TC/G	FA	G by Pos
1899	BOS N	1	.333	.333	3	1	0	0	0	0.0	0	0	0		0	0	0	3	5	1	0	9.0	.889	2B-1

Jim Hickman

HICKMAN, DAVID JAMES BR TR 5′ 7½″ 170 lbs.
B. May 19, 1894, Union City, Tenn. D. Dec. 30, 1965, Brooklyn, N. Y.

Year	Team	Games	BA	SA	AB	H	2B	3B	HR	HR%	R	RBI	BB	SO	SB	Pinch Hit AB	Pinch Hit H	PO	A	E	DP	TC/G	FA	G by Pos
1915	BAL F	20	.210	.321	81	17	4	1	1	1.2	7	7	4		5	0	0	45	7	2	2	2.7	.963	OF-20
1916	BKN N	9	.200	.200	5	1	0	0	0	0.0	3	0	2	0	1	0	0	2	0	0	0	0.7	1.000	OF-3
1917		114	.219	.330	370	81	15	4	6	1.6	46	36	17	66	14	8	1	222	22	15	6	2.6	.942	OF-101
1918		53	.234	.359	167	39	4	7	1	0.6	14	16	8	31	5	3	0	76	9	8	1	2.0	.914	OF-46
1919		57	.192	.240	104	20	3	1	0	0.0	14	11	6	17	2	8	1	47	3	2	1	1.8	.962	OF-29
5 yrs.		253	.217	.322	727	158	26	13	8	1.1	84	70	37	114	27	19	2	392	41	27	10	2.3	.941	OF-199

Jim Hickman

HICKMAN, JAMES LUCIUS BR TR 6′ 3″ 192 lbs.
B. May 10, 1937, Henning, Tenn.

Year	Team	Games	BA	SA	AB	H	2B	3B	HR	HR%	R	RBI	BB	SO	SB	Pinch Hit AB	Pinch Hit H	PO	A	E	DP	TC/G	FA	G by Pos
1962	NY N	140	.245	.401	392	96	18	2	13	3.3	54	46	47	96	4	13	3	265	7	8	0	2.3	.971	OF-124
1963		146	.229	.399	494	113	21	6	17	3.4	53	51	44	120	0	11	1	194	109	20	16	2.3	.938	OF-82, 3B-59
1964		139	.257	.377	409	105	14	1	11	2.7	48	57	36	90	0	31	8	237	8	6	1	2.2	.976	OF-113, 3B-1
1965		141	.236	.407	369	87	18	0	15	4.1	32	40	27	76	3	29	5	386	29	9	22	3.1	.979	OF-91, 1B-30, 3B-14
1966		58	.237	.356	160	38	7	0	4	2.5	15	16	13	34	2	11	1	183	17	2	16	3.3	.990	OF-45, 1B-17
1967	LA N	65	.163	.245	98	16	6	1	0	0.0	7	10	14	28	1	25	3	54	3	0	1	1.4	1.000	OF-37, 3B-2, 1B-2, P-1
1968	CHI N	75	.223	.367	188	42	6	3	5	2.7	22	23	18	38	1	12	2	115	4	3	0	1.8	.975	OF-66
1969		134	.237	.467	338	80	11	2	21	6.2	38	54	47	74	2	18	5	153	6	3	0	1.3	.981	OF-125
1970		149	.315	.582	514	162	33	4	32	6.2	102	115	93	99	0	2	0	706	67	10	47	5.1	.987	OF-79, 1B-74
1971		117	.256	.449	383	98	13	2	19	5.0	50	60	50	61	0	12	2	470	34	3	28	4.5	.994	OF-69, 1B-44
1972		115	.272	.462	368	100	15	2	17	4.6	65	64	52	64	3	13	3	708	70	6	61	7.5	.992	1B-77, OF-27
1973		92	.244	.313	201	49	1	2	3	1.5	27	20	42	42	1	34	6	411	31	5	37	7.0	.989	1B-51, OF-13
1974	STL N	50	.267	.367	60	16	0	0	2	3.3	5	4	8	10	0	30	6	65	7	1	14	4.9	.986	1B-14, 3B-1
13 yrs.		1421	.252	.426	3974	1002	163	25	159	4.0	518	560	491	832	17	241	45	3947	392	76	243	3.5	.983	OF-871, 1B-309, 3B-77, P-1

Piano Legs Hickman

HICKMAN, CHARLES TAYLOR BR TR 5′11½″ 215 lbs.
B. Mar. 4, 1876, Taylortown, Pa. D. Apr. 19, 1934, Morgantown, W. Va.

Year	Team	Games	BA	SA	AB	H	2B	3B	HR	HR%	R	RBI	BB	SO	SB	Pinch Hit AB	Pinch Hit H	PO	A	E	DP	TC/G	FA	G by Pos
1897	BOS N	2	.667	1.667	3	2	0	0	1	33.3	1	2	0		0	0	0	1	1	0	1	1.0	1.000	P-2
1898		19	.259	.293	58	15	2	0	0	0.0	4	7	1		0	0	0	79	5	4	8	4.6	.955	OF-7, 1B-6, P-6
1899		19	.397	.651	63	25	2	7	0	0.0	15	15	2		1	0	0	27	12	6	3	2.4	.867	P-11, OF-7, 1B-1
1900	NY N	127	.313	.482	473	148	19	17	9	1.9	66	91	17		10	0	0	194	277	87	19	4.4	.844	3B-120, OF-7
1901		112	.282	.392	401	113	20	6	4	1.0	44	62	15		5	8	1	154	154	35	10	3.2	.898	OF-50, SS-23, 3B-15, P-9, 2B-7, 1B-2
1902	2 teams	BOS A (28G –.296) CLE A (102G –.380)																						
″	total	130	.363	.541	534	**194**	36	13	11	2.1	74	110	15		9	1	0	1140	55	45	63	9.6	.964	1B-98, OF-27, 2B-3, P-1
1903	CLE A	130	.330	.502	518	171	31	11	12	**2.3**	67	97	17		14	0	0	1323	88	45	69	11.0	.969	1B-125, 2B-7
1904	2 teams	CLE A (86G –.288) DET A (42G –.243)																						
″	total	128	.274	.437	481	132	28	16	6	1.2	52	67	24		12	1	1	874	192	42	42	8.9	.962	1B-79, 2B-45, OF-1
1905	2 teams	DET A (59G –.221) WAS A (88G –.311)																						
″	total	147	.277	.405	573	159	37	12	4	0.7	69	66	21		6	0	0	378	298	49	27	4.9	.932	2B-85, OF-47, 1B-15
1906	WAS A	120	.284	.421	451	128	25	5	9	2.0	53	57	14		9	1	0	305	39	13	10	3.0	.964	OF-95, 1B-18, 3B-5, 2B-1
1907	2 teams	WAS A (60G –.285) CHI A (21G –.261)																						
″	total	81	.282	.389	216	61	12	4	1	0.5	23	24	18		4	**22**	4	312	30	18	13	6.5	.950	1B-30, OF-21, 2B-3, P-1
1908	CLE A	65	.234	.305	197	46	6	1	2	1.0	16	16	9		2	16	4	248	23	13	7	5.8	.954	OF-28, 1B-20, 2B-1
12 yrs.		1080	.301	.447	3968	1194	218	92	59	1.5	484	614	153		72	49	10	5035	1174	357	272	6.4	.946	1B-394, OF-290, 2B-152, 3B-140, P-30, SS-23

Buddy Hicks

HICKS, CLARENCE WALTER BB TR 5′10″ 170 lbs.
B. Feb. 15, 1927, Belvedere, Calif.

Year	Team	Games	BA	SA	AB	H	2B	3B	HR	HR%	R	RBI	BB	SO	SB	Pinch Hit AB	Pinch Hit H	PO	A	E	DP	TC/G	FA	G by Pos
1956	DET A	26	.213	.255	47	10	2	0	0	0.0	5	5	3	2	0	2	0	21	31	0	5	2.3	1.000	SS-16, 2B-6, 3B-1

Jim Hicks

HICKS, JAMES EDWARD — BR TR 6′ 3″ 205 lbs.
B. May 18, 1940, East Chicago, Ind.

Year	Team	Games	BA	SA	AB	H	2B	3B	HR	HR%	R	RBI	BB	SO	SB	Pinch Hit AB	Pinch Hit H	PO	A	E	DP	TC/G	FA	G by Pos
1964	CHI A	2	—	—	0	0	0	0	0	—	0	0	0	0	0	0	0	0	0	0	0	0.0	—	
1965		13	.263	.474	19	5	1	0	1	5.3	2	2	0	9	0	8	2	3	0	1	0	0.8	.750	OF-5
1966		18	.192	.269	26	5	0	1	0	0.0	3	1	1	5	0	2	0	26	0	1	1	2.3	.963	OF-10, 1B-2
1969	2 teams	STL N (19G –.182)	CAL A (37G –.083)																					
″	total	56	.130	.304	92	12	0	2	4	4.3	11	11	17	32	0	17	0	97	3	1	7	3.1	.990	OF-25, 1B-8
1970	CAL A	4	.250	.250	4	1	0	0	0	0.0	0	0	0	2	0	4	1	0	0	0	0	0.0	—	
5 yrs.		93	.163	.319	141	23	1	3	5	3.5	16	14	18	48	0	31	3	126	3	3	8	2.6	.977	OF-40, 1B-10

Joe Hicks

HICKS, WILLIAM JOSEPH — BL TR 6′ 180 lbs.
B. Apr. 7, 1933, Ivy, Va.

Year	Team	Games	BA	SA	AB	H	2B	3B	HR	HR%	R	RBI	BB	SO	SB	Pinch Hit AB	Pinch Hit H	PO	A	E	DP	TC/G	FA	G by Pos
1959	CHI A	6	.429	.429	7	3	0	0	0	0.0	0	0	1	1	0	2	2	3	1	0	0	1.0	1.000	OF-4
1960		36	.191	.213	47	9	1	0	0	0.0	3	2	6	3	0	17	4	14	0	0	0	1.0	1.000	OF-14
1961	WAS A	12	.172	.276	29	5	0	0	1	3.4	2	1	0	4	0	6	2	14	1	0	0	2.1	1.000	OF-7
1962		102	.224	.374	174	39	4	2	6	3.4	20	14	15	34	3	**61**	9	74	1	3	1	1.9	.962	OF-42
1963	NY N	56	.226	.371	159	36	6	1	5	3.1	16	22	7	31	0	16	3	83	1	3	0	2.1	.966	OF-41
5 yrs.		212	.221	.349	416	92	11	3	12	2.9	41	39	29	73	3	102	20	188	4	6	1	1.8	.970	OF-108

Nat Hicks

HICKS, NATHANIEL WOODHULL — BR TR 6′ 1″ 186 lbs.
B. Apr. 19, 1845, Hempstead, N. Y. D. Apr. 21, 1907, Hoboken, N. J.

Year	Team	Games	BA	SA	AB	H	2B	3B	HR	HR%	R	RBI	BB	SO	SB	Pinch Hit AB	Pinch Hit H	PO	A	E	DP	TC/G	FA	G by Pos
1876	NY N	45	.234	.266	188	44	4	1	0	0.0	20	15	3	4		0	0	222	47	94	3	8.1	.741	C-45
1877	CIN N	8	.188	.188	32	6	0	0	0	0.0	3	3	1	2		0	0	32	15	7	3	6.8	.870	C-8
2 yrs.		53	.227	.255	220	50	4	1	0	0.0	23	18	4	6		0	0	254	62	101	6	7.9	.758	C-53

Mahlon Higbee

HIGBEE, MAHLON JESSE — BR TR 5′11″ 165 lbs.
B. Aug. 16, 1901, Louisville, Ky. D. Apr. 7, 1968, DePauw, Ind.

Year	Team	Games	BA	SA	AB	H	2B	3B	HR	HR%	R	RBI	BB	SO	SB	Pinch Hit AB	Pinch Hit H	PO	A	E	DP	TC/G	FA	G by Pos
1922	NY N	3	.400	.700	10	4	0	0	1	10.0	2	5	0	2	0	0	0	2	0	0	0	0.7	1.000	OF-3

Bill Higdon

HIGDON, WILLIAM TRAVIS — BL TR 6′ 1″ 193 lbs.
B. Apr. 27, 1924, Camp Hill, Ala. D. Aug. 30, 1986, Pascagoula, Miss.

Year	Team	Games	BA	SA	AB	H	2B	3B	HR	HR%	R	RBI	BB	SO	SB	Pinch Hit AB	Pinch Hit H	PO	A	E	DP	TC/G	FA	G by Pos
1949	CHI A	11	.304	.435	23	7	3	0	0	0.0	3	1	6	3	1	4	1	9	1	0	0	1.7	1.000	OF-6

Bill Higgins

HIGGINS, WILLIAM EDWARD — TR 5′ 9″ 155 lbs.
B. Sept. 8, 1861, Wilmington, Del. D. Apr. 25, 1919, Wilmington, Del.

Year	Team	Games	BA	SA	AB	H	2B	3B	HR	HR%	R	RBI	BB	SO	SB	Pinch Hit AB	Pinch Hit H	PO	A	E	DP	TC/G	FA	G by Pos
1888	BOS N	14	.185	.204	54	10	1	0	0	0.0	5	4	1	3	1	0	0	44	52	10	12	7.6	.906	2B-14
1890	2 teams	STL AA (67G –.252)	SYR AA (1G –.250)																					
″	total	68	.252	.294	262	66	7	2	0	0.0	40		24		7	0	0	172	208	19	35	5.9	.952	2B-68
2 yrs.		82	.241	.278	316	76	8	2	0	0.0	45	4	25	3	8	0	0	216	260	29	47	6.2	.943	2B-82

Bob Higgins

HIGGINS, ROBERT STONE — BR TR 5′ 8″ 176 lbs.
B. Sept. 23, 1886, Fayetteville, Tenn. D. May 25, 1941, Chattanooga, Tenn.

Year	Team	Games	BA	SA	AB	H	2B	3B	HR	HR%	R	RBI	BB	SO	SB	Pinch Hit AB	Pinch Hit H	PO	A	E	DP	TC/G	FA	G by Pos
1909	CLE A	8	.087	.087	23	2	0	0	0	0.0	0	0	0		0	0	0	38	10	0	1	6.0	1.000	C-8
1911	BKN N	4	.300	.300	10	3	0	0	0	0.0	1	2	1	0	1	1	1	11	3	1	0	5.0	.933	C-2, 3B-1
1912		1	.000	.000	2	0	0	0	0	0.0	0	0	0	1	0	0	0	3	0	1	0	4.0	.750	C-1
3 yrs.		13	.143	.143	35	5	0	0	0	0.0	1	2	1	1	1	1	1	52	13	2	1	5.6	.970	C-11, 3B-1

Kevin Higgins

HIGGINS, KEVIN WAYNE — BL TR 5′11″ 175 lbs.
B. Jan. 22, 1967, San Gabriel, Calif.

Year	Team	Games	BA	SA	AB	H	2B	3B	HR	HR%	R	RBI	BB	SO	SB	Pinch Hit AB	Pinch Hit H	PO	A	E	DP	TC/G	FA	G by Pos
1993	SD N	71	.221	.254	181	40	4	1	0	0.0	17	13	16	17	0	13	2	314	32	6	2	5.0	.983	C-59, 3B-4, 1B-3, OF-3, 2B-1

Mark Higgins

HIGGINS, MARK DOUGLAS — BR TR 6′ 2″ 210 lbs.
B. July 9, 1963, Miami, Fla.

Year	Team	Games	BA	SA	AB	H	2B	3B	HR	HR%	R	RBI	BB	SO	SB	Pinch Hit AB	Pinch Hit H	PO	A	E	DP	TC/G	FA	G by Pos
1989	CLE A	6	.100	.100	10	1	0	0	0	0.0	1	0	1	6	0	1	0	18	3	0	1	4.2	1.000	1B-5

Pinky Higgins

HIGGINS, MICHAEL FRANKLIN — BR TR 6′ 1″ 185 lbs.
B. May 27, 1909, Red Oak, Tex. D. Mar. 21, 1969, Dallas, Tex.
Manager 1955–62.

Year	Team	Games	BA	SA	AB	H	2B	3B	HR	HR%	R	RBI	BB	SO	SB	Pinch Hit AB	Pinch Hit H	PO	A	E	DP	TC/G	FA	G by Pos
1930	PHI A	14	.250	.333	24	6	2	0	0	0.0	1	0	4	5	0	4	0	4	7	0	0	1.4	1.000	3B-5, 2B-2, SS-1
1933		152	.314	.487	567	178	34	11	14	2.5	85	99	61	53	2	0	0	159	270	24	23	3.0	.947	3B-152
1934		144	.330	.508	543	179	37	6	16	2.9	89	90	56	70	9	0	0	147	247	37	34	3.0	.914	3B-144
1935		133	.296	.504	524	155	32	4	23	4.4	69	94	42	62	6	1	1	162	214	21	15	3.0	.947	3B-131
1936		146	.289	.420	550	159	32	2	12	2.2	89	80	67	61	7	1	0	151	266	26	24	3.1	.941	3B-145
1937	BOS A	153	.302	.425	570	172	33	5	9	1.6	88	106	76	51	2	1	1	161	258	29	29	2.9	.935	3B-152
1938		139	.303	.406	524	159	29	5	5	1.0	77	106	71	55	10	1	0	140	272	39	28	3.3	.914	3B-138
1939	DET A	132	.276	.380	489	135	23	2	8	1.6	57	76	56	41	7	2	1	140	241	36	22	3.2	.914	3B-130
1940		131	.271	.415	480	130	24	3	13	2.7	70	76	61	31	4	1	0	133	239	29	16	3.1	.928	3B-129
1941		147	.298	.422	540	161	28	3	11	2.0	79	73	67	45	5	2	0	153	304	26	14	3.3	.946	3B-145
1942		143	.267	.409	499	133	34	2	11	2.2	65	79	72	21	3	5	0	134	243	30	24	3.0	.926	3B-137
1943		138	.277	.377	523	145	20	1	10	1.9	62	84	57	31	2	0	0	156	253	26	22	3.2	.940	3B-138
1944		148	.297	.409	543	161	32	4	7	1.3	79	76	81	34	4	2	1	146	311	22	21	3.3	.954	3B-146
1946	2 teams	DET A (18G –.217)	BOS A (64G –.275)																					
″	total	82	.262	.354	260	68	14	2	2	0.8	20	36	29	30	0	5	1	64	134	11	16	2.8	.947	3B-76
14 yrs.		1802	.292	.428	6636	1941	374	50	141	2.1	930	1075	800	590	61	25	5	1850	3259	356	288	3.1	.935	3B-1768, 2B-2, SS-1
WORLD SERIES																								
1940	DET A	7	.333	.667	24	8	3	1	1	4.2	2	6	3	3	0	0	0	4	30	2	1	5.1	.944	3B-7
1946	BOS A	7	.208	.250	24	5	1	0	0	0.0	1	2	2	0	0	0	0	6	6	2	0	2.0	.857	3B-7
2 yrs.		14	.271	.458	48	13	4	1	1	2.1	3	8	5	3	0	0	0	10	36	4	1	3.6	.920	3B-14

Bobby Higginson

HIGGINSON, ROBERT LEIGH — BL TR 5′11″ 180 lbs.
B. Aug. 18, 1970, Philadelphia, Pa.

Year	Team	Games	BA	SA	AB	H	2B	3B	HR	HR%	R	RBI	BB	SO	SB	Pinch Hit AB	Pinch Hit H	PO	A	E	DP	TC/G	FA	G by Pos
1995	DET A	131	.224	.393	410	92	17	5	14	3.4	61	43	62	107	6	14	3	247	13	4	2	2.1	.985	OF-123, DH-2

Andy High

HIGH, ANDREW AIRD (Handy Andy) BL TR 5′ 6″ 155 lbs.
Brother of Hugh High. Brother of Charlie High.
B. Nov. 21, 1897, Ava, Ill. D. Feb. 22, 1981, Toledo, Ohio.

Year	Team	Games	BA	SA	AB	H	2B	3B	HR	HR%	R	RBI	BB	SO	SB	Pinch Hit AB	Pinch Hit H	PO	A	E	DP	TC/G	FA	G by Pos
1922	BKN N	153	.283	.396	579	164	27	10	6	1.0	82	65	59	26	3	0	0	167	316	23	28	3.3	.955	3B-130, SS-22, 2B-1
1923		123	.270	.387	426	115	23	9	3	0.7	51	37	47	13	4	0	0	194	276	23	38	3.8	.953	3B-80, SS-45, 2B-5
1924		144	.328	.448	582	191	26	13	6	1.0	98	61	57	16	3	0	0	328	478	29	56	5.5	.965	2B-133, SS-17, 3B-1
1925	2 teams	BKN N (44G –.200) BOS N (60G –.288)																						
"	total	104	.257	.350	334	86	15	2	4	1.2	42	34	38	7	3	17	5	80	143	10	15	2.7	.957	3B-71, 2B-12, SS-3
1926	BOS N	130	.296	.387	476	141	17	10	2	0.4	55	66	39	9	4	4	2	200	287	27	36	4.0	.947	3B-81, 2B-49
1927		113	.302	.419	384	116	15	9	4	1.0	59	46	26	11	4	13	6	113	147	20	15	2.8	.929	3B-89, 2B-8, SS-2
1928	STL N	111	.285	.389	368	105	14	3	6	1.6	58	37	37	10	2	17	4	91	164	14	20	2.9	.948	3B-73, 2B-19
1929		146	.295	.411	603	178	32	4	10	1.7	95	63	38	18	7	1	1	150	265	13	33	3.0	.970	3B-123, 2B-22
1930		72	.279	.381	215	60	12	2	2	0.9	34	29	23	6	1	17	5	37	71	1	5	2.1	.991	3B-48, 2B-3
1931		63	.267	.328	131	35	6	1	0	0.0	20	19	24	4	0	19	5	32	64	1	9	2.3	.990	3B-23, 2B-19
1932	CIN N	84	.188	.230	191	36	4	2	0	0.0	16	12	23	6	1	23	7	43	77	7	7	2.2	.945	3B-46, 2B-12
1933		24	.209	.326	43	9	2	0	1	2.3	4	6	5	1	0	10	2	8	21	1	1	2.3	.967	3B-11, 2B-2
1934	PHI N	47	.206	.235	68	14	2	0	0	0.0	4	7	9	3	1	23	5	14	17	3	3	2.1	.912	3B-14, 2B-2
13 yrs.		1314	.284	.388	4400	1250	195	65	44	1.0	618	482	425	130	33	144	42	1457	2326	172	266	3.4	.957	3B-790, 2B-287, SS-89
WORLD SERIES																								
1928	STL N	4	.294	.412	17	5	2	0	0	0.0	1	1	1	3	0	0	0	2	5	0	1	1.8	1.000	3B-4
1930		1	.500	.500	2	1	0	0	0	0.0	1	0	0	0	0	0	0	0	0	0	0	0.0	.000	3B-1
1931		4	.267	.267	15	4	0	0	0	0.0	3	0	0	2	0	0	0	3	9	0	0	3.0	1.000	3B-4
3 yrs.		9	.294	.353	34	10	2	0	0	0.0	5	1	1	5	0	0	0	5	14	0	1	2.1	1.000	3B-9

Charlie High

HIGH, CHARLES EDWIN BL TR 5′ 9″ 170 lbs.
Brother of Hugh High. Brother of Andy High.
B. Dec. 1, 1898, Ava, Ill. D. Sept. 11, 1960, Oak Grove, Ore.

1919	PHI A	11	.069	.069	29	2	0	0	0	0.0	2	1	3	4	2	2	0	16	1	1	0	2.0	.944	OF-9
1920		17	.308	.415	65	20	2	1	1	1.5	7	6	3	6	0	0	0	27	3	4	0	2.0	.882	OF-17
2 yrs.		28	.234	.309	94	22	2	1	1	1.1	9	7	6	10	2	2	0	43	4	5	0	2.0	.904	OF-26

Hugh High

HIGH, HUGH JENKIN (Bunny, Lefty) BL TL 5′ 7½″ 155 lbs.
Brother of Charlie High. Brother of Andy High.
B. Oct. 24, 1887, Pottstown, Pa. D. Nov. 16, 1962, St. Louis, Mo.

1913	DET A	80	.230	.273	183	42	6	1	0	0.0	18	16	28	24	6	19	5	104	8	2	0	2.3	.982	OF-50
1914		80	.266	.326	184	49	5	3	0	0.0	25	17	26	21	7	19	3	92	2	4	1	1.8	.959	OF-53
1915	NY A	119	.258	.342	427	110	19	7	1	0.2	51	43	62	47	22	1	1	254	10	5	1	2.3	.981	OF-117
1916		115	.263	.326	377	99	13	4	1	0.3	44	28	47	44	13	5	1	216	14	12	2	2.2	.950	OF-109
1917		103	.236	.307	365	86	11	6	1	0.3	37	19	48	31	8	2	0	188	16	3	3	2.1	.986	OF-100
1918		7	.000	.000	10	0	0	0	0	0.0	1	0	1	1	0	3	0	6	1	0	1	1.8	1.000	OF-4
6 yrs.		504	.250	.318	1546	386	54	21	3	0.2	176	123	212	168	56	49	10	860	51	26	8	2.2	.972	OF-433

Dick Higham

HIGHAM, RICHARD BL TR
B. July 1851, England D. Mar. 18, 1905, Chicago, Ill.

1876	HAR N	67	.327	.407	312	102	**21**	2	0	0.0	59	35	2	7		0	0	99	35	26	1	2.2	.837	OF-59, C-13, 2B-1, SS-1
1878	PRO N	62	.320	.416	281	90	**22**	1	1	0.4	**60**	29	5	16		0	0	77	28	25	4	2.1	.808	OF-62, C-1
1880	TRO N	1	.200	.200	5	1	0	0	0	0.0	1	0	0	0		0	0	1	0	0	0	0.5	1.000	C-1, OF-1
3 yrs.		130	.323	.410	598	193	43	3	1	0.2	120	64	7	23		0	0	177	63	51	5	2.1	.825	OF-122, C-15, 2B-1, SS-1

John Hiland

HILAND, JOHN WILLIAM BL TL 5′ 8½″ 165 lbs.
B. Sept. 1860, Baltic, R. I. D. Apr. 10, 1901, Philadelphia, Pa.

1885	PHI N	3	.000	.000	9	0	0	0	0	0.0	0		0	4		0	0	6	4	2	0	4.0	.833	2B-3

George Hildebrand

HILDEBRAND, GEORGE ALBERT BR TR 5′ 8″ 170 lbs.
B. Sept. 6, 1878, San Francisco, Calif. D. May 30, 1960, Reseda, Calif.

1902	BKN N	11	.220	.244	41	9	1	0	0	0.0	3	5	3		0	0	0	27	2	0	0	2.6	1.000	OF-11

Palmer Hildebrand

HILDEBRAND, PALMER MARION (Pete) BR TR 5′11″ 170 lbs.
B. Dec. 23, 1884, Schauck, Ohio D. Jan. 25, 1960, North Canton, Ohio.

1913	STL N	26	.164	.200	55	9	2	0	0	0.0	3	1	1	10	1	2	0	71	21	3	5	4.1	.968	C-22, OF-1

R. E. Hildebrand

HILDEBRAND, R. E.
Deceased.

1902	CHI N	1	.000	.000	4	0	0	0	0	0.0	1	0	1		0	0	0	1	0	0	0	1.0	1.000	OF-1

Belden Hill

HILL, BELDEN L. BL TR 6′
B. Aug. 24, 1864, Kewanee, Ill. D. Oct. 22, 1934, Cedar Rapids, Iowa.

1890	BAL AA	9	.167	.233	30	5	2	0	0	0.0	3		3		6	0	0	24	18	7	2	5.4	.857	3B-9

Donnie Hill

HILL, DONALD EARL BB TR 5′10″ 165 lbs.
B. Nov. 12, 1960, Pomona, Calif.

1983	OAK A	53	.266	.348	158	42	7	0	2	1.3	20	15	4	21	1	1	0	87	136	9	24	4.4	.961	SS-53
1984		73	.230	.299	174	40	6	0	2	1.1	21	16	5	12	1	5	0	102	128	12	28	3.3	.950	SS-66, 2B-4, DH-2, 3B-2
1985		123	.285	.351	393	112	13	2	3	0.8	45	48	23	33	8	2	0	228	320	15	56	4.6	.973	2B-122
1986		108	.283	.378	339	96	16	2	4	1.2	37	29	23	38	5	15	4	104	213	9	31	3.1	.972	2B-68, 3B-33, DH-3, SS-2
1987	CHI A	111	.239	.368	410	98	14	6	9	2.2	57	46	30	35	1	3	1	167	278	14	55	3.9	.969	2B-84, 3B-32, DH-1
1988		83	.217	.281	221	48	6	1	2	0.9	17	20	26	32	3	12	3	118	152	8	38	3.7	.971	2B-59, 3B-12, DH-5
1990	CAL A	103	.264	.352	352	93	18	2	3	0.9	36	32	29	27	1	9	2	194	255	11	64	4.2	.976	2B-60, SS-24, 3B-21, 1B-3, DH-1, P-1
1991		77	.239	.301	209	50	8	1	1	0.5	36	20	30	21	1	16	3	127	176	8	36	4.4	.974	2B-39, SS-29, 1B-3
1992	MIN A	25	.294	.353	51	15	3	0	0	0.0	7	2	5	6	0	9	3	21	38	3	5	2.7	.952	SS-10, 2B-7, 3B-5, OF-1
9 yrs.		756	.257	.343	2307	594	91	14	26	1.1	276	228	175	225	21	72	16	1148	1696	89	337	3.9	.970	2B-443, SS-184, 3B-105, DH-12, 1B-6, OF-1, P-1

Glenallen Hill

HILL, GLENALLEN BR TR 6′ 3″ 210 lbs.
B. Mar. 22, 1965, Santa Cruz, Calif.

Year	Team	Games	BA	SA	AB	H	2B	3B	HR	HR%	R	RBI	BB	SO	SB	Pinch Hit AB	Pinch Hit H	PO	A	E	DP	TC/G	FA	G by Pos
1989	TOR A	19	.288	.346	52	15	0	0	1	1.9	4	7	3	12	2	0	0	27	0	1	0	1.5	.964	OF-16, DH-3
1990		84	.231	.435	260	60	11	3	12	4.6	47	32	18	62	8	7	2	115	4	2	0	1.5	.983	OF-60, DH-20
1991	2 teams	TOR A (35G –.253) CLE A (37G –.262)																						
″	total	72	.258	.421	221	57	8	2	8	3.6	29	25	23	54	6	2	0	118	0	3	0	1.9	.975	OF-46, DH-17
1992	CLE A	102	.241	.436	369	89	16	1	18	4.9	38	49	20	73	9	9	1	126	5	6	1	1.5	.956	OF-59, DH-34
1993	2 teams	CLE A (66G –.224) CHI N (31G –.345)																						
″	total	97	.264	.506	261	69	14	2	15	5.7	33	47	17	71	8	19	6	104	3	6	1	1.4	.947	OF-60, DH-18
1994	CHI N	89	.297	.461	269	80	12	1	10	3.7	48	38	29	57	19	20	5	150	0	2	0	1.9	.987	OF-78
1995	SF N	132	.264	.483	497	131	29	4	24	4.8	71	86	39	98	25	7	5	226	10	10	1	2.0	.959	OF-125
7 yrs.		595	.260	.457	1929	501	90	13	88	4.6	270	284	149	427	77	64	19	866	22	30	3	1.7	.967	OF-444, DH-92

Herman Hill

HILL, HERMAN ALEXANDER BL TR 6′ 2″ 190 lbs.
B. Oct. 12, 1945, Tuskegee, Ala. D. Dec. 14, 1970, Valencia, Venezuela.

Year	Team	Games	BA	SA	AB	H	2B	3B	HR	HR%	R	RBI	BB	SO	SB	Pinch Hit AB	Pinch Hit H	PO	A	E	DP	TC/G	FA	G by Pos
1969	MIN A	16	.000	.000	2	0	0	0	0	0.0	4	0	0	1	1	1	0	0	0	0	0	0.0	.000	OF-2
1970		27	.091	.091	22	2	0	0	0	0.0	8	0	0	6	0	4	0	15	1	0	0	1.1	1.000	OF-14
2 yrs.		43	.083	.083	24	2	0	0	0	0.0	12	0	0	7	1	5	0	15	1	0	0	1.0	1.000	OF-16

Hugh Hill

HILL, HUGH ELLIS BL TR 5′11½″ 168 lbs.
Brother of Still Bill Hill.
B. July 21, 1879, Ringgold, Ga. D. Sept. 6, 1958, Cincinnati, Ohio.

Year	Team	Games	BA	SA	AB	H	2B	3B	HR	HR%	R	RBI	BB	SO	SB	Pinch Hit AB	Pinch Hit H	PO	A	E	DP	TC/G	FA	G by Pos
1903	CLE A	1	.000	.000	1	0	0	0	0	0.0	0	0	0		0	1	0	0	0	0	0	0.0	—	
1904	STL N	23	.226	.366	93	21	2	1	3	3.2	13	4	2		3	0	0	41	2	0	1	1.9	1.000	OF-23
2 yrs.		24	.223	.362	94	21	2	1	3	3.2	13	4	2		3	1	0	41	2	0	1	1.9	1.000	OF-23

Hunter Hill

HILL, HUNTER BENJAMIN BR TR
B. June 21, 1879, Austin, Tex. D. Feb. 22, 1959, Austin, Tex.

Year	Team	Games	BA	SA	AB	H	2B	3B	HR	HR%	R	RBI	BB	SO	SB	Pinch Hit AB	Pinch Hit H	PO	A	E	DP	TC/G	FA	G by Pos
1903	STL A	86	.243	.297	317	77	11	3	0	0.0	30	25	8		2	0	0	110	165	23	10	3.5	.923	3B-86
1904	2 teams	STL A (58G –.215) WAS A (77G –.197)																						
″	total	135	.204	.226	509	104	9	1	0	0.0	37	31	17		14	2	0	170	205	59	7	3.3	.864	3B-127, OF-6
1905	WAS A	104	.209	.254	374	78	12	1	1	0.3	37	24	32		10	1	1	130	206	34	10	3.6	.908	3B-103
3 yrs.		325	.216	.253	1200	259	32	5	1	0.1	104	80	57		26	3	1	410	576	116	27	3.4	.895	3B-316, OF-6

Jesse Hill

HILL, JESSE TERRILL BR TR 5′ 9″ 165 lbs.
B. Jan. 20, 1907, Yates, Mo. D. Aug. 31, 1993, Pasadena, Ca.

Year	Team	Games	BA	SA	AB	H	2B	3B	HR	HR%	R	RBI	BB	SO	SB	Pinch Hit AB	Pinch Hit H	PO	A	E	DP	TC/G	FA	G by Pos
1935	NY A	107	.293	.390	392	115	20	3	4	1.0	69	33	42	32	14	7	2	203	9	11	1	2.4	.951	OF-94
1936	WAS A	85	.305	.429	233	71	19	5	0	0.0	50	34	29	23	11	16	3	83	5	3	1	1.5	.967	OF-60
1937	2 teams	WAS A (33G –.217) PHI A (70G –.293)																						
″	total	103	.272	.356	334	91	14	4	2	0.6	56	41	44	36	18	7	0	236	4	9	0	2.8	.964	OF-89
3 yrs.		295	.289	.388	959	277	53	12	6	0.6	175	108	115	91	43	30	5	522	18	23	2	2.3	.959	OF-243

John Hill

HILL, OLIVER CLINTON BL TR 5′11″ 178 lbs.
B. Oct. 16, 1912, Powder Springs, Ga. D. Sept. 20, 1970, Decatur, Ga.

Year	Team	Games	BA	SA	AB	H	2B	3B	HR	HR%	R	RBI	BB	SO	SB	Pinch Hit AB	Pinch Hit H	PO	A	E	DP	TC/G	FA	G by Pos
1939	BOS N	2	.500	1.000	2	1	1	0	0	0.0	1	0	0	0	0	2	1	0	0	0	0	0.0	—	

Marc Hill

HILL, MARC KEVIN (Booter) BR TR 6′ 3″ 205 lbs.
B. Feb. 18, 1952, Elsberry, Mo.

Year	Team	Games	BA	SA	AB	H	2B	3B	HR	HR%	R	RBI	BB	SO	SB	Pinch Hit AB	Pinch Hit H	PO	A	E	DP	TC/G	FA	G by Pos
1973	STL N	1	.000	.000	3	0	0	0	0	0.0	0	0	0	1	0	0	0	5	0	0	0	5.0	1.000	C-1
1974		10	.238	.286	21	5	1	0	0	0.0	2	2	4	5	0	1	0	41	5	0	0	5.1	1.000	C-9
1975	SF N	72	.214	.319	182	39	4	0	5	2.7	14	23	25	27	0	16	3	282	27	2	7	5.1	.994	C-60, 3B-1
1976		54	.183	.290	131	24	5	0	3	2.3	11	15	10	19	0	4	1	186	24	1	3	4.2	.995	C-49, 1B-1
1977		108	.250	.366	320	80	10	0	9	2.8	28	50	34	34	0	7	2	505	57	6	4	5.6	.989	C-102
1978		117	.243	.316	358	87	15	1	3	0.8	20	36	45	39	1	5	3	592	56	9	3	5.6	.986	C-116, 1B-2
1979		63	.207	.278	169	35	3	0	3	1.8	20	15	26	25	0	6	1	285	31	3	5	5.4	.991	C-58, 1B-1
1980	2 teams	SF N (17G –.171) SEA A (29G –.229)																						
″	total	46	.207	.315	111	23	4	1	2	1.8	9	9	4	17	0	3	0	162	18	3	2	4.3	.984	C-43
1981	CHI A	16	.000	.000	6	0	0	0	0	0.0	0	0	0	1	0	3	0	11	1	0	0	0.8	1.000	C-14, 3B-1, 1B-1
1982		53	.261	.386	88	23	2	0	3	3.4	9	13	6	13	0	2	1	136	16	1	2	3.0	.993	C-49, 1B-1, 3B-1
1983		58	.226	.293	133	30	6	0	1	0.8	11	11	9	24	0	4	2	215	12	2	1	3.9	.991	C-55, DH-2, 1B-1
1984		77	.233	.373	193	45	10	1	5	2.6	15	20	9	26	0	5	0	315	17	3	6	4.5	.991	C-72, 1B-2
1985		40	.133	.160	75	10	2	0	0	0.0	5	4	12	9	0	2	0	185	13	3	1	5.3	.985	C-37, 3B-1
1986		22	.158	.158	19	3	0	0	0	0.0	2	0	1	3	0	0	0	59	7	0	0	3.0	1.000	C-22
14 yrs.		737	.223	.317	1809	404	62	3	34	1.9	146	198	185	243	1	58	13	2979	284	33	34	4.7	.990	C-687, 1B-9, 3B-4, DH-2

Homer Hillebrand

HILLEBRAND, HOMER HILLER HENRY BR TL 5′ 8″ 165 lbs.
B. Oct. 10, 1879, Freeport, Ill. D. Jan. 20, 1974, Elsinore, Calif.

Year	Team	Games	BA	SA	AB	H	2B	3B	HR	HR%	R	RBI	BB	SO	SB	Pinch Hit AB	Pinch Hit H	PO	A	E	DP	TC/G	FA	G by Pos
1905	PIT N	39	.236	.300	110	26	3	2	0	0.0	9	7	6		1	1	0	190	20	7	8	6.0	.968	1B-16, P-10, OF-7, C-3
1906		7	.238	.286	21	5	1	0	0	0.0	1	3	1		0	0	0	4	19	0	2	3.3	1.000	P-7
1908		1	—	—	0	0	0	0	0	—	0	0	0		0	0	0	0	0	0	0	0.0	.000	P-1
3 yrs.		47	.237	.298	131	31	4	2	0	0.0	10	10	7		1	1	0	194	39	7	10	5.5	.971	P-18, 1B-16, OF-7, C-3

Chuck Hiller

HILLER, CHARLES JOSEPH BL TR 5′11″ 170 lbs.
B. Oct. 1, 1934, Johnsburg, Ill.

Year	Team	Games	BA	SA	AB	H	2B	3B	HR	HR%	R	RBI	BB	SO	SB	Pinch Hit AB	Pinch Hit H	PO	A	E	DP	TC/G	FA	G by Pos
1961	SF N	70	.237	.321	240	57	12	1	2	0.8	38	12	32	30	4	2	0	133	158	8	34	4.5	.973	2B-67
1962		161	.276	.334	602	166	22	2	3	0.5	94	48	55	49	5	0	0	367	417	29	105	5.0	.964	2B-161
1963		111	.223	.300	417	93	10	2	6	1.4	44	33	20	23	3	5	0	224	277	19	48	4.8	.963	2B-109
1964		80	.180	.244	205	37	8	1	1	0.5	21	17	17	23	1	22	5	113	145	7	29	4.3	.974	2B-60, 3B-1
1965	2 teams	SF N (7G –.143) NY N (100G –.238)																						
″	total	107	.235	.341	293	69	11	1	6	2.0	25	22	14	25	1	33	7	151	183	14	39	4.0	.960	2B-82, OF-4, 3B-2

Chuck Hiller *continued*

Year	Team	Games	BA	SA	AB	H	2B	3B	HR	HR%	R	RBI	BB	SO	SB	Pinch Hit AB	Pinch Hit H	PO	A	E	DP	TC/G	FA	G by Pos
1966	NY N	108	.280	.350	254	71	8	2	2	0.8	25	14	15	22	0	45	**15**	110	153	5	32	3.9	.981	2B-45, 3B-14, OF-9
1967	**2 teams** NY N (25G –.093) PHI N (31G –.302)																							
"	**total**	56	.186	.227	97	18	4	0	0	0.0	4	5	4	15	0	38	7	33	46	3	10	4.1	.963	2B-20
1968	PIT N	11	.385	.462	13	5	1	0	0	0.0	2	1	0	0	0	9	4	4	2	1	0	3.5	.857	2B-2
8 yrs.		704	.243	.316	2121	516	76	9	20	0.9	253	152	157	187	14	154	38	1135	1381	86	297	4.5	.967	2B-546, 3B-17, OF-13
WORLD SERIES																								
1962	SF N	7	.269	.500	26	7	3	0	1	3.8	4	5	3	4	0	0	0	16	22	1	7	5.6	.974	2B-7

Hob Hiller

HILLER, HARVEY MAX BR TR 5′ 8″ 162 lbs.
B. May 12, 1893, East Mauch Chunk, Pa. D. Dec. 27, 1956, Lehighton, Pa.

Year	Team	Games	BA	SA	AB	H	2B	3B	HR	HR%	R	RBI	BB	SO	SB	Pinch Hit AB	Pinch Hit H	PO	A	E	DP	TC/G	FA	G by Pos
1920	BOS A	17	.172	.276	29	5	1	1	0	0.0	4	2	2	5	0	0	0	8	20	2	1	2.1	.933	3B-6, SS-5, 2B-2, OF-1
1921		1	.000	.000	1	0	0	0	0	0.0	0	0	0	0	0	1	0	0	0	0	0	0.0	—	
2 yrs.		18	.167	.267	30	5	1	1	0	0.0	4	2	2	5	0	1	0	8	20	2	1	2.1	.933	3B-6, SS-5, 2B-2, OF-1

Ed Hilley

HILLEY, EDWARD GARFIELD (Whitey) BR TR 5′10½″ 170 lbs.
B. June 17, 1879, Cleveland, Ohio D. Nov. 14, 1956, Cleveland, Ohio.

Year	Team	Games	BA	SA	AB	H	2B	3B	HR	HR%	R	RBI	BB	SO	SB	Pinch Hit AB	Pinch Hit H	PO	A	E	DP	TC/G	FA	G by Pos
1903	PHI A	1	.333	.333	3	1	0	0	0	0.0	1	0	1		0	0	0	3	1	1	1	5.0	.800	3B-1

Mack Hillis

HILLIS, MALCOLM DAVID BR TR 5′10″ 165 lbs.
B. July 23, 1901, Cambridge, Mass. D. June 16, 1961, Cambridge, Mass.

Year	Team	Games	BA	SA	AB	H	2B	3B	HR	HR%	R	RBI	BB	SO	SB	Pinch Hit AB	Pinch Hit H	PO	A	E	DP	TC/G	FA	G by Pos
1924	NY A	1	.000	.000	1	0	0	0	0	0.0	1	0	0	0	0	0	0	0	0	0	0	0.0	.000	2B-1
1928	PIT N	11	.250	.556	36	9	2	3	1	2.8	6	7	0	6	1	2	0	14	25	2	2	4.6	.951	2B-8, 3B-1
2 yrs.		12	.243	.541	37	9	2	3	1	2.7	7	7	0	6	1	2	0	14	25	2	2	4.1	.951	2B-9, 3B-1

Pat Hilly

HILLY, WILLIAM EDWARD BR TR 5′11″ 180 lbs.
Born William Edward Hilgerink.
B. Feb. 24, 1887, Fostoria, Ohio D. July 25, 1953, Eureka, Mo.

Year	Team	Games	BA	SA	AB	H	2B	3B	HR	HR%	R	RBI	BB	SO	SB	Pinch Hit AB	Pinch Hit H	PO	A	E	DP	TC/G	FA	G by Pos
1914	PHI N	8	.300	.300	10	3	0	0	0	0.0	2	1	1	5	0	1	1	6	0	0	0	1.5	1.000	OF-4

Dave Hilton

HILTON, JOHN DAVID BR TR 5′11″ 191 lbs.
B. Sept. 15, 1950, Uvalde, Tex.

Year	Team	Games	BA	SA	AB	H	2B	3B	HR	HR%	R	RBI	BB	SO	SB	Pinch Hit AB	Pinch Hit H	PO	A	E	DP	TC/G	FA	G by Pos
1972	SD N	13	.213	.298	47	10	2	1	0	0.0	2	5	3	6	1	0	0	12	19	2	1	2.5	.939	3B-13
1973		70	.197	.299	234	46	9	0	5	2.1	21	16	19	35	2	0	0	79	141	6	19	3.2	.973	3B-47, 2B-23
1974		74	.240	.309	217	52	8	2	1	0.5	17	12	13	28	3	10	1	70	113	12	17	2.8	.938	3B-55, 2B-15
1975		4	.000	.000	8	0	0	0	0	0.0	0	0	0	0	0	0	0	2	7	1	0	2.5	.900	3B-4
4 yrs.		161	.213	.298	506	108	19	3	6	1.2	40	33	35	69	6	10	1	163	280	21	37	3.0	.955	3B-119, 2B-38

Jack Himes

HIMES, JOHN HERB BL TR 6′ 2″ 180 lbs.
B. Sept. 22, 1878, Bryan, Ohio D. Dec. 16, 1949, Joliet, Ill.

Year	Team	Games	BA	SA	AB	H	2B	3B	HR	HR%	R	RBI	BB	SO	SB	Pinch Hit AB	Pinch Hit H	PO	A	E	DP	TC/G	FA	G by Pos
1905	STL N	12	.146	.146	41	6	0	0	0	0.0	3	0	1		0	1	0	17	1	0	0	1.6	1.000	OF-11
1906		40	.271	.329	155	42	5	2	0	0.0	10	14	7		4	0	0	76	10	2	2	2.2	.977	OF-40
2 yrs.		52	.245	.291	196	48	5	2	0	0.0	13	14	8		4	1	0	93	11	2	2	2.1	.981	OF-51

Bill Hinchman

HINCHMAN, WILLIAM WHITE BR TR 5′11″ 190 lbs.
Brother of Harry Hinchman.
B. Apr. 4, 1883, Philadelphia, Pa. D. Feb. 20, 1963, Columbus, Ohio.

Year	Team	Games	BA	SA	AB	H	2B	3B	HR	HR%	R	RBI	BB	SO	SB	Pinch Hit AB	Pinch Hit H	PO	A	E	DP	TC/G	FA	G by Pos
1905	CIN N	17	.255	.373	51	13	4	1	0	0.0	10	10	13		4	0	0	31	6	5	1	2.5	.881	OF-12, 3B-4, 1B-1
1906		18	.204	.259	54	11	1	1	0	0.0	7	1	8		2	1	1	23	3	1	2	1.7	.963	OF-16
1907	CLE A	152	.228	.305	514	117	19	9	1	0.2	62	50	47		15	0	0	278	22	11	6	2.0	.965	OF-150, 1B-4, 2B-1
1908		137	.231	.353	464	107	23	8	6	**1.3**	55	59	38		9	3	0	236	201	36	27	3.6	.924	OF-75, SS-51, 1B-4
1909		139	.258	.372	457	118	20	13	2	0.4	57	53	41		22	2	1	241	18	24	4	2.1	.915	OF-131, SS-6
1915	PIT N	156	.307	.438	577	177	33	14	5	0.9	72	77	48	75	17	0	0	261	17	9	5	1.8	.969	OF-156
1916		152	.315	.427	555	175	18	**16**	4	0.7	64	76	54	61	10	1	0	496	20	16	12	3.4	.970	OF-124, 1B-31
1917		69	.189	.275	244	46	5	5	2	0.8	27	29	33	27	5	0	0	275	18	11	10	4.5	.964	OF-48, 1B-20
1918		50	.234	.315	111	26	5	2	0	0.0	10	13	15	8	1	19	6	51	10	3	0	1.5	.953	OF-40, 1B-3
1920		18	.188	.188	16	3	0	0	0	0.0	0	1	1	3	0	16	3	0	0	0	0	0.0	—	
10 yrs.		908	.261	.368	3043	793	128	69	20	0.7	364	369	298	174	85	42	11	1892	315	116	67	2.6	.950	OF-752, 1B-63, SS-57, 3B-4, 2B-1

Harry Hinchman

HINCHMAN, HARRY SIBLEY BB TR 5′11″ 165 lbs.
Brother of Bill Hinchman.
B. Aug. 4, 1878, Philadelphia, Pa. D. Jan. 19, 1933, Toledo, Ohio.

Year	Team	Games	BA	SA	AB	H	2B	3B	HR	HR%	R	RBI	BB	SO	SB	Pinch Hit AB	Pinch Hit H	PO	A	E	DP	TC/G	FA	G by Pos
1907	CLE A	15	.216	.314	51	11	3	1	0	0.0	3	9	5		2	0	0	25	60	9	5	6.3	.904	2B-15

Hunkey Hines

HINES, HENRY FRED BR TR 5′ 7″ 165 lbs.
B. Sept. 29, 1867, Elgin, Ill. D. Jan. 2, 1928, Rockford, Ill.

Year	Team	Games	BA	SA	AB	H	2B	3B	HR	HR%	R	RBI	BB	SO	SB	Pinch Hit AB	Pinch Hit H	PO	A	E	DP	TC/G	FA	G by Pos
1895	BKN N	2	.250	.250	8	2	0	0	0	0.0	3	1	2	0	0	0	0	5	0	0	0	2.5	1.000	OF-2

Mike Hines

HINES, MICHAEL P. BR TL 5′10″ 176 lbs.
B. Sept. 1862, Ireland D. Mar. 14, 1910, New Bedford, Mass.

Year	Team	Games	BA	SA	AB	H	2B	3B	HR	HR%	R	RBI	BB	SO	SB	Pinch Hit AB	Pinch Hit H	PO	A	E	DP	TC/G	FA	G by Pos
1883	BOS N	63	.225	.290	231	52	13	1	0	0.0	38	16	7	36		0	0	388	104	62	5	8.4	.888	C-59, OF-7
1884		35	.174	.197	132	23	3	0	0	0.0	16		3	24		0	0	255	64	28	7	9.9	.919	C-35
1885	**3 teams** BOS N (14G –.232) BKN AA (3G –.077) PRO N (1G –.000)																							
"	**total**	18	.194	.278	72	14	4	1	0	0.0	12	4	4	7		0	0	28	9	9	0	2.6	.804	OF-14, C-4
1888	BOS N	4	.125	.250	16	2	0	1	0	0.0	3	2	2	0	0	0	0	16	1	3	0	5.0	.850	OF-3, C-1
4 yrs.		120	.202	.259	451	91	20	3	0	0.0	69	22	16	67	0	0	0	687	178	102	12	7.9	.895	C-99, OF-24

Paul Hines

HINES, PAUL A. BR TR 5′ 9½″ 173 lbs.
B. Mar. 1, 1852, Washington, D. C. D. July 10, 1935, Hyattsville, Md.

Year	Team	Games	BA	SA	AB	H	2B	3B	HR	HR%	R	RBI	BB	SO	SB	Pinch Hit AB	Pinch Hit H	PO	A	E	DP	TC/G	FA	G by Pos
1876	CHI N	64	.331	.439	305	101	**21**	3	2	0.7	62	59	1	3		0	0	159	8	14	4	2.8	.923	OF-64, 2B-1
1877		60	.280	.375	261	73	11	7	0	0.0	44	23	1	8		0	0	102	40	36	5	3.0	.798	OF-49, 2B-11
1878	PRO N	62	**.358**	**.486**	257	92	13	4	**4**	**1.6**	42	**50**	2	10		0	0	109	20	24	4	2.5	.843	OF-61, SS-1
1879		85	**.357**	.482	**409**	**146**	25	10	2	0.5	81	52	8	16		0	0	146	24	26	3	2.3	.867	OF-85
1880		85	.307	.396	374	115	20	2	3	0.8	64	35	13	17		0	0	197	37	15	11	2.9	.940	OF-75, 2B-6, 1B-4

Paul Hines *continued*

Year	Team	Games	BA	SA	AB	H	2B	3B	HR	HR%	R	RBI	BB	SO	SB	Pinch Hit AB	Pinch Hit H	PO	A	E	DP	TC/G	FA	G by Pos
1881		80	.285	.404	361	103	**27**	5	2	0.6	65	31	13	12		0	0	193	23	28	4	2.9	.885	OF-78, 2B-4, 1B-1
1882		84	.309	.467	379	117	28	10	4	1.1	73		10	14		0	0	175	16	29	7	2.6	.868	OF-82, 1B-2
1883		97	.299	.416	442	132	32	4	4	0.9	94		18	23		0	0	268	27	24	10	3.3	.925	OF-89, 1B-9
1884		114	.302	.435	490	148	**36**	10	3	0.6	94		44	28		0	0	266	20	29	9	2.7	.908	OF-108, 1B-7, P-1
1885		98	.270	.345	411	111	20	4	1	0.2	63	35	19	18		0	0	245	25	37	4	3.1	.879	OF-92, 1B-4, SS-1, 3B-1, 2B-1
1886	WAS N	121	.312	.462	487	152	30	8	9	1.8	80	56	35	21		0	0	311	66	47	6	3.4	.889	OF-92, 3B-15, 1B-10, SS-5, 2B-3
1887		123	.308	.458	478	147	32	5	10	2.1	83	72	48	24	46	0	0	270	39	35	7	2.8	.898	OF-109, 1B-7, 2B-5, SS-4
1888	IND N	133	.281	.366	513	144	26	3	4	0.8	84	58	41	45	31	0	0	312	18	30	9	2.7	.917	OF-125, 1B-6, SS-2
1889		121	.305	.401	486	148	27	1	6	1.2	77	72	49	22	34	0	0	1121	61	43	66	10.1	.965	1B-109, OF-12
1890	2 teams	PIT N (31G –.182) BOS N (69G –.264)																						
″	total	100	.239	.302	394	94	13	3	2	0.5	52	57	43	27	15	0	0	318	19	27	11	3.6	.926	OF-83, 1B-18
1891	WAS AA	54	.282	.364	206	58	7	5	0	0.0	25	31	21	16	6	0	0	144	9	17	7	3.1	.900	OF-47, 1B-8
16 yrs.		1481	.301	.413	6253	1881	368	84	56	0.9	1083	631	366	304	132	0	0	4336	452	461	167	3.5	.912	OF-1251, 1B-185, 2B-31, 3B-16, SS-13, P-1

Gordie Hinkle

HINKLE, DANIEL GORDON BR TR 6′ 185 lbs.
B. Apr. 3, 1905, Toronto, Ohio D. Mar. 19, 1972, Houston, Tex.

Year	Team	Games	BA	SA	AB	H	2B	3B	HR	HR%	R	RBI	BB	SO	SB	Pinch Hit AB	Pinch Hit H	PO	A	E	DP	TC/G	FA	G by Pos
1934	BOS A	27	.173	.280	75	13	6	1	0	0.0	7	9	7	23	0	0	0	107	11	1	2	4.6	.992	C-26

George Hinshaw

HINSHAW, GEORGE ADDISON BR TR 6′ 185 lbs.
B. Oct. 23, 1959, Los Angeles, Calif.

Year	Team	Games	BA	SA	AB	H	2B	3B	HR	HR%	R	RBI	BB	SO	SB	Pinch Hit AB	Pinch Hit H	PO	A	E	DP	TC/G	FA	G by Pos
1982	SD N	6	.267	.267	15	4	0	0	0	0.0	1	1	3	5	0	0	0	9	1	0	0	1.7	1.000	OF-6
1983		7	.438	.500	16	7	1	0	0	0.0	1	4	0	4	1	0	0	6	5	0	0	1.8	1.000	3B-5, 2B-1
2 yrs.		13	.355	.387	31	11	1	0	0	0.0	2	5	3	9	1	0	0	15	6	0	0	1.8	1.000	OF-6, 3B-5, 2B-1

Paul Hinson

HINSON, JAMES PAUL BR TR 5′10″ 150 lbs.
B. May 9, 1904, Vanleer, Tenn. D. Sept. 23, 1960, Muskogee, Okla.

Year	Team	Games	BA	SA	AB	H	2B	3B	HR	HR%	R	RBI	BB	SO	SB	Pinch Hit AB	Pinch Hit H	PO	A	E	DP	TC/G	FA	G by Pos
1928	BOS A	3	—	—	0	0	0	0	0	—	1	0	0	0	0	0	0	0	0	0	0	0.0	—	

Chuck Hinton

HINTON, CHARLES EDWARD BR TR 6′ 1″ 180 lbs.
B. May 3, 1934, Rocky Mount, N. C.

Year	Team	Games	BA	SA	AB	H	2B	3B	HR	HR%	R	RBI	BB	SO	SB	Pinch Hit AB	Pinch Hit H	PO	A	E	DP	TC/G	FA	G by Pos
1961	WAS A	106	.260	.381	339	88	13	5	6	1.8	51	34	40	81	22	11	4	175	6	7	4	2.0	.963	OF-92
1962		151	.310	.472	542	168	25	6	17	3.1	73	75	47	66	28	2	0	259	36	4	16	2.0	.987	OF-136, 2B-12, SS-1
1963		150	.269	.426	566	152	20	12	15	2.7	80	55	64	79	25	0	0	345	43	10	9	2.6	.975	OF-125, 3B-19, 1B-6, SS-2
1964		138	.274	.414	514	141	25	7	11	2.1	71	53	57	77	17	5	1	258	7	4	3	2.0	.985	OF-131, 3B-2
1965	CLE A	133	.255	.448	431	110	17	6	18	4.2	59	54	53	65	17	16	2	408	71	13	30	3.6	.974	OF-72, 1B-40, 2B-23, 3B-1
1966		123	.256	.402	348	89	9	3	12	3.4	46	50	35	66	10	17	4	203	6	5	3	1.9	.977	OF-104, 1B-6, 2B-2
1967		147	.245	.355	498	122	19	3	10	2.0	55	37	43	100	6	12	4	243	9	6	2	1.8	.977	OF-136, 2B-5
1968	CAL A	116	.195	.333	267	52	10	3	7	2.6	28	23	24	61	3	32	4	390	60	7	32	4.3	.985	1B-48, OF-37, 3B-13, 2B-9
1969	CLE A	94	.256	.388	121	31	3	2	3	2.5	18	19	8	22	2	40	10	37	15	3	1	1.0	.945	OF-40, 3B-14
1970		107	.318	.477	195	62	4	0	9	4.6	24	29	25	34	0	37	11	229	15	2	14	2.9	.992	1B-40, OF-35, C-4, 2B-3, 3B-2
1971		88	.224	.374	147	33	7	0	5	3.4	13	14	20	34	0	43	5	123	5	0	16	2.8	1.000	1B-20, OF-20, C-5
11 yrs.		1353	.264	.412	3968	1048	152	47	113	2.8	518	443	416	685	130	215	45	2670	273	61	130	2.5	.980	OF-928, 1B-160, 2B-54, 3B-51, C-9, SS-3

John Hinton

HINTON, JOHN ROBERT (Red) BR TR 6′ 200 lbs.
B. June 28, 1876, Pittsburgh, Pa. D. Aug. 8, 1920, Braddock, Pa.

Year	Team	Games	BA	SA	AB	H	2B	3B	HR	HR%	R	RBI	BB	SO	SB	Pinch Hit AB	Pinch Hit H	PO	A	E	DP	TC/G	FA	G by Pos
1901	BOS N	4	.077	.077	13	1	0	0	0	0.0	0	0	2		0	0	0	4	5	3	0	3.0	.750	3B-4

Tommy Hinzo

HINZO, THOMAS LEE BB TR 5′10″ 170 lbs.
B. June 18, 1964, San Diego, Calif.

Year	Team	Games	BA	SA	AB	H	2B	3B	HR	HR%	R	RBI	BB	SO	SB	Pinch Hit AB	Pinch Hit H	PO	A	E	DP	TC/G	FA	G by Pos
1987	CLE A	67	.265	.358	257	68	9	3	3	1.2	31	21	10	47	9	1	0	115	204	9	44	4.9	.973	2B-67
1989		18	.000	.000	17	0	0	0	0	0.0	4	0	2	6	1	1	0	9	7	3	1	2.4	.842	2B-6, SS-1, DH-1
2 yrs.		85	.248	.336	274	68	9	3	3	1.1	35	21	12	53	10	2	0	124	211	12	45	4.6	.965	2B-73, SS-1, DH-1

Gene Hiser

HISER, GENE TAYLOR BL TL 5′11″ 175 lbs.
B. Dec. 11, 1948, Baltimore, Md.

Year	Team	Games	BA	SA	AB	H	2B	3B	HR	HR%	R	RBI	BB	SO	SB	Pinch Hit AB	Pinch Hit H	PO	A	E	DP	TC/G	FA	G by Pos
1971	CHI N	17	.207	.207	29	6	0	0	0	0.0	4	1	4	8	1	5	1	19	0	0	0	2.1	1.000	OF-9
1972		32	.196	.196	46	9	0	0	0	0.0	2	4	6	8	1	11	1	21	2	0	1	1.5	1.000	OF-15
1973		100	.174	.229	109	19	3	0	1	0.9	15	6	11	17	4	37	6	48	0	1	0	0.8	.980	OF-64
1974		12	.235	.294	17	4	1	0	0	0.0	2	1	0	3	0	5	1	8	0	0	0	1.0	1.000	OF-8
1975		45	.242	.290	62	15	3	0	0	0.0	11	6	11	7	0	24	8	28	0	0	1	1.5	1.000	OF-18, 1B-1
5 yrs.		206	.202	.240	263	53	7	0	1	0.4	34	18	32	43	6	82	17	124	2	1	2	1.1	.992	OF-114, 1B-1

Larry Hisle

HISLE, LARRY EUGENE BR TR 6′ 2″ 193 lbs.
B. May 5, 1947, Portsmouth, Ohio.

Year	Team	Games	BA	SA	AB	H	2B	3B	HR	HR%	R	RBI	BB	SO	SB	Pinch Hit AB	Pinch Hit H	PO	A	E	DP	TC/G	FA	G by Pos
1968	PHI N	7	.364	.455	11	4	1	0	0	0.0	1	1	1	4	0	1	0	8	0	0	0	1.3	1.000	OF-6
1969		145	.266	.459	482	128	23	5	20	4.1	75	56	48	152	18	2	0	324	11	8	2	2.5	.977	OF-140
1970		126	.205	.353	405	83	22	4	10	2.5	52	44	53	139	5	3	0	262	5	6	0	2.3	.978	OF-121
1971		36	.197	.237	76	15	3	0	0	0.0	7	3	6	22	1	5	1	48	2	2	0	1.9	.962	OF-27
1973	MIN A	143	.272	.422	545	148	25	6	15	2.8	88	64	64	128	11	1	1	337	11	9	0	2.5	.975	OF-143
1974		143	.286	.465	510	146	20	7	19	3.7	68	79	48	112	12	9	1	279	4	6	1	2.1	.979	OF-137
1975		80	.314	.494	255	80	9	2	11	4.3	37	51	27	39	17	5	3	118	2	3	0	1.7	.976	OF-58, DH-14
1976		155	.272	.394	581	158	19	5	14	2.4	81	96	56	93	31	1	0	361	16	6	1	2.5	.984	OF-154
1977		141	.302	.533	546	165	36	3	28	5.1	95	**119**	56	106	21	2	1	287	11	8	2	2.2	.974	OF-134, DH-6
1978	MIL A	142	.290	.533	520	151	24	0	34	6.5	96	115	67	90	10	4	1	172	6	4	2	1.3	.978	OF-87, DH-51
1979		26	.281	.448	96	27	7	0	3	3.1	18	14	11	19	1	1	1	17	2	0	0	0.8	1.000	DH-15, OF-10
1980		17	.283	.583	60	17	0	0	6	10.0	16	16	14	7	1	0	0	0	0	0	0	0.0	.000	DH-17
1981		27	.230	.414	87	20	4	0	4	4.6	11	11	6	17	0	4	0	0	0	0	0	0.0	.000	DH-24
1982		9	.129	.323	31	4	0	0	2	6.5	7	5	5	13	0	1	1	0	0	0	0	0.0	.000	DH-8
14 yrs.		1197	.273	.452	4205	1146	193	32	166	3.9	652	674	462	941	128	39	10	2213	70	52	8	2.0	.978	OF-1017, DH-135

Billy Hitchcock

HITCHCOCK, WILLIAM CLYDE
Brother of Jim Hitchcock.
B. July 31, 1916, Inverness, Ala.
Manager 1960, 1962–63, 1966–67.

BR TR 6′ 1½″ 185 lbs.

Year	Team	Games	BA	SA	AB	H	2B	3B	HR	HR%	R	RBI	BB	SO	SB	Pinch Hit AB	Pinch Hit H	PO	A	E	DP	TC/G	FA	G by Pos
1942	DET A	85	.211	.246	280	59	8	1	0	0.0	27	29	26	21	2	0	0	157	199	21	39	4.7	.944	SS-80, 3B-1
1946	2 teams	DET A (3G –.000) WAS A (98G –.212)																						
″	total	101	.210	.249	357	75	8	3	0	0.0	27	25	27	52	2	1	0	166	231	21	34	4.2	.950	SS-53, 3B-46, 2B-1
1947	STL A	80	.222	.255	275	61	2	2	1	0.4	25	28	21	34	3	5	0	209	190	14	45	5.5	.966	2B-46, 3B-17, SS-7, 1B-5
1948	BOS A	49	.298	.379	124	37	3	2	1	0.8	15	20	7	9	0	12	3	54	82	4	15	4.7	.971	3B-15, 2B-15
1949		55	.204	.259	147	30	6	1	0	0.0	22	9	17	11	2	16	0	277	30	3	33	8.4	.990	1B-29, 2B-8
1950	PHI A	115	.273	.361	399	109	22	5	1	0.3	35	54	103	32	3	8	3	299	319	22	105	5.9	.966	2B-107, SS-1
1951		77	.306	.401	222	68	10	4	1	0.5	27	36	21	23	2	11	3	100	150	14	31	3.8	.947	3B-45, 2B-23, 1B-1
1952		119	.246	.292	407	100	8	4	1	0.2	45	56	39	45	1	4	0	202	235	22	34	3.9	.952	3B-104, 1B-13
1953	DET A	22	.211	.211	38	8	0	0	0	0.0	8	0	3	3	0	6	1	10	18	2	2	2.1	.933	3B-12, SS-1, 2B-1
9 yrs.		703	.243	.299	2249	547	67	22	5	0.2	231	257	264	230	15	63	10	1474	1454	123	338	4.8	.960	3B-240, 2B-201, SS-142, 1B-48

Jim Hitchcock

HITCHCOCK, JAMES FRANKLIN
Brother of Billy Hitchcock.
B. June 28, 1911, Inverness, Ala. D. June 23, 1959, Montgomery, Ala.

BR TR 5′11″ 175 lbs.

Year	Team	Games	BA	SA	AB	H	2B	3B	HR	HR%	R	RBI	BB	SO	SB	Pinch Hit AB	Pinch Hit H	PO	A	E	DP	TC/G	FA	G by Pos
1938	BOS N	28	.171	.171	76	13	0	0	0	0.0	2	7	2	11	1	0	0	48	61	15	13	4.8	.879	SS-24, 3B-2

Myril Hoag

HOAG, MYRIL OLIVER
B. Mar. 9, 1908, Davis, Calif. D. July 28, 1971, High Springs, Fla.

BR TR 5′11″ 180 lbs.

Year	Team	Games	BA	SA	AB	H	2B	3B	HR	HR%	R	RBI	BB	SO	SB	Pinch Hit AB	Pinch Hit H	PO	A	E	DP	TC/G	FA	G by Pos
1931	NY A	44	.143	.214	28	4	2	0	0	0.0	6	3	1	8	0	10	1	12	2	0	0	0.6	1.000	OF-23, 3B-1
1932		46	.370	.519	54	20	5	0	1	1.9	18	7	7	13	1	3	1	26	3	1	0	0.8	.967	OF-35, 1B-1
1934		97	.267	.351	251	67	8	2	3	1.2	45	34	21	21	1	7	0	142	7	4	2	1.8	.974	OF-86
1935		48	.255	.336	110	28	4	1	1	0.9	13	13	12	19	4	5	0	66	2	1	0	1.9	.986	OF-37
1936		45	.301	.468	156	47	9	4	3	1.9	23	34	7	16	3	3	1	82	2	4	1	2.3	.955	OF-39
1937		106	.301	.423	362	109	19	8	3	0.8	48	46	33	33	4	7	2	181	8	9	2	2.0	.955	OF-99
1938		85	.277	.352	267	74	14	3	0	0.0	28	48	25	31	4	15	3	132	5	5	3	2.0	.965	OF-70
1939	STL A	129	.295	.421	482	142	23	4	10	2.1	58	75	24	35	9	12	4	218	13	7	2	2.0	.971	OF-117, P-1
1940		76	.262	.366	191	50	11	0	3	1.6	20	26	13	30	2	28	5	64	4	2	0	1.5	.971	OF-46
1941	2 teams	STL A (1G –.000) CHI A (106G –.255)																						
″	total	107	.255	.312	381	97	13	3	1	0.3	30	44	27	29	6	6	2	215	6	10	1	2.3	.957	OF-99
1942	CHI A	113	.240	.308	412	99	18	2	2	0.5	47	37	36	21	17	1	1	266	12	8	4	2.6	.972	OF-112
1944	2 teams	CHI A (17G –.229) CLE A (67G –.285)																						
″	total	84	.277	.335	325	90	10	3	1	0.3	38	31	35	24	7	4	0	200	11	11	4	2.8	.950	OF-80
1945	CLE A	40	.211	.297	128	27	5	3	0	0.0	10	3	11	18	1	1	0	73	5	1	1	2.3	.987	OF-33, P-2
13 yrs.		1020	.271	.364	3147	854	141	33	28	0.9	384	401	252	298	59	102	20	1677	80	63	20	2.1	.965	OF-876, P-3, 1B-1, 3B-1
WORLD SERIES																								
1932	NY A	1	—	—	0	0	0	0	0	—	1	0	0	0	0	0	0	0	0	0	0	0.0	—	
1937		5	.300	.500	20	6	1	0	1	5.0	4	2	0	1	0	0	0	11	0	0	0	2.2	1.000	OF-5
1938		2	.400	.600	5	2	1	0	0	0.0	3	1	0	0	0	1	0	1	0	0	0	1.0	1.000	OF-1
3 yrs.		8	.320	.520	25	8	2	0	1	4.0	8	3	0	1	0	1	0	12	0	0	0	2.0	1.000	OF-6

Don Hoak

HOAK, DONALD ALBERT (Tiger)
B. Feb. 5, 1928, Roulette, Pa. D. Oct. 9, 1969, Pittsburgh, Pa.

BR TR 6′ 1″ 170 lbs.

Year	Team	Games	BA	SA	AB	H	2B	3B	HR	HR%	R	RBI	BB	SO	SB	Pinch Hit AB	Pinch Hit H	PO	A	E	DP	TC/G	FA	G by Pos
1954	BKN N	88	.245	.398	261	64	9	5	7	2.7	41	26	25	39	8	11	2	71	139	11	12	2.9	.950	3B-75
1955		94	.240	.362	279	67	13	3	5	1.8	50	19	46	50	9	4	1	82	183	11	15	3.5	.960	3B-78
1956	CHI N	121	.215	.311	424	91	18	4	5	1.2	51	37	41	46	8	5	1	122	158	15	16	2.7	.949	3B-110
1957	CIN N	149	.293	.482	529	155	**39**	2	19	3.6	78	89	74	54	8	0	0	194	270	14	29	3.2	.971	3B-149, 2B-1
1958		114	.261	.376	417	109	30	0	6	1.4	51	50	43	36	6	1	0	133	244	14	29	3.5	.964	3B-112, SS-1
1959	PIT N	155	.294	.399	564	166	29	3	8	1.4	60	65	71	75	9	0	0	169	322	20	31	3.3	.961	3B-155
1960		155	.282	.445	553	156	24	9	16	2.9	97	79	74	74	3	0	0	132	324	25	34	3.1	.948	3B-155
1961		145	.298	.451	503	150	27	7	12	2.4	72	61	73	53	4	2	2	137	267	20	29	3.0	.953	3B-143
1962		121	.241	.350	411	99	14	8	5	1.2	63	48	49	49	4	3	1	93	220	10	19	2.8	.969	3B-116
1963	PHI N	115	.231	.324	377	87	11	3	6	1.6	35	24	27	52	5	9	2	88	205	13	13	2.9	.958	3B-106
1964		6	.000	.000	4	0	0	0	0	0.0	0	0	0	2	0	4	0	0	0	0	0	0.0	—	
11 yrs.		1263	.265	.396	4322	1144	214	44	89	2.1	598	498	523	530	64	39	9	1221	2332	153	227	3.1	.959	3B-1199, SS-1, 2B-1
WORLD SERIES																								
1955	BKN N	3	.333	.333	3	1	0	0	0	0.0	0	0	2	0	0	0	0	1	1	0	0	2.0	1.000	3B-1
1960	PIT N	7	.217	.304	23	5	2	0	0	0.0	3	3	4	1	0	0	0	8	10	1	2	2.7	.947	3B-7
2 yrs.		10	.231	.308	26	6	2	0	0	0.0	3	3	6	1	0	0	0	9	11	1	2	2.6	.952	3B-8

Bill Hobbs

HOBBS, WILLIAM LEE
B. May 7, 1893, Grant's Lick, Ky. D. Jan. 5, 1945, Hamilton, Ohio.

BR TR 5′ 9½″ 155 lbs.

Year	Team	Games	BA	SA	AB	H	2B	3B	HR	HR%	R	RBI	BB	SO	SB	Pinch Hit AB	Pinch Hit H	PO	A	E	DP	TC/G	FA	G by Pos
1913	CIN N	4	.000	.000	4	0	0	0	0	0.0	0	0	0	3	0	1	0	0	3	0	0	1.5	1.000	3B-1, 2B-1
1916		6	.182	.273	11	2	1	0	0	0.0	1	1	2	0	1	0	0	9	27	2	3	6.3	.947	SS-6
2 yrs.		10	.133	.200	15	2	1	0	0	0.0	1	1	2	3	1	1	0	9	30	2	3	5.1	.951	SS-6, 3B-1, 2B-1

Dick Hoblitzell

HOBLITZELL, RICHARD CARLETON
B. Oct. 26, 1888, Waverly, W. Va. D. Nov. 14, 1962, Parkersburg, W. Va.

BL TL 6′ 172 lbs.

Year	Team	Games	BA	SA	AB	H	2B	3B	HR	HR%	R	RBI	BB	SO	SB	Pinch Hit AB	Pinch Hit H	PO	A	E	DP	TC/G	FA	G by Pos
1908	CIN N	32	.254	.316	114	29	3	2	0	0.0	8	8	7		2	0	0	313	24	5	11	10.7	.985	1B-32
1909		142	.308	.418	517	159	23	11	4	0.8	59	67	44		17	0	0	1444	74	28	80	10.9	.982	1B-142
1910		155	.278	.380	**611**	170	24	13	4	0.7	85	70	47	32	28	0	0	1461	83	24	66	10.1	.985	1B-148, 2B-7
1911		158	.289	.415	**622**	180	19	13	11	1.8	81	97	42	44	32	0	0	1442	91	16	81	9.8	.990	1B-158
1912		148	.294	.405	558	164	32	12	2	0.4	73	85	48	28	23	0	0	1326	87	21	73	9.8	.985	1B-147
1913		137	.285	.376	502	143	23	7	3	0.6	59	68	35	26	18	3	2	1373	60	17	76	10.8	.988	1B-134
1914	2 teams	CIN N (78G –.210) BOS A (68G –.319)																						
″	total	146	.262	.342	477	125	18	10	0	0.0	62	62	45	47	19	1	0	1429	61	24	65	10.6	.984	1B-143
1915	BOS A	124	.283	.396	399	113	15	12	2	0.5	54	61	38	26	9	4	0	1095	63	15	51	10.0	.987	1B-117

Dick Hoblitzell *continued*

Year	Team	Games	BA	SA	AB	H	2B	3B	HR	HR%	R	RBI	BB	SO	SB	Pinch Hit AB	Pinch Hit H	PO	A	E	DP	TC/G	FA	G by Pos
1916		130	.259	.305	417	108	17	1	0	0.0	57	50	47	28	10	3	0	1225	67	15	64	10.4	.989	1B-126
1917		120	.257	.343	420	108	19	7	1	0.2	49	47	46	22	12	2	0	1274	52	14	58	11.4	.990	1B-118
1918		25	.159	.174	69	11	1	0	0	0.0	4	4	8	3	3	5	3	209	15	1	18	11.8	.996	1B-19
11 yrs.		1317	.278	.374	4706	1310	194	88	27	0.6	591	619	407	256	173	18	5	12591	677	180	643	10.4	.987	1B-1284, 2B-7
WORLD SERIES																								
1915	BOS A	5	.313	.313	16	5	0	0	0	0.0	1	1	0	1	1	0	0	35	5	1	2	8.2	.976	1B-5
1916		5	.235	.412	17	4	1	1	0	0.0	3	2	6	0	0	0	0	69	4	0	4	14.6	1.000	1B-5
2 yrs.		10	.273	.364	33	9	1	1	0	0.0	4	3	6	1	1	0	0	104	9	1	6	11.4	.991	1B-10

Butch Hobson

HOBSON, CLELL LAVERN, JR. BR TR 6′ 1″ 193 lbs.
B. Aug. 17, 1951, Tuscaloosa, Ala.
Manager 1992–94.

Year	Team	Games	BA	SA	AB	H	2B	3B	HR	HR%	R	RBI	BB	SO	SB	Pinch Hit AB	Pinch Hit H	PO	A	E	DP	TC/G	FA	G by Pos
1975	BOS A	2	.250	.250	4	1	0	0	0	0.0	0	0	0	2	0	0	0	1	3	0	0	4.0	1.000	3B-1
1976		76	.234	.387	269	63	7	5	8	3.0	34	34	15	62	0	0	0	60	146	14	11	2.9	.936	3B-76
1977		159	.265	.489	593	157	33	5	30	5.1	77	112	27	**162**	5	0	0	128	272	23	27	2.7	.946	3B-159
1978		147	.250	.408	512	128	26	2	17	3.3	65	80	50	122	1	0	0	122	261	43	25	2.9	.899	3B-133, DH-14
1979		146	.261	.496	528	138	26	7	28	5.3	74	93	30	78	3	4	0	110	251	25	17	2.7	.935	3B-142, 2B-1
1980		93	.228	.349	324	74	6	0	11	3.4	35	39	25	69	1	1	1	52	109	16	5	1.9	.910	3B-57, DH-36
1981	CAL A	85	.235	.336	268	63	7	4	4	1.5	27	36	35	60	1	0	0	85	139	17	13	2.8	.929	3B-83, DH-2
1982	NY A	30	.172	.207	58	10	2	0	0	0.0	2	3	1	14	0	12	3	37	2	2	3	1.6	.951	DH-15, 1B-11
8 yrs.		738	.248	.423	2556	634	107	23	98	3.8	314	397	183	569	11	17	4	595	1183	140	101	2.6	.927	3B-651, DH-67, 1B-11, 2B-1

Ed Hock

HOCK, EDWARD FRANCIS BL TR 5′10½″ 165 lbs.
B. Mar. 27, 1899, Franklin Furnace, Ohio D. Nov. 21, 1963, Portsmouth, Ohio.

Year	Team	Games	BA	SA	AB	H	2B	3B	HR	HR%	R	RBI	BB	SO	SB	Pinch Hit AB	Pinch Hit H	PO	A	E	DP	TC/G	FA	G by Pos
1920	STL N	1	—	—	0	0	0	0	0	—	0	0	0	0	0	0	0	0	0	0	0	0.0	.000	OF-1
1923	CIN N	2	—	—	0	0	0	0	0	—	0	0	0	0	0	0	0	0	0	0	0	0.0	—	
1924		16	.100	.100	10	1	0	0	0	0.0	7	0	0	2	0	4	1	6	0	0	0	3.0	1.000	OF-2
3 yrs.		19	.100	.100	10	1	0	0	0	0.0	7	0	0	2	0	4	1	6	0	0	0	2.0	1.000	OF-3

Oris Hockett

HOCKETT, ORIS LEON BL TR 5′ 9″ 182 lbs.
B. Sept. 29, 1909, Amboy, Ind. D. Mar. 23, 1969, Torrance, Calif.

Year	Team	Games	BA	SA	AB	H	2B	3B	HR	HR%	R	RBI	BB	SO	SB	Pinch Hit AB	Pinch Hit H	PO	A	E	DP	TC/G	FA	G by Pos
1938	BKN N	21	.329	.471	70	23	5	1	1	1.4	8	8	4	9	0	4	2	24	1	3	0	1.6	.893	OF-17
1939		9	.231	.231	13	3	0	0	0	0.0	3	1	1	1	0	7	2	1	1	0	0	2.0	1.000	OF-1
1941	CLE A	2	.333	.333	6	2	0	0	0	0.0	0	1	2	0	0	0	0	2	0	0	0	1.0	1.000	OF-2
1942		148	.250	.344	601	150	22	7	7	1.2	85	48	45	45	12	1	0	284	12	6	3	2.1	.980	OF-145
1943		141	.276	.354	601	166	33	4	2	0.3	70	51	45	45	13	2	0	347	13	15	3	2.7	.960	OF-139
1944		124	.289	.381	457	132	29	5	1	0.2	47	50	35	27	8	14	2	275	6	5	1	2.6	.983	OF-110
1945	CHI A	106	.293	.381	417	122	23	4	2	0.5	46	55	27	30	10	0	0	273	7	5	3	2.7	.982	OF-106
7 yrs.		551	.276	.365	2165	598	112	21	13	0.6	259	214	159	157	43	28	6	1206	40	34	10	2.5	.973	OF-520

Denny Hocking

HOCKING, DENNIS LEE BB TR 5′10″ 180 lbs.
B. Apr. 2, 1970, Torrance, Calif.

Year	Team	Games	BA	SA	AB	H	2B	3B	HR	HR%	R	RBI	BB	SO	SB	Pinch Hit AB	Pinch Hit H	PO	A	E	DP	TC/G	FA	G by Pos
1993	MIN A	15	.139	.167	36	5	1	0	0	0.0	7	0	6	8	1	5	0	19	23	1	11	3.3	.977	SS-12, 2B-1
1994		11	.323	.419	31	10	3	0	0	0.0	3	2	0	4	2	1	1	11	27	0	5	3.8	1.000	SS-10
1995		9	.200	.360	25	5	0	2	0	0.0	4	3	2	2	1	1	0	13	20	1	4	5.7	.971	SS-6
3 yrs.		35	.217	.304	92	20	4	2	0	0.0	14	5	8	14	4	7	1	43	70	2	20	4.0	.983	SS-28, 2B-1

Johnny Hodapp

HODAPP, URBAN JOHN BR TR 6′ 185 lbs.
B. Sept. 26, 1905, Cincinnati, Ohio D. June 14, 1980, Cincinnati, Ohio.

Year	Team	Games	BA	SA	AB	H	2B	3B	HR	HR%	R	RBI	BB	SO	SB	Pinch Hit AB	Pinch Hit H	PO	A	E	DP	TC/G	FA	G by Pos
1925	CLE A	37	.238	.292	130	31	5	1	0	0.0	12	14	11	7	2	0	0	42	79	5	7	3.4	.960	3B-37
1926		3	.200	.200	5	1	0	0	0	0.0	0	0	0	1	0	0	0	1	2	1	0	1.3	.750	3B-3
1927		75	.304	.454	240	73	15	3	5	2.1	25	40	14	23	2	7	3	111	133	16	19	3.7	.938	3B-67, 1B-4
1928		116	.323	.432	449	145	31	6	2	0.4	51	73	20	20	2	3	2	233	224	20	34	4.2	.958	3B-101, 1B-13
1929		90	.327	.456	294	96	12	7	4	1.4	30	51	15	14	3	16	4	162	271	10	32	6.2	.977	2B-72
1930		154	.354	.502	635	**225**	**51**	8	9	1.4	111	121	32	29	6	0	0	403	557	30	103	6.4	.970	2B-154
1931		122	.295	.365	468	138	19	4	2	0.4	71	56	27	23	1	1	0	274	413	22	73	5.9	.969	2B-121
1932	2 teams	CLE A (7G –.125) CHI A (68G –.227)																						
″	total	75	.219	.313	192	42	9	0	3	1.6	23	20	11	5	1	23	2	82	31	8	5	2.6	.934	OF-31, 2B-12, 3B-4
1933	BOS A	115	.312	.424	413	129	27	5	3	0.7	55	54	33	14	1	6	3	344	335	26	68	6.4	.963	2B-101, 1B-10
9 yrs.		787	.311	.425	2826	880	169	34	28	1.0	378	429	163	136	18	56	14	1652	2045	138	341	5.3	.964	2B-460, 3B-212, OF-31, 1B-27

Mel Hoderlein

HODERLEIN, MELVIN ANTHONY BB TR 5′10″ 185 lbs.
B. June 24, 1923, Mt. Carmel, Ohio.

Year	Team	Games	BA	SA	AB	H	2B	3B	HR	HR%	R	RBI	BB	SO	SB	Pinch Hit AB	Pinch Hit H	PO	A	E	DP	TC/G	FA	G by Pos
1951	BOS A	9	.357	.571	14	5	1	1	0	0.0	1	1	6	2	0	1	0	12	10	2	4	4.0	.917	3B-3, 2B-3
1952	WAS A	72	.269	.327	208	56	8	2	0	0.0	16	17	18	22	2	13	2	138	168	7	43	5.4	.978	2B-58
1953		23	.191	.191	47	9	0	0	0	0.0	5	5	6	9	0	10	2	18	28	2	6	3.7	.958	2B-11, SS-2
1954		14	.160	.200	25	4	1	0	0	0.0	0	1	1	4	0	3	0	13	22	3	5	3.5	.921	SS-6, 2B-5
4 yrs.		118	.252	.306	294	74	10	3	0	0.0	22	24	31	37	2	27	4	181	228	14	58	4.8	.967	2B-77, SS-8, 3B-3

Bert Hodge

HODGE, EDWARD BURTON BL TR 5′11″ 170 lbs.
B. May 25, 1917, Knoxville, Tenn.

Year	Team	Games	BA	SA	AB	H	2B	3B	HR	HR%	R	RBI	BB	SO	SB	Pinch Hit AB	Pinch Hit H	PO	A	E	DP	TC/G	FA	G by Pos
1942	PHI N	8	.182	.182	11	2	0	0	0	0.0	0	0	1	0	0	6	2	1	2	0	0	1.5	1.000	3B-2

Gomer Hodge

HODGE, HAROLD MORRIS BB TR 6′ 2″ 185 lbs.
B. Apr. 3, 1944, Rutherfordton, N. C.

Year	Team	Games	BA	SA	AB	H	2B	3B	HR	HR%	R	RBI	BB	SO	SB	Pinch Hit AB	Pinch Hit H	PO	A	E	DP	TC/G	FA	G by Pos
1971	CLE A	80	.205	.277	83	17	3	0	1	1.2	3	9	4	19	0	**68**	**16**	20	3	0	4	2.9	1.000	1B-3, 3B-3, 2B-2

Gil Hodges

HODGES, GILBERT RAYMOND BR TR 6′ 1½″ 200 lbs.
Born Gilbert Ray Hodge.
B. Apr. 4, 1924, Princeton, Ind. D. Apr. 2, 1972, West Palm Beach, Fla.
Manager 1963–71.

Year	Team	Games	BA	SA	AB	H	2B	3B	HR	HR%	R	RBI	BB	SO	SB	Pinch Hit AB	Pinch Hit H	PO	A	E	DP	TC/G	FA	G by Pos
1943	BKN N	1	.000	.000	2	0	0	0	0	0.0	0	0	1	2	1	0	0	1	2	2	1	5.0	.600	3B-1
1947		28	.156	.260	77	12	3	1	1	1.3	9	7	14	19	0	4	1	79	12	4	2	4.0	.958	C-24
1948		134	.249	.376	481	120	18	5	11	2.3	48	70	43	61	7	2	0	990	72	17	90	8.1	.984	1B-96, C-38
1949		156	.285	.453	596	170	23	4	23	3.9	94	115	66	64	10	0	0	1336	80	7	142	9.1	.995	1B-156
1950		153	.283	.508	561	159	26	2	32	5.7	98	113	73	73	6	0	0	1273	100	8	159	9.0	.994	1B-153
1951		158	.268	.527	582	156	25	3	40	6.9	118	103	93	**99**	9	0	0	1365	126	12	171	9.5	.992	1B-158
1952		153	.254	.500	508	129	27	1	32	6.3	87	102	107	90	2	0	0	1322	116	11	152	9.5	.992	1B-153
1953		141	.302	.550	520	157	22	7	31	6.0	101	122	75	84	1	1	1	1062	101	9	106	7.8	.992	1B-127, OF-24
1954		154	.304	.579	579	176	23	5	42	7.3	106	130	74	84	3	0	0	1381	132	7	129	9.9	.995	1B-154
1955		150	.289	.500	546	158	24	5	27	4.9	75	102	80	91	2	0	0	1291	106	14	126	9.1	.990	1B-139, OF-16
1956		153	.265	.507	550	146	29	4	32	5.8	86	87	76	91	3	1	0	1234	103	12	105	8.0	.991	1B-138, OF-30, C-1
1957		150	.299	.511	579	173	28	7	27	4.7	94	98	63	91	5	0	0	1319	117	14	116	9.5	.990	1B-150, 3B-2, 2B-1
1958	LA N	141	.259	.434	475	123	15	1	22	4.6	68	64	52	87	8	9	1	932	103	9	137	7.1	.991	1B-122, 3B-15, OF-9, C-1
1959		124	.276	.513	413	114	19	2	25	6.1	57	80	58	92	3	7	1	896	74	8	80	8.4	.992	1B-113, 3B-4
1960		101	.198	.371	197	39	8	1	8	4.1	22	30	26	37	0	15	0	411	44	5	42	4.5	.989	1B-92, 3B-10
1961		109	.242	.372	215	52	4	0	8	3.7	25	31	24	43	3	28	7	454	37	1	44	4.9	.998	1B-100
1962	NY N	54	.252	.472	127	32	1	0	9	7.1	15	17	15	27	0	9	2	315	32	5	23	7.5	.986	1B-47
1963		11	.227	.227	22	5	0	0	0	0.0	2	3	3	2	0	1	0	61	8	0	7	6.9	1.000	1B-10
18 yrs.		2071	.273	.487	7030	1921	295	48	370	5.3	1105	1274	943	1137	63	77	13	15722	1365	145	1632	8.3	.992	1B-1908, OF-79, C-64, 3B-32, 2B-1
WORLD SERIES																								
1947	BKN N	1	.000	.000	1	0	0	0	0	0.0	0	0	0	1	0	1	0	0	0	0	0	0.0	—	
1949		5	.235	.412	17	4	0	0	1	5.9	2	4	1	4	0	0	0	38	3	0	0	8.2	1.000	1B-5
1952		7	.000	.000	21	0	0	0	0	0.0	1	1	5	6	0	0	0	60	5	1	4	9.4	.985	1B-7
1953		6	.364	.500	22	8	0	0	1	4.5	3	1	3	3	1	0	0	47	4	1	2	8.7	.981	1B-6
1955		7	.292	.417	24	7	0	0	1	4.2	2	5	3	2	0	0	0	74	4	0	11	11.1	1.000	1B-7
1956		7	.304	.522	23	7	2	0	1	4.3	5	8	4	4	0	0	0	54	5	0	8	8.4	1.000	1B-7
1959	LA N	6	.391	.609	23	9	0	1	1	4.3	2	2	1	2	0	0	0	53	3	0	6	9.3	1.000	1B-6
7 yrs.		39	.267	.412	131	35	2	1	5	3.8	15	21	17	22	1	1	0	326	24	2	31	9.3	.994	1B-38

Ron Hodges

HODGES, RONALD WRAY BL TR 6′ 1″ 185 lbs.
B. June 22, 1949, Rocky Mount, Va.

Year	Team	Games	BA	SA	AB	H	2B	3B	HR	HR%	R	RBI	BB	SO	SB	Pinch Hit AB	Pinch Hit H	PO	A	E	DP	TC/G	FA	G by Pos
1973	NY N	45	.260	.299	127	33	2	0	1	0.8	5	18	11	19	0	5	2	241	13	2	0	6.4	.992	C-40
1974		59	.221	.338	136	30	4	0	4	2.9	16	14	19	11	0	13	2	227	14	12	1	5.8	.953	C-44
1975		9	.206	.412	34	7	1	0	2	5.9	3	4	1	6	0	0	0	69	1	0	0	7.8	1.000	C-9
1976		56	.226	.342	155	35	6	0	4	2.6	21	24	27	16	2	7	2	262	18	7	0	5.5	.976	C-52
1977		66	.265	.325	117	31	4	0	1	0.9	6	5	9	17	0	39	9	112	19	1	3	4.9	.992	C-27
1978		47	.255	.314	102	26	4	1	0	0.0	4	7	10	11	1	16	4	145	20	3	5	5.6	.982	C-30
1979		59	.163	.209	86	14	4	0	0	0.0	4	5	19	16	0	29	3	82	16	2	1	4.5	.980	C-22
1980		36	.238	.286	42	10	2	0	0	0.0	4	5	10	13	1	22	4	47	9	1	0	6.3	.982	C-9
1981		35	.302	.419	43	13	2	0	1	2.3	5	6	5	8	1	25	6	23	1	0	0	3.4	1.000	C-7
1982		80	.246	.373	228	56	12	1	5	2.2	26	27	41	40	4	12	4	362	35	8	4	5.5	.980	C-74
1983		110	.260	.308	250	65	12	0	0	0.0	20	21	49	42	0	14	6	360	45	12	4	4.3	.971	C-96
1984		64	.208	.264	106	22	3	0	1	0.9	5	11	23	18	1	24	6	165	20	4	2	5.4	.979	C-35
12 yrs.		666	.240	.322	1426	342	56	2	19	1.3	119	147	224	217	10	206	48	2095	211	52	20	5.3	.978	C-445
WORLD SERIES																								
1973	NY N	1	—	—	0	0	0	0	0	—	0	0	1	0	0	0	0	0	0	0	0	0.0	—	

Ralph Hodgin

HODGIN, ELMER RALPH BL TR 5′10″ 167 lbs.
B. Feb. 10, 1916, Greensboro, N. C.

Year	Team	Games	BA	SA	AB	H	2B	3B	HR	HR%	R	RBI	BB	SO	SB	Pinch Hit AB	Pinch Hit H	PO	A	E	DP	TC/G	FA	G by Pos
1939	BOS N	32	.208	.229	48	10	1	0	0	0.0	4	4	3	4	0	20	4	15	0	0	0	1.7	1.000	OF-9
1943	CHI A	117	.314	.415	407	128	22	8	1	0.2	52	50	20	24	3	20	8	121	122	9	7	2.6	.964	3B-56, OF-42
1944		121	.295	.385	465	137	25	7	1	0.2	56	51	21	14	3	6	2	170	216	18	22	3.5	.955	3B-82, OF-33
1946		87	.252	.298	258	65	10	1	0	0.0	32	25	19	6	0	29	9	114	3	2	0	2.1	.983	OF-57
1947		59	.294	.400	180	53	10	3	1	0.6	26	24	13	4	1	16	1	99	2	1	0	2.5	.990	OF-41
1948		114	.266	.338	331	88	11	5	1	0.3	28	34	21	11	0	33	7	184	9	6	0	2.5	.970	OF-79
6 yrs.		530	.285	.367	1689	481	79	24	4	0.2	198	188	97	63	7	124	31	703	352	36	29	2.7	.967	OF-261, 3B-138

Paul Hodgson

HODGSON, PAUL JOSEPH DENIS BR TR 6′ 2″ 190 lbs.
B. Apr. 14, 1960, Montreal, Que., Canada.

Year	Team	Games	BA	SA	AB	H	2B	3B	HR	HR%	R	RBI	BB	SO	SB	Pinch Hit AB	Pinch Hit H	PO	A	E	DP	TC/G	FA	G by Pos
1980	TOR A	20	.220	.341	41	9	0	1	1	2.4	5	5	3	12	0	0	0	19	1	0	0	1.4	1.000	OF-11, DH-3

Art Hoelskoetter

HOELSKOETTER, ARTHUR H. BR TR 6′ 2″
B. Sept. 30, 1882, St. Louis, Mo. D. Aug. 3, 1954, St. Louis, Mo.

Year	Team	Games	BA	SA	AB	H	2B	3B	HR	HR%	R	RBI	BB	SO	SB	Pinch Hit AB	Pinch Hit H	PO	A	E	DP	TC/G	FA	G by Pos
1905	STL N	24	.241	.289	83	20	2	1	0	0.0	7	5	3		1	0	0	40	46	4	4	3.8	.956	3B-20, 2B-3, P-1
1906		94	.224	.262	317	71	6	3	0	0.0	21	14	4		2	0	0	109	173	19	10	3.2	.937	3B-53, SS-16, OF-12, P-12, 2B-1
1907		119	.247	.293	396	98	6	3	2	0.5	21	28	27		5	2	0	450	267	42	40	6.3	.945	2B-73, 1B-27, OF-8, C-8, P-2, 3B-2
1908		62	.232	.290	155	36	7	1	0	0.0	10	6	6		1	16	3	187	65	16	7	6.0	.940	C-41, 3B-2, 2B-1, 1B-1
4 yrs.		299	.237	.282	951	225	21	8	2	0.2	59	53	40		9	18	3	786	551	81	61	5.0	.943	2B-78, 3B-77, C-49, 1B-28, OF-20, SS-16, P-15

John Hoey

HOEY, JOHN BERNARD BL TL 5′ 9″ 185 lbs.
B. Nov. 10, 1881, Watertown, Mass. D. Nov. 14, 1947, Waterbury, Conn.

Year	Team	Games	BA	SA	AB	H	2B	3B	HR	HR%	R	RBI	BB	SO	SB	Pinch Hit AB	Pinch Hit H	PO	A	E	DP	TC/G	FA	G by Pos
1906	BOS A	94	.244	.288	361	88	8	4	0	0.0	27	24	14		10	0	0	155	7	15	0	1.9	.915	OF-94
1907		39	.219	.260	96	21	2	1	0	0.0	7	8	1		2	18	**8**	24	0	4	0	1.3	.857	OF-21
1908		13	.163	.163	43	7	0	0	0	0.0	5	3	0		1	2	1	11	2	0	0	1.2	1.000	OF-11
3 yrs.		146	.232	.272	500	116	10	5	0	0.0	39	35	15		13	20	9	190	9	19	0	1.7	.913	OF-126

Stew Hofferth

HOFFERTH, STEWART EDWARD — BR TR 6′ 2″ 195 lbs.
B. Jan. 27, 1913, Logansport, Ind. D. Mar. 7, 1994, Kouts, Ind.

Year	Team	Games	BA	SA	AB	H	2B	3B	HR	HR%	R	RBI	BB	SO	SB	Pinch Hit AB	Pinch Hit H	PO	A	E	DP	TC/G	FA	G by Pos
1944	BOS N	66	.200	.261	180	36	8	0	1	0.6	14	26	11	5	0	16	1	158	22	3	3	3.9	.984	C-47
1945		50	.235	.300	170	40	2	0	3	1.8	13	15	14	11	1	5	1	168	31	4	7	4.5	.980	C-45
1946		20	.207	.259	58	12	1	1	0	0.0	3	10	3	6	0	5	0	66	3	0	0	4.6	1.000	C-15
3 yrs.		136	.216	.277	408	88	11	1	4	1.0	30	51	28	22	1	26	2	392	56	7	10	4.3	.985	C-107

Danny Hoffman

HOFFMAN, DANIEL JOHN — BL TL 5′ 9″ 175 lbs.
B. Mar. 12, 1880, Canton, Conn. D. Mar. 14, 1922, Manchester, Conn.

Year	Team	Games	BA	SA	AB	H	2B	3B	HR	HR%	R	RBI	BB	SO	SB	Pinch Hit AB	Pinch Hit H	PO	A	E	DP	TC/G	FA	G by Pos
1903	PHI A	74	.246	.347	248	61	5	7	2	0.8	29	22	6		7	**11**	**5**	111	4	6	0	1.9	.950	OF-62, P-1
1904		53	.299	.426	204	61	7	5	3	1.5	31	24	5		9	2	0	83	5	6	1	1.8	.936	OF-51
1905		119	.262	.335	454	119	10	10	1	0.2	64	35	33		**46**	1	0	214	12	14	4	2.0	.942	OF-119
1906	2 teams	PHI A (7G –.227) NY A (100G –.256)																						
″	total	107	.254	.319	342	87	10	6	0	0.0	38	23	30		33	2	0	188	9	12	1	2.0	.943	OF-105
1907	NY A	136	.253	.308	517	131	10	3	4	0.8	81	46	42		30	1	0	286	20	15	4	2.4	.953	OF-135
1908	STL A	99	.251	.322	363	91	9	7	1	0.3	41	25	23		17	0	0	185	19	8	8	2.1	.962	OF-99
1909		110	.269	.336	387	104	6	7	2	0.5	44	26	41		24	0	0	230	10	8	6	2.3	.968	OF-109
1910		106	.237	.292	380	90	11	5	0	0.0	20	27	34		16	0	0	202	14	9	5	2.1	.960	OF-106
1911		24	.210	.296	81	17	3	2	0	0.0	11	7	12		3	0	0	63	6	7	1	3.3	.908	OF-23
9 yrs.		828	.256	.328	2976	761	71	52	13	0.4	359	235	226		185	17	5	1562	99	85	30	2.2	.951	OF-809, P-1
WORLD SERIES																								
1905	PHI A	1	.000	.000	1	0	0	0	0	0.0	0	0	0	1	0	1	0	0	0	0	0	0.0	—	

Dutch Hoffman

HOFFMAN, CLARENCE CASPER — BR TR 6′ 175 lbs.
B. Jan. 28, 1904, Freeburg, Ill. D. Dec. 6, 1962, Belleville, Ill.

Year	Team	Games	BA	SA	AB	H	2B	3B	HR	HR%	R	RBI	BB	SO	SB	Pinch Hit AB	Pinch Hit H	PO	A	E	DP	TC/G	FA	G by Pos
1929	CHI A	103	.258	.362	337	87	16	5	3	0.9	27	37	24	28	6	19	6	237	4	4	2	2.8	.984	OF-89

Glenn Hoffman

HOFFMAN, GLENN EDWARD — BR TR 6′ 1″ 175 lbs.
Brother of Trevor Hoffman.
B. July 7, 1958, Orange, Calif.

Year	Team	Games	BA	SA	AB	H	2B	3B	HR	HR%	R	RBI	BB	SO	SB	Pinch Hit AB	Pinch Hit H	PO	A	E	DP	TC/G	FA	G by Pos
1980	BOS A	114	.285	.397	312	89	15	4	4	1.3	37	42	19	41	2	2	1	78	202	17	19	2.5	.943	3B-110, SS-5, 2B-2
1981		78	.231	.285	242	56	10	0	1	0.4	28	20	12	25	0	0	0	132	234	15	62	4.8	.961	SS-78, 3B-1
1982		150	.209	.311	469	98	23	2	7	1.5	53	49	30	69	0	0	0	246	439	20	93	4.7	.972	SS-150
1983		143	.260	.340	473	123	24	1	4	0.8	56	41	30	76	1	0	0	240	417	26	82	4.8	.962	SS-143
1984		64	.189	.243	74	14	4	0	0	0.0	8	4	5	10	0	3	2	43	74	5	18	2.0	.959	SS-56, 3B-4, 2B-2
1985		96	.276	.416	279	77	17	2	6	2.2	40	34	25	40	2	0	0	157	232	11	61	4.0	.973	SS-93, 3B-3, 2B-3
1986		12	.217	.304	23	5	2	0	0	0.0	1	1	2	3	0	0	0	15	11	2	3	1.6	.929	SS-11, 3B-7
1987	2 teams	BOS A (21G –.200) LA N (40G –.220)																						
″	total	61	.214	.257	187	40	8	0	0	0.0	15	16	10	32	0	2	0	85	152	7	28	4.0	.971	SS-56, 3B-3, 2B-2
1989	CAL A	48	.212	.269	104	22	3	0	1	1.0	9	3	3	13	0	1	0	45	75	3	12	2.6	.976	SS-23, 3B-18, 2B-4, 1B-1, DH-1
9 yrs.		766	.242	.331	2163	524	106	9	23	1.1	247	210	136	309	5	8	3	1041	1836	106	378	3.8	.964	SS-615, 3B-146, 2B-13, 1B-1, DH-1

Hickey Hoffman

HOFFMAN, OTTO CHARLES
B. Oct. 27, 1856, Cleveland, Ohio D. Oct. 27, 1915, Peoria, Ill.

Year	Team	Games	BA	SA	AB	H	2B	3B	HR	HR%	R	RBI	BB	SO	SB	Pinch Hit AB	Pinch Hit H	PO	A	E	DP	TC/G	FA	G by Pos
1879	CLE N	2	.000	.000	6	0	0	0	0	0.0	0	0	0	3		0	0	9	4	2	1	5.0	.867	C-2, OF-1

Izzy Hoffman

HOFFMAN, HARRY C. — BL TL 5′ 9″ 160 lbs.
B. Jan. 5, 1875, Bridgeport, N. J. D. Nov. 13, 1942, Philadelphia, Pa.

Year	Team	Games	BA	SA	AB	H	2B	3B	HR	HR%	R	RBI	BB	SO	SB	Pinch Hit AB	Pinch Hit H	PO	A	E	DP	TC/G	FA	G by Pos
1904	WAS A	10	.100	.133	30	3	1	0	0	0.0	1	1	2		0	1	0	19	1	0	1	2.2	1.000	OF-9
1907	BOS N	19	.279	.337	86	24	3	1	0	0.0	17	3	6		2	0	0	22	4	3	1	1.5	.897	OF-19
2 yrs.		29	.233	.284	116	27	4	1	0	0.0	18	4	8		2	1	0	41	5	3	2	1.8	.939	OF-28

John Hoffman

HOFFMAN, JOHN EDWARD (Pork Chop) — BL TR 6′ 190 lbs.
B. Oct. 31, 1943, Aberdeen, S. D.

Year	Team	Games	BA	SA	AB	H	2B	3B	HR	HR%	R	RBI	BB	SO	SB	Pinch Hit AB	Pinch Hit H	PO	A	E	DP	TC/G	FA	G by Pos
1964	HOU N	6	.067	.067	15	1	0	0	0	0.0	1	0	1	7	0	1	0	18	1	0	0	3.8	1.000	C-5
1965		2	.333	.333	6	2	0	0	0	0.0	1	1	0	3	0	0	0	8	0	0	0	4.0	1.000	C-2
2 yrs.		8	.143	.143	21	3	0	0	0	0.0	2	1	1	10	0	1	0	26	1	0	0	3.9	1.000	C-7

Larry Hoffman

HOFFMAN, LAWRENCE CHARLES — BR TR
B. July 18, 1882, Chicago, Ill. D. Dec. 29, 1948, Chicago, Ill.

Year	Team	Games	BA	SA	AB	H	2B	3B	HR	HR%	R	RBI	BB	SO	SB	Pinch Hit AB	Pinch Hit H	PO	A	E	DP	TC/G	FA	G by Pos
1901	CHI N	6	.318	.364	22	7	1	0	0	0.0	2	6	0		1	0	0	6	8	3	0	2.8	.824	3B-5, 2B-1

Ray Hoffman

HOFFMAN, RAYMOND LAMONT — BL TR 6′½″ 175 lbs.
B. June 4, 1917, Detroit, Mich.

Year	Team	Games	BA	SA	AB	H	2B	3B	HR	HR%	R	RBI	BB	SO	SB	Pinch Hit AB	Pinch Hit H	PO	A	E	DP	TC/G	FA	G by Pos
1942	WAS A	7	.053	.053	19	1	0	0	0	0.0	2	2	1	1	0	0	0	6	16	5	0	4.5	.815	3B-6

Tex Hoffman

HOFFMAN, EDWARD ADOLPH — BL TR 6′ 1″ 200 lbs.
B. Nov. 30, 1893, San Antonio, Tex. D. May 19, 1947, New Orleans, La.

Year	Team	Games	BA	SA	AB	H	2B	3B	HR	HR%	R	RBI	BB	SO	SB	Pinch Hit AB	Pinch Hit H	PO	A	E	DP	TC/G	FA	G by Pos
1915	CLE A	9	.154	.154	13	2	0	0	0	0.0	1	2	1	5	0	5	1	1	2	1	0	1.3	.750	3B-3

Jesse Hoffmeister

HOFFMEISTER, JESSE H. — TR
B. Toledo, Ohio Deceased.

Year	Team	Games	BA	SA	AB	H	2B	3B	HR	HR%	R	RBI	BB	SO	SB	Pinch Hit AB	Pinch Hit H	PO	A	E	DP	TC/G	FA	G by Pos
1897	PIT N	48	.309	.484	188	58	6	9	3	1.6	33	36	8		6	0	0	48	70	31	7	3.1	.792	3B-48

Bobby Hofman

HOFMAN, ROBERT GEORGE — BR TR 5′10″ 160 lbs.
B. Oct. 5, 1925, St. Louis, Mo. D. Apr. 5, 1994, Chesterfield, Mo.

Year	Team	Games	BA	SA	AB	H	2B	3B	HR	HR%	R	RBI	BB	SO	SB	Pinch Hit AB	Pinch Hit H	PO	A	E	DP	TC/G	FA	G by Pos
1949	NY N	19	.208	.208	48	10	0	0	0	0.0	4	3	5	6	0	2	0	23	39	4	8	4.1	.939	2B-16
1952		32	.286	.476	63	18	2	2	2	3.2	11	4	8	10	0	7	1	41	46	5	9	3.8	.946	2B-21, 3B-2, 1B-1
1953		74	.266	.544	169	45	7	2	12	7.1	21	34	12	23	1	34	13	55	83	7	18	3.6	.952	3B-23, 2B-17
1954		71	.224	.456	125	28	5	0	8	6.4	12	30	17	15	0	36	10	192	32	4	25	5.8	.982	1B-21, 2B-10, 3B-8
1955		96	.266	.464	207	55	7	2	10	4.8	32	28	22	31	0	40	9	259	59	1	30	4.8	.997	1B-24, 2B-19, C-19, 3B-5
1956		47	.179	.196	56	10	1	0	0	0.0	1	2	6	8	0	26	5	44	12	2	1	3.1	.966	3B-7, C-7, 1B-3, 2B-2
1957		2	.000	.000	2	0	0	0	0	0.0	0	0	0	1	0	2	0	0	0	0	0	0.0	—	
7 yrs.		341	.248	.442	670	166	22	6	32	4.8	81	101	70	94	1	147	38	614	271	23	91	4.4	.975	2B-85, 1B-49, 3B-45, C-26

Solly Hofman

HOFMAN, ARTHUR FREDERICK (Circus Solly) BR TR 6′ 160 lbs.
B. Oct. 29, 1882, St. Louis, Mo. D. Mar. 10, 1956, St. Louis, Mo.

Year	Team	Games	BA	SA	AB	H	2B	3B	HR	HR%	R	RBI	BB	SO	SB	Pinch Hit AB	Pinch Hit H	PO	A	E	DP	TC/G	FA	G by Pos
1903	PIT N	3	.000	.000	2	0	0	0	0	0.0	1	0	0		0	1	0	0	0	0	0	0.0	.000	OF-2
1904	CHI N	7	.269	.385	26	7	0	0	1	3.8	7	4	1		2	0	0	8	4	1	1	1.9	.923	OF-6, SS-1
1905		86	.237	.324	287	68	14	4	1	0.3	43	38	20		15	1	1	248	212	23	18	5.8	.952	2B-59, SS-9, 1B-9, OF-3, 3B-3
1906		64	.256	.328	195	50	2	3	2	1.0	30	20	20		13	3	0	253	52	7	18	5.1	.978	OF-23, 1B-21, SS-9, 2B-4, 3B-4
1907		134	.268	.311	470	126	11	3	1	0.2	67	36	41		29	0	0	433	144	31	36	4.5	.949	OF-68, SS-42, 1B-18, 3B-4, 2B-3
1908		120	.243	.319	411	100	15	5	2	0.5	55	42	33		15	4	2	532	97	23	16	5.5	.965	OF-50, 1B-37, 2B-22, 3B-9
1909		153	.285	.351	527	150	21	4	2	0.4	60	58	53		20	0	0	347	16	13	5	2.5	.965	OF-153
1910		136	.325	.461	477	155	24	16	3	0.6	83	86	65	34	29	0	0	461	28	12	14	3.7	.976	OF-110, 1B-24, 3B-1
1911		143	.252	.305	512	129	17	2	2	0.4	66	70	66	40	30	0	0	583	28	14	22	4.4	.978	OF-107, 1B-36
1912	2 teams	CHI N (36G –.272) PIT N (17G –.283)																						
″	total	53	.275	.371	178	49	15	1	0	0.0	35	20	27	19	5	2	0	183	12	3	11	3.9	.985	OF-42, 1B-9
1913	PIT N	28	.229	.337	83	19	5	2	0	0.0	11	7	8	6	3	4	1	50	3	2	1	2.3	.964	OF-24
1914	BKN F	147	.287	.412	515	148	25	12	5	1.0	65	83	54		34	0	0	443	312	32	54	5.2	.959	2B-108, 1B-22, OF-21, SS-1
1915	BUF F	109	.234	.298	346	81	10	6	0	0.0	29	27	30		12	13	5	231	29	8	7	2.7	.970	OF-82, 1B-11, 3B-4, 2B-2, SS-1
1916	2 teams	NY A (6G –.296) CHI N (5G –.313)																						
″	total	11	.302	.465	43	13	3	2	0	0.0	2	4	3	3	1	1	0	24	3	0	0	2.7	1.000	OF-10
14 yrs.		1194	.269	.352	4072	1095	162	60	19	0.5	554	495	421	102	208	29	9	3796	940	169	203	4.2	.966	OF-701, 2B-198, 1B-187, SS-63, 3B-25
WORLD SERIES																								
1906	CHI N	6	.304	.348	23	7	1	0	0	0.0	3	2	3	4	1	0	0	10	1	0	0	1.8	1.000	OF-6
1908		5	.316	.421	19	6	0	1	0	0.0	2	4	1	4	2	1	0	10	1	0	1	2.2	1.000	OF-5
1910		5	.267	.267	15	4	0	0	0	0.0	2	2	4	3	0	0	0	7	0	1	0	1.6	.875	OF-5
3 yrs.		16	.298	.351	57	17	1	1	0	0.0	7	8	8	11	3	1	0	27	2	1	1	1.9	.967	OF-16

Fred Hofmann

HOFMANN, FRED (Bootnose) BR TR 5′11½″ 175 lbs.
B. June 10, 1894, St. Louis, Mo. D. Nov. 19, 1964, St. Helena, Calif.

Year	Team	Games	BA	SA	AB	H	2B	3B	HR	HR%	R	RBI	BB	SO	SB	Pinch Hit AB	Pinch Hit H	PO	A	E	DP	TC/G	FA	G by Pos
1919	NY A	1	.000	.000	1	0	0	0	0	0.0	0	0	0	0	0	0	0	1	1	0	0	2.0	1.000	C-1
1920		15	.292	.292	24	7	0	0	0	0.0	3	1	1	2	0	1	0	17	2	2	0	1.5	.905	C-14
1921		23	.177	.274	62	11	1	1	1	1.6	7	5	5	13	0	3	1	76	11	4	1	4.8	.956	C-18, 1B-1
1922		37	.297	.484	91	27	5	3	2	2.2	13	10	9	12	0	6	0	91	11	4	0	3.7	.962	C-29
1923		72	.290	.403	238	69	10	4	3	1.3	24	26	18	27	2	2	2	292	34	7	7	4.8	.979	C-70
1924		62	.175	.241	166	29	6	1	1	0.6	17	11	12	15	2	6	1	179	45	2	2	4.2	.991	C-54
1925		3	.000	.000	2	0	0	0	0	0.0	0	0	0	0	0	2	0	0	1	0	0	1.0	1.000	C-1
1927	BOS A	87	.272	.369	217	59	19	1	0	0.0	20	24	21	26	2	5	1	241	59	18	4	3.9	.943	C-81
1928		78	.226	.276	199	45	8	1	0	0.0	14	16	11	25	0	7	0	223	44	5	7	3.8	.982	C-71
9 yrs.		378	.247	.339	1000	247	49	11	7	0.7	98	93	77	120	6	32	5	1120	208	42	21	4.0	.969	C-339, 1B-1
WORLD SERIES																								
1923	NY A	2	.000	.000	1	0	0	0	0	0.0	0	0	1	0	0	1	0	0	0	0	0	0.0	—	

Eddie Hogan

HOGAN, ROBERT EDWARD BR 5′ 7″ 153 lbs.
B. Apr. 1860, St. Louis, Mo. Deceased.

Year	Team	Games	BA	SA	AB	H	2B	3B	HR	HR%	R	RBI	BB	SO	SB	Pinch Hit AB	Pinch Hit H	PO	A	E	DP	TC/G	FA	G by Pos
1882	STL AA	1	.333	.333	3	1	0	0	0	0.0	1		0			0	0	0	1	2	0	3.0	.333	P-1
1884	MIL U	11	.081	.108	37	3	1	0	0	0.0	6		7			0	0	16	9	6	1	2.8	.806	OF-11
1887	NY AA	32	.200	.267	120	24	6	1	0	0.0	22		30		12	0	0	40	13	20	1	2.1	.726	OF-29, SS-4, 3B-1
1888	CLE AA	78	.227	.331	269	61	16	6	0	0.0	60	24	50		30	0	0	104	8	13	1	1.6	.896	OF-78
4 yrs.		122	.207	.294	429	89	23	7	0	0.0	89	24	87		42	0	0	160	31	41	3	1.9	.823	OF-118, SS-4, 3B-1, P-1

Happy Hogan

HOGAN, WILLIAM HENRY BR TR 5′10″ 175 lbs.
Brother of George Hogan.
B. Sept. 14, 1884, North San Juan, Calif. D. Sept. 28, 1974, San Jose, Calif.

Year	Team	Games	BA	SA	AB	H	2B	3B	HR	HR%	R	RBI	BB	SO	SB	Pinch Hit AB	Pinch Hit H	PO	A	E	DP	TC/G	FA	G by Pos
1911	2 teams	PHI A (7G –.105) STL A (123G –.260)																						
″	total	130	.253	.340	462	117	18	8	2	0.4	54	64	43		18	1	0	315	30	25	6	2.9	.932	OF-123, 1B-5
1912	STL A	107	.214	.261	360	77	10	2	1	0.3	32	36	34		17	8	1	229	14	7	6	2.5	.972	OF-99
2 yrs.		237	.236	.305	822	194	28	10	3	0.4	86	100	77		35	9	1	544	44	32	12	2.7	.948	OF-222, 1B-5

Harry Hogan

HOGAN, HARRY S.
B. Nov. 1, 1875, Syracuse, N. Y. D. Jan. 24, 1934, Syracuse, N. Y.

Year	Team	Games	BA	SA	AB	H	2B	3B	HR	HR%	R	RBI	BB	SO	SB	Pinch Hit AB	Pinch Hit H	PO	A	E	DP	TC/G	FA	G by Pos
1901	CLE A	1	.000	.000	4	0	0	0	0	0.0	0	0	0		0	0	0	0	0	0	0	0.0	.000	OF-1

Ken Hogan

HOGAN, KENNETH TIMOTHY BL TR 5′ 9″ 145 lbs.
B. Oct. 9, 1902, Cleveland, Ohio D. Jan. 2, 1980, Cleveland, Ohio.

Year	Team	Games	BA	SA	AB	H	2B	3B	HR	HR%	R	RBI	BB	SO	SB	Pinch Hit AB	Pinch Hit H	PO	A	E	DP	TC/G	FA	G by Pos
1921	CIN N	1	.000	.000	2	0	0	0	0	0.0	0	0	0	1	0	0	0	0	0	0	0	0.0	.000	OF-1
1923	CLE A	1	—	—	0	0	0	0	0	—	0	0	0	0	0	0	0	0	0	0	0	0.0	—	
1924		2	.000	.000	1	0	0	0	0	0.0	0	0	0	0	0	1	0	0	0	0	0	0.0	—	
3 yrs.		4	.000	.000	3	0	0	0	0	0.0	0	0	0	1	0	1	0	0	0	0	0	0.0		OF-1

Marty Hogan

HOGAN, MARTIN F. BR 5′ 8″ 145 lbs.
B. Oct. 25, 1871, Wensbury, England D. Aug. 16, 1923, Youngstown, Ohio.

Year	Team	Games	BA	SA	AB	H	2B	3B	HR	HR%	R	RBI	BB	SO	SB	Pinch Hit AB	Pinch Hit H	PO	A	E	DP	TC/G	FA	G by Pos
1894	2 teams	CIN N (6G –.130) STL N (29G –.280)																						
″	total	35	.252	.341	123	31	3	4	0	0.0	15	16	4	17	9	0	0	52	6	8	5	1.9	.879	OF-35
1895	STL N	5	.167	.222	18	3	1	0	0	0.0	2	2	3	0	2	0	0	13	2	3	0	3.6	.833	OF-5
2 yrs.		40	.241	.326	141	34	4	4	0	0.0	17	18	7	17	11	0	0	65	8	11	5	2.1	.869	OF-40

Shanty Hogan

HOGAN, JAMES FRANCIS BR TR 6′ 1″ 240 lbs.
B. Mar. 21, 1906, Somerville, Mass. D. Apr. 7, 1967, Boston, Mass.

Year	Team	Games	BA	SA	AB	H	2B	3B	HR	HR%	R	RBI	BB	SO	SB	Pinch Hit AB	Pinch Hit H	PO	A	E	DP	TC/G	FA	G by Pos
1925	BOS N	9	.286	.429	21	6	1	1	0	0.0	2	3	1	3	0	4	0	8	0	0	0	1.6	1.000	OF-5
1926		4	.286	.500	14	4	1	1	0	0.0	1	5	0	0	0	0	0	18	5	4	0	6.8	.852	C-4
1927		71	.288	.410	229	66	17	1	3	1.3	24	32	9	23	2	9	1	215	54	4	3	4.5	.985	C-61
1928	NY N	131	.333	.477	411	137	25	2	10	2.4	48	71	42	25	0	6	1	389	57	10	11	3.7	.978	C-124
1929		102	.300	.388	317	95	13	0	5	1.6	19	45	25	22	1	9	2	286	47	7	5	3.7	.979	C-93
1930		122	.339	.517	389	132	26	2	13	3.3	60	75	21	24	2	24	8	386	46	8	5	4.6	.982	C-96
1931		123	.301	.439	396	119	17	1	12	3.0	42	65	29	29	1	10	0	469	54	2	10	4.6	.996	C-113

Shanty Hogan *continued*

Year	Team	Games	BA	SA	AB	H	2B	3B	HR	HR%	R	RBI	BB	SO	SB	Pinch Hit AB	Pinch Hit H	PO	A	E	DP	TC/G	FA	G by Pos
1932		140	.287	.378	502	144	18	2	8	1.6	36	77	26	22	0	4	2	522	71	10	11	4.4	.983	C-136
1933	BOS N	96	.253	.302	328	83	7	0	3	0.9	15	30	13	9	0	1	0	280	56	1	11	3.5	.997	C-95
1934		92	.262	.337	279	73	5	2	4	1.4	20	34	16	13	0	2	0	291	53	5	8	3.9	.986	C-90
1935		59	.301	.387	163	49	8	0	2	1.2	9	25	21	8	0	3	1	175	25	2	2	3.6	.990	C-56
1936	WAS A	19	.323	.431	65	21	4	0	1	1.5	8	7	11	2	0	0	0	83	8	1	5	4.8	.989	C-19
1937		21	.152	.212	66	10	4	0	0	0.0	4	5	6	8	0	0	0	76	17	2	2	4.5	.979	C-21
13 yrs.		989	.295	.406	3180	939	146	12	61	1.9	288	474	220	188	6	72	15	3198	493	56	73	4.1	.985	C-908, OF-5

Bert Hogg

HOGG, WILBERT GEORGE (Sonny) BR TR 5′11½″ 162 lbs.
B. Apr. 21, 1913, Detroit, Mich. D. Nov. 5, 1973, Detroit, Mich.

Year	Team	Games	BA	SA	AB	H	2B	3B	HR	HR%	R	RBI	BB	SO	SB	Pinch Hit AB	Pinch Hit H	PO	A	E	DP	TC/G	FA	G by Pos
1934	BKN N	2	.000	.000	1	0	0	0	0	0.0	0	0	0	0	0	0	0	0	0	0	0	0.0	.000	3B-1

George Hogriever

HOGRIEVER, GEORGE C. BR TR 5′8″ 160 lbs.
B. Mar. 17, 1869, Cincinnati, Ohio D. Jan. 26, 1961, Appleton, Wis.

Year	Team	Games	BA	SA	AB	H	2B	3B	HR	HR%	R	RBI	BB	SO	SB	Pinch Hit AB	Pinch Hit H	PO	A	E	DP	TC/G	FA	G by Pos
1895	CIN N	69	.272	.389	239	65	8	7	2	0.8	61	34	36	17	41	0	0	184	12	19	3	3.1	.912	OF-66, 2B-3
1901	MIL A	54	.235	.299	221	52	10	2	0	0.0	25	16	30		7	0	0	134	3	15	1	2.8	.901	OF-54
2 yrs.		123	.254	.346	460	117	18	9	2	0.4	86	50	66	17	48	0	0	318	15	34	4	3.0	.907	OF-120, 2B-3

Bill Hohman

HOHMAN, WILLIAM HENRY BR TR 6′ 178 lbs.
B. Nov. 27, 1903, Brooklyn, Md. D. Oct. 29, 1968, Baltimore, Md.

Year	Team	Games	BA	SA	AB	H	2B	3B	HR	HR%	R	RBI	BB	SO	SB	Pinch Hit AB	Pinch Hit H	PO	A	E	DP	TC/G	FA	G by Pos
1927	PHI N	7	.278	.278	18	5	0	0	0	0.0	1	0	2	3	0	0	0	10	1	1	0	2.0	.917	OF-6

Eddie Hohnhorst

HOHNHORST, EDWARD HICKS BL TL 6′1″ 175 lbs.
B. Jan. 31, 1885, Ky. D. Mar. 28, 1916, Covington, Ky.

Year	Team	Games	BA	SA	AB	H	2B	3B	HR	HR%	R	RBI	BB	SO	SB	Pinch Hit AB	Pinch Hit H	PO	A	E	DP	TC/G	FA	G by Pos
1910	CLE A	17	.323	.403	62	20	3	1	0	0.0	8	6	4		3	0	0	165	7	5	9	10.4	.972	1B-17
1912		14	.204	.222	54	11	1	0	0	0.0	5	2	2		5	0	0	148	8	6	9	11.6	.963	1B-14
2 yrs.		31	.267	.319	116	31	4	1	0	0.0	13	8	6		8	0	0	313	15	11	18	10.9	.968	1B-31

Chris Hoiles

HOILES, CHRISTOPHER ALLEN BR TR 6′ 195 lbs.
B. Mar. 20, 1965, Bowling Green, Ohio.

Year	Team	Games	BA	SA	AB	H	2B	3B	HR	HR%	R	RBI	BB	SO	SB	Pinch Hit AB	Pinch Hit H	PO	A	E	DP	TC/G	FA	G by Pos
1989	BAL A	6	.111	.222	9	1	1	0	0	0.0	0	1	1	3	0	2	0	11	0	0	0	1.8	1.000	C-3, DH-3
1990		23	.190	.286	63	12	3	0	1	1.6	7	6	5	12	0	3	0	62	6	0	6	3.4	1.000	C-7, DH-7, 1B-6
1991		107	.243	.384	341	83	15	0	11	3.2	36	31	29	61	0	6	1	443	44	1	6	4.7	.998	C-89, DH-13, 1B-2
1992		96	.274	.506	310	85	10	1	20	6.5	49	40	55	60	0	0	0	500	31	3	6	5.6	.994	C-95, DH-1
1993		126	.310	.585	419	130	28	0	29	6.9	80	82	69	94	1	3	0	696	64	5	11	6.1	.993	C-124, DH-2
1994		99	.247	.449	332	82	10	0	19	5.7	45	53	63	73	2	3	0	615	36	7	2	6.7	.989	C-98
1995		114	.250	.460	352	88	15	1	19	5.4	53	58	67	80	1	8	2	658	34	3	3	6.2	.996	C-107, DH-6
7 yrs.		571	.263	.473	1826	481	82	2	99	5.4	270	271	289	383	4	25	3	2985	215	19	34	5.7	.994	C-523, DH-32, 1B-8

Bill Holbert

HOLBERT, WILLIAM HENRY BR TR 197 lbs.
B. Mar. 14, 1855, Baltimore, Md. D. Mar. 20, 1935, Laurel, Md.
Manager 1879.

Year	Team	Games	BA	SA	AB	H	2B	3B	HR	HR%	R	RBI	BB	SO	SB	Pinch Hit AB	Pinch Hit H	PO	A	E	DP	TC/G	FA	G by Pos
1876	LOU N	12	.256	.256	43	11	0	0	0	0.0	3	5	0	3		0	0	62	24	16	3	8.5	.843	C-12
1878	MIL N	45	.185	.197	173	32	2	0	0	0.0	10	12	3	14		0	0	107	47	26	2	3.5	.856	OF-30, C-21
1879	2 teams	SYR N (59G –.201)	TRO N (4G –.267)																					
″	total	63	.205	.205	244	50	0	0	0	0.0	12	23	1	21		0	0	296	73	42	5	6.4	.898	C-60, OF-4
1880	TRO N	60	.189	.222	212	40	5	1	0	0.0	18	8	9	18		0	0	268	107	37	6	6.8	.910	C-58, OF-3
1881		46	.272	.289	180	49	3	0	0	0.0	16	14	3	13		0	0	206	70	26	10	6.6	.914	C-43, OF-3
1882		71	.183	.203	251	46	5	0	0	0.0	24	23	11	22		0	0	269	152	59	14	6.6	.877	C-58, 3B-12, OF-3
1883	NY AA	73	.237	.274	299	71	9	1	0	0.0	26		1			0	0	530	139	60	8	9.9	.918	C-68, OF-5, 2B-1
1884		65	.208	.227	255	53	5	0	0	0.0	28		7			0	0	383	147	55	7	9.0	.906	C-59, OF-5, SS-1
1885		56	.173	.188	202	35	3	0	0	0.0	13		8			0	0	256	96	44	7	6.9	.889	C-39, OF-13, 3B-5
1886		48	.205	.251	171	35	4	2	0	0.0	8		6			0	0	270	106	33	8	8.3	.919	C-45, OF-3, SS-1
1887		69	.227	.267	255	58	4	3	0	0.0	20		7		12	0	0	311	114	46	14	6.6	.902	C-60, 1B-8, SS-2, 2B-1
1888	BKN AA	15	.120	.140	50	6	1	0	0	0.0	4	1	2		0	0	0	74	26	8	2	7.2	.926	C-15
12 yrs.		623	.208	.232	2335	486	41	7	0	0.0	182	86	58	91	12	0	0	3032	1101	452	86	7.2	.901	C-538, OF-69, 3B-17, 1B-8, SS-4, 2B-2

Ray Holbert

HOLBERT, RAY ARTHUR III BR TR 6′ 170 lbs.
B. Sept. 25, 1970, Torrance, Calif.

Year	Team	Games	BA	SA	AB	H	2B	3B	HR	HR%	R	RBI	BB	SO	SB	Pinch Hit AB	Pinch Hit H	PO	A	E	DP	TC/G	FA	G by Pos
1994	SD N	5	.200	.200	5	1	0	0	0	0.0	1	0	0	4	0	4	1	0	0	0	0	0.0	.000	SS-1
1995		63	.178	.315	73	13	2	1	2	2.7	11	5	8	20	4	13	1	27	58	5	13	2.4	.944	SS-30, 2B-7, OF-1
2 yrs.		68	.179	.308	78	14	2	1	2	2.6	12	5	8	24	4	17	2	27	58	5	13	2.3	.944	SS-31, 2B-7, OF-1

Sammy Holbrook

HOLBROOK, JAMES MARBURY BR TR 5′11″ 189 lbs.
B. July 17, 1910, Meridian, Miss. D. Apr. 10, 1991, Jackson, Miss.

Year	Team	Games	BA	SA	AB	H	2B	3B	HR	HR%	R	RBI	BB	SO	SB	Pinch Hit AB	Pinch Hit H	PO	A	E	DP	TC/G	FA	G by Pos
1935	WAS A	52	.259	.348	135	35	2	2	2	1.5	20	25	30	16	0	6	1	145	12	8	0	3.5	.952	C-47

Bill Holden

HOLDEN, WILLIAM PAUL BR TR 6′ 170 lbs.
B. Sept. 7, 1889, Birmingham, Ala. D. Sept. 14, 1971, Pensacola, Fla.

Year	Team	Games	BA	SA	AB	H	2B	3B	HR	HR%	R	RBI	BB	SO	SB	Pinch Hit AB	Pinch Hit H	PO	A	E	DP	TC/G	FA	G by Pos
1913	NY A	18	.302	.396	53	16	3	1	0	0.0	6	8	8	5	0	2	1	37	5	1	0	2.7	.977	OF-16
1914	2 teams	NY A (50G –.182)	CIN N (11G –.214)																					
″	total	61	.187	.223	193	36	3	2	0	0.0	14	13	19	31	2	5	0	110	4	2	0	2.1	.983	OF-55
2 yrs.		79	.211	.260	246	52	6	3	0	0.0	20	21	27	36	2	7	1	147	9	3	0	2.2	.981	OF-71

Joe Holden

HOLDEN, JOSEPH FRANCIS (Socks) BL TR 5′8″ 175 lbs.
B. June 4, 1913, St. Clair, Pa.

Year	Team	Games	BA	SA	AB	H	2B	3B	HR	HR%	R	RBI	BB	SO	SB	Pinch Hit AB	Pinch Hit H	PO	A	E	DP	TC/G	FA	G by Pos
1934	PHI N	10	.071	.071	14	1	0	0	0	0.0	1	0	0	2	0	4	0	15	4	0	0	3.2	1.000	C-6
1935		6	.111	.111	9	1	0	0	0	0.0	0	0	0	3	1	2	0	6	0	0	0	1.5	1.000	C-4
1936		1	.000	.000	1	0	0	0	0	0.0	0	0	0	0	0	1	0	0	0	0	0	0.0	—	
3 yrs.		17	.083	.083	24	2	0	0	0	0.0	1	0	0	5	1	7	0	21	4	0	0	2.5	1.000	C-10

Jim Holdsworth

HOLDSWORTH, JAMES (Long Jim) BR TR
B. July 14, 1850, New York, N. Y. D. Mar. 22, 1918, New York, N. Y.

Year	Team		Games	BA	SA	AB	H	2B	3B	HR	HR%	R	RBI	BB	SO	SB	Pinch Hit AB	Pinch Hit H	PO	A	E	DP	TC/G	FA	G by Pos
1876	**NY**	**N**	52	.266	.295	241	64	3	2	0	0.0	23	19	1	2		0	0	119	14	15	2	2.8	.899	OF-49, 2B-3
1877	**HAR**	**N**	55	.254	.288	260	66	5	2	0	0.0	26	20	2	8		0	0	79	11	18	1	2.0	.833	OF-55
1882	**TRO**	**N**	1	.000	.000	3	0	0	0	0	0.0	0	0	0	1		0	0	1	1	0	0	2.0	1.000	OF-1
1884	**IND**	**AA**	5	.111	.111	18	2	0	0	0	0.0	1		2			0	0	12	1	1	1	2.8	.929	OF-5
4 yrs.			113	.253	.284	522	132	8	4	0	0.0	50	39	5	11		0	0	211	27	34	4	2.4	.875	OF-110, 2B-3

Walter Holke

HOLKE, WALTER HENRY (Union Man) BB TL 6′ 1½″ 185 lbs.
B. Dec. 25, 1892, St. Louis, Mo. D. Oct. 12, 1954, St. Louis, Mo.

Year	Team		Games	BA	SA	AB	H	2B	3B	HR	HR%	R	RBI	BB	SO	SB	Pinch Hit AB	Pinch Hit H	PO	A	E	DP	TC/G	FA	G by Pos
1914	**NY**	**N**	2	.333	.333	6	2	0	0	0	0.0	0	0	0	0	0	0	0	17	2	1	1	10.0	.950	1B-2
1916			34	.351	.423	111	39	4	2	0	0.0	16	13	6	16	10	0	0	331	13	1	15	10.1	.997	1B-34
1917			153	.277	.338	527	146	12	7	2	0.4	55	55	34	54	13	0	0	1635	70	19	104	11.3	.989	1B-153
1918			88	.252	.337	326	82	17	4	1	0.3	38	27	10	26	10	0	0	938	68	10	50	11.5	.990	1B-88
1919	**BOS**	**N**	137	.292	.342	518	151	14	6	0	0.0	48	48	21	25	19	1	0	1474	95	11	86	11.6	.993	1B-136
1920			144	.294	.377	551	162	15	11	3	0.5	53	64	28	31	4	1	1	1528	81	14	97	11.3	.991	1B-143
1921			150	.261	.337	579	151	15	10	3	0.5	60	63	17	41	8	0	0	1471	86	4	100	10.4	.997	1B-150
1922			105	.291	.334	395	115	9	4	0	0.0	35	46	14	23	6	0	0	1017	44	8	65	10.2	.993	1B-105
1923	**PHI**	**N**	147	.311	.418	562	175	31	4	7	1.2	64	70	16	37	7	1	1	1425	69	13	136	10.3	.991	1B-146, P-1
1924			148	.300	.394	563	169	23	6	6	1.1	60	64	25	33	3	0	0	1516	90	12	134	10.9	.993	1B-148
1925	**2 teams**		**PHI N** (39G –.244) **CIN N** (65G –.280)																						
″	**total**		104	.270	.355	318	86	13	4	2	0.6	35	37	20	18	1	15	4	806	47	3	76	9.7	.996	1B-88
11 yrs.			1212	.287	.363	4456	1278	153	58	24	0.5	464	487	191	304	81	18	6	12158	665	96	864	10.8	.993	1B-1193, P-1
WORLD SERIES																									
1917	**NY**	**N**	6	.286	.381	21	6	2	0	0	0.0	2	1	0	6	0	0	0	66	0	1	1	11.2	.985	1B-6

Bill Hollahan

HOLLAHAN, WILLIAM JAMES (Happy) BR TR 5′ 9″ 165 lbs.
B. Nov. 22, 1896, New York, N. Y. D. Nov. 27, 1965, New York, N. Y.

Year	Team		Games	BA	SA	AB	H	2B	3B	HR	HR%	R	RBI	BB	SO	SB	Pinch Hit AB	Pinch Hit H	PO	A	E	DP	TC/G	FA	G by Pos
1920	**WAS**	**A**	3	.250	.250	4	1	0	0	0	0.0	0	1	1	2	1	0	0	5	2	0	0	2.3	1.000	3B-3

Dutch Holland

HOLLAND, ROBERT CLYDE BR TR 6′ 1″ 190 lbs.
B. Oct. 12, 1903, Middlesex, N. C. D. June 16, 1967, Lumberton, N. C.

Year	Team		Games	BA	SA	AB	H	2B	3B	HR	HR%	R	RBI	BB	SO	SB	Pinch Hit AB	Pinch Hit H	PO	A	E	DP	TC/G	FA	G by Pos
1932	**BOS**	**N**	39	.295	.397	156	46	11	1	1	0.6	15	18	12	20	0	0	0	94	3	1	0	2.5	.990	OF-39
1933			13	.258	.355	31	8	3	0	0	0.0	3	3	3	8	1	6	1	13	0	2	0	2.1	.867	OF-7
1934	**CLE**	**A**	50	.250	.406	128	32	12	1	2	1.6	19	13	13	11	0	16	2	44	1	2	0	1.5	.957	OF-31
3 yrs.			102	.273	.397	315	86	26	2	3	1.0	37	34	28	39	1	22	3	151	4	5	0	2.1	.969	OF-77

Will Holland

HOLLAND, WILLARD A. 5′10″ 180 lbs.
B. Fort Wayne, Ind. Deceased.

Year	Team		Games	BA	SA	AB	H	2B	3B	HR	HR%	R	RBI	BB	SO	SB	Pinch Hit AB	Pinch Hit H	PO	A	E	DP	TC/G	FA	G by Pos
1889	**BAL**	**AA**	40	.189	.224	143	27	1	2	0	0.0	13	16	9	28	4	0	0	38	102	24	9	4.1	.854	SS-39, OF-1

Todd Hollandsworth

HOLLANDSWORTH, TODD MATTHEW BL TL 6′ 2″ 193 lbs.
B. Apr. 20, 1973, Dayton, Ohio.

Year	Team		Games	BA	SA	AB	H	2B	3B	HR	HR%	R	RBI	BB	SO	SB	Pinch Hit AB	Pinch Hit H	PO	A	E	DP	TC/G	FA	G by Pos
1995	**LA**	**N**	41	.233	.398	103	24	2	0	5	4.9	16	13	10	29	2	4	0	60	1	4	0	1.8	.938	OF-37
DIVISIONAL PLAYOFF SERIES																									
1995	**LA**	**N**	2	.000	.000	2	0	0	0	0	0.0	0	0	0	0	0	1	0	0	0	0	0	0.0	.000	OF-2

Gary Holle

HOLLE, GARY CHARLES BR TL 6′ 6″ 210 lbs.
B. Aug. 11, 1954, Albany, N. Y.

Year	Team		Games	BA	SA	AB	H	2B	3B	HR	HR%	R	RBI	BB	SO	SB	Pinch Hit AB	Pinch Hit H	PO	A	E	DP	TC/G	FA	G by Pos
1979	**TEX**	**A**	5	.167	.333	6	1	1	0	0	0.0	0	0	1	0	0	4	1	11	0	0	1	11.0	1.000	1B-1

Bug Holliday

HOLLIDAY, JAMES WEAR BR TR 5′11″ 151 lbs.
B. Feb. 8, 1867, St. Louis, Mo. D. Feb. 15, 1910, Cincinnati, Ohio.

Year	Team		Games	BA	SA	AB	H	2B	3B	HR	HR%	R	RBI	BB	SO	SB	Pinch Hit AB	Pinch Hit H	PO	A	E	DP	TC/G	FA	G by Pos
1889	**CIN**	**AA**	135	.321	.497	563	181	28	7	**19**	3.4	107	104	43	59	46	0	0	234	29	22	6	2.1	.923	OF-135
1890	**CIN**	**N**	131	.270	.382	518	140	18	14	4	0.8	93	75	49	36	50	0	0	253	20	15	5	2.2	.948	OF-131
1891			111	.319	.473	442	141	21	10	9	2.0	74	84	37	28	30	0	0	186	13	13	3	1.9	.939	OF-111
1892			152	.292	.449	602	176	23	16	**13**	**2.2**	114	91	57	39	43	0	0	271	21	21	6	2.0	.933	OF-152, P-1
1893			126	.310	.428	500	155	24	10	5	1.0	108	89	73	22	32	0	0	285	14	17	5	2.5	.946	OF-125, 1B-1
1894			122	.372	.523	511	190	24	7	13	2.5	119	119	40	20	29	1	0	251	22	26	5	2.5	.913	OF-119, 1B-1
1895			32	.299	.402	127	38	9	2	0	0.0	25	20	10	3	6	0	0	60	3	4	1	2.1	.940	OF-32
1896			29	.321	.369	84	27	4	0	0	0.0	17	8	9	4	1	6	3	64	6	6	2	3.3	.921	OF-16, 1B-5, P-1, SS-1
1897			61	.313	.431	195	61	9	4	2	1.0	50	20	27		6	8	3	108	22	9	2	2.7	.935	OF-42, SS-4, 1B-3, 2B-3
1898			30	.236	.274	106	25	2	1	0	0.0	21	7	14		5	1	0	61	1	2	1	2.3	.969	OF-28
10 yrs.			929	.311	.448	3648	1134	162	71	65	1.8	728	617	359	211	248	16	6	1773	151	135	36	2.3	.934	OF-891, 1B-10, SS-5, 2B-3, P-2

Dave Hollins

HOLLINS, DAVID MICHAEL BB TR 6′ 1″ 195 lbs.
B. May 25, 1966, Buffalo, N. Y.

Year	Team		Games	BA	SA	AB	H	2B	3B	HR	HR%	R	RBI	BB	SO	SB	Pinch Hit AB	Pinch Hit H	PO	A	E	DP	TC/G	FA	G by Pos
1990	**PHI**	**N**	72	.184	.316	114	21	0	0	5	4.4	14	15	10	28	0	37	8	27	37	4	0	2.2	.941	3B-30, 1B-1
1991			56	.298	.510	151	45	10	2	6	4.0	18	21	17	26	1	14	3	67	62	8	6	3.3	.942	3B-36, 1B-6
1992			156	.270	.469	586	158	28	4	27	4.6	104	93	76	110	9	0	0	120	253	18	22	2.5	.954	3B-156, 1B-1
1993			143	.273	.442	543	148	30	4	18	3.3	104	93	85	109	2	0	0	73	215	27	9	2.2	.914	3B-143
1994			44	.222	.352	162	36	7	1	4	2.5	28	26	23	32	1	0	0	38	47	11	1	2.2	.885	3B-43, OF-1
1995	**2 teams**		**PHI N** (65G –.229) **BOS A** (5G –.154)																						
″	**total**		70	.225	.394	218	49	12	2	7	3.2	48	26	57	45	1	6	1	536	30	7	53	8.7	.988	1B-61, DH-3, OF-2
6 yrs.			541	.258	.435	1774	457	87	13	67	3.8	316	274	268	350	14	57	12	861	644	75	91	3.3	.953	3B-408, 1B-69, DH-3, OF-3
LEAGUE CHAMPIONSHIP SERIES																									
1993	**PHI**	**N**	6	.200	.550	20	4	1	0	2	10.0	2	4	5	4	1	0	0	5	4	0	0	1.5	1.000	3B-6
WORLD SERIES																									
1993	**PHI**	**N**	6	.261	.304	23	6	1	0	0	0.0	5	2	6	5	0	0	0	9	9	0	0	3.0	1.000	3B-6

Stan Hollmig

HOLLMIG, STANLEY ERNEST (Hondo) BR TR 6′ 2½″ 190 lbs.
B. Jan. 2, 1926, Fredericksburg, Tex. D. Dec. 4, 1981, San Antonio, Tex.

Year	Team	Games	BA	SA	AB	H	2B	3B	HR	HR%	R	RBI	BB	SO	SB	Pinch Hit AB	Pinch Hit H	PO	A	E	DP	TC/G	FA	G by Pos
1949	PHI N	81	.255	.371	251	64	11	6	2	0.8	28	26	20	43	1	14	3	108	5	5	1	1.8	.958	OF-66
1950		11	.250	.417	12	3	2	0	0	0.0	1	1	0	3	0	8	2	3	0	0	0	1.0	1.000	OF-3
1951		2	.000	.000	2	0	0	0	0	0.0	0	0	0	0	0	2	0	0	0	0	0	0.0	—	
3 yrs.		94	.253	.370	265	67	13	6	2	0.8	29	27	20	46	1	24	5	111	5	5	1	1.8	.959	OF-69

Charlie Hollocher

HOLLOCHER, CHARLES JACOB BL TR 5′ 7½″ 158 lbs.
B. June 11, 1896, St. Louis, Mo. D. Aug. 14, 1940, Frontenac, Mo.

Year	Team	Games	BA	SA	AB	H	2B	3B	HR	HR%	R	RBI	BB	SO	SB	Pinch Hit AB	Pinch Hit H	PO	A	E	DP	TC/G	FA	G by Pos
1918	CHI N	131	.316	.397	**509**	**161**	23	6	2	0.4	72	38	47	30	26	0	0	278	418	53	39	5.7	.929	SS-131
1919		115	.270	.347	430	116	14	5	3	0.7	51	26	44	19	16	0	0	219	418	40	49	5.9	.941	SS-115
1920		80	.319	.389	301	96	17	2	0	0.0	53	22	41	15	20	0	0	196	280	23	34	6.2	.954	SS-80
1921		140	.289	.384	558	161	28	8	3	0.5	71	37	43	13	5	3	1	282	491	30	72	5.9	.963	SS-137
1922		152	.340	.444	592	201	37	8	3	0.5	90	69	58	5	19	0	0	332	502	30	89	5.7	.965	SS-152
1923		66	.342	.423	260	89	14	2	1	0.4	46	28	26	5	9	1	0	124	212	13	35	5.4	.963	SS-65
1924		76	.245	.336	286	70	12	4	2	0.7	28	21	18	7	4	5	1	156	248	13	42	5.9	.969	SS-71
7 yrs.		760	.304	.392	2936	894	145	35	14	0.5	411	241	277	94	99	9	2	1587	2569	202	360	5.8	.954	SS-751
WORLD SERIES																								
1918	CHI N	6	.190	.286	21	4	0	1	0	0.0	2	0	1	1	2	0	0	12	17	1	6	5.0	.967	SS-6

Ed Holly

HOLLY, EDWARD WILLIAM BR TR 5′10″ 165 lbs.
Born Edward William Ruthlavy.
B. July 6, 1879, Chicago, Ill. D. Nov. 27, 1973, Williamsport, Pa.

Year	Team	Games	BA	SA	AB	H	2B	3B	HR	HR%	R	RBI	BB	SO	SB	Pinch Hit AB	Pinch Hit H	PO	A	E	DP	TC/G	FA	G by Pos
1906	STL N	10	.059	.059	34	2	0	0	0	0.0	1	7	5		0	0	0	24	22	3	7	4.9	.939	SS-10
1907		149	.230	.279	544	125	18	3	1	0.2	55	40	36		16	0	0	326	480	64	45	5.8	.926	SS-147, 2B-3
1914	PIT F	100	.246	.294	350	86	9	4	0	0.0	28	26	17		14	3	2	241	267	31	31	5.6	.942	SS-94, OF-2, 2B-1
1915		16	.262	.310	42	11	2	0	0	0.0	8	5	5		3	1	1	24	26	7	4	4.1	.877	SS-11, 3B-3
4 yrs.		275	.231	.278	970	224	29	7	1	0.1	92	78	63		33	4	3	615	795	105	87	5.6	.931	SS-262, 2B-4, 3B-3, OF-2

Billy Holm

HOLM, WILLIAM FREDERICK BR TR 5′10½″ 168 lbs.
B. July 21, 1912, Chicago, Ill. D. July 27, 1977, East Chicago, Ind.

Year	Team	Games	BA	SA	AB	H	2B	3B	HR	HR%	R	RBI	BB	SO	SB	Pinch Hit AB	Pinch Hit H	PO	A	E	DP	TC/G	FA	G by Pos
1943	CHI N	7	.067	.067	15	1	0	0	0	0.0	0	0	2	4	0	0	0	21	4	0	0	3.6	1.000	C-7
1944		54	.136	.152	132	18	2	0	0	0.0	10	6	16	19	1	3	0	166	18	4	2	3.8	.979	C-50
1945	BOS A	58	.185	.215	135	25	2	1	0	0.0	12	9	23	17	1	1	0	170	30	4	3	3.6	.980	C-57
3 yrs.		119	.156	.177	282	44	4	1	0	0.0	22	15	41	40	2	4	0	357	52	8	5	3.7	.981	C-114

Wattie Holm

HOLM, ROSCOE ALBERT BR TR 5′ 9½″ 160 lbs.
B. Dec. 28, 1901, Peterson, Iowa D. May 19, 1950, Everly, Iowa.

Year	Team	Games	BA	SA	AB	H	2B	3B	HR	HR%	R	RBI	BB	SO	SB	Pinch Hit AB	Pinch Hit H	PO	A	E	DP	TC/G	FA	G by Pos
1924	STL N	81	.294	.355	293	86	10	4	0	0.0	40	23	8	16	1	5	1	178	12	4	2	2.5	.979	OF-64, C-9, 3B-4
1925		13	.207	.259	58	12	1	1	0	0.0	10	2	3	1	1	0	0	40	1	1	1	3.2	.976	OF-13
1926		55	.285	.333	144	41	5	1	0	0.0	18	21	18	14	3	15	5	75	1	3	1	2.0	.962	OF-39
1927		110	.286	.411	419	120	27	8	3	0.7	55	66	24	29	4	4	2	205	25	7	2	2.2	.970	OF-97, 3B-9
1928		102	.277	.394	386	107	24	6	3	0.8	61	47	32	17	1	9	4	118	145	22	9	3.2	.923	3B-83, OF-7
1929		64	.233	.330	176	41	5	6	0	0.0	21	14	12	8	1	17	3	116	4	7	2	2.8	.945	OF-44, 3B-1
1932		11	.176	.235	17	3	1	0	0	0.0	2	1	3	1	0	5	1	9	0	0	0	2.3	1.000	OF-4
7 yrs.		436	.275	.370	1493	410	73	26	6	0.4	207	174	100	86	11	55	16	741	188	44	17	2.6	.955	OF-268, 3B-97, C-9
WORLD SERIES																								
1926	STL N	5	.125	.125	16	2	0	0	0	0.0	1	1	1	2	0	1	0	7	0	0	0	1.8	1.000	OF-4
1928		3	.167	.167	6	1	0	0	0	0.0	0	1	0	1	0	2	0	4	0	0	0	4.0	1.000	OF-1
2 yrs.		8	.136	.136	22	3	0	0	0	0.0	1	2	1	3	0	3	0	11	0	0	0	2.2	1.000	OF-5

Gary Holman

HOLMAN, GARY RICHARD BL TL 6′ 1″ 200 lbs.
B. Jan. 25, 1944, Long Beach, Calif.

Year	Team	Games	BA	SA	AB	H	2B	3B	HR	HR%	R	RBI	BB	SO	SB	Pinch Hit AB	Pinch Hit H	PO	A	E	DP	TC/G	FA	G by Pos
1968	WAS A	75	.294	.376	85	25	5	1	0	0.0	10	7	13	15	0	32	11	75	9	1	3	2.0	.988	1B-33, OF-10
1969		41	.161	.194	31	5	1	0	0	0.0	1	2	4	7	0	26	5	15	0	0	1	1.1	1.000	1B-11, OF-3
2 yrs.		116	.259	.328	116	30	6	1	0	0.0	11	9	17	22	0	58	16	90	9	1	4	1.8	.990	1B-44, OF-13

Ducky Holmes

HOLMES, HOWARD ELBERT BR TR 5′10″ 160 lbs.
B. July 8, 1883, Dayton, Ohio D. Sept. 18, 1945, Dayton, Ohio.

Year	Team	Games	BA	SA	AB	H	2B	3B	HR	HR%	R	RBI	BB	SO	SB	Pinch Hit AB	Pinch Hit H	PO	A	E	DP	TC/G	FA	G by Pos
1906	STL N	9	.185	.185	27	5	0	0	0	0.0	2	2	2		0	0	0	37	9	1	2	5.2	.979	C-9

Ducky Holmes

HOLMES, JAMES WILLIAM BL TR 5′ 6″ 170 lbs.
B. Jan. 28, 1869, Des Moines, Iowa D. Aug. 6, 1932, Truro, Iowa.

Year	Team	Games	BA	SA	AB	H	2B	3B	HR	HR%	R	RBI	BB	SO	SB	Pinch Hit AB	Pinch Hit H	PO	A	E	DP	TC/G	FA	G by Pos
1895	LOU N	40	.373	.516	161	60	10	2	3	1.9	33	20	12	9	9	0	0	49	32	21	2	2.4	.794	OF-29, SS-8, 3B-4, P-2
1896		47	.270	.319	141	38	3	2	0	0.0	22	18	13	5	8	**10**	3	44	14	19	3	2.1	.753	OF-33, P-2, 2B-1, SS-1
1897	2 teams	LOU N (2G –.000) NY N (79G –.268)																						
″	total	81	.265	.339	310	82	8	6	1	0.3	51	44	19		30	2	0	117	19	16	4	1.9	.895	OF-77, SS-2
1898	2 teams	STL N (23G –.238) BAL N (113G –.285)																						
″	total	136	.276	.339	543	150	11	10	1	0.2	63	64	25		29	1	1	286	19	23	7	2.4	.930	OF-135
1899	BAL N	138	.320	.423	553	177	31	7	4	0.7	80	66	39		50	0	0	321	24	27	5	2.7	.927	OF-138
1901	DET A	131	.294	.406	537	158	28	10	4	0.7	90	62	37		35	0	0	217	18	24	5	2.0	.907	OF-131
1902		92	.257	.337	362	93	15	4	2	0.6	50	33	28		16	0	0	155	16	9	5	2.0	.950	OF-92
1903	2 teams	WAS A (21G –.225) CHI A (86G –.279)																						
″	total	107	.270	.330	415	112	10	6	1	0.2	66	26	30		35	3	0	188	34	14	0	2.2	.941	OF-96, 3B-7, 2B-2
1904	CHI A	68	.311	.438	251	78	11	9	1	0.4	42	19	14		13	5	**2**	111	8	3	3	1.9	.975	OF-63
1905		92	.201	.259	328	66	15	2	0	0.0	42	22	19		11	3	2	150	11	11	1	1.9	.936	OF-89
10 yrs.		932	.282	.367	3601	1014	142	58	17	0.5	539	374	236	14	236	24	8	1638	195	167	35	2.2	.916	OF-883, SS-11, 3B-11, P-4, 2B-3

Fred Holmes

HOLMES, FREDERICK C. BR TR
B. July 1, 1878, Chicago, Ill. D. Feb. 13, 1956, Norwood Park, Ill.

Year	Team	Games	BA	SA	AB	H	2B	3B	HR	HR%	R	RBI	BB	SO	SB	Pinch Hit AB	Pinch Hit H	PO	A	E	DP	TC/G	FA	G by Pos
1903	NY A	1	—	—	0	0	0	0	0	—	0	0	1		0	0	0	5	0	1	0	6.0	.833	1B-1
1904	CHI N	1	.333	.667	3	1	1	0	0	0.0	1	0	0		0	0	0	4	1	0	0	5.0	1.000	C-1
2 yrs.		2	.333	.667	3	1	1	0	0	0.0	1	0	1		0	0	0	9	1	1	0	5.5	.909	C-1, 1B-1

Tommy Holmes

HOLMES, THOMAS FRANCIS (Kelly) BL TL 5′10″ 180 lbs.
B. Mar. 29, 1917, Brooklyn, N. Y.
Manager 1951–52.

Year	Team	Games	BA	SA	AB	H	2B	3B	HR	HR%	R	RBI	BB	SO	SB	Pinch Hit AB	Pinch Hit H	PO	A	E	DP	TC/G	FA	G by Pos
1942	BOS N	141	.278	.357	558	155	24	4	4	0.7	56	41	64	10	2	0	0	373	16	4	4	2.8	.990	OF-140
1943		152	.270	.378	**629**	170	33	10	5	0.8	75	41	58	20	7	0	0	408	18	3	3	2.8	.993	OF-152
1944		155	.309	.456	631	195	42	6	13	2.1	93	73	61	11	4	0	0	426	14	4	7	2.9	.991	OF-155
1945		154	.352	**.577**	636	**224**	**47**	6	**28**	4.4	125	117	70	9	15	0	0	334	13	6	4	2.3	.983	OF-154
1946		149	.310	.424	568	176	35	6	6	1.1	80	79	58	14	7	2	1	294	17	4	7	2.2	.987	OF-146
1947		150	.309	.416	618	**191**	33	3	9	1.5	90	53	44	16	3	1	0	336	12	4	4	2.4	.989	OF-147
1948		139	.325	.439	585	190	35	7	6	1.0	85	61	46	20	1	2	1	283	8	5	4	2.2	.983	OF-137
1949		117	.266	.403	380	101	20	4	8	2.1	47	59	39	6	1	12	4	210	10	3	4	2.2	.987	OF-103
1950		105	.298	.450	322	96	20	1	9	2.8	44	51	33	8	0	15	4	151	6	0	0	1.8	1.000	OF-88
1951		27	.172	.241	29	5	2	0	0	0.0	1	5	3	4	0	22	3	2	0	0	0	0.7	1.000	OF-3
1952	BKN N	31	.111	.139	36	4	1	0	0	0.0	2	1	4	4	0	23	2	6	1	0	0	1.2	1.000	OF-6
11 yrs.		1320	.302	.432	4992	1507	292	47	88	1.8	698	581	480	122	40	77	15	2823	115	33	37	2.4	.989	OF-1231
WORLD SERIES																								
1948	BOS N	6	.192	.192	26	5	0	0	0	0.0	3	1	0	0	0	0	0	10	2	0	1	2.0	1.000	OF-6
1952	BKN N	3	.000	.000	1	0	0	0	0	0.0	0	0	0	0	0	0	0	2	0	0	0	0.7	1.000	OF-3
2 yrs.		9	.185	.185	27	5	0	0	0	0.0	3	1	0	0	0	0	0	12	2	0	1	1.6	1.000	OF-9

Jim Holt

HOLT, JAMES WILLIAM BL TR 6′ 180 lbs.
B. May 27, 1944, Graham, N. C.

Year	Team	Games	BA	SA	AB	H	2B	3B	HR	HR%	R	RBI	BB	SO	SB	Pinch Hit AB	Pinch Hit H	PO	A	E	DP	TC/G	FA	G by Pos
1968	MIN A	70	.208	.245	106	22	2	1	0	0.0	9	8	4	20	0	26	4	35	2	1	1	1.0	.974	OF-38, 1B-1
1969		12	.357	.571	14	5	0	0	1	7.1	3	2	0	4	0	7	4	4	0	0	1	0.7	1.000	OF-5, 1B-1
1970		142	.266	.342	319	85	9	3	3	0.9	37	40	17	32	3	14	3	208	2	1	0	1.6	.995	OF-130, 1B-2
1971		126	.259	.318	340	88	11	3	1	0.3	35	29	16	28	5	13	4	219	4	3	3	2.1	.987	OF-106, 1B-3
1972		10	.444	.593	27	12	1	0	1	3.7	6	6	0	1	0	4	1	16	2	1	0	2.4	.947	OF-7, 1B-1
1973		132	.297	.442	441	131	25	3	11	2.5	52	58	29	43	0	11	5	415	26	2	15	3.3	.995	OF-102, 1B-33
1974	2 teams	MIN A (79G –.254) OAK A (30G –.143)																						
″	total	109	.234	.280	239	56	11	0	0	0.0	25	16	15	25	0	24	0	504	49	2	62	6.0	.996	1B-84, OF-5, DH-3
1975	OAK A	102	.220	.293	123	27	3	0	2	1.6	7	16	11	11	0	**43**	**10**	192	18	2	19	3.6	.991	1B-52, DH-4, OF-2, C-1
1976		4	.286	.571	7	2	2	0	0	0.0	0	2	1	2	0	2	1	0	0	0	0	0.0	.000	DH-2
9 yrs.		707	.265	.352	1616	428	64	10	19	1.2	174	177	93	166	8	144	32	1593	103	12	101	2.9	.993	OF-395, 1B-177, DH-9, C-1
LEAGUE CHAMPIONSHIP SERIES																								
1970	MIN A	3	.000	.000	5	0	0	0	0	0.0	0	0	0	2	0	1	0	3	0	1	0	1.3	.750	OF-3
1974	OAK A	2	—	—	0	0	0	0	0	—	0	0	1	0	0	0	0	1	0	0	0	1.0	1.000	1B-1
1975		3	.333	.667	3	1	1	0	0	0.0	0	0	0	0	0	2	1	1	2	0	0	3.0	1.000	1B-1
3 yrs.		8	.125	.250	8	1	1	0	0	0.0	0	0	1	2	0	3	1	5	2	1	0	1.6	.875	OF-3, 1B-2
WORLD SERIES																								
1974	OAK A	4	.667	.667	3	2	0	0	0	0.0	0	2	0	0	0	3	2	1	0	0	1	1.0	1.000	1B-1

Red Holt

HOLT, JAMES EMMETT MADISON BL TL 5′11″ 175 lbs.
B. July 25, 1894, Dayton, Tenn. D. Feb. 2, 1961, Birmingham, Ala.

Year	Team	Games	BA	SA	AB	H	2B	3B	HR	HR%	R	RBI	BB	SO	SB	Pinch Hit AB	Pinch Hit H	PO	A	E	DP	TC/G	FA	G by Pos
1925	PHI A	27	.273	.386	88	24	7	0	1	1.1	13	8	12	9	0	1	0	268	17	4	21	11.6	.986	1B-25

Roger Holt

HOLT, ROGER BOYD BB TR 5′11″ 165 lbs.
B. Apr. 8, 1956, Daytona Beach, Fla.

Year	Team	Games	BA	SA	AB	H	2B	3B	HR	HR%	R	RBI	BB	SO	SB	Pinch Hit AB	Pinch Hit H	PO	A	E	DP	TC/G	FA	G by Pos
1980	NY A	2	.167	.167	6	1	0	0	0	0.0	0	1	1	2	0	0	0	3	9	0	0	6.0	1.000	2B-2

Marty Honan

HONAN, MARTIN WELDON
B. Apr. 1871, Chicago, Ill. D. Aug. 20, 1908, Chicago, Ill.

Year	Team	Games	BA	SA	AB	H	2B	3B	HR	HR%	R	RBI	BB	SO	SB	Pinch Hit AB	Pinch Hit H	PO	A	E	DP	TC/G	FA	G by Pos
1890	CHI N	1	.000	.000	3	0	0	0	0	0.0	0	1	0	2	0	0	0	6	0	1	0	7.0	.857	C-1
1891		5	.167	.333	12	2	0	1	0	0.0	1	3	1	3	0	0	0	18	8	1	0	5.4	.963	C-5
2 yrs.		6	.133	.267	15	2	0	1	0	0.0	1	4	1	5	0	0	0	24	8	2	0	5.7	.941	C-6

Abie Hood

HOOD, ALBIE LARRISON BL TR 5′ 7″ 152 lbs.
B. Jan. 31, 1903, Sanford, N. C. D. Oct. 14, 1988, Chesapeake, Va.

Year	Team	Games	BA	SA	AB	H	2B	3B	HR	HR%	R	RBI	BB	SO	SB	Pinch Hit AB	Pinch Hit H	PO	A	E	DP	TC/G	FA	G by Pos
1925	BOS N	5	.286	.524	21	6	2	0	1	4.8	2	2	1	0	0	0	0	12	11	2	2	5.0	.920	2B-5

Wally Hood

HOOD, WALLACE JAMES, SR. BR TR 5′11½″ 160 lbs.
Father of Wally Hood.
B. Feb. 9, 1895, Whittier, Calif. D. May 2, 1965, Hollywood, Calif.

Year	Team	Games	BA	SA	AB	H	2B	3B	HR	HR%	R	RBI	BB	SO	SB	Pinch Hit AB	Pinch Hit H	PO	A	E	DP	TC/G	FA	G by Pos
1920	2 teams	BKN N (7G –.143) PIT N (2G –.000)																						
″	total	9	.133	.200	15	2	1	0	0	0.0	5	1	5	4	3	1	0	16	1	1	0	3.6	.944	OF-5
1921	BKN N	56	.262	.385	65	17	1	2	1	1.5	16	4	9	14	2	20	4	22	0	1	0	1.1	.957	OF-20
1922		2	—	—	0	0	0	0	0	—	2	0	0	0	0	0	0	0	0	0	0	0.0	—	
3 yrs.		67	.237	.350	80	19	2	2	1	1.3	23	5	14	18	5	21	4	38	1	2	0	1.6	.951	OF-25

Alex Hooks

HOOKS, ALEXANDER MARCUS BL TL 6′ 1″ 183 lbs.
B. Aug. 29, 1906, Edgewood, Tex. D. June 19, 1993, Edgewood, Tex.

Year	Team	Games	BA	SA	AB	H	2B	3B	HR	HR%	R	RBI	BB	SO	SB	Pinch Hit AB	Pinch Hit H	PO	A	E	DP	TC/G	FA	G by Pos
1935	PHI A	15	.227	.295	44	10	3	0	0	0.0	4	4	3	10	0	4	1	85	5	0	11	9.0	1.000	1B-10

Harry Hooper

HOOPER, HARRY BARTHOLOMEW BL TR 5′10″ 168 lbs.
B. Aug. 24, 1887, Bell Station, Calif. D. Dec. 18, 1974, Santa Cruz, Calif.
Hall of Fame 1971.

Year	Team	Games	BA	SA	AB	H	2B	3B	HR	HR%	R	RBI	BB	SO	SB	Pinch Hit AB	Pinch Hit H	PO	A	E	DP	TC/G	FA	G by Pos
1909	BOS A	81	.282	.325	255	72	3	4	0	0.0	29	12	16		15	4	2	124	14	7	3	2.0	.952	OF-74
1910		155	.267	.327	584	156	9	10	2	0.3	81	27	62		40	0	0	241	30	18	7	1.9	.938	OF-155
1911		130	.311	.395	524	163	20	6	4	0.8	93	45	73		38	0	0	181	27	10	1	1.7	.954	OF-130
1912		147	.242	.327	590	143	20	12	2	0.3	98	53	66		29	0	0	220	22	9	6	1.7	.964	OF-147
1913		148	.288	.399	586	169	29	12	4	0.7	100	40	60	51	26	1	0	248	25	9	7	1.9	.968	OF-147, P-1
1914		141	.258	.364	530	137	23	15	1	0.2	85	41	58	47	19	1	0	231	23	7	5	1.9	.973	OF-140
1915		149	.235	.327	566	133	20	13	2	0.4	90	51	89	36	22	0	0	255	23	8	7	1.9	.972	OF-147
1916		151	.271	.350	575	156	20	11	1	0.2	75	37	80	35	27	0	0	266	19	10	5	2.0	.966	OF-151
1917		151	.256	.349	559	143	21	11	3	0.5	89	45	80	40	21	0	0	245	20	8	3	1.8	.971	OF-151
1918		126	.289	.405	474	137	26	13	1	0.2	81	44	75	25	24	0	0	221	16	9	8	2.0	.963	OF-126

Harry Hooper *continued*

Year	Team	Games	BA	SA	AB	H	2B	3B	HR	HR%	R	RBI	BB	SO	SB	Pinch Hit AB	Pinch Hit H	PO	A	E	DP	TC/G	FA	G by Pos
1919		128	.267	.360	491	131	25	6	3	0.6	76	49	79	28	23	0	0	262	19	6	2	2.2	.979	OF-128
1920		139	.312	.470	536	167	30	17	7	1.3	91	53	88	27	16	0	0	263	22	11	2	2.1	.963	OF-139
1921	**CHI A**	108	.327	.470	419	137	26	5	8	1.9	74	58	55	21	13	0	0	182	12	5	3	1.8	.975	OF-108
1922		152	.304	.444	602	183	35	8	11	1.8	111	80	68	33	16	3	0	288	19	12	7	2.1	.962	OF-149
1923		145	.288	.410	576	166	32	4	10	1.7	87	65	68	22	18	2	1	272	15	12	3	2.1	.960	OF-143
1924		130	.328	.481	476	156	27	8	10	2.1	107	62	65	26	16	5	2	251	22	4	8	2.3	.986	OF-123
1925		127	.265	.380	442	117	23	5	6	1.4	62	55	54	21	12	2	0	231	16	6	4	2.0	.976	OF-124
17 yrs.		2308	.281	.387	8785	2466	389	160	75	0.9	1429	817	1136	412	375	18	5	3981	344	151	81	2.0	.966	OF-2282, P-1
WORLD SERIES																								
1912	**BOS A**	8	.290	.419	31	9	2	1	0	0.0	3	2	4	4	2	0	0	16	3	0	1	2.4	1.000	OF-8
1915		5	.350	.650	20	7	0	0	2	10.0	4	3	2	4	0	0	0	8	0	1	0	1.8	.889	OF-5
1916		5	.333	.476	21	7	1	1	0	0.0	6	1	3	1	1	0	0	8	2	0	1	2.0	1.000	OF-5
1918		6	.200	.200	20	4	0	0	0	0.0	0	0	2	2	0	0	0	11	0	0	0	1.8	1.000	OF-6
4 yrs.		24	.293	.435	92	27	3	2	2	2.2	13	6	11	11	3	0	0	43	5	1	2	2.0	.980	OF-24

Buster Hoover

HOOVER, WILLIAM J. BR TR 6′ 1″ 178 lbs.
B. 1863, Philadelphia, Pa. Deceased.

Year	Team	Games	BA	SA	AB	H	2B	3B	HR	HR%	R	RBI	BB	SO	SB	Pinch Hit AB	Pinch Hit H	PO	A	E	DP	TC/G	FA	G by Pos
1884	**2 teams**	**PHI U** (63G –.364) **PHI N** (10G –.190)																						
″	**total**	73	.341	.467	317	108	21	8	1	0.3	82		16	9		0	0	147	77	50	11	3.7	.818	OF-47, SS-15, 2B-6, 1B-6, 3B-1
1886	**BAL AA**	40	.217	.306	157	34	2	6	0	0.0	25		16			0	0	70	3	14	0	2.2	.839	OF-40
1892	**CIN N**	14	.176	.176	51	9	0	0	0	0.0	7	2	5	4	1	0	0	25	3	1	2	2.1	.966	OF-14
3 yrs.		127	.288	.390	525	151	23	14	1	0.2	114	2	37	13	1	0	0	242	83	65	13	3.0	.833	OF-101, SS-15, 2B-6, 1B-6, 3B-1

Charlie Hoover

HOOVER, CHARLES E. BL TR 5′ 8″
B. Sept. 9, 1865, Mound City, Ill. Deceased.

Year	Team	Games	BA	SA	AB	H	2B	3B	HR	HR%	R	RBI	BB	SO	SB	Pinch Hit AB	Pinch Hit H	PO	A	E	DP	TC/G	FA	G by Pos
1888	**KC AA**	3	.300	.300	10	3	0	0	0	0.0	0	1	0		0	0	0	13	5	3	0	7.0	.857	C-3
1889		71	.248	.306	258	64	2	5	1	0.4	44	25	29	38	9	0	0	272	108	40	8	5.8	.905	C-66, 3B-4, OF-3
2 yrs.		74	.250	.306	268	67	2	5	1	0.4	44	26	29	38	9	0	0	285	113	43	8	5.8	.902	C-69, 3B-4, OF-3

Joe Hoover

HOOVER, ROBERT JOSEPH BR TR 5′11″ 175 lbs.
B. Apr. 15, 1915, Brawley, Calif. D. Sept. 2, 1965, Los Angeles, Calif.

Year	Team	Games	BA	SA	AB	H	2B	3B	HR	HR%	R	RBI	BB	SO	SB	Pinch Hit AB	Pinch Hit H	PO	A	E	DP	TC/G	FA	G by Pos
1943	**DET A**	144	.243	.318	575	140	15	8	4	0.7	78	38	36	101	6	0	0	301	393	41	84	5.1	.944	SS-144
1944		120	.236	.290	441	104	20	2	0	0.0	67	29	35	66	7	0	0	258	406	48	103	5.9	.933	SS-119, 2B-1
1945		74	.257	.360	222	57	10	5	1	0.5	33	17	21	35	6	0	0	126	163	17	35	4.5	.944	SS-68
3 yrs.		338	.243	.316	1238	301	45	15	5	0.4	178	84	92	202	19	0	0	685	962	106	222	5.3	.940	SS-331, 2B-1
WORLD SERIES																								
1945	**DET A**	1	.333	.333	3	1	0	0	0	0.0	1	1	0	0	0	0	0	1	1	0	1	2.0	1.000	SS-1

Don Hopkins

HOPKINS, DONALD BL TR 6′ 1″ 175 lbs.
B. Jan. 9, 1952, West Point, Miss.

Year	Team	Games	BA	SA	AB	H	2B	3B	HR	HR%	R	RBI	BB	SO	SB	Pinch Hit AB	Pinch Hit H	PO	A	E	DP	TC/G	FA	G by Pos
1975	**OAK A**	82	.167	.167	6	1	0	0	0	0.0	25	0	2	0	21	3	0	3	0	0	0	0.1	1.000	DH-20, OF-5
1976		3	—	—	0	0	0	0	0	—	0	0	0	0	0	0	0	0	0	0	0	0.0	.000	DH-2
2 yrs.		85	.167	.167	6	1	0	0	0	0.0	25	0	2	0	21	3	0	3	0	0	0	0.1	1.000	DH-22, OF-5
LEAGUE CHAMPIONSHIP SERIES																								
1975	**OAK A**	1	—	—	0	0	0	0	0	—	0	0	0	0	0	0	0	0	0	0	0	0.0	.000	DH-1

Gail Hopkins

HOPKINS, GAIL EASON BL TR 5′10″ 198 lbs.
B. Feb. 19, 1943, Tulsa, Okla.

Year	Team	Games	BA	SA	AB	H	2B	3B	HR	HR%	R	RBI	BB	SO	SB	Pinch Hit AB	Pinch Hit H	PO	A	E	DP	TC/G	FA	G by Pos
1968	**CHI A**	29	.216	.270	37	8	2	0	0	0.0	4	2	6	3	0	20	4	45	1	0	3	6.6	1.000	1B-7
1969		124	.265	.381	373	99	13	3	8	2.1	52	46	50	28	2	21	6	903	51	6	81	9.5	.994	1B-101
1970		116	.286	.383	287	82	8	1	6	2.1	32	29	28	19	0	36	10	645	42	9	67	8.2	.987	1B-77, C-8
1971	**KC A**	103	.278	.431	295	82	16	1	9	3.1	35	47	37	13	3	17	5	669	57	7	76	8.8	.990	1B-83
1972		53	.211	.239	71	15	2	0	0	0.0	1	5	7	4	0	34	6	98	2	1	7	7.2	.990	1B-13, 3B-1
1973		74	.246	.348	138	34	6	1	2	1.4	17	16	29	15	1	19	7	32	3	0	3	0.8	1.000	DH-36, 1B-10
1974	**LA N**	15	.222	.222	18	4	0	0	0	0.0	1	0	3	1	0	11	4	20	3	0	0	5.8	1.000	1B-2, C-2
7 yrs.		514	.266	.376	1219	324	47	6	25	2.1	142	145	160	83	6	158	42	2412	159	23	237	7.6	.991	1B-293, DH-36, C-10, 3B-1

Marty Hopkins

HOPKINS, MEREDITH HILLIARD BR TR 5′11″ 175 lbs.
B. Feb. 22, 1907, Wolfe City, Tex. D. Nov. 20, 1963, Dallas, Tex.

Year	Team	Games	BA	SA	AB	H	2B	3B	HR	HR%	R	RBI	BB	SO	SB	Pinch Hit AB	Pinch Hit H	PO	A	E	DP	TC/G	FA	G by Pos
1934	**2 teams**	**PHI N** (10G –.120) **CHI A** (67G –.214)																						
″	**total**	77	.204	.268	235	48	9	0	2	0.9	28	31	49	31	0	1	0	69	149	9	6	3.2	.960	3B-72
1935	**CHI A**	59	.222	.285	144	32	3	0	2	1.4	20	17	36	23	1	1	0	35	82	8	7	2.3	.936	3B-49, 2B-5
2 yrs.		136	.211	.274	379	80	12	0	4	1.1	48	48	85	54	1	2	0	104	231	17	13	2.8	.952	3B-121, 2B-5

Mike Hopkins

HOPKINS, MICHAEL JOSEPH BR TR 5′ 8″ 160 lbs.
B. Nov. 1, 1872, Glasgow, Scotland D. Feb. 5, 1952, Pittsburgh, Pa.

Year	Team	Games	BA	SA	AB	H	2B	3B	HR	HR%	R	RBI	BB	SO	SB	Pinch Hit AB	Pinch Hit H	PO	A	E	DP	TC/G	FA	G by Pos
1902	**PIT N**	1	1.000	1.500	2	2	1	0	0	0.0	0	0	0		0	0	0	3	1	0	0	4.0	1.000	C-1

Sis Hopkins

HOPKINS, JOHN WINTON (Buck) BL TL 5′10″ 165 lbs.
B. Jan. 3, 1883, Grafton, Va. D. Oct. 2, 1929, Phoebus, Va.

Year	Team	Games	BA	SA	AB	H	2B	3B	HR	HR%	R	RBI	BB	SO	SB	Pinch Hit AB	Pinch Hit H	PO	A	E	DP	TC/G	FA	G by Pos
1907	**STL N**	15	.136	.205	44	6	3	0	0	0.0	7	3	10		2	0	0	21	0	3	0	1.6	.875	OF-15

Johnny Hopp

HOPP, JOHN LEONARD (Hippity) BL TL 5′10″ 170 lbs.
B. July 18, 1916, Hastings, Neb.

Year	Team	Games	BA	SA	AB	H	2B	3B	HR	HR%	R	RBI	BB	SO	SB	Pinch Hit AB	Pinch Hit H	PO	A	E	DP	TC/G	FA	G by Pos
1939	**STL N**	6	.500	.750	4	2	1	0	0	0.0	1	2	1	1	0	3	2	6	1	0	1	7.0	1.000	1B-1
1940		80	.270	.388	152	41	7	4	1	0.7	24	14	9	21	3	23	4	129	4	4	4	2.8	.971	OF-39, 1B-10
1941		134	.303	.436	445	135	25	11	4	0.9	83	50	50	63	15	6	1	542	21	8	24	4.4	.986	OF-91, 1B-39
1942		95	.258	.382	314	81	16	7	3	1.0	41	37	36	40	14	3	1	746	44	14	68	9.1	.983	1B-88
1943		91	.224	.307	241	54	10	2	2	0.8	33	25	24	22	8	4	0	286	17	12	23	4.0	.962	OF-52, 1B-27
1944		139	.336	.499	527	177	35	9	11	2.1	106	72	58	47	15	2	0	352	4	1	1	2.6	.997	OF-131, 1B-6
1945		124	.289	.395	446	129	22	8	3	0.7	67	44	49	24	14	6	1	375	16	7	13	3.3	.982	OF-104, 1B-15

Johnny Hopp *continued*

Year	Team	Games	BA	SA	AB	H	2B	3B	HR	HR%	R	RBI	BB	SO	SB	Pinch Hit AB	Pinch Hit H	PO	A	E	DP	TC/G	FA	G by Pos
1946	BOS N	129	.333	.440	445	148	23	8	3	0.7	71	48	34	34	21	8	3	670	45	11	45	5.8	.985	1B-68, OF-58
1947		134	.288	.358	430	124	20	2	2	0.5	74	32	58	30	13	7	0	296	2	6	0	2.4	.980	OF-125
1948	PIT N	120	.278	.385	392	109	15	12	1	0.3	64	31	40	25	5	14	7	403	21	1	22	4.0	.998	OF-80, 1B-25
1949	2 teams	PIT N (105G –.318)	BKN N (8G –.000)																					
"	total	113	.306	.408	385	118	14	5	5	1.3	55	39	37	32	9	13	5	682	47	8	69	7.4	.989	1B-79, OF-20
1950	2 teams	PIT N (106G –.340)	NY A (19G –.333)																					
"	total	125	.339	.528	345	117	26	6	9	2.6	60	55	51	18	7	28	8	596	35	6	62	6.7	.991	1B-82, OF-13
1951	NY A	46	.206	.317	63	13	1	0	2	3.2	10	4	9	11	2	19	4	121	5	1	10	5.1	.992	1B-25
1952	2 teams	NY A (15G –.160)	DET A (42G –.217)																					
"	total	57	.197	.211	71	14	1	0	0	0.0	9	5	8	10	2	33	8	59	5	0	8	3.8	1.000	1B-13, OF-4
14 yrs.		1393	.296	.414	4260	1262	216	74	46	1.1	698	458	464	378	128	169	44	5263	267	79	350	4.7	.986	OF-717, 1B-478
WORLD SERIES																								
1942	STL N	5	.176	.176	17	3	0	0	0	0.0	3	0	1	1	0	0	0	46	3	1	2	10.0	.980	1B-5
1943		1	.000	.000	4	0	0	0	0	0.0	0	0	0	1	0	0	0	1	0	0	0	1.0	1.000	OF-1
1944		6	.185	.185	27	5	0	0	0	0.0	2	0	0	8	0	0	0	14	0	0	0	2.3	1.000	OF-6
1950	NY A	3	.000	.000	2	0	0	0	0	0.0	0	0	0	0	0	0	0	7	1	0	2	2.7	1.000	1B-3
1951		1	—	—	0	0	0	0	0	—	0	0	1	0	0	0	0	0	0	0	0	0.0	—	
5 yrs.		16	.160	.160	50	8	0	0	0	0.0	5	0	2	10	0	0	0	68	4	1	4	4.9	.986	1B-8, OF-7

Shags Horan

HORAN, JOSEPH PATRICK BR TR 5′10″ 170 lbs.
B. Sept. 6, 1895, St. Louis, Mo. D. Feb. 13, 1969, Torrance, Calif.

Year	Team	Games	BA	SA	AB	H	2B	3B	HR	HR%	R	RBI	BB	SO	SB	Pinch Hit AB	Pinch Hit H	PO	A	E	DP	TC/G	FA	G by Pos
1924	NY A	22	.290	.323	31	9	1	0	0	0.0	4	7	1	5	0	7	2	9	1	0	0	0.8	1.000	OF-13

Sam Horn

HORN, SAMUEL LEE BL TL 6′ 5″ 215 lbs.
B. Nov. 2, 1963, Dallas, Tex.

Year	Team	Games	BA	SA	AB	H	2B	3B	HR	HR%	R	RBI	BB	SO	SB	Pinch Hit AB	Pinch Hit H	PO	A	E	DP	TC/G	FA	G by Pos
1987	BOS A	46	.278	.589	158	44	7	0	14	8.9	31	34	17	55	0	6	1	0	0	0	0	0.0	.000	DH-40
1988		24	.148	.246	61	9	0	0	2	3.3	4	8	11	20	0	4	0	0	0	0	0	0.0	.000	DH-16
1989		33	.148	.185	54	8	2	0	0	0.0	1	4	8	16	0	17	4	5	0	0	0	0.3	1.000	DH-14, 1B-2
1990	BAL A	79	.248	.472	246	61	13	0	14	5.7	30	45	32	62	0	9	4	58	6	2	7	0.9	.970	DH-63, 1B-10
1991		121	.233	.502	317	74	16	0	23	7.3	45	61	41	99	0	24	7	0	0	0	0	0.0	.000	DH-102
1992		63	.235	.401	162	38	10	1	5	3.1	13	19	21	60	0	11	2	0	0	0	0	0.0	.000	DH-46
1993	CLE A	12	.455	.848	33	15	1	0	4	12.1	8	8	1	5	0	1	0	0	0	0	0	0.0	.000	DH-11
1995	TEX A	11	.111	.111	9	1	0	0	0	0.0	0	0	1	6	0	9	1	0	0	0	0	0.0	.000	DH-1
8 yrs.		389	.240	.468	1040	250	49	1	62	6.0	132	179	132	323	0	81	19	63	6	2	7	0.2	.972	DH-293, 1B-12

Bob Horner

HORNER, JAMES ROBERT BR TR 6′ 1″ 195 lbs.
B. Aug. 6, 1957, Junction City, Kans.

Year	Team	Games	BA	SA	AB	H	2B	3B	HR	HR%	R	RBI	BB	SO	SB	Pinch Hit AB	Pinch Hit H	PO	A	E	DP	TC/G	FA	G by Pos
1978	ATL N	89	.266	.539	323	86	17	1	23	7.1	50	63	24	42	0	0	0	81	199	13	17	3.3	.956	3B-89
1979		121	.314	.552	487	153	15	1	33	6.8	66	98	22	74	0	1	0	470	167	22	43	5.2	.967	3B-82, 1B-45
1980		124	.268	.529	463	124	14	1	35	7.6	81	89	27	50	3	3	1	80	253	23	20	2.9	.935	3B-121, 1B-1
1981		79	.277	.460	300	83	10	0	15	5.0	42	42	32	39	2	0	0	51	129	12	6	2.4	.938	3B-79
1982		140	.261	.501	499	130	24	0	32	6.4	85	97	66	75	3	3	0	102	217	10	20	2.4	.970	3B-137
1983		104	.303	.528	386	117	25	1	20	5.2	75	68	50	63	4	0	0	78	153	10	18	2.3	.959	3B-104, 1B-1
1984		32	.274	.425	113	31	8	0	3	2.7	15	19	14	17	0	0	0	21	61	3	6	2.7	.965	3B-32
1985		130	.267	.499	483	129	25	3	27	5.6	61	89	50	57	1	4	1	917	119	11	111	8.2	.989	1B-87, 3B-40
1986		141	.273	.472	517	141	22	0	27	5.2	70	87	52	72	1	2	2	1378	102	8	138	10.7	.995	1B-139
1988	STL N	60	.257	.354	206	53	9	1	3	1.5	15	33	32	23	0	3	2	463	40	5	39	8.9	.990	1B-57
10 yrs.		1020	.277	.499	3777	1047	169	8	218	5.8	560	685	369	512	14	16	6	3641	1440	117	418	5.1	.977	3B-684, 1B-330
LEAGUE CHAMPIONSHIP SERIES																								
1982	ATL N	3	.091	.091	11	1	0	0	0	0.0	0	0	0	2	0	0	0	2	5	0	0	2.3	1.000	3B-3

Rogers Hornsby

HORNSBY, ROGERS (Rajah) BR TR 5′11″ 175 lbs.
B. Apr. 27, 1896, Winters, Tex. D. Jan. 5, 1963, Chicago, Ill.
Manager 1925–28, 1930–37, 1952–53.
Hall of Fame 1942.

Year	Team	Games	BA	SA	AB	H	2B	3B	HR	HR%	R	RBI	BB	SO	SB	Pinch Hit AB	Pinch Hit H	PO	A	E	DP	TC/G	FA	G by Pos
1915	STL N	18	.246	.281	57	14	2	0	0	0.0	5	4	2	6	0	0	0	48	46	8	12	5.7	.922	SS-18
1916		139	.313	.444	495	155	17	15	6	1.2	63	65	40	63	17	1	1	325	315	45	35	4.8	.934	3B-83, SS-45, 1B-15, 2B-1
1917		145	.327	**.484**	523	171	24	**17**	8	1.5	86	66	45	34	17	1	0	268	527	52	82	5.9	.939	SS-144
1918		115	.281	.416	416	117	19	11	5	1.2	51	60	40	43	8	4	2	211	434	46	55	6.2	.933	SS-109, OF-2
1919		138	.318	.430	512	163	15	9	8	1.6	68	71	48	41	17	0	0	233	367	34	39	4.6	.946	3B-72, SS-37, 2B-25, 1B-5
1920		149	**.370**	**.559**	589	**218**	**44**	20	9	1.5	96	**94**	60	50	12	0	0	343	524	34	76	6.0	.962	2B-149
1921		154	**.397**	**.639**	592	**235**	**44**	**18**	21	3.5	**131**	**126**	60	48	13	0	0	340	487	27	63	5.5	.968	2B-142, OF-6, 3B-3, SS-3, 1B-1
1922		154	**.401**	**.722**	623	**250**	**46**	14	**42**	**6.7**	**141**	**152**	65	50	17	0	0	398	473	30	81	5.9	.967	2B-154
1923		107	**.384**	**.627**	424	163	32	10	17	4.0	89	83	55	29	3	1	0	323	299	21	61	6.1	.967	2B-96, 1B-10
1924		143	**.424**	**.696**	536	**227**	**43**	14	25	4.7	**121**	94	**89**	32	5	0	0	301	517	30	102	5.9	.965	2B-143
1925		138	**.403**	**.756**	504	203	41	10	**39**	**7.7**	133	**143**	83	39	5	0	0	287	416	34	95	5.4	.954	2B-136
1926		134	.317	.463	527	167	34	5	11	2.1	96	93	61	39	3	0	0	245	433	27	73	5.3	.962	2B-134
1927	NY N	155	.361	.586	568	205	32	9	26	4.6	**133**	125	**86**	38	9	0	0	299	582	25	98	5.8	.972	2B-155
1928	BOS N	140	**.387**	**.632**	486	188	42	7	21	4.3	99	94	**107**	41	5	0	0	295	450	21	85	5.5	.973	2B-140
1929	CHI N	156	.380	**.679**	602	229	47	8	39	6.5	**156**	149	87	65	2	0	0	286	547	23	106	5.5	.973	2B-156
1930		42	.308	.433	104	32	5	1	2	1.9	15	18	12	12	0	15	2	44	76	11	16	5.2	.916	2B-25
1931		100	.331	.574	357	118	37	1	16	4.5	64	90	56	23	1	4	2	128	255	22	30	4.3	.946	2B-69, 3B-26
1932		19	.224	.310	58	13	2	0	1	1.7	10	7	10	4	0	3	1	17	10	4	0	1.9	.871	OF-10, 3B-6
1933	2 teams	STL N (46G –.325)	STL A (11G –.333)																					
"	total	57	.326	.500	92	30	7	0	3	3.3	11	23	14	7	1	35	11	24	35	2	7	3.6	.967	2B-17
1934	STL A	24	.304	.522	23	7	2	0	1	4.3	2	11	7	4	0	15	5	2	3	0	1	2.5	1.000	OF-1, 3B-1
1935		10	.208	.333	24	5	3	0	0	0.0	1	3	3	6	0	3	1	38	5	0	1	7.2	1.000	1B-3, 2B-2, 3B-1
1936		2	.400	.400	5	2	0	0	0	0.0	1	2	1	0	0	1	1	10	0	0	0	10.0	1.000	1B-1
1937		20	.321	.429	56	18	3	0	1	1.8	7	11	7	5	0	3	0	30	41	4	10	4.4	.947	2B-17
23 yrs.		2259	.358 **2nd**	.577 **7th**	8173	2930	541	169	301	3.7	1579	1584	1038	679	135	86	26	4495	6842	500	1128	5.5	.958	2B-1561, SS-356, 3B-192, 1B-35, OF-19

Rogers Hornsby *continued*

Year	Team	Games	BA	SA	AB	H	2B	3B	HR	HR%	R	RBI	BB	SO	SB	Pinch Hit AB	Pinch Hit H	PO	A	E	DP	TC/G	FA	G by Pos
WORLD SERIES																								
1926	**STL N**	7	.250	.286	28	7	1	0	0	0.0	2	4	2	2	1	0	0	15	21	0	4	5.1	1.000	2B-7
1929	**CHI N**	5	.238	.381	21	5	1	1	0	0.0	4	1	1	8	0	0	0	9	11	1	4	4.2	.952	2B-5
2 yrs.		12	.245	.327	49	12	2	1	0	0.0	6	5	3	10	1	0	0	24	32	1	8	4.8	.982	2B-12

Joe Hornung

HORNUNG, MICHAEL JOSEPH (Ubbo Ubbo) BR TR 5′ 8½″ 164 lbs.
B. June 12, 1857, Carthage, N. Y. D. Oct. 30, 1931, New York, N. Y.

Year	Team	Games	BA	SA	AB	H	2B	3B	HR	HR%	R	RBI	BB	SO	SB	Pinch Hit AB	Pinch Hit H	PO	A	E	DP	TC/G	FA	G by Pos
1879	**BUF N**	78	.266	.367	319	85	18	7	0	0.0	46	38	2	27		0	0	135	12	26	2	2.2	.850	OF-77, 1B-1
1880		85	.266	.363	342	91	8	11	1	0.3	47	42	8	29		0	0	311	36	36	7	4.2	.906	OF-67, 1B-18, 2B-5, P-1
1881	**BOS N**	83	.241	.346	324	78	12	8	2	0.6	40	25	5	25		0	0	198	19	12	5	2.8	.948	OF-83
1882		85	.302	.402	388	117	14	11	1	0.3	67	50	2	25		0	0	196	15	15	4	2.7	.934	OF-84, 1B-1
1883		98	.278	.446	**446**	124	25	13	8	1.8	**107**	66	8	54		0	0	175	15	13	3	2.1	.936	OF-98, 3B-1
1884		115	.268	.400	518	139	27	10	7	1.4	119		17	80		0	0	233	14	21	3	2.3	.922	OF-110, 1B-6
1885		25	.202	.284	109	22	4	1	1	0.9	14	7	1	20		0	0	33	1	3	0	1.5	.919	OF-25
1886		94	.257	.309	424	109	12	2	2	0.5	67	40	10	62		0	0	187	12	11	1	2.2	.948	OF-94
1887		98	.270	.355	437	118	10	6	5	1.1	85	49	17	28	41	0	0	192	23	15	3	2.3	.935	OF-98
1888		107	.239	.318	431	103	11	7	3	0.7	61	53	16	39	29	0	0	151	10	9	0	1.6	.947	OF-107
1889	**BAL AA**	135	.229	.293	533	122	13	9	1	0.2	73	78	22	72	34	0	0	251	32	27	10	2.3	.913	OF-134, 3B-1
1890	**NY N**	120	.238	.292	513	122	18	5	0	0.0	62	65	12	37	39	0	0	488	36	24	28	4.6	.956	OF-77, 1B-36, 3B-5, SS-2
12 yrs.		1123	.257	.350	4784	1230	172	90	31	0.6	788	513	120	498	143	0	0	2550	225	212	66	2.6	.929	OF-1054, 1B-62, 3B-7, 2B-5, SS-2, P-1

Tony Horton

HORTON, ANTHONY DARRIN BR TR 6′ 3″ 210 lbs.
B. Dec. 6, 1944, Santa Monica, Calif.

Year	Team	Games	BA	SA	AB	H	2B	3B	HR	HR%	R	RBI	BB	SO	SB	Pinch Hit AB	Pinch Hit H	PO	A	E	DP	TC/G	FA	G by Pos
1964	**BOS A**	36	.222	.286	126	28	5	0	1	0.8	9	8	3	20	0	6	0	94	5	2	3	3.2	.980	OF-24, 1B-8
1965		60	.294	.485	163	48	8	1	7	4.3	23	23	18	36	0	14	3	311	24	7	30	7.8	.980	1B-44
1966		6	.136	.136	22	3	0	0	0	0.0	0	2	0	5	0	2	0	43	5	0	7	8.0	1.000	1B-6
1967	**2 teams**	**BOS A** (21G –.308)	**CLE A** (106G –.281)																					
″	**total**	127	.284	.418	402	114	16	4	10	2.5	37	53	18	57	3	31	10	811	50	11	66	8.7	.987	1B-100
1968	**CLE A**	133	.249	.411	477	119	29	3	14	2.9	57	59	34	56	3	9	2	972	63	8	80	8.1	.992	1B-128
1969		159	.278	.461	625	174	25	4	27	4.3	77	93	37	91	3	2	0	1179	100	14	130	8.2	.989	1B-157
1970		115	.269	.453	413	111	19	3	17	4.1	48	59	30	54	3	8	3	898	73	6	106	8.7	.994	1B-112
7 yrs.		636	.268	.430	2228	597	102	15	76	3.4	251	297	140	319	12	72	18	4308	320	48	422	8.1	.990	1B-555, OF-24

Willie Horton

HORTON, WILLIE WATTERSON BR TR 5′11″ 209 lbs.
B. Oct. 18, 1942, Arno, Va.

Year	Team	Games	BA	SA	AB	H	2B	3B	HR	HR%	R	RBI	BB	SO	SB	Pinch Hit AB	Pinch Hit H	PO	A	E	DP	TC/G	FA	G by Pos
1963	**DET A**	15	.326	.488	43	14	2	1	1	2.3	6	4	0	8	2	5	3	13	0	0	0	1.4	1.000	OF-9
1964		25	.163	.287	80	13	1	3	1	1.3	6	10	11	20	0	3	1	33	0	2	0	1.5	.943	OF-23
1965		143	.273	.490	512	140	20	2	29	5.7	69	104	48	101	5	3	0	249	9	3	1	1.8	.989	OF-141, 3B-1
1966		146	.262	.481	526	138	22	6	27	5.1	72	100	44	103	1	9	2	233	4	5	1	1.8	.979	OF-137
1967		122	.274	.481	401	110	20	3	19	4.7	47	67	36	80	0	11	3	165	5	5	2	1.6	.971	OF-110
1968		143	.285	.543	512	146	20	2	36	7.0	68	85	49	110	0	5	1	212	6	6	2	1.6	.973	OF-139
1969		141	.262	.465	508	133	17	1	28	5.5	66	91	52	93	3	5	1	272	8	8	0	2.1	.972	OF-136
1970		96	.305	.501	371	113	18	2	17	4.6	53	69	28	43	0	0	0	154	10	3	1	1.7	.982	OF-96
1971		119	.289	.496	450	130	25	1	22	4.9	64	72	37	75	1	2	0	176	8	7	1	1.6	.963	OF-118
1972		108	.231	.387	333	77	9	5	11	3.3	44	36	27	47	0	12	1	131	6	0	0	1.4	1.000	OF-98
1973		111	.316	.501	411	130	19	3	17	4.1	42	53	23	57	1	3	1	160	2	10	0	1.6	.942	OF-107, DH-1
1974		72	.298	.529	238	71	8	1	15	6.3	32	47	21	36	0	6	3	106	2	6	0	1.8	.947	OF-64, DH-1
1975		159	.275	.421	615	169	13	1	25	4.1	62	92	44	109	1	0	0	0	0	0	0	0.0	.000	DH-159
1976		114	.262	.409	401	105	17	0	14	3.5	40	56	49	63	0	6	1	0	0	0	0	0.0	.000	DH-105
1977	**2 teams**	**DET A** (1G –.250)	**TEX A** (139G –.289)																					
″	**total**	140	.289	.430	523	151	23	3	15	2.9	55	75	42	117	2	6	2	16	0	1	0	0.1	.941	DH-128, OF-11
1978	**3 teams**	**CLE A** (50G –.249)	**OAK A** (32G –.314)	**TOR A** (33G –.205)																				
″	**total**	115	.252	.389	393	99	21	0	11	2.8	38	60	28	69	3	9	3	1	0	2	0	0.0	.333	DH-105, OF-1
1979	**SEA A**	162	.279	.458	646	180	19	5	29	4.5	77	106	42	112	1	0	0	0	0	0	0	0.0	.000	DH-162
1980		97	.221	.328	335	74	10	1	8	2.4	32	36	39	70	0	5	2	0	0	0	0	0.0	.000	DH-92
18 yrs.		2028	.273	.457	7298	1993	284	40	325	4.5	873	1163	620	1313	20	90	24	1921	60	58	8	1.0	.972	OF-1190, DH-753, 3B-1
LEAGUE CHAMPIONSHIP SERIES																								
1972	**DET A**	5	.100	.100	10	1	0	0	0	0.0	0	0	1	3	0	2	1	6	0	0	0	2.0	1.000	OF-3
WORLD SERIES																								
1968	**DET A**	7	.304	.565	23	7	1	1	1	4.3	6	3	5	6	0	0	0	5	1	1	0	1.0	.857	OF-7

Dwayne Hosey

HOSEY, DWAYNE SAMUEL BB TR 5′10″ 175 lbs.
B. Mar. 11, 1967, Sharon, Pa.

Year	Team	Games	BA	SA	AB	H	2B	3B	HR	HR%	R	RBI	BB	SO	SB	Pinch Hit AB	Pinch Hit H	PO	A	E	DP	TC/G	FA	G by Pos
1995	**BOS A**	24	.338	.618	68	23	8	1	3	4.4	20	7	8	16	6	2	0	46	1	0	0	2.1	1.000	OF-21, DH-1
DIVISIONAL PLAYOFF SERIES																								
1995	**BOS A**	3	.000	.000	12	0	0	0	0	0.0	1	0	2	3	1	0	0	7	0	0	0	2.3	1.000	OF-3

Steve Hosey

HOSEY, STEVEN BERNARD BR TR 6′ 3″ 215 lbs.
B. Apr. 2, 1969, Oakland, Calif.

Year	Team	Games	BA	SA	AB	H	2B	3B	HR	HR%	R	RBI	BB	SO	SB	Pinch Hit AB	Pinch Hit H	PO	A	E	DP	TC/G	FA	G by Pos
1992	**SF N**	21	.250	.321	56	14	1	0	1	1.8	6	6	0	15	1	3	0	24	0	1	0	1.4	.960	OF-18
1993		3	.500	1.000	2	1	1	0	0	0.0	0	1	1	1	0	1	0	0	0	0	0	0.0	.000	OF-1
2 yrs.		24	.259	.345	58	15	2	0	1	1.7	6	7	1	16	1	4	0	24	0	1	0	1.3	.960	OF-19

Tim Hosley

HOSLEY, TIMOTHY KENNETH BR TR 5′11″ 185 lbs.
B. May 10, 1947, Spartanburg, S. C.

Year	Team	Games	BA	SA	AB	H	2B	3B	HR	HR%	R	RBI	BB	SO	SB	Pinch Hit AB	Pinch Hit H	PO	A	E	DP	TC/G	FA	G by Pos
1970	**DET A**	7	.167	.417	12	2	0	0	1	8.3	1	2	0	6	0	4	1	22	3	0	0	6.3	1.000	C-4
1971		7	.188	.563	16	3	0	0	2	12.5	2	6	0	1	0	4	0	26	0	0	0	5.2	1.000	C-4, 1B-1
1973	**OAK A**	13	.214	.214	14	3	0	0	0	0.0	3	2	2	3	0	4	1	19	1	1	0	1.8	.952	C-12
1974		11	.286	.286	7	2	0	0	0	0.0	3	1	1	2	0	4	1	13	1	0	0	1.6	1.000	C-8, 1B-1
1975	**CHI N**	62	.255	.433	141	36	7	0	6	4.3	22	20	27	25	1	10	2	254	16	9	3	5.3	.968	C-53

Tim Hosley *continued*

Year	Team	Games	BA	SA	AB	H	2B	3B	HR	HR%	R	RBI	BB	SO	SB	Pinch Hit AB	Pinch Hit H	PO	A	E	DP	TC/G	FA	G by Pos
1976	2 teams CHI N (1G –.000) OAK A (37G –.164)																							
"	total	38	.161	.250	56	9	2	0	1	1.8	4	4	8	12	0	12	2	79	13	3	0	2.6	.968	C-37
1977	OAK A	39	.192	.231	78	15	0	0	1	1.3	5	10	16	13	0	5	1	81	13	5	0	2.9	.949	C-19, DH-12, 1B-3
1978		13	.304	.391	23	7	2	0	0	0.0	1	3	1	6	0	7	2	22	3	1	0	8.7	.962	C-2, DH-1
1981		18	.095	.238	21	2	0	0	1	4.8	2	5	2	5	0	14	1	3	0	1	0	0.8	.750	DH-4, 1B-1
9 yrs.		208	.215	.342	368	79	11	0	12	3.3	43	53	57	73	1	64	11	519	50	20	3	3.6	.966	C-139, DH-17, 1B-6

Chuck Hostetler

HOSTETLER, CHARLES CLOYD BL TR 6′ 175 lbs.
B. Sept. 22, 1903, McClellandtown, Pa. D. Feb. 18, 1971, Fort Collins, Colo.

Year	Team	Games	BA	SA	AB	H	2B	3B	HR	HR%	R	RBI	BB	SO	SB	Pinch Hit AB	Pinch Hit H	PO	A	E	DP	TC/G	FA	G by Pos
1944	DET A	90	.298	.347	265	79	9	2	0	0.0	42	20	21	31	4	19	4	129	5	2	1	2.1	.985	OF-65
1945		42	.159	.227	44	7	3	0	0	0.0	3	2	7	8	0	30	6	8	0	1	0	1.1	.889	OF-8
2 yrs.		132	.278	.330	309	86	12	2	0	0.0	45	22	28	39	4	49	10	137	5	3	1	2.0	.979	OF-73
WORLD SERIES																								
1945	DET A	3	.000	.000	3	0	0	0	0	0.0	0	0	0	0	0	3	0	0	0	0	0	0.0	—	

Dave Hostetler

HOSTETLER, DAVID ALAN BR TR 6′ 4″ 215 lbs.
B. Mar. 27, 1956, Pasadena, Calif.

Year	Team	Games	BA	SA	AB	H	2B	3B	HR	HR%	R	RBI	BB	SO	SB	Pinch Hit AB	Pinch Hit H	PO	A	E	DP	TC/G	FA	G by Pos
1981	MON N	5	.500	1.000	6	3	0	0	1	16.7	1	1	0	2	0	3	0	4	0	0	2	2.0	1.000	1B-2
1982	TEX A	113	.232	.433	418	97	12	3	22	5.3	53	67	42	113	2	1	0	1099	48	12	102	10.3	.990	1B-109, DH-3
1983		94	.220	.372	304	67	9	2	11	3.6	31	46	42	103	0	8	1	11	0	0	0	0.1	1.000	DH-88, 1B-2
1984		37	.220	.378	82	18	2	1	3	3.7	7	10	13	27	0	9	2	90	8	0	9	3.6	1.000	1B-14, DH-13
1988	PIT N	6	.250	.250	8	2	0	0	0	0.0	0	0	0	3	0	4	1	15	2	1	0	3.6	.944	1B-4, C-1
5 yrs.		255	.229	.407	818	187	23	6	37	4.5	92	124	97	248	2	25	4	1219	58	13	113	5.5	.990	1B-131, DH-104, C-1

Pete Hotaling

HOTALING, PETER JAMES (Monkey) BR TR 5′ 8″ 166 lbs.
B. Dec. 16, 1856, Mohawk, N. Y. D. July 3, 1928, Cleveland, Ohio.

Year	Team	Games	BA	SA	AB	H	2B	3B	HR	HR%	R	RBI	BB	SO	SB	Pinch Hit AB	Pinch Hit H	PO	A	E	DP	TC/G	FA	G by Pos
1879	CIN N	81	.279	.390	369	103	20	9	1	0.3	64	27	12	17		0	0	158	52	37	8	2.9	.850	OF-69, C-8, 2B-6, 3B-3
1880	CLE N	78	.240	.342	325	78	17	8	0	0.0	40	41	10	30		0	0	120	15	16	5	1.9	.894	OF-78, C-2
1881	WOR N	77	.309	.385	317	98	15	3	1	0.3	51	35	18	12		0	0	153	28	31	2	2.8	.854	OF-74, C-3
1882	BOS N	84	.259	.328	378	98	16	5	0	0.0	64	28	16	21		0	0	150	16	26	5	2.3	.865	OF-84
1883	CLE N	100	.259	.345	417	108	20	8	0	0.0	54		12	31		0	0	181	23	42	5	2.5	.829	OF-100
1884		102	.243	.333	408	99	16	6	3	0.7	69	27	28	50		0	0	174	23	35	5	2.3	.849	OF-102, 2B-1
1885	BKN AA	94	.257	.316	370	95	9	5	1	0.3	73		49			0	0	159	17	21	3	2.1	.893	OF-94
1887	CLE AA	126	.299	.424	505	151	28	13	3	0.6	108		53		43	0	0	267	23	31	5	2.5	.903	OF-126
1888		98	.251	.298	403	101	7	6	0	0.0	67	55	26		35	0	0	170	10	25	7	2.1	.878	OF-98
9 yrs.		840	.267	.353	3492	931	148	63	9	0.3	590	213	224	161	78	0	0	1532	207	264	45	2.4	.868	OF-825, C-13, 2B-7, 3B-3

Ken Hottman

HOTTMAN, KENNETH ROGER BR TR 5′11″ 190 lbs.
B. May 7, 1948, Stockton, Calif.

Year	Team	Games	BA	SA	AB	H	2B	3B	HR	HR%	R	RBI	BB	SO	SB	Pinch Hit AB	Pinch Hit H	PO	A	E	DP	TC/G	FA	G by Pos
1971	CHI A	6	.125	.125	16	2	0	0	0	0.0	1	0	1	2	0	1	0	5	0	0	0	1.0	1.000	OF-5

Sadie Houck

HOUCK, SARGENT PERRY BR TR 5′ 7″ 151 lbs.
B. Mar. 1856, Washington, D. C. D. May 26, 1919, Washington, D. C.

Year	Team	Games	BA	SA	AB	H	2B	3B	HR	HR%	R	RBI	BB	SO	SB	Pinch Hit AB	Pinch Hit H	PO	A	E	DP	TC/G	FA	G by Pos
1879	BOS N	80	.267	.402	356	95	24	9	2	0.6	69	49	4	11		0	0	109	103	46	11	3.2	.822	OF-47, SS-33
1880	2 teams BOS N (12G –.149) PRO N (49G –.201)																							
"	total	61	.190	.294	231	44	7	7	1	0.4	29	24	3	12		0	0	107	11	20	0	2.3	.855	OF-61
1881	DET N	75	.279	.380	308	86	16	6	1	0.3	43	36	6	6		0	0	88	241	50	40	5.1	.868	SS-75
1883		101	.252	.353	416	105	18	12	0	0.0	52		9	18		0	0	162	328	85	36	5.7	.852	SS-101
1884	PHI AA	108	.297	.396	472	140	19	14	0	0.0	93		7			0	0	122	379	60	30	5.1	.893	SS-108, 2B-1
1885		93	.255	.327	388	99	10	9	0	0.0	74		10			0	0	121	362	77	34	6.0	.863	SS-93
1886	2 teams BAL AA (61G –.192) WAS N (52G –.215)																							
"	total	113	.202	.231	455	92	11	1	0	0.0	43	14	6	28		0	0	150	331	83	16	5.0	.853	SS-106, 2B-6, OF-1
1887	NY AA	10	.152	.182	33	5	1	0	0	0.0	3		3		2	0	0	10	42	11	4	5.7	.825	SS-10, 2B-1
8 yrs.		641	.250	.338	2659	666	106	58	4	0.2	406	123	48	75	2	0	0	869	1797	432	171	4.8	.861	SS-526, OF-109, 2B-8

Ralph Houk

HOUK, RALPH GEORGE (Major) BR TR 5′11″ 193 lbs.
B. Aug. 9, 1919, Lawrence, Kans.
Manager 1961–63, 1966–78, 1981–84.

Year	Team	Games	BA	SA	AB	H	2B	3B	HR	HR%	R	RBI	BB	SO	SB	Pinch Hit AB	Pinch Hit H	PO	A	E	DP	TC/G	FA	G by Pos
1947	NY A	41	.272	.326	92	25	3	1	0	0.0	7	12	11	5	0	0	0	138	13	2	0	3.7	.987	C-41
1948		14	.276	.345	29	8	2	0	0	0.0	3	3	0	0	0	0	0	41	5	0	1	3.3	1.000	C-14
1949		5	.571	.571	7	4	0	0	0	0.0	0	1	0	1	0	0	0	8	0	1	0	1.8	.889	C-5
1950		10	.111	.222	9	1	1	0	0	0.0	0	1	0	2	0	1	1	12	1	1	0	1.6	.929	C-9
1951		3	.200	.200	5	1	0	0	0	0.0	0	2	0	1	0	0	0	2	1	0	0	1.0	1.000	C-3
1952		9	.333	.333	6	2	0	0	0	0.0	0	0	1	0	0	0	0	10	1	1	1	1.3	.917	C-9
1953		8	.222	.222	9	2	0	0	0	0.0	2	1	0	1	0	0	0	10	0	0	0	1.3	1.000	C-8
1954		1	.000	.000	1	0	0	0	0	0.0	0	0	0	0	0	1	0	0	0	0	0	0.0	—	
8 yrs.		91	.272	.323	158	43	6	1	0	0.0	12	20	12	10	0	2	1	221	21	5	2	2.8	.980	C-89
WORLD SERIES																								
1947	NY A	1	1.000	1.000	1	1	0	0	0	0.0	0	0	0	0	0	1	1	0	0	0	0	0.0	—	
1952		1	.000	.000	1	0	0	0	0	0.0	0	0	0	0	0	1	0	0	0	0	0	0.0	—	
2 yrs.		2	.500	.500	2	1	0	0	0	0.0	0	0	0	0	0	2	1							

Frank House

HOUSE, HENRY FRANKLIN (Pig) BL TR 6′ 1½″ 190 lbs.
B. Feb. 18, 1930, Bessemer, Ala.

Year	Team	Games	BA	SA	AB	H	2B	3B	HR	HR%	R	RBI	BB	SO	SB	Pinch Hit AB	Pinch Hit H	PO	A	E	DP	TC/G	FA	G by Pos
1950	DET A	5	.400	.600	5	2	1	0	0	0.0	1	0	0	1	0	1	0	4	1	0	0	1.0	1.000	C-5
1951		18	.220	.341	41	9	2	0	1	2.4	3	4	6	2	1	0	0	56	11	3	1	3.9	.957	C-18
1954		114	.250	.366	352	88	12	1	9	2.6	35	38	31	34	2	9	1	434	56	4	7	4.6	.992	C-107
1955		102	.259	.436	328	85	11	1	15	4.6	37	53	22	25	0	12	3	423	35	6	5	5.0	.987	C-93
1956		94	.240	.364	321	77	6	2	10	3.1	44	44	21	19	1	9	3	450	33	7	8	5.6	.986	C-88
1957		106	.259	.345	348	90	9	0	7	2.0	31	36	35	26	1	7	2	535	54	2	5	6.1	.997	C-97
1958	KC A	76	.252	.371	202	51	6	3	4	2.0	16	24	12	13	1	19	7	236	22	2	4	4.7	.992	C-55
1959		98	.236	.303	347	82	14	3	1	0.3	32	30	20	23	0	4	1	447	43	9	7	5.3	.982	C-95

Frank House *continued*

Year	Team	Lg	Games	BA	SA	AB	H	2B	3B	HR	HR%	R	RBI	BB	SO	SB	Pinch Hit AB	Pinch Hit H	PO	A	E	DP	TC/G	FA	G by Pos
1960	CIN	N	23	.179	.250	28	5	2	0	0	0.0	0	3	0	2	0	17	3	21	2	0	1	2.9	1.000	C-8
1961	DET	A	17	.227	.364	22	5	1	1	0	0.0	3	3	4	2	0	3	0	36	1	1	0	2.7	.974	C-14
10 yrs.			653	.248	.362	1994	494	64	11	47	2.4	202	235	151	147	6	81	20	2642	258	34	38	5.1	.988	C-580

Charlie Householder

HOUSEHOLDER, CHARLES F. BR TR 5′ 7″ 150 lbs.
B. 1856, Harrisburg, Pa. Deceased.

Year	Team	Lg	Games	BA	SA	AB	H	2B	3B	HR	HR%	R	RBI	BB	SO	SB	Pinch Hit AB	Pinch Hit H	PO	A	E	DP	TC/G	FA	G by Pos
1884	2 teams		CHI U (66G –.234)	PIT U (17G –.258)																					
″	total		83	.239	.319	310	74	12	5	1	0.3	32		12			0	0	99	66	37	7	2.3	.817	3B-41, OF-40, SS-3, P-2

Charlie Householder

HOUSEHOLDER, CHARLES W. BL TL 5′11″ 158 lbs.
B. 1856, Harrisburg, Pa. D. Dec. 26, 1908, Harrisburg, Pa.

Year	Team	Lg	Games	BA	SA	AB	H	2B	3B	HR	HR%	R	RBI	BB	SO	SB	Pinch Hit AB	Pinch Hit H	PO	A	E	DP	TC/G	FA	G by Pos
1882	BAL	AA	74	.254	.342	307	78	10	7	1	0.3	42		4			0	0	762	20	23	30	10.5	.971	1B-74, C-3
1884	BKN	AA	76	.242	.352	273	66	15	3	3	1.1	28		12			0	0	580	63	43	23	8.8	.937	1B-40, C-31, OF-6, 2B-1
2 yrs.			150	.248	.347	580	144	25	10	4	0.7	70		16			0	0	1342	83	66	53	9.6	.956	1B-114, C-34, OF-6, 2B-1

Ed Householder

HOUSEHOLDER, EDWARD H. TL
B. Oct. 12, 1869, Pittsburgh, Pa. D. July 3, 1924, Los Angeles, Calif.

Year	Team	Lg	Games	BA	SA	AB	H	2B	3B	HR	HR%	R	RBI	BB	SO	SB	Pinch Hit AB	Pinch Hit H	PO	A	E	DP	TC/G	FA	G by Pos
1903	BKN	N	12	.209	.209	43	9	0	0	0	0.0	5	9	2		3	0	0	28	1	1	1	2.5	.967	OF-12

Paul Householder

HOUSEHOLDER, PAUL WESLEY BB TR 6′ 180 lbs.
B. Sept. 4, 1958, Columbus, Ohio.

Year	Team	Lg	Games	BA	SA	AB	H	2B	3B	HR	HR%	R	RBI	BB	SO	SB	Pinch Hit AB	Pinch Hit H	PO	A	E	DP	TC/G	FA	G by Pos
1980	CIN	N	20	.244	.311	45	11	1	1	0	0.0	3	7	1	13	1	7	2	16	2	0	0	1.3	1.000	OF-14
1981			23	.275	.420	69	19	4	0	2	2.9	12	9	10	16	3	4	1	32	1	0	0	1.7	1.000	OF-19
1982			138	.211	.326	417	88	11	5	9	2.2	40	34	30	77	17	10	1	220	14	2	4	1.8	.992	OF-131
1983			123	.255	.387	380	97	24	4	6	1.6	40	43	44	60	12	17	3	221	5	2	0	2.0	.991	OF-112
1984	2 teams		CIN N (14G –.083)	STL N (13G –.143)																					
″	total		27	.115	.154	26	3	1	0	0	0.0	4	0	3	6	1	10	1	9	1	0	0	0.6	1.000	OF-18
1985	MIL	A	95	.258	.418	299	77	15	0	11	3.7	41	34	27	60	1	4	1	202	5	3	0	2.2	.986	OF-91, DH-3
1986			26	.218	.321	78	17	3	1	1	1.3	4	16	7	16	1	2	0	35	1	0	1	1.4	1.000	OF-22, DH-3
1987	HOU	N	14	.083	.167	12	1	1	0	0	0.0	2	1	4	2	0	7	1	3	0	0	0	0.4	1.000	OF-7
8 yrs.			466	.236	.363	1326	313	60	11	29	2.2	146	144	126	250	36	61	10	738	29	7	5	1.8	.991	OF-414, DH-6

John Houseman

HOUSEMAN, JOHN FRANKLIN 160 lbs.
B. Jan. 10, 1870, Holland D. Nov. 4, 1922, Chicago, Ill.

Year	Team	Lg	Games	BA	SA	AB	H	2B	3B	HR	HR%	R	RBI	BB	SO	SB	Pinch Hit AB	Pinch Hit H	PO	A	E	DP	TC/G	FA	G by Pos
1894	CHI	N	4	.400	.733	15	6	3	1	0	0.0	5	4	5	3	2	0	0	8	16	2	4	6.5	.923	SS-3, 2B-1
1897	STL	N	80	.245	.309	278	68	6	6	0	0.0	34	21	28		16	2	1	174	149	27	10	4.3	.923	2B-41, OF-33, SS-5, 3B-3
2 yrs.			84	.253	.331	293	74	9	7	0	0.0	39	25	33	3	18	2	1	182	165	29	14	4.4	.923	2B-42, OF-33, SS-8, 3B-3

Ben Houser

HOUSER, BENJAMIN FRANKLIN BL TL 6′ 1″ 185 lbs.
B. Nov. 30, 1883, Shenandoah, Pa. D. Jan. 15, 1952, Augusta, Me.

Year	Team	Lg	Games	BA	SA	AB	H	2B	3B	HR	HR%	R	RBI	BB	SO	SB	Pinch Hit AB	Pinch Hit H	PO	A	E	DP	TC/G	FA	G by Pos
1910	PHI	A	34	.188	.290	69	13	3	2	0	0.0	9	7	7		0	8	2	160	7	0	10	6.4	1.000	1B-26
1911	BOS	N	20	.254	.310	71	18	1	0	1	1.4	11	9	8	6	2	0	0	160	11	2	13	8.6	.988	1B-20
1912			83	.286	.428	332	95	17	3	8	2.4	38	52	22	29	1	24	9	759	37	11	48	9.7	.986	1B-83
3 yrs.			137	.267	.390	472	126	21	5	9	1.9	58	68	37	35	3	32	11	1079	55	13	71	8.9	.989	1B-129

Wayne Housie

HOUSIE, WAYNE TYRONE BB TR 5′ 9″ 165 lbs.
B. May 20, 1965, Hampton, Va.

Year	Team	Lg	Games	BA	SA	AB	H	2B	3B	HR	HR%	R	RBI	BB	SO	SB	Pinch Hit AB	Pinch Hit H	PO	A	E	DP	TC/G	FA	G by Pos
1991	BOS	A	11	.250	.375	8	2	1	0	0	0.0	2	0	1	3	1	1	1	3	0	0	0	0.5	1.000	OF-4, DH-2
1993	NY	N	18	.188	.250	16	3	1	0	0	0.0	2	1	1	1	0	14	3	0	0	0	0	0.0	.000	OF-2
2 yrs.			29	.208	.292	24	5	2	0	0	0.0	4	1	2	4	1	15	4	3	0	0	0	0.4	1.000	OF-6, DH-2

Fred Houtz

HOUTZ, FRED FRITZ (Lefty) BL TL 5′10″ 170 lbs.
B. Sept. 4, 1875, Connersville, Ind. D. Feb. 15, 1959, Wapakoneta, Ohio.

Year	Team	Lg	Games	BA	SA	AB	H	2B	3B	HR	HR%	R	RBI	BB	SO	SB	Pinch Hit AB	Pinch Hit H	PO	A	E	DP	TC/G	FA	G by Pos
1899	CIN	N	5	.235	.353	17	4	0	1	0	0.0	1	0	4		1	0	0	17	4	0	2	4.2	1.000	OF-5

Steve Hovley

HOVLEY, STEPHEN EUGENE BL TL 5′10″ 188 lbs.
B. Dec. 18, 1944, Ventura, Calif.

Year	Team	Lg	Games	BA	SA	AB	H	2B	3B	HR	HR%	R	RBI	BB	SO	SB	Pinch Hit AB	Pinch Hit H	PO	A	E	DP	TC/G	FA	G by Pos
1969	SEA	A	91	.277	.365	329	91	14	3	3	0.9	41	20	30	34	10	7	0	175	8	2	3	2.2	.989	OF-84
1970	2 teams		MIL A (40G –.281)	OAK A (72G –.190)																					
″	total		112	.243	.285	235	57	10	0	0	0.0	25	17	22	22	8	31	8	126	2	3	1	1.6	.977	OF-80
1971	OAK	A	24	.111	.185	27	3	2	0	0	0.0	3	3	7	9	2	10	2	15	1	0	0	1.5	1.000	OF-11
1972	KC	A	105	.270	.352	196	53	5	1	3	1.5	24	24	24	29	3	**37**	9	103	6	2	0	1.6	.982	OF-68
1973			104	.254	.323	232	59	8	1	2	0.9	29	24	33	34	6	13	2	114	4	3	1	1.3	.975	OF-79, DH-15
5 yrs.			436	.258	.330	1019	263	39	5	8	0.8	122	88	116	128	29	98	21	533	21	10	5	1.7	.982	OF-322, DH-15

Chris Howard

HOWARD, CHRISTOPHER HUGH BR TR 6′ 2″ 200 lbs.
B. Feb. 27, 1966, San Diego, Calif.

Year	Team	Lg	Games	BA	SA	AB	H	2B	3B	HR	HR%	R	RBI	BB	SO	SB	Pinch Hit AB	Pinch Hit H	PO	A	E	DP	TC/G	FA	G by Pos
1991	SEA	A	9	.167	.333	6	1	1	0	0	0.0	1	0	1	2	0	0	0	13	2	0	1	1.7	1.000	C-9
1993			4	.000	.000	1	0	0	0	0	0.0	0	0	0	0	0	0	0	5	0	0	0	1.3	1.000	C-4
1994			9	.200	.240	25	5	1	0	0	0.0	2	2	1	6	0	0	0	44	3	0	0	5.2	1.000	C-9
3 yrs.			22	.188	.250	32	6	2	0	0	0.0	3	2	2	8	0	0	0	62	5	0	1	3.0	1.000	C-22

Dave Howard

HOWARD, DAVID AUSTIN (Del) BR TR 5′11″ 165 lbs.
B. May 1, 1889, Washington, D. C. D. Jan. 26, 1956, Dallas, Tex.

Year	Team	Lg	Games	BA	SA	AB	H	2B	3B	HR	HR%	R	RBI	BB	SO	SB	Pinch Hit AB	Pinch Hit H	PO	A	E	DP	TC/G	FA	G by Pos
1912	WAS	A	1	—	—	0	0	0	0	0	—	1	0	0	0	0	0	0	0	0	0	0	0.0	—	
1915	BKN	F	24	.222	.250	36	8	1	0	0	0.0	5	1	1		0	1	1	20	31	4	0	3.4	.927	2B-12, OF-2, 3B-1, SS-1
2 yrs.			25	.222	.250	36	8	1	0	0	0.0	6	1	1	0	0	1	1	20	31	4	0	3.4	.927	2B-12, OF-2, 3B-1, SS-1

Dave Howard

HOWARD, DAVID WAYNE BB TR 6′ 165 lbs.
Son of Bruce Howard.
B. Feb. 26, 1967, Sarasota, Fla.

Year	Team	Lg	Games	BA	SA	AB	H	2B	3B	HR	HR%	R	RBI	BB	SO	SB	Pinch Hit AB	Pinch Hit H	PO	A	E	DP	TC/G	FA	G by Pos
1991	KC	A	94	.216	.258	236	51	7	0	1	0.4	20	17	16	45	3	1	0	129	248	12	40	4.2	.969	SS-63, 2B-26, OF-1, DH-1, 3B-1
1992			74	.224	.283	219	49	6	2	1	0.5	19	18	15	43	3	0	0	124	204	8	52	4.4	.976	SS-74, OF-2
1993			15	.333	.417	24	8	0	1	0	0.0	5	2	2	5	1	0	0	17	28	3	2	3.7	.938	2B-7, SS-3, 3B-2, OF-1

Dave Howard *continued*

Year	Team	Games	BA	SA	AB	H	2B	3B	HR	HR%	R	RBI	BB	SO	SB	Pinch Hit AB	Pinch Hit H	PO	A	E	DP	TC/G	FA	G by Pos
1994		46	.229	.313	83	19	4	0	1	1.2	9	13	11	23	3	0	0	27	79	1	7	2.3	.991	3B-25, SS-15, 2B-3, DH-2, OF-1, P-1
1995		95	.243	.325	255	62	13	4	0	0.0	23	19	24	41	6	4	1	168	195	6	44	3.5	.984	2B-41, SS-33, OF-30, 1B-1, DH-1
5 yrs.		324	.231	.296	817	189	30	7	3	0.4	76	69	68	157	16	5	1	465	754	30	145	3.7	.976	SS-188, 2B-77, OF-35, 3B-28, DH-4, 1B-1, P-1

Del Howard

HOWARD, GEORGE ELMER BL TR 6′ 180 lbs.
Brother of Ivon Howard.
B. Dec. 24, 1877, Kenney, Ill. D. Dec. 24, 1956, Seattle, Wash.

Year	Team	Games	BA	SA	AB	H	2B	3B	HR	HR%	R	RBI	BB	SO	SB	Pinch Hit AB	Pinch Hit H	PO	A	E	DP	TC/G	FA	G by Pos
1905	**PIT N**	123	.292	.370	435	127	18	5	2	0.5	56	63	27		19	3	0	947	53	23	58	8.6	.978	1B-90, OF-28, P-1
1906	**BOS N**	147	.261	.330	545	142	19	8	1	0.2	46	54	26		17	0	0	280	172	41	16	3.3	.917	OF-87, 2B-45, SS-14, 1B-2
1907	**2 teams**	**BOS N** (50G –.273) **CHI N** (51G –.230)																						
″	**total**	101	.254	.304	335	85	6	4	1	0.3	30	26	17		14	11	3	373	35	13	22	4.7	.969	OF-53, 1B-33, 2B-3
1908	**CHI N**	96	.279	.330	315	88	7	3	1	0.3	42	26	23		11	6	2	155	12	6	1	2.0	.965	OF-81, 1B-5
1909		69	.197	.251	203	40	4	2	1	0.5	25	24	18		6	8	0	593	32	13	29	11.2	.980	1B-57
5 yrs.		536	.263	.326	1833	482	54	22	6	0.3	199	193	111		67	28	5	2348	304	96	126	5.5	.965	OF-249, 1B-187, 2B-48, SS-14, P-1
WORLD SERIES																								
1907	**CHI N**	2	.200	.200	5	1	0	0	0	0.0	0	0	0	2	1	1	0	10	1	0	0	11.0	1.000	1B-1
1908		1	.000	.000	1	0	0	0	0	0.0	0	0	0	0	0	1	0	0	0	0	0	0.0	—	
2 yrs.		3	.167	.167	6	1	0	0	0	0.0	0	0	0	2	1	2	0	10	1	0	0	11.0	1.000	1B-1

Doug Howard

HOWARD, DOUGLAS LYNN BR TR 6′ 3″ 185 lbs.
B. Feb. 6, 1948, Salt Lake City, Utah.

Year	Team	Games	BA	SA	AB	H	2B	3B	HR	HR%	R	RBI	BB	SO	SB	Pinch Hit AB	Pinch Hit H	PO	A	E	DP	TC/G	FA	G by Pos
1972	**CAL A**	11	.263	.289	38	10	1	0	0	0.0	4	2	1	3	0	1	0	18	3	1	3	2.2	.955	OF-8, 3B-1, 1B-1
1973		8	.095	.095	21	2	0	0	0	0.0	2	1	1	6	0	2	0	9	1	0	0	1.3	1.000	OF-6, 3B-1, 1B-1
1974		22	.231	.282	39	9	0	1	0	0.0	5	5	2	1	1	9	3	29	3	0	1	2.0	1.000	OF-8, 1B-5, DH-3
1975	**STL N**	17	.207	.310	29	6	0	0	1	3.4	1	1	0	7	0	10	3	60	6	0	5	9.4	1.000	1B-7
1976	**CLE A**	39	.211	.256	90	19	4	0	0	0.0	7	13	3	13	1	4	1	211	20	2	20	6.1	.991	1B-32, DH-4, OF-2
5 yrs.		97	.212	.258	217	46	5	1	1	0.5	19	22	7	30	2	26	7	327	33	3	29	4.6	.992	1B-46, OF-24, DH-7, 3B-2

Elston Howard

HOWARD, ELSTON GENE (Ellie) BR TR 6′ 2″ 196 lbs.
B. Feb. 23, 1929, St. Louis, Mo. D. Dec. 14, 1980, New York, N. Y.

Year	Team	Games	BA	SA	AB	H	2B	3B	HR	HR%	R	RBI	BB	SO	SB	Pinch Hit AB	Pinch Hit H	PO	A	E	DP	TC/G	FA	G by Pos
1955	**NY A**	97	.290	.477	279	81	8	7	10	3.6	33	43	20	36	0	21	4	147	13	3	5	1.9	.982	OF-75, C-9
1956		98	.262	.362	290	76	8	3	5	1.7	35	34	21	30	0	12	5	205	16	1	5	2.4	.995	OF-65, C-26
1957		110	.253	.379	356	90	13	4	8	2.2	33	44	16	43	2	9	3	266	19	6	5	2.8	.979	OF-71, C-32, 1B-2
1958		103	.314	.479	376	118	19	5	11	2.9	45	66	22	60	1	9	5	447	29	2	13	5.0	.996	C-67, OF-24, 1B-5
1959		125	.273	.476	443	121	24	6	18	4.1	59	73	20	57	0	11	3	712	49	10	41	6.4	.987	1B-50, C-43, OF-28
1960		107	.245	.353	323	79	11	3	6	1.9	29	39	28	43	3	14	5	410	40	6	9	5.0	.987	C-91, OF-1
1961		129	.348	.549	446	155	17	5	21	4.7	64	77	28	65	0	14	4	725	47	6	16	6.5	.992	C-111, 1B-9
1962		136	.279	.474	494	138	23	5	21	4.3	63	91	31	76	1	7	1	713	44	4	12	5.9	.995	C-129
1963		135	.287	.528	487	140	21	6	28	5.7	75	85	35	68	0	5	1	786	51	5	8	6.4	.994	C-132
1964		150	.313	.455	550	172	27	3	15	2.7	63	84	48	73	1	6	1	939	67	2	9	6.9	.998	C-146
1965		110	.233	.345	391	91	15	1	9	2.3	38	45	24	65	0	12	2	644	44	6	8	6.9	.991	C-95, 1B-5, OF-1
1966		126	.256	.356	410	105	19	2	6	1.5	38	35	37	65	0	12	2	665	52	9	17	6.4	.988	C-100, 1B-13
1967	**2 teams**	**NY A** (66G –.196) **BOS A** (42G –.147)																						
″	**total**	108	.178	.244	315	56	9	0	4	1.3	22	28	21	60	0	19	2	536	40	6	9	6.5	.990	C-89, 1B-1
1968	**BOS A**	71	.241	.335	203	49	4	0	5	2.5	22	18	22	45	1	3	0	377	30	2	3	6.0	.995	C-68
14 yrs.		1605	.274	.427	5363	1471	218	50	167	3.1	619	762	373	786	9	154	38	7572	541	68	160	5.5	.992	C-1138, OF-265, 1B-85
WORLD SERIES																								
1955	**NY A**	7	.192	.308	26	5	0	0	1	3.8	3	3	1	8	0	0	0	11	1	0	0	1.7	1.000	OF-7
1956		1	.400	1.200	5	2	1	0	1	20.0	1	1	0	0	0	0	0	2	0	0	0	2.0	1.000	OF-1
1957		6	.273	.545	11	3	0	0	1	9.1	2	3	1	3	0	3	1	22	1	1	1	8.0	.958	1B-3
1958		6	.222	.222	18	4	0	0	0	0.0	4	2	1	4	1	1	0	14	2	0	2	2.7	1.000	OF-6
1960		5	.462	.923	13	6	1	1	1	7.7	4	4	1	4	0	1	1	11	0	0	0	2.8	1.000	C-4
1961		5	.250	.550	20	5	3	0	1	5.0	5	1	2	3	0	0	0	31	0	0	0	6.2	1.000	C-5
1962		6	.143	.190	21	3	1	0	0	0.0	1	1	1	4	0	0	0	37	1	0	1	6.3	1.000	C-6
1963		4	.333	.333	15	5	0	0	0	0.0	0	1	0	3	0	0	0	30	2	0	1	8.0	1.000	C-4
1964		7	.292	.333	24	7	1	0	0	0.0	5	2	4	6	0	0	0	40	2	1	0	6.1	.977	C-7
1967	**BOS A**	7	.111	.111	18	2	0	0	0	0.0	0	1	1	2	0	0	0	23	1	0	0	3.4	1.000	C-7
10 yrs.		54	.246	.386	171	42	7	1	5	2.9	25	19	12	37	1	5	2	221	10	2	5	4.7	.991	C-33, OF-14, 1B-3
		3rd			**8th**	**10th**					**7th**			**2nd**										

Frank Howard

HOWARD, FRANK OLIVER (Hondo, The Capitol Punisher) BR TR 6′ 7″ 255 lbs.
B. Aug. 8, 1936, Columbus, Ohio.
Manager 1981, 1983.

Year	Team	Games	BA	SA	AB	H	2B	3B	HR	HR%	R	RBI	BB	SO	SB	Pinch Hit AB	Pinch Hit H	PO	A	E	DP	TC/G	FA	G by Pos
1958	**LA N**	8	.241	.379	29	7	1	0	1	3.4	3	2	1	11	0	0	0	12	1	0	0	1.6	1.000	OF-8
1959		9	.143	.381	21	3	0	1	1	4.8	2	6	2	9	0	4	1	10	0	0	0	1.7	1.000	OF-6
1960		117	.268	.464	448	120	15	2	23	5.1	55	77	32	108	0	2	0	196	11	4	3	1.8	.981	OF-115, 1B-4
1961		99	.296	.517	267	79	10	2	15	5.6	36	45	21	50	0	19	7	122	10	8	2	1.9	.943	OF-65, 1B-7
1962		141	.296	.560	493	146	25	6	31	6.3	80	119	39	108	1	11	2	187	19	6	4	1.6	.972	OF-131
1963		123	.273	.518	417	114	16	1	28	6.7	58	64	33	116	1	15	3	190	4	8	0	1.8	.960	OF-111
1964		134	.226	.432	433	98	13	2	24	5.5	60	69	51	113	1	10	0	183	2	4	0	1.5	.979	OF-122
1965	**WAS A**	149	.289	.477	516	149	22	6	21	4.1	53	84	55	112	0	10	1	204	5	4	0	1.5	.981	OF-138
1966		146	.278	.442	493	137	19	4	18	3.7	52	71	53	104	1	9	1	216	5	4	1	1.7	.982	OF-135
1967		149	.256	.511	519	133	20	2	36	6.9	71	89	60	**155**	0	5	0	225	6	3	1	1.6	.987	OF-141, 1B-4
1968		158	.274	**.552**	598	164	28	3	**44**	**7.4**	79	106	54	141	0	1	1	576	52	19	39	4.0	.971	OF-107, 1B-55
1969		161	.296	.574	592	175	17	2	48	8.1	111	111	102	96	1	1	0	602	34	14	38	3.5	.978	OF-114, 1B-70
1970		161	.283	.546	566	160	15	1	**44**	7.8	90	**126**	**132**	125	1	0	0	601	31	11	41	3.8	.983	OF-120, 1B-48

Frank Howard *continued*

Year	Team	Games	BA	SA	AB	H	2B	3B	HR	HR%	R	RBI	BB	SO	SB	Pinch Hit AB	Pinch Hit H	PO	A	E	DP	TC/G	FA	G by Pos
1971		153	.279	.474	549	153	25	2	26	4.7	60	83	77	121	1	5	0	555	65	5	40	3.7	.992	OF-100, 1B-68
1972	**2 teams** **TEX A** (95G –.244) **DET A** (14G –.242)																							
"	**total**	109	.244	.369	320	78	10	0	10	3.1	29	38	46	63	1	17	3	521	32	13	44	5.8	.977	1B-76, OF-22
1973	**DET A**	85	.256	.463	227	58	9	1	12	5.3	26	29	24	28	0	7	1	12	0	1	0	0.2	.923	DH-76, 1B-2
16 yrs.		1902	.273	.499	6488	1774	245	35	382	5.9	865	1119	782	1460	8	116	20	4412	277	104	213	2.6	.978	OF-1435, 1B-334, DH-76
WORLD SERIES																								
1963	**LA N**	3	.300	.700	10	3	1	0	1	10.0	2	1	0	2	0	0	0	4	0	0	0	1.3	1.000	OF-3

Ivon Howard

HOWARD, IVON CHESTER BB TR 5′10″ 170 lbs.
Brother of Del Howard.
B. Oct. 12, 1882, Kenney, Ill. D. Mar. 30, 1967, Medford, Ore.

Year	Team	Games	BA	SA	AB	H	2B	3B	HR	HR%	R	RBI	BB	SO	SB	Pinch Hit AB	Pinch Hit H	PO	A	E	DP	TC/G	FA	G by Pos
1914	**STL A**	81	.244	.292	209	51	6	2	0	0.0	21	20	28	42	14	11	3	256	64	10	5	5.0	.970	3B-34, 1B-28, OF-3, SS-1
1915		113	.278	.361	324	90	10	7	1	0.3	43	43	43	48	29	17	3	488	90	12	33	6.4	.980	1B-48, 3B-23, OF-17, SS-2, 2B-2
1916	**CLE A**	81	.187	.272	246	46	11	5	0	0.0	20	23	30	34	9	6	0	167	228	11	20	5.6	.973	2B-65, 1B-7
1917		27	.103	.103	39	4	0	0	0	0.0	7	0	3	5	1	6	0	18	17	2	1	2.6	.946	3B-6, OF-4, 2B-4
4 yrs.		302	.233	.304	818	191	27	14	1	0.1	91	86	104	129	53	40	6	929	399	35	59	5.6	.974	1B-83, 2B-71, 3B-63, OF-24, SS-3

Larry Howard

HOWARD, LAWRENCE RAYFORD BR TR 6′ 3″ 200 lbs.
B. June 6, 1945, Columbus, Ohio.

Year	Team	Games	BA	SA	AB	H	2B	3B	HR	HR%	R	RBI	BB	SO	SB	Pinch Hit AB	Pinch Hit H	PO	A	E	DP	TC/G	FA	G by Pos
1970	**HOU N**	31	.307	.443	88	27	6	0	2	2.3	11	16	10	23	0	4	2	130	12	1	0	4.9	.993	C-26, 1B-2, OF-1
1971		24	.234	.375	64	15	3	0	2	3.1	6	14	3	17	0	5	1	106	12	1	2	5.4	.992	C-22
1972		54	.223	.306	157	35	7	0	2	1.3	16	13	17	30	0	2	0	323	15	7	2	6.4	.980	C-53, OF-1
1973	**2 teams** **HOU N** (20G –.167) **ATL N** (4G –.125)																							
"	**total**	24	.161	.214	56	9	3	0	0	0.0	3	4	7	15	0	2	0	87	8	1	0	4.4	.990	C-22
4 yrs.		133	.236	.337	365	86	19	0	6	1.6	36	47	37	85	0	13	3	646	47	10	4	5.5	.986	C-123, 1B-2, OF-2

Mike Howard

HOWARD, MICHAEL FREDERIC BB TR 6′ 2″ 185 lbs.
B. Apr. 2, 1958, Seattle, Wash.

Year	Team	Games	BA	SA	AB	H	2B	3B	HR	HR%	R	RBI	BB	SO	SB	Pinch Hit AB	Pinch Hit H	PO	A	E	DP	TC/G	FA	G by Pos
1981	**NY N**	14	.167	.208	24	4	1	0	0	0.0	4	3	4	6	2	0	0	18	2	1	0	1.5	.952	OF-14
1982		33	.179	.256	39	7	0	0	1	2.6	5	3	6	7	2	5	2	32	6	0	1	1.5	1.000	OF-22, 2B-3
1983		1	.333	.333	3	1	0	0	0	0.0	0	1	0	1	0	0	0	0	0	0	0	0.0	.000	OF-1
3 yrs.		48	.182	.242	66	12	1	0	1	1.5	9	7	10	14	4	5	2	50	8	1	1	1.5	.983	OF-37, 2B-3

Paul Howard

HOWARD, PAUL JOSEPH (Del) BR TR 5′ 8″ 170 lbs.
B. May 20, 1884, Boston, Mass. D. Aug. 29, 1968, Miami, Fla.

Year	Team	Games	BA	SA	AB	H	2B	3B	HR	HR%	R	RBI	BB	SO	SB	Pinch Hit AB	Pinch Hit H	PO	A	E	DP	TC/G	FA	G by Pos
1909	**BOS A**	6	.200	.267	15	3	1	0	0	0.0	2	2	3		0	0	0	2	1	0	0	0.5	1.000	OF-6

Steve Howard

HOWARD, STEVEN BERNARD BR TR 6′ 2″ 205 lbs.
B. Dec. 7, 1963, Oakland, Calif.

Year	Team	Games	BA	SA	AB	H	2B	3B	HR	HR%	R	RBI	BB	SO	SB	Pinch Hit AB	Pinch Hit H	PO	A	E	DP	TC/G	FA	G by Pos
1990	**OAK A**	21	.231	.308	52	12	4	0	0	0.0	5	1	4	17	0	3	1	14	0	1	0	0.7	.933	OF-14, DH-7

Thomas Howard

HOWARD, THOMAS SYLVESTER BB TR 6′ 2″ 200 lbs.
B. Dec. 11, 1964, Middletown, Ohio.

Year	Team	Games	BA	SA	AB	H	2B	3B	HR	HR%	R	RBI	BB	SO	SB	Pinch Hit AB	Pinch Hit H	PO	A	E	DP	TC/G	FA	G by Pos
1990	**SD N**	20	.273	.318	44	12	2	0	0	0.0	4	0	0	11	0	8	1	19	0	1	0	1.5	.950	OF-13
1991		106	.249	.356	281	70	12	3	4	1.4	30	22	24	57	10	26	3	182	4	1	1	2.2	.995	OF-86
1992	**2 teams** **SD N** (5G –.333) **CLE A** (117G –.277)																							
"	**total**	122	.277	.346	361	100	15	2	2	0.6	37	32	17	60	15	22	7	185	5	2	0	1.9	.990	OF-97, DH-2
1993	**2 teams** **CLE A** (74G –.236) **CIN N** (38G –.277)																							
"	**total**	112	.254	.386	319	81	15	3	7	2.2	48	36	24	63	10	29	6	154	7	3	2	1.8	.982	OF-84, DH-7
1994	**CIN N**	83	.264	.410	178	47	11	0	5	2.8	24	24	10	30	4	32	9	80	2	3	1	1.5	.965	OF-57
1995		113	.302	.402	281	85	15	2	3	1.1	42	26	20	37	17	36	13	127	2	2	0	1.6	.985	OF-82
6 yrs.		556	.270	.374	1464	395	70	10	21	1.4	185	140	95	258	56	153	39	747	20	12	4	1.8	.985	OF-419, DH-9
DIVISIONAL PLAYOFF SERIES																								
1995	**CIN N**	3	.100	.200	10	1	1	0	0	0.0	0	0	0	2	0	0	0	5	0	0	0	1.7	1.000	OF-3
LEAGUE CHAMPIONSHIP SERIES																								
1995	**CIN N**	4	.250	.375	8	2	1	0	0	0.0	0	1	2	0	0	2	1	2	0	0	0	0.7	1.000	OF-3

Wilbur Howard

HOWARD, WILBUR LEON BB TR 6′ 2″ 170 lbs.
B. Jan. 8, 1949, Lowell, N. C.

Year	Team	Games	BA	SA	AB	H	2B	3B	HR	HR%	R	RBI	BB	SO	SB	Pinch Hit AB	Pinch Hit H	PO	A	E	DP	TC/G	FA	G by Pos
1973	**MIL A**	16	.205	.205	39	8	0	0	0	0.0	3	1	2	10	0	0	0	29	2	1	0	2.5	.969	OF-12, DH-1
1974	**HOU N**	64	.216	.306	111	24	4	0	2	1.8	19	5	5	18	4	9	2	65	3	0	1	1.4	1.000	OF-50
1975		121	.283	.365	392	111	16	8	0	0.0	62	21	21	67	32	23	6	194	7	1	0	2.1	.995	OF-95
1976		94	.220	.293	191	42	7	2	1	0.5	26	18	7	28	7	24	6	98	8	5	2	1.7	.955	OF-63, 2B-2
1977		87	.257	.321	187	48	6	0	2	1.1	22	13	5	30	11	24	7	105	5	1	1	1.7	.991	OF-62, 2B-4
1978		84	.230	.291	148	34	4	1	1	0.7	17	13	5	22	6	51	12	43	3	0	0	2.3	1.000	OF-16, C-3, 2B-1
6 yrs.		466	.250	.322	1068	267	37	11	6	0.6	149	71	45	175	60	131	33	534	28	8	4	1.8	.986	OF-298, 2B-7, C-3, DH-1

Jim Howarth

HOWARTH, JAMES EUGENE, JR. BL TL 5′11″ 175 lbs.
B. Mar. 7, 1947, Biloxi, Miss.

Year	Team	Games	BA	SA	AB	H	2B	3B	HR	HR%	R	RBI	BB	SO	SB	Pinch Hit AB	Pinch Hit H	PO	A	E	DP	TC/G	FA	G by Pos
1971	**SF N**	7	.231	.308	13	3	1	0	0	0.0	3	2	3	3	0	1	0	9	0	0	0	1.5	1.000	OF-6
1972		74	.235	.294	119	28	4	0	1	0.8	16	7	16	18	3	39	**13**	70	1	1	0	2.5	.986	OF-25, 1B-4
1973		65	.200	.233	90	18	1	1	0	0.0	8	7	7	8	0	26	6	46	1	0	1	1.4	1.000	OF-33, 1B-1
1974		6	.000	.000	4	0	0	0	0	0.0	0	0	0	0	0	4	0	0	0	0	0	0.0	.000	OF-1
4 yrs.		152	.217	.265	226	49	6	1	1	0.4	27	16	26	29	3	70	19	125	2	1	1	1.8	.992	OF-65, 1B-5

Art Howe

HOWE, ARTHUR HENRY, JR. BR TR 6′ 2″ 190 lbs.
B. Dec. 15, 1946, Pittsburgh, Pa.
Manager 1989–93.

Year	Team	Games	BA	SA	AB	H	2B	3B	HR	HR%	R	RBI	BB	SO	SB	Pinch Hit AB	Pinch Hit H	PO	A	E	DP	TC/G	FA	G by Pos
1974	**PIT N**	29	.243	.365	74	18	4	1	1	1.4	10	5	9	13	0	8	4	11	49	4	8	2.9	.938	3B-20, SS-2
1975		63	.171	.253	146	25	9	0	1	0.7	13	10	15	15	1	18	4	19	89	7	4	2.6	.939	3B-42, SS-3

Art Howe *continued*

Year	Team	Games	BA	SA	AB	H	2B	3B	HR	HR%	R	RBI	BB	SO	SB	Pinch Hit AB	Pinch Hit H	PO	A	E	DP	TC/G	FA	G by Pos
1976	HOU N	21	.138	.172	29	4	1	0	0	0.0	0	0	6	6	0	7	1	7	16	1	3	2.4	.958	3B-8, 2B-2
1977		125	.264	.412	413	109	23	7	8	1.9	44	58	41	60	0	6	3	213	333	8	52	4.4	.986	2B-96, 3B-19, SS-11
1978		119	.293	.436	420	123	33	3	7	1.7	46	55	34	41	2	3	1	240	302	13	51	4.7	.977	2B-107, 3B-11, 1B-1
1979		118	.248	.352	355	88	15	2	6	1.7	32	33	36	37	3	11	1	188	261	7	42	3.5	.985	2B-68, 3B-59, 1B-3
1980		110	.283	.445	321	91	12	5	10	3.1	34	46	34	29	1	18	2	598	86	10	52	6.3	.986	1B-77, 3B-25, SS-5, 2B-3
1981		103	.296	.404	361	107	22	4	3	0.8	43	36	41	23	1	3	1	67	206	9	19	2.8	.968	3B-98, 1B-2
1982		110	.238	.326	365	87	15	1	5	1.4	29	38	41	45	2	3	0	344	174	7	47	4.9	.987	3B-72, 1B-35
1984	STL N	89	.216	.295	139	30	5	0	2	1.4	17	12	18	18	0	21	6	71	80	3	14	2.2	.981	3B-45, 1B-11, 2B-8, SS-5
1985		4	.000	.000	3	0	0	0	0	0.0	0	0	0	0	0	3	0	5	1	0	1	3.0	1.000	3B-1, 1B-1
11 yrs.		891	.260	.379	2626	682	139	23	43	1.6	268	293	275	287	10	101	23	1763	1597	69	293	4.1	.980	3B-400, 2B-284, 1B-130, SS-26
DIVISIONAL PLAYOFF SERIES																								
1981	HOU N	5	.235	.412	17	4	0	0	1	5.9	1	1	2	1	0	0	0	6	9	0	0	3.0	1.000	3B-5
LEAGUE CHAMPIONSHIP SERIES																								
1974	PIT N	1	.000	.000	1	0	0	0	0	0.0	0	0	0	0	0	1	0	0	0	0	0	0.0	—	
1980	HOU N	5	.200	.400	15	3	1	1	0	0.0	0	2	2	2	0	0	0	29	3	0	3	8.0	1.000	1B-4
2 yrs.		6	.188	.375	16	3	1	1	0	0.0	0	2	2	2	0	1	0	29	3	0	3	8.0	1.000	1B-4

Shorty Howe

HOWE, JOHN
B. New York, N. Y. Deceased.

Year	Team	Games	BA	SA	AB	H	2B	3B	HR	HR%	R	RBI	BB	SO	SB	Pinch Hit AB	Pinch Hit H	PO	A	E	DP	TC/G	FA	G by Pos
1890	NY N	19	.172	.172	64	11	0	0	0	0.0	4	4	3	2	3	0	0	36	58	12	3	5.6	.887	2B-18, 3B-1
1893		1	.600	.600	5	3	0	0	0	0.0	1	2	0	0	1	0	0	0	2	3	0	5.0	.400	3B-1
2 yrs.		20	.203	.203	69	14	0	0	0	0.0	5	6	3	2	4	0	0	36	60	15	3	5.6	.865	2B-18, 3B-2

Dixie Howell

HOWELL, HOMER ELLIOTT BR TR 5′11½″ 190 lbs.
B. Apr. 24, 1920, Louisville, Ky. D. Oct. 5, 1990, Binghamton, N. Y. BB 1947

Year	Team	Games	BA	SA	AB	H	2B	3B	HR	HR%	R	RBI	BB	SO	SB	Pinch Hit AB	Pinch Hit H	PO	A	E	DP	TC/G	FA	G by Pos
1947	PIT N	76	.276	.383	214	59	11	0	4	1.9	23	25	27	34	1	1	0	272	30	8	2	4.2	.974	C-74
1949	CIN N	64	.244	.326	172	42	6	1	2	1.2	17	18	8	21	0	8	4	191	35	3	2	4.1	.987	C-56
1950		82	.223	.299	224	50	9	1	2	0.9	30	22	32	31	0	1	0	338	26	5	4	4.6	.986	C-81
1951		77	.251	.319	207	52	6	1	2	1.0	22	18	15	34	0	4	2	275	24	4	5	4.2	.987	C-73
1952		17	.189	.432	37	7	1	1	2	5.4	4	4	3	9	0	5	0	43	9	1	0	4.4	.981	C-12
1953	BKN N	1	.000	.000	1	0	0	0	0	0.0	0	0	0	1	0	1	0	0	0	0	0	0.0	—	
1955		16	.262	.357	42	11	4	0	0	0.0	2	5	1	7	0	4	1	49	4	1	0	4.2	.981	C-13
1956		7	.231	.385	13	3	2	0	0	0.0	0	1	1	3	0	2	0	21	1	0	0	3.7	1.000	C-6
8 yrs.		340	.246	.337	910	224	39	4	12	1.3	98	93	87	140	1	26	7	1189	129	22	13	4.3	.984	C-315

Harry Howell

HOWELL, HENRY HARRY (Handsome Harry) BR TR 5′ 9″
B. Nov. 14, 1876, New Jersey D. May 22, 1956, Spokane, Wash.

Year	Team	Games	BA	SA	AB	H	2B	3B	HR	HR%	R	RBI	BB	SO	SB	Pinch Hit AB	Pinch Hit H	PO	A	E	DP	TC/G	FA	G by Pos
1898	BKN N	2	.250	.250	8	2	0	0	0	0.0	1	1	1		0	0	0	1	5	0	1	3.0	1.000	P-2
1899	BAL N	28	.146	.220	82	12	2	2	0	0.0	4	3	3		0	0	0	10	53	4	1	2.4	.940	P-28
1900	BKN N	22	.286	.405	42	12	2	0	1	2.4	6	6	6		1	0	0	6	31	2	1	1.9	.949	P-21
1901	BAL A	53	.218	.356	188	41	10	5	2	1.1	26	26	5		6	0	0	59	93	16	6	3.1	.905	P-37, OF-9, SS-6, 1B-2, 2B-1
1902		96	.268	.395	347	93	16	11	2	0.6	42	42	18		7	1	0	152	208	26	10	4.0	.933	2B-26, P-26, OF-18, 3B-15, SS-11, 1B-1
1903	NY A	40	.217	.311	106	23	3	2	1	0.9	14	12	5		1	4	0	38	81	7	3	3.2	.944	P-25, 3B-7, SS-5, 2B-1, 1B-1
1904	STL A	36	.221	.327	113	25	5	2	1	0.9	9	6	4		0	2	1	26	143	5	1	5.1	.971	P-34
1905		41	.193	.289	135	26	6	2	1	0.7	9	10	3		0	0	0	26	179	8	3	5.2	.962	P-38, OF-3
1906		35	.125	.173	104	13	3	1	0	0.0	5	6	6		2	0	0	31	111	10	2	4.3	.934	P-35
1907		44	.237	.333	114	27	5	0	2	1.8	12	7	7		2	0	0	42	125	3	4	3.9	.982	P-42, OF-2
1908		41	.183	.267	120	22	7	0	1	0.8	10	9	4		0	0	0	21	101	5	3	3.1	.961	P-41
1909		18	.176	.206	34	6	1	0	0	0.0	5	3	2		0	0	0	15	25	4	2	2.4	.909	P-10, 3B-7, OF-1
1910		1	.000	.000	2	0	0	0	0	0.0	0	0	0		0	0	0	0	1	0	0	1.0	1.000	P-1
13 yrs.		457	.216	.319	1395	302	60	25	11	0.8	143	131	64		19	7	1	427	1156	90	37	3.7	.946	P-340, OF-33, 3B-29, 2B-28, SS-22, 1B-4

Jack Howell

HOWELL, JACK ROBERT BL TR 6′ 185 lbs.
B. Aug. 18, 1961, Tucson, Ariz.

Year	Team	Games	BA	SA	AB	H	2B	3B	HR	HR%	R	RBI	BB	SO	SB	Pinch Hit AB	Pinch Hit H	PO	A	E	DP	TC/G	FA	G by Pos
1985	CAL A	43	.197	.336	137	27	4	0	5	3.6	19	18	16	33	1	2	1	33	75	8	10	2.8	.931	3B-42
1986		63	.272	.470	151	41	14	2	4	2.6	26	21	19	28	2	16	4	38	57	2	5	2.0	.979	3B-39, OF-8, DH-2
1987		138	.245	.461	449	110	18	5	23	5.1	64	64	57	118	4	18	6	185	95	7	15	1.9	.976	OF-89, 3B-48, 2B-13
1988		154	.254	.422	500	127	32	2	16	3.2	59	63	46	130	2	4	1	97	249	17	19	2.4	.953	3B-152, OF-2
1989		144	.228	.411	474	108	19	4	20	4.2	56	52	52	125	0	3	1	97	322	11	27	2.9	.974	3B-142, OF-4
1990		105	.228	.370	316	72	19	1	8	2.5	35	33	46	61	3	6	2	76	196	18	18	2.8	.938	3B-102, SS-1, 1B-1
1991	2 teams	CAL A (32G –.210) SD N (58G –.206)																						
″	total	90	.207	.336	241	50	5	1	8	3.3	35	23	29	44	1	15	4	86	153	4	14	2.9	.984	3B-62, 2B-12, OF-5, 1B-3, DH-1
7 yrs.		737	.236	.409	2268	535	111	15	84	3.7	294	274	265	539	13	64	19	612	1147	67	108	2.5	.963	3B-587, OF-108, 2B-25, 1B-4, DH-3, SS-1
LEAGUE CHAMPIONSHIP SERIES																								
1986	CAL A	2	.000	.000	1	0	0	0	0	0.0	0	0	1	1	0	1	0	0	0	0	0	0.0	—	

Pat Howell

HOWELL, PATRICK O'NEAL BB TR 5′11″ 155 lbs.
B. Aug. 31, 1968, Mobile, Ala.

Year	Team	Games	BA	SA	AB	H	2B	3B	HR	HR%	R	RBI	BB	SO	SB	Pinch Hit AB	Pinch Hit H	PO	A	E	DP	TC/G	FA	G by Pos
1992	NY N	31	.187	.200	75	14	1	0	0	0.0	9	1	2	15	4	0	0	66	0	0	0	2.4	1.000	OF-28

Red Howell

HOWELL, MURRAY DONALD (Porky) BR TR 6′ 215 lbs.
B. Jan. 29, 1909, Atlanta, Ga. D. Oct. 1, 1950, Travelers Rest, S. C.

Year	Team	Games	BA	SA	AB	H	2B	3B	HR	HR%	R	RBI	BB	SO	SB	Pinch Hit AB	Pinch Hit H	PO	A	E	DP	TC/G	FA	G by Pos
1941	CLE A	11	.286	.286	7	2	0	0	0	0.0	0	2	4	2	0	7	2	0	0	0	0	0.0	—	

Roy Howell

HOWELL, ROY LEE BL TR 6′ 1″ 190 lbs.
B. Dec. 18, 1953, Lompoc, Calif.

Year	Team	Games	BA	SA	AB	H	2B	3B	HR	HR%	R	RBI	BB	SO	SB	Pinch Hit AB	Pinch Hit H	PO	A	E	DP	TC/G	FA	G by Pos
1974	TEX A	13	.250	.341	44	11	1	0	1	2.3	2	3	2	10	0	1	0	5	24	3	1	2.7	.906	3B-12
1975		125	.251	.379	383	96	15	2	10	2.6	43	51	39	79	2	12	4	80	214	21	32	2.6	.933	3B-115, DH-5

Roy Howell *continued*

Year	Team	Games	BA	SA	AB	H	2B	3B	HR	HR%	R	RBI	BB	SO	SB	Pinch Hit AB	Pinch Hit H	PO	A	E	DP	TC/G	FA	G by Pos
1976		140	.253	.367	491	124	28	2	8	1.6	55	53	30	106	1	8	1	103	245	28	20	2.7	.926	3B-130, DH-8
1977	**2 teams**	**TEX A** (7G –.000) **TOR A** (96G –.316)																						
"	**total**	103	.302	.430	381	115	17	1	10	2.6	41	44	44	80	4	19	1	94	165	13	13	2.7	.952	3B-88, DH-10, OF-2, 1B-1
1978	**TOR A**	140	.270	.376	551	149	28	3	8	1.5	67	61	44	78	0	2	0	116	306	22	27	3.2	.950	3B-131, OF-5, DH-1
1979		138	.247	.405	511	126	28	4	15	2.9	60	72	42	91	1	2	0	108	290	20	28	3.1	.952	3B-133, DH-4
1980		142	.269	.413	528	142	28	9	10	1.9	51	57	50	92	0	0	0	105	257	16	24	2.7	.958	3B-138, DH-2
1981	**MIL A**	76	.238	.373	244	58	13	1	6	2.5	37	33	23	39	0	8	0	58	100	6	10	2.3	.963	3B-53, DH-13, 1B-3, OF-1
1982		98	.260	.350	300	78	11	2	4	1.3	31	38	21	39	0	12	2	28	2	2	1	0.4	.938	DH-84, 1B-4, OF-2
1983		69	.278	.448	194	54	9	6	4	2.1	23	25	15	29	1	16	4	20	4	1	4	0.4	.960	DH-54, 1B-2
1984		68	.232	.348	164	38	5	1	4	2.4	12	17	8	31	0	16	2	40	69	9	11	2.0	.924	3B-46, DH-8, 1B-4
11 yrs.		1112	.261	.389	3791	991	183	31	80	2.1	422	454	318	674	9	96	14	757	1676	141	171	2.4	.945	3B-846, DH-189, 1B-14, OF-10
DIVISIONAL PLAYOFF SERIES																								
1981	**MIL A**	4	.400	.400	5	2	0	0	0	0.0	0	0	2	2	0	1	1	0	0	0	0	0.0	.000	DH-3
LEAGUE CHAMPIONSHIP SERIES																								
1982	**MIL A**	1	.000	.000	3	0	0	0	0	0.0	0	0	0	1	0	0	0	0	0	0	0	0.0	.000	DH-1
WORLD SERIES																								
1982	**MIL A**	4	.000	.000	11	0	0	0	0	0.0	1	0	0	3	0	0	0	0	0	0	0	0.0	.000	DH-4

Bill Howerton

HOWERTON, WILLIAM RAY (Hopalong)
B. Dec. 12, 1921, Lompoc, Calif.
BL TR 5′11″ 185 lbs.

Year	Team	Games	BA	SA	AB	H	2B	3B	HR	HR%	R	RBI	BB	SO	SB	Pinch Hit AB	Pinch Hit H	PO	A	E	DP	TC/G	FA	G by Pos
1949	**STL N**	9	.308	.385	13	4	1	0	0	0.0	1	1	0	2	0	3	1	9	0	1	0	1.7	.900	OF-6
1950		110	.281	.492	313	88	20	8	10	3.2	50	59	47	60	0	17	5	183	2	6	0	2.0	.969	OF-94
1951	**2 teams**	**STL N** (24G –.262) **PIT N** (80G –.274)																						
"	**total**	104	.271	.475	284	77	16	3	12	4.2	39	41	36	56	1	29	4	130	10	8	2	2.0	.946	OF-70, 3B-4
1952	**2 teams**	**PIT N** (13G –.320) **NY N** (11G –.067)																						
"	**total**	24	.225	.325	40	9	2	1	0	0.0	5	5	9	7	0	13	2	15	1	3	0	2.1	.842	OF-8, 3B-1
4 yrs.		247	.274	.472	650	178	39	12	22	3.4	95	106	92	125	1	62	12	337	13	18	2	2.0	.951	OF-178, 3B-5

Dann Howitt

HOWITT, DANN PAUL JOHN
B. Feb. 13, 1964, Battle Creek, Mich.
BL TR 6′5″ 205 lbs.

Year	Team	Games	BA	SA	AB	H	2B	3B	HR	HR%	R	RBI	BB	SO	SB	Pinch Hit AB	Pinch Hit H	PO	A	E	DP	TC/G	FA	G by Pos
1989	**OAK A**	3	.000	.000	3	0	0	0	0	0.0	0	0	0	2	0	1	0	2	0	0	0	1.0	1.000	1B-1, OF-1
1990		14	.136	.227	22	3	0	1	0	0.0	3	1	3	12	0	2	0	34	1	0	3	2.1	1.000	OF-11, 1B-5, 3B-1
1991		21	.167	.262	42	7	1	0	1	2.4	5	3	1	12	0	6	1	36	0	0	0	1.7	1.000	OF-20, 1B-1
1992	**2 teams**	**OAK A** (22G –.125) **SEA A** (13G –.270)																						
"	**total**	35	.188	.329	85	16	4	1	2	2.4	7	10	8	9	1	2	0	63	5	2	3	2.0	.971	OF-30, 1B-4, DH-1
1993	**SEA A**	32	.211	.355	76	16	3	1	2	2.6	6	8	4	18	0	4	0	42	1	0	0	1.4	1.000	OF-29, DH-2
1994	**CHI A**	10	.357	.571	14	5	3	0	0	0.0	4	0	1	7	0	2	1	15	1	0	1	1.5	1.000	OF-7, 1B-4
6 yrs.		115	.194	.326	242	47	11	3	5	2.1	25	22	17	60	1	17	2	192	8	2	7	1.7	.990	OF-98, 1B-15, DH-3, 3B-1

Dan Howley

HOWLEY, DANIEL PHILIP (Dapper Dan)
B. Oct. 16, 1885, Weymouth, Mass. D. Mar. 10, 1944, Weymouth, Mass.
Manager 1927–32.
BR TR 6′ 187 lbs.

Year	Team	Games	BA	SA	AB	H	2B	3B	HR	HR%	R	RBI	BB	SO	SB	Pinch Hit AB	Pinch Hit H	PO	A	E	DP	TC/G	FA	G by Pos
1913	**PHI N**	26	.125	.188	32	4	2	0	0	0.0	5	2	4	4	3	0	0	48	14	3	2	3.0	.954	C-22

Dick Howser

HOWSER, RICHARD DALTON
B. May 14, 1936, Miami, Fla. D. June 17, 1987, Kansas City, Mo.
Manager 1978, 1980–86.
BR TR 5′8″ 155 lbs.

Year	Team	Games	BA	SA	AB	H	2B	3B	HR	HR%	R	RBI	BB	SO	SB	Pinch Hit AB	Pinch Hit H	PO	A	E	DP	TC/G	FA	G by Pos
1961	**KC A**	158	.280	.362	611	171	29	6	3	0.5	108	45	92	38	37	1	0	299	427	38	85	4.9	.950	SS-157
1962		83	.238	.350	286	68	8	3	6	2.1	53	34	38	8	19	0	0	138	191	13	37	4.8	.962	SS-72
1963	**2 teams**	**KC A** (15G –.195) **CLE A** (49G –.247)																						
"	**total**	64	.236	.276	203	48	5	0	1	0.5	29	11	29	21	9	7	1	101	113	11	21	4.2	.951	SS-54
1964	**CLE A**	162	.256	.319	637	163	23	4	3	0.5	101	52	76	39	20	0	0	291	463	20	100	4.8	.974	SS-162
1965		107	.235	.283	307	72	8	2	1	0.3	47	6	57	25	17	12	3	144	211	7	41	4.0	.981	SS-73, 2B-17
1966		67	.229	.350	140	32	9	1	2	1.4	18	4	15	23	2	8	0	53	95	5	16	2.9	.967	SS-26, 2B-26
1967	**NY A**	63	.268	.309	149	40	6	0	0	0.0	18	10	25	15	1	17	4	64	76	3	18	3.9	.979	2B-22, 3B-12, SS-3
1968		85	.153	.180	150	23	2	1	0	0.0	24	3	35	17	0	40	8	61	106	3	19	5.3	.982	2B-29, 3B-2, SS-1
8 yrs.		789	.248	.318	2483	617	90	17	16	0.6	398	165	367	186	105	85	16	1151	1682	100	337	4.5	.966	SS-548, 2B-94, 3B-14

Dummy Hoy

HOY, WILLIAM ELLSWORTH
B. May 23, 1862, Houcktown, Ohio D. Dec. 15, 1961, Cincinnati, Ohio.
BL TR 5′6″ 160 lbs.

Year	Team	Games	BA	SA	AB	H	2B	3B	HR	HR%	R	RBI	BB	SO	SB	Pinch Hit AB	Pinch Hit H	PO	A	E	DP	TC/G	FA	G by Pos
1888	**WAS N**	136	.274	.338	503	138	10	8	2	0.4	77	29	69	48	**82**	0	0	296	26	37	7	2.6	.897	OF-136
1889		127	.274	.320	507	139	11	6	0	0.0	98	39	75	30	35	0	0	255	29	35	4	2.5	.890	OF-127
1890	**BUF P**	122	.298	.371	493	147	17	8	1	0.2	107	53	94	36	39	0	0	290	25	30	10	2.8	.913	OF-122, 2B-1
1891	**STL AA**	139	.292	.360	559	163	13	5	5	0.9	134	64	**117**	25	59	0	0	251	26	27	3	2.2	.911	OF-139
1892	**WAS N**	152	.280	.354	593	166	19	8	3	0.5	108	75	86	23	60	0	0	275	16	38	3	2.2	.884	OF-152
1893		130	.245	.287	564	138	12	6	0	0.0	106	45	66	9	48	0	0	281	26	37	8	2.6	.892	OF-130
1894	**CIN N**	128	.299	.426	495	148	22	13	5	1.0	114	70	87	18	27	0	0	314	29	40	3	3.0	.896	OF-128
1895		107	.277	.403	429	119	21	12	3	0.7	93	55	52	8	50	0	0	235	14	33	6	2.6	.883	OF-107
1896		121	.298	.409	443	132	23	7	4	0.9	120	57	65	13	50	1	1	303	14	18	3	2.8	.946	OF-120
1897		128	.292	.376	497	145	24	6	2	0.4	87	42	54		37	0	0	359	10	26	5	3.1	.934	OF-128
1898	**LOU N**	148	.304	.416	582	177	15	16	6	1.0	104	66	49		37	0	0	348	19	21	6	2.6	.946	OF-148
1899		154	.306	.398	**633**	194	17	13	5	0.8	116	49	61		32	0	0	321	21	27	8	2.4	.927	OF-154
1901	**CHI A**	132	.294	.400	527	155	28	11	2	0.4	112	60	**86**		27	0	0	278	16	13	6	2.3	.958	OF-132
1902	**CIN N**	72	.290	.384	279	81	16	2	2	0.7	48	20	41		11	0	0	149	4	11	1	2.3	.933	OF-72
14 yrs.		1796	.287	.373	7104	2042	248	121	40	0.6	1424	724	1002	210	594	1	1	3955	275	393	73	2.6	.915	OF-1795, 2B-1

Kent Hrbek

HRBEK, KENT ALLEN (Herbie)
B. May 21, 1960, Minneapolis, Minn.
BL TR 6′4″ 240 lbs.

Year	Team	Games	BA	SA	AB	H	2B	3B	HR	HR%	R	RBI	BB	SO	SB	Pinch Hit AB	Pinch Hit H	PO	A	E	DP	TC/G	FA	G by Pos
1981	**MIN A**	24	.239	.358	67	16	5	0	1	1.5	5	7	5	9	0	5	2	124	4	0	14	6.1	1.000	1B-13, DH-8
1982		140	.301	.485	532	160	21	4	23	4.3	82	92	54	80	3	1	0	1174	88	9	125	9.1	.993	1B-138, DH-2
1983		141	.297	.489	515	153	41	5	16	3.1	75	84	57	71	4	3	0	1151	89	13	125	9.0	.990	1B-137, DH-2

Kent Hrbek *continued*

Year	Team	Games	BA	SA	AB	H	2B	3B	HR	HR%	R	RBI	BB	SO	SB	Pinch Hit AB	Pinch Hit H	PO	A	E	DP	TC/G	FA	G by Pos
1984		149	.311	.522	559	174	31	3	27	4.8	80	107	65	87	1	1	1	1320	99	14	113	9.6	.990	1B-148, DH-1
1985		158	.278	.444	593	165	31	2	21	3.5	78	93	67	87	1	5	2	1339	114	8	114	9.2	.995	1B-156, DH-2
1986		149	.267	.478	550	147	27	1	29	5.3	85	91	71	81	2	3	0	1218	104	10	137	9.0	.992	1B-147, DH-1
1987		143	.285	.545	477	136	20	1	34	7.1	85	90	84	60	5	5	1	1179	68	5	112	9.1	.996	1B-137, DH-1
1988		143	.312	.520	510	159	31	0	25	4.9	75	76	67	54	0	2	1	842	57	3	92	6.4	.997	1B-105, DH-37
1989		109	.272	.517	375	102	17	0	25	6.7	59	84	53	35	3	4	1	723	60	4	66	7.4	.995	1B-89, DH-18
1990		143	.287	.474	492	141	26	0	22	4.5	61	79	69	45	5	4	2	1057	83	3	100	8.1	.997	1B-120, DH-20, 3B-1
1991		132	.284	.461	462	131	20	1	20	4.3	72	89	67	48	4	4	3	1138	95	8	110	9.7	.994	1B-128
1992		112	.244	.409	394	96	20	0	15	3.8	52	58	71	56	5	2	1	954	68	3	75	9.2	.997	1B-104, DH-8
1993		123	.242	.467	392	95	11	1	25	6.4	60	83	71	57	4	8	1	940	81	5	98	8.8	.995	1B-115, DH-2
1994		81	.270	.420	274	74	11	0	10	3.6	34	53	37	28	0	8	5	567	41	2	51	8.0	.997	1B-72, DH-4
14 yrs.		1747	.282	.481	6192	1749	312	18	293	4.7	903	1086	838	798	37	55	20	13726	1051	87	1332	8.7	.994	1B-1609, DH-106, 3B-1
LEAGUE CHAMPIONSHIP SERIES																								
1987	MIN A	5	.150	.300	20	3	0	0	1	5.0	4	1	3	0	0	0	0	40	3	0	3	8.6	1.000	1B-5
1991		5	.143	.143	21	3	0	0	0	0.0	0	3	1	3	0	0	0	40	7	0	3	9.4	1.000	1B-5
2 yrs.		10	.146	.220	41	6	0	0	1	2.4	4	4	4	3	0	0	0	80	10	0	6	9.0	1.000	1B-10
WORLD SERIES																								
1987	MIN A	7	.208	.333	24	5	0	0	1	4.2	4	6	5	3	0	0	0	68	2	0	3	10.0	1.000	1B-7
1991		7	.115	.269	26	3	1	0	1	3.8	2	2	2	6	0	0	0	65	8	0	4	10.4	1.000	1B-7
2 yrs.		14	.160	.300	50	8	1	0	2	4.0	6	8	7	9	0	0	0	133	10	0	7	10.2	1.000	1B-14

Walt Hriniak

HRINIAK, WALTER JOHN BL TR 5′11″ 180 lbs.
B. May 22, 1943, Natick, Mass.

Year	Team	Games	BA	SA	AB	H	2B	3B	HR	HR%	R	RBI	BB	SO	SB	Pinch Hit AB	Pinch Hit H	PO	A	E	DP	TC/G	FA	G by Pos
1968	ATL N	9	.346	.346	26	9	0	0	0	0.0	0	3	0	3	0	0	0	57	1	2	0	6.7	.967	C-9
1969	2 teams	ATL N (7G –.143) SD N (31G –.227)																						
″	total	38	.219	.219	73	16	0	0	0	0.0	4	1	10	12	0	15	2	105	7	2	1	4.6	.982	C-25
2 yrs.		47	.253	.253	99	25	0	0	0	0.0	4	4	10	15	0	15	2	162	8	4	1	5.1	.977	C-34

Al Hubbard

HUBBARD, ALLEN
B. Dec. 9, 1860, Westfield, Mass. D. Dec. 14, 1930, Newton, Mass.

Year	Team	Games	BA	SA	AB	H	2B	3B	HR	HR%	R	RBI	BB	SO	SB	Pinch Hit AB	Pinch Hit H	PO	A	E	DP	TC/G	FA	G by Pos
1883	PHI AA	2	.333	.333	6	2	0	0	0	0.0	2		1			0	0	7	4	4	0	7.5	.733	SS-1, C-1

Glenn Hubbard

HUBBARD, GLENN DEE BR TR 5′ 9″ 150 lbs.
B. Sept. 25, 1957, Hahn, West Germany.

Year	Team	Games	BA	SA	AB	H	2B	3B	HR	HR%	R	RBI	BB	SO	SB	Pinch Hit AB	Pinch Hit H	PO	A	E	DP	TC/G	FA	G by Pos
1978	ATL N	44	.258	.319	163	42	4	0	2	1.2	15	13	10	20	2	0	0	102	130	5	30	5.4	.979	2B-44
1979		97	.231	.295	325	75	12	0	3	0.9	34	29	27	43	0	6	1	193	268	15	57	5.2	.968	2B-91
1980		117	.248	.374	431	107	21	3	9	2.1	55	43	49	69	7	0	0	268	405	15	91	5.9	.978	2B-117
1981		99	.235	.349	361	85	13	5	6	1.7	39	33	33	59	4	0	0	188	344	5	50	5.5	.991	2B-98
1982		145	.248	.350	532	132	25	1	9	1.7	75	59	59	62	4	0	0	312	505	14	111	5.8	.983	2B-144
1983		148	.263	.402	517	136	24	6	12	2.3	65	70	55	71	3	1	0	313	484	12	103	5.5	.985	2B-148
1984		120	.234	.380	397	93	27	2	9	2.3	53	43	55	61	4	4	2	237	405	8	78	5.6	.988	2B-117
1985		142	.232	.314	439	102	21	0	5	1.1	51	39	56	54	4	4	1	339	539	10	127	6.3	.989	2B-140
1986		143	.230	.304	408	94	16	1	4	1.0	42	36	66	74	3	0	0	282	487	19	120	5.5	.976	2B-142
1987		141	.264	.381	443	117	33	2	5	1.1	69	38	77	57	1	2	0	284	478	11	114	5.6	.986	2B-139
1988	OAK A	105	.255	.340	294	75	12	2	3	1.0	35	33	33	50	1	2	0	195	267	6	60	4.5	.987	2B-104, DH-1
1989		53	.198	.313	131	26	6	0	3	2.3	12	12	19	20	2	4	0	82	132	7	34	4.3	.968	2B-48, DH-3
12 yrs.		1354	.244	.349	4441	1084	214	22	70	1.6	545	448	539	640	35	23	4	2795	4444	127	975	5.5	.983	2B-1332, DH-4
LEAGUE CHAMPIONSHIP SERIES																								
1982	ATL N	3	.222	.222	9	2	0	0	0	0.0	1	1	0	3	0	0	0	4	11	0	0	5.0	1.000	2B-3
WORLD SERIES																								
1988	OAK A	4	.250	.250	12	3	0	0	0	0.0	2	0	1	2	1	0	0	5	7	1	0	3.3	.923	2B-4

Mike Hubbard

HUBBARD, MICHAEL WAYNE BR TR 6′ 1″ 180 lbs.
B. Feb. 16, 1971, Lynchburg, Va.

Year	Team	Games	BA	SA	AB	H	2B	3B	HR	HR%	R	RBI	BB	SO	SB	Pinch Hit AB	Pinch Hit H	PO	A	E	DP	TC/G	FA	G by Pos
1995	CHI N	15	.174	.174	23	4	0	0	0	0.0	2	1	2	2	0	6	1	33	0	1	0	3.8	.971	C-9

Trenidad Hubbard

HUBBARD, TRENIDAD AVIEL (Trent) BR TR 5′ 8″ 180 lbs.
B. May 11, 1964, Chicago, Ill.

Year	Team	Games	BA	SA	AB	H	2B	3B	HR	HR%	R	RBI	BB	SO	SB	Pinch Hit AB	Pinch Hit H	PO	A	E	DP	TC/G	FA	G by Pos
1994	CLR N	18	.280	.520	25	7	1	1	1	4.0	3	3	3	4	0	12	5	4	0	0	0	0.8	1.000	OF-5
1995		24	.310	.534	58	18	4	0	3	5.2	13	9	8	6	2	10	3	16	1	0	0	1.1	1.000	OF-16
2 yrs.		42	.301	.530	83	25	5	1	4	4.8	16	12	11	10	2	22	8	20	1	0	0	1.0	1.000	OF-21
DIVISIONAL PLAYOFF SERIES																								
1995	CLR N	3	.000	.000	2	0	0	0	0	0.0	0	0	0	0	0	2	0	0	0	0	0	0.0	—	

Ken Hubbs

HUBBS, KENNETH DOUGLASS BR TR 6′ 2″ 175 lbs.
B. Dec. 23, 1941, Riverside, Calif. D. Feb. 15, 1964, Provo, Utah.

Year	Team	Games	BA	SA	AB	H	2B	3B	HR	HR%	R	RBI	BB	SO	SB	Pinch Hit AB	Pinch Hit H	PO	A	E	DP	TC/G	FA	G by Pos
1961	CHI N	10	.179	.393	28	5	1	1	1	3.6	4	2	0	8	0	2	0	13	15	0	2	3.5	1.000	2B-8
1962		160	.260	.346	661	172	24	9	5	0.8	90	49	35	**129**	3	1	0	363	489	15	103	5.5	.983	2B-159
1963		154	.235	.322	566	133	19	3	8	1.4	54	47	39	93	8	2	1	338	493	22	96	5.6	.974	2B-152
3 yrs.		324	.247	.336	1255	310	44	13	14	1.1	148	98	74	230	11	5	1	714	997	37	201	5.5	.979	2B-319

Clarence Huber

HUBER, CLARENCE BILL (Gilly) BR TR 5′10″ 165 lbs.
B. Oct. 27, 1896, Tyler, Tex. D. Feb. 22, 1965, Laredo, Tex.

Year	Team	Games	BA	SA	AB	H	2B	3B	HR	HR%	R	RBI	BB	SO	SB	Pinch Hit AB	Pinch Hit H	PO	A	E	DP	TC/G	FA	G by Pos
1920	DET A	11	.214	.310	42	9	2	1	0	0.0	4	5	0	5	0	0	0	21	28	5	0	4.9	.907	3B-11
1921		1	—	—	0	0	0	0	0	—	0	0	0	0	0	0	0	1	0	0	0	1.0	1.000	3B-1
1925	PHI N	124	.284	.406	436	124	28	5	5	1.1	46	54	17	33	3	4	2	107	199	17	16	2.7	.947	3B-120
1926		118	.245	.335	376	92	17	7	1	0.3	45	34	42	29	9	2	2	110	214	15	22	2.9	.956	3B-115
4 yrs.		254	.263	.370	854	225	47	13	6	0.7	95	93	59	67	12	6	4	239	441	37	38	2.9	.948	3B-247

Otto Huber

HUBER, OTTO
B. Mar. 12, 1914, Garfield, N. J. D. Apr. 9, 1989, Passaic, N. J.
BR TR 5′10″ 165 lbs.

Year	Team	Games	BA	SA	AB	H	2B	3B	HR	HR%	R	RBI	BB	SO	SB	Pinch Hit AB	Pinch Hit H	PO	A	E	DP	TC/G	FA	G by Pos
1939	BOS N	11	.273	.318	22	6	1	0	0	0.0	2	3	0	1	0	2	1	8	12	1	1	2.6	.952	3B-4, 2B-4

Dave Hudgens

HUDGENS, DAVID MARK
B. Dec. 5, 1956, Oroville, Calif.
BL TL 6′ 2″ 200 lbs.

Year	Team	Games	BA	SA	AB	H	2B	3B	HR	HR%	R	RBI	BB	SO	SB	Pinch Hit AB	Pinch Hit H	PO	A	E	DP	TC/G	FA	G by Pos
1983	OAK A	6	.143	.143	7	1	0	0	0	0.0	0	0	0	3	0	3	0	4	0	0	0	1.0	1.000	1B-3, DH-1

Jimmy Hudgens

HUDGENS, JAMES PRICE
B. Aug. 24, 1902, Newburg, Mo. D. Aug. 26, 1955, St. Louis, Mo.
BL TL 6′ 180 lbs.

Year	Team	Games	BA	SA	AB	H	2B	3B	HR	HR%	R	RBI	BB	SO	SB	Pinch Hit AB	Pinch Hit H	PO	A	E	DP	TC/G	FA	G by Pos
1923	STL N	6	.250	.333	12	3	1	0	0	0.0	2	0	3	3	0	2	0	37	3	1	1	10.3	.976	1B-3, 2B-1
1925	CIN N	3	.429	.857	7	3	1	1	0	0.0	0	0	1	1	0	0	0	34	1	0	2	11.7	1.000	1B-3
1926		17	.250	.300	20	5	1	0	0	0.0	2	1	1	0	0	10	3	33	2	0	1	5.8	1.000	1B-6
3 yrs.		26	.282	.410	39	11	3	1	0	0.0	4	1	5	4	0	12	3	104	6	1	4	8.5	.991	1B-12, 2B-1

Rex Hudler

HUDLER, REX ALLEN
B. Sept. 2, 1960, Tempe, Ariz.
BR TR 6′ 1″ 180 lbs.

Year	Team	Games	BA	SA	AB	H	2B	3B	HR	HR%	R	RBI	BB	SO	SB	Pinch Hit AB	Pinch Hit H	PO	A	E	DP	TC/G	FA	G by Pos
1984	NY A	9	.143	.286	7	1	1	0	0	0.0	2	0	1	5	0	0	0	4	7	0	1	1.2	1.000	2B-9
1985		20	.157	.196	51	8	0	1	0	0.0	4	1	1	9	0	0	0	42	51	2	14	5.3	.979	2B-16, SS-1, 1B-1
1986	BAL A	14	.000	.000	1	0	0	0	0	0.0	1	0	0	0	1	0	0	2	3	1	0	0.4	.833	2B-13, 3B-1
1988	MON N	77	.273	.412	216	59	14	2	4	1.9	38	14	10	34	29	3	0	116	168	10	30	4.1	.966	2B-41, SS-27, OF-4
1989		92	.245	.406	155	38	7	0	6	3.9	21	13	6	23	15	27	4	59	59	7	13	1.6	.944	2B-38, OF-23, SS-18
1990	2 teams	MON N (4G –.333) STL N (89G –.281)																						
″	total	93	.282	.445	220	62	11	2	7	3.2	31	22	12	32	18	21	4	158	42	5	9	3.0	.976	OF-45, 2B-10, 3B-6, 1B-6, SS-1
1991	STL N	101	.227	.309	207	47	10	2	1	0.5	21	15	10	29	12	27	4	130	6	2	6	1.8	.986	OF-58, 1B-12, 2B-5
1992		61	.245	.378	98	24	4	0	3	3.1	17	5	2	23	2	29	7	44	39	3	6	2.4	.965	2B-16, OF-12, 1B-8
1994	CAL A	56	.298	.556	124	37	8	0	8	6.5	17	20	6	28	2	10	0	71	61	5	20	2.8	.964	2B-22, OF-18, 3B-4, DH-4, 1B-1
1995		84	.265	.417	223	59	16	0	6	2.7	30	27	10	48	13	14	2	122	114	4	33	3.0	.983	2B-52, OF-22, DH-3, 1B-2
10 yrs.		607	.257	.403	1302	335	71	7	35	2.7	182	117	58	231	92	131	21	748	550	39	132	2.7	.971	2B-222, OF-182, SS-47, 1B-30, 3B-11, DH-7

Johnny Hudson

HUDSON, JOHN WILSON
B. June 30, 1912, Bryan, Tex. D. Nov. 7, 1970, Bryan, Tex.
BR TR 5′10″ 160 lbs.

Year	Team	Games	BA	SA	AB	H	2B	3B	HR	HR%	R	RBI	BB	SO	SB	Pinch Hit AB	Pinch Hit H	PO	A	E	DP	TC/G	FA	G by Pos
1936	BKN N	6	.167	.167	12	2	0	0	0	0.0	1	0	2	1	0	0	0	10	8	3	1	4.2	.857	SS-4, 2B-1
1937		13	.185	.333	27	5	4	0	0	0.0	3	2	3	9	0	1	0	9	19	4	2	2.7	.875	SS-11, 2B-1
1938		135	.261	.335	498	130	21	5	2	0.4	59	37	39	76	7	1	0	304	398	27	79	5.4	.963	2B-132, SS-3
1939		109	.254	.338	343	87	17	3	2	0.6	46	32	30	36	5	12	3	175	260	18	56	4.7	.960	SS-50, 2B-45, 3B-1
1940		85	.218	.274	179	39	4	3	0	0.0	13	19	9	26	2	4	2	94	146	15	20	3.9	.941	SS-38, 2B-27, 3B-1
1941	CHI N	50	.202	.242	99	20	4	0	0	0.0	8	6	3	15	3	11	0	41	68	9	9	3.0	.924	SS-17, 2B-13, 3B-10
1945	NY N	28	.000	.000	11	0	0	0	0	0.0	8	0	1	1	0	4	0	5	4	1	0	1.4	.900	3B-5, 2B-2
7 yrs.		426	.242	.314	1169	283	50	11	4	0.3	138	96	87	164	17	33	5	638	903	77	167	4.5	.952	2B-221, SS-123, 3B-17

Nat Hudson

HUDSON, NATHANIEL P.
B. Jan. 12, 1869, Chicago, Ill. D. Mar. 14, 1928, Chicago, Ill.
BR TR

Year	Team	Games	BA	SA	AB	H	2B	3B	HR	HR%	R	RBI	BB	SO	SB	Pinch Hit AB	Pinch Hit H	PO	A	E	DP	TC/G	FA	G by Pos
1886	STL AA	43	.233	.273	150	35	4	1	0	0.0	16		11			0	0	53	38	6	2	2.2	.938	P-29, OF-12, 1B-3
1887		13	.250	.333	48	12	2	1	0	0.0	7		4		0	0	0	9	7	3	0	1.3	.842	P-9, OF-6
1888		56	.255	.321	196	50	7	0	2	1.0	27	28	18		9	0	0	89	55	9	4	2.6	.941	P-39, OF-16, 1B-3, SS-1
1889		13	.250	.365	52	13	1	1	1	1.9	6	10	2	11	1	0	0	20	12	3	0	1.9	.914	P-9, OF-6, 1B-3
4 yrs.		125	.247	.312	446	110	14	3	3	0.7	56	38	35	11	10	0	0	171	112	21	6	2.2	.931	P-86, OF-40, 1B-9, SS-1

Frank Huelsman

HUELSMAN, FRANK ELMER
B. June 5, 1874, St. Louis, Mo. D. June 9, 1959, Affton, Mo.
BR TR 6′ 2″ 210 lbs.

Year	Team	Games	BA	SA	AB	H	2B	3B	HR	HR%	R	RBI	BB	SO	SB	Pinch Hit AB	Pinch Hit H	PO	A	E	DP	TC/G	FA	G by Pos
1897	STL N	2	.286	.429	7	2	1	0	0	0.0	0	0	0		0	0	0	0	0	1	0	0.5	.000	OF-2
1904	4 teams	CHI A (4G –.143) DET A (4G –.333) STL A (20G –.221) WAS A (84G –.248)																						
″	total	112	.245	.343	396	97	23	5	2	0.5	28	35	31		7	4	0	162	7	7	2	1.6	.960	OF-107
1905	WAS A	126	.271	.397	421	114	28	8	3	0.7	48	62	31		11	4	1	189	7	15	2	1.7	.929	OF-123
3 yrs.		240	.258	.371	824	213	52	13	5	0.6	76	97	62		18	8	1	351	14	23	4	1.7	.941	OF-232

Mike Huff

HUFF, MICHAEL KALE
B. Aug. 11, 1963, Honolulu, Hawaii.
BR TR 6′ 1″ 180 lbs.

Year	Team	Games	BA	SA	AB	H	2B	3B	HR	HR%	R	RBI	BB	SO	SB	Pinch Hit AB	Pinch Hit H	PO	A	E	DP	TC/G	FA	G by Pos
1989	LA N	12	.200	.360	25	5	1	0	1	4.0	4	2	3	6	0	3	1	18	0	0	0	2.0	1.000	OF-9
1991	2 teams	CLE A (51G –.240) CHI A (51G –.268)																						
″	total	102	.251	.346	243	61	10	2	3	1.2	42	25	37	48	14	12	0	168	7	2	1	1.7	.989	OF-96, 2B-4, DH-2
1992	CHI A	60	.209	.252	115	24	5	0	0	0.0	13	8	10	24	1	16	5	68	2	0	0	1.2	1.000	OF-56, DH-1
1993		43	.182	.295	44	8	2	0	1	2.3	4	6	9	15	1	2	0	40	0	0	0	0.9	1.000	OF-43
1994	TOR A	80	.304	.449	207	63	15	3	3	1.4	31	25	27	27	2	9	3	126	4	1	1	1.7	.992	OF-76
1995		61	.232	.333	138	32	9	1	1	0.7	14	9	22	21	1	14	4	95	3	2	0	1.8	.980	OF-55
6 yrs.		358	.250	.355	772	193	42	6	9	1.2	108	75	108	141	19	56	13	515	16	5	2	1.6	.991	OF-335, 2B-4, DH-3

Ben Huffman

HUFFMAN, BENJAMIN FRANKLIN
B. June 26, 1914, Rileyville, Va.
BL TR 5′11½″ 175 lbs.

Year	Team	Games	BA	SA	AB	H	2B	3B	HR	HR%	R	RBI	BB	SO	SB	Pinch Hit AB	Pinch Hit H	PO	A	E	DP	TC/G	FA	G by Pos
1937	STL A	76	.273	.341	176	48	9	0	1	0.6	18	24	10	7	1	32	7	140	20	5	4	3.9	.970	C-42

Ed Hug

HUG, EDWARD AMBROSE
B. July 14, 1880, Fayetteville, Ohio D. May 11, 1953, Cincinnati, Ohio.
BR TR

Year	Team	Games	BA	SA	AB	H	2B	3B	HR	HR%	R	RBI	BB	SO	SB	Pinch Hit AB	Pinch Hit H	PO	A	E	DP	TC/G	FA	G by Pos
1903	BKN N	1	—	—	0	0	0	0	0	—	0	0	1		0	0	0	0	0	0	0	0.0	.000	C-1

Miller Huggins

HUGGINS, MILLER JAMES (Hug, The Mighty Mite)
B. Mar. 27, 1879, Cincinnati, Ohio D. Sept. 25, 1929, New York, N. Y.
Manager 1913–29.
Hall of Fame 1964.
BB TR 5′ 6½″ 140 lbs.

Year	Team	Games	BA	SA	AB	H	2B	3B	HR	HR%	R	RBI	BB	SO	SB	Pinch Hit AB	Pinch Hit H	PO	A	E	DP	TC/G	FA	G by Pos
1904	CIN N	140	.263	.328	491	129	12	7	2	0.4	96	30	88		13	0	0	337	448	46	32	5.9	.945	2B-140
1905		149	.273	.326	564	154	11	8	1	0.2	117	38	**103**		27	0	0	346	525	51	55	6.2	.945	2B-149
1906		146	.292	.338	545	159	11	7	0	0.0	81	26	71		41	0	0	341	458	44	62	5.8	.948	2B-146
1907		156	.248	.289	561	139	12	4	1	0.2	64	31	**83**		28	0	0	353	443	32	73	5.3	.961	2B-156
1908		135	.239	.287	498	119	14	5	0	0.0	65	23	58		30	4	1	302	406	30	45	5.5	.959	2B-135

Miller Huggins *continued*

Year	Team	Games	BA	SA	AB	H	2B	3B	HR	HR%	R	RBI	BB	SO	SB	Pinch Hit AB	Pinch Hit H	PO	A	E	DP	TC/G	FA	G by Pos
1909		57	.214	.245	159	34	3	1	0	0.0	18	6	28		11	10	1	95	125	16	14	5.1	.932	2B-31, 3B-15
1910	STL N	151	.265	.320	547	145	15	6	1	0.2	101	36	**116**	46	34	0	0	325	452	30	58	5.3	.963	2B-151
1911		138	.261	.312	509	133	19	2	1	0.2	106	24	96	52	37	1	1	281	439	29	62	5.5	.961	2B-136
1912		120	.304	.357	431	131	15	4	0	0.0	82	29	87	31	35	5	0	272	337	37	50	5.7	.943	2B-114
1913		120	.286	.318	381	109	12	0	0	0.0	73	27	91	49	23	5	1	266	339	14	44	5.5	.977	2B-112
1914		148	.263	.318	509	134	17	4	1	0.2	85	24	**105**	63	32	1	0	328	428	28	58	5.3	.964	2B-147
1915		107	.241	.283	353	85	5	2	2	0.6	57	24	74	68	13	0	0	194	315	23	44	5.0	.957	2B-107
1916		18	.333	.333	9	3	0	0	0	0.0	2	0	2	3	0	4	2	10	10	0	0	2.9	1.000	2B-7
13 yrs.		1585	.265	.314	5557	1474	146	50	9	0.2	947	318	1002	312	324	30	6	3450	4725	380	597	5.5	.956	2B-1531, 3B-15

Bill Hughes

HUGHES, WILLIAM R. BL TL
B. Nov. 25, 1866, Bladinsville, Ill. D. Aug. 25, 1943, Santa Ana, Calif.

Year	Team	Games	BA	SA	AB	H	2B	3B	HR	HR%	R	RBI	BB	SO	SB	Pinch Hit AB	Pinch Hit H	PO	A	E	DP	TC/G	FA	G by Pos
1884	WAS U	14	.122	.122	49	6	0	0	0	0.0	5		2			0	0	92	3	7	2	6.8	.931	1B-9, OF-6
1885	PHI AA	4	.188	.375	16	3	1	1	0	0.0	3		1			0	0	4	2	1	0	1.8	.857	OF-2, P-2
2 yrs.		18	.138	.185	65	9	1	1	0	0.0	8		3			0	0	96	5	8	2	5.7	.927	1B-9, OF-8, P-2

Joe Hughes

HUGHES, JOSEPH THOMPSON BR TR 5′10″ 165 lbs.
B. Feb. 21, 1880, Pardo, Pa. D. Mar. 13, 1951, Cleveland, Ohio.

Year	Team	Games	BA	SA	AB	H	2B	3B	HR	HR%	R	RBI	BB	SO	SB	Pinch Hit AB	Pinch Hit H	PO	A	E	DP	TC/G	FA	G by Pos
1902	CHI N	1	.000	.000	3	0	0	0	0	0.0	0	0	0		0	0	0	0	0	0	0	0.0	.000	OF-1

Keith Hughes

HUGHES, KEITH WILLS BL TL 6′ 3″ 210 lbs.
B. Sept. 12, 1963, Bryn Mawr, Pa.

Year	Team	Games	BA	SA	AB	H	2B	3B	HR	HR%	R	RBI	BB	SO	SB	Pinch Hit AB	Pinch Hit H	PO	A	E	DP	TC/G	FA	G by Pos
1987	2 teams	NY A (4G –.000) PHI N (37G –.263)																						
″	total	41	.250	.275	80	20	2	0	0	0.0	8	10	7	13	0	23	8	26	0	1	0	1.4	.963	OF-19
1988	BAL A	41	.194	.324	108	21	4	2	2	1.9	10	14	16	27	1	8	0	59	4	2	2	2.1	.969	OF-31
1990	NY N	8	.000	.000	9	0	0	0	0	0.0	0	0	0	4	0	6	0	5	0	0	0	1.0	1.000	OF-5
1993	CIN N	3	.000	.000	4	0	0	0	0	0.0	0	0	0	0	0	2	0	0	0	0	0	0.0	.000	OF-2
4 yrs.		93	.204	.284	201	41	6	2	2	1.0	18	24	23	44	1	39	8	90	4	3	2	1.7	.969	OF-57

Roy Hughes

HUGHES, ROY JOHN (Jeep, Sage) BR TR 5′10½″ 167 lbs.
B. Jan. 11, 1911, Cincinnati, Ohio D. Mar. 5, 1995, Asheville, N. C.

Year	Team	Games	BA	SA	AB	H	2B	3B	HR	HR%	R	RBI	BB	SO	SB	Pinch Hit AB	Pinch Hit H	PO	A	E	DP	TC/G	FA	G by Pos
1935	CLE A	82	.293	.372	266	78	15	3	0	0.0	40	14	18	17	13	6	0	152	216	17	44	5.5	.956	2B-40, SS-29, 3B-1
1936		152	.295	.378	638	188	35	9	0	0.0	112	63	57	40	20	0	0	421	466	25	98	6.0	.973	2B-152
1937		104	.277	.355	346	96	12	6	1	0.3	57	40	40	22	11	11	4	157	233	13	32	4.5	.968	3B-58, 2B-32
1938	STL A	58	.281	.375	96	27	3	0	2	2.1	16	13	12	11	3	30	6	45	60	4	16	3.9	.963	2B-21, 3B-5, SS-2
1939	2 teams	STL A (17G –.087) PHI N (65G –.228)																						
″	total	82	.215	.254	260	56	5	1	1	0.4	28	17	25	22	4	5	1	194	198	6	34	5.5	.985	2B-71, SS-1
1944	CHI N	126	.287	.351	478	137	16	6	1	0.2	86	28	35	30	16	7	4	220	303	20	54	4.6	.963	3B-66, SS-52
1945		69	.261	.306	222	58	8	1	0	0.0	34	8	16	18	6	5	1	120	157	13	28	4.3	.955	SS-36, 2B-21, 3B-9, 1B-2
1946	PHI N	89	.236	.283	276	65	11	1	0	0.0	23	22	19	15	7	12	3	123	144	11	27	3.8	.960	SS-34, 3B-31, 2B-7, 1B-1
8 yrs.		762	.273	.340	2582	705	105	27	5	0.2	396	205	222	175	80	76	19	1432	1777	109	333	4.9	.967	2B-344, 3B-170, SS-154, 1B-3
WORLD SERIES																								
1945	CHI N	6	.294	.353	17	5	1	0	0	0.0	1	3	4	5	0	0	0	13	17	0	2	5.0	1.000	SS-6

Terry Hughes

HUGHES, TERRY WAYNE BR TR 6′ 1″ 185 lbs.
B. May 13, 1949, Spartanburg, S. C.

Year	Team	Games	BA	SA	AB	H	2B	3B	HR	HR%	R	RBI	BB	SO	SB	Pinch Hit AB	Pinch Hit H	PO	A	E	DP	TC/G	FA	G by Pos
1970	CHI N	2	.333	.333	3	1	0	0	0	0.0	0	0	0	0	0	1	1	0	0	0	0	0.0		OF-1, 3B-1
1973	STL N	11	.214	.286	14	3	1	0	0	0.0	1	1	1	4	0	4	1	9	4	0	1	2.2	1.000	3B-5, 1B-1
1974	BOS A	41	.203	.275	69	14	2	0	1	1.4	5	6	6	18	0	1	0	25	44	3	5	1.9	.958	3B-36, DH-1
3 yrs.		54	.209	.279	86	18	3	0	1	1.2	6	7	7	22	0	6	2	34	48	3	6	1.9	.965	3B-42, 1B-1, DH-1, OF-1

Tom Hughes

HUGHES, THOMAS FRANKLIN BL TR 6′ 1″ 190 lbs.
B. Aug. 6, 1907, Emmet, Ark. D. Aug. 10, 1989, Beaumont, Tex.

Year	Team	Games	BA	SA	AB	H	2B	3B	HR	HR%	R	RBI	BB	SO	SB	Pinch Hit AB	Pinch Hit H	PO	A	E	DP	TC/G	FA	G by Pos
1930	DET A	17	.373	.508	59	22	2	3	0	0.0	8	5	4	8	0	0	0	26	0	3	0	1.8	.897	OF-16

Emil Huhn

HUHN, EMIL HUGO (Hap) BR TR 6′ 180 lbs.
B. Mar. 10, 1892, North Vernon, Ind. D. Sept. 5, 1925, Camden, S. C.

Year	Team	Games	BA	SA	AB	H	2B	3B	HR	HR%	R	RBI	BB	SO	SB	Pinch Hit AB	Pinch Hit H	PO	A	E	DP	TC/G	FA	G by Pos
1915	NWK F	124	.227	.282	415	94	18	1	1	0.2	34	41	28		13	8	1	1071	71	18	70	9.9	.984	1B-101, C-16
1916	CIN N	37	.255	.330	94	24	3	2	0	0.0	4	3	2	11	0	3	1	172	25	1	7	6.0	.995	C-18, 1B-14, OF-1
1917		23	.196	.294	51	10	1	2	0	0.0	2	3	2	5	1	7	1	50	15	2	0	4.5	.970	C-15
3 yrs.		184	.229	.291	560	128	22	5	1	0.2	40	47	32	16	14	18	3	1293	111	21	77	8.6	.985	1B-115, C-49, OF-1

Billy Hulen

HULEN, WILLIAM FRANKLIN BL TL 5′ 8″ 148 lbs.
B. Mar. 12, 1870, Dixon, Calif. D. Oct. 2, 1947, Santa Rosa, Calif.

Year	Team	Games	BA	SA	AB	H	2B	3B	HR	HR%	R	RBI	BB	SO	SB	Pinch Hit AB	Pinch Hit H	PO	A	E	DP	TC/G	FA	G by Pos
1896	PHI N	88	.265	.360	339	90	18	7	0	0.0	87	38	55	20	23	1	1	182	208	56	33	5.1	.874	SS-73, OF-12, 2B-2
1899	WAS N	19	.147	.162	68	10	1	0	0	0.0	10	3	10		5	0	0	25	67	10	2	5.4	.902	SS-19
2 yrs.		107	.246	.327	407	100	19	7	0	0.0	97	41	65	20	28	1	1	207	275	66	35	5.2	.880	SS-92, OF-12, 2B-2

Tim Hulett

HULETT, TIMOTHY CRAIG BR TR 6′ 185 lbs.
B. Jan. 20, 1960, Springfield, Ill.

Year	Team	Games	BA	SA	AB	H	2B	3B	HR	HR%	R	RBI	BB	SO	SB	Pinch Hit AB	Pinch Hit H	PO	A	E	DP	TC/G	FA	G by Pos
1983	CHI A	6	.200	.200	5	1	0	0	0	0.0	0	0	0	0	1	0	0	8	6	2	1	2.7	.875	2B-6
1984		8	.000	.000	7	0	0	0	0	0.0	1	0	1	4	1	1	0	4	15	0	2	2.7	1.000	3B-4, 2B-3
1985		141	.268	.375	395	106	19	4	5	1.3	52	36	30	81	6	2	1	117	256	24	41	2.8	.940	3B-115, 2B-28, OF-1
1986		150	.231	.379	520	120	16	5	17	3.3	53	44	21	91	4	5	1	179	331	15	54	3.4	.971	3B-89, 2B-66
1987		68	.217	.346	240	52	10	0	7	2.9	20	28	10	41	0	0	0	55	142	9	19	3.0	.956	3B-61, 2B-8
1989	BAL A	33	.278	.423	97	27	5	0	3	3.1	12	18	10	17	0	1	0	70	71	4	13	4.3	.972	2B-23, 3B-11
1990		53	.255	.373	153	39	7	1	3	2.0	16	16	15	41	1	9	1	44	101	4	15	3.1	.973	3B-24, 2B-16, DH-8
1991		79	.204	.350	206	42	9	0	7	3.4	29	18	13	49	0	10	2	47	96	4	13	1.8	.973	3B-39, 2B-26, DH-15, SS-1
1992		57	.289	.408	142	41	7	2	2	1.4	11	21	10	31	0	9	2	25	92	7	11	2.3	.944	3B-27, DH-13, 2B-10, SS-5
1993		85	.300	.381	260	78	15	0	2	0.8	40	23	23	56	1	6	1	58	176	8	26	2.7	.967	3B-75, SS-8, 2B-4, DH-2

Tim Hulett *continued*

Year	Team	Lg	Games	BA	SA	AB	H	2B	3B	HR	HR%	R	RBI	BB	SO	SB	Pinch Hit AB	Pinch Hit H	PO	A	E	DP	TC/G	FA	G by Pos
1994			36	.228	.337	92	21	2	1	2	2.2	11	15	12	24	0	2	0	61	93	3	24	4.1	.981	2B-23, 3B-9, SS-6
1995	STL	N	4	.182	.182	11	2	0	0	0	0.0	0	0	0	3	0	2	2	6	13	2	3	7.0	.905	2B-2, SS-1
12 yrs.			720	.249	.371	2128	529	90	13	48	2.3	245	219	145	438	14	47	10	674	1392	82	222	2.9	.962	3B-454, 2B-215, DH-38, SS-21, OF-1

David Hulse

HULSE, DAVID LINDSEY BL TL 5′11″ 170 lbs.
B. Feb. 25, 1968, San Angelo, Texas.

Year	Team	Lg	Games	BA	SA	AB	H	2B	3B	HR	HR%	R	RBI	BB	SO	SB	Pinch Hit AB	Pinch Hit H	PO	A	E	DP	TC/G	FA	G by Pos
1992	TEX	A	32	.304	.348	92	28	4	0	0	0.0	14	2	3	18	3	0	0	61	0	1	0	1.9	.984	OF-31, DH-1
1993			114	.290	.369	407	118	9	10	1	0.2	71	29	26	57	29	6	5	244	3	3	1	2.2	.988	OF-112, DH-2
1994			77	.255	.316	310	79	8	4	1	0.3	58	19	21	53	18	0	0	179	0	4	0	2.4	.978	OF-76
1995	MIL	A	119	.251	.345	339	85	11	6	3	0.9	46	47	18	60	15	7	2	180	2	3	1	1.6	.984	OF-115
4 yrs.			342	.270	.346	1148	310	32	20	5	0.4	189	97	68	188	65	13	7	664	5	11	2	2.0	.984	OF-334, DH-3

Rudy Hulswitt

HULSWITT, RUDOLPH EDWARD BR TR 5′ 8½″ 165 lbs.
B. Feb. 23, 1877, Newport, Ky. D. Jan. 16, 1950, Louisville, Ky.

Year	Team	Lg	Games	BA	SA	AB	H	2B	3B	HR	HR%	R	RBI	BB	SO	SB	Pinch Hit AB	Pinch Hit H	PO	A	E	DP	TC/G	FA	G by Pos
1899	LOU	N	1	—	—	0	0	0	0	0	—	0	0	0		0	0	0	1	1	4	0	6.0	.333	SS-1
1902	PHI	N	128	.272	.322	497	135	11	7	0	0.0	59	38	30		12	0	0	320	405	67	38	6.2	.915	SS-125, 3B-3
1903			138	.247	.329	519	128	22	9	1	0.2	56	58	28		10	0	0	354	430	81	43	6.3	.906	SS-138
1904			113	.244	.298	406	99	11	4	1	0.2	36	36	16		8	0	0	273	310	56	42	5.7	.912	SS-113
1908	CIN	N	119	.228	.285	386	88	5	7	1	0.3	27	28	30		7	0	0	245	370	42	37	5.5	.936	SS-118, 2B-1
1909	STL	N	82	.280	.329	289	81	8	3	0	0.0	21	29	19		7	4	1	166	228	30	20	5.5	.929	SS-65, 2B-12
1910			63	.248	.331	133	33	7	2	0	0.0	9	14	13	10	5	31	6	40	80	21	4	4.4	.851	SS-30, 2B-2
7 yrs.			644	.253	.314	2230	564	64	32	3	0.1	208	203	136	10	49	35	7	1399	1824	301	184	5.8	.915	SS-590, 2B-15, 3B-3

John Hummel

HUMMEL, JOHN EDWIN (Silent John) BR TR 5′11″ 160 lbs.
B. Apr. 4, 1883, Bloomsburg, Pa. D. May 18, 1959, Springfield, Mass.

Year	Team	Lg	Games	BA	SA	AB	H	2B	3B	HR	HR%	R	RBI	BB	SO	SB	Pinch Hit AB	Pinch Hit H	PO	A	E	DP	TC/G	FA	G by Pos
1905	BKN	N	30	.266	.367	109	29	3	4	0	0.0	19	7	9		6	0	0	62	90	6	13	5.3	.962	2B-30
1906			97	.199	.259	286	57	6	4	1	0.3	20	21	36		10	8	2	310	156	18	25	5.6	.963	2B-50, OF-21, 1B-15
1907			107	.234	.313	342	80	12	3	3	0.9	41	31	26		8	10	2	321	162	16	23	5.1	.968	2B-44, OF-33, 1B-12, SS-8
1908			154	.241	.320	594	143	11	12	4	0.7	51	41	34		20	0	0	367	182	18	25	3.7	.968	OF-95, 2B-43, SS-9, 1B-8
1909			146	.280	.363	542	152	15	9	4	0.7	54	52	22		16	2	0	728	207	35	38	6.7	.964	1B-54, 2B-38, SS-36, OF-17
1910			153	.244	.351	578	141	21	13	5	0.9	67	74	57	**81**	21	0	0	344	424	28	67	5.2	.965	2B-153
1911			137	.270	.392	477	129	21	11	5	1.0	54	58	67	66	16	3	0	337	362	21	61	5.4	.971	2B-127, 1B-4, SS-2
1912			122	.282	.404	411	116	21	7	5	1.2	55	54	49	55	7	9	0	297	168	11	22	4.2	.977	2B-58, OF-44, 1B-11
1913			67	.242	.379	198	48	7	7	2	1.0	20	24	13	23	4	15	3	126	66	8	24	3.7	.960	OF-28, SS-17, 1B-6, 2B-3
1914			73	.264	.389	208	55	8	9	0	0.0	25	20	16	25	5	17	2	339	21	6	13	6.4	.984	1B-36, OF-19, SS-1, 2B-1
1915			53	.230	.310	100	23	2	3	0	0.0	6	8	6	11	1	17	2	95	4	0	5	3.1	1.000	OF-20, 1B-11, SS-1
1918	NY	A	22	.295	.377	61	18	1	2	0	0.0	9	4	11	8	3	4	1	58	3	2	3	3.3	.968	OF-15, 1B-3, 2B-1
12 yrs.			1161	.254	.352	3906	991	128	84	29	0.7	421	394	346	269	117	85	12	3384	1845	169	319	5.0	.969	2B-548, OF-292, 1B-160, SS-74

Al Humphrey

HUMPHREY, ALBERT BL TR 5′11″ 180 lbs.
B. Feb. 28, 1886, Ashtabula, Ohio D. May 13, 1961, Ashtabula, Ohio.

Year	Team	Lg	Games	BA	SA	AB	H	2B	3B	HR	HR%	R	RBI	BB	SO	SB	Pinch Hit AB	Pinch Hit H	PO	A	E	DP	TC/G	FA	G by Pos
1911	BKN	N	8	.185	.185	27	5	0	0	0	0.0	4	0	3	7	0	0	0	12	0	1	0	1.6	.923	OF-8

Terry Humphrey

HUMPHREY, TERRYAL GENE BR TR 6′ 3″ 185 lbs.
B. Aug. 4, 1949, Chickasha, Okla.

Year	Team	Lg	Games	BA	SA	AB	H	2B	3B	HR	HR%	R	RBI	BB	SO	SB	Pinch Hit AB	Pinch Hit H	PO	A	E	DP	TC/G	FA	G by Pos
1971	MON	N	9	.192	.231	26	5	1	0	0	0.0	1	1	0	4	0	1	0	50	3	1	0	6.0	.981	C-9
1972			69	.186	.237	215	40	8	0	1	0.5	13	9	16	38	4	4	1	322	37	5	4	5.6	.986	C-65
1973			43	.167	.222	90	15	2	0	1	1.1	5	9	5	16	0	5	0	159	9	0	1	4.8	1.000	C-35
1974			20	.192	.250	52	10	3	0	0	0.0	3	3	4	9	0	2	2	85	15	1	4	5.9	.990	C-17
1975	DET	A	18	.244	.244	41	10	0	0	0	0.0	0	1	2	6	0	0	0	61	9	0	1	3.9	1.000	C-18
1976	CAL	A	71	.245	.311	196	48	10	0	1	0.5	17	19	13	30	0	1	0	397	42	9	4	6.3	.980	C-71
1977			123	.227	.283	304	69	11	0	2	0.7	17	34	21	58	1	0	0	661	63	8	10	6.0	.989	C-123
1978			53	.219	.298	114	25	4	1	1	0.9	11	9	6	12	0	0	0	252	22	6	5	5.2	.979	C-52, 3B-1, 2B-1
1979			9	.059	.059	17	1	0	0	0	0.0	2	0	1	2	0	0	0	55	3	1	1	6.6	.983	C-9
9 yrs.			415	.211	.267	1055	223	39	1	6	0.6	69	85	68	175	5	13	3	2042	203	31	30	5.7	.986	C-399, 3B-1, 2B-1

Mike Humphreys

HUMPHREYS, MICHAEL BUTLER BR TR 6′ 185 lbs.
B. Apr. 10, 1967, Dallas, Tex.

Year	Team	Lg	Games	BA	SA	AB	H	2B	3B	HR	HR%	R	RBI	BB	SO	SB	Pinch Hit AB	Pinch Hit H	PO	A	E	DP	TC/G	FA	G by Pos
1991	NY	A	25	.200	.200	40	8	0	0	0	0.0	9	3	9	7	2	2	0	10	8	1	0	0.9	.947	OF-9, DH-7, 3B-6
1992			4	.100	.100	10	1	0	0	0	0.0	0	0	0	1	0	1	0	7	1	0	0	2.7	1.000	OF-2, DH-1
1993			25	.171	.371	35	6	2	1	1	2.9	6	6	4	11	2	7	1	14	0	0	0	0.6	1.000	OF-21, DH-3
3 yrs.			54	.176	.259	85	15	2	1	1	1.2	15	9	13	19	4	10	1	31	9	1	0	0.8	.976	OF-32, DH-11, 3B-6

John Humphries

HUMPHRIES, JOHN HENRY BL TL 6′ 185 lbs.
B. Nov. 12, 1861, North Gower, Ont., Canada D. Nov. 29, 1933, Salinas, Calif.

Year	Team	Lg	Games	BA	SA	AB	H	2B	3B	HR	HR%	R	RBI	BB	SO	SB	Pinch Hit AB	Pinch Hit H	PO	A	E	DP	TC/G	FA	G by Pos
1883	NY	N	29	.112	.121	107	12	1	0	0	0.0	5		1	22		0	0	84	31	26	0	4.4	.816	C-20, OF-12
1884	2 teams	WAS AA (49G –.176) NY N (20G –.094)																							
″	total		69	.156	.163	257	40	2	0	0	0.0	29		18	19		0	0	394	88	64	8	7.7	.883	C-55, OF-12, 1B-4
2 yrs.			98	.143	.151	364	52	3	0	0	0.0	34		19	41		0	0	478	119	90	8	6.7	.869	C-75, OF-24, 1B-4

Randy Hundley

HUNDLEY, CECIL RANDOLPH BR TR 5′11″ 170 lbs.
Father of Todd Hundley.
B. June 1, 1942, Martinsville, Va.

Year	Team	Lg	Games	BA	SA	AB	H	2B	3B	HR	HR%	R	RBI	BB	SO	SB	Pinch Hit AB	Pinch Hit H	PO	A	E	DP	TC/G	FA	G by Pos
1964	SF	N	2	.000	.000	1	0	0	0	0	0.0	1	0	0	1	0	0	0	0	0	0	0	0.0	.000	C-2
1965			6	.067	.067	15	1	0	0	0	0.0	0	0	0	4	0	0	0	34	9	0	1	7.2	1.000	C-6
1966	CHI	N	149	.236	.397	526	124	22	3	19	3.6	50	63	35	113	1	0	0	871	85	14	8	6.5	.986	C-149
1967			152	.267	.403	539	144	25	3	14	2.6	68	60	44	75	2	2	0	865	59	4	7	6.1	.996	C-152
1968			160	.226	.311	553	125	18	4	7	1.3	41	65	39	69	1	0	0	885	81	5	11	6.1	.995	C-160
1969			151	.255	.391	522	133	15	1	18	3.4	67	64	61	90	2	1	0	978	79	8	17	7.1	.992	C-151
1970			73	.244	.348	250	61	5	0	7	2.8	13	36	16	52	0	0	0	455	26	5	2	6.7	.990	C-73
1971			9	.333	.381	21	7	1	0	0	0.0	1	2	0	2	0	1	0	43	3	1	0	5.9	.979	C-8

Randy Hundley *continued*

Year	Team	Games	BA	SA	AB	H	2B	3B	HR	HR%	R	RBI	BB	SO	SB	Pinch Hit AB	Pinch Hit H	PO	A	E	DP	TC/G	FA	G by Pos
1972		114	.218	.294	357	78	12	0	5	1.4	23	30	22	62	1	2	1	569	53	3	7	5.5	.995	C-113
1973		124	.226	.342	368	83	11	1	10	2.7	35	43	30	51	5	3	1	648	59	5	7	5.8	.993	C-122
1974	MIN A	32	.193	.216	88	17	2	0	0	0.0	2	3	4	12	0	3	0	148	17	6	2	6.1	.965	C-28
1975	SD N	74	.206	.278	180	37	5	1	2	1.1	7	14	19	29	0	18	4	237	20	8	3	5.2	.970	C-51
1976	CHI N	13	.167	.278	18	3	2	0	0	0.0	3	1	1	4	0	4	0	22	2	2	0	2.9	.923	C-9
1977		2	.000	.000	4	0	0	0	0	0.0	0	0	0	1	0	0	0	10	0	0	0	5.0	1.000	C-2
14 yrs.		1061	.236	.350	3442	813	118	13	82	2.4	311	381	271	565	12	34	6	5765	493	61	65	6.2	.990	C-1026

Todd Hundley

HUNDLEY, TODD RANDOLPH BB TR 5′11″ 170 lbs.
Son of Randy Hundley.
B. May 27, 1969, Martinsville, Va.

Year	Team	Games	BA	SA	AB	H	2B	3B	HR	HR%	R	RBI	BB	SO	SB	Pinch Hit AB	Pinch Hit H	PO	A	E	DP	TC/G	FA	G by Pos
1990	NY N	36	.209	.299	67	14	6	0	0	0.0	8	2	6	18	0	3	0	162	8	2	2	4.8	.988	C-36
1991		21	.133	.217	60	8	0	1	1	1.7	5	7	6	14	0	3	1	85	11	0	1	4.8	1.000	C-20
1992		123	.209	.316	358	75	17	0	7	2.0	32	32	19	76	3	7	1	700	48	3	2	6.2	.996	C-121
1993		130	.228	.357	417	95	17	2	11	2.6	40	53	23	62	1	15	3	592	63	8	6	5.4	.988	C-123
1994		91	.237	.443	291	69	10	1	16	5.5	45	42	25	73	2	15	4	448	28	5	0	5.9	.990	C-82
1995		90	.280	.484	275	77	11	0	15	5.5	39	51	42	64	1	12	3	487	28	7	2	5.9	.987	C-89
6 yrs.		491	.230	.379	1468	338	61	4	50	3.4	169	187	121	307	7	55	12	2474	186	25	13	5.7	.991	C-471

Bernie Hungling

HUNGLING, BERNARD HERMAN (Bud) BR TR 6′ 2″ 180 lbs.
B. Mar. 5, 1896, Dayton, Ohio D. Mar. 30, 1968, Dayton, Ohio.

Year	Team	Games	BA	SA	AB	H	2B	3B	HR	HR%	R	RBI	BB	SO	SB	Pinch Hit AB	Pinch Hit H	PO	A	E	DP	TC/G	FA	G by Pos
1922	BKN N	39	.225	.304	102	23	1	2	1	1.0	9	13	6	20	2	3	0	130	23	5	2	4.4	.968	C-36
1923		2	.000	.000	4	0	0	0	0	0.0	0	0	0	2	0	0	0	2	0	1	0	3.0	.667	C-1
1930	STL A	10	.323	.387	31	10	2	0	0	0.0	4	2	5	3	0	0	0	27	2	0	0	2.9	1.000	C-10
3 yrs.		51	.241	.314	137	33	3	2	1	0.7	13	15	11	25	2	3	0	159	25	6	2	4.0	.968	C-47

Bill Hunnefield

HUNNEFIELD, WILLIAM FENTON (Wild Bill) BB TR 5′10″ 165 lbs.
B. Jan. 5, 1899, Dedham, Mass. D. Aug. 28, 1976, Nantucket, Mass.

Year	Team	Games	BA	SA	AB	H	2B	3B	HR	HR%	R	RBI	BB	SO	SB	Pinch Hit AB	Pinch Hit H	PO	A	E	DP	TC/G	FA	G by Pos
1926	CHI A	131	.274	.366	470	129	26	4	3	0.6	81	48	37	28	24	2	0	250	337	36	54	4.8	.942	SS-98, 3B-17, 2B-15
1927		112	.285	.375	365	104	25	1	2	0.5	45	36	25	24	13	13	3	185	243	29	41	4.8	.937	SS-78, 2B-17, 3B-1
1928		94	.294	.354	333	98	8	3	2	0.6	42	24	26	24	16	7	3	168	249	14	48	5.0	.968	2B-83, SS-3, 3B-1
1929		47	.181	.220	127	23	5	0	0	0.0	13	9	7	3	5	10	1	68	96	6	18	5.3	.965	2B-26, 3B-4, SS-2
1930		31	.272	.333	81	22	2	0	1	1.2	11	5	4	10	1	6	1	33	37	5	9	3.3	.933	SS-22, 1B-1
1931	3 teams	CLE A (21G –.239) BOS N (11G –.286) NY N (64G –.270)																						
″	total	96	.264	.313	288	76	9	1	1	0.3	38	22	18	22	6	1	0	161	208	31	37	4.3	.923	2B-61, SS-26, 3B-5
6 yrs.		511	.272	.344	1664	452	75	9	9	0.5	230	144	117	111	65	39	8	865	1170	121	207	4.7	.944	SS-229, 2B-202, 3B-28, 1B-1

Joel Hunt

HUNT, OLIVER JOEL (Jodie) BR TR 5′10″ 165 lbs.
B. Oct. 11, 1905, Texico, N. M. D. July 24, 1978, Teague, Tex.

Year	Team	Games	BA	SA	AB	H	2B	3B	HR	HR%	R	RBI	BB	SO	SB	Pinch Hit AB	Pinch Hit H	PO	A	E	DP	TC/G	FA	G by Pos
1931	STL N	4	.000	.000	1	0	0	0	0	0.0	2	0	0	1	0	1	0	0	0	0	0	0.0	.000	OF-1
1932		12	.190	.238	21	4	1	0	0	0.0	0	3	4	3	0	5	2	13	0	0	0	2.6	1.000	OF-5
2 yrs.		16	.182	.227	22	4	1	0	0	0.0	2	3	4	4	0	6	2	13	0	0	0	2.2	1.000	OF-6

Ken Hunt

HUNT, KENNETH LAWRENCE BR TR 6′ 1″ 205 lbs.
B. July 13, 1934, Grand Forks, N. D.

Year	Team	Games	BA	SA	AB	H	2B	3B	HR	HR%	R	RBI	BB	SO	SB	Pinch Hit AB	Pinch Hit H	PO	A	E	DP	TC/G	FA	G by Pos
1959	NY A	6	.333	.417	12	4	1	0	0	0.0	2	1	0	3	0	1	1	9	0	0	0	1.8	1.000	OF-5
1960		25	.273	.364	22	6	2	0	0	0.0	4	1	4	4	0	1	0	22	0	1	0	1.0	.957	OF-24
1961	LA A	149	.255	.484	479	122	29	3	25	5.2	70	84	49	120	8	20	2	261	7	14	1	2.1	.950	OF-134, 2B-1
1962		13	.182	.455	11	2	0	0	1	9.1	4	1	1	5	1	4	0	13	0	2	0	5.0	.867	1B-3
1963	2 teams	LA A (59G –.183) WAS A (7G –.200)																						
″	total	66	.185	.346	162	30	6	1	6	3.7	18	20	17	55	0	11	1	81	1	2	0	1.5	.976	OF-55
1964	WAS A	51	.135	.208	96	13	4	0	1	1.0	9	4	14	35	0	14	3	68	1	0	1	1.9	1.000	OF-37
6 yrs.		310	.226	.417	782	177	42	4	33	4.2	107	111	85	222	9	51	7	454	9	19	2	1.9	.961	OF-255, 1B-3, 2B-1

Randy Hunt

HUNT, JAMES RANDALL BR TR 6′ 190 lbs.
B. Jan. 3, 1960, Prattville, Ala.

Year	Team	Games	BA	SA	AB	H	2B	3B	HR	HR%	R	RBI	BB	SO	SB	Pinch Hit AB	Pinch Hit H	PO	A	E	DP	TC/G	FA	G by Pos
1985	STL N	14	.158	.158	19	3	0	0	0	0.0	1	1	0	5	0	1	0	33	1	0	0	2.6	1.000	C-13
1986	MON N	21	.208	.333	48	10	0	0	2	4.2	4	5	5	16	0	0	0	135	8	6	2	7.1	.960	C-21
2 yrs.		35	.194	.284	67	13	0	0	2	3.0	5	6	5	21	0	1	0	168	9	6	2	5.4	.967	C-34

Ron Hunt

HUNT, RONALD KENNETH BR TR 6′ 186 lbs.
B. Feb. 23, 1941, St. Louis, Mo.

Year	Team	Games	BA	SA	AB	H	2B	3B	HR	HR%	R	RBI	BB	SO	SB	Pinch Hit AB	Pinch Hit H	PO	A	E	DP	TC/G	FA	G by Pos
1963	NY N	143	.272	.396	533	145	28	4	10	1.9	64	42	40	50	5	1	1	351	416	26	85	5.5	.967	2B-142, 3B-1
1964		127	.303	.406	475	144	19	6	6	1.3	59	42	29	30	6	6	2	258	343	16	76	5.1	.974	2B-109, 3B-12
1965		57	.240	.327	196	47	12	1	1	0.5	21	10	14	19	2	4	0	108	144	8	19	5.0	.969	2B-46, 3B-6
1966		132	.288	.355	479	138	19	2	3	0.6	63	33	41	34	8	8	2	295	388	21	81	5.6	.970	2B-123, SS-1, 3B-1
1967	LA N	110	.263	.345	388	102	17	3	3	0.8	44	33	39	24	2	10	1	215	235	12	51	4.7	.974	2B-90, 3B-8
1968	SF N	148	.250	.297	529	132	19	0	2	0.4	79	28	78	41	6	2	1	289	410	20	66	4.9	.972	2B-147
1969		128	.262	.341	478	125	23	3	3	0.6	72	41	51	47	9	3	0	254	357	13	67	5.0	.979	2B-125, 3B-1
1970		117	.281	.381	367	103	17	1	6	1.6	70	41	44	29	1	23	7	172	206	15	39	3.9	.962	2B-85, 3B-16
1971	MON N	152	.279	.358	520	145	20	3	5	1.0	89	38	58	41	5	5	1	280	400	16	77	4.6	.977	2B-133, 3B-19
1972		129	.253	.298	443	112	20	0	0	0.0	56	18	51	29	9	5	0	261	366	11	61	5.0	.983	2B-122, 3B-5
1973		113	.309	.344	401	124	14	0	0	0.0	61	18	52	19	10	6	2	225	301	11	56	4.6	.980	2B-102, 3B-14
1974	2 teams	MON N (115G –.268) STL N (12G –.174)																						
″	total	127	.263	.298	426	112	15	0	0	0.0	67	26	58	19	2	10	3	114	241	16	35	3.3	.957	3B-75, 2B-36, SS-1
12 yrs.		1483	.273	.347	5235	1429	223	23	39	0.7	745	370	555	382	65	83	20	2822	3807	185	713	4.8	.973	2B-1260, 3B-158, SS-2

Bill Hunter

HUNTER, WILLIAM ELLSWORTH BL TL 5′ 7½″ 155 lbs.
Brother of George Hunter.
B. July 8, 1887, Buffalo, N. Y. D. Apr. 10, 1934, Buffalo, N. Y.

Year	Team	Games	BA	SA	AB	H	2B	3B	HR	HR%	R	RBI	BB	SO	SB	Pinch Hit AB	Pinch Hit H	PO	A	E	DP	TC/G	FA	G by Pos
1912	CLE A	21	.164	.200	55	9	2	0	0	0.0	6	2	10		0	5	0	35	1	0	1	2.3	1.000	OF-16

Bill Hunter

HUNTER, WILLIAM ROBERT 5′ 7½″ 160 lbs.
B. 1855, St. Thomas, Ont., Canada Deceased.

Year	Team	Games	BA	SA	AB	H	2B	3B	HR	HR%	R	RBI	BB	SO	SB	Pinch Hit AB	Pinch Hit H	PO	A	E	DP	TC/G	FA	G by Pos
1884	LOU AA	2	.143	.143	7	1	0	0	0	0.0	1		0			0	0	5	1	3	0	4.5	.667	C-2

Billy Hunter

HUNTER, GORDON WILLIAM BR TR 6′ 180 lbs.
B. June 4, 1928, Punxsutawney, Pa.
Manager 1977–78.

Year	Team	Games	BA	SA	AB	H	2B	3B	HR	HR%	R	RBI	BB	SO	SB	Pinch Hit AB	Pinch Hit H	PO	A	E	DP	TC/G	FA	G by Pos
1953	STL A	154	.219	.259	567	124	18	1	1	0.2	50	37	24	45	3	0	0	284	512	25	99	5.4	.970	SS-152
1954	BAL A	125	.243	.304	411	100	9	5	2	0.5	28	27	21	38	5	1	0	249	333	32	76	5.0	.948	SS-124
1955	NY A	98	.227	.298	255	58	7	1	3	1.2	14	20	15	18	9	1	0	115	249	16	60	3.9	.958	SS-98
1956		39	.280	.427	75	21	3	4	0	0.0	8	11	2	4	0	1	0	51	64	0	22	3.2	1.000	SS-32, 3B-4
1957	KC A	116	.191	.323	319	61	10	4	8	2.5	39	29	27	43	1	4	0	175	263	18	61	3.9	.961	2B-64, SS-35, 3B-17
1958	2 teams	KC A (22G –.155) CLE A (76G –.195)																						
″	total	98	.185	.278	248	46	11	3	2	0.8	27	20	22	44	5	0	0	148	216	19	57	3.9	.950	SS-87, 2B-8, 3B-3
6 yrs.		630	.219	.294	1875	410	58	18	16	0.9	166	144	111	192	23	7	0	1022	1637	110	375	4.4	.960	SS-528, 2B-72, 3B-24

Brian Hunter

HUNTER, BRIAN LEE BR TR 6′ 4″ 180 lbs.
B. Mar. 5, 1971, Portland, Ore.

Year	Team	Games	BA	SA	AB	H	2B	3B	HR	HR%	R	RBI	BB	SO	SB	Pinch Hit AB	Pinch Hit H	PO	A	E	DP	TC/G	FA	G by Pos
1994	HOU N	6	.250	.292	24	6	1	0	0	0.0	2	0	1	6	2	0	0	13	1	1	1	2.5	.933	OF-6
1995		78	.302	.396	321	97	14	5	2	0.6	52	28	21	52	24	3	2	182	8	9	1	2.7	.955	OF-74
2 yrs.		84	.299	.388	345	103	15	5	2	0.6	54	28	22	58	26	3	2	195	9	10	2	2.7	.953	OF-80

Brian Hunter

HUNTER, BRIAN RAYNOLD BR TL 6′ 195 lbs.
B. Mar. 4, 1968, Torrance, Calif.

Year	Team	Games	BA	SA	AB	H	2B	3B	HR	HR%	R	RBI	BB	SO	SB	Pinch Hit AB	Pinch Hit H	PO	A	E	DP	TC/G	FA	G by Pos
1991	ATL N	97	.251	.450	271	68	16	1	12	4.4	32	50	17	48	0	18	3	624	46	8	42	7.5	.988	1B-85, OF-6
1992		102	.239	.487	238	57	13	2	14	5.9	34	41	21	50	1	21	5	542	50	4	35	6.1	.993	1B-92, OF-6
1993		37	.138	.200	80	11	3	1	0	0.0	4	8	2	15	0	11	1	168	13	1	19	5.9	.995	1B-29, OF-2
1994	2 teams	PIT N (76G –.227) CIN N (9G –.304)																						
″	total	85	.234	.480	256	60	16	1	15	5.9	34	57	17	56	0	17	5	515	39	5	48	8.0	.991	1B-60, OF-10
1995	CIN N	40	.215	.329	79	17	6	0	1	1.3	9	9	11	21	2	11	5	171	12	3	19	6.9	.984	1B-23, OF-4
5 yrs.		361	.231	.436	924	213	54	5	42	4.5	113	165	68	190	3	78	19	2020	160	21	163	6.9	.990	1B-289, OF-28
LEAGUE CHAMPIONSHIP SERIES																								
1991	ATL N	5	.333	.611	18	6	2	0	1	5.6	2	4	0	2	0	0	0	30	4	0	3	6.8	1.000	1B-5
1992		3	.200	.200	5	1	0	0	0	0.0	1	0	0	1	0	2	0	7	0	0	0	3.5	1.000	1B-2
2 yrs.		8	.304	.522	23	7	2	0	1	4.3	3	4	0	3	0	2	0	37	4	0	3	5.9	1.000	1B-7
WORLD SERIES																								
1991	ATL N	7	.190	.381	21	4	1	0	1	4.8	2	3	0	2	0	3	1	6	1	1	1	1.0	.875	OF-4, 1B-4
1992		4	.200	.200	5	1	0	0	0	0.0	0	2	0	1	0	1	0	14	1	0	2	5.0	1.000	1B-3
2 yrs.		11	.192	.346	26	5	1	0	1	3.8	2	5	0	3	0	4	1	20	2	1	3	2.1	.957	1B-7, OF-4

Buddy Hunter

HUNTER, HAROLD JAMES BR TR 5′10″ 170 lbs.
B. Aug. 9, 1947, Omaha, Neb.

Year	Team	Games	BA	SA	AB	H	2B	3B	HR	HR%	R	RBI	BB	SO	SB	Pinch Hit AB	Pinch Hit H	PO	A	E	DP	TC/G	FA	G by Pos
1971	BOS A	8	.222	.333	9	2	1	0	0	0.0	2	0	2	1	0	1	0	5	9	0	1	2.3	1.000	2B-6
1973		13	.429	.571	7	3	1	0	0	0.0	3	2	3	1	0	0	0	6	8	0	4	2.3	1.000	3B-3, 2B-2, DH-1
1975		1	.000	.000	1	0	0	0	0	0.0	0	0	0	0	0	0	0	2	1	1	1	4.0	.750	2B-1
3 yrs.		22	.294	.412	17	5	2	0	0	0.0	5	2	5	2	0	1	0	13	18	1	6	2.5	.969	2B-9, 3B-3, DH-1

Eddie Hunter

HUNTER, EDISON FRANKLIN BR TR 5′ 7½″ 150 lbs.
B. Feb. 6, 1905, Bellevue, Ky. D. Mar. 14, 1967, Colerain, Ohio.

Year	Team	Games	BA	SA	AB	H	2B	3B	HR	HR%	R	RBI	BB	SO	SB	Pinch Hit AB	Pinch Hit H	PO	A	E	DP	TC/G	FA	G by Pos
1933	CIN N	1	—	—	0	0	0	0	0	—	0	0	0	0	0	0	0	0	0	0	0	0.0	.000	3B-1

George Hunter

HUNTER, GEORGE HENRY BB TL 5′ 8½″ 165 lbs.
Brother of Bill Hunter.
B. July 8, 1887, Buffalo, N. Y. D. Jan. 11, 1968, Harrisburg, Pa.

Year	Team	Games	BA	SA	AB	H	2B	3B	HR	HR%	R	RBI	BB	SO	SB	Pinch Hit AB	Pinch Hit H	PO	A	E	DP	TC/G	FA	G by Pos
1909	BKN N	44	.228	.285	123	28	7	0	0	0.0	8	8	9		1	3	0	31	32	7	3	1.8	.900	OF-23, P-16
1910		1	—	—	0	0	0	0	0	—	0	0	0	0	0	0	0	0	0	0	0	0.0	.000	OF-1
2 yrs.		45	.228	.285	123	28	7	0	0	0.0	8	8	9	0	1	3	0	31	32	7	3	1.8	.900	OF-24, P-16

Herb Hunter

HUNTER, HERBERT HARRISON BL TR 6′½″ 165 lbs.
B. Dec. 25, 1896, Boston, Mass. D. July 25, 1970, Orlando, Fla.

Year	Team	Games	BA	SA	AB	H	2B	3B	HR	HR%	R	RBI	BB	SO	SB	Pinch Hit AB	Pinch Hit H	PO	A	E	DP	TC/G	FA	G by Pos
1916	2 teams	NY N (21G –.250) CHI N (2G –.000)																						
″	total	23	.219	.313	32	7	0	0	1	3.1	3	4	0	5	0	11	2	22	7	1	0	3.3	.967	3B-7, 1B-2
1917	CHI N	3	.000	.000	3	0	0	0	0	0.0	0	0	0	0	0	1	0	3	2	1	0	3.0	.833	3B-1, 2B-1
1920	BOS A	4	.083	.083	12	1	0	0	0	0.0	2	0	1	1	0	0	0	5	1	1	0	1.8	.857	OF-4
1921	STL N	9	.000	.000	2	0	0	0	0	0.0	3	0	1	0	0	1	0	3	0	0	1	3.0	1.000	1B-1
4 yrs.		39	.163	.224	49	8	0	0	1	2.0	8	4	2	6	0	13	2	33	10	3	1	2.9	.935	3B-8, OF-4, 1B-3, 2B-1

Lem Hunter

HUNTER, ROBERT LEMUEL
B. Jan. 16, 1863, Warren, Ohio D. Nov. 9, 1956, West Lafayette, Ohio.

Year	Team	Games	BA	SA	AB	H	2B	3B	HR	HR%	R	RBI	BB	SO	SB	Pinch Hit AB	Pinch Hit H	PO	A	E	DP	TC/G	FA	G by Pos
1883	CLE N	1	.250	.250	4	1	0	0	0	0.0	1		0	2		0	0	0	1	0	0	0.5	1.000	P-1, OF-1

Newt Hunter

HUNTER, FREDERICK CREIGHTON BR TR 6′ 180 lbs.
B. Jan. 5, 1880, Chillicothe, Ohio D. Oct. 26, 1963, Columbus, Ohio.

Year	Team	Games	BA	SA	AB	H	2B	3B	HR	HR%	R	RBI	BB	SO	SB	Pinch Hit AB	Pinch Hit H	PO	A	E	DP	TC/G	FA	G by Pos
1911	PIT N	65	.254	.388	209	53	10	6	2	1.0	35	24	25	43	9	3	0	504	26	6	44	8.8	.989	1B-61

Steve Huntz

HUNTZ, STEPHEN MICHAEL BB TR 6′ 1″ 204 lbs.
B. Dec. 3, 1945, Cleveland, Ohio.

Year	Team	Games	BA	SA	AB	H	2B	3B	HR	HR%	R	RBI	BB	SO	SB	Pinch Hit AB	Pinch Hit H	PO	A	E	DP	TC/G	FA	G by Pos
1967	STL N	3	.167	.167	6	1	0	0	0	0.0	1	0	1	2	0	1	1	3	2	0	0	2.5	1.000	2B-2
1969		71	.194	.288	139	27	4	0	3	2.2	13	13	27	34	0	3	0	77	121	9	22	3.0	.957	SS-52, 2B-12, 3B-6
1970	SD N	106	.219	.335	352	77	8	0	11	3.1	54	37	66	69	0	9	1	118	257	20	39	3.7	.949	SS-57, 3B-51
1971	CHI A	35	.209	.337	86	18	3	1	2	2.3	10	6	7	9	1	12	0	31	54	0	10	3.1	1.000	2B-14, SS-7, 3B-6
1975	SD N	22	.151	.226	53	8	4	0	0	0.0	3	4	7	8	0	6	0	15	33	3	6	2.8	.941	3B-16, 2B-2
5 yrs.		237	.206	.314	636	131	19	1	16	2.5	81	60	108	122	1	31	2	244	467	32	77	3.3	.957	SS-116, 3B-79, 2B-30

Dave Huppert

HUPPERT, DAVID BLAIN — BR TR 6′ 1″ 190 lbs.
B. Apr. 1, 1957, Southgate, Calif.

Year	Team	Lg	Games	BA	SA	AB	H	2B	3B	HR	HR%	R	RBI	BB	SO	SB	Pinch Hit AB	Pinch Hit H	PO	A	E	DP	TC/G	FA	G by Pos
1983	BAL	A	2	—	—	0	0	0	0	0	—	0	0	0	0	0	0	0	3	0	0	0	1.5	1.000	C-2
1985	MIL	A	15	.048	.048	21	1	0	0	0	0.0	1	0	2	7	0	0	0	45	3	2	2	3.3	.960	C-15
2 yrs.			17	.048	.048	21	1	0	0	0	0.0	1	0	2	7	0	0	0	48	3	2	2	3.1	.962	C-17

Clint Hurdle

HURDLE, CLINTON MERRICK — BL TR 6′ 3″ 195 lbs.
B. July 30, 1957, Big Rapids, Mich.

Year	Team	Lg	Games	BA	SA	AB	H	2B	3B	HR	HR%	R	RBI	BB	SO	SB	Pinch Hit AB	Pinch Hit H	PO	A	E	DP	TC/G	FA	G by Pos
1977	KC	A	9	.308	.538	26	8	0	0	2	7.7	5	7	2	7	0	0	0	17	0	0	0	1.9	1.000	OF-9
1978			133	.264	.398	417	110	25	5	7	1.7	48	56	56	84	1	8	5	544	30	12	48	4.4	.980	OF-78, 1B-52, DH-1, 3B-1
1979			59	.240	.386	171	41	10	3	3	1.8	16	30	28	24	0	7	1	89	2	3	0	1.7	.968	OF-50, DH-4, 3B-1
1980			130	.294	.458	395	116	31	2	10	2.5	50	60	34	61	0	9	3	233	8	10	1	2.0	.960	OF-126
1981			28	.329	.553	76	25	3	1	4	5.3	12	15	13	10	0	2	1	59	1	0	0	2.1	1.000	OF-28
1982	CIN	N	19	.206	.235	34	7	1	0	0	0.0	2	1	2	6	0	3	1	17	2	1	0	1.2	.950	OF-17
1983	NY	N	13	.182	.242	33	6	2	0	0	0.0	3	2	2	10	0	4	0	1	15	4	2	2.0	.800	3B-9, OF-1
1985			43	.195	.354	82	16	4	0	3	3.7	7	7	13	20	0	16	0	89	7	1	0	3.6	.990	C-17, OF-10
1986	STL	N	78	.195	.299	154	30	5	1	3	1.9	18	15	26	38	0	22	6	334	31	3	31	6.3	.992	1B-39, OF-10, C-5, 3B-4
1987	NY	N	3	.333	.333	3	1	0	0	0	0.0	1	0	0	1	0	2	0	1	0	0	0	1.0	1.000	1B-1
10 yrs.			515	.259	.403	1391	360	81	12	32	2.3	162	193	176	261	1	73	17	1384	96	34	82	3.3	.978	OF-329, 1B-92, C-22, 3B-15, DH-5

DIVISIONAL PLAYOFF SERIES

Year	Team	Lg	Games	BA	SA	AB	H	2B	3B	HR	HR%	R	RBI	BB	SO	SB	Pinch Hit AB	Pinch Hit H	PO	A	E	DP	TC/G	FA	G by Pos
1981	KC	A	3	.273	.273	11	3	0	0	0	0.0	0	0	1	1	0	0	0	6	0	0	0	2.0	1.000	OF-3

LEAGUE CHAMPIONSHIP SERIES

Year	Team	Lg	Games	BA	SA	AB	H	2B	3B	HR	HR%	R	RBI	BB	SO	SB	Pinch Hit AB	Pinch Hit H	PO	A	E	DP	TC/G	FA	G by Pos
1978	KC	A	4	.375	.625	8	3	0	1	0	0.0	1	1	2	3	0	1	0	6	1	0	1	3.5	1.000	OF-2
1980			3	.000	.000	2	0	0	0	0	0.0	0	0	0	1	0	0	0	1	0	0	0	0.5	1.000	OF-2
2 yrs.			7	.300	.500	10	3	0	1	0	0.0	1	1	2	4	0	1	0	7	1	0	1	2.0	1.000	OF-4

WORLD SERIES

Year	Team	Lg	Games	BA	SA	AB	H	2B	3B	HR	HR%	R	RBI	BB	SO	SB	Pinch Hit AB	Pinch Hit H	PO	A	E	DP	TC/G	FA	G by Pos
1980	KC	A	4	.417	.500	12	5	1	0	0	0.0	1	0	2	1	1	0	0	8	0	0	0	2.0	1.000	OF-4

Jerry Hurley

HURLEY, JEREMIAH JOSEPH — BR TR 6′ 190 lbs.
B. June 15, 1863, Boston, Mass. D. Sept. 17, 1950, Boston, Mass.

Year	Team	Lg	Games	BA	SA	AB	H	2B	3B	HR	HR%	R	RBI	BB	SO	SB	Pinch Hit AB	Pinch Hit H	PO	A	E	DP	TC/G	FA	G by Pos
1889	BOS	N	1	.000	.000	4	0	0	0	0	0.0	0	0	0	0	0	0	0	2	2	1	0	2.5	.800	C-1, OF-1
1890	PIT	P	8	.273	.318	22	6	1	0	0	0.0	5	2	2	5	0	0	0	27	3	3	0	4.1	.909	C-7, OF-1
1891	CIN	AA	24	.212	.318	66	14	3	2	0	0.0	10	6	12	13	2	0	0	89	11	15	2	4.4	.870	C-24, 1B-1, OF-1
3 yrs.			33	.217	.304	92	20	4	2	0	0.0	15	8	14	18	2	0	0	118	16	19	2	4.3	.876	C-32, OF-3, 1B-1

Pat Hurley

HURLEY, JEREMIAH — BR TR
B. Apr. 1875, New York, N. Y. D. Dec. 27, 1919, New York, N. Y.

Year	Team	Lg	Games	BA	SA	AB	H	2B	3B	HR	HR%	R	RBI	BB	SO	SB	Pinch Hit AB	Pinch Hit H	PO	A	E	DP	TC/G	FA	G by Pos
1901	CIN	N	9	.048	.048	21	1	0	0	0	0.0	1	0	1		1	2	0	39	6	3	0	6.9	.938	C-7
1907	BKN	N	1	.000	.000	2	0	0	0	0	0.0	0	0	1		0	0	0	4	1	0	0	5.0	1.000	C-1
2 yrs.			10	.043	.043	23	1	0	0	0	0.0	1	0	2		1	2	0	43	7	3	0	6.6	.943	C-8

Don Hurst

HURST, FRANK O'DONNELL — BL TL 6′ 215 lbs.
B. Aug. 12, 1905, Maysville, Ky. D. Dec. 6, 1952, Los Angeles, Calif.

Year	Team	Lg	Games	BA	SA	AB	H	2B	3B	HR	HR%	R	RBI	BB	SO	SB	Pinch Hit AB	Pinch Hit H	PO	A	E	DP	TC/G	FA	G by Pos
1928	PHI	N	107	.285	.508	396	113	23	4	19	4.8	73	64	68	40	3	3	0	964	68	12	92	10.0	.989	1B-104
1929			154	.304	.525	589	179	29	4	31	5.3	100	125	80	36	10	0	0	1509	112	24	125	10.7	.985	1B-154
1930			119	.327	.522	391	128	19	3	17	4.3	78	78	46	22	6	13	3	857	59	17	92	9.1	.982	1B-96, OF-7
1931			137	.305	.468	489	149	37	5	11	2.2	63	91	64	28	8	2	0	1206	104	18	117	9.8	.986	1B-135
1932			150	.339	.547	579	196	41	4	24	4.1	109	**143**	65	27	10	0	0	1341	94	10	105	9.6	.993	1B-150
1933			147	.267	.389	550	147	27	8	8	1.5	58	76	48	32	3	5	1	1355	114	23	132	10.5	.985	1B-142
1934	2 teams		PHI N (40G –.262) CHI N (51G –.199)																						
″	total		91	.228	.331	281	64	14	0	5	1.8	29	33	20	25	1	9	2	730	35	8	69	8.9	.990	1B-87
7 yrs.			905	.298	.478	3275	976	190	28	115	3.5	510	610	391	210	41	32	6	7962	586	112	732	9.9	.987	1B-868, OF-7

Butch Huskey

HUSKEY, ROBERT LEON — BR TR 6′ 3″ 244 lbs.
B. Nov. 10, 1971, Anadarko, Okla.

Year	Team	Lg	Games	BA	SA	AB	H	2B	3B	HR	HR%	R	RBI	BB	SO	SB	Pinch Hit AB	Pinch Hit H	PO	A	E	DP	TC/G	FA	G by Pos
1993	NY	N	13	.146	.171	41	6	1	0	0	0.0	2	3	1	13	0	0	0	9	27	3	2	3.0	.923	3B-13
1995			28	.189	.300	90	17	1	0	3	3.3	8	11	10	16	1	0	0	16	59	6	2	2.9	.926	3B-27, OF-1
2 yrs.			41	.176	.260	131	23	2	0	3	2.3	10	14	11	29	1	0	0	25	86	9	4	2.9	.925	3B-40, OF-1

Jeff Huson

HUSON, JEFFREY KENT (Huey) — BL TR 6′ 3″ 180 lbs.
B. Aug. 15, 1964, Scottsdale, Ariz.

Year	Team	Lg	Games	BA	SA	AB	H	2B	3B	HR	HR%	R	RBI	BB	SO	SB	Pinch Hit AB	Pinch Hit H	PO	A	E	DP	TC/G	FA	G by Pos
1988	MON	N	20	.310	.357	42	13	2	0	0	0.0	7	3	4	3	2	2	2	18	41	4	5	3.3	.937	SS-15, 2B-2, 3B-1, OF-1
1989			32	.162	.230	74	12	5	0	0	0.0	1	2	6	6	3	4	1	40	65	8	11	3.8	.929	SS-20, 2B-9, 3B-1
1990	TEX	A	145	.240	.280	396	95	12	2	0	0.0	57	28	46	54	12	18	3	183	304	19	76	3.0	.962	SS-119, 3B-36, 2B-12
1991			119	.213	.287	268	57	8	3	2	0.7	36	26	39	32	8	12	0	141	269	15	43	3.6	.965	SS-116, 2B-2, 3B-1
1992			123	.261	.362	318	83	14	3	4	1.3	49	24	41	43	18	12	1	178	250	9	66	3.3	.979	SS-82, 2B-47, OF-2, DH-1
1993			23	.133	.200	45	6	1	1	0	0.0	3	2	0	10	0	3	0	25	42	6	10	3.5	.918	SS-12, 2B-5, 3B-2, DH-2
1995	BAL	A	66	.248	.317	161	40	4	2	1	0.6	24	19	15	20	5	7	2	59	90	1	19	2.6	.993	3B-33, 2B-21, DH-2, SS-1
7 yrs.			528	.235	.303	1304	306	46	11	7	0.5	177	104	151	168	48	58	9	644	1061	62	230	3.2	.965	SS-365, 2B-98, 3B-74, DH-5, OF-3

Carl Husta

HUSTA, CARL LAWRENCE (Sox) — BR TR 5′11″ 176 lbs.
B. Apr. 8, 1902, Egg Harbor, N. J. D. Nov. 6, 1951, Kingston, N. Y.

Year	Team	Lg	Games	BA	SA	AB	H	2B	3B	HR	HR%	R	RBI	BB	SO	SB	Pinch Hit AB	Pinch Hit H	PO	A	E	DP	TC/G	FA	G by Pos
1925	PHI	A	6	.136	.136	22	3	0	0	0	0.0	2	2	2	3	0	0	0	18	22	1	4	6.8	.976	SS-6

Harry Huston

HUSTON, HARRY EMANUEL KRESS — BR TR 5′ 9″ 168 lbs.
B. Oct. 14, 1883, Bellefontaine, Ohio D. Oct. 13, 1969, Blackwell, Okla.

Year	Team	Lg	Games	BA	SA	AB	H	2B	3B	HR	HR%	R	RBI	BB	SO	SB	Pinch Hit AB	Pinch Hit H	PO	A	E	DP	TC/G	FA	G by Pos
1906	PHI	N	2	.000	.000	4	0	0	0	0	0.0	0	0	1		0	0	0	5	2	0	0	3.5	1.000	C-2

Warren Huston

HUSTON, WARREN LLEWELLYN — BR TR 6′ 170 lbs.
B. Oct. 31, 1913, Newtonville, Mass.

Year	Team	Lg	Games	BA	SA	AB	H	2B	3B	HR	HR%	R	RBI	BB	SO	SB	Pinch Hit AB	Pinch Hit H	PO	A	E	DP	TC/G	FA	G by Pos
1937	PHI	A	38	.130	.185	54	7	3	0	0	0.0	5	3	2	9	0	3	0	40	58	9	17	3.2	.916	2B-16, SS-15, 3B-2
1944	BOS	N	33	.200	.218	55	11	1	0	0	0.0	7	1	8	5	0	0	0	26	44	3	2	2.5	.959	3B-20, 2B-5, SS-4
2 yrs.			71	.165	.202	109	18	4	0	0	0.0	12	4	10	14	0	3	0	66	102	12	19	2.9	.933	3B-22, 2B-21, SS-19

Joe Hutcheson

HUTCHESON, JOSEPH JOHNSON (Poodles) BL TR 6′ 2″ 200 lbs.
B. Feb. 5, 1905, Springtown, Tex. D. Feb. 23, 1993, Tyler, Tex.

Year	Team	Games	BA	SA	AB	H	2B	3B	HR	HR%	R	RBI	BB	SO	SB	Pinch Hit AB	Pinch Hit H	PO	A	E	DP	TC/G	FA	G by Pos
1933	BKN N	55	.234	.364	184	43	4	1	6	3.3	19	21	15	13	1	10	1	84	8	1	2	2.1	.989	OF-45

Ed Hutchinson

HUTCHINSON, EDWIN FORREST BL TR 5′11″ 175 lbs.
B. May 19, 1867, Pittsburgh, Pa. D. July 19, 1934, Colfax, Calif.

Year	Team	Games	BA	SA	AB	H	2B	3B	HR	HR%	R	RBI	BB	SO	SB	Pinch Hit AB	Pinch Hit H	PO	A	E	DP	TC/G	FA	G by Pos
1890	CHI N	4	.059	.118	17	1	1	0	0	0.0	0	0	0	0	0	0	0	6	12	0	1	4.5	1.000	2B-4

Fred Hutchinson

HUTCHINSON, FREDERICK CHARLES BL TR 6′ 2″ 190 lbs.
B. Aug. 12, 1919, Seattle, Wash. D. Nov. 12, 1964, Bradenton, Fla.
Manager 1952–54, 1956–64.

Year	Team	Games	BA	SA	AB	H	2B	3B	HR	HR%	R	RBI	BB	SO	SB	Pinch Hit AB	Pinch Hit H	PO	A	E	DP	TC/G	FA	G by Pos
1939	DET A	13	.382	.412	34	13	1	0	0	0.0	5	6	2	0	0	0	0	6	13	0	1	1.5	1.000	P-13
1940		17	.267	.300	30	8	1	0	0	0.0	1	2	0	0	0	0	0	2	16	2	1	1.2	.900	P-17
1941		2	.000	.000	2	0	0	0	0	0.0	0	0	0	2	0	2	0	0	0	0	0	0.0	—	
1946		40	.315	.360	89	28	4	0	0	0.0	11	13	6	1	0	9	2	11	47	1	3	2.1	.983	P-28
1947		56	.302	.443	106	32	5	2	2	1.9	8	15	6	6	2	22	6	15	40	1	1	1.7	.982	P-33
1948		76	.205	.241	112	23	1	0	1	0.9	11	12	23	9	3	32	7	19	45	0	5	1.9	1.000	P-33
1949		38	.247	.301	73	18	2	1	0	0.0	12	7	8	5	1	4	1	18	39	1	5	1.8	.983	P-33
1950		44	.326	.400	95	31	7	0	0	0.0	15	20	12	3	0	4	1	17	50	4	6	1.8	.944	P-39
1951		47	.188	.212	85	16	2	0	0	0.0	7	7	7	4	0	13	2	17	45	4	1	2.1	.939	P-31
1952		17	.056	.056	18	1	0	0	0	0.0	0	0	3	0	0	5	1	1	15	0	1	1.3	1.000	P-12
1953		4	.167	.667	6	1	0	0	1	16.7	1	1	0	0	0	0	0	6	0	0	0	1.5	1.000	P-3, 1B-1
11 yrs.		354	.263	.326	650	171	23	3	4	0.6	71	83	67	30	6	91	20	112	310	13	24	1.8	.970	P-242, 1B-1
WORLD SERIES																								
1940	DET A	1	—	—	0	0	0	0	0	—	0	0	0	0	0	0	0	0	0	0	0	0.0	.000	P-1

Roy Hutson

HUTSON, ROY LEE BL TR 5′ 9″ 165 lbs.
B. Feb. 27, 1902, Luray, Mo. D. May 20, 1957, La Mesa, Calif.

Year	Team	Games	BA	SA	AB	H	2B	3B	HR	HR%	R	RBI	BB	SO	SB	Pinch Hit AB	Pinch Hit H	PO	A	E	DP	TC/G	FA	G by Pos
1925	BKN N	7	.500	.500	8	4	0	0	0	0.0	1	1	1	1	0	0	0	4	0	0	0	1.0	1.000	OF-4

Jim Hutto

HUTTO, JAMES NEAMON, JR. BR TR 5′11″ 195 lbs.
B. Oct. 17, 1947, Norfolk, Va.

Year	Team	Games	BA	SA	AB	H	2B	3B	HR	HR%	R	RBI	BB	SO	SB	Pinch Hit AB	Pinch Hit H	PO	A	E	DP	TC/G	FA	G by Pos
1970	PHI N	57	.185	.304	92	17	2	0	3	3.3	7	12	5	20	0	26	6	71	4	0	4	1.9	1.000	OF-22, 1B-12, C-5, 3B-1
1975	BAL A	4	.000	.000	5	0	0	0	0	0.0	0	0	0	2	0	1	0	6	0	0	0	2.0	1.000	C-3
2 yrs.		61	.175	.289	97	17	2	0	3	3.1	7	12	5	22	0	27	6	77	4	0	4	1.9	1.000	OF-22, 1B-12, C-8, 3B-1

Tom Hutton

HUTTON, THOMAS GEORGE BL TL 5′11″ 180 lbs.
B. Apr. 20, 1946, Los Angeles, Calif.

Year	Team	Games	BA	SA	AB	H	2B	3B	HR	HR%	R	RBI	BB	SO	SB	Pinch Hit AB	Pinch Hit H	PO	A	E	DP	TC/G	FA	G by Pos
1966	LA N	3	.000	.000	2	0	0	0	0	0.0	0	0	0	0	0	0	0	2	0	0	0	0.7	1.000	1B-3
1969		16	.271	.271	48	13	0	0	0	0.0	2	4	5	7	0	0	0	130	19	1	9	9.4	.993	1B-16
1972	PHI N	134	.260	.344	381	99	16	2	4	1.0	40	38	56	24	5	19	8	648	38	6	47	5.1	.991	1B-87, OF-48
1973		106	.263	.368	247	65	11	0	5	2.0	31	29	32	31	3	37	10	527	43	1	61	8.0	.998	1B-71
1974		96	.240	.356	208	50	6	3	4	1.9	32	33	30	13	2	22	8	285	15	2	25	4.2	.993	1B-39, OF-33
1975		113	.248	.339	165	41	6	0	3	1.8	24	24	27	10	2	36	11	316	33	3	38	4.2	.991	1B-71, OF-12
1976		95	.202	.282	124	25	5	1	1	0.8	15	13	27	11	1	19	5	294	28	0	25	4.4	1.000	1B-72, OF-1
1977		107	.309	.420	81	25	3	0	2	2.5	12	11	12	10	1	34	10	143	15	1	11	1.9	.994	1B-73, OF-9
1978	2 teams	TOR A (64G –.254) MON N (39G –.203)																						
″	total	103	.241	.319	232	56	12	0	2	0.9	23	14	29	16	1	24	4	225	7	1	10	2.7	.996	OF-60, 1B-26
1979	MON N	86	.253	.337	83	21	2	1	1	1.2	14	13	10	7	0	43	11	89	11	0	4	2.9	1.000	1B-25, OF-9
1980		62	.218	.255	55	12	2	0	0	0.0	2	5	4	10	0	43	10	20	1	0	3	1.8	1.000	1B-7, OF-4, P-1
1981		31	.103	.103	29	3	0	0	0	0.0	1	2	2	1	0	17	2	23	2	0	2	2.3	1.000	1B-9, OF-2
12 yrs.		952	.248	.334	1655	410	63	7	22	1.3	196	186	234	140	15	294	79	2702	212	15	235	4.3	.995	1B-499, OF-178, P-1
LEAGUE CHAMPIONSHIP SERIES																								
1976	PHI N	1	.000	.000	1	0	0	0	0	0.0	0	0	0	0	0	1	0	0	0	0	0	0.0	—	
1977		3	.000	.000	3	0	0	0	0	0.0	0	0	0	0	0	2	0	5	0	0	0	5.0	1.000	1B-1
2 yrs.		4	.000	.000	4	0	0	0	0	0.0	0	0	0	0	0	3	0	5	0	0	0	5.0	1.000	1B-1

Ham Hyatt

HYATT, ROBERT HAMILTON BL TR 6′ 1″ 185 lbs.
B. Nov. 1, 1884, Buncombe County, N. C. D. Sept. 11, 1963, Liberty Lake, Wash.

Year	Team	Games	BA	SA	AB	H	2B	3B	HR	HR%	R	RBI	BB	SO	SB	Pinch Hit AB	Pinch Hit H	PO	A	E	DP	TC/G	FA	G by Pos
1909	PIT N	48	.299	.463	67	20	3	4	0	0.0	9	7	3		1	**37**	**9**	28	6	1	3	4.4	.971	OF-6, 1B-2
1910		74	.263	.377	175	46	5	6	1	0.6	19	30	8	14	3	31	6	327	19	5	19	8.4	.986	1B-38, OF-4
1912		46	.289	.340	97	28	3	1	0	0.0	13	22	6	8	2	27	6	26	2	2	2	1.7	.933	OF-15, 1B-3
1913		63	.333	.605	81	27	6	2	4	4.9	8	16	3	8	0	52	15	41	2	2	3	4.5	.956	OF-5, 1B-5
1914		74	.215	.316	79	17	3	1	1	1.3	2	15	7	14	1	**58**	**14**	51	0	1	1	6.5	.981	1B-7, C-1
1915	STL N	106	.268	.376	295	79	8	9	2	0.7	23	46	28	24	3	14	3	656	23	9	32	6.5	.987	1B-81, OF-25
1918	NY A	53	.229	.336	131	30	8	0	2	1.5	11	10	8	8	1	**21**	4	84	6	0	6	3.0	1.000	OF-25, 1B-5
7 yrs.		464	.267	.388	925	247	36	23	10	1.1	85	146	63	76	11	240	57	1213	58	20	66	5.8	.985	1B-141, OF-80, C-1
WORLD SERIES																								
1909	PIT N	2	.000	.000	4	0	0	0	0	0.0	1	1	1	0	0	1	0	0	0	0	0	0.0	.000	OF-1

Tim Hyers

HYERS, TIMOTHY JAMES BL TL 6′ 1″ 185 lbs.
B. Oct. 3, 1971, Atlanta, Ga.

Year	Team	Games	BA	SA	AB	H	2B	3B	HR	HR%	R	RBI	BB	SO	SB	Pinch Hit AB	Pinch Hit H	PO	A	E	DP	TC/G	FA	G by Pos
1994	SD N	52	.254	.280	118	30	3	0	0	0.0	13	7	9	15	3	9	3	258	23	4	19	6.6	.986	1B-41, OF-2
1995		6	.000	.000	5	0	0	0	0	0.0	0	0	0	1	0	5	0	1	1	0	0	2.0	1.000	1B-1
2 yrs.		58	.244	.268	123	30	3	0	0	0.0	13	7	9	16	3	14	3	259	24	4	19	6.5	.986	1B-42, OF-2

Jim Hyndman

HYNDMAN, JAMES WILLIAM
B. July 1865, Kingston, Pa. Deceased.

Year	Team	Games	BA	SA	AB	H	2B	3B	HR	HR%	R	RBI	BB	SO	SB	Pinch Hit AB	Pinch Hit H	PO	A	E	DP	TC/G	FA	G by Pos
1886	PHI AA	1	.000	.000	4	0	0	0	0	0.0	0		0			0	0	3	1	1	0	2.5	.800	P-1, OF-1

Pat Hynes

HYNES, PATRICK J. TL
B. Mar. 12, 1884, St. Louis, Mo. D. Mar. 12, 1907, St. Louis, Mo.

Year	Team	Games	BA	SA	AB	H	2B	3B	HR	HR%	R	RBI	BB	SO	SB	Pinch Hit AB	Pinch Hit H	PO	A	E	DP	TC/G	FA	G by Pos
1903	STL N	1	.000	.000	3	0	0	0	0	0.0	0	0	0		0	0	0	1	0	1	0	2.0	.500	P-1
1904	STL A	66	.236	.287	254	60	7	3	0	0.0	23	15	3		3	0	0	73	5	8	0	1.3	.907	OF-63, P-5
2 yrs.		67	.233	.284	257	60	7	3	0	0.0	23	15	3		3	0	0	74	5	9	0	1.3	.898	OF-63, P-6

Pete Incaviglia

INCAVIGLIA, PETER JOSEPH (Inky) BR TR 6′ 1″ 225 lbs.
B. Apr. 2, 1964, Pebble Beach, Calif.

Year	Team	Games	BA	SA	AB	H	2B	3B	HR	HR%	R	RBI	BB	SO	SB	Pinch Hit AB	Pinch Hit H	PO	A	E	DP	TC/G	FA	G by Pos
1986	TEX A	153	.250	.463	540	135	21	2	30	5.6	82	88	55	**185**	3	4	0	157	6	14	1	1.2	.921	OF-114, DH-36
1987		139	.271	.497	509	138	26	4	27	5.3	85	80	48	168	9	3	0	216	8	13	0	1.7	.945	OF-132, DH-6
1988		116	.249	.467	418	104	19	3	22	5.3	59	54	39	**153**	6	0	0	172	12	2	1	1.6	.989	OF-93, DH-21
1989		133	.236	.453	453	107	27	4	21	4.6	48	81	32	136	5	5	2	213	7	6	2	1.7	.973	OF-125, DH-5
1990		153	.233	.420	529	123	27	0	24	4.5	59	85	45	146	3	13	2	290	12	8	2	2.1	.974	OF-145, DH-2
1991	DET A	97	.214	.353	337	72	12	1	11	3.3	38	38	36	92	1	3	0	106	4	3	2	1.2	.973	OF-54, DH-41
1992	HOU N	113	.266	.430	349	93	22	1	11	3.2	31	44	25	99	2	18	4	188	8	6	1	2.1	.970	OF-98
1993	PHI N	116	.274	.530	368	101	16	3	24	6.5	60	89	21	82	1	24	6	164	4	5	1	1.8	.971	OF-97
1994		80	.230	.439	244	56	10	1	13	5.3	28	32	16	71	1	20	7	90	2	2	0	1.5	.979	OF-63
9 yrs.		1100	.248	.453	3747	929	180	19	183	4.9	490	591	317	1132	31	90	21	1596	63	59	10	1.7	.966	OF-921, DH-111
LEAGUE CHAMPIONSHIP SERIES																								
1993	PHI N	3	.167	.417	12	2	0	0	1	8.3	2	1	0	3	0	0	0	8	0	0	0	2.7	1.000	OF-3
WORLD SERIES																								
1993	PHI N	4	.125	.125	8	1	0	0	0	0.0	0	1	0	4	0	1	0	7	0	0	0	1.8	1.000	OF-4

Alexis Infante

INFANTE, FERMIN ALEXIS BR TR 5′10″ 175 lbs.
Born Fermin Alexis Infante (Carpio).
B. Dec. 4, 1961, Barquisimeto, Venezuela.

Year	Team	Games	BA	SA	AB	H	2B	3B	HR	HR%	R	RBI	BB	SO	SB	Pinch Hit AB	Pinch Hit H	PO	A	E	DP	TC/G	FA	G by Pos
1987	TOR A	1	—	—	0	0	0	0	0	—	0	0	0	0	0	0	0	0	0	0	0	0.0	.000	SS-1
1988		19	.200	.200	15	3	0	0	0	0.0	7	0	2	4	0	0	0	4	6	1	0	1.0	.909	3B-9, SS-2
1989		20	.167	.167	12	2	0	0	0	0.0	1	0	0	1	1	0	0	6	13	0	3	1.1	1.000	SS-9, 3B-4, DH-4, 2B-1
1990	ATL N	20	.036	.071	28	1	1	0	0	0.0	3	0	0	7	0	3	0	22	24	2	4	2.8	.958	2B-10, 3B-4, SS-3
4 yrs.		60	.109	.127	55	6	1	0	0	0.0	11	0	2	12	1	3	0	32	43	3	7	1.7	.962	3B-17, SS-15, 2B-11, DH-4

Scotty Ingerton

INGERTON, WILLIAM JOHN BR TR 6′ 1″ 172 lbs.
B. Apr. 19, 1886, Peninsula, Ohio D. June 15, 1956, Cleveland, Ohio.

Year	Team	Games	BA	SA	AB	H	2B	3B	HR	HR%	R	RBI	BB	SO	SB	Pinch Hit AB	Pinch Hit H	PO	A	E	DP	TC/G	FA	G by Pos
1911	BOS N	136	.250	.340	521	130	24	4	5	1.0	63	61	39	68	6	3	0	367	192	29	24	4.4	.951	3B-58, OF-43, 1B-17, 2B-11, SS-5

Charlie Ingraham

INGRAHAM, CHARLES W. 5′11″ 170 lbs.
B. Apr. 8, 1860, Chicago, Ill. D. Feb. 18, 1906, Chicago, Ill.

Year	Team	Games	BA	SA	AB	H	2B	3B	HR	HR%	R	RBI	BB	SO	SB	Pinch Hit AB	Pinch Hit H	PO	A	E	DP	TC/G	FA	G by Pos
1883	BAL AA	1	.250	.250	4	1	0	0	0	0.0	0		0			0	0	4	1	1	0	6.0	.833	C-1

Garey Ingram

INGRAM, GAREY LAMAR BR TR 5′11″ 180 lbs.
B. July 25, 1970, Columbus, Ga.

Year	Team	Games	BA	SA	AB	H	2B	3B	HR	HR%	R	RBI	BB	SO	SB	Pinch Hit AB	Pinch Hit H	PO	A	E	DP	TC/G	FA	G by Pos
1994	LA N	26	.282	.410	78	22	1	0	3	3.8	10	8	7	22	0	2	1	44	68	2	14	5.0	.982	2B-23
1995		44	.200	.236	55	11	2	0	0	0.0	5	3	9	8	3	14	2	17	26	8	3	2.2	.843	3B-12, 2B-7, OF-4
2 yrs.		70	.248	.338	133	33	3	0	3	2.3	15	11	16	30	3	16	3	61	94	10	17	3.6	.939	2B-30, 3B-12, OF-4

Mel Ingram

INGRAM, MELVIN DAVID BR TR 5′11½″ 175 lbs.
B. July 4, 1904, Asheville, N. C. D. Oct. 28, 1979, Medford, Ore.

Year	Team	Games	BA	SA	AB	H	2B	3B	HR	HR%	R	RBI	BB	SO	SB	Pinch Hit AB	Pinch Hit H	PO	A	E	DP	TC/G	FA	G by Pos
1929	PIT N	3	—	—	0	0	0	0	0	—	1	0	0	0	0	0	0	0	0	0	0	0.0	—	

Riccardo Ingram

INGRAM, RICCARDO BENAY BR TR 6′ 205 lbs.
B. Sept. 10, 1966, Douglas, Ga.

Year	Team	Games	BA	SA	AB	H	2B	3B	HR	HR%	R	RBI	BB	SO	SB	Pinch Hit AB	Pinch Hit H	PO	A	E	DP	TC/G	FA	G by Pos
1994	DET A	12	.217	.217	23	5	0	0	0	0.0	3	2	1	2	0	1	0	13	1	0	0	1.6	1.000	OF-8, DH-1
1995	MIN A	4	.125	.125	8	1	0	0	0	0.0	0	1	2	1	0	1	0	0	0	0	0	0.0	.000	DH-3
2 yrs.		16	.194	.194	31	6	0	0	0	0.0	3	3	3	3	0	2	0	13	1	0	0	1.2	1.000	OF-8, DH-4

Dane Iorg

IORG, DANE CHARLES BL TR 6′ 180 lbs.
Brother of Garth Iorg.
B. May 11, 1950, Eureka, Calif.

Year	Team	Games	BA	SA	AB	H	2B	3B	HR	HR%	R	RBI	BB	SO	SB	Pinch Hit AB	Pinch Hit H	PO	A	E	DP	TC/G	FA	G by Pos
1977	2 teams	PHI N (12G –.167) STL N (30G –.313)																						
″	total	42	.242	.274	62	15	2	0	0	0.0	5	6	6	7	0	21	6	71	4	2	6	4.8	.974	1B-9, OF-7
1978	STL N	35	.271	.341	85	23	4	1	0	0.0	6	4	4	10	0	11	2	33	5	0	0	1.5	1.000	OF-25
1979		79	.291	.380	179	52	11	1	1	0.6	12	21	12	28	1	39	11	121	7	2	2	2.7	.985	OF-39, 1B-10
1980		105	.303	.438	251	76	23	1	3	1.2	33	36	20	34	1	38	10	134	2	1	2	2.0	.993	OF-63, 1B-5, 3B-1
1981		75	.327	.424	217	71	11	2	2	0.9	23	39	7	9	2	14	4	125	7	3	1	2.0	.978	OF-57, 1B-8, 3B-2
1982		102	.294	.361	238	70	14	1	0	0.0	17	34	23	23	0	27	7	177	10	3	6	2.5	.984	OF-63, 1B-10, 3B-2
1983		58	.267	.362	116	31	9	1	0	0.0	6	11	10	11	1	20	6	127	5	3	11	4.1	.978	OF-22, 1B-11
1984	2 teams	STL N (15G –.143) KC A (78G –.255)																						
″	total	93	.243	.384	263	64	18	2	5	1.9	30	33	15	21	0	20	6	434	24	3	37	6.0	.993	1B-49, OF-27, 3B-1
1985	KC A	64	.223	.331	130	29	9	1	1	0.8	7	21	8	16	0	27	4	55	4	0	2	1.6	1.000	OF-32, 1B-2, DH-2, 3B-1
1986	SD N	90	.226	.321	106	24	2	1	2	1.9	10	11	2	21	0	**70**	13	43	2	0	3	2.1	1.000	1B-10, 3B-6, OF-3, P-2
10 yrs.		743	.276	.378	1647	455	103	11	14	0.9	149	216	107	180	5	287	69	1320	70	17	70	3.0	.988	OF-338, 1B-114, 3B-13, P-2, DH-2
LEAGUE CHAMPIONSHIP SERIES																								
1984	KC A	2	.500	.500	2	1	0	0	0	0.0	0	1	0	0	0	2	1	0	0	0	0	0.0	—	
1985		4	.500	1.000	2	1	1	0	0	0.0	0	0	2	0	0	2	1	0	0	0	0	0.0	—	
2 yrs.		6	.500	.750	4	2	1	0	0	0.0	0	1	2	0	0	4	2							
WORLD SERIES																								
1982	STL N	5	.529	.882	17	9	4	1	0	0.0	4	1	0	0	0	0	0	0	0	0	0	0.0	.000	DH-5
1985	KC A	2	.500	.500	2	1	0	0	0	0.0	0	2	0	0	0	2	1	0	0	0	0	0.0	—	
2 yrs.		7	.526	.842	19	10	4	1	0	0.0	4	3	0	0	0	2	1	0	0	0	0	0.0		DH-5

Garth Iorg

IORG, GARTH RAY BR TR 5′11″ 170 lbs.
Brother of Dane Iorg.
B. Oct. 12, 1954, Arcata, Calif.

Year	Team	Games	BA	SA	AB	H	2B	3B	HR	HR%	R	RBI	BB	SO	SB	Pinch Hit AB	Pinch Hit H	PO	A	E	DP	TC/G	FA	G by Pos
1978	TOR A	19	.163	.163	49	8	0	0	0	0.0	3	3	3	4	0	0	0	34	51	3	14	4.9	.966	2B-18
1980		80	.248	.329	222	55	10	1	2	0.9	24	14	12	39	2	7	2	122	155	3	45	3.5	.989	2B-32, 3B-20, OF-14, 1B-11, DH-2, SS-1
1981		70	.242	.293	215	52	11	0	0	0.0	17	10	7	31	2	7	1	98	178	12	33	4.4	.958	2B-46, 3B-17, 1B-1, DH-1
1982		129	.285	.365	417	119	20	5	1	0.2	45	36	12	38	3	22	9	114	236	14	30	2.8	.962	3B-100, 2B-30, DH-1
1983		122	.275	.376	375	103	22	5	2	0.5	40	39	13	45	7	16	5	106	223	9	31	2.7	.973	3B-85, 2B-39, SS-1
1984		121	.227	.304	247	56	10	3	1	0.4	24	25	5	16	1	25	4	66	117	10	18	1.6	.948	3B-112, 2B-7, SS-2, DH-1
1985		131	.313	.469	288	90	22	1	7	2.4	33	37	21	26	2	27	7	71	192	9	24	2.1	.967	3B-104, 2B-23
1986		137	.260	.352	327	85	19	1	3	0.9	30	44	20	47	3	28	10	92	185	12	16	2.0	.958	3B-90, 2B-52, SS-2
1987		122	.210	.284	310	65	11	0	4	1.3	35	30	21	52	2	15	3	149	221	7	36	3.0	.981	2B-91, 3B-28, DH-5
9 yrs.		931	.258	.347	2450	633	125	16	20	0.8	251	238	114	298	22	147	41	852	1558	79	247	2.7	.968	3B-556, 2B-338, OF-14, 1B-12, DH-10, SS-6
LEAGUE CHAMPIONSHIP SERIES																								
1985	TOR A	7	.133	.133	15	2	0	0	0	0.0	1	0	1	3	0	2	0	5	10	0	0	2.5	1.000	3B-6

Happy Iott

IOTT, FREDERICK (Dimples) BR TR 5′10″ 175 lbs.
Born Frederick Hoyot.
B. July 7, 1876, Houlton, Me. D. Feb. 17, 1941, Island Falls, Me.

Year	Team	Games	BA	SA	AB	H	2B	3B	HR	HR%	R	RBI	BB	SO	SB	Pinch Hit AB	Pinch Hit H	PO	A	E	DP	TC/G	FA	G by Pos
1903	CLE A	3	.200	.200	10	2	0	0	0	0.0	1	0	2		1	0	0	7	0	1	0	2.7	.875	OF-3

Hal Irelan

IRELAN, HAROLD (Grump) BB TR 5′ 7″ 165 lbs.
B. Aug. 5, 1890, Burnettsville, Ind. D. July 16, 1944, Carmel, Ind.

Year	Team	Games	BA	SA	AB	H	2B	3B	HR	HR%	R	RBI	BB	SO	SB	Pinch Hit AB	Pinch Hit H	PO	A	E	DP	TC/G	FA	G by Pos
1914	PHI N	67	.236	.303	165	39	8	0	1	0.6	16	16	21	22	3	12	6	118	147	26	14	5.7	.911	2B-44, SS-3, 1B-2, 3B-2

Tim Ireland

IRELAND, TIMOTHY NEAL CHRISTOPHER BR TR 6′ 180 lbs.
B. Mar. 14, 1953, Oakland, Calif. BB 1981

Year	Team	Games	BA	SA	AB	H	2B	3B	HR	HR%	R	RBI	BB	SO	SB	Pinch Hit AB	Pinch Hit H	PO	A	E	DP	TC/G	FA	G by Pos
1981	KC A	4	—	—	0	0	0	0	0	—	1	0	0	0	0	0	0	3	0	0	0	0.8	1.000	1B-4
1982		7	.143	.143	7	1	0	0	0	0.0	2	0	1	1	0	0	0	4	5	1	1	1.4	.900	2B-4, OF-2, 3B-1
2 yrs.		11	.143	.143	7	1	0	0	0	0.0	3	0	1	1	0	0	0	7	5	1	1	1.2	.923	2B-4, 1B-4, OF-2, 3B-1

Ed Irvin

IRVIN, WILLIAM EDWARD BR TR
B. 1882, Philadelphia, Pa. D. Feb. 18, 1916, Philadelphia, Pa.

Year	Team	Games	BA	SA	AB	H	2B	3B	HR	HR%	R	RBI	BB	SO	SB	Pinch Hit AB	Pinch Hit H	PO	A	E	DP	TC/G	FA	G by Pos
1912	DET A	1	.667	2.000	3	2	0	2	0	0.0	0	0	0		0	0	0	0	1	1	0	2.0	.500	3B-1

Monte Irvin

IRVIN, MONFORD MERRILL BR TR 6′ 1″ 195 lbs.
B. Feb. 25, 1919, Columbus, Ala.
Hall of Fame 1973.

Year	Team	Games	BA	SA	AB	H	2B	3B	HR	HR%	R	RBI	BB	SO	SB	Pinch Hit AB	Pinch Hit H	PO	A	E	DP	TC/G	FA	G by Pos
1949	NY N	36	.224	.316	76	17	3	2	0	0.0	7	7	17	11	0	13	0	56	17	1	6	3.7	.986	OF-10, 3B-5, 1B-5
1950		110	.299	.497	374	112	19	5	15	4.0	61	66	52	41	3	4	1	569	51	12	62	5.8	.981	1B-59, OF-49, 3B-1
1951		151	.312	.514	558	174	19	11	24	4.3	94	**121**	89	44	12	1	1	585	60	9	48	4.3	.986	OF-112, 1B-39
1952		46	.310	.437	126	39	2	1	4	3.2	10	21	10	11	0	14	2	44	3	0	1	1.5	1.000	OF-32
1953		124	.329	.541	444	146	21	5	21	4.7	72	97	55	34	2	8	2	244	10	7	4	2.3	.973	OF-113
1954		135	.262	.438	432	113	13	3	19	4.4	62	64	70	23	7	9	3	276	7	8	0	2.2	.973	OF-128, 3B-1, 1B-1
1955		51	.253	.333	150	38	7	1	1	0.7	16	17	17	15	3	6	1	94	4	4	0	2.3	.961	OF-45
1956	CHI N	111	.271	.460	339	92	13	3	15	4.4	44	50	41	41	1	18	7	216	6	2	0	2.3	.991	OF-96
8 yrs.		764	.293	.475	2499	731	97	31	99	4.0	366	443	351	220	28	73	17	2084	158	43	121	3.3	.981	OF-585, 1B-104, 3B-7
WORLD SERIES																								
1951	NY N	6	.458	.542	24	11	0	1	0	0.0	4	2	2	1	2	0	0	17	0	1	0	3.0	.944	OF-6
1954		4	.222	.333	9	2	1	0	0	0.0	1	2	0	3	0	0	0	8	0	1	0	2.3	.889	OF-4
2 yrs.		10	.394	.485	33	13	1	1	0	0.0	5	4	2	4	2	0	0	25	0	2	0	2.7	.926	OF-10

Arthur Irwin

IRWIN, ARTHUR ALBERT BL TR 5′ 8½″ 158 lbs.
Brother of John Irwin.
B. Feb. 14, 1858, Toronto, Ont., Canada D. July 16, 1921, Atlantic Ocean.
Manager 1889, 1891–92, 1894–96, 1898–99.

Year	Team	Games	BA	SA	AB	H	2B	3B	HR	HR%	R	RBI	BB	SO	SB	Pinch Hit AB	Pinch Hit H	PO	A	E	DP	TC/G	FA	G by Pos
1880	WOR N	85	.259	.344	352	91	19	4	1	0.3	53	35	11	27		0	0	98	345	53	27	5.8	.893	SS-82, 3B-3, C-1
1881		50	.267	.325	206	55	8	2	0	0.0	27	24	7	4		0	0	50	155	36	11	4.8	.851	SS-50
1882		84	.219	.279	333	73	12	4	0	0.0	30	30	14	34		0	0	125	270	78	24	5.6	.835	3B-51, SS-33
1883	PRO N	98	.286	.374	406	116	22	7	0	0.0	67		12	38		0	0	100	301	66	29	4.8	.859	SS-94, 2B-4
1884		102	.240	.304	404	97	14	3	2	0.5	73		28	52		0	0	99	308	55	20	4.5	.881	SS-102, P-1
1885		59	.179	.197	218	39	2	1	0	0.0	16	14	14	29		0	0	70	212	43	17	5.4	.868	SS-58, 3B-1, 2B-1
1886	PHI N	101	.233	.282	373	87	6	6	0	0.0	51	34	35	39		0	0	137	323	58	21	5.1	.888	SS-100, 3B-1
1887		100	.254	.350	374	95	14	8	2	0.5	65	56	48	26	19	0	0	178	301	58	30	5.4	.892	SS-100
1888		125	.219	.263	448	98	12	4	0	0.0	51	28	33	56	19	0	0	209	383	64	33	5.2	.902	SS-122, 2B-3
1889	2 teams	PHI N (18G –.219) WAS N (85G –.233)																						
″	total	103	.231	.295	386	89	15	5	0	0.0	58	42	48	43	15	0	0	192	325	65	42	5.5	.888	SS-103, 2B-1, P-1
1890	BOS P	96	.260	.314	354	92	17	1	0	0.0	60	45	57	29	16	0	0	137	331	65	44	5.6	.878	SS-96
1891	BOS AA	6	.118	.118	17	2	0	0	0	0.0	1	0	2	1	0	0	0	7	14	6	5	4.5	.778	SS-6
1894	PHI N	1	—	—	0	0	0	0	0	—	0	0	0	0	0	0	0	0	0	0	0	0.0	.000	SS-1
13 yrs.		1010	.241	.305	3871	934	141	45	5	0.1	552	308	309	378	69	0	0	1402	3268	647	303	5.2	.878	SS-947, 3B-56, 2B-9, P-2, C-1

Charlie Irwin

IRWIN, CHARLES EDWIN BL TR 5′10″ 160 lbs.
B. Feb. 15, 1869, Clinton, Ill. D. Sept. 21, 1925, Chicago, Ill.

Year	Team	Games	BA	SA	AB	H	2B	3B	HR	HR%	R	RBI	BB	SO	SB	Pinch Hit AB	Pinch Hit H	PO	A	E	DP	TC/G	FA	G by Pos
1893	CHI N	21	.305	.427	82	25	6	2	0	0.0	14	13	10	1	4	0	0	55	66	12	10	6.3	.910	SS-21
1894		128	.289	.422	498	144	24	9	8	1.6	84	95	63	23	35	0	0	207	341	89	35	5.0	.860	3B-67, SS-61
1895		3	.200	.200	10	2	0	0	0	0.0	4	0	2	1	0	0	0	3	6	1	1	3.3	.900	SS-3
1896	CIN N	127	.296	.361	476	141	16	6	1	0.2	77	67	26	17	31	0	0	200	262	34	28	3.9	.931	3B-127
1897		134	.289	.364	505	146	26	6	0	0.0	89	74	47		27	0	0	186	236	27	19	3.4	.940	3B-134
1898		136	.240	.305	501	120	14	5	3	0.6	77	55	31		18	0	0	223	305	34	20	4.1	.940	3B-136
1899		90	.232	.306	314	73	4	8	1	0.3	42	52	26		26	2	1	124	165	27	9	3.6	.915	3B-78, SS-6, 2B-3, 1B-1
1900		87	.273	.363	333	91	15	6	1	0.3	59	44	14		9	2	0	125	191	25	14	4.0	.927	3B-61, SS-16, OF-6, 2B-3

Charlie Irwin *continued*

Year	Team	Games	BA	SA	AB	H	2B	3B	HR	HR%	R	RBI	BB	SO	SB	Pinch Hit AB	Pinch Hit H	PO	A	E	DP	TC/G	FA	G by Pos
1901	2 teams	CIN N (67G –.238) BKN N (65G –.215)																						
"	total	132	.227	.293	502	114	25	4	0	0.0	50	45	28		17	0	0	175	245	36	15	3.5	.921	3B-132
1902	BKN N	131	.273	.317	458	125	14	0	2	0.4	59	43	39		13	0	0	174	247	34	21	3.5	.925	3B-130, SS-1
10 yrs.		989	.267	.344	3679	981	144	46	16	0.4	555	488	286	42	180	4	1	1472	2064	319	172	3.9	.917	3B-865, SS-108, OF-6, 2B-6, 1B-1

John Irwin

IRWIN, JOHN BL TR 5′10″ 168 lbs.
Brother of Arthur Irwin.
B. July 21, 1861, Toronto, Ont., Canada D. Feb. 28, 1934, Boston, Mass.

Year	Team	Games	BA	SA	AB	H	2B	3B	HR	HR%	R	RBI	BB	SO	SB	Pinch Hit AB	Pinch Hit H	PO	A	E	DP	TC/G	FA	G by Pos
1882	WOR N	1	.000	.000	4	0	0	0	0	0.0	0	0	0	2		0	0	7	0	4	1	11.0	.636	1B-1
1884	BOS U	105	.234	.319	432	101	22	6	1	0.2	81		15			0	0	117	191	87	7	3.8	.780	3B-105
1886	PHI AA	3	.231	.308	13	3	1	0	0	0.0	4		0			0	0	2	7	2	0	3.7	.818	SS-2, 3B-1
1887	WAS N	8	.355	.613	31	11	2	0	2	6.5	6	3	3	6	6	0	0	13	19	5	1	4.1	.865	SS-5, 3B-4
1888		37	.222	.294	126	28	5	2	0	0.0	14	8	5	18	15	0	0	66	97	30	6	5.2	.845	SS-27, 3B-10
1889		58	.289	.373	228	66	11	4	0	0.0	42	25	25	14	10	0	0	82	129	32	14	4.2	.868	3B-58
1890	BUF P	77	.234	.295	308	72	11	4	0	0.0	62	34	43	19	18	0	0	184	155	32	27	4.8	.914	3B-64, 1B-12, 2B-1
1891	2 teams	BOS AA (19G –.222) LOU AA (14G –.273)																						
"	total	33	.244	.315	127	31	3	3	0	0.0	13	22	11	15	7	0	0	43	33	17	1	2.7	.817	OF-17, 3B-16, SS-1
8 yrs.		322	.246	.326	1269	312	55	19	3	0.2	222	92	102	74	56	0	0	514	631	209	57	4.2	.846	3B-258, SS-35, OF-17, 1B-13, 2B-1

Tommy Irwin

IRWIN, THOMAS ANDREW BR TR 5′11″ 165 lbs.
B. Dec. 20, 1912, Altoona, Pa.

Year	Team	Games	BA	SA	AB	H	2B	3B	HR	HR%	R	RBI	BB	SO	SB	Pinch Hit AB	Pinch Hit H	PO	A	E	DP	TC/G	FA	G by Pos
1938	CLE A	3	.111	.111	9	1	0	0	0	0.0	1	0	3	1	0	0	0	3	8	0	2	3.7	1.000	SS-3

Walt Irwin

IRWIN, WALTER KINGSLEY (Lightning) BR TR 5′10½″ 170 lbs.
B. Sept. 23, 1897, Henrietta, Pa. D. Aug. 18, 1976, Spring Lake, Mich.

Year	Team	Games	BA	SA	AB	H	2B	3B	HR	HR%	R	RBI	BB	SO	SB	Pinch Hit AB	Pinch Hit H	PO	A	E	DP	TC/G	FA	G by Pos
1921	STL N	4	.000	.000	1	0	0	0	0	0.0	1	0	0	1	0	1	0	0	0	0	0	0.0	—	

Orlando Isales

ISALES, ORLANDO BR TR 5′ 9″ 175 lbs.
Born Orlando Isales (Pizarro).
B. Dec. 22, 1959, Santurce, Puerto Rico.

Year	Team	Games	BA	SA	AB	H	2B	3B	HR	HR%	R	RBI	BB	SO	SB	Pinch Hit AB	Pinch Hit H	PO	A	E	DP	TC/G	FA	G by Pos
1980	PHI N	3	.400	.800	5	2	0	1	0	0.0	1	3	1	0	0	0	0	3	0	0	0	1.5	1.000	OF-2

Frank Isbell

ISBELL, WILLIAM FRANK (Bald Eagle) BL TR 5′11″ 190 lbs.
B. Aug. 21, 1875, Delevan, N. Y. D. July 15, 1941, Wichita, Kans.

Year	Team	Games	BA	SA	AB	H	2B	3B	HR	HR%	R	RBI	BB	SO	SB	Pinch Hit AB	Pinch Hit H	PO	A	E	DP	TC/G	FA	G by Pos
1898	CHI N	45	.233	.258	159	37	4	0	0	0.0	17	8	3		3	0	0	54	43	19	5	2.4	.836	OF-28, P-13, 2B-3, 3B-3, SS-2
1901	CHI A	137	.257	.329	556	143	15	8	3	0.5	93	70	36		**52**	0	0	1389	107	32	79	10.8	.979	1B-137, 2B-2, 3B-1, SS-1, P-1
1902		137	.252	.318	515	130	14	4	4	0.8	62	59	14		38	0	0	1405	105	22	100	11.0	.986	1B-133, SS-4, P-1, C-1
1903		138	.242	.332	546	132	25	9	2	0.4	52	59	12		26	0	0	1225	136	35	58	10.0	.975	1B-117, 3B-19, 2B-2, OF-1, SS-1
1904		96	.210	.271	314	66	10	3	1	0.3	27	34	16		19	3	0	663	145	25	29	9.0	.970	1B-57, 2B-27, OF-5, SS-4
1905		94	.296	.440	341	101	21	11	2	0.6	55	45	15		15	0	0	219	136	13	18	4.0	.965	2B-42, OF-40, 1B-9, SS-2
1906		143	.279	.352	549	153	18	11	0	0.0	71	57	30		37	0	0	313	363	36	36	4.8	.949	2B-132, OF-14, P-1, C-1
1907		125	.243	.311	486	118	19	7	0	0.0	60	41	22		22	1	0	285	386	30	42	5.6	.957	2B-119, OF-5, SS-1, P-1
1908		84	.247	.322	320	79	15	3	1	0.3	31	49	19		18	1	0	864	104	18	30	11.9	.982	1B-65, 2B-18
1909		120	.224	.291	433	97	17	6	0	0.0	33	33	23		23	5	2	1226	80	12	51	11.5	.991	1B-101, OF-9, 2B-5
10 yrs.		1119	.250	.326	4219	1056	158	62	13	0.3	501	455	190		253	10	2	7643	1605	242	448	8.4	.974	1B-619, 2B-350, OF-102, 3B-23, P-17, SS-15, C-2
WORLD SERIES																								
1906	CHI A	6	.308	.462	26	8	4	0	0	0.0	4	4	0	6	1	0	0	11	16	5	1	5.3	.844	2B-6

Mike Ivie

IVIE, MICHAEL WILSON BR TR 6′ 3″ 205 lbs.
B. Aug. 8, 1952, Atlanta, Ga.

Year	Team	Games	BA	SA	AB	H	2B	3B	HR	HR%	R	RBI	BB	SO	SB	Pinch Hit AB	Pinch Hit H	PO	A	E	DP	TC/G	FA	G by Pos
1971	SD N	6	.471	.471	17	8	0	0	0	0.0	0	3	1	1	0	1	0	22	2	0	0	4.0	1.000	C-6
1974		12	.088	.176	34	3	0	0	1	2.9	1	3	2	8	0	1	0	67	5	1	9	6.6	.986	1B-11
1975		111	.249	.366	377	94	16	2	8	2.1	36	46	20	63	4	9	3	540	138	23	54	5.0	.967	1B-78, 3B-61, C-1
1976		140	.291	.415	405	118	19	5	7	1.7	51	70	30	41	6	4	0	1032	71	7	90	8.0	.994	1B-135, 3B-2, C-2
1977		134	.272	.395	489	133	29	2	9	1.8	66	66	39	57	3	15	2	886	93	11	79	7.6	.989	1B-105, 3B-25
1978	SF N	117	.308	.475	318	98	14	3	11	3.5	34	55	27	45	3	31	12	579	18	5	33	6.1	.992	1B-76, OF-22
1979		133	.286	.547	402	115	18	3	27	6.7	58	89	47	80	5	23	9	752	47	4	51	6.3	.995	1B-98, OF-24, 3B-4, 2B-1
1980		79	.241	.346	286	69	16	1	4	1.4	21	25	19	40	1	6	1	669	32	5	46	9.8	.993	1B-72
1981	2 teams	SF N (7G –.294) HOU N (19G –.238)																						
"	total	26	.254	.339	59	15	5	0	0	0.0	3	9	2	12	0	13	4	113	15	1	7	8.6	.992	1B-15
1982	2 teams	HOU N (7G –.333) DET A (80G –.232)																						
"	total	87	.234	.445	265	62	12	1	14	5.3	35	38	25	51	0	17	4	0	0	0	0	0.0	.000	DH-79
1983	DET A	12	.214	.310	42	9	4	0	0	0.0	4	7	2	4	0	0	0	86	6	0	6	7.7	1.000	1B-12
11 yrs.		857	.269	.421	2694	724	133	17	81	3.0	309	411	214	402	22	120	35	4746	427	57	375	6.3	.989	1B-602, 3B-92, DH-79, OF-46, C-9, 2B-1

Hank Izquierdo

IZQUIERDO, ENRIQUE ROBERTO BR TR 5′11″ 175 lbs.
Born Enrique Roberto Izquierdo (Valdes).
B. Mar. 20, 1931, Matanzas, Cuba.

Year	Team	Games	BA	SA	AB	H	2B	3B	HR	HR%	R	RBI	BB	SO	SB	Pinch Hit AB	Pinch Hit H	PO	A	E	DP	TC/G	FA	G by Pos
1967	MIN A	16	.269	.346	26	7	2	0	0	0.0	4	2	1	2	0	1	0	65	7	1	1	4.6	.986	C-16

Ray Jablonski

JABLONSKI, RAYMOND LEO (Jabbo) BR TR 5′10″ 175 lbs.
B. Dec. 17, 1926, Chicago, Ill. D. Nov. 25, 1985, Chicago, Ill.

Year	Team	Games	BA	SA	AB	H	2B	3B	HR	HR%	R	RBI	BB	SO	SB	Pinch Hit AB	Pinch Hit H	PO	A	E	DP	TC/G	FA	G by Pos
1953	STL N	157	.268	.427	604	162	23	5	21	3.5	64	112	34	61	2	0	0	94	278	27	27	2.5	.932	3B-157
1954		152	.296	.419	611	181	33	3	12	2.0	80	104	49	42	9	2	2	127	299	34	25	3.1	.926	3B-149, 1B-1
1955	CIN N	74	.240	.403	221	53	9	0	9	4.1	28	28	13	35	0	17	4	69	46	11	3	2.3	.913	OF-28, 3B-28
1956		130	.256	.432	407	104	25	1	15	3.7	42	66	37	57	2	14	5	117	172	9	11	2.3	.970	3B-127, 2B-1
1957	NY N	107	.289	.433	305	88	15	1	9	3.0	37	57	31	47	0	28	6	99	136	12	20	3.2	.951	3B-70, 1B-6, OF-1

Ray Jablonski *continued*

Year	Team	Games	BA	SA	AB	H	2B	3B	HR	HR%	R	RBI	BB	SO	SB	Pinch Hit AB	Pinch Hit H	PO	A	E	DP	TC/G	FA	G by Pos
1958	SF N	82	.230	.461	230	53	15	1	12	5.2	28	46	17	50	2	31	9	49	91	8	2	2.6	.946	3B-57
1959	2 teams	STL N (60G –.253) KC A (25G –.262)																						
"	total	85	.257	.388	152	39	5	0	5	3.3	15	22	11	30	1	53	8	20	43	5	5	1.8	.926	3B-36, SS-1
1960	KC A	21	.219	.250	32	7	1	0	0	0.0	3	3	4	8	0	13	3	4	13	1	0	3.0	.944	3B-6
8 yrs.		808	.268	.423	2562	687	126	11	83	3.2	297	438	196	330	16	158	37	579	1078	107	93	2.6	.939	3B-630, OF-29, 1B-7, SS-1, 2B-1

Fred Jacklitsch

JACKLITSCH, FREDERICK LAWRENCE BR TR 5′ 9″ 180 lbs.
B. May 24, 1876, Brooklyn, N. Y. D. July 18, 1937, Brooklyn, N. Y.

Year	Team	Games	BA	SA	AB	H	2B	3B	HR	HR%	R	RBI	BB	SO	SB	Pinch Hit AB	Pinch Hit H	PO	A	E	DP	TC/G	FA	G by Pos
1900	PHI N	5	.182	.273	11	2	1	0	0	0.0	0	3	0		0	2	0	2	1	0	1	1.0	1.000	C-3
1901		33	.250	.333	120	30	4	3	0	0.0	14	24	12		2	1	0	126	40	5	3	5.5	.971	C-30, 3B-1
1902		38	.202	.237	114	23	4	0	0	0.0	8	8	9		2	8	2	123	31	13	0	5.6	.922	C-29, OF-1
1903	BKN N	60	.267	.364	176	47	8	3	1	0.6	31	21	33		4	6	2	203	72	9	7	5.2	.968	C-53, 2B-1, OF-1
1904		26	.234	.299	77	18	3	1	0	0.0	8	8	7		7	2	0	130	32	14	6	7.3	.920	1B-11, 2B-8, C-5
1905	NY A	1	.000	.000	3	0	0	0	0	0.0	1	1	1		0	0	0	6	1	0	0	7.0	1.000	C-1
1907	PHI N	73	.213	.248	202	43	7	0	0	0.0	19	17	27		7	8	0	314	99	8	18	6.5	.981	C-58, 1B-6, OF-1
1908		37	.221	.256	86	19	3	0	0	0.0	6	7	14		3	5	1	126	38	4	1	5.6	.976	C-30
1909		20	.313	.406	32	10	1	1	0	0.0	6	1	10		1	7	0	45	10	3	0	4.5	.948	C-12, 2B-1
1910		25	.196	.255	51	10	3	0	0	0.0	7	2	5	9	0	7	2	80	24	2	0	6.2	.981	C-13, 1B-2, 3B-1, 2B-1
1914	BAL F	122	.276	.380	337	93	21	4	2	0.6	40	48	52		7	4	1	580	167	9	13	6.4	.988	C-118
1915		49	.237	.348	135	32	9	0	2	1.5	20	13	31		2	2	0	206	51	2	8	5.6	.992	C-45, SS-1
1917	BOS N	1	—	—	0	0	0	0	0	—	0	0	0	0	0	0	0	1	0	0	0	1.0	1.000	C-1
13 yrs.		490	.243	.320	1344	327	64	12	5	0.4	160	153	201	9	35	52	8	1942	566	69	57	5.9	.973	C-398, 1B-19, 2B-11, OF-3, 3B-2, SS-1

Bill Jackson

JACKSON, WILLIAM RILEY BL TL 5′11½″ 160 lbs.
B. Apr. 4, 1881, Pittsburgh, Pa. D. Sept. 24, 1958, Peoria, Ill.

Year	Team	Games	BA	SA	AB	H	2B	3B	HR	HR%	R	RBI	BB	SO	SB	Pinch Hit AB	Pinch Hit H	PO	A	E	DP	TC/G	FA	G by Pos
1914	CHI F	26	.040	.040	25	1	0	0	0	0.0	2	1	3		0	8	0	24	1	1	2	2.6	.962	OF-6, 1B-4
1915		50	.163	.204	98	16	1	0	1	1.0	15	12	14		3	8	1	276	17	5	10	8.1	.983	1B-36, OF-1
2 yrs.		76	.138	.171	123	17	1	0	1	0.8	17	13	17		3	16	1	300	18	6	12	6.9	.981	1B-40, OF-7

Bo Jackson

JACKSON, VINCENT EDWARD BR TR 6′ 1″ 222 lbs.
B. Nov. 30, 1962, Bessemer, Ala.

Year	Team	Games	BA	SA	AB	H	2B	3B	HR	HR%	R	RBI	BB	SO	SB	Pinch Hit AB	Pinch Hit H	PO	A	E	DP	TC/G	FA	G by Pos
1986	KC A	25	.207	.329	82	17	2	1	2	2.4	9	9	7	34	3	0	0	29	2	4	0	1.5	.886	OF-23, DH-1
1987		116	.235	.455	396	93	17	2	22	5.6	46	53	30	158	10	2	0	180	9	9	1	1.7	.955	OF-113, DH-1
1988		124	.246	.472	439	108	16	4	25	5.7	63	68	25	146	27	1	0	246	11	7	2	2.1	.973	OF-121, DH-2
1989		135	.256	.495	515	132	15	6	32	6.2	86	105	39	**172**	26	1	0	224	11	8	2	1.8	.967	OF-110, DH-24
1990		111	.272	.523	405	110	16	1	28	6.9	74	78	44	128	15	4	1	230	8	12	2	2.3	.952	OF-97, DH-10
1991	CHI A	23	.225	.408	71	16	4	0	3	4.2	8	14	12	25	0	2	1	0	0	0	0	0.0	.000	DH-21
1993		85	.232	.433	284	66	9	0	16	5.6	32	45	23	106	0	8	3	89	5	1	1	1.1	.989	OF-47, DH-36
1994	CAL A	75	.279	.507	201	56	7	0	13	6.5	23	43	20	72	1	15	4	77	3	3	0	1.5	.964	OF-46, DH-9
8 yrs.		694	.250	.474	2393	598	86	14	141	5.9	341	415	200	841	82	33	9	1075	49	44	8	1.8	.962	OF-557, DH-104
LEAGUE CHAMPIONSHIP SERIES																								
1993	CHI A	3	.000	.000	10	0	0	0	0	0.0	1	0	3	6	0	0	0	0	0	0	0	0.0	.000	DH-3

Charlie Jackson

JACKSON, CHARLES HERBERT (Lefty) BL TL 5′ 9″ 150 lbs.
B. Feb. 7, 1894, Granite City, Ill. D. May 27, 1968, Radford, Va.

Year	Team	Games	BA	SA	AB	H	2B	3B	HR	HR%	R	RBI	BB	SO	SB	Pinch Hit AB	Pinch Hit H	PO	A	E	DP	TC/G	FA	G by Pos
1915	CHI A	1	.000	.000	1	0	0	0	0	0.0	0	0	0	1	0	1	0	0	0	0	0	0.0	—	
1917	PIT N	41	.240	.298	121	29	3	2	0	0.0	7	1	10	22	4	2	0	65	5	1	0	2.0	.986	OF-36
2 yrs.		42	.238	.295	122	29	3	2	0	0.0	7	1	10	23	4	3	0	65	5	1	0	2.0	.986	OF-36

Chuck Jackson

JACKSON, CHARLES LEO BR TR 6′ 185 lbs.
B. Mar. 19, 1963, Seattle, Wash.

Year	Team	Games	BA	SA	AB	H	2B	3B	HR	HR%	R	RBI	BB	SO	SB	Pinch Hit AB	Pinch Hit H	PO	A	E	DP	TC/G	FA	G by Pos
1987	HOU N	35	.211	.296	71	15	3	0	1	1.4	3	6	7	19	1	5	1	12	39	2	4	1.8	.962	3B-16, OF-13, SS-1
1988		46	.229	.349	83	19	5	1	1	1.2	7	8	7	16	1	9	2	12	51	7	6	1.8	.900	3B-32, SS-3, OF-3
1994	TEX A	1	.000	.000	2	0	0	0	0	0.0	0	0	0	0	0	0	0	0	0	0	0	0.0	.000	3B-1
3 yrs.		82	.218	.321	156	34	8	1	2	1.3	10	14	14	35	2	14	3	24	90	9	10	1.8	.927	3B-49, OF-16, SS-4

Darrin Jackson

JACKSON, DARRIN JAY BR TR 6′ 185 lbs.
B. Aug. 22, 1963, Los Angeles, Calif.

Year	Team	Games	BA	SA	AB	H	2B	3B	HR	HR%	R	RBI	BB	SO	SB	Pinch Hit AB	Pinch Hit H	PO	A	E	DP	TC/G	FA	G by Pos
1985	CHI N	5	.091	.091	11	1	0	0	0	0.0	0	0	0	3	0	1	0	7	0	0	0	1.8	1.000	OF-4
1987		7	.800	1.000	5	4	1	0	0	0.0	2	0	0	0	0	4	3	1	0	0	0	0.2	1.000	OF-5
1988		100	.266	.452	188	50	11	3	6	3.2	29	20	5	28	4	21	5	116	1	2	0	1.6	.983	OF-74
1989	2 teams	CHI N (45G –.229) SD N (25G –.207)																						
"	total	70	.218	.329	170	37	7	0	4	2.4	17	20	13	34	1	14	1	121	5	5	4	2.1	.962	OF-63
1990	SD N	58	.257	.363	113	29	3	0	3	2.7	10	9	5	24	3	18	4	63	1	1	1	1.7	.985	OF-39
1991		122	.262	.476	359	94	12	1	21	5.8	51	49	27	66	5	23	3	243	2	2	2	2.5	.992	OF-98, P-1
1992		155	.249	.392	587	146	23	5	17	2.9	72	70	26	106	14	2	0	436	18	2	9	3.0	.996	OF-153
1993	2 teams	TOR A (46G –.216) NY N (31G –.195)																						
"	total	77	.209	.312	263	55	9	0	6	2.3	19	26	10	75	0	8	2	137	6	1	2	2.0	.993	OF-72
1994	CHI A	104	.312	.455	369	115	17	3	10	2.7	43	51	27	56	7	8	3	225	2	1	1	2.2	.996	OF-102
9 yrs.		698	.257	.406	2065	531	83	12	67	3.2	243	245	113	392	34	99	21	1349	35	14	19	2.3	.990	OF-610, P-1

George Jackson

JACKSON, GEORGE CHRISTOPHER (Hickory) BR TR 6′½″ 180 lbs.
B. Oct. 14, 1882, Springfield, Mo. D. Nov. 25, 1972, Cleburne, Tex.

Year	Team	Games	BA	SA	AB	H	2B	3B	HR	HR%	R	RBI	BB	SO	SB	Pinch Hit AB	Pinch Hit H	PO	A	E	DP	TC/G	FA	G by Pos
1911	BOS N	39	.347	.449	147	51	11	2	0	0.0	28	25	12	21	12	0	0	74	4	6	1	2.2	.929	OF-39
1912		110	.262	.350	397	104	13	5	4	1.0	55	48	38	72	22	2	0	230	20	15	3	2.5	.943	OF-107
1913		3	.300	.300	10	3	0	0	0	0.0	2	0	0	2	0	0	0	6	1	1	0	2.7	.875	OF-3
3 yrs.		152	.285	.375	554	158	24	7	4	0.7	85	73	50	95	34	2	0	310	25	22	4	2.4	.938	OF-149

Henry Jackson

JACKSON, HENRY EVERETT — BR TR 6′ 2″ 185 lbs.
B. June 23, 1861, Union City, Ind. D. Sept. 14, 1932, Chicago, Ill.

Year	Team	Games	BA	SA	AB	H	2B	3B	HR	HR%	R	RBI	BB	SO	SB	Pinch Hit AB	Pinch Hit H	PO	A	E	DP	TC/G	FA	G by Pos
1887	IND N	10	.263	.289	38	10	1	0	0	0.0	1	3	0	12	2	0	0	108	3	8	7	11.9	.933	1B-10

Jim Jackson

JACKSON, JAMES BENNER — BR TR
B. Nov. 28, 1877, Philadelphia, Pa. D. Oct. 9, 1955, Philadelphia, Pa.

Year	Team	Games	BA	SA	AB	H	2B	3B	HR	HR%	R	RBI	BB	SO	SB	Pinch Hit AB	Pinch Hit H	PO	A	E	DP	TC/G	FA	G by Pos
1901	BAL A	99	.250	.330	364	91	17	3	2	0.5	42	50	20		11	3	0	234	4	7	1	2.6	.971	OF-96
1902	NY N	35	.182	.245	110	20	5	1	0	0.0	14	13	15		6	1	0	57	4	7	0	2.0	.897	OF-34
1905	CLE A	108	.257	.318	421	108	12	4	2	0.5	58	31	34		15	0	0	196	21	13	3	2.1	.943	OF-105, 3B-3
1906		105	.214	.270	374	80	13	4	0	0.0	44	38	38		25	1	0	189	5	5	2	1.9	.975	OF-105
4 yrs.		347	.236	.301	1269	299	47	12	4	0.3	158	132	107		57	5	0	676	34	32	6	2.2	.957	OF-340, 3B-3

Joe Jackson

JACKSON, JOSEPH JEFFERSON (Shoeless Joe) — BL TR 6′ 1″ 200 lbs.
B. July 16, 1889, Pickens County, S. C. D. Dec. 5, 1951, Greenville, S. C.

Year	Team	Games	BA	SA	AB	H	2B	3B	HR	HR%	R	RBI	BB	SO	SB	Pinch Hit AB	Pinch Hit H	PO	A	E	DP	TC/G	FA	G by Pos
1908	PHI A	5	.130	.130	23	3	0	0	0	0.0	0	3	0		0	0	0	6	1	1	0	1.6	.875	OF-5
1909		5	.294	.294	17	5	0	0	0	0.0	3	3	1		0	1	0	10	0	2	0	3.0	.833	OF-4
1910	CLE A	20	.387	.587	75	29	2	5	1	1.3	15	11	8		4	0	0	40	2	1	1	2.2	.977	OF-20
1911		147	.408	.590	571	233	45	19	7	1.2	126	83	56		41	0	0	242	32	12	8	1.9	.958	OF-147
1912		152	.395	.579	572	226	44	**26**	3	0.5	121	90	54		35	2	1	273	30	16	2	2.1	.950	OF-150
1913		148	.373	**.551**	528	**197**	**39**	17	7	1.3	109	71	80	26	26	0	0	211	28	18	5	1.7	.930	OF-148
1914		122	.338	.464	453	153	22	13	3	0.7	61	53	41	34	22	2	1	195	13	7	4	1.8	.967	OF-119
1915	2 teams	CLE A (82G –.331)	CHI A (46G –.265)																					
″	total	128	.308	.445	461	142	20	14	5	1.1	63	81	52	23	16	4	2	436	27	15	13	3.9	.969	OF-95, 1B-27
1916	CHI A	155	.341	.495	592	202	40	**21**	3	0.5	91	78	46	25	24	0	0	290	17	8	5	2.0	.975	OF-155
1917		146	.301	.429	538	162	20	17	5	0.9	91	75	57	25	13	1	0	341	18	6	4	2.5	.984	OF-145
1918		17	.354	.492	65	23	2	2	1	1.5	9	20	8	1	3	0	0	36	1	0	0	2.2	1.000	OF-17
1919		139	.351	.506	516	181	31	14	7	1.4	79	96	60	10	9	0	0	252	15	9	4	2.0	.967	OF-139
1920		146	.382	.589	570	218	42	**20**	12	2.1	105	121	56	14	9	1	0	314	14	12	2	2.3	.965	OF-145
13 yrs.		1330	.356 **3rd**	.518	4981	1774	307	168	54	1.1	873	785	519	158	202	11	4	2646	198	107	48	2.2	.964	OF-1289, 1B-27
WORLD SERIES																								
1917	CHI A	6	.304	.304	23	7	0	0	0	0.0	4	2	1	0	1	0	0	9	1	0	0	1.7	1.000	OF-6
1919		8	.375	.563	32	12	3	0	1	3.1	5	6	1	2	0	0	0	16	1	0	1	2.1	1.000	OF-8
2 yrs.		14	.345	.455	55	19	3	0	1	1.8	9	8	2	2	1	0	0	25	2	0	1	1.9	1.000	OF-14

Ken Jackson

JACKSON, KENNETH BERNARD — BR TR 6′ 1″ 190 lbs.
B. Aug. 21, 1963, Shreveport, La.

Year	Team	Games	BA	SA	AB	H	2B	3B	HR	HR%	R	RBI	BB	SO	SB	Pinch Hit AB	Pinch Hit H	PO	A	E	DP	TC/G	FA	G by Pos
1987	PHI N	8	.250	.375	16	4	2	0	0	0.0	1	2	1	4	0	0	0	6	15	1	1	2.8	.955	SS-8

Lou Jackson

JACKSON, LOUIS CLARENCE — BL TR 5′10″ 168 lbs.
B. July 26, 1935, Riverton, La. D. May 27, 1969, Tokyo, Japan.

Year	Team	Games	BA	SA	AB	H	2B	3B	HR	HR%	R	RBI	BB	SO	SB	Pinch Hit AB	Pinch Hit H	PO	A	E	DP	TC/G	FA	G by Pos
1958	CHI N	24	.171	.371	35	6	2	1	1	2.9	5	6	1	9	0	11	1	9	0	0	0	0.8	1.000	OF-12
1959		6	.250	.250	4	1	0	0	0	0.0	2	1	0	2	0	4	1	0	0	0	0	0.0	—	
1964	BAL A	4	.375	.375	8	3	0	0	0	0.0	0	0	0	2	0	3	0	4	0	0	0	4.0	1.000	OF-1
3 yrs.		34	.213	.362	47	10	2	1	1	2.1	7	7	1	13	0	18	2	13	0	0	0	1.0	1.000	OF-13

Randy Jackson

JACKSON, RANSOM JOSEPH (Handsome Ransom) — BR TR 6′ 1½″ 180 lbs.
B. Feb. 10, 1926, Little Rock, Ark.

Year	Team	Games	BA	SA	AB	H	2B	3B	HR	HR%	R	RBI	BB	SO	SB	Pinch Hit AB	Pinch Hit H	PO	A	E	DP	TC/G	FA	G by Pos
1950	CHI N	34	.225	.396	111	25	4	3	3	2.7	13	6	7	25	4	7	0	26	56	8	3	3.3	.911	3B-27
1951		145	.275	.425	557	153	24	6	16	2.9	78	76	47	44	14	2	1	198	323	24	32	3.8	.956	3B-143
1952		116	.232	.351	379	88	8	5	9	2.4	44	34	27	42	6	10	2	93	203	13	13	2.9	.958	3B-104, OF-1
1953		139	.285	.476	498	142	22	8	19	3.8	61	66	42	61	8	7	0	141	265	22	24	3.2	.949	3B-133
1954		126	.273	.450	484	132	17	6	19	3.9	77	67	44	55	2	2	0	118	266	18	21	3.2	.955	3B-124
1955		138	.265	.445	499	132	13	7	21	4.2	73	70	58	58	0	3	1	125	247	20	26	2.9	.949	3B-134
1956	BKN N	101	.274	.446	307	84	15	7	8	2.6	37	53	28	38	2	21	5	84	184	2	19	3.4	.993	3B-80
1957		48	.198	.252	131	26	1	0	2	1.5	7	16	9	20	0	4	2	27	53	2	7	2.4	.976	3B-34
1958	2 teams	LA N (35G –.185)	CLE A (29G –.242)																					
″	total	64	.218	.365	156	34	6	1	5	3.2	15	17	8	28	0	21	4	38	98	11	10	3.6	.925	3B-41
1959	2 teams	CLE A (3G –.143)	CHI N (41G –.243)																					
″	total	44	.235	.358	81	19	5	1	1	1.2	7	10	11	11	0	16	1	20	30	3	2	2.1	.943	3B-24, OF-1
10 yrs.		955	.261	.421	3203	835	115	44	103	3.2	412	415	281	382	36	93	16	870	1725	123	157	3.2	.955	3B-844, OF-2
WORLD SERIES																								
1956	BKN N	3	.000	.000	3	0	0	0	0	0.0	0	0	0	2	0	3	0	0	0	0	0	0.0	—	

Reggie Jackson

JACKSON, REGINALD MARTINEZ (Mr. October) — BL TL 6′ 195 lbs.
B. May 18, 1946, Wyncote, Pa.
Hall of Fame 1993.

Year	Team	Games	BA	SA	AB	H	2B	3B	HR	HR%	R	RBI	BB	SO	SB	Pinch Hit AB	Pinch Hit H	PO	A	E	DP	TC/G	FA	G by Pos
1967	KC A	35	.178	.305	118	21	4	4	1	0.8	13	6	10	46	1	2	0	55	1	4	0	1.8	.933	OF-34
1968	OAK A	154	.250	.452	553	138	13	6	29	5.2	82	74	50	**171**	14	1	0	269	14	12	5	2.0	.959	OF-151
1969		152	.275	**.608**	549	151	36	3	47	8.6	**123**	118	114	**142**	13	2	1	278	14	11	2	2.0	.964	OF-150
1970		149	.237	.458	426	101	21	2	23	5.4	57	66	75	**135**	26	7	2	251	8	12	0	1.9	.956	OF-142
1971		150	.277	.508	567	157	29	3	32	5.6	87	80	63	**161**	16	5	1	285	15	7	3	2.1	.977	OF-145
1972		135	.265	.473	499	132	25	2	25	5.0	72	75	59	125	9	0	0	301	5	9	5	2.3	.971	OF-135
1973		151	.293	**.531**	539	158	28	2	**32**	**5.9**	**99**	**117**	76	111	22	4	0	302	4	9	0	2.1	.971	OF-145, DH-3
1974		148	.289	.514	506	146	25	1	29	5.7	90	93	86	105	25	3	0	296	8	10	2	2.2	.968	OF-127, DH-19
1975		157	.253	.511	593	150	39	3	**36**	6.1	91	104	67	133	17	1	0	315	13	12	5	2.2	.965	OF-147, DH-9
1976	BAL A	134	.277	**.502**	498	138	27	2	27	5.4	84	91	54	108	28	2	1	284	8	11	3	2.3	.964	OF-121, DH-11
1977	NY A	146	.286	.550	525	150	39	2	32	6.1	93	110	74	129	17	3	0	236	7	13	0	1.8	.949	OF-127, DH-18
1978		139	.274	.477	511	140	13	5	27	5.3	82	97	58	133	14	1	1	212	6	3	1	1.6	.986	OF-104, DH-35
1979		131	.297	.544	465	138	24	2	29	6.2	78	89	65	107	9	3	1	274	7	4	2	2.1	.986	OF-125, DH-11
1980		143	.300	.597	514	154	22	4	**41**	**8.0**	94	111	83	122	1	3	1	174	3	7	0	1.3	.962	OF-94, DH-46
1981		94	.237	.428	334	79	17	1	15	4.5	33	54	46	82	0	1	1	111	3	3	0	1.2	.974	OF-61, DH-33
1982	CAL A	153	.275	.532	530	146	17	1	**39**	**7.4**	92	101	85	**156**	4	11	6	200	6	6	1	1.5	.972	OF-139, DH-5
1983		116	.194	.340	397	77	14	1	14	3.5	43	49	52	140	0	10	2	66	4	1	1	0.7	.986	DH-62, OF-47

Reggie Jackson *continued*

Year	Team	Games	BA	SA	AB	H	2B	3B	HR	HR%	R	RBI	BB	SO	SB	Pinch Hit AB	Pinch Hit H	PO	A	E	DP	TC/G	FA	G by Pos
1984		143	.223	.406	525	117	17	2	25	4.8	67	81	55	141	8	7	1	7	0	0	0	0.1	1.000	DH-134, OF-3
1985		143	.252	.487	460	116	27	0	27	5.9	64	85	78	138	1	12	2	112	6	7	1	0.9	.944	OF-81, DH-52
1986		132	.241	.408	419	101	12	2	18	4.3	65	58	92	115	1	14	4	4	1	1	0	0.0	.833	DH-121, OF-4
1987	OAK A	115	.220	.402	336	74	14	1	15	4.5	42	43	33	97	2	29	7	30	0	0	0	0.3	1.000	DH-79, OF-20
21 yrs.		2820	.262	.490	9864	2584	463	49	563	5.7	1551	1702	1375	2597	228	121	31	4062	133	142	31	1.6	.967	OF-2102, DH-638
									6th					**1st**										
DIVISIONAL PLAYOFF SERIES																								
1981	NY A	5	.300	.600	20	6	0	0	2	10.0	4	4	1	5	0	0	0	7	0	0	0	1.4	1.000	OF-5
LEAGUE CHAMPIONSHIP SERIES																								
1971	OAK A	3	.333	.917	12	4	1	0	2	16.7	2	2	0	1	0	0	0	9	1	0	0	3.3	1.000	OF-3
1972		5	.278	.333	18	5	1	0	0	0.0	1	2	1	6	2	0	0	14	0	1	0	3.0	.933	OF-5
1973		5	.143	.143	21	3	0	0	0	0.0	0	0	0	6	0	0	0	19	0	0	0	3.8	1.000	OF-5
1974		4	.167	.250	12	2	1	0	0	0.0	0	1	5	2	0	0	0	0	0	0	0	0.0		DH-3, OF-1
1975		3	.417	.667	12	5	0	0	1	8.3	1	3	0	2	0	0	0	5	1	0	1	2.0	1.000	OF-3
1977	NY A	5	.125	.125	16	2	0	0	0	0.0	1	1	2	2	1	1	1	10	1	0	0	2.2	1.000	OF-4, DH-1
1978		4	.462	1.000	13	6	1	0	2	15.4	5	6	3	4	0	0	0	4	0	0	0	1.0	1.000	DH-3, OF-1
1980		3	.273	.364	11	3	1	0	0	0.0	1	0	1	4	0	0	0	5	0	0	0	1.7	1.000	OF-3
1981		2	.000	.000	4	0	0	0	0	0.0	1	1	1	0	1	0	0	1	0	0	0	0.5	1.000	OF-2
1982	CAL A	5	.111	.278	18	2	0	0	1	5.6	2	2	2	7	0	0	0	2	0	0	0	0.4	1.000	OF-5
1986		6	.192	.269	26	5	2	0	0	0.0	2	2	2	7	0	0	0	0	0	0	0	0.0	.000	DH-6
11 yrs.		45	.227	.380	163	37	7	0	6	3.7	16	20	17	41	4	1	1	69	3	1	1	1.6	.986	OF-32, DH-13
		1st			**1st**	**2nd**	**1st**		**3rd**		**4th**	**2nd**	**2nd**	**1st**										
WORLD SERIES																								
1973	OAK A	7	.310	.586	29	9	3	1	1	3.4	3	6	2	7	0	0	0	17	0	0	0	2.4	1.000	OF-7
1974		5	.286	.571	14	4	1	0	1	7.1	3	1	5	3	1	0	0	6	1	1	0	1.6	.875	OF-5
1977	NY A	6	.450	1.250	20	9	1	0	5	25.0	10	8	3	4	0	0	0	9	0	0	0	1.5	1.000	OF-6
1978		6	.391	.696	23	9	1	0	2	8.7	2	8	3	7	0	0	0	0	0	0	0	0.0	.000	DH-6
1981		3	.333	.667	12	4	1	0	1	8.3	3	1	2	3	0	0	0	5	0	1	0	2.0	.833	OF-3
5 yrs.		27	.357	.755	98	35	7	1	10	10.2	21	24	15	24	1	0	0	37	1	2	0	1.5	.950	OF-21, DH-6
				1st					**5th**	**3rd**	**10th**	**8th**		**8th**										

Ron Jackson

JACKSON, RONALD HARRIS
B. Oct. 22, 1933, Kalamazoo, Mich.

BR TR 6′ 7″ 225 lbs.

Year	Team	Games	BA	SA	AB	H	2B	3B	HR	HR%	R	RBI	BB	SO	SB	Pinch Hit AB	Pinch Hit H	PO	A	E	DP	TC/G	FA	G by Pos
1954	CHI A	40	.280	.452	93	26	4	0	4	4.3	10	10	6	20	2	7	1	244	9	3	15	7.3	.988	1B-35
1955		40	.203	.324	74	15	1	1	2	2.7	10	7	8	22	1	7	4	162	9	2	14	6.0	.988	1B-29
1956		22	.214	.321	56	12	3	0	1	1.8	7	4	10	13	1	3	0	138	11	0	16	7.8	1.000	1B-19
1957		13	.317	.467	60	19	3	0	2	3.3	4	8	1	12	0	0	0	125	5	1	10	10.1	.992	1B-13
1958		61	.233	.404	146	34	4	0	7	4.8	19	21	18	46	2	22	4	289	16	1	29	8.1	.997	1B-38
1959		10	.214	.500	14	3	1	0	1	7.1	3	2	1	0	0	5	1	30	1	0	3	6.2	1.000	1B-5
1960	BOS A	10	.226	.290	31	7	2	0	0	0.0	1	0	1	6	0	1	0	66	5	2	10	8.1	.973	1B-9
7 yrs.		196	.245	.395	474	116	18	1	17	3.6	54	52	45	119	6	45	10	1054	56	9	97	7.6	.992	1B-148

Ron Jackson

JACKSON, RONNIE DAMIEN
B. May 9, 1953, Birmingham, Ala.

BR TR 6′ 200 lbs.

Year	Team	Games	BA	SA	AB	H	2B	3B	HR	HR%	R	RBI	BB	SO	SB	Pinch Hit AB	Pinch Hit H	PO	A	E	DP	TC/G	FA	G by Pos
1975	CAL A	13	.231	.282	39	9	2	0	0	0.0	2	2	2	10	1	1	0	19	4	2	0	1.9	.920	OF-9, 3B-3, DH-1
1976		127	.227	.344	410	93	18	3	8	2.0	44	40	30	58	5	5	1	91	225	16	20	2.5	.952	3B-114, 2B-7, DH-6, OF-4
1977		106	.243	.390	292	71	15	2	8	2.7	38	28	24	42	3	20	8	314	75	6	33	4.1	.985	1B-43, 3B-30, DH-20, OF-3, SS-1
1978		105	.297	.421	387	115	18	6	6	1.6	49	57	16	31	2	5	1	606	88	8	56	6.5	.989	1B-75, 3B-31, DH-1, OF-1
1979	MIN A	159	.271	.429	583	158	40	5	14	2.4	85	68	51	59	3	4	0	1448	140	9	175	10.0	.994	1B-157, 3B-1, SS-1, OF-1
1980		131	.265	.391	396	105	29	3	5	1.3	48	42	28	41	1	21	4	1000	74	10	105	7.9	.991	1B-119, OF-15, 3B-2, DH-1
1981	2 teams	MIN A (54G –.263)	DET A (31G –.284)																					
″	total	85	.270	.396	270	73	17	1	5	1.9	29	40	18	26	6	10	1	547	45	5	46	7.4	.992	1B-65, OF-7, DH-6, 3B-3
1982	CAL A	53	.331	.415	142	47	6	0	2	1.4	15	19	10	12	0	8	4	317	31	2	37	7.6	.994	1B-37, 3B-9
1983		102	.230	.351	348	80	16	1	8	2.3	41	39	27	33	2	12	2	402	114	13	43	5.1	.975	3B-38, 1B-35, DH-16, OF-15
1984	2 teams	CAL A (33G –.165)	BAL A (12G –.286)																					
″	total	45	.193	.244	119	23	4	1	0	0.0	5	7	7	17	0	8	1	208	35	4	22	6.0	.984	1B-21, 3B-19, OF-1
10 yrs.		926	.259	.385	2986	774	165	22	56	1.9	356	342	213	329	23	94	22	4952	831	75	537	6.4	.987	1B-552, 3B-250, OF-56, DH-51, 2B-7, SS-2
LEAGUE CHAMPIONSHIP SERIES																								
1982	CAL A	1	1.000	1.000	1	1	0	0	0	0.0	0	0	0	0	0	1	1	0	0	0	0	0.0	—	

Sonny Jackson

JACKSON, ROLAND THOMAS
B. July 9, 1944, Washington, D. C.

BL TR 5′ 9″ 150 lbs.

Year	Team	Games	BA	SA	AB	H	2B	3B	HR	HR%	R	RBI	BB	SO	SB	Pinch Hit AB	Pinch Hit H	PO	A	E	DP	TC/G	FA	G by Pos
1963	HOU N	1	.000	.000	3	0	0	0	0	0.0	0	0	0	1	0	0	0	0	5	1	0	6.0	.833	SS-1
1964		9	.348	.391	23	8	1	0	0	0.0	3	1	2	3	1	1	0	8	12	3	1	3.3	.870	SS-7
1965		10	.130	.130	23	3	0	0	0	0.0	1	0	1	1	1	1	0	16	15	1	3	3.6	.969	SS-8, 3B-1
1966		150	.292	.334	596	174	6	5	3	0.5	80	25	42	53	49	0	0	270	449	37	73	5.0	.951	SS-150
1967		129	.237	.283	520	123	18	3	0	0.0	67	25	36	45	22	2	0	204	379	35	63	4.8	.943	SS-128
1968	ATL N	105	.226	.268	358	81	8	2	1	0.3	37	19	25	35	16	2	1	132	307	22	35	4.7	.952	SS-99
1969		98	.239	.289	318	76	3	5	1	0.3	41	27	35	33	12	2	0	161	254	17	48	4.5	.961	SS-97
1970		103	.259	.320	328	85	14	3	0	0.0	60	20	45	27	11	8	1	123	240	26	40	4.5	.933	SS-87
1971		149	.258	.324	547	141	20	5	2	0.4	58	25	35	45	7	2	0	336	8	7	0	2.4	.980	OF-145
1972		60	.238	.333	126	30	6	3	0	0.0	20	8	7	9	1	23	8	47	62	3	9	3.4	.973	SS-17, OF-10, 3B-6
1973		117	.209	.252	206	43	5	2	0	0.0	29	12	22	13	6	27	8	93	89	6	10	2.0	.968	OF-56, SS-36
1974		5	.429	.429	7	3	0	0	0	0.0	0	0	0	0	0	4	2	2	0	0	0	2.0	1.000	OF-1
12 yrs.		936	.251	.303	3055	767	81	28	7	0.2	396	162	250	265	126	72	20	1392	1820	158	282	4.0	.953	SS-630, OF-212, 3B-7
LEAGUE CHAMPIONSHIP SERIES																								
1969	ATL N	1	—	—	0	0	0	0	0	—	0	0	0	0	0	0	0	0	0	0	0	0.0	.000	SS-1

Travis Jackson

JACKSON, TRAVIS CALVIN (Stonewall) BR TR 5′10½″ 160 lbs.
B. Nov. 2, 1903, Waldo, Ark. D. July 27, 1987, Waldo, Ark.
Hall of Fame 1982.

Year	Team		Games	BA	SA	AB	H	2B	3B	HR	HR%	R	RBI	BB	SO	SB	Pinch Hit AB	Pinch Hit H	PO	A	E	DP	TC/G	FA	G by Pos
1922	NY	N	3	.000	.000	8	0	0	0	0	0.0	1	0	0	2	0	0	0	3	7	1	1	3.7	.909	SS-3
1923			96	.275	.391	327	90	12	7	4	1.2	45	37	22	40	3	4	2	107	265	23	31	4.3	.942	SS-60, 3B-31, 2B-1
1924			151	.302	.428	596	180	26	8	11	1.8	81	76	21	56	6	0	0	332	534	58	101	6.1	.937	SS-151
1925			112	.285	.397	411	117	15	2	9	2.2	51	59	24	43	8	2	0	277	366	40	64	6.2	.941	SS-110
1926			111	.327	.494	385	126	24	8	8	2.1	64	51	20	26	2	2	1	259	352	24	72	5.8	.962	SS-108, OF-1
1927			127	.318	.486	469	149	29	4	14	3.0	67	98	32	30	8	1	0	292	449	37	85	6.2	.952	SS-124, 3B-2
1928			150	.270	.436	537	145	35	6	14	2.6	73	77	56	46	8	1	0	354	547	45	112	6.3	.952	SS-149
1929			149	.294	.490	551	162	21	12	21	3.8	92	94	64	56	10	0	0	329	552	28	110	6.1	.969	SS-149
1930			116	.339	.529	431	146	27	8	13	3.0	70	82	32	25	6	1	0	218	441	30	72	6.0	.956	SS-115
1931			145	.310	.420	555	172	26	10	5	0.9	65	71	36	23	13	0	0	303	496	25	79	5.7	.970	SS-145
1932			52	.256	.415	195	50	17	1	4	2.1	23	38	13	16	1	0	0	106	166	22	31	5.7	.925	SS-52
1933			53	.246	.287	122	30	5	0	0	0.0	11	12	8	11	2	9	1	52	87	11	16	3.6	.927	SS-21, 3B-21
1934			137	.268	.436	523	140	26	7	16	3.1	75	101	37	71	1	0	0	292	477	43	61	5.8	.947	SS-130, 3B-9
1935			128	.301	.440	511	154	20	12	9	1.8	74	80	29	64	3	0	0	139	220	20	13	3.0	.947	3B-128
1936			126	.230	.297	465	107	8	1	7	1.5	41	53	18	56	0	3	1	110	218	16	10	2.8	.953	3B-116, SS-9
15 yrs.			1656	.291	.433	6086	1768	291	86	135	2.2	833	929	412	565	71	23	5	3173	5177	423	858	5.4	.952	SS-1326, 3B-307, OF-1, 2B-1
WORLD SERIES																									
1923	NY	N	1	.000	.000	1	0	0	0	0	0.0	0	0	0	0	0	1	0	0	0	0	0	0.0	—	
1924			7	.074	.074	27	2	0	0	0	0.0	3	1	1	4	1	0	0	8	20	3	3	4.4	.903	SS-7
1933			5	.222	.278	18	4	1	0	0	0.0	3	2	1	3	0	0	0	3	16	1	2	4.0	.950	3B-5
1936			6	.190	.190	21	4	0	0	0	0.0	1	1	1	3	0	0	0	2	8	3	1	2.2	.769	3B-6
4 yrs.			19	.149	.164	67	10	1	0	0	0.0	7	4	3	10	1	1	0	13	44	7	6	3.6	.891	3B-11, SS-7

Lamar Jacobs

JACOBS, LAMAR GARY (Jake) BR TR 6′ 175 lbs.
B. June 9, 1937, Youngstown, Ohio.

Year	Team		Games	BA	SA	AB	H	2B	3B	HR	HR%	R	RBI	BB	SO	SB	Pinch Hit AB	Pinch Hit H	PO	A	E	DP	TC/G	FA	G by Pos
1960	WAS	A	6	.000	.000	2	0	0	0	0	0.0	0	0	0	0	0	2	0	0	0	0	0	0.0	—	
1961	MIN	A	4	.250	.250	8	2	0	0	0	0.0	0	0	0	2	0	1	0	2	0	0	0	0.7	1.000	OF-3
2 yrs.			10	.200	.200	10	2	0	0	0	0.0	0	0	0	2	0	3	0	2	0	0	0	0.7	1.000	OF-3

Mike Jacobs

JACOBS, MORRIS ELMORE
B. Dec. 1877, Louisville, Ky. D. Mar. 21, 1949, Louisville, Ky.

Year	Team		Games	BA	SA	AB	H	2B	3B	HR	HR%	R	RBI	BB	SO	SB	Pinch Hit AB	Pinch Hit H	PO	A	E	DP	TC/G	FA	G by Pos
1902	CHI	N	5	.211	.211	19	4	0	0	0	0.0	1	2	0		0	0	0	9	13	3	1	5.0	.880	SS-5

Otto Jacobs

JACOBS, OTTO ALBERT BR TR 5′9″ 180 lbs.
B. Apr. 19, 1889, Chicago, Ill. D. Nov. 19, 1955, Chicago, Ill.

Year	Team		Games	BA	SA	AB	H	2B	3B	HR	HR%	R	RBI	BB	SO	SB	Pinch Hit AB	Pinch Hit H	PO	A	E	DP	TC/G	FA	G by Pos
1918	CHI	A	29	.205	.274	73	15	3	1	0	0.0	4	3	5	8	0	7	1	64	21	4	3	4.2	.955	C-21

Ray Jacobs

JACOBS, RAYMOND F. BR TR 6′ 160 lbs.
B. Jan. 2, 1902, Salt Lake City, Utah D. Apr. 4, 1952, Los Angeles, Calif.

Year	Team		Games	BA	SA	AB	H	2B	3B	HR	HR%	R	RBI	BB	SO	SB	Pinch Hit AB	Pinch Hit H	PO	A	E	DP	TC/G	FA	G by Pos
1928	CHI	N	2	.000	.000	2	0	0	0	0	0.0	0	0	0	1	0	2	0	0	0	0	0	0.0	—	

Spook Jacobs

JACOBS, FORREST VANDERGRIFT BR TR 5′8½″ 155 lbs.
B. Nov. 4, 1925, Cheswold, Del.

Year	Team		Games	BA	SA	AB	H	2B	3B	HR	HR%	R	RBI	BB	SO	SB	Pinch Hit AB	Pinch Hit H	PO	A	E	DP	TC/G	FA	G by Pos
1954	PHI	A	132	.258	.283	508	131	11	1	0	0.0	63	26	60	22	17	0	0	347	300	17	98	5.1	.974	2B-131
1955	KC	A	13	.261	.261	23	6	0	0	0	0.0	7	1	3	0	1	1	0	9	9	0	4	2.6	1.000	2B-7
1956	2 teams		KC A (32G –.216) PIT N (11G –.162)																						
″	total		43	.201	.239	134	27	5	0	0	0.0	17	6	17	10	4	0	0	104	95	9	31	5.0	.957	2B-42
3 yrs.			188	.247	.274	665	164	16	1	0	0.0	87	33	80	32	22	1	0	460	404	26	133	4.9	.971	2B-180

Baby Doll Jacobson

JACOBSON, WILLIAM CHESTER BR TR 6′3″ 215 lbs.
B. Aug. 16, 1890, Cable, Ill. D. Jan. 16, 1977, Orion, Ill.

Year	Team		Games	BA	SA	AB	H	2B	3B	HR	HR%	R	RBI	BB	SO	SB	Pinch Hit AB	Pinch Hit H	PO	A	E	DP	TC/G	FA	G by Pos
1915	2 teams		DET A (37G –.215) STL A (34G –.209)																						
″	total		71	.211	.344	180	38	12	3	2	1.1	18	13	15	40	3	22	5	172	7	3	6	3.7	.984	OF-39, 1B-10
1917	STL	A	148	.248	.340	529	131	23	7	4	0.8	53	55	31	67	10	6	1	411	25	15	10	3.2	.967	OF-131, 1B-11
1919			120	.323	.453	455	147	31	8	4	0.9	70	51	24	47	9	5	2	345	11	16	4	3.3	.957	OF-105, 1B-8
1920			154	.355	.501	609	216	34	14	9	1.5	97	122	46	37	11	0	0	394	18	9	5	2.7	.979	OF-154, 1B-1
1921			151	.352	.487	599	211	38	14	5	0.8	90	90	42	30	8	0	0	469	19	7	11	3.3	.986	OF-141, 1B-11
1922			145	.317	.463	555	176	22	16	9	1.6	88	102	46	36	19	1	0	431	11	16	12	3.2	.965	OF-137, 1B-7
1923			147	.309	.419	592	183	29	6	8	1.4	76	81	29	27	6	1	0	409	10	11	4	2.9	.974	OF-146
1924			152	.318	.528	579	184	41	12	19	3.3	103	97	35	45	6	0	0	484	7	7	4	3.3	.986	OF-151
1925			142	.341	.513	540	184	30	9	15	2.8	103	76	45	26	8	2	1	383	18	13	9	3.0	.969	OF-139
1926	2 teams		STL A (50G –.286) BOS A (98G –.305)																						
″	total		148	.299	.436	576	172	51	2	8	1.4	62	90	31	36	5	0	0	298	9	8	1	2.1	.975	OF-148
1927	3 teams		BOS A (45G –.245) CLE A (32G –.252) PHI A (17G –.229)																						
″	total		94	.246	.334	293	72	17	3	1	0.3	27	42	11	19	1	9	0	181	5	8	0	2.3	.959	OF-84
11 yrs.			1472	.311	.451	5507	1714	328	94	84	1.5	787	819	355	410	86	46	9	3977	140	113	66	3.0	.973	OF-1375, 1B-48

Merwin Jacobson

JACOBSON, MERWIN JOHN WILLIAM (Jake) BL TL 5′11½″ 165 lbs.
B. Mar. 7, 1894, New Britain, Conn. D. Jan. 13, 1978, Baltimore, Md.

Year	Team		Games	BA	SA	AB	H	2B	3B	HR	HR%	R	RBI	BB	SO	SB	Pinch Hit AB	Pinch Hit H	PO	A	E	DP	TC/G	FA	G by Pos
1915	NY	N	8	.083	.083	24	2	0	0	0	0.0	0	0	1	5	0	2	0	9	1	1	0	2.2	.909	OF-5
1916	CHI	N	4	.231	.231	13	3	0	0	0	0.0	2	0	1	4	2	0	0	8	0	0	0	2.0	1.000	OF-4
1926	BKN	N	110	.247	.292	288	71	9	2	0	0.0	41	23	36	24	5	17	5	191	5	5	2	2.3	.975	OF-86
1927			11	.000	.000	6	0	0	0	0	0.0	4	1	0	1	0	5	0	1	0	0	0	0.3	1.000	OF-3
4 yrs.			133	.230	.269	331	76	9	2	0	0.0	47	24	38	34	7	24	5	209	6	6	2	2.3	.973	OF-98

Brook Jacoby

JACOBY, BROOK WALLACE BR TR 5′11″ 175 lbs.
B. Nov. 23, 1959, Philadelphia, Pa.

Year	Team		Games	BA	SA	AB	H	2B	3B	HR	HR%	R	RBI	BB	SO	SB	Pinch Hit AB	Pinch Hit H	PO	A	E	DP	TC/G	FA	G by Pos
1981	ATL	N	11	.200	.200	10	2	0	0	0	0.0	0	1	0	3	0	8	2	3	4	0	1	2.3	1.000	3B-3
1983			4	.000	.000	8	0	0	0	0	0.0	0	0	0	1	0	2	0	0	2	0	0	1.0	1.000	3B-2
1984	CLE	A	126	.264	.369	439	116	19	3	7	1.6	64	40	32	73	3	0	0	86	188	14	17	2.3	.951	3B-126, SS-1
1985			161	.274	.426	606	166	26	3	20	3.3	72	87	48	120	2	1	0	114	319	19	26	2.8	.958	3B-161, 2B-1
1986			158	.288	.441	583	168	30	4	17	2.9	83	80	56	137	2	0	0	109	292	25	24	2.7	.941	3B-158

Brook Jacoby *continued*

Year	Team	Games	BA	SA	AB	H	2B	3B	HR	HR%	R	RBI	BB	SO	SB	Pinch Hit AB	Pinch Hit H	PO	A	E	DP	TC/G	FA	G by Pos
1987		155	.300	.541	540	162	26	4	32	5.9	73	69	75	73	2	2	1	192	261	22	24	3.1	.954	3B-144, 1B-7, DH-4
1988		152	.241	.335	552	133	25	0	9	1.6	59	49	48	101	2	1	0	99	298	10	23	2.7	.975	3B-151
1989		147	.272	.416	519	141	26	5	13	2.5	49	64	62	90	2	0	0	92	268	17	15	2.6	.955	3B-144, DH-3
1990		155	.293	.427	553	162	24	4	14	2.5	77	75	63	58	1	3	2	628	186	6	75	4.6	.993	3B-99, 1B-78
1991	**2 teams**	**CLE A** (66G –.234) **OAK A** (56G –.213)																						
"	**total**	122	.224	.308	419	94	21	1	4	1.0	28	44	27	54	2	6	0	453	136	7	42	4.8	.988	3B-67, 1B-58
1992	**CLE A**	120	.261	.326	291	76	7	0	4	1.4	30	36	28	54	0	9	5	91	177	10	24	2.3	.964	3B-111, 1B-10
11 yrs.		1311	.270	.405	4520	1220	204	24	120	2.7	535	545	439	764	16	32	10	1867	2131	130	271	3.1	.969	3B-1166, 1B-153, DH-7, 2B-1, SS-1

Harry Jacoby

JACOBY, HARRY
B. Philadelphia, Pa. Deceased.

Year	Team	Games	BA	SA	AB	H	2B	3B	HR	HR%	R	RBI	BB	SO	SB	Pinch Hit AB	Pinch Hit H	PO	A	E	DP	TC/G	FA	G by Pos
1882	**BAL AA**	31	.174	.223	121	21	1	1	1	0.8	17		7			0	0	46	59	26	3	4.1	.802	3B-19, OF-13
1885		11	.140	.186	43	6	2	0	0	0.0	4		2			0	0	21	22	5	2	4.4	.896	2B-11
2 yrs.		42	.165	.213	164	27	3	1	1	0.6	21		9			0	0	67	81	31	5	4.2	.827	3B-19, OF-13, 2B-11

John Jaha

JAHA, JOHN EMIL BR TR 6′ 1″ 195 lbs.
B. May 27, 1966, Portland, Ore.

Year	Team	Games	BA	SA	AB	H	2B	3B	HR	HR%	R	RBI	BB	SO	SB	Pinch Hit AB	Pinch Hit H	PO	A	E	DP	TC/G	FA	G by Pos
1992	**MIL A**	47	.226	.308	133	30	3	1	2	1.5	17	10	12	30	10	3	2	286	22	0	22	6.6	1.000	1B-38, DH-8, OF-1
1993		153	.264	.416	515	136	21	0	19	3.7	78	70	51	109	13	4	0	1187	128	10	116	8.7	.992	1B-150, 2B-1, 3B-1
1994		84	.241	.412	291	70	14	0	12	4.1	45	39	32	75	3	1	0	660	47	8	60	8.5	.989	1B-73, DH-11
1995		88	.313	.579	316	99	20	2	20	6.3	59	65	36	66	2	1	1	648	62	2	86	8.2	.997	1B-81, DH-6
4 yrs.		372	.267	.445	1255	335	58	3	53	4.2	199	184	131	280	28	9	3	2781	259	20	284	8.3	.993	1B-342, DH-25, 3B-1, 2B-1, OF-1

Art Jahn

JAHN, ARTHUR CHARLES BR TR 6′ 180 lbs.
B. Dec. 2, 1895, Struble, Iowa D. Jan. 9, 1948, Little Rock, Ark.

Year	Team	Games	BA	SA	AB	H	2B	3B	HR	HR%	R	RBI	BB	SO	SB	Pinch Hit AB	Pinch Hit H	PO	A	E	DP	TC/G	FA	G by Pos
1925	**CHI N**	58	.301	.416	226	68	10	8	0	0.0	30	37	11	20	2	0	0	124	5	2	3	2.3	.985	OF-58
1928	**2 teams**	**NY N** (10G –.276) **PHI N** (36G –.223)																						
"	**total**	46	.236	.301	123	29	5	0	1	0.8	15	18	6	16	0	8	1	63	2	1	1	1.7	.985	OF-39
2 yrs.		104	.278	.375	349	97	15	8	1	0.3	45	55	17	36	2	8	1	187	7	3	4	2.0	.985	OF-97

Art James

JAMES, ARTHUR, JR. BL TL 6′ 170 lbs.
B. Aug. 2, 1952, Detroit, Mich.

Year	Team	Games	BA	SA	AB	H	2B	3B	HR	HR%	R	RBI	BB	SO	SB	Pinch Hit AB	Pinch Hit H	PO	A	E	DP	TC/G	FA	G by Pos
1975	**DET A**	11	.225	.275	40	9	2	0	0	0.0	2	1	1	3	1	0	0	33	0	0	0	3.0	1.000	OF-11

Bernie James

JAMES, ROBERT BYRNE BB TR 5′ 9½″ 150 lbs.
B. Sept. 2, 1905, Angleton, Tex. D. Aug. 1, 1994, San Antonio, Tex. BR 1929
BL 1930

Year	Team	Games	BA	SA	AB	H	2B	3B	HR	HR%	R	RBI	BB	SO	SB	Pinch Hit AB	Pinch Hit H	PO	A	E	DP	TC/G	FA	G by Pos
1929	**BOS N**	46	.307	.376	101	31	3	2	0	0.0	12	9	9	13	3	7	1	70	56	8	11	4.1	.940	2B-32, OF-1
1930		8	.182	.273	11	2	1	0	0	0.0	1	1	0	1	0	1	0	5	11	1	1	2.4	.941	2B-7
1933	**NY N**	60	.224	.280	125	28	2	1	1	0.8	22	10	8	12	5	5	2	76	94	10	20	4.9	.944	2B-26, SS-6, 3B-5
3 yrs.		114	.257	.321	237	61	6	3	1	0.4	35	20	17	26	8	13	3	151	161	19	32	4.3	.943	2B-65, SS-6, 3B-5, OF-1

Bert James

JAMES, BERTON HULON (Jesse) BL TR 5′11″ 185 lbs.
B. July 7, 1886, Coopertown, Tenn. D. Jan. 2, 1959, Adairville, Ky.

Year	Team	Games	BA	SA	AB	H	2B	3B	HR	HR%	R	RBI	BB	SO	SB	Pinch Hit AB	Pinch Hit H	PO	A	E	DP	TC/G	FA	G by Pos
1909	**STL N**	6	.286	.286	21	6	0	0	0	0.0	1	0	4		1	0	0	9	1	1	1	1.8	.909	OF-6

Charlie James

JAMES, CHARLES WESLEY BR TR 6′ 1″ 195 lbs.
B. Dec. 22, 1937, St. Louis, Mo.

Year	Team	Games	BA	SA	AB	H	2B	3B	HR	HR%	R	RBI	BB	SO	SB	Pinch Hit AB	Pinch Hit H	PO	A	E	DP	TC/G	FA	G by Pos
1960	**STL N**	43	.180	.320	50	9	1	0	2	4.0	5	5	1	12	0	9	1	21	1	2	1	0.6	.917	OF-37
1961		108	.255	.355	349	89	19	2	4	1.1	43	44	15	59	2	19	3	151	3	6	1	1.8	.963	OF-90
1962		129	.276	.392	388	107	13	4	8	2.1	50	59	10	58	3	12	4	156	7	2	1	1.4	.988	OF-116
1963		116	.268	.406	347	93	14	2	10	2.9	34	45	10	64	2	18	10	169	4	1	1	1.7	.994	OF-101
1964		88	.223	.335	233	52	9	1	5	2.1	24	17	11	58	0	31	8	76	3	3	0	1.4	.963	OF-60
1965	**CIN N**	26	.205	.205	39	8	0	0	0	0.0	2	2	1	9	0	19	4	10	0	1	0	1.6	.909	OF-7
6 yrs.		510	.255	.369	1406	358	56	9	29	2.1	158	172	48	260	7	108	30	583	18	15	4	1.5	.976	OF-411
WORLD SERIES																								
1964	**STL N**	3	.000	.000	3	0	0	0	0	0.0	0	0	0	1	0	3	0	0	0	0	0	0.0	—	

Chris James

JAMES, DONALD CHRIS BR TR 6′ 1″ 190 lbs.
B. Oct. 4, 1962, Rusk, Tex.

Year	Team	Games	BA	SA	AB	H	2B	3B	HR	HR%	R	RBI	BB	SO	SB	Pinch Hit AB	Pinch Hit H	PO	A	E	DP	TC/G	FA	G by Pos
1986	**PHI N**	16	.283	.413	46	13	3	0	1	2.2	5	5	1	13	0	6	2	19	0	0	0	1.7	1.000	OF-11
1987		115	.293	.525	358	105	20	6	17	4.7	48	54	27	67	3	9	5	198	5	2	1	1.9	.990	OF-108
1988		150	.242	.389	566	137	24	1	19	3.4	57	66	31	73	7	4	1	282	51	9	6	2.3	.974	OF-116, 3B-31
1989	**2 teams**	**PHI N** (45G –.207) **SD N** (87G –.264)																						
"	**total**	132	.243	.367	482	117	17	2	13	2.7	55	65	26	68	5	8	2	215	27	7	4	1.9	.972	OF-116, 3B-17
1990	**CLE A**	140	.299	.443	528	158	32	4	12	2.3	62	70	31	71	4	6	2	25	1	0	0	0.2	1.000	DH-124, OF-14
1991		115	.238	.318	437	104	16	2	5	1.1	31	41	18	61	3	7	2	173	10	0	8	1.6	1.000	DH-60, OF-39, 1B-15
1992	**SF N**	111	.242	.375	248	60	10	4	5	2.0	25	32	14	45	2	44	9	112	2	3	2	1.9	.974	OF-62
1993	**2 teams**	**HOU N** (65G –.256) **TEX A** (8G –.355)																						
"	**total**	73	.275	.525	160	44	11	1	9	5.6	24	26	18	40	2	28	7	79	4	3	1	2.1	.965	OF-41
1994	**TEX A**	52	.256	.534	133	34	8	4	7	5.3	28	19	20	38	0	12	3	63	2	0	0	1.4	1.000	OF-48
1995	**2 teams**	**KC A** (26G –.310) **BOS A** (16G –.167)																						
"	**total**	42	.268	.390	82	22	4	0	2	2.4	8	8	7	14	1	9	2	23	0	0	0	0.7	1.000	DH-19, OF-13
10 yrs.		946	.261	.413	3040	794	145	24	90	3.0	343	386	193	490	27	133	35	1189	102	24	22	1.6	.982	OF-568, DH-203, 3B-48, 1B-15

Cleo James

JAMES, CLEO JOEL BR TR 5′10″ 176 lbs.
B. Aug. 31, 1940, Clarksdale, Miss.

Year	Team	Games	BA	SA	AB	H	2B	3B	HR	HR%	R	RBI	BB	SO	SB	Pinch Hit AB	Pinch Hit H	PO	A	E	DP	TC/G	FA	G by Pos
1968	**LA N**	10	.200	.300	10	2	1	0	0	0.0	2	0	0	6	0	6	1	2	0	0	0	1.0	1.000	OF-2
1970	**CHI N**	100	.210	.324	176	37	7	2	3	1.7	33	14	17	24	5	6	0	115	5	0	1	1.3	1.000	OF-90

Cleo James *continued*

Year	Team	Games	BA	SA	AB	H	2B	3B	HR	HR%	R	RBI	BB	SO	SB	Pinch Hit AB	Pinch Hit H	PO	A	E	DP	TC/G	FA	G by Pos
1971		54	.287	.373	150	43	7	0	2	1.3	25	13	10	16	6	3	1	90	5	2	2	1.9	.979	OF-48, 3B-2
1973		44	.111	.111	45	5	0	0	0	0.0	9	0	1	6	5	10	1	23	1	1	0	1.1	.960	OF-22
4 yrs.		208	.228	.318	381	87	15	2	5	1.3	69	27	28	52	16	25	3	230	11	3	3	1.5	.988	OF-162, 3B-2

Dion James

JAMES, DION
B. Nov. 9, 1962, Philadelphia, Pa.
BL TL 6′ 1″ 170 lbs.

Year	Team	Games	BA	SA	AB	H	2B	3B	HR	HR%	R	RBI	BB	SO	SB	Pinch Hit AB	Pinch Hit H	PO	A	E	DP	TC/G	FA	G by Pos
1983	MIL A	11	.100	.100	20	2	0	0	0	0.0	1	1	2	2	1	0	0	12	1	0	0	1.2	1.000	OF-9, DH-2
1984		128	.295	.377	387	114	19	5	1	0.3	52	30	32	41	10	17	3	252	7	3	1	2.2	.989	OF-118
1985		18	.224	.245	49	11	1	0	0	0.0	5	3	6	6	0	4	0	20	0	0	0	1.4	1.000	OF-11, DH-3
1987	ATL N	134	.312	.472	494	154	37	6	10	2.0	80	61	70	63	10	11	1	262	4	1	1	2.1	.996	OF-126
1988		132	.256	.350	386	99	17	5	3	0.8	46	30	58	59	9	15	3	222	5	3	0	1.9	.987	OF-120
1989	2 teams	ATL N (63G –.259) CLE A (71G –.306)																						
″	total	134	.287	.366	415	119	18	0	5	1.2	41	40	49	49	2	28	5	211	8	3	5	1.9	.986	OF-83, DH-27, 1B-10
1990	CLE A	87	.274	.363	248	68	15	2	1	0.4	28	22	27	23	5	14	3	282	17	4	21	3.9	.987	1B-35, OF-33, DH-10
1992	NY A	67	.262	.379	145	38	8	0	3	2.1	24	17	22	15	1	17	2	62	1	0	0	1.2	1.000	OF-46, DH-5
1993		115	.332	.466	343	114	21	2	7	2.0	62	36	31	31	0	22	9	141	4	5	1	1.4	.967	OF-103, 1B-1, DH-1
1995		85	.287	.354	209	60	6	1	2	1.0	22	26	20	16	4	25	7	61	4	1	1	1.1	.985	OF-29, DH-27, 1B-6
10 yrs.		911	.289	.393	2696	779	142	21	32	1.2	361	266	317	305	42	153	33	1525	51	20	30	2.0	.987	OF-678, DH-75, 1B-52
DIVISIONAL PLAYOFF SERIES																								
1995	NY A	4	.083	.083	12	1	0	0	0	0.0	0	0	1	1	0	0	0	6	0	0	0	1.5	1.000	OF-4

Skip James

JAMES, PHILIP ROBERT
B. Oct. 21, 1949, Elmhurst, Ill.
BL TL 6′ 185 lbs.

Year	Team	Games	BA	SA	AB	H	2B	3B	HR	HR%	R	RBI	BB	SO	SB	Pinch Hit AB	Pinch Hit H	PO	A	E	DP	TC/G	FA	G by Pos
1977	SF N	10	.267	.333	15	4	1	0	0	0.0	3	3	2	3	0	2	0	46	4	0	2	5.6	1.000	1B-9
1978		41	.095	.143	21	2	1	0	0	0.0	5	3	4	5	1	10	1	58	6	0	5	2.4	1.000	1B-27
2 yrs.		51	.167	.222	36	6	2	0	0	0.0	8	6	6	8	1	12	1	104	10	0	7	3.2	1.000	1B-36

Charlie Jamieson

JAMIESON, CHARLES DEVINE
B. Feb. 7, 1893, Paterson, N. J. D. Oct. 27, 1969, Paterson, N. J.
BL TL 5′ 8½″ 165 lbs.

Year	Team	Games	BA	SA	AB	H	2B	3B	HR	HR%	R	RBI	BB	SO	SB	Pinch Hit AB	Pinch Hit H	PO	A	E	DP	TC/G	FA	G by Pos
1915	WAS A	17	.279	.382	68	19	3	2	0	0.0	9	7	6	9	0	0	0	36	5	0	0	2.4	1.000	OF-17
1916		64	.248	.276	145	36	4	0	0	0.0	16	13	18	18	5	13	4	90	7	8	4	2.3	.924	OF-41, 1B-4, P-1
1917	2 teams	WAS A (20G –.171) PHI A (85G –.265)																						
″	total	105	.257	.288	382	98	8	2	0	0.0	45	29	43	41	8	12	5	135	12	11	4	1.7	.930	OF-92, P-1
1918	PHI A	110	.202	.238	416	84	11	2	0	0.0	50	11	54	30	11	4	1	184	21	10	4	2.0	.953	OF-102, P-5
1919	CLE A	26	.353	.588	17	6	2	1	0	0.0	3	2	0	2	2	9	3	5	2	1	0	1.1	.875	P-4, OF-3
1920		108	.319	.411	370	118	17	7	1	0.3	69	40	41	26	2	2	0	194	15	8	0	2.1	.963	OF-98, 1B-4
1921		140	.310	.414	536	166	33	10	1	0.2	94	45	67	27	8	2	2	277	17	8	3	2.2	.974	OF-137
1922		145	.323	.429	567	183	29	11	3	0.5	87	57	54	22	15	1	0	289	18	7	5	2.2	.978	OF-144, P-2
1923		152	.345	.447	**644**	**222**	36	12	2	0.3	130	51	80	37	19	0	0	360	18	10	1	2.6	.974	OF-152
1924		143	.359	.458	594	213	34	8	3	0.5	98	53	47	15	21	1	0	330	11	9	6	2.5	.974	OF-139
1925		138	.296	.379	557	165	24	5	4	0.7	109	42	72	26	14	3	1	324	16	16	4	2.6	.955	OF-135
1926		143	.299	.395	555	166	33	7	2	0.4	89	45	53	22	9	0	0	293	15	13	5	2.2	.960	OF-143
1927		127	.309	.380	489	151	23	6	0	0.0	73	36	64	14	7	0	0	300	13	10	2	2.5	.969	OF-127
1928		112	.307	.374	433	133	18	4	1	0.2	63	37	56	20	3	0	0	282	22	5	1	2.8	.984	OF-111
1929		102	.291	.357	364	106	22	1	0	0.0	56	26	50	12	2	4	2	192	8	4	1	2.2	.980	OF-93
1930		103	.301	.374	366	110	22	1	1	0.3	64	52	36	20	5	6	1	162	7	8	0	1.9	.955	OF-95
1931		28	.302	.395	43	13	2	1	0	0.0	7	4	5	1	1	19	6	11	0	2	0	1.9	.846	OF-7
1932		16	.063	.125	16	1	1	0	0	0.0	0	0	2	3	0	11	0	3	1	0	0	2.0	1.000	OF-2
18 yrs.		1779	.303	.385	6562	1990	322	80	18	0.3	1062	550	748	345	132	87	25	3467	208	130	40	2.3	.966	OF-1638, P-13, 1B-8
WORLD SERIES																								
1920	CLE A	6	.333	.400	15	5	1	0	0	0.0	2	1	1	0	1	1	0	8	1	0	1	1.8	1.000	OF-5

Vic Janowicz

JANOWICZ, VICTOR FELIX
B. Feb. 26, 1930, Elyria, Ohio D. Feb. 27, 1996, Columbus, Ohio.
BR TR 5′ 9″ 185 lbs.

Year	Team	Games	BA	SA	AB	H	2B	3B	HR	HR%	R	RBI	BB	SO	SB	Pinch Hit AB	Pinch Hit H	PO	A	E	DP	TC/G	FA	G by Pos
1953	PIT N	42	.252	.341	123	31	3	1	2	1.6	10	8	5	31	0	5	1	104	15	8	2	3.6	.937	C-35
1954		41	.151	.192	73	11	3	0	0	0.0	10	2	7	24	0	11	2	16	32	5	3	2.8	.906	3B-18, OF-1
2 yrs.		83	.214	.286	196	42	6	1	2	1.0	20	10	12	55	0	16	3	120	47	13	5	3.3	.928	C-35, 3B-18, OF-1

Ray Jansen

JANSEN, RAYMOND WILLIAM
B. Jan. 16, 1889, St. Louis, Mo. D. Mar. 19, 1934, St. Louis, Mo.
BR TR 5′11″ 155 lbs.

Year	Team	Games	BA	SA	AB	H	2B	3B	HR	HR%	R	RBI	BB	SO	SB	Pinch Hit AB	Pinch Hit H	PO	A	E	DP	TC/G	FA	G by Pos
1910	STL A	1	.800	.800	5	4	0	0	0	0.0	0	0	0		0	0	0	2	5	3	0	10.0	.700	3B-1

Heinie Jantzen

JANTZEN, WALTER C.
B. Apr. 9, 1890, Chicago, Ill. D. Apr. 1, 1948, Hines, Ill.
BR TR 5′11½″ 170 lbs.

Year	Team	Games	BA	SA	AB	H	2B	3B	HR	HR%	R	RBI	BB	SO	SB	Pinch Hit AB	Pinch Hit H	PO	A	E	DP	TC/G	FA	G by Pos
1912	STL A	31	.185	.227	119	22	0	1	1	0.8	10	8	4		3	0	0	53	6	0	3	1.9	1.000	OF-31

Hal Janvrin

JANVRIN, HAROLD CHANDLER (Childe Harold)
B. Aug. 27, 1892, Haverhill, Mass. D. Mar. 1, 1962, Boston, Mass.
BR TR 5′11½″ 168 lbs.

Year	Team	Games	BA	SA	AB	H	2B	3B	HR	HR%	R	RBI	BB	SO	SB	Pinch Hit AB	Pinch Hit H	PO	A	E	DP	TC/G	FA	G by Pos
1911	BOS A	9	.148	.185	27	4	1	0	0	0.0	2	1	3		0	0	0	43	7	6	1	6.2	.893	3B-5, 1B-4
1913		86	.207	.264	276	57	5	1	3	1.1	18	25	23	27	17	5	0	172	177	26	17	4.6	.931	SS-48, 3B-19, 2B-8, 1B-6
1914		143	.238	.305	492	117	18	6	1	0.2	65	51	38	50	29	0	0	669	237	43	50	6.8	.955	2B-57, 1B-56, SS-20, 3B-6
1915		99	.269	.304	316	85	9	1	0	0.0	41	37	14	27	8	3	1	135	204	32	18	4.0	.914	SS-64, 3B-20, 2B-8
1916		117	.223	.284	310	69	11	4	0	0.0	32	26	32	32	6	7	1	203	233	28	37	4.4	.940	SS-59, 2B-39, 1B-4, 3B-3
1917		55	.197	.220	127	25	3	0	0	0.0	21	8	11	13	2	4	1	63	108	11	17	3.7	.940	2B-38, SS-10, 1B-1
1919	2 teams	WAS A (61G –.178) STL N (7G –.214)																						
″	total	68	.180	.225	222	40	5	1	1	0.5	18	14	21	19	8	3	1	122	128	24	14	4.4	.912	2B-58, SS-3, 3B-1
1920	STL N	87	.274	.344	270	74	8	4	1	0.4	33	28	17	19	5	4	1	307	93	13	33	5.3	.969	SS-27, 1B-25, OF-20, 2B-6
1921	2 teams	STL N (18G –.281) BKN N (44G –.196)																						
″	total	62	.218	.258	124	27	5	0	0	0.0	13	19	8	6	4	8	1	98	59	12	7	4.0	.929	SS-17, 2B-11, 1B-8, 3B-5, OF-1
1922	BKN N	30	.298	.386	57	17	3	1	0	0.0	7	1	4	4	0	5	2	22	38	9	4	3.0	.870	2B-15, SS-4, 3B-2, OF-1, 1B-1
10 yrs.		756	.232	.287	2221	515	68	18	6	0.3	250	210	171	197	79	39	8	1834	1284	204	198	4.9	.939	SS-252, 2B-240, 1B-105, 3B-61, OF-22

Year	Team	Games	BA	SA	AB	H	2B	3B	HR	HR%	R	RBI	BB	SO	SB	Pinch Hit AB	Pinch Hit H	PO	A	E	DP	TC/G	FA	G by Pos

Hal Janvrin *continued*

WORLD SERIES																								
1915	**BOS A**	1	.000	.000	1	0	0	0	0	0.0	0	0	0	0	0	0	0	1	0	0	0	1.0	1.000	SS-1
1916		5	.217	.348	23	5	3	0	0	0.0	2	1	0	6	0	0	0	8	16	2	4	5.2	.923	2B-5
2 yrs.		6	.208	.333	24	5	3	0	0	0.0	2	1	0	6	0	0	0	9	16	2	4	4.5	.926	2B-5, SS-1

Roy Jarvis

JARVIS, LeROY GILBERT BR TR 5′ 9″ 160 lbs.
B. June 27, 1926, Shawnee, Okla. D. Jan. 13, 1990, Oklahoma City, Okla.

1944	**BKN N**	1	.000	.000	1	0	0	0	0	0.0	0	0	0	1	0	0	0	1	0	0	0	1.0	1.000	C-1
1946	**PIT N**	2	.250	.250	4	1	0	0	0	0.0	0	0	1	1	0	1	0	4	0	1	0	5.0	.800	C-1
1947		18	.156	.244	45	7	1	0	1	2.2	4	4	6	5	0	2	0	50	8	2	1	4.0	.967	C-15
3 yrs.		21	.160	.240	50	8	1	0	1	2.0	4	4	7	7	0	3	0	55	8	3	1	3.9	.955	C-17

Paul Jata

JATA, PAUL BR TR 6′ 1″ 190 lbs.
B. Sept. 4, 1949, Astoria, N. Y.

1972	**DET A**	32	.230	.257	74	17	2	0	0	0.0	8	3	7	14	0	12	4	116	6	1	6	5.3	.992	1B-12, OF-10, C-1

Alfredo Javier

JAVIER, IGNACIO ALFREDO BR TR 5′11″ 170 lbs.
Born Ignacio Alfredo Wilkes (Javier).
B. Feb. 4, 1954, San Pedro de Macoris, Dominican Republic.

1976	**HOU N**	8	.208	.208	24	5	0	0	0	0.0	1	0	2	5	0	1	0	7	0	0	0	1.0	1.000	OF-7

Julian Javier

JAVIER, MANUEL JULIAN (Hoolie, The Phantom) BR TR 6′ 1″ 175 lbs.
Born Manuel Julian Javier (Liranzo).
Father of Stan Javier.
B. Aug. 9, 1936, San Francisco De Macoris, Dominican Republic.

1960	**STL N**	119	.237	.341	451	107	19	8	4	0.9	55	21	21	72	19	0	0	272	338	24	71	5.3	.962	2B-119
1961		113	.279	.337	445	124	14	3	2	0.4	58	41	30	51	11	0	0	239	332	20	82	5.2	.966	2B-113
1962		155	.263	.356	598	157	25	5	7	1.2	97	39	47	73	26	0	0	344	416	19	96	5.0	.976	2B-151, SS-4
1963		161	.263	.381	609	160	27	9	9	1.5	82	46	24	86	18	0	0	377	415	25	93	5.1	.969	2B-161
1964		155	.241	.363	535	129	19	5	12	2.2	66	65	30	82	9	0	0	360	401	27	97	5.1	.966	2B-154
1965		77	.227	.314	229	52	6	4	2	0.9	34	23	8	44	5	0	0	128	179	8	40	4.6	.975	2B-69
1966		147	.228	.324	460	105	13	5	7	1.5	52	31	26	63	11	0	0	306	364	13	89	4.7	.981	2B-145
1967		140	.281	.404	520	146	16	3	14	2.7	68	64	25	92	6	2	0	311	352	24	72	5.0	.965	2B-138
1968		139	.260	.347	519	135	25	4	4	0.8	54	52	24	61	10	0	0	304	339	16	68	4.7	.976	2B-139
1969		143	.282	.408	493	139	28	2	10	2.0	59	42	40	74	8	4	1	244	374	21	70	4.5	.967	2B-141
1970		139	.251	.306	513	129	16	3	2	0.4	62	42	24	70	6	3	2	329	413	15	84	5.5	.980	2B-137
1971		90	.259	.347	259	67	6	4	3	1.2	32	28	9	33	5	9	2	164	188	8	45	4.4	.978	2B-80, 3B-1
1972	**CIN N**	44	.209	.297	91	19	2	0	2	2.2	3	12	6	11	1	20	4	15	38	5	4	2.3	.914	3B-19, 2B-5, 1B-1
13 yrs.		1622	.257	.355	5722	1469	216	55	78	1.4	722	506	314	812	135	38	9	3393	4149	225	911	4.9	.971	2B-1552, 3B-20, SS-4, 1B-1
WORLD SERIES																								
1964	**STL N**	1	—	—	0	0	0	0	0	—	1	0	0	0	0	0	0	0	1	0	0	1.0	1.000	2B-1
1967		7	.360	.600	25	9	3	0	1	4.0	2	4	0	6	0	0	0	12	20	1	4	4.7	.970	2B-7
1968		7	.333	.370	27	9	1	0	0	0.0	1	3	3	4	1	0	0	14	14	0	3	4.0	1.000	2B-7
1972	**CIN N**	4	.000	.000	2	0	0	0	0	0.0	0	0	0	0	0	2	0	0	0	0	0	0.0	—	
4 yrs.		19	.333	.463	54	18	4	0	1	1.9	4	7	3	10	1	2	0	26	35	1	7	4.1	.984	2B-15

Stan Javier

JAVIER, STANLEY JULIAN BB TR 6′ 180 lbs.
Born Stanley Julian Javier (DeJavier).
Son of Julian Javier.
B. Jan. 9, 1964, San Francisco De Macoris, Dominican Republic.

1984	**NY A**	7	.143	.143	7	1	0	0	0	0.0	1	0	0	1	0	0	0	3	0	0	0	0.6	1.000	OF-5
1986	**OAK A**	59	.202	.272	114	23	8	0	0	0.0	13	8	16	27	8	0	0	118	1	0	1	2.2	1.000	OF-51, DH-2
1987		81	.185	.258	151	28	3	1	2	1.3	22	9	19	33	3	7	0	149	5	3	4	2.0	.981	OF-71, 1B-6, DH-1
1988		125	.257	.320	397	102	13	3	2	0.5	49	35	32	63	20	9	2	274	7	5	5	2.4	.983	OF-115, 1B-4, DH-2
1989		112	.248	.316	310	77	12	3	1	0.3	42	28	31	45	12	7	0	221	8	2	2	2.1	.991	OF-107, 2B-1, 1B-1
1990	**2 teams**	**OAK A** (19G –.242) **LA N** (104G –.304)																						
″	**total**	123	.298	.395	309	92	9	6	3	1.0	60	27	40	50	15	31	8	223	2	0	1	2.2	1.000	OF-100, DH-2
1991	**LA N**	121	.205	.284	176	36	5	3	1	0.6	21	11	16	36	7	52	5	90	4	3	1	1.4	.969	OF-69, 1B-2
1992	**2 teams**	**LA N** (56G –.190) **PHI N** (74G –.261)																						
″	**total**	130	.249	.314	334	83	17	1	1	0.3	42	29	37	54	18	30	7	229	7	3	1	2.4	.987	OF-101
1993	**CAL A**	92	.291	.405	237	69	10	4	3	1.3	33	28	27	33	12	27	7	167	4	4	2	2.2	.977	OF-64, 1B-12, 2B-2, DH-1
1994	**OAK A**	109	.272	.399	419	114	23	0	10	2.4	75	44	49	76	24	1	0	274	4	4	0	2.6	.986	OF-108, 3B-1, 1B-1
1995		130	.278	.387	442	123	20	2	8	1.8	81	56	49	63	36	11	3	332	3	0	1	2.7	1.000	OF-124, 3B-1
11 yrs.		1089	.258	.348	2896	748	120	23	31	1.1	439	275	316	481	155	175	32	2080	45	24	18	2.3	.989	OF-915, 1B-26, DH-8, 2B-3, 3B-2
LEAGUE CHAMPIONSHIP SERIES																								
1988	**OAK A**	2	.500	.500	4	2	0	0	0	0.0	0	1	1	0	0	0	0	5	0	0	0	2.5	1.000	OF-2
1989		1	.000	.000	2	0	0	0	0	0.0	0	0	0	1	0	0	0	1	0	0	0	1.0	1.000	OF-1
2 yrs.		3	.333	.333	6	2	0	0	0	0.0	0	1	1	1	0	0	0	6	0	0	0	2.0	1.000	OF-3
WORLD SERIES																								
1988	**OAK A**	3	.500	.500	4	2	0	0	0	0.0	0	2	0	1	0	0	0	1	0	0	0	0.5	1.000	OF-2
1989		1	—	—	0	0	0	0	0	—	0	0	0	0	0	0	0	0	0	0	0	0.0	.000	OF-1
2 yrs.		4	.500	.500	4	2	0	0	0	0.0	0	2	0	1	0	0	0	1	0	0	0	0.3	1.000	OF-3

Tex Jeanes

JEANES, ERNEST LEE BR TR 6′ 176 lbs.
B. Dec. 19, 1900, Maypearl, Tex. D. Apr. 5, 1973, Longview, Tex.

1921	**CLE A**	4	.500	.500	2	1	0	0	0	0.0	2	2	1	0	0	0	0	1	1	0	0	0.5	1.000	OF-4
1922		1	.000	.000	1	0	0	0	0	0.0	0	0	1	0	0	0	0	0	0	0	0	0.0		OF-1, P-1
1925	**WAS A**	15	.263	.474	19	5	1	0	1	5.3	2	4	3	2	1	2	1	9	0	0	0	0.7	1.000	OF-13
1926		21	.233	.300	30	7	2	0	0	0.0	6	3	0	3	0	7	2	21	0	0	0	1.5	1.000	OF-14
1927	**NY N**	11	.300	.300	20	6	0	0	0	0.0	5	0	2	2	0	3	1	15	1	0	0	2.3	1.000	OF-6, P-1
5 yrs.		52	.264	.347	72	19	3	0	1	1.4	15	9	7	7	1	12	4	46	2	0	0	1.2	1.000	OF-38, P-2

Hal Jeffcoat

JEFFCOAT, HAROLD BENTLEY — BR TR 5′10½″ 185 lbs.
Brother of George Jeffcoat.
B. Sept. 6, 1924, West Columbia, S. C.

Year	Team	Lg	Games	BA	SA	AB	H	2B	3B	HR	HR%	R	RBI	BB	SO	SB	Pinch Hit AB	Pinch Hit H	PO	A	E	DP	TC/G	FA	G by Pos
1948	CHI	N	134	.279	.355	473	132	16	4	4	0.8	53	42	24	68	8	14	6	307	12	8	3	2.7	.976	OF-119
1949			108	.245	.344	363	89	18	6	2	0.6	43	26	20	48	12	5	2	250	12	10	2	2.7	.963	OF-101
1950			66	.235	.352	179	42	13	1	2	1.1	21	18	6	23	7	8	1	83	6	3	0	1.7	.967	OF-53
1951			113	.273	.403	278	76	20	2	4	1.4	44	27	16	23	8	9	3	166	11	2	5	2.1	.989	OF-87
1952			102	.219	.330	297	65	17	2	4	1.3	29	30	15	40	7	1	0	218	16	1	2	2.5	.996	OF-95
1953			106	.235	.328	183	43	3	1	4	2.2	22	22	21	26	5	2	0	175	6	5	2	1.9	.973	OF-100
1954			56	.258	.484	31	8	2	1	1	3.2	13	6	1	7	2	0	0	13	20	4	1	0.8	.892	P-43, OF-3
1955			52	.174	.304	23	4	0	0	1	4.3	3	1	2	9	0	0	0	4	24	3	1	0.6	.903	P-50
1956	CIN	N	49	.148	.185	54	8	2	0	0	0.0	5	5	3	20	0	0	0	21	42	2	4	1.7	.969	P-38
1957			53	.203	.449	69	14	3	1	4	5.8	13	11	5	20	0	0	0	16	30	2	5	1.3	.958	P-37
1958			50	.556	.556	9	5	0	0	0	0.0	2	0	1	2	0	0	0	9	19	0	2	0.6	1.000	P-49, OF-1
1959	2 teams		CIN N (17G –1.000)			STL N (12G –.000)																			
″	total		29	.250	.500	4	1	1	0	0	0.0	1	0	0	3	0	0	0	5	5	0	1	0.4	1.000	P-28
12 yrs.			918	.248	.355	1963	487	95	18	26	1.3	249	188	114	289	49	39	12	1267	203	40	28	1.9	.974	OF-559, P-245

Gregg Jefferies

JEFFERIES, GREGORY SCOTT — BB TR 5′11″ 175 lbs.
B. Aug. 1, 1967, Burlingame, Calif.

Year	Team	Lg	Games	BA	SA	AB	H	2B	3B	HR	HR%	R	RBI	BB	SO	SB	Pinch Hit AB	Pinch Hit H	PO	A	E	DP	TC/G	FA	G by Pos
1987	NY	N	6	.500	.667	6	3	1	0	0	0.0	0	2	0	0	0	6	3	0	0	0	0	0.0	—	
1988			29	.321	.596	109	35	8	2	6	5.5	19	17	8	10	5	1	0	33	46	2	9	2.7	.975	3B-20, 2B-10
1989			141	.258	.392	508	131	28	2	12	2.4	72	56	39	46	21	7	1	242	280	14	44	3.7	.974	2B-123, 3B-20
1990			153	.283	.434	604	171	**40**	3	15	2.5	96	68	46	40	11	4	1	242	341	16	54	3.9	.973	2B-118, 3B-34
1991			136	.272	.374	486	132	19	2	9	1.9	59	62	47	38	26	9	2	170	271	17	21	3.6	.963	2B-77, 3B-51
1992	KC	A	152	.285	.404	604	172	36	3	10	1.7	66	75	43	29	19	3	0	96	304	26	22	2.9	.939	3B-146, DH-1, 2B-1
1993	STL	N	142	.342	.485	544	186	24	3	16	2.9	89	83	62	32	46	1	1	1281	77	9	115	9.7	.993	1B-140, 2B-1
1994			103	.325	.489	397	129	27	1	12	3.0	52	55	45	26	12	3	2	890	52	7	91	9.3	.993	1B-102
1995	PHI	N	114	.306	.448	480	147	31	2	11	2.3	69	56	35	26	9	1	0	578	36	3	53	5.4	.995	1B-59, OF-55
9 yrs.			976	.296	.436	3738	1106	214	18	91	2.4	522	474	325	247	149	35	10	3532	1407	94	409	5.3	.981	2B-330, 1B-301, 3B-271, OF-55, DH-1
LEAGUE CHAMPIONSHIP SERIES																									
1988	NY	N	7	.333	.407	27	9	2	0	0	0.0	2	1	4	0	0	0	0	5	8	1	0	2.0	.929	3B-7

Reggie Jefferson

JEFFERSON, REGINALD JIROD — BB TL 6′4″ 210 lbs.
B. Sept. 25, 1968, Tallahassee, Fla.

Year	Team	Lg	Games	BA	SA	AB	H	2B	3B	HR	HR%	R	RBI	BB	SO	SB	Pinch Hit AB	Pinch Hit H	PO	A	E	DP	TC/G	FA	G by Pos
1991	2 teams		CIN N (5G –.143)			CLE A (26G –.198)																			
″	total		31	.194	.306	108	21	3	0	3	2.8	11	13	4	24	0	2	0	266	25	2	31	10.5	.993	1B-28
1992	CLE	A	24	.337	.483	89	30	6	2	1	1.1	8	6	1	17	0	2	1	129	12	1	9	6.5	.993	1B-15, DH-7
1993			113	.249	.372	366	91	11	2	10	2.7	35	34	28	78	1	17	3	112	10	3	10	1.2	.976	DH-88, 1B-15
1994	SEA	A	63	.327	.543	162	53	11	0	8	4.9	24	32	17	32	0	16	7	95	10	2	14	2.3	.981	DH-32, 1B-13, OF-2
1995	BOS	A	46	.289	.479	121	35	8	0	5	4.1	21	26	9	24	0	8	3	28	4	0	4	0.8	1.000	DH-32, 1B-7, OF-2
5 yrs.			277	.272	.423	846	230	39	4	27	3.2	99	111	59	175	1	45	14	630	61	8	68	2.9	.989	DH-159, 1B-78, OF-4
DIVISIONAL PLAYOFF SERIES																									
1995	BOS	A	1	.250	.250	4	1	0	0	0	0.0	1	0	0	1	0	0	0	0	0	0	0	0.0	.000	DH-1

Stan Jefferson

JEFFERSON, STANLEY — BB TR 5′11″ 175 lbs.
B. Dec. 4, 1962, New York, N. Y.

Year	Team	Lg	Games	BA	SA	AB	H	2B	3B	HR	HR%	R	RBI	BB	SO	SB	Pinch Hit AB	Pinch Hit H	PO	A	E	DP	TC/G	FA	G by Pos
1986	NY	N	14	.208	.375	24	5	1	0	1	4.2	6	3	2	8	0	5	0	13	0	0	0	1.9	1.000	OF-7
1987	SD	N	116	.230	.339	422	97	8	7	8	1.9	59	29	39	92	34	9	0	232	3	3	1	2.2	.987	OF-107
1988			49	.144	.216	111	16	1	2	1	0.9	16	4	9	22	5	3	0	62	0	0	0	1.6	1.000	OF-38
1989	2 teams		NY A (10G –.083)			BAL A (35G –.260)																			
″	total		45	.245	.381	139	34	7	0	4	2.9	20	21	4	26	10	6	1	82	3	1	1	2.0	.988	OF-39, DH-3
1990	2 teams		BAL A (10G –.000)			CLE A (49G –.276)																			
″	total		59	.231	.350	117	27	8	0	2	1.7	22	10	10	26	9	5	0	70	4	1	1	1.7	.987	OF-39, DH-6
1991	CIN	N	13	.053	.053	19	1	0	0	0	0.0	2	0	1	3	2	4	0	4	0	0	0	0.8	1.000	OF-5
6 yrs.			296	.216	.326	832	180	25	9	16	1.9	125	67	65	177	60	32	1	463	10	5	3	2.0	.990	OF-235, DH-9

Irv Jeffries

JEFFRIES, IRVINE FRANKLIN — BR TR 5′10″ 175 lbs.
B. Sept. 10, 1905, Louisville, Ky. D. June 8, 1982, Louisville, Ky.

Year	Team	Lg	Games	BA	SA	AB	H	2B	3B	HR	HR%	R	RBI	BB	SO	SB	Pinch Hit AB	Pinch Hit H	PO	A	E	DP	TC/G	FA	G by Pos
1930	CHI	A	40	.237	.330	97	23	3	0	2	2.1	14	11	3	2	1	1	0	31	56	6	6	4.0	.935	SS-13, 3B-10
1931			79	.224	.296	223	50	10	0	2	0.9	29	16	14	9	3	5	0	83	130	14	9	3.2	.938	3B-61, 2B-6, SS-5
1934	PHI	N	56	.246	.349	175	43	6	0	4	2.3	28	19	15	10	2	2	0	123	157	11	42	5.5	.962	2B-52, 3B-1
3 yrs.			175	.234	.321	495	116	19	0	8	1.6	71	46	32	21	6	8	0	237	343	31	57	4.1	.949	3B-72, 2B-58, SS-18

Chris Jelic

JELIC, CHRISTOPHER JOHN — BR TR 5′11″ 180 lbs.
B. Dec. 16, 1963, Bethlehem, Pa.

Year	Team	Lg	Games	BA	SA	AB	H	2B	3B	HR	HR%	R	RBI	BB	SO	SB	Pinch Hit AB	Pinch Hit H	PO	A	E	DP	TC/G	FA	G by Pos
1990	NY	N	4	.091	.364	11	1	0	0	1	9.1	2	1	0	3	0	1	0	1	0	0	0	0.3	1.000	OF-4

Frank Jelincich

JELINCICH, FRANK ANTHONY (Jelly) — BR TR 6′2″ 198 lbs.
B. Sept. 3, 1919, San Jose, Calif. D. June 27, 1992, Rochester, Minn.

Year	Team	Lg	Games	BA	SA	AB	H	2B	3B	HR	HR%	R	RBI	BB	SO	SB	Pinch Hit AB	Pinch Hit H	PO	A	E	DP	TC/G	FA	G by Pos
1941	CHI	N	4	.125	.125	8	1	0	0	0	0.0	0	2	1	2	0	2	0	1	0	0	0	0.5	1.000	OF-2

Greg Jelks

JELKS, GREGORY DION — BR TR 6′2″ 190 lbs.
B. Aug. 16, 1961, Cherokee, Ala.

Year	Team	Lg	Games	BA	SA	AB	H	2B	3B	HR	HR%	R	RBI	BB	SO	SB	Pinch Hit AB	Pinch Hit H	PO	A	E	DP	TC/G	FA	G by Pos
1987	PHI	N	10	.091	.182	11	1	1	0	0	0.0	2	0	3	4	0	1	0	19	2	1	0	3.1	.955	3B-4, 1B-2, OF-1

Steve Jeltz

JELTZ, LARRY STEVEN — BB TR 5′11″ 180 lbs.; BR 1983–1985
B. May 28, 1959, Paris, France.

Year	Team	Lg	Games	BA	SA	AB	H	2B	3B	HR	HR%	R	RBI	BB	SO	SB	Pinch Hit AB	Pinch Hit H	PO	A	E	DP	TC/G	FA	G by Pos
1983	PHI	N	13	.125	.375	8	1	0	1	0	0.0	0	1	1	2	0	3	0	4	5	0	1	1.1	1.000	2B-4, SS-2, 3B-2
1984			28	.206	.279	68	14	0	1	1	1.5	7	7	7	11	2	0	0	37	93	1	8	4.7	.992	SS-27, 3B-1
1985			89	.189	.219	196	37	4	1	0	0.0	17	12	26	55	1	0	0	106	215	14	38	3.9	.958	SS-86
1986			145	.219	.262	439	96	11	4	0	0.0	44	36	65	97	6	5	2	229	406	22	81	4.7	.967	SS-141
1987			114	.232	.304	293	68	9	6	0	0.0	37	12	39	54	1	1	1	192	271	14	55	4.1	.971	SS-114, OF-1

Steve Jeltz *continued*

Year	Team		Games	BA	SA	AB	H	2B	3B	HR	HR%	R	RBI	BB	SO	SB	Pinch Hit AB	Pinch Hit H	PO	A	E	DP	TC/G	FA	G by Pos
1988			148	.187	.237	379	71	11	4	0	0.0	39	27	59	58	3	3	0	195	368	14	73	3.9	.976	SS-148
1989			116	.243	.338	263	64	7	3	4	1.5	28	25	45	44	4	13	2	111	205	6	33	2.8	.981	SS-63, 3B-30, 2B-23, OF-1
1990	**KC**	**A**	74	.155	.194	103	16	4	0	0	0.0	11	10	6	21	1	1	0	58	98	4	21	2.1	.975	2B-34, SS-23, OF-13, 3B-3, DH-3
8 yrs.			727	.210	.268	1749	367	46	20	5	0.3	183	130	248	342	18	26	5	932	1661	75	310	3.7	.972	SS-604, 2B-61, 3B-36, OF-15, DH-3

Joe Jenkins

JENKINS, JOSEPH DANIEL BR TR 5′11″ 170 lbs.
B. Oct. 12, 1890, Shelbyville, Tenn. D. June 21, 1974, Fresno, Calif.

Year	Team		Games	BA	SA	AB	H	2B	3B	HR	HR%	R	RBI	BB	SO	SB	Pinch Hit AB	Pinch Hit H	PO	A	E	DP	TC/G	FA	G by Pos
1914	**STL**	**A**	19	.125	.219	32	4	1	1	0	0.0	0	0	1	11	2	9	1	24	3	2	0	3.2	.931	C-9
1917	**CHI**	**A**	10	.111	.111	9	1	0	0	0	0.0	0	2	0	5	0	9	1	0	0	0	0	0.0	—	
1919			11	.158	.211	19	3	1	0	0	0.0	0	1	1	1	1	7	1	10	4	3	0	4.3	.824	C-4
3 yrs.			40	.133	.200	60	8	2	1	0	0.0	0	3	2	17	3	25	3	34	7	5	0	3.5	.891	C-13

John Jenkins

JENKINS, JOHN ROBERT BR TR 5′8″ 160 lbs.
B. July 7, 1896, Bosworth, Mo. D. Aug. 3, 1968, Columbia, Mo.

Year	Team		Games	BA	SA	AB	H	2B	3B	HR	HR%	R	RBI	BB	SO	SB	Pinch Hit AB	Pinch Hit H	PO	A	E	DP	TC/G	FA	G by Pos
1922	**CHI**	**A**	5	.000	.000	3	0	0	0	0	0.0	0	1	0	2	0	1	0	1	1	1	0	1.5	.667	SS-1, 2B-1

Tom Jenkins

JENKINS, THOMAS GRIFFITH (Tut) BL TR 6′ 1½″ 174 lbs.
B. Apr. 10, 1898, Camden, Ala. D. May 3, 1979, Weymouth, Mass.

Year	Team		Games	BA	SA	AB	H	2B	3B	HR	HR%	R	RBI	BB	SO	SB	Pinch Hit AB	Pinch Hit H	PO	A	E	DP	TC/G	FA	G by Pos
1925	**BOS**	**A**	15	.297	.359	64	19	2	1	0	0.0	9	5	3	4	0	0	0	30	0	2	0	2.1	.938	OF-15
1926	**2 teams**		**BOS A** (21G –.180) **PHI A** (6G –.174)																						
″	**total**		27	.178	.247	73	13	3	1	0	0.0	6	6	3	9	0	8	2	39	0	0	0	2.1	1.000	OF-19
1929	**STL**	**A**	21	.182	.273	22	4	0	1	0	0.0	1	0	4	8	0	15	2	2	0	0	0	0.7	1.000	OF-3
1930			2	.250	.625	8	2	1	1	0	0.0	1	3	0	1	0	0	0	4	0	0	0	2.0	1.000	OF-2
1931			81	.265	.352	230	61	7	2	3	1.3	20	25	17	25	1	23	7	93	6	5	1	1.8	.952	OF-58
1932			25	.323	.339	62	20	1	0	0	0.0	5	5	1	6	0	13	5	29	2	2	0	2.8	.939	OF-12
6 yrs.			171	.259	.336	459	119	14	6	3	0.7	42	44	28	53	1	59	16	197	8	9	1	2.0	.958	OF-109

Alamazoo Jennings

JENNINGS, ALFRED GORDEN
B. Nov. 30, 1850, Newport, Ky. D. Nov. 2, 1894, Cincinnati, Ohio.

Year	Team		Games	BA	SA	AB	H	2B	3B	HR	HR%	R	RBI	BB	SO	SB	Pinch Hit AB	Pinch Hit H	PO	A	E	DP	TC/G	FA	G by Pos
1878	**MIL**	**N**	1	.000	.000	2	0	0	0	0	0.0	0	0	1	0		0	0	2	1	4	0	7.0	.429	C-1

Bill Jennings

JENNINGS, WILLIAM LEE BR TR 6′2″ 175 lbs.
B. Sept. 28, 1925, St. Louis, Mo.

Year	Team		Games	BA	SA	AB	H	2B	3B	HR	HR%	R	RBI	BB	SO	SB	Pinch Hit AB	Pinch Hit H	PO	A	E	DP	TC/G	FA	G by Pos
1951	**STL**	**A**	64	.179	.251	195	35	10	2	0	0.0	20	13	26	42	1	0	0	141	165	15	39	5.0	.953	SS-64

Doug Jennings

JENNINGS, JAMES DOUGLAS BL TL 5′10″ 175 lbs.
B. Sept. 30, 1964, Atlanta, Ga.

Year	Team		Games	BA	SA	AB	H	2B	3B	HR	HR%	R	RBI	BB	SO	SB	Pinch Hit AB	Pinch Hit H	PO	A	E	DP	TC/G	FA	G by Pos
1988	**OAK**	**A**	71	.208	.297	101	21	6	0	1	1.0	9	15	21	28	0	27	5	85	5	1	8	2.3	.989	OF-23, 1B-14, DH-2
1989			4	.000	.000	4	0	0	0	0	0.0	0	0	0	2	0	1	0	2	0	0	0	0.7	1.000	OF-3
1990			64	.192	.301	156	30	7	2	2	1.3	19	14	17	48	0	14	2	90	1	1	5	1.6	.989	OF-45, DH-8, 1B-4
1991			8	.111	.111	9	1	0	0	0	0.0	0	0	2	2	0	1	0	8	0	0	0	1.3	1.000	OF-6
1993	**CHI**	**N**	42	.250	.462	52	13	3	1	2	3.8	8	8	3	10	0	30	5	80	2	0	8	8.2	1.000	1B-10
5 yrs.			189	.202	.317	322	65	16	3	5	1.6	36	37	43	90	0	73	12	265	8	2	21	2.4	.993	OF-77, 1B-28, DH-10
LEAGUE CHAMPIONSHIP SERIES																									
1990	**OAK**	**A**	1	.000	.000	1	0	0	0	0	0.0	0	0	0	0	0	0	0	0	0	0	0	0.0	.000	OF-1
WORLD SERIES																									
1990	**OAK**	**A**	1	1.000	1.000	1	1	0	0	0	0.0	0	0	0	0	0	1	1	0	0	0	0	0.0	—	

Hughie Jennings

JENNINGS, HUGH AMBROSE (Hustling Hughie) BR TR 5′ 8½″ 165 lbs.
B. Apr. 2, 1869, Pittston, Pa. D. Feb. 1, 1928, Scranton, Pa.
Manager 1907–20, 1924–25.
Hall of Fame 1945.

Year	Team		Games	BA	SA	AB	H	2B	3B	HR	HR%	R	RBI	BB	SO	SB	Pinch Hit AB	Pinch Hit H	PO	A	E	DP	TC/G	FA	G by Pos
1891	**LOU**	**AA**	88	.293	.376	351	103	10	8	1	0.3	53	58	17	35	12	0	0	358	232	57	38	7.4	.912	SS-68, 1B-17, 3B-3
1892	**LOU**	**N**	152	.222	.273	594	132	16	4	2	0.3	65	61	30	30	28	0	0	343	537	90	59	6.4	.907	SS-152
1893	**2 teams**		**LOU N** (23G –.136) **BAL N** (16G –.255)																						
″	**total**		39	.182	.224	143	26	3	0	1	0.7	12	15	7	6	0	0	0	86	126	25	15	6.1	.895	SS-38, OF-1
1894	**BAL**	**N**	128	.335	.479	501	168	28	16	4	0.8	134	109	37	17	37	0	0	307	499	63	69	6.8	.928	SS-128
1895			131	.386	.512	529	204	41	7	4	0.8	159	125	24	17	53	0	0	425	457	56	71	7.2	.940	SS-131
1896			130	.401	.488	521	209	27	9	0	0.0	125	121	19	11	70	0	0	377	476	66	70	7.1	.928	SS-130
1897			117	.355	.469	439	156	26	9	2	0.5	133	79	42		60	1	0	335	425	55	54	7.0	.933	SS-116
1898			143	.328	.421	534	175	25	11	1	0.2	135	87	78		28	0	0	365	440	62	51	6.1	.928	SS-115, 2B-27, OF-1
1899	**2 teams**		**BAL N** (2G –.375) **BKN N** (67G –.296)																						
″	**total**		69	.299	.420	224	67	3	12	0	0.0	44	42	22		18	1	1	480	56	19	28	8.5	.966	1B-50, SS-12, 2B-3
1900	**BKN**	**N**	115	.272	.347	441	120	18	6	1	0.2	61	69	31		31	1	1	1053	84	23	71	10.2	.980	1B-112, 2B-2
1901	**PHI**	**N**	82	.275	.368	302	83	21	2	1	0.3	38	39	25		13	0	0	750	46	18	21	9.9	.978	1B-80, SS-1, 2B-1
1902			78	.277	.363	289	80	16	3	1	0.3	31	32	14		8	0	0	677	63	15	33	9.7	.980	1B-69, SS-5, 2B-4
1903	**BKN**	**N**	6	.235	.235	17	4	0	0	0	0.0	2	1	1		1	2	0	7	0	0	0	1.8	1.000	OF-4
1907	**DET**	**A**	1	.250	.500	4	1	1	0	0	0.0	0	0	0		0	0	0	2	3	3	0	4.0	.625	SS-1, 2B-1
1909			2	.500	.500	4	2	0	0	0	0.0	1	2	0		0	0	0	9	1	0	2	5.0	1.000	1B-2
1912			1	.000	.000	1	0	0	0	0	0.0	0	0	0		0	1	0	0	0	0	0	0.0	—	
1918			1	—	—	0	0	0	0	0	—	0	0	0	0	0	0	0	2	0	0	0	2.0	1.000	1B-1
17 yrs.			1283	.313	.407	4894	1530	235	87	18	0.4	993	840	347	116	359	6	2	5576	3445	552	582	7.5	.942	SS-897, 1B-331, 2B-38, OF-6, 3B-3

Jackie Jensen

JENSEN, JACK EUGENE BR TR 5′11″ 190 lbs.
B. Mar. 9, 1927, San Francisco, Calif. D. July 14, 1982, Charlottesville, Va.

Year	Team		Games	BA	SA	AB	H	2B	3B	HR	HR%	R	RBI	BB	SO	SB	Pinch Hit AB	Pinch Hit H	PO	A	E	DP	TC/G	FA	G by Pos
1950	**NY**	**A**	45	.171	.300	70	12	2	2	1	1.4	13	5	7	8	4	6	1	36	0	2	0	1.7	.947	OF-23
1951			56	.298	.500	168	50	8	1	8	4.8	30	25	18	18	8	6	1	106	6	3	1	2.4	.974	OF-48
1952	**2 teams**		**NY A** (7G –.105) **WAS A** (144G –.286)																						
″	**total**		151	.280	.402	589	165	30	6	10	1.7	83	82	67	44	18	3	1	291	17	7	1	2.1	.978	OF-148

Jackie Jensen *continued*

Year	Team	Lg	Games	BA	SA	AB	H	2B	3B	HR	HR%	R	RBI	BB	SO	SB	Pinch Hit AB	Pinch Hit H	PO	A	E	DP	TC/G	FA	G by Pos
1953	WAS	A	147	.266	.408	552	147	32	8	10	1.8	87	84	73	51	18	1	0	274	9	5	0	2.0	.983	OF-146
1954	BOS	A	152	.276	.472	580	160	25	7	25	4.3	92	117	79	52	**22**	1	0	331	12	5	0	2.3	.986	OF-151
1955			152	.275	.479	574	158	27	6	26	4.5	95	**116**	89	63	16	0	0	281	11	7	3	2.0	.977	OF-150
1956			151	.315	.497	578	182	23	**11**	20	3.5	80	97	89	43	11	0	0	291	13	12	2	2.1	.962	OF-151
1957			145	.281	.469	544	153	29	2	23	4.2	82	103	75	66	8	1	1	251	16	11	4	1.9	.960	OF-144
1958			154	.286	.535	548	157	31	0	35	6.4	83	**122**	99	65	9	1	0	293	14	6	3	2.0	.981	OF-153
1959			148	.277	.492	535	148	31	0	28	5.2	101	**112**	88	67	20	2	0	311	12	6	4	2.3	.982	OF-146
1961			137	.263	.392	498	131	21	2	13	2.6	64	66	66	69	9	6	0	274	14	4	2	2.2	.986	OF-131
11 yrs.			1438	.279	.460	5236	1463	259	45	199	3.8	810	929	750	546	143	27	4	2739	124	68	20	2.1	.977	OF-1391
WORLD SERIES																									
1950	NY	A	1	—	—	0	0	0	0	0	—	0	0	0	0	0	0	0	0	0	0	0	0.0	—	

Woody Jensen

JENSEN, FORREST DOCENUS BL TL 5′10½″ 160 lbs.
B. Aug. 11, 1907, Bremerton, Wash.

Year	Team	Lg	Games	BA	SA	AB	H	2B	3B	HR	HR%	R	RBI	BB	SO	SB	Pinch Hit AB	Pinch Hit H	PO	A	E	DP	TC/G	FA	G by Pos
1931	PIT	N	73	.243	.326	267	65	5	4	3	1.1	43	17	10	18	4	3	1	182	2	5	1	2.8	.974	OF-67
1932			7	.000	.000	5	0	0	0	0	0.0	2	0	0	2	0	5	0	0	0	0	0	0.0	.000	OF-1
1933			70	.296	.362	196	58	7	3	0	0.0	29	15	8	2	1	23	6	95	1	2	0	2.5	.980	OF-40
1934			88	.290	.364	283	82	13	4	0	0.0	34	27	4	13	2	21	6	143	1	1	0	2.2	.993	OF-66
1935			143	.324	.429	627	203	28	7	8	1.3	97	62	15	14	9	3	2	290	6	7	1	2.1	.977	OF-143
1936			153	.283	.404	**696**	197	34	10	10	1.4	98	58	16	19	2	0	0	338	6	9	1	2.3	.975	OF-153
1937			124	.279	.389	509	142	23	9	5	1.0	77	45	15	29	2	3	1	256	5	10	1	2.3	.963	OF-120
1938			68	.200	.232	125	25	4	0	0	0.0	12	10	1	3	0	23	4	45	0	5	0	1.3	.900	OF-38
1939			12	.167	.167	12	2	0	0	0	0.0	0	1	0	0	0	6	1	0	1	0	0	0.3	1.000	OF-3
9 yrs.			738	.285	.382	2720	774	114	37	26	1.0	392	235	69	100	20	87	21	1349	22	39	4	2.2	.972	OF-631

Dan Jessee

JESSEE, DANIEL EDWARD BL TR 5′10″ 165 lbs.
B. Feb. 22, 1901, Olive Hill, Ky. D. Apr. 30, 1970, Venice, Fla.

Year	Team	Lg	Games	BA	SA	AB	H	2B	3B	HR	HR%	R	RBI	BB	SO	SB	Pinch Hit AB	Pinch Hit H	PO	A	E	DP	TC/G	FA	G by Pos
1929	CLE	A	1	—	—	0	0	0	0	0	—	0	0	0	0	0	0	0	0	0	0	0	0.0	—	

Garry Jestadt

JESTADT, GARRY ARTHUR BR TR 6′2″ 188 lbs.
B. Mar. 19, 1947, Chicago, Ill.

Year	Team	Lg	Games	BA	SA	AB	H	2B	3B	HR	HR%	R	RBI	BB	SO	SB	Pinch Hit AB	Pinch Hit H	PO	A	E	DP	TC/G	FA	G by Pos
1969	MON	N	6	.000	.000	6	0	0	0	0	0.0	1	1	0	0	0	4	0	2	0	1	0	3.0	.667	SS-1
1971	2 teams		CHI N (3G –.000) SD N (75G –.291)																						
″	total		78	.286	.354	192	55	13	0	0	0.0	17	13	11	24	1	4	1	66	142	13	11	3.0	.941	3B-50, 2B-23, SS-1
1972	SD	N	92	.246	.344	256	63	5	1	6	2.3	15	22	13	21	0	23	5	106	134	13	27	3.3	.949	2B-48, 3B-25, SS-3
3 yrs.			176	.260	.344	454	118	18	1	6	1.3	33	36	24	45	1	31	6	174	276	27	38	3.2	.943	3B-75, 2B-71, SS-5

Derek Jeter

JETER, DEREK SANDERSON BR TR 6′3″ 175 lbs.
B. June 26, 1974, Pequannock, N. J.

Year	Team	Lg	Games	BA	SA	AB	H	2B	3B	HR	HR%	R	RBI	BB	SO	SB	Pinch Hit AB	Pinch Hit H	PO	A	E	DP	TC/G	FA	G by Pos
1995	NY	A	15	.250	.375	48	12	4	1	0	0.0	5	7	3	11	0	0	0	17	34	2	6	3.5	.962	SS-15

John Jeter

JETER, JOHN (The Jet) BR TR 6′1″ 180 lbs.
Father of Shawn Jeter.
B. Oct. 24, 1944, Shreveport, La.

Year	Team	Lg	Games	BA	SA	AB	H	2B	3B	HR	HR%	R	RBI	BB	SO	SB	Pinch Hit AB	Pinch Hit H	PO	A	E	DP	TC/G	FA	G by Pos
1969	PIT	N	28	.310	.517	29	9	1	1	1	3.4	7	6	3	15	1	3	1	12	1	0	0	0.6	1.000	OF-20
1970			85	.238	.341	126	30	3	2	2	1.6	27	12	13	34	9	17	5	53	2	0	0	1.0	1.000	OF-56
1971	SD	N	18	.320	.413	75	24	4	0	1	1.3	8	3	2	16	2	1	0	57	1	2	1	3.5	.967	OF-17
1972			110	.221	.316	326	72	4	3	7	2.1	25	21	18	92	11	20	5	222	1	3	0	2.5	.987	OF-91
1973	CHI	A	89	.240	.383	300	72	14	4	7	2.3	38	26	9	74	4	8	1	144	3	7	0	2.1	.955	OF-72, DH-3
1974	CLE	A	6	.353	.412	17	6	1	0	0	0.0	3	1	1	6	1	1	0	5	0	1	0	1.0	.833	OF-6
6 yrs.			336	.244	.360	873	213	27	10	18	2.1	108	69	46	237	28	50	12	493	8	13	1	1.9	.975	OF-262, DH-3
LEAGUE CHAMPIONSHIP SERIES																									
1970	PIT	N	3	.000	.000	2	0	0	0	0	0.0	0	0	0	2	0	1	0	2	0	0	0	2.0	1.000	OF-1

Shawn Jeter

JETER, SHAWN DARRELL BL TR 6′2″ 185 lbs.
Son of John Jeter.
B. June 28, 1966, Shreveport, La.

Year	Team	Lg	Games	BA	SA	AB	H	2B	3B	HR	HR%	R	RBI	BB	SO	SB	Pinch Hit AB	Pinch Hit H	PO	A	E	DP	TC/G	FA	G by Pos
1992	CHI	A	13	.111	.111	18	2	0	0	0	0.0	1	0	0	7	0	2	0	10	0	1	0	1.1	.909	OF-8, DH-2

Sam Jethroe

JETHROE, SAMUEL (Jet) BB TR 6′1″ 178 lbs.
B. Jan. 20, 1918, East St. Louis, Ill.

Year	Team	Lg	Games	BA	SA	AB	H	2B	3B	HR	HR%	R	RBI	BB	SO	SB	Pinch Hit AB	Pinch Hit H	PO	A	E	DP	TC/G	FA	G by Pos
1950	BOS	N	141	.273	.442	582	159	28	8	18	3.1	100	58	52	93	**35**	0	0	355	17	12	6	2.7	.969	OF-141
1951			148	.280	.460	572	160	29	10	18	3.1	101	65	57	88	**35**	5	2	356	18	10	5	2.7	.974	OF-140
1952			151	.232	.357	608	141	23	7	13	2.1	79	58	68	112	28	0	0	413	10	13	3	2.9	.970	OF-151
1954	PIT	N	2	.000	.000	1	0	0	0	0	0.0	0	0	0	0	0	1	0	1	0	0	0	1.0	1.000	OF-1
4 yrs.			442	.261	.418	1763	460	80	25	49	2.8	280	181	177	293	98	6	2	1125	45	35	14	2.8	.971	OF-433

Elvio Jimenez

JIMENEZ, FELIX ELVIO BR TR 5′9″ 170 lbs.
Born Felix Elvio Jimenez (Rivera).
Brother of Manny Jimenez.
B. Jan. 6, 1940, San Pedro de Macoris, Dominican Republic.

Year	Team	Lg	Games	BA	SA	AB	H	2B	3B	HR	HR%	R	RBI	BB	SO	SB	Pinch Hit AB	Pinch Hit H	PO	A	E	DP	TC/G	FA	G by Pos
1964	NY	A	1	.333	.333	6	2	0	0	0	0.0	0	0	0	0	0	0	0	4	0	0	0	4.0	1.000	OF-1

Houston Jimenez

JIMENEZ, ALFONSO BR TR 5′8″ 144 lbs.
Born Alfonso Jimenez (Gonzalez).
B. Oct. 30, 1957, Navojoa, Mexico.

Year	Team	Lg	Games	BA	SA	AB	H	2B	3B	HR	HR%	R	RBI	BB	SO	SB	Pinch Hit AB	Pinch Hit H	PO	A	E	DP	TC/G	FA	G by Pos
1983	MIN	A	36	.174	.256	86	15	5	1	0	0.0	5	9	4	11	0	0	0	43	83	4	20	3.6	.969	SS-36
1984			108	.201	.245	298	60	11	1	0	0.0	28	19	15	34	0	0	0	145	273	18	59	4.1	.959	SS-107
1987	PIT	N	5	.000	.000	6	0	0	0	0	0.0	0	0	1	2	0	1	0	3	8	0	1	2.8	1.000	SS-2, 2B-2
1988	CLE	A	9	.048	.048	21	1	0	0	0	0.0	1	1	0	2	0	0	0	13	28	1	5	4.7	.976	2B-7, SS-2
4 yrs.			158	.185	.234	411	76	16	2	0	0.0	34	29	20	49	0	1	0	204	392	23	85	4.0	.963	SS-147, 2B-9

Manny Jimenez

JIMENEZ, MANUEL EMILIO BL TR 6′ 1″ 185 lbs.
Born Manuel Emilio Jimenez (Rivera).
Brother of Elvio Jimenez.
B. Nov. 19, 1938, San Pedro de Macoris, Dominican Republic.

Year	Team		Games	BA	SA	AB	H	2B	3B	HR	HR%	R	RBI	BB	SO	SB	Pinch Hit AB	Pinch Hit H	PO	A	E	DP	TC/G	FA	G by Pos
1962	KC	A	139	.301	.428	479	144	24	2	11	2.3	48	69	31	34	0	17	7	185	7	3	0	1.6	.985	OF-122
1963			60	.280	.338	157	44	9	0	0	0.0	12	15	16	14	0	15	2	66	6	3	0	1.9	.960	OF-40
1964			95	.225	.436	204	46	7	0	12	5.9	19	38	15	24	0	41	9	59	3	4	1	1.3	.939	OF-49
1966			13	.114	.171	35	4	0	1	0	0.0	1	1	6	4	0	2	0	9	1	1	0	0.9	.909	OF-12
1967	PIT	N	50	.250	.393	56	14	2	0	2	3.6	3	10	1	4	0	42	**12**	4	0	0	0	0.7	1.000	OF-6
1968			66	.303	.394	66	20	1	1	1	1.5	7	11	6	15	0	**53**	10	6	0	1	0	1.4	.857	OF-5
1969	CHI	N	6	.167	.167	6	1	0	0	0	0.0	0	0	0	2	0	6	1	0	0	0	0	0.0	—	
7 yrs.			429	.272	.401	1003	273	43	4	26	2.6	90	144	75	97	0	176	41	329	17	12	1	1.5	.966	OF-234

Pete Johns

JOHNS, WILLIAM R. BR TR 5′10″ 165 lbs.
B. Jan. 17, 1889, Cleveland, Ohio D. Aug. 9, 1964, Cleveland, Ohio.

Year	Team		Games	BA	SA	AB	H	2B	3B	HR	HR%	R	RBI	BB	SO	SB	Pinch Hit AB	Pinch Hit H	PO	A	E	DP	TC/G	FA	G by Pos
1915	CHI	A	28	.210	.250	100	21	2	1	0	0.0	7	11	8	11	2	0	0	37	62	6	5	3.8	.943	3B-28
1918	STL	A	46	.180	.213	89	16	1	1	0	0.0	5	11	4	6	0	20	2	105	22	5	5	5.5	.962	1B-10, 3B-4, OF-4, SS-4, 2B-2
2 yrs.			74	.196	.233	189	37	3	2	0	0.0	12	22	12	17	2	20	2	142	84	11	10	4.6	.954	3B-32, 1B-10, OF-4, SS-4, 2B-2

Abbie Johnson

JOHNSON, ALBERT J. 5′ 9½″ 165 lbs.
B. July 26, 1872, London, Ont., Canada Deceased.

Year	Team		Games	BA	SA	AB	H	2B	3B	HR	HR%	R	RBI	BB	SO	SB	Pinch Hit AB	Pinch Hit H	PO	A	E	DP	TC/G	FA	G by Pos
1896	LOU	N	25	.230	.276	87	20	2	1	0	0.0	10	14	4	6	0	0	0	57	61	8	9	5.0	.937	2B-25
1897			48	.242	.292	161	39	6	1	0	0.0	16	23	13		2	2	0	96	119	27	15	5.4	.888	2B-33, SS-12
2 yrs.			73	.238	.286	248	59	8	2	0	0.0	26	37	17	6	2	2	0	153	180	35	24	5.3	.905	2B-58, SS-12

Alex Johnson

JOHNSON, ALEXANDER BR TR 6′ 205 lbs.
B. Dec. 7, 1942, Helena, Ark.

Year	Team		Games	BA	SA	AB	H	2B	3B	HR	HR%	R	RBI	BB	SO	SB	Pinch Hit AB	Pinch Hit H	PO	A	E	DP	TC/G	FA	G by Pos
1964	PHI	N	43	.303	.495	109	33	7	1	4	3.7	18	18	6	26	1	7	2	47	1	1	0	1.4	.980	OF-35
1965			97	.294	.443	262	77	9	3	8	3.1	27	28	15	60	4	27	8	109	3	4	0	1.4	.966	OF-82
1966	STL	N	25	.186	.279	86	16	0	1	2	2.3	7	6	5	18	1	2	0	23	2	1	0	1.2	.962	OF-22
1967			81	.223	.314	175	39	9	2	1	0.6	20	12	9	26	6	20	5	91	7	3	2	1.8	.970	OF-57
1968	CIN	N	149	.312	.395	603	188	32	6	2	0.3	79	58	26	71	16	9	1	243	8	14	2	1.9	.947	OF-140
1969			139	.315	.463	523	165	18	4	17	3.3	86	88	25	69	11	9	3	222	5	18	1	1.9	.927	OF-132
1970	CAL	A	156	**.329**	.459	614	202	26	6	14	2.3	85	86	35	68	17	0	0	269	11	12	0	1.9	.959	OF-156
1971			65	.260	.318	242	63	8	0	2	0.8	19	21	15	34	5	5	0	84	3	7	0	1.5	.926	OF-61
1972	CLE	A	108	.239	.340	356	85	10	1	8	2.2	31	37	22	40	6	10	0	145	4	7	1	1.6	.955	OF-95
1973	TEX	A	158	.287	.377	624	179	26	3	8	1.3	62	68	32	82	10	1	1	72	4	1	0	0.5	.987	DH-116, OF-47
1974	2 teams		TEX A (114G –.291)	NY A (10G –.214)																					
″	total		124	.287	.362	481	138	15	3	5	1.0	60	43	28	62	20	6	0	168	6	8	2	1.5	.956	OF-82, DH-36
1975	NY	A	52	.261	.345	119	31	5	1	1	0.8	15	15	7	21	2	14	5	9	0	0	0	0.3	1.000	DH-28, OF-7
1976	DET	A	125	.268	.354	429	115	15	2	6	1.4	41	45	19	49	14	16	5	159	7	8	1	1.6	.954	OF-90, DH-19
13 yrs.			1322	.288	.392	4623	1331	180	33	78	1.7	550	525	244	626	113	126	30	1641	61	84	9	1.5	.953	OF-1006, DH-199

Bill Johnson

JOHNSON, WILLIAM F. (Sleepy Bill) BL TL
B. Sept. 1862, N. J. D. July 17, 1942, Chester, Pa.

Year	Team		Games	BA	SA	AB	H	2B	3B	HR	HR%	R	RBI	BB	SO	SB	Pinch Hit AB	Pinch Hit H	PO	A	E	DP	TC/G	FA	G by Pos
1884	PHI	U	1	.000	.000	4	0	0	0	0	0.0	0		0			0	0	0	0	0	0	0.0	.000	OF-1
1887	IND	N	11	.190	.190	42	8	0	0	0	0.0	3	3	0	6	5	0	0	11	2	4	0	1.5	.765	OF-11
1890	BAL	AA	24	.295	.379	95	28	2	3	0	0.0	15		7		8	0	0	39	6	7	3	2.2	.865	OF-24
1891			129	.271	.369	480	130	13	14	2	0.4	101	79	89	55	32	0	0	235	28	37	5	2.3	.877	OF-129
1892	BAL	N	4	.133	.133	15	2	0	0	0	0.0	2	2	2	0	0	0	0	4	0	2	0	1.5	.667	OF-4
5 yrs.			169	.264	.351	636	168	15	17	2	0.3	121	84	98	61	45	0	0	289	36	50	8	2.2	.867	OF-169

Bill Johnson

JOHNSON, WILLIAM LAWRENCE BL TR 5′11″ 170 lbs.
B. Oct. 18, 1892, Chicago, Ill. D. Nov. 3, 1950, Los Angeles, Calif.

Year	Team		Games	BA	SA	AB	H	2B	3B	HR	HR%	R	RBI	BB	SO	SB	Pinch Hit AB	Pinch Hit H	PO	A	E	DP	TC/G	FA	G by Pos
1916	PHI	A	4	.267	.333	15	4	1	0	0	0.0	1	1	0	4	0	0	0	4	0	0	0	1.0	1.000	OF-4
1917			48	.174	.257	109	19	2	2	1	0.9	7	8	8	14	4	16	2	31	5	4	2	1.3	.900	OF-30
2 yrs.			52	.185	.266	124	23	3	2	1	0.8	8	9	8	18	4	16	2	35	5	4	2	1.3	.909	OF-34

Billy Johnson

JOHNSON, WILLIAM RUSSELL (Bull) BR TR 5′10″ 180 lbs.
B. Aug. 30, 1918, Montclair, N. J.

Year	Team		Games	BA	SA	AB	H	2B	3B	HR	HR%	R	RBI	BB	SO	SB	Pinch Hit AB	Pinch Hit H	PO	A	E	DP	TC/G	FA	G by Pos
1943	NY	A	155	.280	.367	592	166	24	6	5	0.8	70	94	53	30	3	0	0	183	326	18	32	3.4	.966	3B-155
1946			85	.260	.382	296	77	14	5	4	1.4	51	35	31	42	1	10	1	71	163	11	15	3.3	.955	3B-74
1947			132	.285	.417	494	141	19	8	10	2.0	67	95	44	43	1	0	0	136	204	17	12	2.7	.952	3B-132
1948			127	.294	.446	446	131	20	6	12	2.7	59	64	41	30	0	8	2	147	213	20	25	3.2	.947	3B-118
1949			113	.249	.374	329	82	11	3	8	2.4	48	56	48	44	1	13	6	207	146	13	26	3.6	.964	3B-81, 1B-21, 2B-1
1950			108	.260	.376	327	85	16	2	6	1.8	44	40	42	30	1	4	1	96	169	12	21	2.6	.957	3B-100, 1B-5
1951	2 teams		NY A (15G –.300)	STL N (124G –.262)																					
″	total		139	.266	.411	482	128	26	1	14	2.9	57	68	53	49	5	1	0	107	332	11	32	3.3	.976	3B-137
1952	STL	N	94	.252	.323	282	71	10	2	2	0.7	23	34	34	21	1	5	0	56	177	12	10	2.8	.951	3B-89
1953			11	.200	.400	5	1	1	0	0	0.0	0	1	1	1	0	0	0	1	8	0	1	0.8	1.000	3B-11
9 yrs.			964	.271	.391	3253	882	141	33	61	1.9	419	487	347	290	13	41	10	1004	1738	114	174	3.1	.960	3B-897, 1B-26, 2B-1
WORLD SERIES																									
1943	NY	A	5	.300	.450	20	6	1	1	0	0.0	3	3	0	3	0	0	0	2	9	1	0	2.4	.917	3B-5
1947			7	.269	.500	26	7	0	3	0	0.0	8	2	3	4	0	0	0	11	14	0	1	3.6	1.000	3B-7
1949			2	.143	.143	7	1	0	0	0	0.0	0	0	0	2	1	0	0	2	5	0	0	3.5	1.000	3B-2
1950			4	.000	.000	6	0	0	0	0	0.0	0	0	0	3	0	0	0	1	5	0	1	1.5	1.000	3B-4
4 yrs.			18	.237	.390	59	14	1	4 1st	0	0.0	11	5	3	12	1	0	0	16	33	1	2	2.8	.980	3B-18

Bob Johnson

JOHNSON, ROBERT LEE (Indian Bob) BR TR 6′ 180 lbs.
Brother of Roy Johnson.
B. Nov. 26, 1906, Pryor, Okla. D. July 6, 1982, Tacoma, Wash.

Year	Team		Games	BA	SA	AB	H	2B	3B	HR	HR%	R	RBI	BB	SO	SB	Pinch Hit AB	Pinch Hit H	PO	A	E	DP	TC/G	FA	G by Pos
1933	PHI	A	142	.290	.505	535	155	44	4	21	3.9	103	93	85	74	8	0	0	298	16	16	3	2.3	.952	OF-142
1934			141	.307	.563	547	168	26	6	34	6.2	111	92	58	60	12	1	0	304	17	11	3	2.4	.967	OF-139
1935			147	.299	.510	582	174	29	5	28	4.8	103	109	78	76	2	0	0	337	13	20	4	2.5	.946	OF-147
1936			153	.292	.525	566	165	29	14	25	4.4	91	121	88	71	6	0	0	345	82	19	25	2.9	.957	OF-131, 2B-22, 1B-1
1937			138	.306	.556	477	146	32	6	25	5.2	91	108	98	65	9	3	0	314	15	8	3	2.5	.976	OF-133, 2B-2

Bob Johnson *continued*

Year	Team	Games	BA	SA	AB	H	2B	3B	HR	HR%	R	RBI	BB	SO	SB	Pinch Hit AB	Pinch Hit H	PO	A	E	DP	TC/G	FA	G by Pos
1938		152	.313	.552	563	176	27	9	30	5.3	114	113	87	73	9	0	0	406	27	18	6	2.9	.960	OF-150, 2B-3, 3B-1
1939		150	.338	.553	544	184	30	9	23	4.2	115	114	99	59	15	0	0	369	15	13	3	2.6	.967	OF-150, 2B-1
1940		138	.268	.514	512	137	25	4	31	6.1	93	103	83	64	8	2	0	310	15	13	4	2.5	.962	OF-136
1941		149	.275	.478	552	152	30	8	22	4.0	98	107	95	75	6	0	0	541	35	8	29	3.9	.986	OF-122, 1B-28
1942		149	.291	.451	550	160	35	7	13	2.4	78	80	82	61	3	0	0	318	18	13	1	2.3	.963	OF-149
1943	WAS A	117	.265	.400	438	116	22	8	7	1.6	65	63	62	50	11	0	0	308	61	9	14	3.2	.976	OF-88, 3B-19, 1B-10
1944	BOS A	144	.324	.528	525	170	40	8	17	3.2	106	106	95	67	2	2	0	270	23	7	3	2.1	.977	OF-142
1945		143	.280	.425	529	148	27	7	12	2.3	71	74	63	56	5	3	1	296	15	8	4	2.3	.975	OF-140
13 yrs.		1863	.296	.506	6920	2051	396	95	288	4.2	1239	1283	1073	851	96	11	1	4416	352	163	102	2.7	.967	OF-1769, 1B-39, 2B-28, 3B-20

Bob Johnson

JOHNSON, ROBERT WALLACE
B. Mar. 4, 1936, Omaha, Neb.
BR TR 5′10″ 175 lbs.

Year	Team	Games	BA	SA	AB	H	2B	3B	HR	HR%	R	RBI	BB	SO	SB	Pinch Hit AB	Pinch Hit H	PO	A	E	DP	TC/G	FA	G by Pos
1960	KC A	76	.205	.253	146	30	4	0	1	0.7	12	9	19	23	2	5	0	102	134	7	23	3.6	.971	SS-30, 2B-27, 3B-11
1961	WAS A	61	.295	.442	224	66	13	1	6	2.7	27	28	19	26	4	1	0	111	178	13	31	5.0	.957	SS-57, 3B-2, 2B-2
1962		135	.288	.416	466	134	20	2	12	2.6	58	43	32	50	9	12	4	164	288	22	39	3.8	.954	3B-72, SS-50, 2B-3, OF-1
1963	BAL A	82	.295	.429	254	75	10	0	8	3.1	34	32	18	35	5	14	6	182	163	7	41	5.0	.980	2B-50, 1B-8, SS-7, 3B-5
1964		93	.248	.348	210	52	8	2	3	1.4	18	29	9	37	0	**45**	**15**	164	77	5	27	4.9	.980	SS-18, 2B-15, 1B-15, OF-1, 3B-1
1965		87	.242	.359	273	66	13	2	5	1.8	36	27	15	34	1	15	1	310	106	9	29	5.7	.979	1B-34, SS-23, 3B-13, 2B-5
1966		71	.217	.268	157	34	5	0	1	0.6	13	10	12	24	0	30	7	155	65	4	21	5.6	.982	2B-20, 1B-17, 3B-3
1967	2 teams	BAL A (4G –.333)	NY N (90G –.348)																					
″	total	94	.348	.472	233	81	8	3	5	2.1	27	27	13	30	1	34	**13**	222	105	7	37	4.3	.979	2B-39, 1B-23, SS-14, 3B-1
1968	2 teams	CIN N (16G –.267)	ATL N (59G –.262)																					
″	total	75	.262	.297	202	53	5	1	0	0.0	17	12	11	22	0	18	3	55	107	10	11	3.1	.942	3B-48, 2B-4, SS-2, 1B-1
1969	2 teams	STL N (19G –.207)	OAK A (51G –.343)																					
″	total	70	.302	.375	96	29	1	0	2	2.1	6	11	5	8	0	50	14	64	13	2	9	5.6	.975	1B-8, 3B-4, 2B-2
1970	OAK A	30	.174	.261	46	8	1	0	1	2.2	6	2	3	2	2	19	3	11	17	1	2	3.2	.966	3B-6, SS-2, 1B-1
11 yrs.		874	.272	.377	2307	628	88	11	44	1.9	254	230	156	291	24	243	66	1540	1253	87	270	4.5	.970	SS-203, 2B-167, 3B-166, 1B-107, OF-2

Bobby Johnson

JOHNSON, BOBBY EARL
B. July 31, 1959, Dallas, Tex.
BR TR 6′3″ 195 lbs.

Year	Team	Games	BA	SA	AB	H	2B	3B	HR	HR%	R	RBI	BB	SO	SB	Pinch Hit AB	Pinch Hit H	PO	A	E	DP	TC/G	FA	G by Pos
1981	TEX A	6	.278	.611	18	5	0	0	2	11.1	2	4	1	3	0	0	0	31	0	0	0	5.2	1.000	C-5, 1B-1
1982		20	.125	.268	56	7	2	0	2	3.6	4	7	3	22	0	4	0	92	5	0	1	5.7	1.000	C-14, 1B-3
1983		72	.211	.343	175	37	6	1	5	2.9	18	16	16	55	3	0	0	346	19	2	15	5.1	.995	C-62, 1B-10
3 yrs.		98	.197	.345	249	49	8	1	9	3.6	24	27	20	80	3	4	0	469	24	2	16	5.2	.996	C-81, 1B-14

Brian Johnson

JOHNSON, BRIAN DAVID
B. Jan. 8, 1968, Oakland, Calif.
BR TR 6′2″ 210 lbs.

Year	Team	Games	BA	SA	AB	H	2B	3B	HR	HR%	R	RBI	BB	SO	SB	Pinch Hit AB	Pinch Hit H	PO	A	E	DP	TC/G	FA	G by Pos
1994	SD N	36	.247	.409	93	23	4	1	3	3.2	7	16	5	21	0	10	4	185	15	0	1	6.9	1.000	C-24, 1B-5
1995		68	.251	.338	207	52	9	0	3	1.4	20	29	11	39	0	13	5	403	31	4	2	7.7	.991	C-55, 1B-2
2 yrs.		104	.250	.360	300	75	13	1	6	2.0	27	45	16	60	0	23	9	588	46	4	3	7.4	.994	C-79, 1B-7

Charles Johnson

JOHNSON, CHARLES EDWARD, JR.
B. July 20, 1971, Fort Pierce, Fla.
BR TR 6′2″ 215 lbs.

Year	Team	Games	BA	SA	AB	H	2B	3B	HR	HR%	R	RBI	BB	SO	SB	Pinch Hit AB	Pinch Hit H	PO	A	E	DP	TC/G	FA	G by Pos
1994	FLA N	4	.455	.818	11	5	1	0	1	9.1	5	4	1	4	0	0	0	18	2	0	0	5.0	1.000	C-4
1995		97	.251	.410	315	79	15	1	11	3.5	40	39	46	71	0	0	0	641	63	6	3	7.3	.992	C-97
2 yrs.		101	.258	.423	326	84	16	1	12	3.7	45	43	47	75	0	0	0	659	65	6	3	7.2	.992	C-101

Charlie Johnson

JOHNSON, CHARLES CLEVELAND (Home Run)
B. Mar. 12, 1885, Slatington, Pa. D. Aug. 28, 1940, Marcus Hook, Pa.
BL TL 5′9″ 150 lbs.

Year	Team	Games	BA	SA	AB	H	2B	3B	HR	HR%	R	RBI	BB	SO	SB	Pinch Hit AB	Pinch Hit H	PO	A	E	DP	TC/G	FA	G by Pos
1908	PHI N	6	.250	.375	16	4	0	1	0	0.0	2	2	1		0	2	0	8	0	0	0	2.0	1.000	OF-4

Cliff Johnson

JOHNSON, CLIFFORD, JR. (Heathcliff)
B. July 22, 1947, San Antonio, Tex.
BR TR 6′4″ 215 lbs.

Year	Team	Games	BA	SA	AB	H	2B	3B	HR	HR%	R	RBI	BB	SO	SB	Pinch Hit AB	Pinch Hit H	PO	A	E	DP	TC/G	FA	G by Pos
1972	HOU N	5	.250	.250	4	1	0	0	0	0.0	0	0	2	0	0	3	0	6	0	0	0	6.0	1.000	C-1
1973		7	.300	.700	20	6	2	0	2	10.0	6	6	1	7	0	2	0	47	2	0	7	9.8	1.000	1B-5
1974		83	.228	.439	171	39	4	1	10	5.8	26	29	33	45	0	38	13	270	18	4	17	6.0	.986	C-28, 1B-21
1975		122	.276	.506	340	94	16	1	20	5.9	52	65	46	64	1	33	5	604	38	12	37	7.3	.982	1B-47, C-41, OF-1
1976		108	.226	.399	318	72	21	2	10	3.1	36	49	62	59	0	9	2	468	35	9	10	5.0	.982	C-66, OF-20, 1B-16
1977	2 teams	HOU N (51G –.299)	NY A (56G –.296)																					
″	total	107	.297	.584	286	85	16	0	22	7.7	46	54	43	53	0	22	8	258	25	4	21	3.0	.986	OF-34, DH-25, 1B-21, C-15
1978	NY A	76	.184	.351	174	32	9	1	6	3.4	20	19	30	32	0	15	2	71	10	2	1	1.3	.976	DH-39, C-22, 1B-1
1979	2 teams	NY A (28G –.266)	CLE A (72G –.271)																					
″	total	100	.270	.520	304	82	16	0	20	6.6	48	67	34	46	2	17	4	10	1	0	0	0.1	1.000	DH-82, C-5
1980	2 teams	CLE A (54G –.230)	CHI N (68G –.235)																					
″	total	122	.232	.397	370	86	11	1	16	4.3	53	62	54	65	0	23	4	471	16	5	34	5.2	.990	1B-46, DH-45, OF-3, C-1
1981	OAK A	84	.260	.476	273	71	8	0	17	6.2	40	59	28	60	5	17	2	42	1	0	2	0.6	1.000	DH-68, 1B-9
1982		73	.238	.383	214	51	10	0	7	3.3	19	31	26	41	1	20	5	66	8	1	7	1.3	.987	DH-48, 1B-11
1983	TOR A	142	.265	.489	407	108	23	1	22	5.4	59	76	67	69	0	24	4	47	4	0	5	0.4	1.000	DH-130, 1B-6
1984		127	.304	.507	359	109	23	1	16	4.5	51	61	50	62	0	34	11	26	0	0	0	0.2	1.000	DH-109, 1B-2
1985	2 teams	TEX A (82G –.257)	TOR A (24G –.274)																					
″	total	106	.260	.417	369	96	17	1	13	3.5	35	66	40	59	0	8	3	17	1	1	4	0.2	.947	DH-103, 1B-3
1986	TOR A	107	.250	.426	336	84	12	1	15	4.5	48	55	52	57	0	12	5	8	1	0	2	0.1	1.000	DH-95, 1B-1
15 yrs.		1369	.258	.459	3945	1016	188	10	196	5.0	539	699	568	719	9	277	68	2411	160	38	147	2.2	.985	DH-744, 1B-189, C-179, OF-58
DIVISIONAL PLAYOFF SERIES																								
1981	OAK A	2	.286	.429	7	2	1	0	0	0.0	0	0	0	1	0	0	0	0	0	0	0	0.0	.000	DH-2
LEAGUE CHAMPIONSHIP SERIES																								
1977	NY A	5	.400	.733	15	6	2	0	1	6.7	2	2	1	2	0	1	0	0	0	0	0	0.0	.000	DH-4
1978		1	.000	.000	1	0	0	0	0	0.0	0	0	0	0	0	1	0	0	0	0	0	0.0	—	

Cliff Johnson *continued*

Year	Team	Games	BA	SA	AB	H	2B	3B	HR	HR%	R	RBI	BB	SO	SB	Pinch Hit AB	Pinch Hit H	PO	A	E	DP	TC/G	FA	G by Pos
1981	OAK A	2	.000	.000	6	0	0	0	0	0.0	0	0	2	2	0	0	0	0	0	0	0	0.0	.000	DH-2
1985	TOR A	7	.368	.474	19	7	2	0	0	0.0	1	2	1	4	0	3	2	0	0	0	0	0.0	.000	DH-7
4 yrs.		15	.317	.488	41	13	4	0	1	2.4	3	4	4	8	0	5	2	0	0	0	0	0.0		DH-13
WORLD SERIES																								
1977	NY A	2	.000	.000	1	0	0	0	0	0.0	0	0	0	0	0	1	0	0	0	0	0	0.0	.000	C-1
1978		2	.000	.000	2	0	0	0	0	0.0	0	0	0	1	0	2	0	0	0	0	0	0.0	—	
2 yrs.		4	.000	.000	3	0	0	0	0	0.0	0	0	0	1	0	3	0	0	0	0	0	0.0		C-1

Darrell Johnson

JOHNSON, DARRELL DEAN
B. Aug. 25, 1928, Horace, Neb.
Manager 1974–80, 1982.

BR TR 6′ 1″ 180 lbs.

Year	Team	Games	BA	SA	AB	H	2B	3B	HR	HR%	R	RBI	BB	SO	SB	Pinch Hit AB	Pinch Hit H	PO	A	E	DP	TC/G	FA	G by Pos
1952	2 teams	STL A (29G –.282) CHI A (22G –.108)																						
″	total	51	.226	.261	115	26	2	1	0	0.0	12	10	16	13	1	10	4	161	23	5	4	4.4	.974	C-43
1957	NY A	21	.217	.304	46	10	1	0	1	2.2	4	8	3	10	0	1	0	75	8	0	1	4.2	1.000	C-20
1958		5	.250	.250	16	4	0	0	0	0.0	1	0	0	2	0	1	0	22	3	0	1	6.3	1.000	C-4
1960	STL N	8	.000	.000	2	0	0	0	0	0.0	0	0	1	0	0	0	0	10	1	0	0	1.4	1.000	C-8
1961	2 teams	PHI N (21G –.230) CIN N (20G –.315)																						
″	total	41	.270	.322	115	31	3	0	1	0.9	7	9	4	10	0	0	0	198	23	2	4	5.4	.991	C-41
1962	2 teams	CIN N (2G –.000) BAL A (6G –.182)																						
″	total	8	.154	.154	26	4	0	0	0	0.0	0	1	2	4	0	0	0	46	4	0	1	6.3	1.000	C-8
6 yrs.		134	.234	.278	320	75	6	1	2	0.6	24	28	26	39	1	12	4	512	62	7	11	4.7	.988	C-124
WORLD SERIES																								
1961	CIN N	2	.500	.500	4	2	0	0	0	0.0	0	0	0	0	0	0	0	8	1	0	1	4.5	1.000	C-2

Davey Johnson

JOHNSON, DAVID ALLEN
B. Jan. 30, 1943, Orlando, Fla.
Manager 1984–90, 1993–95.

BR TR 6′ 1″ 170 lbs.

Year	Team	Games	BA	SA	AB	H	2B	3B	HR	HR%	R	RBI	BB	SO	SB	Pinch Hit AB	Pinch Hit H	PO	A	E	DP	TC/G	FA	G by Pos
1965	BAL A	20	.170	.234	47	8	3	0	0	0.0	5	1	5	6	3	4	1	11	37	3	7	3.6	.941	3B-9, 2B-3, SS-2
1966		131	.257	.351	501	129	20	3	7	1.4	47	56	31	64	3	2	0	294	357	20	77	5.2	.970	2B-126, SS-3
1967		148	.247	.376	510	126	30	3	10	2.0	62	64	59	82	4	2	0	344	351	14	76	4.8	.980	2B-144, 3B-3
1968		145	.242	.359	504	122	24	4	9	1.8	50	56	44	80	7	2	1	294	370	15	74	4.2	.978	2B-127, SS-34
1969		142	.280	.391	511	143	34	1	7	1.4	52	57	57	52	3	0	0	358	370	12	93	5.1	.984	2B-142, SS-2
1970		149	.281	.392	530	149	27	1	10	1.9	68	53	66	68	2	0	0	382	391	8	102	5.2	.990	2B-149, SS-2
1971		142	.282	.443	510	144	26	1	18	3.5	67	72	51	55	3	1	0	361	367	12	103	5.3	.984	2B-140
1972		118	.221	.335	376	83	22	3	5	1.3	31	32	52	68	1	2	1	286	307	6	81	5.2	.990	2B-116
1973	ATL N	157	.270	.546	559	151	25	0	43	7.7	84	99	81	93	5	2	1	383	464	30	106	5.7	.966	2B-155
1974		136	.251	.390	454	114	18	0	15	3.3	56	62	75	59	1	4	2	789	231	11	100	7.2	.989	1B-73, 2B-71
1975		1	1.000	2.000	1	1	1	0	0	0.0	0	1	0	0	0	1	1	0	0	0	0	0.0	—	
1977	PHI N	78	.321	.545	156	50	9	1	8	5.1	23	36	23	20	1	26	9	299	31	0	30	5.7	1.000	1B-43, 2B-9, 3B-6
1978	2 teams	PHI N (44G –.191) CHI N (24G –.306)																						
″	total	68	.232	.355	138	32	3	1	4	2.9	19	20	15	28	0	30	10	61	63	11	11	3.1	.919	3B-21, 2B-15, 1B-7
13 yrs.		1435	.261	.404	4797	1252	242	18	136	2.8	564	609	559	675	33	76	26	3862	3339	142	860	5.2	.981	2B-1197, 1B-123, SS-43, 3B-39
LEAGUE CHAMPIONSHIP SERIES																								
1969	BAL A	3	.231	.231	13	3	0	0	0	0.0	2	0	2	1	0	0	0	5	11	0	2	5.3	1.000	2B-3
1970		3	.364	.909	11	4	0	0	2	18.2	4	4	1	1	0	0	0	11	4	0	3	5.0	1.000	2B-3
1971		3	.300	.500	10	3	2	0	0	0.0	2	0	3	1	0	0	0	5	6	1	3	4.0	.917	2B-3
1977	PHI N	1	.250	.250	4	1	0	0	0	0.0	0	2	0	1	0	0	0	8	0	0	0	8.0	1.000	1B-1
4 yrs.		10	.289	.500	38	11	2	0	2	5.3	8	6	6	4	0	0	0	29	21	1	8	5.1	.980	2B-9, 1B-1
WORLD SERIES																								
1966	BAL A	4	.286	.357	14	4	1	0	0	0.0	1	1	0	1	0	0	0	12	12	0	4	6.0	1.000	2B-4
1969		5	.063	.063	16	1	0	0	0	0.0	1	0	2	1	0	0	0	7	15	0	4	4.4	1.000	2B-5
1970		5	.313	.438	16	5	2	0	0	0.0	2	2	5	2	0	0	0	15	9	0	1	4.8	1.000	2B-5
1971		7	.148	.148	27	4	0	0	0	0.0	1	3	0	1	0	0	0	18	12	0	2	4.3	1.000	2B-7
4 yrs.		21	.192	.233	73	14	3	0	0	0.0	5	6	7	5	0	0	0	52	48	0	11	4.8	1.000	2B-21

Deron Johnson

JOHNSON, DERON ROGER
B. July 17, 1938, San Diego, Calif. D. Apr. 23, 1992, Poway, Calif.

BR TR 6′ 2″ 200 lbs.

Year	Team	Games	BA	SA	AB	H	2B	3B	HR	HR%	R	RBI	BB	SO	SB	Pinch Hit AB	Pinch Hit H	PO	A	E	DP	TC/G	FA	G by Pos
1960	NY A	6	.500	.750	4	2	1	0	0	0.0	0	0	0	0	0	1	0	0	3	1	0	0.8	.750	3B-5
1961	2 teams	NY A (13G –.105) KC A (83G –.216)																						
″	total	96	.209	.344	302	63	11	3	8	2.6	32	44	16	49	0	10	2	134	66	9	7	2.3	.957	OF-59, 3B-27, 1B-3
1962	KC A	17	.105	.158	19	2	1	0	0	0.0	1	0	3	8	0	9	0	5	1	1	0	1.2	.857	3B-2, OF-2, 1B-2
1964	CIN N	140	.273	.472	477	130	24	4	21	4.4	63	79	37	98	4	13	5	952	84	10	82	7.4	.990	1B-131, OF-10, 3B-1
1965		159	.287	.515	616	177	30	7	32	5.2	92	**130**	52	97	0	0	0	132	266	22	26	2.6	.948	3B-159
1966		142	.257	.461	505	130	25	3	24	4.8	75	81	39	87	1	5	1	339	36	5	21	1.9	.987	OF-106, 1B-71, 3B-18
1967		108	.224	.388	361	81	18	1	13	3.6	39	53	22	104	0	10	3	606	73	4	51	6.5	.994	1B-81, 3B-24
1968	ATL N	127	.208	.316	342	71	11	1	8	2.3	29	33	35	79	0	13	3	759	78	4	66	7.1	.995	1B-97, 3B-21
1969	PHI N	138	.255	.419	475	121	19	4	17	3.6	51	80	60	111	4	6	1	250	99	11	12	2.6	.969	OF-72, 3B-50, 1B-18
1970		159	.256	.456	574	147	28	3	27	4.7	66	93	72	132	0	5	2	1180	74	6	104	8.0	.995	1B-154, 3B-3
1971		158	.265	.490	582	154	29	0	34	5.8	74	95	72	146	0	3	1	1233	123	12	125	8.7	.991	1B-136, 3B-22
1972		96	.213	.357	230	49	4	1	9	3.9	19	31	26	69	0	30	6	479	24	9	43	8.3	.982	1B-62
1973	2 teams	PHI N (12G –.167) OAK A (131G –.246)																						
″	total	143	.240	.400	500	120	16	2	20	4.0	64	86	64	126	0	3	0	244	12	3	32	1.9	.988	DH-107, 1B-33
1974	3 teams	OAK A (50G –.195) MIL A (49G –.151) BOS A (11G –.120)																						
″	total	110	.171	.305	351	60	4	2	13	3.7	30	43	32	84	2	6	0	220	10	4	17	2.2	.983	DH-77, 1B-30
1975	2 teams	CHI A (148G –.232) BOS A (3G –.600)																						
″	total	151	.239	.388	565	135	25	1	19	3.4	68	75	50	117	0	3	2	475	24	3	40	3.3	.994	DH-94, 1B-57
1976	BOS A	15	.132	.211	38	5	1	1	0	0.0	3	0	5	11	0	3	0	30	1	0	3	6.2	1.000	OF-5
16 yrs.		1765	.244	.420	5941	1447	247	33	245	4.1	706	923	585	1318	11	120	26	7038	974	104	629	4.7	.987	1B-875, 3B-332, DH-278, OF-254
LEAGUE CHAMPIONSHIP SERIES																								
1973	OAK A	4	.100	.100	10	1	0	0	0	0.0	0	0	0	0	0	0	0	0	0	0	0	0.0	.000	DH-4

Deron Johnson *continued*

Year	Team	Games	BA	SA	AB	H	2B	3B	HR	HR%	R	RBI	BB	SO	SB	Pinch Hit AB	Pinch Hit H	PO	A	E	DP	TC/G	FA	G by Pos
WORLD SERIES																								
1973	**OAK A**	6	.300	.400	10	3	1	0	0	0.0	0	0	1	4	0	3	2	8	1	0	0	4.5	1.000	1B-2

Dick Johnson

JOHNSON, RICHARD ALLAN (Footer, Treads)
B. Feb. 15, 1932, Dayton, Ohio.
BL TL 5′11″ 175 lbs.

Year	Team	Games	BA	SA	AB	H	2B	3B	HR	HR%	R	RBI	BB	SO	SB	Pinch Hit AB	Pinch Hit H	PO	A	E	DP	TC/G	FA	G by Pos
1958	**CHI N**	8	.000	.000	5	0	0	0	0	0.0	1	0	0	1	0	5	0	0	0	0	0	0.0	—	

Don Johnson

JOHNSON, DONALD SPORE (Pep)
Son of Ernie Johnson.
B. Dec. 7, 1911, Chicago, Ill.
BR TR 6′ 170 lbs.

Year	Team	Games	BA	SA	AB	H	2B	3B	HR	HR%	R	RBI	BB	SO	SB	Pinch Hit AB	Pinch Hit H	PO	A	E	DP	TC/G	FA	G by Pos
1943	**CHI N**	10	.190	.238	42	8	2	0	0	0.0	5	1	2	4	0	0	0	32	35	3	8	7.0	.957	2B-10
1944		154	.278	.352	608	169	37	1	2	0.3	50	71	28	48	8	0	0	385	462	47	85	5.8	.947	2B-154
1945		138	.302	.361	557	168	23	2	2	0.4	94	58	32	34	9	0	0	309	440	19	74	5.6	.975	2B-138
1946		83	.242	.290	314	76	10	1	1	0.3	37	19	26	39	6	0	0	192	228	8	34	5.2	.981	2B-83
1947		120	.259	.333	402	104	17	2	3	0.7	33	26	24	45	2	5	1	260	302	17	69	5.1	.971	2B-108, 3B-6
1948		6	.250	.250	12	3	0	0	0	0.0	0	0	0	1	1	2	0	3	3	2	2	2.0	.750	3B-2, 2B-2
6 yrs.		511	.273	.337	1935	528	89	6	8	0.4	219	175	112	171	26	7	1	1181	1470	96	272	5.5	.965	2B-495, 3B-8
WORLD SERIES																								
1945	**CHI N**	7	.172	.310	29	5	2	1	0	0.0	4	0	0	8	0	0	0	11	24	1	5	5.1	.972	2B-7

Ed Johnson

JOHNSON, EDWIN CYRIL
B. Mar. 31, 1899, Morganfield, Ky. D. July 3, 1975, Morganfield, Ky.
BL TR 5′9″ 160 lbs.

Year	Team	Games	BA	SA	AB	H	2B	3B	HR	HR%	R	RBI	BB	SO	SB	Pinch Hit AB	Pinch Hit H	PO	A	E	DP	TC/G	FA	G by Pos
1920	**WAS A**	2	.250	.250	8	2	0	0	0	0.0	0	1	0	0	0	0	0	3	0	1	0	2.0	.750	OF-2

Elmer Johnson

JOHNSON, ELMER ELLSWORTH (Hickory)
B. June 12, 1884, Beard, Ind. D. Oct. 31, 1966, Hollywood, Fla.
BR TR 5′9″ 185 lbs.

Year	Team	Games	BA	SA	AB	H	2B	3B	HR	HR%	R	RBI	BB	SO	SB	Pinch Hit AB	Pinch Hit H	PO	A	E	DP	TC/G	FA	G by Pos
1914	**NY N**	11	.167	.250	12	2	1	0	0	0.0	0	0	1	3	0	0	0	14	4	1	0	1.7	.947	C-11

Erik Johnson

JOHNSON, ERIK ANTHONY
B. Oct. 11, 1965, Oakland, Calif.
BR TR 5′11″ 175 lbs.

Year	Team	Games	BA	SA	AB	H	2B	3B	HR	HR%	R	RBI	BB	SO	SB	Pinch Hit AB	Pinch Hit H	PO	A	E	DP	TC/G	FA	G by Pos
1993	**SF N**	4	.400	.800	5	2	2	0	0	0.0	1	0	0	1	0	1	0	1	1	0	0	0.5	1.000	2B-2, 3B-1, SS-1
1994		5	.154	.154	13	2	0	0	0	0.0	0	0	0	4	0	2	0	8	7	0	3	5.0	1.000	2B-2, SS-1
2 yrs.		9	.222	.333	18	4	2	0	0	0.0	1	0	0	5	0	3	0	9	8	0	3	2.4	1.000	2B-4, SS-2, 3B-1

Ernie Johnson

JOHNSON, ERNEST RUDOLPH
Father of Don Johnson.
B. Apr. 29, 1888, Chicago, Ill. D. May 1, 1952, Monrovia, Calif.
BL TR 5′9″ 151 lbs.

Year	Team	Games	BA	SA	AB	H	2B	3B	HR	HR%	R	RBI	BB	SO	SB	Pinch Hit AB	Pinch Hit H	PO	A	E	DP	TC/G	FA	G by Pos
1912	**CHI A**	18	.262	.310	42	11	0	1	0	0.0	7	5	1		0	1	1	23	37	1	3	3.8	.984	SS-16
1915	**STL F**	152	.240	.355	512	123	18	10	7	1.4	58	67	46		32	0	0	348	477	51	64	5.8	.942	SS-152
1916	**STL A**	74	.229	.292	236	54	9	3	0	0.0	29	19	30	23	13	1	0	126	209	24	20	5.0	.933	SS-60, 3B-12
1917		80	.246	.327	199	49	6	2	2	1.0	28	20	12	16	13	2	0	122	197	25	19	4.8	.927	SS-39, 2B-18, 3B-14
1918		29	.265	.294	34	9	1	0	0	0.0	7	0	0	2	4	9	2	6	17	5	1	2.3	.821	SS-11, 3B-1
1921	**CHI A**	142	.295	.369	613	181	28	7	1	0.2	93	51	29	24	22	1	1	291	494	44	80	5.9	.947	SS-141
1922		145	.254	.292	603	153	17	3	0	0.0	85	56	40	30	21	2	0	259	468	37	74	5.4	.952	SS-141
1923	**2 teams**	**CHI A** (12G –.189) **NY A** (17G –.354)																						
″	**total**	29	.267	.347	101	27	3	1	1	1.0	11	9	4	6	2	3	3	46	58	6	13	4.4	.945	SS-24, 3B-1
1924	**NY A**	64	.353	.597	119	42	4	8	3	2.5	24	12	11	7	1	13	3	60	81	7	13	3.9	.953	2B-27, SS-9, 3B-2
1925		76	.282	.412	170	48	5	1	5	2.9	30	17	8	10	6	14	1	87	108	9	21	3.2	.956	2B-34, SS-28, 3B-2
10 yrs.		809	.265	.349	2629	697	91	36	19	0.7	372	256	181	118	114	46	11	1368	2146	209	308	5.1	.944	SS-621, 2B-79, 3B-32
WORLD SERIES																								
1923	**NY A**	2	—	—	0	0	0	0	0	—	1	0	0	0	0	0	0	0	1	0	0	1.0	1.000	SS-1

Frank Johnson

JOHNSON, FRANK HERBERT
B. July 22, 1942, El Paso, Tex.
BR TR 6′1″ 155 lbs.

Year	Team	Games	BA	SA	AB	H	2B	3B	HR	HR%	R	RBI	BB	SO	SB	Pinch Hit AB	Pinch Hit H	PO	A	E	DP	TC/G	FA	G by Pos
1966	**SF N**	15	.219	.219	32	7	0	0	0	0.0	2	0	2	7	0	1	0	15	0	0	0	1.2	1.000	OF-13
1967		8	.300	.300	10	3	0	0	0	0.0	3	0	1	2	0	2	0	8	0	1	0	3.0	.889	OF-3
1968		67	.190	.218	174	33	2	0	1	0.6	11	7	12	23	1	8	0	61	83	9	6	2.9	.941	3B-36, OF-8, SS-5, 2B-3
1969		7	.100	.100	10	1	0	0	0	0.0	2	0	0	1	0	0	0	7	0	0	0	1.0	1.000	OF-7
1970		67	.273	.360	161	44	1	2	3	1.9	25	31	19	18	1	11	3	199	14	5	16	3.6	.977	OF-33, 1B-27
1971		32	.082	.102	49	4	1	0	0	0.0	4	5	3	9	0	21	2	40	1	1	3	3.2	.976	1B-9, OF-4
6 yrs.		196	.211	.257	436	92	4	2	4	0.9	47	43	37	60	2	43	5	330	98	16	25	3.0	.964	OF-68, 3B-36, 1B-36, SS-5, 2B-3

Howard Johnson

JOHNSON, HOWARD MICHAEL (Hojo)
B. Nov. 29, 1960, Clearwater, Fla.
BB TR 5′11″ 175 lbs.

Year	Team	Games	BA	SA	AB	H	2B	3B	HR	HR%	R	RBI	BB	SO	SB	Pinch Hit AB	Pinch Hit H	PO	A	E	DP	TC/G	FA	G by Pos
1982	**DET A**	54	.316	.426	155	49	5	0	4	2.6	23	14	16	30	7	7	1	36	40	7	6	1.6	.916	3B-33, DH-10, OF-9
1983		27	.212	.348	66	14	0	0	3	4.5	11	5	7	10	0	6	2	10	30	7	2	2.0	.851	3B-21, DH-2
1984		116	.248	.394	355	88	14	1	12	3.4	43	50	40	67	10	7	2	63	150	14	21	1.8	.938	3B-108, SS-9, DH-4, OF-1, 1B-1
1985	**NY N**	126	.242	.393	389	94	18	4	11	2.8	38	46	34	78	6	12	4	78	190	18	27	2.4	.937	3B-113, SS-7, OF-1
1986		88	.245	.445	220	54	14	0	10	4.5	30	39	31	64	8	17	2	52	136	20	24	2.6	.904	3B-45, SS-34, OF-1
1987		157	.265	.504	554	147	22	1	36	6.5	93	99	83	113	32	2	1	118	305	26	27	2.5	.942	3B-140, SS-38, OF-2
1988		148	.230	.422	495	114	21	1	24	4.8	85	68	86	104	23	3	1	110	274	18	37	2.2	.955	3B-131, SS-52
1989		153	.287	.559	571	164	41	3	36	6.3	**104**	101	77	126	41	0	0	97	217	24	22	1.9	.929	3B-143, SS-31
1990		154	.244	.434	590	144	37	3	23	3.9	89	90	69	100	34	1	0	150	335	28	39	3.1	.945	3B-92, SS-73
1991		156	.259	.535	564	146	34	4	**38**	**6.7**	108	**117**	78	120	30	1	0	161	264	31	26	2.8	.932	3B-104, OF-30, SS-28
1992		100	.223	.337	350	78	19	0	7	2.0	48	43	55	79	22	3	0	206	3	4	0	2.2	.981	OF-98
1993		72	.238	.379	235	56	8	2	7	3.0	32	26	43	43	6	3	0	52	135	11	11	3.0	.944	3B-67
1994	**CLR N**	93	.211	.405	227	48	10	2	10	4.4	30	40	39	73	11	33	10	98	2	2	0	1.6	.980	OF-62, 1B-1
1995	**CHI N**	87	.195	.355	169	33	4	1	7	4.1	26	22	34	46	1	28	7	45	64	7	10	2.0	.940	3B-34, OF-13, 2B-8, 1B-3, SS-1
14 yrs.		1531	.249	.446	4940	1229	247	22	228	4.6	760	760	692	1053	231	123	30	1276	2145	217	252	2.3	.940	3B-1031, SS-273, OF-217, DH-16, 2B-8, 1B-5

Howard Johnson *continued*

Year	Team	Games	BA	SA	AB	H	2B	3B	HR	HR%	R	RBI	BB	SO	SB	Pinch Hit AB	Pinch Hit H	PO	A	E	DP	TC/G	FA	G by Pos
LEAGUE CHAMPIONSHIP SERIES																								
1986	NY N	2	.000	.000	2	0	0	0	0	0.0	0	0	0	0	0	2	0	0	0	0	0	0.0	—	
1988		6	.056	.056	18	1	0	0	0	0.0	3	0	1	6	1	2	0	6	9	1	0	2.7	.938	SS-5, 3B-1
2 yrs.		8	.050	.050	20	1	0	0	0	0.0	3	0	1	6	1	4	0	6	9	1	0	2.7	.938	SS-5, 3B-1
WORLD SERIES																								
1984	DET A	1	.000	.000	1	0	0	0	0	0.0	0	0	0	0	0	1	0	0	0	0	0	0.0	—	
1986	NY N	2	.000	.000	5	0	0	0	0	0.0	0	0	0	2	0	1	0	1	0	0	0	0.5	1.000	3B-1, SS-1
2 yrs.		3	.000	.000	6	0	0	0	0	0.0	0	0	0	2	0	2	0	1	0	0	0	0.5	1.000	3B-1, SS-1

Lamar Johnson

JOHNSON, LAMAR BR TR 6′ 2″ 215 lbs.
B. Sept. 2, 1950, Bessemer, Ala.

Year	Team	Games	BA	SA	AB	H	2B	3B	HR	HR%	R	RBI	BB	SO	SB	Pinch Hit AB	Pinch Hit H	PO	A	E	DP	TC/G	FA	G by Pos
1974	CHI A	10	.345	.345	29	10	0	0	0	0.0	1	2	0	3	0	0	0	40	2	0	8	4.2	1.000	1B-7, DH-3
1975		8	.200	.400	30	6	3	0	1	3.3	2	1	1	5	0	1	0	46	2	2	4	6.3	.960	1B-6, DH-2
1976		82	.320	.432	222	71	11	1	4	1.8	29	33	19	37	2	18	4	210	18	4	20	3.3	.983	DH-35, 1B-34, OF-1
1977		118	.302	.505	374	113	12	5	18	4.8	52	65	24	53	1	26	**10**	346	32	4	31	3.4	.990	DH-68, 1B-45
1978		148	.273	.376	498	136	23	2	8	1.6	52	72	43	46	6	10	2	887	71	8	74	6.7	.992	1B-108, DH-36
1979		133	.309	.449	479	148	29	1	12	2.5	60	74	41	56	8	7	1	748	63	11	62	6.3	.987	1B-94, DH-37
1980		147	.277	.409	541	150	26	3	13	2.4	51	81	47	53	2	5	1	671	56	7	70	5.0	.990	1B-80, DH-66
1981		41	.276	.351	134	37	7	0	1	0.7	10	15	5	14	0	6	1	264	15	3	31	7.4	.989	1B-36, DH-2
1982	TEX A	105	.259	.358	324	84	11	0	7	2.2	37	38	31	40	3	19	5	105	4	2	6	1.2	.982	DH-77, 1B-12
9 yrs.		792	.287	.415	2631	755	122	12	64	2.4	294	381	211	307	22	92	24	3317	263	41	306	4.8	.989	1B-422, DH-326, OF-1

Lance Johnson

JOHNSON, KENNETH LANCE BL TL 5′10″ 160 lbs.
B. July 6, 1963, Cincinnati, Ohio.

Year	Team	Games	BA	SA	AB	H	2B	3B	HR	HR%	R	RBI	BB	SO	SB	Pinch Hit AB	Pinch Hit H	PO	A	E	DP	TC/G	FA	G by Pos
1987	STL N	33	.220	.288	59	13	2	1	0	0.0	4	7	4	6	6	8	2	27	0	2	0	1.2	.931	OF-25
1988	CHI A	33	.185	.234	124	23	4	1	0	0.0	11	6	6	11	6	3	0	63	1	2	0	2.1	.970	OF-31, DH-1
1989		50	.300	.367	180	54	8	2	0	0.0	28	16	17	24	16	3	1	113	0	2	0	2.5	.983	OF-45, DH-1
1990		151	.285	.357	541	154	18	9	1	0.2	76	51	33	45	36	17	4	353	5	10	3	2.5	.973	OF-148, DH-1
1991		160	.274	.342	588	161	14	**13**	0	0.0	72	49	26	58	26	4	2	425	11	2	3	2.8	.995	OF-158
1992		157	.279	.363	567	158	15	**12**	3	0.5	67	47	34	33	41	3	1	433	11	6	3	2.9	.987	OF-157
1993		147	.311	.396	540	168	18	**14**	0	0.0	75	47	36	33	35	2	0	427	7	9	1	3.0	.980	OF-146
1994		106	.277	.393	412	114	11	**14**	3	0.7	56	54	26	23	26	3	0	317	1	0	0	3.1	1.000	OF-103, DH-1
1995		142	.306	.425	**607**	**186**	18	12	10	1.6	98	57	32	31	40	5	2	335	8	3	2	2.5	.991	OF-140, DH-1
9 yrs.		979	.285	.372	3618	1031	108	78	17	0.5	487	334	214	264	232	48	12	2493	44	36	12	2.7	.986	OF-953, DH-5
LEAGUE CHAMPIONSHIP SERIES																								
1987	STL N	1	—	—	0	0	0	0	0	—	1	0	0	0	1	0	0	0	0	0	0	0.0	—	
1993	CHI A	6	.217	.478	23	5	1	1	1	4.3	2	6	2	1	1	0	0	15	0	0	0	2.5	1.000	OF-6
2 yrs.		7	.217	.478	23	5	1	1	1	4.3	3	6	2	1	2	0	0	15	0	0	0	2.5	1.000	OF-6
WORLD SERIES																								
1987	STL N	1	—	—	0	0	0	0	0	—	0	0	0	0	1	0	0	0	0	0	0	0.0	—	

Larry Johnson

JOHNSON, LARRY DOBY BR TR 6′ 185 lbs.
B. Aug. 17, 1950, Cleveland, Ohio.

Year	Team	Games	BA	SA	AB	H	2B	3B	HR	HR%	R	RBI	BB	SO	SB	Pinch Hit AB	Pinch Hit H	PO	A	E	DP	TC/G	FA	G by Pos
1972	CLE A	1	.500	.500	2	1	0	0	0	0.0	0	0	0	1	0	1	0	4	0	0	0	4.0	1.000	C-1
1974		1	—	—	0	0	0	0	0	—	1	0	0	0	0	0	0	0	0	0	0	0.0	—	
1975	MON N	1	.333	.667	3	1	1	0	0	0.0	0	1	1	1	0	1	0	4	1	0	0	5.0	1.000	C-1
1976		6	.154	.231	13	2	1	0	0	0.0	0	0	0	2	0	0	0	22	2	0	0	4.8	1.000	C-5
1978	CHI A	3	.125	.125	8	1	0	0	0	0.0	0	0	1	4	0	0	0	5	1	1	0	2.3	.857	C-2, DH-1
5 yrs.		12	.192	.269	26	5	2	0	0	0.0	1	1	2	8	0	2	0	35	4	1	0	4.0	.975	C-9, DH-1

Lou Johnson

JOHNSON, LOUIS BROWN (Slick, Sweet Lou) BR TR 5′11″ 170 lbs.
B. Sept. 22, 1934, Lexington, Ky.

Year	Team	Games	BA	SA	AB	H	2B	3B	HR	HR%	R	RBI	BB	SO	SB	Pinch Hit AB	Pinch Hit H	PO	A	E	DP	TC/G	FA	G by Pos
1960	CHI N	34	.206	.265	68	14	2	1	0	0.0	6	1	5	19	3	6	0	43	4	0	0	1.9	1.000	OF-25
1961	LA A	1	—	—	0	0	0	0	0	—	0	0	0	0	0	0	0	0	0	0	0	0.0	.000	OF-1
1962	MIL N	61	.282	.453	117	33	4	5	2	1.7	22	13	11	27	6	9	1	61	1	0	1	1.1	1.000	OF-55
1965	LA N	131	.259	.391	468	121	24	1	12	2.6	57	58	24	81	15	2	0	199	3	3	2	1.6	.985	OF-128
1966		152	.272	.414	526	143	20	2	17	3.2	71	73	21	75	8	1	0	249	8	4	2	1.8	.985	OF-148
1967		104	.270	.418	330	89	14	1	11	3.3	39	41	24	52	4	16	5	153	7	4	0	1.8	.976	OF-91
1968	2 teams	CHI N (62G –.244) CLE A (65G –.257)																						
″	total	127	.251	.376	407	102	25	4	6	1.5	39	37	15	47	9	14	7	184	5	4	1	1.7	.979	OF-114
1969	CAL A	67	.203	.263	133	27	8	0	0	0.0	10	9	10	19	5	22	3	56	2	4	0	1.4	.935	OF-44
8 yrs.		677	.258	.389	2049	529	97	14	48	2.3	244	232	110	320	50	70	16	945	30	19	6	1.6	.981	OF-606
WORLD SERIES																								
1965	LA N	7	.296	.593	27	8	2	0	2	7.4	3	4	1	3	0	0	0	13	1	1	0	2.1	.933	OF-7
1966		4	.267	.333	15	4	1	0	0	0.0	1	0	1	1	0	0	0	9	0	0	0	2.3	1.000	OF-4
2 yrs.		11	.286	.500	42	12	3	0	2	4.8	4	4	2	4	0	0	0	22	1	1	0	2.2	.958	OF-11

Mark Johnson

JOHNSON, MARK PATRICK BL TL 6′ 4″ 230 lbs.
B. Oct. 17, 1967, Worcester, Mass.

Year	Team	Games	BA	SA	AB	H	2B	3B	HR	HR%	R	RBI	BB	SO	SB	Pinch Hit AB	Pinch Hit H	PO	A	E	DP	TC/G	FA	G by Pos
1995	PIT N	79	.208	.421	221	46	6	1	13	5.9	32	28	37	66	5	12	2	527	34	8	53	8.1	.986	1B-70

Otis Johnson

JOHNSON, OTIS L. BB TR 5′ 9″ 185 lbs.
B. Nov. 5, 1883, Fowler, Ind. D. Nov. 9, 1915, Johnson City, N. Y.

Year	Team	Games	BA	SA	AB	H	2B	3B	HR	HR%	R	RBI	BB	SO	SB	Pinch Hit AB	Pinch Hit H	PO	A	E	DP	TC/G	FA	G by Pos
1911	NY A	71	.234	.378	209	49	9	6	3	1.4	21	36	39		12	4	0	115	177	31	23	5.0	.904	SS-47, 2B-15, 3B-3

Paul Johnson

JOHNSON, PAUL OSCAR BR TR 5′ 8″ 160 lbs.
B. Sept. 2, 1896, N. Grosvenordale, Conn. D. Feb. 14, 1973, McAllen, Tex.

Year	Team	Games	BA	SA	AB	H	2B	3B	HR	HR%	R	RBI	BB	SO	SB	Pinch Hit AB	Pinch Hit H	PO	A	E	DP	TC/G	FA	G by Pos
1920	PHI A	18	.208	.208	72	15	0	0	0	0.0	6	5	4	8	1	0	0	26	2	2	0	1.7	.933	OF-18
1921		48	.315	.417	127	40	6	2	1	0.8	17	10	9	17	0	14	7	62	1	2	1	2.0	.969	OF-32
2 yrs.		66	.276	.342	199	55	6	2	1	0.5	23	15	13	25	1	14	7	88	3	4	1	1.9	.958	OF-50

Randy Johnson

JOHNSON, RANDALL GLENN BR TR 6′ 1″ 185 lbs.
B. June 10, 1956, Escondido, Calif.

Year	Team	Games	BA	SA	AB	H	2B	3B	HR	HR%	R	RBI	BB	SO	SB	Pinch Hit AB	Pinch Hit H	PO	A	E	DP	TC/G	FA	G by Pos
1982	ATL N	27	.239	.348	46	11	5	0	0	0.0	5	6	6	4	0	7	1	21	47	3	7	4.2	.958	2B-13, 3B-4
1983		86	.250	.292	144	36	3	0	1	0.7	22	17	20	27	1	25	8	44	72	1	13	2.1	.991	3B-53, 2B-4
1984		91	.279	.374	294	82	13	0	5	1.7	28	30	21	21	4	13	3	44	171	14	14	2.8	.939	3B-81
3 yrs.		204	.267	.347	484	129	21	0	6	1.2	55	53	47	52	5	45	12	109	290	18	34	2.7	.957	3B-138, 2B-17

Randy Johnson

JOHNSON, RANDALL STUART BL TL 6′ 2″ 195 lbs.
B. Aug. 15, 1958, Miami, Fla.

Year	Team	Games	BA	SA	AB	H	2B	3B	HR	HR%	R	RBI	BB	SO	SB	Pinch Hit AB	Pinch Hit H	PO	A	E	DP	TC/G	FA	G by Pos
1980	CHI A	12	.200	.200	20	4	0	0	0	0.0	0	3	2	4	0	5	2	2	0	0	0	0.3	1.000	DH-4, OF-1, 1B-1
1982	MIN A	89	.248	.419	234	58	10	0	10	4.3	26	33	30	46	0	22	2	2	0	0	0	0.0	1.000	DH-67, OF-2
2 yrs.		101	.244	.402	254	62	10	0	10	3.9	26	36	32	50	0	27	4	4	0	0	0	0.1	1.000	DH-71, OF-3, 1B-1

Randy Johnson

JOHNSON, RONDIN ALLEN BB TR 5′10″ 160 lbs.
B. Dec. 16, 1958, Bremerton, Wash.

Year	Team	Games	BA	SA	AB	H	2B	3B	HR	HR%	R	RBI	BB	SO	SB	Pinch Hit AB	Pinch Hit H	PO	A	E	DP	TC/G	FA	G by Pos
1986	KC A	11	.258	.323	31	8	0	1	0	0.0	1	2	0	3	0	0	0	14	32	0	5	4.2	1.000	2B-11

Ron Johnson

JOHNSON, RONALD DAVID BR TR 6′ 2″ 223 lbs.
B. Mar. 23, 1956, Long Beach, Calif.

Year	Team	Games	BA	SA	AB	H	2B	3B	HR	HR%	R	RBI	BB	SO	SB	Pinch Hit AB	Pinch Hit H	PO	A	E	DP	TC/G	FA	G by Pos
1982	KC A	8	.286	.429	14	4	2	0	0	0.0	2	0	4	3	0	0	0	39	2	1	3	6.0	.976	1B-7
1983		9	.259	.259	27	7	0	0	0	0.0	2	1	3	1	0	0	0	66	3	2	9	7.9	.972	1B-7, C-2
1984	MON N	5	.200	.200	5	1	0	0	0	0.0	0	1	0	2	0	2	0	5	0	0	0	1.7	1.000	1B-2, OF-1
3 yrs.		22	.261	.304	46	12	2	0	0	0.0	4	2	7	6	0	2	0	110	5	3	12	6.2	.975	1B-16, C-2, OF-1

Roy Johnson

JOHNSON, ROY CLEVELAND BL TR 5′ 9″ 175 lbs.
Brother of Bob Johnson.
B. Feb. 23, 1903, Pryor, Okla. D. Sept. 10, 1973, Tacoma, Wash.

Year	Team	Games	BA	SA	AB	H	2B	3B	HR	HR%	R	RBI	BB	SO	SB	Pinch Hit AB	Pinch Hit H	PO	A	E	DP	TC/G	FA	G by Pos
1929	DET A	146	.314	.475	**640**	201	**45**	14	10	1.6	128	69	67	60	20	2	0	377	25	31	5	3.0	.928	OF-146
1930		125	.275	.409	462	127	30	13	2	0.4	84	35	40	46	17	6	2	218	15	16	4	2.1	.936	OF-118
1931		151	.279	.438	621	173	37	**19**	8	1.3	107	55	72	51	33	1	1	332	25	15	8	2.5	.960	OF-150
1932	2 teams	DET A (49G –.251) BOS A (94G –.299)																						
″	total	143	.282	.451	543	153	38	6	14	2.6	103	69	64	67	20	9	4	269	9	21	0	2.2	.930	OF-133
1933	BOS A	133	.313	.466	483	151	30	7	10	2.1	88	95	55	36	13	7	1	280	14	25	3	2.6	.922	OF-125
1934		143	.320	.467	569	182	43	10	7	1.2	85	119	54	36	11	5	1	260	12	15	1	2.1	.948	OF-137
1935		145	.315	.423	553	174	33	9	3	0.5	70	66	74	34	11	3	2	267	21	17	1	2.1	.944	OF-142
1936	NY A	63	.265	.367	147	39	8	2	1	0.7	21	19	21	14	3	20	3	66	2	4	0	2.2	.944	OF-33
1937	2 teams	NY A (12G –.294) BOS N (85G –.277)																						
″	total	97	.280	.363	311	87	11	3	3	1.0	29	28	41	31	6	20	4	152	5	10	0	2.2	.940	OF-75, 3B-1
1938	BOS N	7	.172	.172	29	5	0	0	0	0.0	2	1	1	5	1	0	0	10	0	3	0	1.9	.769	OF-7
10 yrs.		1153	.296	.438	4358	1292	275	83	58	1.3	717	556	489	380	135	73	18	2231	128	157	22	2.4	.938	OF-1066, 3B-1
WORLD SERIES																								
1936	NY A	2	.000	.000	1	0	0	0	0	0.0	0	0	0	1	0	1	0	0	0	0	0	0.0	—	

Roy Johnson

JOHNSON, ROY EDWARD BL TL 6′ 5″ 205 lbs.
B. June 27, 1959, Parkin, Ark.

Year	Team	Games	BA	SA	AB	H	2B	3B	HR	HR%	R	RBI	BB	SO	SB	Pinch Hit AB	Pinch Hit H	PO	A	E	DP	TC/G	FA	G by Pos
1982	MON N	17	.219	.281	32	7	2	0	0	0.0	2	2	1	6	0	5	1	18	0	0	0	1.6	1.000	OF-11
1984		16	.152	.303	33	5	2	0	1	3.0	2	2	7	10	1	6	2	15	0	1	0	1.6	.938	OF-10
1985		3	.000	.000	5	0	0	0	0	0.0	0	0	0	3	0	0	0	0	0	0	0	0.0	.000	OF-3
3 yrs.		36	.171	.271	70	12	4	0	1	1.4	4	4	8	19	1	11	3	33	0	1	0	1.4	.971	OF-24

Spud Johnson

JOHNSON, JOHN RALPH BL TL 5′ 9″ 175 lbs.
B. 1860 Deceased.

Year	Team	Games	BA	SA	AB	H	2B	3B	HR	HR%	R	RBI	BB	SO	SB	Pinch Hit AB	Pinch Hit H	PO	A	E	DP	TC/G	FA	G by Pos
1889	COL AA	116	.283	.370	459	130	14	10	2	0.4	91	79	39	47	34	0	0	156	87	41	10	2.4	.856	OF-69, 3B-44, 1B-2, SS-1
1890		135	.346	.461	538	186	23	18	1	0.2	106		48		43	0	0	164	12	14	1	1.4	.926	OF-135
1891	CLE N	80	.257	.309	327	84	8	3	1	0.3	49	46	22	23	16	0	0	110	10	17	1	1.7	.876	OF-79, 1B-1
3 yrs.		331	.302	.392	1324	400	45	31	4	0.3	246	125	109	70	93	0	0	430	109	72	12	1.8	.882	OF-283, 3B-44, 1B-3, SS-1

Stan Johnson

JOHNSON, STANLEY LUCIUS BL TL 5′10″ 180 lbs.
B. Feb. 12, 1937, Dallas, Tex.

Year	Team	Games	BA	SA	AB	H	2B	3B	HR	HR%	R	RBI	BB	SO	SB	Pinch Hit AB	Pinch Hit H	PO	A	E	DP	TC/G	FA	G by Pos
1960	CHI A	5	.167	.667	6	1	0	0	1	16.7	1	1	0	1	0	5	1	1	0	0	0	0.5	1.000	OF-2
1961	KC A	3	.000	.000	3	0	0	0	0	0.0	1	0	2	1	0	1	0	0	0	0	0	0.0	.000	OF-2
2 yrs.		8	.111	.444	9	1	0	0	1	11.1	2	1	2	2	0	6	1	1	0	0	0	0.3	1.000	OF-4

Tim Johnson

JOHNSON, TIMOTHY EVALD BL TR 6′ 1″ 170 lbs.
B. July 22, 1949, Grand Forks, N. D.

Year	Team	Games	BA	SA	AB	H	2B	3B	HR	HR%	R	RBI	BB	SO	SB	Pinch Hit AB	Pinch Hit H	PO	A	E	DP	TC/G	FA	G by Pos
1973	MIL A	136	.213	.243	465	99	10	2	0	0.0	39	32	29	93	6	2	0	253	381	25	88	4.9	.962	SS-135
1974		93	.245	.331	245	60	7	7	0	0.0	25	25	11	48	4	4	1	139	230	9	51	4.1	.976	SS-64, 2B-26, DH-1, OF-1, 3B-1
1975		38	.141	.153	85	12	1	0	0	0.0	6	2	6	17	3	5	2	38	63	5	8	2.9	.953	2B-11, 3B-11, SS-10, DH-3, 1B-2
1976		105	.275	.311	273	75	4	3	0	0.0	25	14	19	32	4	1	0	167	238	8	42	3.5	.981	2B-100, 3B-17, SS-1, 1B-1
1977		30	.061	.091	33	2	1	0	0	0.0	5	2	5	10	1	10	1	17	19	2	5	1.5	.947	2B-10, SS-6, DH-4, 3B-4, OF-1
1978	2 teams	MIL A (3G –.000) TOR A (68G –.241)																						
″	total	71	.232	.256	82	19	2	0	0	0.0	10	3	10	16	0	4	0	38	92	2	17	2.1	.985	SS-51, 2B-13
1979	TOR A	43	.186	.233	86	16	2	1	0	0.0	6	6	8	15	0	1	0	91	70	7	24	4.1	.958	2B-25, 3B-9, 1B-7
7 yrs.		516	.223	.265	1269	283	27	13	0	0.0	116	84	88	231	18	27	4	743	1093	58	235	3.7	.969	SS-267, 2B-185, 3B-42, 1B-10, DH-8, OF-2

Tony Johnson

JOHNSON, ANTHONY CLAIR BR TR 6′ 3″ 195 lbs.
B. June 23, 1956, Memphis, Tenn.

Year	Team	Games	BA	SA	AB	H	2B	3B	HR	HR%	R	RBI	BB	SO	SB	Pinch Hit AB	Pinch Hit H	PO	A	E	DP	TC/G	FA	G by Pos
1981	MON N	2	.000	.000	1	0	0	0	0	0.0	0	0	0	0	0	0	0	0	0	0	0	0.0	.000	OF-1
1982	TOR A	70	.235	.367	98	23	2	1	3	3.1	17	14	11	26	3	10	3	45	2	1	0	0.9	.979	OF-28, DH-28
2 yrs.		72	.232	.364	99	23	2	1	3	3.0	17	14	11	26	3	10	3	45	2	1	0	0.8	.979	OF-29, DH-28

Wallace Johnson

JOHNSON, WALLACE DARNELL BB TR 6′ 173 lbs.
B. Dec. 25, 1956, Gary, Ind.

Year	Team	Games	BA	SA	AB	H	2B	3B	HR	HR%	R	RBI	BB	SO	SB	Pinch Hit AB	Pinch Hit H	PO	A	E	DP	TC/G	FA	G by Pos
1981	MON N	11	.222	.444	9	2	0	1	0	0.0	1	3	1	1	1	7	2	1	2	0	1	3.0	1.000	2B-1
1982		36	.193	.263	57	11	0	2	0	0.0	5	2	5	5	4	21	4	22	18	2	4	3.2	.952	2B-13
1983	2 teams	MON N (3G –.500) SF N (7G –.125)																						
″	total	10	.200	.200	10	2	0	0	0	0.0	1	1	1	0	1	7	1	3	2	0	1	5.0	1.000	2B-1
1984	MON N	17	.208	.208	24	5	0	0	0	0.0	3	4	5	4	0	10	3	27	3	1	3	7.8	.968	1B-4
1986		61	.283	.346	127	36	3	1	1	0.8	13	10	7	9	6	37	11	204	17	2	15	8.3	.991	1B-27
1987		75	.247	.341	85	21	5	0	1	1.2	7	14	7	6	5	61	**17**	68	2	2	4	8.0	.972	1B-9
1988		86	.309	.383	94	29	5	1	0	0.0	7	3	12	15	0	**64**	**22**	80	9	1	3	6.4	.989	1B-13, 2B-1
1989		85	.272	.368	114	31	3	1	2	1.8	9	17	7	12	1	59	14	130	7	4	8	7.8	.972	1B-18
1990		47	.163	.245	49	8	1	0	1	2.0	6	5	7	6	1	34	4	39	0	0	7	5.6	1.000	1B-7
9 yrs.		428	.255	.332	569	145	17	6	5	0.9	52	59	52	58	19	300	78	574	60	12	46	6.9	.981	1B-78, 2B-16
DIVISIONAL PLAYOFF SERIES																								
1981	MON N	2	.500	.500	2	1	0	0	0	0.0	0	1	0	0	0	2	1	0	0	0	0	0.0	—	

Walter Johnson

JOHNSON, WALTER PERRY (Barney, The Big Train) BR TR 6′ 1″ 200 lbs.
B. Nov. 6, 1887, Humboldt, Kans. D. Dec. 10, 1946, Washington, D. C.
Manager 1929–35.
Hall of Fame 1936.

Year	Team	Games	BA	SA	AB	H	2B	3B	HR	HR%	R	RBI	BB	SO	SB	Pinch Hit AB	Pinch Hit H	PO	A	E	DP	TC/G	FA	G by Pos
1907	WAS A	14	.111	.167	36	4	0	1	0	0.0	3	1	1		0	0	0	5	20	3	1	2.0	.893	P-14
1908		36	.165	.253	79	13	3	2	0	0.0	7	5	6		0	0	0	4	56	4	3	1.8	.938	P-36
1909		40	.129	.188	101	13	3	0	1	1.0	6	6	1		0	0	0	15	73	7	2	2.4	.926	P-40
1910		45	.175	.277	137	24	6	1	2	1.5	14	12	4		2	0	0	23	90	6	3	2.6	.950	P-45
1911		42	.234	.344	128	30	5	3	1	0.8	18	15	0		1	2	1	14	95	4	8	2.8	.965	P-40
1912		55	.264	.403	144	38	6	4	2	1.4	16	20	7		2	5	0	15	93	4	4	2.2	.964	P-50
1913		54	.261	.433	134	35	5	6	2	1.5	12	14	5	14	2	5	2	22	82	0	7	2.2	1.000	P-47, OF-1
1914		55	.221	.331	136	30	4	1	3	2.2	23	16	10	27	2	3	0	30	102	5	6	2.6	.964	P-51, OF-1
1915		64	.231	.374	147	34	7	4	2	1.4	14	17	8	34	0	12	2	23	95	6	7	2.4	.952	P-47, OF-4
1916		58	.232	.324	142	33	2	4	1	0.7	14	7	11	28	0	9	2	17	72	6	2	2.0	.937	P-48
1917		57	.254	.362	130	33	12	1	0	0.0	15	15	9	30	1	9	1	16	82	0	2	2.1	1.000	P-47
1918		65	.267	.367	150	40	4	4	1	0.7	10	18	9	18	2	20	5	22	71	2	4	2.2	.979	P-39, OF-4
1919		56	.192	.272	125	24	1	3	1	0.8	13	8	12	17	1	14	3	23	69	1	5	2.2	.989	P-39, OF-3
1920		35	.261	.406	69	18	1	3	1	1.4	7	8	6	12	0	11	2	7	28	3	0	1.7	.921	P-21, OF-2
1921		38	.270	.333	111	30	7	0	0	0.0	10	10	6	14	0	2	0	4	51	1	1	1.6	.982	P-35
1922		43	.204	.259	108	22	3	0	1	0.9	8	15	2	12	0	2	0	11	66	0	2	1.9	1.000	P-41
1923		43	.194	.290	93	18	3	3	0	0.0	11	13	4	15	0	0	0	13	51	2	7	1.5	.970	P-43
1924		39	.283	.389	113	32	9	0	1	0.9	18	14	3	11	0	1	0	9	53	0	2	1.6	1.000	P-38
1925		36	.433	.577	97	42	6	1	2	2.1	12	20	3	6	0	6	2	5	37	0	2	1.4	1.000	P-30
1926		35	.194	.272	103	20	5	0	1	1.0	6	12	3	11	0	2	0	11	38	1	1	1.5	.980	P-33
1927		26	.348	.522	46	16	2	0	2	4.3	6	10	3	4	0	7	1	5	25	0	3	1.7	1.000	P-18
21 yrs.		936	.236	.342	2329	549	94	41	24	1.0	243	256	113	253	13	110	21	294	1349	55	72	2.1	.968	P-802, OF-15
WORLD SERIES																								
1924	WAS A	3	.111	.111	9	1	0	0	0	0.0	0	0	0	0	0	0	0	1	4	1	2	2.0	.833	P-3
1925		3	.091	.091	11	1	0	0	0	0.0	0	0	0	3	0	0	0	0	4	0	0	1.3	1.000	P-3
2 yrs.		6	.100	.100	20	2	0	0	0	0.0	0	0	0	3	0	0	0	1	8	1	2	1.7	.900	P-6

Dick Johnston

JOHNSTON, RICHARD FREDERICK BR TR 5′ 8″ 155 lbs.
B. Apr. 6, 1863, Kingston, N. Y. D. Apr. 4, 1934, Detroit, Mich.

Year	Team	Games	BA	SA	AB	H	2B	3B	HR	HR%	R	RBI	BB	SO	SB	Pinch Hit AB	Pinch Hit H	PO	A	E	DP	TC/G	FA	G by Pos
1884	RIC AA	39	.281	.425	146	41	5	5	2	1.4	23		2			0	0	87	13	17	3	3.0	.855	OF-37, SS-2
1885	BOS N	26	.234	.369	111	26	6	3	1	0.9	17	23	0	15		0	0	40	8	9	2	2.2	.842	OF-26
1886		109	.240	.334	413	99	18	9	1	0.2	48	57	3	70		0	0	243	29	33	4	2.8	.892	OF-109
1887		127	.258	.393	507	131	13	20	5	1.0	87	77	16	35	52	0	0	339	34	27	9	3.1	.933	OF-127
1888		135	.296	.472	**585**	173	31	**18**	12	2.1	102	68	15	33	35	0	0	286	30	36	3	2.6	.898	OF-135
1889		132	.228	.301	539	123	16	4	5	0.9	80	67	41	60	34	0	0	267	22	26	6	2.4	.917	OF-132
1890	2 teams	BOS P (2G –.111) NY P (77G –.242)																						
″	total	79	.238	.321	315	75	9	7	1	0.3	37	43	18	26	7	0	0	169	19	22	3	2.6	.895	OF-78, SS-2
1891	CIN AA	99	.221	.309	376	83	11	2	6	1.6	59	51	38	44	12	0	0	193	20	25	4	2.4	.895	OF-99
8 yrs.		746	.251	.366	2992	751	109	68	33	1.1	453	386	133	283	140	0	0	1624	175	195	34	2.7	.902	OF-743, SS-4

Doc Johnston

JOHNSTON, WHEELER ROGER BL TL 6′ 170 lbs.
Brother of Jimmy Johnston.
B. Sept. 9, 1887, Cleveland, Tenn. D. Feb. 17, 1961, Chattanooga, Tenn.

Year	Team	Games	BA	SA	AB	H	2B	3B	HR	HR%	R	RBI	BB	SO	SB	Pinch Hit AB	Pinch Hit H	PO	A	E	DP	TC/G	FA	G by Pos
1909	CIN N	3	.000	.000	10	0	0	0	0	0.0	1	1	0		0	0	0	25	2	0	0	9.0	1.000	1B-3
1912	CLE A	43	.280	.390	164	46	7	4	1	0.6	22	11	11		8	2	0	330	17	3	27	8.5	.991	1B-41
1913		133	.255	.347	530	135	19	12	2	0.4	74	39	35	65	19	0	0	1319	76	15	76	10.6	.989	1B-133
1914		103	.244	.294	340	83	15	1	0	0.0	43	23	28	46	14	7	2	853	36	12	43	9.9	.987	1B-89, OF-2
1915	PIT N	147	.265	.372	543	144	19	12	5	0.9	71	64	38	40	26	0	0	1453	48	13	65	10.3	.991	1B-147
1916		114	.213	.287	404	86	10	10	0	0.0	33	39	20	42	17	3	0	1042	47	14	44	10.0	.987	1B-110
1918	CLE A	74	.227	.286	273	62	12	2	0	0.0	30	25	26	19	12	1	0	738	40	9	25	10.8	.989	1B-73
1919		102	.305	.384	331	101	17	3	1	0.3	42	33	25	18	21	4	1	957	57	16	57	10.5	.984	1B-98
1920		147	.292	.385	535	156	24	10	2	0.4	68	71	28	32	13	0	0	1427	91	12	83	10.4	.992	1B-147
1921		118	.297	.401	384	114	20	7	2	0.5	53	44	29	15	2	3	1	960	62	12	72	8.9	.988	1B-116
1922	PHI A	71	.250	.358	260	65	11	7	1	0.4	41	29	24	15	7	6	0	641	31	7	34	10.4	.990	1B-65
11 yrs.		1055	.263	.351	3774	992	154	68	14	0.4	478	379	264	292	139	26	4	9745	507	113	526	10.1	.989	1B-1022, OF-2
WORLD SERIES																								
1920	CLE A	5	.273	.273	11	3	0	0	0	0.0	1	0	2	1	1	1	0	27	6	0	3	6.6	1.000	1B-5

Fred Johnston

JOHNSTON, WILFRED IVY (Red Top) BR TR 5′10½″ 160 lbs.
B. July 9, 1899, Charlotte, N. C. D. July 14, 1959, Tyler, Tex.

Year	Team	Games	BA	SA	AB	H	2B	3B	HR	HR%	R	RBI	BB	SO	SB	Pinch Hit AB	Pinch Hit H	PO	A	E	DP	TC/G	FA	G by Pos
1924	BKN N	4	.250	.250	4	1	0	0	0	0.0	1	0	0	1	0	0	0	1	2	1	0	2.0	.750	3B-1, 2B-1

Greg Johnston

JOHNSTON, GREGORY BERNARD BL TL 6′ 175 lbs.
B. Feb. 12, 1955, Los Angeles, Calif.

Year	Team		Games	BA	SA	AB	H	2B	3B	HR	HR%	R	RBI	BB	SO	SB	Pinch Hit AB	Pinch Hit H	PO	A	E	DP	TC/G	FA	G by Pos
1979	SF	N	42	.203	.270	74	15	2	0	1	1.4	5	7	2	17	0	27	6	27	1	1	0	1.6	.966	OF-18
1980	MIN	A	14	.185	.296	27	5	3	0	0	0.0	3	1	2	4	0	3	1	25	0	0	0	1.8	1.000	OF-14
1981			7	.125	.125	16	2	0	0	0	0.0	2	0	2	5	0	0	0	11	1	0	1	2.0	1.000	OF-6
3 yrs.			63	.188	.256	117	22	5	0	1	0.9	10	8	6	26	0	30	7	63	2	1	1	1.7	.985	OF-38

Jimmy Johnston

JOHNSTON, JAMES HARLE BR TR 5′10″ 160 lbs.
Brother of Doc Johnston.
B. Dec. 10, 1889, Cleveland, Tenn. D. Feb. 14, 1967, Chattanooga, Tenn.

Year	Team		Games	BA	SA	AB	H	2B	3B	HR	HR%	R	RBI	BB	SO	SB	Pinch Hit AB	Pinch Hit H	PO	A	E	DP	TC/G	FA	G by Pos
1911	CHI	A	1	.000	.000	2	0	0	0	0	0.0	0	2	0		0	0	0	1	0	0	0	1.0	1.000	OF-1
1914	CHI	N	50	.228	.327	101	23	3	2	1	1.0	9	8	4	9	3	11	2	69	16	8	3	2.9	.914	OF-28, 2B-4
1916	BKN	N	118	.252	.327	425	107	13	8	1	0.2	58	26	35	38	22	1	1	224	16	9	3	2.3	.964	OF-106
1917			103	.270	.324	330	89	10	4	0	0.0	33	25	23	28	16	8	1	269	37	17	5	2.8	.947	OF-92, 1B-14, SS-4, 2B-3, 3B-3
1918			123	.281	.347	484	136	16	8	0	0.0	54	27	33	31	22	1	0	382	48	13	13	3.6	.971	OF-96, 1B-21, 3B-4, 2B-1
1919			117	.281	.336	405	114	11	4	1	0.2	56	23	29	26	11	9	1	201	302	20	32	5.0	.962	2B-87, OF-14, 1B-2, SS-1
1920			155	.291	.361	635	185	17	12	1	0.2	87	52	43	23	19	0	0	171	289	32	22	3.2	.935	3B-146, OF-7, SS-3
1921			152	.325	.460	624	203	41	14	5	0.8	104	56	45	26	28	0	0	168	321	35	37	3.4	.933	3B-150, SS-3
1922			138	.319	.400	567	181	20	7	4	0.7	110	49	38	17	18	0	0	300	434	42	71	5.6	.946	2B-62, SS-50, 3B-26
1923			151	.325	.426	625	203	29	11	4	0.6	111	60	53	15	16	1	0	369	532	51	63	6.3	.946	2B-84, SS-52, 3B-14
1924			86	.298	.365	315	94	11	2	2	0.6	51	29	27	10	5	7	4	171	219	24	32	5.3	.942	SS-63, 3B-10, 1B-4, OF-1
1925			123	.297	.355	431	128	13	3	2	0.5	63	43	45	15	7	12	4	189	119	34	15	3.1	.901	3B-81, OF-20, 1B-8, SS-2
1926	2 teams	BOS N (23G –.246) NY N (37G –.232)																							
″	total		60	.238	.270	126	30	1	0	1	0.8	18	10	16	8	2	25	5	25	24	5	3	1.7	.907	OF-15, 3B-14, 2B-2
13 yrs.			1377	.294	.374	5070	1493	185	75	22	0.4	754	410	391	246	169	75	18	2539	2357	290	299	4.0	.944	3B-448, OF-380, 2B-243, SS-178, 1B-49
WORLD SERIES																									
1916	BKN	N	3	.300	.500	10	3	0	1	0	0.0	1	0	1	0	0	1	1	1	0	1	0	1.0	.500	OF-2
1920			4	.214	.214	14	3	0	0	0	0.0	2	0	0	2	1	0	0	2	8	0	1	2.5	1.000	3B-4
2 yrs.			7	.250	.333	24	6	0	1	0	0.0	3	0	1	2	1	1	1	3	8	1	1	2.0	.917	3B-4, OF-2

Johnny Johnston

JOHNSTON, JOHN THOMAS BL TR 5′11″ 172 lbs.
B. Mar. 28, 1890, Longview, Tex. D. Mar. 7, 1940, San Diego, Calif.

Year	Team		Games	BA	SA	AB	H	2B	3B	HR	HR%	R	RBI	BB	SO	SB	Pinch Hit AB	Pinch Hit H	PO	A	E	DP	TC/G	FA	G by Pos
1913	STL	A	109	.224	.297	380	85	14	4	2	0.5	37	27	42	51	11	3	0	222	23	9	3	2.4	.965	OF-106

Rex Johnston

JOHNSTON, REX DAVID BB TR 6′ 1½″ 202 lbs.
B. Nov. 8, 1937, Colton, Calif.

Year	Team		Games	BA	SA	AB	H	2B	3B	HR	HR%	R	RBI	BB	SO	SB	Pinch Hit AB	Pinch Hit H	PO	A	E	DP	TC/G	FA	G by Pos
1964	PIT	N	14	.000	.000	7	0	0	0	0	0.0	1	0	3	0	0	3	0	2	0	0	0	0.3	1.000	OF-8

Jay Johnstone

JOHNSTONE, JOHN WILLIAM BL TR 6′ 1″ 175 lbs.
B. Nov. 20, 1945, Manchester, Conn. BB 1966

Year	Team		Games	BA	SA	AB	H	2B	3B	HR	HR%	R	RBI	BB	SO	SB	Pinch Hit AB	Pinch Hit H	PO	A	E	DP	TC/G	FA	G by Pos
1966	CAL	A	61	.264	.378	254	67	12	4	3	1.2	35	17	11	36	3	0	0	114	2	3	1	2.0	.975	OF-61
1967			79	.209	.274	230	48	7	1	2	0.9	18	10	5	37	3	21	5	141	3	4	0	2.3	.973	OF-63
1968			41	.261	.313	115	30	4	1	0	0.0	11	3	7	15	2	8	0	58	4	1	1	2.2	.984	OF-29
1969			148	.270	.381	540	146	20	5	10	1.9	64	59	38	75	3	4	1	331	12	6	4	2.4	.983	OF-144
1970			119	.237	.403	320	76	10	5	11	3.4	34	39	24	53	1	23	5	200	7	4	3	2.1	.981	OF-100
1971	CHI	A	124	.260	.425	388	101	14	1	16	4.1	53	40	38	50	10	11	3	232	9	8	1	2.1	.968	OF-119
1972			113	.188	.268	261	49	9	0	4	1.5	27	17	25	42	2	19	6	154	5	2	1	1.7	.988	OF-97
1973	OAK	A	23	.107	.143	28	3	1	0	0	0.0	1	3	2	4	0	11	0	7	0	0	0	0.5	1.000	OF-7, DH-4, 2B-2
1974	PHI	N	64	.295	.475	200	59	10	4	6	3.0	30	30	24	28	5	6	4	88	4	3	1	1.6	.968	OF-59
1975			122	.329	.454	350	115	19	2	7	2.0	50	54	42	39	7	25	10	152	10	4	3	1.6	.976	OF-101
1976			129	.318	.457	440	140	38	4	5	1.1	62	53	41	39	5	12	2	293	10	8	2	2.4	.974	OF-122, 1B-6
1977			112	.284	.479	363	103	18	4	15	4.1	64	59	38	38	3	14	5	294	15	1	17	2.8	.997	OF-91, 1B-19
1978	2 teams	PHI N (35G –.179) NY A (36G –.262)																							
″	total		71	.223	.264	121	27	2	0	1	0.8	9	10	10	19	0	28	2	108	7	1	9	2.8	.991	OF-29, 1B-8, DH-5
1979	2 teams	NY A (23G –.208) SD N (75G –.294)																							
″	total		98	.277	.341	249	69	9	2	1	0.4	17	39	20	28	2	25	6	217	18	4	10	2.7	.983	OF-64, 1B-22, DH-3
1980	LA	N	109	.307	.406	251	77	15	2	2	0.8	31	20	24	29	3	41	11	100	9	4	0	1.9	.965	OF-61
1981			61	.205	.349	83	17	3	0	3	3.6	8	6	7	13	0	38	11	33	4	1	2	2.1	.974	OF-16, 1B-2
1982	2 teams	LA N (21G –.077) CHI N (98G –.249)																							
″	total		119	.241	.404	282	68	14	1	10	3.5	40	45	45	43	0	26	3	154	8	3	0	1.9	.982	OF-86
1983	CHI	N	86	.257	.436	140	36	7	0	6	4.3	16	22	20	24	1	38	6	55	3	4	1	1.4	.935	OF-44
1984			52	.288	.370	73	21	2	2	0	0.0	8	3	7	18	0	39	10	12	0	0	0	0.8	1.000	OF-15
1985	LA	N	17	.133	.200	15	2	1	0	0	0.0	0	2	1	2	0	15	2	0	0	0	0	0.0	—	
20 yrs.			1748	.267	.394	4703	1254	215	38	102	2.2	578	531	429	632	50	404	92	2743	130	61	56	2.1	.979	OF-1308, 1B-57, DH-12, 2B-2
DIVISIONAL PLAYOFF SERIES																									
1981	LA	N	1	.000	.000	1	0	0	0	0	0.0	0	0	0	0	0	1	0	0	0	0	0	0.0	—	
LEAGUE CHAMPIONSHIP SERIES																									
1976	PHI	N	3	.778	1.111	9	7	1	1	0	0.0	1	2	1	0	0	1	1	3	0	0	0	1.5	1.000	OF-2
1977			2	.200	.200	5	1	0	0	0	0.0	0	0	0	1	0	1	0	4	0	0	0	2.0	1.000	OF-2
1981	LA	N	2	.000	.000	2	0	0	0	0	0.0	0	0	0	0	0	2	0	0	0	0	0	0.0	—	
1985			1	.000	.000	1	0	0	0	0	0.0	0	0	0	0	0	1	0	0	0	0	0	0.0	—	
4 yrs.			8	.471	.647	17	8	1	1	0	0.0	1	2	1	1	0	5	1	7	0	0	0	1.8	1.000	OF-4
WORLD SERIES																									
1978	NY	A	2	—	—	0	0	0	0	0	—	0	0	0	0	0	0	0	1	0	0	0	0.5	1.000	OF-2
1981	LA	N	3	.667	1.667	3	2	0	0	1	33.3	1	3	0	0	0	3	2	0	0	0	0	0.0	—	
2 yrs.			5	.667	1.667	3	2	0	0	1	33.3	1	3	0	0	0	3	2	1	0	0	0	0.5	1.000	OF-2

Stan Jok

JOK, STANLEY EDWARD (Tucker) BR TR 6′ 190 lbs.
B. May 3, 1926, Buffalo, N. Y. D. Mar. 6, 1972, Buffalo, N. Y.

Year	Team	Games	BA	SA	AB	H	2B	3B	HR	HR%	R	RBI	BB	SO	SB	Pinch Hit AB	Pinch Hit H	PO	A	E	DP	TC/G	FA	G by Pos
1954	**2 teams**	**PHI N** (3G –.000) **CHI A** (3G –.167)																						
″	**total**	6	.133	.133	15	2	0	0	0	0.0	1	2	1	4	0	3	0	3	7	0	1	3.3	1.000	3B-3
1955	**CHI A**	6	.250	1.000	4	1	0	0	1	25.0	3	2	1	1	0	0	0	2	4	1	0	1.8	.857	3B-3, OF-1
2 yrs.		12	.158	.316	19	3	0	0	1	5.3	4	4	2	5	0	3	0	5	11	1	1	2.4	.941	3B-6, OF-1

Smead Jolley

JOLLEY, SMEAD POWELL (Smudge) BL TR 6′ 3½″ 210 lbs.
B. Jan. 14, 1902, Wesson, Ark. D. Nov. 17, 1991, Alameda, Calif.

Year	Team	Games	BA	SA	AB	H	2B	3B	HR	HR%	R	RBI	BB	SO	SB	Pinch Hit AB	Pinch Hit H	PO	A	E	DP	TC/G	FA	G by Pos
1930	**CHI A**	152	.313	.492	616	193	38	12	16	2.6	76	114	28	52	3	1	1	249	17	14	4	1.9	.950	OF-151
1931		54	.300	.482	110	33	11	0	3	2.7	5	28	7	4	0	30	**14**	29	1	5	1	1.5	.857	OF-23
1932	**2 teams**	**CHI A** (12G –.357) **BOS A** (137G –.309)																						
″	**total**	149	.312	.476	573	179	30	5	18	3.1	60	106	30	29	1	6	1	266	15	16	3	2.1	.946	OF-137, C-6
1933	**BOS A**	118	.282	.445	411	116	32	4	9	2.2	47	65	24	20	1	15	4	178	12	9	3	2.0	.955	OF-102
4 yrs.		473	.305	.475	1710	521	111	21	46	2.7	188	313	89	105	5	52	20	722	45	44	11	1.9	.946	OF-413, C-6

Jones

JONES
B. Johnstown, Pa. Deceased.

Year	Team	Games	BA	SA	AB	H	2B	3B	HR	HR%	R	RBI	BB	SO	SB	Pinch Hit AB	Pinch Hit H	PO	A	E	DP	TC/G	FA	G by Pos
1884	**WAS AA**	4	.294	.294	17	5	0	0	0	0.0	2		1		0	0	0	6	0	0	0	1.5	1.000	OF-4

Jones

JONES
Deceased.

Year	Team	Games	BA	SA	AB	H	2B	3B	HR	HR%	R	RBI	BB	SO	SB	Pinch Hit AB	Pinch Hit H	PO	A	E	DP	TC/G	FA	G by Pos
1885	**NY AA**	1	.250	.250	4	1	0	0	0	0.0	0		0			0	0	2	4	0	0	6.0	1.000	3B-1

Bill Jones

JONES, WILLIAM
B. Syracuse, N. Y.

Year	Team	Games	BA	SA	AB	H	2B	3B	HR	HR%	R	RBI	BB	SO	SB	Pinch Hit AB	Pinch Hit H	PO	A	E	DP	TC/G	FA	G by Pos
1882	**BAL AA**	4	.067	.067	15	1	0	0	0	0.0	1		0			0	0	9	5	2	0	4.0	.875	OF-2, C-2
1884	**PHI U**	4	.143	.143	14	2	0	0	0	0.0	2		1			0	0	23	4	7	1	6.8	.794	C-4, OF-1
2 yrs.		8	.103	.103	29	3	0	0	0	0.0	3		1			0	0	32	9	9	1	5.6	.820	C-6, OF-3

Bill Jones

JONES, WILLIAM DENNIS (Midget) BL TR 5′ 6½″ 157 lbs.
B. Apr. 8, 1887, Hartland, N. B., Canada D. Oct. 10, 1946, Boston, Mass.

Year	Team	Games	BA	SA	AB	H	2B	3B	HR	HR%	R	RBI	BB	SO	SB	Pinch Hit AB	Pinch Hit H	PO	A	E	DP	TC/G	FA	G by Pos
1911	**BOS N**	24	.216	.294	51	11	2	1	0	0.0	6	3	15	7	1	3	1	36	3	6	0	2.5	.867	OF-18
1912		3	.500	.500	2	1	0	0	0	0.0	0	2	0	1	0	2	1	0	0	0	0	0.0	—	
2 yrs.		27	.226	.302	53	12	2	1	0	0.0	6	5	15	8	1	5	2	36	3	6	0	2.5	.867	OF-18

Binky Jones

JONES, JOHN JOSEPH BR TR 5′ 9″ 154 lbs.
B. July 11, 1899, St. Louis, Mo. D. May 13, 1961, St. Louis, Mo.

Year	Team	Games	BA	SA	AB	H	2B	3B	HR	HR%	R	RBI	BB	SO	SB	Pinch Hit AB	Pinch Hit H	PO	A	E	DP	TC/G	FA	G by Pos
1924	**BKN N**	10	.108	.135	37	4	1	0	0	0.0	0	2	0	3	0	0	0	17	27	5	6	4.9	.898	SS-10

Bob Jones

JONES, ROBERT WALTER (Ducky) BL TR 6′ 170 lbs.
B. Dec. 2, 1889, Clayton, Calif. D. Aug. 30, 1964, San Diego, Calif.

Year	Team	Games	BA	SA	AB	H	2B	3B	HR	HR%	R	RBI	BB	SO	SB	Pinch Hit AB	Pinch Hit H	PO	A	E	DP	TC/G	FA	G by Pos
1917	**DET A**	46	.156	.221	77	12	1	2	0	0.0	16	2	4	8	3	10	2	26	57	6	2	3.4	.933	2B-18, 3B-8
1918		74	.275	.352	287	79	14	4	0	0.0	43	21	17	16	7	3	1	143	83	11	8	3.4	.954	3B-63, 1B-6
1919		127	.260	.335	439	114	18	6	1	0.2	37	57	34	39	11	0	0	134	219	21	14	2.9	.944	3B-127
1920		81	.249	.306	265	66	6	3	1	0.4	35	18	22	13	3	5	0	90	158	15	9	3.6	.943	3B-67, 2B-5, SS-1
1921		141	.303	.383	554	168	23	9	1	0.2	82	72	37	24	8	0	0	194	324	27	12	3.9	.950	3B-141
1922		124	.257	.325	455	117	10	6	3	0.7	65	44	36	18	8	3	0	161	267	17	22	3.7	.962	3B-119
1923		100	.250	.320	372	93	15	4	1	0.3	51	40	29	13	7	0	0	109	224	16	17	3.6	.954	3B-97
1924		110	.272	.361	393	107	27	4	0	0.0	52	47	20	20	1	3	1	108	196	14	12	3.0	.956	3B-106
1925		50	.236	.277	148	35	6	0	0	0.0	18	15	9	5	1	3	1	43	91	2	5	3.0	.985	3B-46
9 yrs.		853	.265	.337	2990	791	120	38	7	0.2	399	316	208	156	49	27	5	1008	1619	129	101	3.4	.953	3B-774, 2B-23, 1B-6, SS-1

Bobby Jones

JONES, ROBERT OLIVER BL TL 6′ 2″ 195 lbs.
B. Oct. 11, 1949, Elkton, Md.

Year	Team	Games	BA	SA	AB	H	2B	3B	HR	HR%	R	RBI	BB	SO	SB	Pinch Hit AB	Pinch Hit H	PO	A	E	DP	TC/G	FA	G by Pos
1974	**TEX A**	2	.000	.000	5	0	0	0	0	0.0	0	0	0	1	0	0	0	5	0	0	0	2.5	1.000	OF-2
1975		9	.091	.091	11	1	0	0	0	0.0	2	0	3	3	0	1	0	6	0	0	0	1.0	1.000	OF-5, DH-1
1976	**CAL A**	78	.211	.355	166	35	6	0	6	3.6	22	17	14	30	3	17	2	98	6	1	0	1.6	.990	OF-62, DH-2
1977		14	.176	.353	17	3	0	0	1	5.9	3	3	4	5	0	6	1	0	0	0	0	0.0	.000	DH-6
1981	**TEX A**	10	.265	.559	34	9	1	0	3	8.8	4	7	1	7	0	0	0	20	4	0	0	2.4	1.000	OF-10
1983		41	.222	.319	72	16	4	0	1	1.4	5	11	5	17	0	23	4	24	0	0	0	1.0	1.000	DH-11, OF-11, 1B-1
1984		64	.259	.371	143	37	4	0	4	2.8	14	22	10	19	1	24	5	139	7	1	8	3.6	.993	OF-22, 1B-15, DH-4
1985		83	.224	.351	134	30	2	0	5	3.7	14	23	11	30	1	42	10	44	0	0	1	1.0	1.000	OF-30, DH-10, 1B-4
1986		13	.095	.095	21	2	0	0	0	0.0	1	3	2	5	0	2	1	29	1	1	2	2.8	.968	OF-9, 1B-2
9 yrs.		314	.221	.348	603	133	17	0	20	3.3	65	86	50	117	5	115	23	365	18	3	11	1.9	.992	OF-151, DH-34, 1B-22

Charley Jones

JONES, CHARLES WESLEY (Long Charley) BR TR 5′11½″ 202 lbs.
Born Benjamin Wesley Rippay.
B. Apr. 3, 1850, Alamance County, N. C. Deceased.

Year	Team	Games	BA	SA	AB	H	2B	3B	HR	HR%	R	RBI	BB	SO	SB	Pinch Hit AB	Pinch Hit H	PO	A	E	DP	TC/G	FA	G by Pos
1876	**CIN N**	64	.286	.420	276	79	17	4	4	1.4	40	38	7	17		0	0	151	11	27	2	3.0	.857	OF-64
1877	**3 teams**	**CIN N** (17G –.304) **CHI N** (2G –.375) **CIN N** (38G –.313)																						
″	**total**	57	.313	.471	240	75	12	10	2	0.8	53	38	15	25		0	0	238	15	37	6	5.0	.872	OF-48, 1B-10
1878	**CIN N**	61	.310	.441	261	81	11	7	3	1.1	50	39	4	17		0	0	120	9	15	1	2.4	.896	OF-61
1879	**BOS N**	83	.315	.510	355	112	22	10	**9**	**2.5**	**85**	**62**	**29**	38		0	0	162	20	13	1	2.3	.933	OF-83
1880		66	.300	.429	280	84	15	3	5	**1.8**	44	38	11	27		0	0	108	11	25	3	2.2	.826	OF-66
1883	**CIN AA**	90	.294	.473	391	115	15	11	11	2.8	84		20			0	0	172	12	26	1	2.3	.876	OF-90
1884		113	.314	.470	472	148	19	17	7	1.5	117		37			0	0	207	12	28	0	2.2	.887	OF-113
1885		112	.322	.456	**487**	157	19	17	4	0.8	108		21			0	0	214	22	29	6	2.4	.891	OF-112
1886		127	.270	.388	500	135	22	11	5	1.0	87		61			0	0	217	23	33	1	2.1	.879	OF-127
1887	**2 teams**	**CIN AA** (41G –.314) **NY AA** (62G –.255)																						
″	**total**	103	.278	.395	400	111	18	7	5	1.3	58		31		15	0	0	188	25	23	8	2.2	.903	OF-103, P-2, 1B-1
1888	**KC AA**	6	.160	.240	25	4	0	1	0	0.0	2	5	1		1	0	0	8	1	3	0	2.0	.750	OF-6
11 yrs.		882	.299	.443	3687	1101	170	98	55	1.5	728	220	237	124	16	0	0	1785	161	259	29	2.5	.883	OF-873, 1B-11, P-2

Charlie Jones

JONES, CHARLES C. (Casey)
B. June 2, 1876, Butler, Pa. D. Apr. 2, 1947, Lusten, Minn.
BR TR 6′ 1″

Year	Team	Games	BA	SA	AB	H	2B	3B	HR	HR%	R	RBI	BB	SO	SB	Pinch Hit AB	Pinch Hit H	PO	A	E	DP	TC/G	FA	G by Pos
1901	BOS A	10	.146	.195	41	6	2	0	0	0.0	6	6	1		2	0	0	13	0	1	0	1.4	.929	OF-10
1905	WAS A	142	.208	.267	544	113	18	4	2	0.4	68	41	31		24	0	0	240	24	11	6	1.9	.960	OF-142
1906		131	.241	.326	497	120	11	11	3	0.6	56	42	24		34	2	0	282	20	12	7	2.4	.962	OF-128, 2B-1
1907		121	.265	.343	437	116	14	10	0	0.0	48	37	22		26	2	0	267	14	8	4	2.4	.972	OF-111, 2B-5, 1B-4, SS-2
1908	STL A	74	.232	.289	263	61	11	2	0	0.0	37	17	14		14	2	0	116	13	5	2	1.9	.963	OF-72
5 yrs.		478	.233	.304	1782	416	56	27	5	0.3	215	143	92		100	6	0	918	71	37	19	2.2	.964	OF-463, 2B-6, 1B-4, SS-2

Charlie Jones

JONES, CHARLES F.
B. New York, N. Y. Deceased.

Year	Team	Games	BA	SA	AB	H	2B	3B	HR	HR%	R	RBI	BB	SO	SB	Pinch Hit AB	Pinch Hit H	PO	A	E	DP	TC/G	FA	G by Pos
1884	BKN AA	25	.178	.189	90	16	1	0	0	0.0	10		5			0	0	38	49	13	5	3.8	.870	2B-13, 3B-11, OF-2

Chipper Jones

JONES, LARRY WAYNE
B. Apr. 24, 1972, Deland, Fla.
BB TR 6′ 3″ 185 lbs.

Year	Team	Games	BA	SA	AB	H	2B	3B	HR	HR%	R	RBI	BB	SO	SB	Pinch Hit AB	Pinch Hit H	PO	A	E	DP	TC/G	FA	G by Pos
1993	ATL N	8	.667	1.000	3	2	1	0	0	0.0	2	0	1	1	0	2	1	1	1	0	0	0.7	1.000	SS-3
1995		140	.265	.450	524	139	22	3	23	4.4	87	86	73	99	8	1	0	102	259	25	19	2.7	.935	3B-123, OF-20
2 yrs.		148	.268	.454	527	141	23	3	23	4.4	89	86	74	100	8	3	1	103	260	25	19	2.7	.936	3B-123, OF-20, SS-3
DIVISIONAL PLAYOFF SERIES																								
1995	ATL N	4	.389	.833	18	7	2	0	2	11.1	4	4	2	2	0	0	0	3	4	0	0	1.8	1.000	3B-4
LEAGUE CHAMPIONSHIP SERIES																								
1995	ATL N	4	.438	.625	16	7	0	0	1	6.3	3	3	3	1	1	0	0	4	13	0	2	4.3	1.000	3B-4
WORLD SERIES																								
1995	ATL N	6	.286	.429	21	6	3	0	0	0.0	3	1	4	3	0	0	0	6	12	1	1	3.2	.947	3B-6

Chris Jones

JONES, CHRISTOPHER CARLOS
B. Dec. 16, 1965, Utica, N. Y.
BR TR 6′ 2″ 200 lbs.

Year	Team	Games	BA	SA	AB	H	2B	3B	HR	HR%	R	RBI	BB	SO	SB	Pinch Hit AB	Pinch Hit H	PO	A	E	DP	TC/G	FA	G by Pos
1991	CIN N	52	.292	.416	89	26	1	2	2	2.2	14	6	2	31	2	26	8	27	1	0	0	1.1	1.000	OF-26
1992	HOU N	54	.190	.302	63	12	2	1	1	1.6	7	4	7	21	3	14	1	27	0	2	0	0.7	.931	OF-43
1993	CLR N	86	.273	.450	209	57	11	4	6	2.9	29	31	10	48	9	22	8	114	2	2	0	1.7	.983	OF-70
1994		21	.300	.400	40	12	2	1	0	0.0	6	2	2	14	0	9	1	16	0	1	0	1.2	.941	OF-14
1995	NY N	79	.280	.467	182	51	6	2	8	4.4	33	31	13	45	2	25	10	122	6	2	4	2.3	.985	OF-52, 1B-5
5 yrs.		292	.271	.431	583	158	22	10	17	2.9	89	74	34	159	16	96	28	306	9	7	4	1.5	.978	OF-205, 1B-5

Chris Jones

JONES, CHRISTOPHER DALE
B. July 13, 1957, Los Angeles, Calif.
BL TL 6′ 183 lbs.

Year	Team	Games	BA	SA	AB	H	2B	3B	HR	HR%	R	RBI	BB	SO	SB	Pinch Hit AB	Pinch Hit H	PO	A	E	DP	TC/G	FA	G by Pos
1985	HOU N	31	.200	.200	25	5	0	0	0	0.0	0	1	3	7	0	14	3	15	0	0	0	1.0	1.000	OF-15
1986	SF N	3	.000	.000	1	0	0	0	0	0.0	0	0	0	0	1	1	0	0	0	0	0	0.0	—	
2 yrs.		34	.192	.192	26	5	0	0	0	0.0	0	1	3	7	1	15	3	15	0	0	0	1.0	1.000	OF-15

Clarence Jones

JONES, CLARENCE WOODROW
B. Nov. 7, 1941, Zanesville, Ohio.
BL TL 6′ 2″ 185 lbs.

Year	Team	Games	BA	SA	AB	H	2B	3B	HR	HR%	R	RBI	BB	SO	SB	Pinch Hit AB	Pinch Hit H	PO	A	E	DP	TC/G	FA	G by Pos
1967	CHI N	53	.252	.348	135	34	7	0	2	1.5	13	16	14	33	0	9	3	133	5	3	7	3.2	.979	OF-31, 1B-13
1968		5	.000	.000	2	0	0	0	0	0.0	0	0	2	1	0	2	0	2	0	0	0	2.0	1.000	1B-1
2 yrs.		58	.248	.343	137	34	7	0	2	1.5	13	16	16	34	0	11	3	135	5	3	7	3.2	.979	OF-31, 1B-14

Cleon Jones

JONES, CLEON JOSEPH
B. Aug. 4, 1942, Plateau, Ala.
BR TL 6′ 185 lbs.

Year	Team	Games	BA	SA	AB	H	2B	3B	HR	HR%	R	RBI	BB	SO	SB	Pinch Hit AB	Pinch Hit H	PO	A	E	DP	TC/G	FA	G by Pos
1963	NY N	6	.133	.133	15	2	0	0	0	0.0	1	1	0	4	0	2	0	6	0	0	0	1.2	1.000	OF-5
1965		30	.149	.203	74	11	1	0	1	1.4	2	9	2	23	1	9	2	36	2	0	0	1.7	1.000	OF-23
1966		139	.275	.372	495	136	16	4	8	1.6	74	57	30	62	16	11	0	275	10	6	2	2.3	.979	OF-129
1967		129	.246	.331	411	101	10	5	5	1.2	46	30	19	57	12	13	2	210	5	5	3	1.9	.977	OF-115
1968		147	.297	.452	509	151	29	4	14	2.8	63	55	31	98	23	10	1	226	7	9	0	1.7	.963	OF-139
1969		137	.340	.482	483	164	25	4	12	2.5	92	75	64	60	16	4	2	322	11	2	3	2.4	.994	OF-122, 1B-15
1970		134	.277	.417	506	140	25	8	10	2.0	71	63	57	87	12	5	0	243	10	5	3	2.0	.981	OF-130
1971		136	.319	.473	505	161	24	6	14	2.8	63	69	53	87	6	5	1	248	4	5	1	1.9	.981	OF-132
1972		106	.245	.331	375	92	15	1	5	1.3	39	52	30	83	1	3	0	310	20	6	10	3.2	.982	OF-84, 1B-20
1973		92	.260	.395	339	88	13	0	11	3.2	48	48	28	51	1	4	3	168	6	6	0	2.0	.967	OF-92
1974		124	.282	.421	461	130	23	1	13	2.8	62	60	38	79	3	6	1	220	8	7	0	2.0	.970	OF-120
1975		21	.240	.260	50	12	1	0	0	0.0	2	2	3	6	0	9	3	9	0	0	0	0.8	1.000	OF-12
1976	CHI A	12	.200	.225	40	8	1	0	0	0.0	2	3	5	5	0	1	0	7	0	0	0	0.6	1.000	OF-8, DH-3
13 yrs.		1213	.281	.404	4263	1196	183	33	93	2.2	565	524	360	702	91	82	15	2280	83	51	22	2.1	.979	OF-1111, 1B-35, DH-3
LEAGUE CHAMPIONSHIP SERIES																								
1969	NY N	3	.429	.786	14	6	2	0	1	7.1	4	4	1	2	2	0	0	11	0	0	0	3.7	1.000	OF-3
1973		5	.300	.400	20	6	2	0	0	0.0	3	3	2	4	0	0	0	10	0	1	0	2.2	.909	OF-5
2 yrs.		8	.353	.559	34	12	4	0	1	2.9	7	7	3	6	2	0	0	21	0	1	0	2.8	.955	OF-8
WORLD SERIES																								
1969	NY N	5	.158	.211	19	3	1	0	0	0.0	2	0	0	1	0	0	0	7	0	0	0	1.4	1.000	OF-5
1973		7	.286	.464	28	8	2	0	1	3.6	5	1	4	2	0	0	0	11	1	1	0	1.9	.923	OF-7
2 yrs.		12	.234	.362	47	11	3	0	1	2.1	7	1	4	3	0	0	0	18	1	1	0	1.7	.950	OF-12

Cobe Jones

JONES, COBURN DYAS
B. Aug. 21, 1907, Denver, Colo. D. June 3, 1969, Denver, Colo.
BB TR 5′ 7″ 155 lbs.

Year	Team	Games	BA	SA	AB	H	2B	3B	HR	HR%	R	RBI	BB	SO	SB	Pinch Hit AB	Pinch Hit H	PO	A	E	DP	TC/G	FA	G by Pos
1928	PIT N	2	.500	.500	2	1	0	0	0	0.0	0	0	0	0	0	0	0	0	1	0	0	0.5	1.000	SS-2
1929		25	.254	.365	63	16	5	1	0	0.0	6	4	1	5	1	9	2	28	29	5	6	4.1	.919	SS-15
2 yrs.		27	.262	.369	65	17	5	1	0	0.0	6	4	1	5	1	9	2	28	30	5	6	3.7	.921	SS-17

Dalton Jones

JONES, JAMES DALTON
B. Dec. 10, 1943, McComb, Miss.
BL TR 6′ 1″ 180 lbs.

Year	Team	Games	BA	SA	AB	H	2B	3B	HR	HR%	R	RBI	BB	SO	SB	Pinch Hit AB	Pinch Hit H	PO	A	E	DP	TC/G	FA	G by Pos
1964	BOS A	118	.230	.342	374	86	16	4	6	1.6	37	39	22	38	6	35	11	182	196	17	41	4.5	.957	2B-85, SS-1, 3B-1
1965		112	.270	.373	367	99	13	5	5	1.4	41	37	28	45	8	28	4	80	177	17	18	3.1	.938	3B-81, 2B-8
1966		115	.234	.365	252	59	11	5	4	1.6	26	23	22	27	1	48	13	133	126	12	26	3.7	.956	2B-70, 3B-3
1967		89	.289	.409	159	46	6	2	3	1.9	18	25	11	23	0	47	**13**	23	61	6	6	1.8	.933	3B-30, 2B-19, 1B-1
1968		111	.234	.314	354	83	13	0	5	1.4	38	29	17	53	1	28	11	491	80	7	55	6.4	.988	1B-56, 2B-26, 3B-8

Dalton Jones *continued*

Year	Team	Games	BA	SA	AB	H	2B	3B	HR	HR%	R	RBI	BB	SO	SB	Pinch Hit AB	Pinch Hit H	PO	A	E	DP	TC/G	FA	G by Pos
1969		111	.220	.318	336	74	18	3	3	0.9	50	33	39	36	1	18	3	702	64	7	61	8.5	.991	1B-81, 3B-9, 2B-1
1970	DET A	89	.220	.351	191	42	7	0	6	3.1	29	21	33	33	1	29	11	111	99	4	26	3.4	.981	2B-35, 3B-18, 1B-10
1971		83	.254	.399	138	35	5	0	5	3.6	15	11	9	21	1	45	13	25	17	2	3	1.3	.955	OF-16, 3B-13, 1B-3, 2B-1
1972	2 teams	DET A (7G –.000) TEX A (72G –.159)																						
″	total	79	.152	.241	158	24	2	0	4	2.5	14	19	10	33	1	32	2	58	63	3	11	2.5	.976	3B-23, 2B-17, 1B-7, OF-2
9 yrs.		907	.235	.343	2329	548	91	19	41	1.8	268	237	191	309	20	310	81	1805	883	75	247	4.4	.973	2B-262, 3B-186, 1B-158, OF-18, SS-1
WORLD SERIES																								
1967	BOS A	6	.389	.389	18	7	0	0	0	0.0	2	1	1	3	0	1	1	4	8	0	2	3.0	1.000	3B-4

Darryl Jones

JONES, DARRYL LEE BR TR 5′10″ 175 lbs.
Brother of Lynn Jones.
B. June 5, 1951, Meadville, Pa.

1979	NY A	18	.255	.404	47	12	5	1	0	0.0	6	6	2	7	0	2	2	1	0	0	0	0.1	1.000	DH-15, OF-2

Davy Jones

JONES, DAVID JEFFERSON (Kangaroo) BL TR 5′10″ 165 lbs.
B. June 30, 1880, Cambria, Wis. D. Mar. 30, 1972, Mankato, Minn.

1901	MIL A	14	.173	.346	52	9	0	0	3	5.8	12	5	11		4	0	0	41	0	4	0	3.2	.911	OF-14
1902	2 teams	STL A (15G –.224) CHI N (64G –.305)																						
″	total	79	.291	.363	292	85	13	4	0	0.0	45	17	44		17	0	0	177	8	8	4	2.4	.959	OF-79
1903	CHI N	130	.282	.336	497	140	18	3	1	0.2	64	62	53		15	0	0	249	14	8	3	2.1	.970	OF-130
1904		98	.244	.333	336	82	11	5	3	0.9	44	39	41		14	0	0	128	8	10	0	1.5	.932	OF-97
1906	DET A	84	.260	.310	323	84	12	2	0	0.0	41	24	41		21	0	0	193	10	4	3	2.5	.981	OF-84
1907		126	.273	.318	491	134	10	6	0	0.0	101	27	60		30	0	0	282	15	9	2	2.4	.971	OF-126
1908		56	.207	.240	121	25	2	1	0	0.0	17	10	13		11	21	3	67	5	3	2	2.3	.960	OF-32
1909		69	.279	.309	204	57	2	2	0	0.0	44	10	28		12	10	1	103	4	2	1	1.9	.982	OF-57
1910		113	.265	.313	377	100	6	6	0	0.0	77	24	51		25	9	0	181	13	9	2	2.0	.956	OF-101
1911		98	.273	.302	341	93	10	0	0	0.0	78	19	41		25	4	1	156	15	9	3	2.0	.950	OF-92
1912		97	.294	.323	316	93	5	2	0	0.0	54	24	38		16	15	4	141	13	6	4	2.0	.963	OF-81
1913	CHI A	10	.286	.286	21	6	0	0	0	0.0	2	0	9	0	1	1	0	11	2	2	0	1.9	.867	OF-8
1914	PIT F	97	.273	.361	352	96	9	8	2	0.6	58	24	42		15	4	2	216	11	7	1	2.5	.970	OF-93
1915		14	.327	.367	49	16	0	1	0	0.0	6	4	6		1	0	0	24	1	2	0	2.1	.926	OF-13
14 yrs.		1085	.270	.325	3772	1020	98	40	9	0.2	643	289	478	0	207	64	11	1969	119	83	25	2.2	.962	OF-1007
WORLD SERIES																								
1907	DET A	5	.353	.353	17	6	0	0	0	0.0	1	0	4	0	3	0	0	10	2	1	0	2.6	.923	OF-5
1908		3	.000	.000	2	0	0	0	0	0.0	1	0	1	1	0	2	0	0	0	0	0	0.0	—	
1909		7	.233	.333	30	7	0	0	1	3.3	6	2	2	1	1	0	0	14	0	1	0	2.1	.933	OF-7
3 yrs.		15	.265	.327	49	13	0	0	1	2.0	8	2	7	2	4	2	0	24	2	2	0	2.3	.929	OF-12

Deacon Jones

JONES, GROVER WILLIAM BL TR 5′10″ 185 lbs.
B. Apr. 18, 1934, White Plains, N. Y.

1962	CHI A	18	.321	.393	28	9	2	0	0	0.0	3	8	4	6	0	8	4	46	4	2	3	8.7	.962	1B-6
1963		17	.188	.500	16	3	0	1	1	6.3	4	2	2	2	0	12	1	6	1	0	4	7.0	1.000	1B-1
1966		5	.400	.400	5	2	0	0	0	0.0	0	0	0	0	0	5	2	0	0	0	0	0.0	—	
3 yrs.		40	.286	.429	49	14	2	1	1	2.0	7	10	6	8	0	25	7	52	5	2	7	8.4	.966	1B-7

Fielder Jones

JONES, FIELDER ALLISON BL TR 5′11″ 180 lbs.
B. Aug. 13, 1871, Shinglehouse, Pa. D. Mar. 13, 1934, Portland, Ore.
Manager 1904–08, 1914–18.

1896	BKN N	104	.354	.443	395	140	10	8	3	0.8	82	46	48	15	18	0	0	171	10	14	6	1.9	.928	OF-103
1897		135	.314	.378	548	172	15	10	0	0.0	134	49	61		48	0	0	233	22	16	8	2.0	.941	OF-135
1898		146	.304	.364	596	181	15	9	1	0.2	89	69	46		36	0	0	233	20	20	7	1.9	.927	OF-144, SS-2
1899		102	.285	.334	365	104	8	2	2	0.5	75	38	54		18	5	2	199	11	12	2	2.3	.946	OF-96
1900		136	.310	.393	552	171	26	4	4	0.7	108	54	57		33	0	0	315	15	15	3	2.5	.957	OF-136
1901	CHI A	133	.311	.365	521	162	16	3	2	0.4	120	65	84		38	0	0	216	20	16	5	1.9	.937	OF-133
1902		135	.321	.370	532	171	16	5	0	0.0	98	54	57		33	0	0	323	25	10	11	2.7	.972	OF-135
1903		136	.287	.340	530	152	18	5	0	0.0	71	45	47		21	0	0	324	11	5	3	2.5	.985	OF-136
1904		154	.243	.305	564	137	14	6	3	0.5	74	43	54		25	0	0	325	15	8	4	2.3	.977	OF-154
1905		153	.245	.327	568	139	17	12	2	0.4	91	38	73		20	0	0	337	21	11	5	2.4	.970	OF-153
1906		144	.230	.302	496	114	22	4	2	0.4	77	34	83		26	0	0	312	23	4	5	2.4	.988	OF-144
1907		154	.261	.297	559	146	18	1	0	0.0	72	47	67		17	0	0	307	18	9	6	2.2	.973	OF-154
1908		149	.253	.306	529	134	11	7	1	0.2	92	50	86		26	0	0	288	17	10	5	2.1	.968	OF-149
1914	STL F	5	.333	.333	3	1	0	0	0	0.0	0	0	1		0	3	1	0	0	0	0	0.0	—	
1915		7	.000	.000	6	0	0	0	0	0.0	1	0	0		0	3	0	1	0	0	0	0.3	1.000	OF-3
15 yrs.		1793	.284	.346	6764	1924	206	76	20	0.3	1184	632	818	15	359	11	3	3584	228	150	70	2.2	.962	OF-1775, SS-2
WORLD SERIES																								
1906	CHI A	6	.095	.095	21	2	0	0	0	0.0	4	0	3	3	0	0	0	9	0	0	0	1.5	1.000	OF-6

Frank Jones

JONES, FRANK M. BL
B. Aug. 25, 1858, Princeton, Ill. D. Feb. 4, 1936, Marietta, Ohio.

1884	DET N	2	.333	.333	6	2	0	0	0	0.0	1	0	0	0	0	0	0	4	3	0	0	3.5	1.000	SS-1, OF-1

Hal Jones

JONES, HAROLD MARION BR TR 6′2″ 194 lbs.
B. Apr. 9, 1936, Louisiana, Mo.

1961	CLE A	12	.171	.343	35	6	0	0	2	5.7	2	4	2	12	0	2	0	73	3	2	12	7.8	.974	1B-10
1962		5	.313	.375	16	5	1	0	0	0.0	2	1	0	4	0	1	0	28	3	1	1	8.0	.969	1B-4
2 yrs.		17	.216	.353	51	11	1	0	2	3.9	4	5	2	16	0	3	0	101	6	3	13	7.9	.973	1B-14

Henry Jones

JONES, HENRY MONROE BB 5′6″ 149 lbs.
B. May 10, 1857, New York, N. Y. D. May 31, 1955, Manistee, Mich.

1884	DET N	34	.209	.248	129	27	3	1	0	0.0	23		16	19		0	0	52	90	17	1	4.4	.893	2B-16, OF-12, SS-8

Howie Jones

JONES, HOWARD (Cotton) BL TL 5′11″ 165 lbs.
Born Howard Painter.
B. Mar. 1, 1897, Irwin, Pa. D. July 15, 1972, Jeannette, Pa.

Year	Team		Games	BA	SA	AB	H	2B	3B	HR	HR%	R	RBI	BB	SO	SB	Pinch Hit AB	Pinch Hit H	PO	A	E	DP	TC/G	FA	G by Pos
1921	STL	N	3	.000	.000	2	0	0	0	0	0.0	0	0	0	1	0	2	0	0	0	0	0	0.0	.000	OF-1

Jack Jones

JONES, RYERSON L. (Angel Sleeves) TR
B. Cincinnati, Ohio Deceased.

Year	Team		Games	BA	SA	AB	H	2B	3B	HR	HR%	R	RBI	BB	SO	SB	Pinch Hit AB	Pinch Hit H	PO	A	E	DP	TC/G	FA	G by Pos
1883	LOU	AA	2	.000	.000	7	0	0	0	0	0.0	1		0			0	0	1	3	2	0	2.0	.667	OF-2, SS-1
1884	CIN	U	69	.261	.309	272	71	5	1	2	0.7	36		12			0	0	104	200	59	16	5.2	.837	SS-41, 2B-19, 3B-10
2 yrs.			71	.254	.301	279	71	5	1	2	0.7	37		12			0	0	105	203	61	16	5.1	.835	SS-42, 2B-19, 3B-10, OF-2

Jake Jones

JONES, JAMES MURRELL BR TR 6′ 3″ 197 lbs.
B. Nov. 23, 1920, Epps, La.

Year	Team		Games	BA	SA	AB	H	2B	3B	HR	HR%	R	RBI	BB	SO	SB	Pinch Hit AB	Pinch Hit H	PO	A	E	DP	TC/G	FA	G by Pos
1941	CHI	A	3	.000	.000	11	0	0	0	0	0.0	0	0	0	4	0	0	0	25	0	0	0	8.3	1.000	1B-3
1942			7	.150	.200	20	3	1	0	0	0.0	2	0	2	2	1	2	0	47	2	2	2	10.2	.961	1B-5
1946			24	.266	.468	79	21	5	1	3	3.8	10	13	2	13	0	4	0	201	5	3	18	10.4	.986	1B-20
1947	2 teams	CHI A (45G –.240) BOS A (109G –.235)																							
″	total		154	.237	.386	575	136	21	4	19	3.3	65	96	54	85	6	2	0	1462	104	16	60	10.4	.990	1B-152
1948	BOS	A	36	.200	.267	105	21	4	0	1	1.0	3	8	11	26	1	4	0	275	22	2	30	9.6	.993	1B-31
5 yrs.			224	.229	.368	790	181	31	5	23	2.9	80	117	69	130	8	12	0	2010	133	23	110	10.3	.989	1B-211

Jeff Jones

JONES, JEFFRY RAYMOND BR TR 6′ 2″ 200 lbs.
B. Oct. 22, 1957, Philadelphia, Pa.

Year	Team		Games	BA	SA	AB	H	2B	3B	HR	HR%	R	RBI	BB	SO	SB	Pinch Hit AB	Pinch Hit H	PO	A	E	DP	TC/G	FA	G by Pos
1983	CIN	N	16	.227	.295	44	10	3	0	0	0.0	6	5	11	13	2	2	0	33	1	0	0	2.4	1.000	OF-13, 1B-1

Jim Jones

JONES, JAMES TILFORD (Sheriff) BR TR 5′10″ 162 lbs.
B. Dec. 25, 1876, London, Ky. D. May 6, 1953, London, Ky.

Year	Team		Games	BA	SA	AB	H	2B	3B	HR	HR%	R	RBI	BB	SO	SB	Pinch Hit AB	Pinch Hit H	PO	A	E	DP	TC/G	FA	G by Pos
1897	LOU	N	2	.250	.500	4	1	1	0	0	0.0	2	0	1		0	1	0	0	0	0	0	0.0	.000	P-1
1901	NY	N	21	.209	.319	91	19	4	3	0	0.0	10	5	4		2	0	0	33	6	5	1	2.1	.886	OF-20, P-1
1902			67	.237	.289	249	59	11	1	0	0.0	16	19	13		7	0	0	122	9	15	2	2.2	.897	OF-67
3 yrs.			90	.230	.299	344	79	16	4	0	0.0	28	24	18		9	1	0	155	15	20	3	2.1	.895	OF-87, P-2

John Jones

JONES, JOHN WILLIAM (Skins) BL TL 5′11″ 185 lbs.
B. May 13, 1901, Coatesville, Pa. D. Nov. 3, 1956, Baltimore, Md.

Year	Team		Games	BA	SA	AB	H	2B	3B	HR	HR%	R	RBI	BB	SO	SB	Pinch Hit AB	Pinch Hit H	PO	A	E	DP	TC/G	FA	G by Pos
1923	PHI	A	1	.250	.250	4	1	0	0	0	0.0	0	1	0	1	0	0	0	4	0	0	0	4.0	1.000	OF-1
1932			4	.167	.167	6	1	0	0	0	0.0	0	0	0	3	0	3	0	1	0	0	0	1.0	1.000	OF-1
2 yrs.			5	.200	.200	10	2	0	0	0	0.0	0	1	0	4	0	3	0	5	0	0	0	2.5	1.000	OF-2

Lynn Jones

JONES, LYNN MORRIS BR TR 5′ 9″ 175 lbs.
Brother of Darryl Jones.
B. Jan. 1, 1953, Meadville, Pa.

Year	Team		Games	BA	SA	AB	H	2B	3B	HR	HR%	R	RBI	BB	SO	SB	Pinch Hit AB	Pinch Hit H	PO	A	E	DP	TC/G	FA	G by Pos
1979	DET	A	95	.296	.390	213	63	8	0	4	1.9	33	26	17	22	9	11	2	142	3	3	1	1.6	.980	OF-84, DH-6
1980			30	.255	.364	55	14	2	2	0	0.0	9	6	10	5	1	4	1	31	0	0	0	1.3	1.000	OF-17, DH-6
1981			71	.259	.322	174	45	5	0	2	1.1	19	19	18	10	1	13	4	85	5	1	2	1.4	.989	OF-60, DH-4
1982			58	.223	.259	139	31	3	1	0	0.0	15	14	7	14	0	7	2	86	3	0	2	1.6	1.000	OF-56, DH-1
1983			49	.266	.344	64	17	1	2	0	0.0	9	6	3	6	1	15	3	28	2	1	0	0.8	.968	OF-31, DH-6
1984	KC	A	47	.301	.388	103	31	6	0	1	1.0	11	10	4	9	1	7	2	51	0	2	0	1.2	.962	OF-45
1985			110	.211	.257	152	32	7	0	0	0.0	12	9	8	15	0	13	0	115	2	2	1	1.2	.983	OF-100, DH-2
1986			67	.128	.170	47	6	2	0	0	0.0	1	1	6	5	0	2	0	34	0	1	0	0.5	.971	OF-62, DH-3, 2B-1
8 yrs.			527	.252	.321	947	239	34	5	7	0.7	109	91	73	86	13	72	14	572	15	10	6	1.2	.983	OF-455, DH-28, 2B-1
LEAGUE CHAMPIONSHIP SERIES																									
1984	KC	A	3	.200	.200	5	1	0	0	0	0.0	1	0	0	0	0	3	1	2	0	0	0	1.0	1.000	OF-2
1985			5	—	—	0	0	0	0	0	—	0	0	0	0	0	0	0	2	0	0	0	0.4	1.000	OF-5
2 yrs.			8	.200	.200	5	1	0	0	0	0.0	1	0	0	0	0	3	1	4	0	0	0	0.6	1.000	OF-7
WORLD SERIES																									
1985	KC	A	5	.667	1.667	3	2	1	1	0	0.0	0	0	0	0	0	2	2	4	0	0	0	4.0	1.000	OF-1

Mack Jones

JONES, MACK (Mack The Knife) BL TR 6′ 1″ 180 lbs.
B. Nov. 6, 1938, Atlanta, Ga.

Year	Team		Games	BA	SA	AB	H	2B	3B	HR	HR%	R	RBI	BB	SO	SB	Pinch Hit AB	Pinch Hit H	PO	A	E	DP	TC/G	FA	G by Pos
1961	MIL	N	28	.231	.298	104	24	3	2	0	0.0	13	12	12	28	4	1	0	45	2	0	1	1.8	1.000	OF-26
1962			91	.255	.420	333	85	17	4	10	3.0	51	36	44	100	5	1	0	142	3	4	0	1.6	.973	OF-91
1963			93	.219	.342	228	50	11	4	3	1.3	36	22	26	59	8	17	4	135	1	3	0	1.7	.978	OF-80
1965			143	.262	.510	504	132	18	7	31	6.2	78	75	29	122	8	10	2	239	2	5	2	1.8	.980	OF-133
1966	ATL	N	118	.264	.468	417	110	14	1	23	5.5	60	66	39	85	16	5	1	251	1	5	0	2.3	.981	OF-112, 1B-1
1967			140	.253	.434	454	115	23	4	17	3.7	72	50	64	108	10	13	4	252	7	4	1	2.1	.985	OF-126
1968	CIN	N	103	.252	.427	234	59	9	1	10	4.3	40	34	28	46	2	38	9	82	1	1	0	1.4	.988	OF-60
1969	MON	N	135	.270	.488	455	123	23	5	22	4.8	73	79	67	110	6	5	1	226	6	10	0	1.9	.959	OF-129
1970			108	.240	.458	271	65	11	3	14	5.2	51	32	59	74	5	27	10	118	3	4	1	1.4	.968	OF-87
1971			43	.165	.297	91	15	3	0	3	3.3	11	9	15	24	1	16	2	39	1	2	0	1.6	.952	OF-27
10 yrs.			1002	.252	.444	3091	778	132	31	133	4.3	485	415	383	756	65	133	33	1529	27	38	5	1.8	.976	OF-871, 1B-1

Nippy Jones

JONES, VERNAL LEROY BR TR 6′ 1″ 185 lbs.
B. June 29, 1925, Los Angeles, Calif. D. Oct. 3, 1995, Sacramento, Calif.

Year	Team		Games	BA	SA	AB	H	2B	3B	HR	HR%	R	RBI	BB	SO	SB	Pinch Hit AB	Pinch Hit H	PO	A	E	DP	TC/G	FA	G by Pos
1946	STL	N	16	.333	.333	12	4	0	0	0	0.0	3	1	2	2	0	9	4	2	2	1	1	1.7	.800	2B-3
1947			23	.247	.342	73	18	4	0	1	1.4	6	5	2	10	0	7	1	34	40	5	5	5.3	.937	2B-13, OF-2
1948			132	.254	.397	481	122	21	9	10	2.1	58	81	36	45	2	2	0	1148	63	17	98	9.6	.986	1B-128
1949			110	.300	.426	380	114	20	2	8	2.1	51	62	16	20	1	11	2	876	40	15	85	9.5	.984	1B-98
1950			13	.231	.269	26	6	1	0	0	0.0	0	6	3	1	0	4	2	54	3	1	8	7.3	.983	1B-8
1951			80	.263	.333	300	79	12	0	3	1.0	20	41	9	13	1	9	1	698	48	7	7	10.6	.991	1B-71
1952	PHI	N	8	.167	.267	30	5	0	0	1	3.3	3	5	0	4	0	0	0	73	7	2	8	10.3	.976	1B-8
1957	MIL	N	30	.266	.392	79	21	2	1	2	2.5	5	8	3	7	0	10	2	144	12	1	12	7.5	.994	1B-20, OF-1
8 yrs.			412	.267	.382	1381	369	60	12	25	1.8	146	209	71	102	4	52	12	3029	215	49	224	9.4	.985	1B-333, 2B-16, OF-3

Nippy Jones *continued*

Year	Team		Games	BA	SA	AB	H	2B	3B	HR	HR%	R	RBI	BB	SO	SB	Pinch Hit AB	Pinch Hit H	PO	A	E	DP	TC/G	FA	G by Pos
WORLD SERIES																									
1946	STL	N	1	.000	.000	1	0	0	0	0	0.0	0	0	0	1	0	1	0	0	0	0	0	0.0	—	
1957	MIL	N	3	.000	.000	2	0	0	0	0	0.0	0	0	0	0	0	2	0	0	0	0	0	0.0	—	
2 yrs.			4	.000	.000	3	0	0	0	0	0.0	0	0	0	1	0	3	0							

Red Jones

JONES, MAURICE MORRIS — BL TR 6′ 3″ 190 lbs.
B. Nov. 2, 1914, Timpson, Tex. D. June 30, 1975, Lincoln, Calif.

Year	Team		Games	BA	SA	AB	H	2B	3B	HR	HR%	R	RBI	BB	SO	SB	Pinch Hit AB	Pinch Hit H	PO	A	E	DP	TC/G	FA	G by Pos
1940	STL	N	12	.091	.091	11	1	0	0	0	0.0	0	1	1	2	0	10	1	1	0	0	0	1.0	1.000	OF-1

Ricky Jones

JONES, RICKY MIRON — BR TR 6′ 3″ 186 lbs.
B. June 4, 1958, Tupelo, Miss.

Year	Team		Games	BA	SA	AB	H	2B	3B	HR	HR%	R	RBI	BB	SO	SB	Pinch Hit AB	Pinch Hit H	PO	A	E	DP	TC/G	FA	G by Pos
1986	BAL	A	16	.182	.242	33	6	2	0	0	0.0	2	4	7	8	0	0	0	19	38	0	9	3.4	1.000	2B-11, 3B-6

Ron Jones

JONES, RONALD GLEN — BL TR 5′10″ 195 lbs.
B. June 11, 1964, Seguin, Tex.

Year	Team		Games	BA	SA	AB	H	2B	3B	HR	HR%	R	RBI	BB	SO	SB	Pinch Hit AB	Pinch Hit H	PO	A	E	DP	TC/G	FA	G by Pos
1988	PHI	N	33	.290	.548	124	36	6	1	8	6.5	15	26	2	14	0	1	0	70	1	0	0	2.2	1.000	OF-32
1989			12	.290	.484	31	9	0	0	2	6.5	7	4	9	1	1	0	0	27	1	0	1	2.3	1.000	OF-12
1990			24	.276	.466	58	16	2	0	3	5.2	5	7	9	9	0	8	2	25	1	0	0	1.6	1.000	OF-16
1991			28	.154	.231	26	4	2	0	0	0.0	0	3	2	9	0	26	4	0	0	0	0	0.0	—	
4 yrs.			97	.272	.485	239	65	10	1	13	5.4	27	40	22	33	1	35	6	122	3	0	1	2.1	1.000	OF-60

Ross Jones

JONES, ROSS A. — BR TR 6′ 2″ 185 lbs.
B. Jan. 14, 1960, Miami, Fla.

Year	Team		Games	BA	SA	AB	H	2B	3B	HR	HR%	R	RBI	BB	SO	SB	Pinch Hit AB	Pinch Hit H	PO	A	E	DP	TC/G	FA	G by Pos
1984	NY	N	17	.100	.200	10	1	1	0	0	0.0	2	1	3	4	0	3	0	0	7	1	2	0.9	.875	SS-7, 2B-1, 3B-1
1986	SEA	A	11	.095	.095	21	2	0	0	0	0.0	0	0	0	4	0	0	0	9	11	0	2	2.0	1.000	SS-4, 2B-3, 3B-2, DH-1
1987	KC	A	39	.254	.325	114	29	4	2	0	0.0	10	10	5	15	1	0	0	46	111	4	15	4.1	.975	SS-36, 2B-3
3 yrs.			67	.221	.283	145	32	5	2	0	0.0	12	11	8	23	1	3	0	55	129	5	19	3.3	.974	SS-47, 2B-7, 3B-3, DH-1

Ruppert Jones

JONES, RUPPERT SANDERSON — BL TL 5′10″ 170 lbs.
B. Mar. 12, 1955, Dallas, Tex.

Year	Team		Games	BA	SA	AB	H	2B	3B	HR	HR%	R	RBI	BB	SO	SB	Pinch Hit AB	Pinch Hit H	PO	A	E	DP	TC/G	FA	G by Pos
1976	KC	A	28	.216	.333	51	11	1	1	1	2.0	9	7	3	16	0	9	1	21	0	0	0	1.0	1.000	OF-17, DH-3
1977	SEA	A	160	.263	.454	597	157	26	8	24	4.0	85	76	55	120	13	1	0	465	11	9	3	3.1	.981	OF-155, DH-4
1978			129	.235	.337	472	111	24	3	6	1.3	48	46	55	85	22	1	0	393	10	6	2	3.2	.985	OF-128
1979			162	.267	.444	622	166	29	9	21	3.4	109	78	85	78	33	1	0	453	13	5	4	2.9	.989	OF-161
1980	NY	A	83	.223	.357	328	73	11	3	9	2.7	38	42	34	50	18	0	0	246	4	3	1	3.1	.988	OF-82
1981	SD	N	105	.249	.370	397	99	34	1	4	1.0	53	39	43	66	7	0	0	295	9	2	3	2.9	.993	OF-104
1982			116	.283	.425	424	120	20	2	12	2.8	69	61	62	90	18	2	0	314	3	5	1	2.8	.984	OF-114
1983			133	.233	.394	335	78	12	3	12	3.6	42	49	35	58	11	18	3	268	6	6	3	2.4	.979	OF-111, 1B-5
1984	DET	A	79	.284	.516	215	61	12	1	12	5.6	26	37	21	47	2	15	6	150	4	0	1	2.1	1.000	OF-73, DH-2
1985	CAL	A	125	.231	.447	389	90	17	2	21	5.4	66	67	57	82	7	13	0	179	12	1	5	1.7	.995	OF-73, DH-43
1986			126	.229	.427	393	90	21	3	17	4.3	73	49	64	87	10	12	3	205	5	4	0	1.8	.981	OF-121
1987			85	.245	.432	192	47	8	2	8	4.2	25	28	20	38	2	27	6	81	1	3	0	1.2	.965	OF-66, DH-3
12 yrs.			1331	.250	.416	4415	1103	215	38	147	3.3	643	579	534	817	143	99	19	3070	78	44	23	2.5	.986	OF-1205, DH-55, 1B-5
LEAGUE CHAMPIONSHIP SERIES																									
1984	DET	A	2	.000	.000	5	0	0	0	0	0.0	1	0	1	1	0	1	0	5	0	0	0	2.5	1.000	OF-2
1986	CAL	A	6	.176	.235	17	3	1	0	0	0.0	4	2	5	2	0	0	0	6	0	0	0	1.2	1.000	OF-5
2 yrs.			8	.136	.182	22	3	1	0	0	0.0	5	2	6	3	0	1	0	11	0	0	0	1.6	1.000	OF-7
WORLD SERIES																									
1984	DET	A	2	.000	.000	3	0	0	0	0	0.0	0	0	0	1	0	0	0	3	0	0	0	1.5	1.000	OF-2

Tex Jones

JONES, WILLIAM RODERICK — BR TR 6′ 192 lbs.
B. Aug. 4, 1885, Marion, Kans. D. Feb. 26, 1938, Wichita, Kans.

Year	Team		Games	BA	SA	AB	H	2B	3B	HR	HR%	R	RBI	BB	SO	SB	Pinch Hit AB	Pinch Hit H	PO	A	E	DP	TC/G	FA	G by Pos
1911	CHI	A	9	.194	.226	31	6	1	0	0	0.0	4	4	3		1	0	0	96	12	0	6	12.0	1.000	1B-9

Tim Jones

JONES, WILLIAM TIMOTHY — BL TR 5′10″ 172 lbs.
B. Dec. 1, 1962, Sumter, S. C.

Year	Team		Games	BA	SA	AB	H	2B	3B	HR	HR%	R	RBI	BB	SO	SB	Pinch Hit AB	Pinch Hit H	PO	A	E	DP	TC/G	FA	G by Pos
1988	STL	N	31	.269	.269	52	14	0	0	0	0.0	2	3	4	10	4	9	1	26	40	1	7	3.7	.985	SS-9, 2B-8, 3B-1
1989			42	.293	.373	75	22	6	0	0	0.0	11	7	7	8	1	10	2	33	48	2	4	2.7	.976	2B-12, SS-12, 3B-5, OF-1, C-1
1990			67	.219	.313	128	28	7	1	1	0.8	9	12	12	20	3	14	4	43	105	7	15	2.8	.955	SS-29, 2B-19, 3B-6, P-1
1991			16	.167	.250	24	4	2	0	0	0.0	1	2	2	6	0	0	0	5	16	0	3	1.2	1.000	SS-14, 2B-4
1992			67	.200	.228	145	29	4	0	0	0.0	9	3	11	29	5	1	0	76	114	4	32	3.0	.979	SS-34, 2B-28, 3B-2, OF-1
1993			29	.262	.361	61	16	6	0	0	0.0	13	1	9	8	2	0	0	34	63	2	9	3.5	.980	SS-21, 2B-7
6 yrs.			252	.233	.295	485	113	25	1	1	0.2	45	28	45	81	15	34	7	217	386	16	70	2.9	.974	SS-119, 2B-78, 3B-14, OF-2, P-1, C-1

Tom Jones

JONES, THOMAS — BR TR 6′ 1″ 195 lbs.
B. Jan. 22, 1877, Honesdale, Pa. D. June 21, 1923, Danville, Pa.

Year	Team		Games	BA	SA	AB	H	2B	3B	HR	HR%	R	RBI	BB	SO	SB	Pinch Hit AB	Pinch Hit H	PO	A	E	DP	TC/G	FA	G by Pos
1902	BAL	A	37	.283	.384	159	45	8	4	0	0.0	22	14	2		1	0	0	341	22	17	23	10.0	.955	1B-37, 2B-1
1904	STL	A	156	.243	.309	625	152	15	10	2	0.3	53	68	15		16	0	0	1485	149	21	54	10.3	.987	1B-134, 2B-23, OF-4
1905			135	.242	.282	504	122	16	2	0	0.0	45	48	30		5	0	0	1502	105	25	52	12.1	.985	1B-135
1906			144	.252	.315	539	136	22	6	0	0.0	51	30	24		27	1	0	1476	116	25	55	11.3	.985	1B-143
1907			155	.250	.291	549	137	17	3	0	0.0	53	34	34		24	0	0	1687	103	31	69	11.7	.983	1B-155
1908			155	.246	.284	549	135	14	2	1	0.2	43	50	30		18	0	0	1616	90	24	79	11.2	.986	1B-155
1909	2 teams		STL A (97G –.249) DET A (44G –.281)																						
″	total		141	.259	.308	490	127	18	3	0	0.0	43	47	23		22	0	0	1402	103	19	77	10.8	.988	1B-139, 3B-2
1910	DET	A	135	.255	.303	432	110	13	4	0	0.0	32	45	35		22	0	0	1405	67	23	50	11.1	.985	1B-135
8 yrs.			1058	.251	.303	3847	964	123	34	3	0.1	342	336	193		135	1	0	10914	755	185	459	11.2	.984	1B-1033, 2B-24, OF-4, 3B-2
WORLD SERIES																									
1909	DET	A	7	.250	.292	24	6	1	0	0	0.0	3	2	2	0	1	0	0	71	1	1	1	10.4	.986	1B-7

Tracy Jones

JONES, TRACY DONALD
B. Mar. 31, 1961, Hawthorne, Calif.

BR TR 6′ 3″ 180 lbs.

Year	Team	Games	BA	SA	AB	H	2B	3B	HR	HR%	R	RBI	BB	SO	SB	Pinch Hit AB	Pinch Hit H	PO	A	E	DP	TC/G	FA	G by Pos
1986	CIN N	46	.349	.453	86	30	3	0	2	2.3	16	10	9	5	7	12	2	46	1	0	0	1.8	1.000	OF-24, 1B-2
1987		117	.290	.437	359	104	17	3	10	2.8	53	44	23	40	31	25	6	189	2	2	0	2.0	.990	OF-95
1988	2 teams	CIN N (37G –.229) MON N (53G –.333)																						
″	total	90	.295	.371	224	66	6	1	3	1.3	29	24	20	18	18	23	6	96	2	2	0	1.5	.980	OF-68
1989	2 teams	SF N (40G –.186) DET A (46G –.259)																						
″	total	86	.231	.322	255	59	14	0	3	1.2	22	38	21	30	3	16	3	107	0	1	0	1.5	.991	OF-66, DH-8
1990	2 teams	DET A (50G –.229) SEA A (25G –.302)																						
″	total	75	.260	.397	204	53	8	1	6	2.9	23	24	9	25	1	16	3	68	3	2	0	0.9	.973	OF-45, DH-40
1991	SEA A	79	.251	.360	175	44	8	1	3	1.7	30	24	18	22	2	20	6	49	0	0	0	0.7	1.000	DH-37, OF-36
6 yrs.		493	.273	.388	1303	356	56	6	27	2.1	173	164	100	140	62	112	26	555	8	7	0	1.4	.988	OF-334, DH-85, 1B-2

Willie Jones

JONES, WILLIE EDWARD (Puddin' Head)
B. Aug. 16, 1925, Dillon, S. C. D. Oct. 18, 1983, Cincinnati, Ohio.

BR TR 6′ 2″ 205 lbs.

Year	Team	Games	BA	SA	AB	H	2B	3B	HR	HR%	R	RBI	BB	SO	SB	Pinch Hit AB	Pinch Hit H	PO	A	E	DP	TC/G	FA	G by Pos
1947	PHI N	18	.226	.258	62	14	0	1	0	0.0	5	10	7	0	2	1	0	19	41	6	3	3.9	.909	3B-17
1948		17	.333	.467	60	20	2	0	2	3.3	9	9	3	5	0	0	0	30	33	5	1	4.0	.926	3B-17
1949		149	.244	.421	532	130	35	1	19	3.6	71	77	65	66	3	3	0	181	308	27	19	3.6	.948	3B-145
1950		157	.267	.456	610	163	28	6	25	4.1	100	88	61	40	5	0	0	190	323	25	30	3.4	.954	3B-157
1951		148	.285	.470	564	161	28	5	22	3.9	79	81	60	47	6	0	0	190	286	17	33	3.4	.966	3B-147
1952		147	.250	.383	541	135	12	3	18	3.3	60	72	53	36	5	0	0	216	281	16	31	3.5	.969	3B-147
1953		149	.225	.385	481	108	16	2	19	4.0	61	70	85	45	1	1	1	176	253	11	36	3.0	.975	3B-147
1954		142	.271	.402	535	145	28	3	12	2.2	64	56	61	54	4	1	1	184	277	15	23	3.4	.968	3B-141
1955		146	.258	.401	516	133	20	3	16	3.1	65	81	77	51	6	0	0	202	235	18	22	3.1	.960	3B-146
1956		149	.277	.429	520	144	20	4	17	3.3	88	78	92	49	5	0	0	202	264	13	23	3.2	.973	3B-149
1957		133	.218	.332	440	96	19	2	9	2.0	58	47	61	41	1	7	2	140	197	12	18	2.8	.966	3B-126
1958		118	.271	.420	398	108	15	1	14	3.5	52	60	49	45	1	5	2	141	186	11	13	3.0	.967	3B-110, 1B-1
1959	3 teams	PHI N (47G –.269) CLE A (11G –.222) CIN N (72G –.249)																						
″	total	130	.255	.421	411	105	22	2	14	3.4	57	56	48	43	0	11	2	135	191	11	16	2.9	.967	3B-118
1960	CIN N	79	.268	.376	149	40	7	0	3	2.0	16	27	31	16	1	27	10	44	59	4	5	2.3	.963	3B-46, 2B-1
1961		9	.000	.000	7	0	0	0	0	0.0	1	0	2	3	0	6	0	0	0	1	0	1.0	.000	3B-1
15 yrs.		1691	.258	.410	5826	1502	252	33	190	3.3	786	812	755	541	40	62	18	2050	2934	192	273	3.2	.963	3B-1614, 2B-1, 1B-1
WORLD SERIES																								
1950	PHI N	4	.286	.357	14	4	1	0	0	0.0	1	0	0	3	0	0	0	8	9	1	0	4.5	.944	3B-4

Bubber Jonnard

JONNARD, CLARENCE JAMES
Brother of Claude Jonnard.
B. Nov. 23, 1897, Nashville, Tenn. D. Aug. 23, 1977, New York, N. Y.

BR TR 6′ 1″ 185 lbs.

Year	Team	Games	BA	SA	AB	H	2B	3B	HR	HR%	R	RBI	BB	SO	SB	Pinch Hit AB	Pinch Hit H	PO	A	E	DP	TC/G	FA	G by Pos
1920	CHI A	2	.000	.000	5	0	0	0	0	0.0	0	0	0	1	0	1	0	4	2	1	1	7.0	.857	C-1
1922	PIT N	10	.238	.333	21	5	0	1	0	0.0	4	2	2	4	0	0	0	30	7	1	0	3.8	.974	C-10
1926	PHI N	19	.118	.147	34	4	1	0	0	0.0	3	2	3	4	0	4	0	30	7	2	1	2.6	.949	C-15
1927		53	.294	.336	143	42	6	0	0	0.0	18	14	7	7	0	7	5	93	24	4	3	3.0	.967	C-41
1929	STL N	18	.097	.097	31	3	0	0	0	0.0	1	2	0	6	0	0	0	39	5	2	1	2.6	.957	C-18
1935	PHI N	1	.000	.000	1	0	0	0	0	0.0	0	0	0	1	0	0	0	1	0	0	0	1.0	1.000	C-1
6 yrs.		103	.230	.268	235	54	7	1	0	0.0	26	20	12	23	0	12	5	197	45	10	6	2.9	.960	C-86

Eddie Joost

JOOST, EDWIN DAVID
B. June 5, 1916, San Francisco, Calif.
Manager 1954.

BR TR 6′ 175 lbs.

Year	Team	Games	BA	SA	AB	H	2B	3B	HR	HR%	R	RBI	BB	SO	SB	Pinch Hit AB	Pinch Hit H	PO	A	E	DP	TC/G	FA	G by Pos
1936	CIN N	13	.154	.192	26	4	1	0	0	0.0	1	1	2	5	0	0	0	15	22	1	4	3.2	.974	SS-7, 2B-5
1937		6	.083	.083	12	1	0	0	0	0.0	0	0	0	0	0	0	0	8	13	3	2	4.0	.875	2B-6
1939		42	.252	.336	143	36	6	3	0	0.0	23	14	12	15	1	4	0	94	101	12	23	5.4	.942	2B-32, SS-6
1940		88	.216	.266	278	60	7	2	1	0.4	24	24	32	40	4	0	0	161	270	16	51	5.0	.964	SS-78, 2B-7, 3B-4
1941		152	.253	.337	537	136	25	4	4	0.7	67	40	69	59	9	0	0	326	429	46	88	5.2	.943	SS-147, 2B-4, 1B-2, 3B-1
1942		142	.224	.320	562	126	30	3	6	1.1	65	41	62	57	9	0	0	299	434	50	93	5.4	.936	SS-130, 2B-15
1943	BOS N	124	.185	.252	421	78	16	3	2	0.5	34	20	68	80	5	0	0	247	341	33	53	4.9	.947	3B-67, 2B-60, SS-1
1945		35	.248	.312	141	35	7	1	0	0.0	16	9	13	7	0	0	0	64	76	12	13	4.3	.921	2B-19, 3B-16
1947	PHI A	151	.206	.330	540	111	22	3	13	2.4	76	64	114	**110**	6	0	0	370	452	38	100	5.7	.956	SS-151
1948		135	.250	.395	509	127	22	2	16	3.1	99	55	119	87	2	0	0	325	409	20	115	5.6	.973	SS-135
1949		144	.263	.453	525	138	25	3	23	4.4	128	81	149	80	2	0	0	352	442	25	126	5.7	.969	SS-144
1950		131	.233	.384	476	111	12	3	18	3.8	79	58	101	68	5	0	0	241	389	29	117	5.0	.956	SS-131
1951		140	.289	.461	553	160	28	5	19	3.4	107	78	106	70	10	0	0	325	422	20	115	5.5	.974	SS-140
1952		146	.244	.415	540	132	26	3	20	3.7	94	75	122	94	5	0	0	278	431	28	81	5.0	.962	SS-146
1953		51	.249	.384	177	44	6	0	6	3.4	39	15	45	24	3	0	0	102	147	11	33	5.1	.958	SS-51
1954		19	.362	.489	47	17	3	0	1	2.1	7	9	10	10	0	2	0	14	32	1	5	3.1	.979	SS-9, 3B-5, 2B-1
1955	BOS A	55	.193	.336	119	23	2	0	5	4.2	15	17	17	21	0	17	5	55	92	12	23	4.1	.925	SS-20, 2B-17, 3B-2
17 yrs.		1574	.239	.366	5606	1339	238	35	134	2.4	874	601	1041	827	61	23	5	3276	4502	357	1042	5.2	.956	SS-1296, 2B-166, 3B-95, 1B-2
WORLD SERIES																								
1940	CIN N	7	.200	.200	25	5	0	0	0	0.0	0	2	1	2	0	0	0	14	12	0	6	3.7	1.000	2B-7

Brian Jordan

JORDAN, BRIAN O'NEAL
B. Mar. 29, 1967, Baltimore, Md.

BR TR 6′ 1″ 205 lbs.

Year	Team	Games	BA	SA	AB	H	2B	3B	HR	HR%	R	RBI	BB	SO	SB	Pinch Hit AB	Pinch Hit H	PO	A	E	DP	TC/G	FA	G by Pos
1992	STL N	55	.207	.373	193	40	9	4	5	2.6	17	22	10	48	7	5	1	101	4	1	0	2.0	.991	OF-53
1993		67	.309	.543	223	69	10	6	10	4.5	33	44	12	35	6	2	0	140	4	4	0	2.3	.973	OF-65
1994		53	.258	.410	178	46	8	2	5	2.8	14	15	16	40	4	5	3	105	6	1	1	2.4	.991	OF-46, 1B-1
1995		131	.296	.488	490	145	20	4	22	4.5	83	81	22	79	24	6	3	268	4	1	2	2.2	.996	OF-126
4 yrs.		306	.277	.466	1084	300	47	16	42	3.9	147	162	60	202	41	18	7	614	18	7	3	2.2	.989	OF-290, 1B-1

Buck Jordan

JORDAN, BAXTER BYERLY
B. Jan. 16, 1907, Cooleemee, N. C. D. Mar. 18, 1993, Salisbury, N. C.

BL TR 6′ 170 lbs.

Year	Team	Games	BA	SA	AB	H	2B	3B	HR	HR%	R	RBI	BB	SO	SB	Pinch Hit AB	Pinch Hit H	PO	A	E	DP	TC/G	FA	G by Pos
1927	NY N	5	.200	.200	5	1	0	0	0	0.0	0	0	0	3	0	5	1	0	0	0	0	0.0	—	
1929		2	.500	1.000	2	1	1	0	0	0.0	1	0	0	0	0	1	0	1	0	0	1	1.0	1.000	1B-1
1931	WAS A	9	.222	.333	18	4	2	0	0	0.0	3	1	1	3	0	1	0	45	0	1	3	6.6	.978	1B-7

Buck Jordan *continued*

Year	Team	Games	BA	SA	AB	H	2B	3B	HR	HR%	R	RBI	BB	SO	SB	Pinch Hit AB	Pinch Hit H	PO	A	E	DP	TC/G	FA	G by Pos
1932	BOS N	49	.321	.434	212	68	12	3	2	0.9	27	29	4	5	1	0	0	514	31	5	48	11.2	.991	1B-49
1933		152	.286	.386	588	168	29	9	4	0.7	77	46	34	22	4	2	0	1513	88	14	117	10.8	.991	1B-150
1934		124	.311	.413	489	152	26	9	2	0.4	68	58	35	19	3	7	6	1165	66	14	85	10.6	.989	1B-117
1935		130	.279	.383	470	131	24	5	5	1.1	62	35	19	17	3	19	5	876	79	17	59	9.3	.983	1B-95, 3B-8, OF-2
1936		138	.323	.405	555	179	27	5	3	0.5	81	66	45	22	2	2	0	1307	96	10	137	10.4	.993	1B-136
1937	**2 teams**	**BOS N** (8G –.250) **CIN N** (98G –.282)																						
"	**total**	106	.281	.352	324	91	14	3	1	0.3	46	28	25	14	6	28	7	669	46	8	55	9.5	.989	1B-76
1938	**2 teams**	**CIN N** (9G –.286) **PHI N** (87G –.300)																						
"	**total**	96	.300	.363	317	95	18	1	0	0.0	31	18	19	4	1	19	6	176	115	4	24	3.9	.986	3B-58, 1B-17
10 yrs.		811	.299	.391	2980	890	153	35	17	0.6	396	281	182	109	20	84	25	6266	521	73	529	9.6	.989	1B-648, 3B-66, OF-2

Dutch Jordan

JORDAN, ADOLPH OTTO BR TR 5′10″ 185 lbs.
B. Jan. 5, 1880, Pittsburgh, Pa. D. Dec. 23, 1972, West Allegheny, Pa.

Year	Team	Games	BA	SA	AB	H	2B	3B	HR	HR%	R	RBI	BB	SO	SB	Pinch Hit AB	Pinch Hit H	PO	A	E	DP	TC/G	FA	G by Pos
1903	BKN N	78	.236	.285	267	63	11	1	0	0.0	27	21	19		9	1	0	145	161	27	15	4.3	.919	2B-54, 3B-18, OF-4, 1B-1
1904		87	.179	.234	252	45	10	2	0	0.0	21	19	13		7	2	1	167	196	17	17	4.5	.955	2B-70, 3B-11, 1B-4
2 yrs.		165	.208	.260	519	108	21	3	0	0.0	48	40	32		16	3	1	312	357	44	32	4.4	.938	2B-124, 3B-29, 1B-5, OF-4

Jimmy Jordan

JORDAN, JAMES WILLIAM (Lord) BR TR 5′9″ 157 lbs.
B. Jan. 13, 1908, Tucapau, S. C. D. Dec. 4, 1957, Gastonia, N. C.

Year	Team	Games	BA	SA	AB	H	2B	3B	HR	HR%	R	RBI	BB	SO	SB	Pinch Hit AB	Pinch Hit H	PO	A	E	DP	TC/G	FA	G by Pos
1933	BKN N	70	.256	.322	211	54	12	1	0	0.0	16	17	4	6	3	2	1	122	203	12	27	5.4	.964	SS-51, 2B-11
1934		97	.266	.322	369	98	17	2	0	0.0	34	43	9	32	1	1	0	171	256	21	50	4.4	.953	SS-51, 2B-41, 3B-9
1935		94	.278	.302	295	82	7	0	0	0.0	26	30	9	17	3	14	5	177	279	14	39	5.9	.970	2B-46, SS-28, 3B-5
1936		115	.234	.291	398	93	15	1	2	0.5	26	28	15	21	1	4	1	235	275	15	44	5.0	.971	2B-98, 3B-6, SS-1
4 yrs.		376	.257	.308	1273	327	51	4	2	0.2	102	118	37	76	8	21	7	705	1013	62	160	5.1	.965	2B-196, SS-131, 3B-20

Kevin Jordan

JORDAN, KEVIN WAYNE BR TR 6′1″ 185 lbs.
B. Oct. 9, 1969, San Francisco, Calif.

Year	Team	Games	BA	SA	AB	H	2B	3B	HR	HR%	R	RBI	BB	SO	SB	Pinch Hit AB	Pinch Hit H	PO	A	E	DP	TC/G	FA	G by Pos
1995	PHI N	24	.185	.315	54	10	1	0	2	3.7	6	6	2	9	0	10	1	29	35	1	8	6.5	.985	2B-9, 3B-1

Mike Jordan

JORDAN, MICHAEL HENRY 5′7½″ 155 lbs.
B. Feb. 7, 1863, Lawrence, Mass. D. Sept. 25, 1940, Lawrence, Mass.

Year	Team	Games	BA	SA	AB	H	2B	3B	HR	HR%	R	RBI	BB	SO	SB	Pinch Hit AB	Pinch Hit H	PO	A	E	DP	TC/G	FA	G by Pos
1890	PIT N	37	.096	.104	125	12	1	0	0	0.0	8	6	15	19	5	0	0	62	9	4	0	2.0	.947	OF-37

Ricky Jordan

JORDAN, PAUL SCOTT BR TR 6′5″ 210 lbs.
B. May 26, 1965, Richmond, Calif.

Year	Team	Games	BA	SA	AB	H	2B	3B	HR	HR%	R	RBI	BB	SO	SB	Pinch Hit AB	Pinch Hit H	PO	A	E	DP	TC/G	FA	G by Pos
1988	PHI N	69	.308	.491	273	84	15	1	11	4.0	41	43	7	39	1	0	0	579	35	5	41	9.0	.992	1B-69
1989		144	.285	.407	523	149	22	3	12	2.3	63	75	23	62	4	10	4	1271	61	9	99	9.6	.993	1B-140
1990		92	.241	.352	324	78	21	0	5	1.5	32	44	13	39	2	8	2	743	37	4	65	9.3	.995	1B-84
1991		101	.272	.452	301	82	21	3	9	3.0	38	49	14	49	0	28	9	626	37	9	37	9.3	.987	1B-72
1992		94	.304	.417	276	84	19	0	4	1.4	33	34	5	44	3	28	8	427	27	2	34	7.0	.996	1B-54, OF-11
1993		90	.289	.421	159	46	4	1	5	3.1	21	18	8	32	0	53	16	201	4	2	20	6.3	.990	1B-33
1994		72	.282	.473	220	62	14	2	8	3.6	29	37	6	32	0	23	4	430	14	3	41	9.1	.993	1B-49
7 yrs.		662	.282	.425	2076	585	116	10	54	2.6	257	300	76	297	10	150	43	4277	215	34	337	8.8	.992	1B-501, OF-11
LEAGUE CHAMPIONSHIP SERIES																								
1993	PHI N	2	.000	.000	1	0	0	0	0	0.0	0	0	1	0	0	1	0	0	0	0	0	0.0	—	
WORLD SERIES																								
1993	PHI N	3	.200	.200	10	2	0	0	0	0.0	0	0	0	2	0	1	0	0	0	0	0	0.0	.000	DH-2

Scott Jordan

JORDAN, SCOTT ALLAN BR TR 6′ 175 lbs.
B. May 27, 1963, Waco, Tex.

Year	Team	Games	BA	SA	AB	H	2B	3B	HR	HR%	R	RBI	BB	SO	SB	Pinch Hit AB	Pinch Hit H	PO	A	E	DP	TC/G	FA	G by Pos
1988	CLE A	7	.111	.111	9	1	0	0	0	0.0	0	1	0	3	0	0	0	10	0	0	0	1.7	1.000	OF-6

Slats Jordan

JORDAN, CLARENCE VEASEY BL TL 6′1″ 190 lbs.
B. Sept. 26, 1879, Baltimore, Md. D. Dec. 7, 1953, Catonsville, Md.

Year	Team	Games	BA	SA	AB	H	2B	3B	HR	HR%	R	RBI	BB	SO	SB	Pinch Hit AB	Pinch Hit H	PO	A	E	DP	TC/G	FA	G by Pos
1901	BAL A	1	.000	.000	3	0	0	0	0	0.0	0	0	0	0	0	0	0	13	0	2	0	15.0	.867	1B-1
1902		1	.000	.000	4	0	0	0	0	0.0	0	0	0	0	0	0	0	0	0	0	0	0.0	.000	OF-1
2 yrs.		2	.000	.000	7	0	0	0	0	0.0	0	0	0	0	0	0	0	13	0	2	0	7.5	.867	OF-1, 1B-1

Tim Jordan

JORDAN, TIMOTHY JOSEPH (Hoboken) BL TL 6′1″ 170 lbs.
B. Feb. 14, 1879, New York, N. Y. D. Sept. 13, 1949, Bronx, N. Y.

Year	Team	Games	BA	SA	AB	H	2B	3B	HR	HR%	R	RBI	BB	SO	SB	Pinch Hit AB	Pinch Hit H	PO	A	E	DP	TC/G	FA	G by Pos
1901	WAS A	6	.200	.250	20	4	1	0	0	0.0	2	2	3		0	0	0	62	2	4	2	11.3	.941	1B-6
1903	NY A	2	.125	.125	8	1	0	0	0	0.0	2	0	0		0	0	0	16	0	2	3	9.0	.889	1B-2
1906	BKN N	129	.262	.422	450	118	20	8	**12**	**2.7**	67	78	59		16	3	0	1240	64	30	44	10.6	.978	1B-126
1907		147	.274	.363	485	133	15	8	4	0.8	43	53	74		10	3	0	1417	78	31	71	10.7	.980	1B-143
1908		148	.247	.371	515	127	18	5	**12**	**2.3**	58	60	59		9	1	0	1462	55	28	52	10.6	.982	1B-146
1909		103	.273	.379	330	90	20	3	3	0.9	47	36	59		13	7	1	937	29	17	36	10.3	.983	1B-95
1910		5	.200	.800	5	1	0	0	1	20.0	1	3	0	2	0	5	1	0	0	0	0	0.0	—	
7 yrs.		540	.261	.382	1813	474	74	24	32	1.8	220	232	254	2	48	19	2	5134	228	112	208	10.6	.980	1B-518

Tom Jordan

JORDAN, THOMAS JEFFERSON BR TR 6′1½″ 195 lbs.
B. Sept. 5, 1919, Lawton, Okla.

Year	Team	Games	BA	SA	AB	H	2B	3B	HR	HR%	R	RBI	BB	SO	SB	Pinch Hit AB	Pinch Hit H	PO	A	E	DP	TC/G	FA	G by Pos
1944	CHI A	14	.267	.333	45	12	1	1	0	0.0	2	3	1	0	0	0	0	48	6	3	0	4.1	.947	C-14
1946	**2 teams**	**CHI A** (10G –.267) **CLE A** (14G –.200)																						
"	**total**	24	.220	.380	50	11	3	1	1	2.0	3	3	3	2	1	10	1	43	6	1	1	3.3	.980	C-15
1948	STL A	1	.000	.000	1	0	0	0	0	0.0	0	0	0	0	0	1	0	0	0	0	0	0.0	—	
3 yrs.		39	.240	.354	96	23	4	2	1	1.0	5	6	4	2	1	11	1	91	12	4	1	3.7	.963	C-29

Arndt Jorgens

JORGENS, ARNDT LUDWIG BR TR 5′9″ 160 lbs.
Brother of Orville Jorgens.
B. May 18, 1905, Modum, Norway D. Mar. 1, 1980, Wilmette, Ill.

Year	Team	Games	BA	SA	AB	H	2B	3B	HR	HR%	R	RBI	BB	SO	SB	Pinch Hit AB	Pinch Hit H	PO	A	E	DP	TC/G	FA	G by Pos
1929	NY A	18	.324	.412	34	11	3	0	0	0.0	6	4	6	7	0	2	0	41	6	1	1	3.2	.979	C-15
1930		16	.367	.467	30	11	3	0	0	0.0	7	1	2	4	0	0	0	43	5	2	1	3.1	.960	C-16

Arndt Jorgens *continued*

Year	Team	Games	BA	SA	AB	H	2B	3B	HR	HR%	R	RBI	BB	SO	SB	Pinch Hit AB	Pinch Hit H	PO	A	E	DP	TC/G	FA	G by Pos
1931		46	.270	.320	100	27	1	2	0	0.0	12	14	9	3	0	4	0	144	10	6	0	4.0	.963	C-40
1932		55	.219	.318	151	33	7	1	2	1.3	13	19	14	11	0	0	0	240	20	9	3	4.9	.967	C-55
1933		21	.220	.400	50	11	3	0	2	4.0	9	13	12	3	1	3	0	108	2	2	2	5.9	.982	C-19
1934		58	.208	.251	183	38	6	1	0	0.0	14	20	23	24	2	2	1	288	20	5	7	5.6	.984	C-56
1935		36	.238	.262	84	20	2	0	0	0.0	6	8	12	10	0	3	0	130	12	0	5	4.3	1.000	C-33
1936		31	.273	.348	66	18	3	1	0	0.0	5	5	2	3	0	1	1	87	9	1	0	3.2	.990	C-30
1937		13	.130	.174	23	3	1	0	0	0.0	3	3	2	5	0	1	0	27	2	0	0	2.6	1.000	C-11
1938		9	.235	.353	17	4	2	0	0	0.0	3	2	3	3	0	1	0	18	6	2	0	3.3	.923	C-8
1939		3	—	—	0	0	0	0	0	—	1	0	0	0	0	0	0	2	0	0	0	1.0	1.000	C-2
11 yrs.		306	.238	.310	738	176	31	5	4	0.5	79	89	85	73	3	17	2	1128	92	28	19	4.4	.978	C-285

Mike Jorgensen

JORGENSEN, MICHAEL
B. Aug. 16, 1948, Passaic, N. J.
Manager 1995.

BL TL 6′ 195 lbs.

Year	Team	Games	BA	SA	AB	H	2B	3B	HR	HR%	R	RBI	BB	SO	SB	Pinch Hit AB	Pinch Hit H	PO	A	E	DP	TC/G	FA	G by Pos
1968	NY N	8	.143	.214	14	2	1	0	0	0.0	0	0	0	4	0	4	0	32	1	0	3	8.3	1.000	1B-4
1970		76	.195	.356	87	17	3	1	3	3.4	15	4	10	23	2	15	2	145	12	3	9	2.7	.981	1B-50, OF-10
1971		45	.220	.373	118	26	1	1	5	4.2	16	11	11	24	1	13	2	64	2	3	1	2.2	.957	OF-31, 1B-1
1972	MON N	113	.231	.384	372	86	12	3	13	3.5	48	47	53	75	12	10	2	801	57	6	66	8.3	.993	1B-76, OF-28
1973		138	.230	.344	413	95	16	2	9	2.2	49	47	64	49	16	13	4	1002	80	5	88	8.1	.995	1B-123, OF-11
1974		131	.310	.488	287	89	16	1	11	3.8	45	59	70	39	3	26	8	653	54	1	47	5.9	.999	1B-91, OF-29
1975		144	.261	.422	445	116	18	0	18	4.0	58	67	79	75	3	17	4	1153	91	7	123	9.0	.994	1B-133, OF-6
1976		125	.254	.344	343	87	13	0	6	1.7	36	23	52	48	7	14	0	651	58	8	59	5.9	.989	1B-81, OF-41
1977	2 teams	MON N (19G –.200) OAK A (66G –.246)																						
″	total	85	.242	.381	223	54	5	1	8	3.6	21	32	28	48	3	18	1	388	36	4	27	5.7	.991	1B-53, OF-20, DH-2
1978	TEX A	96	.196	.258	97	19	3	0	1	1.0	20	9	18	10	3	3	0	317	31	2	23	4.0	.994	1B-78, OF-9, DH-1
1979		90	.223	.382	157	35	7	0	6	3.8	21	16	14	29	0	19	2	320	31	4	28	4.3	.989	1B-60, OF-20, DH-2
1980	NY N	119	.255	.355	321	82	11	0	7	2.2	43	43	46	55	0	19	2	562	37	4	33	5.9	.993	1B-72, OF-31
1981		86	.205	.352	122	25	5	2	3	2.5	8	15	12	24	4	29	5	143	9	1	8	2.6	.993	1B-40, OF-19
1982		120	.254	.360	114	29	6	0	2	1.8	16	14	21	24	2	48	15	131	5	2	14	1.9	.986	1B-56, OF-16
1983	2 teams	NY N (38G –.250) ATL N (57G –.250)																						
″	total	95	.250	.389	72	18	4	0	2	2.8	10	11	10	12	0	45	12	81	6	0	11	2.0	1.000	1B-38, OF-6
1984	2 teams	ATL N (31G –.269) STL N (59G –.245)																						
″	total	90	.250	.347	124	31	5	2	1	0.8	9	17	13	23	0	38	10	222	19	2	30	4.8	.992	1B-47, OF-4
1985	STL N	72	.196	.250	112	22	6	0	0	0.0	14	11	31	27	2	22	3	318	17	2	32	6.6	.994	1B-49, OF-2
17 yrs.		1633	.243	.373	3421	833	132	13	95	2.8	429	426	532	589	58	353	72	6983	546	54	602	5.7	.993	1B-1052, OF-283, DH-5
LEAGUE CHAMPIONSHIP SERIES																								
1985	STL N	2	.000	.000	2	0	0	0	0	0.0	0	0	0	1	0	2	0	0	0	0	0	0.0	—	
WORLD SERIES																								
1985	STL N	2	.000	.000	3	0	0	0	0	0.0	0	0	0	0	0	2	0	1	0	0	0	1.0	1.000	OF-1

Pinky Jorgensen

JORGENSEN, CARL
B. Nov. 21, 1914, Laton, Calif.

BR TR 6′ 1″ 195 lbs.

Year	Team	Games	BA	SA	AB	H	2B	3B	HR	HR%	R	RBI	BB	SO	SB	Pinch Hit AB	Pinch Hit H	PO	A	E	DP	TC/G	FA	G by Pos
1937	CIN N	6	.286	.286	14	4	0	0	0	0.0	1	1	1	2	0	1	0	6	1	1	0	2.0	.875	OF-4

Spider Jorgensen

JORGENSEN, JOHN DONALD
B. Nov. 3, 1919, Folsom, Calif.

BL TR 5′ 9″ 155 lbs.

Year	Team	Games	BA	SA	AB	H	2B	3B	HR	HR%	R	RBI	BB	SO	SB	Pinch Hit AB	Pinch Hit H	PO	A	E	DP	TC/G	FA	G by Pos
1947	BKN N	129	.274	.410	441	121	29	8	5	1.1	57	67	58	45	4	1	1	116	235	19	26	2.9	.949	3B-128
1948		31	.300	.444	90	27	6	2	1	1.1	15	13	16	13	1	5	3	22	33	7	3	2.6	.887	3B-24
1949		53	.269	.343	134	36	5	1	1	0.7	15	14	23	13	0	13	2	28	59	5	5	2.6	.946	3B-36
1950	2 teams	BKN N (2G –.000) NY N (24G –.135)																						
″	total	26	.128	.128	39	5	0	0	0	0.0	5	5	6	2	0	17	2	7	15	2	1	4.0	.917	3B-6
1951	NY N	28	.235	.353	51	12	0	0	2	3.9	5	8	3	2	0	16	3	14	1	0	0	1.3	1.000	OF-11, 3B-1
5 yrs.		267	.266	.384	755	201	40	11	9	1.2	97	107	106	75	5	52	11	187	343	33	35	2.7	.941	3B-195, OF-11
WORLD SERIES																								
1947	BKN N	7	.200	.300	20	4	2	0	0	0.0	1	3	2	4	0	0	0	8	12	2	1	3.1	.909	3B-7
1949		4	.182	.364	11	2	2	0	0	0.0	1	0	2	2	0	1	0	1	6	0	0	2.3	1.000	3B-3
2 yrs.		11	.194	.323	31	6	4	0	0	0.0	2	3	4	6	0	1	0	9	18	2	1	2.9	.931	3B-10

Terry Jorgensen

JORGENSEN, TERRY ALLEN
B. Sept. 2, 1966, Kewaunee, Wis.

BR TR 6′ 4″ 208 lbs.

Year	Team	Games	BA	SA	AB	H	2B	3B	HR	HR%	R	RBI	BB	SO	SB	Pinch Hit AB	Pinch Hit H	PO	A	E	DP	TC/G	FA	G by Pos
1989	MIN A	10	.174	.217	23	4	1	0	0	0.0	1	2	4	5	0	0	0	4	19	1	3	2.7	.958	3B-9
1992		22	.310	.328	58	18	1	0	0	0.0	5	5	3	11	1	1	0	103	25	1	14	5.4	.992	1B-13, 3B-9, SS-2
1993		59	.224	.289	152	34	7	0	1	0.7	15	12	10	21	1	3	0	65	95	3	13	2.7	.982	3B-45, 1B-9, SS-6
3 yrs.		91	.240	.292	233	56	9	0	1	0.4	21	19	17	37	2	4	0	172	139	5	30	3.4	.984	3B-63, 1B-22, SS-8

Felix Jose

JOSE, DOMINGO FELIX
Born Domingo Felix Andujar (Felix).
B. May 8, 1965, Santo Domingo, Dominican Republic.

BB TR 6′ 1″ 190 lbs.

Year	Team	Games	BA	SA	AB	H	2B	3B	HR	HR%	R	RBI	BB	SO	SB	Pinch Hit AB	Pinch Hit H	PO	A	E	DP	TC/G	FA	G by Pos
1988	OAK A	8	.333	.500	6	2	1	0	0	0.0	2	1	0	1	1	2	0	8	0	0	0	1.3	1.000	OF-6
1989		20	.193	.228	57	11	2	0	0	0.0	3	5	4	13	0	3	1	35	2	1	0	2.0	.974	OF-19
1990	2 teams	OAK A (101G –.264) STL N (25G –.271)																						
″	total	126	.265	.385	426	113	16	1	11	2.6	54	52	24	81	12	13	2	254	5	5	1	2.2	.981	OF-115, DH-7
1991	STL N	154	.305	.438	568	173	40	6	8	1.4	69	77	50	113	20	1	1	268	15	3	2	1.9	.990	OF-153
1992		131	.295	.432	509	150	22	3	14	2.8	62	75	40	100	28	5	2	273	11	6	1	2.3	.979	OF-127
1993	KC A	149	.253	.349	499	126	24	3	6	1.2	64	43	36	95	31	9	2	237	6	7	3	1.7	.972	OF-144, DH-1
1994		99	.303	.475	366	111	28	1	11	3.0	56	55	35	75	10	2	1	193	7	4	1	2.1	.980	OF-98
1995		9	.133	.167	30	4	1	0	0	0.0	2	1	2	9	0	2	0	15	2	0	0	2.4	1.000	OF-7
8 yrs.		696	.280	.407	2461	690	134	14	50	2.0	312	309	191	487	102	37	9	1283	48	26	8	2.0	.981	OF-669, DH-8

Rick Joseph

JOSEPH, RICARDO EMELINDO BR TR 6′ 1″ 192 lbs.
Born Ricardo Emilindo Joseph (Harrigan).
B. Aug. 24, 1939, San Pedro de Macoris, Dominican Republic
D. Sept. 8, 1979, Santo Domingo, Dominican Republic.

Year	Team	Games	BA	SA	AB	H	2B	3B	HR	HR%	R	RBI	BB	SO	SB	Pinch Hit AB	Pinch Hit H	PO	A	E	DP	TC/G	FA	G by Pos
1964	KC A	17	.222	.259	54	12	2	0	0	0.0	3	1	3	11	0	4	0	102	12	5	14	7.9	.958	1B-12, 3B-3
1967	PHI N	17	.220	.341	41	9	2	0	1	2.4	4	5	4	10	0	5	1	94	9	0	7	7.9	1.000	1B-13
1968		66	.219	.310	155	34	5	0	3	1.9	20	12	16	35	0	24	7	256	38	5	24	6.6	.983	1B-30, 3B-14, OF-1
1969		99	.273	.398	264	72	15	0	6	2.3	35	37	22	57	2	25	3	162	112	11	21	3.8	.961	3B-58, 1B-17, 2B-1
1970		71	.227	.336	119	27	2	1	3	2.5	7	10	6	28	0	37	11	68	8	5	5	2.6	.938	OF-12, 1B-10, 3B-9
5 yrs.		270	.243	.349	633	154	26	1	13	2.1	69	65	51	141	2	95	22	682	179	26	71	4.9	.971	3B-84, 1B-82, OF-13, 2B-1

Duane Josephson

JOSEPHSON, DUANE CHARLES BR TR 6′ 190 lbs.
B. June 3, 1942, New Hampton, Iowa.

Year	Team	Games	BA	SA	AB	H	2B	3B	HR	HR%	R	RBI	BB	SO	SB	Pinch Hit AB	Pinch Hit H	PO	A	E	DP	TC/G	FA	G by Pos
1965	CHI A	4	.111	.111	9	1	0	0	0	0.0	2	0	2	4	0	0	0	21	1	0	0	5.5	1.000	C-4
1966		11	.237	.263	38	9	1	0	0	0.0	3	3	3	3	0	0	0	66	8	2	1	6.9	.974	C-11
1967		62	.238	.291	189	45	5	1	1	0.5	11	9	6	24	0	5	0	292	24	0	3	5.4	1.000	C-59
1968		128	.247	.353	434	107	16	6	6	1.4	35	45	18	52	2	11	3	641	86	7	15	6.0	.990	C-122
1969		52	.241	.321	162	39	6	2	1	0.6	19	20	13	17	0	7	3	227	27	4	1	5.5	.984	C-47
1970		96	.316	.407	285	90	12	1	4	1.4	28	41	24	28	1	14	5	353	38	6	7	4.7	.985	C-84
1971	BOS A	91	.245	.395	306	75	14	1	10	3.3	38	39	22	35	2	5	1	491	32	6	5	6.1	.989	C-87
1972		26	.268	.378	82	22	4	1	1	1.2	11	7	4	11	0	4	1	155	9	3	8	7.6	.982	1B-16, C-6
8 yrs.		470	.258	.358	1505	388	58	12	23	1.5	147	164	92	174	5	46	13	2246	225	28	40	5.7	.989	C-420, 1B-16

Von Joshua

JOSHUA, VON EVERETT BL TL 5′10″ 170 lbs.
B. May 1, 1948, Oakland, Calif.

Year	Team	Games	BA	SA	AB	H	2B	3B	HR	HR%	R	RBI	BB	SO	SB	Pinch Hit AB	Pinch Hit H	PO	A	E	DP	TC/G	FA	G by Pos
1969	LA N	14	.250	.250	8	2	0	0	0	0.0	2	0	0	2	1	1	0	4	0	1	0	0.6	.800	OF-8
1970		72	.266	.358	109	29	1	3	1	0.9	23	8	6	24	2	21	5	47	1	3	1	1.2	.941	OF-41
1971		11	.000	.000	7	0	0	0	0	0.0	2	0	0	1	0	5	0	7	0	0	0	1.4	1.000	OF-5
1973		75	.252	.327	159	40	4	1	2	1.3	19	17	8	29	7	25	8	61	2	1	0	1.4	.984	OF-46
1974		81	.234	.315	124	29	5	1	1	0.8	11	16	7	17	3	45	8	33	0	2	0	1.0	.943	OF-35
1975	SF N	129	.318	.448	507	161	25	10	7	1.4	75	43	32	75	20	11	4	279	10	2	3	2.5	.993	OF-117
1976	2 teams	SF N (42G –.263) MIL A (107G –.267)																						
″	total	149	.266	.347	579	154	18	7	5	0.9	57	30	22	78	9	10	3	338	13	9	5	2.6	.975	OF-140, DH-1
1977	MIL A	144	.261	.384	536	140	25	7	9	1.7	58	49	21	74	12	12	1	311	8	10	0	2.3	.970	OF-140
1979	LA N	94	.282	.408	142	40	7	1	3	2.1	22	14	7	23	1	48	9	56	2	2	0	1.3	.967	OF-46
1980	SD N	53	.238	.397	63	15	2	1	2	3.2	8	7	5	15	0	39	9	26	1	0	1	1.9	1.000	OF-12, 1B-2
10 yrs.		822	.273	.380	2234	610	87	31	30	1.3	277	184	108	338	55	217	47	1162	37	30	10	2.1	.976	OF-590, 1B-2, DH-1
LEAGUE CHAMPIONSHIP SERIES																								
1974	LA N	1	—	—	0	0	0	0	0	—	0	0	1	0	0	0	0	0	0	0	0	0.0	—	
WORLD SERIES																								
1974	LA N	4	.000	.000	4	0	0	0	0	0.0	0	0	0	0	0	4	0	0	0	0	0	0.0	—	

Ted Jourdan

JOURDAN, THEODORE CHARLES BL TL 6′ 175 lbs.
B. Sept. 5, 1895, New Orleans, La. D. Sept. 23, 1961, New Orleans, La.

Year	Team	Games	BA	SA	AB	H	2B	3B	HR	HR%	R	RBI	BB	SO	SB	Pinch Hit AB	Pinch Hit H	PO	A	E	DP	TC/G	FA	G by Pos
1916	CHI A	3	.000	.000	2	0	0	0	0	0.0	0	0	1	1	2	2	0	0	0	0	0	0.0	—	
1917		17	.147	.206	34	5	0	1	0	0.0	2	2	1	3	0	3	0	68	5	2	2	5.4	.973	1B-14
1918		7	.100	.100	10	1	0	0	0	0.0	1	1	0	0	0	5	1	12	0	0	0	6.0	1.000	1B-2
1920		48	.240	.293	150	36	6	1	0	0.0	16	8	17	17	3	8	1	369	18	7	35	9.9	.982	1B-40
4 yrs.		75	.214	.265	196	42	6	2	0	0.0	19	11	19	21	5	18	2	449	23	9	37	8.6	.981	1B-56

Pop Joy

JOY, ALOYSIUS C.
B. June 11, 1860, Washington, D. C. D. June 28, 1937, Washington, D. C.

Year	Team	Games	BA	SA	AB	H	2B	3B	HR	HR%	R	RBI	BB	SO	SB	Pinch Hit AB	Pinch Hit H	PO	A	E	DP	TC/G	FA	G by Pos
1884	WAS U	36	.215	.215	130	28	0	0	0	0.0	12		2			0	0	331	7	12	14	9.7	.966	1B-36

Joyce

JOYCE,
Deceased.

Year	Team	Games	BA	SA	AB	H	2B	3B	HR	HR%	R	RBI	BB	SO	SB	Pinch Hit AB	Pinch Hit H	PO	A	E	DP	TC/G	FA	G by Pos
1886	WAS N	1	—	—	0	0	0	0	0	—	0	0	0	0		0	0	0	0	0	0	0.0	.000	OF-1

Bill Joyce

JOYCE, WILLIAM MICHAEL (Scrappy Bill) BL TR 5′11″ 185 lbs.
B. Sept. 21, 1865, St. Louis, Mo. D. May 8, 1941, St. Louis, Mo.
Manager 1896–98.

Year	Team	Games	BA	SA	AB	H	2B	3B	HR	HR%	R	RBI	BB	SO	SB	Pinch Hit AB	Pinch Hit H	PO	A	E	DP	TC/G	FA	G by Pos
1890	BKN P	133	.252	.368	489	123	18	18	1	0.2	121	78	**123**	77	43	0	0	176	284	107	22	4.3	.811	3B-133
1891	BOS AA	65	.309	.506	243	75	9	15	3	1.2	76	51	63	27	36	0	0	90	149	41	12	4.3	.854	3B-64, 1B-1
1892	BKN N	97	.245	.398	372	91	15	12	6	1.6	89	45	82	55	23	0	0	148	164	50	8	3.7	.862	3B-94, OF-3
1894	WAS N	99	.355	.648	355	126	25	14	17	**4.8**	103	89	87	33	21	0	0	152	183	52	20	3.9	.866	3B-99
1895		126	.312	.527	474	148	25	13	17	3.6	110	95	**96**	54	29	0	0	186	232	77	16	3.9	.844	3B-126
1896	2 teams	WAS N (81G –.313) NY N (49G –.370)																						
″	total	130	.333	.524	475	158	25	12	**14**	**2.9**	121	94	101	34	45	0	0	205	296	62	22	4.3	.890	3B-97, 2B-33
1897	NY N	109	.304	.433	388	118	15	13	3	0.8	109	64	78		33	0	0	187	199	66	19	4.2	.854	3B-106, 1B-2
1898		145	.258	.392	508	131	20	9	10	2.0	91	91	88		34	0	0	1271	121	54	73	9.9	.963	1B-130, 3B-14, 2B-2
8 yrs.		904	.294	.468	3304	970	152	106	71	2.1	820	607	718	280	264	0	0	2415	1628	509	192	5.0	.888	3B-733, 1B-133, 2B-35, OF-3

Mike Joyce

Playing record listed under Mike O'Neill.

Wally Joyner

JOYNER, WALLACE KEITH (Wally World) BL TL 6′ 2″ 185 lbs.
B. June 16, 1962, Atlanta, Ga.

Year	Team	Games	BA	SA	AB	H	2B	3B	HR	HR%	R	RBI	BB	SO	SB	Pinch Hit AB	Pinch Hit H	PO	A	E	DP	TC/G	FA	G by Pos
1986	CAL A	154	.290	.457	593	172	27	3	22	3.7	82	100	57	58	5	4	1	1222	139	15	128	9.1	.989	1B-152
1987		149	.285	.528	564	161	33	1	34	6.0	100	117	72	64	8	2	0	1276	92	10	133	9.2	.993	1B-149
1988		158	.295	.419	597	176	31	2	13	2.2	81	85	55	51	8	4	2	1369	143	8	148	9.7	.995	1B-156
1989		159	.282	.420	593	167	30	2	16	2.7	78	79	46	58	3	2	1	1487	99	4	146	10.0	.997	1B-159
1990		83	.268	.394	310	83	15	0	8	2.6	35	41	41	34	2	1	0	727	62	4	78	9.6	.995	1B-83

Wally Joyner *continued*

Year	Team	Lg	Games	BA	SA	AB	H	2B	3B	HR	HR%	R	RBI	BB	SO	SB	Pinch Hit AB	Pinch Hit H	PO	A	E	DP	TC/G	FA	G by Pos
1991			143	.301	.488	551	166	34	3	21	3.8	79	96	52	66	2	2	0	1335	98	8	124	10.2	.994	1B-141
1992	KC	A	149	.269	.386	572	154	36	2	9	1.6	66	66	55	50	11	1	0	1236	137	10	138	9.3	.993	1B-145, DH-4
1993			141	.292	.467	497	145	36	3	15	3.0	83	65	66	67	5	1	0	1116	145	7	116	9.1	.994	1B-140
1994			97	.311	.449	363	113	20	3	8	2.2	52	57	47	43	3	0	0	779	64	8	67	8.8	.991	1B-86, DH-11
1995			131	.310	.447	465	144	28	0	12	2.6	69	83	69	65	3	7	1	1111	118	3	119	9.6	.998	1B-126, DH-2
10 yrs.			1364	.290	.447	5105	1481	290	19	158	3.1	725	789	560	556	50	24	5	11658	1097	77	1197	9.5	.994	1B-1337, DH-17
LEAGUE CHAMPIONSHIP SERIES																									
1986	CAL	A	3	.455	.909	11	5	2	0	1	9.1	3	2	2	0	0	0	0	26	1	0	2	9.0	1.000	1B-3

Oscar Judd

JUDD, THOMAS WILLIAM OSCAR (Ossie) BL TL 6′½″ 180 lbs.
B. Feb. 14, 1908, London, Ont., Canada D. Dec. 27, 1995, Ingersoll, Ont., Canada.

Year	Team	Lg	Games	BA	SA	AB	H	2B	3B	HR	HR%	R	RBI	BB	SO	SB	Pinch Hit AB	Pinch Hit H	PO	A	E	DP	TC/G	FA	G by Pos
1941	BOS	A	10	.500	.750	4	2	1	0	0	0.0	2	2	3	0	0	1	0	0	4	1	0	0.7	.800	P-7
1942			36	.269	.418	67	18	2	1	2	3.0	10	4	3	7	0	5	1	6	29	1	1	1.2	.972	P-31
1943			27	.259	.315	54	14	1	1	0	0.0	2	0	5	4	0	2	0	9	41	3	4	2.3	.943	P-23
1944			10	.182	.182	11	2	0	0	0	0.0	4	1	3	0	0	1	0	1	4	0	0	0.6	1.000	P-9
1945	2 teams		BOS A (2G –.500) PHI N (27G –.267)																						
″	total		29	.281	.344	32	9	2	0	0	0.0	4	2	4	4	0	3	0	4	23	0	0	1.1	1.000	P-25
1946	PHI	N	46	.316	.405	79	25	2	1	1	1.3	7	8	4	4	0	14	2	10	50	0	0	2.0	1.000	P-30
1947			44	.188	.281	64	12	2	2	0	0.0	6	2	4	16	0	10	2	7	33	1	3	1.3	.976	P-32
1948			4	.167	.333	6	1	1	0	0	0.0	1	0	1	2	0	0	0	1	2	1	0	1.0	.750	P-4
8 yrs.			206	.262	.356	317	83	11	5	3	0.9	36	19	27	37	0	36	5	38	186	7	8	1.4	.970	P-161

Frank Jude

JUDE, FRANK BR TR 5′7″ 150 lbs.
B. 1884, Libby, Minn. D. May 4, 1961, Brownsville, Tex.

Year	Team	Lg	Games	BA	SA	AB	H	2B	3B	HR	HR%	R	RBI	BB	SO	SB	Pinch Hit AB	Pinch Hit H	PO	A	E	DP	TC/G	FA	G by Pos
1906	CIN	N	80	.208	.263	308	64	6	4	1	0.3	31	31	16		7	0	0	95	14	4	1	1.4	.965	OF-80

Joe Judge

JUDGE, JOSEPH IGNATIUS BL TL 5′8½″ 155 lbs.
B. May 25, 1894, Brooklyn, N. Y. D. Mar. 11, 1963, Washington, D. C.

Year	Team	Lg	Games	BA	SA	AB	H	2B	3B	HR	HR%	R	RBI	BB	SO	SB	Pinch Hit AB	Pinch Hit H	PO	A	E	DP	TC/G	FA	G by Pos
1915	WAS	A	12	.415	.463	41	17	2	0	0	0.0	7	9	4	6	2	0	0	97	5	1	7	8.6	.990	1B-10, OF-2
1916			103	.220	.298	336	74	10	8	0	0.0	42	31	54	44	18	0	0	935	69	14	53	9.9	.986	1B-103
1917			102	.285	.415	393	112	15	15	2	0.5	62	30	50	40	17	0	0	906	60	12	59	9.8	.988	1B-100
1918			130	.261	.341	502	131	23	7	1	0.2	56	46	49	32	20	0	0	1304	92	21	71	10.9	.985	1B-130
1919			135	.288	.409	521	150	33	12	2	0.4	83	31	81	35	23	2	0	1177	78	15	66	9.5	.988	1B-133
1920			126	.333	.462	493	164	19	15	5	1.0	103	51	65	34	12	1	0	1194	62	10	67	10.2	.992	1B-124
1921			153	.301	.412	622	187	26	11	7	1.1	87	72	68	35	21	0	0	1417	89	6	109	9.9	.996	1B-152
1922			148	.294	.450	591	174	32	15	10	1.7	84	81	50	20	5	1	1	1413	101	6	131	10.3	.996	1B-148
1923			113	.314	.417	405	127	24	6	2	0.5	56	63	58	20	11	1	0	1070	88	8	113	10.4	.993	1B-112
1924			140	.324	.450	516	167	38	9	3	0.6	71	79	53	21	13	0	0	1276	86	8	108	9.8	.994	1B-140
1925			112	.314	.487	376	118	31	5	8	2.1	65	66	55	21	7	2	0	901	71	7	92	9.0	.993	1B-109
1926			134	.291	.442	453	132	25	11	7	1.5	70	92	53	25	7	6	3	1145	95	8	90	9.8	.994	1B-128
1927			137	.308	.418	522	161	29	11	2	0.4	68	71	45	22	10	1	0	1309	71	6	79	10.2	.996	1B-136
1928			153	.306	.417	542	166	31	10	3	0.6	78	93	80	19	16	3	1	1412	92	6	118	10.1	.996	1B-149
1929			143	.315	.442	543	171	35	8	6	1.1	83	71	73	33	12	1	0	1323	88	6	116	10.0	.996	1B-142
1930			126	.326	.509	442	144	29	11	10	2.3	83	80	60	29	13	9	3	1050	67	2	95	9.6	.998	1B-117
1931			35	.284	.324	74	21	3	0	0	0.0	11	9	8	8	0	18	4	155	10	1	9	11.1	.994	1B-15
1932			82	.258	.364	291	75	16	3	3	1.0	45	29	37	19	3	4	0	668	46	2	71	9.2	.997	1B-78
1933	2 teams		BKN N (42G –.214) BOS A (35G –.296)																						
″	total		77	.255	.318	220	56	10	2	0	0.0	27	31	20	14	3	18	4	502	29	3	45	9.5	.994	1B-56
1934	BOS	A	10	.333	.467	15	5	2	0	0	0.0	3	2	2	1	0	8	2	24	1	0	1	12.5	1.000	1B-2
20 yrs.			2171	.298	.420	7898	2352	433	159	71	0.9	1184	1037	965	478	213	75	18	19278	1300	142	1500	9.9	.993	1B-2084, OF-2
WORLD SERIES																									
1924	WAS	A	7	.385	.423	26	10	1	0	0	0.0	4	0	5	2	0	0	0	62	4	1	8	9.6	.985	1B-7
1925			7	.174	.348	23	4	1	0	1	4.3	2	4	3	2	0	0	0	59	2	0	8	8.7	1.000	1B-7
2 yrs.			14	.286	.388	49	14	2	0	1	2.0	6	4	8	4	0	0	0	121	6	1	16	9.1	.992	1B-14

Walt Judnich

JUDNICH, WALTER FRANKLIN BL TL 6′1″ 205 lbs.
B. Jan. 24, 1917, San Francisco, Calif. D. July 12, 1971, Glendale, Calif.

Year	Team	Lg	Games	BA	SA	AB	H	2B	3B	HR	HR%	R	RBI	BB	SO	SB	Pinch Hit AB	Pinch Hit H	PO	A	E	DP	TC/G	FA	G by Pos
1940	STL	A	137	.303	.520	519	157	27	7	24	4.6	97	89	54	71	8	4	1	356	7	4	4	2.8	.989	OF-133
1941			146	.284	.456	546	155	40	6	14	2.6	90	83	80	45	5	6	3	383	11	8	3	2.9	.980	OF-140
1942			132	.313	.499	457	143	22	6	17	3.7	78	82	74	41	3	9	4	330	4	3	0	2.8	.991	OF-122
1946			142	.262	.411	511	134	23	4	15	2.9	60	72	60	54	0	3	0	409	6	2	2	3.0	.995	OF-137
1947			144	.258	.426	500	129	24	3	18	3.6	58	64	60	62	2	2	1	1105	77	13	118	8.3	.989	1B-129, OF-15
1948	CLE	A	79	.257	.372	218	56	13	3	2	0.9	36	29	56	23	2	10	2	240	11	4	19	3.7	.984	OF-49, 1B-20
1949	PIT	N	10	.229	.257	35	8	1	0	0	0.0	5	1	1	2	0	2	0	27	0	0	0	3.4	1.000	OF-8
7 yrs.			790	.281	.452	2786	782	150	29	90	3.2	424	420	385	298	20	36	11	2850	116	34	146	4.0	.989	OF-604, 1B-149
WORLD SERIES																									
1948	CLE	A	4	.077	.077	13	1	0	0	0	0.0	1	1	1	4	0	0	0	7	0	0	0	1.8	1.000	OF-4

Lyle Judy

JUDY, LYLE LeROY (Punch) BR TR 5′10″ 150 lbs.
B. Nov. 15, 1913, Lawrenceville, Ill. D. Jan. 15, 1991, Ormond Beach, Fla.

Year	Team	Lg	Games	BA	SA	AB	H	2B	3B	HR	HR%	R	RBI	BB	SO	SB	Pinch Hit AB	Pinch Hit H	PO	A	E	DP	TC/G	FA	G by Pos
1935	STL	N	8	.000	.000	11	0	0	0	0	0.0	2	0	2	2	2	0	0	9	7	0	2	3.2	1.000	2B-5

Red Juelich

JUELICH, JOHN SAMUEL BR TR 5′11½″ 168 lbs.
B. Sept. 20, 1916, St. Louis, Mo. D. Dec. 25, 1970, St. Louis, Mo.

Year	Team	Lg	Games	BA	SA	AB	H	2B	3B	HR	HR%	R	RBI	BB	SO	SB	Pinch Hit AB	Pinch Hit H	PO	A	E	DP	TC/G	FA	G by Pos
1939	PIT	N	17	.239	.326	46	11	0	2	0	0.0	5	4	2	4	0	3	0	21	24	3	5	4.0	.938	2B-10, 3B-2

George Jumonville

JUMONVILLE, GEORGE BENEDICT BR TR 6′ 175 lbs.
B. May 16, 1917, Mobile, Ala.

Year	Team	Lg	Games	BA	SA	AB	H	2B	3B	HR	HR%	R	RBI	BB	SO	SB	Pinch Hit AB	Pinch Hit H	PO	A	E	DP	TC/G	FA	G by Pos
1940	PHI	N	11	.088	.088	34	3	0	0	0	0.0	0	0	1	6	0	0	0	20	21	2	3	3.9	.953	SS-10, 3B-1
1941			6	.429	.857	7	3	0	0	1	14.3	1	2	0	0	0	3	2	1	4	0	0	2.5	1.000	SS-1, 2B-1
2 yrs.			17	.146	.220	41	6	0	0	1	2.4	1	2	1	6	0	3	2	21	25	2	3	3.7	.958	SS-11, 2B-1, 3B-1

Ed Jurak

JURAK, EDWARD JAMES (Lizard)
B. Oct. 24, 1957, Hollywood, Calif.
BR TR 6′ 2″ 185 lbs.

Year	Team	Lg	Games	BA	SA	AB	H	2B	3B	HR	HR%	R	RBI	BB	SO	SB	Pinch Hit AB	Pinch Hit H	PO	A	E	DP	TC/G	FA	G by Pos
1982	**BOS**	**A**	12	.333	.333	21	7	0	0	0	0.0	3	7	2	4	0	0	0	7	17	2	1	2.2	.923	3B-11, OF-1
1983			75	.277	.377	159	44	8	4	0	0.0	19	18	18	25	1	4	2	197	117	11	34	4.3	.966	SS-38, 1B-19, 3B-12, DH-5, 2B-1
1984			47	.242	.364	66	16	3	1	1	1.5	6	7	12	12	0	3	1	92	40	3	20	3.1	.978	1B-19, 2B-14, 3B-9, SS-2
1985			26	.231	.231	13	3	0	0	0	0.0	4	0	1	3	0	3	0	5	10	2	0	1.2	.882	3B-7, SS-3, DH-2, OF-1, 1B-1
1988	**OAK**	**A**	3	.000	.000	1	0	0	0	0	0.0	1	0	0	0	0	1	0	0	0	0	0	0.0	.000	3B-1
1989	**SF**	**N**	30	.238	.238	42	10	0	0	0	0.0	2	1	5	5	0	18	4	20	17	5	2	2.3	.881	SS-6, 3B-5, 2B-4, OF-2, 1B-1
6 yrs.			193	.265	.344	302	80	11	5	1	0.3	35	33	38	49	1	29	7	321	201	23	57	3.3	.958	SS-49, 3B-45, 1B-40, 2B-19, DH-7, OF-4

Bill Jurges

JURGES, WILLIAM FREDERICK
B. May 9, 1908, Bronx, N. Y.
Manager 1959–60.
BR TR 5′11″ 175 lbs.

Year	Team	Lg	Games	BA	SA	AB	H	2B	3B	HR	HR%	R	RBI	BB	SO	SB	Pinch Hit AB	Pinch Hit H	PO	A	E	DP	TC/G	FA	G by Pos
1931	**CHI**	**N**	88	.201	.287	293	59	15	5	0	0.0	34	23	25	41	2	1	0	113	202	11	32	3.6	.966	3B-54, 2B-33, SS-3
1932			115	.253	.348	396	100	24	4	2	0.5	40	52	19	26	1	1	0	227	401	23	70	6.0	.965	SS-103, 3B-5
1933			143	.269	.359	487	131	17	6	5	1.0	49	50	26	39	3	0	0	298	476	34	95	5.7	.958	SS-143
1934			100	.246	.366	358	88	15	2	8	2.2	43	33	19	34	1	2	1	205	334	19	63	5.7	.966	SS-98
1935			146	.241	.314	519	125	33	1	1	0.2	69	59	42	39	3	0	0	348	484	31	99	5.9	.964	SS-146
1936			118	.280	.350	429	120	25	1	1	0.2	51	42	23	25	4	0	0	249	379	26	80	5.6	.960	SS-116
1937			129	.298	.389	450	134	18	10	1	0.2	53	65	42	41	2	0	0	258	370	16	74	5.0	.975	SS-128
1938			137	.245	.303	465	114	18	3	1	0.2	53	47	58	53	3	0	0	277	417	34	82	5.4	.953	SS-136
1939	**NY**	**N**	138	.285	.398	543	155	21	11	6	1.1	84	63	47	34	3	0	0	295	482	28	95	5.9	.965	SS-137
1940			63	.252	.322	214	54	3	3	2	0.9	23	36	25	14	2	0	0	123	196	11	36	5.2	.967	SS-63
1941			134	.293	.386	471	138	25	2	5	1.1	50	61	47	36	0	0	0	230	432	30	82	5.2	.957	SS-134
1942			127	.256	.289	464	119	7	1	2	0.4	45	30	43	42	1	3	1	251	401	15	67	5.4	.978	SS-124
1943			136	.229	.279	481	110	8	2	4	0.8	46	29	53	38	2	8	3	236	359	25	54	4.9	.960	SS-99, 3B-28
1944			85	.211	.240	246	52	2	1	1	0.4	28	23	23	20	4	14	2	64	149	8	13	3.1	.964	3B-61, SS-10, 2B-1
1945			61	.324	.403	176	57	3	1	3	1.7	22	24	24	11	2	7	2	55	116	10	4	3.5	.945	3B-44, SS-8
1946	**CHI**	**N**	82	.222	.281	221	49	9	2	0	0.0	26	17	43	28	3	0	0	127	212	8	26	4.2	.977	SS-73, 3B-7, 2B-2
1947			14	.200	.325	40	8	2	0	1	2.5	5	2	9	9	0	0	0	13	36	4	10	3.8	.925	SS-14
17 yrs.			1816	.258	.335	6253	1613	245	55	43	0.7	721	656	568	530	36	36	9	3369	5446	333	982	5.2	.964	SS-1535, 3B-199, 2B-36
WORLD SERIES																									
1932	**CHI**	**N**	3	.364	.455	11	4	1	0	0	0.0	1	1	0	1	1	0	0	12	8	2	5	7.3	.909	SS-3
1935			6	.250	.250	16	4	0	0	0	0.0	3	1	4	4	0	0	0	16	15	1	4	5.3	.969	SS-6
1938			4	.231	.308	13	3	1	0	0	0.0	0	0	1	3	0	0	0	11	7	1	2	4.8	.947	SS-4
3 yrs.			13	.275	.325	40	11	2	0	0	0.0	4	2	5	8	1	0	0	39	30	4	11	5.6	.945	SS-13

Joe Just

JUST, JOSEPH ERWIN
Born Joseph Erwin Juszczak.
B. Jan. 8, 1916, Milwaukee, Wis.
BR TR 5′11″ 185 lbs.

Year	Team	Lg	Games	BA	SA	AB	H	2B	3B	HR	HR%	R	RBI	BB	SO	SB	Pinch Hit AB	Pinch Hit H	PO	A	E	DP	TC/G	FA	G by Pos
1944	**CIN**	**N**	11	.182	.182	11	2	0	0	0	0.0	0	0	0	2	0	1	0	12	0	1	0	1.3	.923	C-10
1945			14	.147	.147	34	5	0	0	0	0.0	2	2	4	7	0	0	0	31	5	2	0	2.7	.947	C-14
2 yrs.			25	.156	.156	45	7	0	0	0	0.0	2	2	4	9	0	1	0	43	5	3	0	2.1	.941	C-24

David Justice

JUSTICE, DAVID CHRISTOPHER
B. Apr. 14, 1966, Cincinnati, Ohio.
BL TL 6′ 3″ 195 lbs.

Year	Team	Lg	Games	BA	SA	AB	H	2B	3B	HR	HR%	R	RBI	BB	SO	SB	Pinch Hit AB	Pinch Hit H	PO	A	E	DP	TC/G	FA	G by Pos
1989	**ATL**	**N**	16	.235	.353	51	12	3	0	1	2.0	7	3	3	9	2	0	0	24	0	0	0	1.5	1.000	OF-16
1990			127	.282	.535	439	124	23	2	28	6.4	76	78	64	92	11	5	2	604	42	14	44	5.1	.979	1B-69, OF-61
1991			109	.275	.503	396	109	25	1	21	5.3	67	87	65	81	8	3	0	204	9	7	0	2.1	.968	OF-106
1992			144	.256	.446	484	124	19	5	21	4.3	78	72	79	85	2	3	0	313	8	8	2	2.3	.976	OF-140
1993			157	.270	.515	585	158	15	4	40	6.8	90	120	78	90	3	0	0	323	9	5	2	2.1	.985	OF-157
1994			104	.313	.531	352	110	16	2	19	5.4	61	59	69	45	2	2	1	193	6	11	0	2.1	.948	OF-102
1995			120	.253	.479	411	104	17	2	24	5.8	73	78	73	68	4	0	0	233	8	4	0	2.0	.984	OF-120
7 yrs.			777	.273	.498	2718	741	118	16	154	5.7	452	497	431	470	32	13	3	1894	82	49	48	2.6	.976	OF-702, 1B-69
DIVISIONAL PLAYOFF SERIES																									
1995	**ATL**	**N**	4	.231	.231	13	3	0	0	0	0.0	2	0	5	2	0	0	0	6	0	1	0	1.8	.857	OF-4
LEAGUE CHAMPIONSHIP SERIES																									
1991	**ATL**	**N**	7	.200	.360	25	5	1	0	1	4.0	4	2	3	7	0	0	0	17	0	1	0	2.6	.944	OF-7
1992			7	.280	.560	25	7	1	0	2	8.0	5	6	6	2	0	0	0	19	3	0	0	3.1	1.000	OF-7
1993			6	.143	.190	21	3	1	0	0	0.0	2	4	3	3	0	0	0	14	0	1	0	2.5	.933	OF-6
1995			3	.273	.273	11	3	0	0	0	0.0	1	1	2	1	0	0	0	4	0	0	0	1.3	1.000	OF-3
4 yrs.			23	.220	.366	82	18	3	0	3	3.7	12	13	14	13	0	0	0	54	3	2	0	2.6	.966	OF-23
													9th	**5th**											
WORLD SERIES																									
1991	**ATL**	**N**	7	.259	.481	27	7	0	0	2	7.4	5	6	5	5	2	0	0	21	1	1	0	3.3	.957	OF-7
1992			6	.158	.316	19	3	0	0	1	5.3	4	3	6	5	1	0	0	15	0	1	0	2.7	.938	OF-6
1995			6	.250	.450	20	5	1	0	1	5.0	3	5	5	1	0	0	0	16	0	0	0	2.7	1.000	OF-6
3 yrs.			19	.227	.424	66	15	1	0	4	6.1	12	14	16	11	3	0	0	52	1	2	0	2.9	.964	OF-19

Skip Jutze

JUTZE, ALFRED HENRY
B. May 28, 1946, Bayside, N. Y.
BR TR 5′11″ 190 lbs.

Year	Team	Lg	Games	BA	SA	AB	H	2B	3B	HR	HR%	R	RBI	BB	SO	SB	Pinch Hit AB	Pinch Hit H	PO	A	E	DP	TC/G	FA	G by Pos
1972	**STL**	**N**	21	.239	.268	71	17	2	0	0	0.0	1	5	1	16	0	4	0	93	15	4	1	6.6	.964	C-17
1973	**HOU**	**N**	90	.223	.245	278	62	6	0	0	0.0	18	18	19	37	0	3	0	450	31	8	4	5.7	.984	C-86
1974			8	.231	.231	13	3	0	0	0	0.0	0	1	1	1	0	0	0	16	2	0	0	2.6	1.000	C-7
1975			51	.226	.247	93	21	2	0	0	0.0	9	6	2	4	1	2	0	147	15	2	3	3.5	.988	C-47
1976			42	.152	.239	92	14	2	3	0	0.0	7	6	4	16	0	2	1	125	21	2	5	3.5	.986	C-42
1977	**SEA**	**A**	42	.220	.321	109	24	2	0	3	2.8	10	15	7	12	0	3	0	170	15	3	3	4.7	.984	C-40
6 yrs.			254	.215	.259	656	141	14	3	3	0.5	45	51	34	86	1	14	1	1001	99	19	16	4.7	.983	C-239

Jack Kading

KADING, JOHN FREDERICK BR TR 6′ 3″ 190 lbs.
B. Nov. 27, 1884, Waukesha, Wis. D. June 2, 1964, Chicago, Ill.

Year	Team	Games	BA	SA	AB	H	2B	3B	HR	HR%	R	RBI	BB	SO	SB	Pinch Hit AB	Pinch Hit H	PO	A	E	DP	TC/G	FA	G by Pos
1910	PIT N	8	.304	.478	23	7	2	1	0	0.0	5	4	4	5	0	0	0	70	7	0	5	9.6	1.000	1B-8
1914	CHI F	3	.000	.000	3	0	0	0	0	0.0	0	0	0		0	3	0	0	0	0	0	0.0	—	
2 yrs.		11	.269	.423	26	7	2	1	0	0.0	5	4	4	5	0	3	0	70	7	0	5	9.6	1.000	1B-8

Jake Kafora

KAFORA, FRANK JACOB (Tomatoes) BR TR 6′ 180 lbs.
B. Oct. 16, 1888, Chicago, Ill. D. Mar. 23, 1928, Chicago, Ill.

Year	Team	Games	BA	SA	AB	H	2B	3B	HR	HR%	R	RBI	BB	SO	SB	Pinch Hit AB	Pinch Hit H	PO	A	E	DP	TC/G	FA	G by Pos
1913	PIT N	1	.000	.000	1	0	0	0	0	0.0	1	0	0	1	0	0	0	1	0	0	0	1.0	1.000	C-1
1914		21	.130	.130	23	3	0	0	0	0.0	2	0	0	6	0	3	0	27	5	0	0	1.9	1.000	C-17
2 yrs.		22	.125	.125	24	3	0	0	0	0.0	3	0	0	7	0	3	0	28	5	0	0	1.8	1.000	C-18

Ike Kahdot

KAHDOT, ISAAC LEONARD (Chief) BR TR 5′ 5½″ 145 lbs.
B. Oct. 22, 1901, Georgetown, Okla.

Year	Team	Games	BA	SA	AB	H	2B	3B	HR	HR%	R	RBI	BB	SO	SB	Pinch Hit AB	Pinch Hit H	PO	A	E	DP	TC/G	FA	G by Pos
1922	CLE A	4	.000	.000	2	0	0	0	0	0.0	0	0	0	1	0	0	0	1	2	0	1	1.5	1.000	3B-2

Nick Kahl

KAHL, NICHOLAS ALEXANDER BR TR 5′ 9″ 185 lbs.
B. Apr. 10, 1879, Coulterville, Ill. D. July 13, 1959, Sparta, Ill.

Year	Team	Games	BA	SA	AB	H	2B	3B	HR	HR%	R	RBI	BB	SO	SB	Pinch Hit AB	Pinch Hit H	PO	A	E	DP	TC/G	FA	G by Pos
1905	CLE A	39	.221	.267	131	29	4	1	0	0.0	16	21	4		1	6	1	62	95	10	3	5.1	.940	2B-31, SS-1, OF-1

Bob Kahle

KAHLE, ROBERT WAYNE BR TR 6′ 170 lbs.
B. Nov. 23, 1915, Newcastle, Ind. D. Dec. 16, 1988, Inglewood, Calif.

Year	Team	Games	BA	SA	AB	H	2B	3B	HR	HR%	R	RBI	BB	SO	SB	Pinch Hit AB	Pinch Hit H	PO	A	E	DP	TC/G	FA	G by Pos
1938	BOS N	8	.333	.333	3	1	0	0	0	0.0	2	0	0	0	0	3	1	0	0	0	0	0.0	—	

Owen Kahn

KAHN, OWEN EARLE (Jack) BR TR 5′11″ 160 lbs.
B. June 5, 1905, Richmond, Va. D. Jan. 17, 1981, Richmond, Va.

Year	Team	Games	BA	SA	AB	H	2B	3B	HR	HR%	R	RBI	BB	SO	SB	Pinch Hit AB	Pinch Hit H	PO	A	E	DP	TC/G	FA	G by Pos
1930	BOS N	1	—	—	0	0	0	0	0	—	1	0	0	0	0	0	0	0	0	0	0	0.0	—	

Mike Kahoe

KAHOE, MICHAEL JOSEPH BR TR 6′ 185 lbs.
B. Sept. 3, 1873, Yellow Springs, Ohio D. May 14, 1949, Akron, Ohio.

Year	Team	Games	BA	SA	AB	H	2B	3B	HR	HR%	R	RBI	BB	SO	SB	Pinch Hit AB	Pinch Hit H	PO	A	E	DP	TC/G	FA	G by Pos
1895	CIN N	3	.000	.000	4	0	0	0	0	0.0	0	0	0	0	0	0	0	2	0	0	0	0.7	1.000	C-3
1899		14	.167	.238	42	7	1	1	0	0.0	2	4	0		1	1	0	48	18	3	3	5.3	.957	C-13
1900		52	.189	.257	175	33	3	3	1	0.6	18	9	4		3	0	0	207	80	15	6	5.8	.950	C-51, SS-1
1901	2 teams	CIN N (4G –.308) CHI N (67G –.224)																						
″	total	71	.228	.304	250	57	12	2	1	0.4	21	21	9		5	0	0	418	81	17	11	7.1	.967	C-67, 1B-6
1902	2 teams	CHI N (7G –.222) STL A (55G –.244)																						
″	total	62	.242	.335	215	52	10	2	2	0.9	21	30	6		4	2	1	231	59	13	5	5.1	.957	C-57, 3B-2, SS-1
1903	STL A	77	.189	.258	244	46	7	5	0	0.0	26	23	11		1	4	0	333	64	12	8	5.6	.971	C-71, OF-2
1904		72	.216	.250	236	51	6	1	0	0.0	9	12	8		4	2	0	307	91	13	3	6.0	.968	C-69
1905	PHI N	16	.255	.294	51	13	2	0	0	0.0	2	4	1		1	1	0	58	20	2	2	5.3	.975	C-15
1907	2 teams	CHI N (5G –.400) WAS A (17G –.191)																						
″	total	22	.228	.246	57	13	1	0	0	0.0	3	2	0		0	3	1	70	20	2	2	4.8	.978	C-18, 1B-1
1908	WAS A	17	.185	.222	27	5	1	0	0	0.0	1	0	0		0	6	1	51	7	1	1	5.4	.983	C-11
1909		4	.125	.125	8	1	0	0	0	0.0	0	0	0		2	1	0	9	4	2	0	5.0	.867	C-3
11 yrs.		410	.212	.276	1309	278	43	14	4	0.3	103	105	39	0	21	20	3	1734	444	80	41	5.8	.965	C-378, 1B-7, 3B-2, OF-2, SS-2

Al Kaiser

KAISER, ALFRED EDWARD (Deerfoot) BR TR 5′ 9″ 165 lbs.
B. Aug. 3, 1886, Cincinnati, Ohio D. Apr. 11, 1969, Cincinnati, Ohio.

Year	Team	Games	BA	SA	AB	H	2B	3B	HR	HR%	R	RBI	BB	SO	SB	Pinch Hit AB	Pinch Hit H	PO	A	E	DP	TC/G	FA	G by Pos
1911	2 teams	CHI N (27G –.250) BOS N (65G –.203)																						
″	total	92	.217	.306	281	61	5	7	2	0.7	36	22	17	38	10	10	2	136	9	13	3	2.0	.918	OF-81
1912	BOS N	4	.000	.000	13	0	0	0	0	0.0	0	0	0	3	0	0	0	8	1	1	0	2.5	.900	OF-4
1914	IND F	59	.230	.299	187	43	10	0	1	0.5	22	16	17		6	7	2	107	4	13	0	2.4	.895	OF-50, 1B-1
3 yrs.		155	.216	.295	481	104	15	7	3	0.6	58	38	34	41	16	17	4	251	14	27	3	2.1	.908	OF-135, 1B-1

John Kalahan

KALAHAN, JOHN JOSEPH BR TR 6′ 165 lbs.
B. Sept. 30, 1878, Philadelphia, Pa. D. June 20, 1952, Philadelphia, Pa.

Year	Team	Games	BA	SA	AB	H	2B	3B	HR	HR%	R	RBI	BB	SO	SB	Pinch Hit AB	Pinch Hit H	PO	A	E	DP	TC/G	FA	G by Pos
1903	PHI A	1	.000	.000	5	0	0	0	0	0.0	0	0	0		0	0	0	5	1	0	0	6.0	1.000	C-1

Charlie Kalbfus

KALBFUS, CHARLES HENRY BR TR 5′11″ 145 lbs.
B. Dec. 28, 1864, Washington, D. C. D. Nov. 18, 1941, Washington, D. C.

Year	Team	Games	BA	SA	AB	H	2B	3B	HR	HR%	R	RBI	BB	SO	SB	Pinch Hit AB	Pinch Hit H	PO	A	E	DP	TC/G	FA	G by Pos
1884	WAS U	1	.200	.200	5	1	0	0	0	0.0	1		0			0	0	0	0	0	0	0.0	.000	OF-1

Frank Kalin

KALIN, FRANK BRUNO (Fats) BR TR 6′ 200 lbs.
Born Frank Bruno Kalinkiewicz.
B. Oct. 3, 1917, Steubenville, Ohio D. Jan. 12, 1975, Weirton, W. Va.

Year	Team	Games	BA	SA	AB	H	2B	3B	HR	HR%	R	RBI	BB	SO	SB	Pinch Hit AB	Pinch Hit H	PO	A	E	DP	TC/G	FA	G by Pos
1940	PIT N	3	.000	.000	3	0	0	0	0	0.0	0	1	2	0	0	1	0	2	0	1	0	1.5	.667	OF-2
1943	CHI A	4	.000	.000	4	0	0	0	0	0.0	0	0	0	0	0	4	0	0	0	0	0	0.0	—	
2 yrs.		7	.000	.000	7	0	0	0	0	0.0	0	1	2	0	0	5	0	2	0	1	0	1.5	.667	OF-2

Al Kaline

KALINE, ALBERT WILLIAM BR TR 6′ 1½″ 175 lbs.
B. Dec. 19, 1934, Baltimore, Md.
Hall of Fame 1980.

Year	Team	Games	BA	SA	AB	H	2B	3B	HR	HR%	R	RBI	BB	SO	SB	Pinch Hit AB	Pinch Hit H	PO	A	E	DP	TC/G	FA	G by Pos
1953	DET A	30	.250	.357	28	7	0	0	1	3.6	9	2	1	5	1	1	0	11	1	0	0	0.6	1.000	OF-20
1954		138	.276	.347	504	139	18	3	4	0.8	42	43	22	45	9	3	1	283	16	9	0	2.3	.971	OF-135
1955		152	**.340**	.546	588	**200**	24	8	27	4.6	121	102	82	57	6	0	0	306	14	7	4	2.2	.979	OF-152
1956		153	.314	.530	617	194	32	10	27	4.4	96	128	70	55	7	0	0	343	18	6	4	2.4	.984	OF-153
1957		149	.295	.478	577	170	29	4	23	4.0	83	90	43	38	11	5	1	319	13	5	2	2.3	.985	OF-145
1958		146	.313	.490	543	170	34	7	16	2.9	84	85	54	47	7	2	0	316	23	2	4	2.4	.994	OF-145
1959		136	.327	**.530**	511	167	19	2	27	5.3	86	94	72	42	10	0	0	364	4	4	0	2.7	.989	OF-136
1960		147	.278	.426	551	153	29	4	15	2.7	77	68	65	47	19	4	2	367	5	5	1	2.7	.987	OF-142
1961		153	.324	.515	586	190	**41**	7	19	3.2	116	82	66	42	14	5	3	379	10	4	3	2.7	.990	OF-147, 3B-1
1962		100	.304	.593	398	121	16	6	29	7.3	78	94	47	39	4	0	0	225	8	4	1	2.4	.983	OF-100
1963		145	.312	.514	551	172	24	3	27	4.9	89	101	54	48	6	5	3	257	5	2	0	1.9	.992	OF-140
1964		146	.293	.469	525	154	31	5	17	3.2	77	68	75	51	4	9	2	278	6	3	2	2.1	.990	OF-136

Al Kaline *continued*

Year	Team	Games	BA	SA	AB	H	2B	3B	HR	HR%	R	RBI	BB	SO	SB	Pinch Hit AB	Pinch Hit H	PO	A	E	DP	TC/G	FA	G by Pos
1965		125	.281	.471	399	112	18	2	18	4.5	72	72	72	49	6	11	4	195	3	3	0	1.8	.985	OF-112, 3B-1
1966		142	.288	.534	479	138	29	1	29	6.1	85	88	81	66	5	3	1	279	7	2	1	2.1	.993	OF-136
1967		131	.308	.541	458	141	28	2	25	5.5	94	78	83	47	8	1	0	217	14	4	2	1.8	.983	OF-130
1968		102	.287	.428	327	94	14	1	10	3.1	49	53	55	39	6	10	5	283	14	7	15	3.2	.977	OF-74, 1B-22
1969		131	.272	.447	456	124	17	0	21	4.6	74	69	54	61	1	7	2	257	11	7	7	2.2	.975	OF-118, 1B-9
1970		131	.278	.450	467	130	24	4	16	3.4	64	71	77	49	2	3	0	530	34	6	40	4.0	.989	OF-91, 1B-52
1971		133	.294	.462	405	119	19	2	15	3.7	69	54	82	57	4	12	3	234	7	0	3	1.8	1.000	OF-129, 1B-5
1972		106	.313	.475	278	87	11	2	10	3.6	46	32	28	33	1	24	**10**	148	9	1	5	1.7	.994	OF-84, 1B-11
1973		91	.255	.394	310	79	13	0	10	3.2	40	45	29	28	4	9	0	347	13	1	32	3.6	.997	OF-63, 1B-36
1974		147	.262	.389	558	146	28	2	13	2.3	71	64	65	75	2	1	0	0	0	0	0	0.0	.000	DH-146
22 yrs.		2834	.297	.480	10116	3007	498	75	399	3.9	1622	1583	1277	1020	137	115	37	5938	235	82	126	2.3	.987	OF-2488, DH-146, 1B-135, 3B-2
LEAGUE CHAMPIONSHIP SERIES																								
1972	DET A	5	.263	.421	19	5	0	0	1	5.3	3	1	2	2	0	0	0	12	0	1	0	2.6	.923	OF-5
WORLD SERIES																								
1968	DET A	7	.379	.655	29	11	2	0	2	6.9	6	8	0	7	0	0	0	18	0	0	0	2.6	1.000	OF-7

Willie Kamm

KAMM, WILLIAM EDWARD BR TR 5′10½″ 170 lbs.
B. Feb. 2, 1900, San Francisco, Calif. D. Dec. 21, 1988, Belmont, Calif.

Year	Team	Games	BA	SA	AB	H	2B	3B	HR	HR%	R	RBI	BB	SO	SB	Pinch Hit AB	Pinch Hit H	PO	A	E	DP	TC/G	FA	G by Pos
1923	CHI A	149	.292	.430	544	159	39	9	6	1.1	57	87	62	82	17	0	0	173	352	22	29	3.7	.960	3B-149
1924		147	.254	.364	528	134	28	6	6	1.1	58	93	64	59	9	0	0	190	312	15	31	3.6	.971	3B-145
1925		152	.279	.393	509	142	32	4	6	1.2	82	83	**90**	36	11	0	0	182	310	22	32	3.4	.957	3B-152
1926		143	.294	.385	480	141	24	10	0	0.0	63	62	77	24	14	1	0	177	323	11	16	3.6	.978	3B-142
1927		148	.270	.378	540	146	32	13	0	0.0	85	59	70	18	7	2	0	236	279	15	21	3.6	.972	3B-146
1928		155	.308	.411	552	170	30	12	1	0.2	70	84	73	22	17	0	0	243	278	12	33	3.4	.977	3B-155
1929		147	.268	.369	523	140	32	6	3	0.6	72	63	75	23	12	2	1	221	270	11	27	3.5	.978	3B-145
1930		112	.269	.396	331	89	21	6	3	0.9	49	47	51	20	5	5	0	142	209	23	17	3.6	.939	3B-105
1931	2 teams	CHI A (18G –.254) CLE A (114G –.295)																						
″	total	132	.290	.386	469	136	35	5	0	0.0	77	75	71	19	14	0	0	158	240	23	33	3.2	.945	3B-132
1932	CLE A	148	.286	.403	524	150	34	9	3	0.6	76	83	75	36	6	0	0	164	299	16	20	3.2	.967	3B-148
1933		133	.282	.336	447	126	17	2	1	0.2	59	47	54	27	7	2	0	153	221	6	16	2.9	.984	3B-131
1934		121	.269	.345	386	104	23	3	0	0.0	52	42	62	38	7	4	2	109	248	8	24	3.1	.978	3B-118
1935		6	.333	.333	18	6	0	0	0	0.0	2	1	0	1	0	2	0	3	4	1	0	2.0	.875	3B-4
13 yrs.		1693	.281	.384	5851	1643	347	85	29	0.5	802	826	824	405	126	18	3	2151	3345	185	299	3.4	.967	3B-1672

Alex Kampouris

KAMPOURIS, ALEXIS WILLIAM BR TR 5′ 8″ 155 lbs.
B. Nov. 13, 1912, Sacramento, Calif. D. May 29, 1993, Sacramento, Calif.

Year	Team	Games	BA	SA	AB	H	2B	3B	HR	HR%	R	RBI	BB	SO	SB	Pinch Hit AB	Pinch Hit H	PO	A	E	DP	TC/G	FA	G by Pos
1934	CIN N	19	.197	.212	66	13	1	0	0	0.0	6	3	3	18	2	2	0	35	53	5	7	5.8	.946	2B-16
1935		148	.246	.361	499	123	26	5	7	1.4	46	62	32	84	8	2	0	381	426	41	88	5.8	.952	2B-141, SS-6
1936		122	.239	.332	355	85	10	4	5	1.4	43	46	24	46	3	1	0	271	376	21	71	5.6	.969	2B-119, OF-1
1937		146	.249	.424	458	114	21	4	17	3.7	62	71	60	65	2	0	0	367	439	33	87	5.7	.961	2B-146
1938	2 teams	CIN N (21G –.257) NY N (82G –.246)																						
″	total	103	.249	.345	342	85	10	1	7	2.0	48	44	37	63	0	3	0	241	321	16	63	5.8	.972	2B-100
1939	NY N	74	.249	.403	201	50	12	2	5	2.5	23	29	30	41	0	1	0	154	193	11	35	4.9	.969	2B-62, 3B-11
1941	BKN N	16	.314	.588	51	16	4	2	2	3.9	8	9	11	8	0	1	0	31	45	1	7	5.1	.987	2B-15
1942		10	.238	.429	21	5	2	1	0	0.0	3	3	0	4	0	1	0	16	16	1	5	3.7	.970	2B-9
1943	2 teams	BKN N (19G –.227) WAS A (51G –.207)																						
″	total	70	.212	.296	189	40	8	1	2	1.1	33	17	47	31	7	6	2	109	127	14	21	4.0	.944	3B-33, 2B-28, OF-1
9 yrs.		708	.243	.367	2182	531	94	20	45	2.1	272	284	244	360	22	17	2	1605	1996	143	384	5.4	.962	2B-636, 3B-44, SS-6, OF-2

Frank Kane

KANE, FRANCIS THOMAS (Sugar) BL TR 5′11½″ 175 lbs.
Played as Frank Kiley 1915.
Born Francis Thomas Kiley.
B. Mar. 9, 1895, Whitman, Mass. D. Dec. 2, 1962, Brockton, Mass.

Year	Team	Games	BA	SA	AB	H	2B	3B	HR	HR%	R	RBI	BB	SO	SB	Pinch Hit AB	Pinch Hit H	PO	A	E	DP	TC/G	FA	G by Pos
1915	BKN F	3	.200	.400	10	2	0	1	0	0.0	2	2	0		0	1	0	5	1	0	0	3.0	1.000	OF-2
1919	NY A	1	.000	.000	1	0	0	0	0	0.0	0	0	0	0	0	1	0	0	0	0	0	0.0	—	
2 yrs.		4	.182	.364	11	2	0	1	0	0.0	2	2	0	0	0	2	0	5	1	0	0	3.0	1.000	OF-2

Jere Kane

KANE, WILLIAM JEREMIAH BR TR 6′ 175 lbs.
B. Apr. 1869, Baltimore, Md. D. June 16, 1949, East St. Louis, Ill.

Year	Team	Games	BA	SA	AB	H	2B	3B	HR	HR%	R	RBI	BB	SO	SB	Pinch Hit AB	Pinch Hit H	PO	A	E	DP	TC/G	FA	G by Pos
1890	STL AA	8	.200	.200	25	5	0	0	0	0.0	3		2		0	0	0	46	5	4	1	6.1	.927	1B-5, C-4

Jim Kane

KANE, JAMES JOSEPH (Shamus) BL TL 6′ 2″ 225 lbs.
B. Nov. 27, 1881, Scranton, Pa. D. Oct. 2, 1947, Omaha, Neb.

Year	Team	Games	BA	SA	AB	H	2B	3B	HR	HR%	R	RBI	BB	SO	SB	Pinch Hit AB	Pinch Hit H	PO	A	E	DP	TC/G	FA	G by Pos
1908	PIT N	55	.241	.303	145	35	3	3	0	0.0	16	22	12		5	14	1	378	24	14	19	10.4	.966	1B-40

John Kane

KANE, JOHN FRANCIS BR TR 5′ 6″ 138 lbs.
B. Sept. 24, 1882, Chicago, Ill. D. Jan. 28, 1934, St. Anthony, Ida.

Year	Team	Games	BA	SA	AB	H	2B	3B	HR	HR%	R	RBI	BB	SO	SB	Pinch Hit AB	Pinch Hit H	PO	A	E	DP	TC/G	FA	G by Pos
1907	CIN N	79	.248	.347	262	65	9	4	3	1.1	40	19	22		20	2	1	120	80	19	2	2.9	.913	OF-42, 3B-25, SS-6, 2B-2
1908		130	.213	.288	455	97	11	7	3	0.7	61	23	43		30	1	0	298	17	6	2	2.5	.981	OF-127, 2B-1
1909	CHI N	20	.089	.111	45	4	1	0	0	0.0	6	5	2		1	2	0	26	24	3	3	3.3	.943	OF-8, SS-3, 3B-3, 2B-2
1910		32	.242	.290	62	15	0	0	1	1.6	11	12	9	10	2	0	0	31	14	3	1	1.6	.938	OF-18, 2B-6, 3B-4, SS-2
4 yrs.		261	.220	.297	824	181	21	11	7	0.8	118	59	76	10	53	5	1	475	135	31	8	2.6	.952	OF-195, 3B-32, SS-11, 2B-11
WORLD SERIES																								
1910	CHI N	1	—	—	0	0	0	0	0	—	0	0	0	0	0	0	0	0	0	0	0	0.0	—	

Johnny Kane

KANE, JOHN FRANCIS BB TR 5′10½″ 162 lbs.
B. Feb. 19, 1900, Chicago, Ill. D. June 25, 1956, Chicago, Ill.

Year	Team	Games	BA	SA	AB	H	2B	3B	HR	HR%	R	RBI	BB	SO	SB	Pinch Hit AB	Pinch Hit H	PO	A	E	DP	TC/G	FA	G by Pos
1925	CHI A	14	.179	.196	56	10	1	0	0	0.0	6	3	0	3	0	0	0	22	49	3	6	5.3	.959	SS-8, 2B-6

Tom Kane

KANE, THOMAS JOSEPH (Sugar) BR TR 5′10½″ 160 lbs.
B. Dec. 15, 1906, Chicago, Ill. D. Nov. 26, 1973, Chicago, Ill.

Year	Team		Games	BA	SA	AB	H	2B	3B	HR	HR%	R	RBI	BB	SO	SB	Pinch Hit AB	Pinch Hit H	PO	A	E	DP	TC/G	FA	G by Pos
1938	BOS	N	2	.000	.000	2	0	0	0	0	0.0	0	0	2	0	0	0	0	2	2	0	0	2.0	1.000	2B-2

Rod Kanehl

KANEHL, RODERICK EDWIN (Hot Rod) BR TR 6′ 1″ 180 lbs.
B. Apr. 1, 1934, Wichita, Kans.

Year	Team		Games	BA	SA	AB	H	2B	3B	HR	HR%	R	RBI	BB	SO	SB	Pinch Hit AB	Pinch Hit H	PO	A	E	DP	TC/G	FA	G by Pos
1962	NY	N	133	.248	.322	351	87	10	2	4	1.1	52	27	23	36	8	11	3	235	230	32	57	4.2	.936	2B-62, 3B-30, OF-20, 1B-3, SS-2
1963			109	.241	.288	191	46	6	0	1	0.5	26	9	5	26	6	21	5	128	35	12	7	2.0	.931	OF-58, 3B-13, 2B-12, 1B-3
1964			98	.232	.280	254	59	7	1	1	0.4	25	11	7	18	3	15	3	161	125	6	26	3.7	.979	2B-34, OF-25, 3B-19, 1B-2
3 yrs.			340	.241	.300	796	192	23	3	6	0.8	103	47	35	80	17	47	11	524	390	50	90	3.4	.948	2B-108, OF-103, 3B-62, 1B-8, SS-2

Heinie Kappel

KAPPEL, HENRY BR TR 5′ 8″ 160 lbs.
Brother of Joe Kappel.
B. Sept. 1863, Philadelphia, Pa. D. Aug. 27, 1905, Philadelphia, Pa.

Year	Team		Games	BA	SA	AB	H	2B	3B	HR	HR%	R	RBI	BB	SO	SB	Pinch Hit AB	Pinch Hit H	PO	A	E	DP	TC/G	FA	G by Pos
1887	CIN	AA	23	.282	.372	78	22	3	2	0	0.0	11		2		3	0	0	35	42	14	3	4.0	.846	3B-9, OF-7, 2B-6, SS-1
1888			36	.259	.364	143	37	4	4	1	0.7	18	15	2		20	0	0	50	91	39	11	5.0	.783	SS-25, 2B-10, 3B-1
1889	COL	AA	46	.272	.422	173	47	7	5	3	1.7	25	21	21	28	10	0	0	69	128	40	7	5.2	.831	SS-23, 3B-23
3 yrs.			105	.269	.391	394	106	14	11	4	1.0	54	36	25	28	33	0	0	154	261	93	21	4.8	.817	SS-49, 3B-33, 2B-16, OF-7

Joe Kappel

KAPPEL, JOSEPH BR 5′10″ 165 lbs.
Brother of Heinie Kappel.
B. Apr. 27, 1857, Philadelphia, Pa. D. July 8, 1929, Philadelphia, Pa.

Year	Team		Games	BA	SA	AB	H	2B	3B	HR	HR%	R	RBI	BB	SO	SB	Pinch Hit AB	Pinch Hit H	PO	A	E	DP	TC/G	FA	G by Pos
1884	PHI	N	4	.067	.067	15	1	0	0	0	0.0	1		0	2		0	0	16	8	9	0	8.3	.727	C-4
1890	PHI	AA	56	.240	.303	208	50	8	1	1	0.5	29		20		12	0	0	75	92	31	8	3.5	.843	OF-23, SS-18, 3B-11, C-3, 2B-2
2 yrs.			60	.229	.287	223	51	8	1	1	0.4	30		20	2	12	0	0	91	100	40	8	3.8	.827	OF-23, SS-18, 3B-11, C-7, 2B-2

Ron Karkovice

KARKOVICE, RONALD JOSEPH BR TR 6′ 1″ 210 lbs.
B. Aug. 8, 1963, Union, N. J.

Year	Team		Games	BA	SA	AB	H	2B	3B	HR	HR%	R	RBI	BB	SO	SB	Pinch Hit AB	Pinch Hit H	PO	A	E	DP	TC/G	FA	G by Pos
1986	CHI	A	37	.247	.443	97	24	7	0	4	4.1	13	13	9	37	1	0	0	227	19	1	4	6.7	.996	C-37
1987			39	.071	.141	85	6	0	0	2	2.4	7	7	7	40	3	0	0	147	20	3	3	4.6	.982	C-37
1988			46	.174	.287	115	20	4	0	3	2.6	10	9	7	30	4	0	0	190	24	1	4	4.7	.995	C-46
1989			71	.264	.385	182	48	9	2	3	1.6	21	24	10	56	0	0	0	299	47	5	6	5.0	.986	C-68, DH-2
1990			68	.246	.399	183	45	10	0	6	3.3	30	20	16	52	2	4	2	296	31	2	4	5.1	.994	C-64, DH-1
1991			75	.246	.413	167	41	13	0	5	3.0	25	22	15	42	0	4	0	309	28	4	6	4.9	.988	C-69, OF-1
1992			123	.237	.392	342	81	12	1	13	3.8	39	50	30	89	10	4	0	536	53	6	8	5.0	.990	C-119, OF-1
1993			128	.228	.424	403	92	17	1	20	5.0	60	54	29	126	2	2	0	769	63	5	4	6.6	.994	C-127
1994			77	.213	.425	207	44	9	1	11	5.3	33	29	36	68	0	6	0	417	19	3	1	5.8	.993	C-76
1995			113	.217	.387	323	70	14	1	13	4.0	44	51	39	84	2	4	1	629	42	6	1	6.0	.991	C-113
10 yrs.			777	.224	.389	2104	471	95	6	80	3.8	282	279	198	624	24	24	3	3819	346	36	41	5.5	.991	C-756, DH-3, OF-2
LEAGUE CHAMPIONSHIP SERIES																									
1993	CHI	A	6	.000	.000	15	0	0	0	0	0.0	0	0	1	7	0	0	0	30	2	0	0	5.3	1.000	C-6

Bill Karlon

KARLON, WILLIAM JOHN (Hank) BR TR 6′ 1″ 190 lbs.
B. Jan. 21, 1909, Palmer, Mass. D. Dec. 7, 1964, Ware, Mass.

Year	Team		Games	BA	SA	AB	H	2B	3B	HR	HR%	R	RBI	BB	SO	SB	Pinch Hit AB	Pinch Hit H	PO	A	E	DP	TC/G	FA	G by Pos
1930	NY	A	2	.000	.000	5	0	0	0	0	0.0	0	0	0	1	0	1	0	1	0	0	0	1.0	1.000	OF-1

Marty Karow

KAROW, MARTIN GREGORY BR TR 5′10½″ 170 lbs.
Born Martin Gregory Karowsky.
B. July 18, 1904, Braddock, Pa. D. Apr. 27, 1986, Bryan, Tex.

Year	Team		Games	BA	SA	AB	H	2B	3B	HR	HR%	R	RBI	BB	SO	SB	Pinch Hit AB	Pinch Hit H	PO	A	E	DP	TC/G	FA	G by Pos
1927	BOS	A	6	.200	.300	10	2	1	0	0	0.0	0	0	0	2	0	1	1	2	6	0	3	1.6	1.000	SS-3, 3B-2

Benn Karr

KARR, BENJAMIN JOYCE (Baldy) BL TR 6′ 175 lbs.
B. Nov. 28, 1893, Mt. Pleasant, Miss. D. Dec. 8, 1968, Memphis, Tenn.

Year	Team		Games	BA	SA	AB	H	2B	3B	HR	HR%	R	RBI	BB	SO	SB	Pinch Hit AB	Pinch Hit H	PO	A	E	DP	TC/G	FA	G by Pos
1920	BOS	A	57	.280	.387	75	21	5	0	1	1.3	8	15	6	18	0	29	9	5	18	2	0	1.0	.920	P-26
1921			43	.258	.290	62	16	2	0	0	0.0	7	9	3	16	1	14	1	2	30	2	0	1.3	.941	P-26
1922			66	.214	.235	98	21	2	0	0	0.0	7	4	4	7	1	22	2	9	44	5	3	1.4	.914	P-41
1925	CLE	A	46	.261	.348	92	24	5	0	1	1.1	11	17	7	8	0	13	3	14	57	4	5	2.3	.947	P-32
1926			31	.222	.333	45	10	5	0	0	0.0	8	4	3	4	0	1	0	6	35	2	0	1.4	.953	P-30
1927			22	.200	.250	20	4	1	0	0	0.0	2	0	4	6	1	0	0	4	29	2	0	1.6	.943	P-22
6 yrs.			265	.245	.311	392	96	20	0	2	0.5	43	49	27	59	3	79	15	40	213	17	8	1.5	.937	P-177

Eric Karros

KARROS, ERIC PETER BR TR 6′ 4″ 205 lbs.
B. Nov. 4, 1967, Hackensack, N. J.

Year	Team		Games	BA	SA	AB	H	2B	3B	HR	HR%	R	RBI	BB	SO	SB	Pinch Hit AB	Pinch Hit H	PO	A	E	DP	TC/G	FA	G by Pos
1991	LA	N	14	.071	.143	14	1	1	0	0	0.0	0	1	1	6	0	4	1	33	2	0	5	3.5	1.000	1B-10
1992			149	.257	.426	545	140	30	1	20	3.7	63	88	37	103	2	7	4	1211	126	9	98	9.4	.993	1B-143
1993			158	.247	.409	619	153	27	2	23	3.7	74	80	34	82	0	1	0	1335	147	12	118	9.5	.992	1B-157
1994			111	.266	.426	406	108	21	1	14	3.4	51	46	29	53	2	2	0	896	116	9	79	9.4	.991	1B-109
1995			143	.298	.535	551	164	29	3	32	5.8	83	105	61	115	4	0	0	1234	109	7	100	9.4	.995	1B-143
5 yrs.			575	.265	.447	2135	566	108	7	89	4.2	271	320	162	359	8	14	5	4709	500	37	400	9.3	.993	1B-562
DIVISIONAL PLAYOFF SERIES																									
1995	LA	N	3	.500	1.083	12	6	1	0	2	16.7	3	4	1	0	0	0	0	14	0	0	2	4.7	1.000	1B-3

John Karst

KARST, JOHN GOTTLIEB (King) BL TR 5′11½″ 175 lbs.
B. Oct. 15, 1893, Philadelphia, Pa. D. May 21, 1976, Cape May, N. J.

Year	Team		Games	BA	SA	AB	H	2B	3B	HR	HR%	R	RBI	BB	SO	SB	Pinch Hit AB	Pinch Hit H	PO	A	E	DP	TC/G	FA	G by Pos
1915	BKN	N	1	—	—	0	0	0	0	0	—	0	0	0	0	0	0	0	0	1	0	1	1.0	1.000	3B-1

Eddie Kasko

KASKO, EDWARD MICHAEL BR TR 6′ 180 lbs.
B. June 27, 1932, Linden, N. J.
Manager 1970–73.

Year	Team		Games	BA	SA	AB	H	2B	3B	HR	HR%	R	RBI	BB	SO	SB	Pinch Hit AB	Pinch Hit H	PO	A	E	DP	TC/G	FA	G by Pos
1957	STL	N	134	.273	.334	479	131	16	5	1	0.2	59	35	33	53	6	5	1	118	248	15	26	2.8	.961	3B-120, SS-13, 2B-1
1958			104	.220	.282	259	57	8	1	2	0.8	20	22	21	25	1	10	3	136	218	13	54	4.1	.965	SS-77, 2B-12, 3B-1
1959	CIN	N	118	.283	.350	329	93	14	1	2	0.6	39	31	14	38	2	2	0	192	295	13	63	4.3	.974	SS-84, 3B-31, 2B-2
1960			126	.292	.378	479	140	21	1	6	1.3	56	51	46	37	9	7	2	194	287	15	47	3.7	.970	3B-86, 2B-33, SS-15
1961			126	.271	.335	469	127	22	1	2	0.4	64	27	32	36	4	7	2	214	301	18	60	4.1	.966	SS-112, 3B-12, 2B-6

Eddie Kasko *continued*

Year	Team	Games	BA	SA	AB	H	2B	3B	HR	HR%	R	RBI	BB	SO	SB	Pinch Hit AB	Pinch Hit H	PO	A	E	DP	TC/G	FA	G by Pos
1962		134	.278	.356	533	148	26	2	4	0.8	74	41	35	44	3	4	1	120	253	23	31	2.9	.942	3B-114, SS-21
1963		76	.241	.332	199	48	9	0	3	1.5	25	10	21	29	0	14	3	57	108	7	13	2.7	.959	3B-48, SS-15, 2B-1
1964	**HOU N**	133	.243	.283	448	109	16	1	0	0.0	45	22	37	52	4	4	2	229	388	15	72	4.9	.976	SS-128, 3B-2
1965		68	.247	.302	215	53	7	1	1	0.5	18	10	11	20	1	8	2	98	155	6	27	4.2	.977	SS-59, 3B-2
1966	**BOS A**	58	.213	.287	136	29	7	0	1	0.7	11	12	15	19	1	20	3	55	96	4	16	4.1	.974	SS-20, 3B-10, 2B-8
10 yrs.		1077	.264	.331	3546	935	146	13	22	0.6	411	261	265	353	31	81	19	1413	2349	129	409	3.8	.967	SS-544, 3B-426, 2B-63
WORLD SERIES																								
1961	**CIN N**	5	.318	.318	22	7	0	0	0	0.0	1	1	0	2	0	0	0	13	13	1	5	5.4	.963	SS-5

Ray Katt

KATT, RAYMOND FREDERICK BR TR 6′ 2″ 190 lbs.
B. May 9, 1927, New Braunfels, Tex.

Year	Team	Games	BA	SA	AB	H	2B	3B	HR	HR%	R	RBI	BB	SO	SB	Pinch Hit AB	Pinch Hit H	PO	A	E	DP	TC/G	FA	G by Pos
1952	**NY N**	9	.222	.222	27	6	0	0	0	0.0	4	1	1	5	0	0	0	39	4	0	0	5.4	1.000	C-8
1953		8	.172	.207	29	5	1	0	0	0.0	2	1	1	3	0	0	0	33	6	1	0	5.0	.975	C-8
1954		86	.255	.435	200	51	7	1	9	4.5	26	33	19	29	1	5	0	265	23	8	4	3.6	.973	C-82
1955		124	.215	.313	326	70	7	2	7	2.1	27	28	22	38	0	3	2	482	45	7	7	4.4	.987	C-122
1956	**2 teams**	**NY N** (37G –.228) **STL N** (47G –.259)																						
″	**total**	84	.247	.429	259	64	8	0	13	5.0	21	34	12	40	0	0	0	395	34	8	1	5.2	.982	C-84
1957	**NY N**	72	.230	.297	165	38	3	1	2	1.2	11	17	15	35	1	7	2	238	25	5	4	3.9	.981	C-68
1958	**STL N**	19	.171	.268	41	7	1	0	1	2.4	1	4	4	6	0	5	0	63	4	2	2	4.9	.971	C-14
1959		15	.292	.375	24	7	2	0	0	0.0	0	2	0	8	0	1	0	38	2	1	0	2.9	.976	C-14
8 yrs.		417	.232	.356	1071	248	29	4	32	3.0	92	120	74	164	2	21	4	1553	143	32	18	4.3	.981	C-400

Benny Kauff

KAUFF, BENJAMIN MICHAEL BL TL 5′ 8″ 157 lbs.
B. Jan. 5, 1890, Pomeroy, Ohio D. Nov. 17, 1961, Columbus, Ohio.

Year	Team	Games	BA	SA	AB	H	2B	3B	HR	HR%	R	RBI	BB	SO	SB	Pinch Hit AB	Pinch Hit H	PO	A	E	DP	TC/G	FA	G by Pos
1912	**NY A**	5	.273	.273	11	3	0	0	0	0.0	4	2	3		1	0	0	4	0	0	0	1.0	1.000	OF-4
1914	**IND F**	154	**.370**	.534	571	**211**	**44**	13	8	1.4	**120**	95	72		**75**	0	0	310	31	17	5	2.3	.953	OF-154
1915	**BKN F**	136	**.342**	**.509**	483	165	23	11	12	2.5	92	83	85		**55**	0	0	317	32	15	7	2.7	.959	OF-136
1916	**NY N**	154	.264	.408	552	146	22	15	9	1.6	71	74	68	65	40	0	0	329	22	14	6	2.4	.962	OF-154
1917		153	.308	.388	559	172	22	4	5	0.9	89	68	59	54	30	0	0	357	12	9	4	2.5	.976	OF-153
1918		67	.315	.437	270	85	19	4	2	0.7	41	39	16	30	9	0	0	147	11	8	4	2.5	.952	OF-67
1919		135	.277	.422	491	136	27	7	10	2.0	73	67	39	45	21	1	1	306	18	17	3	2.5	.950	OF-134
1920		55	.274	.446	157	43	12	3	3	1.9	31	26	25	14	3	3	1	111	10	5	0	2.5	.960	OF-51
8 yrs.		859	.311	.450	3094	961	169	57	49	1.6	521	454	367	208	234	4	2	1881	136	85	29	2.5	.960	OF-853
WORLD SERIES																								
1917	**NY N**	6	.160	.440	25	4	1	0	2	8.0	2	5	0	2	1	0	0	7	0	1	0	1.3	.875	OF-6

Dick Kauffman

KAUFFMAN, HOWARD RICHARD BB TR 6′ 3″ 190 lbs.
B. June 22, 1888, East Lewisburg, Pa. D. Apr. 16, 1948, Mifflinburg, Pa.

Year	Team	Games	BA	SA	AB	H	2B	3B	HR	HR%	R	RBI	BB	SO	SB	Pinch Hit AB	Pinch Hit H	PO	A	E	DP	TC/G	FA	G by Pos
1914	**STL A**	7	.267	.333	15	4	1	0	0	0.0	1	2	0	3	0	1	0	29	0	1	0	5.0	.967	1B-6
1915		37	.258	.355	124	32	8	2	0	0.0	9	14	5	27	0	4	1	293	16	5	22	9.5	.984	1B-32, OF-1
2 yrs.		44	.259	.353	139	36	9	2	0	0.0	10	16	5	30	0	5	1	322	16	6	22	8.8	.983	1B-38, OF-1

Charlie Kavanagh

KAVANAGH, CHARLES HUGH (Silk) BR TR 5′ 9″ 165 lbs.
B. June 9, 1893, Chicago, Ill. D. Sept. 6, 1973, Reedsburg, Wis.

Year	Team	Games	BA	SA	AB	H	2B	3B	HR	HR%	R	RBI	BB	SO	SB	Pinch Hit AB	Pinch Hit H	PO	A	E	DP	TC/G	FA	G by Pos
1914	**CHI A**	5	.200	.200	5	1	0	0	0	0.0	0	0	0	2	0	5	1	0	0	0	0	0.0	—	

Leo Kavanagh

KAVANAGH, LEO DANIEL BR TR 5′ 9″ 180 lbs.
B. Aug. 9, 1894, Chicago, Ill. D. Aug. 10, 1950, Chicago, Ill.

Year	Team	Games	BA	SA	AB	H	2B	3B	HR	HR%	R	RBI	BB	SO	SB	Pinch Hit AB	Pinch Hit H	PO	A	E	DP	TC/G	FA	G by Pos
1914	**CHI F**	5	.273	.273	11	3	0	0	0	0.0	0	1	1		0	0	0	7	6	0	1	2.6	1.000	SS-5

Marty Kavanagh

KAVANAGH, MARTIN JOSEPH BR TR 6′ 187 lbs.
B. June 13, 1891, Harrison, N. J. D. July 28, 1960, Eloise, Mich.

Year	Team	Games	BA	SA	AB	H	2B	3B	HR	HR%	R	RBI	BB	SO	SB	Pinch Hit AB	Pinch Hit H	PO	A	E	DP	TC/G	FA	G by Pos
1914	**DET A**	127	.248	.351	439	109	21	6	4	0.9	60	35	41	42	16	8	1	264	334	45	30	5.4	.930	2B-115, 1B-4
1915		113	.295	.452	332	98	14	13	4	1.2	55	49	42	44	8	20	**10**	563	121	19	24	7.8	.973	1B-44, 2B-42, OF-2, SS-2
1916	**2 teams**	**DET A** (58G –.141) **CLE A** (19G –.250)																						
″	**total**	77	.180	.270	122	22	6	1	1	0.8	10	15	11	20	0	**46**	7	34	35	7	3	2.9	.908	OF-11, 2B-11, 3B-3, 1B-1
1917	**CLE A**	14	.000	.000	14	0	0	0	0	0.0	1	0	3	2	0	9	0	2	1	0	1	1.5	1.000	OF-2
1918	**3 teams**	**CLE A** (13G –.211) **STL N** (12G –.182) **DET A** (13G –.273)																						
″	**total**	38	.222	.294	126	28	6	0	1	0.8	12	23	21	14	2	2	0	267	23	11	13	8.4	.963	1B-24, OF-8, 2B-4
5 yrs.		369	.249	.362	1033	257	47	20	10	1.0	138	122	118	122	26	85	18	1130	514	82	71	6.3	.952	2B-172, 1B-73, OF-23, 3B-3, SS-2

Bill Kay

KAY, WALTER BROCTON (King Bill) BL TR 6′ 2″ 180 lbs.
B. Feb. 14, 1878, New Castle, Va. D. Dec. 3, 1945, Roanoke, Va.

Year	Team	Games	BA	SA	AB	H	2B	3B	HR	HR%	R	RBI	BB	SO	SB	Pinch Hit AB	Pinch Hit H	PO	A	E	DP	TC/G	FA	G by Pos
1907	**WAS A**	25	.333	.383	60	20	1	1	0	0.0	8	7	0		0	11	3	19	1	0	0	1.7	1.000	OF-12

Eddie Kazak

KAZAK, EDWARD TERRANCE BR TR 6′ 175 lbs.
Born Edward Terrance Tkaczuk.
B. July 18, 1920, Steubenville, Ohio.

Year	Team	Games	BA	SA	AB	H	2B	3B	HR	HR%	R	RBI	BB	SO	SB	Pinch Hit AB	Pinch Hit H	PO	A	E	DP	TC/G	FA	G by Pos
1948	**STL N**	6	.273	.409	22	6	3	0	0	0.0	1	2	0	2	0	0	0	7	11	2	2	3.3	.900	3B-6
1949		92	.304	.423	326	99	15	3	6	1.8	43	42	29	17	0	7	2	74	187	23	22	3.3	.919	3B-80, 2B-5
1950		93	.256	.357	207	53	2	2	5	2.4	21	23	18	19	0	**42**	10	36	95	9	7	2.9	.936	3B-48
1951		11	.182	.242	33	6	2	0	0	0.0	2	4	5	5	0	1	0	11	17	2	1	3.0	.933	3B-10
1952	**2 teams**	**STL N** (3G –.000) **CIN N** (13G –.067)																						
″	**total**	16	.059	.176	17	1	0	1	0	0.0	2	0	0	2	0	9	1	5	2	1	0	1.6	.875	3B-4, 1B-1
5 yrs.		218	.273	.383	605	165	22	6	11	1.8	69	71	52	45	0	59	13	133	312	37	32	3.1	.923	3B-148, 2B-5, 1B-1

Ted Kazanski

KAZANSKI, THEODORE STANLEY BR TR 6′ 1″ 175 lbs.
B. Jan. 25, 1934, Hamtramck, Mich.

Year	Team	Games	BA	SA	AB	H	2B	3B	HR	HR%	R	RBI	BB	SO	SB	Pinch Hit AB	Pinch Hit H	PO	A	E	DP	TC/G	FA	G by Pos
1953	**PHI N**	95	.217	.308	360	78	17	5	2	0.6	39	27	26	53	1	0	0	185	239	23	53	4.7	.949	SS-95
1954		39	.135	.183	104	14	2	0	1	1.0	7	8	4	14	0	1	0	43	77	7	18	3.3	.945	SS-38
1955		9	.083	.333	12	1	0	0	1	8.3	1	1	1	1	0	1	0	5	9	0	1	1.8	1.000	SS-4, 3B-4

Ted Kazanski *continued*

Year	Team	Lg	Games	BA	SA	AB	H	2B	3B	HR	HR%	R	RBI	BB	SO	SB	Pinch Hit AB	Pinch Hit H	PO	A	E	DP	TC/G	FA	G by Pos
1956			117	.211	.277	379	80	11	1	4	1.1	35	34	20	41	0	1	0	246	261	11	68	4.4	.979	2B-116, SS-1
1957			62	.265	.362	185	49	7	1	3	1.6	15	11	17	20	1	5	1	64	95	5	21	2.7	.970	3B-36, 2B-22, SS-3
1958			95	.228	.315	289	66	12	2	3	1.0	21	35	22	34	2	5	1	140	175	8	41	3.3	.975	2B-59, SS-22, 3B-16
6 yrs.			417	.217	.299	1329	288	49	9	14	1.1	118	116	90	163	4	13	2	683	856	54	202	3.8	.966	2B-197, SS-163, 3B-56

Bob Kearney

KEARNEY, ROBERT HENRY BR TR 6′ 190 lbs.
B. Oct. 3, 1956, San Antonio, Tex.

Year	Team	Lg	Games	BA	SA	AB	H	2B	3B	HR	HR%	R	RBI	BB	SO	SB	Pinch Hit AB	Pinch Hit H	PO	A	E	DP	TC/G	FA	G by Pos
1979	**SF**	**N**	2	—	—	0	0	0	0	0	—	0	0	1	0	0	0	0	0	0	0	0	0.0	.000	C-1
1981	**OAK**	**A**	1	—	—	0	0	0	0	0	—	0	0	0	0	0	0	0	0	0	0	0	0.0	.000	C-1
1982			22	.169	.211	71	12	3	0	0	0.0	7	5	3	10	0	0	0	114	14	4	1	6.0	.970	C-22
1983			108	.255	.372	298	76	11	0	8	2.7	33	32	21	50	1	8	0	437	41	9	5	4.7	.982	C-101, DH-3
1984	**SEA**	**A**	133	.225	.334	431	97	24	1	7	1.6	39	43	18	72	7	0	0	823	63	11	9	6.7	.988	C-133
1985			108	.243	.354	305	74	14	1	6	2.0	24	27	11	59	1	0	0	529	50	3	7	5.4	.995	C-108
1986			81	.240	.377	204	49	10	0	6	2.9	23	25	12	35	0	4	0	419	46	5	3	5.9	.989	C-79
1987			24	.170	.298	47	8	4	1	0	0.0	5	1	1	9	0	0	0	94	10	2	0	4.4	.981	C-24
8 yrs.			479	.233	.346	1356	316	66	3	27	2.0	131	133	67	235	9	12	0	2416	224	34	25	5.7	.987	C-469, DH-3

Ted Kearns

KEARNS, EDWARD JOSEPH BR TR 5′11″ 185 lbs.
B. Jan. 1, 1900, Trenton, N. J. D. Dec. 21, 1949, Trenton, N. J.

Year	Team	Lg	Games	BA	SA	AB	H	2B	3B	HR	HR%	R	RBI	BB	SO	SB	Pinch Hit AB	Pinch Hit H	PO	A	E	DP	TC/G	FA	G by Pos
1920	**PHI**	**A**	1	.000	.000	1	0	0	0	0	0.0	0	0	0	0	0	1	0	0	0	0	0	0.0	—	
1924	**CHI**	**N**	4	.250	.375	16	4	0	1	0	0.0	0	1	1	1	0	0	0	29	2	0	3	7.8	1.000	1B-4
1925			3	.500	.500	2	1	0	0	0	0.0	0	0	0	0	0	0	0	3	0	0	1	1.0	1.000	1B-3
3 yrs.			8	.263	.368	19	5	0	1	0	0.0	0	1	1	1	0	1	0	32	2	0	4	4.9	1.000	1B-7

Tom Kearns

KEARNS, THOMAS J. (Dasher) BR TR 5′ 7″ 160 lbs.
B. Nov. 9, 1860, Rochester, N. Y. D. Dec. 7, 1938, Buffalo, N. Y.

Year	Team	Lg	Games	BA	SA	AB	H	2B	3B	HR	HR%	R	RBI	BB	SO	SB	Pinch Hit AB	Pinch Hit H	PO	A	E	DP	TC/G	FA	G by Pos
1880	**BUF**	**N**	2	.000	.000	7	0	0	0	0	0.0	0	0	0	0		0	0	10	2	6	0	9.0	.667	C-2
1882	**DET**	**N**	4	.308	.462	13	4	2	0	0	0.0	2	1	0	4		0	0	3	8	4	0	3.8	.733	2B-4
1884			21	.203	.228	79	16	0	1	0	0.0	9		2	10		0	0	48	50	23	5	5.8	.810	2B-21
3 yrs.			27	.202	.242	99	20	2	1	0	0.0	11	1	2	14		0	0	61	60	33	5	5.7	.786	2B-25, C-2

Eddie Kearse

KEARSE, EDWARD PAUL (Truck) BR TR 6′ 1″ 195 lbs.
B. Feb. 23, 1916, San Francisco, Calif. D. July 15, 1968, Eureka, Calif.

Year	Team	Lg	Games	BA	SA	AB	H	2B	3B	HR	HR%	R	RBI	BB	SO	SB	Pinch Hit AB	Pinch Hit H	PO	A	E	DP	TC/G	FA	G by Pos
1942	**NY**	**A**	11	.192	.192	26	5	0	0	0	0.0	2	2	3	1	1	0	0	42	7	0	0	4.5	1.000	C-11

Chick Keating

KEATING, WALTER FRANCIS BR TR 5′ 9½″ 155 lbs.
B. Aug. 8, 1891, Philadelphia, Pa. D. July 13, 1959, Philadelphia, Pa.

Year	Team	Lg	Games	BA	SA	AB	H	2B	3B	HR	HR%	R	RBI	BB	SO	SB	Pinch Hit AB	Pinch Hit H	PO	A	E	DP	TC/G	FA	G by Pos
1913	**CHI**	**N**	2	.200	.400	5	1	1	0	0	0.0	1	0	0	1	0	0	0	6	1	0	0	3.5	1.000	SS-2
1914			20	.100	.167	30	3	0	1	0	0.0	3	0	6	9	0	0	0	15	24	2	2	2.6	.951	SS-16
1915			4	.000	.000	8	0	0	0	0	0.0	1	0	0	3	1	1	0	4	5	3	0	6.0	.750	SS-2
1926	**PHI**	**N**	4	.000	.000	2	0	0	0	0	0.0	0	0	0	0	0	0	0	1	2	1	0	0.8	.750	2B-2, SS-2, 3B-1
4 yrs.			30	.089	.156	45	4	1	1	0	0.0	5	0	6	13	1	1	0	26	32	6	2	2.6	.906	SS-22, 2B-2, 3B-1

Greg Keatley

KEATLEY, GREGORY STEVEN BR TR 6′ 2″ 200 lbs.
B. Sept. 12, 1953, Princeton, W. Va.

Year	Team	Lg	Games	BA	SA	AB	H	2B	3B	HR	HR%	R	RBI	BB	SO	SB	Pinch Hit AB	Pinch Hit H	PO	A	E	DP	TC/G	FA	G by Pos
1981	**KC**	**A**	2	—	—	0	0	0	0	0	—	0	0	0	0	0	0	0	1	0	0	0	0.5	1.000	C-2

Pat Keedy

KEEDY, CHARLES PATRICK BR TR 6′ 4″ 205 lbs.
B. Jan. 10, 1958, Birmingham, Ala.

Year	Team	Lg	Games	BA	SA	AB	H	2B	3B	HR	HR%	R	RBI	BB	SO	SB	Pinch Hit AB	Pinch Hit H	PO	A	E	DP	TC/G	FA	G by Pos
1985	**CAL**	**A**	3	.500	1.500	4	2	1	0	1	25.0	1	1	0	0	0	0	0	1	0	0	0	0.3	1.000	3B-2, OF-1
1987	**CHI**	**A**	17	.171	.341	41	7	1	0	2	4.9	6	2	2	14	1	0	0	17	32	2	5	3.2	.961	3B-11, 1B-2, OF-1, SS-1, 2B-1
1989	**CLE**	**A**	9	.214	.357	14	3	2	0	0	0.0	3	1	2	5	0	2	0	4	7	1	1	1.5	.917	OF-3, 3B-2, DH-1, SS-1, 1B-1
3 yrs.			29	.203	.424	59	12	4	0	3	5.1	10	4	4	19	1	2	0	22	39	3	6	2.4	.953	3B-15, OF-5, 1B-3, SS-2, DH-1, 2B-1

Tim Keefe

KEEFE, TIMOTHY JOHN (Sir Timothy) BR TR 5′10½″ 185 lbs.
B. Jan. 1, 1857, Cambridge, Mass. D. Apr. 23, 1933, Cambridge, Mass.
Hall of Fame 1964.

Year	Team	Lg	Games	BA	SA	AB	H	2B	3B	HR	HR%	R	RBI	BB	SO	SB	Pinch Hit AB	Pinch Hit H	PO	A	E	DP	TC/G	FA	G by Pos
1880	**TRO**	**N**	12	.233	.302	43	10	3	0	0	0.0	4	3	1	12		0	0	7	22	0	0	2.4	1.000	P-12
1881			46	.230	.289	152	35	7	1	0	0.0	18	19	21	26		0	0	23	79	17	5	2.6	.857	P-45, OF-1
1882			53	.228	.360	189	43	8	7	1	0.5	24	19	17	46		0	0	52	102	14	6	3.1	.917	P-43, OF-8, 3B-3
1883	**NY**	**AA**	70	.220	.313	259	57	6	9	0	0.0	39		14			0	0	38	152	61	3	3.6	.757	P-68, OF-1, 2B-1
1884			63	.235	.347	213	50	3	6	3	1.4	27		18			0	0	26	97	32	3	2.5	.794	P-58, OF-5
1885	**NY**	**N**	47	.163	.229	166	27	1	5	0	0.0	20		13	22		0	0	30	80	13	0	2.6	.894	P-46, OF-2
1886			64	.171	.244	205	35	10	1	1	0.5	26	20	17	42		0	0	29	107	15	3	2.3	.901	P-64, OF-1
1887			56	.220	.351	191	42	7	6	2	1.0	27	23	20	41	2	0	0	18	102	15	1	2.3	.889	P-56, OF-2
1888			51	.127	.177	181	23	3	0	2	1.1	10	8	4	56	3	0	0	30	79	11	1	2.3	.908	P-51, OF-1
1889			47	.154	.215	149	23	5	2	0	0.0	17	8	8	40	2	0	0	10	78	8	3	2.0	.917	P-47
1890	**NY**	**P**	30	.109	.185	92	10	1	0	2	2.2	18	11	13	26	0	0	0	15	61	4	2	2.7	.950	P-30
1891	**2 teams**		**NY N** (8G –.095) **PHI N** (11G –.172)																						
″	**total**		19	.140	.180	50	7	0	1	0	0.0	2	2	7	29	1	0	0	6	28	2	1	1.9	.944	P-19
1892	**PHI**	**N**	39	.085	.128	117	10	2	0	1	0.9	6	3	13	47	1	0	0	8	68	13	2	2.3	.854	P-39
1893			22	.228	.278	79	18	4	0	0	0.0	10	6	9	24	1	0	0	5	32	6	1	2.0	.860	P-22
14 yrs.			619	.187	.269	2086	390	60	38	12	0.6	248	122	175	411	10	0	0	297	1087	211	31	2.6	.868	P-600, OF-21, 3B-3, 2B-1

Willie Keeler

KEELER, WILLIAM HENRY (Wee Willie) BL TL 5′ 4½″ 140 lbs.
Born William Henry O'Kelleher.
B. Mar. 3, 1872, Brooklyn, N. Y. D. Jan. 1, 1923, Brooklyn, N. Y.
Hall of Fame 1939.

Year	Team	Lg	Games	BA	SA	AB	H	2B	3B	HR	HR%	R	RBI	BB	SO	SB	Pinch Hit AB	Pinch Hit H	PO	A	E	DP	TC/G	FA	G by Pos
1892	**NY**	**N**	14	.321	.377	53	17	3	0	0	0.0	7	6	3	3	5	0	0	15	21	5	1	2.9	.878	3B-14
1893	**2 teams**		**NY N** (7G –.333) **BKN N** (20G –.313)																						
″	**total**		27	.317	.442	104	33	3	2	2	1.9	19	16	9	5	5	0	0	34	39	16	2	3.3	.820	3B-12, OF-11, SS-2, 2B-2

Willie Keeler *continued*

Year	Team	Lg	Games	BA	SA	AB	H	2B	3B	HR	HR%	R	RBI	BB	SO	SB	Pinch Hit AB	Pinch Hit H	PO	A	E	DP	TC/G	FA	G by Pos
1894	**BAL**	**N**	129	.371	.517	590	219	27	22	5	0.8	165	94	40	6	32	0	0	217	26	16	4	2.0	.938	OF-128, 2B-1
1895			131	.377	.494	**565**	213	24	15	4	0.7	162	78	37	12	47	0	0	244	21	10	5	2.1	.964	OF-131
1896			127	.386	.496	544	210	22	13	4	0.7	153	82	37	9	67	0	0	227	20	8	6	2.0	.969	OF-126
1897			129	**.424**	.544	564	**239**	27	19	1	0.2	145	74	35		64	0	0	217	12	7	2	1.8	.970	OF-129
1898			128	**.385**	.410	561	**216**	7	2	1	0.2	126	44	31		28	1	0	211	14	9	2	1.8	.962	OF-128, 3B-1
1899	**BKN**	**N**	141	.379	.451	570	216	12	13	1	0.2	**140**	61	37		45	0	0	208	21	5	4	1.7	.979	OF-141
1900			136	.362	.449	563	**204**	13	12	4	0.7	106	68	30		41	0	0	227	23	16	4	1.9	.940	OF-136, 2B-1
1901			136	.355	.443	589	209	16	15	2	0.3	123	43	21		23	0	0	194	36	9	6	1.7	.962	OF-125, 3B-10, 2B-3
1902			132	.338	.396	556	188	18	7	0	0.0	86	38	21		19	0	0	208	14	5	4	1.7	.978	OF-132
1903	**NY**	**A**	132	.318	.373	515	164	14	7	0	0.0	95	32	32		24	0	0	183	15	15	4	1.6	.930	OF-128, 3B-4
1904			143	.343	.409	543	186	14	8	2	0.4	78	40	35		21	1	1	186	16	14	7	1.5	.935	OF-142
1905			149	.302	.362	560	169	14	4	4	0.7	81	38	43		19	0	0	207	38	11	2	1.7	.957	OF-139, 2B-12, 3B-3
1906			152	.304	.338	592	180	8	3	2	0.3	96	33	40		23	0	0	213	16	3	3	1.5	.987	OF-152
1907			107	.234	.255	423	99	5	2	0	0.0	50	17	15		7	0	0	144	13	5	5	1.5	.969	OF-107
1908			91	.263	.288	323	85	3	1	1	0.3	38	14	31		14	3	0	123	9	9	2	1.6	.936	OF-88
1909			99	.264	.319	360	95	7	5	1	0.3	44	32	24		10	3	0	111	9	4	2	1.3	.968	OF-95
1910	**NY**	**N**	19	.300	.300	10	3	0	0	0	0.0	5	0	3	1	1	9	2	1	0	0	0	0.5	1.000	OF-2
19 yrs.			2122	.343 **8th**	.417	8585	2945	237	150	34	0.4	1719	810	524	36	495	17	3	3170	363	167	65	1.8	.955	OF-2040, 3B-44, 2B-19, SS-2

Bob Keely

KEELY, ROBERT WILLIAM BR TR 6′ 175 lbs.
B. Aug. 22, 1909, St. Louis, Mo.

Year	Team	Lg	Games	BA	SA	AB	H	2B	3B	HR	HR%	R	RBI	BB	SO	SB	Pinch Hit AB	Pinch Hit H	PO	A	E	DP	TC/G	FA	G by Pos
1944	**STL**	**N**	1	—	—	0	0	0	0	0	—	0	0	0	0	0	0	0	1	0	0	0	1.0	1.000	C-1
1945			1	.000	.000	1	0	0	0	0	0.0	0	0	0	0	0	0	0	1	0	0	0	1.0	1.000	C-1
2 yrs.			2	.000	.000	1	0	0	0	0	0.0	0	0	0	0	0	0	0	2	0	0	0	1.0	1.000	C-2

Bill Keen

KEEN, WILLIAM BROWN (Buster) BR TR 6′ 181 lbs.
B. Aug. 16, 1892, Oglethorpe, Ga. D. July 16, 1947, South Point, Ohio.

Year	Team	Lg	Games	BA	SA	AB	H	2B	3B	HR	HR%	R	RBI	BB	SO	SB	Pinch Hit AB	Pinch Hit H	PO	A	E	DP	TC/G	FA	G by Pos
1911	**PIT**	**N**	6	.000	.000	7	0	0	0	0	0.0	0	0	1	4	0	5	0	6	0	0	0	6.0	1.000	1B-1

Jim Keenan

KEENAN, JAMES WILLIAM BR TR 5′10″ 186 lbs.
B. Feb. 10, 1858, New Haven, Conn. D. Sept. 21, 1926, Cincinnati, Ohio.

Year	Team	Lg	Games	BA	SA	AB	H	2B	3B	HR	HR%	R	RBI	BB	SO	SB	Pinch Hit AB	Pinch Hit H	PO	A	E	DP	TC/G	FA	G by Pos
1880	**BUF**	**N**	2	.143	.143	7	1	0	0	0	0.0	1	0	1	1		0	0	11	7	1	0	9.5	.947	C-2
1882	**PIT**	**AA**	25	.219	.323	96	21	7	0	1	1.0	10		1			0	0	145	22	19	3	7.2	.898	C-22, OF-3, SS-1
1884	**IND**	**AA**	68	.293	.418	249	73	14	4	3	1.2	36		16			0	0	462	80	45	6	8.5	.923	C-59, 1B-6, OF-2, SS-1, P-1
1885	**CIN**	**AA**	36	.265	.333	132	35	2	2	1	0.8	16		8			0	0	191	38	19	2	6.5	.923	C-33, 1B-4, P-1
1886			44	.270	.399	148	40	4	3	3	2.0	31		18			0	0	220	54	24	6	6.2	.919	C-30, OF-7, 3B-5, 1B-4, P-2
1887			47	.253	.287	174	44	4	1	0	0.0	19		11		7	0	0	252	68	21	15	7.0	.938	C-38, 1B-11
1888			85	.233	.323	313	73	9	8	1	0.3	38	40	22		9	0	0	506	120	30	13	7.7	.954	C-69, 1B-16
1889			87	.287	.453	300	86	10	11	6	2.0	52	60	48	35	18	0	0	503	99	22	25	7.1	.965	C-66, 1B-21, 3B-1
1890	**CIN**	**N**	54	.139	.223	202	28	4	2	3	1.5	21	19	19	36	5	0	0	271	64	16	6	6.5	.954	C-50, 1B-2, OF-1, 3B-1
1891			75	.202	.317	252	51	7	5	4	1.6	30	33	33	39	2	0	0	590	53	31	22	8.9	.954	1B-41, C-34, 3B-1
10 yrs.			523	.241	.348	1873	452	61	36	22	1.2	254	152	177	111	41	0	0	3151	605	228	98	7.4	.943	C-403, 1B-105, OF-13, 3B-8, P-4, SS-2

Jim Keesey

KEESEY, JAMES WARD BR TR 6′½″ 170 lbs.
B. Oct. 27, 1902, Perryville, Mo. D. Sept. 5, 1951, Boise, Ida.

Year	Team	Lg	Games	BA	SA	AB	H	2B	3B	HR	HR%	R	RBI	BB	SO	SB	Pinch Hit AB	Pinch Hit H	PO	A	E	DP	TC/G	FA	G by Pos
1925	**PHI**	**A**	5	.400	.400	5	2	0	0	0	0.0	1	1	0	2	0	3	2	2	0	0	0	1.0	1.000	1B-2
1930			11	.250	.333	12	3	1	0	0	0.0	2	2	1	2	0	8	2	10	0	1	2	3.7	.909	1B-3
2 yrs.			16	.294	.353	17	5	1	0	0	0.0	3	3	1	4	0	11	4	12	0	1	2	2.6	.923	1B-5

Bill Keinzil

KEINZIL, WILLIAM BL TL
B. Philadelphia, Pa. Deceased.

Year	Team	Lg	Games	BA	SA	AB	H	2B	3B	HR	HR%	R	RBI	BB	SO	SB	Pinch Hit AB	Pinch Hit H	PO	A	E	DP	TC/G	FA	G by Pos
1882	**PHI**	**AA**	9	.333	.545	33	11	3	2	0	0.0	8		5			0	0	15	1	3	0	2.1	.842	OF-9
1884	**PHI**	**U**	67	.254	.351	299	76	13	8	0	0.0	76		21			0	0	87	18	31	2	2.0	.772	OF-67
2 yrs.			76	.262	.370	332	87	16	10	0	0.0	84		26			0	0	102	19	34	2	2.0	.781	OF-76

Bill Keister

KEISTER, WILLIAM HOFFMAN (Wagon Tongue) BL TR 5′ 5½″ 168 lbs.
B. Aug. 17, 1874, Baltimore, Md. D. Aug. 19, 1924, Baltimore, Md.

Year	Team	Lg	Games	BA	SA	AB	H	2B	3B	HR	HR%	R	RBI	BB	SO	SB	Pinch Hit AB	Pinch Hit H	PO	A	E	DP	TC/G	FA	G by Pos
1896	**BAL**	**N**	15	.241	.293	58	14	3	0	0	0.0	8	5	3	5	4	1	0	16	27	8	2	3.6	.843	2B-8, 3B-6
1898	**BOS**	**N**	10	.167	.233	30	5	2	0	0	0.0	5	4	0		0	1	0	10	16	0	2	2.9	1.000	2B-4, SS-4, OF-1
1899	**BAL**	**N**	136	.329	.449	523	172	22	16	3	0.6	96	73	16		33	0	0	265	401	66	36	5.3	.910	SS-90, 2B-46, OF-1
1900	**STL**	**N**	126	.300	.398	497	149	26	10	1	0.2	78	72	25		32	1	1	224	345	50	27	4.9	.919	2B-116, SS-7, 3B-3
1901	**BAL**	**A**	115	.328	.482	442	145	20	**21**	2	0.5	78	93	18		24	2	0	231	322	97	30	5.8	.851	SS-112
1902	**WAS**	**A**	119	.300	.462	483	145	33	9	9	1.9	82	90	14		27	1	0	229	166	34	14	3.5	.921	OF-65, 2B-40, 3B-14, SS-2
1903	**PHI**	**N**	100	.320	.445	400	128	27	7	3	0.8	53	63	14		11	0	0	133	22	10	1	1.6	.939	OF-100
7 yrs.			621	.312	.440	2433	758	133	63	18	0.7	400	400	90	5	131	6	1	1108	1299	265	112	4.3	.901	SS-215, 2B-214, OF-167, 3B-23

Mickey Keliher

KELIHER, MAURICE MICHAEL BL TL 6′ 175 lbs.
B. Jan. 11, 1890, Washington, D. C. D. Sept. 7, 1930, Washington, D. C.

Year	Team	Lg	Games	BA	SA	AB	H	2B	3B	HR	HR%	R	RBI	BB	SO	SB	Pinch Hit AB	Pinch Hit H	PO	A	E	DP	TC/G	FA	G by Pos
1911	**PIT**	**N**	2	.000	.000	7	0	0	0	0	0.0	0	0	0	5	0	1	0	6	1	1	1	4.0	.875	1B-2
1912			2	—	—	0	0	0	0	0	—	1	0	0	0	0	0	0	0	0	0	0	0.0	—	
2 yrs.			4	.000	.000	7	0	0	0	0	0.0	1	0	0	5	0	1	0	6	1	1	1	4.0	.875	1B-2

George Kell

KELL, GEORGE CLYDE BR TR 5′ 9″ 175 lbs.
Brother of Skeeter Kell.
B. Aug. 23, 1922, Swifton, Ark.
Hall of Fame 1983.

Year	Team	Lg	Games	BA	SA	AB	H	2B	3B	HR	HR%	R	RBI	BB	SO	SB	Pinch Hit AB	Pinch Hit H	PO	A	E	DP	TC/G	FA	G by Pos
1943	**PHI**	**A**	1	.200	.600	5	1	0	1	0	0.0	1	1	0	0	0	0	0	1	3	0	0	4.0	1.000	3B-1
1944			139	.268	.309	514	138	15	3	0	0.0	51	44	22	23	5	0	0	167	289	20	25	3.4	.958	3B-139
1945			147	.272	.356	567	154	30	3	4	0.7	50	56	27	15	2	0	0	186	345	20	32	3.7	.964	3B-147

George Kell *continued*

Year	Team	Games	BA	SA	AB	H	2B	3B	HR	HR%	R	RBI	BB	SO	SB	Pinch Hit AB	Pinch Hit H	PO	A	E	DP	TC/G	FA	G by Pos
1946	**2 teams**	**PHI A** (26G –.299) **DET A** (105G –.327)																						
″	**total**	131	.322	.432	521	168	25	10	4	0.8	70	52	40	20	3	0	0	143	267	7	27	3.2	.983	3B-131, 1B-1
1947	**DET A**	152	.320	.412	588	188	29	5	5	0.9	75	93	61	16	9	0	0	167	333	20	25	3.4	.962	3B-152
1948		92	.304	.402	368	112	24	3	2	0.5	47	44	33	15	2	0	0	108	146	8	15	2.8	.969	3B-92
1949		134	**.343**	.467	522	179	38	9	3	0.6	97	59	71	13	7	0	0	154	271	11	23	3.3	.975	3B-134
1950		157	.340	.484	**641**	**218**	**56**	6	8	1.2	114	101	66	18	3	0	0	186	315	9	30	3.2	.982	3B-157
1951		147	.319	.400	598	**191**	**36**	3	2	0.3	92	59	61	18	10	0	0	175	310	20	34	3.4	.960	3B-147
1952	**2 teams**	**DET A** (39G –.296) **BOS A** (75G –.319)																						
″	**total**	114	.311	.423	428	133	23	2	7	1.6	52	57	45	23	0	1	0	113	216	14	21	3.1	.959	3B-112
1953	**BOS A**	134	.307	.483	460	141	41	2	12	2.6	68	73	52	22	5	8	4	118	231	10	23	2.7	.972	3B-124, OF-7
1954	**2 teams**	**BOS A** (26G –.258) **CHI A** (71G –.283)																						
″	**total**	97	.276	.362	326	90	13	0	5	1.5	40	58	33	15	1	9	1	306	105	11	36	4.7	.974	3B-56, 1B-32, OF-2
1955	**CHI A**	128	.312	.429	429	134	24	1	8	1.9	44	81	51	36	2	8	2	216	170	7	20	3.0	.982	3B-105, 1B-24, OF-1
1956	**2 teams**	**CHI A** (21G –.313) **BAL A** (102G –.261)																						
″	**total**	123	.271	.395	425	115	22	2	9	2.1	52	48	33	37	0	6	0	138	198	7	24	2.8	.980	3B-115, 1B-6, 2B-1
1957	**BAL A**	99	.297	.413	310	92	9	0	9	2.9	28	44	25	16	2	11	4	212	127	4	25	3.4	.988	3B-80, 1B-22
15 yrs.		1795	.306	.414	6702	2054	385	50	78	1.2	881	870	620	287	51	43	11	2390	3326	168	360	3.3	.971	3B-1692, 1B-85, OF-10, 2B-1

Skeeter Kell

KELL, EVERETT LEE BR TR 5′ 9″ 160 lbs.
Brother of George Kell.
B. Oct. 11, 1929, Swifton, Ark.

Year	Team	Games	BA	SA	AB	H	2B	3B	HR	HR%	R	RBI	BB	SO	SB	Pinch Hit AB	Pinch Hit H	PO	A	E	DP	TC/G	FA	G by Pos
1952	**PHI A**	75	.221	.286	213	47	8	3	0	0.0	24	17	14	18	5	1	0	143	169	12	35	4.8	.963	2B-68

Duke Kelleher

KELLEHER, ALBERT ALOYSIUS TR
B. Sept. 30, 1893, New York, N. Y. D. Sept. 28, 1947, Staten Island, N. Y.

Year	Team	Games	BA	SA	AB	H	2B	3B	HR	HR%	R	RBI	BB	SO	SB	Pinch Hit AB	Pinch Hit H	PO	A	E	DP	TC/G	FA	G by Pos
1916	**NY N**	1	—	—	0	0	0	0	0	—	0	0	0	0	0	0	0	0	0	0	0	0.0	.000	C-1

Frankie Kelleher

KELLEHER, FRANCIS EUGENE BR TR 6′ 1″ 195 lbs.
B. Aug. 22, 1916, San Francisco, Calif. D. Apr. 13, 1979, Stockton, Calif.

Year	Team	Games	BA	SA	AB	H	2B	3B	HR	HR%	R	RBI	BB	SO	SB	Pinch Hit AB	Pinch Hit H	PO	A	E	DP	TC/G	FA	G by Pos
1942	**CIN N**	38	.182	.309	110	20	3	1	3	2.7	13	12	16	20	0	7	3	67	1	1	1	2.3	.986	OF-30
1943		9	.000	.000	10	0	0	0	0	0.0	1	0	2	0	0	7	0	2	0	0	0	2.0	1.000	OF-1
2 yrs.		47	.167	.283	120	20	3	1	3	2.5	14	12	18	20	0	14	3	69	1	1	1	2.3	.986	OF-31

John Kelleher

KELLEHER, JOHN PATRICK BR TR 5′11″ 150 lbs.
B. Sept. 13, 1893, Brookline, Mass. D. Aug. 21, 1960, Brighton, Mass.

Year	Team	Games	BA	SA	AB	H	2B	3B	HR	HR%	R	RBI	BB	SO	SB	Pinch Hit AB	Pinch Hit H	PO	A	E	DP	TC/G	FA	G by Pos
1912	**STL N**	8	.333	.417	12	4	1	0	0	0.0	0	1	0	2	0	4	1	3	4	0	1	2.3	1.000	3B-3
1916	**BKN N**	2	.000	.000	3	0	0	0	0	0.0	0	0	0	0	0	0	0	1	1	0	0	1.0	1.000	SS-1, 3B-1
1921	**CHI N**	95	.309	.432	301	93	11	7	4	1.3	31	47	16	16	2	9	5	192	194	15	31	4.6	.963	3B-37, 2B-27, SS-11, 1B-11, OF-1
1922		63	.259	.306	193	50	7	1	0	0.0	23	20	15	14	5	6	0	94	112	12	13	3.8	.945	3B-46, SS-7, 1B-4
1923		66	.306	.451	193	59	10	0	6	3.1	27	21	14	9	2	15	6	228	84	22	21	6.3	.934	1B-22, SS-14, 3B-11, 2B-6
1924	**BOS N**	1	.000	.000	1	0	0	0	0	0.0	0	0	0	1	0	1	0	0	0	0	0	0.0	—	
6 yrs.		235	.293	.400	703	206	29	8	10	1.4	81	89	45	42	9	35	12	518	395	49	66	4.8	.949	3B-98, 1B-37, 2B-33, SS-33, OF-1

Mick Kelleher

KELLEHER, MICHAEL DENNIS BR TR 5′ 9″ 176 lbs.
B. July 25, 1947, Seattle, Wash.

Year	Team	Games	BA	SA	AB	H	2B	3B	HR	HR%	R	RBI	BB	SO	SB	Pinch Hit AB	Pinch Hit H	PO	A	E	DP	TC/G	FA	G by Pos
1972	**STL N**	23	.159	.222	63	10	2	1	0	0.0	5	1	6	15	0	0	0	60	61	2	14	5.3	.984	SS-23
1973		43	.184	.237	38	7	2	0	0	0.0	4	2	4	11	0	0	0	30	55	4	10	2.1	.955	SS-42
1974	**HOU N**	19	.158	.158	57	9	0	0	0	0.0	4	2	5	10	1	0	0	23	62	5	10	5.0	.944	SS-18
1975	**STL N**	7	.000	.000	4	0	0	0	0	0.0	0	0	0	1	0	0	0	3	7	1	1	1.6	.909	SS-7
1976	**CHI N**	124	.228	.270	337	77	12	1	0	0.0	28	22	15	32	0	3	1	167	324	12	57	3.9	.976	SS-101, 3B-22, 2B-5
1977		63	.230	.303	122	28	5	2	0	0.0	14	11	9	12	0	0	0	78	126	4	21	3.8	.981	2B-40, SS-14, 3B-1
1978		68	.253	.263	95	24	1	0	0	0.0	8	6	7	11	4	3	1	52	100	0	10	2.4	1.000	3B-37, 2B-17, SS-10
1979		73	.254	.296	142	36	4	1	0	0.0	14	10	7	9	2	0	0	78	148	6	24	3.1	.974	3B-32, 2B-29, SS-14
1980		105	.146	.177	96	14	1	1	0	0.0	12	4	9	17	1	3	1	82	129	7	23	2.1	.968	2B-57, 3B-31, SS-17
1981	**DET A**	61	.221	.273	77	17	4	0	0	0.0	10	6	7	10	0	3	1	30	75	4	12	1.8	.963	3B-39, 2B-11, SS-9
1982	**2 teams**	**DET A** (2G –.000) **CAL A** (34G –.163)																						
″	**total**	36	.160	.180	50	8	1	0	0	0.0	9	1	5	5	1	1	0	34	61	3	8	2.7	.969	SS-28, 3B-7, 2B-1
11 yrs.		622	.213	.253	1081	230	32	6	0	0.0	108	65	74	133	9	13	4	637	1148	48	190	3.0	.974	SS-283, 3B-169, 2B-160

Charlie Keller

KELLER, CHARLES ERNEST (King Kong) BL TR 5′10″ 185 lbs.
Brother of Hal Keller.
B. Sept. 12, 1916, Middletown, Md. D. May 23, 1990, Frederick, Md.

Year	Team	Games	BA	SA	AB	H	2B	3B	HR	HR%	R	RBI	BB	SO	SB	Pinch Hit AB	Pinch Hit H	PO	A	E	DP	TC/G	FA	G by Pos
1939	**NY A**	111	.334	.500	398	133	21	6	11	2.8	87	83	81	49	6	4	2	213	5	7	1	2.1	.969	OF-105
1940		138	.286	.508	500	143	18	15	21	4.2	102	93	**106**	65	8	0	0	317	5	11	2	2.4	.967	OF-136
1941		140	.298	.580	507	151	24	10	33	6.5	102	122	102	65	6	3	0	328	7	7	2	2.5	.980	OF-137
1942		152	.292	.513	544	159	24	9	26	4.8	106	108	114	61	14	0	0	321	10	5	1	2.2	.985	OF-152
1943		141	.271	.525	512	139	15	11	31	**6.1**	97	86	**106**	60	7	0	0	338	8	2	0	2.5	.994	OF-141
1945		44	.301	.577	163	49	7	4	10	6.1	26	34	31	21	0	0	0	110	4	0	0	2.6	1.000	OF-44
1946		150	.275	.533	538	148	29	10	30	5.6	98	101	113	**101**	1	1	0	324	4	7	0	2.2	.979	OF-149
1947		45	.238	.550	151	36	6	1	13	8.6	36	36	41	18	0	2	0	85	2	3	0	2.1	.967	OF-43
1948		83	.267	.417	247	66	15	2	6	2.4	41	44	41	25	1	15	2	126	1	3	0	2.0	.977	OF-66
1949		60	.250	.379	116	29	4	1	3	2.6	17	16	25	15	2	27	3	41	0	1	0	1.4	.976	OF-31
1950	**DET A**	50	.314	.569	51	16	1	3	2	3.9	7	16	13	6	0	32	9	10	0	0	0	1.7	1.000	OF-6
1951		54	.258	.435	62	16	2	0	3	4.8	6	21	11	12	0	**38**	**9**	22	0	0	0	2.8	1.000	OF-8
1952	**NY A**	2	.000	.000	1	0	0	0	0	0.0	0	0	0	1	0	1	0	0	0	0	0	0.0	.000	OF-1
13 yrs.		1170	.286	.518	3790	1085	166	72	189	5.0	725	760	784	499	45	123	25	2235	46	46	6	2.3	.980	OF-1019
WORLD SERIES																								
1939	**NY A**	4	.438	1.188	16	7	1	1	3	18.8	8	6	1	2	0	0	0	6	0	0	0	1.5	1.000	OF-4
1941		5	.389	.500	18	7	2	0	0	0.0	5	5	3	1	0	0	0	12	0	0	0	2.4	1.000	OF-5

Charlie Keller *continued*

Year	Team	Games	BA	SA	AB	H	2B	3B	HR	HR%	R	RBI	BB	SO	SB	Pinch Hit AB	Pinch Hit H	PO	A	E	DP	TC/G	FA	G by Pos
1942		5	.200	.500	20	4	0	0	2	10.0	2	5	1	3	0	0	0	12	1	0	1	2.6	1.000	OF-5
1943		5	.222	.333	18	4	0	1	0	0.0	3	2	2	5	1	0	0	10	1	0	0	2.2	1.000	OF-5
4 yrs.		19	.306	.611 **10th**	72	22	3	2	5	6.9	18	18	7	11	1	0	0	40	2	0	1	2.2	1.000	OF-19

Hal Keller

KELLER, HAROLD KEFAUVER BL TR 6′ 1″ 200 lbs.
Brother of Charlie Keller.
B. July 7, 1927, Middletown, Md.

Year	Team	Games	BA	SA	AB	H	2B	3B	HR	HR%	R	RBI	BB	SO	SB	Pinch Hit AB	Pinch Hit H	PO	A	E	DP	TC/G	FA	G by Pos
1949	WAS A	3	.333	.333	3	1	0	0	0	0.0	1	0	0	0	0	3	1	0	0	0	0	0.0	—	
1950		11	.214	.429	28	6	3	0	1	3.6	1	5	2	2	0	2	1	25	1	0	0	3.3	1.000	C-8
1952		11	.174	.261	23	4	2	0	0	0.0	2	0	1	1	0	0	0	25	4	1	1	2.7	.967	C-11
3 yrs.		25	.204	.352	54	11	5	0	1	1.9	4	5	3	3	0	5	2	50	5	1	1	2.9	.982	C-19

Frank Kellert

KELLERT, FRANK WILLIAM BR TR 6′ 2½″ 185 lbs.
B. July 6, 1924, Oklahoma City, Okla. D. Nov. 19, 1976, Oklahoma City, Okla.

Year	Team	Games	BA	SA	AB	H	2B	3B	HR	HR%	R	RBI	BB	SO	SB	Pinch Hit AB	Pinch Hit H	PO	A	E	DP	TC/G	FA	G by Pos
1953	STL A	2	.000	.000	4	0	0	0	0	0.0	0	0	0	0	0	1	0	8	0	0	0	8.0	1.000	1B-1
1954	BAL A	10	.206	.265	34	7	2	0	0	0.0	3	1	5	4	0	1	0	74	2	0	6	8.4	1.000	1B-9
1955	BKN N	39	.325	.575	80	26	4	2	4	5.0	12	19	9	10	0	13	3	159	12	3	9	7.9	.983	1B-22
1956	CHI N	71	.186	.318	129	24	3	1	4	3.1	10	17	12	22	0	41	10	209	24	2	22	8.7	.991	1B-27
4 yrs.		122	.231	.389	247	57	9	3	8	3.2	25	37	26	36	0	56	13	450	38	5	37	8.4	.990	1B-59
WORLD SERIES																								
1955	BKN N	3	.333	.333	3	1	0	0	0	0.0	0	0	0	0	0	3	1	0	0	0	0	0.0	—	

Red Kellett

KELLETT, DONALD STAFFORD BR TR 6′ 185 lbs.
B. July 15, 1909, Brooklyn, N. Y. D. Nov. 3, 1970, Ft. Lauderdale, Fla.

Year	Team	Games	BA	SA	AB	H	2B	3B	HR	HR%	R	RBI	BB	SO	SB	Pinch Hit AB	Pinch Hit H	PO	A	E	DP	TC/G	FA	G by Pos
1934	BOS A	9	.000	.000	9	0	0	0	0	0.0	0	0	1	5	0	1	0	5	8	2	1	2.1	.867	SS-4, 2B-2, 3B-1

Joe Kelley

KELLEY, JOSEPH JAMES BR TR 5′11″ 190 lbs.
B. Dec. 9, 1871, Cambridge, Mass. D. Aug. 14, 1943, Baltimore, Md.
Manager 1902–05, 1908.
Hall of Fame 1971.

Year	Team	Games	BA	SA	AB	H	2B	3B	HR	HR%	R	RBI	BB	SO	SB	Pinch Hit AB	Pinch Hit H	PO	A	E	DP	TC/G	FA	G by Pos
1891	2 teams	BOS N (12G –.244) PIT N (2G –.143)																						
″	total	14	.231	.288	52	12	1	1	0	0.0	7	3	2	7	0	0	0	6	0	1	0	0.5	.857	OF-14
1892	2 teams	PIT N (56G –.239) BAL N (10G –.212)																						
″	total	66	.235	.324	238	56	7	7	0	0.0	29	32	21	28	10	0	0	115	13	13	4	2.1	.908	OF-66
1893	BAL N	125	.305	.476	502	153	27	16	9	1.8	120	76	77	44	33	0	0	307	22	21	4	2.8	.940	OF-125
1894		129	.393	.602	507	199	48	20	6	1.2	165	111	107	36	46	0	0	276	16	15	3	2.4	.951	OF-129
1895		131	.365	.546	518	189	26	19	10	1.9	148	134	77	29	54	0	0	260	20	16	5	2.3	.946	OF-131
1896		131	.364	.543	519	189	31	19	8	1.5	148	100	91	19	**87**	0	0	280	20	13	3	2.4	.958	OF-130
1897		131	.362	.489	505	183	31	9	5	1.0	113	118	70		44	0	0	242	23	12	3	2.1	.957	OF-130, SS-3, 3B-2
1898		124	.321	.438	464	149	18	15	2	0.4	71	110	56		24	1	0	235	19	9	4	2.1	.966	OF-122, 3B-2
1899	BKN N	143	.325	.450	538	175	21	14	6	1.1	108	93	70		31	0	0	307	26	8	7	2.4	.977	OF-143
1900		121	.319	.485	454	145	23	17	6	1.3	92	91	53		26	1	1	450	49	18	18	4.2	.965	OF-77, 1B-32, 3B-13
1901		120	.309	.427	492	152	22	12	4	0.8	77	65	40		18	0	0	988	92	29	63	9.2	.974	1B-115, 3B-5
1902	2 teams	BAL A (60G –.311) CIN N (40G –.321)																						
″	total	100	.315	.442	378	119	24	9	2	0.5	74	46	49		15	1	1	231	84	12	16	3.2	.963	OF-68, 3B-17, 2B-10, 1B-5, SS-2
1903	CIN N	105	.316	.418	383	121	22	4	3	0.8	85	45	51		18	1	0	239	86	22	11	3.3	.937	OF-67, SS-12, 2B-11, 3B-8, 1B-6
1904		123	.281	.385	449	126	21	13	0	0.0	75	63	49		15	0	0	1059	78	14	48	9.3	.988	1B-117, OF-6, 2B-1
1905		90	.277	.346	321	89	7	6	1	0.3	43	37	27		8	3	0	151	11	4	2	1.9	.976	OF-85, 1B-2
1906		129	.228	.323	465	106	19	11	1	0.2	43	53	44		9	2	1	212	20	8	7	1.9	.967	OF-122, 1B-3, 3B-1, SS-1
1908	BOS N	62	.259	.338	228	59	8	2	2	0.9	25	17	27		5	10	1	189	20	8	3	4.5	.963	OF-38, 1B-10
17 yrs.		1844	.317	.451	7013	2222	356	194 **9th**	65	0.9	1423	1194	911	163	443	19	4	5547	599	223	201	3.5	.965	OF-1453, 1B-290, 3B-48, 2B-22, SS-18

Mike Kelley

KELLEY, MICHAEL JOSEPH BR TR 6′ 210 lbs.
B. Dec. 2, 1875, Templeton, Mass. D. June 6, 1955, Minneapolis, Minn.

Year	Team	Games	BA	SA	AB	H	2B	3B	HR	HR%	R	RBI	BB	SO	SB	Pinch Hit AB	Pinch Hit H	PO	A	E	DP	TC/G	FA	G by Pos
1899	LOU N	76	.241	.326	282	68	11	2	3	1.1	48	33	21		10	0	0	745	38	21	37	10.6	.974	1B-76

Frank Kelliher

KELLIHER, FRANCIS MORTIMER (Yucca) BL TL 5′ 9½″ 175 lbs.
B. May 23, 1899, Somerville, Mass. D. Mar. 4, 1956, Somerville, Mass.

Year	Team	Games	BA	SA	AB	H	2B	3B	HR	HR%	R	RBI	BB	SO	SB	Pinch Hit AB	Pinch Hit H	PO	A	E	DP	TC/G	FA	G by Pos
1919	WAS A	1	.000	.000	1	0	0	0	0	0.0	0	0	0	0	0	1	0	0	0	0	0	0.0	—	

Bill Kellogg

KELLOGG, WILLIAM DEARSTYNE BR TR 5′10″ 153 lbs.
B. May 25, 1884, Albany, N. Y. D. Dec. 12, 1971, Baltimore, Md.

Year	Team	Games	BA	SA	AB	H	2B	3B	HR	HR%	R	RBI	BB	SO	SB	Pinch Hit AB	Pinch Hit H	PO	A	E	DP	TC/G	FA	G by Pos
1914	CIN N	71	.175	.190	126	22	0	1	0	0.0	14	7	14	28	7	7	1	332	35	6	18	7.2	.984	1B-38, 2B-11, OF-2, 3B-1

Nat Kellogg

KELLOGG, NATHANIEL MONROE 5′ 9″ 175 lbs.
B. Sept. 28, 1858, Dorchester, Iowa Deceased.

Year	Team	Games	BA	SA	AB	H	2B	3B	HR	HR%	R	RBI	BB	SO	SB	Pinch Hit AB	Pinch Hit H	PO	A	E	DP	TC/G	FA	G by Pos
1885	DET N	5	.118	.176	17	2	1	0	0	0.0	4	0	1	5		0	0	6	12	5	1	4.6	.783	SS-5

Bill Kelly

KELLY, WILLIAM HENRY (Big Bill) BR TR 6′ 190 lbs.
B. Dec. 28, 1898, Syracuse, N. Y. D. Apr. 8, 1990, Syracuse, N. Y.

Year	Team	Games	BA	SA	AB	H	2B	3B	HR	HR%	R	RBI	BB	SO	SB	Pinch Hit AB	Pinch Hit H	PO	A	E	DP	TC/G	FA	G by Pos
1920	PHI A	9	.231	.308	13	3	1	0	0	0.0	0	0	0	2	0	7	2	11	1	0	0	6.0	1.000	1B-2
1928	PHI N	23	.169	.211	71	12	1	1	0	0.0	6	5	7	20	0	0	0	216	14	2	19	10.1	.991	1B-23
2 yrs.		32	.179	.226	84	15	2	1	0	0.0	6	5	7	22	0	7	2	227	15	2	19	9.8	.992	1B-25

Bill Kelly

KELLY, WILLIAM JOSEPH BR TR 6′½″ 183 lbs.
B. May 1, 1886, Baltimore, Md. D. June 3, 1940, Detroit, Mich.

Year	Team	Games	BA	SA	AB	H	2B	3B	HR	HR%	R	RBI	BB	SO	SB	Pinch Hit AB	Pinch Hit H	PO	A	E	DP	TC/G	FA	G by Pos
1910	STL N	2	.000	.000	2	0	0	0	0	0.0	1	0	1	0	0	1	0	0	0	0	0	0.0	.000	C-1
1911	PIT N	6	.125	.125	8	1	0	0	0	0.0	0	0	0	2	0	5	1	11	0	0	0	11.0	1.000	C-1

Bill Kelly *continued*

Year	Team	Games	BA	SA	AB	H	2B	3B	HR	HR%	R	RBI	BB	SO	SB	Pinch Hit AB	Pinch Hit H	PO	A	E	DP	TC/G	FA	G by Pos
1912		48	.318	.394	132	42	3	2	1	0.8	20	11	2	16	8	3	0	174	29	2	1	5.3	.990	C-39
1913		48	.268	.341	82	22	2	2	0	0.0	11	9	2	12	1	5	2	135	31	7	3	4.3	.960	C-40
4 yrs.		104	.290	.362	224	65	5	4	1	0.4	32	20	5	30	9	14	3	320	60	9	4	4.8	.977	C-81

Bob Kelly

KELLY, JAMES ROBERT BL TR 5′11″ 180 lbs.
Born Robert John Taggert.
B. Feb. 1, 1884, Bloomfield, N. J. D. Apr. 10, 1961, Kingsport, Tenn.

Year	Team	Games	BA	SA	AB	H	2B	3B	HR	HR%	R	RBI	BB	SO	SB	Pinch Hit AB	Pinch Hit H	PO	A	E	DP	TC/G	FA	G by Pos
1914	PIT N	32	.227	.318	44	10	2	1	0	0.0	4	3	2	3	0	22	7	12	1	0	0	1.9	1.000	OF-7
1915	PIT F	148	.294	.405	524	154	12	17	4	0.8	68	50	35		38	0	0	292	27	16	5	2.3	.952	OF-148
1918	BOS N	35	.329	.390	146	48	1	4	0	0.0	19	4	9	9	4	0	0	82	2	4	0	2.5	.955	OF-35
3 yrs.		215	.297	.396	714	212	15	22	4	0.6	91	57	46	12	42	22	7	386	30	20	5	2.3	.954	OF-190

Bob Kelly

KELLY, ROBERT BROWN (Speed) BR TR 6′ 2″ 185 lbs.
B. Aug. 19, 1884, Bryan, Ohio D. May 6, 1949, Goshen, Ind.

Year	Team	Games	BA	SA	AB	H	2B	3B	HR	HR%	R	RBI	BB	SO	SB	Pinch Hit AB	Pinch Hit H	PO	A	E	DP	TC/G	FA	G by Pos
1909	WAS A	17	.143	.238	42	6	2	1	0	0.0	3	1	3		1	2	0	10	27	9	2	3.3	.804	3B-10, 2B-3, OF-1

Charlie Kelly

KELLY, CHARLES H.
Deceased.

Year	Team	Games	BA	SA	AB	H	2B	3B	HR	HR%	R	RBI	BB	SO	SB	Pinch Hit AB	Pinch Hit H	PO	A	E	DP	TC/G	FA	G by Pos
1883	PHI N	2	.143	.429	7	1	0	1	0	0.0	1		0	3		0	0	3	4	3	1	5.0	.700	3B-2
1886	PHI AA	1	.000	.000	3	0	0	0	0	0.0	0		0			0	0	0	2	4	0	6.0	.333	SS-1
2 yrs.		3	.100	.300	10	1	0	1	0	0.0	1		0	3		0	0	3	6	7	1	5.3	.563	3B-2, SS-1

Dale Kelly

KELLY, DALE PATRICK BR TR 6′ 3″ 210 lbs.
B. Aug. 27, 1955, Santa Maria, Calif.

Year	Team	Games	BA	SA	AB	H	2B	3B	HR	HR%	R	RBI	BB	SO	SB	Pinch Hit AB	Pinch Hit H	PO	A	E	DP	TC/G	FA	G by Pos
1980	TOR A	3	.286	.286	7	2	0	0	0	0.0	0	0	0	4	0	0	0	17	0	0	0	5.7	1.000	C-3

George Kelly

KELLY, GEORGE LANGE (Highpockets) BR TR 6′ 4″ 190 lbs.
Brother of Ren Kelly.
B. Sept. 10, 1895, San Francisco, Calif. D. Oct. 13, 1984, Burlingame, Calif.
Hall of Fame 1973.

Year	Team	Games	BA	SA	AB	H	2B	3B	HR	HR%	R	RBI	BB	SO	SB	Pinch Hit AB	Pinch Hit H	PO	A	E	DP	TC/G	FA	G by Pos
1915	NY N	17	.158	.237	38	6	0	0	1	2.6	2	4	1	9	0	2	0	62	4	2	1	5.2	.971	1B-9, OF-4
1916		49	.158	.211	76	12	2	1	0	0.0	4	3	6	24	1	23	5	107	2	2	5	4.3	.982	1B-13, OF-12, 3B-1
1917	**2 teams**	**NY N** (11G –.000) **PIT N** (8G –.087)																						
″	**total**	19	.067	.133	30	2	0	1	0	0.0	2	0	1	12	0	3	0	70	4	2	4	5.4	.974	1B-9, OF-3, P-1, 2B-1
1919	NY N	32	.290	.411	107	31	6	2	1	0.9	12	14	3	15	1	0	0	341	11	2	17	11.1	.994	1B-32
1920		155	.266	.397	590	157	22	11	11	1.9	69	**94**	41	**92**	6	0	0	1759	103	11	115	12.1	.994	1B-155
1921		149	.308	.528	587	181	42	9	**23**	**3.9**	95	122	40	73	4	0	0	1552	115	17	132	11.3	.990	1B-149
1922		151	.328	.497	592	194	33	8	17	2.9	96	107	30	65	12	0	0	1642	103	13	123	11.6	.993	1B-151
1923		145	.307	.452	560	172	23	5	16	2.9	82	103	47	64	14	0	0	1568	60	12	111	11.3	.993	1B-145
1924		144	.324	.531	571	185	37	9	21	3.7	91	**136**	38	52	7	2	0	1357	79	13	107	10.0	.991	1B-125, OF-14, 2B-5, 3B-1
1925		147	.309	.471	586	181	29	3	20	3.4	87	99	35	54	5	0	0	567	411	18	81	6.6	.982	2B-108, 1B-25, OF-17
1926		136	.303	.445	499	151	24	4	13	2.6	70	80	36	52	4	5	0	1233	144	15	101	10.5	.989	1B-114, 2B-18
1927	CIN N	61	.270	.446	222	60	16	4	5	2.3	27	21	11	23	1	1	0	476	64	8	49	8.6	.985	1B-49, 2B-13, OF-2
1928		116	.296	.435	402	119	33	7	3	0.7	46	58	28	35	2	2	0	927	70	11	100	9.0	.989	1B-99, OF-13
1929		147	.293	.428	577	169	45	9	5	0.9	73	103	33	61	7	0	0	1537	103	11	127	11.2	.993	1B-147
1930	**2 teams**	**CIN N** (51G –.287) **CHI N** (39G –.331)																						
″	**total**	90	.308	.432	354	109	16	2	8	2.3	40	54	14	36	1	1	0	917	67	5	75	11.1	.995	1B-89
1932	BKN N	64	.243	.356	202	49	9	1	4	2.0	23	22	22	27	0	1	0	576	36	10	48	9.9	.984	1B-62, OF-1
16 yrs.		1622	.297	.452	5993	1778	337	76	148	2.5	819	1020	386	694	65	40	5	14691	1376	152	1196	10.2	.991	1B-1373, 2B-145, OF-66, 3B-2, P-1
WORLD SERIES																								
1921	NY N	8	.233	.267	30	7	1	0	0	0.0	3	3	3	10	0	0	0	86	7	0	3	11.6	1.000	1B-8
1922		5	.278	.278	18	5	0	0	0	0.0	0	2	0	3	0	0	0	61	1	0	2	12.4	1.000	1B-5
1923		6	.182	.182	22	4	0	0	0	0.0	1	1	1	2	0	0	0	63	4	1	5	11.3	.985	1B-6
1924		7	.290	.419	31	9	1	0	1	3.2	7	4	1	8	0	0	0	52	5	1	2	6.4	.983	1B-4, OF-4, 2B-1
4 yrs.		26	.248	.297	101	25	2	0	1	1.0	11	10	5	23	0	0	0	262	17	2	12	10.0	.993	1B-23, OF-4, 2B-1
														10th										

Honest John Kelly

KELLY, JOHN O. 6′½″ 185 lbs.
B. Oct. 31, 1856, New York, N. Y. D. Mar. 27, 1926, Malba, N. Y.
Manager 1887–88.

Year	Team	Games	BA	SA	AB	H	2B	3B	HR	HR%	R	RBI	BB	SO	SB	Pinch Hit AB	Pinch Hit H	PO	A	E	DP	TC/G	FA	G by Pos
1879	**2 teams**	**SYR N** (10G –.111) **TRO N** (6G –.227)																						
″	**total**	16	.155	.172	58	9	1	0	0	0.0	5	2	0	7		0	0	57	17	18	1	5.8	.804	C-11, OF-2, 1B-2, 3B-1

Joe Kelly

KELLY, JOSEPH HENRY BR TR 5′ 9″ 172 lbs.
B. Sept. 23, 1886, Weir City, Kans. D. Aug. 16, 1977, St. Joseph, Mo.

Year	Team	Games	BA	SA	AB	H	2B	3B	HR	HR%	R	RBI	BB	SO	SB	Pinch Hit AB	Pinch Hit H	PO	A	E	DP	TC/G	FA	G by Pos
1914	PIT N	141	.222	.301	508	113	19	9	1	0.2	47	48	39	59	21	2	0	319	15	19	3	2.6	.946	OF-138
1916	CHI N	54	.254	.343	169	43	7	1	2	1.2	18	15	9	16	10	8	1	98	4	5	0	2.3	.953	OF-46
1917	BOS N	116	.222	.299	445	99	9	8	3	0.7	41	36	26	45	21	0	0	284	16	17	8	2.7	.946	OF-116
1918		47	.232	.297	155	36	2	4	0	0.0	20	15	6	12	12	2	1	93	4	7	0	2.3	.933	OF-45
1919		18	.141	.156	64	9	1	0	0	0.0	3	3	0	11	2	2	1	30	3	2	0	2.2	.943	OF-16
5 yrs.		376	.224	.298	1341	300	38	22	6	0.4	129	117	80	143	66	14	3	824	42	50	11	2.5	.945	OF-361

Joe Kelly

KELLY, JOSEPH JAMES BL TL 6′ 180 lbs.
B. Apr. 23, 1900, New York, N. Y. D. Nov. 24, 1967, Lynbrook, N. Y.

Year	Team	Games	BA	SA	AB	H	2B	3B	HR	HR%	R	RBI	BB	SO	SB	Pinch Hit AB	Pinch Hit H	PO	A	E	DP	TC/G	FA	G by Pos
1926	CHI N	65	.335	.455	176	59	15	3	0	0.0	16	32	7	11	0	24	9	58	3	3	0	1.6	.953	OF-39
1928		32	.212	.288	52	11	1	0	1	1.9	3	7	1	3	0	21	3	105	6	3	8	11.4	.974	1B-10
2 yrs.		97	.307	.417	228	70	16	3	1	0.4	19	39	8	14	0	45	12	163	9	6	8	3.6	.966	OF-39, 1B-10

John Kelly

KELLY, JOHN B. 5′ 9″ 165 lbs.
B. Mar. 13, 1879, Clifton Heights, Pa. D. Mar. 19, 1944, Baltimore, Md.

Year	Team	Games	BA	SA	AB	H	2B	3B	HR	HR%	R	RBI	BB	SO	SB	Pinch Hit AB	Pinch Hit H	PO	A	E	DP	TC/G	FA	G by Pos
1907	STL N	53	.188	.213	197	37	5	0	0	0.0	12	6	13		7	1	0	85	7	3	4	1.8	.968	OF-52

Kick Kelly

KELLY, JOHN FRANCIS (Father) BR TR 6′ 185 lbs.
B. Mar. 3, 1859, Patterson, N. J. D. Apr. 13, 1908, Patterson, N. J.

Year	Team	Lg	Games	BA	SA	AB	H	2B	3B	HR	HR%	R	RBI	BB	SO	SB	Pinch Hit AB	Pinch Hit H	PO	A	E	DP	TC/G	FA	G by Pos
1882	**CLE**	**N**	30	.135	.154	104	14	2	0	0	0.0	6	5	1	24		0	0	113	35	37	2	6.2	.800	C-30
1883	**2 teams**	**BAL AA** (48G –.228)	**PHI N** (1G –.000)																						
″	**total**		49	.224	.288	205	46	9	2	0	0.0	18		3	2		0	0	189	39	58	3	5.5	.797	C-38, OF-14
1884	**2 teams**	**CIN U** (38G –.282)	**WAS U** (4G –.357)																						
″	**total**		42	.288	.359	156	45	6	1	1	0.6	24		6			0	0	239	67	44	3	8.1	.874	C-40, OF-3
3 yrs.			121	.226	.282	465	105	17	3	1	0.2	48	5	10	26		0	0	541	141	139	8	6.6	.831	C-108, OF-17

King Kelly

KELLY, MICHAEL JOSEPH BR TR 5′10″ 170 lbs.
B. Dec. 31, 1857, Troy, N. Y. D. Nov. 8, 1894, Boston, Mass.
Manager 1887, 1890–91.
Hall of Fame 1945.

Year	Team	Lg	Games	BA	SA	AB	H	2B	3B	HR	HR%	R	RBI	BB	SO	SB	Pinch Hit AB	Pinch Hit H	PO	A	E	DP	TC/G	FA	G by Pos
1878	**CIN**	**N**	60	.283	.321	237	67	7	1	0	0.0	29	27	7	7		0	0	150	65	43	5	3.9	.833	OF-47, C-17, 3B-2
1879			77	.348	.493	345	120	20	12	2	0.6	78	47	8	14		0	0	164	139	58	4	4.3	.839	3B-33, OF-29, C-21, 2B-1
1880	**CHI**	**N**	84	.291	.401	344	100	17	9	1	0.3	72	60	12	22		0	0	111	68	42	3	2.3	.810	OF-64, C-17, 3B-14, SS-1, 2B-1, P-1
1881			82	.323	.433	353	114	**27**	3	2	0.6	84	55	16	14		0	0	121	52	33	3	2.3	.840	OF-72, C-11, 3B-8
1882			84	.305	.432	377	115	**37**	4	1	0.3	81	55	10	27		0	0	133	149	59	12	3.6	.827	SS-42, OF-38, C-12, 3B-3, 1B-1
1883			98	.255	.388	428	109	28	10	3	0.7	92		16	35		0	0	183	91	63	7	2.7	.813	OF-82, C-38, 2B-3, 3B-2, P-1
1884			108	**.354**	.524	452	160	28	5	13	2.9	**120**		46	24		0	0	201	141	86	10	3.7	.799	OF-63, C-28, SS-12, 3B-10, 1B-2, P-2
1885			107	.288	.436	438	126	24	7	9	2.1	**124**	74	46	24		0	0	259	112	58	5	3.7	.865	OF-69, C-37, 2B-6, 3B-2, 1B-2
1886			118	**.388**	.534	451	175	32	11	4	0.9	**155**	79	83	33		0	0	387	141	59	11	4.3	.899	OF-56, C-53, 1B-9, 3B-8, 2B-6, SS-5
1887	**BOS**	**N**	116	.322	.488	484	156	34	11	8	1.7	120	63	55	40	84	0	0	252	163	72	24	4.0	.852	OF-61, 2B-30, C-24, P-3, SS-2, 3B-2
1888			107	.318	.480	440	140	22	11	9	2.0	85	71	31	39	56	0	0	395	150	66	10	5.6	.892	C-76, OF-34
1889			125	.294	.448	507	149	**41**	5	9	1.8	120	78	65	40	68	0	0	211	53	44	6	2.3	.857	OF-113, C-23
1890	**BOS**	**P**	89	.326	.450	340	111	18	6	4	1.2	83	66	52	22	51	0	0	274	145	55	12	4.9	.884	C-56, SS-27, OF-6, 1B-4, 3B-2, P-1
1891	**3 teams**	**CIN AA** (82G –.297)	**BOS AA** (4G –.267)	**BOS N** (16G –.231)																					
″	**total**		102	.286	.389	350	100	16	7	2	0.6	65	62	57	40	29	0	0	351	159	59	19	4.6	.896	C-81, OF-21, 3B-8, 2B-6, 1B-5, P-3, SS-1
1892	**BOS**	**N**	78	.189	.235	281	53	7	0	2	0.7	40	41	39	31	24	0	0	340	101	47	13	6.2	.904	C-72, OF-2, 1B-2, 3B-2, P-1
1893	**NY**	**N**	20	.269	.284	67	18	1	0	0	0.0	9	15	6	5	3	2	0	55	22	10	1	4.8	.885	C-17, OF-1
16 yrs.			1455	.308	.438	5894	1813	359	102	69	1.2	1357	793	549	417	315	2	0	3587	1751	854	145	3.8	.862	OF-758, C-583, 3B-96, SS-90, 2B-53, 1B-25, P-12

Mike Kelly

KELLY, MICHAEL RAYMOND BR TR 6′ 4″ 195 lbs.
B. June 2, 1970, Los Angeles, Calif.

Year	Team	Lg	Games	BA	SA	AB	H	2B	3B	HR	HR%	R	RBI	BB	SO	SB	Pinch Hit AB	Pinch Hit H	PO	A	E	DP	TC/G	FA	G by Pos
1994	**ATL**	**N**	30	.273	.506	77	21	10	1	2	2.6	14	9	2	17	0	6	0	25	0	1	0	1.0	.962	OF-25
1995			97	.190	.314	137	26	6	1	3	2.2	26	17	11	49	7	14	3	63	0	4	0	0.8	.940	OF-83
2 yrs.			127	.220	.383	214	47	16	2	5	2.3	40	26	13	66	7	20	3	88	0	5	0	0.9	.946	OF-108

Pat Kelly

KELLY, HAROLD PATRICK BL TL 6′ 1″ 185 lbs.
B. July 30, 1944, Philadelphia, Pa.

Year	Team	Lg	Games	BA	SA	AB	H	2B	3B	HR	HR%	R	RBI	BB	SO	SB	Pinch Hit AB	Pinch Hit H	PO	A	E	DP	TC/G	FA	G by Pos
1967	**MIN**	**A**	8	.000	.000	1	0	0	0	0	0.0	1	0	0	1	0	1	0	0	0	0	0	0.0	—	
1968			12	.114	.257	35	4	2	0	1	2.9	2	2	3	10	0	2	0	20	1	1	0	2.2	.955	OF-10
1969	**KC**	**A**	112	.264	.388	417	110	20	4	8	1.9	61	32	49	70	40	3	0	237	12	5	3	2.4	.980	OF-107
1970			136	.235	.314	452	106	16	1	6	1.3	56	38	76	105	34	17	1	254	8	10	2	2.3	.963	OF-118
1971	**CHI**	**A**	67	.291	.390	213	62	6	3	3	1.4	32	22	36	29	14	7	4	100	7	1	0	1.8	.991	OF-61
1972			119	.261	.368	402	105	14	7	5	1.2	57	24	55	69	32	17	3	173	8	6	3	1.7	.968	OF-109
1973			144	.280	.347	550	154	24	5	1	0.2	77	44	65	91	22	7	2	254	9	6	2	1.9	.978	OF-141, DH-1
1974			122	.281	.361	424	119	16	3	4	0.9	60	21	46	58	18	3	0	79	2	2	2	0.7	.976	DH-67, OF-53
1975			133	.274	.406	471	129	21	7	9	1.9	73	45	58	69	18	5	1	222	4	2	1	1.8	.991	OF-115, DH-14
1976			107	.254	.386	311	79	20	3	5	1.6	42	34	45	45	15	20	7	37	1	2	0	0.4	.950	DH-63, OF-26
1977	**BAL**	**A**	120	.256	.375	360	92	13	0	10	2.8	50	49	53	75	25	11	5	181	2	3	1	1.7	.984	OF-109, DH-1
1978			100	.274	.445	274	75	12	1	11	4.0	38	40	34	58	10	18	6	123	3	4	1	1.6	.969	OF-80, DH-2
1979			68	.288	.536	153	44	11	0	9	5.9	25	25	20	25	4	23	11	36	0	0	0	0.9	1.000	OF-24, DH-18
1980			89	.260	.365	200	52	10	1	3	1.5	38	26	34	54	16	29	8	48	4	0	0	0.8	1.000	OF-36, DH-30
1981	**CLE**	**A**	48	.213	.307	75	16	4	0	1	1.3	8	16	14	9	2	24	3	6	0	0	0	0.2	1.000	DH-18, OF-8
15 yrs.			1385	.264	.377	4338	1147	189	35	76	1.8	620	418	588	768	250	187	51	1770	61	42	15	1.5	.978	OF-997, DH-214
LEAGUE CHAMPIONSHIP SERIES																									
1979	**BAL**	**A**	3	.364	.636	11	4	0	0	1	9.1	3	4	1	3	2	0	0	3	0	0	0	1.0	1.000	OF-2, DH-1
WORLD SERIES																									
1979	**BAL**	**A**	5	.250	.250	4	1	0	0	0	0.0	0	0	1	1	0	4	1	0	0	0	0	0.0	—	

Pat Kelly

KELLY, PATRICK FRANKLIN BR TR 6′ 180 lbs.
B. Oct. 14, 1967, Philadelphia, Pa.

Year	Team	Lg	Games	BA	SA	AB	H	2B	3B	HR	HR%	R	RBI	BB	SO	SB	Pinch Hit AB	Pinch Hit H	PO	A	E	DP	TC/G	FA	G by Pos
1991	**NY**	**A**	96	.242	.339	298	72	12	4	3	1.0	35	23	15	52	12	0	0	78	204	18	29	3.0	.940	3B-80, 2B-19
1992			106	.226	.374	318	72	22	2	7	2.2	38	27	25	72	8	0	0	203	296	11	64	5.0	.978	2B-101, DH-1
1993			127	.273	.389	406	111	24	1	7	1.7	49	51	24	68	14	2	0	245	369	14	84	5.0	.978	2B-125
1994			93	.280	.399	286	80	21	2	3	1.0	35	41	19	51	6	1	0	182	257	10	69	4.8	.978	2B-93
1995			89	.237	.333	270	64	12	1	4	1.5	32	29	23	65	8	2	0	161	255	7	52	4.8	.983	2B-87, DH-1
5 yrs.			511	.253	.369	1578	399	91	10	24	1.5	189	171	106	308	48	5	0	869	1381	60	298	4.6	.974	2B-425, 3B-80, DH-2
DIVISIONAL PLAYOFF SERIES																									
1995	**NY**	**A**	5	.000	.000	3	0	0	0	0	0.0	3	1	1	3	0	0	0	2	4	0	2	1.5	1.000	2B-4

Red Kelly

KELLY, ALBERT MICHAEL BR TR 5′11½″ 165 lbs.
B. Nov. 15, 1884, Union, Ill. D. Feb. 4, 1961, Zephyrhills, Fla.

Year	Team	Lg	Games	BA	SA	AB	H	2B	3B	HR	HR%	R	RBI	BB	SO	SB	Pinch Hit AB	Pinch Hit H	PO	A	E	DP	TC/G	FA	G by Pos
1910	**CHI**	**A**	14	.156	.200	45	7	0	1	0	0.0	6	1	7		0	0	0	18	1	0	0	1.4	1.000	OF-14

Roberto Kelly

KELLY, ROBERTO CONRADO BR TR 6′ 2″ 180 lbs.
Born Roberto Conrado Kelly (Gray).
B. Oct. 1, 1964, Panama City, Panama.

Year	Team	Games	BA	SA	AB	H	2B	3B	HR	HR%	R	RBI	BB	SO	SB	Pinch Hit AB	Pinch Hit H	PO	A	E	DP	TC/G	FA	G by Pos
1987	NY A	23	.269	.385	52	14	3	0	1	1.9	12	7	5	15	9	0	0	42	0	2	0	2.6	.955	OF-17
1988		38	.247	.364	77	19	4	1	1	1.3	9	7	3	15	5	1	1	70	1	1	0	2.4	.986	OF-30
1989		137	.302	.417	441	133	18	3	9	2.0	65	48	41	89	35	2	2	353	9	6	2	2.7	.984	OF-137
1990		162	.285	.418	641	183	32	4	15	2.3	85	61	33	148	42	4	1	420	5	5	0	2.7	.988	OF-160, DH-1
1991		126	.267	.444	486	130	22	2	20	4.1	68	69	45	77	32	2	1	268	8	4	1	2.2	.986	OF-125
1992		152	.272	.384	580	158	31	2	10	1.7	81	66	41	96	28	5	0	389	8	7	3	2.8	.983	OF-146
1993	CIN N	78	.319	.475	320	102	17	3	9	2.8	44	35	17	43	21	0	0	198	3	1	1	2.6	.995	OF-77
1994	2 teams	CIN N (47G –.302) ATL N (63G –.286)																						
″	total	110	.293	.422	434	127	23	3	9	2.1	73	45	35	71	19	0	0	247	5	3	0	2.3	.988	OF-110
1995	2 teams	MON N (24G –.274) LA N (112G –.279)																						
″	total	136	.278	.373	504	140	23	2	7	1.4	58	57	22	79	19	3	1	225	3	6	0	1.7	.974	OF-134
9 yrs.		962	.285	.414	3535	1006	173	20	81	2.3	495	395	242	633	210	17	6	2212	42	35	7	2.4	.985	OF-936, DH-1
DIVISIONAL PLAYOFF SERIES																								
1995	LA N	3	.364	.364	11	4	0	0	0	0.0	0	0	1	0	0	0	0	8	0	1	0	3.0	.889	OF-3

Tom Kelly

KELLY, JAY THOMAS BL TL 5′11″ 188 lbs.
B. Aug. 15, 1950, Graceville, Minn.
Manager 1986–95.

Year	Team	Games	BA	SA	AB	H	2B	3B	HR	HR%	R	RBI	BB	SO	SB	Pinch Hit AB	Pinch Hit H	PO	A	E	DP	TC/G	FA	G by Pos
1975	MIN A	49	.181	.244	127	23	5	0	1	0.8	11	11	15	22	0	5	1	360	28	6	27	8.8	.985	1B-43, OF-2

Van Kelly

KELLY, VAN HOWARD BL TR 5′11″ 180 lbs.
B. Mar. 18, 1946, Charlotte, N. C.

Year	Team	Games	BA	SA	AB	H	2B	3B	HR	HR%	R	RBI	BB	SO	SB	Pinch Hit AB	Pinch Hit H	PO	A	E	DP	TC/G	FA	G by Pos
1969	SD N	73	.244	.330	209	51	7	1	3	1.4	16	15	12	24	0	16	4	47	104	6	10	2.7	.962	3B-49, 2B-10
1970		38	.169	.236	89	15	3	0	1	1.1	9	9	15	21	0	11	1	23	46	2	3	2.5	.972	3B-27, 2B-1
2 yrs.		111	.221	.302	298	66	10	1	4	1.3	25	24	27	45	0	27	5	70	150	8	13	2.6	.965	3B-76, 2B-11

Billy Kelsey

KELSEY, GEORGE WILLIAM BR TR 5′10″ 150 lbs.
B. Aug. 24, 1881, Covington, Ohio D. Apr. 25, 1968, Springfield, Ohio.

Year	Team	Games	BA	SA	AB	H	2B	3B	HR	HR%	R	RBI	BB	SO	SB	Pinch Hit AB	Pinch Hit H	PO	A	E	DP	TC/G	FA	G by Pos
1907	PIT N	2	.400	.400	5	2	0	0	0	0.0	1	0	0		0	0	0	5	2	0	0	3.5	1.000	C-2

Ken Keltner

KELTNER, KENNETH FREDERICK BR TR 6′ 190 lbs.
B. Oct. 31, 1916, Milwaukee, Wis. D. Dec. 12, 1991, New Berlin, Wis.

Year	Team	Games	BA	SA	AB	H	2B	3B	HR	HR%	R	RBI	BB	SO	SB	Pinch Hit AB	Pinch Hit H	PO	A	E	DP	TC/G	FA	G by Pos
1937	CLE A	1	.000	.000	1	0	0	0	0	0.0	0	1	0	0	0	0	0	0	1	0	0	1.0	1.000	3B-1
1938		149	.276	.497	576	159	31	9	26	4.5	86	113	33	75	4	0	0	141	271	19	19	2.9	.956	3B-149
1939		154	.325	.489	587	191	35	11	13	2.2	84	97	51	41	6	0	0	187	297	13	40	3.2	.974	3B-154
1940		149	.254	.418	543	138	24	10	15	2.8	67	77	51	56	10	1	0	170	277	22	27	3.2	.953	3B-148
1941		149	.269	.485	581	156	31	13	23	4.0	83	84	51	56	2	0	0	181	346	16	36	3.6	.971	3B-149
1942		152	.287	.383	624	179	34	4	6	1.0	72	78	20	36	4	1	0	166	353	30	38	3.6	.945	3B-151
1943		110	.260	.375	427	111	31	3	4	0.9	47	39	36	20	2	3	1	113	228	11	24	3.3	.969	3B-107
1944		149	.295	.466	573	169	41	9	13	2.3	74	91	53	29	4	0	0	168	369	18	37	3.7	.968	3B-149
1946		116	.241	.387	398	96	17	1	13	3.3	47	45	30	38	0	4	1	112	195	11	18	2.8	.965	3B-112
1947		151	.257	.383	541	139	29	3	11	2.0	49	76	59	45	5	1	0	156	266	12	29	2.9	.972	3B-150
1948		153	.297	.522	558	166	24	4	31	5.6	91	119	89	52	2	0	0	123	312	14	27	2.9	.969	3B-153
1949		80	.232	.382	246	57	9	2	8	3.3	35	30	38	26	0	10	2	51	145	4	11	2.9	.980	3B-69
1950	BOS A	13	.321	.393	28	9	2	0	0	0.0	2	2	3	6	0	4	1	9	10	1	1	2.2	.950	3B-8, 1B-1
13 yrs.		1526	.276	.441	5683	1570	308	69	163	2.9	737	852	514	480	39	24	5	1577	3070	171	307	3.2	.965	3B-1500, 1B-1
WORLD SERIES																								
1948	CLE A	6	.095	.095	21	2	0	0	0	0.0	3	0	2	3	0	0	0	3	11	1	1	2.5	.933	3B-6

John Kelty

KELTY, JOHN JAMES (Chief) 5′10″ 175 lbs.
B. June 1866, Jersey City, N. J. Deceased.

Year	Team	Games	BA	SA	AB	H	2B	3B	HR	HR%	R	RBI	BB	SO	SB	Pinch Hit AB	Pinch Hit H	PO	A	E	DP	TC/G	FA	G by Pos
1890	PIT N	59	.237	.319	207	49	10	2	1	0.5	24	27	22	42	10	0	0	100	6	12	1	2.0	.898	OF-59

Billie Kemmer

KEMMER, WILLIAM EDWARD BR TR 6′ 2″
Born William Edward Kemmerer.
B. Nov. 15, 1873, Pa. D. June 8, 1945, Washington, D. C.

Year	Team	Games	BA	SA	AB	H	2B	3B	HR	HR%	R	RBI	BB	SO	SB	Pinch Hit AB	Pinch Hit H	PO	A	E	DP	TC/G	FA	G by Pos
1895	LOU N	11	.184	.263	38	7	0	0	1	2.6	5	3	2	4	0	0	0	34	23	10	4	6.1	.851	3B-9, 1B-2

Rudy Kemmler

KEMMLER, RUDOLPH BR TR
Born Rudolph Kemler.
B. 1860, Chicago, Ill. D. June 20, 1909, Chicago, Ill.

Year	Team	Games	BA	SA	AB	H	2B	3B	HR	HR%	R	RBI	BB	SO	SB	Pinch Hit AB	Pinch Hit H	PO	A	E	DP	TC/G	FA	G by Pos
1879	PRO N	2	.143	.143	7	1	0	0	0	0.0	0	0	0	1		0	0	13	7	4	0	12.0	.833	C-2
1881	CLE N	1	.000	.000	3	0	0	0	0	0.0	0	0	0	1		0	0	5	2	0	1	7.0	1.000	C-1
1882	2 teams	CIN AA (3G –.091) PIT AA (24G –.253)																						
″	total	27	.236	.282	110	26	5	0	0	0.0	7		1			0	0	131	39	15	1	6.6	.919	C-26, OF-2
1883	COL AA	84	.208	.239	318	66	6	2	0	0.0	27		13			0	0	390	99	73	11	6.7	.870	C-82, OF-2
1884		61	.199	.242	211	42	3	3	0	0.0	28		15			0	0	293	77	37	4	6.7	.909	C-58, 1B-2, OF-1
1885	PIT AA	18	.203	.266	64	13	2	1	0	0.0	2		2			0	0	86	28	17	0	7.3	.870	C-18
1886	STL AA	35	.138	.154	123	17	2	0	0	0.0	13		8			0	0	182	65	23	4	7.7	.915	C-32, 1B-3
1889	COL AA	8	.115	.115	26	3	0	0	0	0.0	2	0	3	3	0	0	0	35	18	4	1	7.1	.930	C-8
8 yrs.		236	.195	.230	862	168	18	6	0	0.0	79	0	42	5	0	0	0	1135	335	173	22	6.9	.895	C-227, 1B-5, OF-5

Steve Kemp

KEMP, STEVEN F. BL TL 6′ 195 lbs.
B. Aug. 7, 1954, San Angelo, Tex.

Year	Team	Games	BA	SA	AB	H	2B	3B	HR	HR%	R	RBI	BB	SO	SB	Pinch Hit AB	Pinch Hit H	PO	A	E	DP	TC/G	FA	G by Pos
1977	DET A	151	.257	.422	552	142	29	4	18	3.3	75	88	71	93	3	3	0	252	10	5	1	1.8	.981	OF-148
1978		159	.277	.399	582	161	18	4	15	2.6	75	79	97	87	2	2	1	325	11	8	2	2.2	.977	OF-157
1979		134	.318	.543	490	156	26	3	26	5.3	88	105	68	70	5	4	1	229	12	6	2	1.9	.976	OF-120, DH-11
1980		135	.293	.474	508	149	23	3	21	4.1	88	101	69	64	5	6	2	197	4	1	3	1.5	.995	OF-85, DH-46
1981		105	.277	.419	372	103	18	4	9	2.4	52	49	70	48	9	3	1	207	4	3	0	2.1	.986	OF-92, DH-12
1982	CHI A	160	.286	.428	580	166	23	1	19	3.3	91	98	89	83	7	3	1	280	6	7	1	1.9	.976	OF-154, DH-2
1983	NY A	109	.241	.399	373	90	17	3	12	3.2	53	49	41	37	1	9	2	215	5	3	3	2.2	.987	OF-101, DH-2

Steve Kemp *continued*

Year	Team	Lg	Games	BA	SA	AB	H	2B	3B	HR	HR%	R	RBI	BB	SO	SB	Pinch Hit AB	Pinch Hit H	PO	A	E	DP	TC/G	FA	G by Pos
1984			94	.291	.403	313	91	12	1	7	2.2	37	41	40	54	4	9	2	138	2	4	0	1.7	.972	OF-75, DH-12
1985	PIT	N	92	.250	.347	236	59	13	2	2	0.8	19	21	25	54	1	27	9	105	1	0	0	1.7	1.000	OF-63
1986			13	.188	.375	16	3	0	0	1	6.3	1	1	4	6	1	5	0	9	0	0	0	2.3	1.000	OF-4
1988	TEX	A	16	.222	.222	36	8	0	0	0	0.0	2	2	2	9	1	5	1	6	0	0	0	0.5	1.000	DH-7, OF-5, 1B-1
11 yrs.			1168	.278	.431	4058	1128	179	25	130	3.2	581	634	576	605	39	76	20	1963	55	37	12	1.9	.982	OF-1004, DH-92, 1B-1

Fred Kendall

KENDALL, FRED LYN BR TR 6′ 1″ 185 lbs.
B. Jan. 31, 1949, Torrance, Calif.

Year	Team	Lg	Games	BA	SA	AB	H	2B	3B	HR	HR%	R	RBI	BB	SO	SB	Pinch Hit AB	Pinch Hit H	PO	A	E	DP	TC/G	FA	G by Pos
1969	SD	N	10	.154	.154	26	4	0	0	0	0.0	2	0	2	5	0	1	0	37	5	0	0	4.7	1.000	C-9
1970			4	.000	.000	9	0	0	0	0	0.0	0	1	0	0	0	1	0	7	1	0	0	2.0	1.000	C-2, OF-1, 1B-1
1971			49	.171	.207	111	19	1	0	1	0.9	2	7	7	16	1	7	1	184	14	0	1	4.8	1.000	C-39, 3B-1, 1B-1
1972			91	.216	.322	273	59	3	4	6	2.2	18	18	11	42	0	8	1	506	41	3	11	6.6	.995	C-82, 1B-1
1973			145	.282	.396	507	143	22	3	10	2.0	39	59	30	35	3	5	1	749	64	13	7	6.0	.984	C-138
1974			141	.231	.333	424	98	15	2	8	1.9	32	45	49	33	0	21	6	631	64	12	12	5.3	.983	C-133
1975			103	.199	.248	286	57	12	1	0	0.0	16	24	26	28	0	18	4	337	38	9	6	4.5	.977	C-85
1976			146	.246	.296	456	112	17	0	2	0.4	30	39	36	42	1	1	0	582	54	4	6	4.4	.994	C-146
1977	CLE	A	103	.249	.325	317	79	13	1	3	0.9	18	39	16	27	0	1	0	506	35	5	5	5.3	.991	C-102, DH-1
1978	BOS	A	20	.195	.220	41	8	1	0	0	0.0	3	4	1	2	0	2	0	107	11	2	7	6.7	.983	1B-13, C-5
1979	SD	N	46	.167	.216	102	17	2	0	1	1.0	8	6	11	7	0	8	4	162	19	4	3	4.4	.978	C-40, 1B-2
1980			19	.292	.292	24	7	0	0	0	0.0	2	2	0	3	0	5	2	31	1	2	0	2.3	.941	C-14, 1B-1
12 yrs.			877	.234	.312	2576	603	86	11	31	1.2	170	244	189	240	5	78	19	3839	347	54	58	5.2	.987	C-795, 1B-19, 3B-1, DH-1, OF-1

Al Kenders

KENDERS, ALBERT DANIEL GEORGE BR TR 6′ 185 lbs.
B. Apr. 4, 1937, Barrington, N. J.

Year	Team	Lg	Games	BA	SA	AB	H	2B	3B	HR	HR%	R	RBI	BB	SO	SB	Pinch Hit AB	Pinch Hit H	PO	A	E	DP	TC/G	FA	G by Pos
1961	PHI	N	10	.174	.217	23	4	1	0	0	0.0	0	1	1	0	0	0	0	27	3	0	1	3.0	1.000	C-10

Ed Kenna

KENNA, EDWARD ALOYISIUS (Scrap Iron) BR TR 5′ 7½″ 150 lbs.
B. Sept. 30, 1897, San Francisco, Calif. D. Aug. 21, 1972, San Francisco, Calif.

Year	Team	Lg	Games	BA	SA	AB	H	2B	3B	HR	HR%	R	RBI	BB	SO	SB	Pinch Hit AB	Pinch Hit H	PO	A	E	DP	TC/G	FA	G by Pos
1928	WAS	A	41	.297	.390	118	35	4	2	1	0.8	14	20	14	8	1	7	2	104	26	8	3	4.1	.942	C-34

Bob Kennedy

KENNEDY, ROBERT DANIEL BR TR 6′ 2″ 193 lbs.
Father of Terry Kennedy.
B. Aug. 18, 1920, Chicago, Ill.
Manager 1963–65, 1968.

Year	Team	Lg	Games	BA	SA	AB	H	2B	3B	HR	HR%	R	RBI	BB	SO	SB	Pinch Hit AB	Pinch Hit H	PO	A	E	DP	TC/G	FA	G by Pos
1939	CHI	A	3	.250	.250	8	2	0	0	0	0.0	0	1	0	0	0	1	0	0	3	1	0	2.0	.750	3B-2
1940			154	.252	.315	606	153	23	3	3	0.5	74	52	42	58	3	0	0	178	322	33	25	3.5	.938	3B-154
1941			76	.206	.276	257	53	9	3	1	0.4	16	29	17	23	5	0	0	88	153	17	12	3.6	.934	3B-71
1942			113	.231	.299	412	95	18	5	0	0.0	37	38	22	41	11	1	0	130	209	15	17	3.2	.958	3B-96, OF-16
1946			113	.258	.350	411	106	13	5	5	1.2	43	34	24	42	6	5	2	176	87	16	7	2.7	.943	OF-75, 3B-29
1947			115	.262	.362	428	112	19	3	6	1.4	47	48	18	38	3	4	0	205	10	7	3	2.1	.968	OF-106, 3B-1
1948	2 teams		CHI A (30G –.248) CLE A (66G –.301)																						
″	total		96	.269	.360	186	50	11	3	0	0.0	14	19	8	23	0	12	6	103	10	2	3	1.4	.983	OF-80, 2B-2, 1B-1
1949	CLE	A	121	.276	.417	424	117	23	5	9	2.1	49	57	37	40	5	2	0	203	56	3	8	2.2	.989	OF-98, 3B-21
1950			146	.291	.409	540	157	27	5	9	1.7	79	54	53	31	3	2	0	294	13	4	3	2.2	.987	OF-144
1951			108	.246	.383	321	79	15	4	7	2.2	30	29	34	33	4	4	0	174	9	6	2	1.8	.968	OF-106
1952			22	.300	.425	40	12	3	1	0	0.0	6	12	9	5	1	5	0	25	12	0	1	2.3	1.000	OF-13, 3B-3
1953			100	.236	.323	161	38	5	0	3	1.9	22	22	19	11	0	6	2	91	2	0	0	1.0	1.000	OF-89
1954	2 teams		CLE A (1G –.000) BAL A (106G –.251)																						
″	total		107	.251	.359	323	81	13	2	6	1.9	37	45	28	43	2	17	4	121	131	15	10	2.9	.944	3B-71, OF-22
1955	2 teams		BAL A (26G –.143) CHI A (83G –.304)																						
″	total		109	.264	.412	284	75	11	2	9	3.2	38	48	26	26	0	23	4	129	77	7	17	2.2	.967	3B-56, OF-34, 1B-9
1956	2 teams		CHI A (8G –.077) DET A (69G –.232)																						
″	total		77	.221	.311	190	42	5	0	4	2.1	17	22	26	23	2	19	2	91	43	12	5	2.4	.918	3B-33, OF-29
1957	2 teams		CHI A (4G –.000) BKN N (19G –.129)																						
″	total		23	.121	.242	33	4	1	0	1	3.0	5	4	1	6	0	7	1	8	2	0	0	0.8	1.000	OF-9, 3B-3
16 yrs.			1483	.254	.355	4624	1176	196	41	63	1.4	514	514	364	443	45	108	21	2016	1139	138	113	2.4	.958	OF-821, 3B-540, 1B-10, 2B-2
WORLD SERIES																									
1948	CLE	A	3	.500	.500	2	1	0	0	0	0.0	0	1	0	1	0	0	0	2	0	0	0	0.7	1.000	OF-3

Doc Kennedy

KENNEDY, MICHAEL JOSEPH BR TR 5′ 9½″ 185 lbs.
B. Aug. 11, 1853, Brooklyn, N. Y. D. May 25, 1920, Grove, N. Y.

Year	Team	Lg	Games	BA	SA	AB	H	2B	3B	HR	HR%	R	RBI	BB	SO	SB	Pinch Hit AB	Pinch Hit H	PO	A	E	DP	TC/G	FA	G by Pos
1879	CLE	N	49	.290	.368	193	56	8	2	1	0.5	19	18	2	10		0	0	318	52	42	4	8.2	.898	C-46, 1B-4
1880			66	.200	.248	250	50	10	1	0	0.0	26	18	5	12		0	0	398	68	52	9	7.7	.900	C-65, OF-2
1881			39	.313	.373	150	47	7	1	0	0.0	19	15	5	13		0	0	215	38	23	4	7.1	.917	C-35, OF-3, 3B-1
1882			1	.333	.333	3	1	0	0	0	0.0	0	0	1	0		0	0	9	9	3	0	21.0	.857	C-1
1883	BUF	N	5	.316	.316	19	6	0	0	0	0.0	3		2	2		0	0	21	0	5	2	5.2	.808	OF-4, 1B-1
5 yrs.			160	.260	.319	615	160	25	4	1	0.2	67	51	15	37		0	0	961	167	125	19	7.7	.900	C-147, OF-9, 1B-5, 3B-1

Ed Kennedy

KENNEDY, EDWARD 5′ 6″ 150 lbs.
B. Apr. 1, 1856, Carbondale, Pa. D. May 20, 1905, New York, N. Y.

Year	Team	Lg	Games	BA	SA	AB	H	2B	3B	HR	HR%	R	RBI	BB	SO	SB	Pinch Hit AB	Pinch Hit H	PO	A	E	DP	TC/G	FA	G by Pos
1883	NY	AA	94	.219	.292	356	78	6	7	2	0.6	57		17			0	0	112	10	16	0	1.5	.884	OF-94
1884			103	.190	.225	378	72	6	2	1	0.3	49		16			0	0	142	18	14	5	1.7	.920	OF-100, SS-1, C-1, 2B-1
1885			96	.203	.266	349	71	8	4	2	0.6	35		12			0	0	154	15	32	1	2.1	.841	OF-96
1886	BKN	AA	6	.182	.182	22	4	0	0	0	0.0	1		2			0	0	10	0	1	0	1.8	.909	OF-6
4 yrs.			299	.204	.259	1105	225	20	13	5	0.5	142		47			0	0	418	43	63	6	1.8	.880	OF-296, SS-1, C-1, 2B-1

Ed Kennedy

KENNEDY, WILLIAM EDWARD BR TR 5′ 7″ 160 lbs.
B. Apr. 5, 1861, Bellevue, Ky. D. Dec. 22, 1912, Cheyenne, Wyo.

Year	Team	Lg	Games	BA	SA	AB	H	2B	3B	HR	HR%	R	RBI	BB	SO	SB	Pinch Hit AB	Pinch Hit H	PO	A	E	DP	TC/G	FA	G by Pos
1884	CIN	U	13	.208	.271	48	10	1	1	0	0.0	6		1			0	0	14	24	5	1	3.3	.884	3B-8, SS-4, OF-1

Jim Kennedy

KENNEDY, JAMES EARL BL TR 5′ 9″ 160 lbs.
Brother of Junior Kennedy.
B. Nov. 1, 1946, Tulsa, Okla.

Year	Team		Games	BA	SA	AB	H	2B	3B	HR	HR%	R	RBI	BB	SO	SB	Pinch Hit AB	Pinch Hit H	PO	A	E	DP	TC/G	FA	G by Pos
1970	STL	N	12	.125	.125	24	3	0	0	0	0.0	1	0	0	0	0	1	0	19	20	4	5	3.6	.907	SS-7, 2B-5

John Kennedy

KENNEDY, JOHN EDWARD BR TR 6′ 185 lbs.
B. May 29, 1941, Chicago, Ill.

Year	Team		Games	BA	SA	AB	H	2B	3B	HR	HR%	R	RBI	BB	SO	SB	Pinch Hit AB	Pinch Hit H	PO	A	E	DP	TC/G	FA	G by Pos
1962	WAS	A	14	.262	.381	42	11	0	1	1	2.4	6	2	2	7	0	3	2	15	30	3	4	4.4	.938	SS-9, 3B-2
1963			36	.177	.226	62	11	1	1	0	0.0	3	4	6	22	2	3	0	19	49	4	5	2.6	.944	3B-26, SS-2
1964			148	.230	.324	482	111	16	4	7	1.5	55	35	29	119	3	3	0	168	322	25	42	3.3	.951	3B-106, SS-49, 2B-2
1965	LA	N	104	.171	.229	105	18	3	0	1	1.0	12	5	8	33	1	3	0	40	74	4	6	1.2	.966	3B-95, SS-5
1966			125	.201	.281	274	55	9	2	3	1.1	15	24	10	64	1	1	0	102	210	8	32	2.5	.975	3B-87, SS-28, 2B-15
1967	NY	A	78	.196	.235	179	35	4	0	1	0.6	22	17	17	35	2	5	2	83	152	16	21	3.5	.936	SS-36, 3B-34, 2B-2
1969	SEA	A	61	.234	.367	128	30	3	1	4	3.1	18	14	14	25	4	5	0	63	82	10	13	2.8	.935	SS-33, 3B-23
1970	2 teams		MIL A (25G –.255) BOS A (43G –.256)																						
″	total		68	.255	.413	184	47	9	1	6	3.3	23	23	11	23	0	8	1	71	112	9	14	3.1	.953	3B-38, 2B-18, SS-4, 1B-1
1971	BOS	A	74	.276	.412	272	75	12	5	5	1.8	41	22	14	42	1	2	1	114	163	13	35	3.9	.955	2B-37, SS-33, 3B-5
1972			71	.245	.335	212	52	11	1	2	0.9	22	22	18	40	0	5	0	110	141	13	34	3.8	.951	2B-32, SS-27, 3B-11
1973			67	.181	.271	155	28	9	1	1	0.6	17	16	12	45	0	1	0	92	108	6	30	3.2	.971	2B-31, 3B-24, DH-9
1974			10	.133	.333	15	2	0	0	1	6.7	3	1	1	6	0	0	0	8	11	4	3	2.3	.826	2B-6, 3B-4
12 yrs.			856	.225	.323	2110	475	77	17	32	1.5	237	185	142	461	14	39	6	885	1454	115	239	2.9	.953	3B-455, SS-226, 2B-143, DH-9, 1B-1
WORLD SERIES																									
1965	LA	N	4	.000	.000	1	0	0	0	0	0.0	0	0	0	0	0	0	0	0	2	1	0	0.8	.667	3B-4
1966			2	.200	.200	5	1	0	0	0	0.0	0	0	0	0	0	0	0	0	3	0	0	1.5	1.000	3B-2
2 yrs.			6	.167	.167	6	1	0	0	0	0.0	0	0	0	0	0	0	0	0	5	1	0	1.0	.833	3B-6

John Kennedy

KENNEDY, JOHN IRVIN BR TR 5′10″ 175 lbs.
B. Oct. 12, 1926, Jacksonville, Fla.

Year	Team		Games	BA	SA	AB	H	2B	3B	HR	HR%	R	RBI	BB	SO	SB	Pinch Hit AB	Pinch Hit H	PO	A	E	DP	TC/G	FA	G by Pos
1957	PHI	N	5	.000	.000	2	0	0	0	0	0.0	1	0	0	1	0	0	0	0	1	1	1	1.0	.500	3B-2

Junior Kennedy

KENNEDY, JUNIOR RAYMOND BR TR 5′11″ 175 lbs.
Brother of Jim Kennedy.
B. Aug. 9, 1950, Fort Gibson, Okla.

Year	Team		Games	BA	SA	AB	H	2B	3B	HR	HR%	R	RBI	BB	SO	SB	Pinch Hit AB	Pinch Hit H	PO	A	E	DP	TC/G	FA	G by Pos
1974	CIN	N	22	.158	.158	19	3	0	0	0	0.0	2	0	6	4	0	2	0	15	13	2	1	1.4	.933	2B-17, 3B-5
1978			89	.255	.293	157	40	2	2	0	0.0	22	11	31	28	4	13	2	94	142	5	28	3.2	.979	2B-71, 3B-4
1979			83	.273	.318	220	60	7	0	1	0.5	29	17	28	31	4	17	4	105	162	5	30	4.0	.982	2B-59, SS-5, 3B-4
1980			104	.261	.335	337	88	16	3	1	0.3	31	34	36	34	3	1	0	200	303	6	53	4.9	.988	2B-103
1981			27	.250	.273	44	11	1	0	0	0.0	5	5	1	5	0	6	1	22	32	1	8	2.6	.982	2B-16, 3B-5
1982	CHI	N	105	.219	.264	242	53	3	1	2	0.8	22	25	21	34	1	4	0	138	228	12	35	3.6	.968	2B-71, SS-28, 3B-7
1983			17	.136	.136	22	3	0	0	0	0.0	3	3	1	6	0	2	0	12	17	0	3	2.4	1.000	2B-7, 3B-4, SS-1
7 yrs.			447	.248	.299	1041	258	29	6	4	0.4	114	95	124	142	12	45	7	586	897	31	158	3.7	.980	2B-344, SS-34, 3B-29

Ray Kennedy

KENNEDY, RAYMOND LINCOLN BR TR 5′ 9″ 165 lbs.
B. May 19, 1895, Pittsburgh, Pa. D. Jan. 18, 1969, Casselberry, Fla.

Year	Team		Games	BA	SA	AB	H	2B	3B	HR	HR%	R	RBI	BB	SO	SB	Pinch Hit AB	Pinch Hit H	PO	A	E	DP	TC/G	FA	G by Pos
1916	STL	A	1	.000	.000	1	0	0	0	0	0.0	0	0	0	0	0	1	0	0	0	0	0	0.0	—	

Snapper Kennedy

KENNEDY, SHERMAN MONTGOMERY BB TR 5′10″ 165 lbs.
B. Nov. 1, 1878, Conneaut, Ohio D. Aug. 15, 1945, Pasadena, Tex.

Year	Team		Games	BA	SA	AB	H	2B	3B	HR	HR%	R	RBI	BB	SO	SB	Pinch Hit AB	Pinch Hit H	PO	A	E	DP	TC/G	FA	G by Pos
1902	CHI	N	1	.000	.000	5	0	0	0	0	0.0	0	0	0		0	0	0	5	0	0	0	5.0	1.000	OF-1

Terry Kennedy

KENNEDY, TERRENCE EDWARD BL TR 6′ 3″ 220 lbs.
Son of Bob Kennedy.
B. June 4, 1956, Euclid, Ohio.

Year	Team		Games	BA	SA	AB	H	2B	3B	HR	HR%	R	RBI	BB	SO	SB	Pinch Hit AB	Pinch Hit H	PO	A	E	DP	TC/G	FA	G by Pos
1978	STL	N	10	.172	.172	29	5	0	0	0	0.0	0	2	4	3	0	1	0	46	4	1	1	5.1	.980	C-10
1979			33	.284	.404	109	31	7	0	2	1.8	11	17	6	20	0	5	1	135	7	1	1	4.5	.993	C-32
1980			84	.254	.375	248	63	12	3	4	1.6	28	34	28	34	0	12	2	231	22	7	3	3.8	.973	C-41, OF-28
1981	SD	N	101	.301	.385	382	115	24	1	2	0.5	32	41	22	53	0	3	0	465	63	20	12	5.5	.964	C-100
1982			153	.295	.486	562	166	42	1	21	3.7	75	97	26	91	1	5	2	777	66	9	18	5.6	.989	C-139, 1B-12
1983			149	.284	.434	549	156	27	2	17	3.1	47	98	51	89	1	4	2	807	82	12	12	6.1	.987	C-143, 1B-4
1984			148	.240	.353	530	127	16	1	14	2.6	54	57	33	99	1	5	0	708	54	14	6	5.3	.982	C-147
1985			143	.261	.372	532	139	27	1	10	1.9	54	74	31	102	0	5	2	662	68	10	12	5.1	.986	C-140, 1B-5
1986			141	.264	.403	432	114	22	1	12	2.8	46	57	37	74	0	23	11	692	70	8	13	6.3	.990	C-123
1987	BAL	A	143	.250	.385	512	128	13	1	18	3.5	51	62	35	112	1	5	0	750	58	6	11	5.7	.993	C-142
1988			85	.226	.298	265	60	10	0	3	1.1	20	16	15	53	0	8	1	332	23	2	3	4.5	.994	C-79
1989	SF	N	125	.239	.324	355	85	15	0	5	1.4	19	34	35	56	1	11	3	519	47	8	6	4.7	.986	C-121, 1B-2
1990			107	.277	.370	303	84	22	0	2	0.7	25	26	31	38	1	12	4	390	38	4	3	4.2	.991	C-103
1991			69	.234	.339	171	40	7	1	3	1.8	12	13	11	31	0	13	4	240	36	6	2	4.7	.979	C-58, 1B-2
14 yrs.			1491	.264	.386	4979	1313	244	12	113	2.3	474	628	365	855	6	112	32	6754	638	108	103	5.2	.986	C-1378, OF-28, 1B-25
LEAGUE CHAMPIONSHIP SERIES																									
1984	SD	N	5	.222	.222	18	4	0	0	0	0.0	2	1	1	3	0	0	0	28	4	0	1	6.4	1.000	C-5
1989	SF	N	5	.188	.250	16	3	1	0	0	0.0	0	0	1	4	0	0	0	26	1	0	2	5.4	1.000	C-5
2 yrs.			10	.206	.235	34	7	1	0	0	0.0	2	1	2	7	0	0	0	54	5	0	3	5.9	1.000	C-10
WORLD SERIES																									
1984	SD	N	5	.211	.421	19	4	1	0	1	5.3	2	3	1	1	0	0	0	30	2	0	1	6.4	1.000	C-5
1989	SF	N	4	.167	.167	12	2	0	0	0	0.0	1	2	1	3	0	0	0	23	1	1	1	6.3	.960	C-4
2 yrs.			9	.194	.323	31	6	1	0	1	3.2	3	5	2	4	0	0	0	53	3	1	2	6.3	.982	C-9

Jerry Kenney

KENNEY, GERALD TENNYSON, JR. BL TR 6′ 1″ 170 lbs.
B. June 30, 1945, St. Louis, Mo.

Year	Team		Games	BA	SA	AB	H	2B	3B	HR	HR%	R	RBI	BB	SO	SB	Pinch Hit AB	Pinch Hit H	PO	A	E	DP	TC/G	FA	G by Pos
1967	NY	A	20	.310	.397	58	18	2	0	1	1.7	4	5	10	8	2	2	0	29	50	4	5	4.6	.952	SS-18
1969			130	.257	.311	447	115	14	2	2	0.4	49	34	48	36	25	11	4	146	236	7	29	3.1	.982	3B-83, OF-31, SS-10
1970			140	.193	.282	404	78	10	7	4	1.0	46	35	52	44	20	1	0	114	307	17	19	3.2	.961	3B-135, 2B-2

Jerry Kenney *continued*

Year	Team	Games	BA	SA	AB	H	2B	3B	HR	HR%	R	RBI	BB	SO	SB	Pinch Hit AB	Pinch Hit H	PO	A	E	DP	TC/G	FA	G by Pos
1971		120	.262	.311	325	85	10	3	0	0.0	50	20	56	38	9	4	0	74	249	15	24	2.9	.956	3B-109, SS-5, 1B-1
1972		50	.210	.227	119	25	2	0	0	0.0	16	7	16	13	3	4	1	57	132	6	30	4.2	.969	SS-45, 3B-1
1973	CLE A	5	.250	.375	16	4	0	1	0	0.0	0	2	2	0	0	0	0	9	12	0	1	4.2	1.000	2B-5
6 yrs.		465	.237	.299	1369	325	38	13	7	0.5	165	103	184	139	59	22	5	429	986	49	108	3.3	.967	3B-328, SS-78, OF-31, 2B-7, 1B-1

Jeff Kent

KENT, JEFFREY FRANKLIN BR TR 6′ 1″ 185 lbs.
B. Mar. 7, 1968, Bellflower, Calif.

Year	Team	Games	BA	SA	AB	H	2B	3B	HR	HR%	R	RBI	BB	SO	SB	Pinch Hit AB	Pinch Hit H	PO	A	E	DP	TC/G	FA	G by Pos
1992	2 teams	TOR A (65G –.240) NY N (37G –.239)																						
″	total	102	.239	.430	305	73	21	2	11	3.6	52	50	27	76	2	3	1	124	205	14	23	3.3	.959	2B-51, 3B-50, 1B-3, SS-1
1993	NY N	140	.270	.446	496	134	24	0	21	4.2	65	80	30	88	4	1	0	261	341	22	73	4.4	.965	2B-127, 3B-12, SS-2
1994		107	.292	.475	415	121	24	5	14	3.4	53	68	23	84	1	0	0	221	338	14	76	5.4	.976	2B-107
1995		125	.278	.464	472	131	22	3	20	4.2	65	65	29	89	3	3	0	246	354	10	66	5.0	.984	2B-122
4 yrs.		474	.272	.455	1688	459	91	10	66	3.9	235	263	109	337	10	7	1	852	1238	60	238	4.5	.972	2B-407, 3B-62, SS-3, 1B-3

Dick Kenworthy

KENWORTHY, RICHARD LEE BR TR 5′ 9″ 170 lbs.
B. Apr. 1, 1941, Red Oak, Iowa.

Year	Team	Games	BA	SA	AB	H	2B	3B	HR	HR%	R	RBI	BB	SO	SB	Pinch Hit AB	Pinch Hit H	PO	A	E	DP	TC/G	FA	G by Pos
1962	CHI A	3	.000	.000	4	0	0	0	0	0.0	0	0	0	3	0	1	0	1	4	0	2	2.5	1.000	2B-2
1964		2	.000	.000	2	0	0	0	0	0.0	0	0	0	1	0	2	0	0	0	0	0	0.0	—	
1965		3	.000	.000	1	0	0	0	0	0.0	0	0	1	0	0	1	0	0	0	0	0	0.0	—	
1966		9	.200	.200	25	5	0	0	0	0.0	1	0	0	0	0	3	1	0	7	1	0	1.3	.875	3B-6
1967		50	.227	.412	97	22	4	1	4	4.1	9	11	4	17	0	15	0	16	51	2	1	2.0	.971	3B-35
1968		58	.221	.238	122	27	2	0	0	0.0	2	2	5	21	0	19	5	21	70	6	3	2.6	.938	3B-38
6 yrs.		125	.215	.295	251	54	6	1	4	1.6	12	13	10	42	0	41	6	38	132	9	6	2.2	.950	3B-79, 2B-2

Duke Kenworthy

KENWORTHY, WILLIAM JENNINGS (Iron Duke) BB TR 5′ 7″ 165 lbs.
B. July 4, 1886, Cambridge, Ohio D. Sept. 21, 1950, Eureka, Calif.

Year	Team	Games	BA	SA	AB	H	2B	3B	HR	HR%	R	RBI	BB	SO	SB	Pinch Hit AB	Pinch Hit H	PO	A	E	DP	TC/G	FA	G by Pos
1912	WAS A	12	.237	.263	38	9	1	0	0	0.0	6	2	2		3	2	0	14	3	0	0	1.7	1.000	OF-10
1914	KC F	146	.317	.525	545	173	40	14	**15**	**2.8**	93	91	36		37	1	0	437	407	43	79	6.1	.952	2B-145
1915		122	.298	.432	396	118	30	7	3	0.8	59	52	28		20	6	1	237	285	35	35	4.8	.937	2B-108, OF-7
1917	STL A	5	.100	.100	10	1	0	0	0	0.0	1	1	1	1	1	1	0	6	10	2	3	4.5	.889	2B-4
4 yrs.		285	.304	.473	989	301	71	21	18	1.8	159	146	67	1	61	10	1	694	705	80	117	5.4	.946	2B-257, OF-17

Joe Keough

KEOUGH, JOSEPH WILLIAM BL TL 6′ 185 lbs.
Brother of Marty Keough.
B. Jan. 7, 1946, Pomona, Calif.

Year	Team	Games	BA	SA	AB	H	2B	3B	HR	HR%	R	RBI	BB	SO	SB	Pinch Hit AB	Pinch Hit H	PO	A	E	DP	TC/G	FA	G by Pos
1968	OAK A	34	.214	.316	98	21	2	1	2	2.0	7	18	8	11	1	3	1	51	2	2	0	1.8	.964	OF-29, 1B-1
1969	KC A	70	.187	.199	166	31	2	0	0	0.0	17	7	13	13	5	20	3	83	2	0	1	1.7	1.000	OF-49, 1B-1
1970		57	.322	.443	183	59	6	2	4	2.2	28	21	23	18	1	8	2	176	13	4	13	3.7	.979	OF-34, 1B-18
1971		110	.248	.325	351	87	14	2	3	0.9	34	30	35	26	0	11	4	164	4	3	1	1.7	.982	OF-100
1972		56	.219	.250	64	14	2	0	0	0.0	8	5	8	7	2	31	8	12	1	0	1	0.8	1.000	OF-16
1973	CHI A	5	.000	.000	1	0	0	0	0	0.0	1	0	0	0	0	1	0	0	0	0	0	0.0	—	
6 yrs.		332	.246	.319	863	212	26	5	9	1.0	95	81	87	75	9	74	18	486	22	9	16	2.1	.983	OF-228, 1B-20

Marty Keough

KEOUGH, RICHARD MARTIN BL TL 6′ 180 lbs.
Father of Matt Keough. Brother of Joe Keough.
B. Apr. 14, 1935, Oakland, Calif.

Year	Team	Games	BA	SA	AB	H	2B	3B	HR	HR%	R	RBI	BB	SO	SB	Pinch Hit AB	Pinch Hit H	PO	A	E	DP	TC/G	FA	G by Pos
1956	BOS A	3	.000	.000	2	0	0	0	0	0.0	1	1	1	0	0	2	0	0	0	0	0	0.0	—	
1957		9	.059	.059	17	1	0	0	0	0.0	1	0	4	3	0	1	0	16	0	0	0	2.3	1.000	OF-7
1958		68	.220	.322	118	26	3	3	1	0.8	21	9	7	29	1	34	5	54	0	2	1	2.1	.964	OF-25, 1B-2
1959		96	.243	.418	251	61	13	5	7	2.8	40	27	26	40	3	27	7	164	5	1	2	2.4	.994	OF-69, 1B-3
1960	2 teams	BOS A (38G –.248) CLE A (65G –.248)																						
″	total	103	.248	.346	254	63	11	1	4	1.6	34	20	17	31	4	32	5	125	5	1	0	1.8	.992	OF-71
1961	WAS A	135	.249	.410	390	97	18	9	9	2.3	57	34	32	60	12	17	4	308	13	6	10	3.0	.982	OF-100, 1B-10
1962	CIN N	111	.278	.422	230	64	8	2	7	3.0	34	27	21	31	3	20	4	236	22	5	12	2.6	.981	OF-71, 1B-29
1963		95	.227	.401	172	39	8	2	6	3.5	21	21	25	37	1	24	4	250	24	2	25	3.7	.993	1B-46, OF-28
1964		109	.257	.395	276	71	9	1	9	3.3	29	28	22	58	1	34	9	119	5	1	4	1.5	.992	OF-81, 1B-4
1965		62	.116	.116	43	5	0	0	0	0.0	14	3	3	14	0	21	4	75	5	1	4	2.3	.988	1B-32, OF-4
1966	2 teams	ATL N (17G –.059) CHI N (33G –.231)																						
″	total	50	.163	.186	43	7	1	0	0	0.0	4	6	6	15	1	31	5	29	0	1	0	2.5	.967	OF-8, 1B-4
11 yrs.		841	.242	.379	1796	434	71	23	43	2.4	256	176	164	318	26	243	47	1376	79	20	58	2.5	.986	OF-464, 1B-130

John Kerins

KERINS, JOHN NELSON BR TR 5′10″ 177 lbs.
B. July 15, 1858, Indianapolis, Ind. D. Sept. 8, 1919, Louisville, Ky.
Manager 1888.

Year	Team	Games	BA	SA	AB	H	2B	3B	HR	HR%	R	RBI	BB	SO	SB	Pinch Hit AB	Pinch Hit H	PO	A	E	DP	TC/G	FA	G by Pos
1884	IND AA	93	.216	.310	361	78	10	3	6	1.7	58		6			0	0	896	43	31	20	10.0	.968	1B-87, C-5, OF-4, 3B-1
1885	LOU AA	112	.243	.353	456	111	9	16	3	0.7	65		20			0	0	1071	74	65	52	10.2	.946	1B-96, C-19, OF-3, 3B-1
1886		120	.269	.370	487	131	19	9	4	0.8	113		66			0	0	991	183	67	37	10.3	.946	C-65, 1B-47, OF-7, SS-1
1887		112	.294	.443	476	140	18	**19**	5	1.1	101		38		49	0	0	964	111	55	33	9.9	.951	1B-74, C-35, OF-5
1888		83	.235	.313	319	75	11	4	2	0.6	38	41	25		16	0	0	344	70	55	6	5.4	.883	OF-47, C-33, 1B-4, 3B-2, 2B-1
1889	2 teams	LOU AA (2G –.333) BAL AA (16G –.283)																						
″	total	18	.290	.339	62	18	3	0	0	0.0	9	15	2	5	2	0	0	74	11	6	1	4.8	.934	1B-9, C-5, OF-4, SS-1
1890	STL AA	18	.127	.159	63	8	2	0	0	0.0	8		8		2	0	0	172	10	6	12	10.4	.968	1B-17, C-1
7 yrs.		556	.252	.357	2224	561	72	51	20	0.9	392	56	165	5	69	0	0	4512	502	285	161	9.2	.946	1B-334, C-163, OF-70, 3B-4, SS-2, 2B-1

Orie Kerlin

KERLIN, ORIE MILTON (Cy) BL TR 5′ 7″ 149 lbs.
B. Jan. 23, 1891, Summerfield, La. D. Oct. 29, 1974, Shreveport, La.

Year	Team	Games	BA	SA	AB	H	2B	3B	HR	HR%	R	RBI	BB	SO	SB	Pinch Hit AB	Pinch Hit H	PO	A	E	DP	TC/G	FA	G by Pos
1915	PIT F	3	.000	.000	1	0	0	0	0	0.0	0	0	0		0	0	0	0	0	0	0	0.0	.000	C-3

Bill Kern

KERN, WILLIAM GEORGE BR TR 6′ 2″ 184 lbs.
B. Feb. 28, 1933, Coplay, Pa.

Year	Team		Games	BA	SA	AB	H	2B	3B	HR	HR%	R	RBI	BB	SO	SB	Pinch Hit AB	Pinch Hit H	PO	A	E	DP	TC/G	FA	G by Pos
1962	KC	A	8	.250	.438	16	4	0	0	1	6.3	1	1	0	3	0	5	2	3	2	0	0	1.7	1.000	OF-3

George Kernek

KERNEK, GEORGE BOYD BL TL 6′ 3″ 170 lbs.
B. Jan. 12, 1940, Holdenville, Okla.

Year	Team		Games	BA	SA	AB	H	2B	3B	HR	HR%	R	RBI	BB	SO	SB	Pinch Hit AB	Pinch Hit H	PO	A	E	DP	TC/G	FA	G by Pos
1965	STL	N	10	.290	.452	31	9	3	1	0	0.0	6	3	2	4	0	3	0	65	5	2	9	10.3	.972	1B-7
1966			20	.240	.280	50	12	0	1	0	0.0	5	3	4	9	1	4	1	114	8	2	14	7.8	.984	1B-16
2 yrs.			30	.259	.346	81	21	3	2	0	0.0	11	6	6	13	1	7	1	179	13	4	23	8.5	.980	1B-23

Russ Kerns

KERNS, RUSSELL ELDON BL TR 6′ 188 lbs.
B. Nov. 10, 1920, Fremont, Ohio.

Year	Team		Games	BA	SA	AB	H	2B	3B	HR	HR%	R	RBI	BB	SO	SB	Pinch Hit AB	Pinch Hit H	PO	A	E	DP	TC/G	FA	G by Pos
1945	DET	A	1	.000	.000	1	0	0	0	0	0.0	0	0	0	0	0	1	0	0	0	0	0	0.0	—	

Buddy Kerr

KERR, JOHN JOSEPH BR TR 6′ 2″ 175 lbs.
B. Nov. 6, 1922, Astoria, N. Y.

Year	Team		Games	BA	SA	AB	H	2B	3B	HR	HR%	R	RBI	BB	SO	SB	Pinch Hit AB	Pinch Hit H	PO	A	E	DP	TC/G	FA	G by Pos
1943	NY	N	27	.286	.378	98	28	3	0	2	2.0	14	12	8	5	1	0	0	60	90	7	10	5.8	.955	SS-27
1944			150	.266	.387	548	146	31	4	9	1.6	68	63	37	32	14	0	0	328	507	40	81	5.9	.954	SS-149
1945			149	.249	.319	546	136	20	3	4	0.7	53	40	41	34	5	1	0	333	515	32	81	5.9	.964	SS-148
1946			145	.249	.338	497	124	20	3	6	1.2	50	40	53	31	7	1	1	264	428	14	68	4.9	.980	SS-126, 3B-18
1947			138	.287	.386	547	157	23	5	7	1.3	73	49	36	49	2	0	0	270	460	17	77	5.4	.977	SS-138
1948			144	.240	.288	496	119	16	4	0	0.0	41	46	56	36	9	1	1	269	456	25	72	5.2	.967	SS-143
1949			90	.209	.227	220	46	4	0	0	0.0	16	19	21	23	0	0	0	125	224	15	33	4.1	.959	SS-89
1950	BOS	N	155	.227	.310	507	115	24	6	2	0.4	45	46	50	50	0	0	0	310	471	28	97	5.2	.965	SS-155
1951			69	.186	.227	172	32	4	0	1	0.6	18	18	22	20	0	0	0	115	177	9	37	4.4	.970	SS-63, 2B-5
9 yrs.			1067	.249	.328	3631	903	145	25	31	0.9	378	333	324	280	38	3	2	2074	3328	187	556	5.3	.967	SS-1038, 3B-18, 2B-5

Doc Kerr

KERR, JOHN JONAS BB TR 5′10½″ 190 lbs.
B. Jan. 17, 1882, Dellroy, Ohio D. June 9, 1937, Baltimore, Md.

Year	Team		Games	BA	SA	AB	H	2B	3B	HR	HR%	R	RBI	BB	SO	SB	Pinch Hit AB	Pinch Hit H	PO	A	E	DP	TC/G	FA	G by Pos
1914	2 teams		PIT F (42G –.239) BAL F (14G –.265)																						
″	total		56	.248	.381	105	26	5	3	1	1.0	7	8	11		1	20	4	147	43	5	2	6.1	.974	C-31, 1B-1
1915	BAL	F	3	.333	.333	6	2	0	0	0	0.0	1	0	1		0	0	0	9	1	0	0	3.3	1.000	C-2, 1B-1
2 yrs.			59	.252	.378	111	28	5	3	1	0.9	8	8	12		1	20	4	156	44	5	2	5.9	.976	C-33, 1B-2

John Kerr

KERR, JOHN FRANCIS BR TR 5′ 8″ 158 lbs.
B. Nov. 26, 1898, San Francisco, Calif. D. Oct. 19, 1993, Long Beach, Calif. BB 1923–1924

Year	Team		Games	BA	SA	AB	H	2B	3B	HR	HR%	R	RBI	BB	SO	SB	Pinch Hit AB	Pinch Hit H	PO	A	E	DP	TC/G	FA	G by Pos
1923	DET	A	19	.214	.238	42	9	1	0	0	0.0	4	1	4	5	0	1	0	19	45	9	5	4.9	.877	SS-15
1924			17	.273	.273	11	3	0	0	0	0.0	3	1	0	0	0	7	2	1	0	0	0	0.2	1.000	3B-3, OF-2
1929	CHI	A	127	.258	.332	419	108	20	4	1	0.2	50	39	31	24	9	1	1	307	459	23	84	6.5	.971	2B-122
1930			70	.289	.410	266	77	11	6	3	1.1	37	27	21	23	4	0	0	172	218	9	40	5.7	.977	2B-51, SS-19
1931			128	.268	.329	444	119	17	2	2	0.5	51	50	35	22	9	4	1	307	383	25	79	5.7	.965	2B-117, 3B-7, SS-1
1932	WAS	A	51	.273	.333	132	36	6	1	0	0.0	14	15	13	3	3	10	1	73	97	9	17	4.6	.950	2B-17, SS-14, 3B-8
1933			28	.200	.200	40	8	0	0	0	0.0	5	0	3	2	0	5	1	25	31	2	4	3.4	.966	2B-16, 3B-1
1934			31	.272	.311	103	28	4	0	0	0.0	8	12	8	13	1	1	1	63	76	4	10	4.8	.972	3B-17, 2B-13
8 yrs.			471	.266	.337	1457	388	59	13	6	0.4	172	145	115	92	26	29	7	967	1309	81	239	5.6	.966	2B-336, SS-49, 3B-36, OF-2
WORLD SERIES																									
1933	WAS	A	1	—	—	0	0	0	0	0	—	0	0	0	0	0	0	0	0	0	0	0	0.0	—	

Mel Kerr

KERR, JOHN MELVILLE BL TL 5′11½″ 155 lbs.
B. May 22, 1903, Souris, Man., Canada D. Aug. 9, 1980, Vero Beach, Fla.

Year	Team		Games	BA	SA	AB	H	2B	3B	HR	HR%	R	RBI	BB	SO	SB	Pinch Hit AB	Pinch Hit H	PO	A	E	DP	TC/G	FA	G by Pos
1925	CHI	N	1	—	—	0	0	0	0	0	—	1	0	0	0	0	0	0	0	0	0	0	0.0	—	

Dan Kerwin

KERWIN, DANIEL PATRICK BL TL 5′ 9″ 164 lbs.
B. July 9, 1879, Philadelphia, Pa. D. July 13, 1960, Philadelphia, Pa.

Year	Team		Games	BA	SA	AB	H	2B	3B	HR	HR%	R	RBI	BB	SO	SB	Pinch Hit AB	Pinch Hit H	PO	A	E	DP	TC/G	FA	G by Pos
1903	CIN	N	2	.667	.833	6	4	1	0	0	0.0	1	1	2		0	0	0	1	0	1	0	1.0	.500	OF-2

Don Kessinger

KESSINGER, DONALD EULON BB TR 6′ 1″ 170 lbs.
Father of Keith Kessinger. BR 1964–1965
B. July 17, 1942, Forrest City, Ark.
Manager 1979.

Year	Team		Games	BA	SA	AB	H	2B	3B	HR	HR%	R	RBI	BB	SO	SB	Pinch Hit AB	Pinch Hit H	PO	A	E	DP	TC/G	FA	G by Pos
1964	CHI	N	4	.167	.167	12	2	0	0	0	0.0	1	0	0	1	0	2	0	3	7	0	1	2.5	1.000	SS-4
1965			106	.201	.233	309	62	4	3	0	0.0	19	14	20	44	1	0	0	176	338	28	69	5.2	.948	SS-105
1966			150	.274	.302	533	146	8	2	1	0.2	50	43	26	46	13	0	0	202	474	35	68	4.8	.951	SS-148
1967			145	.231	.272	580	134	10	7	0	0.0	61	42	33	80	6	0	0	215	457	19	77	4.8	.973	SS-143
1968			160	.240	.287	655	157	14	7	1	0.2	63	32	38	86	9	1	0	263	573	33	97	5.5	.962	SS-159
1969			158	.273	.366	664	181	38	6	4	0.6	109	53	61	70	11	1	0	266	542	20	101	5.3	.976	SS-157
1970			154	.266	.349	631	168	21	14	1	0.2	100	39	66	59	12	0	0	257	501	22	86	5.1	.972	SS-154
1971			155	.258	.316	617	159	18	6	2	0.3	77	38	52	54	15	2	0	263	512	27	97	5.2	.966	SS-154
1972			149	.274	.334	577	158	20	6	1	0.2	77	39	67	44	8	3	0	259	504	28	90	5.4	.965	SS-146
1973			160	.262	.310	577	151	22	3	0	0.0	52	43	57	44	6	2	0	274	526	30	109	5.3	.964	SS-158
1974			153	.259	.321	599	155	20	7	1	0.2	83	42	62	54	7	3	0	259	476	32	87	5.1	.958	SS-150
1975			154	.243	.319	601	146	26	10	0	0.0	77	46	68	47	4	2	0	210	464	24	103	4.6	.966	SS-140, 3B-13
1976	STL	N	145	.239	.313	502	120	22	6	1	0.2	55	40	61	51	3	1	0	266	435	24	105	5.0	.967	SS-113, 2B-31, 3B-2
1977	2 teams		STL N (59G –.239) CHI A (39G –.235)																						
″	total		98	.237	.281	253	60	7	2	0	0.0	26	18	27	33	2	15	0	135	200	13	46	3.6	.963	SS-47, 2B-37, 3B-13
1978	CHI	A	131	.255	.309	431	110	18	1	1	0.2	35	31	36	34	2	1	0	183	335	13	62	4.0	.976	SS-123, 2B-9
1979			56	.200	.282	110	22	6	0	1	0.9	14	7	10	12	1	0	0	61	109	2	17	3.1	.988	SS-54, 2B-1, 1B-1
16 yrs.			2078	.252	.312	7651	1931	254	80	14	0.2	899	527	684	759	100	33	0	3292	6453	350	1215	4.9	.965	SS-1955, 2B-78, 3B-28, 1B-1

Keith Kessinger

KESSINGER, ROBERT KEITH BB TR 6′ 2″ 185 lbs.
Son of Don Kessinger.
B. Feb. 19, 1967, Forest City, Ark.

Year	Team		Games	BA	SA	AB	H	2B	3B	HR	HR%	R	RBI	BB	SO	SB	Pinch Hit AB	Pinch Hit H	PO	A	E	DP	TC/G	FA	G by Pos
1993	CIN	N	11	.259	.407	27	7	1	0	1	3.7	4	3	4	4	0	0	0	7	22	2	5	2.8	.935	SS-11

Henry Kessler

KESSLER, HENRY (Lucky) BR TR 5′10″ 144 lbs.
B. 1847, Brooklyn, N. Y. D. Jan. 9, 1900, Franklin, Pa.

Year	Team	Games	BA	SA	AB	H	2B	3B	HR	HR%	R	RBI	BB	SO	SB	Pinch Hit AB	Pinch Hit H	PO	A	E	DP	TC/G	FA	G by Pos
1876	**CIN N**	59	.258	.278	248	64	5	0	0	0.0	26	11	7	10		0	0	77	125	52	13	4.1	.795	SS-46, OF-16
1877		6	.100	.100	20	2	0	0	0	0.0	0	0	2	1		0	0	13	8	15	2	6.0	.583	C-5, 1B-1
2 yrs.		65	.246	.265	268	66	5	0	0	0.0	26	11	9	11		0	0	90	133	67	15	4.3	.769	SS-46, OF-16, C-5, 1B-1

Fred Ketcham

KETCHAM, FREDERICK L. BL TR 5′ 8″ 157 lbs.
B. July 27, 1875, Elmira, N. Y. D. Mar. 12, 1908, Cortland, N. Y.

Year	Team	Games	BA	SA	AB	H	2B	3B	HR	HR%	R	RBI	BB	SO	SB	Pinch Hit AB	Pinch Hit H	PO	A	E	DP	TC/G	FA	G by Pos
1899	**LOU N**	15	.295	.311	61	18	1	0	0	0.0	13	5	0		2	0	0	17	0	0	0	1.1	1.000	OF-15
1901	**PHI A**	5	.227	.227	22	5	0	0	0	0.0	5	2	0		0	0	0	7	0	1	0	1.6	.875	OF-5
2 yrs.		20	.277	.289	83	23	1	0	0	0.0	18	7	0		2	0	0	24	0	1	0	1.3	.960	OF-20

Phil Ketter

KETTER, PHILIP TR
Born Philip Ketterer.
B. Apr. 13, 1884, St. Louis, Mo. D. Apr. 9, 1965, St. Louis, Mo.

Year	Team	Games	BA	SA	AB	H	2B	3B	HR	HR%	R	RBI	BB	SO	SB	Pinch Hit AB	Pinch Hit H	PO	A	E	DP	TC/G	FA	G by Pos
1912	**STL A**	2	.333	.333	6	2	0	0	0	0.0	1	0	0		0	0	0	3	3	0	0	3.0	1.000	C-2

Sam Khalifa

KHALIFA, SAM BR TR 5′10″ 160 lbs.
B. Dec. 5, 1963, Fontana, Calif.

Year	Team	Games	BA	SA	AB	H	2B	3B	HR	HR%	R	RBI	BB	SO	SB	Pinch Hit AB	Pinch Hit H	PO	A	E	DP	TC/G	FA	G by Pos
1985	**PIT N**	95	.237	.319	320	76	14	3	2	0.6	30	31	34	56	5	0	0	156	316	16	45	5.1	.967	SS-95
1986		64	.185	.225	151	28	6	0	0	0.0	8	4	19	28	0	1	0	94	168	10	25	4.1	.963	SS-60, 2B-6
1987		5	.176	.176	17	3	0	0	0	0.0	1	2	0	2	0	0	0	5	6	1	1	2.4	.917	SS-5
3 yrs.		164	.219	.285	488	107	20	3	2	0.4	39	37	53	86	5	1	0	255	490	27	71	4.7	.965	SS-160, 2B-6

Hod Kibbie

KIBBIE, HORACE KENT BR TR 5′10″ 150 lbs.
B. July 18, 1903, Fort Worth, Tex. D. Oct. 19, 1975, Fort Worth, Tex.

Year	Team	Games	BA	SA	AB	H	2B	3B	HR	HR%	R	RBI	BB	SO	SB	Pinch Hit AB	Pinch Hit H	PO	A	E	DP	TC/G	FA	G by Pos
1925	**BOS N**	11	.268	.317	41	11	2	0	0	0.0	5	2	5	6	0	0	0	23	40	5	5	6.2	.926	2B-8, SS-3

Jack Kibble

KIBBLE, JOHN WESTLY (Happy) BB TR 5′ 9½″ 154 lbs.
B. Jan. 2, 1892, Seatonville, Ill. D. Dec. 13, 1969, Roundup, Mont.

Year	Team	Games	BA	SA	AB	H	2B	3B	HR	HR%	R	RBI	BB	SO	SB	Pinch Hit AB	Pinch Hit H	PO	A	E	DP	TC/G	FA	G by Pos
1912	**CLE A**	5	.000	.000	8	0	0	0	0	0.0	1	0	0		0	0	0	5	11	0	3	3.2	1.000	3B-4, 2B-1

Steve Kiefer

KIEFER, STEVEN GEORGE BR TR 6′ 1″ 175 lbs.
Brother of Mark Kiefer.
B. Oct. 18, 1960, Chicago, Ill.

Year	Team	Games	BA	SA	AB	H	2B	3B	HR	HR%	R	RBI	BB	SO	SB	Pinch Hit AB	Pinch Hit H	PO	A	E	DP	TC/G	FA	G by Pos
1984	**OAK A**	23	.175	.300	40	7	1	2	0	0.0	7	2	2	10	2	1	1	15	35	5	5	2.5	.909	SS-17, DH-3, 3B-2
1985		40	.197	.288	66	13	1	1	1	1.5	8	10	1	18	0	1	0	15	37	7	5	1.6	.881	3B-34, DH-2
1986	**MIL A**	2	.000	.000	6	0	0	0	0	0.0	0	0	0	4	0	0	0	7	8	0	2	7.5	1.000	SS-2
1987		28	.202	.394	99	20	4	0	5	5.1	17	17	7	28	0	2	1	16	50	2	4	2.3	.971	3B-26, 2B-4
1988		7	.300	.700	10	3	1	0	1	10.0	2	1	2	3	0	1	0	4	8	1	2	1.6	.923	3B-4, 2B-4
1989	**NY A**	5	.125	.125	8	1	0	0	0	0.0	0	0	0	5	0	0	0	1	1	0	0	0.4	1.000	3B-5
6 yrs.		105	.192	.341	229	44	7	3	7	3.1	34	30	12	68	2	5	2	58	139	15	18	2.1	.929	3B-71, SS-19, 2B-8, DH-5

Pete Kilduff

KILDUFF, PETER JOHN BR TR 5′ 7″ 155 lbs.
B. Apr. 4, 1893, Weir City, Kans. D. Feb. 14, 1930, Pittsburg, Kans.

Year	Team	Games	BA	SA	AB	H	2B	3B	HR	HR%	R	RBI	BB	SO	SB	Pinch Hit AB	Pinch Hit H	PO	A	E	DP	TC/G	FA	G by Pos
1917	**2 teams**	**NY N** (31G –.205) **CHI N** (56G –.277)																						
″	**total**	87	.257	.346	280	72	12	5	1	0.4	35	27	16	30	13	0	0	141	203	25	33	4.4	.932	SS-56, 2B-26, 3B-1
1918	**CHI N**	30	.204	.269	93	19	2	2	0	0.0	7	13	7	7	1	0	0	72	72	10	18	5.1	.935	2B-30
1919	**2 teams**	**CHI N** (31G –.273) **BKN N** (32G –.301)																						
″	**total**	63	.286	.366	161	46	7	3	0	0.0	14	16	22	16	6	2	1	51	103	17	11	3.1	.901	3B-40, 2B-9, SS-7
1920	**BKN N**	141	.272	.360	478	130	26	8	0	0.0	62	58	58	43	2	2	1	322	463	28	71	5.8	.966	2B-134, 3B-5
1921		107	.288	.406	372	107	15	10	3	0.8	45	45	31	36	6	1	0	243	383	24	58	6.1	.963	2B-105, 3B-1
5 yrs.		428	.270	.364	1384	374	62	28	4	0.3	163	159	134	132	28	5	2	829	1224	104	191	5.2	.952	2B-304, SS-63, 3B-47
WORLD SERIES																								
1920	**BKN N**	7	.095	.095	21	2	0	0	0	0.0	0	0	1	4	0	0	0	15	28	0	4	6.1	1.000	2B-7

Frank Kiley

Playing record listed under Frank Kane.

John Kiley

KILEY, JOHN FREDERICK BL TL 5′ 7″ 147 lbs.
B. July 1, 1859, South Dedham, Mass. D. Dec. 18, 1940, Norwood, Mass.

Year	Team	Games	BA	SA	AB	H	2B	3B	HR	HR%	R	RBI	BB	SO	SB	Pinch Hit AB	Pinch Hit H	PO	A	E	DP	TC/G	FA	G by Pos
1884	**WAS AA**	14	.214	.321	56	12	2	2	0	0.0	9		3			0	0	15	1	12	0	2.0	.571	OF-14
1891	**BOS N**	1	.000	.000	2	0	0	0	0	0.0	0	0	1	1	0	0	0	0	2	0	0	2.0	1.000	P-1
2 yrs.		15	.207	.310	58	12	2	2	0	0.0	9	0	4	1	0	0	0	15	3	12	0	2.0	.600	OF-14, P-1

Pat Kilhullen

KILHULLEN, JOSEPH ISADORE BR TR 5′ 9″ 175 lbs.
B. Aug. 10, 1890, Carbondale, Pa. D. Nov. 2, 1922, Oakland, Calif.

Year	Team	Games	BA	SA	AB	H	2B	3B	HR	HR%	R	RBI	BB	SO	SB	Pinch Hit AB	Pinch Hit H	PO	A	E	DP	TC/G	FA	G by Pos
1914	**PIT N**	1	.000	.000	1	0	0	0	0	0.0	0	0	0	0	0	0	0	0	0	0	0	0.0	.000	C-1

Harmon Killebrew

KILLEBREW, HARMON CLAYTON (Killer) BR TR 5′11″ 195 lbs.
B. June 29, 1936, Payette, Ida.
Hall of Fame 1984.

Year	Team	Games	BA	SA	AB	H	2B	3B	HR	HR%	R	RBI	BB	SO	SB	Pinch Hit AB	Pinch Hit H	PO	A	E	DP	TC/G	FA	G by Pos
1954	**WAS A**	9	.308	.385	13	4	1	0	0	0.0	1	3	2	3	0	2	0	5	2	0	0	2.3	1.000	2B-3
1955		38	.200	.362	80	16	1	0	4	5.0	12	7	9	31	0	13	1	24	49	5	3	3.0	.936	3B-23, 2B-3
1956		44	.222	.394	99	22	2	0	5	5.1	10	13	10	39	0	21	2	24	44	4	4	3.0	.944	3B-20, 2B-4
1957		9	.290	.548	31	9	2	0	2	6.5	4	5	2	8	0	2	1	2	16	1	2	2.4	.947	3B-7, 2B-1
1958		13	.194	.194	31	6	0	0	0	0.0	2	2	0	12	0	4	1	8	13	0	1	2.3	1.000	3B-9
1959		153	.242	.516	546	132	20	2	**42**	**7.7**	98	105	90	116	3	0	0	135	325	30	18	3.2	.939	3B-150, OF-4
1960		124	.276	.534	442	122	19	1	31	7.0	84	80	71	106	1	4	2	629	135	17	76	5.7	.978	1B-71, 3B-65
1961	**MIN A**	150	.288	.606	541	156	20	7	46	8.5	94	122	107	109	1	0	0	1003	143	23	101	7.0	.980	1B-119, 3B-45, OF-2
1962		155	.243	.545	552	134	21	1	**48**	**8.7**	85	**126**	106	**142**	1	1	1	241	5	9	4	1.6	.965	OF-151, 1B-4
1963		142	.258	**.555**	515	133	18	0	**45**	**8.7**	88	96	72	105	0	3	1	219	7	3	0	1.7	.987	OF-137

Harmon Killebrew *continued*

Year	Team	Games	BA	SA	AB	H	2B	3B	HR	HR%	R	RBI	BB	SO	SB	Pinch Hit AB	Pinch Hit H	PO	A	E	DP	TC/G	FA	G by Pos
1964		158	.270	.548	577	156	11	1	**49**	8.5	95	111	93	135	0	1	0	232	1	7	0	1.5	.971	OF-157
1965		113	.269	.501	401	108	16	1	25	6.2	78	75	72	69	0	2	1	743	113	12	67	7.4	.986	1B-72, 3B-44, OF-1
1966		162	.281	.538	569	160	27	1	39	6.9	89	110	**103**	98	0	1	0	435	205	18	41	3.9	.973	3B-108, 1B-42, OF-18
1967		163	.269	.558	547	147	24	1	**44**	**8.0**	105	113	**131**	111	1	0	0	1285	89	12	100	8.5	.991	1B-160, 3B-3
1968		100	.210	.420	295	62	7	2	17	5.8	40	40	70	70	0	9	1	601	71	7	51	7.7	.990	1B-77, 3B-11
1969		162	.276	.584	555	153	20	2	**49**	**8.8**	106	**140**	**145**	84	8	0	0	639	219	22	67	4.8	.975	3B-105, 1B-80
1970		157	.271	.546	527	143	20	1	41	**7.8**	96	113	128	84	0	2	0	312	212	20	28	3.3	.963	3B-138, 1B-28
1971		147	.254	.464	500	127	19	1	28	5.6	61	**119**	**114**	96	3	4	1	700	149	13	55	5.6	.985	1B-90, 3B-64
1972		139	.231	.450	433	100	13	2	26	6.0	53	74	94	91	0	8	0	995	99	9	82	8.5	.992	1B-130
1973		69	.242	.347	248	60	9	1	5	2.0	29	32	41	59	0	2	0	431	45	1	42	7.2	.998	1B-57, DH-9
1974		122	.222	.360	333	74	7	0	13	3.9	28	54	45	61	0	30	11	218	21	2	21	2.7	.992	DH-57, 1B-33
1975	**KC A**	106	.199	.375	312	62	13	0	14	4.5	25	44	54	70	1	9	1	28	0	0	4	0.3	1.000	DH-92, 1B-6
22 yrs.		2435	.256	.509	8147	2086	290	24	573 **5th**	7.0 **3rd**	1283	1584	1559	1699 **10th**	19	118	24	8909	1963	215	767	4.6	.981	1B-969, 3B-792, OF-470, DH-158, 2B-11
LEAGUE CHAMPIONSHIP SERIES																								
1969	**MIN A**	3	.125	.250	8	1	1	0	0	0.0	2	0	6	2	0	0	0	6	3	0	0	3.0	1.000	3B-3
1970		3	.273	.818	11	3	0	0	2	18.2	2	4	2	4	0	0	0	8	4	1	1	4.3	.923	3B-2, 1B-1
2 yrs.		6	.211	.579	19	4	1	0	2	10.5	4	4	8	6	0	0	0	14	7	1	1	3.7	.955	3B-5, 1B-1
WORLD SERIES																								
1965	**MIN A**	7	.286	.429	21	6	0	0	1	4.8	2	2	6	4	0	0	0	11	7	1	0	2.7	.947	3B-7

Bill Killefer

KILLEFER, WILLIAM LAVIER (Reindeer Bill) BR TR 5′10½″ 200 lbs.
Brother of Red Killefer.
B. Oct. 10, 1887, Bloomingdale, Mich. D. July 3, 1960, Elsmere, Del.
Manager 1921–25, 1930–33.

Year	Team	Games	BA	SA	AB	H	2B	3B	HR	HR%	R	RBI	BB	SO	SB	Pinch Hit AB	Pinch Hit H	PO	A	E	DP	TC/G	FA	G by Pos
1909	**STL A**	11	.138	.138	29	4	0	0	0	0.0	0	1	0		2	0	0	36	21	6	2	5.7	.905	C-11
1910		74	.124	.155	193	24	2	2	0	0.0	14	7	12		0	1	0	311	124	29	16	6.4	.938	C-73
1911	**PHI N**	6	.188	.188	16	3	0	0	0	0.0	3	2	0	2	0	0	0	29	10	1	1	6.7	.975	C-6
1912		85	.224	.280	268	60	6	3	1	0.4	18	21	4	14	6	0	0	407	134	15	17	6.5	.973	C-85
1913		120	.244	.300	360	88	14	3	0	0.0	25	24	4	17	2	1	0	570	166	9	16	6.3	.988	C-118, 1B-1
1914		98	.234	.274	299	70	10	1	0	0.0	27	27	8	17	3	8	3	464	154	14	11	7.0	.978	C-90
1915		105	.237	.278	320	76	9	2	0	0.0	26	24	18	14	5	1	0	539	126	19	6	6.5	.972	C-105
1916		97	.217	.294	286	62	5	4	3	1.0	22	27	8	14	2	4	0	443	89	8	15	5.9	.985	C-91
1917		125	.274	.303	409	112	12	0	0	0.0	28	31	15	21	4	4	0	617	138	12	14	6.4	.984	C-120
1918	**CHI N**	104	.233	.281	331	77	10	3	0	0.0	30	22	17	10	5	0	0	487	110	11	12	5.8	.982	C-104
1919		103	.286	.330	315	90	10	2	0	0.0	17	22	15	8	5	3	0	478	124	8	7	6.1	.987	C-100
1920		62	.220	.267	191	42	7	1	0	0.0	16	16	8	5	2	1	0	304	80	9	6	6.4	.977	C-61
1921		45	.323	.331	133	43	1	0	0	0.0	11	16	4	4	3	3	1	147	43	7	6	4.7	.964	C-42
13 yrs.		1035	.238	.283	3150	751	86	21	4	0.1	237	240	113	126	39	26	4	4832	1319	148	129	6.3	.977	C-1006, 1B-1
WORLD SERIES																								
1915	**PHI N**	1	.000	.000	1	0	0	0	0	0.0	0	0	0	0	0	1	0	0	0	0	0	0.0	—	
1918	**CHI N**	6	.118	.176	17	2	1	0	0	0.0	2	2	2	0	0	0	0	26	6	0	1	5.3	1.000	C-6
2 yrs.		7	.111	.167	18	2	1	0	0	0.0	2	2	2	0	0	1	0	26	6	0	1	5.3	1.000	C-6

Red Killefer

KILLEFER, WADE HAMPTON (Lollypop) BR TR 5′ 9½″ 175 lbs.
Brother of Bill Killefer.
B. Apr. 13, 1885, Bloomingdale, Mich. D. Sept. 4, 1958, Los Angeles, Calif.

Year	Team	Games	BA	SA	AB	H	2B	3B	HR	HR%	R	RBI	BB	SO	SB	Pinch Hit AB	Pinch Hit H	PO	A	E	DP	TC/G	FA	G by Pos
1907	**DET A**	1	.000	.000	4	0	0	0	0	0.0	0	0	0		0	0	0	2	0	0	0	2.0	1.000	OF-1
1908		28	.213	.227	75	16	1	0	0	0.0	9	11	3		4	0	0	48	54	12	9	4.2	.895	2B-16, SS-7, 3B-4
1909	**2 teams**	**DET A** (23G –.279) **WAS A** (40G –.174)																						
″	**total**	63	.209	.264	182	38	3	2	1	0.5	17	9	16		6	7	3	103	77	20	9	3.6	.900	OF-25, 2B-20, 3B-6, C-3, SS-1
1910	**WAS A**	106	.229	.284	345	79	17	1	0	0.0	35	24	29		17	4	1	190	234	29	27	4.5	.936	2B-88, OF-12
1914	**CIN N**	42	.277	.333	141	39	6	1	0	0.0	16	12	20	18	11	1	0	60	12	4	0	1.8	.947	OF-37, 2B-5, 3B-1
1915		155	.272	.362	555	151	25	11	1	0.2	75	41	38	33	12	2	0	339	17	11	6	2.4	.970	OF-153, 1B-2
1916	**2 teams**	**CIN N** (70G –.244) **NY N** (2G –1.000)																						
″	**total**	72	.247	.306	235	58	9	1	1	0.4	29	19	22	8	7	3	2	138	6	5	2	2.2	.966	OF-68
7 yrs.		467	.248	.314	1537	381	61	16	3	0.2	181	116	128	59	57	17	6	880	400	81	53	3.0	.940	OF-296, 2B-129, 3B-11, SS-8, C-3, 1B-2

Matt Kilroy

KILROY, MATTHEW ALOYSIUS (Matches) BL TL 5′ 9″ 175 lbs.
Brother of Mike Kilroy.
B. June 21, 1866, Philadelphia, Pa. D. Mar. 2, 1940, Philadelphia, Pa.

Year	Team	Games	BA	SA	AB	H	2B	3B	HR	HR%	R	RBI	BB	SO	SB	Pinch Hit AB	Pinch Hit H	PO	A	E	DP	TC/G	FA	G by Pos
1886	**BAL AA**	68	.174	.197	218	38	3	1	0	0.0	33		21			0	0	32	116	28	1	2.5	.841	P-68, OF-2
1887		72	.247	.318	239	59	5	6	0	0.0	46		31		12	0	0	39	167	22	2	3.1	.904	P-69, OF-4, SS-1
1888		43	.179	.241	145	26	5	2	0	0.0	13	19	11		10	0	0	21	61	6	2	1.9	.932	P-40, OF-7
1889		65	.274	.361	208	57	3	6	1	0.5	32	26	23	26	13	0	0	30	142	18	4	2.8	.905	P-59, OF-8
1890	**BOS P**	31	.215	.247	93	20	1	1	0	0.0	11	8	12	9	11	0	0	28	60	10	2	2.9	.898	P-30, OF-2, 3B-1, SS-1
1891	**CIN AA**	8	.150	.150	20	3	0	0	0	0.0	2	0	4	2	0	0	0	3	14	2	0	2.4	.895	P-7, OF-1
1892	**WAS N**	4	.200	.200	10	2	0	0	0	0.0	0	0	1	0	0	0	0	3	14	2	0	4.8	.895	P-4
1893	**LOU N**	5	.438	.625	16	7	3	0	0	0.0	4	3	1	3	0	0	0	1	12	1	0	2.8	.929	P-5
1894		8	.118	.118	17	2	0	0	0	0.0	2	1	1	6	1	0	0	6	13	4	0	2.9	.826	P-8
1898	**CHI N**	26	.229	.292	96	22	4	1	0	0.0	20	10	13		0	1	0	21	31	4	2	2.2	.929	P-13, OF-12
10 yrs.		330	.222	.280	1062	236	24	17	1	0.1	163	67	118	46	47	1	0	184	630	97	13	2.7	.894	P-303, OF-36, SS-2, 3B-1

Dick Kimble

KIMBLE, RICHARD LEWIS BL TR 5′ 9″ 160 lbs.
B. July 27, 1915, Buchtel, Ohio.

Year	Team	Games	BA	SA	AB	H	2B	3B	HR	HR%	R	RBI	BB	SO	SB	Pinch Hit AB	Pinch Hit H	PO	A	E	DP	TC/G	FA	G by Pos
1945	**WAS A**	20	.245	.306	49	12	1	1	0	0.0	5	1	5	2	0	4	0	19	38	3	5	4.0	.950	SS-15

Bruce Kimm

KIMM, BRUCE EDWARD
B. June 29, 1951, Cedar Rapids, Iowa.
BR TR 5'11" 175 lbs.

Year	Team	Games	BA	SA	AB	H	2B	3B	HR	HR%	R	RBI	BB	SO	SB	Pinch Hit AB	Pinch Hit H	PO	A	E	DP	TC/G	FA	G by Pos
1976	DET A	63	.263	.336	152	40	8	0	1	0.7	13	6	15	20	4	0	0	256	33	9	5	4.7	.970	C-61, DH-2
1977		14	.080	.120	25	2	1	0	0	0.0	2	1	0	4	0	0	0	43	3	2	0	3.4	.958	C-12, DH-2
1979	CHI N	9	.091	.091	11	1	0	0	0	0.0	0	0	0	0	0	0	0	30	1	1	0	3.6	.969	C-9
1980	CHI A	100	.243	.291	251	61	10	1	0	0.0	20	19	17	26	1	3	0	375	26	6	2	4.2	.985	C-98
4 yrs.		186	.237	.292	439	104	19	1	1	0.2	35	26	32	50	5	3	0	704	63	18	7	4.3	.977	C-180, DH-4

Wally Kimmick

KIMMICK, WALTER LYONS
B. May 30, 1897, Turtle Creek, Pa. D. July 24, 1989, Boswell, Pa.
BR TR 5'11" 174 lbs.

Year	Team	Games	BA	SA	AB	H	2B	3B	HR	HR%	R	RBI	BB	SO	SB	Pinch Hit AB	Pinch Hit H	PO	A	E	DP	TC/G	FA	G by Pos
1919	STL N	2	.000	.000	1	0	0	0	0	0.0	1	0	1	0	1	1	0	0	1	0	0	1.0	1.000	SS-1
1921	CIN N	3	.167	.167	6	1	0	0	0	0.0	0	1	0	1	0	1	0	1	3	2	1	3.0	.667	3B-2
1922		39	.247	.292	89	22	2	1	0	0.0	11	12	3	12	0	3	0	44	87	4	11	4.0	.970	SS-30, 2B-3, 3B-1
1923		29	.225	.275	80	18	2	1	0	0.0	11	6	5	15	3	2	0	41	78	3	10	5.5	.975	2B-17, 3B-4, SS-1
1925	PHI N	70	.305	.376	141	43	3	2	1	0.7	16	10	22	26	0	11	4	62	95	9	9	2.7	.946	SS-28, 3B-21, 2B-13
1926		20	.214	.357	28	6	2	1	0	0.0	0	2	3	7	0	6	1	25	8	4	1	2.6	.892	1B-5, 3B-4, SS-4, 2B-1
6 yrs.		163	.261	.325	345	90	9	5	1	0.3	39	31	34	61	4	24	5	173	272	22	32	3.5	.953	SS-64, 2B-34, 3B-32, 1B-5

Chad Kimsey

KIMSEY, CLYDE ELIAS
B. Aug. 6, 1906, Copperhill, Tenn. D. Dec. 3, 1942, Pryor, Okla.
BL TR 6'3½" 200 lbs.

Year	Team	Games	BA	SA	AB	H	2B	3B	HR	HR%	R	RBI	BB	SO	SB	Pinch Hit AB	Pinch Hit H	PO	A	E	DP	TC/G	FA	G by Pos
1929	STL A	29	.267	.533	30	8	2	0	2	6.7	6	4	1	8	0	5	1	7	25	1	2	1.4	.970	P-24
1930		60	.343	.514	70	24	4	1	2	2.9	14	14	5	16	1	16	2	2	32	2	0	0.9	.944	P-42
1931		47	.270	.459	37	10	1	0	2	5.4	5	5	8	11	1	4	0	6	31	3	1	1.0	.925	P-42
1932	2 teams	STL A (34G –.333) CHI A (7G –.000)																						
"	total	41	.300	.350	20	6	1	0	0	0.0	1	1	1	4	0	1	0	4	30	2	2	0.9	.944	P-40
1933	CHI A	28	.152	.152	33	5	0	0	0	0.0	1	1	0	9	0	1	0	2	28	0	2	1.1	1.000	P-28
1936	DET A	22	.313	.500	16	5	1	1	0	0.0	3	1	1	5	0	0	0	3	18	1	0	1.0	.955	P-22
6 yrs.		227	.282	.432	206	58	9	2	6	2.9	30	26	16	53	2	27	3	24	164	9	7	1.0	.954	P-198

Jerry Kindall

KINDALL, GERALD DONALD (Slim)
B. May 27, 1935, St. Paul, Minn.
BR TR 6'2½" 175 lbs.
BB 1960

Year	Team	Games	BA	SA	AB	H	2B	3B	HR	HR%	R	RBI	BB	SO	SB	Pinch Hit AB	Pinch Hit H	PO	A	E	DP	TC/G	FA	G by Pos
1956	CHI N	32	.164	.218	55	9	1	1	0	0.0	7	0	6	17	1	0	0	33	53	4	12	5.0	.956	SS-18
1957		72	.160	.276	181	29	3	0	6	3.3	18	12	8	48	1	10	2	73	109	15	10	3.5	.924	2B-28, 3B-19, SS-9
1958		3	.167	.333	6	1	1	0	0	0.0	0	0	0	3	0	0	0	6	5	0	2	3.7	1.000	2B-3
1960		89	.240	.346	246	59	16	2	2	0.8	17	23	5	52	4	3	0	147	222	13	45	4.5	.966	2B-82, SS-2
1961		96	.242	.419	310	75	22	3	9	2.9	37	44	18	89	2	7	1	206	233	26	61	4.8	.944	2B-50, SS-47
1962	CLE A	154	.232	.349	530	123	21	1	13	2.5	51	55	45	107	4	0	0	358	494	19	114	5.7	.978	2B-154
1963		86	.205	.295	234	48	4	1	5	2.1	27	20	18	71	3	3	1	134	183	9	31	3.7	.972	SS-46, 2B-37, 1B-4
1964	2 teams	CLE A (23G –.360) MIN A (62G –.148)																						
"	total	85	.183	.261	153	28	3	0	3	2.0	13	8	9	51	0	0	0	161	116	7	28	3.5	.975	2B-51, 1B-24, SS-7
1965	MIN A	125	.196	.289	342	67	12	1	6	1.8	41	36	36	97	2	2	1	246	266	23	63	4.3	.957	2B-106, 3B-10, SS-7
9 yrs.		742	.213	.327	2057	439	83	9	44	2.1	211	198	145	535	17	25	5	1364	1681	116	366	4.5	.963	2B-511, SS-136, 3B-29, 1B-28

Ralph Kiner

KINER, RALPH McPHERRAN
B. Oct. 27, 1922, Santa Rita, N. M.
Hall of Fame 1975.
BR TR 6'2" 195 lbs.

Year	Team	Games	BA	SA	AB	H	2B	3B	HR	HR%	R	RBI	BB	SO	SB	Pinch Hit AB	Pinch Hit H	PO	A	E	DP	TC/G	FA	G by Pos
1946	PIT N	144	.247	.430	502	124	17	3	**23**	**4.6**	63	81	74	**109**	3	3	0	339	6	11	0	2.5	.969	OF-140
1947		152	.313	**.639**	565	177	23	4	**51**	**9.0**	118	127	98	81	1	0	0	390	8	7	1	2.7	.983	OF-152
1948		156	.265	.533	555	147	19	5	**40**	**7.2**	104	123	112	61	1	1	1	382	6	10	1	2.6	.975	OF-154
1949		152	.310	**.658**	549	170	19	5	**54**	**9.8**	116	**127**	**117**	61	6	0	0	311	12	7	3	2.2	.979	OF-152
1950		150	.272	.590	547	149	21	6	**47**	**8.6**	112	118	122	79	2	0	0	287	13	11	2	2.1	.965	OF-150
1951		151	.309	**.627**	531	164	31	6	**42**	**7.9**	**124**	109	**137**	57	2	0	0	751	36	18	60	5.3	.978	OF-94, 1B-58
1952		149	.244	.500	516	126	17	2	**37**	**7.2**	90	87	**110**	77	3	0	0	250	9	8	0	1.8	.970	OF-149
1953	2 teams	PIT N (41G –.270) CHI N (117G –.283)																						
"	total	158	.279	.512	562	157	20	3	35	6.2	100	116	100	88	2	1	0	282	11	8	3	1.9	.973	OF-157
1954	CHI N	147	.285	.487	557	159	36	5	22	3.9	88	73	76	90	2	0	0	298	6	9	1	2.1	.971	OF-147
1955	CLE A	113	.243	.452	321	78	13	0	18	5.6	56	54	65	46	0	28	11	141	2	2	0	1.7	.986	OF-87
10 yrs.		1472	.279	.548	5205	1451	216	39	369	7.1 **2nd**	971	1015	1011	749	22	33	12	3431	109	91	71	2.5	.975	OF-1382, 1B-58

Charlie King

KING, CHARLES GILBERT (Chick)
B. Nov. 10, 1930, Paris, Tenn.
BR TR 6'2" 190 lbs.

Year	Team	Games	BA	SA	AB	H	2B	3B	HR	HR%	R	RBI	BB	SO	SB	Pinch Hit AB	Pinch Hit H	PO	A	E	DP	TC/G	FA	G by Pos
1954	DET A	11	.214	.286	28	6	0	1	0	0.0	4	3	3	8	0	4	0	22	1	1	1	3.4	.958	OF-7
1955		7	.238	.238	21	5	0	0	0	0.0	3	0	1	2	0	0	0	12	0	1	0	2.2	.923	OF-6
1956		7	.222	.222	9	2	0	0	0	0.0	0	0	1	4	0	2	0	4	0	1	0	1.3	.800	OF-4
1958	CHI N	8	.250	.250	8	2	0	0	0	0.0	1	1	3	1	0	1	0	6	0	0	0	0.9	1.000	OF-7
1959	2 teams	CHI N (7G –.000) STL N (5G –.429)																						
"	total	12	.300	.300	10	3	0	0	0	0.0	3	1	0	3	0	0	0	9	0	0	0	1.8	1.000	OF-5
5 yrs.		45	.237	.263	76	18	0	1	0	0.0	11	5	8	18	0	7	0	53	1	3	1	2.0	.947	OF-29

Fred King

Playing record listed under John Butler.

Hal King

KING, HAROLD
B. Feb. 1, 1944, Oviedo, Fla.
BL TR 6'1" 200 lbs.

Year	Team	Games	BA	SA	AB	H	2B	3B	HR	HR%	R	RBI	BB	SO	SB	Pinch Hit AB	Pinch Hit H	PO	A	E	DP	TC/G	FA	G by Pos
1967	HOU N	15	.250	.364	44	11	1	2	0	0.0	2	6	2	9	0	4	1	62	8	0	1	6.4	1.000	C-11
1968		27	.145	.218	55	8	2	1	0	0.0	4	2	7	16	0	11	1	83	8	3	0	4.9	.968	C-19
1970	ATL N	89	.260	.461	204	53	8	0	11	5.4	29	30	32	41	1	26	6	316	14	5	1	5.4	.985	C-62
1971		86	.207	.328	198	41	9	0	5	2.5	14	19	29	43	0	26	6	274	23	5	0	5.0	.983	C-60
1972	TEX A	50	.180	.320	122	22	5	0	4	3.3	12	12	25	35	0	12	0	181	16	6	3	5.3	.970	C-38
1973	CIN N	35	.186	.465	43	8	0	0	4	9.3	5	10	6	10	0	26	5	26	1	0	1	3.0	1.000	C-9
1974		20	.176	.235	17	3	1	0	0	0.0	1	3	3	4	0	14	3	6	1	0	0	1.4	1.000	C-5
7 yrs.		322	.214	.366	683	146	26	3	24	3.5	67	82	104	158	1	119	22	948	71	19	6	5.1	.982	C-204

Hal King *continued*

Year	Team	Games	BA	SA	AB	H	2B	3B	HR	HR%	R	RBI	BB	SO	SB	Pinch Hit AB	Pinch Hit H	PO	A	E	DP	TC/G	FA	G by Pos
LEAGUE CHAMPIONSHIP SERIES																								
1973	CIN N	3	.500	.500	2	1	0	0	0	0.0	0	0	1	1	0	2	1	0	0	0	0	0.0	—	

Jeff King

KING, JEFFREY WAYNE BR TR 6′ 1″ 175 lbs.
B. Dec. 26, 1964, Marion, Ind.

Year	Team	Games	BA	SA	AB	H	2B	3B	HR	HR%	R	RBI	BB	SO	SB	Pinch Hit AB	Pinch Hit H	PO	A	E	DP	TC/G	FA	G by Pos
1989	PIT N	75	.195	.353	215	42	13	3	5	2.3	31	19	20	34	4	15	3	403	59	4	36	7.0	.991	1B-46, 3B-13, 2B-7, SS-1
1990		127	.245	.410	371	91	17	1	14	3.8	46	53	21	50	3	19	5	61	215	18	15	2.5	.939	3B-115, 1B-1
1991		33	.239	.376	109	26	1	1	4	3.7	16	18	14	15	3	0	0	15	62	2	0	2.4	.975	3B-33
1992		130	.231	.371	480	111	21	2	14	2.9	56	65	27	56	4	7	1	368	234	12	58	4.3	.980	3B-73, 1B-32, 2B-32, SS-6, OF-1
1993		158	.295	.406	611	180	35	3	9	1.5	82	98	59	54	8	1	0	108	362	18	30	3.0	.963	3B-156, SS-2, 2B-2
1994		94	.263	.375	339	89	23	0	5	1.5	36	42	30	38	3	1	0	61	198	13	26	3.0	.952	3B-91, 2B-1
1995		122	.265	.456	445	118	27	2	18	4.0	61	87	55	63	7	3	2	350	204	17	40	4.4	.970	3B-84, 1B-35, 2B-8, SS-2
7 yrs.		739	.256	.399	2570	657	137	12	69	2.7	328	382	226	310	32	46	11	1366	1334	84	205	3.8	.970	3B-565, 1B-114, 2B-50, SS-11, OF-1
LEAGUE CHAMPIONSHIP SERIES																								
1990	PIT N	5	.100	.100	10	1	0	0	0	0.0	0	0	1	5	0	2	0	1	4	0	0	1.3	1.000	3B-4
1992		7	.241	.379	29	7	4	0	0	0.0	4	2	0	1	0	0	0	11	19	1	5	4.4	.968	3B-7
2 yrs.		12	.205	.308	39	8	4	0	0	0.0	4	2	1	6	0	2	0	12	23	1	5	3.3	.972	3B-11

Jim King

KING, JAMES HUBERT BL TR 6′ 185 lbs.
B. Aug. 27, 1932, Elkins, Ark.

Year	Team	Games	BA	SA	AB	H	2B	3B	HR	HR%	R	RBI	BB	SO	SB	Pinch Hit AB	Pinch Hit H	PO	A	E	DP	TC/G	FA	G by Pos
1955	CHI N	113	.256	.425	301	77	12	3	11	3.7	43	45	24	39	2	18	4	184	10	2	2	2.1	.990	OF-93
1956		118	.249	.445	317	79	13	2	15	4.7	32	54	30	40	1	34	6	187	10	2	2	2.4	.990	OF-82
1957	STL N	22	.314	.314	35	11	0	0	0	0.0	1	2	4	2	0	16	4	7	0	0	0	0.9	1.000	OF-8
1958	SF N	34	.214	.393	56	12	2	1	2	3.6	8	8	10	8	0	14	3	18	0	0	0	1.2	1.000	OF-15
1961	WAS A	110	.270	.449	263	71	12	1	11	4.2	43	46	38	45	4	17	1	139	7	3	2	1.6	.980	OF-91, C-1
1962		132	.243	.387	333	81	15	0	11	3.3	39	35	55	37	4	31	8	178	9	4	4	1.9	.979	OF-101
1963		136	.231	.444	459	106	16	5	24	5.2	61	62	45	43	3	22	4	213	13	3	2	1.9	.987	OF-123
1964		134	.241	.412	415	100	15	1	18	4.3	46	56	55	65	3	22	7	240	10	7	0	2.1	.973	OF-121
1965		120	.213	.430	258	55	10	2	14	5.4	46	49	44	50	1	37	8	127	7	1	1	1.5	.993	OF-88
1966		117	.248	.403	310	77	14	2	10	3.2	41	30	38	41	4	34	7	147	4	2	0	1.8	.987	OF-85
1967	3 teams	WAS A (47G –.210) CHI A (23G –.120) CLE A (19G –.143)																						
″	total	89	.175	.234	171	30	3	2	1	0.6	14	14	20	31	1	42	11	66	0	2	0	1.5	.971	OF-44, C-1
11 yrs.		1125	.240	.411	2918	699	112	19	117	4.0	374	401	363	401	23	287	63	1506	70	26	13	1.9	.984	OF-851, C-2

Lee King

KING, EDWARD LEE BR TR 5′ 8″ 160 lbs.
B. Dec. 26, 1892, Hundred, W. Va. D. Sept. 16, 1967, Shinnston, W. Va.

Year	Team	Games	BA	SA	AB	H	2B	3B	HR	HR%	R	RBI	BB	SO	SB	Pinch Hit AB	Pinch Hit H	PO	A	E	DP	TC/G	FA	G by Pos
1916	PIT N	8	.111	.111	18	2	0	0	0	0.0	0	1	0	7	0	2	0	4	1	2	0	0.9	.714	OF-8
1917		111	.249	.320	381	95	14	5	1	0.3	32	35	15	58	8	9	3	198	16	7	6	2.2	.968	OF-102
1918		36	.232	.321	112	26	3	2	1	0.9	9	11	11	15	3	0	0	50	0	5	0	1.5	.909	OF-36
1919	NY N	21	.100	.150	20	2	1	0	0	0.0	5	1	1	6	0	9	1	2	0	1	0	0.4	.667	OF-7
1920		93	.276	.429	261	72	11	4	7	2.7	32	42	21	38	3	12	2	167	8	9	1	2.2	.951	OF-84
1921	2 teams	NY N (39G –.223) PHI N (64G –.269)																						
″	total	103	.255	.406	310	79	23	6	4	1.3	42	39	21	43	1	7	2	167	15	17	0	2.1	.915	OF-92, 1B-1
1922	2 teams	PHI N (19G –.226) NY N (20G –.176)																						
″	total	39	.207	.391	87	18	8	1	2	2.3	14	15	13	8	1	7	1	102	3	2	3	4.3	.981	OF-20, 1B-5
7 yrs.		411	.247	.366	1189	294	60	18	15	1.3	134	144	82	175	16	46	9	690	43	43	10	2.2	.945	OF-349, 1B-6
WORLD SERIES																								
1922	NY N	2	1.000	1.000	1	1	0	0	0	0.0	0	1	0	0	0	0	0	0	0	0	0	0.0	.000	OF-2

Lee King

KING, EDWARD LEE BR TR 5′10″ 150 lbs.
B. Mar. 28, 1894, Waltham, Mass. D. Sept. 7, 1938, Newton Centre, Mass.

Year	Team	Games	BA	SA	AB	H	2B	3B	HR	HR%	R	RBI	BB	SO	SB	Pinch Hit AB	Pinch Hit H	PO	A	E	DP	TC/G	FA	G by Pos
1916	PHI A	42	.188	.222	144	27	1	2	0	0.0	13	8	7	15	4	2	0	53	44	13	5	2.8	.882	OF-22, SS-11, 3B-5, 2B-2
1919	BOS N	2	.000	.000	1	0	0	0	0	0.0	0	0	0	0	0	1	0	0	0	0	0	0.0	—	
2 yrs.		44	.186	.221	145	27	1	2	0	0.0	13	8	7	15	4	3	0	53	44	13	5	2.8	.882	OF-22, SS-11, 3B-5, 2B-2

Lynn King

KING, LYNN PAUL (Dig) BL TR 5′ 9″ 165 lbs.
B. Nov. 28, 1907, Villisca, Iowa D. May 11, 1972, Atlantic, Iowa.

Year	Team	Games	BA	SA	AB	H	2B	3B	HR	HR%	R	RBI	BB	SO	SB	Pinch Hit AB	Pinch Hit H	PO	A	E	DP	TC/G	FA	G by Pos
1935	STL N	8	.182	.182	22	4	0	0	0	0.0	6	0	4	1	2	1	0	26	0	0	0	4.3	1.000	OF-6
1936		78	.190	.230	100	19	2	1	0	0.0	12	10	9	14	2	25	5	59	1	1	1	1.8	.984	OF-34
1939		89	.235	.259	85	20	2	0	0	0.0	10	11	15	3	2	35	10	53	1	1	0	1.3	.982	OF-44
3 yrs.		175	.208	.237	207	43	4	1	0	0.0	28	21	28	18	6	61	15	138	2	2	1	1.7	.986	OF-84

Sam King

KING, SAMUEL WARREN BL TL 6′
B. May 17, 1852, Peabody, Mass. D. Aug. 11, 1922, Peabody, Mass.

Year	Team	Games	BA	SA	AB	H	2B	3B	HR	HR%	R	RBI	BB	SO	SB	Pinch Hit AB	Pinch Hit H	PO	A	E	DP	TC/G	FA	G by Pos
1884	WAS AA	12	.178	.222	45	8	2	0	0	0.0	3		1			0	0	121	4	12	6	11.4	.912	1B-12

Silver King

KING, CHARLES FREDERICK BR TR 6′ 170 lbs.
Born Charles Frederick Koenig.
B. Jan. 11, 1868, St. Louis, Mo. D. May 21, 1938, St. Louis, Mo.

Year	Team	Games	BA	SA	AB	H	2B	3B	HR	HR%	R	RBI	BB	SO	SB	Pinch Hit AB	Pinch Hit H	PO	A	E	DP	TC/G	FA	G by Pos
1886	KC N	7	.045	.045	22	1	0	0	0	0.0	0	1	2	12		0	0	0	13	3	0	2.3	.813	P-5, OF-2
1887	STL AA	62	.207	.243	222	46	6	1	0	0.0	28		24		10	0	0	35	70	16	1	1.9	.868	P-46, OF-17
1888		66	.208	.300	207	43	4	6	1	0.5	25	14	40		6	0	0	33	119	12	4	2.4	.927	P-66, OF-2
1889		56	.228	.296	189	43	7	3	0	0.0	37	30	22	40	3	0	0	19	91	5	2	1.9	.957	P-56, 1B-2, OF-1
1890	CHI P	58	.168	.249	185	31	2	5	1	0.5	24	16	13	22	3	0	0	22	139	6	5	2.9	.964	P-56, OF-1, 1B-1
1891	PIT N	49	.169	.223	148	25	2	3	0	0.0	12	9	14	31	0	0	0	19	67	10	5	2.0	.896	P-48, 3B-1
1892	NY N	52	.210	.311	167	35	3	4	2	1.2	27	23	16	26	1	0	0	22	81	11	4	2.2	.904	P-52
1893	2 teams	NY N (7G –.176) CIN N (17G –.162)																						
″	total	24	.167	.222	54	9	1	1	0	0.0	13	4	15	16	0	0	0	8	32	3	1	1.8	.930	P-24
1896	WAS N	22	.276	.379	58	16	6	0	0	0.0	9	12	8	15	1	0	0	6	19	1	0	1.2	.962	P-22
1897		24	.193	.228	57	11	2	0	0	0.0	8	7	12		0	0	0	2	40	2	1	1.9	.955	P-23
10 yrs.		420	.199	.268	1309	260	33	23	4	0.3	183	116	166	162	24	0	0	166	671	69	23	2.1	.924	P-398, OF-23, 1B-3, 3B-1

Wes Kingdon

KINGDON, WESCOTT WILLIAM BR TR 5′ 8″ 148 lbs.
B. July 4, 1900, Los Angeles, Calif. D. Apr. 19, 1975, Capistrano, Calif.

Year	Team	Games	BA	SA	AB	H	2B	3B	HR	HR%	R	RBI	BB	SO	SB	Pinch Hit AB	Pinch Hit H	PO	A	E	DP	TC/G	FA	G by Pos
1932	WAS A	18	.324	.471	34	11	3	1	0	0.0	10	3	5	2	0	5	1	8	15	1	2	2.0	.958	3B-8, SS-4

Mike Kingery

KINGERY, MICHAEL SCOTT BL TL 6′ 180 lbs.
B. Mar. 29, 1961, St. James, Minn.

Year	Team	Games	BA	SA	AB	H	2B	3B	HR	HR%	R	RBI	BB	SO	SB	Pinch Hit AB	Pinch Hit H	PO	A	E	DP	TC/G	FA	G by Pos
1986	KC A	62	.258	.388	209	54	8	5	3	1.4	25	14	12	30	7	5	2	102	6	3	2	1.9	.973	OF-59
1987	SEA A	120	.280	.449	354	99	25	4	9	2.5	38	52	27	43	7	9	3	226	15	2	3	2.1	.992	OF-114, DH-4
1988		57	.203	.276	123	25	6	0	1	0.8	21	9	19	23	3	5	0	102	6	2	1	2.0	.982	OF-44, 1B-10
1989		31	.224	.342	76	17	3	0	2	2.6	14	6	7	14	1	6	0	70	0	0	0	3.0	1.000	OF-23
1990	SF N	105	.295	.338	207	61	7	1	0	0.0	24	24	12	19	6	17	7	126	7	3	2	1.4	.978	OF-95
1991		91	.182	.236	110	20	2	2	0	0.0	13	8	15	21	1	44	11	60	2	1	2	1.4	.984	OF-38, 1B-6
1992	OAK A	12	.107	.107	28	3	0	0	0	0.0	3	1	1	3	0	3	0	14	0	0	0	1.4	1.000	OF-10
1994	CLR N	105	.349	.532	301	105	27	8	4	1.3	56	41	30	26	5	12	3	187	5	4	1	2.0	.980	OF-98, 1B-1
1995		119	.269	.411	350	94	18	4	8	2.3	66	37	45	40	13	15	4	205	5	5	0	1.9	.977	OF-108, 1B-5
9 yrs.		702	.272	.400	1758	478	96	24	27	1.5	260	192	168	219	43	116	30	1092	46	20	11	1.9	.983	OF-589, 1B-22, DH-4
DIVISIONAL PLAYOFF SERIES																								
1995	CLR N	4	.200	.200	10	2	0	0	0	0.0	1	0	0	1	0	0	0	5	0	0	0	1.3	1.000	OF-4

Dave Kingman

KINGMAN, DAVID ARTHUR (Kong) BR TR 6′ 6″ 210 lbs.
B. Dec. 21, 1948, Pendleton, Ore.

Year	Team	Games	BA	SA	AB	H	2B	3B	HR	HR%	R	RBI	BB	SO	SB	Pinch Hit AB	Pinch Hit H	PO	A	E	DP	TC/G	FA	G by Pos
1971	SF N	41	.278	.557	115	32	10	2	6	5.2	17	24	9	35	5	7	1	168	9	4	9	5.3	.978	1B-20, OF-14
1972		135	.225	.462	472	106	17	4	29	6.1	65	83	51	140	16	5	0	496	159	22	49	4.9	.968	3B-59, 1B-56, OF-22
1973		112	.203	.479	305	62	10	1	24	7.9	54	55	41	122	8	7	1	313	146	22	30	4.5	.954	3B-60, 1B-46, P-2
1974		121	.223	.440	350	78	18	2	18	5.1	41	55	37	125	8	11	3	696	98	25	69	7.2	.969	1B-91, 3B-21, OF-2
1975	NY N	134	.231	.494	502	116	22	1	36	**7.2**	65	88	34	153	7	5	0	526	69	14	37	4.3	.977	OF-71, 1B-58, 3B-12
1976		123	.238	.506	474	113	14	1	37	**7.8**	70	86	28	135	7	1	0	293	18	9	11	2.5	.972	OF-111, 1B-16
1977	4 teams	NY N (58G –.209) SD N (56G –.238) CAL A (10G –.194) NY A (8G –.250)																						
″	total	132	.221	.444	439	97	20	0	26	5.9	47	78	28	143	5	23	4	406	29	9	16	3.7	.980	OF-75, 1B-38, DH-6, 3B-2
1978	CHI N	119	.266	.542	395	105	17	4	28	7.1	65	79	39	111	3	8	1	226	10	6	6	2.3	.975	OF-100, 1B-6
1979		145	.288	**.613**	532	153	19	5	**48**	**9.0**	97	115	45	**131**	4	5	3	240	11	12	3	1.9	.954	OF-139
1980		81	.278	.522	255	71	8	0	18	7.1	31	57	21	44	2	16	6	119	10	8	0	2.2	.942	OF-61, 1B-2
1981	NY N	100	.221	.456	353	78	11	3	22	6.2	40	59	55	**105**	6	1	0	548	34	20	39	5.8	.967	1B-56, OF-48
1982		149	.204	.432	535	109	9	1	**37**	**6.9**	80	99	59	**156**	4	5	0	1232	69	18	88	9.2	.986	1B-143
1983		100	.198	.383	248	49	7	0	13	5.2	25	29	22	57	2	39	7	450	28	3	43	8.7	.994	1B-50, OF-5
1984	OAK A	147	.268	.505	549	147	23	1	35	6.4	68	118	44	119	2	0	0	55	2	0	3	0.4	1.000	DH-139, 1B-9
1985		158	.238	.417	592	141	16	0	30	5.1	66	91	62	114	3	2	1	50	1	0	3	0.3	1.000	DH-149, 1B-9
1986		144	.210	.431	561	118	19	0	35	6.2	70	94	33	126	3	2	0	17	0	2	2	0.1	.895	DH-140, 1B-3
16 yrs.		1941	.236	.478	6677	1575	240	25	442	6.6	901	1210	608	1816	85	137	27	5835	693	174	408	3.6	.974	OF-648, 1B-603, DH-434, 3B-154, P-2
										5th				**5th**										
LEAGUE CHAMPIONSHIP SERIES																								
1971	SF N	4	.111	.111	9	1	0	0	0	0.0	0	0	1	3	0	1	0	5	0	0	0	2.5	1.000	OF-2

Henry Kingman

KINGMAN, HENRY LEES BL TL 6′ 1½″ 165 lbs.
B. Apr. 3, 1892, Tientsin, China D. Dec. 27, 1982, Oakland, Calif.

Year	Team	Games	BA	SA	AB	H	2B	3B	HR	HR%	R	RBI	BB	SO	SB	Pinch Hit AB	Pinch Hit H	PO	A	E	DP	TC/G	FA	G by Pos
1914	NY A	4	.000	.000	3	0	0	0	0	0.0	0	0	1	2	0	3	0	1	0	0	0	1.0	1.000	1B-1

Walt Kinlock

KINLOCK, WALTER
B. 1878, St. Joseph, Mo. Deceased.

Year	Team	Games	BA	SA	AB	H	2B	3B	HR	HR%	R	RBI	BB	SO	SB	Pinch Hit AB	Pinch Hit H	PO	A	E	DP	TC/G	FA	G by Pos
1895	STL N	1	.333	.333	3	1	0	0	0	0.0	0	0	0	2	0	0	0	4	1	0	1	5.0	1.000	3B-1

Bob Kinsella

KINSELLA, ROBERT FRANCIS (Red) BL TR 5′ 9½″ 165 lbs.
B. Jan. 5, 1899, Springfield, Ill. D. Dec. 30, 1951, Los Angeles, Calif.

Year	Team	Games	BA	SA	AB	H	2B	3B	HR	HR%	R	RBI	BB	SO	SB	Pinch Hit AB	Pinch Hit H	PO	A	E	DP	TC/G	FA	G by Pos
1919	NY N	3	.222	.222	9	2	0	0	0	0.0	1	0	0	3	1	0	0	1	0	1	0	0.7	.500	OF-3
1920		1	.333	.333	3	1	0	0	0	0.0	0	1	0	2	0	0	0	1	0	1	0	2.0	.500	OF-1
2 yrs.		4	.250	.250	12	3	0	0	0	0.0	1	1	0	5	1	0	0	2	0	2	0	1.0	.500	OF-4

Kinsler

KINSLER
B. Staten Island, N. Y. Deceased.

Year	Team	Games	BA	SA	AB	H	2B	3B	HR	HR%	R	RBI	BB	SO	SB	Pinch Hit AB	Pinch Hit H	PO	A	E	DP	TC/G	FA	G by Pos
1893	NY N	1	.000	.000	3	0	0	0	0	0.0	1	0	1	1	0	0	0	1	0	0	0	1.0	1.000	OF-1

Tom Kinslow

KINSLOW, THOMAS F. BR TR 5′10″ 160 lbs.
B. Jan. 12, 1866, Washington, D. C. D. Feb. 22, 1901, Washington, D. C.

Year	Team	Games	BA	SA	AB	H	2B	3B	HR	HR%	R	RBI	BB	SO	SB	Pinch Hit AB	Pinch Hit H	PO	A	E	DP	TC/G	FA	G by Pos
1886	WAS N	3	.250	.250	8	2	0	0	0	0.0	1	1	0	1		0	0	11	4	0	0	5.0	1.000	C-3
1887	NY AA	2	.000	.000	6	0	0	0	0	0.0	0		0		0	0	0	6	3	0	0	4.5	1.000	C-2
1890	BKN P	64	.264	.409	242	64	11	6	4	1.7	30	46	10	22	2	0	0	298	72	37	7	6.4	.909	C-64
1891	BKN N	61	.237	.263	228	54	6	0	0	0.0	22	33	9	22	3	0	0	252	54	26	6	5.4	.922	C-61
1892		66	.305	.443	246	75	6	11	2	0.8	37	40	13	16	4	0	0	355	89	32	6	7.2	.933	C-66
1893		78	.244	.333	312	76	8	4	4	1.3	38	45	11	13	4	0	0	291	80	27	11	5.1	.932	C-76, OF-2
1894		62	.305	.408	223	68	5	6	2	0.9	39	41	20	11	4	0	0	219	47	27	4	4.7	.908	C-61, 1B-1
1895	PIT N	19	.226	.258	62	14	2	0	0	0.0	10	5	2	2	1	1	0	67	10	3	1	4.4	.963	C-18
1896	LOU N	8	.280	.360	25	7	0	1	0	0.0	4	7	1	5	0	2	0	23	4	4	2	5.2	.871	C-5, 1B-1
1898	2 teams	WAS N (3G –.111) STL N (14G –.283)																						
″	total	17	.258	.323	62	16	2	1	0	0.0	5	4	1		0	0	0	49	21	7	4	4.3	.909	C-17, 1B-1
10 yrs.		380	.266	.361	1414	376	40	29	12	0.8	186	222	67	92	18	3	0	1571	384	163	41	5.6	.923	C-373, 1B-3, OF-2

Walt Kinzie

KINZIE, WALTER HARRIS BR 5′10½″ 161 lbs.
B. Mar. 16, 1857, Chicago, Ill. D. Nov. 5, 1909, Chicago, Ill.

Year	Team	Games	BA	SA	AB	H	2B	3B	HR	HR%	R	RBI	BB	SO	SB	Pinch Hit AB	Pinch Hit H	PO	A	E	DP	TC/G	FA	G by Pos
1882	DET N	13	.094	.132	53	5	0	1	0	0.0	5	2	0	8		0	0	8	38	8	1	4.2	.852	SS-13
1884	2 teams	CHI N (19G –.159) STL AA (2G –.111)																						
″	total	21	.154	.253	91	14	3	0	2	2.2	4		0	13		0	0	26	55	17	4	4.7	.827	SS-17, 2B-2, 3B-2
2 yrs.		34	.132	.208	144	19	3	1	2	1.4	9	2	0	21		0	0	34	93	25	5	4.5	.836	SS-30, 2B-2, 3B-2

Ed Kippert

KIPPERT, EDWARD AUGUST BR TR 5′10½″ 180 lbs.
B. Jan. 3, 1880, Detroit, Mich. D. June 3, 1960, Detroit, Mich.

Year	Team	Games	BA	SA	AB	H	2B	3B	HR	HR%	R	RBI	BB	SO	SB	Pinch Hit AB	Pinch Hit H	PO	A	E	DP	TC/G	FA	G by Pos
1914	CIN N	2	.000	.000	2	0	0	0	0	0.0	0	0	0	0	0	0	0	1	0	0	0	0.5	1.000	OF-2

Jim Kirby

KIRBY, JAMES HERSCHEL BR TR 5′11″ 175 lbs.
B. May 5, 1923, Nashville, Tenn.

Year	Team	Games	BA	SA	AB	H	2B	3B	HR	HR%	R	RBI	BB	SO	SB	Pinch Hit AB	Pinch Hit H	PO	A	E	DP	TC/G	FA	G by Pos
1949	CHI N	3	.500	.500	2	1	0	0	0	0.0	0	0	0	0	0	2	1	0	0	0	0	0.0	—	

LaRue Kirby

KIRBY, LaRUE BB TR 6′ 185 lbs.
B. Dec. 30, 1889, Eureka, Mich. D. June 10, 1961, Lansing, Mich.

Year	Team	Games	BA	SA	AB	H	2B	3B	HR	HR%	R	RBI	BB	SO	SB	Pinch Hit AB	Pinch Hit H	PO	A	E	DP	TC/G	FA	G by Pos
1912	NY N	3	.200	.400	5	1	1	0	0	0.0	1	0	0	0	0	0	0	2	3	0	0	1.7	1.000	P-3
1914	STL F	52	.246	.338	195	48	6	3	2	1.0	21	18	14		5	0	0	100	7	3	2	2.2	.973	OF-50
1915		61	.213	.275	178	38	7	2	0	0.0	15	16	17		3	5	1	88	8	4	2	1.9	.960	OF-52, P-1
3 yrs.		116	.230	.310	378	87	14	5	2	0.5	37	34	31	0	8	5	1	190	18	7	4	2.0	.967	OF-102, P-4

Wayne Kirby

KIRBY, WAYNE LEONARD BL TR 5′11″ 185 lbs.
B. Jan. 22, 1964, Williamsburg, Va.

Year	Team	Games	BA	SA	AB	H	2B	3B	HR	HR%	R	RBI	BB	SO	SB	Pinch Hit AB	Pinch Hit H	PO	A	E	DP	TC/G	FA	G by Pos
1991	CLE A	21	.209	.256	43	9	2	0	0	0.0	4	5	2	6	1	1	0	40	1	0	0	2.0	1.000	OF-21
1992		21	.167	.389	18	3	1	0	1	5.6	9	1	3	2	0	9	2	3	0	0	0	0.5	1.000	DH-4, OF-2
1993		131	.269	.371	458	123	19	5	6	1.3	71	60	37	58	17	10	0	273	19	5	5	2.3	.983	OF-123, DH-5
1994		78	.293	.403	191	56	6	0	5	2.6	33	23	13	30	11	15	5	92	2	4	1	1.4	.959	OF-68, DH-2
1995		101	.207	.298	188	39	10	2	1	0.5	29	14	13	32	10	27	5	95	2	1	1	1.3	.990	OF-68, DH-7
5 yrs.		352	.256	.357	898	230	38	7	13	1.4	146	103	68	128	39	62	12	503	24	10	7	1.8	.981	OF-282, DH-18
DIVISIONAL PLAYOFF SERIES																								
1995	CLE A	3	1.000	1.000	1	1	0	0	0	0.0	0	0	0	0	0	0	0	0	0	0	0	0.0	.000	OF-2
LEAGUE CHAMPIONSHIP SERIES																								
1995	CLE A	5	.200	.200	5	1	0	0	0	0.0	2	0	0	0	1	0	0	3	0	0	0	0.8	1.000	OF-4
WORLD SERIES																								
1995	CLE A	3	.000	.000	1	0	0	0	0	0.0	0	0	0	1	0	1	0	1	0	0	0	1.0	1.000	OF-1

Tom Kirk

KIRK, THOMAS DANIEL BL TL 5′10½″ 182 lbs.
B. Sept. 27, 1927, Philadelphia, Pa. D. Aug. 1, 1974, Philadelphia, Pa.

Year	Team	Games	BA	SA	AB	H	2B	3B	HR	HR%	R	RBI	BB	SO	SB	Pinch Hit AB	Pinch Hit H	PO	A	E	DP	TC/G	FA	G by Pos
1947	PHI A	1	.000	.000	1	0	0	0	0	0.0	0	0	0	0	0	1	0	0	0	0	0	0.0	—	

Jay Kirke

KIRKE, JUDSON FABIAN BL TR 6′ 195 lbs.
B. June 16, 1888, Fleischmanns, N. Y. D. Aug. 31, 1968, New Orleans, La.

Year	Team	Games	BA	SA	AB	H	2B	3B	HR	HR%	R	RBI	BB	SO	SB	Pinch Hit AB	Pinch Hit H	PO	A	E	DP	TC/G	FA	G by Pos
1910	DET A	8	.200	.240	25	5	1	0	0	0.0	3	3	1		1	0	0	16	17	3	1	4.5	.917	2B-7, OF-1
1911	BOS N	20	.360	.528	89	32	5	5	0	0.0	9	12	2	6	3	0	0	68	11	4	2	4.2	.952	OF-14, 1B-3, SS-1, 3B-1, 2B-1
1912		103	.320	.407	359	115	11	4	4	1.1	53	62	9	46	7	17	4	108	45	23	6	1.7	.869	OF-71, 3B-32, 1B-1
1913		18	.237	.289	38	9	2	0	0	0.0	3	3	1	6	0	5	1	19	5	2	0	2.0	.923	OF-13
1914	CLE A	67	.273	.343	242	66	10	2	1	0.4	18	25	7	30	5	7	3	235	15	4	10	4.2	.984	OF-42, 1B-18
1915		87	.310	.395	339	105	19	2	2	0.6	35	40	14	21	5	0	0	886	52	13	37	10.9	.986	1B-87
1918	NY N	17	.250	.268	56	14	1	0	0	0.0	1	3	1	3	0	1	0	165	12	4	7	11.3	.978	1B-16
7 yrs.		320	.301	.385	1148	346	49	13	7	0.6	122	148	35	112	21	30	8	1497	157	53	63	5.5	.969	OF-141, 1B-125, 3B-33, 2B-8, SS-1

Willie Kirkland

KIRKLAND, WILLIE CHARLES BL TR 6′ 1″ 206 lbs.
B. Feb. 17, 1934, Siluria, Ala.

Year	Team	Games	BA	SA	AB	H	2B	3B	HR	HR%	R	RBI	BB	SO	SB	Pinch Hit AB	Pinch Hit H	PO	A	E	DP	TC/G	FA	G by Pos
1958	SF N	122	.258	.447	418	108	25	6	14	3.3	48	56	43	69	3	9	3	187	12	8	4	1.8	.961	OF-115
1959		126	.272	.475	463	126	22	3	22	4.8	64	68	42	84	5	8	2	212	8	7	0	1.9	.969	OF-117
1960		146	.252	.454	515	130	21	10	21	4.1	59	65	44	86	12	5	0	252	16	6	5	1.9	.978	OF-143
1961	CLE A	146	.259	.474	525	136	22	5	27	5.1	84	95	48	77	7	13	2	290	12	8	5	2.2	.974	OF-138
1962		137	.200	.377	419	84	9	1	21	5.0	56	72	43	62	9	13	1	233	11	7	0	2.0	.972	OF-125
1963		127	.230	.375	427	98	13	2	15	3.5	51	47	45	99	8	21	8	234	11	4	2	2.2	.984	OF-112
1964	2 teams	BAL A (66G –.200) WAS A (32G –.216)																						
″	total	98	.206	.345	252	52	11	0	8	3.2	22	35	23	56	3	13	2	125	7	5	3	1.6	.964	OF-85
1965	WAS A	123	.231	.401	312	72	9	1	14	4.5	38	54	19	65	3	35	6	151	3	2	0	1.7	.987	OF-92
1966		124	.190	.325	163	31	2	1	6	3.7	21	17	16	50	2	51	12	56	3	1	0	0.9	.983	OF-68
9 yrs.		1149	.240	.422	3494	837	134	29	148	4.2	443	509	323	648	52	168	36	1740	83	48	19	1.9	.974	OF-995

Ed Kirkpatrick

KIRKPATRICK, EDGAR LEON BL TR 5′11½″ 195 lbs.
B. Oct. 8, 1944, Spokane, Wash.

Year	Team	Games	BA	SA	AB	H	2B	3B	HR	HR%	R	RBI	BB	SO	SB	Pinch Hit AB	Pinch Hit H	PO	A	E	DP	TC/G	FA	G by Pos
1962	LA A	3	.000	.000	6	0	0	0	0	0.0	0	0	0	2	0	2	0	10	0	0	0	10.0	1.000	C-1
1963		34	.195	.338	77	15	5	0	2	2.6	4	7	6	19	1	14	1	82	5	1	1	3.7	.989	C-14, OF-10
1964		75	.242	.356	219	53	13	3	2	0.9	20	22	23	30	2	13	4	90	3	3	0	1.5	.969	OF-63
1965	CAL A	19	.260	.452	73	19	5	0	3	4.1	8	8	3	9	1	0	0	28	3	1	0	1.7	.969	OF-19
1966		117	.192	.327	312	60	7	4	9	2.9	31	44	51	67	7	17	5	169	5	1	1	1.7	.994	OF-102, 1B-3
1967		3	.000	.000	8	0	0	0	0	0.0	0	0	0	2	0	1	0	4	0	0	0	1.3	1.000	C-2, OF-1
1968		89	.230	.273	161	37	4	0	1	0.6	23	15	25	32	1	43	14	62	5	3	1	1.4	.957	OF-45, C-4, 1B-2
1969	KC A	120	.257	.451	315	81	11	4	14	4.4	40	49	43	42	3	34	5	204	13	1	1	2.3	.995	OF-82, C-8, 1B-2, 3B-2, 2B-1
1970		134	.229	.406	424	97	17	2	18	4.2	59	62	55	65	4	21	4	626	70	12	25	5.7	.983	C-89, OF-19, 1B-16
1971		120	.219	.332	365	80	12	1	9	2.5	46	46	48	60	3	9	5	412	30	8	6	3.8	.982	OF-61, C-59
1972		113	.275	.396	364	100	15	1	9	2.5	43	43	51	50	3	5	2	590	49	6	5	5.9	.991	C-108, 1B-1
1973		126	.263	.375	429	113	24	3	6	1.4	61	45	46	48	3	2	0	264	11	4	0	2.1	.986	OF-108, C-14, DH-8
1974	PIT N	116	.247	.347	271	67	9	0	6	2.2	32	38	51	30	1	33	5	561	32	6	55	7.6	.990	1B-59, OF-14, C-6
1975		89	.236	.375	144	34	5	0	5	3.5	15	16	18	22	1	42	13	167	9	0	10	4.2	1.000	1B-28, OF-14
1976		83	.233	.295	146	34	9	0	0	0.0	14	16	14	15	1	40	6	205	17	4	15	6.5	.982	1B-25, OF-9, 3B-1
1977	3 teams	PIT N (21G –.143) TEX A (20G –.188) MIL A (29G –.273)																						
″	total	70	.222	.288	153	34	7	0	1	0.7	15	13	22	25	3	18	7	145	7	4	8	2.9	.974	OF-30, 1B-13, DH-8, 3B-2, C-1
16 yrs.		1311	.238	.363	3467	824	143	18	85	2.5	411	424	456	518	34	294	71	3619	259	54	128	3.7	.986	OF-577, C-306, 1B-149, DH-16, 3B-5, 2B-1

Ed Kirkpatrick *continued*

LEAGUE CHAMPIONSHIP SERIES

Year	Team	Games	BA	SA	AB	H	2B	3B	HR	HR%	R	RBI	BB	SO	SB	Pinch Hit AB	Pinch Hit H	PO	A	E	DP	TC/G	FA	G by Pos
1974	PIT N	3	.000	.000	9	0	0	0	0	0.0	0	0	2	0	0	0	0	22	0	0	2	7.3	1.000	1B-3
1975		2	.000	.000	2	0	0	0	0	0.0	0	0	0	0	0	2	0	0	0	0	0	0.0	—	
2 yrs.		5	.000	.000	11	0	0	0	0	0.0	0	0	2	0	0	2	0	22	0	0	2	7.3	1.000	1B-3

Enos Kirkpatrick

KIRKPATRICK, ENOS CLAIRE BR TR 5′10″ 175 lbs.
B. Dec. 8, 1885, Pittsburgh, Pa. D. Apr. 14, 1964, Pittsburgh, Pa.

Year	Team	Games	BA	SA	AB	H	2B	3B	HR	HR%	R	RBI	BB	SO	SB	Pinch Hit AB	Pinch Hit H	PO	A	E	DP	TC/G	FA	G by Pos
1912	BKN N	32	.191	.223	94	18	1	1	0	0.0	13	6	9	15	5	1	0	29	67	4	3	3.1	.960	3B-29, SS-3
1913		48	.247	.348	89	22	4	1	1	1.1	13	5	3	18	5	13	2	110	36	7	6	5.5	.954	SS-10, 1B-8, 2B-6, 3B-4
1914	BAL F	55	.253	.351	174	44	7	2	2	1.1	22	16	18		10	2	1	47	88	11	3	2.9	.925	3B-36, SS-11, OF-3, 1B-1
1915		68	.240	.310	171	41	8	2	0	0.0	22	19	24		12	5	1	101	108	20	11	3.9	.913	3B-28, 2B-21, SS-5, 1B-5
4 yrs.		203	.237	.314	528	125	20	6	3	0.6	70	46	54	33	32	21	4	287	299	42	23	3.7	.933	3B-97, SS-29, 2B-27, 1B-14, OF-3

Joe Kirrene

KIRRENE, JOSEPH JOHN BR TR 6′2″ 195 lbs.
B. Oct. 4, 1931, San Francisco, Calif.

Year	Team	Games	BA	SA	AB	H	2B	3B	HR	HR%	R	RBI	BB	SO	SB	Pinch Hit AB	Pinch Hit H	PO	A	E	DP	TC/G	FA	G by Pos
1950	CHI A	1	.250	.250	4	1	0	0	0	0.0	0	0	0	1	0	0	0	1	1	0	0	2.0	1.000	3B-1
1954		9	.304	.348	23	7	1	0	0	0.0	4	4	5	2	1	1	0	7	11	1	2	2.1	.947	3B-9
2 yrs.		10	.296	.333	27	8	1	0	0	0.0	4	4	5	3	1	1	0	8	12	1	2	2.1	.952	3B-10

Ernie Kish

KISH, ERNEST ALEXANDER BL TR 5′9½″ 170 lbs.
B. Feb. 6, 1918, Washington, D. C. D. Dec. 21, 1993, Kirtland, Ohio.

Year	Team	Games	BA	SA	AB	H	2B	3B	HR	HR%	R	RBI	BB	SO	SB	Pinch Hit AB	Pinch Hit H	PO	A	E	DP	TC/G	FA	G by Pos
1945	PHI A	43	.245	.309	110	27	5	1	0	0.0	10	10	9	9	0	9	2	52	3	4	0	2.0	.932	OF-30

Frank Kitson

KITSON, FRANK R. BL TR 5′11″ 165 lbs.
B. Sept. 11, 1869, Hopkins, Mich. D. Apr. 14, 1930, Allegan, Mich.

Year	Team	Games	BA	SA	AB	H	2B	3B	HR	HR%	R	RBI	BB	SO	SB	Pinch Hit AB	Pinch Hit H	PO	A	E	DP	TC/G	FA	G by Pos
1898	BAL N	31	.314	.395	86	27	1	3	0	0.0	13	16	5		2	3	2	16	33	6	0	2.0	.891	P-17, OF-11
1899		45	.201	.269	134	27	7	1	0	0.0	13	8	6		7	4	0	12	69	2	1	2.1	.976	P-40
1900	BKN N	43	.294	.358	109	32	5	1	0	0.0	20	16	6		2	2	0	13	39	5	0	1.4	.912	P-40, OF-1
1901		47	.263	.353	133	35	5	2	1	0.8	22	16	4		0	6	2	19	56	4	2	1.9	.949	P-38, OF-2, 1B-1
1902		39	.265	.389	113	30	3	4	1	0.9	9	11	3		0	7	**3**	7	69	3	1	2.5	.962	P-31
1903	DET A	36	.181	.216	116	21	0	2	0	0.0	12	4	2		2	0	0	15	69	3	0	2.4	.966	P-31, OF-5
1904		27	.208	.250	72	15	0	0	1	1.4	9	4	1		0	1	0	6	68	4	2	3.0	.949	P-26
1905		33	.184	.207	87	16	2	0	0	0.0	8	4	3		0	0	0	5	65	7	0	2.3	.909	P-33
1906	WAS A	31	.244	.411	90	22	4	4	1	1.1	9	12	8		1	1	0	5	62	3	1	2.3	.957	P-30
1907	2 teams	WAS A (5G –.125) NY A (12G –.261)																						
″	total	17	.226	.226	31	7	0	0	0	0.0	4	4	1		0	0	0	4	21	3	0	1.8	.893	P-16
10 yrs.		349	.239	.314	971	232	27	17	4	0.4	119	95	39		14	24	7	102	551	40	7	2.2	.942	P-302, OF-19, 1B-1

Chris Kitsos

KITSOS, CHRISTOPHER ANESTOS BB TR 5′9″ 165 lbs.
B. Feb. 11, 1928, New York, N. Y.

Year	Team	Games	BA	SA	AB	H	2B	3B	HR	HR%	R	RBI	BB	SO	SB	Pinch Hit AB	Pinch Hit H	PO	A	E	DP	TC/G	FA	G by Pos
1954	CHI N	1	—	—	0	0	0	0	0	—	0	0	0	0	0	0	0	0	2	0	0	2.0	1.000	SS-1

Ron Kittle

KITTLE, RONALD DALE (Kitty) BR TR 6′4″ 200 lbs.
B. Jan. 5, 1958, Gary, Ind.

Year	Team	Games	BA	SA	AB	H	2B	3B	HR	HR%	R	RBI	BB	SO	SB	Pinch Hit AB	Pinch Hit H	PO	A	E	DP	TC/G	FA	G by Pos
1982	CHI A	20	.241	.414	29	7	2	0	1	3.4	3	7	3	12	0	13	2	3	0	0	0	0.4	1.000	OF-5, DH-3
1983		145	.254	.504	520	132	19	3	35	**6.7**	75	100	39	**150**	8	6	0	234	7	9	0	1.8	.964	OF-139, DH-2
1984		139	.215	.453	466	100	15	0	32	**6.9**	67	74	49	137	3	13	4	226	14	7	2	1.9	.972	OF-124, DH-7
1985		116	.230	.467	379	87	12	0	26	6.9	51	58	31	92	1	9	0	88	2	1	1	0.8	.989	OF-57, DH-57
1986	2 teams	CHI A (86G –.213) NY A (30G –.237)																						
″	total	116	.218	.420	376	82	13	0	21	5.6	42	60	35	110	4	12	2	39	3	0	0	0.4	1.000	DH-86, OF-21
1987	NY A	59	.277	.535	159	44	5	0	12	7.5	21	28	10	36	0	13	1	4	1	0	0	0.1	1.000	DH-49, OF-2
1988	CLE A	75	.258	.533	225	58	8	0	18	8.0	31	43	16	65	0	13	5	0	0	0	0	0.0	.000	DH-63
1989	CHI A	51	.302	.556	169	51	10	0	11	6.5	26	37	22	42	0	3	1	216	12	4	28	4.7	.983	1B-27, DH-17, OF-5
1990	2 teams	CHI A (83G –.245) BAL A (22G –.164)																						
″	total	105	.231	.438	338	78	16	0	18	5.3	33	46	26	91	0	14	4	176	6	2	19	1.9	.989	DH-67, 1B-30
1991	CHI A	17	.191	.319	47	9	0	0	2	4.3	7	7	5	9	0	2	0	101	6	2	8	7.3	.982	1B-15
10 yrs.		843	.239	.473	2708	648	100	3	176	6.5	356	460	236	744	16	98	19	1087	51	25	58	1.5	.979	OF-353, DH-351, 1B-72

LEAGUE CHAMPIONSHIP SERIES

Year	Team	Games	BA	SA	AB	H	2B	3B	HR	HR%	R	RBI	BB	SO	SB	Pinch Hit AB	Pinch Hit H	PO	A	E	DP	TC/G	FA	G by Pos
1983	CHI A	3	.286	.429	7	2	1	0	0	0.0	1	0	1	2	0	0	0	0	0	0	0	0.0	.000	OF-3

Mal Kittridge

KITTRIDGE, MALACHI JEDDIDAH BR TR 5′7″ 170 lbs.
B. Oct. 12, 1869, Clinton, Mass. D. June 23, 1928, Gary, Ind.
Manager 1904.

Year	Team	Games	BA	SA	AB	H	2B	3B	HR	HR%	R	RBI	BB	SO	SB	Pinch Hit AB	Pinch Hit H	PO	A	E	DP	TC/G	FA	G by Pos
1890	CHI N	96	.201	.270	333	67	8	3	3	0.9	46	35	39	53	7	0	0	458	113	34	9	6.3	.944	C-96
1891		79	.209	.291	296	62	8	5	2	0.7	26	27	17	28	4	0	0	384	87	30	5	6.3	.940	C-79
1892		69	.179	.201	229	41	5	0	0	0.0	19	10	11	27	2	0	0	359	87	26	5	6.8	.945	C-69
1893		70	.231	.329	255	59	9	5	2	0.8	32	30	17	15	3	0	0	260	81	22	4	5.2	.939	C-70
1894		51	.315	.387	168	53	8	2	0	0.0	36	23	26	20	2	0	0	209	36	20	4	5.2	.925	C-51
1895		60	.226	.325	212	48	6	3	3	1.4	30	29	16	9	6	0	0	197	48	6	4	4.3	.976	C-59
1896		65	.223	.265	215	48	4	1	1	0.5	17	19	14	14	6	0	0	251	56	12	12	4.9	.962	C-64, P-1
1897		79	.202	.271	262	53	5	5	1	0.4	25	30	22		9	0	0	324	75	20	6	5.3	.952	C-79
1898	LOU N	86	.244	.317	287	70	8	5	1	0.3	27	31	15		9	0	0	258	80	20	10	4.2	.944	C-86
1899	2 teams	LOU N (45G –.202) WAS N (44G –.150)																						
″	total	89	.176	.202	262	46	5	1	0	0.0	25	23	36		5	3	1	280	117	16	9	4.8	.961	C-86
1901	BOS N	114	.252	.304	381	96	14	0	2	0.5	24	40	32		2	0	0	581	136	12	7	6.5	.984	C-113
1902		80	.235	.286	255	60	7	0	2	0.8	18	30	24		4	7	1	363	99	9	5	6.5	.981	C-72
1903	2 teams	BOS N (32G –.212) WAS A (60G –.214)																						
″	total	92	.213	.241	291	62	6	1	0	0.0	18	22	21		2	2	0	398	118	11	7	5.9	.979	C-90

Mal Kittridge *continued*

Year	Team	Games	BA	SA	AB	H	2B	3B	HR	HR%	R	RBI	BB	SO	SB	Pinch Hit AB	Pinch Hit H	PO	A	E	DP	TC/G	FA	G by Pos
1904	**WAS A**	81	.242	.268	265	64	7	0	0	0.0	11	24	8		2	2	0	346	99	8	4	5.7	.982	C-79
1905		76	.164	.197	238	39	8	0	0	0.0	13	14	15		1	0	0	323	113	10	8	5.9	.978	C-75
1906	**2 teams**	**WAS A** (27G –.179) **CLE A** (1G –.000)																						
″	**total**	28	.173	.173	81	14	0	0	0	0.0	5	3	1		0	0	0	124	18	7	1	5.3	.953	C-28
16 yrs.		1215	.219	.274	4030	882	108	31	17	0.4	372	390	314	166	64	14	2	5115	1363	263	100	5.6	.961	C-1196, P-1

Billy Klaus

KLAUS, WILLIAM JOSEPH BL TR 5′ 9″ 160 lbs.
Brother of Bobby Klaus.
B. Dec. 9, 1928, Fox Lake, Ill.

Year	Team	Games	BA	SA	AB	H	2B	3B	HR	HR%	R	RBI	BB	SO	SB	Pinch Hit AB	Pinch Hit H	PO	A	E	DP	TC/G	FA	G by Pos
1952	**BOS N**	7	.000	.000	4	0	0	0	0	0.0	3	0	1	1	0	3	0	1	0	1	0	0.5	.500	SS-4
1953	**MIL N**	2	.000	.000	2	0	0	0	0	0.0	1	1	0	0	0	2	0	0	0	0	0	0.0	—	
1955	**BOS A**	135	.283	.377	541	153	26	2	7	1.3	83	60	60	44	6	2	0	214	411	31	55	4.9	.953	SS-126, 3B-8
1956		135	.271	.387	520	141	29	5	7	1.3	91	59	90	43	1	5	1	155	306	27	26	3.7	.945	3B-106, SS-26
1957		127	.252	.369	477	120	18	4	10	2.1	76	42	55	53	2	8	2	204	417	25	93	5.5	.961	SS-118
1958		61	.159	.239	88	14	4	0	1	1.1	5	7	5	16	0	39	6	18	35	7	2	2.2	.883	SS-27
1959	**BAL A**	104	.249	.312	321	80	11	0	3	0.9	33	25	51	38	2	4	0	120	231	13	28	3.3	.964	SS-59, 3B-49, 2B-1
1960		46	.209	.326	43	9	2	0	1	2.3	8	6	9	9	0	3	0	29	52	2	14	1.9	.976	2B-30, SS-12, 3B-2
1961	**WAS A**	91	.227	.359	251	57	8	2	7	2.8	26	30	30	34	2	18	3	64	155	8	11	3.2	.965	3B-51, SS-18, OF-1, 2B-1
1962	**PHI N**	102	.206	.302	248	51	8	2	4	1.6	30	20	29	43	1	28	5	93	142	9	21	2.6	.963	3B-53, SS-30, 2B-11
1963		11	.056	.056	18	1	0	0	0	0.0	1	0	1	4	0	8	1	1	7	0	1	1.0	1.000	SS-5, 3B-3
11 yrs.		821	.249	.351	2513	626	106	15	40	1.6	357	250	331	285	14	120	18	899	1756	123	251	3.7	.956	SS-425, 3B-272, 2B-43, OF-1

Bobby Klaus

KLAUS, ROBERT FRANCIS BR TR 5′10″ 170 lbs.
Brother of Billy Klaus.
B. Dec. 27, 1937, Spring Grove, Ill.

Year	Team	Games	BA	SA	AB	H	2B	3B	HR	HR%	R	RBI	BB	SO	SB	Pinch Hit AB	Pinch Hit H	PO	A	E	DP	TC/G	FA	G by Pos
1964	**2 teams**	**CIN N** (40G –.183) **NY N** (56G –.244)																						
″	**total**	96	.225	.334	302	68	13	4	4	1.3	35	17	29	43	4	7	0	127	186	10	22	3.6	.969	2B-43, 3B-39, SS-8
1965	**NY N**	119	.191	.253	288	55	12	0	2	0.7	30	12	45	49	1	4	1	179	254	11	54	3.6	.975	2B-72, SS-28, 3B-25
2 yrs.		215	.208	.295	590	123	25	4	6	1.0	65	29	74	92	5	11	1	306	440	21	76	3.6	.973	2B-115, 3B-64, SS-36

Ollie Klee

KLEE, OLLIE CHESTER (Babe) BL TL 5′ 9½″ 160 lbs.
B. May 20, 1900, Piqua, Ohio D. Feb. 9, 1977, Toledo, Ohio.

Year	Team	Games	BA	SA	AB	H	2B	3B	HR	HR%	R	RBI	BB	SO	SB	Pinch Hit AB	Pinch Hit H	PO	A	E	DP	TC/G	FA	G by Pos
1925	**CIN N**	3	.000	.000	1	0	0	0	0	0.0	0	0	0	1	0	0	0	0	0	0	0	0.0	.000	OF-1

Chuck Klein

KLEIN, CHARLES HERBERT BL TR 6′ 185 lbs.
B. Oct. 7, 1904, Indianapolis, Ind. D. Mar. 28, 1958, Indianapolis, Ind.
Hall of Fame 1980.

Year	Team	Games	BA	SA	AB	H	2B	3B	HR	HR%	R	RBI	BB	SO	SB	Pinch Hit AB	Pinch Hit H	PO	A	E	DP	TC/G	FA	G by Pos
1928	**PHI N**	64	.360	.577	253	91	14	4	11	4.3	41	34	14	22	0	1	0	128	7	3	0	2.2	.978	OF-63
1929		149	.356	.657	616	219	45	6	**43**	7.0	126	145	54	61	5	0	0	321	18	12	3	2.4	.966	OF-149
1930		156	.386	.687	648	250	**59**	8	40	6.2	**158**	170	54	50	4	0	0	362	44	17	10	2.7	.960	OF-156
1931		148	.337	**.584**	594	200	34	10	**31**	5.2	**121**	**121**	59	49	7	0	0	292	13	9	0	2.1	.971	OF-148
1932		154	.348	**.646**	650	**226**	50	15	**38**	5.8	**152**	137	60	49	**20**	0	0	331	29	15	3	2.4	.960	OF-154
1933		152	**.368**	**.602**	606	**223**	**44**	7	**28**	4.6	101	**120**	56	36	15	0	0	339	21	5	5	2.4	.986	OF-152
1934	**CHI N**	115	.301	.510	435	131	27	2	20	4.6	78	80	47	38	3	5	2	222	6	9	2	2.2	.962	OF-110
1935		119	.293	.488	434	127	14	4	21	4.8	71	73	41	42	4	6	1	215	11	10	7	2.1	.958	OF-111
1936	**2 teams**	**CHI N** (29G –.294) **PHI N** (117G –.309)																						
″	**total**	146	.306	.512	601	184	35	7	25	4.2	102	105	49	59	6	0	0	276	16	23	2	2.2	.927	OF-146
1937	**PHI N**	115	.325	.495	406	132	20	2	15	3.7	74	57	39	21	3	13	3	175	11	10	3	1.9	.949	OF-102
1938		129	.247	.356	458	113	22	2	8	1.7	53	61	38	30	7	10	1	229	8	10	1	2.1	.960	OF-119
1939	**2 teams**	**PHI N** (25G –.191) **PIT N** (85G –.300)																						
″	**total**	110	.284	.486	317	90	18	5	12	3.8	45	56	36	21	2	26	**11**	153	5	7	1	2.1	.958	OF-77, 1B-1
1940	**PHI N**	116	.218	.333	354	77	16	2	7	2.0	39	37	44	30	2	18	2	180	4	3	2	1.6	.984	OF-116
1941		50	.123	.164	73	9	0	0	1	1.4	6	3	10	6	0	31	5	22	1	1	0	1.7	.958	OF-14
1942		14	.071	.071	14	1	0	0	0	0.0	0	0	0	2	0	14	1	0	0	0	0	0.0	—	
1943		12	.100	.100	20	2	0	0	0	0.0	0	3	0	3	1	10	1	0	0	1	0	0.5	.000	OF-2
1944		4	.143	.143	7	1	0	0	0	0.0	1	0	0	2	0	3	1	5	0	0	0	5.0	1.000	OF-1
17 yrs.		1753	.320	.543	6486	2076	398	74	300	4.6	1168	1202	601	521	79	137	28	3250	194	135	39	2.2	.962	OF-1620, 1B-1
WORLD SERIES																								
1935	**CHI N**	5	.333	.583	12	4	0	0	1	8.3	2	2	0	2	0	3	1	4	0	0	0	1.3	1.000	OF-3

Lou Klein

KLEIN, LOUIS FRANK BR TR 5′11″ 167 lbs.
B. Oct. 22, 1918, New Orleans, La. D. June 20, 1976, Metairie, La.
Manager 1961–62, 1965.

Year	Team	Games	BA	SA	AB	H	2B	3B	HR	HR%	R	RBI	BB	SO	SB	Pinch Hit AB	Pinch Hit H	PO	A	E	DP	TC/G	FA	G by Pos
1943	**STL N**	154	.287	.410	627	180	28	14	7	1.1	91	62	50	70	9	0	0	356	444	27	118	4.7	.967	2B-126, SS-51
1945		19	.228	.386	57	13	4	1	1	1.8	12	6	14	9	0	0	0	38	23	3	4	3.2	.953	SS-7, OF-7, 3B-4, 2B-2
1946		23	.194	.258	93	18	3	0	1	1.1	12	4	9	7	1	0	0	58	60	3	18	5.3	.975	2B-23
1949		58	.219	.325	114	25	6	0	2	1.8	25	12	22	20	0	18	3	33	85	11	10	3.5	.915	SS-21, 2B-9, 3B-7
1951	**2 teams**	**CLE A** (2G –.000) **PHI A** (49G –.229)																						
″	**total**	51	.226	.377	146	33	7	0	5	3.4	22	17	10	13	0	9	0	85	107	5	32	4.7	.975	2B-42
5 yrs.		305	.259	.381	1037	269	48	15	16	1.5	162	101	105	119	10	27	3	570	719	49	182	4.5	.963	2B-202, SS-79, 3B-11, OF-7
WORLD SERIES																								
1943	**STL N**	5	.136	.136	22	3	0	0	0	0.0	0	0	1	2	0	0	0	10	13	2	4	5.0	.920	2B-5

Red Kleinow

KLEINOW, JOHN PETER BR TR 5′10″ 165 lbs.
B. July 20, 1879, Milwaukee, Wis. D. Oct. 9, 1929, New York, N. Y.

Year	Team	Games	BA	SA	AB	H	2B	3B	HR	HR%	R	RBI	BB	SO	SB	Pinch Hit AB	Pinch Hit H	PO	A	E	DP	TC/G	FA	G by Pos
1904	**NY A**	68	.206	.282	209	43	8	4	0	0.0	12	16	15		4	2	0	278	71	12	5	5.6	.967	C-62, 3B-2, OF-1
1905		88	.221	.281	253	56	6	3	1	0.4	23	24	20		7	2	0	389	85	11	4	5.6	.977	C-83, 1B-3
1906		96	.220	.276	268	59	9	3	0	0.0	30	31	24		8	0	0	382	102	14	8	5.2	.972	C-95, 1B-1
1907		90	.264	.316	269	71	6	4	0	0.0	30	26	24		5	3	0	326	97	14	5	5.0	.968	C-86, 1B-1
1908		96	.168	.204	279	47	3	2	1	0.4	16	13	22		5	5	2	283	118	15	5	4.6	.964	C-89, 2B-2

Red Kleinow *continued*

Year	Team	Games	BA	SA	AB	H	2B	3B	HR	HR%	R	RBI	BB	SO	SB	Pinch Hit AB	Pinch Hit H	PO	A	E	DP	TC/G	FA	G by Pos
1909		78	.228	.320	206	47	11	4	0	0.0	24	15	25		7	1	0	343	83	15	6	5.7	.966	C-77
1910	**2 teams**	**NY A** (6G –.417) **BOS A** (50G –.150)																						
"	**total**	56	.170	.195	159	27	1	0	1	0.6	11	10	21		5	3	0	285	69	11	12	6.8	.970	C-54
1911	**2 teams**	**BOS A** (8G –.214) **PHI N** (4G –.125)																						
"	**total**	12	.182	.227	22	4	1	0	0	0.0	0	0	2	1	1	0	0	32	11	0	0	3.6	1.000	C-12
8 yrs.		584	.213	.269	1665	354	45	20	3	0.2	146	135	153	1	42	16	2	2318	636	92	45	5.4	.970	C-558, 1B-5, 3B-2, 2B-2, OF-1

Ryan Klesko

KLESKO, RYAN ANTHONY BL TL 6′ 3″ 220 lbs.
B. June 12, 1971, Westminster, Calif.

Year	Team	Games	BA	SA	AB	H	2B	3B	HR	HR%	R	RBI	BB	SO	SB	Pinch Hit AB	Pinch Hit H	PO	A	E	DP	TC/G	FA	G by Pos
1992	**ATL N**	13	.000	.000	14	0	0	0	0	0.0	0	1	0	5	0	7	0	25	0	0	2	5.0	1.000	1B-5
1993		22	.353	.765	17	6	1	0	2	11.8	3	5	3	4	0	15	6	8	0	0	0	1.6	1.000	1B-3, OF-2
1994		92	.278	.563	245	68	13	3	17	6.9	42	47	26	48	1	14	3	89	3	7	1	1.2	.929	OF-74, 1B-6
1995		107	.310	.608	329	102	25	2	23	7.0	48	70	47	72	5	6	2	131	4	8	0	1.3	.944	OF-102, 1B-4
4 yrs.		234	.291	.580	605	176	39	5	42	6.9	93	123	76	129	6	42	11	253	7	15	3	1.4	.945	OF-178, 1B-18
DIVISIONAL PLAYOFF SERIES																								
1995	**ATL N**	4	.467	.533	15	7	1	0	0	0.0	5	1	0	3	0	0	0	3	0	0	0	0.8	1.000	OF-4
LEAGUE CHAMPIONSHIP SERIES																								
1995	**ATL N**	4	.000	.000	7	0	0	0	0	0.0	0	0	3	4	0	2	0	1	0	0	0	0.3	1.000	OF-3
WORLD SERIES																								
1995	**ATL N**	6	.313	.875	16	5	0	0	3	18.8	4	4	3	4	0	0	0	1	0	0	0	0.2	1.000	OF-3, DH-3

Jay Kleven

KLEVEN, JAY ALLEN BR TR 6′ 2″ 190 lbs.
B. Dec. 2, 1949, Oakland, Calif.

Year	Team	Games	BA	SA	AB	H	2B	3B	HR	HR%	R	RBI	BB	SO	SB	Pinch Hit AB	Pinch Hit H	PO	A	E	DP	TC/G	FA	G by Pos
1976	**NY N**	2	.200	.200	5	1	0	0	0	0.0	0	2	0	1	0	0	0	10	0	0	0	5.0	1.000	C-2

Lou Klimchock

KLIMCHOCK, LOUIS STEPHEN BL TR 5′11″ 180 lbs.
B. Oct. 15, 1939, Hostetter, Pa.

Year	Team	Games	BA	SA	AB	H	2B	3B	HR	HR%	R	RBI	BB	SO	SB	Pinch Hit AB	Pinch Hit H	PO	A	E	DP	TC/G	FA	G by Pos
1958	**KC A**	2	.200	.500	10	2	0	0	1	10.0	2	1	0	1	0	0	0	2	6	0	1	4.0	1.000	2B-2
1959		17	.273	.470	66	18	1	0	4	6.1	10	13	1	6	0	1	0	34	41	4	11	4.9	.949	2B-16
1960		10	.300	.300	10	3	0	0	0	0.0	0	0	0	0	0	9	2	0	0	0	0	0.0	.000	2B-1
1961		57	.215	.289	121	26	4	1	1	0.8	8	16	5	13	0	32	6	92	11	6	4	4.4	.945	1B-11, OF-7, 3B-6, 2B-1
1962	**MIL N**	8	.000	.000	8	0	0	0	0	0.0	0	0	0	2	0	8	0	0	0	0	0	0.0	—	
1963	**2 teams**	**WAS A** (9G –.143) **MIL N** (24G –.196)																						
"	**total**	33	.183	.200	60	11	1	0	0	0.0	7	3	0	13	0	20	3	79	15	1	12	6.3	.989	1B-12, 2B-3
1964	**MIL N**	10	.333	.429	21	7	2	0	0	0.0	3	2	1	2	0	5	2	3	4	0	0	1.2	1.000	3B-4, 2B-2
1965		34	.077	.077	39	3	0	0	0	0.0	3	3	2	8	0	29	2	20	4	2	0	6.5	.923	1B-4
1966	**NY N**	5	.000	.000	5	0	0	0	0	0.0	0	0	0	3	0	5	0	0	0	0	0	0.0	—	
1968	**CLE A**	11	.133	.133	15	2	0	0	0	0.0	0	3	1	0	0	7	0	1	2	2	0	0.8	.600	3B-4, 1B-1, 2B-1
1969		90	.287	.422	258	74	13	2	6	2.3	26	26	18	14	0	15	2	83	116	10	15	2.7	.952	3B-56, 2B-21, C-1
1970		41	.161	.214	56	9	0	0	1	1.8	5	2	3	9	0	30	4	39	9	0	6	4.8	1.000	2B-5, 1B-5
12 yrs.		318	.232	.330	669	155	21	3	13	1.9	64	69	31	71	0	161	21	353	208	25	49	3.6	.957	3B-70, 2B-52, 1B-33, OF-7, C-1

Bobby Kline

KLINE, JOHN ROBERT BR TR 6′ 179 lbs.
B. Jan. 27, 1929, St. Petersburg, Fla.

Year	Team	Games	BA	SA	AB	H	2B	3B	HR	HR%	R	RBI	BB	SO	SB	Pinch Hit AB	Pinch Hit H	PO	A	E	DP	TC/G	FA	G by Pos
1955	**WAS A**	77	.221	.257	140	31	5	0	0	0.0	12	9	11	27	0	0	0	107	164	16	38	3.7	.944	SS-69, 2B-4, 3B-3, P-1

Johnny Kling

KLING, JOHN (Noisy) BR TR 5′ 9½″ 160 lbs.
Brother of Bill Kling.
B. Feb. 25, 1875, Kansas City, Mo. D. Jan. 31, 1947, Kansas City, Mo.
Manager 1912.

Year	Team	Games	BA	SA	AB	H	2B	3B	HR	HR%	R	RBI	BB	SO	SB	Pinch Hit AB	Pinch Hit H	PO	A	E	DP	TC/G	FA	G by Pos
1900	**CHI N**	15	.294	.392	51	15	3	1	0	0.0	8	7	2		0	0	0	49	15	7	2	4.7	.901	C-15
1901		74	.277	.324	253	70	6	3	0	0.0	26	21	9		7	4	1	328	75	21	7	6.0	.950	C-69, OF-1, 1B-1
1902		114	.286	.343	434	124	19	3	0	0.0	50	57	29		23	1	0	472	160	19	17	5.8	.971	C-112, SS-1
1903		132	.297	.428	491	146	29	13	3	0.6	67	68	22		23	0	0	565	189	24	13	5.9	.969	C-132
1904		123	.243	.296	452	110	18	0	2	0.4	41	46	16		7	2	0	560	135	20	8	6.0	.972	C-104, OF-10, 1B-6
1905		111	.218	.279	380	83	8	6	1	0.3	26	52	28		13	1	0	549	137	24	12	6.4	.966	C-106, OF-4, 1B-1
1906		107	.312	.420	343	107	15	8	2	0.6	45	46	23		14	7	2	520	127	12	7	6.7	.982	C-96, OF-3
1907		104	.284	.386	334	95	15	8	1	0.3	44	43	27		9	3	0	509	111	8	12	6.3	.987	C-98, 1B-2
1908		126	.276	.382	424	117	23	5	4	0.9	51	59	21		16	2	0	607	153	17	12	6.2	.978	C-117, OF-6, 1B-2
1910		91	.269	.360	297	80	17	2	2	0.7	31	32	37	27	3	4	0	407	118	11	10	6.2	.979	C-86
1911	**2 teams**	**CHI N** (27G –.175) **BOS N** (75G –.224)																						
"	**total**	102	.212	.293	321	68	11	3	3	0.9	40	29	38	43	1	4	1	424	140	26	8	6.1	.956	C-96, 3B-1
1912	**BOS N**	81	.317	.405	252	80	10	3	2	0.8	26	30	15	30	3	7	2	322	108	19	20	6.1	.958	C-74
1913	**CIN N**	80	.273	.364	209	57	7	6	0	0.0	20	23	14	14	2	15	3	259	94	9	3	5.7	.975	C-63
13 yrs.		1260	.272	.357	4241	1152	181	61	20	0.5	475	513	281	114	121	50	9	5571	1562	217	131	6.1	.970	C-1168, OF-24, 1B-12, 3B-1, SS-1
WORLD SERIES																								
1906	**CHI N**	6	.176	.235	17	3	1	0	0	0.0	2	0	4	3	0	0	0	46	10	1	3	9.5	.982	C-6
1907		5	.211	.211	19	4	0	0	0	0.0	2	1	1	4	0	0	0	25	9	1	0	7.0	.971	C-5
1908		5	.250	.313	16	4	1	0	0	0.0	2	1	2	2	0	0	0	32	6	0	1	7.6	1.000	C-5
1910		5	.077	.077	13	1	0	0	0	0.0	0	1	1	2	0	2	0	11	7	0	0	6.0	1.000	C-3
4 yrs.		21	.185	.215	65	12	2	0	0	0.0	6	3	8	11	0	2	0	114	32	2	4	7.8	.986	C-19

Rudy Kling

KLING, RUDOLPH A. BR TR 5′10″ 178 lbs.
B. Mar. 23, 1870, St. Louis, Mo. D. Mar. 14, 1937, St. Louis, Mo.

Year	Team	Games	BA	SA	AB	H	2B	3B	HR	HR%	R	RBI	BB	SO	SB	Pinch Hit AB	Pinch Hit H	PO	A	E	DP	TC/G	FA	G by Pos
1902	**STL N**	4	.200	.200	10	2	0	0	0	0.0	1	0	4		1	0	0	9	7	3	2	4.8	.842	SS-4

Joe Klinger

KLINGER, JOSEPH JOHN BR TR 6′ 190 lbs.
B. Aug. 2, 1902, Canonsburg, Pa. D. July 31, 1960, Little Rock, Ark.

Year	Team	Games	BA	SA	AB	H	2B	3B	HR	HR%	R	RBI	BB	SO	SB	Pinch Hit AB	Pinch Hit H	PO	A	E	DP	TC/G	FA	G by Pos
1927	**NY N**	3	.400	.400	5	2	0	0	0	0.0	0	0	0	2	0	2	0	3	0	0	0	3.0	1.000	OF-1
1930	**CHI A**	4	.375	.375	8	3	0	0	0	0.0	0	1	0	0	0	0	0	14	0	0	2	3.5	1.000	1B-2, C-2
2 yrs.		7	.385	.385	13	5	0	0	0	0.0	0	1	0	2	0	2	0	17	0	0	2	3.4	1.000	C-2, 1B-2, OF-1

Nap Kloza

KLOZA, JOHN CLARENCE BR TR 5′11″ 180 lbs.
B. Sept. 7, 1903, Milwaukee, Wis. D. June 11, 1962, Milwaukee, Wis.

Year	Team	Games	BA	SA	AB	H	2B	3B	HR	HR%	R	RBI	BB	SO	SB	Pinch Hit AB	Pinch Hit H	PO	A	E	DP	TC/G	FA	G by Pos
1931	STL A	3	.143	.143	7	1	0	0	0	0.0	1	0	1	4	0	0	0	1	1	0	0	0.7	1.000	OF-3
1932		19	.154	.308	13	2	0	1	0	0.0	4	2	4	4	0	10	1	2	0	0	0	0.7	1.000	OF-3
2 yrs.		22	.150	.250	20	3	0	1	0	0.0	5	2	5	8	0	10	1	3	1	0	0	0.7	1.000	OF-6

Joe Klugmann

KLUGMANN, JOE BR TR 5′11″ 175 lbs.
B. Mar. 26, 1895, St. Louis, Mo. D. July 18, 1951, Moberly, Mo.

Year	Team	Games	BA	SA	AB	H	2B	3B	HR	HR%	R	RBI	BB	SO	SB	Pinch Hit AB	Pinch Hit H	PO	A	E	DP	TC/G	FA	G by Pos
1921	CHI N	6	.286	.286	21	6	0	0	0	0.0	3	2	1	2	0	1	1	15	16	1	1	6.4	.969	2B-5
1922		2	.000	.000	2	0	0	0	0	0.0	0	0	0	0	0	0	0	2	3	0	1	2.5	1.000	2B-2
1924	BKN N	31	.165	.215	79	13	2	1	0	0.0	7	3	2	9	0	1	0	52	65	9	14	4.3	.929	2B-28, SS-1
1925	CLE A	38	.329	.482	85	28	9	2	0	0.0	12	12	8	4	3	3	1	64	67	7	10	3.9	.949	2B-29, 1B-4, 3B-2
4 yrs.		77	.251	.342	187	47	11	3	0	0.0	22	17	11	15	3	5	2	133	151	17	26	4.2	.944	2B-64, 1B-4, 3B-2, SS-1

Elmer Klumpp

KLUMPP, ELMER EDWARD BR TR 6′ 184 lbs.
B. Aug. 26, 1906, St. Louis, Mo.

Year	Team	Games	BA	SA	AB	H	2B	3B	HR	HR%	R	RBI	BB	SO	SB	Pinch Hit AB	Pinch Hit H	PO	A	E	DP	TC/G	FA	G by Pos
1934	WAS A	12	.133	.133	15	2	0	0	0	0.0	2	0	0	1	0	1	0	15	1	2	0	1.6	.889	C-11
1937	BKN N	5	.091	.091	11	1	0	0	0	0.0	0	2	1	4	0	1	0	16	1	0	0	5.7	1.000	C-3
2 yrs.		17	.115	.115	26	3	0	0	0	0.0	2	2	1	5	0	2	0	31	2	2	0	2.5	.943	C-14

Billy Klusman

KLUSMAN, WILLIAM F. BR TR 5′10½″ 185 lbs.
B. Mar. 24, 1865, Cincinnati, Ohio D. June 24, 1907, Cincinnati, Ohio.

Year	Team	Games	BA	SA	AB	H	2B	3B	HR	HR%	R	RBI	BB	SO	SB	Pinch Hit AB	Pinch Hit H	PO	A	E	DP	TC/G	FA	G by Pos
1888	BOS N	28	.168	.262	107	18	4	0	2	1.9	9	11	5	13	3	0	0	63	75	13	6	5.4	.914	2B-28
1890	STL AA	15	.277	.415	65	18	4	1	1	1.5	9		1		1	0	0	16	44	7	3	4.5	.896	2B-15
2 yrs.		43	.209	.320	172	36	8	1	3	1.7	18	11	6	13	4	0	0	79	119	20	9	5.1	.908	2B-43

Ted Kluszewski

KLUSZEWSKI, THEODORE BERNARD (Klu) BL TL 6′ 2″ 225 lbs.
B. Sept. 10, 1924, Argo, Ill. D. Mar. 29, 1988, Cincinnati, Ohio.

Year	Team	Games	BA	SA	AB	H	2B	3B	HR	HR%	R	RBI	BB	SO	SB	Pinch Hit AB	Pinch Hit H	PO	A	E	DP	TC/G	FA	G by Pos
1947	CIN N	9	.100	.100	10	1	0	0	0	0.0	1	2	1	2	0	5	0	10	0	0	1	5.0	1.000	1B-2
1948		113	.274	.451	379	104	23	4	12	3.2	49	57	18	32	1	15	5	833	65	9	60	9.3	.990	1B-98
1949		136	.309	.411	531	164	26	2	8	1.5	63	68	19	24	3	2	1	1140	65	14	109	9.1	.989	1B-134
1950		134	.307	.515	538	165	37	0	25	4.6	76	111	33	28	3	2	0	1123	61	15	101	9.2	.987	1B-131
1951		154	.259	.387	607	157	35	2	13	2.1	74	77	35	33	6	1	0	1381	88	5	115	9.6	.997	1B-154
1952		135	.320	.509	497	159	24	11	16	3.2	62	86	47	28	3	3	1	1121	66	8	116	9.0	.993	1B-133
1953		149	.316	.570	570	180	25	0	40	7.0	97	108	55	34	2	1	0	1285	58	7	149	9.2	.995	1B-147
1954		149	.326	.642	573	187	28	3	**49**	**8.6**	104	**141**	78	35	0	0	0	1237	101	5	166	9.0	.996	1B-149
1955		153	.314	.585	612	**192**	25	0	47	7.7	116	113	66	40	1	0	0	1388	86	8	153	9.7	.995	1B-153
1956		138	.302	.536	517	156	14	1	35	6.8	91	102	49	31	1	7	1	1166	89	13	110	9.7	.990	1B-131
1957		69	.268	.465	127	34	7	0	6	4.7	12	21	5	5	0	47	12	161	15	2	11	7.7	.989	1B-23
1958	PIT N	100	.292	.402	301	88	13	4	4	1.3	29	37	26	16	0	24	9	591	36	4	62	8.8	.994	1B-72
1959	2 teams	PIT N (60G –.262) CHI A (31G –.297)																						
″	total	91	.278	.404	223	62	12	2	4	1.8	22	27	14	24	0	39	7	371	22	0	27	8.0	1.000	1B-49
1960	CHI A	81	.293	.425	181	53	9	0	5	2.8	20	39	22	10	0	34	8	325	19	1	38	8.8	.997	1B-39
1961	LA A	107	.243	.460	263	64	12	0	15	5.7	32	39	24	23	0	43	9	520	28	6	51	8.4	.989	1B-66
15 yrs.		1718	.298	.498	5929	1766	290	29	279	4.7	848	1028	492	365	20	223	53	12652	799	97	1269	9.1	.993	1B-1481
WORLD SERIES																								
1959	CHI A	6	.391	.826	23	9	1	0	3	13.0	5	10	2	0	0	0	0	59	3	0	2	10.3	1.000	1B-6

Mickey Klutts

KLUTTS, GENE ELLIS BR TR 5′11″ 170 lbs.
B. Sept. 20, 1954, Montebello, Calif.

Year	Team	Games	BA	SA	AB	H	2B	3B	HR	HR%	R	RBI	BB	SO	SB	Pinch Hit AB	Pinch Hit H	PO	A	E	DP	TC/G	FA	G by Pos
1976	NY A	2	.000	.000	3	0	0	0	0	0.0	0	0	0	1	0	0	0	4	3	1	0	4.0	.875	SS-2
1977		5	.267	.533	15	4	1	0	1	6.7	3	4	2	1	0	0	0	5	15	0	1	4.0	1.000	3B-4, SS-1
1978		1	1.000	1.500	2	2	1	0	0	0.0	1	0	0	0	0	0	0	1	2	1	1	4.0	.750	3B-1
1979	OAK A	24	.192	.288	73	14	2	1	1	1.4	3	4	7	20	0	0	0	35	50	7	6	3.5	.924	SS-10, 2B-8, 3B-6, DH-2
1980		75	.269	.401	197	53	14	0	4	2.0	20	21	13	41	1	5	3	63	104	9	8	2.3	.949	3B-62, SS-8, 2B-7, DH-1
1981		15	.370	.696	46	17	0	0	5	10.9	9	11	2	9	0	1	1	7	15	1	1	1.6	.957	3B-14
1982		55	.178	.229	157	28	8	0	0	0.0	10	14	9	18	0	9	2	41	82	7	6	2.7	.946	3B-49
1983	TOR A	22	.256	.465	43	11	0	0	3	7.0	3	5	1	11	0	7	3	4	11	0	2	0.8	1.000	3B-17, DH-2
8 yrs.		199	.241	.371	536	129	26	1	14	2.6	49	59	34	101	1	22	9	160	282	26	25	2.4	.944	3B-153, SS-21, 2B-15, DH-5
DIVISIONAL PLAYOFF SERIES																								
1981	OAK A	2	.143	.143	7	1	0	0	0	0.0	0	0	0	1	0	0	0	0	2	0	0	1.0	1.000	3B-2
LEAGUE CHAMPIONSHIP SERIES																								
1981	OAK A	3	.429	.429	7	3	0	0	0	0.0	1	0	0	1	0	0	0	3	5	1	0	3.0	.889	3B-3

Clyde Kluttz

KLUTTZ, CLYDE FRANKLIN BR TR 6′ 193 lbs.
B. Dec. 12, 1917, Rockwell, N. C. D. May 12, 1979, Salisbury, N. C.

Year	Team	Games	BA	SA	AB	H	2B	3B	HR	HR%	R	RBI	BB	SO	SB	Pinch Hit AB	Pinch Hit H	PO	A	E	DP	TC/G	FA	G by Pos
1942	BOS N	72	.267	.338	210	56	10	1	1	0.5	21	31	7	13	0	15	6	200	29	5	5	4.1	.979	C-57
1943		66	.246	.280	207	51	7	0	0	0.0	13	20	15	9	0	9	1	176	43	6	5	4.1	.973	C-55
1944		81	.279	.376	229	64	12	2	2	0.9	20	19	13	14	0	23	4	199	40	5	5	4.2	.980	C-58
1945	2 teams	BOS N (25G –.296) NY N (73G –.279)																						
″	total	98	.284	.389	303	86	18	1	4	1.3	34	31	17	16	1	20	3	259	43	6	6	4.1	.981	C-76
1946	2 teams	NY N (5G –.375) STL N (52G –.265)																						
″	total	57	.271	.319	144	39	7	0	0	0.0	8	15	10	11	0	5	3	183	24	5	4	4.2	.976	C-51
1947	PIT N	73	.302	.435	232	70	9	2	6	2.6	26	42	17	18	1	4	1	247	55	4	7	4.4	.987	C-69
1948		94	.221	.325	271	60	12	2	4	1.5	26	20	20	19	3	3	1	298	54	8	8	4.0	.978	C-91
1951	2 teams	STL A (4G –.500) WAS A (53G –.308)																						
″	total	57	.313	.393	163	51	10	0	1	0.6	17	23	21	8	0	9	2	168	16	6	2	4.0	.968	C-47
1952	WAS A	58	.229	.285	144	33	5	0	1	0.7	7	11	12	11	0	6	1	163	27	4	4	3.7	.979	C-52
9 yrs.		656	.268	.354	1903	510	90	8	19	1.0	172	212	132	119	5	94	22	1893	331	49	46	4.1	.978	C-556

Joe Kmak

KMAK, JOSEPH ROBERT BR TR 6′ 200 lbs.
B. May 3, 1963, Napa, Calif.

Year	Team	Games	BA	SA	AB	H	2B	3B	HR	HR%	R	RBI	BB	SO	SB	Pinch Hit AB	Pinch Hit H	PO	A	E	DP	TC/G	FA	G by Pos
1993	MIL A	51	.218	.264	110	24	5	0	0	0.0	9	7	14	13	6	1	0	172	23	0	4	3.9	1.000	C-50
1995	CHI N	19	.245	.358	53	13	3	0	1	1.9	7	6	6	12	0	2	1	93	9	0	0	5.4	1.000	C-18, 3B-1
2 yrs.		70	.227	.294	163	37	8	0	1	0.6	16	13	20	25	6	3	1	265	32	0	4	4.3	1.000	C-68, 3B-1

Otto Knabe

KNABE, FRANZ OTTO (Dutch) BR TR 5′ 8″ 175 lbs.
B. June 12, 1884, Carrick, Pa. D. May 17, 1961, Philadelphia, Pa.
Manager 1914–15.

Year	Team	Games	BA	SA	AB	H	2B	3B	HR	HR%	R	RBI	BB	SO	SB	Pinch Hit AB	Pinch Hit H	PO	A	E	DP	TC/G	FA	G by Pos
1905	PIT N	3	.300	.400	10	3	1	0	0	0.0	0	2	3		0	0	0	2	9	3	1	4.7	.786	3B-3
1907	PHI N	129	.255	.338	444	113	16	9	1	0.2	67	34	52		18	2	0	301	338	26	54	5.3	.961	2B-121, OF-5
1908		151	.218	.294	555	121	26	8	0	0.0	63	27	49		27	0	0	344	470	26	42	5.6	.969	2B-151
1909		114	.234	.281	402	94	13	3	0	0.0	40	33	35		9	2	0	237	312	36	38	5.3	.938	2B-109, OF-1
1910		137	.261	.325	510	133	18	6	1	0.2	73	44	47	42	15	1	0	383	381	37	72	5.9	.954	2B-136
1911		142	.237	.294	528	125	15	6	1	0.2	99	42	94	35	23	0	0	310	412	38	54	5.4	.950	2B-142
1912		126	.282	.326	426	120	11	4	0	0.0	56	46	55	20	16	3	1	258	342	30	45	5.1	.952	2B-123
1913		148	.263	.342	571	150	25	7	2	0.4	70	53	45	26	14	0	0	311	466	33	58	5.5	.959	2B-148
1914	BAL F	147	.226	.303	469	106	26	2	2	0.4	45	42	53		10	3	1	287	389	31	49	4.9	.956	2B-144
1915		103	.253	.325	320	81	16	2	1	0.3	38	25	37		7	8	2	203	264	12	52	5.0	.975	2B-94, OF-1
1916	2 teams	PIT N (28G –.191) CHI N (57G –.276)																						
″	total	85	.244	.299	234	57	11	1	0	0.0	21	16	15	24	4	5	2	117	212	18	20	4.8	.948	2B-70, SS-1, 3B-1, OF-1
11 yrs.		1285	.247	.313	4469	1103	178	48	8	0.2	572	364	485	147	143	24	6	2753	3595	290	485	5.3	.956	2B-1238, OF-8, 3B-4, SS-1

Cotton Knaupp

KNAUPP, HENRY ANTONE BR TR 5′ 9″ 165 lbs.
B. Aug. 13, 1889, San Antonio, Tex. D. July 6, 1967, New Orleans, La.

Year	Team	Games	BA	SA	AB	H	2B	3B	HR	HR%	R	RBI	BB	SO	SB	Pinch Hit AB	Pinch Hit H	PO	A	E	DP	TC/G	FA	G by Pos
1910	CLE A	18	.237	.322	59	14	3	1	0	0.0	3	11	8		1	0	0	27	57	11	6	5.3	.884	SS-18
1911		13	.103	.128	39	4	1	0	0	0.0	2	0	0		3	0	0	17	36	2	2	4.2	.964	SS-13
2 yrs.		31	.184	.245	98	18	4	1	0	0.0	5	11	8		4	0	0	44	93	13	8	4.8	.913	SS-31

Alan Knicely

KNICELY, ALAN LEE BR TR 6′ 190 lbs.
B. May 19, 1955, Harrisonburg, Va.

Year	Team	Games	BA	SA	AB	H	2B	3B	HR	HR%	R	RBI	BB	SO	SB	Pinch Hit AB	Pinch Hit H	PO	A	E	DP	TC/G	FA	G by Pos
1979	HOU N	7	.000	.000	6	0	0	0	0	0.0	0	0	2	3	0	3	0	2	0	0	0	0.7	1.000	C-3
1980		1	.000	.000	1	0	0	0	0	0.0	0	0	0	1	0	1	0	0	0	0	0	0.0	—	
1981		3	.571	1.429	7	4	0	0	2	28.6	2	2	0	1	0	1	1	11	2	0	0	4.3	1.000	C-2, OF-1
1982		59	.188	.248	133	25	2	0	2	1.5	10	12	14	30	0	17	1	128	15	4	2	3.7	.973	C-23, OF-16, 3B-1
1983	CIN N	59	.224	.316	98	22	3	0	2	2.0	11	10	16	28	0	19	4	124	13	0	3	3.3	1.000	C-31, OF-8, 1B-2
1984		10	.138	.138	29	4	0	0	0	0.0	0	5	3	6	0	0	0	60	5	1	5	7.3	.985	1B-8, C-1
1985	2 teams	CIN N (48G –.253) PHI N (7G –.000)																						
″	total	55	.242	.388	165	40	9	0	5	3.0	17	26	16	38	0	8	0	235	13	8	2	5.4	.969	C-46, 1B-1
1986	STL N	34	.195	.268	82	16	3	0	1	1.2	8	6	17	21	1	5	1	187	16	1	20	6.6	.995	1B-29, C-2
8 yrs.		228	.213	.315	521	111	17	0	12	2.3	48	61	68	128	1	54	7	747	64	14	32	4.7	.983	C-108, 1B-40, OF-25, 3B-1

Austin Knickerbocker

KNICKERBOCKER, AUSTIN JAY BR TR 5′11″ 185 lbs.
B. Oct. 15, 1918, Bangall, N. Y.

Year	Team	Games	BA	SA	AB	H	2B	3B	HR	HR%	R	RBI	BB	SO	SB	Pinch Hit AB	Pinch Hit H	PO	A	E	DP	TC/G	FA	G by Pos
1947	PHI A	21	.250	.396	48	12	3	2	0	0.0	8	2	3	4	0	2	2	32	1	2	0	2.5	.943	OF-14

Bill Knickerbocker

KNICKERBOCKER, WILLIAM HART BR TR 5′11″ 170 lbs.
B. Dec. 29, 1911, Los Angeles, Calif. D. Sept. 8, 1963, Sebastopol, Calif.

Year	Team	Games	BA	SA	AB	H	2B	3B	HR	HR%	R	RBI	BB	SO	SB	Pinch Hit AB	Pinch Hit H	PO	A	E	DP	TC/G	FA	G by Pos
1933	CLE A	80	.226	.326	279	63	16	3	2	0.7	20	32	11	30	1	1	0	151	233	25	37	5.1	.939	SS-80
1934		146	.317	.408	593	188	32	5	4	0.7	82	67	25	40	6	0	0	262	451	28	106	5.1	.962	SS-146
1935		132	.298	.380	540	161	34	5	0	0.0	77	55	27	31	2	3	0	247	453	32	82	5.7	.956	SS-128
1936		155	.294	.400	618	182	35	3	8	1.3	81	73	56	30	5	0	0	313	486	40	97	5.4	.952	SS-155
1937	STL A	121	.261	.365	491	128	29	5	4	0.8	53	61	30	32	3	0	0	220	379	26	64	5.2	.958	SS-115, 2B-6
1938	NY A	46	.250	.383	128	32	8	3	1	0.8	15	21	11	10	0	9	1	82	89	3	25	4.7	.983	2B-34, SS-3
1939		6	.154	.231	13	2	1	0	0	0.0	2	1	0	0	0	2	0	6	12	0	1	4.5	1.000	SS-2, 2B-2
1940		45	.242	.347	124	30	8	1	1	0.8	17	10	14	8	1	7	2	33	77	6	18	3.2	.948	SS-19, 3B-17
1941	CHI A	89	.245	.385	343	84	23	2	7	2.0	51	29	41	27	6	1	0	204	221	13	58	5.0	.970	2B-88
1942	PHI A	87	.253	.304	289	73	12	0	1	0.3	25	19	29	30	1	6	0	178	220	16	45	5.0	.961	2B-81, SS-1
10 yrs.		907	.276	.374	3418	943	198	27	28	0.8	423	368	244	238	25	29	3	1696	2621	189	533	5.1	.958	SS-649, 2B-211, 3B-17

Joe Knight

KNIGHT, JOSEPH WILLIAM (Quiet Joe) BL TL 5′11″ 185 lbs.
B. Sept. 28, 1859, Port Stanley, Ont., Canada D. Oct. 16, 1938, Lynhurst, Ont., Canada.

Year	Team	Games	BA	SA	AB	H	2B	3B	HR	HR%	R	RBI	BB	SO	SB	Pinch Hit AB	Pinch Hit H	PO	A	E	DP	TC/G	FA	G by Pos
1884	PHI N	6	.250	.375	24	6	3	0	0	0.0	2		0	2		0	0	3	12	4	0	3.2	.789	P-6
1890	CIN N	127	.312	.424	481	150	26	8	4	0.8	67	67	38	31	17	0	0	224	11	19	0	2.0	.925	OF-127
2 yrs.		133	.309	.422	505	156	29	8	4	0.8	69	67	38	33	17	0	0	227	23	23	0	2.1	.916	OF-127, P-6

John Knight

KNIGHT, JOHN WESLEY (Schoolboy) BR TR 6′ 2½″ 180 lbs.
B. Oct. 6, 1885, Philadelphia, Pa. D. Dec. 19, 1965, Walnut Creek, Calif.

Year	Team	Games	BA	SA	AB	H	2B	3B	HR	HR%	R	RBI	BB	SO	SB	Pinch Hit AB	Pinch Hit H	PO	A	E	DP	TC/G	FA	G by Pos
1905	PHI A	88	.203	.274	325	66	12	1	3	0.9	28	29	9		4	5	0	145	189	40	9	4.5	.893	SS-81, 3B-2
1906		74	.194	.273	253	49	7	2	3	1.2	29	20	19		6	0	0	82	149	19	6	3.4	.924	3B-67, 2B-7
1907	2 teams	PHI A (38G –.222) BOS A (100G –.212)																						
″	total	138	.214	.275	499	107	16	4	2	0.4	37	41	29		9	2	0	189	304	53	23	4.0	.903	3B-134, SS-4
1909	NY A	116	.236	.286	360	85	8	5	0	0.0	46	40	37		15	1	0	369	269	48	34	6.0	.930	SS-78, 1B-19, 2B-18
1910		117	.312	.413	414	129	25	4	3	0.7	58	45	34		23	2	1	439	281	37	48	6.6	.951	SS-79, 1B-23, 2B-7, 3B-4, OF-1
1911		132	.268	.351	470	126	16	7	3	0.6	69	62	42		18	1	0	491	354	68	53	7.0	.926	SS-82, 1B-27, 2B-21, 3B-1
1912	WAS A	32	.161	.204	93	15	2	1	0	0.0	10	9	16		4	0	0	95	49	8	10	4.8	.947	2B-27, 1B-5
1913	NY A	70	.236	.276	250	59	10	0	0	0.0	24	24	25	27	7	0	0	544	115	17	32	9.5	.975	1B-50, 2B-21
8 yrs.		767	.239	.309	2664	636	96	24	14	0.5	301	270	211	27	86	11	1	2354	1710	290	215	5.7	.933	SS-324, 3B-208, 1B-124, 2B-101, OF-1

Lon Knight

KNIGHT, ALONZO P. BR TR 5′11½″ 165 lbs.
B. June 16, 1853, Philadelphia, Pa. D. Apr. 23, 1932, Philadelphia, Pa.
Manager 1883–84.

Year	Team	Games	BA	SA	AB	H	2B	3B	HR	HR%	R	RBI	BB	SO	SB	Pinch Hit AB	Pinch Hit H	PO	A	E	DP	TC/G	FA	G by Pos
1876	PHI N	55	.250	.313	240	60	9	3	0	0.0	32	24	2	2		0	0	156	48	40	10	3.9	.836	P-34, 1B-13, OF-9, 2B-6
1880	WOR N	49	.239	.323	201	48	11	3	0	0.0	31	21	5	8		0	0	47	22	11	1	1.6	.863	OF-49

Lon Knight *continued*

Year	Team	Games	BA	SA	AB	H	2B	3B	HR	HR%	R	RBI	BB	SO	SB	Pinch Hit AB	Pinch Hit H	PO	A	E	DP	TC/G	FA	G by Pos
1881	**DET N**	83	.271	.344	340	92	16	3	1	0.3	67	52	23	21		0	0	119	24	18	6	1.9	.888	OF-82, 2B-1, 1B-1
1882		86	.207	.277	347	72	12	6	0	0.0	39	24	16	21		0	0	129	25	24	2	2.1	.865	OF-84, 1B-2
1883	**PHI AA**	97	.252	.354	429	108	23	9	1	0.2	98		21			0	0	129	37	28	5	2.0	.856	OF-93, 3B-3, 2B-2
1884		108	.271	.364	484	131	18	12	1	0.2	94		10			0	0	165	39	19	6	2.0	.915	OF-108, P-2, 1B-1
1885	**2 teams**	**PHI AA** (29G –.210) **PRO N** (25G –.160)																						
″	**total**	54	.190	.210	200	38	2	1	0	0.0	25	8	20	17		0	0	88	17	7	5	2.0	.938	OF-54, P-2
7 yrs.		532	.245	.323	2241	549	91	37	3	0.1	386	129	97	69		0	0	833	212	147	35	2.2	.877	OF-479, P-38, 1B-17, 2B-9, 3B-3

Ray Knight

KNIGHT, CHARLES RAY BR TR 6′ 1″ 185 lbs.
B. Dec. 28, 1952, Albany, Ga.

Year	Team	Games	BA	SA	AB	H	2B	3B	HR	HR%	R	RBI	BB	SO	SB	Pinch Hit AB	Pinch Hit H	PO	A	E	DP	TC/G	FA	G by Pos
1974	**CIN N**	14	.182	.273	11	2	1	0	0	0.0	1	2	1	2	0	0	0	2	8	0	0	0.7	1.000	3B-14
1977		80	.261	.370	92	24	5	1	1	1.1	8	13	9	16	1	26	6	45	46	4	8	1.5	.958	3B-37, 2B-17, OF-5, SS-3
1978		83	.200	.292	65	13	3	0	1	1.5	7	4	3	13	0	16	2	13	41	7	1	0.9	.885	3B-60, 2B-4, OF-3, SS-1, 1B-1
1979		150	.318	.454	551	175	37	4	10	1.8	64	79	38	57	4	1	0	120	262	15	26	2.7	.962	3B-149
1980		162	.264	.417	618	163	39	7	14	2.3	71	78	36	62	1	1	0	120	291	13	19	2.6	.969	3B-162
1981		106	.259	.370	386	100	23	1	6	1.6	43	34	33	51	2	1	0	69	176	11	18	2.4	.957	3B-105
1982	**HOU N**	158	.294	.402	609	179	36	6	6	1.0	72	70	48	58	2	0	0	1002	186	17	94	7.4	.986	1B-96, 3B-67
1983		145	.304	.444	507	154	36	4	9	1.8	43	70	42	62	0	4	0	1285	73	9	131	9.6	.993	1B-143
1984	**2 teams**	**HOU N** (88G –.223) **NY N** (27G –.280)																						
″	**total**	115	.237	.299	371	88	14	0	3	0.8	28	35	21	43	0	10	4	256	132	9	27	3.7	.977	3B-81, 1B-27
1985	**NY N**	90	.218	.328	271	59	12	0	6	2.2	22	36	13	32	1	16	1	56	113	7	5	2.3	.960	3B-73, 2B-2, 1B-1
1986		137	.298	.424	486	145	24	2	11	2.3	51	76	40	63	2	6	2	94	204	16	17	2.4	.949	3B-132, 1B-1
1987	**BAL A**	150	.256	.373	563	144	24	0	14	2.5	46	65	39	90	0	1	1	169	284	19	35	3.1	.960	3B-130, DH-14, 1B-6
1988	**DET A**	105	.217	.301	299	65	12	2	3	1.0	34	33	20	30	1	23	2	438	42	4	40	6.3	.992	1B-64, 3B-11, OF-2
13 yrs.		1495	.271	.390	4829	1311	266	27	84	1.7	490	595	343	579	14	105	18	3669	1858	131	421	4.0	.977	3B-1021, 1B-339, 2B-23, DH-14, OF-10, SS-4
LEAGUE CHAMPIONSHIP SERIES																								
1979	**CIN N**	3	.286	.357	14	4	1	0	0	0.0	0	0	0	2	1	0	0	0	5	0	0	1.7	1.000	3B-3
1986	**NY N**	6	.167	.167	24	4	0	0	0	0.0	1	2	1	5	0	0	0	5	19	1	0	4.2	.960	3B-6
2 yrs.		9	.211	.237	38	8	1	0	0	0.0	1	2	1	7	1	0	0	5	24	1	0	3.3	.967	3B-9
WORLD SERIES																								
1986	**NY N**	6	.391	.565	23	9	1	0	1	4.3	4	5	2	2	0	0	0	5	6	1	0	2.0	.917	3B-6

Pete Knisely

KNISELY, PETER COLE BR TR 5′ 9″ 185 lbs.
B. Aug. 11, 1887, Waynesburg, Pa. D. July 1, 1948, Brownsville, Pa.

Year	Team	Games	BA	SA	AB	H	2B	3B	HR	HR%	R	RBI	BB	SO	SB	Pinch Hit AB	Pinch Hit H	PO	A	E	DP	TC/G	FA	G by Pos
1912	**CIN N**	21	.328	.522	67	22	7	3	0	0.0	10	7	4	5	3	3	0	32	10	3	2	2.6	.933	OF-13, 2B-3, SS-1
1913	**CHI N**	2	.000	.000	2	0	0	0	0	0.0	0	0	0	1	0	2	0	0	0	0	0	0.0	—	
1914		37	.130	.159	69	9	0	1	0	0.0	5	5	5	6	0	19	4	36	3	1	2	2.5	.975	OF-16
1915		64	.246	.313	134	33	9	0	0	0.0	12	17	15	18	1	17	4	59	16	8	4	1.9	.904	OF-34, 2B-9
4 yrs.		124	.235	.324	272	64	16	4	0	0.0	27	29	24	30	4	41	8	127	29	12	8	2.2	.929	OF-63, 2B-12, SS-1

Chuck Knoblauch

KNOBLAUCH, EDWARD CHARLES BR TR 5′ 9″ 175 lbs.
B. July 7, 1968, Houston, Tex.

Year	Team	Games	BA	SA	AB	H	2B	3B	HR	HR%	R	RBI	BB	SO	SB	Pinch Hit AB	Pinch Hit H	PO	A	E	DP	TC/G	FA	G by Pos
1991	**MIN A**	151	.281	.350	565	159	24	6	1	0.2	78	50	59	40	25	3	2	249	460	18	94	4.8	.975	2B-148, SS-2
1992		155	.297	.358	600	178	19	6	2	0.3	104	56	88	60	34	1	0	306	415	6	104	4.7	.992	2B-154, SS-1, DH-1
1993		153	.277	.346	602	167	27	4	2	0.3	82	41	65	44	29	4	0	302	431	9	99	4.8	.988	2B-148, SS-6, OF-1
1994		109	.312	.461	445	139	**45**	3	5	1.1	85	51	41	56	35	0	0	190	285	3	60	4.3	.994	2B-109, SS-1
1995		136	.333	.487	538	179	34	8	11	2.0	107	63	78	95	46	0	0	254	400	10	85	4.8	.985	2B-136, SS-2
5 yrs.		704	.299	.396	2750	822	149	27	21	0.8	456	261	331	295	169	8	2	1301	1991	46	442	4.7	.986	2B-695, SS-12, OF-1, DH-1
LEAGUE CHAMPIONSHIP SERIES																								
1991	**MIN A**	5	.350	.450	20	7	2	0	0	0.0	5	3	3	3	2	0	0	8	14	0	3	4.4	1.000	2B-5
WORLD SERIES																								
1991	**MIN A**	7	.308	.346	26	8	1	0	0	0.0	3	2	4	2	4	0	0	15	14	1	1	4.3	.967	2B-7

Mike Knode

KNODE, KENNETH THOMSON BL TR 5′10″ 160 lbs.
Brother of Ray Knode.
B. Nov. 8, 1895, Westminster, Md. D. Dec. 20, 1980, South Bend, Ind.

Year	Team	Games	BA	SA	AB	H	2B	3B	HR	HR%	R	RBI	BB	SO	SB	Pinch Hit AB	Pinch Hit H	PO	A	E	DP	TC/G	FA	G by Pos
1920	**STL N**	42	.231	.277	65	15	1	1	0	0.0	11	12	5	6	0	18	4	22	17	5	0	2.6	.886	OF-9, 2B-4, 3B-2, SS-2

Ray Knode

KNODE, ROBERT TROXELL (Bob) BL TL 5′10″ 160 lbs.
Brother of Mike Knode.
B. Jan. 28, 1901, Westminster, Md. D. Apr. 13, 1982, Battle Creek, Mich.

Year	Team	Games	BA	SA	AB	H	2B	3B	HR	HR%	R	RBI	BB	SO	SB	Pinch Hit AB	Pinch Hit H	PO	A	E	DP	TC/G	FA	G by Pos
1923	**CLE A**	22	.289	.447	38	11	0	0	2	5.3	7	4	2	4	1	0	0	112	7	1	8	5.7	.992	1B-21
1924		11	.243	.270	37	9	1	0	0	0.0	6	4	3	0	2	0	0	110	9	1	11	12.0	.992	1B-10
1925		45	.250	.296	108	27	5	0	0	0.0	13	11	10	4	3	3	0	270	19	3	27	8.6	.990	1B-34
1926		31	.333	.458	24	8	1	1	0	0.0	6	2	2	3	0	5	2	57	4	1	3	5.6	.984	1B-11
4 yrs.		109	.266	.338	207	55	7	1	2	1.0	32	21	17	11	6	8	2	549	39	6	49	7.8	.990	1B-76

Punch Knoll

KNOLL, CHARLES ELMER BR TR 5′ 7½″ 170 lbs.
B. Oct. 7, 1881, Evansville, Ind. D. Feb. 8, 1960, Evansville, Ind.

Year	Team	Games	BA	SA	AB	H	2B	3B	HR	HR%	R	RBI	BB	SO	SB	Pinch Hit AB	Pinch Hit H	PO	A	E	DP	TC/G	FA	G by Pos
1905	**WAS A**	85	.213	.295	244	52	10	5	0	0.0	24	29	9		3	8	3	135	9	8	1	2.0	.947	OF-70, C-5, 1B-2

Bobby Knoop

KNOOP, ROBERT FRANK BR TR 6′ 1″ 170 lbs.
B. Oct. 18, 1938, Sioux City, Iowa.
Manager 1994.

Year	Team	Games	BA	SA	AB	H	2B	3B	HR	HR%	R	RBI	BB	SO	SB	Pinch Hit AB	Pinch Hit H	PO	A	E	DP	TC/G	FA	G by Pos
1964	**LA A**	162	.216	.280	486	105	8	1	7	1.4	42	38	46	109	3	1	0	357	522	20	123	5.6	.978	2B-161
1965	**CAL A**	142	.269	.383	465	125	24	4	7	1.5	47	43	31	101	3	0	0	331	402	22	89	5.3	.971	2B-142
1966		161	.232	.386	590	137	18	**11**	17	2.9	54	72	43	144	1	0	0	381	488	17	135	5.5	.981	2B-161
1967		159	.245	.352	511	125	18	5	9	1.8	51	38	44	136	2	0	0	376	392	11	91	4.9	.986	2B-159
1968		152	.249	.324	494	123	20	4	3	0.6	48	39	35	128	3	1	1	350	425	15	94	5.2	.981	2B-151

Bobby Knoop *continued*

Year	Team	Games	BA	SA	AB	H	2B	3B	HR	HR%	R	RBI	BB	SO	SB	Pinch Hit AB	Pinch Hit H	PO	A	E	DP	TC/G	FA	G by Pos
1969	2 teams	CAL A (27G –.197) CHI A (104G –.229)																						
"	total	131	.224	.315	416	93	15	1	7	1.7	39	47	48	84	3	1	0	335	386	12	90	5.6	.984	2B-131
1970	CHI A	130	.229	.308	402	92	13	2	5	1.2	34	36	34	79	0	3	1	276	403	11	102	5.5	.984	2B-126
1971	KC A	72	.205	.286	161	33	8	1	1	0.6	14	11	15	36	1	16	3	89	120	7	31	4.1	.968	2B-52, 3B-1
1972		44	.237	.289	97	23	5	0	0	0.0	8	7	9	16	0	9	2	61	80	4	24	3.9	.972	2B-33, 3B-4
9 yrs.		1153	.236	.334	3622	856	129	29	56	1.5	337	331	305	833	16	31	7	2556	3218	119	779	5.3	.980	2B-1116, 3B-5

Randy Knorr

KNORR, RANDY DUANE BR TR 6′ 2″ 205 lbs.
B. Nov. 12, 1968, San Gabriel, Calif.

Year	Team	Games	BA	SA	AB	H	2B	3B	HR	HR%	R	RBI	BB	SO	SB	Pinch Hit AB	Pinch Hit H	PO	A	E	DP	TC/G	FA	G by Pos
1991	TOR A	3	.000	.000	1	0	0	0	0	0.0	0	0	1	1	0	0	0	6	1	0	0	2.3	1.000	C-3
1992		8	.263	.421	19	5	0	0	1	5.3	1	2	1	5	0	0	0	33	3	0	0	4.0	1.000	C-8, DH-1
1993		39	.248	.436	101	25	3	2	4	4.0	11	20	9	29	0	1	0	168	20	0	4	4.8	1.000	C-39
1994		40	.242	.427	124	30	2	0	7	5.6	20	19	10	35	0	1	0	247	21	2	1	6.8	.993	C-40
1995		45	.212	.341	132	28	8	0	3	2.3	18	16	11	28	0	2	1	243	22	8	1	6.1	.971	C-45
5 yrs.		135	.233	.398	377	88	13	2	15	4.0	50	57	32	98	0	4	1	697	67	10	6	5.7	.987	C-135, DH-1
WORLD SERIES																								
1993	TOR A	1	—	—	0	0	0	0	0	—	0	0	0	0	0	0	0	3	0	0	0	3.0	1.000	C-1

Fritz Knothe

KNOTHE, WILFRED EDGAR BR TR 5′10½″ 180 lbs.
Brother of George Knothe.
B. May 1, 1903, Passaic, N. J. D. Mar. 27, 1963, Passaic, N. J.

Year	Team	Games	BA	SA	AB	H	2B	3B	HR	HR%	R	RBI	BB	SO	SB	Pinch Hit AB	Pinch Hit H	PO	A	E	DP	TC/G	FA	G by Pos
1932	BOS N	89	.238	.308	344	82	19	1	1	0.3	45	36	39	37	5	1	1	81	168	14	7	3.0	.947	3B-87
1933	2 teams	BOS N (44G –.228) PHI N (41G –.150)																						
"	total	85	.196	.247	271	53	7	2	1	0.4	25	17	19	44	3	5	0	98	165	11	18	3.5	.960	3B-65, SS-9, 2B-4
2 yrs.		174	.220	.281	615	135	26	3	2	0.3	70	53	58	81	8	6	1	179	333	25	25	3.3	.953	3B-152, SS-9, 2B-4

George Knothe

KNOTHE, GEORGE BERTRAM BR TR 5′10″ 165 lbs.
Brother of Fritz Knothe.
B. Jan. 12, 1898, Bayonne, N. J. D. July 3, 1981, Dover, N. J.

Year	Team	Games	BA	SA	AB	H	2B	3B	HR	HR%	R	RBI	BB	SO	SB	Pinch Hit AB	Pinch Hit H	PO	A	E	DP	TC/G	FA	G by Pos
1932	PHI N	6	.083	.167	12	1	1	0	0	0.0	2	0	0	0	0	0	0	4	8	1	2	2.6	.923	2B-5

Joe Knotts

KNOTTS, JOSEPH STEVEN BR TR
B. Mar. 3, 1884, Greensboro, Pa. D. Sept. 15, 1950, Philadelphia, Pa.

Year	Team	Games	BA	SA	AB	H	2B	3B	HR	HR%	R	RBI	BB	SO	SB	Pinch Hit AB	Pinch Hit H	PO	A	E	DP	TC/G	FA	G by Pos
1907	BOS N	3	.000	.000	8	0	0	0	0	0.0	0	0	1		0	0	0	10	4	0	0	4.7	1.000	C-3

Jake Knowdell

KNOWDELL, JACOB AUGUSTUS 5′ 7½″ 148 lbs.
B. July 27, 1840, Brooklyn, N. Y. Deceased.

Year	Team	Games	BA	SA	AB	H	2B	3B	HR	HR%	R	RBI	BB	SO	SB	Pinch Hit AB	Pinch Hit H	PO	A	E	DP	TC/G	FA	G by Pos
1878	MIL N	4	.214	.286	14	3	1	0	0	0.0	2	2	0	3		0	0	13	5	4	0	5.5	.818	C-2, SS-1, OF-1

Jimmy Knowles

KNOWLES, JAMES 5′ 9″ 160 lbs.
B. Sept. 1856, Toronto, Ont., Canada D. Feb. 11, 1912, Jersey City, N. J.

Year	Team	Games	BA	SA	AB	H	2B	3B	HR	HR%	R	RBI	BB	SO	SB	Pinch Hit AB	Pinch Hit H	PO	A	E	DP	TC/G	FA	G by Pos
1884	2 teams	PIT AA (46G –.231) BKN AA (41G –.235)																						
"	total	87	.233	.319	335	78	10	8	1	0.3	38		8			0	0	818	51	45	38	10.5	.951	1B-75, 3B-11, SS-1
1886	WAS N	115	.212	.318	443	94	16	11	3	0.7	43	35	15	73		0	0	264	346	81	41	6.0	.883	2B-62, 3B-53
1887	NY AA	16	.250	.300	60	15	1	1	0	0.0	12		1		6	0	0	49	37	7	4	5.5	.925	2B-16, 3B-1
1890	ROC AA	123	.281	.369	491	138	12	8	5	1.0	83		59		55	0	0	162	303	63	19	4.3	.881	3B-123
1892	NY N	16	.153	.169	59	9	1	0	0	0.0	9	7	6	8	2	0	0	14	26	10	2	3.1	.800	3B-15, SS-1
5 yrs.		357	.241	.329	1388	334	40	28	9	0.6	185	42	89	81	63	0	0	1307	763	206	104	6.4	.909	3B-203, 2B-78, 1B-75, SS-2

Andy Knox

KNOX, ANDREW JACKSON (Dasher) BR TR
B. Jan. 5, 1864, Philadelphia, Pa. D. Sept. 14, 1940, Philadelphia, Pa.

Year	Team	Games	BA	SA	AB	H	2B	3B	HR	HR%	R	RBI	BB	SO	SB	Pinch Hit AB	Pinch Hit H	PO	A	E	DP	TC/G	FA	G by Pos
1890	PHI AA	21	.253	.293	75	19	3	0	0	0.0	6		9		5	0	0	205	5	8	8	10.4	.963	1B-21

Cliff Knox

KNOX, CLIFFORD HIRAM (Bud) BB TR 5′11½″ 178 lbs.
B. Jan. 7, 1902, Coalville, Iowa D. Sept. 24, 1965, Oskaloosa, Iowa.

Year	Team	Games	BA	SA	AB	H	2B	3B	HR	HR%	R	RBI	BB	SO	SB	Pinch Hit AB	Pinch Hit H	PO	A	E	DP	TC/G	FA	G by Pos
1924	PIT N	6	.222	.222	18	4	0	0	0	0.0	1	2	2	0	0	0	0	23	10	3	2	6.0	.917	C-6

John Knox

KNOX, JOHN CLINTON BL TR 6′ 170 lbs.
B. July 26, 1948, Newark, N. J.

Year	Team	Games	BA	SA	AB	H	2B	3B	HR	HR%	R	RBI	BB	SO	SB	Pinch Hit AB	Pinch Hit H	PO	A	E	DP	TC/G	FA	G by Pos
1972	DET A	14	.077	.154	13	1	1	0	0	0.0	1	0	1	2	0	9	1	3	10	0	3	3.3	1.000	2B-4
1973		12	.281	.313	32	9	1	0	0	0.0	1	3	3	3	1	0	0	17	17	0	3	3.8	1.000	2B-9
1974		55	.307	.341	88	27	1	1	0	0.0	11	6	6	13	5	4	1	55	54	5	20	3.3	.956	2B-33, 3B-1, DH-1
1975		43	.267	.279	86	23	1	0	0	0.0	8	2	10	9	1	5	2	38	62	5	10	3.6	.952	2B-23, 3B-3, DH-3
4 yrs.		124	.274	.301	219	60	4	1	0	0.0	21	11	20	27	7	18	4	113	143	10	36	3.5	.962	2B-69, 3B-4, DH-4
LEAGUE CHAMPIONSHIP SERIES																								
1972	DET A	1	—	—	0	0	0	0	0	—	0	0	0	0	0	0	0	0	0	0	0	0.0	—	

Nick Koback

KOBACK, NICHOLAS NICHOLIE BR TR 6′ 187 lbs.
B. July 19, 1935, Hartford, Conn.

Year	Team	Games	BA	SA	AB	H	2B	3B	HR	HR%	R	RBI	BB	SO	SB	Pinch Hit AB	Pinch Hit H	PO	A	E	DP	TC/G	FA	G by Pos
1953	PIT N	7	.125	.250	16	2	0	1	0	0.0	1	0	1	4	0	1	1	8	2	0	0	1.7	1.000	C-6
1954		4	.000	.000	10	0	0	0	0	0.0	0	0	0	8	0	0	0	14	0	0	0	3.5	1.000	C-4
1955		5	.286	.286	7	2	0	0	0	0.0	0	0	0	1	0	3	1	4	1	0	0	2.5	1.000	C-2
3 yrs.		16	.121	.182	33	4	0	1	0	0.0	1	0	1	13	0	4	2	26	3	0	0	2.4	1.000	C-12

Barney Koch

KOCH, BARNETT BR TR 5′ 8″ 140 lbs.
B. Mar. 23, 1923, Campbell, Neb. D. June 6, 1987, Tacoma, Wash.

Year	Team	Games	BA	SA	AB	H	2B	3B	HR	HR%	R	RBI	BB	SO	SB	Pinch Hit AB	Pinch Hit H	PO	A	E	DP	TC/G	FA	G by Pos
1944	BKN N	33	.219	.240	96	21	2	0	0	0.0	11	1	3	9	0	1	1	65	65	6	10	4.5	.956	2B-29, SS-1

Brad Kocher

KOCHER, BRADLEY WILSON BR TR 5′11″ 188 lbs.
B. Jan. 16, 1888, White Haven, Pa. D. Jan. 13, 1965, White Haven, Pa.

Year	Team	Games	BA	SA	AB	H	2B	3B	HR	HR%	R	RBI	BB	SO	SB	Pinch Hit AB	Pinch Hit H	PO	A	E	DP	TC/G	FA	G by Pos
1912	DET A	24	.206	.286	63	13	3	1	0	0.0	5	9	2		0	1	0	68	26	10	3	4.5	.904	C-23
1915	NY N	4	.455	.636	11	5	0	1	0	0.0	3	2	0	1	0	1	0	12	4	0	0	5.3	1.000	C-3
1916		34	.108	.138	65	7	2	0	0	0.0	1	1	2	10	0	4	1	75	15	2	1	3.1	.978	C-30
3 yrs.		62	.180	.245	139	25	5	2	0	0.0	9	12	4	11	0	6	1	155	45	12	4	3.8	.943	C-56

Pete Koegel

KOEGEL, PETER JOHN — BR TR 6′ 6½″ 230 lbs.
B. July 31, 1947, Mineola, N. Y.

Year	Team	Games	BA	SA	AB	H	2B	3B	HR	HR%	R	RBI	BB	SO	SB	Pinch Hit AB	Pinch Hit H	PO	A	E	DP	TC/G	FA	G by Pos
1970	MIL A	7	.250	.625	8	2	0	0	1	12.5	2	1	1	3	0	6	2	1	0	0	0	1.0	1.000	OF-1
1971	2 teams	MIL A (2G –.000) PHI N (12G –.231)																						
″	total	14	.207	.241	29	6	1	0	0	0.0	1	3	4	9	0	4	1	28	3	0	2	3.4	1.000	C-7, OF-1, 1B-1
1972	PHI N	41	.143	.184	49	7	2	0	0	0.0	3	1	6	16	0	21	2	43	5	1	3	2.6	.980	1B-8, C-5, 3B-4, OF-2
3 yrs.		62	.174	.244	86	15	3	0	1	1.2	6	5	11	28	0	31	5	72	8	1	5	2.8	.988	C-12, 1B-9, 3B-4, OF-4

Ben Koehler

KOEHLER, BERNARD JAMES — BR TR 5′10½″ 175 lbs.
B. Jan. 26, 1877, Schoerndorn, Germany D. May 21, 1961, South Bend, Ind.

Year	Team	Games	BA	SA	AB	H	2B	3B	HR	HR%	R	RBI	BB	SO	SB	Pinch Hit AB	Pinch Hit H	PO	A	E	DP	TC/G	FA	G by Pos
1905	STL A	142	.237	.297	536	127	14	6	2	0.4	55	47	32		22	0	0	347	41	10	18	2.7	.975	OF-127, 1B-12, 2B-6
1906		66	.220	.237	186	41	1	1	0	0.0	27	15	24		9	5	1	95	26	8	7	2.1	.938	OF-52, 2B-7, SS-1, 3B-1
2 yrs.		208	.233	.281	722	168	15	7	2	0.3	82	62	56		31	5	1	442	67	18	25	2.6	.966	OF-179, 2B-13, 1B-12, SS-1, 3B-1

Pip Koehler

KOEHLER, HORACE LEVERING — BR TR 5′10″ 165 lbs.
B. Jan. 16, 1902, Gilbert, Pa. D. Dec. 8, 1986, Tacoma, Wash.

Year	Team	Games	BA	SA	AB	H	2B	3B	HR	HR%	R	RBI	BB	SO	SB	Pinch Hit AB	Pinch Hit H	PO	A	E	DP	TC/G	FA	G by Pos
1925	NY N	12	.000	.000	2	0	0	0	0	0.0	1	0	0	1	0	0	0	3	0	0	0	1.0	1.000	OF-3

Brian Koelling

KOELLING, BRIAN WAYNE — BR TR 6′ 1″ 187 lbs.
B. June 11, 1969, Cincinnati, Ohio.

Year	Team	Games	BA	SA	AB	H	2B	3B	HR	HR%	R	RBI	BB	SO	SB	Pinch Hit AB	Pinch Hit H	PO	A	E	DP	TC/G	FA	G by Pos
1993	CIN N	7	.067	.067	15	1	0	0	0	0.0	2	0	0	2	0	1	0	6	12	1	1	3.8	.947	2B-3, SS-2

Len Koenecke

KOENECKE, LEONARD GEORGE — BL TR 5′11½″ 192 lbs.
B. Jan. 18, 1904, Baraboo, Wis. D. Sept. 17, 1935, Toronto, Ont., Canada.

Year	Team	Games	BA	SA	AB	H	2B	3B	HR	HR%	R	RBI	BB	SO	SB	Pinch Hit AB	Pinch Hit H	PO	A	E	DP	TC/G	FA	G by Pos
1932	NY N	42	.255	.380	137	35	5	0	4	2.9	33	14	11	13	3	1	0	61	0	5	0	1.9	.924	OF-35
1934	BKN N	123	.320	.509	460	147	31	7	14	3.0	79	73	70	38	8	2	0	310	6	2	0	2.6	.994	OF-121
1935		100	.283	.372	325	92	13	2	4	1.2	43	27	43	45	0	8	0	222	3	8	0	2.6	.966	OF-91
3 yrs.		265	.297	.441	922	274	49	9	22	2.4	155	114	124	96	11	11	0	593	9	15	0	2.5	.976	OF-247

Mark Koenig

KOENIG, MARK ANTHONY — BB TR 6′ 180 lbs.
B. July 19, 1904, San Francisco, Calif. D. Apr. 22, 1993, Willows, Calif.

Year	Team	Games	BA	SA	AB	H	2B	3B	HR	HR%	R	RBI	BB	SO	SB	Pinch Hit AB	Pinch Hit H	PO	A	E	DP	TC/G	FA	G by Pos
1925	NY A	28	.209	.282	110	23	6	1	0	0.0	14	4	5	4	0	0	0	53	81	8	16	5.1	.944	SS-28
1926		147	.271	.363	617	167	26	8	5	0.8	93	62	43	37	4	6	1	281	422	52	66	5.4	.931	SS-141
1927		123	.285	.382	526	150	20	11	3	0.6	99	62	25	21	3	1	0	262	423	47	76	6.0	.936	SS-122
1928		132	.319	.415	533	170	19	10	4	0.8	89	63	32	19	3	7	3	260	328	49	69	5.1	.923	SS-125
1929		116	.292	.416	373	109	27	5	3	0.8	44	41	23	17	1	16	1	137	216	32	34	3.9	.917	SS-61, 3B-37, 2B-1
1930	2 teams	NY A (21G –.230) DET A (76G –.240)																						
″	total	97	.238	.299	341	81	14	2	1	0.3	46	25	26	20	2	4	0	153	244	35	54	4.6	.919	SS-89, 3B-2, P-2, OF-1
1931	DET A	106	.253	.349	364	92	24	4	1	0.3	33	39	14	12	8	15	4	191	238	28	41	4.9	.939	2B-55, SS-35, P-3
1932	CHI N	33	.353	.510	102	36	5	1	3	2.9	15	11	3	5	0	2	0	58	106	12	21	5.3	.932	SS-33
1933		80	.284	.390	218	62	12	1	3	1.4	32	25	15	9	5	15	4	72	134	14	25	3.4	.936	3B-37, SS-26, 2B-2
1934	CIN N	151	.272	.336	633	172	26	6	1	0.2	60	67	15	24	5	2	0	321	405	48	59	5.1	.938	3B-64, SS-58, 2B-26, 1B-4
1935	NY N	107	.283	.336	396	112	12	0	3	0.8	40	37	13	18	0	9	1	178	294	18	39	4.9	.963	2B-64, SS-21, 3B-15
1936		42	.276	.397	58	16	4	0	1	1.7	7	7	8	4	0	17	4	21	38	7	14	3.1	.894	SS-10, 2B-8, 3B-3
12 yrs.		1162	.279	.367	4271	1190	195	49	28	0.7	572	443	222	190	31	94	18	1987	2929	350	514	4.9	.934	SS-749, 3B-158, 2B-156, P-5, 1B-4, OF-1
WORLD SERIES																								
1926	NY A	7	.125	.156	32	4	1	0	0	0.0	2	2	0	6	0	0	0	12	24	4	3	5.7	.900	SS-7
1927		4	.500	.611	18	9	2	0	0	0.0	5	2	0	2	0	0	0	6	8	0	1	3.5	1.000	SS-4
1928		4	.158	.158	19	3	0	0	0	0.0	1	0	0	1	0	0	0	8	11	2	3	5.3	.905	SS-4
1932	CHI N	2	.250	.750	4	1	0	1	0	0.0	1	1	1	0	0	0	0	4	3	0	1	7.0	1.000	SS-1
1936	NY N	3	.333	.333	3	1	0	0	0	0.0	0	0	0	1	0	3	1	1	0	0	0	1.0	1.000	2B-1
5 yrs.		20	.237	.303	76	18	3	1	0	0.0	9	5	1	10	0	3	1	31	46	6	8	4.9	.928	SS-16, 2B-1

Dick Kokos

KOKOS, RICHARD JEROME — BL TL 5′ 8½″ 170 lbs.
Born Richard Jerome Kokoszka.
B. Feb. 28, 1928, Chicago, Ill. D. Apr. 9, 1986, Chicago, Ill.

Year	Team	Games	BA	SA	AB	H	2B	3B	HR	HR%	R	RBI	BB	SO	SB	Pinch Hit AB	Pinch Hit H	PO	A	E	DP	TC/G	FA	G by Pos
1948	STL A	71	.298	.426	258	77	15	3	4	1.6	40	40	28	32	4	1	0	126	8	5	2	2.0	.964	OF-71
1949		143	.261	.459	501	131	28	1	23	4.6	80	77	66	**91**	3	6	2	290	16	6	5	2.3	.981	OF-138
1950		143	.261	.447	490	128	27	5	18	3.7	77	67	88	73	8	14	2	342	8	11	2	2.8	.970	OF-127
1953		107	.241	.411	299	72	12	0	13	4.3	41	38	56	53	0	25	6	152	5	6	1	2.0	.963	OF-83
1954	BAL A	11	.200	.500	10	2	0	0	1	10.0	1	1	4	3	0	8	2	3	0	0	0	3.0	1.000	OF-1
5 yrs.		475	.263	.441	1558	410	82	9	59	3.8	239	223	242	252	15	54	12	913	37	28	10	2.3	.971	OF-420

Gary Kolb

KOLB, GARY ALAN — BL TR 6′ 194 lbs.
B. Mar. 13, 1940, Rock Falls, Ill.

Year	Team	Games	BA	SA	AB	H	2B	3B	HR	HR%	R	RBI	BB	SO	SB	Pinch Hit AB	Pinch Hit H	PO	A	E	DP	TC/G	FA	G by Pos
1960	STL N	9	.000	.000	3	0	0	0	0	0.0	1	0	0	0	0	0	0	4	0	0	0	2.0	1.000	OF-2
1962		6	.357	.357	14	5	0	0	0	0.0	1	0	1	3	0	0	0	9	0	0	0	1.5	1.000	OF-6
1963		75	.271	.479	96	26	1	5	3	3.1	23	10	22	26	2	6	0	52	1	1	1	0.9	.981	OF-58, C-1, 3B-1
1964	MIL N	36	.188	.203	64	12	1	0	0	0.0	7	2	6	10	3	5	0	26	17	4	2	1.6	.915	OF-14, 3B-7, 2B-6, C-2
1965	2 teams	MIL N (24G –.259) NY N (40G –.167)																						
″	total	64	.188	.231	117	22	2	0	1	0.9	11	8	4	34	3	20	5	51	5	2	2	1.3	.966	OF-42, 3B-1, 1B-1
1968	PIT N	74	.218	.319	119	26	4	1	2	1.7	16	6	11	17	2	31	6	56	11	5	3	1.8	.931	OF-25, C-10, 3B-4, 2B-1
1969		29	.081	.108	37	3	1	0	0	0.0	4	3	2	14	0	20	1	29	4	0	0	4.7	1.000	C-7
7 yrs.		293	.209	.296	450	94	9	6	6	1.3	63	29	46	104	10	82	12	227	38	12	8	1.5	.957	OF-147, C-20, 3B-13, 2B-7, 1B-1

Don Kolloway

KOLLOWAY, DONALD MARTIN (Butch, Cab) — BR TR 6′ 3″ 200 lbs.
B. Aug. 4, 1918, Posen, Ill. D. June 30, 1994, Blue Island, Ill.

Year	Team	Games	BA	SA	AB	H	2B	3B	HR	HR%	R	RBI	BB	SO	SB	Pinch Hit AB	Pinch Hit H	PO	A	E	DP	TC/G	FA	G by Pos
1940	CHI A	10	.225	.250	40	9	1	0	0	0.0	5	3	0	3	1	0	0	19	28	4	7	5.1	.922	2B-10
1941		71	.271	.354	280	76	8	3	3	1.1	33	24	6	12	11	3	1	152	185	18	29	5.4	.949	2B-62, 1B-4
1942		147	.273	.368	601	164	**40**	4	3	0.5	72	60	30	39	16	0	0	636	360	28	108	6.9	.973	2B-116, 1B-33
1943		85	.216	.287	348	75	14	4	1	0.3	29	33	9	30	11	0	0	246	240	16	71	5.9	.968	2B-85
1946		123	.280	.363	482	135	23	4	3	0.6	45	53	9	29	14	1	0	267	353	24	82	5.3	.963	2B-90, 3B-31

Don Kolloway *continued*

Year	Team	Games	BA	SA	AB	H	2B	3B	HR	HR%	R	RBI	BB	SO	SB	Pinch Hit AB	Pinch Hit H	PO	A	E	DP	TC/G	FA	G by Pos
1947		124	.278	.359	485	135	25	4	2	0.4	49	35	17	34	11	7	2	378	331	27	86	6.2	.963	2B-99, 1B-11, 3B-8
1948		119	.273	.369	417	114	14	4	6	1.4	60	38	18	18	2	12	3	264	303	22	63	5.8	.963	2B-83, 3B-18
1949	**2 teams**	**CHI A** (4G –.000) **DET A** (126G –.294)																						
"	**total**	130	.292	.355	487	142	19	3	2	0.4	71	47	49	26	7	12	2	613	196	18	94	6.5	.978	2B-62, 1B-57, 3B-9
1950	**DET A**	125	.289	.388	467	135	20	4	6	1.3	55	62	29	28	1	5	1	1088	88	13	133	10.0	.989	1B-118, 2B-1
1951		78	.255	.302	212	54	7	0	1	0.5	28	17	15	12	2	17	4	452	49	4	53	8.6	.992	1B-59
1952		65	.243	.329	173	42	9	0	2	1.2	19	21	7	19	0	25	5	266	44	7	19	7.9	.978	1B-32, 2B-8
1953	**PHI A**	2	.000	.000	1	0	0	0	0	0.0	0	0	0	1	0	1	0	0	0	0	0	0.0	.000	3B-1
12 yrs.		1079	.271	.353	3993	1081	180	30	29	0.7	466	393	189	251	76	83	18	4381	2177	181	745	6.8	.973	2B-616, 1B-314, 3B-67

Karl Kolseth

KOLSETH, KARL DICKEY BL TR 6′ 182 lbs.
B. Dec. 25, 1892, Somerville, Mass. D. May 3, 1956, Cumberland, Md.

Year	Team	Games	BA	SA	AB	H	2B	3B	HR	HR%	R	RBI	BB	SO	SB	Pinch Hit AB	Pinch Hit H	PO	A	E	DP	TC/G	FA	G by Pos
1915	**BAL F**	6	.261	.391	23	6	1	1	0	0.0	1	1	1		0	0	0	63	2	6	5	11.8	.915	1B-6

Fred Kommers

KOMMERS, FREDERICK RAYMOND (Bugs) BL TR 6′ 175 lbs.
B. Mar. 31, 1886, Chicago, Ill. D. June 14, 1943, Chicago, Ill.

Year	Team	Games	BA	SA	AB	H	2B	3B	HR	HR%	R	RBI	BB	SO	SB	Pinch Hit AB	Pinch Hit H	PO	A	E	DP	TC/G	FA	G by Pos
1913	**PIT N**	40	.232	.316	155	36	5	4	0	0.0	14	22	10	29	1	0	0	94	1	2	0	2.4	.979	OF-40
1914	**2 teams**	**STL F** (76G –.307) **BAL F** (16G –.214)																						
"	**total**	92	.294	.427	286	84	10	8	4	1.4	38	42	31		7	10	4	122	11	13	1	1.8	.911	OF-79
2 yrs.		132	.272	.388	441	120	15	12	4	0.9	52	64	41	29	8	10	4	216	12	15	1	2.0	.938	OF-119

Brad Komminsk

KOMMINSK, BRAD LYNN BR TR 6′ 2″ 202 lbs.
B. Apr. 4, 1961, Lima, Ohio.

Year	Team	Games	BA	SA	AB	H	2B	3B	HR	HR%	R	RBI	BB	SO	SB	Pinch Hit AB	Pinch Hit H	PO	A	E	DP	TC/G	FA	G by Pos
1983	**ATL N**	19	.222	.278	36	8	2	0	0	0.0	2	4	5	7	0	7	2	16	1	1	0	1.4	.944	OF-13
1984		90	.203	.316	301	61	10	0	8	2.7	37	36	29	77	18	10	4	135	2	1	0	1.7	.993	OF-80
1985		106	.227	.327	300	68	12	3	4	1.3	52	21	38	71	10	15	0	161	2	7	0	1.8	.959	OF-92
1986		5	.400	.400	5	2	0	0	0	0.0	1	1	0	1	0	1	0	1	2	0	0	0.8	1.000	OF-2, 3B-2
1987	**MIL A**	7	.067	.067	15	1	0	0	0	0.0	0	0	1	7	1	1	0	10	0	0	0	1.7	1.000	OF-5, DH-1
1989	**CLE A**	71	.237	.419	198	47	8	2	8	4.0	27	33	24	55	8	5	1	181	3	1	1	2.7	.995	OF-68
1990	**2 teams**	**SF N** (8G –.200) **BAL A** (46G –.238)																						
"	**total**	54	.236	.358	106	25	4	0	3	2.8	20	8	15	31	1	11	2	70	2	0	0	1.5	1.000	OF-47, DH-2
1991	**OAK A**	24	.120	.160	25	3	1	0	0	0.0	1	2	2	9	1	2	1	18	1	0	0	0.9	1.000	OF-22
8 yrs.		376	.218	.336	986	215	37	5	23	2.3	140	105	114	258	39	52	10	592	13	10	1	1.8	.984	OF-329, DH-3, 3B-2

Ed Konetchy

KONETCHY, EDWARD JOSEPH (Big Ed) BR TR 6′ 2½″ 195 lbs.
B. Sept. 3, 1885, LaCrosse, Wis. D. May 27, 1947, Fort Worth, Tex.

Year	Team	Games	BA	SA	AB	H	2B	3B	HR	HR%	R	RBI	BB	SO	SB	Pinch Hit AB	Pinch Hit H	PO	A	E	DP	TC/G	FA	G by Pos
1907	**STL N**	90	.252	.361	330	83	11	8	3	0.9	34	30	26		13	0	0	922	71	25	46	11.3	.975	1B-90
1908		154	.248	.354	545	135	19	12	5	0.9	46	50	38		16	0	0	1610	122	24	61	11.4	.986	1B-154
1909		152	.286	.396	576	165	23	14	4	0.7	88	80	65		25	0	0	1584	97	26	71	11.2	.985	1B-152
1910		144	.302	.425	520	157	23	16	3	0.6	87	78	78	59	18	0	0	1499	98	15	81	11.1	.991	1B-144, P-1
1911		158	.289	.433	571	165	**38**	13	6	1.1	90	88	81	63	27	0	0	1652	71	16	85	11.0	.991	1B-158
1912		143	.314	.455	538	169	26	13	8	1.5	81	82	62	66	25	0	0	1396	91	13	77	10.5	.991	1B-142, OF-1
1913		139	.273	.418	502	137	18	17	7	1.4	74	68	53	41	27	0	0	1432	91	7	71	10.9	.995	1B-139, P-1
1914	**PIT N**	154	.249	.343	563	140	23	9	4	0.7	56	51	32	48	20	0	0	1576	93	8	70	10.9	.995	1B-154
1915	**PIT F**	152	.314	.483	576	181	31	18	10	1.7	79	93	41		27	0	0	1536	81	10	83	10.7	.994	1B-152
1916	**BOS N**	158	.260	.373	566	147	29	13	3	0.5	76	70	43	46	13	0	0	1626	96	18	96	11.0	.990	1B-158
1917		130	.272	.380	474	129	19	13	2	0.4	56	54	36	40	16	1	0	1351	70	8	65	11.1	.994	1B-129
1918		119	.236	.307	437	103	15	5	2	0.5	33	56	32	35	5	0	0	1239	65	11	70	11.1	.992	1B-112, OF-6, P-1
1919	**BKN N**	132	.298	.391	486	145	24	9	1	0.2	46	47	29	39	14	0	0	1288	89	9	62	10.5	.994	1B-132
1920		131	.308	.431	497	153	22	12	5	1.0	62	63	33	18	3	1	0	1332	79	14	70	11.0	.990	1B-130
1921	**2 teams**	**BKN N** (55G –.269) **PHI N** (72G –.321)																						
"	**total**	127	.299	.458	465	139	23	9	11	2.4	63	82	40	38	6	2	0	1335	83	20	79	11.5	.986	1B-125
15 yrs.		2083	.281	.402	7646	2148	344	181	74	1.0	971	992	689	493	255	4	0	21378	1297	224	1087	11.0	.990	1B-2071, OF-7, P-3
WORLD SERIES																								
1920	**BKN N**	7	.174	.261	23	4	0	1	0	0.0	0	2	3	2	0	0	0	70	8	1	4	11.3	.987	1B-7

Mike Konnick

KONNICK, MICHAEL ALOYSIUS BR TR 5′ 9″ 180 lbs.
B. Jan. 13, 1889, Glen Lyon, Pa. D. July 9, 1971, Wilkes-Barre, Pa.

Year	Team	Games	BA	SA	AB	H	2B	3B	HR	HR%	R	RBI	BB	SO	SB	Pinch Hit AB	Pinch Hit H	PO	A	E	DP	TC/G	FA	G by Pos
1909	**CIN N**	2	.400	.600	5	2	1	0	0	0.0	0	1	0		0	0	0	6	1	0	0	3.5	1.000	C-2
1910		1	.000	.000	3	0	0	0	0	0.0	0	0	1	0	0	0	0	2	2	0	0	4.0	1.000	SS-1
2 yrs.		3	.250	.375	8	2	1	0	0	0.0	0	1	1	0	0	0	0	8	3	0	0	3.7	1.000	C-2, SS-1

Bruce Konopka

KONOPKA, BRUNO BRUCE BL TL 6′ 2″ 190 lbs.
B. Sept. 16, 1919, Hammond, Ind.

Year	Team	Games	BA	SA	AB	H	2B	3B	HR	HR%	R	RBI	BB	SO	SB	Pinch Hit AB	Pinch Hit H	PO	A	E	DP	TC/G	FA	G by Pos
1942	**PHI A**	5	.300	.300	10	3	0	0	0	0.0	2	1	1	1	0	2	1	17	1	0	2	6.0	1.000	1B-3
1943		2	.000	.000	2	0	0	0	0	0.0	0	0	0	1	0	2	0	0	0	0	0	0.0	—	
1946		38	.237	.301	93	22	4	1	0	0.0	7	9	4	8	0	17	5	148	17	1	13	7.9	.994	1B-20, OF-1
3 yrs.		45	.238	.295	105	25	4	1	0	0.0	9	10	5	10	0	21	6	165	18	1	15	7.7	.995	1B-23, OF-1

Harry Koons

KOONS, HENRY M. BR TR 5′ 8″ 174 lbs.
B. 1863, Philadelphia, Pa. Deceased.

Year	Team	Games	BA	SA	AB	H	2B	3B	HR	HR%	R	RBI	BB	SO	SB	Pinch Hit AB	Pinch Hit H	PO	A	E	DP	TC/G	FA	G by Pos
1884	**2 teams**	**ALT U** (21G –.231) **CHI U** (1G –.000)																						
"	**total**	22	.222	.272	81	18	2	1	0	0.0	8		2			0	0	45	45	14	1	4.5	.865	3B-22, C-1

George Kopacz

KOPACZ, GEORGE FELIX (Sonny) BL TL 6′ 1″ 195 lbs.
B. Feb. 26, 1941, Chicago, Ill.

Year	Team	Games	BA	SA	AB	H	2B	3B	HR	HR%	R	RBI	BB	SO	SB	Pinch Hit AB	Pinch Hit H	PO	A	E	DP	TC/G	FA	G by Pos
1966	**ATL N**	6	.000	.000	9	0	0	0	0	0.0	1	0	1	5	0	4	0	10	0	1	0	5.5	.909	1B-2
1970	**PIT N**	10	.188	.188	16	3	0	0	0	0.0	1	0	0	5	0	7	1	17	0	0	2	5.7	1.000	1B-3
2 yrs.		16	.120	.120	25	3	0	0	0	0.0	2	0	1	10	0	11	1	27	0	1	2	5.6	.964	1B-5

Year	Team		Games	BA	SA	AB	H	2B	3B	HR	HR%	R	RBI	BB	SO	SB	Pinch Hit AB	Pinch Hit H	PO	A	E	DP	TC/G	FA	G by Pos

Larry Kopf

KOPF, WILLIAM LORENZ BB TR 5′ 9″ 160 lbs.
Played as Fred Brady 1913.
Brother of Wally Kopf.
B. Nov. 3, 1890, Bristol, Conn. D. Oct. 15, 1986, Hamilton County, Ohio.

Year	Team		Games	BA	SA	AB	H	2B	3B	HR	HR%	R	RBI	BB	SO	SB	Pinch Hit AB	Pinch Hit H	PO	A	E	DP	TC/G	FA	G by Pos
1913	CLE	A	5	.222	.222	9	2	0	0	0	0.0	1	1	0	0	0	0	0	5	10	1	1	4.0	.938	2B-3, 3B-1
1914	PHI	A	35	.188	.275	69	13	2	2	0	0.0	8	12	8	14	6	5	1	52	51	13	3	4.5	.888	SS-13, 3B-8, 2B-5
1915			118	.225	.269	386	87	10	2	1	0.3	39	33	41	45	5	0	0	205	279	48	30	4.5	.910	SS-74, 3B-42, 2B-2
1916	CIN	N	11	.275	.325	40	11	2	0	0	0.0	2	5	1	8	1	0	0	16	33	3	4	4.7	.942	SS-11
1917			148	.255	.326	573	146	19	8	2	0.3	81	26	28	48	17	2	1	276	470	68	59	5.6	.916	SS-145
1919			135	.270	.326	503	136	18	5	0	0.0	51	58	28	27	18	0	0	273	407	41	39	5.3	.943	SS-135
1920			126	.245	.303	458	112	15	6	0	0.0	56	59	35	24	14	1	1	251	371	47	0	5.2	.930	SS-123, 3B-2, 2B-2, OF-1
1921			107	.218	.264	367	80	8	3	1	0.3	36	25	43	20	3	6	1	207	322	31	39	5.5	.945	SS-93, 2B-4, 3B-3, OF-1
1922	BOS	N	126	.266	.298	466	124	6	3	1	0.2	59	37	45	22	8	1	1	259	382	45	58	5.5	.934	2B-78, SS-33, 3B-13
1923			39	.275	.312	138	38	3	1	0	0.0	15	10	13	6	0	0	0	86	133	23	26	5.9	.905	SS-37, 2B-4
10 yrs.			850	.249	.301	3009	749	83	30	5	0.2	348	266	242	214	72	15	5	1630	2458	320	259	5.3	.927	SS-664, 2B-98, 3B-69, OF-2
WORLD SERIES																									
1919	CIN	N	8	.222	.370	27	6	0	2	0	0.0	3	3	3	2	0	0	0	10	29	1	4	5.0	.975	SS-8

Wally Kopf

KOPF, WALTER HENRY BB TR 5′11″ 168 lbs.
Brother of Larry Kopf.
B. July 10, 1899, Stonington, Conn. D. Apr. 30, 1979, Cincinnati, Ohio.

Year	Team		Games	BA	SA	AB	H	2B	3B	HR	HR%	R	RBI	BB	SO	SB	Pinch Hit AB	Pinch Hit H	PO	A	E	DP	TC/G	FA	G by Pos
1921	NY	N	2	.333	.333	3	1	0	0	0	0.0	0	0	1	1	0	0	0	0	6	0	1	3.0	1.000	3B-2

Merlin Kopp

KOPP, MERLIN HENRY (Manny) BB TR 5′ 8″ 158 lbs.
BR 1915
B. Jan. 2, 1892, Toledo, Ohio D. May 6, 1960, Sacramento, Calif.

Year	Team		Games	BA	SA	AB	H	2B	3B	HR	HR%	R	RBI	BB	SO	SB	Pinch Hit AB	Pinch Hit H	PO	A	E	DP	TC/G	FA	G by Pos
1915	WAS	A	16	.250	.250	32	8	0	0	0	0.0	2	0	5	7	1	6	2	14	0	1	0	1.7	.933	OF-9
1918	PHI	A	96	.234	.292	363	85	7	7	0	0.0	60	18	42	55	22	0	0	221	20	7	6	2.6	.972	OF-96
1919			75	.226	.281	235	53	2	4	1	0.4	34	12	42	43	16	4	0	127	7	11	0	2.2	.924	OF-65
3 yrs.			187	.232	.286	630	146	9	11	1	0.2	96	30	89	105	39	10	2	362	27	19	6	2.4	.953	OF-170

Joe Koppe

KOPPE, JOSEPH BR TR 5′10″ 165 lbs.
Born Joseph Kopchia.
B. Oct. 19, 1930, Detroit, Mich.

Year	Team		Games	BA	SA	AB	H	2B	3B	HR	HR%	R	RBI	BB	SO	SB	Pinch Hit AB	Pinch Hit H	PO	A	E	DP	TC/G	FA	G by Pos
1958	MIL	N	16	.444	.444	9	4	0	0	0	0.0	3	0	1	1	0	0	0	5	10	3	3	6.0	.833	SS-3
1959	PHI	N	126	.261	.386	422	110	18	7	7	1.7	68	28	41	80	7	0	0	225	362	27	67	5.0	.956	SS-113, 2B-11
1960			58	.171	.235	170	29	6	1	1	0.6	13	13	23	47	3	1	0	107	136	13	24	4.5	.949	SS-55, 3B-2
1961	2 teams		PHI N (6G –.000) LA A (91G –.251)																						
″	total		97	.249	.340	341	85	12	2	5	1.5	47	40	45	77	3	0	0	137	258	22	52	4.3	.947	SS-93, 2B-3, 3B-1
1962	LA	A	128	.227	.301	375	85	16	0	4	1.1	47	40	73	84	2	2	0	203	369	27	66	4.7	.955	SS-118, 2B-5, 3B-4
1963			76	.210	.273	143	30	4	1	1	0.7	11	12	9	30	0	20	4	69	94	6	17	3.1	.964	SS-19, 3B-18, 2B-14, OF-3
1964			54	.257	.310	113	29	4	1	0	0.0	10	6	14	16	0	3	1	61	118	12	22	4.1	.937	SS-31, 2B-13, 3B-3
1965	CAL	A	23	.212	.333	33	7	1	0	1	3.0	3	2	3	10	1	3	1	23	40	1	6	3.6	.984	2B-10, SS-4, 3B-4
8 yrs.			578	.236	.324	1606	379	61	12	19	1.2	202	141	209	345	16	29	6	830	1387	111	257	4.4	.952	SS-436, 2B-56, 3B-32, OF-3

George Kopshaw

KOPSHAW, GEORGE KARL BR TR 5′11½″ 176 lbs.
B. July 5, 1895, Passaic, N. J. D. Dec. 26, 1934, Lynchburg, Va.

Year	Team		Games	BA	SA	AB	H	2B	3B	HR	HR%	R	RBI	BB	SO	SB	Pinch Hit AB	Pinch Hit H	PO	A	E	DP	TC/G	FA	G by Pos
1923	STL	N	2	.200	.400	5	1	1	0	0	0.0	1	0	0	1	0	0	0	2	0	0	0	2.0	1.000	C-1

Steve Korcheck

KORCHECK, STEPHEN JOSEPH (Hoss) BR TR 6′ 1″ 205 lbs.
B. Aug. 11, 1932, McClellandtown, Pa.

Year	Team		Games	BA	SA	AB	H	2B	3B	HR	HR%	R	RBI	BB	SO	SB	Pinch Hit AB	Pinch Hit H	PO	A	E	DP	TC/G	FA	G by Pos
1954	WAS	A	2	.143	.143	7	1	0	0	0	0.0	0	0	0	2	0	0	0	5	1	1	0	3.5	.857	C-2
1955			13	.278	.333	36	10	2	0	0	0.0	3	2	0	5	0	3	1	46	7	0	2	4.4	1.000	C-12
1958			21	.078	.157	51	4	2	1	0	0.0	6	1	1	16	0	1	0	68	9	2	2	4.0	.975	C-20
1959			22	.157	.196	51	8	2	0	0	0.0	3	4	5	13	0	0	0	103	8	3	3	5.2	.974	C-22
4 yrs.			58	.159	.214	145	23	6	1	0	0.0	12	7	6	36	0	4	1	222	25	6	7	4.5	.976	C-56

Art Kores

KORES, ARTHUR EMIL (Dutch) BR TR 5′ 9″ 167 lbs.
B. July 22, 1886, Milwaukee, Wis. D. Mar. 26, 1974, Milwaukee, Wis.

Year	Team		Games	BA	SA	AB	H	2B	3B	HR	HR%	R	RBI	BB	SO	SB	Pinch Hit AB	Pinch Hit H	PO	A	E	DP	TC/G	FA	G by Pos
1915	STL	F	60	.234	.313	201	47	9	2	1	0.5	18	22	21		6	0	0	80	161	10	12	4.2	.960	3B-60

Andy Kosco

KOSCO, ANDREW JOHN BR TR 6′ 3″ 205 lbs.
B. Oct. 5, 1941, Youngstown, Ohio.

Year	Team		Games	BA	SA	AB	H	2B	3B	HR	HR%	R	RBI	BB	SO	SB	Pinch Hit AB	Pinch Hit H	PO	A	E	DP	TC/G	FA	G by Pos
1965	MIN	A	23	.236	.364	55	13	4	0	1	1.8	3	6	1	15	0	8	3	35	3	0	1	2.4	1.000	OF-14, 1B-2
1966			57	.222	.291	158	35	5	0	2	1.3	11	13	7	31	0	14	6	99	2	2	3	2.3	.981	OF-40, 1B-5
1967			9	.143	.179	28	4	1	0	0	0.0	4	4	2	4	0	3	1	12	0	1	0	1.9	.923	OF-7
1968	NY	A	131	.240	.382	466	112	19	1	15	3.2	47	59	16	71	2	11	4	403	24	9	18	3.5	.979	OF-95, 1B-28
1969	LA	N	120	.248	.422	424	105	13	2	19	4.5	51	74	21	66	0	13	5	161	6	3	3	1.5	.982	OF-109, 1B-3
1970			74	.228	.388	224	51	12	0	8	3.6	21	27	1	40	1	16	2	102	2	2	0	1.8	.981	OF-58, 1B-1
1971	MIL	A	98	.227	.379	264	60	6	2	10	3.8	27	39	24	57	1	28	8	264	25	3	23	3.4	.990	OF-45, 1B-29, 3B-12
1972	2 teams		CAL A (49G –.239) BOS A (17G –.213)																						
″	total		66	.233	.439	189	44	6	3	9	4.8	20	19	7	32	1	17	3	81	3	1	0	1.8	.988	OF-48
1973	CIN	N	47	.280	.568	118	33	7	0	9	7.6	17	21	13	26	0	13	3	59	1	0	0	1.6	1.000	OF-36, 1B-1
1974			33	.189	.243	37	7	2	0	0	0.0	3	5	7	8	0	20	4	4	7	2	0	1.4	.846	3B-8, OF-1
10 yrs.			658	.236	.394	1963	464	75	8	73	3.7	204	267	99	350	5	143	39	1220	73	23	48	2.4	.983	OF-453, 1B-69, 3B-20
LEAGUE CHAMPIONSHIP SERIES																									
1973	CIN	N	3	.300	.300	10	3	0	0	0	0.0	0	0	2	3	0	0	0	12	0	1	0	4.3	.923	OF-3

Clem Koshorek

KOSHOREK, CLEMENT JOHN (Scooter) BR TR 5′ 6″ 165 lbs.
B. June 20, 1925, Royal Oak, Mich. D. Sept. 8, 1991, Royal Oak, Mich.

Year	Team		Games	BA	SA	AB	H	2B	3B	HR	HR%	R	RBI	BB	SO	SB	Pinch Hit AB	Pinch Hit H	PO	A	E	DP	TC/G	FA	G by Pos
1952	PIT	N	98	.261	.314	322	84	17	0	0	0.0	27	15	26	39	4	8	1	149	232	18	47	4.6	.955	SS-33, 2B-27, 3B-26
1953			1	.000	.000	1	0	0	0	0	0.0	0	0	0	1	0	1	0	0	0	0	0	0.0	—	
2 yrs.			99	.260	.313	323	84	17	0	0	0.0	27	15	26	40	4	9	1	149	232	18	47	4.6	.955	SS-33, 2B-27, 3B-26

Kevin Koslofski

KOSLOFSKI, KEVIN CRAIG BL TR 5′ 8″ 165 lbs.
B. Sept. 24, 1966, Decatur, Ill.

Year	Team	Games	BA	SA	AB	H	2B	3B	HR	HR%	R	RBI	BB	SO	SB	Pinch Hit AB	Pinch Hit H	PO	A	E	DP	TC/G	FA	G by Pos
1992	KC A	55	.248	.346	133	33	0	2	3	2.3	20	13	12	23	2	5	2	107	5	1	0	2.2	.991	OF-52
1993		15	.269	.385	26	7	0	0	1	3.8	4	2	4	5	0	1	0	20	2	0	2	1.6	1.000	OF-13, DH-1
1994		2	.250	.250	4	1	0	0	0	0.0	2	0	2	1	0	1	1	2	1	1	0	2.0	.750	OF-2
3 yrs.		72	.252	.350	163	41	0	2	4	2.5	26	15	18	29	2	7	3	129	8	2	2	2.0	.986	OF-67, DH-1

Mike Kosman

KOSMAN, MICHAEL THOMAS BR TR 5′ 9″ 160 lbs.
B. Dec. 10, 1917, Hamtramck, Mich.

Year	Team	Games	BA	SA	AB	H	2B	3B	HR	HR%	R	RBI	BB	SO	SB	Pinch Hit AB	Pinch Hit H	PO	A	E	DP	TC/G	FA	G by Pos
1944	CIN N	1	—	—	0	0	0	0	0	—	0	0	0	0	0	0	0	0	0	0	0	0.0	—	

Fred Koster

KOSTER, FREDERICK CHARLES (Fritz) BL TL 5′10½″ 165 lbs.
B. Dec. 21, 1905, Louisville, Ky. D. Apr. 24, 1979, St. Matthews, Ky.

Year	Team	Games	BA	SA	AB	H	2B	3B	HR	HR%	R	RBI	BB	SO	SB	Pinch Hit AB	Pinch Hit H	PO	A	E	DP	TC/G	FA	G by Pos
1931	PHI N	76	.225	.265	151	34	2	2	0	0.0	21	8	14	21	4	19	3	80	4	7	1	2.2	.923	OF-41

Frank Kostro

KOSTRO, FRANK JERRY BR TR 6′ 2″ 190 lbs.
B. Aug. 4, 1937, Windber, Pa.

Year	Team	Games	BA	SA	AB	H	2B	3B	HR	HR%	R	RBI	BB	SO	SB	Pinch Hit AB	Pinch Hit H	PO	A	E	DP	TC/G	FA	G by Pos
1962	DET A	16	.268	.341	41	11	3	0	0	0.0	5	3	1	6	0	4	1	9	20	1	2	2.7	.967	3B-11
1963	2 teams	DET A (31G –.231) LA A (43G –.222)																						
″	total	74	.225	.298	151	34	3	1	2	1.3	10	10	15	30	0	36	7	85	44	4	8	3.4	.970	3B-25, 1B-8, OF-6
1964	MIN A	59	.272	.408	103	28	5	0	3	2.9	10	12	4	21	0	35	10	17	33	4	2	2.5	.926	3B-12, 2B-7, OF-2, 1B-1
1965		20	.161	.226	31	5	2	0	0	0.0	2	1	4	5	0	6	0	10	18	5	6	2.2	.848	2B-7, 3B-6, OF-2
1967		32	.323	.323	31	10	0	0	0	0.0	4	2	3	2	0	23	9	1	0	0	0	0.3	1.000	OF-3, 3B-1
1968		63	.241	.296	108	26	4	1	0	0.0	9	9	6	20	0	36	7	54	2	0	1	1.9	1.000	OF-24, 1B-5
1969		2	.000	.000	2	0	0	0	0	0.0	0	0	0	1	0	2	0	0	0	0	0	0.0	—	
7 yrs.		266	.244	.321	467	114	17	2	5	1.1	40	37	33	85	0	142	34	176	117	14	19	2.6	.954	3B-55, OF-37, 2B-14, 1B-14

Brian Kowitz

KOWITZ, BRIAN MARK BL TL 5′10″ 182 lbs.
B. Aug. 7, 1969, Baltimore, Md.

Year	Team	Games	BA	SA	AB	H	2B	3B	HR	HR%	R	RBI	BB	SO	SB	Pinch Hit AB	Pinch Hit H	PO	A	E	DP	TC/G	FA	G by Pos
1995	ATL N	10	.167	.208	24	4	1	0	0	0.0	3	3	2	5	0	1	1	6	0	0	0	0.8	1.000	OF-8

Ernie Koy

KOY, ERNEST ANYZ (Chief) BR TR 6′ 200 lbs.
B. Sept. 17, 1909, Sealy, Tex.

Year	Team	Games	BA	SA	AB	H	2B	3B	HR	HR%	R	RBI	BB	SO	SB	Pinch Hit AB	Pinch Hit H	PO	A	E	DP	TC/G	FA	G by Pos
1938	BKN N	142	.299	.468	521	156	29	13	11	2.1	78	76	38	76	15	3	1	306	7	5	4	2.3	.984	OF-135, 3B-1
1939		123	.278	.445	425	118	37	5	8	1.9	57	67	39	64	11	9	1	252	4	10	1	2.3	.962	OF-114
1940	2 teams	BKN N (24G –.229) STL N (93G –.310)																						
″	total	117	.301	.452	396	119	21	6	9	2.3	53	60	31	62	13	7	0	217	2	6	0	2.0	.973	OF-110
1941	2 teams	STL N (13G –.200) CIN N (67G –.250)																						
″	total	80	.242	.357	244	59	12	2	4	1.6	29	31	15	30	1	13	3	110	3	1	1	1.9	.991	OF-61
1942	2 teams	CIN N (3G –.000) PHI N (91G –.244)																						
″	total	94	.242	.346	260	63	9	3	4	1.5	21	26	14	52	0	9	2	149	4	3	1	2.0	.981	OF-78
5 yrs.		556	.279	.427	1846	515	108	29	36	2.0	238	260	137	284	40	41	7	1034	20	25	7	2.2	.977	OF-498, 3B-1

Al Kozar

KOZAR, ALBERT KENNETH BR TR 5′ 9½″ 173 lbs.
B. July 5, 1921, McKees Rocks, Pa.

Year	Team	Games	BA	SA	AB	H	2B	3B	HR	HR%	R	RBI	BB	SO	SB	Pinch Hit AB	Pinch Hit H	PO	A	E	DP	TC/G	FA	G by Pos
1948	WAS A	150	.250	.326	577	144	25	8	1	0.2	61	58	66	52	4	0	0	348	444	27	89	5.5	.967	2B-149
1949		105	.269	.357	350	94	15	2	4	1.1	46	31	25	23	2	4	0	232	235	11	57	4.7	.977	2B-102
1950	2 teams	WAS A (20G –.200) CHI A (10G –.300)																						
″	total	30	.215	.277	65	14	1	0	1	1.5	11	5	5	11	0	6	1	39	51	3	11	4.7	.968	2B-19, 3B-1
3 yrs.		285	.254	.334	992	252	41	10	6	0.6	118	94	96	86	6	10	1	619	730	41	157	5.1	.971	2B-270, 3B-1

Joe Kracher

KRACHER, JOSEPH PETER (Jug) BR TR 5′11″ 185 lbs.
B. Nov. 4, 1915, Philadelphia, Pa. D. Dec. 24, 1981, San Angelo, Tex.

Year	Team	Games	BA	SA	AB	H	2B	3B	HR	HR%	R	RBI	BB	SO	SB	Pinch Hit AB	Pinch Hit H	PO	A	E	DP	TC/G	FA	G by Pos
1939	PHI N	5	.200	.200	5	1	0	0	0	0.0	1	0	2	1	0	2	1	1	0	0	0	0.5	1.000	C-2

Clarence Kraft

KRAFT, CLARENCE OTTO (Big Boy) BR TR 6′ 190 lbs.
B. June 9, 1887, Evansville, Ind. D. Mar. 26, 1958, Fort Worth, Tex.

Year	Team	Games	BA	SA	AB	H	2B	3B	HR	HR%	R	RBI	BB	SO	SB	Pinch Hit AB	Pinch Hit H	PO	A	E	DP	TC/G	FA	G by Pos
1914	BOS N	3	.333	.333	3	1	0	0	0	0.0	0	0	0	1	0	2	0	4	0	0	0	4.0	1.000	1B-1

Ed Kranepool

KRANEPOOL, EDWARD EMIL (The Krane) BL TL 6′ 3″ 205 lbs.
B. Nov. 8, 1944, New York, N. Y.

Year	Team	Games	BA	SA	AB	H	2B	3B	HR	HR%	R	RBI	BB	SO	SB	Pinch Hit AB	Pinch Hit H	PO	A	E	DP	TC/G	FA	G by Pos
1962	NY N	3	.167	.333	6	1	1	0	0	0.0	0	0	0	1	0	0	0	9	3	0	0	4.0	1.000	1B-3
1963		86	.209	.289	273	57	12	2	2	0.7	22	14	18	50	4	13	3	228	18	4	17	3.3	.984	OF-55, 1B-20
1964		119	.257	.393	420	108	19	4	10	2.4	47	45	32	50	0	10	2	983	80	10	78	9.8	.991	1B-104, OF-6
1965		153	.253	.371	525	133	24	4	10	1.9	44	53	39	71	1	11	4	1375	93	12	116	10.1	.992	1B-147
1966		146	.254	.399	464	118	15	2	16	3.4	51	57	41	66	1	7	1	1180	86	12	100	8.9	.991	1B-132, OF-11
1967		141	.269	.373	469	126	17	1	10	2.1	37	54	37	51	0	9	1	1137	87	10	103	8.9	.992	1B-139
1968		127	.231	.295	373	86	13	1	3	0.8	29	20	19	39	0	16	3	924	75	6	76	8.7	.994	1B-113, OF-2
1969		112	.238	.368	353	84	9	2	11	3.1	36	49	37	32	3	7	1	812	64	6	76	8.2	.993	1B-106, OF-2
1970		43	.170	.170	47	8	0	0	0	0.0	2	3	5	2	0	31	4	47	3	0	5	6.3	1.000	1B-8
1971		122	.280	.447	421	118	20	4	14	3.3	61	58	38	33	0	8	2	795	61	2	67	7.2	.998	1B-108, OF-11
1972		122	.269	.394	327	88	15	1	8	2.4	28	34	34	35	1	16	4	705	48	3	65	6.9	.996	1B-108, OF-1
1973		100	.239	.306	284	68	12	2	1	0.4	28	35	30	28	1	16	2	448	28	2	39	5.8	.996	1B-51, OF-32
1974		94	.300	.415	217	65	11	1	4	1.8	20	24	18	14	1	35	**17**	207	9	5	18	3.9	.977	OF-33, 1B-24
1975		106	.323	.409	325	105	16	0	4	1.2	42	43	27	21	1	20	8	671	46	2	51	8.4	.997	1B-82, OF-4
1976		123	.292	.410	415	121	17	1	10	2.4	47	49	35	38	1	10	4	721	35	3	48	6.5	.996	1B-86, OF-31
1977		108	.281	.448	281	79	17	0	10	3.6	28	40	23	20	1	29	13	347	30	4	21	4.6	.990	OF-42, 1B-41
1978		66	.210	.346	81	17	2	0	3	3.7	7	19	8	12	0	50	15	36	4	0	3	2.7	1.000	OF-12, 1B-3
1979		82	.232	.303	155	36	5	0	2	1.3	7	17	13	18	0	37	6	215	19	0	18	6.3	1.000	1B-29, OF-8
18 yrs.		1853	.261	.377	5436	1418	225	25	118	2.2	536	614	454	581	15	325	90	10840	789	81	901	7.5	.993	1B-1304, OF-250
LEAGUE CHAMPIONSHIP SERIES																								
1969	NY N	3	.250	.333	12	3	1	0	0	0.0	2	1	1	2	0	0	0	20	3	0	2	7.7	1.000	1B-3
1973		1	.500	.500	2	1	0	0	0	0.0	0	2	0	0	0	0	0	2	0	0	0	2.0	1.000	OF-1
2 yrs.		4	.286	.357	14	4	1	0	0	0.0	2	3	1	2	0	0	0	22	3	0	2	6.3	1.000	1B-3, OF-1

Ed Kranepool *continued*

Year	Team	Games	BA	SA	AB	H	2B	3B	HR	HR%	R	RBI	BB	SO	SB	Pinch Hit AB	Pinch Hit H	PO	A	E	DP	TC/G	FA	G by Pos
WORLD SERIES																								
1969	NY N	1	.250	1.000	4	1	0	0	1	25.0	1	1	0	0	0	0	0	7	0	0	0	7.0	1.000	1B-1
1973		4	.000	.000	3	0	0	0	0	0.0	0	0	0	0	0	3	0	0	0	0	0	0.0	—	
2 yrs.		5	.143	.571	7	1	0	0	1	14.3	1	1	0	0	0	3	0	7	0	0	0	7.0	1.000	1B-1

Charlie Krause

KRAUSE, CHARLES TR
Also appeared in box score as Krouse.
B. Oct. 2, 1873, Detroit, Mich. D. Mar. 30, 1948, Eloise, Mich.

Year	Team	Games	BA	SA	AB	H	2B	3B	HR	HR%	R	RBI	BB	SO	SB	Pinch Hit AB	Pinch Hit H	PO	A	E	DP	TC/G	FA	G by Pos
1901	CIN N	1	.250	.250	4	1	0	0	0	0.0	0	0	0		0	0	0	1	2	2	0	5.0	.600	2B-1

Danny Kravitz

KRAVITZ, DANIEL (Beak, Dusty) BL TR 5′11″ 195 lbs.
B. Dec. 21, 1930, Lopez, Pa.

Year	Team	Games	BA	SA	AB	H	2B	3B	HR	HR%	R	RBI	BB	SO	SB	Pinch Hit AB	Pinch Hit H	PO	A	E	DP	TC/G	FA	G by Pos
1956	PIT N	32	.265	.441	68	18	2	2	2	2.9	6	10	5	9	1	12	0	93	10	6	2	3.9	.945	C-26, 3B-2
1957		19	.146	.171	41	6	1	0	0	0.0	2	4	2	10	0	9	1	45	9	0	1	3.6	1.000	C-15
1958		45	.240	.340	100	24	3	2	1	1.0	9	5	11	10	0	8	1	103	16	4	3	3.3	.967	C-37
1959		52	.253	.377	162	41	9	1	3	1.9	18	21	5	14	0	8	3	198	19	3	3	4.9	.986	C-45
1960	2 teams	PIT N (8G –.000) KC A (59G –.234)																						
″	total	67	.227	.354	181	41	7	2	4	2.2	17	14	12	21	0	18	4	217	16	7	3	5.0	.971	C-48
5 yrs.		215	.236	.355	552	130	22	7	10	1.8	52	54	35	64	1	55	9	656	70	20	12	4.3	.973	C-171, 3B-2

Mike Kreevich

KREEVICH, MICHAEL ANDREAS BR TR 5′ 7½″ 168 lbs.
B. June 10, 1908, Mount Olive, Ill. D. Apr. 25, 1994, Pana, Ill.

Year	Team	Games	BA	SA	AB	H	2B	3B	HR	HR%	R	RBI	BB	SO	SB	Pinch Hit AB	Pinch Hit H	PO	A	E	DP	TC/G	FA	G by Pos
1931	CHI N	5	.167	.167	12	2	0	0	0	0.0	0	0	0	6	1	1	0	5	1	0	0	1.5	1.000	OF-4
1935	CHI A	6	.435	.522	23	10	2	0	0	0.0	3	2	1	0	1	0	0	8	4	0	0	2.0	1.000	3B-6
1936		137	.307	.433	550	169	32	11	5	0.9	99	69	61	46	10	3	2	300	17	12	5	2.5	.964	OF-133
1937		144	.302	.468	583	176	29	**16**	12	2.1	94	73	43	45	10	3	1	401	13	5	4	3.0	.988	OF-138
1938		129	.297	.436	489	145	26	12	6	1.2	73	73	55	23	13	3	0	379	7	10	2	3.1	.975	OF-127
1939		145	.323	.436	541	175	30	8	5	0.9	85	77	59	40	23	3	0	425	26	12	4	3.2	.974	OF-139, 3B-4
1940		144	.265	.387	582	154	27	10	8	1.4	86	55	34	49	15	0	0	428	12	8	3	3.1	.982	OF-144
1941		121	.232	.305	436	101	16	8	0	0.0	44	37	35	26	17	7	4	302	7	2	2	2.8	.994	OF-113
1942	PHI A	116	.255	.309	444	113	19	1	1	0.2	57	30	47	31	7	6	2	314	4	6	0	3.0	.981	OF-107
1943	STL A	60	.255	.292	161	41	6	0	0	0.0	24	10	26	13	4	7	1	146	5	1	1	3.0	.993	OF-51
1944		105	.301	.405	402	121	15	6	5	1.2	55	44	27	24	3	5	0	282	4	4	0	2.9	.986	OF-100
1945	2 teams	STL A (81G –.237) WAS A (45G –.278)																						
″	total	126	.252	.327	453	114	19	3	3	0.7	56	44	58	38	11	7	2	328	6	5	0	2.9	.985	OF-118
12 yrs.		1238	.283	.391	4676	1321	221	75	45	1.0	676	514	446	341	115	45	12	3318	106	65	21	2.9	.981	OF-1174, 3B-10
WORLD SERIES																								
1944	STL A	6	.231	.346	26	6	3	0	0	0.0	0	0	0	5	0	0	0	20	2	0	0	3.7	1.000	OF-6

Charlie Krehmeyer

KREHMEYER, CHARLES L. BL TL 5′11″ 179 lbs.
B. July 5, 1863, St. Louis, Mo. D. Feb. 10, 1926, St. Louis, Mo.

Year	Team	Games	BA	SA	AB	H	2B	3B	HR	HR%	R	RBI	BB	SO	SB	Pinch Hit AB	Pinch Hit H	PO	A	E	DP	TC/G	FA	G by Pos
1884	STL AA	21	.229	.257	70	16	0	1	0	0.0	3		2			0	0	56	7	12	1	3.3	.840	OF-15, C-7, 1B-1
1885	2 teams	LOU AA (7G –.226) STL N (1G –.000)																						
″	total	8	.206	.294	34	7	1	1	0	0.0	4	0	1	2		0	0	32	8	11	0	6.4	.784	C-5, OF-2, 1B-1
2 yrs.		29	.221	.269	104	23	1	2	0	0.0	7	0	3	2		0	0	88	15	23	1	4.1	.817	OF-17, C-12, 1B-2

Ralph Kreitz

KREITZ, RALPH WESLEY (Red) BR TR 5′ 9½″ 175 lbs.
B. Nov. 13, 1885, Plum Creek, Neb. D. July 20, 1941, Portland, Ore.

Year	Team	Games	BA	SA	AB	H	2B	3B	HR	HR%	R	RBI	BB	SO	SB	Pinch Hit AB	Pinch Hit H	PO	A	E	DP	TC/G	FA	G by Pos
1911	CHI A	7	.235	.294	17	4	1	0	0	0.0	0	0	2		0	0	0	24	4	0	1	4.0	1.000	C-7

Jimmy Kremers

KREMERS, JAMES EDWARD BL TR 6′ 3″ 205 lbs.
B. Oct. 8, 1965, Little Rock, Ark.

Year	Team	Games	BA	SA	AB	H	2B	3B	HR	HR%	R	RBI	BB	SO	SB	Pinch Hit AB	Pinch Hit H	PO	A	E	DP	TC/G	FA	G by Pos
1990	ATL N	29	.110	.192	73	8	1	1	1	1.4	7	2	6	27	0	5	0	107	10	1	2	4.4	.992	C-27

Wayne Krenchicki

KRENCHICKI, WAYNE RICHARD BL TR 6′ 1″ 180 lbs.
B. Sept. 17, 1954, Trenton, N. J.

Year	Team	Games	BA	SA	AB	H	2B	3B	HR	HR%	R	RBI	BB	SO	SB	Pinch Hit AB	Pinch Hit H	PO	A	E	DP	TC/G	FA	G by Pos
1979	BAL A	16	.190	.238	21	4	1	0	0	0.0	1	0	0	0	0	0	0	12	12	2	1	2.0	.923	SS-7, 2B-6
1980		9	.143	.143	14	2	0	0	0	0.0	1	0	1	3	0	1	0	9	9	0	2	2.3	1.000	SS-6, 2B-1, DH-1
1981		33	.214	.286	56	12	4	0	0	0.0	7	6	4	9	0	1	0	23	56	3	12	2.7	.963	SS-16, 2B-7, 3B-6, DH-1
1982	CIN N	94	.283	.358	187	53	6	1	2	1.1	19	21	13	23	5	28	7	40	103	6	10	1.9	.960	3B-70, 2B-9
1983	2 teams	CIN N (51G –.273) DET A (59G –.278)																						
″	total	110	.276	.333	210	58	9	0	1	0.5	24	27	19	31	0	18	2	50	116	9	14	1.7	.949	3B-87, 2B-7, SS-6, 1B-3
1984	CIN N	97	.298	.470	181	54	9	2	6	3.3	18	22	19	23	0	36	7	35	92	5	6	1.9	.962	3B-62, 2B-3, 1B-3
1985		90	.272	.393	173	47	9	0	4	2.3	16	25	28	20	0	32	5	35	87	4	9	2.3	.968	3B-52, 2B-3
1986	MON N	101	.240	.312	221	53	6	2	2	0.9	21	23	22	32	2	31	7	325	59	6	26	5.8	.985	1B-41, 3B-24, OF-1, 2B-1
8 yrs.		550	.266	.359	1063	283	44	5	15	1.4	107	124	106	141	7	147	28	529	534	35	80	2.6	.968	3B-301, 1B-47, 2B-37, SS-35, DH-2, OF-1

Charlie Kress

KRESS, CHARLES STEVEN (Chuck) BL TL 6′ 190 lbs.
B. Dec. 9, 1921, Philadelphia, Pa.

Year	Team	Games	BA	SA	AB	H	2B	3B	HR	HR%	R	RBI	BB	SO	SB	Pinch Hit AB	Pinch Hit H	PO	A	E	DP	TC/G	FA	G by Pos
1947	CIN N	11	.148	.148	27	4	0	0	0	0.0	4	0	6	4	0	2	1	52	7	1	5	7.5	.983	1B-8
1949	2 teams	CIN N (27G –.207) CHI A (97G –.278)																						
″	total	124	.272	.364	382	104	20	6	1	0.3	48	47	42	49	6	11	3	979	70	8	109	9.5	.992	1B-111
1950	CHI A	3	.000	.000	8	0	0	0	0	0.0	0	0	0	2	0	1	0	19	1	0	2	10.0	1.000	1B-2
1954	2 teams	DET A (24G –.189) BKN N (13G –.083)																						
″	total	37	.163	.204	49	8	0	1	0	0.0	5	5	1	4	0	27	3	64	5	3	5	8.0	.958	1B-8, OF-1
4 yrs.		175	.249	.328	466	116	20	7	1	0.2	57	52	49	59	6	41	7	1114	83	12	121	9.3	.990	1B-129, OF-1

Red Kress

KRESS, RALPH BR TR 5′11½″ 165 lbs.
B. Jan. 2, 1907, Columbia, Calif. D. Nov. 29, 1962, Los Angeles, Calif.

Year	Team	Games	BA	SA	AB	H	2B	3B	HR	HR%	R	RBI	BB	SO	SB	Pinch Hit AB	Pinch Hit H	PO	A	E	DP	TC/G	FA	G by Pos
1927	STL A	7	.304	.609	23	7	2	1	1	4.3	3	3	3	3	0	0	0	12	25	1	4	5.4	.974	SS-7
1928		150	.273	.371	560	153	26	10	3	0.5	78	81	48	70	5	0	0	318	400	55	99	5.2	.929	SS-150

Red Kress *continued*

Year	Team	Games	BA	SA	AB	H	2B	3B	HR	HR%	R	RBI	BB	SO	SB	Pinch Hit AB	Pinch Hit H	PO	A	E	DP	TC/G	FA	G by Pos
1929		147	.305	.436	557	170	38	4	9	1.6	82	107	52	54	5	1	0	312	441	43	94	5.5	.946	SS-146
1930		154	.313	.487	614	192	43	8	16	2.6	94	112	50	56	3	0	0	306	406	51	87	5.0	.933	SS-123, 3B-31
1931		150	.311	.493	605	188	46	8	16	2.6	87	114	46	48	3	1	0	305	206	31	28	3.2	.943	3B-84, OF-40, SS-38, 1B-10
1932	2 teams	STL A (14G –.173) CHI A (135G –.285)																						
"	total	149	.275	.425	567	156	42	5	11	1.9	85	66	51	42	7	0	0	304	228	37	46	3.8	.935	OF-64, SS-53, 3B-33
1933	CHI A	129	.248	.377	467	116	20	5	10	2.1	47	78	37	40	4	12	6	1185	60	29	83	10.7	.977	1B-111, OF-8
1934	2 teams	CHI A (8G –.286) WAS A (56G –.228)																						
"	total	64	.232	.351	185	43	4	3	4	2.2	21	25	20	22	3	9	2	333	35	2	21	7.3	.995	1B-30, OF-10, 2B-9, SS-1, 3B-1
1935	WAS A	84	.298	.405	252	75	13	4	2	0.8	32	42	25	16	3	18	4	157	211	14	61	6.0	.963	SS-53, 1B-5, P-3, OF-2, 2B-1
1936		109	.284	.427	391	111	20	6	8	2.0	51	51	39	25	6	5	0	266	315	30	75	6.0	.951	SS-64, 2B-33, 1B-5
1938	STL A	150	.302	.408	566	171	33	3	7	1.2	74	79	69	47	5	1	1	321	388	26	100	4.9	.965	SS-150
1939	2 teams	STL A (13G –.279) DET A (51G –.242)																						
"	total	64	.250	.305	200	50	8	0	1	0.5	24	30	23	18	3	6	4	111	152	16	39	4.8	.943	SS-38, 2B-16, 3B-4
1940	DET A	33	.222	.303	99	22	3	1	1	1.0	13	11	10	12	0	5	3	45	74	8	6	4.4	.937	3B-17, SS-12
1946	NY N	1	.000	.000	1	0	0	0	0	0.0	0	0	1	0	0	0	0	2	3	0	0	5.0	1.000	P-1
14 yrs.		1391	.286	.420	5087	1454	298	58	89	1.7	691	799	474	453	47	58	20	3977	2944	343	743	5.4	.953	SS-835, 3B-170, 1B-161, OF-124, 2B-59, P-4

Chad Kreuter

KREUTER, CHADDEN MICHAEL BB TR 6′ 2″ 190 lbs.
B. Aug. 26, 1964, Greenbrae, Calif.

Year	Team	Games	BA	SA	AB	H	2B	3B	HR	HR%	R	RBI	BB	SO	SB	Pinch Hit AB	Pinch Hit H	PO	A	E	DP	TC/G	FA	G by Pos
1988	TEX A	16	.275	.412	51	14	2	1	1	2.0	3	5	7	13	0	0	0	93	8	1	0	6.4	.990	C-16
1989		87	.152	.266	158	24	3	0	5	3.2	16	9	27	40	0	1	0	453	26	4	4	5.7	.992	C-85
1990		22	.045	.091	22	1	1	0	0	0.0	2	2	8	9	0	0	0	39	4	1	0	2.1	.977	C-20, DH-1
1991		3	.000	.000	4	0	0	0	0	0.0	0	0	0	1	0	1	0	5	0	0	0	5.0	1.000	C-1
1992	DET A	67	.253	.332	190	48	9	0	2	1.1	22	16	20	38	0	3	2	271	22	5	6	4.7	.983	C-62, DH-1
1993		119	.286	.484	374	107	23	3	15	4.0	59	51	49	92	2	8	4	522	70	7	10	5.2	.988	C-112, DH-2, 1B-1
1994		65	.224	.288	170	38	8	0	1	0.6	17	19	28	36	0	1	1	280	22	4	1	4.6	.987	C-64, OF-1, 1B-1
1995	SEA A	26	.227	.333	75	17	5	0	1	1.3	12	8	5	22	0	5	4	151	12	4	1	7.3	.976	C-23
8 yrs.		405	.239	.367	1044	249	51	4	25	2.4	131	110	144	251	2	19	11	1814	164	26	22	5.1	.987	C-383, DH-4, 1B-2, OF-1

Paul Krichell

KRICHELL, PAUL BERNARD BR TR 5′ 7″ 150 lbs.
B. Dec. 19, 1882, New York, N. Y. D. June 4, 1957, New York, N. Y.

Year	Team	Games	BA	SA	AB	H	2B	3B	HR	HR%	R	RBI	BB	SO	SB	Pinch Hit AB	Pinch Hit H	PO	A	E	DP	TC/G	FA	G by Pos
1911	STL A	28	.232	.268	82	19	3	0	0	0.0	6	8	4		2	3	0	80	36	7	2	4.9	.943	C-25
1912		57	.217	.255	161	35	6	0	0	0.0	19	8	19		2	0	0	255	72	14	9	6.0	.959	C-57
2 yrs.		85	.222	.259	243	54	9	0	0	0.0	25	16	23		4	3	0	335	108	21	11	5.7	.955	C-82

Bill Krieg

KRIEG, WILLIAM FREDERICK BR TR 5′ 8″ 180 lbs.
B. Jan. 29, 1859, Petersburg, Ill. D. Mar. 25, 1930, Chillicothe, Ill.

Year	Team	Games	BA	SA	AB	H	2B	3B	HR	HR%	R	RBI	BB	SO	SB	Pinch Hit AB	Pinch Hit H	PO	A	E	DP	TC/G	FA	G by Pos
1884	2 teams	CHI U (61G –.229) PIT U (10G –.359)																						
"	total	71	.247	.330	279	69	15	4	0	0.0	35		11			0	0	471	117	57	4	8.7	.912	C-52, OF-20, SS-1, 1B-1
1885	2 teams	CHI N (1G –.000) BKN AA (17G –.150)																						
"	total	18	.143	.254	63	9	4	0	1	1.6	7	0	2	2		0	0	100	18	12	3	7.2	.908	C-12, 1B-5, OF-1
1886	WAS N	27	.255	.408	98	25	6	3	1	1.0	11	15	3	12		0	0	227	5	6	7	8.8	.975	1B-27
1887		25	.253	.379	95	24	4	1	2	2.1	9	17	7	5	2	0	0	148	5	5	5	6.3	.968	1B-16, OF-9
4 yrs.		141	.237	.344	535	127	29	8	4	0.7	62	32	23	19	2	0	0	946	145	80	19	8.1	.932	C-64, 1B-49, OF-30, SS-1

Krieger

KRIEGER
Deceased.

Year	Team	Games	BA	SA	AB	H	2B	3B	HR	HR%	R	RBI	BB	SO	SB	Pinch Hit AB	Pinch Hit H	PO	A	E	DP	TC/G	FA	G by Pos
1884	KC U	1	.000	.000	3	0	0	0	0	0.0	0		0			0	0	1	1	0	0	1.0	1.000	P-1, OF-1

Mickey Krietner

KRIETNER, ALBERT JOSEPH BR TR 6′ 3″ 190 lbs.
B. Oct. 10, 1922, Nashville, Tenn.

Year	Team	Games	BA	SA	AB	H	2B	3B	HR	HR%	R	RBI	BB	SO	SB	Pinch Hit AB	Pinch Hit H	PO	A	E	DP	TC/G	FA	G by Pos
1943	CHI N	3	.375	.375	8	3	0	0	0	0.0	0	2	1	2	0	0	0	8	1	0	0	3.0	1.000	C-3
1944		39	.153	.176	85	13	2	0	0	0.0	3	1	8	16	0	0	0	104	13	1	3	3.0	.992	C-39
2 yrs.		42	.172	.194	93	16	2	0	0	0.0	3	3	9	18	0	0	0	112	14	1	3	3.0	.992	C-42

John Kroner

KRONER, JOHN HAROLD BR TR 6′ 165 lbs.
B. Nov. 13, 1908, St. Louis, Mo. D. Apr. 26, 1968, St. Louis, Mo.

Year	Team	Games	BA	SA	AB	H	2B	3B	HR	HR%	R	RBI	BB	SO	SB	Pinch Hit AB	Pinch Hit H	PO	A	E	DP	TC/G	FA	G by Pos
1935	BOS A	2	.250	.250	4	1	0	0	0	0.0	1	0	1	1	0	0	0	0	1	0	0	0.5	1.000	3B-2
1936		84	.292	.443	298	87	17	8	4	1.3	40	62	26	24	2	1	0	146	211	18	36	4.4	.952	2B-38, 3B-28, SS-18, OF-1
1937	CLE A	86	.237	.314	283	67	14	1	2	0.7	29	26	22	25	1	9	2	157	203	14	46	5.0	.963	2B-64, 3B-11
1938		51	.248	.410	117	29	16	0	1	0.9	13	17	19	6	0	7	1	107	91	7	25	4.9	.966	2B-31, 1B-7, 3B-3, SS-1
4 yrs.		223	.262	.385	702	184	47	9	7	1.0	83	105	68	56	3	17	3	410	506	39	107	4.7	.959	2B-133, 3B-44, SS-19, 1B-7, OF-1

Mike Krsnich

KRSNICH, MICHAEL BR TR 6′ 1″ 190 lbs.
Brother of Rocky Krsnich.
B. Sept. 24, 1931, West Allis, Wis.

Year	Team	Games	BA	SA	AB	H	2B	3B	HR	HR%	R	RBI	BB	SO	SB	Pinch Hit AB	Pinch Hit H	PO	A	E	DP	TC/G	FA	G by Pos
1960	MIL N	4	.333	.444	9	3	1	0	0	0.0	0	2	0	0	0	2	1	5	0	0	0	1.7	1.000	OF-3
1962		11	.083	.167	12	1	1	0	0	0.0	0	2	0	4	0	6	1	2	1	0	1	0.6	1.000	OF-3, 3B-1, 1B-1
2 yrs.		15	.190	.286	21	4	2	0	0	0.0	0	4	0	4	0	8	2	7	1	0	1	1.0	1.000	OF-6, 3B-1, 1B-1

Rocky Krsnich

KRSNICH, ROCCO PETER BR TR 6′ 1″ 174 lbs.
Brother of Mike Krsnich.
B. Aug. 5, 1927, West Allis, Wis.

Year	Team	Games	BA	SA	AB	H	2B	3B	HR	HR%	R	RBI	BB	SO	SB	Pinch Hit AB	Pinch Hit H	PO	A	E	DP	TC/G	FA	G by Pos
1949	CHI A	16	.218	.364	55	12	3	1	1	1.8	7	9	6	4	0	0	0	18	40	4	4	3.9	.935	2B-16
1952		40	.231	.385	91	21	7	2	1	1.1	11	15	12	9	0	2	0	45	72	5	6	3.3	.959	3B-37
1953		64	.202	.287	129	26	8	0	1	0.8	9	14	12	11	0	6	1	31	100	10	7	2.5	.929	3B-57
3 yrs.		120	.215	.335	275	59	18	3	3	1.1	27	38	30	24	0	8	1	94	212	19	17	3.0	.942	3B-94, 2B-16

Ernie Krueger

KRUEGER, ERNEST GEORGE
B. Dec. 27, 1890, Chicago, Ill. D. Apr. 22, 1976, Waukegan, Ill.
BR TR 5′10½″ 185 lbs.

Year	Team	Games	BA	SA	AB	H	2B	3B	HR	HR%	R	RBI	BB	SO	SB	Pinch Hit AB	Pinch Hit H	PO	A	E	DP	TC/G	FA	G by Pos
1913	CLE A	5	.000	.000	6	0	0	0	0	0.0	0	0	0	2	0	1	0	4	3	0	0	1.8	1.000	C-4
1915	NY A	10	.172	.207	29	5	1	0	0	0.0	3	0	0	5	0	2	0	30	8	4	1	5.3	.905	C-8
1917	2 teams	NY N (8G –.000) BKN N (31G –.272)																						
"	total	39	.242	.341	91	22	2	2	1	1.1	10	6	5	11	1	9	1	121	25	4	4	5.2	.973	C-29
1918	BKN N	30	.287	.379	87	25	4	2	0	0.0	4	7	4	9	2	7	2	104	38	2	3	6.3	.986	C-23
1919		80	.248	.381	226	56	7	4	5	2.2	24	36	19	25	4	10	2	305	88	15	2	6.2	.963	C-66
1920		52	.288	.363	146	42	4	2	1	0.7	21	17	16	13	2	5	1	165	46	9	4	4.8	.959	C-46
1921		65	.264	.436	163	43	11	4	3	1.8	18	20	14	12	2	14	3	179	39	7	4	4.3	.969	C-52
1925	CIN N	37	.307	.386	88	27	4	0	1	1.1	7	7	6	8	1	6	0	75	12	5	3	3.1	.946	C-30
8 yrs.		318	.263	.376	836	220	33	14	11	1.3	87	93	64	85	12	54	9	983	259	46	21	5.0	.964	C-258
WORLD SERIES																								
1920	BKN N	4	.167	.167	6	1	0	0	0	0.0	0	0	0	0	0	1	0	10	2	0	1	4.0	1.000	C-3

Otto Krueger

KRUEGER, ARTHUR WILLIAM (Oom Paul)
B. Sept. 17, 1876, Chicago, Ill. D. Feb. 20, 1961, St. Louis, Mo.
BR TR 5′ 7″ 165 lbs.

Year	Team	Games	BA	SA	AB	H	2B	3B	HR	HR%	R	RBI	BB	SO	SB	Pinch Hit AB	Pinch Hit H	PO	A	E	DP	TC/G	FA	G by Pos
1899	CLE N	13	.227	.250	44	10	1	0	0	0.0	4	2	8		1	0	0	22	27	10	4	4.5	.831	3B-9, SS-2, 2B-2
1900	STL N	12	.400	.686	35	14	3	2	1	2.9	8	3	10		0	0	0	20	26	8	2	4.5	.852	2B-12
1901		142	.275	.363	520	143	16	12	2	0.4	77	79	50		19	0	0	171	275	60	11	3.6	.881	3B-142
1902		128	.266	.315	467	124	7	8	0	0.0	55	46	29		14	3	0	206	426	75	48	5.7	.894	SS-107, 3B-18
1903	PIT N	80	.246	.344	256	63	6	8	1	0.4	42	28	21		5	4	1	109	113	20	17	3.3	.917	SS-29, OF-28, 3B-13, 2B-3
1904		86	.194	.243	268	52	6	2	1	0.4	34	26	29		8	8	1	115	117	23	10	3.4	.910	OF-33, SS-32, 3B-10
1905	PHI N	46	.184	.211	114	21	1	1	0	0.0	10	12	13		1	**16**	3	44	66	8	10	3.9	.932	SS-23, OF-6, 3B-1
7 yrs.		507	.251	.322	1704	427	40	33	5	0.3	230	196	160		48	31	5	687	1050	204	102	4.1	.895	SS-193, 3B-193, OF-67, 2B-17

Chris Krug

KRUG, EVERETT BEN
B. Dec. 25, 1939, Los Angeles, Calif.
BR TR 6′ 4″ 200 lbs.

Year	Team	Games	BA	SA	AB	H	2B	3B	HR	HR%	R	RBI	BB	SO	SB	Pinch Hit AB	Pinch Hit H	PO	A	E	DP	TC/G	FA	G by Pos
1965	CHI N	60	.201	.320	169	34	5	0	5	3.0	16	24	13	52	0	3	0	273	27	6	5	5.3	.980	C-58
1966		11	.214	.250	28	6	1	0	0	0.0	1	1	1	8	0	1	0	55	5	0	2	6.0	1.000	C-10
1969	SD N	8	.059	.059	17	1	0	0	0	0.0	0	0	1	6	0	1	0	28	2	2	0	4.6	.938	C-7
3 yrs.		79	.192	.290	214	41	6	0	5	2.3	17	25	15	66	0	5	0	356	34	8	7	5.3	.980	C-75

Gary Krug

KRUG, GARY EUGENE
B. Feb. 12, 1955, Garden City, Kans.
BL TL 6′ 4″ 225 lbs.

Year	Team	Games	BA	SA	AB	H	2B	3B	HR	HR%	R	RBI	BB	SO	SB	Pinch Hit AB	Pinch Hit H	PO	A	E	DP	TC/G	FA	G by Pos
1981	CHI N	7	.400	.400	5	2	0	0	0	0.0	0	0	1	1	0	5	2	0	0	0	0	0.0	—	

Henry Krug

KRUG, HENRY CHARLES
B. Dec. 4, 1876, San Francisco, Calif. D. Jan. 14, 1908, San Francisco, Calif.
BR TR

Year	Team	Games	BA	SA	AB	H	2B	3B	HR	HR%	R	RBI	BB	SO	SB	Pinch Hit AB	Pinch Hit H	PO	A	E	DP	TC/G	FA	G by Pos
1902	PHI N	53	.227	.273	198	45	3	3	0	0.0	20	14	7		2	0	0	116	62	12	10	3.4	.937	OF-28, 2B-13, SS-9, 3B-6

Marty Krug

KRUG, MARTIN JOHN
B. Sept. 10, 1888, Koblenz, Germany D. June 27, 1966, Glendale, Calif.
BR TR 5′ 9″ 165 lbs.

Year	Team	Games	BA	SA	AB	H	2B	3B	HR	HR%	R	RBI	BB	SO	SB	Pinch Hit AB	Pinch Hit H	PO	A	E	DP	TC/G	FA	G by Pos
1912	BOS A	16	.308	.410	39	12	2	1	0	0.0	6	7	5		2	2	0	19	26	5	4	3.8	.900	SS-9, 2B-4
1922	CHI N	127	.276	.371	450	124	23	4	4	0.9	67	60	43	43	7	0	0	174	255	32	30	3.6	.931	3B-104, 2B-23, SS-1
2 yrs.		143	.278	.374	489	136	25	5	4	0.8	73	67	48	43	9	2	0	193	281	37	34	3.6	.928	3B-104, 2B-27, SS-10

Art Kruger

KRUGER, ARTHUR T.
B. Mar. 16, 1881, San Antonio, Tex. D. Nov. 28, 1949, Hondo, Calif.
BR TR 6′ 185 lbs.

Year	Team	Games	BA	SA	AB	H	2B	3B	HR	HR%	R	RBI	BB	SO	SB	Pinch Hit AB	Pinch Hit H	PO	A	E	DP	TC/G	FA	G by Pos
1907	CIN N	100	.233	.322	317	74	10	9	0	0.0	25	28	18		10	4	0	199	11	6	3	2.3	.972	OF-96
1910	2 teams	CLE A (62G –.170) BOS N (1G –.000)																						
"	total	63	.170	.223	224	38	6	3	0	0.0	19	14	20	0	12	1	0	116	10	6	3	2.1	.955	OF-62
1914	KC F	122	.259	.372	441	114	24	7	4	0.9	45	47	23		11	2	0	249	14	10	1	2.3	.963	OF-120
1915		80	.237	.317	240	57	9	2	2	0.8	24	26	12		5	14	4	116	8	2	2	1.9	.984	OF-66
4 yrs.		365	.232	.321	1222	283	49	21	6	0.5	113	115	73	0	38	21	4	680	43	24	9	2.2	.968	OF-344

John Kruk

KRUK, JOHN MARTIN
B. Feb. 9, 1961, Charleston, W. Va.
BL TL 5′10″ 220 lbs.

Year	Team	Games	BA	SA	AB	H	2B	3B	HR	HR%	R	RBI	BB	SO	SB	Pinch Hit AB	Pinch Hit H	PO	A	E	DP	TC/G	FA	G by Pos
1986	SD N	122	.309	.424	278	86	16	2	4	1.4	33	38	45	58	2	32	8	139	6	3	3	1.8	.980	OF-74, 1B-9
1987		138	.313	.488	447	140	14	2	20	4.5	72	91	73	93	18	12	6	911	78	5	74	7.6	.995	1B-101, OF-29
1988		120	.241	.362	378	91	17	1	9	2.4	54	44	80	68	5	7	2	634	37	3	45	5.7	.996	1B-63, OF-55
1989	2 teams	SD N (31G –.184) PHI N (81G –.331)																						
"	total	112	.300	.437	357	107	13	6	8	2.2	53	44	44	53	3	8	1	212	9	4	4	2.1	.982	OF-99, 1B-7
1990	PHI N	142	.291	.431	443	129	25	8	7	1.6	52	67	69	70	10	13	5	543	45	4	34	4.0	.993	OF-87, 1B-61
1991		152	.294	.483	538	158	27	6	21	3.9	84	92	67	100	7	9	2	848	53	3	55	5.9	.997	1B-102, OF-52
1992		144	.323	.458	507	164	30	4	10	2.0	86	70	92	88	3	1	0	1037	58	8	76	7.1	.993	1B-121, OF-35
1993		150	.316	.475	535	169	33	5	14	2.6	100	85	111	87	6	7	1	1149	69	8	79	8.5	.993	1B-144
1994		75	.302	.427	255	77	17	0	5	2.0	35	38	42	51	4	4	3	540	46	3	45	8.5	.995	1B-69
1995	CHI A	45	.308	.390	159	49	7	0	2	1.3	13	23	26	33	0	2	0	10	0	1	1	0.3	.909	DH-42, 1B-1
10 yrs.		1200	.300	.446	3897	1170	199	34	100	2.6	582	592	649	701	58	95	28	6023	401	42	416	5.6	.994	1B-678, OF-431, DH-42
LEAGUE CHAMPIONSHIP SERIES																								
1993	PHI N	6	.250	.542	24	6	2	1	1	4.2	4	5	4	5	0	0	0	44	2	0	2	7.7	1.000	1B-6
WORLD SERIES																								
1993	PHI N	6	.348	.391	23	8	1	0	0	0.0	4	4	7	7	0	0	0	42	3	0	4	7.5	1.000	1B-6

Dick Kryhoski

KRYHOSKI, RICHARD DAVID
B. Mar. 24, 1925, Leonia, N. J.
BL TL 6′ 2″ 182 lbs.

Year	Team	Games	BA	SA	AB	H	2B	3B	HR	HR%	R	RBI	BB	SO	SB	Pinch Hit AB	Pinch Hit H	PO	A	E	DP	TC/G	FA	G by Pos
1949	NY A	54	.294	.401	177	52	10	3	1	0.6	18	27	9	17	2	2	0	363	31	7	39	7.9	.983	1B-51
1950	DET A	53	.219	.349	169	37	10	0	4	2.4	20	19	8	11	0	5	2	409	27	4	44	9.4	.991	1B-47
1951		119	.287	.437	421	121	19	4	12	2.9	58	57	28	29	1	10	4	964	81	9	95	9.4	.991	1B-112
1952	STL A	111	.243	.383	342	83	13	1	11	3.2	38	42	23	42	2	25	8	680	49	8	80	8.6	.989	1B-86
1953		104	.278	.497	338	94	18	4	16	4.7	35	50	26	33	0	19	4	685	66	6	7	8.6	.992	1B-88

Dick Kryhoski *continued*

Year	Team	Games	BA	SA	AB	H	2B	3B	HR	HR%	R	RBI	BB	SO	SB	Pinch Hit AB	Pinch Hit H	PO	A	E	DP	TC/G	FA	G by Pos
1954	BAL A	100	.260	.327	300	78	13	2	1	0.3	32	34	19	24	0	23	3	591	52	5	52	9.4	.992	1B-69
1955	KC A	28	.213	.255	47	10	2	0	0	0.0	2	2	6	7	0	13	3	76	6	1	7	5.9	.988	1B-14
7 yrs.		569	.265	.403	1794	475	85	14	45	2.5	203	231	119	163	5	97	24	3768	312	40	324	8.8	.990	1B-467

Tony Kubek

KUBEK, ANTHONY CHRISTOPHER
B. Oct. 12, 1936, Milwaukee, Wis.
BL TR 6′ 3″ 190 lbs.

Year	Team	Games	BA	SA	AB	H	2B	3B	HR	HR%	R	RBI	BB	SO	SB	Pinch Hit AB	Pinch Hit H	PO	A	E	DP	TC/G	FA	G by Pos
1957	NY A	127	.297	.381	431	128	21	3	3	0.7	56	39	24	48	6	8	1	189	183	20	33	3.0	.949	OF-50, SS-41, 3B-38, 2B-1
1958		138	.265	.317	559	148	21	1	2	0.4	66	48	25	57	5	1	0	249	453	28	98	5.3	.962	SS-134, OF-3, 1B-1, 2B-1
1959		132	.279	.391	512	143	25	7	6	1.2	67	51	24	46	3	4	1	219	256	15	49	3.6	.969	SS-67, OF-53, 3B-17, 2B-1
1960		147	.273	.401	568	155	25	3	14	2.5	77	62	31	42	3	6	2	251	444	22	84	4.3	.969	SS-136, OF-29
1961		153	.276	.395	617	170	38	6	8	1.3	84	46	27	60	1	8	2	261	449	30	107	5.1	.959	SS-145
1962		45	.314	.432	169	53	6	1	4	2.4	28	17	12	17	2	2	1	88	117	9	27	5.2	.958	SS-35, OF-6
1963		135	.257	.343	557	143	21	3	7	1.3	72	44	28	68	4	1	1	227	403	13	80	4.8	.980	SS-132, OF-1
1964		106	.229	.340	415	95	16	3	8	1.9	46	31	26	55	4	2	0	186	307	11	52	5.1	.978	SS-99
1965		109	.218	.295	339	74	5	3	5	1.5	26	35	20	48	1	12	4	138	238	14	53	4.0	.964	SS-93, OF-3, 1B-1
9 yrs.		1092	.266	.364	4167	1109	178	30	57	1.4	522	373	217	441	29	44	12	1808	2850	162	583	4.4	.966	SS-882, OF-145, 3B-55, 2B-3, 1B-2
WORLD SERIES																								
1957	NY A	7	.286	.500	28	8	0	0	2	7.1	4	4	0	4	0	0	0	17	5	2	0	3.4	.917	OF-5, 3B-2
1958		7	.048	.048	21	1	0	0	0	0.0	0	1	1	7	0	0	0	9	15	2	2	3.7	.923	SS-7
1960		7	.333	.367	30	10	1	0	0	0.0	6	3	2	2	0	0	0	10	21	3	4	3.8	.912	SS-7, OF-2
1961		5	.227	.227	22	5	0	0	0	0.0	3	1	1	4	0	0	0	5	11	0	1	3.2	1.000	SS-5
1962		7	.276	.310	29	8	1	0	0	0.0	2	1	1	3	0	0	0	12	17	1	3	4.3	.967	SS-7
1963		4	.188	.188	16	3	0	0	0	0.0	1	0	0	3	0	0	0	5	13	0	5	4.5	1.000	SS-4
6 yrs.		37	.240	.295	146	35	2	0	2	1.4	16	10	5	23 **10th**	0	0	0	58	82	8	15	3.8	.946	SS-30, OF-7, 3B-2

Ted Kubiak

KUBIAK, THEODORE RODGER
B. May 12, 1942, New Brunswick, N. J.
BB TR 6′ 175 lbs.
BB 1968

Year	Team	Games	BA	SA	AB	H	2B	3B	HR	HR%	R	RBI	BB	SO	SB	Pinch Hit AB	Pinch Hit H	PO	A	E	DP	TC/G	FA	G by Pos
1967	KC A	53	.157	.196	102	16	2	1	0	0.0	6	5	12	20	0	15	2	37	58	3	7	2.8	.969	SS-20, 2B-10, 3B-5
1968	OAK A	48	.250	.325	120	30	5	2	0	0.0	10	8	8	18	1	13	2	60	78	11	13	4.1	.926	2B-24, SS-12
1969		92	.249	.305	305	76	9	1	2	0.7	38	27	25	35	2	14	3	153	215	10	41	5.0	.974	SS-42, 2B-33
1970	MIL A	158	.252	.313	540	136	9	6	4	0.7	63	41	72	51	4	0	0	361	412	19	98	4.8	.976	2B-91, SS-73
1971	2 teams	MIL A (89G –.227) STL N (32G –.250)																						
″	total	121	.232	.337	332	77	9	7	4	1.2	34	27	52	43	1	12	2	220	278	18	52	4.4	.965	2B-62, SS-56
1972	2 teams	TEX A (46G –.224) OAK A (51G –.181)																						
″	total	97	.205	.248	210	43	7	1	0	0.0	19	15	21	23	0	9	1	156	165	4	38	3.6	.988	2B-74, SS-15, 3B-2
1973	OAK A	106	.220	.313	182	40	6	1	3	1.6	15	17	12	19	1	4	1	117	186	8	41	2.8	.974	2B-83, SS-26, 3B-2
1974		99	.209	.223	220	46	3	0	0	0.0	22	18	18	15	1	4	0	129	175	6	38	2.9	.981	2B-71, SS-19, 3B-14, DH-2
1975	2 teams	OAK A (20G –.250) SD N (87G –.224)																						
″	total	107	.228	.254	224	51	6	0	0	0.0	15	18	26	20	3	13	2	63	157	7	17	2.4	.969	3B-71, 2B-17, SS-7, 1B-1
1976	SD N	96	.236	.278	212	50	5	2	0	0.0	16	26	25	28	0	39	2	77	110	4	21	3.2	.979	3B-27, 2B-25, SS-6, 1B-1
10 yrs.		977	.231	.289	2447	565	61	21	13	0.5	238	202	271	272	13	123	15	1373	1834	90	366	3.7	.973	2B-490, SS-276, 3B-121, 1B-2, DH-2
LEAGUE CHAMPIONSHIP SERIES																								
1972	OAK A	4	.500	.500	4	2	0	0	0	0.0	0	1	0	0	0	0	0	3	8	1	0	3.0	.917	2B-3, SS-1
1973		3	.000	.000	2	0	0	0	0	0.0	0	0	0	1	0	0	0	0	1	0	0	0.3	1.000	2B-3
2 yrs.		7	.333	.333	6	2	0	0	0	0.0	0	1	0	1	0	0	0	3	9	1	0	1.9	.923	2B-6, SS-1
WORLD SERIES																								
1972	OAK A	4	.333	.333	3	1	0	0	0	0.0	0	0	0	0	0	0	0	4	3	0	0	1.8	1.000	2B-4
1973		4	.000	.000	3	0	0	0	0	0.0	1	0	1	1	0	0	0	5	7	0	1	3.0	1.000	2B-4
2 yrs.		8	.167	.167	6	1	0	0	0	0.0	1	0	1	1	0	0	0	9	10	0	1	2.4	1.000	2B-8

Jack Kubiszyn

KUBISZYN, JOHN HENRY
B. Dec. 19, 1936, Buffalo, N. Y.
BR TR 5′11″ 170 lbs.

Year	Team	Games	BA	SA	AB	H	2B	3B	HR	HR%	R	RBI	BB	SO	SB	Pinch Hit AB	Pinch Hit H	PO	A	E	DP	TC/G	FA	G by Pos
1961	CLE A	25	.214	.214	42	9	0	0	0	0.0	4	0	2	5	0	6	0	15	28	0	3	2.5	1.000	3B-8, SS-7, 2B-2
1962		25	.169	.254	59	10	2	0	1	1.7	3	2	5	7	0	5	1	32	48	3	14	4.4	.964	SS-18, 3B-1
2 yrs.		50	.188	.238	101	19	2	0	1	1.0	7	2	7	12	0	11	1	47	76	3	17	3.5	.976	SS-25, 3B-9, 2B-2

Gil Kubski

KUBSKI, GILBERT THOMAS
B. Oct. 12, 1954, Longview, Tex.
BL TR 6′ 3″ 185 lbs.

Year	Team	Games	BA	SA	AB	H	2B	3B	HR	HR%	R	RBI	BB	SO	SB	Pinch Hit AB	Pinch Hit H	PO	A	E	DP	TC/G	FA	G by Pos
1980	CAL A	22	.254	.302	63	16	3	0	0	0.0	11	6	6	10	1	1	0	36	2	0	0	1.9	1.000	OF-20

Steve Kuczek

KUCZEK, STANISLAW LEO
B. Dec. 28, 1924, Amsterdam, N. Y.
BR TR 6′ 160 lbs.

Year	Team	Games	BA	SA	AB	H	2B	3B	HR	HR%	R	RBI	BB	SO	SB	Pinch Hit AB	Pinch Hit H	PO	A	E	DP	TC/G	FA	G by Pos
1949	BOS N	1	1.000	2.000	1	1	1	0	0	0.0	0	0	0	0	0	1	1	0	0	0	0	0.0	—	

Willie Kuehne

KUEHNE, WILLIAM J.
B. Oct. 24, 1858, Leipzig, Germany D. Oct. 27, 1921, Sulphur Springs, Ohio.
BR TR 185 lbs.

Year	Team	Games	BA	SA	AB	H	2B	3B	HR	HR%	R	RBI	BB	SO	SB	Pinch Hit AB	Pinch Hit H	PO	A	E	DP	TC/G	FA	G by Pos
1883	COL AA	95	.227	.332	374	85	8	14	1	0.3	38		2			0	0	132	212	72	21	4.3	.827	3B-69, 2B-18, SS-7, OF-3
1884		110	.236	.381	415	98	13	16	5	1.2	48		9			0	0	120	219	46	13	3.5	.881	3B-109, OF-1
1885	PIT AA	104	.226	.341	411	93	9	19	0	0.0	54		15			0	0	109	214	51	16	3.6	.864	3B-97, SS-7
1886		117	.204	.314	481	98	16	17	1	0.2	73		19			0	0	303	99	29	11	3.6	.933	OF-54, 3B-47, 1B-18
1887	PIT N	102	.299	.425	402	120	18	15	1	0.2	68	41	14	39	17	0	0	166	321	62	31	5.4	.887	SS-91, 3B-4, 1B-4, OF-3
1888		138	.235	.336	524	123	22	11	3	0.6	60	62	9	68	34	0	0	208	327	51	29	4.2	.913	3B-75, SS-63
1889		97	.246	.362	390	96	20	5	5	1.3	43	57	9	36	15	0	0	147	187	34	17	3.8	.908	3B-75, OF-13, 2B-5, SS-2, 1B-2
1890	PIT P	126	.239	.352	528	126	21	12	5	0.9	66	73	28	37	21	0	0	159	304	82	18	4.3	.850	3B-126
1891	2 teams	COL AA (68G –.215) LOU AA (39G –.270)																						
″	total	107	.235	.291	413	97	12	1	3	0.7	57	39	17	35	30	0	0	137	232	46	22	3.9	.889	3B-107
1892	3 teams	LOU N (76G –.167) STL N (7G –.143) CIN N (6G –.208)																						
″	total	89	.168	.224	339	57	6	5	1	0.3	26	40	14	45	7	0	0	128	195	46	23	4.1	.875	3B-86, 2B-2, SS-1
10 yrs.		1085	.232	.337	4277	993	145	115	25	0.6	533	312	136	260	124	0	0	1609	2310	519	201	4.1	.883	3B-795, SS-171, OF-74, 2B-25, 1B-24

Harvey Kuenn

KUENN, HARVEY EDWARD
B. Dec. 4, 1930, West Allis, Wis. D. Feb. 28, 1988, Peoria, Ariz.
Manager 1975, 1982–83.

BR TR 6′ 2″ 187 lbs.

Year	Team	Lg	Games	BA	SA	AB	H	2B	3B	HR	HR%	R	RBI	BB	SO	SB	Pinch Hit AB	Pinch Hit H	PO	A	E	DP	TC/G	FA	G by Pos
1952	DET	A	19	.325	.400	80	26	2	2	0	0.0	2	8	2	1	2	0	0	44	57	4	12	5.5	.962	SS-19
1953			155	.308	.386	**679**	**209**	33	7	2	0.3	94	48	50	31	6	0	0	308	441	21	78	5.0	.973	SS-155
1954			155	.306	.390	**656**	**201**	28	6	5	0.8	81	48	29	13	9	0	0	294	496	28	85	5.3	.966	SS-155
1955			145	.306	.423	620	190	**38**	5	8	1.3	101	62	40	27	8	4	1	253	378	29	83	4.7	.956	SS-141
1956			146	.332	.470	591	**196**	32	7	12	2.0	96	88	55	34	9	6	1	219	388	20	86	4.4	.968	SS-141, OF-1
1957			151	.277	.388	624	173	30	6	9	1.4	74	44	47	28	5	1	0	251	387	30	91	4.3	.955	SS-136, 3B-17, 1B-1
1958			139	.319	.442	561	179	**39**	3	8	1.4	73	54	51	34	5	1	1	358	9	6	1	2.7	.984	OF-138
1959			139	**.353**	.501	561	**198**	**42**	7	9	1.6	99	71	48	37	7	1	0	247	6	3	0	1.9	.988	OF-137
1960	CLE	A	126	.308	.416	474	146	24	0	9	1.9	65	54	55	25	3	4	1	222	13	9	3	2.0	.963	OF-119, 3B-5
1961	SF	N	131	.265	.361	471	125	22	4	5	1.1	60	46	47	34	5	10	4	190	43	10	5	1.9	.959	OF-93, 3B-32, SS-1
1962			130	.304	.433	487	148	23	5	10	2.1	73	68	49	37	3	9	2	180	47	8	5	1.7	.966	OF-105, 3B-30
1963			120	.290	.374	417	121	13	2	6	1.4	61	31	44	38	2	15	2	115	60	13	3	1.6	.931	OF-64, 3B-53
1964			111	.262	.353	351	92	16	2	4	1.1	42	22	35	32	0	17	5	136	9	6	4	1.5	.960	OF-88, 1B-11, 3B-2
1965	2 teams		SF N (23G –.237) CHI N (54G –.217)																						
″	total		77	.223	.251	179	40	5	0	0	0.0	15	12	32	16	4	25	7	81	8	3	1	1.6	.967	OF-49, 1B-8
1966	2 teams		CHI N (3G –.333) PHI N (86G –.296)																						
″	total		89	.296	.352	162	48	9	0	0	0.0	15	15	10	17	0	48	11	130	3	1	11	2.9	.993	OF-32, 1B-13, 3B-1
15 yrs.			1833	.303	.408	6913	2092	356	56	87	1.3	951	671	594	404	68	141	35	3028	2345	191	468	3.2	.966	OF-826, SS-748, 3B-140, 1B-33
WORLD SERIES																									
1962	SF	N	4	.083	.083	12	1	0	0	0	0.0	1	0	1	1	0	0	0	11	0	0	0	2.8	1.000	OF-4

Joe Kuhel

KUHEL, JOSEPH ANTHONY
B. June 25, 1906, Cleveland, Ohio D. Feb. 26, 1984, Kansas City, Kans.
Manager 1948–49.

BL TL 6′ 180 lbs.

Year	Team	Lg	Games	BA	SA	AB	H	2B	3B	HR	HR%	R	RBI	BB	SO	SB	Pinch Hit AB	Pinch Hit H	PO	A	E	DP	TC/G	FA	G by Pos
1930	WAS	A	18	.286	.429	63	18	3	3	0	0.0	9	17	5	6	1	1	0	149	8	3	10	10.0	.981	1B-16
1931			139	.269	.410	524	141	34	8	8	1.5	70	85	47	45	7	0	0	1255	57	12	119	9.5	.991	1B-139
1932			101	.291	.415	347	101	21	5	4	1.2	52	52	32	19	5	9	1	761	45	5	64	9.5	.994	1B-85
1933			153	.322	.467	602	194	34	10	11	1.8	89	107	59	48	17	0	0	1498	61	7	126	10.2	.996	1B-153
1934			63	.289	.392	263	76	12	3	3	1.1	49	25	30	14	2	0	0	618	23	4	62	10.2	.994	1B-63
1935			151	.261	.338	633	165	25	9	2	0.3	99	74	78	44	5	0	0	1425	87	14	150	10.1	.991	1B-151
1936			149	.321	.502	588	189	42	8	16	2.7	107	118	64	30	15	0	0	1452	75	11	138	10.3	.993	1B-149, 3B-1
1937			136	.283	.400	547	155	24	11	6	1.1	73	61	63	39	6	0	0	1242	85	9	141	9.8	.993	1B-136
1938	CHI	A	117	.267	.410	412	110	27	4	8	1.9	67	51	72	35	9	6	0	1136	59	14	97	10.9	.988	1B-111
1939			139	.300	.460	546	164	24	9	15	2.7	107	56	64	51	18	3	0	1256	72	11	113	9.8	.992	1B-136
1940			155	.280	.488	603	169	28	8	27	4.5	111	94	87	59	12	0	0	1395	91	18	112	9.7	.988	1B-155
1941			153	.250	.392	600	150	39	5	12	2.0	99	63	70	55	20	1	0	1444	108	10	113	10.3	.994	1B-151
1942			115	.249	.332	413	103	14	4	4	1.0	60	52	60	22	22	3	0	1085	70	11	94	10.4	.991	1B-112
1943			153	.213	.284	531	113	21	1	5	0.9	55	46	76	45	14	0	0	1471	106	8	143	10.4	.995	1B-153
1944	WAS	A	139	.278	.378	518	144	26	7	4	0.8	90	51	68	40	11	1	1	1251	83	17	119	9.8	.987	1B-138
1945			142	.285	.400	533	152	29	13	2	0.4	73	75	79	31	10	1	0	1323	94	16	101	10.2	.989	1B-141
1946	2 teams		WAS A (14G –.150) CHI A (64G –.273)																						
″	total		78	.264	.368	258	68	9	3	4	1.6	26	22	26	26	4	8	2	625	41	4	67	9.9	.994	1B-68
1947	CHI	A	3	.000	.000	3	0	0	0	0	0.0	0	0	0	3	0	3	0	0	0	0	0	0.0	—	
18 yrs.			2104	.277	.406	7984	2212	412	111	131	1.6	1236	1049	980	612	178	36	4	19386	1165	174	1769	10.1	.992	1B-2057, 3B-1
WORLD SERIES																									
1933	WAS	A	5	.150	.150	20	3	0	0	0	0.0	1	1	1	4	0	0	0	59	3	0	4	12.4	1.000	1B-5

Kenny Kuhn

KUHN, KENNETH HAROLD
B. Mar. 20, 1937, Louisville, Ky.

BL TR 5′10½″ 175 lbs.

Year	Team	Lg	Games	BA	SA	AB	H	2B	3B	HR	HR%	R	RBI	BB	SO	SB	Pinch Hit AB	Pinch Hit H	PO	A	E	DP	TC/G	FA	G by Pos
1955	CLE	A	4	.333	.333	6	2	0	0	0	0.0	0	0	1	0	1	0	0	1	3	0	0	1.0	1.000	SS-4
1956			27	.273	.318	22	6	1	0	0	0.0	7	2	0	4	0	4	1	13	14	1	4	1.3	.964	SS-17, 2B-5
1957			40	.170	.170	53	9	0	0	0	0.0	5	5	4	9	0	14	1	26	15	2	2	2.5	.953	2B-14, 3B-2, SS-1
3 yrs.			71	.210	.222	81	17	1	0	0	0.0	12	7	5	13	1	18	2	40	32	3	6	1.7	.960	SS-22, 2B-19, 3B-2

Walt Kuhn

KUHN, WALTER CHARLES (Red)
B. Feb. 2, 1884, Fresno, Calif. D. June 14, 1935, Fresno, Calif.

BR TR 5′ 7″ 162 lbs.

Year	Team	Lg	Games	BA	SA	AB	H	2B	3B	HR	HR%	R	RBI	BB	SO	SB	Pinch Hit AB	Pinch Hit H	PO	A	E	DP	TC/G	FA	G by Pos
1912	CHI	A	75	.202	.242	178	36	7	0	0	0.0	16	10	20		5	0	0	318	104	15	8	5.8	.966	C-75
1913			26	.160	.180	50	8	1	0	0	0.0	5	5	13	8	1	2	0	75	22	2	1	4.1	.980	C-24
1914			17	.275	.300	40	11	1	0	0	0.0	4	0	8	11	2	0	0	60	17	1	3	4.9	.987	C-16
3 yrs.			118	.205	.239	268	55	9	0	0	0.0	25	15	41	19	8	2	0	453	143	18	12	5.3	.971	C-115

Charlie Kuhns

KUHNS, CHARLES B.
B. Oct. 27, 1877, Freeport, Pa. D. July 15, 1922, Pittsburgh, Pa.

5′ 9″ 160 lbs.

Year	Team	Lg	Games	BA	SA	AB	H	2B	3B	HR	HR%	R	RBI	BB	SO	SB	Pinch Hit AB	Pinch Hit H	PO	A	E	DP	TC/G	FA	G by Pos
1897	PIT	N	1	.000	.000	3	0	0	0	0	0.0	0	0	1		0	0	0	1	3	2	0	6.0	.667	3B-1
1899	BOS	N	7	.278	.278	18	5	0	0	0	0.0	2	3	2		0	0	0	6	14	5	2	4.2	.800	SS-3, 3B-3
2 yrs.			8	.238	.238	21	5	0	0	0	0.0	2	3	3		0	0	0	7	17	7	2	4.4	.774	3B-4, SS-3

Duane Kuiper

KUIPER, DUANE EUGENE
B. June 19, 1950, Racine, Wis.

BL TR 6′ 175 lbs.

Year	Team	Lg	Games	BA	SA	AB	H	2B	3B	HR	HR%	R	RBI	BB	SO	SB	Pinch Hit AB	Pinch Hit H	PO	A	E	DP	TC/G	FA	G by Pos
1974	CLE	A	10	.500	.591	22	11	2	0	0	0.0	7	4	2	2	1	1	1	16	19	0	3	4.4	1.000	2B-8
1975			90	.292	.329	346	101	11	1	0	0.0	42	25	30	26	19	0	0	192	230	12	65	4.9	.972	2B-87, DH-1
1976			135	.263	.312	506	133	13	6	0	0.0	47	37	30	42	10	4	0	321	367	11	95	5.2	.984	2B-128, 1B-5, DH-2
1977			148	.277	.333	610	169	15	8	1	0.2	62	50	37	55	11	0	0	334	449	12	104	5.4	.985	2B-148
1978			149	.283	.338	547	155	18	6	0	0.0	52	43	19	35	4	0	0	341	408	16	91	5.1	.979	2B-149
1979			140	.255	.294	479	122	9	5	0	0.0	46	39	37	27	4	0	0	345	380	9	89	5.2	.988	2B-140
1980			42	.282	.315	149	42	5	0	0	0.0	10	9	13	8	0	0	0	87	111	1	28	4.7	.995	2B-42
1981			72	.257	.286	206	53	6	0	0	0.0	15	14	8	13	1	4	2	118	174	5	24	4.1	.983	2B-72
1982	SF	N	107	.280	.330	218	61	9	1	0	0.0	26	17	32	24	2	44	14	101	124	5	24	4.5	.978	2B-51
1983			72	.250	.284	176	44	2	2	0	0.0	14	14	27	13	0	10	2	107	140	3	17	3.9	.988	2B-64

Duane Kuiper *continued*

Year	Team	Games	BA	SA	AB	H	2B	3B	HR	HR%	R	RBI	BB	SO	SB	Pinch Hit AB	Pinch Hit H	PO	A	E	DP	TC/G	FA	G by Pos
1984		83	.200	.209	115	23	1	0	0	0.0	8	11	12	10	0	47	9	62	66	4	14	4.1	.970	2B-31, 1B-1
1985		9	.600	.600	5	3	0	0	0	0.0	0	0	1	0	0	5	3	0	0	0	0	0.0	—	
12 yrs.		1057	.271	.316	3379	917	91	29	1	0.0	329	263	248	255	52	115	31	2024	2468	78	554	4.9	.983	2B-920, 1B-6, DH-3

Jeff Kunkel

KUNKEL, JEFFREY WILLIAM BR TR 6′ 2″ 175 lbs.
Son of Bill Kunkel.
B. Mar. 25, 1962, West Palm Beach, Fla.

Year	Team	Games	BA	SA	AB	H	2B	3B	HR	HR%	R	RBI	BB	SO	SB	Pinch Hit AB	Pinch Hit H	PO	A	E	DP	TC/G	FA	G by Pos
1984	TEX A	50	.204	.324	142	29	2	3	3	2.1	13	7	2	35	4	0	0	81	120	17	22	4.4	.922	SS-48, DH-1
1985		2	.250	.250	4	1	0	0	0	0.0	1	0	0	3	0	0	0	2	5	0	1	3.5	1.000	SS-2
1986		8	.231	.462	13	3	0	0	1	7.7	3	2	0	2	0	1	0	4	6	3	0	2.2	.769	SS-5, DH-1
1987		15	.219	.313	32	7	0	0	1	3.1	1	2	0	10	0	1	0	19	27	3	8	2.6	.939	2B-10, 3B-3, OF-3, SS-1, DH-1, 1B-1
1988		55	.227	.357	154	35	8	3	2	1.3	14	15	4	35	0	3	0	78	119	8	23	3.1	.961	2B-28, SS-19, 3B-10, OF-6, DH-3, P-1
1989		108	.270	.437	293	79	21	2	8	2.7	39	29	20	75	3	6	1	143	168	22	27	3.1	.934	SS-59, OF-30, 2B-8, DH-5, 3B-4, P-1
1990		99	.170	.280	200	34	11	1	3	1.5	17	17	11	66	2	6	1	101	172	11	34	2.8	.961	SS-67, 3B-15, 2B-13, OF-5, DH-1
1992	CHI N	20	.138	.207	29	4	2	0	0	0.0	0	1	0	8	0	8	1	18	14	1	2	2.8	.970	SS-6, OF-3, 2B-3
8 yrs.		357	.221	.355	867	192	44	9	18	2.1	88	73	37	234	9	25	3	446	631	65	117	3.1	.943	SS-207, 2B-62, OF-47, 3B-32, DH-12, P-2, 1B-1

Rusty Kuntz

KUNTZ, RUSSELL JAY BR TR 6′ 3″ 190 lbs.
B. Feb. 4, 1955, Orange, Calif.

Year	Team	Games	BA	SA	AB	H	2B	3B	HR	HR%	R	RBI	BB	SO	SB	Pinch Hit AB	Pinch Hit H	PO	A	E	DP	TC/G	FA	G by Pos
1979	CHI A	5	.091	.091	11	1	0	0	0	0.0	0	0	2	6	0	0	0	12	1	0	1	2.6	1.000	OF-5
1980		36	.226	.290	62	14	4	0	0	0.0	5	3	5	13	1	3	2	45	2	1	1	1.4	.979	OF-34
1981		67	.255	.291	55	14	2	0	0	0.0	15	4	6	8	1	3	0	54	0	0	0	1.0	1.000	OF-51, DH-5
1982		21	.192	.231	26	5	1	0	0	0.0	4	3	2	8	0	0	0	21	0	0	0	1.0	1.000	OF-21
1983	2 teams	CHI A (28G –.262)	MIN A (31G –.190)																					
″	total	59	.211	.303	142	30	4	0	3	2.1	19	6	18	41	1	4	1	106	3	2	1	1.9	.982	OF-57, DH-1
1984	DET A	84	.286	.414	140	40	12	0	2	1.4	32	22	25	28	2	12	5	74	2	1	1	1.0	.987	OF-67, DH-10
1985		5	.000	.000	5	0	0	0	0	0.0	0	0	2	2	0	4	0	0	0	1	0	0.3	.000	DH-3, 1B-1
7 yrs.		277	.236	.322	441	104	23	0	5	1.1	75	38	60	106	5	26	8	312	8	5	4	1.3	.985	OF-235, DH-19, 1B-1
LEAGUE CHAMPIONSHIP SERIES																								
1984	DET A	1	.000	.000	1	0	0	0	0	0.0	0	0	0	0	0	1	0	0	0	0	0	0.0	.000	OF-1
WORLD SERIES																								
1984	DET A	2	.000	.000	1	0	0	0	0	0.0	0	1	0	1	0	1	0	0	0	0	0	0.0	—	

Whitey Kurowski

KUROWSKI, GEORGE JOHN BR TR 5′11″ 193 lbs.
B. Apr. 19, 1918, Reading, Pa.

Year	Team	Games	BA	SA	AB	H	2B	3B	HR	HR%	R	RBI	BB	SO	SB	Pinch Hit AB	Pinch Hit H	PO	A	E	DP	TC/G	FA	G by Pos
1941	STL N	5	.333	.556	9	3	2	0	0	0.0	1	2	0	2	0	1	0	2	3	0	0	1.3	1.000	3B-4
1942		115	.254	.391	366	93	17	3	9	2.5	51	42	33	60	7	9	0	124	194	19	19	3.2	.944	3B-104, SS-1, OF-1
1943		139	.287	.439	522	150	24	8	13	2.5	69	70	31	54	3	1	0	167	257	21	29	3.2	.953	3B-137, SS-2
1944		149	.270	.449	555	150	25	7	20	3.6	95	87	58	40	2	2	0	192	290	17	21	3.2	.966	3B-146, 2B-9, SS-1
1945		133	.323	.511	511	165	27	3	21	4.1	84	102	45	45	1	1	0	174	238	16	28	3.1	.963	3B-131, SS-6
1946		142	.301	.462	519	156	32	5	14	2.7	76	89	72	47	2	3	1	175	249	15	17	3.2	.966	3B-138
1947		146	.310	.544	513	159	27	6	27	5.3	108	104	87	56	4	4	1	140	250	19	17	2.9	.954	3B-141
1948		77	.214	.277	220	47	8	0	2	0.9	34	33	42	28	0	9	1	55	100	10	7	2.5	.939	3B-65
1949		10	.143	.143	14	2	0	0	0	0.0	0	0	1	0	0	8	2	3	2	0	0	2.5	1.000	3B-2
9 yrs.		916	.286	.455	3229	925	162	32	106	3.3	518	529	369	332	19	38	5	1032	1583	117	138	3.1	.957	3B-868, SS-10, 2B-9, OF-1
WORLD SERIES																								
1942	STL N	5	.267	.600	15	4	0	1	1	6.7	3	5	2	3	0	0	0	7	4	1	0	2.4	.917	3B-5
1943		5	.222	.278	18	4	1	0	0	0.0	2	1	0	3	0	0	0	8	8	2	0	3.6	.889	3B-5
1944		6	.217	.261	23	5	1	0	0	0.0	2	1	1	4	0	0	0	4	15	0	1	3.2	1.000	3B-6
1946		7	.296	.407	27	8	3	0	0	0.0	5	2	0	3	0	0	0	13	9	1	2	3.3	.957	3B-7
4 yrs.		23	.253	.373	83	21	5	1	1	1.2	12	9	3	13	0	0	0	32	36	4	3	3.1	.944	3B-23

Craig Kusick

KUSICK, CRAIG ROBERT BR TR 6′ 3″ 210 lbs.
B. Sept. 30, 1948, Milwaukee, Wis.

Year	Team	Games	BA	SA	AB	H	2B	3B	HR	HR%	R	RBI	BB	SO	SB	Pinch Hit AB	Pinch Hit H	PO	A	E	DP	TC/G	FA	G by Pos
1973	MIN A	15	.250	.292	48	12	2	0	0	0.0	4	4	7	9	0	1	0	89	5	1	7	6.3	.989	1B-11, OF-2, DH-2
1974		76	.239	.403	201	48	7	1	8	4.0	36	26	35	36	0	7	2	479	42	2	45	7.0	.996	1B-75
1975		57	.237	.404	156	37	8	0	6	3.8	14	27	21	23	0	9	3	372	31	4	45	8.0	.990	1B-51
1976		109	.259	.432	266	69	13	0	11	4.1	33	36	35	44	5	35	3	109	17	3	16	1.3	.977	DH-79, 1B-23
1977		115	.254	.433	268	68	12	0	12	4.5	34	45	49	60	3	**38**	**10**	133	7	4	9	1.3	.972	DH-85, 1B-23
1978		77	.173	.272	191	33	3	2	4	2.1	23	20	37	38	3	24	4	228	22	4	14	3.6	.984	DH-35, 1B-27, OF-9
1979	2 teams	MIN A (24G –.241)	TOR A (24G –.204)																					
″	total	48	.222	.407	108	24	5	0	5	4.6	11	13	10	18	0	10	1	209	18	4	20	5.5	.983	1B-28, DH-13, P-1
7 yrs.		497	.235	.392	1238	291	50	3	46	3.7	155	171	194	228	11	124	23	1619	142	22	156	3.8	.988	1B-238, DH-214, OF-11, P-1

Art Kusnyer

KUSNYER, ARTHUR WILLIAM BR TR 6′ 2″ 197 lbs.
B. Dec. 19, 1945, Akron, Ohio.

Year	Team	Games	BA	SA	AB	H	2B	3B	HR	HR%	R	RBI	BB	SO	SB	Pinch Hit AB	Pinch Hit H	PO	A	E	DP	TC/G	FA	G by Pos
1970	CHI A	4	.100	.100	10	1	0	0	0	0.0	0	0	0	4	0	1	0	12	4	1	0	5.7	.941	C-3
1971	CAL A	6	.154	.154	13	2	0	0	0	0.0	0	0	0	3	0	0	0	19	4	1	0	4.0	.958	C-6
1972		64	.207	.263	179	37	2	1	2	1.1	13	13	16	33	0	2	0	362	33	10	3	6.4	.975	C-63
1973		41	.125	.156	64	8	2	0	0	0.0	5	3	2	12	0	0	0	130	13	3	2	3.6	.979	C-41
1976	MIL A	15	.118	.147	34	4	1	0	0	0.0	2	3	1	5	1	0	0	41	4	3	2	3.4	.938	C-14
1978	KC A	9	.231	.538	13	3	1	0	1	7.7	1	2	2	4	0	0	0	32	3	2	0	4.1	.946	C-9
6 yrs.		139	.176	.230	313	55	6	1	3	1.0	21	21	21	61	1	3	0	596	61	20	7	5.0	.970	C-136

Joe Kustus

KUSTUS, JOSEPH JULIUS BR TR 5′10″
B. Sept. 5, 1882, Detroit, Mich. D. Apr. 27, 1916, Eloise, Mich.

Year	Team	Games	BA	SA	AB	H	2B	3B	HR	HR%	R	RBI	BB	SO	SB	Pinch Hit AB	Pinch Hit H	PO	A	E	DP	TC/G	FA	G by Pos
1909	BKN N	53	.145	.191	173	25	5	0	1	0.6	12	11	11		9	3	0	92	6	5	1	2.1	.951	OF-50

Randy Kutcher

KUTCHER, RANDY SCOTT
B. Apr. 30, 1960, Anchorage, Alaska.
BR TR 5′11″ 170 lbs.

Year	Team	Games	BA	SA	AB	H	2B	3B	HR	HR%	R	RBI	BB	SO	SB	Pinch Hit AB	Pinch Hit H	PO	A	E	DP	TC/G	FA	G by Pos
1986	SF N	71	.237	.409	186	44	9	1	7	3.8	28	16	11	41	6	13	1	111	11	1	3	1.7	.992	OF-51, SS-13, 3B-4, 2B-3
1987		14	.188	.375	16	3	1	1	0	0.0	7	1	1	5	1	2	0	14	5	0	1	1.7	1.000	OF-6, 3B-2, 2B-2, SS-1
1988	BOS A	19	.167	.250	12	2	1	0	0	0.0	2	0	0	2	0	0	0	6	5	1	0	1.3	.917	OF-7, 3B-2
1989		77	.225	.362	160	36	10	3	2	1.3	28	18	11	46	3	5	2	112	8	3	0	1.8	.976	OF-57, 3B-6, DH-6, C-1
1990		63	.230	.351	74	17	4	1	1	1.4	18	5	13	18	3	1	0	55	26	0	2	1.5	1.000	OF-34, 3B-11, 2B-5, DH-5
5 yrs.		244	.228	.377	448	102	25	6	10	2.2	83	40	36	112	13	21	3	298	55	5	6	1.7	.986	OF-155, 3B-25, SS-14, DH-11, 2B-10, C-1
LEAGUE CHAMPIONSHIP SERIES																								
1990	BOS A	2	—	—	0	0	0	0	0	—	0	0	0	0	0	0	0	0	0	0	0	0.0	—	

Joe Kutina

KUTINA, JOSEPH PETER
B. Jan. 16, 1885, Chicago, Ill. D. Apr. 13, 1945, Chicago, Ill.
BR TR 6′ 2″ 205 lbs.

Year	Team	Games	BA	SA	AB	H	2B	3B	HR	HR%	R	RBI	BB	SO	SB	Pinch Hit AB	Pinch Hit H	PO	A	E	DP	TC/G	FA	G by Pos
1911	STL A	26	.257	.446	101	26	6	2	3	3.0	12	15	2		2	0	0	250	15	5	16	10.4	.981	1B-26
1912		67	.205	.293	205	42	9	3	1	0.5	18	18	13		0	15	2	491	24	8	28	10.1	.985	1B-51, OF-1
2 yrs.		93	.222	.343	306	68	15	5	4	1.3	30	33	15		2	15	2	741	39	13	44	10.2	.984	1B-77, OF-1

Al Kvasnak

KVASNAK, ALEXANDER
B. Jan. 11, 1921, Sagamore, Pa.
BR TR 6′ 1″ 170 lbs.

Year	Team	Games	BA	SA	AB	H	2B	3B	HR	HR%	R	RBI	BB	SO	SB	Pinch Hit AB	Pinch Hit H	PO	A	E	DP	TC/G	FA	G by Pos
1942	WAS A	5	.182	.182	11	2	0	0	0	0.0	3	0	2	1	0	2	1	5	0	0	0	1.7	1.000	OF-3

Cass Kwietniewski

Playing record listed under Cass Michaels.

Andy Kyle

KYLE, ANDREW EWING
B. Oct. 29, 1889, Toronto, Ont., Canada D. Sept. 6, 1971, Toronto, Ont., Canada.
BL TL 5′ 8″ 160 lbs.

Year	Team	Games	BA	SA	AB	H	2B	3B	HR	HR%	R	RBI	BB	SO	SB	Pinch Hit AB	Pinch Hit H	PO	A	E	DP	TC/G	FA	G by Pos
1912	CIN N	9	.333	.381	21	7	1	0	0	0.0	3	4	4	2	0	2	0	15	1	0	0	2.3	1.000	OF-7

Chet Laabs

LAABS, CHESTER PETER
B. Apr. 30, 1912, Milwaukee, Wis. D. Jan. 26, 1983, Warren, Mich.
BR TR 5′ 8″ 175 lbs.

Year	Team	Games	BA	SA	AB	H	2B	3B	HR	HR%	R	RBI	BB	SO	SB	Pinch Hit AB	Pinch Hit H	PO	A	E	DP	TC/G	FA	G by Pos
1937	DET A	72	.240	.434	242	58	13	5	8	3.3	31	37	24	66	6	9	2	133	2	4	0	2.2	.971	OF-62
1938		64	.237	.398	211	50	7	3	7	3.3	26	37	15	52	3	11	3	128	4	4	1	2.6	.971	OF-53
1939	2 teams	DET A (5G –.313) STL A (95G –.300)																						
″	total	100	.300	.489	333	100	21	6	10	3.0	53	64	35	62	4	16	4	212	8	7	0	2.7	.969	OF-84
1940	STL A	105	.271	.505	218	59	11	5	10	4.6	32	40	34	59	3	35	**14**	124	3	4	1	2.1	.969	OF-63
1941		118	.278	.482	392	109	23	6	15	3.8	64	59	51	59	5	16	5	217	6	4	2	2.3	.982	OF-100
1942		144	.275	.498	520	143	21	7	27	5.2	90	99	88	88	0	3	1	276	13	9	3	2.1	.970	OF-139
1943		151	.250	.409	580	145	27	7	17	2.9	83	85	73	**105**	5	1	0	346	16	9	4	2.5	.976	OF-150
1944		66	.234	.378	201	47	10	2	5	2.5	28	23	29	33	3	11	0	108	3	0	2	2.0	1.000	OF-55
1945		35	.239	.358	109	26	4	3	1	0.9	15	8	16	17	0	0	0	68	1	1	0	2.0	.986	OF-35
1946		80	.261	.492	264	69	13	0	16	6.1	40	52	20	50	3	6	0	151	5	2	2	2.2	.987	OF-72
1947	PHI A	15	.219	.344	32	7	1	0	1	3.1	5	5	4	4	0	7	1	17	1	0	0	2.6	1.000	OF-7
11 yrs.		950	.262	.452	3102	813	151	44	117	3.8	467	509	389	595	32	115	30	1780	62	44	15	2.3	.977	OF-820
WORLD SERIES																								
1944	STL A	5	.200	.400	15	3	1	1	0	0.0	1	0	2	6	0	1	0	5	1	0	0	1.5	1.000	OF-4

Coco Laboy

LABOY, JOSE ALBERTO
B. July 3, 1940, Ponce, Puerto Rico.
BR TR 5′10″ 165 lbs.

Year	Team	Games	BA	SA	AB	H	2B	3B	HR	HR%	R	RBI	BB	SO	SB	Pinch Hit AB	Pinch Hit H	PO	A	E	DP	TC/G	FA	G by Pos
1969	MON N	157	.258	.409	562	145	29	1	18	3.2	53	83	40	96	0	1	0	115	307	25	28	2.9	.944	3B-156
1970		137	.199	.299	432	86	26	1	5	1.2	37	53	31	81	0	7	0	107	200	17	20	2.4	.948	3B-132, 2B-3
1971		76	.252	.298	151	38	4	0	1	0.7	10	14	11	19	0	15	5	40	68	7	4	1.7	.939	3B-65, 2B-2
1972		28	.261	.420	69	18	2	0	3	4.3	6	14	10	16	0	2	0	18	34	1	2	1.8	.981	3B-24, 2B-3, SS-2
1973		22	.121	.242	33	4	1	0	1	3.0	2	2	5	8	0	3	0	13	19	4	2	1.6	.889	3B-20, OF-1, 2B-1
5 yrs.		420	.233	.354	1247	291	62	2	28	2.2	108	166	97	220	0	28	5	293	628	54	56	2.4	.945	3B-397, 2B-9, SS-2, OF-1

Candy LaChance

LaCHANCE, GEORGE JOSEPH
B. Feb. 15, 1870, Putnam, Conn. D. Aug. 18, 1932, Waterville, Conn.
BB TR 6′ 1″ 183 lbs.

Year	Team	Games	BA	SA	AB	H	2B	3B	HR	HR%	R	RBI	BB	SO	SB	Pinch Hit AB	Pinch Hit H	PO	A	E	DP	TC/G	FA	G by Pos
1893	BKN N	11	.171	.200	35	6	1	0	0	0.0	1	6	2	12	0	0	0	18	4	10	0	2.9	.688	C-6, OF-5
1894		68	.323	.494	257	83	13	8	5	1.9	48	52	16	32	20	0	0	525	19	15	26	8.1	.973	1B-56, C-10, OF-3
1895		127	.312	.427	536	167	22	8	8	1.5	99	108	29	48	37	0	0	1290	53	24	68	10.7	.982	1B-125, OF-3
1896		89	.284	.448	348	99	10	13	7	2.0	60	58	23	32	17	0	0	956	37	14	62	11.3	.986	1B-89
1897		126	.308	.446	520	160	28	16	4	0.8	86	90	15		26	0	0	1289	64	30	76	11.0	.978	1B-126
1898		136	.247	.346	526	130	23	7	5	1.0	62	65	31		23	1	0	934	163	49	73	8.5	.957	1B-74, SS-48, OF-13
1899	BAL N	125	.307	.405	472	145	23	10	1	0.2	65	75	21		31	0	0	1272	40	21	72	10.7	.984	1B-125
1901	CLE A	133	.303	.381	548	166	22	9	1	0.2	81	75	7		11	0	0	1342	58	30	73	10.8	.979	1B-133
1902	BOS A	138	.279	.351	541	151	13	4	6	1.1	60	56	18		8	0	0	1544	46	27	80	11.7	.983	1B-138
1903		141	.257	.328	522	134	22	6	1	0.2	60	53	28		12	0	0	1471	57	25	68	11.0	.984	1B-141
1904		157	.227	.283	573	130	19	5	1	0.2	55	47	23		7	0	0	1691	59	14	65	11.2	.992	1B-157
1905		12	.146	.171	41	6	1	0	0	0.0	1	5	6		0	0	0	154	7	2	6	13.6	.988	1B-12
12 yrs.		1263	.280	.379	4919	1377	197	86	39	0.8	678	690	219	124	192	1	0	12486	607	261	669	10.6	.980	1B-1176, SS-48, OF-24, C-16
WORLD SERIES																								
1903	BOS A	8	.222	.370	27	6	2	1	0	0.0	5	4	3	2	0	0	0	79	3	3	3	10.6	.965	1B-8

Rene Lachemann

LACHEMANN, RENE GEORGE
Brother of Marcel Lachemann.
B. May 4, 1945, Los Angeles, Calif.
Manager 1981–84, 1993–95.
BR TR 6′ 198 lbs.

Year	Team	Games	BA	SA	AB	H	2B	3B	HR	HR%	R	RBI	BB	SO	SB	Pinch Hit AB	Pinch Hit H	PO	A	E	DP	TC/G	FA	G by Pos
1965	KC A	92	.227	.394	216	49	7	1	9	4.2	20	29	12	57	0	23	4	361	27	8	3	5.3	.980	C-75
1966		7	.200	.400	5	1	1	0	0	0.0	0	0	0	1	0	1	0	10	1	0	1	1.8	1.000	C-6
1968	OAK A	19	.150	.167	60	9	1	0	0	0.0	3	4	1	11	0	4	0	82	5	3	0	5.6	.967	C-16
3 yrs.		118	.210	.345	281	59	9	1	9	3.2	23	33	13	69	0	28	4	453	33	11	4	5.1	.978	C-97

Year	Team		Games	BA	SA	AB	H	2B	3B	HR	HR%	R	RBI	BB	SO	SB	Pinch Hit AB	Pinch Hit H	PO	A	E	DP	TC/G	FA	G by Pos
Pete LaCock																									
LaCOCK, RALPH PIERRE II — B. Jan. 17, 1952, Burbank, Calif. — BL TL 6′ 2″ 200 lbs.																									
1972	CHI	N	5	.500	.500	6	3	0	0	0	0.0	3	4	0	1	1	1	1	2	0	0	0	0.7	1.000	OF-3
1973			11	.250	.313	16	4	1	0	0	0.0	1	3	1	2	0	7	3	5	1	0	0	1.2	1.000	OF-5
1974			35	.182	.264	110	20	4	1	1	0.9	9	8	12	16	0	4	1	134	12	2	5	4.5	.986	OF-22, 1B-11
1975			106	.229	.341	249	57	8	1	6	2.4	30	30	37	27	0	26	9	479	45	6	39	6.7	.989	1B-53, OF-26
1976			106	.221	.373	244	54	9	2	8	3.3	34	28	42	37	1	39	7	454	33	13	47	6.8	.974	1B-54, OF-19
1977	KC	A	88	.303	.408	218	66	12	1	3	1.4	25	29	15	25	2	22	8	203	19	2	16	3.3	.991	1B-29, DH-26, OF-12
1978			118	.295	.419	322	95	21	2	5	1.6	44	48	21	27	1	23	3	700	39	5	67	7.0	.993	1B-106
1979			132	.277	.380	408	113	25	4	3	0.7	54	56	37	26	2	18	3	829	68	3	79	7.3	.997	1B-108, DH-16
1980			114	.205	.263	156	32	6	0	1	0.6	14	18	17	10	1	12	5	311	22	2	28	2.9	.994	1B-86, OF-29
9 yrs.			715	.257	.366	1729	444	86	11	27	1.6	214	224	182	171	8	152	40	3117	239	33	281	5.6	.990	1B-447, OF-116, DH-42
LEAGUE CHAMPIONSHIP SERIES																									
1977	KC	A	1	.000	.000	1	0	0	0	0	0.0	0	0	1	1	0	1	0	4	0	0	0	4.0	1.000	1B-1
1978			4	.364	.727	11	4	2	1	0	0.0	1	1	3	1	1	1	0	25	1	0	3	8.7	1.000	1B-3
1980			1	—	—	0	0	0	0	0	—	0	0	0	0	0	0	0	0	0	0	0	0.0	.000	1B-1
3 yrs.			6	.333	.667	12	4	2	1	0	0.0	1	1	4	2	1	2	0	29	1	0	3	6.0	1.000	1B-5
WORLD SERIES																									
1980	KC	A	1	—	—	0	0	0	0	0	—	0	0	0	0	0	0	0	2	0	0	1	2.0	1.000	1B-1
Guy Lacy																									
LACY, OSCEOLA GUY — B. June 12, 1897, Cleveland, Tenn. D. Nov. 19, 1953, Cleveland, Tenn. — BL TR 5′11½″ 170 lbs.																									
1926	CLE	A	13	.167	.292	24	4	0	0	1	4.2	2	2	2	2	0	0	0	18	24	2	3	3.4	.955	2B-11, 3B-2
Lee Lacy																									
LACY, LEONDAUS — B. Apr. 10, 1948, Longview, Tex. — BR TR 6′ 1″ 175 lbs.																									
1972	LA	N	60	.259	.313	243	63	7	3	0	0.0	34	12	19	37	5	2	1	125	161	8	38	5.1	.973	2B-58
1973			57	.207	.222	135	28	2	0	0	0.0	14	8	15	34	2	13	1	80	85	6	22	4.2	.965	2B-41
1974			48	.282	.359	78	22	6	0	0	0.0	13	8	2	14	2	11	3	38	53	3	8	2.7	.968	2B-34, 3B-1
1975			101	.314	.451	306	96	11	5	7	2.3	44	40	22	29	5	21	4	152	75	13	11	2.8	.946	2B-43, OF-43, SS-1
1976	2 teams	ATL N (50G –.272) LA N (53G –.266)																							
″	total		103	.269	.346	338	91	11	3	3	0.9	42	34	22	25	3	17	5	193	111	9	28	3.4	.971	2B-46, OF-42, 3B-4
1977	LA	N	75	.266	.414	169	45	7	0	6	3.6	28	21	10	21	4	24	6	56	69	4	11	2.0	.969	OF-32, 2B-22, 3B-12
1978			103	.261	.518	245	64	16	4	13	5.3	29	40	27	30	7	34	13	114	64	9	7	2.4	.952	OF-44, 2B-24, 3B-9, SS-1
1979	PIT	N	84	.247	.412	182	45	9	3	5	2.7	17	15	22	36	6	33	6	77	8	3	1	1.9	.966	OF-41, 2B-5
1980			109	.335	.511	278	93	20	4	7	2.5	45	33	28	33	18	16	5	175	11	3	1	2.1	.984	OF-88, 3B-3
1981			78	.268	.385	213	57	11	4	2	0.9	31	10	11	29	24	13	3	121	8	3	1	2.1	.977	OF-63, 3B-1
1982			121	.312	.415	359	112	16	3	5	1.4	66	31	32	57	40	13	3	186	9	7	1	1.8	.965	OF-113, 3B-2
1983			108	.302	.406	288	87	12	3	4	1.4	40	13	22	36	31	20	6	167	2	0	0	1.7	1.000	OF-98
1984			138	.321	.464	474	152	26	3	12	2.5	66	70	32	61	21	8	0	272	18	2	4	2.3	.993	OF-127, 2B-2
1985	BAL	A	121	.293	.409	492	144	22	4	9	1.8	69	48	39	95	10	4	2	231	9	4	0	2.0	.984	OF-115, DH-5
1986			130	.287	.391	491	141	18	0	11	2.2	77	47	37	71	4	11	3	239	8	2	4	2.0	.992	OF-120, DH-3
1987			87	.244	.399	258	63	13	3	7	2.7	35	28	32	49	3	12	4	135	11	4	2	1.8	.973	OF-80, DH-4
16 yrs.			1523	.286	.410	4549	1303	207	42	91	2.0	650	458	372	657	185	252	65	2361	702	80	139	2.4	.975	OF-1006, 2B-275, 3B-32, DH-12, SS-2
LEAGUE CHAMPIONSHIP SERIES																									
1974	LA	N	1	—	—	0	0	0	0	0	—	0	0	0	0	0	0	0	0	0	0	0	0.0	—	
1977			1	1.000	1.000	1	1	0	0	0	0.0	1	0	0	0	0	1	1	0	0	0	0	0.0	—	
1978			2	.000	.000	2	0	0	0	0	0.0	0	0	0	0	0	2	0	0	0	0	0	0.0	—	
3 yrs.			4	.333	.333	3	1	0	0	0	0.0	1	0	0	0	0	3	1							
WORLD SERIES																									
1974	LA	N	1	.000	.000	1	0	0	0	0	0.0	0	0	0	1	0	1	0	0	0	0	0	0.0	—	
1977			4	.429	.429	7	3	0	0	0	0.0	1	2	1	1	0	2	1	2	0	0	0	1.0	1.000	OF-2
1978			4	.143	.143	14	2	0	0	0	0.0	0	1	1	3	0	0	0	0	0	0	0	0.0	.000	DH-4
1979	PIT	N	4	.250	.250	4	1	0	0	0	0.0	0	0	0	1	0	4	1	0	0	0	0	0.0	—	
4 yrs.			13	.231	.231	26	6	0	0	0	0.0	1	3	2	6	0	7	2	2	0	0	0	0.3	1.000	DH-4, OF-2
Hi Ladd																									
LADD, ARTHUR CLIFFORD (Uncle Hiram) — B. Feb. 9, 1870, Willimantic, Conn. D. May 7, 1948, Cranston, R. I. — BL TR 6′ 4″ 180 lbs.																									
1898	2 teams	PIT N (1G –.000) BOS N (1G –.250)																							
″	total		2	.200	.200	5	1	0	0	0	0.0	1	0	0		0	1	0	2	0	0	0	2.0	1.000	OF-1
Steve Ladew																									
LADEW, STEPHEN — B. St. Louis, Mo. Deceased.																									
1889	KC	AA	2	.000	.000	4	0	0	0	0	0.0	0	0	0	3	0	0	0	1	1	0	0	1.0	1.000	OF-1, P-1
Joe Lafata																									
LAFATA, JOSEPH JOSEPH — B. Aug. 3, 1921, Detroit, Mich. — BL TL 6′ 163 lbs.																									
1947	NY	N	62	.221	.295	95	21	1	0	2	2.1	13	18	15	18	1	31	6	46	3	1	2	2.4	.980	OF-19, 1B-2
1948			1	.000	.000	1	0	0	0	0	0.0	0	0	0	1	0	1	0	0	0	0	0	0.0	—	
1949			64	.236	.343	140	33	2	2	3	2.1	18	16	9	23	1	14	6	296	10	5	25	6.6	.984	1B-47
3 yrs.			127	.229	.322	236	54	3	2	5	2.1	31	34	24	42	2	46	12	342	13	6	27	5.3	.983	1B-49, OF-19
Flip Lafferty																									
LAFFERTY, FRANK BERNARD — B. May 4, 1854, Scranton, Pa. D. Feb. 8, 1910, Wilmington, Del. — TR																									
1876	PHI	N	1	.000	.000	3	0	0	0	0	0.0	0	0	0	0		0	0	1	2	1	1	4.0	.750	P-1
1877	LOU	N	4	.059	.118	17	1	1	0	0	0.0	2	0	0	4		0	0	3	0	1	0	1.0	.750	OF-4
2 yrs.			5	.050	.100	20	1	1	0	0	0.0	2	0	0	4		0	0	4	2	2	1	1.6	.750	OF-4, P-1
Ty LaForest																									
LaFOREST, BYRON JOSEPH — B. Apr. 18, 1917, Edmondston, N. B., Canada D. May 5, 1947, Arlington, Mass. — BR TR 5′ 8″ 160 lbs.																									
1945	BOS	A	52	.250	.353	204	51	7	4	2	1.0	25	16	10	35	4	0	0	51	97	5	11	3.1	.967	3B-45, OF-5

Roger LaFrancois

LaFRANCOIS, ROGER VICTOR
B. Aug. 2, 1954, Norwich, Conn.
BL TR 6′ 2″ 202 lbs.

Year	Team	Games	BA	SA	AB	H	2B	3B	HR	HR%	R	RBI	BB	SO	SB	Pinch Hit AB	Pinch Hit H	PO	A	E	DP	TC/G	FA	G by Pos
1982	BOS A	8	.400	.500	10	4	1	0	0	0.0	1	1	0	0	0	2	1	15	0	0	0	1.9	1.000	C-8

Mike Laga

LAGA, MICHAEL RUSSELL
B. June 14, 1960, Ridgewood, N. J.
BL TL 6′ 2″ 210 lbs.

Year	Team	Games	BA	SA	AB	H	2B	3B	HR	HR%	R	RBI	BB	SO	SB	Pinch Hit AB	Pinch Hit H	PO	A	E	DP	TC/G	FA	G by Pos
1982	DET A	27	.261	.466	88	23	9	0	3	3.4	6	11	4	23	1	4	1	163	4	1	18	6.2	.994	1B-19, DH-8
1983		12	.190	.190	21	4	0	0	0	0.0	2	2	1	9	0	3	1	9	1	0	2	0.9	1.000	DH-6, 1B-5
1984		9	.545	.545	11	6	0	0	0	0.0	1	1	1	2	0	3	3	12	1	0	1	1.6	1.000	1B-4, DH-4
1985		9	.167	.361	36	6	1	0	2	5.6	3	6	0	9	0	0	0	33	5	1	4	4.3	.974	DH-5, 1B-4
1986	2 teams	DET A (15G –.200) STL N (18G –.217)																						
″	total	33	.209	.462	91	19	5	0	6	6.6	13	16	10	31	0	5	0	207	21	0	19	7.4	1.000	1B-28, DH-3
1987	STL N	17	.138	.276	29	4	1	0	1	3.4	4	4	2	7	0	5	1	66	7	2	10	6.3	.973	1B-12
1988		41	.130	.160	100	13	0	0	1	1.0	5	4	2	21	0	5	0	293	17	0	26	8.4	1.000	1B-37
1989	SF N	17	.200	.400	20	4	1	0	1	5.0	1	7	1	6	0	11	2	16	1	0	0	4.3	1.000	1B-4
1990		23	.185	.444	27	5	1	0	2	7.4	4	4	1	7	0	11	2	33	5	0	4	3.8	1.000	1B-10
9 yrs.		188	.199	.355	423	84	18	0	16	3.8	39	55	22	115	1	47	10	832	62	4	84	6.0	.996	1B-123, DH-26

Joe Lahoud

LAHOUD, JOSEPH MICHAEL (Duck)
B. Apr. 14, 1947, Danbury, Conn.
BL TL 6′ 1″ 198 lbs.

Year	Team	Games	BA	SA	AB	H	2B	3B	HR	HR%	R	RBI	BB	SO	SB	Pinch Hit AB	Pinch Hit H	PO	A	E	DP	TC/G	FA	G by Pos
1968	BOS A	29	.192	.244	78	15	1	0	1	1.3	5	6	16	16	0	6	2	23	2	2	0	1.1	.926	OF-25
1969		101	.188	.335	218	41	5	0	9	4.1	32	21	40	43	2	25	2	91	3	2	0	1.4	.979	OF-66, 1B-1
1970		17	.245	.388	49	12	1	0	2	4.1	6	5	7	6	0	4	2	23	3	1	0	2.1	.963	OF-13
1971		107	.215	.438	256	55	9	3	14	5.5	39	32	40	45	2	29	8	139	4	1	3	2.1	.993	OF-69
1972	MIL A	111	.237	.399	316	75	9	3	12	3.8	35	34	45	54	3	11	4	189	2	5	0	2.0	.974	OF-97
1973		96	.204	.311	225	46	9	0	5	2.2	29	26	27	36	5	15	4	85	2	0	1	1.1	1.000	DH-41, OF-40
1974	CAL A	127	.271	.458	325	88	16	3	13	4.0	46	44	47	57	4	14	4	156	6	4	2	1.4	.976	OF-106, DH-10
1975		76	.214	.359	192	41	6	2	6	3.1	21	33	48	33	2	9	2	41	1	0	0	0.7	1.000	DH-35, OF-29
1976	2 teams	CAL A (42G –.177) TEX A (38G –.225)																						
″	total	80	.200	.265	185	37	7	1	1	0.5	18	9	28	32	1	21	3	54	0	2	0	0.7	.964	DH-50, OF-31
1977	KC A	34	.262	.431	65	17	5	0	2	3.1	8	8	11	16	1	12	3	18	2	1	0	1.1	.952	OF-15, DH-4
1978		13	.125	.125	16	2	0	0	0	0.0	0	0	0	1	0	12	2	0	0	0	0	0.0		OF-1, DH-1
11 yrs.		791	.223	.372	1925	429	68	12	65	3.4	239	218	309	339	20	158	36	819	25	18	6	1.4	.979	OF-492, DH-141, 1B-1
LEAGUE CHAMPIONSHIP SERIES																								
1977	KC A	1	.000	.000	1	0	0	0	0	0.0	2	0	2	0	0	0	0	0	0	0	0	0.0	.000	DH-1

Dick Lajeskie

LAJESKIE, RICHARD EDWARD
B. Jan. 8, 1926, Passaic, N. J. D. Aug. 15, 1976, Ramsey, N. J.
BR TR 5′11″ 175 lbs.

Year	Team	Games	BA	SA	AB	H	2B	3B	HR	HR%	R	RBI	BB	SO	SB	Pinch Hit AB	Pinch Hit H	PO	A	E	DP	TC/G	FA	G by Pos
1946	NY N	6	.200	.200	10	2	0	0	0	0.0	3	0	3	2	0	0	0	7	20	1	1	7.0	.964	2B-4

Nap Lajoie

LAJOIE, NAPOLEON (Larry)
B. Sept. 5, 1874, Woonsocket, R. I. D. Feb. 7, 1959, Daytona Beach, Fla.
Manager 1905–09.
Hall of Fame 1937.
BR TR 6′ 1″ 195 lbs.

Year	Team	Games	BA	SA	AB	H	2B	3B	HR	HR%	R	RBI	BB	SO	SB	Pinch Hit AB	Pinch Hit H	PO	A	E	DP	TC/G	FA	G by Pos
1896	PHI N	39	.326	.543	175	57	12	7	4	2.3	36	42	1	11	7	0	0	363	11	2	27	9.6	.995	1B-39
1897		126	.361	**.569**	545	197	40	23	9	1.7	107	127	15		20	0	0	1117	45	20	45	9.2	.983	1B-108, OF-19, 3B-2
1898		147	.324	.461	608	197	**43**	11	6	1.0	113	**127**	21		25	0	0	449	407	46	60	6.1	.949	2B-146, 1B-1
1899		76	.378	.554	312	118	19	9	6	1.9	70	70	12		13	4	2	236	232	22	39	6.8	.955	2B-67, OF-5
1900		102	.337	.510	451	152	33	12	7	1.6	95	92	10		22	0	0	287	341	30	69	6.4	.954	2B-102, 3B-1
1901	PHI A	131	**.422**	**.635**	543	**229**	**48**	13	**14**	2.6	**145**	**125**	24		27	0	0	430	424	34	63	6.8	.962	2B-119, SS-12
1902	2 teams	PHI A (1G –.250) CLE A (86G –.368)																						
″	total	87	.366	.551	352	129	34	5	7	2.0	81	65	19		19	0	0	272	286	15	49	6.6	.974	2B-87
1903	CLE A	126	**.355**	**.533**	488	173	40	13	7	1.4	90	93	24		22	1	0	378	407	36	61	6.6	.956	2B-123, 3B-1, 1B-1
1904		140	**.381**	**.554**	554	**211**	**50**	14	6	1.1	92	**102**	27		31	0	0	378	386	38	52	5.7	.953	2B-95, SS-44, 1B-2
1905		65	.329	.422	249	82	13	2	2	0.8	29	41	17		11	1	0	198	179	3	27	5.9	.992	2B-59, 1B-5
1906		152	.355	.460	602	**214**	**49**	7	0	0.0	88	91	30		20	0	0	389	479	28	81	5.9	.969	2B-130, 3B-15, SS-7
1907		137	.299	.393	509	152	30	6	2	0.4	53	63	30		24	0	0	409	472	26	87	6.6	.971	2B-128, 1B-9
1908		157	.289	.375	581	168	32	6	2	0.3	77	74	47		15	0	0	460	543	37	78	6.6	.964	2B-156, 1B-1
1909		128	.324	.431	469	152	33	7	1	0.2	56	47	35		13	0	0	282	373	28	60	5.3	.959	2B-120, 1B-8
1910		159	.384	.514	**591**	**227**	**51**	7	4	0.7	92	76	60		26	0	0	512	438	31	63	6.0	.968	2B-149, 1B-10, SS-4
1911		90	.365	.454	315	115	20	1	2	0.6	36	60	26		13	9	4	479	109	14	33	7.7	.977	1B-41, 2B-37
1912		117	.368	.462	448	165	34	4	0	0.0	66	90	28		18	0	0	412	261	24	62	6.0	.966	2B-97, 1B-20
1913		137	.335	.404	465	156	25	2	1	0.2	67	68	33	17	17	9	2	279	363	20	59	5.3	.970	2B-126
1914		121	.258	.305	419	108	14	3	0	0.0	37	50	32	15	14	9	1	487	233	22	67	6.7	.970	2B-80, 1B-31
1915	PHI A	129	.280	.355	490	137	24	5	1	0.2	40	61	11	16	10	1	0	318	373	26	67	5.6	.964	2B-110, SS-10, 1B-5, 3B-2
1916		113	.246	.312	426	105	14	4	2	0.5	33	35	14	26	15	1	0	307	332	17	62	5.9	.974	2B-105, 1B-5, OF-2
21 yrs.		2479	.338	.466	9592	3244 **10th**	658 **6th**	161	83	0.9	1503	1599	516	85	382	35	9	8442	6694	519	1211	6.4	.967	2B-2036, 1B-286, SS-77, OF-26, 3B-21

Eddie Lake

LAKE, EDWARD ERVING
B. Mar. 18, 1916, Antioch, Calif. D. June 7, 1995, Castro Valley, Calif.
BR TR 5′ 7″ 159 lbs.

Year	Team	Games	BA	SA	AB	H	2B	3B	HR	HR%	R	RBI	BB	SO	SB	Pinch Hit AB	Pinch Hit H	PO	A	E	DP	TC/G	FA	G by Pos
1939	STL N	2	.250	.250	4	1	0	0	0	0.0	0	0	1	0	0	0	0	3	3	1	1	3.5	.857	SS-2
1940		32	.212	.348	66	14	3	0	2	3.0	12	7	12	17	1	5	0	35	39	3	4	3.3	.961	2B-17, SS-6
1941		45	.105	.132	76	8	2	0	0	0.0	9	0	15	22	3	6	1	40	56	9	11	3.0	.914	3B-15, SS-15, 2B-5
1943	BOS A	75	.199	.287	216	43	10	0	3	1.4	26	16	47	35	3	2	0	128	195	13	43	5.3	.961	SS-63
1944		57	.206	.246	126	26	5	0	0	0.0	21	8	23	22	5	1	0	54	117	13	29	3.6	.929	SS-41, P-6, 2B-3, 3B-1
1945		133	.279	.410	473	132	27	1	11	2.3	81	51	106	37	9	1	0	265	459	40	112	5.8	.948	SS-130, 2B-1
1946	DET A	155	.254	.339	587	149	24	1	8	1.4	105	31	103	69	15	0	0	232	391	35	85	4.2	.947	SS-155
1947		158	.211	.322	602	127	19	6	12	2.0	96	46	120	54	11	0	0	268	441	43	94	4.8	.943	SS-158

Eddie Lake *continued*

Year	Team	Games	BA	SA	AB	H	2B	3B	HR	HR%	R	RBI	BB	SO	SB	Pinch Hit AB	Pinch Hit H	PO	A	E	DP	TC/G	FA	G by Pos
1948		64	.263	.323	198	52	6	0	2	1.0	51	18	57	20	3	0	0	122	147	8	31	4.5	.971	2B-45, 3B-17
1949		94	.196	.254	240	47	9	1	1	0.4	38	15	61	33	2	12	2	113	167	10	37	3.9	.966	SS-38, 2B-19, 3B-18
1950		20	.000	.000	7	0	0	0	0	0.0	3	1	1	3	0	7	0	0	0	0	0	0.0		SS-1, 3B-1
11 yrs.		835	.231	.323	2595	599	105	9	39	1.5	442	193	546	312	52	34	3	1260	2015	175	447	4.6	.949	SS-609, 2B-90, 3B-52, P-6

Fred Lake

LAKE, FREDERICK LOVETT BR TR 5′10″ 170 lbs.
B. Oct. 16, 1866, Nova Scotia, Canada D. Nov. 24, 1931, Boston, Mass.
Manager 1908–10.

Year	Team	Games	BA	SA	AB	H	2B	3B	HR	HR%	R	RBI	BB	SO	SB	Pinch Hit AB	Pinch Hit H	PO	A	E	DP	TC/G	FA	G by Pos
1891	**BOS N**	5	.143	.143	7	1	0	0	0	0.0	1	0	2	4	0	0	0	3	2	0	0	1.0	1.000	C-4, OF-1
1894	**LOU N**	16	.286	.405	42	12	2	0	1	2.4	8	10	11	6	2	0	0	36	21	11	5	4.3	.838	2B-6, SS-5, C-5
1897	**BOS N**	19	.242	.306	62	15	4	0	0	0.0	2	5	1		2	1	0	49	15	2	0	3.7	.970	C-18
1898	**PIT N**	5	.077	.077	13	1	0	0	0	0.0	1	1	2		0	1	0	33	1	0	3	11.3	1.000	1B-3
1910	**BOS N**	3	.000	.000	1	0	0	0	0	0.0	0	0	1	0	0	1	0	0	0	0	0	0.0	—	
5 yrs.		48	.232	.304	125	29	6	0	1	0.8	12	16	17	10	4	3	0	121	39	13	8	4.1	.925	C-27, 2B-6, SS-5, 1B-3, OF-1

Steve Lake

LAKE, STEVEN MICHAEL BR TR 6′ 1″ 180 lbs.
B. Mar. 14, 1957, Inglewood, Calif.

Year	Team	Games	BA	SA	AB	H	2B	3B	HR	HR%	R	RBI	BB	SO	SB	Pinch Hit AB	Pinch Hit H	PO	A	E	DP	TC/G	FA	G by Pos
1983	**CHI N**	38	.259	.365	85	22	4	1	1	1.2	9	7	2	6	0	5	0	115	22	0	3	4.3	1.000	C-32
1984		25	.222	.407	54	12	4	0	2	3.7	4	7	0	7	0	1	0	72	13	4	0	3.7	.955	C-24
1985		58	.151	.193	119	18	2	0	1	0.8	5	11	3	21	1	4	1	182	25	1	1	3.8	.995	C-55
1986	**2 teams**	**CHI N** (10G –.421) **STL N** (26G –.245)																						
″	**total**	36	.294	.412	68	20	2	0	2	2.9	8	14	3	7	0	0	0	105	9	2	3	3.2	.983	C-36
1987	**STL N**	74	.251	.346	179	45	7	2	2	1.1	19	19	10	18	0	14	4	253	21	1	2	4.7	.996	C-59
1988		36	.278	.389	54	15	3	0	1	1.9	5	4	3	15	0	17	5	51	8	1	1	3.2	.983	C-19
1989	**PHI N**	58	.252	.335	155	39	5	1	2	1.3	9	14	12	20	0	7	3	262	33	3	3	5.4	.990	C-55
1990		29	.250	.275	80	20	2	0	0	0.0	4	6	3	12	0	1	0	115	19	1	1	4.8	.993	C-28
1991		58	.228	.285	158	36	4	1	1	0.6	12	11	2	26	0	0	0	277	25	2	1	5.2	.993	C-58
1992		20	.245	.340	53	13	2	0	1	1.9	3	2	1	8	0	3	0	71	8	2	1	4.8	.975	C-17
1993	**CHI N**	44	.225	.400	120	27	6	0	5	4.2	11	13	4	19	0	3	1	168	27	3	1	4.8	.985	C-41
11 yrs.		476	.237	.331	1125	267	41	5	18	1.6	89	108	43	159	1	55	14	1671	210	20	17	4.5	.989	C-424
LEAGUE CHAMPIONSHIP SERIES																								
1984	**CHI N**	1	1.000	2.000	1	1	1	0	0	0.0	0	0	0	0	0	0	0	0	0	0	0	0.0	.000	C-1
WORLD SERIES																								
1987	**STL N**	3	.333	.333	3	1	0	0	0	0.0	0	1	0	0	0	0	0	8	1	0	0	3.0	1.000	C-3

Al Lakeman

LAKEMAN, ALBERT WESLEY (Moose) BR TR 6′ 2″ 195 lbs.
B. Dec. 31, 1918, Cincinnati, Ohio D. May 25, 1976, Spartanburg, S. C.

Year	Team	Games	BA	SA	AB	H	2B	3B	HR	HR%	R	RBI	BB	SO	SB	Pinch Hit AB	Pinch Hit H	PO	A	E	DP	TC/G	FA	G by Pos
1942	**CIN N**	20	.158	.184	38	6	1	0	0	0.0	0	2	3	10	0	2	0	57	7	2	2	3.9	.970	C-17
1943		22	.255	.327	55	14	2	1	0	0.0	5	6	3	11	0	1	0	55	8	0	2	3.0	1.000	C-21
1944		1	.000	.000	1	0	0	0	0	0.0	0	0	0	1	0	1	0	0	0	0	0	0.0	.000	
1945		76	.256	.415	258	66	9	4	8	3.1	22	31	17	45	0	2	1	226	31	10	4	3.6	.963	C-74
1946		23	.133	.133	30	4	0	0	0	0.0	0	4	2	7	0	16	1	12	2	0	0	2.3	1.000	C-6
1947	**2 teams**	**CIN N** (2G –.000) **PHI N** (55G –.159)																						
″	**total**	57	.158	.272	184	29	3	0	6	3.3	11	19	5	40	0	5	0	286	18	4	16	5.9	.987	1B-29, C-23
1948	**PHI N**	32	.162	.235	68	11	2	0	1	1.5	2	4	5	22	0	9	1	73	4	0	0	3.3	1.000	C-22, P-1
1949	**BOS N**	3	.167	.167	6	1	0	0	0	0.0	0	0	1	0	0	1	0	19	2	0	2	10.5	1.000	1B-2
1954	**DET A**	5	.000	.000	6	0	0	0	0	0.0	0	0	0	1	0	1	0	10	0	0	0	2.5	1.000	C-4
9 yrs.		239	.203	.314	646	131	17	5	15	2.3	40	66	36	137	0	38	3	738	72	16	26	4.1	.981	C-167, 1B-31, P-1

Tim Laker

LAKER, TIMOTHY JOHN BR TR 6′ 2″ 185 lbs.
B. Nov. 27, 1969, Encino, Calif.

Year	Team	Games	BA	SA	AB	H	2B	3B	HR	HR%	R	RBI	BB	SO	SB	Pinch Hit AB	Pinch Hit H	PO	A	E	DP	TC/G	FA	G by Pos
1992	**MON N**	28	.217	.283	46	10	3	0	0	0.0	8	4	2	14	1	0	0	102	8	1	1	4.0	.991	C-28
1993		43	.198	.244	86	17	2	1	0	0.0	3	7	2	16	2	3	1	136	18	2	2	3.6	.987	C-43
1995		64	.234	.369	141	33	8	1	3	2.1	17	20	14	38	0	1	0	265	27	7	1	4.9	.977	C-61
3 yrs.		135	.220	.315	273	60	13	2	3	1.1	28	31	18	68	3	4	1	503	53	10	4	4.3	.982	C-132

Bud Lally

LALLY, DANIEL J. BL TR 5′11½″ 210 lbs.
B. Aug. 12, 1867, Jersey City, N. J. D. Apr. 14, 1936, Milwaukee, Wis.

Year	Team	Games	BA	SA	AB	H	2B	3B	HR	HR%	R	RBI	BB	SO	SB	Pinch Hit AB	Pinch Hit H	PO	A	E	DP	TC/G	FA	G by Pos
1891	**PIT N**	41	.224	.315	143	32	6	2	1	0.7	24	17	16	20	0	0	0	45	2	9	0	1.4	.839	OF-41
1897	**STL N**	87	.279	.366	355	99	15	5	2	0.6	56	42	9		12	0	0	223	12	25	3	3.0	.904	OF-84, 1B-3
2 yrs.		128	.263	.351	498	131	21	7	3	0.6	80	59	25	20	12	0	0	268	14	34	3	2.5	.892	OF-125, 1B-3

Ray Lamanno

LAMANNO, RAYMOND SIMOND BR TR 6′ 185 lbs.
B. Nov. 17, 1919, Oakland, Calif. D. Feb. 9, 1994, Berkeley, Calif.

Year	Team	Games	BA	SA	AB	H	2B	3B	HR	HR%	R	RBI	BB	SO	SB	Pinch Hit AB	Pinch Hit H	PO	A	E	DP	TC/G	FA	G by Pos
1941	**CIN N**	1	—	—	0	0	0	0	0	—	0	0	0	0	0	0	0	1	0	0	0	1.0	1.000	C-1
1942		111	.264	.404	371	98	12	2	12	3.2	40	43	31	54	0	7	1	421	59	11	7	4.7	.978	C-104
1946		85	.243	.305	239	58	12	0	1	0.4	18	30	11	26	0	21	4	222	37	7	6	4.4	.974	C-61
1947		118	.257	.358	413	106	21	3	5	1.2	33	50	28	39	0	9	2	556	62	9	6	5.8	.986	C-109
1948		127	.242	.273	385	93	12	0	0	0.0	31	27	48	32	2	3	0	537	49	13	11	4.8	.978	C-125
5 yrs.		442	.252	.338	1408	355	57	5	18	1.3	122	150	118	151	2	40	7	1737	207	40	30	5.0	.980	C-400

Bill Lamar

LAMAR, WILLIAM HARMONG (Good Time Bill) BL TR 6′ 1″ 185 lbs.
B. Mar. 21, 1897, Rockville, Md. D. May 24, 1970, Rockport, Mass. BB 1927

Year	Team	Games	BA	SA	AB	H	2B	3B	HR	HR%	R	RBI	BB	SO	SB	Pinch Hit AB	Pinch Hit H	PO	A	E	DP	TC/G	FA	G by Pos
1917	**NY A**	11	.244	.244	41	10	0	0	0	0.0	2	3	0	2	1	0	0	26	1	0	0	2.5	1.000	OF-11
1918		28	.227	.255	110	25	3	0	0	0.0	12	2	6	2	2	1	1	58	3	8	2	2.6	.884	OF-27
1919	**2 teams**	**NY A** (11G –.188) **BOS A** (48G –.291)																						
″	**total**	59	.280	.329	164	46	6	1	0	0.0	19	14	7	10	4	19	3	69	7	6	1	2.0	.927	OF-39, 1B-1
1920	**BKN N**	24	.273	.364	44	12	4	0	0	0.0	5	4	0	1	0	10	3	12	1	0	0	1.1	1.000	OF-12
1921		3	.333	.333	3	1	0	0	0	0.0	2	0	0	0	0	2	1	0	0	0	0	0.0	.000	OF-1
1924	**PHI A**	87	.330	.474	367	121	22	5	7	1.9	68	48	18	21	8	0	0	184	13	6	4	2.3	.970	OF-87
1925		138	.356	.468	568	202	39	8	3	0.5	85	77	21	17	2	6	1	283	18	15	4	2.4	.953	OF-131

Bill Lamar *continued*

Year	Team	Games	BA	SA	AB	H	2B	3B	HR	HR%	R	RBI	BB	SO	SB	Pinch Hit AB	Pinch Hit H	PO	A	E	DP	TC/G	FA	G by Pos
1926		116	.284	.389	419	119	17	6	5	1.2	62	50	18	15	4	8	3	199	10	10	2	2.1	.954	OF-105
1927		84	.299	.426	324	97	23	3	4	1.2	48	47	16	10	4	5	1	148	9	8	1	2.1	.952	OF-79
9 yrs.		550	.310	.417	2040	633	114	23	19	0.9	303	245	86	78	25	51	13	979	62	53	14	2.2	.952	OF-492, 1B-1
WORLD SERIES																								
1920	BKN N	3	.000	.000	3	0	0	0	0	0.0	0	0	0	0	0	3	0	0	0	0	0	0.0	—	

Lyman Lamb

LAMB, LAYMON RAYMOND BR TR 5′ 7″ 150 lbs.
B. Mar. 17, 1895, Lincoln, Neb. D. Oct. 5, 1955, Fayetteville, Ark.

Year	Team	Games	BA	SA	AB	H	2B	3B	HR	HR%	R	RBI	BB	SO	SB	Pinch Hit AB	Pinch Hit H	PO	A	E	DP	TC/G	FA	G by Pos
1920	STL A	9	.375	.458	24	9	2	0	0	0.0	4	4	0	7	2	2	1	10	0	0	0	1.4	1.000	OF-7
1921		45	.254	.373	134	34	9	2	1	0.7	18	17	4	12	0	5	1	38	62	6	3	2.9	.943	3B-23, 2B-7, OF-6
2 yrs.		54	.272	.386	158	43	11	2	1	0.6	22	21	4	19	2	7	2	48	62	6	3	2.7	.948	3B-23, OF-13, 2B-7

Pete Lamer

LAMER, PIERRE TR 5′10″ 170 lbs.
Born Pierre Lamere.
B. Dec. 1873, New York, N. Y. D. Oct. 24, 1931, Brooklyn, N. Y.

Year	Team	Games	BA	SA	AB	H	2B	3B	HR	HR%	R	RBI	BB	SO	SB	Pinch Hit AB	Pinch Hit H	PO	A	E	DP	TC/G	FA	G by Pos
1902	CHI N	2	.222	.222	9	2	0	0	0	0.0	2	0	0		0	0	0	9	3	2	1	7.0	.857	C-2
1907	CIN N	1	.000	.000	2	0	0	0	0	0.0	0	0	0		0	0	0	0	1	0	0	1.0	1.000	C-1
2 yrs.		3	.182	.182	11	2	0	0	0	0.0	2	0	0		0	0	0	9	4	2	1	5.0	.867	C-3

Gene Lamont

LAMONT, GENE WILLIAM BL TR 6′ 1″ 195 lbs.
B. Dec. 25, 1946, Rockford, Ill.
Manager 1992–95.

Year	Team	Games	BA	SA	AB	H	2B	3B	HR	HR%	R	RBI	BB	SO	SB	Pinch Hit AB	Pinch Hit H	PO	A	E	DP	TC/G	FA	G by Pos
1970	DET A	15	.295	.477	44	13	3	1	1	2.3	3	4	2	9	0	0	0	87	8	0	0	6.3	1.000	C-15
1971		7	.067	.067	15	1	0	0	0	0.0	2	1	0	5	0	0	0	38	2	2	0	6.0	.952	C-7
1972		1	—	—	0	0	0	0	0	—	0	0	0	0	0	0	0	1	0	0	0	1.0	1.000	C-1
1974		60	.217	.359	92	20	4	0	3	3.3	9	8	7	19	0	0	0	204	21	6	0	3.8	.974	C-60
1975		4	.375	.500	8	3	1	0	0	0.0	1	1	0	2	1	0	0	14	3	1	0	4.5	.944	C-4
5 yrs.		87	.233	.371	159	37	8	1	4	2.5	15	14	9	35	1	0	0	344	34	9	0	4.4	.977	C-87

Bobby LaMotte

LaMOTTE, ROBERT EUGENE BR TR 5′11″ 160 lbs.
B. Feb. 15, 1898, Savannah, Ga. D. Nov. 2, 1970, Chatham, Ga.

Year	Team	Games	BA	SA	AB	H	2B	3B	HR	HR%	R	RBI	BB	SO	SB	Pinch Hit AB	Pinch Hit H	PO	A	E	DP	TC/G	FA	G by Pos
1920	WAS A	4	.000	.000	3	0	0	0	0	0.0	0	0	1	1	0	0	0	0	4	1	0	2.5	.800	SS-1, 3B-1
1921		16	.195	.195	41	8	0	0	0	0.0	5	2	5	0	0	0	0	20	43	4	0	5.6	.940	SS-12
1922		68	.252	.332	214	54	10	2	1	0.5	22	23	15	21	6	0	0	101	147	11	17	3.8	.958	3B-62, SS-6
1925	STL A	97	.272	.368	356	97	20	4	2	0.6	61	51	34	22	5	2	0	223	275	39	57	5.6	.927	SS-93, 3B-3
1926		36	.203	.329	79	16	4	3	0	0.0	11	9	11	6	0	4	0	47	66	10	15	4.0	.919	SS-30, 3B-1
5 yrs.		221	.253	.341	693	175	34	9	3	0.4	99	85	66	50	11	6	0	391	535	65	89	4.7	.934	SS-142, 3B-67

Keith Lampard

LAMPARD, CHRISTOPHER KEITH BL TR 6′ 2″ 197 lbs.
B. Dec. 20, 1945, Warrington, England.

Year	Team	Games	BA	SA	AB	H	2B	3B	HR	HR%	R	RBI	BB	SO	SB	Pinch Hit AB	Pinch Hit H	PO	A	E	DP	TC/G	FA	G by Pos
1969	HOU N	9	.250	.500	12	3	0	0	1	8.3	2	2	0	3	0	7	3	3	1	0	0	4.0	1.000	OF-1
1970		53	.236	.375	72	17	8	1	0	0.0	8	5	5	24	0	38	9	25	2	0	0	1.5	1.000	OF-16, 1B-2
2 yrs.		62	.238	.393	84	20	8	1	1	1.2	10	7	5	27	0	45	12	28	3	0	0	1.6	1.000	OF-17, 1B-2

Tom Lampkin

LAMPKIN, THOMAS MICHAEL BL TR 5′11″ 180 lbs.
B. Mar. 4, 1964, Cincinnati, Ohio.

Year	Team	Games	BA	SA	AB	H	2B	3B	HR	HR%	R	RBI	BB	SO	SB	Pinch Hit AB	Pinch Hit H	PO	A	E	DP	TC/G	FA	G by Pos
1988	CLE A	4	.000	.000	4	0	0	0	0	0.0	0	0	1	0	0	1	0	3	0	0	0	1.0	1.000	C-3
1990	SD N	26	.222	.302	63	14	0	1	1	1.6	4	4	4	9	0	6	1	91	10	3	1	5.2	.971	C-20
1991		38	.190	.276	58	11	3	1	0	0.0	4	3	3	9	0	24	5	49	5	0	0	4.9	1.000	C-11
1992		9	.235	.235	17	4	0	0	0	0.0	3	0	6	1	2	1	0	30	3	0	0	4.1	1.000	C-7, OF-1
1993	MIL A	73	.198	.321	162	32	8	0	4	2.5	22	25	20	26	7	13	2	242	24	6	2	4.3	.978	C-60, OF-3, DH-1
1995	SF N	65	.276	.342	76	21	2	0	1	1.3	8	9	9	8	2	39	8	62	5	0	0	2.9	1.000	C-17, OF-6
6 yrs.		215	.216	.308	380	82	13	2	6	1.6	41	41	43	53	11	84	16	477	47	9	3	4.1	.983	C-118, OF-10, DH-1

Rick Lancellotti

LANCELLOTTI, RICHARD ANTHONY BL TL 6′ 3″ 195 lbs.
B. July 5, 1956, Providence, R. I.

Year	Team	Games	BA	SA	AB	H	2B	3B	HR	HR%	R	RBI	BB	SO	SB	Pinch Hit AB	Pinch Hit H	PO	A	E	DP	TC/G	FA	G by Pos
1982	SD N	17	.179	.231	39	7	2	0	0	0.0	2	4	2	8	0	8	1	63	2	1	7	6.6	.985	1B-7, OF-3
1986	SF N	15	.222	.556	18	4	0	0	2	11.1	2	6	0	7	0	13	4	7	0	0	0	3.5	1.000	OF-1, 1B-1
1990	BOS A	4	.000	.000	8	0	0	0	0	0.0	0	1	0	3	0	1	0	20	2	0	3	11.0	1.000	1B-2
3 yrs.		36	.169	.292	65	11	2	0	2	3.1	4	11	2	18	0	22	5	90	4	1	10	6.8	.989	1B-10, OF-4

Doc Land

LAND, WILLIAM GILBERT BL TL 5′11″ 165 lbs.
Born Doc Burrell Land.
B. May 14, 1903, Bennsville, Miss. D. Apr. 14, 1986, Livingston, Ala.

Year	Team	Games	BA	SA	AB	H	2B	3B	HR	HR%	R	RBI	BB	SO	SB	Pinch Hit AB	Pinch Hit H	PO	A	E	DP	TC/G	FA	G by Pos
1929	WAS A	1	.000	.000	3	0	0	0	0	0.0	0	0	1	0	0	0	0	1	0	0	0	1.0	1.000	OF-1

Grover Land

LAND, GROVER CLEVELAND BR TR 6′ 190 lbs.
B. Sept. 22, 1884, Frankfort, Ky. D. July 22, 1958, Phoenix, Ariz.

Year	Team	Games	BA	SA	AB	H	2B	3B	HR	HR%	R	RBI	BB	SO	SB	Pinch Hit AB	Pinch Hit H	PO	A	E	DP	TC/G	FA	G by Pos
1908	CLE A	8	.188	.188	16	3	0	0	0	0.0	1	2	0		0	0	0	18	3	1	0	2.8	.955	C-8
1910		34	.207	.207	111	23	0	0	0	0.0	4	7	2		1	0	0	169	47	4	3	6.7	.982	C-33
1911		35	.140	.187	107	15	1	2	0	0.0	5	10	3		2	0	0	148	50	8	5	5.9	.961	C-34, 1B-1
1913		17	.234	.255	47	11	1	0	0	0.0	3	9	4	1	1	1	1	83	26	9	3	6.9	.924	C-17
1914	BKN F	102	.275	.304	335	92	6	2	0	0.0	24	29	12		7	5	1	490	147	20	11	6.8	.970	C-97
1915		96	.259	.317	290	75	13	2	0	0.0	25	22	6		3	14	3	314	114	18	13	5.5	.960	C-81
6 yrs.		292	.242	.278	906	219	21	6	0	0.0	62	79	27	1	14	20	5	1222	387	60	35	6.2	.964	C-270, 1B-1

Ken Landenberger

LANDENBERGER, KENNETH HENRY (Red) BL TL 6′ 3″ 200 lbs.
B. July 29, 1928, Lyndhurst, Ohio D. July 28, 1960, Cleveland, Ohio.

Year	Team	Games	BA	SA	AB	H	2B	3B	HR	HR%	R	RBI	BB	SO	SB	Pinch Hit AB	Pinch Hit H	PO	A	E	DP	TC/G	FA	G by Pos
1952	CHI A	2	.200	.200	5	1	0	0	0	0.0	0	0	0	2	0	1	0	8	1	0	0	9.0	1.000	1B-1

Rafael Landestoy

LANDESTOY, RAFAEL SILVALDO
Born Rafael Silvaldo Landestoy (Santana).
B. May 28, 1953, Bani, Dominican Republic.

BB TR 5'10" 165 lbs.
BR 1977

Year	Team	Games	BA	SA	AB	H	2B	3B	HR	HR%	R	RBI	BB	SO	SB	Pinch Hit AB	Pinch Hit H	PO	A	E	DP	TC/G	FA	G by Pos
1977	LA N	15	.278	.278	18	5	0	0	0	0.0	6	0	3	2	2	0	0	8	18	0	2	2.4	1.000	2B-8, SS-3
1978	HOU N	59	.266	.298	218	58	5	1	0	0.0	18	9	8	23	7	9	1	66	132	4	19	3.9	.980	SS-50, 2B-2
1979		129	.270	.344	282	76	9	6	0	0.0	33	30	29	24	13	14	2	168	237	12	54	3.6	.971	2B-114, SS-3
1980		149	.247	.328	393	97	13	8	1	0.3	42	27	31	37	23	26	3	185	295	9	67	3.0	.982	2B-94, SS-65, 3B-3
1981	**2 teams**	**HOU N** (35G –.149)	**CIN N** (12G –.182)																					
"	**total**	47	.153	.188	85	13	1	1	0	0.0	8	5	17	9	5	10	1	55	64	4	11	3.6	.967	2B-34
1982	CIN N	73	.189	.243	111	21	3	0	1	0.9	11	9	8	14	2	35	11	41	54	0	11	2.3	1.000	3B-21, 2B-16, OF-3, SS-2
1983	**2 teams**	**CIN N** (7G –.000)	**LA N** (64G –.172)																					
"	**total**	71	.159	.246	69	11	1	1	1	1.4	6	1	3	8	0	33	4	34	28	3	7	1.7	.954	2B-14, OF-11, 3B-11, 1B-2, SS-1
1984	LA N	53	.185	.241	54	10	0	0	1	1.9	10	2	1	6	2	18	3	22	24	6	5	1.7	.885	2B-14, 3B-11, OF-5
8 yrs.		596	.237	.300	1230	291	32	17	4	0.3	134	83	100	123	54	145	25	579	852	38	176	3.0	.974	2B-296, SS-124, 3B-46, OF-19, 1B-2
LEAGUE CHAMPIONSHIP SERIES																								
1980	HOU N	5	.222	.222	9	2	0	0	0	0.0	3	2	1	0	1	0	0	5	8	1	0	3.5	.929	2B-3, SS-1
1983	LA N	2	.000	.000	2	0	0	0	0	0.0	0	0	0	1	0	2	0	0	0	0	0	0.0	—	
2 yrs.		7	.182	.182	11	2	0	0	0	0.0	3	2	1	1	1	2	0	5	8	1	0	3.5	.929	2B-3, SS-1
WORLD SERIES																								
1977	LA N	1	—	—	0	0	0	0	0	—	0	0	0	0	0	0	0	0	0	0	0	0.0	—	

Jim Landis

LANDIS, JAMES HENRY
B. Mar. 9, 1934, Fresno, Calif.

BR TR 6'1" 180 lbs.

Year	Team	Games	BA	SA	AB	H	2B	3B	HR	HR%	R	RBI	BB	SO	SB	Pinch Hit AB	Pinch Hit H	PO	A	E	DP	TC/G	FA	G by Pos
1957	CHI A	96	.212	.296	274	58	11	3	2	0.7	38	16	45	61	14	4	1	192	8	3	4	2.3	.985	OF-90
1958		142	.277	.434	523	145	23	7	15	2.9	72	64	52	80	19	1	0	331	9	5	1	2.4	.986	OF-142
1959		149	.272	.379	515	140	26	7	5	1.0	78	60	78	68	20	0	0	420	10	3	2	2.9	.993	OF-148
1960		148	.253	.389	494	125	25	6	10	2.0	89	49	80	84	23	0	0	372	10	6	3	2.6	.985	OF-147
1961		140	.283	.470	534	151	18	8	22	4.1	87	85	65	71	19	2	0	389	9	5	3	2.9	.988	OF-139
1962		149	.228	.375	534	122	21	6	15	2.8	82	61	80	105	19	4	1	360	2	2	1	2.5	.995	OF-144
1963		133	.225	.369	396	89	6	6	13	3.3	56	45	47	75	8	11	3	264	6	2	0	2.2	.993	OF-124
1964		106	.208	.272	298	62	8	4	1	0.3	30	18	36	64	5	7	1	183	7	1	2	1.9	.995	OF-101
1965	KC A	118	.239	.310	364	87	15	1	3	0.8	46	36	57	84	8	13	3	258	0	4	0	2.4	.985	OF-108
1966	CLE A	85	.222	.323	158	35	5	1	3	1.9	23	14	20	25	2	22	4	86	0	0	0	1.4	1.000	OF-61
1967	**3 teams**	**HOU N** (50G –.252)	**DET A** (25G –.208)	**BOS A** (5G –.143)																				
"	**total**	80	.237	.364	198	47	11	1	4	2.0	24	19	28	50	2	16	1	72	8	1	1	1.3	.988	OF-61
11 yrs.		1346	.247	.375	4288	1061	169	50	93	2.2	625	467	588	767	139	80	14	2927	69	32	17	2.4	.989	OF-1265
WORLD SERIES																								
1959	CHI A	6	.292	.292	24	7	0	0	0	0.0	6	1	1	7	1	0	0	9	0	1	0	1.7	.900	OF-6

Ken Landreaux

LANDREAUX, KENNETH FRANCIS
B. Dec. 22, 1954, Los Angeles, Calif.

BL TR 5'10" 165 lbs.

Year	Team	Games	BA	SA	AB	H	2B	3B	HR	HR%	R	RBI	BB	SO	SB	Pinch Hit AB	Pinch Hit H	PO	A	E	DP	TC/G	FA	G by Pos
1977	CAL A	23	.250	.342	76	19	5	1	0	0.0	6	5	5	15	1	0	0	59	5	2	2	3.0	.970	OF-22
1978		93	.223	.346	260	58	7	5	5	1.9	37	23	20	20	7	7	2	138	6	2	0	1.7	.986	OF-83, DH-1
1979	MIN A	151	.305	.450	564	172	27	5	15	2.7	81	83	37	57	10	7	1	292	10	6	1	2.1	.981	OF-147
1980		129	.281	.417	484	136	23	11	7	1.4	56	62	39	42	8	3	2	231	8	6	0	1.9	.976	OF-120, DH-6
1981	LA N	99	.251	.367	390	98	16	4	7	1.8	48	41	25	42	18	4	1	210	4	0	0	2.3	1.000	OF-95
1982		129	.284	.410	461	131	23	7	7	1.5	71	50	39	54	31	11	1	281	3	4	1	2.5	.986	OF-117
1983		141	.281	.451	481	135	25	3	17	3.5	63	66	34	52	30	4	1	299	4	3	1	2.2	.990	OF-137
1984		134	.251	.374	438	110	11	5	11	2.5	39	47	29	35	10	16	3	212	3	3	2	1.7	.986	OF-129
1985		147	.268	.405	482	129	26	2	12	2.5	70	50	33	37	15	22	4	267	4	7	1	2.0	.975	OF-140
1986		103	.261	.364	283	74	13	2	4	1.4	34	29	22	39	10	31	6	145	5	7	0	1.8	.955	OF-85
1987		115	.203	.324	182	37	4	0	6	3.3	17	23	16	28	5	50	10	72	5	4	3	1.3	.951	OF-63
11 yrs.		1264	.268	.400	4101	1099	180	45	91	2.2	522	479	299	421	145	155	31	2206	57	44	11	2.0	.981	OF-1138, DH-7
DIVISIONAL PLAYOFF SERIES																								
1981	LA N	5	.200	.250	20	4	1	0	0	0.0	1	1	0	1	0	0	0	16	0	0	0	3.2	1.000	OF-5
LEAGUE CHAMPIONSHIP SERIES																								
1981	LA N	5	.100	.200	10	1	1	0	0	0.0	0	0	3	2	0	0	0	4	0	0	0	0.8	1.000	OF-5
1983		4	.143	.143	14	2	0	0	0	0.0	0	1	1	3	0	0	0	12	0	0	0	3.0	1.000	OF-4
1985		5	.389	.556	18	7	3	0	0	0.0	4	2	1	1	0	1	0	7	0	0	0	1.8	1.000	OF-4
3 yrs.		14	.238	.333	42	10	4	0	0	0.0	4	3	5	6	0	1	0	23	0	0	0	1.8	1.000	OF-13
WORLD SERIES																								
1981	LA N	5	.167	.333	6	1	1	0	0	0.0	1	0	0	2	1	2	1	6	0	0	0	2.0	1.000	OF-3

Hobie Landrith

LANDRITH, HOBERT NEAL
B. Mar. 16, 1930, Decatur, Ill.

BL TR 5'10" 170 lbs.

Year	Team	Games	BA	SA	AB	H	2B	3B	HR	HR%	R	RBI	BB	SO	SB	Pinch Hit AB	Pinch Hit H	PO	A	E	DP	TC/G	FA	G by Pos
1950	CIN N	4	.214	.214	14	3	0	0	0	0.0	1	1	2	1	0	0	0	15	2	0	0	4.3	1.000	C-4
1951		4	.385	.462	13	5	1	0	0	0.0	3	0	1	1	0	0	0	23	2	0	0	6.3	1.000	C-4
1952		15	.260	.340	50	13	4	0	0	0.0	1	4	0	4	0	1	1	56	7	0	0	4.5	1.000	C-14
1953		52	.240	.331	154	37	3	1	3	1.9	15	16	12	8	2	4	2	179	13	3	4	4.1	.985	C-47
1954		48	.198	.383	81	16	0	0	5	6.2	12	14	18	9	1	5	2	123	15	2	1	3.3	.986	C-42
1955		43	.253	.425	87	22	3	0	4	4.6	9	7	10	14	0	16	3	86	14	0	3	3.7	1.000	C-27
1956	CHI N	111	.221	.311	312	69	10	3	4	1.3	22	32	39	38	0	15	4	483	55	14	9	5.6	.975	C-99
1957	STL N	75	.243	.313	214	52	6	0	3	1.4	18	26	25	27	1	10	1	339	29	5	3	5.6	.987	C-67
1958		70	.215	.306	144	31	4	0	3	2.1	9	13	26	21	0	24	5	227	16	2	3	5.4	.992	C-45
1959	SF N	109	.251	.332	283	71	14	0	3	1.1	30	29	43	23	0	2	1	576	45	5	5	5.7	.992	C-109
1960		71	.242	.311	190	46	10	0	1	0.5	18	20	23	11	1	2	0	346	23	13	5	5.5	.966	C-70
1961		43	.239	.380	71	17	4	0	2	2.8	11	10	12	7	0	13	2	126	9	2	2	4.6	.985	C-30

Hobie Landrith *continued*

Year	Team	Games	BA	SA	AB	H	2B	3B	HR	HR%	R	RBI	BB	SO	SB	Pinch Hit AB	Pinch Hit H	PO	A	E	DP	TC/G	FA	G by Pos
1962	2 teams NY N (23G –.289) BAL A (60G –.222)																							
"	total	83	.236	.349	212	50	7	1	5	2.4	24	24	27	12	0	2	0	376	37	9	5	5.2	.979	C-81
1963	2 teams BAL A (2G –.000) WAS A (42G –.175)																							
"	total	44	.173	.231	104	18	3	0	1	1.0	6	7	15	12	0	7	0	161	17	4	3	4.8	.978	C-38
14 yrs.		772	.233	.327	1929	450	69	5	34	1.8	179	203	253	188	5	101	21	3116	284	59	43	5.1	.983	C-677

Ced Landrum

LANDRUM, CEDRIC BERNARD
B. Sept. 3, 1963, Butler, Ala.
BL TR 5′9″ 165 lbs.

Year	Team	Games	BA	SA	AB	H	2B	3B	HR	HR%	R	RBI	BB	SO	SB	Pinch Hit AB	Pinch Hit H	PO	A	E	DP	TC/G	FA	G by Pos
1991	CHI N	56	.233	.279	86	20	2	1	0	0.0	28	6	10	18	27	2	0	61	0	2	0	1.4	.968	OF-44
1993	NY N	22	.263	.316	19	5	1	0	0	0.0	2	1	0	5	0	18	5	0	0	0	0	0.0	.000	OF-3
2 yrs.		78	.238	.286	105	25	3	1	0	0.0	30	7	10	23	27	20	5	61	0	2	0	1.3	.968	OF-47

Don Landrum

LANDRUM, DONALD LeROY
B. Feb. 16, 1936, Santa Rosa, Calif.
BL TR 6′ 180 lbs.

Year	Team	Games	BA	SA	AB	H	2B	3B	HR	HR%	R	RBI	BB	SO	SB	Pinch Hit AB	Pinch Hit H	PO	A	E	DP	TC/G	FA	G by Pos
1957	PHI N	2	.143	.286	7	1	1	0	0	0.0	1	0	2	1	0	0	0	9	0	0	0	4.5	1.000	OF-2
1960	STL N	13	.245	.408	49	12	0	1	2	4.1	7	3	4	6	3	0	0	34	1	0	0	2.7	1.000	OF-13
1961		28	.167	.242	66	11	2	0	1	1.5	5	3	5	14	1	1	0	42	3	0	1	1.7	1.000	OF-25, 2B-1
1962	2 teams STL N (32G –.314) CHI N (83G –.282)																							
"	total	115	.286	.330	273	78	5	2	1	0.4	40	18	34	33	11	20	2	141	3	4	3	1.7	.973	OF-85
1963	CHI N	84	.242	.282	227	55	4	1	1	0.4	27	10	13	42	6	24	3	100	3	3	0	1.9	.972	OF-57
1964		11	.000	.000	11	0	0	0	0	0.0	2	0	1	2	0	8	0	1	1	0	0	2.0	1.000	OF-1
1965		131	.226	.334	425	96	20	4	6	1.4	60	34	36	84	14	15	2	241	3	3	0	2.1	.988	OF-115
1966	SF N	72	.186	.255	102	19	4	0	1	1.0	9	7	9	18	1	18	2	55	6	2	0	1.2	.968	OF-54
8 yrs.		456	.234	.310	1160	272	36	8	12	1.0	151	75	104	200	36	86	9	623	20	12	4	1.9	.982	OF-352, 2B-1

Jesse Landrum

LANDRUM, JESSE GLENN
B. July 31, 1912, Crockett, Tex. D. June 27, 1983, Beaumont, Tex.
BR TR 5′11½″ 175 lbs.

Year	Team	Games	BA	SA	AB	H	2B	3B	HR	HR%	R	RBI	BB	SO	SB	Pinch Hit AB	Pinch Hit H	PO	A	E	DP	TC/G	FA	G by Pos
1938	CHI A	4	.000	.000	6	0	0	0	0	0.0	0	1	0	2	0	1	0	0	3	0	1	1.0	1.000	2B-3

Tito Landrum

LANDRUM, TERRY LEE
B. Oct. 25, 1954, Joplin, Mo.
BR TR 5′11″ 175 lbs.

Year	Team	Games	BA	SA	AB	H	2B	3B	HR	HR%	R	RBI	BB	SO	SB	Pinch Hit AB	Pinch Hit H	PO	A	E	DP	TC/G	FA	G by Pos
1980	STL N	35	.247	.325	77	19	2	2	0	0.0	6	7	6	17	3	5	1	40	1	1	0	1.4	.976	OF-29
1981		81	.261	.370	119	31	5	4	0	0.0	13	10	6	14	4	11	3	72	6	0	1	1.2	1.000	OF-67
1982		79	.278	.403	72	20	3	0	2	2.8	12	14	8	18	0	18	4	50	2	0	1	0.9	1.000	OF-56
1983	2 teams STL N (6G –.200) BAL A (26G –.310)																							
"	total	32	.298	.447	47	14	2	1	1	2.1	8	4	2	13	1	9	2	40	0	0	0	1.3	1.000	OF-31
1984	STL N	105	.272	.387	173	47	9	1	3	1.7	21	26	10	27	3	23	9	93	1	2	0	1.1	.979	OF-88
1985		85	.280	.429	161	45	8	2	4	2.5	21	21	19	30	1	24	8	91	2	0	1	1.3	1.000	OF-73
1986		96	.210	.283	205	43	7	1	2	1.0	24	17	20	41	3	28	5	131	6	1	1	1.8	.993	OF-78
1987	2 teams STL N (30G –.200) LA N (51G –.239)																							
"	total	81	.222	.282	117	26	4	0	1	0.9	13	10	10	30	2	35	8	77	2	1	0	1.5	.988	OF-54, 1B-1
1988	BAL A	13	.125	.208	24	3	0	1	0	0.0	2	2	4	6	0	1	0	15	0	0	0	1.2	1.000	OF-12, DH-1
9 yrs.		607	.249	.353	995	248	40	12	13	1.3	120	111	85	196	17	154	40	609	20	5	4	1.3	.992	OF-488, DH-1, 1B-1
LEAGUE CHAMPIONSHIP SERIES																								
1983	BAL A	4	.200	.500	10	2	0	0	1	10.0	2	1	0	2	0	1	0	5	0	0	0	1.7	1.000	OF-3
1985	STL N	6	.429	.429	14	6	0	0	0	0.0	2	4	1	1	1	1	1	6	0	0	0	1.2	1.000	OF-5
2 yrs.		10	.333	.458	24	8	0	0	1	4.2	4	5	1	3	1	2	1	11	0	0	0	1.4	1.000	OF-8
WORLD SERIES																								
1983	BAL A	3	—	—	0	0	0	0	0	—	0	0	0	0	1	0	0	1	0	0	0	0.3	1.000	OF-3
1985	STL N	7	.360	.560	25	9	2	0	1	4.0	3	1	0	2	0	0	0	12	1	0	1	1.9	1.000	OF-7
2 yrs.		10	.360	.560	25	9	2	0	1	4.0	3	1	0	2	1	0	0	13	1	0	1	1.4	1.000	OF-10

Chappy Lane

LANE, GEORGE M.
B. Pittsburgh, Pa. Deceased.
BR 165 lbs.

Year	Team	Games	BA	SA	AB	H	2B	3B	HR	HR%	R	RBI	BB	SO	SB	Pinch Hit AB	Pinch Hit H	PO	A	E	DP	TC/G	FA	G by Pos
1882	PIT AA	57	.178	.276	214	38	8	2	3	1.4	26		5			0	0	516	22	18	21	9.6	.968	1B-43, OF-13, C-2
1884	TOL AA	57	.228	.330	215	49	9	5	1	0.5	26		2			0	0	493	32	34	18	9.6	.939	1B-46, OF-9, 3B-2, C-1
2 yrs.		114	.203	.303	429	87	17	7	4	0.9	52		7			0	0	1009	54	52	39	9.6	.953	1B-89, OF-22, C-3, 3B-2

Dick Lane

LANE, RICHARD HARRISON
B. June 28, 1927, Highland Park, Mich.
BR TR 5′11″ 178 lbs.

Year	Team	Games	BA	SA	AB	H	2B	3B	HR	HR%	R	RBI	BB	SO	SB	Pinch Hit AB	Pinch Hit H	PO	A	E	DP	TC/G	FA	G by Pos
1949	CHI A	12	.119	.119	42	5	0	0	0	0.0	4	4	5	3	0	1	0	25	2	0	0	2.5	1.000	OF-11

Hunter Lane

LANE, JAMES HUNTER (Dodo)
B. July 20, 1900, Pulaski, Tenn. D. Sept. 12, 1994, Memphis, Tenn.
BR TR 5′11″ 165 lbs.

Year	Team	Games	BA	SA	AB	H	2B	3B	HR	HR%	R	RBI	BB	SO	SB	Pinch Hit AB	Pinch Hit H	PO	A	E	DP	TC/G	FA	G by Pos
1924	BOS N	7	.067	.067	15	1	0	0	0	0.0	0	0	1	1	0	2	0	7	4	1	0	2.4	.917	3B-4, 2B-1

Marv Lane

LANE, MARVIN
B. Jan. 18, 1950, Sandersville, Ga.
BR TR 5′11″ 180 lbs.

Year	Team	Games	BA	SA	AB	H	2B	3B	HR	HR%	R	RBI	BB	SO	SB	Pinch Hit AB	Pinch Hit H	PO	A	E	DP	TC/G	FA	G by Pos
1971	DET A	8	.143	.143	14	2	0	0	0	0.0	0	1	1	3	0	2	0	6	0	0	0	1.0	1.000	OF-6
1972		8	.000	.000	6	0	0	0	0	0.0	2	0	0	2	0	1	0	3	0	0	0	1.0	1.000	OF-3
1973		6	.250	.625	8	2	0	0	1	12.5	2	2	2	2	0	0	0	7	0	0	0	1.8	1.000	OF-4
1974		50	.233	.350	103	24	4	1	2	1.9	16	9	19	24	2	5	3	70	3	1	0	1.6	.986	OF-46, DH-1
1976		18	.188	.208	48	9	1	0	0	0.0	3	5	6	11	0	3	0	23	1	1	0	1.7	.960	OF-15
5 yrs.		90	.207	.296	179	37	5	1	3	1.7	23	17	28	42	2	11	3	109	4	2	0	1.5	.983	OF-74, DH-1

Don Lang

LANG, DONALD CHARLES
B. Mar. 15, 1915, Selma, Calif.
BR TR 6′ 175 lbs.

Year	Team	Games	BA	SA	AB	H	2B	3B	HR	HR%	R	RBI	BB	SO	SB	Pinch Hit AB	Pinch Hit H	PO	A	E	DP	TC/G	FA	G by Pos
1938	CIN N	21	.260	.420	50	13	3	1	1	2.0	5	11	2	7	0	2	2	17	26	2	3	2.6	.956	3B-15, SS-1, 2B-1
1948	STL N	117	.269	.356	323	87	14	1	4	1.2	30	31	47	38	2	16	1	86	191	11	15	3.0	.962	3B-95, 2B-2
2 yrs.		138	.268	.365	373	100	17	2	5	1.3	35	42	49	45	2	18	3	103	217	13	18	2.9	.961	3B-110, 2B-3, SS-1

Bill Lange

LANGE, WILLIAM ALEXANDER (Little Eva) BR TR 6′ 1½″ 190 lbs.
B. June 6, 1871, San Francisco, Calif. D. July 23, 1950, San Francisco, Calif.

Year	Team	Lg	Games	BA	SA	AB	H	2B	3B	HR	HR%	R	RBI	BB	SO	SB	Pinch Hit AB	Pinch Hit H	PO	A	E	DP	TC/G	FA	G by Pos
1893	CHI	N	117	.281	.380	469	132	8	7	8	1.7	92	88	52	20	47	0	0	303	250	60	28	5.2	.902	2B-57, OF-40, 3B-8, SS-7, C-7
1894			111	.328	.446	442	145	16	9	6	1.4	84	90	56	18	65	0	0	270	29	36	10	3.0	.893	OF-109, SS-2, 3B-1
1895			123	.389	.575	478	186	27	16	10	2.1	120	98	55	24	67	0	0	298	28	27	6	2.9	.924	OF-123
1896			122	.326	.465	469	153	21	16	4	0.9	114	92	65	24	84	0	0	314	18	24	3	2.9	.933	OF-121, C-1
1897			118	.340	.480	479	163	24	14	5	1.0	119	83	48		**73**	0	0	264	17	16	4	2.5	.946	OF-118
1898			113	.319	.441	442	141	16	10	6	1.4	79	69	36		22	0	0	286	19	9	5	2.8	.971	OF-111, 1B-2
1899			107	.325	.416	416	135	21	7	1	0.2	81	58	38		41	0	0	373	26	11	20	3.8	.973	OF-94, 1B-14
7 yrs.			811	.330	.459	3195	1055	133	79	40	1.3	689	578	350	86	399	0	0	2108	387	183	76	3.3	.932	OF-716, 2B-57, 1B-16, SS-9, 3B-9, C-8

Frank Lange

LANGE, FRANK HERMAN (Seagan) BR TR 5′11″ 180 lbs.
B. Oct. 28, 1883, Columbus, Wis. D. Dec. 26, 1945, Madison, Wis.

Year	Team	Lg	Games	BA	SA	AB	H	2B	3B	HR	HR%	R	RBI	BB	SO	SB	Pinch Hit AB	Pinch Hit H	PO	A	E	DP	TC/G	FA	G by Pos
1910	CHI	A	23	.255	.333	51	13	4	0	0	0.0	3	8	2		0	0	0	5	29	5	1	1.7	.872	P-23
1911			54	.289	.421	76	22	6	2	0	0.0	7	16	7		0	19	8	7	41	9	2	2.0	.842	P-29
1912			40	.215	.308	65	14	4	1	0	0.0	4	7	4		0	9	2	6	42	5	1	1.7	.906	P-31
1913			17	.167	.222	18	3	1	0	0	0.0	1	1	3	5	0	5	1	1	17	0	3	1.5	1.000	P-12
4 yrs.			134	.248	.348	210	52	15	3	0	0.0	15	32	16	5	0	33	11	19	129	19	7	1.8	.886	P-95

Sam Langford

LANGFORD, ELTON J. BL TR 6′ 180 lbs.
B. May 21, 1899, Briggs, Tex. D. July 31, 1993, Plainview, Tex.

Year	Team	Lg	Games	BA	SA	AB	H	2B	3B	HR	HR%	R	RBI	BB	SO	SB	Pinch Hit AB	Pinch Hit H	PO	A	E	DP	TC/G	FA	G by Pos
1926	BOS	A	1	.000	.000	1	0	0	0	0	0.0	1	0	0	0	0	1	0	0	0	0	0	0.0	—	
1927	CLE	A	20	.269	.388	67	18	5	0	1	1.5	10	7	5	7	0	0	0	39	1	0	0	2.0	1.000	OF-20
1928			110	.276	.382	427	118	17	8	4	0.9	50	50	21	35	3	3	1	239	5	7	2	2.3	.972	OF-107
3 yrs.			131	.275	.382	495	136	22	8	5	1.0	61	57	26	42	3	4	1	278	6	7	2	2.3	.976	OF-127

Bob Langsford

LANGSFORD, ROBERT WILLIAM BR TR
Born Robert Hugo Lankswert.
B. Aug. 5, 1865, Louisville, Ky. D. Jan. 10, 1907, Louisville, Ky.

Year	Team	Lg	Games	BA	SA	AB	H	2B	3B	HR	HR%	R	RBI	BB	SO	SB	Pinch Hit AB	Pinch Hit H	PO	A	E	DP	TC/G	FA	G by Pos
1899	LOU	N	1	.000	.000	4	0	0	0	0	0.0	0	0	0		0	0	0	3	2	0	0	5.0	1.000	SS-1

Hal Lanier

LANIER, HAROLD CLIFTON BR TR 6′ 2″ 180 lbs.
BB 1967
Son of Max Lanier.
B. July 4, 1942, Denton, N. C.
Manager 1986–88.

Year	Team	Lg	Games	BA	SA	AB	H	2B	3B	HR	HR%	R	RBI	BB	SO	SB	Pinch Hit AB	Pinch Hit H	PO	A	E	DP	TC/G	FA	G by Pos
1964	SF	N	98	.274	.347	383	105	16	3	2	0.5	40	28	5	44	2	2	0	226	298	11	48	5.3	.979	2B-98, SS-3
1965			159	.226	.289	522	118	15	9	0	0.0	41	39	21	67	2	1	0	294	445	18	75	4.8	.976	2B-158, SS-1
1966			149	.231	.290	459	106	14	2	3	0.7	37	37	16	49	1	1	0	303	423	13	80	4.8	.982	2B-112, SS-41
1967			151	.213	.255	525	112	16	3	0	0.0	37	42	16	61	2	0	0	253	519	20	92	4.6	.975	SS-137, 2B-34
1968			151	.206	.239	486	100	14	1	0	0.0	37	27	12	57	2	1	0	282	496	17	72	5.3	.979	SS-150
1969			150	.228	.251	495	113	9	1	0	0.0	37	35	25	68	0	0	0	252	530	25	98	5.4	.969	SS-150
1970			134	.231	.279	438	101	13	1	2	0.5	33	41	21	41	1	0	0	263	399	22	85	5.0	.968	SS-130, 2B-4, 1B-2
1971			109	.233	.286	206	48	8	0	1	0.5	21	13	15	26	0	3	0	91	130	6	19	2.1	.974	3B-83, 2B-13, SS-8, 1B-3
1972	NY	A	60	.214	.243	103	22	3	0	0	0.0	5	6	2	13	1	3	2	32	87	4	13	2.1	.967	3B-47, SS-9, 2B-3
1973			35	.209	.244	86	18	3	0	0	0.0	9	5	3	10	0	0	0	45	81	4	16	3.7	.969	SS-26, 2B-8, 3B-1
10 yrs.			1196	.228	.275	3703	843	111	20	8	0.2	297	273	136	436	11	11	2	2041	3408	140	598	4.6	.975	SS-655, 2B-430, 3B-131, 1B-5
LEAGUE CHAMPIONSHIP SERIES																									
1971	SF	N	1	.000	.000	1	0	0	0	0	0.0	0	0	0	0	0	0	0	1	0	0	0	1.0	1.000	3B-1

Rimp Lanier

LANIER, LORENZO BL TR 5′ 8″ 150 lbs.
B. Oct. 19, 1948, Tuskegee, Ala.

Year	Team	Lg	Games	BA	SA	AB	H	2B	3B	HR	HR%	R	RBI	BB	SO	SB	Pinch Hit AB	Pinch Hit H	PO	A	E	DP	TC/G	FA	G by Pos
1971	PIT	N	6	.000	.000	4	0	0	0	0	0.0	0	0	0	1	0	4	0	0	0	0	0	0.0	—	

Ray Lankford

LANKFORD, RAYMOND LEWIS BL TL 5′11″ 180 lbs.
B. June 5, 1967, Los Angeles, Calif.

Year	Team	Lg	Games	BA	SA	AB	H	2B	3B	HR	HR%	R	RBI	BB	SO	SB	Pinch Hit AB	Pinch Hit H	PO	A	E	DP	TC/G	FA	G by Pos
1990	STL	N	39	.286	.452	126	36	10	1	3	2.4	12	12	13	27	8	7	3	92	1	1	0	2.7	.989	OF-35
1991			151	.251	.392	566	142	23	**15**	9	1.6	83	69	41	114	44	5	1	367	7	6	2	2.6	.984	OF-149
1992			153	.293	.480	598	175	40	6	20	3.3	87	86	72	**147**	42	1	0	438	5	2	0	2.9	.996	OF-153
1993			127	.238	.346	407	97	17	3	7	1.7	64	45	81	111	14	8	1	312	6	7	0	2.7	.978	OF-121
1994			109	.267	.488	416	111	25	5	19	4.6	89	57	58	113	11	5	0	259	5	6	1	2.6	.978	OF-104
1995			132	.277	.513	483	134	35	2	25	5.2	81	82	63	110	24	3	1	300	7	3	1	2.4	.990	OF-129
6 yrs.			711	.268	.446	2596	695	150	32	83	3.2	416	351	328	622	143	29	6	1768	31	25	4	2.6	.986	OF-691

Les Lanning

LANNING, LESTER ALFRED (Red) BL TL 5′ 9″ 165 lbs.
B. May 13, 1895, Harvard, Ill. D. June 13, 1962, Bristol, Conn.

Year	Team	Lg	Games	BA	SA	AB	H	2B	3B	HR	HR%	R	RBI	BB	SO	SB	Pinch Hit AB	Pinch Hit H	PO	A	E	DP	TC/G	FA	G by Pos
1916	PHI	A	19	.182	.242	33	6	2	0	0	0.0	5	1	10	9	0	3	0	10	8	1	0	1.3	.947	OF-9, P-6

Carney Lansford

LANSFORD, CARNEY RAY BR TR 6′ 2″ 195 lbs.
Brother of Joe Lansford.
B. Feb. 7, 1957, San Jose, Calif.

Year	Team	Lg	Games	BA	SA	AB	H	2B	3B	HR	HR%	R	RBI	BB	SO	SB	Pinch Hit AB	Pinch Hit H	PO	A	E	DP	TC/G	FA	G by Pos
1978	CAL	A	121	.294	.406	453	133	23	2	8	1.8	63	52	31	67	20	2	0	94	186	18	18	2.5	.940	3B-117, SS-2, DH-1
1979			157	.287	.436	654	188	30	5	19	2.9	114	79	39	115	20	0	0	135	263	7	29	2.6	.983	3B-157
1980			151	.261	.390	602	157	27	3	15	2.5	87	80	50	93	14	1	1	151	250	19	29	2.8	.955	3B-150
1981	BOS	A	102	**.336**	.439	399	134	23	3	4	1.0	61	52	34	28	15	1	0	70	180	13	17	2.6	.951	3B-86, DH-16
1982			128	.301	.444	482	145	28	4	11	2.3	65	63	46	48	9	1	0	83	216	10	19	2.4	.968	3B-114, DH-13
1983	OAK	A	80	.308	.475	299	92	16	2	10	3.3	43	45	22	33	3	3	1	60	163	10	19	2.9	.957	3B-78, SS-1
1984			151	.300	.439	597	179	31	5	14	2.3	70	74	40	62	9	0	0	137	268	18	27	2.8	.957	3B-151
1985			98	.277	.429	401	111	18	2	13	3.2	51	46	18	27	2	1	0	85	119	5	11	2.2	.976	3B-97
1986			151	.284	.421	591	168	16	4	19	3.2	80	72	39	51	16	1	0	480	170	6	37	4.0	.991	3B-100, 1B-60, DH-2, 2B-1
1987			151	.289	.455	554	160	27	4	19	3.4	89	76	60	44	27	2	1	156	258	7	20	2.6	.983	3B-142, 1B-17, DH-4
1988			150	.279	.360	556	155	20	2	7	1.3	80	57	35	35	29	4	0	125	221	7	18	2.3	.980	3B-143, 1B-9, 2B-1
1989			148	.336	.405	551	185	28	2	2	0.4	81	52	51	25	37	0	0	195	188	13	20	2.6	.967	3B-136, 1B-15, DH-3
1990			134	.268	.320	507	136	15	1	3	0.6	58	50	45	50	16	2	0	128	195	9	24	2.4	.973	3B-126, 1B-5, DH-5

Carney Lansford *continued*

Year	Team	Games	BA	SA	AB	H	2B	3B	HR	HR%	R	RBI	BB	SO	SB	Pinch Hit AB	Pinch Hit H	PO	A	E	DP	TC/G	FA	G by Pos
1991		5	.063	.063	16	1	0	0	0	0.0	0	1	0	2	0	1	0	0	3	0	0	0.6	1.000	3B-4, DH-1
1992		135	.262	.369	496	130	30	1	7	1.4	65	75	43	39	7	5	1	199	167	11	23	2.7	.971	3B-119, 1B-18, DH-2, SS-1
15 yrs.		1862	.290	.411	7158	2074	332	40	151	2.1	1007	874	553	719	224	24	4	2098	2847	153	311	2.7	.970	3B-1720, 1B-124, DH-47, SS-4, 2B-2
LEAGUE CHAMPIONSHIP SERIES																								
1979	CAL A	4	.294	.294	17	5	0	0	0	0.0	2	3	1	2	1	0	0	4	8	0	3	3.0	1.000	3B-4
1988	OAK A	4	.294	.529	17	5	1	0	1	5.9	4	2	0	2	0	0	0	7	8	0	2	3.8	1.000	3B-4
1989		3	.455	.455	11	5	0	0	0	0.0	2	4	2	1	2	0	0	1	2	0	0	1.0	1.000	3B-3
1990		4	.438	.500	16	7	1	0	0	0.0	2	2	0	1	0	0	0	3	11	0	1	3.5	1.000	3B-4
1992		5	.167	.167	18	3	0	0	0	0.0	0	1	1	1	0	0	0	2	9	1	0	2.4	.917	3B-5
5 yrs.		20	.316	.380	79	25	2	0	1	1.3	10	12	4	7	3	0	0	17	38	1	6	2.8	.982	3B-20
WORLD SERIES																								
1988	OAK A	5	.167	.167	18	3	0	0	0	0.0	2	1	2	2	0	0	0	8	7	0	1	3.0	1.000	3B-5
1989		4	.438	.688	16	7	1	0	1	6.3	5	4	3	1	0	0	0	5	5	0	0	2.5	1.000	3B-4
1990		4	.267	.267	15	4	0	0	0	0.0	0	1	1	0	1	0	0	1	14	0	0	3.8	1.000	3B-4
3 yrs.		13	.286	.367	49	14	1	0	1	2.0	7	6	6	3	1	0	0	14	26	0	1	3.1	1.000	3B-13

Joe Lansford

LANSFORD, JOSEPH DALE
Brother of Carney Lansford.
B. Jan. 15, 1961, Santa Clara, Calif.

BR TR 6′ 5″ 225 lbs.

Year	Team	Games	BA	SA	AB	H	2B	3B	HR	HR%	R	RBI	BB	SO	SB	Pinch Hit AB	Pinch Hit H	PO	A	E	DP	TC/G	FA	G by Pos
1982	SD N	13	.182	.182	22	4	0	0	0	0.0	6	3	6	4	0	3	0	69	3	1	9	8.1	.986	1B-9
1983		12	.250	.625	8	2	0	0	1	12.5	1	2	0	3	0	6	1	11	1	0	1	1.5	1.000	1B-8
2 yrs.		25	.200	.300	30	6	0	0	1	3.3	7	5	6	7	0	9	1	80	4	1	10	5.0	.988	1B-17

Mike Lansing

LANSING, MICHAEL THOMAS (The Laser)
B. Apr. 3, 1968, Rawlins, Wyo.

BR TR 6′ 175 lbs.

Year	Team	Games	BA	SA	AB	H	2B	3B	HR	HR%	R	RBI	BB	SO	SB	Pinch Hit AB	Pinch Hit H	PO	A	E	DP	TC/G	FA	G by Pos
1993	MON N	141	.287	.369	491	141	29	1	3	0.6	64	45	46	56	23	4	1	136	336	24	53	3.2	.952	3B-81, SS-51, 2B-25
1994		106	.266	.368	394	105	21	2	5	1.3	44	35	30	37	12	0	0	164	283	10	54	3.7	.978	2B-82, 3B-28, SS-12
1995		127	.255	.392	467	119	30	2	10	2.1	47	62	28	65	27	0	0	307	373	6	77	5.3	.991	2B-127, SS-2
3 yrs.		374	.270	.376	1352	365	80	5	18	1.3	155	142	104	158	62	4	1	607	992	40	184	4.0	.976	2B-234, 3B-109, SS-65

Pete Lapan

LAPAN, PETER NELSON
B. June 25, 1891, Easthampton, Mass. D. Jan. 5, 1953, Norwalk, Calif.

BR TR 5′ 7″ 165 lbs.

Year	Team	Games	BA	SA	AB	H	2B	3B	HR	HR%	R	RBI	BB	SO	SB	Pinch Hit AB	Pinch Hit H	PO	A	E	DP	TC/G	FA	G by Pos
1922	WAS A	11	.324	.441	34	11	1	0	1	2.9	7	6	3	4	1	0	0	36	10	2	0	4.4	.958	C-11
1923		2	.000	.000	2	0	0	0	0	0.0	0	0	0	0	0	2	0	0	0	0	0	0.0	—	
2 yrs.		13	.306	.417	36	11	1	0	1	2.8	7	6	3	4	1	2	0	36	10	2	0	4.4	.958	C-11

Ralph LaPointe

LaPOINTE, RALPH ROBERT
B. Jan. 8, 1922, Winooski, Vt. D. Sept. 13, 1967, Burlington, Vt.

BR TR 5′11″ 185 lbs.

Year	Team	Games	BA	SA	AB	H	2B	3B	HR	HR%	R	RBI	BB	SO	SB	Pinch Hit AB	Pinch Hit H	PO	A	E	DP	TC/G	FA	G by Pos
1947	PHI N	56	.308	.355	211	65	7	0	1	0.5	33	15	17	15	8	2	1	82	158	11	25	4.6	.956	SS-54
1948	STL N	87	.225	.239	222	50	3	0	0	0.0	27	15	18	19	1	2	0	143	158	12	36	4.5	.962	2B-44, SS-25, 3B-1
2 yrs.		143	.266	.296	433	115	10	0	1	0.2	60	30	35	34	9	4	1	225	316	23	61	4.5	.959	SS-79, 2B-44, 3B-1

Frank LaPorte

LaPORTE, FRANK BREYFOGLE (Pot)
B. Feb. 6, 1880, Uhrichsville, Ohio D. Sept. 25, 1939, Newcomerstown, Ohio.

BR TR 5′ 8″ 175 lbs.

Year	Team	Games	BA	SA	AB	H	2B	3B	HR	HR%	R	RBI	BB	SO	SB	Pinch Hit AB	Pinch Hit H	PO	A	E	DP	TC/G	FA	G by Pos
1905	NY A	11	.400	.500	40	16	1	0	1	2.5	4	12	1		1	0	0	19	26	4	4	4.5	.918	2B-11
1906		123	.264	.368	454	120	23	9	2	0.4	60	54	22		10	3	1	133	229	35	16	3.3	.912	3B-114, 2B-5, OF-1
1907		130	.270	.360	470	127	20	11	0	0.0	56	48	27		10	2	0	157	125	30	6	2.4	.904	3B-64, OF-63, 1B-1
1908	2 teams	BOS A (62G –.237) NY A (39G –.262)																						
″	total	101	.249	.316	301	75	4	8	0	0.0	21	30	20		6	19	5	130	192	19	17	4.2	.944	2B-53, OF-16, 3B-12
1909	NY A	89	.298	.379	309	92	19	3	0	0.0	35	31	18		5	5	2	142	208	23	30	4.5	.938	2B-83
1910		124	.264	.338	432	114	14	6	2	0.5	43	67	33		16	6	1	175	246	21	21	3.7	.952	2B-79, OF-24, 3B-15
1911	STL A	136	.314	.446	507	159	37	12	2	0.4	71	82	34		4	0	0	289	409	36	59	5.4	.951	2B-133, 3B-3
1912	2 teams	STL A (80G –.312) WAS A (39G –.309)																						
″	total	119	.311	.393	402	125	20	5	1	0.2	45	55	32		10	11	0	183	215	27	34	3.9	.936	2B-76, OF-32
1913	WAS A	79	.252	.306	242	61	5	4	0	0.0	25	18	17	16	10	8	1	83	114	9	13	2.9	.956	3B-46, 2B-13, OF-12
1914	IND F	133	.311	.436	505	157	27	12	4	0.8	86	**107**	36		15	1	0	300	373	31	61	5.3	.956	2B-132
1915	NWK F	148	.253	.351	550	139	28	10	2	0.4	55	56	48		14	2	0	330	431	32	69	5.4	.960	2B-146
11 yrs.		1193	.281	.376	4212	1185	198	80	14	0.3	501	560	288	16	101	57	10	1941	2568	267	330	4.2	.944	2B-731, 3B-254, OF-148, 1B-1

Jack Lapp

LAPP, JOHN WALKER
B. Sept. 10, 1884, Frazer, Pa. D. Feb. 6, 1920, Philadelphia, Pa.

BL TR 5′ 8″ 160 lbs.

Year	Team	Games	BA	SA	AB	H	2B	3B	HR	HR%	R	RBI	BB	SO	SB	Pinch Hit AB	Pinch Hit H	PO	A	E	DP	TC/G	FA	G by Pos
1908	PHI A	13	.143	.200	35	5	0	1	0	0.0	4	1	5		0	0	0	55	16	4	0	5.8	.947	C-13
1909		21	.339	.429	56	19	3	1	0	0.0	8	10	3		1	2	0	95	26	8	2	6.8	.938	C-19
1910		71	.234	.286	192	45	4	3	0	0.0	18	17	20		0	7	3	361	88	9	6	7.3	.980	C-63
1911		68	.353	.467	167	59	10	3	1	0.6	35	26	24		4	6	3	296	51	9	8	5.8	.975	C-57, 1B-4
1912		90	.292	.399	281	82	15	6	1	0.4	26	35	19		3	8	4	354	105	20	10	5.8	.958	C-82
1913		81	.227	.290	238	54	4	4	1	0.4	23	20	37	26	1	2	0	315	110	14	5	5.6	.968	C-77, 1B-1
1914		69	.231	.286	199	46	7	2	0	0.0	22	19	31	14	1	3	1	330	88	10	4	6.4	.977	C-67
1915		112	.272	.375	312	85	16	5	2	0.6	26	31	30	29	5	10	4	470	118	19	23	6.0	.969	C-89, 1B-12
1916	CHI A	40	.208	.228	101	21	0	1	0	0.0	6	7	8	10	1	4	0	131	41	2	2	5.1	.989	C-34
9 yrs.		565	.263	.343	1581	416	59	26	5	0.3	168	166	177	79	16	42	15	2407	643	95	60	6.1	.970	C-501, 1B-17
WORLD SERIES																								
1910	PHI A	1	.250	.250	4	1	0	0	0	0.0	0	1	0	2	0	0	0	4	2	0	0	6.0	1.000	C-1
1911		2	.250	.250	8	2	0	0	0	0.0	1	0	0	1	0	0	0	18	8	0	0	13.0	1.000	C-2
1913		1	.250	.250	4	1	0	0	0	0.0	0	0	0	1	0	0	0	7	1	0	0	8.0	1.000	C-1
1914		1	.000	.000	1	0	0	0	0	0.0	0	0	0	0	0	0	0	2	1	0	0	3.0	1.000	C-1
4 yrs.		5	.235	.235	17	4	0	0	0	0.0	1	1	0	4	0	0	0	31	12	0	0	8.6	1.000	C-5

Norm Larker

LARKER, NORMAN HOWARD JOHN
B. Dec. 27, 1930, Beaver Meadows, Pa.

BL TL 6′ 185 lbs.

Year	Team	Games	BA	SA	AB	H	2B	3B	HR	HR%	R	RBI	BB	SO	SB	Pinch Hit AB	Pinch Hit H	PO	A	E	DP	TC/G	FA	G by Pos
1958	LA N	99	.277	.427	253	70	16	5	4	1.6	32	29	29	21	1	29	7	239	17	5	18	3.8	.981	OF-43, 1B-25
1959		108	.289	.418	311	90	14	1	8	2.6	37	49	26	25	0	24	7	491	48	5	53	6.4	.991	1B-55, OF-30

Norm Larker *continued*

Year	Team	Games	BA	SA	AB	H	2B	3B	HR	HR%	R	RBI	BB	SO	SB	Pinch Hit AB	Pinch Hit H	PO	A	E	DP	TC/G	FA	G by Pos
1960		133	.323	.430	440	142	26	3	5	1.1	55	78	36	24	1	15	6	917	80	7	81	8.3	.993	1B-119, OF-2
1961		97	.270	.387	282	76	16	1	5	1.8	29	38	24	22	0	10	2	589	52	3	68	7.4	.995	1B-86, OF-1
1962	**HOU N**	147	.263	.374	506	133	19	5	9	1.8	58	63	70	47	1	10	6	1153	103	11	103	9.0	.991	1B-135, OF-6
1963	**2 teams**	**MIL N** (64G –.177) **SF N** (19G –.071)																						
"	**total**	83	.168	.224	161	27	6	0	1	0.6	15	14	26	26	0	30	4	344	35	5	26	7.2	.987	1B-53
6 yrs.		667	.275	.390	1953	538	97	15	32	1.6	226	271	211	165	3	118	32	3733	335	36	349	7.4	.991	1B-473, OF-82
WORLD SERIES																								
1959	**LA N**	6	.188	.188	16	3	0	0	0	0.0	2	0	2	3	0	0	0	12	1	0	0	2.2	1.000	OF-6

Barry Larkin

LARKIN, BARRY LOUIS BR TR 6′ 185 lbs.
B. Apr. 28, 1964, Cincinnati, Ohio.

Year	Team	Games	BA	SA	AB	H	2B	3B	HR	HR%	R	RBI	BB	SO	SB	Pinch Hit AB	Pinch Hit H	PO	A	E	DP	TC/G	FA	G by Pos
1986	**CIN N**	41	.283	.403	159	45	4	3	3	1.9	27	19	9	21	8	4	0	51	125	4	22	4.6	.978	SS-36, 2B-3
1987		125	.244	.371	439	107	16	2	12	2.7	64	43	36	52	21	4	1	168	358	19	72	4.6	.965	SS-119
1988		151	.296	.429	588	174	32	5	12	2.0	91	56	41	24	40	2	0	231	470	29	67	4.9	.960	SS-148
1989		97	.342	.446	325	111	14	4	4	1.2	47	36	20	23	10	10	4	142	267	10	31	5.1	.976	SS-82
1990		158	.301	.396	614	185	25	6	7	1.1	85	67	49	49	30	3	1	254	469	17	86	4.7	.977	SS-156
1991		123	.302	.506	464	140	27	4	20	4.3	88	69	55	64	24	2	0	226	372	15	65	5.2	.976	SS-119
1992		140	.304	.454	533	162	32	6	12	2.3	76	78	63	58	15	0	0	233	408	11	67	4.7	.983	SS-140
1993		100	.315	.445	384	121	20	3	8	2.1	57	51	51	33	14	0	0	159	281	16	56	4.6	.965	SS-99
1994		110	.279	.419	427	119	23	5	9	2.1	78	52	64	58	26	0	0	178	312	10	56	4.5	.980	SS-110
1995		131	.319	.492	496	158	29	6	15	3.0	98	66	61	49	51	0	0	192	342	11	71	4.2	.980	SS-131
10 yrs.		1176	.298	.438	4429	1322	222	44	102	2.3	711	537	449	431	239	25	6	1834	3404	142	593	4.7	.974	SS-1140, 2B-3
DIVISIONAL PLAYOFF SERIES																								
1995	**CIN N**	3	.385	.385	13	5	0	0	0	0.0	2	1	1	2	4	0	0	3	8	0	1	3.7	1.000	SS-3
LEAGUE CHAMPIONSHIP SERIES																								
1990	**CIN N**	6	.261	.348	23	6	2	0	0	0.0	5	1	3	1	3	0	0	21	15	1	2	6.2	.973	SS-6
1995		4	.389	.611	18	7	2	1	0	0.0	1	0	1	1	1	0	0	10	15	1	2	6.5	.962	SS-4
2 yrs.		10	.317	.463	41	13	4	1	0	0.0	6	1	4	2	4	0	0	31	30	2	4	6.3	.968	SS-10
WORLD SERIES																								
1990	**CIN N**	4	.353	.529	17	6	1	1	0	0.0	3	1	2	0	0	0	0	1	14	0	2	3.8	1.000	SS-4

Ed Larkin

LARKIN, EDWARD FRANCIS BR TR 5′ 8″
B. July 1, 1885, Wyalusing, Pa. D. Mar. 28, 1934, Wyalusing, Pa.

Year	Team	Games	BA	SA	AB	H	2B	3B	HR	HR%	R	RBI	BB	SO	SB	Pinch Hit AB	Pinch Hit H	PO	A	E	DP	TC/G	FA	G by Pos
1909	**PHI A**	2	.167	.167	6	1	0	0	0	0.0	0	1	1		0	0	0	9	1	3	0	6.5	.769	C-2

Gene Larkin

LARKIN, EUGENE THOMAS BB TR 6′ 3″ 195 lbs.
B. Oct. 24, 1962, Flushing, N. Y.

Year	Team	Games	BA	SA	AB	H	2B	3B	HR	HR%	R	RBI	BB	SO	SB	Pinch Hit AB	Pinch Hit H	PO	A	E	DP	TC/G	FA	G by Pos
1987	**MIN A**	85	.266	.382	233	62	11	2	4	1.7	23	28	25	31	1	17	5	165	10	2	12	2.7	.989	DH-40, 1B-26
1988		149	.267	.382	505	135	30	2	8	1.6	56	70	68	55	3	4	0	466	28	3	46	3.4	.994	DH-86, 1B-60
1989		136	.267	.368	446	119	25	1	6	1.3	61	46	54	57	5	11	3	524	28	4	45	4.0	.993	1B-67, DH-41, OF-32
1990		119	.269	.392	401	108	26	4	5	1.2	46	42	42	55	5	5	0	299	18	2	29	2.7	.994	OF-47, DH-43, 1B-28
1991		98	.286	.373	255	73	14	1	2	0.8	34	19	30	21	2	19	3	340	20	3	23	3.9	.992	OF-47, 1B-39, DH-4, 3B-1, 2B-1
1992		115	.246	.359	337	83	18	1	6	1.8	38	42	28	43	7	24	8	509	35	5	50	5.4	.991	1B-55, OF-43, DH-4
1993		56	.264	.347	144	38	7	1	1	0.7	17	19	21	16	0	14	4	156	7	2	11	3.2	.988	OF-28, 1B-18, DH-3, 3B-2
7 yrs.		758	.266	.374	2321	618	131	12	32	1.4	275	266	268	278	23	94	23	2459	146	21	216	3.7	.992	1B-293, DH-221, OF-197, 3B-3, 2B-1
LEAGUE CHAMPIONSHIP SERIES																								
1987	**MIN A**	1	1.000	2.000	1	1	1	0	0	0.0	0	1	0	0	0	1	1	0	0	0	0	0.0	—	
1991		3	.000	.000	3	0	0	0	0	0.0	0	0	0	1	0	3	0	0	0	0	0	0.0	—	
2 yrs.		4	.250	.500	4	1	1	0	0	0.0	0	1	0	1	0	4	1							
WORLD SERIES																								
1987	**MIN A**	5	.000	.000	3	0	0	0	0	0.0	1	0	1	0	0	3	0	1	0	0	0	0.5	1.000	1B-1, DH-1
1991		4	.500	.500	4	2	0	0	0	0.0	0	1	0	0	0	4	2	0	0	0	0	0.0	.000	DH-1
2 yrs.		9	.286	.286	7	2	0	0	0	0.0	1	1	1	0	0	7	2	1	0	0	0	0.3	1.000	DH-2, 1B-1

Henry Larkin

LARKIN, HENRY E. (Ted) BR TR 5′10″ 170 lbs.
B. Jan. 12, 1860, Reading, Pa. D. Jan. 31, 1942, Reading, Pa.
Manager 1890.

Year	Team	Games	BA	SA	AB	H	2B	3B	HR	HR%	R	RBI	BB	SO	SB	Pinch Hit AB	Pinch Hit H	PO	A	E	DP	TC/G	FA	G by Pos
1884	**PHI AA**	85	.276	.423	326	90	21	9	3	0.9	59		15			0	0	107	11	20	1	1.6	.855	OF-85, 2B-2
1885		108	.329	.525	453	149	**37**	14	8	1.8	114		26			0	0	208	23	31	9	2.4	.882	OF-108
1886		139	.319	.450	565	180	**36**	16	2	0.4	133		59			0	0	264	21	44	2	2.4	.866	OF-139
1887		126	.310	.421	497	154	22	12	3	0.6	105		48		37	0	0	416	47	36	23	4.0	.928	OF-93, 1B-23, 2B-10
1888		135	.269	.403	546	147	28	12	7	1.3	92	101	33		20	0	0	1263	69	56	51	10.2	.960	1B-122, 2B-14
1889		133	.318	.426	516	164	23	12	3	0.6	105	74	83	41	11	0	0	1234	38	38	89	9.8	.971	1B-131, 3B-1, 2B-1
1890	**CLE P**	125	.332	.484	506	168	32	15	5	1.0	93	112	65	18	5	0	0	1268	40	30	63	10.6	.978	1B-125, OF-1
1891	**PHI AA**	133	.279	.441	526	147	27	14	10	1.9	94	93	66	56	2	0	0	1029	34	31	56	8.2	.972	1B-111, OF-23
1892	**WAS N**	119	.280	.390	464	130	13	7	8	1.7	76	96	39	21	21	0	0	1122	69	39	77	10.3	.968	1B-117, OF-2
1893		81	.317	.436	319	101	20	3	4	1.3	54	73	50	5	1	0	0	781	29	31	48	10.4	.963	1B-81
10 yrs.		1184	.303	.440	4718	1430	259	114	53	1.1	925	549	484	141	97	0	0	7692	381	356	419	7.1	.958	1B-710, OF-451, 2B-27, 3B-1

Terry Larkin

LARKIN, FRANK S. BR TR
B. 1856, Brooklyn, N. Y. D. Sept. 16, 1894, Brooklyn, N. Y.

Year	Team	Games	BA	SA	AB	H	2B	3B	HR	HR%	R	RBI	BB	SO	SB	Pinch Hit AB	Pinch Hit H	PO	A	E	DP	TC/G	FA	G by Pos
1876	**NY N**	1	.000	.000	4	0	0	0	0	0.0	0	0	0	0		0	0	0	2	2	0	4.0	.500	P-1
1877	**HAR N**	58	.228	.311	228	52	6	5	1	0.4	28	18	5	23		0	0	31	99	20	1	2.5	.867	P-56, 3B-2, 2B-1
1878	**CHI N**	58	.288	.363	226	65	9	4	0	0.0	33	32	**17**	17		0	0	20	95	21	0	2.3	.846	P-56, OF-1, 3B-1
1879		60	.219	.289	228	50	12	2	0	0.0	26	18	8	24		0	0	10	80	9	1	1.6	.909	P-58, OF-3
1880	**TRO N**	6	.150	.200	20	3	1	0	0	0.0	1	1	3	4		0	0	5	11	1	2	2.1	.941	P-5, OF-2, SS-1
1884	**2 teams**	**WAS U** (17G –.243) **RIC AA** (40G –.201)																						
"	**total**	57	.215	.258	209	45	1	4	0	0.0	28		13			0	0	123	145	40	16	5.4	.870	2B-40, 3B-17
6 yrs.		240	.235	.303	915	215	29	15	1	0.1	116	69	46	68		0	0	189	432	93	20	2.9	.870	P-176, 2B-41, 3B-20, OF-6, SS-1

Year	Team	Lg	Games	BA	SA	AB	H	2B	3B	HR	HR%	R	RBI	BB	SO	SB	Pinch Hit AB	Pinch Hit H	PO	A	E	DP	TC/G	FA	G by Pos

Bob Larmore

LARMORE, ROBERT McKAHAN (Red) BR TR 5′10½″ 185 lbs.
B. Dec. 6, 1896, Anderson, Ind. D. Jan. 15, 1964, St. Louis, Mo.

Year	Team	Lg	Games	BA	SA	AB	H	2B	3B	HR	HR%	R	RBI	BB	SO	SB	Pinch Hit AB	Pinch Hit H	PO	A	E	DP	TC/G	FA	G by Pos
1918	STL	N	4	.286	.286	7	2	0	0	0	0.0	0	1	0	2	0	2	2	3	4	2	0	4.5	.778	SS-2

Sam LaRoque

LaROQUE, SAMUEL H. J. TR 5′11″ 190 lbs.
B. Feb. 26, 1863, St. Mathias, Que., Canada Deceased.

Year	Team	Lg	Games	BA	SA	AB	H	2B	3B	HR	HR%	R	RBI	BB	SO	SB	Pinch Hit AB	Pinch Hit H	PO	A	E	DP	TC/G	FA	G by Pos
1888	DET	N	2	.444	.444	9	4	0	0	0	0.0	1	2	1	1	0	0	0	7	8	4	3	9.5	.789	2B-2
1890	PIT	N	111	.242	.313	434	105	20	4	1	0.2	59	40	35	29	27	0	0	292	321	76	35	6.2	.890	2B-78, SS-31, 1B-2, OF-1
1891	2 teams		PIT N (1G –.000) LOU AA (10G –.314)																						
″	total		11	.282	.462	39	11	2	1	1	2.6	6	8	5	9	1	0	0	31	25	9	4	5.4	.862	2B-10, 1B-1, 3B-1
3 yrs.			124	.249	.328	482	120	22	5	2	0.4	66	50	41	39	28	0	0	330	354	89	42	6.1	.885	2B-90, SS-31, 1B-3, 3B-1, OF-1

Vic LaRose

LaROSE, VICTOR RAYMOND BR TR 5′11″ 180 lbs.
B. Dec. 23, 1944, Los Angeles, Calif.

Year	Team	Lg	Games	BA	SA	AB	H	2B	3B	HR	HR%	R	RBI	BB	SO	SB	Pinch Hit AB	Pinch Hit H	PO	A	E	DP	TC/G	FA	G by Pos
1968	CHI	N	4	.000	.000	2	0	0	0	0	0.0	0	0	0	1	0	0	0	1	5	1	0	1.8	.857	SS-2, 2B-2

Harry LaRoss

LaROSS, HARRY RAYMOND (Spike) BR TR 5′11½″ 170 lbs.
B. Jan. 12, 1888, Easton, Pa. D. May 22, 1954, Chicago, Ill.

Year	Team	Lg	Games	BA	SA	AB	H	2B	3B	HR	HR%	R	RBI	BB	SO	SB	Pinch Hit AB	Pinch Hit H	PO	A	E	DP	TC/G	FA	G by Pos
1914	CIN	N	22	.229	.250	48	11	1	0	0	0.0	7	5	2	10	4	0	0	15	2	6	0	1.1	.739	OF-20

Don Larsen

LARSEN, DON JAMES BR TR 6′4″ 215 lbs.
B. Aug. 7, 1929, Michigan City, Ind.

Year	Team	Lg	Games	BA	SA	AB	H	2B	3B	HR	HR%	R	RBI	BB	SO	SB	Pinch Hit AB	Pinch Hit H	PO	A	E	DP	TC/G	FA	G by Pos
1953	STL	A	50	.284	.457	81	23	3	1	3	3.7	11	10	4	14	0	10	1	8	29	2	1	1.0	.949	P-38, OF-1
1954	BAL	A	44	.250	.409	88	22	5	3	1	1.1	6	4	5	15	0	15	0	14	34	1	3	1.7	.980	P-29
1955	NY	A	21	.146	.317	41	6	1	0	2	4.9	4	7	4	13	0	3	1	5	13	1	3	1.0	.947	P-19
1956			45	.241	.380	79	19	5	0	2	2.5	10	12	6	17	0	7	2	13	23	3	3	1.0	.923	P-38
1957			31	.250	.339	56	14	5	0	0	0.0	6	5	6	11	0	1	0	10	20	2	2	1.2	.938	P-27
1958			28	.306	.571	49	15	1	0	4	8.2	9	13	5	9	0	7	2	5	14	2	2	1.1	.905	P-19
1959			29	.255	.298	47	12	2	0	0	0.0	8	8	7	15	0	3	1	5	22	2	1	1.2	.931	P-25
1960	KC	A	23	.207	.241	29	6	1	0	0	0.0	3	3	0	11	0	1	0	4	8	1	1	0.6	.923	P-22
1961	2 teams		KC A (18G –.300) CHI A (25G –.320)																						
″	total		43	.311	.444	45	14	0	0	2	4.4	4	8	1	10	0	12	5	8	17	0	0	0.7	1.000	P-33, OF-1
1962	SF	N	52	.200	.280	25	5	0	1	0	0.0	3	1	0	7	0	4	0	4	15	0	3	0.4	1.000	P-49
1963			46	.182	.182	11	2	0	0	0	0.0	1	0	1	1	0	0	0	4	12	1	0	0.4	.941	P-46
1964	2 teams		SF N (6G –.000) HOU N (31G –.097)																						
″	total		37	.094	.125	32	3	1	0	0	0.0	0	0	4	10	0	3	0	9	19	1	1	0.8	.966	P-36
1965	2 teams		HOU N (1G –.000) BAL A (27G –.273)																						
″	total		28	.231	.308	13	3	1	0	0	0.0	0	1	0	5	0	0	0	6	16	1	1	0.8	.957	P-28
1967	CHI	N	3	—	—	0	0	0	0	0	—	0	0	0	0	0	0	0	0	2	0	1	0.7	1.000	P-3
14 yrs.			480	.242	.371	596	144	25	5	14	2.3	65	72	43	138	0	66	12	95	244	17	22	0.9	.952	P-412, OF-2
WORLD SERIES																									
1955	NY	A	1	.000	.000	2	0	0	0	0	0.0	0	0	0	0	0	0	0	0	1	0	0	1.0	1.000	P-1
1956			2	.333	.333	3	1	0	0	0	0.0	1	1	0	1	0	0	0	0	1	0	0	0.5	1.000	P-2
1957			2	.000	.000	2	0	0	0	0	0.0	1	0	2	1	0	0	0	0	1	0	0	0.5	1.000	P-2
1958			2	.000	.000	2	0	0	0	0	0.0	0	0	1	0	0	0	0	1	0	0	0	0.5	1.000	P-2
1962	SF	N	3	—	—	0	0	0	0	0	—	0	0	0	0	0	0	0	1	0	0	0	0.3	1.000	P-3
5 yrs.			10	.111	.111	9	1	0	0	0	0.0	2	1	3	2	0	0	0	2	3	0	0	0.5	1.000	P-10

Swede Larsen

LARSEN, ERLING ADELL BR TR 5′11″ 175 lbs.
B. Nov. 15, 1913, Jersey City, N. J.

Year	Team	Lg	Games	BA	SA	AB	H	2B	3B	HR	HR%	R	RBI	BB	SO	SB	Pinch Hit AB	Pinch Hit H	PO	A	E	DP	TC/G	FA	G by Pos
1936	BOS	N	3	.000	.000	1	0	0	0	0	0.0	0	0	0	0	0	0	0	1	0	0	0	0.5	1.000	2B-2

Tony LaRussa

LaRUSSA, ANTHONY BR TR 6′ 175 lbs.
B. Oct. 4, 1944, Tampa, Fla.
Manager 1979–95.

Year	Team	Lg	Games	BA	SA	AB	H	2B	3B	HR	HR%	R	RBI	BB	SO	SB	Pinch Hit AB	Pinch Hit H	PO	A	E	DP	TC/G	FA	G by Pos
1963	KC	A	34	.250	.318	44	11	1	1	0	0.0	4	1	7	12	0	1	1	29	25	2	8	3.3	.964	SS-14, 2B-3
1968	OAK	A	5	.333	.333	3	1	0	0	0	0.0	0	0	0	0	0	3	1	0	0	0	0	0.0	—	
1969			8	.000	.000	8	0	0	0	0	0.0	0	0	0	1	0	8	0	0	0	0	0	0.0	—	
1970			52	.198	.255	106	21	4	1	0	0.0	6	6	15	19	0	11	2	67	89	5	21	3.7	.969	2B-44
1971	2 teams		OAK A (23G –.000) ATL N (9G –.286)																						
″	total		32	.133	.133	15	2	0	0	0	0.0	4	0	1	5	0	6	0	16	13	3	5	1.5	.906	2B-16, SS-4, 3B-2
1973	CHI	N	1	—	—	0	0	0	0	0	—	1	0	0	0	0	0	0	0	0	0	0	0.0	—	
6 yrs.			132	.199	.250	176	35	5	2	0	0.0	15	7	23	37	0	29	4	112	127	10	34	3.0	.960	2B-63, SS-18, 3B-2

Lyn Lary

LARY, LYNFORD HOBART BR TR 6′ 165 lbs.
B. Jan. 28, 1906, Armona, Calif. D. Jan. 9, 1973, Downey, Calif.

Year	Team	Lg	Games	BA	SA	AB	H	2B	3B	HR	HR%	R	RBI	BB	SO	SB	Pinch Hit AB	Pinch Hit H	PO	A	E	DP	TC/G	FA	G by Pos
1929	NY	A	80	.309	.428	236	73	9	2	5	2.1	48	26	24	15	4	7	0	67	147	11	19	3.2	.951	3B-55, SS-14, 2B-2
1930			117	.289	.386	464	134	20	8	3	0.6	93	52	45	40	14	3	0	224	324	35	58	5.2	.940	SS-113
1931			155	.280	.416	610	171	35	9	10	1.6	100	107	88	54	13	0	0	321	484	46	85	5.5	.946	SS-155
1932			91	.232	.343	280	65	14	4	3	1.1	56	39	52	28	9	1	0	180	223	25	42	4.8	.942	SS-80, 1B-5, 3B-2, 2B-2, OF-1
1933			52	.220	.291	127	28	3	3	0	0.0	25	13	28	17	2	4	0	55	72	7	10	2.8	.948	3B-28, SS-16, 1B-3, OF-1
1934	2 teams		NY A (1G –.000) BOS A (129G –.241)																						
″	total		130	.241	.322	419	101	20	4	2	0.5	58	54	67	51	12	0	0	264	396	25	67	5.3	.964	SS-129, 1B-1
1935	2 teams		WAS A (39G –.194) STL A (93G –.288)																						
″	total		132	.268	.371	474	127	29	7	2	0.4	86	42	76	53	28	3	1	321	384	29	79	6.0	.960	SS-123
1936	STL	A	155	.289	.366	620	179	30	6	2	0.3	112	52	117	54	**37**	0	0	339	495	38	88	5.6	.956	SS-155
1937	CLE	A	156	.290	.421	644	187	46	7	8	1.2	110	77	88	64	18	0	0	325	489	31	95	5.4	.963	SS-156
1938			141	.268	.361	568	152	36	4	3	0.5	94	51	88	65	23	0	0	296	399	26	88	5.1	.964	SS-141
1939	3 teams		CLE A (3G –.000) BKN N (29G –.161) STL N (34G –.187)																						
″	total		66	.176	.231	108	19	4	1	0	0.0	18	10	28	22	2	3	0	77	95	10	14	3.4	.945	SS-44, 3B-10
1940	STL	A	27	.056	.111	54	3	1	1	0	0.0	5	3	4	7	0	6	0	29	33	3	7	5.0	.954	SS-12, 2B-1
12 yrs.			1302	.269	.372	4604	1239	247	56	38	0.8	805	526	705	470	162	27	1	2498	3541	286	652	5.1	.955	SS-1138, 3B-95, 1B-9, 2B-5, OF-2

Don Lassetter

LASSETTER, DONALD O'NEAL BR TR 6' 3" 200 lbs.
B. Mar. 27, 1933, Newnan, Ga.

Year	Team	Games	BA	SA	AB	H	2B	3B	HR	HR%	R	RBI	BB	SO	SB	Pinch Hit AB	Pinch Hit H	PO	A	E	DP	TC/G	FA	G by Pos
1957	STL N	4	.154	.308	13	2	0	1	0	0.0	2	0	1	3	0	1	0	9	0	0	0	3.0	1.000	OF-3

Arlie Latham

LATHAM, WALTER ARLINGTON (The Freshest Man on Earth) BR TR 5' 8" 150 lbs.
B. Mar. 15, 1860, W. Lebanon, N. H. D. Nov. 29, 1952, Garden City, N. Y.
Manager 1896.

Year	Team	Games	BA	SA	AB	H	2B	3B	HR	HR%	R	RBI	BB	SO	SB	Pinch Hit AB	Pinch Hit H	PO	A	E	DP	TC/G	FA	G by Pos
1880	BUF N	22	.127	.190	79	10	3	1	0	0.0	9	3	1	8		0	0	31	36	7	1	3.2	.905	SS-12, OF-10, C-1
1883	STL AA	98	.236	.300	406	96	12	7	0	0.0	86		18			0	0	120	256	58	14	4.4	.866	3B-98, C-1
1884		110	.274	.367	474	130	17	12	1	0.2	115		19			0	0	142	302	70	16	4.6	.864	3B-110, C-1
1885		110	.206	.256	485	100	15	3	1	0.2	84		18			0	0	116	224	49	16	3.5	.874	3B-109, C-2
1886		134	.301	.374	578	174	23	8	1	0.2	**152**		55			0	0	139	290	88	22	3.9	.830	3B-133, 2B-1
1887		136	.316	.413	**627**	198	35	10	2	0.3	163		45		129	0	0	169	305	66	19	3.9	.878	3B-132, 2B-5, C-2
1888		133	.265	.326	570	151	19	5	2	0.4	119	31	43		**109**	0	0	178	287	62	19	3.9	.882	3B-133, SS-1
1889		118	.246	.307	512	126	13	3	4	0.8	110	49	42	30	69	0	0	204	256	59	23	4.4	.886	3B-116, 2B-3
1890	2 teams	CHI P (52G –.229) CIN N (41G –.250)																						
"	total	93	.238	.302	378	90	13	4	1	0.3	82	35	45	40	52	0	0	119	222	52	19	4.2	.868	3B-93, OF-1
1891	CIN N	135	.272	.386	533	145	20	10	7	1.3	119	53	74	35	87	0	0	177	370	75	24	4.6	.879	3B-135, C-1
1892		152	.238	.283	622	148	20	4	0	0.0	111	44	60	54	66	0	0	192	354	71	29	4.1	.885	3B-142, 2B-9, OF-1
1893		127	.282	.350	531	150	18	6	2	0.4	101	49	62	20	57	0	0	172	281	55	23	4.0	.892	3B-127
1894		129	.313	.403	524	164	23	6	4	0.8	129	60	60	24	59	0	0	163	255	67	23	3.8	.862	3B-127, 2B-2
1895		112	.311	.380	460	143	14	6	2	0.4	93	69	42	25	48	0	0	141	200	55	16	3.5	.861	3B-108, 1B-3, 2B-1
1896	STL N	8	.200	.200	35	7	0	0	0	0.0	3	5	4	3	2	0	0	14	15	10	2	4.9	.744	3B-8
1899	WAS N	6	.167	.167	6	1	0	0	0	0.0	1	0	1		0	2	1	2	0	0	1	1.0	1.000	OF-1, 2B-1
1909	NY N	4	.000	.000	2	0	0	0	0	0.0	1	0	0		1	1	0	0	2	0	0	1.0	1.000	2B-2
17 yrs.		1627	.269	.341	6822	1833	245	85	27	0.4	1478	398	589	239	679	3	1	2079	3655	844	267	4.0	.872	3B-1571, 2B-24, SS-13, OF-13, C-8, 1B-3

Juice Latham

LATHAM, GEORGE WARREN (Jumbo) BR TR 5' 8" 164 lbs.
B. Sept. 6, 1852, Utica, N. Y. D. May 26, 1914, Utica, N. Y.
Manager 1882.

Year	Team	Games	BA	SA	AB	H	2B	3B	HR	HR%	R	RBI	BB	SO	SB	Pinch Hit AB	Pinch Hit H	PO	A	E	DP	TC/G	FA	G by Pos
1877	LOU N	59	.291	.371	278	81	10	6	0	0.0	42	22	5	6		0	0	659	24	36	28	12.2	.950	1B-59
1882	PHI AA	74	.285	.328	323	92	10	2	0	0.0	47		10			0	0	792	12	23	28	11.2	.972	1B-74
1883	LOU AA	88	.250	.302	368	92	7	6	0	0.0	60		12			0	0	676	82	55	49	9.0	.932	1B-67, 2B-14, SS-9
1884		77	.169	.198	308	52	3	3	0	0.0	31		8			0	0	790	32	33	48	11.1	.961	1B-76, 3B-1
4 yrs.		298	.248	.298	1277	317	30	17	0	0.0	180	22	35	6		0	0	2917	150	147	153	10.7	.954	1B-276, 2B-14, SS-9, 3B-1

Chick Lathers

LATHERS, CHARLES TEN EYCK BL TR 6' 180 lbs.
B. Oct. 22, 1888, Detroit, Mich. D. July 26, 1971, Petoskey, Mich.

Year	Team	Games	BA	SA	AB	H	2B	3B	HR	HR%	R	RBI	BB	SO	SB	Pinch Hit AB	Pinch Hit H	PO	A	E	DP	TC/G	FA	G by Pos
1910	DET A	41	.232	.256	82	19	2	0	0	0.0	4	3	8		0	14	3	30	60	10	5	4.2	.900	3B-13, 2B-7, SS-4
1911		29	.222	.244	45	10	1	0	0	0.0	5	4	5		0	4	2	21	33	5	2	2.5	.915	2B-9, 3B-8, SS-4, 1B-3
2 yrs.		70	.228	.252	127	29	3	0	0	0.0	9	7	13		0	18	5	51	93	15	7	3.3	.906	3B-21, 2B-16, SS-8, 1B-3

Tacks Latimer

LATIMER, CLIFFORD WESLEY BR TR 6' 160 lbs.
B. Nov. 30, 1877, Loveland, Ohio D. Apr. 24, 1936, Loveland, Ohio.

Year	Team	Games	BA	SA	AB	H	2B	3B	HR	HR%	R	RBI	BB	SO	SB	Pinch Hit AB	Pinch Hit H	PO	A	E	DP	TC/G	FA	G by Pos
1898	NY N	5	.294	.353	17	5	1	0	0	0.0	1	1	0		0	0	0	16	8	4	1	4.7	.857	C-4, OF-2
1899	LOU N	9	.276	.310	29	8	1	0	0	0.0	3	4	2		1	0	0	38	10	3	0	5.7	.941	C-8, 1B-1
1900	PIT N	4	.333	.417	12	4	1	0	0	0.0	1	2	0		0	0	0	14	4	1	0	4.8	.947	C-4
1901	BAL A	1	.250	.250	4	1	0	0	0	0.0	0	0	0		0	0	0	4	0	0	0	4.0	1.000	C-1
1902	BKN N	8	.042	.042	24	1	0	0	0	0.0	0	0	0		0	0	0	26	10	2	0	4.8	.947	C-8
5 yrs.		27	.221	.256	86	19	3	0	0	0.0	5	7	2		1	0	0	98	32	10	1	5.0	.929	C-25, OF-2, 1B-1

Charlie Lau

LAU, CHARLES RICHARD BL TR 6' 190 lbs.
B. Apr. 12, 1933, Romulus, Mich. D. Mar. 18, 1984, Key Colony Beach, Fla.

Year	Team	Games	BA	SA	AB	H	2B	3B	HR	HR%	R	RBI	BB	SO	SB	Pinch Hit AB	Pinch Hit H	PO	A	E	DP	TC/G	FA	G by Pos
1956	DET A	3	.222	.222	9	2	0	0	0	0.0	1	0	0	1	0	0	0	17	0	0	0	5.7	1.000	C-3
1958		30	.147	.221	68	10	1	2	0	0.0	8	6	12	15	0	4	1	120	10	2	3	4.9	.985	C-27
1959		2	.167	.167	6	1	0	0	0	0.0	0	0	0	2	0	1	0	11	1	0	1	6.0	1.000	C-2
1960	MIL N	21	.189	.226	53	10	2	0	0	0.0	4	2	6	10	0	7	0	94	11	0	2	6.6	1.000	C-16
1961	2 teams	MIL N (28G –.207) BAL A (17G –.170)																						
"	total	45	.194	.256	129	25	5	0	1	0.8	6	9	15	14	1	2	0	204	13	5	4	5.3	.977	C-42
1962	BAL A	81	.294	.462	197	58	11	2	6	3.0	21	37	7	11	1	30	11	269	15	1	1	5.1	.996	C-56
1963	2 teams	BAL A (29G –.188) KC A (62G –.294)																						
"	total	91	.272	.366	235	64	13	0	3	1.3	19	32	15	22	1	29	4	306	20	7	3	5.7	.979	C-58
1964	2 teams	KC A (43G –.271) BAL A (62G –.259)																						
"	total	105	.264	.391	276	73	22	2	3	1.1	27	23	27	45	0	28	7	422	25	4	2	5.5	.991	C-82
1965	BAL A	68	.295	.409	132	39	5	2	2	1.5	15	18	17	18	0	29	8	165	9	2	1	5.0	.989	C-35
1966		18	.500	.833	12	6	2	1	0	0.0	1	5	4	1	0	12	6	0	0	0	0	0.0	—	
1967	2 teams	BAL A (11G –.125) ATL N (52G –.200)																						
"	total	63	.189	.283	53	10	2	0	1	1.9	3	8	6	11	0	53	10	0	0	0	0	0.0	—	
11 yrs.		527	.255	.365	1170	298	63	9	16	1.4	105	140	109	150	3	195	47	1608	104	21	17	5.4	.988	C-321

Billy Lauder

LAUDER, WILLIAM BR TR 5'10" 160 lbs.
B. Feb. 23, 1874, New York, N. Y. D. May 20, 1933, Norwalk, Conn.

Year	Team	Games	BA	SA	AB	H	2B	3B	HR	HR%	R	RBI	BB	SO	SB	Pinch Hit AB	Pinch Hit H	PO	A	E	DP	TC/G	FA	G by Pos
1898	PHI N	97	.263	.357	361	95	14	7	2	0.6	42	67	19		6	0	0	132	171	47	6	3.6	.866	3B-97
1899		151	.268	.333	583	156	17	6	3	0.5	74	90	34		15	0	0	210	307	62	22	3.8	.893	3B-151
1901	PHI A	2	.125	.125	8	1	0	0	0	0.0	1	0	0		0	0	0	4	6	2	0	6.0	.833	3B-2
1902	NY N	125	.237	.288	482	114	20	1	1	0.2	41	44	10		19	0	0	195	252	45	17	3.9	.909	3B-121, OF-4
1903		108	.281	.314	395	111	13	0	0	0.0	52	53	14		19	0	0	140	194	34	10	3.4	.908	3B-108
5 yrs.		483	.261	.321	1829	477	64	14	6	0.3	210	254	77		59	0	0	681	930	190	55	3.7	.895	3B-479, OF-4

Tim Laudner

LAUDNER, TIMOTHY JON BR TR 6' 3" 212 lbs.
B. June 7, 1958, Mason City, Iowa.

Year	Team	Games	BA	SA	AB	H	2B	3B	HR	HR%	R	RBI	BB	SO	SB	Pinch Hit AB	Pinch Hit H	PO	A	E	DP	TC/G	FA	G by Pos
1981	MIN A	14	.163	.349	43	7	2	0	2	4.7	4	5	3	17	0	0	0	49	5	0	0	3.9	1.000	C-12, DH-2
1982		93	.255	.392	306	78	19	1	7	2.3	37	33	34	74	0	0	0	454	41	12	5	5.5	.976	C-93
1983		62	.185	.345	168	31	9	0	6	3.6	20	18	15	49	0	4	2	259	22	4	5	4.7	.986	C-57, DH-4

Tim Laudner *continued*

Year	Team	Games	BA	SA	AB	H	2B	3B	HR	HR%	R	RBI	BB	SO	SB	Pinch Hit AB	Pinch Hit H	PO	A	E	DP	TC/G	FA	G by Pos
1984		87	.206	.389	262	54	16	1	10	3.8	31	35	18	78	0	8	2	362	38	9	2	4.9	.978	C-81, DH-2
1985		72	.238	.396	164	39	5	0	7	4.3	16	19	12	45	0	6	0	236	19	8	3	3.8	.970	C-68, 1B-1
1986		76	.244	.451	193	47	10	0	10	5.2	21	29	24	56	1	15	2	299	13	5	3	4.7	.984	C-68
1987		113	.191	.389	288	55	7	1	16	5.6	30	43	23	80	1	7	1	547	29	7	5	5.3	.988	C-101, 1B-7, DH-2
1988		117	.251	.408	375	94	18	1	13	3.5	38	54	36	89	0	4	0	624	35	5	8	5.7	.992	C-109, DH-4, 1B-3
1989		100	.222	.351	239	53	11	1	6	2.5	24	27	25	65	1	11	5	347	16	3	5	3.7	.992	C-68, DH-19, 1B-11
9 yrs.		734	.225	.391	2038	458	97	5	77	3.8	221	263	190	553	3	55	12	3177	218	53	36	4.8	.985	C-657, DH-33, 1B-22
LEAGUE CHAMPIONSHIP SERIES																								
1987	**MIN A**	5	.071	.143	14	1	1	0	0	0.0	1	2	2	5	0	0	0	31	2	0	0	6.6	1.000	C-5
WORLD SERIES																								
1987	**MIN A**	7	.318	.500	22	7	1	0	1	4.5	4	4	5	4	0	0	0	46	2	0	1	6.9	1.000	C-7

Chuck Lauer

LAUER, JOHN CHARLES TR
B. 1865, Pittsburgh, Pa. Deceased.

Year	Team	Games	BA	SA	AB	H	2B	3B	HR	HR%	R	RBI	BB	SO	SB	Pinch Hit AB	Pinch Hit H	PO	A	E	DP	TC/G	FA	G by Pos
1884	**PIT AA**	13	.114	.114	44	5	0	0	0	0.0	5		0			0	0	16	3	3	0	1.6	.864	OF-10, P-3, 1B-1
1889	**PIT N**	4	.188	.188	16	3	0	0	0	0.0	2	1	0	5	0	0	0	16	8	5	0	7.3	.828	C-3, OF-1
1890	**CHI N**	2	.250	.375	8	2	1	0	0	0.0	1	2	0	0	0	0	0	12	3	3	0	9.0	.833	C-2
3 yrs.		19	.147	.162	68	10	1	0	0	0.0	8	3	0	5	0	0	0	44	14	11	0	3.5	.841	OF-11, C-5, P-3, 1B-1

Bill Lauterborn

LAUTERBORN, WILLIAM BERNARD BR TR 5′ 6″ 140 lbs.
B. June 9, 1879, Hornell, N. Y. D. Apr. 19, 1965, Andover, N. Y.

Year	Team	Games	BA	SA	AB	H	2B	3B	HR	HR%	R	RBI	BB	SO	SB	Pinch Hit AB	Pinch Hit H	PO	A	E	DP	TC/G	FA	G by Pos
1904	**BOS N**	20	.275	.304	69	19	2	0	0	0.0	7	2	1		1	0	0	39	60	6	2	5.3	.943	2B-20
1905		67	.185	.200	200	37	1	1	0	0.0	11	9	12		1	9	2	89	132	32	4	4.4	.874	3B-29, 2B-23, SS-3, OF-2
2 yrs.		87	.208	.227	269	56	3	1	0	0.0	18	11	13		2	9	2	128	192	38	6	4.6	.894	2B-43, 3B-29, SS-3, OF-2

Cookie Lavagetto

LAVAGETTO, HARRY ARTHUR BR TR 6′ 170 lbs.
B. Dec. 1, 1912, Oakland, Calif. D. Aug. 10, 1990, Orinda, Calif.
Manager 1957–61.

Year	Team	Games	BA	SA	AB	H	2B	3B	HR	HR%	R	RBI	BB	SO	SB	Pinch Hit AB	Pinch Hit H	PO	A	E	DP	TC/G	FA	G by Pos
1934	**PIT N**	87	.220	.322	304	67	16	3	3	1.0	41	46	32	39	6	2	1	214	234	18	39	5.6	.961	2B-83
1935		78	.290	.364	231	67	9	4	0	0.0	27	19	18	15	1	16	3	100	143	15	10	4.5	.942	2B-42, 3B-15
1936		60	.244	.371	197	48	15	2	2	1.0	21	26	15	13	0	9	0	100	132	16	25	4.9	.935	2B-37, 3B-13, SS-1
1937	**BKN N**	149	.282	.406	503	142	26	6	8	1.6	64	70	74	41	13	4	0	281	368	34	64	4.7	.950	2B-100, 3B-45
1938		137	.273	.405	487	133	34	6	6	1.2	68	79	68	31	15	3	0	142	240	28	28	3.0	.932	3B-132, 2B-4
1939		153	.300	.416	587	176	28	5	10	1.7	93	87	78	30	14	4	2	163	278	24	28	3.1	.948	3B-149
1940		118	.257	.344	448	115	21	3	4	0.9	56	43	70	32	4	1	0	137	191	24	12	3.0	.932	3B-116
1941		132	.277	.370	441	122	24	7	1	0.2	75	78	80	21	7	10	0	117	215	22	17	3.0	.938	3B-120
1946		88	.236	.318	242	57	9	1	3	1.2	36	27	38	17	3	11	2	70	108	14	11	2.9	.927	3B-67
1947		41	.261	.406	69	18	1	0	3	4.3	6	11	12	5	0	17	4	40	31	2	3	3.5	.973	3B-18, 1B-3
10 yrs.		1043	.269	.377	3509	945	183	37	40	1.1	487	486	485	244	63	77	12	1364	1940	197	237	3.7	.944	3B-675, 2B-266, 1B-3, SS-1
WORLD SERIES																								
1941	**BKN N**	3	.100	.100	10	1	0	0	0	0.0	1	0	2	0	0	0	0	2	1	0	0	1.0	1.000	3B-3
1947		5	.143	.286	7	1	1	0	0	0.0	0	3	0	2	0	5	1	0	1	0	0	0.3	1.000	3B-3
2 yrs.		8	.118	.176	17	2	1	0	0	0.0	1	3	2	2	0	5	1	2	2	0	0	0.7	1.000	3B-6

Mike LaValliere

LaVALLIERE, MICHAEL EUGENE (Spanky) BL TR 5′10″ 180 lbs.
B. Aug. 18, 1960, Charlotte, N. C.

Year	Team	Games	BA	SA	AB	H	2B	3B	HR	HR%	R	RBI	BB	SO	SB	Pinch Hit AB	Pinch Hit H	PO	A	E	DP	TC/G	FA	G by Pos
1984	**PHI N**	6	.000	.000	7	0	0	0	0	0.0	0	0	2	2	0	0	0	20	2	0	0	3.7	1.000	C-6
1985	**STL N**	12	.147	.176	34	5	1	0	0	0.0	2	6	7	3	0	0	0	48	5	0	3	4.4	1.000	C-12
1986		110	.234	.310	303	71	10	2	3	1.0	18	30	36	37	0	4	0	468	47	6	8	4.8	.988	C-108
1987	**PIT N**	121	.300	.365	340	102	19	0	1	0.3	33	36	43	32	0	14	5	584	70	5	11	5.9	.992	C-112
1988		120	.261	.330	352	92	18	0	2	0.6	24	47	50	34	3	10	1	565	55	8	6	5.5	.987	C-114
1989		68	.316	.400	190	60	10	0	2	1.1	15	23	29	24	0	3	0	306	24	3	3	5.1	.991	C-65
1990		96	.258	.344	279	72	15	0	3	1.1	27	31	44	20	0	2	1	478	36	5	6	5.5	.990	C-95
1991		108	.289	.360	336	97	11	2	3	0.9	25	41	33	27	2	3	0	565	46	1	4	5.8	.998	C-105
1992		95	.256	.328	293	75	13	1	2	0.7	22	29	44	21	0	1	0	421	63	3	6	5.2	.994	C-92, 3B-1
1993	**2 teams**	**PIT N** (1G –.200) **CHI A** (37G –.258)																						
″	**total**	38	.255	.275	102	26	2	0	0	0.0	6	8	4	14	0	0	0	176	28	0	2	5.4	1.000	C-38
1994	**CHI A**	59	.281	.331	139	39	4	0	1	0.7	6	24	20	15	0	2	0	305	21	3	1	5.7	.991	C-58
1995		46	.245	.337	98	24	6	0	1	1.0	7	19	9	15	0	1	0	202	19	1	1	4.8	.995	C-46
12 yrs.		879	.268	.338	2473	663	109	5	18	0.7	185	294	321	244	5	40	7	4138	416	35	51	5.4	.992	C-851, 3B-1
LEAGUE CHAMPIONSHIP SERIES																								
1990	**PIT N**	3	.000	.000	6	0	0	0	0	0.0	1	0	3	1	0	0	0	17	2	0	0	6.3	1.000	C-3
1991		3	.333	.333	6	2	0	0	0	0.0	0	1	2	0	0	1	1	14	3	0	0	5.7	1.000	C-3
1992		3	.200	.200	10	2	0	0	0	0.0	1	0	0	3	0	0	0	14	0	0	0	4.7	1.000	C-3
1993	**CHI A**	2	.333	.333	3	1	0	0	0	0.0	0	0	1	0	0	0	0	8	0	0	0	4.0	1.000	C-2
4 yrs.		11	.200	.200	25	5	0	0	0	0.0	2	1	6	4	0	1	1	53	5	0	0	5.3	1.000	C-11

Doc Lavan

LAVAN, JOHN LEONARD BR TR 5′ 8½″ 151 lbs.
Born John Leonard Laven.
B. Oct. 28, 1890, Grand Rapids, Mich. D. May 29, 1952, Detroit, Mich.

Year	Team	Games	BA	SA	AB	H	2B	3B	HR	HR%	R	RBI	BB	SO	SB	Pinch Hit AB	Pinch Hit H	PO	A	E	DP	TC/G	FA	G by Pos
1913	**2 teams**	**STL A** (46G –.141) **PHI A** (5G –.071)																						
″	**total**	51	.135	.172	163	22	2	2	0	0.0	9	5	10	46	3	0	0	88	153	25	24	5.2	.906	SS-51
1914	**STL A**	74	.264	.339	239	63	7	4	1	0.4	21	21	17	39	6	0	0	178	193	34	17	5.5	.916	SS-73
1915		157	.218	.284	514	112	17	7	1	0.2	44	48	42	**83**	13	0	0	313	475	75	81	5.5	.913	SS-157
1916		110	.236	.280	343	81	13	1	0	0.0	32	19	32	38	7	3	1	217	386	32	52	6.0	.950	SS-106
1917		118	.239	.290	355	85	8	5	0	0.0	19	30	19	34	5	1	0	244	354	50	70	5.5	.923	SS-110, 2B-7
1918	**WAS A**	117	.278	.323	464	129	17	2	0	0.0	44	45	14	21	12	0	0	275	354	57	43	5.8	.917	SS-117, OF-1
1919	**STL N**	100	.242	.295	356	86	12	2	1	0.3	25	25	11	30	4	1	0	207	352	43	49	6.1	.929	SS-99
1920		142	.289	.374	516	149	21	10	1	0.2	52	63	19	38	11	4	1	327	489	50	77	6.3	.942	SS-138
1921		150	.259	.350	560	145	23	11	2	0.4	58	82	23	30	7	0	0	382	540	49	88	6.5	.950	SS-150
1922		89	.227	.265	264	60	8	1	0	0.0	24	27	13	10	3	1	0	172	258	30	40	5.3	.935	SS-82, 3B-5

Doc Lavan *continued*

Year	Team	Games	BA	SA	AB	H	2B	3B	HR	HR%	R	RBI	BB	SO	SB	Pinch Hit AB	Pinch Hit H	PO	A	E	DP	TC/G	FA	G by Pos
1923		50	.198	.279	111	22	6	0	1	0.9	10	12	9	7	0	2	1	83	104	14	0	4.2	.930	SS-40, 3B-4, 1B-3, 2B-1
1924		4	.000	.000	6	0	0	0	0	0.0	0	0	0	0	0	0	0	3	10	2	2	3.8	.867	SS-2, 2B-2
12 yrs.		1162	.245	.308	3891	954	134	45	7	0.2	338	377	209	376	71	12	3	2489	3668	461	543	5.8	.930	SS-1125, 2B-10, 3B-9, 1B-3, OF-1

Art LaVigne

LaVIGNE, ARTHUR DAVID BR TR 5′10″ 162 lbs.
B. Jan. 26, 1885, Worcester, Mass. D. July 18, 1950, Worcester, Mass.

Year	Team	Games	BA	SA	AB	H	2B	3B	HR	HR%	R	RBI	BB	SO	SB	Pinch Hit AB	Pinch Hit H	PO	A	E	DP	TC/G	FA	G by Pos
1914	BUF F	51	.156	.178	90	14	2	0	0	0.0	10	4	7		0	7	1	151	45	6	4	5.5	.970	C-34, 1B-3

Johnny Lavin

LAVIN, JOHN 5′11″ 175 lbs.
B. Troy, N. Y. Deceased.

Year	Team	Games	BA	SA	AB	H	2B	3B	HR	HR%	R	RBI	BB	SO	SB	Pinch Hit AB	Pinch Hit H	PO	A	E	DP	TC/G	FA	G by Pos
1884	STL AA	16	.212	.250	52	11	2	0	0	0.0	9		3			0	0	17	1	6	0	1.5	.750	OF-16

Rudy Law

LAW, RUDY KARL BL TL 6′ 1″ 165 lbs.
B. Oct. 7, 1956, Waco, Tex.

Year	Team	Games	BA	SA	AB	H	2B	3B	HR	HR%	R	RBI	BB	SO	SB	Pinch Hit AB	Pinch Hit H	PO	A	E	DP	TC/G	FA	G by Pos
1978	LA N	11	.250	.250	12	3	0	0	0	0.0	2	1	1	2	3	1	0	3	0	0	0	0.5	1.000	OF-6
1980		128	.260	.302	388	101	5	4	1	0.3	55	23	23	27	40	16	4	233	6	3	3	2.3	.988	OF-106
1982	CHI A	121	.318	.438	336	107	15	8	3	0.9	55	32	23	41	36	17	3	215	2	6	0	2.3	.973	OF-94, DH-3
1983		141	.283	.369	501	142	20	7	3	0.6	95	34	42	36	77	13	4	302	5	2	2	2.3	.994	OF-132, DH-3
1984		136	.251	.345	487	122	14	7	6	1.2	68	37	39	42	29	11	5	322	5	5	2	2.6	.985	OF-130
1985		125	.259	.374	390	101	21	6	4	1.0	62	35	27	40	29	17	6	226	7	3	3	1.9	.987	OF-120, DH-3
1986	KC A	87	.261	.388	307	80	26	5	1	0.3	42	36	29	22	14	8	1	145	2	2	0	1.9	.987	OF-77, DH-2
7 yrs.		749	.271	.366	2421	656	101	37	18	0.7	379	198	184	210	228	83	23	1446	27	21	10	2.2	.986	OF-665, DH-11
LEAGUE CHAMPIONSHIP SERIES																								
1983	CHI A	4	.389	.444	18	7	1	0	0	0.0	1	0	0	1	2	0	0	10	0	0	0	2.5	1.000	OF-4

Vance Law

LAW, VANCE AARON BR TR 6′ 2″ 185 lbs.
Son of Vern Law.
B. Oct. 1, 1956, Boise, Ida.

Year	Team	Games	BA	SA	AB	H	2B	3B	HR	HR%	R	RBI	BB	SO	SB	Pinch Hit AB	Pinch Hit H	PO	A	E	DP	TC/G	FA	G by Pos
1980	PIT N	25	.230	.311	74	17	2	2	0	0.0	11	3	3	7	2	3	1	31	54	3	8	4.4	.966	2B-11, SS-8, 3B-1
1981		30	.134	.164	67	9	0	1	0	0.0	1	3	2	15	1	2	0	50	58	0	10	3.9	1.000	2B-19, SS-7, 3B-2
1982	CHI A	114	.281	.384	359	101	20	1	5	1.4	40	54	26	46	4	1	1	156	313	26	52	3.7	.947	SS-85, 3B-39, 2B-10, OF-1
1983		145	.243	.348	408	99	21	5	4	1.0	55	42	51	56	3	0	0	94	311	14	28	2.9	.967	3B-139, 2B-3, SS-2, DH-1, OF-1
1984		151	.252	.403	481	121	18	2	17	3.5	60	59	41	75	4	4	2	119	246	16	32	2.3	.958	3B-137, 2B-22, OF-5, SS-4
1985	MON N	147	.266	.405	519	138	30	6	10	1.9	75	52	86	96	6	5	0	420	402	12	98	5.3	.986	2B-126, 1B-20, 3B-11, OF-1
1986		112	.225	.325	360	81	17	2	5	1.4	37	44	37	66	3	6	1	273	299	4	59	4.4	.993	2B-94, 1B-20, 3B-13, P-3, OF-1
1987		133	.273	.422	436	119	27	1	12	2.8	52	56	51	62	8	5	1	258	308	11	54	3.9	.981	2B-106, 3B-22, 1B-17, P-3
1988	CHI N	151	.293	.412	556	163	29	2	11	2.0	73	78	55	79	1	1	0	112	272	19	22	2.7	.953	3B-150, OF-1
1989		130	.235	.355	408	96	22	3	7	1.7	38	42	38	73	2	10	0	76	168	13	13	2.1	.949	3B-119, OF-1
1991	OAK A	74	.209	.276	134	28	7	1	0	0.0	11	9	18	27	0	9	4	39	66	5	7	1.5	.955	3B-67, SS-3, OF-3, 1B-1, P-1
11 yrs.		1212	.256	.376	3802	972	193	26	71	1.9	453	442	408	602	34	46	10	1628	2497	123	383	3.3	.971	3B-700, 2B-391, SS-109, 1B-58, OF-14, P-7, DH-1
LEAGUE CHAMPIONSHIP SERIES																								
1983	CHI A	4	.182	.182	11	2	0	0	0	0.0	0	1	1	3	0	0	0	2	9	1	1	3.0	.917	3B-4
1989	CHI N	2	.000	.000	3	0	0	0	0	0.0	0	0	0	3	0	1	0	0	0	0	0	0.0	.000	3B-1
2 yrs.		6	.143	.143	14	2	0	0	0	0.0	0	1	1	6	0	1	0	2	9	1	1	2.4	.917	3B-5

Garland Lawing

LAWING, GARLAND FREDERICK (Knobby) BR TR 6′ 1″ 180 lbs.
B. Aug. 26, 1919, Gastonia, N. C.

Year	Team	Games	BA	SA	AB	H	2B	3B	HR	HR%	R	RBI	BB	SO	SB	Pinch Hit AB	Pinch Hit H	PO	A	E	DP	TC/G	FA	G by Pos
1946	2 teams	CIN N (2G –.000) NY N (8G –.167)																						
″	total	10	.133	.133	15	2	0	0	0	0.0	2	0	0	5	0	3	1	6	0	0	0	1.2	1.000	OF-5

Tom Lawless

LAWLESS, THOMAS JAMES BR TR 5′11″ 170 lbs.
B. Dec. 19, 1956, Erie, Pa.

Year	Team	Games	BA	SA	AB	H	2B	3B	HR	HR%	R	RBI	BB	SO	SB	Pinch Hit AB	Pinch Hit H	PO	A	E	DP	TC/G	FA	G by Pos
1982	CIN N	49	.212	.248	165	35	6	0	0	0.0	19	4	9	30	16	1	0	87	136	5	35	4.9	.978	2B-47
1984	2 teams	CIN N (43G –.250) MON N (11G –.176)																						
″	total	54	.237	.299	97	23	3	0	1	1.0	11	2	8	16	7	5	1	50	52	1	8	2.7	.990	2B-32, 3B-6
1985	STL N	47	.207	.293	58	12	3	1	0	0.0	8	8	5	4	2	9	2	19	44	1	4	2.7	.984	3B-13, 2B-11
1986		46	.282	.308	39	11	1	0	0	0.0	5	3	2	8	8	12	2	11	15	2	1	1.4	.929	3B-12, 2B-7, OF-1
1987		19	.080	.120	25	2	1	0	0	0.0	5	0	3	5	2	5	0	5	15	0	3	1.8	1.000	2B-7, 3B-3, OF-1
1988		54	.154	.262	65	10	2	1	1	1.5	9	3	7	9	6	10	1	23	29	0	3	1.4	1.000	3B-24, OF-6, 2B-5, 1B-1
1989	TOR A	59	.229	.243	70	16	1	0	0	0.0	20	3	7	12	12	7	3	39	26	3	6	1.4	.956	OF-16, 3B-12, DH-12, 2B-7, C-1
1990		15	.083	.083	12	1	0	0	0	0.0	1	1	0	1	0	0	0	11	4	1	1	1.3	.938	DH-5, 3B-4, OF-2, 2B-1
8 yrs.		343	.207	.258	531	110	17	2	2	0.4	78	24	41	85	53	49	9	245	321	13	61	2.5	.978	2B-117, 3B-74, OF-26, DH-17, C-1, 1B-1
LEAGUE CHAMPIONSHIP SERIES																								
1987	STL N	3	.333	.333	6	2	0	0	0	0.0	0	0	1	1	0	2	1	1	4	0	0	1.7	1.000	3B-2, OF-1
WORLD SERIES																								
1985	STL N	1	—	—	0	0	0	0	0	—	0	0	0	0	0	0	0	0	0	0	0	0.0	—	
1987		3	.100	.400	10	1	0	0	1	10.0	1	3	0	4	0	0	0	3	6	1	1	3.3	.900	3B-3
2 yrs.		4	.100	.400	10	1	0	0	1	10.0	1	3	0	4	0	0	0	3	6	1	1	3.3	.900	3B-3

Mike Lawlor

LAWLOR, MICHAEL H. TR 6′ 180 lbs.
B. Mar. 11, 1854, Troy, N. Y. D. Aug. 3, 1918, Troy, N. Y.

Year	Team	Games	BA	SA	AB	H	2B	3B	HR	HR%	R	RBI	BB	SO	SB	Pinch Hit AB	Pinch Hit H	PO	A	E	DP	TC/G	FA	G by Pos
1880	TRO N	4	.111	.111	9	1	0	0	0	0.0	1	0	1	1		0	0	18	8	4	0	7.5	.867	C-4
1884	WAS U	2	.000	.000	7	0	0	0	0	0.0	0		0			0	0	15	5	0	0	10.0	1.000	C-2
2 yrs.		6	.063	.063	16	1	0	0	0	0.0	1	0	1	1		0	0	33	13	4	0	8.3	.920	C-6

Bill Lawrence

LAWRENCE, WILLIAM HENRY BR TR 6′ 4″ 194 lbs.
B. Mar. 11, 1906, San Mateo, Calif.

Year	Team	Games	BA	SA	AB	H	2B	3B	HR	HR%	R	RBI	BB	SO	SB	Pinch Hit AB	Pinch Hit H	PO	A	E	DP	TC/G	FA	G by Pos
1932	DET A	25	.217	.239	46	10	1	0	0	0.0	10	3	5	5	0	2	0	39	2	0	1	2.7	1.000	OF-15

Jim Lawrence

LAWRENCE, JAMES ROSS
B. Feb. 12, 1939, Hamilton, Ont., Canada.
BL TR 6′ 1″ 185 lbs.

Year	Team	Games	BA	SA	AB	H	2B	3B	HR	HR%	R	RBI	BB	SO	SB	Pinch Hit AB	Pinch Hit H	PO	A	E	DP	TC/G	FA	G by Pos
1963	CLE A	2	—	—	0	0	0	0	0	—	0	0	0	0	0	0	0	3	0	1	0	2.0	.750	C-2

Otis Lawry

LAWRY, OTIS CARROLL (Rabbit)
B. Nov. 1, 1893, Fairfield, Me. D. Oct. 23, 1965, China, Me.
BL TR 5′ 8″ 133 lbs.

Year	Team	Games	BA	SA	AB	H	2B	3B	HR	HR%	R	RBI	BB	SO	SB	Pinch Hit AB	Pinch Hit H	PO	A	E	DP	TC/G	FA	G by Pos
1916	PHI A	41	.203	.203	123	25	0	0	0	0.0	10	4	9	21	4	5	0	39	71	11	8	3.6	.909	2B-29, OF-5
1917		30	.164	.182	55	9	1	0	0	0.0	7	1	2	9	1	4	1	24	35	5	2	3.6	.922	2B-17, OF-1
2 yrs.		71	.191	.197	178	34	1	0	0	0.0	17	5	11	30	5	9	1	63	106	16	10	3.6	.914	2B-46, OF-6

Marcus Lawton

LAWTON, MARCUS DWAYNE
Brother of Matt Lawton.
B. Aug. 18, 1965, Gulfport, Miss.
BB TR 6′ 1″ 160 lbs.

Year	Team	Games	BA	SA	AB	H	2B	3B	HR	HR%	R	RBI	BB	SO	SB	Pinch Hit AB	Pinch Hit H	PO	A	E	DP	TC/G	FA	G by Pos
1989	NY A	10	.214	.214	14	3	0	0	0	0.0	1	0	0	3	1	2	0	9	0	2	0	1.2	.818	OF-8, DH-1

Matt Lawton

LAWTON, MATTHEW
Brother of Marcus Lawton.
B. Nov. 3, 1971, Gulfport, Miss.
BL TR 5′10″ 180 lbs.

Year	Team	Games	BA	SA	AB	H	2B	3B	HR	HR%	R	RBI	BB	SO	SB	Pinch Hit AB	Pinch Hit H	PO	A	E	DP	TC/G	FA	G by Pos
1995	MIN A	21	.317	.467	60	19	4	1	1	1.7	11	12	7	11	1	4	0	34	1	1	0	1.8	.972	OF-19, DH-1

Gene Layden

LAYDEN, EUGENE FRANCIS
B. Mar. 14, 1894, Pittsburgh, Pa. D. Dec. 12, 1984, Pittsburgh, Pa.
BL TL 5′10″ 160 lbs.

Year	Team	Games	BA	SA	AB	H	2B	3B	HR	HR%	R	RBI	BB	SO	SB	Pinch Hit AB	Pinch Hit H	PO	A	E	DP	TC/G	FA	G by Pos
1915	NY A	3	.286	.286	7	2	0	0	0	0.0	2	0	0	1	0	0	0	3	0	1	0	2.0	.750	OF-2

Pete Layden

LAYDEN, PETER JOHN
B. Dec. 30, 1919, Dallas, Tex. D. July 18, 1982, Edna, Tex.
BR TR 5′11″ 185 lbs.

Year	Team	Games	BA	SA	AB	H	2B	3B	HR	HR%	R	RBI	BB	SO	SB	Pinch Hit AB	Pinch Hit H	PO	A	E	DP	TC/G	FA	G by Pos
1948	STL A	41	.250	.288	104	26	2	1	0	0.0	11	4	6	10	4	8	2	69	3	2	0	2.5	.973	OF-30

Herman Layne

LAYNE, HERMAN
B. Feb. 13, 1901, New Haven, W. Va. D. Aug. 27, 1973, Gallipolis, Ohio.
BR TR 5′11″ 165 lbs.

Year	Team	Games	BA	SA	AB	H	2B	3B	HR	HR%	R	RBI	BB	SO	SB	Pinch Hit AB	Pinch Hit H	PO	A	E	DP	TC/G	FA	G by Pos
1927	PIT N	11	.000	.000	6	0	0	0	0	0.0	3	0	1	0	0	1	0	0	0	1	0	0.5	.000	OF-2

Hilly Layne

LAYNE, IVORIA HILLIS (Tony)
B. Feb. 23, 1918, Whitwell, Tenn.
BL TR 6′ 170 lbs.

Year	Team	Games	BA	SA	AB	H	2B	3B	HR	HR%	R	RBI	BB	SO	SB	Pinch Hit AB	Pinch Hit H	PO	A	E	DP	TC/G	FA	G by Pos
1941	WAS A	13	.280	.320	50	14	2	0	0	0.0	8	6	4	5	1	0	0	12	29	2	1	3.3	.953	3B-13
1944		33	.195	.218	87	17	2	0	0	0.0	6	8	6	10	2	13	2	27	49	3	5	3.8	.962	3B-18, 2B-3
1945		61	.299	.408	147	44	5	4	1	0.7	23	14	10	7	0	23	4	34	53	4	3	2.8	.956	3B-33
3 yrs.		107	.264	.335	284	75	9	4	1	0.4	37	28	20	22	3	36	6	73	131	9	9	3.2	.958	3B-64, 2B-3

Les Layton

LAYTON, LESTER LEE
B. Nov. 18, 1921, Nardin, Okla.
BR TR 6′ 165 lbs.

Year	Team	Games	BA	SA	AB	H	2B	3B	HR	HR%	R	RBI	BB	SO	SB	Pinch Hit AB	Pinch Hit H	PO	A	E	DP	TC/G	FA	G by Pos
1948	NY N	63	.231	.429	91	21	4	4	2	2.2	14	12	6	21	1	32	8	38	1	2	0	2.0	.951	OF-20

Johnny Lazor

LAZOR, JOHN PAUL
B. Sept. 9, 1912, Taylor, Wash.
BL TR 5′ 9½″ 180 lbs.

Year	Team	Games	BA	SA	AB	H	2B	3B	HR	HR%	R	RBI	BB	SO	SB	Pinch Hit AB	Pinch Hit H	PO	A	E	DP	TC/G	FA	G by Pos
1943	BOS A	83	.226	.293	208	47	10	2	0	0.0	21	13	21	25	5	17	2	135	7	3	0	2.3	.979	OF-63
1944		16	.083	.125	24	2	1	0	0	0.0	0	0	1	0	0	8	1	8	2	0	0	1.4	1.000	OF-6, C-1
1945		101	.310	.424	335	104	19	2	5	1.5	35	45	18	17	3	17	5	141	6	6	0	1.9	.961	OF-81
1946		23	.138	.241	29	4	0	0	1	3.4	1	4	0	11	0	16	1	6	0	0	0	0.9	1.000	OF-7
4 yrs.		223	.263	.357	596	157	30	4	6	1.0	57	62	40	53	8	58	9	290	15	9	0	2.0	.971	OF-157, C-1

Tony Lazzeri

LAZZERI, ANTHONY MICHAEL (Poosh 'Em Up)
B. Dec. 6, 1903, San Francisco, Calif. D. Aug. 6, 1946, San Francisco, Calif.
Hall of Fame 1991.
BR TR 5′11½″ 170 lbs.

Year	Team	Games	BA	SA	AB	H	2B	3B	HR	HR%	R	RBI	BB	SO	SB	Pinch Hit AB	Pinch Hit H	PO	A	E	DP	TC/G	FA	G by Pos
1926	NY A	155	.275	.462	589	162	28	14	18	3.1	79	114	54	**96**	16	0	0	309	478	35	74	5.3	.957	2B-149, SS-5, 3B-1
1927		153	.309	.482	570	176	29	8	18	3.2	92	102	69	82	22	0	0	281	525	29	75	5.2	.965	2B-113, SS-38, 3B-9
1928		116	.332	.535	404	134	30	11	10	2.5	62	82	43	50	15	4	1	236	331	26	56	5.1	.956	2B-116
1929		147	.354	.561	545	193	37	11	18	3.3	101	106	69	45	9	0	0	475	627	53	131	5.6	.954	2B-147, SS-61
1930		143	.303	.462	571	173	34	15	9	1.6	109	121	60	62	4	1	0	294	382	26	59	4.8	.963	2B-77, 3B-60, SS-8, OF-1, 1B-1
1931		135	.267	.401	484	129	27	7	8	1.7	67	83	79	80	18	7	5	255	341	26	56	4.8	.958	2B-90, 3B-39
1932		141	.300	.506	510	153	28	16	15	2.9	79	113	82	64	11	3	1	364	412	17	70	5.7	.979	2B-133, 3B-5
1933		139	.294	.486	523	154	22	12	18	3.4	94	104	73	62	15	1	0	338	407	25	71	5.6	.968	2B-138
1934		123	.267	.445	438	117	24	6	14	3.2	59	67	71	64	11	1	1	254	316	18	59	4.8	.969	2B-92, 3B-30
1935		130	.273	.417	477	130	18	6	13	2.7	72	83	63	75	11	5	3	303	354	22	76	5.3	.968	2B-118, SS-9
1936		150	.287	.441	537	154	29	6	14	2.6	82	109	97	65	8	0	0	348	418	25	88	5.3	.968	2B-148, SS-2
1937		126	.244	.399	446	109	21	3	14	3.1	56	70	71	76	7	1	0	251	382	22	64	5.2	.966	2B-125
1938	CHI N	54	.267	.433	120	32	5	0	5	4.2	21	23	22	30	0	14	2	49	75	7	12	3.5	.947	SS-25, 3B-7, 2B-4, OF-1
1939	2 teams	BKN N (14G –.282) NY N (13G –.295)																						
″	total	27	.289	.458	83	24	2	0	4	4.8	13	14	17	13	1	1	0	40	59	10	10	4.2	.908	3B-15, 2B-11
14 yrs.		1739	.292	.467	6297	1840	334	115	178	2.8	986	1191	870	864	148	38	13	3797	5107	341	901	5.2	.963	2B-1461, 3B-166, SS-148, OF-2, 1B-1

WORLD SERIES

Year	Team	Games	BA	SA	AB	H	2B	3B	HR	HR%	R	RBI	BB	SO	SB	Pinch Hit AB	Pinch Hit H	PO	A	E	DP	TC/G	FA	G by Pos
1926	NY A	7	.192	.231	26	5	1	0	0	0.0	2	3	1	6	0	0	0	14	19	1	2	4.9	.971	2B-7
1927		4	.267	.333	15	4	1	0	0	0.0	1	2	1	4	0	0	0	10	18	1	4	7.3	.966	2B-4
1928		4	.250	.333	12	3	1	0	0	0.0	2	0	1	0	2	0	0	2	7	2	1	2.8	.818	2B-4
1932		4	.294	.647	17	5	0	0	2	11.8	4	5	2	1	0	0	0	8	11	1	1	5.0	.950	2B-4
1936		6	.250	.400	20	5	0	0	1	5.0	4	7	4	4	0	0	0	13	17	0	1	5.0	1.000	2B-6
1937		5	.400	.733	15	6	0	1	1	6.7	3	2	3	3	0	0	0	11	16	0	1	5.4	1.000	2B-5
1938	CHI N	2	.000	.000	2	0	0	0	0	0.0	0	0	0	1	0	2	0	0	0	0	0	0.0	—	
7 yrs.		32	.262	.421	107	28	3	1	4	3.7	16	19	12	19	2	2	0	58	88	5	10	5.0	.967	2B-30

Freddy Leach

LEACH, FREDERICK
B. Nov. 23, 1897, Springfield, Mo. D. Dec. 10, 1981, Hagerman, Ida.
BL TR 5′11″ 183 lbs.

Year	Team	Games	BA	SA	AB	H	2B	3B	HR	HR%	R	RBI	BB	SO	SB	Pinch Hit AB	Pinch Hit H	PO	A	E	DP	TC/G	FA	G by Pos
1923	PHI N	52	.260	.327	104	27	4	0	1	1.0	5	16	3	14	1	23	4	38	0	2	0	1.5	.950	OF-26
1924		8	.464	.821	28	13	2	1	2	7.1	6	7	2	1	0	0	0	8	1	0	0	1.3	1.000	OF-7

Freddy Leach *continued*

Year	Team	Games	BA	SA	AB	H	2B	3B	HR	HR%	R	RBI	BB	SO	SB	Pinch Hit AB	Pinch Hit H	PO	A	E	DP	TC/G	FA	G by Pos
1925		65	.312	.442	292	91	15	4	5	1.7	47	28	5	21	1	0	0	178	2	9	1	2.9	.952	OF-65
1926		129	.329	.484	492	162	29	7	11	2.2	73	71	16	33	6	5	1	313	15	7	2	2.7	.979	OF-123
1927		140	.306	.444	536	164	30	4	12	2.2	69	83	21	32	2	1	0	385	26	8	10	3.0	.981	OF-139
1928		145	.304	.469	588	179	36	11	13	2.2	83	96	30	30	4	0	0	545	29	8	33	4.0	.986	OF-120, 1B-25
1929	NY N	113	.290	.431	411	119	22	6	8	1.9	74	47	17	14	10	17	5	149	2	4	0	1.6	.974	OF-95
1930		126	.327	.482	544	178	19	13	13	2.4	90	71	22	25	3	2	0	208	11	5	4	1.8	.978	OF-124
1931		129	.309	.421	515	159	30	5	6	1.2	75	61	29	9	4	2	0	239	6	6	1	2.0	.976	OF-125
1932	BOS N	84	.247	.318	223	55	9	2	1	0.4	21	29	18	10	1	30	8	126	2	3	0	2.6	.977	OF-50
10 yrs.		991	.307	.446	3733	1147	196	53	72	1.9	543	509	163	189	32	80	18	2189	94	52	51	2.6	.978	OF-874, 1B-25

Rick Leach

LEACH, RICHARD MAX BL TL 6′ 1″ 180 lbs.
B. May 4, 1957, Ann Arbor, Mich.

Year	Team	Games	BA	SA	AB	H	2B	3B	HR	HR%	R	RBI	BB	SO	SB	Pinch Hit AB	Pinch Hit H	PO	A	E	DP	TC/G	FA	G by Pos
1981	DET A	54	.193	.289	83	16	3	1	1	1.2	9	11	16	15	0	10	2	149	14	0	15	3.3	1.000	1B-32, OF-15, DH-2
1982		82	.239	.330	218	52	7	2	3	1.4	23	12	21	29	4	14	2	430	29	2	36	6.2	.996	1B-56, OF-14, DH-4
1983		99	.248	.355	242	60	17	0	3	1.2	22	26	19	21	2	18	4	465	45	4	37	5.8	.992	1B-73, OF-13, DH-3
1984	TOR A	65	.261	.375	88	23	6	2	0	0.0	11	7	8	14	0	22	8	92	14	0	9	2.4	1.000	OF-23, 1B-15, DH-6, P-1
1985		16	.200	.257	35	7	0	1	0	0.0	2	1	3	9	0	4	1	78	6	1	8	6.1	.988	1B-10, OF-4
1986		110	.309	.435	246	76	14	1	5	2.0	35	39	13	24	0	31	10	107	5	3	11	1.3	.974	DH-42, OF-39, 1B-7
1987		98	.282	.405	195	55	13	1	3	1.5	26	25	25	25	0	28	7	57	1	1	0	0.7	.983	OF-43, DH-42, 1B-5
1988		87	.276	.352	199	55	13	1	0	0.0	21	23	18	27	0	19	1	93	5	0	1	1.3	1.000	OF-49, DH-25, 1B-4
1989	TEX A	110	.272	.351	239	65	14	1	1	0.4	32	23	32	33	2	30	6	74	2	3	2	0.9	.962	DH-44, OF-41, 1B-4
1990	SF N	78	.293	.402	174	51	13	0	2	1.1	24	16	21	20	0	20	7	123	5	1	4	2.2	.992	OF-52, 1B-7
10 yrs.		799	.268	.369	1719	460	100	10	18	1.0	205	183	176	217	8	196	48	1668	126	15	123	2.7	.992	OF-293, 1B-213, DH-168, P-1

Tommy Leach

LEACH, THOMAS WILLIAM BR TR 5′ 6½″ 150 lbs.
B. Nov. 4, 1877, French Creek, N. Y. D. Sept. 29, 1969, Haines City, Fla.

Year	Team	Games	BA	SA	AB	H	2B	3B	HR	HR%	R	RBI	BB	SO	SB	Pinch Hit AB	Pinch Hit H	PO	A	E	DP	TC/G	FA	G by Pos
1898	LOU N	3	.100	.100	10	1	0	0	0	0.0	0	0	0		0	0	0	2	7	3	0	3.0	.750	3B-3, 2B-1
1899		106	.288	.379	406	117	10	6	5	1.2	75	57	37		19	0	0	194	278	61	17	5.0	.886	3B-80, SS-25, 2B-2
1900	PIT N	51	.212	.263	160	34	1	2	1	0.6	20	16	21		8	1	0	74	117	24	9	4.3	.888	3B-31, SS-8, 2B-7, OF-4
1901		98	.305	.414	374	114	12	13	1	0.3	64	44	20		16	2	1	130	208	35	11	3.9	.906	3B-92, SS-4
1902		135	.280	.442	514	144	21	22	**6**	**1.2**	97	85	45		25	1	0	170	316	39	10	3.9	.926	3B-134
1903		127	.298	.438	507	151	16	17	7	1.4	97	87	40		22	0	0	178	292	65	16	4.2	.879	3B-127
1904		146	.257	.335	579	149	15	12	2	0.3	92	56	45		23	0	0	212	371	60	18	4.4	.907	3B-146
1905		131	.257	.345	499	128	10	14	2	0.4	71	53	37		17	0	0	245	141	16	15	3.0	.960	OF-71, 3B-58, 2B-2, SS-2
1906		133	.286	.342	476	136	10	7	1	0.2	66	39	33		21	6	3	209	143	20	4	3.0	.946	3B-65, OF-60, SS-1
1907		149	.303	.404	547	166	19	12	4	0.7	102	43	40		43	0	0	332	95	24	12	3.0	.947	OF-111, 3B-33, SS-6, 2B-1
1908		152	.259	.381	583	151	24	16	5	0.9	93	41	54		24	0	0	205	295	33	19	3.5	.938	3B-150, OF-2
1909		151	.261	.368	587	153	29	8	6	1.0	**126**	43	66		27	0	0	355	38	13	5	2.7	.968	OF-138, 3B-13
1910		135	.270	.357	529	143	24	5	4	0.8	83	52	38	62	18	1	0	358	17	14	5	2.9	.964	OF-131, SS-2, 2B-1
1911		108	.238	.324	386	92	12	6	3	0.8	60	43	46	50	19	4	0	226	42	7	6	2.7	.975	OF-89, SS-13, 3B-1
1912	2 teams	PIT N (28G –.299) CHI N (82G –.242)																						
″	total	110	.257	.340	362	93	14	5	2	0.6	74	51	67	29	20	4	2	255	22	7	7	2.8	.975	OF-97, 3B-4
1913	CHI N	130	.289	.423	454	131	23	10	6	1.3	**99**	32	77	44	21	7	3	276	17	6	5	2.5	.980	OF-119, 3B-2
1914		153	.263	.373	577	152	24	9	7	1.2	80	46	79	50	16	1	0	346	42	18	5	2.7	.956	OF-137, 3B-16
1915	CIN N	107	.224	.275	335	75	7	5	0	0.0	42	17	56	38	20	9	1	200	9	9	2	2.3	.959	OF-96
1918	PIT N	30	.194	.306	72	14	2	3	0	0.0	14	5	19	5	2	2	0	40	10	5	2	2.1	.909	OF-23, SS-3
19 yrs.		2155	.269	.370	7957	2144	273	172	62	0.8	1355	810	820	278	361	38	10	4007	2460	459	168	3.3	.934	OF-1078, 3B-955, SS-64, 2B-14
WORLD SERIES																								
1903	PIT N	8	.273	.515	33	9	0	4	0	0.0	3	7	1	4	2	0	0	5	16	4	0	3.1	.840	3B-8
1909		7	.320	.480	25	8	4	0	0	0.0	8	2	2	1	1	0	0	20	3	0	0	3.3	1.000	OF-6, 3B-1
2 yrs.		15	.293	.500	58	17	4	4 **1st**	0	0.0	11	9	3	5	3	0	0	25	19	4	0	3.2	.917	3B-9, OF-6

Dan Leahy

LEAHY, DANIEL C. 5′ 9″ 155 lbs.
B. Aug. 8, 1870, Nashville, Tenn. D. Dec. 25, 1915, Nashville, Tenn.

Year	Team	Games	BA	SA	AB	H	2B	3B	HR	HR%	R	RBI	BB	SO	SB	Pinch Hit AB	Pinch Hit H	PO	A	E	DP	TC/G	FA	G by Pos
1896	PHI N	2	.333	.500	6	2	1	0	0	0.0	0	1	1	2	0	0	0	4	8	2	0	7.0	.857	SS-2

Tom Leahy

LEAHY, THOMAS JOSEPH TR
B. June 2, 1869, New Haven, Conn. D. June 11, 1951, New Haven, Conn.

Year	Team	Games	BA	SA	AB	H	2B	3B	HR	HR%	R	RBI	BB	SO	SB	Pinch Hit AB	Pinch Hit H	PO	A	E	DP	TC/G	FA	G by Pos
1897	2 teams	PIT N (24G –.261) WAS N (19G –.385)																						
″	total	43	.306	.396	144	44	5	4	0	0.0	22	19	16		9	0	0	63	37	16	2	2.6	.862	OF-23, 3B-11, C-7, 2B-3
1898	WAS N	15	.182	.218	55	10	2	0	0	0.0	10	5	8		6	0	0	26	34	4	3	4.3	.938	3B-12, 2B-3
1901	2 teams	MIL A (33G –.242) PHI A (5G –.333)																						
″	total	38	.254	.351	114	29	7	2	0	0.0	19	11	12		3	3	2	102	41	9	5	4.3	.941	C-29, OF-4, SS-1, 2B-1
1905	STL N	35	.227	.299	97	22	1	3	0	0.0	3	7	8		0	6	1	91	31	7	1	4.4	.946	C-29
4 yrs.		131	.256	.337	410	105	15	9	0	0.0	54	42	44		18	9	3	282	143	36	11	3.7	.922	C-65, OF-27, 3B-23, 2B-7, SS-1

Fred Lear

LEAR, FREDERICK FRANCIS (King) BR TR 6′½″ 180 lbs.
B. Apr. 7, 1894, New York, N. Y. D. Oct. 13, 1955, East Orange, N. J.

Year	Team	Games	BA	SA	AB	H	2B	3B	HR	HR%	R	RBI	BB	SO	SB	Pinch Hit AB	Pinch Hit H	PO	A	E	DP	TC/G	FA	G by Pos
1915	PHI A	2	.000	.000	2	0	0	0	0	0.0	0	0	0	2	0	0	0	3	0	2	0	2.5	.600	3B-2
1918	CHI N	2	.000	.000	1	0	0	0	0	0.0	0	0	1	0	0	1	0	0	0	0	0	0.0	—	
1919		40	.224	.329	76	17	3	1	1	1.3	8	11	8	11	2	14	2	121	27	5	6	7.3	.967	1B-9, 2B-9, SS-3
1920	NY N	31	.253	.310	87	22	0	1	1	1.1	12	7	8	15	0	4	1	20	39	3	5	2.5	.952	3B-24, 2B-1
4 yrs.		75	.235	.313	166	39	3	2	2	1.2	20	18	17	28	2	19	3	144	66	10	11	4.6	.955	3B-26, 2B-10, 1B-9, SS-3

Bill Leard

LEARD, WILLIAM WALLACE (Wild Bill) BR TR 5′10″ 155 lbs.
B. Oct. 14, 1885, Oneida, N. Y. D. Jan. 15, 1970, San Francisco, Calif.

Year	Team	Games	BA	SA	AB	H	2B	3B	HR	HR%	R	RBI	BB	SO	SB	Pinch Hit AB	Pinch Hit H	PO	A	E	DP	TC/G	FA	G by Pos
1917	BKN N	3	.000	.000	3	0	0	0	0	0.0	0	0	0	1	0	1	0	0	0	0	0	0.0	.000	2B-1

Jack Leary

LEARY, JOHN J. TL 5′11″ 186 lbs.
B. 1858, New Haven, Conn. Deceased.

Year	Team	Games	BA	SA	AB	H	2B	3B	HR	HR%	R	RBI	BB	SO	SB	Pinch Hit AB	Pinch Hit H	PO	A	E	DP	TC/G	FA	G by Pos
1880	**BOS N**	1	.000	.000	3	0	0	0	0	0.0	1	0	1	0		0	0	0	2	0	0	1.0	1.000	OF-1, P-1
1881	**DET N**	3	.273	.545	11	3	1	1	0	0.0	2	4	1	1		0	0	5	2	2	0	2.3	.778	OF-2, P-2
1882	**2 teams**	**PIT AA** (60G –.292) **BAL AA** (4G –.222)																						
″	**total**	64	.287	.360	275	79	8	3	2	0.7	35		5			0	0	78	81	49	2	3.0	.764	3B-33, OF-28, P-6, 2B-1, 1B-1
1883	**2 teams**	**LOU AA** (40G –.188) **BAL AA** (3G –.182)																						
″	**total**	43	.188	.301	176	33	1	5	3	1.7	17		2			0	0	72	112	44	14	5.3	.807	SS-40, 2B-3
1884	**2 teams**	**ALT U** (8G –.091) **CHI U** (10G –.175)																						
″	**total**	18	.137	.151	73	10	1	0	0	0.0	1		1			0	0	36	20	20	0	3.5	.737	OF-9, P-5, 2B-4, 3B-4
5 yrs.		129	.232	.314	538	125	11	9	5	0.9	56	4	10	1		0	0	191	217	115	16	3.7	.780	OF-40, SS-40, 3B-37, P-14, 2B-8, 1B-1

John Leary

LEARY, JOHN LOUIS (Jack) BR TR 5′11½″ 180 lbs.
B. May 2, 1891, Waltham, Mass. D. Aug. 18, 1961, Waltham, Mass.

Year	Team	Games	BA	SA	AB	H	2B	3B	HR	HR%	R	RBI	BB	SO	SB	Pinch Hit AB	Pinch Hit H	PO	A	E	DP	TC/G	FA	G by Pos
1914	**STL A**	144	.265	.343	533	141	28	7	0	0.0	35	45	10	71	9	2	1	1323	91	20	68	9.9	.986	1B-130, C-15
1915		75	.242	.286	227	55	10	0	0	0.0	19	15	5	36	2	11	4	469	41	13	42	8.2	.975	1B-53, C-11
2 yrs.		219	.258	.326	760	196	38	7	0	0.0	54	60	15	107	11	13	5	1792	132	33	110	9.4	.983	1B-183, C-26

Hal Leathers

LEATHERS, HAROLD LANGFORD (Chuck) BL TR 5′ 8″ 152 lbs.
B. Dec. 2, 1898, Selma, Calif. D. Apr. 12, 1977, Modesto, Calif.

Year	Team	Games	BA	SA	AB	H	2B	3B	HR	HR%	R	RBI	BB	SO	SB	Pinch Hit AB	Pinch Hit H	PO	A	E	DP	TC/G	FA	G by Pos
1920	**CHI N**	9	.304	.478	23	7	1	0	1	4.3	3	1	1	1	1	1	0	15	21	7	0	4.8	.837	SS-6, 2B-3

Emil Leber

LEBER, EMIL BOHMIEL BR TR 5′11″ 170 lbs.
B. May 15, 1881, Cleveland, Ohio D. Nov. 6, 1924, Cleveland, Ohio.

Year	Team	Games	BA	SA	AB	H	2B	3B	HR	HR%	R	RBI	BB	SO	SB	Pinch Hit AB	Pinch Hit H	PO	A	E	DP	TC/G	FA	G by Pos
1905	**CLE A**	2	.000	.000	6	0	0	0	0	0.0	1	0	1		0	0	0	0	4	0	0	2.0	1.000	3B-2

Bevo LeBourveau

LeBOURVEAU, DeWITT WILEY BL TR 5′11″ 175 lbs.
B. Aug. 24, 1894, Dana, Calif. D. Dec. 9, 1947, Nevada City, Calif.

Year	Team	Games	BA	SA	AB	H	2B	3B	HR	HR%	R	RBI	BB	SO	SB	Pinch Hit AB	Pinch Hit H	PO	A	E	DP	TC/G	FA	G by Pos
1919	**PHI N**	17	.270	.270	63	17	0	0	0	0.0	4	0	10	8	2	0	0	27	6	0	0	1.9	1.000	OF-17
1920		84	.257	.333	261	67	7	2	3	1.1	29	12	11	36	9	8	1	133	16	8	1	2.2	.949	OF-72
1921		93	.295	.438	281	83	12	5	6	2.1	42	35	29	51	4	16	9	126	7	13	2	1.9	.911	OF-76
1922		74	.269	.389	167	45	8	3	2	1.2	24	20	24	29	0	25	4	77	4	7	1	2.1	.920	OF-42
1929	**PHI A**	12	.313	.438	16	5	0	1	0	0.0	1	2	5	1	0	9	1	8	0	0	0	2.7	1.000	OF-3
5 yrs.		280	.275	.379	788	217	27	11	11	1.4	100	69	79	125	15	58	15	371	33	28	4	2.1	.935	OF-210

Aaron Ledesma

LEDESMA, AARON DAVID BR TR 6′ 2″ 200 lbs.
B. June 3, 1971, Union City, Calif.

Year	Team	Games	BA	SA	AB	H	2B	3B	HR	HR%	R	RBI	BB	SO	SB	Pinch Hit AB	Pinch Hit H	PO	A	E	DP	TC/G	FA	G by Pos
1995	**NY N**	21	.242	.242	33	8	0	0	0	0.0	4	3	6	7	0	9	3	5	12	2	0	1.4	.895	3B-10, 1B-2, SS-2

Bill Lee

LEE, WILLIAM JOSEPH BR TR 5′ 9″ 165 lbs.
B. Jan. 9, 1892, Bayonne, N. J. D. Jan. 6, 1984, West Hazleton, Pa.

Year	Team	Games	BA	SA	AB	H	2B	3B	HR	HR%	R	RBI	BB	SO	SB	Pinch Hit AB	Pinch Hit H	PO	A	E	DP	TC/G	FA	G by Pos
1915	**STL A**	18	.186	.203	59	11	1	0	0	0.0	2	4	6	5	1	2	1	40	5	1	1	2.9	.978	OF-15, 3B-1
1916		7	.182	.182	11	2	0	0	0	0.0	1	0	1	1	0	3	2	5	0	0	0	1.7	1.000	OF-3
2 yrs.		25	.186	.200	70	13	1	0	0	0.0	3	4	7	6	1	5	3	45	5	1	1	2.7	.980	OF-18, 3B-1

Cliff Lee

LEE, CLIFFORD WALKER BR TR 6′ 1″ 175 lbs.
B. Aug. 4, 1896, Lexington, Neb. D. Aug. 25, 1980, Denver, Colo.

Year	Team	Games	BA	SA	AB	H	2B	3B	HR	HR%	R	RBI	BB	SO	SB	Pinch Hit AB	Pinch Hit H	PO	A	E	DP	TC/G	FA	G by Pos
1919	**PIT N**	42	.196	.286	112	22	2	4	0	0.0	5	2	6	8	2	8	1	96	17	5	0	3.5	.958	C-28, OF-6
1920		37	.237	.316	76	18	2	2	0	0.0	9	8	4	14	0	16	3	55	24	2	3	3.9	.975	C-19, OF-2
1921	**PHI N**	88	.308	.427	286	88	14	4	4	1.4	31	29	13	34	5	10	6	546	25	10	35	7.5	.983	1B-48, OF-27, C-2
1922		122	.322	.540	422	136	29	6	17	4.0	65	77	32	43	2	13	3	340	17	10	19	3.4	.973	OF-89, 1B-18, 3B-1
1923		107	.321	.493	355	114	20	4	11	3.1	54	47	20	39	3	12	1	267	13	8	11	2.9	.972	OF-83, 1B-16
1924	**2 teams**	**PHI N** (21G –.250) **CIN N** (6G –.333)																						
″	**total**	27	.258	.435	62	16	4	2	1	1.6	5	9	2	7	0	7	2	64	3	0	4	3.7	1.000	OF-14, 1B-4
1925	**CLE A**	77	.322	.491	230	74	15	6	4	1.7	43	42	21	33	2	7	2	129	7	7	2	2.0	.951	OF-70
1926		21	.175	.275	40	7	1	0	1	2.5	4	2	6	8	0	8	1	25	0	0	0	2.1	1.000	OF-9, C-3
8 yrs.		521	.300	.462	1583	475	87	28	38	2.4	216	216	104	186	14	81	19	1522	106	42	74	3.8	.975	OF-300, 1B-86, C-52, 3B-1

Derek Lee

LEE, DEREK GERALD BL TR 6′ 1″ 200 lbs.
B. July 28, 1966, Chicago, Ill.

Year	Team	Games	BA	SA	AB	H	2B	3B	HR	HR%	R	RBI	BB	SO	SB	Pinch Hit AB	Pinch Hit H	PO	A	E	DP	TC/G	FA	G by Pos
1993	**MIN A**	15	.152	.182	33	5	1	0	0	0.0	3	4	1	4	0	5	1	15	0	0	0	1.2	1.000	OF-13

Dud Lee

LEE, ERNEST DUDLEY BL TR 5′ 9″ 150 lbs.
Played as Dud Dudley in 1920 and 1921.
B. Aug. 22, 1899, Denver, Colo. D. Jan. 7, 1971, Denver, Colo.

Year	Team	Games	BA	SA	AB	H	2B	3B	HR	HR%	R	RBI	BB	SO	SB	Pinch Hit AB	Pinch Hit H	PO	A	E	DP	TC/G	FA	G by Pos
1920	**STL A**	1	1.000	1.000	2	2	0	0	0	0.0	2	1	0	0	1	0	0	0	1	2	0	3.0	.333	SS-1
1921		72	.167	.211	180	30	4	2	0	0.0	18	11	14	34	1	0	0	138	152	19	30	4.8	.939	SS-31, 2B-30, 3B-3
1924	**BOS A**	94	.253	.313	288	73	9	4	0	0.0	36	29	40	17	8	3	0	198	246	30	43	5.3	.937	SS-90
1925		84	.224	.275	255	57	7	3	0	0.0	22	19	34	19	2	0	0	188	260	37	64	5.8	.924	SS-84
1926		2	.143	.143	7	1	0	0	0	0.0	2	0	0	0	0	0	0	4	3	0	1	3.5	1.000	SS-2
5 yrs.		253	.223	.275	732	163	20	9	0	0.0	80	60	88	70	12	3	0	528	662	88	138	5.3	.931	SS-208, 2B-30, 3B-3

Hal Lee

LEE, HAROLD BURNHAM (Sheriff) BR TR 5′11″ 180 lbs.
B. Feb. 15, 1905, Ludlow, Miss. D. Sept. 4, 1989, Pascagoula, Miss.

Year	Team	Games	BA	SA	AB	H	2B	3B	HR	HR%	R	RBI	BB	SO	SB	Pinch Hit AB	Pinch Hit H	PO	A	E	DP	TC/G	FA	G by Pos
1930	**BKN N**	22	.162	.243	37	6	0	0	1	2.7	5	4	4	5	0	7	1	17	0	0	0	1.4	1.000	OF-12
1931	**PHI N**	44	.221	.344	131	29	10	0	2	1.5	13	12	10	18	0	5	1	86	1	3	1	2.4	.967	OF-38
1932		149	.303	.497	595	180	42	10	18	3.0	76	85	36	45	6	0	0	380	11	14	3	2.7	.965	OF-148
1933	**2 teams**	**PHI N** (46G –.287) **BOS N** (88G –.221)																						
″	**total**	134	.244	.353	479	117	27	11	1	0.2	57	40	36	39	2	1	0	304	11	7	2	2.4	.978	OF-132
1934	**BOS N**	139	.292	.405	521	152	23	6	8	1.5	70	79	47	43	3	7	1	327	14	10	5	2.7	.972	OF-128, 2B-4
1935		112	.303	.374	422	128	18	6	0	0.0	49	39	18	25	0	2	0	273	7	11	0	2.6	.962	OF-110
1936		152	.253	.336	565	143	24	7	3	0.5	46	64	52	50	4	1	0	319	5	9	1	2.2	.973	OF-150
7 yrs.		752	.275	.392	2750	755	144	40	33	1.2	316	323	203	225	15	23	3	1706	49	54	12	2.5	.970	OF-718, 2B-4

Leonidas Lee

LEE, LEONIDAS PYRRHUS
Born Leonidas Pyrrhus Funkhouser.
B. Dec. 13, 1860, St. Louis, Mo. D. June 11, 1912, Hendersonville, N. C.

Year	Team	Games	BA	SA	AB	H	2B	3B	HR	HR%	R	RBI	BB	SO	SB	Pinch Hit AB	Pinch Hit H	PO	A	E	DP	TC/G	FA	G by Pos
1877	STL N	4	.278	.333	18	5	1	0	0	0.0	0	0	0	1		0	0	6	1	4	0	2.2	.636	OF-4, SS-1

Leron Lee

LEE, LERON BL TR 6′ 196 lbs.
B. Mar. 4, 1948, Bakersfield, Calif.

Year	Team	Games	BA	SA	AB	H	2B	3B	HR	HR%	R	RBI	BB	SO	SB	Pinch Hit AB	Pinch Hit H	PO	A	E	DP	TC/G	FA	G by Pos
1969	STL N	7	.217	.261	23	5	1	0	0	0.0	3	0	3	8	0	0	0	7	1	0	0	1.1	1.000	OF-7
1970		121	.227	.352	264	60	13	1	6	2.3	28	23	24	66	5	38	9	120	3	4	0	1.6	.969	OF-77
1971	2 teams	STL N (25G –.179) SD N (79G –.273)																						
"	total	104	.264	.405	284	75	21	2	5	1.8	32	23	22	57	4	26	3	90	6	9	1	1.4	.914	OF-76
1972	SD N	101	.300	.497	370	111	23	7	12	3.2	50	47	29	58	2	4	2	186	6	5	2	2.1	.975	OF-96
1973		118	.237	.297	333	79	7	2	3	0.9	36	30	33	61	4	30	7	154	7	5	0	2.0	.970	OF-84
1974	CLE A	79	.233	.353	232	54	13	0	5	2.2	18	25	15	42	3	17	2	131	5	6	1	2.2	.958	OF-62, DH-2
1975	2 teams	CLE A (13G –.130) LA N (48G –.256)																						
"	total	61	.212	.288	66	14	5	0	0	0.0	5	2	5	14	1	46	10	8	0	0	0	0.7	1.000	OF-9, DH-3
1976	LA N	23	.133	.178	45	6	0	1	0	0.0	1	2	2	9	0	14	3	12	0	0	0	1.2	1.000	OF-10
8 yrs.		614	.250	.375	1617	404	83	13	31	1.9	173	152	133	315	19	175	36	708	28	29	4	1.8	.962	OF-421, DH-5

Manny Lee

LEE, MANUEL BB TR 5′ 9″ 150 lbs.
Born Manuel Lora (Lee).
B. June 17, 1965, San Pedro de Macoris, Dominican Republic.

Year	Team	Games	BA	SA	AB	H	2B	3B	HR	HR%	R	RBI	BB	SO	SB	Pinch Hit AB	Pinch Hit H	PO	A	E	DP	TC/G	FA	G by Pos
1985	TOR A	64	.200	.200	40	8	0	0	0	0.0	9	0	2	9	1	3	1	34	56	3	11	1.6	.968	2B-38, SS-8, DH-8, 3B-5
1986		35	.205	.269	78	16	0	1	1	1.3	8	7	4	10	0	0	0	36	76	2	11	3.2	.982	2B-29, SS-5, 3B-2
1987		56	.256	.347	121	31	2	3	1	0.8	14	11	6	13	2	3	2	77	110	5	26	3.6	.974	2B-27, SS-26
1988		116	.291	.365	381	111	16	3	2	0.5	38	38	26	64	3	2	0	250	308	12	71	4.4	.979	2B-98, SS-23, 3B-8
1989		99	.260	.333	300	78	9	2	3	1.0	27	34	20	60	4	13	1	152	201	11	51	3.7	.970	2B-40, SS-28, 3B-17, DH-13, OF-1
1990		117	.243	.340	391	95	12	4	6	1.5	45	41	26	90	3	3	0	265	301	4	66	4.7	.993	2B-112, SS-9
1991		138	.234	.288	445	104	18	3	0	0.0	41	29	24	107	7	0	0	194	360	19	52	4.2	.967	SS-138
1992		128	.263	.316	396	104	10	1	3	0.8	49	39	50	73	6	0	0	187	331	7	67	4.1	.987	SS-128
1993	TEX A	73	.220	.259	205	45	3	1	1	0.5	31	12	22	39	2	0	0	96	205	10	35	4.3	.968	SS-72
1994		95	.278	.361	335	93	18	2	2	0.6	41	38	21	66	3	0	0	152	281	13	53	4.6	.971	SS-85, 2B-13
1995	STL N	1	1.000	1.000	1	1	0	0	0	0.0	1	0	0	0	0	0	0	2	2	1	0	5.0	.800	2B-1
11 yrs.		922	.255	.323	2693	686	88	20	19	0.7	304	249	201	531	31	24	4	1445	2231	87	443	4.0	.977	SS-522, 2B-358, 3B-32, DH-21, OF-1
LEAGUE CHAMPIONSHIP SERIES																								
1985	TOR A	1	—	—	0	0	0	0	0	—	0	0	0	0	0	0	0	0	0	0	0	0.0	.000	2B-1
1989		2	.250	.250	8	2	0	0	0	0.0	2	0	0	1	0	0	0	4	1	0	1	2.5	1.000	2B-2
1991		5	.125	.125	16	2	0	0	0	0.0	3	0	1	5	0	0	0	8	16	1	3	5.0	.960	SS-5
1992		6	.278	.444	18	5	1	1	0	0.0	2	3	1	2	0	0	0	12	15	3	5	5.0	.900	SS-6
4 yrs.		14	.214	.286	42	9	1	1	0	0.0	7	3	2	8	0	0	0	24	32	4	9	4.3	.933	SS-11, 2B-3
WORLD SERIES																								
1992	TOR A	6	.105	.105	19	2	0	0	0	0.0	1	0	1	2	0	0	0	14	10	1	4	4.2	.960	SS-6

Terry Lee

LEE, TERRY JAMES BR TR 6′ 5″ 215 lbs.
B. Mar. 13, 1962, Los Angeles, Calif.

Year	Team	Games	BA	SA	AB	H	2B	3B	HR	HR%	R	RBI	BB	SO	SB	Pinch Hit AB	Pinch Hit H	PO	A	E	DP	TC/G	FA	G by Pos
1990	CIN N	12	.211	.263	19	4	1	0	0	0.0	1	3	2	2	0	6	2	28	3	0	1	5.2	1.000	1B-6
1991		3	.000	.000	6	0	0	0	0	0.0	0	0	0	2	0	1	0	8	4	0	0	6.0	1.000	1B-2
2 yrs.		15	.160	.200	25	4	1	0	0	0.0	1	3	2	4	0	7	2	36	7	0	1	5.4	1.000	1B-8

Watty Lee

LEE, WYATT ARNOLD (Indian) BL TL 5′10½″ 171 lbs.
B. Aug. 12, 1879, Lynch Station, Va. D. Mar. 6, 1936, Washington, D. C.

Year	Team	Games	BA	SA	AB	H	2B	3B	HR	HR%	R	RBI	BB	SO	SB	Pinch Hit AB	Pinch Hit H	PO	A	E	DP	TC/G	FA	G by Pos
1901	WAS A	43	.256	.349	129	33	6	3	0	0.0	15	12	7		0	2	0	16	82	7	3	2.4	.933	P-36, OF-7
1902		109	.256	.366	391	100	21	5	4	1.0	61	45	33		8	3	0	176	46	19	1	2.2	.921	OF-95, P-13
1903		75	.208	.277	231	48	8	4	0	0.0	17	13	18		5	5	1	113	64	9	5	2.7	.952	OF-47, P-22
1904	PIT N	8	.333	.500	12	4	0	1	0	0.0	1	0	0		0	3	2	1	7	1	0	1.8	.889	P-5
4 yrs.		235	.242	.338	763	185	35	13	4	0.5	94	70	58		13	13	3	306	199	36	9	2.4	.933	OF-149, P-76

Gene Leek

LEEK, EUGENE HAROLD BR TR 6′ 185 lbs.
B. July 15, 1936, San Diego, Calif.

Year	Team	Games	BA	SA	AB	H	2B	3B	HR	HR%	R	RBI	BB	SO	SB	Pinch Hit AB	Pinch Hit H	PO	A	E	DP	TC/G	FA	G by Pos
1959	CLE A	13	.222	.389	36	8	3	0	1	2.8	7	5	2	7	0	0	0	8	19	2	0	2.1	.931	3B-13, SS-1
1961	LA A	57	.226	.357	199	45	9	1	5	2.5	16	20	7	54	0	0	0	71	146	12	17	4.0	.948	3B-49, SS-7, OF-1
1962		7	.143	.143	14	2	0	0	0	0.0	0	0	0	6	0	2	1	5	4	0	1	2.3	1.000	3B-4
3 yrs.		77	.221	.349	249	55	12	1	6	2.4	23	25	9	67	0	2	1	84	169	14	18	3.6	.948	3B-66, SS-8, OF-1

Dave Leeper

LEEPER, DAVID DALE BL TL 5′11″ 170 lbs.
B. Oct. 30, 1959, Santa Ana, Calif.

Year	Team	Games	BA	SA	AB	H	2B	3B	HR	HR%	R	RBI	BB	SO	SB	Pinch Hit AB	Pinch Hit H	PO	A	E	DP	TC/G	FA	G by Pos
1984	KC A	4	.000	.000	6	0	0	0	0	0.0	1	0	0	1	0	1	0	4	0	0	0	1.3	1.000	OF-2, DH-1
1985		15	.088	.088	34	3	0	0	0	0.0	1	4	1	3	0	8	1	13	0	1	0	1.8	.929	OF-8
2 yrs.		19	.075	.075	40	3	0	0	0	0.0	2	4	1	4	0	9	1	17	0	1	0	1.6	.944	OF-10, DH-1

George Lees

LEES, GEORGE EDWARD BR TR 5′ 9″ 150 lbs.
B. Feb. 2, 1895, Bethlehem, Pa. D. Jan. 2, 1980, Mechanicsburg, Pa.

Year	Team	Games	BA	SA	AB	H	2B	3B	HR	HR%	R	RBI	BB	SO	SB	Pinch Hit AB	Pinch Hit H	PO	A	E	DP	TC/G	FA	G by Pos
1921	CHI A	20	.214	.262	42	9	2	0	0	0.0	3	4	0	3	0	4	0	32	7	2	1	2.6	.951	C-16

Bill Lefebvre

LEFEBVRE, WILFRID HENRY (Lefty) BL TL 5′11½″ 180 lbs.
B. Nov. 11, 1915, Natick, R. I.

Year	Team	Games	BA	SA	AB	H	2B	3B	HR	HR%	R	RBI	BB	SO	SB	Pinch Hit AB	Pinch Hit H	PO	A	E	DP	TC/G	FA	G by Pos
1938	BOS A	1	1.000	4.000	1	1	0	0	1	100.0	1	1	0	0	0	0	0	0	0	0	0	0.0	.000	P-1
1939		7	.300	.300	10	3	0	0	0	0.0	3	1	2	2	0	2	1	1	2	0	0	0.6	1.000	P-5
1943	WAS A	7	.286	.500	14	4	3	0	0	0.0	0	1	1	0	0	1	1	1	6	0	1	1.2	1.000	P-6
1944		60	.258	.355	62	16	2	2	0	0.0	4	8	12	9	0	29	**10**	17	14	1	3	1.2	.969	P-24, 1B-2
4 yrs.		75	.276	.414	87	24	5	2	1	1.1	8	11	15	11	0	32	12	19	22	1	4	1.1	.976	P-36, 1B-2

Jim Lefebvre

LEFEBVRE, JAMES KENNETH (Frenchy) BB TR 6′ 180 lbs.
B. Jan. 7, 1942, Inglewood, Calif.
Manager 1989–93.

Year	Team	Games	BA	SA	AB	H	2B	3B	HR	HR%	R	RBI	BB	SO	SB	Pinch Hit AB	Pinch Hit H	PO	A	E	DP	TC/G	FA	G by Pos
1965	LA N	157	.250	.369	544	136	21	4	12	2.2	57	69	71	92	3	2	1	349	429	24	91	5.1	.970	2B-156
1966		152	.274	.460	544	149	23	3	24	4.4	69	74	48	72	1	3	1	268	389	16	63	4.2	.976	2B-119, 3B-40
1967		136	.261	.366	494	129	18	5	8	1.6	51	50	44	64	1	7	0	173	321	18	39	3.9	.965	3B-92, 2B-34, 1B-5
1968		84	.241	.343	286	69	12	1	5	1.7	23	31	26	55	0	5	1	179	161	8	33	4.0	.977	2B-62, 3B-16, OF-5, 1B-3
1969		95	.236	.349	275	65	15	2	4	1.5	29	44	48	37	2	11	4	154	185	6	26	4.0	.983	3B-44, 2B-37, 1B-6
1970		109	.252	.344	314	79	15	1	4	1.3	33	44	29	42	1	17	3	168	212	6	41	4.2	.984	2B-70, 3B-20, 1B-1
1971		119	.245	.384	388	95	14	2	12	3.1	40	68	39	55	0	15	4	247	274	9	71	4.9	.983	2B-102, 3B-7
1972		70	.201	.337	169	34	8	0	5	3.0	11	24	17	30	0	25	6	70	99	4	24	3.9	.977	2B-33, 3B-11
8 yrs.		922	.251	.378	3014	756	126	18	74	2.5	313	404	322	447	8	85	20	1608	2070	91	388	4.4	.976	2B-613, 3B-230, 1B-15, OF-5
WORLD SERIES																								
1965	LA N	3	.400	.400	10	4	0	0	0	0.0	2	0	0	0	0	0	0	3	7	1	0	3.7	.909	2B-3
1966		4	.167	.417	12	2	0	0	1	8.3	1	1	3	4	0	0	0	10	10	0	3	5.0	1.000	2B-4
2 yrs.		7	.273	.409	22	6	0	0	1	4.5	3	1	3	4	0	0	0	13	17	1	3	4.4	.968	2B-7

Joe Lefebvre

LEFEBVRE, JOSEPH HENRY BL TR 5′10″ 170 lbs.
B. Feb. 22, 1956, Concord, N. H.

Year	Team	Games	BA	SA	AB	H	2B	3B	HR	HR%	R	RBI	BB	SO	SB	Pinch Hit AB	Pinch Hit H	PO	A	E	DP	TC/G	FA	G by Pos
1980	NY A	74	.227	.407	150	34	1	1	8	5.3	26	21	27	30	0	4	2	75	3	2	1	1.1	.975	OF-71
1981	SD N	86	.256	.439	246	63	13	4	8	3.3	31	31	35	33	6	5	2	167	6	1	2	2.1	.994	OF-84
1982		102	.238	.326	239	57	9	0	4	1.7	25	21	18	50	0	34	8	72	74	3	6	1.9	.980	3B-39, OF-36, C-3
1983	2 teams	SD N (18G –.250) PHI N (101G –.310)																						
″	total	119	.306	.522	278	85	20	8	8	2.9	35	39	33	49	5	40	11	105	22	5	1	1.3	.962	OF-80, 3B-13, C-5
1984	PHI N	52	.250	.362	160	40	9	0	3	1.9	22	18	23	37	0	8	4	83	4	3	1	1.9	.967	OF-47, 3B-1
1986		14	.111	.111	18	2	0	0	0	0.0	0	0	3	5	0	9	1	4	0	0	0	1.3	1.000	OF-3
6 yrs.		447	.258	.414	1091	281	52	13	31	2.8	139	130	139	204	11	100	28	506	109	14	11	1.6	.978	OF-321, 3B-53, C-8
LEAGUE CHAMPIONSHIP SERIES																								
1980	NY A	1	—	—	0	0	0	0	0	—	0	0	0	0	0	0	0	0	0	0	0	0.0	.000	OF-1
1983	PHI N	2	.000	.000	2	0	0	0	0	0.0	0	1	0	1	0	1	0	2	0	0	0	2.0	1.000	OF-1
2 yrs.		3	.000	.000	2	0	0	0	0	0.0	0	1	0	1	0	1	0	2	0	0	0	1.0	1.000	OF-2
WORLD SERIES																								
1983	PHI N	3	.200	.400	5	1	1	0	0	0.0	0	2	0	1	0	0	0	3	0	0	0	1.5	1.000	OF-2

Al LeFevre

LeFEVRE, ALFREDO MODESTO BR TR 5′10½″ 160 lbs.
B. Sept. 16, 1898, New York, N. Y. D. Jan. 21, 1982, Glen Cove, N. Y.

Year	Team	Games	BA	SA	AB	H	2B	3B	HR	HR%	R	RBI	BB	SO	SB	Pinch Hit AB	Pinch Hit H	PO	A	E	DP	TC/G	FA	G by Pos
1920	NY N	17	.148	.222	27	4	0	1	0	0.0	5	0	0	13	0	1	0	12	29	0	4	2.6	1.000	SS-9, 2B-6, 3B-1

Wade Lefler

LEFLER, WADE HAMPTON BL TR 5′11″ 162 lbs.
B. June 5, 1896, Cooleemee, N. C. D. Mar. 6, 1981, Hickory, N. C.

Year	Team	Games	BA	SA	AB	H	2B	3B	HR	HR%	R	RBI	BB	SO	SB	Pinch Hit AB	Pinch Hit H	PO	A	E	DP	TC/G	FA	G by Pos
1924	2 teams	BOS N (1G –.000) WAS A (5G –.625)																						
″	total	6	.556	.889	9	5	3	0	0	0.0	0	4	0	1	0	5	3	2	0	0	0	2.0	1.000	OF-1

Ron LeFlore

LeFLORE, RONALD BR TR 6′ 200 lbs.
B. June 16, 1948, Detroit, Mich.

Year	Team	Games	BA	SA	AB	H	2B	3B	HR	HR%	R	RBI	BB	SO	SB	Pinch Hit AB	Pinch Hit H	PO	A	E	DP	TC/G	FA	G by Pos
1974	DET A	59	.260	.323	254	66	8	1	2	0.8	37	13	13	58	23	0	0	151	8	11	3	2.9	.935	OF-59
1975		136	.258	.347	550	142	13	6	8	1.5	66	37	33	139	28	0	0	317	13	9	3	2.5	.973	OF-134
1976		135	.316	.410	544	172	23	8	4	0.7	93	39	51	111	58	1	0	381	14	11	1	3.1	.973	OF-132, DH-1
1977		154	.325	.475	652	212	30	10	16	2.5	100	57	37	121	39	3	2	365	12	11	0	2.5	.972	OF-154
1978		155	.297	.405	666	198	30	3	12	1.8	**126**	62	65	104	**68**	0	0	440	9	11	4	3.0	.976	OF-155
1979		148	.300	.415	600	180	22	10	9	1.5	110	57	52	95	78	1	1	293	6	3	3	2.1	.990	OF-113, DH-34
1980	MON N	139	.257	.363	521	134	21	11	4	0.8	95	39	62	99	**97**	1	1	233	14	11	1	2.0	.957	OF-130
1981	CHI A	82	.246	.300	337	83	10	4	0	0.0	46	24	28	70	36	0	0	162	6	7	2	2.1	.960	OF-82
1982		91	.287	.392	334	96	15	4	4	1.2	58	25	22	91	28	5	1	179	7	12	1	2.3	.939	OF-83, DH-2
9 yrs.		1099	.288	.392	4458	1283	172	57	59	1.3	731	353	363	888	455	11	5	2521	89	86	18	2.5	.968	OF-1042, DH-37

Lou Legett

LEGETT, LOUIS ALFRED (Doc) BR TR 5′10″ 166 lbs.
B. June 1, 1901, New Orleans, La. D. Mar. 6, 1988, New Orleans, La.

Year	Team	Games	BA	SA	AB	H	2B	3B	HR	HR%	R	RBI	BB	SO	SB	Pinch Hit AB	Pinch Hit H	PO	A	E	DP	TC/G	FA	G by Pos
1929	BOS N	39	.160	.185	81	13	2	0	0	0.0	7	6	3	18	2	9	2	58	16	7	1	2.9	.914	C-28
1933	BOS A	8	.200	.400	5	1	1	0	0	0.0	1	1	0	0	0	2	0	4	0	0	0	2.0	1.000	C-2
1934		19	.289	.289	38	11	0	0	0	0.0	4	1	2	4	0	1	1	36	7	1	0	2.6	.977	C-17
1935		2	—	—	0	0	0	0	0	—	1	0	0	0	0	0	0	0	0	0	0	0.0	—	
4 yrs.		68	.202	.226	124	25	3	0	0	0.0	13	8	5	22	2	12	3	98	23	8	1	2.7	.938	C-47

Greg Legg

LEGG, GREGORY LYNN BR TR 6′ 1″ 185 lbs.
B. Apr. 21, 1960, San Jose, Calif.

Year	Team	Games	BA	SA	AB	H	2B	3B	HR	HR%	R	RBI	BB	SO	SB	Pinch Hit AB	Pinch Hit H	PO	A	E	DP	TC/G	FA	G by Pos
1986	PHI N	11	.450	.500	20	9	1	0	0	0.0	2	1	0	3	0	6	2	4	16	1	1	4.2	.952	2B-4, SS-1
1987		3	.000	.000	2	0	0	0	0	0.0	1	0	0	0	0	0	0	3	1	0	1	1.3	1.000	SS-1, 2B-1, 3B-1
2 yrs.		14	.409	.455	22	9	1	0	0	0.0	3	1	0	3	0	6	2	7	17	1	2	3.1	.960	2B-5, SS-2, 3B-1

Mickey Lehane

LEHANE, MICHAEL PATRICK BR 6′ 1½″ 180 lbs.
B. Apr. 15, 1865, New York, N. Y. Deceased.

Year	Team	Games	BA	SA	AB	H	2B	3B	HR	HR%	R	RBI	BB	SO	SB	Pinch Hit AB	Pinch Hit H	PO	A	E	DP	TC/G	FA	G by Pos
1884	WAS U	3	.333	.500	12	4	2	0	0	0.0	1		0			0	0	1	10	5	0	3.2	.688	SS-3, OF-1, 3B-1
1890	COL AA	140	.211	.268	512	108	19	5	0	0.0	54		43		13	0	0	1430	73	27	80	10.9	.982	1B-140
1891		137	.215	.272	511	110	12	7	1	0.2	59	52	34	77	16	0	0	1362	71	28	98	10.7	.981	1B-137
3 yrs.		280	.214	.272	1035	222	33	12	1	0.1	114	52	77	77	29	0	0	2793	154	60	178	10.7	.980	1B-277, SS-3, OF-1, 3B-1

Paul Lehner

LEHNER, PAUL EUGENE (Gulliver) BL TL 5′ 9″ 160 lbs.
B. July 1, 1920, Dolomite, Ala. D. Dec. 27, 1967, Birmingham, Ala.

Year	Team	Games	BA	SA	AB	H	2B	3B	HR	HR%	R	RBI	BB	SO	SB	Pinch Hit AB	Pinch Hit H	PO	A	E	DP	TC/G	FA	G by Pos
1946	STL A	16	.222	.333	45	10	1	2	0	0.0	6	5	1	5	0	4	1	15	1	1	0	1.4	.941	OF-12
1947		135	.248	.381	483	120	25	9	7	1.4	59	48	28	29	5	6	2	344	1	7	0	2.8	.980	OF-127
1948		103	.276	.363	333	92	15	4	2	0.6	23	46	30	19	0	13	6	235	5	6	3	2.7	.976	OF-89, 1B-2
1949		104	.229	.303	297	68	13	0	3	1.0	25	37	16	20	0	26	7	314	14	4	13	4.5	.988	OF-55, 1B-18
1950	PHI A	114	.309	.436	427	132	17	5	9	2.1	48	52	32	33	1	8	3	247	10	5	1	2.6	.981	OF-101

Paul Lehner *continued*

Year	Team	Games	BA	SA	AB	H	2B	3B	HR	HR%	R	RBI	BB	SO	SB	Pinch Hit AB	Pinch Hit H	PO	A	E	DP	TC/G	FA	G by Pos
1951	**4 teams**	**PHI A** (9G –.143) **CHI A** (23G –.208) **STL A** (21G –.134) **CLE A** (12G –.231)																						
"	**total**	65	.172	.250	180	31	9	1	1	0.6	14	7	18	12	0	19	4	108	5	1	0	2.5	.991	OF-45
1952	**BOS A**	3	.667	.667	3	2	0	0	0	0.0	0	2	2	0	0	1	1	3	0	0	0	1.5	1.000	OF-2
7 yrs.		540	.257	.364	1768	455	80	21	22	1.2	175	197	127	118	6	77	24	1266	36	24	17	2.9	.982	OF-431, 1B-20

Clarence Lehr

LEHR, CLARENCE EMANUEL (King) BR TR 5′11″ 165 lbs.
B. May 16, 1886, Escanaba, Mich. D. Jan. 31, 1948, Highland Park, Mich.

Year	Team	Games	BA	SA	AB	H	2B	3B	HR	HR%	R	RBI	BB	SO	SB	Pinch Hit AB	Pinch Hit H	PO	A	E	DP	TC/G	FA	G by Pos
1911	**PHI N**	23	.148	.148	27	4	0	0	0	0.0	2	2	0	7	0	6	1	10	8	1	4	1.6	.947	OF-4, SS-4, 2B-4

Hank Leiber

LEIBER, HENRY EDWARD BR TR 6′ 1½″ 205 lbs.
B. Jan. 17, 1911, Phoenix, Ariz. D. Nov. 8, 1993, Tucson, Ariz.

Year	Team	Games	BA	SA	AB	H	2B	3B	HR	HR%	R	RBI	BB	SO	SB	Pinch Hit AB	Pinch Hit H	PO	A	E	DP	TC/G	FA	G by Pos
1933	**NY N**	6	.200	.200	10	2	0	0	0	0.0	1	0	0	2	0	5	0	3	1	0	0	4.0	1.000	OF-1
1934		63	.241	.332	187	45	5	3	2	1.1	17	25	4	13	1	12	2	99	3	3	1	2.1	.971	OF-51
1935		154	.331	.512	613	203	37	4	22	3.6	110	107	48	29	0	0	0	357	5	13	2	2.4	.965	OF-154
1936		101	.279	.457	337	94	19	7	9	2.7	44	67	37	41	1	12	1	165	9	7	3	2.1	.961	OF-86, 1B-1
1937		51	.293	.429	184	54	7	3	4	2.2	24	32	15	27	1	5	1	78	1	1	0	1.7	.988	OF-46
1938		98	.269	.442	360	97	18	4	12	3.3	50	65	31	45	0	8	3	181	6	5	3	2.2	.974	OF-89
1939	**CHI N**	112	.310	.556	365	113	16	1	24	6.6	65	88	59	42	1	8	1	249	5	6	0	2.7	.977	OF-98
1940		117	.302	.482	440	133	24	2	17	3.9	68	86	45	68	1	3	0	302	19	5	10	2.8	.985	OF-103, 1B-12
1941		53	.216	.377	162	35	5	0	7	4.3	20	25	16	25	0	9	0	192	8	5	13	4.7	.976	OF-29, 1B-15
1942	**NY N**	58	.218	.340	147	32	6	0	4	2.7	11	23	19	27	0	14	4	93	6	2	1	2.4	.980	OF-41, P-1
10 yrs.		813	.288	.462	2805	808	137	24	101	3.6	410	518	274	319	5	76	12	1719	63	47	33	2.5	.974	OF-698, 1B-28, P-1
WORLD SERIES																								
1936	**NY N**	2	.000	.000	6	0	0	0	0	0.0	0	0	2	2	0	0	0	13	1	0	1	7.0	1.000	OF-2
1937		3	.364	.364	11	4	0	0	0	0.0	2	2	1	1	0	0	0	7	0	0	0	2.3	1.000	OF-3
2 yrs.		5	.235	.235	17	4	0	0	0	0.0	2	2	3	3	0	0	0	20	1	0	1	4.2	1.000	OF-5

Nemo Leibold

LEIBOLD, HARRY LORAN BL TR 5′ 6½″ 157 lbs.
B. Feb. 17, 1892, Butler, Ind. D. Feb. 4, 1977, Detroit, Mich.

Year	Team	Games	BA	SA	AB	H	2B	3B	HR	HR%	R	RBI	BB	SO	SB	Pinch Hit AB	Pinch Hit H	PO	A	E	DP	TC/G	FA	G by Pos
1913	**CLE A**	84	.259	.339	286	74	11	6	0	0.0	37	12	21	43	16	10	1	142	12	9	1	2.3	.945	OF-72
1914		114	.264	.311	402	106	13	3	0	0.0	46	32	54	56	12	6	1	221	22	18	4	2.4	.931	OF-107
1915	**2 teams**	**CLE A** (57G –.256) **CHI A** (36G –.230)																						
"	**total**	93	.249	.299	281	70	6	4	0	0.0	38	15	39	27	6	14	5	204	15	5	0	3.0	.978	OF-75
1916	**CHI A**	45	.244	.305	82	20	1	2	0	0.0	5	13	7	7	7	20	4	31	1	0	2	1.3	1.000	OF-24
1917		125	.236	.292	428	101	12	6	0	0.0	59	29	74	34	27	3	0	204	18	9	3	1.9	.961	OF-122
1918		116	.250	.316	440	110	14	6	1	0.2	57	31	63	32	13	1	0	259	16	6	5	2.5	.979	OF-114
1919		122	.302	.353	434	131	18	2	0	0.0	81	26	72	30	17	0	0	218	26	19	4	2.2	.928	OF-122
1920		108	.220	.281	413	91	16	3	1	0.2	61	28	55	30	7	3	1	190	18	5	5	2.0	.977	OF-108
1921	**BOS A**	123	.306	.388	467	143	26	6	0	0.0	88	30	41	27	13	5	0	283	15	16	9	2.7	.949	OF-117
1922		81	.258	.306	271	70	8	1	1	0.4	42	18	41	14	1	9	3	190	10	7	3	2.9	.966	OF-71
1923	**2 teams**	**BOS A** (12G –.111) **WAS A** (95G –.305)																						
"	**total**	107	.294	.366	333	98	13	4	1	0.3	69	22	54	18	7	9	2	195	14	5	3	2.3	.977	OF-94
1924	**WAS A**	84	.293	.350	246	72	6	4	0	0.0	41	20	42	10	6	11	1	148	7	1	0	2.2	.994	OF-70
1925		56	.274	.310	84	23	1	1	0	0.0	14	7	8	7	1	19	3	34	3	1	1	1.4	.974	OF-26, 3B-1
13 yrs.		1258	.266	.327	4167	1109	145	48	4	0.1	638	283	571	335	133	110	21	2319	177	101	40	2.3	.961	OF-1122, 3B-1
WORLD SERIES																								
1917	**CHI A**	2	.400	.400	5	2	0	0	0	0.0	1	2	1	1	0	2	0	1	0	0	0	0.5	1.000	OF-2
1919		5	.056	.056	18	1	0	0	0	0.0	0	0	2	3	1	1	0	5	2	0	0	1.4	1.000	OF-5
1924	**WAS A**	3	.167	.333	6	1	1	0	0	0.0	1	0	1	0	0	2	1	2	0	0	0	2.0	1.000	OF-1
1925		3	.500	1.000	2	1	1	0	0	0.0	1	0	1	0	0	2	1	0	0	0	0	0.0	—	
4 yrs.		13	.161	.226	31	5	2	0	0	0.0	3	2	5	4	1	7	2	8	2	0	0	1.3	1.000	OF-8

Elmer Leifer

LEIFER, ELMER EDWIN BL TR 5′ 9½″ 170 lbs.
B. May 23, 1893, Clarington, Ohio D. Sept. 26, 1948, Everett, Wash.

Year	Team	Games	BA	SA	AB	H	2B	3B	HR	HR%	R	RBI	BB	SO	SB	Pinch Hit AB	Pinch Hit H	PO	A	E	DP	TC/G	FA	G by Pos
1921	**CHI A**	9	.300	.300	10	3	0	0	0	0.0	0	1	0	4	0	7	2	1	1	0	0	1.0	1.000	3B-1, OF-1

John Leighton

LEIGHTON, JOHN ATKINSON 5′11″ 170 lbs.
B. Oct. 4, 1861, Peabody, Mass. D. Oct. 31, 1956, Lynn, Mass.

Year	Team	Games	BA	SA	AB	H	2B	3B	HR	HR%	R	RBI	BB	SO	SB	Pinch Hit AB	Pinch Hit H	PO	A	E	DP	TC/G	FA	G by Pos
1890	**SYR AA**	7	.296	.370	27	8	2	0	0	0.0	6		3		2	0	0	15	0	1	0	2.3	.938	OF-7

Bill Leinhauser

LEINHAUSER, WILLIAM CHARLES BR TR 5′10″ 150 lbs.
B. Nov. 4, 1893, Philadelphia, Pa. D. Apr. 14, 1978, Elkins Park, Pa.

Year	Team	Games	BA	SA	AB	H	2B	3B	HR	HR%	R	RBI	BB	SO	SB	Pinch Hit AB	Pinch Hit H	PO	A	E	DP	TC/G	FA	G by Pos
1912	**DET A**	1	.000	.000	4	0	0	0	0	0.0	0	0	0		0	0	0	0	1	0	0	1.0	1.000	OF-1

Ed Leip

LEIP, EDGAR ELLSWORTH BR TR 5′ 9″ 160 lbs.
B. Nov. 29, 1910, Trenton, N. J. D. Nov. 24, 1983, Zephyrhills, Fla.

Year	Team	Games	BA	SA	AB	H	2B	3B	HR	HR%	R	RBI	BB	SO	SB	Pinch Hit AB	Pinch Hit H	PO	A	E	DP	TC/G	FA	G by Pos
1939	**WAS A**	9	.344	.375	32	11	1	0	0	0.0	4	2	2	4	0	1	0	15	24	2	5	5.1	.951	2B-8
1940	**PIT N**	3	.200	.200	5	1	0	0	0	0.0	2	0	0	0	0	0	0	2	2	0	1	2.0	1.000	2B-2
1941		15	.200	.360	25	5	0	2	0	0.0	1	3	1	2	1	3	0	10	19	4	2	4.1	.879	2B-7, 3B-1
1942		3	—	—	0	0	0	0	0	—	0	0	0	0	0	0	0	0	0	0	0	0.0	—	
4 yrs.		30	.274	.355	62	17	1	2	0	0.0	7	5	3	6	1	4	0	27	45	6	8	4.3	.923	2B-17, 3B-1

Scott Leius

LEIUS, SCOTT THOMAS BR TR 6′ 3″ 180 lbs.
B. Sept. 24, 1965, Yonkers, N. Y.

Year	Team	Games	BA	SA	AB	H	2B	3B	HR	HR%	R	RBI	BB	SO	SB	Pinch Hit AB	Pinch Hit H	PO	A	E	DP	TC/G	FA	G by Pos
1990	**MIN A**	14	.240	.400	25	6	1	0	1	4.0	4	4	2	2	0	0	0	20	25	0	10	3.5	1.000	SS-12, 3B-1
1991		109	.286	.417	199	57	7	2	5	2.5	35	20	30	35	5	25	11	56	129	7	15	1.9	.964	3B-79, SS-19, OF-2
1992		129	.249	.318	409	102	18	2	2	0.5	50	35	34	61	6	3	2	63	261	15	13	2.5	.956	3B-125, SS-10
1993		10	.167	.167	18	3	0	0	0	0.0	4	2	2	4	0	0	0	10	26	2	7	4.2	.947	SS-9
1994		97	.246	.417	350	86	16	1	14	4.0	57	49	37	58	2	5	1	63	184	8	13	2.6	.969	3B-95, SS-2
1995		117	.247	.349	372	92	16	5	4	1.1	51	45	49	54	2	8	3	60	185	14	21	2.1	.946	3B-112, SS-7, DH-3
6 yrs.		476	.252	.366	1373	346	58	10	26	1.9	201	155	154	214	15	41	17	272	810	46	79	2.4	.959	3B-412, SS-59, DH-3, OF-2

Scott Leius *continued*

LEAGUE CHAMPIONSHIP SERIES

Year	Team	Games	BA	SA	AB	H	2B	3B	HR	HR%	R	RBI	BB	SO	SB	Pinch Hit AB	Pinch Hit H	PO	A	E	DP	TC/G	FA	G by Pos
1991	MIN A	3	.000	.000	4	0	0	0	0	0.0	0	0	1	1	0	1	0	1	4	0	1	1.7	1.000	3B-3

WORLD SERIES

Year	Team	Games	BA	SA	AB	H	2B	3B	HR	HR%	R	RBI	BB	SO	SB	Pinch Hit AB	Pinch Hit H	PO	A	E	DP	TC/G	FA	G by Pos
1991	MIN A	7	.357	.571	14	5	0	0	1	7.1	2	2	1	2	0	1	0	5	8	1	0	2.0	.929	3B-6, SS-1

Frank Leja

LEJA, FRANK JOHN BL TL 6′ 4″ 205 lbs.
B. Feb. 7, 1936, Holyoke, Mass. D. May 3, 1991, Boston, Mass.

Year	Team	Games	BA	SA	AB	H	2B	3B	HR	HR%	R	RBI	BB	SO	SB	Pinch Hit AB	Pinch Hit H	PO	A	E	DP	TC/G	FA	G by Pos
1954	NY A	12	.200	.200	5	1	0	0	0	0.0	2	0	0	1	0	3	0	3	0	0	0	0.5	1.000	1B-6
1955		7	.000	.000	2	0	0	0	0	0.0	1	0	0	1	0	1	0	2	0	0	1	1.0	1.000	1B-2
1962	LA A	7	.000	.000	16	0	0	0	0	0.0	0	0	1	6	0	2	0	38	3	2	4	10.8	.953	1B-4
3 yrs.		26	.043	.043	23	1	0	0	0	0.0	3	0	1	8	0	6	0	43	3	2	5	4.0	.958	1B-12

Larry LeJeune

LeJEUNE, SHELDON ALDENBERT BR TR 6′ 180 lbs.
B. July 22, 1885, Chicago, Ill. D. Apr. 21, 1952, Eloise, Mich.

Year	Team	Games	BA	SA	AB	H	2B	3B	HR	HR%	R	RBI	BB	SO	SB	Pinch Hit AB	Pinch Hit H	PO	A	E	DP	TC/G	FA	G by Pos
1911	BKN N	6	.158	.158	19	3	0	0	0	0.0	2	2	2	8	2	0	0	9	0	2	0	1.8	.818	OF-6
1915	PIT N	18	.169	.200	65	11	0	1	0	0.0	4	2	2	7	4	0	0	43	4	3	1	2.8	.940	OF-18
2 yrs.		24	.167	.190	84	14	0	1	0	0.0	6	4	4	15	6	0	0	52	4	5	1	2.5	.918	OF-24

Don LeJohn

LeJOHN, DONALD EVERETT BR TR 5′10″ 175 lbs.
B. May 13, 1934, Daisytown, Pa.

Year	Team	Games	BA	SA	AB	H	2B	3B	HR	HR%	R	RBI	BB	SO	SB	Pinch Hit AB	Pinch Hit H	PO	A	E	DP	TC/G	FA	G by Pos
1965	LA N	34	.256	.282	78	20	2	0	0	0.0	2	7	5	13	0	10	2	9	38	2	2	1.9	.959	3B-26

WORLD SERIES

Year	Team	Games	BA	SA	AB	H	2B	3B	HR	HR%	R	RBI	BB	SO	SB	Pinch Hit AB	Pinch Hit H	PO	A	E	DP	TC/G	FA	G by Pos
1965	LA N	1	.000	.000	1	0	0	0	0	0.0	0	0	0	1	0	1	0	0	0	0	0	0.0	—	

Jack Lelivelt

LELIVELT, JOHN FRANK BL TL 5′11″ 175 lbs.
Brother of Bill Lelivelt.
B. Nov. 14, 1885, Chicago, Ill. D. Jan. 20, 1941, Seattle, Wash.

Year	Team	Games	BA	SA	AB	H	2B	3B	HR	HR%	R	RBI	BB	SO	SB	Pinch Hit AB	Pinch Hit H	PO	A	E	DP	TC/G	FA	G by Pos
1909	WAS A	91	.292	.355	318	93	8	6	0	0.0	25	24	19		8	0	0	179	14	6	3	2.2	.970	OF-91
1910		110	.265	.311	347	92	10	3	0	0.0	40	33	40		20	13	2	217	17	10	7	2.5	.959	OF-89, 1B-7
1911		72	.320	.409	225	72	12	4	0	0.0	29	22	22		7	16	6	142	18	9	2	3.0	.947	OF-49, 1B-7
1912	NY A	36	.362	.537	149	54	6	7	2	1.3	12	23	4		7	0	0	75	4	3	2	2.3	.963	OF-36
1913	**2 teams**	**NY A** (17G –.214) **CLE A** (23G –.391)																						
″	**total**	40	.294	.373	51	15	2	1	0	0.0	2	11	2	5	2	35	**12**	12	1	0	0	2.6	1.000	OF-5
1914	CLE A	32	.328	.438	64	21	5	1	0	0.0	6	13	2	10	2	19	5	15	0	1	0	1.2	.938	OF-12, 1B-1
6 yrs.		381	.301	.381	1154	347	43	22	2	0.2	114	126	89	15	46	83	25	640	54	29	14	2.4	.960	OF-282, 1B-15

Johnnie LeMaster

LeMASTER, JOHNNIE LEE BR TR 6′ 2″ 165 lbs.
B. June 19, 1954, Portsmouth, Ohio.

Year	Team	Games	BA	SA	AB	H	2B	3B	HR	HR%	R	RBI	BB	SO	SB	Pinch Hit AB	Pinch Hit H	PO	A	E	DP	TC/G	FA	G by Pos
1975	SF N	22	.189	.324	74	14	4	0	2	2.7	4	9	4	15	2	0	0	26	62	3	12	4.1	.967	SS-22
1976		33	.210	.280	100	21	3	2	0	0.0	9	9	2	21	2	2	0	54	109	11	17	5.6	.937	SS-31
1977		68	.149	.201	134	20	5	1	0	0.0	13	8	13	27	2	2	0	66	134	14	16	3.8	.935	SS-54, 3B-2
1978		101	.235	.335	272	64	18	3	1	0.4	23	14	21	45	6	0	0	135	261	14	40	4.2	.966	SS-96, 2B-2
1979		108	.254	.324	343	87	11	2	3	0.9	42	29	23	55	9	2	0	160	303	20	32	4.6	.959	SS-106
1980		135	.215	.306	405	87	16	6	3	0.7	33	31	25	57	0	0	0	200	372	26	54	4.5	.957	SS-134
1981		104	.253	.287	324	82	9	1	0	0.0	27	28	24	46	3	0	0	166	294	17	57	4.6	.964	SS-103
1982		130	.216	.266	436	94	14	1	2	0.5	34	30	31	78	13	0	0	223	382	23	63	4.8	.963	SS-130
1983		141	.240	.307	534	128	16	1	6	1.1	81	30	60	96	39	1	0	215	402	23	58	4.6	.964	SS-139
1984		132	.217	.282	451	98	13	2	4	0.9	46	32	31	97	17	1	1	222	391	23	70	4.9	.964	SS-129
1985	**3 teams**	**SF N** (12G –.000) **CLE A** (11G –.150) **PIT N** (22G –.155)																						
″	**total**	45	.128	.160	94	12	0	0	1	1.1	5	8	6	23	1	1	0	74	98	5	20	4.3	.972	SS-41
1987	OAK A	20	.083	.083	24	2	0	0	0	0.0	3	1	1	4	0	0	0	14	24	1	5	2.0	.974	3B-8, SS-7, 2B-5
12 yrs.		1039	.222	.289	3191	709	109	19	22	0.7	320	229	241	564	94	9	1	1555	2832	180	444	4.5	.961	SS-992, 3B-10, 2B-7

Steve Lembo

LEMBO, STEPHEN NEAL BR TR 6′ 1″ 185 lbs.
B. Nov. 13, 1926, Brooklyn, N. Y. D. Dec. 4, 1989, Flushing, N. Y.

Year	Team	Games	BA	SA	AB	H	2B	3B	HR	HR%	R	RBI	BB	SO	SB	Pinch Hit AB	Pinch Hit H	PO	A	E	DP	TC/G	FA	G by Pos
1950	BKN N	5	.167	.167	6	1	0	0	0	0.0	0	0	1	0	0	0	0	16	3	0	1	3.8	1.000	C-5
1952		2	.200	.200	5	1	0	0	0	0.0	0	1	0	1	0	0	0	9	0	0	0	4.5	1.000	C-2
2 yrs.		7	.182	.182	11	2	0	0	0	0.0	0	1	1	1	0	0	0	25	3	0	1	4.0	1.000	C-7

Mark Lemke

LEMKE, MARK ALAN BB TR 5′10″ 167 lbs.
B. Aug. 13, 1965, Utica, N. Y.

Year	Team	Games	BA	SA	AB	H	2B	3B	HR	HR%	R	RBI	BB	SO	SB	Pinch Hit AB	Pinch Hit H	PO	A	E	DP	TC/G	FA	G by Pos
1988	ATL N	16	.224	.293	58	13	4	0	0	0.0	8	2	4	5	0	0	0	47	51	3	11	6.3	.970	2B-16
1989		14	.182	.364	55	10	2	1	2	3.6	4	10	5	7	0	1	1	25	40	0	7	4.6	1.000	2B-14
1990		102	.226	.280	239	54	13	0	0	0.0	22	21	21	22	0	15	2	90	193	4	29	3.2	.986	3B-45, 2B-44, SS-1
1991		136	.234	.312	269	63	11	2	2	0.7	36	23	29	27	1	27	9	162	215	10	40	3.1	.974	2B-110, 3B-15
1992		155	.227	.304	427	97	7	4	6	1.4	38	26	50	39	0	10	0	236	335	9	56	3.7	.984	2B-145, 3B-13
1993		151	.252	.341	493	124	19	2	7	1.4	52	49	65	50	1	1	0	329	442	14	100	5.2	.982	2B-150
1994		104	.294	.363	350	103	15	0	3	0.9	40	31	38	37	0	2	0	208	300	3	54	5.0	.994	2B-103
1995		116	.253	.356	399	101	16	5	5	1.3	42	38	44	40	2	1	0	205	305	5	61	4.5	.990	2B-115
8 yrs.		794	.247	.330	2290	565	87	14	25	1.1	242	200	256	227	4	57	12	1302	1881	48	358	4.2	.985	2B-697, 3B-73, SS-1

DIVISIONAL PLAYOFF SERIES

Year	Team	Games	BA	SA	AB	H	2B	3B	HR	HR%	R	RBI	BB	SO	SB	Pinch Hit AB	Pinch Hit H	PO	A	E	DP	TC/G	FA	G by Pos
1995	ATL N	4	.211	.263	19	4	1	0	0	0.0	3	1	1	3	0	0	0	8	16	0	3	6.0	1.000	2B-4

LEAGUE CHAMPIONSHIP SERIES

Year	Team	Games	BA	SA	AB	H	2B	3B	HR	HR%	R	RBI	BB	SO	SB	Pinch Hit AB	Pinch Hit H	PO	A	E	DP	TC/G	FA	G by Pos
1991	ATL N	7	.200	.250	20	4	1	0	0	0.0	1	1	4	0	0	0	0	12	10	1	2	3.3	.957	2B-7
1992		7	.333	.381	21	7	1	0	0	0.0	2	2	5	3	0	0	0	11	16	0	3	3.4	1.000	2B-7, 3B-1
1993		6	.208	.292	24	5	2	0	0	0.0	2	4	1	6	0	0	0	6	19	2	1	4.5	.926	2B-6
1995		4	.167	.167	18	3	0	0	0	0.0	2	1	1	0	0	0	0	13	16	0	5	7.3	1.000	2B-4
4 yrs.		24	.229	.277	83	19	4	0	0	0.0	7	8	11	9	0	0	0	42	61	3	11	4.2	.972	2B-24, 3B-1
													9th											

Mark Lemke *continued*

Year	Team	Games	BA	SA	AB	H	2B	3B	HR	HR%	R	RBI	BB	SO	SB	Pinch Hit AB	Pinch Hit H	PO	A	E	DP	TC/G	FA	G by Pos
WORLD SERIES																								
1991	ATL N	6	.417	.708	24	10	1	3	0	0.0	4	4	2	4	0	0	0	14	19	1	4	5.7	.971	2B-6
1992		6	.211	.211	19	4	0	0	0	0.0	0	2	1	3	0	0	0	19	12	0	5	5.2	1.000	2B-6
1995		6	.273	.273	22	6	0	0	0	0.0	1	0	3	2	0	0	0	10	24	1	2	5.8	.971	2B-6
3 yrs.		18	.308	.415	65	20	1	3 **4th**	0	0.0	5	6	6	9	0	0	0	43	55	2	11	5.6	.980	2B-18

Bob Lemon

LEMON, ROBERT GRANVILLE BL TR 6′ 180 lbs.
B. Sept. 22, 1920, San Bernardino, Calif.
Manager 1970–72, 1977–79, 1981–82.
Hall of Fame 1976.

Year	Team	Games	BA	SA	AB	H	2B	3B	HR	HR%	R	RBI	BB	SO	SB	Pinch Hit AB	Pinch Hit H	PO	A	E	DP	TC/G	FA	G by Pos
1941	CLE A	5	.250	.250	4	1	0	0	0	0.0	0	0	0	1	0	3	1	1	1	0	0	2.0	1.000	3B-1
1942		5	.000	.000	5	0	0	0	0	0.0	0	0	0	3	0	3	0	0	1	1	0	2.0	.500	3B-1
1946		55	.180	.247	89	16	3	0	1	1.1	9	4	7	18	0	7	1	46	30	2	7	1.8	.974	P-32, OF-12
1947		47	.321	.607	56	18	4	3	2	3.6	11	5	6	9	0	3	1	13	46	1	4	1.5	.983	P-37, OF-2
1948		52	.286	.487	119	34	9	0	5	4.2	20	21	8	23	0	4	1	23	86	4	8	2.6	.965	P-43
1949		46	.269	.556	108	29	6	2	7	6.5	17	19	10	20	0	8	4	34	71	4	5	2.9	.963	P-37
1950		72	.272	.485	136	37	9	1	6	4.4	21	26	13	25	0	26	6	22	66	4	6	2.1	.957	P-44
1951		56	.206	.353	102	21	4	1	3	2.9	11	13	9	22	0	14	4	21	60	2	5	2.0	.976	P-42
1952		54	.226	.315	124	28	5	0	2	1.6	14	9	4	21	0	8	1	32	79	2	7	2.7	.982	P-42
1953		51	.232	.384	112	26	9	1	2	1.8	12	17	7	20	2	6	1	31	74	3	15	2.6	.972	P-41
1954		40	.214	.337	98	21	4	1	2	2.0	11	10	6	24	0	3	1	22	57	3	8	2.3	.963	P-36
1955		49	.244	.282	78	19	0	0	1	1.3	11	9	13	16	0	9	4	16	43	1	3	1.7	.983	P-35
1956		43	.194	.355	93	18	0	0	5	5.4	8	12	9	21	0	5	3	24	61	6	6	2.3	.934	P-39
1957		25	.065	.152	46	3	1	0	1	2.2	2	1	0	14	0	4	0	12	31	0	5	2.0	1.000	P-21
1958		15	.231	.231	13	3	0	0	0	0.0	1	1	1	4	0	6	3	1	7	0	1	0.7	1.000	P-11
15 yrs.		615	.232	.386	1183	274	54	9	37	3.1	148	147	93	241	2	109	31	298	713	33	80	2.2	.968	P-460, OF-14, 3B-2
WORLD SERIES																								
1948	CLE A	2	.000	.000	7	0	0	0	0	0.0	0	0	0	0	0	0	0	3	9	0	1	6.0	1.000	P-2
1954		3	.000	.000	6	0	0	0	0	0.0	0	0	1	1	0	1	0	2	2	0	0	2.0	1.000	P-2
2 yrs.		5	.000	.000	13	0	0	0	0	0.0	0	0	1	1	0	1	0	5	11	0	1	4.0	1.000	P-4

Chet Lemon

LEMON, CHESTER EARL BR TR 6′ 185 lbs.
B. Feb. 12, 1955, Jackson, Miss.

Year	Team	Games	BA	SA	AB	H	2B	3B	HR	HR%	R	RBI	BB	SO	SB	Pinch Hit AB	Pinch Hit H	PO	A	E	DP	TC/G	FA	G by Pos
1975	CHI A	9	.257	.314	35	9	2	0	0	0.0	2	1	2	6	1	1	0	5	7	1	0	1.4	.923	3B-6, DH-2, OF-1
1976		132	.246	.328	451	111	15	5	4	0.9	46	38	28	65	13	1	0	353	12	3	1	2.8	.992	OF-131
1977		150	.273	.459	553	151	38	4	19	3.4	99	67	52	88	8	0	0	512	12	12	2	3.6	.978	OF-149
1978		105	.300	.510	357	107	24	6	13	3.6	51	55	39	46	5	1	0	284	8	5	2	2.8	.983	OF-95, DH-10
1979		148	.318	.496	556	177	**44**	2	17	3.1	79	86	56	68	7	0	0	411	10	10	2	2.9	.977	OF-147, DH-1
1980		147	.292	.442	514	150	32	6	11	2.1	76	51	71	56	6	1	0	347	11	7	2	2.5	.981	OF-139, DH-6, 2B-1
1981		94	.302	.491	328	99	23	6	9	2.7	50	50	33	48	5	0	0	240	2	4	1	2.6	.984	OF-93
1982	DET A	125	.266	.447	436	116	20	1	19	4.4	75	52	56	69	1	2	1	242	11	4	2	2.1	.984	OF-121, DH-1
1983		145	.255	.464	491	125	21	5	24	4.9	78	69	54	70	0	2	1	406	6	5	3	2.9	.988	OF-145
1984		141	.287	.495	509	146	34	6	20	3.9	77	76	51	83	5	3	1	427	6	2	1	3.1	.995	OF-140, DH-1
1985		145	.265	.439	517	137	28	4	18	3.5	69	68	45	93	0	1	0	411	6	4	3	2.9	.990	OF-144
1986		126	.251	.407	403	101	21	3	12	3.0	45	53	39	53	2	8	2	316	6	5	1	2.6	.985	OF-124
1987		146	.277	.481	470	130	30	3	20	4.3	75	75	70	82	0	11	5	350	4	3	1	2.5	.992	OF-145
1988		144	.264	.436	512	135	29	4	17	3.3	67	64	59	65	1	2	0	296	8	8	3	2.2	.974	OF-144
1989		127	.237	.343	414	98	19	2	7	1.7	45	47	46	71	1	13	4	189	6	3	0	1.6	.985	OF-111, DH-13
1990		104	.258	.379	322	83	16	4	5	1.6	39	32	48	61	3	9	2	209	7	6	1	2.2	.973	OF-96, DH-6
16 yrs.		1988	.273	.442	6868	1875	396	61	215	3.1	973	884	749	1024	58	55	16	4998	122	82	25	2.6	.984	OF-1925, DH-40, 3B-6, 2B-1
LEAGUE CHAMPIONSHIP SERIES																								
1984	DET A	3	.000	.000	13	0	0	0	0	0.0	1	0	0	1	0	0	0	9	0	0	0	3.0	1.000	OF-3
1987		5	.278	.611	18	5	0	0	2	11.1	4	4	1	4	0	0	0	13	0	0	0	2.6	1.000	OF-5
2 yrs.		8	.161	.355	31	5	0	0	2	6.5	5	4	1	5	0	0	0	22	0	0	0	2.8	1.000	OF-8
WORLD SERIES																								
1984	DET A	5	.294	.294	17	5	0	0	0	0.0	1	1	2	2	2	0	0	15	0	0	0	3.0	1.000	OF-5

Jim Lemon

LEMON, JAMES ROBERT BR TR 6′ 4″ 200 lbs.
B. Mar. 23, 1928, Covington, Va.
Manager 1968.

Year	Team	Games	BA	SA	AB	H	2B	3B	HR	HR%	R	RBI	BB	SO	SB	Pinch Hit AB	Pinch Hit H	PO	A	E	DP	TC/G	FA	G by Pos
1950	CLE A	12	.176	.294	34	6	1	0	1	2.9	4	1	3	12	0	3	1	13	1	3	1	1.7	.824	OF-10
1953		16	.174	.261	46	8	1	0	1	2.2	5	5	3	15	0	3	0	26	1	4	0	2.4	.871	OF-11, 1B-2
1954	WAS A	37	.234	.344	128	30	2	3	2	1.6	12	13	9	34	0	4	1	58	0	3	0	1.8	.951	OF-33
1955		10	.200	.400	25	5	2	0	1	4.0	3	3	3	4	0	3	2	12	0	1	0	2.2	.923	OF-6
1956		146	.271	.502	538	146	21	**11**	27	5.0	77	96	65	**138**	2	4	1	301	11	12	6	2.3	.963	OF-141
1957		137	.284	.448	518	147	22	6	17	3.3	58	64	49	**94**	1	4	1	253	8	10	2	2.0	.963	OF-131, 1B-3
1958		142	.246	.467	501	123	15	9	26	5.2	65	75	50	**120**	2	8	3	255	8	6	2	2.0	.978	OF-137
1959		147	.279	.510	531	148	18	3	33	6.2	73	100	46	99	5	5	1	281	4	9	0	2.1	.969	OF-142
1960		148	.269	.508	528	142	10	1	38	7.2	81	100	67	114	2	5	1	251	11	11	1	1.9	.960	OF-145
1961	MIN A	129	.258	.423	423	109	26	1	14	3.3	57	52	44	98	1	10	2	182	7	12	0	1.7	.940	OF-120
1962		12	.176	.353	17	3	0	0	1	5.9	1	5	3	4	0	8	3	1	0	0	0	0.3	1.000	OF-3
1963	3 teams	**MIN A** (7G –.118) **PHI N** (31G –.271) **CHI A** (36G –.200)																						
″	total	74	.218	.301	156	34	2	1	3	1.9	10	15	21	55	0	26	6	166	7	5	18	3.8	.972	1B-25, OF-22
12 yrs.		1010	.262	.460	3445	901	120	35	164	4.8	446	529	363	787	13	83	22	1799	58	76	30	2.1	.961	OF-901, 1B-30

Don Lenhardt

LENHARDT, DONALD EUGENE (Footsie) B. Oct. 4, 1922, Alton, Ill. BR TR 6′ 3″ 190 lbs.

Year	Team	Games	BA	SA	AB	H	2B	3B	HR	HR%	R	RBI	BB	SO	SB	Pinch Hit AB	Pinch Hit H	PO	A	E	DP	TC/G	FA	G by Pos
1950	STL A	139	.273	.481	480	131	22	6	22	4.6	75	81	90	94	3	10	3	709	58	11	79	5.8	.986	1B-86, OF-39, 3B-10
1951	2 teams	STL A (31G –.262) CHI A (64G –.266)																						
″	total	95	.265	.460	302	80	12	1	15	5.0	32	63	30	38	2	13	3	179	2	3	0	2.2	.984	OF-80, 1B-3
1952	3 teams	BOS A (30G –.295) DET A (45G –.188) STL A (18G –.271)																						
″	total	93	.239	.397	297	71	10	2	11	3.7	41	42	47	44	0	10	2	177	7	2	6	2.2	.989	OF-81, 1B-2
1953	STL A	97	.317	.465	303	96	15	0	10	3.3	37	35	41	41	1	17	4	153	16	6	1	2.1	.966	OF-77, 3B-6
1954	2 teams	BAL A (13G –.152) BOS A (44G –.273)																						
″	total	57	.232	.374	99	23	5	0	3	3.0	7	18	6	18	0	35	6	37	6	0	0	1.9	1.000	OF-20, 1B-2, 3B-1
5 yrs.		481	.271	.450	1481	401	64	9	61	4.1	192	239	214	235	6	85	18	1255	89	22	86	3.4	.984	OF-297, 1B-93, 3B-17

Bob Lennon

LENNON, ROBERT ALBERT (Arch) B. Sept. 15, 1928, Brooklyn, N. Y. BL TL 6′ 200 lbs.

Year	Team	Games	BA	SA	AB	H	2B	3B	HR	HR%	R	RBI	BB	SO	SB	Pinch Hit AB	Pinch Hit H	PO	A	E	DP	TC/G	FA	G by Pos
1954	NY N	3	.000	.000	3	0	0	0	0	0.0	0	0	0	0	0	3	0	0	0	0	0	0.0	—	
1956		26	.182	.200	55	10	1	0	0	0.0	3	1	4	17	0	3	0	21	2	3	2	1.2	.885	OF-21
1957	CHI N	9	.143	.333	21	3	1	0	1	4.8	2	3	1	9	0	5	0	4	0	0	0	1.0	1.000	OF-4
3 yrs.		38	.165	.228	79	13	2	0	1	1.3	5	4	5	26	0	11	0	25	2	3	2	1.2	.900	OF-25

Patrick Lennon

LENNON, PATRICK ORLANDO B. Apr. 27, 1968, Whiteville, N. C. BR TR 6′ 2″ 200 lbs.

Year	Team	Games	BA	SA	AB	H	2B	3B	HR	HR%	R	RBI	BB	SO	SB	Pinch Hit AB	Pinch Hit H	PO	A	E	DP	TC/G	FA	G by Pos
1991	SEA A	9	.125	.250	8	1	1	0	0	0.0	2	1	3	1	0	4	1	2	0	0	0	0.3	1.000	DH-5, OF-1
1992		1	.000	.000	2	0	0	0	0	0.0	0	0	0	0	0	0	0	5	0	0	1	5.0	1.000	1B-1
2 yrs.		10	.100	.200	10	1	1	0	0	0.0	2	1	3	1	0	4	1	7	0	0	1	1.0	1.000	DH-5, 1B-1, OF-1

Ed Lennox

LENNOX, JAMES EDGAR (Eggie) B. Nov. 3, 1885, Camden, N. J. D. Oct. 26, 1939, Camden, N. J. BR TR 5′10″ 174 lbs.

Year	Team	Games	BA	SA	AB	H	2B	3B	HR	HR%	R	RBI	BB	SO	SB	Pinch Hit AB	Pinch Hit H	PO	A	E	DP	TC/G	FA	G by Pos
1906	PHI A	6	.059	.118	17	1	1	0	0	0.0	1	0	1		0	0	0	9	21	3	0	5.5	.909	3B-6
1909	BKN N	126	.262	.359	435	114	18	9	2	0.5	33	44	47		11	5	1	167	210	16	18	3.2	.959	3B-121
1910		110	.259	.357	367	95	19	4	3	0.8	19	32	36	39	7	10	1	135	149	15	14	3.0	.950	3B-100
1912	CHI N	27	.235	.346	81	19	4	1	1	1.2	13	16	12	10	1	2	1	25	32	4	1	2.5	.934	3B-24
1914	PIT F	124	.312	.493	430	134	25	10	11	2.6	71	84	71		19	1	0	136	193	16	12	2.8	.954	3B-123
1915		55	.302	.453	53	16	3	1	1	1.9	1	9	7		0	**45**	**14**	5	10	0	0	5.0	1.000	3B-3
6 yrs.		448	.274	.400	1383	379	70	25	18	1.3	138	185	174	49	38	63	17	477	615	54	45	3.0	.953	3B-377

Jim Lentine

LENTINE, JAMES MATTHEW B. July 16, 1954, Los Angeles, Calif. BR TR 6′ 175 lbs.

Year	Team	Games	BA	SA	AB	H	2B	3B	HR	HR%	R	RBI	BB	SO	SB	Pinch Hit AB	Pinch Hit H	PO	A	E	DP	TC/G	FA	G by Pos
1978	STL N	8	.182	.182	11	2	0	0	0	0.0	1	1	0	0	1	1	0	4	0	0	0	1.3	1.000	OF-3
1979		11	.391	.435	23	9	1	0	0	0.0	2	1	3	6	0	3	2	12	1	0	1	1.6	1.000	OF-8
1980	2 teams	STL N (9G –.100) DET A (67G –.261)																						
″	total	76	.251	.327	171	43	8	1	1	0.6	20	18	28	32	2	10	2	102	5	4	0	1.6	.964	OF-61, DH-9
3 yrs.		95	.263	.332	205	54	9	1	1	0.5	23	20	31	38	3	14	4	118	6	4	1	1.6	.969	OF-72, DH-9

Eddie Leon

LEON, EDUARDO ANTONIO B. Aug. 11, 1946, Tucson, Ariz. BR TR 6′ 170 lbs.

Year	Team	Games	BA	SA	AB	H	2B	3B	HR	HR%	R	RBI	BB	SO	SB	Pinch Hit AB	Pinch Hit H	PO	A	E	DP	TC/G	FA	G by Pos
1968	CLE A	6	.000	.000	1	0	0	0	0	0.0	0	0	0	1	0	0	0	3	5	0	3	1.3	1.000	SS-6
1969		64	.239	.310	213	51	6	0	3	1.4	20	19	19	37	2	0	0	114	185	15	43	4.9	.952	SS-64
1970		152	.248	.353	549	136	20	4	10	1.8	58	56	47	89	1	0	0	368	419	18	112	4.9	.978	2B-141, SS-23, 3B-1
1971		131	.261	.326	429	112	12	2	4	0.9	35	35	34	69	3	4	1	271	325	12	84	4.6	.980	2B-107, SS-24
1972		89	.200	.271	225	45	2	1	4	1.8	14	16	20	47	0	23	5	103	179	6	39	4.1	.979	2B-36, SS-35
1973	CHI A	127	.228	.291	399	91	10	3	3	0.8	37	30	34	103	1	2	0	202	392	17	80	4.9	.972	SS-122, 2B-3
1974		31	.109	.130	46	5	1	0	0	0.0	1	3	2	12	0	0	0	37	49	3	18	2.9	.966	SS-21, 2B-7, 3B-2, DH-1
1975	NY A	1	—	—	0	0	0	0	0	—	0	0	0	0	0	0	0	0	0	0	0	0.0	.000	SS-1
8 yrs.		601	.236	.313	1862	440	51	10	24	1.3	165	159	156	358	7	29	6	1098	1554	71	379	4.6	.974	SS-296, 2B-294, 3B-3, DH-1

Leonard

LEONARD Deceased.

Year	Team	Games	BA	SA	AB	H	2B	3B	HR	HR%	R	RBI	BB	SO	SB	Pinch Hit AB	Pinch Hit H	PO	A	E	DP	TC/G	FA	G by Pos
1892	STL N	1	—	—	0	0	0	0	0	—	0	0	0	0	0	0	0	0	0	0	0	0.0	.000	OF-1

Andy Leonard

LEONARD, ANDREW JACKSON B. June 1, 1846, County Cavan, Ireland D. Aug. 21, 1903, Boston, Mass. BR TR 5′ 7″ 168 lbs.

Year	Team	Games	BA	SA	AB	H	2B	3B	HR	HR%	R	RBI	BB	SO	SB	Pinch Hit AB	Pinch Hit H	PO	A	E	DP	TC/G	FA	G by Pos
1876	BOS N	64	.281	.327	303	85	10	2	0	0.0	53	27	4	6		0	0	157	87	35	12	4.3	.875	OF-35, 2B-30
1877		58	.287	.305	272	78	5	0	0	0.0	46	27	5	5		0	0	107	53	24	5	3.2	.870	OF-37, SS-21
1878		60	.260	.328	262	68	8	5	0	0.0	41	16	3	19		0	0	65	8	21	1	1.6	.777	OF-60
1880	CIN N	33	.211	.256	133	28	3	0	1	0.8	15	17	8	11		0	0	29	75	21	4	3.8	.832	SS-23, 3B-10
4 yrs.		215	.267	.311	970	259	26	7	1	0.1	155	87	20	41		0	0	358	223	101	22	3.2	.852	OF-132, SS-44, 2B-30, 3B-10

Jeffrey Leonard

LEONARD, JEFFREY (Hac-Man) B. Sept. 22, 1955, Philadelphia, Pa. BR TR 6′ 2″ 200 lbs.

Year	Team	Games	BA	SA	AB	H	2B	3B	HR	HR%	R	RBI	BB	SO	SB	Pinch Hit AB	Pinch Hit H	PO	A	E	DP	TC/G	FA	G by Pos
1977	LA N	11	.300	.500	10	3	0	1	0	0.0	1	2	1	4	0	3	0	7	0	0	0	0.7	1.000	OF-10
1978	HOU N	8	.385	.462	26	10	2	0	0	0.0	2	4	1	2	0	1	0	16	1	0	1	2.1	1.000	OF-8
1979		134	.290	.350	411	119	15	5	0	0.0	47	47	46	68	23	11	2	227	6	10	1	2.0	.959	OF-123
1980		88	.213	.333	216	46	7	5	3	1.4	29	20	19	46	4	24	6	161	9	3	7	2.6	.983	OF-56, 1B-11
1981	2 teams	HOU N (7G –.167) SF N (37G –.307)																						
″	total	44	.290	.510	145	42	12	4	4	2.8	21	29	12	25	5	6	1	152	5	1	5	4.3	.994	1B-30, OF-7
1982	SF N	80	.259	.421	278	72	16	1	9	3.2	32	49	19	65	18	2	1	137	2	9	0	2.0	.939	OF-74, 1B-1
1983		139	.279	.461	516	144	17	7	21	4.1	74	87	35	116	26	4	2	253	17	7	2	2.0	.975	OF-136
1984		136	.302	.484	514	155	27	2	21	4.1	76	86	47	123	17	4	0	247	14	8	4	2.1	.970	OF-131
1985		133	.241	.393	507	122	20	3	17	3.4	49	62	21	107	11	7	1	203	10	5	0	1.7	.977	OF-126
1986		89	.279	.381	341	95	11	3	6	1.8	48	42	20	62	16	4	2	158	4	5	1	1.9	.970	OF-87
1987		131	.280	.467	503	141	29	4	19	3.8	70	63	21	68	16	11	6	193	7	7	2	1.6	.966	OF-127
1988	2 teams	SF N (44G –.256) MIL A (94G –.235)																						
″	total	138	.242	.352	534	129	27	1	10	1.9	57	64	25	92	17	3	0	265	4	4	1	2.0	.985	OF-134, DH-2

Jeffrey Leonard *continued*

Year	Team	Games	BA	SA	AB	H	2B	3B	HR	HR%	R	RBI	BB	SO	SB	Pinch Hit AB	Pinch Hit H	PO	A	E	DP	TC/G	FA	G by Pos
1989	SEA A	150	.254	.420	566	144	20	1	24	4.2	69	93	38	125	6	2	0	54	2	1	0	0.4	.982	DH-123, OF-26
1990		134	.251	.356	478	120	20	0	10	2.1	39	75	37	97	4	9	2	118	0	2	0	0.9	.983	OF-79, DH-48
14 yrs.		1415	.266	.411	5045	1342	223	37	144	2.9	614	723	342	1000	163	91	23	2191	81	62	24	1.7	.973	OF-1124, DH-173, 1B-42
LEAGUE CHAMPIONSHIP SERIES																								
1980	HOU N	3	.000	.000	3	0	0	0	0	0.0	0	0	0	2	0	2	0	2	1	0	1	3.0	1.000	OF-1
1987	SF N	7	.417	.917	24	10	0	0	4	16.7	5	5	3	4	0	0	0	14	1	0	0	2.1	1.000	OF-7
2 yrs.		10	.370	.815	27	10	0	0	4	14.8	5	5	3	6	0	2	0	16	2	0	1	2.3	1.000	OF-8

Joe Leonard

LEONARD, JOSEPH HOWARD BL TR 5′7½″ 156 lbs.
B. Nov. 15, 1894, West Chicago, Ill. D. May 1, 1920, Washington, D. C.

Year	Team	Games	BA	SA	AB	H	2B	3B	HR	HR%	R	RBI	BB	SO	SB	Pinch Hit AB	Pinch Hit H	PO	A	E	DP	TC/G	FA	G by Pos
1914	PIT N	53	.198	.246	126	25	2	2	0	0.0	17	4	12	21	4	7	0	29	52	8	2	2.3	.910	3B-38, SS-1
1916	2 teams	CLE A (3G –.000) WAS A (42G –.274)																						
″	total	45	.271	.312	170	46	7	0	0	0.0	21	14	22	24	4	1	0	54	66	6	6	2.9	.952	3B-42, 2B-1
1917	WAS A	99	.192	.259	297	57	6	7	0	0.0	30	23	45	40	6	9	3	252	134	16	32	4.5	.960	3B-67, 1B-20, SS-1, OF-1
1919		71	.258	.359	198	51	8	3	2	1.0	26	20	20	28	3	6	1	112	99	8	14	3.8	.963	2B-28, 3B-25, 1B-4, OF-1
1920		1	—	—	0	0	0	0	0	—	0		0			0	0	0	0	0	0	0.0	—	
5 yrs.		269	.226	.293	791	179	23	12	2	0.3	94	61	99	113	17	23	4	447	351	38	54	3.7	.955	3B-172, 2B-29, 1B-24, OF-2, SS-2

Mark Leonard

LEONARD, MARK DAVID BL TR 6′1″ 195 lbs.
B. Aug. 14, 1964, Mountain View, Calif.

Year	Team	Games	BA	SA	AB	H	2B	3B	HR	HR%	R	RBI	BB	SO	SB	Pinch Hit AB	Pinch Hit H	PO	A	E	DP	TC/G	FA	G by Pos
1990	SF N	11	.176	.412	17	3	1	0	1	5.9	3	2	3	8	0	4	0	10	0	0	0	1.4	1.000	OF-7
1991		64	.240	.357	129	31	7	1	2	1.6	14	14	12	25	0	26	7	41	0	0	0	1.2	1.000	OF-34
1992		55	.234	.383	128	30	7	0	4	3.1	13	16	16	31	0	14	3	61	2	1	2	1.7	.984	OF-37
1993	BAL A	10	.067	.133	15	1	1	0	0	0.0	1	3	3	7	0	2	0	5	0	1	0	0.9	.833	OF-4, DH-3
1994	SF N	14	.364	.636	11	4	1	1	0	0.0	2	2	3	2	0	10	4	1	0	0	0	0.5	1.000	OF-2
1995		14	.190	.381	21	4	1	0	1	4.8	4	4	5	2	0	6	1	9	0	0	1	1.5	1.000	OF-6
6 yrs.		168	.227	.371	321	73	18	2	8	2.5	37	41	42	75	0	62	15	127	2	2	3	1.4	.985	OF-90, DH-3

John Leovich

LEOVICH, JOHN JOSEPH BR TR 6′½″ 200 lbs.
B. May 5, 1918, Portland, Ore.

Year	Team	Games	BA	SA	AB	H	2B	3B	HR	HR%	R	RBI	BB	SO	SB	Pinch Hit AB	Pinch Hit H	PO	A	E	DP	TC/G	FA	G by Pos
1941	PHI A	1	.500	1.000	2	1	1	0	0	0.0	0	0	0	0	0	0	0	0	0	0	0	0.0	.000	C-1

Ted Lepcio

LEPCIO, THADDEUS STANLEY BR TR 5′10″ 177 lbs.
B. July 28, 1930, Utica, N. Y.

Year	Team	Games	BA	SA	AB	H	2B	3B	HR	HR%	R	RBI	BB	SO	SB	Pinch Hit AB	Pinch Hit H	PO	A	E	DP	TC/G	FA	G by Pos
1952	BOS A	84	.263	.394	274	72	17	2	5	1.8	34	26	24	41	3	0	0	164	212	14	46	4.7	.964	2B-57, 3B-25, SS-1
1953		66	.236	.360	161	38	4	2	4	2.5	17	11	17	24	0	4	1	96	155	6	37	4.0	.977	2B-34, SS-20, 3B-11
1954		116	.256	.384	398	102	19	4	8	2.0	42	45	42	62	3	2	0	276	297	21	64	5.0	.965	2B-80, 3B-24, SS-14
1955		51	.231	.433	134	31	9	0	6	4.5	19	15	13	36	1	4	0	48	84	8	6	3.1	.943	3B-45
1956		83	.261	.454	284	74	10	0	15	5.3	34	51	30	77	1	9	3	170	206	13	51	4.9	.967	2B-57, 3B-22
1957		79	.241	.418	232	56	10	2	9	3.9	24	37	29	61	0	10	2	136	194	8	58	5.0	.976	2B-68
1958		50	.199	.353	136	27	3	0	6	4.4	10	14	12	47	0	10	3	93	99	4	27	4.9	.980	2B-40
1959	2 teams	BOS A (3G –.333) DET A (76G –.279)																						
″	total	79	.280	.417	218	61	9	0	7	3.2	26	25	17	51	2	16	5	96	144	11	30	3.5	.956	SS-35, 2B-25, 3B-11
1960	PHI N	69	.227	.319	141	32	7	0	2	1.4	16	8	17	41	0	9	1	50	74	9	6	1.9	.932	3B-50, SS-14, 2B-5
1961	2 teams	CHI A (5G –.000) MIN A (47G –.170)																						
″	total	52	.167	.395	114	19	3	1	7	6.1	11	19	9	31	1	5	0	53	77	7	20	2.1	.949	3B-36, 2B-22, SS-6
10 yrs.		729	.245	.398	2092	512	91	11	69	3.3	233	251	210	471	11	69	15	1182	1542	101	345	4.0	.964	2B-388, 3B-224, SS-90

Pete LePine

LePINE, LOUIS JOSEPH BL TL 5′10″ 142 lbs.
B. Sept. 5, 1876, Montreal, Que., Canada D. Dec. 3, 1949, Woonsocket, R. I.

Year	Team	Games	BA	SA	AB	H	2B	3B	HR	HR%	R	RBI	BB	SO	SB	Pinch Hit AB	Pinch Hit H	PO	A	E	DP	TC/G	FA	G by Pos
1902	DET A	30	.208	.313	96	20	3	2	1	1.0	8	19	8		1	2	0	77	9	3	6	3.3	.966	OF-19, 1B-8

Don Leppert

LEPPERT, DON EUGENE (Tiger) BL TR 5′8″ 175 lbs.
B. Nov. 20, 1930, Memphis, Tenn.

Year	Team	Games	BA	SA	AB	H	2B	3B	HR	HR%	R	RBI	BB	SO	SB	Pinch Hit AB	Pinch Hit H	PO	A	E	DP	TC/G	FA	G by Pos
1955	BAL A	40	.114	.143	70	8	0	1	0	0.0	6	2	9	10	1	2	0	52	37	6	11	2.7	.937	2B-35

Don Leppert

LEPPERT, DONALD GEORGE BL TR 6′2″ 220 lbs.
B. Oct. 19, 1931, Indianapolis, Ind.

Year	Team	Games	BA	SA	AB	H	2B	3B	HR	HR%	R	RBI	BB	SO	SB	Pinch Hit AB	Pinch Hit H	PO	A	E	DP	TC/G	FA	G by Pos
1961	PIT N	22	.267	.483	60	16	2	1	3	5.0	6	5	1	11	0	2	0	80	11	3	1	4.5	.968	C-21
1962		45	.266	.388	139	37	6	1	3	2.2	14	18	12	21	0	1	0	243	23	3	2	6.1	.989	C-44
1963	WAS A	73	.237	.374	211	50	11	0	6	2.8	20	24	20	29	0	14	6	281	20	5	4	5.1	.984	C-60
1964		50	.156	.254	122	19	3	0	3	2.5	6	12	11	32	0	7	1	191	14	2	2	4.8	.990	C-43
4 yrs.		190	.229	.363	532	122	22	2	15	2.8	46	59	44	93	0	24	7	795	68	13	9	5.2	.985	C-168

Dutch Lerchen

LERCHEN, BERTRAM ROE BR TR 5′8″ 160 lbs.
Father of George Lerchen.
B. Apr. 4, 1889, Detroit, Mich. D. Jan. 7, 1962, Detroit, Mich.

Year	Team	Games	BA	SA	AB	H	2B	3B	HR	HR%	R	RBI	BB	SO	SB	Pinch Hit AB	Pinch Hit H	PO	A	E	DP	TC/G	FA	G by Pos
1910	BOS A	6	.000	.000	15	0	0	0	0	0.0	1	0	1		0	0	0	9	4	1	1	2.3	.929	SS-6

George Lerchen

LERCHEN, GEORGE EDWARD BB TR 5′11″ 175 lbs.
BL 1953
Son of Dutch Lerchen.
B. Dec. 1, 1922, Detroit, Mich.

Year	Team	Games	BA	SA	AB	H	2B	3B	HR	HR%	R	RBI	BB	SO	SB	Pinch Hit AB	Pinch Hit H	PO	A	E	DP	TC/G	FA	G by Pos
1952	DET A	14	.156	.281	32	5	1	0	1	3.1	1	3	7	10	1	7	2	15	0	0	0	2.1	1.000	OF-7
1953	CIN N	22	.294	.353	17	5	1	0	0	0.0	2	2	5	6	0	17	6	1	0	0	0	1.0	1.000	OF-1
2 yrs.		36	.204	.306	49	10	2	0	1	2.0	3	5	12	16	1	24	8	16	0	0	0	2.0	1.000	OF-8

Walt Lerian

LERIAN, WALTER IRVIN (Peck) BR TR 6′ 190 lbs.
B. Feb. 10, 1903, Baltimore, Md. D. Oct. 22, 1929, Baltimore, Md.

Year	Team	Games	BA	SA	AB	H	2B	3B	HR	HR%	R	RBI	BB	SO	SB	Pinch Hit AB	Pinch Hit H	PO	A	E	DP	TC/G	FA	G by Pos
1928	PHI N	96	.272	.381	239	65	16	2	2	0.8	28	25	41	29	1	17	4	239	61	7	12	4.1	.977	C-74
1929		105	.223	.363	273	61	13	2	7	2.6	28	25	53	37	0	2	0	271	69	5	13	3.3	.986	C-103
2 yrs.		201	.246	.371	512	126	29	4	9	1.8	56	50	94	66	1	19	4	510	130	12	25	3.7	.982	C-177

Roy Leslie

LESLIE, ROY REID BR TR 6′ 1″ 175 lbs.
B. Aug. 23, 1894, Bailey, Tex. D. Apr. 9, 1972, Sherman, Tex.

Year	Team	Lg	Games	BA	SA	AB	H	2B	3B	HR	HR%	R	RBI	BB	SO	SB	Pinch Hit AB	Pinch Hit H	PO	A	E	DP	TC/G	FA	G by Pos
1917	CHI	N	7	.211	.211	19	4	0	0	0	0.0	1	1	1	5	1	1	0	59	3	2	3	10.7	.969	1B-6
1919	STL	N	12	.208	.250	24	5	1	0	0	0.0	2	4	4	3	0	1	0	62	4	3	5	7.7	.957	1B-9
1922	PHI	N	141	.271	.359	513	139	23	2	6	1.2	44	50	37	49	3	2	2	1517	63	16	110	11.5	.990	1B-139
3 yrs.			160	.266	.349	556	148	24	2	6	1.1	47	55	42	57	4	4	2	1638	70	21	118	11.2	.988	1B-154

Sam Leslie

LESLIE, SAMUEL ANDREW (Sambo) BL TL 6′ 192 lbs.
B. July 26, 1905, Moss Point, Miss. D. Jan. 21, 1979, Pascagoula, Miss.

Year	Team	Lg	Games	BA	SA	AB	H	2B	3B	HR	HR%	R	RBI	BB	SO	SB	Pinch Hit AB	Pinch Hit H	PO	A	E	DP	TC/G	FA	G by Pos
1929	NY	N	1	.000	.000	1	0	0	0	0	0.0	0	1	0	0	0	0	0	1	0	0	0	1.0	1.000	OF-1
1930			2	.500	.500	2	1	0	0	0	0.0	0	0	0	1	0	2	1	0	0	0	0	0.0	—	
1931			53	.302	.547	53	16	4	0	3	5.7	11	5	1	2	3	45	12	16	1	0	0	2.8	1.000	1B-6
1932			77	.293	.387	75	22	4	0	1	1.3	5	15	2	5	0	**72**	**22**	7	0	0	0	3.5	1.000	1B-2
1933	2 teams		NY N (40G –.321) BKN N (96G –.286)																						
″	total		136	.295	.417	501	148	23	7	8	1.6	62	73	35	23	1	6	3	1226	70	21	72	10.1	.984	1B-130
1934	BKN	N	146	.332	.456	546	181	29	6	9	1.6	75	102	69	34	5	6	1	1262	93	9	104	9.9	.993	1B-138
1935			142	.308	.421	520	160	30	7	5	1.0	72	93	55	19	4	4	1	1233	81	14	106	9.6	.989	1B-138
1936	NY	N	117	.295	.408	417	123	19	5	6	1.4	49	54	23	16	0	15	5	1030	68	10	81	11.2	.991	1B-99
1937			72	.309	.414	191	59	7	2	3	1.6	25	30	20	12	1	26	8	444	38	5	45	11.1	.990	1B-44
1938			76	.253	.331	154	39	7	1	1	0.6	12	16	11	6	0	40	6	304	15	4	21	10.1	.988	1B-32
10 yrs.			822	.304	.421	2460	749	123	28	36	1.5	311	389	216	118	14	216	59	5523	366	63	429	10.1	.989	1B-589, OF-1
WORLD SERIES																									
1936	NY	N	3	.667	.667	3	2	0	0	0	0.0	0	0	0	0	0	3	2	0	0	0	0	0.0	—	
1937			2	.000	.000	1	0	0	0	0	0.0	0	0	1	0	0	1	0	0	0	0	0	0.0	—	
2 yrs.			5	.500	.500	4	2	0	0	0	0.0	0	0	1	0	0	4	2							

Charlie Letchas

LETCHAS, CHARLIE BR TR 5′10″ 150 lbs.
B. Oct. 3, 1915, Thomasville, Ga. D. Mar. 14, 1995, Tampa, Fla.

Year	Team	Lg	Games	BA	SA	AB	H	2B	3B	HR	HR%	R	RBI	BB	SO	SB	Pinch Hit AB	Pinch Hit H	PO	A	E	DP	TC/G	FA	G by Pos
1939	PHI	N	12	.227	.341	44	10	2	0	1	2.3	2	3	1	2	0	0	0	24	32	4	9	5.0	.933	2B-12
1941	WAS	A	2	.125	.125	8	1	0	0	0	0.0	0	1	1	1	0	0	0	1	7	2	1	5.0	.800	2B-2
1944	PHI	N	116	.237	.258	396	94	8	0	0	0.0	29	33	32	27	0	9	2	219	300	16	54	5.0	.970	2B-47, 3B-32, SS-29
1946			6	.231	.231	13	3	0	0	0	0.0	1	0	1	1	0	1	0	10	8	0	4	4.5	1.000	2B-4
4 yrs.			136	.234	.262	461	108	10	0	1	0.2	32	37	35	31	0	10	2	254	347	22	68	4.9	.965	2B-65, 3B-32, SS-29

Tom Letcher

LETCHER, FREDERICK THOMAS (Grandpa, Old Emergency No. 1, Uncle Tom) BL
B. Jan. 1868, Bryan, Ohio Deceased.

Year	Team	Lg	Games	BA	SA	AB	H	2B	3B	HR	HR%	R	RBI	BB	SO	SB	Pinch Hit AB	Pinch Hit H	PO	A	E	DP	TC/G	FA	G by Pos
1891	MIL	AA	6	.190	.238	21	4	1	0	0	0.0	3	2	0	1	1	0	0	4	2	1	2	1.2	.857	OF-6

Jesse Levan

LEVAN, JESSE ROY BL TR 6′ 172 lbs.
B. July 15, 1926, Reading, Pa.

Year	Team	Lg	Games	BA	SA	AB	H	2B	3B	HR	HR%	R	RBI	BB	SO	SB	Pinch Hit AB	Pinch Hit H	PO	A	E	DP	TC/G	FA	G by Pos
1947	PHI	N	2	.444	.444	9	4	0	0	0	0.0	3	1	0	0	0	0	0	2	0	0	0	1.0	1.000	OF-2
1954	WAS	A	7	.300	.300	10	3	0	0	0	0.0	1	0	0	0	0	2	1	6	1	0	1	1.4	1.000	3B-4, 1B-1
1955			16	.188	.375	16	3	0	0	1	6.3	1	4	0	2	0	16	3	0	0	0	0	0.0	—	
3 yrs.			25	.286	.371	35	10	0	0	1	2.9	5	5	0	2	0	18	4	8	1	0	1	1.3	1.000	3B-4, OF-2, 1B-1

Jim Levey

LEVEY, JAMES JULIUS BB TR 5′10½″ 154 lbs.
BR 1930–1931
B. Sept. 13, 1906, Pittsburgh, Pa. D. Mar. 14, 1970, Dallas, Tex.

Year	Team	Lg	Games	BA	SA	AB	H	2B	3B	HR	HR%	R	RBI	BB	SO	SB	Pinch Hit AB	Pinch Hit H	PO	A	E	DP	TC/G	FA	G by Pos
1930	STL	A	8	.243	.297	37	9	2	0	0	0.0	7	3	3	2	0	0	0	20	26	2	6	6.0	.958	SS-8
1931			139	.209	.285	498	104	19	2	5	1.0	53	38	35	83	13	0	0	269	398	58	92	5.2	.920	SS-139
1932			152	.280	.382	568	159	30	8	4	0.7	59	63	21	48	6	0	0	284	439	47	83	5.1	.939	SS-152
1933			141	.195	.240	529	103	10	4	2	0.4	43	36	26	68	4	2	0	298	428	42	73	5.6	.945	SS-138
4 yrs.			440	.230	.305	1632	375	61	14	11	0.7	162	140	85	201	23	2	0	871	1291	149	254	5.3	.936	SS-437

Charlie Levis

LEVIS, CHARLES H. BR
B. June 21, 1860, St. Louis, Mo. D. Oct. 16, 1926, St. Louis, Mo.

Year	Team	Lg	Games	BA	SA	AB	H	2B	3B	HR	HR%	R	RBI	BB	SO	SB	Pinch Hit AB	Pinch Hit H	PO	A	E	DP	TC/G	FA	G by Pos
1884	3 teams		BAL U (87G –.228) WAS U (1G –.000) IND AA (3G –.200)																						
″	total		91	.225	.321	386	87	11	4	6	1.6	59		3			0	0	957	25	45	34	11.3	.956	1B-91
1885	BAL	AA	1	.250	.250	4	1	0	0	0	0.0	2		0			0	0	8	0	1	0	9.0	.889	1B-1
2 yrs.			92	.226	.321	390	88	11	4	6	1.5	61		3			0	0	965	25	46	34	11.3	.956	1B-92

Jesse Levis

LEVIS, JESSE BL TR 5′ 9″ 180 lbs.
B. Apr. 14, 1968, Philadelphia, Pa.

Year	Team	Lg	Games	BA	SA	AB	H	2B	3B	HR	HR%	R	RBI	BB	SO	SB	Pinch Hit AB	Pinch Hit H	PO	A	E	DP	TC/G	FA	G by Pos
1992	CLE	A	28	.279	.442	43	12	4	0	1	2.3	2	3	0	5	0	12	1	59	5	1	0	3.0	.985	C-21, DH-1
1993			31	.175	.206	63	11	2	0	0	0.0	7	4	2	10	0	8	1	109	7	1	3	4.0	.991	C-29
1994			1	1.000	1.000	1	1	0	0	0	0.0	0	0	0	0	0	1	1	0	0	0	0	0.0	—	
1995			12	.333	.444	18	6	2	0	0	0.0	1	3	1	0	0	1	0	33	5	0	0	3.2	1.000	C-12
4 yrs.			72	.240	.328	125	30	8	0	1	0.8	10	10	3	15	0	22	3	201	17	2	3	3.5	.991	C-62, DH-1

Ed Levy

LEVY, EDWARD CLARENCE BR TR 6′ 5½″ 190 lbs.
B. Oct. 28, 1916, Birmingham, Ala.

Year	Team	Lg	Games	BA	SA	AB	H	2B	3B	HR	HR%	R	RBI	BB	SO	SB	Pinch Hit AB	Pinch Hit H	PO	A	E	DP	TC/G	FA	G by Pos
1940	PHI	N	1	.000	.000	1	0	0	0	0	0.0	0	0	0	0	0	1	0	0	0	0	0	0.0	—	
1942	NY	A	13	.122	.122	41	5	0	0	0	0.0	5	3	4	5	1	0	0	114	11	1	12	9.7	.992	1B-13
1944			40	.242	.418	153	37	11	2	4	2.6	12	29	6	19	1	4	2	75	2	3	0	2.2	.963	OF-36
3 yrs.			54	.215	.354	195	42	11	2	4	2.1	17	32	10	24	2	5	2	189	13	4	12	4.2	.981	OF-36, 1B-13

Lewis

LEWIS
B. Brooklyn, N. Y. Deceased.

Year	Team	Lg	Games	BA	SA	AB	H	2B	3B	HR	HR%	R	RBI	BB	SO	SB	Pinch Hit AB	Pinch Hit H	PO	A	E	DP	TC/G	FA	G by Pos
1890	BUF	P	1	.200	.200	5	1	0	0	0	0.0	1	0	0	0	0	0	0	2	3	0	0	2.5	1.000	P-1, OF-1

Allan Lewis

LEWIS, ALLAN SYDNEY (Panamanian Express) BB TR 6′ 170 lbs.
B. Dec. 12, 1941, Colon, Panama.

Year	Team	Lg	Games	BA	SA	AB	H	2B	3B	HR	HR%	R	RBI	BB	SO	SB	Pinch Hit AB	Pinch Hit H	PO	A	E	DP	TC/G	FA	G by Pos
1967	KC	A	34	.167	.167	6	1	0	0	0	0.0	7	0	0	3	14	6	1	0	0	0	0	0.0	—	
1968	OAK	A	26	.250	.250	4	1	0	0	0	0.0	9	0	1	0	8	3	1	0	0	0	0	0.0	.000	OF-1
1969			12	.000	.000	1	0	0	0	0	0.0	2	0	0	0	3	1	0	0	0	0	0	0.0	—	

Allan Lewis *continued*

Year	Team	Games	BA	SA	AB	H	2B	3B	HR	HR%	R	RBI	BB	SO	SB	Pinch Hit AB	Pinch Hit H	PO	A	E	DP	TC/G	FA	G by Pos
1970		25	.250	.625	8	2	0	0	1	12.5	8	1	0	0	7	0	0	2	0	0	0	1.0	1.000	OF-2
1972		24	.200	.300	10	2	1	0	0	0.0	5	2	0	1	8	0	0	9	0	1	0	1.7	.900	OF-6
1973		35	—	—	0	0	0	0	0	—	16	0	0	0	7	0	0	1	0	0	0	0.1	1.000	DH-6, OF-1
6 yrs.		156	.207	.345	29	6	1	0	1	3.4	47	3	1	4	44	10	2	12	0	1	0	0.8	.923	OF-10, DH-6
LEAGUE CHAMPIONSHIP SERIES																								
1973	**OAK A**	2	—	—	0	0	0	0	0	—	1	0	0	0	0	0	0	0	0	0	0	0.0	—	
WORLD SERIES																								
1972	**OAK A**	6	—	—	0	0	0	0	0	—	2	0	0	0	0	0	0	0	0	0	0	0.0	—	
1973		3	—	—	0	0	0	0	0	—	1	0	0	0	0	0	0	0	0	0	0	0.0	—	
2 yrs.		9			0	0	0	0	0		3	0	0	0	0	0	0							

Bill Lewis

LEWIS, WILLIAM HENRY (Buddy) BR TR 5′9″ 165 lbs.
B. Oct. 15, 1904, Ripley, Tenn. D. Oct. 24, 1977, Memphis, Tenn.

Year	Team	Games	BA	SA	AB	H	2B	3B	HR	HR%	R	RBI	BB	SO	SB	Pinch Hit AB	Pinch Hit H	PO	A	E	DP	TC/G	FA	G by Pos
1933	**STL N**	15	.400	.514	35	14	1	0	1	2.9	8	8	2	3	0	6	2	44	4	0	0	6.0	1.000	C-8
1935	**BOS N**	6	.000	.000	4	0	0	0	0	0.0	1	0	1	1	0	4	0	0	0	0	0	0.0	.000	C-1
1936		29	.306	.339	62	19	2	0	0	0.0	11	3	12	7	0	8	2	49	9	2	1	2.9	.967	C-21
3 yrs.		50	.327	.386	101	33	3	0	1	1.0	20	11	15	11	0	18	4	93	13	2	1	3.6	.981	C-30

Buddy Lewis

LEWIS, JOHN KELLY BL TR 6′1″ 175 lbs.
B. Aug. 10, 1916, Gastonia, N. C.

Year	Team	Games	BA	SA	AB	H	2B	3B	HR	HR%	R	RBI	BB	SO	SB	Pinch Hit AB	Pinch Hit H	PO	A	E	DP	TC/G	FA	G by Pos
1935	**WAS A**	8	.107	.107	28	3	0	0	0	0.0	0	2	0	5	0	1	0	5	11	1	1	2.8	.941	3B-6
1936		143	.291	.399	601	175	21	13	6	1.0	100	67	47	46	6	1	0	152	297	32	24	3.5	.933	3B-139
1937		156	.314	.425	**668**	210	32	6	10	1.5	107	79	52	44	11	0	0	146	293	29	32	3.0	.938	3B-156
1938		151	.296	.431	656	194	35	9	12	1.8	122	91	58	35	17	0	0	161	329	47	32	3.6	.912	3B-151
1939		140	.319	.478	536	171	23	**16**	10	1.9	87	75	72	27	10	4	1	122	326	32	31	3.6	.933	3B-134
1940		148	.317	.443	600	190	38	10	6	1.0	101	63	74	36	15	0	0	248	83	15	12	2.3	.957	OF-112, 3B-36
1941		149	.297	.434	569	169	29	11	9	1.6	97	72	82	30	10	4	3	280	103	24	13	2.8	.941	OF-96, 3B-49
1945		69	.333	.465	258	86	14	7	2	0.8	42	37	37	15	1	0	0	151	8	3	3	2.3	.981	OF-69
1946		150	.292	.421	582	170	28	13	7	1.2	82	45	59	26	5	5	1	304	16	10	5	2.3	.970	OF-145
1947		140	.261	.342	506	132	15	4	6	1.2	67	48	51	27	6	9	2	259	11	9	2	2.1	.968	OF-130
1949		95	.245	.366	257	63	14	4	3	1.2	25	28	41	12	2	24	**9**	136	4	3	1	2.1	.979	OF-67
11 yrs.		1349	.297	.420	5261	1563	249	93	71	1.3	830	607	573	303	83	48	16	1964	1481	205	156	2.8	.944	3B-671, OF-619

Darren Lewis

LEWIS, DARREN JOEL BR TR 6′ 180 lbs.
B. Aug. 28, 1967, Berkeley, Calif.

Year	Team	Games	BA	SA	AB	H	2B	3B	HR	HR%	R	RBI	BB	SO	SB	Pinch Hit AB	Pinch Hit H	PO	A	E	DP	TC/G	FA	G by Pos
1990	**OAK A**	25	.229	.229	35	8	0	0	0	0.0	4	1	7	4	2	4	0	33	0	0	0	1.3	1.000	OF-23, DH-2
1991	**SF N**	72	.248	.311	222	55	5	3	1	0.5	41	15	36	30	13	4	1	159	2	0	0	2.4	1.000	OF-68
1992		100	.231	.272	320	74	8	1	1	0.3	38	18	29	46	28	6	1	225	3	0	2	2.4	1.000	OF-94
1993		136	.253	.324	522	132	17	7	2	0.4	84	48	30	40	46	9	2	344	4	0	3	2.7	1.000	OF-131
1994		114	.257	.357	451	116	15	**9**	4	0.9	70	29	53	50	30	1	0	281	5	2	1	2.5	.993	OF-113
1995	**2 teams**	**SF N** (74G –.252) **CIN N** (58G –.245)																						
″	**total**	132	.250	.297	472	118	13	3	1	0.2	66	24	34	57	32	9	1	321	5	2	0	2.5	.994	OF-130
6 yrs.		579	.249	.314	2022	503	58	23	9	0.4	303	135	189	227	151	33	5	1363	19	4	6	2.5	.997	OF-559, DH-2
DIVISIONAL PLAYOFF SERIES																								
1995	**CIN N**	3	.000	.000	3	0	0	0	0	0.0	0	0	0	1	0	1	0	3	0	0	0	1.0	1.000	OF-3
LEAGUE CHAMPIONSHIP SERIES																								
1995	**CIN N**	2	.000	.000	1	0	0	0	0	0.0	0	0	0	0	0	0	0	2	0	0	0	1.0	1.000	OF-2

Duffy Lewis

LEWIS, GEORGE EDWARD BR TR 5′10½″ 165 lbs.
B. Apr. 18, 1888, San Francisco, Calif. D. June 17, 1979, Salem, N. H.

Year	Team	Games	BA	SA	AB	H	2B	3B	HR	HR%	R	RBI	BB	SO	SB	Pinch Hit AB	Pinch Hit H	PO	A	E	DP	TC/G	FA	G by Pos
1910	**BOS A**	151	.283	.407	541	153	29	7	8	1.5	64	68	32		10	2	1	261	28	17	9	2.1	.944	OF-149
1911		130	.307	.437	469	144	32	4	7	1.5	64	86	25		11	4	1	203	27	15	4	2.0	.939	OF-125
1912		154	.284	.408	581	165	36	9	6	1.0	85	109	52		9	0	0	301	23	18	4	2.2	.947	OF-154
1913		149	.298	.397	551	164	31	12	0	0.0	54	90	30	55	12	6	1	262	29	12	3	2.1	.960	OF-142, P-1
1914		146	.278	.398	510	142	37	9	2	0.4	53	79	57	41	22	2	0	254	22	14	2	2.0	.952	OF-142
1915		152	.291	.382	557	162	31	7	2	0.4	69	76	45	63	14	0	0	263	15	14	3	1.9	.952	OF-152
1916		152	.268	.343	563	151	29	5	1	0.2	56	56	33	56	16	1	0	306	16	10	4	2.2	.970	OF-151
1917		150	.302	.392	553	167	29	9	1	0.2	55	65	29	54	8	0	0	324	20	10	6	2.4	.972	OF-150
1919	**NY A**	141	.272	.365	559	152	23	4	7	1.3	67	89	17	42	8	0	0	254	13	4	4	1.9	.985	OF-141
1920		107	.271	.332	365	99	8	1	4	1.1	34	61	24	32	2	7	1	182	14	8	1	2.1	.961	OF-99
1921	**WAS A**	27	.186	.245	102	19	4	1	0	0.0	11	14	8	10	1	0	0	47	3	1	0	1.9	.980	OF-27
11 yrs.		1459	.284	.384	5351	1518	289	68	38	0.7	612	793	352	353	113	22	4	2657	210	123	40	2.1	.959	OF-1432, P-1
WORLD SERIES																								
1912	**BOS A**	8	.156	.250	32	5	3	0	0	0.0	4	2	2	2	0	0	0	14	0	1	0	1.9	.933	OF-8
1915		5	.444	.667	18	8	1	0	1	5.6	1	5	1	4	0	0	0	10	1	0	0	2.2	1.000	OF-5
1916		5	.353	.588	17	6	2	1	0	0.0	3	1	2	1	0	0	0	9	1	0	0	2.0	1.000	OF-5
3 yrs.		18	.284	.448	67	19	6	1	1	1.5	8	8	5	7	0	0	0	33	2	1	0	2.0	.972	OF-18

Fred Lewis

LEWIS, FREDERICK MILLER BB TR 5′10½″ 194 lbs.
B. Oct. 13, 1858, Buffalo, N. Y. D. June 5, 1945, Utica, N. Y.

Year	Team	Games	BA	SA	AB	H	2B	3B	HR	HR%	R	RBI	BB	SO	SB	Pinch Hit AB	Pinch Hit H	PO	A	E	DP	TC/G	FA	G by Pos
1881	**BOS N**	27	.219	.272	114	25	6	0	0	0.0	17	9	7	5		0	0	35	6	8	1	1.8	.837	OF-27
1883	**2 teams**	**PHI N** (38G –.250) **STL AA** (49G –.301)																						
″	**total**	87	.279	.350	369	103	15	4	1	0.3	58		5	13		0	0	173	14	38	1	2.6	.831	OF-87
1884	**2 teams**	**STL AA** (73G –.323) **STL U** (8G –.300)																						
″	**total**	81	.321	.418	330	106	26	3	0	0.0	65		19			0	0	128	15	24	1	2.1	.856	OF-81
1885	**STL N**	45	.293	.359	181	53	9	0	1	0.6	12	27	9	10		0	0	71	18	4	2	2.1	.957	OF-45
1886	**CIN AA**	77	.318	.417	324	103	14	6	2	0.6	72		20			0	0	126	12	19	1	2.0	.879	OF-76, 3B-1
5 yrs.		317	.296	.378	1318	390	70	13	4	0.3	224	36	60	28		0	0	533	65	93	6	2.2	.865	OF-316, 3B-1

Jack Lewis

LEWIS, JOHN DAVID BR TR 5′ 8″ 158 lbs.
B. Feb. 12, 1884, Pittsburgh, Pa. D. Feb. 25, 1956, Steubenville, Ohio.

Year	Team	Lg	Games	BA	SA	AB	H	2B	3B	HR	HR%	R	RBI	BB	SO	SB	Pinch Hit AB	Pinch Hit H	PO	A	E	DP	TC/G	FA	G by Pos
1911	BOS	A	18	.271	.271	59	16	0	0	0	0.0	7	6	7		2	0	0	30	51	6	5	4.8	.931	2B-18
1914	PIT	F	117	.234	.302	394	92	14	5	1	0.3	32	48	17		9	1	0	304	332	34	33	5.8	.949	2B-115, SS-1
1915			82	.264	.333	231	61	6	5	0	0.0	24	26	8		7	13	2	150	152	11	20	4.6	.965	2B-45, SS-11, OF-6, 1B-5, 3B-1
3 yrs.			217	.247	.310	684	169	20	10	1	0.1	63	80	32		18	14	2	484	535	51	58	5.3	.952	2B-178, SS-12, OF-6, 1B-5, 3B-1

Johnny Lewis

LEWIS, JOHNNY JOE BL TR 6′ 1″ 189 lbs.
B. Aug. 10, 1939, Greenville, Ala.

Year	Team	Lg	Games	BA	SA	AB	H	2B	3B	HR	HR%	R	RBI	BB	SO	SB	Pinch Hit AB	Pinch Hit H	PO	A	E	DP	TC/G	FA	G by Pos
1964	STL	N	40	.234	.362	94	22	2	2	2	2.1	10	7	13	23	2	3	0	53	3	2	1	1.6	.966	OF-36
1965	NY	N	148	.245	.384	477	117	15	3	15	3.1	64	45	59	117	4	14	4	257	14	7	3	2.0	.975	OF-142
1966			65	.193	.331	166	32	6	1	5	3.0	21	20	21	43	2	16	2	77	2	1	1	1.6	.988	OF-49
1967			13	.118	.147	34	4	1	0	0	0.0	2	2	2	11	0	4	0	15	1	0	0	1.6	1.000	OF-10
4 yrs.			266	.227	.359	771	175	24	6	22	2.9	97	74	95	194	8	37	6	402	20	10	5	1.8	.977	OF-237

Mark Lewis

LEWIS, MARK DAVID BR TR 6′ 1″ 190 lbs.
B. Nov. 30, 1969, Hamilton, Ohio

Year	Team	Lg	Games	BA	SA	AB	H	2B	3B	HR	HR%	R	RBI	BB	SO	SB	Pinch Hit AB	Pinch Hit H	PO	A	E	DP	TC/G	FA	G by Pos
1991	CLE	A	84	.264	.318	314	83	15	1	0	0.0	29	30	15	45	2	2	2	129	231	9	47	4.3	.976	2B-50, SS-36
1992			122	.264	.351	413	109	21	0	5	1.2	44	30	25	69	4	0	0	184	336	26	71	4.5	.952	SS-121, 3B-1
1993			14	.250	.346	52	13	2	0	1	1.9	6	5	0	7	3	0	0	22	31	2	10	4.2	.964	SS-13
1994			20	.205	.315	73	15	5	0	1	1.4	6	8	2	13	1	0	0	17	40	6	4	3.2	.905	SS-13, 3B-6, 2B-1
1995	CIN	N	81	.339	.480	171	58	13	1	3	1.8	25	30	21	33	0	17	4	19	108	4	4	1.7	.969	3B-72, SS-2, 2B-2
5 yrs.			321	.272	.360	1023	278	56	2	10	1.0	110	103	63	167	10	19	6	371	746	47	136	3.7	.960	SS-185, 3B-79, 2B-53
DIVISIONAL PLAYOFF SERIES																									
1995	CIN	N	2	.500	2.000	2	1	0	0	1	50.0	2	5	1	0	0	2	1	0	0	1	0	0.5	.000	3B-2
LEAGUE CHAMPIONSHIP SERIES																									
1995	CIN	N	2	.250	.250	4	1	0	0	0	0.0	0	0	1	1	0	0	0	2	3	0	0	2.5	1.000	3B-2

Phil Lewis

LEWIS, PHILIP BR TR 6′ 195 lbs.
B. Oct. 7, 1883, Pittsburgh, Pa. D. Aug. 8, 1959, Port Wentworth, Ga.

Year	Team	Lg	Games	BA	SA	AB	H	2B	3B	HR	HR%	R	RBI	BB	SO	SB	Pinch Hit AB	Pinch Hit H	PO	A	E	DP	TC/G	FA	G by Pos
1905	BKN	N	118	.254	.305	433	110	9	2	3	0.7	32	33	16		16	0	0	253	371	66	63	5.8	.904	SS-118
1906			136	.243	.279	452	110	8	4	0	0.0	40	37	43		14	1	1	244	393	54	35	5.1	.922	SS-135
1907			136	.248	.276	475	118	11	1	0	0.0	52	30	23		16	0	0	277	372	43	37	5.1	.938	SS-136
1908			118	.219	.267	415	91	5	6	1	0.2	22	30	13		9	3	0	227	352	35	33	5.3	.943	SS-116
4 yrs.			508	.242	.282	1775	429	33	13	4	0.2	146	130	95		55	4	1	1001	1488	198	168	5.3	.926	SS-505

Jim Leyritz

LEYRITZ, JAMES JOSEPH BR TR 6′ 190 lbs.
B. Dec. 27, 1963, Lakewood, Ohio.

Year	Team	Lg	Games	BA	SA	AB	H	2B	3B	HR	HR%	R	RBI	BB	SO	SB	Pinch Hit AB	Pinch Hit H	PO	A	E	DP	TC/G	FA	G by Pos
1990	NY	A	92	.257	.356	303	78	13	1	5	1.7	28	25	27	51	2	4	2	117	107	13	5	2.5	.945	3B-69, OF-14, C-11
1991			32	.182	.221	77	14	3	0	0	0.0	8	4	13	15	0	9	2	38	21	3	3	2.3	.952	3B-18, C-5, 1B-3, DH-1
1992			63	.257	.444	144	37	6	0	7	4.9	17	26	14	22	0	10	1	96	15	1	2	2.0	.991	DH-31, C-18, 1B-2, 3B-2, OF-2, 2B-1
1993			95	.309	.525	259	80	14	0	14	5.4	43	53	37	59	0	13	4	333	15	2	22	3.9	.994	1B-29, OF-28, DH-21, C-12
1994			75	.265	.518	249	66	12	0	17	6.8	47	58	35	61	0	7	1	282	15	0	6	4.1	1.000	C-37, DH-25, 1B-10
1995			77	.269	.394	264	71	12	0	7	2.7	37	37	37	73	1	3	0	418	23	3	12	5.6	.993	C-46, 1B-18, DH-15
6 yrs.			434	.267	.431	1296	346	60	1	50	3.9	180	203	163	281	3	46	10	1284	196	22	50	3.6	.985	C-129, DH-93, 3B-89, 1B-62, OF-44, 2B-1
DIVISIONAL PLAYOFF SERIES																									
1995	NY	A	2	.143	.571	7	1	0	0	1	14.3	1	2	0	1	0	1	0	13	0	0	0	6.5	1.000	C-2

Carlos Lezcano

LEZCANO, CARLOS MANUEL BR TR 6′ 2″ 185 lbs.
Born Carlos Manuel Lezcano (Rubio).
B. Sept. 30, 1955, Arecibo, Puerto Rico.

Year	Team	Lg	Games	BA	SA	AB	H	2B	3B	HR	HR%	R	RBI	BB	SO	SB	Pinch Hit AB	Pinch Hit H	PO	A	E	DP	TC/G	FA	G by Pos
1980	CHI	N	42	.205	.375	88	18	4	1	3	3.4	15	12	11	29	1	2	0	70	3	4	0	2.0	.948	OF-39
1981			7	.071	.071	14	1	0	0	0	0.0	1	2	0	4	0	2	0	7	0	0	0	1.4	1.000	OF-5
2 yrs.			49	.186	.333	102	19	4	1	3	2.9	16	14	11	33	1	4	0	77	3	4	0	1.9	.952	OF-44

Sixto Lezcano

LEZCANO, SIXTO JOAQUIN BR TR 5′10″ 165 lbs.
Born Sixto Joaquin Lezcano (Curras).
B. Nov. 28, 1953, Arecibo, Puerto Rico.

Year	Team	Lg	Games	BA	SA	AB	H	2B	3B	HR	HR%	R	RBI	BB	SO	SB	Pinch Hit AB	Pinch Hit H	PO	A	E	DP	TC/G	FA	G by Pos
1974	MIL	A	15	.241	.389	54	13	2	0	2	3.7	5	9	4	9	1	0	0	32	3	1	1	2.4	.972	OF-15
1975			134	.247	.382	429	106	19	3	11	2.6	55	43	46	93	5	4	0	240	10	6	1	2.0	.977	OF-129, DH-2
1976			145	.285	.382	513	146	19	5	7	1.4	53	56	51	112	14	0	0	345	10	10	3	2.5	.973	OF-142, DH-3
1977			109	.273	.502	400	109	21	4	21	5.3	50	49	52	78	6	0	0	238	11	3	2	2.3	.988	OF-108
1978			132	.292	.459	442	129	21	4	15	3.4	62	61	64	83	3	2	1	262	18	6	5	2.2	.979	OF-127, DH-3
1979			138	.321	.573	473	152	29	3	28	5.9	84	101	77	74	4	1	0	281	10	4	2	2.2	.986	OF-135, DH-1
1980			112	.229	.421	411	94	19	3	18	4.4	51	55	39	75	1	0	0	228	8	4	4	2.1	.983	OF-108, DH-4
1981	STL	N	72	.266	.393	214	57	8	2	5	2.3	26	28	40	40	0	4	1	103	5	3	1	1.7	.973	OF-65
1982	SD	N	138	.289	.472	470	136	26	6	16	3.4	73	84	78	69	2	2	0	275	16	3	8	2.2	.990	OF-134
1983	2 teams		SD N (97G –.233) PHI N (18G –.282)																						
″	total		115	.239	.351	356	85	12	2	8	2.2	49	56	52	75	1	14	5	189	10	6	1	1.9	.971	OF-106
1984	PHI	N	109	.277	.480	256	71	6	2	14	5.5	36	40	38	43	0	27	6	151	3	3	0	1.8	.981	OF-87
1985	PIT	N	72	.207	.302	116	24	2	0	3	2.6	16	9	35	17	0	27	6	57	2	2	0	1.5	.967	OF-40
12 yrs.			1291	.271	.440	4134	1122	184	34	148	3.6	560	591	576	768	37	81	19	2401	106	51	28	2.1	.980	OF-1196, DH-13
LEAGUE CHAMPIONSHIP SERIES																									
1983	PHI	N	4	.308	.538	13	4	0	0	1	7.7	2	2	1	1	0	1	0	5	1	1	0	1.8	.857	OF-4
WORLD SERIES																									
1983	PHI	N	4	.125	.125	8	1	0	0	0	0.0	0	0	0	2	0	1	0	2	0	0	0	0.7	1.000	OF-3

Steve Libby

LIBBY, STEPHEN AUGUSTUS 6′ 1½″ 168 lbs.
B. Dec. 8, 1853, Scarborough, Me. D. Mar. 31, 1935, Milford, Conn.

Year	Team	Lg	Games	BA	SA	AB	H	2B	3B	HR	HR%	R	RBI	BB	SO	SB	Pinch Hit AB	Pinch Hit H	PO	A	E	DP	TC/G	FA	G by Pos
1879	BUF	N	1	.000	.000	2	0	0	0	0	0.0	0	0	0	1		0	0	8	0	0	0	8.0	1.000	1B-1

Al Libke

LIBKE, ALBERT WALTER (Big Al) BL TR 6′ 4″ 215 lbs.
B. Sept. 12, 1918, Tacoma, Wash.

Year	Team	Lg	Games	BA	SA	AB	H	2B	3B	HR	HR%	R	RBI	BB	SO	SB	Pinch Hit AB	Pinch Hit H	PO	A	E	DP	TC/G	FA	G by Pos
1945	CIN	N	130	.283	.383	449	127	23	5	4	0.9	41	53	34	62	6	15	3	236	15	9	7	2.3	.965	OF-108, P-4, 1B-2
1946			124	.253	.343	431	109	22	1	5	1.2	32	42	43	50	0	8	2	191	14	6	4	1.8	.972	OF-115, P-1
2 yrs.			254	.268	.364	880	236	45	6	9	1.0	73	95	77	112	6	23	5	427	29	15	11	2.0	.968	OF-223, P-5, 1B-2

Francisco Libran

LIBRAN, FRANCISCO BR TR 6′ 168 lbs.
Born Francisco Libran (Rosas).
B. May 6, 1948, Mayaguez, Puerto Rico.

Year	Team	Lg	Games	BA	SA	AB	H	2B	3B	HR	HR%	R	RBI	BB	SO	SB	Pinch Hit AB	Pinch Hit H	PO	A	E	DP	TC/G	FA	G by Pos
1969	SD	N	10	.100	.200	10	1	1	0	0	0.0	1	1	1	2	0	0	0	4	10	0	1	1.6	1.000	SS-9

John Lickert

LICKERT, JOHN WILBUR BR TR 5′11″ 175 lbs.
B. Apr. 4, 1960, Pittsburgh, Pa.

Year	Team	Lg	Games	BA	SA	AB	H	2B	3B	HR	HR%	R	RBI	BB	SO	SB	Pinch Hit AB	Pinch Hit H	PO	A	E	DP	TC/G	FA	G by Pos
1981	BOS	A	1	—	—	0	0	0	0	0	—	0	0	0	0	0	0	0	1	0	0	0	1.0	1.000	C-1

Dave Liddell

LIDDELL, DAVID ALEXANDER BR TR 6′ 190 lbs.
Born Desmond Lane Liddell.
B. June 15, 1966, Los Angeles, Calif.

Year	Team	Lg	Games	BA	SA	AB	H	2B	3B	HR	HR%	R	RBI	BB	SO	SB	Pinch Hit AB	Pinch Hit H	PO	A	E	DP	TC/G	FA	G by Pos
1990	NY	N	1	1.000	1.000	1	1	0	0	0	0.0	1	0	0	0	0	1	1	1	0	0	0	1.0	1.000	C-1

Mike Lieberthal

LIEBERTHAL, MICHAEL SCOTT BR TR 6′ 170 lbs.
B. Jan. 18, 1972, Glendale, Calif.

Year	Team	Lg	Games	BA	SA	AB	H	2B	3B	HR	HR%	R	RBI	BB	SO	SB	Pinch Hit AB	Pinch Hit H	PO	A	E	DP	TC/G	FA	G by Pos
1994	PHI	N	24	.266	.367	79	21	3	1	1	1.3	6	5	3	5	0	2	0	122	5	4	0	6.0	.969	C-22
1995			16	.255	.298	47	12	2	0	0	0.0	1	4	5	5	0	2	0	95	10	1	1	7.6	.991	C-14
2 yrs.			40	.262	.341	126	33	5	1	1	0.8	7	9	8	10	0	4	0	217	15	5	1	6.6	.979	C-36

Fred Liese

LIESE, FREDERICK RICHARD BL TL 5′ 8″ 150 lbs.
B. Oct. 7, 1885, Wis. D. June 30, 1967, Los Angeles, Calif.

Year	Team	Lg	Games	BA	SA	AB	H	2B	3B	HR	HR%	R	RBI	BB	SO	SB	Pinch Hit AB	Pinch Hit H	PO	A	E	DP	TC/G	FA	G by Pos
1910	BOS	N	5	.000	.000	4	0	0	0	0	0.0	0	0	1	2	0	4	0	0	0	0	0	0.0	—	

Bill Lillard

LILLARD, WILLIAM BEVERLY BR TR 5′10″ 170 lbs.
Brother of Gene Lillard.
B. Jan. 10, 1918, Goleta, Calif.

Year	Team	Lg	Games	BA	SA	AB	H	2B	3B	HR	HR%	R	RBI	BB	SO	SB	Pinch Hit AB	Pinch Hit H	PO	A	E	DP	TC/G	FA	G by Pos
1939	PHI	A	7	.316	.368	19	6	1	0	0	0.0	4	1	3	1	0	0	0	12	25	1	3	5.4	.974	SS-7
1940			73	.238	.311	206	49	8	2	1	0.5	26	21	28	28	0	1	0	113	157	23	28	4.2	.922	SS-69, 2B-1
2 yrs.			80	.244	.316	225	55	9	2	1	0.4	30	22	31	29	0	1	0	125	182	24	31	4.3	.927	SS-76, 2B-1

Gene Lillard

LILLARD, ROBERT EUGENE BR TR 5′10½″ 178 lbs.
Brother of Bill Lillard.
B. Nov. 12, 1913, Santa Barbara, Calif. D. Apr. 12, 1991, Goleta, Calif.

Year	Team	Lg	Games	BA	SA	AB	H	2B	3B	HR	HR%	R	RBI	BB	SO	SB	Pinch Hit AB	Pinch Hit H	PO	A	E	DP	TC/G	FA	G by Pos
1936	CHI	N	19	.206	.235	34	7	1	0	0	0.0	6	2	3	8	0	10	3	11	13	2	2	3.7	.923	SS-4, 3B-3
1939			23	.100	.100	10	1	0	0	0	0.0	3	0	6	3	0	0	0	2	11	0	0	0.6	1.000	P-20
1940	STL	N	2	—	—	0	0	0	0	0	—	0	0	0	0	0	0	0	0	1	0	0	0.5	1.000	P-2
3 yrs.			44	.182	.205	44	8	1	0	0	0.0	9	2	9	11	0	10	3	13	25	2	2	1.4	.950	P-22, SS-4, 3B-3

Jim Lillie

LILLIE, JAMES J. (Grasshopper)
Born James J. Lilly.
B. July 27, 1861, New Haven, Conn. D. Nov. 9, 1890, Kansas City, Mo.

Year	Team	Lg	Games	BA	SA	AB	H	2B	3B	HR	HR%	R	RBI	BB	SO	SB	Pinch Hit AB	Pinch Hit H	PO	A	E	DP	TC/G	FA	G by Pos
1883	BUF	N	50	.234	.313	201	47	7	3	1	0.5	25		1	31		0	0	84	13	22	3	2.2	.815	OF-47, P-3, C-2, SS-1, 3B-1, 2B-1
1884			114	.223	.289	471	105	12	5	3	0.6	68		5	71		0	0	190	46	40	7	2.4	.855	OF-114, P-2
1885			112	.249	.307	430	107	13	3	2	0.5	49	30	6	39		0	0	196	31	35	5	2.3	.866	OF-112, SS-3, 1B-1
1886	KC	N	114	.175	.197	416	73	9	0	0	0.0	37	22	11	80		0	0	199	32	30	3	2.3	.885	OF-114, P-1
4 yrs.			390	.219	.272	1518	332	41	11	6	0.4	179	52	23	221		0	0	669	122	127	18	2.3	.862	OF-387, P-6, SS-4, C-2, 3B-1, 1B-1, 2B-1

Bob Lillis

LILLIS, ROBERT PERRY (Flea) BR TR 5′11″ 160 lbs.
B. June 2, 1930, Altadena, Calif.
Manager 1982–85.

Year	Team	Lg	Games	BA	SA	AB	H	2B	3B	HR	HR%	R	RBI	BB	SO	SB	Pinch Hit AB	Pinch Hit H	PO	A	E	DP	TC/G	FA	G by Pos
1958	LA	N	20	.391	.507	69	27	3	1	1	1.4	10	5	4	2	1	1	1	29	52	3	10	4.4	.964	SS-19
1959			30	.229	.271	48	11	2	0	0	0.0	7	2	3	4	0	1	1	27	52	7	10	4.3	.919	SS-20
1960			48	.267	.333	60	16	4	0	0	0.0	6	6	2	6	2	3	0	40	52	1	11	2.4	.989	SS-23, 3B-14, 2B-1
1961	2 teams		LA N (19G –.111) STL N (86G –.217)																						
″	total		105	.213	.230	239	51	4	0	0	0.0	24	22	8	14	3	3	0	123	201	19	33	3.6	.945	SS-57, 2B-25, 3B-12
1962	HOU	N	129	.249	.300	457	114	12	4	1	0.2	38	30	28	23	7	1	1	223	378	15	72	4.4	.976	SS-99, 2B-33, 3B-9
1963			147	.198	.237	469	93	13	1	1	0.2	31	19	15	35	3	3	0	249	375	26	59	4.4	.960	SS-124, 2B-19, 3B-6
1964			109	.268	.313	332	89	11	2	0	0.0	31	17	11	10	4	13	3	169	236	10	40	3.9	.976	2B-52, SS-43, 3B-12
1965			124	.221	.255	408	90	12	1	0	0.0	34	20	20	10	2	5	3	206	304	16	52	4.4	.970	SS-104, 3B-9, 2B-6
1966			68	.232	.268	164	38	6	0	0	0.0	14	11	7	4	1	8	1	99	109	10	24	3.7	.954	2B-35, SS-18, 3B-6
1967			37	.244	.256	82	20	1	0	0	0.0	3	5	1	8	0	9	1	27	66	7	9	3.6	.930	SS-23, 2B-3, 3B-2
10 yrs.			817	.236	.277	2328	549	68	9	3	0.1	198	137	99	116	23	47	11	1192	1825	114	320	4.0	.964	SS-530, 2B-174, 3B-70

Lou Limmer

LIMMER, LOUIS BL TL 6′ 2″ 190 lbs.
B. Mar. 10, 1925, New York, N. Y.

Year	Team	Lg	Games	BA	SA	AB	H	2B	3B	HR	HR%	R	RBI	BB	SO	SB	Pinch Hit AB	Pinch Hit H	PO	A	E	DP	TC/G	FA	G by Pos
1951	PHI	A	94	.159	.280	214	34	9	1	5	2.3	25	30	28	40	1	31	5	450	40	6	54	8.6	.988	1B-58
1954			115	.231	.415	316	73	10	3	14	4.4	41	32	35	37	2	30	8	597	56	8	63	8.4	.988	1B-79
2 yrs.			209	.202	.360	530	107	19	4	19	3.6	66	62	63	77	3	61	13	1047	96	14	117	8.4	.988	1B-137

Rufino Linares

LINARES, RUFINO BR TR 6′ 170 lbs.
Born Rufino de la Cruz (Linares).
B. Feb. 28, 1951, Ingerio Quiqueya, Dominican Republic.

Year	Team	Lg	Games	BA	SA	AB	H	2B	3B	HR	HR%	R	RBI	BB	SO	SB	Pinch Hit AB	Pinch Hit H	PO	A	E	DP	TC/G	FA	G by Pos
1981	ATL	N	78	.265	.375	253	67	9	2	5	2.0	27	25	9	28	8	24	5	124	6	5	1	2.3	.963	OF-60
1982			77	.298	.377	191	57	7	1	2	1.0	28	17	7	29	5	31	8	92	4	0	1	1.8	1.000	OF-53
1984			34	.207	.310	58	12	3	0	1	1.7	4	10	6	12	0	20	5	21	2	1	0	1.8	.958	OF-13
1985	CAL	A	18	.256	.512	43	11	2	0	3	7.0	7	11	2	5	2	5	1	1	0	0	0	0.1	1.000	DH-14, OF-2
4 yrs.			207	.270	.380	545	147	21	3	11	2.0	66	63	24	74	15	80	19	238	12	6	2	1.8	.977	OF-128, DH-14

Carl Lind

LIND, HENRY CARL BR TR 6′ 160 lbs.
B. Sept. 19, 1903, New Orleans, La. D. Aug. 2, 1946, New York, N. Y.

Year	Team	Games	BA	SA	AB	H	2B	3B	HR	HR%	R	RBI	BB	SO	SB	Pinch Hit AB	Pinch Hit H	PO	A	E	DP	TC/G	FA	G by Pos
1927	**CLE A**	12	.135	.135	37	5	0	0	0	0.0	2	1	5	7	1	0	0	21	41	2	6	5.3	.969	2B-11, SS-1
1928		154	.294	.375	**650**	191	42	4	1	0.2	102	54	36	48	8	0	0	390	505	37	116	6.1	.960	2B-154
1929		66	.241	.286	224	54	8	1	0	0.0	19	13	13	17	0	1	0	190	211	18	60	6.4	.957	2B-64, 3B-1
1930		24	.246	.290	69	17	3	0	0	0.0	8	6	3	7	0	1	0	48	77	8	19	5.8	.940	SS-22, 2B-1
4 yrs.		256	.272	.340	980	267	53	5	1	0.1	131	74	57	79	9	2	0	649	834	65	201	6.1	.958	2B-230, SS-23, 3B-1

Jack Lind

LIND, JACKSON HUGH BB TR 6′ 170 lbs.
B. June 8, 1946, Denver, Colo.

Year	Team	Games	BA	SA	AB	H	2B	3B	HR	HR%	R	RBI	BB	SO	SB	Pinch Hit AB	Pinch Hit H	PO	A	E	DP	TC/G	FA	G by Pos
1974	**MIL A**	9	.235	.353	17	4	2	0	0	0.0	4	1	3	2	0	0	0	15	16	1	3	3.6	.969	SS-5, 2B-4
1975		17	.050	.050	20	1	0	0	0	0.0	1	0	2	12	1	0	0	19	27	3	3	3.1	.939	SS-9, 3B-6, 1B-1
2 yrs.		26	.135	.189	37	5	2	0	0	0.0	5	1	5	14	1	0	0	34	43	4	6	3.2	.951	SS-14, 3B-6, 2B-4, 1B-1

Jose Lind

LIND, JOSE BR TR 5′11″ 155 lbs.
Born Jose Lind (Salgado).
B. May 1, 1964, Toabaja, Puerto Rico.

Year	Team	Games	BA	SA	AB	H	2B	3B	HR	HR%	R	RBI	BB	SO	SB	Pinch Hit AB	Pinch Hit H	PO	A	E	DP	TC/G	FA	G by Pos
1987	**PIT N**	35	.322	.434	143	46	8	4	0	0.0	21	11	8	12	2	0	0	53	139	1	12	5.5	.995	2B-35
1988		154	.262	.324	611	160	24	4	2	0.3	82	49	42	75	15	4	2	333	473	11	73	5.3	.987	2B-153
1989		153	.232	.289	578	134	21	3	2	0.3	52	48	39	64	15	5	2	309	438	18	81	5.1	.976	2B-151
1990		152	.261	.340	514	134	28	5	1	0.2	46	48	35	52	8	0	0	330	449	7	74	5.2	.991	2B-152
1991		150	.265	.339	502	133	16	6	3	0.6	53	54	30	56	7	1	0	349	438	9	79	5.3	.989	2B-149
1992		135	.235	.269	468	110	14	1	0	0.0	38	39	26	29	3	1	0	311	428	6	78	5.6	.992	2B-134
1993	**KC A**	136	.248	.288	431	107	13	2	0	0.0	33	37	13	36	3	1	1	269	362	4	75	4.7	.994	2B-136
1994		85	.269	.348	290	78	16	2	1	0.3	34	31	16	34	9	1	0	149	252	5	44	4.8	.988	2B-84, DH-1
1995	**2 teams**	**KC A** (29G –.268) **CAL A** (15G –.163)																						
″	**total**	44	.236	.271	140	33	5	0	0	0.0	9	7	6	12	0	1	0	80	115	1	27	4.5	.995	2B-44
9 yrs.		1044	.254	.316	3677	935	145	27	9	0.2	368	324	215	370	62	14	5	2183	3094	62	543	5.1	.988	2B-1038, DH-1
LEAGUE CHAMPIONSHIP SERIES																								
1990	**PIT N**	6	.238	.524	21	5	1	1	1	4.8	1	2	1	4	0	0	0	19	19	0	4	6.3	1.000	2B-6
1991		7	.160	.160	25	4	0	0	0	0.0	0	3	0	6	0	0	0	12	24	1	1	5.3	.973	2B-7
1992		7	.222	.481	27	6	2	1	1	3.7	5	5	1	4	0	0	0	16	23	2	3	5.9	.951	2B-7
3 yrs.		20	.205	.384	73	15	3	2 **4th**	2	2.7	6	10	2	14	0	0	0	47	66	3	8	5.8	.974	2B-20

Em Lindbeck

LINDBECK, EMERIT DESMOND BL TR 6′ 185 lbs.
B. Aug. 27, 1935, Kewanee, Ill.

Year	Team	Games	BA	SA	AB	H	2B	3B	HR	HR%	R	RBI	BB	SO	SB	Pinch Hit AB	Pinch Hit H	PO	A	E	DP	TC/G	FA	G by Pos
1960	**DET A**	2	.000	.000	1	0	0	0	0	0.0	0	0	1	0	0	1	0	0	0	0	0	0.0	—	

Johnny Lindell

LINDELL, JOHN HARLAN BR TR 6′4½″ 217 lbs.
B. Aug. 30, 1916, Greeley, Colo. D. Aug. 27, 1985, Newport Beach, Calif.

Year	Team	Games	BA	SA	AB	H	2B	3B	HR	HR%	R	RBI	BB	SO	SB	Pinch Hit AB	Pinch Hit H	PO	A	E	DP	TC/G	FA	G by Pos
1941	**NY A**	1	.000	.000	1	0	0	0	0	0.0	0	0	0	0	0	1	0	0	0	0	0	0.0	—	
1942		27	.250	.292	24	6	1	0	0	0.0	1	4	0	5	0	5	2	5	7	1	2	0.6	.923	P-23
1943		122	.245	.365	441	108	17	**12**	4	0.9	53	51	51	55	2	1	0	269	11	10	1	2.4	.966	OF-122
1944		149	.300	.500	594	178	33	**16**	18	3.0	91	103	44	56	5	0	0	468	9	7	3	3.2	.986	OF-149
1945		41	.283	.377	159	45	6	3	1	0.6	26	20	17	10	2	0	0	108	2	2	0	2.7	.982	OF-41
1946		102	.259	.410	332	86	10	5	10	3.0	41	40	32	47	4	14	3	275	12	6	18	3.3	.980	OF-74, 1B-14
1947		127	.275	.412	476	131	18	7	11	2.3	66	67	32	70	1	7	3	308	6	7	1	2.7	.978	OF-118
1948		88	.317	.511	309	98	17	2	13	4.2	58	55	35	50	0	7	0	165	7	1	1	2.2	.994	OF-79
1949		78	.242	.374	211	51	10	0	6	2.8	33	27	35	27	3	13	2	114	4	2	1	1.8	.983	OF-65
1950	**2 teams**	**NY A** (7G –.190) **STL N** (36G –.186)																						
″	**total**	43	.187	.366	134	25	5	2	5	3.7	18	18	19	26	0	4	0	67	1	2	1	1.8	.971	OF-39
1953	**2 teams**	**PIT N** (58G –.286) **PHI N** (11G –.389)																						
″	**total**	69	.303	.495	109	33	7	1	4	3.7	14	17	22	17	0	26	8	22	45	4	2	2.0	.944	P-32, OF-2, 1B-2
1954	**PHI N**	7	.200	.200	5	1	0	0	0	0.0	0	2	2	3	0	5	1	0	0	0	0	0.0	—	
12 yrs.		854	.273	.429	2795	762	124	48	72	2.6	401	404	289	366	17	83	19	1801	104	42	30	2.6	.978	OF-689, P-55, 1B-16
WORLD SERIES																								
1943	**NY A**	4	.111	.111	9	1	0	0	0	0.0	1	0	1	4	0	0	0	8	0	0	0	2.0	1.000	OF-4
1947		6	.500	.778	18	9	3	1	0	0.0	3	7	5	2	0	0	0	11	0	0	0	1.8	1.000	OF-6
1949		2	.143	.143	7	1	0	0	0	0.0	0	0	0	2	0	0	0	2	1	1	0	2.0	.750	OF-2
3 yrs.		12	.324	.471	34	11	3	1	0	0.0	4	7	6	8	0	0	0	21	1	1	0	1.9	.957	OF-12

Jim Lindeman

LINDEMAN, JAMES WILLIAM BR TR 6′1″ 200 lbs.
B. Jan. 10, 1962, Evanston, Ill.

Year	Team	Games	BA	SA	AB	H	2B	3B	HR	HR%	R	RBI	BB	SO	SB	Pinch Hit AB	Pinch Hit H	PO	A	E	DP	TC/G	FA	G by Pos
1986	**STL N**	19	.255	.327	55	14	1	0	1	1.8	7	6	2	10	1	2	1	118	10	1	8	6.8	.992	1B-17, OF-1, 3B-1
1987		75	.208	.386	207	43	13	0	8	3.9	20	28	11	56	3	13	2	196	14	3	13	3.1	.986	OF-49, 1B-20
1988		17	.209	.372	43	9	1	0	2	4.7	3	7	2	9	0	4	2	36	2	1	2	2.6	.974	OF-12, 1B-3
1989		73	.111	.133	45	5	1	0	0	0.0	8	2	3	18	0	26	2	93	6	1	7	2.1	.990	1B-42, OF-5
1990	**DET A**	12	.219	.438	32	7	1	0	2	6.3	5	8	2	13	0	5	0	5	0	0	0	0.4	1.000	DH-10, 1B-1, OF-1
1991	**PHI N**	65	.337	.389	95	32	5	0	0	0.0	13	12	13	14	0	36	13	35	1	0	1	1.2	1.000	OF-30, 1B-1
1992		29	.256	.359	39	10	1	0	1	2.6	6	6	3	11	0	21	8	6	0	0	0	0.7	1.000	OF-9
1993	**HOU N**	9	.348	.478	23	8	3	0	0	0.0	2	0	0	7	0	4	0	40	5	0	6	5.0	1.000	1B-9
1994	**NY N**	52	.270	.496	137	37	8	1	7	5.1	18	20	6	35	0	15	4	74	2	4	4	2.2	.950	OF-33, 1B-4
9 yrs.		351	.244	.391	676	165	34	1	21	3.1	82	89	42	173	4	126	32	603	40	10	41	2.6	.985	OF-140, 1B-97, DH-10, 3B-1
LEAGUE CHAMPIONSHIP SERIES																								
1987	**STL N**	5	.308	.538	13	4	0	0	1	7.7	1	3	0	3	0	1	0	33	2	0	3	7.0	1.000	1B-5
WORLD SERIES																								
1987	**STL N**	6	.333	.400	15	5	1	0	0	0.0	3	2	0	3	0	1	0	28	2	3	2	4.7	.909	1B-6, OF-1

Bob Lindemann

LINDEMANN, JOHN FREDERICK MANN BB TR 6′ 175 lbs.
B. June 5, 1881, Philadelphia, Pa. D. Dec. 19, 1951, Williamsport, Pa.

Year	Team	Games	BA	SA	AB	H	2B	3B	HR	HR%	R	RBI	BB	SO	SB	Pinch Hit AB	Pinch Hit H	PO	A	E	DP	TC/G	FA	G by Pos
1901	**PHI A**	3	.111	.111	9	1	0	0	0	0.0	0	0	0		0	0	0	2	1	2	0	1.7	.600	OF-3

Walt Linden

LINDEN, WALTER CHARLES BR TR 6′ 1″ 190 lbs.
B. Mar. 27, 1924, Chicago, Ill.

Year	Team	Games	BA	SA	AB	H	2B	3B	HR	HR%	R	RBI	BB	SO	SB	Pinch Hit AB	Pinch Hit H	PO	A	E	DP	TC/G	FA	G by Pos
1950	BOS N	3	.400	.600	5	2	1	0	0	0.0	0	0	1	0	0	0	0	5	0	0	0	1.7	1.000	C-3

Bill Lindsay

LINDSAY, WILLIAM GIBBONS BL TR 5′10½″ 165 lbs.
B. Feb. 24, 1881, Madison, N. C. D. July 14, 1963, Greensboro, N. C.

Year	Team	Games	BA	SA	AB	H	2B	3B	HR	HR%	R	RBI	BB	SO	SB	Pinch Hit AB	Pinch Hit H	PO	A	E	DP	TC/G	FA	G by Pos
1911	CLE A	19	.242	.273	66	16	2	0	0	0.0	6	5	1		2	2	1	14	41	7	1	3.9	.887	3B-15, 2B-1

Pinky Lindsay

LINDSAY, CHRISTIAN HALLER (Chris Crab) BR TR 6′ 190 lbs.
B. July 24, 1878, Baker's Yard, Pa. D. Jan. 25, 1941, Cleveland, Ohio.

Year	Team	Games	BA	SA	AB	H	2B	3B	HR	HR%	R	RBI	BB	SO	SB	Pinch Hit AB	Pinch Hit H	PO	A	E	DP	TC/G	FA	G by Pos
1905	DET A	88	.267	.316	329	88	14	1	0	0.0	38	31	18		10	0	0	761	57	18	40	9.5	.978	1B-88
1906		141	.224	.265	499	112	16	2	0	0.0	59	33	45		18	2	0	1162	104	36	59	9.3	.972	1B-122, 2B-17, 3B-1
2 yrs.		229	.242	.285	828	200	30	3	0	0.0	97	64	63		28	2	0	1923	161	54	99	9.4	.975	1B-210, 2B-17, 3B-1

Bill Lindsey

LINDSEY, WILLIAM DONALD BR TR 6′ 3″ 195 lbs.
B. Apr. 12, 1960, Staten Island, N. Y.

Year	Team	Games	BA	SA	AB	H	2B	3B	HR	HR%	R	RBI	BB	SO	SB	Pinch Hit AB	Pinch Hit H	PO	A	E	DP	TC/G	FA	G by Pos
1987	CHI A	9	.188	.188	16	3	0	0	0	0.0	2	1	0	3	0	0	0	28	4	0	1	3.6	1.000	C-9

Doug Lindsey

LINDSEY, MICHAEL DOUGLAS BR TR 6′ 2″ 200 lbs.
B. Sept. 22, 1967, Austin, Tex.

Year	Team	Games	BA	SA	AB	H	2B	3B	HR	HR%	R	RBI	BB	SO	SB	Pinch Hit AB	Pinch Hit H	PO	A	E	DP	TC/G	FA	G by Pos
1991	PHI N	1	.000	.000	3	0	0	0	0	0.0	0	0	0	3	0	0	0	8	0	0	0	8.0	1.000	C-1
1993	2 teams	PHI N (2G –.500) CHI A (2G –.000)																						
″	total	4	.333	.333	3	1	0	0	0	0.0	0	0	0	1	0	0	0	6	0	0	0	1.5	1.000	C-4
2 yrs.		5	.167	.167	6	1	0	0	0	0.0	0	0	0	4	0	0	0	14	0	0	0	2.8	1.000	C-5

Charlie Lindstrom

LINDSTROM, CHARLES WILLIAM BR TR 5′11″ 175 lbs.
Son of Freddie Lindstrom.
B. Sept. 7, 1936, Chicago, Ill.

Year	Team	Games	BA	SA	AB	H	2B	3B	HR	HR%	R	RBI	BB	SO	SB	Pinch Hit AB	Pinch Hit H	PO	A	E	DP	TC/G	FA	G by Pos
1958	CHI A	1	1.000	3.000	1	1	0	1	0	0.0	1	1	1	0	0	0	0	2	0	0	0	2.0	1.000	C-1

Freddie Lindstrom

LINDSTROM, FREDERICK CHARLES (Lindy) BR TR 5′11″ 170 lbs.
Father of Charlie Lindstrom.
B. Nov. 21, 1905, Chicago, Ill. D. Oct. 4, 1981, Chicago, Ill.
Hall of Fame 1976.

Year	Team	Games	BA	SA	AB	H	2B	3B	HR	HR%	R	RBI	BB	SO	SB	Pinch Hit AB	Pinch Hit H	PO	A	E	DP	TC/G	FA	G by Pos
1924	NY N	52	.253	.316	79	20	3	1	0	0.0	19	4	6	10	3	6	2	34	53	6	7	2.7	.935	2B-23, 3B-11
1925		104	.287	.430	356	102	15	12	4	1.1	43	33	22	20	5	2	1	127	154	14	10	3.0	.953	3B-96, SS-1, 2B-1
1926		140	.302	.420	543	164	19	9	9	1.7	90	76	39	21	11	1	1	152	251	16	23	3.0	.962	3B-138, OF-1
1927		138	.306	.436	562	172	36	8	7	1.2	107	58	40	40	10	1	0	182	181	12	12	2.7	.968	3B-87, OF-51
1928		153	.358	.511	646	**231**	39	9	14	2.2	99	107	25	21	15	0	0	145	340	21	34	3.3	.958	3B-153
1929		130	.319	.464	549	175	23	6	15	2.7	99	91	30	28	10	2	0	134	258	14	24	3.2	.966	3B-128
1930		148	.379	.575	609	231	39	7	22	3.6	127	106	48	33	15	0	0	132	291	21	24	3.0	.953	3B-148
1931		78	.300	.429	303	91	12	6	5	1.7	38	36	26	12	5	1	0	158	8	7	3	2.2	.960	OF-73, 2B-4
1932		144	.271	.407	595	161	26	5	15	2.5	83	92	27	28	6	0	0	326	33	10	3	2.6	.973	OF-128, 3B-15
1933	PIT N	138	.310	.448	538	167	39	10	5	0.9	70	55	33	22	1	8	3	388	7	5	2	3.1	.988	OF-130
1934		97	.290	.405	383	111	24	4	4	1.0	59	49	23	21	1	4	1	181	8	2	1	2.1	.990	OF-92
1935	CHI N	90	.275	.389	342	94	22	4	3	0.9	49	62	10	13	1	6	1	167	40	7	7	2.6	.967	OF-50, 3B-33
1936	BKN N	26	.264	.302	106	28	4	0	0	0.0	12	10	5	7	1	0	0	51	4	1	0	2.2	.982	OF-26
13 yrs.		1438	.311	.449	5611	1747	301	81	103	1.8	895	779	334	276	84	31	9	2177	1628	136	150	2.8	.965	3B-809, OF-551, 2B-28, SS-1
WORLD SERIES																								
1924	NY N	7	.333	.400	30	10	2	0	0	0.0	1	4	3	6	0	0	0	7	18	0	0	3.6	1.000	3B-7
1935	CHI N	4	.200	.267	15	3	1	0	0	0.0	0	0	1	1	0	0	0	1	0	1	0	0.4	.500	OF-4, 3B-1
2 yrs.		11	.289	.356	45	13	3	0	0	0.0	1	4	4	7	0	0	0	8	18	1	0	2.3	.963	3B-8, OF-4

Carl Linhart

LINHART, CARL JAMES BL TR 5′11″ 184 lbs.
B. Dec. 14, 1929, Zborov, Czechoslovakia.

Year	Team	Games	BA	SA	AB	H	2B	3B	HR	HR%	R	RBI	BB	SO	SB	Pinch Hit AB	Pinch Hit H	PO	A	E	DP	TC/G	FA	G by Pos
1952	DET A	3	.000	.000	2	0	0	0	0	0.0	0	0	0	0	0	2	0	0	0	0	0	0.0	—	

Bob Linton

LINTON, CLAUD CLARENCE BL TR 6′ 185 lbs.
B. Apr. 18, 1903, Emerson, Ark. D. Apr. 3, 1980, Destin, Fla.

Year	Team	Games	BA	SA	AB	H	2B	3B	HR	HR%	R	RBI	BB	SO	SB	Pinch Hit AB	Pinch Hit H	PO	A	E	DP	TC/G	FA	G by Pos
1929	PIT N	17	.111	.111	18	2	0	0	0	0.0	0	1	1	2	0	8	1	6	3	0	0	1.1	1.000	C-8

Larry Lintz

LINTZ, LARRY BB TR 5′10″ 150 lbs.
B. Oct. 10, 1949, Martinez, Calif.

Year	Team	Games	BA	SA	AB	H	2B	3B	HR	HR%	R	RBI	BB	SO	SB	Pinch Hit AB	Pinch Hit H	PO	A	E	DP	TC/G	FA	G by Pos
1973	MON N	52	.250	.259	116	29	1	0	0	0.0	20	3	17	18	12	2	1	63	114	9	19	3.8	.952	2B-34, SS-15
1974		113	.238	.276	319	76	10	1	0	0.0	60	20	44	50	50	0	0	169	252	18	48	4.4	.959	2B-67, SS-31, 3B-1
1975	2 teams	MON N (46G –.197) STL N (27G –.278)																						
″	total	73	.207	.213	150	31	1	0	0	0.0	24	4	26	20	21	0	0	101	132	9	21	4.6	.963	2B-45, SS-8
1976	OAK A	68	.000	.000	1	0	0	0	0	0.0	21	0	2	0	31	0	0	2	2	0	0	0.1	1.000	DH-19, 2B-5, OF-3
1977		41	.133	.167	30	4	1	0	0	0.0	11	0	8	13	13	0	0	29	37	1	9	1.9	.985	2B-28, DH-5, SS-2, 3B-1
1978	CLE A	3	—	—	0	0	0	0	0	—	1	0	0	0	1	0	0	0	0	0	0	0.0	.000	DH-1
6 yrs.		350	.227	.252	616	140	13	1	0	0.0	137	27	97	101	128	2	1	364	537	37	97	3.5	.961	2B-179, SS-56, DH-25, OF-3, 3B-2

Phil Linz

LINZ, PHILIP FRANCIS (Supersub) BR TR 6′ 1″ 180 lbs.
B. June 4, 1939, Baltimore, Md.

Year	Team	Games	BA	SA	AB	H	2B	3B	HR	HR%	R	RBI	BB	SO	SB	Pinch Hit AB	Pinch Hit H	PO	A	E	DP	TC/G	FA	G by Pos
1962	NY A	71	.287	.372	129	37	8	0	1	0.8	28	14	6	17	6	16	7	53	59	9	10	3.4	.926	SS-21, 3B-8, 2B-5, OF-2
1963		72	.269	.349	186	50	9	0	2	1.1	22	12	15	18	1	15	2	69	103	4	17	3.3	.977	SS-22, 3B-13, OF-12, 2B-6
1964		112	.250	.364	368	92	21	3	5	1.4	63	25	43	61	3	9	0	126	282	20	43	4.1	.953	SS-55, 3B-41, 2B-5, OF-3
1965		99	.207	.277	285	59	12	1	2	0.7	37	16	30	33	2	8	1	144	221	17	30	4.8	.955	SS-71, 3B-4, OF-4, 2B-1
1966	PHI N	40	.200	.243	70	14	3	0	0	0.0	4	6	2	14	0	15	0	18	29	2	4	2.1	.959	SS-14, SS-6, 2B-3
1967	2 teams	PHI N (23G –.222) NY N (24G –.207)																						
″	total	47	.211	.303	76	16	4	0	1	1.3	12	6	6	11	0	15	2	40	39	3	8	2.8	.963	SS-15, 2B-11, 3B-2, OF-1
1968	NY N	78	.209	.236	258	54	7	0	0	0.0	19	17	10	41	1	9	1	136	162	10	36	4.3	.968	2B-71
7 yrs.		519	.235	.311	1372	322	64	4	11	0.8	185	96	112	195	13	87	13	586	895	65	148	3.9	.958	SS-190, 2B-102, 3B-82, OF-22

Phil Linz *continued*

WORLD SERIES

Year	Team	Lg	Games	BA	SA	AB	H	2B	3B	HR	HR%	R	RBI	BB	SO	SB	Pinch Hit AB	Pinch Hit H	PO	A	E	DP	TC/G	FA	G by Pos
1963	NY	A	3	.333	.333	3	1	0	0	0	0.0	0	0	0	1	0	3	1	0	0	0	0	0.0	—	
1964			7	.226	.452	31	7	1	0	2	6.5	5	2	2	5	0	0	0	7	21	2	5	4.3	.933	SS-7
2 yrs.			10	.235	.441	34	8	1	0	2	5.9	5	2	2	6	0	3	1	7	21	2	5	4.3	.933	SS-7

Johnny Lipon

LIPON, JOHN JOSEPH (Skids) BR TR 6′ 175 lbs.
B. Nov. 10, 1922, Martins Ferry, Ohio.
Manager 1971.

Year	Team	Lg	Games	BA	SA	AB	H	2B	3B	HR	HR%	R	RBI	BB	SO	SB	Pinch Hit AB	Pinch Hit H	PO	A	E	DP	TC/G	FA	G by Pos
1942	DET	A	34	.191	.206	131	25	2	0	0	0.0	5	9	7	7	1	0	0	85	103	11	24	5.9	.945	SS-34
1946			14	.300	.300	20	6	0	0	0	0.0	4	1	5	3	0	1	0	14	15	2	5	3.4	.935	SS-8, 3B-1
1948			121	.290	.397	458	133	18	8	5	1.1	65	52	68	22	4	1	0	212	347	17	63	4.8	.970	SS-117, 3B-1, 2B-1
1949			127	.251	.330	439	110	14	6	3	0.7	57	59	75	24	2	5	0	240	364	22	92	5.2	.965	SS-120
1950			147	.293	.368	601	176	27	6	2	0.3	104	63	81	26	9	0	0	273	483	33	126	5.4	.958	SS-147
1951			129	.265	.300	487	129	15	1	0	0.0	56	38	49	27	7	2	0	244	364	33	80	5.1	.949	SS-125
1952	2 teams		DET A (39G –.221) BOS A (79G –.205)																						
″	total		118	.211	.259	370	78	12	3	0	0.0	42	30	48	26	4	1	0	202	330	11	67	4.7	.980	SS-108, 3B-7
1953	2 teams		BOS A (60G –.214) STL A (7G –.222)																						
″	total		67	.214	.260	154	33	7	0	0	0.0	18	14	14	17	1	2	0	89	154	12	26	3.9	.953	SS-58, 3B-6, 2B-1
1954	CIN	N	1	.000	.000	1	0	0	0	0	0.0	0	0	0	0	0	1	0	0	0	0	0	0.0	—	
9 yrs.			758	.259	.324	2661	690	95	24	10	0.4	351	266	347	152	28	13	0	1359	2160	141	483	5.0	.961	SS-717, 3B-15, 2B-2

Nig Lipscomb

LIPSCOMB, GERARD BR TR 6′ 175 lbs.
B. Feb. 24, 1911, Rutherfordton, N. C. D. Feb. 27, 1978, Huntersville, N. C.

Year	Team	Lg	Games	BA	SA	AB	H	2B	3B	HR	HR%	R	RBI	BB	SO	SB	Pinch Hit AB	Pinch Hit H	PO	A	E	DP	TC/G	FA	G by Pos
1937	STL	A	36	.323	.438	96	31	9	1	0	0.0	11	8	11	10	0	4	1	73	82	6	28	5.2	.963	2B-27, P-3, 3B-1

Bob Lipski

LIPSKI, ROBERT PETER BL TR 6′ 1″ 180 lbs.
B. July 7, 1938, Scranton, Pa.

Year	Team	Lg	Games	BA	SA	AB	H	2B	3B	HR	HR%	R	RBI	BB	SO	SB	Pinch Hit AB	Pinch Hit H	PO	A	E	DP	TC/G	FA	G by Pos
1963	CLE	A	2	.000	.000	1	0	0	0	0	0.0	0	0	0	1	0	0	0	3	0	0	0	1.5	1.000	C-2

Nelson Liriano

LIRIANO, NELSON ARTURO BB TR 5′10″ 165 lbs.
Born Nelson Arturo Liriano (Bonilla).
B. June 3, 1964, Puerto Plata, Dominican Republic.

Year	Team	Lg	Games	BA	SA	AB	H	2B	3B	HR	HR%	R	RBI	BB	SO	SB	Pinch Hit AB	Pinch Hit H	PO	A	E	DP	TC/G	FA	G by Pos
1987	TOR	A	37	.241	.342	158	38	6	2	2	1.3	29	10	16	22	13	1	1	83	107	1	28	5.2	.995	2B-37
1988			99	.264	.333	276	73	6	2	3	1.1	36	23	11	40	12	16	4	121	177	12	48	3.4	.961	2B-80, DH-11, 3B-1
1989			132	.263	.376	418	110	26	3	5	1.2	51	53	43	51	16	7	4	267	330	12	76	4.8	.980	2B-122, DH-5
1990	2 teams		TOR A (50G –.212) MIN A (53G –.254)																						
″	total		103	.234	.327	355	83	12	9	1	0.3	46	28	38	44	8	5	2	176	260	11	53	4.4	.975	2B-99, DH-2, SS-1
1991	KC	A	10	.409	.409	22	9	0	0	0	0.0	5	1	0	2	0	0	0	11	23	0	3	3.4	1.000	2B-10
1993	CLR	N	48	.305	.424	151	46	6	3	2	1.3	28	15	18	22	6	3	2	65	103	6	20	3.3	.966	SS-35, 2B-16, 3B-1
1994			87	.255	.396	255	65	17	5	3	1.2	39	31	42	44	0	3	1	146	225	10	42	4.5	.974	2B-79, SS-3, 3B-2
1995	PIT	N	107	.286	.398	259	74	12	1	5	1.9	29	38	24	34	2	37	9	130	137	5	31	3.7	.982	2B-67, 3B-5, SS-1
8 yrs.			623	.263	.367	1894	498	85	25	21	1.1	263	199	192	259	57	72	23	999	1362	57	301	4.2	.976	2B-510, SS-40, DH-18, 3B-9

LEAGUE CHAMPIONSHIP SERIES

Year	Team	Lg	Games	BA	SA	AB	H	2B	3B	HR	HR%	R	RBI	BB	SO	SB	Pinch Hit AB	Pinch Hit H	PO	A	E	DP	TC/G	FA	G by Pos
1989	TOR	A	3	.429	.429	7	3	0	0	0	0.0	1	1	2	0	3	0	0	4	3	1	1	2.7	.875	2B-3

Joe Lis

LIS, JOSEPH ANTHONY BR TR 6′ 195 lbs.
B. Aug. 15, 1946, Somerville, N. J.

Year	Team	Lg	Games	BA	SA	AB	H	2B	3B	HR	HR%	R	RBI	BB	SO	SB	Pinch Hit AB	Pinch Hit H	PO	A	E	DP	TC/G	FA	G by Pos
1970	PHI	N	13	.189	.324	37	7	2	0	1	2.7	1	4	5	11	0	4	0	18	0	1	0	2.1	.947	OF-9
1971			59	.211	.407	123	26	6	0	6	4.9	16	10	16	43	0	22	3	42	2	1	0	1.3	.978	OF-35
1972			62	.243	.414	140	34	6	0	6	4.3	13	18	30	34	0	19	4	242	16	2	19	5.9	.992	1B-30, OF-14
1973	MIN	A	103	.245	.403	253	62	11	1	9	3.6	37	25	28	66	0	4	1	626	48	9	59	7.0	.987	1B-96, DH-1
1974	2 teams		MIN A (24G –.195) CLE A (57G –.202)																						
″	total		81	.200	.340	150	30	3	0	6	4.0	20	19	19	42	1	15	4	297	27	4	24	4.8	.988	1B-49, 3B-9, DH-9, OF-1
1975	CLE	A	9	.308	.923	13	4	2	0	2	15.4	4	8	3	3	0	0	0	39	2	0	2	4.6	1.000	1B-8, DH-1
1976			20	.314	.451	51	16	1	0	2	3.9	4	7	8	8	0	3	0	107	8	0	10	6.4	1.000	1B-17, DH-1
1977	SEA	A	9	.231	.231	13	3	0	0	0	0.0	1	1	1	2	0	2	1	24	1	0	3	5.0	1.000	1B-4, C-1
8 yrs.			356	.233	.399	780	182	31	1	32	4.1	96	92	110	209	1	69	13	1395	104	17	117	5.3	.989	1B-204, OF-59, DH-12, 3B-9, C-1

Rick Lisi

LISI, RICARDO PATRICK EMILO BR TR 6′ 175 lbs.
B. Mar. 17, 1956, Halifax, Nova Scotia, Canada.

Year	Team	Lg	Games	BA	SA	AB	H	2B	3B	HR	HR%	R	RBI	BB	SO	SB	Pinch Hit AB	Pinch Hit H	PO	A	E	DP	TC/G	FA	G by Pos
1981	TEX	A	9	.313	.313	16	5	0	0	0	0.0	6	1	4	0	0	2	0	9	0	0	0	1.1	1.000	OF-8

Pat Listach

LISTACH, PATRICK ALAN BR TR 5′ 9″ 170 lbs.
B. Sept. 12, 1967, Natchitoches, La.

Year	Team	Lg	Games	BA	SA	AB	H	2B	3B	HR	HR%	R	RBI	BB	SO	SB	Pinch Hit AB	Pinch Hit H	PO	A	E	DP	TC/G	FA	G by Pos
1992	MIL	A	149	.290	.349	579	168	19	6	1	0.2	93	47	55	124	54	1	0	238	449	24	89	4.7	.966	SS-148, OF-1, 2B-1
1993			98	.244	.317	356	87	15	1	3	0.8	50	30	37	70	18	2	1	135	267	10	53	4.1	.976	SS-95, OF-6
1994			16	.296	.352	54	16	3	0	0	0.0	8	2	3	8	2	1	0	19	51	3	10	4.6	.959	SS-16
1995			101	.219	.254	334	73	8	2	0	0.0	35	25	25	61	13	3	1	169	273	6	73	4.1	.987	2B-59, SS-36, OF-11, 3B-2
4 yrs.			364	.260	.317	1323	344	45	9	4	0.3	186	104	120	263	87	7	2	561	1040	43	225	4.4	.974	SS-295, 2B-60, OF-18, 3B-2

Pete Lister

LISTER, MORRIS ELMER BR TR
B. July 21, 1881, Savanna, Ill. D. Mar. 27, 1947, St. Petersburg, Fla.

Year	Team	Lg	Games	BA	SA	AB	H	2B	3B	HR	HR%	R	RBI	BB	SO	SB	Pinch Hit AB	Pinch Hit H	PO	A	E	DP	TC/G	FA	G by Pos
1907	CLE	A	22	.277	.308	65	18	2	0	0	0.0	5	4	3		2	0	0	219	10	6	12	10.7	.974	1B-22

Bryan Little

LITTLE, RICHARD BRYAN BB TR 5′11″ 155 lbs.
B. Oct. 8, 1959, Houston, Tex.

Year	Team	Lg	Games	BA	SA	AB	H	2B	3B	HR	HR%	R	RBI	BB	SO	SB	Pinch Hit AB	Pinch Hit H	PO	A	E	DP	TC/G	FA	G by Pos
1982	MON	N	29	.214	.214	42	9	0	0	0	0.0	6	3	4	6	2	2	0	21	32	1	2	2.1	.981	2B-16, SS-10
1983			106	.260	.329	350	91	15	3	1	0.3	48	36	50	22	4	4	1	181	248	9	44	3.7	.979	SS-66, 2B-51
1984			85	.244	.293	266	65	11	1	0	0.0	31	9	34	19	2	7	3	137	199	6	44	4.3	.982	2B-77, SS-2

Bryan Little *continued*

Year	Team	Games	BA	SA	AB	H	2B	3B	HR	HR%	R	RBI	BB	SO	SB	Pinch Hit AB	Pinch Hit H	PO	A	E	DP	TC/G	FA	G by Pos
1985	CHI A	73	.250	.340	188	47	9	1	2	1.1	35	27	26	21	0	3	0	101	165	5	33	3.8	.982	2B-68, 3B-2, SS-1
1986	2 teams	CHI A (20G –.171) NY A (14G –.195)																						
"	total	34	.184	.211	76	14	2	0	0	0.0	6	2	6	11	0	3	0	69	69	2	15	4.1	.986	2B-26, SS-7, 3B-1
5 yrs.		327	.245	.306	922	226	37	5	3	0.3	126	77	120	79	8	19	4	509	713	23	138	3.8	.982	2B-238, SS-86, 3B-3

Harry Little

LITTLE, HARRY A. TR
B. St. Louis, Mo. Deceased.

Year	Team	Games	BA	SA	AB	H	2B	3B	HR	HR%	R	RBI	BB	SO	SB	Pinch Hit AB	Pinch Hit H	PO	A	E	DP	TC/G	FA	G by Pos
1877	2 teams	STL N (3G –.167) LOU N (1G –.000)																						
"	total	4	.133	.133	15	2	0	0	0	0.0	2	0	2	7		0	0	7	5	1	0	3.3	.923	OF-3, 2B-1

Jack Little

LITTLE, WILLIAM ARTHUR BR TR 5′11″ 175 lbs.
B. Mar. 12, 1891, Mart, Tex. D. July 27, 1961, Dallas, Tex.

Year	Team	Games	BA	SA	AB	H	2B	3B	HR	HR%	R	RBI	BB	SO	SB	Pinch Hit AB	Pinch Hit H	PO	A	E	DP	TC/G	FA	G by Pos
1912	NY A	3	.250	.250	12	3	0	0	0	0.0	2	0	1	0	2	0	0	6	1	0	0	2.3	1.000	OF-3

Scott Little

LITTLE, DENNIS SCOTT BR TR 6′ 198 lbs.
B. Jan. 19, 1963, East St. Louis, Ill.

Year	Team	Games	BA	SA	AB	H	2B	3B	HR	HR%	R	RBI	BB	SO	SB	Pinch Hit AB	Pinch Hit H	PO	A	E	DP	TC/G	FA	G by Pos
1989	PIT N	3	.250	.250	4	1	0	0	0	0.0	0	0	0	1	0	2	0	1	1	0	1	2.0	1.000	OF-1

Dennis Littlejohn

LITTLEJOHN, DENNIS GERALD BR TR 6′ 2″ 200 lbs.
B. Oct. 4, 1954, Santa Monica, Calif.

Year	Team	Games	BA	SA	AB	H	2B	3B	HR	HR%	R	RBI	BB	SO	SB	Pinch Hit AB	Pinch Hit H	PO	A	E	DP	TC/G	FA	G by Pos
1978	SF N	2	—	—	0	0	0	0	0	—	0	0	0	0	0	0	0	0	0	0	0	0.0	.000	C-2
1979		63	.197	.254	193	38	6	1	1	0.5	15	13	21	46	0	0	0	366	43	6	7	6.6	.986	C-63
1980		13	.241	.276	29	7	1	0	0	0.0	2	2	7	7	0	3	0	51	8	1	1	6.0	.983	C-10
3 yrs.		78	.203	.257	222	45	7	1	1	0.5	17	15	28	53	0	3	0	417	51	7	8	6.3	.985	C-75

Larry Littleton

LITTLETON, LARRY MARVIN BR TR 6′ 1″ 185 lbs.
B. Apr. 3, 1954, Charlotte, N. C.

Year	Team	Games	BA	SA	AB	H	2B	3B	HR	HR%	R	RBI	BB	SO	SB	Pinch Hit AB	Pinch Hit H	PO	A	E	DP	TC/G	FA	G by Pos
1981	CLE A	26	.000	.000	23	0	0	0	0	0.0	2	1	3	6	0	4	0	11	0	0	0	0.5	1.000	OF-24

Greg Litton

LITTON, JON GREGORY BR TR 6′ 175 lbs.
B. July 13, 1964, New Orleans, La.

Year	Team	Games	BA	SA	AB	H	2B	3B	HR	HR%	R	RBI	BB	SO	SB	Pinch Hit AB	Pinch Hit H	PO	A	E	DP	TC/G	FA	G by Pos
1989	SF N	71	.252	.413	143	36	5	3	4	2.8	12	17	7	29	0	27	9	44	66	3	5	1.7	.973	3B-34, 2B-15, SS-9, OF-6, C-2
1990		93	.245	.314	204	50	9	1	1	0.5	17	24	11	45	1	35	5	90	43	1	10	1.6	.993	OF-56, 2B-18, SS-7, 3B-5
1991		59	.181	.276	127	23	7	1	1	0.8	13	15	11	25	0	13	3	121	65	2	21	3.2	.989	1B-15, 2B-15, 3B-11, SS-9, OF-6, C-1, P-1
1992		68	.229	.350	140	32	5	0	4	2.9	9	15	11	33	0	16	4	82	85	4	26	3.2	.977	2B-31, 3B-10, 1B-8, SS-3, OF-1
1993	SEA A	72	.299	.448	174	52	17	0	3	1.7	25	25	18	30	0	15	6	135	52	0	28	2.5	1.000	OF-22, 2B-17, 1B-13, DH-12, 3B-7, SS-5
1994	BOS A	11	.095	.095	21	2	0	0	0	0.0	2	1	0	5	0	1	1	14	12	0	1	2.4	1.000	2B-4, 3B-3, 1B-3, DH-1
6 yrs.		374	.241	.355	809	195	43	5	13	1.6	78	97	58	167	1	107	28	486	323	10	91	2.3	.988	2B-100, OF-91, 3B-70, 1B-39, SS-33, DH-13, C-3, P-1
LEAGUE CHAMPIONSHIP SERIES																								
1989	SF N	1	1.000	1.000	1	1	0	0	0	0.0	0	0	0	0	0	1	1	0	0	0	0	0.0	—	
WORLD SERIES																								
1989	SF N	2	.500	1.167	6	3	1	0	1	16.7	1	3	0	0	0	1	1	2	3	0	0	1.7	1.000	2B-2, 3B-1

Jack Littrell

LITTRELL, JACK NAPIER BR TR 6′ 179 lbs.
B. Jan. 22, 1929, Louisville, Ky.

Year	Team	Games	BA	SA	AB	H	2B	3B	HR	HR%	R	RBI	BB	SO	SB	Pinch Hit AB	Pinch Hit H	PO	A	E	DP	TC/G	FA	G by Pos
1952	PHI A	4	.000	.000	2	0	0	0	0	0.0	0	0	1	2	0	1	0	0	2	0	1	0.7	1.000	SS-2, 3B-1
1954		9	.300	.467	30	9	2	0	1	3.3	7	3	6	3	1	0	0	19	22	1	8	4.7	.976	SS-9
1955	KC A	37	.200	.229	70	14	0	1	0	0.0	7	1	4	12	0	6	0	55	51	6	12	3.5	.946	SS-22, 1B-6, 2B-4
1957	CHI N	61	.190	.261	153	29	4	2	1	0.7	8	13	9	43	0	2	1	84	131	12	23	3.9	.947	SS-47, 2B-6, 3B-5
4 yrs.		111	.204	.275	255	52	6	3	2	0.8	22	17	20	60	1	9	1	158	206	19	44	3.8	.950	SS-80, 2B-10, 1B-6, 3B-6

Danny Litwhiler

LITWHILER, DANIEL WEBSTER BR TR 5′10½″ 198 lbs.
B. Aug. 31, 1916, Ringtown, Pa.

Year	Team	Games	BA	SA	AB	H	2B	3B	HR	HR%	R	RBI	BB	SO	SB	Pinch Hit AB	Pinch Hit H	PO	A	E	DP	TC/G	FA	G by Pos
1940	PHI N	36	.345	.493	142	49	2	2	5	3.5	10	17	3	13	1	2	0	68	4	1	1	2.0	.986	OF-36
1941		151	.305	.466	590	180	29	6	18	3.1	72	66	39	43	1	1	0	393	12	15	3	2.8	.964	OF-150
1942		151	.271	.389	591	160	25	9	9	1.5	59	56	27	42	2	0	0	308	9	0	0	2.1	1.000	OF-151
1943	2 teams	PHI N (36G –.259) STL N (80G –.279)																						
"	total	116	.272	.428	397	108	20	3	12	3.0	63	48	30	45	2	8	0	225	12	1	2	2.3	.996	OF-104
1944	STL N	140	.264	.427	492	130	25	5	15	3.0	53	82	37	56	2	3	1	294	6	8	1	2.3	.974	OF-136
1946	2 teams	STL N (6G –.000) BOS N (79G –.291)																						
"	total	85	.286	.444	252	72	12	2	8	3.2	29	38	20	24	1	17	5	128	4	2	0	2.0	.985	OF-65, 3B-2
1947	BOS N	91	.261	.394	226	59	5	2	7	3.1	38	31	25	43	1	23	4	119	2	3	0	1.9	.976	OF-66
1948	2 teams	BOS N (13G –.273) CIN N (106G –.275)																						
"	total	119	.275	.456	371	102	21	2	14	3.8	51	50	52	43	1	15	5	200	38	3	4	2.3	.988	OF-91, 3B-15
1949	CIN N	102	.291	.473	292	85	18	1	11	3.8	35	48	44	42	0	14	3	147	12	3	2	1.9	.981	OF-82, 3B-3
1950		54	.259	.455	112	29	4	0	6	5.4	15	12	20	21	0	19	4	46	0	2	0	1.7	.958	OF-29
1951		12	.276	.517	29	8	1	0	2	6.9	3	3	2	5	0	4	2	14	0	1	0	2.1	.933	OF-7
11 yrs.		1057	.281	.438	3494	982	162	32	107	3.1	428	451	299	377	11	106	24	1942	99	39	13	2.2	.981	OF-917, 3B-20
WORLD SERIES																								
1943	STL N	5	.267	.333	15	4	1	0	0	0.0	0	2	2	4	0	1	1	11	0	0	0	2.8	1.000	OF-4
1944		5	.200	.400	20	4	1	0	1	5.0	2	1	2	7	0	0	0	5	0	0	0	1.0	1.000	OF-5
2 yrs.		10	.229	.371	35	8	2	0	1	2.9	2	3	4	11	0	1	1	16	0	0	0	1.8	1.000	OF-9

Mickey Livingston

LIVINGSTON, THOMPSON ORVILLE BR TR 6′ 1½″ 185 lbs.
B. Nov. 15, 1914, Newberry, S. C. D. Apr. 3, 1983, Newberry, S. C.

Year	Team	Games	BA	SA	AB	H	2B	3B	HR	HR%	R	RBI	BB	SO	SB	Pinch Hit AB	Pinch Hit H	PO	A	E	DP	TC/G	FA	G by Pos
1938	WAS A	2	.750	1.250	4	3	2	0	0	0.0	0	1	0	1	0	0	0	2	0	1	0	1.5	.667	C-2
1941	PHI N	95	.203	.242	207	42	6	1	0	0.0	16	18	20	38	2	18	4	263	34	8	5	4.2	.974	C-71, 1B-1
1942		89	.205	.264	239	49	6	1	2	0.8	20	22	25	20	0	6	2	334	37	5	13	4.5	.987	C-78, 1B-6
1943	2 teams	PHI N (84G –.249) CHI N (36G –.261)																						
"	total	120	.253	.362	376	95	14	3	7	1.9	36	34	31	26	2	2	0	422	66	4	11	4.1	.992	C-115, 1B-6
1945	CHI N	71	.254	.317	224	57	4	2	2	0.9	19	23	19	6	2	2	0	264	27	3	2	4.3	.990	C-68, 1B-1

Mickey Livingston *continued*

Year	Team	Games	BA	SA	AB	H	2B	3B	HR	HR%	R	RBI	BB	SO	SB	Pinch Hit AB	Pinch Hit H	PO	A	E	DP	TC/G	FA	G by Pos
1946		66	.256	.369	176	45	14	0	2	1.1	14	20	20	19	0	8	1	239	25	5	3	4.8	.981	C-56
1947	**2 teams**	**CHI N** (19G –.212) **NY N** (5G –.167)																						
″	**total**	24	.205	.256	39	8	2	0	0	0.0	2	3	2	7	0	14	5	30	2	1	0	3.7	.970	C-9
1948	**NY N**	45	.212	.333	99	21	4	1	2	2.0	9	12	21	11	1	3	1	135	10	3	2	3.5	.980	C-42
1949	**2 teams**	**NY N** (19G –.298) **BOS N** (28G –.234)																						
″	**total**	47	.264	.413	121	32	4	1	4	3.3	12	18	5	13	0	6	0	136	14	3	0	3.7	.980	C-41
1951	**BKN N**	2	.400	.400	5	2	0	0	0	0.0	0	2	1	0	0	0	0	3	2	0	1	2.5	1.000	C-2
10 yrs.		561	.238	.326	1490	354	56	9	19	1.3	128	153	144	141	7	59	13	1828	217	33	37	4.2	.984	C-484, 1B-14
WORLD SERIES																								
1945	**CHI N**	6	.364	.500	22	8	3	0	0	0.0	3	4	1	1	0	0	0	22	4	0	0	4.3	1.000	C-6

Paddy Livingston

LIVINGSTON, PATRICK JOSEPH BR TR 5′ 8″ 197 lbs.
B. Jan. 14, 1880, Cleveland, Ohio D. Sept. 19, 1977, Cleveland, Ohio.

Year	Team	Games	BA	SA	AB	H	2B	3B	HR	HR%	R	RBI	BB	SO	SB	Pinch Hit AB	Pinch Hit H	PO	A	E	DP	TC/G	FA	G by Pos
1901	**CLE A**	1	.000	.000	2	0	0	0	0	0.0	0	0	0		0	0	0	0	1	0	0	1.0	1.000	C-1
1906	**CIN N**	50	.158	.223	139	22	1	4	0	0.0	8	8	12		0	3	0	202	62	11	5	5.9	.960	C-47
1909	**PHI A**	64	.234	.314	175	41	6	4	0	0.0	15	15	15		4	0	0	306	106	13	6	6.6	.969	C-64
1910		37	.208	.292	120	25	4	3	0	0.0	11	9	6		2	0	0	205	68	9	5	7.6	.968	C-37
1911		27	.239	.296	71	17	4	0	0	0.0	9	8	7		1	1	0	133	36	4	1	6.7	.977	C-26
1912	**CLE A**	19	.234	.319	47	11	2	1	0	0.0	5	3	1		0	6	0	63	18	2	0	6.4	.976	C-13
1917	**STL N**	7	.200	.200	20	4	0	0	0	0.0	0	2	0	1	2	1	0	26	6	0	0	5.3	1.000	C-6
7 yrs.		205	.209	.280	574	120	17	12	0	0.0	48	45	41	1	9	11	0	935	297	39	17	6.6	.969	C-194

Scott Livingstone

LIVINGSTONE, SCOTT LOUIS BL TR 6′ 190 lbs.
B. July 15, 1965, Dallas, Tex.

Year	Team	Games	BA	SA	AB	H	2B	3B	HR	HR%	R	RBI	BB	SO	SB	Pinch Hit AB	Pinch Hit H	PO	A	E	DP	TC/G	FA	G by Pos
1991	**DET A**	44	.291	.378	127	37	5	0	2	1.6	19	11	10	25	2	2	1	32	67	2	6	2.3	.980	3B-43
1992		117	.282	.376	354	100	21	0	4	1.1	43	46	21	36	1	13	3	67	189	10	15	2.4	.962	3B-112
1993		98	.293	.359	304	89	10	2	2	0.7	39	39	19	32	1	9	3	33	94	6	6	1.4	.955	3B-62, DH-32
1994	**2 teams**	**DET A** (15G –.217) **SD N** (57G –.272)																						
″	**total**	72	.266	.369	203	54	13	1	2	1.0	11	11	7	26	2	9	3	26	81	6	7	1.8	.947	3B-51, 1B-6, DH-5
1995	**SD N**	99	.337	.490	196	66	15	0	5	2.6	26	32	15	22	2	43	14	301	33	3	26	5.6	.991	1B-43, 3B-13, 2B-4
5 yrs.		430	.292	.389	1184	346	64	3	15	1.3	138	139	72	141	8	76	24	459	464	27	60	2.6	.972	3B-281, 1B-49, DH-37, 2B-4

Abel Lizotte

LIZOTTE, ABEL 5′ 8″ 174 lbs.
B. Apr. 13, 1870, Lewiston, Me. D. Dec. 4, 1926, Wilkes-Barre, Pa.

Year	Team	Games	BA	SA	AB	H	2B	3B	HR	HR%	R	RBI	BB	SO	SB	Pinch Hit AB	Pinch Hit H	PO	A	E	DP	TC/G	FA	G by Pos
1896	**PIT N**	7	.103	.103	29	3	0	0	0	0.0	3	3	2	2	1	0	0	53	6	3	3	8.9	.952	1B-7

Winston Llenas

LLENAS, WINSTON ENRIQUILLO (Chilote) BR TR 5′10″ 165 lbs.
Born Winston Enriquillo Llenas (Davilla).
B. Sept. 23, 1943, Santiago, Dominican Republic.

Year	Team	Games	BA	SA	AB	H	2B	3B	HR	HR%	R	RBI	BB	SO	SB	Pinch Hit AB	Pinch Hit H	PO	A	E	DP	TC/G	FA	G by Pos
1968	**CAL A**	16	.128	.154	39	5	1	0	0	0.0	5	1	2	5	0	7	0	9	15	6	0	3.3	.800	3B-9
1969		34	.170	.213	47	8	2	0	0	0.0	4	0	2	10	0	26	7	2	11	1	1	1.6	.929	3B-9
1972		44	.266	.313	64	17	3	0	0	0.0	3	7	3	8	0	28	7	7	16	2	2	1.8	.920	3B-10, OF-2, 2B-2
1973		78	.269	.300	130	35	1	0	1	0.8	16	25	10	16	0	**56**	**16**	42	37	1	3	2.3	.988	2B-20, 3B-11, OF-4
1974		72	.261	.348	138	36	6	0	2	1.4	16	17	11	19	0	33	7	48	11	0	2	1.0	1.000	OF-32, 2B-15, DH-10, 3B-2
1975		56	.186	.221	113	21	4	0	0	0.0	6	11	10	11	0	24	7	76	36	0	16	3.0	1.000	2B-12, OF-10, DH-6, 1B-6, 3B-3
6 yrs.		300	.230	.279	531	122	17	0	3	0.6	50	61	38	69	0	174	44	184	126	10	24	2.0	.969	2B-49, OF-48, 3B-44, DH-16, 1B-6

Mike Loan

LOAN, WILLIAM JOSEPH BR TR 5′11″ 185 lbs.
B. Sept. 27, 1894, Philadelphia, Pa. D. Nov. 21, 1966, Springfield, Pa.

Year	Team	Games	BA	SA	AB	H	2B	3B	HR	HR%	R	RBI	BB	SO	SB	Pinch Hit AB	Pinch Hit H	PO	A	E	DP	TC/G	FA	G by Pos
1912	**PHI N**	1	.500	.500	2	1	0	0	0	0.0	1	0	0	0	0	0	0	1	0	0	0	1.0	1.000	C-1

Bobby Loane

LOANE, ROBERT KENNETH BR TR 6′ 190 lbs.
B. Aug. 6, 1914, Berkeley, Calif.

Year	Team	Games	BA	SA	AB	H	2B	3B	HR	HR%	R	RBI	BB	SO	SB	Pinch Hit AB	Pinch Hit H	PO	A	E	DP	TC/G	FA	G by Pos
1939	**WAS A**	3	.000	.000	9	0	0	0	0	0.0	2	1	4	4	0	0	0	8	2	1	1	3.7	.909	OF-3
1940	**BOS N**	13	.227	.364	22	5	3	0	0	0.0	4	1	2	5	2	1	1	19	2	0	1	2.1	1.000	OF-10
2 yrs.		16	.161	.258	31	5	3	0	0	0.0	6	2	6	9	2	1	1	27	4	1	2	2.5	.969	OF-13

Frank Lobert

LOBERT, FRANK JOHN BR TR 6′ 180 lbs.
Brother of Hans Lobert.
B. Nov. 26, 1883, Williamsport, Pa. D. May 29, 1932, Pittsburgh, Pa.

Year	Team	Games	BA	SA	AB	H	2B	3B	HR	HR%	R	RBI	BB	SO	SB	Pinch Hit AB	Pinch Hit H	PO	A	E	DP	TC/G	FA	G by Pos
1914	**BAL F**	11	.200	.267	30	6	0	1	0	0.0	3	2	0		0	1	0	17	5	3	1	3.1	.880	3B-7, 2B-1

Hans Lobert

LOBERT, JOHN BERNARD (Honus) BR TR 5′ 9″ 170 lbs.
Brother of Frank Lobert.
B. Oct. 18, 1881, Wilmington, Del. D. Sept. 14, 1968, Philadelphia, Pa.
Manager 1938, 1942.

Year	Team	Games	BA	SA	AB	H	2B	3B	HR	HR%	R	RBI	BB	SO	SB	Pinch Hit AB	Pinch Hit H	PO	A	E	DP	TC/G	FA	G by Pos
1903	**PIT N**	5	.077	.154	13	1	1	0	0	0.0	1	0	1		1	0	0	6	8	3	1	3.4	.824	3B-3, SS-1, 2B-1
1905	**CHI N**	14	.196	.239	46	9	2	0	0	0.0	7	1	3		4	0	0	20	25	4	2	3.5	.918	3B-13, OF-1
1906	**CIN N**	79	.310	.366	268	83	5	5	0	0.0	39	19	19		20	4	1	118	178	20	8	4.1	.937	3B-35, SS-31, 2B-10, OF-1
1907		148	.246	.313	537	132	9	12	1	0.2	61	41	37		30	1	0	311	392	46	53	5.1	.939	SS-142, 3B-5
1908		155	.293	.407	570	167	17	18	4	0.7	71	63	46		47	0	0	222	270	42	16	3.4	.921	3B-99, SS-35, OF-21
1909		122	.212	.294	425	90	13	5	4	0.9	50	52	48		30	0	0	182	204	33	16	3.4	.921	3B-122
1910		93	.309	.395	314	97	6	6	3	1.0	43	40	30	9	41	0	0	123	164	21	11	3.4	.932	3B-90
1911	**PHI N**	147	.285	.405	541	154	20	9	9	1.7	94	72	66	31	40	0	0	202	213	20	13	3.0	.954	3B-147
1912		65	.327	.436	257	84	12	5	2	0.8	37	33	19	13	13	1	0	80	86	4	3	2.7	.976	3B-64
1913		150	.300	.424	573	172	28	11	7	1.2	98	55	42	34	41	1	0	184	228	11	13	2.8	.974	3B-145, SS-3, 2B-1
1914		135	.275	.349	505	139	24	5	1	0.2	83	52	49	32	31	0	0	194	178	22	10	2.9	.944	3B-133, SS-2
1915	**NY N**	106	.251	.319	386	97	18	4	0	0.0	46	38	25	24	14	3	1	109	192	16	9	3.0	.950	3B-106
1916		48	.224	.316	76	17	3	2	0	0.0	6	11	5	8	2	24	6	14	35	2	2	2.5	.961	3B-20
1917		50	.192	.269	52	10	1	0	1	1.9	4	5	5	5	2	24	3	10	19	3	2	1.5	.906	3B-21
14 yrs.		1317	.274	.366	4563	1252	159	82	32	0.7	640	482	395	156	316	58	11	1775	2192	247	159	3.4	.941	3B-1003, SS-214, OF-23, 2B-12

Harry Lochhead

LOCHHEAD, ROBERT HENRY BR TR 5'11" 172 lbs.
B. Mar. 29, 1876, Stockton, Calif. D. Aug. 22, 1909, Stockton, Calif.

Year	Team	Games	BA	SA	AB	H	2B	3B	HR	HR%	R	RBI	BB	SO	SB	Pinch Hit AB	Pinch Hit H	PO	A	E	DP	TC/G	FA	G by Pos
1899	CLE N	148	.238	.261	541	129	7	1	1	0.2	52	43	21		23	0	0	320	493	81	54	6.0	.909	SS-146, 2B-1, P-1
1901	2 teams	DET A (1G –.500) PHI A (9G –.088)																						
"	total	10	.132	.132	38	5	0	0	0	0.0	5	2	3		0	0	0	12	22	10	1	4.4	.773	SS-10
2 yrs.		158	.231	.252	579	134	7	1	1	0.2	57	45	24		23	0	0	332	515	91	55	5.9	.903	SS-156, 2B-1, P-1

Don Lock

LOCK, DON WILSON BR TR 6' 2" 195 lbs.
B. July 27, 1936, Wichita, Kans.

Year	Team	Games	BA	SA	AB	H	2B	3B	HR	HR%	R	RBI	BB	SO	SB	Pinch Hit AB	Pinch Hit H	PO	A	E	DP	TC/G	FA	G by Pos
1962	WAS A	71	.253	.458	225	57	6	2	12	5.3	30	37	30	63	4	3	1	144	2	4	0	2.2	.973	OF-67
1963		149	.252	.446	531	134	20	1	27	5.1	71	82	70	151	7	5	2	377	14	8	6	2.7	.980	OF-146
1964		152	.248	.461	512	127	17	4	28	5.5	73	80	79	137	4	6	1	354	19	5	3	2.5	.987	OF-149
1965		143	.215	.371	418	90	15	1	16	3.8	52	39	57	115	1	8	3	278	6	9	3	2.2	.969	OF-136
1966		138	.233	.396	386	90	13	1	16	4.1	52	48	57	126	2	13	5	295	8	7	1	2.4	.977	OF-129
1967	PHI N	112	.252	.435	313	79	13	1	14	4.5	46	51	43	98	9	25	2	172	8	5	2	1.9	.973	OF-97
1968		99	.210	.351	248	52	7	2	8	3.2	27	34	26	64	3	25	3	145	2	7	1	2.0	.955	OF-78
1969	2 teams	PHI N (4G –.000) BOS A (53G –.224)																						
"	total	57	.210	.274	62	13	1	0	1	1.6	8	2	11	22	0	22	2	34	2	0	0	1.1	1.000	OF-29, 1B-4
8 yrs.		921	.238	.417	2695	642	92	12	122	4.5	359	373	373	776	30	107	19	1799	61	45	16	2.3	.976	OF-831, 1B-4

Marshall Locke

LOCKE, MARSHALL PINKNEY WILDER
B. Mar. 12, 1857, Ashland, Ohio D. Mar. 6, 1940, Ashland, Ohio.

Year	Team	Games	BA	SA	AB	H	2B	3B	HR	HR%	R	RBI	BB	SO	SB	Pinch Hit AB	Pinch Hit H	PO	A	E	DP	TC/G	FA	G by Pos
1884	IND AA	7	.241	.310	29	7	0	1	0	0.0	5		0			0	0	7	1	2	0	1.4	.800	OF-7

Keith Lockhart

LOCKHART, KEITH VIRGIL BL TR 5'10" 170 lbs.
B. Nov. 10, 1964, Whittier, Calif.

Year	Team	Games	BA	SA	AB	H	2B	3B	HR	HR%	R	RBI	BB	SO	SB	Pinch Hit AB	Pinch Hit H	PO	A	E	DP	TC/G	FA	G by Pos
1994	SD N	27	.209	.349	43	9	0	0	2	4.7	4	6	4	10	1	13	3	10	21	1	3	1.6	.969	3B-13, 2B-5, SS-1, OF-1
1995	KC A	94	.321	.478	274	88	19	3	6	2.2	41	33	14	21	8	21	6	112	178	8	44	3.2	.973	2B-61, 3B-17, DH-14
2 yrs.		121	.306	.461	317	97	19	3	8	2.5	45	39	18	31	9	34	9	122	199	9	47	2.9	.973	2B-66, 3B-30, DH-14, SS-1, OF-1

Gene Locklear

LOCKLEAR, GENE BL TR 5'10" 165 lbs.
B. July 19, 1949, Lumberton, N. C.

Year	Team	Games	BA	SA	AB	H	2B	3B	HR	HR%	R	RBI	BB	SO	SB	Pinch Hit AB	Pinch Hit H	PO	A	E	DP	TC/G	FA	G by Pos
1973	2 teams	CIN N (29G –.192) SD N (67G –.240)																						
"	total	96	.233	.328	180	42	6	1	3	1.7	26	25	23	27	9	44	9	81	2	4	0	2.1	.954	OF-42
1974	SD N	39	.270	.405	74	20	3	2	1	1.4	7	3	4	12	0	25	7	22	1	0	0	1.9	1.000	OF-12
1975		100	.321	.439	237	76	11	1	5	2.1	31	27	22	26	4	48	14	92	4	3	1	1.9	.970	OF-51
1976	2 teams	SD N (43G –.224) NY A (13G –.219)																						
"	total	56	.222	.263	99	22	4	0	0	0.0	11	9	6	22	0	33	9	24	0	1	0	1.3	.960	OF-14, DH-6
1977	NY A	1	.600	.600	5	3	0	0	0	0.0	1	2	0	0	0	0	0	2	0	1	0	3.0	.667	OF-1
5 yrs.		292	.274	.373	595	163	24	4	9	1.5	76	66	55	87	13	150	39	221	7	9	1	1.9	.962	OF-120, DH-6

Stu Locklin

LOCKLIN, STUART CARLTON BL TL 6' 1½" 190 lbs.
B. July 22, 1928, Appleton, Wis.

Year	Team	Games	BA	SA	AB	H	2B	3B	HR	HR%	R	RBI	BB	SO	SB	Pinch Hit AB	Pinch Hit H	PO	A	E	DP	TC/G	FA	G by Pos
1955	CLE A	16	.167	.222	18	3	1	0	0	0.0	4	0	3	4	0	6	1	3	0	0	0	0.4	1.000	OF-7
1956		9	.167	.167	6	1	0	0	0	0.0	0	0	0	1	0	4	0	1	0	0	0	1.0	1.000	OF-1
2 yrs.		25	.167	.208	24	4	1	0	0	0.0	4	0	3	5	0	10	1	4	0	0	0	0.5	1.000	OF-8

Whitey Lockman

LOCKMAN, CARROLL WALTER BL TR 6' 1" 175 lbs.
B. July 25, 1926, Lowell, N. C.
Manager 1972–74.

Year	Team	Games	BA	SA	AB	H	2B	3B	HR	HR%	R	RBI	BB	SO	SB	Pinch Hit AB	Pinch Hit H	PO	A	E	DP	TC/G	FA	G by Pos
1945	NY N	32	.341	.481	129	44	9	0	3	2.3	16	18	13	10	1	0	0	72	1	3	1	2.4	.961	OF-32
1947		2	.500	.500	2	1	0	0	0	0.0	0	1	0	0	0	2	1	0	0	0	0	0.0	—	
1948		146	.286	.454	584	167	24	10	18	3.1	117	59	68	63	8	1	0	388	6	5	0	2.8	.987	OF-144
1949		151	.301	.429	617	186	32	7	11	1.8	97	65	62	31	12	0	0	353	10	10	1	2.5	.973	OF-151
1950		129	.295	.400	532	157	28	5	6	1.1	72	52	42	29	1	1	0	305	11	7	3	2.5	.978	OF-128
1951		153	.282	.407	614	173	27	7	12	2.0	85	73	50	32	4	0	0	1120	92	17	115	8.0	.986	1B-119, OF-34
1952		154	.290	.396	606	176	17	4	13	2.1	99	58	67	52	2	0	0	1435	111	13	155	10.1	.992	1B-154
1953		150	.295	.389	607	179	22	4	9	1.5	85	61	52	36	3	3	1	1106	102	13	96	8.1	.989	1B-120, OF-30
1954		148	.251	.375	570	143	17	3	16	2.8	73	60	59	31	2	1	0	1265	88	18	122	9.3	.987	1B-145, OF-2
1955		147	.273	.384	576	157	19	0	15	2.6	76	49	39	34	3	2	0	780	38	6	62	5.5	.993	OF-81, 1B-68
1956	2 teams	NY N (48G –.272) STL N (70G –.249)																						
"	total	118	.260	.304	362	94	7	3	1	0.3	27	20	34	25	2	17	4	234	7	11	3	2.4	.956	OF-96, 1B-9
1957	NY N	133	.248	.331	456	113	9	4	7	1.5	51	30	39	19	5	8	0	1022	72	14	94	8.6	.987	1B-102, OF-27
1958	SF N	92	.238	.328	122	29	5	0	2	1.6	15	7	13	8	0	45	11	100	21	2	10	2.6	.984	OF-25, 2B-15, 1B-7
1959	2 teams	BAL A (38G –.217) CIN N (52G –.262)																						
"	total	90	.242	.307	153	37	6	2	0	0.0	17	9	12	10	0	33	4	227	33	5	30	4.7	.981	1B-42, 2B-11, OF-2, 3B-1
1960	CIN N	21	.200	.500	10	2	0	0	1	10.0	6	1	2	3	0	8	1	10	0	0	2	2.0	1.000	1B-5
15 yrs.		1666	.279	.391	5940	1658	222	49	114	1.9	836	563	552	383	43	121	22	8417	592	124	694	5.9	.986	1B-771, OF-752, 2B-26, 3B-1
WORLD SERIES																								
1951	NY N	6	.240	.440	25	6	2	0	1	4.0	1	4	1	2	0	0	0	48	5	2	4	9.2	.964	1B-6
1954		4	.111	.111	18	2	0	0	0	0.0	2	0	1	2	0	0	0	40	0	0	2	10.0	1.000	1B-4
2 yrs.		10	.186	.302	43	8	2	0	1	2.3	3	4	2	4	0	0	0	88	5	2	6	9.5	.979	1B-10

Milo Lockwood

LOCKWOOD, MILO HATHAWAY 5'10" 160 lbs.
B. Apr. 7, 1858, Solon, Ohio D. Oct. 9, 1897, Economy, Pa.

Year	Team	Games	BA	SA	AB	H	2B	3B	HR	HR%	R	RBI	BB	SO	SB	Pinch Hit AB	Pinch Hit H	PO	A	E	DP	TC/G	FA	G by Pos
1884	WAS U	20	.209	.224	67	14	1	0	0	0.0	9		8			0	0	27	28	13	2	2.7	.809	OF-11, P-11, 3B-3

Skip Lockwood

LOCKWOOD, CLAUDE EDWARD BR TR 6' 1" 175 lbs.
B. Aug. 17, 1946, Roslindale, Mass.

Year	Team	Games	BA	SA	AB	H	2B	3B	HR	HR%	R	RBI	BB	SO	SB	Pinch Hit AB	Pinch Hit H	PO	A	E	DP	TC/G	FA	G by Pos
1965	KC A	42	.121	.121	33	4	0	0	0	0.0	4	0	7	11	0	25	3	9	4	0	1	1.9	1.000	3B-7
1969	SEA A	6	.000	.000	7	0	0	0	0	0.0	0	0	0	2	0	0	0	2	5	0	1	1.2	1.000	P-6
1970	MIL A	27	.226	.302	53	12	1	0	1	1.9	2	2	1	11	0	0	0	14	18	1	1	1.2	.970	P-27
1971		36	.081	.145	62	5	1	0	1	1.6	2	4	5	20	0	0	0	9	18	0	2	0.8	1.000	P-33
1972		31	.132	.132	53	7	0	0	0	0.0	3	0	3	12	0	0	0	10	13	1	1	0.8	.958	P-29

Skip Lockwood *continued*

Year	Team	Lg	Games	BA	SA	AB	H	2B	3B	HR	HR%	R	RBI	BB	SO	SB	Pinch Hit AB	Pinch Hit H	PO	A	E	DP	TC/G	FA	G by Pos
1973			37	—	—	0	0	0	0	0	—	0	0	0	0	0	0	0	11	23	2	1	1.0	.944	P-37
1974	CAL	A	37	—	—	0	0	0	0	0	—	0	0	0	0	0	0	0	3	11	0	1	0.4	1.000	P-37
1975	NY	N	24	.167	.167	6	1	0	0	0	0.0	0	1	0	0	0	0	0	1	3	1	0	0.2	.800	P-24
1976			56	.333	.389	18	6	1	0	0	0.0	2	2	2	3	0	0	0	2	11	2	1	0.3	.867	P-56
1977			63	.200	.200	15	3	0	0	0	0.0	1	1	0	1	0	0	0	1	6	1	0	0.1	.875	P-63
1978			57	.182	.545	11	2	1	0	1	9.1	1	1	0	5	0	0	0	4	5	1	1	0.2	.900	P-57
1979			28	.000	.000	2	0	0	0	0	0.0	0	0	0	1	0	0	0	1	3	1	1	0.2	.800	P-27
1980	BOS	A	24	—	—	0	0	0	0	0	—	0	0	0	0	0	0	0	3	3	0	0	0.3	1.000	P-24
13 yrs.			468	.154	.204	260	40	4	0	3	1.2	15	11	18	66	0	25	3	70	123	10	11	0.5	.951	P-420, 3B-7

Dario Lodigiani

LODIGIANI, DARIO ANTONIO (Lodi) BR TR 5′ 8″ 150 lbs.
B. July 16, 1916, San Francisco, Calif.

Year	Team	Lg	Games	BA	SA	AB	H	2B	3B	HR	HR%	R	RBI	BB	SO	SB	Pinch Hit AB	Pinch Hit H	PO	A	E	DP	TC/G	FA	G by Pos
1938	PHI	A	93	.280	.388	325	91	15	1	6	1.8	36	44	34	25	3	0	0	210	259	25	48	5.3	.949	2B-80, 3B-13
1939			121	.260	.382	393	102	22	4	6	1.5	46	44	42	18	2	4	1	159	263	27	24	3.8	.940	3B-89, 2B-28
1940			1	.000	.000	1	0	0	0	0	0.0	0	0	0	0	0	1	0	0	0	0	0	0.0	—	
1941	CHI	A	87	.239	.348	322	77	19	2	4	1.2	39	40	31	19	0	0	0	120	187	12	22	3.7	.962	3B-86
1942			59	.280	.321	168	47	7	0	0	0.0	9	15	18	10	3	5	1	55	118	9	9	3.6	.951	3B-43, 2B-7
1946			44	.245	.297	155	38	8	0	0	0.0	12	13	16	14	4	0	0	41	88	9	4	3.1	.935	3B-44
6 yrs.			405	.260	.358	1364	355	71	7	16	1.2	142	156	141	86	12	10	2	585	915	82	107	4.1	.948	3B-275, 2B-115

George Loepp

LOEPP, GEORGE HERBERT BR TR 5′11″ 170 lbs.
B. Sept. 11, 1901, Detroit, Mich. D. Sept. 4, 1967, Los Angeles, Calif.

Year	Team	Lg	Games	BA	SA	AB	H	2B	3B	HR	HR%	R	RBI	BB	SO	SB	Pinch Hit AB	Pinch Hit H	PO	A	E	DP	TC/G	FA	G by Pos
1928	BOS	A	15	.176	.275	51	9	3	1	0	0.0	6	3	5	12	0	1	0	35	2	2	1	2.8	.949	OF-14
1930	WAS	A	50	.276	.343	134	37	7	1	0	0.0	23	14	20	9	0	1	0	89	3	4	0	2.0	.958	OF-48
2 yrs.			65	.249	.324	185	46	10	2	0	0.0	29	17	25	21	0	2	0	124	5	6	1	2.2	.956	OF-62

Kenny Lofton

LOFTON, KENNETH BL TL 6′ 180 lbs.
B. May 31, 1967, East Chicago, Ind.

Year	Team	Lg	Games	BA	SA	AB	H	2B	3B	HR	HR%	R	RBI	BB	SO	SB	Pinch Hit AB	Pinch Hit H	PO	A	E	DP	TC/G	FA	G by Pos
1991	HOU	N	20	.203	.216	74	15	1	0	0	0.0	9	0	5	19	2	1	0	41	1	1	0	2.2	.977	OF-20
1992	CLE	A	148	.285	.365	576	164	15	8	5	0.9	96	42	68	54	**66**	2	0	420	14	8	3	3.1	.982	OF-143
1993			148	.325	.408	569	185	28	8	1	0.2	116	42	81	83	**70**	2	0	402	11	9	3	2.9	.979	OF-146
1994			112	.349	.536	459	**160**	32	9	12	2.6	105	57	52	56	**60**	0	0	276	13	2	3	2.6	.993	OF-112
1995			118	.310	.453	481	149	22	**13**	7	1.5	93	53	40	49	**54**	1	0	248	11	8	2	2.3	.970	OF-114, DH-2
5 yrs.			546	.312	.427	2159	673	98	38	25	1.2	419	194	246	261	252	6	0	1387	50	28	11	2.7	.981	OF-535, DH-2
DIVISIONAL PLAYOFF SERIES																									
1995	CLE	A	3	.154	.154	13	2	0	0	0	0.0	1	0	1	3	0	0	0	9	0	2	0	3.7	.818	OF-3
LEAGUE CHAMPIONSHIP SERIES																									
1995	CLE	A	6	.458	.625	24	11	0	2 **4th**	0	0.0	4	3	4	6	5	0	0	15	0	0	0	2.5	1.000	OF-6
WORLD SERIES																									
1995	CLE	A	6	.200	.240	25	5	1	0	0	0.0	6	0	3	1	6	0	0	12	0	0	0	2.0	1.000	OF-6

Dick Loftus

LOFTUS, RICHARD JOSEPH BL TR 6′ 155 lbs.
B. Mar. 7, 1901, Concord, Mass. D. Jan. 21, 1972, Concord, Mass.

Year	Team	Lg	Games	BA	SA	AB	H	2B	3B	HR	HR%	R	RBI	BB	SO	SB	Pinch Hit AB	Pinch Hit H	PO	A	E	DP	TC/G	FA	G by Pos
1924	BKN	N	46	.272	.346	81	22	6	0	0	0.0	18	8	7	2	1	7	3	51	1	0	1	1.7	1.000	OF-29, 1B-1
1925			51	.237	.282	131	31	6	0	0	0.0	16	13	5	5	2	10	1	82	4	2	1	2.3	.977	OF-38
2 yrs.			97	.250	.307	212	53	12	0	0	0.0	34	21	12	7	3	17	4	133	5	2	2	2.1	.986	OF-67, 1B-1

Tom Loftus

LOFTUS, THOMAS JOSEPH BR 168 lbs.
B. Nov. 15, 1856, St. Louis, Mo. D. Apr. 16, 1910, Dubuque, Iowa.
Manager 1884, 1888–91, 1900–03.

Year	Team	Lg	Games	BA	SA	AB	H	2B	3B	HR	HR%	R	RBI	BB	SO	SB	Pinch Hit AB	Pinch Hit H	PO	A	E	DP	TC/G	FA	G by Pos
1877	STL	N	3	.182	.182	11	2	0	0	0	0.0	2	0	0	1		0	0	4	3	2	0	3.0	.778	OF-3
1883	STL	AA	6	.182	.182	22	4	0	0	0	0.0	1		2			0	0	15	0	2	0	2.8	.882	OF-6
2 yrs.			9	.182	.182	33	6	0	0	0	0.0	3	0	2	1		0	0	19	3	4	0	2.9	.846	OF-9

Johnny Logan

LOGAN, JOHN (Yatcha) BR TR 5′11″ 175 lbs.
B. Mar. 23, 1927, Endicott, N. Y.

Year	Team	Lg	Games	BA	SA	AB	H	2B	3B	HR	HR%	R	RBI	BB	SO	SB	Pinch Hit AB	Pinch Hit H	PO	A	E	DP	TC/G	FA	G by Pos
1951	BOS	N	62	.219	.272	169	37	7	1	0	0.0	14	16	18	13	0	3	0	98	155	11	31	4.6	.958	SS-58
1952			117	.283	.368	456	129	21	3	4	0.9	56	42	31	33	1	0	0	247	385	18	81	5.6	.972	SS-117
1953	MIL	N	150	.273	.398	611	167	27	8	11	1.8	100	73	41	33	2	0	0	295	481	20	104	5.3	.975	SS-150
1954			154	.275	.373	560	154	17	7	8	1.4	66	66	51	51	2	0	0	324	489	26	104	5.4	.969	SS-154
1955			154	.297	.442	595	177	**37**	5	13	2.2	95	83	58	58	3	0	0	268	511	30	100	5.3	.963	SS-154
1956			148	.281	.431	545	153	27	5	15	2.8	69	46	46	49	3	0	0	266	467	24	94	5.1	.968	SS-148
1957			129	.273	.401	494	135	19	7	10	2.0	59	49	31	49	5	1	1	263	440	29	94	5.7	.960	SS-129
1958			145	.226	.326	530	120	20	0	11	2.1	54	53	40	57	1	1	1	273	481	32	99	5.5	.959	SS-144
1959			138	.291	.411	470	137	17	0	13	2.8	59	50	57	45	1	0	0	260	431	18	78	5.1	.975	SS-138
1960			136	.245	.334	482	118	14	4	7	1.5	52	42	43	40	1	0	0	235	417	30	77	5.0	.956	SS-136
1961	2 teams		MIL N (18G –.105)			PIT N (27G –.231)																			
″	total		45	.197	.268	71	14	5	0	0	0.0	5	6	5	11	0	30	8	12	29	1	6	2.8	.976	SS-8, 3B-7
1962	PIT	N	44	.300	.375	80	24	3	0	1	1.3	7	12	7	6	0	23	3	13	35	1	5	2.6	.980	3B-19
1963			81	.232	.254	181	42	2	1	0	0.0	15	9	23	27	0	30	7	77	126	17	29	4.6	.923	SS-44, 3B-4
13 yrs.			1503	.268	.378	5244	1407	216	41	93	1.8	651	547	451	472	19	88	20	2631	4447	257	902	5.2	.965	SS-1380, 3B-30
WORLD SERIES																									
1957	MIL	N	7	.185	.333	27	5	1	0	1	3.7	5	2	3	6	0	0	0	13	25	0	6	5.4	1.000	SS-7
1958			7	.120	.200	25	3	2	0	0	0.0	3	2	2	4	0	0	0	10	24	2	2	5.1	.944	SS-7
2 yrs.			14	.154	.269	52	8	3	0	1	1.9	8	4	5	10	0	0	0	23	49	2	8	5.3	.973	SS-14

Pete Lohman

LOHMAN, GEORGE F.
B. Oct. 21, 1864, Lake Elmo, Minn. D. Nov. 21, 1928, Los Angeles, Calif.

Year	Team	Lg	Games	BA	SA	AB	H	2B	3B	HR	HR%	R	RBI	BB	SO	SB	Pinch Hit AB	Pinch Hit H	PO	A	E	DP	TC/G	FA	G by Pos
1891	WAS	AA	32	.193	.303	109	21	1	4	1	0.9	18	11	16	17	1	0	0	125	35	18	4	5.1	.899	C-21, OF-8, 3B-4, SS-1, 2B-1

Howard Lohr

LOHR, HOWARD SYLVESTER BR TR 6′ 165 lbs.
B. June 3, 1892, Philadelphia, Pa. D. June 9, 1977, Philadelphia, Pa.

Year	Team	Games	BA	SA	AB	H	2B	3B	HR	HR%	R	RBI	BB	SO	SB	Pinch Hit AB	Pinch Hit H	PO	A	E	DP	TC/G	FA	G by Pos
1914	**CIN N**	18	.213	.277	47	10	1	1	0	0.0	6	7	0	8	2	1	0	24	1	2	1	1.6	.926	OF-17
1916	**CLE A**	3	.143	.143	7	1	0	0	0	0.0	0	1	0	1	1	0	0	3	0	0	0	1.0	1.000	OF-3
2 yrs.		21	.204	.259	54	11	1	1	0	0.0	6	8	0	9	3	1	0	27	1	2	1	1.5	.933	OF-20

Lucky Lohrke

LOHRKE, JACK WAYNE BR TR 6′ 180 lbs.
B. Feb. 25, 1924, Los Angeles, Calif.

Year	Team	Games	BA	SA	AB	H	2B	3B	HR	HR%	R	RBI	BB	SO	SB	Pinch Hit AB	Pinch Hit H	PO	A	E	DP	TC/G	FA	G by Pos
1947	**NY N**	112	.240	.401	329	79	12	4	11	3.3	44	35	46	29	3	1	0	118	187	20	20	2.9	.938	3B-111
1948		97	.250	.364	280	70	15	1	5	1.8	35	31	30	30	3	9	0	125	170	22	21	3.7	.931	3B-50, 2B-36
1949		55	.267	.456	180	48	11	4	5	2.8	32	22	16	12	3	3	1	86	143	9	13	4.2	.962	2B-23, 3B-19, SS-15
1950		30	.186	.186	43	8	0	0	0	0.0	4	4	4	8	0	13	2	10	18	1	3	1.7	.966	3B-16, 2B-1
1951		23	.200	.275	40	8	0	0	1	2.5	3	3	10	2	0	5	0	11	23	2	2	2.0	.944	3B-17, SS-1
1952	**PHI N**	25	.207	.207	29	6	0	0	0	0.0	4	1	4	3	0	12	4	7	15	1	3	2.6	.957	SS-5, 3B-3, 2B-1
1953		12	.154	.154	13	2	0	0	0	0.0	3	0	1	2	0	5	2	2	8	2	1	2.4	.833	2B-2, SS-2, 3B-1
7 yrs.		354	.242	.375	914	221	38	9	22	2.4	125	96	111	86	9	48	9	359	564	57	63	3.2	.942	3B-217, 2B-63, SS-23
WORLD SERIES																								
1951	**NY N**	2	.000	.000	2	0	0	0	0	0.0	0	0	0	1	0	2	0	0	0	0	0	0.0	—	

Al Lois

LOIS, ALBERTO BR TR 5′ 9″ 175 lbs.
Born Alberto Louis (Pie).
B. May 6, 1956, Hato Mayor, Dominican Republic.

Year	Team	Games	BA	SA	AB	H	2B	3B	HR	HR%	R	RBI	BB	SO	SB	Pinch Hit AB	Pinch Hit H	PO	A	E	DP	TC/G	FA	G by Pos
1978	**PIT N**	3	.250	.750	4	1	0	1	0	0.0	0	0	0	1	0	0	0	4	0	0	0	2.0	1.000	OF-2
1979		11	—	—	0	0	0	0	0	—	6	0	0	0	1	0	0	0	0	0	0	0.0	—	
2 yrs.		14	.250	.750	4	1	0	1	0	0.0	6	0	0	1	1	0	0	4	0	0	0	2.0	1.000	OF-2

Ron Lolich

LOLICH, RONALD JOHN BR TR 6′ 1″ 185 lbs.
B. Sept. 19, 1946, Portland, Ore.

Year	Team	Games	BA	SA	AB	H	2B	3B	HR	HR%	R	RBI	BB	SO	SB	Pinch Hit AB	Pinch Hit H	PO	A	E	DP	TC/G	FA	G by Pos
1971	**CHI A**	2	.125	.250	8	1	1	0	0	0.0	0	0	0	2	0	0	0	1	0	0	0	0.5	1.000	OF-2
1972	**CLE A**	24	.188	.275	80	15	1	0	2	2.5	4	8	4	20	0	3	0	39	1	0	0	1.8	1.000	OF-22
1973		61	.229	.321	140	32	7	0	2	1.4	16	15	7	27	0	19	4	38	2	4	0	1.0	.909	OF-32, DH-12
3 yrs.		87	.211	.303	228	48	9	0	4	1.8	20	23	11	49	0	22	4	78	3	4	0	1.3	.953	OF-56, DH-12

Sherm Lollar

LOLLAR, JOHN SHERMAN BR TR 6′ 1″ 185 lbs.
B. Aug. 23, 1924, Durham, Ark. D. Sept. 24, 1977, Springfield, Mo.

Year	Team	Games	BA	SA	AB	H	2B	3B	HR	HR%	R	RBI	BB	SO	SB	Pinch Hit AB	Pinch Hit H	PO	A	E	DP	TC/G	FA	G by Pos
1946	**CLE A**	28	.242	.387	62	15	6	0	1	1.6	7	9	5	9	0	4	1	89	9	1	1	4.1	.990	C-24
1947	**NY A**	11	.219	.375	32	7	0	1	1	3.1	4	6	1	5	0	2	0	44	3	0	0	5.2	1.000	C-9
1948		22	.211	.211	38	8	0	0	0	0.0	0	4	1	6	0	12	4	36	4	1	1	4.1	.976	C-10
1949	**STL A**	109	.261	.384	284	74	9	1	8	2.8	28	49	32	22	0	15	2	279	39	4	3	3.5	.988	C-93
1950		126	.280	.449	396	111	22	3	13	3.3	55	65	64	25	2	13	4	367	48	8	9	3.9	.981	C-109
1951		98	.252	.397	310	78	21	0	8	2.6	44	44	43	26	1	10	2	361	48	2	8	4.8	.995	C-85, 3B-1
1952	**CHI A**	132	.240	.384	375	90	15	0	13	3.5	35	50	54	34	1	11	2	590	53	7	4	5.4	.989	C-120
1953		113	.287	.416	334	96	19	0	8	2.4	46	54	47	29	1	5	1	473	51	3	2	4.9	.994	C-107, 1B-1
1954		107	.244	.351	316	77	13	0	7	2.2	31	34	37	28	0	15	3	395	38	3	8	4.7	.993	C-93
1955		138	.261	.408	426	111	13	1	16	3.8	67	61	68	34	2	4	1	664	62	4	12	5.4	.995	C-136
1956		136	.293	.438	450	132	28	2	11	2.4	55	75	53	34	2	5	2	679	40	5	6	5.5	.993	C-132
1957		101	.256	.393	351	90	11	2	11	3.1	33	70	35	24	2	9	3	454	45	1	5	5.2	.998	C-96
1958		127	.273	.454	421	115	16	0	20	4.8	53	84	57	37	2	13	5	597	63	9	8	5.8	.987	C-116
1959		140	.265	.451	505	134	22	3	22	4.4	63	84	55	49	4	5	3	800	68	6	33	6.0	.993	C-122, 1B-24
1960		129	.252	.356	421	106	23	0	7	1.7	43	46	42	39	2	7	2	555	54	3	12	5.0	.995	C-123
1961		116	.282	.380	337	95	10	1	7	2.1	38	41	37	22	0	10	4	464	48	1	6	4.8	.998	C-107
1962		84	.268	.350	220	59	12	0	2	0.9	17	26	32	23	1	19	2	298	23	3	0	4.9	.991	C-66
1963		35	.233	.288	73	17	4	0	0	0.0	4	6	8	7	0	11	2	98	9	2	2	4.4	.982	C-23, 1B-2
18 yrs.		1752	.264	.402	5351	1415	244	14	155	2.9	623	808	671	453	20	170	43	7243	705	63	120	5.0	.992	C-1571, 1B-27, 3B-1
WORLD SERIES																								
1947	**NY A**	2	.750	1.250	4	3	2	0	0	0.0	3	1	0	0	0	0	0	2	1	0	0	1.5	1.000	C-2
1959	**CHI A**	6	.227	.364	22	5	0	0	1	4.5	3	5	1	3	0	0	0	28	5	0	0	5.5	1.000	C-6
2 yrs.		8	.308	.500	26	8	2	0	1	3.8	6	6	1	3	0	0	0	30	6	0	0	4.5	1.000	C-8

Doug Loman

LOMAN, DOUGLAS EDWARD BL TL 5′11½″ 185 lbs.
B. May 9, 1958, Bakersfield, Calif.

Year	Team	Games	BA	SA	AB	H	2B	3B	HR	HR%	R	RBI	BB	SO	SB	Pinch Hit AB	Pinch Hit H	PO	A	E	DP	TC/G	FA	G by Pos
1984	**MIL A**	23	.276	.408	76	21	4	0	2	2.6	13	12	15	7	0	0	0	54	4	2	0	2.6	.967	OF-23
1985		24	.212	.318	66	14	3	2	0	0.0	10	7	1	12	0	7	2	41	4	0	2	2.3	1.000	OF-20
2 yrs.		47	.246	.366	142	35	7	2	2	1.4	23	19	16	19	0	7	2	95	8	2	2	2.4	.981	OF-43

Ernie Lombardi

LOMBARDI, ERNESTO NATALI (Bocci, Schnozz) BR TR 6′ 3″ 230 lbs.
B. Apr. 6, 1908, Oakland, Calif. D. Sept. 26, 1977, Santa Cruz, Calif.
Hall of Fame 1986.

Year	Team	Games	BA	SA	AB	H	2B	3B	HR	HR%	R	RBI	BB	SO	SB	Pinch Hit AB	Pinch Hit H	PO	A	E	DP	TC/G	FA	G by Pos
1931	**BKN N**	73	.297	.412	182	54	7	1	4	2.2	20	23	12	12	1	21	7	218	23	4	5	4.9	.984	C-50
1932	**CIN N**	118	.303	.479	413	125	22	9	11	2.7	43	68	41	19	0	7	2	288	76	14	6	3.5	.963	C-108
1933		107	.283	.383	350	99	21	1	4	1.1	30	47	16	17	2	10	2	223	52	8	3	3.0	.972	C-95
1934		132	.305	.434	417	127	19	4	9	2.2	42	62	16	22	0	19	4	383	61	5	8	4.0	.989	C-111
1935		120	.343	.539	332	114	23	3	12	3.6	36	64	16	6	0	**36**	8	298	49	6	4	4.3	.983	C-82
1936		121	.333	.496	387	129	23	2	12	3.1	42	68	19	16	1	15	3	330	54	15	10	3.8	.962	C-105
1937		120	.334	.473	368	123	22	1	9	2.4	41	59	14	17	1	28	5	333	58	11	3	4.5	.973	C-90
1938		129	**.342**	.524	489	167	30	1	19	3.9	60	95	40	14	0	6	3	512	73	9	8	4.8	.985	C-123
1939		130	.287	.487	450	129	26	2	20	4.4	43	85	35	19	0	8	1	536	63	10	7	5.1	.984	C-120
1940		109	.319	.489	376	120	22	0	14	3.7	50	74	31	14	0	7	2	397	46	5	5	4.4	.989	C-101
1941		117	.264	.374	398	105	12	1	10	2.5	33	60	36	14	1	1	0	496	70	10	9	5.0	.983	C-116
1942	**BOS N**	105	**.330**	.482	309	102	14	0	11	3.6	32	46	37	12	1	16	2	251	41	6	3	3.5	.980	C-85
1943	**NY N**	104	.305	.431	295	90	7	0	10	3.4	19	51	16	11	1	28	7	296	36	10	8	4.7	.971	C-73
1944		117	.255	.370	373	95	13	0	10	2.7	37	58	33	25	0	14	3	350	47	13	11	4.1	.968	C-100
1945		115	.307	.486	368	113	7	1	19	5.2	46	70	43	11	0	18	4	425	49	8	8	5.0	.983	C-96

Year	Team	Games	BA	SA	AB	H	2B	3B	HR	HR%	R	RBI	BB	SO	SB	Pinch Hit AB	Pinch Hit H	PO	A	E	DP	TC/G	FA	G by Pos

Ernie Lombardi *continued*

Year	Team	Games	BA	SA	AB	H	2B	3B	HR	HR%	R	RBI	BB	SO	SB	Pinch Hit AB	Pinch Hit H	PO	A	E	DP	TC/G	FA	G by Pos
1946		88	.290	.466	238	69	4	1	12	5.0	19	39	18	24	0	24	6	272	36	7	7	5.0	.978	C-63
1947		48	.282	.436	110	31	5	0	4	3.6	8	21	7	9	0	23	7	86	11	2	2	4.1	.980	C-24
17 yrs.		1853	.306	.460	5855	1792	277	27	190	3.2	601	990	430	262	8	281	66	5694	845	143	107	4.3	.979	C-1542
WORLD SERIES																								
1939	**CIN N**	4	.214	.214	14	3	0	0	0	0.0	0	2	0	1	0	0	0	22	1	1	0	6.0	.958	C-4
1940		2	.333	.667	3	1	1	0	0	0.0	0	0	1	0	0	0	0	4	0	0	0	4.0	1.000	C-1
2 yrs.		6	.235	.294	17	4	1	0	0	0.0	0	2	1	1	0	0	0	26	1	1	0	5.6	.964	C-5

Phil Lombardi

LOMBARDI, PHILLIP ARDEN BR TR 6′ 2″ 200 lbs.
B. Feb. 20, 1963, Abilene, Tex.

Year	Team	Games	BA	SA	AB	H	2B	3B	HR	HR%	R	RBI	BB	SO	SB	Pinch Hit AB	Pinch Hit H	PO	A	E	DP	TC/G	FA	G by Pos
1986	**NY A**	20	.278	.528	36	10	3	0	2	5.6	6	6	4	7	0	9	3	22	3	3	0	2.5	.893	OF-8, C-3
1987		5	.125	.125	8	1	0	0	0	0.0	0	0	0	2	0	5	0	7	1	0	0	2.7	1.000	C-3
1989	**NY N**	18	.229	.313	48	11	1	0	1	2.1	4	3	5	8	0	3	0	93	5	2	1	5.9	.980	C-16, 1B-1
3 yrs.		43	.239	.380	92	22	4	0	3	3.3	10	9	9	17	0	17	3	122	9	5	1	4.4	.963	C-22, OF-8, 1B-1

Steve Lombardozzi

LOMBARDOZZI, STEPHEN PAUL (Lombo) BR TR 6′ 175 lbs.
B. Apr. 26, 1960, Malden, Mass.

Year	Team	Games	BA	SA	AB	H	2B	3B	HR	HR%	R	RBI	BB	SO	SB	Pinch Hit AB	Pinch Hit H	PO	A	E	DP	TC/G	FA	G by Pos
1985	**MIN A**	28	.370	.481	54	20	4	1	0	0.0	10	6	6	6	3	1	0	31	80	2	16	4.3	.982	2B-26
1986		156	.227	.347	453	103	20	5	8	1.8	53	33	52	76	3	0	0	289	407	6	102	4.5	.991	2B-155
1987		136	.238	.352	432	103	19	3	8	1.9	51	38	33	66	5	0	0	245	356	14	77	4.6	.977	2B-133
1988		103	.209	.307	287	60	15	2	3	1.0	34	27	35	48	2	1	1	152	237	5	54	3.7	.987	2B-90, SS-12, 3B-5
1989	**HOU N**	21	.216	.432	37	8	3	1	1	2.7	5	3	4	9	0	2	0	20	28	4	5	2.7	.923	2B-18, 3B-1
1990		2	.000	.000	1	0	0	0	0	0.0	0	0	1	1	0	1	0	0	0	0	0	0.0	—	
6 yrs.		446	.233	.347	1264	294	61	12	20	1.6	153	107	131	206	13	5	1	737	1108	31	254	4.3	.983	2B-422, SS-12, 3B-6
LEAGUE CHAMPIONSHIP SERIES																								
1987	**MIN A**	5	.267	.267	15	4	0	0	0	0.0	2	1	2	2	0	0	0	8	9	1	3	3.6	.944	2B-5
WORLD SERIES																								
1987	**MIN A**	6	.412	.647	17	7	1	0	1	5.9	3	4	2	2	0	0	0	9	24	0	3	5.5	1.000	2B-6

Walt Lonergan

LONERGAN, WALTER E. BR TR 5′ 7″ 156 lbs.
B. Sept. 22, 1885, Boston, Mass. D. Jan. 23, 1958, Lexington, Mass.

Year	Team	Games	BA	SA	AB	H	2B	3B	HR	HR%	R	RBI	BB	SO	SB	Pinch Hit AB	Pinch Hit H	PO	A	E	DP	TC/G	FA	G by Pos
1911	**BOS A**	10	.269	.269	26	7	0	0	0	0.0	2	1	1		1	0	0	19	17	3	2	4.3	.923	2B-7, SS-1, 3B-1

Long

LONG
Deceased.

Year	Team	Games	BA	SA	AB	H	2B	3B	HR	HR%	R	RBI	BB	SO	SB	Pinch Hit AB	Pinch Hit H	PO	A	E	DP	TC/G	FA	G by Pos
1888	**LOU AA**	1	.000	.000	2	0	0	0	0	0.0	0	0	1		0	0	0	0	0	0	0	0.0	.000	OF-1

Dale Long

LONG, RICHARD DALE BL TL 6′ 4″ 205 lbs.
B. Feb. 6, 1926, Springfield, Mo. D. Jan. 27, 1991, Palm Coast, Fla.

Year	Team	Games	BA	SA	AB	H	2B	3B	HR	HR%	R	RBI	BB	SO	SB	Pinch Hit AB	Pinch Hit H	PO	A	E	DP	TC/G	FA	G by Pos
1951	**2 teams**	**PIT N** (10G –.167) **STL A** (34G –.238)																						
″	**total**	44	.231	.368	117	27	5	1	3	2.6	12	12	10	25	0	13	1	235	19	3	23	8.6	.988	1B-29, OF-1
1955	**PIT N**	131	.291	.513	419	122	19	**13**	16	3.8	59	79	48	72	0	13	4	968	97	13	114	9.1	.988	1B-119
1956		148	.263	.485	517	136	20	7	27	5.2	64	91	54	85	1	12	2	1201	99	24	92	9.6	.982	1B-138
1957	**2 teams**	**PIT N** (7G –.182) **CHI N** (123G –.305)																						
″	**total**	130	.298	.496	419	125	20	0	21	5.0	55	67	56	73	1	18	6	962	77	5	87	9.4	.995	1B-111
1958	**CHI N**	142	.271	.467	480	130	26	4	20	4.2	68	75	66	64	2	5	2	1173	85	10	130	9.1	.992	1B-137, C-2
1959		110	.236	.432	296	70	10	3	14	4.7	34	37	31	53	0	27	6	731	49	12	63	9.3	.985	1B-85
1960	**2 teams**	**SF N** (37G –.167) **NY A** (26G –.366)																						
″	**total**	63	.253	.495	95	24	3	1	6	6.3	10	16	12	13	0	39	11	151	10	1	8	7.7	.994	1B-21
1961	**WAS A**	123	.249	.459	377	94	20	4	17	4.5	52	49	39	41	0	24	3	827	62	15	87	9.5	.983	1B-95
1962	**2 teams**	**WAS A** (67G –.241) **NY A** (41G –.298)																						
″	**total**	108	.260	.386	285	74	12	0	8	2.8	29	41	36	31	6	28	3	701	53	4	88	9.2	.995	1B-82
1963	**NY A**	14	.200	.200	15	3	0	0	0	0.0	1	0	1	3	0	11	2	11	0	1	1	6.0	.917	1B-2
10 yrs.		1013	.267	.464	3020	805	135	33	132	4.4	384	467	353	460	10	190	40	6960	551	88	693	9.2	.988	1B-819, C-2, OF-1
WORLD SERIES																								
1960	**NY A**	3	.333	.333	3	1	0	0	0	0.0	0	0	0	0	0	3	1	0	0	0	0	0.0	—	
1962		2	.200	.200	5	1	0	0	0	0.0	0	1	0	1	0	0	0	9	3	0	1	6.0	1.000	1B-2
2 yrs.		5	.250	.250	8	2	0	0	0	0.0	0	1	0	1	0	3	1	9	3	0	1	6.0	1.000	1B-2

Dan Long

LONG, DANIEL W.
B. Aug. 27, 1867, Boston, Mass. D. Apr. 30, 1929, Sausalito, Calif.

Year	Team	Games	BA	SA	AB	H	2B	3B	HR	HR%	R	RBI	BB	SO	SB	Pinch Hit AB	Pinch Hit H	PO	A	E	DP	TC/G	FA	G by Pos
1890	**BAL AA**	21	.156	.156	77	12	0	0	0	0.0	19		14		16	0	0	26	5	2	0	1.6	.939	OF-21

Herman Long

LONG, HERMAN C. (Germany) BL TR 5′ 8½″ 160 lbs.
B. Apr. 13, 1866, Chicago, Ill. D. Sept. 17, 1909, Denver, Colo.

Year	Team	Games	BA	SA	AB	H	2B	3B	HR	HR%	R	RBI	BB	SO	SB	Pinch Hit AB	Pinch Hit H	PO	A	E	DP	TC/G	FA	G by Pos
1889	**KC AA**	136	.275	.368	574	158	32	6	3	0.5	137	60	64	63	89	0	0	355	506	122	59	7.2	.876	SS-128, 2B-8, OF-1
1890	**BOS N**	101	.251	.355	431	108	15	3	8	1.9	95	52	40	34	49	0	0	230	352	66	40	6.4	.898	SS-101
1891		139	.282	.400	577	163	21	13	7	1.2	129	74	80	51	60	0	0	345	441	85	60	6.3	.902	SS-139
1892		151	.280	.378	646	181	33	6	6	0.9	115	78	44	36	57	0	0	313	502	102	65	6.0	.889	SS-141, OF-12, 3B-1
1893		128	.288	.382	552	159	22	6	6	1.1	**149**	58	73	32	38	0	0	282	487	100	68	6.8	.885	SS-123, 2B-5
1894		104	.324	.505	475	154	28	11	12	2.5	137	79	35	17	24	0	0	239	365	78	53	6.4	.886	SS-98, OF-5, 2B-3
1895		124	.316	.447	535	169	23	10	9	1.7	109	75	31	12	35	0	0	289	412	84	49	6.3	.893	SS-122, 2B-2
1896		120	.343	.463	501	172	26	8	6	1.2	105	100	26	16	36	0	0	311	415	83	52	6.7	.897	SS-120
1897		107	.322	.444	450	145	32	7	3	0.7	89	69	23		22	0	0	274	353	66	40	6.4	.905	SS-107, OF-1
1898		144	.265	.365	589	156	21	10	6	1.0	99	99	39		20	0	0	333	479	67	65	6.1	.924	SS-142, 2B-2
1899		145	.265	.375	578	153	30	8	6	1.0	91	100	45		20	0	0	371	437	60	69	6.0	.931	SS-143, 1B-2
1900		125	.261	.391	486	127	19	4	**12**	**2.5**	80	66	44		26	0	0	257	454	48	34	6.1	.937	SS-125
1901		138	.228	.295	518	118	14	6	3	0.6	55	68	25		20	0	0	304	468	44	55	5.9	.946	SS-138

Herman Long *continued*

Year	Team	Games	BA	SA	AB	H	2B	3B	HR	HR%	R	RBI	BB	SO	SB	Pinch Hit AB	Pinch Hit H	PO	A	E	DP	TC/G	FA	G by Pos
1902		118	.228	.268	429	98	11	0	2	0.5	39	44	31		24	0	0	320	395	44	52	6.4	.942	SS-105, 2B-13
1903	**2 teams**	**NY A** (22G –.188) **DET A** (69G –.222)																						
"	**total**	91	.213	.260	319	68	15	0	0	0.0	27	31	12		14	1	1	213	258	46	24	5.7	.911	SS-60, 2B-31
1904	**PHI N**	1	.250	.250	4	1	0	0	0	0.0	0	0	0		0	0	0	4	4	1	0	9.0	.889	2B-1
16 yrs.		1872	.278	.383	7664	2130	342	98	89	1.2	1456	1053	612	261	534	1	1	4440	6328	1096	785	6.3	.908	SS-1792, 2B-65, OF-19, 1B-2, 3B-1

Jeoff Long

LONG, JEOFFREY KEITH BR TR 6′ 1″ 200 lbs.
B. Oct. 9, 1941, Covington, Ky.

Year	Team	Games	BA	SA	AB	H	2B	3B	HR	HR%	R	RBI	BB	SO	SB	Pinch Hit AB	Pinch Hit H	PO	A	E	DP	TC/G	FA	G by Pos
1963	**STL N**	5	.200	.200	5	1	0	0	0	0.0	0	0	0	1	0	5	1	0	0	0	0	0.0	—	
1964	**2 teams**	**STL N** (28G –.233) **CHI A** (23G –.143)																						
"	**total**	51	.192	.244	78	15	1	0	1	1.3	5	9	10	33	0	28	4	69	4	3	7	4.5	.961	OF-9, 1B-8
2 yrs.		56	.193	.241	83	16	1	0	1	1.2	5	9	10	34	0	33	5	69	4	3	7	4.5	.961	OF-9, 1B-8

Jim Long

LONG, JAMES ALBERT BR TR 5′11″ 160 lbs.
B. June 29, 1898, Fort Dodge, Iowa D. Sept. 14, 1970, Fort Dodge, Iowa.

Year	Team	Games	BA	SA	AB	H	2B	3B	HR	HR%	R	RBI	BB	SO	SB	Pinch Hit AB	Pinch Hit H	PO	A	E	DP	TC/G	FA	G by Pos
1922	**CHI A**	3	.000	.000	3	0	0	0	0	0.0	0	0	1	0	0	1	0	1	0	0	0	0.5	1.000	C-2

Jim Long

LONG, JAMES M.
B. Nov. 15, 1862, Louisville, Ky. D. Dec. 12, 1932, Louisville, Ky.

Year	Team	Games	BA	SA	AB	H	2B	3B	HR	HR%	R	RBI	BB	SO	SB	Pinch Hit AB	Pinch Hit H	PO	A	E	DP	TC/G	FA	G by Pos
1891	**LOU AA**	6	.240	.240	25	6	0	0	0	0.0	5	4	3	6	1	0	0	10	2	2	1	2.3	.857	OF-6
1893	**BAL N**	55	.212	.283	226	48	8	1	2	0.9	31	25	16	27	23	0	0	109	8	14	1	2.4	.893	OF-55
2 yrs.		61	.215	.279	251	54	8	1	2	0.8	36	29	19	33	24	0	0	119	10	16	2	2.4	.890	OF-61

Red Long

LONG, NELSON BR TR 6′ 1″ 190 lbs.
B. Sept. 28, 1876, Burlington, Ont., Canada D. Aug. 11, 1929, Hamilton, Ont., Canada.

Year	Team	Games	BA	SA	AB	H	2B	3B	HR	HR%	R	RBI	BB	SO	SB	Pinch Hit AB	Pinch Hit H	PO	A	E	DP	TC/G	FA	G by Pos
1902	**BOS N**	3	.273	.273	11	3	0	0	0	0.0	1	0	0		0	0	0	8	6	0	0	4.7	1.000	SS-2, P-1

Tommy Long

LONG, THOMAS AUGUSTUS BR TR 5′10½″ 165 lbs.
B. June 1, 1890, Mitchum, Ala. D. June 15, 1972, Mobile, Ala.

Year	Team	Games	BA	SA	AB	H	2B	3B	HR	HR%	R	RBI	BB	SO	SB	Pinch Hit AB	Pinch Hit H	PO	A	E	DP	TC/G	FA	G by Pos
1911	**WAS A**	14	.229	.292	48	11	3	0	0	0.0	1	5	1		4	1	0	13	1	2	0	1.2	.875	OF-13
1912		1	.000	.000	1	0	0	0	0	0.0	0	0	0		0	1	0	0	0	0	0	0.0	—	
1915	**STL N**	140	.294	.446	507	149	21	**25**	2	0.4	61	61	31	50	19	4	2	236	18	20	1	2.0	.927	OF-140
1916		119	.293	.377	403	118	11	10	1	0.2	37	33	10	43	21	12	2	143	13	9	2	1.6	.945	OF-106
1917		144	.232	.325	530	123	12	14	3	0.6	49	41	37	44	21	7	1	173	9	16	2	1.4	.919	OF-137
5 yrs.		418	.269	.379	1489	401	47	49	6	0.4	148	140	79	137	65	25	5	565	41	47	5	1.6	.928	OF-396

Tony Longmire

LONGMIRE, ANTHONY EUGENE BL TR 6′ 1″ 197 lbs.
B. Aug. 12, 1968, Vallejo, Calif.

Year	Team	Games	BA	SA	AB	H	2B	3B	HR	HR%	R	RBI	BB	SO	SB	Pinch Hit AB	Pinch Hit H	PO	A	E	DP	TC/G	FA	G by Pos
1993	**PHI N**	11	.231	.231	13	3	0	0	0	0.0	1	1	0	1	0	8	3	4	0	0	0	2.0	1.000	OF-2
1994		69	.237	.317	139	33	11	0	0	0.0	10	17	10	27	2	31	8	45	3	3	1	1.6	.941	OF-32
1995		59	.356	.510	104	37	7	0	3	2.9	21	19	11	19	1	33	10	33	2	0	0	1.5	1.000	OF-23
3 yrs.		139	.285	.391	256	73	18	0	3	1.2	32	37	21	47	3	72	21	82	5	3	1	1.6	.967	OF-57
LEAGUE CHAMPIONSHIP SERIES																								
1993	**PHI N**	1	.000	.000	1	0	0	0	0	0.0	0	0	0	1	0	1	0	0	0	0	0	0.0	—	

Joe Lonnett

LONNETT, JOSEPH PAUL BR TR 5′10″ 180 lbs.
B. Feb. 7, 1927, Beaver Falls, Pa.

Year	Team	Games	BA	SA	AB	H	2B	3B	HR	HR%	R	RBI	BB	SO	SB	Pinch Hit AB	Pinch Hit H	PO	A	E	DP	TC/G	FA	G by Pos
1956	**PHI N**	16	.182	.182	22	4	0	0	0	0.0	2	0	2	7	0	8	1	24	2	0	1	3.7	1.000	C-7
1957		67	.169	.294	160	27	5	0	5	3.1	12	15	22	39	0	2	0	305	16	1	3	5.0	.997	C-65
1958		17	.140	.180	50	7	2	0	0	0.0	0	2	2	11	0	2	0	78	7	1	3	5.7	.988	C-15
1959		43	.172	.215	93	16	1	0	1	1.1	8	10	14	17	0	0	0	171	4	3	0	4.1	.983	C-43
4 yrs.		143	.166	.246	325	54	8	0	6	1.8	22	27	40	74	0	12	1	578	29	5	7	4.7	.992	C-130

Bruce Look

LOOK, BRUCE MICHAEL BL TR 5′11″ 183 lbs.
Brother of Dean Look.
B. June 9, 1943, Lansing, Mich.

Year	Team	Games	BA	SA	AB	H	2B	3B	HR	HR%	R	RBI	BB	SO	SB	Pinch Hit AB	Pinch Hit H	PO	A	E	DP	TC/G	FA	G by Pos
1968	**MIN A**	59	.246	.280	118	29	4	0	0	0.0	7	9	20	24	0	16	3	202	20	1	5	5.4	.996	C-41

Dean Look

LOOK, DEAN ZACHARY BR TR 5′11″ 185 lbs.
Brother of Bruce Look.
B. July 23, 1937, Lansing, Mich.

Year	Team	Games	BA	SA	AB	H	2B	3B	HR	HR%	R	RBI	BB	SO	SB	Pinch Hit AB	Pinch Hit H	PO	A	E	DP	TC/G	FA	G by Pos
1961	**CHI A**	3	.000	.000	6	0	0	0	0	0.0	0	0	0	1	0	2	0	1	0	0	0	1.0	1.000	OF-1

Stan Lopata

LOPATA, STANLEY EDWARD BR TR 6′ 2″ 210 lbs.
B. Sept. 12, 1925, Delray, Mich.

Year	Team	Games	BA	SA	AB	H	2B	3B	HR	HR%	R	RBI	BB	SO	SB	Pinch Hit AB	Pinch Hit H	PO	A	E	DP	TC/G	FA	G by Pos
1948	**PHI N**	6	.133	.200	15	2	1	0	0	0.0	2	2	0	4	0	2	0	17	1	0	1	4.5	1.000	C-4
1949		83	.271	.425	240	65	9	2	8	3.3	31	27	21	44	1	19	4	236	19	7	2	4.5	.973	C-58
1950		58	.209	.279	129	27	2	2	1	0.8	10	11	22	25	1	5	1	176	13	5	3	3.8	.974	C-51
1951		3	.000	.000	5	0	0	0	0	0.0	0	0	0	0	0	2	0	6	0	0	0	6.0	1.000	C-1
1952		57	.274	.402	179	49	9	1	4	2.2	25	27	36	33	1	3	0	274	21	4	6	5.4	.987	C-55
1953		81	.239	.419	234	56	12	3	8	3.4	34	31	28	39	3	1	0	344	27	5	2	4.7	.987	C-80
1954		86	.290	.544	259	75	14	5	14	5.4	42	42	33	37	1	8	3	336	27	4	1	4.8	.989	C-75, 1B-1
1955		99	.271	.538	303	82	9	3	22	7.3	49	58	58	62	4	8	2	480	50	3	16	5.9	.994	C-66, 1B-24
1956		146	.267	.535	535	143	33	7	32	6.0	96	95	75	93	5	5	2	873	40	16	41	6.6	.983	C-102, 1B-39
1957		116	.237	.433	388	92	18	2	18	4.6	50	67	56	81	2	7	2	634	36	8	9	6.3	.988	C-108
1958		86	.248	.388	258	64	9	0	9	3.5	36	33	60	63	0	6	2	418	28	6	6	5.7	.987	C-80
1959	**MIL N**	25	.104	.104	48	5	0	0	0	0.0	0	4	3	13	0	11	2	49	0	0	1	3.8	1.000	C-11, 1B-2
1960		7	.125	.125	8	1	0	0	0	0.0	0	0	1	3	0	3	1	17	0	1	0	4.5	.944	C-4
13 yrs.		853	.254	.452	2601	661	116	25	116	4.5	375	397	393	497	18	80	19	3860	262	59	88	5.5	.986	C-695, 1B-66
WORLD SERIES																								
1950	**PHI N**	2	.000	.000	1	0	0	0	0	0.0	0	0	0	1	0	1	0	1	0	0	0	1.0	1.000	C-1

Davey Lopes

LOPES, DAVID EARL
B. May 3, 1945, East Providence, R. I.
BR TR 5′ 9″ 170 lbs.

Year	Team	Games	BA	SA	AB	H	2B	3B	HR	HR%	R	RBI	BB	SO	SB	Pinch Hit AB	Pinch Hit H	PO	A	E	DP	TC/G	FA	G by Pos
1972	LA N	11	.214	.310	42	9	4	0	0	0.0	6	1	7	6	4	0	0	27	27	2	5	5.1	.964	2B-11
1973		142	.275	.351	535	147	13	5	6	1.1	77	37	62	77	36	1	0	323	380	11	90	5.0	.985	2B-135, OF-5, SS-2, 3B-1
1974		145	.266	.383	530	141	26	3	10	1.9	95	35	66	71	59	0	0	309	360	24	71	4.8	.965	2B-143
1975		155	.262	.359	618	162	24	6	8	1.3	108	41	91	93	**77**	0	0	360	386	16	60	4.4	.979	2B-137, OF-24, SS-14
1976		117	.241	.342	427	103	17	7	4	0.9	72	20	56	49	**63**	0	0	254	268	19	56	4.5	.965	2B-100, OF-19
1977		134	.283	.406	502	142	19	5	11	2.2	85	53	73	69	47	1	1	287	380	14	74	5.2	.979	2B-130
1978		151	.278	.421	587	163	25	4	17	2.9	93	58	71	70	45	1	1	340	424	20	88	5.3	.974	2B-147, OF-2
1979		153	.265	.464	582	154	20	6	28	4.8	109	73	97	88	44	1	0	341	384	14	82	4.9	.981	2B-152
1980		141	.251	.344	553	139	15	3	10	1.8	79	49	58	71	23	0	0	304	416	15	85	5.3	.980	2B-140
1981		58	.206	.285	214	44	2	0	5	2.3	35	17	22	35	20	3	0	129	161	2	30	5.3	.993	2B-55
1982	OAK A	128	.242	.371	450	109	19	3	11	2.4	58	42	40	51	28	0	0	295	338	15	82	4.9	.977	2B-125, OF-6
1983		147	.277	.423	494	137	13	4	17	3.4	64	67	51	61	22	10	3	267	287	9	83	3.8	.984	2B-123, DH-12, OF-7, 3B-5
1984	2 teams	OAK A (72G –.257) CHI N (16G –.235)																						
″	total	88	.255	.421	247	63	12	1	9	3.6	37	36	37	41	15	7	2	105	49	6	10	1.9	.962	OF-51, 2B-19, DH-9, 3B-5
1985	CHI N	99	.284	.444	275	78	11	0	11	4.0	52	44	46	37	47	22	4	115	6	1	1	1.5	.992	OF-79, 3B-4, 2B-1
1986	2 teams	CHI N (59G –.299) HOU N (37G –.235)																						
″	total	96	.275	.420	255	70	10	3	7	2.7	49	35	43	25	25	19	4	96	65	8	5	2.2	.953	OF-41, 3B-37
1987	HOU N	47	.233	.349	43	10	2	0	1	2.3	4	6	13	8	2	28	7	6	0	1	0	1.4	.857	OF-5
16 yrs.		1812	.263	.388	6354	1671	232	50	155	2.4	1023	614	833	852	557	93	22	3558	3931	177	822	4.4	.977	2B-1418, OF-239, 3B-52, DH-21, SS-16
DIVISIONAL PLAYOFF SERIES																								
1981	LA N	5	.200	.250	20	4	1	0	0	0.0	1	0	3	7	1	0	0	7	12	0	0	3.8	1.000	2B-5
LEAGUE CHAMPIONSHIP SERIES																								
1974	LA N	4	.267	.400	15	4	0	1	0	0.0	4	3	5	1	3	0	0	9	18	1	4	7.0	.964	2B-4
1977		4	.235	.235	17	4	0	0	0	0.0	2	3	2	0	0	0	0	9	10	1	1	5.0	.950	2B-4
1978		4	.389	.889	18	7	1	1	2	11.1	3	5	0	1	1	0	0	10	10	2	3	5.5	.909	2B-4
1981		5	.278	.278	18	5	0	0	0	0.0	0	0	1	3	5	0	0	13	13	0	5	5.2	1.000	2B-5
1984	CHI N	2	.000	.000	1	0	0	0	0	0.0	0	0	0	0	0	1	0	0	0	0	0	0.0	.000	OF-1
1986	HOU N	3	.000	.000	2	0	0	0	0	0.0	1	0	1	0	0	2	0	0	0	0	0	0.0	—	
6 yrs.		22	.282	.437	71	20	1	2	2	2.8	10	11	9	5	9	3	0	41	51	4	13	5.3	.958	2B-17, OF-1
								4th							**3rd**									
WORLD SERIES																								
1974	LA N	5	.111	.111	18	2	0	0	0	0.0	2	0	3	4	2	0	0	19	9	0	3	5.6	1.000	2B-5
1977		6	.167	.375	24	4	0	1	1	4.2	3	2	4	3	2	0	0	12	22	0	2	5.7	1.000	2B-6
1978		6	.308	.654	26	8	0	0	3	11.5	7	7	2	1	2	0	0	10	19	1	4	5.0	.967	2B-6
1981		6	.227	.273	22	5	1	0	0	0.0	6	2	4	3	4	0	0	26	14	6	5	7.7	.870	2B-6
4 yrs.		23	.211	.378	90	19	1	1	4	4.4	18	11	13	11	10	0	0	67	64	7	14	6.0	.949	2B-23
															3rd									

Al Lopez

LOPEZ, ALFONSO RAYMOND
B. Aug. 20, 1908, Tampa, Fla.
Manager 1951–65, 1968–69.
Hall of Fame 1977.
BR TR 5′11″ 165 lbs.

Year	Team	Games	BA	SA	AB	H	2B	3B	HR	HR%	R	RBI	BB	SO	SB	Pinch Hit AB	Pinch Hit H	PO	A	E	DP	TC/G	FA	G by Pos
1928	BKN N	3	.000	.000	12	0	0	0	0	0.0	0	0	0	0	0	0	0	9	0	0	0	3.0	1.000	C-3
1930		128	.309	.418	421	130	20	4	6	1.4	60	57	33	35	3	1	1	465	66	9	9	4.3	.983	C-126
1931		111	.269	.328	360	97	13	4	0	0.0	38	40	28	33	1	5	1	390	69	11	6	4.5	.977	C-105
1932		126	.275	.356	404	111	18	6	1	0.2	44	43	34	35	3	1	0	456	82	13	10	4.4	.976	C-125
1933		126	.301	.376	372	112	11	4	3	0.8	39	41	21	39	10	1	1	452	88	5	15	4.4	.991	C-124, 2B-1
1934		140	.273	.383	439	120	23	2	7	1.6	58	54	49	44	2	1	0	548	68	11	6	4.4	.982	C-137, 3B-2, 2B-2
1935		128	.251	.327	379	95	12	4	3	0.8	50	39	35	36	2	1	0	472	65	11	8	4.3	.980	C-126
1936	BOS N	128	.242	.345	426	103	12	4	8	1.9	46	50	41	41	1	1	0	448	107	14	9	4.4	.975	C-127, 1B-1
1937		105	.204	.269	334	68	11	1	3	0.9	31	38	35	57	3	1	1	342	83	7	5	4.2	.984	C-102
1938		71	.267	.314	236	63	6	1	1	0.4	19	14	11	24	5	0	0	240	42	3	4	4.0	.989	C-71
1939		131	.252	.369	412	104	22	1	8	1.9	32	49	40	45	1	0	0	424	72	7	11	3.9	.986	C-129
1940	2 teams	BOS N (36G –.294) PIT N (59G –.259)																						
″	total	95	.273	.355	293	80	9	3	3	1.0	35	41	19	21	6	0	0	343	62	4	11	4.3	.990	C-95
1941	PIT N	114	.265	.347	317	84	9	1	5	1.6	33	43	31	23	0	0	0	345	54	8	5	3.6	.980	C-114
1942		103	.256	.308	289	74	8	2	1	0.3	17	26	34	17	0	2	2	327	53	2	14	3.9	.995	C-99
1943		118	.263	.317	372	98	9	4	1	0.3	40	39	49	25	2	1	0	378	67	5	9	3.8	.989	C-116, 3B-1
1944		115	.230	.281	331	76	12	1	1	0.3	27	34	34	24	4	0	0	372	52	7	6	3.7	.984	C-115
1945		91	.218	.251	243	53	8	0	0	0.0	22	18	35	12	1	0	0	326	38	3	7	4.0	.992	C-91
1946		56	.307	.340	150	46	2	0	1	0.7	13	12	23	14	1	0	0	173	30	3	4	3.7	.985	C-56
1947	CLE A	61	.262	.270	126	33	1	0	0	0.0	9	14	9	13	1	4	0	144	28	0	1	3.0	1.000	C-57
19 yrs.		1950	.261	.337	5916	1547	206	42	52	0.9	613	652	561	538	46	19	6	6654	1126	123	140	4.1	.984	C-1918, 3B-3, 2B-3, 1B-1

Art Lopez

LOPEZ, ARTURO
Born Arturo Lopez (Rodriguez).
B. June 8, 1937, Mayaguez, Puerto Rico.
BL TL 5′ 9″ 170 lbs.

Year	Team	Games	BA	SA	AB	H	2B	3B	HR	HR%	R	RBI	BB	SO	SB	Pinch Hit AB	Pinch Hit H	PO	A	E	DP	TC/G	FA	G by Pos
1965	NY A	38	.143	.143	49	7	0	0	0	0.0	5	0	1	6	0	13	1	23	0	1	0	1.5	.958	OF-16

Carlos Lopez

LOPEZ, CARLOS ANTONIO
Born Carlos Antonio Lopez (Morales).
B. Sept. 27, 1950, Mazatlan, Mexico.
BR TR 6′ 190 lbs.

Year	Team	Games	BA	SA	AB	H	2B	3B	HR	HR%	R	RBI	BB	SO	SB	Pinch Hit AB	Pinch Hit H	PO	A	E	DP	TC/G	FA	G by Pos
1976	CAL A	9	.000	.000	10	0	0	0	0	0.0	1	0	2	3	2	0	0	4	0	0	0	0.8	1.000	OF-4, DH-1
1977	SEA A	99	.283	.431	297	84	18	1	8	2.7	39	34	14	61	16	5	1	160	11	5	3	1.9	.972	OF-90, DH-2
1978	BAL A	129	.238	.332	193	46	6	0	4	2.1	21	20	9	34	5	14	1	151	7	2	2	1.4	.988	OF-114, DH-1
3 yrs.		237	.260	.384	500	130	24	1	12	2.4	61	54	25	98	23	19	2	315	18	7	5	1.6	.979	OF-208, DH-4

Hector Lopez

LOPEZ, HECTOR HEADLEY BR TR 5'11" 182 lbs.
Born Hector Headley Lopez (Swainson).
B. July 9, 1929, Colon, Panama.

Year	Team	Lg	Games	BA	SA	AB	H	2B	3B	HR	HR%	R	RBI	BB	SO	SB	Pinch Hit AB	Pinch Hit H	PO	A	E	DP	TC/G	FA	G by Pos
1955	KC	A	128	.290	.422	483	140	15	2	15	3.1	50	68	33	58	1	1	0	197	331	29	58	4.3	.948	3B-93, 2B-36
1956			151	.273	.428	561	153	27	3	18	3.2	91	69	63	73	4	5	2	218	282	30	32	3.5	.943	3B-121, OF-20, 2B-8, SS-4
1957			121	.294	.448	391	115	19	4	11	2.8	51	35	41	66	1	8	3	125	229	23	21	3.2	.939	3B-111, 2B-4, OF-3
1958			151	.261	.415	564	147	28	4	17	3.0	84	73	49	61	2	4	1	309	377	21	86	4.6	.970	2B-96, 3B-55, OF-1, SS-1
1959	2 teams	KC A (36G –.281) NY A (112G –.283)																							
"	total		148	.283	.471	541	153	26	5	22	4.1	82	93	36	77	4	5	0	209	219	31	31	3.2	.932	3B-76, OF-35, 2B-33
1960	NY	A	131	.284	.414	408	116	14	6	9	2.2	66	42	46	64	1	26	2	204	9	7	2	2.0	.968	OF-106, 2B-5, 3B-1
1961			93	.222	.305	243	54	7	2	3	1.2	27	22	24	38	1	16	4	123	7	3	0	1.8	.977	OF-72
1962			106	.275	.391	335	92	19	1	6	1.8	45	48	33	53	0	24	5	177	5	3	0	2.2	.984	OF-84, 3B-1, 2B-1
1963			130	.249	.395	433	108	13	4	14	3.2	54	52	35	71	1	9	2	188	11	9	2	1.7	.957	OF-124, 2B-1
1964			127	.260	.418	285	74	9	3	10	3.5	34	34	24	54	1	22	7	131	4	4	1	1.3	.971	OF-103, 3B-1
1965			111	.261	.392	283	74	12	2	7	2.5	25	39	26	61	0	28	5	100	3	7	1	1.4	.936	OF-75, 1B-2
1966			54	.214	.368	117	25	4	1	4	3.4	14	16	8	20	0	20	7	43	1	3	0	1.6	.936	OF-29
12 yrs.			1451	.269	.415	4644	1251	193	37	136	2.9	623	591	418	696	16	168	38	2024	1478	170	234	2.8	.954	OF-652, 3B-459, 2B-184, SS-5, 1B-2
WORLD SERIES																									
1960	NY	A	3	.429	.429	7	3	0	0	0	0.0	0	0	0	0	0	2	2	0	1	0	0	1.0	1.000	OF-1
1961			4	.333	.889	9	3	0	1	1	11.1	3	7	2	3	0	0	0	8	0	0	0	2.7	1.000	OF-3
1962			2	.000	.000	2	0	0	0	0	0.0	0	0	0	0	0	2	0	0	0	0	0	0.0	—	
1963			3	.250	.500	8	2	2	0	0	0.0	1	0	0	1	0	1	0	2	0	0	0	1.0	1.000	OF-2
1964			3	.000	.000	2	0	0	0	0	0.0	0	0	0	2	0	2	0	0	0	0	0	0.0	.000	OF-1
5 yrs.			15	.286	.536	28	8	2	1	1	3.6	4	7	2	6	0	7	2	10	1	0	0	1.6	1.000	OF-7

Javier Lopez

LOPEZ, JAVIER BR TR 6' 3" 185 lbs.
Born Javier Lopez (Torres).
B. Nov. 5, 1970, Ponce, Puerto Rico.

Year	Team	Lg	Games	BA	SA	AB	H	2B	3B	HR	HR%	R	RBI	BB	SO	SB	Pinch Hit AB	Pinch Hit H	PO	A	E	DP	TC/G	FA	G by Pos
1992	ATL	N	9	.375	.500	16	6	2	0	0	0.0	3	2	0	1	0	2	1	28	2	0	0	3.3	1.000	C-9
1993			8	.375	.750	16	6	1	1	1	6.3	1	2	0	2	0	2	0	37	2	1	0	5.7	.975	C-7
1994			80	.245	.419	277	68	9	0	13	4.7	27	35	17	61	0	6	1	560	35	3	0	8.0	.995	C-75
1995			100	.315	.498	333	105	11	4	14	4.2	37	51	14	57	0	11	1	625	50	8	2	7.3	.988	C-93
4 yrs.			197	.288	.470	642	185	23	5	28	4.4	68	90	31	121	0	21	3	1250	89	12	2	7.3	.991	C-184
DIVISIONAL PLAYOFF SERIES																									
1995	ATL	N	3	.444	.444	9	4	0	0	0	0.0	0	3	0	3	0	0	0	22	3	0	1	8.3	1.000	C-3
LEAGUE CHAMPIONSHIP SERIES																									
1992	ATL	N	1	.000	.000	1	0	0	0	0	0.0	0	0	0	0	0	0	0	2	0	0	0	2.0	1.000	C-1
1995			3	.357	.643	14	5	1	0	1	7.1	2	3	0	1	0	0	0	28	2	0	0	10.0	1.000	C-3
2 yrs.			4	.333	.600	15	5	1	0	1	6.7	2	3	0	1	0	0	0	30	2	0	0	8.0	1.000	C-4
WORLD SERIES																									
1995	ATL	N	6	.176	.471	17	3	2	0	1	5.9	1	3	1	1	0	1	0	32	4	0	0	6.0	1.000	C-6

Luis Lopez

LOPEZ, LUIS ANTONIO BR TR 6' 1" 190 lbs.
B. Sept. 1, 1964, Brooklyn, N. Y.

Year	Team	Lg	Games	BA	SA	AB	H	2B	3B	HR	HR%	R	RBI	BB	SO	SB	Pinch Hit AB	Pinch Hit H	PO	A	E	DP	TC/G	FA	G by Pos
1990	LA	N	6	.000	.000	6	0	0	0	0	0.0	0	0	0	2	0	5	0	4	0	0	1	4.0	1.000	1B-1
1991	CLE	A	35	.220	.293	82	18	4	1	0	0.0	7	7	4	7	0	10	4	109	9	2	7	4.0	.983	C-12, 1B-10, DH-6, OF-1, 3B-1
2 yrs.			41	.205	.273	88	18	4	1	0	0.0	7	7	4	9	0	15	4	113	9	2	8	4.0	.984	C-12, 1B-11, DH-6, OF-1, 3B-1

Luis Lopez

LOPEZ, LUIS MANUEL BB TR 5'11" 175 lbs.
Born Luis Manuel Lopez (Santos).
B. Sept. 4, 1970, Cidra, Puerto Rico.

Year	Team	Lg	Games	BA	SA	AB	H	2B	3B	HR	HR%	R	RBI	BB	SO	SB	Pinch Hit AB	Pinch Hit H	PO	A	E	DP	TC/G	FA	G by Pos
1993	SD	N	17	.116	.140	43	5	1	0	0	0.0	1	1	0	8	0	1	1	23	34	1	5	3.9	.983	2B-15
1994			77	.277	.379	235	65	16	1	2	0.9	29	20	15	39	3	8	1	101	174	14	23	3.8	.952	SS-43, 2B-29, 3B-5
2 yrs.			94	.252	.342	278	70	17	1	2	0.7	30	21	15	47	3	9	2	124	208	15	28	3.8	.957	2B-44, SS-43, 3B-5

Bris Lord

LORD, BRISCOE ROBOTHAM (The Human Eyeball) BR TR 5' 9" 185 lbs.
B. Sept. 21, 1883, Upland, Pa. D. Nov. 13, 1964, Annapolis, Md.

Year	Team	Lg	Games	BA	SA	AB	H	2B	3B	HR	HR%	R	RBI	BB	SO	SB	Pinch Hit AB	Pinch Hit H	PO	A	E	DP	TC/G	FA	G by Pos
1905	PHI	A	66	.239	.298	238	57	14	0	0	0.0	41	13	14		3	5	1	94	9	4	3	1.8	.963	OF-60, 3B-1
1906			118	.233	.302	434	101	13	7	1	0.2	50	44	27		12	2	1	212	13	14	4	2.1	.941	OF-115
1907			57	.182	.218	170	31	3	0	1	0.6	12	11	14		2	4	1	91	6	5	0	1.9	.951	OF-53, P-1
1909	CLE	A	69	.269	.333	249	67	7	3	1	0.4	26	25	8		10	2	0	110	13	1	4	1.8	.992	OF-69
1910	2 teams	CLE A (56G –.219) PHI A (72G –.278)																							
"	total		128	.254	.376	489	124	21	18	1	0.2	76	37	35		10	2	1	219	20	7	6	2.0	.972	OF-126
1911	PHI	A	134	.310	.429	574	178	37	11	3	0.5	92	55	35		15	2	1	271	17	11	5	2.3	.963	OF-132
1912			96	.238	.317	378	90	12	9	0	0.0	63	25	34		15	0	0	148	15	10	5	1.8	.942	OF-96
1913	BOS	N	73	.251	.387	235	59	12	1	6	2.6	22	26	8	22	7	11	1	81	4	8	0	1.5	.914	OF-62
8 yrs.			741	.256	.348	2767	707	119	49	13	0.5	382	236	175	22	74	28	6	1226	97	60	27	1.9	.957	OF-713, P-1, 3B-1
WORLD SERIES																									
1905	PHI	A	5	.100	.100	20	2	0	0	0	0.0	0	2	0	5	0	0	0	11	1	0	0	2.4	1.000	OF-5
1910			5	.182	.273	22	4	2	0	0	0.0	3	1	1	3	0	0	0	8	0	0	0	1.6	1.000	OF-5
1911			6	.185	.259	27	5	2	0	0	0.0	2	1	0	5	0	0	0	14	1	0	0	2.5	1.000	OF-6
3 yrs.			16	.159	.217	69	11	4	0	0	0.0	5	4	1	13	0	0	0	33	2	0	0	2.2	1.000	OF-16

Carlton Lord

LORD, WILLIAM CARLTON BR TR 5'11" 170 lbs.
B. Jan. 7, 1900, Philadelphia, Pa. D. Aug. 15, 1947, Chester, Pa.

Year	Team	Lg	Games	BA	SA	AB	H	2B	3B	HR	HR%	R	RBI	BB	SO	SB	Pinch Hit AB	Pinch Hit H	PO	A	E	DP	TC/G	FA	G by Pos
1923	PHI	N	17	.234	.277	47	11	2	0	0	0.0	3	2	2	3	0	3	1	12	23	7	1	3.0	.833	3B-14

Harry Lord

LORD, HARRY DONALD BL TR 5'10½" 165 lbs.
B. Mar. 8, 1882, Porter, Me. D. Aug. 9, 1948, Westbrook, Me.
Manager 1915.

Year	Team	Lg	Games	BA	SA	AB	H	2B	3B	HR	HR%	R	RBI	BB	SO	SB	Pinch Hit AB	Pinch Hit H	PO	A	E	DP	TC/G	FA	G by Pos
1907	BOS	A	10	.158	.184	38	6	1	0	0	0.0	4	3	1		1	0	0	12	22	3	0	3.7	.919	3B-10
1908			145	.260	.319	558	145	15	6	2	0.4	61	37	22		23	1	0	181	271	47	13	3.5	.906	3B-143
1909			136	.311	.360	534	166	12	7	0	0.0	85	31	20		36	1	0	180	268	34	10	3.6	.929	3B-134

Harry Lord *continued*

Year	Team	Games	BA	SA	AB	H	2B	3B	HR	HR%	R	RBI	BB	SO	SB	Pinch Hit AB	Pinch Hit H	PO	A	E	DP	TC/G	FA	G by Pos
1910	2 teams	BOS A (77G –.250)	CHI A (44G –.297)																					
"	total	121	.267	.333	453	121	11	8	1	0.2	51	42	28		34	3	1	136	219	27	15	3.3	.929	3B-114, SS-1
1911	CHI A	141	.321	.433	561	180	18	18	3	0.5	103	61	32		43	2	0	175	226	25	21	3.1	.941	3B-138
1912		151	.267	.368	570	152	19	12	5	0.9	81	54	52		28	0	0	188	177	38	14	2.7	.906	3B-106, OF-45
1913		150	.263	.346	547	144	18	12	1	0.2	62	42	45	39	24	0	0	142	221	30	13	2.6	.924	3B-150
1914		21	.188	.275	69	13	1	1	1	1.4	8	3	5	3	2	0	0	10	32	3	0	2.3	.933	3B-19, OF-1
1915	BUF F	97	.270	.345	359	97	12	6	1	0.3	50	21	21		15	3	1	86	158	14	13	2.8	.946	3B-92, OF-1
9 yrs.		972	.278	.356	3689	1024	107	70	14	0.4	505	294	226	42	206	10	2	1110	1594	221	99	3.1	.924	3B-906, OF-47, SS-1

Mark Loretta

LORETTA, MARK DAVID BR TR 6′ 175 lbs.
B. Aug. 14, 1971, Santa Monica, Calif.

Year	Team	Games	BA	SA	AB	H	2B	3B	HR	HR%	R	RBI	BB	SO	SB	Pinch Hit AB	Pinch Hit H	PO	A	E	DP	TC/G	FA	G by Pos
1995	MIL A	19	.260	.380	50	13	3	0	1	2.0	13	3	4	7	1	4	2	19	42	1	8	3.4	.984	SS-13, 2B-4, DH-1

Scott Loucks

LOUCKS, SCOTT GREGORY BR TR 6′ 178 lbs.
B. Nov. 11, 1956, Anchorage, Alaska.

Year	Team	Games	BA	SA	AB	H	2B	3B	HR	HR%	R	RBI	BB	SO	SB	Pinch Hit AB	Pinch Hit H	PO	A	E	DP	TC/G	FA	G by Pos
1980	HOU N	8	.333	.333	3	1	0	0	0	0.0	4	0	0	2	0	2	1	1	0	0	0	0.3	1.000	OF-4
1981		10	.571	.571	7	4	0	0	0	0.0	2	0	1	3	1	0	0	5	0	0	0	1.0	1.000	OF-5
1982		44	.224	.265	49	11	2	0	0	0.0	6	3	3	17	4	5	0	41	3	1	1	1.2	.978	OF-37
1983		7	.214	.214	14	3	0	0	0	0.0	2	0	1	4	2	1	0	12	1	0	0	2.2	1.000	OF-6
1985	PIT N	4	.286	.571	7	2	2	0	0	0.0	1	1	2	2	0	0	0	2	0	0	0	0.5	1.000	OF-4
5 yrs.		73	.262	.313	80	21	4	0	0	0.0	15	4	7	28	7	8	1	61	4	1	1	1.2	.985	OF-56

Baldy Louden

LOUDEN, WILLIAM P. BR TR 5′11″ 175 lbs.
B. Aug. 27, 1885, Piedmont, W. Va. D. Dec. 8, 1935, Piedmont, W. Va.

Year	Team	Games	BA	SA	AB	H	2B	3B	HR	HR%	R	RBI	BB	SO	SB	Pinch Hit AB	Pinch Hit H	PO	A	E	DP	TC/G	FA	G by Pos
1907	NY A	5	.111	.111	9	1	0	0	0	0.0	4	0	2		1	0	0	4	8	4	0	5.3	.750	3B-3
1912	DET A	121	.241	.298	403	97	12	4	1	0.2	57	36	58		28	2	1	242	370	39	25	5.6	.940	2B-86, 3B-26, SS-5
1913		72	.241	.314	191	46	4	5	0	0.0	28	23	24	22	6	2	0	76	146	17	11	3.5	.929	2B-32, 3B-26, SS-6, OF-5
1914	BUF F	126	.313	.399	431	135	11	4	6	1.4	73	63	52		35	10	4	299	285	43	34	5.5	.931	SS-115
1915		141	.281	.367	469	132	18	5	4	0.9	67	48	64		30	2	0	283	391	27	51	5.2	.961	2B-88, SS-27, 3B-19
1916	CIN N	134	.219	.280	439	96	16	4	1	0.2	38	32	54	54	12	5	0	279	417	25	51	5.5	.965	2B-108, SS-23
6 yrs.		599	.261	.334	1942	507	61	22	12	0.6	267	202	254	76	112	21	5	1183	1617	155	172	5.2	.948	2B-314, SS-176, 3B-74, OF-5

Charlie Loudenslager

LOUDENSLAGER, CHARLES EDWARD TR 5′ 9″ 186 lbs.
B. May 21, 1881, Baltimore, Md. D. Oct. 31, 1933, Baltimore, Md.

Year	Team	Games	BA	SA	AB	H	2B	3B	HR	HR%	R	RBI	BB	SO	SB	Pinch Hit AB	Pinch Hit H	PO	A	E	DP	TC/G	FA	G by Pos
1904	BKN N	1	.000	.000	2	0	0	0	0	0.0	0	0	0		0	0	0	0	1	0	0	1.0	1.000	2B-1

Bill Loughlin

LOUGHLIN, WILLIAM H.
B. Baltimore, Md. Deceased.

Year	Team	Games	BA	SA	AB	H	2B	3B	HR	HR%	R	RBI	BB	SO	SB	Pinch Hit AB	Pinch Hit H	PO	A	E	DP	TC/G	FA	G by Pos
1883	BAL AA	1	.400	.400	5	2	0	0	0	0.0	0		0			0	0	0	0	0	0	0.0	.000	OF-1

Loughran

LOUGHRAN
B. New York, N. Y. Deceased.

Year	Team	Games	BA	SA	AB	H	2B	3B	HR	HR%	R	RBI	BB	SO	SB	Pinch Hit AB	Pinch Hit H	PO	A	E	DP	TC/G	FA	G by Pos
1884	NY N	9	.103	.207	29	3	1	1	0	0.0	4		7	11		0	0	46	8	10	1	6.4	.844	C-9, OF-1

Tom Lovelace

LOVELACE, THOMAS RIVERS BR TR 5′11″ 170 lbs.
B. Oct. 19, 1897, Wolfe City, Tex. D. July 12, 1979, Dallas, Tex.

Year	Team	Games	BA	SA	AB	H	2B	3B	HR	HR%	R	RBI	BB	SO	SB	Pinch Hit AB	Pinch Hit H	PO	A	E	DP	TC/G	FA	G by Pos
1922	PIT N	1	.000	.000	1	0	0	0	0	0.0	0	0	0	0	0	1	0	0	0	0	0	0.0	—	

Mem Lovett

LOVETT, MERRITT MARWOOD BR TR 5′9½″ 165 lbs.
B. June 15, 1912, Chicago, Ill.

Year	Team	Games	BA	SA	AB	H	2B	3B	HR	HR%	R	RBI	BB	SO	SB	Pinch Hit AB	Pinch Hit H	PO	A	E	DP	TC/G	FA	G by Pos
1933	CHI A	1	.000	.000	1	0	0	0	0	0.0	0	0	0	0	0	1	0	0	0	0	0	0.0	—	

Jay Loviglio

LOVIGLIO, JOHN PAUL BR TR 5′ 9″ 160 lbs.
B. May 30, 1956, Freeport, N. Y.

Year	Team	Games	BA	SA	AB	H	2B	3B	HR	HR%	R	RBI	BB	SO	SB	Pinch Hit AB	Pinch Hit H	PO	A	E	DP	TC/G	FA	G by Pos
1980	PHI N	16	.000	.000	5	0	0	0	0	0.0	7	0	1	0	1	0	0	3	2	0	0	5.0	1.000	2B-1
1981	CHI A	14	.267	.267	15	4	0	0	0	0.0	5	2	1	1	2	0	0	9	10	3	2	2.4	.864	3B-4, 2B-3, DH-2
1982		15	.194	.194	31	6	0	0	0	0.0	5	2	1	4	2	0	0	24	30	2	5	3.7	.964	2B-13, DH-2
1983	CHI N	1	.000	.000	1	0	0	0	0	0.0	0	0	0	1	0	1	0	0	0	0	0	0.0	—	
4 yrs.		46	.192	.192	52	10	0	0	0	0.0	17	4	3	6	5	1	0	36	42	5	7	3.3	.940	2B-17, 3B-4, DH-4

Joe Lovitto

LOVITTO, JOSEPH, JR. BB TR 6′ 185 lbs.
B. Jan. 6, 1951, San Pedro, Calif.

Year	Team	Games	BA	SA	AB	H	2B	3B	HR	HR%	R	RBI	BB	SO	SB	Pinch Hit AB	Pinch Hit H	PO	A	E	DP	TC/G	FA	G by Pos
1972	TEX A	117	.224	.267	330	74	9	1	1	0.3	23	19	37	54	13	7	1	233	7	6	2	2.4	.976	OF-103
1973		26	.136	.159	44	6	1	0	0	0.0	3	0	5	7	1	0	0	26	21	5	3	2.3	.904	3B-20, OF-3
1974		113	.223	.297	283	63	9	3	2	0.7	27	26	25	36	6	1	0	224	7	6	4	2.1	.975	OF-107, 1B-5
1975		50	.208	.264	106	22	3	0	1	0.9	17	8	13	16	2	7	1	71	3	1	1	1.8	.987	OF-38, DH-2, 1B-1, C-1
4 yrs.		306	.216	.271	763	165	22	4	4	0.5	70	53	80	113	22	15	2	554	38	18	10	2.2	.970	OF-251, 3B-20, 1B-6, DH-2, C-1

Torey Lovullo

LOVULLO, SALVATORE ANTHONY BB TR 6′ 185 lbs.
B. July 25, 1965, Santa Monica, Calif.

Year	Team	Games	BA	SA	AB	H	2B	3B	HR	HR%	R	RBI	BB	SO	SB	Pinch Hit AB	Pinch Hit H	PO	A	E	DP	TC/G	FA	G by Pos
1988	DET A	12	.381	.667	21	8	1	1	1	4.8	2	2	1	2	0	0	0	12	19	0	2	2.6	1.000	2B-9, 3B-3
1989		29	.115	.172	87	10	2	0	1	1.1	8	4	14	20	0	4	0	134	24	1	15	5.5	.994	1B-18, 3B-11
1991	NY A	22	.176	.216	51	9	2	0	0	0.0	0	2	5	7	0	0	0	14	33	3	1	2.3	.940	3B-22
1993	CAL A	116	.251	.354	367	92	20	0	6	1.6	42	30	36	49	7	12	5	208	249	11	70	4.0	.976	2B-91, 3B-14, SS-9, OF-2, 1B-1
1994	SEA A	36	.222	.375	72	16	5	0	2	2.8	9	7	9	13	1	8	2	19	49	1	8	2.7	.986	2B-20, 3B-5, DH-1
5 yrs.		215	.226	.329	598	135	30	1	10	1.7	61	45	65	91	8	24	7	387	374	16	96	3.8	.979	2B-120, 3B-55, 1B-19, SS-9, OF-2, DH-1

Fletcher Low

LOW, FLETCHER BR TR 5′10½″ 175 lbs.
B. Apr. 7, 1893, Essex, Mass. D. June 6, 1973, Hanover, N. H.

Year	Team	Games	BA	SA	AB	H	2B	3B	HR	HR%	R	RBI	BB	SO	SB	Pinch Hit AB	Pinch Hit H	PO	A	E	DP	TC/G	FA	G by Pos
1915	BOS N	1	.250	.750	4	1	0	1	0	0.0	1	1	0	0	0	0	0	2	1	0	0	3.0	1.000	3B-1

Bobby Lowe

LOWE, ROBERT LINCOLN (Link) BR TR 5′10″ 150 lbs.
B. July 10, 1868, Pittsburgh, Pa. D. Dec. 8, 1951, Detroit, Mich.
Manager 1904.

Year	Team	Games	BA	SA	AB	H	2B	3B	HR	HR%	R	RBI	BB	SO	SB	Pinch Hit AB	Pinch Hit H	PO	A	E	DP	TC/G	FA	G by Pos
1890	BOS N	52	.280	.391	207	58	13	2	2	1.0	35	21	26	32	15	0	0	103	82	11	2	3.8	.944	SS-24, OF-15, 3B-12
1891		125	.260	.354	497	129	19	5	6	1.2	92	74	53	54	43	**1**	0	214	70	24	5	2.4	.922	OF-107, 2B-17, SS-2, 3B-1, P-1
1892		124	.242	.324	475	115	16	7	3	0.6	79	57	37	46	36	0	0	264	119	37	18	3.3	.912	OF-90, 3B-14, SS-13, 2B-10
1893		126	.298	.433	526	157	19	5	14	2.7	130	89	55	29	22	0	0	320	425	52	59	6.3	.935	2B-121, SS-5
1894		133	.346	.520	**613**	212	34	11	17	2.8	158	115	50	25	23	0	0	348	408	59	63	6.1	.928	2B-130, SS-2, 3B-1
1895		99	.296	.410	412	122	12	7	7	1.7	101	62	40	16	24	0	0	265	336	29	50	6.4	.954	2B-99
1896		73	.321	.403	305	98	11	4	2	0.7	59	48	20	11	15	0	0	193	280	17	31	6.7	.965	2B-73
1897		123	.309	.419	499	154	24	8	5	1.0	87	106	32		16	0	0	270	404	34	33	5.8	.952	2B-123
1898		147	.272	.338	559	152	11	7	4	0.7	65	94	29		12	0	0	405	467	38	64	6.2	.958	2B-145, SS-2
1899		152	.272	.335	559	152	5	9	4	0.7	81	88	35		17	0	0	366	473	40	66	5.8	.954	2B-148, SS-4
1900		127	.278	.342	474	132	11	5	3	0.6	65	71	26		15	0	0	323	335	34	38	5.4	.951	2B-127
1901		129	.255	.299	491	125	11	1	3	0.6	47	47	17		22	0	0	201	244	38	21	3.7	.921	3B-111, 2B-18
1902	CHI N	121	.246	.286	472	116	13	3	0	0.0	41	31	11		16	0	0	329	410	33	59	6.5	.957	2B-117, 3B-2
1903		32	.267	.371	105	28	5	3	0	0.0	14	15	4		5	1	1	91	80	11	13	6.3	.940	2B-22, 1B-6, 3B-1
1904	2 teams	PIT N (1G –.000) DET A (140G –.208)																						
″	total	141	.207	.258	507	105	14	6	0	0.0	47	40	17		15	1	0	328	402	27	44	5.4	.964	2B-140
1905	DET A	60	.193	.254	181	35	7	2	0	0.0	17	9	13		3	2	0	93	54	4	1	2.6	.974	OF-25, 3B-22, 2B-6, SS-4, 1B-1
1906		41	.207	.248	145	30	3	0	1	0.7	11	12	4		3	2	0	99	136	16	3	6.1	.936	SS-19, 2B-17, 3B-5
1907		17	.243	.297	37	9	2	0	0	0.0	2	5	4		0	2	0	7	17	3	0	1.7	.889	3B-10, OF-4, SS-2
18 yrs.		1822	.273	.360	7064	1929	230	85	71	1.0	1131	984	473	213	302	9	1	4219	4742	507	570	5.2	.946	2B-1313, OF-241, 3B-179, SS-77, 1B-7, P-1

Dickie Lowe

LOWE, RICHARD ALVERN
B. Jan. 28, 1854, Evansville, Wis. D. June 28, 1922, Janesville, Wis.

Year	Team	Games	BA	SA	AB	H	2B	3B	HR	HR%	R	RBI	BB	SO	SB	Pinch Hit AB	Pinch Hit H	PO	A	E	DP	TC/G	FA	G by Pos
1884	DET N	1	.333	.333	3	1	0	0	0	0.0	0		0	1		0	0	0	1	7	0	8.0	.125	C-1

John Lowenstein

LOWENSTEIN, JOHN LEE BL TR 6′ 175 lbs.
B. Jan. 27, 1947, Wolf Point, Mont.

Year	Team	Games	BA	SA	AB	H	2B	3B	HR	HR%	R	RBI	BB	SO	SB	Pinch Hit AB	Pinch Hit H	PO	A	E	DP	TC/G	FA	G by Pos
1970	CLE A	17	.256	.442	43	11	3	1	1	2.3	5	6	1	9	1	3	0	15	37	2	6	3.6	.963	2B-10, OF-2, 3B-2, SS-1
1971		58	.186	.307	140	26	5	0	4	2.9	15	9	16	28	1	9	2	103	66	4	18	3.5	.977	2B-29, OF-18, SS-3
1972		68	.212	.397	151	32	8	1	6	4.0	16	21	20	43	2	11	3	82	7	0	3	1.5	1.000	OF-58, 1B-2
1973		98	.292	.410	305	89	16	1	6	2.0	42	40	23	41	5	20	7	124	85	7	22	2.0	.968	OF-51, 2B-25, DH-25, 3B-8, 1B-1
1974		140	.242	.325	508	123	14	2	8	1.6	65	48	53	85	36	2	1	314	84	6	11	2.8	.985	OF-100, 3B-28, 1B-12, 2B-4
1975		91	.242	.404	265	64	5	1	12	4.5	37	33	28	28	15	14	4	61	16	2	1	1.0	.975	OF-36, DH-31, 3B-8, 2B-2
1976		93	.205	.284	229	47	8	2	2	0.9	33	14	25	35	11	16	2	178	10	7	9	2.4	.964	OF-61, DH-11, 1B-9
1977		81	.242	.376	149	36	6	1	4	2.7	24	12	21	29	1	25	4	63	1	0	0	1.1	1.000	OF-39, DH-19, 1B-1
1978	TEX A	77	.222	.386	176	39	8	3	5	2.8	28	21	37	29	16	22	4	34	42	6	2	1.3	.927	3B-25, DH-21, OF-16
1979	BAL A	97	.254	.482	197	50	8	2	11	5.6	33	34	30	37	16	23	5	124	7	1	3	1.7	.992	OF-72, DH-3, 3B-1, 1B-1
1980		104	.311	.413	196	61	8	0	4	2.0	38	27	32	29	7	12	5	128	3	1	0	1.4	.992	OF-91, DH-3
1981		83	.249	.381	189	47	7	0	6	3.2	19	20	22	32	7	10	3	100	3	1	0	1.4	.990	OF-73, DH-4
1982		122	.320	.602	322	103	15	2	24	7.5	69	66	54	59	7	17	5	202	2	0	0	1.8	1.000	OF-111
1983		122	.281	.481	310	87	13	2	15	4.8	52	60	49	55	2	16	4	155	8	3	1	1.5	.982	OF-107, DH-1, 2B-1
1984		105	.237	.374	270	64	13	0	8	3.0	34	28	33	54	1	26	6	113	5	3	2	1.3	.975	OF-67, DH-22, 1B-2
1985		12	.077	.077	26	2	0	0	0	0.0	0	2	2	3	0	3	0	7	0	0	0	0.7	1.000	DH-6, OF-4
16 yrs.		1368	.253	.403	3476	881	137	18	116	3.3	510	441	446	596	128	229	55	1803	376	43	78	1.8	.981	OF-906, DH-146, 3B-72, 2B-71, 1B-28, SS-4
LEAGUE CHAMPIONSHIP SERIES																								
1979	BAL A	4	.167	.667	6	1	0	0	1	16.7	2	3	2	2	0	2	1	6	0	0	0	2.0	1.000	OF-3
1983		2	.167	.333	6	1	1	0	0	0.0	0	2	1	2	0	0	0	4	0	0	0	1.3	1.000	OF-2, DH-1
2 yrs.		6	.167	.500	12	2	1	0	1	8.3	2	5	3	4	0	2	1	10	0	0	0	1.7	1.000	OF-5, DH-1
WORLD SERIES																								
1979	BAL A	6	.231	.308	13	3	1	0	0	0.0	2	3	1	3	0	3	2	6	0	1	0	2.3	.857	OF-3
1983		4	.385	.692	13	5	1	0	1	7.7	2	1	0	3	0	0	0	4	0	1	0	1.3	.800	OF-4
2 yrs.		10	.308	.500	26	8	2	0	1	3.8	4	4	1	6	0	3	2	10	0	2	0	1.7	.833	OF-7

Peanuts Lowrey

LOWREY, HARRY LEE BR TR 5′ 8½″ 170 lbs.
B. Aug. 27, 1918, Culver City, Calif. D. July 2, 1986, Inglewood, Calif.

Year	Team	Games	BA	SA	AB	H	2B	3B	HR	HR%	R	RBI	BB	SO	SB	Pinch Hit AB	Pinch Hit H	PO	A	E	DP	TC/G	FA	G by Pos
1942	CHI N	27	.190	.241	58	11	0	0	1	1.7	4	4	4	4	0	3	0	43	2	1	1	2.4	.978	OF-19
1943		130	.292	.400	480	140	25	12	1	0.2	59	63	35	24	13	4	1	341	62	10	11	3.1	.976	OF-113, SS-16, 2B-3
1945		143	.283	.392	523	148	22	7	7	1.3	72	89	48	27	11	5	1	281	19	5	1	2.2	.984	OF-138, SS-2
1946		144	.257	.343	540	139	24	5	4	0.7	75	54	56	22	10	0	0	330	49	12	5	2.7	.969	OF-126, 3B-20
1947		115	.281	.375	448	126	17	5	5	1.1	56	37	38	26	2	1	0	138	200	17	21	2.9	.952	3B-91, OF-25, 2B-6
1948		129	.294	.349	435	128	12	3	2	0.5	47	54	34	31	2	13	3	238	29	5	4	2.4	.982	OF-103, 3B-9, 2B-2, SS-1
1949	2 teams	CHI N (38G –.270) CIN N (89G –.275)																						
″	total	127	.274	.362	420	115	21	2	4	1.0	66	35	46	19	4	16	6	259	9	4	2	2.5	.985	OF-109, 3B-1
1950	2 teams	CIN N (91G –.227) STL N (17G –.268)																						
″	total	108	.234	.297	320	75	14	0	2	0.6	44	15	42	8	0	14	2	184	36	4	8	2.5	.982	OF-76, 2B-7, 3B-5
1951	STL N	114	.303	.422	370	112	19	5	5	1.4	52	40	35	12	0	19	5	230	25	9	5	2.7	.966	OF-85, 3B-11, 2B-3
1952		132	.286	.353	374	107	18	2	1	0.3	48	48	34	13	3	27	**13**	176	20	7	2	1.8	.966	OF-106, 3B-6
1953		104	.269	.423	182	49	9	2	5	2.7	26	27	15	21	1	**59**	**22**	64	20	3	6	1.8	.966	OF-38, 2B-10, 3B-1
1954		74	.115	.197	61	7	1	2	0	0.0	6	5	9	9	0	53	7	5	0	0	0	0.4	1.000	OF-12
1955	PHI N	54	.189	.226	106	20	4	0	0	0.0	9	8	7	10	2	16	2	44	6	1	2	1.6	.980	OF-28, 2B-2, 1B-1
13 yrs.		1401	.273	.362	4317	1177	186	45	37	0.9	564	479	403	226	48	230	62	2333	477	78	68	2.5	.973	OF-978, 3B-144, 2B-33, SS-19, 1B-1
WORLD SERIES																								
1945	CHI N	7	.310	.345	29	9	1	0	0	0.0	4	0	1	2	1	0	0	21	1	0	0	3.1	1.000	OF-7

Dwight Lowry

LOWRY, DWIGHT
Born Dwight Lowery.
B. Oct. 23, 1957, Lumberton, N. C.
BL TR 6′ 3″ 210 lbs.

Year	Team	Games	BA	SA	AB	H	2B	3B	HR	HR%	R	RBI	BB	SO	SB	Pinch Hit AB	Pinch Hit H	PO	A	E	DP	TC/G	FA	G by Pos
1984	DET A	32	.244	.422	45	11	2	0	2	4.4	8	7	3	11	0	4	1	87	8	0	2	3.1	1.000	C-31
1986		56	.307	.393	150	46	4	0	3	2.0	21	18	17	19	0	0	0	250	17	2	2	4.7	.993	C-55, OF-1, 1B-1
1987		13	.200	.280	25	5	2	0	0	0.0	0	1	0	6	0	1	0	40	2	0	0	3.2	1.000	C-12, 1B-1
1988	MIN A	7	.000	.000	7	0	0	0	0	0.0	0	0	0	2	0	2	0	12	1	0	0	2.6	1.000	C-5
4 yrs.		108	.273	.374	227	62	8	0	5	2.2	29	26	20	38	0	7	1	389	28	2	4	4.0	.995	C-103, 1B-2, OF-1

Willie Lozado

LOZADO, WILLIAM
B. May 12, 1959, New York, N. Y.
BR TR 6′ 1″ 170 lbs.

Year	Team	Games	BA	SA	AB	H	2B	3B	HR	HR%	R	RBI	BB	SO	SB	Pinch Hit AB	Pinch Hit H	PO	A	E	DP	TC/G	FA	G by Pos
1984	MIL A	43	.271	.411	107	29	8	2	1	0.9	15	20	12	23	0	2	0	26	61	7	7	2.1	.926	3B-36, SS-6, DH-1, 2B-1

Steve Lubratich

LUBRATICH, STEVEN GEORGE
B. May 1, 1955, Oakland, Calif.
BR TR 6′ 170 lbs.

Year	Team	Games	BA	SA	AB	H	2B	3B	HR	HR%	R	RBI	BB	SO	SB	Pinch Hit AB	Pinch Hit H	PO	A	E	DP	TC/G	FA	G by Pos
1981	CAL A	7	.143	.190	21	3	1	0	0	0.0	2	1	0	2	1	0	0	2	17	0	2	3.2	1.000	3B-6
1983		57	.218	.276	156	34	9	0	0	0.0	12	7	4	17	0	0	0	91	149	7	34	4.2	.972	SS-23, 3B-22, 2B-14
2 yrs.		64	.209	.266	177	37	10	0	0	0.0	14	8	4	19	1	0	0	93	166	7	36	4.1	.974	3B-28, SS-23, 2B-14

Hugh Luby

LUBY, HUGH MAX (Hal)
B. June 13, 1913, Blackfoot, Ida. D. May 4, 1986, Eugene, Ore.
BR TR 5′10″ 185 lbs.

Year	Team	Games	BA	SA	AB	H	2B	3B	HR	HR%	R	RBI	BB	SO	SB	Pinch Hit AB	Pinch Hit H	PO	A	E	DP	TC/G	FA	G by Pos
1936	PHI A	9	.184	.211	38	7	1	0	0	0.0	3	3	0	7	2	0	0	16	28	6	3	5.6	.880	2B-9
1944	NY N	111	.254	.316	323	82	10	2	2	0.6	30	35	52	15	2	2	0	179	244	19	35	4.0	.957	3B-65, 2B-45, 1B-1
2 yrs.		120	.247	.305	361	89	11	2	2	0.6	33	38	52	22	4	2	0	195	272	25	38	4.1	.949	3B-65, 2B-54, 1B-1

Pat Luby

LUBY, JOHN PERKINS
B. June 1869, Charleston, S. C. D. Apr. 24, 1899, Charleston, S. C.
TR 6′ 185 lbs.

Year	Team	Games	BA	SA	AB	H	2B	3B	HR	HR%	R	RBI	BB	SO	SB	Pinch Hit AB	Pinch Hit H	PO	A	E	DP	TC/G	FA	G by Pos
1890	CHI N	36	.267	.440	116	31	5	3	3	2.6	27	17	9	6	3	0	0	31	44	3	0	2.2	.962	P-34, 1B-2
1891		32	.245	.408	98	24	2	4	2	2.0	19	24	8	16	3	0	0	14	42	3	2	1.8	.949	P-30, OF-2, 1B-1
1892		45	.190	.270	163	31	3	2	2	1.2	14	20	12	27	3	0	0	28	62	9	3	2.1	.909	P-31, OF-16
1895	LOU N	19	.283	.396	53	15	2	2	0	0.0	6	9	8	3	2	0	0	54	25	5	5	4.7	.940	P-11, 1B-5, OF-2
4 yrs.		132	.235	.363	430	101	12	11	7	1.6	66	70	37	52	11	0	0	127	173	20	10	2.4	.938	P-106, OF-20, 1B-8

Johnny Lucadello

LUCADELLO, JOHN
B. Feb. 22, 1919, Thurber, Tex.
BB TR 5′11″ 160 lbs.

Year	Team	Games	BA	SA	AB	H	2B	3B	HR	HR%	R	RBI	BB	SO	SB	Pinch Hit AB	Pinch Hit H	PO	A	E	DP	TC/G	FA	G by Pos
1938	STL A	7	.150	.200	20	3	1	0	0	0.0	1	0	0	0	0	1	0	5	5	1	0	1.8	.909	3B-6
1939		9	.233	.300	30	7	2	0	0	0.0	0	4	2	4	0	2	1	16	15	3	3	4.9	.912	2B-7
1940		17	.317	.540	63	20	4	2	2	3.2	15	10	6	4	1	1	0	37	53	3	14	5.8	.968	2B-16
1941		107	.279	.382	351	98	22	4	2	0.6	58	31	48	23	5	22	2	195	209	22	40	4.8	.948	2B-70, SS-12, 3B-6, OF-1
1946		87	.248	.305	210	52	7	1	1	0.5	21	15	36	20	0	25	7	84	102	7	14	3.4	.964	3B-37, 2B-19
1947	NY A	12	.083	.083	12	1	0	0	0	0.0	0	0	1	5	0	7	1	3	0	0	0	0.6	1.000	2B-5
6 yrs.		239	.264	.359	686	181	36	7	5	0.7	95	60	93	56	6	58	11	340	384	36	71	4.2	.953	2B-117, 3B-49, SS-12, OF-1

Fritz Lucas

LUCAS, FREDERICK WARRINGTON
B. Jan. 19, 1903, Vineland, N. J. D. Mar. 11, 1987, Cambridge, Md.
BR TR 5′10″ 165 lbs.

Year	Team	Games	BA	SA	AB	H	2B	3B	HR	HR%	R	RBI	BB	SO	SB	Pinch Hit AB	Pinch Hit H	PO	A	E	DP	TC/G	FA	G by Pos
1935	PHI N	20	.265	.265	34	9	0	0	0	0.0	1	2	3	6	0	8	1	17	0	1	0	1.8	.944	OF-10

Johnny Lucas

LUCAS, JOHN CHARLES (Buster)
B. Feb. 10, 1903, Glen Carbon, Ill. D. Oct. 31, 1970, Maryville, Ill.
BR TL 5′10″ 186 lbs.

Year	Team	Games	BA	SA	AB	H	2B	3B	HR	HR%	R	RBI	BB	SO	SB	Pinch Hit AB	Pinch Hit H	PO	A	E	DP	TC/G	FA	G by Pos
1931	BOS A	3	.000	.000	2	0	0	0	0	0.0	0	0	0	1	0	0	0	0	0	0	0	0.0	.000	OF-2
1932		1	.000	.000	1	0	0	0	0	0.0	0	0	0	0	0	1	0	0	0	0	0	0.0	—	
2 yrs.		4	.000	.000	3	0	0	0	0	0.0	0	0	0	1	0	1	0	0	0	0	0	0.0		OF-2

Red Lucas

LUCAS, CHARLES FREDERICK (The Nashville Narcissus)
B. Apr. 28, 1902, Columbia, Tenn. D. July 9, 1986, Nashville, Tenn.
BL TR 5′ 9½″ 170 lbs.

Year	Team	Games	BA	SA	AB	H	2B	3B	HR	HR%	R	RBI	BB	SO	SB	Pinch Hit AB	Pinch Hit H	PO	A	E	DP	TC/G	FA	G by Pos
1923	NY N	3	.000	.000	2	0	0	0	0	0.0	0	0	0	1	0	0	0	1	3	0	0	1.3	1.000	P-3
1924	BOS N	33	.333	.364	33	11	1	0	0	0.0	5	5	1	4	0	3	0	5	23	0	1	1.0	1.000	P-27, 3B-2
1925		6	.150	.150	20	3	0	0	0	0.0	1	2	2	4	0	0	0	9	21	1	3	5.2	.968	2B-6
1926	CIN N	66	.303	.461	76	23	4	4	0	0.0	15	14	10	13	0	21	5	6	36	0	1	1.0	1.000	P-39, 2B-1
1927		80	.313	.373	150	47	5	2	0	0.0	14	28	12	10	0	27	6	14	63	4	4	1.8	.951	P-37, 2B-5, SS-3, OF-1
1928		39	.315	.370	73	23	2	1	0	0.0	8	7	4	6	0	12	4	8	37	0	3	1.7	1.000	P-27
1929		76	.293	.336	140	41	6	0	0	0.0	15	13	13	15	1	42	**13**	12	63	4	3	2.5	.949	P-32
1930		80	.336	.442	113	38	4	1	2	1.8	18	19	17	4	0	**39**	**14**	8	30	0	0	1.2	1.000	P-33
1931		97	.281	.307	153	43	4	0	0	0.0	15	17	12	9	0	**60**	**15**	8	54	1	3	2.2	.984	P-29
1932		76	.287	.387	150	43	11	2	0	0.0	13	19	10	9	0	42	10	17	55	2	4	2.4	.973	P-31
1933		75	.287	.377	122	35	6	1	1	0.8	14	15	12	6	0	41	13	3	52	0	5	1.9	1.000	P-29
1934	PIT N	68	.219	.286	105	23	5	1	0	0.0	11	8	6	16	1	34	8	7	24	2	2	1.1	.939	P-29
1935		47	.318	.409	66	21	6	0	0	0.0	6	10	7	11	0	22	8	7	23	1	1	1.5	.968	P-20
1936		69	.241	.296	108	26	4	1	0	0.0	11	14	8	17	0	40	9	8	33	1	4	1.6	.976	P-27
1937		59	.268	.305	82	22	3	0	0	0.0	8	17	7	6	0	**37**	**9**	9	19	0	1	1.4	1.000	P-20
1938		33	.109	.109	46	5	0	0	0	0.0	1	2	3	2	0	17	0	3	14	0	1	1.3	1.000	P-13
16 yrs.		907	.281	.347	1439	404	61	13	3	0.2	155	190	124	133	2	437	114 **6th**	125	550	16	36	1.7	.977	P-396, 2B-12, SS-3, 3B-2, OF-1

Frank Luce

LUCE, FRANK EDWARD
B. Dec. 6, 1896, Spencer, Ohio D. Feb. 3, 1942, Milwaukee, Wis.
BL TR 5′11″ 180 lbs.

Year	Team	Games	BA	SA	AB	H	2B	3B	HR	HR%	R	RBI	BB	SO	SB	Pinch Hit AB	Pinch Hit H	PO	A	E	DP	TC/G	FA	G by Pos
1923	PIT N	9	.500	.500	12	6	0	0	0	0.0	2	3	2	2	2	3	0	4	0	0	0	0.8	1.000	OF-5

Fred Luderus

LUDERUS, FREDERICK WILLIAM
B. Sept. 12, 1885, Milwaukee, Wis. D. Jan. 5, 1961, Three Lakes, Wis.
BL TR 5′11½″ 185 lbs.

Year	Team	Games	BA	SA	AB	H	2B	3B	HR	HR%	R	RBI	BB	SO	SB	Pinch Hit AB	Pinch Hit H	PO	A	E	DP	TC/G	FA	G by Pos
1909	CHI N	11	.297	.459	37	11	1	1	1	2.7	8	9	3		0	0	0	110	4	6	4	10.9	.950	1B-11
1910	2 teams	CHI N (24G –.204) PHI N (21G –.294)																						
″	total	45	.254	.352	122	31	6	3	0	0.0	15	17	13	8	2	8	2	335	19	7	22	10.0	.981	1B-36
1911	PHI N	146	.301	.472	551	166	24	11	16	2.9	69	99	40	76	6	0	0	1373	77	22	85	10.1	.985	1B-146
1912		148	.257	.381	572	147	31	5	10	1.7	77	69	44	65	8	2	0	1421	104	15	77	10.5	.990	1B-146
1913		155	.262	.432	588	154	32	7	18	3.1	67	86	34	51	5	0	0	1533	92	26	76	10.7	.984	1B-155

Fred Luderus *continued*

Year	Team	Games	BA	SA	AB	H	2B	3B	HR	HR%	R	RBI	BB	SO	SB	Pinch Hit AB	Pinch Hit H	PO	A	E	DP	TC/G	FA	G by Pos
1914		121	.248	.388	443	110	16	5	12	2.7	55	55	33	31	2	0	0	1102	76	30	49	10.0	.975	1B-121
1915		141	.315	.457	499	157	36	7	7	1.4	55	62	42	36	9	0	0	1409	99	11	76	10.8	.993	1B-141
1916		146	.281	.374	508	143	26	3	5	1.0	52	53	41	32	8	0	0	1499	71	28	83	10.9	.982	1B-146
1917		154	.261	.351	522	136	24	4	5	1.0	57	72	65	35	5	0	0	1597	91	16	91	11.1	.991	1B-154
1918		125	.288	.378	468	135	23	2	5	1.1	54	67	42	33	4	0	0	1307	98	17	74	11.4	.988	1B-125
1919		138	.293	.405	509	149	30	6	5	1.0	60	54	54	48	6	0	0	1385	108	22	82	11.0	.985	1B-138
1920		16	.156	.219	32	5	2	0	0	0.0	1	4	3	6	0	9	2	55	4	1	6	8.6	.983	1B-7
12 yrs.		1346	.277	.403	4851	1344	251	54	84	1.7	570	647	414	421	55	19	4	13126	843	201	725	10.7	.986	1B-1326
WORLD SERIES																								
1915	**PHI N**	5	.438	.750	16	7	2	0	1	6.3	1	6	1	4	0	0	0	40	4	1	2	9.0	.978	1B-5

Bill Ludwig

LUDWIG, WILLIAM LAWRENCE BR TR
B. May 27, 1882, Louisville, Ky. D. Sept. 5, 1947, Louisville, Ky.

Year	Team	Games	BA	SA	AB	H	2B	3B	HR	HR%	R	RBI	BB	SO	SB	Pinch Hit AB	Pinch Hit H	PO	A	E	DP	TC/G	FA	G by Pos
1908	**STL N**	66	.182	.214	187	34	2	2	0	0.0	15	8	16		3	4	0	227	87	16	2	5.3	.952	C-62

Roy Luebbe

LUEBBE, ROY JOHN BB TR 6′ 175 lbs.
B. Sept. 17, 1900, Parkersburg, Iowa D. Aug. 21, 1985, Papillon, Neb.

Year	Team	Games	BA	SA	AB	H	2B	3B	HR	HR%	R	RBI	BB	SO	SB	Pinch Hit AB	Pinch Hit H	PO	A	E	DP	TC/G	FA	G by Pos
1925	**NY A**	8	.000	.000	15	0	0	0	0	0.0	1	3	2	6	0	0	0	26	4	0	0	3.8	1.000	C-8

Henry Luff

LUFF, HENRY T. 5′11″ 175 lbs.
B. Sept. 14, 1856, Philadelphia, Pa. D. Oct. 11, 1916, Philadelphia, Pa.

Year	Team	Games	BA	SA	AB	H	2B	3B	HR	HR%	R	RBI	BB	SO	SB	Pinch Hit AB	Pinch Hit H	PO	A	E	DP	TC/G	FA	G by Pos
1882	**2 teams**	**DET N** (3G –.273) **CIN AA** (28G –.233)																						
″	**total**	31	.237	.298	131	31	4	2	0	0.0	17	1	2	0		0	0	273	15	29	15	9.9	.909	1B-27, 2B-3, OF-2
1883	**LOU AA**	6	.174	.174	23	4	0	0	0	0.0	1		0			0	0	36	1	7	1	7.3	.841	1B-4, OF-2
1884	**2 teams**	**PHI U** (26G –.270) **KC U** (5G –.053)																						
″	**total**	31	.238	.300	130	31	4	2	0	0.0	9		5			0	0	95	26	40	4	4.7	.752	OF-16, 3B-9, 1B-6, 2B-3
3 yrs.		68	.232	.289	284	66	8	4	0	0.0	27	1	7	0		0	0	404	42	76	20	7.3	.854	1B-37, OF-20, 3B-9, 2B-6

Eddie Lukon

LUKON, EDWARD PAUL (Mongoose) BL TL 5′10″ 168 lbs.
B. Aug. 5, 1920, Burgettstown, Pa.

Year	Team	Games	BA	SA	AB	H	2B	3B	HR	HR%	R	RBI	BB	SO	SB	Pinch Hit AB	Pinch Hit H	PO	A	E	DP	TC/G	FA	G by Pos
1941	**CIN N**	23	.267	.302	86	23	3	0	0	0.0	6	3	6	6	1	0	0	47	2	1	1	2.3	.980	OF-22
1945		2	.125	.125	8	1	0	0	0	0.0	1	0	0	1	0	0	0	6	0	0	0	3.0	1.000	OF-2
1946		102	.250	.442	312	78	8	8	12	3.8	31	34	26	29	3	18	2	190	5	3	1	2.4	.985	OF-83
1947		86	.205	.410	200	41	6	1	11	5.5	26	33	28	36	0	28	6	103	4	0	2	1.9	1.000	OF-55
4 yrs.		213	.236	.408	606	143	17	9	23	3.8	64	70	60	72	4	46	8	346	11	4	4	2.2	.989	OF-162

Mike Lum

LUM, MICHAEL KEN-WAI BL TL 6′ 180 lbs.
B. Oct. 27, 1945, Honolulu, Hawaii.

Year	Team	Games	BA	SA	AB	H	2B	3B	HR	HR%	R	RBI	BB	SO	SB	Pinch Hit AB	Pinch Hit H	PO	A	E	DP	TC/G	FA	G by Pos
1967	**ATL N**	9	.231	.231	26	6	0	0	0	0.0	1	1	1	4	0	3	1	16	1	1	0	3.0	.944	OF-6
1968		122	.224	.319	232	52	7	3	3	1.3	22	21	14	35	3	27	8	115	7	3	0	1.3	.976	OF-95
1969		121	.268	.333	168	45	8	0	1	0.6	20	22	16	18	0	31	9	119	2	1	1	1.4	.992	OF-89
1970		123	.254	.399	291	74	17	2	7	2.4	25	28	17	43	3	28	9	168	3	2	0	1.8	.988	OF-98
1971		145	.269	.390	454	122	14	1	13	2.9	56	55	47	43	0	14	2	287	11	3	2	2.4	.990	OF-125, 1B-1
1972		123	.228	.350	369	84	14	2	9	2.4	40	38	50	52	1	15	6	247	6	6	1	2.3	.977	OF-109, 1B-2
1973		138	.294	.462	513	151	26	6	16	3.1	74	82	41	89	2	9	0	833	45	9	64	6.0	.990	1B-84, OF-64
1974		106	.233	.366	361	84	11	2	11	3.0	50	50	45	49	0	10	1	554	26	4	44	5.3	.993	1B-60, OF-50
1975		124	.228	.327	364	83	8	2	8	2.2	32	36	39	38	2	26	4	657	34	5	41	7.1	.993	1B-60, OF-38
1976	**CIN N**	84	.228	.346	136	31	5	1	3	2.2	15	20	22	24	0	39	10	48	0	0	0	1.3	1.000	OF-38
1977		81	.160	.288	125	20	1	0	5	4.0	14	16	9	33	2	47	5	83	2	1	4	2.7	.988	OF-24, 1B-8
1978		86	.267	.452	146	39	7	1	6	4.1	15	23	22	18	0	36	11	100	8	2	2	2.2	.982	OF-43, 1B-7
1979	**ATL N**	111	.249	.359	217	54	6	0	6	2.8	27	27	18	34	0	**52**	**17**	420	30	1	36	8.4	.998	1B-51, OF-3
1980		93	.205	.241	83	17	3	0	0	0.0	7	5	18	19	0	50	12	58	4	0	1	2.1	1.000	OF-19, 1B-10
1981	**2 teams**	**ATL N** (10G –.091) **CHI N** (41G –.241)																						
″	**total**	51	.217	.319	69	15	1	0	2	2.9	6	7	7	7	0	31	8	16	0	1	0	1.1	.941	OF-15, 1B-1
15 yrs.		1517	.247	.370	3554	877	128	20	90	2.5	404	431	366	506	13	418	103	3721	179	39	196	3.6	.990	OF-816, 1B-284
LEAGUE CHAMPIONSHIP SERIES																								
1969	**ATL N**	2	1.000	1.500	2	2	1	0	0	0.0	0	0	0	0	0	1	1	0	0	0	0	0.0	.000	OF-1
1976	**CIN N**	1	.000	.000	1	0	0	0	0	0.0	0	0	0	0	0	1	0	0	0	0	0	0.0	—	
2 yrs.		3	.667	1.000	3	2	1	0	0	0.0	0	0	0	0	0	2	1	0	0	0	0	0.0		OF-1

Harry Lumley

LUMLEY, HARRY G BL TR 5′10″ 183 lbs.
B. Sept. 29, 1880, Forest City, Pa. D. May 22, 1938, Binghamton, N. Y.
Manager 1909.

Year	Team	Games	BA	SA	AB	H	2B	3B	HR	HR%	R	RBI	BB	SO	SB	Pinch Hit AB	Pinch Hit H	PO	A	E	DP	TC/G	FA	G by Pos
1904	**BKN N**	150	.279	.428	577	161	23	**18**	**9**	1.6	79	78	41		30	0	0	228	26	12	8	1.8	.955	OF-150
1905		130	.293	.412	505	148	19	10	7	1.4	50	47	36		22	1	1	177	21	19	4	1.7	.912	OF-129
1906		133	.324	**.477**	484	157	23	12	9	1.9	72	61	48		35	2	0	231	13	13	5	2.0	.949	OF-131
1907		127	.267	.425	454	121	23	11	9	**2.0**	47	66	31		18	9	1	171	15	8	7	1.6	.959	OF-118
1908		127	.216	.327	440	95	13	12	4	0.9	36	39	29		4	11	2	157	13	8	6	1.5	.955	OF-116
1909		55	.250	.331	172	43	8	3	0	0.0	13	14	16		1	3	1	83	9	5	1	1.9	.948	OF-52
1910		8	.143	.143	21	3	0	0	0	0.0	3	0	3	6	0	2	0	5	0	1	0	1.5	.833	OF-4
7 yrs.		730	.274	.408	2653	728	109	66	38	1.4	300	305	204	6	110	28	5	1052	97	66	31	1.7	.946	OF-700

Jerry Lumpe

LUMPE, JERRY DEAN BL TR 6′ 2″ 185 lbs.
B. June 2, 1933, Lincoln, Mo.

Year	Team	Games	BA	SA	AB	H	2B	3B	HR	HR%	R	RBI	BB	SO	SB	Pinch Hit AB	Pinch Hit H	PO	A	E	DP	TC/G	FA	G by Pos
1956	**NY A**	20	.258	.306	62	16	3	0	0	0.0	12	4	5	11	1	4	0	33	56	8	15	5.4	.918	SS-17, 3B-1
1957		40	.340	.437	103	35	6	2	0	0.0	15	11	9	13	2	7	2	22	57	4	8	2.3	.952	3B-30, SS-6
1958		81	.254	.362	232	59	8	4	3	1.3	34	32	23	21	1	16	4	63	135	11	15	3.0	.947	3B-65, SS-5
1959	**2 teams**	**NY A** (18G –.222) **KC A** (108G –.243)																						
″	**total**	126	.241	.308	448	108	11	5	3	0.7	49	30	47	39	2	4	1	231	343	13	86	4.3	.978	2B-62, SS-60, 3B-16
1960	**KC A**	146	.272	.357	574	156	19	3	8	1.4	69	53	48	49	1	5	0	383	408	16	112	5.4	.980	2B-134, SS-15

Jerry Lumpe *continued*

Year	Team	Games	BA	SA	AB	H	2B	3B	HR	HR%	R	RBI	BB	SO	SB	Pinch Hit AB	Pinch Hit H	PO	A	E	DP	TC/G	FA	G by Pos
1961		148	.293	.392	569	167	29	9	3	0.5	81	54	48	39	1	1	0	403	426	18	105	5.8	.979	2B-147
1962		156	.301	.432	641	193	34	10	10	1.6	89	83	44	38	0	1	1	344	435	11	97	5.0	.986	2B-156, SS-2
1963		157	.271	.363	595	161	26	7	5	0.8	75	59	58	44	3	2	0	341	452	10	92	5.2	.988	2B-155
1964	DET A	158	.256	.338	624	160	21	6	6	1.0	75	46	50	61	2	0	0	339	394	13	95	4.7	.983	2B-158
1965		145	.257	.323	502	129	15	3	4	0.8	72	39	56	34	7	10	1	281	308	9	69	4.3	.985	2B-139
1966		113	.231	.291	385	89	14	3	1	0.3	30	26	24	44	0	20	2	202	223	4	51	4.5	.991	2B-95
1967		81	.232	.322	177	41	4	0	4	2.3	19	17	16	18	0	29	3	73	93	7	12	2.9	.960	2B-54, 3B-6
12 yrs.		1371	.268	.356	4912	1314	190	52	47	1.0	620	454	428	411	20	99	14	2715	3330	124	757	4.7	.980	2B-1100, 3B-118, SS-105
WORLD SERIES																								
1957	NY A	6	.286	.286	14	4	0	0	0	0.0	0	2	1	1	0	3	2	3	6	0	0	3.0	1.000	3B-3
1958		6	.167	.167	12	2	0	0	0	0.0	0	0	1	2	0	3	0	2	4	0	0	1.2	1.000	3B-3, SS-2
2 yrs.		12	.231	.231	26	6	0	0	0	0.0	0	2	2	3	0	6	2	5	10	0	0	1.9	1.000	3B-6, SS-2

Don Lund

LUND, DONALD ANDREW BR TR 6′ 200 lbs.
B. May 18, 1923, Detroit, Mich.

Year	Team	Games	BA	SA	AB	H	2B	3B	HR	HR%	R	RBI	BB	SO	SB	Pinch Hit AB	Pinch Hit H	PO	A	E	DP	TC/G	FA	G by Pos
1945	BKN N	4	.000	.000	3	0	0	0	0	0.0	0	0	1	1	0	3	0	0	0	0	0	0.0	—	
1947		11	.300	.700	20	6	2	0	2	10.0	5	5	3	7	0	5	2	11	0	0	0	2.2	1.000	OF-5
1948	2 teams	BKN N (27G –.188) STL A (63G –.248)																						
"	total	90	.230	.365	230	53	11	4	4	1.7	30	30	15	33	1	16	0	113	5	1	0	1.7	.992	OF-70
1949	DET A	2	.000	.000	2	0	0	0	0	0.0	0	0	0	1	0	2	0	0	0	0	0	0.0	—	
1952		8	.304	.304	23	7	0	0	0	0.0	1	1	3	3	0	1	0	10	1	0	0	1.6	1.000	OF-7
1953		131	.257	.390	421	108	21	4	9	2.1	51	47	39	65	3	8	2	275	12	6	0	2.4	.980	OF-123
1954		35	.130	.167	54	7	2	0	0	0.0	4	3	4	3	1	9	1	32	1	1	0	1.1	.971	OF-31
7 yrs.		281	.240	.369	753	181	36	8	15	2.0	91	86	65	113	5	44	5	441	19	8	0	2.0	.983	OF-236

Gordon Lund

LUND, GORDON THOMAS BR TR 5′11″ 170 lbs.
B. Feb. 23, 1941, Iron Mountain, Mich.

Year	Team	Games	BA	SA	AB	H	2B	3B	HR	HR%	R	RBI	BB	SO	SB	Pinch Hit AB	Pinch Hit H	PO	A	E	DP	TC/G	FA	G by Pos
1967	CLE A	3	.250	.375	8	2	1	0	0	0.0	1	0	0	2	0	1	0	1	3	2	2	3.0	.667	SS-2
1969	SEA A	20	.263	.263	38	10	0	0	0	0.0	4	1	5	7	1	0	0	15	38	5	7	3.1	.914	SS-17, 2B-1, 3B-1
2 yrs.		23	.261	.283	46	12	1	0	0	0.0	5	1	5	9	1	1	0	16	41	7	9	3.0	.891	SS-19, 2B-1, 3B-1

Tom Lundstedt

LUNDSTEDT, THOMAS ROBERT BB TR 6′4″ 195 lbs.
B. Apr. 10, 1949, Davenport, Iowa.

Year	Team	Games	BA	SA	AB	H	2B	3B	HR	HR%	R	RBI	BB	SO	SB	Pinch Hit AB	Pinch Hit H	PO	A	E	DP	TC/G	FA	G by Pos
1973	CHI N	4	.000	.000	5	0	0	0	0	0.0	0	0	0	1	0	0	0	10	1	0	0	2.8	1.000	C-4
1974		22	.094	.094	32	3	0	0	0	0.0	1	0	5	7	0	0	0	70	4	1	0	3.4	.987	C-22
1975	MIN A	18	.107	.107	28	3	0	0	0	0.0	2	1	4	5	0	3	1	46	3	0	2	3.1	1.000	C-14, DH-2
3 yrs.		44	.092	.092	65	6	0	0	0	0.0	3	1	9	13	0	3	1	126	8	1	2	3.2	.993	C-40, DH-2

Harry Lunte

LUNTE, HARRY AUGUST BR TR 5′11½″ 165 lbs.
B. Sept. 15, 1892, St. Louis, Mo. D. July 27, 1965, St. Louis, Mo.

Year	Team	Games	BA	SA	AB	H	2B	3B	HR	HR%	R	RBI	BB	SO	SB	Pinch Hit AB	Pinch Hit H	PO	A	E	DP	TC/G	FA	G by Pos
1919	CLE A	26	.195	.221	77	15	2	0	0	0.0	2	2	1	7	0	2	0	37	64	7	5	4.5	.935	SS-24
1920		28	.197	.197	71	14	0	0	0	0.0	6	7	5	6	0	0	0	31	66	2	7	4.1	.980	SS-21, 2B-3
2 yrs.		54	.196	.209	148	29	2	0	0	0.0	8	9	6	13	0	2	0	68	130	9	12	4.3	.957	SS-45, 2B-3
WORLD SERIES																								
1920	CLE A	1	—	—	0	0	0	0	0	—	0	0	0	0	0	0	0	0	0	0	0	0.0	.000	SS-1

Tony Lupien

LUPIEN, ULYSSES JOHN BL TL 5′10½″ 185 lbs.
B. Apr. 23, 1917, Chelmsford, Mass.

Year	Team	Games	BA	SA	AB	H	2B	3B	HR	HR%	R	RBI	BB	SO	SB	Pinch Hit AB	Pinch Hit H	PO	A	E	DP	TC/G	FA	G by Pos
1940	BOS A	10	.474	.842	19	9	3	2	0	0.0	5	4	1	1	0	2	1	37	2	0	4	4.9	1.000	1B-8
1942		128	.281	.384	463	130	25	7	3	0.6	63	70	50	20	10	6	0	1091	68	9	99	9.7	.992	1B-121
1943		154	.255	.339	608	155	21	9	4	0.7	65	47	54	23	16	1	0	1487	118	12	149	10.6	.993	1B-153
1944	PHI N	153	.283	.377	597	169	23	9	5	0.8	82	52	56	29	18	1	1	1453	103	13	114	10.4	.992	1B-151
1945		15	.315	.333	54	17	1	0	0	0.0	1	3	6	0	2	0	0	129	16	0	11	9.7	1.000	1B-15
1948	CHI A	154	.246	.316	617	152	19	3	6	1.0	69	54	74	38	11	0	0	1436	92	11	155	10.0	.993	1B-154
6 yrs.		614	.268	.355	2358	632	92	30	18	0.8	285	230	241	111	57	10	2	5633	399	45	532	10.1	.993	1B-602

Al Luplow

LUPLOW, ALVIN DAVID BL TR 5′10″ 175 lbs.
B. Mar. 13, 1939, Saginaw, Mich.

Year	Team	Games	BA	SA	AB	H	2B	3B	HR	HR%	R	RBI	BB	SO	SB	Pinch Hit AB	Pinch Hit H	PO	A	E	DP	TC/G	FA	G by Pos
1961	CLE A	5	.056	.056	18	1	0	0	0	0.0	0	0	2	6	0	0	0	9	2	0	1	2.2	1.000	OF-5
1962		97	.277	.475	318	88	15	3	14	4.4	54	45	36	44	1	13	4	162	4	7	0	2.0	.960	OF-86
1963		100	.234	.339	295	69	6	2	7	2.4	34	27	33	62	4	18	1	157	7	1	1	1.9	.994	OF-85
1964		19	.111	.111	18	2	0	0	0	0.0	1	1	1	8	0	15	1	5	0	0	0	1.0	1.000	OF-5
1965		53	.133	.244	45	6	2	0	1	2.2	3	4	3	14	0	44	6	3	0	0	0	0.5	1.000	OF-6
1966	NY N	111	.251	.347	334	84	9	1	7	2.1	31	31	38	46	2	19	5	147	4	2	1	1.5	.987	OF-101
1967	2 teams	NY N (41G –.205) PIT N (55G –.184)																						
"	total	96	.195	.260	215	42	2	0	4	1.9	24	17	14	33	1	41	7	100	5	4	1	1.9	.963	OF-58
7 yrs.		481	.235	.352	1243	292	34	6	33	2.7	147	125	127	213	8	150	24	583	22	14	4	1.8	.977	OF-346

Scott Lusader

LUSADER, SCOTT EDWARD BL TL 5′10″ 165 lbs.
B. Sept. 30, 1964, Chicago, Ill.

Year	Team	Games	BA	SA	AB	H	2B	3B	HR	HR%	R	RBI	BB	SO	SB	Pinch Hit AB	Pinch Hit H	PO	A	E	DP	TC/G	FA	G by Pos
1987	DET A	23	.319	.489	47	15	3	1	1	2.1	8	8	5	7	1	0	0	29	0	1	0	1.3	.967	OF-22, DH-1
1988		16	.063	.250	16	1	0	0	1	6.3	3	3	1	4	0	5	0	7	0	0	0	0.7	1.000	DH-6, OF-4
1989		40	.252	.320	103	26	4	0	1	1.0	15	8	9	21	3	8	1	56	0	4	0	1.8	.933	OF-33, DH-1
1990		45	.241	.333	87	21	2	0	2	2.3	13	16	12	8	0	1	0	53	1	1	0	1.3	.982	OF-42, DH-2
1991	NY A	11	.143	.143	7	1	0	0	0	0.0	2	1	1	3	0	3	1	3	0	0	0	0.6	1.000	OF-4, DH-1
5 yrs.		135	.246	.346	260	64	9	1	5	1.9	41	36	28	43	4	17	2	148	1	6	0	1.3	.961	OF-105, DH-11

Billy Lush

LUSH, WILLIAM LUCAS BB TR 5′8″ 165 lbs.
Brother of Ernie Lush.
B. Nov. 10, 1873, Bridgeport, Conn. D. Aug. 28, 1951, Hawthorne, N. Y.

Year	Team	Games	BA	SA	AB	H	2B	3B	HR	HR%	R	RBI	BB	SO	SB	Pinch Hit AB	Pinch Hit H	PO	A	E	DP	TC/G	FA	G by Pos
1895	WAS N	5	.333	.333	18	6	0	0	0	0.0	2	2	2	1	0	0	0	9	0	4	0	2.6	.692	OF-5
1896		97	.247	.369	352	87	9	11	4	1.1	74	45	66	49	28	3	1	145	23	23	4	2.0	.880	OF-91, 2B-3

Billy Lush *continued*

Year	Team	Games	BA	SA	AB	H	2B	3B	HR	HR%	R	RBI	BB	SO	SB	Pinch Hit AB	Pinch Hit H	PO	A	E	DP	TC/G	FA	G by Pos
1897		3	.000	.000	12	0	0	0	0	0.0	1	0	2		0	0	0	5	1	0	0	2.0	1.000	OF-3
1901	BOS N	7	.185	.296	27	5	1	1	0	0.0	2	3	3		0	0	0	22	2	1	1	3.6	.960	OF-7
1902		120	.223	.262	413	92	8	1	2	0.5	68	19	76		30	3	1	251	26	14	5	2.5	.952	OF-116, 3B-1
1903	DET A	119	.274	.390	423	116	18	14	1	0.2	71	33	70		14	1	0	257	43	15	6	2.6	.952	OF-101, 3B-12, SS-3, 2B-3
1904	CLE A	138	.258	.325	477	123	13	8	1	0.2	76	50	72		12	0	0	269	11	12	4	2.1	.959	OF-138
7 yrs.		489	.249	.332	1722	429	49	35	8	0.5	294	152	291	50	84	7	2	958	106	69	20	2.3	.939	OF-461, 3B-13, 2B-6, SS-3

Ernie Lush

LUSH, ERNEST BENJAMIN BR TL
Brother of Billy Lush.
B. Oct. 31, 1884, Bridgeport, Conn. D. Feb. 26, 1937, Detroit, Mich.

Year	Team	Games	BA	SA	AB	H	2B	3B	HR	HR%	R	RBI	BB	SO	SB	Pinch Hit AB	Pinch Hit H	PO	A	E	DP	TC/G	FA	G by Pos
1910	STL N	1	.000	.000	4	0	0	0	0	0.0	0	0	1	1	0	0	0	1	0	0	0	1.0	1.000	OF-1

Johnny Lush

LUSH, JOHN CHARLES BL TL 5′ 9½″ 165 lbs.
B. Oct. 8, 1885, Williamsport, Pa. D. Nov. 18, 1946, Beverly Hills, Calif.

Year	Team	Games	BA	SA	AB	H	2B	3B	HR	HR%	R	RBI	BB	SO	SB	Pinch Hit AB	Pinch Hit H	PO	A	E	DP	TC/G	FA	G by Pos
1904	PHI N	106	.276	.369	369	102	22	3	2	0.5	39	42	27		12	4	1	583	44	35	28	6.5	.947	1B-62, OF-33, P-7
1905		6	.313	.313	16	5	0	0	0	0.0	3	1	1		0	1	1	6	6	4	0	3.2	.750	OF-3, P-2
1906		76	.264	.307	212	56	7	1	0	0.0	28	15	14		6	**14**	1	75	95	13	3	3.0	.929	P-37, OF-22, 1B-2
1907	2 teams	PHI N (17G –.200) STL N (27G –.280)																						
″	total	44	.254	.344	122	31	3	4	0	0.0	11	10	6		5	13	2	19	54	7	4	2.1	.913	P-28, OF-11
1908	STL N	45	.169	.191	89	15	2	0	0	0.0	7	2	7		1	6	1	15	73	7	0	2.5	.926	P-38
1909		45	.239	.293	92	22	5	0	0	0.0	11	14	6		2	7	0	9	64	4	0	2.1	.948	P-34, OF-3
1910		47	.226	.301	93	21	1	3	0	0.0	8	10	8	11	2	10	4	8	56	5	2	1.9	.928	P-36
7 yrs.		369	.254	.322	993	252	40	11	2	0.2	107	94	69	11	28	55	10	715	392	75	37	3.7	.937	P-182, OF-72, 1B-64

Charlie Luskey

LUSKEY, CHARLES MELTON BR TR 5′ 7″ 165 lbs.
B. Apr. 6, 1876, Washington, D. C. D. Dec. 20, 1962, Bethesda, Md.

Year	Team	Games	BA	SA	AB	H	2B	3B	HR	HR%	R	RBI	BB	SO	SB	Pinch Hit AB	Pinch Hit H	PO	A	E	DP	TC/G	FA	G by Pos
1901	WAS A	11	.195	.317	41	8	3	1	0	0.0	8	3	2		0	0	0	25	1	7	0	3.0	.788	OF-8, C-3

Luke Lutenberg

LUTENBERG, CHARLES WILLIAM BR TR 6′ 2″ 225 lbs.
B. Oct. 4, 1864, Quincy, Ill. D. Dec. 24, 1938, Quincy, Ill.

Year	Team	Games	BA	SA	AB	H	2B	3B	HR	HR%	R	RBI	BB	SO	SB	Pinch Hit AB	Pinch Hit H	PO	A	E	DP	TC/G	FA	G by Pos
1894	LOU N	69	.192	.264	250	48	10	4	0	0.0	42	23	23	21	4	0	0	597	43	15	55	9.5	.977	1B-67, 2B-2

Lyle Luttrell

LUTTRELL, LYLE KENNETH BR TR 6′ 180 lbs.
B. Feb. 22, 1930, Bloomington, Ill. D. July 11, 1984, Chattanooga, Tenn.

Year	Team	Games	BA	SA	AB	H	2B	3B	HR	HR%	R	RBI	BB	SO	SB	Pinch Hit AB	Pinch Hit H	PO	A	E	DP	TC/G	FA	G by Pos
1956	WAS A	38	.189	.328	122	23	5	3	2	1.6	17	9	8	19	5	1	0	69	100	11	19	4.9	.939	SS-37
1957		19	.200	.289	45	9	4	0	0	0.0	4	5	3	8	0	2	0	23	28	4	5	3.2	.927	SS-17
2 yrs.		57	.192	.317	167	32	9	3	2	1.2	21	14	11	27	5	3	0	92	128	15	24	4.4	.936	SS-54

Joe Lutz

LUTZ, ROLLIN JOSEPH BL TL 6′ 195 lbs.
B. Feb. 18, 1925, Keokuk, Iowa.

Year	Team	Games	BA	SA	AB	H	2B	3B	HR	HR%	R	RBI	BB	SO	SB	Pinch Hit AB	Pinch Hit H	PO	A	E	DP	TC/G	FA	G by Pos
1951	STL A	14	.167	.222	36	6	0	1	0	0.0	7	2	6	9	0	3	1	76	4	0	9	7.3	1.000	1B-11

Red Lutz

LUTZ, LOUIS WILLIAM BR TR 5′10″ 170 lbs.
B. Dec. 17, 1898, Cincinnati, Ohio D. Feb. 22, 1984, Cincinnati, Ohio.

Year	Team	Games	BA	SA	AB	H	2B	3B	HR	HR%	R	RBI	BB	SO	SB	Pinch Hit AB	Pinch Hit H	PO	A	E	DP	TC/G	FA	G by Pos
1922	CIN N	1	1.000	2.000	1	1	1	0	0	0.0	0	0	0	0	0	0	0	0	0	0	0	0.0	.000	C-1

Rube Lutzke

LUTZKE, WALTER JOHN BR TR 5′11″ 175 lbs.
B. Nov. 17, 1897, Milwaukee, Wis. D. Mar. 6, 1938, Granville, Wis.

Year	Team	Games	BA	SA	AB	H	2B	3B	HR	HR%	R	RBI	BB	SO	SB	Pinch Hit AB	Pinch Hit H	PO	A	E	DP	TC/G	FA	G by Pos
1923	CLE A	143	.256	.337	511	131	20	6	3	0.6	71	65	59	57	10	0	0	186	358	35	23	4.0	.940	3B-143
1924		106	.243	.314	341	83	18	3	0	0.0	37	42	38	46	4	0	0	161	241	22	26	4.0	.948	3B-103, 2B-3
1925		81	.218	.269	238	52	9	0	1	0.4	31	16	26	29	2	2	1	83	156	14	14	3.2	.945	3B-69, 2B-10
1926		142	.261	.345	475	124	28	6	0	0.0	42	59	34	35	6	0	0	160	302	19	27	3.4	.960	3B-142
1927		100	.251	.309	311	78	12	3	0	0.0	35	41	22	29	2	2	0	120	199	21	24	3.5	.938	3B-98
5 yrs.		572	.249	.321	1876	468	87	18	4	0.2	216	223	179	196	24	4	1	710	1256	111	114	3.7	.947	3B-555, 2B-13

Greg Luzinski

LUZINSKI, GREGORY MICHAEL (The Bull) BR TR 6′ 1″ 220 lbs.
B. Nov. 22, 1950, Chicago, Ill.

Year	Team	Games	BA	SA	AB	H	2B	3B	HR	HR%	R	RBI	BB	SO	SB	Pinch Hit AB	Pinch Hit H	PO	A	E	DP	TC/G	FA	G by Pos
1970	PHI N	8	.167	.167	12	2	0	0	0	0.0	0	0	3	5	0	5	1	20	3	0	1	7.7	1.000	1B-3
1971		28	.300	.470	100	30	8	0	3	3.0	13	15	12	32	2	0	0	247	34	1	16	10.1	.996	1B-28
1972		150	.281	.453	563	158	33	5	18	3.2	66	68	42	114	0	4	1	257	9	12	2	1.9	.957	OF-145, 1B-2
1973		161	.285	.484	610	174	26	4	29	4.8	76	97	51	135	3	4	2	262	7	2	1	1.7	.993	OF-159
1974		85	.272	.394	302	82	14	1	7	2.3	29	48	29	76	3	4	0	146	10	3	0	1.9	.981	OF-82
1975		161	.300	.540	596	179	35	3	34	5.7	85	**120**	89	151	3	2	0	248	10	9	0	1.7	.966	OF-159
1976		149	.304	.478	533	162	28	1	21	3.9	74	95	50	107	1	5	0	204	8	8	0	1.5	.964	OF-144
1977		149	.309	.594	554	171	35	3	39	7.0	99	130	80	**140**	3	1	0	205	11	8	2	1.5	.964	OF-148
1978		155	.265	.526	540	143	32	2	35	6.5	85	101	100	135	8	1	0	232	7	4	2	1.6	.984	OF-154
1979		137	.252	.427	452	114	23	1	18	4.0	47	81	56	103	3	9	1	156	3	9	1	1.3	.946	OF-125
1980		106	.228	.440	368	84	19	1	19	5.2	44	56	60	100	3	1	0	137	2	1	0	1.3	.993	OF-105
1981	CHI A	104	.265	.476	378	100	15	1	21	5.6	55	62	58	80	0	0	0	0	0	0	0	0.0	.000	DH-103
1982		159	.292	.451	583	170	37	1	18	3.1	87	102	89	120	1	2	1	0	0	0	0	0.0	.000	DH-156
1983		144	.255	.502	502	128	26	1	32	6.4	73	95	70	117	2	2	0	6	1	0	1	0.0	1.000	DH-139, 1B-2
1984		125	.238	.364	412	98	13	0	13	3.2	47	58	56	80	5	11	3	0	0	0	0	0.0	.000	DH-114
15 yrs.		1821	.276	.478	6505	1795	344	24	307	4.7	880	1128	845	1495	37	51	9	2120	105	57	26	1.3	.975	OF-1221, DH-512, 1B-35

LEAGUE CHAMPIONSHIP SERIES

Year	Team	Games	BA	SA	AB	H	2B	3B	HR	HR%	R	RBI	BB	SO	SB	Pinch Hit AB	Pinch Hit H	PO	A	E	DP	TC/G	FA	G by Pos
1976	PHI N	3	.273	.727	11	3	2	0	1	9.1	2	3	1	4	0	0	0	6	0	0	0	2.0	1.000	OF-3
1977		4	.286	.571	14	4	1	0	1	7.1	2	2	3	3	1	0	0	4	1	0	0	1.3	1.000	OF-4
1978		4	.375	.875	16	6	0	1	2	12.5	3	3	1	2	0	0	0	5	0	0	0	1.3	1.000	OF-4
1980		5	.294	.588	17	5	2	0	1	5.9	3	4	0	6	0	1	1	5	0	1	0	1.5	.833	OF-4
1983	CHI A	4	.133	.200	15	2	1	0	0	0.0	0	0	1	5	0	0	0	0	0	0	0	0.0	.000	DH-4
5 yrs.		20	.274	.589	73	20	6	1	5	6.8	10	12	6	20	1	1	1	20	1	1	0	1.2	.955	OF-15, DH-4
				7th			**7th**		**4th**	**4th**				**4th**										

Greg Luzinski *continued*

Year	Team	Games	BA	SA	AB	H	2B	3B	HR	HR%	R	RBI	BB	SO	SB	Pinch Hit AB	Pinch Hit H	PO	A	E	DP	TC/G	FA	G by Pos
WORLD SERIES																								
1980	PHI N	3	.000	.000	9	0	0	0	0	0.0	0	0	1	5	0	0	0	1	0	0	0	0.3	1.000	DH-2, OF-1

Mitch Lyden

LYDEN, MITCHELL SCOTT BR TR 6′ 3″ 225 lbs.
B. Dec. 14, 1964, Portland, Ore.

Year	Team	Games	BA	SA	AB	H	2B	3B	HR	HR%	R	RBI	BB	SO	SB	Pinch Hit AB	Pinch Hit H	PO	A	E	DP	TC/G	FA	G by Pos
1993	FLA N	6	.300	.600	10	3	0	0	1	10.0	2	1	0	3	0	4	1	4	0	0	0	2.0	1.000	C-2

Scott Lydy

LYDY, DONALD SCOTT BR TR 6′ 5″ 190 lbs.
B. Oct. 26, 1968, Mesa, Ariz.

Year	Team	Games	BA	SA	AB	H	2B	3B	HR	HR%	R	RBI	BB	SO	SB	Pinch Hit AB	Pinch Hit H	PO	A	E	DP	TC/G	FA	G by Pos
1993	OAK A	41	.225	.333	102	23	5	0	2	2.0	11	7	8	39	2	1	0	67	2	3	0	1.8	.958	OF-38, DH-2

Dummy Lynch

LYNCH, MATTHEW DANIEL BR TR 5′11″ 174 lbs.
B. Feb. 7, 1927, Dallas, Tex. D. June 30, 1978, Plano, Tex.

Year	Team	Games	BA	SA	AB	H	2B	3B	HR	HR%	R	RBI	BB	SO	SB	Pinch Hit AB	Pinch Hit H	PO	A	E	DP	TC/G	FA	G by Pos
1948	CHI N	7	.286	.714	7	2	0	0	1	14.3	3	1	1	1	0	4	1	0	2	0	0	2.0	1.000	2B-1

Henry Lynch

LYNCH, HENRY W. 5′ 7″ 143 lbs.
B. Apr. 8, 1866, Worcester, Mass. D. Nov. 23, 1925, Worcester, Mass.

Year	Team	Games	BA	SA	AB	H	2B	3B	HR	HR%	R	RBI	BB	SO	SB	Pinch Hit AB	Pinch Hit H	PO	A	E	DP	TC/G	FA	G by Pos
1893	CHI N	4	.214	.357	14	3	2	0	0	0.0	0	2	1	1	0	0	0	5	0	1	0	1.5	.833	OF-4

Jerry Lynch

LYNCH, GERALD THOMAS BL TR 6′ 1″ 185 lbs.
B. July 17, 1930, Bay City, Mich.

Year	Team	Games	BA	SA	AB	H	2B	3B	HR	HR%	R	RBI	BB	SO	SB	Pinch Hit AB	Pinch Hit H	PO	A	E	DP	TC/G	FA	G by Pos
1954	PIT N	98	.239	.373	284	68	4	5	8	2.8	27	36	20	43	2	15	2	127	10	5	2	1.7	.965	OF-83
1955		88	.284	.443	282	80	18	6	5	1.8	43	28	22	33	2	18	4	112	13	6	3	1.8	.954	OF-71, C-2
1956		19	.158	.263	19	3	0	1	0	0.0	1	0	1	4	0	16	3	3	0	0	0	3.0	1.000	OF-1
1957	CIN N	67	.258	.403	124	32	4	1	4	3.2	11	13	6	18	0	42	8	40	0	0	0	1.5	1.000	OF-24, C-2
1958		122	.312	.498	420	131	20	5	16	3.8	58	68	18	54	1	25	9	154	5	5	2	1.6	.970	OF-101
1959		117	.269	.462	379	102	16	3	17	4.5	49	58	29	50	2	19	7	180	5	4	3	1.9	.979	OF-98
1960		102	.289	.478	159	46	8	2	6	3.8	23	27	16	25	0	**66**	**19**	41	1	4	1	1.4	.913	OF-32
1961		96	.315	.624	181	57	13	2	13	7.2	33	50	27	25	2	47	**19**	53	2	3	0	1.3	.948	OF-44
1962		114	.281	.486	288	81	15	4	12	4.2	41	57	24	38	3	38	9	89	7	3	1	1.4	.970	OF-73
1963	2 teams	CIN N (22G –.250) PIT N (88G –.266)																						
″	total	110	.264	.454	269	71	9	3	12	4.5	31	45	23	33	0	37	12	75	2	3	0	1.1	.962	OF-71
1964	PIT N	114	.273	.495	297	81	14	2	16	5.4	35	66	26	57	0	34	7	59	0	1	0	0.8	.983	OF-78
1965		73	.281	.413	121	34	1	0	5	4.1	7	16	8	26	0	41	7	27	1	3	0	1.2	.903	OF-26
1966		64	.214	.286	56	12	1	0	1	1.8	5	6	4	10	0	**49**	10	5	0	0	0	1.3	1.000	OF-4
13 yrs.		1184	.277	.463	2879	798	123	34	115	4.0	364	470	224	416	12	447	116 **5th**	965	46	37	12	1.5	.965	OF-706, C-4
WORLD SERIES																								
1961	CIN N	4	.000	.000	3	0	0	0	0	0.0	0	0	1	1	0	3	0	0	0	0	0	0.0	—	

Mike Lynch

LYNCH, MICHAEL JOSEPH TR 5′10″ 155 lbs.
B. Sept. 10, 1875, St. Paul, Minn. D. Apr. 1, 1947, Jennings Lodge, Ore.

Year	Team	Games	BA	SA	AB	H	2B	3B	HR	HR%	R	RBI	BB	SO	SB	Pinch Hit AB	Pinch Hit H	PO	A	E	DP	TC/G	FA	G by Pos
1902	CHI N	7	.143	.143	28	4	0	0	0	0.0	4	0	2		0	0	0	12	1	1	0	2.0	.929	OF-7

Thomas Lynch

LYNCH, THOMAS S. BL 5′11″ 175 lbs.
B. 1863, Peru, Ill. D. May 13, 1923, Peru, Ill.

Year	Team	Games	BA	SA	AB	H	2B	3B	HR	HR%	R	RBI	BB	SO	SB	Pinch Hit AB	Pinch Hit H	PO	A	E	DP	TC/G	FA	G by Pos
1884	CHI N	1	.000	.000	4	0	0	0	0	0.0	0	0	0	2		0	0	8	1	0	0	4.5	1.000	1B-1, P-1

Tom Lynch

LYNCH, THOMAS JAMES BL TR 5′10½″ 170 lbs.
B. Apr. 3, 1860, Bennington, Vt. D. Mar. 28, 1955, Cohoes, N. Y.

Year	Team	Games	BA	SA	AB	H	2B	3B	HR	HR%	R	RBI	BB	SO	SB	Pinch Hit AB	Pinch Hit H	PO	A	E	DP	TC/G	FA	G by Pos
1884	2 teams	WIL U (16G –.276) PHI N (13G –.313)																						
″	total	29	.292	.415	106	31	7	3	0	0.0	13	0	9	5	0	0	0	101	29	17	3	4.7	.884	OF-15, C-15, 1B-1
1885	PHI N	13	.189	.245	53	10	3	0	0	0.0	7		10	3		0	0	26	5	6	1	2.8	.838	OF-13
2 yrs.		42	.258	.358	159	41	10	3	0	0.0	20	0	19	8	0	0	0	127	34	23	4	4.2	.875	OF-28, C-15, 1B-1

Walt Lynch

LYNCH, WALTER EDWARD BR TR 6′ 176 lbs.
B. Apr. 15, 1897, Buffalo, N. Y. D. Dec. 21, 1976, Daytona Beach, Fla.

Year	Team	Games	BA	SA	AB	H	2B	3B	HR	HR%	R	RBI	BB	SO	SB	Pinch Hit AB	Pinch Hit H	PO	A	E	DP	TC/G	FA	G by Pos
1922	BOS A	3	.500	.500	2	1	0	0	0	0.0	1	0	0	0	0	0	0	1	1	0	0	0.7	1.000	C-3

Byrd Lynn

LYNN, BYRD BR TR 5′11″ 165 lbs.
B. Mar. 13, 1889, Unionville, Ill. D. Feb. 5, 1940, Napa, Calif.

Year	Team	Games	BA	SA	AB	H	2B	3B	HR	HR%	R	RBI	BB	SO	SB	Pinch Hit AB	Pinch Hit H	PO	A	E	DP	TC/G	FA	G by Pos
1916	CHI A	31	.225	.250	40	9	1	0	0	0.0	4	3	4	7	2	15	3	56	24	4	0	6.5	.952	C-13
1917		35	.222	.250	72	16	2	0	0	0.0	7	5	7	11	1	6	1	104	13	5	4	4.2	.959	C-29
1918		5	.250	.250	8	2	0	0	0	0.0	0	0	2	1	0	1	1	6	3	0	0	2.3	1.000	C-4
1919		29	.227	.288	66	15	4	0	0	0.0	4	4	4	9	0	1	1	87	20	2	5	3.9	.982	C-28
1920		16	.320	.480	25	8	2	1	0	0.0	0	3	1	3	0	2	2	27	5	0	0	2.3	1.000	C-14
5 yrs.		116	.237	.289	211	50	9	1	0	0.0	15	15	18	31	3	25	8	280	65	11	9	4.0	.969	C-88
WORLD SERIES																								
1917	CHI A	1	.000	.000	1	0	0	0	0	0.0	0	0	0	1	0	1	0	0	0	0	0	0.0	—	
1919		1	.000	.000	1	0	0	0	0	0.0	0	0	0	0	0	0	0	1	0	0	0	1.0	1.000	C-1
2 yrs.		2	.000	.000	2	0	0	0	0	0.0	0	0	0	1	0	1	0	1	0	0	0	1.0	1.000	C-1

Fred Lynn

LYNN, FREDRIC MICHAEL BL TL 6′ 1″ 185 lbs.
B. Feb. 3, 1952, Chicago, Ill.

Year	Team	Games	BA	SA	AB	H	2B	3B	HR	HR%	R	RBI	BB	SO	SB	Pinch Hit AB	Pinch Hit H	PO	A	E	DP	TC/G	FA	G by Pos
1974	BOS A	15	.419	.698	43	18	2	2	2	4.7	5	10	6	6	0	2	0	18	2	0	0	1.3	1.000	OF-15, DH-1
1975		145	.331	**.566**	528	175	**47**	7	21	4.0	**103**	105	62	90	10	2	1	404	11	7	1	2.9	.983	OF-144
1976		132	.314	.467	507	159	32	8	10	2.0	76	65	48	67	14	1	0	367	13	6	4	2.9	.984	OF-128, DH-5
1977		129	.260	.447	497	129	29	5	18	3.6	81	76	51	63	2	3	0	333	7	2	1	2.7	.994	OF-125, DH-1
1978		150	.298	.492	541	161	33	3	22	4.1	75	82	75	50	3	0	0	408	11	7	2	2.9	.984	OF-149
1979		147	**.333**	**.637**	531	177	42	1	39	7.3	116	122	82	79	2	4	1	381	10	5	4	2.8	.987	OF-143, DH-1
1980		110	.301	.480	415	125	32	3	12	2.9	67	61	58	39	12	0	0	302	11	2	4	2.9	.994	OF-110
1981	CAL A	76	.219	.316	256	56	8	1	5	2.0	28	31	38	42	1	9	1	176	4	4	1	2.7	.978	OF-69

Fred Lynn *continued*

Year	Team	Games	BA	SA	AB	H	2B	3B	HR	HR%	R	RBI	BB	SO	SB	Pinch Hit AB	Pinch Hit H	PO	A	E	DP	TC/G	FA	G by Pos
1982		138	.299	.517	472	141	38	1	21	4.4	89	86	58	72	7	10	5	317	6	3	3	2.5	.991	OF-133
1983		117	.272	.483	437	119	20	3	22	5.0	56	74	55	83	2	3	0	274	8	2	4	2.5	.993	OF-113, DH-2
1984		142	.271	.474	517	140	28	4	23	4.4	84	79	77	98	2	5	2	321	12	6	5	2.4	.982	OF-140
1985	**BAL A**	124	.263	.449	448	118	12	1	23	5.1	59	68	53	100	7	1	0	314	6	2	2	2.6	.994	OF-123
1986		112	.287	.499	397	114	13	1	23	5.8	67	67	53	59	2	7	3	244	2	4	1	2.3	.984	OF-107, DH-1
1987		111	.253	.487	396	100	24	0	23	5.8	49	60	39	72	3	4	1	229	2	2	1	2.1	.991	OF-101, DH-8
1988	**2 teams**	**BAL A** (87G –.252) **DET A** (27G –.222)																						
"	**total**	114	.246	.478	391	96	14	1	25	6.4	46	56	33	82	2	7	2	257	3	2	0	2.4	.992	OF-105, DH-5
1989	**DET A**	117	.241	.371	353	85	11	1	11	3.1	44	46	47	71	1	17	3	119	5	1	0	1.1	.992	OF-68, DH-46
1990	**SD N**	90	.240	.357	196	47	3	1	6	3.1	18	23	22	44	2	32	11	92	1	0	0	1.7	1.000	OF-55
17 yrs.		1969	.283	.484	6925	1960	388	43	306	4.4	1063	1111	857	1117	72	107	30	4556	114	55	33	2.5	.988	OF-1828, DH-70
LEAGUE CHAMPIONSHIP SERIES																								
1975	**BOS A**	3	.364	.455	11	4	1	0	0	0.0	1	3	0	0	0	0	0	12	1	1	1	4.7	.929	OF-3
1982	**CAL A**	5	.611	.889	18	11	2	0	1	5.6	4	5	2	3	0	0	0	16	0	1	0	3.4	.941	OF-5
2 yrs.		8	.517	.724	29	15	3	0	1	3.4	5	8	2	3	0	0	0	28	1	2	1	3.9	.935	OF-8
WORLD SERIES																								
1975	**BOS A**	7	.280	.440	25	7	1	0	1	4.0	3	5	3	5	0	0	0	23	1	0	0	3.4	1.000	OF-7

Jerry Lynn

LYNN, JEROME EDWARD BR TR 5′10″ 164 lbs.
B. Apr. 14, 1916, Scranton, Pa. D. Sept. 25, 1972, Scranton, Pa.

Year	Team	Games	BA	SA	AB	H	2B	3B	HR	HR%	R	RBI	BB	SO	SB	Pinch Hit AB	Pinch Hit H	PO	A	E	DP	TC/G	FA	G by Pos
1937	**WAS A**	1	.667	1.000	3	2	1	0	0	0.0	0	0	0	0	0	0	0	4	3	0	2	7.0	1.000	2B-1

Russ Lyon

LYON, RUSSELL MAYO BR TR 6′ 1″ 230 lbs.
B. June 26, 1913, Ball Ground, Ga. D. Dec. 24, 1975, Charleston, S. C.

Year	Team	Games	BA	SA	AB	H	2B	3B	HR	HR%	R	RBI	BB	SO	SB	Pinch Hit AB	Pinch Hit H	PO	A	E	DP	TC/G	FA	G by Pos
1944	**CLE A**	7	.182	.182	11	2	0	0	0	0.0	1	0	1	1	0	4	0	7	3	1	0	3.7	.909	C-3

Barry Lyons

LYONS, BARRY STEPHEN BR TR 6′ 1″ 205 lbs.
B. June 3, 1960, Biloxi, Miss.

Year	Team	Games	BA	SA	AB	H	2B	3B	HR	HR%	R	RBI	BB	SO	SB	Pinch Hit AB	Pinch Hit H	PO	A	E	DP	TC/G	FA	G by Pos
1986	**NY N**	6	.000	.000	9	0	0	0	0	0.0	1	2	1	2	0	2	0	16	0	1	0	5.7	.941	C-3
1987		53	.254	.392	130	33	4	1	4	3.1	15	24	8	24	0	4	1	223	17	4	0	5.0	.984	C-49
1988		50	.231	.330	91	21	7	1	0	0.0	5	11	3	12	0	18	3	130	9	3	0	4.3	.979	C-32, 1B-1
1989		79	.247	.340	235	58	13	0	3	1.3	15	27	11	28	0	8	2	463	29	10	4	6.6	.980	C-76
1990	**2 teams**	**NY N** (24G –.237) **LA N** (3G –.200)																						
"	**total**	27	.235	.341	85	20	0	0	3	3.5	9	9	2	10	0	4	1	183	12	4	1	8.0	.980	C-25
1991	**2 teams**	**LA N** (9G –.000) **CAL A** (2G –.200)																						
"	**total**	11	.071	.071	14	1	0	0	0	0.0	0	0	0	2	0	4	0	22	2	0	1	3.0	1.000	C-6, 1B-2
1995	**CHI A**	27	.266	.531	64	17	2	0	5	7.8	8	16	4	14	0	5	0	91	13	2	3	4.1	.981	C-16, DH-7, 1B-3
7 yrs.		253	.239	.358	628	150	26	2	15	2.4	53	89	29	92	0	45	7	1128	82	24	9	5.6	.981	C-207, DH-7, 1B-6

Bill Lyons

LYONS, WILLIAM ALLEN BR TR 6′ 1″ 175 lbs.
B. Apr. 26, 1958, Alton, Ill.

Year	Team	Games	BA	SA	AB	H	2B	3B	HR	HR%	R	RBI	BB	SO	SB	Pinch Hit AB	Pinch Hit H	PO	A	E	DP	TC/G	FA	G by Pos
1983	**STL N**	42	.167	.217	60	10	1	1	0	0.0	3	3	1	11	3	11	1	30	44	1	7	2.3	.987	2B-23, 3B-8, SS-2
1984		46	.219	.260	73	16	3	0	0	0.0	13	3	9	13	3	8	1	58	74	1	21	3.4	.992	2B-25, SS-11, 3B-3
2 yrs.		88	.195	.241	133	26	4	1	0	0.0	16	6	10	24	6	19	2	88	118	2	28	2.9	.990	2B-48, SS-13, 3B-11

Denny Lyons

LYONS, DENNIS PATRICK ALOYSIUS BR TR 5′10″ 185 lbs.
B. Mar. 12, 1866, Cincinnati, Ohio D. Jan. 3, 1929, West Covington, Ky.

Year	Team	Games	BA	SA	AB	H	2B	3B	HR	HR%	R	RBI	BB	SO	SB	Pinch Hit AB	Pinch Hit H	PO	A	E	DP	TC/G	FA	G by Pos
1885	**PRO N**	4	.125	.188	16	2	1	0	0	0.0	3	1	0	3		0	0	6	8	3	0	4.3	.824	3B-4
1886	**PHI AA**	32	.211	.252	123	26	3	1	0	0.0	22		8			0	0	35	53	21	1	3.4	.807	3B-32
1887		137	.367	.523	570	209	43	14	6	1.1	128		47		73	0	0	255	215	73	29	4.0	.866	3B-137
1888		111	.296	.406	456	135	22	5	6	1.3	93	83	41		39	0	0	159	193	49	11	3.6	.878	3B-111
1889		131	.329	.469	510	168	36	4	9	1.8	135	82	79	44	10	0	0	209	291	81	29	4.4	.861	3B-130, 1B-1
1890		88	.354	**.531**	339	120	29	5	7	**2.1**	79		57		21	0	0	147	203	35	14	4.4	.909	3B-88
1891	**STL AA**	120	.315	.455	451	142	24	3	11	2.4	124	84	88	58	9	0	0	151	246	59	16	3.8	.871	3B-120
1892	**NY N**	108	.257	.396	389	100	16	7	8	2.1	71	51	59	36	11	0	0	152	206	53	13	3.8	.871	3B-108
1893	**PIT N**	131	.306	.429	490	150	19	16	3	0.6	103	105	97	29	19	0	0	214	303	46	23	4.3	.918	3B-131
1894		71	.323	.457	254	82	14	4	4	1.6	51	50	42	12	14	0	0	119	155	31	11	4.3	.898	3B-71
1895	**STL N**	33	.295	.388	129	38	6	0	2	1.6	24	25	14	5	3	0	0	61	49	13	2	3.7	.894	3B-33
1896	**PIT N**	118	.307	.420	436	134	25	6	4	0.9	77	71	67	25	13	2	0	165	201	44	15	3.5	.893	3B-116
1897		37	.206	.359	131	27	6	4	2	1.5	22	17	22		5	0	0	345	19	4	14	9.9	.989	1B-35, 3B-2
13 yrs.		1121	.310	.443	4294	1333	244	69	62	1.4	932	569	621	212	217	2	0	2018	2142	512	178	4.2	.890	3B-1083, 1B-36

Ed Lyons

LYONS, EDWARD HOYTE (Mouse) BR TR 5′ 9″ 165 lbs.
B. May 12, 1923, Winston-Salem, N. C.

Year	Team	Games	BA	SA	AB	H	2B	3B	HR	HR%	R	RBI	BB	SO	SB	Pinch Hit AB	Pinch Hit H	PO	A	E	DP	TC/G	FA	G by Pos
1947	**WAS A**	7	.154	.154	26	4	0	0	0	0.0	2	0	2	2	0	0	0	19	28	0	7	6.7	1.000	2B-7

Harry Lyons

LYONS, HARRY P. BR TR 5′10½″ 157 lbs.
B. Mar. 25, 1866, Chester, Pa. D. June 30, 1912, Mauricetown, N. J.

Year	Team	Games	BA	SA	AB	H	2B	3B	HR	HR%	R	RBI	BB	SO	SB	Pinch Hit AB	Pinch Hit H	PO	A	E	DP	TC/G	FA	G by Pos
1887	**2 teams**	**PHI N** (1G –.000) **STL AA** (2G –.125)																						
"	**total**	3	.083	.083	12	1	0	0	0	0.0	2	0	1	0	2	0	0	4	5	1	1	3.3	.900	OF-2, 2B-1
1888	**STL AA**	123	.194	.259	499	97	10	5	4	0.8	66	63	20		36	0	0	237	35	36	4	2.4	.883	OF-122, 3B-2, 2B-1, SS-1
1889	**NY N**	5	.100	.200	20	2	0	1	0	0.0	1	2	2	0	0	0	0	5	0	0	0	1.0	1.000	OF-5
1890	**ROC AA**	133	.260	.332	**584**	152	11	11	3	0.5	83		27		47	0	0	265	30	27	4	2.4	.916	OF-132, 3B-2, C-1, P-1
1892	**NY N**	96	.238	.260	411	98	5	2	0	0.0	67	53	33	29	25	0	0	186	16	20	1	2.3	.910	OF-96
1893		47	.273	.321	187	51	5	2	0	0.0	27	21	14	6	10	0	0	113	9	11	3	2.8	.917	OF-47
6 yrs.		407	.234	.289	1713	401	31	21	7	0.4	246	139	97	35	120	0	0	810	95	95	13	2.4	.905	OF-404, 3B-4, 2B-2, P-1, C-1, SS-1

Pat Lyons

LYONS, PATRICK JERRY TR
B. Mar. 1860 D. Jan. 20, 1914, Springfield, Ohio.

Year	Team	Games	BA	SA	AB	H	2B	3B	HR	HR%	R	RBI	BB	SO	SB	Pinch Hit AB	Pinch Hit H	PO	A	E	DP	TC/G	FA	G by Pos
1890	**CLE N**	11	.053	.079	38	2	1	0	0	0.0	2	1	4	4	0	0	0	24	28	10	2	5.6	.839	2B-11

Steve Lyons

LYONS, STEPHEN JOHN (Psycho)
B. June 3, 1960, Tacoma, Wash.
BL TR 6′ 3″ 190 lbs.

Year	Team	Games	BA	SA	AB	H	2B	3B	HR	HR%	R	RBI	BB	SO	SB	Pinch Hit AB	Pinch Hit H	PO	A	E	DP	TC/G	FA	G by Pos
1985	BOS A	133	.264	.358	371	98	14	3	5	1.3	52	30	32	64	12	13	2	253	6	7	0	2.2	.974	OF-114, DH-5, 3B-1, SS-1
1986	2 teams	BOS A (59G –.250) CHI A (42G –.203)																						
″	total	101	.227	.300	247	56	9	3	1	0.4	30	20	19	47	4	7	1	175	11	4	1	2.0	.979	OF-90, 3B-3, DH-1, 1B-1
1987	CHI A	76	.280	.363	193	54	11	1	1	0.5	26	19	12	37	3	4	0	69	101	4	12	2.6	.977	3B-51, OF-15, 2B-1
1988		146	.269	.373	472	127	28	3	5	1.1	59	45	32	59	1	3	1	128	243	29	38	2.7	.928	3B-128, OF-14, 2B-4, C-2, 1B-1
1989		140	.264	.339	443	117	21	3	2	0.5	51	50	35	68	9	14	5	414	245	15	73	4.1	.978	2B-70, 1B-40, 3B-28, OF-20, SS-3, DH-1, C-1
1990		94	.192	.267	146	28	6	1	1	0.7	22	11	10	41	1	21	3	244	54	5	33	3.3	.983	1B-61, 2B-15, OF-7, 3B-5, DH-3, SS-1, P-1
1991	BOS A	87	.241	.354	212	51	10	1	4	1.9	15	17	11	35	10	21	1	118	43	3	6	2.1	.982	OF-45, 2B-16, 3B-12, DH-2, 1B-2, SS-1, P-1
1992	3 teams	ATL N (11G –.071) MON N (16G –.231) BOS A (21G –.250)																						
″	total	48	.200	.273	55	11	0	2	0	0.0	5	4	3	8	1	12	3	65	9	0	5	2.2	1.000	OF-19, 1B-9, 2B-3, DH-2
1993	BOS A	28	.130	.174	23	3	1	0	0	0.0	4	0	2	5	1	5	1	11	15	0	2	1.1	1.000	OF-10, 2B-9, DH-1, 3B-1, 1B-1, C-1
9 yrs.		853	.252	.340	2162	545	100	17	19	0.9	264	196	156	364	42	100	17	1477	727	67	170	2.8	.970	OF-334, 3B-229, 2B-118, 1B-115, DH-15, SS-6, C-4, P-2

Ted Lyons

LYONS, THEODORE AMAR
B. Dec. 28, 1900, Lake Charles, La. D. July 25, 1986, Sulphur, La.
Manager 1946–48.
Hall of Fame 1955.
BB TR 5′11″ 200 lbs.

Year	Team	Games	BA	SA	AB	H	2B	3B	HR	HR%	R	RBI	BB	SO	SB	Pinch Hit AB	Pinch Hit H	PO	A	E	DP	TC/G	FA	G by Pos
1923	CHI A	9	.200	.200	5	1	0	0	0	0.0	0	1	1	3	0	0	0	3	7	0	1	1.1	1.000	P-9
1924		41	.221	.247	77	17	0	1	0	0.0	10	6	5	13	0	0	0	3	45	5	2	1.3	.906	P-41
1925		43	.186	.216	97	18	3	0	0	0.0	6	7	3	13	0	0	0	8	80	4	3	2.1	.957	P-43
1926		41	.212	.240	104	22	1	1	0	0.0	7	3	1	10	0	1	0	16	91	5	3	2.9	.955	P-39
1927		41	.255	.373	110	28	6	2	1	0.9	16	9	6	17	0	0	0	13	79	2	3	2.4	.979	P-39
1928		49	.253	.275	91	23	2	0	0	0.0	10	8	1	9	0	0	0	20	60	7	6	2.2	.920	P-39
1929		40	.220	.264	91	20	4	0	0	0.0	7	11	9	13	0	0	0	21	66	5	4	2.4	.946	P-37, OF-1
1930		57	.311	.434	122	38	6	3	1	0.8	20	15	2	18	0	9	3	14	77	6	5	2.3	.938	P-42
1931		42	.152	.152	33	5	0	0	0	0.0	6	3	2	1	0	2	1	4	18	1	3	1.0	.957	P-22
1932		49	.260	.356	73	19	2	1	1	1.4	11	10	4	10	0	1	0	11	42	2	1	1.7	.964	P-33
1933		51	.286	.363	91	26	2	1	1	1.1	11	11	4	6	0	7	1	10	49	1	3	1.7	.983	P-36
1934		50	.206	.278	97	20	4	0	1	1.0	9	16	3	19	0	17	3	12	50	4	4	2.2	.939	P-30
1935		29	.220	.268	82	18	4	0	0	0.0	5	6	3	4	0	6	1	9	31	0	2	1.7	1.000	P-23
1936		26	.157	.157	70	11	0	0	0	0.0	2	5	5	12	0	0	0	12	38	0	2	1.9	1.000	P-26
1937		23	.211	.211	57	12	0	0	0	0.0	6	3	9	14	0	0	0	6	33	0	3	1.8	1.000	P-22
1938		24	.194	.222	72	14	2	0	0	0.0	9	4	2	9	0	1	0	9	46	1	1	2.4	.982	P-23
1939		21	.295	.344	61	18	3	0	0	0.0	5	8	5	7	0	0	0	9	22	3	3	1.6	.912	P-21
1940		22	.240	.293	75	18	4	0	0	0.0	4	7	2	7	0	0	0	12	24	3	1	1.8	.923	P-22
1941		22	.270	.297	74	20	2	0	0	0.0	8	6	2	6	0	0	0	17	36	1	3	2.5	.981	P-22
1942		20	.239	.299	67	16	4	0	0	0.0	10	10	3	7	0	0	0	8	41	1	4	2.5	.980	P-20
1946		5	.000	.000	14	0	0	0	0	0.0	0	0	1	3	0	0	0	2	10	0	0	2.4	1.000	P-5
21 yrs.		705	.233	.285	1563	364	49	9	5	0.3	162	149	73	201	0	44	9	219	945	51	57	2.0	.958	P-594, OF-1

Terry Lyons

LYONS, TERENCE HILBERT
B. Dec. 14, 1908, New Holland, Ohio D. Sept. 9, 1959, Dayton, Ohio.
BR TR 6′½″ 165 lbs.

Year	Team	Games	BA	SA	AB	H	2B	3B	HR	HR%	R	RBI	BB	SO	SB	Pinch Hit AB	Pinch Hit H	PO	A	E	DP	TC/G	FA	G by Pos
1929	PHI N	1	—	—	0	0	0	0	0	—	0	0	0	0	0	0	0	0	0	0	0	0.0	.000	1B-1

Pop Lytle

LYTLE, EDWARD BENSON (Dad)
B. Mar. 10, 1862, Racine, Wis. D. Dec. 21, 1950, Long Beach, Calif.
BR TR 5′11″ 160 lbs.

Year	Team	Games	BA	SA	AB	H	2B	3B	HR	HR%	R	RBI	BB	SO	SB	Pinch Hit AB	Pinch Hit H	PO	A	E	DP	TC/G	FA	G by Pos
1890	2 teams	CHI N (1G –.000) PIT N (15G –.145)																						
″	total	16	.136	.153	59	8	1	0	0	0.0	3	0	8	10	0	0	0	28	22	10	0	3.8	.833	2B-8, OF-8

Jim Lyttle

LYTTLE, JAMES LAWRENCE
B. May 20, 1946, Hamilton, Ohio.
BL TR 6′ 180 lbs.

Year	Team	Games	BA	SA	AB	H	2B	3B	HR	HR%	R	RBI	BB	SO	SB	Pinch Hit AB	Pinch Hit H	PO	A	E	DP	TC/G	FA	G by Pos
1969	NY A	28	.181	.229	83	15	4	0	0	0.0	7	4	4	19	1	1	0	55	3	1	1	2.1	.983	OF-28
1970		87	.310	.452	126	39	7	1	3	2.4	20	14	10	26	3	7	3	84	2	1	0	1.2	.989	OF-70
1971		49	.198	.291	86	17	5	0	1	1.2	7	7	8	18	0	15	1	47	1	0	0	1.7	1.000	OF-29
1972	CHI A	44	.232	.341	82	19	5	2	0	0.0	8	5	1	28	0	21	6	32	1	0	1	1.6	1.000	OF-21
1973	MON N	49	.259	.422	116	30	5	1	4	3.4	12	19	9	14	0	11	2	73	3	2	1	2.2	.974	OF-36
1974		25	.333	.333	9	3	0	0	0	0.0	1	2	1	3	0	6	2	6	1	0	0	0.4	1.000	OF-18
1975		44	.273	.345	55	15	4	0	0	0.0	7	6	13	6	0	19	4	17	1	0	0	1.1	1.000	OF-16
1976	2 teams	MON N (42G –.271) LA N (23G –.221)																						
″	total	65	.248	.327	153	38	7	1	1	0.7	9	13	15	25	0	20	5	87	8	1	4	2.0	.990	OF-47
8 yrs.		391	.248	.352	710	176	37	5	9	1.3	71	70	61	139	4	100	23	401	20	5	7	1.6	.988	OF-265

Kevin Maas

MAAS, KEVIN CHRISTIAN
B. Jan. 20, 1965, Castro Valley, Calif.
BL TL 6′ 3″ 195 lbs.

Year	Team	Games	BA	SA	AB	H	2B	3B	HR	HR%	R	RBI	BB	SO	SB	Pinch Hit AB	Pinch Hit H	PO	A	E	DP	TC/G	FA	G by Pos
1990	NY A	79	.252	.535	254	64	9	0	21	8.3	42	41	43	76	1	5	0	486	35	9	45	7.1	.983	1B-57, DH-18
1991		148	.220	.390	500	110	14	1	23	4.6	69	63	83	128	5	9	2	317	23	6	22	2.4	.983	DH-109, 1B-36
1992		98	.248	.406	286	71	12	0	11	3.8	35	35	25	63	3	19	7	142	4	2	11	1.8	.986	DH-62, 1B-22
1993		59	.205	.411	151	31	4	0	9	6.0	20	25	24	32	1	12	3	115	5	2	13	2.5	.984	DH-31, 1B-17
1995	MIN A	22	.193	.316	57	11	4	0	1	1.8	5	5	7	11	0	6	0	43	1	3	4	2.3	.936	DH-12, 1B-8
5 yrs.		406	.230	.422	1248	287	43	1	65	5.2	171	169	182	310	10	51	12	1103	68	22	95	3.2	.982	DH-232, 1B-140

John Mabry

MABRY, JOHN STEVEN
B. Oct. 17, 1970, Wilmington, Del.
BL TR 6′ 4″ 195 lbs.

Year	Team	Games	BA	SA	AB	H	2B	3B	HR	HR%	R	RBI	BB	SO	SB	Pinch Hit AB	Pinch Hit H	PO	A	E	DP	TC/G	FA	G by Pos
1994	STL N	6	.304	.435	23	7	3	0	0	0.0	2	3	2	4	0	0	0	16	0	0	0	2.7	1.000	OF-6
1995		129	.307	.405	388	119	21	1	5	1.3	35	41	24	45	0	27	8	652	56	4	65	6.4	.994	1B-73, OF-39
2 yrs.		135	.307	.406	411	126	24	1	5	1.2	37	44	26	49	0	27	8	668	56	4	65	6.2	.995	1B-73, OF-45

Harvey MacDonald

MacDONALD, HARVEY FORSYTH BL TL 5′11″ 170 lbs.
B. May 18, 1898, New York, N. Y. D. Oct. 4, 1965, Manoa, Pa.

Year	Team		Games	BA	SA	AB	H	2B	3B	HR	HR%	R	RBI	BB	SO	SB	Pinch Hit AB	Pinch Hit H	PO	A	E	DP	TC/G	FA	G by Pos
1928	PHI	N	13	.250	.250	16	4	0	0	0	0.0	0	2	2	3	0	9	4	3	0	0	0	1.5	1.000	OF-2

Macey

MACEY
B. Columbus, Ohio Deceased.

Year	Team		Games	BA	SA	AB	H	2B	3B	HR	HR%	R	RBI	BB	SO	SB	Pinch Hit AB	Pinch Hit H	PO	A	E	DP	TC/G	FA	G by Pos
1890	PHI	AA	1	.000	.000	1	0	0	0	0	0.0	0		0		0	0	0	1	0	0	0	1.0	1.000	C-1

Mike Macfarlane

MACFARLANE, MICHAEL ANDREW (Mac) BR TR 6′ 1″ 200 lbs.
B. Apr. 12, 1964, Stockton, Calif.

Year	Team		Games	BA	SA	AB	H	2B	3B	HR	HR%	R	RBI	BB	SO	SB	Pinch Hit AB	Pinch Hit H	PO	A	E	DP	TC/G	FA	G by Pos
1987	KC	A	8	.211	.263	19	4	1	0	0	0.0	0	3	2	2	0	0	0	29	2	0	0	3.9	1.000	C-8
1988			70	.265	.393	211	56	15	0	4	1.9	25	26	21	37	0	4	0	309	18	2	3	4.8	.994	C-68
1989			69	.223	.299	157	35	6	0	2	1.3	13	19	7	27	0	12	2	249	17	1	4	4.2	.996	C-59, DH-4
1990			124	.255	.380	400	102	24	4	6	1.5	37	58	25	69	1	13	3	660	23	6	9	5.9	.991	C-112, DH-5
1991			84	.277	.506	267	74	18	2	13	4.9	34	41	17	52	1	13	4	391	28	3	4	5.8	.993	C-69, DH-4
1992			129	.234	.445	402	94	28	3	17	4.2	51	48	30	89	1	16	4	527	43	4	7	4.9	.993	C-104, DH-13
1993			117	.273	.497	388	106	27	0	20	5.2	55	67	40	83	2	12	5	647	68	11	11	6.4	.985	C-114
1994			92	.255	.462	314	80	17	3	14	4.5	53	47	35	71	1	6	1	498	39	4	2	6.1	.993	C-81, DH-8
1995	BOS	A	115	.225	.404	364	82	18	1	15	4.1	45	51	38	78	2	3	0	618	49	5	3	5.9	.993	C-111, DH-3
9 yrs.			808	.251	.431	2522	633	154	13	91	3.6	313	360	215	508	8	79	19	3928	287	36	43	5.6	.992	C-726, DH-37
DIVISIONAL PLAYOFF SERIES																									
1995	BOS	A	3	.333	.333	9	3	0	0	0	0.0	0	1	0	3	0	0	0	18	0	2	0	6.7	.900	C-3

Ed MacGamwell

MacGAMWELL, EDWARD M. BL TL
B. Jan. 10, 1879, Buffalo, N. Y. D. May 26, 1924, Albany, N. Y.

Year	Team		Games	BA	SA	AB	H	2B	3B	HR	HR%	R	RBI	BB	SO	SB	Pinch Hit AB	Pinch Hit H	PO	A	E	DP	TC/G	FA	G by Pos
1905	BKN	N	4	.250	.250	16	4	0	0	0	0.0	0	0	1		0	0	0	37	2	2	0	10.3	.951	1B-4

Ken Macha

MACHA, KENNETH EDWARD BR TR 6′ 2″ 215 lbs.
Brother of Mike Macha.
B. Sept. 29, 1950, Monroeville, Pa.

Year	Team		Games	BA	SA	AB	H	2B	3B	HR	HR%	R	RBI	BB	SO	SB	Pinch Hit AB	Pinch Hit H	PO	A	E	DP	TC/G	FA	G by Pos
1974	PIT	N	5	.600	.800	5	3	1	0	0	0.0	1	1	0	0	0	5	3	1	0	0	0	1.0	1.000	C-1
1977			35	.274	.316	95	26	4	0	0	0.0	2	11	6	17	1	6	0	72	25	1	5	3.1	.990	3B-17, 1B-11, OF-4
1978			29	.212	.269	52	11	1	1	0	0.0	5	5	12	10	2	7	1	11	21	1	3	1.6	.970	3B-21
1979	MON	N	25	.278	.417	36	10	3	1	0	0.0	8	4	2	9	0	7	1	22	18	0	2	2.2	1.000	3B-13, 1B-2, OF-2, C-1
1980			49	.290	.383	107	31	5	1	1	0.9	10	8	11	17	0	11	2	31	43	6	5	2.2	.925	3B-33, 1B-2, C-1, OF-1
1981	TOR	A	37	.200	.224	85	17	2	0	0	0.0	4	6	8	15	1	1	0	99	36	5	17	3.7	.964	3B-19, 1B-16, DH-2, C-1
6 yrs.			180	.258	.324	380	98	16	3	1	0.3	30	35	39	68	4	37	7	236	143	13	32	2.7	.967	3B-103, 1B-31, OF-7, C-4, DH-2

Mike Macha

MACHA, MICHAEL WILLIAM BR TR 5′11″ 180 lbs.
Brother of Ken Macha.
B. Feb. 17, 1954, Victoria, Tex.

Year	Team		Games	BA	SA	AB	H	2B	3B	HR	HR%	R	RBI	BB	SO	SB	Pinch Hit AB	Pinch Hit H	PO	A	E	DP	TC/G	FA	G by Pos
1979	ATL	N	6	.154	.154	13	2	0	0	0	0.0	2	1	1	5	0	2	0	2	8	3	0	4.3	.769	3B-3
1980	TOR	A	5	.000	.000	8	0	0	0	0	0.0	0	0	0	1	0	2	0	2	5	2	1	3.0	.778	3B-2, C-1
2 yrs.			11	.095	.095	21	2	0	0	0	0.0	2	1	1	6	0	4	0	4	13	5	1	3.7	.773	3B-5, C-1

Dave Machemer

MACHEMER, DAVID RITCHIE BR TR 5′11½″ 180 lbs.
B. May 24, 1951, St. Joseph, Mich.

Year	Team		Games	BA	SA	AB	H	2B	3B	HR	HR%	R	RBI	BB	SO	SB	Pinch Hit AB	Pinch Hit H	PO	A	E	DP	TC/G	FA	G by Pos
1978	CAL	A	10	.273	.455	22	6	1	0	1	4.5	6	2	2	1	0	0	0	6	12	2	0	2.2	.900	2B-5, 3B-3, SS-1
1979	DET	A	19	.192	.231	26	5	1	0	0	0.0	8	2	3	2	0	0	0	18	20	1	6	3.0	.974	2B-11, OF-1, DH-1
2 yrs.			29	.229	.333	48	11	2	0	1	2.1	14	4	5	3	0	0	0	24	32	3	6	2.7	.949	2B-16, 3B-3, DH-1, OF-1, SS-1

Connie Mack

MACK, CORNELIUS ALEXANDER (The Tall Tactician) BR TR 6′ 1″ 170 lbs.
Born Cornelius Alexander McGillicuddy.
Father of Earle Mack.
B. Dec. 22, 1862, E. Brookfield, Mass. D. Feb. 8, 1956, Philadelphia, Pa.
Manager 1894–96, 1901–50.
Hall of Fame 1937.

Year	Team		Games	BA	SA	AB	H	2B	3B	HR	HR%	R	RBI	BB	SO	SB	Pinch Hit AB	Pinch Hit H	PO	A	E	DP	TC/G	FA	G by Pos
1886	WAS	N	10	.361	.472	36	13	2	1	0	0.0	4	5	0	2		0	0	88	22	5	2	11.5	.957	C-10
1887			82	.201	.226	314	63	6	1	0	0.0	35	20	8	17	26	0	0	403	127	55	16	7.0	.906	C-76, OF-5, 2B-2
1888			85	.187	.273	300	56	5	6	3	1.0	49	29	17	18	31	0	0	384	155	48	8	6.9	.918	C-79, OF-4, SS-1, 1B-1
1889			98	.293	.339	386	113	16	1	0	0.0	51	42	15	12	26	0	0	432	100	57	22	5.8	.903	C-45, OF-34, 1B-22
1890	BUF	P	123	.266	.344	503	134	15	12	0	0.0	95	53	47	13	16	0	0	500	147	50	14	5.5	.928	C-112, OF-9, 1B-5
1891	PIT	N	75	.214	.250	280	60	10	0	0	0.0	43	29	19	11	4	0	0	385	79	35	1	6.7	.930	C-72, 1B-3
1892			97	.243	.301	346	84	9	4	1	0.3	39	31	21	22	11	1	**1**	415	143	29	11	6.1	.951	C-92, OF-3, 1B-1
1893			37	.286	.323	133	38	3	1	0	0.0	22	15	10	9	4	0	0	128	47	11	5	5.0	.941	C-37
1894			69	.250	.303	228	57	7	1	1	0.4	32	21	20	14	8	0	0	274	67	19	6	5.2	.947	C-69
1895			14	.306	.347	49	15	2	0	0	0.0	12	4	7	1	1	1	0	48	10	2	2	4.6	.967	C-12, 1B-1
1896			33	.217	.267	120	26	4	1	0	0.0	9	16	5	8	0	0	0	261	19	7	14	8.7	.976	1B-28, C-5
11 yrs.			723	.245	.300	2695	659	79	28	5	0.2	391	265	169	127	127	2	1	3318	916	318	101	6.3	.930	C-609, 1B-61, OF-55, 2B-2, SS-1

Denny Mack

MACK, DENNIS JOSEPH BR TR 5′ 7″ 164 lbs.
Born Dennis Joseph McGee.
B. 1851, Easton, Pa. D. Apr. 10, 1888, Wilkes-Barre, Pa.
Manager 1882.

Year	Team		Games	BA	SA	AB	H	2B	3B	HR	HR%	R	RBI	BB	SO	SB	Pinch Hit AB	Pinch Hit H	PO	A	E	DP	TC/G	FA	G by Pos
1876	STL	N	48	.217	.261	180	39	5	0	1	0.6	32	7	11	5		0	0	59	124	26	8	4.4	.876	SS-41, 2B-5, OF-2
1880	BUF	N	17	.203	.203	59	12	0	0	0	0.0	5	3	5	7		0	0	19	46	4	3	4.1	.942	SS-16, 2B-1
1882	LOU	AA	72	.182	.201	264	48	3	1	0	0.0	41		16			0	0	108	220	49	20	4.8	.870	SS-49, 2B-24, OF-5
1883	PIT	AA	60	.196	.246	224	44	5	3	0	0.0	26		13			0	0	256	123	34	18	6.5	.918	SS-38, 1B-25, 2B-1
4 yrs.			197	.197	.230	727	143	13	4	1	0.1	104	10	45	12		0	0	442	513	113	49	5.2	.894	SS-144, 2B-31, 1B-25, OF-7

Year	Team	Games	BA	SA	AB	H	2B	3B	HR	HR%	R	RBI	BB	SO	SB	Pinch Hit AB	Pinch Hit H	PO	A	E	DP	TC/G	FA	G by Pos

Earle Mack

MACK, EARLE THADDEUS BL TR 5′ 8″ 140 lbs.
Born Earle Thaddeus McGillicuddy.
Son of Connie Mack.
B. Feb. 1, 1890, Spencer, Mass. D. Feb. 4, 1967, Upper Darby, Pa.
Manager 1937, 1939.

Year	Team	Games	BA	SA	AB	H	2B	3B	HR	HR%	R	RBI	BB	SO	SB	PH AB	PH H	PO	A	E	DP	TC/G	FA	G by Pos
1910	PHI A	1	.500	1.000	4	2	0	1	0	0.0	0	0	0		0	0	0	3	2	0	0	5.0	1.000	C-1
1911		2	.000	.000	4	0	0	0	0	0.0	0	0	0		0	0	0	0	0	0	0	0.0	.000	3B-2
1914		2	.000	.000	8	0	0	0	0	0.0	0	1	0	0	1	0	0	19	1	0	0	10.0	1.000	1B-2
3 yrs.		5	.125	.250	16	2	0	1	0	0.0	0	1	0	0	1	0	0	22	3	0	0	5.0	1.000	3B-2, 1B-2, C-1

Joe Mack

MACK, JOSEPH JOHN BB TL 5′11½″ 185 lbs.
Born Joseph John Maciarz.
B. Jan. 4, 1912, Chicago, Ill.

Year	Team	Games	BA	SA	AB	H	2B	3B	HR	HR%	R	RBI	BB	SO	SB	PH AB	PH H	PO	A	E	DP	TC/G	FA	G by Pos
1945	BOS N	66	.231	.323	260	60	13	1	3	1.2	30	44	34	39	1	1	0	635	48	6	48	10.6	.991	1B-65

Quinn Mack

MACK, QUINN DAVID BL TL 5′10″ 185 lbs.
Brother of Shane Mack.
B. Sept. 11, 1965, Los Angeles, Calif.

Year	Team	Games	BA	SA	AB	H	2B	3B	HR	HR%	R	RBI	BB	SO	SB	PH AB	PH H	PO	A	E	DP	TC/G	FA	G by Pos
1994	SEA A	5	.238	.381	21	5	3	0	0	0.0	1	2	1	3	2	0	0	6	0	0	0	1.2	1.000	OF-4, DH-1

Ray Mack

MACK, RAYMOND JAMES BR TR 6′ 200 lbs.
Born Raymond James Mlckovsky.
B. Aug. 31, 1916, Cleveland, Ohio D. May 7, 1969, Bucyrus, Ohio.

Year	Team	Games	BA	SA	AB	H	2B	3B	HR	HR%	R	RBI	BB	SO	SB	PH AB	PH H	PO	A	E	DP	TC/G	FA	G by Pos
1938	CLE A	2	.333	.667	6	2	0	1	0	0.0	2	2	0	1	0	0	0	8	6	0	0	7.0	1.000	2B-2
1939		36	.152	.232	112	17	4	1	1	0.9	12	6	12	19	0	2	0	80	87	4	25	4.9	.977	2B-34, 3B-1
1940		146	.283	.409	530	150	21	5	12	2.3	60	69	51	77	4	0	0	323	417	27	109	5.3	.965	2B-146
1941		145	.228	.341	501	114	22	4	9	1.8	54	44	54	69	8	0	0	363	386	23	109	5.3	.970	2B-145
1942		143	.225	.291	481	108	14	6	2	0.4	43	45	41	51	9	0	0	340	434	25	105	5.6	.969	2B-143
1943		153	.220	.312	545	120	25	2	7	1.3	56	62	47	61	8	0	0	381	444	28	123	5.6	.967	2B-153
1944		83	.232	.306	284	66	15	3	0	0.0	24	29	28	45	4	0	0	226	243	24	73	5.9	.951	2B-83
1946		61	.205	.281	171	35	6	2	1	0.6	13	9	23	27	2	0	0	118	142	8	37	4.4	.970	2B-61
1947	2 teams NY A (1G –.000) CHI N (21G –.218)																							
″	total	22	.218	.372	78	17	6	0	2	2.6	9	12	5	15	0	0	0	58	78	5	15	6.7	.965	2B-21
9 yrs.		791	.232	.329	2708	629	113	24	34	1.3	273	278	261	365	35	2	0	1897	2237	144	596	5.4	.966	2B-788, 3B-1

Reddy Mack

MACK, JOSEPH
Born Joseph McNamara.
B. May 2, 1866, Ireland D. Dec. 30, 1916, Newport, Ky.

Year	Team	Games	BA	SA	AB	H	2B	3B	HR	HR%	R	RBI	BB	SO	SB	PH AB	PH H	PO	A	E	DP	TC/G	FA	G by Pos
1885	LOU AA	11	.244	.268	41	10	1	0	0	0.0	7		2			0	0	33	36	9	9	7.1	.885	2B-11
1886		137	.244	.344	483	118	23	11	1	0.2	82		68			0	0	350	446	88	60	6.5	.900	2B-137
1887		128	.308	.395	478	147	23	8	1	0.2	117		83		22	0	0	366	395	73	48	6.5	.912	2B-128
1888		112	.217	.289	446	97	13	5	3	0.7	77	34	52		18	0	0	307	344	67	35	6.4	.907	2B-112
1889	BAL AA	136	.241	.320	519	125	24	7	1	0.2	84	87	60	69	23	0	0	372	358	83	70	6.0	.898	2B-135, OF-1
1890		26	.284	.421	95	27	3	5	0	0.0	14		10		7	0	0	62	76	10	7	5.7	.932	2B-26
6 yrs.		550	.254	.340	2062	524	87	36	6	0.3	381	121	275	69	70	0	0	1490	1655	330	229	6.3	.905	2B-549, OF-1

Shane Mack

MACK, SHANE LEE BR TR 6′ 185 lbs.
Brother of Quinn Mack.
B. Dec. 7, 1963, Los Angeles, Calif.

Year	Team	Games	BA	SA	AB	H	2B	3B	HR	HR%	R	RBI	BB	SO	SB	PH AB	PH H	PO	A	E	DP	TC/G	FA	G by Pos
1987	SD N	105	.239	.361	238	57	11	3	4	1.7	28	25	18	47	4	20	3	159	1	3	0	1.8	.982	OF-91
1988		56	.244	.269	119	29	3	0	0	0.0	13	12	14	21	5	0	0	110	4	2	1	2.1	.983	OF-55
1990	MIN A	125	.326	.460	313	102	10	4	8	2.6	50	44	29	69	13	16	7	230	8	3	1	2.1	.988	OF-109, DH-4
1991		143	.310	.529	442	137	27	8	18	4.1	79	74	34	79	13	8	3	290	6	7	2	2.1	.977	OF-140, DH-1
1992		156	.315	.467	600	189	31	6	16	2.7	101	75	64	106	26	2	1	322	9	4	2	2.2	.988	OF-155
1993		128	.276	.412	503	139	30	4	10	2.0	66	61	41	76	15	1	0	347	8	5	1	2.8	.986	OF-128
1994		81	.333	.564	303	101	21	2	15	5.0	55	61	32	51	4	2	1	201	2	2	0	2.6	.990	OF-75, DH-4
7 yrs.		794	.299	.458	2518	754	133	27	71	2.8	392	352	232	449	80	49	15	1659	38	26	7	2.3	.985	OF-753, DH-9
LEAGUE CHAMPIONSHIP SERIES																								
1991	MIN A	5	.333	.500	18	6	1	1	0	0.0	4	3	2	4	2	0	0	3	0	1	0	0.8	.750	OF-5
WORLD SERIES																								
1991	MIN A	6	.130	.174	23	3	1	0	0	0.0	0	1	0	7	0	0	0	11	0	0	0	1.8	1.000	OF-6

Pete Mackanin

MACKANIN, PETER, JR. BR TR 6′ 2″ 190 lbs.
B. Aug. 1, 1951, Chicago, Ill.

Year	Team	Games	BA	SA	AB	H	2B	3B	HR	HR%	R	RBI	BB	SO	SB	PH AB	PH H	PO	A	E	DP	TC/G	FA	G by Pos
1973	TEX A	44	.100	.122	90	9	2	0	0	0.0	3	2	4	26	0	2	0	39	88	7	15	3.1	.948	SS-33, 3B-10
1974		2	.167	.500	6	1	0	1	0	0.0	0	0	0	2	0	1	0	3	8	0	3	5.5	1.000	SS-2
1975	MON N	130	.225	.375	448	101	19	6	12	2.7	59	44	31	99	11	4	0	300	411	26	100	5.7	.965	2B-127, 3B-1, SS-1
1976		114	.224	.337	380	85	15	2	8	2.1	36	33	15	66	6	4	1	203	307	19	64	4.7	.964	2B-100, 3B-8, SS-3, OF-1
1977		55	.224	.329	85	19	2	2	1	1.2	9	6	4	17	3	29	7	34	44	4	11	3.2	.951	2B-9, SS-8, 3B-5, OF-4
1978	PHI N	5	.250	.250	8	2	0	0	0	0.0	0	1	0	4	0	4	1	6	2	0	0	4.0	1.000	3B-1, 1B-1
1979		13	.111	.444	9	1	0	0	1	11.1	2	2	1	2	0	6	0	1	9	0	0	1.7	1.000	3B-2, SS-2, 2B-2
1980	MIN A	108	.266	.361	319	85	18	0	4	1.3	31	35	14	34	6	15	5	168	285	18	75	4.2	.962	2B-71, SS-30, DH-5, 1B-4, 3B-3
1981		77	.231	.324	225	52	7	1	4	1.8	21	18	7	40	1	9	2	171	149	12	40	4.2	.964	2B-31, SS-28, 1B-10, DH-6, 3B-4
9 yrs.		548	.226	.339	1570	355	63	12	30	1.9	161	141	76	290	27	74	16	925	1303	86	308	4.5	.963	2B-340, SS-107, 3B-34, 1B-15, DH-11, OF-5

Eric MacKenzie

MacKENZIE, ERIC HUGH BL TR 6′ 185 lbs.
B. Aug. 29, 1932, Glendon, Alta., Canada.

Year	Team	Games	BA	SA	AB	H	2B	3B	HR	HR%	R	RBI	BB	SO	SB	PH AB	PH H	PO	A	E	DP	TC/G	FA	G by Pos
1955	KC A	1	.000	.000	1	0	0	0	0	0.0	0	0	0	0	0	0	0	0	0	0	0	0.0	.000	C-1

Gordon MacKenzie

MacKENZIE, HENRY GORDON BR TR 5′11″ 175 lbs.
B. July 9, 1937, St. Petersburg, Fla.

Year	Team	Games	BA	SA	AB	H	2B	3B	HR	HR%	R	RBI	BB	SO	SB	PH AB	PH H	PO	A	E	DP	TC/G	FA	G by Pos
1961	KC A	11	.125	.125	24	3	0	0	0	0.0	1	1	1	6	0	6	1	22	3	0	2	3.6	1.000	C-7

Felix Mackiewicz

MACKIEWICZ, FELIX THADDEUS BR TR 6' 2" 195 lbs.
B. Nov. 20, 1917, Chicago, Ill. D. Dec. 20, 1993, Olivette, Mo.

Year	Team	Lg	Games	BA	SA	AB	H	2B	3B	HR	HR%	R	RBI	BB	SO	SB	Pinch Hit AB	Pinch Hit H	PO	A	E	DP	TC/G	FA	G by Pos
1941	PHI	A	5	.286	.429	14	4	0	1	0	0.0	3	0	1	0	0	1	0	5	0	0	0	1.7	1.000	OF-3
1942			6	.214	.357	14	3	2	0	0	0.0	3	2	0	4	0	3	1	6	1	0	0	2.3	1.000	OF-3
1943			9	.063	.063	16	1	0	0	0	0.0	1	0	2	8	0	3	0	9	0	0	0	3.0	1.000	OF-3
1945	CLE	A	120	.273	.368	359	98	14	7	2	0.6	42	37	44	41	5	7	0	288	11	4	4	2.7	.987	OF-112
1946			78	.260	.349	258	67	15	4	0	0.0	35	16	16	32	5	5	1	172	2	3	1	2.5	.983	OF-72
1947	2 teams		CLE A (2G –.000) WAS A (3G –.167)																						
"	total		5	.091	.182	11	1	1	0	0	0.0	1	0	0	3	0	0	0	8	0	0	0	1.6	1.000	OF-5
6 yrs.			223	.259	.351	672	174	32	12	2	0.3	85	55	63	88	10	19	2	488	14	7	5	2.6	.986	OF-198

Steve Macko

MACKO, STEVEN JOSEPH BL TR 5'10" 160 lbs.
B. Sept. 6, 1954, Burlington, Iowa D. Nov. 15, 1981, Arlington, Tex.

Year	Team	Lg	Games	BA	SA	AB	H	2B	3B	HR	HR%	R	RBI	BB	SO	SB	Pinch Hit AB	Pinch Hit H	PO	A	E	DP	TC/G	FA	G by Pos
1979	CHI	N	19	.225	.250	40	9	1	0	0	0.0	2	3	4	8	0	5	0	21	33	0	4	3.9	1.000	2B-10, 3B-4
1980			6	.300	.400	20	6	2	0	0	0.0	2	2	0	3	0	0	0	11	14	0	4	4.2	1.000	SS-3, 3B-2, 2B-1
2 yrs.			25	.250	.300	60	15	3	0	0	0.0	4	5	4	11	0	5	0	32	47	0	8	4.0	1.000	2B-11, 3B-6, SS-3

Lonnie Maclin

MACLIN, LONNIE LEE, JR. BL TL 6' 185 lbs.
B. Feb. 17, 1967, St. Louis, Mo.

Year	Team	Lg	Games	BA	SA	AB	H	2B	3B	HR	HR%	R	RBI	BB	SO	SB	Pinch Hit AB	Pinch Hit H	PO	A	E	DP	TC/G	FA	G by Pos
1993	STL	N	12	.077	.077	13	1	0	0	0	0.0	2	1	0	5	1	5	0	3	0	0	0	0.6	1.000	OF-5

Max Macon

MACON, MAX CULLEN BL TL 6' 3" 175 lbs.
B. Oct. 14, 1915, Pensacola, Fla. D. Aug. 5, 1989, Jupiter, Fla.

Year	Team	Lg	Games	BA	SA	AB	H	2B	3B	HR	HR%	R	RBI	BB	SO	SB	Pinch Hit AB	Pinch Hit H	PO	A	E	DP	TC/G	FA	G by Pos
1938	STL	N	46	.306	.306	36	11	0	0	0	0.0	5	3	2	4	0	2	0	3	32	2	2	0.9	.946	P-38, OF-1
1940	BKN	N	2	1.000	1.000	1	1	0	0	0	0.0	0	0	0	0	0	0	0	0	0	0	0	0.0	.000	P-2
1942			26	.279	.372	43	12	2	1	0	0.0	4	1	2	4	1	11	5	9	15	1	0	1.8	.960	P-14
1943			45	.164	.164	55	9	0	0	0	0.0	7	6	0	1	1	13	1	14	19	1	4	1.2	.971	P-25, 1B-3
1944	BOS	N	106	.273	.355	366	100	15	3	3	0.8	38	36	12	23	7	10	2	671	51	17	62	7.8	.977	1B-72, OF-22, P-1
1947			1	.000	.000	1	0	0	0	0	0.0	0	0	0	0	0	0	0	0	1	0	0	1.0	1.000	P-1
6 yrs.			226	.265	.333	502	133	17	4	3	0.6	54	46	16	32	9	36	8	697	118	21	68	4.7	.975	P-81, 1B-75, OF-23

Waddy MacPhee

MacPHEE, WALTER SCOTT BR TR 5' 8" 140 lbs.
B. Dec. 23, 1899, Brooklyn, N. Y. D. Jan. 20, 1980, Charlotte, N. C.

Year	Team	Lg	Games	BA	SA	AB	H	2B	3B	HR	HR%	R	RBI	BB	SO	SB	Pinch Hit AB	Pinch Hit H	PO	A	E	DP	TC/G	FA	G by Pos
1922	NY	N	2	.286	.571	7	2	0	1	0	0.0	2	0	1	0	0	0	0	3	5	1	0	4.5	.889	3B-2

Jimmy Macullar

MACULLAR, JAMES F. (Little Mac) BR TL 5' 6" 155 lbs.
B. Jan. 16, 1855, Boston, Mass. D. Apr. 8, 1924, Baltimore, Md.
Manager 1879.

Year	Team	Lg	Games	BA	SA	AB	H	2B	3B	HR	HR%	R	RBI	BB	SO	SB	Pinch Hit AB	Pinch Hit H	PO	A	E	DP	TC/G	FA	G by Pos
1879	SYR	N	64	.211	.248	246	52	9	0	0	0.0	24	13	3	27		0	0	139	120	42	9	4.4	.860	SS-37, OF-26, 2B-4, 3B-1
1882	CIN	AA	79	.234	.294	299	70	6	6	0	0.0	44		14			0	0	141	13	13	2	2.1	.922	OF-79
1883			14	.167	.208	48	8	2	0	0	0.0	4		4			0	0	17	2	4	0	1.5	.826	OF-14, SS-1
1884	BAL	AA	107	.204	.316	358	73	16	6	4	1.1	73		35			0	0	119	317	67	23	4.7	.867	SS-107
1885			100	.191	.278	320	61	7	6	3	0.9	52		49			0	0	178	311	68	28	5.6	.878	SS-98, OF-2
1886			85	.205	.239	268	55	7	1	0	0.0	49		49			0	0	120	213	58	19	4.5	.852	SS-82, OF-2, P-1, 2B-1
6 yrs.			449	.207	.276	1539	319	47	19	7	0.5	246	13	154	27		0	0	714	976	252	81	4.3	.870	SS-325, OF-123, 2B-5, P-1, 3B-1

Bunny Madden

MADDEN, THOMAS JOSEPH BL TL 5'11" 160 lbs.
B. July 31, 1883, Philadelphia, Pa. D. July 26, 1930, Philadelphia, Pa.

Year	Team	Lg	Games	BA	SA	AB	H	2B	3B	HR	HR%	R	RBI	BB	SO	SB	Pinch Hit AB	Pinch Hit H	PO	A	E	DP	TC/G	FA	G by Pos
1906	BOS	N	4	.267	.267	15	4	0	0	0	0.0	1	0	1		0	0	0	3	1	0	0	1.0	1.000	OF-4
1910	NY	A	1	.000	.000	1	0	0	0	0	0.0	0	0	0		0	1	0	0	0	0	0	0.0	—	
2 yrs.			5	.250	.250	16	4	0	0	0	0.0	1	0	1		0	1	0	3	1	0	0	1.0	1.000	OF-4

Gene Madden

MADDEN, EUGENE BL TR 5'10" 155 lbs.
B. June 5, 1890, Elm Grove, W. Va. D. Apr. 6, 1949, Utica, N. Y.

Year	Team	Lg	Games	BA	SA	AB	H	2B	3B	HR	HR%	R	RBI	BB	SO	SB	Pinch Hit AB	Pinch Hit H	PO	A	E	DP	TC/G	FA	G by Pos
1916	PIT	N	1	.000	.000	1	0	0	0	0	0.0	0	0	0	0	0	1	0	0	0	0	0	0.0	—	

Red Madden

MADDEN, FRANCIS A.
B. Oct. 17, 1892, Pittsburgh, Pa. D. Apr. 30, 1952, Pittsburgh, Pa.

Year	Team	Lg	Games	BA	SA	AB	H	2B	3B	HR	HR%	R	RBI	BB	SO	SB	Pinch Hit AB	Pinch Hit H	PO	A	E	DP	TC/G	FA	G by Pos
1914	PIT	F	2	.500	.500	2	1	0	0	0	0.0	0	1	0		0	1	0	0	0	0	0	0.0	.000	C-1

Tom Madden

MADDEN, THOMAS FRANCIS BR TR 5'10" 190 lbs.
B. Sept. 14, 1882, Boston, Mass. D. Jan. 20, 1954, Cambridge, Mass.

Year	Team	Lg	Games	BA	SA	AB	H	2B	3B	HR	HR%	R	RBI	BB	SO	SB	Pinch Hit AB	Pinch Hit H	PO	A	E	DP	TC/G	FA	G by Pos
1909	BOS	A	10	.235	.235	17	4	0	0	0	0.0	0	1	0		0	3	1	27	5	2	0	4.9	.941	C-7
1910			14	.371	.457	35	13	3	0	0	0.0	4	4	3		0	2	1	50	11	4	0	5.4	.938	C-12
1911	2 teams		BOS A (4G –.200) PHI N (28G –.276)																						
"	total		32	.264	.297	91	24	1	1	0	0.0	6	6	2	13	0	1	1	130	36	12	3	6.8	.933	C-26
3 yrs.			56	.287	.329	143	41	4	1	0	0.0	10	11	5	13	0	6	3	207	52	18	3	6.2	.935	C-45

Clarence Maddern

MADDERN, CLARENCE JAMES BR TR 6' 1" 185 lbs.
B. Sept. 26, 1921, Bisbee, Ariz. D. Aug. 9, 1986, Tucson, Ariz.

Year	Team	Lg	Games	BA	SA	AB	H	2B	3B	HR	HR%	R	RBI	BB	SO	SB	Pinch Hit AB	Pinch Hit H	PO	A	E	DP	TC/G	FA	G by Pos
1946	CHI	N	3	.000	.000	3	0	0	0	0	0.0	0	0	0	0	0	1	0	4	0	0	0	2.0	1.000	OF-2
1948			80	.252	.374	214	54	12	1	4	1.9	16	27	10	25	0	23	5	98	6	2	0	1.9	.981	OF-55
1949			10	.333	.667	9	3	0	0	1	11.1	1	2	2	0	0	7	1	2	1	0	0	3.0	1.000	1B-1
1951	CLE	A	11	.167	.167	12	2	0	0	0	0.0	0	0	0	1	0	9	1	2	0	1	0	3.0	.667	OF-1
4 yrs.			104	.248	.370	238	59	12	1	5	2.1	17	29	12	26	0	40	7	106	7	3	0	2.0	.974	OF-58, 1B-1

Elliott Maddox

MADDOX, ELLIOTT BR TR 5'11" 180 lbs.
B. Dec. 21, 1947, East Orange, N. J.

Year	Team	Lg	Games	BA	SA	AB	H	2B	3B	HR	HR%	R	RBI	BB	SO	SB	Pinch Hit AB	Pinch Hit H	PO	A	E	DP	TC/G	FA	G by Pos
1970	DET	A	109	.248	.364	258	64	13	4	3	1.2	30	24	30	42	2	20	2	104	100	14	10	2.2	.936	3B-40, OF-37, SS-19, 2B-1
1971	WAS	A	128	.217	.275	258	56	8	2	1	0.4	38	18	51	42	10	19	7	201	21	3	4	2.0	.987	OF-103, 3B-12
1972	TEX	A	98	.252	.289	294	74	7	2	0	0.0	40	10	49	53	20	1	0	199	7	2	4	2.2	.990	OF-94
1973			100	.238	.262	172	41	1	0	1	0.6	24	17	29	28	5	3	0	148	14	3	2	1.7	.982	OF-89, 3B-7, DH-1
1974	NY	A	137	.303	.386	466	141	26	2	3	0.6	75	45	69	48	6	3	2	336	19	5	4	2.6	.986	OF-135, 2B-2, 3B-1

Elliott Maddox *continued*

Year	Team	Games	BA	SA	AB	H	2B	3B	HR	HR%	R	RBI	BB	SO	SB	Pinch Hit AB	Pinch Hit H	PO	A	E	DP	TC/G	FA	G by Pos
1975		55	.307	.394	218	67	10	3	1	0.5	36	23	21	24	9	0	0	158	5	0	3	2.9	1.000	OF-55, 2B-1
1976		18	.217	.261	46	10	2	0	0	0.0	4	3	4	3	0	2	1	21	2	0	1	1.5	1.000	OF-13, DH-2
1977	**BAL A**	49	.262	.383	107	28	7	0	2	1.9	14	9	13	9	2	2	0	99	0	1	0	2.2	.990	OF-45, 3B-1
1978	**NY N**	119	.257	.329	389	100	18	2	2	0.5	43	39	71	38	2	7	0	196	80	9	8	2.3	.968	OF-79, 3B-43, 1B-1
1979		86	.268	.339	224	60	13	0	1	0.4	21	12	20	27	3	21	8	131	22	3	1	2.1	.981	OF-65, 3B-11
1980		130	.246	.319	411	101	16	1	4	1.0	35	34	52	44	1	11	2	111	211	14	19	2.8	.958	3B-115, OF-4, 1B-2
11 yrs.		1029	.261	.334	2843	742	121	16	18	0.6	360	234	409	358	60	89	22	1704	481	54	56	2.3	.976	OF-719, 3B-230, SS-19, 2B-4, 1B-3, DH-3
LEAGUE CHAMPIONSHIP SERIES																								
1976	**NY A**	3	.222	.333	9	2	1	0	0	0.0	0	1	0	1	0	0	0	9	0	0	0	3.0	1.000	OF-3
WORLD SERIES																								
1976	**NY A**	2	.200	.600	5	1	0	1	0	0.0	0	0	1	2	0	0	0	0	0	0	0	0.0		OF-1, DH-1

Garry Maddox

MADDOX, GARRY LEE BR TR 6′ 3″ 175 lbs.
B. Sept. 1, 1949, Cincinnati, Ohio.

Year	Team	Games	BA	SA	AB	H	2B	3B	HR	HR%	R	RBI	BB	SO	SB	Pinch Hit AB	Pinch Hit H	PO	A	E	DP	TC/G	FA	G by Pos
1972	**SF N**	125	.266	.432	458	122	26	7	12	2.6	62	58	14	97	13	2	0	279	7	6	3	2.4	.979	OF-121
1973		144	.319	.460	587	187	30	10	11	1.9	81	76	24	73	24	2	1	370	4	12	0	2.8	.969	OF-140
1974		135	.284	.398	538	153	31	3	8	1.5	74	50	29	64	21	6	2	345	3	5	0	2.7	.986	OF-131
1975	**2 teams**	**SF N** (17G –.135) **PHI N** (99G –.291)																						
″	**total**	116	.272	.406	426	116	26	8	5	1.2	54	50	42	57	25	5	0	325	13	5	4	3.1	.985	OF-110
1976	**PHI N**	146	.330	.456	531	175	37	6	6	1.1	75	68	42	59	29	2	0	441	10	5	0	3.2	.989	OF-144
1977		139	.292	.448	571	167	27	10	14	2.5	85	74	24	58	22	2	0	383	7	9	2	2.9	.977	OF-138
1978		155	.288	.410	598	172	34	3	11	1.8	62	68	39	89	33	1	0	444	7	8	1	3.0	.983	OF-154
1979		148	.281	.425	548	154	28	6	13	2.4	70	61	17	71	26	6	1	433	13	2	2	3.2	.996	OF-140
1980		143	.259	.386	549	142	31	3	11	2.0	59	73	18	52	25	1	0	405	7	10	0	3.0	.976	OF-143
1981		94	.263	.337	323	85	7	1	5	1.5	37	40	17	42	9	1	0	251	8	6	4	2.8	.977	OF-94
1982		119	.284	.417	412	117	27	2	8	1.9	39	61	12	32	7	9	2	253	8	2	4	2.4	.992	OF-111
1983		97	.275	.367	324	89	14	2	4	1.2	27	32	17	31	7	11	3	216	1	5	0	2.3	.977	OF-95
1984		77	.282	.390	241	68	11	0	5	2.1	29	19	13	29	3	14	0	160	3	0	1	2.4	1.000	OF-69
1985		105	.239	.339	218	52	8	1	4	1.8	22	23	13	26	4	25	4	143	3	3	0	1.6	.980	OF-94
1986		6	.429	.429	7	3	0	0	0	0.0	1	1	2	1	0	3	1	1	0	0	0	0.3	1.000	OF-3
15 yrs.		1749	.285	.413	6331	1802	337	62	117	1.8	777	754	323	781	248	90	14	4449	94	78	21	2.7	.983	OF-1687
DIVISIONAL PLAYOFF SERIES																								
1981	**PHI N**	2	.333	.667	3	1	1	0	0	0.0	0	0	0	0	0	0	0	3	0	0	0	1.5	1.000	OF-2
LEAGUE CHAMPIONSHIP SERIES																								
1976	**PHI N**	3	.231	.308	13	3	1	0	0	0.0	2	1	1	0	0	0	0	9	0	0	0	3.0	1.000	OF-3
1977		4	.429	.429	7	3	0	0	0	0.0	1	2	0	1	0	0	0	6	0	0	0	3.0	1.000	OF-2
1978		4	.263	.263	19	5	0	0	0	0.0	1	2	0	3	0	0	0	16	0	1	0	4.3	.941	OF-4
1980		5	.300	.400	20	6	2	0	0	0.0	2	3	2	2	2	0	0	23	0	0	0	4.6	1.000	OF-5
1983		3	.273	.364	11	3	1	0	0	0.0	0	1	0	1	0	0	0	8	0	1	0	3.0	.889	OF-3
5 yrs.		19	.286	.343	70	20	4	0	0	0.0	6	9	3	7	2	0	0	62	0	2	0	3.8	.969	OF-17
WORLD SERIES																								
1980	**PHI N**	6	.227	.318	22	5	2	0	0	0.0	1	1	1	3	0	0	0	11	1	0	1	2.0	1.000	OF-6
1983		4	.250	.583	12	3	1	0	1	8.3	1	1	0	2	0	1	0	7	0	0	0	2.3	1.000	OF-3
2 yrs.		10	.235	.412	34	8	3	0	1	2.9	2	2	1	5	0	1	0	18	1	0	1	2.1	1.000	OF-9

Jerry Maddox

MADDOX, JERRY GLENN BR TR 6′ 2″ 200 lbs.
B. July 28, 1953, Whittier, Calif.

Year	Team	Games	BA	SA	AB	H	2B	3B	HR	HR%	R	RBI	BB	SO	SB	Pinch Hit AB	Pinch Hit H	PO	A	E	DP	TC/G	FA	G by Pos
1978	**ATL N**	7	.214	.214	14	3	0	0	0	0.0	1	1	1	2	0	2	1	3	7	1	0	2.2	.909	3B-5

Art Madison

MADISON, ARTHUR M. BR TR 5′ 9″ 165 lbs.
B. Jan. 14, 1872, Clarksburg, Mass. D. Jan. 27, 1933, North Adams, Mass.

Year	Team	Games	BA	SA	AB	H	2B	3B	HR	HR%	R	RBI	BB	SO	SB	Pinch Hit AB	Pinch Hit H	PO	A	E	DP	TC/G	FA	G by Pos
1895	**PHI N**	11	.353	.441	34	12	3	0	0	0.0	6	8	1	1	4	0	0	17	23	6	2	4.2	.870	SS-6, 2B-3, 3B-2
1899	**PIT N**	42	.271	.356	118	32	2	4	0	0.0	20	19	11		1	6	**3**	72	87	12	10	4.8	.930	2B-19, SS-15, 3B-2
2 yrs.		53	.289	.375	152	44	5	4	0	0.0	26	27	12	1	5	6	3	89	110	18	12	4.6	.917	2B-22, SS-21, 3B-4

Scotti Madison

MADISON, CHARLES SCOTT BB TR 5′11″ 185 lbs.
B. Sept. 12, 1959, Pensacola, Fla.

Year	Team	Games	BA	SA	AB	H	2B	3B	HR	HR%	R	RBI	BB	SO	SB	Pinch Hit AB	Pinch Hit H	PO	A	E	DP	TC/G	FA	G by Pos
1985	**DET A**	6	.000	.000	11	0	0	0	0	0.0	0	1	2	0	0	2	0	1	0	0	0	0.3	1.000	DH-3, C-1
1986		2	.000	.000	7	0	0	0	0	0.0	0	1	0	3	0	0	0	1	1	1	1	1.5	.667	3B-1, DH-1
1987	**KC A**	7	.267	.467	15	4	3	0	0	0.0	4	0	1	5	0	1	0	28	3	3	4	4.9	.912	1B-4, C-3
1988		16	.171	.229	35	6	2	0	0	0.0	4	2	4	5	1	6	0	23	1	0	0	2.7	1.000	C-4, OF-3, 1B-2
1989	**CIN N**	40	.173	.276	98	17	7	0	1	1.0	13	7	8	9	0	16	1	19	44	0	3	2.4	1.000	3B-26
5 yrs.		71	.163	.253	166	27	12	0	1	0.6	21	11	15	22	1	25	1	72	49	4	8	2.6	.968	3B-27, C-8, 1B-6, DH-4, OF-3

Ed Madjeski

MADJESKI, EDWARD WILLIAM BR TR 5′11″ 178 lbs.
Born Edward William Majewski.
B. July 20, 1908, Far Rockaway, N. Y. D. Nov. 11, 1994, Montgomery, Ohio.

Year	Team	Games	BA	SA	AB	H	2B	3B	HR	HR%	R	RBI	BB	SO	SB	Pinch Hit AB	Pinch Hit H	PO	A	E	DP	TC/G	FA	G by Pos
1932	**PHI A**	17	.229	.229	35	8	0	0	0	0.0	4	3	3	6	0	8	2	30	7	0	3	4.6	1.000	C-8
1933		51	.282	.310	142	40	4	0	0	0.0	17	17	4	21	0	12	4	122	14	6	3	3.5	.958	C-41
1934	**2 teams**	**PHI A** (8G –.375) **CHI A** (85G –.221)																						
″	**total**	93	.225	.343	289	65	15	2	5	1.7	37	34	14	32	2	11	3	348	49	12	11	5.1	.971	C-80
1937	**NY N**	5	.200	.200	15	3	0	0	0	0.0	0	2	0	2	0	0	0	8	2	0	1	2.0	1.000	C-5
4 yrs.		166	.241	.320	481	116	19	2	5	1.0	58	56	21	61	2	31	9	508	72	18	18	4.5	.970	C-134

Bill Madlock

MADLOCK, WILLIAM, JR. (Mad Dog) BR TR 5′11″ 185 lbs.
B. Jan. 2, 1951, Memphis, Tenn.

Year	Team	Games	BA	SA	AB	H	2B	3B	HR	HR%	R	RBI	BB	SO	SB	Pinch Hit AB	Pinch Hit H	PO	A	E	DP	TC/G	FA	G by Pos
1973	**TEX A**	21	.351	.532	77	27	5	3	1	1.3	16	5	7	9	3	0	0	13	32	4	2	2.3	.918	3B-21
1974	**CHI N**	128	.313	.442	453	142	21	5	9	2.0	65	54	42	39	11	8	4	84	229	18	14	2.7	.946	3B-121
1975		130	**.354**	.479	514	182	29	7	7	1.4	77	64	42	34	9	0	0	79	250	20	14	2.7	.943	3B-128
1976		142	**.339**	.500	514	174	36	1	15	2.9	68	84	56	27	15	5	1	107	234	14	21	2.6	.961	3B-136
1977	**SF N**	140	.302	.426	533	161	28	1	12	2.3	70	46	43	33	13	8	1	101	234	18	18	2.7	.949	3B-126, 2B-6

Bill Madlock *continued*

Year	Team	Games	BA	SA	AB	H	2B	3B	HR	HR%	R	RBI	BB	SO	SB	Pinch Hit AB	Pinch Hit H	PO	A	E	DP	TC/G	FA	G by Pos
1978		122	.309	.481	447	138	26	3	15	3.4	76	44	48	39	16	8	1	234	300	14	49	4.7	.974	2B-114, 1B-3
1979	**2 teams**	**SF N** (69G –.261) **PIT N** (85G –.328)																						
″	**total**	154	.298	.438	560	167	26	5	14	2.5	85	85	52	41	32	5	2	209	297	14	47	3.4	.973	3B-85, 2B-63, 1B-5
1980	**PIT N**	137	.277	.399	494	137	22	4	10	2.0	62	53	45	33	16	3	1	159	217	17	25	2.8	.957	3B-127, 1B-12
1981		82	**.341**	.495	279	95	23	1	6	2.2	35	45	34	17	18	4	0	50	147	9	17	2.6	.956	3B-78
1982		154	.319	.488	568	181	33	3	19	3.3	92	95	48	39	18	7	2	114	267	18	25	2.7	.955	3B-146, 1B-3
1983		130	**.323**	.444	473	153	21	0	12	2.5	68	68	49	24	3	4	1	59	193	11	20	2.1	.958	3B-126
1984		103	.253	.323	403	102	16	0	4	1.0	38	44	26	29	3	3	0	76	176	15	17	2.7	.944	3B-98, 1B-1
1985	**2 teams**	**PIT N** (110G –.251) **LA N** (34G –.360)																						
″	**total**	144	.275	.402	513	141	27	1	12	2.3	69	56	49	53	10	5	4	155	243	19	20	2.9	.954	3B-130, 1B-12
1986	**LA N**	111	.280	.404	379	106	17	0	10	2.6	38	60	30	43	3	9	1	79	171	26	8	2.7	.906	3B-101, 1B-2
1987	**2 teams**	**LA N** (21G –.180) **DET A** (87G –.279)																						
″	**total**	108	.264	.442	387	102	18	0	17	4.4	61	57	34	50	4	6	0	175	35	5	16	2.1	.977	DH-64, 1B-23, 3B-17
15 yrs.		1806	.305	.442	6594	2008	348	34	163	2.5	920	860	605	510	174	75	18	1694	3025	222	313	2.8	.955	3B-1440, 2B-183, DH-64, 1B-61
LEAGUE CHAMPIONSHIP SERIES																								
1979	**PIT N**	3	.250	.500	12	3	0	0	1	8.3	1	2	2	0	2	0	0	1	7	0	1	2.7	1.000	3B-3
1985	**LA N**	6	.333	.750	24	8	1	0	3	12.5	5	7	0	2	1	0	0	6	9	0	0	2.5	1.000	3B-6
1987	**DET A**	1	.000	.000	5	0	0	0	0	0.0	0	0	0	3	0	0	0	0	0	0	0	0.0	.000	DH-1
3 yrs.		10	.268	.585	41	11	1	0	4	9.8	6	9	2	5	3	0	0	7	16	0	1	2.3	1.000	3B-9, DH-1
WORLD SERIES																								
1979	**PIT N**	7	.375	.417	24	9	1	0	0	0.0	2	3	5	1	0	0	0	3	10	1	4	2.0	.929	3B-7

Sal Madrid

MADRID, SALVATOR BR TR 5′9″ 165 lbs.
B. June 9, 1920, El Paso, Tex. D. Feb. 24, 1977, Fort Wayne, Ind.

Year	Team	Games	BA	SA	AB	H	2B	3B	HR	HR%	R	RBI	BB	SO	SB	Pinch Hit AB	Pinch Hit H	PO	A	E	DP	TC/G	FA	G by Pos
1947	**CHI N**	8	.125	.167	24	3	1	0	0	0.0	0	1	1	6	0	0	0	16	27	2	5	5.6	.956	SS-8

Dave Magadan

MAGADAN, DAVID JOSEPH BL TR 6′3″ 190 lbs.
B. Sept. 30, 1962, Tampa, Fla.

Year	Team	Games	BA	SA	AB	H	2B	3B	HR	HR%	R	RBI	BB	SO	SB	Pinch Hit AB	Pinch Hit H	PO	A	E	DP	TC/G	FA	G by Pos
1986	**NY N**	10	.444	.444	18	8	0	0	0	0.0	3	3	3	1	0	1	1	48	5	0	5	5.9	1.000	1B-9
1987		85	.318	.443	192	61	13	1	3	1.6	21	24	22	22	0	30	6	88	92	4	9	2.9	.978	3B-50, 1B-13
1988		112	.277	.334	314	87	15	0	1	0.3	39	35	60	39	0	12	1	459	99	10	42	4.8	.982	1B-71, 3B-48
1989		127	.286	.393	374	107	22	3	4	1.1	47	41	49	37	1	23	5	587	89	7	54	5.9	.990	1B-87, 3B-28
1990		144	.328	.457	451	148	28	6	6	1.3	74	72	74	55	2	22	9	837	99	3	53	7.1	.997	1B-113, 3B-19
1991		124	.258	.342	418	108	23	0	4	1.0	58	51	83	50	1	4	3	1035	90	5	73	9.3	.996	1B-122
1992		99	.283	.346	321	91	9	1	3	0.9	33	28	56	44	1	5	0	54	136	11	11	2.1	.945	3B-93, 1B-2
1993	**2 teams**	**FLA N** (66G –.286) **SEA A** (71G –.259)																						
″	**total**	137	.273	.356	455	124	23	0	5	1.1	49	50	80	63	2	10	3	380	194	12	50	4.3	.980	3B-90, 1B-43, DH-2
1994	**FLA N**	74	.275	.322	211	58	7	0	1	0.5	30	17	39	25	0	14	6	127	78	4	12	3.3	.981	3B-48, 1B-16
1995	**HOU N**	127	.313	.399	348	109	24	0	2	0.6	44	51	71	56	2	20	6	121	165	18	13	2.7	.941	3B-100, 1B-11
10 yrs.		1039	.290	.378	3102	901	164	11	29	0.9	398	372	537	392	9	141	40	3736	1047	74	322	5.0	.985	1B-487, 3B-476, DH-2
LEAGUE CHAMPIONSHIP SERIES																								
1988	**NY N**	3	.000	.000	3	0	0	0	0	0.0	0	0	0	2	0	3	0	0	0	0	0	0.0	—	

Ever Magallanes

MAGALLANES, EVERADO BL TR 5′10″ 165 lbs.
Born Everado Magallanes (Espinoza).
B. Nov. 6, 1965, Chihuahua, Mexico.

Year	Team	Games	BA	SA	AB	H	2B	3B	HR	HR%	R	RBI	BB	SO	SB	Pinch Hit AB	Pinch Hit H	PO	A	E	DP	TC/G	FA	G by Pos
1991	**CLE A**	3	.000	.000	2	0	0	0	0	0.0	0	0	1	1	0	1	0	0	1	0	0	0.5	1.000	SS-2

Lee Magee

MAGEE, LEO CHRISTOPHER BB TR 5′11″ 165 lbs.
Born Leopold Christopher Hoernschemeyer.
B. June 4, 1889, Cincinnati, Ohio D. Mar. 14, 1966, Columbus, Ohio.
Manager 1915.

Year	Team	Games	BA	SA	AB	H	2B	3B	HR	HR%	R	RBI	BB	SO	SB	Pinch Hit AB	Pinch Hit H	PO	A	E	DP	TC/G	FA	G by Pos
1911	**STL N**	26	.261	.304	69	18	1	1	0	0.0	9	8	8	8	4	2	0	45	44	5	6	4.5	.947	2B-18, SS-3
1912		128	.290	.354	458	133	13	8	0	0.0	60	40	39	29	16	8	3	299	101	20	17	3.7	.952	OF-85, 2B-23, 1B-6, SS-1
1913		136	.265	.327	529	140	13	7	2	0.4	53	31	34	30	23	0	0	374	86	9	17	3.4	.981	OF-107, 2B-21, 1B-6, SS-2
1914		162	.284	.353	529	150	23	4	2	0.4	59	40	42	24	36	0	0	626	51	8	25	4.6	.988	OF-102, 1B-40, 2B-6
1915	**BKN F**	121	.323	.436	452	146	19	10	4	0.9	87	49	22		34	4	0	290	322	41	47	5.6	.937	2B-115, 1B-2
1916	**NY A**	131	.257	.325	510	131	18	4	3	0.6	57	45	50	31	29	1	0	305	26	8	3	2.6	.976	OF-128, 2B-2
1917	**2 teams**	**NY A** (51G –.220) **STL A** (36G –.170)																						
″	**total**	87	.200	.225	285	57	5	1	0	0.0	28	12	19	24	6	3	1	164	80	8	9	3.1	.968	OF-51, 3B-20, 2B-6, 1B-5
1918	**CIN N**	119	.290	.394	459	133	22	13	0	0.0	62	28	28	19	19	1	0	281	364	29	74	5.8	.957	2B-114, 3B-3
1919	**2 teams**	**BKN N** (45G –.238) **CHI N** (79G –.292)																						
″	**total**	124	.270	.346	448	121	19	6	1	0.2	52	24	23	24	19	7	2	213	226	27	15	3.9	.942	OF-44, 2B-43, 3B-19, SS-13
9 yrs.		1034	.275	.349	3739	1029	133	54	12	0.3	467	277	265	189	186	26	6	2597	1300	155	213	4.1	.962	OF-517, 2B-348, 1B-59, 3B-42, SS-19

Sherry Magee

MAGEE, SHERWOOD ROBERT BR TR 5′11″ 179 lbs.
B. Aug. 6, 1884, Clarendon, Pa. D. Mar. 13, 1929, Philadelphia, Pa.

Year	Team	Games	BA	SA	AB	H	2B	3B	HR	HR%	R	RBI	BB	SO	SB	Pinch Hit AB	Pinch Hit H	PO	A	E	DP	TC/G	FA	G by Pos
1904	**PHI N**	95	.277	.409	364	101	15	12	3	0.8	51	57	14		11	0	0	156	19	15	3	2.0	.921	OF-94, 1B-1
1905		155	.299	.420	603	180	24	17	5	0.8	100	98	44		48	0	0	341	19	14	6	2.4	.963	OF-155
1906		154	.282	.407	563	159	36	8	6	1.1	77	67	52		55	0	0	316	18	6	2	2.2	.982	OF-154
1907		140	.328	.455	503	165	28	12	4	0.8	75	**85**	53		46	1	0	297	13	7	7	2.3	.978	OF-139
1908		143	.283	.417	508	144	30	16	2	0.4	79	57	49		40	1	0	279	15	9	5	2.1	.970	OF-142
1909		143	.270	.398	522	141	33	14	2	0.4	60	66	43		38	0	0	283	11	9	0	2.1	.970	OF-143
1910		154	**.331**	**.507**	519	172	39	17	6	1.2	**110**	**123**	94	36	49	0	0	285	9	8	2	2.0	.974	OF-154
1911		121	.288	.483	445	128	32	5	15	3.4	79	94	49	33	22	1	0	248	14	5	3	2.2	.981	OF-120
1912		132	.306	.438	464	142	25	9	6	1.3	79	72	55	54	30	5	2	312	8	12	4	2.6	.964	OF-124, 1B-6
1913		138	.306	.479	470	144	36	6	11	2.3	92	70	38	36	23	12	3	257	8	9	4	2.2	.967	OF-123, 1B-4
1914		146	.314	**.509**	544	**171**	**39**	11	15	2.8	96	**103**	55	42	25	2	2	549	187	37	20	5.3	.952	OF-67, SS-39, 1B-32, 2B-8
1915	**BOS N**	156	.280	.392	571	160	34	12	2	0.4	72	87	54	39	15	0	0	524	26	7	11	3.6	.987	OF-134, 1B-22

Sherry Magee *continued*

Year	Team	Games	BA	SA	AB	H	2B	3B	HR	HR%	R	RBI	BB	SO	SB	Pinch Hit AB	Pinch Hit H	PO	A	E	DP	TC/G	FA	G by Pos
1916		120	.241	.327	419	101	17	5	3	0.7	44	54	44	52	10	1	0	231	9	5	0	2.0	.980	OF-120, 1B-2, SS-1
1917	**2 teams**	**BOS N** (72G –.256) **CIN N** (45G –.321)																						
"	**total**	117	.279	.371	383	107	16	8	1	0.3	41	52	29	30	11	5	1	253	17	9	7	2.5	.968	OF-106, 1B-4
1918	**CIN N**	115	.297	.415	400	119	15	13	2	0.5	46	**76**	37	18	14	5	1	692	56	15	41	6.9	.980	1B-66, OF-38, 2B-6
1919		56	.215	.264	163	35	6	1	0	0.0	11	21	26	19	4	6	2	102	4	1	1	2.2	.991	OF-47, 3B-1, 2B-1
16 yrs.		2085	.291	.427	7441	2169	425	166	83	1.1	1112	1182	736	359	441	39	11	5125	433	168	116	2.8	.971	OF-1860, 1B-137, SS-40, 2B-15, 3B-1
WORLD SERIES																								
1919	**CIN N**	2	.500	.500	2	1	0	0	0	0.0	0	0	0	0	0	2	1	0	0	0	0	0.0	—	

Harl Maggert

MAGGERT, HARL VESTIN BL TR 5′ 8″ 155 lbs.
Father of Harl Maggert.
B. Feb. 13, 1883, Cromwell, Ind. D. Jan. 7, 1963, Fresno, Calif.

Year	Team	Games	BA	SA	AB	H	2B	3B	HR	HR%	R	RBI	BB	SO	SB	Pinch Hit AB	Pinch Hit H	PO	A	E	DP	TC/G	FA	G by Pos
1907	**PIT N**	3	.000	.000	6	0	0	0	0	0.0	1	0	2		1	1	0	6	0	0	0	3.0	1.000	OF-2
1912	**PHI A**	72	.256	.351	242	62	8	6	1	0.4	39	13	36		10	11	3	103	5	7	0	1.9	.939	OF-61
2 yrs.		75	.250	.343	248	62	8	6	1	0.4	40	13	38		11	12	3	109	5	7	0	1.9	.942	OF-63

Harl Maggert

MAGGERT, HARL WARREN BR TR 6′ 190 lbs.
Son of Harl Maggert.
B. May 14, 1914, Los Angeles, Calif. D. July 10, 1986, Citrus Heights, Calif.

Year	Team	Games	BA	SA	AB	H	2B	3B	HR	HR%	R	RBI	BB	SO	SB	Pinch Hit AB	Pinch Hit H	PO	A	E	DP	TC/G	FA	G by Pos
1938	**BOS N**	66	.281	.416	89	25	3	0	3	3.4	12	19	10	20	0	**43**	10	24	13	2	1	2.2	.949	OF-10, 3B-8

John Magner

MAGNER, WILLIAM JOHN
B. 1855

Year	Team	Games	BA	SA	AB	H	2B	3B	HR	HR%	R	RBI	BB	SO	SB	Pinch Hit AB	Pinch Hit H	PO	A	E	DP	TC/G	FA	G by Pos
1879	**CIN N**	1	.000	.000	4	0	0	0	0	0.0	0	1	0	1		0	0	1	0	1	0	2.0	.500	OF-1

Stubby Magner

MAGNER, EDMUND BURKE BR TR 5′ 3″ 135 lbs.
B. Feb. 20, 1888, Kalamazoo, Mich. D. Sept. 6, 1956, Chillicothe, Ohio.

Year	Team	Games	BA	SA	AB	H	2B	3B	HR	HR%	R	RBI	BB	SO	SB	Pinch Hit AB	Pinch Hit H	PO	A	E	DP	TC/G	FA	G by Pos
1911	**NY A**	13	.212	.212	33	7	0	0	0	0.0	3	4	4		1	0	0	15	32	2	3	4.5	.959	SS-6, 2B-5

George Magoon

MAGOON, GEORGE HENRY (Topsy, Maggie) BR TR 5′10″ 165 lbs.
B. Mar. 27, 1875, St. Albans, Me. D. Dec. 6, 1943, Rochester, N. H.

Year	Team	Games	BA	SA	AB	H	2B	3B	HR	HR%	R	RBI	BB	SO	SB	Pinch Hit AB	Pinch Hit H	PO	A	E	DP	TC/G	FA	G by Pos
1898	**BKN N**	93	.224	.254	343	77	7	0	1	0.3	35	39	30		7	0	0	199	357	45	38	6.5	.925	SS-93
1899	**2 teams**	**BAL N** (62G –.256) **CHI N** (59G –.228)																						
"	**total**	121	.242	.295	396	96	13	4	0	0.0	50	52	50		12	0	0	281	431	71	53	6.5	.909	SS-121
1901	**CIN N**	127	.252	.324	460	116	16	7	1	0.2	47	53	52		15	0	0	284	382	57	42	5.7	.921	SS-112, 2B-15
1902		45	.272	.352	162	44	9	2	0	0.0	29	23	13		7	1	0	92	152	20	19	6.0	.924	2B-41, SS-3
1903	**2 teams**	**CIN N** (42G –.216) **CHI A** (94G –.228)																						
"	**total**	136	.224	.273	473	106	17	3	0	0.0	38	34	49		6	1	0	287	366	40	37	5.1	.942	2B-126, 3B-9
5 yrs.		522	.239	.294	1834	439	62	16	2	0.1	199	201	194		47	2	0	1143	1688	233	189	5.9	.924	SS-329, 2B-182, 3B-9

Tom Magrann

MAGRANN, THOMAS JOSEPH BR TR 6′ 3″ 177 lbs.
B. Dec. 9, 1963, Hollywood, Fla.

Year	Team	Games	BA	SA	AB	H	2B	3B	HR	HR%	R	RBI	BB	SO	SB	Pinch Hit AB	Pinch Hit H	PO	A	E	DP	TC/G	FA	G by Pos
1989	**CLE A**	9	.000	.000	10	0	0	0	0	0.0	0	0	0	4	0	0	0	30	2	0	0	3.6	1.000	C-9

Freddie Maguire

MAGUIRE, FREDERICK EDWARD BR TR 5′11″ 155 lbs.
B. May 10, 1899, Roxbury, Mass. D. Nov. 3, 1961, Boston, Mass.

Year	Team	Games	BA	SA	AB	H	2B	3B	HR	HR%	R	RBI	BB	SO	SB	Pinch Hit AB	Pinch Hit H	PO	A	E	DP	TC/G	FA	G by Pos
1922	**NY N**	5	.333	.333	12	4	0	0	0	0.0	4	1	0	1	1	1	0	4	13	1	1	6.0	.944	2B-3
1923		41	.200	.233	30	6	1	0	0	0.0	11	2	2	4	1	1	0	21	31	7	7	3.5	.881	2B-16, 3B-1
1928	**CHI N**	140	.279	.350	574	160	24	7	1	0.2	67	41	25	38	6	2	1	410	524	23	126	6.9	.976	2B-138
1929	**BOS N**	138	.252	.337	496	125	26	8	0	0.0	54	41	19	40	8	0	0	335	438	23	94	5.7	.971	2B-138, SS-1
1930		146	.267	.328	516	138	21	5	0	0.0	54	52	20	22	4	0	0	387	476	28	104	6.1	.969	2B-146
1931		148	.228	.272	492	112	18	2	0	0.0	36	26	16	26	3	0	0	372	478	21	94	5.9	.976	2B-148
6 yrs.		618	.257	.322	2120	545	90	22	1	0.0	226	163	82	131	23	4	1	1529	1960	103	426	6.1	.971	2B-589, SS-1, 3B-1
WORLD SERIES																								
1923	**NY N**	2	—	—	0	0	0	0	0	—	1	0	0	0	0	0	0	0	0	0	0	0.0	—	

Jack Maguire

MAGUIRE, JACK BR TR 5′11″ 165 lbs.
B. Feb. 5, 1925, St. Louis, Mo.

Year	Team	Games	BA	SA	AB	H	2B	3B	HR	HR%	R	RBI	BB	SO	SB	Pinch Hit AB	Pinch Hit H	PO	A	E	DP	TC/G	FA	G by Pos
1950	**NY N**	29	.175	.225	40	7	2	0	0	0.0	3	3	3	13	0	16	3	31	5	0	2	3.3	1.000	OF-9, 1B-2
1951	**3 teams**	**NY N** (16G –.400) **PIT N** (8G –.000) **STL A** (41G –.244)																						
"	**total**	65	.257	.342	152	39	3	2	2	1.3	22	18	15	23	1	13	2	85	18	4	1	2.5	.963	OF-34, 3B-6, 2B-3
2 yrs.		94	.240	.318	192	46	5	2	2	1.0	25	21	18	36	1	29	5	116	23	4	3	2.6	.972	OF-43, 3B-6, 2B-3, 1B-2

Jim Mahady

MAHADY, JAMES BERNARD BR TR 5′11″ 170 lbs.
B. Apr. 22, 1901, Cortland, N. Y. D. Aug. 9, 1936, Cortland, N. Y.

Year	Team	Games	BA	SA	AB	H	2B	3B	HR	HR%	R	RBI	BB	SO	SB	Pinch Hit AB	Pinch Hit H	PO	A	E	DP	TC/G	FA	G by Pos
1921	**NY N**	1	—	—	0	0	0	0	0	—	0	0	0	0	0	0	0	0	1	0	0	1.0	1.000	2B-1

Art Mahan

MAHAN, ARTHUR LEO BL TL 5′11″ 178 lbs.
B. June 8, 1913, Somerville, Mass.

Year	Team	Games	BA	SA	AB	H	2B	3B	HR	HR%	R	RBI	BB	SO	SB	Pinch Hit AB	Pinch Hit H	PO	A	E	DP	TC/G	FA	G by Pos
1940	**PHI N**	146	.244	.318	544	133	24	5	2	0.4	55	39	40	37	4	0	0	1380	102	12	120	10.2	.992	1B-145, P-1

Frank Mahar

MAHAR, FRANK EDWARD TR 5′10½″
B. Dec. 4, 1878, Natick, Mass. D. Dec. 5, 1961, Somerville, Mass.

Year	Team	Games	BA	SA	AB	H	2B	3B	HR	HR%	R	RBI	BB	SO	SB	Pinch Hit AB	Pinch Hit H	PO	A	E	DP	TC/G	FA	G by Pos
1902	**PHI N**	1	.000	.000	1	0	0	0	0	0.0	0	0	0		0	1	0	0	0	0	0	0.0	—	

Billy Maharg

MAHARG, WILLIAM JOSEPH BR TR 5′ 4½″ 155 lbs.
Born William Joseph Graham.
B. Mar. 19, 1881, Philadelphia, Pa. D. Nov. 20, 1953, Philadelphia, Pa.

Year	Team	Games	BA	SA	AB	H	2B	3B	HR	HR%	R	RBI	BB	SO	SB	Pinch Hit AB	Pinch Hit H	PO	A	E	DP	TC/G	FA	G by Pos
1912	**DET A**	1	.000	.000	1	0	0	0	0	0.0	0	0	0		0	0	0	0	2	0	0	2.0	1.000	3B-1
1916	**PHI N**	1	.000	.000	1	0	0	0	0	0.0	0	0	0	0	0	0	0	0	0	0	0	0.0	.000	OF-1
2 yrs.		2	.000	.000	2	0	0	0	0	0.0	0	0	0	0	0	0	0	0	2	0	0	1.0	1.000	OF-1, 3B-1

Ron Mahay

MAHAY, RONALD MATTHEW BL TL 6′ 2″ 185 lbs.
B. June 28, 1971, Crestwood, Ill.

Year	Team		Games	BA	SA	AB	H	2B	3B	HR	HR%	R	RBI	BB	SO	SB	Pinch Hit AB	Pinch Hit H	PO	A	E	DP	TC/G	FA	G by Pos
1995	BOS	A	5	.200	.450	20	4	2	0	1	5.0	3	3	1	6	0	0	0	9	0	0	0	1.8	1.000	OF-5

Tom Maher

MAHER, THOMAS FRANCIS
B. Philadelphia, Pa. Deceased.

Year	Team		Games	BA	SA	AB	H	2B	3B	HR	HR%	R	RBI	BB	SO	SB	Pinch Hit AB	Pinch Hit H	PO	A	E	DP	TC/G	FA	G by Pos
1902	PHI	N	1	—	—	0	0	0	0	0	—	0	0	0		0	0	0	0	0	0	0	0.0	—	

Greg Mahlberg

MAHLBERG, GREGORY JOHN BR TR 5′10″ 180 lbs.
B. Aug. 8, 1952, Milwaukee, Wis.

Year	Team		Games	BA	SA	AB	H	2B	3B	HR	HR%	R	RBI	BB	SO	SB	Pinch Hit AB	Pinch Hit H	PO	A	E	DP	TC/G	FA	G by Pos
1978	TEX	A	1	.000	.000	1	0	0	0	0	0.0	0	0	0	0	0	0	0	2	0	0	0	2.0	1.000	C-1
1979			7	.118	.294	17	2	0	0	1	5.9	2	1	2	4	0	0	0	22	1	0	0	3.3	1.000	C-7
2 yrs.			8	.111	.278	18	2	0	0	1	5.6	2	1	2	4	0	0	0	24	1	0	0	3.1	1.000	C-8

Dan Mahoney

MAHONEY, DANIEL J. BR TR 5′ 9½″ 165 lbs.
B. Mar. 20, 1864, Springfield, Mass. D. Feb. 1, 1904, Springfield, Mass.

Year	Team		Games	BA	SA	AB	H	2B	3B	HR	HR%	R	RBI	BB	SO	SB	Pinch Hit AB	Pinch Hit H	PO	A	E	DP	TC/G	FA	G by Pos
1892	CIN	N	5	.190	.286	21	4	0	1	0	0.0	1	1	1	4	0	0	0	23	10	2	0	7.0	.943	C-5
1895	WAS	N	6	.167	.167	12	2	0	0	0	0.0	2	1	0	0	0	3	1	14	1	1	1	5.3	.938	C-2, 1B-1
2 yrs.			11	.182	.242	33	6	0	1	0	0.0	3	2	1	4	0	3	1	37	11	3	1	6.4	.941	C-7, 1B-1

Danny Mahoney

MAHONEY, DANIEL JOSEPH BR TR 5′ 6½″ 145 lbs.
B. Sept. 6, 1888, Haverhill, Mass. D. Sept. 28, 1960, Utica, N. Y.

Year	Team		Games	BA	SA	AB	H	2B	3B	HR	HR%	R	RBI	BB	SO	SB	Pinch Hit AB	Pinch Hit H	PO	A	E	DP	TC/G	FA	G by Pos
1911	CIN	N	1	—	—	0	0	0	0	0	—	0	0	0	0	0	0	0	0	0	0	0	0.0	—	

Jim Mahoney

MAHONEY, JAMES THOMAS (Moe) BR TR 6′ 175 lbs.
B. May 26, 1934, Englewood, N. J.

Year	Team		Games	BA	SA	AB	H	2B	3B	HR	HR%	R	RBI	BB	SO	SB	Pinch Hit AB	Pinch Hit H	PO	A	E	DP	TC/G	FA	G by Pos
1959	BOS	A	31	.130	.261	23	3	0	0	1	4.3	10	4	3	7	0	0	0	24	39	4	5	2.2	.940	SS-30
1961	WAS	A	43	.241	.259	108	26	0	1	0	0.0	10	6	5	23	1	1	0	59	97	5	26	4.9	.969	SS-31, 2B-2
1962	CLE	A	41	.243	.419	74	18	4	0	3	4.1	12	5	3	14	0	1	0	44	70	3	14	3.7	.974	SS-23, 2B-8, 3B-1
1965	HOU	N	5	.200	.200	5	1	0	0	0	0.0	0	0	0	3	0	0	0	5	2	0	3	1.4	1.000	SS-5
4 yrs.			120	.229	.314	210	48	4	1	4	1.9	32	15	11	47	1	2	0	132	208	12	48	3.5	.966	SS-89, 2B-10, 3B-1

Mike Mahoney

MAHONEY, GEORGE W. BR 6′ 4″ 220 lbs.
B. Dec. 5, 1873, Boston, Mass. D. Jan. 3, 1940, Boston, Mass.

Year	Team		Games	BA	SA	AB	H	2B	3B	HR	HR%	R	RBI	BB	SO	SB	Pinch Hit AB	Pinch Hit H	PO	A	E	DP	TC/G	FA	G by Pos
1897	BOS	N	2	.500	.500	2	1	0	0	0	0.0	1	1	0		0	0	0	1	1	0	0	1.0	1.000	P-1, C-1
1898	STL	N	2	.000	.000	7	0	0	0	0	0.0	0	0	0		0	0	0	22	1	2	1	12.5	.920	1B-2
2 yrs.			4	.111	.111	9	1	0	0	0	0.0	1	1	0		0	0	0	23	2	2	1	6.8	.926	1B-2, P-1, C-1

Bob Maier

MAIER, ROBERT PHILLIP BR TR 5′ 8″ 180 lbs.
B. Sept. 5, 1915, Dunellen, N. J. D. Aug. 4, 1993, South Plainfield, N. J.

Year	Team		Games	BA	SA	AB	H	2B	3B	HR	HR%	R	RBI	BB	SO	SB	Pinch Hit AB	Pinch Hit H	PO	A	E	DP	TC/G	FA	G by Pos
1945	DET	A	132	.263	.350	486	128	25	7	1	0.2	58	34	37	32	7	2	1	144	226	25	19	3.1	.937	3B-124, OF-5
WORLD SERIES																									
1945	DET	A	1	1.000	1.000	1	1	0	0	0	0.0	0	0	0	0	0	1	1	0	0	0	0	0.0	—	

Emil Mailho

MAILHO, EMIL PIERRE (Lefty) BL TL 5′10″ 165 lbs.
B. Dec. 16, 1909, Berkeley, Calif.

Year	Team		Games	BA	SA	AB	H	2B	3B	HR	HR%	R	RBI	BB	SO	SB	Pinch Hit AB	Pinch Hit H	PO	A	E	DP	TC/G	FA	G by Pos
1936	PHI	A	21	.056	.056	18	1	0	0	0	0.0	5	0	5	3	0	16	1	2	0	0	0	2.0	1.000	OF-1

Charlie Maisel

MAISEL, CHARLES LOUIS BR TR 6′ 1″
B. Apr. 21, 1894, Catonsville, Md. D. Aug. 25, 1953, Baltimore, Md.

Year	Team		Games	BA	SA	AB	H	2B	3B	HR	HR%	R	RBI	BB	SO	SB	Pinch Hit AB	Pinch Hit H	PO	A	E	DP	TC/G	FA	G by Pos
1915	BAL	F	1	.000	.000	4	0	0	0	0	0.0	0	0	0		0	0	0	6	2	0	0	8.0	1.000	C-1

Fritz Maisel

MAISEL, FREDERICK CHARLES (Flash) BR TR 5′ 7½″ 170 lbs.
Brother of George Maisel.
B. Dec. 23, 1889, Catonsville, Md. D. Apr. 22, 1967, Baltimore, Md.

Year	Team		Games	BA	SA	AB	H	2B	3B	HR	HR%	R	RBI	BB	SO	SB	Pinch Hit AB	Pinch Hit H	PO	A	E	DP	TC/G	FA	G by Pos
1913	NY	A	51	.257	.310	187	48	4	3	0	0.0	33	12	34	20	25	0	0	70	83	8	3	3.2	.950	3B-51
1914			149	.239	.325	548	131	23	9	2	0.4	78	47	76	69	**74**	0	0	206	245	35	17	3.3	.928	3B-148
1915			135	.281	.357	530	149	16	6	4	0.8	77	46	48	35	51	1	1	184	223	26	20	3.2	.940	3B-134
1916			53	.228	.259	158	36	5	0	0	0.0	18	7	20	18	4	6	1	71	32	4	4	2.6	.963	OF-26, 3B-11, 2B-4
1917			113	.198	.228	404	80	4	4	0	0.0	46	20	36	18	29	5	2	231	295	19	37	5.1	.965	2B-100, 3B-7
1918	STL	A	90	.232	.261	284	66	4	2	0	0.0	43	16	46	17	11	5	0	108	154	14	10	3.5	.949	3B-79, OF-1
6 yrs.			591	.242	.299	2111	510	56	24	6	0.3	295	148	260	177	194	17	4	870	1032	106	91	3.6	.947	3B-430, 2B-104, OF-27

George Maisel

MAISEL, GEORGE JOHN BR TR 5′10½″ 180 lbs.
Brother of Fritz Maisel.
B. Mar. 12, 1892, Catonsville, Md. D. Nov. 20, 1968, Baltimore, Md.

Year	Team		Games	BA	SA	AB	H	2B	3B	HR	HR%	R	RBI	BB	SO	SB	Pinch Hit AB	Pinch Hit H	PO	A	E	DP	TC/G	FA	G by Pos
1913	STL	A	11	.167	.278	18	3	2	0	0	0.0	2	1	1	7	0	5	1	5	0	1	0	1.2	.833	OF-5
1916	DET	A	7	.000	.000	5	0	0	0	0	0.0	2	0	0	2	0	0	0	1	5	1	1	2.3	.857	3B-3
1921	CHI	N	111	.310	.338	393	122	7	2	0	0.0	54	43	11	13	17	1	1	259	12	6	2	2.6	.978	OF-108
1922			38	.190	.226	84	16	1	1	0	0.0	9	6	8	2	1	5	1	50	2	0	0	1.4	1.000	OF-38
4 yrs.			167	.282	.314	500	141	10	3	0	0.0	67	50	20	24	18	11	3	315	19	8	3	2.2	.977	OF-151, 3B-3

Hank Majeski

MAJESKI, HENRY (Heeney) BR TR 5′ 9″ 174 lbs.
B. Dec. 13, 1916, Staten Island, N. Y. D. Aug. 9, 1991, Staten Island, N. Y.

Year	Team		Games	BA	SA	AB	H	2B	3B	HR	HR%	R	RBI	BB	SO	SB	Pinch Hit AB	Pinch Hit H	PO	A	E	DP	TC/G	FA	G by Pos
1939	BOS	N	106	.272	.379	367	100	16	1	7	1.9	35	54	18	30	2	7	2	111	196	18	19	3.3	.945	3B-99
1940			3	.000	.000	3	0	0	0	0	0.0	0	0	0	0	0	3	0	0	0	0	0	0.0	—	
1941			19	.145	.236	55	8	5	0	0	0.0	5	3	1	13	0	8	1	15	26	4	2	4.1	.911	3B-11
1946	2 teams		NY A (8G –.083) PHI A (78G –.250)																						
″	total		86	.243	.333	276	67	14	4	1	0.4	26	25	26	16	3	11	0	79	161	9	22	3.4	.964	3B-74
1947	PHI	A	141	.280	.405	479	134	26	5	8	1.7	54	72	53	31	1	2	0	170	283	5	32	3.3	.989	3B-134, SS-4, 2B-1
1948			148	.310	.454	590	183	41	4	12	2.0	88	120	48	43	2	0	0	176	292	12	23	3.2	.975	3B-142, SS-8
1949			114	.277	.417	448	124	26	5	9	2.0	62	67	29	23	0	1	0	117	219	15	37	3.1	.957	3B-113
1950	CHI	A	122	.309	.406	414	128	18	2	6	1.4	47	46	42	34	1	9	1	115	246	11	31	3.3	.970	3B-112
1951	2 teams		CHI A (12G –.257) PHI A (89G –.285)																						
″	total		101	.282	.411	358	101	23	4	5	1.4	45	48	36	24	1	5	2	86	232	9	19	3.4	.972	3B-97
1952	2 teams		PHI A (34G –.256) CLE A (36G –.296)																						
″	total		70	.269	.351	171	46	4	2	2	1.2	21	29	26	17	0	23	6	48	105	5	16	3.3	.968	3B-45, 2B-3

Hank Majeski *continued*

Year	Team	Games	BA	SA	AB	H	2B	3B	HR	HR%	R	RBI	BB	SO	SB	Pinch Hit AB	Pinch Hit H	PO	A	E	DP	TC/G	FA	G by Pos
1953	CLE A	50	.300	.440	50	15	1	0	2	4.0	6	12	3	8	0	31	11	9	11	0	2	1.1	1.000	2B-10, 3B-7, OF-1
1954		57	.281	.388	121	34	4	0	3	2.5	10	17	7	14	0	26	8	67	64	3	11	3.8	.978	2B-25, 3B-10
1955	2 teams	CLE A (36G –.188) BAL A (16G –.171)																						
"	total	52	.180	.281	89	16	3	0	2	2.2	5	8	10	7	0	23	1	22	29	0	4	2.0	1.000	3B-17, 2B-9
13 yrs.		1069	.279	.398	3421	956	181	27	57	1.7	404	501	299	260	10	149	32	1015	1864	91	218	3.2	.969	3B-861, 2B-48, SS-12, OF-1
WORLD SERIES																								
1954	CLE A	4	.167	.667	6	1	0	0	1	16.7	1	3	0	1	0	2	1	2	1	0	0	3.0	1.000	3B-1

Mike Maksudian

MAKSUDIAN, MICHAEL BRYANT BL TR 5′11″ 220 lbs.
B. May 28, 1966, Belleville, Ill.

Year	Team	Games	BA	SA	AB	H	2B	3B	HR	HR%	R	RBI	BB	SO	SB	Pinch Hit AB	Pinch Hit H	PO	A	E	DP	TC/G	FA	G by Pos
1992	TOR A	3	.000	.000	3	0	0	0	0	0.0	0	0	0	0	0	3	0	0	0	0	0	0.0	.000	1B-1
1993	MIN A	5	.167	.250	12	2	1	0	0	0.0	2	2	4	2	0	1	0	28	6	0	3	6.8	1.000	1B-4, 3B-1
1994	CHI N	26	.269	.346	26	7	2	0	0	0.0	6	4	10	4	0	13	4	18	5	0	3	3.3	1.000	1B-3, 3B-2, C-2
3 yrs.		34	.220	.293	41	9	3	0	0	0.0	8	6	14	6	0	17	4	46	11	0	6	4.4	1.000	1B-8, 3B-3, C-2

Charlie Malay

MALAY, CHARLES FRANCIS BB TR 5′11½″ 175 lbs.
Father of Joe Malay.
B. June 13, 1879, Brooklyn, N. Y. D. Sept. 18, 1949, Brooklyn, N. Y.

Year	Team	Games	BA	SA	AB	H	2B	3B	HR	HR%	R	RBI	BB	SO	SB	Pinch Hit AB	Pinch Hit H	PO	A	E	DP	TC/G	FA	G by Pos
1905	BKN N	102	.252	.292	349	88	7	2	1	0.3	33	31	22		13	1	0	188	220	32	17	4.4	.927	2B-75, OF-25, SS-1

Joe Malay

MALAY, JOSEPH CHARLES BL TL 6′ 175 lbs.
Son of Charlie Malay.
B. Oct. 25, 1905, Brooklyn, N. Y. D. Mar. 19, 1989, Bridgeport, Conn.

Year	Team	Games	BA	SA	AB	H	2B	3B	HR	HR%	R	RBI	BB	SO	SB	Pinch Hit AB	Pinch Hit H	PO	A	E	DP	TC/G	FA	G by Pos
1933	NY N	8	.125	.125	24	3	0	0	0	0.0	0	2	0	0	0	0	0	56	7	0	2	7.9	1.000	1B-8
1935		1	1.000	1.000	1	1	0	0	0	0.0	0	0	0	0	0	1	1	0	0	0	0	0.0	—	
2 yrs.		9	.160	.160	25	4	0	0	0	0.0	0	2	0	0	0	1	1	56	7	0	2	7.9	1.000	1B-8

Candy Maldonado

MALDONADO, CANDIDO BR TR 6′ 185 lbs.
Born Candido Maldonado (Guadarrama).
B. Sept. 5, 1960, Humacao, Puerto Rico.

Year	Team	Games	BA	SA	AB	H	2B	3B	HR	HR%	R	RBI	BB	SO	SB	Pinch Hit AB	Pinch Hit H	PO	A	E	DP	TC/G	FA	G by Pos
1981	LA N	11	.083	.083	12	1	0	0	0	0.0	0	0	0	5	0	4	0	8	0	0	0	0.9	1.000	OF-9
1982		6	.000	.000	4	0	0	0	0	0.0	0	0	1	2	0	2	0	5	0	0	0	1.7	1.000	OF-3
1983		42	.194	.290	62	12	1	1	1	1.6	5	6	5	14	0	9	2	26	0	0	0	0.8	1.000	OF-33
1984		116	.268	.382	254	68	14	0	5	2.0	25	28	19	29	0	31	9	124	5	8	0	1.3	.942	OF-102, 3B-4
1985		121	.225	.338	213	48	7	1	5	2.3	20	19	19	40	1	31	7	121	6	2	0	1.1	.984	OF-113
1986	SF N	133	.252	.477	405	102	31	3	18	4.4	49	85	20	77	4	40	17	161	11	3	0	1.7	.983	OF-101, 3B-1
1987		118	.292	.509	442	129	28	4	20	4.5	69	85	34	78	8	4	1	176	7	5	0	1.6	.973	OF-116
1988		142	.255	.377	499	127	23	1	12	2.4	53	68	37	89	6	5	0	251	5	10	1	1.9	.962	OF-139
1989		129	.217	.362	345	75	23	0	9	2.6	39	41	37	69	4	30	7	181	6	5	1	1.7	.974	OF-116
1990	CLE A	155	.273	.446	590	161	32	2	22	3.7	76	95	49	134	3	1	0	293	9	2	1	2.0	.993	OF-134, DH-20
1991	2 teams	MIL A (34G –.207) TOR A (52G –.277)																						
"	total	86	.250	.427	288	72	15	0	12	4.2	37	48	36	76	4	3	0	139	2	2	0	1.7	.986	OF-76, DH-9
1992	TOR A	137	.272	.462	489	133	25	4	20	4.1	64	66	59	112	2	2	0	260	12	6	1	2.0	.978	OF-132, DH-4
1993	2 teams	CHI N (70G –.186) CLE A (28G –.247)																						
"	total	98	.208	.348	221	46	7	0	8	3.6	19	35	24	58	0	36	8	89	4	6	2	1.4	.939	OF-67, DH-2
1994	CLE A	42	.196	.435	92	18	5	1	5	5.4	14	12	19	31	1	12	2	6	0	0	0	0.2	1.000	DH-25, OF-5
1995	2 teams	TOR A (61G –.269) TEX A (13G –.233)																						
"	total	74	.263	.489	190	50	16	0	9	4.7	28	30	32	50	1	11	1	98	3	1	0	1.5	.990	OF-69, DH-1
15 yrs.		1410	.254	.424	4106	1042	227	17	146	3.6	498	618	391	864	34	221	54	1938	70	50	6	1.6	.976	OF-1215, DH-61, 3B-5
LEAGUE CHAMPIONSHIP SERIES																								
1983	LA N	2	.000	.000	2	0	0	0	0	0.0	0	0	0	1	0	2	0	0	0	0	0	0.0	—	
1985		4	.143	.143	7	1	0	0	0	0.0	0	1	0	3	0	1	0	4	0	1	0	1.7	.800	OF-3
1987	SF N	5	.211	.263	19	4	1	0	0	0.0	2	2	0	3	0	0	0	7	0	0	0	1.4	1.000	OF-5
1989		3	.000	.000	3	0	0	0	0	0.0	1	1	2	0	0	1	0	2	0	0	0	0.7	1.000	OF-3
1991	TOR A	5	.100	.150	20	2	1	0	0	0.0	1	1	1	6	0	0	0	4	0	0	0	1.3	1.000	OF-3
1992		6	.273	.545	22	6	0	0	2	9.1	3	6	3	4	0	0	0	9	1	0	1	1.7	1.000	OF-6
6 yrs.		25	.178	.288	73	13	2	0	2	2.7	7	11	6	17 **10th**	0	4	0	26	1	1	1	1.4	.964	OF-20
WORLD SERIES																								
1989	SF N	4	.091	.273	11	1	0	1	0	0.0	1	0	0	4	0	1	1	5	0	0	0	1.7	1.000	OF-3
1992	TOR A	6	.158	.316	19	3	0	0	1	5.3	1	2	2	5	0	1	0	8	2	0	1	2.0	1.000	OF-5
2 yrs.		10	.133	.300	30	4	0	1	1	3.3	2	2	2	9	0	2	1	13	2	0	1	1.9	1.000	OF-8

Jim Maler

MALER, JAMES MICHAEL BR TR 6′ 4″ 230 lbs.
B. Aug. 16, 1958, New York, N. Y.

Year	Team	Games	BA	SA	AB	H	2B	3B	HR	HR%	R	RBI	BB	SO	SB	Pinch Hit AB	Pinch Hit H	PO	A	E	DP	TC/G	FA	G by Pos
1981	SEA A	12	.348	.391	23	8	1	0	0	0.0	1	2	2	1	1	7	3	36	2	0	5	5.4	1.000	1B-5, DH-2
1982		64	.226	.344	221	50	8	3	4	1.8	18	26	12	35	0	5	1	529	41	5	45	9.3	.991	1B-57, DH-5
1983		26	.182	.242	66	12	1	0	1	1.5	5	3	5	11	0	4	1	152	9	0	8	6.7	1.000	1B-19, DH-5
3 yrs.		102	.226	.326	310	70	10	3	5	1.6	24	31	19	47	1	16	5	717	52	5	58	8.3	.994	1B-81, DH-12

Tony Malinosky

MALINOSKY, ANTHONY FRANCIS BR TR 5′10½″ 165 lbs.
B. Oct. 5, 1909, Collinsville, Ill.

Year	Team	Games	BA	SA	AB	H	2B	3B	HR	HR%	R	RBI	BB	SO	SB	Pinch Hit AB	Pinch Hit H	PO	A	E	DP	TC/G	FA	G by Pos
1937	BKN N	35	.228	.253	79	18	2	0	0	0.0	7	3	9	11	0	9	1	15	28	9	2	2.2	.827	3B-13, SS-11

Bobby Malkmus

MALKMUS, ROBERT EDWARD BR TR 5′ 9″ 175 lbs.
B. July 4, 1931, Newark, N. J.

Year	Team	Games	BA	SA	AB	H	2B	3B	HR	HR%	R	RBI	BB	SO	SB	Pinch Hit AB	Pinch Hit H	PO	A	E	DP	TC/G	FA	G by Pos
1957	MIL N	13	.091	.182	22	2	0	1	0	0.0	6	0	3	3	0	3	0	16	19	1	4	5.1	.972	2B-7
1958	WAS A	41	.186	.243	70	13	2	1	0	0.0	5	3	4	15	0	11	4	55	54	4	14	3.9	.965	2B-26, 3B-2, SS-1
1959		6	—	—	0	0	0	0	0	—	0	0	0	0	0	0	0	0	0	0	0	0.0	.000	

Bobby Malkmus *continued*

Year	Team	Games	BA	SA	AB	H	2B	3B	HR	HR%	R	RBI	BB	SO	SB	Pinch Hit AB	Pinch Hit H	PO	A	E	DP	TC/G	FA	G by Pos
1960	PHI N	79	.211	.278	133	28	4	1	1	0.8	16	12	11	28	2	5	0	68	101	2	20	2.7	.988	SS-29, 2B-23, 3B-12
1961		121	.231	.327	342	79	8	2	7	2.0	39	31	20	43	1	6	0	210	299	12	67	4.5	.977	2B-58, SS-34, 3B-25
1962		8	.200	.400	5	1	1	0	0	0.0	3	0	0	1	0	3	0	1	4	0	1	5.0	1.000	SS-1
6 yrs.		268	.215	.301	572	123	15	5	8	1.4	69	46	38	90	3	28	4	350	477	19	106	3.9	.978	2B-114, SS-65, 3B-39

Jerry Mallett

MALLETT, GERALD GORDON BR TR 6′5″ 208 lbs.
B. Sept. 18, 1935, Bonne Terre, Mo.

Year	Team	Games	BA	SA	AB	H	2B	3B	HR	HR%	R	RBI	BB	SO	SB	Pinch Hit AB	Pinch Hit H	PO	A	E	DP	TC/G	FA	G by Pos
1959	BOS A	4	.267	.267	15	4	0	0	0	0.0	1	1	1	3	0	0	0	14	2	0	2	4.0	1.000	OF-4

Les Mallon

MALLON, LESLIE CLYDE BR TR 5′8″ 160 lbs.
B. Nov. 21, 1905, Sweetwater, Tex. D. Apr. 17, 1991, Granbury, Tex.

Year	Team	Games	BA	SA	AB	H	2B	3B	HR	HR%	R	RBI	BB	SO	SB	Pinch Hit AB	Pinch Hit H	PO	A	E	DP	TC/G	FA	G by Pos
1931	PHI N	122	.309	.379	375	116	19	2	1	0.3	41	45	29	40	0	9	2	270	308	28	62	5.6	.954	2B-97, 1B-5, SS-3, 3B-3
1932		103	.259	.349	347	90	16	0	5	1.4	44	31	28	28	1	9	3	202	233	22	42	4.9	.952	2B-88, 3B-5
1934	BOS N	42	.295	.343	166	49	6	1	0	0.0	23	18	15	12	0	0	0	92	145	8	17	5.8	.967	2B-42
1935		116	.274	.357	412	113	24	2	2	0.5	48	25	28	37	3	5	3	201	281	18	34	4.5	.964	2B-73, 3B-36, OF-1
4 yrs.		383	.283	.359	1300	368	65	5	8	0.6	156	119	100	117	4	23	8	765	967	76	155	5.1	.958	2B-300, 3B-44, 1B-5, SS-3, OF-1

Ben Mallonee

MALLONEE, HOWARD BENNETT (Lefty) BL TL 5′6″ 150 lbs.
B. Mar. 31, 1894, Baltimore, Md. D. Feb. 19, 1978, Baltimore, Md.

Year	Team	Games	BA	SA	AB	H	2B	3B	HR	HR%	R	RBI	BB	SO	SB	Pinch Hit AB	Pinch Hit H	PO	A	E	DP	TC/G	FA	G by Pos
1921	PHI A	6	.250	.292	24	6	1	0	0	0.0	2	0	1	1	1	0	0	15	1	0	0	2.7	1.000	OF-6

Jule Mallonee

MALLONEE, JULIUS NORRIS BL TR 6′2″ 180 lbs.
B. Apr. 4, 1900, Charlotte, N. C. D. Oct. 26, 1934, Charlotte, N. C.

Year	Team	Games	BA	SA	AB	H	2B	3B	HR	HR%	R	RBI	BB	SO	SB	Pinch Hit AB	Pinch Hit H	PO	A	E	DP	TC/G	FA	G by Pos
1925	CHI A	2	.000	.000	3	0	0	0	0	0.0	1	0	1	0	0	1	0	1	0	0	0	1.0	1.000	OF-1

Jim Mallory

MALLORY, JAMES BAUGH (Sunny Jim) BR TR 6′1″ 170 lbs.
B. Sept. 1, 1918, Lawrenceville, Va.

Year	Team	Games	BA	SA	AB	H	2B	3B	HR	HR%	R	RBI	BB	SO	SB	Pinch Hit AB	Pinch Hit H	PO	A	E	DP	TC/G	FA	G by Pos
1940	WAS A	4	.167	.167	12	2	0	0	0	0.0	2	0	1	1	0	0	0	10	0	0	0	3.3	1.000	OF-3
1945	2 teams	STL N (13G –.233) NY N (37G –.298)																						
″	total	50	.277	.299	137	38	3	0	0	0.0	13	14	6	9	1	11	3	67	3	3	1	2.3	.959	OF-32
2 yrs.		54	.268	.289	149	40	3	0	0	0.0	15	14	7	10	1	11	3	77	3	3	1	2.4	.964	OF-35

Sheldon Mallory

MALLORY, SHELDON BL TL 6′2″ 175 lbs.
B. July 16, 1953, Argo, Ill.

Year	Team	Games	BA	SA	AB	H	2B	3B	HR	HR%	R	RBI	BB	SO	SB	Pinch Hit AB	Pinch Hit H	PO	A	E	DP	TC/G	FA	G by Pos
1977	OAK A	64	.214	.262	126	27	4	1	0	0.0	19	5	11	18	12	6	2	96	3	3	0	1.8	.971	OF-45, DH-7, 1B-4

Harry Malmberg

MALMBERG, HARRY WILLIAM (Swede) BR TR 6′1″ 170 lbs.
B. July 31, 1926, Fairfield, Ala. D. Oct. 29, 1976, San Francisco, Calif.

Year	Team	Games	BA	SA	AB	H	2B	3B	HR	HR%	R	RBI	BB	SO	SB	Pinch Hit AB	Pinch Hit H	PO	A	E	DP	TC/G	FA	G by Pos
1955	DET A	67	.216	.260	208	45	5	2	0	0.0	25	19	29	19	0	0	0	155	181	5	42	5.2	.985	2B-65

Eddie Malone

MALONE, EDWARD RUSSELL BR TR 5′10″ 175 lbs.
B. June 16, 1920, Chicago, Ill.

Year	Team	Games	BA	SA	AB	H	2B	3B	HR	HR%	R	RBI	BB	SO	SB	Pinch Hit AB	Pinch Hit H	PO	A	E	DP	TC/G	FA	G by Pos
1949	CHI A	55	.271	.353	170	46	7	2	1	0.6	17	16	29	19	2	3	1	186	22	2	2	4.1	.990	C-51
1950		31	.225	.254	71	16	2	0	0	0.0	2	10	10	8	0	10	2	79	10	0	3	4.2	1.000	C-21
2 yrs.		86	.257	.324	241	62	9	2	1	0.4	19	26	39	27	2	13	3	265	32	2	5	4.2	.993	C-72

Fergy Malone

MALONE, FERGUSON G. BR TL 5′8″ 156 lbs.
B. 1842, Ireland D. Jan. 1, 1905, Seattle, Wash.
Manager 1884.

Year	Team	Games	BA	SA	AB	H	2B	3B	HR	HR%	R	RBI	BB	SO	SB	Pinch Hit AB	Pinch Hit H	PO	A	E	DP	TC/G	FA	G by Pos
1876	PHI N	22	.229	.250	96	22	2	0	0	0.0	14	6	0	1		0	0	82	32	32	0	6.1	.781	C-20, OF-3, SS-1
1884	PHI U	1	.250	.250	4	1	0	0	0	0.0	0		0			0	0	9	0	2	0	11.0	.818	C-1
2 yrs.		23	.230	.250	100	23	2	0	0	0.0	14	6	0	1		0	0	91	32	34	0	6.3	.783	C-21, OF-3, SS-1

Lew Malone

MALONE, LEWIS ALOYSIUS BR TR 5′11″ 175 lbs.
Played as Lew Ryan in 1915.
B. Mar. 13, 1897, Baltimore, Md. D. Feb. 17, 1972, Brooklyn, N. Y.

Year	Team	Games	BA	SA	AB	H	2B	3B	HR	HR%	R	RBI	BB	SO	SB	Pinch Hit AB	Pinch Hit H	PO	A	E	DP	TC/G	FA	G by Pos
1915	PHI A	76	.204	.279	201	41	4	4	1	0.5	17	17	21	40	7	12	3	133	126	28	10	4.7	.902	2B-43, 3B-12, OF-4, SS-2
1916		5	.000	.000	4	0	0	0	0	0.0	1	0	1	2	0	3	0	1	0	0	0	1.0	1.000	SS-1
1917	BKN N	1	—	—	0	0	0	0	0	—	1	0	0	0	0	1	0	0	0	0	0	0.0	—	
1919		51	.204	.284	162	33	7	3	0	0.0	9	11	6	18	1	0	0	62	82	11	5	3.0	.929	3B-47, SS-2, 2B-2
4 yrs.		133	.202	.278	367	74	11	7	1	0.3	28	28	28	60	8	16	3	196	208	39	15	3.9	.912	3B-59, 2B-45, SS-5, OF-4

Billy Maloney

MALONEY, WILLIAM ALPHONSE BL TR 5′10″ 177 lbs.
B. June 5, 1878, Lewiston, Me. D. Sept. 2, 1960, Breckenridge, Tex.

Year	Team	Games	BA	SA	AB	H	2B	3B	HR	HR%	R	RBI	BB	SO	SB	Pinch Hit AB	Pinch Hit H	PO	A	E	DP	TC/G	FA	G by Pos
1901	MIL A	86	.293	.331	290	85	3	4	0	0.0	42	22	7		11	5	2	302	111	23	6	5.4	.947	C-72, OF-8
1902	2 teams	STL A (30G –.205) CIN N (27G –.247)																						
″	total	57	.224	.274	201	45	7	0	1	0.5	21	18	8		8	3	0	103	19	13	3	2.5	.904	OF-41, C-14
1905	CHI N	145	.260	.351	558	145	17	14	2	0.4	78	56	43		**59**	0	0	251	18	13	4	1.9	.954	OF-145
1906	BKN N	151	.221	.272	566	125	15	7	0	0.0	71	32	49		38	0	0	355	19	13	6	2.6	.966	OF-151
1907		144	.229	.283	502	115	7	10	0	0.0	51	32	31		25	0	0	336	18	12	5	2.5	.967	OF-144
1908		113	.195	.273	359	70	5	7	3	0.8	31	17	24		14	6	1	255	19	14	4	2.7	.951	OF-103, C-4
6 yrs.		696	.236	.299	2476	585	54	42	6	0.2	294	177	162		155	14	3	1602	204	88	28	2.8	.954	OF-592, C-90

John Maloney

MALONEY, JOHN
Deceased.

Year	Team	Games	BA	SA	AB	H	2B	3B	HR	HR%	R	RBI	BB	SO	SB	Pinch Hit AB	Pinch Hit H	PO	A	E	DP	TC/G	FA	G by Pos
1876	NY N	2	.286	.571	7	2	0	1	0	0.0	1	2	0	1		0	0	4	0	1	0	2.5	.800	OF-2
1877	HAR N	1	.250	.250	4	1	0	0	0	0.0	0	0	0	0		0	0	1	0	3	0	4.0	.250	OF-1
2 yrs.		3	.273	.455	11	3	0	1	0	0.0	1	2	0	1		0	0	5	0	4	0	3.0	.556	OF-3

Pat Maloney

MALONEY, PATRICK WILLIAM BR TR 6′ 150 lbs.
B. Jan. 19, 1888, Grosvenordale, Conn. D. June 27, 1979, Pawtucket, R. I.

Year	Team	Games	BA	SA	AB	H	2B	3B	HR	HR%	R	RBI	BB	SO	SB	Pinch Hit AB	Pinch Hit H	PO	A	E	DP	TC/G	FA	G by Pos
1912	NY A	22	.215	.228	79	17	1	0	0	0.0	9	4	6		3	0	0	61	2	5	0	3.4	.926	OF-20

Frank Malzone

MALZONE, FRANK JAMES BR TR 5′10″ 180 lbs.
B. Feb. 28, 1930, Bronx, N. Y.

Year	Team	Games	BA	SA	AB	H	2B	3B	HR	HR%	R	RBI	BB	SO	SB	Pinch Hit AB	Pinch Hit H	PO	A	E	DP	TC/G	FA	G by Pos
1955	BOS A	6	.350	.400	20	7	1	0	0	0.0	2	1	1	3	0	1	0	2	15	0	1	4.3	1.000	3B-4
1956		27	.165	.272	103	17	3	1	2	1.9	15	11	9	8	1	0	0	24	57	6	4	3.3	.931	3B-26
1957		153	.292	.427	634	185	31	5	15	2.4	82	103	31	41	2	0	0	151	370	25	31	3.6	.954	3B-153
1958		155	.295	.421	**627**	185	30	2	15	2.4	76	87	33	53	1	0	0	139	378	27	36	3.5	.950	3B-155
1959		154	.280	.437	604	169	34	2	19	3.1	90	92	42	58	6	0	0	134	357	24	40	3.3	.953	3B-154
1960		152	.271	.398	595	161	30	2	14	2.4	60	79	36	42	2	1	0	159	318	26	36	3.3	.948	3B-151
1961		151	.266	.386	590	157	21	4	14	2.4	74	87	44	49	1	2	0	136	304	23	45	3.1	.950	3B-149
1962		156	.283	.426	619	175	20	3	21	3.4	74	95	35	43	0	0	0	154	313	16	32	3.1	.967	3B-156
1963		151	.291	.419	580	169	25	2	15	2.6	66	71	31	45	0	3	0	151	283	16	18	3.0	.964	3B-148
1964		148	.264	.372	537	142	19	0	13	2.4	62	56	37	43	0	5	1	141	259	17	24	2.9	.959	3B-143
1965		106	.239	.319	364	87	20	0	3	0.8	40	34	28	38	1	16	3	79	170	8	19	2.7	.969	3B-96
1966	CAL A	82	.206	.277	155	32	5	0	2	1.3	6	12	10	11	0	43	10	38	60	8	3	3.0	.925	3B-35
12 yrs.		1441	.274	.399	5428	1486	239	21	133	2.5	647	728	337	434	14	71	14	1308	2884	196	289	3.2	.955	3B-1370

Frank Mancuso

MANCUSO, FRANK OCTAVIUS BR TR 6′ 195 lbs.
Brother of Gus Mancuso.
B. May 23, 1918, Houston, Tex.

Year	Team	Games	BA	SA	AB	H	2B	3B	HR	HR%	R	RBI	BB	SO	SB	Pinch Hit AB	Pinch Hit H	PO	A	E	DP	TC/G	FA	G by Pos
1944	STL A	88	.205	.262	244	50	11	0	1	0.4	19	24	20	32	1	1	0	311	35	17	9	4.2	.953	C-87
1945		119	.268	.329	365	98	13	3	1	0.3	39	38	46	44	0	3	0	467	55	6	10	4.6	.989	C-115
1946		87	.240	.328	262	63	8	3	3	1.1	22	23	30	31	1	1	0	298	31	9	3	4.0	.973	C-85
1947	WAS A	43	.229	.282	131	30	5	1	0	0.0	5	13	5	11	0	7	2	144	15	7	1	4.7	.958	C-35
4 yrs.		337	.241	.306	1002	241	37	7	5	0.5	85	98	101	118	2	12	2	1220	136	39	23	4.3	.972	C-322
WORLD SERIES																								
1944	STL A	2	.667	.667	3	2	0	0	0	0.0	0	1	0	0	0	1	1	3	0	0	0	3.0	1.000	C-1

Gus Mancuso

MANCUSO, AUGUST RODNEY (Blackie) BR TR 5′10″ 185 lbs.
Brother of Frank Mancuso.
B. Dec. 5, 1905, Galveston, Tex. D. Oct. 26, 1984, Houston, Tex.

Year	Team	Games	BA	SA	AB	H	2B	3B	HR	HR%	R	RBI	BB	SO	SB	Pinch Hit AB	Pinch Hit H	PO	A	E	DP	TC/G	FA	G by Pos
1928	STL N	11	.184	.237	38	7	0	1	0	0.0	2	3	0	5	0	0	0	54	7	1	0	5.6	.984	C-11
1930		76	.366	.551	227	83	17	2	7	3.1	39	59	18	16	1	12	3	277	33	10	2	5.2	.969	C-61
1931		67	.262	.374	187	49	16	1	1	0.5	13	23	18	13	2	10	1	239	40	8	6	5.1	.972	C-56
1932		103	.284	.413	310	88	23	1	5	1.6	25	43	30	15	0	19	6	454	53	12	7	6.3	.977	C-82
1933	NY N	144	.264	.345	481	127	17	2	6	1.2	39	56	48	21	0	2	1	580	83	19	15	4.8	.972	C-142
1934		122	.245	.337	383	94	14	0	7	1.8	32	46	27	19	0	0	0	448	67	12	7	4.3	.977	C-122
1935		128	.298	.380	447	133	18	2	5	1.1	33	56	30	16	1	2	0	484	71	16	4	4.5	.972	C-126
1936		139	.301	.405	519	156	21	3	9	1.7	55	63	39	28	0	1	0	524	104	15	15	4.7	.977	C-138
1937		86	.279	.387	287	80	17	1	4	1.4	30	39	17	20	1	5	0	410	69	9	4	6.0	.982	C-81
1938		52	.348	.437	158	55	8	0	2	1.3	19	15	17	13	0	8	2	184	24	5	5	4.8	.977	C-44
1939	CHI N	80	.231	.295	251	58	10	0	2	0.8	17	17	24	19	0	3	0	333	36	7	6	4.9	.981	C-76
1940	BKN N	60	.229	.285	144	33	8	0	0	0.0	16	16	13	7	0	4	1	193	26	4	6	4.0	.982	C-56
1941	STL N	106	.229	.293	328	75	13	1	2	0.6	25	37	37	19	0	1	0	482	58	6	6	5.2	.989	C-105
1942	2 teams	STL N (5G –.077) NY N (39G –.193)																						
"	total	44	.180	.205	122	22	1	1	0	0.0	4	9	14	7	1	3	0	151	21	4	2	4.3	.977	C-41
1943	NY N	94	.198	.242	252	50	5	0	2	0.8	11	20	28	16	0	15	3	336	40	10	1	5.0	.974	C-77
1944		78	.251	.297	195	49	4	1	1	0.5	15	25	30	20	0	4	2	249	37	7	4	4.1	.976	C-72
1945	PHI N	70	.199	.227	176	35	5	0	0	0.0	11	16	28	10	2	0	0	215	34	3	4	3.6	.988	C-70
17 yrs.		1460	.265	.351	4505	1194	197	16	53	1.2	386	543	418	264	8	89	19	5613	803	148	94	4.8	.977	C-1360
WORLD SERIES																								
1930	STL N	2	.286	.286	7	2	0	0	0	0.0	1	0	1	2	0	0	0	12	1	0	0	6.5	1.000	C-2
1931		2	.000	.000	1	0	0	0	0	0.0	0	0	0	0	0	1	0	2	0	0	0	2.0	1.000	C-1
1933	NY N	5	.118	.176	17	2	1	0	0	0.0	2	2	3	0	0	0	0	31	4	0	2	7.0	1.000	C-5
1936		6	.263	.368	19	5	2	0	0	0.0	3	1	3	3	0	0	0	40	5	0	2	7.5	1.000	C-6
1937		3	.000	.000	8	0	0	0	0	0.0	0	1	0	1	0	1	0	8	1	0	0	4.5	1.000	C-2
5 yrs.		18	.173	.231	52	9	3	0	0	0.0	6	4	7	6	0	2	0	93	11	0	4	6.5	1.000	C-16

Carl Manda

MANDA, CARL ALAN BR TR 5′10″ 170 lbs.
B. Nov. 16, 1888, Little River, Kans. D. Mar. 9, 1983, Artesia, N. M.

Year	Team	Games	BA	SA	AB	H	2B	3B	HR	HR%	R	RBI	BB	SO	SB	Pinch Hit AB	Pinch Hit H	PO	A	E	DP	TC/G	FA	G by Pos
1914	CHI A	9	.267	.267	15	4	0	0	0	0.0	2	1	3	3	1	0	0	10	23	1	1	4.9	.971	2B-7

Jim Mangan

MANGAN, JAMES DANIEL BR TR 5′10″ 190 lbs.
B. Sept. 24, 1929, San Francisco, Calif.

Year	Team	Games	BA	SA	AB	H	2B	3B	HR	HR%	R	RBI	BB	SO	SB	Pinch Hit AB	Pinch Hit H	PO	A	E	DP	TC/G	FA	G by Pos
1952	PIT N	11	.154	.154	13	2	0	0	0	0.0	1	2	1	3	0	7	0	3	2	1	0	1.5	.833	C-4
1954		14	.192	.192	26	5	0	0	0	0.0	2	2	4	9	0	7	1	24	3	0	1	3.9	1.000	C-7
1956	NY N	20	.100	.100	20	2	0	0	0	0.0	2	1	4	6	0	3	1	34	1	0	1	2.3	1.000	C-15
3 yrs.		45	.153	.153	59	9	0	0	0	0.0	5	5	9	18	0	17	2	61	6	1	2	2.6	.985	C-26

Angel Mangual

MANGUAL, ANGEL LUIS BR TR 5′10″ 178 lbs.
Born Angel Luis Mangual (Guilbe).
Brother of Pepe Mangual.
B. Mar. 19, 1947, Juana Diaz, Puerto Rico.

Year	Team	Games	BA	SA	AB	H	2B	3B	HR	HR%	R	RBI	BB	SO	SB	Pinch Hit AB	Pinch Hit H	PO	A	E	DP	TC/G	FA	G by Pos
1969	PIT N	6	.250	.500	4	1	1	0	0	0.0	1	0	0	0	0	3	1	0	0	1	0	0.3	.000	OF-3
1971	OAK A	94	.286	.362	287	82	8	1	4	1.4	32	30	17	27	1	14	2	163	3	2	1	2.1	.988	OF-81
1972		91	.246	.364	272	67	13	2	5	1.8	19	32	14	48	0	16	6	166	4	5	2	2.4	.971	OF-74
1973		74	.224	.302	192	43	4	1	3	1.6	20	13	8	34	1	13	0	88	2	5	0	1.8	.947	OF-50, 1B-2, 2B-1
1974		115	.233	.367	365	85	14	4	9	2.5	37	43	17	59	3	11	3	142	5	6	0	1.4	.961	OF-74, DH-37, 3B-1
1975		62	.220	.275	109	24	3	0	1	0.9	13	6	3	18	0	17	4	44	1	1	0	0.9	.978	OF-39, DH-15
1976		8	.167	.250	12	2	1	0	0	0.0	0	1	0	1	0	1	0	4	1	0	0	0.7	1.000	OF-7
7 yrs.		450	.245	.346	1241	304	44	8	22	1.8	122	125	59	187	5	75	16	607	16	20	3	1.7	.969	OF-328, DH-52, 1B-2, 3B-1, 2B-1

Angel Mangual *continued*

LEAGUE CHAMPIONSHIP SERIES

Year	Team	Games	BA	SA	AB	H	2B	3B	HR	HR%	R	RBI	BB	SO	SB	Pinch Hit AB	Pinch Hit H	PO	A	E	DP	TC/G	FA	G by Pos
1971	**OAK A**	3	.167	.417	12	2	1	1	0	0.0	1	2	0	1	0	0	0	6	0	0	0	2.0	1.000	OF-3
1972		3	.000	.000	3	0	0	0	0	0.0	0	0	0	1	0	3	0	0	0	0	0	0.0	—	
1973		3	.111	.111	9	1	0	0	0	0.0	1	0	0	3	0	1	0	2	0	0	0	0.7	1.000	OF-3
1974		1	.250	.250	4	1	0	0	0	0.0	0	0	0	0	0	0	0	0	0	0	0	0.0	.000	DH-1
4 yrs.		10	.143	.250	28	4	1	1	0	0.0	2	2	0	5	0	4	0	8	0	0	0	1.1	1.000	OF-6, DH-1

WORLD SERIES

Year	Team	Games	BA	SA	AB	H	2B	3B	HR	HR%	R	RBI	BB	SO	SB	Pinch Hit AB	Pinch Hit H	PO	A	E	DP	TC/G	FA	G by Pos
1972	**OAK A**	4	.300	.300	10	3	0	0	0	0.0	1	1	0	0	0	2	1	6	0	1	0	3.5	.857	OF-2
1973		5	.000	.000	6	0	0	0	0	0.0	0	0	0	3	0	5	0	1	0	0	0	1.0	1.000	OF-1
1974		1	.000	.000	1	0	0	0	0	0.0	0	0	0	1	0	1	0	0	0	0	0	0.0	—	
3 yrs.		10	.176	.176	17	3	0	0	0	0.0	1	1	0	4	0	8	1	7	0	1	0	2.7	.875	OF-3

Pepe Mangual

MANGUAL, JOSE MANUEL BR TR 5′10″ 157 lbs.
Born Jose Manuel Mangual (Guilbe).
Brother of Angel Mangual.
B. May 23, 1952, Ponce, Puerto Rico.

Year	Team	Games	BA	SA	AB	H	2B	3B	HR	HR%	R	RBI	BB	SO	SB	Pinch Hit AB	Pinch Hit H	PO	A	E	DP	TC/G	FA	G by Pos
1972	**MON N**	8	.273	.273	11	3	0	0	0	0.0	2	0	1	5	0	1	0	2	0	0	0	0.7	1.000	OF-3
1973		33	.177	.387	62	11	2	1	3	4.8	9	7	6	18	2	7	1	28	0	1	0	1.3	.966	OF-22
1974		23	.311	.361	61	19	3	0	0	0.0	10	4	5	15	5	2	1	22	0	0	0	1.0	1.000	OF-22
1975		140	.245	.337	514	126	16	2	9	1.8	84	45	74	115	33	6	3	308	8	9	2	2.4	.972	OF-138
1976	**2 teams**	**MON N** (66G –.260) **NY N** (41G –.186)																						
″	**total**	107	.237	.338	317	75	14	3	4	1.3	49	25	60	81	24	4	0	210	5	6	2	2.2	.973	OF-100
1977	**NY N**	8	.143	.143	7	1	0	0	0	0.0	1	2	1	4	0	0	0	5	0	1	0	1.5	.833	OF-4
6 yrs.		319	.242	.340	972	235	35	6	16	1.6	155	83	147	238	64	20	5	575	13	17	4	2.1	.972	OF-289

George Mangus

MANGUS, GEORGE GRAHAM BL TR 5′11½″ 165 lbs.
B. May 22, 1890, Red Creek, N. Y. D. Aug. 10, 1933, Rutland, Mass.

Year	Team	Games	BA	SA	AB	H	2B	3B	HR	HR%	R	RBI	BB	SO	SB	Pinch Hit AB	Pinch Hit H	PO	A	E	DP	TC/G	FA	G by Pos
1912	**PHI N**	10	.200	.320	25	5	3	0	0	0.0	2	3	1	6	0	4	0	9	0	3	0	2.4	.750	OF-5

Clyde Manion

MANION, CLYDE JENNINGS (Pete) BR TR 5′11″ 175 lbs.
B. Oct. 30, 1896, Jefferson City, Mo. D. Sept. 4, 1967, Detroit, Mich.

Year	Team	Games	BA	SA	AB	H	2B	3B	HR	HR%	R	RBI	BB	SO	SB	Pinch Hit AB	Pinch Hit H	PO	A	E	DP	TC/G	FA	G by Pos
1920	**DET A**	32	.275	.350	80	22	4	1	0	0.0	4	8	4	7	0	2	1	83	27	7	3	3.9	.940	C-30
1921		12	.111	.111	18	2	0	0	0	0.0	0	2	2	2	0	6	1	5	3	0	0	2.0	1.000	C-4
1922		42	.275	.362	69	19	4	1	0	0.0	9	12	4	6	0	13	4	61	8	5	0	3.4	.932	C-21, 1B-1
1923		23	.136	.136	22	3	0	0	0	0.0	0	2	2	2	0	17	2	5	1	1	0	1.8	.857	C-3, 1B-1
1924		14	.231	.231	13	3	0	0	0	0.0	1	2	1	1	0	9	3	4	0	1	0	1.3	.800	C-3, 1B-1
1926		75	.199	.222	176	35	4	0	0	0.0	15	14	24	16	1	1	0	227	48	8	2	3.8	.972	C-74
1927		1	—	—	0	0	0	0	0	—	0	0	1	0	0	1	0	0	0	0	0	0.0	—	
1928	**STL A**	76	.226	.280	243	55	5	1	2	0.8	25	31	15	18	3	5	2	302	49	7	10	5.0	.980	C-71
1929		35	.243	.261	111	27	2	0	0	0.0	16	11	15	3	1	1	0	141	22	4	2	4.9	.976	C-34
1930		57	.216	.243	148	32	1	0	1	0.7	12	11	24	17	0	1	0	214	44	4	4	4.7	.985	C-56
1932	**CIN N**	49	.207	.237	135	28	4	0	0	0.0	7	12	14	16	0	1	0	137	23	5	3	3.5	.970	C-47
1933		36	.167	.179	84	14	1	0	0	0.0	3	3	8	7	0	2	0	84	19	2	2	3.1	.981	C-34
1934		25	.185	.185	54	10	0	0	0	0.0	4	4	4	7	0	1	0	57	13	0	2	2.9	1.000	C-24
13 yrs.		477	.217	.252	1153	250	25	3	3	0.3	96	112	118	102	5	60	13	1320	257	44	28	4.0	.973	C-401, 1B-3

Phil Mankowski

MANKOWSKI, PHILLIP ANTHONY BL TR 6′ 180 lbs.
B. Jan. 9, 1953, Buffalo, N. Y.

Year	Team	Games	BA	SA	AB	H	2B	3B	HR	HR%	R	RBI	BB	SO	SB	Pinch Hit AB	Pinch Hit H	PO	A	E	DP	TC/G	FA	G by Pos
1976	**DET A**	24	.271	.353	85	23	2	1	1	1.2	9	4	4	8	0	1	0	20	47	2	8	3.0	.971	3B-23
1977		94	.276	.353	286	79	7	3	3	1.0	21	27	16	41	1	10	3	73	196	10	15	3.2	.964	3B-85, 2B-1
1978		88	.275	.365	222	61	8	0	4	1.8	28	20	22	28	2	9	2	42	129	5	17	2.2	.972	3B-80, DH-1
1979		42	.222	.263	99	22	4	0	0	0.0	11	8	10	16	0	9	1	22	56	3	6	2.2	.963	3B-36, DH-1
1980	**NY N**	8	.167	.250	12	2	1	0	0	0.0	1	1	2	4	0	4	0	0	4	3	0	2.3	.571	3B-3
1982		13	.229	.257	35	8	1	0	0	0.0	2	4	1	6	0	0	0	2	20	1	2	1.8	.957	3B-13
6 yrs.		269	.264	.338	739	195	23	4	8	1.1	72	64	55	103	3	33	6	159	452	24	48	2.6	.962	3B-240, DH-2, 2B-1

Charlie Manlove

MANLOVE, CHARLES HENRY WEEKS (Chick) BR TR 5′ 9″ 165 lbs.
B. Oct. 8, 1862, Philadelphia, Pa. D. Feb. 12, 1952, Altoona, Pa.

Year	Team	Games	BA	SA	AB	H	2B	3B	HR	HR%	R	RBI	BB	SO	SB	Pinch Hit AB	Pinch Hit H	PO	A	E	DP	TC/G	FA	G by Pos
1884	**2 teams**	**ALT U** (2G –.429) **NY N** (3G –.000)																						
″	**total**	5	.176	.176	17	3	0	0	0	0.0	1		0	4		0	0	17	5	4	2	4.3	.846	C-4, OF-2

Ben Mann

MANN, BEN GARTH (Red) BR TR 6′ 155 lbs.
B. Nov. 16, 1915, Brandon, Tex. D. Sept. 11, 1980, Italy, Tex.

Year	Team	Games	BA	SA	AB	H	2B	3B	HR	HR%	R	RBI	BB	SO	SB	Pinch Hit AB	Pinch Hit H	PO	A	E	DP	TC/G	FA	G by Pos
1944	**CHI N**	1	—	—	0	0	0	0	0	—	1	0	0	0	0	0	0	0	0	0	0	0.0	—	

Fred Mann

MANN, FRED J. BL 5′10½″ 178 lbs.
B. Apr. 1, 1858, Sutton, Vt. D. Apr. 16, 1916, Springfield, Mass.

Year	Team	Games	BA	SA	AB	H	2B	3B	HR	HR%	R	RBI	BB	SO	SB	Pinch Hit AB	Pinch Hit H	PO	A	E	DP	TC/G	FA	G by Pos
1882	**2 teams**	**WOR N** (19G –.234) **PHI AA** (29G –.231)																						
″	**total**	48	.232	.333	198	46	12	4	0	0.0	25	0	6	15		0	0	67	68	40	5	3.6	.771	3B-47, 1B-1
1883	**COL AA**	96	.249	.368	394	98	18	13	1	0.3	61		18			0	0	217	29	38	5	2.9	.866	OF-82, 1B-9, 3B-6, SS-1
1884		99	.276	.464	366	101	12	18	7	1.9	70		25			0	0	126	18	23	3	1.7	.862	OF-97, 2B-2
1885	**PIT AA**	99	.253	.327	391	99	17	6	0	0.0	60		31			0	0	159	13	18	2	1.9	.905	OF-97, 3B-3
1886		116	.250	.364	440	110	16	14	2	0.5	85		45			0	0	203	13	30	2	2.1	.878	OF-116
1887	**2 teams**	**CLE AA** (64G –.309) **PHI AA** (55G –.275)																						
″	**total**	119	.293	.418	488	143	29	13	2	0.4	87		38		41	0	0	215	18	27	6	2.2	.896	OF-119
6 yrs.		577	.262	.383	2277	597	104	68	12	0.5	388	0	163	15	41	0	0	987	159	176	23	2.3	.867	OF-511, 3B-56, 1B-10, 2B-2, SS-1

Johnny Mann

MANN, JOHN LEO BR TR 5′11″ 160 lbs.
B. Feb. 4, 1898, Fontanet, Ind. D. Mar. 31, 1977, Terre Haute, Ind.

Year	Team	Games	BA	SA	AB	H	2B	3B	HR	HR%	R	RBI	BB	SO	SB	Pinch Hit AB	Pinch Hit H	PO	A	E	DP	TC/G	FA	G by Pos
1928	**CHI A**	6	.333	.333	6	2	0	0	0	0.0	0	1	1	0	0	6	2	1	2	0	0	1.5	1.000	3B-2

Kelly Mann

MANN, KELLY JOHN BR TR 6′ 3″ 215 lbs.
B. Aug. 17, 1967, Santa Monica, Calif.

Year	Team		Games	BA	SA	AB	H	2B	3B	HR	HR%	R	RBI	BB	SO	SB	Pinch Hit AB	Pinch Hit H	PO	A	E	DP	TC/G	FA	G by Pos
1989	**ATL**	**N**	7	.208	.292	24	5	2	0	0	0.0	1	1	0	6	0	0	0	48	5	0	0	7.6	1.000	C-7
1990			11	.143	.286	28	4	1	0	1	3.6	2	2	0	6	0	1	0	40	3	0	1	4.3	1.000	C-10
2 yrs.			18	.173	.288	52	9	3	0	1	1.9	3	3	0	12	0	1	0	88	8	0	1	5.6	1.000	C-17

Les Mann

MANN, LESLIE BR TR 5′ 9″ 172 lbs.
B. Nov. 18, 1893, Lincoln, Neb. D. Jan. 14, 1962, Pasadena, Calif.

Year	Team		Games	BA	SA	AB	H	2B	3B	HR	HR%	R	RBI	BB	SO	SB	Pinch Hit AB	Pinch Hit H	PO	A	E	DP	TC/G	FA	G by Pos
1913	**BOS**	**N**	120	.253	.369	407	103	24	7	3	0.7	54	51	18	73	7	0	0	250	14	11	2	2.3	.960	OF-120
1914			126	.247	.375	389	96	16	11	4	1.0	44	40	24	50	9	3	0	273	24	15	8	2.5	.952	OF-123
1915	**CHI**	**F**	135	.306	.438	470	144	12	**19**	4	0.9	74	58	36		18	4	2	269	17	9	3	2.3	.969	OF-130, SS-1
1916	**CHI**	**N**	127	.272	.361	415	113	13	9	2	0.5	46	29	19	31	11	9	1	200	9	6	1	1.9	.972	OF-115
1917			117	.273	.367	444	121	19	10	1	0.2	63	44	27	46	14	1	0	203	20	11	2	2.0	.953	OF-116
1918			129	.288	.384	489	141	27	7	2	0.4	69	55	38	45	21	0	0	229	15	10	3	2.0	.961	OF-129
1919	**2 teams**		**CHI N** (80G –.227) **BOS N** (40G –.283)																						
″	**total**		120	.245	.358	444	109	14	12	4	0.9	46	42	20	43	19	1	0	237	19	10	3	2.3	.962	OF-118
1920	**BOS**	**N**	110	.276	.351	424	117	7	8	3	0.7	48	32	38	42	7	3	0	228	13	5	1	2.2	.980	OF-110
1921	**STL**	**N**	97	.328	.512	256	84	12	7	7	2.7	57	30	23	28	5	5	1	174	11	6	2	2.4	.969	OF-79
1922			84	.347	.497	147	51	14	1	2	1.4	42	20	16	12	0	2	0	87	3	2	1	1.6	.978	OF-57
1923	**2 teams**		**STL N** (38G –.371) **CIN N** (8G –.000)																						
″	**total**		46	.367	.633	90	33	5	2	5	5.6	21	11	9	5	0	1	0	44	3	1	0	1.8	.979	OF-26
1924	**BOS**	**N**	32	.275	.422	102	28	7	4	0	0.0	13	10	8	10	1	3	1	59	4	0	0	2.3	1.000	OF-28
1925			60	.342	.478	184	63	11	4	2	1.1	27	20	5	11	6	2	1	116	7	1	1	2.2	.992	OF-57
1926			50	.302	.419	129	39	8	2	1	0.8	23	20	9	9	5	3	0	79	5	3	0	1.9	.966	OF-46
1927	**2 teams**		**BOS N** (29G –.258) **NY N** (29G –.328)																						
″	**total**		58	.293	.421	133	39	7	2	2	1.5	21	16	16	10	4	5	1	65	6	2	1	1.6	.973	OF-46
1928	**NY**	**N**	82	.264	.342	193	51	7	1	2	1.0	29	25	18	9	2	1	0	97	3	5	1	1.5	.952	OF-68
16 yrs.			1493	.282	.398	4716	1332	203	106	44	0.9	677	503	324	424	129	43	7	2610	173	97	29	2.1	.966	OF-1368, SS-1
WORLD SERIES																									
1914	**BOS**	**N**	3	.286	.286	7	2	0	0	0	0.0	1	1	0	1	0	1	0	1	0	0	0	0.5	1.000	OF-2
1918	**CHI**	**N**	6	.227	.318	22	5	2	0	0	0.0	0	2	0	0	0	0	0	7	0	0	0	1.2	1.000	OF-6
2 yrs.			9	.241	.310	29	7	2	0	0	0.0	1	3	0	1	0	1	0	8	0	0	0	1.0	1.000	OF-8

Jack Manning

MANNING, JOHN E. BR TR 5′ 8½″ 158 lbs.
B. Dec. 20, 1853, Braintree, Mass. D. Aug. 15, 1929, Boston, Mass.
Manager 1877.

Year	Team		Games	BA	SA	AB	H	2B	3B	HR	HR%	R	RBI	BB	SO	SB	Pinch Hit AB	Pinch Hit H	PO	A	E	DP	TC/G	FA	G by Pos
1876	**BOS**	**N**	70	.264	.330	288	76	13	0	2	0.7	52	25	7	5		0	0	85	37	26	3	1.6	.824	OF-56, P-34, SS-1, 2B-1
1877	**CIN**	**N**	57	.317	.437	252	80	16	7	0	0.0	47	36	5	6		0	0	233	84	51	8	5.5	.861	SS-26, 1B-17, OF-12, P-10, 2B-2
1878	**BOS**	**N**	60	.254	.302	248	63	10	1	0	0.0	41	23	10	16		0	0	61	12	23	1	1.5	.760	OF-59, P-3
1880	**CIN**	**N**	48	.216	.311	190	41	6	3	2	1.1	20	17	7	15		0	0	64	12	20	1	2.0	.792	OF-47, 1B-1
1881	**BUF**	**N**	1	.000	.000	1	0	0	0	0	0.0	0	0	0	0		0	0	0	1	0	0	1.0	1.000	OF-1
1883	**PHI**	**N**	98	.267	.364	420	112	31	5	0	0.0	60		20	37		0	0	155	37	33	5	2.3	.853	OF-98
1884			104	.271	.394	424	115	29	4	5	1.2	71		40	67		0	0	140	26	30	7	1.9	.847	OF-104
1885			107	.256	.348	445	114	24	4	3	0.7	61		37	27		0	0	134	21	18	3	1.6	.896	OF-107
1886	**BAL**	**AA**	137	.223	.286	556	124	18	7	1	0.2	78		50			0	0	165	16	23	3	1.5	.887	OF-137
9 yrs.			682	.257	.345	2824	725	147	31	13	0.5	430	101	176	173		0	0	1037	246	224	31	2.1	.851	OF-621, P-47, SS-27, 1B-18, 2B-3

Jimmy Manning

MANNING, JAMES H. BB TR 5′ 7″ 157 lbs.
B. Jan. 31, 1862, Fall River, Mass. D. Oct. 22, 1929, Edinburg, Tex.
Manager 1901.

Year	Team		Games	BA	SA	AB	H	2B	3B	HR	HR%	R	RBI	BB	SO	SB	Pinch Hit AB	Pinch Hit H	PO	A	E	DP	TC/G	FA	G by Pos
1884	**BOS**	**N**	89	.241	.316	345	83	8	6	2	0.6	52		19	47		0	0	139	61	29	7	2.4	.873	OF-73, SS-9, 2B-9, 3B-3
1885	**2 teams**		**BOS N** (84G –.206) **DET N** (20G –.269)																						
″	**total**		104	.219	.320	384	84	12	9	3	0.8	49	36	23	46		0	0	184	75	40	10	2.9	.866	OF-83, SS-21
1886	**DET**	**N**	26	.186	.268	97	18	2	3	0	0.0	14	7	6	10		0	0	32	5	2	1	1.4	.949	OF-26, SS-1
1887			13	.192	.212	52	10	1	0	0	0.0	5	3	5	4	3	0	0	16	7	8	0	2.4	.742	OF-10, SS-3
1889	**KC**	**AA**	132	.204	.281	506	103	16	7	3	0.6	68	68	54	61	58	0	0	238	206	44	25	3.6	.910	OF-69, 2B-63, 3B-1, SS-1
5 yrs.			364	.215	.297	1384	298	39	25	8	0.6	188	114	107	168	61	0	0	609	354	123	43	2.9	.887	OF-261, 2B-72, SS-35, 3B-4

Rick Manning

MANNING, RICHARD EUGENE BL TR 6′ 1″ 180 lbs.
B. Sept. 2, 1954, Niagara Falls, N. Y.

Year	Team		Games	BA	SA	AB	H	2B	3B	HR	HR%	R	RBI	BB	SO	SB	Pinch Hit AB	Pinch Hit H	PO	A	E	DP	TC/G	FA	G by Pos
1975	**CLE**	**A**	120	.285	.358	480	137	16	5	3	0.6	69	35	44	62	19	1	0	331	12	9	2	3.0	.974	OF-118, DH-1
1976			138	.292	.393	552	161	24	7	6	1.1	73	43	41	75	16	2	1	359	8	5	1	2.7	.987	OF-136
1977			68	.226	.337	252	57	7	3	5	2.0	33	18	21	35	9	0	0	191	2	2	0	2.9	.990	OF-68
1978			148	.263	.337	566	149	27	3	3	0.5	65	50	38	62	12	7	2	377	7	2	1	2.7	.995	OF-144
1979			144	.259	.304	560	145	12	2	3	0.5	67	51	55	48	30	3	1	417	9	6	2	3.0	.986	OF-141, DH-1
1980			140	.234	.306	471	110	17	4	3	0.6	55	52	63	66	12	0	0	379	7	4	1	2.8	.990	OF-139
1981			103	.244	.336	360	88	15	3	4	1.1	47	33	40	57	25	0	0	305	6	4	3	3.1	.987	OF-103
1982			152	.270	.352	562	152	18	2	8	1.4	71	44	54	60	12	0	0	387	10	9	1	2.7	.978	OF-152
1983	**2 teams**		**CLE A** (50G –.278) **MIL A** (108G –.229)																						
″	**total**		158	.246	.316	569	140	20	4	4	0.7	60	43	38	62	18	0	0	471	2	5	0	3.0	.990	OF-158
1984	**MIL**	**A**	119	.249	.370	341	85	10	5	7	2.1	53	31	34	32	5	11	3	231	2	3	2	2.1	.987	OF-114, DH-1
1985			79	.218	.296	216	47	9	1	2	0.9	19	18	14	19	1	9	0	160	2	4	0	2.2	.976	OF-74, DH-2
1986			89	.254	.434	205	52	7	3	8	3.9	31	27	17	20	5	2	0	155	3	2	0	1.8	.988	OF-83, DH-5
1987			97	.228	.307	114	26	7	1	0	0.0	21	13	12	18	4	16	6	68	1	3	0	0.9	.958	OF-78, DH-2
13 yrs.			1555	.257	.341	5248	1349	189	43	56	1.1	664	458	471	616	168	51	13	3831	71	58	13	2.6	.985	OF-1508, DH-12

Tim Manning

MANNING, TIMOTHY EDWARD BR TR 5′10″ 170 lbs.
B. Dec. 3, 1853, Henley-On-Thames, England D. June 11, 1934, Oak Park, Ill.

Year	Team		Games	BA	SA	AB	H	2B	3B	HR	HR%	R	RBI	BB	SO	SB	Pinch Hit AB	Pinch Hit H	PO	A	E	DP	TC/G	FA	G by Pos
1882	**PRO**	**N**	21	.105	.105	76	8	0	0	0	0.0	7		5	13		0	0	32	42	20	3	4.5	.787	SS-17, C-4
1883	**BAL**	**AA**	35	.215	.256	121	26	5	0	0	0.0	23		14			0	0	105	106	20	8	6.6	.913	2B-35

Tim Manning *continued*

Year	Team	Games	BA	SA	AB	H	2B	3B	HR	HR%	R	RBI	BB	SO	SB	Pinch Hit AB	Pinch Hit H	PO	A	E	DP	TC/G	FA	G by Pos
1884		91	.205	.293	341	70	14	5	2	0.6	49		26			0	0	228	277	52	28	6.1	.907	2B-91
1885	2 teams	BAL AA (43G –.204) PRO N (10G –.057)																						
″	total	53	.177	.234	192	34	9	1	0	0.0	20	0	11	11		0	0	139	159	29	21	6.1	.911	2B-41, SS-10, 3B-3
4 yrs.		200	.189	.252	730	138	28	6	2	0.3	99	0	56	24		0	0	504	584	121	60	6.0	.900	2B-167, SS-27, C-4, 3B-3

Don Manno

MANNO, DONALD D. BR TR 6′ 1″ 190 lbs.
B. May 15, 1915, Williamsport, Pa.

Year	Team	Games	BA	SA	AB	H	2B	3B	HR	HR%	R	RBI	BB	SO	SB	Pinch Hit AB	Pinch Hit H	PO	A	E	DP	TC/G	FA	G by Pos
1940	BOS N	3	.286	.714	7	2	0	0	1	14.3	1	4	0	2	0	1	0	5	0	0	0	2.5	1.000	OF-2
1941		22	.167	.200	30	5	1	0	0	0.0	2	4	3	7	0	13	2	13	0	0	0	1.4	1.000	OF-5, 3B-3, 1B-1
2 yrs.		25	.189	.297	37	7	1	0	1	2.7	3	8	3	9	0	14	2	18	0	0	0	1.6	1.000	OF-7, 3B-3, 1B-1

Fred Manrique

MANRIQUE, FRED ELOY BR TR 6′ 1″ 175 lbs.
Born Fred Eloy Manrique (Reyes).
B. Nov. 5, 1961, Edo Bolivar, Venezuela.

Year	Team	Games	BA	SA	AB	H	2B	3B	HR	HR%	R	RBI	BB	SO	SB	Pinch Hit AB	Pinch Hit H	PO	A	E	DP	TC/G	FA	G by Pos
1981	TOR A	14	.143	.143	28	4	0	0	0	0.0	1	1	0	12	0	2	1	10	27	3	7	2.9	.925	SS-11, 3B-2, DH-1
1984		10	.333	.333	9	3	0	0	0	0.0	0	1	0	1	0	1	0	5	10	1	3	1.6	.938	2B-9, DH-1
1985	MON N	9	.308	.769	13	4	1	1	1	7.7	5	1	1	3	0	4	2	5	10	0	1	3.0	1.000	2B-2, SS-2, 3B-1
1986	STL N	13	.176	.353	17	3	0	0	1	5.9	2	1	1	1	1	7	1	1	3	0	0	0.8	1.000	3B-4, 2B-1
1987	CHI A	115	.258	.362	298	77	13	3	4	1.3	30	29	19	69	5	1	0	176	286	7	64	4.1	.985	2B-92, SS-23
1988		140	.235	.342	345	81	10	6	5	1.4	43	37	21	54	6	5	1	241	343	13	83	4.2	.978	2B-129, SS-12
1989	2 teams	CHI A (65G –.299) TEX A (54G –.288)																						
″	total	119	.294	.397	378	111	25	1	4	1.1	46	52	17	63	4	8	3	177	250	21	61	3.7	.953	2B-74, SS-39, 3B-7, DH-1
1990	MIN A	69	.237	.346	228	54	10	0	5	2.2	22	29	4	35	2	5	1	104	155	7	40	3.9	.974	2B-67, DH-1
1991	OAK A	9	.143	.143	21	3	0	0	0	0.0	2	0	2	1	0	0	0	10	20	1	3	3.4	.968	SS-7, 2B-2
9 yrs.		498	.254	.360	1337	340	59	11	20	1.5	151	151	65	239	18	33	9	729	1104	53	262	3.9	.972	2B-376, SS-94, 3B-14, DH-4

John Mansell

MANSELL, JOHN BL 5′10″ 168 lbs.
Brother of Tom Mansell. Brother of Mike Mansell.
B. 1861, Auburn, N. Y. D. Feb. 20, 1925, Willard, N. Y.

Year	Team	Games	BA	SA	AB	H	2B	3B	HR	HR%	R	RBI	BB	SO	SB	Pinch Hit AB	Pinch Hit H	PO	A	E	DP	TC/G	FA	G by Pos
1882	PHI AA	31	.238	.278	126	30	3	1	0	0.0	17		4			0	0	49	4	14	0	2.2	.791	OF-31

Mike Mansell

MANSELL, MICHAEL R. BL 5′11″ 175 lbs.
Brother of Tom Mansell. Brother of John Mansell.
B. Jan. 15, 1858, Auburn, N. Y. D. Dec. 4, 1902, Auburn, N. Y.

Year	Team	Games	BA	SA	AB	H	2B	3B	HR	HR%	R	RBI	BB	SO	SB	Pinch Hit AB	Pinch Hit H	PO	A	E	DP	TC/G	FA	G by Pos
1879	SYR N	67	.215	.260	242	52	4	2	1	0.4	24	13	5	45		0	0	204	11	29	2	3.6	.881	OF-67
1880	CIN N	53	.193	.278	187	36	6	2	2	1.1	22	12	4	37		0	0	147	13	25	5	3.5	.865	OF-53
1882	PIT AA	79	.277	.438	347	96	**18**	**16**	2	0.6	59		7			0	0	159	16	36	1	2.7	.829	OF-79
1883		96	.257	.371	412	106	12	13	3	0.7	90		25			0	0	186	11	26	1	2.3	.883	OF-96
1884	3 teams	PIT AA (27G –.140) PHI AA (20G –.200) RIC AA (29G –.301)																						
″	total	76	.219	.304	283	62	3	9	1	0.4	42		20			0	0	92	10	29	2	1.7	.779	OF-76, 1B-1
5 yrs.		371	.239	.344	1471	352	43	42	9	0.6	237	25	61	82		0	0	788	61	145	11	2.7	.854	OF-371, 1B-1

Tom Mansell

MANSELL, THOMAS E. BL TR 5′ 8″ 160 lbs.
Brother of Mike Mansell. Brother of John Mansell.
B. Jan. 1, 1855, Auburn, N. Y. D. Oct. 6, 1934, Auburn, N. Y.

Year	Team	Games	BA	SA	AB	H	2B	3B	HR	HR%	R	RBI	BB	SO	SB	Pinch Hit AB	Pinch Hit H	PO	A	E	DP	TC/G	FA	G by Pos
1879	2 teams	TRO N (40G –.243) SYR N (1G –.250)																						
″	total	41	.243	.276	181	44	6	0	0	0.0	29	11	3	9		0	0	65	3	23	1	2.2	.747	OF-41
1883	2 teams	DET N (34G –.221) STL AA (28G –.402)																						
″	total	62	.305	.370	243	74	12	2	0	0.0	45		15	13		0	0	68	13	25	1	1.7	.764	OF-62, P-1
1884	2 teams	CIN AA (65G –.248) COL AA (23G –.195)																						
″	total	88	.236	.303	343	81	5	9	0	0.0	58		21			0	0	99	6	37	0	1.6	.739	OF-87, 3B-1
3 yrs.		191	.259	.318	767	199	23	11	0	0.0	132	11	39	22		0	0	232	22	85	2	1.8	.749	OF-190, 3B-1, P-1

Felix Mantilla

MANTILLA, FELIX BR TR 6′ 160 lbs.
Born Felix Mantilla (Lamela).
B. July 29, 1934, Isabela, Puerto Rico.

Year	Team	Games	BA	SA	AB	H	2B	3B	HR	HR%	R	RBI	BB	SO	SB	Pinch Hit AB	Pinch Hit H	PO	A	E	DP	TC/G	FA	G by Pos
1956	MIL N	35	.283	.340	53	15	1	1	0	0.0	9	3	1	8	0	5	2	21	45	1	8	3.7	.985	SS-15, 3B-3
1957		71	.236	.363	182	43	9	1	4	2.2	28	21	14	34	2	7	0	87	136	12	28	4.2	.949	SS-35, 2B-13, 3B-7, OF-1
1958		85	.221	.345	226	50	5	1	7	3.1	37	19	20	20	2	7	1	122	61	4	15	2.6	.979	OF-43, 2B-21, SS-5, 3B-2
1959		103	.215	.271	251	54	5	0	3	1.2	26	19	16	31	6	4	0	136	211	17	40	3.7	.953	2B-60, SS-23, 3B-9, OF-7
1960		63	.257	.365	148	38	7	0	3	2.0	21	11	7	16	3	7	2	80	85	9	15	2.9	.948	2B-26, SS-25, OF-8
1961		45	.215	.280	93	20	3	0	1	1.1	13	5	10	16	1	5	0	47	48	3	7	2.2	.969	SS-19, 2B-10, OF-10, 3B-6
1962	NY N	141	.275	.399	466	128	17	4	11	2.4	54	59	37	51	3	17	3	139	251	20	36	3.1	.951	3B-95, SS-25, 2B-14
1963	BOS A	66	.315	.461	178	56	8	0	6	3.4	27	15	20	14	2	16	2	83	74	4	19	3.7	.975	SS-27, OF-11, 2B-5
1964		133	.289	.553	425	123	20	1	30	7.1	69	64	41	46	0	25	6	173	146	5	29	3.1	.985	OF-48, 2B-45, 3B-7, SS-6
1965		150	.275	.416	534	147	17	2	18	3.4	60	92	79	84	7	1	1	296	288	16	64	3.9	.973	2B-123, OF-27, 1B-2
1966	HOU N	77	.219	.371	151	33	5	0	6	4.0	16	22	11	32	1	38	10	124	46	4	11	4.6	.977	1B-14, 3B-14, 2B-9, OF-1
11 yrs.		969	.261	.403	2707	707	97	10	89	3.3	360	330	256	352	27	132	27	1308	1391	95	272	3.4	.966	2B-326, SS-180, OF-156, 3B-143, 1B-16
WORLD SERIES																								
1957	MIL N	4	.000	.000	10	0	0	0	0	0.0	1	0	1	0	0	0	0	6	8	0	1	4.7	1.000	2B-3
1958		4	—	—	0	0	0	0	0	—	1	0	0	0	0	0	0	0	0	0	0	0.0	.000	SS-1
2 yrs.		8	.000	.000	10	0	0	0	0	0.0	2	0	1	0	0	0	0	6	8	0	1	3.5	1.000	2B-3, SS-1

Mickey Mantle

MANTLE, MICKEY CHARLES (The Commerce Comet) BB TR 5′11½″ 195 lbs.
B. Oct. 20, 1931, Spavinaw, Okla. D. Aug. 13, 1995, Dallas, Tex.
Hall of Fame 1974.

Year	Team	Games	BA	SA	AB	H	2B	3B	HR	HR%	R	RBI	BB	SO	SB	Pinch Hit AB	Pinch Hit H	PO	A	E	DP	TC/G	FA	G by Pos
1951	NY A	96	.267	.443	341	91	11	5	13	3.8	61	65	43	74	8	8	1	135	4	6	1	1.7	.959	OF-86
1952		142	.311	.530	549	171	37	7	23	4.2	94	87	75	**111**	4	1	0	348	16	14	5	2.7	.963	OF-141, 3B-1
1953		127	.295	.497	461	136	24	3	21	4.6	105	92	79	90	8	8	4	322	10	6	2	2.8	.982	OF-121, SS-1
1954		146	.300	.525	543	163	17	12	27	5.0	**129**	102	102	**107**	5	1	0	334	25	9	6	2.5	.976	OF-144, SS-4, 2B-1
1955		147	.306	**.611**	517	158	25	**11**	**37**	7.2	121	99	**113**	97	8	3	1	376	11	2	2	2.6	.995	OF-145, SS-2

Mickey Mantle *continued*

Year	Team	Games	BA	SA	AB	H	2B	3B	HR	HR%	R	RBI	BB	SO	SB	Pinch Hit AB	Pinch Hit H	PO	A	E	DP	TC/G	FA	G by Pos
1956		150	**.353**	**.705**	533	188	22	5	**52**	**9.8**	**132**	**130**	112	99	10	4	1	370	10	4	3	2.7	.990	OF-144
1957		144	.365	.665	474	173	28	6	34	7.2	**121**	94	**146**	75	16	4	1	324	6	7	1	2.4	.979	OF-139
1958		150	.304	.592	519	158	21	1	**42**	8.1	**127**	97	**129**	**120**	18	0	0	331	5	8	2	2.3	.977	OF-150
1959		144	.285	.514	541	154	23	4	31	5.7	104	75	94	**126**	21	0	0	366	7	2	3	2.6	.995	OF-143
1960		153	.275	.558	527	145	17	6	**40**	7.6	**119**	94	111	**125**	14	2	0	326	9	3	1	2.3	.991	OF-150
1961		153	.317	**.687**	514	163	16	6	54	**10.5**	**132**	128	**126**	112	12	2	0	351	6	6	0	2.4	.983	OF-150
1962		123	.321	**.605**	377	121	15	1	30	8.0	96	89	**122**	78	9	6	1	214	4	5	1	1.9	.978	OF-117
1963		65	.314	.622	172	54	8	0	15	8.7	40	35	40	32	2	10	3	99	2	1	0	2.0	.990	OF-52
1964		143	.303	.591	465	141	25	2	35	7.5	92	111	99	102	6	11	2	217	3	5	1	1.7	.978	OF-132
1965		122	.255	.452	361	92	12	1	19	5.3	44	46	73	76	4	14	0	165	3	6	0	1.6	.966	OF-108
1966		108	.288	.538	333	96	12	1	23	6.9	40	56	57	76	1	11	2	172	2	0	0	1.8	1.000	OF-97
1967		144	.245	.434	440	108	17	0	22	5.0	63	55	107	113	1	12	5	1089	91	8	82	9.1	.993	1B-131
1968		144	.237	.398	435	103	14	1	18	4.1	57	54	106	97	6	9	4	1195	76	15	91	9.8	.988	1B-131
18 yrs.		2401	.298	.557	8102	2415	344	72	536	6.6	1677	1509	1734	1710	153	106	25	6734	290	107	201	3.1	.985	OF-2019, 1B-262, SS-7, 2B-1, 3B-1
									8th	**6th**			**5th**	**9th**										
WORLD SERIES																								
1951	**NY A**	2	.200	.200	5	1	0	0	0	0.0	1	0	2	1	0	0	0	4	0	0	0	2.0	1.000	OF-2
1952		7	.345	.655	29	10	1	1	2	6.9	5	3	3	4	0	0	0	16	0	0	0	2.3	1.000	OF-7
1953		6	.208	.458	24	5	0	0	2	8.3	3	7	3	8	0	0	0	14	0	0	0	2.3	1.000	OF-6
1955		3	.200	.500	10	2	0	0	1	10.0	1	1	0	2	0	1	0	4	0	0	0	2.0	1.000	OF-2
1956		7	.250	.667	24	6	1	0	3	12.5	6	4	6	5	1	0	0	18	1	0	0	2.7	1.000	OF-7
1957		6	.263	.421	19	5	0	0	1	5.3	3	2	3	1	0	0	0	8	0	1	0	1.8	.889	OF-5
1958		7	.250	.583	24	6	0	1	2	8.3	4	3	7	4	0	0	0	16	0	0	0	2.3	1.000	OF-7
1960		7	.400	.800	25	10	1	0	3	12.0	8	11	8	9	0	0	0	15	0	0	0	2.1	1.000	OF-7
1961		2	.167	.167	6	1	0	0	0	0.0	0	0	0	2	0	0	0	2	0	0	0	1.0	1.000	OF-2
1962		7	.120	.160	25	3	1	0	0	0.0	2	0	4	5	2	0	0	11	0	0	0	1.6	1.000	OF-7
1963		4	.133	.333	15	2	0	0	1	6.7	1	1	1	5	0	0	0	6	0	0	0	1.5	1.000	OF-4
1964		7	.333	.792	24	8	2	0	3	12.5	8	8	6	8	0	0	0	13	0	2	0	2.1	.867	OF-7
12 yrs.		65	.257	.535	230	59	6	2	18	7.8	42	40	43	54	3	1	0	127	1	3	0	2.1	.977	OF-63
		2nd			**2nd**	**2nd**			**1st**	**10th**	**1st**	**1st**	**1st**	**1st**										

Jeff Manto

MANTO, JEFFREY PAUL BR TR 6′ 3″ 210 lbs.
B. Aug. 23, 1964, Bristol, Pa.

Year	Team	Games	BA	SA	AB	H	2B	3B	HR	HR%	R	RBI	BB	SO	SB	Pinch Hit AB	Pinch Hit H	PO	A	E	DP	TC/G	FA	G by Pos
1990	**CLE A**	30	.224	.395	76	17	5	1	2	2.6	12	14	21	18	0	1	0	185	24	2	18	7.0	.991	1B-25, 3B-5
1991		47	.211	.313	128	27	7	0	2	1.6	15	13	14	22	2	0	0	109	63	8	17	3.5	.956	3B-32, 1B-14, C-5, OF-1
1993	**PHI N**	8	.056	.056	18	1	0	0	0	0.0	0	0	0	3	0	1	0	2	8	0	0	1.4	1.000	3B-6, SS-1
1995	**BAL A**	89	.256	.492	254	65	9	0	17	6.7	31	38	24	69	0	12	5	68	102	6	16	2.0	.966	3B-69, DH-13, 1B-4
4 yrs.		174	.231	.412	476	110	21	1	21	4.4	58	65	59	112	2	14	5	364	197	16	51	3.3	.972	3B-112, 1B-43, DH-13, C-5, SS-1, OF-1

Chuck Manuel

MANUEL, CHARLES FUQUA BL TR 6′ 4″ 195 lbs.
B. Jan. 4, 1944, Northfork, W. Va.

Year	Team	Games	BA	SA	AB	H	2B	3B	HR	HR%	R	RBI	BB	SO	SB	Pinch Hit AB	Pinch Hit H	PO	A	E	DP	TC/G	FA	G by Pos
1969	**MIN A**	83	.207	.280	164	34	6	0	2	1.2	14	24	28	33	1	37	3	57	2	2	0	1.3	.967	OF-46
1970		59	.188	.234	64	12	0	0	1	1.6	4	7	6	17	0	43	9	7	0	0	0	0.6	1.000	OF-11
1971		18	.125	.188	16	2	1	0	0	0.0	1	1	1	8	0	16	2	0	0	0	0	0.0	.000	OF-1
1972		63	.205	.270	122	25	5	0	1	0.8	6	8	4	16	0	33	7	39	4	1	0	1.6	.977	OF-28
1974	**LA N**	4	.333	.333	3	1	0	0	0	0.0	0	1	1	0	0	3	1	0	0	0	0	0.0	—	
1975		15	.133	.133	15	2	0	0	0	0.0	0	2	0	3	0	15	2	0	0	0	0	0.0	—	
6 yrs.		242	.198	.260	384	76	12	0	4	1.0	25	43	40	77	1	147	24	103	6	3	0	1.3	.973	OF-86
LEAGUE CHAMPIONSHIP SERIES																								
1969	**MIN A**	1	—	—	0	0	0	0	0	—	0	0	1	0	0	0	0	0	0	0	0	0.0	—	
1970		1	.000	.000	1	0	0	0	0	0.0	0	0	0	1	0	1	0	0	0	0	0	0.0	—	
2 yrs.		2	.000	.000	1	0	0	0	0	0.0	0	0	1	1	0	1	0							

Jerry Manuel

MANUEL, JERRY BB TR 6′ 158 lbs.
B. Dec. 23, 1953, Hahira, Ga. BR 1981–1982

Year	Team	Games	BA	SA	AB	H	2B	3B	HR	HR%	R	RBI	BB	SO	SB	Pinch Hit AB	Pinch Hit H	PO	A	E	DP	TC/G	FA	G by Pos
1975	**DET A**	6	.056	.056	18	1	0	0	0	0.0	0	0	0	4	0	0	0	11	23	2	4	6.0	.944	2B-6
1976		54	.140	.163	43	6	1	0	0	0.0	4	2	3	9	1	0	0	40	64	8	8	2.2	.929	2B-47, SS-4, DH-1
1980	**MON N**	7	.000	.000	6	0	0	0	0	0.0	0	0	0	2	0	0	0	5	11	1	0	2.4	.941	SS-7
1981		27	.200	.455	55	11	5	0	3	5.5	10	10	6	11	0	0	0	37	41	1	10	3.2	.987	2B-23, SS-2
1982	**SD N**	2	.200	.600	5	1	0	1	0	0.0	0	1	1	0	0	0	0	1	1	0	1	0.7	1.000	2B-1, 3B-1, SS-1
5 yrs.		96	.150	.283	127	19	6	1	3	2.4	14	13	10	26	1	0	0	94	140	12	23	2.6	.951	2B-77, SS-14, 3B-1, DH-1
DIVISIONAL PLAYOFF SERIES																								
1981	**MON N**	5	.071	.071	14	1	0	0	0	0.0	0	0	2	5	0	0	0	13	19	3	0	7.0	.914	2B-5
LEAGUE CHAMPIONSHIP SERIES																								
1981	**MON N**	1	—	—	0	0	0	0	0	—	0	0	0	0	0	0	0	0	0	0	0	0.0	—	

Frank Manush

MANUSH, FRANK BENJAMIN BR TR 5′10½″ 175 lbs.
Brother of Heinie Manush.
B. Sept. 18, 1883, Tuscumbia, Ala. D. Jan. 5, 1965, Laguna Beach, Calif.

Year	Team	Games	BA	SA	AB	H	2B	3B	HR	HR%	R	RBI	BB	SO	SB	Pinch Hit AB	Pinch Hit H	PO	A	E	DP	TC/G	FA	G by Pos
1908	**PHI A**	23	.156	.208	77	12	2	1	0	0.0	6	0	2		2	1	0	28	29	6	3	2.9	.905	3B-20, 2B-2

Heinie Manush

MANUSH, HENRY EMMETT BL TL 6′ 1″ 200 lbs.
Brother of Frank Manush.
B. July 20, 1901, Tuscumbia, Ala. D. May 12, 1971, Sarasota, Fla.
Hall of Fame 1964.

Year	Team	Games	BA	SA	AB	H	2B	3B	HR	HR%	R	RBI	BB	SO	SB	Pinch Hit AB	Pinch Hit H	PO	A	E	DP	TC/G	FA	G by Pos
1923	**DET A**	109	.334	.471	308	103	20	5	4	1.3	59	54	20	21	3	27	6	158	6	8	0	2.2	.953	OF-79
1924		120	.289	.448	422	122	24	8	9	2.1	83	68	27	30	14	11	1	225	4	5	1	2.2	.979	OF-106, 1B-1
1925		99	.303	.430	277	84	14	3	5	1.8	46	47	24	21	8	22	6	153	7	3	0	2.2	.982	OF-73
1926		136	**.378**	.564	498	188	35	8	14	2.8	95	86	31	28	11	14	5	283	7	10	3	2.5	.967	OF-120
1927		152	.298	.442	593	177	31	18	6	1.0	102	80	47	29	12	1	1	361	9	11	3	2.5	.971	OF-150

Heinie Manush *continued*

Year	Team	Games	BA	SA	AB	H	2B	3B	HR	HR%	R	RBI	BB	SO	SB	Pinch Hit AB	Pinch Hit H	PO	A	E	DP	TC/G	FA	G by Pos
1928	**STL A**	154	.378	.575	638	**241**	**47**	20	13	2.0	104	108	39	14	17	0	0	355	6	3	2	2.4	.992	OF-154
1929		142	.355	.500	574	204	**45**	10	6	1.0	85	81	43	24	9	1	0	293	11	4	3	2.2	.987	OF-141
1930	**2 teams**	**STL A** (49G –.328)	**WAS A** (88G –.362)																					
"	**total**	137	.350	.531	554	194	49	12	9	1.6	100	94	31	24	7	3	0	255	10	3	0	2.0	.989	OF-134
1931	**WAS A**	146	.307	.438	616	189	41	11	6	1.0	110	70	36	27	3	3	0	245	5	6	1	1.8	.977	OF-143
1932		149	.342	.520	625	214	41	14	14	2.2	121	116	36	29	7	3	1	318	6	4	3	2.2	.988	OF-146
1933		153	.336	.459	658	**221**	32	**17**	5	0.8	115	95	36	18	6	3	2	325	10	6	1	2.3	.982	OF-150
1934		137	.349	.523	556	194	42	11	11	2.0	88	89	36	23	7	7	1	293	5	6	2	2.3	.980	OF-131
1935		119	.273	.390	479	131	26	9	4	0.8	68	56	35	17	2	7	1	251	8	4	5	2.4	.985	OF-111
1936	**BOS A**	82	.291	.371	313	91	15	5	0	0.0	43	45	17	11	1	9	4	110	3	4	1	1.6	.966	OF-72
1937	**BKN N**	132	.333	.442	466	155	25	7	4	0.9	57	73	40	24	6	9	3	187	7	6	1	1.6	.970	OF-123
1938	**2 teams**	**BKN N** (17G –.235)	**PIT N** (15G –.308)																					
"	**total**	32	.250	.375	64	16	4	2	0	0.0	11	10	7	4	1	18	5	29	1	0	0	2.5	1.000	OF-12
1939	**PIT N**	10	.000	.000	12	0	0	0	0	0.0	0	1	1	1	0	8	0	1	0	0	0	1.0	1.000	OF-1
17 yrs.		2009	.330	.479	7653	2524	491	160	110	1.4	1287	1173	506	345	114	146	36	3842	105	83	26	2.2	.979	OF-1846, 1B-1
WORLD SERIES																								
1933	**WAS A**	5	.111	.111	18	2	0	0	0	0.0	2	0	2	1	0	0	0	10	0	0	0	2.0	1.000	OF-5

Kirt Manwaring

MANWARING, KIRT DEAN
B. July 15, 1965, Elmira, N. Y.
BR TR 5′11″ 185 lbs.

Year	Team	Games	BA	SA	AB	H	2B	3B	HR	HR%	R	RBI	BB	SO	SB	Pinch Hit AB	Pinch Hit H	PO	A	E	DP	TC/G	FA	G by Pos
1987	**SF N**	6	.143	.143	7	1	0	0	0	0.0	0	0	0	1	0	0	0	9	1	1	0	1.8	.909	C-6
1988		40	.250	.336	116	29	7	0	1	0.9	12	15	2	21	0	0	0	162	24	4	2	4.8	.979	C-40
1989		85	.210	.250	200	42	4	2	0	0.0	14	18	11	28	2	9	2	289	32	6	3	4.0	.982	C-81
1990		8	.154	.308	13	2	0	1	0	0.0	0	1	0	3	0	0	0	22	3	0	1	3.1	1.000	C-8
1991		67	.225	.275	178	40	9	0	0	0.0	16	19	9	22	1	1	1	315	28	4	7	5.2	.988	C-67
1992		109	.244	.335	349	85	10	5	4	1.1	24	26	29	42	2	2	1	564	68	4	12	5.9	.994	C-108
1993		130	.275	.350	432	119	15	1	5	1.2	48	49	41	76	1	0	0	739	70	2	12	6.2	.998	C-130
1994		97	.250	.320	316	79	17	1	1	0.3	30	29	25	50	1	0	0	540	53	4	4	6.2	.993	C-97
1995		118	.251	.332	379	95	15	2	4	1.1	21	36	27	72	1	1	0	607	55	7	5	5.7	.990	C-118
9 yrs.		660	.247	.321	1990	492	77	12	15	0.8	165	193	144	315	8	13	4	3247	334	32	46	5.5	.991	C-655
LEAGUE CHAMPIONSHIP SERIES																								
1989	**SF N**	3	.000	.000	2	0	0	0	0	0.0	0	0	0	0	0	1	0	5	0	0	0	1.7	1.000	C-3
WORLD SERIES																								
1989	**SF N**	1	1.000	2.000	1	1	1	0	0	0.0	1	0	0	0	0	0	0	0	0	0	0	0.0	.000	C-1

Cliff Mapes

MAPES, CLIFFORD FRANKLIN (Tiger)
B. Mar. 13, 1922, Sutherland, Neb.
BL TR 6′ 3″ 205 lbs.

Year	Team	Games	BA	SA	AB	H	2B	3B	HR	HR%	R	RBI	BB	SO	SB	Pinch Hit AB	Pinch Hit H	PO	A	E	DP	TC/G	FA	G by Pos
1948	**NY A**	53	.250	.432	88	22	11	1	1	1.1	19	12	6	13	1	26	4	42	4	2	1	2.3	.958	OF-21
1949		111	.247	.378	304	75	13	3	7	2.3	56	38	58	50	6	4	0	228	14	6	4	2.3	.976	OF-108
1950		108	.247	.421	356	88	14	6	12	3.4	60	61	47	61	1	6	2	183	8	10	4	2.0	.950	OF-102
1951	**2 teams**	**NY A** (45G –.216)	**STL A** (56G –.274)																					
"	**total**	101	.262	.433	252	66	10	3	9	3.6	38	38	30	47	0	13	5	136	4	2	1	1.6	.986	OF-87
1952	**DET A**	86	.197	.373	193	38	7	0	9	4.7	26	23	27	42	0	23	6	86	3	3	1	1.5	.967	OF-62
5 yrs.		459	.242	.406	1193	289	55	13	38	3.2	199	172	168	213	8	72	17	675	33	23	11	1.9	.969	OF-380
WORLD SERIES																								
1949	**NY A**	4	.100	.200	10	1	1	0	0	0.0	3	2	2	4	0	0	0	8	0	1	0	2.3	.889	OF-4
1950		1	.000	.000	4	0	0	0	0	0.0	0	0	0	1	0	0	0	3	0	0	0	3.0	1.000	OF-1
2 yrs.		5	.071	.143	14	1	1	0	0	0.0	3	2	2	5	0	0	0	11	0	1	0	2.4	.917	OF-5

Howard Maple

MAPLE, HOWARD ALBERT
B. July 20, 1903, Adrian, Mo. D. Nov. 9, 1970, Portland, Ore.
BL TR 5′7″ 175 lbs.

Year	Team	Games	BA	SA	AB	H	2B	3B	HR	HR%	R	RBI	BB	SO	SB	Pinch Hit AB	Pinch Hit H	PO	A	E	DP	TC/G	FA	G by Pos
1932	**WAS A**	44	.244	.293	41	10	0	1	0	0.0	6	7	7	7	0	2	0	34	5	0	2	1.0	1.000	C-41

George Mappes

MAPPES, GEORGE RICHARD (Dick)
B. Dec. 25, 1865, St. Louis, Mo. D. Feb. 20, 1934, St. Louis, Mo.

Year	Team	Games	BA	SA	AB	H	2B	3B	HR	HR%	R	RBI	BB	SO	SB	Pinch Hit AB	Pinch Hit H	PO	A	E	DP	TC/G	FA	G by Pos
1885	**BAL AA**	6	.211	.316	19	4	0	1	0	0.0	2		1			0	0	16	12	4	1	5.3	.875	2B-6
1886	**STL N**	6	.143	.143	14	2	0	0	0	0.0	1	0	1	5		0	0	18	5	4	0	4.5	.852	C-3, 3B-2, 2B-1
2 yrs.		12	.182	.242	33	6	0	1	0	0.0	3	0	2	5		0	0	34	17	8	1	4.9	.864	2B-7, C-3, 3B-2

Rabbit Maranville

MARANVILLE, WALTER JAMES VINCENT
B. Nov. 11, 1891, Springfield, Mass. D. Jan. 5, 1954, New York, N. Y.
Manager 1925.
Hall of Fame 1954.
BR TR 5′ 5″ 155 lbs.

Year	Team	Games	BA	SA	AB	H	2B	3B	HR	HR%	R	RBI	BB	SO	SB	Pinch Hit AB	Pinch Hit H	PO	A	E	DP	TC/G	FA	G by Pos
1912	**BOS N**	26	.209	.233	86	18	2	0	0	0.0	8	8	9	14	1	0	0	46	97	11	11	5.9	.929	SS-26
1913		143	.247	.308	571	141	13	8	2	0.4	68	48	68	62	25	0	0	317	475	43	49	5.8	.949	SS-143
1914		156	.246	.326	586	144	23	6	4	0.7	74	78	45	56	28	0	0	407	574	65	92	6.7	.938	SS-156
1915		149	.244	.324	509	124	23	6	2	0.4	51	43	45	65	18	0	0	391	486	55	63	6.3	.941	SS-149
1916		155	.235	.325	604	142	16	13	4	0.7	79	38	50	69	32	0	0	386	515	50	79	6.1	.947	SS-155
1917		142	.260	.357	561	146	19	13	3	0.5	69	43	40	47	27	0	0	341	474	46	67	6.1	.947	SS-142
1918		11	.316	.368	38	12	0	1	0	0.0	3	3	4	0	0	0	0	34	34	5	2	6.6	.932	SS-11
1919		131	.267	.377	480	128	18	10	5	1.0	44	43	36	23	12	0	0	361	488	53	74	6.9	.941	SS-131
1920		134	.266	.371	493	131	19	15	1	0.2	48	43	28	24	14	1	0	354	462	45	62	6.5	.948	SS-133
1921	**PIT N**	153	.294	.379	612	180	25	12	1	0.2	90	70	47	38	25	0	0	325	529	34	72	5.8	.962	SS-153
1922		155	.295	.378	**672**	198	26	15	0	0.0	115	63	61	43	24	0	0	419	512	36	93	6.2	.963	SS-138, 2B-18
1923		141	.277	.346	581	161	19	9	1	0.2	78	41	42	34	14	0	0	332	505	30	94	6.1	.965	SS-141
1924		152	.266	.399	594	158	33	20	2	0.3	62	71	35	53	18	0	0	365	568	26	109	6.3	.973	2B-152
1925	**CHI N**	75	.233	.293	266	62	10	3	0	0.0	37	23	29	20	6	1	0	162	261	20	51	6.0	.955	SS-74
1926	**BKN N**	78	.235	.312	234	55	8	5	0	0.0	32	24	26	24	7	0	0	161	246	19	30	5.5	.955	SS-60, 2B-18
1927	**STL N**	9	.241	.276	29	7	1	0	0	0.0	0	0	2	2	0	0	0	17	34	2	6	5.9	.962	SS-9
1928		112	.240	.342	366	88	14	10	1	0.3	40	34	36	27	3	0	0	237	364	19	58	5.4	.969	SS-112, 2B-2
1929	**BOS N**	146	.284	.366	560	159	26	10	0	0.0	87	55	47	33	13	0	0	324	537	35	104	6.1	.961	SS-146, 2B-1

Rabbit Maranville *continued*

Year	Team	Games	BA	SA	AB	H	2B	3B	HR	HR%	R	RBI	BB	SO	SB	Pinch Hit AB	Pinch Hit H	PO	A	E	DP	TC/G	FA	G by Pos
1930		142	.281	.367	558	157	26	8	2	0.4	85	43	48	23	9	0	0	349	450	29	98	5.8	.965	SS-138, 3B-4
1931		145	.260	.317	562	146	22	5	0	0.0	69	33	56	34	9	1	0	289	453	41	98	5.3	.948	SS-137, 2B-11
1932		149	.235	.284	571	134	20	4	0	0.0	67	37	46	28	4	0	0	402	473	22	91	6.0	.975	2B-149
1933		143	.218	.266	478	104	15	4	0	0.0	46	38	36	34	2	1	1	362	384	22	82	5.4	.971	2B-142
1935		23	.149	.179	67	10	2	0	0	0.0	3	5	3	3	0	3	0	32	46	3	10	4.1	.963	2B-20
23 yrs.		2670	.258	.340	10078	2605	380	177	28	0.3	1255	884	839	756	291	7	1	6413	8967	711	1495	6.0	.956	SS-2154, 2B-513, 3B-4
WORLD SERIES																								
1914	BOS N	4	.308	.308	13	4	0	0	0	0.0	1	3	1	1	2	0	0	7	13	1	2	5.3	.952	SS-4
1928	STL N	4	.308	.385	13	4	1	0	0	0.0	2	0	1	1	1	0	0	11	3	1	2	3.8	.933	SS-4
2 yrs.		8	.308	.346	26	8	1	0	0	0.0	3	3	2	2	3	0	0	18	16	2	4	4.5	.944	SS-8

Johnny Marcum

MARCUM, JOHN ALFRED (Footsie) BL TR 5′11″ 197 lbs.
B. Sept. 9, 1909, Campbellsburg, Ky. D. Sept. 10, 1984, Louisville, Ky.

Year	Team	Games	BA	SA	AB	H	2B	3B	HR	HR%	R	RBI	BB	SO	SB	Pinch Hit AB	Pinch Hit H	PO	A	E	DP	TC/G	FA	G by Pos
1933	PHI A	5	.167	.167	12	2	0	0	0	0.0	2	0	2	1	0	0	0	5	6	0	0	2.2	1.000	P-5
1934		58	.268	.330	112	30	4	0	1	0.9	10	13	3	5	0	20	3	14	42	3	2	1.6	.949	P-37
1935		64	.311	.395	119	37	2	1	2	1.7	13	17	9	5	0	23	7	11	32	5	1	1.2	.896	P-39
1936	BOS A	48	.205	.307	88	18	3	0	2	2.3	6	7	3	5	0	18	0	7	31	2	3	1.3	.950	P-31
1937		51	.267	.360	86	23	8	0	0	0.0	12	13	7	4	0	13	2	13	38	1	1	1.4	.981	P-37
1938		19	.135	.135	37	5	0	0	0	0.0	3	3	6	9	0	3	0	3	15	0	0	1.2	1.000	P-15
1939	2 teams	STL A (16G –.455)	CHI A (38G –.281)																					
″	total	54	.329	.342	79	26	1	0	0	0.0	10	17	6	3	0	22	5	8	17	1	2	0.8	.962	P-31
7 yrs.		299	.265	.330	533	141	18	1	5	0.9	56	70	36	32	0	99	17	61	181	12	9	1.3	.953	P-195

Marty Marion

MARION, MARTIN WHITEFORD (Slats, The Octopus) BR TR 6′ 2″ 170 lbs.
Brother of Red Marion.
B. Dec. 1, 1917, Richburg, S. C.
Manager 1951–56.

Year	Team	Games	BA	SA	AB	H	2B	3B	HR	HR%	R	RBI	BB	SO	SB	Pinch Hit AB	Pinch Hit H	PO	A	E	DP	TC/G	FA	G by Pos
1940	STL N	125	.278	.345	435	121	18	1	3	0.7	44	46	21	34	9	0	0	245	366	33	76	5.2	.949	SS-125
1941		155	.252	.320	547	138	22	3	3	0.5	50	58	42	48	8	0	0	299	489	38	85	5.3	.954	SS-155
1942		147	.276	.375	485	134	**38**	5	0	0.0	66	54	48	50	8	0	0	296	448	31	87	5.3	.960	SS-147
1943		129	.280	.337	418	117	15	3	1	0.2	38	52	32	37	1	1	0	232	424	20	93	5.3	.970	SS-128
1944		144	.267	.362	506	135	26	2	6	1.2	50	63	43	50	1	0	0	268	461	21	90	5.2	.972	SS-144
1945		123	.277	.370	430	119	27	5	1	0.2	63	59	39	39	2	0	0	237	372	21	70	5.2	.967	SS-122
1946		146	.233	.325	498	116	29	4	3	0.6	51	46	59	53	1	1	0	290	480	21	105	5.5	.973	SS-145
1947		149	.272	.352	540	147	19	6	4	0.7	57	74	49	58	3	0	0	329	452	15	104	5.3	.981	SS-149
1948		144	.252	.333	567	143	26	4	4	0.7	70	43	37	54	1	2	0	263	445	19	80	5.1	.974	SS-142
1949		134	.272	.369	515	140	31	2	5	1.0	61	70	37	42	1	0	0	242	441	17	74	5.2	.976	SS-134
1950		106	.247	.317	372	92	10	2	4	1.1	36	40	44	55	1	5	1	180	313	11	73	5.0	.978	SS-101
1952	STL A	67	.247	.339	186	46	11	0	2	1.1	16	19	19	17	0	4	2	105	138	5	41	3.9	.980	SS-63
1953		3	.000	.000	7	0	0	0	0	0.0	0	0	0	0	0	1	0	1	0	0	0	0.5	1.000	3B-2
13 yrs.		1572	.263	.345	5506	1448	272	37	36	0.7	602	624	470	537	35	14	3	2987	4829	252	978	5.2	.969	SS-1555, 3B-2
WORLD SERIES																								
1942	STL N	5	.111	.222	18	2	0	1	0	0.0	2	3	1	2	0	0	0	13	16	0	3	5.8	1.000	SS-5
1943		5	.357	.714	14	5	2	0	1	7.1	1	2	3	1	1	0	0	8	14	1	4	4.6	.957	SS-5
1944		6	.227	.364	22	5	3	0	0	0.0	1	2	2	3	0	0	0	7	22	0	2	4.8	1.000	SS-6
1946		7	.250	.333	24	6	2	0	0	0.0	1	4	1	1	0	0	0	12	22	2	3	5.1	.944	SS-7
4 yrs.		23	.231	.385	78	18	7	1	1	1.3	5	11	7	7	1	0	0	40	74	3	12	5.1	.974	SS-23

Red Marion

MARION, JOHN WYETH BR TR 6′ 2″ 175 lbs.
Brother of Marty Marion.
B. Mar. 14, 1914, Richburg, S. C. D. Mar. 13, 1975, San Jose, Calif.

Year	Team	Games	BA	SA	AB	H	2B	3B	HR	HR%	R	RBI	BB	SO	SB	Pinch Hit AB	Pinch Hit H	PO	A	E	DP	TC/G	FA	G by Pos
1935	WAS A	4	.182	.545	11	2	1	0	1	9.1	1	1	0	2	0	0	0	4	1	1	0	2.0	.833	OF-3
1943		14	.176	.176	17	3	0	0	0	0.0	2	1	3	1	0	9	1	7	0	0	0	1.8	1.000	OF-4
2 yrs.		18	.179	.321	28	5	1	0	1	3.6	3	2	3	3	0	9	1	11	1	1	0	1.9	.923	OF-7

Roger Maris

MARIS, ROGER EUGENE BL TR 6′ 197 lbs.
Born Roger Eugene Maras.
B. Sept. 10, 1934, Hibbing, Minn. D. Dec. 14, 1985, Houston, Tex.

Year	Team	Games	BA	SA	AB	H	2B	3B	HR	HR%	R	RBI	BB	SO	SB	Pinch Hit AB	Pinch Hit H	PO	A	E	DP	TC/G	FA	G by Pos
1957	CLE A	116	.235	.405	358	84	9	5	14	3.9	61	51	60	79	8	5	2	266	10	7	2	2.5	.975	OF-112
1958	2 teams	CLE A (51G –.225)	KC A (99G –.247)																					
″	total	150	.240	.431	583	140	19	4	28	4.8	87	80	45	85	4	6	0	303	15	9	4	2.2	.972	OF-146
1959	KC A	122	.273	.464	433	118	21	7	16	3.7	69	72	58	53	2	5	2	231	7	6	4	2.1	.975	OF-117
1960	NY A	136	.283	**.581**	499	141	18	7	39	**7.8**	98	**112**	70	65	2	4	1	263	6	4	1	2.1	.985	OF-131
1961		161	.269	.620	590	159	16	4	**61**[1]	10.3	**132**	**141**	94	67	0	1	0	266	9	9	1	1.8	.968	OF-160
1962		157	.256	.485	590	151	34	1	33	5.6	92	100	87	78	1	3	0	316	4	3	0	2.1	.991	OF-154
1963		90	.269	.542	312	84	14	1	23	7.4	53	53	35	40	1	5	2	162	6	2	1	2.0	.988	OF-86
1964		141	.281	.464	513	144	12	2	26	5.1	86	71	62	78	3	6	1	250	6	1	0	1.9	.996	OF-137
1965		46	.239	.439	155	37	7	0	8	5.2	22	27	29	29	0	4	1	66	1	2	0	1.6	.971	OF-43
1966		119	.233	.382	348	81	9	2	13	3.7	37	43	36	60	0	20	6	133	3	1	0	1.4	.993	OF-95
1967	STL N	125	.261	.405	410	107	18	7	9	2.2	64	55	52	61	0	19	2	224	5	2	1	2.0	.991	OF-118
1968		100	.255	.374	310	79	18	2	5	1.6	25	45	24	38	0	21	6	169	4	3	1	2.1	.983	OF-84
12 yrs.		1463	.260	.476	5101	1325	195	42	275	5.4	826	850	652	733	21	99	23	2649	76	49	15	2.0	.982	OF-1383
WORLD SERIES																								
1960	NY A	7	.267	.500	30	8	1	0	2	6.7	6	2	2	4	0	0	0	11	0	1	0	1.7	.917	OF-7
1961		5	.105	.316	19	2	1	0	1	5.3	4	2	4	6	0	0	0	11	1	0	0	2.4	1.000	OF-5
1962		7	.174	.348	23	4	1	0	1	4.3	4	5	5	2	0	0	0	11	1	0	0	1.7	1.000	OF-7
1963		2	.000	.000	5	0	0	0	0	0.0	0	0	0	1	0	0	0	3	0	0	0	1.5	1.000	OF-2
1964		7	.200	.300	30	6	0	0	1	3.3	4	1	1	4	0	0	0	19	0	0	0	2.7	1.000	OF-7

Roger Maris *continued*

Year	Team	Lg	Games	BA	SA	AB	H	2B	3B	HR	HR%	R	RBI	BB	SO	SB	Pinch Hit AB	Pinch Hit H	PO	A	E	DP	TC/G	FA	G by Pos
1967	STL	N	7	.385	.538	26	10	1	0	1	3.8	3	7	3	1	0	0	0	15	0	1	0	2.3	.938	OF-7
1968			6	.158	.211	19	3	1	0	0	0.0	5	1	3	3	0	1	0	8	0	0	0	1.6	1.000	OF-5
7 yrs.			41	.217	.368	152	33	5	0	6	3.9	26	18	18	21	0	1	0	78	2	2	0	2.0	.976	OF-40
			10th			10th						6th													

Gene Markland

MARKLAND, CLENETH EUGENE (Mousey)
B. Dec. 26, 1919, Detroit, Mich.
BR TR 5′10″ 160 lbs.

Year	Team	Lg	Games	BA	SA	AB	H	2B	3B	HR	HR%	R	RBI	BB	SO	SB	Pinch Hit AB	Pinch Hit H	PO	A	E	DP	TC/G	FA	G by Pos
1950	PHI	A	5	.125	.125	8	1	0	0	0	0.0	2	0	3	0	0	0	0	12	9	0	1	4.2	1.000	2B-5

Hal Marnie

MARNIE, HARRY SYLVESTER
B. July 6, 1918, Philadelphia, Pa.
BR TR 6′ 1″ 178 lbs.

Year	Team	Lg	Games	BA	SA	AB	H	2B	3B	HR	HR%	R	RBI	BB	SO	SB	Pinch Hit AB	Pinch Hit H	PO	A	E	DP	TC/G	FA	G by Pos
1940	PHI	N	11	.176	.176	34	6	0	0	0	0.0	4	4	4	2	0	0	0	19	42	1	8	5.6	.984	2B-11
1941			61	.241	.297	158	38	3	3	0	0.0	12	11	13	25	0	2	0	129	108	3	24	4.1	.988	2B-39, SS-16, 3B-3
1942			24	.167	.167	30	5	0	0	0	0.0	3	0	1	1	1	2	0	30	32	4	9	3.5	.939	2B-11, SS-7, 3B-1
3 yrs.			96	.221	.261	222	49	3	3	0	0.0	19	15	18	28	1	4	0	178	182	8	41	4.2	.978	2B-61, SS-23, 3B-4

Fred Marolewski

MAROLEWSKI, FRED DANIEL (Fritz)
B. Oct. 6, 1928, Chicago, Ill.
BR TR 6′ 2½″ 205 lbs.

Year	Team	Lg	Games	BA	SA	AB	H	2B	3B	HR	HR%	R	RBI	BB	SO	SB	Pinch Hit AB	Pinch Hit H	PO	A	E	DP	TC/G	FA	G by Pos
1953	STL	N	1	—	—	0	0	0	0	0	—	0	0	0	0	0	0	0	0	0	0	0	0.0	.000	1B-1

Ollie Marquardt

MARQUARDT, ALBERT LUDWIG
B. Sept. 22, 1902, Toledo, Ohio D. Feb. 7, 1968, Port Clinton, Ohio.
BR TR 5′ 9″ 156 lbs.

Year	Team	Lg	Games	BA	SA	AB	H	2B	3B	HR	HR%	R	RBI	BB	SO	SB	Pinch Hit AB	Pinch Hit H	PO	A	E	DP	TC/G	FA	G by Pos
1931	BOS	A	17	.179	.205	39	7	1	0	0	0.0	4	2	3	4	0	1	0	20	33	3	4	4.3	.946	2B-13

Gonzalo Marquez

MARQUEZ, GONZALO ENRIQUE
Born Gonzalo Enrique Marquez (Mora).
B. Mar. 31, 1946, Carupano, Venezuela D. Dec. 20, 1984, Valencia, Venezuela.
BL TL 5′11″ 180 lbs.

Year	Team	Lg	Games	BA	SA	AB	H	2B	3B	HR	HR%	R	RBI	BB	SO	SB	Pinch Hit AB	Pinch Hit H	PO	A	E	DP	TC/G	FA	G by Pos
1972	OAK	A	23	.381	.381	21	8	0	0	0	0.0	2	4	3	4	1	16	7	12	1	1	1	7.0	.929	1B-2
1973	2 teams	OAK A (23G –.240) CHI N (19G –.224)																							
″	total		42	.229	.301	83	19	3	0	1	1.2	6	6	3	8	0	20	5	156	15	1	14	8.2	.994	1B-19, 2B-2
1974	CHI	N	11	.000	.000	11	0	0	0	0	0.0	1	0	1	2	0	10	0	2	0	0	0	2.0	1.000	1B-1
3 yrs.			76	.235	.287	115	27	3	0	1	0.9	9	10	7	14	1	46	12	170	16	2	15	7.8	.989	1B-22, 2B-2
LEAGUE CHAMPIONSHIP SERIES																									
1972	OAK	A	3	.667	.667	3	2	0	0	0	0.0	1	1	0	0	0	3	2	0	0	0	0	0.0	—	
WORLD SERIES																									
1972	OAK	A	5	.600	.600	5	3	0	0	0	0.0	0	1	0	0	0	5	3	0	0	0	0	0.0	—	

Luis Marquez

MARQUEZ, LUIS ANGEL (Canena)
Born Luis Angel Marquez (Sanchez).
B. Oct. 28, 1925, Aguadilla, Puerto Rico D. Mar. 1, 1988, Aguadilla, Puerto Rico.
BR TR 5′10½″ 174 lbs.

Year	Team	Lg	Games	BA	SA	AB	H	2B	3B	HR	HR%	R	RBI	BB	SO	SB	Pinch Hit AB	Pinch Hit H	PO	A	E	DP	TC/G	FA	G by Pos
1951	BOS	N	68	.197	.254	122	24	5	1	0	0.0	19	11	10	20	4	9	2	100	2	0	0	2.4	1.000	OF-43
1954	2 teams	CHI N (17G –.083) PIT N (14G –.111)																							
″	total		31	.095	.095	21	2	0	0	0	0.0	5	0	6	4	3	5	1	20	0	0	0	1.1	1.000	OF-18
2 yrs.			99	.182	.231	143	26	5	1	0	0.0	24	11	16	24	7	14	3	120	2	0	0	2.0	1.000	OF-61

Bob Marquis

MARQUIS, ROBERT RUDOLPH
B. Dec. 23, 1924, Oklahoma City, Okla.
BL TL 6′ 1″ 170 lbs.

Year	Team	Lg	Games	BA	SA	AB	H	2B	3B	HR	HR%	R	RBI	BB	SO	SB	Pinch Hit AB	Pinch Hit H	PO	A	E	DP	TC/G	FA	G by Pos
1953	CIN	N	40	.273	.477	44	12	1	1	2	4.5	9	3	4	11	0	26	5	19	0	2	0	2.1	.905	OF-10

Roger Marquis

MARQUIS, ROGER JULIAN (Noonie)
B. Apr. 5, 1937, Holyoke, Mass.
BL TL 6′ 190 lbs.

Year	Team	Lg	Games	BA	SA	AB	H	2B	3B	HR	HR%	R	RBI	BB	SO	SB	Pinch Hit AB	Pinch Hit H	PO	A	E	DP	TC/G	FA	G by Pos
1955	BAL	A	1	.000	.000	1	0	0	0	0	0.0	0	0	0	0	0	0	0	0	0	0	0	0.0	.000	OF-1

Lefty Marr

MARR, CHARLES W.
B. Sept. 19, 1862, Cincinnati, Ohio D. Jan. 11, 1912, New Britain, Conn.
BL TL

Year	Team	Lg	Games	BA	SA	AB	H	2B	3B	HR	HR%	R	RBI	BB	SO	SB	Pinch Hit AB	Pinch Hit H	PO	A	E	DP	TC/G	FA	G by Pos
1886	CIN	AA	8	.276	.379	29	8	1	1	0	0.0	2		1			0	0	15	1	7	0	2.9	.696	OF-8
1889	COL	AA	139	.306	.414	546	167	26	**15**	1	0.2	110	75	87	32	29	0	0	254	253	90	22	4.2	.849	3B-66, OF-47, SS-26, 1B-1, C-1
1890	CIN	N	130	.300	.389	527	158	17	12	2	0.4	91	73	46	29	44	0	0	140	144	39	8	2.5	.879	OF-64, 3B-63, SS-3
1891	2 teams	CIN N (72G –.259) CIN AA (14G –.193)																							
″	total		86	.248	.318	343	85	10	7	0	0.0	41	36	32	19	18	0	0	98	7	18	2	1.4	.854	OF-86
4 yrs.			363	.289	.381	1445	418	54	35	3	0.2	244	184	166	80	91	0	0	507	405	154	32	2.9	.856	OF-205, 3B-129, SS-29, 1B-1, C-1

Oreste Marrero

MARRERO, ORESTE VILATO
Born Oreste Vilato Marrero (Vazquez).
B. Oct. 31, 1969, Bayamon, Puerto Rico.
BL TL 6′ 195 lbs.

Year	Team	Lg	Games	BA	SA	AB	H	2B	3B	HR	HR%	R	RBI	BB	SO	SB	Pinch Hit AB	Pinch Hit H	PO	A	E	DP	TC/G	FA	G by Pos
1993	MON	N	32	.210	.333	81	17	5	1	1	1.2	10	4	14	16	1	0	0	194	15	2	21	6.6	.991	1B-32

Bill Marriott

MARRIOTT, WILLIAM EARL
B. Apr. 18, 1893, Pratt, Kans. D. Aug. 11, 1969, Berkeley, Calif.
BL TR 6′ 170 lbs.

Year	Team	Lg	Games	BA	SA	AB	H	2B	3B	HR	HR%	R	RBI	BB	SO	SB	Pinch Hit AB	Pinch Hit H	PO	A	E	DP	TC/G	FA	G by Pos
1917	CHI	N	2	.000	.000	6	0	0	0	0	0.0	0	0	0	1	0	2	0	2	0	1	0	3.0	.667	OF-1
1920			14	.279	.465	43	12	4	2	0	0.0	7	5	6	5	1	0	0	26	40	8	2	5.3	.892	2B-14
1921			30	.316	.395	38	12	1	1	0	0.0	3	7	4	1	0	20	4	11	13	5	2	3.2	.828	2B-6, OF-1, SS-1, 3B-1
1925	BOS	N	103	.268	.305	370	99	9	1	1	0.3	37	40	28	26	3	8	1	100	187	22	13	3.4	.929	3B-89, OF-1
1926	BKN	N	109	.267	.378	360	96	13	9	3	0.8	39	42	17	20	12	4	0	80	173	20	6	2.6	.927	3B-104
1927			6	.111	.333	9	1	0	1	0	0.0	0	1	2	2	0	4	0	3	5	1	0	4.5	.889	3B-2
6 yrs.			264	.266	.347	826	220	27	14	4	0.5	86	95	57	55	16	38	5	222	418	57	23	3.2	.918	3B-196, 2B-20, OF-3, SS-1

Armando Marsans

MARSANS, ARMANDO
B. Oct. 3, 1887, Matanzas, Cuba D. Sept. 3, 1960, Havana, Cuba.
BR TR 5′10″ 157 lbs.

Year	Team	Lg	Games	BA	SA	AB	H	2B	3B	HR	HR%	R	RBI	BB	SO	SB	Pinch Hit AB	Pinch Hit H	PO	A	E	DP	TC/G	FA	G by Pos
1911	CIN	N	58	.261	.304	138	36	2	2	0	0.0	17	11	15	11	11	19	3	64	2	3	0	1.9	.957	OF-34, 3B-1, 1B-1
1912			110	.317	.404	416	132	19	7	1	0.2	59	38	20	17	35	2	2	265	12	8	2	2.7	.972	OF-98, 1B-6
1913			118	.297	.340	435	129	7	6	0	0.0	49	38	17	25	37	1	0	402	26	15	21	3.7	.966	OF-94, 1B-22, 3B-2, SS-1

Armando Marsans *continued*

Year	Team	Games	BA	SA	AB	H	2B	3B	HR	HR%	R	RBI	BB	SO	SB	Pinch Hit AB	Pinch Hit H	PO	A	E	DP	TC/G	FA	G by Pos
1914	2 teams CIN N (36G –.298) STL F (9G –.350)																							
″	total	45	.311	.354	164	51	3	2	0	0.0	21	24	17	6	17	0	0	98	28	12	9	3.1	.913	OF-36, 2B-7, SS-2
1915	STL F	36	.177	.202	124	22	3	0	0	0.0	16	6	14		5	1	0	71	8	2	3	2.3	.975	OF-35
1916	STL A	151	.254	.286	528	134	12	1	1	0.2	51	60	57	41	46	1	1	351	25	9	7	2.6	.977	OF-150
1917	2 teams STL A (75G –.230) NY A (25G –.227)																							
″	total	100	.229	.275	345	79	16	0	0	0.0	41	35	28	9	17	1	1	232	24	9	3	2.7	.966	OF-92, 3B-5, 2B-1
1918	NY A	37	.236	.293	123	29	5	1	0	0.0	13	9	5	3	3	1	0	64	2	4	0	1.9	.943	OF-36
8 yrs.		655	.269	.318	2273	612	67	19	2	0.1	267	221	173	112	171	26	7	1547	127	62	45	2.8	.964	OF-575, 1B-29, 2B-8, 3B-8, SS-3

Freddie Marsh

MARSH, FRED FRANCIS BR TR 5′10″ 180 lbs.
B. Jan. 5, 1924, Valley Falls, Kans.

Year	Team	Games	BA	SA	AB	H	2B	3B	HR	HR%	R	RBI	BB	SO	SB	Pinch Hit AB	Pinch Hit H	PO	A	E	DP	TC/G	FA	G by Pos
1949	CLE A	1	—	—	0	0	0	0	0	—	0	0	0	0	0	0	0	0	0	0	0	0.0	—	
1951	STL A	130	.243	.335	445	108	21	4	4	0.9	44	43	36	56	4	10	2	141	231	29	33	3.3	.928	3B-117, SS-3, 2B-2
1952	3 teams STL A (11G –.217) WAS A (9G –.042) STL A (76G –.286)																							
″	total	96	.258	.321	271	70	9	1	2	0.7	29	28	28	37	3	3	2	114	183	19	45	3.3	.940	SS-60, 3B-21, 2B-14, OF-2
1953	CHI A	67	.200	.274	95	19	1	0	2	2.1	22	2	13	26	0	11	2	61	71	6	12	2.5	.957	3B-32, SS-17, 1B-5, 2B-2
1954		62	.306	.398	98	30	5	2	0	0.0	21	4	9	16	4	2	0	41	86	4	8	3.1	.969	3B-36, SS-3, 1B-2, OF-1
1955	BAL A	89	.218	.267	303	66	7	1	2	0.7	30	19	35	33	1	1	0	216	193	14	55	3.8	.967	2B-76, 3B-18, SS-16
1956		20	.125	.125	24	3	0	0	0	0.0	2	0	4	3	1	0	0	17	18	3	5	1.8	.921	3B-8, SS-8, 2B-5
7 yrs.		465	.239	.311	1236	296	43	8	10	0.8	148	96	125	171	13	27	6	590	782	75	158	3.2	.948	3B-232, SS-107, 2B-99, 1B-7, OF-3

Tom Marsh

MARSH, THOMAS OWEN BR TR 6′ 2″ 180 lbs.
B. Dec. 27, 1965, Toledo, Ohio.

Year	Team	Games	BA	SA	AB	H	2B	3B	HR	HR%	R	RBI	BB	SO	SB	Pinch Hit AB	Pinch Hit H	PO	A	E	DP	TC/G	FA	G by Pos
1992	PHI N	42	.200	.304	125	25	3	2	2	1.6	7	16	2	23	0	8	2	66	0	2	0	1.9	.971	OF-35
1994		8	.278	.444	18	5	1	1	0	0.0	3	3	1	1	0	3	1	8	0	1	0	1.3	.889	OF-7
1995		43	.294	.422	109	32	3	1	3	2.8	13	15	4	25	0	14	3	44	2	3	0	1.7	.939	OF-29
3 yrs.		93	.246	.365	252	62	7	4	5	2.0	23	34	7	49	0	25	6	118	2	6	0	1.8	.952	OF-71

Bill Marshall

MARSHALL, WILLIAM HENRY BR TR 5′ 8½″ 156 lbs.
B. Feb. 14, 1911, Dorchester, Mass. D. May 5, 1977, Sacramento, Calif.

Year	Team	Games	BA	SA	AB	H	2B	3B	HR	HR%	R	RBI	BB	SO	SB	Pinch Hit AB	Pinch Hit H	PO	A	E	DP	TC/G	FA	G by Pos
1931	BOS A	1	—	—	0	0	0	0	0	—	1	0	0	0	0	0	0	0	0	0	0	0.0	—	
1934	CIN N	6	.125	.125	8	1	0	0	0	0.0	0	0	0	2	0	3	1	2	5	1	0	4.0	.875	2B-2
2 yrs.		7	.125	.125	8	1	0	0	0	0.0	1	0	0	2	0	3	1	2	5	1	0	4.0	.875	2B-2

Charlie Marshall

MARSHALL, CHARLES ANTHONY BR TR 5′10½″ 178 lbs.
Born Charles Anthony Marcziewicz.
B. Aug. 28, 1919, Wilmington, Del.

Year	Team	Games	BA	SA	AB	H	2B	3B	HR	HR%	R	RBI	BB	SO	SB	Pinch Hit AB	Pinch Hit H	PO	A	E	DP	TC/G	FA	G by Pos
1941	STL N	1	—	—	0	0	0	0	0	—	0	0	0	0	0	0	0	1	0	0	0	1.0	1.000	C-1

Dave Marshall

MARSHALL, DAVID LEWIS BL TR 6′ 1″ 182 lbs.
B. Jan. 14, 1943, Artesia, Calif.

Year	Team	Games	BA	SA	AB	H	2B	3B	HR	HR%	R	RBI	BB	SO	SB	Pinch Hit AB	Pinch Hit H	PO	A	E	DP	TC/G	FA	G by Pos
1967	SF N	1	—	—	0	0	0	0	0	—	0	0	0	0	0	0	0	0	0	0	0	0.0	—	
1968		76	.264	.322	174	46	5	1	1	0.6	17	16	20	37	2	23	7	58	3	5	3	1.3	.924	OF-50
1969		110	.232	.288	267	62	7	1	2	0.7	32	33	40	68	1	20	4	106	3	5	0	1.3	.956	OF-87
1970	NY N	92	.243	.402	189	46	10	1	6	3.2	21	29	17	43	4	44	11	71	2	2	0	1.7	.973	OF-43
1971		100	.238	.332	214	51	9	1	3	1.4	28	21	26	54	3	36	8	92	2	1	0	1.5	.989	OF-64
1972		72	.250	.359	156	39	5	0	4	2.6	21	11	22	28	3	29	3	70	0	2	0	1.7	.972	OF-42
1973	SD N	39	.286	.388	49	14	5	0	0	0.0	4	4	8	9	0	24	5	14	0	0	0	1.8	1.000	OF-8
7 yrs.		490	.246	.338	1049	258	41	4	16	1.5	123	114	133	239	13	176	38	411	10	15	3	1.5	.966	OF-294

Doc Marshall

MARSHALL, EDWARD HERBERT BR TR 5′11″ 150 lbs.
B. June 4, 1906, New Albany, Miss.

Year	Team	Games	BA	SA	AB	H	2B	3B	HR	HR%	R	RBI	BB	SO	SB	Pinch Hit AB	Pinch Hit H	PO	A	E	DP	TC/G	FA	G by Pos
1929	NY N	5	.400	.533	15	6	2	0	0	0.0	6	2	1	0	0	0	0	7	11	0	0	3.6	1.000	2B-5
1930		78	.309	.359	223	69	5	3	0	0.0	33	21	13	9	0	5	3	109	179	13	29	4.5	.957	SS-45, 2B-17, 3B-5
1931		68	.201	.253	194	39	6	2	0	0.0	15	10	8	8	1	3	1	124	160	14	31	4.9	.953	2B-47, SS-11, 3B-3
1932		68	.248	.292	226	56	8	1	0	0.0	18	28	6	11	1	0	0	119	199	27	37	5.5	.922	SS-63
4 yrs.		219	.258	.309	658	170	21	6	0	0.0	72	61	28	28	2	8	4	359	549	54	97	4.9	.944	SS-119, 2B-69, 3B-8

Doc Marshall

MARSHALL, WILLIAM RIDDLE BR TR 6′ 185 lbs.
B. Sept. 22, 1875, Butler, Pa. D. Dec. 11, 1959, Clinton, Ill.

Year	Team	Games	BA	SA	AB	H	2B	3B	HR	HR%	R	RBI	BB	SO	SB	Pinch Hit AB	Pinch Hit H	PO	A	E	DP	TC/G	FA	G by Pos
1904	3 teams PHI N (8G –.100) NY N (11G –.353) BOS N (13G –.209)																							
″	total	32	.213	.250	80	17	1	1	0	0.0	7	5	3		2	7	0	82	42	8	4	5.5	.939	C-20, OF-3, 2B-1
1906	2 teams NY N (38G –.167) STL N (39G –.276)																							
″	total	77	.227	.284	225	51	7	3	0	0.0	14	17	13		8	9	1	270	73	10	5	5.1	.972	C-51, OF-16, 1B-2
1907	STL N	84	.201	.269	268	54	8	2	2	0.7	19	18	12		2	1	0	374	142	26	9	6.5	.952	C-83
1908	2 teams STL N (6G –.071) CHI N (12G –.300)																							
″	total	18	.206	.265	34	7	0	1	0	0.0	4	4	0		0	2	1	48	10	1	2	4.5	.983	C-10, OF-3
1909	BKN N	50	.201	.262	149	30	7	1	0	0.0	7	10	6		3	1	0	110	61	9	2	3.6	.950	C-49, OF-1
5 yrs.		261	.210	.270	756	159	23	8	2	0.3	51	54	34		15	20	2	884	328	54	22	5.3	.957	C-213, OF-23, 1B-2, 2B-1

Jim Marshall

MARSHALL, RUFUS JAMES BL TL 6′ 1″ 190 lbs.
B. May 25, 1931, Danville, Ill.
Manager 1974–76, 1979.

Year	Team	Games	BA	SA	AB	H	2B	3B	HR	HR%	R	RBI	BB	SO	SB	Pinch Hit AB	Pinch Hit H	PO	A	E	DP	TC/G	FA	G by Pos
1958	2 teams BAL A (85G –.215) CHI N (26G –.272)																							
″	total	111	.232	.386	272	63	6	3	10	3.7	29	30	30	43	4	36	6	504	27	1	48	6.2	.998	1B-67, OF-19
1959	CHI N	108	.252	.405	294	74	10	1	11	3.7	39	40	33	39	0	33	8	565	52	2	52	7.7	.997	1B-72, OF-8
1960	SF N	75	.237	.339	118	28	2	2	2	1.7	19	13	17	24	0	38	8	177	9	6	13	5.6	.969	1B-28, OF-6
1961		44	.222	.306	36	8	0	0	1	2.8	5	7	3	8	0	32	7	9	1	0	1	1.7	1.000	1B-4, OF-2
1962	2 teams NY N (17G –.344) PIT N (55G –.220)																							
″	total	72	.250	.424	132	33	6	1	5	3.8	19	16	18	25	1	32	6	229	20	0	27	7.8	1.000	1B-31, OF-1
5 yrs.		410	.242	.388	852	206	24	7	29	3.4	111	106	101	139	5	171	35	1484	109	9	141	6.7	.994	1B-202, OF-36

Joe Marshall

MARSHALL, JOSEPH HANLEY (Home Run Joe) BR TR 5′ 8″ 170 lbs.
B. Feb. 19, 1876, Audubon, Minn. D. Sept. 11, 1931, Santa Monica, Calif.

Year	Team	Games	BA	SA	AB	H	2B	3B	HR	HR%	R	RBI	BB	SO	SB	Pinch Hit AB	Pinch Hit H	PO	A	E	DP	TC/G	FA	G by Pos
1903	PIT N	10	.261	.478	23	6	1	2	0	0.0	2	2	0		0	3	0	8	8	1	1	2.4	.941	SS-3, OF-3, 2B-1
1906	STL N	33	.158	.211	95	15	1	2	0	0.0	2	7	6		0	5	1	54	9	6	3	2.6	.913	OF-23, 1B-4
2 yrs.		43	.178	.263	118	21	2	4	0	0.0	4	9	6		0	8	1	62	17	7	4	2.5	.919	OF-26, 1B-4, SS-3, 2B-1

Keith Marshall

MARSHALL, KEITH ALAN BR TR 6′ 2″ 175 lbs.
B. July 2, 1951, San Francisco, Calif.

Year	Team	Games	BA	SA	AB	H	2B	3B	HR	HR%	R	RBI	BB	SO	SB	Pinch Hit AB	Pinch Hit H	PO	A	E	DP	TC/G	FA	G by Pos
1973	KC A	8	.222	.333	9	2	1	0	0	0.0	0	3	1	4	0	0	0	6	0	0	0	0.8	1.000	OF-8

Max Marshall

MARSHALL, MILO MAX BL TR 6′ 1″ 180 lbs.
B. Sept. 18, 1913, Shenandoah, Iowa.

Year	Team	Games	BA	SA	AB	H	2B	3B	HR	HR%	R	RBI	BB	SO	SB	Pinch Hit AB	Pinch Hit H	PO	A	E	DP	TC/G	FA	G by Pos
1942	CIN N	131	.255	.349	530	135	17	6	7	1.3	49	43	34	38	4	1	0	245	3	6	2	2.0	.976	OF-129
1943		132	.236	.313	508	120	11	8	4	0.8	55	39	34	52	8	3	1	240	12	5	4	2.0	.981	OF-129
1944		66	.245	.371	229	56	13	2	4	1.7	36	23	21	10	3	7	1	131	6	5	3	2.4	.965	OF-59
3 yrs.		329	.245	.339	1267	311	41	16	15	1.2	140	105	89	100	15	11	2	616	21	16	9	2.1	.975	OF-317

Mike Marshall

MARSHALL, MICHAEL ALLEN (Moose) BR TR 6′ 5″ 215 lbs.
B. Jan. 12, 1960, Libertyville, Ill.

Year	Team	Games	BA	SA	AB	H	2B	3B	HR	HR%	R	RBI	BB	SO	SB	Pinch Hit AB	Pinch Hit H	PO	A	E	DP	TC/G	FA	G by Pos
1981	LA N	14	.200	.320	25	5	3	0	0	0.0	2	1	1	4	0	7	3	14	2	0	2	2.0	1.000	1B-3, 3B-3, OF-2
1982		49	.242	.432	95	23	3	0	5	5.3	10	9	13	23	2	20	3	122	5	2	6	4.0	.984	OF-19, 1B-13
1983		140	.284	.434	465	132	17	1	17	3.7	47	65	43	127	7	6	1	395	21	6	16	3.0	.986	OF-109, 1B-33
1984		134	.257	.438	495	127	27	0	21	4.2	69	65	40	93	4	7	2	331	17	5	12	2.7	.986	OF-118, 1B-15
1985		135	.293	.515	518	152	27	2	28	5.4	72	95	37	137	3	3	0	265	12	4	9	2.1	.986	OF-125, 1B-7
1986		103	.233	.439	330	77	11	0	19	5.8	47	53	27	90	4	1	0	149	8	6	1	1.7	.963	OF-97
1987		104	.294	.460	402	118	19	0	16	4.0	45	72	18	79	0	2	1	147	4	2	0	1.5	.987	OF-102
1988		144	.277	.445	542	150	27	2	20	3.7	63	82	24	93	4	4	0	605	49	7	31	4.6	.989	OF-90, 1B-53
1989		105	.260	.408	377	98	21	1	11	2.9	41	42	33	78	2	5	2	179	2	4	0	1.8	.978	OF-102
1990	2 teams	NY N (53G –.239) BOS A (30G –.286)																						
″	total	83	.258	.433	275	71	14	2	10	3.6	34	39	11	66	0	9	1	332	31	3	24	5.0	.992	1B-50, DH-14, OF-9
1991	2 teams	BOS A (22G –.290) CAL A (2G –.000)																						
″	total	24	.261	.362	69	18	4	0	1	1.4	4	7	0	20	0	7	1	63	1	1	6	3.6	.985	DH-8, 1B-6, OF-4
11 yrs.		1035	.270	.446	3593	971	173	8	148	4.1	434	530	247	810	26	71	14	2602	152	40	107	2.8	.986	OF-777, 1B-180, DH-22, 3B-3
DIVISIONAL PLAYOFF SERIES																								
1981	LA N	1	.000	.000	1	0	0	0	0	0.0	0	0	0	1	0	1	0	0	0	0	0	0.0	—	
LEAGUE CHAMPIONSHIP SERIES																								
1983	LA N	4	.133	.400	15	2	1	0	1	6.7	1	2	1	6	0	0	0	22	2	0	0	4.8	1.000	1B-3, OF-2
1985		6	.217	.435	23	5	2	0	1	4.3	1	3	1	3	0	0	0	8	0	0	0	1.3	1.000	OF-6
1988		7	.233	.333	30	7	1	1	0	0.0	3	5	2	9	0	0	0	14	0	0	0	2.0	1.000	OF-7
1990	BOS A	3	.333	.333	3	1	0	0	0	0.0	0	0	0	0	0	3	1	0	0	0	0	0.0	—	
4 yrs.		20	.211	.380	71	15	4	1	2	2.8	5	10	4	18	0	3	1	44	2	0	0	2.6	1.000	OF-15, 1B-3
														7th										
WORLD SERIES																								
1988	LA N	5	.231	.615	13	3	0	1	1	7.7	2	3	0	5	0	0	0	6	0	0	0	1.2	1.000	OF-5

Willard Marshall

MARSHALL, WILLARD WARREN BL TR 6′ 1″ 205 lbs.
B. Feb. 8, 1921, Richmond, Va.

Year	Team	Games	BA	SA	AB	H	2B	3B	HR	HR%	R	RBI	BB	SO	SB	Pinch Hit AB	Pinch Hit H	PO	A	E	DP	TC/G	FA	G by Pos
1942	NY N	116	.257	.372	401	103	9	2	11	2.7	41	59	26	20	1	8	2	222	13	6	4	2.3	.975	OF-107
1946		131	.282	.406	510	144	18	3	13	2.5	63	48	33	29	3	7	2	253	14	6	2	2.2	.978	OF-125
1947		155	.291	.528	587	171	19	6	36	6.1	102	107	67	30	3	0	0	334	19	10	6	2.3	.972	OF-155
1948		143	.272	.419	537	146	21	8	14	2.6	72	86	64	34	2	0	0	266	16	5	2	2.0	.983	OF-142
1949		141	.307	.429	499	153	19	3	12	2.4	81	70	78	20	4	3	1	292	13	8	3	2.3	.974	OF-138
1950	BOS N	105	.235	.332	298	70	10	2	5	1.7	38	40	36	5	1	20	4	150	11	7	2	2.0	.958	OF-85
1951		136	.281	.433	469	132	24	7	11	2.3	65	62	48	18	0	7	1	220	11	0	3	1.8	1.000	OF-127
1952	2 teams	BOS N (21G –.227) CIN N (107G –.267)																						
″	total	128	.261	.393	463	121	27	2	10	2.2	57	57	41	25	0	9	0	215	16	5	5	2.0	.979	OF-121
1953	CIN N	122	.266	.482	357	95	14	6	17	4.8	51	62	41	28	0	33	4	187	11	1	1	2.1	.995	OF-95
1954	CHI A	47	.254	.324	71	18	2	0	1	1.4	7	7	11	9	0	19	4	23	1	1	0	0.9	.960	OF-29
1955		22	.171	.171	41	7	0	0	0	0.0	6	6	13	1	0	7	0	22	0	1	0	1.9	.957	OF-12
11 yrs.		1246	.274	.423	4233	1160	163	39	130	3.1	583	604	458	219	14	113	18	2184	125	50	28	2.1	.979	OF-1136

Marty Martel

MARTEL, LEON ALPHONSE (Doc) BR TR 6′ 185 lbs.
B. Jan. 29, 1883, Weymouth, Mass. D. Oct. 11, 1947, Washington, D. C.

Year	Team	Games	BA	SA	AB	H	2B	3B	HR	HR%	R	RBI	BB	SO	SB	Pinch Hit AB	Pinch Hit H	PO	A	E	DP	TC/G	FA	G by Pos
1909	PHI N	24	.268	.390	41	11	3	1	0	0.0	1	7	4		0	10	3	56	19	2	1	5.9	.974	C-13
1910	BOS N	10	.129	.129	31	4	0	0	0	0.0	0	1	2	3	0	1	0	92	5	2	5	9.9	.980	1B-10
2 yrs.		34	.208	.278	72	15	3	1	0	0.0	1	8	6	3	0	11	3	148	24	4	6	7.7	.977	C-13, 1B-10

Al Martin

MARTIN, ALBERT LEE BL TL 6′ 2″ 220 lbs.
B. Nov. 24, 1967, West Covina, Calif.

Year	Team	Games	BA	SA	AB	H	2B	3B	HR	HR%	R	RBI	BB	SO	SB	Pinch Hit AB	Pinch Hit H	PO	A	E	DP	TC/G	FA	G by Pos
1992	PIT N	12	.167	.333	12	2	0	1	0	0.0	1	2	0	5	0	6	1	6	0	0	0	0.9	1.000	OF-7
1993		143	.281	.481	480	135	26	8	18	3.8	85	64	42	122	16	14	5	268	6	7	0	2.1	.975	OF-136
1994		82	.286	.457	276	79	12	4	9	3.3	48	33	34	56	15	3	0	129	8	3	1	1.8	.979	OF-77
1995		124	.282	.442	439	124	25	3	13	3.0	70	41	44	92	20	12	2	205	8	5	2	1.8	.977	OF-121
4 yrs.		361	.282	.460	1207	340	63	16	40	3.3	204	140	120	275	51	35	8	608	22	15	3	1.9	.977	OF-341

Babe Martin

MARTIN, BORIS MICHAEL BR TR 5′11½″ 194 lbs.
Born Boris Michael Martinovich.
B. Mar. 28, 1920, Seattle, Wash.

Year	Team	Games	BA	SA	AB	H	2B	3B	HR	HR%	R	RBI	BB	SO	SB	Pinch Hit AB	Pinch Hit H	PO	A	E	DP	TC/G	FA	G by Pos
1944	STL A	2	.750	1.000	4	3	1	0	0	0.0	0	1	0	0	0	1	1	1	0	0	0	1.0	1.000	OF-1
1945		54	.200	.281	185	37	5	2	2	1.1	13	16	11	24	0	1	1	152	11	3	3	3.1	.982	OF-48, 1B-6
1946		3	.222	.222	9	2	0	0	0	0.0	0	1	1	2	0	1	1	18	0	0	0	9.0	1.000	C-2

Babe Martin *continued*

Year	Team	Games	BA	SA	AB	H	2B	3B	HR	HR%	R	RBI	BB	SO	SB	Pinch Hit AB	Pinch Hit H	PO	A	E	DP	TC/G	FA	G by Pos
1948	**BOS A**	4	.500	.500	4	2	0	0	0	0.0	0	0	0	1	0	3	1	0	0	0	0	0.0	.000	C-1
1949		2	.000	.000	2	0	0	0	0	0.0	0	0	0	0	0	1	0	0	0	0	0	0.0	.000	C-1
1953	**STL A**	4	.000	.000	2	0	0	0	0	0.0	0	0	1	0	0	2	0	0	0	0	0	0.0	.000	C-1
6 yrs.		69	.214	.291	206	44	6	2	2	1.0	13	18	13	27	0	9	4	171	11	3	3	3.1	.984	OF-49, 1B-6, C-5

Bill Martin

MARTIN, WILLIAM LLOYD BR TR 5′ 8½″ 170 lbs.
B. Feb. 13, 1894, Washington, D. C. D. Sept. 14, 1949, Arlington, Va.

Year	Team	Games	BA	SA	AB	H	2B	3B	HR	HR%	R	RBI	BB	SO	SB	Pinch Hit AB	Pinch Hit H	PO	A	E	DP	TC/G	FA	G by Pos
1914	**BOS N**	1	.000	.000	3	0	0	0	0	0.0	0	0	0	0	0	0	0	0	1	1	0	2.0	.500	SS-1

Billy Martin

MARTIN, ALFRED MANUEL (The Kid) BR TR 5′11½″ 165 lbs.
B. May 16, 1928, Berkeley, Calif. D. Dec. 25, 1989, Johnson City, N. Y.
Manager 1969, 1971–83, 1985, 1988.

Year	Team	Games	BA	SA	AB	H	2B	3B	HR	HR%	R	RBI	BB	SO	SB	Pinch Hit AB	Pinch Hit H	PO	A	E	DP	TC/G	FA	G by Pos
1950	**NY A**	34	.250	.361	36	9	1	0	1	2.8	10	8	3	3	0	10	2	24	16	1	5	1.8	.976	2B-22, 3B-1
1951		51	.259	.345	58	15	1	2	0	0.0	10	2	4	9	0	10	0	45	62	4	17	3.5	.964	2B-23, SS-6, 3B-2, OF-1
1952		109	.267	.344	363	97	13	3	3	0.8	32	33	22	31	3	1	0	244	323	9	92	5.4	.984	2B-107
1953		149	.257	.395	587	151	24	6	15	2.6	72	75	43	56	6	1	0	389	409	14	126	5.0	.983	2B-146, SS-18
1955		20	.300	.371	70	21	2	0	1	1.4	8	9	7	9	1	0	0	46	50	3	20	4.9	.970	2B-17, SS-3
1956		121	.264	.397	458	121	24	5	9	2.0	76	49	30	56	7	1	0	253	288	15	87	4.6	.973	2B-105, 3B-16
1957	**2 teams**	**NY A** (43G –.241) **KC A** (73G –.257)																						
″	**total**	116	.251	.383	410	103	14	5	10	2.4	45	39	15	34	9	5	0	220	232	13	53	4.1	.972	2B-78, 3B-33, SS-2
1958	**DET A**	131	.255	.339	498	127	19	1	7	1.4	56	42	16	62	5	2	0	206	288	20	63	4.0	.961	SS-88, 3B-41
1959	**CLE A**	73	.260	.401	242	63	7	0	9	3.7	37	24	7	18	0	1	0	150	153	2	37	4.3	.993	2B-67, 3B-4
1960	**CIN N**	103	.246	.334	317	78	17	1	3	0.9	34	16	27	34	0	4	0	228	207	11	52	4.6	.975	2B-97
1961	**2 teams**	**MIL N** (6G –.000) **MIN A** (108G –.246)																						
″	**total**	114	.242	.355	380	92	15	5	6	1.6	45	36	13	43	3	9	1	217	224	17	61	4.3	.963	2B-105, SS-1
11 yrs.		1021	.257	.369	3419	877	137	28	64	1.9	425	333	187	355	34	44	3	2022	2252	109	613	4.5	.975	2B-767, SS-118, 3B-97, OF-1
WORLD SERIES																								
1951	**NY A**	1	—	—	0	0	0	0	0	—	1	0	0	0	0	0	0	0	0	0	0	0.0	—	
1952		7	.217	.348	23	5	0	0	1	4.3	2	4	2	2	0	0	0	16	16	1	5	4.7	.970	2B-7
1953		6	.500	.958	24	12	1	2	2	8.3	5	8	1	2	1	0	0	13	15	0	3	4.7	1.000	2B-6
1955		7	.320	.440	25	8	1	1	0	0.0	2	4	1	5	0	0	0	17	20	0	7	5.3	1.000	2B-7
1956		7	.296	.519	27	8	0	0	2	7.4	5	3	1	6	0	0	0	12	18	0	4	3.3	1.000	2B-7, 3B-2
5 yrs.		28	.333	.566	99	33	2	3	5	5.1	15	19	5	15	1	0	0	58	69	1	19	4.4	.992	2B-27, 3B-2
								4th																

Frank Martin

MARTIN, FRANK
B. Feb. 28, 1879, Chicago, Ill. D. Sept. 30, 1924, Chicago, Ill.

Year	Team	Games	BA	SA	AB	H	2B	3B	HR	HR%	R	RBI	BB	SO	SB	Pinch Hit AB	Pinch Hit H	PO	A	E	DP	TC/G	FA	G by Pos
1897	**LOU N**	2	.250	.250	8	2	0	0	0	0.0	1	0	0		0	0	0	4	9	3	0	8.0	.813	2B-2
1898	**CHI N**	1	.000	.000	4	0	0	0	0	0.0	0	0	0		0	0	0	5	2	0	0	7.0	1.000	2B-1
1899	**NY N**	17	.259	.296	54	14	2	0	0	0.0	5	1	2		0	0	0	24	37	13	5	4.4	.824	3B-17
3 yrs.		20	.242	.273	66	16	2	0	0	0.0	6	1	2		0	0	0	33	48	16	5	4.8	.835	3B-17, 2B-3

Gene Martin

MARTIN, THOMAS EUGENE BL TR 6′½″ 190 lbs.
B. Jan. 12, 1947, Americus, Ga.

Year	Team	Games	BA	SA	AB	H	2B	3B	HR	HR%	R	RBI	BB	SO	SB	Pinch Hit AB	Pinch Hit H	PO	A	E	DP	TC/G	FA	G by Pos
1968	**WAS A**	9	.364	.727	11	4	1	0	1	9.1	1	1	0	1	0	7	3	0	0	0	0	0.0	.000	OF-2

Hersh Martin

MARTIN, HERSHEL RAY BB TR 6′ 2″ 190 lbs.
B. Sept. 19, 1909, Birmingham, Ala. D. Nov. 17, 1980, Cuba, Mo.

Year	Team	Games	BA	SA	AB	H	2B	3B	HR	HR%	R	RBI	BB	SO	SB	Pinch Hit AB	Pinch Hit H	PO	A	E	DP	TC/G	FA	G by Pos
1937	**PHI N**	141	.283	.409	579	164	35	7	8	1.4	102	49	69	66	11	2	0	353	9	8	1	2.7	.978	OF-139
1938		120	.298	.421	466	139	36	6	3	0.6	58	39	34	48	8	4	3	298	7	11	2	2.7	.965	OF-116
1939		111	.282	.387	393	111	28	5	1	0.3	59	22	42	27	4	14	3	276	5	7	1	3.0	.976	OF-95
1940		33	.253	.349	83	21	6	1	0	0.0	10	5	9	9	1	10	4	42	4	1	0	2.0	.979	OF-23
1944	**NY A**	85	.302	.445	328	99	12	4	9	2.7	49	47	34	26	5	5	1	177	8	7	4	2.4	.964	OF-80
1945		117	.267	.392	408	109	18	6	7	1.7	53	53	65	31	4	14	5	233	8	4	1	2.4	.984	OF-102
6 yrs.		607	.285	.408	2257	643	135	29	28	1.2	331	215	253	207	33	49	16	1379	41	38	9	2.6	.974	OF-555

J. C. Martin

MARTIN, JOSEPH CLIFTON BL TR 6′ 2″ 188 lbs.
B. Dec. 13, 1936, Axton, Va.

Year	Team	Games	BA	SA	AB	H	2B	3B	HR	HR%	R	RBI	BB	SO	SB	Pinch Hit AB	Pinch Hit H	PO	A	E	DP	TC/G	FA	G by Pos
1959	**CHI A**	3	.250	.250	4	1	0	0	0	0.0	0	1	0	1	0	1	0	0	2	1	0	1.5	.667	3B-2
1960		4	.100	.150	20	2	1	0	0	0.0	0	2	0	6	0	0	0	8	8	0	0	2.7	1.000	3B-5, 1B-1
1961		110	.230	.336	274	63	8	3	5	1.8	26	32	21	31	1	11	2	353	118	10	38	5.0	.979	1B-60, 3B-36
1962		18	.077	.077	26	2	0	0	0	0.0	0	2	0	3	0	11	0	19	2	0	0	2.6	1.000	C-6, 3B-1, 1B-1
1963		105	.205	.313	259	53	11	1	5	1.9	25	28	26	35	0	12	3	476	49	9	9	5.2	.983	C-98, 1B-3, 3B-1
1964		122	.197	.279	294	58	10	1	4	1.4	23	22	16	30	0	6	0	530	43	8	6	4.8	.986	C-120
1965		119	.261	.339	230	60	12	0	2	0.9	21	21	24	29	2	15	3	385	43	7	7	3.7	.984	C-112, 1B-4, 3B-2
1966		67	.255	.363	157	40	5	3	2	1.3	13	20	14	24	0	4	1	243	23	5	3	4.3	.982	C-63
1967		101	.234	.337	252	59	12	1	4	1.6	22	22	30	41	4	6	1	479	39	7	3	5.4	.987	C-96, 1B-1
1968	**NY N**	78	.225	.316	244	55	9	2	3	1.2	20	31	21	31	0	8	1	458	31	6	11	7.4	.988	C-53, 1B-14
1969		66	.209	.316	177	37	5	1	4	2.3	12	21	12	32	0	18	3	279	9	1	2	5.8	.997	C-48, 1B-2
1970	**CHI N**	40	.156	.208	77	12	1	0	1	1.3	11	4	20	11	0	3	0	164	16	5	2	4.7	.973	C-36, 1B-3
1971		47	.264	.352	125	33	5	0	2	1.6	13	17	12	16	1	5	0	218	21	1	2	5.5	.996	C-43, OF-1
1972		25	.240	.300	50	12	3	0	0	0.0	3	7	5	9	1	9	2	60	4	2	1	3.9	.970	C-17
14 yrs.		905	.222	.315	2189	487	82	12	32	1.5	189	230	201	299	9	109	16	3672	408	62	84	5.0	.985	C-692, 1B-89, 3B-47, OF-1
LEAGUE CHAMPIONSHIP SERIES																								
1969	**NY N**	2	.500	.500	2	1	0	0	0	0.0	0	2	0	0	0	2	1	0	0	0	0	0.0	—	
WORLD SERIES																								
1969	**NY N**	1	—	—	0	0	0	0	0	—	0	0	0	0	0	0	0	0	0	0	0	0.0	—	

Jack Martin

MARTIN, JOHN CHRISTOPHER BR TR 5′ 9″ 159 lbs.
B. Apr. 19, 1887, Plainfield, N. J. D. July 4, 1980, Bronx, N. Y.

Year	Team	Games	BA	SA	AB	H	2B	3B	HR	HR%	R	RBI	BB	SO	SB	Pinch Hit AB	Pinch Hit H	PO	A	E	DP	TC/G	FA	G by Pos
1912	NY A	69	.225	.260	231	52	6	1	0	0.0	30	17	37		14	0	0	127	217	39	18	5.6	.898	SS-64, 3B-4, 2B-1
1914	2 teams	BOS N (33G –.212) PHI N (83G –.253)																						
″	total	116	.244	.279	377	92	7	3	0	0.0	36	26	33	36	6	3	0	217	294	38	29	4.9	.931	SS-83, 3B-27, 1B-1, 2B-1
2 yrs.		185	.237	.271	608	144	13	4	0	0.0	66	43	70	36	20	3	0	344	511	77	47	5.1	.917	SS-147, 3B-31, 2B-2, 1B-1

Jerry Martin

MARTIN, JERRY LINDSEY BR TR 6′ 1″ 195 lbs.
Son of Barney Martin.
B. May 11, 1949, Columbia, S. C.

Year	Team	Games	BA	SA	AB	H	2B	3B	HR	HR%	R	RBI	BB	SO	SB	Pinch Hit AB	Pinch Hit H	PO	A	E	DP	TC/G	FA	G by Pos
1974	PHI N	13	.214	.286	14	3	1	0	0	0.0	2	1	1	5	0	4	1	5	0	0	0	0.5	1.000	OF-11
1975		57	.212	.345	113	24	7	1	2	1.8	15	11	11	16	2	9	1	90	3	2	1	1.9	.979	OF-49
1976		130	.248	.355	121	30	7	0	2	1.7	30	15	7	28	3	22	6	85	0	2	2	0.8	.977	OF-110, 1B-1
1977		116	.260	.447	215	56	16	3	6	2.8	34	28	18	42	6	18	5	117	4	2	1	1.1	.984	OF-106, 1B-1
1978		128	.271	.451	266	72	13	4	9	3.4	40	36	28	65	9	24	5	148	8	2	1	1.4	.987	OF-112
1979	CHI N	150	.272	.453	534	145	34	3	19	3.6	74	73	38	85	2	8	1	297	11	6	4	2.2	.981	OF-144
1980		141	.227	.419	494	112	22	2	23	4.7	57	73	38	107	8	11	2	262	8	6	0	2.1	.978	OF-129
1981	SF N	72	.241	.336	241	58	5	3	4	1.7	23	25	21	52	6	7	0	138	4	1	1	2.2	.993	OF-64
1982	KC A	147	.266	.399	519	138	22	1	15	2.9	52	65	38	138	1	7	2	333	4	7	2	2.4	.980	OF-142, DH-3
1983		13	.318	.500	44	14	2	0	2	4.5	4	13	1	7	1	0	0	22	0	1	0	1.8	.957	OF-13
1984	NY N	51	.154	.264	91	14	1	0	3	3.3	6	5	6	29	0	24	3	56	3	0	5	1.8	1.000	OF-30, 1B-3
11 yrs.		1018	.251	.409	2652	666	130	17	85	3.2	337	345	207	574	38	134	26	1553	45	29	17	1.8	.982	OF-910, 1B-5, DH-3
LEAGUE CHAMPIONSHIP SERIES																								
1976	PHI N	1	.000	.000	1	0	0	0	0	0.0	1	0	0	0	0	0	0	1	0	0	0	1.0	1.000	OF-1
1977		3	.000	.000	4	0	0	0	0	0.0	0	0	0	2	0	1	0	1	0	0	0	1.0	1.000	OF-1
1978		4	.222	.667	9	2	1	0	1	11.1	1	2	1	3	0	2	1	7	0	0	0	2.3	1.000	OF-3
3 yrs.		8	.143	.429	14	2	1	0	1	7.1	2	2	1	5	0	3	1	9	0	0	0	1.8	1.000	OF-5

Joe Martin

MARTIN, JOSEPH SAMUEL (Silent Joe) BL TR 5′ 9½″ 155 lbs.
B. Jan. 1, 1876, Hollidaysburg, Pa. D. May 25, 1964, Altoona, Pa.

Year	Team	Games	BA	SA	AB	H	2B	3B	HR	HR%	R	RBI	BB	SO	SB	Pinch Hit AB	Pinch Hit H	PO	A	E	DP	TC/G	FA	G by Pos
1903	2 teams	WAS A (35G –.227) STL A (44G –.214)																						
″	total	79	.219	.315	292	64	10	9	0	0.0	29	14	11		2	1	1	119	82	21	9	2.8	.905	OF-45, 2B-21, 3B-14

Joe Martin

MARTIN, WILLIAM JOSEPH (Smokey Joe) BR TR 5′11½″ 181 lbs.
B. Aug. 28, 1911, Seymour, Mo. D. Sept. 28, 1960, Buffalo, N. Y.

Year	Team	Games	BA	SA	AB	H	2B	3B	HR	HR%	R	RBI	BB	SO	SB	Pinch Hit AB	Pinch Hit H	PO	A	E	DP	TC/G	FA	G by Pos
1936	NY N	7	.267	.333	15	4	1	0	0	0.0	0	2	0	4	0	0	0	5	8	0	1	1.9	1.000	3B-7
1938	CHI A	1	—	—	0	0	0	0	0	—	0	0	0	0	0	0	0	0	0	0	0	0.0	—	
2 yrs.		8	.267	.333	15	4	1	0	0	0.0	0	2	0	4	0	0	0	5	8	0	1	1.9	1.000	3B-7

Mike Martin

MARTIN, JOSEPH MICHAEL BL TR 6′ 2″ 193 lbs.
B. Dec. 3, 1958, Portland, Ore.

Year	Team	Games	BA	SA	AB	H	2B	3B	HR	HR%	R	RBI	BB	SO	SB	Pinch Hit AB	Pinch Hit H	PO	A	E	DP	TC/G	FA	G by Pos
1986	CHI N	8	.077	.154	13	1	1	0	0	0.0	1	0	2	4	0	1	0	18	5	0	0	2.9	1.000	C-8

Norberto Martin

MARTIN, NORBERTO ENRIQUE (Paco) BR TR 5′10″ 175 lbs.
Born Norberto Enrique Martin (McDonald).
B. Dec. 10, 1966, San Pedro de Macoris, Dominican Republic.

Year	Team	Games	BA	SA	AB	H	2B	3B	HR	HR%	R	RBI	BB	SO	SB	Pinch Hit AB	Pinch Hit H	PO	A	E	DP	TC/G	FA	G by Pos
1993	CHI A	8	.357	.357	14	5	0	0	0	0.0	3	2	1	1	0	1	0	13	9	1	4	3.8	.957	2B-5, DH-1
1994		45	.275	.366	131	36	7	1	1	0.8	19	16	9	16	4	5	1	58	77	2	11	3.3	.985	2B-28, SS-6, 3B-5, OF-2, DH-1
1995		72	.269	.400	160	43	7	4	2	1.3	17	17	3	25	5	18	6	52	67	7	16	2.3	.944	2B-17, OF-12, DH-10, 3B-9, SS-7
3 yrs.		125	.275	.384	305	84	14	5	3	1.0	39	35	13	42	9	24	7	123	153	10	31	2.8	.965	2B-50, OF-14, 3B-14, SS-13, DH-12

Pepper Martin

MARTIN, JOHN LEONARD ROOSEVELT (The Wild Hoss Of The Osage) BR TR 5′ 8″ 170 lbs.
B. Feb. 29, 1904, Temple, Okla. D. Mar. 5, 1965, McAlester, Okla.

Year	Team	Games	BA	SA	AB	H	2B	3B	HR	HR%	R	RBI	BB	SO	SB	Pinch Hit AB	Pinch Hit H	PO	A	E	DP	TC/G	FA	G by Pos
1928	STL N	39	.308	.308	13	4	0	0	0	0.0	11	0	1	2	2	12	3	2	0	0	0	0.5	1.000	OF-4
1930		6	.000	.000	1	0	0	0	0	0.0	5	0	0	0	0	1	0	0	0	0	0	0.0	—	
1931		123	.300	.467	413	124	32	8	7	1.7	68	75	30	40	16	7	4	282	10	10	2	2.7	.967	OF-110
1932		85	.238	.372	323	77	19	6	4	1.2	47	34	30	31	9	0	0	169	28	5	4	2.4	.975	OF-69, 3B-15
1933		145	.316	.456	599	189	36	12	8	1.3	**122**	57	67	46	**26**	0	0	139	273	25	14	3.0	.943	3B-145
1934		110	.289	.425	454	131	25	11	5	1.1	76	49	32	41	**23**	1	0	85	196	19	7	2.8	.937	3B-107, P-1
1935		135	.299	.447	539	161	41	6	9	1.7	121	54	33	58	20	5	0	145	171	32	17	2.7	.908	3B-114, OF-16
1936		143	.309	.469	572	177	36	11	11	1.9	121	76	58	66	**23**	1	0	239	25	13	6	1.9	.953	OF-127, 3B-15, P-1
1937		98	.304	.475	339	103	27	8	5	1.5	60	38	33	50	9	9	2	210	20	7	5	2.7	.970	OF-82, 3B-5
1938		91	.294	.398	269	79	18	2	2	0.7	34	38	18	34	4	23	5	139	4	2	1	2.2	.986	OF-62, 3B-4
1939		88	.306	.448	281	86	17	7	3	1.1	48	37	30	35	6	10	0	128	34	7	2	2.3	.959	OF-51, 3B-22
1940		86	.316	.456	228	72	15	4	3	1.3	28	39	22	24	6	17	4	106	13	3	0	1.9	.975	OF-63, 3B-2
1944		40	.279	.395	86	24	4	0	2	2.3	15	4	15	11	2	5	1	48	1	1	0	1.7	.980	OF-29
13 yrs.		1189	.298	.443	4117	1227	270	75	59	1.4	756	501	369	438	146	91	19	1692	775	124	58	2.5	.952	OF-613, 3B-429, P-2
WORLD SERIES																								
1928	STL N	1	—	—	0	0	0	0	0	—	1	0	0	0	0	0	0	0	0	0	0	0.0	—	
1931		7	.500	.792	24	12	4	0	1	4.2	5	5	2	3	5	0	0	10	0	0	0	1.4	1.000	OF-7
1934		7	.355	.516	31	11	3	1	0	0.0	8	3	3	3	2	0	0	6	9	4	0	2.7	.789	3B-7
3 yrs.		15	.418	.636	55	23	7	1	1	1.8	14	8	5	6	7	0	0	16	9	4	0	2.1	.862	3B-7, OF-7
			1st	**7th**											**9th**									

Stu Martin

MARTIN, STUART McGUIRE BL TR 6′ 155 lbs.
B. Nov. 17, 1913, Rich Square, N. C.

Year	Team	Games	BA	SA	AB	H	2B	3B	HR	HR%	R	RBI	BB	SO	SB	Pinch Hit AB	Pinch Hit H	PO	A	E	DP	TC/G	FA	G by Pos
1936	STL N	92	.298	.440	332	99	21	4	6	1.8	63	41	29	27	17	4	0	173	250	22	52	5.2	.951	2B-83, SS-3
1937		90	.260	.309	223	58	6	1	1	0.4	34	17	32	18	3	28	6	168	138	14	30	5.5	.956	2B-48, 1B-9, SS-1
1938		114	.278	.357	417	116	26	2	1	0.2	54	27	30	28	4	15	3	225	301	18	59	5.5	.967	2B-99
1939		120	.268	.384	425	114	26	7	3	0.7	60	30	33	40	4	11	0	249	305	13	62	5.3	.977	2B-107, 1B-1
1940		112	.238	.336	369	88	12	6	4	1.1	45	32	33	35	4	9	1	99	160	7	14	2.5	.974	3B-73, 2B-33

Stu Martin *continued*

Year	Team	Games	BA	SA	AB	H	2B	3B	HR	HR%	R	RBI	BB	SO	SB	Pinch Hit AB	Pinch Hit H	PO	A	E	DP	TC/G	FA	G by Pos
1941	PIT N	88	.305	.378	233	71	13	2	0	0.0	37	19	10	17	2	28	6	134	157	9	26	5.4	.970	2B-53, 3B-2, 1B-1
1942		42	.225	.317	120	27	4	2	1	0.8	16	12	8	10	1	10	0	69	70	3	14	4.4	.979	2B-30, 1B-1, SS-1
1943	CHI N	64	.220	.254	118	26	4	0	0	0.0	13	5	15	10	1	25	5	64	69	2	11	4.2	.985	2B-22, 3B-8, 1B-2
8 yrs.		722	.268	.361	2237	599	112	24	16	0.7	322	183	190	185	36	130	21	1181	1450	88	268	4.7	.968	2B-475, 3B-83, 1B-14, SS-5

Buck Martinez

MARTINEZ, JOHN ALBERT BR TR 5′10″ 190 lbs.
B. Nov. 7, 1948, Redding, Calif.

Year	Team	Games	BA	SA	AB	H	2B	3B	HR	HR%	R	RBI	BB	SO	SB	Pinch Hit AB	Pinch Hit H	PO	A	E	DP	TC/G	FA	G by Pos
1969	KC A	72	.229	.327	205	47	6	1	4	2.0	14	23	8	25	0	18	4	292	26	9	8	5.8	.972	C-55, OF-1
1970		6	.111	.111	9	1	0	0	0	0.0	1	0	2	1	0	1	0	20	3	1	0	4.8	.958	C-5
1971		22	.152	.196	46	7	2	0	0	0.0	3	1	5	9	0	1	0	84	6	3	0	4.4	.968	C-21
1973		14	.250	.375	32	8	1	0	1	3.1	2	6	4	5	0	0	0	52	4	2	1	4.1	.966	C-14
1974		43	.215	.290	107	23	3	1	1	0.9	10	8	14	19	0	4	2	151	16	4	1	4.5	.977	C-38
1975		80	.226	.323	226	51	9	2	3	1.3	15	23	21	28	1	1	0	361	39	8	4	5.2	.980	C-79
1976		95	.228	.356	267	61	13	3	5	1.9	24	34	16	45	0	4	1	420	40	4	4	4.9	.991	C-94
1977		29	.225	.313	80	18	4	0	1	1.3	3	9	3	12	0	2	0	133	8	1	0	4.9	.993	C-29
1978	MIL A	89	.219	.277	256	56	10	1	1	0.4	26	20	14	42	1	0	0	327	32	8	7	4.1	.978	C-89
1979		69	.270	.372	196	53	8	0	4	2.0	17	26	8	25	0	0	0	198	39	8	2	3.6	.967	C-68, P-1
1980		76	.224	.306	219	49	9	0	3	1.4	16	17	12	33	1	0	0	293	33	5	0	4.4	.985	C-76
1981	TOR A	45	.227	.398	128	29	8	1	4	3.1	13	21	11	16	1	0	0	192	22	2	3	4.8	.991	C-45
1982		96	.242	.423	260	63	17	0	10	3.8	26	37	24	34	1	10	4	382	35	5	8	4.5	.988	C-93
1983		88	.253	.452	221	56	14	0	10	4.5	27	33	29	39	0	12	4	331	25	4	3	4.2	.989	C-85
1984		102	.220	.349	232	51	13	1	5	2.2	24	37	29	49	0	18	1	360	34	2	5	4.0	.995	C-98, DH-1
1985		42	.162	.313	99	16	3	0	4	4.0	11	14	10	12	0	4	1	155	16	2	5	4.1	.988	C-42
1986		81	.181	.269	160	29	8	0	2	1.3	13	12	20	25	0	17	4	289	19	2	6	3.9	.994	C-78, DH-1
17 yrs.		1049	.225	.343	2743	618	128	10	58	2.1	245	321	230	419	5	92	21	4040	397	70	57	4.4	.984	C-1009, DH-2, P-1, OF-1
LEAGUE CHAMPIONSHIP SERIES																								
1976	KC A	5	.333	.333	15	5	0	0	0	0.0	0	4	1	3	0	0	0	15	4	0	1	3.8	1.000	C-5

Carlos Martinez

MARTINEZ, CARLOS ALBERTO BR TR 6′ 5″ 175 lbs.
Born Carlos Alberto Escobar (Martinez).
B. Aug. 11, 1964, LaGuaira, Venezuela.

Year	Team	Games	BA	SA	AB	H	2B	3B	HR	HR%	R	RBI	BB	SO	SB	Pinch Hit AB	Pinch Hit H	PO	A	E	DP	TC/G	FA	G by Pos
1988	CHI A	17	.164	.182	55	9	1	0	0	0.0	5	0	0	12	1	0	0	7	33	4	1	2.9	.909	3B-15
1989		109	.300	.406	350	105	22	0	5	1.4	44	32	21	57	4	5	2	283	134	20	25	3.9	.954	3B-68, 1B-34, OF-10, DH-1
1990		92	.224	.327	272	61	6	5	4	1.5	18	24	10	40	0	10	3	632	38	8	50	7.9	.988	1B-82, DH-3, OF-1
1991	CLE A	72	.284	.397	257	73	14	0	5	1.9	22	30	10	43	3	2	0	229	12	8	30	3.5	.968	DH-41, 1B-31
1992		69	.263	.377	228	60	9	1	5	2.2	23	35	7	21	1	9	3	276	57	4	46	4.9	.988	1B-37, 3B-28, DH-4
1993		80	.244	.340	262	64	10	0	5	1.9	26	31	20	29	1	9	1	162	51	9	17	2.9	.959	3B-35, 1B-22, DH-19
1995	CAL A	26	.180	.246	61	11	1	0	1	1.6	7	9	6	7	0	4	1	25	25	1	8	2.3	.980	3B-16, 1B-4, DH-2
7 yrs.		465	.258	.359	1485	383	63	6	25	1.7	145	161	74	209	10	39	10	1614	350	54	177	4.5	.973	1B-210, 3B-162, DH-70, OF-11

Carmelo Martinez

MARTINEZ, CARMELO BR TR 6′ 2″ 185 lbs.
Born Carmelo Martinez (Salgado).
B. July 28, 1960, Dorado, Puerto Rico.

Year	Team	Games	BA	SA	AB	H	2B	3B	HR	HR%	R	RBI	BB	SO	SB	Pinch Hit AB	Pinch Hit H	PO	A	E	DP	TC/G	FA	G by Pos
1983	CHI N	29	.258	.494	89	23	3	0	6	6.7	8	16	4	19	0	4	1	233	17	2	18	9.0	.992	1B-26, OF-1, 3B-1
1984	SD N	149	.250	.395	488	122	28	2	13	2.7	64	66	68	82	1	4	0	317	15	8	4	2.4	.976	OF-142, 1B-2
1985		150	.253	.434	514	130	28	1	21	4.1	64	72	87	82	0	0	0	302	14	7	5	2.1	.978	OF-150, 1B-3
1986		113	.238	.389	244	58	10	0	9	3.7	28	25	35	46	1	36	8	142	14	2	4	1.8	.987	OF-60, 1B-26, 3B-1
1987		139	.273	.430	447	122	21	2	15	3.4	59	70	70	82	5	7	1	591	42	9	41	4.5	.986	OF-78, 1B-65
1988		121	.236	.416	365	86	12	0	18	4.9	48	65	35	57	1	28	8	430	32	4	31	4.4	.991	OF-64, 1B-41
1989		111	.221	.348	267	59	12	2	6	2.2	23	39	32	54	0	32	7	225	18	2	11	2.5	.992	OF-65, 1B-32
1990	2 teams	PHI N (71G –.242) PIT N (12G –.211)																						
″	total	83	.240	.419	217	52	9	0	10	4.6	26	35	30	42	2	17	4	374	29	2	35	5.8	.995	1B-48, OF-22
1991	3 teams	PIT N (11G –.250) KC A (44G –.207) CIN N (53G –.232)																						
″	total	108	.222	.371	275	61	11	0	10	3.6	30	36	43	64	0	19	5	581	48	9	45	6.9	.986	1B-76, OF-16, DH-1
9 yrs.		1003	.245	.408	2906	713	134	7	108	3.7	350	424	404	528	10	147	34	3195	229	45	194	3.8	.987	OF-598, 1B-319, 3B-2, DH-1
LEAGUE CHAMPIONSHIP SERIES																								
1984	SD N	5	.176	.176	17	3	0	0	0	0.0	1	0	2	4	0	0	0	6	0	0	0	1.2	1.000	OF-5
1990	PIT N	2	.250	.500	8	2	2	0	0	0.0	0	2	0	1	0	0	0	15	1	0	1	8.0	1.000	1B-2
2 yrs.		7	.200	.280	25	5	2	0	0	0.0	1	2	2	5	0	0	0	21	1	0	1	3.1	1.000	OF-5, 1B-2
WORLD SERIES																								
1984	SD N	5	.176	.176	17	3	0	0	0	0.0	0	0	1	9	0	0	0	7	0	1	0	1.6	.875	OF-5

Chito Martinez

MARTINEZ, REYENALDO IGNACIO BL TL 5′10″ 180 lbs.
B. Dec. 19, 1965, Belize, British Honduras.

Year	Team	Games	BA	SA	AB	H	2B	3B	HR	HR%	R	RBI	BB	SO	SB	Pinch Hit AB	Pinch Hit H	PO	A	E	DP	TC/G	FA	G by Pos
1991	BAL A	67	.269	.514	216	58	12	1	13	6.0	32	33	11	51	1	8	1	112	4	2	2	2.0	.983	OF-54, DH-4, 1B-1
1992		83	.268	.404	198	53	10	1	5	2.5	26	25	31	47	0	22	4	104	4	3	1	2.0	.973	OF-52, DH-4
1993		8	.000	.000	15	0	0	0	0	0.0	0	0	4	4	0	3	0	2	0	0	0	0.3	1.000	OF-5, DH-2
3 yrs.		158	.259	.445	429	111	22	2	18	4.2	58	58	46	102	1	33	5	218	8	5	3	1.9	.978	OF-111, DH-10, 1B-1

Dave Martinez

MARTINEZ, DAVID BL TL 5′10″ 150 lbs.
B. Sept. 26, 1964, New York, N. Y.

Year	Team	Games	BA	SA	AB	H	2B	3B	HR	HR%	R	RBI	BB	SO	SB	Pinch Hit AB	Pinch Hit H	PO	A	E	DP	TC/G	FA	G by Pos
1986	CHI N	53	.139	.194	108	15	1	1	1	0.9	13	7	6	22	4	5	1	77	2	1	1	1.7	.988	OF-46
1987		142	.292	.418	459	134	18	8	8	1.7	70	36	57	96	16	11	3	283	10	6	1	2.2	.980	OF-139
1988	2 teams	CHI N (75G –.254) MON N (63G –.257)																						
″	total	138	.255	.351	447	114	13	6	6	1.3	51	46	38	94	23	11	1	281	4	6	1	2.2	.979	OF-132
1989	MON N	126	.274	.382	361	99	16	7	3	0.8	41	27	27	57	23	11	3	199	7	7	1	1.8	.967	OF-118
1990		118	.279	.422	391	109	13	5	11	2.8	60	39	24	48	13	14	3	257	6	3	1	2.4	.989	OF-108, P-1
1991		124	.295	.419	396	117	18	5	7	1.8	47	42	20	54	16	11	4	213	10	4	0	2.0	.982	OF-112
1992	CIN N	135	.254	.354	393	100	20	5	3	0.8	47	31	42	54	12	12	0	382	18	6	23	3.1	.985	OF-111, 1B-21
1993	SF N	91	.241	.361	241	58	12	1	5	2.1	28	27	27	39	6	20	3	131	6	1	2	1.9	.993	OF-73

Dave Martinez *continued*

Year	Team	Games	BA	SA	AB	H	2B	3B	HR	HR%	R	RBI	BB	SO	SB	Pinch Hit AB	Pinch Hit H	PO	A	E	DP	TC/G	FA	G by Pos
1994		97	.247	.362	235	58	9	3	4	1.7	23	27	21	22	3	25	8	255	18	3	17	3.3	.989	OF-58, 1B-25
1995	CHI A	118	.307	.436	303	93	16	4	5	1.7	49	37	32	41	8	16	6	392	25	3	38	3.8	.993	OF-59, 1B-48, DH-4, P-1
10 yrs.		1142	.269	.385	3334	897	136	45	53	1.6	429	319	294	527	124	136	32	2470	106	40	85	2.5	.985	OF-956, 1B-94, DH-4, P-2

Domingo Martinez

MARTINEZ, DOMINGO EMILIO BR TR 6′ 2″ 215 lbs.
Born Domingo Emilio Martinez (La Fontaine).
B. Aug. 4, 1967, Santo Domingo, Dominican Republic.

Year	Team	Games	BA	SA	AB	H	2B	3B	HR	HR%	R	RBI	BB	SO	SB	Pinch Hit AB	Pinch Hit H	PO	A	E	DP	TC/G	FA	G by Pos
1992	TOR A	7	.625	1.000	8	5	0	0	1	12.5	2	3	0	1	0	2	2	12	0	0	2	1.7	1.000	1B-7
1993		8	.286	.500	14	4	0	0	1	7.1	2	3	1	7	0	2	1	25	4	0	2	3.6	1.000	1B-7, 3B-1
2 yrs.		15	.409	.682	22	9	0	0	2	9.1	4	6	1	8	0	4	3	37	4	0	4	2.7	1.000	1B-14, 3B-1

Edgar Martinez

MARTINEZ, EDGAR BR TR 6′ 175 lbs.
B. Jan. 2, 1963, New York, N. Y.

Year	Team	Games	BA	SA	AB	H	2B	3B	HR	HR%	R	RBI	BB	SO	SB	Pinch Hit AB	Pinch Hit H	PO	A	E	DP	TC/G	FA	G by Pos
1987	SEA A	13	.372	.581	43	16	5	2	0	0.0	6	5	2	5	0	1	0	13	19	0	1	2.5	1.000	3B-12, DH-1
1988		14	.281	.406	32	9	4	0	0	0.0	0	5	4	7	0	1	1	5	8	1	1	1.1	.929	3B-13
1989		65	.240	.304	171	41	5	0	2	1.2	20	20	17	26	2	8	1	40	72	6	9	1.9	.949	3B-61
1990		144	.302	.433	487	147	27	2	11	2.3	71	49	74	62	1	1	0	89	259	27	16	2.6	.928	3B-143, DH-2
1991		150	.307	.452	544	167	35	1	14	2.6	98	52	84	72	0	3	1	84	299	15	25	2.7	.962	3B-144, DH-2
1992		135	**.343**	.544	528	181	**46**	3	18	3.4	100	73	54	61	14	3	0	88	211	17	25	2.4	.946	3B-103, DH-28, 1B-2
1993		42	.237	.378	135	32	7	0	4	3.0	20	13	28	19	0	2	1	5	11	2	1	0.4	.889	DH-24, 3B-16
1994		89	.285	.482	326	93	23	1	13	4.0	47	51	53	42	6	0	0	44	127	9	8	2.0	.950	3B-65, DH-23
1995		145	**.356**	.628	511	182	**52**	0	29	5.7	**121**	113	116	87	4	0	0	30	4	2	0	0.2	.944	DH-138, 3B-4, 1B-3
9 yrs.		797	.313	.491	2777	868	204	9	91	3.3	483	381	432	381	27	19	4	398	1010	79	86	1.9	.947	3B-561, DH-218, 1B-5
DIVISIONAL PLAYOFF SERIES																								
1995	SEA A	5	.571	1.000	21	12	3	0	2	9.5	6	10	6	2	0	0	0	0	0	0	0	0.0	.000	DH-5
LEAGUE CHAMPIONSHIP SERIES																								
1995	SEA A	6	.087	.087	23	2	0	0	0	0.0	0	0	2	5	1	0	0	0	0	0	0	0.0	.000	DH-6

Hector Martinez

MARTINEZ, RODOLFO HECTOR BR TR 5′10″ 160 lbs.
B. May 11, 1939, Las Villas, Cuba.

Year	Team	Games	BA	SA	AB	H	2B	3B	HR	HR%	R	RBI	BB	SO	SB	Pinch Hit AB	Pinch Hit H	PO	A	E	DP	TC/G	FA	G by Pos
1962	KC A	1	.000	.000	1	0	0	0	0	0.0	0	0	0	1	0	1	0	0	0	0	0	0.0	—	
1963		6	.286	.500	14	4	0	0	1	7.1	2	3	1	3	0	3	0	7	0	0	0	2.3	1.000	OF-3
2 yrs.		7	.267	.467	15	4	0	0	1	6.7	2	3	1	4	0	4	0	7	0	0	0	2.3	1.000	OF-3

Jose Martinez

MARTINEZ, JOSE BR TR 6′ 178 lbs.
Born Jose Martinez (Azcuiz).
B. July 26, 1942, Cardenas, Cuba.

Year	Team	Games	BA	SA	AB	H	2B	3B	HR	HR%	R	RBI	BB	SO	SB	Pinch Hit AB	Pinch Hit H	PO	A	E	DP	TC/G	FA	G by Pos
1969	PIT N	77	.268	.321	168	45	6	0	1	0.6	20	16	9	32	1	6	2	86	132	6	31	3.2	.973	2B-42, SS-20, 3B-5, OF-2
1970		19	.050	.050	20	1	0	0	0	0.0	1	0	1	5	0	3	0	12	17	3	4	2.7	.906	3B-7, 2B-4, SS-1
2 yrs.		96	.245	.293	188	46	6	0	1	0.5	21	16	10	37	1	9	2	98	149	9	35	3.2	.965	2B-46, SS-21, 3B-12, OF-2

Marty Martinez

MARTINEZ, ORLANDO BB TR 6′ 170 lbs.
BR 1962
Born Orlando Martinez Oliva.
B. Aug. 23, 1941, Havana, Cuba.
Manager 1986.

Year	Team	Games	BA	SA	AB	H	2B	3B	HR	HR%	R	RBI	BB	SO	SB	Pinch Hit AB	Pinch Hit H	PO	A	E	DP	TC/G	FA	G by Pos
1962	MIN A	37	.167	.278	18	3	0	1	0	0.0	13	3	3	4	0	0	0	6	18	2	2	2.2	.923	SS-11, 3B-1
1967	ATL N	44	.288	.342	73	21	2	1	0	0.0	14	5	11	11	0	0	0	45	73	9	16	3.2	.929	SS-25, 2B-9, C-3, 3B-2, 1B-1
1968		113	.230	.261	356	82	5	3	0	0.0	34	12	29	28	6	1	0	169	264	18	44	3.7	.960	SS-54, 3B-37, 2B-16, C-14
1969	HOU N	78	.308	.374	198	61	5	4	0	0.0	14	15	10	21	0	18	4	77	66	11	8	2.5	.929	OF-21, SS-17, 3B-15, C-7, 2B-1, P-1
1970		75	.220	.240	150	33	3	0	0	0.0	12	12	9	22	0	38	9	57	78	2	10	2.8	.985	SS-29, 3B-10, C-6, 2B-4
1971		32	.258	.339	62	16	3	1	0	0.0	4	4	3	6	1	13	4	29	37	1	7	2.9	.985	2B-9, SS-7, 1B-4, 3B-3
1972	3 teams	STL N (9G –.429) TEX A (26G –.146) OAK A (22G –.125)																						
″	total	57	.159	.193	88	14	1	1	0	0.0	6	6	5	15	0	19	4	44	56	7	11	2.7	.935	2B-20, SS-14, 3B-6
7 yrs.		436	.243	.287	945	230	19	11	0	0.0	97	57	70	107	7	89	21	427	592	50	98	3.1	.953	SS-157, 3B-74, 2B-59, C-30, OF-21, 1B-5, P-1

Sandy Martinez

MARTINEZ, ANGEL SANDY BL TR 6′ 2″ 200 lbs.
Born Angel Sandy Martinez (Martinez).
B. Oct. 3, 1972, Villa Mella, Dominican Republic.

Year	Team	Games	BA	SA	AB	H	2B	3B	HR	HR%	R	RBI	BB	SO	SB	Pinch Hit AB	Pinch Hit H	PO	A	E	DP	TC/G	FA	G by Pos
1995	TOR A	62	.241	.335	191	46	12	0	2	1.0	12	25	7	45	0	3	0	329	28	5	5	5.9	.986	C-61

Teddy Martinez

MARTINEZ, TEODORO NOEL BR TR 6′ 165 lbs.
BB 1973
Born Teodoro Noel Martinez (Encarnacion).
B. Dec. 10, 1947, Barahona, Dominican Republic.

Year	Team	Games	BA	SA	AB	H	2B	3B	HR	HR%	R	RBI	BB	SO	SB	Pinch Hit AB	Pinch Hit H	PO	A	E	DP	TC/G	FA	G by Pos
1970	NY N	4	.063	.063	16	1	0	0	0	0.0	0	0	0	3	0	0	0	9	11	0	4	4.0	1.000	2B-4, SS-1
1971		38	.288	.384	125	36	5	2	1	0.8	16	10	4	22	6	1	0	45	80	3	17	3.2	.977	SS-23, 2B-13, 3B-3, OF-1
1972		103	.224	.279	330	74	5	5	1	0.3	22	19	12	49	7	4	0	175	194	5	30	3.5	.987	2B-47, SS-42, OF-15, 3B-2
1973		92	.255	.308	263	67	11	0	1	0.4	34	14	13	38	3	1	0	119	139	12	15	3.2	.956	SS-44, OF-21, 3B-14, 2B-5
1974		116	.219	.323	334	73	15	7	2	0.6	32	43	14	40	3	8	1	164	257	20	38	4.1	.955	SS-75, 3B-12, 2B-11, OF-10
1975	2 teams	STL N (16G –.190) OAK A (86G –.172)																						
″	total	102	.176	.194	108	19	2	0	0	0.0	8	5	2	11	1	11	1	72	84	5	16	1.6	.969	SS-46, 2B-33, 3B-15, OF-7
1977	LA N	67	.299	.380	137	41	6	1	1	0.7	21	10	2	20	3	4	0	80	96	3	29	3.4	.983	2B-27, SS-13, 3B-12
1978		54	.255	.327	55	14	1	0	1	1.8	13	5	4	14	3	4	0	39	51	5	7	2.2	.947	SS-17, 3B-16, 2B-10
1979		81	.268	.330	112	30	5	1	0	0.0	19	2	4	16	3	4	0	45	69	5	7	1.9	.958	3B-23, SS-21, 2B-18
9 yrs.		657	.240	.309	1480	355	50	16	7	0.5	165	108	55	213	29	37	2	748	981	58	163	3.0	.968	SS-282, 2B-168, 3B-97, OF-54
LEAGUE CHAMPIONSHIP SERIES																								
1975	OAK A	3	—	—	0	0	0	0	0	—	0	0	0	0	0	0	0	1	1	0	0	0.7	1.000	2B-3
WORLD SERIES																								
1973	NY N	2	—	—	0	0	0	0	0	—	0	0	0	0	0	0	0	0	0	0	0	0.0	—	

Tino Martinez

MARTINEZ, CONSTANTINO BL TR 6′ 2″ 205 lbs.
B. Dec. 7, 1967, Tampa, Fla.

Year	Team	Games	BA	SA	AB	H	2B	3B	HR	HR%	R	RBI	BB	SO	SB	Pinch Hit AB	Pinch Hit H	PO	A	E	DP	TC/G	FA	G by Pos
1990	SEA A	24	.221	.279	68	15	4	0	0	0.0	4	5	9	9	0	2	0	155	12	0	25	7.3	1.000	1B-23
1991		36	.205	.330	112	23	2	0	4	3.6	11	9	11	24	0	5	2	249	22	2	24	8.0	.993	1B-29, DH-5
1992		136	.257	.411	460	118	19	2	16	3.5	53	66	42	77	2	11	1	678	58	4	62	5.9	.995	1B-78, DH-47
1993		109	.265	.456	408	108	25	1	17	4.2	48	60	45	56	0	0	0	932	60	3	89	9.1	.997	1B-103, DH-6
1994		97	.261	.508	329	86	21	0	20	6.1	42	61	29	52	1	5	1	705	45	2	62	8.4	.997	1B-82, DH-8
1995		141	.293	.551	519	152	35	3	31	6.0	92	111	62	91	0	3	1	1043	103	8	86	8.2	.993	1B-139, DH-1
6 yrs.		543	.265	.466	1896	502	106	6	88	4.6	250	312	198	309	3	26	5	3762	300	19	348	7.8	.995	1B-454, DH-67
DIVISIONAL PLAYOFF SERIES																								
1995	SEA A	5	.409	.591	22	9	1	0	1	4.5	4	5	3	4	0	0	0	39	5	0	4	8.8	1.000	1B-5
LEAGUE CHAMPIONSHIP SERIES																								
1995	SEA A	6	.136	.136	22	3	0	0	0	0.0	1	0	3	7	0	0	0	45	5	1	6	8.5	.980	1B-6

Tony Martinez

MARTINEZ, GABRIEL ANTONIO BR TR 5′10″ 165 lbs.
Born Gabriel Antonio Martinez (Diaz).
B. Mar. 18, 1940, Perico, Cuba D. Aug. 24, 1991, Miami, Fla.

Year	Team	Games	BA	SA	AB	H	2B	3B	HR	HR%	R	RBI	BB	SO	SB	Pinch Hit AB	Pinch Hit H	PO	A	E	DP	TC/G	FA	G by Pos
1963	CLE A	43	.156	.184	141	22	4	0	0	0.0	10	8	5	18	1	0	0	59	90	6	17	3.8	.961	SS-41
1964		9	.214	.286	14	3	1	0	0	0.0	1	2	0	2	0	1	0	11	11	0	6	4.4	1.000	2B-4, SS-1
1965		4	.000	.000	3	0	0	0	0	0.0	0	0	0	0	0	3	0	0	0	0	0	0.0	—	
1966		17	.294	.294	17	5	0	0	0	0.0	2	0	1	6	1	6	3	10	8	1	1	2.1	.947	SS-5, 2B-4
4 yrs.		73	.171	.200	175	30	5	0	0	0.0	13	10	6	26	2	10	3	80	109	7	24	3.6	.964	SS-47, 2B-8

Joe Marty

MARTY, JOSEPH ANTON BR TR 6′ 182 lbs.
B. Sept. 1, 1913, Sacramento, Calif. D. Oct. 4, 1984, Sacramento, Calif.

Year	Team	Games	BA	SA	AB	H	2B	3B	HR	HR%	R	RBI	BB	SO	SB	Pinch Hit AB	Pinch Hit H	PO	A	E	DP	TC/G	FA	G by Pos
1937	CHI N	88	.290	.414	290	84	17	2	5	1.7	41	44	28	30	3	3	2	196	4	5	0	2.4	.976	OF-84
1938		76	.243	.391	235	57	8	3	7	3.0	32	35	18	26	0	7	0	143	6	2	1	2.2	.987	OF-68
1939	2 teams	CHI N (23G –.132) PHI N (91G –.254)																						
″	total	114	.229	.384	375	86	13	6	11	2.9	38	54	28	40	3	12	3	200	13	7	3	2.2	.968	OF-100, P-1
1940	PHI N	123	.270	.437	455	123	21	8	13	2.9	52	50	17	50	2	4	1	296	7	8	0	2.6	.974	OF-118
1941		137	.268	.371	477	128	19	3	8	1.7	60	39	51	41	6	5	0	286	7	11	0	2.3	.964	OF-132
5 yrs.		538	.261	.400	1832	478	78	22	44	2.4	223	222	142	187	14	31	6	1121	37	33	4	2.4	.972	OF-502, P-1
WORLD SERIES																								
1938	CHI N	3	.500	.833	12	6	1	0	1	8.3	1	5	0	2	0	0	0	7	0	0	0	2.3	1.000	OF-3

Bob Martyn

MARTYN, ROBERT GORDON BL TR 6′ 176 lbs.
B. Aug. 15, 1930, Weiser, Ida.

Year	Team	Games	BA	SA	AB	H	2B	3B	HR	HR%	R	RBI	BB	SO	SB	Pinch Hit AB	Pinch Hit H	PO	A	E	DP	TC/G	FA	G by Pos
1957	KC A	58	.267	.366	131	35	2	4	1	0.8	10	12	11	20	1	8	0	77	3	2	0	1.7	.976	OF-49
1958		95	.261	.394	226	59	10	7	2	0.9	25	23	26	36	1	28	7	112	4	4	2	1.9	.967	OF-63
1959		1	.000	.000	1	0	0	0	0	0.0	0	0	0	0	0	1	0	0	0	0	0	0.0	—	
3 yrs.		154	.263	.383	358	94	12	11	3	0.8	35	35	37	56	2	37	7	189	7	6	2	1.8	.970	OF-112

Gary Martz

MARTZ, GARY ARTHUR BR TR 6′ 4″ 210 lbs.
B. Jan. 10, 1951, Spokane, Wash.

Year	Team	Games	BA	SA	AB	H	2B	3B	HR	HR%	R	RBI	BB	SO	SB	Pinch Hit AB	Pinch Hit H	PO	A	E	DP	TC/G	FA	G by Pos
1975	KC A	1	.000	.000	1	0	0	0	0	0.0	0	0	0	0	0	1	0	1	0	0	0	1.0	1.000	OF-1

John Marzano

MARZANO, JOHN ROBERT BR TR 5′11″ 185 lbs.
B. Feb. 14, 1963, Philadelphia, Pa.

Year	Team	Games	BA	SA	AB	H	2B	3B	HR	HR%	R	RBI	BB	SO	SB	Pinch Hit AB	Pinch Hit H	PO	A	E	DP	TC/G	FA	G by Pos
1987	BOS A	52	.244	.399	168	41	11	0	5	3.0	20	24	7	41	0	1	0	337	24	5	7	7.0	.986	C-52
1988		10	.138	.172	29	4	1	0	0	0.0	3	1	1	3	0	0	0	77	4	0	0	8.1	1.000	C-10
1989		7	.444	.778	18	8	3	0	1	5.6	5	3	0	2	0	1	1	29	4	0	0	4.7	1.000	C-7
1990		32	.241	.289	83	20	4	0	0	0.0	8	6	5	10	0	0	0	153	14	0	3	5.2	1.000	C-32
1991		49	.263	.333	114	30	8	0	0	0.0	10	9	1	16	0	1	1	174	20	3	0	4.1	.985	C-48
1992		19	.080	.160	50	4	2	1	0	0.0	4	1	2	12	0	1	0	81	9	3	1	4.9	.968	C-18, DH-1
1995	TEX A	2	.333	.333	6	2	0	0	0	0.0	1	0	0	0	0	0	0	7	1	0	0	4.0	1.000	C-2
7 yrs.		171	.233	.338	468	109	29	1	6	1.3	51	44	16	84	0	4	2	858	76	11	11	5.6	.988	C-169, DH-1

Clyde Mashore

MASHORE, CLYDE WAYNE BR TR 6′ 182 lbs.
B. May 29, 1945, Concord, Calif.

Year	Team	Games	BA	SA	AB	H	2B	3B	HR	HR%	R	RBI	BB	SO	SB	Pinch Hit AB	Pinch Hit H	PO	A	E	DP	TC/G	FA	G by Pos
1969	CIN N	2	.000	.000	1	0	0	0	0	0.0	1	0	0	0	0	1	0	0	0	0	0	0.0	—	
1970	MON N	13	.160	.280	25	4	0	0	1	4.0	2	3	4	11	0	4	0	12	0	0	0	1.2	1.000	OF-10
1971		66	.193	.263	114	22	5	0	1	0.9	20	7	10	22	1	12	2	60	0	2	0	1.3	.968	OF-47, 3B-1
1972		93	.227	.330	176	40	7	1	3	1.7	23	23	14	41	6	19	3	80	3	1	0	1.1	.988	OF-74
1973		67	.204	.320	103	21	3	0	3	2.9	12	14	15	28	4	15	3	65	4	3	0	1.6	.958	OF-44, 2B-1
5 yrs.		241	.208	.305	419	87	15	1	8	1.9	58	47	43	102	11	51	8	217	7	6	0	1.3	.974	OF-175, 2B-1, 3B-1

Phil Masi

MASI, PHILIP SAMUEL BR TR 5′10″ 177 lbs.
B. Jan. 6, 1916, Chicago, Ill. D. Mar. 29, 1990, Mount Prospect, Ill.

Year	Team	Games	BA	SA	AB	H	2B	3B	HR	HR%	R	RBI	BB	SO	SB	Pinch Hit AB	Pinch Hit H	PO	A	E	DP	TC/G	FA	G by Pos
1939	BOS N	46	.254	.377	114	29	7	2	1	0.9	14	14	9	15	0	3	0	104	15	5	0	3.0	.960	C-42
1940		63	.196	.261	138	27	4	1	1	0.7	11	14	14	14	0	9	3	137	32	6	2	3.4	.966	C-52
1941		87	.222	.339	180	40	8	2	3	1.7	17	18	16	13	4	3	1	194	31	5	3	2.8	.978	C-83
1942		57	.218	.276	87	19	3	1	0	0.0	14	9	12	4	2	1	0	82	21	4	1	2.5	.963	C-39, OF-4
1943		80	.273	.345	238	65	9	1	2	0.8	27	28	27	20	7	1	1	192	40	2	1	3.2	.991	C-73
1944		89	.275	.402	251	69	13	5	3	1.2	33	23	31	20	4	8	1	298	46	7	12	4.6	.980	C-63, 1B-12, 3B-2
1945		111	.272	.418	371	101	25	4	7	1.9	55	46	42	32	9	9	1	390	54	10	8	4.5	.978	C-95, 1B-7
1946		133	.267	.358	397	106	17	5	3	0.8	52	62	55	41	5	5	2	470	56	10	5	4.3	.981	C-124
1947		126	.304	.443	411	125	22	4	9	2.2	54	50	47	27	7	3	1	411	58	5	1	3.9	.989	C-123
1948		113	.253	.343	376	95	19	0	5	1.3	43	44	35	26	2	1	0	458	39	6	5	4.6	.988	C-109
1949	2 teams	BOS N (37G –.210) PIT N (48G –.274)																						
″	total	85	.246	.313	240	59	8	1	2	0.8	29	19	31	26	2	3	0	308	37	2	11	4.2	.994	C-81, 1B-2
1950	CHI A	122	.279	.390	377	105	17	2	7	1.9	38	55	49	36	2	9	1	440	52	2	9	4.3	.996	C-114
1951		84	.271	.391	225	61	11	2	4	1.8	24	28	32	27	1	3	0	299	24	7	7	4.2	.979	C-78
1952		30	.254	.302	63	16	1	1	0	0.0	9	7	10	10	0	3	1	101	7	5	2	4.5	.956	C-25
14 yrs.		1226	.264	.370	3468	917	164	31	47	1.4	420	417	410	311	45	61	12	3884	512	76	67	4.0	.983	C-1101, 1B-21, OF-4, 3B-2

Phil Masi *continued*

WORLD SERIES

Year	Team	Games	BA	SA	AB	H	2B	3B	HR	HR%	R	RBI	BB	SO	SB	Pinch Hit AB	Pinch Hit H	PO	A	E	DP	TC/G	FA	G by Pos
1948	BOS N	5	.125	.250	8	1	1	0	0	0.0	1	1	0	0	0	1	1	10	1	0	0	2.2	1.000	C-5

Harry Maskrey

MASKREY, HARRY H.
Brother of Leech Maskrey.
B. Dec. 21, 1861, Mercer, Pa. D. Aug. 17, 1930, Mercer, Pa.

Year	Team	Games	BA	SA	AB	H	2B	3B	HR	HR%	R	RBI	BB	SO	SB	Pinch Hit AB	Pinch Hit H	PO	A	E	DP	TC/G	FA	G by Pos
1882	LOU AA	1	.000	.000	4	0	0	0	0	0.0	0		0			0	0	0	0	1	0	1.0	.000	OF-1

Leech Maskrey

MASKREY, SAMUEL LEECH BR TR 5′ 8″ 150 lbs.
Brother of Harry Maskrey.
B. Feb. 11, 1854, Mercer, Pa. D. Apr. 1, 1922, Mercer, Pa.

Year	Team	Games	BA	SA	AB	H	2B	3B	HR	HR%	R	RBI	BB	SO	SB	Pinch Hit AB	Pinch Hit H	PO	A	E	DP	TC/G	FA	G by Pos
1882	LOU AA	76	.226	.288	288	65	14	2	0	0.0	30		9			0	0	137	13	18	1	2.2	.893	OF-76, 2B-1
1883		96	.202	.291	361	73	13	8	1	0.3	50		10			0	0	193	19	20	1	2.4	.914	OF-96, SS-1
1884		105	.250	.301	412	103	13	4	0	0.0	48		17			0	0	141	20	19	2	1.7	.894	OF-103, 3B-3, SS-1
1885		109	.229	.307	423	97	8	11	1	0.2	54		19			0	0	169	12	21	2	1.8	.896	OF-108, 3B-3
1886	2 teams	LOU AA (5G –.158) CIN AA (27G –.194)																						
″	total	32	.188	.239	117	22	4	1	0	0.0	8		6			0	0	54	9	8	1	2.2	.887	OF-31, 3B-2
5 yrs.		418	.225	.294	1601	360	52	26	2	0.1	190		61			0	0	694	73	86	7	2.0	.899	OF-414, 3B-8, SS-2, 2B-1

Charlie Mason

MASON, CHARLES E. BR TR
B. June 25, 1853, New Orleans, La. D. Oct. 21, 1936, Philadelphia, Pa.
Manager 1887.

Year	Team	Games	BA	SA	AB	H	2B	3B	HR	HR%	R	RBI	BB	SO	SB	Pinch Hit AB	Pinch Hit H	PO	A	E	DP	TC/G	FA	G by Pos
1883	PHI AA	1	.500	.500	2	1	0	0	0	0.0	0		0			0	0	0	0	0	0	0.0	.000	OF-1

Don Mason

MASON, DONALD STETSON BL TR 5′11″ 160 lbs.
B. Dec. 20, 1944, Boston, Mass.

Year	Team	Games	BA	SA	AB	H	2B	3B	HR	HR%	R	RBI	BB	SO	SB	Pinch Hit AB	Pinch Hit H	PO	A	E	DP	TC/G	FA	G by Pos
1966	SF N	42	.120	.240	25	3	0	0	1	4.0	8	1	0	2	0	13	1	10	9	2	1	2.3	.905	2B-9
1967		4	.000	.000	3	0	0	0	0	0.0	0	0	0	0	0	0	0	0	3	0	0	1.5	1.000	2B-2
1968		10	.158	.158	19	3	0	0	0	0.0	3	1	1	4	1	0	0	9	9	0	0	1.6	1.000	2B-5, SS-4, 3B-2
1969		104	.228	.260	250	57	4	2	0	0.0	43	13	36	29	1	18	5	135	179	20	37	4.2	.940	2B-51, 3B-21, SS-7
1970		46	.139	.139	36	5	0	0	0	0.0	4	1	5	7	0	20	1	11	8	1	1	1.4	.950	2B-14
1971	SD N	113	.212	.270	344	73	12	1	2	0.6	43	11	27	35	6	17	6	189	233	16	47	4.7	.963	2B-90, 3B-3
1972		9	.182	.182	11	2	0	0	0	0.0	1	0	1	1	0	4	1	3	6	4	0	4.3	.692	2B-3
1973		8	.000	.000	8	0	0	0	0	0.0	0	0	0	2	0	6	0	1	2	1	1	4.0	.750	2B-1
8 yrs.		336	.205	.250	696	143	16	3	3	0.4	102	27	70	80	8	78	14	358	449	44	87	4.0	.948	2B-175, 3B-26, SS-11

Jim Mason

MASON, JAMES PERCY BL TR 6′ 2″ 185 lbs.
B. Aug. 14, 1950, Mobile, Ala.

Year	Team	Games	BA	SA	AB	H	2B	3B	HR	HR%	R	RBI	BB	SO	SB	Pinch Hit AB	Pinch Hit H	PO	A	E	DP	TC/G	FA	G by Pos
1971	WAS A	3	.333	.333	9	3	0	0	0	0.0	0	0	1	3	0	0	0	8	13	1	1	7.3	.955	SS-3
1972	TEX A	46	.197	.218	147	29	3	0	0	0.0	10	10	9	39	0	3	0	58	106	10	14	4.1	.943	SS-32, 3B-10
1973		92	.206	.290	238	49	7	2	3	1.3	23	19	23	48	0	1	0	143	230	20	51	4.2	.949	SS-74, 2B-19, 3B-1
1974	NY A	152	.250	.352	440	110	18	6	5	1.1	41	37	35	87	1	0	0	241	430	25	87	4.6	.964	SS-152
1975		94	.152	.211	223	34	3	2	2	0.9	17	16	22	49	0	0	0	134	209	16	45	3.8	.955	SS-93, 2B-1
1976		93	.180	.235	217	39	7	1	1	0.5	17	14	9	37	0	0	0	128	245	13	47	4.2	.966	SS-93
1977	2 teams	TOR A (22G –.165) TEX A (36G –.218)																						
″	total	58	.187	.254	134	25	6	0	1	0.7	19	9	13	20	1	1	0	75	108	6	20	3.3	.968	SS-54, DH-3, 3B-1
1978	TEX A	55	.190	.229	105	20	4	0	0	0.0	10	3	5	17	0	2	0	47	92	10	14	2.7	.933	SS-42, 3B-11, DH-1, 2B-1
1979	MON N	40	.183	.282	71	13	5	1	0	0.0	3	6	7	16	0	4	0	35	62	3	10	2.6	.970	SS-33, 3B-6
9 yrs.		633	.203	.275	1584	322	53	12	12	0.8	140	114	124	316	2	11	0	869	1495	104	289	3.9	.958	SS-576, 3B-29, 2B-21, DH-4

LEAGUE CHAMPIONSHIP SERIES

Year	Team	Games	BA	SA	AB	H	2B	3B	HR	HR%	R	RBI	BB	SO	SB	Pinch Hit AB	Pinch Hit H	PO	A	E	DP	TC/G	FA	G by Pos
1976	NY A	2	—	—	0	0	0	0	0	—	0	0	0	0	0	0	0	1	2	0	0	1.5	1.000	SS-2

WORLD SERIES

Year	Team	Games	BA	SA	AB	H	2B	3B	HR	HR%	R	RBI	BB	SO	SB	Pinch Hit AB	Pinch Hit H	PO	A	E	DP	TC/G	FA	G by Pos
1976	NY A	3	1.000	4.000	1	1	0	0	1	100.0	1	1	0	0	0	0	0	1	2	0	0	1.0	1.000	SS-3

Gordon Massa

MASSA, GORDON RICHARD (Duke, Moose) BL TR 6′ 3″ 210 lbs.
B. Sept. 2, 1935, Cincinnati, Ohio.

Year	Team	Games	BA	SA	AB	H	2B	3B	HR	HR%	R	RBI	BB	SO	SB	Pinch Hit AB	Pinch Hit H	PO	A	E	DP	TC/G	FA	G by Pos
1957	CHI N	6	.467	.533	15	7	1	0	0	0.0	2	3	4	3	0	0	0	21	0	0	0	3.5	1.000	C-6
1958		2	.000	.000	2	0	0	0	0	0.0	0	0	0	2	0	2	0	0	0	0	0	0.0	—	
2 yrs.		8	.412	.471	17	7	1	0	0	0.0	2	3	4	5	0	2	0	21	0	0	0	3.5	1.000	C-6

Bill Massey

MASSEY, WILLIAM HENRY (Big Bill) BR 5′11″ 168 lbs.
B. Jan. 1871, Philadelphia, Pa. D. Oct. 9, 1940, Manila, Philippines.

Year	Team	Games	BA	SA	AB	H	2B	3B	HR	HR%	R	RBI	BB	SO	SB	Pinch Hit AB	Pinch Hit H	PO	A	E	DP	TC/G	FA	G by Pos
1894	CIN N	13	.283	.340	53	15	3	0	0	0.0	7	5	3	2	0	0	0	123	11	6	17	10.8	.957	1B-10, 2B-2, 3B-1

Mike Massey

MASSEY, WILLIAM HERBERT BB TR 6′ 195 lbs.
B. Sept. 28, 1893, Galveston, Tex. D. Oct. 17, 1971, Shreveport, La.

Year	Team	Games	BA	SA	AB	H	2B	3B	HR	HR%	R	RBI	BB	SO	SB	Pinch Hit AB	Pinch Hit H	PO	A	E	DP	TC/G	FA	G by Pos
1917	BOS N	31	.198	.198	91	18	0	0	0	0.0	12	2	15	15	2	0	0	40	68	12	10	4.8	.900	2B-25

Roy Massey

MASSEY, ROY HARDEE (Red) BL TR 5′11″ 170 lbs.
B. Oct. 9, 1890, Sevierville, Tenn. D. June 23, 1954, Atlanta, Ga.

Year	Team	Games	BA	SA	AB	H	2B	3B	HR	HR%	R	RBI	BB	SO	SB	Pinch Hit AB	Pinch Hit H	PO	A	E	DP	TC/G	FA	G by Pos
1918	BOS N	66	.291	.340	203	59	6	2	0	0.0	20	18	23	20	1	12	0	107	6	6	3	2.3	.950	OF-45, 1B-4, SS-1, 3B-1

Dan Masteller

MASTELLER, DAN PATRICK BL TL 6′ 185 lbs.
B. Mar. 17, 1968, Toledo, Ohio.

Year	Team	Games	BA	SA	AB	H	2B	3B	HR	HR%	R	RBI	BB	SO	SB	Pinch Hit AB	Pinch Hit H	PO	A	E	DP	TC/G	FA	G by Pos
1995	MIN A	71	.237	.343	198	47	12	0	3	1.5	21	21	18	19	1	13	4	365	21	2	35	5.0	.995	1B-48, OF-22, DH-8

Vic Mata

MATA, VICTOR JOSE BR TR 6′ 1″ 165 lbs.
Born Victor Jose Mata (Abreu).
B. June 17, 1961, Santiago, Dominican Republic.

Year	Team	Games	BA	SA	AB	H	2B	3B	HR	HR%	R	RBI	BB	SO	SB	Pinch Hit AB	Pinch Hit H	PO	A	E	DP	TC/G	FA	G by Pos
1984	NY A	30	.329	.443	70	23	5	0	1	1.4	8	6	0	12	1	4	2	49	0	3	0	1.9	.942	OF-28
1985		6	.143	.143	7	1	0	0	0	0.0	1	0	0	0	0	2	0	1	0	0	0	0.3	1.000	OF-3
2 yrs.		36	.312	.416	77	24	5	0	1	1.3	9	6	0	12	1	6	2	50	0	3	0	1.7	.943	OF-31

Tom Matchick

MATCHICK, JOHN THOMAS
B. Sept. 7, 1943, Hazelton, Pa.

BL TR 6′ 1″ 173 lbs.

Year	Team	Games	BA	SA	AB	H	2B	3B	HR	HR%	R	RBI	BB	SO	SB	Pinch Hit AB	Pinch Hit H	PO	A	E	DP	TC/G	FA	G by Pos
1967	DET A	8	.167	.167	6	1	0	0	0	0.0	1	0	0	2	0	5	0	1	0	0	0	1.0	1.000	SS-1
1968		80	.203	.286	227	46	6	2	3	1.3	18	14	10	46	0	13	5	106	154	10	31	3.5	.963	SS-59, 2B-13, 1B-6
1969		94	.242	.292	298	72	11	2	0	0.0	25	32	15	51	3	16	8	121	176	8	36	3.7	.974	2B-47, 3B-27, SS-6, 1B-2
1970	2 teams	KC A (55G –.196) BOS A (10G –.071)																						
″	total	65	.186	.227	172	32	3	2	0	0.0	13	11	7	25	0	12	0	87	155	3	39	4.2	.988	SS-44, 2B-11, 3B-3
1971	MIL A	42	.219	.254	114	25	1	0	1	0.9	6	7	7	23	3	0	0	31	62	2	6	2.3	.979	3B-41, 2B-1
1972	BAL A	3	.222	.222	9	2	0	0	0	0.0	0	0	0	1	0	0	0	2	4	1	0	2.3	.857	3B-3
6 yrs.		292	.215	.270	826	178	21	6	4	0.5	63	64	39	148	6	46	13	348	551	24	112	3.5	.974	SS-110, 3B-74, 2B-72, 1B-8
WORLD SERIES																								
1968	DET A	3	.000	.000	3	0	0	0	0	0.0	0	0	0	1	0	3	0	0	0	0	0	0.0	—	

Mike Matheny

MATHENY, MICHAEL SCOTT
B. Sept. 22, 1970, Columbus, Ohio.

BR TR 6′ 3″ 205 lbs.

Year	Team	Games	BA	SA	AB	H	2B	3B	HR	HR%	R	RBI	BB	SO	SB	Pinch Hit AB	Pinch Hit H	PO	A	E	DP	TC/G	FA	G by Pos
1994	MIL A	28	.226	.340	53	12	3	0	1	1.9	3	2	3	13	0	2	0	81	8	1	1	3.3	.989	C-27
1995		80	.247	.313	166	41	9	1	0	0.0	13	21	12	28	2	1	0	261	18	4	2	3.5	.986	C-80
2 yrs.		108	.242	.320	219	53	12	1	1	0.5	16	23	15	41	2	3	0	342	26	5	3	3.5	.987	C-107

Joe Mathes

MATHES, JOSEPH JOHN
B. July 28, 1891, Milwaukee, Wis. D. Dec. 21, 1978, St. Louis, Mo.

BB TR 6′½″ 180 lbs.

Year	Team	Games	BA	SA	AB	H	2B	3B	HR	HR%	R	RBI	BB	SO	SB	Pinch Hit AB	Pinch Hit H	PO	A	E	DP	TC/G	FA	G by Pos
1912	PHI A	4	.143	.143	14	2	0	0	0	0.0	0	0	0		0	0	0	1	7	1	0	2.3	.889	3B-4
1914	STL F	26	.294	.329	85	25	3	0	0	0.0	10	6	9		1	1	1	48	57	7	5	4.9	.938	2B-23
1916	BOS N	2	—	—	0	0	0	0	0	—	0	0	0	0	0	0	0	0	0	2	0	1.0	.000	2B-2
3 yrs.		32	.273	.303	99	27	3	0	0	0.0	10	6	9	0	1	1	1	49	64	10	5	4.2	.919	2B-25, 3B-4

Bobby Mathews

MATHEWS, ROBERT T.
B. Nov. 21, 1851, Baltimore, Md. D. Apr. 17, 1898, Baltimore, Md.

BR TR 5′ 5½″ 140 lbs.

Year	Team	Games	BA	SA	AB	H	2B	3B	HR	HR%	R	RBI	BB	SO	SB	Pinch Hit AB	Pinch Hit H	PO	A	E	DP	TC/G	FA	G by Pos
1876	NY N	56	.183	.211	218	40	4	1	0	0.0	19	9	3	2		0	0	41	78	28	0	2.6	.810	P-56, OF-1
1877	CIN N	15	.169	.169	59	10	0	0	0	0.0	5	0	1	2		0	0	8	19	7	0	2.0	.794	P-15, SS-1, OF-1
1879	PRO N	43	.202	.231	173	35	2	0	1	0.6	25	10	7	12		0	0	24	46	13	1	1.6	.843	P-27, OF-21, 3B-5
1881	2 teams	PRO N (16G –.193) BOS N (19G –.169)																						
″	total	35	.180	.203	128	23	3	0	0	0.0	8	8	5	11		0	0	30	21	11	2	1.5	.823	OF-23, P-19
1882	BOS N	45	.225	.260	169	38	6	0	0	0.0	17	13	8	18		0	0	11	34	12	1	1.2	.789	P-34, OF-13, SS-1
1883	PHI AA	45	.186	.198	167	31	2	0	0	0.0	15		4			0	0	15	68	12	2	2.0	.874	P-44, OF-3
1884		49	.185	.223	184	34	5	1	0	0.0	26		7			0	0	8	78	25	1	2.2	.775	P-49, OF-1
1885		48	.168	.184	179	30	3	0	0	0.0	22		10			0	0	8	67	10	1	1.7	.882	P-48, OF-1
1886		24	.239	.273	88	21	3	0	0	0.0	16		3			0	0	5	46	9	3	2.4	.850	P-24, OF-1
1887		7	.200	.200	25	5	0	0	0	0.0	5		4		0	0	0	2	14	2	1	2.6	.889	P-7
10 yrs.		367	.192	.217	1390	267	28	2	1	0.1	158	40	52	45	0	0	0	152	471	129	12	1.9	.828	P-323, OF-65, 3B-5, SS-2

Eddie Mathews

MATHEWS, EDWIN LEE
B. Oct. 13, 1931, Texarkana, Tex.
Manager 1972–74.
Hall of Fame 1978.

BL TR 6′ 1″ 190 lbs.

Year	Team	Games	BA	SA	AB	H	2B	3B	HR	HR%	R	RBI	BB	SO	SB	Pinch Hit AB	Pinch Hit H	PO	A	E	DP	TC/G	FA	G by Pos
1952	BOS N	145	.242	.447	528	128	23	5	25	4.7	80	58	59	**115**	6	2	0	160	259	19	21	3.1	.957	3B-142
1953	MIL N	154	.302	.627	579	175	31	8	**47**	**8.1**	110	135	99	83	1	0	0	154	311	30	33	3.2	.939	3B-157
1954		138	.290	.603	476	138	21	4	40	8.4	96	103	113	61	10	2	0	133	254	15	28	2.9	.963	3B-127, OF-10
1955		141	.289	.601	499	144	23	5	41	8.2	108	101	**109**	98	3	2	1	140	280	21	23	3.2	.952	3B-137
1956		151	.272	.518	552	150	21	2	37	6.7	103	95	91	86	6	2	0	133	287	25	22	3.0	.944	3B-150
1957		148	.292	.540	572	167	28	9	32	5.6	109	94	90	79	3	0	0	131	299	16	27	3.0	.964	3B-147
1958		149	.251	.458	546	137	18	1	31	5.7	97	77	85	85	5	0	0	116	351	22	24	3.3	.955	3B-149
1959		148	.306	.593	594	182	16	8	**46**	**7.7**	118	114	80	71	2	0	0	144	305	18	21	3.2	.961	3B-148
1960		153	.277	.551	548	152	19	7	39	**7.1**	108	124	111	113	7	0	0	141	280	22	23	2.9	.950	3B-153
1961		152	.306	.535	572	175	23	6	32	5.6	103	91	**93**	95	12	1	0	168	281	18	30	3.1	.961	3B-151
1962		152	.265	.496	536	142	25	6	29	5.4	106	90	**101**	90	4	3	0	208	285	16	29	3.5	.969	3B-140, 1B-7
1963		158	.263	.453	547	144	27	4	23	4.2	82	84	**124**	119	3	1	0	176	277	19	23	2.9	.960	3B-121, OF-42
1964		141	.233	.412	502	117	19	1	23	4.6	83	74	85	100	2	6	1	184	252	17	23	3.4	.962	3B-128, 1B-7
1965		156	.251	.469	546	137	23	0	32	5.9	77	95	73	110	1	8	1	113	301	19	19	2.8	.956	3B-153
1966	ATL N	134	.250	.420	452	113	21	4	16	3.5	72	53	63	82	1	12	4	114	237	20	31	2.9	.946	3B-127
1967	2 teams	HOU N (101G –.238) DET A (36G –.231)																						
″	total	137	.236	.392	436	103	16	2	16	3.7	53	57	63	88	2	15	2	714	113	15	62	6.1	.982	1B-92, 3B-45
1968	DET A	31	.212	.385	52	11	0	0	3	5.8	4	8	5	12	0	16	3	37	14	1	5	4.3	.981	3B-6, 1B-6
17 yrs.		2388	.271	.509	8537	2315	354	72	512	6.0	1509	1453	1444	1487	68	70	12	2966	4386	313	444	3.3	.959	3B-2181, 1B-112, OF-52
WORLD SERIES																								
1957	MIL N	7	.227	.500	22	5	3	0	1	4.5	4	4	8	5	0	0	0	9	19	1	1	4.1	.966	3B-7
1958		7	.160	.240	25	4	2	0	0	0.0	3	3	6	11	1	0	0	5	13	1	0	2.7	.947	3B-7
1968	DET A	2	.333	.333	3	1	0	0	0	0.0	0	0	1	1	0	1	0	0	1	1	0	2.0	.500	3B-1
3 yrs.		16	.200	.360	50	10	5	0	1	2.0	7	7	15	17	1	1	0	14	33	3	1	3.3	.940	3B-15

Nelson Mathews

MATHEWS, NELSON ELMER
Father of T. J. Mathews.
B. July 21, 1941, Columbia, Ill.

BR TR 6′ 4″ 195 lbs.

Year	Team	Games	BA	SA	AB	H	2B	3B	HR	HR%	R	RBI	BB	SO	SB	Pinch Hit AB	Pinch Hit H	PO	A	E	DP	TC/G	FA	G by Pos
1960	CHI N	3	.250	.250	8	2	0	0	0	0.0	1	0	0	2	0	1	1	5	0	0	0	2.5	1.000	OF-2
1961		3	.111	.111	9	1	0	0	0	0.0	0	0	0	2	0	1	0	5	0	0	0	2.5	1.000	OF-2
1962		15	.306	.469	49	15	2	0	2	4.1	5	13	5	4	3	1	0	25	0	1	0	1.9	.962	OF-14
1963		61	.155	.277	155	24	3	2	4	2.6	12	10	16	48	3	8	0	91	1	2	1	2.0	.979	OF-46
1964	KC A	157	.239	.377	573	137	27	5	14	2.4	58	60	43	**143**	2	1	0	384	5	13	2	2.6	.968	OF-154
1965		67	.212	.359	184	39	7	7	2	1.1	17	15	24	49	0	10	1	103	1	2	0	1.9	.981	OF-57
6 yrs.		306	.223	.359	978	218	39	14	22	2.2	93	98	88	248	8	22	2	613	7	18	3	2.3	.972	OF-275

Jimmy Mathison

MATHISON, JAMES MICHAEL IGNATIUS
B. Nov. 11, 1878, Baltimore, Md. D. July 4, 1911, Baltimore, Md.

TR

Year	Team	Games	BA	SA	AB	H	2B	3B	HR	HR%	R	RBI	BB	SO	SB	Pinch Hit AB	Pinch Hit H	PO	A	E	DP	TC/G	FA	G by Pos
1902	BAL A	29	.264	.308	91	24	2	1	0	0.0	12	7	9		2	0	0	43	53	12	4	3.7	.889	3B-28, SS-1

John Matias

MATIAS, JOHN ROY BL TL 5′11″ 170 lbs.
B. Aug. 15, 1944, Honolulu, Hawaii.

Year	Team	Games	BA	SA	AB	H	2B	3B	HR	HR%	R	RBI	BB	SO	SB	Pinch Hit AB	Pinch Hit H	PO	A	E	DP	TC/G	FA	G by Pos
1970	CHI A	58	.188	.256	117	22	2	0	2	1.7	7	6	3	22	1	27	5	132	12	3	14	3.7	.980	OF-22, 1B-18

Francisco Matos

MATOS, FRANCISCO AGUIRRE BR TR 6′1″ 160 lbs.
Born Francisco Aguirre Matos (Mancebo).
B. July 23, 1969, Santo Domingo, Dominican Republic.

Year	Team	Games	BA	SA	AB	H	2B	3B	HR	HR%	R	RBI	BB	SO	SB	Pinch Hit AB	Pinch Hit H	PO	A	E	DP	TC/G	FA	G by Pos
1994	OAK A	14	.250	.286	28	7	1	0	0	0.0	1	2	1	2	1	2	0	13	24	3	4	2.9	.925	2B-12, DH-2

C. V. Matterson

MATTERSON, C. V.
B. Ohio Deceased.

Year	Team	Games	BA	SA	AB	H	2B	3B	HR	HR%	R	RBI	BB	SO	SB	Pinch Hit AB	Pinch Hit H	PO	A	E	DP	TC/G	FA	G by Pos
1884	STL U	1	.000	.000	4	0	0	0	0	0.0	0		0			0	0	0	0	0	0	0.0		OF-1, P-1

Bob Matthews

MATTHEWS, ROBERT
B. Camden, N. J. Deceased.

Year	Team	Games	BA	SA	AB	H	2B	3B	HR	HR%	R	RBI	BB	SO	SB	Pinch Hit AB	Pinch Hit H	PO	A	E	DP	TC/G	FA	G by Pos
1891	PHI AA	1	.333	.333	3	1	0	0	0	0.0	1	0	0	1	0	0	0	0	0	0	0	0.0	.000	OF-1

Gary Matthews

MATTHEWS, GARY NATHANIEL (Sarge) BR TR 6′2″ 185 lbs.
B. July 5, 1950, San Fernando, Calif.

Year	Team	Games	BA	SA	AB	H	2B	3B	HR	HR%	R	RBI	BB	SO	SB	Pinch Hit AB	Pinch Hit H	PO	A	E	DP	TC/G	FA	G by Pos
1972	SF N	20	.290	.532	62	18	1	1	4	6.5	11	14	7	13	0	1	0	34	0	1	0	1.8	.971	OF-19
1973		148	.300	.444	540	162	22	10	12	2.2	74	58	58	83	17	1	1	277	11	5	0	2.0	.983	OF-145
1974		154	.287	.442	561	161	27	6	16	2.9	87	82	70	69	11	4	0	281	9	9	2	2.0	.970	OF-151
1975		116	.280	.431	425	119	22	3	12	2.8	67	58	65	53	13	3	1	225	11	8	2	2.2	.967	OF-113
1976		156	.279	.443	587	164	28	4	20	3.4	79	84	75	94	12	1	0	265	8	7	0	1.8	.975	OF-156
1977	ATL N	148	.283	.438	555	157	25	5	17	3.1	89	64	67	90	22	2	1	262	11	10	1	2.0	.965	OF-145
1978		129	.285	.462	474	135	20	5	18	3.8	75	62	61	92	8	3	0	238	10	8	0	2.0	.969	OF-127
1979		156	.304	.502	631	192	34	5	27	4.3	97	90	60	75	18	0	0	292	12	8	4	2.0	.974	OF-156
1980		155	.278	.419	571	159	17	3	19	3.3	79	75	42	93	11	8	2	258	8	11	0	1.9	.960	OF-143
1981	PHI N	101	.301	.451	359	108	21	3	9	2.5	62	67	59	42	15	2	0	170	11	7	1	1.9	.963	OF-100
1982		162	.281	.427	616	173	31	1	19	3.1	89	83	66	87	21	1	0	268	14	10	2	1.8	.966	OF-162
1983		132	.258	.374	446	115	18	2	10	2.2	66	50	69	81	13	9	2	174	11	5	2	1.6	.974	OF-122
1984	CHI N	147	.291	.428	491	143	21	2	14	2.9	101	82	**103**	97	17	3	0	224	7	11	0	1.7	.955	OF-145
1985		97	.235	.406	298	70	12	0	13	4.4	45	40	59	64	2	11	2	119	7	3	2	1.5	.977	OF-85
1986		123	.259	.478	370	96	16	1	21	5.7	49	46	60	59	3	16	0	137	5	9	1	1.4	.940	OF-105
1987	2 teams	CHI N (44G –.262) SEA A (45G –.235)																						
″	total	89	.242	.323	161	39	4	0	3	1.9	13	23	19	33	0	49	11	2	0	0	0	0.0	1.000	DH-45, OF-2
16 yrs.		2033	.281	.439	7147	2011	319	51	234	3.3	1083	978	940	1125	183	114	20	3226	135	112	17	1.8	.968	OF-1876, DH-45
DIVISIONAL PLAYOFF SERIES																								
1981	PHI N	5	.400	.650	20	8	0	1	1	5.0	3	1	0	2	0	0	0	6	0	0	0	1.2	1.000	OF-5
LEAGUE CHAMPIONSHIP SERIES																								
1983	PHI N	4	.429	1.071	14	6	0	0	3	21.4	4	8	2	1	1	0	0	6	0	0	0	1.5	1.000	OF-4
1984	CHI N	5	.200	.600	15	3	0	0	2	13.3	4	5	6	4	1	0	0	10	0	0	0	2.0	1.000	OF-5
2 yrs.		9	.310	.828	29	9	0	0	5	17.2	8	13	8	5	2	0	0	16	0	0	0	1.8	1.000	OF-9
									4th			9th												
WORLD SERIES																								
1983	PHI N	5	.250	.438	16	4	0	0	1	6.3	1	1	2	2	0	0	0	15	0	0	0	3.0	1.000	OF-5

Wid Matthews

MATTHEWS, WID CURRY BL TL 5′8½″ 155 lbs.
B. Oct. 20, 1896, Raleigh, Ill. D. Oct. 5, 1965, Hollywood, Calif.

Year	Team	Games	BA	SA	AB	H	2B	3B	HR	HR%	R	RBI	BB	SO	SB	Pinch Hit AB	Pinch Hit H	PO	A	E	DP	TC/G	FA	G by Pos
1923	PHI A	129	.274	.328	485	133	11	6	1	0.2	52	25	50	27	16	1	0	316	3	18	0	2.7	.947	OF-127
1924	WAS A	53	.302	.408	169	51	10	4	0	0.0	25	13	11	4	3	6	4	121	7	2	2	3.0	.985	OF-44
1925		10	.444	.444	9	4	0	0	0	0.0	2	1	0	1	0	7	3	1	0	0	0	1.0	1.000	OF-1
3 yrs.		192	.284	.350	663	188	21	10	1	0.2	79	39	61	32	19	14	7	438	10	20	2	2.7	.957	OF-172

Steve Matthias

MATTHIAS, STEPHEN J. 5′8″ 160 lbs.
B. 1860, Mitchellville, Md. Deceased.

Year	Team	Games	BA	SA	AB	H	2B	3B	HR	HR%	R	RBI	BB	SO	SB	Pinch Hit AB	Pinch Hit H	PO	A	E	DP	TC/G	FA	G by Pos
1884	CHI U	37	.275	.338	142	39	7	1	0	0.0	24		5			0	0	33	101	25	5	4.2	.843	SS-36, OF-2

Bobby Mattick

MATTICK, ROBERT JAMES BR TR 5′11″ 178 lbs.
Son of Wally Mattick.
B. Dec. 5, 1915, Sioux City, Iowa.
Manager 1980–81.

Year	Team	Games	BA	SA	AB	H	2B	3B	HR	HR%	R	RBI	BB	SO	SB	Pinch Hit AB	Pinch Hit H	PO	A	E	DP	TC/G	FA	G by Pos
1938	CHI N	1	1.000	1.000	1	1	0	0	0	0.0	0	1	0	0	0	0	0	0	0	0	0	0.0	.000	SS-1
1939		51	.287	.365	178	51	12	1	0	0.0	16	23	6	19	1	1	0	102	179	22	28	6.3	.927	SS-48
1940		128	.218	.252	441	96	15	0	0	0.0	30	33	19	33	5	1	0	233	431	38	76	5.5	.946	SS-126, 3B-1
1941	CIN N	20	.183	.233	60	11	3	0	0	0.0	8	7	8	7	1	2	0	28	42	1	6	3.9	.986	SS-12, 3B-5, 2B-1
1942		6	.200	.300	10	2	1	0	0	0.0	0	0	0	1	0	0	0	7	6	0	1	4.3	1.000	SS-3
5 yrs.		206	.233	.281	690	161	31	1	0	0.0	54	64	33	60	7	4	0	370	658	61	111	5.5	.944	SS-190, 3B-6, 2B-1

Wally Mattick

MATTICK, WALTER JOSEPH (Chick) BR TR 5′10″ 180 lbs.
Father of Bobby Mattick.
B. Mar. 12, 1887, St. Louis, Mo. D. Nov. 5, 1968, Los Altos, Calif.

Year	Team	Games	BA	SA	AB	H	2B	3B	HR	HR%	R	RBI	BB	SO	SB	Pinch Hit AB	Pinch Hit H	PO	A	E	DP	TC/G	FA	G by Pos
1912	CHI A	88	.260	.358	285	74	7	9	1	0.4	45	35	27		15	8	3	154	8	3	1	2.1	.982	OF-78
1913		68	.188	.237	207	39	8	1	0	0.0	15	11	18	16	3	3	1	116	14	3	2	2.1	.977	OF-63
1918	STL N	8	.143	.143	14	2	0	0	0	0.0	0	1	2	3	0	5	1	5	1	0	0	2.0	1.000	OF-3
3 yrs.		164	.227	.302	506	115	15	10	1	0.2	60	47	47	19	18	16	5	275	23	6	3	2.1	.980	OF-144

Mike Mattimore

MATTIMORE, MICHAEL JOSEPH BL TL 5′8½″ 160 lbs.
B. 1859, Renovo, Pa. D. Apr. 28, 1931, Butte, Mont.

Year	Team	Games	BA	SA	AB	H	2B	3B	HR	HR%	R	RBI	BB	SO	SB	Pinch Hit AB	Pinch Hit H	PO	A	E	DP	TC/G	FA	G by Pos
1887	NY N	8	.250	.281	32	8	1	0	0	0.0	5	4	0	6	1	0	0	8	5	1	0	1.6	.929	P-7, OF-2
1888	PHI AA	41	.268	.380	142	38	6	5	0	0.0	22	12	12		16	0	0	32	71	10	6	2.7	.912	P-26, OF-16
1889	2 teams	PHI AA (23G –.233) KC AA (19G –.160)																						
″	total	42	.196	.270	148	29	2	3	1	0.7	16	13	12	23	6	0	0	98	12	15	2	2.8	.880	OF-31, 1B-7, P-6
1890	BKN AA	33	.132	.155	129	17	1	1	0	0.0	14		16		11	0	0	20	38	12	0	2.1	.829	P-19, OF-14
4 yrs.		124	.204	.273	451	92	10	9	1	0.2	57	29	40	29	34	0	0	158	126	38	8	2.5	.882	OF-63, P-58, 1B-7

Don Mattingly

MATTINGLY, DONALD ARTHUR BL TL 6′ 185 lbs.
B. Apr. 20, 1961, Evansville, Ind.

Year	Team	Games	BA	SA	AB	H	2B	3B	HR	HR%	R	RBI	BB	SO	SB	Pinch Hit AB	Pinch Hit H	PO	A	E	DP	TC/G	FA	G by Pos
1982	NY A	7	.167	.167	12	2	0	0	0	0.0	0	1	0	1	0	1	0	15	1	0	0	2.3	1.000	OF-6, 1B-1
1983		91	.283	.409	279	79	15	4	4	1.4	34	32	21	31	0	8	1	350	15	3	31	4.0	.992	OF-48, 1B-42, 2B-1
1984		153	**.343**	.537	603	**207**	**44**	2	23	3.8	91	110	41	33	1	3	1	1143	126	6	136	8.4	.995	1B-133, OF-19
1985		159	.324	.567	652	211	**48**	3	35	5.4	107	**145**	56	41	2	0	0	1318	87	7	154	8.9	.995	1B-159
1986		162	.352	**.573**	677	**238**	**53**	2	31	4.6	117	113	53	35	0	0	0	1378	111	7	134	9.1	.995	1B-160, 3B-3, DH-1
1987		141	.327	.559	569	186	38	2	30	5.3	93	115	51	38	1	1	0	1239	91	5	122	9.5	.996	1B-140, DH-1
1988		144	.311	.462	599	186	37	0	18	3.0	94	88	41	29	1	1	0	1250	99	9	131	9.4	.993	1B-143, OF-1, DH-1
1989		158	.303	.477	631	191	37	2	23	3.6	79	113	51	30	3	0	0	1276	87	7	143	8.4	.995	1B-145, DH-17, OF-1
1990		102	.256	.335	394	101	16	0	5	1.3	40	42	28	20	1	4	2	800	78	3	81	8.6	.997	1B-89, DH-13, OF-1
1991		152	.288	.394	587	169	35	0	9	1.5	64	68	46	42	2	4	1	1119	77	5	135	8.1	.996	1B-127, DH-22
1992		157	.287	.416	640	184	40	0	14	2.2	89	86	39	43	3	2	0	1209	116	4	129	8.4	.997	1B-143, DH-15
1993		134	.291	.445	530	154	27	2	17	3.2	78	86	61	42	0	2	1	1258	84	3	123	10.0	.998	1B-130, DH-5
1994		97	.304	.411	372	113	20	1	6	1.6	62	51	60	24	0	2	1	916	66	2	95	10.1	.998	1B-97
1995		128	.288	.413	458	132	32	2	7	1.5	59	49	40	35	0	6	2	994	82	7	90	8.6	.994	1B-125, DH-1
14 yrs.		1785	.307	.471	7003	2153	442	20	222	3.2	1007	1099	588	444	14	34	9	14265	1120	68	1504	8.6	.996	1B-1634, DH-76, OF-76, 3B-3, 2B-1
DIVISIONAL PLAYOFF SERIES																								
1995	NY A	5	.417	.708	24	10	4	0	1	4.2	3	6	1	5	0	0	0	36	4	1	3	8.2	.976	1B-5

Ralph Mattis

MATTIS, RALPH L. (Matty) BR TR 5′11″ 172 lbs.
B. Aug. 24, 1890, Roxborough, Pa. D. Sept. 13, 1960, Williamsport, Pa.

Year	Team	Games	BA	SA	AB	H	2B	3B	HR	HR%	R	RBI	BB	SO	SB	Pinch Hit AB	Pinch Hit H	PO	A	E	DP	TC/G	FA	G by Pos
1914	PIT F	36	.247	.318	85	21	4	1	0	0.0	14	8	9		2	11	3	39	6	3	1	2.0	.938	OF-24

Cloy Mattox

MATTOX, CLOY MITCHELL (Monk) BL TL 5′ 8″ 168 lbs.
Brother of Jim Mattox.
B. Nov. 24, 1902, Leesville, Va. D. Aug. 31, 1985, Danville, Va.

Year	Team	Games	BA	SA	AB	H	2B	3B	HR	HR%	R	RBI	BB	SO	SB	Pinch Hit AB	Pinch Hit H	PO	A	E	DP	TC/G	FA	G by Pos
1929	PHI A	3	.167	.167	6	1	0	0	0	0.0	0	0	1	1	0	0	0	5	2	1	0	2.7	.875	C-3

Jim Mattox

MATTOX, JAMES POWELL BL TR 5′ 9½″ 168 lbs.
Brother of Cloy Mattox.
B. Dec. 17, 1896, Leesville, Va. D. Oct. 12, 1973, Myrtle Beach, S. C.

Year	Team	Games	BA	SA	AB	H	2B	3B	HR	HR%	R	RBI	BB	SO	SB	Pinch Hit AB	Pinch Hit H	PO	A	E	DP	TC/G	FA	G by Pos
1922	PIT N	29	.294	.353	51	15	1	1	0	0.0	11	3	1	3	0	4	3	52	11	1	2	3.0	.984	C-21
1923		22	.188	.281	32	6	1	1	0	0.0	4	1	0	5	0	14	2	16	8	1	0	3.1	.960	C-8
2 yrs.		51	.253	.325	83	21	2	2	0	0.0	15	4	1	8	0	18	5	68	19	2	2	3.1	.978	C-29

Len Matuszek

MATUSZEK, LEONARD JAMES BL TR 6′ 2″ 190 lbs.
B. Sept. 27, 1954, Toledo, Ohio.

Year	Team	Games	BA	SA	AB	H	2B	3B	HR	HR%	R	RBI	BB	SO	SB	Pinch Hit AB	Pinch Hit H	PO	A	E	DP	TC/G	FA	G by Pos
1981	PHI N	13	.273	.364	11	3	1	0	0	0.0	1	1	3	1	0	9	3	5	4	0	1	4.5	1.000	3B-1, 1B-1
1982		25	.077	.103	39	3	1	0	0	0.0	1	3	1	10	0	17	1	12	8	3	1	2.1	.870	3B-8, 1B-3
1983		28	.275	.525	80	22	6	1	4	5.0	12	16	4	14	0	6	1	144	9	0	8	7.3	1.000	1B-21
1984		101	.248	.458	262	65	17	1	12	4.6	40	43	39	54	4	24	10	644	55	8	40	8.6	.989	1B-81, OF-1
1985	2 teams	TOR A (62G –.212) LA N (43G –.222)																						
″	total	105	.215	.350	214	46	8	3	5	2.3	33	28	19	38	2	29	4	66	4	0	3	0.8	1.000	DH-54, OF-17, 1B-15, 3B-1
1986	LA N	91	.261	.432	199	52	7	0	9	4.5	26	28	21	47	2	25	4	235	22	5	18	3.9	.981	OF-37, 1B-31
1987		16	.067	.067	15	1	0	0	0	0.0	0	0	1	4	0	13	0	4	1	0	0	1.7	1.000	1B-3
7 yrs.		379	.234	.405	820	192	40	5	30	3.7	113	119	88	168	8	123	23	1110	103	16	71	4.5	.987	1B-155, OF-55, DH-54, 3B-10
LEAGUE CHAMPIONSHIP SERIES																								
1985	LA N	3	1.000	1.000	1	1	0	0	0	0.0	1	0	0	0	0	1	1	0	0	0	0	0.0		OF-1, 1B-1

Gene Mauch

MAUCH, GENE WILLIAM (Skip) BR TR 5′10″ 165 lbs.
B. Nov. 18, 1925, Salina, Kans.
Manager 1960–82, 1985–87.

Year	Team	Games	BA	SA	AB	H	2B	3B	HR	HR%	R	RBI	BB	SO	SB	Pinch Hit AB	Pinch Hit H	PO	A	E	DP	TC/G	FA	G by Pos
1944	BKN N	5	.133	.200	15	2	1	0	0	0.0	2	2	2	3	0	0	0	7	9	0	3	3.2	1.000	SS-5
1947	PIT N	16	.300	.300	30	9	0	0	0	0.0	8	1	7	6	0	0	0	18	20	3	1	4.1	.927	2B-6, SS-4
1948	2 teams	BKN N (12G –.154) CHI N (53G –.203)																						
″	total	65	.199	.265	151	30	3	2	1	0.7	19	7	27	14	1	11	0	90	105	12	26	3.9	.942	2B-33, SS-20
1949	CHI N	72	.247	.333	150	37	6	2	1	0.7	15	7	21	15	3	13	4	98	125	9	27	4.5	.961	2B-25, SS-19, 3B-7
1950	BOS N	48	.231	.298	121	28	5	0	1	0.8	17	15	14	9	1	3	2	83	85	7	18	4.4	.960	2B-28, 3B-7, SS-5
1951		19	.100	.100	20	2	0	0	0	0.0	5	1	7	4	0	2	0	16	16	1	2	2.2	.970	SS-10, 3B-3, 2B-2
1952	STL N	7	.000	.000	3	0	0	0	0	0.0	0	0	1	2	0	1	0	1	0	1	0	1.0	.500	SS-2
1956	BOS A	7	.320	.320	25	8	0	0	0	0.0	4	1	3	3	0	1	0	12	17	2	4	5.2	.935	2B-6
1957		65	.270	.369	222	60	10	3	2	0.9	23	28	22	26	1	7	3	127	153	11	41	5.0	.962	2B-58
9 yrs.		304	.239	.312	737	176	25	7	5	0.7	93	62	104	82	6	38	9	452	530	46	122	4.3	.955	2B-158, SS-65, 3B-17

Al Maul

MAUL, ALBERT JOSEPH (Smiling Al) BR TR 6′ 175 lbs.
B. Oct. 9, 1865, Philadelphia, Pa. D. May 3, 1958, Philadelphia, Pa.

Year	Team	Games	BA	SA	AB	H	2B	3B	HR	HR%	R	RBI	BB	SO	SB	Pinch Hit AB	Pinch Hit H	PO	A	E	DP	TC/G	FA	G by Pos
1884	PHI U	1	.000	.000	4	0	0	0	0	0.0	0		0			0	0	0	1	0	0	1.0	1.000	P-1
1887	PHI N	16	.304	.464	56	17	2	2	1	1.8	15	4	15	10	5	0	0	30	10	5	2	2.6	.889	OF-8, P-7, 1B-2
1888	PIT N	74	.208	.274	259	54	9	4	0	0.0	21	31	21	45	9	0	0	450	20	16	22	6.5	.967	1B-38, OF-34, P-3
1889		68	.276	.393	257	71	6	6	4	1.6	37	44	29	41	18	0	0	125	32	10	5	2.4	.940	OF-64, P-6
1890	PIT P	45	.259	.321	162	42	6	2	0	0.0	31	21	22	12	5	0	0	51	84	16	5	3.3	.894	P-30, OF-15, SS-1
1891	PIT N	47	.188	.255	149	28	2	4	0	0.0	15	14	20	28	4	0	0	61	13	9	3	1.7	.892	OF-40, P-8
1893	WAS N	44	.254	.373	134	34	8	4	0	0.0	10	12	33	14	1	2	0	28	70	12	1	2.5	.891	P-37, OF-7
1894		41	.242	.363	124	30	3	3	2	1.6	23	20	14	11	1	2	0	30	51	9	1	2.3	.900	P-28, OF-12
1895		22	.250	.375	72	18	5	2	0	0.0	9	16	6	7	0	2	1	18	32	4	3	2.7	.926	P-16, OF-4
1896		8	.286	.393	28	8	1	1	0	0.0	6	5	3	2	0	0	0	2	10	1	1	1.6	.923	P-8
1897	2 teams	WAS N (1G –.000) BAL N (2G –.333)																						
″	total	3	.250	.250	4	1	0	0	0	0.0	0	0	0		0	0	0	0	2	0	0	0.7	1.000	P-3
1898	BAL N	29	.204	.280	93	19	3	2	0	0.0	21	10	16		1	0	0	9	38	2	0	1.7	.959	P-28, OF-1
1899	BKN N	4	.273	.273	11	3	0	0	0	0.0	2	0	1		0	0	0	0	9	1	0	2.5	.900	P-4

Al Maul *continued*

Year	Team	Games	BA	SA	AB	H	2B	3B	HR	HR%	R	RBI	BB	SO	SB	Pinch Hit AB	Pinch Hit H	PO	A	E	DP	TC/G	FA	G by Pos
1900	PHI N	5	.200	.200	15	3	0	0	0	0.0	2	1	2		0	0	0	0	11	1	0	2.4	.917	P-5
1901	NY N	3	.375	.375	8	3	0	0	0	0.0	1	1	0		0	0	0	1	7	0	0	2.7	1.000	P-3
15 yrs.		410	.241	.332	1376	331	45	30	7	0.5	193	179	182	170	44	6	1	805	390	86	43	3.1	.933	P-187, OF-185, 1B-40, SS-1

Mark Mauldin

MAULDIN, MARSHALL REESE BR TR 5′11″ 170 lbs.
B. Nov. 5, 1914, Atlanta, Ga. D. Sept. 2, 1990, Union City, Ga.

Year	Team	Games	BA	SA	AB	H	2B	3B	HR	HR%	R	RBI	BB	SO	SB	Pinch Hit AB	Pinch Hit H	PO	A	E	DP	TC/G	FA	G by Pos
1934	CHI A	10	.263	.395	38	10	2	0	1	2.6	3	3	0	3	0	0	0	12	17	3	3	3.2	.906	3B-10

Rob Maurer

MAURER, ROBERT JOHN BL TL 6′ 3″ 200 lbs.
B. Jan. 7, 1967, Evansville, Ind.

Year	Team	Games	BA	SA	AB	H	2B	3B	HR	HR%	R	RBI	BB	SO	SB	Pinch Hit AB	Pinch Hit H	PO	A	E	DP	TC/G	FA	G by Pos
1991	TEX A	13	.063	.125	16	1	1	0	0	0.0	0	2	2	6	0	6	0	7	3	0	2	1.7	1.000	1B-4, DH-2
1992		8	.222	.222	9	2	0	0	0	0.0	1	1	1	2	0	5	1	9	1	0	0	2.5	1.000	1B-3, DH-1
2 yrs.		21	.120	.160	25	3	1	0	0	0.0	1	3	3	8	0	11	1	16	4	0	2	2.0	1.000	1B-7, DH-3

Carmen Mauro

MAURO, CARMEN LOUIS BL TR 6′ 167 lbs.
B. Nov. 10, 1926, St. Paul, Minn.

Year	Team	Games	BA	SA	AB	H	2B	3B	HR	HR%	R	RBI	BB	SO	SB	Pinch Hit AB	Pinch Hit H	PO	A	E	DP	TC/G	FA	G by Pos
1948	CHI N	3	.200	.800	5	1	0	0	1	20.0	2	1	2	0	0	0	0	7	0	0	0	3.5	1.000	OF-2
1950		62	.227	.297	185	42	4	3	1	0.5	19	10	13	31	3	9	1	86	2	5	0	1.9	.946	OF-49
1951		13	.172	.207	29	5	1	0	0	0.0	3	3	2	6	0	6	1	17	1	2	0	3.3	.900	OF-6
1953	3 teams BKN N (8G –.000) WAS A (17G –.174) PHI A (64G –.267)																							
″	total	89	.244	.315	197	48	4	5	0	0.0	16	19	20	28	3	31	8	130	6	4	0	2.5	.971	OF-56, 3B-1
4 yrs.		167	.231	.305	416	96	9	8	2	0.5	40	33	37	65	6	46	10	240	9	11	0	2.3	.958	OF-113, 3B-1

Bob Mavis

MAVIS, ROBERT HENRY BL TR 5′ 7″ 160 lbs.
B. Apr. 8, 1918, Milwaukee, Wis.

Year	Team	Games	BA	SA	AB	H	2B	3B	HR	HR%	R	RBI	BB	SO	SB	Pinch Hit AB	Pinch Hit H	PO	A	E	DP	TC/G	FA	G by Pos
1949	DET A	1	—	—	0	0	0	0	0	—	0	0	0	0	0	0	0	0	0	0	0	0.0	—	

Dal Maxvill

MAXVILL, CHARLES DALLAN BR TR 5′11″ 157 lbs.
B. Feb. 18, 1939, Granite City, Ill.

Year	Team	Games	BA	SA	AB	H	2B	3B	HR	HR%	R	RBI	BB	SO	SB	Pinch Hit AB	Pinch Hit H	PO	A	E	DP	TC/G	FA	G by Pos
1962	STL N	79	.222	.265	189	42	3	1	1	0.5	20	18	17	39	1	3	0	111	169	11	41	3.8	.962	SS-76, 3B-1
1963		53	.235	.275	51	12	2	0	0	0.0	12	3	6	11	0	3	0	25	40	2	10	1.9	.970	SS-24, 2B-9, 3B-3
1964		37	.231	.231	26	6	0	0	0	0.0	4	4	0	7	1	1	0	27	19	1	5	1.6	.979	2B-15, SS-13, OF-1, 3B-1
1965		68	.135	.202	89	12	2	2	0	0.0	10	10	7	15	0	2	0	74	86	2	23	2.7	.988	2B-49, SS-12
1966		134	.244	.294	394	96	14	3	0	0.0	25	24	37	61	3	2	0	223	434	22	91	5.1	.968	SS-128, 2B-5, OF-1
1967		152	.227	.279	476	108	14	4	1	0.2	37	41	48	66	0	0	0	241	486	19	78	4.8	.975	SS-148, 2B-7
1968		151	.253	.298	459	116	8	5	1	0.2	51	24	52	71	0	0	0	232	458	22	81	4.7	.969	SS-151
1969		132	.175	.228	372	65	10	2	2	0.5	27	32	44	52	1	0	0	216	408	20	78	4.9	.969	SS-131
1970		152	.201	.223	399	80	5	2	0	0.0	35	28	51	56	0	0	0	260	485	13	91	4.8	.983	SS-136, 2B-22
1971		142	.225	.258	356	80	10	1	0	0.0	31	24	43	45	1	1	0	188	413	13	71	4.4	.979	SS-140
1972	2 teams STL N (105G –.221) OAK A (27G –.250)																							
″	total	132	.224	.263	312	70	7	1	1	0.3	24	24	32	58	0	1	0	201	313	11	69	3.9	.979	SS-99, 2B-35
1973	2 teams OAK A (29G –.211) PIT N (74G –.189)																							
″	total	103	.191	.233	236	45	4	3	0	0.0	19	18	23	43	0	2	0	119	257	12	51	3.7	.969	SS-92, 2B-11, 3B-1
1974	2 teams PIT N (8G –.182) OAK A (60G –.192)																							
″	total	68	.189	.189	74	14	0	0	0	0.0	6	2	10	14	0	0	0	47	103	4	24	2.3	.974	SS-37, 2B-30, 3B-1
1975	OAK A	20	.200	.200	10	2	0	0	0	0.0	1	0	0	0	0	0	0	10	13	1	1	1.1	.958	SS-20, 2B-2
14 yrs.		1423	.217	.259	3443	748	79	24	6	0.2	302	252	370	538	7	15	0	1974	3684	153	714	4.1	.974	SS-1207, 2B-185, 3B-7, OF-2
LEAGUE CHAMPIONSHIP SERIES																								
1972	OAK A	5	.125	.125	8	1	0	0	0	0.0	0	0	1	2	1	0	0	0	1	0	0	0.2	1.000	SS-4, 2B-1
1974		1	.000	.000	1	0	0	0	0	0.0	0	0	0	1	0	0	0	2	1	0	1	3.0	1.000	2B-1
2 yrs.		6	.111	.111	9	1	0	0	0	0.0	0	0	1	3	1	0	0	2	2	0	1	0.7	1.000	SS-4, 2B-2
WORLD SERIES																								
1964	STL N	7	.200	.250	20	4	1	0	0	0.0	0	1	1	4	0	0	0	13	15	0	5	4.0	1.000	2B-7
1967		7	.158	.263	19	3	0	1	0	0.0	1	1	4	1	0	0	0	13	17	0	3	4.3	1.000	SS-7
1968		7	.000	.000	22	0	0	0	0	0.0	1	0	3	5	0	0	0	15	14	0	6	4.1	1.000	SS-7
1974	OAK A	2	—	—	0	0	0	0	0	—	0	0	0	0	0	0	0	0	0	0	0	0.0	.000	2B-2
4 yrs.		23	.115	.164	61	7	1	1	0	0.0	2	2	8	10	0	0	0	41	46	0	14	3.8	1.000	SS-14, 2B-9

Charlie Maxwell

MAXWELL, CHARLES RICHARD (Smokey) BL TL 5′11″ 185 lbs.
B. Apr. 8, 1927, Lawton, Mich.

Year	Team	Games	BA	SA	AB	H	2B	3B	HR	HR%	R	RBI	BB	SO	SB	Pinch Hit AB	Pinch Hit H	PO	A	E	DP	TC/G	FA	G by Pos
1950	BOS A	3	.000	.000	8	0	0	0	0	0.0	1	0	1	3	0	1	0	6	0	0	0	3.0	1.000	OF-2
1951		49	.188	.313	80	15	1	0	3	3.8	8	12	9	18	0	31	7	25	0	2	0	2.1	.926	OF-13
1952		8	.067	.133	15	1	1	0	0	0.0	0	0	3	11	0	3	0	30	5	1	1	6.0	.972	OF-3, 1B-3
1954		74	.250	.308	104	26	4	1	0	0.0	9	5	12	21	3	45	12	25	1	0	0	1.0	1.000	OF-27
1955	2 teams BAL A (4G –.000) DET A (55G –.266)																							
″	total	59	.257	.522	113	29	7	1	7	6.2	19	18	8	21	0	30	7	76	5	3	0	3.0	.964	OF-26, 1B-2
1956	DET A	141	.326	.534	500	163	14	3	28	5.6	96	87	79	74	1	7	4	281	12	4	1	2.2	.987	OF-136
1957		138	.276	.482	492	136	23	3	24	4.9	75	82	76	84	3	3	3	317	6	1	1	2.4	.997	OF-137
1958		131	.272	.426	397	108	14	4	13	3.3	56	65	64	54	6	8	1	290	8	4	9	2.4	.987	OF-114, 1B-14
1959		145	.251	.461	518	130	12	2	31	6.0	81	95	81	91	0	8	3	285	6	4	1	2.2	.986	OF-136
1960		134	.237	.440	482	114	16	5	24	5.0	70	81	58	75	5	14	1	254	5	1	0	2.2	.996	OF-120
1961		79	.229	.405	131	30	4	2	5	3.8	11	18	20	24	0	45	12	53	2	2	0	2.3	.965	OF-25
1962	2 teams DET A (30G –.194) CHI A (69G –.296)																							
″	total	99	.271	.440	273	74	10	3	10	3.7	35	52	42	42	0	20	3	176	6	3	7	2.4	.984	OF-71, 1B-7
1963	CHI A	71	.231	.362	130	30	4	2	3	2.3	17	17	31	27	0	21	3	136	7	0	15	3.5	1.000	OF-24, 1B-17
1964		2	.000	.000	2	0	0	0	0	0.0	0	0	0	0	0	2	0	0	0	0	0	0.0	—	
14 yrs.		1133	.264	.451	3245	856	110	26	148	4.6	478	532	484	545	18	238	56	1954	63	25	35	2.3	.988	OF-834, 1B-43

Carlos May

MAY, CARLOS BL TR 5′11″ 200 lbs.
Brother of Lee May.
B. May 17, 1948, Birmingham, Ala.

Year	Team	Games	BA	SA	AB	H	2B	3B	HR	HR%	R	RBI	BB	SO	SB	Pinch Hit AB	Pinch Hit H	PO	A	E	DP	TC/G	FA	G by Pos
1968	CHI A	17	.179	.194	67	12	1	0	0	0.0	4	1	3	15	0	0	0	24	0	1	0	1.5	.960	OF-17
1969		100	.281	.488	367	103	18	2	18	4.9	62	62	58	66	1	2	1	154	10	3	0	1.7	.982	OF-100

Carlos May *continued*

Year	Team	Games	BA	SA	AB	H	2B	3B	HR	HR%	R	RBI	BB	SO	SB	Pinch Hit AB	Pinch Hit H	PO	A	E	DP	TC/G	FA	G by Pos
1970		150	.285	.414	555	158	28	4	12	2.2	83	68	79	96	12	2	0	276	23	4	8	2.0	.987	OF-141, 1B-7
1971		141	.294	.406	500	147	21	7	7	1.4	64	70	62	61	16	5	2	1206	72	19	90	9.3	.985	1B-130, OF-9
1972		148	.308	.438	523	161	26	3	12	2.3	83	68	79	70	23	0	0	247	15	5	2	1.8	.981	OF-145, 1B-5
1973		149	.268	.412	553	148	20	0	20	3.6	62	96	53	73	8	2	0	129	8	1	0	0.9	.993	DH-75, OF-70, 1B-2
1974		149	.249	.334	551	137	19	2	8	1.5	66	58	46	76	8	10	0	245	11	3	1	1.8	.988	OF-129, DH-13
1975		128	.271	.374	454	123	19	2	8	1.8	55	53	67	46	12	1	0	580	52	8	55	5.0	.988	1B-63, OF-46, DH-19
1976	**2 teams**	**CHI A** (20G –.175) **NY A** (87G –.278)																						
″	**total**	107	.259	.333	351	91	13	2	3	0.9	45	43	43	37	5	15	5	41	0	1	0	0.4	.976	DH-81, OF-16, 1B-1
1977	**2 teams**	**NY A** (65G –.227) **CAL A** (11G –.333)																						
″	**total**	76	.236	.312	199	47	7	1	2	1.0	21	17	22	25	0	14	6	18	2	0	1	0.3	1.000	DH-54, OF-4, 1B-3
10 yrs.		1165	.274	.392	4120	1127	172	23	90	2.2	545	536	512	565	85	51	14	2920	193	45	157	2.8	.986	OF-677, DH-242, 1B-211
LEAGUE CHAMPIONSHIP SERIES																								
1976	**NY A**	3	.200	.300	10	2	1	0	0	0.0	1	0	1	4	0	1	0	0	0	0	0	0.0	.000	DH-3
WORLD SERIES																								
1976	**NY A**	4	.000	.000	9	0	0	0	0	0.0	0	0	0	1	0	2	0	0	0	0	0	0.0	.000	DH-4

Dave May

MAY, DAVID LaFRANCE BL TR 5′10½″ 186 lbs.
Father of Derrick May.
B. Dec. 23, 1943, New Castle, Del.

Year	Team	Games	BA	SA	AB	H	2B	3B	HR	HR%	R	RBI	BB	SO	SB	Pinch Hit AB	Pinch Hit H	PO	A	E	DP	TC/G	FA	G by Pos
1967	**BAL A**	36	.235	.306	85	20	1	1	1	1.2	12	7	6	13	0	15	3	30	1	1	0	1.7	.969	OF-19
1968		84	.191	.270	152	29	6	3	0	0.0	15	7	19	27	3	26	3	62	1	1	0	1.0	.984	OF-61
1969		78	.242	.367	120	29	6	0	3	2.5	8	10	9	23	2	32	8	43	4	3	0	1.3	.940	OF-40
1970	**2 teams**	**BAL A** (25G –.194) **MIL A** (101G –.240)																						
″	**total**	126	.236	.332	373	88	8	2	8	2.1	42	37	48	60	8	15	1	260	6	3	0	2.5	.989	OF-108
1971	**MIL A**	144	.277	.425	501	139	20	3	16	3.2	74	65	50	59	15	3	0	342	10	9	3	2.5	.975	OF-142
1972		143	.238	.340	500	119	20	2	9	1.8	49	45	47	56	11	7	3	376	9	6	3	2.8	.985	OF-138
1973		156	.303	.473	624	189	23	4	25	4.0	96	93	44	78	6	3	3	401	9	9	3	2.7	.979	OF-152, DH-2
1974		135	.226	.325	477	108	15	1	10	2.1	56	42	28	73	4	8	1	249	10	3	2	2.0	.989	OF-121, DH-8
1975	**ATL N**	82	.276	.493	203	56	8	0	12	5.9	28	40	25	27	1	26	7	103	3	4	2	2.1	.964	OF-53
1976		105	.215	.308	214	46	5	3	3	1.4	27	23	26	31	5	44	8	98	5	3	1	1.8	.972	OF-60
1977	**TEX A**	120	.241	.350	340	82	14	1	7	2.1	46	42	32	43	4	11	2	181	8	6	2	1.7	.969	OF-111, DH-5
1978	**2 teams**	**MIL A** (39G –.195) **PIT N** (5G –.000)																						
″	**total**	44	.185	.309	81	15	4	0	2	2.5	9	11	10	11	1	18	4	32	2	2	1	1.5	.944	OF-16, DH-8
12 yrs.		1253	.251	.375	3670	920	130	20	96	2.6	462	422	344	501	60	208	43	2177	68	50	17	2.2	.978	OF-1021, DH-23
LEAGUE CHAMPIONSHIP SERIES																								
1969	**BAL A**	1	.000	.000	1	0	0	0	0	0.0	0	0	0	0	0	1	0	0	0	0	0	0.0	—	
WORLD SERIES																								
1969	**BAL A**	2	.000	.000	1	0	0	0	0	0.0	0	0	1	1	0	1	0	0	0	0	0	0.0	—	

Derrick May

MAY, DERRICK BRANT BL TR 6′4″ 210 lbs.
Son of Dave May.
B. July 14, 1968, Rochester, N. Y.

Year	Team	Games	BA	SA	AB	H	2B	3B	HR	HR%	R	RBI	BB	SO	SB	Pinch Hit AB	Pinch Hit H	PO	A	E	DP	TC/G	FA	G by Pos
1990	**CHI N**	17	.246	.344	61	15	3	0	1	1.6	8	11	2	7	1	0	0	34	1	1	0	2.1	.972	OF-17
1991		15	.227	.455	22	5	2	0	1	4.5	4	3	2	1	0	7	1	11	1	0	0	1.7	1.000	OF-7
1992		124	.274	.373	351	96	11	0	8	2.3	33	45	14	40	5	21	6	153	3	5	0	1.5	.969	OF-108
1993		128	.295	.422	465	137	25	2	10	2.2	62	77	31	41	10	10	1	220	8	7	1	1.9	.970	OF-122
1994		100	.284	.420	345	98	19	2	8	2.3	43	51	30	34	3	11	1	154	4	1	0	1.7	.994	OF-92
1995	**2 teams**	**MIL A** (32G –.248) **HOU N** (78G –.301)																						
″	**total**	110	.282	.436	319	90	18	2	9	2.8	44	50	24	42	5	23	9	141	1	4	0	1.7	.973	OF-87, 1B-1
6 yrs.		494	.282	.411	1563	441	78	6	37	2.4	194	237	103	165	24	72	18	713	18	18	1	1.7	.976	OF-433, 1B-1

Jerry May

MAY, JERRY LEE BR TR 6′2″ 190 lbs.
B. Dec. 14, 1943, Staunton, Va.

Year	Team	Games	BA	SA	AB	H	2B	3B	HR	HR%	R	RBI	BB	SO	SB	Pinch Hit AB	Pinch Hit H	PO	A	E	DP	TC/G	FA	G by Pos
1964	**PIT N**	11	.258	.258	31	8	0	0	0	0.0	1	3	3	9	0	0	0	80	5	1	0	7.8	.988	C-11
1965		4	.500	.500	2	1	0	0	0	0.0	0	1	0	0	0	0	0	2	0	0	0	0.5	1.000	C-4
1966		42	.250	.385	52	13	4	0	1	1.9	6	2	2	15	0	4	0	114	12	2	3	3.1	.984	C-41
1967		110	.271	.351	325	88	13	2	3	0.9	23	22	36	55	0	1	0	550	52	4	9	5.5	.993	C-110
1968		137	.219	.272	416	91	15	2	1	0.2	26	33	41	80	0	1	0	752	70	10	10	6.2	.988	C-135
1969		62	.232	.384	190	44	8	0	7	3.7	21	23	9	53	1	11	2	325	22	2	3	6.7	.994	C-52
1970		51	.209	.288	139	29	4	2	1	0.7	13	16	21	25	0	4	2	280	32	2	2	7.0	.994	C-45
1971	**KC A**	71	.252	.344	218	55	13	2	1	0.5	16	24	27	37	0	2	0	314	38	1	6	5.0	.997	C-71
1972		53	.190	.276	116	22	5	1	1	0.9	10	4	14	13	0	11	1	175	13	4	1	4.7	.979	C-41
1973	**2 teams**	**KC A** (11G –.133) **NY N** (4G –.250)																						
″	**total**	15	.158	.237	38	6	1	1	0	0.0	4	2	4	6	0	0	0	57	4	3	2	4.3	.953	C-15
10 yrs.		556	.234	.318	1527	357	63	10	15	1.0	120	130	157	293	1	34	5	2649	248	29	36	5.6	.990	C-525

Lee May

MAY, LEE ANDREW BR TR 6′3″ 195 lbs.
Brother of Carlos May.
B. Mar. 23, 1943, Birmingham, Ala.

Year	Team	Games	BA	SA	AB	H	2B	3B	HR	HR%	R	RBI	BB	SO	SB	Pinch Hit AB	Pinch Hit H	PO	A	E	DP	TC/G	FA	G by Pos
1965	**CIN N**	5	.000	.000	4	0	0	0	0	0.0	1	0	0	1	0	4	0	0	0	0	0	0.0	—	
1966		25	.333	.507	75	25	5	1	2	2.7	14	10	0	14	0	9	1	132	9	4	15	9.1	.972	1B-16
1967		127	.265	.422	438	116	29	2	12	2.7	54	57	19	80	4	8	0	703	46	6	50	5.9	.992	1B-81, OF-48
1968		146	.290	.469	559	162	32	1	22	3.9	78	80	34	100	4	3	1	1094	73	5	86	7.6	.996	1B-122, OF-33
1969		158	.278	.529	607	169	32	3	38	6.3	85	110	45	142	5	1	0	1395	102	11	128	9.3	.993	1B-156, OF-7
1970		153	.253	.484	605	153	34	2	34	5.6	78	94	38	125	1	0	0	1362	109	10	143	9.7	.993	1B-153
1971		147	.278	.532	553	154	17	3	39	7.1	85	98	42	135	3	4	1	1261	78	8	118	9.4	.994	1B-143
1972	**HOU N**	148	.284	.490	592	168	31	2	29	4.9	87	98	52	**145**	3	2	1	1318	76	6	133	9.6	.996	1B-146
1973		148	.270	.479	545	147	24	3	28	5.1	65	105	34	122	1	4	0	1220	78	9	112	9.1	.993	1B-144
1974		152	.268	.444	556	149	26	0	24	4.3	59	85	17	97	3	8	1	1253	88	8	116	9.3	.994	1B-145
1975	**BAL A**	146	.262	.424	580	152	28	3	20	3.4	67	99	36	91	1	1	1	1312	106	10	138	9.8	.993	1B-144, DH-2
1976		148	.258	.447	530	137	17	4	25	4.7	61	**109**	41	104	4	4	1	722	62	3	61	5.4	.996	1B-94, DH-52

Lee May *continued*

Year	Team	Games	BA	SA	AB	H	2B	3B	HR	HR%	R	RBI	BB	SO	SB	Pinch Hit AB	Pinch Hit H	PO	A	E	DP	TC/G	FA	G by Pos
1977		150	.253	.426	585	148	16	2	27	4.6	75	99	38	119	2	2	0	907	56	5	101	6.5	.995	1B-110, DH-39
1978		148	.246	.414	556	137	16	1	25	4.5	56	80	31	110	5	6	1	34	2	1	3	0.3	.973	DH-140, 1B-4
1979		124	.254	.412	456	116	15	0	19	4.2	59	69	28	100	3	7	3	21	0	2	2	0.2	.913	DH-117, 1B-2
1980		78	.243	.401	222	54	10	2	7	3.2	20	31	15	53	2	27	11	57	3	0	4	0.9	1.000	DH-58, 1B-7
1981	**KC A**	26	.291	.345	55	16	3	0	0	0.0	3	8	3	14	0	13	4	63	2	0	8	5.4	1.000	1B-8, DH-4
1982		42	.308	.505	91	28	5	2	3	3.3	12	12	14	18	0	9	1	175	10	2	18	5.5	.989	1B-32, DH-2
18 yrs.		2071	.267	.459	7609	2031	340	31	354	4.7	959	1244	487	1570	39	112	27	13029	900	90	1236	7.0	.994	1B-1507, DH-414, OF-88
DIVISIONAL PLAYOFF SERIES																								
1981	**KC A**	1	—	—	0	0	0	0	0	—	0	0	0	0	0	0	0	2	0	0	0	2.0	1.000	1B-1
LEAGUE CHAMPIONSHIP SERIES																								
1970	**CIN N**	3	.167	.250	12	2	1	0	0	0.0	0	2	0	2	0	0	0	31	1	0	1	10.7	1.000	1B-3
1979	**BAL A**	2	.143	.143	7	1	0	0	0	0.0	0	1	1	3	0	0	0	0	0	0	0	0.0	.000	DH-2
2 yrs.		5	.158	.211	19	3	1	0	0	0.0	0	3	1	5	0	0	0	31	1	0	1	6.4	1.000	1B-3, DH-2
WORLD SERIES																								
1970	**CIN N**	5	.389	.833	18	7	2	0	2	11.1	6	8	2	2	0	0	0	48	3	0	3	10.2	1.000	1B-5
1979	**BAL A**	2	.000	.000	1	0	0	0	0	0.0	0	0	1	1	0	1	0	0	0	0	0	0.0	—	
2 yrs.		7	.368	.789	19	7	2	0	2	10.5	6	8	3	3	0	1	0	48	3	0	3	10.2	1.000	1B-5

Milt May

MAY, MILTON SCOTT
Son of Pinky May.
B. Aug. 1, 1950, Gary, Ind.

BL TR 6′ 190 lbs.

Year	Team	Games	BA	SA	AB	H	2B	3B	HR	HR%	R	RBI	BB	SO	SB	Pinch Hit AB	Pinch Hit H	PO	A	E	DP	TC/G	FA	G by Pos
1970	**PIT N**	5	.500	.750	4	2	1	0	0	0.0	1	2	0	0	0	4	2	0	0	0	0	0.0	—	
1971		49	.278	.429	126	35	1	0	6	4.8	15	25	9	16	0	17	3	168	12	0	3	5.8	1.000	C-31
1972		57	.281	.353	139	39	10	0	0	0.0	12	14	10	13	0	18	4	179	21	3	2	6.2	.985	C-33
1973		101	.269	.378	283	76	8	1	7	2.5	29	31	34	26	0	18	2	402	36	12	4	5.7	.973	C-79
1974	**HOU N**	127	.289	.402	405	117	17	4	7	1.7	47	54	39	33	0	9	2	525	63	4	10	5.1	.993	C-116
1975		111	.241	.316	386	93	15	1	4	1.0	29	52	26	41	1	8	3	568	70	9	8	6.3	.986	C-102
1976	**DET A**	6	.280	.320	25	7	1	0	0	0.0	2	1	0	1	0	0	0	33	5	0	0	6.3	1.000	C-6
1977		115	.249	.378	397	99	9	3	12	3.0	32	46	26	31	0	5	2	551	78	9	12	5.7	.986	C-111
1978		105	.250	.361	352	88	9	0	10	2.8	24	37	27	26	0	12	1	406	58	10	5	5.0	.979	C-94
1979	**2 teams**	**DET A** (6G –.273) **CHI A** (65G –.252)																						
″	**total**	71	.254	.423	213	54	15	0	7	3.3	24	31	15	28	0	2	0	296	28	6	1	4.7	.982	C-70
1980	**SF N**	111	.260	.366	358	93	16	2	6	1.7	27	50	25	40	0	15	6	500	59	8	12	5.5	.986	C-103
1981		97	.310	.383	316	98	17	0	2	0.6	20	33	34	29	1	9	5	468	48	6	4	5.6	.989	C-93
1982		114	.263	.380	395	104	19	0	9	2.3	29	39	28	38	0	13	6	552	61	8	5	5.6	.987	C-110
1983	**2 teams**	**SF N** (66G –.247) **PIT N** (7G –.250)																						
″	**total**	73	.247	.369	198	49	6	0	6	3.0	18	20	22	24	2	13	3	308	35	6	5	5.8	.983	C-60
1984	**PIT N**	50	.177	.240	96	17	3	0	1	1.0	4	8	10	15	0	18	3	135	15	1	2	5.8	.993	C-26
15 yrs.		1192	.263	.371	3693	971	147	11	77	2.1	313	443	305	361	4	161	42	5091	589	82	73	5.6	.986	C-1034
LEAGUE CHAMPIONSHIP SERIES																								
1971	**PIT N**	1	.000	.000	1	0	0	0	0	0.0	0	0	0	0	0	1	0	0	0	0	0	0.0	—	
1972		1	.500	.500	2	1	0	0	0	0.0	0	1	0	0	0	0	0	8	1	0	1	9.0	1.000	C-1
2 yrs.		2	.333	.333	3	1	0	0	0	0.0	0	1	0	0	0	1	0	8	1	0	1	9.0	1.000	C-1
WORLD SERIES																								
1971	**PIT N**	2	.500	.500	2	1	0	0	0	0.0	0	1	0	0	0	2	1	0	0	0	0	0.0	—	

Pinky May

MAY, MERRILL GLEND
Father of Milt May.
B. Jan. 18, 1911, Laconia, Ind.

BR TR 5′11½″ 165 lbs.

Year	Team	Games	BA	SA	AB	H	2B	3B	HR	HR%	R	RBI	BB	SO	SB	Pinch Hit AB	Pinch Hit H	PO	A	E	DP	TC/G	FA	G by Pos
1939	**PHI N**	135	.287	.371	464	133	27	3	2	0.4	49	62	41	20	4	3	1	153	263	19	28	3.3	.956	3B-132
1940		136	.293	.355	501	147	24	2	1	0.2	59	48	58	33	2	0	0	140	303	22	13	3.4	.953	3B-135, SS-1
1941		142	.267	.318	490	131	17	4	0	0.0	46	39	55	30	2	2	1	194	324	15	31	3.8	.972	3B-140
1942		115	.238	.281	345	82	15	0	0	0.0	25	18	51	17	3	7	0	109	227	13	23	3.3	.963	3B-107
1943		137	.282	.345	415	117	19	2	1	0.2	31	48	56	21	2	5	3	142	280	16	20	3.3	.963	3B-132
5 yrs.		665	.275	.337	2215	610	102	11	4	0.2	210	215	261	121	13	17	5	738	1397	85	115	3.4	.962	3B-646, SS-1

John Mayberry

MAYBERRY, JOHN CLAIBORN
B. Feb. 18, 1949, Detroit, Mich.

BL TL 6′3″ 215 lbs.

Year	Team	Games	BA	SA	AB	H	2B	3B	HR	HR%	R	RBI	BB	SO	SB	Pinch Hit AB	Pinch Hit H	PO	A	E	DP	TC/G	FA	G by Pos
1968	**HOU N**	4	.000	.000	9	0	0	0	0	0.0	0	0	0	2	0	2	0	25	0	0	1	12.5	1.000	1B-2
1969		5	.000	.000	4	0	0	0	0	0.0	0	0	1	1	0	3	0	0	0	0	0	0.0	—	
1970		50	.216	.365	148	32	3	2	5	3.4	23	14	21	33	1	6	1	371	35	2	29	9.1	.995	1B-45
1971		46	.182	.350	137	25	0	1	7	5.1	16	14	13	32	0	10	4	317	15	1	20	9.0	.997	1B-37
1972	**KC A**	149	.298	.507	503	150	24	3	25	5.0	65	100	78	74	0	4	2	1338	82	7	141	9.8	.995	1B-146
1973		152	.278	.478	510	142	20	2	26	5.1	87	100	**122**	79	3	4	2	1457	81	9	156	10.3	.994	1B-149, DH-1
1974		126	.234	.424	427	100	13	1	22	5.2	63	69	77	72	4	7	2	963	61	10	101	8.5	.990	1B-106, DH-16
1975		156	.291	.547	554	161	38	1	34	6.1	95	106	**119**	73	5	0	0	1199	100	16	105	8.3	.988	1B-131, DH-27
1976		161	.232	.342	594	138	22	2	13	2.2	76	95	82	73	3	1	0	1484	105	7	132	9.4	.996	1B-160, DH-9
1977		153	.230	.401	543	125	22	1	23	4.2	73	82	83	86	1	2	1	1296	81	7	118	9.0	.995	1B-145, DH-8
1978	**TOR A**	152	.250	.416	515	129	15	2	22	4.3	51	70	60	57	1	10	2	1143	52	8	120	8.2	.993	1B-139, DH-7
1979		137	.274	.461	464	127	22	1	21	4.5	61	74	69	60	1	6	2	1192	74	6	129	9.4	.995	1B-135
1980		149	.248	.473	501	124	19	2	30	6.0	62	82	77	80	0	5	1	1243	79	8	138	9.2	.994	1B-136, DH-8
1981		94	.248	.452	290	72	6	1	17	5.9	34	43	44	45	1	7	2	647	36	5	65	7.6	.993	1B-80, DH-10
1982	**2 teams**	**TOR A** (17G –.273) **NY A** (69G –.209)																						
″	**total**	86	.218	.367	248	54	7	0	10	4.0	27	30	35	43	0	6	1	494	26	2	52	6.2	.996	1B-67, DH-17
15 yrs.		1620	.253	.439	5447	1379	211	19	255	4.7	733	879	881	810	20	73	20	13169	827	88	1307	8.9	.994	1B-1478, DH-103
LEAGUE CHAMPIONSHIP SERIES																								
1976	**KC A**	5	.222	.389	18	4	0	0	1	5.6	4	3	1	0	0	0	0	48	1	0	4	9.8	1.000	1B-5
1977		4	.167	.500	12	2	1	0	1	8.3	1	3	1	2	0	0	0	29	1	2	0	8.0	.938	1B-4
2 yrs.		9	.200	.433	30	6	1	0	2	6.7	5	6	2	2	0	0	0	77	2	2	4	9.0	.975	1B-9

Lee Maye

MAYE, ARTHUR LEE BL TR 6′ 2″ 190 lbs.
B. Dec. 11, 1934, Tuscaloosa, Ala.

Year	Team	Lg	Games	BA	SA	AB	H	2B	3B	HR	HR%	R	RBI	BB	SO	SB	Pinch Hit AB	Pinch Hit H	PO	A	E	DP	TC/G	FA	G by Pos
1959	MIL	N	51	.300	.436	140	42	5	1	4	2.9	17	16	7	26	2	7	4	80	3	2	1	1.9	.976	OF-44
1960			41	.301	.373	83	25	6	0	0	0.0	14	2	7	21	5	17	2	29	1	1	0	1.6	.968	OF-19
1961			110	.271	.440	373	101	11	5	14	3.8	68	41	36	50	10	17	5	169	6	5	0	1.9	.972	OF-96
1962			99	.244	.358	349	85	10	0	10	2.9	40	41	25	58	9	8	1	209	2	5	1	2.3	.977	OF-94
1963			124	.271	.428	442	120	22	7	11	2.5	67	34	36	52	14	18	3	231	4	4	1	2.2	.983	OF-111
1964			153	.304	.447	588	179	**44**	5	10	1.7	96	74	34	54	5	13	2	268	9	11	1	2.1	.962	OF-135, 3B-5
1965	2 teams		MIL N (15G –.302) HOU N (108G –.251)																						
″	total		123	.256	.359	468	120	19	7	5	1.1	46	43	22	43	1	8	1	200	8	10	1	1.9	.954	OF-116
1966	HOU	N	115	.288	.419	358	103	12	4	9	2.5	38	36	20	26	4	20	4	145	4	8	0	1.6	.949	OF-97
1967	CLE	A	115	.259	.444	297	77	20	4	9	3.0	43	27	26	47	3	42	10	102	2	2	0	1.4	.981	OF-77, 2B-1
1968			109	.281	.378	299	84	13	2	4	1.3	20	26	15	24	0	30	9	123	4	3	0	1.6	.977	OF-80, 1B-1
1969	2 teams		CLE A (43G –.250) WAS A (71G –.290)																						
″	total		114	.277	.422	346	96	14	3	10	2.9	50	41	28	40	2	24	4	155	2	7	1	1.7	.957	OF-93, 3B-1
1970	2 teams		WAS A (96G –.263) CHI A (6G –.167)																						
″	total		102	.261	.395	261	68	12	1	7	2.7	28	31	21	33	4	39	7	75	5	0	1	1.2	1.000	OF-68, 3B-1
1971	CHI	A	32	.205	.318	44	9	2	0	1	2.3	6	7	5	7	0	17	5	11	1	0	0	1.2	1.000	OF-10
13 yrs.			1288	.274	.410	4048	1109	190	39	94	2.3	533	419	282	481	59	260	57	1797	51	58	7	1.8	.970	OF-1040, 3B-7, 1B-1, 2B-1

Ed Mayer

MAYER, EDWARD H 5′ 8½″ 155 lbs.
B. Aug. 16, 1866, Marshall, Ill. D. May 18, 1913, Chicago, Ill.

Year	Team	Lg	Games	BA	SA	AB	H	2B	3B	HR	HR%	R	RBI	BB	SO	SB	Pinch Hit AB	Pinch Hit H	PO	A	E	DP	TC/G	FA	G by Pos
1890	PHI	N	117	.242	.320	484	117	25	5	1	0.2	49	70	22	36	20	0	0	173	224	55	22	3.9	.878	3B-117
1891			68	.187	.224	268	50	2	4	0	0.0	24	31	14	29	7	0	0	100	105	29	4	3.4	.876	3B-31, OF-29, SS-7, 2B-1
2 yrs.			185	.222	.286	752	167	27	9	1	0.1	73	101	36	65	27	0	0	273	329	84	26	3.7	.878	3B-148, OF-29, SS-7, 2B-1

Sam Mayer

MAYER, SAMUEL FRANKEL BR TL 5′10″ 164 lbs.
Born Samuel Frankel Erskine.
Brother of Erskine Mayer.
B. Feb. 28, 1893, Atlanta, Ga. D. July 1, 1962, Atlanta, Ga.

Year	Team	Lg	Games	BA	SA	AB	H	2B	3B	HR	HR%	R	RBI	BB	SO	SB	Pinch Hit AB	Pinch Hit H	PO	A	E	DP	TC/G	FA	G by Pos
1915	WAS	A	11	.241	.345	29	7	0	0	1	3.4	5	4	4	2	1	0	0	14	1	0	1	1.3	1.000	OF-10, 1B-1, P-1

Wally Mayer

MAYER, WALTER A. BR TR 5′11″ 168 lbs.
B. July 8, 1890, Cincinnati, Ohio D. Nov. 18, 1951, Minnetonka, Minn.

Year	Team	Lg	Games	BA	SA	AB	H	2B	3B	HR	HR%	R	RBI	BB	SO	SB	Pinch Hit AB	Pinch Hit H	PO	A	E	DP	TC/G	FA	G by Pos
1911	CHI	A	1	.000	.000	3	0	0	0	0	0.0	0	0	2		0	0	0	7	2	1	0	10.0	.900	C-1
1912			7	.000	.000	9	0	0	0	0	0.0	1	0	1		0	1	0	13	1	0	0	2.3	1.000	C-6
1914			39	.165	.224	85	14	3	1	0	0.0	7	5	14	23	1	5	0	138	47	7	3	5.6	.964	C-33, 3B-1
1915			22	.222	.315	54	12	3	1	0	0.0	3	5	5	8	0	2	0	89	15	1	0	5.3	.990	C-20
1917	BOS	A	4	.167	.167	12	2	0	0	0	0.0	2	0	5	2	0	0	0	19	8	1	1	7.0	.964	C-4
1918			26	.224	.306	49	11	4	0	0	0.0	7	5	7	7	0	3	0	63	18	3	0	3.7	.964	C-23
1919	STL	A	30	.226	.323	62	14	4	1	0	0.0	2	5	8	11	0	5	1	84	33	5	1	4.9	.959	C-25
7 yrs.			129	.193	.266	274	53	14	3	0	0.0	22	20	42	51	1	16	1	413	124	18	5	4.9	.968	C-112, 3B-1

Paddy Mayes

MAYES, ADAIR BUSHYHEAD BL TR 5′11″ 160 lbs.
B. Mar. 17, 1885, Locust Grove, Okla. D. May 28, 1962, Fayetteville, Ark.

Year	Team	Lg	Games	BA	SA	AB	H	2B	3B	HR	HR%	R	RBI	BB	SO	SB	Pinch Hit AB	Pinch Hit H	PO	A	E	DP	TC/G	FA	G by Pos
1911	PHI	N	5	.000	.000	5	0	0	0	0	0.0	1	0	1	2	0	1	0	2	0	0	0	1.0	1.000	OF-2

Buster Maynard

MAYNARD, JAMES WALTER BR TR 5′11″ 170 lbs.
B. Mar. 25, 1913, Henderson, N. C. D. Sept. 7, 1977, Durham, N. C.

Year	Team	Lg	Games	BA	SA	AB	H	2B	3B	HR	HR%	R	RBI	BB	SO	SB	Pinch Hit AB	Pinch Hit H	PO	A	E	DP	TC/G	FA	G by Pos
1940	NY	N	7	.276	.586	29	8	2	2	1	3.4	6	2	2	6	0	0	0	13	0	1	0	2.0	.929	OF-7
1942			89	.247	.342	190	47	4	1	4	2.1	17	32	19	19	3	15	3	116	28	5	5	2.2	.966	OF-58, 3B-10, 2B-1
1943			121	.206	.305	393	81	8	2	9	2.3	43	32	24	27	3	19	1	177	57	7	2	2.5	.971	OF-74, 3B-22
1946			7	.000	.000	4	0	0	0	0	0.0	2	0	1	1	0	1	0	3	0	1	0	1.3	.750	OF-3
4 yrs.			224	.221	.328	616	136	14	5	14	2.3	68	66	46	53	6	35	4	309	85	14	7	2.3	.966	OF-142, 3B-32, 2B-1

Chick Maynard

MAYNARD, LEROY EVANS BL TR 5′ 9″ 150 lbs.
B. Nov. 2, 1896, Turners Falls, Mass. D. Jan. 31, 1957, Bangor, Me.

Year	Team	Lg	Games	BA	SA	AB	H	2B	3B	HR	HR%	R	RBI	BB	SO	SB	Pinch Hit AB	Pinch Hit H	PO	A	E	DP	TC/G	FA	G by Pos
1922	BOS	A	12	.125	.125	24	3	0	0	0	0.0	1	0	3	2	0	0	0	13	21	5	1	3.3	.872	SS-12

Brent Mayne

MAYNE, BRENT DANEM BL TR 6′ 1″ 195 lbs.
B. Apr. 19, 1968, Loma Linda, Calif.

Year	Team	Lg	Games	BA	SA	AB	H	2B	3B	HR	HR%	R	RBI	BB	SO	SB	Pinch Hit AB	Pinch Hit H	PO	A	E	DP	TC/G	FA	G by Pos
1990	KC	A	5	.231	.231	13	3	0	0	0	0.0	2	1	3	3	0	1	0	29	3	1	0	6.6	.970	C-5
1991			85	.251	.325	231	58	8	0	3	1.3	22	31	23	42	2	8	2	425	38	6	4	5.8	.987	C-80, DH-1
1992			82	.225	.272	213	48	10	0	0	0.0	16	18	11	26	0	14	4	281	33	3	2	4.5	.991	C-62, 3B-8, DH-1
1993			71	.254	.337	205	52	9	1	2	1.0	22	22	18	31	3	4	1	356	27	2	1	5.6	.995	C-68, DH-1
1994			46	.257	.347	144	37	5	1	2	1.4	19	20	14	27	1	4	0	246	13	1	1	5.8	.996	C-42, DH-3
1995			110	.251	.326	307	77	18	1	1	0.3	23	27	25	41	0	7	0	540	39	3	8	5.7	.995	C-103
6 yrs.			399	.247	.319	1113	275	50	3	8	0.7	104	119	94	170	6	38	7	1877	153	16	16	5.5	.992	C-360, 3B-8, DH-6

Eddie Mayo

MAYO, EDWARD JOSEPH BL TR 5′11″ 178 lbs.
Born Edward Joseph Mayoski.
B. Apr. 15, 1910, Holyoke, Mass.

Year	Team	Lg	Games	BA	SA	AB	H	2B	3B	HR	HR%	R	RBI	BB	SO	SB	Pinch Hit AB	Pinch Hit H	PO	A	E	DP	TC/G	FA	G by Pos
1936	NY	N	46	.199	.262	141	28	4	1	1	0.7	11	8	11	12	0	3	1	32	69	2	8	2.6	.981	3B-40
1937	BOS	N	65	.227	.291	172	39	6	1	1	0.6	19	18	15	20	1	14	4	57	73	6	2	2.7	.956	3B-50
1938			8	.214	.429	14	3	0	0	1	7.1	2	4	1	0	0	0	0	6	10	1	3	2.1	.941	3B-6, SS-2
1943	PHI	A	128	.219	.244	471	103	10	1	0	0.0	49	28	34	32	2	5	0	176	223	10	18	3.3	.976	3B-123
1944	DET	A	154	.249	.313	607	151	18	3	5	0.8	76	63	57	23	9	0	0	401	498	21	125	6.0	.977	2B-143, SS-11
1945			134	.285	.405	501	143	24	3	10	2.0	71	54	48	29	7	9	4	326	393	15	91	5.9	.980	2B-124
1946			51	.252	.317	202	51	9	2	0	0.0	21	22	14	12	6	2	0	96	125	8	28	4.7	.965	2B-49
1947			142	.279	.379	535	149	28	4	6	1.1	66	48	48	28	3	1	1	326	365	12	80	5.0	.983	2B-142
1948			106	.249	.324	370	92	20	1	2	0.5	35	42	30	19	1	10	2	211	242	11	49	4.8	.976	2B-86, 3B-10
9 yrs.			834	.252	.328	3013	759	119	16	26	0.9	350	287	258	175	29	44	12	1631	1998	86	404	4.7	.977	2B-544, 3B-229, SS-13

Eddie Mayo *continued*

Year	Team		Games	BA	SA	AB	H	2B	3B	HR	HR%	R	RBI	BB	SO	SB	Pinch Hit AB	Pinch Hit H	PO	A	E	DP	TC/G	FA	G by Pos
WORLD SERIES																									
1936	**NY**	**N**	1	.000	.000	1	0	0	0	0	0.0	0	0	0	0	0	0	0	0	0	0	0	0.0	.000	3B-1
1945	**DET**	**A**	7	.250	.286	28	7	1	0	0	0.0	4	2	2	2	0	0	0	18	13	1	4	4.6	.969	2B-7
2 yrs.			8	.241	.276	29	7	1	0	0	0.0	4	2	2	2	0	0	0	18	13	1	4	4.0	.969	2B-7, 3B-1

Jackie Mayo

MAYO, JOHN LEWIS
B. July 26, 1925, Litchfield, Ill.
BL TR 6′ 1″ 190 lbs.

Year	Team		Games	BA	SA	AB	H	2B	3B	HR	HR%	R	RBI	BB	SO	SB	Pinch Hit AB	Pinch Hit H	PO	A	E	DP	TC/G	FA	G by Pos
1948	**PHI**	**N**	12	.229	.343	35	8	2	1	0	0.0	7	3	7	7	1	1	0	27	1	0	0	2.5	1.000	OF-11
1949			45	.128	.128	39	5	0	0	0	0.0	3	2	4	5	0	15	1	23	1	3	0	1.1	.889	OF-25
1950			18	.222	.306	36	8	3	0	0	0.0	1	3	2	5	0	3	0	23	0	1	0	1.6	.958	OF-15
1951			9	.143	.143	7	1	0	0	0	0.0	1	0	0	0	0	4	0	4	0	0	0	0.8	1.000	OF-5
1952			50	.244	.311	119	29	5	0	1	0.8	13	4	12	17	1	15	0	108	10	0	4	3.6	1.000	OF-27, 1B-6
1953			5	.000	.000	4	0	0	0	0	0.0	0	0	0	1	0	4	0	0	0	0	0	0.0	.000	OF-1
6 yrs.			139	.213	.275	240	51	10	1	1	0.4	25	12	25	35	2	42	1	185	12	4	4	2.2	.980	OF-84, 1B-6
WORLD SERIES																									
1950	**PHI**	**N**	3	—	—	0	0	0	0	0	—	0	0	1	0	0	0	0	1	0	0	0	1.0	1.000	OF-1

Willie Mays

MAYS, WILLIE HOWARD (Say Hey)
B. May 6, 1931, Westfield, Ala.
Hall of Fame 1979.
BR TR 5′10½″ 170 lbs.

Year	Team		Games	BA	SA	AB	H	2B	3B	HR	HR%	R	RBI	BB	SO	SB	Pinch Hit AB	Pinch Hit H	PO	A	E	DP	TC/G	FA	G by Pos
1951	**NY**	**N**	121	.274	.472	464	127	22	5	20	4.3	59	68	56	60	7	0	0	353	12	9	2	3.1	.976	OF-121
1952			34	.236	.409	127	30	2	4	4	3.1	17	23	16	17	4	0	0	109	6	1	2	3.4	.991	OF-34
1954			151	**.345**	**.667**	565	195	33	**13**	41	7.3	119	110	66	57	8	0	0	448	13	7	9	3.1	.985	OF-151
1955			152	.319	**.659**	580	185	18	**13**	**51**	**8.8**	123	127	79	60	24	0	0	407	23	8	8	2.9	.982	OF-152
1956			152	.296	.557	578	171	27	8	36	6.2	101	84	68	65	**40**	0	0	415	14	9	6	2.9	.979	OF-152
1957			152	.333	**.626**	585	195	26	**20**	35	6.0	112	97	76	62	**38**	1	0	422	14	9	5	3.0	.980	OF-150
1958	**SF**	**N**	152	.347	.583	600	208	33	11	29	4.8	**121**	96	78	56	**31**	2	0	429	17	9	2	3.0	.980	OF-151
1959			151	.313	.583	575	180	43	5	34	5.9	125	104	65	58	**27**	4	2	353	6	6	2	2.5	.984	OF-147
1960			153	.319	.555	595	**190**	29	12	29	4.9	107	103	61	70	25	1	0	392	12	8	2	2.7	.981	OF-152
1961			154	.308	.584	572	176	32	3	40	7.0	**129**	123	81	77	18	1	1	385	7	8	3	2.6	.980	OF-153
1962			162	.304	.615	621	189	36	5	**49**	**7.9**	130	141	78	85	18	1	0	429	6	4	1	2.7	.991	OF-161
1963			157	.314	.582	596	187	32	7	38	6.4	115	103	66	83	8	2	0	397	7	8	1	2.6	.981	OF-157, SS-1
1964			157	.296	**.607**	578	171	21	9	**47**	**8.1**	121	111	82	72	19	3	1	376	12	6	5	2.5	.985	OF-155, 3B-1, 1B-1, SS-1
1965			157	.317	**.645**	558	177	21	3	**52**	**9.3**	118	112	76	71	9	6	0	337	13	6	4	2.4	.983	OF-151
1966			152	.288	.556	552	159	29	4	37	6.7	99	103	70	81	5	4	1	370	8	7	2	2.6	.982	OF-150
1967			141	.263	.453	486	128	22	2	22	4.5	83	70	51	92	6	11	1	277	3	7	0	2.1	.976	OF-134
1968			148	.289	.488	498	144	20	5	23	4.6	84	79	67	81	12	3	2	310	7	7	3	2.3	.978	OF-142, 1B-1
1969			117	.283	.437	403	114	17	3	13	3.2	64	58	49	71	6	12	3	205	4	5	1	1.9	.977	OF-109, 1B-1
1970			139	.291	.506	478	139	15	2	28	5.9	94	83	79	90	5	10	2	303	9	7	6	2.4	.978	OF-129, 1B-5
1971			136	.271	.482	417	113	24	5	18	4.3	82	61	**112**	123	23	15	4	576	29	17	44	4.7	.973	OF-84, 1B-48
1972	**2 teams**		**SF N** (19G –.184) **NY N** (69G –.267)																						
″	**total**		88	.250	.402	244	61	11	1	8	3.3	35	22	60	48	4	11	4	213	5	4	4	3.0	.982	OF-63, 1B-11
1973	**NY**	**N**	66	.211	.344	209	44	10	0	6	2.9	24	25	27	47	1	7	2	246	6	4	9	4.1	.984	OF-45, 1B-17
22 yrs.			2992	.302	.557	10881	3283	523	140	660	6.1	2062	1903	1463	1526	338	94	23	7752	233	156	121	2.8	.981	OF-2843, 1B-84, SS-2, 3B-1
			6th		**10th**	**8th**	**9th**			**3rd**		**5th**	**7th**												
LEAGUE CHAMPIONSHIP SERIES																									
1971	**SF**	**N**	4	.267	.600	15	4	2	0	1	6.7	2	3	3	3	1	0	0	5	0	0	0	1.3	1.000	OF-4
1973	**NY**	**N**	1	.333	.333	3	1	0	0	0	0.0	1	1	0	0	0	1	1	1	0	0	0	1.0	1.000	OF-1
2 yrs.			5	.278	.556	18	5	2	0	1	5.6	3	4	3	3	1	1	1	6	0	0	0	1.2	1.000	OF-5
WORLD SERIES																									
1951	**NY**	**N**	6	.182	.182	22	4	0	0	0	0.0	1	1	2	2	0	0	0	16	1	0	0	2.8	1.000	OF-6
1954			4	.286	.357	14	4	1	0	0	0.0	4	3	4	1	1	0	0	10	0	0	0	2.5	1.000	OF-4
1962	**SF**	**N**	7	.250	.321	28	7	2	0	0	0.0	3	1	1	5	1	0	0	19	0	0	0	2.7	1.000	OF-7
1973	**NY**	**N**	3	.286	.286	7	2	0	0	0	0.0	1	1	0	1	0	1	0	1	0	1	0	1.0	.500	OF-2
4 yrs.			20	.239	.282	71	17	3	0	0	0.0	9	6	7	9	2	1	0	46	1	1	0	2.5	.979	OF-19

Bill Mazeroski

MAZEROSKI, WILLIAM STANLEY (Maz)
B. Sept. 5, 1936, Wheeling, W. Va.
BR TR 5′11½″ 183 lbs.

Year	Team		Games	BA	SA	AB	H	2B	3B	HR	HR%	R	RBI	BB	SO	SB	Pinch Hit AB	Pinch Hit H	PO	A	E	DP	TC/G	FA	G by Pos
1956	**PIT**	**N**	81	.243	.318	255	62	8	1	3	1.2	30	14	18	24	0	0	0	163	242	8	56	5.1	.981	2B-81
1957			148	.283	.407	526	149	27	7	8	1.5	59	54	27	49	3	4	1	308	443	17	96	5.3	.978	2B-144
1958			152	.275	.439	567	156	24	6	19	3.4	69	68	25	71	1	0	0	344	496	17	118	5.6	.980	2B-152
1959			135	.241	.339	493	119	15	6	7	1.4	50	59	29	54	1	2	0	303	373	13	100	5.2	.981	2B-133
1960			151	.273	.392	538	147	21	5	11	2.0	58	64	40	50	4	1	0	413	449	10	127	5.8	.989	2B-151
1961			152	.265	.380	558	148	21	2	13	2.3	71	59	26	55	2	0	0	410	505	23	144	6.2	.975	2B-152
1962			159	.271	.418	572	155	24	9	14	2.4	55	81	37	47	0	0	0	425	509	14	138	6.0	.985	2B-159
1963			142	.245	.343	534	131	22	3	8	1.5	43	52	32	46	2	3	1	340	506	14	131	6.2	.984	2B-138
1964			162	.268	.381	601	161	22	8	10	1.7	66	64	29	52	1	0	0	346	543	23	122	5.6	.975	2B-162
1965			130	.271	.346	494	134	17	1	6	1.2	52	54	18	34	2	4	0	290	439	9	113	5.8	.988	2B-127
1966			162	.262	.398	621	163	22	7	16	2.6	56	82	31	62	4	0	0	411	538	8	161	5.9	.992	2B-162
1967			163	.261	.352	639	167	25	3	9	1.4	62	77	30	55	1	0	0	417	498	18	131	5.7	.981	2B-163
1968			143	.251	.312	506	127	18	2	3	0.6	36	42	38	38	3	1	0	319	467	15	107	5.6	.981	2B-142
1969			67	.229	.308	227	52	7	1	3	1.3	13	25	22	16	1	2	0	134	192	4	46	5.1	.988	2B-65
1970			112	.229	.324	367	84	14	0	7	1.9	29	39	27	40	2	9	4	227	325	7	87	5.5	.987	2B-102
1971			70	.254	.295	193	49	3	1	1	0.5	17	16	15	8	0	20	6	97	126	3	22	4.3	.987	2B-46, 3B-7
1972			34	.188	.250	64	12	4	0	0	0.0	3	3	3	5	0	14	1	29	43	1	7	4.1	.986	2B-15, 3B-3
17 yrs.			2163	.260	.367	7755	2016	294	62	138	1.8	769	853	447	706	27	60	13	4976	6694	204	1706	5.6	.983	2B-2094, 3B-10
LEAGUE CHAMPIONSHIP SERIES																									
1970	**PIT**	**N**	1	.000	.000	2	0	0	0	0	0.0	0	0	2	0	0	0	0	1	4	0	0	5.0	1.000	2B-1
1971			1	1.000	1.000	1	1	0	0	0	0.0	1	0	0	0	0	1	1	0	0	0	0	0.0	—	
1972			2	.500	.500	2	1	0	0	0	0.0	0	0	0	1	0	2	1	0	0	0	0	0.0	—	
3 yrs.			4	.400	.400	5	2	0	0	0	0.0	1	0	2	1	0	3	2	1	4	0	0	5.0	1.000	2B-1

Bill Mazeroski *continued*

Year	Team		Games	BA	SA	AB	H	2B	3B	HR	HR%	R	RBI	BB	SO	SB	Pinch Hit AB	Pinch Hit H	PO	A	E	DP	TC/G	FA	G by Pos
WORLD SERIES																									
1960	PIT	N	7	.320	.640	25	8	2	0	2	8.0	4	5	0	3	0	0	0	16	23	0	6	5.6	1.000	2B-7
1971			1	.000	.000	1	0	0	0	0	0.0	0	0	0	0	0	1	0	0	0	0	0	0.0	—	
2 yrs.			8	.308	.615	26	8	2	0	2	7.7	4	5	0	3	0	1	0	16	23	0	6	5.6	1.000	2B-7

Mel Mazzera

MAZZERA, MELVIN LEONARD (Mike)
B. Jan. 31, 1914, Stockton, Calif.
BL TL 5′11″ 180 lbs.

Year	Team		Games	BA	SA	AB	H	2B	3B	HR	HR%	R	RBI	BB	SO	SB	Pinch Hit AB	Pinch Hit H	PO	A	E	DP	TC/G	FA	G by Pos
1935	STL	A	12	.233	.400	30	7	2	0	1	3.3	4	2	4	9	0	2	0	18	1	1	0	2.0	.950	OF-10
1937			7	.286	.571	7	2	2	0	0	0.0	1	0	0	2	0	7	2	0	0	0	0	0.0	—	
1938			86	.279	.426	204	57	8	2	6	2.9	33	29	12	25	1	37	9	74	7	2	1	1.8	.976	OF-47
1939			34	.297	.459	111	33	5	2	3	2.7	21	22	10	20	0	6	1	56	1	1	0	2.3	.983	OF-25
1940	PHI	N	69	.237	.321	156	37	5	4	0	0.0	16	13	19	15	1	17	3	90	6	1	3	1.8	.990	OF-42, 1B-11
5 yrs.			208	.268	.402	508	136	22	8	10	2.0	75	66	45	71	2	69	15	238	15	5	4	1.9	.981	OF-124, 1B-11

Lee Mazzilli

MAZZILLI, LEE LOUIS (Maz)
B. Mar. 25, 1955, New York, N. Y.
BB TR 6′ 1″ 180 lbs.

Year	Team		Games	BA	SA	AB	H	2B	3B	HR	HR%	R	RBI	BB	SO	SB	Pinch Hit AB	Pinch Hit H	PO	A	E	DP	TC/G	FA	G by Pos
1976	NY	N	24	.195	.299	77	15	2	0	2	2.6	9	7	14	10	5	2	1	55	2	1	2	2.5	.983	OF-23
1977			159	.250	.339	537	134	24	3	6	1.1	66	46	72	72	22	5	2	386	9	3	1	2.6	.992	OF-156
1978			148	.273	.432	542	148	28	5	16	3.0	78	61	69	82	20	5	1	386	8	5	3	2.8	.987	OF-144
1979			158	.303	.449	597	181	34	4	15	2.5	78	79	93	74	34	1	0	480	24	5	16	3.2	.990	OF-143, 1B-15
1980			152	.280	.431	578	162	31	4	16	2.8	82	76	82	92	41	2	0	874	53	14	68	6.0	.985	1B-92, OF-66
1981			95	.228	.358	324	74	14	5	6	1.9	36	34	46	53	17	6	2	192	5	6	1	2.3	.970	OF-89
1982	2 teams	TEX A (58G –.241) NY A (37G –.266)																							
″	total		95	.251	.375	323	81	10	0	10	3.1	43	34	43	41	13	11	1	234	8	4	27	2.9	.984	DH-33, OF-28, 1B-23
1983	PIT	N	109	.240	.337	246	59	9	0	5	2.0	37	24	49	43	15	41	6	173	3	4	6	2.8	.978	OF-57, 1B-7
1984			111	.237	.331	266	63	11	1	4	1.5	37	21	40	42	8	32	6	103	2	1	0	1.3	.991	OF-74, 1B-5
1985			92	.282	.376	117	33	8	0	1	0.9	20	9	29	17	4	56	16	152	6	3	15	6.7	.981	1B-19, OF-5
1986	2 teams	PIT N (61G –.226) NY N (39G –.276)																							
″	total		100	.245	.351	151	37	5	1	3	2.0	28	15	38	36	4	54	8	128	2	0	3	3.0	1.000	OF-28, 1B-15
1987	NY	N	88	.306	.460	124	38	8	1	3	2.4	26	24	21	14	5	55	**17**	82	3	0	1	2.2	1.000	OF-25, 1B-13
1988			68	.147	.164	116	17	2	0	0	0.0	9	12	12	16	4	30	7	114	4	3	5	3.6	.975	OF-18, 1B-16
1989	2 teams	NY N (48G –.183) TOR A (28G –.227)																							
″	total		76	.206	.389	126	26	5	0	6	4.8	22	18	34	35	5	32	9	66	2	2	3	1.7	.971	DH-19, OF-12, 1B-10
14 yrs.			1475	.259	.385	4124	1068	191	24	93	2.3	571	460	642	627	197	332	76	3425	131	51	151	3.2	.986	OF-868, 1B-215, DH-52
LEAGUE CHAMPIONSHIP SERIES																									
1986	NY	N	5	.200	.200	5	1	0	0	0	0.0	0	0	0	3	0	5	1	0	0	0	0	0.0	—	
1988			3	.500	.500	2	1	0	0	0	0.0	0	0	0	0	1	2	1	0	0	0	0	0.0	—	
1989	TOR	A	3	.000	.000	8	0	0	0	0	0.0	0	0	0	2	0	1	0	0	0	0	0	0.0	.000	DH-2
3 yrs.			11	.133	.133	15	2	0	0	0	0.0	0	0	0	5	1	8	2	0	0	0	0	0.0		DH-2
WORLD SERIES																									
1986	NY	N	4	.400	.400	5	2	0	0	0	0.0	2	0	0	0	0	4	2	1	0	0	0	0.5	1.000	OF-1, DH-1

Jimmy McAleer

McALEER, JAMES ROBERT
B. July 10, 1864, Youngstown, Ohio D. Apr. 29, 1931, Youngstown, Ohio.
Manager 1901–11.
BR TR 6′ 175 lbs.

Year	Team		Games	BA	SA	AB	H	2B	3B	HR	HR%	R	RBI	BB	SO	SB	Pinch Hit AB	Pinch Hit H	PO	A	E	DP	TC/G	FA	G by Pos
1889	CLE	N	110	.235	.282	447	105	6	6	1	0.2	66	35	30	49	37	0	0	247	29	13	9	2.6	.955	OF-110
1890	CLE	P	86	.267	.340	341	91	8	7	1	0.3	58	42	37	33	21	0	0	249	15	17	4	3.3	.940	OF-86
1891	CLE	N	136	.237	.312	565	134	16	10	2	0.4	97	61	49	47	51	0	0	284	19	25	1	2.4	.924	OF-136
1892			149	.238	.329	571	136	26	7	4	0.7	92	70	63	54	40	0	0	367	25	16	0	2.7	.961	OF-149
1893			91	.237	.274	350	83	5	1	2	0.6	63	41	35	21	32	0	0	230	16	19	3	2.9	.928	OF-91
1894			64	.289	.379	253	73	15	1	2	0.8	36	40	13	17	14	0	0	175	9	9	3	3.0	.953	OF-64
1895			131	.271	.311	528	143	17	2	0	0.0	84	68	38	37	32	0	0	341	14	25	1	2.9	.934	OF-132
1896			116	.288	.347	455	131	16	4	1	0.2	70	54	47	32	24	0	0	278	18	13	5	2.7	.958	OF-116
1897			24	.220	.242	91	20	2	0	0	0.0	6	10	7		4	0	0	51	3	3	0	2.4	.947	OF-24
1898			106	.238	.246	366	87	3	0	0	0.0	47	48	46		7	0	0	243	14	10	4	2.5	.963	OF-104, 2B-2
1901	CLE	A	3	.143	.143	7	1	0	0	0	0.0	0	0	0		0	0	0	3	0	0	0	0.8	1.000	OF-2, 3B-1, P-1
1902	STL	A	2	.667	.667	3	2	0	0	0	0.0	0	0	0		0	0	0	0	0	0	0	0.0	.000	OF-2
1907			2	—	—	0	0	0	0	0	—	0	0	0	0	0	0	0	0	0	0	0	0.0	—	
13 yrs.			1020	.253	.311	3977	1006	114	38	13	0.3	619	469	365	290	262	0	0	2468	162	150	30	2.7	.946	OF-1016, 2B-2, 3B-1, P-1

John McAleese

McALEESE, JOHN JAMES
B. Aug. 22, 1878, Sharon, Pa. D. Nov. 14, 1950, New York, N. Y.
BR TR 5′ 8″

Year	Team		Games	BA	SA	AB	H	2B	3B	HR	HR%	R	RBI	BB	SO	SB	Pinch Hit AB	Pinch Hit H	PO	A	E	DP	TC/G	FA	G by Pos
1901	CHI	A	1	.000	.000	1	0	0	0	0	0.0	0	0	0		0	0	0	0	1	0	0	1.0	1.000	P-1
1909	STL	A	85	.213	.240	267	57	7	0	0	0.0	33	12	32		18	2	0	121	15	14	2	1.9	.907	OF-79, 3B-2
2 yrs.			86	.213	.239	268	57	7	0	0	0.0	33	12	32		18	2	0	121	16	14	2	1.8	.907	OF-79, 3B-2, P-1

Bill McAllester

McALLESTER, WILLIAM LUSK
B. Dec. 29, 1888, Chattanooga, Tenn. D. Mar. 3, 1970, Chattanooga, Tenn.
BR TR 5′11½″ 170 lbs.

Year	Team		Games	BA	SA	AB	H	2B	3B	HR	HR%	R	RBI	BB	SO	SB	Pinch Hit AB	Pinch Hit H	PO	A	E	DP	TC/G	FA	G by Pos
1913	STL	A	47	.153	.200	85	13	4	0	0	0.0	3	6	11	12	2	8	2	103	35	14	4	4.1	.908	C-37

Sport McAllister

McALLISTER, LEWIS WILLIAM
B. July 23, 1874, Austin, Miss. D. July 17, 1962, Wyandotte, Mich.
BB TR 5′11″ 180 lbs.

Year	Team		Games	BA	SA	AB	H	2B	3B	HR	HR%	R	RBI	BB	SO	SB	Pinch Hit AB	Pinch Hit H	PO	A	E	DP	TC/G	FA	G by Pos
1896	CLE	N	8	.222	.296	27	6	2	0	0	0.0	2	1	0	2	1	0	0	6	2	1	0	1.3	.889	OF-4, C-2, P-1
1897			43	.219	.270	137	30	5	1	0	0.0	23	11	12		3	0	0	74	21	9	1	2.5	.913	OF-28, SS-4, P-4, 1B-3, C-2, 2B-1
1898			17	.228	.316	57	13	3	1	0	0.0	8	9	5		0	0	0	15	17	2	0	2.0	.941	P-9, OF-8
1899			113	.237	.297	418	99	6	8	1	0.2	29	31	19		5	2	0	218	59	28	11	2.6	.908	OF-79, C-17, 3B-7, 1B-6, SS-3, P-3, 2B-1
1901	DET	A	90	.301	.386	306	92	9	4	3	1.0	45	57	15		17	4	2	381	66	42	19	5.6	.914	C-35, 1B-28, OF-11, 3B-10, SS-3

Sport McAllister *continued*

Year	Team	Games	BA	SA	AB	H	2B	3B	HR	HR%	R	RBI	BB	SO	SB	Pinch Hit AB	Pinch Hit H	PO	A	E	DP	TC/G	FA	G by Pos
1902	2 teams DET A (66G –.210) BAL A (3G –.091)																							
"	total	69	.204	.254	240	49	5	2	1	0.4	19	33	6		1	5	0	312	75	15	20	6.2	.963	1B-27, OF-12, C-9, SS-6, 3B-6, 2B-5
1903	DET A	78	.260	.306	265	69	8	2	0	0.0	31	22	10		5	5	1	170	169	33	14	5.0	.911	SS-46, C-18, OF-5, 3B-4, 1B-1
7 yrs.		418	.247	.308	1450	358	38	18	5	0.3	157	164	67	2	32	16	3	1176	409	130	65	4.2	.924	OF-147, C-83, 1B-65, SS-62, 3B-27, P-17, 2B-7

Jim McAnany

McANANY, JAMES BR TR 5′10″ 196 lbs.
B. Sept. 4, 1936, Los Angeles, Calif.

Year	Team	Games	BA	SA	AB	H	2B	3B	HR	HR%	R	RBI	BB	SO	SB	Pinch Hit AB	Pinch Hit H	PO	A	E	DP	TC/G	FA	G by Pos
1958	CHI A	5	.000	.000	13	0	0	0	0	0.0	0	0	0	5	0	1	0	9	0	0	0	3.0	1.000	OF-3
1959		67	.276	.348	210	58	9	3	0	0.0	22	27	19	26	2	0	0	106	6	4	4	1.7	.966	OF-67
1960		3	.000	.000	2	0	0	0	0	0.0	0	0	0	2	0	2	0	0	0	0	0	0.0	—	
1961	CHI N	11	.300	.400	10	3	1	0	0	0.0	1	0	1	3	0	10	3	0	0	0	0	0.0	.000	OF-1
1962		7	.000	.000	6	0	0	0	0	0.0	0	0	1	2	0	6	0	0	0	0	0	0.0	—	
5 yrs.		93	.253	.320	241	61	10	3	0	0.0	23	27	21	38	2	19	3	115	6	4	4	1.8	.968	OF-71
WORLD SERIES																								
1959	CHI A	3	.000	.000	5	0	0	0	0	0.0	0	0	1	0	0	0	0	5	0	0	0	1.7	1.000	OF-3

Ike McAuley

McAULEY, JAMES EARL BR TR 5′ 9½″ 150 lbs.
B. Aug. 19, 1891, Wichita, Kans. D. Apr. 6, 1928, Des Moines, Iowa.

Year	Team	Games	BA	SA	AB	H	2B	3B	HR	HR%	R	RBI	BB	SO	SB	Pinch Hit AB	Pinch Hit H	PO	A	E	DP	TC/G	FA	G by Pos
1914	PIT N	15	.125	.125	24	3	0	0	0	0.0	3	0	0	8	0	1	0	9	19	4	4	3.2	.875	SS-5, 3B-3, 2B-2
1915		5	.133	.200	15	2	1	0	0	0.0	0	0	0	6	0	2	0	3	8	1	1	2.4	.917	SS-5
1916		4	.250	.250	8	2	0	0	0	0.0	1	1	0	1	0	0	0	8	7	1	2	4.0	.938	SS-4
1917	STL N	3	.286	.286	7	2	0	0	0	0.0	0	1	0	1	0	0	0	2	3	1	0	2.0	.833	SS-3
1925	CHI N	37	.280	.368	125	35	7	2	0	0.0	10	11	11	12	1	0	0	94	93	10	21	5.3	.949	SS-37
5 yrs.		64	.246	.313	179	44	8	2	0	0.0	14	13	11	28	1	3	0	116	130	17	28	4.5	.935	SS-54, 3B-3, 2B-2

Dick McAuliffe

McAULIFFE, RICHARD JOHN BL TR 5′11″ 176 lbs.
B. Nov. 29, 1939, Hartford, Conn.

Year	Team	Games	BA	SA	AB	H	2B	3B	HR	HR%	R	RBI	BB	SO	SB	Pinch Hit AB	Pinch Hit H	PO	A	E	DP	TC/G	FA	G by Pos
1960	DET A	8	.259	.333	27	7	0	1	0	0.0	2	1	2	6	0	0	0	12	26	5	7	6.1	.884	SS-7
1961		80	.256	.389	285	73	12	4	6	2.1	36	33	24	39	2	7	3	92	154	19	32	3.4	.928	SS-55, 3B-22
1962		139	.263	.403	471	124	20	5	12	2.5	50	63	64	76	4	6	1	260	257	30	45	4.1	.945	2B-70, 3B-49, SS-16
1963		150	.262	.384	568	149	18	6	13	2.3	77	61	64	75	11	2	1	256	388	24	76	4.5	.964	SS-133, 2B-15
1964		162	.241	.427	557	134	18	7	24	4.3	85	66	77	96	8	2	1	262	467	32	84	4.8	.958	SS-160
1965		113	.260	.433	404	105	13	6	15	3.7	61	54	49	62	6	2	0	190	286	22	58	4.4	.956	SS-112
1966		124	.274	.509	430	118	16	8	23	5.3	83	56	66	80	5	8	2	174	321	19	52	4.3	.963	SS-105, 3B-15
1967		153	.239	.411	557	133	16	7	22	3.9	92	65	105	118	6	0	0	300	374	28	82	3.7	.960	2B-145, SS-43
1968		151	.249	.411	570	142	24	10	16	2.8	**95**	56	82	99	8	3	2	292	352	9	80	4.3	.986	2B-148, SS-5
1969		74	.262	.458	271	71	10	5	11	4.1	49	33	47	41	2	2	1	167	196	9	40	5.2	.976	2B-72
1970		146	.234	.345	530	124	21	1	12	2.3	73	50	101	62	5	8	0	299	391	21	83	4.6	.970	2B-127, SS-15, 3B-12
1971		128	.208	.379	477	99	16	6	18	3.8	67	57	53	67	4	4	2	326	310	8	87	5.0	.988	2B-123, SS-7
1972		122	.240	.353	408	98	16	3	8	2.0	47	30	59	59	0	8	0	267	251	13	63	4.4	.976	2B-116, SS-3, 3B-1
1973		106	.274	.437	343	94	18	1	12	3.5	39	47	49	52	0	6	2	217	266	7	63	4.7	.986	2B-102, SS-2, DH-1
1974	BOS A	100	.210	.320	272	57	13	1	5	1.8	32	24	39	40	2	9	1	151	178	11	38	3.4	.968	2B-53, 3B-40, DH-3, SS-3
1975		7	.133	.133	15	2	0	0	0	0.0	0	1	1	2	0	0	0	2	8	3	1	1.9	.769	3B-7
16 yrs.		1763	.247	.403	6185	1530	231	71	197	3.2	888	697	882	974	63	67	16	3267	4225	260	891	4.3	.966	2B-971, SS-666, 3B-146, DH-4
LEAGUE CHAMPIONSHIP SERIES																								
1972	DET A	5	.200	.350	20	4	0	0	1	5.0	3	1	1	4	0	0	0	12	7	4	1	4.6	.826	SS-4, 2B-1
WORLD SERIES																								
1968	DET A	7	.222	.333	27	6	0	0	1	3.7	5	3	4	6	0	0	0	11	16	0	2	3.9	1.000	2B-7

Gene McAuliffe

McAULIFFE, EUGENE LEO BR TR 6′ 1″ 180 lbs.
B. Feb. 28, 1872, Randolph, Mass. D. Apr. 29, 1953, Randolph, Mass.

Year	Team	Games	BA	SA	AB	H	2B	3B	HR	HR%	R	RBI	BB	SO	SB	Pinch Hit AB	Pinch Hit H	PO	A	E	DP	TC/G	FA	G by Pos
1904	BOS N	1	.500	.500	2	1	0	0	0	0.0	0	0	0		0	0	0	1	1	1	0	3.0	.667	C-1

George McAvoy

McAVOY, GEORGE ROBERT
B. Mar. 12, 1884 Deceased.

Year	Team	Games	BA	SA	AB	H	2B	3B	HR	HR%	R	RBI	BB	SO	SB	Pinch Hit AB	Pinch Hit H	PO	A	E	DP	TC/G	FA	G by Pos
1914	PHI N	1	.000	.000	1	0	0	0	0	0.0	0	0	0	0	0	1	0	0	0	0	0	0.0	—	

Wickey McAvoy

McAVOY, JAMES EUGENE BR TR 5′11″ 172 lbs.
B. Oct. 20, 1894, Rochester, N. Y. D. July 6, 1973, Rochester, N. Y.

Year	Team	Games	BA	SA	AB	H	2B	3B	HR	HR%	R	RBI	BB	SO	SB	Pinch Hit AB	Pinch Hit H	PO	A	E	DP	TC/G	FA	G by Pos
1913	PHI A	4	.111	.111	9	1	0	0	0	0.0	0	0	0	4	0	0	0	14	7	0	0	5.3	1.000	C-4
1914		8	.125	.250	16	2	0	1	0	0.0	1	0	0	4	0	0	0	25	8	1	1	4.3	.971	C-8
1915		68	.190	.250	184	35	7	2	0	0.0	12	6	11	32	0	4	0	235	130	25	8	6.1	.936	C-64
1917		10	.250	.417	24	6	1	0	1	4.2	1	4	0	3	0	2	0	27	15	2	0	5.5	.955	C-8
1918		83	.244	.284	271	66	5	3	0	0.0	14	32	13	23	5	6	1	242	123	15	15	4.9	.961	C-74, OF-1, P-1, 1B-1
1919		62	.141	.194	170	24	5	2	0	0.0	10	11	14	21	1	4	0	182	73	7	6	4.6	.973	C-57
6 yrs.		235	.199	.254	674	134	18	8	1	0.1	38	53	38	87	6	16	1	725	356	50	30	5.2	.956	C-215, OF-1, P-1, 1B-1

Algie McBride

McBRIDE, ALGERNON GRIGGS BL TL 5′ 9″ 152 lbs.
B. May 23, 1869, Washington, D. C. D. Jan. 10, 1956, Georgetown, Ohio.

Year	Team	Games	BA	SA	AB	H	2B	3B	HR	HR%	R	RBI	BB	SO	SB	Pinch Hit AB	Pinch Hit H	PO	A	E	DP	TC/G	FA	G by Pos
1896	CHI N	9	.241	.448	29	7	1	1	1	3.4	2	7	7	3	0	0	0	21	1	2	0	2.7	.917	OF-9
1898	CIN N	120	.302	.393	486	147	14	12	2	0.4	94	43	51		16	0	0	288	18	13	3	2.7	.959	OF-120
1899		64	.347	.446	251	87	12	5	1	0.4	57	23	30		5	0	0	124	8	7	2	2.2	.950	OF-64
1900		112	.275	.374	436	120	15	8	4	0.9	57	59	25		12	3	0	163	10	16	5	1.7	.915	OF-109
1901	2 teams CIN N (30G –.236) NY N (68G –.280)																							
"	total	98	.266	.344	387	103	18	0	4	1.0	46	47	19		3	5	2	143	9	7	3	1.7	.956	OF-93
5 yrs.		403	.292	.385	1589	464	60	26	12	0.8	256	179	132	3	36	8	2	739	46	45	13	2.1	.946	OF-395

Bake McBride

McBRIDE, ARNOLD RAY
B. Feb. 3, 1949, Fulton, Mo.
BL TR 6′ 2″ 190 lbs.

Year	Team	Games	BA	SA	AB	H	2B	3B	HR	HR%	R	RBI	BB	SO	SB	Pinch Hit AB	Pinch Hit H	PO	A	E	DP	TC/G	FA	G by Pos
1973	STL N	40	.302	.349	63	19	3	0	0	0.0	8	5	4	10	0	17	6	39	1	1	0	2.4	.976	OF-17
1974		150	.309	.394	559	173	19	5	6	1.1	81	56	43	57	30	7	3	395	9	4	1	2.8	.990	OF-144
1975		116	.300	.404	413	124	10	9	5	1.2	70	36	34	52	26	11	3	289	4	3	1	2.8	.990	OF-107
1976		72	.335	.445	272	91	13	4	3	1.1	40	24	18	28	10	7	2	201	5	4	0	3.2	.981	OF-66
1977	2 teams	STL N (43G –.262) PHI N (85G –.339)																						
″	total	128	.316	.520	402	127	25	6	15	3.7	76	61	32	44	36	21	5	188	8	2	1	1.9	.990	OF-106
1978	PHI N	122	.269	.392	472	127	20	4	10	2.1	68	49	28	68	28	6	1	234	8	1	3	2.0	.996	OF-119
1979		151	.280	.411	582	163	16	12	12	2.1	82	60	41	77	25	9	3	341	12	4	3	2.4	.989	OF-147
1980		137	.309	.453	554	171	33	10	9	1.6	68	87	26	58	13	3	2	282	6	3	1	2.2	.990	OF-133
1981		58	.271	.385	221	60	17	1	2	0.9	26	21	11	25	5	9	3	76	2	1	1	1.4	.987	OF-56
1982	CLE A	27	.365	.471	85	31	3	3	0	0.0	8	13	2	12	2	5	2	37	0	0	0	1.7	1.000	OF-22
1983		70	.291	.348	230	67	8	1	1	0.4	21	18	9	26	8	10	2	81	4	2	1	1.4	.977	OF-46, DH-15
11 yrs.		1071	.299	.420	3853	1153	167	55	63	1.6	548	430	248	457	183	105	32	2163	59	25	12	2.3	.989	OF-963, DH-15
DIVISIONAL PLAYOFF SERIES																								
1981	PHI N	4	.200	.267	15	3	1	0	0	0.0	1	0	0	5	0	0	0	6	0	0	0	1.5	1.000	OF-4
LEAGUE CHAMPIONSHIP SERIES																								
1977	PHI N	4	.222	.389	18	4	0	0	1	5.6	2	2	0	2	0	0	0	6	2	0	1	2.0	1.000	OF-4
1978		3	.222	.556	9	2	0	0	1	11.1	2	1	0	2	0	1	1	1	0	0	0	0.5	1.000	OF-2
1980		5	.238	.238	21	5	0	0	0	0.0	0	0	1	5	2	0	0	11	3	1	2	3.0	.933	OF-5
3 yrs.		12	.229	.354	48	11	0	0	2	4.2	4	3	1	9	2	1	1	18	5	1	3	2.2	.958	OF-11
WORLD SERIES																								
1980	PHI N	6	.304	.478	23	7	1	0	1	4.3	3	5	2	1	0	0	0	13	1	0	0	2.3	1.000	OF-6

George McBride

McBRIDE, GEORGE FLORIAN
B. Nov. 20, 1880, Milwaukee, Wis. D. July 2, 1973, Milwaukee, Wis.
Manager 1921.
BR TR 5′11″ 170 lbs.

Year	Team	Games	BA	SA	AB	H	2B	3B	HR	HR%	R	RBI	BB	SO	SB	Pinch Hit AB	Pinch Hit H	PO	A	E	DP	TC/G	FA	G by Pos
1901	MIL A	3	.167	.167	12	2	0	0	0	0.0	0	0	1		0	0	0	5	7	0	2	4.0	1.000	SS-3
1905	2 teams	PIT N (27G –.218) STL N (81G –.217)																						
″	total	108	.217	.258	368	80	5	2	2	0.5	31	41	20		12	2	0	176	321	36	35	5.0	.932	SS-88, 3B-17, 1B-1
1906	STL N	90	.169	.208	313	53	8	2	0	0.0	24	13	17		5	0	0	194	310	30	33	5.9	.944	SS-90
1908	WAS A	155	.232	.274	518	120	10	6	0	0.0	47	34	41		12	0	0	372	568	52	58	6.4	.948	SS-155
1909		155	.234	.266	504	118	16	0	0	0.0	38	34	36		17	0	0	341	499	58	56	5.8	.935	SS-155
1910		154	.230	.288	514	118	19	4	1	0.2	54	55	61		11	0	0	370	518	58	57	6.1	.939	SS-154
1911		154	.235	.269	557	131	11	4	0	0.0	58	59	52		15	0	0	353	546	56	60	6.2	.941	SS-154
1912		152	.226	.284	521	118	13	7	1	0.2	56	52	38		17	0	0	349	498	53	55	5.9	.941	SS-152
1913		150	.214	.285	499	107	18	7	1	0.2	52	52	43	46	12	0	0	316	490	34	62	5.6	.960	SS-150
1914		156	.203	.243	503	102	12	4	0	0.0	49	24	43	70	12	0	0	367	460	36	72	5.5	.958	SS-156
1915		146	.204	.252	476	97	8	6	1	0.2	54	30	29	60	10	0	0	326	422	25	47	5.3	.968	SS-146
1916		139	.227	.283	466	106	15	4	1	0.2	36	36	23	58	8	0	0	282	438	32	53	5.4	.957	SS-139
1917		50	.191	.213	141	27	3	0	0	0.0	6	9	10	17	1	1	0	78	122	11	15	4.3	.948	SS-41, 3B-6, 2B-2
1918		18	.132	.132	53	7	0	0	0	0.0	2	1	0	11	1	1	0	29	45	1	4	4.7	.987	SS-14, 2B-2
1919		15	.200	.275	40	8	1	1	0	0.0	3	4	3	6	0	0	0	29	40	5	2	4.9	.932	SS-15
1920		13	.220	.244	41	9	1	0	0	0.0	6	3	2	3	0	0	0	24	32	2	3	4.5	.966	SS-13
16 yrs.		1658	.218	.264	5526	1203	140	47	7	0.1	516	447	419	271	133	4	0	3611	5316	489	614	5.7	.948	SS-1625, 3B-23, 2B-4, 1B-1

John McBride

McBRIDE, JOHN F.
Deceased.

Year	Team	Games	BA	SA	AB	H	2B	3B	HR	HR%	R	RBI	BB	SO	SB	Pinch Hit AB	Pinch Hit H	PO	A	E	DP	TC/G	FA	G by Pos
1890	PHI AA	1	.000	.000	2	0	0	0	0	0.0	0		0		0	0	0	1	1	0	0	2.0	1.000	OF-1

Tom McBride

McBRIDE, THOMAS RAYMOND
B. Nov. 2, 1914, Bonham, Tex.
BR TR 6′½″ 188 lbs.

Year	Team	Games	BA	SA	AB	H	2B	3B	HR	HR%	R	RBI	BB	SO	SB	Pinch Hit AB	Pinch Hit H	PO	A	E	DP	TC/G	FA	G by Pos
1943	BOS A	26	.240	.292	96	23	3	1	0	0.0	11	7	7	3	2	2	0	60	2	1	1	2.6	.984	OF-24
1944		71	.245	.306	216	53	7	3	0	0.0	29	24	8	13	4	7	3	159	10	2	7	2.8	.988	OF-57, 1B-5
1945		100	.305	.387	344	105	11	7	1	0.3	38	47	26	17	2	9	2	281	18	3	15	3.3	.990	OF-81, 1B-11
1946		61	.301	.359	153	46	5	2	0	0.0	21	19	9	6	0	17	5	61	1	0	0	1.4	1.000	OF-43
1947	2 teams	BOS A (2G –.200) WAS A (56G –.271)																						
″	total	58	.269	.316	171	46	4	2	0	0.0	19	15	15	9	3	8	2	105	3	3	0	2.1	.973	OF-52, 3B-1
1948	WAS A	92	.257	.325	206	53	9	1	1	0.5	22	29	28	15	2	33	5	108	7	2	3	2.1	.983	OF-55
6 yrs.		408	.275	.340	1186	326	39	16	2	0.2	140	141	93	63	13	76	17	774	41	11	26	2.5	.987	OF-312, 1B-16, 3B-1
WORLD SERIES																								
1946	BOS A	5	.167	.167	12	2	0	0	0	0.0	0	1	0	1	0	3	0	4	0	1	0	2.5	.800	OF-2

Bill McCabe

McCABE, WILLIAM FRANCIS
B. Oct. 28, 1892, Chicago, Ill. D. Sept. 2, 1966, Chicago, Ill.
BB TR 5′ 9½″ 180 lbs.
BL 1918

Year	Team	Games	BA	SA	AB	H	2B	3B	HR	HR%	R	RBI	BB	SO	SB	Pinch Hit AB	Pinch Hit H	PO	A	E	DP	TC/G	FA	G by Pos
1918	CHI N	29	.178	.222	45	8	0	1	0	0.0	9	5	4	7	2	6	1	23	42	4	1	4.1	.942	2B-13, OF-4
1919		33	.155	.214	84	13	3	1	0	0.0	8	5	9	15	3	3	0	43	10	4	3	2.4	.930	OF-19, SS-4, 3B-1
1920	2 teams	CHI N (3G –.500) BKN N (41G –.147)																						
″	total	44	.157	.157	70	11	0	0	0	0.0	11	3	2	6	1	4	1	37	47	11	5	4.0	.884	SS-12, OF-6, 2B-5, 3B-1
3 yrs.		106	.161	.196	199	32	3	2	0	0.0	28	13	15	28	6	13	2	103	99	19	9	3.4	.914	OF-29, 2B-18, SS-16, 3B-2
WORLD SERIES																								
1918	CHI N	3	.000	.000	1	0	0	0	0	0.0	1	0	0	0	0	1	0	0	0	0	0	0.0	—	
1920	BKN N	1	—	—	0	0	0	0	0	—	0	0	0	0	0	0	0	0	0	0	0	0.0	—	
2 yrs.		4	.000	.000	1	0	0	0	0	0.0	1	0	0	0	0	1	0							

Joe McCabe

McCABE, JOSEPH ROBERT
B. Aug. 27, 1938, Indianapolis, Ind.
BR TR 6′ 190 lbs.

Year	Team	Games	BA	SA	AB	H	2B	3B	HR	HR%	R	RBI	BB	SO	SB	Pinch Hit AB	Pinch Hit H	PO	A	E	DP	TC/G	FA	G by Pos
1964	MIN A	14	.158	.158	19	3	0	0	0	0.0	1	2	0	8	0	1	0	34	2	0	1	3.0	1.000	C-12
1965	WAS A	14	.185	.296	27	5	0	0	1	3.7	1	5	4	13	1	4	2	30	5	1	0	3.3	.972	C-11
2 yrs.		28	.174	.239	46	8	0	0	1	2.2	2	7	4	21	1	5	2	64	7	1	1	3.1	.986	C-23

Swat McCabe
McCABE, JAMES ARTHUR BL TR 5′10″
B. Nov. 20, 1881, Towanda, Pa. D. Dec. 9, 1944, Bristol, Conn.

Year	Team	Games	BA	SA	AB	H	2B	3B	HR	HR%	R	RBI	BB	SO	SB	Pinch Hit AB	Pinch Hit H	PO	A	E	DP	TC/G	FA	G by Pos
1909	CIN N	3	.545	.636	11	6	1	0	0	0.0	2	0	0		1	0	0	5	0	3	0	2.7	.625	OF-3
1910		13	.257	.286	35	9	1	0	0	0.0	3	5	1	2	0	4	1	14	2	0	1	1.8	1.000	OF-9
2 yrs.		16	.326	.370	46	15	2	0	0	0.0	5	5	1	2	1	4	1	19	2	3	1	2.0	.875	OF-12

Harry McCaffrey
McCAFFREY, HARRY CHARLES BR TR 5′10½″ 185 lbs.
B. Nov. 25, 1858, St. Louis, Mo. D. Apr. 19, 1928, St. Louis, Mo.

Year	Team	Games	BA	SA	AB	H	2B	3B	HR	HR%	R	RBI	BB	SO	SB	Pinch Hit AB	Pinch Hit H	PO	A	E	DP	TC/G	FA	G by Pos
1882	2 teams	STL AA (38G –.275) LOU AA (1G –.250)																						
″	total	39	.274	.401	157	43	8	6	0	0.0	24		3			0	0	74	50	17	5	3.5	.879	OF-23, 2B-9, 3B-7, 1B-1
1883	STL AA	5	.056	.056	18	1	0	0	0	0.0	0		1			0	0	6	3	1	2	2.0	.900	OF-5
1885	CIN AA	1	.000	.000	5	0	0	0	0	0.0	0		0			0	0	0	0	1	0	1.0	.000	P-1
3 yrs.		45	.244	.356	180	44	8	6	0	0.0	24		4			0	0	80	53	19	7	3.3	.875	OF-28, 2B-9, 3B-7, P-1, 1B-1

Sparrow McCaffrey
McCAFFREY, CHARLES P. 120 lbs.
B. 1868, Philadelphia, Pa. D. Apr. 29, 1894, Philadelphia, Pa.

Year	Team	Games	BA	SA	AB	H	2B	3B	HR	HR%	R	RBI	BB	SO	SB	Pinch Hit AB	Pinch Hit H	PO	A	E	DP	TC/G	FA	G by Pos
1889	COL AA	2	1.000	1.000	1	1	0	0	0	0.0	1	0	1	0	0	0	0	0	0	0	0	0.0	.000	C-2

Brian McCall
McCALL, BRIAN ALLEN (Bam) BL TL 5′10″ 170 lbs.
B. June 25, 1943, Kentfield, Calif.

Year	Team	Games	BA	SA	AB	H	2B	3B	HR	HR%	R	RBI	BB	SO	SB	Pinch Hit AB	Pinch Hit H	PO	A	E	DP	TC/G	FA	G by Pos
1962	CHI A	4	.375	1.125	8	3	0	0	2	25.0	2	3	0	2	0	3	1	4	0	0	0	4.0	1.000	OF-1
1963		3	.000	.000	7	0	0	0	0	0.0	1	0	1	2	0	0	0	3	0	0	0	1.5	1.000	OF-2
2 yrs.		7	.200	.600	15	3	0	0	2	13.3	3	3	1	4	0	3	1	7	0	0	0	2.3	1.000	OF-3

Scott McCandless
McCANDLESS, SCOTT COOK (Cook) BL TR 6′ 170 lbs.
B. May 5, 1891, Pittsburgh, Pa. D. Aug. 17, 1961, Pittsburgh, Pa.

Year	Team	Games	BA	SA	AB	H	2B	3B	HR	HR%	R	RBI	BB	SO	SB	Pinch Hit AB	Pinch Hit H	PO	A	E	DP	TC/G	FA	G by Pos
1914	BAL F	11	.258	.323	31	8	0	1	0	0.0	5	1	3		0	2	0	10	1	0	0	1.4	1.000	OF-8
1915		117	.214	.300	406	87	6	7	5	1.2	47	34	41		9	9	1	209	16	13	8	2.3	.945	OF-105
2 yrs.		128	.217	.302	437	95	6	8	5	1.1	52	35	44		9	11	1	219	17	13	8	2.2	.948	OF-113

Emmett McCann
McCANN, ROBERT EMMETT BR TR 6′ 175 lbs.
B. Mar. 4, 1902, Philadelphia, Pa. D. Apr. 15, 1937, Philadelphia, Pa.

Year	Team	Games	BA	SA	AB	H	2B	3B	HR	HR%	R	RBI	BB	SO	SB	Pinch Hit AB	Pinch Hit H	PO	A	E	DP	TC/G	FA	G by Pos
1920	PHI A	13	.265	.353	34	9	1	1	0	0.0	4	3	3	1	0	1	0	20	29	5	3	4.9	.907	SS-11
1921		52	.223	.255	157	35	5	0	0	0.0	15	15	4	6	2	6	1	65	119	11	14	4.3	.944	SS-32, 3B-9, 2B-2, 1B-1, C-1
1926	BOS A	6	.000	.000	3	0	0	0	0	0.0	0	0	1	1	0	1	0	2	0	0	0	1.0	1.000	SS-1, 3B-1
3 yrs.		71	.227	.268	194	44	6	1	0	0.0	19	18	8	8	2	8	1	87	148	16	17	4.3	.936	SS-44, 3B-10, 2B-2, 1B-1, C-1

Roger McCardell
McCARDELL, ROGER MORTON BR TR 6′ 200 lbs.
B. Aug. 29, 1932, Gorsuch Mills, Md.

Year	Team	Games	BA	SA	AB	H	2B	3B	HR	HR%	R	RBI	BB	SO	SB	Pinch Hit AB	Pinch Hit H	PO	A	E	DP	TC/G	FA	G by Pos
1959	SF N	4	.000	.000	4	0	0	0	0	0.0	0	0	0	0	0	1	0	5	1	0	0	2.0	1.000	C-3

Bill McCarren
McCARREN, WILLIAM JOSEPH BR TR 5′11½″ 170 lbs.
B. Nov. 4, 1895, Fortenia, Pa. D. Sept. 11, 1983, Denver, Colo.

Year	Team	Games	BA	SA	AB	H	2B	3B	HR	HR%	R	RBI	BB	SO	SB	Pinch Hit AB	Pinch Hit H	PO	A	E	DP	TC/G	FA	G by Pos
1923	BKN N	69	.245	.343	216	53	10	1	3	1.4	28	27	22	39	0	1	0	72	106	14	11	2.9	.927	3B-66, OF-1

Alex McCarthy
McCARTHY, ALEXANDER GEORGE BR TR 5′9″ 150 lbs.
B. May 12, 1888, Chicago, Ill. D. Mar. 12, 1978, Salisbury, Md.

Year	Team	Games	BA	SA	AB	H	2B	3B	HR	HR%	R	RBI	BB	SO	SB	Pinch Hit AB	Pinch Hit H	PO	A	E	DP	TC/G	FA	G by Pos
1910	PIT N	3	.083	.250	12	1	0	1	0	0.0	1	0	0	2	0	0	0	4	10	2	2	5.3	.875	SS-3
1911		50	.240	.327	150	36	5	1	2	1.3	18	31	14	24	4	2	0	94	127	5	20	4.9	.978	SS-33, 2B-11, 3B-1, OF-1
1912		111	.277	.334	401	111	12	4	1	0.2	53	41	30	36	8	2	0	242	325	22	53	5.4	.963	2B-105, 3B-4
1913		31	.203	.270	74	15	5	0	0	0.0	7	10	7	7	1	1	0	33	55	5	4	3.1	.946	3B-12, SS-12, 2B-6
1914		57	.150	.179	173	26	0	1	1	0.6	14	14	6	17	2	1	0	63	136	11	10	4.0	.948	3B-36, 2B-10, SS-6
1915	2 teams	PIT N (21G –.204) CHI N (23G –.264)																						
″	total	44	.240	.306	121	29	3	1	1	0.8	7	9	10	17	3	2	1	83	109	5	17	4.5	.975	2B-21, 3B-16, SS-6, 1B-1
1916	2 teams	CHI N (37G –.243) PIT N (50G –.199)																						
″	total	87	.217	.261	253	55	5	3	0	0.0	21	9	26	17	4	2	0	156	212	21	27	4.4	.946	SS-42, 2B-41, 3B-5
1917	PIT N	49	.219	.245	151	33	4	0	0	0.0	15	8	11	13	1	0	0	85	115	6	18	4.3	.971	3B-26, 2B-13, SS-9
8 yrs.		432	.229	.282	1335	306	34	11	5	0.4	136	122	104	133	23	10	1	760	1089	77	151	4.6	.960	2B-207, SS-111, 3B-100, 1B-1, OF-1

Bill McCarthy
McCARTHY, WILLIAM JOHN TR
B. Feb. 14, 1886, Boston, Mass. D. Feb. 4, 1928, Washington, D. C.

Year	Team	Games	BA	SA	AB	H	2B	3B	HR	HR%	R	RBI	BB	SO	SB	Pinch Hit AB	Pinch Hit H	PO	A	E	DP	TC/G	FA	G by Pos
1905	BOS N	1	.000	.000	3	0	0	0	0	0.0	0	0	0		0	0	0	5	1	3	0	9.0	.667	C-1
1907	CIN N	3	.125	.125	8	1	0	0	0	0.0	1	0	0		0	0	0	6	4	0	0	3.3	1.000	C-3
2 yrs.		4	.091	.091	11	1	0	0	0	0.0	1	0	0		0	0	0	11	5	3	0	4.8	.842	C-4

Jack McCarthy
McCARTHY, JOHN ARTHUR BL TL 5′9″ 155 lbs.
B. Mar. 26, 1869, Gilbertville, Mass. D. Sept. 11, 1931, Chicago, Ill.

Year	Team	Games	BA	SA	AB	H	2B	3B	HR	HR%	R	RBI	BB	SO	SB	Pinch Hit AB	Pinch Hit H	PO	A	E	DP	TC/G	FA	G by Pos
1893	CIN N	49	.282	.354	195	55	8	3	0	0.0	28	22	22	7	6	0	0	111	9	13	1	2.7	.902	OF-47, 1B-2
1894		40	.269	.335	167	45	9	1	0	0.0	29	21	17	6	3	0	0	193	19	13	12	5.6	.942	OF-25, 1B-15
1898	PIT N	137	.289	.380	537	155	13	12	4	0.7	75	78	34		7	0	0	296	19	22	4	2.5	.935	OF-137
1899		138	.305	.421	560	171	22	17	3	0.5	108	67	39		28	0	0	281	18	12	5	2.3	.961	OF-138
1900	CHI N	124	.294	.354	503	148	16	7	0	0.0	68	48	24		22	1	0	233	20	15	4	2.2	.944	OF-123
1901	CLE A	86	.321	.402	343	110	14	7	0	0.0	60	32	30		9	0	0	157	9	9	5	2.0	.949	OF-86
1902		95	.284	.398	359	102	31	5	0	0.0	45	41	24		12	0	0	178	6	11	0	2.1	.944	OF-95
1903	2 teams	CLE A (108G –.265) CHI N (24G –.277)																						
″	total	132	.267	.347	516	138	25	8	0	0.0	58	57	23		23	0	0	211	13	9	6	1.8	.961	OF-132
1904	CHI N	115	.264	.306	432	114	14	2	0	0.0	36	51	23		14	0	0	213	8	9	0	2.0	.961	OF-115
1905		59	.276	.335	170	47	4	3	0	0.0	16	14	10		8	15	6	107	12	4	9	2.9	.967	OF-37, 1B-6
1906	BKN N	91	.304	.351	322	98	13	1	0	0.0	23	35	20		9	5	1	158	13	14	1	2.2	.924	OF-86
1907		25	.220	.242	91	20	2	0	0	0.0	4	8	2		4	0	0	38	0	0	0	1.5	1.000	OF-25
12 yrs.		1091	.287	.364	4195	1203	171	66	7	0.2	550	474	268	13	145	21	7	2176	146	131	47	2.3	.947	OF-1046, 1B-23

Jerry McCarthy

McCARTHY, JEROME FRANCIS BL TL 6′ 1″ 205 lbs.
B. May 23, 1923, Brooklyn, N. Y. D. Oct. 3, 1965, Oceanside, N. Y.

Year	Team		Games	BA	SA	AB	H	2B	3B	HR	HR%	R	RBI	BB	SO	SB	Pinch Hit AB	Pinch Hit H	PO	A	E	DP	TC/G	FA	G by Pos
1948	**STL**	**A**	2	.333	.333	3	1	0	0	0	0.0	0	0	0	0	0	1	0	3	0	2	0	2.5	.600	1B-2

Joe McCarthy

McCARTHY, JOSEPH N. BR TR
B. Dec. 25, 1881, Syracuse, N. Y. D. Jan. 12, 1937, Syracuse, N. Y.

Year	Team		Games	BA	SA	AB	H	2B	3B	HR	HR%	R	RBI	BB	SO	SB	Pinch Hit AB	Pinch Hit H	PO	A	E	DP	TC/G	FA	G by Pos
1905	**NY**	**A**	1	.000	.000	2	0	0	0	0	0.0	0	0	0		0	0	0	2	1	0	0	3.0	1.000	C-1
1906	**STL**	**N**	15	.243	.297	37	9	2	0	0	0.0	3	2	2		0	0	0	47	14	1	2	4.4	.984	C-14
2 yrs.			16	.231	.282	39	9	2	0	0	0.0	3	2	2		0	0	0	49	15	1	2	4.3	.985	C-15

Johnny McCarthy

McCARTHY, JOHN JOSEPH BL TL 6′ 1½″ 185 lbs.
B. Jan. 7, 1910, Chicago, Ill. D. Sept. 13, 1973, Mundelein, Ill.

Year	Team		Games	BA	SA	AB	H	2B	3B	HR	HR%	R	RBI	BB	SO	SB	Pinch Hit AB	Pinch Hit H	PO	A	E	DP	TC/G	FA	G by Pos
1934	**BKN**	**N**	17	.179	.308	39	7	2	0	1	2.6	7	5	2	2	0	3	0	89	9	4	13	7.8	.961	1B-13
1935			22	.250	.313	48	12	1	1	0	0.0	9	4	2	9	0	3	0	110	0	2	11	5.9	.982	1B-19
1936	**NY**	**N**	4	.438	.625	16	7	0	0	1	6.3	1	2	0	1	1	0	0	45	6	1	5	13.0	.981	1B-4
1937			114	.279	.410	420	117	19	3	10	2.4	53	65	24	37	2	4	0	1123	82	16	89	11.1	.987	1B-110
1938			134	.272	.368	470	128	13	4	8	1.7	55	59	39	28	3	8	3	1315	77	10	111	11.2	.993	1B-125
1939			50	.263	.400	80	21	6	1	1	1.3	12	11	3	8	0	33	8	114	4	0	13	6.9	1.000	1B-12, OF-4, P-1
1940			51	.239	.299	67	16	4	0	0	0.0	6	5	2	8	0	**43**	**11**	57	5	0	6	10.3	1.000	1B-6
1941			14	.325	.400	40	13	3	0	0	0.0	1	12	3	0	0	5	2	68	7	1	4	8.4	.987	1B-8, OF-1
1943	**BOS**	**N**	78	.304	.438	313	95	24	6	2	0.6	32	33	10	19	1	0	0	839	53	4	51	11.5	.996	1B-78
1946			2	.143	.143	7	1	0	0	0	0.0	0	1	2	0	0	0	0	18	0	0	0	9.0	1.000	1B-2
1948	**NY**	**N**	56	.263	.404	57	15	0	1	2	3.5	6	12	3	2	0	**45**	**13**	27	1	1	2	4.8	.966	1B-6
11 yrs.			542	.277	.392	1557	432	72	16	25	1.6	182	209	90	114	7	144	37	3805	244	39	305	10.5	.990	1B-383, OF-5, P-1
WORLD SERIES																									
1937	**NY**	**N**	5	.211	.263	19	4	1	0	0	0.0	1	1	1	2	0	0	0	38	1	2	4	8.2	.951	1B-5

Tommy McCarthy

McCARTHY, THOMAS FRANCIS MICHAEL BR TR 5′ 7″ 170 lbs.
B. July 24, 1863, Boston, Mass. D. Aug. 5, 1922, Boston, Mass.
Manager 1890.
Hall of Fame 1946.

Year	Team		Games	BA	SA	AB	H	2B	3B	HR	HR%	R	RBI	BB	SO	SB	Pinch Hit AB	Pinch Hit H	PO	A	E	DP	TC/G	FA	G by Pos
1884	**BOS**	**U**	53	.215	.249	209	45	3	2	0	0.0	37		6			0	0	45	30	18	2	1.7	.806	OF-48, P-7
1885	**BOS**	**N**	40	.182	.196	148	27	2	0	0	0.0	16	11	5	25		0	0	69	8	12	0	2.2	.865	OF-40
1886	**PHI**	**N**	8	.185	.333	27	5	2	1	0	0.0	6	3	2	3		0	0	8	1	2	0	1.2	.818	OF-8, P-1
1887			18	.186	.243	70	13	4	0	0	0.0	7	6	2	5	15	0	0	40	11	17	1	3.8	.750	OF-8, 2B-5, SS-3, 3B-2
1888	**STL**	**AA**	131	.274	.331	511	140	20	3	1	0.2	107	68	38		93	0	0	243	44	21	12	2.3	.932	OF-131, P-2
1889			140	.291	.364	**604**	176	24	7	2	0.3	136	63	46	26	57	0	0	230	39	33	11	2.1	.891	OF-140, 2B-2, P-1
1890			133	.350	.467	548	192	28	9	6	1.1	137		66		**83**	0	0	205	95	43	11	2.5	.875	OF-102, 3B-32, 2B-1
1891			134	.309	.409	570	176	21	6	8	1.4	124	92	49	19	37	0	0	225	92	47	14	2.6	.871	OF-112, 2B-14, SS-12, 3B-2, P-1
1892	**BOS**	**N**	152	.242	.310	603	146	19	5	4	0.7	119	63	93	29	53	0	0	219	29	33	4	1.8	.883	OF-152
1893			116	.346	.465	462	160	28	6	5	1.1	107	111	64	10	46	0	0	228	49	32	9	2.6	.896	OF-108, 2B-7, SS-3
1894			127	.349	.490	539	188	21	8	13	2.4	118	126	59	17	43	0	0	291	33	34	10	2.7	.905	OF-127, SS-2, 2B-1, P-1
1895			117	.290	.341	452	131	13	2	2	0.4	90	73	72	12	18	0	0	212	35	33	3	2.4	.882	OF-109, 2B-9
1896	**BKN**	**N**	104	.249	.316	377	94	8	4	3	0.8	62	47	34	17	22	0	0	175	20	17	6	2.1	.920	OF-103
13 yrs.			1273	.292	.376	5120	1493	193	53	44	0.9	1066	663	536	163	467	0	0	2190	486	342	83	2.3	.887	OF-1188, 2B-39, 3B-36, SS-20, P-13

David McCarty

McCARTY, DAVID ANDREW BR TL 6′ 5″ 210 lbs.
B. Nov. 23, 1969, Houston, Tex.

Year	Team		Games	BA	SA	AB	H	2B	3B	HR	HR%	R	RBI	BB	SO	SB	Pinch Hit AB	Pinch Hit H	PO	A	E	DP	TC/G	FA	G by Pos
1993	**MIN**	**A**	98	.214	.286	350	75	15	2	2	0.6	36	21	19	80	2	5	1	412	38	8	25	4.4	.983	OF-67, 1B-36, DH-2
1994			44	.260	.374	131	34	8	2	1	0.8	21	12	7	32	2	3	0	244	27	5	19	6.0	.982	1B-32, OF-14
1995	**2 teams**	**MIN A** (25G –.218) **SF N** (12G –.250)																							
″	**total**		37	.227	.307	75	17	4	1	0	0.0	11	6	6	22	1	9	4	149	10	2	13	5.6	.988	1B-20, OF-9
3 yrs.			179	.227	.309	556	126	27	5	3	0.5	68	39	32	134	5	17	5	805	75	15	57	5.0	.983	OF-90, 1B-88, DH-2

Lew McCarty

McCARTY, GEORGE LEWIS BR TR 5′11½″ 192 lbs.
B. Nov. 17, 1888, Milton, Pa. D. June 9, 1930, Reading, Pa.

Year	Team		Games	BA	SA	AB	H	2B	3B	HR	HR%	R	RBI	BB	SO	SB	Pinch Hit AB	Pinch Hit H	PO	A	E	DP	TC/G	FA	G by Pos
1913	**BKN**	**N**	9	.231	.231	26	6	0	0	0	0.0	1	2	2	2	0	0	0	37	10	0	1	5.2	1.000	C-9
1914			90	.254	.327	284	72	14	2	1	0.4	20	30	14	22	1	6	2	398	117	16	9	6.3	.970	C-84
1915			84	.239	.301	276	66	9	4	0	0.0	19	19	7	23	7	3	1	310	101	13	5	5.0	.969	C-84
1916	**2 teams**	**BKN N** (55G –.313) **NY N** (25G –.397)																							
″	**total**		80	.339	.427	218	74	9	5	0	0.0	23	22	21	25	4	10	4	357	68	6	13	6.3	.986	C-51, 1B-17
1917	**NY**	**N**	56	.247	.327	162	40	3	2	2	1.2	15	19	14	6	1	2	1	235	43	6	0	5.3	.979	C-54
1918			86	.268	.319	257	69	7	3	0	0.0	16	24	17	13	3	7	2	288	67	9	3	4.9	.975	C-75
1919			85	.281	.371	210	59	5	4	2	1.0	17	21	18	15	2	24	7	203	56	8	1	4.5	.970	C-59
1920	**2 teams**	**NY N** (36G –.132) **STL N** (5G –.286)																							
″	**total**		41	.156	.156	45	7	0	0	0	0.0	2	0	9	2	2	29	5	21	10	0	1	3.9	1.000	C-8
1921	**STL**	**N**	1	.000	.000	1	0	0	0	0	0.0	0	0	0	1	0	1	0	0	0	0	0	0.0	—	
9 yrs.			532	.266	.335	1479	393	47	20	5	0.3	113	137	102	109	20	82	22	1849	472	58	33	5.4	.976	C-424, 1B-17
WORLD SERIES																									
1917	**NY**	**N**	3	.400	.800	5	2	0	1	0	0.0	1	1	0	0	0	1	0	7	1	1	0	4.5	.889	C-2

Tim McCarver

McCARVER, JAMES TIMOTHY BL TR 6′ 183 lbs.
B. Oct. 16, 1941, Memphis, Tenn.

Year	Team		Games	BA	SA	AB	H	2B	3B	HR	HR%	R	RBI	BB	SO	SB	Pinch Hit AB	Pinch Hit H	PO	A	E	DP	TC/G	FA	G by Pos
1959	**STL**	**N**	8	.167	.208	24	4	1	0	0	0.0	3	0	2	1	0	1	0	32	2	1	0	5.8	.971	C-6
1960			10	.200	.200	10	2	0	0	0	0.0	3	0	0	2	0	4	1	9	0	0	0	1.8	1.000	C-5
1961			22	.239	.343	67	16	2	1	1	1.5	5	6	0	5	0	2	2	86	9	3	0	4.9	.969	C-20
1963			127	.289	.383	405	117	12	7	4	1.0	39	51	27	43	5	5	1	722	55	5	7	6.2	.994	C-126
1964			143	.288	.400	465	134	19	3	9	1.9	53	52	40	44	2	7	1	762	43	11	9	6.0	.987	C-137
1965			113	.276	.408	409	113	17	2	11	2.7	48	48	31	26	5	5	2	687	43	4	4	6.6	.995	C-111
1966			150	.274	.424	543	149	19	**13**	12	2.2	50	68	36	38	9	5	1	841	62	7	7	6.1	.992	C-148
1967			138	.295	.452	471	139	26	3	14	3.0	68	69	54	32	8	11	4	819	67	3	10	6.8	.997	C-130
1968			128	.253	.350	434	110	15	6	5	1.2	35	48	26	31	4	19	4	708	54	11	6	7.1	.986	C-109
1969			138	.260	.365	515	134	27	3	7	1.4	46	51	49	26	4	1	0	925	66	14	10	7.4	.986	C-136

Tim McCarver *continued*

Year	Team	Games	BA	SA	AB	H	2B	3B	HR	HR%	R	RBI	BB	SO	SB	Pinch Hit AB	Pinch Hit H	PO	A	E	DP	TC/G	FA	G by Pos
1970	PHI N	44	.287	.439	164	47	11	1	4	2.4	16	14	14	10	2	0	0	314	18	3	2	7.6	.991	C-44
1971		134	.278	.392	474	132	20	5	8	1.7	51	46	43	26	5	14	3	673	51	11	8	5.9	.985	C-125
1972	2 teams	PHI N (45G –.237) MON N (77G –.251)																						
″	total	122	.246	.338	391	96	13	1	7	1.8	33	34	36	29	5	18	2	561	47	8	3	5.9	.987	C-85, OF-14, 3B-6
1973	STL N	130	.266	.366	331	88	16	4	3	0.9	30	49	38	31	2	39	8	608	34	9	48	7.4	.986	1B-77, C-11
1974	2 teams	STL N (74G –.217) BOS A (11G –.250)																						
″	total	85	.224	.246	134	30	1	1	0	0.0	16	12	26	7	1	43	7	163	16	4	1	4.9	.978	C-29, 1B-6, DH-2
1975	2 teams	BOS A (12G –.381) PHI N (47G –.254)																						
″	total	59	.287	.400	80	23	4	1	1	1.3	7	10	15	10	0	39	10	83	9	2	2	4.9	.979	C-17, 1B-2
1976	PHI N	90	.277	.432	155	43	11	2	3	1.9	26	29	35	14	2	42	9	265	9	0	1	6.4	1.000	C-41, 1B-2
1977		93	.320	.527	169	54	13	2	6	3.6	28	30	28	11	3	36	9	238	14	3	5	5.7	.988	C-42, 1B-3
1978		90	.247	.342	146	36	9	1	1	0.7	18	14	28	24	2	41	8	215	14	2	5	5.1	.991	C-34, 1B-11
1979		79	.241	.314	137	33	5	1	1	0.7	13	12	19	12	2	39	10	174	12	2	0	5.9	.989	C-31, OF-1
1980		6	.200	.400	5	1	1	0	0	0.0	2	2	1	0	0	2	0	8	0	0	0	4.0	1.000	1B-2
21 yrs.		1909	.271	.388	5529	1501	242	57	97	1.8	590	645	548	422	61	373	82	8893	625	103	128	6.4	.989	C-1387, 1B-103, OF-15, 3B-6, DH-2

LEAGUE CHAMPIONSHIP SERIES

Year	Team	Games	BA	SA	AB	H	2B	3B	HR	HR%	R	RBI	BB	SO	SB	Pinch Hit AB	Pinch Hit H	PO	A	E	DP	TC/G	FA	G by Pos
1976	PHI N	2	.000	.000	4	0	0	0	0	0.0	0	0	0	1	0	1	0	6	0	0	0	6.0	1.000	C-1
1977		3	.167	.167	6	1	0	0	0	0.0	1	0	1	3	0	1	0	7	0	0	0	3.5	1.000	C-2
1978		2	.000	.000	4	0	0	0	0	0.0	2	1	2	0	0	1	0	8	0	0	0	8.0	1.000	C-1
3 yrs.		7	.071	.071	14	1	0	0	0	0.0	3	1	3	4	0	3	0	21	0	0	0	5.3	1.000	C-4

WORLD SERIES

Year	Team	Games	BA	SA	AB	H	2B	3B	HR	HR%	R	RBI	BB	SO	SB	Pinch Hit AB	Pinch Hit H	PO	A	E	DP	TC/G	FA	G by Pos
1964	STL N	7	.478	.739	23	11	1	1	1	4.3	4	5	5	1	1	0	0	57	1	0	0	8.3	1.000	C-7
1967		7	.125	.167	24	3	1	0	0	0.0	3	2	2	2	0	0	0	55	4	0	1	8.4	1.000	C-7
1968		7	.333	.593	27	9	0	2	1	3.7	3	4	3	2	0	0	0	61	1	0	0	8.9	1.000	C-7
3 yrs.		21	.311	.500	74	23	2	3 4th	2	2.7	10	11	10	5	1	0	0	173	6	0	1	8.5	1.000	C-21

Al McCauley

McCAULEY, ALLEN A. BL TL 6′ 180 lbs.
B. Mar. 4, 1863, Indianapolis, Ind. D. Aug. 24, 1917, Indianapolis, Ind.

Year	Team	Games	BA	SA	AB	H	2B	3B	HR	HR%	R	RBI	BB	SO	SB	Pinch Hit AB	Pinch Hit H	PO	A	E	DP	TC/G	FA	G by Pos
1884	IND AA	17	.189	.226	53	10	0	1	0	0.0	7		12			0	0	40	23	4	4	3.7	.940	P-10, 1B-5, OF-3
1890	PHI N	112	.244	.344	418	102	25	7	1	0.2	63	42	57	38	8	0	0	1053	26	30	68	9.9	.973	1B-112
1891	WAS AA	59	.282	.398	206	58	5	8	1	0.5	36	31	30	13	9	0	0	541	22	18	27	9.8	.969	1B-59
3 yrs.		188	.251	.352	677	170	30	16	2	0.3	106	73	99	51	17	0	0	1634	71	52	99	9.3	.970	1B-176, P-10, OF-3

Bill McCauley

McCAULEY, WILLIAM H.
B. Dec. 20, 1869, Washington, D. C. D. Jan. 27, 1926, Washington, D. C.

Year	Team	Games	BA	SA	AB	H	2B	3B	HR	HR%	R	RBI	BB	SO	SB	Pinch Hit AB	Pinch Hit H	PO	A	E	DP	TC/G	FA	G by Pos
1895	WAS N	1	.000	.000	2	0	0	0	0	0.0	0	0	0	0	0	0	0	1	4	2	0	7.0	.714	SS-1

Jim McCauley

McCAULEY, JAMES A. BL TR 6′ 180 lbs.
B. Mar. 24, 1863, Stanley, N. Y. D. Sept. 14, 1930, Canandaigua, N. Y.

Year	Team	Games	BA	SA	AB	H	2B	3B	HR	HR%	R	RBI	BB	SO	SB	Pinch Hit AB	Pinch Hit H	PO	A	E	DP	TC/G	FA	G by Pos
1884	STL AA	1	.000	.000	2	0	0	0	0	0.0	0		0			0	0	7	2	2	0	11.0	.818	C-1
1885	2 teams	BUF N (24G –.179) CHI N (3G –.167)																						
″	total	27	.178	.222	90	16	2	1	0	0.0	5	7	13	15		0	0	104	39	11	1	5.3	.929	C-23, OF-6
1886	BKN AA	11	.233	.267	30	7	1	0	0	0.0	5		11			0	0	61	16	14	2	8.3	.846	C-11
3 yrs.		39	.189	.230	122	23	3	1	0	0.0	10	7	24	15		0	0	172	57	27	3	6.2	.895	C-35, OF-6

Pat McCauley

McCAULEY, PATRICK M. TR 5′10½″ 156 lbs.
B. June 10, 1870, Ware, Mass. D. Jan. 23, 1917, Newark, N. J.

Year	Team	Games	BA	SA	AB	H	2B	3B	HR	HR%	R	RBI	BB	SO	SB	Pinch Hit AB	Pinch Hit H	PO	A	E	DP	TC/G	FA	G by Pos
1893	STL N	5	.063	.063	16	1	0	0	0	0.0	0	0	0	1	0	0	0	15	6	5	1	5.2	.808	C-5
1896	WAS N	26	.250	.357	84	21	3	0	2	2.4	14	11	7	8	3	1	0	73	27	9	2	4.4	.917	C-24, OF-1
1903	NY A	6	.053	.053	19	1	0	0	0	0.0	0	1	0		0	0	0	20	3	2	0	4.2	.920	C-6
3 yrs.		37	.193	.269	119	23	3	0	2	1.7	14	12	7	9	3	1	0	108	36	16	3	4.4	.900	C-35, OF-1

Harry McChesney

McCHESNEY, HARRY VINCENT (Pud) BR TR 5′ 9″ 165 lbs.
B. June 1, 1880, Pittsburgh, Pa. D. Aug. 11, 1960, Pittsburgh, Pa.

Year	Team	Games	BA	SA	AB	H	2B	3B	HR	HR%	R	RBI	BB	SO	SB	Pinch Hit AB	Pinch Hit H	PO	A	E	DP	TC/G	FA	G by Pos
1904	CHI N	22	.261	.375	88	23	6	2	0	0.0	9	11	4		2	0	0	27	2	1	1	1.4	.967	OF-22

Pete McClanahan

McCLANAHAN, ROBERT HUGH BR TR 5′ 9″ 170 lbs.
B. Oct. 24, 1906, Cold Springs, Tex. D. Oct. 28, 1987, Mont Belvieu, Tex.

Year	Team	Games	BA	SA	AB	H	2B	3B	HR	HR%	R	RBI	BB	SO	SB	Pinch Hit AB	Pinch Hit H	PO	A	E	DP	TC/G	FA	G by Pos
1931	PIT N	7	.500	.500	4	2	0	0	0	0.0	2	0	2	0	0	4	2	0	0	0	0	0.0	—	

Bill McClellan

McCLELLAN, WILLIAM HENRY BL TL 5′ 5½″ 156 lbs.
B. Mar. 22, 1856, Chicago, Ill. D. July 2, 1929, Chicago, Ill.

Year	Team	Games	BA	SA	AB	H	2B	3B	HR	HR%	R	RBI	BB	SO	SB	Pinch Hit AB	Pinch Hit H	PO	A	E	DP	TC/G	FA	G by Pos
1878	CHI N	48	.224	.263	205	46	6	1	0	0.0	26	29	2	13		0	0	89	159	40	15	6.0	.861	2B-42, SS-5, OF-1
1881	PRO N	68	.166	.185	259	43	3	1	0	0.0	30	16	15	21		0	0	82	153	39	18	4.0	.858	SS-50, OF-17, 2B-1
1883	PHI N	80	.230	.328	326	75	21	4	1	0.3	42		19	18		0	0	157	256	75	25	6.0	.846	SS-78, OF-2, 3B-1
1884		111	.258	.316	450	116	13	2	3	0.7	71		28	43		0	0	165	313	84	22	5.0	.851	SS-111, OF-1
1885	BKN AA	112	.267	.345	464	124	22	7	0	0.0	85		28			0	0	237	261	67	29	5.0	.881	3B-57, 2B-55
1886		141	.255	.346	595	152	33	9	1	0.2	131		56			0	0	423	435	88	64	6.7	.907	2B-141
1887		136	.263	.334	548	144	24	6	1	0.2	109		80		70	0	0	366	397	105	52	6.4	.879	2B-136
1888	2 teams	BKN AA (74G –.205) CLE AA (22G –.222)																						
″	total	96	.209	.246	350	73	7	3	0	0.0	39	26	46		19	0	0	202	175	44	26	4.4	.895	2B-61, OF-33, SS-2
8 yrs.		792	.242	.308	3197	773	129	33	6	0.2	533	71	274	95	89	0	0	1721	2149	542	251	5.6	.877	2B-436, SS-246, 3B-58, OF-54

Harvey McClellan

McCLELLAN, HARVEY McDOWELL (Little Mac) BR TR 5′ 9½″ 143 lbs.
B. Dec. 22, 1894, Cynthiana, Ky. D. Nov. 6, 1925, Cynthiana, Ky.

Year	Team	Games	BA	SA	AB	H	2B	3B	HR	HR%	R	RBI	BB	SO	SB	Pinch Hit AB	Pinch Hit H	PO	A	E	DP	TC/G	FA	G by Pos
1919	CHI A	7	.333	.333	12	4	0	0	0	0.0	2	1	1	1	0	1	0	6	7	1	1	2.8	.929	3B-3, SS-2
1920		10	.333	.500	18	6	1	1	0	0.0	4	5	4	1	2	2	0	7	6	1	0	2.3	.929	SS-4, 3B-2
1921		63	.179	.224	196	35	4	1	1	0.5	20	14	14	18	2	3	0	112	141	8	23	4.7	.969	2B-20, SS-15, OF-15, 3B-5

Harvey McClellan *continued*

Year	Team	Games	BA	SA	AB	H	2B	3B	HR	HR%	R	RBI	BB	SO	SB	Pinch Hit AB	Pinch Hit H	PO	A	E	DP	TC/G	FA	G by Pos
1922		91	.226	.322	301	68	17	3	2	0.7	28	28	16	32	3	5	4	94	180	12	17	3.5	.958	3B-71, SS-8, 2B-2, OF-1
1923		141	.235	.304	550	129	29	3	1	0.2	67	41	27	44	14	1	1	222	399	27	65	4.6	.958	SS-138, 2B-2
1924		32	.176	.212	85	15	3	0	0	0.0	9	9	6	7	2	1	0	36	87	7	7	4.3	.946	SS-21, 2B-7, OF-1, 3B-1
6 yrs.		344	.221	.292	1162	257	54	8	4	0.3	130	98	68	103	23	13	5	477	820	56	113	4.3	.959	SS-188, 3B-82, 2B-31, OF-17

Lloyd McClendon

McCLENDON, LLOYD GLENN BR TR 5′10″ 190 lbs.
B. Jan. 11, 1959, Gary, Ind.

Year	Team	Games	BA	SA	AB	H	2B	3B	HR	HR%	R	RBI	BB	SO	SB	Pinch Hit AB	Pinch Hit H	PO	A	E	DP	TC/G	FA	G by Pos
1987	**CIN N**	45	.208	.361	72	15	5	0	2	2.8	8	13	4	15	1	24	6	80	5	2	3	4.6	.977	C-12, 1B-5, OF-1, 3B-1
1988		72	.219	.314	137	30	4	0	3	2.2	9	14	15	22	4	24	6	197	13	4	11	4.0	.981	C-23, OF-17, 1B-12, 3B-2
1989	**CHI N**	92	.286	.479	259	74	12	1	12	4.6	47	40	37	31	6	16	5	310	18	6	21	4.0	.982	OF-45, 1B-28, 3B-6, C-5
1990	**2 teams**	**CHI N** (49G –.159) **PIT N** (4G –.333)																						
″	**total**	53	.164	.245	110	18	3	0	2	1.8	6	12	14	22	1	16	2	120	9	1	5	3.3	.992	OF-24, 1B-8, C-8
1991	**PIT N**	85	.288	.460	163	47	7	0	7	4.3	24	24	18	23	2	33	9	163	12	3	13	3.2	.983	OF-32, 1B-22, C-2
1992		84	.253	.353	190	48	8	1	3	1.6	26	20	28	24	1	16	5	136	9	3	3	1.9	.980	OF-60, 1B-18
1993		88	.221	.326	181	40	11	1	2	1.1	21	19	23	17	0	32	6	98	5	3	2	1.6	.972	OF-61, 1B-6
1994		51	.239	.413	92	22	4	0	4	4.3	9	12	4	11	0	29	8	46	2	1	5	2.2	.980	OF-20, 1B-2
8 yrs.		570	.244	.381	1204	294	54	3	35	2.9	150	154	143	165	15	190	47	1150	73	23	63	3.0	.982	OF-260, 1B-101, C-50, 3B-9
LEAGUE CHAMPIONSHIP SERIES																								
1989	**CHI N**	3	.667	.667	3	2	0	0	0	0.0	0	0	1	0	0	2	1	3	0	0	0	1.0	1.000	C-2, OF-1
1991	**PIT N**	3	.000	.000	2	0	0	0	0	0.0	0	0	1	0	0	2	0	0	0	0	0	0.0	.000	1B-1
1992		5	.727	1.182	11	8	2	0	1	9.1	4	4	4	1	0	0	0	10	0	0	0	2.0	1.000	OF-5
3 yrs.		11	.625	.938	16	10	2	0	1	6.3	4	4	6	1	0	4	1	13	0	0	0	1.4	1.000	OF-6, C-2, 1B-1

Jeff McCleskey

McCLESKEY, JEFFERSON LAMAR BL TR 5′11″ 160 lbs.
B. Nov. 6, 1891, Americus, Ga. D. May 11, 1971, Americus, Ga.

Year	Team	Games	BA	SA	AB	H	2B	3B	HR	HR%	R	RBI	BB	SO	SB	Pinch Hit AB	Pinch Hit H	PO	A	E	DP	TC/G	FA	G by Pos
1913	**BOS N**	2	.000	.000	3	0	0	0	0	0.0	0	0	1	0	0	0	0	2	1	1	0	2.0	.750	3B-2

Bill McCloskey

McCLOSKEY, WILLIAM GEORGE 5′ 8″ 155 lbs.
B. May 1854, Philadelphia, Pa. Deceased.

Year	Team	Games	BA	SA	AB	H	2B	3B	HR	HR%	R	RBI	BB	SO	SB	Pinch Hit AB	Pinch Hit H	PO	A	E	DP	TC/G	FA	G by Pos
1884	**WIL U**	9	.100	.100	30	3	0	0	0	0.0	0		0			0	0	38	7	13	1	5.8	.776	OF-5, C-5

Hal McClure

McCLURE, HAROLD MURRAY (Mac) BR TR 6′ 165 lbs.
B. Aug. 8, 1859, Lewisburg, Pa. D. June 5, 1919, Wilkes-Barre, Pa.

Year	Team	Games	BA	SA	AB	H	2B	3B	HR	HR%	R	RBI	BB	SO	SB	Pinch Hit AB	Pinch Hit H	PO	A	E	DP	TC/G	FA	G by Pos
1882	**BOS N**	2	.333	.333	6	2	0	0	0	0.0	1	0	0	1		0	0	3	0	1	0	2.0	.750	OF-2

Larry McClure

McCLURE, LAWRENCE LEDWITH BR TR 5′ 6½″ 130 lbs.
B. Oct. 3, 1885, Wayne, W. Va. D. Aug. 31, 1949, Huntington, W. Va.

Year	Team	Games	BA	SA	AB	H	2B	3B	HR	HR%	R	RBI	BB	SO	SB	Pinch Hit AB	Pinch Hit H	PO	A	E	DP	TC/G	FA	G by Pos
1910	**NY A**	1	.000	.000	1	0	0	0	0	0.0	0	0	0		0	0	0	0	0	0	0	0.0	.000	OF-1

Amby McConnell

McCONNELL, AMBROSE MOSES BL TR 5′ 7″ 150 lbs.
B. Apr. 29, 1883, North Powell, Vt. D. May 20, 1942, Utica, N. Y.

Year	Team	Games	BA	SA	AB	H	2B	3B	HR	HR%	R	RBI	BB	SO	SB	Pinch Hit AB	Pinch Hit H	PO	A	E	DP	TC/G	FA	G by Pos
1908	**BOS A**	140	.279	.335	502	140	10	6	2	0.4	77	43	38		31	10	5	238	355	41	33	4.9	.935	2B-126, SS-3
1909		121	.238	.289	453	108	7	8	0	0.0	59	36	34		26	0	0	251	389	31	43	5.5	.954	2B-121
1910	**2 teams**	**BOS A** (12G –.167) **CHI A** (32G –.277)																						
″	**total**	44	.252	.303	155	39	2	3	0	0.0	19	6	12		8	2	0	78	108	9	10	4.6	.954	2B-42
1911	**CHI A**	104	.280	.341	396	111	11	5	1	0.3	45	34	23		7	1	0	189	280	13	31	4.7	.973	2B-103
4 yrs.		409	.264	.319	1506	398	30	22	3	0.2	200	119	107		72	13	5	756	1132	94	117	5.0	.953	2B-392, SS-3

George McConnell

McCONNELL, GEORGE NEELY BR TR 6′ 3″ 190 lbs.
B. Sept. 16, 1877, Shelbyville, Tenn. D. May 10, 1964, Chattanooga, Tenn.

Year	Team	Games	BA	SA	AB	H	2B	3B	HR	HR%	R	RBI	BB	SO	SB	Pinch Hit AB	Pinch Hit H	PO	A	E	DP	TC/G	FA	G by Pos
1909	**NY A**	13	.209	.256	43	9	0	1	0	0.0	4	5	1		1	0	0	124	14	5	7	11.0	.965	1B-11, P-2
1912		42	.297	.385	91	27	4	2	0	0.0	11	8	4		0	17	6	24	75	8	3	4.3	.925	P-23, 1B-2
1913		39	.179	.209	67	12	2	0	0	0.0	4	2	0	11	0	3	0	11	74	3	2	2.4	.966	P-35, 1B-1
1914	**CHI N**	1	.000	.000	2	0	0	0	0	0.0	0	0	0	1	0	0	0	0	3	0	0	3.0	1.000	P-1
1915	**CHI F**	53	.248	.352	125	31	6	2	1	0.8	14	18	0		2	8	2	8	105	3	4	2.6	.974	P-44
1916	**CHI N**	48	.158	.158	57	9	0	0	0	0.0	2	0	2	4	0	0	0	9	50	3	3	2.2	.952	P-28
6 yrs.		196	.229	.294	385	88	12	5	1	0.3	35	33	7	16	3	28	8	176	321	22	19	3.5	.958	P-133, 1B-14

Sammy McConnell

McCONNELL, SAMUEL FAULKNER BL TR 5′ 6½″ 150 lbs.
B. June 8, 1895, Philadelphia, Pa. D. June 27, 1981, Phoenixville, Pa.

Year	Team	Games	BA	SA	AB	H	2B	3B	HR	HR%	R	RBI	BB	SO	SB	Pinch Hit AB	Pinch Hit H	PO	A	E	DP	TC/G	FA	G by Pos
1915	**PHI A**	6	.182	.273	11	2	1	0	0	0.0	1	0	1	3	0	0	0	6	10	3	0	3.8	.842	3B-5

Don McCormack

McCORMACK, DONALD ROSS BR TR 6′ 3″ 205 lbs.
B. Sept. 18, 1955, Omak, Wash.

Year	Team	Games	BA	SA	AB	H	2B	3B	HR	HR%	R	RBI	BB	SO	SB	Pinch Hit AB	Pinch Hit H	PO	A	E	DP	TC/G	FA	G by Pos
1980	**PHI N**	2	1.000	1.000	1	1	0	0	0	0.0	0	0	0	0	0	0	0	6	0	0	0	3.0	1.000	C-2
1981		3	.250	.250	4	1	0	0	0	0.0	0	0	0	1	0	0	0	4	2	0	0	2.0	1.000	C-3
2 yrs.		5	.400	.400	5	2	0	0	0	0.0	0	0	0	1	0	0	0	10	2	0	0	2.4	1.000	C-5

Barry McCormick

McCORMICK, WILLIAM J. TR 5′ 9″
B. Dec. 25, 1874, Maysville, Ky. D. Jan. 28, 1956, Cincinnati, Ohio.

Year	Team	Games	BA	SA	AB	H	2B	3B	HR	HR%	R	RBI	BB	SO	SB	Pinch Hit AB	Pinch Hit H	PO	A	E	DP	TC/G	FA	G by Pos
1895	**LOU N**	3	.250	.417	12	3	0	1	0	0.0	2	0	0	0	1	0	0	4	7	1	1	4.0	.917	SS-2, 2B-1
1896	**CHI N**	45	.220	.268	168	37	3	1	1	0.6	22	23	14	30	9	0	0	51	98	31	12	4.0	.828	3B-35, SS-6, 2B-3, OF-1
1897		101	.267	.348	419	112	8	10	2	0.5	87	55	33		44	0	0	171	269	59	26	4.8	.882	3B-56, SS-46, 2B-1
1898		137	.247	.321	530	131	15	9	2	0.4	76	78	47		15	0	0	155	326	63	31	3.9	.884	3B-136, SS-1, 2B-1
1899		102	.258	.324	376	97	15	2	2	0.5	48	52	25		14	0	0	205	351	37	49	5.8	.938	2B-99, SS-3
1900		110	.219	.303	379	83	13	5	3	0.8	35	48	38		8	0	0	198	378	64	34	5.8	.900	SS-84, 3B-21, 2B-5
1901		115	.234	.304	427	100	15	6	1	0.2	45	32	31		12	0	0	206	411	60	47	5.9	.911	SS-112, 3B-3
1902	**STL A**	139	.246	.308	504	124	14	4	3	0.6	55	51	37		10	0	0	159	298	45	28	3.6	.910	3B-132, SS-7, OF-1
1903	**2 teams**	**STL A** (61G –.217) **WAS A** (63G –.215)																						
″	**total**	124	.216	.282	426	92	16	3	2	0.5	27	40	28		8	0	0	217	347	25	43	4.8	.958	2B-91, 3B-28, SS-4
1904	**WAS A**	113	.218	.250	404	88	11	1	0	0.0	36	39	27		9	0	0	204	355	37	39	5.3	.938	2B-113
10 yrs.		989	.238	.304	3645	867	110	42	16	0.4	433	418	280	30	130	0	0	1570	2840	422	310	4.9	.913	3B-411, 2B-314, SS-265, OF-2

Frank McCormick

McCORMICK, FRANK ANDREW (Buck) BR TR 6′ 4″ 205 lbs.
B. June 9, 1911, New York, N. Y. D. Nov. 21, 1982, Manhasset, N. Y.

Year	Team	Games	BA	SA	AB	H	2B	3B	HR	HR%	R	RBI	BB	SO	SB	Pinch Hit AB	Pinch Hit H	PO	A	E	DP	TC/G	FA	G by Pos
1934	CIN N	12	.313	.563	16	5	2	1	0	0.0	1	5	0	1	0	10	4	16	0	1	1	8.5	.941	1B-2
1937		24	.325	.386	83	27	5	0	0	0.0	5	9	2	4	1	0	0	199	18	1	20	8.7	.995	1B-20, 2B-4, OF-1
1938		151	.327	.425	**640**	**209**	40	4	5	0.8	89	106	18	17	1	0	0	1441	95	7	127	10.2	.995	1B-151
1939		156	.332	.495	630	**209**	41	4	18	2.9	99	**128**	40	16	1	0	0	1518	100	7	153	10.4	.996	1B-156
1940		155	.309	.482	**618**	**191**	**44**	3	19	3.1	93	127	52	26	2	0	0	1587	98	8	146	10.9	.995	1B-155
1941		154	.269	.421	603	162	31	5	17	2.8	77	97	40	13	2	0	0	1464	92	8	130	10.2	.995	1B-154
1942		145	.277	.388	564	156	24	0	13	2.3	58	89	45	18	1	1	0	1403	101	10	132	10.5	.993	1B-144
1943		126	.303	.413	472	143	28	0	8	1.7	56	59	29	15	2	6	0	1156	85	6	116	10.4	.995	1B-120
1944		153	.305	.482	581	177	37	3	20	3.4	85	102	57	17	7	0	0	1508	135	13	130	10.8	.992	1B-153
1945		152	.276	.384	580	160	33	0	10	1.7	68	81	56	22	6	1	0	1469	118	9	104	10.6	.994	1B-151
1946	PHI N	135	.284	.397	504	143	20	2	11	2.2	46	66	36	21	2	1	0	1185	98	1	92	9.6	.999	1B-134
1947	2 teams	PHI N (15G –.225) BOS N (81G –.354)																						
″	total	96	.333	.464	252	84	20	2	3	1.2	31	51	14	10	2	36	**13**	514	30	3	40	9.1	.995	1B-60
1948	BOS N	75	.250	.389	180	45	9	2	4	2.2	14	34	10	9	0	22	4	343	33	5	30	7.6	.987	1B-50
13 yrs.		1534	.299	.434	5723	1711	334	26	128	2.2	722	954	399	189	27	77	21	13803	1003	79	1221	10.2	.995	1B-1450, 2B-4, OF-1
WORLD SERIES																								
1939	CIN N	4	.400	.467	15	6	1	0	0	0.0	1	1	0	1	0	0	0	32	2	0	1	8.5	1.000	1B-4
1940		7	.214	.250	28	6	1	0	0	0.0	2	0	1	1	0	0	0	59	4	2	7	9.3	.969	1B-7
1948	BOS N	3	.200	.200	5	1	0	0	0	0.0	0	0	0	2	0	2	0	5	1	0	1	6.0	1.000	1B-1
3 yrs.		14	.271	.313	48	13	2	0	0	0.0	3	1	1	4	0	2	0	96	7	2	9	8.8	.981	1B-12

Jerry McCormick

McCORMICK, JOHN
B. Philadelphia, Pa. D. Sept. 19, 1905, Philadelphia, Pa.

Year	Team	Games	BA	SA	AB	H	2B	3B	HR	HR%	R	RBI	BB	SO	SB	Pinch Hit AB	Pinch Hit H	PO	A	E	DP	TC/G	FA	G by Pos
1883	BAL AA	93	.262	.334	389	102	16	6	0	0.0	40		2			0	0	138	196	84	10	4.5	.799	3B-93
1884	2 teams	PHI U (67G –.285) WAS U (42G –.217)																						
″	total	109	.261	.323	452	118	20	4	0	0.0	64		5			0	0	161	208	82	18	4.1	.818	3B-92, SS-7, 2B-5, OF-5, P-1
2 yrs.		202	.262	.328	841	220	36	10	0	0.0	104		7			0	0	299	404	166	28	4.3	.809	3B-185, SS-7, 2B-5, OF-5, P-1

Jim McCormick

McCORMICK, JAMES BR TR 5′10½″ 215 lbs.
B. Nov. 3, 1856, Glasgow, Scotland D. Mar. 10, 1918, Paterson, N. J.
Manager 1879–80, 1882.

Year	Team	Games	BA	SA	AB	H	2B	3B	HR	HR%	R	RBI	BB	SO	SB	Pinch Hit AB	Pinch Hit H	PO	A	E	DP	TC/G	FA	G by Pos
1878	IND N	15	.143	.161	56	8	1	0	0	0.0	5	0	0	2		0	0	9	33	3	3	2.6	.933	P-14, OF-3
1879	CLE N	75	.220	.270	282	62	10	2	0	0.0	35	20	1	9		0	0	97	120	15	4	2.9	.935	P-62, OF-13, 1B-4
1880		78	.246	.284	289	71	11	0	0	0.0	34	26	5	5		0	0	38	135	26	4	2.5	.869	P-74, OF-5
1881		70	.256	.311	309	79	9	4	0	0.0	45	26	5	16		0	0	55	92	18	4	2.3	.891	P-59, OF-10, 2B-1, 3B-1
1882		70	.218	.290	262	57	7	3	2	0.8	35	15	2	22		0	0	45	100	15	1	2.2	.906	P-68, OF-4
1883		43	.236	.274	157	37	2	2	0	0.0	21		2	14		0	0	28	101	17	4	3.3	.884	P-43, OF-1
1884	2 teams	CLE N (49G –.263) CIN U (27G –.245)																						
″	total	76	.257	.317	300	77	8	5	0	0.0	27	23	1	11		0	0	54	119	9	6	2.3	.951	P-68, OF-11
1885	2 teams	PRO N (4G –.214) CHI N (25G –.223)																						
″	total	29	.222	.308	117	26	2	4	0	0.0	15	16	2	18		0	0	23	75	5	3	3.6	.951	P-28, OF-1
1886	CHI N	42	.236	.345	174	41	9	2	2	1.1	17	21	2	30		0	0	22	75	6	3	2.2	.942	P-42, OF-4
1887	PIT N	36	.243	.294	136	33	7	0	0	0.0	12	18	2	0	9	0	0	13	88	8	1	3.0	.927	P-36
10 yrs.		534	.236	.294	2082	491	66	22	4	0.2	246	165	22	127	9	0	0	384	938	122	33	2.6	.916	P-494, OF-52, 1B-4, 2B-1, 3B-1

Jim McCormick

McCORMICK, JAMES AMBROSE BR TR 6′ 1″ 160 lbs.
B. Nov. 2, 1868, Spencer, Mass. D. Feb. 1, 1948, Saco, Me.

Year	Team	Games	BA	SA	AB	H	2B	3B	HR	HR%	R	RBI	BB	SO	SB	Pinch Hit AB	Pinch Hit H	PO	A	E	DP	TC/G	FA	G by Pos
1892	STL N	3	.000	.000	11	0	0	0	0	0.0	0	0	1	5	0	0	0	4	8	0	0	4.0	1.000	2B-2, 3B-1

Mike McCormick

McCORMICK, MICHAEL J. BR TR 5′ 3″ 155 lbs.
B. May 1883, Jersey City, N. J. D. Nov. 18, 1953, Jersey City, N. J.

Year	Team	Games	BA	SA	AB	H	2B	3B	HR	HR%	R	RBI	BB	SO	SB	Pinch Hit AB	Pinch Hit H	PO	A	E	DP	TC/G	FA	G by Pos
1904	BKN N	105	.184	.222	347	64	5	4	0	0.0	28	27	43		22	0	0	139	190	31	21	3.4	.914	3B-104, 2B-1

Mike McCormick

McCORMICK, MYRON WINTHROP BR TR 6′ 195 lbs.
B. May 6, 1917, Angel's Camp, Calif. D. Apr. 14, 1976, Ventura, Calif.

Year	Team	Games	BA	SA	AB	H	2B	3B	HR	HR%	R	RBI	BB	SO	SB	Pinch Hit AB	Pinch Hit H	PO	A	E	DP	TC/G	FA	G by Pos
1940	CIN N	110	.300	.355	417	125	20	0	1	0.2	48	30	13	36	8	2	0	266	9	4	2	2.6	.986	OF-107
1941		110	.287	.382	369	106	17	3	4	1.1	52	31	30	24	4	4	0	240	9	6	2	2.5	.976	OF-101
1942		40	.237	.319	135	32	2	3	1	0.7	18	11	13	7	0	1	0	93	2	1	1	2.5	.990	OF-38
1943		4	.133	.133	15	2	0	0	0	0.0	0	0	2	0	0	0	0	10	0	1	0	2.8	.909	OF-4
1946	2 teams	CIN N (23G –.216) BOS N (59G –.262)																						
″	total	82	.248	.311	238	59	8	2	1	0.4	33	21	19	12	0	10	2	165	2	3	0	2.5	.982	OF-69
1947	BOS N	92	.285	.412	284	81	13	7	3	1.1	42	36	20	21	1	12	4	155	4	3	0	2.1	.981	OF-79
1948		115	.303	.417	343	104	22	7	1	0.3	45	39	32	34	1	14	6	187	7	5	3	2.0	.975	OF-100
1949	BKN N	55	.209	.302	139	29	5	1	2	1.4	17	14	14	12	1	6	2	75	3	0	0	1.6	1.000	OF-49
1950	2 teams	NY N (4G –.000) CHI A (55G –.232)																						
″	total	59	.225	.296	142	32	4	3	0	0.0	16	10	16	8	0	11	1	105	4	2	2	2.5	.982	OF-44
1951	WAS A	81	.288	.362	243	70	9	3	1	0.4	31	23	29	20	1	15	7	134	7	5	0	2.4	.966	OF-62
10 yrs.		748	.275	.361	2325	640	100	29	14	0.6	302	215	188	174	16	75	22	1430	47	30	10	2.3	.980	OF-653
WORLD SERIES																								
1940	CIN N	7	.310	.414	29	9	3	0	0	0.0	1	2	1	6	0	0	0	24	1	1	0	3.7	.962	OF-7
1948	BOS N	6	.261	.261	23	6	0	0	0	0.0	1	2	0	4	0	0	0	17	0	0	0	2.8	1.000	OF-6
1949	BKN N	1	—	—	0	0	0	0	0	—	0	0	0	0	0	0	0	1	0	0	0	1.0	1.000	OF-1
3 yrs.		14	.288	.346	52	15	3	0	0	0.0	2	4	1	10	0	0	0	42	1	1	0	3.1	.977	OF-14

Moose McCormick

McCORMICK, HARRY ELWOOD BL TL 5′11″ 180 lbs.
B. Feb. 28, 1881, Philadelphia, Pa. D. July 9, 1962, Lewisburg, Pa.

Year	Team	Games	BA	SA	AB	H	2B	3B	HR	HR%	R	RBI	BB	SO	SB	Pinch Hit AB	Pinch Hit H	PO	A	E	DP	TC/G	FA	G by Pos
1904	2 teams	NY N (59G –.266) PIT N (66G –.290)																						
″	total	125	.279	.392	441	123	19	11	3	0.7	53	49	26		19	4	2	182	10	15	2	1.7	.928	OF-121
1908	2 teams	PHI N (11G –.091) NY N (73G –.302)																						
″	total	84	.285	.365	274	78	16	3	0	0.0	31	34	6		6	10	3	108	3	11	2	1.7	.910	OF-70
1909	NY N	110	.291	.402	413	120	21	8	3	0.7	68	27	49		4	10	2	144	13	13	6	1.6	.924	OF-109

Moose McCormick *continued*

Year	Team		Games	BA	SA	AB	H	2B	3B	HR	HR%	R	RBI	BB	SO	SB	Pinch Hit AB	Pinch Hit H	PO	A	E	DP	TC/G	FA	G by Pos
1912			42	.333	.487	39	13	4	1	0	0.0	4	8	6	9	1	**30**	**11**	3	0	1	0	0.6	.750	OF-6, 1B-1
1913			57	.275	.375	80	22	2	3	0	0.0	9	15	5	13	0	39	10	19	1	2	1	1.5	.909	OF-15
5 yrs.			418	.285	.391	1247	356	62	26	6	0.5	165	133	92	22	30	93	28	456	27	42	11	1.6	.920	OF-321, 1B-1
WORLD SERIES																									
1912	NY	N	5	.250	.250	4	1	0	0	0	0.0	0	1	0	0	0	4	1	0	0	0	0	0.0	—	
1913			2	.500	.500	2	1	0	0	0	0.0	1	0	0	0	0	2	1	0	0	0	0	0.0	—	
2 yrs.			7	.333	.333	6	2	0	0	0	0.0	1	1	0	0	0	6	2							

Barney McCosky

McCOSKY, WILLIAM BARNEY
B. Apr. 11, 1917, Coal Run, Pa.

BL TR 6′ 1″ 184 lbs.

Year	Team		Games	BA	SA	AB	H	2B	3B	HR	HR%	R	RBI	BB	SO	SB	Pinch Hit AB	Pinch Hit H	PO	A	E	DP	TC/G	FA	G by Pos
1939	DET	A	147	.311	.430	611	190	33	14	4	0.7	120	58	70	45	20	2	1	428	7	6	2	3.0	.986	OF-145
1940			143	.340	.491	589	**200**	39	**19**	4	0.7	123	57	67	41	13	2	1	349	7	6	2	2.6	.983	OF-141
1941			127	.324	.425	494	160	25	8	3	0.6	80	55	61	33	8	4	4	328	6	5	2	2.8	.985	OF-122
1942			154	.293	.412	600	176	28	11	7	1.2	75	50	68	37	11	0	0	351	7	7	2	2.4	.981	OF-154
1946	2 teams		DET A (25G –.198) PHI A (92G –.354)																						
″	total		117	.318	.409	399	127	22	4	2	0.5	44	45	60	22	2	5	1	263	3	6	0	2.5	.978	OF-109
1947	PHI	A	137	.328	.399	546	179	22	7	1	0.2	77	52	57	29	1	1	0	346	8	6	2	2.6	.983	OF-136
1948			135	.326	.386	515	168	21	5	0	0.0	95	46	68	22	1	1	1	277	9	3	1	2.2	.990	OF-134
1950			66	.240	.307	179	43	10	1	0	0.0	19	11	22	12	0	23	5	73	1	1	1	1.8	.987	OF-42
1951	3 teams		PHI A (12G –.296) CIN N (25G –.320) CLE A (31G –.213)																						
″	total		68	.268	.377	138	37	7	1	2	1.4	14	14	15	11	1	32	7	58	0	0	0	1.7	1.000	OF-34
1952	CLE	A	54	.212	.325	80	17	4	1	1	1.3	14	6	8	5	1	30	9	17	0	1	0	0.9	.944	OF-19
1953			22	.190	.333	21	4	3	0	0	0.0	3	3	1	4	0	21	4	0	0	0	0	0.0	—	
11 yrs.			1170	.312	.414	4172	1301	214	71	24	0.6	664	397	497	261	58	121	33	2490	48	41	12	2.5	.984	OF-1036
WORLD SERIES																									
1940	DET	A	7	.304	.348	23	7	1	0	0	0.0	5	1	7	0	0	0	0	19	0	0	0	2.7	1.000	OF-7

Willie McCovey

McCOVEY, WILLIE LEE (Stretch)
B. Jan. 10, 1938, Mobile, Ala.
Hall of Fame 1986.

BL TL 6′ 4″ 198 lbs.

Year	Team		Games	BA	SA	AB	H	2B	3B	HR	HR%	R	RBI	BB	SO	SB	Pinch Hit AB	Pinch Hit H	PO	A	E	DP	TC/G	FA	G by Pos
1959	SF	N	52	.354	.656	192	68	9	5	13	6.8	32	38	22	35	2	2	2	424	29	5	29	9.0	.989	1B-51
1960			101	.238	.469	260	62	15	3	13	5.0	37	51	45	53	1	32	7	557	39	9	42	8.5	.985	1B-71
1961			106	.271	.491	328	89	12	3	18	5.5	59	50	37	60	1	21	4	669	55	11	55	8.8	.985	1B-84
1962			91	.293	.590	229	67	6	1	20	8.7	41	54	29	35	3	17	4	186	9	3	13	2.7	.985	OF-57, 1B-17
1963			152	.280	.566	564	158	19	5	**44**	**7.8**	103	102	50	119	1	5	0	363	21	15	5	2.5	.962	OF-135, 1B-23
1964			130	.220	.412	364	80	14	1	18	4.9	55	54	61	73	2	23	4	273	19	14	20	2.8	.954	OF-83, 1B-26
1965			160	.276	.539	540	149	17	4	39	7.2	93	92	88	118	0	6	1	1310	87	13	93	9.0	.991	1B-156
1966			150	.295	.586	502	148	26	6	36	7.2	85	96	76	100	2	7	2	1287	81	22	91	9.6	.984	1B-145
1967			135	.276	.535	456	126	17	4	31	**6.8**	73	91	71	110	3	9	2	1221	81	15	102	10.4	.989	1B-127
1968			148	.293	**.545**	523	153	16	4	**36**	**6.9**	81	**105**	72	71	4	2	1	1305	103	21	91	9.8	.985	1B-146
1969			149	.320	**.656**	491	157	26	2	**45**	**9.2**	101	**126**	121	66	0	1	0	1392	79	12	116	10.0	.992	1B-148
1970			152	.289	**.612**	495	143	39	2	39	**7.9**	98	126	**137**	75	0	5	2	1217	134	15	117	9.4	.989	1B-146
1971			105	.277	.480	329	91	13	0	18	5.5	45	70	64	57	0	8	3	828	63	15	80	9.5	.983	1B-95
1972			81	.213	.403	263	56	8	0	14	5.3	30	35	38	45	0	7	2	617	32	9	52	8.9	.986	1B-74
1973			130	.266	.546	383	102	14	3	29	7.6	52	75	105	78	1	8	2	930	76	12	89	8.7	.988	1B-117
1974	SD	N	128	.253	.506	344	87	19	1	22	6.4	53	63	96	76	1	18	7	815	47	11	59	8.4	.987	1B-104
1975			122	.252	.460	413	104	17	0	23	5.6	43	68	57	80	1	4	2	979	73	15	94	9.3	.986	1B-115
1976	2 teams		SD N (71G –.203) OAK A (11G –.208)																						
″	total		82	.204	.336	226	46	9	0	7	3.1	20	36	24	43	0	21	6	420	44	4	39	7.8	.991	1B-51, DH-9
1977	SF	N	141	.280	.500	478	134	21	0	28	5.9	54	86	67	106	3	4	0	1072	60	13	93	8.4	.989	1B-136
1978			108	.228	.396	351	80	19	2	12	3.4	32	64	36	57	1	9	2	721	44	10	49	8.0	.987	1B-97
1979			117	.249	.402	353	88	9	0	15	4.2	34	57	36	70	0	28	11	740	48	10	60	9.0	.987	1B-89
1980			48	.204	.301	113	23	8	0	1	0.9	8	16	13	23	0	17	2	241	12	2	18	9.4	.992	1B-27
22 yrs.			2588	.270	.515	8197	2211	353	46	521 **10th**	6.4	1229	1555	1345	1550	26	254	66	17567	1236	256	1407	8.2	.987	1B-2045, OF-275, DH-9
LEAGUE CHAMPIONSHIP SERIES																									
1971	SF	N	4	.429	.857	14	6	0	0	2	14.3	2	6	4	2	0	0	0	34	3	1	0	9.5	.974	1B-4
WORLD SERIES																									
1962	SF	N	4	.200	.533	15	3	0	1	1	6.7	2	1	1	3	0	0	0	23	4	2	2	7.3	.931	OF-2, 1B-2

Art McCoy

McCOY, ARTHUR GRAY
B. July 1864, Danville, Pa. D. Mar. 22, 1904, Danville, Pa.

168 lbs.

Year	Team		Games	BA	SA	AB	H	2B	3B	HR	HR%	R	RBI	BB	SO	SB	Pinch Hit AB	Pinch Hit H	PO	A	E	DP	TC/G	FA	G by Pos
1889	WAS	N	2	.000	.000	6	0	0	0	0	0.0	0	0	2	1	0	0	0	6	2	1	0	4.5	.889	2B-2

Benny McCoy

McCOY, BENJAMIN JENISON
B. Nov. 9, 1915, Jenison, Mich.

BL TR 5′ 9″ 170 lbs.

Year	Team		Games	BA	SA	AB	H	2B	3B	HR	HR%	R	RBI	BB	SO	SB	Pinch Hit AB	Pinch Hit H	PO	A	E	DP	TC/G	FA	G by Pos
1938	DET	A	7	.200	.267	15	3	1	0	0	0.0	2	0	1	2	0	0	0	10	16	3	4	4.1	.897	2B-6, 3B-1
1939			55	.302	.448	192	58	13	6	1	0.5	38	33	29	26	3	5	0	108	150	11	25	5.4	.959	2B-34, SS-16
1940	PHI	A	134	.257	.373	490	126	26	5	7	1.4	56	62	65	44	2	4	2	262	393	35	82	5.3	.949	2B-130, 3B-1
1941			141	.271	.368	517	140	12	7	8	1.5	86	61	95	50	3	5	0	285	423	27	87	5.4	.963	2B-135
4 yrs.			337	.269	.381	1214	327	52	18	16	1.3	182	156	190	122	8	14	2	665	982	76	198	5.3	.956	2B-305, SS-16, 3B-2

Quinton McCracken

McCRACKEN, QUINTON ANTOINE
B. Mar. 16, 1970, Wilmington, N. C.

BB TR 5′ 7″ 170 lbs.

Year	Team		Games	BA	SA	AB	H	2B	3B	HR	HR%	R	RBI	BB	SO	SB	Pinch Hit AB	Pinch Hit H	PO	A	E	DP	TC/G	FA	G by Pos
1995	CLR	N	3	.000	.000	1	0	0	0	0	0.0	0	0	0	1	0	1	0	0	0	0	0	0.0	.000	OF-1

Tom McCraw

McCRAW, TOMMY LEE
B. Nov. 21, 1940, Malvern, Ark.

BL TL 6′ 183 lbs.

Year	Team		Games	BA	SA	AB	H	2B	3B	HR	HR%	R	RBI	BB	SO	SB	Pinch Hit AB	Pinch Hit H	PO	A	E	DP	TC/G	FA	G by Pos
1963	CHI	A	102	.254	.379	280	71	11	3	6	2.1	38	33	21	46	15	3	1	673	47	5	65	7.5	.993	1B-97
1964			125	.261	.367	368	96	11	5	6	1.6	47	36	32	65	15	20	2	637	41	7	57	5.7	.990	1B-84, OF-36
1965			133	.238	.344	273	65	12	1	5	1.8	38	21	25	48	12	22	7	336	24	4	18	2.7	.989	1B-72, OF-64

Tom McCraw *continued*

Year	Team	Games	BA	SA	AB	H	2B	3B	HR	HR%	R	RBI	BB	SO	SB	Pinch Hit AB	Pinch Hit H	PO	A	E	DP	TC/G	FA	G by Pos
1966		151	.229	.329	389	89	16	4	5	1.3	49	48	29	40	20	7	1	893	68	9	56	6.0	.991	1B-121, OF-41
1967		125	.236	.362	453	107	18	3	11	2.4	55	45	33	55	24	2	0	1177	110	11	92	10.1	.992	1B-123, OF-6
1968		136	.235	.375	477	112	16	12	9	1.9	51	44	36	58	20	3	0	1285	93	20	103	10.4	.986	1B-135
1969		93	.258	.350	240	62	12	2	2	0.8	21	25	21	24	1	17	4	302	15	3	21	3.8	.991	1B-44, OF-41
1970		129	.220	.319	332	73	11	2	6	1.8	39	31	21	50	12	32	8	427	35	9	34	4.4	.981	1B-59, OF-49
1971	WAS A	122	.213	.382	207	44	6	4	7	3.4	33	25	19	38	3	40	9	134	2	5	3	1.6	.965	OF-60, 1B-30
1972	CLE A	129	.258	.371	391	101	13	5	7	1.8	43	33	41	47	12	12	2	504	28	3	29	4.4	.994	OF-84, 1B-38
1973	CAL A	99	.265	.326	264	70	7	0	3	1.1	25	24	30	42	3	23	5	268	25	1	28	4.4	.997	OF-34, 1B-25, DH-8
1974	2 teams	CAL A (56G –.286)			CLE A (45G –.304)																			
"	total	101	.294	.442	231	68	16	0	6	2.6	38	34	17	24	2	23	6	448	38	3	39	6.0	.994	1B-67, OF-13, DH-2
1975	CLE A	23	.275	.451	51	14	1	1	2	3.9	7	5	7	7	4	4	2	112	6	1	9	6.3	.992	1B-16, OF-3
13 yrs.		1468	.246	.362	3956	972	150	42	75	1.9	484	404	332	544	143	208	47	7196	532	81	554	5.8	.990	1B-911, OF-431, DH-10

Rodney McCray

McCRAY, RODNEY DUNCAN BR TR 5′10″ 175 lbs.
B. Sept. 13, 1963, Detroit, Mich.

Year	Team	Games	BA	SA	AB	H	2B	3B	HR	HR%	R	RBI	BB	SO	SB	Pinch Hit AB	Pinch Hit H	PO	A	E	DP	TC/G	FA	G by Pos
1990	CHI A	32	.000	.000	6	0	0	0	0	0.0	8	0	1	4	6	2	0	8	0	0	0	0.4	1.000	OF-13, DH-7
1991		17	.286	.286	7	2	0	0	0	0.0	2	0	0	2	1	0	0	10	0	0	0	0.7	1.000	OF-8, DH-6
1992	NY N	18	1.000	1.000	1	1	0	0	0	0.0	3	1	0	0	2	0	0	6	0	0	0	0.5	1.000	OF-13
3 yrs.		67	.214	.214	14	3	0	0	0	0.0	13	1	1	6	9	2	0	24	0	0	0	0.5	1.000	OF-34, DH-13

Frank McCrea

McCREA, FRANCIS WILLIAM BR TR 5′9″ 155 lbs.
B. Sept. 6, 1896, Jersey City, N. J. D. Feb. 25, 1981, Dover, N. J.

Year	Team	Games	BA	SA	AB	H	2B	3B	HR	HR%	R	RBI	BB	SO	SB	Pinch Hit AB	Pinch Hit H	PO	A	E	DP	TC/G	FA	G by Pos
1925	CLE A	1	.200	.200	5	1	0	0	0	0.0	1	0	0	0	0	0	0	4	0	0	0	4.0	1.000	C-1

Walt McCreedie

McCREEDIE, WALTER HENRY BL TR 6′2″ 195 lbs.
B. Nov. 29, 1876, Manchester, Iowa D. July 29, 1934, Portland, Ore.

Year	Team	Games	BA	SA	AB	H	2B	3B	HR	HR%	R	RBI	BB	SO	SB	Pinch Hit AB	Pinch Hit H	PO	A	E	DP	TC/G	FA	G by Pos
1903	BKN N	56	.324	.347	213	69	5	0	0	0.0	40	20	24		10	0	0	68	6	6	3	1.4	.925	OF-56

Tom McCreery

McCREERY, THOMAS LIVINGSTON BB TR 5′11″ 180 lbs.
B. Oct. 19, 1874, Beaver, Pa. D. July 3, 1941, Beaver, Pa.

Year	Team	Games	BA	SA	AB	H	2B	3B	HR	HR%	R	RBI	BB	SO	SB	Pinch Hit AB	Pinch Hit H	PO	A	E	DP	TC/G	FA	G by Pos
1895	LOU N	31	.324	.370	108	35	3	1	0	0.0	18	10	8	15	3	0	0	31	23	10	4	2.0	.844	OF-18, P-8, SS-4, 3B-1, 1B-1
1896		115	.351	.546	441	155	23	**21**	7	1.6	87	65	42	**58**	26	2	1	180	22	18	5	1.9	.918	OF-111, 2B-1, P-1
1897	2 teams	LOU N (89G –.284)			NY N (49G –.299)																			
"	total	138	.289	.386	515	149	13	11	5	1.0	91	68	60		28	2	0	186	32	33	4	1.8	.869	OF-134, 2B-3
1898	2 teams	NY N (35G –.198)			PIT N (53G –.311)																			
"	total	88	.267	.389	311	83	9	10	3	1.0	48	37	45		6	2	1	144	10	17	1	2.0	.901	OF-86
1899	PIT N	118	.323	.422	455	147	21	9	2	0.4	76	64	47		11	5	2	234	55	34	5	2.9	.895	OF-97, SS-9, 2B-7
1900		43	.220	.318	132	29	4	3	1	0.8	20	13	16		2	5	0	62	10	9	2	2.3	.889	OF-35, P-1
1901	BKN N	91	.290	.433	335	97	11	14	3	0.9	47	53	32		13	3	1	217	15	14	6	2.8	.943	OF-82, 1B-4, SS-2
1902		112	.244	.309	430	105	8	4	4	0.9	49	57	29		16	0	0	1036	60	23	54	10.0	.979	1B-108, OF-4
1903	2 teams	BKN N (40G –.262)			BOS N (23G –.217)																			
"	total	63	.246	.317	224	55	7	3	1	0.4	28	20	29		11	2	2	106	6	13	3	2.0	.896	OF-61
9 yrs.		799	.290	.401	2951	855	99	76	26	0.9	464	387	308	73	116	21	7	2196	233	171	84	3.3	.934	OF-628, 1B-113, SS-15, 2B-11, P-10, 3B-1

Frank McCue

McCUE, FRANK ALOYSIUS BB TR 5′9″ 150 lbs.
B. Oct. 4, 1898, Chicago, Ill. D. July 5, 1953, Evergreen Park, Ill.

Year	Team	Games	BA	SA	AB	H	2B	3B	HR	HR%	R	RBI	BB	SO	SB	Pinch Hit AB	Pinch Hit H	PO	A	E	DP	TC/G	FA	G by Pos
1922	PHI A	2	.000	.000	5	0	0	0	0	0.0	0	0	0	0	0	0	0	0	0	0	0	0.0	.000	3B-2

Clyde McCullough

McCULLOUGH, CLYDE EDWARD BR TR 5′11½″ 180 lbs.
B. Mar. 4, 1917, Nashville, Tenn. D. Sept. 18, 1982, San Francisco, Calif.

Year	Team	Games	BA	SA	AB	H	2B	3B	HR	HR%	R	RBI	BB	SO	SB	Pinch Hit AB	Pinch Hit H	PO	A	E	DP	TC/G	FA	G by Pos
1940	CHI N	9	.154	.192	26	4	1	0	0	0.0	4	1	5	5	0	2	0	44	4	0	1	6.9	1.000	C-7
1941		125	.227	.323	418	95	9	2	9	2.2	41	53	34	67	5	5	1	481	64	10	6	4.7	.982	C-119
1942		109	.282	.398	337	95	22	1	5	1.5	39	31	25	47	7	8	2	386	61	9	10	4.7	.980	C-97
1943		87	.237	.293	266	63	5	2	2	0.8	20	23	24	33	6	4	0	271	25	7	2	3.7	.977	C-81
1946		95	.287	.417	307	88	18	5	4	1.3	38	34	22	39	2	5	0	390	40	4	4	4.9	.991	C-89
1947		86	.252	.376	234	59	12	4	3	1.3	25	30	20	20	1	17	3	280	35	5	3	5.0	.984	C-64
1948		69	.209	.273	172	36	4	2	1	0.6	10	7	15	25	0	15	2	225	25	7	5	5.0	.973	C-51
1949	PIT N	91	.237	.349	241	57	9	3	4	1.7	30	21	24	30	1	0	0	363	39	6	8	4.5	.985	C-90
1950		103	.254	.405	279	71	16	4	6	2.2	28	34	31	35	3	2	0	362	45	6	3	4.1	.985	C-100
1951		92	.297	.440	259	77	9	2	8	3.1	26	39	27	31	2	7	4	364	52	5	10	4.9	.988	C-86
1952		66	.233	.291	172	40	5	1	1	0.6	10	15	10	18	0	5	1	227	38	5	4	4.4	.981	C-61, 1B-1
1953	CHI N	77	.258	.367	229	59	3	2	6	2.6	21	23	15	23	0	4	1	273	31	4	7	4.2	.987	C-73
1954		31	.259	.457	81	21	7	0	3	3.7	9	17	5	5	0	2	0	105	7	2	4	3.9	.982	C-26, 3B-3
1955		44	.198	.198	81	16	0	0	0	0.0	7	10	8	15	0	7	3	160	12	2	0	4.7	.989	C-37
1956		14	.211	.263	19	4	1	0	0	0.0	0	1	0	5	0	7	1	24	3	0	0	3.9	1.000	C-7
15 yrs.		1098	.252	.358	3121	785	121	28	52	1.7	308	339	265	398	27	90	18	3955	481	72	67	4.5	.984	C-988, 3B-3, 1B-1
WORLD SERIES																								
1945	CHI N	1	.000	.000	1	0	0	0	0	0.0	0	0	0	0	0	1	0	0	0	0	0	0.0	—	

Harry McCurdy

McCURDY, HARRY HENRY BL TR 5′11″ 187 lbs.
B. Sept. 15, 1899, Stevens Point, Wis. D. July 21, 1972, Houston, Tex.

Year	Team	Games	BA	SA	AB	H	2B	3B	HR	HR%	R	RBI	BB	SO	SB	Pinch Hit AB	Pinch Hit H	PO	A	E	DP	TC/G	FA	G by Pos
1922	STL N	13	.296	.519	27	8	2	2	0	0.0	3	5	1	1	0	3	0	24	5	1	2	2.7	.967	C-9, 1B-2
1923		67	.265	.346	185	49	11	2	0	0.0	17	15	11	11	3	9	0	157	30	6	4	3.3	.969	C-58
1926	CHI A	44	.326	.488	86	28	7	2	1	1.2	16	11	6	10	0	11	2	84	13	3	3	3.0	.970	C-25, 1B-8
1927		86	.286	.393	262	75	19	3	1	0.4	34	27	32	24	6	3	0	261	55	9	8	4.0	.972	C-82
1928		49	.262	.417	103	27	10	0	2	1.9	12	13	8	15	1	14	3	95	11	4	2	3.2	.964	C-34
1930	PHI N	80	.331	.419	148	49	6	2	1	0.7	23	25	15	12	0	32	8	97	16	4	1	2.9	.966	C-41
1931		66	.287	.367	150	43	9	0	1	0.7	21	25	23	16	2	17	7	157	27	6	1	4.2	.968	C-45
1932		62	.235	.316	136	32	6	1	1	0.7	13	14	17	13	0	15	2	132	17	4	3	3.6	.974	C-42

Harry McCurdy *continued*

Year	Team		Games	BA	SA	AB	H	2B	3B	HR	HR%	R	RBI	BB	SO	SB	Pinch Hit AB	Pinch Hit H	PO	A	E	DP	TC/G	FA	G by Pos
1933			73	.278	.407	54	15	1	0	2	3.7	9	12	16	6	0	**52**	**15**	0	0	0	0	0.0	.000	C-2
1934	CIN	N	3	.000	.000	6	0	0	0	0	0.0	0	1	0	0	0	2	0	11	2	0	2	4.3	1.000	1B-3
10 yrs.			543	.282	.387	1157	326	71	12	9	0.8	148	148	129	108	12	158	37	1018	176	37	26	3.5	.970	C-338, 1B-13

Terry McDaniel

McDANIEL, TERRENCE KEITH
B. Dec. 6, 1966, Kansas City, Mo.
BB TR 5′ 9″ 195 lbs.

Year	Team		Games	BA	SA	AB	H	2B	3B	HR	HR%	R	RBI	BB	SO	SB	Pinch Hit AB	Pinch Hit H	PO	A	E	DP	TC/G	FA	G by Pos
1991	NY	N	23	.207	.241	29	6	1	0	0	0.0	3	2	1	11	2	5	1	18	0	0	0	1.3	1.000	OF-14

Ray McDavid

McDAVID, RAY DARNELL
B. July 20, 1971, San Diego, Calif.
BL TR 6′ 3″ 190 lbs.

Year	Team		Games	BA	SA	AB	H	2B	3B	HR	HR%	R	RBI	BB	SO	SB	Pinch Hit AB	Pinch Hit H	PO	A	E	DP	TC/G	FA	G by Pos
1994	SD	N	9	.250	.286	28	7	1	0	0	0.0	2	2	1	8	1	2	1	11	0	0	0	1.6	1.000	OF-7
1995			11	.176	.176	17	3	0	0	0	0.0	2	0	2	6	1	3	1	5	0	0	0	0.7	1.000	OF-7
2 yrs.			20	.222	.244	45	10	1	0	0	0.0	4	2	3	14	2	5	2	16	0	0	0	1.1	1.000	OF-14

Mickey McDermott

McDERMOTT, MAURICE JOSEPH
B. Aug. 29, 1928, Poughkeepsie, N. Y.
BL TL 6′ 2″ 170 lbs.

Year	Team		Games	BA	SA	AB	H	2B	3B	HR	HR%	R	RBI	BB	SO	SB	Pinch Hit AB	Pinch Hit H	PO	A	E	DP	TC/G	FA	G by Pos
1948	BOS	A	7	.375	.500	8	3	1	0	0	0.0	2	0	0	0	0	0	0	1	8	0	0	1.3	1.000	P-7
1949			13	.212	.303	33	7	3	0	0	0.0	3	6	3	6	0	0	0	2	14	1	0	1.4	.941	P-12
1950			39	.364	.477	44	16	5	0	0	0.0	11	12	9	3	0	0	0	5	25	2	1	0.8	.938	P-38
1951			43	.273	.364	66	18	1	1	1	1.5	8	6	3	14	0	3	0	4	34	2	5	1.2	.950	P-34
1952			36	.226	.323	62	14	1	1	1	1.6	10	7	4	11	0	1	0	10	24	2	1	1.2	.944	P-30
1953			45	.301	.419	93	28	8	0	1	1.1	9	13	2	13	0	12	1	5	40	2	3	1.5	.957	P-32
1954	WAS	A	54	.200	.232	95	19	3	0	0	0.0	7	4	7	12	0	19	3	3	39	2	2	1.5	.955	P-30
1955			70	.263	.337	95	25	4	0	1	1.1	10	10	6	16	1	38	9	3	30	2	1	1.1	.943	P-31
1956	NY	A	46	.212	.269	52	11	0	0	1	1.9	4	4	8	13	0	19	4	2	13	0	2	0.7	1.000	P-23
1957	KC	A	58	.245	.510	49	12	1	0	4	8.2	6	7	9	16	0	24	5	12	17	2	0	1.0	.935	P-29, 1B-2
1958	DET	A	4	.333	.333	3	1	0	0	0	0.0	0	1	0	2	0	2	1	0	0	0	0	0.0	.000	P-2
1961	2 teams		STL N (22G –.071)		KC A (7G –.200)																				
″	total		29	.105	.211	19	2	2	0	0	0.0	1	4	1	6	0	9	2	2	3	1	0	0.3	.833	P-23
12 yrs.			444	.252	.349	619	156	29	2	9	1.5	71	74	52	112	1	127	25	49	247	16	15	1.1	.949	P-291, 1B-2
WORLD SERIES																									
1956	NY	A	1	1.000	1.000	1	1	0	0	0	0.0	0	0	0	0	0	0	0	0	0	0	0	0.0	.000	P-1

Red McDermott

McDERMOTT, FRANK A.
B. Nov. 12, 1889, Philadelphia, Pa. D. Sept. 11, 1964, Philadelphia, Pa.
BR TR 5′ 6″ 150 lbs.

Year	Team		Games	BA	SA	AB	H	2B	3B	HR	HR%	R	RBI	BB	SO	SB	Pinch Hit AB	Pinch Hit H	PO	A	E	DP	TC/G	FA	G by Pos
1912	DET	A	5	.267	.333	15	4	1	0	0	0.0	2	0	0		1	0	0	7	1	0	0	1.6	1.000	OF-5

Terry McDermott

McDERMOTT, TERRENCE MICHAEL
B. Mar. 20, 1951, Rockville Centre, N. Y.
BR TR 6′ 3″ 205 lbs.

Year	Team		Games	BA	SA	AB	H	2B	3B	HR	HR%	R	RBI	BB	SO	SB	Pinch Hit AB	Pinch Hit H	PO	A	E	DP	TC/G	FA	G by Pos
1972	LA	N	9	.130	.130	23	3	0	0	0	0.0	2	0	2	8	0	3	1	46	2	0	4	6.9	1.000	1B-7

Tom McDermott

McDERMOTT, THOMAS NATHANIEL
B. Mar. 15, 1856, Zanesville, Ohio D. Nov. 23, 1922, Mansfield, Ohio.

Year	Team		Games	BA	SA	AB	H	2B	3B	HR	HR%	R	RBI	BB	SO	SB	Pinch Hit AB	Pinch Hit H	PO	A	E	DP	TC/G	FA	G by Pos
1885	BAL	AA	1	—	—	0	0	0	0	0	—	0		0			0	0	0	0	0	0	0.0	.000	2B-1

Dave McDonald

McDONALD, DAVID BRUCE
B. May 20, 1943, New Albany, Ind.
BL TR 6′ 3″ 215 lbs.

Year	Team		Games	BA	SA	AB	H	2B	3B	HR	HR%	R	RBI	BB	SO	SB	Pinch Hit AB	Pinch Hit H	PO	A	E	DP	TC/G	FA	G by Pos
1969	NY	A	9	.217	.261	23	5	1	0	0	0.0	0	2	2	5	0	3	0	45	3	2	2	7.1	.960	1B-7
1971	MON	N	24	.103	.231	39	4	2	0	1	2.6	3	4	4	14	0	17	1	53	4	1	9	6.4	.983	1B-8, OF-1
2 yrs.			33	.145	.242	62	9	3	0	1	1.6	3	6	6	19	0	20	1	98	7	3	11	6.8	.972	1B-15, OF-1

Ed McDonald

McDONALD, EDWARD C.
B. Oct. 28, 1886, Albany, N. Y. D. Mar. 11, 1946, Albany, N. Y.
BR TR 6′ 180 lbs.

Year	Team		Games	BA	SA	AB	H	2B	3B	HR	HR%	R	RBI	BB	SO	SB	Pinch Hit AB	Pinch Hit H	PO	A	E	DP	TC/G	FA	G by Pos
1911	BOS	N	54	.206	.297	175	36	7	3	1	0.6	28	21	40	39	11	0	0	65	86	7	10	2.9	.956	3B-53, SS-1
1912			121	.259	.349	459	119	23	6	2	0.4	70	34	70	**91**	22	3	1	147	216	23	18	3.3	.940	3B-118
1913	CHI	N	1	—	—	0	0	0	0	0	—	0	0	0	0	0	0	0	0	0	0	0	0.0	—	
3 yrs.			176	.244	.334	634	155	30	9	3	0.5	98	55	110	130	33	3	1	212	302	30	28	3.2	.945	3B-171, SS-1

Jim McDonald

McDONALD, JAMES
B. Philadelphia, Pa. Deceased.
BR TR 6′ 180 lbs.

Year	Team		Games	BA	SA	AB	H	2B	3B	HR	HR%	R	RBI	BB	SO	SB	Pinch Hit AB	Pinch Hit H	PO	A	E	DP	TC/G	FA	G by Pos
1902	NY	N	2	.333	.333	9	3	0	0	0	0.0	0	1	0		0	0	0	2	0	0	0	1.0	1.000	OF-2

Jim McDonald

McDONALD, JAMES A.
B. Aug. 6, 1860, San Francisco, Calif. D. Sept. 14, 1914, San Francisco, Calif.

Year	Team		Games	BA	SA	AB	H	2B	3B	HR	HR%	R	RBI	BB	SO	SB	Pinch Hit AB	Pinch Hit H	PO	A	E	DP	TC/G	FA	G by Pos
1884	2 teams		PIT AA (38G –.159)		WAS U (2G –.167)																				
″	total		40	.159	.179	151	24	3	0	0	0.0	11		2			0	0	50	42	24	2	2.9	.793	3B-22, OF-16, C-1, 2B-1
1885	BUF	N	5	.000	.000	14	0	0	0	0	0.0	0	0	0	4		0	0	6	12	2	1	4.0	.900	SS-4, OF-1
2 yrs.			45	.145	.164	165	24	3	0	0	0.0	11	0	2	4		0	0	56	54	26	3	3.0	.809	3B-22, OF-17, SS-4, C-1, 2B-1

Joe McDonald

McDONALD, MALCOLM JOSEPH (Tex)
B. Apr. 9, 1888, Galveston, Tex. D. May 30, 1963, Baytown, Tex.
BR TR 5′11″ 175 lbs.

Year	Team		Games	BA	SA	AB	H	2B	3B	HR	HR%	R	RBI	BB	SO	SB	Pinch Hit AB	Pinch Hit H	PO	A	E	DP	TC/G	FA	G by Pos
1910	STL	A	10	.156	.156	32	5	0	0	0	0.0	4	1	1		0	0	0	10	13	5	2	2.8	.821	3B-10

Tex McDonald

McDONALD, CHARLES C.
Born Charles C. Crabtree.
B. Jan. 31, 1891, Farmersville, Tex. D. Mar. 31, 1943, Houston, Tex.
BL TR 5′10″ 160 lbs.

Year	Team		Games	BA	SA	AB	H	2B	3B	HR	HR%	R	RBI	BB	SO	SB	Pinch Hit AB	Pinch Hit H	PO	A	E	DP	TC/G	FA	G by Pos
1912	CIN	N	61	.257	.357	140	36	3	4	1	0.7	16	15	13	24	5	15	5	84	89	16	7	4.5	.915	SS-42
1913	2 teams		CIN N (11G –.300)		BOS N (62G –.359)																				
″	total		73	.355	.432	155	55	4	4	0	0.0	25	20	15	18	4	26	9	39	76	16	9	3.4	.878	3B-31, 2B-6, OF-1, SS-1

Tex McDonald *continued*

Year	Team	Games	BA	SA	AB	H	2B	3B	HR	HR%	R	RBI	BB	SO	SB	Pinch Hit AB	Pinch Hit H	PO	A	E	DP	TC/G	FA	G by Pos
1914	2 teams PIT F (67G –.318) BUF F (69G –.296)																							
″	total	136	.307	.461	473	145	29	13	6	1.3	59	61	33		20	8	1	201	126	22	15	2.6	.937	OF-90, 2B-37, SS-5
1915	BUF F	87	.271	.426	251	68	9	6	6	2.4	31	39	27		5	20	7	93	4	8	1	1.6	.924	OF-65
4 yrs.		357	.298	.434	1019	304	45	27	13	1.3	131	135	88	42	34	69	22	417	295	62	32	2.8	.920	OF-156, SS-48, 2B-43, 3B-31

Jim McDonnell

McDONNELL, JAMES WILLIAM (Mack) BL TR 5′11″ 165 lbs.
B. Aug. 15, 1922, Gagetown, Mich.

Year	Team	Games	BA	SA	AB	H	2B	3B	HR	HR%	R	RBI	BB	SO	SB	Pinch Hit AB	Pinch Hit H	PO	A	E	DP	TC/G	FA	G by Pos
1943	CLE A	2	.000	.000	1	0	0	0	0	0.0	1	0	2	1	0	0	0	1	0	0	0	1.0	1.000	C-1
1944		20	.233	.233	43	10	0	0	0	0.0	5	4	4	3	0	7	0	40	5	5	1	3.8	.900	C-13
1945		28	.196	.235	51	10	2	0	0	0.0	3	8	2	4	0	5	0	85	12	2	4	4.3	.980	C-23
3 yrs.		50	.211	.232	95	20	2	0	0	0.0	9	12	8	8	0	12	0	126	17	7	5	4.1	.953	C-37

Ed McDonough

McDONOUGH, EDWARD SEBASTIAN BR TR 6′ 160 lbs.
B. Sept. 11, 1886, Elgin, Ill. D. Sept. 2, 1926, Elgin, Ill.

Year	Team	Games	BA	SA	AB	H	2B	3B	HR	HR%	R	RBI	BB	SO	SB	Pinch Hit AB	Pinch Hit H	PO	A	E	DP	TC/G	FA	G by Pos
1909	PHI N	1	.000	.000	1	0	0	0	0	0.0	0	0	0		0	0	0	1	1	0	0	2.0	1.000	C-1
1910		5	.111	.111	9	1	0	0	0	0.0	1	0	0	1	0	1	0	11	1	0	0	3.0	1.000	C-4
2 yrs.		6	.100	.100	10	1	0	0	0	0.0	1	0	0	1	0	1	0	12	2	0	0	2.8	1.000	C-5

Gil McDougald

McDOUGALD, GILBERT JAMES BR TR 6′ 175 lbs.
B. May 19, 1928, San Francisco, Calif.

Year	Team	Games	BA	SA	AB	H	2B	3B	HR	HR%	R	RBI	BB	SO	SB	Pinch Hit AB	Pinch Hit H	PO	A	E	DP	TC/G	FA	G by Pos
1951	NY A	131	.306	.488	402	123	23	4	14	3.5	72	63	56	54	14	4	0	174	249	14	46	3.2	.968	3B-82, 2B-55
1952		152	.263	.369	555	146	16	5	11	2.0	65	78	57	73	6	1	0	233	372	18	69	4.0	.971	3B-117, 2B-38
1953		141	.285	.416	541	154	27	7	10	1.8	82	83	60	65	3	1	0	170	332	23	45	3.2	.956	3B-136, 2B-26
1954		126	.259	.416	394	102	22	2	12	3.0	66	48	62	64	3	4	0	240	286	8	88	4.2	.985	2B-92, 3B-35
1955		141	.285	.407	533	152	10	8	13	2.4	79	53	65	77	6	0	0	367	382	13	123	5.3	.983	2B-126, 3B-17
1956		120	.311	.443	438	136	13	3	13	3.0	79	56	68	59	3	2	0	239	363	17	109	4.8	.973	SS-92, 2B-31, 3B-5
1957		141	.289	.442	539	156	25	**9**	13	2.4	87	62	59	71	2	1	0	313	451	17	123	5.2	.978	SS-121, 2B-21, 3B-7
1958		138	.250	.376	503	126	19	1	14	2.8	69	65	59	75	6	6	1	299	357	16	111	5.0	.976	2B-115, SS-19
1959		127	.251	.353	434	109	16	8	4	0.9	44	34	35	40	0	2	0	190	345	10	70	4.2	.982	2B-53, SS-52, 3B-25
1960		119	.258	.401	337	87	16	4	8	2.4	54	34	38	45	2	20	9	127	236	13	31	3.0	.965	3B-84, 2B-42
10 yrs.		1336	.276	.410	4676	1291	187	51	112	2.4	697	576	559	623	45	41	10	2352	3373	149	815	4.2	.975	2B-599, 3B-508, SS-284
WORLD SERIES																								
1951	NY A	6	.261	.435	23	6	1	0	1	4.3	2	7	2	2	0	0	0	10	14	1	4	2.8	.960	3B-5, 2B-4
1952		7	.200	.320	25	5	0	0	1	4.0	5	3	5	2	1	0	0	4	15	4	2	3.3	.826	3B-7
1953		6	.167	.500	24	4	0	1	2	8.3	2	4	1	3	0	0	0	5	14	0	0	3.2	1.000	3B-6
1955		7	.259	.370	27	7	0	0	1	3.7	2	1	2	6	0	0	0	6	13	1	1	2.9	.950	3B-7
1956		7	.143	.143	21	3	0	0	0	0.0	0	1	3	6	0	0	0	16	16	0	4	4.6	1.000	SS-7
1957		7	.250	.250	24	6	0	0	0	0.0	3	2	3	3	1	0	0	13	24	1	5	5.4	.974	SS-7
1958		7	.321	.607	28	9	2	0	2	7.1	5	4	2	4	0	0	0	18	23	0	3	5.9	1.000	2B-7
1960		6	.278	.333	18	5	1	0	0	0.0	4	2	2	3	0	0	0	5	7	1	0	2.2	.923	3B-6
8 yrs.		53	.237	.379	190	45	4	1	7	3.7	23	24	20	29	2	0	0	77	126	8	19	3.8	.962	3B-31, SS-14, 2B-11
		4th			**5th**	**7th**			**10th**		**8th**	**8th**	**9th**	**5th**										

Oddibe McDowell

McDOWELL, ODDIBE, JR. BL TL 5′ 9″ 165 lbs.
B. Aug. 25, 1962, Hollywood, Fla.

Year	Team	Games	BA	SA	AB	H	2B	3B	HR	HR%	R	RBI	BB	SO	SB	Pinch Hit AB	Pinch Hit H	PO	A	E	DP	TC/G	FA	G by Pos
1985	TEX A	111	.239	.431	406	97	14	5	18	4.4	63	42	36	85	25	8	2	282	9	2	2	2.7	.993	OF-103, DH-4
1986		154	.266	.427	572	152	24	7	18	3.1	105	49	65	112	33	8	2	325	13	3	3	2.3	.991	OF-148, DH-1
1987		128	.241	.428	407	98	26	4	14	3.4	65	52	51	99	24	11	1	263	5	3	1	2.2	.989	OF-125
1988		120	.247	.355	437	108	19	5	6	1.4	55	37	41	89	33	9	2	267	2	3	1	2.3	.989	OF-113, DH-3
1989	2 teams CLE A (69G –.222) ATL N (76G –.304)																							
″	total	145	.266	.391	519	138	23	6	10	1.9	89	46	52	73	27	9	3	303	7	5	1	2.4	.984	OF-132, DH-2
1990	ATL N	113	.243	.357	305	74	14	0	7	2.3	47	25	21	53	13	34	7	134	2	4	0	1.9	.971	OF-72
1994	TEX A	59	.262	.317	183	48	5	1	1	0.5	34	15	28	39	14	5	0	113	2	2	0	2.1	.983	OF-53, DH-2
7 yrs.		830	.253	.395	2829	715	125	28	74	2.6	458	266	294	550	169	84	17	1687	40	22	8	2.3	.987	OF-746, DH-12

Pryor McElveen

McELVEEN, PRYOR MYNATT (Humpy) BR TR 5′10″ 168 lbs.
B. Nov. 5, 1881, Atlanta, Ga. D. Oct. 27, 1951, Pleasant Hill, Tenn.

Year	Team	Games	BA	SA	AB	H	2B	3B	HR	HR%	R	RBI	BB	SO	SB	Pinch Hit AB	Pinch Hit H	PO	A	E	DP	TC/G	FA	G by Pos
1909	BKN N	81	.198	.271	258	51	8	1	3	1.2	22	25	14		6	13	4	147	107	14	11	3.9	.948	3B-37, SS-11, OF-10, 2B-5, 1B-5
1910		74	.225	.305	213	48	8	3	1	0.5	19	26	22	47	6	9	3	89	105	12	14	3.2	.942	3B-54, SS-6, 2B-3, C-1
1911		16	.194	.194	31	6	0	0	0	0.0	1	5	0	3	0	10	3	16	10	2	4	4.7	.929	2B-5, SS-1
3 yrs.		171	.209	.281	502	105	16	4	4	0.8	42	56	36	50	12	32	10	252	222	28	29	3.6	.944	3B-91, SS-18, 2B-13, OF-10, 1B-5, C-1

Lee McElwee

McELWEE, LELAND STANFORD (Mac) BR TR 5′10½″ 160 lbs.
B. May 23, 1894, La Mesa, Calif. D. Feb. 8, 1957, Union, Me.

Year	Team	Games	BA	SA	AB	H	2B	3B	HR	HR%	R	RBI	BB	SO	SB	Pinch Hit AB	Pinch Hit H	PO	A	E	DP	TC/G	FA	G by Pos
1916	PHI A	54	.265	.284	155	41	3	0	0	0.0	9	10	8	17	0	9	1	57	68	14	7	3.2	.899	3B-30, OF-9, 2B-3, SS-1, 1B-1

Frank McElyea

McELYEA, FRANK BR TR 6′ 6″ 221 lbs.
B. Aug. 4, 1918, White County, Ill. D. Apr. 19, 1987, Evansville, Ind.

Year	Team	Games	BA	SA	AB	H	2B	3B	HR	HR%	R	RBI	BB	SO	SB	Pinch Hit AB	Pinch Hit H	PO	A	E	DP	TC/G	FA	G by Pos
1942	BOS N	7	.000	.000	4	0	0	0	0	0.0	2	0	0	0	0	1	0	2	0	0	0	2.0	1.000	OF-1

Guy McFadden

McFADDEN, GUY G.
B. Sept. 3, 1872, Topeka, Kans. D. Mar. 10, 1911, Topeka, Kans.

Year	Team	Games	BA	SA	AB	H	2B	3B	HR	HR%	R	RBI	BB	SO	SB	Pinch Hit AB	Pinch Hit H	PO	A	E	DP	TC/G	FA	G by Pos
1895	STL N	4	.214	.214	14	3	0	0	0	0.0	1	2	0	2	0	0	0	30	0	1	3	7.8	.968	1B-4

Leon McFadden

McFADDEN, LEON BR TR 6′ 2″ 195 lbs.
B. Apr. 26, 1944, Little Rock, Ark.

Year	Team	Games	BA	SA	AB	H	2B	3B	HR	HR%	R	RBI	BB	SO	SB	Pinch Hit AB	Pinch Hit H	PO	A	E	DP	TC/G	FA	G by Pos
1968	HOU N	16	.277	.298	47	13	1	0	0	0.0	2	1	6	10	1	1	1	16	44	2	3	3.9	.968	SS-16
1969		44	.176	.203	74	13	2	0	0	0.0	3	3	4	9	1	11	1	25	17	2	0	1.8	.955	OF-17, SS-8
1970		2	—	—	0	0	0	0	0	—	0	0	0	0	0	0	0	0	0	0	0	0.0	—	
3 yrs.		62	.215	.240	121	26	3	0	0	0.0	5	4	10	19	2	12	2	41	61	4	3	2.6	.962	SS-24, OF-17

Alex McFarlan

McFARLAN, ALEXANDER SHEPERD
Brother of Dan McFarlan.
B. Oct. 11, 1869, St. Louis, Mo. D. Mar. 2, 1939, Pewee Valley, Ky.

Year	Team	Games	BA	SA	AB	H	2B	3B	HR	HR%	R	RBI	BB	SO	SB	Pinch Hit AB	Pinch Hit H	PO	A	E	DP	TC/G	FA	G by Pos
1892	LOU N	14	.167	.167	42	7	0	0	0	0.0	2	1	8	11	1	0	0	21	6	7	1	2.4	.794	OF-12, 2B-2

Chris McFarland

McFARLAND, CHRISTOPHER 5′ 9″ 170 lbs.
B. Aug. 17, 1861, Fall River, Mass. D. May 24, 1918, New Bedford, Mass.

Year	Team	Games	BA	SA	AB	H	2B	3B	HR	HR%	R	RBI	BB	SO	SB	Pinch Hit AB	Pinch Hit H	PO	A	E	DP	TC/G	FA	G by Pos
1884	BAL U	3	.214	.286	14	3	1	0	0	0.0	2		0			0	0	4	0	3	0	1.8	.571	OF-3, P-1

Ed McFarland

McFARLAND, EDWARD WILLIAM BR TR 5′10″ 180 lbs.
B. Aug. 3, 1874, Cleveland, Ohio D. Nov. 28, 1959, Cleveland, Ohio.

Year	Team	Games	BA	SA	AB	H	2B	3B	HR	HR%	R	RBI	BB	SO	SB	Pinch Hit AB	Pinch Hit H	PO	A	E	DP	TC/G	FA	G by Pos
1893	CLE N	8	.409	.591	22	9	2	1	0	0.0	5	6	1	2	0	0	0	4	4	1	0	1.1	.889	OF-5, 3B-2, C-1
1896	STL N	83	.241	.345	290	70	13	4	3	1.0	48	36	15	17	7	1	0	276	117	16	6	5.0	.961	C-80, OF-2
1897	2 teams	STL N (31G –.327) PHI N (38G –.223)																						
″	total	69	.270	.388	237	64	8	7	2	0.8	32	33	22		4	2	0	228	77	18	4	4.8	.944	C-60, OF-3, 1B-3, 2B-1
1898	PHI N	121	.282	.375	429	121	21	5	3	0.7	65	71	44		4	0	0	420	136	23	7	4.8	.960	C-121
1899		96	.333	.472	324	108	22	10	1	0.3	59	57	36		9	2	0	305	125	14	14	4.7	.968	C-94
1900		94	.305	.392	344	105	14	8	0	0.0	50	38	29		9	1	0	280	137	16	9	4.6	.963	C-93, 3B-1
1901		74	.285	.356	295	84	14	2	1	0.3	33	32	18		11	0	0	316	102	13	2	5.8	.970	C-74
1902	CHI A	73	.230	.295	244	56	9	2	1	0.4	29	25	19		8	2	0	291	71	12	7	5.3	.968	C-69, 1B-1
1903		61	.209	.279	201	42	7	2	1	0.5	15	19	14		3	4	1	244	65	10	7	5.6	.969	C-56, 1B-1
1904		50	.275	.381	160	44	11	3	0	0.0	22	20	17		2	1	1	195	39	6	2	4.9	.975	C-49
1905		80	.280	.364	250	70	13	4	0	0.0	24	31	23		5	9	4	343	88	12	8	6.3	.973	C-70
1906		7	.136	.182	22	3	1	0	0	0.0	0	3	3		0	3	1	32	4	1	0	12.3	.973	C-3
1907		52	.283	.362	138	39	9	1	0	0.0	11	8	12		3	7	2	192	47	7	4	5.7	.972	C-43
1908	BOS A	19	.208	.292	48	10	2	1	0	0.0	5	4	1		0	6	2	63	24	2	3	6.8	.978	C-13
14 yrs.		887	.275	.369	3004	825	146	50	12	0.4	398	383	254	19	65	38	11	3189	1036	151	73	5.2	.965	C-826, OF-10, 1B-5, 3B-3, 2B-1
WORLD SERIES																								
1906	CHI A	1	.000	.000	1	0	0	0	0	0.0	0	0	0	0	0	1	0	0	0	0	0	0.0	—	

Herm McFarland

McFARLAND, HERMAS WALTER BL TR 5′ 6″ 150 lbs.
B. Mar. 11, 1870, Des Moines, Iowa D. Sept. 21, 1935, Richmond, Va.

Year	Team	Games	BA	SA	AB	H	2B	3B	HR	HR%	R	RBI	BB	SO	SB	Pinch Hit AB	Pinch Hit H	PO	A	E	DP	TC/G	FA	G by Pos
1896	LOU N	30	.191	.273	110	21	4	1	1	0.9	11	12	9	14	4	1	0	54	6	15	3	2.6	.800	OF-28, C-1
1898	CIN N	19	.281	.391	64	18	1	3	0	0.0	10	11	7		3	1	0	29	1	1	0	1.8	.968	OF-17
1901	CHI A	132	.275	.383	473	130	21	9	4	0.8	83	59	75		33	0	0	283	14	17	3	2.4	.946	OF-132
1902	2 teams	CHI A (9G –.172) BAL A (61G –.322)																						
″	total	70	.306	.454	271	83	19	6	3	1.1	59	40	38		11	2	0	165	12	6	1	2.7	.967	OF-68
1903	NY A	103	.243	.378	362	88	16	9	5	1.4	41	45	46		13	0	0	207	9	14	2	2.2	.939	OF-103
5 yrs.		354	.266	.387	1280	340	61	28	13	1.0	204	167	175	14	64	4	0	738	42	53	9	2.4	.936	OF-348, C-1

Howie McFarland

McFARLAND, HOWARD ALEXANDER BR TR 6′ 175 lbs.
B. Mar. 7, 1911, El Reno, Okla.

Year	Team	Games	BA	SA	AB	H	2B	3B	HR	HR%	R	RBI	BB	SO	SB	Pinch Hit AB	Pinch Hit H	PO	A	E	DP	TC/G	FA	G by Pos
1945	WAS A	6	.091	.091	11	1	0	0	0	0.0	0	2	0	3	0	3	0	2	1	0	0	1.0	1.000	OF-3

Orlando McFarlane

McFARLANE, ORLANDO DeJESUS BR TR 6′ 180 lbs.
Born Orlando DeJesus McFarlane (Quesada).
B. June 28, 1938, Oriente, Cuba.

Year	Team	Games	BA	SA	AB	H	2B	3B	HR	HR%	R	RBI	BB	SO	SB	Pinch Hit AB	Pinch Hit H	PO	A	E	DP	TC/G	FA	G by Pos
1962	PIT N	8	.087	.087	23	2	0	0	0	0.0	0	1	1	4	0	0	0	44	5	0	1	6.1	1.000	C-8
1964		37	.244	.308	78	19	5	0	0	0.0	5	1	4	27	0	3	1	106	12	2	2	3.3	.983	C-35, OF-1
1966	DET A	49	.254	.413	138	35	7	0	5	3.6	16	13	9	46	0	15	2	205	21	2	2	6.9	.991	C-33
1967	CAL A	12	.227	.227	22	5	0	0	0	0.0	0	3	1	7	0	5	1	28	1	2	0	5.2	.935	C-6
1968		18	.290	.290	31	9	0	0	0	0.0	1	2	5	9	0	10	3	36	6	1	1	4.8	.977	C-9
5 yrs.		124	.240	.332	292	70	12	0	5	1.7	22	20	20	93	0	33	7	419	45	7	6	5.1	.985	C-91, OF-1

Patsy McGaffigan

McGAFFIGAN, MARK ANDREW BR TR 5′ 8″ 140 lbs.
B. Sept. 12, 1888, Carlyle, Ill. D. Dec. 22, 1940, Carlyle, Ill.

Year	Team	Games	BA	SA	AB	H	2B	3B	HR	HR%	R	RBI	BB	SO	SB	Pinch Hit AB	Pinch Hit H	PO	A	E	DP	TC/G	FA	G by Pos
1917	PHI N	19	.167	.183	60	10	1	0	0	0.0	5	6	0	7	1	0	0	32	49	7	5	4.9	.920	SS-17, OF-1
1918		54	.203	.255	192	39	3	2	1	0.5	17	8	16	23	3	0	0	100	158	14	19	5.0	.949	2B-53, SS-1
2 yrs.		73	.194	.238	252	49	4	2	1	0.4	22	14	16	30	4	0	0	132	207	21	24	5.0	.942	2B-53, SS-18, OF-1

Ed McGah

McGAH, EDWARD JOSEPH BR TR 6′ 183 lbs.
B. Sept. 30, 1921, Oakland, Calif.

Year	Team	Games	BA	SA	AB	H	2B	3B	HR	HR%	R	RBI	BB	SO	SB	Pinch Hit AB	Pinch Hit H	PO	A	E	DP	TC/G	FA	G by Pos
1946	BOS A	15	.216	.297	37	8	1	1	0	0.0	2	1	7	7	0	1	0	47	5	1	0	3.8	.981	C-14
1947		9	.000	.000	14	0	0	0	0	0.0	1	2	3	0	0	1	0	24	3	1	1	4.0	.964	C-7
2 yrs.		24	.157	.216	51	8	1	1	0	0.0	3	3	10	7	0	2	0	71	8	2	1	3.9	.975	C-21

Ambrose McGann

McGANN, AMROSE 170 lbs.
B. 1875 Deceased.

Year	Team	Games	BA	SA	AB	H	2B	3B	HR	HR%	R	RBI	BB	SO	SB	Pinch Hit AB	Pinch Hit H	PO	A	E	DP	TC/G	FA	G by Pos
1895	LOU N	20	.288	.411	73	21	5	2	0	0.0	9	9	8	6	6	1	0	35	39	12	1	4.5	.860	SS-8, 3B-6, OF-5

Dan McGann

McGANN, DENNIS LAWRENCE (Cap) BB TR 6′ 190 lbs.
B. July 15, 1871, Shelbyville, Ky. D. Dec. 13, 1910, Louisville, Ky.

Year	Team	Games	BA	SA	AB	H	2B	3B	HR	HR%	R	RBI	BB	SO	SB	Pinch Hit AB	Pinch Hit H	PO	A	E	DP	TC/G	FA	G by Pos
1896	BOS N	43	.322	.474	171	55	6	7	2	1.2	25	30	12	10	2	0	0	88	111	21	10	5.1	.905	2B-43
1898	BAL N	145	.301	.393	535	161	18	8	5	0.9	99	106	53		33	0	0	1416	68	26	78	10.4	.983	1B-145
1899	2 teams	BKN N (63G –.243) WAS N (76G –.343)																						
″	total	139	.300	.431	494	148	20	12	7	1.4	114	90	35		27	2	0	1312	67	17	86	10.2	.988	1B-137
1900	STL N	121	.297	.387	444	132	10	9	4	0.9	79	58	32		26	0	0	1215	59	13	41	10.5	.990	1B-121, 2B-1
1901		103	.289	.411	426	123	14	10	6	1.4	73	56	16		17	0	0	1030	50	18	64	10.7	.984	1B-103
1902	2 teams	BAL A (68G –.316) NY N (61G –.300)																						
″	total	129	.308	.403	477	147	15	15	0	0.0	67	63	31		29	0	0	1292	80	22	90	10.8	.984	1B-129
1903	NY N	129	.270	.357	482	130	21	6	3	0.6	75	50	32		36	0	0	1188	64	15	58	9.8	.988	1B-129
1904		141	.286	.387	517	148	22	6	6	1.2	81	71	36		42	0	0	1481	94	15	62	11.3	.991	1B-141
1905		136	.299	.434	491	147	23	14	5	1.0	88	75	55		22	0	0	1350	86	13	59	10.7	.991	1B-136
1906		134	.237	.304	451	107	14	8	0	0.0	62	37	60		30	1	0	1391	83	8	61	11.1	.995	1B-133

Dan McGann *continued*

Year	Team	Games	BA	SA	AB	H	2B	3B	HR	HR%	R	RBI	BB	SO	SB	Pinch Hit AB	Pinch Hit H	PO	A	E	DP	TC/G	FA	G by Pos
1907		81	.298	.363	262	78	9	1	2	0.8	29	36	29		9	0	0	781	55	5	36	10.4	.994	1B-81
1908	BOS N	135	.240	.291	475	114	8	5	2	0.4	52	55	38		9	5	1	1247	117	18	66	10.6	.987	1B-121, 2B-9
12 yrs.		1436	.285	.382	5225	1490	180	101	42	0.8	844	727	429	10	282	8	1	13791	934	191	711	10.4	.987	1B-1376, 2B-53
WORLD SERIES																								
1905	NY N	5	.235	.353	17	4	2	0	0	0.0	1	4	2	7	0	0	0	55	2	1	2	11.6	.983	1B-5

Chippy McGarr

McGARR, JAMES B. BR TR 5′7″ 168 lbs.
B. May 10, 1863, Worcester, Mass. D. June 6, 1904, Worcester, Mass.

Year	Team	Games	BA	SA	AB	H	2B	3B	HR	HR%	R	RBI	BB	SO	SB	Pinch Hit AB	Pinch Hit H	PO	A	E	DP	TC/G	FA	G by Pos
1884	CHI U	19	.157	.186	70	11	2	0	0	0.0	10		0			0	0	35	25	8	2	3.6	.882	2B-13, OF-6
1886	PHI AA	71	.266	.345	267	71	9	3	2	0.7	41		9			0	0	109	231	60	25	5.6	.850	SS-71
1887		137	.295	.366	536	158	23	6	1	0.2	93		23		84	0	0	198	402	86	42	5.0	.875	SS-137
1888	STL AA	34	.235	.242	132	31	1	0	0	0.0	17	13	6		25	0	0	70	102	22	11	5.7	.887	2B-33, SS-1
1889	2 teams	KC AA (25G –.287) BAL AA (3G –.143)																						
″	total	28	.278	.304	115	32	3	0	0	0.0	23	16	7	12	12	0	0	51	47	20	12	4.2	.831	3B-11, OF-6, SS-6, 2B-5
1890	BOS N	121	.236	.296	487	115	12	7	1	0.2	68	51	34	38	39	0	0	160	243	30	15	3.6	.931	3B-115, SS-5, OF-1
1893	CLE N	63	.309	.357	249	77	12	0	0	0.0	38	28	20	15	24	0	0	93	147	31	7	4.3	.886	3B-63
1894		128	.275	.356	523	144	24	6	2	0.4	94	74	28	29	31	0	0	170	242	45	17	3.6	.902	3B-128
1895		112	.265	.322	419	111	14	2	2	0.5	85	59	34	33	19	0	0	137	222	52	14	3.7	.873	3B-108, 2B-4
1896		113	.268	.327	455	122	16	4	1	0.2	68	53	22	30	16	0	0	123	228	29	20	3.3	.924	3B-113, C-1
10 yrs.		826	.268	.329	3253	872	116	28	9	0.3	537	294	183	157	250	0	0	1146	1889	383	165	4.1	.888	3B-538, SS-220, 2B-55, OF-13, C-1

Jim McGarr

McGARR, JAMES VINCENT (Reds) BR TR 5′9½″ 170 lbs.
B. Nov. 9, 1888, Philadelphia, Pa. D. July 21, 1981, Miami, Fla.

Year	Team	Games	BA	SA	AB	H	2B	3B	HR	HR%	R	RBI	BB	SO	SB	Pinch Hit AB	Pinch Hit H	PO	A	E	DP	TC/G	FA	G by Pos
1912	DET A	1	.000	.000	4	0	0	0	0	0.0	0	0	0		0	0	0	1	3	1	0	5.0	.800	2B-1

Dan McGarvey

McGARVEY, DANIEL FRANCIS BR
B. Dec. 2, 1887, Philadelphia, Pa. D. Mar. 7, 1947, Philadelphia, Pa.

Year	Team	Games	BA	SA	AB	H	2B	3B	HR	HR%	R	RBI	BB	SO	SB	Pinch Hit AB	Pinch Hit H	PO	A	E	DP	TC/G	FA	G by Pos
1912	DET A	1	.000	.000	3	0	0	0	0	0.0	0	0	1		0	0	0	1	1	1	0	3.0	.667	OF-1

Jack McGeachy

McGEACHY, JOHN CHARLES BR TR 5′8″ 165 lbs.
B. May 13, 1864, Clinton, Mass. D. Apr. 5, 1930, Cambridge, Mass.

Year	Team	Games	BA	SA	AB	H	2B	3B	HR	HR%	R	RBI	BB	SO	SB	Pinch Hit AB	Pinch Hit H	PO	A	E	DP	TC/G	FA	G by Pos
1886	2 teams	DET N (6G –.333) STL N (59G –.204)																						
″	total	65	.217	.320	253	55	12	4	2	0.8	34	28	1	40		0	0	102	28	22	5	2.3	.855	OF-61, 3B-2, 2B-2
1887	IND N	99	.269	.333	405	109	17	3	1	0.2	49	56	5	16	27	0	0	231	25	33	3	2.9	.886	OF-98, 3B-1, P-1
1888		118	.219	.261	452	99	15	2	0	0.0	45	30	5	21	49	0	0	194	28	16	5	2.0	.933	OF-117, P-1, SS-1
1889		131	.267	.342	532	142	32	1	2	0.4	83	63	9	39	37	0	0	189	36	20	8	1.8	.918	OF-131, P-3
1890	BKN P	104	.244	.323	443	108	24	4	1	0.2	84	65	19	12	21	0	0	206	16	23	1	2.4	.906	OF-104
1891	2 teams	PHI AA (50G –.229) BOS AA (41G –.253)																						
″	total	91	.240	.301	379	91	6	4	3	0.8	50	34	18	20	20	0	0	139	14	14	0	1.8	.916	OF-91
6 yrs.		608	.245	.314	2464	604	106	18	9	0.4	345	276	57	148	154	0	0	1061	147	128	22	2.2	.904	OF-602, P-5, 3B-3, 2B-2, SS-1

Mike McGeary

McGEARY, MICHAEL HENRY BR TR 5′7″ 138 lbs.
B. 1851, Philadelphia, Pa. Deceased.
Manager 1880–81.

Year	Team	Games	BA	SA	AB	H	2B	3B	HR	HR%	R	RBI	BB	SO	SB	Pinch Hit AB	Pinch Hit H	PO	A	E	DP	TC/G	FA	G by Pos
1876	STL N	61	.261	.272	276	72	3	0	0	0.0	48	30	2	1		0	0	146	185	44	17	6.0	.883	2B-56, C-5, OF-1, 3B-1
1877		57	.252	.279	258	65	3	2	0	0.0	35	20	2	6		0	0	164	181	42	12	6.7	.887	2B-39, 3B-19
1879	PRO N	85	.275	.305	374	103	7	2	0	0.0	62	35	5	13		0	0	238	290	67	25	7.0	.887	2B-73, 3B-12
1880	2 teams	PRO N (18G –.136) CLE N (31G –.252)																						
″	total	49	.212	.235	170	36	2	1	0	0.0	19	4	4	9		0	0	57	95	22	6	3.4	.874	3B-46, 2B-2, OF-2, SS-1
1881	CLE N	11	.220	.220	41	9	0	0	0	0.0	1	5	0	6		0	0	8	13	8	1	2.6	.724	3B-11
1882	DET N	34	.143	.188	133	19	4	1	0	0.0	14	2	2	20		0	0	64	120	16	5	5.6	.920	SS-33, 2B-3
6 yrs.		297	.243	.268	1252	304	19	6	0	0.0	179	96	15	55		0	0	677	884	199	66	5.8	.887	2B-173, 3B-89, SS-34, C-5, OF-3

Dan McGee

McGEE, DANIEL ALOYSIUS BR TR 5′8½″ 152 lbs.
B. Sept. 29, 1911, New York, N. Y. D. Dec. 4, 1991, Lakehurst, N. J.

Year	Team	Games	BA	SA	AB	H	2B	3B	HR	HR%	R	RBI	BB	SO	SB	Pinch Hit AB	Pinch Hit H	PO	A	E	DP	TC/G	FA	G by Pos
1934	BOS N	7	.136	.136	22	3	0	0	0	0.0	2	1	3	6	0	0	0	14	25	2	3	5.9	.951	SS-7

Tubby McGee

McGEE, FRANCIS D. BR TR 5′11½″ 175 lbs.
B. Apr. 28, 1899, Columbus, Ohio D. Jan. 30, 1934, Columbus, Ohio.

Year	Team	Games	BA	SA	AB	H	2B	3B	HR	HR%	R	RBI	BB	SO	SB	Pinch Hit AB	Pinch Hit H	PO	A	E	DP	TC/G	FA	G by Pos
1925	WAS A	2	.000	.000	3	0	0	0	0	0.0	0	0	0	1	0	0	0	11	1	0	1	6.0	1.000	1B-2

Willie McGee

McGEE, WILLIE DEAN BB TR 6′1″ 176 lbs.
B. Nov. 2, 1958, San Francisco, Calif.

Year	Team	Games	BA	SA	AB	H	2B	3B	HR	HR%	R	RBI	BB	SO	SB	Pinch Hit AB	Pinch Hit H	PO	A	E	DP	TC/G	FA	G by Pos
1982	STL N	123	.296	.391	422	125	12	8	4	0.9	43	56	12	58	24	15	6	245	3	11	0	2.2	.958	OF-117
1983		147	.286	.374	601	172	22	8	5	0.8	75	75	26	98	39	3	2	385	7	5	1	2.7	.987	OF-145
1984		145	.291	.394	571	166	19	11	6	1.1	82	50	29	80	43	5	0	374	10	6	4	2.8	.985	OF-141
1985		152	**.353**	.503	612	**216**	26	**18**	10	1.6	114	82	34	86	56	4	2	382	11	9	2	2.7	.978	OF-149
1986		124	.256	.370	497	127	22	7	7	1.4	65	48	37	82	19	2	0	325	9	3	0	2.8	.991	OF-121
1987		153	.285	.434	620	177	37	11	11	1.8	76	105	24	90	16	2	1	354	10	7	1	2.4	.981	OF-152, SS-1
1988		137	.292	.372	562	164	24	6	3	0.5	73	50	32	84	41	2	1	348	9	9	0	2.7	.975	OF-135
1989		58	.236	.352	199	47	10	2	3	1.5	23	17	10	34	8	10	2	118	2	3	0	2.6	.976	OF-47
1990	2 teams	STL N (125G –.335) OAK A (29G –.274)																						
″	total	154	**.324**	.419	614	199	35	7	3	0.5	99	77	48	104	31	2	0	413	14	17	5	2.9	.962	OF-152, DH-1
1991	SF N	131	.312	.408	497	155	30	3	4	0.8	67	43	34	74	17	4	2	259	6	6	3	2.1	.978	OF-128
1992		138	.297	.354	474	141	20	2	1	0.2	56	36	29	88	13	21	11	231	11	6	2	2.1	.976	OF-119
1993		130	.301	.389	475	143	28	1	4	0.8	53	46	38	67	10	7	1	224	9	5	1	1.9	.979	OF-126
1994		45	.282	.397	156	44	3	0	5	3.2	19	23	15	24	3	4	0	79	2	1	0	2.0	.988	OF-42
1995	BOS A	67	.285	.400	200	57	11	3	2	1.0	32	15	9	41	5	14	4	101	7	3	1	1.7	.973	OF-64
14 yrs.		1704	.297	.402	6500	1933	299	87	68	1.0	877	723	377	1010	325	95	32	3838	110	91	20	2.5	.977	OF-1638, DH-1, SS-1

Willie McGee *continued*

DIVISIONAL PLAYOFF SERIES

Year	Team		Games	BA	SA	AB	H	2B	3B	HR	HR%	R	RBI	BB	SO	SB	Pinch Hit AB	Pinch Hit H	PO	A	E	DP	TC/G	FA	G by Pos
1995	BOS	A	2	.250	.250	4	1	0	0	0	0.0	0	1	0	2	0	1	0	0	0	0	0	0.0	.000	OF-2

LEAGUE CHAMPIONSHIP SERIES

Year	Team		Games	BA	SA	AB	H	2B	3B	HR	HR%	R	RBI	BB	SO	SB	Pinch Hit AB	Pinch Hit H	PO	A	E	DP	TC/G	FA	G by Pos
1982	STL	N	3	.308	.846	13	4	0	2	1	7.7	4	5	0	5	0	0	0	12	0	1	0	4.3	.923	OF-3
1985			6	.269	.308	26	7	1	0	0	0.0	6	3	3	6	2	0	0	17	0	0	0	2.8	1.000	OF-6
1987			7	.308	.423	26	8	1	1	0	0.0	2	2	0	5	0	0	0	16	0	0	0	2.3	1.000	OF-7
1990	OAK	A	3	.222	.333	9	2	1	0	0	0.0	3	0	1	2	2	0	0	2	0	0	0	1.0	1.000	OF-2
4 yrs.			19	.284	.446	74	21	3	3 2nd	1	1.4	15 5th	10	4	18 7th	4	0	0	47	0	1	0	2.7	.979	OF-18

WORLD SERIES

Year	Team		Games	BA	SA	AB	H	2B	3B	HR	HR%	R	RBI	BB	SO	SB	Pinch Hit AB	Pinch Hit H	PO	A	E	DP	TC/G	FA	G by Pos
1982	STL	N	6	.240	.480	25	6	0	0	2	8.0	6	5	1	3	2	0	0	24	0	0	0	4.0	1.000	OF-6
1985			7	.259	.444	27	7	2	0	1	3.7	2	2	1	3	1	0	0	15	0	0	0	2.1	1.000	OF-7
1987			7	.370	.444	27	10	2	0	0	0.0	2	4	0	9	0	0	0	21	1	1	0	3.3	.957	OF-7
1990	OAK	A	4	.200	.300	10	2	1	0	0	0.0	1	0	0	2	1	1	0	5	0	0	0	1.7	1.000	OF-3
4 yrs.			24	.281	.438	89	25	5	0	3	3.4	11	11	2	17	4	1	0	65	1	1	0	2.9	.985	OF-23

Dan McGeehan

McGEEHAN, DANIEL DeSALES BR TR 5′ 6″ 135 lbs.
Brother of Connie McGeehan.
B. June 7, 1885, Jeddo, Pa. D. July 12, 1955, Hazleton, Pa.

Year	Team		Games	BA	SA	AB	H	2B	3B	HR	HR%	R	RBI	BB	SO	SB	Pinch Hit AB	Pinch Hit H	PO	A	E	DP	TC/G	FA	G by Pos
1911	STL	N	3	.222	.222	9	2	0	0	0	0.0	0	1	0	1	0	0	0	4	5	2	0	3.7	.818	2B-3

Bill McGhee

McGHEE, WILLIAM MAC (Fibber) BL TL 5′10½″ 185 lbs.
B. Sept. 5, 1905, Shawmut, Ala. D. Mar. 10, 1984, Decatur, Ga.

Year	Team		Games	BA	SA	AB	H	2B	3B	HR	HR%	R	RBI	BB	SO	SB	Pinch Hit AB	Pinch Hit H	PO	A	E	DP	TC/G	FA	G by Pos
1944	PHI	A	77	.289	.341	287	83	12	0	1	0.3	27	19	21	20	2	2	0	701	46	8	51	10.1	.989	1B-75
1945			93	.252	.284	250	63	6	1	0	0.0	24	19	24	16	3	31	9	143	9	1	7	2.7	.993	OF-48, 1B-8
2 yrs.			170	.272	.315	537	146	18	1	1	0.2	51	38	45	36	5	33	9	844	55	9	58	6.9	.990	1B-83, OF-48

Ed McGhee

McGHEE, WARREN EDWARD BR TR 5′11″ 170 lbs.
B. Sept. 29, 1924, Perry, Ark. D. Feb. 13, 1986, Memphis, Tenn.

Year	Team		Games	BA	SA	AB	H	2B	3B	HR	HR%	R	RBI	BB	SO	SB	Pinch Hit AB	Pinch Hit H	PO	A	E	DP	TC/G	FA	G by Pos
1950	CHI	A	3	.167	.500	6	1	0	1	0	0.0	0	0	0	1	0	1	0	1	0	0	0	1.0	1.000	OF-1
1953	PHI	A	104	.263	.324	358	94	11	4	1	0.3	36	29	32	43	4	7	2	319	4	6	0	3.3	.982	OF-99
1954	2 teams		PHI A (21G –.208) CHI A (42G –.227)																						
"	total		63	.219	.289	128	28	3	0	2	1.6	17	14	16	16	5	11	1	93	4	4	1	2.1	.960	OF-47
1955	CHI	A	26	.077	.077	13	1	0	0	0	0.0	6	0	6	1	2	2	1	12	0	1	0	0.8	.923	OF-17
4 yrs.			196	.246	.311	505	124	14	5	3	0.6	59	43	54	61	11	21	4	425	8	11	1	2.7	.975	OF-164

Bill McGilvray

McGILVRAY, WILLIAM ALEXANDER (Big Bill) BL TL 6′ 160 lbs.
B. Apr. 29, 1883, Portland, Ore. D. May 23, 1952, Denver, Colo.

Year	Team		Games	BA	SA	AB	H	2B	3B	HR	HR%	R	RBI	BB	SO	SB	Pinch Hit AB	Pinch Hit H	PO	A	E	DP	TC/G	FA	G by Pos
1908	CIN	N	2	.000	.000	2	0	0	0	0	0.0	0	0	0		0	2	0	0	0	0	0	0.0	—	

Tim McGinley

McGINLEY, TIMOTHY S. 5′ 9½″ 155 lbs.
B. Philadelphia, Pa. D. Nov. 2, 1899, Oakland, Calif.

Year	Team		Games	BA	SA	AB	H	2B	3B	HR	HR%	R	RBI	BB	SO	SB	Pinch Hit AB	Pinch Hit H	PO	A	E	DP	TC/G	FA	G by Pos
1876	BOS	N	9	.150	.150	40	6	0	0	0	0.0	5	2	0	1		0	0	26	3	16	1	5.0	.644	OF-6, C-3

Frank McGinn

McGINN, FRANK J.
B. 1869, Cincinnati, Ohio D. Nov. 19, 1897, Cincinnati, Ohio.

Year	Team		Games	BA	SA	AB	H	2B	3B	HR	HR%	R	RBI	BB	SO	SB	Pinch Hit AB	Pinch Hit H	PO	A	E	DP	TC/G	FA	G by Pos
1890	PIT	N	1	.000	.000	4	0	0	0	0	0.0	0	0	0	2	0	0	0	1	0	0	0	1.0	1.000	OF-1

Russ McGinnis

McGINNIS, RUSSELL BRENT BR TR 6′ 3″ 225 lbs.
B. June 18, 1963, Coffeyville, Kans.

Year	Team		Games	BA	SA	AB	H	2B	3B	HR	HR%	R	RBI	BB	SO	SB	Pinch Hit AB	Pinch Hit H	PO	A	E	DP	TC/G	FA	G by Pos
1992	TEX	A	14	.242	.364	33	8	4	0	0	0.0	2	4	3	7	0	2	0	45	4	0	3	3.5	1.000	C-10, 3B-2, 1B-2
1995	KC	A	3	.000	.000	5	0	0	0	0	0.0	1	0	1	1	0	2	0	9	0	0	0	3.0	1.000	1B-1, 3B-1, OF-1
2 yrs.			17	.211	.316	38	8	4	0	0	0.0	3	4	4	8	0	4	0	54	4	0	3	3.4	1.000	C-10, 3B-3, 1B-3, OF-1

John McGlone

McGLONE, JOHN T. 5′10″ 165 lbs.
B. 1864, Brooklyn, N. Y. D. Nov. 24, 1927, Brooklyn, N. Y.

Year	Team		Games	BA	SA	AB	H	2B	3B	HR	HR%	R	RBI	BB	SO	SB	Pinch Hit AB	Pinch Hit H	PO	A	E	DP	TC/G	FA	G by Pos
1886	WAS	N	4	.067	.067	15	1	0	0	0	0.0	2	1	0	3		0	0	7	4	2	0	3.3	.846	3B-4
1887	CLE	AA	21	.253	.304	79	20	2	1	0	0.0	14		7		15	0	0	42	40	14	3	4.6	.854	3B-21
1888			55	.182	.232	203	37	1	3	1	0.5	22	22	16		26	0	0	81	95	45	5	4.0	.796	3B-48, OF-7
3 yrs.			80	.195	.242	297	58	3	4	1	0.3	38	23	23	3	41	0	0	130	139	61	8	4.1	.815	3B-73, OF-7

Art McGovern

McGOVERN, ARTHUR JOHN BR TR 160 lbs.
B. Feb. 27, 1882, St. John, N. B., Canada D. Nov. 14, 1915, Thornton, R. I.

Year	Team		Games	BA	SA	AB	H	2B	3B	HR	HR%	R	RBI	BB	SO	SB	Pinch Hit AB	Pinch Hit H	PO	A	E	DP	TC/G	FA	G by Pos
1905	BOS	A	15	.114	.136	44	5	1	0	0	0.0	1	1	4		0	0	0	67	11	4	1	5.5	.951	C-15

Frank McGowan

McGOWAN, FRANK BERNARD (Beauty) BL TR 5′11″ 190 lbs.
B. Nov. 8, 1901, Branford, Conn. D. May 6, 1982, Hamden, Conn.

Year	Team		Games	BA	SA	AB	H	2B	3B	HR	HR%	R	RBI	BB	SO	SB	Pinch Hit AB	Pinch Hit H	PO	A	E	DP	TC/G	FA	G by Pos
1922	PHI	A	99	.230	.307	300	69	10	5	1	0.3	36	20	40	46	6	12	4	210	13	8	2	2.8	.965	OF-82
1923			95	.254	.303	287	73	9	1	1	0.3	41	19	36	25	4	7	0	154	12	5	1	2.2	.971	OF-79
1928	STL	A	47	.363	.524	168	61	13	4	2	1.2	35	18	16	15	2	0	0	99	3	4	1	2.3	.962	OF-47
1929			125	.254	.354	441	112	26	6	2	0.5	62	51	61	34	5	7	0	257	16	7	5	2.4	.975	OF-117
1937	BOS	N	9	.083	.083	12	1	0	0	0	0.0	0	0	1	2	0	6	0	2	0	0	0	1.0	1.000	OF-2
5 yrs.			375	.262	.351	1208	316	58	16	6	0.5	174	108	154	122	17	32	4	722	44	24	9	2.4	.970	OF-327

John McGraw

McGRAW, JOHN JOSEPH (Little Napoleon) BL TR 5′ 7″ 155 lbs.
B. Apr. 7, 1873, Truxton, N. Y. D. Feb. 25, 1934, New Rochelle, N. Y.
Manager 1899, 1901–32.
Hall of Fame 1937.

Year	Team		Games	BA	SA	AB	H	2B	3B	HR	HR%	R	RBI	BB	SO	SB	Pinch Hit AB	Pinch Hit H	PO	A	E	DP	TC/G	FA	G by Pos
1891	BAL	AA	33	.270	.383	115	31	3	5	0	0.0	17	14	12	17	4	0	0	47	52	21	7	3.6	.825	SS-21, OF-9, 2B-3
1892	BAL	N	79	.269	.339	286	77	13	2	1	0.3	41	26	32	21	15	0	0	165	144	28	16	4.3	.917	2B-34, OF-34, SS-8, 3B-3
1893			127	.321	.412	480	154	9	10	5	1.0	123	64	101	11	38	0	0	234	350	68	40	5.1	.896	SS-117, OF-11
1894			124	.340	.436	512	174	18	14	1	0.2	156	92	91	12	78	0	0	143	265	48	17	3.7	.895	3B-118, 2B-6
1895			96	.369	.448	388	143	13	6	2	0.5	110	48	60	9	61	0	0	100	239	47	19	4.0	.878	3B-95, 2B-1

Year	Team	Lg	Games	BA	SA	AB	H	2B	3B	HR	HR%	R	RBI	BB	SO	SB	Pinch Hit AB	Pinch Hit H	PO	A	E	DP	TC/G	FA	G by Pos

John McGraw *continued*

Year	Team	Lg	Games	BA	SA	AB	H	2B	3B	HR	HR%	R	RBI	BB	SO	SB	Pinch Hit AB	Pinch Hit H	PO	A	E	DP	TC/G	FA	G by Pos
1896			23	.325	.403	77	25	2	2	0	0.0	20	14	11	4	13	3	0	32	38	12	4	4.3	.854	3B-18, 1B-1
1897			106	.325	.379	391	127	15	3	0	0.0	90	48	99		44	1	0	112	182	38	16	3.2	.886	3B-105
1898			143	.342	.396	515	176	8	10	0	0.0	**143**	53	**112**		43	1	0	148	271	47	16	3.3	.899	3B-137, OF-3
1899			117	.391	.446	399	156	13	3	1	0.3	**140**	33	**124**		73	0	0	142	270	24	14	3.7	.945	3B-117
1900	**STL**	**N**	99	.344	.416	334	115	10	4	2	0.6	84	33	85		29	0	0	106	213	32	7	3.5	.909	3B-99
1901	**BAL**	**A**	73	.349	.487	232	81	14	9	0	0.0	71	28	61		24	3	0	80	107	23	5	3.0	.890	3B-69
1902	**2 teams**		**BAL A** (20G –.286)		**NY N** (35G –.224)																				
″	**total**		55	.247	.306	170	42	3	2	1	0.6	27	8	43		12	2	0	85	140	22	18	4.7	.911	SS-34, 3B-19
1903	**NY**	**N**	12	.273	.273	11	3	0	0	0	0.0	2	1	1		1	6	2	2	1	1	0	0.7	.750	OF-2, 2B-2, SS-1, 3B-1
1904			5	.333	.333	12	4	0	0	0	0.0	0	0	3		0	1	0	12	17	2	3	7.8	.935	SS-2, 2B-2
1905			3	—	—	0	0	0	0	0	—	0	0	0		1	0	0	0	0	0	0	0.0	.000	OF-1
1906			4	.000	.000	2	0	0	0	0	0.0	0	0	1		0	2	0	0	0	0	0	0.0	.000	3B-1
16 yrs.			1099	.333	.410	3924	1308	121	70	13	0.3	1024	462	836	74	436	19	2	1408	2289	413	182	3.8	.900	3B-782, SS-183, OF-60, 2B-48, 1B-1

Fred McGriff

McGRIFF, FREDERICK STANLEY (Crime Dog)
B. Oct. 31, 1963, Tampa, Fla.
BL TL 6′ 3″ 200 lbs.

Year	Team	Lg	Games	BA	SA	AB	H	2B	3B	HR	HR%	R	RBI	BB	SO	SB	Pinch Hit AB	Pinch Hit H	PO	A	E	DP	TC/G	FA	G by Pos
1986	**TOR**	**A**	3	.200	.200	5	1	0	0	0	0.0	1	0	0	2	0	0	0	3	0	0	0	1.0	1.000	DH-2, 1B-1
1987			107	.247	.505	295	73	16	0	20	6.8	58	43	60	104	3	14	1	108	7	2	5	1.1	.983	DH-90, 1B-14
1988			154	.282	.552	536	151	35	4	34	6.3	100	82	79	149	6	5	2	1344	93	5	143	9.4	.997	1B-153
1989			161	.269	.525	551	148	27	3	**36**	6.5	98	92	119	132	7	1	0	1460	115	17	148	9.9	.989	1B-159, DH-2
1990			153	.300	.530	557	167	21	1	35	6.3	91	88	94	108	5	0	0	1246	126	6	119	9.0	.996	1B-147, DH-6
1991	**SD**	**N**	153	.278	.494	528	147	19	1	31	5.9	84	106	105	135	4	0	0	1370	87	14	111	9.6	.990	1B-153
1992			152	.286	.556	531	152	30	4	**35**	6.6	79	104	96	108	8	1	0	1219	108	12	95	8.9	.991	1B-151
1993	**2 teams**		**SD N** (83G –.275)		**ATL N** (68G –.310)																				
″	**total**		151	.291	.549	557	162	29	2	37	6.6	111	101	76	106	5	2	1	1203	92	17	102	8.8	.987	1B-149
1994	**ATL**	**N**	113	.318	.623	424	135	25	1	34	8.0	81	94	50	76	7	1	0	1004	66	7	73	9.6	.994	1B-112
1995			144	.280	.489	528	148	27	1	27	5.1	85	93	65	99	3	0	0	1286	93	5	104	9.6	.996	1B-144
10 yrs.			1291	.285	.535	4512	1284	229	17	289 **9th**	6.4	788	803	744	1019	48	24	4	10243	787	85	900	8.7	.992	1B-1183, DH-100
DIVISIONAL PLAYOFF SERIES																									
1995	**ATL**	**N**	4	.333	.667	18	6	0	0	2	11.1	4	6	2	3	0	0	0	39	2	0	5	10.3	1.000	1B-4
LEAGUE CHAMPIONSHIP SERIES																									
1989	**TOR**	**A**	5	.143	.143	21	3	0	0	0	0.0	1	3	0	4	0	0	0	35	2	1	3	7.6	.974	1B-5
1993	**ATL**	**N**	6	.435	.652	23	10	2	0	1	4.3	6	4	4	7	0	0	0	50	3	0	1	8.8	1.000	1B-6
1995			4	.438	.688	16	7	4	0	0	0.0	5	0	3	0	0	0	0	42	4	0	8	11.5	1.000	1B-4
3 yrs.			15	.333	.483	60	20	6 **7th**	0	1	1.7	12	7	7	11	0	0	0	127	9	1	12	9.1	.993	1B-15
WORLD SERIES																									
1995	**ATL**	**N**	6	.261	.609	23	6	2	0	2	8.7	5	3	3	7	1	0	0	68	2	1	2	11.8	.986	1B-6

Terry McGriff

McGRIFF, TERENCE ROY
B. Sept. 23, 1963, Fort Pierce, Fla.
BR TR 6′ 2″ 190 lbs.

Year	Team	Lg	Games	BA	SA	AB	H	2B	3B	HR	HR%	R	RBI	BB	SO	SB	Pinch Hit AB	Pinch Hit H	PO	A	E	DP	TC/G	FA	G by Pos
1987	**CIN**	**N**	34	.225	.326	89	20	3	0	2	2.2	6	11	8	17	0	0	0	160	14	3	1	5.4	.983	C-33
1988			35	.198	.260	96	19	3	0	1	1.0	9	4	12	31	1	1	0	177	14	2	1	6.0	.990	C-32
1989			6	.273	.273	11	3	0	0	0	0.0	1	2	2	3	0	0	0	23	3	2	0	4.7	.929	C-6
1990	**2 teams**		**CIN N** (2G –.000)		**HOU N** (4G –.000)																				
″	**total**		6	.000	.000	9	0	0	0	0	0.0	0	0	0	1	0	1	0	13	2	1	1	3.2	.938	C-5
1993	**FLA**	**N**	3	.000	.000	7	0	0	0	0	0.0	0	0	1	2	0	1	0	12	0	0	0	4.0	1.000	C-3
1994	**STL**	**N**	42	.219	.272	114	25	6	0	0	0.0	10	13	13	11	0	2	1	207	23	2	0	5.9	.991	C-39
6 yrs.			126	.206	.270	326	67	12	0	3	0.9	26	30	36	65	1	5	1	592	56	10	3	5.6	.985	C-118

Mark McGrillis

McGRILLIS, MARK A.
B. Oct. 22, 1872, Philadelphia, Pa. D. May 16, 1935, Philadelphia, Pa.

Year	Team	Lg	Games	BA	SA	AB	H	2B	3B	HR	HR%	R	RBI	BB	SO	SB	Pinch Hit AB	Pinch Hit H	PO	A	E	DP	TC/G	FA	G by Pos
1892	**STL**	**N**	1	.000	.000	3	0	0	0	0	0.0	0	0	0	1	0	0	0	0	2	0	0	2.0	1.000	3B-1

Joe McGuckin

McGUCKIN, JOSEPH W.
B. Mar. 13, 1862, Paterson, N. J. D. Dec. 31, 1903, Yonkers, N. Y.
5′ 8½″ 160 lbs.

Year	Team	Lg	Games	BA	SA	AB	H	2B	3B	HR	HR%	R	RBI	BB	SO	SB	Pinch Hit AB	Pinch Hit H	PO	A	E	DP	TC/G	FA	G by Pos
1890	**BAL**	**AA**	11	.108	.108	37	4	0	0	0	0.0	2		6		3	0	0	21	4	1	1	2.4	.962	OF-11

John McGuinness

McGUINNESS, JOHN JAMES
B. 1857, Ireland D. Dec. 19, 1916, Binghamton, N. Y.
5′10½″ 150 lbs.

Year	Team	Lg	Games	BA	SA	AB	H	2B	3B	HR	HR%	R	RBI	BB	SO	SB	Pinch Hit AB	Pinch Hit H	PO	A	E	DP	TC/G	FA	G by Pos
1876	**NY**	**N**	1	.000	.000	4	0	0	0	0	0.0	0	0	0	0		0	0	1	1	4	0	3.0	.333	2B-1, C-1
1879	**SYR**	**N**	12	.294	.353	51	15	1	1	0	0.0	7	4	0	6		0	0	113	3	9	8	10.4	.928	1B-12
1884	**PHI**	**U**	53	.236	.282	220	52	8	1	0	0.0	25		5			0	0	569	25	28	22	11.5	.955	1B-48, 2B-5, SS-1
3 yrs.			66	.244	.291	275	67	9	2	0	0.0	32	4	5	6		0	0	683	29	41	30	11.1	.946	1B-60, 2B-6, SS-1, C-1

Bill McGuire

McGUIRE, WILLIAM PATRICK (Moose)
B. Feb. 14, 1964, Omaha, Neb.
BR TR 6′ 3″ 205 lbs.

Year	Team	Lg	Games	BA	SA	AB	H	2B	3B	HR	HR%	R	RBI	BB	SO	SB	Pinch Hit AB	Pinch Hit H	PO	A	E	DP	TC/G	FA	G by Pos
1988	**SEA**	**A**	9	.188	.188	16	3	0	0	0	0.0	1	2	3	2	0	0	0	29	3	0	0	3.6	1.000	C-9
1989			14	.179	.286	28	5	0	0	1	3.6	2	4	2	6	0	0	0	62	6	0	0	4.9	1.000	C-14
2 yrs.			23	.182	.250	44	8	0	0	1	2.3	3	6	5	8	0	0	0	91	9	0	0	4.3	1.000	C-23

Deacon McGuire

McGUIRE, JAMES THOMAS
B. Nov. 18, 1863, Youngstown, Ohio D. Oct. 31, 1936, Duck Lake, Mich.
Manager 1898, 1907–11.
BR TR 6′ 1″ 185 lbs.

Year	Team	Lg	Games	BA	SA	AB	H	2B	3B	HR	HR%	R	RBI	BB	SO	SB	Pinch Hit AB	Pinch Hit H	PO	A	E	DP	TC/G	FA	G by Pos
1884	**TOL**	**AA**	45	.185	.252	151	28	7	0	1	0.7	12		5			0	0	231	61	32	1	6.8	.901	C-41, OF-4, SS-3
1885	**DET**	**N**	34	.190	.256	121	23	4	2	0	0.0	11	9	5	23		0	0	252	52	26	2	9.7	.921	C-31, OF-3
1886	**PHI**	**N**	50	.198	.287	167	33	7	1	2	1.2	25	18	19	25		0	0	299	51	41	3	7.8	.895	C-49, OF-1
1887			41	.307	.467	150	46	6	6	2	1.3	22	23	11	8	3	0	0	214	52	35	6	7.3	.884	C-41
1888	**3 teams**		**PHI N** (12G –.333)		**DET N** (3G –.000)		**CLE AA** (26G –.255)																		
″	**total**		41	.259	.373	158	41	5	5	1	0.6	22	24	11	13	2	0	0	223	47	38	4	7.5	.877	C-30, 1B-6, OF-3, 3B-2

Deacon McGuire *continued*

Year	Team	Games	BA	SA	AB	H	2B	3B	HR	HR%	R	RBI	BB	SO	SB	Pinch Hit AB	Pinch Hit H	PO	A	E	DP	TC/G	FA	G by Pos
1890	ROC AA	87	.299	.408	331	99	16	4	4	1.2	46		21		8	0	0	543	103	35	15	7.6	.949	C-71, 1B-15, OF-3, P-1
1891	WAS AA	114	.303	.426	413	125	22	10	3	0.7	55	66	43	34	10	0	0	463	140	65	9	5.6	.903	C-98, OF-18, 3B-3, 1B-1
1892	WAS N	97	.232	.340	315	73	14	4	4	1.3	46	43	61	48	7	0	0	453	101	33	10	6.0	.944	C-89, 1B-8, OF-1
1893		63	.262	.359	237	62	14	3	1	0.4	29	26	26	12	3	0	0	287	56	34	14	6.1	.910	C-50, 1B-12
1894		104	.306	.419	425	130	18	6	6	1.4	67	78	33	19	11	0	0	288	114	36	8	4.2	.918	C-104
1895		132	.336	.478	533	179	30	8	10	1.9	89	97	40	18	16	0	0	408	181	41	11	4.7	.935	C-132, SS-1
1896		108	.321	.416	389	125	25	3	2	0.5	60	70	30	14	12	9	2	351	88	30	14	4.7	.936	C-98, 1B-1
1897		93	.343	.474	327	112	17	7	4	1.2	51	53	21		9	11	3	355	88	22	8	5.9	.953	C-73, 1B-6
1898		131	.268	.323	489	131	18	3	1	0.2	59	57	24		10	3	2	707	120	29	37	6.6	.966	C-93, 1B-37
1899	2 teams	WAS N (59G –.271) BKN N (46G –.318)																						
"	total	105	.292	.371	356	104	15	5	1	0.3	47	35	28		7	2	0	334	129	14	5	4.6	.971	C-102, 1B-1
1900	BKN N	71	.286	.365	241	69	15	2	0	0.0	20	34	19		2	2	1	218	77	15	7	4.5	.952	C-69
1901		85	.296	.375	301	89	16	4	0	0.0	28	40	18		4	1	0	439	94	21	6	6.6	.962	C-81, 1B-3
1902	DET A	73	.227	.323	229	52	14	1	2	0.9	27	23	24		0	2	0	210	65	14	6	4.1	.952	C-70
1903		72	.250	.306	248	62	12	1	0	0.0	15	21	19		3	2	0	331	73	18	9	6.0	.957	C-69, 1B-1
1904	NY A	101	.208	.258	322	67	12	2	0	0.0	17	20	27		2	2	**2**	536	120	20	11	6.9	.970	C-97, 1B-1
1905		72	.219	.268	228	50	7	2	0	0.0	9	33	18		3	1	1	366	69	11	4	6.3	.975	C-71
1906		51	.299	.333	144	43	5	0	0	0.0	11	14	12		3	1	0	226	38	10	2	5.5	.964	C-49, 1B-1
1907	2 teams	NY A (1G –.000) BOS A (6G –.750)																						
"	total	7	.600	1.200	5	3	0	0	1	20.0	1	1	0		0	4	3	3	1	0	0	4.0	1.000	C-1
1908	2 teams	BOS A (1G –.000) CLE A (1G –.250)																						
"	total	2	.200	.400	5	1	1	0	0	0.0	0	2	0		0	1	0	10	0	0	0	10.0	1.000	1B-1
1910	CLE A	1	.333	.333	3	1	0	0	0	0.0	0	0	0		0	0	0	2	1	0	0	3.0	1.000	C-1
1912	DET A	1	.500	.500	2	1	0	0	0	0.0	1	0	0		0	0	0	2	3	2	0	7.0	.714	C-1
26 yrs.		1781	.278	.372	6290	1749	300	79	45	0.7	770	787	515	214	115	41	14	7751	1924	622	192	5.9	.940	C-1611, 1B-94, OF-33, 3B-5, SS-4, P-1

Jim McGuire

McGUIRE, JAMES A.
B. Feb. 4, 1875, Dunkirk, N. Y. D. Jan. 26, 1917, Buffalo, N. Y.
TR

Year	Team	Games	BA	SA	AB	H	2B	3B	HR	HR%	R	RBI	BB	SO	SB	Pinch Hit AB	Pinch Hit H	PO	A	E	DP	TC/G	FA	G by Pos
1901	CLE A	18	.232	.261	69	16	2	0	0	0.0	4	3	0		0	0	0	40	54	9	10	5.7	.913	SS-18

Mickey McGuire

McGUIRE, MICKEY C.
B. Jan. 18, 1941, Dayton, Ohio.
BR TR 5′10″ 170 lbs.

Year	Team	Games	BA	SA	AB	H	2B	3B	HR	HR%	R	RBI	BB	SO	SB	Pinch Hit AB	Pinch Hit H	PO	A	E	DP	TC/G	FA	G by Pos
1962	BAL A	6	.000	.000	4	0	0	0	0	0.0	0	0	0	0	0	1	0	2	2	0	0	0.8	1.000	SS-5
1967		10	.235	.235	17	4	0	0	0	0.0	2	2	0	2	0	6	1	3	3	0	0	1.5	1.000	2B-4
2 yrs.		16	.190	.190	21	4	0	0	0	0.0	2	2	0	2	0	7	1	5	5	0	0	1.1	1.000	SS-5, 2B-4

Bill McGunnigle

McGUNNIGLE, WILLIAM HENRY (Gunner)
B. Jan. 1, 1855, Boston, Mass. D. Mar. 9, 1899, Brockton, Mass.
Manager 1888–91, 1896.
BR TR 5′ 9″ 155 lbs.

Year	Team	Games	BA	SA	AB	H	2B	3B	HR	HR%	R	RBI	BB	SO	SB	Pinch Hit AB	Pinch Hit H	PO	A	E	DP	TC/G	FA	G by Pos
1879	BUF N	47	.175	.187	171	30	0	1	0	0.0	22	5	5	24		0	0	64	35	9	2	2.3	.917	OF-34, P-14
1880	2 teams	BUF N (7G –.182) WOR N (1G –.000)																						
"	total	8	.154	.154	26	4	0	0	0	0.0	0	1	0	6		0	0	6	4	2	0	1.3	.833	P-5, OF-4
1882	CLE N	1	.200	.200	5	1	0	0	0	0.0	2	0	0	1		0	0	0	0	0	0	0.0	.000	OF-1
3 yrs.		56	.173	.183	202	35	0	1	0	0.0	24	6	5	31		0	0	70	39	11	2	2.1	.908	OF-39, P-19

Mark McGwire

McGWIRE, MARK DAVID
B. Oct. 1, 1963, Pomona, Calif.
BR TR 6′ 5″ 215 lbs.

Year	Team	Games	BA	SA	AB	H	2B	3B	HR	HR%	R	RBI	BB	SO	SB	Pinch Hit AB	Pinch Hit H	PO	A	E	DP	TC/G	FA	G by Pos
1986	OAK A	18	.189	.377	53	10	1	0	3	5.7	10	9	4	18	0	3	1	10	20	6	1	2.3	.833	3B-16
1987		151	.289	**.618**	557	161	28	4	**49**	**8.8**	97	118	71	131	1	2	1	1176	101	13	91	8.3	.990	1B-145, 3B-8, OF-3
1988		155	.260	.478	550	143	22	1	32	5.8	87	99	76	117	0	4	2	1228	88	9	118	8.5	.993	1B-154, OF-1
1989		143	.231	.467	490	113	17	0	33	**6.7**	74	95	83	94	1	1	0	1170	114	6	122	9.0	.995	1B-141, DH-2
1990		156	.235	.489	523	123	16	0	39	7.5	87	108	**110**	116	2	1	0	1329	95	5	126	9.2	.997	1B-154, DH-2
1991		154	.201	.383	483	97	22	0	22	4.6	62	75	93	116	2	4	1	1191	101	4	120	8.5	.997	1B-152
1992		139	.268	**.585**	467	125	22	0	42	**9.0**	87	104	90	105	0	1	0	1118	71	6	118	8.5	.995	1B-139, DH-1
1993		27	.333	.726	84	28	6	0	9	10.7	16	24	21	19	0	1	0	197	14	0	20	8.4	1.000	1B-25
1994		47	.252	.474	135	34	3	0	9	6.7	26	25	37	40	0	2	0	311	17	4	25	7.4	.988	1B-40, DH-5
1995		104	.274	.685	317	87	13	0	39	**12.3**	75	90	88	77	1	1	0	775	63	12	64	8.4	.986	1B-91, DH-10
10 yrs.		1094	.252	.523	3659	921	150	5	277	7.6	621	747	673	833	7	20	5	8505	684	65	805	8.5	.993	1B-1041, 3B-24, DH-20, OF-4
LEAGUE CHAMPIONSHIP SERIES																								
1988	OAK A	4	.333	.533	15	5	0	0	1	6.7	4	3	1	5	0	0	0	24	2	0	4	6.5	1.000	1B-4
1989		5	.389	.611	18	7	1	0	1	5.6	3	3	1	4	0	0	0	46	1	1	4	9.6	.979	1B-5
1990		4	.154	.154	13	2	0	0	0	0.0	2	2	3	3	0	0	0	40	0	0	3	10.0	1.000	1B-4
1992		6	.150	.300	20	3	0	0	1	5.0	1	3	5	4	0	0	0	46	2	1	3	8.2	.980	1B-6
4 yrs.		19	.258	.409	66	17	1	0	3	4.5	10	11	10	16	0	0	0	156	5	2	14	8.6	.988	1B-19
WORLD SERIES																								
1988	OAK A	5	.059	.235	17	1	0	0	1	5.9	1	1	3	4	0	0	0	40	3	0	2	8.6	1.000	1B-5
1989		4	.294	.353	17	5	1	0	0	0.0	0	1	1	3	0	0	0	28	2	0	1	7.5	1.000	1B-4
1990		4	.214	.214	14	3	0	0	0	0.0	1	0	2	4	0	0	0	42	1	2	5	11.3	.956	1B-4
3 yrs.		13	.188	.271	48	9	1	0	1	2.1	2	2	6	11	0	0	0	110	6	2	8	9.1	.983	1B-13

Bob McHale

McHALE, ROBERT EMMET
B. Feb. 7, 1870, Sacramento, Calif. D. June 9, 1952, Sacramento, Calif.

Year	Team	Games	BA	SA	AB	H	2B	3B	HR	HR%	R	RBI	BB	SO	SB	Pinch Hit AB	Pinch Hit H	PO	A	E	DP	TC/G	FA	G by Pos
1898	WAS N	11	.182	.242	33	6	2	0	0	0.0	5	7	1		1	0	0	19	2	3	2	2.2	.875	OF-9, SS-1, 1B-1

Jim McHale

McHALE, JAMES BERNARD
B. Dec. 17, 1875, Miners Mills, Pa. D. June 17, 1959, Los Angeles, Calif.
BR TR 5′11″ 165 lbs.

Year	Team	Games	BA	SA	AB	H	2B	3B	HR	HR%	R	RBI	BB	SO	SB	Pinch Hit AB	Pinch Hit H	PO	A	E	DP	TC/G	FA	G by Pos
1908	BOS A	21	.224	.313	67	15	2	2	0	0.0	9	7	4		4	0	0	30	2	1	0	1.7	.970	OF-19

John McHale

McHALE, JOHN JOSEPH BL TR 6′ 200 lbs.
B. Sept. 21, 1921, Detroit, Mich.

Year	Team	Lg	Games	BA	SA	AB	H	2B	3B	HR	HR%	R	RBI	BB	SO	SB	Pinch Hit AB	Pinch Hit H	PO	A	E	DP	TC/G	FA	G by Pos
1943	DET	A	4	.000	.000	3	0	0	0	0	0.0	0	0	1	1	0	3	0	0	0	0	0	0.0	—	
1944			1	.000	.000	1	0	0	0	0	0.0	0	0	0	0	0	1	1	0	0	0	0	0.0	—	
1945			19	.143	.143	14	2	0	0	0	0.0	0	1	1	4	0	14	2	5	1	0	0	2.0	1.000	1B-3
1947			39	.211	.316	95	20	1	0	3	3.2	10	11	7	24	1	15	4	195	12	1	12	8.3	.995	1B-25
1948			1	.000	.000	1	0	0	0	0	0.0	0	0	0	0	0	1	0	0	0	0	0	0.0	—	
5 yrs.			64	.193	.281	114	22	1	0	3	2.6	10	12	9	29	1	34	7	200	13	1	12	7.6	.995	1B-28
WORLD SERIES																									
1945	DET	A	3	.000	.000	3	0	0	0	0	0.0	0	0	0	1	0	3	0	0	0	0	0	0.0	—	

Austin McHenry

McHENRY, AUSTIN BUSH (Mac) BR TR 6′ 175 lbs.
B. Sept. 22, 1895, Wrightsville, Ohio D. Nov. 27, 1922, Jefferson, Ohio.

Year	Team	Lg	Games	BA	SA	AB	H	2B	3B	HR	HR%	R	RBI	BB	SO	SB	Pinch Hit AB	Pinch Hit H	PO	A	E	DP	TC/G	FA	G by Pos
1918	STL	N	80	.261	.360	272	71	12	6	1	0.4	32	29	21	24	8	0	0	145	14	8	3	2.1	.952	OF-80
1919			110	.286	.404	371	106	19	11	1	0.3	41	47	19	57	7	4	0	183	20	3	3	2.0	.985	OF-103
1920			137	.282	.423	504	142	19	11	10	2.0	66	65	25	73	8	3	1	297	21	16	1	2.5	.952	OF-133
1921			152	.350	.531	574	201	37	8	17	3.0	92	102	38	48	10	0	0	371	13	14	3	2.6	.965	OF-152
1922			64	.303	.466	238	72	18	3	5	2.1	31	43	14	27	2	2	1	132	13	10	3	2.5	.935	OF-61
5 yrs.			543	.302	.448	1959	592	105	39	34	1.7	262	286	117	229	35	9	2	1128	81	51	13	2.4	.960	OF-529

Vance McHenry

McHENRY, VANCE LOREN BR TR 5′ 9″ 165 lbs.
B. July 10, 1956, Chico, Calif.

Year	Team	Lg	Games	BA	SA	AB	H	2B	3B	HR	HR%	R	RBI	BB	SO	SB	Pinch Hit AB	Pinch Hit H	PO	A	E	DP	TC/G	FA	G by Pos
1981	SEA	A	15	.222	.222	18	4	0	0	0	0.0	3	2	1	1	0	2	1	7	18	3	6	2.0	.893	SS-13, DH-1
1982			3	.000	.000	1	0	0	0	0	0.0	0	0	0	0	0	1	0	1	0	1	0	1.0	.500	SS-1, DH-1
2 yrs.			18	.211	.211	19	4	0	0	0	0.0	3	2	1	1	0	3	1	8	18	4	6	1.9	.867	SS-14, DH-2

Irish McIlveen

McILVEEN, HENRY COOKE BL TL 5′11½″ 180 lbs.
B. July 27, 1880, Belfast, Ireland D. Oct. 18, 1960, Lorain, Ohio.

Year	Team	Lg	Games	BA	SA	AB	H	2B	3B	HR	HR%	R	RBI	BB	SO	SB	Pinch Hit AB	Pinch Hit H	PO	A	E	DP	TC/G	FA	G by Pos
1906	PIT	N	5	.400	.400	5	2	0	0	0	0.0	1	0	0		0	2	1	1	2	0	0	1.5	1.000	P-2
1908	NY	A	44	.213	.266	169	36	3	3	0	0.0	17	8	14		6	0	0	70	4	4	0	1.8	.949	OF-44
1909			4	.000	.000	3	0	0	0	0	0.0	0	0	1		0	3	0	0	0	0	0	0.0	—	
3 yrs.			53	.215	.266	177	38	3	3	0	0.0	18	8	15		6	5	1	71	6	4	0	1.8	.951	OF-44, P-2

Stuffy McInnis

McINNIS, JOHN PHALEN BR TR 5′ 9½″ 162 lbs.
B. Sept. 19, 1890, Gloucester, Mass. D. Feb. 16, 1960, Ipswich, Mass.
Manager 1927.

Year	Team	Lg	Games	BA	SA	AB	H	2B	3B	HR	HR%	R	RBI	BB	SO	SB	Pinch Hit AB	Pinch Hit H	PO	A	E	DP	TC/G	FA	G by Pos
1909	PHI	A	19	.239	.304	46	11	0	0	1	2.2	4	4	2		0	5	2	34	44	10	5	6.3	.886	SS-14
1910			38	.301	.438	73	22	2	4	0	0.0	10	12	7		3	10	3	33	39	5	3	2.9	.935	SS-17, 2B-5, 3B-4, OF-1
1911			126	.321	.425	468	150	20	10	3	0.6	76	77	25		23	4	1	1105	101	35	58	10.3	.972	1B-97, SS-24
1912			153	.327	.433	568	186	25	13	3	0.5	83	101	49		27	0	0	1533	100	27	88	10.8	.984	1B-153
1913			148	.326	.418	543	177	30	4	4	0.7	79	90	45	31	16	0	0	1504	80	12	85	10.8	.992	1B-148
1914			149	.314	.368	576	181	12	8	1	0.2	74	95	19	27	25	0	0	1423	85	7	89	10.2	.995	1B-149
1915			119	.314	.362	456	143	14	4	0	0.0	44	49	14	17	8	0	0	1123	83	13	63	10.2	.989	1B-119
1916			140	.295	.361	512	151	25	3	1	0.2	42	60	25	19	7	0	0	1404	96	12	87	10.8	.992	1B-140
1917			150	.303	.351	567	172	19	4	0	0.0	50	44	33	19	18	0	0	1658	95	12	81	11.8	.993	1B-150
1918	BOS	A	117	.272	.322	423	115	11	5	0	0.0	40	56	19	10	10	0	0	1100	113	10	53	10.5	.992	1B-94, 3B-23
1919			120	.305	.361	440	134	12	5	1	0.2	32	58	23	11	8	2	1	1236	82	7	84	11.2	.995	1B-118
1920			148	.297	.356	559	166	21	3	2	0.4	50	71	18	19	6	0	0	1586	91	7	101	11.4	.996	1B-148
1921			152	.307	.394	584	179	31	10	0	0.0	72	74	21	9	2	0	0	1549	102	1	109	10.9	.999	1B-152
1922	CLE	A	142	.305	.389	537	164	28	7	1	0.2	58	78	15	5	1	1	0	1376	73	5	96	10.3	.997	1B-140, C-1
1923	BOS	N	154	.315	.392	607	191	23	9	2	0.3	70	95	26	12	7	0	0	1500	89	14	136	10.4	.991	1B-154
1924			146	.291	.360	581	169	23	7	1	0.2	57	59	15	6	9	0	0	1435	95	10	129	10.5	.994	1B-146
1925	PIT	N	59	.368	.484	155	57	10	4	0	0.0	19	24	17	1	1	13	4	377	24	3	40	8.8	.993	1B-46
1926			47	.299	.362	127	38	6	1	0	0.0	12	13	7	3	1	7	2	300	17	4	32	8.0	.988	1B-40
1927	PHI	N	1	—	—	0	0	0	0	0	—	0	0	0	0	0	0	0	1	0	0	0	1.0	1.000	1B-1
19 yrs.			2128	.308	.381	7822	2406	312	101	20	0.3	872	1060	380	189	172	42	13	20277	1409	194	1339	10.5	.991	1B-1995, SS-55, 3B-27, 2B-5, C-1, OF-1
WORLD SERIES																									
1911	PHI	A	1	—	—	0	0	0	0	0	—	0	0	0	0	0	0	0	1	0	0	0	1.0	1.000	1B-1
1913			5	.118	.176	17	2	1	0	0	0.0	1	2	0	2	0	0	0	45	0	0	4	9.0	1.000	1B-5
1914			4	.143	.214	14	2	1	0	0	0.0	2	0	3	3	0	0	0	50	2	1	4	13.3	.981	1B-4
1918	BOS	A	6	.250	.250	20	5	0	0	0	0.0	2	1	1	1	0	0	0	71	2	0	3	12.2	1.000	1B-6
1925	PIT	N	4	.286	.286	14	4	0	0	0	0.0	0	1	0	2	0	1	0	30	3	0	0	11.0	1.000	1B-3
5 yrs.			20	.200	.231	65	13	2	0	0	0.0	5	4	4	8	0	1	0	197	7	1	11	10.8	.995	1B-19

Harry McIntire

McINTIRE, JOHN REID (Rocks) BR TR 5′11″ 180 lbs.
B. Jan. 11, 1879, Dayton, Ohio D. Jan. 9, 1949, Daytona Beach, Fla.

Year	Team	Lg	Games	BA	SA	AB	H	2B	3B	HR	HR%	R	RBI	BB	SO	SB	Pinch Hit AB	Pinch Hit H	PO	A	E	DP	TC/G	FA	G by Pos
1905	BKN	N	45	.246	.312	138	34	6	0	1	0.7	16	11	3		2	5	0	13	73	11	2	2.2	.887	P-40, OF-5
1906			45	.175	.204	103	18	1	1	0	0.0	5	3	6		0	3	1	10	78	3	4	2.2	.967	P-39, OF-3
1907			30	.217	.290	69	15	3	1	0	0.0	6	3	7		0	2	0	7	56	6	2	2.5	.913	P-28
1908			40	.200	.250	100	20	3	1	0	0.0	5	4	2		0	0	0	6	76	4	5	2.2	.953	P-40
1909			32	.171	.276	76	13	4	2	0	0.0	9	4	1		0	0	0	6	62	4	3	2.3	.944	P-32
1910	CHI	N	30	.258	.333	66	17	2	0	1	1.5	3	8	4	13	0	2	0	4	48	3	0	2.0	.945	P-28
1911			26	.264	.340	53	14	4	0	0	0.0	9	2	5	10	0	1	1	1	42	0	0	1.7	1.000	P-25
1912			8	.300	.500	10	3	0	1	0	0.0	1	5	1	1	0	4	3	1	6	1	0	2.0	.875	P-4
1913	CIN	N	1	—	—	0	0	0	0	0	—	0	0	0	0	0	0	0	0	0	0	0	0.0	.000	P-1
9 yrs.			257	.218	.285	615	134	23	6	2	0.3	54	40	29	24	2	17	5	48	441	32	16	2.1	.939	P-237, OF-8
WORLD SERIES																									
1910	CHI	N	2	.000	.000	1	0	0	0	0	0.0	0	0	0	1	0	0	0	0	2	1	0	1.5	.667	P-2

Tim McIntosh

McINTOSH, TIMOTHY ALLEN BR TR 5′11″ 195 lbs.
B. Mar. 21, 1965, Minneapolis, Minn.

Year	Team	Lg	Games	BA	SA	AB	H	2B	3B	HR	HR%	R	RBI	BB	SO	SB	Pinch Hit AB	Pinch Hit H	PO	A	E	DP	TC/G	FA	G by Pos
1990	MIL	A	5	.200	.800	5	1	0	0	1	20.0	1	1	0	2	0	1	0	6	1	1	0	2.0	.875	C-4
1991			7	.364	.727	11	4	1	0	1	9.1	2	1	0	4	0	1	0	1	0	0	0	0.1	1.000	OF-4, DH-2, 1B-1

Tim McIntosh *continued*

Year	Team	Games	BA	SA	AB	H	2B	3B	HR	HR%	R	RBI	BB	SO	SB	Pinch Hit AB	Pinch Hit H	PO	A	E	DP	TC/G	FA	G by Pos
1992		35	.182	.221	77	14	3	0	0	0.0	7	6	3	9	1	2	0	122	10	1	6	3.9	.992	C-14, OF-10, 1B-7, DH-3
1993	**2 teams**	**MIL A** (1G –.000) **MON N** (20G –.095)																						
"	**total**	21	.095	.143	21	2	1	0	0	0.0	2	2	0	7	0	11	1	8	1	0	0	0.7	1.000	OF-7, C-6
4 yrs.		68	.184	.281	114	21	5	0	2	1.8	12	10	3	22	1	15	1	137	12	2	6	2.6	.987	C-24, OF-21, 1B-8, DH-5

Matty McIntyre

McINTYRE, MATTHEW W. BL TL 5′11″ 175 lbs.
B. June 12, 1880, Stonington, Conn. D. Apr. 2, 1920, Detroit, Mich.

Year	Team	Games	BA	SA	AB	H	2B	3B	HR	HR%	R	RBI	BB	SO	SB	Pinch Hit AB	Pinch Hit H	PO	A	E	DP	TC/G	FA	G by Pos
1901	**PHI A**	82	.276	.341	308	85	12	4	0	0.0	38	46	30		11	0	0	155	8	14	0	2.2	.921	OF-82
1904	**DET A**	152	.253	.317	578	146	11	10	2	0.3	74	46	44		11	0	0	334	16	15	4	2.4	.959	OF-152
1905		131	.263	.325	495	130	21	5	0	0.0	59	30	48		9	0	0	286	18	10	6	2.4	.968	OF-131
1906		133	.260	.343	493	128	19	11	0	0.0	63	39	56		29	0	0	254	25	5	8	2.1	.982	OF-133
1907		20	.284	.321	81	23	1	1	0	0.0	6	9	7		3	0	0	43	3	0	1	2.3	1.000	OF-20
1908		151	.295	.383	569	168	24	13	0	0.0	**105**	28	83		20	0	0	329	17	8	4	2.3	.977	OF-151
1909		125	.244	.326	476	116	18	9	1	0.2	65	34	54		13	2	0	217	14	6	1	1.9	.975	OF-122
1910		83	.236	.318	305	72	15	5	0	0.0	40	25	39		4	6	1	147	12	9	2	2.2	.946	OF-77
1911	**CHI A**	146	.323	.401	569	184	19	11	1	0.2	102	52	64		17	0	0	235	18	14	5	1.8	.948	OF-146
1912		45	.167	.167	84	14	0	0	0	0.0	10	10	14		3	0	0	37	2	0	0	0.9	1.000	OF-45
10 yrs.		1068	.269	.343	3958	1066	140	69	4	0.1	562	319	439		120	8	1	2037	133	81	31	2.1	.964	OF-1059
WORLD SERIES																								
1908	**DET A**	5	.222	.278	18	4	1	0	0	0.0	2	0	3	2	1	0	0	10	0	1	0	2.2	.909	OF-5
1909		4	.000	.000	3	0	0	0	0	0.0	0	0	0	1	0	3	0	0	0	0	0	0.0	.000	OF-1
2 yrs.		9	.190	.238	21	4	1	0	0	0.0	2	0	3	3	1	3	0	10	0	1	0	1.8	.909	OF-6

Otto McIvor

McIVOR, EDWARD OTTO BB TL 5′11½″ 175 lbs.
B. July 26, 1884, Greenville, Tex. D. May 4, 1954, Dallas, Tex.

Year	Team	Games	BA	SA	AB	H	2B	3B	HR	HR%	R	RBI	BB	SO	SB	Pinch Hit AB	Pinch Hit H	PO	A	E	DP	TC/G	FA	G by Pos
1911	**STL N**	30	.226	.339	62	14	2	1	1	1.6	11	9	9	14	0	7	0	24	1	2	0	1.6	.926	OF-17

Dave McKay

McKAY, DAVID LAWRENCE BB TR 6′ 1″ 195 lbs.
B. Mar. 14, 1950, Vancouver, B.C., Canada. BR 1975–1976

Year	Team	Games	BA	SA	AB	H	2B	3B	HR	HR%	R	RBI	BB	SO	SB	Pinch Hit AB	Pinch Hit H	PO	A	E	DP	TC/G	FA	G by Pos
1975	**MIN A**	33	.256	.352	125	32	4	1	2	1.6	8	16	6	14	1	0	0	38	70	9	12	3.5	.923	3B-33
1976		45	.203	.217	138	28	2	0	0	0.0	8	8	9	27	1	3	1	27	77	10	13	2.6	.912	3B-41, SS-2, DH-1
1977	**TOR A**	95	.197	.266	274	54	4	3	3	1.1	18	22	7	51	2	0	0	141	205	14	36	3.8	.961	2B-40, 3B-32, SS-20, DH-2
1978		145	.238	.351	504	120	20	8	7	1.4	59	45	20	91	4	0	0	310	414	12	96	5.0	.984	2B-140, SS-3, 3B-2, DH-1
1979		47	.218	.276	156	34	9	0	0	0.0	19	12	7	19	1	0	0	119	150	7	37	5.8	.975	2B-46, 3B-2
1980	**OAK A**	123	.244	.315	295	72	16	1	1	0.3	29	29	10	57	1	1	1	155	242	10	33	3.2	.975	2B-62, 3B-54, SS-10
1981		79	.263	.375	224	59	11	1	4	1.8	25	21	16	43	4	3	0	118	172	13	26	3.4	.957	3B-43, 2B-38, SS-7
1982		78	.198	.283	212	42	4	1	4	1.9	25	17	11	35	6	2	0	120	153	11	24	3.6	.961	2B-59, 3B-16, SS-3
8 yrs.		645	.229	.313	1928	441	70	15	21	1.1	191	170	86	337	20	9	2	1028	1483	86	277	4.0	.967	2B-385, 3B-223, SS-45, DH-4
DIVISIONAL PLAYOFF SERIES																								
1981	**OAK A**	3	.273	.545	11	3	0	0	1	9.1	1	1	1	1	0	0	0	9	6	1	0	5.3	.938	2B-3
LEAGUE CHAMPIONSHIP SERIES																								
1981	**OAK A**	3	.273	.273	11	3	0	0	0	0.0	0	1	0	2	0	0	0	7	6	1	0	4.7	.929	2B-3

Ed McKean

McKEAN, EDWIN JOHN (Mack) BR TR 5′ 9″ 160 lbs.
B. June 6, 1864, Grafton, Ohio D. Aug. 16, 1919, Cleveland, Ohio.

Year	Team	Games	BA	SA	AB	H	2B	3B	HR	HR%	R	RBI	BB	SO	SB	Pinch Hit AB	Pinch Hit H	PO	A	E	DP	TC/G	FA	G by Pos
1887	**CLE AA**	132	.286	.375	539	154	16	13	2	0.4	97		60		76	0	0	220	369	105	34	5.1	.849	SS-123, 2B-8, OF-4
1888		131	.299	.425	548	164	21	15	6	1.1	94	68	28		52	0	0	226	271	56	19	4.1	.899	SS-78, OF-48, 2B-9, 3B-1
1889	**CLE N**	123	.318	.418	500	159	22	8	4	0.8	88	75	42	25	35	0	0	209	401	62	42	5.5	.908	SS-122, 2B-1
1890		136	.296	.417	530	157	15	14	7	1.3	95	61	87	25	23	0	0	268	439	75	47	5.7	.904	SS-134, 2B-3
1891		141	.282	.373	**603**	170	13	12	6	1.0	115	69	64	19	14	0	0	248	463	91	42	5.7	.887	SS-141
1892		129	.262	.326	531	139	14	10	0	0.0	76	93	49	28	19	0	0	207	369	92	29	5.2	.862	SS-129
1893		125	.310	.473	545	169	29	24	4	0.7	103	133	50	14	16	0	0	247	431	74	55	6.0	.902	SS-125
1894		130	.357	.509	554	198	30	15	8	1.4	116	128	49	12	33	0	0	269	411	71	43	5.8	.905	SS-130
1895		131	.342	.501	**565**	193	32	17	8	1.4	131	119	45	25	12	0	0	246	424	67	42	5.6	.909	SS-131
1896		133	.338	.468	571	193	29	12	7	1.2	100	112	45	9	13	0	0	214	400	57	57	5.0	.915	SS-133
1897		125	.273	.379	523	143	21	14	2	0.4	83	78	40		15	0	0	226	385	53	36	5.3	.920	SS-125
1898		151	.285	.371	604	172	23	1	9	1.5	89	94	56		11	0	0	304	425	53	47	5.2	.932	SS-151
1899	**STL N**	67	.260	.339	277	72	7	3	3	1.1	40	40	20		4	0	0	254	156	34	25	6.6	.923	SS-42, 1B-15, 2B-10
13 yrs.		1654	.302	.416	6890	2083	272	158	66	1.0	1227	1070	635	157	323	0	0	3138	4944	890	518	5.4	.901	SS-1564, OF-52, 2B-31, 1B-15, 3B-1

Bill McKechnie

McKECHNIE, WILLIAM BOYD (Deacon) BB TR 5′10″ 160 lbs.
B. Aug. 7, 1886, Wilkinsburg, Pa. D. Oct. 29, 1965, Bradenton, Fla.
Manager 1915, 1922–26, 1928–46.
Hall of Fame 1962.

Year	Team	Games	BA	SA	AB	H	2B	3B	HR	HR%	R	RBI	BB	SO	SB	Pinch Hit AB	Pinch Hit H	PO	A	E	DP	TC/G	FA	G by Pos
1907	**PIT N**	3	.125	.125	8	1	0	0	0	0.0	0	0	0		0	0	0	1	4	0	0	1.7	1.000	3B-2, 2B-1
1910		71	.217	.241	212	46	1	2	0	0.0	23	12	11	23	4	8	2	146	166	12	20	5.2	.963	2B-36, SS-14, 3B-8, 1B-4
1911		104	.227	.315	321	73	8	7	2	0.6	40	37	28	18	9	5	2	598	109	21	49	7.9	.971	1B-57, 2B-17, SS-12, 3B-6
1912		24	.247	.274	73	18	0	1	0	0.0	8	4	2	1	2	1	0	23	42	3	4	2.8	.956	3B-15, SS-4, 2B-3, 1B-2
1913	**2 teams**	**BOS N** (1G –.000) **NY A** (44G –.134)																						
"	**total**	45	.129	.129	116	15	0	0	0	0.0	8	8	8	18	2	4	0	77	94	12	13	4.9	.934	2B-27, SS-7, 3B-2, OF-1
1914	**IND F**	149	.304	.377	570	173	24	6	2	0.4	107	38	53		47	0	0	195	327	34	28	3.7	.939	3B-149
1915	**NWK F**	127	.251	.328	451	113	22	5	1	0.2	49	43	41		28	8	3	184	226	19	17	3.6	.956	3B-117, OF-1
1916	**2 teams**	**NY N** (71G –.246) **CIN N** (37G –.277)																						
"	**total**	108	.256	.292	390	100	12	1	0	0.0	26	27	10	32	11	2	0	108	193	17	14	3.0	.947	3B-106
1917	**CIN N**	48	.254	.291	134	34	3	1	0	0.0	11	15	7	7	5	4	1	76	94	15	15	4.3	.919	2B-26, SS-13, 3B-4
1918	**PIT N**	126	.255	.340	435	111	13	9	2	0.5	34	43	24	22	12	0	0	162	261	15	26	3.5	.966	3B-126
1920		40	.218	.278	133	29	3	1	1	0.8	13	13	4	7	7	3	0	56	84	8	11	4.0	.946	3B-20, SS-10, 2B-6, 1B-1
11 yrs.		845	.251	.313	2843	713	86	33	8	0.3	319	240	188	128	127	35	8	1626	1600	156	197	4.2	.954	3B-555, 2B-116, 1B-64, SS-60, OF-2

Frank McKee

McKEE, FRANK
B. Philadelphia, Pa. Deceased.

Year	Team	Games	BA	SA	AB	H	2B	3B	HR	HR%	R	RBI	BB	SO	SB	Pinch Hit AB	Pinch Hit H	PO	A	E	DP	TC/G	FA	G by Pos
1884	WAS U	4	.176	.176	17	3	0	0	0	0.0	2	0	1	0	0	0	0	1	1	4	0	1.0	.333	OF-3, 3B-2, C-1

Red McKee

McKEE, RAYMOND ELLIS BL TR 5′11″ 180 lbs.
B. July 20, 1890, Shawnee, Ohio D. Aug. 5, 1972, Saginaw, Mich.

Year	Team	Games	BA	SA	AB	H	2B	3B	HR	HR%	R	RBI	BB	SO	SB	Pinch Hit AB	Pinch Hit H	PO	A	E	DP	TC/G	FA	G by Pos
1913	DET A	67	.283	.358	187	53	3	4	1	0.5	18	20	21	21	7	6	0	237	84	17	5	5.5	.950	C-61
1914		32	.188	.234	64	12	1	1	0	0.0	7	8	14	16	1	5	1	87	20	4	2	4.1	.964	C-27
1915		55	.274	.349	106	29	5	0	1	0.9	10	17	13	16	1	15	2	116	30	7	4	4.4	.954	C-35
1916		32	.211	.276	76	16	1	2	0	0.0	3	4	6	11	0	6	2	76	31	5	3	4.3	.955	C-26
4 yrs.		186	.254	.323	433	110	10	7	2	0.5	38	49	54	64	9	32	5	516	165	33	14	4.8	.954	C-149

Jim McKeever

McKEEVER, JAMES 5′10″ 170 lbs.
B. Apr. 19, 1861, St. John, N. B., Canada D. Aug. 19, 1897, Boston, Mass.

Year	Team	Games	BA	SA	AB	H	2B	3B	HR	HR%	R	RBI	BB	SO	SB	Pinch Hit AB	Pinch Hit H	PO	A	E	DP	TC/G	FA	G by Pos
1884	BOS U	16	.136	.136	66	9	0	0	0	0.0	13		0			0	0	96	12	16	1	7.8	.871	C-12, OF-4

Russ McKelvy

McKELVY, RUSSELL ERRETT BR TR
B. Sept. 8, 1854, Swissvale, Pa. D. Oct. 19, 1915, Omaha, Neb.

Year	Team	Games	BA	SA	AB	H	2B	3B	HR	HR%	R	RBI	BB	SO	SB	Pinch Hit AB	Pinch Hit H	PO	A	E	DP	TC/G	FA	G by Pos
1878	IND N	63	.225	.289	253	57	4	3	2	0.8	33	36	5	38		0	0	121	27	28	2	2.7	.841	OF-62, P-4
1882	PIT AA	1	.000	.000	4	0	0	0	0	0.0	0		0			0	0	0	0	0	0	0.0	.000	OF-1
2 yrs.		64	.222	.284	257	57	4	3	2	0.8	33	36	5	38		0	0	121	27	28	2	2.6	.841	OF-63, P-4

Ed McKenna

McKENNA, EDWARD J.
B. St. Louis, Mo. Deceased.

Year	Team	Games	BA	SA	AB	H	2B	3B	HR	HR%	R	RBI	BB	SO	SB	Pinch Hit AB	Pinch Hit H	PO	A	E	DP	TC/G	FA	G by Pos
1877	STL N	1	.200	.200	5	1	0	0	0	0.0	0	0	0	1		0	0	1	0	0	0	1.0	1.000	OF-1
1884	WAS U	32	.188	.197	117	22	1	0	0	0.0	19		4			0	0	124	46	35	5	5.1	.829	C-23, OF-10, 3B-7
2 yrs.		33	.189	.197	122	23	1	0	0	0.0	19	0	4	1		0	0	125	46	35	5	5.0	.830	C-23, OF-11, 3B-7

Dave McKeough

McKEOUGH, DAVID J. 5′ 7″ 158 lbs.
B. Dec. 1, 1863, Utica, N. Y. D. July 11, 1901, Utica, N. Y.

Year	Team	Games	BA	SA	AB	H	2B	3B	HR	HR%	R	RBI	BB	SO	SB	Pinch Hit AB	Pinch Hit H	PO	A	E	DP	TC/G	FA	G by Pos
1890	ROC AA	62	.225	.248	218	49	5	0	0	0.0	38		29		14	0	0	205	124	31	8	5.7	.914	C-47, SS-13, 2B-2, 3B-1
1891	PHI AA	15	.259	.315	54	14	1	1	0	0.0	4	3	8	6	0	0	0	55	17	13	5	5.7	.847	C-14, SS-1
2 yrs.		77	.232	.261	272	63	6	1	0	0.0	42	3	37	6	14	0	0	260	141	44	13	5.7	.901	C-61, SS-14, 2B-2, 3B-1

Bob McKinney

McKINNEY, ROBERT FRANCIS BR TR 5′ 7″ 165 lbs.
B. Oct. 4, 1875, McSherrystown, Pa. D. Aug. 19, 1946, Chicago, Ill.

Year	Team	Games	BA	SA	AB	H	2B	3B	HR	HR%	R	RBI	BB	SO	SB	Pinch Hit AB	Pinch Hit H	PO	A	E	DP	TC/G	FA	G by Pos
1901	PHI A	2	.000	.000	2	0	0	0	0	0.0	0	0	0		0	0	0	0	0	1	0	0.5	.000	3B-1, 2B-1

Rich McKinney

McKINNEY, CHARLES RICHARD BR TR 5′11″ 185 lbs.
B. Nov. 22, 1946, Piqua, Ohio.

Year	Team	Games	BA	SA	AB	H	2B	3B	HR	HR%	R	RBI	BB	SO	SB	Pinch Hit AB	Pinch Hit H	PO	A	E	DP	TC/G	FA	G by Pos
1970	CHI A	43	.168	.311	119	20	5	0	4	3.4	12	17	11	25	3	8	1	34	81	6	9	3.6	.950	3B-23, SS-11
1971		114	.271	.377	369	100	11	2	8	2.2	35	46	35	37	0	19	11	195	171	11	34	3.9	.971	2B-67, OF-25, 3B-5
1972	NY A	37	.215	.256	121	26	2	0	1	0.8	10	7	7	13	1	4	0	17	71	8	5	2.9	.917	3B-33
1973	OAK A	48	.246	.338	65	16	3	0	1	1.5	9	7	7	4	0	19	2	13	19	2	4	1.0	.941	3B-17, 2B-7, DH-6, OF-3
1974		5	.143	.143	7	1	0	0	0	0.0	0	0	0	0	0	3	0	1	0	0	0	0.3	1.000	2B-3
1975		8	.143	.143	7	1	0	0	0	0.0	0	2	1	2	0	4	0	1	0	0	0	0.3	1.000	DH-2, 1B-1
1977		86	.177	.303	198	35	7	0	6	3.0	13	21	16	43	0	31	6	213	27	9	22	3.8	.964	1B-32, DH-18, 3B-7, OF-5, 2B-3
7 yrs.		341	.225	.328	886	199	28	2	20	2.3	79	100	77	124	4	88	20	474	369	36	74	3.3	.959	3B-85, 2B-80, OF-33, 1B-33, DH-26, SS-11

Alex McKinnon

McKINNON, ALEXANDER J. BR 5′11½″ 170 lbs.
B. Aug. 14, 1856, Boston, Mass. D. July 24, 1887, Charlestown, Mass.
Manager 1885.

Year	Team	Games	BA	SA	AB	H	2B	3B	HR	HR%	R	RBI	BB	SO	SB	Pinch Hit AB	Pinch Hit H	PO	A	E	DP	TC/G	FA	G by Pos
1884	NY N	116	.272	.394	470	128	21	12	4	0.9	66		8	62		0	0	1097	31	53	57	10.2	.955	1B-116
1885	STL N	100	.294	.382	411	121	21	6	1	0.2	42	44	8	31		0	0	1102	26	25	50	11.5	.978	1B-100
1886		122	.301	.428	491	148	24	7	8	1.6	75	72	21	23		0	0	1175	35	47	61	10.3	.963	1B-119, OF-3
1887	PIT N	48	.340	.475	200	68	16	4	1	0.5	26	30	8	9	6	0	0	483	25	12	27	10.8	.977	1B-48
4 yrs.		386	.296	.412	1572	465	82	29	14	0.9	209	146	45	125	6	0	0	3857	117	137	195	10.7	.967	1B-383, OF-3

Jeff McKnight

McKNIGHT, JEFFERSON ALAN BB TR 6′ 170 lbs.
Son of Jim McKnight.
B. Feb. 18, 1963, Conway, Ark.

Year	Team	Games	BA	SA	AB	H	2B	3B	HR	HR%	R	RBI	BB	SO	SB	Pinch Hit AB	Pinch Hit H	PO	A	E	DP	TC/G	FA	G by Pos
1989	NY N	6	.250	.250	12	3	0	0	0	0.0	2	0	2	1	0	3	1	4	5	1	1	1.4	.900	2B-4, 1B-1, SS-1, 3B-1
1990	BAL A	29	.200	.267	75	15	2	0	1	1.3	11	4	5	17	0	2	0	106	20	0	11	4.2	1.000	1B-15, OF-8, 2B-5, SS-1, DH-1
1991		16	.171	.195	41	7	1	0	0	0.0	2	2	2	7	1	4	1	22	2	0	1	1.8	1.000	OF-7, DH-4, 1B-2
1992	NY N	31	.271	.400	85	23	3	1	2	2.4	10	13	2	8	0	13	3	82	40	3	8	4.2	.976	2B-14, 1B-9, SS-3, 3B-3, OF-1
1993		105	.256	.323	164	42	3	1	2	1.2	19	13	13	31	0	59	19	86	88	10	19	2.9	.946	SS-29, 2B-15, 1B-10, 3B-9, C-1
1994		31	.148	.185	27	4	1	0	0	0.0	1	2	4	12	0	26	4	8	0	0	0	4.0	1.000	1B-2
6 yrs.		218	.233	.304	404	94	10	2	5	1.2	45	34	28	76	1	107	28	308	155	14	40	3.3	.971	1B-39, 2B-38, SS-34, OF-16, 3B-13, DH-5, C-1

Jim McKnight

McKNIGHT, JAMES ARTHUR BR TR 6′ 1″ 185 lbs.
Father of Jeff McKnight.
B. July 1, 1936, Bee Branch, Ark. D. Feb. 24, 1994, Van Buren County, Ark.

Year	Team	Games	BA	SA	AB	H	2B	3B	HR	HR%	R	RBI	BB	SO	SB	Pinch Hit AB	Pinch Hit H	PO	A	E	DP	TC/G	FA	G by Pos
1960	CHI N	3	.333	.333	6	2	0	0	0	0.0	0	1	0	1	0	1	0	0	2	1	1	1.5	.667	2B-1, OF-1
1962		60	.224	.247	85	19	0	1	0	0.0	6	5	2	13	0	49	11	17	20	2	5	2.4	.949	3B-9, OF-5, 2B-2
2 yrs.		63	.231	.253	91	21	0	1	0	0.0	6	6	2	14	0	50	11	17	22	3	6	2.3	.929	3B-9, OF-6, 2B-3

Ed McLane

McLANE, EDWARD CAMERON 5′10″ 179 lbs.
B. Aug. 20, 1881, Weston, Mass. D. Aug. 21, 1975, Baltimore, Md.

Year	Team	Games	BA	SA	AB	H	2B	3B	HR	HR%	R	RBI	BB	SO	SB	Pinch Hit AB	Pinch Hit H	PO	A	E	DP	TC/G	FA	G by Pos
1907	BKN N	1	.000	.000	2	0	0	0	0	0.0	0	0	0		0	0	0	1	0	2	0	3.0	.333	OF-1

Art McLarney

McLARNEY, ARTHUR JAMES BB TR 6′ 168 lbs.
B. Dec. 20, 1908, Fort Worden, Wash. D. Dec. 20, 1984, Seattle, Wash.

Year	Team	Games	BA	SA	AB	H	2B	3B	HR	HR%	R	RBI	BB	SO	SB	Pinch Hit AB	Pinch Hit H	PO	A	E	DP	TC/G	FA	G by Pos
1932	NY N	9	.130	.174	23	3	1	0	0	0.0	2	3	1	3	0	0	0	13	17	0	3	3.3	1.000	SS-9

Year	Team	Games	BA	SA	AB	H	2B	3B	HR	HR%	R	RBI	BB	SO	SB	Pinch Hit AB	Pinch Hit H	PO	A	E	DP	TC/G	FA	G by Pos

Polly McLarry

McLARRY, HOWARD ZELL
B. Mar. 25, 1891, Leonard, Tex. D. Nov. 4, 1971, Bonham, Tex.
BL TR 6′ 185 lbs.

Year	Team	Games	BA	SA	AB	H	2B	3B	HR	HR%	R	RBI	BB	SO	SB	Pinch Hit AB	Pinch Hit H	PO	A	E	DP	TC/G	FA	G by Pos
1912	CHI A	2	.000	.000	2	0	0	0	0	0.0	0	0	0		0	2	0	0	0	0	0	0.0	—	
1915	CHI N	68	.197	.244	127	25	3	0	1	0.8	16	12	14	20	2	21	2	208	55	8	8	6.0	.970	1B-25, 2B-20
2 yrs.		70	.194	.240	129	25	3	0	1	0.8	16	12	14	20	2	23	2	208	55	8	8	6.0	.970	1B-25, 2B-20

Barney McLaughlin

McLAUGHLIN, BERNARD
Brother of Frank McLaughlin.
B. 1857, Ireland D. Feb. 13, 1921, Lowell, Mass.
BR TR 5′ 8″ 163 lbs.

Year	Team	Games	BA	SA	AB	H	2B	3B	HR	HR%	R	RBI	BB	SO	SB	Pinch Hit AB	Pinch Hit H	PO	A	E	DP	TC/G	FA	G by Pos
1884	KC U	42	.228	.309	162	37	7	3	0	0.0	15		9			0	0	58	49	24	8	2.9	.817	OF-24, 2B-12, P-7, SS-2
1887	PHI N	50	.220	.302	205	45	8	3	1	0.5	26	26	11	27	2	0	0	106	156	36	15	6.0	.879	2B-50
1890	SYR AA	86	.264	.313	329	87	8	1	2	0.6	43		47		13	0	0	120	258	41	22	4.9	.902	SS-86
3 yrs.		178	.243	.309	696	169	23	7	3	0.4	84	26	67	27	15	0	0	284	463	101	45	4.7	.881	SS-88, 2B-62, OF-24, P-7

Frank McLaughlin

McLAUGHLIN, FRANCIS EDWARD
Brother of Barney McLaughlin.
B. June 19, 1856, Lowell, Mass. D. Apr. 5, 1917, Lowell, Mass.
BR TR 5′ 9″ 160 lbs.

Year	Team	Games	BA	SA	AB	H	2B	3B	HR	HR%	R	RBI	BB	SO	SB	Pinch Hit AB	Pinch Hit H	PO	A	E	DP	TC/G	FA	G by Pos
1882	WOR N	15	.218	.345	55	12	0	2	1	1.8	7	4	0	11		0	0	17	40	20	2	5.1	.740	SS-14, OF-1
1883	PIT AA	29	.219	.263	114	25	2	0	1	0.9	15		6			0	0	24	85	25	4	4.1	.813	SS-25, OF-4, P-2, 2B-2
1884	3 teams CIN U (16G –.239) CHI U (15G –.239) KC U (32G –.228)																							
″	total	63	.233	.358	257	60	19	2	3	1.2	38		12			0	0	114	133	62	15	4.5	.799	2B-24, SS-22, OF-11, 3B-9, P-2
3 yrs.		107	.228	.331	426	97	21	4	5	1.2	60	4	18	11		0	0	155	258	107	21	4.5	.794	SS-61, 2B-26, OF-16, 3B-9, P-4

Jim McLaughlin

McLAUGHLIN, JAMES
B. San Francisco, Calif. Deceased.

Year	Team	Games	BA	SA	AB	H	2B	3B	HR	HR%	R	RBI	BB	SO	SB	Pinch Hit AB	Pinch Hit H	PO	A	E	DP	TC/G	FA	G by Pos
1884	WAS U	10	.189	.270	37	7	3	0	0	0.0	3		0			0	0	12	21	17	0	5.0	.660	SS-9, 3B-1

Jim McLaughlin

McLAUGHLIN, JAMES ROBERT
B. Jan. 3, 1902, St. Louis, Mo. D. Dec. 18, 1968, Mount Vernon, Ill.
BR TR 5′10½″ 170 lbs.

Year	Team	Games	BA	SA	AB	H	2B	3B	HR	HR%	R	RBI	BB	SO	SB	Pinch Hit AB	Pinch Hit H	PO	A	E	DP	TC/G	FA	G by Pos
1932	STL A	1	.000	.000	1	0	0	0	0	0.0	0	1	0	0	0	0	0	0	0	0	0	0.0	.000	3B-1

Jim McLaughlin

McLAUGHLIN, JAMES THOMAS
B. Nov. 18, 1860, Cleveland, Ohio D. Nov. 16, 1895, Cleveland, Ohio.
BL TL 157 lbs.

Year	Team	Games	BA	SA	AB	H	2B	3B	HR	HR%	R	RBI	BB	SO	SB	Pinch Hit AB	Pinch Hit H	PO	A	E	DP	TC/G	FA	G by Pos
1884	BAL AA	5	.227	.364	22	5	1	1	0	0.0	3		0			0	0	3	7	1	0	1.8	.909	OF-3, P-3

Kid McLaughlin

McLAUGHLIN, JAMES ANSON (Sunshine)
B. Apr. 12, 1888, Randolph, N. Y. D. Nov. 13, 1934, Allegany, N. Y.
BL TR 5′ 8½″ 158 lbs.

Year	Team	Games	BA	SA	AB	H	2B	3B	HR	HR%	R	RBI	BB	SO	SB	Pinch Hit AB	Pinch Hit H	PO	A	E	DP	TC/G	FA	G by Pos
1914	CIN N	3	.000	.000	2	0	0	0	0	0.0	1	0	0	0	0	1	0	1	0	0	0	0.5	1.000	OF-2

Tom McLaughlin

McLAUGHLIN, THOMAS
B. Mar. 28, 1860, Louisville, Ky. D. July 21, 1921, Louisville, Ky.
TR

Year	Team	Games	BA	SA	AB	H	2B	3B	HR	HR%	R	RBI	BB	SO	SB	Pinch Hit AB	Pinch Hit H	PO	A	E	DP	TC/G	FA	G by Pos
1883	LOU AA	42	.192	.226	146	28	1	2	0	0.0	16		5			0	0	105	72	27	8	4.5	.868	SS-19, OF-17, 1B-5, 3B-2, 2B-2
1884		98	.200	.272	335	67	11	5	1	0.3	41		22			0	0	126	346	57	36	5.3	.892	SS-93, 3B-4, 2B-2
1885		112	.212	.302	411	87	13	9	2	0.5	49		15			0	0	351	330	88	50	6.9	.886	2B-93, SS-19
1886	NY AA	74	.136	.156	250	34	3	1	0	0.0	27		26			0	0	126	233	43	17	5.4	.893	SS-63, 2B-10, OF-1
1891	WAS AA	14	.268	.317	41	11	0	1	0	0.0	9	3	7	6	3	0	0	25	36	9	6	5.0	.871	SS-14
5 yrs.		340	.192	.254	1183	227	28	18	3	0.3	142	3	75	6	3	0	0	733	1017	224	117	5.7	.887	SS-208, 2B-107, OF-18, 3B-6, 1B-5

Ralph McLaurin

McLAURIN, RALPH EDGAR
B. May 23, 1885, Kissimmee, Fla. D. Feb. 11, 1943, McColl, S. C.

Year	Team	Games	BA	SA	AB	H	2B	3B	HR	HR%	R	RBI	BB	SO	SB	Pinch Hit AB	Pinch Hit H	PO	A	E	DP	TC/G	FA	G by Pos
1908	STL N	8	.227	.227	22	5	0	0	0	0.0	2	0	0		0	2	0	14	0	2	0	2.7	.875	OF-6

Larry McLean

McLEAN, JOHN BANNERMAN
B. July 18, 1881, Frederickton, N. B., Canada D. Mar. 24, 1921, Boston, Mass.
BR TR 6′ 5″ 228 lbs.

Year	Team	Games	BA	SA	AB	H	2B	3B	HR	HR%	R	RBI	BB	SO	SB	Pinch Hit AB	Pinch Hit H	PO	A	E	DP	TC/G	FA	G by Pos
1901	BOS A	9	.211	.263	19	4	1	0	0	0.0	4	2	0		1	4	2	38	2	0	2	8.0	1.000	1B-5
1903	CHI N	1	.000	.000	4	0	0	0	0	0.0	0	1	1		0	0	0	7	1	1	0	9.0	.889	C-1
1904	STL N	27	.167	.214	84	14	2	1	0	0.0	5	4	4		1	2	0	126	20	7	1	6.4	.954	C-24
1906	CIN N	12	.200	.257	35	7	2	0	0	0.0	3	2	4		0	0	0	49	13	3	0	5.4	.954	C-12
1907		113	.289	.361	374	108	9	9	0	0.0	35	54	13		4	11	2	476	113	15	22	5.9	.975	C-89, 1B-13
1908		99	.217	.282	309	67	9	4	1	0.3	24	28	15		2	10	2	445	87	22	11	6.3	.960	C-69, 1B-19
1909		95	.256	.324	324	83	12	2	2	0.6	26	36	21		1	0	0	379	119	11	16	5.4	.978	C-95
1910		127	.298	.378	423	126	14	7	2	0.5	27	71	26	23	4	9	2	485	158	11	18	5.5	.983	C-119
1911		107	.287	.320	328	94	7	2	0	0.0	24	34	20	18	1	8	0	414	138	18	16	5.8	.968	C-98
1912		102	.243	.303	333	81	15	1	1	0.3	17	27	18	15	1	4	2	425	124	15	16	5.8	.973	C-98
1913	2 teams STL N (48G –.270) NY N (30G –.320)																							
″	total	78	.286	.344	227	65	13	0	0	0.0	10	21	10	13	1	8	2	244	80	10	9	4.8	.970	C-70
1914	NY N	79	.260	.299	154	40	6	0	0	0.0	8	14	4	9	4	4	0	211	42	7	8	3.5	.973	C-74
1915		13	.152	.152	33	5	0	0	0	0.0	0	4	0	1	0	1	0	47	18	1	0	5.5	.985	C-12
13 yrs.		862	.262	.323	2647	694	90	26	6	0.2	183	298	136	79	20	61	12	3346	915	121	119	5.5	.972	C-761, 1B-37
WORLD SERIES																								
1913	NY N	5	.500	.500	12	6	0	0	0	0.0	0	2	0	0	0	1	0	12	4	0	0	4.0	1.000	C-4

Mark McLemore

McLEMORE, MARK TREMELL
B. Oct. 4, 1964, San Diego, Calif.
BB TR 5′11″ 175 lbs.

Year	Team	Games	BA	SA	AB	H	2B	3B	HR	HR%	R	RBI	BB	SO	SB	Pinch Hit AB	Pinch Hit H	PO	A	E	DP	TC/G	FA	G by Pos
1986	CAL A	5	.000	.000	4	0	0	0	0	0.0	0	0	1	2	0	0	0	3	10	0	1	6.5	1.000	2B-2
1987		138	.236	.300	433	102	13	3	3	0.7	61	41	48	72	25	1	0	293	363	17	98	4.8	.975	2B-132, SS-6, DH-3
1988		77	.240	.330	233	56	11	2	2	0.9	38	16	25	28	13	9	3	108	178	6	53	4.2	.979	2B-63, 3B-5, DH-1
1989		32	.243	.291	103	25	3	1	0	0.0	12	14	7	19	6	1	0	55	88	5	24	5.3	.966	2B-27, DH-1
1990	2 teams CAL A (20G –.146) CLE A (8G –.167)																							
″	total	28	.150	.183	60	9	2	0	0	0.0	6	2	4	15	1	2	0	37	39	4	10	3.2	.950	2B-11, SS-8, 3B-4, DH-2
1991	HOU N	21	.148	.164	61	9	1	0	0	0.0	6	2	6	13	0	2	0	25	54	2	8	4.3	.975	2B-19
1992	BAL A	101	.246	.294	228	56	7	2	0	0.0	40	27	21	26	11	11	4	126	186	7	47	3.7	.978	2B-70, DH-16
1993		148	.284	.368	581	165	27	5	4	0.7	81	72	64	92	21	0	0	335	80	6	23	2.7	.986	OF-124, 2B-25, 3B-4, DH-1

Mark McLemore *continued*

Year	Team	Games	BA	SA	AB	H	2B	3B	HR	HR%	R	RBI	BB	SO	SB	Pinch Hit AB	Pinch Hit H	PO	A	E	DP	TC/G	FA	G by Pos
1994		104	.257	.321	343	88	11	1	3	0.9	44	29	51	50	20	4	0	220	270	9	53	4.8	.982	2B-96, OF-7, DH-1
1995	TEX A	129	.261	.358	467	122	20	5	5	1.1	73	41	59	71	21	3	1	246	184	4	40	3.1	.991	OF-73, 2B-66, DH-1
10 yrs.		783	.251	.325	2513	632	95	19	17	0.7	361	244	286	388	118	33	8	1448	1452	60	357	3.9	.980	2B-511, OF-204, DH-26, SS-14, 3B-13

Jim McLeod

McLEOD, SOULE JAMES BR TR 6′ 187 lbs.
B. Sept. 12, 1908, Jones, La. D. Aug. 3, 1981, Little Rock, Ark.

Year	Team	Games	BA	SA	AB	H	2B	3B	HR	HR%	R	RBI	BB	SO	SB	Pinch Hit AB	Pinch Hit H	PO	A	E	DP	TC/G	FA	G by Pos
1930	WAS A	18	.265	.294	34	9	1	0	0	0.0	3	1	1	5	1	0	0	10	19	2	1	1.8	.935	3B-10, SS-7
1932		7	—	—	0	0	0	0	0	—	1	0	1	0	0	0	0	0	1	0	0	1.0	1.000	SS-1
1933	PHI N	67	.194	.228	232	45	6	1	0	0.0	20	15	12	25	1	0	0	60	120	17	8	2.9	.914	3B-67, SS-1
3 yrs.		92	.203	.237	266	54	7	1	0	0.0	24	16	14	30	2	0	0	70	140	19	9	2.7	.917	3B-77, SS-9

Ralph McLeod

McLEOD, RALPH ALTON BL TL 6′ 170 lbs.
B. Oct. 19, 1916, West Quincy, Mass.

Year	Team	Games	BA	SA	AB	H	2B	3B	HR	HR%	R	RBI	BB	SO	SB	Pinch Hit AB	Pinch Hit H	PO	A	E	DP	TC/G	FA	G by Pos
1938	BOS N	6	.286	.429	7	2	1	0	0	0.0	1	0	0	2	0	5	2	1	0	0	0	1.0	1.000	OF-1

Jack McMahon

McMAHON, JOHN HENRY BR TL 5′10″ 165 lbs.
B. Oct. 15, 1869, Waterbury, Conn. D. Dec. 30, 1894, Bridgeport, Conn.

Year	Team	Games	BA	SA	AB	H	2B	3B	HR	HR%	R	RBI	BB	SO	SB	Pinch Hit AB	Pinch Hit H	PO	A	E	DP	TC/G	FA	G by Pos
1892	NY N	40	.224	.374	147	33	5	7	1	0.7	21	24	10	9	3	0	0	331	16	11	14	8.7	.969	1B-36, C-5
1893		11	.333	.467	30	10	2	1	0	0.0	5	4	2	0	0	0	0	33	8	5	0	4.2	.891	C-11
2 yrs.		51	.243	.390	177	43	7	8	1	0.6	26	28	12	9	3	0	0	364	24	16	14	7.8	.960	1B-36, C-16

Frank McManus

McMANUS, FRANCIS E. TR 5′10″
B. Sept. 21, 1875, Lawrence, Mass. D. Sept. 1, 1923, Syracuse, N. Y.

Year	Team	Games	BA	SA	AB	H	2B	3B	HR	HR%	R	RBI	BB	SO	SB	Pinch Hit AB	Pinch Hit H	PO	A	E	DP	TC/G	FA	G by Pos
1899	WAS N	7	.381	.429	21	8	1	0	0	0.0	3	2	2		3	0	0	15	12	2	1	4.1	.931	C-7
1903	BKN N	2	.000	.000	7	0	0	0	0	0.0	0	0	0		0	0	0	9	4	1	0	7.0	.929	C-2
1904	2 teams	DET A (1G –.000) NY A (4G –.000)																						
″	total	5	.000	.000	7	0	0	0	0	0.0	0	0	0		0	0	0	9	0	1	0	2.0	.900	C-5
3 yrs.		14	.229	.257	35	8	1	0	0	0.0	3	2	2		3	0	0	33	16	4	1	3.8	.925	C-14

Jim McManus

McMANUS, JAMES MICHAEL BL TL 6′ 4″ 215 lbs.
B. July 20, 1936, Brookline, Mass.

Year	Team	Games	BA	SA	AB	H	2B	3B	HR	HR%	R	RBI	BB	SO	SB	Pinch Hit AB	Pinch Hit H	PO	A	E	DP	TC/G	FA	G by Pos
1960	KC A	5	.308	.538	13	4	0	0	1	7.7	3	2	1	2	0	2	0	29	1	0	1	10.0	1.000	1B-3

Marty McManus

McMANUS, MARTIN JOSEPH BR TR 5′10½″ 160 lbs.
B. Mar. 14, 1900, Chicago, Ill. D. Feb. 18, 1966, St. Louis, Mo.
Manager 1932–33.

Year	Team	Games	BA	SA	AB	H	2B	3B	HR	HR%	R	RBI	BB	SO	SB	Pinch Hit AB	Pinch Hit H	PO	A	E	DP	TC/G	FA	G by Pos
1920	STL A	1	.333	1.000	3	1	0	1	0	0.0	0	1	0	0	0	0	0	0	2	1	0	3.0	.667	3B-1
1921		121	.260	.367	412	107	19	8	3	0.7	49	64	27	30	5	0	0	290	312	32	54	5.2	.950	2B-96, 3B-13, 1B-10, SS-2
1922		154	.312	.459	606	189	34	11	11	1.8	88	109	38	41	9	0	0	404	468	33	103	5.9	.964	2B-153, 1B-1
1923		154	.309	.481	582	180	35	10	15	2.6	86	94	49	50	14	1	0	555	385	32	102	6.4	.967	2B-133, 1B-20
1924		123	.333	.441	442	147	23	5	5	1.1	71	80	54	40	13	4	1	324	365	20	67	6.0	.972	2B-118
1925		154	.288	.457	587	169	**44**	8	13	2.2	108	90	73	**69**	5	0	0	430	479	31	93	6.1	.967	2B-154, OF-1
1926		149	.284	.424	549	156	30	10	9	1.6	102	68	55	62	5	0	0	332	399	27	68	5.1	.964	3B-84, 2B-61, 1B-4
1927	DET A	108	.268	.431	369	99	19	7	9	2.4	60	69	34	38	8	9	4	245	263	17	54	5.1	.968	SS-39, 2B-35, 3B-22, 1B-6
1928		139	.288	.430	500	144	37	5	8	1.6	78	73	51	32	11	4	1	490	213	19	45	5.2	.974	3B-92, 1B-45, SS-1
1929		154	.280	.451	599	168	32	8	18	3.0	99	90	60	52	17	0	0	219	308	15	31	3.4	.972	3B-150, SS-9
1930		132	.320	.475	484	155	40	4	9	1.9	74	89	59	28	**23**	0	0	156	249	14	26	3.1	.967	3B-130, SS-3, 1B-1
1931	2 teams	DET A (107G –.271) BOS A (17G –.290)																						
″	total	124	.274	.366	424	116	21	3	4	0.9	47	62	57	23	8	5	0	162	303	21	37	4.1	.957	3B-90, 2B-28, 1B-1
1932	BOS A	93	.235	.374	302	71	19	4	5	1.7	39	24	36	30	1	15	1	151	228	18	28	4.8	.955	2B-49, 3B-30, SS-2, 1B-1
1933		106	.284	.413	366	104	30	4	3	0.8	51	36	49	21	3	3	1	143	207	14	20	3.4	.962	3B-76, 2B-26, 1B-4
1934	BOS N	119	.276	.372	435	120	18	0	8	1.8	56	47	32	42	5	8	2	188	326	22	45	4.9	.959	2B-73, 3B-37
15 yrs.		1831	.289	.430	6660	1926	401	88	120	1.8	1008	996	674	558	127	49	10	4089	4507	316	773	4.9	.965	2B-926, 3B-725, 1B-93, SS-56, OF-1

Jimmy McMath

McMATH, JIMMY LEE BL TL 6′ 1½″ 195 lbs.
B. Aug. 10, 1949, Tuscaloosa, Ala.

Year	Team	Games	BA	SA	AB	H	2B	3B	HR	HR%	R	RBI	BB	SO	SB	Pinch Hit AB	Pinch Hit H	PO	A	E	DP	TC/G	FA	G by Pos
1968	CHI N	6	.143	.143	14	2	0	0	0	0.0	0	2	0	6	0	3	0	6	0	0	0	2.0	1.000	OF-3

George McMillan

McMILLAN, GEORGE A. (Reddy) 5′ 8″ 175 lbs.
B. Evansville, Ind. Deceased.

Year	Team	Games	BA	SA	AB	H	2B	3B	HR	HR%	R	RBI	BB	SO	SB	Pinch Hit AB	Pinch Hit H	PO	A	E	DP	TC/G	FA	G by Pos
1890	NY N	10	.143	.143	35	5	0	0	0	0.0	4	1	7	4	1	0	0	11	1	3	0	1.5	.800	OF-10

Norm McMillan

McMILLAN, NORMAN ALEXIS (Bub) BR TR 6′ 175 lbs.
B. Oct. 5, 1895, Latta, S. C. D. Sept. 28, 1969, Marion, S. C.

Year	Team	Games	BA	SA	AB	H	2B	3B	HR	HR%	R	RBI	BB	SO	SB	Pinch Hit AB	Pinch Hit H	PO	A	E	DP	TC/G	FA	G by Pos
1922	NY A	33	.256	.321	78	20	1	2	0	0.0	7	11	6	10	4	1	0	37	1	3	0	1.5	.927	OF-23, 3B-5
1923	BOS A	131	.253	.327	459	116	24	5	0	0.0	37	42	28	44	13	2	0	261	327	35	48	4.8	.944	3B-67, 2B-35, SS-28
1924	STL A	76	.279	.358	201	56	12	2	0	0.0	25	27	12	17	6	8	4	132	122	11	19	4.3	.958	2B-37, 3B-17, SS-6, 1B-2
1928	CHI N	49	.220	.293	123	27	2	2	1	0.8	11	12	13	19	0	9	1	44	84	5	13	3.6	.962	2B-19, 3B-18
1929		124	.271	.392	495	134	35	5	5	1.0	77	55	36	43	13	3	2	131	226	21	21	3.2	.944	3B-120
5 yrs.		413	.260	.352	1356	353	74	16	6	0.4	157	147	95	133	36	23	7	605	760	75	101	3.8	.948	3B-227, 2B-91, SS-34, OF-23, 1B-2
WORLD SERIES																								
1922	NY A	1	.000	.000	2	0	0	0	0	0.0	0	0	0	0	0	1	0	1	0	0	0	1.0	1.000	OF-1
1929	CHI N	5	.100	.100	20	2	0	0	0	0.0	0	0	2	6	1	0	0	6	9	0	0	3.0	1.000	3B-5
2 yrs.		6	.091	.091	22	2	0	0	0	0.0	0	0	2	6	1	1	0	7	9	0	0	2.7	1.000	3B-5, OF-1

Roy McMillan

McMILLAN, ROY DAVID BR TR 5′11″ 170 lbs.
B. July 17, 1930, Bonham, Tex.
Manager 1972, 1975.

Year	Team	Games	BA	SA	AB	H	2B	3B	HR	HR%	R	RBI	BB	SO	SB	Pinch Hit AB	Pinch Hit H	PO	A	E	DP	TC/G	FA	G by Pos
1951	CIN N	85	.211	.246	199	42	4	0	1	0.5	21	8	17	26	0	8	3	92	160	9	28	3.9	.966	SS-54, 3B-12, 2B-1
1952		154	.244	.350	540	132	32	2	7	1.3	60	57	45	81	4	0	0	297	495	24	101	5.3	.971	SS-154

Roy McMillan *continued*

Year	Team	Games	BA	SA	AB	H	2B	3B	HR	HR%	R	RBI	BB	SO	SB	Pinch Hit AB	Pinch Hit H	PO	A	E	DP	TC/G	FA	G by Pos
1953		155	.233	.302	557	130	15	4	5	0.9	51	43	43	52	2	0	0	288	519	23	114	5.4	.972	SS-155
1954		154	.250	.313	588	147	21	2	4	0.7	86	42	47	54	4	0	0	341	464	34	129	5.4	.959	SS-154
1955		151	.268	.328	470	126	21	2	1	0.2	50	37	66	33	4	0	0	290	495	25	111	5.4	.969	SS-150
1956		150	.263	.344	479	126	16	7	3	0.6	51	62	76	54	4	0	0	319	511	21	105	5.7	.975	SS-150
1957		151	.272	.357	448	122	25	5	1	0.2	50	55	66	44	5	0	0	253	418	16	86	4.5	.977	SS-151
1958		145	.229	.298	393	90	18	3	1	0.3	48	25	47	33	5	0	0	278	394	14	81	4.7	.980	SS-145
1959		79	.264	.447	246	65	14	2	9	3.7	38	24	27	27	0	0	0	163	205	10	50	5.2	.974	SS-73
1960		124	.236	.351	399	94	12	2	10	2.5	42	42	35	40	2	0	0	174	329	19	70	4.1	.964	SS-116, 2B-10
1961	MIL N	154	.220	.293	505	111	16	0	7	1.4	42	48	61	86	2	0	0	257	496	19	110	5.0	.975	SS-154
1962		137	.246	.350	468	115	13	0	12	2.6	66	41	60	53	2	2	1	243	424	19	85	5.1	.972	SS-135
1963		100	.250	.325	320	80	10	1	4	1.3	35	29	17	25	1	4	2	143	283	9	60	4.6	.979	SS-94
1964	2 teams	MIL N (8G –.308) NY N (113G –.211)																						
"	total	121	.214	.253	392	84	8	2	1	0.3	31	27	14	18	4	2	0	224	360	15	66	5.0	.975	SS-119
1965	NY N	157	.242	.292	528	128	19	2	1	0.2	44	42	24	60	1	4	0	248	477	27	80	4.9	.964	SS-153
1966		76	.214	.277	220	47	9	1	1	0.5	24	12	20	25	1	5	2	112	203	8	35	4.5	.975	SS-71
16 yrs.		2093	.243	.321	6752	1639	253	35	68	1.0	739	594	665	711	41	25	8	3722	6233	292	1311	5.0	.972	SS-2028, 3B-12, 2B-11

Tommy McMillan

McMILLAN, THOMAS ERWIN
B. Sept. 13, 1951, Richmond, Va.
BR TR 5′ 9″ 165 lbs.

Year	Team	Games	BA	SA	AB	H	2B	3B	HR	HR%	R	RBI	BB	SO	SB	Pinch Hit AB	Pinch Hit H	PO	A	E	DP	TC/G	FA	G by Pos
1977	SEA A	2	.000	.000	5	0	0	0	0	0.0	0	0	0	0	0	0	0	2	3	0	1	2.5	1.000	SS-2

Tommy McMillan

McMILLAN, THOMAS LAW (Rebel)
B. Apr. 18, 1888, Pittston, Pa. D. July 15, 1966, Orlando, Fla.
BR TR 5′ 5″ 130 lbs.

Year	Team	Games	BA	SA	AB	H	2B	3B	HR	HR%	R	RBI	BB	SO	SB	Pinch Hit AB	Pinch Hit H	PO	A	E	DP	TC/G	FA	G by Pos
1908	BKN N	43	.238	.259	147	35	3	0	0	0.0	9	3	9		5	0	0	82	86	22	10	4.4	.884	SS-29, OF-14
1909		108	.212	.257	373	79	15	1	0	0.0	18	24	20		11	1	0	197	314	48	33	5.2	.914	SS-105, 2B-2, 3B-1
1910	2 teams	BKN N (23G –.176) CIN N (82G –.185)																						
"	total	105	.183	.205	322	59	1	3	0	0.0	22	15	37	33	11	0	0	210	336	47	39	5.6	.921	SS-105
1912	NY A	41	.228	.242	149	34	2	0	0	0.0	24	12	15		18	0	0	74	109	10	12	4.7	.948	SS-41
4 yrs.		297	.209	.238	991	207	21	4	0	0.0	73	54	81	33	45	1	0	563	845	127	94	5.2	.917	SS-280, OF-14, 2B-2, 3B-1

Hugh McMullen

McMULLEN, HUGH RAPHAEL
B. Dec. 16, 1901, La Cygne, Kans. D. May 23, 1986, Whittier, Calif.
BB TR 6′ 1″ 180 lbs.
BB 1928–1929

Year	Team	Games	BA	SA	AB	H	2B	3B	HR	HR%	R	RBI	BB	SO	SB	Pinch Hit AB	Pinch Hit H	PO	A	E	DP	TC/G	FA	G by Pos
1925	NY N	5	.133	.200	15	2	1	0	0	0.0	1	0	0	3	0	0	0	12	0	0	0	2.4	1.000	C-5
1926		57	.187	.209	91	17	2	0	0	0.0	5	6	2	18	1	1	0	107	22	8	3	2.4	.942	C-56
1928	WAS A	1	.000	.000	1	0	0	0	0	0.0	0	0	0	1	0	1	0	0	0	0	0	0.0	—	
1929	CIN N	1	.000	.000	1	0	0	0	0	0.0	0	0	0	0	0	0	0	2	0	0	0	2.0	1.000	C-1
4 yrs.		64	.176	.204	108	19	3	0	0	0.0	6	6	2	22	1	2	0	121	22	8	3	2.4	.947	C-62

Ken McMullen

McMULLEN, KENNETH LEE
B. June 1, 1942, Oxnard, Calif.
BR TR 6′ 3″ 190 lbs.

Year	Team	Games	BA	SA	AB	H	2B	3B	HR	HR%	R	RBI	BB	SO	SB	Pinch Hit AB	Pinch Hit H	PO	A	E	DP	TC/G	FA	G by Pos
1962	LA N	6	.273	.273	11	3	0	0	0	0.0	0	0	0	3	0	4	1	1	0	0	0	0.5	1.000	OF-2
1963		79	.236	.339	233	55	9	0	5	2.1	16	28	20	46	1	8	1	48	134	13	8	2.7	.933	3B-71, OF-1, 2B-1
1964		24	.209	.254	67	14	0	0	1	1.5	3	2	3	7	0	6	0	106	9	3	7	5.9	.975	1B-13, 3B-4, OF-3
1965	WAS A	150	.263	.414	555	146	18	6	18	3.2	75	54	47	90	2	5	0	169	300	22	29	3.3	.955	3B-142, OF-8, 1B-1
1966		147	.233	.359	524	122	19	4	13	2.5	48	54	44	89	3	2	1	190	284	21	33	3.3	.958	3B-141, 1B-8, OF-1
1967		146	.245	.377	563	138	22	2	16	2.8	73	67	46	84	5	0	0	153	348	18	38	3.6	.965	3B-145
1968		151	.248	.382	557	138	11	2	20	3.6	66	62	63	66	1	5	1	194	302	19	26	3.3	.963	3B-145, SS-11
1969		158	.272	.425	562	153	25	2	19	3.4	83	87	70	103	4	5	1	185	347	13	35	3.5	.976	3B-154
1970	2 teams	WAS A (15G –.203) CAL A (124G –.232)																						
"	total	139	.229	.351	481	110	11	3	14	2.9	55	64	64	91	1	4	1	154	306	19	39	3.5	.960	3B-137
1971	CAL A	160	.250	.395	593	148	19	2	21	3.5	63	68	53	74	1	3	0	137	344	17	27	3.2	.966	3B-158
1972		137	.269	.369	472	127	18	1	9	1.9	36	34	48	59	1	0	0	89	267	11	26	2.7	.970	3B-137
1973	LA N	42	.247	.482	85	21	5	0	5	5.9	6	18	6	13	0	19	6	5	54	5	2	2.7	.922	3B-24
1974		44	.250	.417	60	15	1	0	3	5.0	5	12	2	12	0	35	9	10	14	0	1	2.4	1.000	3B-7, 2B-3
1975		39	.239	.435	46	11	1	1	2	4.3	4	14	7	12	0	25	6	26	12	0	1	2.7	1.000	3B-11, 1B-3
1976	OAK A	98	.220	.355	186	41	6	2	5	2.7	20	23	22	33	1	31	**9**	222	39	2	20	2.9	.992	3B-35, 1B-26, DH-23, OF-5, 2B-1
1977	MIL A	63	.228	.404	136	31	7	1	5	3.7	15	19	15	33	0	24	5	80	15	2	10	2.1	.979	DH-29, 1B-11, 3B-7
16 yrs.		1583	.248	.383	5131	1273	172	26	156	3.0	568	606	510	815	20	176	41	1769	2775	165	302	3.2	.965	3B-1318, 1B-62, DH-52, OF-20, SS-11, 2B-5
LEAGUE CHAMPIONSHIP SERIES																								
1974	LA N	1	.000	.000	1	0	0	0	0	0.0	0	0	0	1	0	1	0	0	0	0	0	0.0	—	

Fred McMullin

McMULLIN, FREDERICK WILLIAM
B. Oct. 13, 1891, Scammon, Kans. D. Nov. 21, 1952, Los Angeles, Calif.
BR TR 5′11″ 170 lbs.

Year	Team	Games	BA	SA	AB	H	2B	3B	HR	HR%	R	RBI	BB	SO	SB	Pinch Hit AB	Pinch Hit H	PO	A	E	DP	TC/G	FA	G by Pos
1914	DET A	1	.000	.000	1	0	0	0	0	0.0	0	0	0	1	0	0	0	1	1	1	0	3.0	.667	SS-1
1916	CHI A	68	.257	.273	187	48	3	0	0	0.0	8	10	19	30	9	2	1	78	116	10	11	3.1	.951	3B-63, SS-2, 2B-1
1917		59	.237	.258	194	46	2	1	0	0.0	35	12	27	17	9	5	1	63	92	15	4	3.1	.912	3B-52, SS-2
1918		70	.277	.319	235	65	7	0	1	0.4	32	16	25	26	7	0	0	74	151	14	9	3.4	.941	3B-69, 2B-1
1919		60	.294	.388	170	50	8	4	0	0.0	31	19	11	18	4	8	4	54	96	11	11	3.2	.932	3B-46, 2B-5
1920		46	.197	.268	127	25	1	4	0	0.0	14	13	9	13	1	11	1	31	56	3	5	2.7	.967	3B-29, 2B-3, SS-1
6 yrs.		304	.256	.302	914	234	21	9	1	0.1	120	70	91	105	30	26	7	301	512	54	40	3.2	.938	3B-259, 2B-10, SS-6
WORLD SERIES																								
1917	CHI A	6	.125	.167	24	3	1	0	0	0.0	1	2	1	6	0	0	0	2	14	0	2	2.7	1.000	3B-6
1919		2	.500	.500	2	1	0	0	0	0.0	0	0	0	0	0	2	1	0	0	0	0	0.0	—	
2 yrs.		8	.154	.192	26	4	1	0	0	0.0	1	2	1	6	0	2	1	2	14	0	2	2.7	1.000	3B-6

Carl McNabb

McNABB, CARL MAC (Skinny)
B. Jan. 25, 1917, Stevenson, Ala.
BR TR 5′ 9″ 155 lbs.

Year	Team	Games	BA	SA	AB	H	2B	3B	HR	HR%	R	RBI	BB	SO	SB	Pinch Hit AB	Pinch Hit H	PO	A	E	DP	TC/G	FA	G by Pos
1945	DET A	1	.000	.000	1	0	0	0	0	0.0	0	0	0	1	0	1	0	0	0	0	0	0.0	—	

Eric McNair

McNAIR, DONALD ERIC (Boob) BR TR 5′ 8″ 160 lbs.
B. Apr. 12, 1909, Meridian, Miss. D. Mar. 11, 1949, Meridian, Miss.

Year	Team	Games	BA	SA	AB	H	2B	3B	HR	HR%	R	RBI	BB	SO	SB	Pinch Hit AB	Pinch Hit H	PO	A	E	DP	TC/G	FA	G by Pos
1929	PHI A	4	.500	.625	8	4	1	0	0	0.0	2	3	0	0	1	0	0	6	5	0	0	2.8	1.000	SS-4
1930		78	.266	.333	237	63	12	2	0	0.0	27	34	9	19	5	7	1	100	110	17	13	3.4	.925	SS-31, 3B-29, 2B-5, OF-1
1931		79	.271	.368	280	76	10	1	5	1.8	41	33	11	19	1	3	1	97	155	19	36	3.6	.930	3B-47, 2B-16, SS-13
1932		135	.285	.478	554	158	**47**	3	18	3.2	87	95	28	29	8	2	0	242	391	31	89	5.0	.953	SS-133
1933		89	.261	.403	310	81	15	4	7	2.3	57	48	15	32	2	16	5	169	216	17	39	5.4	.958	SS-46, 2B-28
1934		151	.280	.412	599	168	20	4	17	2.8	80	82	35	42	7	0	0	305	489	41	109	5.5	.951	SS-151
1935		137	.270	.342	526	142	22	2	4	0.8	55	57	35	33	3	3	0	270	364	28	80	4.9	.958	SS-121, 3B-11, 1B-2
1936	BOS A	128	.285	.391	494	141	36	2	4	0.8	68	74	27	34	3	0	0	272	346	23	67	4.9	.964	SS-84, 2B-35, 3B-11
1937		126	.292	.453	455	133	29	4	12	2.6	60	76	30	33	10	9	2	256	344	27	72	5.2	.957	2B-106, SS-9, 3B-4, 1B-1
1938		46	.156	.188	96	15	1	1	0	0.0	9	7	3	6	0	14	2	43	69	10	15	3.8	.918	SS-15, 2B-14, 3B-3
1939	CHI A	129	.324	.426	479	155	18	5	7	1.5	62	82	38	41	17	1	0	151	299	25	43	3.6	.947	3B-103, 2B-19, SS-9
1940		66	.227	.371	251	57	13	1	7	2.8	26	31	12	26	1	0	0	130	171	17	27	4.8	.947	2B-65, 3B-1
1941	DET A	23	.186	.203	59	11	1	0	0	0.0	5	3	4	4	0	9	3	14	24	2	1	2.9	.950	3B-11, SS-3
1942	2 teams	DET A (26G –.162)			PHI A (34G –.243)																			
″	total	60	.211	.251	171	36	4	0	1	0.6	13	8	14	10	1	8	1	77	101	15	16	3.8	.922	SS-50, 2B-1
14 yrs.		1251	.274	.392	4519	1240	229	29	82	1.8	592	633	261	328	59	72	15	2132	3084	272	607	4.6	.950	SS-669, 2B-289, 3B-220, 1B-3, OF-1
WORLD SERIES																								
1930	PHI A	1	.000	.000	1	0	0	0	0	0.0	0	0	0	0	0	1	0	0	0	0	0	0.0	—	
1931		2	.000	.000	2	0	0	0	0	0.0	1	0	0	1	0	1	0	1	1	0	0	2.0	1.000	2B-1
2 yrs.		3	.000	.000	3	0	0	0	0	0.0	1	0	0	1	0	2	0	1	1	0	0	2.0	1.000	2B-1

Mike McNally

McNALLY, MICHAEL JOSEPH BR TR 5′11″ 150 lbs.
B. Sept. 9, 1892, Minooka, Pa. D. May 29, 1965, Bethlehem, Pa.

Year	Team	Games	BA	SA	AB	H	2B	3B	HR	HR%	R	RBI	BB	SO	SB	Pinch Hit AB	Pinch Hit H	PO	A	E	DP	TC/G	FA	G by Pos
1915	BOS A	23	.151	.189	53	8	0	1	0	0.0	7	0	3	7	0	0	0	20	28	5	4	2.3	.906	3B-18, 2B-5
1916		87	.170	.170	135	23	0	0	0	0.0	28	9	10	19	9	2	0	63	112	11	10	3.3	.941	2B-35, 3B-14, SS-7, OF-1
1917		42	.300	.320	50	15	1	0	0	0.0	9	2	6	3	3	1	1	21	48	3	3	2.5	.958	3B-14, SS-9, 2B-6
1919		33	.262	.357	42	11	4	0	0	0.0	10	6	1	2	4	1	0	21	42	3	6	2.6	.955	3B-11, SS-11, 2B-3
1920		93	.256	.279	312	80	5	1	0	0.0	42	23	31	24	13	1	1	230	246	32	40	5.6	.937	2B-76, SS-8, 1B-6
1921	NY A	71	.260	.312	215	56	4	2	1	0.5	36	24	14	15	5	1	0	80	169	9	12	4.0	.965	3B-48, 2B-16
1922		52	.252	.294	143	36	2	2	0	0.0	20	18	16	14	2	0	0	61	96	4	7	3.5	.975	3B-32, 2B-9, SS-4, 1B-1
1923		30	.211	.211	38	8	0	0	0	0.0	5	1	3	4	2	3	0	10	27	2	1	1.6	.949	SS-13, 3B-7, 2B-5
1924		49	.246	.246	69	17	0	0	0	0.0	11	2	7	5	1	2	1	48	62	2	7	2.5	.982	2B-25, 3B-13, SS-6
1925	WAS A	12	.143	.143	21	3	0	0	0	0.0	1	0	1	4	0	0	0	11	10	2	1	2.3	.913	3B-7, SS-2, 2B-1
10 yrs.		492	.238	.267	1078	257	16	6	1	0.1	169	85	92	97	39	11	3	565	840	73	91	3.6	.951	2B-181, 3B-164, SS-60, 1B-7, OF-1
WORLD SERIES																								
1916	BOS A	1	—	—	0	0	0	0	0	—	1	0	0	0	0	0	0	0	0	0	0	0.0	—	
1921	NY A	7	.200	.250	20	4	1	0	0	0.0	3	1	1	3	2	0	0	5	10	3	2	2.6	.833	3B-7
1922		1	—	—	0	0	0	0	0	—	0	0	0	0	0	0	0	1	1	0	0	2.0	1.000	2B-1
3 yrs.		9	.200	.250	20	4	1	0	0	0.0	4	1	1	3	2	0	0	6	11	3	2	2.5	.850	3B-7, 2B-1

Bob McNamara

McNAMARA, ROBERT MAXEY BR TR 5′10″ 170 lbs.
B. Sept. 19, 1916, Denver, Colo.

Year	Team	Games	BA	SA	AB	H	2B	3B	HR	HR%	R	RBI	BB	SO	SB	Pinch Hit AB	Pinch Hit H	PO	A	E	DP	TC/G	FA	G by Pos
1939	PHI A	9	.222	.333	9	2	1	0	0	0.0	0	3	1	1	0	0	0	5	5	0	0	1.1	1.000	3B-5, SS-2, 2B-1, 1B-1

Dinny McNamara

McNAMARA, JOHN RAYMOND BL TR 5′ 9″ 165 lbs.
B. Sept. 16, 1905, Lexington, Mass. D. Dec. 20, 1963, Arlington, Mass.

Year	Team	Games	BA	SA	AB	H	2B	3B	HR	HR%	R	RBI	BB	SO	SB	Pinch Hit AB	Pinch Hit H	PO	A	E	DP	TC/G	FA	G by Pos
1927	BOS N	11	.000	.000	9	0	0	0	0	0.0	3	0	0	3	0	0	0	10	0	0	0	3.3	1.000	OF-3
1928		9	.250	.250	4	1	0	0	0	0.0	2	0	0	1	0	1	0	7	0	0	0	2.3	1.000	OF-3
2 yrs.		20	.077	.077	13	1	0	0	0	0.0	5	0	0	4	0	1	0	17	0	0	0	2.8	1.000	OF-6

George McNamara

McNAMARA, GEORGE FRANCIS BL TR 6′ 175 lbs.
B. Jan. 11, 1901, Chicago, Ill. D. June 12, 1990, Hinsdale, Ill.

Year	Team	Games	BA	SA	AB	H	2B	3B	HR	HR%	R	RBI	BB	SO	SB	Pinch Hit AB	Pinch Hit H	PO	A	E	DP	TC/G	FA	G by Pos
1922	WAS A	3	.273	.273	11	3	0	0	0	0.0	3	1	1	2	0	0	0	3	0	0	0	1.0	1.000	OF-3

Jim McNamara

McNAMARA, JAMES PATRICK BL TR 6′ 4″ 210 lbs.
B. June 10, 1965, Nashua, N. H.

Year	Team	Games	BA	SA	AB	H	2B	3B	HR	HR%	R	RBI	BB	SO	SB	Pinch Hit AB	Pinch Hit H	PO	A	E	DP	TC/G	FA	G by Pos
1992	SF N	30	.216	.270	74	16	1	0	1	1.4	6	9	6	25	0	1	0	131	8	1	1	4.7	.993	C-30
1993		4	.143	.143	7	1	0	0	0	0.0	0	1	0	1	0	1	0	12	0	0	0	3.0	1.000	C-4
2 yrs.		34	.210	.259	81	17	1	0	1	1.2	6	10	6	26	0	2	0	143	8	1	1	4.5	.993	C-34

Tom McNamara

McNAMARA, THOMAS HENRY BR TR 6′ 2″ 200 lbs.
B. Nov. 5, 1895, Roxbury, Mass. D. May 5, 1974, Danvers, Mass.

Year	Team	Games	BA	SA	AB	H	2B	3B	HR	HR%	R	RBI	BB	SO	SB	Pinch Hit AB	Pinch Hit H	PO	A	E	DP	TC/G	FA	G by Pos
1922	PIT N	1	.000	.000	1	0	0	0	0	0.0	0	0	0	0	0	1	0	0	0	0	0	0.0	—	

Rusty McNealy

McNEALY, ROBERT LEE BL TL 5′ 8″ 160 lbs.
B. Aug. 12, 1958, Sacramento, Calif.

Year	Team	Games	BA	SA	AB	H	2B	3B	HR	HR%	R	RBI	BB	SO	SB	Pinch Hit AB	Pinch Hit H	PO	A	E	DP	TC/G	FA	G by Pos
1983	OAK A	15	.000	.000	4	0	0	0	0	0.0	5	0	0	0	0	0	0	6	0	0	0	0.5	1.000	DH-7, OF-5

Earl McNeely

McNEELY, GEORGE EARL BR TR 5′ 9″ 155 lbs.
B. May 12, 1898, Sacramento, Calif. D. July 16, 1971, Sacramento, Calif.

Year	Team	Games	BA	SA	AB	H	2B	3B	HR	HR%	R	RBI	BB	SO	SB	Pinch Hit AB	Pinch Hit H	PO	A	E	DP	TC/G	FA	G by Pos
1924	WAS A	43	.330	.425	179	59	5	6	0	0.0	31	15	5	21	3	1	0	105	3	3	1	2.6	.973	OF-42
1925		122	.286	.356	385	110	14	2	3	0.8	76	37	48	54	14	1	0	262	13	7	3	2.5	.975	OF-112, 1B-1
1926		124	.303	.403	442	134	20	12	0	0.0	84	48	44	28	18	2	0	274	9	9	3	2.4	.969	OF-120
1927		73	.276	.373	185	51	10	4	0	0.0	40	16	11	13	11	11	2	118	5	4	1	2.5	.969	OF-47, 1B-4
1928	STL A	127	.236	.319	496	117	27	7	0	0.0	66	44	37	39	8	7	2	229	19	4	2	2.1	.984	OF-120
1929		69	.243	.300	230	56	8	1	1	0.4	27	18	7	13	2	6	0	96	4	2	0	1.6	.980	OF-62
1930		76	.272	.362	235	64	19	1	0	0.0	33	20	22	14	8	3	1	302	18	8	30	5.0	.976	OF-38, 1B-27
1931		49	.225	.265	102	23	4	0	0	0.0	12	15	9	5	4	4	0	59	3	2	1	1.8	.969	OF-36
8 yrs.		683	.272	.354	2254	614	107	33	4	0.2	369	213	183	187	68	35	5	1445	74	39	41	2.6	.975	OF-577, 1B-32

Earl McNeely *continued*

Year	Team	Games	BA	SA	AB	H	2B	3B	HR	HR%	R	RBI	BB	SO	SB	Pinch Hit AB	Pinch Hit H	PO	A	E	DP	TC/G	FA	G by Pos
WORLD SERIES																								
1924	WAS A	7	.222	.333	27	6	3	0	0	0.0	4	1	4	4	1	1	0	8	0	1	0	1.5	.889	OF-6
1925		4	—	—	0	0	0	0	0	—	2	0	0	0	1	0	0	3	0	0	0	1.5	1.000	OF-2
2 yrs.		11	.222	.333	27	6	3	0	0	0.0	6	1	4	4	2	1	0	11	0	1	0	1.5	.917	OF-8

Jeff McNeely

McNEELY, JEFFREY LAVERN BR TR 6′ 2″ 190 lbs.
B. Oct. 18, 1969, Monroe, N. C.

Year	Team	Games	BA	SA	AB	H	2B	3B	HR	HR%	R	RBI	BB	SO	SB	Pinch Hit AB	Pinch Hit H	PO	A	E	DP	TC/G	FA	G by Pos
1993	BOS A	21	.297	.378	37	11	1	1	0	0.0	10	1	7	9	6	1	0	22	0	2	0	1.6	.917	OF-13, DH-2

Norm McNeil

McNEIL, NORMAN FRANCIS BR TR 5′11″ 180 lbs.
B. Oct. 22, 1892, Chicago, Ill. D. Apr. 11, 1942, Buffalo, N. Y.

Year	Team	Games	BA	SA	AB	H	2B	3B	HR	HR%	R	RBI	BB	SO	SB	Pinch Hit AB	Pinch Hit H	PO	A	E	DP	TC/G	FA	G by Pos
1919	BOS A	5	.333	.333	9	3	0	0	0	0.0	0	1	1	0	0	0	0	8	1	2	0	2.2	.818	C-5

Jerry McNertney

McNERTNEY, GERALD EDWARD BR TR 6′ 180 lbs.
B. Aug. 7, 1936, Boone, Iowa.

Year	Team	Games	BA	SA	AB	H	2B	3B	HR	HR%	R	RBI	BB	SO	SB	Pinch Hit AB	Pinch Hit H	PO	A	E	DP	TC/G	FA	G by Pos
1964	CHI A	73	.215	.290	186	40	5	0	3	1.6	16	23	19	24	0	6	0	360	30	5	5	5.7	.987	C-69
1966		44	.220	.220	59	13	0	0	0	0.0	3	1	7	6	1	5	0	112	14	4	0	3.5	.969	C-37
1967		56	.228	.350	123	28	6	0	3	2.4	8	13	6	14	0	1	1	229	41	1	4	5.2	.996	C-52
1968		74	.219	.308	169	37	4	1	3	1.8	18	18	18	29	0	11	3	301	39	5	9	5.3	.986	C-64, 1B-1
1969	SEA A	128	.241	.349	410	99	18	1	8	2.0	39	55	29	63	1	7	3	697	67	9	13	6.3	.988	C-122
1970	MIL A	111	.243	.348	296	72	11	1	6	2.0	27	22	22	33	1	18	4	461	53	8	6	4.9	.985	C-94, 1B-13
1971	STL N	56	.289	.445	128	37	4	2	4	3.1	15	22	12	14	0	16	5	192	7	3	1	5.6	.985	C-36
1972		39	.208	.313	48	10	3	1	0	0.0	3	9	6	16	0	28	4	50	4	1	0	5.5	.982	C-10
1973	PIT N	9	.250	.250	4	1	0	0	0	0.0	0	0	0	0	0	0	0	11	0	0	0	1.2	1.000	C-9
9 yrs.		590	.237	.338	1423	337	51	6	27	1.9	129	163	119	199	3	92	20	2413	255	36	38	5.3	.987	C-493, 1B-14

Bill McNulty

McNULTY, WILLIAM FRANCIS BR TR 6′ 4″ 205 lbs.
B. Aug. 29, 1946, Sacramento, Calif.

Year	Team	Games	BA	SA	AB	H	2B	3B	HR	HR%	R	RBI	BB	SO	SB	Pinch Hit AB	Pinch Hit H	PO	A	E	DP	TC/G	FA	G by Pos
1969	OAK A	5	.000	.000	17	0	0	0	0	0.0	0	0	0	10	0	0	0	9	2	0	0	2.2	1.000	OF-5
1972		4	.100	.100	10	1	0	0	0	0.0	0	0	2	1	0	1	0	2	2	1	0	1.7	.800	3B-3
2 yrs.		9	.037	.037	27	1	0	0	0	0.0	0	0	2	11	0	1	0	11	4	1	0	2.0	.938	OF-5, 3B-3

Pat McNulty

McNULTY, PATRICK HOWARD BL TR 5′11″ 160 lbs.
B. Feb. 27, 1899, Cleveland, Ohio D. May 4, 1963, Hollywood, Calif.

Year	Team	Games	BA	SA	AB	H	2B	3B	HR	HR%	R	RBI	BB	SO	SB	Pinch Hit AB	Pinch Hit H	PO	A	E	DP	TC/G	FA	G by Pos
1922	CLE A	22	.271	.339	59	16	2	1	0	0.0	10	5	9	5	4	0	0	43	0	2	0	2.0	.956	OF-22
1924		101	.268	.347	291	78	13	5	0	0.0	46	26	33	22	10	15	3	137	9	6	2	2.0	.961	OF-75
1925		118	.314	.421	373	117	18	2	6	1.6	70	43	47	23	7	5	3	206	16	8	2	2.1	.965	OF-111
1926		48	.250	.321	56	14	2	1	0	0.0	3	6	5	9	0	31	7	8	2	1	0	1.2	.909	OF-9
1927		19	.317	.341	41	13	1	0	0	0.0	3	4	4	3	1	5	2	28	1	3	1	2.7	.906	OF-12
5 yrs.		308	.290	.378	820	238	36	9	6	0.7	132	84	98	62	22	56	15	422	28	20	5	2.1	.957	OF-229

Bid McPhee

McPHEE, JOHN ALEXANDER BR TR 5′ 8″ 152 lbs.
B. Nov. 1, 1859, Massena, N. Y. D. Jan. 3, 1943, San Diego, Calif.
Manager 1901–02.

Year	Team	Games	BA	SA	AB	H	2B	3B	HR	HR%	R	RBI	BB	SO	SB	Pinch Hit AB	Pinch Hit H	PO	A	E	DP	TC/G	FA	G by Pos
1882	CIN AA	78	.228	.309	311	71	8	7	1	0.3	43		11			0	0	274	207	42	36	6.7	.920	2B-78
1883		96	.245	.343	367	90	10	10	2	0.5	61		18			0	0	314	277	46	48	6.6	.928	2B-96
1884		112	.278	.360	450	125	8	7	5	1.1	107		27			0	0	415	365	64	74	7.5	.924	2B-112
1885		110	.265	.311	431	114	12	4	0	0.0	78		19			0	0	339	354	47	57	6.7	.936	2B-110
1886		140	.266	.388	560	149	23	12	**7**	1.3	139		59			0	0	529	464	65	90	7.6	.939	2B-140
1887		129	.289	.407	540	156	20	**19**	2	0.4	137		55		95	0	0	442	434	72	76	7.3	.924	2B-129
1888		111	.240	.336	458	110	12	10	4	0.9	88	51	43		54	0	0	369	365	47	65	7.0	.940	2B-109, OF-1, 3B-1
1889		135	.269	.369	540	145	25	7	5	0.9	109	57	60	29	63	0	0	430	450	52	85	6.9	.944	2B-135, 3B-1
1890	CIN N	132	.256	.386	528	135	16	22	3	0.6	125	39	82	26	55	0	0	404	431	51	62	6.7	.942	2B-132
1891		138	.256	.370	562	144	14	16	6	1.1	107	38	74	35	33	0	0	389	492	42	72	6.7	.954	2B-138
1892		144	.274	.370	573	157	19	12	4	0.7	111	60	84	48	44	0	0	451	471	51	86	6.8	.948	2B-144
1893		127	.281	.379	491	138	17	11	3	0.6	101	68	94	20	25	0	0	396	455	41	101	7.0	.954	2B-127
1894		128	.304	.418	474	144	21	9	5	1.1	107	88	90	23	33	0	0	389	446	49	72	7.0	.945	2B-126
1895		115	.299	.417	432	129	24	12	1	0.2	107	75	73	30	30	0	0	355	366	34	57	6.6	.955	2B-115
1896		117	.305	.386	433	132	18	7	1	0.2	81	87	51	18	48	0	0	297	357	15	56	5.7	.978	2B-117
1897		81	.301	.408	282	85	13	7	1	0.4	45	39	35		9	0	0	209	267	17	34	6.1	.966	2B-81
1898		133	.249	.346	486	121	26	9	1	0.2	72	60	66		21	0	0	302	396	34	74	5.5	.954	2B-130, OF-3
1899		111	.279	.370	373	104	17	7	1	0.3	60	65	40		18	5	**3**	245	312	26	41	5.5	.955	2B-106
18 yrs.		2137	.271	.372	8291	2249	303	188	52	0.6	1678	727	981	229	528	5	3	6549	6909	795	1186	6.7	.944	2B-2125, OF-4, 3B-2

Marty McQuaid

McQUAID, MORTIMER MARTIN
B. June 28, 1861, Chicago, Ill. D. Mar. 5, 1928, Chicago, Ill.

Year	Team	Games	BA	SA	AB	H	2B	3B	HR	HR%	R	RBI	BB	SO	SB	Pinch Hit AB	Pinch Hit H	PO	A	E	DP	TC/G	FA	G by Pos
1891	STL AA	4	.364	.545	11	4	2	0	0	0.0	1	1	0	1	1	0	0	6	6	0	1	3.0	1.000	2B-3, OF-1
1898	WAS N	1	.000	.000	4	0	0	0	0	0.0	0	0	0		0	0	0	1	0	2	0	3.0	.333	OF-1
2 yrs.		5	.267	.400	15	4	2	0	0	0.0	1	1	0	1	1	0	0	7	6	2	1	3.0	.867	2B-3, OF-2

Jerry McQuaig

McQUAIG, GERALD JOSEPH BR TR 5′11″ 183 lbs.
B. Jan. 31, 1912, Douglas, Ga.

Year	Team	Games	BA	SA	AB	H	2B	3B	HR	HR%	R	RBI	BB	SO	SB	Pinch Hit AB	Pinch Hit H	PO	A	E	DP	TC/G	FA	G by Pos
1934	PHI A	7	.063	.063	16	1	0	0	0	0.0	2	1	2	4	0	0	0	8	0	1	0	1.5	.889	OF-6

Mox McQuery

McQUERY, WILLIAM THOMAS 6′ 4″
B. June 28, 1861, Garrard County, Ky. D. June 12, 1900, Cincinnati, Ohio.

Year	Team	Games	BA	SA	AB	H	2B	3B	HR	HR%	R	RBI	BB	SO	SB	Pinch Hit AB	Pinch Hit H	PO	A	E	DP	TC/G	FA	G by Pos
1884	CIN U	35	.280	.364	132	37	5	0	2	1.5	31		8			0	0	340	8	8	9	10.2	.978	1B-35
1885	DET N	70	.273	.388	278	76	15	4	3	1.1	34	30	8	29		0	0	714	29	18	33	10.9	.976	1B-69, OF-1
1886	KC N	122	.247	.352	449	111	27	4	4	0.9	62	38	36	44		0	0	1295	50	43	61	11.4	.969	1B-122
1890	SYR AA	122	.308	.384	461	142	17	6	2	0.4	64		53		26	0	0	1146	45	34	63	10.0	.972	1B-122
1891	WAS AA	68	.241	.330	261	63	9	4	2	0.8	40	37	18	19	3	0	0	701	30	17	39	11.0	.977	1B-68
5 yrs.		417	.271	.365	1581	429	73	18	13	0.8	231	105	123	92	29	0	0	4196	162	120	205	10.7	.973	1B-416, OF-1

Glenn McQuillen

McQUILLEN, GLENN RICHARD (Red) BR TR 6′ 198 lbs.
B. Apr. 19, 1915, Strasburg, Va. D. June 8, 1989, Gardenville, Md.

Year	Team		Games	BA	SA	AB	H	2B	3B	HR	HR%	R	RBI	BB	SO	SB	Pinch Hit AB	Pinch Hit H	PO	A	E	DP	TC/G	FA	G by Pos
1938	**STL**	**A**	43	.284	.319	116	33	4	0	0	0.0	14	13	4	12	0	12	3	66	0	2	0	2.3	.971	OF-30
1941			7	.333	.524	21	7	2	1	0	0.0	4	3	1	2	0	1	0	14	0	1	0	2.5	.933	OF-6
1942			100	.283	.425	339	96	15	12	3	0.9	40	47	10	17	1	23	4	156	2	5	0	2.1	.969	OF-77
1946			59	.241	.313	166	40	3	3	1	0.6	24	12	19	18	0	9	1	77	8	2	0	1.8	.977	OF-48
1947			1	.000	.000	1	0	0	0	0	0.0	0	0	0	0	0	1	0	0	0	0	0	0.0	—	
5 yrs.			210	.274	.379	643	176	24	16	4	0.6	82	75	34	49	1	46	8	313	10	10	0	2.1	.970	OF-161

George McQuinn

McQUINN, GEORGE HARTLEY BL TL 5′11″ 165 lbs.
B. May 29, 1910, Arlington, Va. D. Dec. 24, 1978, Alexandria, Va.

Year	Team		Games	BA	SA	AB	H	2B	3B	HR	HR%	R	RBI	BB	SO	SB	Pinch Hit AB	Pinch Hit H	PO	A	E	DP	TC/G	FA	G by Pos
1936	**CIN**	**N**	38	.201	.284	134	27	3	4	0	0.0	5	13	10	22	0	0	0	336	27	3	30	9.6	.992	1B-38
1938	**STL**	**A**	148	.324	.477	602	195	42	7	12	2.0	100	82	58	49	4	0	0	1207	90	10	134	8.8	.992	1B-148
1939			154	.316	.515	617	195	37	13	20	3.2	101	94	65	42	6	0	0	1377	116	11	122	9.8	.993	1B-154
1940			151	.279	.460	594	166	39	10	16	2.7	78	84	57	58	3	1	0	1436	124	13	157	10.5	.992	1B-150
1941			130	.297	.479	495	147	28	4	18	3.6	93	80	74	30	5	4	0	1138	109	6	109	10.0	.995	1B-125
1942			145	.262	.403	554	145	32	5	12	2.2	86	78	60	77	1	1	0	1384	105	13	116	10.4	.991	1B-144
1943			125	.243	.374	449	109	19	2	12	2.7	53	74	56	65	4	3	0	1072	86	9	88	9.6	.992	1B-122
1944			146	.250	.376	516	129	26	3	11	2.1	83	72	85	74	4	0	0	1332	72	9	116	9.7	.994	1B-146
1945			139	.277	.398	483	134	31	3	7	1.4	69	61	65	51	1	4	4	1143	105	11	87	9.3	.991	1B-136
1946	**PHI**	**A**	136	.225	.316	484	109	23	6	3	0.6	47	35	64	62	4	2	1	1098	99	15	107	9.0	.988	1B-134
1947	**NY**	**A**	144	.304	.437	517	157	24	3	13	2.5	84	80	78	66	0	2	1	1198	93	8	120	9.1	.994	1B-142
1948			94	.248	.421	302	75	11	4	11	3.6	33	41	40	38	0	7	1	693	48	5	79	8.3	.993	1B-90
12 yrs.			1550	.276	.424	5747	1588	315	64	135	2.3	832	794	712	634	32	24	7	13414	1074	113	1265	9.5	.992	1B-1529
WORLD SERIES																									
1944	**STL**	**A**	6	.438	.750	16	7	2	0	1	6.3	2	5	7	2	0	0	0	50	2	0	3	8.7	1.000	1B-6
1947	**NY**	**A**	7	.130	.130	23	3	0	0	0	0.0	3	1	5	8	0	0	0	48	4	1	3	7.6	.981	1B-7
2 yrs.			13	.256	.385	39	10	2	0	1	2.6	5	6	12	10	0	0	0	98	6	1	6	8.1	.990	1B-13

Brian McRae

McRAE, BRIAN WESLEY BB TR 6′ 175 lbs.
Son of Hal McRae.
B. Aug. 27, 1967, Bradenton, Fla.

Year	Team		Games	BA	SA	AB	H	2B	3B	HR	HR%	R	RBI	BB	SO	SB	Pinch Hit AB	Pinch Hit H	PO	A	E	DP	TC/G	FA	G by Pos
1990	**KC**	**A**	46	.286	.405	168	48	8	3	2	1.2	21	23	9	29	4	1	1	120	1	0	0	2.7	1.000	OF-45
1991			152	.261	.372	629	164	28	9	8	1.3	86	64	24	99	20	2	1	405	2	3	0	2.7	.993	OF-150
1992			149	.223	.308	533	119	23	5	4	0.8	63	52	42	88	18	5	2	419	8	3	2	2.9	.993	OF-148, DH-1
1993			153	.282	.413	627	177	28	9	12	1.9	78	69	37	105	23	3	0	394	4	7	3	2.6	.983	OF-153
1994			114	.273	.378	436	119	22	6	4	0.9	71	40	54	67	28	1	0	252	2	3	0	2.3	.988	OF-110, DH-4
1995	**CHI**	**N**	137	.288	.440	**580**	167	38	7	12	2.1	92	48	47	92	27	1	0	345	4	3	0	2.6	.991	OF-137
6 yrs.			751	.267	.385	2973	794	147	39	42	1.4	411	296	213	480	120	13	4	1935	21	19	5	2.6	.990	OF-743, DH-5

Hal McRae

McRAE, HAROLD ABRAHAM BR TR 5′11″ 180 lbs.
Father of Brian McRae.
B. July 10, 1945, Avon Park, Fla.
Manager 1991–94.

Year	Team		Games	BA	SA	AB	H	2B	3B	HR	HR%	R	RBI	BB	SO	SB	Pinch Hit AB	Pinch Hit H	PO	A	E	DP	TC/G	FA	G by Pos
1968	**CIN**	**N**	17	.196	.216	51	10	1	0	0	0.0	1	2	4	14	1	1	0	33	30	5	8	4.3	.926	2B-16
1970			70	.248	.442	165	41	6	1	8	4.8	18	23	15	23	0	19	5	53	7	1	1	1.2	.984	OF-46, 3B-6, 2B-1
1971			99	.264	.427	337	89	24	2	9	2.7	39	34	11	35	3	13	2	167	6	6	1	2.0	.966	OF-91
1972			61	.278	.474	97	27	4	0	5	5.2	9	26	2	10	0	40	10	16	14	6	1	1.6	.833	OF-12, 3B-11
1973	**KC**	**A**	106	.234	.385	338	79	18	3	9	2.7	36	50	34	38	2	10	2	101	6	5	2	1.1	.955	OF-64, DH-37, 3B-2
1974			148	.310	.475	539	167	36	4	15	2.8	71	88	54	68	11	2	0	132	3	7	2	1.0	.951	DH-90, OF-56, 3B-1
1975			126	.306	.442	480	147	38	6	5	1.0	58	71	47	47	11	0	0	207	7	3	2	1.7	.986	OF-114, DH-12, 3B-1
1976			149	.332	.461	527	175	34	5	8	1.5	75	73	64	43	22	3	1	63	2	2	0	0.5	.970	DH-117, OF-31
1977			162	.298	.515	641	191	**54**	11	21	3.3	104	92	59	43	18	1	1	81	8	4	1	0.6	.957	DH-116, OF-46
1978			156	.273	.429	623	170	39	5	16	2.6	90	72	51	62	17	0	0	3	1	0	0	0.0	1.000	DH-153, OF-3
1979			101	.288	.466	393	113	32	4	10	2.5	55	74	38	46	5	2	1	0	0	0	0	0.0	.000	DH-100
1980			124	.297	.483	489	145	39	5	14	2.9	73	83	29	56	10	4	2	17	0	0	0	0.1	1.000	DH-110, OF-9
1981			101	.272	.396	389	106	23	2	7	1.8	38	36	34	33	3	0	0	10	0	1	0	0.1	.909	DH-97, OF-4
1982			159	.308	.542	613	189	**46**	8	27	4.4	91	**133**	55	61	4	0	0	1	0	1	0	0.0	.500	DH-158, OF-1
1983			157	.311	.462	589	183	41	6	12	2.0	84	82	50	68	2	1	0	0	0	0	0	0.0	.000	DH-156
1984			106	.303	.397	317	96	13	4	3	0.9	30	42	34	47	0	20	4	0	0	0	0	0.0	.000	DH-94
1985			112	.259	.450	320	83	19	0	14	4.4	41	70	44	45	0	24	4	0	0	0	0	0.0	.000	DH-106
1986			112	.252	.378	278	70	14	0	7	2.5	22	37	18	39	0	**47**	**15**	0	0	0	0	0.0	.000	DH-75
1987			18	.313	.500	32	10	3	0	1	3.1	5	9	5	1	0	11	4	0	0	0	0	0.0	.000	DH-7
19 yrs.			2084	.290	.454	7218	2091	484	66	191	2.6	940	1097	648	779	109	198	51	884	84	41	18	0.5	.959	DH-1428, OF-477, 3B-21, 2B-17
DIVISIONAL PLAYOFF SERIES																									
1981	**KC**	**A**	3	.091	.182	11	1	1	0	0	0.0	0	0	1	1	0	0	0	0	0	0	0	0.0	.000	DH-3
LEAGUE CHAMPIONSHIP SERIES																									
1970	**CIN**	**N**	2	.000	.000	4	0	0	0	0	0.0	0	0	0	1	0	1	0	2	0	0	0	2.0	1.000	OF-1
1972			1	—	—	0	0	0	0	0	—	0	0	0	0	0	0	0	0	0	0	0	0.0	—	
1976	**KC**	**A**	5	.118	.294	17	2	1	1	0	0.0	2	1	1	4	0	0	0	5	1	0	0	1.2	1.000	DH-3, OF-2
1977			5	.444	.778	18	8	3	0	1	5.6	6	2	3	1	0	0	0	2	1	0	0	0.6	1.000	DH-3, OF-2
1978			4	.214	.214	14	3	0	0	0	0.0	0	2	2	2	1	0	0	0	0	0	0	0.0	.000	DH-4
1980			3	.200	.200	10	2	0	0	0	0.0	0	0	1	3	0	0	0	0	0	0	0	0.0	.000	DH-3
1984			2	1.000	1.500	2	2	1	0	0	0.0	0	1	0	0	0	2	2	0	0	0	0	0.0	—	
1985			6	.261	.348	23	6	2	0	0	0.0	1	3	1	6	0	0	0	0	0	0	0	0.0	.000	DH-6
8 yrs.			28	.261	.398	88	23	7	1	1	1.1	9	9	8	17	1	3	2	9	2	0	0	0.5	1.000	DH-19, OF-5
			3rd					**1st**							**10th**										
WORLD SERIES																									
1970	**CIN**	**N**	3	.455	.636	11	5	2	0	0	0.0	1	3	0	1	0	0	0	2	1	0	0	1.0	1.000	OF-3
1972			5	.444	.556	9	4	1	0	0	0.0	1	2	0	1	0	2	2	4	0	0	0	2.0	1.000	OF-2

Hal McRae *continued*

Year	Team		Games	BA	SA	AB	H	2B	3B	HR	HR%	R	RBI	BB	SO	SB	Pinch Hit AB	Pinch Hit H	PO	A	E	DP	TC/G	FA	G by Pos
1980	KC	A	6	.375	.500	24	9	3	0	0	0.0	3	1	2	2	0	0	0	0	0	0	0	0.0	.000	DH-6
1985			3	.000	.000	1	0	0	0	0	0.0	0	0	1	0	0	1	0	0	0	0	0	0.0	—	
4 yrs.			17	.400 3rd	.533	45	18	6	0	0	0.0	5	6	3	4	0	3	2	6	1	0	0	0.6	1.000	DH-6, OF-5

McRemer

McREMER
Deceased.

Year	Team		Games	BA	SA	AB	H	2B	3B	HR	HR%	R	RBI	BB	SO	SB	Pinch Hit AB	Pinch Hit H	PO	A	E	DP	TC/G	FA	G by Pos
1884	WAS	U	1	.000	.000	3	0	0	0	0	0.0	0		0			0	0	2	0	0	0	2.0	1.000	OF-1

Kevin McReynolds

McREYNOLDS, WALTER KEVIN (Big Mac) BR TR 6′ 1″ 205 lbs.
B. Oct. 16, 1959, Little Rock, Ark.

Year	Team		Games	BA	SA	AB	H	2B	3B	HR	HR%	R	RBI	BB	SO	SB	Pinch Hit AB	Pinch Hit H	PO	A	E	DP	TC/G	FA	G by Pos
1983	SD	N	39	.221	.343	140	31	3	1	4	2.9	15	14	12	29	2	2	1	87	4	1	1	2.4	.989	OF-38
1984			147	.278	.465	525	146	26	6	20	3.8	68	75	34	69	3	5	1	422	10	4	1	3.0	.991	OF-143
1985			152	.234	.371	564	132	24	4	15	2.7	61	75	43	81	4	2	0	430	12	3	3	3.0	.993	OF-150
1986			158	.287	.504	560	161	31	6	26	4.6	89	96	66	83	8	4	1	332	9	8	4	2.3	.977	OF-154
1987	NY	N	151	.276	.495	590	163	32	5	29	4.9	86	95	39	70	14	3	2	286	8	4	0	2.0	.987	OF-150
1988			147	.288	.496	552	159	30	2	27	4.9	82	99	38	56	21	3	1	252	18	4	5	1.9	.985	OF-147
1989			148	.272	.450	545	148	25	3	22	4.0	74	85	46	74	15	3	1	307	10	10	3	2.3	.969	OF-145
1990			147	.269	.455	521	140	23	1	24	4.6	75	82	71	61	9	2	1	237	14	3	2	1.8	.988	OF-144
1991			143	.259	.416	522	135	32	1	16	3.1	65	74	49	46	6	4	2	281	9	2	1	2.1	.993	OF-141
1992	KC	A	109	.247	.418	373	92	25	0	13	3.5	45	49	67	48	7	4	0	204	4	3	0	2.0	.986	OF-106, DH-1
1993			110	.245	.425	351	86	22	4	11	3.1	44	42	37	56	2	16	2	191	5	2	0	1.9	.990	OF-104, DH-1
1994	NY	N	51	.256	.406	180	46	11	2	4	2.2	23	21	20	34	2	4	0	91	1	0	1	2.0	1.000	OF-47
12 yrs.			1502	.265	.447	5423	1439	284	35	211	3.9	727	807	522	707	93	52	12	3120	104	44	21	2.2	.987	OF-1469, DH-2
LEAGUE CHAMPIONSHIP SERIES																									
1984	SD	N	4	.300	.600	10	3	0	0	1	10.0	2	4	3	1	0	0	0	10	0	0	0	2.5	1.000	OF-4
1988	NY	N	7	.250	.536	28	7	2	0	2	7.1	4	4	3	5	2	0	0	19	0	0	0	2.7	1.000	OF-7
2 yrs.			11	.263	.553	38	10	2	0	3	7.9	6	8	6	6	2	0	0	29	0	0	0	2.6	1.000	OF-11

Pete McShannic

McSHANNIC, PETER ROBERT BB TR 5′ 7″ 190 lbs.
B. Mar. 20, 1864, Pittsburgh, Pa. D. Nov. 30, 1946, Toledo, Ohio.

Year	Team		Games	BA	SA	AB	H	2B	3B	HR	HR%	R	RBI	BB	SO	SB	Pinch Hit AB	Pinch Hit H	PO	A	E	DP	TC/G	FA	G by Pos
1888	PIT	N	26	.194	.204	98	19	1	0	0	0.0	5	5	1	9	3	0	0	39	49	9	1	3.7	.907	3B-26

Trick McSorley

McSORLEY, JOHN BERNARD BR TR 5′ 4″ 142 lbs.
B. Dec. 16, 1852, St. Louis, Mo. D. Feb. 9, 1936, St. Louis, Mo.

Year	Team		Games	BA	SA	AB	H	2B	3B	HR	HR%	R	RBI	BB	SO	SB	Pinch Hit AB	Pinch Hit H	PO	A	E	DP	TC/G	FA	G by Pos
1884	TOL	AA	21	.250	.265	68	17	1	0	0	0.0	12		3			0	0	154	10	7	13	7.4	.959	1B-16, OF-5, P-1, 3B-1
1885	STL	N	2	.500	.667	6	3	1	0	0	0.0	2	1	2	1		0	0	1	1	3	0	2.5	.400	3B-2
1886	STL	AA	5	.150	.300	20	3	3	0	0	0.0	1		0			0	0	4	9	4	0	3.4	.765	SS-5
3 yrs.			28	.245	.298	94	23	5	0	0	0.0	15	1	5	1		0	0	159	20	14	13	6.4	.927	1B-16, OF-5, SS-5, 3B-3, P-1

Paul McSweeney

McSWEENEY, PAUL A.
B. Apr. 3, 1867, St. Louis, Mo. D. Aug. 12, 1951, St. Louis, Mo.

Year	Team		Games	BA	SA	AB	H	2B	3B	HR	HR%	R	RBI	BB	SO	SB	Pinch Hit AB	Pinch Hit H	PO	A	E	DP	TC/G	FA	G by Pos
1891	STL	AA	3	.250	.333	12	3	1	0	0	0.0	2	2	0	0	1	0	0	7	6	8	0	5.3	.619	2B-3, 3B-1

Jim McTamany

McTAMANY, JAMES EDWARD BR TR 5′ 8″ 190 lbs.
B. July 1, 1863, Philadelphia, Pa. D. Apr. 16, 1916, Lenni, Pa.

Year	Team		Games	BA	SA	AB	H	2B	3B	HR	HR%	R	RBI	BB	SO	SB	Pinch Hit AB	Pinch Hit H	PO	A	E	DP	TC/G	FA	G by Pos
1885	BKN	AA	35	.275	.382	131	36	7	2	1	0.8	21		9			0	0	43	0	5	0	1.4	.896	OF-35
1886			111	.254	.371	418	106	23	10	2	0.5	86		54			0	0	215	27	29	5	2.4	.893	OF-111
1887			134	.258	.344	520	134	22	10	1	0.2	123		76		66	0	0	281	32	28	8	2.5	.918	OF-134
1888	KC	AA	130	.246	.331	516	127	12	10	4	0.8	94	41	67		55	0	0	245	27	26	5	2.3	.913	OF-130
1889	COL	AA	139	.276	.365	529	146	21	7	4	0.8	113	52	116	66	40	0	0	247	28	30	8	2.2	.902	OF-139
1890			125	.258	.352	466	120	27	7	1	0.2	**140**		**112**		43	0	0	232	17	16	8	2.1	.940	OF-125
1891	2 teams		COL AA (81G –.250) PHI AA (58G –.225)																						
″	total		139	.239	.364	522	125	23	12	6	1.1	116	56	101	92	33	0	0	279	20	27	5	2.3	.917	OF-139
7 yrs.			813	.256	.355	3102	794	135	58	19	0.6	693	149	535	158	237	0	0	1542	151	161	39	2.3	.913	OF-813

Cal McVey

McVEY, CALVIN ALEXANDER BR TR 5′ 9″ 170 lbs.
B. Aug. 30, 1850, Montrose, Iowa D. Aug. 20, 1926, San Francisco, Calif.
Manager 1878–79.

Year	Team		Games	BA	SA	AB	H	2B	3B	HR	HR%	R	RBI	BB	SO	SB	Pinch Hit AB	Pinch Hit H	PO	A	E	DP	TC/G	FA	G by Pos
1876	CHI	N	63	.347	.406	308	107	15	0	1	0.3	62	53	2	4		0	0	511	24	27	21	7.6	.952	1B-55, P-11, C-6, 3B-1, OF-1
1877			60	.368	.455	266	98	9	7	0	0.0	58	36	8	11		0	0	179	75	42	4	3.9	.858	C-40, 3B-17, P-17, 2B-1, 1B-1
1878	CIN	N	61	.306	.395	271	83	10	4	2	0.7	43	28	5	10		0	0	83	107	42	6	3.6	.819	3B-61, C-3
1879			81	.297	.381	354	105	18	6	0	0.0	64	55	8	13		0	0	752	8	44	33	9.6	.945	1B-72, OF-7, P-3, 3B-1, C-1
4 yrs.			265	.328	.407	1199	393	52	17	3	0.3	227	172	23	38		0	0	1525	214	155	64	6.4	.918	1B-128, 3B-80, C-50, P-31, OF-8, 2B-1

George McVey

McVEY, GEORGE W. BR TR 6′ 1″ 185 lbs.
B. Sept. 16, 1865, Port Jervis, N. Y. D. May 3, 1896, Quincy, Ill.

Year	Team		Games	BA	SA	AB	H	2B	3B	HR	HR%	R	RBI	BB	SO	SB	Pinch Hit AB	Pinch Hit H	PO	A	E	DP	TC/G	FA	G by Pos
1885	BKN	AA	6	.143	.143	21	3	0	0	0	0.0	2		2			0	0	45	4	3	3	8.7	.942	1B-3, C-3

Bill McWilliams

McWILLIAMS, WILLIAM HENRY BR TR 6′ 1″ 180 lbs.
B. Nov. 28, 1910, Dubuque, Iowa.

Year	Team		Games	BA	SA	AB	H	2B	3B	HR	HR%	R	RBI	BB	SO	SB	Pinch Hit AB	Pinch Hit H	PO	A	E	DP	TC/G	FA	G by Pos
1931	BOS	A	2	.000	.000	2	0	0	0	0	0.0	0	0	0	1	0	2	0	0	0	0	0	0.0	—	

Bobby Meacham

MEACHAM, ROBERT ANDREW BB TR 6′ 1″ 180 lbs.
B. Aug. 25, 1960, Los Angeles, Calif. BR 1987–1988

Year	Team		Games	BA	SA	AB	H	2B	3B	HR	HR%	R	RBI	BB	SO	SB	Pinch Hit AB	Pinch Hit H	PO	A	E	DP	TC/G	FA	G by Pos
1983	NY	A	22	.235	.275	51	12	2	0	0	0.0	5	4	4	10	8	0	0	16	64	6	9	3.9	.930	SS-18, 3B-4
1984			99	.253	.328	360	91	13	4	2	0.6	62	25	32	70	9	0	0	140	272	19	52	4.4	.956	SS-96, 2B-2
1985			156	.218	.266	481	105	16	2	1	0.2	70	47	54	102	25	0	0	236	390	24	103	4.2	.963	SS-155

Bobby Meacham *continued*

Year	Team	Games	BA	SA	AB	H	2B	3B	HR	HR%	R	RBI	BB	SO	SB	Pinch Hit AB	Pinch Hit H	PO	A	E	DP	TC/G	FA	G by Pos
1986		56	.224	.280	161	36	7	1	0	0.0	19	10	17	39	3	0	0	70	149	12	31	4.1	.948	SS-56
1987		77	.271	.409	203	55	11	1	5	2.5	28	21	19	33	6	1	1	110	184	10	36	3.8	.967	SS-56, 2B-25
1988		47	.217	.296	115	25	9	0	0	0.0	18	7	14	22	7	1	0	56	85	7	19	3.0	.953	SS-24, 2B-21, 3B-5
6 yrs.		457	.236	.308	1371	324	58	8	8	0.6	202	114	140	276	58	2	1	628	1144	78	250	4.0	.958	SS-405, 2B-48, 3B-9

Charlie Mead

MEAD, CHARLES RICHARD BL TR 6′ 1″ 185 lbs.
B. Apr. 9, 1921, Vermilion, Alta., Canada.

Year	Team	Games	BA	SA	AB	H	2B	3B	HR	HR%	R	RBI	BB	SO	SB	Pinch Hit AB	Pinch Hit H	PO	A	E	DP	TC/G	FA	G by Pos
1943	NY N	37	.274	.349	146	40	6	1	1	0.7	9	13	10	15	3	0	0	77	3	2	3	2.2	.976	OF-37
1944		39	.179	.231	78	14	1	0	1	1.3	5	8	5	7	0	14	2	47	4	1	2	2.3	.981	OF-23
1945		11	.270	.378	37	10	1	0	1	2.7	4	6	5	2	0	0	0	22	3	1	1	2.4	.962	OF-11
3 yrs.		87	.245	.318	261	64	8	1	3	1.1	18	27	20	24	3	14	2	146	10	4	6	2.3	.975	OF-71

Louie Meadows

MEADOWS, MICHAEL RAY BL TL 5′11″ 190 lbs.
B. Apr. 29, 1961, Maysville, N. C.

Year	Team	Games	BA	SA	AB	H	2B	3B	HR	HR%	R	RBI	BB	SO	SB	Pinch Hit AB	Pinch Hit H	PO	A	E	DP	TC/G	FA	G by Pos
1986	HOU N	6	.333	.333	6	2	0	0	0	0.0	1	0	0	0	1	6	2	0	0	0	0	0.0	.000	OF-1
1988		35	.190	.381	42	8	0	1	2	4.8	5	3	6	8	4	18	3	18	1	0	0	1.9	1.000	OF-10
1989		31	.176	.353	51	9	0	0	3	5.9	5	10	1	14	1	20	2	13	0	0	0	0.9	1.000	OF-14, 1B-1
1990	2 teams	HOU N (15G –.143) PHI N (15G –.071)																						
″	total	30	.107	.107	28	3	0	0	0	0.0	4	0	3	6	0	16	0	8	0	0	0	0.6	1.000	OF-13
4 yrs.		102	.173	.307	127	22	0	1	5	3.9	15	13	10	28	6	60	7	39	1	0	0	1.0	1.000	OF-38, 1B-1

Pat Meaney

MEANEY, PATRICK J. BR TL
B. July 1871, Philadelphia, Pa. D. Oct. 20, 1922, Philadelphia, Pa.

Year	Team	Games	BA	SA	AB	H	2B	3B	HR	HR%	R	RBI	BB	SO	SB	Pinch Hit AB	Pinch Hit H	PO	A	E	DP	TC/G	FA	G by Pos
1912	DET A	1	.000	.000	2	0	0	0	0	0.0	0	0	1		0	0	0	3	2	1	1	6.0	.833	SS-1

Charlie Meara

MEARA, CHARLES EDWARD (Goggy) BL TR 5′10″ 160 lbs.
B. Apr. 13, 1891, New York, N. Y. D. Feb. 8, 1962, Bronx, N. Y.

Year	Team	Games	BA	SA	AB	H	2B	3B	HR	HR%	R	RBI	BB	SO	SB	Pinch Hit AB	Pinch Hit H	PO	A	E	DP	TC/G	FA	G by Pos
1914	NY A	4	.286	.286	7	2	0	0	0	0.0	2	1	2	2	0	0	0	4	0	0	0	1.3	1.000	OF-3

Pat Meares

MEARES, PATRICK JAMES BR TR 6′ 185 lbs.
B. Sept. 6, 1968, Salina, Kans.

Year	Team	Games	BA	SA	AB	H	2B	3B	HR	HR%	R	RBI	BB	SO	SB	Pinch Hit AB	Pinch Hit H	PO	A	E	DP	TC/G	FA	G by Pos
1993	MIN A	111	.251	.309	346	87	14	3	0	0.0	33	33	7	52	4	1	0	165	304	19	70	4.4	.961	SS-111
1994		80	.266	.354	229	61	12	1	2	0.9	29	24	14	50	5	1	0	134	209	13	45	4.5	.963	SS-79
1995		116	.269	.431	390	105	19	4	12	3.1	57	49	15	68	10	3	1	186	317	18	67	4.5	.965	SS-114, OF-3
3 yrs.		307	.262	.369	965	253	45	8	14	1.5	119	106	36	170	19	5	1	485	830	50	182	4.4	.963	SS-304, OF-3

Ray Medeiros

MEDEIROS, RAY ANTONE (Pep) BR TR 5′10″ 163 lbs.
B. May 9, 1926, Oakland, Calif.

Year	Team	Games	BA	SA	AB	H	2B	3B	HR	HR%	R	RBI	BB	SO	SB	Pinch Hit AB	Pinch Hit H	PO	A	E	DP	TC/G	FA	G by Pos
1945	CIN N	1	—	—	0	0	0	0	0	—	0	0	0	0	0	0	0	0	0	0	0	0.0	—	

Luis Medina

MEDINA, LUIS MAIN BR TL 6′ 4″ 200 lbs.
B. Mar. 26, 1963, Santa Monica, Calif.

Year	Team	Games	BA	SA	AB	H	2B	3B	HR	HR%	R	RBI	BB	SO	SB	Pinch Hit AB	Pinch Hit H	PO	A	E	DP	TC/G	FA	G by Pos
1988	CLE A	16	.255	.608	51	13	0	0	6	11.8	10	8	2	18	0	1	0	137	9	0	14	9.1	1.000	1B-16
1989		30	.205	.361	83	17	1	0	4	4.8	8	8	6	35	0	3	2	4	0	2	0	0.2	.667	DH-25, OF-3, 1B-1
1991		5	.063	.063	16	1	0	0	0	0.0	0	0	1	7	0	0	0	0	0	0	0	0.0	.000	DH-5
3 yrs.		51	.207	.413	150	31	1	0	10	6.7	18	16	9	60	0	4	2	141	9	2	14	3.0	.987	DH-30, 1B-17, OF-3

Joe Medwick

MEDWICK, JOSEPH MICHAEL (Ducky, Muscles) BR TR 5′10″ 187 lbs.
B. Nov. 24, 1911, Carteret, N. J. D. Mar. 21, 1975, St. Petersburg, Fla.
Hall of Fame 1968.

Year	Team	Games	BA	SA	AB	H	2B	3B	HR	HR%	R	RBI	BB	SO	SB	Pinch Hit AB	Pinch Hit H	PO	A	E	DP	TC/G	FA	G by Pos
1932	STL N	26	.349	.538	106	37	12	1	2	1.9	13	12	2	10	3	0	0	63	2	2	1	2.6	.970	OF-26
1933		148	.306	.497	595	182	40	10	18	3.0	92	98	26	56	5	1	0	318	17	7	2	2.3	.980	OF-147
1934		149	.319	.529	620	198	40	**18**	18	2.9	110	106	21	83	3	0	0	322	10	14	1	2.3	.960	OF-149
1935		154	.353	.576	634	224	46	13	23	3.6	132	126	30	59	4	0	0	352	8	13	0	2.4	.965	OF-154
1936		155	.351	.577	636	**223**	**64**	13	18	2.8	115	**138**	34	33	3	0	0	367	16	6	4	2.5	.985	OF-155
1937		156	**.374**	**.641**	**633**	**237**	**56**	10	**31**	4.9	**111**	**154**	41	50	4	0	0	329	9	4	1	2.2	.988	OF-156
1938		146	.322	.536	590	190	**47**	8	21	3.6	100	**122**	42	41	0	2	0	330	12	9	6	2.4	.974	OF-144
1939		150	.332	.507	606	201	48	8	14	2.3	98	117	45	44	6	1	0	313	10	8	1	2.2	.976	OF-149
1940	2 teams	STL N (37G –.304) BKN N (106G –.300)																						
″	total	143	.301	.482	581	175	30	12	17	2.9	83	86	32	36	2	3	0	321	8	6	0	2.4	.982	OF-140
1941	BKN N	133	.318	.517	538	171	33	10	18	3.3	100	88	38	35	2	2	1	270	11	5	2	2.2	.983	OF-131
1942		142	.300	.403	553	166	37	4	4	0.7	69	96	32	25	2	2	0	287	5	3	1	2.1	.990	OF-140
1943	2 teams	BKN N (48G –.272) NY N (78G –.281)																						
″	total	126	.278	.380	497	138	30	3	5	1.0	54	70	19	22	1	6	2	221	12	7	3	2.0	.971	OF-117, 1B-3
1944	NY N	128	.337	.441	490	165	24	3	7	1.4	64	85	38	24	2	6	1	290	8	2	2	2.5	.993	OF-122
1945	2 teams	NY N (26G –.304) BOS N (66G –.284)																						
″	total	92	.290	.374	310	90	17	0	3	1.0	31	37	14	14	5	17	3	248	11	1	8	3.4	.996	OF-61, 1B-15
1946	BKN N	41	.312	.442	77	24	4	0	2	2.6	7	18	6	5	0	18	4	38	0	2	2	2.1	.950	OF-18, 1B-1
1947	STL N	75	.307	.467	150	46	12	0	4	2.7	19	28	16	12	0	31	7	56	3	0	2	1.4	1.000	OF-43
1948		20	.211	.211	19	4	0	0	0	0.0	0	2	1	2	0	18	4	0	0	0	0	0.0	.000	OF-1
17 yrs.		1984	.324	.505	7635	2471	540	113	205	2.7	1198	1383	437	551	42	107	22	4125	142	89	36	2.3	.980	OF-1853, 1B-19
WORLD SERIES																								
1934	STL N	7	.379	.552	29	11	0	1	1	3.4	4	5	1	7	0	0	0	9	0	0	0	1.3	1.000	OF-7
1941	BKN N	5	.235	.294	17	4	1	0	0	0.0	1	0	1	2	0	0	0	8	0	0	0	1.6	1.000	OF-5
2 yrs.		12	.326	.457	46	15	1	1	1	2.2	5	5	2	9	0	0	0	17	0	0	0	1.4	1.000	OF-12

Tommy Mee

MEE, THOMAS WILLIAM (Judge) BR TR 5′ 8″ 165 lbs.
B. Mar. 18, 1890, Chicago, Ill. D. May 16, 1981, Chicago, Ill.

Year	Team	Games	BA	SA	AB	H	2B	3B	HR	HR%	R	RBI	BB	SO	SB	Pinch Hit AB	Pinch Hit H	PO	A	E	DP	TC/G	FA	G by Pos
1910	STL A	8	.158	.263	19	3	2	0	0	0.0	1	1	0		0	0	0	8	18	5	0	3.9	.839	SS-6, 3B-1, 2B-1

Dad Meek

MEEK, FRANK J.
B. Mar. 14, 1867, St. Louis, Mo. D. Dec. 22, 1922, St. Louis, Mo.

Year	Team	Games	BA	SA	AB	H	2B	3B	HR	HR%	R	RBI	BB	SO	SB	Pinch Hit AB	Pinch Hit H	PO	A	E	DP	TC/G	FA	G by Pos
1889	STL AA	2	.500	.500	2	1	0	0	0	0.0	2	1	0	0	1	0	0	0	2	1	0	1.5	.667	C-2
1890		4	.313	.313	16	5	0	0	0	0.0	3		0		1	0	0	33	9	4	0	11.5	.913	C-4
2 yrs.		6	.333	.333	18	6	0	0	0	0.0	5	1	0	0	2	0	0	33	11	5	0	8.2	.898	C-6

Sammy Meeks

MEEKS, SAMUEL MACK BR TR 5′ 9″ 160 lbs.
B. Apr. 23, 1923, Anderson, S. C.

Year	Team	Games	BA	SA	AB	H	2B	3B	HR	HR%	R	RBI	BB	SO	SB	Pinch Hit AB	Pinch Hit H	PO	A	E	DP	TC/G	FA	G by Pos
1948	WAS A	24	.121	.152	33	4	1	0	0	0.0	4	2	1	12	0	9	0	13	18	2	6	3.0	.939	SS-10, 2B-1
1949	CIN N	16	.306	.528	36	11	2	0	2	5.6	10	6	2	6	1	3	1	24	33	0	12	5.2	1.000	2B-8, SS-3
1950		39	.284	.368	95	27	5	0	1	1.1	7	8	6	14	1	7	3	35	68	5	13	3.5	.954	SS-29, 3B-2
1951		23	.229	.229	35	8	0	0	0	0.0	4	2	0	4	1	18	3	9	4	1	2	2.8	.929	3B-4, SS-1
4 yrs.		102	.251	.337	199	50	8	0	3	1.5	25	18	9	36	3	37	7	81	123	8	33	3.7	.962	SS-43, 2B-9, 3B-6

Dave Meier

MEIER, DAVID KEITH BR TR 6′ 195 lbs.
B. Aug. 8, 1959, Helena, Mont.

Year	Team	Games	BA	SA	AB	H	2B	3B	HR	HR%	R	RBI	BB	SO	SB	Pinch Hit AB	Pinch Hit H	PO	A	E	DP	TC/G	FA	G by Pos
1984	MIN A	59	.238	.306	147	35	8	1	0	0.0	18	13	6	9	0	9	1	87	2	2	0	1.7	.978	OF-50, DH-4, 3B-1
1985		71	.260	.346	104	27	6	0	1	1.0	15	8	18	12	0	11	0	77	1	1	1	1.2	.987	OF-63, DH-3
1987	TEX A	13	.286	.333	21	6	1	0	0	0.0	4	0	0	4	0	3	0	11	0	1	0	1.5	.917	OF-8
1988	CHI N	2	.400	.400	5	2	0	0	0	0.0	0	1	0	1	0	1	1	1	0	0	0	1.0	1.000	3B-1
4 yrs.		145	.253	.325	277	70	15	1	1	0.4	37	22	24	26	0	24	2	176	3	4	1	1.4	.978	OF-121, DH-7, 3B-2

Dutch Meier

MEIER, ARTHUR ERNST BR TR 5′10″ 175 lbs.
B. Mar. 30, 1879, St. Louis, Mo. D. Mar. 23, 1948, Chicago, Ill.

Year	Team	Games	BA	SA	AB	H	2B	3B	HR	HR%	R	RBI	BB	SO	SB	Pinch Hit AB	Pinch Hit H	PO	A	E	DP	TC/G	FA	G by Pos
1906	PIT N	82	.256	.326	273	70	11	4	0	0.0	32	16	13		4	13	2	115	43	11	6	2.4	.935	OF-52, SS-17

Walt Meinert

MEINERT, WALTER HENRY BL TL 5′ 7½″ 150 lbs.
B. Dec. 11, 1890, New York, N. Y. D. Nov. 9, 1958, Decatur, Ill.

Year	Team	Games	BA	SA	AB	H	2B	3B	HR	HR%	R	RBI	BB	SO	SB	Pinch Hit AB	Pinch Hit H	PO	A	E	DP	TC/G	FA	G by Pos
1913	STL A	4	.375	.375	8	3	0	0	0	0.0	1	0	1	3	1	1	1	3	0	0	0	1.5	1.000	OF-2

Bob Meinke

MEINKE, ROBERT BERNARD BR TR 5′10″ 135 lbs.
Son of Frank Meinke.
B. June 25, 1887, Chicago, Ill. D. Dec. 29, 1952, Chicago, Ill.

Year	Team	Games	BA	SA	AB	H	2B	3B	HR	HR%	R	RBI	BB	SO	SB	Pinch Hit AB	Pinch Hit H	PO	A	E	DP	TC/G	FA	G by Pos
1910	CIN N	2	.000	.000	1	0	0	0	0	0.0	0	0	1	0	0	0	0	3	4	0	0	3.5	1.000	SS-2

Frank Meinke

MEINKE, FRANK LOUIS BR 5′10½″ 172 lbs.
Father of Bob Meinke.
B. Oct. 18, 1863, Chicago, Ill. D. Nov. 8, 1931, Chicago, Ill.

Year	Team	Games	BA	SA	AB	H	2B	3B	HR	HR%	R	RBI	BB	SO	SB	Pinch Hit AB	Pinch Hit H	PO	A	E	DP	TC/G	FA	G by Pos
1884	DET N	92	.164	.273	341	56	5	7	6	1.8	28		6	89		0	0	80	214	44	20	3.5	.870	SS-51, P-35, OF-4, 3B-3, 2B-3
1885		1	.000	.000	3	0	0	0	0	0.0	0	0	0	1		0	0	1	2	0	0	1.5	1.000	OF-1, P-1
2 yrs.		93	.163	.270	344	56	5	7	6	1.7	28	0	6	90		0	0	81	216	44	20	3.5	.871	SS-51, P-36, OF-5, 3B-3, 2B-3

George Meister

MEISTER, GEORGE B.
B. June 5, 1864, Dorzbach, Germany D. Aug. 24, 1908, Glenwood, Pa.

Year	Team	Games	BA	SA	AB	H	2B	3B	HR	HR%	R	RBI	BB	SO	SB	Pinch Hit AB	Pinch Hit H	PO	A	E	DP	TC/G	FA	G by Pos
1884	TOL AA	34	.193	.244	119	23	6	0	0	0.0	9		3			0	0	27	40	15	3	2.4	.817	3B-34

John Meister

MEISTER, JOHN F. 5′ 8″ 175 lbs.
B. May 10, 1863, Altoona, Pa. D. Jan. 28, 1923, Philadelphia, Pa.

Year	Team	Games	BA	SA	AB	H	2B	3B	HR	HR%	R	RBI	BB	SO	SB	Pinch Hit AB	Pinch Hit H	PO	A	E	DP	TC/G	FA	G by Pos
1886	NY AA	45	.237	.339	186	44	7	3	2	1.1	35		4			0	0	130	121	26	18	6.2	.906	2B-45
1887		39	.222	.304	158	35	6	2	1	0.6	24		16		9	0	0	68	43	13	9	3.1	.895	OF-22, 2B-14, 3B-3, SS-1
2 yrs.		84	.230	.323	344	79	13	5	3	0.9	59		20		9	0	0	198	164	39	27	4.7	.903	2B-59, OF-22, 3B-3, SS-1

Karl Meister

MEISTER, KARL DANIEL (Dutch) BR TR 6′ 178 lbs.
B. May 15, 1891, Marietta, Ohio D. Aug. 15, 1967, Marietta, Ohio.

Year	Team	Games	BA	SA	AB	H	2B	3B	HR	HR%	R	RBI	BB	SO	SB	Pinch Hit AB	Pinch Hit H	PO	A	E	DP	TC/G	FA	G by Pos
1913	CIN N	4	.286	.429	7	2	1	0	0	0.0	1	2	0	4	0	0	0	2	0	1	0	0.8	.667	OF-4

Moxie Meixell

MEIXELL, MERTON MERRILL BL TL 5′10″ 168 lbs.
B. Oct. 18, 1887, Lake Crystal, Minn. D. Aug. 17, 1982, Los Angeles, Calif.

Year	Team	Games	BA	SA	AB	H	2B	3B	HR	HR%	R	RBI	BB	SO	SB	Pinch Hit AB	Pinch Hit H	PO	A	E	DP	TC/G	FA	G by Pos
1912	CLE A	2	.500	.500	2	1	0	0	0	0.0	0	0	0		0	2	1	0	0	0	0	0.0	—	

Roberto Mejia

MEJIA, ROBERTO ANTONIO BR TR 5′11″ 160 lbs.
Born Roberto Antonio (Diaz).
B. Apr. 14, 1972, Hato Mayor, Dominican Republic.

Year	Team	Games	BA	SA	AB	H	2B	3B	HR	HR%	R	RBI	BB	SO	SB	Pinch Hit AB	Pinch Hit H	PO	A	E	DP	TC/G	FA	G by Pos
1993	CLR N	65	.231	.402	229	53	14	5	5	2.2	31	20	13	63	4	0	0	126	184	12	38	5.0	.963	2B-65
1994		38	.241	.431	116	28	8	1	4	3.4	11	14	15	33	3	3	0	70	93	7	19	5.0	.959	2B-34
1995		23	.154	.231	52	8	1	0	1	1.9	5	4	0	17	0	4	1	35	30	2	4	4.2	.970	2B-16
3 yrs.		126	.224	.388	397	89	23	6	10	2.5	47	38	28	113	7	7	1	231	307	21	61	4.9	.962	2B-115

Roman Mejias

MEJIAS, ROMAN BR TR 6′ 175 lbs.
Born Roman Mejias (Gomez).
B. Aug. 9, 1930, Abreus, Cuba.

Year	Team	Games	BA	SA	AB	H	2B	3B	HR	HR%	R	RBI	BB	SO	SB	Pinch Hit AB	Pinch Hit H	PO	A	E	DP	TC/G	FA	G by Pos
1955	PIT N	71	.216	.329	167	36	8	1	3	1.8	14	21	9	13	1	20	4	67	8	6	2	1.9	.926	OF-43
1957		58	.275	.423	142	39	7	4	2	1.4	12	15	6	13	2	17	3	60	6	0	0	1.6	1.000	OF-42
1958		76	.268	.408	157	42	3	2	5	3.2	17	19	2	27	0	21	5	104	3	3	0	1.9	.973	OF-57
1959		96	.236	.341	276	65	6	1	7	2.5	28	28	21	48	1	4	1	155	8	5	2	2.0	.970	OF-85
1960		3	.000	.000	1	0	0	0	0	0.0	1	0	0	1	0	1	0	0	0	0	0	0.0	—	
1961		4	.000	.000	1	0	0	0	0	0.0	1	0	0	1	0	1	0	1	0	0	0	0.5	1.000	OF-2
1962	HOU N	146	.286	.445	566	162	12	3	24	4.2	82	76	30	83	12	5	0	217	10	13	2	1.7	.946	OF-142
1963	BOS A	111	.227	.370	357	81	18	0	11	3.1	43	39	14	36	4	24	4	177	6	5	1	2.2	.973	OF-86
1964		62	.238	.347	101	24	3	1	2	2.0	14	4	7	16	0	16	4	49	2	2	0	1.4	.962	OF-37
9 yrs.		627	.254	.391	1768	449	57	12	54	3.1	212	202	89	238	20	109	21	830	43	34	7	1.8	.963	OF-494

Sam Mejias

MEJIAS, SAMUEL ELIAS BR TR 6′ 170 lbs.
B. May 9, 1952, Santiago, Dominican Republic.

Year	Team	Games	BA	SA	AB	H	2B	3B	HR	HR%	R	RBI	BB	SO	SB	Pinch Hit AB	Pinch Hit H	PO	A	E	DP	TC/G	FA	G by Pos
1976	STL N	18	.143	.190	21	3	1	0	0	0.0	1	0	2	2	2	1	0	19	1	0	0	1.2	1.000	OF-17
1977	MON N	74	.228	.376	101	23	4	1	3	3.0	14	8	2	17	1	20	4	55	2	2	1	1.1	.966	OF-56

Sam Mejias *continued*

Year	Team		Games	BA	SA	AB	H	2B	3B	HR	HR%	R	RBI	BB	SO	SB	Pinch Hit AB	Pinch Hit H	PO	A	E	DP	TC/G	FA	G by Pos
1978			67	.232	.250	56	13	1	0	0	0.0	9	6	2	5	0	10	3	35	2	2	0	0.7	.949	OF-52, P-1
1979	**2 teams**		**CHI N** (31G –.182)			**CIN N** (7G –.500)																			
″	**total**		38	.231	.231	13	3	0	0	0	0.0	5	0	2	5	0	7	1	8	0	1	0	0.3	.889	OF-28
1980	**CIN**	**N**	71	.278	.370	108	30	5	1	1	0.9	16	10	6	13	4	7	2	89	4	1	1	1.4	.989	OF-67
1981			66	.286	.327	49	14	2	0	0	0.0	6	7	2	9	1	8	2	34	1	1	0	0.6	.972	OF-58
6 yrs.			334	.247	.330	348	86	13	2	4	1.1	51	31	16	51	8	53	12	240	10	7	2	0.9	.973	OF-278, P-1

Dutch Mele

MELE, ALBERT ERNEST BL TL 6′½″ 195 lbs.
B. Jan. 11, 1915, New York, N. Y. D. Feb. 12, 1975, Hollywood, Calif.

Year	Team		Games	BA	SA	AB	H	2B	3B	HR	HR%	R	RBI	BB	SO	SB	Pinch Hit AB	Pinch Hit H	PO	A	E	DP	TC/G	FA	G by Pos
1937	**CIN**	**N**	6	.143	.214	14	2	1	0	0	0.0	1	1	1	1	0	1	0	1	0	0	0	0.2	1.000	OF-5

Sam Mele

MELE, SABATH ANTHONY BR TR 6′ 1″ 183 lbs.
B. Jan. 21, 1923, Astoria, N. Y.
Manager 1961–67.

Year	Team		Games	BA	SA	AB	H	2B	3B	HR	HR%	R	RBI	BB	SO	SB	Pinch Hit AB	Pinch Hit H	PO	A	E	DP	TC/G	FA	G by Pos
1947	**BOS**	**A**	123	.302	.448	453	137	14	8	12	2.6	71	73	37	35	0	6	3	238	10	2	1	2.2	.992	OF-115, 1B-1
1948			66	.233	.344	180	42	12	1	2	1.1	25	25	13	21	1	9	1	99	2	3	0	1.9	.971	OF-55
1949	**2 teams**		**BOS A** (18G –.196)			**WAS A** (78G –.242)																			
″	**total**		96	.235	.326	310	73	13	3	3	1.0	22	32	24	48	4	15	2	207	13	6	12	2.7	.973	OF-74, 1B-11
1950	**WAS**	**A**	126	.274	.432	435	119	21	6	12	2.8	57	86	51	40	2	10	4	341	26	4	13	3.2	.989	OF-99, 1B-16
1951			143	.274	.391	558	153	**36**	7	5	0.9	58	94	32	31	2	6	1	385	15	2	12	2.9	.995	OF-124, 1B-15
1952	**2 teams**		**WAS A** (9G –.429)			**CHI A** (123G –.248)																			
″	**total**		132	.259	.421	451	117	21	2	16	3.5	48	69	49	42	1	12	2	178	8	1	1	1.5	.995	OF-119, 1B-3
1953	**CHI**	**A**	140	.274	.437	481	132	26	8	12	2.5	64	82	58	47	3	6	3	217	14	1	1	1.7	.996	OF-138, 1B-2
1954	**2 teams**		**BAL A** (72G –.239)			**BOS A** (42G –.318)																			
″	**total**		114	.268	.431	362	97	15	4	12	3.3	39	55	30	38	1	19	7	285	14	6	19	3.1	.980	OF-75, 1B-22
1955	**2 teams**		**BOS A** (14G –.129)			**CIN N** (35G –.210)																			
″	**total**		49	.183	.280	93	17	3	0	2	2.2	5	8	5	20	1	25	1	38	3	1	0	2.0	.976	OF-20, 1B-1
1956	**CLE**	**A**	57	.254	.421	114	29	7	0	4	3.5	17	20	12	20	0	28	8	88	7	1	5	3.4	.990	OF-20, 1B-8
10 yrs.			1046	.267	.408	3437	916	168	39	80	2.3	406	544	311	342	15	136	32	2076	112	27	64	2.4	.988	OF-839, 1B-79

Francisco Melendez

MELENDEZ, FRANCISCO JAVIER BL TL 6′ 170 lbs.
Born Francisco Javier Melendez (Villegas).
B. Jan. 25, 1964, Rio Piedras, Puerto Rico.

Year	Team		Games	BA	SA	AB	H	2B	3B	HR	HR%	R	RBI	BB	SO	SB	Pinch Hit AB	Pinch Hit H	PO	A	E	DP	TC/G	FA	G by Pos
1984	**PHI**	**N**	21	.130	.130	23	3	0	0	0	0.0	0	2	1	5	0	13	1	37	4	0	1	4.1	1.000	1B-10
1986			9	.250	.250	8	2	0	0	0	0.0	0	0	0	2	0	7	1	1	0	0	0	0.5	1.000	1B-2
1987	**SF**	**N**	12	.313	.500	16	5	0	0	1	6.3	2	1	0	3	0	10	1	19	0	0	0	3.8	1.000	1B-5
1988			23	.192	.192	26	5	0	0	0	0.0	1	3	3	2	0	16	4	27	0	0	2	3.9	1.000	1B-6, OF-1
1989	**BAL**	**A**	9	.273	.273	11	3	0	0	0	0.0	1	3	1	2	0	4	1	25	2	0	4	5.4	1.000	1B-5
5 yrs.			74	.214	.250	84	18	0	0	1	1.2	4	9	5	14	0	50	8	109	6	0	7	4.0	1.000	1B-28, OF-1

Luis Melendez

MELENDEZ, LUIS ANTONIO BR TR 6′ 165 lbs.
Born Luis Antonio Melendez (Santana).
B. Aug. 11, 1949, Aibonito, Puerto Rico.

Year	Team		Games	BA	SA	AB	H	2B	3B	HR	HR%	R	RBI	BB	SO	SB	Pinch Hit AB	Pinch Hit H	PO	A	E	DP	TC/G	FA	G by Pos
1970	**STL**	**N**	21	.300	.314	70	21	1	0	0	0.0	11	8	2	12	3	3	0	31	2	0	0	1.8	1.000	OF-18
1971			88	.225	.254	173	39	3	1	0	0.0	25	11	24	29	2	22	4	90	3	4	0	1.5	.959	OF-66
1972			118	.238	.334	332	79	11	3	5	1.5	32	28	25	34	5	21	2	206	5	9	0	2.1	.959	OF-105
1973			121	.267	.343	341	91	18	1	2	0.6	35	35	27	50	2	21	8	196	8	2	4	2.2	.990	OF-95
1974			83	.218	.298	124	27	4	3	0	0.0	15	8	11	9	2	31	4	84	1	2	0	1.9	.977	OF-46, SS-1
1975			110	.265	.347	291	77	8	5	2	0.7	33	27	16	25	3	35	8	169	3	3	1	2.0	.983	OF-89
1976	**2 teams**		**STL N** (20G –.125)			**SD N** (72G –.244)																			
″	**total**		92	.224	.259	143	32	5	0	0	0.0	15	5	3	15	1	25	4	99	0	1	0	1.5	.990	OF-68
1977	**SD**	**N**	8	.000	.000	3	0	0	0	0	0.0	1	0	1	1	0	3	0	1	0	0	0	0.5	1.000	OF-2
8 yrs.			641	.248	.318	1477	366	50	13	9	0.6	167	122	109	175	18	161	30	876	22	21	5	1.9	.977	OF-489, SS-1

Oscar Melillo

MELILLO, OSCAR DONALD (Ski, Spinach) BR TR 5′ 8″ 150 lbs.
B. Aug. 4, 1899, Chicago, Ill. D. Nov. 14, 1963, Chicago, Ill.
Manager 1938.

Year	Team		Games	BA	SA	AB	H	2B	3B	HR	HR%	R	RBI	BB	SO	SB	Pinch Hit AB	Pinch Hit H	PO	A	E	DP	TC/G	FA	G by Pos
1926	**STL**	**A**	99	.255	.335	385	98	18	5	1	0.3	54	30	32	31	6	0	0	238	324	22	71	5.9	.962	2B-88, 3B-11
1927			107	.225	.287	356	80	18	2	0	0.0	45	26	25	28	3	5	1	229	293	36	72	5.5	.935	2B-101
1928			51	.189	.205	132	25	2	0	0	0.0	9	9	9	11	2	2	0	79	104	6	15	4.0	.968	2B-28, 3B-19
1929			141	.296	.401	494	146	17	10	5	1.0	57	67	29	30	11	0	0	342	519	24	98	6.3	.973	2B-141
1930			149	.256	.369	574	147	30	10	5	0.9	62	59	23	44	15	1	0	384	572	21	107	6.6	.979	2B-148
1931			151	.306	.407	617	189	34	11	2	0.3	89	75	37	29	7	0	0	428	543	32	118	6.6	.968	2B-151
1932			154	.242	.324	612	148	19	11	3	0.5	71	66	36	42	6	1	0	393	526	18	110	6.1	.981	2B-153
1933			132	.292	.381	496	145	23	6	3	0.6	50	79	29	18	12	0	0	362	451	7	110	6.3	.991	2B-130
1934			144	.241	.297	552	133	19	3	2	0.4	54	55	28	27	4	3	0	412	462	17	110	6.3	.981	2B-141
1935	**2 teams**		**STL A** (19G –.206)			**BOS A** (106G –.261)																			
″	**total**		125	.253	.303	462	117	16	2	1	0.2	53	44	46	26	3	1	0	324	432	21	94	6.3	.973	2B-123
1936	**BOS**	**A**	98	.226	.287	327	74	12	4	0	0.0	39	32	28	16	0	4	2	239	242	10	59	5.3	.980	2B-93
1937			26	.250	.286	56	14	2	0	0	0.0	8	6	5	4	0	2	1	33	35	4	8	3.1	.944	2B-19, SS-2, 3B-2
12 yrs.			1377	.260	.340	5063	1316	210	64	22	0.4	591	548	327	306	69	19	4	3463	4503	218	972	6.1	.973	2B-1316, 3B-32, SS-2

Joe Mellana

MELLANA, JOSEPH PETER BR TR 5′10″ 180 lbs.
B. Mar. 11, 1905, Oakland, Calif. D. Nov. 1, 1969, Larkspur, Calif.

Year	Team		Games	BA	SA	AB	H	2B	3B	HR	HR%	R	RBI	BB	SO	SB	Pinch Hit AB	Pinch Hit H	PO	A	E	DP	TC/G	FA	G by Pos
1927	**PHI**	**A**	4	.286	.286	7	2	0	0	0	0.0	1	2	0	1	0	0	0	0	8	1	1	4.5	.889	3B-2

Bill Mellor

MELLOR, WILLIAM HARPIN BR TR 6′ 190 lbs.
B. June 6, 1874, Camden, N. J. D. Nov. 5, 1940, Bridgeton, R. I.

Year	Team		Games	BA	SA	AB	H	2B	3B	HR	HR%	R	RBI	BB	SO	SB	Pinch Hit AB	Pinch Hit H	PO	A	E	DP	TC/G	FA	G by Pos
1902	**BAL**	**A**	10	.361	.444	36	13	3	0	0	0.0	4	5	3		1	0	0	87	2	2	1	9.1	.978	1B-10

Paul Meloan

MELOAN, PAUL B. (Molly) BL TR 5′10½″ 175 lbs.
B. Aug. 23, 1888, Paynesville, Mo. D. Feb. 11, 1950, Taft, Calif.

Year	Team	Games	BA	SA	AB	H	2B	3B	HR	HR%	R	RBI	BB	SO	SB	Pinch Hit AB	Pinch Hit H	PO	A	E	DP	TC/G	FA	G by Pos
1910	CHI A	65	.243	.324	222	54	6	6	0	0.0	23	23	17		4	0	0	76	16	5	1	1.5	.948	OF-65
1911	2 teams	CHI A (1G –.333) STL A (64G –.262)																						
″	total	65	.263	.378	209	55	11	2	3	1.4	30	15	15		7	9	0	69	6	9	1	1.5	.893	OF-55
2 yrs.		130	.253	.350	431	109	17	8	3	0.7	53	38	32		11	9	0	145	22	14	2	1.5	.923	OF-120

Bill Melton

MELTON, WILLIAM EDWIN BR TR 6′ 2″ 200 lbs.
B. July 7, 1945, Gulfport, Miss.

Year	Team	Games	BA	SA	AB	H	2B	3B	HR	HR%	R	RBI	BB	SO	SB	Pinch Hit AB	Pinch Hit H	PO	A	E	DP	TC/G	FA	G by Pos
1968	CHI A	34	.266	.394	109	29	8	0	2	1.8	5	16	10	32	1	1	0	17	75	3	5	2.9	.968	3B-33
1969		157	.255	.433	556	142	26	2	23	4.1	67	87	56	106	1	4	1	125	325	22	36	3.0	.953	3B-148, OF-11
1970		141	.263	.488	514	135	15	1	33	6.4	74	96	56	107	2	0	0	158	187	18	22	2.6	.950	OF-71, 3B-70
1971		150	.269	.492	543	146	18	2	**33**	6.1	72	86	61	87	3	0	0	116	371	16	26	3.4	.968	3B-148
1972		57	.245	.370	208	51	5	0	7	3.4	22	30	23	31	1	1	0	47	125	12	12	3.3	.935	3B-56
1973		152	.277	.439	560	155	29	1	20	3.6	83	87	75	66	4	0	0	115	347	23	31	3.2	.953	3B-151, DH-1
1974		136	.242	.404	495	120	17	0	21	4.2	63	63	59	60	3	1	0	100	272	24	29	3.0	.939	3B-123, DH-11
1975		149	.240	.359	512	123	16	0	15	2.9	62	70	78	106	5	0	0	131	313	26	23	3.2	.945	3B-138, DH-11
1976	CAL A	118	.208	.328	341	71	17	3	6	1.8	31	42	44	53	2	26	7	227	36	3	22	2.6	.989	DH-51, 1B-30, 3B-21
1977	CLE A	50	.241	.323	133	32	11	0	0	0.0	17	14	17	21	1	10	3	142	28	2	11	4.1	.988	1B-15, DH-14, 3B-13
10 yrs.		1144	.253	.419	3971	1004	162	9	160	4.0	496	591	479	669	23	43	11	1178	2079	149	217	3.1	.956	3B-901, DH-88, OF-82, 1B-45

Dave Melton

MELTON, DAVID OLIN BR TR 6′ 185 lbs.
B. Oct. 3, 1928, Pampa, Tex.

Year	Team	Games	BA	SA	AB	H	2B	3B	HR	HR%	R	RBI	BB	SO	SB	Pinch Hit AB	Pinch Hit H	PO	A	E	DP	TC/G	FA	G by Pos
1956	KC A	3	.333	.333	3	1	0	0	0	0.0	0	0	0	0	0	0	0	3	0	0	0	1.0	1.000	OF-3
1958		9	.000	.000	6	0	0	0	0	0.0	0	0	0	5	0	6	0	2	0	0	0	1.0	1.000	OF-2
2 yrs.		12	.111	.111	9	1	0	0	0	0.0	0	0	0	5	0	6	0	5	0	0	0	1.0	1.000	OF-5

Bob Melvin

MELVIN, ROBERT PAUL BR TR 6′ 4″ 205 lbs.
B. Oct. 28, 1961, Palo Alto, Calif.

Year	Team	Games	BA	SA	AB	H	2B	3B	HR	HR%	R	RBI	BB	SO	SB	Pinch Hit AB	Pinch Hit H	PO	A	E	DP	TC/G	FA	G by Pos
1985	DET A	41	.220	.293	82	18	4	1	0	0.0	10	4	3	21	0	0	0	175	13	2	1	4.6	.989	C-41
1986	SF N	89	.224	.347	268	60	14	2	5	1.9	24	25	15	69	3	6	1	443	60	6	7	6.0	.988	C-84, 3B-1
1987		84	.199	.366	246	49	8	0	11	4.5	31	31	17	44	0	8	1	414	44	1	8	5.8	.998	C-78, 1B-1
1988		92	.234	.377	273	64	13	1	8	2.9	23	27	13	46	0	4	1	406	31	7	4	4.9	.984	C-89, 1B-1
1989	BAL A	85	.241	.295	278	67	10	1	1	0.4	22	32	15	53	1	5	0	303	20	3	1	3.9	.991	C-75, DH-9
1990		93	.243	.346	301	73	14	1	5	1.7	30	37	11	53	0	11	2	365	26	1	2	4.5	.997	C-76, DH-10, 1B-1
1991		79	.250	.307	228	57	10	0	1	0.4	11	23	11	46	0	5	2	383	31	1	8	5.5	.998	C-72, DH-4
1992	KC A	32	.314	.386	70	22	5	0	0	0.0	5	6	5	13	0	8	2	99	9	1	5	4.5	.991	C-21, 1B-3
1993	BOS A	77	.222	.313	176	39	7	0	3	1.7	13	23	7	44	0	3	1	309	19	2	5	4.3	.994	C-76, 1B-1
1994	2 teams	NY A (9G –.286) CHI A (11G –.158)																						
″	total	20	.212	.303	33	7	0	0	1	3.0	5	4	1	7	0	1	0	64	0	0	2	3.2	1.000	C-15, 1B-4, DH-1
10 yrs.		692	.233	.337	1955	456	85	6	35	1.8	174	212	98	396	4	51	10	2961	253	24	43	4.9	.993	C-627, DH-24, 1B-11, 3B-1
LEAGUE CHAMPIONSHIP SERIES																								
1987	SF N	3	.429	.429	7	3	0	0	0	0.0	0	0	1	1	0	1	0	14	1	0	0	7.5	1.000	C-2

Mario Mendoza

MENDOZA, MARIO BR TR 5′11″ 170 lbs.
Born Mario Mendoza (Aizpuru).
B. Dec. 26, 1950, Chihuahua, Mexico.

Year	Team	Games	BA	SA	AB	H	2B	3B	HR	HR%	R	RBI	BB	SO	SB	Pinch Hit AB	Pinch Hit H	PO	A	E	DP	TC/G	FA	G by Pos
1974	PIT N	91	.221	.252	163	36	1	2	0	0.0	10	15	8	35	1	1	0	77	187	10	21	3.1	.964	SS-87
1975		56	.180	.200	50	9	1	0	0	0.0	8	2	3	17	0	0	0	29	70	5	10	1.9	.952	SS-53, 3B-1
1976		50	.185	.239	92	17	5	0	0	0.0	6	12	4	15	0	1	0	42	105	5	19	3.2	.967	SS-45, 3B-2, 2B-1
1977		70	.198	.235	81	16	3	0	0	0.0	5	4	3	10	0	4	2	41	87	10	13	2.1	.928	SS-45, 3B-19, P-1
1978		57	.218	.291	55	12	1	0	1	1.8	5	3	2	9	3	2	1	28	61	5	4	1.8	.947	2B-21, 3B-18, SS-14
1979	SEA A	148	.198	.249	373	74	10	3	1	0.3	26	29	9	62	3	0	0	177	422	20	91	4.2	.968	SS-148
1980		114	.245	.310	277	68	6	3	2	0.7	27	14	16	42	3	0	0	149	290	19	68	4.0	.959	SS-114
1981	TEX A	88	.231	.266	229	53	6	1	0	0.0	18	22	7	25	2	0	0	114	270	12	47	4.5	.970	SS-88
1982		12	.118	.118	17	2	0	0	0	0.0	1	0	0	4	0	0	0	14	16	4	6	2.8	.882	SS-12
9 yrs.		686	.215	.262	1337	287	33	9	4	0.3	106	101	52	219	12	8	3	671	1508	90	279	3.4	.960	SS-606, 3B-40, 2B-22, P-1
LEAGUE CHAMPIONSHIP SERIES																								
1974	PIT N	3	.200	.200	5	1	0	0	0	0.0	0	1	1	0	0	0	0	4	7	0	0	3.7	1.000	SS-3

Mike Mendoza

MENDOZA, MICHAEL JOSEPH BR TR 6′ 5″ 215 lbs.
B. Nov. 26, 1955, Inglewood, Calif.

Year	Team	Games	BA	SA	AB	H	2B	3B	HR	HR%	R	RBI	BB	SO	SB	Pinch Hit AB	Pinch Hit H	PO	A	E	DP	TC/G	FA	G by Pos
1979	HOU N	2	—	—	0	0	0	0	0	—	0	0	0	0	0	0	0	0	0	0	0	0.0	.000	P-1

Minnie Mendoza

MENDOZA, CRISTOBAL RIGOBERTO BR TR 6′ 180 lbs.
Born Cristobal Rigoberto Mendoza (Carreras).
B. Nov. 16, 1933, Ceiba Del Agua, Cuba.

Year	Team	Games	BA	SA	AB	H	2B	3B	HR	HR%	R	RBI	BB	SO	SB	Pinch Hit AB	Pinch Hit H	PO	A	E	DP	TC/G	FA	G by Pos
1970	MIN A	16	.188	.188	16	3	0	0	0	0.0	2	2	0	1	0	9	2	8	5	0	0	1.4	1.000	3B-5, 2B-4

Jock Menefee

MENEFEE, JOHN BR TR 6′ 165 lbs.
B. Jan. 15, 1868, Rowlesburg, West Virginia D. Mar. 11, 1953, Belle Vernon, Pa.

Year	Team	Games	BA	SA	AB	H	2B	3B	HR	HR%	R	RBI	BB	SO	SB	Pinch Hit AB	Pinch Hit H	PO	A	E	DP	TC/G	FA	G by Pos
1892	PIT N	2	.000	.000	3	0	0	0	0	0.0	0	0	0	0	0	0	0	1	2	0	0	1.5	1.000	OF-1, P-1
1893	LOU N	22	.274	.329	73	20	2	1	0	0.0	10	12	13	5	2	0	0	19	38	5	2	2.8	.919	P-15, OF-7
1894	2 teams	LOU N (29G –.165) PIT N (13G –.255)																						
″	total	42	.198	.246	126	25	2	2	0	0.0	13	11	11	10	4	0	0	30	79	8	0	2.8	.932	P-41, 2B-1
1895	PIT N	2	—	—	0	0	0	0	0	—	0	0	0	0	0	0	0	1	1	1	0	1.5	.667	P-2
1898	NY N	1	.000	.000	5	0	0	0	0	0.0	0	0	0		0	0	0	0	3	1	0	4.0	.750	P-1
1900	CHI N	17	.109	.109	46	5	0	0	0	0.0	5	4	2		0	1	0	3	21	3	1	1.7	.889	P-16
1901		48	.257	.329	152	39	5	3	0	0.0	19	13	8		4	1	0	67	48	12	2	2.6	.906	OF-24, P-21, 1B-2, 2B-1
1902		65	.231	.259	216	50	4	1	0	0.0	24	15	15		4	0	0	230	57	13	7	4.5	.957	OF-23, P-22, 1B-18, 3B-2, 2B-1
1903		22	.203	.250	64	13	3	0	0	0.0	3	2	3		0	0	0	31	56	8	0	4.3	.916	P-20, 1B-2
9 yrs.		221	.222	.266	685	152	16	7	0	0.0	74	57	52	15	14	2	0	382	305	51	12	3.3	.931	P-139, OF-55, 1B-22, 2B-3, 3B-2

Year	Team	Games	BA	SA	AB	H	2B	3B	HR	HR%	R	RBI	BB	SO	SB	Pinch Hit AB	Pinch Hit H	PO	A	E	DP	TC/G	FA	G by Pos

Denis Menke

MENKE, DENIS JOHN BR TR 6′ 185 lbs.
B. July 21, 1940, Algona, Iowa.

Year	Team	Games	BA	SA	AB	H	2B	3B	HR	HR%	R	RBI	BB	SO	SB	Pinch Hit AB	Pinch Hit H	PO	A	E	DP	TC/G	FA	G by Pos
1962	MIL N	50	.192	.267	146	28	3	1	2	1.4	12	16	16	38	0	2	0	87	109	8	23	4.3	.961	2B-20, 3B-15, SS-9, 1B-2, OF-1
1963		146	.234	.344	518	121	16	4	11	2.1	58	50	37	106	6	2	0	234	398	24	67	4.2	.963	SS-82, 3B-51, 2B-22, OF-1, 1B-1
1964		151	.283	.479	505	143	29	5	20	4.0	79	65	68	77	4	2	1	283	455	27	84	4.7	.965	SS-141, 2B-15, 3B-6
1965		71	.243	.392	181	44	13	1	4	2.2	16	18	18	28	1	12	2	110	146	9	27	4.0	.966	SS-54, 1B-8, 3B-4
1966	ATL N	138	.251	.412	454	114	20	4	15	3.3	55	60	71	87	0	3	1	228	341	24	56	3.9	.960	SS-106, 3B-39, 1B-7
1967		129	.227	.325	418	95	14	3	7	1.7	37	39	65	62	5	0	0	183	350	19	65	4.3	.966	SS-124, 3B-3
1968	HOU N	150	.249	.347	542	135	23	6	6	1.1	56	56	64	81	5	1	0	346	384	15	71	4.6	.980	2B-119, SS-35, 1B-5, 3B-4
1969		154	.269	.387	553	149	25	5	10	1.8	72	90	87	87	2	0	0	257	414	27	75	4.3	.961	SS-131, 2B-23, 1B-9, 3B-1
1970		154	.304	.441	562	171	26	6	13	2.3	82	92	82	80	6	1	0	262	460	30	81	4.5	.960	SS-133, 2B-21, 1B-5, 3B-5, OF-3
1971		146	.246	.320	475	117	26	3	1	0.2	57	43	59	68	4	9	1	892	151	10	88	6.8	.991	1B-101, 3B-32, SS-17, 2B-5
1972	CIN N	140	.233	.345	447	104	19	2	9	2.0	41	50	58	76	0	3	1	125	260	16	25	2.8	.960	3B-130, 1B-11
1973		139	.191	.270	241	46	10	0	3	1.2	38	26	69	53	1	8	1	80	197	9	20	2.1	.969	3B-123, SS-7, 2B-5, 1B-1
1974	HOU N	30	.103	.138	29	3	1	0	0	0.0	2	1	4	10	0	8	2	21	23	0	5	1.8	1.000	1B-12, 3B-7, 2B-3, SS-2
13 yrs.		1598	.250	.370	5071	1270	225	40	101	2.0	605	606	698	853	34	51	9	3108	3688	218	687	4.2	.969	SS-841, 3B-420, 2B-233, 1B-162, OF-5
LEAGUE CHAMPIONSHIP SERIES																								
1972	CIN N	5	.250	.313	16	4	1	0	0	0.0	1	0	4	3	0	0	0	3	11	0	0	2.8	1.000	3B-5
1973		3	.222	.556	9	2	0	0	1	11.1	1	1	1	2	0	1	0	0	4	0	0	1.3	1.000	3B-2, SS-1
2 yrs.		8	.240	.400	25	6	1	0	1	4.0	2	1	5	5	0	1	0	3	15	0	0	2.3	1.000	3B-7, SS-1
WORLD SERIES																								
1972	CIN N	7	.083	.208	24	2	0	0	1	4.2	1	2	2	6	0	0	0	6	23	0	0	4.1	1.000	3B-7

Mike Menosky

MENOSKY, MICHAEL WILLIAM (Leaping Mike) BL TR 5′10″ 163 lbs.
B. Oct. 16, 1894, Glen Campbell, Pa. D. Apr. 11, 1983, Detroit, Mich.

Year	Team	Games	BA	SA	AB	H	2B	3B	HR	HR%	R	RBI	BB	SO	SB	Pinch Hit AB	Pinch Hit H	PO	A	E	DP	TC/G	FA	G by Pos
1914	PIT F	68	.264	.350	140	37	4	1	2	1.4	26	9	16		5	17	6	60	5	4	0	1.7	.942	OF-41
1915		17	.095	.095	21	2	0	0	0	0.0	3	1	2		2	5	0	11	0	1	0	1.3	.917	OF-9
1916	WAS A	10	.162	.243	37	6	1	1	0	0.0	5	3	1	10	1	1	0	17	3	1	2	2.3	.952	OF-9
1917		114	.258	.366	322	83	12	10	1	0.3	46	34	45	55	22	13	4	208	15	4	3	2.4	.982	OF-94
1919		116	.287	.401	342	98	15	3	6	1.8	62	39	44	46	13	7	3	222	7	5	1	2.3	.979	OF-103
1920	BOS A	141	.297	.393	532	158	24	9	3	0.6	80	64	65	52	23	0	0	281	17	12	2	2.2	.961	OF-141
1921		133	.300	.377	477	143	18	5	3	0.6	77	43	60	45	12	0	0	278	12	9	3	2.2	.970	OF-133
1922		126	.283	.369	406	115	16	5	3	0.7	61	32	40	33	9	21	7	240	14	6	3	2.5	.977	OF-103
1923		84	.229	.314	188	43	8	4	0	0.0	22	25	22	19	3	23	6	103	12	10	1	2.6	.920	OF-49
9 yrs.		809	.278	.370	2465	685	98	38	18	0.7	382	250	295	260	90	87	26	1420	85	52	15	2.3	.967	OF-682

Ed Mensor

MENSOR, EDWARD (The Midget) BB TR 5′6″ 145 lbs.
B. Nov. 7, 1886, Woodville, Ont., Canada D. Apr. 20, 1970, Salem, Ore.

Year	Team	Games	BA	SA	AB	H	2B	3B	HR	HR%	R	RBI	BB	SO	SB	Pinch Hit AB	Pinch Hit H	PO	A	E	DP	TC/G	FA	G by Pos
1912	PIT N	39	.263	.333	99	26	3	2	0	0.0	19	1	23	12	10	5	1	60	3	3	0	2.1	.955	OF-32
1913		44	.179	.196	56	10	1	0	0	0.0	9	1	8	13	2	15	4	31	4	1	1	1.8	.972	OF-18, SS-1, 2B-1
1914		44	.202	.281	89	18	2	1	1	1.1	15	6	22	13	2	6	0	61	2	2	0	2.6	.969	OF-25
3 yrs.		127	.221	.283	244	54	6	3	1	0.4	43	8	53	38	14	26	5	152	9	6	1	2.2	.964	OF-75, SS-1, 2B-1

Ted Menze

MENZE, THEODORE CHARLES BR TR 5′9″ 172 lbs.
B. Nov. 4, 1897, St. Louis, Mo. D. Dec. 23, 1969, St. Louis, Mo.

Year	Team	Games	BA	SA	AB	H	2B	3B	HR	HR%	R	RBI	BB	SO	SB	Pinch Hit AB	Pinch Hit H	PO	A	E	DP	TC/G	FA	G by Pos
1918	STL N	1	.000	.000	3	0	0	0	0	0.0	0	0	0	2	0	0	0	1	0	0	0	1.0	1.000	OF-1

Rudi Meoli

MEOLI, RUDOLPH BARTHOLOMEW BL TR 5′9″ 165 lbs.
B. May 1, 1951, Troy, N. Y.

Year	Team	Games	BA	SA	AB	H	2B	3B	HR	HR%	R	RBI	BB	SO	SB	Pinch Hit AB	Pinch Hit H	PO	A	E	DP	TC/G	FA	G by Pos
1971	CAL A	7	.000	.000	3	0	0	0	0	0.0	0	0	0	1	0	3	0	0	0	0	0	0.0	—	
1973		120	.223	.289	305	68	12	1	2	0.7	36	23	31	38	2	1	1	142	284	30	57	3.9	.934	SS-95, 3B-13, 2B-8
1974		36	.244	.267	90	22	2	0	0	0.0	9	3	8	10	2	5	0	15	67	5	6	2.9	.943	3B-20, SS-8, 1B-1, 2B-1
1975		70	.214	.246	126	27	2	1	0	0.0	12	6	15	20	3	8	1	39	97	10	13	2.6	.932	SS-28, 3B-15, 2B-11, DH-3
1978	CHI N	47	.103	.172	29	3	0	1	0	0.0	10	2	6	4	1	19	2	6	14	1	0	1.9	.952	2B-6, 3B-5
1979	PHI N	30	.178	.260	73	13	4	1	0	0.0	2	6	9	15	2	2	0	37	75	2	12	3.6	.982	SS-16, 2B-15, 3B-1
6 yrs.		310	.212	.267	626	133	20	4	2	0.3	69	40	69	88	10	38	4	239	537	48	88	3.3	.942	SS-147, 3B-54, 2B-41, DH-3, 1B-1

Orlando Mercado

MERCADO, ORLANDO BR TR 6′ 180 lbs.
Born Orlando Mercado (Rodriguez).
B. Nov. 7, 1961, Arecibo, Puerto Rico.

Year	Team	Games	BA	SA	AB	H	2B	3B	HR	HR%	R	RBI	BB	SO	SB	Pinch Hit AB	Pinch Hit H	PO	A	E	DP	TC/G	FA	G by Pos
1982	SEA A	9	.118	.294	17	2	0	0	1	5.9	1	6	0	5	0	0	0	31	1	0	0	3.6	1.000	C-8, DH-1
1983		66	.197	.298	178	35	11	2	1	0.6	10	16	14	27	2	2	0	342	27	2	2	5.7	.995	C-65
1984		30	.218	.282	78	17	3	1	0	0.0	5	5	4	12	1	3	1	118	10	1	0	4.4	.992	C-29
1986	TEX A	46	.235	.294	102	24	1	1	1	1.0	7	7	6	13	0	1	0	240	25	1	5	5.9	.996	C-45
1987	2 teams	DET A (10G –.136) LA N (7G –.600)																						
″	total	17	.222	.259	27	6	1	0	0	0.0	3	2	3	1	0	0	0	53	8	1	1	3.6	.984	C-17
1988	OAK A	16	.125	.250	24	3	0	0	1	4.2	3	1	3	8	0	0	0	45	2	2	0	3.1	.959	C-16
1989	MIN A	19	.105	.105	38	4	0	0	0	0.0	1	1	4	4	1	0	0	73	9	0	2	4.3	1.000	C-19
1990	2 teams	NY N (42G –.211) MON N (8G –.250)																						
″	total	50	.214	.316	98	21	1	0	3	3.1	10	7	8	12	0	4	0	239	9	2	2	5.2	.992	C-48
8 yrs.		253	.199	.281	562	112	17	4	7	1.2	40	45	42	82	4	10	1	1141	91	9	12	5.0	.993	C-247, DH-1

Orlando Merced

MERCED, ORLANDO LUIS BB TR 6′ 180 lbs.
Born Orlando Luis Merced (Villanueva).
B. Nov. 2, 1966, Hato Rey, Puerto Rico.

Year	Team	Games	BA	SA	AB	H	2B	3B	HR	HR%	R	RBI	BB	SO	SB	Pinch Hit AB	Pinch Hit H	PO	A	E	DP	TC/G	FA	G by Pos
1990	PIT N	25	.208	.250	24	5	1	0	0	0.0	3	0	1	9	0	24	5	0	0	0	0	0.0		OF-1, C-1
1991		120	.275	.399	411	113	17	2	10	2.4	83	50	64	81	8	17	6	916	60	12	64	8.8	.988	1B-105, OF-7
1992		134	.247	.385	405	100	28	5	6	1.5	50	60	52	63	5	25	10	906	75	5	74	7.5	.995	1B-114, OF-17

Orlando Merced *continued*

Year	Team	Games	BA	SA	AB	H	2B	3B	HR	HR%	R	RBI	BB	SO	SB	Pinch Hit AB	Pinch Hit H	PO	A	E	DP	TC/G	FA	G by Pos
1993		137	.313	.443	447	140	26	4	8	1.8	68	70	77	64	3	15	9	485	31	10	27	3.5	.981	OF-109, 1B-42
1994		108	.272	.412	386	105	21	3	9	2.3	48	51	42	58	4	2	0	509	29	5	46	4.4	.991	OF-68, 1B-55
1995		132	.300	.468	487	146	29	4	15	3.1	75	83	52	74	7	9	2	375	23	6	24	2.8	.985	OF-107, 1B-35
6 yrs.		656	.282	.422	2160	609	122	18	48	2.2	327	314	288	349	27	92	32	3191	218	38	235	5.2	.989	1B-351, OF-309, C-1
LEAGUE CHAMPIONSHIP SERIES																								
1991	**PIT N**	3	.222	.556	9	2	0	0	1	11.1	1	1	0	1	0	0	0	13	0	1	0	7.0	.929	1B-2
1992		4	.100	.200	10	1	1	0	0	0.0	0	2	2	4	0	1	0	27	2	1	3	7.5	.967	1B-4
2 yrs.		7	.158	.368	19	3	1	0	1	5.3	1	3	2	5	0	1	0	40	2	2	3	7.3	.955	1B-6

Henry Mercedes

MERCEDES, HENRY FELIPE BR TR 5′11″ 185 lbs.
Born Henry Felipe Mercedes (Perez).
B. July 23, 1969, Santo Domingo, Dominican Republic.

Year	Team	Games	BA	SA	AB	H	2B	3B	HR	HR%	R	RBI	BB	SO	SB	Pinch Hit AB	Pinch Hit H	PO	A	E	DP	TC/G	FA	G by Pos
1992	**OAK A**	9	.800	1.200	5	4	0	1	0	0.0	1	1	0	1	0	2	1	7	0	1	0	0.9	.875	C-9
1993		20	.213	.255	47	10	2	0	0	0.0	5	3	2	15	1	2	0	66	10	1	1	4.1	.987	C-18, DH-1
1995	**KC A**	23	.256	.302	43	11	2	0	0	0.0	7	9	8	13	0	1	0	62	8	1	1	3.2	.986	C-22
3 yrs.		52	.263	.326	95	25	4	1	0	0.0	13	13	10	29	1	5	1	135	18	3	2	3.1	.981	C-49, DH-1

Luis Mercedes

MERCEDES, LUIS ROBERTO BR TR 6′ 180 lbs.
Born Luis Roberto Mercedes (Santana).
B. Feb. 15, 1968, San Pedro de Macoris, Dominican Republic.

Year	Team	Games	BA	SA	AB	H	2B	3B	HR	HR%	R	RBI	BB	SO	SB	Pinch Hit AB	Pinch Hit H	PO	A	E	DP	TC/G	FA	G by Pos
1991	**BAL A**	19	.204	.241	54	11	2	0	0	0.0	10	2	4	9	0	2	1	20	0	0	0	1.3	1.000	OF-15, DH-1
1992		23	.140	.180	50	7	2	0	0	0.0	7	4	8	9	0	2	0	41	2	2	0	2.0	.956	OF-16, DH-7
1993	**2 teams**	**BAL A** (10G –.292) **SF N** (18G –.160)																						
″	**total**	28	.224	.306	49	11	2	1	0	0.0	2	3	6	7	1	12	0	16	1	0	1	1.1	1.000	OF-13, DH-2
3 yrs.		70	.190	.242	153	29	6	1	0	0.0	19	9	18	25	1	16	1	77	3	2	1	1.5	.976	OF-44, DH-10

John Mercer

MERCER, JOHN LOCKE BL TL 5′10½″ 155 lbs.
B. June 22, 1892, Taylortown, La. D. Dec. 22, 1982, Shreveport, La.

Year	Team	Games	BA	SA	AB	H	2B	3B	HR	HR%	R	RBI	BB	SO	SB	Pinch Hit AB	Pinch Hit H	PO	A	E	DP	TC/G	FA	G by Pos
1912	**STL N**	1	.000	.000	1	0	0	0	0	0.0	0	0	0	0	0	0	0	1	0	1	0	2.0	.500	1B-1

Win Mercer

MERCER, GEORGE BARCLAY BR TR 5′ 7″ 140 lbs.
B. June 20, 1874, Chester, W. Va. D. Jan. 12, 1903, San Francisco, Calif.

Year	Team	Games	BA	SA	AB	H	2B	3B	HR	HR%	R	RBI	BB	SO	SB	Pinch Hit AB	Pinch Hit H	PO	A	E	DP	TC/G	FA	G by Pos
1894	**WAS N**	52	.284	.377	162	46	5	2	2	1.2	27	29	9	20	9	0	0	20	69	6	1	1.8	.937	P-49, OF-4
1895		63	.255	.327	196	50	9	1	1	0.5	26	26	12	32	7	**5**	**2**	44	76	25	3	2.5	.828	P-43, SS-7, OF-5, 3B-3, 2B-1
1896		49	.244	.282	156	38	1	1	1	0.6	23	14	9	18	9	2	1	37	89	21	3	3.1	.857	P-46, OF-1
1897		48	.319	.407	135	43	2	5	0	0.0	22	19	6		7	2	0	0	0	0	0	0.0	.000	P-45
1898		80	.321	.398	249	80	3	5	2	0.8	38	25	18		14	2	1	91	116	29	8	2.9	.877	P-33, SS-23, OF-19, 3B-5, 2B-1
1899		108	.299	.360	375	112	6	7	1	0.3	73	35	32		16	6	0	109	156	40	8	3.0	.869	3B-62, P-23, OF-16, 1B-1, SS-1
1900	**NY N**	75	.294	.310	248	73	4	0	0	0.0	31	27	26		15	1	0	75	149	32	11	3.4	.875	P-32, 3B-19, OF-14, SS-7, 2B-3
1901	**WAS A**	51	.300	.379	140	42	7	2	0	0.0	26	16	23		10	4	0	92	57	15	10	3.3	.909	P-24, OF-16, 1B-7, 3B-1, SS-1
1902	**DET A**	35	.180	.200	100	18	2	0	0	0.0	8	6	6		1	0	0	13	103	8	2	3.5	.935	P-35
9 yrs.		561	.285	.345	1761	502	39	23	7	0.4	274	197	141	70	88	22	4	481	815	176	46	2.7	.880	P-330, 3B-90, OF-75, SS-39, 1B-8, 2B-5

Andy Merchant

MERCHANT, JAMES ANDERSON BL TR 5′11″ 185 lbs.
B. Aug. 30, 1950, Mobile, Ala.

Year	Team	Games	BA	SA	AB	H	2B	3B	HR	HR%	R	RBI	BB	SO	SB	Pinch Hit AB	Pinch Hit H	PO	A	E	DP	TC/G	FA	G by Pos
1975	**BOS A**	1	.500	.500	4	2	0	0	0	0.0	1	0	1	0	0	0	0	2	1	0	0	3.0	1.000	C-1
1976		2	.000	.000	2	0	0	0	0	0.0	0	0	0	2	0	2	0	1	0	0	0	1.0	1.000	C-1
2 yrs.		3	.333	.333	6	2	0	0	0	0.0	1	0	1	2	0	2	0	3	1	0	0	2.0	1.000	C-2

Art Merewether

MEREWETHER, ARTHUR FRANCIS (Merry) BR TR 5′ 9½″ 155 lbs.
B. July 7, 1902, East Providence, R. I.

Year	Team	Games	BA	SA	AB	H	2B	3B	HR	HR%	R	RBI	BB	SO	SB	Pinch Hit AB	Pinch Hit H	PO	A	E	DP	TC/G	FA	G by Pos
1922	**PIT N**	1	.000	.000	1	0	0	0	0	0.0	0	0	0	0	0	1	0	0	0	0	0	0.0	—	

Fred Merkle

MERKLE, FREDERICK CHARLES BR TR 6′ 1″ 190 lbs.
B. Dec. 20, 1888, Watertown, Wis. D. Mar. 2, 1956, Daytona Beach, Fla.

Year	Team	Games	BA	SA	AB	H	2B	3B	HR	HR%	R	RBI	BB	SO	SB	Pinch Hit AB	Pinch Hit H	PO	A	E	DP	TC/G	FA	G by Pos
1907	**NY N**	15	.255	.277	47	12	1	0	0	0.0	0	5	1		0	0	0	122	7	7	4	9.1	.949	1B-15
1908		38	.268	.439	41	11	2	1	1	2.4	6	7	4		0	16	2	65	3	0	3	3.8	1.000	1B-11, OF-5, 3B-1, 2B-1
1909		78	.191	.237	236	45	9	1	0	0.0	15	20	16		7	8	3	622	30	16	29	9.5	.976	1B-69, 2B-1
1910		144	.292	.441	506	148	35	14	4	0.8	75	70	44	59	23	0	0	1390	84	29	87	10.4	.981	1B-144
1911		149	.283	.438	541	153	24	12	12	2.2	80	84	43	60	49	0	0	1375	117	22	73	10.2	.985	1B-148
1912		129	.309	.449	479	148	22	6	11	2.3	82	84	42	70	37	0	0	1229	72	27	77	10.3	.980	1B-129
1913		153	.261	.373	563	147	30	12	3	0.5	78	69	41	60	35	0	0	1463	76	22	86	10.2	.986	1B-153
1914		146	.258	.375	512	132	25	7	7	1.4	71	63	52	**80**	23	0	0	1463	88	16	80	10.7	.990	1B-146
1915		140	.299	.384	505	151	25	3	4	0.8	52	62	36	39	20	1	0	1191	58	15	63	9.0	.988	1B-111, OF-29
1916	**2 teams**	**NY N** (112G –.237) **BKN N** (23G –.232)																						
″	**total**	135	.236	.336	470	111	20	3	7	1.5	51	46	40	50	19	5	2	1314	63	21	64	10.7	.985	1B-127, OF-4
1917	**2 teams**	**BKN N** (2G –.125) **CHI N** (146G –.266)																						
″	**total**	148	.264	.368	557	147	31	9	3	0.5	66	57	42	61	13	1	0	1453	69	26	86	10.5	.983	1B-142, OF-6
1918	**CHI N**	129	.297	.388	482	143	25	5	3	0.6	55	65	35	36	21	0	0	1388	82	15	69	11.5	.990	1B-129
1919		133	.267	.349	498	133	20	6	3	0.6	52	62	33	35	20	1	0	1494	56	23	66	11.9	.985	1B-132
1920		92	.285	.397	330	94	20	4	3	0.9	33	38	24	32	3	6	0	906	54	15	52	11.3	.985	1B-85, OF-1
1925	**NY A**	7	.385	.462	13	5	1	0	0	0.0	4	1	1	1	1	2	1	28	1	0	3	5.8	1.000	1B-5
1926		1	.000	.000	2	0	0	0	0	0.0	0	0	0	0	0	0	0	6	0	0	0	6.0	1.000	1B-1
16 yrs.		1637	.273	.384	5782	1580	290	83	61	1.1	720	733	454	583	271	39	8	15509	860	254	842	10.4	.985	1B-1547, OF-45, 2B-2, 3B-1
WORLD SERIES																								
1911	**NY N**	6	.150	.200	20	3	1	0	0	0.0	1	1	2	6	0	0	0	62	4	2	0	11.3	.971	1B-6
1912		8	.273	.394	33	9	2	1	0	0.0	5	3	0	7	1	0	0	83	1	3	2	10.9	.966	1B-8
1913		4	.231	.462	13	3	0	0	1	7.7	3	3	1	2	0	0	0	38	1	2	0	10.3	.951	1B-4
1916	**BKN N**	3	.250	.250	4	1	0	0	0	0.0	0	0	2	0	0	1	0	9	1	1	0	11.0	.909	1B-1
1918	**CHI N**	6	.278	.278	18	5	0	0	0	0.0	1	1	4	3	0	0	0	52	9	0	6	10.2	1.000	1B-6
5 yrs.		27	.239	.330	88	21	3	1	1	1.1	10	8	9	18	1	1	0	244	16	8	8	10.7	.970	1B-25

Ed Merrill

MERRILL, EDWARD MASON 5′11″ 176 lbs.
B. May 1860, Maysville, Ky. D. Aug. 18, 1924, Chicago, Ill.

Year	Team	Games	BA	SA	AB	H	2B	3B	HR	HR%	R	RBI	BB	SO	SB	Pinch Hit AB	Pinch Hit H	PO	A	E	DP	TC/G	FA	G by Pos
1882	2 teams	LOU AA (1G –.000)	WOR N (2G –.125)																					
″	total	3	.125	.125	8	1	0	0	0	0.0	0	4	0	1		0	0	1	4	2	0	2.3	.714	3B-2, OF-1
1884	IND AA	55	.179	.204	196	35	3	1	0	0.0	14		6			0	0	144	162	34	15	6.2	.900	2B-55
2 yrs.		58	.176	.201	204	36	3	1	0	0.0	14	4	6	1		0	0	145	166	36	15	6.0	.896	2B-55, 3B-2, OF-1

Lloyd Merriman

MERRIMAN, LLOYD ARCHER (Citation) BL TL 6′ 190 lbs.
B. Aug. 2, 1924, Clovis, Calif.

Year	Team	Games	BA	SA	AB	H	2B	3B	HR	HR%	R	RBI	BB	SO	SB	Pinch Hit AB	Pinch Hit H	PO	A	E	DP	TC/G	FA	G by Pos
1949	CIN N	103	.230	.348	287	66	12	5	4	1.4	35	26	21	36	2	11	1	214	7	7	1	2.7	.969	OF-86
1950		92	.258	.349	298	77	15	3	2	0.7	44	31	30	23	6	4	1	181	4	2	1	2.2	.989	OF-84
1951		114	.242	.359	359	87	23	2	5	1.4	34	36	31	34	8	14	4	309	5	1	2	3.1	.997	OF-102
1954		73	.268	.357	112	30	8	1	0	0.0	12	16	23	10	3	38	11	51	0	1	0	2.1	.981	OF-25
1955	2 teams	CHI A (1G –.000)	CHI N (72G –.214)																					
″	total	73	.212	.288	146	31	6	1	1	0.7	15	8	21	21	1	20	4	82	2	2	2	1.8	.977	OF-49
5 yrs.		455	.242	.345	1202	291	64	12	12	1.0	140	117	126	124	20	87	21	837	18	13	6	2.5	.985	OF-346

Bill Merritt

MERRITT, WILLIAM HENRY BR TR 5′ 7″ 160 lbs.
B. July 30, 1870, Lowell, Mass. D. Nov. 17, 1937, Lowell, Mass.

Year	Team	Games	BA	SA	AB	H	2B	3B	HR	HR%	R	RBI	BB	SO	SB	Pinch Hit AB	Pinch Hit H	PO	A	E	DP	TC/G	FA	G by Pos
1891	CHI N	11	.214	.238	42	9	1	0	0	0.0	4	4	2	2	0	0	0	41	11	3	2	4.6	.945	C-11, 1B-1
1892	LOU N	46	.196	.262	168	33	4	2	1	0.6	22	13	11	15	3	0	0	175	58	15	6	5.4	.940	C-46
1893	BOS N	39	.348	.496	141	49	6	3	3	2.1	30	26	13	13	3	0	0	130	25	9	6	4.2	.945	C-37, OF-2
1894	3 teams	BOS N (10G –.231)	PIT N (36G –.275)	CIN N (29G –.327)																				
″	total	75	.294	.375	248	73	8	3	2	0.8	38	45	32	10	6	4	0	202	78	17	8	4.1	.943	C-60, 1B-5, OF-4, 3B-3
1895	2 teams	CIN N (22G –.177)	PIT N (67G –.285)																					
″	total	89	.258	.286	318	82	7	1	0	0.0	41	39	24	21	4	1	0	342	79	27	12	5.2	.940	C-83, 1B-2, 2B-1
1896	PIT N	77	.291	.344	282	82	8	2	1	0.4	26	42	18	10	3	3	1	286	95	25	8	5.4	.938	C-62, 3B-5, 2B-3, 1B-3, SS-2
1897		62	.263	.316	209	55	6	1	1	0.5	21	26	9		2	2	0	270	47	15	10	5.5	.955	C-53, 1B-7
1899	BOS N	1	.000	.000	2	0	0	0	0	0.0	0	0	0		0	0	0	2	2	0	0	4.0	1.000	C-1
8 yrs.		400	.272	.334	1410	383	40	12	8	0.6	182	195	109	71	21	10	1	1448	395	111	52	5.0	.943	C-353, 1B-18, 3B-8, OF-6, 2B-4, SS-2

George Merritt

MERRITT, GEORGE WASHINGTON TR 6′ 160 lbs.
B. Apr. 14, 1880, Paterson, N. J. D. Feb. 21, 1938, Memphis, Tenn.

Year	Team	Games	BA	SA	AB	H	2B	3B	HR	HR%	R	RBI	BB	SO	SB	Pinch Hit AB	Pinch Hit H	PO	A	E	DP	TC/G	FA	G by Pos
1901	PIT N	4	.273	.455	11	3	0	1	0	0.0	2	0	0		0	1	0	1	5	0	0	2.0	1.000	P-3
1902		2	.333	.444	9	3	1	0	0	0.0	2	2	0		0	0	0	4	1	0	0	2.5	1.000	OF-2
1903		9	.148	.222	27	4	0	1	0	0.0	4	3	2		1	0	0	9	0	1	0	1.3	.900	OF-7, P-1
3 yrs.		15	.213	.319	47	10	1	2	0	0.0	8	5	2		1	1	0	14	6	1	0	1.6	.952	OF-9, P-4

Herm Merritt

MERRITT, HERMAN G. BR TR
B. Nov. 12, 1900, Independence, Kans. D. May 26, 1957, Kansas City, Mo.

Year	Team	Games	BA	SA	AB	H	2B	3B	HR	HR%	R	RBI	BB	SO	SB	Pinch Hit AB	Pinch Hit H	PO	A	E	DP	TC/G	FA	G by Pos
1921	DET A	20	.370	.478	46	17	1	2	0	0.0	3	6	1	5	1	1	0	25	20	6	0	3.0	.882	SS-17

Howard Merritt

MERRITT, JOHN HOWARD (Lefty) BR TL 5′11″ 170 lbs.
B. Oct. 6, 1894, Tupelo, Miss. D. Nov. 3, 1955, Tupelo, Miss.

Year	Team	Games	BA	SA	AB	H	2B	3B	HR	HR%	R	RBI	BB	SO	SB	Pinch Hit AB	Pinch Hit H	PO	A	E	DP	TC/G	FA	G by Pos
1913	NY N	1	—	—	0	0	0	0	0	—	0	0	0	0	0	0	0	0	0	0	0	0.0	.000	OF-1

Jack Merson

MERSON, JOHN WARREN BR TR 5′11″ 175 lbs.
B. Jan. 17, 1922, Elk Ridge, Md.

Year	Team	Games	BA	SA	AB	H	2B	3B	HR	HR%	R	RBI	BB	SO	SB	Pinch Hit AB	Pinch Hit H	PO	A	E	DP	TC/G	FA	G by Pos
1951	PIT N	13	.360	.540	50	18	2	2	1	2.0	6	14	1	7	0	0	0	30	46	1	7	5.9	.987	2B-13
1952		111	.246	.344	398	98	20	2	5	1.3	41	38	22	38	1	3	0	220	266	12	62	4.6	.976	2B-81, 3B-27
1953	BOS A	1	.000	.000	4	0	0	0	0	0.0	0	0	0	0	0	0	0	3	4	1	0	8.0	.875	2B-1
3 yrs.		125	.257	.363	452	116	22	4	6	1.3	47	52	23	45	1	3	0	253	316	14	69	4.8	.976	2B-95, 3B-27

Sam Mertes

MERTES, SAMUEL BLAIR (Sandow) BR TR 5′10″ 185 lbs.
B. Aug. 6, 1872, San Francisco, Calif. D. Mar. 11, 1945, San Francisco, Calif.

Year	Team	Games	BA	SA	AB	H	2B	3B	HR	HR%	R	RBI	BB	SO	SB	Pinch Hit AB	Pinch Hit H	PO	A	E	DP	TC/G	FA	G by Pos
1896	PHI N	37	.238	.322	143	34	4	4	0	0.0	20	14	8	10	19	1	0	86	5	9	1	2.7	.910	OF-35, SS-1, 2B-1
1898	CHI N	83	.297	.383	269	80	4	8	1	0.4	45	47	34		27	5	0	128	53	27	16	2.6	.870	OF-60, SS-14, 2B-4, 1B-2
1899		117	.298	.467	426	127	13	16	9	2.1	83	81	33		45	5	1	223	27	21	9	2.4	.923	OF-108, 1B-3, SS-1
1900		127	.295	.407	481	142	25	4	7	1.5	72	60	42		38	0	0	532	49	28	22	4.8	.954	OF-88, 1B-33, SS-7
1901	CHI A	137	.277	.396	545	151	16	17	5	0.9	94	98	52		46	0	0	357	396	47	54	5.8	.941	2B-132, OF-5
1902		129	.282	.362	497	140	23	7	1	0.2	60	79	37		46	0	0	263	45	23	9	2.5	.931	OF-120, SS-5, C-2, 1B-1, 2B-1, P-1, 3B-1
1903	NY N	138	.280	.437	517	145	**32**	14	7	1.4	100	**104**	61		45	0	0	274	25	9	5	2.2	.971	OF-137, 1B-1, C-1
1904		148	.276	.393	532	147	28	11	4	0.8	83	78	54		47	0	0	248	19	12	1	1.9	.957	OF-147, SS-1
1905		150	.279	.417	551	154	27	17	5	0.9	81	108	56		52	0	0	230	10	10	3	1.7	.960	OF-150
1906	2 teams	NY N (71G –.237)	STL N (53G –.246)																					
″	total	124	.241	.329	444	107	16	10	1	0.2	57	52	45		31	0	0	196	14	14	0	1.8	.938	OF-124
10 yrs.		1190	.279	.398	4405	1227	188	108	40	0.9	695	721	422	10	396	11	1	2537	643	200	120	2.8	.941	OF-974, 2B-138, 1B-40, SS-29, C-3, P-1, 3B-1
WORLD SERIES																								
1905	NY N	5	.176	.235	17	3	1	0	0	0.0	2	3	2	5	0	0	0	3	1	0	0	0.8	1.000	OF-5

Lennie Merullo

MERULLO, LEONARD RICHARD BR TR 5′11½″ 166 lbs.
B. May 5, 1917, Boston, Mass.

Year	Team	Games	BA	SA	AB	H	2B	3B	HR	HR%	R	RBI	BB	SO	SB	Pinch Hit AB	Pinch Hit H	PO	A	E	DP	TC/G	FA	G by Pos
1941	CHI N	7	.353	.412	17	6	1	0	0	0.0	3	1	2	0	1	0	0	12	18	1	5	4.4	.968	SS-7
1942		143	.256	.324	515	132	23	3	2	0.4	53	37	35	45	14	0	0	299	438	42	80	5.4	.946	SS-143
1943		129	.254	.313	453	115	18	3	1	0.2	37	25	26	42	7	0	0	222	396	39	68	5.1	.941	SS-125, 3B-2, 2B-1
1944		66	.212	.280	193	41	8	1	1	0.5	20	16	16	18	3	6	1	116	167	19	26	5.3	.937	SS-56, 1B-1
1945		121	.239	.299	394	94	18	0	2	0.5	40	37	31	30	7	0	0	209	336	30	49	4.9	.948	SS-118
1946		65	.151	.214	126	19	8	0	0	0.0	14	7	11	13	2	1	0	78	131	12	23	5.0	.946	SS-44
1947		108	.241	.290	373	90	16	1	0	0.0	24	29	15	26	4	0	0	219	322	29	77	5.3	.949	SS-108
7 yrs.		639	.240	.301	2071	497	92	8	6	0.3	191	152	136	174	38	7	1	1155	1808	172	328	5.2	.945	SS-601, 3B-2, 1B-1, 2B-1
WORLD SERIES																								
1945	CHI N	3	.000	.000	2	0	0	0	0	0.0	0	0	0	1	0	0	0	4	2	0	2	2.0	1.000	SS-3

Matt Merullo

MERULLO, MATTHEW BATES BL TR 6' 2" 200 lbs.
B. Aug. 4, 1965, Winchester, Mass.

Year	Team	Games	BA	SA	AB	H	2B	3B	HR	HR%	R	RBI	BB	SO	SB	Pinch Hit AB	Pinch Hit H	PO	A	E	DP	TC/G	FA	G by Pos
1989	CHI A	31	.222	.272	81	18	1	0	1	1.2	5	8	6	14	0	7	3	100	10	3	0	4.0	.973	C-27, DH-1
1991		80	.229	.343	140	32	1	0	5	3.6	8	21	9	18	0	**41**	7	159	14	2	11	3.6	.989	C-27, 1B-16, DH-6
1992		24	.180	.240	50	9	1	1	0	0.0	3	3	1	8	0	7	0	64	3	2	0	4.1	.971	C-16, DH-1
1993		8	.050	.050	20	1	0	0	0	0.0	1	0	0	1	0	3	0	0	0	0	0	0.0	.000	DH-6
1994	CLE A	4	.100	.100	10	1	0	0	0	0.0	1	0	2	1	0	0	0	22	0	1	0	5.8	.957	C-4
1995	MIN A	76	.282	.379	195	55	14	1	1	0.5	19	27	14	27	0	19	3	215	12	3	0	3.8	.987	C-46, DH-13, 1B-2
6 yrs.		223	.234	.319	496	116	17	2	7	1.4	37	59	32	69	0	77	13	560	39	11	11	3.7	.982	C-120, DH-27, 1B-18

Steve Mesner

MESNER, STEPHEN MATHIAS BR TR 5' 9" 178 lbs.
B. Jan. 13, 1918, Los Angeles, Calif. D. Apr. 6, 1981, San Diego, Calif.

Year	Team	Games	BA	SA	AB	H	2B	3B	HR	HR%	R	RBI	BB	SO	SB	Pinch Hit AB	Pinch Hit H	PO	A	E	DP	TC/G	FA	G by Pos
1938	CHI N	2	.250	.250	4	1	0	0	0	0.0	2	0	1	1	0	1	0	0	2	1	0	3.0	.667	SS-1
1939		17	.279	.372	43	12	4	0	0	0.0	7	6	3	4	0	3	0	16	43	4	8	4.5	.937	SS-12, 3B-1, 2B-1
1941	STL N	24	.145	.159	69	10	1	0	0	0.0	8	10	5	6	0	1	0	23	45	3	8	3.2	.958	3B-22
1943	CIN N	137	.272	.327	504	137	26	1	0	0.0	53	52	26	20	6	7	4	132	274	24	29	3.3	.944	3B-130
1944		121	.242	.309	414	100	17	4	1	0.2	31	47	34	20	1	1	0	120	246	19	21	3.2	.951	3B-120
1945		150	.254	.298	540	137	19	1	1	0.2	52	52	52	18	4	0	0	173	329	15	36	3.4	.971	3B-148, 2B-3
6 yrs.		451	.252	.306	1574	397	67	6	2	0.1	153	167	121	69	11	13	4	464	939	66	102	3.4	.955	3B-421, SS-13, 2B-4

Bobby Messenger

MESSENGER, CHARLES WALTER BB TR 5'10½" 165 lbs.
B. Mar. 19, 1884, Bangor, Me. D. July 10, 1951, Bath, Me.

Year	Team	Games	BA	SA	AB	H	2B	3B	HR	HR%	R	RBI	BB	SO	SB	Pinch Hit AB	Pinch Hit H	PO	A	E	DP	TC/G	FA	G by Pos
1909	CHI A	31	.170	.196	112	19	1	1	0	0.0	18	0	13		7	0	0	34	4	2	1	1.3	.950	OF-31
1910		9	.231	.308	26	6	0	1	0	0.0	7	4	4		3	1	0	9	2	2	0	1.4	.846	OF-9
1911		13	.118	.235	17	2	0	1	0	0.0	4	0	3		0	9	2	7	0	1	0	2.0	.875	OF-4
1914	STL A	1	.000	.000	2	0	0	0	0	0.0	0	0	0	0	0	0	0	0	0	0	0	0.0	.000	OF-1
4 yrs.		54	.172	.217	157	27	1	3	0	0.0	29	4	20	0	10	10	2	50	6	5	1	1.4	.918	OF-45

Tom Messitt

MESSITT, THOMAS JOHN 5' 9" 177 lbs.
B. July 27, 1874, Frankfort, Pa. D. Sept. 22, 1934, Chicago, Ill.

Year	Team	Games	BA	SA	AB	H	2B	3B	HR	HR%	R	RBI	BB	SO	SB	Pinch Hit AB	Pinch Hit H	PO	A	E	DP	TC/G	FA	G by Pos
1899	LOU N	3	.091	.091	11	1	0	0	0	0.0	0	0	0		0	0	0	5	7	0	0	4.0	1.000	C-3

Scat Metha

METHA, FRANK JOSEPH BR TR 5'11" 165 lbs.
B. Dec. 13, 1913, Los Angeles, Calif. D. Mar. 2, 1975, Fountain Valley, Calif.

Year	Team	Games	BA	SA	AB	H	2B	3B	HR	HR%	R	RBI	BB	SO	SB	Pinch Hit AB	Pinch Hit H	PO	A	E	DP	TC/G	FA	G by Pos
1940	DET A	26	.243	.297	37	9	0	1	0	0.0	6	3	2	8	0	2	0	10	27	2	3	2.4	.949	2B-10, 3B-6

Bud Metheny

METHENY, ARTHUR BEAUREGARD BL TL 5'11" 190 lbs.
B. June 1, 1915, St. Louis, Mo.

Year	Team	Games	BA	SA	AB	H	2B	3B	HR	HR%	R	RBI	BB	SO	SB	Pinch Hit AB	Pinch Hit H	PO	A	E	DP	TC/G	FA	G by Pos
1943	NY A	103	.261	.397	360	94	18	2	9	2.5	51	36	39	34	2	10	1	156	1	6	0	1.8	.963	OF-91
1944		137	.239	.355	518	124	16	1	14	2.7	72	67	56	57	5	4	0	232	8	11	2	1.9	.956	OF-132
1945		133	.248	.338	509	126	18	2	8	1.6	64	53	54	31	5	4	0	227	12	4	2	1.9	.984	OF-128
1946		3	.000	.000	3	0	0	0	0	0.0	0	0	0	0	0	3	0	0	0	0	0	0.0	—	
4 yrs.		376	.247	.359	1390	344	52	5	31	2.2	187	156	149	122	12	21	1	615	21	21	4	1.9	.968	OF-351
WORLD SERIES																								
1943	NY A	2	.125	.125	8	1	0	0	0	0.0	0	0	0	2	0	0	0	3	0	0	0	1.5	1.000	OF-2

Catfish Metkovich

METKOVICH, GEORGE MICHAEL BL TL 6' 1" 185 lbs.
B. Oct. 8, 1921, Angel's Camp, Calif. D. May 17, 1995, Costa Mesa, Calif.

Year	Team	Games	BA	SA	AB	H	2B	3B	HR	HR%	R	RBI	BB	SO	SB	Pinch Hit AB	Pinch Hit H	PO	A	E	DP	TC/G	FA	G by Pos
1943	BOS A	78	.246	.361	321	79	14	4	5	1.6	34	27	19	38	1	0	0	206	9	9	5	2.9	.960	OF-76, 1B-2
1944		134	.277	.406	549	152	28	8	9	1.6	94	59	31	57	13	2	1	711	41	17	40	5.8	.978	OF-82, 1B-50
1945		138	.260	.347	539	140	26	3	5	0.9	65	62	51	70	19	3	0	1022	78	16	96	8.0	.986	1B-97, OF-42
1946		86	.246	.356	281	69	15	2	4	1.4	42	25	36	39	8	3	0	125	3	7	0	1.7	.948	OF-81
1947	CLE A	126	.254	.362	473	120	22	7	5	1.1	68	40	32	51	5	6	2	350	3	4	2	3.0	.989	OF-119, 1B-1
1949	CHI A	93	.237	.331	338	80	9	4	5	1.5	50	45	41	24	5	5	1	212	1	7	0	2.5	.968	OF-87
1951	PIT N	120	.293	.378	423	124	21	3	3	0.7	51	40	28	23	3	13	6	477	31	4	32	4.8	.992	OF-69, 1B-37
1952		125	.271	.391	373	101	18	3	7	1.9	41	41	32	29	5	20	4	602	34	7	59	6.1	.989	1B-72, OF-33
1953	2 teams	PIT N (26G –.146) CHI N (61G –.234)																						
"	total	87	.212	.333	165	35	9	1	3	1.8	24	19	22	13	2	33	8	158	3	2	4	3.0	.988	OF-42, 1B-12
1954	MIL N	68	.276	.358	123	34	5	1	1	0.8	7	15	15	15	0	31	9	160	17	0	15	5.7	1.000	1B-18, OF-13
10 yrs.		1055	.261	.367	3585	934	167	36	47	1.3	476	373	307	359	61	116	31	4023	220	73	253	4.6	.983	OF-644, 1B-289
WORLD SERIES																								
1946	BOS A	2	.500	1.000	2	1	1	0	0	0.0	1	0	0	0	0	2	1	0	0	0	0	0.0	—	

Charlie Metro

METRO, CHARLES BR TR 5'11½" 178 lbs.
Born Charles Moreskonich.
B. Apr. 28, 1919, Nanty Glo, Pa.
Manager 1962, 1970.

Year	Team	Games	BA	SA	AB	H	2B	3B	HR	HR%	R	RBI	BB	SO	SB	Pinch Hit AB	Pinch Hit H	PO	A	E	DP	TC/G	FA	G by Pos
1943	DET A	44	.200	.200	40	8	0	0	0	0.0	12	2	3	6	1	2	0	28	0	1	0	2.1	.966	OF-14
1944	2 teams	DET A (38G –.192) PHI A (24G –.100)																						
"	total	62	.161	.178	118	19	0	1	0	0.0	12	6	10	16	1	8	2	64	11	1	3	2.0	.987	OF-31, 3B-5, 2B-2
1945	PHI A	65	.210	.315	200	42	10	1	3	1.5	18	15	23	33	1	9	3	100	5	3	0	1.9	.972	OF-57
3 yrs.		171	.193	.257	358	69	10	2	3	0.8	42	23	36	55	3	19	5	192	16	5	3	2.0	.977	OF-102, 3B-5, 2B-2

Lenny Metz

METZ, LEONARD RAYMOND BR TR 5'10½" 170 lbs.
B. July 6, 1899, Louisville, Colo. D. Feb. 24, 1953, Denver, Colo.

Year	Team	Games	BA	SA	AB	H	2B	3B	HR	HR%	R	RBI	BB	SO	SB	Pinch Hit AB	Pinch Hit H	PO	A	E	DP	TC/G	FA	G by Pos
1923	PHI N	12	.216	.216	37	8	0	0	0	0.0	4	3	4	3	0	0	0	28	32	2	7	5.2	.968	SS-6, 2B-6
1924		7	.286	.286	7	2	0	0	0	0.0	1	1	1	0	0	0	0	3	8	2	1	2.2	.846	SS-6
1925		11	.000	.000	14	0	0	0	0	0.0	1	0	0	2	0	0	0	9	16	1	0	2.4	.962	SS-9, 2B-2
3 yrs.		30	.172	.172	58	10	0	0	0	0.0	6	4	5	5	0	0	0	40	56	5	8	3.5	.950	SS-21, 2B-8

Roger Metzger

METZGER, ROGER HENRY BB TR 6' 165 lbs.
B. Oct. 10, 1947, Fredericksburg, Tex. BL 1970, 1980

Year	Team	Games	BA	SA	AB	H	2B	3B	HR	HR%	R	RBI	BB	SO	SB	Pinch Hit AB	Pinch Hit H	PO	A	E	DP	TC/G	FA	G by Pos
1970	CHI N	1	.000	.000	2	0	0	0	0	0.0	0	0	0	0	0	0	0	1	4	1	1	6.0	.833	SS-1
1971	HOU N	150	.235	.299	562	132	14	**11**	0	0.0	64	26	44	50	15	1	1	275	459	17	91	5.1	.977	SS-148
1972		153	.222	.259	641	142	12	3	2	0.3	84	38	60	71	23	0	0	238	504	22	101	5.0	.971	SS-153

Roger Metzger *continued*

Year	Team	Lg	Games	BA	SA	AB	H	2B	3B	HR	HR%	R	RBI	BB	SO	SB	Pinch Hit AB	Pinch Hit H	PO	A	E	DP	TC/G	FA	G by Pos
1973			154	.250	.322	580	145	11	**14**	1	0.2	67	35	39	70	10	1	0	231	429	12	83	4.5	.982	SS-149
1974			143	.253	.320	572	145	18	10	0	0.0	66	30	37	73	9	0	0	238	451	17	85	4.9	.976	SS-143
1975			127	.227	.296	450	102	7	9	2	0.4	54	26	41	39	4	2	1	186	441	15	83	5.1	.977	SS-126
1976			152	.210	.270	481	101	13	8	0	0.0	37	29	52	63	1	0	0	258	468	10	93	4.8	.986	SS-150, 2B-2
1977			97	.186	.264	269	50	9	6	0	0.0	24	16	32	24	2	1	0	130	260	11	45	4.1	.973	SS-96, 2B-1
1978	2 teams		HOU N (45G –.220)		SF N (75G –.260)																				
"	total		120	.246	.285	358	88	10	2	0	0.0	28	23	24	26	8	4	1	171	289	14	51	4.1	.970	SS-116, 2B-1
1979	SF	N	94	.251	.340	259	65	7	8	0	0.0	24	31	23	31	11	6	1	122	237	15	38	4.2	.960	SS-78, 2B-10, 3B-1
1980			28	.074	.074	27	2	0	0	0	0.0	5	0	3	2	0	8	1	14	19	1	4	2.4	.971	SS-13, 2B-1
11 yrs.			1219	.231	.293	4201	972	101	71	5	0.1	453	254	355	449	83	23	5	1864	3561	135	675	4.7	.976	SS-1173, 2B-15, 3B-1

Bill Metzig

METZIG, WILLIAM ANDREW BR TR 6′ 1″ 180 lbs.
B. Dec. 4, 1918, Fort Dodge, Iowa.

Year	Team	Lg	Games	BA	SA	AB	H	2B	3B	HR	HR%	R	RBI	BB	SO	SB	Pinch Hit AB	Pinch Hit H	PO	A	E	DP	TC/G	FA	G by Pos
1944	CHI	A	5	.125	.125	16	2	0	0	0	0.0	1	1	1	4	0	0	0	13	15	0	2	5.6	1.000	2B-5

Alex Metzler

METZLER, ALEXANDER BL TR 5′ 9″ 167 lbs.
B. Jan. 4, 1903, Fresno, Calif. D. Nov. 30, 1973, Fresno, Calif.

Year	Team	Lg	Games	BA	SA	AB	H	2B	3B	HR	HR%	R	RBI	BB	SO	SB	Pinch Hit AB	Pinch Hit H	PO	A	E	DP	TC/G	FA	G by Pos
1925	CHI	N	9	.184	.237	38	7	2	0	0	0.0	2	2	3	7	0	0	0	24	3	0	0	3.0	1.000	OF-9
1926	PHI	A	20	.239	.284	67	16	3	0	0	0.0	8	12	7	5	1	3	1	34	3	0	1	2.2	1.000	OF-17
1927	CHI	A	134	.319	.429	543	173	29	11	3	0.6	87	61	61	39	15	0	0	397	16	15	6	3.2	.965	OF-134
1928			139	.304	.422	464	141	18	14	3	0.6	71	55	77	30	16	6	2	288	11	10	3	2.3	.968	OF-134
1929			146	.275	.371	568	156	23	13	2	0.4	80	49	80	45	11	4	0	316	16	14	3	2.5	.960	OF-141
1930	2 teams		CHI A (56G –.177)		STL A (56G –.258)																				
"	total		112	.236	.302	288	68	10	3	1	0.3	42	28	32	18	5	24	4	144	3	7	0	1.9	.955	OF-83
6 yrs.			560	.285	.384	1968	561	85	41	9	0.5	290	207	260	144	48	37	7	1203	52	46	13	2.5	.965	OF-518

Hensley Meulens

MEULENS, HENSLEY FILEMON ACASIO (Bam-Bam) BR TR 6′ 4″ 200 lbs.
B. June 23, 1967, Curacao, Netherlands Antilles.

Year	Team	Lg	Games	BA	SA	AB	H	2B	3B	HR	HR%	R	RBI	BB	SO	SB	Pinch Hit AB	Pinch Hit H	PO	A	E	DP	TC/G	FA	G by Pos
1989	NY	A	8	.179	.179	28	5	0	0	0	0.0	2	1	2	8	0	0	0	5	23	4	1	4.0	.875	3B-8
1990			23	.241	.434	83	20	7	0	3	3.6	12	10	9	25	1	0	0	49	3	2	1	2.3	.963	OF-23
1991			96	.222	.319	288	64	8	1	6	2.1	37	29	18	97	3	11	4	179	5	6	7	2.0	.968	OF-73, DH-13, 1B-7
1992			2	.600	1.200	5	3	0	0	1	20.0	1	1	1	0	0	0	0	0	3	0	2	1.5	1.000	3B-2
1993			30	.170	.340	53	9	1	1	2	3.8	8	5	8	19	0	7	1	32	0	0	0	1.1	1.000	OF-24, 1B-3, 3B-1
5 yrs.			159	.221	.344	457	101	16	2	12	2.6	60	46	38	149	4	18	5	265	34	12	11	2.0	.961	OF-120, DH-13, 3B-11, 1B-10

Bob Meusel

MEUSEL, ROBERT WILLIAM (Long Bob) BR TR 6′ 3″ 190 lbs.
Brother of Irish Meusel.
B. July 19, 1896, San Jose, Calif. D. Nov. 28, 1977, Downey, Calif.

Year	Team	Lg	Games	BA	SA	AB	H	2B	3B	HR	HR%	R	RBI	BB	SO	SB	Pinch Hit AB	Pinch Hit H	PO	A	E	DP	TC/G	FA	G by Pos
1920	NY	A	119	.328	.517	460	151	40	7	11	2.4	75	83	20	72	4	8	5	162	85	20	17	2.4	.925	OF-64, 3B-45, 1B-2
1921			149	.318	.559	598	190	40	16	24	4.0	104	135	34	**88**	17	2	2	253	28	20	8	2.0	.934	OF-147
1922			121	.319	.522	473	151	26	11	16	3.4	61	84	40	58	13	0	0	202	24	12	0	2.0	.950	OF-121
1923			132	.313	.478	460	144	29	10	9	2.0	59	91	31	52	13	9	4	206	17	11	2	1.9	.953	OF-121
1924			143	.325	.494	579	188	40	11	12	2.1	93	120	32	43	26	0	0	252	17	14	4	2.0	.951	OF-143, 3B-2
1925			156	.290	.542	624	181	34	12	**33**	5.3	101	**138**	54	55	10	0	0	271	55	6	8	2.1	.982	OF-131, 3B-27
1926			108	.315	.470	413	130	22	3	12	2.9	73	81	37	32	16	1	0	211	4	9	1	2.1	.960	OF-107
1927			135	.337	.510	516	174	47	9	8	1.6	75	103	45	58	24	3	1	249	15	14	1	2.1	.950	OF-131
1928			131	.297	.467	518	154	45	5	11	2.1	77	113	39	56	6	0	0	259	16	7	6	2.2	.975	OF-131
1929			100	.261	.391	391	102	15	3	10	2.6	46	57	17	42	2	3	0	206	9	7	2	2.3	.968	OF-96
1930	CIN	N	113	.289	.460	443	128	30	8	10	2.3	62	62	26	63	9	1	0	223	8	9	3	2.1	.963	OF-112
11 yrs.			1407	.309	.497	5475	1693	368	95	156	2.8	826	1067	375	619	140	27	12	2494	278	129	52	2.1	.956	OF-1304, 3B-74, 1B-2
WORLD SERIES																									
1921	NY	A	8	.200	.267	30	6	2	0	0	0.0	3	3	2	5	1	0	0	10	2	0	0	1.5	1.000	OF-8
1922			5	.300	.350	20	6	1	0	0	0.0	2	2	1	3	1	0	0	7	1	0	0	1.6	1.000	OF-5
1923			6	.269	.462	26	7	1	2	0	0.0	1	8	0	3	0	0	0	14	0	0	0	2.3	1.000	OF-6
1926			7	.238	.381	21	5	1	1	0	0.0	3	0	6	1	0	0	0	13	0	1	0	2.0	.929	OF-7
1927			4	.118	.118	17	2	0	0	0	0.0	1	1	1	7	1	0	0	8	0	1	0	2.3	.889	OF-4
1928			4	.200	.467	15	3	1	0	1	6.7	5	3	2	5	2	0	0	4	0	0	0	1.0	1.000	OF-4
6 yrs.			34	.225	.341	129	29	6	3	1	0.8	15	17	12	24	5	0	0	56	3	2	0	1.8	.967	OF-34
									4th						**8th**										

Irish Meusel

MEUSEL, EMIL FREDERICK BR TR 5′11½″ 178 lbs.
Brother of Bob Meusel.
B. June 9, 1893, Oakland, Calif. D. Mar. 1, 1963, Long Beach, Calif.

Year	Team	Lg	Games	BA	SA	AB	H	2B	3B	HR	HR%	R	RBI	BB	SO	SB	Pinch Hit AB	Pinch Hit H	PO	A	E	DP	TC/G	FA	G by Pos
1914	WAS	A	1	.000	.000	2	0	0	0	0	0.0	0	0	0	0	0	0	0	1	0	0	0	1.0	1.000	OF-1
1918	PHI	N	124	.279	.383	473	132	25	6	4	0.8	48	62	30	21	18	0	0	303	25	12	4	2.7	.965	OF-120, 2B-4
1919			135	.305	.411	521	159	26	7	5	1.0	65	59	15	13	24	5	1	256	14	9	4	2.2	.968	OF-128
1920			138	.309	.473	518	160	27	8	14	**2.7**	75	69	32	27	17	7	1	283	17	21	8	2.4	.935	OF-129, 1B-3
1921	2 teams		PHI N (89G –.353)		NY N (62G –.329)																				
"	total		151	.343	.515	586	201	33	13	14	2.4	96	87	33	29	13	0	0	275	28	17	4	2.2	.947	OF-147
1922	NY	N	154	.331	.509	617	204	28	17	16	2.6	100	132	35	33	12	0	0	279	15	6	1	1.9	.980	OF-154
1923			146	.297	.477	595	177	22	14	19	3.2	102	**125**	38	16	8	1	0	268	10	15	2	2.0	.949	OF-145
1924			139	.310	.423	549	170	26	9	6	1.1	75	102	33	18	11	1	1	287	4	10	0	2.2	.967	OF-138
1925			135	.328	.548	516	169	35	8	21	4.1	82	111	26	19	5	8	2	244	16	11	2	2.2	.959	OF-126
1926			129	.292	.432	449	131	25	10	6	1.3	51	65	16	18	5	15	2	197	10	9	1	1.9	.958	OF-112
1927	BKN	N	42	.243	.351	74	18	3	1	1	1.4	7	7	11	5	0	23	6	28	2	0	1	1.8	1.000	OF-17
11 yrs.			1294	.310	.464	4900	1521	250	93	106	2.2	701	819	269	199	113	60	13	2421	141	110	27	2.2	.959	OF-1217, 2B-4, 1B-3
WORLD SERIES																									
1921	NY	N	8	.345	.586	29	10	2	1	1	3.4	4	7	2	3	1	0	0	8	2	0	0	1.3	1.000	OF-8
1922			5	.250	.400	20	5	0	0	1	5.0	3	7	0	1	0	0	0	3	0	0	0	0.6	1.000	OF-5

Irish Meusel *continued*

Year	Team	Games	BA	SA	AB	H	2B	3B	HR	HR%	R	RBI	BB	SO	SB	Pinch Hit AB	Pinch Hit H	PO	A	E	DP	TC/G	FA	G by Pos
1923		6	.280	.520	25	7	1	1	1	4.0	3	2	0	2	0	0	0	13	0	0	0	2.2	1.000	OF-6
1924		4	.154	.154	13	2	0	0	0	0.0	0	1	2	0	0	1	0	5	0	1	0	1.5	.833	OF-4
4 yrs.		23	.276	.460	87	24	3	2	3	3.4	10	17	4	6	1	1	0	29	2	1	0	1.4	.969	OF-23

Benny Meyer

MEYER, BERNHARD (Earache) BR TR 5′ 9″ 170 lbs.
B. Jan. 1, 1888, Hematite, Mo. D. Feb. 6, 1974, Festus, Mo.

Year	Team	Games	BA	SA	AB	H	2B	3B	HR	HR%	R	RBI	BB	SO	SB	Pinch Hit AB	Pinch Hit H	PO	A	E	DP	TC/G	FA	G by Pos
1913	BKN N	38	.195	.253	87	17	0	1	1	1.1	12	10	10	14	8	2	0	47	3	3	0	1.9	.943	OF-27, C-1
1914	BAL F	143	.304	.410	500	152	18	10	5	1.0	76	40	71		23	5	1	179	22	18	6	1.6	.918	OF-132, SS-4
1915	2 teams	BAL F (35G –.242)	BUF F (93G –.231)																					
″	total	128	.234	.289	453	106	10	6	1	0.2	57	34	77		15	7	2	187	10	12	1	1.7	.943	OF-122
1925	PHI N	1	1.000	2.000	1	1	1	0	0	0.0	1	0	0	0	0	0	0	0	0	0	0	0.0	.000	2B-1
4 yrs.		310	.265	.346	1041	276	29	17	7	0.7	146	84	158	14	46	14	3	413	35	33	7	1.7	.931	OF-281, SS-4, 2B-1, C-1

Billy Meyer

MEYER, WILLIAM ADAM BR TR 5′ 9½″ 170 lbs.
B. Jan. 14, 1892, Knoxville, Tenn. D. Mar. 31, 1957, Knoxville, Tenn.
Manager 1948–52.

Year	Team	Games	BA	SA	AB	H	2B	3B	HR	HR%	R	RBI	BB	SO	SB	Pinch Hit AB	Pinch Hit H	PO	A	E	DP	TC/G	FA	G by Pos
1913	CHI A	1	1.000	1.000	1	1	0	0	0	0.0	0	0	0	0	0	0	0	5	1	1	0	7.0	.857	C-1
1916	PHI A	50	.232	.297	138	32	2	2	1	0.7	6	12	8	11	3	2	0	217	79	12	5	6.4	.961	C-48
1917		62	.235	.278	162	38	5	1	0	0.0	9	9	7	14	0	7	0	235	66	12	2	5.7	.962	C-55
3 yrs.		113	.236	.289	301	71	7	3	1	0.3	15	21	15	25	3	9	0	457	146	25	7	6.0	.960	C-104

Dan Meyer

MEYER, DANIEL THOMAS BL TR 5′11″ 180 lbs.
B. Aug. 3, 1952, Hamilton, Ohio.

Year	Team	Games	BA	SA	AB	H	2B	3B	HR	HR%	R	RBI	BB	SO	SB	Pinch Hit AB	Pinch Hit H	PO	A	E	DP	TC/G	FA	G by Pos
1974	DET A	13	.200	.440	50	10	1	1	3	6.0	5	7	1	1	1	1	0	29	0	1	0	2.5	.967	OF-12
1975		122	.236	.336	470	111	17	3	8	1.7	56	47	26	25	8	2	1	571	41	12	39	5.2	.981	OF-74, 1B-46
1976		105	.252	.327	294	74	8	4	2	0.7	37	16	17	22	10	36	8	244	14	2	16	3.9	.992	OF-47, 1B-19
1977	SEA A	159	.273	.442	582	159	24	4	22	3.8	75	90	43	51	11	2	0	1407	109	12	134	9.6	.992	1B-159
1978		123	.227	.327	444	101	18	1	8	1.8	38	56	24	39	7	1	0	1107	79	13	119	9.7	.989	1B-121, OF-2, DH-1
1979		144	.278	.459	525	146	21	7	20	3.8	72	74	29	35	11	7	2	198	205	22	27	2.9	.948	3B-101, OF-31, 1B-15
1980		146	.275	.407	531	146	25	6	11	2.1	56	71	31	42	8	17	3	219	22	10	7	1.8	.960	OF-123, DH-7, 3B-5, 1B-4
1981		83	.262	.345	252	66	10	1	3	1.2	26	22	10	16	4	19	3	79	88	7	15	2.5	.960	3B-49, OF-14, DH-3, 1B-3
1982	OAK A	120	.240	.363	383	92	17	3	8	2.1	28	59	19	33	1	29	4	387	32	5	38	4.0	.988	1B-58, DH-38, OF-11
1983		69	.189	.260	169	32	9	0	1	0.6	15	13	19	11	0	7	1	305	16	4	28	5.0	.988	1B-41, DH-12, OF-11, 3B-1
1984		20	.318	.545	22	7	3	1	0	0.0	1	4	0	2	0	17	4	15	2	1	1	3.6	.944	1B-3, DH-2
1985		14	.000	.000	12	0	0	0	0	0.0	2	0	1	0	0	12	0	1	0	0	0	0.3	1.000	DH-1, OF-1, 3B-1
12 yrs.		1118	.253	.379	3734	944	153	31	86	2.3	411	459	220	277	61	150	26	4562	608	89	424	5.2	.983	1B-469, OF-326, 3B-157, DH-64

Dutch Meyer

MEYER, LAMBERT DALTON BR TR 5′10½″ 181 lbs.
B. Oct. 6, 1915, Waco, Tex.

Year	Team	Games	BA	SA	AB	H	2B	3B	HR	HR%	R	RBI	BB	SO	SB	Pinch Hit AB	Pinch Hit H	PO	A	E	DP	TC/G	FA	G by Pos
1937	CHI N	1	—	—	0	0	0	0	0	—	0	0	0	0	0	0	0	0	0	0	0	0.0	—	
1940	DET A	23	.259	.310	58	15	3	0	0	0.0	12	6	4	10	2	3	0	28	44	3	6	3.6	.960	2B-21
1941		46	.190	.281	153	29	9	1	1	0.7	12	14	8	13	1	6	2	107	101	6	19	5.3	.972	2B-40
1942		14	.327	.500	52	17	3	0	2	3.8	5	9	4	4	0	0	0	31	56	1	14	6.3	.989	2B-14
1945	CLE A	130	.292	.418	524	153	29	8	7	1.3	71	48	40	32	2	0	0	317	313	14	66	5.0	.978	2B-130
1946		72	.232	.285	207	48	5	3	0	0.0	13	16	26	16	0	7	1	110	150	6	26	4.2	.977	2B-64
6 yrs.		286	.264	.367	994	262	49	12	10	1.0	113	93	82	75	5	16	3	593	664	30	131	4.8	.977	2B-269

George Meyer

MEYER, GEORGE FRANCIS BR TR 5′ 9″ 160 lbs.
B. Aug. 3, 1909, Chicago, Ill. D. Jan. 3, 1992, Hoffman Estates, Ill.

Year	Team	Games	BA	SA	AB	H	2B	3B	HR	HR%	R	RBI	BB	SO	SB	Pinch Hit AB	Pinch Hit H	PO	A	E	DP	TC/G	FA	G by Pos
1938	CHI A	24	.296	.370	81	24	2	2	0	0.0	10	9	11	17	3	0	0	61	86	5	12	6.3	.967	2B-24

Joey Meyer

MEYER, TANNER JOE BR TR 6′ 3″ 260 lbs.
B. May 10, 1962, Honolulu, Hawaii.

Year	Team	Games	BA	SA	AB	H	2B	3B	HR	HR%	R	RBI	BB	SO	SB	Pinch Hit AB	Pinch Hit H	PO	A	E	DP	TC/G	FA	G by Pos
1988	MIL A	103	.263	.419	327	86	18	0	11	3.4	22	45	23	88	0	4	1	190	18	3	19	2.1	.986	DH-66, 1B-33
1989		53	.224	.408	147	33	6	0	7	4.8	13	29	12	36	1	6	1	100	7	2	14	2.2	.982	DH-31, 1B-18
2 yrs.		156	.251	.416	474	119	24	0	18	3.8	35	74	35	124	1	10	2	290	25	5	33	2.2	.984	DH-97, 1B-51

Leo Meyer

MEYER, LEO TR
B. Mar. 29, 1888, Iowa D. Sept. 2, 1968, Smyrna, Del.

Year	Team	Games	BA	SA	AB	H	2B	3B	HR	HR%	R	RBI	BB	SO	SB	Pinch Hit AB	Pinch Hit H	PO	A	E	DP	TC/G	FA	G by Pos
1909	BKN N	7	.130	.130	23	3	0	0	0	0.0	1	0	2		0	0	0	22	23	6	2	7.3	.882	SS-7

Scott Meyer

MEYER, SCOTT WILLIAM BR TR 6′ 1″ 195 lbs.
B. Aug. 19, 1957, Evergreen Park, Ill.

Year	Team	Games	BA	SA	AB	H	2B	3B	HR	HR%	R	RBI	BB	SO	SB	Pinch Hit AB	Pinch Hit H	PO	A	E	DP	TC/G	FA	G by Pos
1978	OAK A	8	.111	.222	9	1	1	0	0	0.0	1	0	0	4	0	2	0	11	0	0	0	1.4	1.000	C-7, DH-1

Levi Meyerle

MEYERLE, LEVI SAMUEL (Long Levi) BR TR 6′ 1″ 177 lbs.
B. July 1845, Philadelphia, Pa. D. Nov. 4, 1921, Philadelphia, Pa.

Year	Team	Games	BA	SA	AB	H	2B	3B	HR	HR%	R	RBI	BB	SO	SB	Pinch Hit AB	Pinch Hit H	PO	A	E	DP	TC/G	FA	G by Pos
1876	PHI N	55	.340	.449	256	87	12	8	0	0.0	46	34	3	2		0	0	98	110	52	5	4.6	.800	3B-49, 2B-3, OF-3, P-2
1877	CIN N	27	.327	.430	107	35	7	2	0	0.0	11	15	0	4		0	0	55	86	24	5	5.3	.855	SS-18, 2B-12, OF-1
1884	PHI U	3	.091	.182	11	1	1	0	0	0.0	0		0			0	0	15	0	4	1	6.3	.789	1B-2, OF-1
3 yrs.		85	.329	.436	374	123	20	10	0	0.0	57	49	3	6		0	0	168	196	80	11	4.9	.820	3B-49, SS-18, 2B-15, OF-5, 1B-2, P-2

Chief Meyers

MEYERS, JOHN TORTES BR TR 5′11″ 194 lbs.
B. July 29, 1880, Riverside, Calif. D. July 25, 1971, San Bernardino, Calif.

Year	Team	Games	BA	SA	AB	H	2B	3B	HR	HR%	R	RBI	BB	SO	SB	Pinch Hit AB	Pinch Hit H	PO	A	E	DP	TC/G	FA	G by Pos
1909	NY N	90	.277	.382	220	61	10	5	1	0.5	15	30	22		3	24	8	376	71	17	4	7.3	.963	C-64
1910		127	.285	.342	365	104	18	0	1	0.3	25	62	40	18	5	9	1	638	154	25	16	7.0	.969	C-117
1911		133	.332	.432	391	130	18	9	1	0.3	48	61	25	33	7	4	1	729	108	18	11	6.7	.979	C-128
1912		126	.358	.477	371	133	16	5	6	1.6	60	54	47	20	8	2	1	576	111	19	10	5.8	.973	C-122
1913		120	.312	.410	378	118	18	5	3	0.8	37	47	37	22	7	2	1	579	143	25	12	6.4	.967	C-116

Chief Meyers *continued*

Year	Team	Games	BA	SA	AB	H	2B	3B	HR	HR%	R	RBI	BB	SO	SB	Pinch Hit AB	Pinch Hit H	PO	A	E	DP	TC/G	FA	G by Pos
1914		134	.286	.354	381	109	13	5	1	0.3	33	55	34	25	4	7	3	487	150	20	16	5.2	.970	C-126
1915		110	.232	.311	289	67	10	5	1	0.3	24	26	26	18	4	11	1	464	90	8	15	5.1	.986	C-110
1916	BKN N	80	.247	.314	239	59	10	3	0	0.0	21	21	26	15	2	5	0	389	95	8	9	6.6	.984	C-74
1917	2 teams	BKN N (47G –.212) BOS N (25G –.250)																						
"	total	72	.225	.300	200	45	7	4	0	0.0	13	7	17	11	4	4	0	299	74	6	6	5.6	.984	C-68
9 yrs.		992	.291	.378	2834	826	120	41	14	0.5	276	363	274	162	44	68	16	4537	996	146	99	6.1	.974	C-925
WORLD SERIES																								
1911	NY N	6	.300	.400	20	6	2	0	0	0.0	2	2	0	3	0	0	0	37	12	0	1	8.2	1.000	C-6
1912		8	.357	.429	28	10	0	1	0	0.0	2	3	2	3	1	0	0	42	4	1	0	5.9	.979	C-8
1913		1	.000	.000	4	0	0	0	0	0.0	0	0	0	0	0	0	0	4	2	0	0	6.0	1.000	C-1
1916	BKN N	3	.200	.400	10	2	0	1	0	0.0	0	1	1	0	0	0	0	21	8	0	0	9.7	1.000	C-3
4 yrs.		18	.290	.387	62	18	2	2	0	0.0	4	6	3	6	1	0	0	104	26	1	1	7.3	.992	C-18

Henry Meyers

MEYERS, HENRY L.
B. 1860, Philadelphia, Pa. D. June 28, 1898, Harrisburg, Pa.

Year	Team	Games	BA	SA	AB	H	2B	3B	HR	HR%	R	RBI	BB	SO	SB	Pinch Hit AB	Pinch Hit H	PO	A	E	DP	TC/G	FA	G by Pos
1890	PHI AA	5	.158	.158	19	3	0	0	0	0.0	2		1		2	0	0	6	7	6	0	3.8	.684	3B-5

Lew Meyers

MEYERS, LEWIS HENRY BR TR 5′11″ 165 lbs.
B. Dec. 9, 1859, Cincinnati, Ohio D. Nov. 30, 1920, Cincinnati, Ohio.

Year	Team	Games	BA	SA	AB	H	2B	3B	HR	HR%	R	RBI	BB	SO	SB	Pinch Hit AB	Pinch Hit H	PO	A	E	DP	TC/G	FA	G by Pos
1884	CIN U	2	.000	.000	3	0	0	0	0	0.0	1		1			0	0	2	0	1	0	1.0	.667	C-2, OF-1

Bob Micelotta

MICELOTTA, ROBERT PETER (Mickey) BR TR 5′11″ 185 lbs.
B. Oct. 20, 1928, Corona, N. Y.

Year	Team	Games	BA	SA	AB	H	2B	3B	HR	HR%	R	RBI	BB	SO	SB	Pinch Hit AB	Pinch Hit H	PO	A	E	DP	TC/G	FA	G by Pos
1954	PHI N	13	.000	.000	3	0	0	0	0	0.0	2	0	1	1	0	2	0	0	1	0	0	1.0	1.000	SS-1
1955		4	.000	.000	4	0	0	0	0	0.0	0	0	0	0	0	2	0	2	2	0	1	2.0	1.000	SS-2
2 yrs.		17	.000	.000	7	0	0	0	0	0.0	2	0	1	1	0	4	0	2	3	0	1	1.7	1.000	SS-3

Gene Michael

MICHAEL, EUGENE RICHARD (Stick) BB TR 6′2″ 183 lbs.
B. June 2, 1938, Kent, Ohio.
Manager 1981–82, 1986–87.

Year	Team	Games	BA	SA	AB	H	2B	3B	HR	HR%	R	RBI	BB	SO	SB	Pinch Hit AB	Pinch Hit H	PO	A	E	DP	TC/G	FA	G by Pos
1966	PIT N	30	.152	.273	33	5	2	1	0	0.0	9	2	0	7	0	10	3	10	20	3	7	3.0	.909	SS-8, 2B-2, 3B-1
1967	LA N	98	.202	.224	223	45	3	1	0	0.0	20	7	11	30	1	2	0	117	204	17	30	4.1	.950	SS-83
1968	NY A	61	.198	.250	116	23	3	0	1	0.9	8	8	2	23	3	0	0	68	103	11	15	4.1	.940	SS-43, P-1
1969		119	.272	.364	412	112	24	4	2	0.5	41	31	43	56	7	1	0	205	365	19	64	5.0	.968	SS-118
1970		134	.214	.255	435	93	10	1	2	0.5	42	38	50	93	3	6	4	259	390	28	79	5.2	.959	SS-123, 3B-4, 2B-3
1971		139	.224	.276	456	102	15	0	3	0.7	36	35	48	64	3	6	2	243	474	20	88	5.4	.973	SS-136
1972		126	.233	.279	391	91	7	4	1	0.3	29	32	32	45	4	5	2	218	437	21	89	5.6	.969	SS-121
1973		129	.225	.278	418	94	11	1	3	0.7	30	47	26	51	1	0	0	208	433	23	84	5.1	.965	SS-129
1974		81	.260	.311	177	46	9	0	0	0.0	19	13	14	24	0	1	1	122	170	9	40	3.5	.970	2B-45, SS-39, 3B-2
1975	DET A	56	.214	.290	145	31	2	0	3	2.1	15	13	8	28	0	1	1	63	125	10	28	3.6	.949	SS-44, 2B-7, 3B-4
10 yrs.		973	.229	.284	2806	642	86	12	15	0.5	249	226	234	421	22	32	13	1513	2721	161	524	4.8	.963	SS-844, 2B-57, 3B-11, P-1

Cass Michaels

MICHAELS, CASIMIR EUGENE BR TR 5′11″ 175 lbs.
Played as Cass Kwietniewski in 1943 and 1944.
Born Casimir Eugene Kwietniewski.
B. Mar. 4, 1926, Detroit, Mich. D. Nov. 12, 1982, Grosse Pointe, Mich.

Year	Team	Games	BA	SA	AB	H	2B	3B	HR	HR%	R	RBI	BB	SO	SB	Pinch Hit AB	Pinch Hit H	PO	A	E	DP	TC/G	FA	G by Pos
1943	CHI A	2	.000	.000	7	0	0	0	0	0.0	0	0	0	0	0	0	0	1	1	0	0	1.0	1.000	3B-2
1944		27	.176	.265	68	12	4	1	0	0.0	4	5	2	5	0	1	0	37	71	8	12	4.8	.931	SS-21, 3B-3
1945		129	.245	.299	445	109	8	5	2	0.4	47	54	37	28	8	2	0	260	428	47	74	5.8	.936	SS-126, 2B-1
1946		91	.258	.296	291	75	8	0	1	0.3	37	22	29	36	9	3	0	213	235	22	62	5.5	.953	2B-66, 3B-13, SS-6
1947		110	.273	.363	355	97	15	4	3	0.8	31	34	39	28	10	3	0	210	267	15	61	4.6	.970	2B-60, 3B-44, SS-2
1948		145	.248	.329	484	120	12	6	5	1.0	47	56	69	42	8	4	2	313	456	28	115	5.7	.965	SS-85, 2B-55, OF-1
1949		154	.308	.421	561	173	27	9	6	1.1	73	83	101	50	5	0	0	392	484	22	135	5.8	.976	2B-154
1950	2 teams	CHI A (36G –.312) WAS A (106G –.250)																						
"	total	142	.266	.365	526	140	14	7	8	1.5	69	66	68	47	2	3	2	399	401	23	127	5.9	.972	2B-139
1951	WAS A	138	.258	.340	485	125	20	4	4	0.8	59	45	61	41	1	7	2	258	391	24	86	5.3	.964	2B-128
1952	3 teams	WAS A (22G –.233) STL A (55G –.265) PHI A (55G –.250)																						
"	total	132	.252	.356	452	114	16	8	5	1.1	53	50	53	42	4	6	2	258	308	17	62	4.6	.971	2B-85, 3B-42
1953	PHI A	117	.251	.363	411	103	10	0	12	2.9	53	42	51	56	7	6	2	304	302	19	81	5.7	.970	2B-110
1954	CHI A	101	.262	.397	282	74	13	2	7	2.5	35	44	56	31	10	7	0	96	182	12	10	3.1	.959	3B-91, 2B-2
12 yrs.		1288	.262	.353	4367	1142	147	46	53	1.2	508	501	566	406	64	42	10	2741	3526	237	825	5.3	.964	2B-800, SS-240, 3B-195, OF-1

Ralph Michaels

MICHAELS, RALPH JOSEPH BR TR 5′10½″ 178 lbs.
B. May 3, 1902, Etna, Pa. D. Aug. 5, 1988, Monroeville, Pa.

Year	Team	Games	BA	SA	AB	H	2B	3B	HR	HR%	R	RBI	BB	SO	SB	Pinch Hit AB	Pinch Hit H	PO	A	E	DP	TC/G	FA	G by Pos
1924	CHI N	8	.364	.364	11	4	0	0	0	0.0	0	2	0	1	0	3	1	6	7	1	1	3.5	.929	SS-4
1925		22	.280	.300	50	14	1	0	0	0.0	10	6	6	9	1	3	0	26	26	1	4	2.9	.981	3B-15, 2B-1, SS-1, 1B-1
1926		2	—	—	0	0	0	0	0	—	1	0	0	0	0	0	0	0	0	0	0	0.0	—	
3 yrs.		32	.295	.311	61	18	1	0	0	0.0	11	8	6	10	1	6	1	32	33	2	5	3.0	.970	3B-15, SS-5, 2B-1, 1B-1

Ed Mickelson

MICKELSON, EDWARD ALLEN BR TR 6′3″ 205 lbs.
B. Sept. 9, 1926, Ottawa, Ill.

Year	Team	Games	BA	SA	AB	H	2B	3B	HR	HR%	R	RBI	BB	SO	SB	Pinch Hit AB	Pinch Hit H	PO	A	E	DP	TC/G	FA	G by Pos
1950	STL N	5	.100	.100	10	1	0	0	0	0.0	1	0	2	3	0	1	0	36	4	0	1	10.0	1.000	1B-4
1953	STL A	7	.133	.200	15	2	1	0	0	0.0	1	2	2	6	0	3	0	20	2	0	2	7.3	1.000	1B-3
1957	CHI N	6	.000	.000	12	0	0	0	0	0.0	0	1	0	4	0	4	0	21	3	0	3	12.0	1.000	1B-2
3 yrs.		18	.081	.108	37	3	1	0	0	0.0	2	3	4	13	0	8	0	77	9	0	6	9.6	1.000	1B-9

Ezra Midkiff

MIDKIFF, EZRA MILLINGTON (Salt Rock) BL TR 5′10″ 180 lbs.
B. Nov. 13, 1882, Salt Rock, W. Va. D. Mar. 20, 1957, Huntington, W. Va.

Year	Team	Games	BA	SA	AB	H	2B	3B	HR	HR%	R	RBI	BB	SO	SB	Pinch Hit AB	Pinch Hit H	PO	A	E	DP	TC/G	FA	G by Pos
1909	CIN N	1	.000	.000	2	0	0	0	0	0.0	0	0	0		0	0	0	0	0	1	0	1.0	.000	3B-1
1912	NY A	21	.244	.256	86	21	1	0	0	0.0	9	9	7		4	0	0	21	52	8	1	3.9	.901	3B-21
1913		83	.197	.236	284	56	9	1	0	0.0	22	14	12	33	9	1	0	113	193	13	12	3.9	.959	3B-76, SS-4, 2B-2
3 yrs.		105	.207	.239	372	77	10	1	0	0.0	31	23	19	33	13	1	0	134	245	22	13	3.9	.945	3B-98, SS-4, 2B-2

Ed Mierkowicz

MIERKOWICZ, EDWARD FRANK (Butch) BR TR 6′ 4″ 205 lbs.
B. Mar. 6, 1924, Wyandotte, Mich.

Year	Team	Games	BA	SA	AB	H	2B	3B	HR	HR%	R	RBI	BB	SO	SB	Pinch Hit AB	Pinch Hit H	PO	A	E	DP	TC/G	FA	G by Pos
1945	DET A	10	.133	.267	15	2	2	0	0	0.0	0	2	1	3	0	3	1	8	0	0	0	1.3	1.000	OF-6
1947		21	.190	.286	42	8	1	0	1	2.4	6	1	1	12	1	9	1	18	0	1	0	1.9	.947	OF-10
1948		3	.200	.200	5	1	0	0	0	0.0	0	1	2	2	0	2	0	4	0	0	0	4.0	1.000	OF-1
1950	STL N	1	.000	.000	1	0	0	0	0	0.0	0	0	0	1	0	1	0	0	0	0	0	0.0	—	
4 yrs.		35	.175	.270	63	11	3	0	1	1.6	6	4	4	18	1	15	2	30	0	1	0	1.8	.968	OF-17
WORLD SERIES																								
1945	DET A	1	—	—	0	0	0	0	0	—	0	0	0	0	0	0	0	0	0	0	0	0.0	.000	OF-1

Matt Mieske

MIESKE, MATTHEW TODD BR TR 6′ 185 lbs.
B. Feb. 13, 1968, Midland, Mich.

Year	Team	Games	BA	SA	AB	H	2B	3B	HR	HR%	R	RBI	BB	SO	SB	Pinch Hit AB	Pinch Hit H	PO	A	E	DP	TC/G	FA	G by Pos
1993	MIL A	23	.241	.397	58	14	0	0	3	5.2	9	7	4	14	0	0	0	43	1	3	0	2.1	.936	OF-22
1994		84	.259	.432	259	67	13	1	10	3.9	39	38	21	62	3	0	0	155	7	4	1	2.0	.976	OF-80, DH-1
1995		117	.251	.442	267	67	13	1	12	4.5	42	48	27	45	2	11	2	177	7	4	0	1.7	.979	OF-108, DH-2
3 yrs.		224	.253	.433	584	148	26	2	25	4.3	90	93	52	121	5	11	2	375	15	11	1	1.9	.973	OF-210, DH-3

Larry Miggins

MIGGINS, LAWRENCE EDWARD (Irish) BR TR 6′ 4″ 198 lbs.
B. Aug. 20, 1925, Bronx, N. Y.

Year	Team	Games	BA	SA	AB	H	2B	3B	HR	HR%	R	RBI	BB	SO	SB	Pinch Hit AB	Pinch Hit H	PO	A	E	DP	TC/G	FA	G by Pos
1948	STL N	1	.000	.000	1	0	0	0	0	0.0	1	0	0	0	0	1	0	0	0	0	0	0.0	—	
1952		42	.229	.365	96	22	5	1	2	2.1	7	10	3	19	0	16	4	30	0	1	0	1.2	.968	OF-25, 1B-1
2 yrs.		43	.227	.361	97	22	5	1	2	2.1	8	10	3	19	0	17	4	30	0	1	0	1.2	.968	OF-25, 1B-1

John Mihalic

MIHALIC, JOHN MICHAEL BR TR 5′11″ 172 lbs.
B. Nov. 13, 1911, Cleveland, Ohio D. Apr. 24, 1987, Ft. Oglethorpe, Ga.

Year	Team	Games	BA	SA	AB	H	2B	3B	HR	HR%	R	RBI	BB	SO	SB	Pinch Hit AB	Pinch Hit H	PO	A	E	DP	TC/G	FA	G by Pos
1935	WAS A	6	.227	.364	22	5	3	0	0	0.0	4	6	2	3	1	0	0	11	17	1	5	4.8	.966	SS-6
1936		25	.239	.284	88	21	2	1	0	0.0	15	8	14	14	2	0	0	59	79	4	23	5.7	.972	2B-25
1937		38	.252	.336	107	27	5	2	0	0.0	13	8	17	9	2	5	0	75	90	3	25	5.4	.982	2B-28, SS-3
3 yrs.		69	.244	.318	217	53	10	3	0	0.0	32	22	33	26	5	5	0	145	186	8	53	5.5	.976	2B-53, SS-9

Eddie Miksis

MIKSIS, EDWARD THOMAS BR TR 6′½″ 185 lbs.
B. Sept. 11, 1926, Burlington, N. J.

Year	Team	Games	BA	SA	AB	H	2B	3B	HR	HR%	R	RBI	BB	SO	SB	Pinch Hit AB	Pinch Hit H	PO	A	E	DP	TC/G	FA	G by Pos
1944	BKN N	26	.220	.242	91	20	2	0	0	0.0	12	11	6	11	4	1	0	41	44	8	13	3.7	.914	3B-15, SS-10
1946		23	.146	.146	48	7	0	0	0	0.0	3	5	3	3	0	3	0	13	20	1	0	2.4	.971	3B-13, 2B-1
1947		45	.267	.419	86	23	1	0	4	4.7	18	10	9	8	0	12	1	54	29	1	4	2.7	.988	2B-13, OF-11, 3B-5, SS-2
1948		86	.213	.281	221	47	7	1	2	0.9	28	16	19	27	5	3	1	125	148	9	20	3.5	.968	2B-54, 3B-22, SS-5
1949		50	.221	.292	113	25	5	0	1	0.9	17	6	7	8	3	8	0	33	66	2	4	2.7	.980	3B-29, SS-4, 2B-3, 1B-1
1950		51	.250	.382	76	19	2	1	2	2.6	13	10	5	10	3	4	1	57	55	6	10	3.2	.949	2B-15, SS-15, 3B-7
1951	2 teams	BKN N (19G –.200) CHI N (102G –.266)																						
″	total	121	.265	.339	431	114	14	3	4	0.9	54	35	34	38	11	5	1	282	321	19	73	5.7	.969	2B-103, 3B-6
1952	CHI N	93	.232	.305	383	89	20	1	2	0.5	44	19	20	32	4	1	0	207	254	18	43	5.1	.962	2B-54, SS-40
1953		142	.251	.343	577	145	17	6	8	1.4	61	39	33	59	13	0	0	315	406	35	96	5.2	.954	2B-92, SS-53
1954		38	.202	.293	99	20	3	0	2	2.0	9	3	3	9	1	10	0	64	63	5	16	5.5	.962	2B-21, 3B-2, OF-1
1955		131	.235	.328	481	113	14	2	9	1.9	52	41	32	55	3	2	0	290	52	6	6	2.7	.983	OF-111, 3B-18
1956		114	.239	.360	356	85	10	3	9	2.5	54	27	32	40	4	13	6	144	151	7	14	3.0	.977	3B-48, OF-33, 2B-19, SS-2
1957	2 teams	STL N (49G –.211) BAL A (1G –.000)																						
″	total	50	.205	.282	39	8	0	0	1	2.6	3	2	7	7	0	15	3	13	0	0	0	0.4	1.000	OF-31
1958	2 teams	BAL A (3G –.000) CIN N (69G –.140)																						
″	total	72	.135	.135	52	7	0	0	0	0.0	15	4	5	6	1	5	0	41	32	4	2	1.3	.948	OF-32, 3B-14, 2B-7, SS-6, 1B-1
14 yrs.		1042	.236	.322	3053	722	95	17	44	1.4	383	228	215	313	52	82	13	1679	1641	121	301	3.7	.965	2B-382, OF-219, 3B-179, SS-137, 1B-2
WORLD SERIES																								
1947	BKN N	5	.250	.250	4	1	0	0	0	0.0	1	0	0	1	0	3	0	3	1	1	2	1.7	.800	OF-2, 2B-1
1949		3	.286	.429	7	2	1	0	0	0.0	0	0	0	1	0	1	1	3	3	1	0	3.5	.857	3B-2
2 yrs.		8	.273	.364	11	3	1	0	0	0.0	1	0	0	2	0	4	1	6	4	2	2	2.4	.833	OF-2, 3B-2, 2B-1

Clyde Milan

MILAN, JESSE CLYDE (Deerfoot) BL TR 5′ 9″ 168 lbs.
Brother of Horace Milan.
B. Mar. 25, 1887, Linden, Tenn. D. Mar. 3, 1953, Orlando, Fla.
Manager 1922.

Year	Team	Games	BA	SA	AB	H	2B	3B	HR	HR%	R	RBI	BB	SO	SB	Pinch Hit AB	Pinch Hit H	PO	A	E	DP	TC/G	FA	G by Pos
1907	WAS A	48	.279	.328	183	51	5	2	0	0.0	22	9	8		8	1	0	80	12	7	1	2.1	.929	OF-47
1908		130	.239	.315	485	116	10	12	1	0.2	55	32	38		29	8	1	265	18	12	6	2.4	.959	OF-122
1909		130	.200	.258	400	80	12	4	1	0.3	36	15	31		10	9	3	222	19	7	3	2.1	.972	OF-120
1910		142	.279	.333	531	148	17	6	0	0.0	89	16	71		44	1	0	267	30	17	10	2.2	.946	OF-142
1911		154	.315	.394	**616**	194	24	8	3	0.5	109	35	74		58	0	0	347	33	17	2	2.6	.957	OF-154
1912		154	.306	.379	601	184	19	11	1	0.2	105	79	63		**88**	0	0	326	31	25	6	2.5	.935	OF-154
1913		154	.301	.378	579	174	18	9	3	0.5	92	54	58	25	**75**	0	0	296	20	23	7	2.2	.932	OF-154
1914		115	.295	.396	437	129	19	11	1	0.2	63	39	32	26	38	2	0	230	10	13	0	2.2	.949	OF-113
1915		153	.288	.346	573	165	13	7	2	0.3	83	66	53	32	40	1	0	352	13	21	3	2.6	.946	OF-151
1916		150	.273	.313	565	154	14	3	1	0.2	58	45	56	31	34	0	0	372	27	16	8	2.8	.961	OF-149
1917		155	.294	.333	579	170	15	4	0	0.0	60	48	58	26	20	2	0	339	18	14	3	2.4	.962	OF-153
1918		128	.290	.346	503	146	18	5	0	0.0	56	56	36	14	26	4	1	299	17	9	3	2.6	.972	OF-124
1919		88	.287	.361	321	92	12	6	0	0.0	43	37	40	16	11	2	1	195	9	10	2	2.5	.953	OF-86
1920		126	.322	.403	506	163	22	5	3	0.6	70	41	28	12	10	3	0	291	15	9	1	2.6	.971	OF-123
1921		112	.288	.397	406	117	19	11	1	0.2	55	40	37	13	4	12	4	196	19	16	2	2.4	.931	OF-98
1922		42	.230	.297	74	17	5	0	0	0.0	8	5	2	2	0	29	4	18	3	0	1	1.9	1.000	OF-11
16 yrs.		1981	.285	.353	7359	2100	242	104	17	0.2	1004	617	685	197	495	74	14	4095	294	216	58	2.4	.953	OF-1901

Horace Milan

MILAN, HORACE ROBERT BR TR 5′ 9″ 175 lbs.
Brother of Clyde Milan.
B. Apr. 7, 1894, Linden, Tenn. D. June 29, 1955, Texarkana, Ark.

Year	Team	Games	BA	SA	AB	H	2B	3B	HR	HR%	R	RBI	BB	SO	SB	Pinch Hit AB	Pinch Hit H	PO	A	E	DP	TC/G	FA	G by Pos
1915	WAS A	11	.407	.519	27	11	1	1	0	0.0	6	7	8	7	2	0	0	10	0	0	0	1.0	1.000	OF-10
1917		31	.288	.356	73	21	3	1	0	0.0	8	9	4	9	4	8	2	41	0	3	0	1.9	.932	OF-23
2 yrs.		42	.320	.400	100	32	4	2	0	0.0	14	16	12	16	6	8	2	51	0	3	0	1.6	.944	OF-33

Larry Milbourne

MILBOURNE, LAWRENCE WILLIAM BB TR 6′ 161 lbs.
B. Feb. 14, 1951, Port Norris, N. J.

Year	Team		Games	BA	SA	AB	H	2B	3B	HR	HR%	R	RBI	BB	SO	SB	Pinch Hit AB	Pinch Hit H	PO	A	E	DP	TC/G	FA	G by Pos
1974	**HOU**	**N**	112	.279	.309	136	38	2	1	0	0.0	31	9	10	14	6	1	0	102	148	7	24	2.6	.973	2B-87, SS-8, OF-4
1975			73	.212	.265	151	32	1	2	1	0.7	17	9	6	14	1	4	1	95	136	10	35	3.7	.959	2B-43, SS-22
1976			59	.248	.276	145	36	4	0	0	0.0	22	7	14	10	6	18	3	67	100	6	19	5.4	.965	2B-32
1977	**SEA**	**A**	86	.219	.285	242	53	10	0	2	0.8	24	21	6	20	3	9	1	120	209	11	46	4.1	.968	2B-41, SS-40, DH-1, 3B-1
1978			93	.226	.295	234	53	6	2	2	0.9	31	20	9	6	5	3	2	92	169	9	27	3.4	.967	3B-32, SS-23, 2B-15, DH-10
1979			123	.278	.354	356	99	13	4	2	0.6	40	26	19	20	5	30	**12**	144	265	12	57	3.4	.971	SS-65, 2B-49, 3B-11
1980			106	.264	.333	258	68	6	6	0	0.0	31	26	19	13	7	19	3	103	195	8	50	3.6	.974	2B-38, SS-34, DH-8, 3B-6
1981	**NY**	**A**	61	.313	.399	163	51	7	2	1	0.6	24	12	9	14	2	3	2	74	121	8	26	3.4	.961	SS-39, 2B-14, DH-3, 3B-3
1982	**3 teams**		**NY A** (14G –.148) **MIN A** (29G –.235) **CLE A** (82G –.275)																						
″	**total**		125	.257	.327	416	107	13	5	2	0.5	40	26	20	32	3	8	1	210	297	18	59	3.9	.966	2B-92, SS-30, 3B-12, DH-1
1983	**2 teams**		**PHI N** (41G –.242) **NY A** (31G –.200)																						
″	**total**		72	.221	.265	136	30	4	1	0	0.0	8	6	9	17	3	9	1	86	105	4	17	2.9	.979	2B-46, SS-14, 3B-7
1984	**SEA**	**A**	79	.265	.313	211	56	5	1	1	0.5	22	22	12	16	0	23	8	53	86	12	14	2.3	.921	3B-40, 2B-14, DH-6, SS-5
11 yrs.			989	.254	.317	2448	623	71	24	11	0.4	290	184	133	176	41	127	34	1146	1831	105	374	3.4	.966	2B-471, SS-280, 3B-112, DH-29, OF-4
DIVISIONAL PLAYOFF SERIES																									
1981	**NY**	**A**	5	.316	.368	19	6	1	0	0	0.0	4	0	0	1	0	0	0	5	14	0	0	3.8	1.000	SS-5
LEAGUE CHAMPIONSHIP SERIES																									
1981	**NY**	**A**	3	.462	.462	13	6	0	0	0	0.0	4	1	0	0	0	0	0	2	7	0	2	3.0	1.000	SS-3
WORLD SERIES																									
1981	**NY**	**A**	6	.250	.350	20	5	2	0	0	0.0	2	3	4	0	0	0	0	5	16	2	1	3.8	.913	SS-6

Dee Miles

MILES, WILSON DANIEL BL TR 6′ 175 lbs.
B. Feb. 15, 1909, Kellerman, Ala. D. Nov. 2, 1976, Birmingham, Ala.

Year	Team		Games	BA	SA	AB	H	2B	3B	HR	HR%	R	RBI	BB	SO	SB	Pinch Hit AB	Pinch Hit H	PO	A	E	DP	TC/G	FA	G by Pos
1935	**WAS**	**A**	60	.264	.306	216	57	5	2	0	0.0	28	29	7	13	6	13	4	92	5	3	1	2.2	.970	OF-45
1936			25	.237	.322	59	14	1	2	0	0.0	8	7	1	5	0	14	1	22	1	1	0	2.4	.958	OF-10
1939	**PHI**	**A**	106	.300	.400	320	96	17	6	1	0.3	49	37	15	17	3	29	7	146	4	5	1	2.0	.968	OF-77
1940			88	.301	.403	236	71	9	6	1	0.4	26	23	8	18	1	33	8	117	3	7	0	2.5	.945	OF-50
1941			80	.312	.365	170	53	7	1	0	0.0	14	15	4	8	0	**45**	**15**	79	2	0	1	2.3	1.000	OF-35
1942			99	.272	.335	346	94	12	5	0	0.0	41	22	12	10	5	10	3	177	6	3	0	2.3	.984	OF-81
1943	**BOS**	**A**	45	.215	.264	121	26	2	2	0	0.0	9	10	3	3	0	21	5	58	3	2	1	2.5	.968	OF-25
7 yrs.			503	.280	.353	1468	411	53	24	2	0.1	175	143	50	74	15	165	43	691	24	21	4	2.3	.971	OF-323

Don Miles

MILES, DONALD RAY BL TL 6′ 1″ 210 lbs.
B. Mar. 13, 1936, Indianapolis, Ind.

Year	Team		Games	BA	SA	AB	H	2B	3B	HR	HR%	R	RBI	BB	SO	SB	Pinch Hit AB	Pinch Hit H	PO	A	E	DP	TC/G	FA	G by Pos
1958	**LA**	**N**	8	.182	.182	22	4	0	0	0	0.0	2	0	0	6	0	3	0	16	0	0	0	3.2	1.000	OF-5

Mike Miley

MILEY, MICHAEL WILFRED BB TR 6′ 1″ 185 lbs.
B. Mar. 30, 1953, Yazoo City, Miss. D. Jan. 6, 1977, Baton Rouge, La.

Year	Team		Games	BA	SA	AB	H	2B	3B	HR	HR%	R	RBI	BB	SO	SB	Pinch Hit AB	Pinch Hit H	PO	A	E	DP	TC/G	FA	G by Pos
1975	**CAL**	**A**	70	.174	.259	224	39	3	2	4	1.8	17	26	16	54	0	0	0	107	186	19	53	4.5	.939	SS-70
1976			14	.184	.237	38	7	2	0	0	0.0	4	4	4	8	1	0	0	22	30	1	9	3.8	.981	SS-14
2 yrs.			84	.176	.256	262	46	5	2	4	1.5	21	30	20	62	1	0	0	129	216	20	62	4.3	.945	SS-84

Felix Millan

MILLAN, FELIX BERNARDO BR TR 5′11″ 172 lbs.
Born Felix Bernardo Millan (Martinez).
B. Aug. 21, 1943, Yabucoa, Puerto Rico.

Year	Team		Games	BA	SA	AB	H	2B	3B	HR	HR%	R	RBI	BB	SO	SB	Pinch Hit AB	Pinch Hit H	PO	A	E	DP	TC/G	FA	G by Pos
1966	**ATL**	**N**	37	.275	.341	91	25	6	0	0	0.0	20	5	2	6	3	3	0	57	56	3	13	4.3	.974	2B-25, SS-1, 3B-1
1967			41	.235	.346	136	32	3	3	2	1.5	13	6	4	10	0	0	0	84	125	6	24	5.2	.972	2B-41
1968			149	.289	.340	570	165	22	2	1	0.2	49	33	22	26	6	0	0	330	438	16	91	5.4	.980	2B-145
1969			162	.267	.345	652	174	23	5	6	0.9	98	57	34	35	14	0	0	373	444	17	72	5.1	.980	2B-162
1970			142	.310	.380	590	183	25	5	2	0.3	100	37	35	23	16	0	0	337	359	15	83	5.0	.979	2B-142
1971			143	.289	.362	577	167	20	8	2	0.3	65	45	37	22	11	1	1	373	437	15	120	5.9	.982	2B-141
1972			125	.257	.313	498	128	19	3	1	0.2	46	38	23	28	6	5	1	273	339	8	67	5.2	.987	2B-120
1973	**NY**	**N**	153	.290	.353	638	185	23	4	3	0.5	82	37	35	22	2	0	0	410	411	9	99	5.4	.989	2B-153
1974			136	.268	.311	518	139	15	2	1	0.2	50	33	31	14	5	1	1	374	315	15	81	5.3	.979	2B-134
1975			162	.283	.348	676	191	37	2	1	0.1	81	56	36	28	1	0	0	379	420	23	95	5.1	.972	2B-162
1976			139	.282	.343	531	150	25	2	1	0.2	55	35	41	19	2	4	1	311	315	15	68	4.7	.977	2B-136
1977			91	.248	.315	314	78	11	2	2	0.6	40	21	18	9	1	0	0	197	188	9	43	4.4	.977	2B-89
12 yrs.			1480	.279	.343	5791	1617	229	38	22	0.4	699	403	318	242	67	14	4	3498	3847	151	856	5.2	.980	2B-1450, SS-1, 3B-1
LEAGUE CHAMPIONSHIP SERIES																									
1969	**ATL**	**N**	3	.333	.417	12	4	1	0	0	0.0	2	0	3	0	0	0	0	3	9	1	1	4.3	.923	2B-3
1973	**NY**	**N**	5	.316	.316	19	6	0	0	0	0.0	5	2	3	1	0	0	0	9	11	0	2	4.0	1.000	2B-5
2 yrs.			8	.323	.355	31	10	1	0	0	0.0	7	2	6	1	0	0	0	12	20	1	3	4.1	.970	2B-8
WORLD SERIES																									
1973	**NY**	**N**	7	.188	.281	32	6	1	1	0	0.0	3	1	1	1	0	0	0	16	13	3	3	4.6	.906	2B-7

Frank Millard

MILLARD, FRANK E.
B. July 4, 1865, E. St. Louis, Ill. D. July 4, 1892, Galveston, Tex.

Year	Team		Games	BA	SA	AB	H	2B	3B	HR	HR%	R	RBI	BB	SO	SB	Pinch Hit AB	Pinch Hit H	PO	A	E	DP	TC/G	FA	G by Pos
1890	**STL**	**AA**	1	.000	.000	1	0	0	0	0	0.0	0		1		0	0	0	1	4	3	0	8.0	.625	2B-1

Bill Miller

MILLER, WILLIAM ALEXANDER BL TL 6′ 2″ 170 lbs.
Born William Alexander Moeller.
B. May 23, 1879, Germany D. Sept. 8, 1957, Ashtabula, Ohio.

Year	Team		Games	BA	SA	AB	H	2B	3B	HR	HR%	R	RBI	BB	SO	SB	Pinch Hit AB	Pinch Hit H	PO	A	E	DP	TC/G	FA	G by Pos
1902	**PIT**	**N**	1	.200	.200	5	1	0	0	0	0.0	0	2	0		0	0	0	0	0	0	0	0.0	.000	OF-1

Bing Miller

MILLER, EDMUND JOHN BR TR 6′ 185 lbs.
Brother of Ralph Miller.
B. Aug. 30, 1894, Vinton, Iowa D. May 7, 1966, Philadelphia, Pa.

Year	Team		Games	BA	SA	AB	H	2B	3B	HR	HR%	R	RBI	BB	SO	SB	Pinch Hit AB	Pinch Hit H	PO	A	E	DP	TC/G	FA	G by Pos
1921	**WAS**	**A**	114	.288	.457	420	121	28	8	9	2.1	57	71	25	50	3	5	2	247	13	15	4	2.5	.945	OF-109
1922	**PHI**	**A**	143	.336	.553	535	180	29	12	21	3.9	90	90	24	42	10	4	1	314	19	8	3	2.5	.977	OF-139
1923			123	.299	.450	458	137	25	4	12	2.6	68	64	27	34	9	3	0	262	10	6	0	2.3	.978	OF-119

Bing Miller *continued*

Year	Team	Games	BA	SA	AB	H	2B	3B	HR	HR%	R	RBI	BB	SO	SB	Pinch Hit AB	Pinch Hit H	PO	A	E	DP	TC/G	FA	G by Pos
1924		113	.342	.462	398	136	22	4	6	1.5	62	62	12	24	11	9	3	238	18	7	11	2.6	.973	OF-94, 1B-7
1925		124	.319	.485	474	151	29	10	10	2.1	78	81	19	14	11	3	0	245	13	7	7	2.1	.974	OF-115, 1B-12
1926	**2 teams**	**PHI A** (38G –.291) **STL A** (94G –.331)																						
"	**total**	132	.322	.462	463	149	33	7	6	1.3	73	63	33	18	11	2	1	273	13	15	3	2.3	.950	OF-128, 1B-1
1927	**STL A**	144	.325	.449	492	160	32	7	5	1.0	83	75	30	26	9	16	6	309	9	10	3	2.6	.970	OF-126
1928	**PHI A**	139	.329	.471	510	168	34	7	8	1.6	76	85	27	24	10	5	0	298	8	10	2	2.4	.968	OF-133
1929		147	.335	.493	556	186	32	16	8	1.4	84	93	40	25	24	1	0	311	10	10	4	2.3	.970	OF-145
1930		154	.303	.438	585	177	38	7	9	1.5	89	100	47	22	13	0	0	309	10	8	3	2.1	.976	OF-154
1931		137	.281	.425	534	150	43	5	8	1.5	76	77	36	16	5	0	0	305	7	4	1	2.3	.987	OF-137
1932		95	.295	.449	305	90	17	3	8	2.6	40	58	20	11	7	8	2	180	3	4	0	2.2	.979	OF-84
1933		67	.275	.400	120	33	7	1	2	1.7	22	17	12	7	4	**30**	7	62	2	1	2	1.8	.985	OF-30, 1B-6
1934		81	.243	.339	177	43	10	2	1	0.6	22	22	16	14	1	**33**	**10**	72	2	0	1	1.6	1.000	OF-46
1935	**BOS A**	78	.304	.442	138	42	8	1	3	2.2	18	26	10	8	0	**43**	**13**	48	2	2	0	1.8	.962	OF-29
1936		30	.298	.447	47	14	2	1	1	2.1	9	6	5	5	0	13	1	14	1	0	1	1.2	1.000	OF-13
16 yrs.		1821	.312	.462	6212	1937	389	95	117	1.9	947	990	383	340	128	175	46	3487	140	107	45	2.3	.971	OF-1601, 1B-26
WORLD SERIES																								
1929	**PHI A**	5	.368	.421	19	7	1	0	0	0.0	1	4	0	2	0	0	0	13	0	1	0	2.8	.929	OF-5
1930		6	.143	.238	21	3	2	0	0	0.0	0	3	0	4	0	0	0	12	0	0	0	2.0	1.000	OF-6
1931		7	.269	.308	26	7	1	0	0	0.0	3	1	0	4	0	0	0	12	0	0	0	1.7	1.000	OF-7
3 yrs.		18	.258	.318	66	17	4	0	0	0.0	4	8	0	10	0	0	0	37	0	1	0	2.1	.974	OF-18

Bruce Miller

MILLER, CHARLES BRUCE BR TR 6′ 1″ 185 lbs.
B. Mar. 4, 1947, Ft. Wayne, Ind.

Year	Team	Games	BA	SA	AB	H	2B	3B	HR	HR%	R	RBI	BB	SO	SB	Pinch Hit AB	Pinch Hit H	PO	A	E	DP	TC/G	FA	G by Pos
1973	**SF N**	12	.143	.143	21	3	0	0	0	0.0	1	2	2	3	0	4	0	7	14	2	0	2.9	.913	3B-4, 2B-3, SS-1
1974		73	.278	.323	198	55	7	1	0	0.0	19	16	11	15	1	10	3	55	161	12	11	3.6	.947	3B-41, SS-13, 2B-9
1975		99	.239	.288	309	74	6	3	1	0.3	22	31	15	26	0	12	1	114	186	15	31	3.3	.952	3B-68, 2B-21, SS-6
1976		12	.160	.200	25	4	1	0	0	0.0	1	2	2	5	0	2	0	9	16	2	3	2.7	.926	2B-8, 3B-2
4 yrs.		196	.246	.291	553	136	14	4	1	0.2	43	51	30	49	1	28	4	185	377	31	45	3.4	.948	3B-115, 2B-41, SS-20

Charlie Miller

MILLER, CHARLES ELMER TR
B. Jan. 4, 1892, Warrensburg, Mo. D. Apr. 23, 1972, Warrensburg, Mo.

Year	Team	Games	BA	SA	AB	H	2B	3B	HR	HR%	R	RBI	BB	SO	SB	Pinch Hit AB	Pinch Hit H	PO	A	E	DP	TC/G	FA	G by Pos
1912	**STL A**	1	.000	.000	2	0	0	0	0	0.0	0	0	0		0	0	0	0	2	0	0	2.0	1.000	SS-1

Charlie Miller

MILLER, CHARLES HESS BR TR 6′ 190 lbs.
B. Dec. 30, 1877, Conestoga Center, Pa. D. Jan. 13, 1951, Millersville, Pa.

Year	Team	Games	BA	SA	AB	H	2B	3B	HR	HR%	R	RBI	BB	SO	SB	Pinch Hit AB	Pinch Hit H	PO	A	E	DP	TC/G	FA	G by Pos
1915	**BAL F**	1	.000	.000	1	0	0	0	0	0.0	0	0	0		0	1	0	0	0	0	0	0.0	—	

Charlie Miller

MILLER, CHARLES MARION BL TL 5′ 8½″ 155 lbs.
B. Sept. 18, 1889, Woodville, Ohio D. June 16, 1961, Houston, Tex.

Year	Team	Games	BA	SA	AB	H	2B	3B	HR	HR%	R	RBI	BB	SO	SB	Pinch Hit AB	Pinch Hit H	PO	A	E	DP	TC/G	FA	G by Pos
1913	**STL N**	4	.167	.167	12	2	0	0	0	0.0	0	1	0	2	0	1	0	4	0	0	0	1.3	1.000	OF-3
1914		36	.194	.222	36	7	1	0	0	0.0	4	2	3	9	2	11	2	11	1	0	0	0.6	1.000	OF-19
2 yrs.		40	.188	.208	48	9	1	0	0	0.0	4	3	3	11	2	12	2	15	1	0	0	0.7	1.000	OF-22

Dakin Miller

MILLER, DAKIN EVANS BL TR 5′10″ 175 lbs.
B. Sept. 3, 1876, Malvern, Iowa D. Apr. 19, 1950, Stockton, Calif.

Year	Team	Games	BA	SA	AB	H	2B	3B	HR	HR%	R	RBI	BB	SO	SB	Pinch Hit AB	Pinch Hit H	PO	A	E	DP	TC/G	FA	G by Pos
1902	**CHI N**	51	.246	.278	187	46	4	1	0	0.0	17	13	7		10	0	0	97	9	5	0	2.2	.955	OF-51

Darrell Miller

MILLER, DARRELL KEITH BR TR 6′ 2″ 200 lbs.
B. Feb. 26, 1958, Washington, D. C.

Year	Team	Games	BA	SA	AB	H	2B	3B	HR	HR%	R	RBI	BB	SO	SB	Pinch Hit AB	Pinch Hit H	PO	A	E	DP	TC/G	FA	G by Pos
1984	**CAL A**	17	.171	.171	41	7	0	0	0	0.0	5	1	4	9	0	1	0	92	7	1	12	5.9	.990	1B-16, OF-1
1985		51	.375	.583	48	18	2	1	2	4.2	8	7	1	10	0	6	3	39	3	2	0	0.9	.955	OF-45, DH-4, 3B-1, C-1
1986		33	.228	.298	57	13	2	1	0	0.0	6	4	4	8	0	5	2	30	3	0	0	0.9	1.000	OF-23, C-10, DH-2
1987		53	.241	.398	108	26	5	0	4	3.7	14	16	9	13	1	9	4	131	15	2	1	2.8	.986	C-33, OF-18, 3B-1
1988		70	.221	.307	140	31	4	1	2	1.4	21	7	9	29	2	9	2	229	18	4	1	4.0	.984	C-53, OF-8, DH-1
5 yrs.		224	.241	.350	394	95	13	3	8	2.0	54	35	27	69	3	30	11	521	46	9	14	2.7	.984	C-97, OF-95, 1B-16, DH-7, 3B-2

Doc Miller

MILLER, ROY OSCAR BL TL 5′10½″ 170 lbs.
B. Feb. 4, 1883, Chatham, Ont., Canada D. July 31, 1938, Jersey City, N. J.

Year	Team	Games	BA	SA	AB	H	2B	3B	HR	HR%	R	RBI	BB	SO	SB	Pinch Hit AB	Pinch Hit H	PO	A	E	DP	TC/G	FA	G by Pos
1910	**2 teams**	**CHI N** (1G –.000) **BOS N** (130G –.286)																						
"	**total**	131	.286	.377	483	138	27	4	3	0.6	48	55	33	52	17	1	0	203	9	11	3	1.7	.951	OF-130
1911	**BOS N**	146	.333	.442	577	**192**	36	3	7	1.2	69	91	43	43	32	0	0	243	26	11	4	1.9	.961	OF-146
1912	**2 teams**	**BOS N** (51G –.234) **PHI N** (67G –.288)																						
"	**total**	118	.259	.360	378	98	20	6	2	0.5	50	45	23	30	9	28	7	140	21	6	5	1.9	.964	OF-90
1913	**PHI N**	69	.345	.414	87	30	6	0	0	0.0	9	11	6	6	2	**56**	**20**	8	0	2	0	0.8	.800	OF-12
1914	**CIN N**	47	.255	.313	192	49	7	2	0	0.0	8	33	16	18	4	35	12	79	2	2	1	1.8	.976	OF-47
5 yrs.		511	.295	.390	1717	507	96	15	12	0.7	184	235	121	149	64	120	39	673	58	32	13	1.8	.958	OF-425

Doggie Miller

MILLER, GEORGE FREDERICK (Calliope, Foghorn) BR TR 5′ 6″ 145 lbs.
B. Aug. 15, 1864, Brooklyn, N. Y. D. Apr. 6, 1909, Brooklyn, N. Y.
Manager 1894.

Year	Team	Games	BA	SA	AB	H	2B	3B	HR	HR%	R	RBI	BB	SO	SB	Pinch Hit AB	Pinch Hit H	PO	A	E	DP	TC/G	FA	G by Pos
1884	**PIT AA**	89	.225	.265	347	78	10	2	0	0.0	46		13			0	0	252	62	49	4	4.1	.865	OF-49, C-36, 3B-3, 2B-1
1885		42	.163	.193	166	27	3	1	0	0.0	19		4			0	0	185	60	33	4	6.5	.881	C-33, OF-6, 3B-2, SS-2
1886		83	.252	.325	317	80	15	1	2	0.6	70		43			0	0	286	63	34	1	4.5	.911	C-61, OF-23, 2B-1
1887	**PIT N**	87	.243	.325	342	83	17	4	1	0.3	58	34	35	13	33	0	0	294	61	31	2	4.4	.920	C-73, OF-14, 3B-1
1888		103	.277	.344	404	112	17	5	0	0.0	50	36	18	16	27	0	0	331	92	44	8	4.5	.906	C-68, OF-32, 3B-4
1889		104	.268	.384	422	113	25	3	6	1.4	77	56	31	11	16	0	0	357	101	53	9	4.8	.896	C-76, OF-27, 3B-3
1890		138	.273	.350	549	150	24	3	4	0.7	85	66	68	11	32	0	0	236	285	82	21	4.2	.864	3B-88, OF-25, SS-13, C-10, 2B-6
1891		135	.285	.363	548	156	19	6	4	0.7	80	57	59	26	35	0	0	339	238	80	13	4.8	.878	C-41, SS-37, 3B-34, OF-24, 1B-1
1892		149	.254	.326	623	158	15	12	2	0.3	103	59	69	14	28	0	0	413	145	44	22	3.8	.927	OF-76, C-63, SS-19, 3B-2
1893		41	.182	.234	154	28	6	1	0	0.0	23	17	17	8	3	1	0	141	45	17	3	5.1	.916	C-40

Doggie Miller *continued*

Year	Team		Games	BA	SA	AB	H	2B	3B	HR	HR%	R	RBI	BB	SO	SB	Pinch Hit AB	Pinch Hit H	PO	A	E	DP	TC/G	FA	G by Pos
1894	**STL**	**N**	127	.339	.453	481	163	9	11	8	1.7	93	86	58	9	17	2	0	361	191	60	17	4.8	.902	3B-52, C-41, 2B-18, 1B-12, OF-4, SS-1
1895			121	.292	.369	490	143	15	4	5	1.0	81	74	25	12	18	0	0	276	145	55	16	3.7	.884	3B-46, C-46, OF-21, SS-9, 1B-6
1896	**LOU**	**N**	98	.275	.361	324	89	17	4	1	0.3	54	33	27	9	16	9	**6**	202	130	31	14	3.9	.915	C-48, 2B-25, OF-8, 3B-8, 1B-3, SS-2
13 yrs.			1317	.267	.345	5167	1380	192	57	33	0.6	839	518	467	129	225	12	6	3673	1618	613	134	4.4	.896	C-636, OF-309, 3B-243, SS-83, 2B-51, 1B-22

Dots Miller

MILLER, JOHN BARNEY BR TR 5′11½″ 170 lbs.
B. Sept. 9, 1886, Kearny, N. J. D. Sept. 5, 1923, Saranac Lake, N. Y.

Year	Team		Games	BA	SA	AB	H	2B	3B	HR	HR%	R	RBI	BB	SO	SB	Pinch Hit AB	Pinch Hit H	PO	A	E	DP	TC/G	FA	G by Pos
1909	**PIT**	**N**	151	.279	.396	560	156	31	13	3	0.5	71	87	39		14	1	0	260	426	34	50	4.8	.953	2B-150
1910			120	.227	.309	444	101	13	10	1	0.2	45	48	33	41	11	1	0	266	321	33	45	5.2	.947	2B-117, SS-2
1911			137	.268	.377	470	126	17	8	6	1.3	82	78	51	48	17	5	1	273	357	38	65	5.2	.943	2B-129
1912			148	.275	.397	567	156	33	12	4	0.7	74	87	37	45	18	1	0	1385	85	23	93	10.2	.985	1B-147
1913			154	.272	.419	580	158	24	20	7	1.2	75	90	37	52	20	0	0	1406	82	25	68	9.9	.983	1B-150, SS-3
1914	**STL**	**N**	155	.290	.393	573	166	27	10	4	0.7	67	88	34	52	16	0	0	1176	247	30	67	9.3	.979	1B-98, SS-53, 2B-5
1915			150	.264	.342	553	146	17	10	2	0.4	73	72	43	48	27	0	0	1142	215	20	83	9.2	.985	1B-83, 2B-55, 3B-9, SS-3
1916			143	.238	.315	505	120	22	7	1	0.2	47	46	40	49	18	0	0	1056	200	19	84	8.3	.985	1B-93, 2B-38, SS-21, 3B-1
1917			148	.248	.320	544	135	15	9	2	0.4	61	45	33	52	14	0	0	755	362	28	100	7.7	.976	2B-92, 1B-46, SS-11
1919			101	.231	.292	346	80	10	4	1	0.3	38	24	13	23	6	5	2	756	127	22	47	9.4	.976	1B-68, 2B-28
1920	**PHI**	**N**	98	.254	.309	343	87	12	2	1	0.3	41	27	16	17	13	2	0	254	234	27	48	5.3	.948	2B-59, 3B-17, SS-12, 1B-9, OF-1
1921			84	.297	.350	320	95	11	3	0	0.0	37	23	15	27	3	1	0	441	113	19	36	6.7	.967	3B-41, 1B-38, 2B-6
12 yrs.			1589	.263	.357	5805	1526	232	108	32	0.6	711	715	391	454	177	16	3	9170	2769	318	786	7.7	.974	1B-732, 2B-679, SS-105, 3B-68, OF-1
WORLD SERIES																									
1909	**PIT**	**N**	7	.250	.286	28	7	1	0	0	0.0	2	4	2	4	3	0	0	17	13	3	1	4.7	.909	2B-7

Dusty Miller

MILLER, CHARLES BRADLEY BL TR 5′11½″ 170 lbs.
B. Sept. 10, 1868, Oil City, Pa. D. Sept. 3, 1945, Memphis, Tenn.

Year	Team		Games	BA	SA	AB	H	2B	3B	HR	HR%	R	RBI	BB	SO	SB	Pinch Hit AB	Pinch Hit H	PO	A	E	DP	TC/G	FA	G by Pos
1889	**BAL**	**AA**	11	.150	.225	40	6	1	1	0	0.0	4	6	2	11	3	0	0	11	21	16	0	4.4	.667	SS-8, OF-3
1890	**STL**	**AA**	26	.219	.365	96	21	5	3	1	1.0	17		8		4	0	0	35	16	7	3	2.1	.879	OF-24, SS-3
1895	**CIN**	**N**	132	.335	.507	529	177	31	18	8	1.5	103	112	33	34	43	0	0	243	25	18	8	2.2	.937	OF-132
1896			125	.321	.468	504	162	38	12	4	0.8	91	93	33	30	76	0	0	199	21	24	7	2.0	.902	OF-125
1897			119	.316	.409	440	139	27	1	4	0.9	83	70	48		29	0	0	203	18	17	2	2.0	.929	OF-119
1898			152	.299	.396	586	175	24	12	3	0.5	99	90	38		32	0	0	292	23	24	4	2.2	.929	OF-152
1899	**2 teams**		**CIN N** (80G –.251) **STL N** (10G –.205)																						
″	**total**		90	.246	.309	362	89	13	5	0	0.0	47	40	12		19	0	0	168	19	16	5	2.3	.921	OF-90
7 yrs.			655	.301	.419	2557	769	139	52	20	0.8	444	411	174	75	206	0	0	1151	143	122	29	2.2	.914	OF-645, SS-11

Ed Miller

MILLER, EDWIN J. BR TR 6′ 180 lbs.
B. Nov. 24, 1888, Annville, Pa. D. Apr. 17, 1980, Lebanon, Pa.

Year	Team		Games	BA	SA	AB	H	2B	3B	HR	HR%	R	RBI	BB	SO	SB	Pinch Hit AB	Pinch Hit H	PO	A	E	DP	TC/G	FA	G by Pos
1912	**STL**	**A**	13	.196	.217	46	9	1	0	0	0.0	4	5	2		1	0	0	90	11	8	3	7.8	.927	1B-8, SS-6
1914			34	.138	.172	58	8	0	1	0	0.0	8	4	4	13	1	8	0	60	14	6	4	4.0	.925	1B-8, OF-5, 2B-5, 3B-2
1918	**CLE**	**A**	32	.229	.333	96	22	4	3	0	0.0	9	3	12	10	2	2	0	236	20	6	16	10.1	.977	1B-22, OF-4
3 yrs.			79	.195	.260	200	39	5	4	0	0.0	21	12	18	23	4	10	0	386	45	20	23	7.5	.956	1B-38, OF-9, SS-6, 2B-5, 3B-2

Ed Miller

MILLER, L. EDWARD
B. Tecumseh, Mich. Deceased.

Year	Team		Games	BA	SA	AB	H	2B	3B	HR	HR%	R	RBI	BB	SO	SB	Pinch Hit AB	Pinch Hit H	PO	A	E	DP	TC/G	FA	G by Pos
1884	**TOL**	**AA**	8	.250	.250	24	6	0	0	0	0.0	2		1			0	0	5	3	5	0	1.6	.615	OF-8

Eddie Miller

MILLER, EDWARD LEE BB TR 5′ 9″ 175 lbs.
B. June 29, 1957, San Pablo, Calif.

Year	Team		Games	BA	SA	AB	H	2B	3B	HR	HR%	R	RBI	BB	SO	SB	Pinch Hit AB	Pinch Hit H	PO	A	E	DP	TC/G	FA	G by Pos
1977	**TEX**	**A**	17	.333	.333	6	2	0	0	0	0.0	7	1	1	1	3	0	0	4	0	0	0	0.8	1.000	DH-3, OF-2
1978	**ATL**	**N**	6	.143	.190	21	3	1	0	0	0.0	5	2	2	4	3	0	0	7	0	0	0	1.4	1.000	OF-5
1979			27	.310	.319	113	35	1	0	0	0.0	12	5	5	24	15	0	0	79	1	1	0	3.0	.988	OF-27
1980			11	.158	.158	19	3	0	0	0	0.0	3	0	0	5	1	0	0	6	0	0	0	0.7	1.000	OF-9
1981			50	.231	.269	134	31	3	1	0	0.0	29	7	7	29	23	6	2	65	2	1	0	1.9	.985	OF-36
1982	**DET**	**A**	14	.040	.040	25	1	0	0	0	0.0	3	0	4	4	0	1	0	13	1	0	0	1.6	1.000	OF-8, DH-1
1984	**SD**	**N**	13	.286	.643	14	4	0	1	1	7.1	4	2	0	4	4	1	0	5	2	0	0	0.9	1.000	OF-8
7 yrs.			138	.238	.274	332	79	5	2	1	0.3	63	17	19	71	49	8	2	179	6	2	0	1.9	.989	OF-95, DH-4

Eddie Miller

MILLER, EDWARD ROBERT (Eppie) BR TR 5′ 9″ 180 lbs.
B. Nov. 26, 1916, Pittsburgh, Pa.

Year	Team		Games	BA	SA	AB	H	2B	3B	HR	HR%	R	RBI	BB	SO	SB	Pinch Hit AB	Pinch Hit H	PO	A	E	DP	TC/G	FA	G by Pos
1936	**CIN**	**N**	5	.100	.100	10	1	0	0	0	0.0	0	0	1	1	0	0	0	5	10	1	1	3.2	.938	SS-4, 2B-1
1937			36	.150	.233	60	9	3	1	0	0.0	3	5	3	8	0	2	0	46	69	9	16	3.6	.927	SS-30, 3B-4
1939	**BOS**	**N**	77	.267	.361	296	79	12	2	4	1.4	32	31	16	21	4	0	0	183	275	14	76	6.1	.970	SS-77
1940			151	.276	.418	569	157	33	3	14	2.5	78	79	41	43	8	0	0	405	487	28	122	6.1	.970	SS-151
1941			154	.239	.326	585	140	27	3	6	1.0	54	68	35	72	8	0	0	336	485	29	112	5.5	.966	SS-154
1942			144	.243	.337	534	130	28	2	6	1.1	47	47	22	42	11	0	0	285	450	13	78	5.2	.983	SS-144
1943	**CIN**	**N**	154	.224	.293	576	129	26	4	2	0.3	49	71	33	43	8	0	0	335	543	19	123	5.8	.979	SS-154
1944			155	.209	.289	536	112	21	5	4	0.7	48	55	41	41	9	0	0	357	544	27	100	6.0	.971	SS-155
1945			115	.238	.404	421	100	27	2	13	3.1	46	49	18	38	4	0	0	245	382	16	61	5.6	.975	SS-115
1946			91	.194	.288	299	58	10	0	6	2.0	30	36	25	34	5	3	1	184	297	15	79	5.6	.970	SS-88
1947			151	.268	.457	545	146	**38**	4	19	3.5	69	87	49	40	5	0	0	295	445	21	88	5.0	.972	SS-151
1948	**PHI**	**N**	130	.246	.382	468	115	20	1	14	3.0	45	61	19	40	1	7	0	229	341	20	63	4.8	.966	SS-122
1949			85	.207	.320	266	55	10	1	6	2.3	21	29	29	21	1	3	1	240	189	6	54	5.2	.986	2B-82, SS-1
1950	**STL**	**N**	64	.227	.326	172	39	8	0	3	1.7	17	22	19	21	0	11	1	75	176	5	31	4.9	.980	SS-51, 2B-1
14 yrs.			1512	.238	.352	5337	1270	263	28	97	1.8	539	640	351	465	64	26	3	3220	4693	223	1004	5.5	.973	SS-1397, 2B-84, 3B-4

Elmer Miller

MILLER, ELMER BR TR 6′ 175 lbs.
B. July 28, 1890, Sandusky, Ohio D. Nov. 28, 1944, Beloit, Wis.

Year	Team	Games	BA	SA	AB	H	2B	3B	HR	HR%	R	RBI	BB	SO	SB	Pinch Hit AB	Pinch Hit H	PO	A	E	DP	TC/G	FA	G by Pos
1912	**STL N**	12	.189	.216	37	7	1	0	0	0.0	5	3	4	9	1	1	0	24	1	0	1	2.3	1.000	OF-11
1915	**NY A**	26	.145	.157	83	12	1	0	0	0.0	4	3	4	14	0	0	0	41	1	2	0	1.7	.955	OF-26
1916		43	.224	.289	152	34	3	2	1	0.7	12	18	11	18	8	0	0	84	9	3	5	2.3	.969	OF-42
1917		114	.251	.319	379	95	11	3	3	0.8	43	35	40	44	11	1	0	204	16	9	2	2.0	.961	OF-112
1918		67	.243	.322	202	49	9	2	1	0.5	18	22	19	17	2	4	0	149	13	9	0	2.8	.947	OF-62
1921		56	.298	.450	242	72	9	8	4	1.7	41	36	19	16	2	0	0	134	10	8	2	2.7	.947	OF-56
1922	**2 teams**	**NY A** (51G –.267) **BOS A** (44G –.190)																						
″	**total**	95	.232	.357	319	74	9	5	7	2.2	47	34	16	22	5	9	1	186	10	6	2	2.4	.970	OF-83
7 yrs.		413	.243	.335	1414	343	43	20	16	1.1	170	151	113	140	29	15	1	822	60	37	12	2.3	.960	OF-392
WORLD SERIES																								
1921	**NY A**	8	.161	.194	31	5	1	0	0	0.0	3	2	2	5	0	0	0	10	1	0	0	1.4	1.000	OF-8

Elmer Miller

MILLER, ELMER JOSEPH BL TL 5′11″ 189 lbs.
B. Apr. 17, 1904, Detroit, Mich. D. Jan. 8, 1987, Corona, Calif.

Year	Team	Games	BA	SA	AB	H	2B	3B	HR	HR%	R	RBI	BB	SO	SB	Pinch Hit AB	Pinch Hit H	PO	A	E	DP	TC/G	FA	G by Pos
1929	**PHI N**	31	.237	.342	38	9	1	0	1	2.6	3	4	1	5	0	17	2	11	5	1	0	1.4	.941	P-8, OF-4

George Miller

MILLER, GEORGE C. BR TR 5′ 5″ 160 lbs.
B. Feb. 19, 1853, Newport, Ky. D. July 24, 1929, Norwood, Ohio.

Year	Team	Games	BA	SA	AB	H	2B	3B	HR	HR%	R	RBI	BB	SO	SB	Pinch Hit AB	Pinch Hit H	PO	A	E	DP	TC/G	FA	G by Pos
1877	**CIN N**	11	.162	.189	37	6	1	0	0	0.0	4	3	5	2		0	0	56	11	6	0	6.6	.918	C-11
1884	**CIN AA**	6	.250	.400	20	5	1	1	0	0.0	6		1			0	0	30	9	1	1	6.7	.975	C-6
2 yrs.		17	.193	.263	57	11	2	1	0	0.0	10	3	6	2		0	0	86	20	7	1	6.6	.938	C-17

Hack Miller

MILLER, JAMES ELDRIDGE BR TR 5′11½″ 215 lbs.
B. Feb. 13, 1913, Celeste, Tex. D. Nov. 21, 1966, Dallas, Tex.

Year	Team	Games	BA	SA	AB	H	2B	3B	HR	HR%	R	RBI	BB	SO	SB	Pinch Hit AB	Pinch Hit H	PO	A	E	DP	TC/G	FA	G by Pos
1944	**DET A**	5	.200	.800	5	1	0	0	1	20.0	1	3	1	1	0	0	0	7	1	0	0	1.6	1.000	C-5
1945		2	.750	.750	4	3	0	0	0	0.0	0	1	0	0	0	0	0	4	1	0	0	2.5	1.000	C-2
2 yrs.		7	.444	.778	9	4	0	0	1	11.1	1	4	1	1	0	0	0	11	2	0	0	1.9	1.000	C-7

Hack Miller

MILLER, LAWRENCE H. BR TR 5′ 9″ 195 lbs.
B. Jan. 1, 1894, New York, N. Y. D. Sept. 17, 1971, Oakland, Calif.

Year	Team	Games	BA	SA	AB	H	2B	3B	HR	HR%	R	RBI	BB	SO	SB	Pinch Hit AB	Pinch Hit H	PO	A	E	DP	TC/G	FA	G by Pos
1916	**BKN N**	3	.333	1.000	3	1	0	1	0	0.0	0	1	1	1	0	0	0	1	0	0	0	0.3	1.000	OF-3
1918	**BOS A**	12	.276	.345	29	8	2	0	0	0.0	2	4	0	4	0	2	0	10	0	0	0	1.0	1.000	OF-10
1922	**CHI N**	122	.352	.511	466	164	28	5	12	2.6	61	78	26	39	3	6	2	219	15	10	3	2.1	.959	OF-116
1923		135	.301	.482	485	146	24	2	20	4.1	74	88	27	39	6	4	4	256	17	6	4	2.2	.978	OF-129
1924		53	.336	.504	131	44	8	1	4	3.1	17	25	8	11	1	20	7	54	1	3	0	1.8	.948	OF-32
1925		24	.279	.430	86	24	3	2	2	2.3	10	9	2	9	0	3	2	35	1	5	0	2.0	.878	OF-21
6 yrs.		349	.322	.490	1200	387	65	11	38	3.2	164	205	64	103	10	35	15	575	34	24	7	2.0	.962	OF-311
WORLD SERIES																								
1918	**BOS A**	1	.000	.000	1	0	0	0	0	0.0	0	0	0	0	0	1	0	0	0	0	0	0.0	—	

Hughie Miller

MILLER, HUGH STANLEY (Cotton) BR TR 6′ 1½″ 175 lbs.
B. Dec. 28, 1887, St. Louis, Mo. D. Dec. 24, 1945, Jefferson Barracks, Mo.

Year	Team	Games	BA	SA	AB	H	2B	3B	HR	HR%	R	RBI	BB	SO	SB	Pinch Hit AB	Pinch Hit H	PO	A	E	DP	TC/G	FA	G by Pos
1911	**PHI N**	1	—	—	0	0	0	0	0	—	0	0	0	0	0	0	0	0	0	0	0	0.0	—	
1914	**STL F**	132	.222	.284	490	109	20	5	0	0.0	51	46	27		4	2	1	1256	65	14	48	10.3	.990	1B-130
1915		7	.500	.667	6	3	1	0	0	0.0	0	3	0		0	1	0	13	0	0	0	2.2	1.000	1B-6
3 yrs.		140	.226	.288	496	112	21	5	0	0.0	51	49	27	0	4	3	1	1269	65	14	48	9.9	.990	1B-136

Jake Miller

MILLER, JACOB GEORGE BR TR 5′10″ 170 lbs.
Born Jacob George Munzing.
B. Dec. 1, 1895, Baltimore, Md. D. Aug. 24, 1974, Towson, Md.

Year	Team	Games	BA	SA	AB	H	2B	3B	HR	HR%	R	RBI	BB	SO	SB	Pinch Hit AB	Pinch Hit H	PO	A	E	DP	TC/G	FA	G by Pos
1922	**PIT N**	3	.091	.091	11	1	0	0	0	0.0	0	0	2	0	1	0	0	8	0	1	0	3.0	.889	OF-3

Jim Miller

MILLER, JAMES McCURDY (Rabbit) BR TR 5′ 8″ 165 lbs.
B. Oct. 2, 1880, Pittsburgh, Pa. D. Feb. 7, 1937, Pittsburgh, Pa.

Year	Team	Games	BA	SA	AB	H	2B	3B	HR	HR%	R	RBI	BB	SO	SB	Pinch Hit AB	Pinch Hit H	PO	A	E	DP	TC/G	FA	G by Pos
1901	**NY N**	18	.138	.138	58	8	0	0	0	0.0	3	3	6		1	0	0	26	47	5	6	4.3	.936	2B-18

Joe Miller

MILLER, JOSEPH A. BR 5′ 9½″ 165 lbs.
B. Feb. 17, 1861, Baltimore, Md. D. Apr. 23, 1928, Wheeling, W. Va.

Year	Team	Games	BA	SA	AB	H	2B	3B	HR	HR%	R	RBI	BB	SO	SB	Pinch Hit AB	Pinch Hit H	PO	A	E	DP	TC/G	FA	G by Pos
1884	**TOL AA**	105	.239	.312	423	101	12	8	1	0.2	46		26			0	0	125	320	70	26	4.9	.864	SS-105
1885	**LOU AA**	98	.183	.239	339	62	9	5	0	0.0	44		28			0	0	123	329	68	26	5.3	.869	SS-79, 3B-11, 2B-8
2 yrs.		203	.214	.280	762	163	21	13	1	0.1	90		54			0	0	248	649	138	52	5.1	.867	SS-184, 3B-11, 2B-8

John Miller

MILLER, JOHN ALLEN BR TR 5′11″ 195 lbs.
B. Mar. 14, 1944, Alhambra, Calif.

Year	Team	Games	BA	SA	AB	H	2B	3B	HR	HR%	R	RBI	BB	SO	SB	Pinch Hit AB	Pinch Hit H	PO	A	E	DP	TC/G	FA	G by Pos
1966	**NY A**	6	.087	.217	23	2	0	0	1	4.3	1	2	0	9	0	0	0	20	0	0	1	3.3	1.000	OF-3, 1B-3
1969	**LA N**	26	.211	.316	38	8	1	0	1	2.6	3	1	2	9	0	15	3	30	4	0	2	2.4	1.000	OF-6, 1B-5, 3B-2, 2B-1
2 yrs.		32	.164	.279	61	10	1	0	2	3.3	4	3	2	18	0	15	3	50	4	0	3	2.7	1.000	OF-9, 1B-8, 3B-2, 2B-1

Keith Miller

MILLER, KEITH ALAN BR TR 5′11″ 175 lbs.
B. June 12, 1963, Midland, Mich.

Year	Team	Games	BA	SA	AB	H	2B	3B	HR	HR%	R	RBI	BB	SO	SB	Pinch Hit AB	Pinch Hit H	PO	A	E	DP	TC/G	FA	G by Pos
1987	**NY N**	25	.373	.490	51	19	2	2	0	0.0	14	1	2	6	8	0	0	21	38	2	6	3.8	.967	2B-16
1988		40	.214	.300	70	15	1	1	1	1.4	9	5	6	10	0	9	2	34	24	5	3	2.0	.921	2B-16, SS-8, 3B-6, OF-1
1989		57	.231	.301	143	33	7	0	1	0.7	15	7	5	27	6	7	2	90	52	5	8	3.1	.966	2B-23, OF-14, SS-8, 3B-2
1990		88	.258	.305	233	60	8	0	1	0.4	42	12	23	46	16	16	4	168	21	4	8	2.5	.979	OF-61, 2B-11, SS-4
1991		98	.280	.411	275	77	22	1	4	1.5	41	23	23	44	14	11	2	165	154	10	30	3.6	.970	2B-60, OF-28, SS-2, 3B-2
1992	**KC A**	106	.284	.389	416	118	24	4	4	1.0	57	38	31	46	16	2	0	230	250	15	60	4.5	.970	2B-93, OF-16, DH-1
1993		37	.167	.194	108	18	3	0	0	0.0	9	3	8	19	3	5	0	18	35	6	3	1.7	.898	3B-21, DH-6, OF-4, 2B-3
1994		5	.133	.133	15	2	0	0	0	0.0	1	0	0	3	0	0	0	7	2	0	0	1.5	1.000	OF-4, 3B-2
1995		9	.333	.533	15	5	0	0	1	6.7	2	3	2	4	0	5	1	5	1	0	0	0.8	1.000	OF-4, DH-4
9 yrs.		465	.262	.351	1326	347	67	8	12	0.9	190	92	100	205	63	55	11	738	577	47	118	3.2	.965	2B-222, OF-132, 3B-33, SS-22, DH-11

Keith Miller

MILLER, NEAL KEITH BB TR 5′11″ 175 lbs.
B. Mar. 7, 1963, Dallas, Tex.

Year	Team	Games	BA	SA	AB	H	2B	3B	HR	HR%	R	RBI	BB	SO	SB	Pinch Hit AB	Pinch Hit H	PO	A	E	DP	TC/G	FA	G by Pos
1988	PHI N	47	.167	.229	48	8	3	0	0	0.0	4	6	5	13	0	37	6	3	2	1	1	0.8	.833	OF-4, 3B-3, SS-1
1989		8	.300	.400	10	3	1	0	0	0.0	0	0	0	3	0	6	1	2	0	0	0	1.0	1.000	OF-2
2 yrs.		55	.190	.259	58	11	4	0	0	0.0	4	6	5	16	0	43	7	5	2	1	1	0.8	.875	OF-6, 3B-3, SS-1

Kohly Miller

MILLER, FRANK A.
B. Jan. 1874, Cumru Township, Pa. D. Mar. 29, 1951, Reading, Pa.

Year	Team	Games	BA	SA	AB	H	2B	3B	HR	HR%	R	RBI	BB	SO	SB	Pinch Hit AB	Pinch Hit H	PO	A	E	DP	TC/G	FA	G by Pos
1892	**2 teams**	**WAS N** (1G –.000) **STL N** (1G –.000)																						
″	**total**	2	.000	.000	7	0	0	0	0	0.0	0	0	0	1	0	0	0	1	2	4	0	3.5	.429	3B-1, SS-1
1897	PHI N	3	.182	.182	11	2	0	0	0	0.0	2	1	2	0	0	0	0	8	4	2	1	4.7	.857	2B-3
2 yrs.		5	.111	.111	18	2	0	0	0	0.0	2	1	2	1	0	0	0	9	6	6	1	4.2	.714	2B-3, 3B-1, SS-1

Lemmie Miller

MILLER, LEMMIE EARL BR TR 6′ 1″ 190 lbs.
B. June 2, 1960, Dallas, Tex.

Year	Team	Games	BA	SA	AB	H	2B	3B	HR	HR%	R	RBI	BB	SO	SB	Pinch Hit AB	Pinch Hit H	PO	A	E	DP	TC/G	FA	G by Pos
1984	LA N	8	.167	.167	12	2	0	0	0	0.0	1	0	1	2	0	5	1	3	0	0	0	0.6	1.000	OF-5

Norm Miller

MILLER, NORMAN CALVIN BL TR 5′10″ 185 lbs.
B. Feb. 5, 1946, Los Angeles, Calif.

Year	Team	Games	BA	SA	AB	H	2B	3B	HR	HR%	R	RBI	BB	SO	SB	Pinch Hit AB	Pinch Hit H	PO	A	E	DP	TC/G	FA	G by Pos
1965	HOU N	11	.200	.333	15	3	0	1	0	0.0	2	1	1	7	0	7	1	2	0	0	0	1.0	1.000	OF-2
1966		11	.147	.235	34	5	0	0	1	2.9	1	3	2	8	0	2	0	15	4	1	2	2.0	.950	OF-8, 3B-2
1967		64	.205	.300	190	39	9	3	1	0.5	15	14	19	42	2	13	2	84	3	3	1	1.7	.967	OF-53
1968		79	.237	.393	257	61	18	2	6	2.3	35	28	22	48	6	6	2	131	1	4	1	1.8	.971	OF-74
1969		119	.264	.364	409	108	21	4	4	1.0	58	50	47	77	4	2	0	172	7	3	3	1.6	.984	OF-114
1970		90	.239	.332	226	54	9	0	4	1.8	29	29	41	33	3	19	5	103	6	6	1	1.6	.948	OF-72, C-1
1971		45	.257	.405	74	19	5	0	2	2.7	5	10	5	13	0	28	9	23	0	0	0	1.1	1.000	OF-20, C-1
1972		67	.243	.393	107	26	4	0	4	3.7	18	13	13	23	1	31	10	35	1	0	1	1.2	1.000	OF-29
1973	**2 teams**	**HOU N** (3G –.000) **ATL N** (9G –.375)																						
″	**total**	12	.273	.636	11	3	1	0	1	9.1	2	6	3	5	0	8	1	2	0	1	0	1.5	.667	OF-2
1974	ATL N	42	.171	.268	41	7	1	0	1	2.4	1	5	7	9	0	31	6	3	1	0	0	1.0	1.000	OF-4
10 yrs.		540	.238	.356	1364	325	68	10	24	1.8	166	159	160	265	16	147	36	570	23	18	9	1.6	.971	OF-378, C-2, 3B-2

Orlando Miller

MILLER, ORLANDO BR TR 6′ 1″ 180 lbs.
Born Orlando Miller (Salmon).
B. Jan. 13, 1969, Changuinola, Panama.

Year	Team	Games	BA	SA	AB	H	2B	3B	HR	HR%	R	RBI	BB	SO	SB	Pinch Hit AB	Pinch Hit H	PO	A	E	DP	TC/G	FA	G by Pos
1994	HOU N	16	.325	.525	40	13	0	1	2	5.0	3	9	2	12	1	3	0	12	30	0	4	3.0	1.000	SS-11, 2B-3
1995		92	.262	.377	324	85	20	1	5	1.5	36	36	22	71	3	3	1	133	269	15	49	4.7	.964	SS-89
2 yrs.		108	.269	.393	364	98	20	2	7	1.9	39	45	24	83	4	6	1	145	299	15	53	4.5	.967	SS-100, 2B-3

Otto Miller

MILLER, LOWELL OTTO (Moonie) BR TR 6′ 196 lbs.
B. June 1, 1889, Minden, Neb. D. Mar. 29, 1962, Brooklyn, N. Y.

Year	Team	Games	BA	SA	AB	H	2B	3B	HR	HR%	R	RBI	BB	SO	SB	Pinch Hit AB	Pinch Hit H	PO	A	E	DP	TC/G	FA	G by Pos
1910	BKN N	31	.167	.212	66	11	3	0	0	0.0	5	2	2	19	1	3	0	116	37	2	2	5.5	.987	C-28
1911		25	.210	.306	62	13	2	2	0	0.0	7	8	0	4	2	2	0	61	28	7	0	4.4	.927	C-22
1912		98	.278	.351	316	88	18	1	1	0.3	35	31	18	50	11	2	2	455	141	15	11	6.5	.975	C-94
1913		104	.272	.350	320	87	11	7	0	0.0	26	26	10	31	7	0	0	460	148	18	14	6.0	.971	C-103, 1B-1
1914		54	.231	.278	169	39	6	1	0	0.0	17	9	7	20	0	3	1	236	66	11	5	6.3	.965	C-50
1915		84	.224	.287	254	57	4	6	0	0.0	20	25	6	28	3	1	0	363	91	9	8	5.5	.981	C-84
1916		73	.255	.329	216	55	9	2	1	0.5	16	17	7	29	6	4	2	311	85	13	6	5.9	.968	C-69
1917		92	.230	.288	274	63	5	4	1	0.4	19	17	14	29	5	0	0	412	95	11	8	5.7	.979	C-91
1918		75	.193	.228	228	44	6	1	0	0.0	8	8	9	20	1	11	1	289	78	10	7	6.0	.973	C-62, 1B-1
1919		51	.226	.256	164	37	5	0	0	0.0	18	5	7	14	2	0	0	223	58	10	5	5.7	.966	C-51
1920		90	.289	.332	301	87	9	2	0	0.0	16	33	9	18	0	1	0	418	65	7	8	5.5	.986	C-89
1921		91	.234	.315	286	67	8	6	1	0.3	22	27	9	26	2	0	0	338	107	13	10	5.0	.972	C-91
1922		59	.261	.350	180	47	11	1	1	0.6	20	23	6	13	0	2	1	216	56	9	3	4.9	.968	C-57
13 yrs.		927	.245	.308	2836	695	97	33	5	0.2	229	231	104	301	40	29	7	3898	1055	135	87	5.7	.973	C-891, 1B-2
WORLD SERIES																								
1916	BKN N	2	.125	.125	8	1	0	0	0	0.0	0	0	0	1	0	0	0	8	3	0	1	5.5	1.000	C-2
1920		6	.143	.143	14	2	0	0	0	0.0	0	0	1	2	0	0	0	17	6	0	0	3.8	1.000	C-6
2 yrs.		8	.136	.136	22	3	0	0	0	0.0	0	0	1	3	0	0	0	25	9	0	1	4.3	1.000	C-8

Otto Miller

MILLER, OTIS LOUIS BR TR 5′10½″ 168 lbs.
B. Feb. 2, 1901, Belleville, Ill. D. July 26, 1959, Belleville, Ill.

Year	Team	Games	BA	SA	AB	H	2B	3B	HR	HR%	R	RBI	BB	SO	SB	Pinch Hit AB	Pinch Hit H	PO	A	E	DP	TC/G	FA	G by Pos
1927	STL A	51	.224	.289	76	17	5	0	0	0.0	8	8	8	5	0	5	0	29	54	6	9	1.9	.933	SS-35, 3B-11
1930	BOS A	112	.286	.373	370	106	22	5	0	0.0	49	40	26	21	2	13	5	97	201	17	20	3.2	.946	3B-83, 2B-15
1931		107	.272	.308	389	106	12	1	0	0.0	38	43	15	20	1	10	1	135	230	16	27	3.8	.958	3B-75, 2B-25
1932		2	.000	.000	2	0	0	0	0	0.0	0	0	0	0	0	2	0	0	0	0	0	0.0	—	
4 yrs.		272	.274	.335	837	229	39	6	0	0.0	95	91	49	46	3	30	6	261	485	39	56	3.2	.950	3B-169, 2B-40, SS-35

Ralph Miller

MILLER, RALPH JOSEPH BR TR 6′ 190 lbs.
B. Feb. 29, 1896, Fort Wayne, Ind. D. Mar. 18, 1939, Fort Wayne, Ind.

Year	Team	Games	BA	SA	AB	H	2B	3B	HR	HR%	R	RBI	BB	SO	SB	Pinch Hit AB	Pinch Hit H	PO	A	E	DP	TC/G	FA	G by Pos
1920	PHI N	97	.219	.266	338	74	14	1	0	0.0	28	28	11	32	3	0	0	105	183	18	16	3.2	.941	3B-91, 1B-3, SS-2, OF-1
1921		57	.304	.397	204	62	10	0	3	1.5	19	26	6	10	3	2	1	107	164	30	24	5.4	.900	SS-46, 3B-10
1924	WAS A	9	.133	.133	15	2	0	0	0	0.0	1	0	1	1	0	6	0	5	11	1	1	5.7	.941	2B-3
3 yrs.		163	.248	.311	557	138	24	1	3	0.5	48	54	18	43	6	8	1	217	358	49	41	4.0	.921	3B-101, SS-48, 2B-3, 1B-3, OF-1
WORLD SERIES																								
1924	WAS A	4	.182	.182	11	2	0	0	0	0.0	0	2	1	0	0	0	0	6	4	2	0	3.0	.833	3B-4

Ray Miller

MILLER, RAYMOND PETER BL TL 5′10″ 168 lbs.
B. Feb. 12, 1888, Pittsburgh, Pa. D. Apr. 7, 1927, Pittsburgh, Pa.

Year	Team	Games	BA	SA	AB	H	2B	3B	HR	HR%	R	RBI	BB	SO	SB	Pinch Hit AB	Pinch Hit H	PO	A	E	DP	TC/G	FA	G by Pos
1917	**2 teams**	**CLE A** (19G –.190) **PIT N** (6G –.148)																						
″	**total**	25	.167	.208	48	8	2	0	0	0.0	2	2	10	6	0	12	2	94	9	0	5	10.3	1.000	1B-10

Rick Miller

MILLER, RICHARD ALAN BL TL 6′ 175 lbs.
B. Apr. 19, 1948, Grand Rapids, Mich.

Year	Team	Games	BA	SA	AB	H	2B	3B	HR	HR%	R	RBI	BB	SO	SB	Pinch Hit AB	Pinch Hit H	PO	A	E	DP	TC/G	FA	G by Pos
1971	**BOS A**	15	.333	.576	33	11	5	0	1	3.0	9	7	8	8	0	0	0	30	1	1	0	2.3	.969	OF-14
1972		89	.214	.367	98	21	4	1	3	3.1	13	15	11	27	0	7	0	80	7	3	0	1.2	.967	OF-75
1973		143	.261	.372	441	115	17	7	6	1.4	65	43	51	59	12	3	1	301	4	7	1	2.3	.978	OF-137
1974		114	.261	.350	280	73	8	1	5	1.8	41	22	37	47	13	1	0	253	7	3	3	2.5	.989	OF-105
1975		77	.194	.231	108	21	2	1	0	0.0	21	15	21	20	3	9	1	101	2	2	1	1.6	.981	OF-65
1976		105	.283	.361	269	76	15	3	0	0.0	40	27	34	47	11	17	5	220	4	2	1	2.6	.991	OF-82, DH-4
1977		86	.254	.333	189	48	9	3	0	0.0	34	24	22	30	11	6	2	118	5	1	3	1.5	.992	OF-79, DH-1
1978	**CAL A**	132	.263	.339	475	125	25	4	1	0.2	66	37	54	70	3	5	1	353	9	4	5	2.8	.989	OF-129
1979		120	.293	.365	427	125	15	5	2	0.5	60	28	50	69	5	1	0	349	3	4	1	3.0	.989	OF-117, DH-2
1980		129	.274	.337	412	113	14	3	2	0.5	52	38	48	71	7	10	4	299	11	5	3	2.7	.984	OF-118
1981	**BOS A**	97	.291	.377	316	92	17	2	2	0.6	38	33	28	36	3	3	1	219	5	3	0	2.4	.987	OF-95
1982		135	.254	.325	409	104	13	2	4	1.0	50	38	40	41	5	8	2	277	6	5	2	2.3	.983	OF-127
1983		104	.286	.363	262	75	10	2	2	0.8	41	21	28	30	3	35	16	151	5	1	2	2.2	.994	OF-66, 1B-2, DH-2
1984		95	.260	.317	123	32	5	1	0	0.0	17	12	17	22	1	53	14	80	5	1	1	2.2	.988	OF-31, 1B-8
1985		41	.333	.378	45	15	2	0	0	0.0	5	9	5	6	1	31	7	9	0	0	0	0.8	1.000	OF-8, DH-4
15 yrs.		1482	.269	.350	3887	1046	161	35	28	0.7	552	369	454	583	78	189	54	2840	74	42	23	2.3	.986	OF-1248, DH-13, 1B-10
LEAGUE CHAMPIONSHIP SERIES																								
1979	**CAL A**	4	.250	.250	16	4	0	0	0	0.0	2	0	0	1	0	0	0	14	2	0	2	4.0	1.000	OF-4
WORLD SERIES																								
1975	**BOS A**	3	.000	.000	2	0	0	0	0	0.0	0	0	0	0	0	0	0	1	0	0	0	0.5	1.000	OF-2

Rod Miller

MILLER, RODNEY CARTER BL TR 5′10″ 160 lbs.
B. Jan. 16, 1940, Portland, Ore.

Year	Team	Games	BA	SA	AB	H	2B	3B	HR	HR%	R	RBI	BB	SO	SB	Pinch Hit AB	Pinch Hit H	PO	A	E	DP	TC/G	FA	G by Pos
1957	**BKN N**	1	.000	.000	1	0	0	0	0	0.0	0	0	0	1	0	1	0	0	0	0	0	0.0	—	

Rudy Miller

MILLER, RUDEL CHARLES BR TR 6′ 1″ 180 lbs.
B. July 12, 1900, Kalamazoo, Mich. D. Jan. 22, 1994, Kalamazoo, Mich.

Year	Team	Games	BA	SA	AB	H	2B	3B	HR	HR%	R	RBI	BB	SO	SB	Pinch Hit AB	Pinch Hit H	PO	A	E	DP	TC/G	FA	G by Pos
1929	**PHI A**	2	.250	.250	4	1	0	0	0	0.0	1	1	3	0	0	0	0	3	3	2	0	4.0	.750	3B-2

Tom Miller

MILLER, THOMAS ROYALL BL TR 5′11″ 180 lbs.
B. July 5, 1897, Powhatan Court House, Va. D. Aug. 13, 1980, Richmond, Va.

Year	Team	Games	BA	SA	AB	H	2B	3B	HR	HR%	R	RBI	BB	SO	SB	Pinch Hit AB	Pinch Hit H	PO	A	E	DP	TC/G	FA	G by Pos
1918	**BOS N**	2	.000	.000	2	0	0	0	0	0.0	0	0	0	0	1	2	0	0	0	0	0	0.0	—	
1919		7	.333	.333	6	2	0	0	0	0.0	2	0	0	1	0	6	2	0	0	0	0	0.0	—	
2 yrs.		9	.250	.250	8	2	0	0	0	0.0	2	0	0	1	1	8	2							

Ward Miller

MILLER, WARD TAYLOR (Windy) BL TR 5′11″ 177 lbs.
B. July 5, 1884, Mt. Carroll, Ill. D. Sept. 4, 1958, Dixon, Ill.

Year	Team	Games	BA	SA	AB	H	2B	3B	HR	HR%	R	RBI	BB	SO	SB	Pinch Hit AB	Pinch Hit H	PO	A	E	DP	TC/G	FA	G by Pos
1909	**2 teams**	**PIT N** (15G –.143)	**CIN N** (43G –.310)																					
″	**total**	58	.254	.296	169	43	3	2	0	0.0	19	8	10		11	13	1	79	3	2	0	2.1	.976	OF-40
1910	**CIN N**	81	.238	.286	126	30	6	0	0	0.0	21	10	22	13	10	**40**	**11**	44	7	3	1	2.1	.944	OF-26
1912	**CHI N**	86	.307	.386	241	74	11	4	0	0.0	45	22	26	18	11	15	6	109	6	7	2	1.9	.943	OF-64
1913		80	.236	.345	203	48	5	7	1	0.5	23	16	34	33	13	13	8	136	9	3	5	2.3	.980	OF-63
1914	**STL F**	121	.294	.400	402	118	17	7	4	1.0	49	50	59		18	8	3	248	15	13	3	2.5	.953	OF-111
1915		154	.306	.381	536	164	19	9	1	0.2	80	63	79		33	0	0	299	16	12	3	2.1	.963	OF-154
1916	**STL A**	146	.266	.328	485	129	17	5	1	0.2	72	50	72	76	25	9	3	218	12	14	0	1.8	.943	OF-135, 2B-1
1917		43	.207	.280	82	17	1	1	1	1.2	13	2	16	15	7	12	4	24	4	1	1	1.2	.966	OF-25
8 yrs.		769	.278	.355	2244	623	79	35	8	0.4	322	221	318	155	128	110	36	1157	72	55	15	2.1	.957	OF-618, 2B-1

Warren Miller

MILLER, WARREN LEMUEL (Gitz) BL TL 5′10″ 160 lbs.
B. July 14, 1885, Philadelphia, Pa. D. Aug. 12, 1956, Philadelphia, Pa.

Year	Team	Games	BA	SA	AB	H	2B	3B	HR	HR%	R	RBI	BB	SO	SB	Pinch Hit AB	Pinch Hit H	PO	A	E	DP	TC/G	FA	G by Pos
1909	**WAS A**	26	.216	.216	51	11	0	0	0	0.0	5	1	4		0	0	0	18	2	0	0	1.3	1.000	OF-15
1911		21	.147	.147	34	5	0	0	0	0.0	3	0	0		0	11	1	6	1	2	1	1.0	.778	OF-9
2 yrs.		47	.188	.188	85	16	0	0	0	0.0	8	1	4		0	11	1	24	3	2	1	1.2	.931	OF-24

Joe Millette

MILLETTE, JOSEPH ANTHONY BR TR 6′ 1″ 180 lbs.
B. Aug. 12, 1966, Walnut Creek, Calif.

Year	Team	Games	BA	SA	AB	H	2B	3B	HR	HR%	R	RBI	BB	SO	SB	Pinch Hit AB	Pinch Hit H	PO	A	E	DP	TC/G	FA	G by Pos
1992	**PHI N**	33	.205	.205	78	16	0	0	0	0.0	5	2	5	10	1	1	0	33	86	3	15	4.1	.975	SS-26, 3B-3, 2B-1
1993		10	.200	.200	10	2	0	0	0	0.0	3	2	1	2	0	0	0	3	18	0	1	2.1	1.000	SS-7, 3B-3
2 yrs.		43	.205	.205	88	18	0	0	0	0.0	8	4	6	12	1	1	0	36	104	3	16	3.6	.979	SS-33, 3B-6, 2B-1

Wally Millies

MILLIES, WALTER LOUIS BR TR 5′10½″ 170 lbs.
B. Oct. 18, 1906, Chicago, Ill. D. Feb. 28, 1995, Oak Lawn, Ill.

Year	Team	Games	BA	SA	AB	H	2B	3B	HR	HR%	R	RBI	BB	SO	SB	Pinch Hit AB	Pinch Hit H	PO	A	E	DP	TC/G	FA	G by Pos
1934	**BKN N**	2	.000	.000	7	0	0	0	0	0.0	0	0	0	0	0	0	0	10	1	0	1	5.5	1.000	C-2
1936	**WAS A**	74	.312	.377	215	67	10	2	0	0.0	26	25	11	8	1	1	0	205	40	8	3	3.5	.968	C-72
1937		59	.223	.274	179	40	7	1	0	0.0	21	28	9	15	1	4	1	199	33	7	7	4.3	.971	C-56
1939	**PHI N**	84	.234	.249	205	48	3	0	0	0.0	12	12	9	5	0	0	0	229	37	10	3	3.3	.964	C-84
1940		26	.070	.070	43	3	0	0	0	0.0	1	0	4	4	0	2	0	59	9	3	0	3.0	.958	C-24
1941		1	.000	.000	2	0	0	0	0	0.0	0	0	0	0	0	0	0	2	2	1	0	5.0	.800	C-1
6 yrs.		246	.243	.283	651	158	20	3	0	0.0	60	65	33	32	2	7	1	704	122	29	14	3.6	.966	C-239

Jocko Milligan

MILLIGAN, JOHN BR TR 6′ 195 lbs.
B. Aug. 8, 1861, Philadelphia, Pa. D. Aug. 29, 1923, Philadelphia, Pa.

Year	Team	Games	BA	SA	AB	H	2B	3B	HR	HR%	R	RBI	BB	SO	SB	Pinch Hit AB	Pinch Hit H	PO	A	E	DP	TC/G	FA	G by Pos
1884	**PHI AA**	66	.287	.418	268	77	20	3	3	1.1	39		8			0	0	477	101	37	5	9.3	.940	C-65, OF-1
1885		67	.268	.377	265	71	15	4	2	0.8	35		7			0	0	478	85	37	14	8.7	.938	C-61, 1B-6, OF-2
1886		75	.252	.379	301	76	17	3	5	1.7	52		21			0	0	538	68	36	13	8.4	.944	C-40, 1B-29, OF-5, 3B-2
1887		95	.302	.411	377	114	27	4	2	0.5	54		21		8	0	0	698	92	51	31	8.6	.939	1B-50, C-47, OF-1
1888	**STL AA**	63	.251	.365	219	55	6	2	5	2.3	19	37	17		3	0	0	355	86	25	12	7.4	.946	C-58, 1B-5
1889		72	.366	.623	273	100	30	2	12	4.4	53	76	16	19	2	0	0	425	107	36	10	7.6	.937	C-66, 1B-9
1890	**PHI P**	62	.295	.397	234	69	9	3	3	1.3	38	57	19	19	2	0	0	286	66	40	14	6.2	.898	C-59, 1B-3, P-1
1891	**PHI AA**	118	.303	.505	455	138	**35**	12	11	2.4	75	106	56	51	2	0	0	763	112	43	27	7.7	.953	C-87, 1B-32

Jocko Milligan *continued*

Year	Team	Games	BA	SA	AB	H	2B	3B	HR	HR%	R	RBI	BB	SO	SB	Pinch Hit AB	Pinch Hit H	PO	A	E	DP	TC/G	FA	G by Pos
1892	WAS N	88	.276	.437	323	89	19	9	5	1.5	40	43	26	24	2	1	0	522	99	24	22	7.4	.963	C-59, 1B-28
1893	2 teams	BAL N (24G –.245) NY N (42G –.231)																						
"	total	66	.237	.365	249	59	10	8	2	0.8	35	44	19	20	4	1	0	380	84	23	15	7.5	.953	C-43, 1B-22
10 yrs.		772	.286	.434	2964	848	188	50	50	1.7	440	363	210	133	23	2	0	4922	900	352	163	7.9	.943	C-585, 1B-184, OF-9, 3B-2, P-1

Randy Milligan

MILLIGAN, RANDY ANDRE (Moose) BR TR 6′ 2″ 200 lbs.
B. Nov. 27, 1961, San Diego, Calif.

Year	Team	Games	BA	SA	AB	H	2B	3B	HR	HR%	R	RBI	BB	SO	SB	Pinch Hit AB	Pinch Hit H	PO	A	E	DP	TC/G	FA	G by Pos
1987	NY N	3	.000	.000	1	0	0	0	0	0.0	0	0	1	1	0	1	0	0	0	0	0	0.0	—	
1988	PIT N	40	.220	.390	82	18	5	0	3	3.7	10	8	20	24	1	13	3	213	15	3	19	8.9	.987	1B-25, OF-1
1989	BAL A	124	.268	.458	365	98	23	5	12	3.3	56	45	74	75	9	11	2	914	83	5	92	8.5	.995	1B-117, DH-1
1990		109	.265	.492	362	96	20	1	20	5.5	64	60	88	68	6	0	0	846	87	9	94	8.8	.990	1B-98, DH-9
1991		141	.263	.406	483	127	17	2	16	3.3	57	70	84	108	0	6	1	948	81	11	92	7.4	.989	1B-106, DH-25, OF-9
1992		137	.240	.361	462	111	21	1	11	2.4	71	53	106	81	0	3	0	1009	76	7	110	8.1	.994	1B-129, DH-6
1993	2 teams	CIN N (83G –.274) CLE A (19G –.426)																						
"	total	102	.299	.434	281	84	18	1	6	2.1	37	36	60	53	0	18	7	578	64	5	63	7.3	.992	1B-79, OF-9, DH-1
1994	MON N	47	.232	.329	82	19	2	0	2	2.4	10	12	14	21	0	12	2	157	19	4	16	5.5	.978	1B-33
8 yrs.		703	.261	.420	2118	553	106	10	70	3.3	305	284	447	431	16	64	15	4665	425	44	486	7.9	.991	1B-587, DH-42, OF-19

Bill Mills

MILLS, WILLIAM HENRY BR TR 5′10″ 175 lbs.
B. Nov. 2, 1920, Boston, Mass.

Year	Team	Games	BA	SA	AB	H	2B	3B	HR	HR%	R	RBI	BB	SO	SB	Pinch Hit AB	Pinch Hit H	PO	A	E	DP	TC/G	FA	G by Pos
1944	PHI A	5	.250	.250	4	1	0	0	0	0.0	0	0	1	1	0	3	1	0	0	0	0	0.0	.000	C-1

Brad Mills

MILLS, JAMES BRADLEY BL TR 6′ 195 lbs.
B. Jan. 19, 1957, Exeter, Calif.

Year	Team	Games	BA	SA	AB	H	2B	3B	HR	HR%	R	RBI	BB	SO	SB	Pinch Hit AB	Pinch Hit H	PO	A	E	DP	TC/G	FA	G by Pos
1980	MON N	21	.300	.317	60	18	1	0	0	0.0	1	8	5	6	0	4	2	19	24	1	3	2.4	.977	3B-18
1981		17	.238	.286	21	5	1	0	0	0.0	3	1	2	1	0	9	3	6	6	0	1	1.3	1.000	3B-7, 2B-2
1982		54	.224	.313	67	15	3	0	1	1.5	6	2	5	11	0	40	10	4	9	2	1	1.2	.867	3B-13
1983		14	.250	.250	20	5	0	0	0	0.0	1	1	2	3	0	9	2	1	4	1	0	1.5	.833	3B-3, 1B-1
4 yrs.		106	.256	.304	168	43	5	0	1	0.6	11	12	14	21	0	62	17	30	43	4	5	1.8	.948	3B-41, 2B-2, 1B-1
DIVISIONAL PLAYOFF SERIES																								
1981	MON N	1	—	—	0	0	0	0	0	—	0	0	1	0	0	0	0	0	0	0	0	0.0	—	

Buster Mills

MILLS, COLONEL BUSTER BR TR 5′11½″ 195 lbs.
B. Sept. 16, 1908, Ranger, Tex. D. Dec. 1, 1991, Arlington, Tex.
Manager 1953.

Year	Team	Games	BA	SA	AB	H	2B	3B	HR	HR%	R	RBI	BB	SO	SB	Pinch Hit AB	Pinch Hit H	PO	A	E	DP	TC/G	FA	G by Pos
1934	STL N	29	.236	.361	72	17	4	1	1	1.4	7	8	4	11	0	9	3	45	0	0	0	2.5	1.000	OF-18
1935	BKN N	17	.214	.339	56	12	2	1	1	1.8	12	7	5	11	1	0	0	33	0	1	0	2.0	.971	OF-17
1937	BOS A	123	.295	.418	505	149	25	8	7	1.4	85	58	46	41	11	3	1	239	8	14	0	2.2	.946	OF-120
1938	STL A	123	.285	.373	466	133	24	4	3	0.6	66	46	43	46	7	10	1	235	9	9	2	2.2	.964	OF-113
1940	NY A	34	.397	.587	63	25	3	3	1	1.6	10	15	7	5	0	18	6	22	0	0	0	1.6	1.000	OF-14
1942	CLE A	80	.277	.333	195	54	4	2	1	0.5	19	26	23	18	5	24	4	142	4	4	2	2.8	.973	OF-53
1946		9	.273	.273	22	6	0	0	0	0.0	1	3	3	5	0	3	0	11	0	0	0	1.8	1.000	OF-6
7 yrs.		415	.287	.390	1379	396	62	19	14	1.0	200	163	131	137	24	67	15	727	21	28	4	2.3	.964	OF-341

Everett Mills

MILLS, EVERETT 6′ 1″ 174 lbs.
B. Jan. 20, 1845, Newark, N. J. D. June 22, 1908, Newark, N. J.

Year	Team	Games	BA	SA	AB	H	2B	3B	HR	HR%	R	RBI	BB	SO	SB	Pinch Hit AB	Pinch Hit H	PO	A	E	DP	TC/G	FA	G by Pos
1876	HAR N	63	.260	.299	254	66	8	1	0	0.0	28	23	1	3		0	0	644	7	42	13	11.0	.939	1B-63

Frank Mills

MILLS, FRANK LeMOYNE BL TR 6′ 180 lbs.
B. May 13, 1895, Knoxville, Ohio D. Aug. 31, 1983, Youngstown, Ohio.

Year	Team	Games	BA	SA	AB	H	2B	3B	HR	HR%	R	RBI	BB	SO	SB	Pinch Hit AB	Pinch Hit H	PO	A	E	DP	TC/G	FA	G by Pos
1914	CLE A	4	.125	.125	8	1	0	0	0	0.0	0	0	1	2	0	1	1	5	4	1	0	5.0	.900	C-2

Jack Mills

MILLS, ABBOTT PAIGE BL TR 6′ 165 lbs.
B. Oct. 23, 1889, S. Williamstown, Mass. D. June 3, 1973, Washington, D. C.

Year	Team	Games	BA	SA	AB	H	2B	3B	HR	HR%	R	RBI	BB	SO	SB	Pinch Hit AB	Pinch Hit H	PO	A	E	DP	TC/G	FA	G by Pos
1911	CLE A	13	.294	.294	17	5	0	0	0	0.0	5	1	1		1	0	0	3	11	0	1	2.0	1.000	3B-7

Rupert Mills

MILLS, RUPERT FRANK BR TR 6′ 2″ 185 lbs.
B. Oct. 12, 1892, Newark, N. J. D. July 20, 1929, Lake Hopatcong, N. J.

Year	Team	Games	BA	SA	AB	H	2B	3B	HR	HR%	R	RBI	BB	SO	SB	Pinch Hit AB	Pinch Hit H	PO	A	E	DP	TC/G	FA	G by Pos
1915	NWK F	41	.201	.254	134	27	5	1	0	0.0	12	16	6		6	3	0	385	23	10	23	11.3	.976	1B-37

Pete Milne

MILNE, WILLIAM JAMES BL TR 6′ 1″ 180 lbs.
B. Apr. 10, 1925, Mobile, Ala.

Year	Team	Games	BA	SA	AB	H	2B	3B	HR	HR%	R	RBI	BB	SO	SB	Pinch Hit AB	Pinch Hit H	PO	A	E	DP	TC/G	FA	G by Pos
1948	NY N	12	.222	.296	27	6	0	1	0	0.0	0	2	1	6	0	1	0	13	0	2	0	1.7	.867	OF-9
1949		31	.241	.379	29	7	1	0	1	3.4	5	6	3	6	0	24	6	2	0	0	0	2.0	1.000	OF-1
1950		4	.250	.750	4	1	0	1	0	0.0	1	1	0	1	0	4	1	0	0	0	0	0.0	—	
3 yrs.		47	.233	.367	60	14	1	2	1	1.7	6	9	4	13	0	29	7	15	0	2	0	1.7	.882	OF-10

Brian Milner

MILNER, BRIAN TATE BR TR 6′ 2″ 200 lbs.
B. Nov. 17, 1959, Ft. Worth, Tex.

Year	Team	Games	BA	SA	AB	H	2B	3B	HR	HR%	R	RBI	BB	SO	SB	Pinch Hit AB	Pinch Hit H	PO	A	E	DP	TC/G	FA	G by Pos
1978	TOR A	2	.444	.667	9	4	0	1	0	0.0	3	2	0	1	0	0	0	4	0	1	0	2.5	.800	C-2

Eddie Milner

MILNER, EDWARD JAMES (Greyhound) BL TL 5′11″ 173 lbs.
B. May 21, 1955, Columbus, Ohio.

Year	Team	Games	BA	SA	AB	H	2B	3B	HR	HR%	R	RBI	BB	SO	SB	Pinch Hit AB	Pinch Hit H	PO	A	E	DP	TC/G	FA	G by Pos
1980	CIN N	6	.000	.000	3	0	0	0	0	0.0	1	0	0	0	0	3	0	0	0	0	0	0.0	—	
1981		8	.200	.400	5	1	1	0	0	0.0	0	1	1	1	0	3	0	2	0	0	0	0.5	1.000	OF-4
1982		113	.268	.378	407	109	23	5	4	1.0	61	31	41	40	18	6	2	215	8	3	1	2.1	.987	OF-107
1983		146	.261	.384	502	131	23	6	9	1.8	77	33	68	60	41	8	2	392	9	4	0	2.9	.990	OF-139
1984		117	.232	.342	336	78	8	4	7	2.1	44	29	51	50	21	14	2	285	8	5	4	2.8	.983	OF-108
1985		145	.254	.347	453	115	19	7	3	0.7	82	33	61	31	35	12	5	340	12	6	3	2.7	.983	OF-135
1986		145	.259	.446	424	110	22	6	15	3.5	70	47	36	56	18	15	3	292	6	3	0	2.4	.990	OF-127

Eddie Milner *continued*

Year	Team	Games	BA	SA	AB	H	2B	3B	HR	HR%	R	RBI	BB	SO	SB	Pinch Hit AB	Pinch Hit H	PO	A	E	DP	TC/G	FA	G by Pos
1987	**SF N**	101	.252	.374	214	54	14	0	4	1.9	38	19	24	33	10	19	4	135	0	1	0	1.6	.993	OF-84
1988	**CIN N**	23	.176	.196	51	9	1	0	0	0.0	3	2	4	9	2	7	0	29	1	1	0	2.1	.968	OF-15
9 yrs.		804	.253	.376	2395	607	111	28	42	1.8	376	195	286	280	145	87	18	1690	44	23	8	2.4	.987	OF-719
LEAGUE CHAMPIONSHIP SERIES																								
1987	**SF N**	6	.143	.143	7	1	0	0	0	0.0	0	0	0	3	0	1	1	8	0	0	0	2.0	1.000	OF-4

John Milner

MILNER, JOHN DAVID (Hammer)
B. Dec. 28, 1949, Atlanta, Ga.
BL TL 6′ 185 lbs.

Year	Team	Games	BA	SA	AB	H	2B	3B	HR	HR%	R	RBI	BB	SO	SB	Pinch Hit AB	Pinch Hit H	PO	A	E	DP	TC/G	FA	G by Pos
1971	**NY N**	9	.167	.222	18	3	1	0	0	0.0	1	1	0	3	0	6	0	8	1	0	0	3.0	1.000	OF-3
1972		117	.238	.423	362	86	12	2	17	4.7	52	38	51	74	2	12	3	233	13	6	9	2.5	.976	OF-91, 1B-10
1973		129	.239	.432	451	108	12	3	23	5.1	69	72	62	84	1	4	0	804	51	11	66	7.0	.987	1B-95, OF-29
1974		137	.252	.408	507	128	19	0	20	3.9	70	63	66	77	10	2	2	1147	77	7	103	9.3	.994	1B-133
1975		91	.191	.336	220	42	11	0	7	3.2	24	29	33	22	1	32	3	267	27	3	21	4.9	.990	OF-31, 1B-29
1976		127	.271	.447	443	120	25	4	15	3.4	56	78	65	53	0	12	6	239	9	3	6	2.0	.988	OF-112, 1B-12
1977		131	.255	.415	388	99	20	3	12	3.1	43	57	61	55	6	21	2	700	50	5	65	6.9	.993	1B-87, OF-22
1978	**PIT N**	108	.271	.390	295	80	17	0	6	2.0	39	38	34	25	5	15	4	287	14	3	15	3.1	.990	OF-69, 1B-28
1979		128	.276	.475	326	90	9	4	16	4.9	52	60	53	37	3	26	7	367	20	8	28	3.5	.980	OF-64, 1B-48
1980		114	.244	.370	238	58	6	0	8	3.4	31	34	52	29	2	33	8	510	32	6	48	6.8	.989	1B-70, OF-11
1981	**2 teams**	**PIT N** (34G –.237) **MON N** (31G –.237)																						
″	**total**	65	.237	.393	135	32	6	0	5	3.7	12	18	17	9	0	26	9	225	17	5	16	6.7	.980	1B-29, OF-8
1982	**2 teams**	**MON N** (26G –.107) **PIT N** (33G –.240)																						
″	**total**	59	.170	.321	53	9	2	0	2	3.8	6	10	10	5	1	43	7	24	2	0	5	4.3	1.000	1B-6
12 yrs.		1215	.249	.413	3436	855	140	16	131	3.8	455	498	504	473	31	232	51	4811	313	57	382	5.2	.989	1B-547, OF-440
DIVISIONAL PLAYOFF SERIES																								
1981	**MON N**	2	.500	.500	2	1	0	0	0	0.0	0	1	0	0	0	2	1	0	0	0	0	0.0	—	
LEAGUE CHAMPIONSHIP SERIES																								
1973	**NY N**	5	.176	.176	17	3	0	0	0	0.0	2	1	5	3	0	0	0	37	6	0	3	8.6	1.000	1B-5
1979	**PIT N**	3	.000	.000	9	0	0	0	0	0.0	0	0	2	0	0	0	0	1	0	0	0	0.3	1.000	OF-3
1981	**MON N**	1	.000	.000	1	0	0	0	0	0.0	0	0	0	1	0	1	0	0	0	0	0	0.0	—	
3 yrs.		9	.111	.111	27	3	0	0	0	0.0	2	1	7	4	0	1	0	38	6	0	3	5.5	1.000	1B-5, OF-3
WORLD SERIES																								
1973	**NY N**	7	.296	.296	27	8	0	0	0	0.0	2	2	5	1	0	0	0	66	1	0	2	9.6	1.000	1B-7
1979	**PIT N**	3	.333	.444	9	3	1	0	0	0.0	2	1	2	0	0	0	0	5	0	0	0	1.7	1.000	OF-3
2 yrs.		10	.306	.333	36	11	1	0	0	0.0	4	3	7	1	0	0	0	71	1	0	2	7.2	1.000	1B-7, OF-3

Mike Milosevich

MILOSEVICH, MICHAEL (Mollie)
B. Jan. 13, 1915, Zeigler, Ill. D. Feb. 3, 1966, E. Chicago, Ind.
BR TR 5′10½″ 172 lbs.

Year	Team	Games	BA	SA	AB	H	2B	3B	HR	HR%	R	RBI	BB	SO	SB	Pinch Hit AB	Pinch Hit H	PO	A	E	DP	TC/G	FA	G by Pos
1944	**NY A**	94	.247	.308	312	77	11	4	0	0.0	27	32	30	37	1	2	0	176	281	22	68	5.3	.954	SS-91
1945		30	.217	.246	69	15	2	0	0	0.0	5	7	6	6	0	6	0	37	55	4	11	4.2	.958	SS-22, 2B-1
2 yrs.		124	.241	.297	381	92	13	4	0	0.0	32	39	36	43	1	8	0	213	336	26	79	5.0	.955	SS-113, 2B-1

Don Mincher

MINCHER, DONALD RAY
B. June 24, 1938, Huntsville, Ala.
BL TR 6′ 3″ 205 lbs.

Year	Team	Games	BA	SA	AB	H	2B	3B	HR	HR%	R	RBI	BB	SO	SB	Pinch Hit AB	Pinch Hit H	PO	A	E	DP	TC/G	FA	G by Pos
1960	**WAS A**	27	.241	.392	79	19	4	1	2	2.5	10	5	11	11	0	7	2	209	5	5	14	10.9	.977	1B-20
1961	**MIN A**	35	.188	.406	101	19	5	1	5	5.0	18	11	22	11	0	8	0	234	18	8	28	9.0	.969	1B-29
1962		86	.240	.488	121	29	1	1	9	7.4	20	29	34	24	0	45	9	211	13	5	17	9.2	.978	1B-25
1963		82	.258	.520	225	58	8	0	17	7.6	41	42	30	51	0	14	0	446	27	8	34	8.0	.983	1B-60
1964		120	.237	.547	287	68	12	4	23	8.0	45	56	27	51	0	41	7	549	43	5	50	7.9	.992	1B-76
1965		128	.251	.509	346	87	17	3	22	6.4	43	65	49	73	1	29	6	818	45	7	64	8.7	.992	1B-99, OF-1
1966		139	.251	.418	431	108	30	0	14	3.2	53	62	58	68	3	8	3	995	85	9	62	8.4	.992	1B-130
1967	**CAL A**	147	.273	.487	487	133	23	3	25	5.1	81	76	69	69	0	6	1	1178	88	8	92	8.9	.994	1B-142, OF-1
1968		120	.236	.368	399	94	12	1	13	3.3	35	48	43	65	0	9	3	949	59	9	90	9.0	.991	1B-113
1969	**SEA A**	140	.246	.454	427	105	14	0	25	5.9	53	78	78	69	10	9	2	1033	93	6	98	9.3	.995	1B-122
1970	**OAK A**	140	.246	.460	463	114	18	0	27	5.8	62	74	56	71	5	3	0	1109	91	12	107	8.8	.990	1B-137
1971	**2 teams**	**OAK A** (28G –.239) **WAS A** (100G –.291)																						
″	**total**	128	.280	.427	415	116	21	2	12	2.9	44	53	73	66	3	12	2	907	82	9	91	8.7	.991	1B-115
1972	**2 teams**	**TEX A** (61G –.236) **OAK A** (47G –.148)																						
″	**total**	108	.216	.335	245	53	11	0	6	2.4	25	44	56	39	2	30	7	544	47	4	49	8.5	.993	1B-70
13 yrs.		1400	.249	.450	4026	1003	176	16	200	5.0	530	643	606	668	24	221	42	9182	696	95	796	8.7	.990	1B-1138, OF-2
LEAGUE CHAMPIONSHIP SERIES																								
1972	**OAK A**	1	.000	.000	1	0	0	0	0	0.0	0	0	0	1	0	1	0	0	0	0	0	0.0	—	
WORLD SERIES																								
1965	**MIN A**	7	.130	.261	23	3	0	0	1	4.3	3	1	2	7	0	0	0	51	4	0	0	7.9	1.000	1B-7
1972	**OAK A**	3	1.000	1.000	1	1	0	0	0	0.0	0	1	0	0	0	1	1	0	0	0	0	0.0	—	
2 yrs.		10	.167	.292	24	4	0	0	1	4.2	3	2	2	7	0	1	1	51	4	0	0	7.9	1.000	1B-7

Dan Minnehan

MINNEHAN, DANIEL JOSEPH
B. Nov. 28, 1865, Troy, N. Y. D. Aug. 8, 1929, Troy, N. Y.
BR TR 5′10″ 145 lbs.

Year	Team	Games	BA	SA	AB	H	2B	3B	HR	HR%	R	RBI	BB	SO	SB	Pinch Hit AB	Pinch Hit H	PO	A	E	DP	TC/G	FA	G by Pos
1895	**LOU N**	8	.382	.382	34	13	0	0	0	0.0	6	6	1	1	0	0	0	14	12	3	3	3.2	.897	3B-7, OF-2

Minnie Minoso

MINOSO, SATURNINO ORESTES ARMAS
Born Saturnino Orestes Armas Minoso (Arrieta).
B. Nov. 29, 1922, Havana, Cuba.
BR TR 5′10″ 175 lbs.

Year	Team	Games	BA	SA	AB	H	2B	3B	HR	HR%	R	RBI	BB	SO	SB	Pinch Hit AB	Pinch Hit H	PO	A	E	DP	TC/G	FA	G by Pos
1949	**CLE A**	9	.188	.375	16	3	0	0	1	6.3	2	1	2	2	0	1	0	11	0	0	0	1.6	1.000	OF-7
1951	**2 teams**	**CLE A** (8G –.429) **CHI A** (138G –.324)																						
″	**total**	146	.326	.500	530	173	34	**14**	10	1.9	112	76	72	42	**31**	2	0	266	130	22	11	2.6	.947	OF-82, 3B-68, 1B-7, SS-1
1952	**CHI A**	147	.281	.424	569	160	24	9	13	2.3	96	61	71	46	**22**	0	0	323	22	7	3	2.3	.980	OF-143, 3B-9, SS-1
1953		157	.313	.466	556	174	24	8	15	2.7	104	104	74	43	**25**	0	0	282	29	12	3	2.1	.963	OF-147, 3B-10
1954		153	.320	.535	568	182	29	**18**	19	3.3	119	116	77	46	18	0	0	347	25	9	4	2.5	.976	OF-146, 3B-9
1955		139	.288	.424	517	149	26	7	10	1.9	79	70	76	43	19	1	0	289	21	9	4	2.3	.972	OF-138, 3B-2
1956		151	.316	.525	545	172	29	**11**	21	3.9	106	88	86	40	12	3	1	287	16	10	1	2.0	.968	OF-148, 3B-8, 1B-1

Minnie Minoso *continued*

Year	Team	Games	BA	SA	AB	H	2B	3B	HR	HR%	R	RBI	BB	SO	SB	Pinch Hit AB	Pinch Hit H	PO	A	E	DP	TC/G	FA	G by Pos
1957		153	.310	.454	568	176	**36**	5	12	2.1	96	103	79	54	18	0	0	293	9	5	2	2.0	.984	OF-152, 3B-1
1958	**CLE A**	149	.302	.484	556	168	25	2	24	4.3	94	80	59	53	14	3	1	301	13	8	1	2.2	.975	OF-147, 3B-1
1959		148	.302	.468	570	172	32	0	21	3.7	92	92	54	46	8	0	0	314	14	5	1	2.3	.985	OF-148
1960	**CHI A**	154	.311	.481	591	**184**	32	4	20	3.4	89	105	52	63	17	0	0	282	14	6	3	2.0	.980	OF-154
1961		152	.280	.420	540	151	28	3	14	2.6	91	82	67	46	9	1	1	273	10	13	2	2.0	.956	OF-147
1962	**STL N**	39	.196	.278	97	19	5	0	1	1.0	14	10	7	17	4	6	0	33	2	1	0	1.3	.972	OF-27
1963	**WAS A**	109	.229	.317	315	72	12	2	4	1.3	38	30	33	38	8	26	4	108	26	5	1	1.7	.964	OF-74, 3B-8
1964	**CHI A**	30	.226	.323	31	7	0	0	1	3.2	4	5	5	3	0	22	4	9	0	0	0	1.8	1.000	OF-5
1976		3	.125	.125	8	1	0	0	0	0.0	0	0	0	2	0	0	0	0	0	0	0	0.0	.000	DH-3
1980		2	.000	.000	2	0	0	0	0	0.0	0	0	0	0	0	2	0	0	0	0	0	0.0	—	
17 yrs.		1841	.298	.459	6579	1963	336	83	186	2.8	1136	1023	814	584	205	67	11	3418	331	112	36	2.2	.971	OF-1665, 3B-116, 1B-8, DH-3, SS-2

Willie Miranda

MIRANDA, GUILLERMO BB TR 5′ 9½″ 150 lbs.
Born Guillermo Miranda (Perez).
B. May 24, 1926, Velasco, Cuba.

Year	Team	Games	BA	SA	AB	H	2B	3B	HR	HR%	R	RBI	BB	SO	SB	Pinch Hit AB	Pinch Hit H	PO	A	E	DP	TC/G	FA	G by Pos
1951	**WAS A**	7	.444	.444	9	4	0	0	0	0.0	2	0	0	0	0	2	2	9	2	2	0	4.3	.846	SS-2, 1B-1
1952	**3 teams** **CHI A** (12G –.250) **STL A** (7G –.091) **CHI A** (58G –.218)																							
″	**total**	77	.211	.261	161	34	4	2	0	0.0	16	8	16	15	1	1	0	80	162	8	30	3.7	.968	SS-61, 3B-5, 2B-2
1953	**2 teams** **STL A** (17G –.167) **NY A** (48G –.224)																							
″	**total**	65	.219	.266	64	14	0	0	1	1.6	14	5	6	11	2	0	0	61	82	3	20	2.5	.979	SS-53, 3B-6
1954	**NY A**	92	.250	.345	116	29	4	2	1	0.9	12	12	10	10	0	1	0	91	133	12	36	2.5	.949	SS-88, 2B-4, 3B-1
1955	**BAL A**	153	.255	.310	487	124	12	6	1	0.2	42	38	42	58	4	0	0	300	482	34	101	5.3	.958	SS-153, 2B-1
1956		148	.217	.282	461	100	16	4	2	0.4	38	34	46	73	3	0	0	229	436	26	91	4.7	.962	SS-147
1957		115	.194	.204	314	61	3	0	0	0.0	29	20	24	42	2	0	0	166	324	17	59	4.4	.966	SS-115
1958		102	.201	.243	214	43	6	0	1	0.5	15	8	14	25	1	0	0	137	216	14	53	3.6	.962	SS-102
1959		65	.159	.216	88	14	5	0	0	0.0	8	7	7	16	0	0	0	60	108	5	25	2.7	.971	SS-47, 3B-11, 2B-5
9 yrs.		824	.221	.271	1914	423	50	14	6	0.3	176	132	165	250	13	4	2	1133	1945	121	415	4.0	.962	SS-768, 3B-23, 2B-12, 1B-1

John Misse

MISSE, JOHN BEVERLEY BR TR 5′ 8″ 150 lbs.
B. May 30, 1885, Highland, Kans. D. Mar. 18, 1970, St. Joseph, Mo.

Year	Team	Games	BA	SA	AB	H	2B	3B	HR	HR%	R	RBI	BB	SO	SB	Pinch Hit AB	Pinch Hit H	PO	A	E	DP	TC/G	FA	G by Pos
1914	**STL F**	99	.196	.229	306	60	8	1	0	0.0	28	22	36		3	0	0	229	281	43	29	5.5	.922	2B-50, SS-48, 3B-2

Bobby Mitchell

MITCHELL, ROBERT VAN BL TL 5′10″ 170 lbs.
B. Apr. 7, 1955, Salt Lake City, Utah.

Year	Team	Games	BA	SA	AB	H	2B	3B	HR	HR%	R	RBI	BB	SO	SB	Pinch Hit AB	Pinch Hit H	PO	A	E	DP	TC/G	FA	G by Pos
1980	**LA N**	9	.333	.333	3	1	0	0	0	0.0	1	0	1	0	0	1	1	5	0	0	0	0.6	1.000	OF-8
1981		10	.125	.125	8	1	0	0	0	0.0	0	0	1	4	0	2	0	6	0	0	0	0.9	1.000	OF-7
1982	**MIN A**	124	.249	.313	454	113	11	6	2	0.4	48	28	54	53	8	3	1	350	8	1	3	3.0	.997	OF-121
1983		59	.230	.303	152	35	4	2	1	0.7	26	15	28	21	1	13	3	94	2	1	1	2.2	.990	OF-44
4 yrs.		202	.243	.308	617	150	15	8	3	0.5	75	43	84	78	9	19	5	455	10	2	4	2.6	.996	OF-180

Bobby Mitchell

MITCHELL, ROBERT VANCE BR TR 6′ 3″ 185 lbs.
B. Oct. 22, 1943, Norristown, Pa.

Year	Team	Games	BA	SA	AB	H	2B	3B	HR	HR%	R	RBI	BB	SO	SB	Pinch Hit AB	Pinch Hit H	PO	A	E	DP	TC/G	FA	G by Pos
1970	**NY A**	10	.227	.318	22	5	2	0	0	0.0	1	4	2	3	0	3	1	20	0	0	0	2.9	1.000	OF-7
1971	**MIL A**	35	.182	.345	55	10	1	1	2	3.6	7	6	6	18	0	12	2	35	2	1	1	2.0	.974	OF-19
1973		47	.223	.385	130	29	6	0	5	3.8	12	20	5	32	4	7	2	24	0	1	0	0.6	.960	OF-20, DH-19
1974		88	.243	.387	173	42	6	2	5	2.9	27	20	18	46	7	9	2	30	1	1	0	0.4	.969	DH-53, OF-26
1975		93	.249	.454	229	57	14	3	9	3.9	39	41	25	69	3	13	2	128	2	1	1	1.6	.992	OF-72, DH-11
5 yrs.		273	.235	.406	609	143	29	6	21	3.4	86	91	56	168	14	44	9	237	5	4	2	1.1	.984	OF-144, DH-83

Clarence Mitchell

MITCHELL, CLARENCE ELMER BL TL 5′11½″ 190 lbs.
B. Feb. 22, 1891, Franklin, Neb. D. Nov. 6, 1963, Grand Island, Neb.

Year	Team	Games	BA	SA	AB	H	2B	3B	HR	HR%	R	RBI	BB	SO	SB	Pinch Hit AB	Pinch Hit H	PO	A	E	DP	TC/G	FA	G by Pos
1911	**DET A**	5	.500	.500	4	2	0	0	0	0.0	2	0	1		0	0	0	0	2	0	0	0.4	1.000	P-5
1916	**CIN N**	56	.239	.274	117	28	2	1	0	0.0	11	11	4	6	1	14	4	70	56	3	9	3.4	.977	P-29, 1B-6, OF-3
1917		47	.278	.311	90	25	3	0	0	0.0	13	5	5	5	0	1	0	73	49	4	5	2.9	.968	P-32, OF-6, 1B-6
1918	**BKN N**	10	.250	.375	24	6	1	1	0	0.0	2	2	0	3	0	2	0	6	0	1	0	0.8	.857	OF-6, 1B-2, P-1
1919		34	.367	.449	49	18	1	0	1	2.0	7	2	4	4	0	9	3	4	36	1	1	1.8	.976	P-23
1920		55	.234	.290	107	25	2	2	0	0.0	9	11	8	9	1	18	6	98	36	2	8	4.0	.985	P-19, 1B-11, OF-4
1921		46	.264	.319	91	24	5	0	0	0.0	11	12	5	7	3	3	0	30	64	4	7	2.4	.959	P-37, 1B-4
1922		55	.290	.426	155	45	6	3	3	1.9	21	28	19	6	0	9	4	366	34	3	32	8.6	.993	1B-42, P-5
1923	**PHI N**	53	.269	.397	78	21	3	2	1	1.3	10	9	4	11	0	24	6	4	18	3	2	0.9	.880	P-29
1924		69	.255	.284	102	26	3	0	0	0.0	7	13	2	7	1	37	6	10	51	0	3	2.0	1.000	P-30
1925		52	.196	.217	92	18	2	0	0	0.0	7	13	5	9	2	17	1	20	62	0	9	2.4	1.000	P-32, 1B-2
1926		39	.244	.295	78	19	4	0	0	0.0	8	6	5	5	0	7	1	18	62	1	3	2.5	.988	P-28, 1B-4
1927		18	.238	.357	42	10	2	0	1	2.4	5	6	2	1	0	3	0	1	25	1	1	2.1	.963	P-13
1928	**2 teams** **PHI N** (5G –.250) **STL N** (19G –.125)																							
″	**total**	24	.133	.150	60	8	1	0	0	0.0	0	1	0	3	0	1	0	6	51	1	3	2.6	.983	P-22
1929	**STL N**	26	.273	.348	66	18	3	1	0	0.0	9	9	4	6	1	0	0	1	37	1	1	1.6	.974	P-25
1930	**2 teams** **STL N** (1G –.500) **NY N** (24G –.255)																							
″	**total**	25	.265	.286	49	13	1	0	0	0.0	9	1	1	5	0	0	0	10	35	0	1	1.8	1.000	P-25
1931	**NY N**	27	.219	.288	73	16	2	0	1	1.4	5	4	2	4	0	0	0	13	33	6	2	1.9	.885	P-27
1932		8	.200	.200	10	2	0	0	0	0.0	2	0	1	1	0	0	0	2	3	1	0	0.8	.833	P-8
18 yrs.		649	.252	.315	1287	324	41	10	7	0.5	138	133	72	92	9	145	31	732	654	32	87	2.9	.977	P-390, 1B-77, OF-19
WORLD SERIES																								
1920	**BKN N**	2	.333	.333	3	1	0	0	0	0.0	0	0	0	0	0	1	1	1	0	0	0	1.0	1.000	P-1
1928	**STL N**	1	.000	.000	2	0	0	0	0	0.0	0	0	0	0	0	0	0	0	1	1	0	2.0	.500	P-1
2 yrs.		3	.200	.200	5	1	0	0	0	0.0	0	0	0	0	0	1	1	1	1	1	0	1.5	.667	P-2

Dale Mitchell

MITCHELL, LOREN DALE BL TL 6′ 1″ 195 lbs.
B. Aug. 23, 1921, Colony, Okla. D. Jan. 5, 1987, Tulsa, Okla.

Year	Team	Games	BA	SA	AB	H	2B	3B	HR	HR%	R	RBI	BB	SO	SB	Pinch Hit AB	Pinch Hit H	PO	A	E	DP	TC/G	FA	G by Pos
1946	**CLE A**	11	.432	.500	44	19	3	0	0	0.0	7	5	1	2	1	0	0	28	0	0	0	2.5	1.000	OF-11
1947		123	.316	.396	493	156	16	10	1	0.2	69	34	23	14	2	8	3	252	8	6	1	2.3	.977	OF-115

Dale Mitchell *continued*

Year	Team	Games	BA	SA	AB	H	2B	3B	HR	HR%	R	RBI	BB	SO	SB	Pinch Hit AB	Pinch Hit H	PO	A	E	DP	TC/G	FA	G by Pos
1948		141	.336	.431	608	204	30	8	4	0.7	82	56	45	17	13	2	1	307	12	3	3	2.3	.991	OF-140
1949		149	.317	.428	**640**	**203**	16	**23**	3	0.5	81	56	43	11	10	0	0	337	10	2	2	2.3	.994	OF-149
1950		130	.308	.399	506	156	27	5	3	0.6	81	49	67	21	3	4	1	236	3	7	1	1.9	.972	OF-127
1951		134	.290	.424	510	148	21	7	11	2.2	83	62	53	16	7	10	2	253	3	2	0	2.1	.992	OF-124
1952		134	.323	.415	511	165	26	3	5	1.0	61	58	52	9	6	5	1	258	2	2	0	2.0	.992	OF-128
1953		134	.300	.446	500	150	26	4	13	2.6	76	60	42	20	3	13	2	224	2	7	1	1.9	.970	OF-125
1954		53	.283	.350	60	17	1	0	1	1.7	6	6	9	1	0	44	14	9	1	1	0	1.6	.909	OF-6, 1B-1
1955		61	.259	.328	58	15	2	1	0	0.0	4	10	4	3	0	**45**	13	27	2	0	5	2.6	1.000	1B-8, OF-3
1956	**2 teams**	**CLE A** (38G –.133)		**BKN N** (19G –.292)																				
"	**total**	57	.204	.222	54	11	1	0	0	0.0	5	7	7	5	0	46	10	3	0	0	0	1.0	1.000	OF-3
11 yrs.		1127	.312	.416	3984	1244	169	61	41	1.0	555	403	346	119	45	177	47	1934	43	30	13	2.1	.985	OF-931, 1B-9
WORLD SERIES																								
1948	**CLE A**	6	.174	.348	23	4	1	0	1	4.3	4	1	2	0	0	0	0	13	0	0	0	2.2	1.000	OF-6
1954		3	.000	.000	2	0	0	0	0	0.0	0	0	1	0	0	2	0	0	0	0	0	0.0	—	
1956	**BKN N**	4	.000	.000	4	0	0	0	0	0.0	0	0	0	1	0	4	0	0	0	0	0	0.0	—	
3 yrs.		13	.138	.276	29	4	1	0	1	3.4	4	1	3	1	0	6	0	13	0	0	0	2.2	1.000	OF-6

Fred Mitchell

MITCHELL, FREDERICK FRANCIS BR TR 5′ 9½″ 185 lbs.
Born Frederick Francis Yapp.
B. June 5, 1878, Cambridge, Mass. D. Oct. 13, 1970, Newton, Mass.
Manager 1917–23.

Year	Team	Games	BA	SA	AB	H	2B	3B	HR	HR%	R	RBI	BB	SO	SB	Pinch Hit AB	Pinch Hit H	PO	A	E	DP	TC/G	FA	G by Pos
1901	**BOS A**	20	.159	.250	44	7	0	2	0	0.0	5	4	2		0	0	0	2	34	6	2	2.1	.857	P-17, 2B-2, SS-1
1902	**2 teams**	**BOS A** (1G –.000)		**PHI A** (20G –.188)																				
"	**total**	21	.184	.245	49	9	1	1	0	0.0	7	3	1		1	1	0	6	45	4	4	2.8	.927	P-19, OF-1
1903	**PHI N**	29	.200	.242	95	19	4	0	0	0.0	11	10	0		0	1	1	10	50	10	3	2.5	.857	P-28
1904	**2 teams**	**PHI N** (25G –.207)		**BKN N** (8G –.292)																				
"	**total**	33	.226	.302	106	24	4	2	0	0.0	12	9	6		1	0	0	85	83	11	5	5.4	.939	P-21, 1B-9, 3B-2, OF-1
1905	**BKN N**	27	.190	.190	79	15	0	0	0	0.0	4	8	4		0	2	1	71	44	13	2	5.1	.898	P-12, 1B-7, 3B-4, SS-1, OF-1
1910	**NY A**	68	.230	.286	196	45	7	2	0	0.0	16	18	9		6	6	2	262	69	11	2	5.0	.968	C-68
1913	**BOS N**	4	.333	.333	3	1	0	0	0	0.0	0	0	0	2	0	3	1	0	0	0	0	0.0	—	
7 yrs.		202	.210	.262	572	120	16	7	0	0.0	55	52	22	2	8	13	5	436	325	55	18	4.2	.933	P-97, C-68, 1B-16, 3B-6, OF-3, 2B-2, SS-2

Johnny Mitchell

MITCHELL, JOHN FRANKLIN BB TR 5′ 8″ 155 lbs.
B. Aug. 9, 1894, Detroit, Mich. D. Nov. 4, 1965, Birmingham, Mich.

Year	Team	Games	BA	SA	AB	H	2B	3B	HR	HR%	R	RBI	BB	SO	SB	Pinch Hit AB	Pinch Hit H	PO	A	E	DP	TC/G	FA	G by Pos
1921	**NY A**	13	.262	.286	42	11	1	0	0	0.0	4	2	4	4	1	0	0	13	26	6	1	3.8	.867	SS-7, 2B-5
1922	**2 teams**	**NY A** (4G –.000)		**BOS A** (59G –.251)																				
"	**total**	63	.246	.290	207	51	4	1	1	0.5	21	8	16	18	1	1	0	98	185	11	31	4.7	.963	SS-62
1923	**BOS A**	92	.225	.291	347	78	15	4	0	0.0	40	19	34	18	7	0	0	194	271	18	40	5.3	.963	SS-87, 2B-5
1924	**BKN N**	64	.263	.317	243	64	10	0	1	0.4	42	16	37	22	3	0	0	131	216	18	30	5.7	.951	SS-64
1925		97	.250	.292	336	84	8	3	0	0.0	45	18	28	19	2	1	0	184	266	25	49	5.3	.947	SS-90
5 yrs.		329	.245	.296	1175	288	38	8	2	0.2	152	63	119	81	14	2	0	620	964	78	151	5.2	.953	SS-310, 2B-10

Keith Mitchell

MITCHELL, KEITH ALEXANDER BR TR 5′10″ 180 lbs.
B. Aug. 6, 1969, San Diego, Calif.

Year	Team	Games	BA	SA	AB	H	2B	3B	HR	HR%	R	RBI	BB	SO	SB	Pinch Hit AB	Pinch Hit H	PO	A	E	DP	TC/G	FA	G by Pos
1991	**ATL N**	48	.318	.409	66	21	0	0	2	3.0	11	5	8	12	3	10	2	31	1	1	0	1.0	.970	OF-34
1994	**SEA A**	46	.227	.359	128	29	2	0	5	3.9	21	15	18	22	0	6	1	49	0	1	0	1.1	.980	OF-39, DH-6
2 yrs.		94	.258	.376	194	50	2	0	7	3.6	32	20	26	34	3	16	3	80	1	2	0	1.1	.976	OF-73, DH-6
LEAGUE CHAMPIONSHIP SERIES																								
1991	**ATL N**	5	.000	.000	4	0	0	0	0	0.0	0	0	0	1	0	1	0	2	0	0	0	0.4	1.000	OF-5
WORLD SERIES																								
1991	**ATL N**	3	.000	.000	2	0	0	0	0	0.0	0	0	0	1	0	0	0	0	0	0	0	0.0	.000	OF-3

Kevin Mitchell

MITCHELL, KEVIN DARNELL (Mitch, World) BR TR 5′10″ 210 lbs.
B. Jan. 13, 1962, San Diego, Calif.

Year	Team	Games	BA	SA	AB	H	2B	3B	HR	HR%	R	RBI	BB	SO	SB	Pinch Hit AB	Pinch Hit H	PO	A	E	DP	TC/G	FA	G by Pos
1984	**NY N**	7	.214	.214	14	3	0	0	0	0.0	0	1	0	3	0	4	1	1	4	1	2	1.2	.833	3B-5
1986		108	.277	.466	328	91	22	2	12	3.7	51	43	33	61	3	20	3	158	69	10	10	2.3	.958	OF-68, SS-24, 3B-7, 1B-2
1987	**2 teams**	**SD N** (62G –.245)		**SF N** (69G –.306)																				
"	**total**	131	.280	.474	464	130	20	2	22	4.7	68	70	48	88	9	9	2	76	240	15	19	2.6	.955	3B-119, OF-6, SS-1
1988	**SF N**	148	.251	.442	505	127	25	7	19	3.8	60	80	48	85	5	10	2	118	205	22	18	2.4	.936	3B-102, OF-40
1989		154	.291	**.635**	543	158	34	6	**47**	**8.7**	100	**125**	87	115	3	3	1	305	10	7	0	2.2	.978	OF-147, 3B-2
1990		140	.290	.544	524	152	24	2	35	6.7	90	93	58	87	4	2	1	295	9	9	3	2.3	.971	OF-138
1991		113	.256	.515	371	95	13	1	27	7.3	52	69	43	57	2	13	0	188	6	6	1	2.0	.970	OF-100, 1B-1
1992	**SEA A**	99	.286	.428	360	103	24	0	9	2.5	48	67	35	46	0	5	3	130	4	0	0	1.4	1.000	OF-69, DH-26
1993	**CIN N**	93	.341	.601	323	110	21	3	19	5.9	56	64	25	48	1	3	0	149	7	7	2	1.9	.957	OF-87
1994		95	.326	.681	310	101	18	1	30	9.7	57	77	59	62	2	4	1	139	10	4	2	1.7	.974	OF-89, 1B-1
10 yrs.		1088	.286	.529	3742	1070	201	24	220	5.9	582	689	436	652	29	73	14	1559	564	81	57	2.1	.963	OF-744, 3B-235, DH-26, SS-25, 1B-4
LEAGUE CHAMPIONSHIP SERIES																								
1986	**NY N**	2	.250	.250	8	2	0	0	0	0.0	1	0	0	1	0	0	0	3	0	0	0	1.5	1.000	OF-2
1987	**SF N**	7	.267	.400	30	8	1	0	1	3.3	2	2	0	3	1	0	0	4	10	1	1	2.1	.933	3B-7
1989		5	.353	.706	17	6	0	0	2	11.8	5	7	3	3	0	0	0	15	1	1	1	3.4	.941	OF-5
3 yrs.		14	.291	.473	55	16	1	0	3	5.5	8	9	3	7	1	0	0	22	11	2	2	2.5	.943	3B-7, OF-7
WORLD SERIES																								
1986	**NY N**	5	.250	.250	8	2	0	0	0	0.0	1	0	0	3	0	2	1	0	2	0	0	0.7	1.000	OF-2, DH-1
1989	**SF N**	4	.294	.471	17	5	0	0	1	5.9	2	2	0	3	0	0	0	10	0	1	0	2.8	.909	OF-4
2 yrs.		9	.280	.400	25	7	0	0	1	4.0	3	2	0	6	0	2	1	10	2	1	0	1.9	.923	OF-6, DH-1

Mike Mitchell

MITCHELL, MICHAEL FRANCIS BR TR 6′ 1″ 185 lbs.
B. Dec. 12, 1879, Springfield, Ohio D. July 16, 1961, Phoenix, Ariz.

Year	Team	Games	BA	SA	AB	H	2B	3B	HR	HR%	R	RBI	BB	SO	SB	Pinch Hit AB	Pinch Hit H	PO	A	E	DP	TC/G	FA	G by Pos
1907	**CIN N**	148	.292	.382	558	163	17	12	3	0.5	64	47	37		17	0	0	280	39	14	10	2.3	.958	OF-146, 1B-2
1908		119	.222	.281	406	90	9	6	1	0.2	41	37	46		18	0	0	201	16	9	2	1.9	.960	OF-118, 1B-1

Mike Mitchell *continued*

Year	Team	Games	BA	SA	AB	H	2B	3B	HR	HR%	R	RBI	BB	SO	SB	Pinch Hit AB	Pinch Hit H	PO	A	E	DP	TC/G	FA	G by Pos
1909		145	.310	.430	523	162	17	**17**	4	0.8	83	86	57		37	0	0	262	20	11	3	2.0	.962	OF-144, 1B-1
1910		156	.286	.401	583	167	16	**18**	5	0.9	79	88	59	56	35	0	0	314	22	13	9	2.2	.963	OF-149, 1B-7
1911		142	.291	.427	529	154	22	22	2	0.4	74	84	44	34	35	2	0	280	23	9	8	2.2	.971	OF-140
1912		157	.283	.377	552	156	14	13	4	0.7	60	78	41	43	23	2	1	251	18	15	8	2.0	.947	OF-144
1913	**2 teams**	**CHI N** (81G –.259)		**PIT N** (54G –.271)																				
"	**total**	135	.264	.369	477	126	19	8	5	1.0	62	51	46	48	23	0	0	326	23	21	0	2.7	.943	OF-135
1914	**2 teams**	**PIT N** (76G –.234)		**WAS A** (55G –.285)																				
"	**total**	131	.255	.343	466	119	16	8	3	0.6	51	43	38	35	14	2	0	273	22	8	6	2.3	.974	OF-129
8 yrs.		1133	.278	.380	4094	1137	130	104	27	0.7	514	514	368	216	202	6	1	2187	183	100	46	2.2	.960	OF-1105, 1B-11

Ralph Mitterling

MITTERLING, RALPH (Sarge) BR TR 5′10″ 165 lbs.
B. Apr. 19, 1890, Freeburg, Pa. D. Jan. 22, 1956, Pittsburgh, Pa.

Year	Team	Games	BA	SA	AB	H	2B	3B	HR	HR%	R	RBI	BB	SO	SB	Pinch Hit AB	Pinch Hit H	PO	A	E	DP	TC/G	FA	G by Pos
1916	**PHI A**	13	.154	.154	39	6	0	0	0	0.0	1	2	3	6	0	1	0	16	1	1	1	1.5	.944	OF-12

George Mitterwald

MITTERWALD, GEORGE EUGENE BR TR 6′ 2″ 195 lbs.
B. June 7, 1945, Berkeley, Calif.

Year	Team	Games	BA	SA	AB	H	2B	3B	HR	HR%	R	RBI	BB	SO	SB	Pinch Hit AB	Pinch Hit H	PO	A	E	DP	TC/G	FA	G by Pos
1966	**MIN A**	3	.200	.200	5	1	0	0	0	0.0	1	0	0	0	0	0	0	13	0	0	0	4.3	1.000	C-3
1968		11	.206	.235	34	7	1	0	0	0.0	1	1	3	8	0	1	0	69	4	3	0	7.6	.961	C-10
1969		69	.257	.380	187	48	8	0	5	2.7	18	13	17	47	0	6	1	340	33	5	6	5.9	.987	C-63, OF-1
1970		117	.222	.388	369	82	12	2	15	4.1	36	46	34	84	3	1	0	740	62	3	8	6.9	.996	C-117
1971		125	.250	.389	388	97	13	1	13	3.4	38	44	39	104	3	7	2	656	53	10	7	6.0	.986	C-120
1972		64	.184	.239	163	30	4	1	1	0.6	12	8	9	37	0	4	1	272	33	5	4	5.1	.984	C-61
1973		125	.259	.405	432	112	15	0	16	3.7	50	64	39	111	3	3	0	676	59	6	6	5.9	.992	C-122, DH-3
1974	**CHI N**	78	.251	.381	215	54	7	0	7	3.3	17	28	18	42	1	11	3	335	40	10	4	5.7	.974	C-68
1975		84	.220	.345	200	44	4	3	5	2.5	19	26	19	42	0	15	3	315	38	8	10	5.2	.978	C-59, 1B-10
1976		101	.215	.287	303	65	7	0	5	1.7	19	28	16	63	1	16	1	512	50	8	13	6.4	.986	C-64, 1B-25
1977		110	.238	.378	349	83	22	0	9	2.6	40	43	28	69	3	2	0	623	78	8	13	6.4	.989	C-109, 1B-1
11 yrs.		887	.236	.362	2645	623	93	7	76	2.9	251	301	222	607	14	66	11	4551	450	66	71	6.1	.987	C-796, 1B-36, DH-3, OF-1
LEAGUE CHAMPIONSHIP SERIES																								
1969	**MIN A**	2	.143	.143	7	1	0	0	0	0.0	0	0	1	3	0	0	0	10	4	0	0	7.0	1.000	C-2
1970		3	.500	.625	8	4	1	0	0	0.0	2	2	0	2	0	0	0	16	1	0	2	8.5	1.000	C-2
2 yrs.		5	.333	.400	15	5	1	0	0	0.0	2	2	1	5	0	0	0	26	5	0	2	7.8	1.000	C-4

Johnny Mize

MIZE, JOHN ROBERT (The Big Cat) BL TR 6′ 2″ 215 lbs.
B. Jan. 7, 1913, Demorest, Ga. D. June 2, 1993, Demorest, Ga.
Hall of Fame 1981.

Year	Team	Games	BA	SA	AB	H	2B	3B	HR	HR%	R	RBI	BB	SO	SB	Pinch Hit AB	Pinch Hit H	PO	A	E	DP	TC/G	FA	G by Pos
1936	**STL N**	126	.329	.577	414	136	30	8	19	4.6	76	93	50	32	1	15	7	909	67	6	63	9.4	.994	1B-97, OF-8
1937		145	.364	.595	560	204	40	7	25	4.5	103	113	56	57	2	1	0	1308	67	17	104	9.7	.988	1B-144
1938		149	.337	**.614**	531	179	34	**16**	27	5.1	85	102	74	47	0	7	1	1297	93	15	117	10.0	.989	1B-140
1939		153	**.349**	**.626**	564	197	44	14	**28**	5.0	104	108	92	49	0	1	0	1348	90	19	123	9.6	.987	1B-152
1940		155	.314	**.636**	579	182	31	13	**43**	**7.4**	111	**137**	82	49	7	2	1	1376	80	14	105	9.6	.990	1B-153
1941		126	.317	.535	473	150	**39**	8	16	3.4	67	100	70	45	4	4	1	1157	82	8	104	10.2	.994	1B-122
1942	**NY N**	142	.305	**.521**	541	165	25	7	26	4.8	97	**110**	60	39	3	3	0	1393	74	8	98	10.7	.995	1B-138
1946		101	.337	.576	377	127	18	3	22	5.8	70	70	62	26	3	0	0	928	83	11	80	10.1	.989	1B-101
1947		154	.302	.614	586	177	26	2	**51**	8.7	**137**	**138**	74	42	2	0	0	1380	117	6	120	9.8	.996	1B-154
1948		152	.289	.564	560	162	26	4	**40**	7.1	110	125	94	37	4	0	0	1359	111	13	114	9.8	.991	1B-152
1949	**2 teams**	**NY N** (106G –.263)		**NY A** (13G –.261)																				
"	**total**	119	.263	.440	411	108	16	0	19	4.6	63	64	54	21	1	8	2	953	68	7	82	9.6	.993	1B-107
1950	**NY A**	90	.277	.595	274	76	12	0	25	9.1	43	72	29	24	0	16	3	490	31	2	73	7.3	.996	1B-72
1951		113	.259	.398	332	86	14	1	10	3.0	37	49	36	24	1	21	**9**	632	44	4	86	7.3	.994	1B-93
1952		78	.263	.416	137	36	9	0	4	2.9	9	29	11	15	0	48	**10**	218	18	3	32	8.9	.987	1B-27
1953		81	.250	.394	104	26	3	0	4	3.8	6	27	12	17	0	**61**	**19**	113	7	0	19	8.0	1.000	1B-15
15 yrs.		1884	.312	.562 **8th**	6443	2011	367	83	359	5.6	1118	1337	856	524	28	187	53	14861	1032	133	1320	9.6	.992	1B-1667, OF-8
WORLD SERIES																								
1949	**NY A**	2	1.000	1.000	2	2	0	0	0	0.0	0	2	0	0	0	2	2	0	0	0	0	0.0	—	
1950		4	.133	.133	15	2	0	0	0	0.0	0	0	0	1	0	0	0	27	3	0	2	7.5	1.000	1B-4
1951		4	.286	.429	7	2	1	0	0	0.0	2	1	2	0	0	2	0	12	0	0	4	6.0	1.000	1B-2
1952		5	.400	1.067	15	6	1	0	3	20.0	3	6	3	1	0	1	1	25	3	0	4	7.0	1.000	1B-4
1953		3	.000	.000	3	0	0	0	0	0.0	0	0	0	1	0	3	0	0	0	0	0	0.0	—	
5 yrs.		18	.286	.548	42	12	2	0	3	7.1	5	9	5	3	0	8	3	64	6	0	10	7.0	1.000	1B-10

John Mizerock

MIZEROCK, JOHN JOSEPH BL TR 6′ 180 lbs.
B. Dec. 8, 1960, Punxsutawney, Pa.

Year	Team	Games	BA	SA	AB	H	2B	3B	HR	HR%	R	RBI	BB	SO	SB	Pinch Hit AB	Pinch Hit H	PO	A	E	DP	TC/G	FA	G by Pos
1983	**HOU N**	33	.153	.259	85	13	4	1	1	1.2	8	10	12	15	0	0	0	154	24	6	5	5.6	.967	C-33
1985		15	.237	.342	38	9	4	0	0	0.0	6	6	2	8	0	0	0	77	8	3	1	5.9	.966	C-15
1986		44	.185	.259	81	15	1	1	1	1.2	9	6	24	16	0	3	0	221	12	3	0	5.6	.987	C-42
1989	**ATL N**	11	.222	.222	27	6	0	0	0	0.0	1	2	0	3	0	0	0	48	4	0	0	4.7	1.000	C-11
4 yrs.		103	.186	.268	231	43	9	2	2	0.9	24	24	38	42	0	3	0	500	48	12	6	5.5	.979	C-101

Bill Mizeur

MIZEUR, WILLIAM FRANCIS (Bad Bill) BL TR 6′ 180 lbs.
B. June 22, 1897, Nokomis, Ill. D. Aug. 27, 1976, Decatur, Ill.

Year	Team	Games	BA	SA	AB	H	2B	3B	HR	HR%	R	RBI	BB	SO	SB	Pinch Hit AB	Pinch Hit H	PO	A	E	DP	TC/G	FA	G by Pos
1923	**STL A**	1	.000	.000	1	0	0	0	0	0.0	0	0	0	0	0	1	0	0	0	0	0	0.0	—	
1924		1	.000	.000	1	0	0	0	0	0.0	0	0	0	0	0	1	0	0	0	0	0	0.0	—	
2 yrs.		2	.000	.000	2	0	0	0	0	0.0	0	0	0	0	0	2	0							

Dave Moates

MOATES, DAVID ALLEN BL TL 5′ 9″ 163 lbs.
B. Jan. 30, 1948, Great Lakes, Ill.

Year	Team	Games	BA	SA	AB	H	2B	3B	HR	HR%	R	RBI	BB	SO	SB	Pinch Hit AB	Pinch Hit H	PO	A	E	DP	TC/G	FA	G by Pos
1974	**TEX A**	1	—	—	0	0	0	0	0	—	0	0	0	0	0	0	0	0	0	0	0	0.0	—	
1975		54	.274	.377	175	48	9	0	3	1.7	21	14	13	15	9	0	0	114	6	2	1	2.3	.984	OF-51, DH-1
1976		85	.241	.307	137	33	7	1	0	0.0	21	13	11	18	6	7	3	106	4	1	2	1.5	.991	OF-66, DH-7
3 yrs.		140	.260	.346	312	81	16	1	3	1.0	42	27	24	33	15	7	3	220	10	3	3	1.9	.987	OF-117, DH-8

Danny Moeller

MOELLER, DANIEL EDWARD BB TR 5′11″ 165 lbs.
B. Mar. 23, 1885, DeWitt, Iowa D. Apr. 14, 1951, Florence, Ala.

Year	Team	Games	BA	SA	AB	H	2B	3B	HR	HR%	R	RBI	BB	SO	SB	Pinch Hit AB	Pinch Hit H	PO	A	E	DP	TC/G	FA	G by Pos
1907	**PIT N**	11	.286	.357	42	12	1	1	0	0.0	4	3	4		2	0	0	11	1	3	1	1.4	.800	OF-11
1908		36	.193	.239	109	21	3	1	0	0.0	14	9	9		4	7	0	38	0	2	0	1.5	.950	OF-27
1912	**WAS A**	132	.276	.399	519	143	26	10	6	1.2	90	46	52		30	0	0	227	25	15	5	2.0	.944	OF-132
1913		153	.236	.321	589	139	15	10	5	0.8	88	42	72	**103**	62	0	0	249	27	22	4	1.9	.926	OF-153
1914		151	.250	.324	571	143	19	10	1	0.2	83	45	71	89	26	1	0	208	19	17	4	1.6	.930	OF-150
1915		118	.226	.311	438	99	11	10	2	0.5	65	23	59	63	32	1	0	167	13	9	6	1.6	.952	OF-116
1916	**2 teams**	**WAS A** (78G –.246)	**CLE A** (25G –.067)																					
″	**total**	103	.226	.274	270	61	8	1	1	0.4	35	24	35	41	15	21	4	105	13	4	4	1.6	.967	OF-73, 2B-1
7 yrs.		704	.243	.328	2538	618	83	43	15	0.6	379	192	302	296	171	30	4	1005	98	72	24	1.8	.939	OF-662, 2B-1

Joe Moffett

MOFFETT, JOSEPH W. 6′ 179 lbs.
Brother of Sam Moffett.
B. June 1859, Wheeling, W. Va. Deceased.

Year	Team	Games	BA	SA	AB	H	2B	3B	HR	HR%	R	RBI	BB	SO	SB	Pinch Hit AB	Pinch Hit H	PO	A	E	DP	TC/G	FA	G by Pos
1884	**TOL AA**	56	.201	.255	204	41	5	3	0	0.0	17		2			0	0	421	42	33	23	8.9	.933	1B-38, 3B-12, OF-3, 2B-3

Sam Moffett

MOFFETT, SAMUEL R. BR TR 6′ 175 lbs.
Brother of Joe Moffett.
B. Mar. 14, 1857, Wheeling, W. Va. D. May 5, 1907, Butte, Mont.

Year	Team	Games	BA	SA	AB	H	2B	3B	HR	HR%	R	RBI	BB	SO	SB	Pinch Hit AB	Pinch Hit H	PO	A	E	DP	TC/G	FA	G by Pos
1884	**CLE N**	67	.184	.246	256	47	12	2	0	0.0	26	14	8	56		0	0	102	68	23	4	2.8	.881	OF-42, P-24, 1B-2, 3B-1, 2B-1
1887	**IND N**	11	.122	.146	41	5	1	0	0	0.0	6	1	1	6	2	0	0	8	7	3	0	1.6	.833	P-6, OF-5
1888		10	.114	.114	35	4	0	0	0	0.0	6	0	5	4	0	0	0	4	5	3	1	1.2	.750	P-7, OF-3
3 yrs.		88	.169	.220	332	56	13	2	0	0.0	38	15	14	66	2	0	0	114	80	29	5	2.5	.870	OF-50, P-37, 1B-2, 3B-1, 2B-1

John Mohardt

MOHARDT, JOHN HENRY BR TR 5′10″ 165 lbs.
B. Jan. 21, 1898, Pittsburgh, Pa. D. Nov. 24, 1961, La Jolla, Calif.

Year	Team	Games	BA	SA	AB	H	2B	3B	HR	HR%	R	RBI	BB	SO	SB	Pinch Hit AB	Pinch Hit H	PO	A	E	DP	TC/G	FA	G by Pos
1922	**DET A**	5	1.000	1.000	1	1	0	0	0	0.0	2	0	1	0	0	0	0	1	0	0	0	0.3	1.000	OF-3

Kid Mohler

MOHLER, ERNEST FOLLETTE BL TL 5′ 4½″ 145 lbs.
B. Dec. 13, 1874, Oneida, Ill. D. Nov. 4, 1961, San Francisco, Calif.

Year	Team	Games	BA	SA	AB	H	2B	3B	HR	HR%	R	RBI	BB	SO	SB	Pinch Hit AB	Pinch Hit H	PO	A	E	DP	TC/G	FA	G by Pos
1894	**WAS N**	3	.111	.111	9	1	0	0	0	0.0	0	0	2	4	0	0	0	10	10	1	1	7.0	.952	2B-3

Johnny Mokan

MOKAN, JOHN LEO BR TR 5′ 7″ 165 lbs.
B. Sept. 23, 1895, Buffalo, N. Y. D. Feb. 10, 1985, Buffalo, N. Y.

Year	Team	Games	BA	SA	AB	H	2B	3B	HR	HR%	R	RBI	BB	SO	SB	Pinch Hit AB	Pinch Hit H	PO	A	E	DP	TC/G	FA	G by Pos
1921	**PIT N**	19	.269	.404	52	14	3	2	0	0.0	7	9	5	3	0	3	0	35	0	2	0	2.8	.946	OF-13
1922	**2 teams**	**PIT N** (31G –.258)	**PHI N** (47G –.252)																					
″	**total**	78	.254	.350	240	61	10	2	3	1.3	29	35	25	28	1	14	3	90	9	11	3	2.0	.900	OF-54, 3B-2
1923	**PHI N**	113	.313	.460	400	125	23	3	10	2.5	76	48	53	31	6	6	1	237	19	8	0	2.5	.970	OF-105, 3B-1
1924		96	.260	.363	366	95	15	1	7	1.9	50	44	30	27	7	2	1	195	9	3	1	2.2	.986	OF-94
1925		75	.330	.488	209	69	11	2	6	2.9	30	42	27	9	3	6	1	120	1	2	0	1.8	.984	OF-68
1926		127	.303	.414	456	138	23	5	6	1.3	68	62	41	31	4	2	1	221	16	8	4	2.0	.967	OF-123
1927		74	.286	.366	213	61	13	2	0	0.0	22	33	25	21	5	9	2	97	5	4	0	1.7	.962	OF-63
7 yrs.		582	.291	.409	1936	563	98	17	32	1.7	282	273	206	150	26	42	9	995	59	38	8	2.1	.965	OF-520, 3B-3

Fenton Mole

MOLE, FENTON LeROY (Muscles) BL TL 6′ 1½″ 200 lbs.
B. June 14, 1925, San Leandro, Calif.

Year	Team	Games	BA	SA	AB	H	2B	3B	HR	HR%	R	RBI	BB	SO	SB	Pinch Hit AB	Pinch Hit H	PO	A	E	DP	TC/G	FA	G by Pos
1949	**NY A**	10	.185	.333	27	5	2	1	0	0.0	2	2	3	5	0	2	1	59	6	0	12	8.1	1.000	1B-8

Bob Molinaro

MOLINARO, ROBERT JOSEPH (Molly) BL TR 6′ 180 lbs.
B. May 21, 1950, Newark, N. J.

Year	Team	Games	BA	SA	AB	H	2B	3B	HR	HR%	R	RBI	BB	SO	SB	Pinch Hit AB	Pinch Hit H	PO	A	E	DP	TC/G	FA	G by Pos
1975	**DET A**	6	.263	.368	19	5	0	1	0	0.0	2	1	1	0	0	0	0	8	1	0	0	1.5	1.000	OF-6
1977	**2 teams**	**DET A** (4G –.250)	**CHI A** (1G –.500)																					
″	**total**	5	.333	.500	6	2	1	0	0	0.0	0	0	0	3	1	4	1	1	0	0	0	1.0	1.000	OF-1
1978	**CHI A**	105	.262	.378	286	75	5	5	6	2.1	39	27	19	12	22	12	4	88	2	0	0	1.0	1.000	OF-62, DH-32
1979	**BAL A**	8	.000	.000	6	0	0	0	0	0.0	0	0	1	3	1	1	0	7	0	0	0	1.4	1.000	OF-5
1980	**CHI A**	119	.291	.404	344	100	16	4	5	1.5	48	36	26	29	18	21	7	85	3	4	0	1.0	.957	OF-49, DH-47
1981		47	.262	.405	42	11	1	1	1	2.4	7	9	8	1	1	**35**	**9**	3	0	0	0	0.5	1.000	DH-4, OF-2
1982	**2 teams**	**CHI N** (65G –.197)	**PHI N** (19G –.286)																					
″	**total**	84	.213	.262	80	17	1	0	1	1.3	6	14	9	6	2	**67**	14	2	0	0	0	0.5	1.000	OF-4
1983	**2 teams**	**PHI N** (19G –.111)	**DET A** (8G –.000)																					
″	**total**	27	.100	.300	20	2	1	0	1	5.0	4	3	1	3	1	20	2	0	0	0	0	0.0	.000	DH-1
8 yrs.		401	.264	.375	803	212	25	11	14	1.7	106	90	65	57	46	160	37	194	6	4	0	1.0	.980	OF-129, DH-84

Paul Molitor

MOLITOR, PAUL LEO BR TR 6′ 185 lbs.
B. Aug. 22, 1956, St. Paul, Minn.

Year	Team	Games	BA	SA	AB	H	2B	3B	HR	HR%	R	RBI	BB	SO	SB	Pinch Hit AB	Pinch Hit H	PO	A	E	DP	TC/G	FA	G by Pos
1978	**MIL A**	125	.273	.372	521	142	26	4	6	1.2	73	45	19	54	30	3	0	253	401	22	74	5.4	.967	2B-91, SS-31, DH-2, 3B-1
1979		140	.322	.469	584	188	27	16	9	1.5	88	62	48	48	33	2	0	309	440	16	84	5.5	.979	2B-122, SS-10, DH-8
1980		111	.304	.438	450	137	29	2	9	2.0	81	37	48	48	34	2	1	260	336	20	90	5.5	.968	2B-91, SS-12, DH-7, 3B-1
1981		64	.267	.335	251	67	11	0	2	0.8	45	19	25	29	10	1	0	119	4	3	1	2.0	.976	OF-46, DH-16
1982		160	.302	.450	**666**	201	26	8	19	2.9	**136**	71	69	93	41	0	0	134	350	32	48	3.2	.938	3B-150, DH-6, SS-4
1983		152	.270	.410	608	164	28	6	15	2.5	95	47	59	74	41	2	0	105	343	16	37	3.1	.966	3B-146, DH-2
1984		13	.217	.239	46	10	1	0	0	0.0	3	6	2	8	1	2	0	7	21	2	3	2.7	.933	3B-7, DH-4
1985		140	.297	.408	576	171	28	3	10	1.7	93	48	54	80	21	1	0	126	263	19	30	2.9	.953	3B-135, DH-4
1986		105	.281	.426	437	123	24	6	9	2.1	62	55	40	81	20	0	0	86	171	15	25	2.6	.945	3B-91, DH-10, OF-4
1987		118	.353	.566	465	164	**41**	5	16	3.4	**114**	75	69	67	45	1	0	60	113	5	24	1.5	.972	DH-58, 3B-41, 2B-19
1988		154	.312	.452	609	190	34	6	13	2.1	115	60	71	54	41	0	0	87	188	17	15	1.9	.942	3B-105, DH-49, 2B-1
1989		155	.315	.439	615	194	35	4	11	1.8	84	56	64	67	27	0	0	106	287	18	27	2.6	.956	3B-112, DH-28, 2B-16
1990		103	.285	.464	418	119	27	6	12	2.9	64	45	37	51	18	1	0	463	222	10	65	6.7	.986	2B-60, 1B-37, DH-4, 3B-2
1991		158	.325	.489	**665**	**216**	32	**13**	17	2.6	**133**	75	77	62	19	0	0	389	32	6	52	2.7	.986	DH-112, 1B-46
1992		158	.320	.461	609	195	36	7	12	2.0	89	89	73	66	31	2	0	461	26	2	44	3.1	.996	DH-108, 1B-48

Paul Molitor *continued*

Year	Team	Games	BA	SA	AB	H	2B	3B	HR	HR%	R	RBI	BB	SO	SB	Pinch Hit AB	Pinch Hit H	PO	A	E	DP	TC/G	FA	G by Pos
1993	TOR A	160	.332	.509	636	**211**	37	5	22	3.5	121	111	77	71	22	0	0	178	14	3	16	1.2	.985	DH-137, 1B-23
1994		115	.341	.518	454	155	30	4	14	3.1	86	75	55	48	20	0	0	47	3	0	6	0.4	1.000	DH-110, 1B-5
1995		130	.270	.423	525	142	31	2	15	2.9	63	60	61	57	12	0	0	0	0	0	0	0.0	.000	DH-129
18 yrs.		2261	.305	.451	9135	2789	503	97	211	2.3	1545	1036	948	1058	466	17	1	3190	3214	206	641	2.9	.969	DH-794, 3B-791, 2B-400, 1B-159, SS-57, OF-50
DIVISIONAL PLAYOFF SERIES																								
1981	MIL A	5	.250	.400	20	5	0	0	1	5.0	2	1	2	5	0	0	0	12	0	0	0	2.4	1.000	OF-5
LEAGUE CHAMPIONSHIP SERIES																								
1982	MIL A	5	.316	.684	19	6	1	0	2	10.5	4	5	2	3	1	0	0	4	11	2	2	3.4	.882	3B-5
1993	TOR A	6	.391	.696	23	9	2	1	1	4.3	7	5	3	3	0	0	0	0	0	0	0	0.0	.000	DH-6
2 yrs.		11	.357	.690	42	15	3	1	3	7.1	11	10	5	6	1	0	0	4	11	2	2	1.5	.882	DH-6, 3B-5
WORLD SERIES																								
1982	MIL A	7	.355	.355	31	11	0	0	0	0.0	5	2	2	4	1	0	0	4	9	0	1	1.9	1.000	3B-7
1993	TOR A	6	.500	1.000	24	12	2	2	2	8.3	10	8	3	0	1	0	0	7	3	0	2	1.7	1.000	DH-3, 3B-2, 1B-1
2 yrs.		13	.418	.636	55	23	2	2	2	3.6	15	10	5	4	2	0	0	11	12	0	3	1.8	1.000	3B-9, DH-3, 1B-1
			1st	**7th**																				

Fred Mollenkamp

MOLLENKAMP, FREDERICK HENRY
B. Mar. 15, 1890, Cincinnati, Ohio D. Nov. 1, 1948, Cincinnati, Ohio.

Year	Team	Games	BA	SA	AB	H	2B	3B	HR	HR%	R	RBI	BB	SO	SB	Pinch Hit AB	Pinch Hit H	PO	A	E	DP	TC/G	FA	G by Pos
1914	PHI N	3	.125	.125	8	1	0	0	0	0.0	0	0	2	0	0	0	0	23	5	0	2	9.3	1.000	1B-3

Fritz Mollwitz

MOLLWITZ, FREDERICK AUGUST (Zip) BR TR 6′ 2″ 170 lbs.
B. June 16, 1890, Koburg, Germany D. Oct. 3, 1967, Bradenton, Fla.

Year	Team	Games	BA	SA	AB	H	2B	3B	HR	HR%	R	RBI	BB	SO	SB	Pinch Hit AB	Pinch Hit H	PO	A	E	DP	TC/G	FA	G by Pos
1913	CHI N	2	.429	.429	7	3	0	0	0	0.0	1	0	0	0	0	0	0	19	0	0	0	9.5	1.000	1B-2
1914	2 teams	CHI N (13G –.150) CIN N (32G –.162)																						
″	total	45	.160	.176	131	21	2	0	0	0.0	12	6	3	12	3	6	0	339	21	4	19	9.8	.989	1B-36, OF-1
1915	CIN N	153	.259	.316	525	136	21	3	1	0.2	36	51	15	49	19	0	0	1545	79	7	107	10.7	.996	1B-153
1916	2 teams	CIN N (65G –.224) CHI N (33G –.268)																						
″	total	98	.236	.291	254	60	6	4	0	0.0	13	27	12	18	10	20	5	606	30	14	35	8.2	.978	1B-73, OF-6
1917	PIT N	36	.257	.300	140	36	4	1	0	0.0	15	12	8	8	4	0	0	341	17	2	16	9.7	.994	1B-36, 2B-1
1918		119	.269	.329	432	116	12	7	0	0.0	43	45	23	24	23	0	0	1252	73	13	67	11.2	.990	1B-119
1919	2 teams	PIT N (56G –.173) STL N (25G –.229)																						
″	total	81	.191	.243	251	48	5	4	0	0.0	18	17	22	21	11	2	1	778	34	5	41	10.3	.994	1B-77, OF-2
7 yrs.		534	.241	.294	1740	420	50	19	1	0.1	138	158	83	132	70	28	6	4880	254	45	285	10.2	.991	1B-496, OF-9, 2B-1

Blas Monaco

MONACO, BLAS BB TR 5′11″ 170 lbs.
B. Nov. 16, 1915, San Antonio, Tex.

Year	Team	Games	BA	SA	AB	H	2B	3B	HR	HR%	R	RBI	BB	SO	SB	Pinch Hit AB	Pinch Hit H	PO	A	E	DP	TC/G	FA	G by Pos
1937	CLE A	5	.286	.571	7	2	0	1	0	0.0	0	2	0	2	0	2	1	4	5	0	0	3.0	1.000	2B-3
1946		12	.000	.000	6	0	0	0	0	0.0	2	0	1	1	0	6	0	0	0	0	0	0.0	—	
2 yrs.		17	.154	.308	13	2	0	1	0	0.0	2	2	1	3	0	8	1	4	5	0	0	3.0	1.000	2B-3

Freddie Moncewicz

MONCEWICZ, FREDERICK ALFRED BR TR 5′ 8½″ 175 lbs.
B. Sept. 1, 1903, Brockton, Mass. D. Apr. 23, 1969, Brockton, Mass.

Year	Team	Games	BA	SA	AB	H	2B	3B	HR	HR%	R	RBI	BB	SO	SB	Pinch Hit AB	Pinch Hit H	PO	A	E	DP	TC/G	FA	G by Pos
1928	BOS A	3	.000	.000	1	0	0	0	0	0.0	0	0	0	1	0	0	0	1	1	0	0	1.0	1.000	SS-2

Al Monchak

MONCHAK, ALEX BR TR 6′ 180 lbs.
B. Mar. 5, 1917, Bayonne, N. J.

Year	Team	Games	BA	SA	AB	H	2B	3B	HR	HR%	R	RBI	BB	SO	SB	Pinch Hit AB	Pinch Hit H	PO	A	E	DP	TC/G	FA	G by Pos
1940	PHI N	19	.143	.143	14	2	0	0	0	0.0	1	0	0	6	1	1	0	5	5	2	1	1.2	.833	SS-9, 2B-1

Rick Monday

MONDAY, ROBERT JAMES BL TL 6′ 3″ 195 lbs.
B. Nov. 20, 1945, Batesville, Ark.

Year	Team	Games	BA	SA	AB	H	2B	3B	HR	HR%	R	RBI	BB	SO	SB	Pinch Hit AB	Pinch Hit H	PO	A	E	DP	TC/G	FA	G by Pos
1966	KC A	17	.098	.171	41	4	1	1	0	0.0	4	2	6	16	1	1	0	26	1	1	0	1.9	.964	OF-15
1967		124	.251	.419	406	102	14	6	14	3.4	52	58	42	107	3	13	2	260	14	8	6	2.5	.972	OF-113
1968	OAK A	148	.274	.402	482	132	24	7	8	1.7	56	49	72	143	14	6	2	299	11	7	3	2.2	.978	OF-144
1969		122	.271	.424	399	108	17	4	12	3.0	57	54	72	100	12	5	1	262	3	10	0	2.3	.964	OF-119
1970		112	.290	.457	376	109	19	7	10	2.7	63	37	58	99	17	1	0	257	3	5	2	2.4	.981	OF-109
1971		116	.245	.439	355	87	9	3	18	5.1	53	56	49	93	6	7	2	238	6	4	1	2.2	.984	OF-111
1972	CHI N	138	.249	.399	434	108	22	5	11	2.5	68	42	78	102	12	3	0	268	6	1	2	2.1	.996	OF-134
1973		149	.267	.469	554	148	24	5	26	4.7	93	56	92	124	5	3	1	317	9	9	2	2.3	.973	OF-148
1974		142	.294	.467	538	158	19	7	20	3.7	84	58	70	94	7	4	0	302	10	5	5	2.3	.984	OF-139
1975		136	.267	.446	491	131	29	4	17	3.5	89	60	83	95	8	4	1	315	6	9	0	2.5	.973	OF-131
1976		137	.272	.507	534	145	20	5	32	6.0	107	77	60	125	5	4	1	587	26	5	17	4.6	.992	OF-103, 1B-32
1977	LA N	118	.230	.383	392	90	13	1	15	3.8	47	48	60	109	1	6	0	221	5	2	0	1.9	.991	OF-115, 1B-3
1978		119	.254	.468	342	87	14	1	19	5.6	54	57	49	100	2	16	2	217	3	1	1	2.1	.995	OF-103, 1B-1
1979		12	.303	.303	33	10	0	0	0	0.0	2	2	5	6	0	1	1	27	0	1	0	2.8	.964	OF-10
1980		96	.268	.469	194	52	7	1	10	5.2	35	25	28	49	2	36	8	92	1	3	0	1.9	.969	OF-50
1981		66	.315	.608	130	41	1	2	11	8.5	24	25	24	42	1	23	8	50	1	2	0	1.3	.962	OF-41
1982		104	.257	.481	210	54	6	4	11	5.2	37	42	39	51	2	35	4	86	7	4	2	1.6	.959	OF-57, 1B-4
1983		99	.247	.399	178	44	7	1	6	3.4	21	20	29	42	0	42	8	80	2	3	1	1.8	.965	OF-44, 1B-4
1984		31	.191	.298	47	9	2	0	1	2.1	4	7	8	16	0	17	3	74	4	1	3	6.6	.987	1B-10, OF-2
19 yrs.		1986	.264	.443	6136	1619	248	64	241	3.9	950	775	924	1513	98	227	44	3978	118	81	45	2.4	.981	OF-1688, 1B-54
DIVISIONAL PLAYOFF SERIES																								
1981	LA N	5	.214	.214	14	3	0	0	0	0.0	1	1	2	4	0	0	0	12	0	0	0	2.4	1.000	OF-5
LEAGUE CHAMPIONSHIP SERIES																								
1971	OAK A	1	.000	.000	3	0	0	0	0	0.0	0	0	1	2	0	0	0	4	0	0	0	4.0	1.000	OF-1
1977	LA N	3	.286	.429	7	2	1	0	0	0.0	1	0	2	1	0	1	0	6	0	0	0	2.0	1.000	OF-3
1978		3	.200	.400	10	2	0	1	0	0.0	2	0	1	5	0	1	0	6	0	0	0	2.0	1.000	OF-3
1981		3	.333	.667	9	3	0	0	1	11.1	2	1	0	4	0	1	0	2	0	0	0	1.0	1.000	OF-2
1983		1	—	—	0	0	0	0	0	—	0	0	0	0	0	0	0	0	0	0	0	0.0	—	
5 yrs.		11	.241	.448	29	7	1	1	1	3.4	5	1	4	12	0	3	0	18	0	0	0	2.0	1.000	OF-9

Rick Monday *continued*

Year	Team	Games	BA	SA	AB	H	2B	3B	HR	HR%	R	RBI	BB	SO	SB	Pinch Hit AB	Pinch Hit H	PO	A	E	DP	TC/G	FA	G by Pos
WORLD SERIES																								
1977	LA N	4	.167	.167	12	2	0	0	0	0.0	0	0	0	3	0	0	0	5	0	0	0	1.3	1.000	OF-4
1978		5	.154	.231	13	2	1	0	0	0.0	2	0	4	3	0	0	0	5	0	0	0	1.0	1.000	OF-4, DH-1
1981		5	.231	.308	13	3	1	0	0	0.0	1	0	3	6	0	1	0	9	0	0	0	2.3	1.000	OF-4
3 yrs.		14	.184	.237	38	7	2	0	0	0.0	3	0	7	12	0	1	0	19	0	0	0	1.5	1.000	OF-12, DH-1

Raul Mondesi

MONDESI, RAUL RAMON BR TR 5′11″ 202 lbs.
Born Raul Ramon Mondesi (Avelino).
B. Mar. 12, 1971, San Cristobal, Dominican Republic.

Year	Team	Games	BA	SA	AB	H	2B	3B	HR	HR%	R	RBI	BB	SO	SB	Pinch Hit AB	Pinch Hit H	PO	A	E	DP	TC/G	FA	G by Pos
1993	LA N	42	.291	.488	86	25	3	1	4	4.7	13	10	4	16	4	7	3	55	3	3	1	1.5	.951	OF-40
1994		112	.306	.516	434	133	27	8	16	3.7	63	56	16	78	11	0	0	206	16	8	1	2.1	.965	OF-112
1995		139	.285	.496	536	153	23	6	26	4.9	91	88	33	96	27	1	0	281	16	6	2	2.2	.980	OF-138
3 yrs.		293	.295	.504	1056	311	53	15	46	4.4	167	154	53	190	42	8	3	542	35	17	4	2.0	.971	OF-290
DIVISIONAL PLAYOFF SERIES																								
1995	LA N	3	.222	.222	9	2	0	0	0	0.0	0	1	0	2	0	0	0	8	0	0	0	2.7	1.000	OF-3

Don Money

MONEY, DONALD WAYNE (Brooks) BR TR 6′ 1″ 170 lbs.
B. June 7, 1947, Washington, D. C.

Year	Team	Games	BA	SA	AB	H	2B	3B	HR	HR%	R	RBI	BB	SO	SB	Pinch Hit AB	Pinch Hit H	PO	A	E	DP	TC/G	FA	G by Pos
1968	PHI N	4	.231	.385	13	3	2	0	0	0.0	1	2	2	4	0	0	0	6	8	0	3	3.5	1.000	SS-4
1969		127	.229	.327	450	103	22	2	6	1.3	41	42	43	83	1	1	0	212	443	21	82	5.4	.969	SS-126
1970		120	.295	.463	447	132	25	4	14	3.1	66	66	43	68	4	0	0	133	236	15	28	3.2	.961	3B-119, SS-2
1971		121	.223	.358	439	98	22	8	7	1.6	40	38	31	80	4	5	1	167	197	11	21	2.9	.971	3B-68, OF-40, 2B-20
1972		152	.222	.343	536	119	16	2	15	2.8	54	52	41	92	5	1	0	140	316	10	31	3.0	.979	3B-151, SS-2
1973	MIL A	145	.284	.401	556	158	28	2	11	2.0	75	61	53	53	22	2	0	146	276	13	41	3.0	.970	3B-124, SS-21
1974		159	.283	.415	**629**	178	32	3	15	2.4	85	65	62	80	19	0	0	131	336	5	42	3.0	.989	3B-157, DH-1, 2B-1
1975		109	.277	.432	405	112	16	1	15	3.7	58	43	31	51	7	5	1	109	194	15	24	3.0	.953	3B-99, SS-7
1976		117	.267	.408	439	117	18	4	12	2.7	51	62	47	50	6	8	1	96	202	13	21	2.7	.958	3B-103, DH-10, SS-1
1977		152	.279	.470	570	159	28	3	25	4.4	86	83	57	70	8	2	2	306	390	16	83	4.4	.978	2B-116, OF-23, 3B-15, DH-7
1978		137	.293	.440	518	152	30	2	14	2.7	88	54	48	70	3	5	2	705	216	9	88	6.7	.990	1B-61, 2B-36, 3B-25, DH-15, SS-2
1979		92	.237	.351	350	83	20	1	6	1.7	52	38	40	47	1	3	1	240	117	2	33	3.8	.994	DH-33, 3B-26, 1B-19, 2B-16
1980		86	.256	.498	289	74	17	1	17	5.9	39	46	40	36	0	5	2	176	129	12	35	3.7	.962	3B-55, 1B-14, DH-14, 2B-2
1981		60	.216	.286	185	40	7	0	2	1.1	17	14	19	27	0	3	1	33	100	3	9	2.3	.978	3B-56, DH-2, 1B-1
1982		96	.284	.531	275	78	14	3	16	5.8	40	55	32	38	0	21	2	72	49	4	11	1.3	.968	DH-66, 3B-16, 1B-11, 2B-1
1983		43	.149	.219	114	17	5	0	1	0.9	5	8	11	17	0	12	1	25	33	1	2	1.4	.983	DH-28, 3B-11, 1B-2
16 yrs.		1720	.261	.406	6215	1623	302	36	176	2.8	798	729	600	866	80	73	14	2697	3242	150	554	3.5	.975	3B-1025, 2B-192, DH-176, SS-165, 1B-108, OF-63
DIVISIONAL PLAYOFF SERIES																								
1981	MIL A	2	.000	.000	3	0	0	0	0	0.0	0	0	0	0	0	2	0	1	1	0	0	1.0	1.000	2B-1, DH-1
LEAGUE CHAMPIONSHIP SERIES																								
1982	MIL A	4	.182	.182	11	2	0	0	0	0.0	2	1	3	1	0	0	0	0	0	0	0	0.0	.000	DH-4
WORLD SERIES																								
1982	MIL A	5	.231	.308	13	3	1	0	0	0.0	4	1	2	3	0	1	0	0	0	0	0	0.0	.000	DH-4

Frank Monroe

MONROE, FRANK W.
B. Hamilton, Ohio Deceased.

Year	Team	Games	BA	SA	AB	H	2B	3B	HR	HR%	R	RBI	BB	SO	SB	Pinch Hit AB	Pinch Hit H	PO	A	E	DP	TC/G	FA	G by Pos
1884	IND AA	2	.000	.000	8	0	0	0	0	0.0	1		0			0	0	6	1	1	0	4.0	.875	OF-1, C-1

John Monroe

MONROE, JOHN ALLEN BL TR 5′ 8″ 160 lbs.
B. Aug. 24, 1898, Farmersville, Tex. D. June 19, 1956, Conroe, Tex.

Year	Team	Games	BA	SA	AB	H	2B	3B	HR	HR%	R	RBI	BB	SO	SB	Pinch Hit AB	Pinch Hit H	PO	A	E	DP	TC/G	FA	G by Pos
1921	**2 teams**	**NY N** (19G –.143) **PHI N** (41G –.286)																						
″	**total**	60	.266	.357	154	41	4	2	2	1.3	17	11	14	15	2	5	1	81	134	19	12	5.1	.919	2B-36, 3B-9, SS-1

Ed Montague

MONTAGUE, EDWARD FRANCIS BR TR 5′10″ 165 lbs.
B. July 24, 1905, San Francisco, Calif. D. June 17, 1988, Daly City, Calif.

Year	Team	Games	BA	SA	AB	H	2B	3B	HR	HR%	R	RBI	BB	SO	SB	Pinch Hit AB	Pinch Hit H	PO	A	E	DP	TC/G	FA	G by Pos
1928	CLE A	32	.235	.275	51	12	0	1	0	0.0	12	3	6	7	0	1	1	32	45	11	10	3.7	.875	SS-15, 3B-9
1930		58	.263	.330	179	47	5	2	1	0.6	37	16	37	38	1	0	0	97	125	17	20	4.1	.929	SS-46, 3B-13
1931		64	.285	.373	193	55	8	3	1	0.5	27	26	21	22	3	0	0	127	202	27	30	5.6	.924	SS-64
1932		66	.245	.281	192	47	5	1	0	0.0	29	24	21	24	3	0	0	96	142	29	24	3.9	.891	SS-57, 3B-11
4 yrs.		220	.262	.324	615	161	18	7	2	0.3	105	69	85	91	7	1	1	352	514	84	84	4.4	.912	SS-182, 3B-33

Willie Montanez

MONTANEZ, GUILLERMO BL TL 6′ 170 lbs.
Born Guillermo Montanez (Naranjo).
B. Apr. 1, 1948, Catano, Puerto Rico.

Year	Team	Games	BA	SA	AB	H	2B	3B	HR	HR%	R	RBI	BB	SO	SB	Pinch Hit AB	Pinch Hit H	PO	A	E	DP	TC/G	FA	G by Pos
1966	CAL A	8	.000	.000	2	0	0	0	0	0.0	2	0	0	2	1	2	0	1	0	0	1	0.5	1.000	1B-2
1970	PHI N	18	.240	.240	25	6	0	0	0	0.0	3	3	1	4	0	6	3	15	3	0	3	1.2	1.000	OF-10, 1B-5
1971		158	.255	.471	599	153	27	6	30	5.0	78	99	67	105	4	1	1	377	12	11	4	2.4	.973	OF-158, 1B-9
1972		147	.247	.405	531	131	**39**	3	13	2.4	60	64	58	108	1	5	4	429	22	6	18	3.2	.987	OF-130, 1B-14
1973		146	.263	.370	552	145	16	5	11	2.0	69	65	46	80	2	6	3	852	58	6	89	6.1	.993	1B-99, OF-51
1974		143	.304	.410	527	160	33	1	7	1.3	55	79	32	57	3	6	2	1217	79	10	126	9.5	.992	1B-137, OF-1
1975	**2 teams**	**PHI N** (21G –.286) **SF N** (135G –.305)																						
″	**total**	156	.302	.415	602	182	34	2	10	1.7	61	101	49	62	6	2	1	1333	98	10	134	9.3	.993	1B-155
1976	**2 teams**	**SF N** (60G –.309) **ATL N** (103G –.321)																						
″	**total**	163	.317	.418	650	206	29	2	11	1.7	74	84	36	47	2	2	1	1569	107	22	141	10.5	.987	1B-161
1977	ATL N	136	.287	.458	544	156	31	1	20	3.7	70	68	35	60	1	2	1	1129	70	10	88	9.0	.992	1B-134
1978	NY N	159	.256	.392	609	156	32	0	17	2.8	66	96	60	92	9	1	0	1350	104	8	138	9.3	.995	1B-158
1979	**2 teams**	**NY N** (109G –.234) **TEX A** (38G –.319)																						
″	**total**	147	.256	.372	554	142	25	0	13	2.3	55	71	33	62	0	4	1	1096	92	12	109	8.3	.990	1B-127, DH-17
1980	**2 teams**	**SD N** (128G –.274) **MON N** (14G –.211)																						
″	**total**	142	.272	.348	500	136	12	4	6	1.2	40	64	39	55	3	11	3	1214	86	8	105	10.2	.994	1B-128

Willie Montanez *continued*

Year	Team	Games	BA	SA	AB	H	2B	3B	HR	HR%	R	RBI	BB	SO	SB	Pinch Hit AB	Pinch Hit H	PO	A	E	DP	TC/G	FA	G by Pos
1981	2 teams MON N (26G –.177) PIT N (29G –.263)																							
"	total	55	.210	.260	100	21	0	1	1	1.0	8	6	5	11	0	30	9	173	13	1	12	6.9	.995	1B-27
1982	2 teams PIT N (36G –.281) PHI N (18G –.063)																							
"	total	54	.208	.229	48	10	1	0	0	0.0	4	2	4	6	0	43	9	9	3	0	1	1.2	1.000	1B-8, OF-2
14 yrs.		1632	.275	.402	5843	1604	279	25	139	2.4	645	802	465	751	32	121	38	10764	747	104	969	7.6	.991	1B-1164, OF-352, DH-17

Rene Monteagudo

MONTEAGUDO, RENE BL TL 5′ 7″ 165 lbs.
Born Rene Monteagudo (Miranda).
Father of Aurelio Monteagudo.
B. Mar. 12, 1916, Havana, Cuba D. Sept. 14, 1973, Hialeah, Fla.

Year	Team	Games	BA	SA	AB	H	2B	3B	HR	HR%	R	RBI	BB	SO	SB	Pinch Hit AB	Pinch Hit H	PO	A	E	DP	TC/G	FA	G by Pos
1938	WAS A	5	.500	.500	6	3	0	0	0	0.0	0	1	0	0	0	0	0	0	1	0	0	0.2	1.000	P-5
1940		27	.182	.273	33	6	1	1	0	0.0	4	1	1	4	0	0	0	5	11	1	1	0.6	.941	P-27
1944		10	.289	.342	38	11	2	0	0	0.0	2	4	0	1	0	1	1	12	1	1	0	1.6	.929	OF-9
1945	PHI N	114	.301	.332	193	58	6	0	0	0.0	26	15	28	7	2	**52**	**18**	62	12	8	3	1.7	.902	OF-35, P-14
4 yrs.		156	.289	.330	270	78	9	1	0	0.0	32	21	29	12	2	53	19	79	25	10	4	1.3	.912	P-46, OF-44

Felipe Montemayor

MONTEMAYOR, FELIPE ANGEL (Monty) BL TL 6′ 2″ 185 lbs.
B. Feb. 7, 1930, Monterrey, Mexico.

Year	Team	Games	BA	SA	AB	H	2B	3B	HR	HR%	R	RBI	BB	SO	SB	Pinch Hit AB	Pinch Hit H	PO	A	E	DP	TC/G	FA	G by Pos
1953	PIT N	28	.109	.182	55	6	4	0	0	0.0	5	2	4	13	0	13	1	29	2	0	0	2.6	1.000	OF-12
1955		36	.211	.347	95	20	1	3	2	2.1	10	8	18	24	1	8	1	44	0	2	0	1.6	.957	OF-28
2 yrs.		64	.173	.287	150	26	5	3	2	1.3	15	10	22	37	1	21	2	73	2	2	0	1.9	.974	OF-40

Al Montgomery

MONTGOMERY, ALVIN ATLAS BR TR 5′10½″ 185 lbs.
B. July 3, 1920, Loving, N. M. D. Apr. 26, 1942, Waverly, Va.

Year	Team	Games	BA	SA	AB	H	2B	3B	HR	HR%	R	RBI	BB	SO	SB	Pinch Hit AB	Pinch Hit H	PO	A	E	DP	TC/G	FA	G by Pos
1941	BOS N	42	.192	.212	52	10	1	0	0	0.0	4	4	9	8	0	10	0	34	6	1	0	1.4	.976	C-30

Bob Montgomery

MONTGOMERY, ROBERT EDWARD BR TR 6′ 1″ 195 lbs.
B. Apr. 16, 1944, Nashville, Tenn.

Year	Team	Games	BA	SA	AB	H	2B	3B	HR	HR%	R	RBI	BB	SO	SB	Pinch Hit AB	Pinch Hit H	PO	A	E	DP	TC/G	FA	G by Pos
1970	BOS A	22	.179	.244	78	14	2	0	1	1.3	8	4	6	20	0	1	0	143	13	3	3	7.2	.981	C-22
1971		67	.239	.341	205	49	11	2	2	1.0	19	24	16	43	1	2	0	361	15	4	3	5.8	.989	C-66
1972		24	.286	.377	77	22	1	0	2	2.6	7	7	3	17	0	2	1	120	10	2	2	6.0	.985	C-22
1973		34	.320	.563	128	41	6	2	7	5.5	18	25	7	36	0	1	0	168	19	5	2	5.8	.974	C-33
1974		88	.252	.339	254	64	10	0	4	1.6	26	38	13	50	3	5	2	318	28	8	3	4.2	.977	C-79, DH-5
1975		62	.226	.318	195	44	10	1	2	1.0	16	26	4	37	1	3	0	239	25	5	7	4.3	.981	C-53, 1B-6, DH-3
1976		31	.247	.398	93	23	3	1	3	3.2	10	13	5	20	0	1	0	106	12	2	2	3.9	.983	C-30, DH-1
1977		17	.300	.500	40	12	2	0	2	5.0	6	7	4	9	0	2	1	50	6	1	0	3.8	.982	C-15
1978		10	.241	.345	29	7	1	1	0	0.0	2	5	2	12	0	0	0	35	5	1	0	4.1	.976	C-10
1979		32	.349	.419	86	30	4	1	0	0.0	13	7	4	24	1	0	0	121	5	2	0	4.1	.984	C-31
10 yrs.		387	.258	.372	1185	306	50	8	23	1.9	125	156	64	268	6	17	4	1661	138	33	22	4.9	.982	C-361, DH-9, 1B-6
WORLD SERIES																								
1975	BOS A	1	.000	.000	1	0	0	0	0	0.0	0	0	0	0	0	1	0	0	0	0	0	0.0	—	

Charlie Montoyo

MONTOYO, JOSE CARLOS BR TR 5′10″ 170 lbs.
Born Jose Carlos Montoyo (Diaz).
B. Oct. 17, 1965, Florida, Puerto Rico.

Year	Team	Games	BA	SA	AB	H	2B	3B	HR	HR%	R	RBI	BB	SO	SB	Pinch Hit AB	Pinch Hit H	PO	A	E	DP	TC/G	FA	G by Pos
1993	MON N	4	.400	.600	5	2	1	0	0	0.0	1	3	0	0	0	3	1	0	0	0	0	0.0	.000	2B-3

Allan Montreuil

MONTREUIL, ALLAN ARTHUR BR TR 5′ 5″ 158 lbs.
B. Aug. 23, 1943, New Orleans, La.

Year	Team	Games	BA	SA	AB	H	2B	3B	HR	HR%	R	RBI	BB	SO	SB	Pinch Hit AB	Pinch Hit H	PO	A	E	DP	TC/G	FA	G by Pos
1972	CHI N	5	.091	.091	11	1	0	0	0	0.0	0	0	1	4	0	0	0	8	8	0	1	3.2	1.000	2B-5

Danny Monzon

MONZON, DANIEL FRANCISCO BR TR 5′10″ 182 lbs.
B. May 17, 1946, Bronx, N. Y. D. Jan. 21, 1996, Santo Domingo, Dominican Republic.

Year	Team	Games	BA	SA	AB	H	2B	3B	HR	HR%	R	RBI	BB	SO	SB	Pinch Hit AB	Pinch Hit H	PO	A	E	DP	TC/G	FA	G by Pos
1972	MIN A	55	.273	.291	55	15	1	0	0	0.0	13	5	8	12	1	13	1	29	38	1	7	3.1	.985	2B-13, 3B-5, SS-3, OF-1
1973		39	.224	.263	76	17	1	1	0	0.0	10	4	11	9	1	3	0	40	61	6	11	3.3	.944	2B-17, 3B-14, OF-1
2 yrs.		94	.244	.275	131	32	2	1	0	0.0	23	9	19	21	2	16	1	69	99	7	18	3.2	.960	2B-30, 3B-19, SS-3, OF-2

Joe Moock

MOOCK, JOSEPH GEOFFREY BL TR 6′ 1″ 180 lbs.
B. Mar. 12, 1944, Plaquemine, La.

Year	Team	Games	BA	SA	AB	H	2B	3B	HR	HR%	R	RBI	BB	SO	SB	Pinch Hit AB	Pinch Hit H	PO	A	E	DP	TC/G	FA	G by Pos
1967	NY N	13	.225	.275	40	9	2	0	0	0.0	2	5	0	7	0	1	0	10	23	3	3	3.0	.917	3B-12

George Moolic

MOOLIC, GEORGE HENRY (Prunes) BR TR 5′ 7″ 145 lbs.
B. Mar. 12, 1867, Lawrence, Mass. D. Feb. 19, 1915, Methuen, Mass.

Year	Team	Games	BA	SA	AB	H	2B	3B	HR	HR%	R	RBI	BB	SO	SB	Pinch Hit AB	Pinch Hit H	PO	A	E	DP	TC/G	FA	G by Pos
1886	CHI N	16	.143	.196	56	8	3	0	0	0.0	9	2	2	17		0	0	96	25	7	3	7.5	.945	C-15, OF-2

Wally Moon

MOON, WALLACE WADE BL TR 6′ 169 lbs.
B. Apr. 3, 1930, Bay, Ark.

Year	Team	Games	BA	SA	AB	H	2B	3B	HR	HR%	R	RBI	BB	SO	SB	Pinch Hit AB	Pinch Hit H	PO	A	E	DP	TC/G	FA	G by Pos
1954	STL N	151	.304	.435	635	193	29	9	12	1.9	106	76	71	73	18	2	0	387	11	9	2	2.8	.978	OF-148
1955		152	.295	.459	593	175	24	8	19	3.2	86	76	47	65	11	8	2	633	39	12	41	4.5	.982	OF-100, 1B-51
1956		149	.298	.469	540	161	22	11	16	3.0	86	68	80	50	12	0	0	657	55	11	54	4.9	.985	OF-97, 1B-52
1957		142	.295	.508	516	152	28	5	24	4.7	86	73	62	57	5	9	1	245	8	9	1	2.0	.966	OF-133
1958		108	.238	.366	290	69	10	3	7	2.4	36	38	47	30	2	23	2	122	5	2	0	1.6	.984	OF-82
1959	LA N	145	.302	.495	543	164	26	**11**	19	3.5	93	74	81	64	15	3	2	226	13	4	2	1.7	.984	OF-143, 1B-1
1960		138	.299	.452	469	140	21	6	13	2.8	74	69	67	53	6	12	3	194	15	3	3	1.7	.986	OF-127
1961		134	.328	.505	463	152	25	3	17	3.7	79	88	89	79	7	3	0	186	5	6	1	1.5	.970	OF-133
1962		95	.242	.336	244	59	9	1	4	1.6	36	31	30	33	5	32	6	300	20	7	29	4.8	.979	OF-36, 1B-32
1963		122	.262	.382	343	90	13	2	8	2.3	41	48	45	43	5	25	6	125	2	5	0	1.4	.962	OF-96
1964		68	.220	.305	118	26	2	1	2	1.7	8	9	12	22	1	43	8	33	0	0	0	1.4	1.000	OF-23
1965		53	.202	.270	89	18	3	0	1	1.1	6	11	13	22	2	25	5	25	1	0	0	1.1	1.000	OF-23
12 yrs.		1457	.289	.445	4843	1399	212	60	142	2.9	737	661	644	591	89	185	35	3133	174	68	133	2.6	.980	OF-1141, 1B-136

Wally Moon *continued*

Year	Team	Games	BA	SA	AB	H	2B	3B	HR	HR%	R	RBI	BB	SO	SB	Pinch Hit AB	Pinch Hit H	PO	A	E	DP	TC/G	FA	G by Pos
WORLD SERIES																								
1959	LA N	6	.261	.391	23	6	0	0	1	4.3	3	2	2	2	1	0	0	10	1	0	0	1.8	1.000	OF-6
1965		2	.000	.000	2	0	0	0	0	0.0	0	0	0	0	0	2	0	0	0	0	0	0.0	—	
2 yrs.		8	.240	.360	25	6	0	0	1	4.0	3	2	2	2	1	2	0	10	1	0	0	1.8	1.000	OF-6

Al Moore

MOORE, ALBERT JAMES BR TR 5′10″ 174 lbs.
B. Aug. 4, 1902, Brooklyn, N. Y. D. Nov. 29, 1974, Atlantic Ocean.

Year	Team	Games	BA	SA	AB	H	2B	3B	HR	HR%	R	RBI	BB	SO	SB	Pinch Hit AB	Pinch Hit H	PO	A	E	DP	TC/G	FA	G by Pos
1925	NY N	2	.125	.125	8	1	0	0	0	0.0	0	0	1	2	0	0	0	4	0	0	0	2.0	1.000	OF-2
1926		28	.222	.272	81	18	4	0	0	0.0	12	10	5	7	2	4	0	52	4	2	3	2.9	.966	OF-20
2 yrs.		30	.213	.258	89	19	4	0	0	0.0	12	10	6	9	2	4	0	56	4	2	3	2.8	.968	OF-22

Anse Moore

MOORE, ANSEL WINN BL TR 6′ 1″ 190 lbs.
B. Sept. 22, 1917, Delhi, La. D. Oct. 29, 1993, Pearl, Miss.

Year	Team	Games	BA	SA	AB	H	2B	3B	HR	HR%	R	RBI	BB	SO	SB	Pinch Hit AB	Pinch Hit H	PO	A	E	DP	TC/G	FA	G by Pos
1946	DET A	51	.209	.261	134	28	4	0	1	0.7	16	8	12	9	1	16	4	65	2	2	1	2.2	.971	OF-32

Archie Moore

MOORE, ARCHIE FRANCIS BL TL 6′ 2″ 190 lbs.
B. Aug. 30, 1941, Upper Darby, Pa.

Year	Team	Games	BA	SA	AB	H	2B	3B	HR	HR%	R	RBI	BB	SO	SB	Pinch Hit AB	Pinch Hit H	PO	A	E	DP	TC/G	FA	G by Pos
1964	NY A	31	.174	.261	23	4	2	0	0	0.0	4	1	2	9	0	13	3	18	2	0	2	1.3	1.000	OF-8, 1B-7
1965		9	.412	.706	17	7	2	0	1	5.9	1	4	4	4	0	4	1	7	1	1	0	1.8	.889	OF-5
2 yrs.		40	.275	.450	40	11	4	0	1	2.5	5	5	6	13	0	17	4	25	3	1	2	1.5	.966	OF-13, 1B-7

Bill Moore

MOORE, WILLIAM HENRY BL TR 5′11″ 170 lbs.
B. Dec. 12, 1901, Kansas City, Mo. D. May 24, 1972, Kansas City, Mo.

Year	Team	Games	BA	SA	AB	H	2B	3B	HR	HR%	R	RBI	BB	SO	SB	Pinch Hit AB	Pinch Hit H	PO	A	E	DP	TC/G	FA	G by Pos
1926	BOS A	5	.167	.167	18	3	0	0	0	0.0	2	0	0	4	0	0	0	12	6	0	2	3.6	1.000	C-5
1927		44	.217	.246	69	15	2	0	0	0.0	7	4	13	8	0	1	0	75	30	7	0	2.7	.938	C-42
2 yrs.		49	.207	.230	87	18	2	0	0	0.0	9	4	13	12	0	1	0	87	36	7	2	2.8	.946	C-47

Billy Moore

MOORE, WILLIAM ROSS BR TL 6′ 1″ 185 lbs.
B. Oct. 10, 1960, Los Angeles, Calif.

Year	Team	Games	BA	SA	AB	H	2B	3B	HR	HR%	R	RBI	BB	SO	SB	Pinch Hit AB	Pinch Hit H	PO	A	E	DP	TC/G	FA	G by Pos
1986	MON N	6	.167	.167	12	2	0	0	0	0.0	0	0	0	4	0	3	0	22	1	0	1	5.8	1.000	1B-3, OF-1

Bobby Moore

MOORE, ROBERT VINCENT BR TR 5′11″ 165 lbs.
B. Oct. 27, 1965, Cincinnati, Ohio.

Year	Team	Games	BA	SA	AB	H	2B	3B	HR	HR%	R	RBI	BB	SO	SB	Pinch Hit AB	Pinch Hit H	PO	A	E	DP	TC/G	FA	G by Pos
1991	KC A	18	.357	.429	14	5	1	0	0	0.0	3	0	1	2	3	2	0	11	0	0	0	0.8	1.000	OF-13

Charley Moore

MOORE, CHARLES WESLEY BR TR 5′10″ 160 lbs.
B. Dec. 1, 1884, Jackson County, Ind. D. July 29, 1970, Portland, Ore.

Year	Team	Games	BA	SA	AB	H	2B	3B	HR	HR%	R	RBI	BB	SO	SB	Pinch Hit AB	Pinch Hit H	PO	A	E	DP	TC/G	FA	G by Pos
1912	CHI N	5	.222	.444	9	2	0	1	0	0.0	2	2	0	1	0	0	0	3	6	1	0	2.5	.900	SS-2, 3B-1, 2B-1

Charlie Moore

MOORE, CHARLES WILLIAM, JR. BR TR 5′11″ 190 lbs.
B. June 21, 1953, Birmingham, Ala.

Year	Team	Games	BA	SA	AB	H	2B	3B	HR	HR%	R	RBI	BB	SO	SB	Pinch Hit AB	Pinch Hit H	PO	A	E	DP	TC/G	FA	G by Pos
1973	MIL A	8	.185	.259	27	5	0	1	0	0.0	0	3	2	4	0	0	0	48	5	1	0	6.8	.981	C-8
1974		72	.245	.333	204	50	10	4	0	0.0	17	19	21	34	3	6	3	229	28	4	5	3.9	.985	C-61, DH-6
1975		73	.290	.394	241	70	20	1	1	0.4	26	29	17	31	1	7	3	234	23	10	2	3.8	.963	C-47, OF-22, DH-1
1976		87	.191	.290	241	46	7	4	3	1.2	33	16	43	45	1	2	0	249	45	9	1	3.8	.970	C-49, OF-28, DH-2, 3B-1
1977		138	.248	.360	375	93	15	6	5	1.3	42	45	31	39	1	4	3	566	78	13	10	4.8	.980	C-137
1978		96	.269	.358	268	72	7	1	5	1.9	30	31	12	24	4	1	0	314	41	6	3	3.8	.983	C-95
1979		111	.300	.404	337	101	16	2	5	1.5	45	38	29	32	8	19	6	414	60	10	7	4.5	.979	C-106, 2B-2
1980		111	.291	.362	320	93	13	2	2	0.6	42	30	24	28	10	27	8	319	28	4	3	3.3	.989	C-105
1981		48	.301	.410	156	47	8	3	1	0.6	16	9	12	13	1	4	1	160	17	5	0	3.8	.973	C-34, OF-8, DH-6
1982		133	.254	.360	456	116	22	4	6	1.3	53	45	29	49	2	10	3	317	23	7	8	2.6	.980	OF-115, C-20, 2B-1
1983		151	.284	.369	529	150	27	6	2	0.4	65	49	55	42	11	0	0	309	10	7	1	2.1	.979	OF-150, C-7, DH-1
1984		70	.234	.314	188	44	7	1	2	1.1	13	17	10	26	0	5	2	145	3	3	0	2.2	.980	OF-61, C-7
1985		105	.232	.292	349	81	13	4	0	0.0	35	31	27	53	4	1	0	511	54	13	7	5.5	.978	C-102, OF-3
1986		80	.260	.374	235	61	12	3	3	1.3	24	39	21	38	5	2	1	429	45	4	7	6.1	.992	C-72, OF-4, DH-2, 2B-1
1987	TOR A	51	.215	.355	107	23	10	1	1	0.9	15	7	13	12	0	3	2	237	11	5	0	5.2	.980	C-44, OF-5
15 yrs.		1334	.261	.355	4033	1052	187	43	36	0.9	456	408	346	470	51	91	32	4481	471	101	54	3.8	.980	C-894, OF-396, DH-18, 2B-4, 3B-1
DIVISIONAL PLAYOFF SERIES																								
1981	MIL A	4	.222	.222	9	2	0	0	0	0.0	0	1	1	2	0	0	0	7	0	0	0	1.8	1.000	OF-2, DH-2
LEAGUE CHAMPIONSHIP SERIES																								
1982	MIL A	5	.462	.462	13	6	0	0	0	0.0	3	0	1	2	0	0	0	7	1	0	0	1.6	1.000	OF-5
WORLD SERIES																								
1982	MIL A	7	.346	.462	26	9	3	0	0	0.0	3	2	1	0	0	0	0	13	0	0	0	1.9	1.000	OF-7

Dee Moore

MOORE, D. C. BR TR 6′ 200 lbs.
B. Apr. 6, 1914, Hedley, Tex.

Year	Team	Games	BA	SA	AB	H	2B	3B	HR	HR%	R	RBI	BB	SO	SB	Pinch Hit AB	Pinch Hit H	PO	A	E	DP	TC/G	FA	G by Pos
1936	CIN N	6	.400	.800	10	4	2	1	0	0.0	4	1	0	3	0	4	1	5	3	1	0	3.0	.889	P-2, C-1
1937		7	.077	.077	13	1	0	0	0	0.0	2	0	1	2	0	1	0	23	4	2	1	4.8	.931	C-6
1943	2 teams	BKN N (37G –.253) PHI N (37G –.239)																						
″	total	74	.245	.307	192	47	7	1	1	0.5	21	20	26	16	1	13	1	156	41	8	7	3.6	.961	C-36, 3B-14, OF-6, 1B-1
1946	PHI N	11	.077	.077	13	1	0	0	0	0.0	2	1	7	3	0	2	0	24	2	1	3	3.4	.963	C-6, 1B-2
4 yrs.		98	.232	.303	228	53	9	2	1	0.4	29	22	34	24	1	20	2	208	50	12	11	3.6	.956	C-49, 3B-14, OF-6, 1B-3, P-2

Eddie Moore

MOORE, GRAHAM EDWARD BR TR 5′ 7″ 165 lbs.
B. Jan. 18, 1899, Barlow, Ky. D. Feb. 10, 1976, Ft. Myers, Fla.

Year	Team	Games	BA	SA	AB	H	2B	3B	HR	HR%	R	RBI	BB	SO	SB	Pinch Hit AB	Pinch Hit H	PO	A	E	DP	TC/G	FA	G by Pos
1923	PIT N	6	.269	.308	26	7	1	0	0	0.0	6	1	2	3	1	0	0	12	12	2	2	4.3	.923	SS-6
1924		72	.359	.464	209	75	8	4	2	1.0	47	13	27	12	6	8	4	93	34	1	2	2.4	.992	OF-35, 3B-14, 2B-4
1925		142	.298	.413	547	163	29	8	6	1.1	106	77	73	26	19	2	2	340	407	39	82	5.6	.950	2B-122, OF-15, 3B-3
1926	2 teams	PIT N (43G –.227) BOS N (54G –.266)																						
″	total	97	.250	.304	316	79	11	3	0	0.0	36	34	28	18	9	9	3	170	245	25	49	5.1	.943	2B-62, SS-15, 3B-10
1927	BOS N	112	.302	.363	411	124	14	4	1	0.2	53	32	39	17	5	6	3	200	223	16	36	4.1	.964	3B-52, 2B-39, OF-16, SS-1

Eddie Moore *continued*

Year	Team	Games	BA	SA	AB	H	2B	3B	HR	HR%	R	RBI	BB	SO	SB	Pinch Hit AB	Pinch Hit H	PO	A	E	DP	TC/G	FA	G by Pos
1928		68	.237	.307	215	51	9	0	2	0.9	27	18	19	12	7	5	0	131	8	6	3	2.6	.959	OF-54, 2B-1
1929	BKN N	111	.296	.371	402	119	18	6	0	0.0	48	48	44	16	3	1	1	205	348	28	52	5.1	.952	2B-74, SS-36, OF-2, 3B-1
1930		76	.281	.372	196	55	13	1	1	0.5	24	20	21	7	1	9	5	117	115	10	23	3.8	.959	2B-23, OF-23, SS-17, 3B-1
1932	NY N	37	.264	.333	87	23	3	0	1	1.1	9	6	9	6	1	4	0	52	81	9	13	4.4	.937	SS-21, 3B-6, 2B-5
1934	CLE A	27	.154	.185	65	10	2	0	0	0.0	4	8	10	4	0	3	0	56	47	7	11	4.8	.936	2B-18, 3B-3, SS-2
10 yrs.		748	.285	.366	2474	706	108	26	13	0.5	360	257	272	121	52	47	18	1376	1520	143	273	4.5	.953	2B-348, OF-145, SS-98, 3B-90
WORLD SERIES																								
1925	PIT N	7	.231	.385	26	6	1	0	1	3.8	7	2	5	2	0	0	0	16	13	1	2	4.3	.967	2B-7

Ferdie Moore

MOORE, FERDINAND DePAGE
B. Feb. 21, 1896, Camden, N. J. D. May 6, 1947, Atlantic City, N. J.

Year	Team	Games	BA	SA	AB	H	2B	3B	HR	HR%	R	RBI	BB	SO	SB	Pinch Hit AB	Pinch Hit H	PO	A	E	DP	TC/G	FA	G by Pos
1914	PHI A	2	.500	.500	4	2	0	0	0	0.0	1	1	0	2	0	0	0	17	0	2	0	9.5	.895	1B-2

Gary Moore

MOORE, GARY DOUGLAS BR TL 5′10″ 175 lbs.
B. Feb. 24, 1945, Tulsa, Okla.

Year	Team	Games	BA	SA	AB	H	2B	3B	HR	HR%	R	RBI	BB	SO	SB	Pinch Hit AB	Pinch Hit H	PO	A	E	DP	TC/G	FA	G by Pos
1970	LA N	7	.188	.438	16	3	0	2	0	0.0	2	0	0	1	1	2	1	9	0	0	0	1.5	1.000	OF-5, 1B-1

Gene Moore

MOORE, EUGENE, JR. (Rowdy) BL TL 5′11″ 175 lbs.
Son of Gene Moore.
B. Aug. 26, 1909, Lancaster, Tex. D. Mar. 12, 1978, Jackson, Miss.

Year	Team	Games	BA	SA	AB	H	2B	3B	HR	HR%	R	RBI	BB	SO	SB	Pinch Hit AB	Pinch Hit H	PO	A	E	DP	TC/G	FA	G by Pos
1931	CIN N	4	.143	.214	14	2	1	0	0	0.0	2	1	0	0	0	1	0	8	0	0	0	2.7	1.000	OF-3
1933	STL N	11	.395	.579	38	15	3	2	0	0.0	6	8	4	10	1	1	0	29	0	1	0	3.0	.967	OF-10
1934		9	.278	.333	18	5	1	0	0	0.0	2	1	2	2	0	6	2	12	0	1	0	4.3	.923	OF-3
1935		3	.000	.000	3	0	0	0	0	0.0	0	0	0	1	0	3	0	0	0	0	0	0.0	—	
1936	BOS N	151	.290	.449	637	185	38	12	13	2.0	91	67	40	80	6	0	0	314	32	8	0	2.3	.977	OF-151
1937		148	.283	.456	561	159	29	10	16	2.9	88	70	61	73	11	0	0	340	21	8	1	2.5	.978	OF-148
1938		54	.272	.400	180	49	8	3	3	1.7	27	19	16	20	1	5	1	97	4	2	0	2.2	.981	OF-47
1939	BKN N	107	.225	.337	306	69	13	6	3	1.0	45	39	40	50	4	18	3	141	8	6	3	1.8	.961	OF-86, 1B-1
1940	2 teams	BKN N (10G –.269) BOS N (103G –.292)																						
″	total	113	.290	.401	389	113	26	1	5	1.3	49	41	26	35	2	11	1	206	11	3	3	2.2	.986	OF-100
1941	BOS N	129	.272	.393	397	108	17	8	5	1.3	42	43	45	37	5	16	3	229	13	8	2	2.3	.968	OF-110
1942	WAS A	1	.000	.000	2	0	0	0	0	0.0	0	0	0	1	0	0	0	0	0	0	0	0.0	.000	OF-1
1943		92	.268	.370	254	68	14	3	2	0.8	41	39	19	29	0	30	12	125	5	2	0	2.3	.985	OF-57, 1B-1
1944	STL A	110	.238	.349	390	93	13	6	6	1.5	56	58	24	37	0	11	5	210	5	8	3	2.3	.964	OF-98, 1B-1
1945		110	.260	.359	354	92	16	2	5	1.4	48	50	40	26	1	10	0	184	10	6	0	2.0	.970	OF-100
14 yrs.		1042	.270	.400	3543	958	179	53	58	1.6	497	436	317	401	31	112	27	1895	109	53	12	2.2	.974	OF-914, 1B-3
WORLD SERIES																								
1944	STL A	6	.182	.182	22	4	0	0	0	0.0	4	0	3	6	0	0	0	8	0	0	0	1.3	1.000	OF-6

Henry Moore

MOORE, HENRY S.
Deceased.

Year	Team	Games	BA	SA	AB	H	2B	3B	HR	HR%	R	RBI	BB	SO	SB	Pinch Hit AB	Pinch Hit H	PO	A	E	DP	TC/G	FA	G by Pos
1884	WAS U	111	.336	.414	461	155	23	5	1	0.2	77		19			0	0	141	24	45	6	1.9	.786	OF-105, SS-8

Jackie Moore

MOORE, JACKIE SPENCER BR TR 6′ 180 lbs.
B. Feb. 19, 1939, Jay, Fla.
Manager 1984–86.

Year	Team	Games	BA	SA	AB	H	2B	3B	HR	HR%	R	RBI	BB	SO	SB	Pinch Hit AB	Pinch Hit H	PO	A	E	DP	TC/G	FA	G by Pos
1965	DET A	21	.094	.094	53	5	0	0	0	0.0	2	2	6	12	0	1	0	128	6	2	1	6.8	.985	C-20

Jerry Moore

MOORE, JEREMIAH S. BL 5′11″ 170 lbs.
B. Detroit, Mich. D. Sept. 26, 1890, Wayne, Mich.

Year	Team	Games	BA	SA	AB	H	2B	3B	HR	HR%	R	RBI	BB	SO	SB	Pinch Hit AB	Pinch Hit H	PO	A	E	DP	TC/G	FA	G by Pos
1884	2 teams	ALT U (20G –.313) CLE N (9G –.200)																						
″	total	29	.282	.355	110	31	3	1	1	0.9	11	10	0	5		0	0	118	27	29	0	5.8	.833	C-21, OF-9
1885	DET N	6	.174	.217	23	4	1	0	0	0.0	2	0	1	3		0	0	24	12	9	0	7.5	.800	C-6
2 yrs.		35	.263	.331	133	35	4	1	1	0.8	13	10	1	8		0	0	142	39	38	0	6.1	.826	C-27, OF-9

Jimmy Moore

MOORE, JAMES WILLIAM BR TR 6′½″ 187 lbs.
B. Apr. 24, 1903, Paris, Tenn. D. Mar. 7, 1986, Memphis, Tenn.

Year	Team	Games	BA	SA	AB	H	2B	3B	HR	HR%	R	RBI	BB	SO	SB	Pinch Hit AB	Pinch Hit H	PO	A	E	DP	TC/G	FA	G by Pos
1930	2 teams	CHI A (16G –.205) PHI A (15G –.380)																						
″	total	31	.303	.427	89	27	5	0	2	2.2	14	14	8	7	1	9	4	38	3	3	2	2.0	.932	OF-22
1931	PHI A	49	.224	.315	143	32	5	1	2	1.4	18	21	11	13	0	11	0	70	3	2	2	2.1	.973	OF-36
2 yrs.		80	.254	.358	232	59	10	1	4	1.7	32	35	19	20	1	20	4	108	6	5	4	2.1	.958	OF-58
WORLD SERIES																								
1930	PHI A	3	.333	.333	3	1	0	0	0	0.0	0	0	1	1	0	1	1	0	0	0	0	0.0	.000	OF-1
1931		2	.333	.333	3	1	0	0	0	0.0	0	0	0	1	0	1	0	1	0	0	0	1.0	1.000	OF-1
2 yrs.		5	.333	.333	6	2	0	0	0	0.0	0	0	1	2	0	2	1	1	0	0	0	0.5	1.000	OF-2

Joe Moore

MOORE, JOSEPH GREGG (Jo-Jo, The Gause Ghost) BL TR 5′11″ 155 lbs.
B. Dec. 25, 1908, Gause, Tex.

Year	Team	Games	BA	SA	AB	H	2B	3B	HR	HR%	R	RBI	BB	SO	SB	Pinch Hit AB	Pinch Hit H	PO	A	E	DP	TC/G	FA	G by Pos
1930	NY N	3	.200	.200	5	1	0	0	0	0.0	1	0	0	1	0	2	1	2	0	0	0	2.0	1.000	OF-1
1931		4	.250	.375	8	2	1	0	0	0.0	0	3	0	1	1	3	0	2	0	0	0	2.0	1.000	OF-1
1932		86	.305	.374	361	110	15	2	2	0.6	53	27	20	18	4	0	0	160	6	3	10	2.0	.982	OF-86
1933		132	.292	.342	524	153	16	5	0	0.0	56	42	21	27	4	0	0	266	19	10	6	2.2	.966	OF-132
1934		139	.331	.486	580	192	37	4	15	2.6	106	61	31	23	5	8	1	242	8	12	1	2.0	.954	OF-131
1935		155	.295	.429	**681**	201	28	9	15	2.2	108	71	53	24	5	0	0	342	11	10	2	2.3	.972	OF-155
1936		152	.316	.421	649	205	29	9	7	1.1	110	63	37	27	2	3	0	291	25	6	3	2.2	.981	OF-149
1937		142	.310	.440	580	180	37	10	6	1.0	89	57	46	37	7	2	0	226	12	6	0	1.7	.975	OF-140
1938		125	.302	.437	506	153	23	6	11	2.2	76	56	22	27	2	10	1	214	8	5	1	2.0	.978	OF-114
1939		138	.269	.370	562	151	23	2	10	1.8	80	47	45	17	5	2	1	260	13	4	2	2.0	.986	OF-136
1940		138	.276	.385	543	150	33	4	6	1.1	83	46	43	30	7	3	0	259	9	5	1	2.1	.982	OF-133
1941		121	.273	.369	428	117	16	2	7	1.6	47	40	30	15	4	3	1	237	5	7	0	2.1	.972	OF-116
12 yrs.		1335	.298	.408	5427	1615	258	53	79	1.5	809	513	348	247	46	36	5	2501	116	68	26	2.1	.975	OF-1294

Joe Moore *continued*

Year	Team	Games	BA	SA	AB	H	2B	3B	HR	HR%	R	RBI	BB	SO	SB	Pinch Hit		PO	A	E	DP	TC/G	FA	G by Pos
																AB	H							
WORLD SERIES																								
1933	NY N	5	.227	.273	22	5	1	0	0	0.0	1	1	1	3	0	0	0	13	1	0	1	2.8	1.000	OF-5
1936		6	.214	.393	28	6	2	0	1	3.6	4	1	1	4	0	0	0	9	0	0	0	1.5	1.000	OF-6
1937		5	.391	.435	23	9	1	0	0	0.0	1	1	0	1	0	0	0	13	0	0	0	2.6	1.000	OF-5
3 yrs.		16	.274	.370	73	20	4	0	1	1.4	6	3	2	8	0	0	0	35	1	0	1	2.3	1.000	OF-16

Johnny Moore

MOORE, JOHN FRANCIS
B. Mar. 23, 1902, Waterville, Conn. D. Apr. 4, 1991, Bradenton, Fla.
BL TR 5′10½″ 175 lbs.

Year	Team	Games	BA	SA	AB	H	2B	3B	HR	HR%	R	RBI	BB	SO	SB	Pinch Hit AB	Pinch Hit H	PO	A	E	DP	TC/G	FA	G by Pos
1928	CHI N	4	.000	.000	4	0	0	0	0	0.0	0	0	0	0	0	4	0	0	0	0	0	0.0	—	
1929		37	.286	.397	63	18	1	0	2	3.2	13	8	4	6	0	15	5	32	1	1	0	2.3	.971	OF-15
1931		39	.240	.346	104	25	3	1	2	1.9	19	16	7	5	1	15	3	51	3	2	0	2.5	.964	OF-22
1932		119	.305	.470	443	135	24	5	13	2.9	59	64	22	38	4	10	4	272	12	5	2	2.7	.983	OF-109
1933	CIN N	135	.263	.325	514	135	19	5	1	0.2	60	44	29	16	4	3	1	329	12	9	4	2.7	.974	OF-132
1934	**2 teams**	**CIN N** (16G –.190) **PHI N** (116G –.343)																						
″	**total**	132	.330	.494	500	165	35	7	11	2.2	73	98	43	20	7	6	1	267	18	5	2	2.3	.983	OF-125
1935	PHI N	153	.323	.483	600	194	33	3	19	3.2	84	93	45	50	4	3	0	233	18	7	6	1.7	.973	OF-150
1936		124	.328	.494	472	155	24	3	16	3.4	85	68	26	22	1	10	4	214	5	12	1	2.1	.948	OF-112
1937		96	.319	.472	307	98	16	2	9	2.9	46	59	18	18	2	20	7	124	9	8	1	2.0	.943	OF-72
1945	CHI N	7	.167	.167	6	1	0	0	0	0.0	0	2	1	1	0	6	1	0	0	0	0	0.0	—	
10 yrs.		846	.307	.449	3013	926	155	26	73	2.4	439	452	195	176	23	92	26	1522	78	49	16	2.2	.970	OF-737
WORLD SERIES																								
1932	CHI N	2	.000	.000	7	0	0	0	0	0.0	1	0	2	1	0	0	0	4	0	0	0	2.0	1.000	OF-2

Junior Moore

MOORE, ALVIN EARL
B. Jan. 25, 1953, Waskom, Tex.
BR TR 5′11″ 195 lbs.

Year	Team	Games	BA	SA	AB	H	2B	3B	HR	HR%	R	RBI	BB	SO	SB	Pinch Hit AB	Pinch Hit H	PO	A	E	DP	TC/G	FA	G by Pos
1976	ATL N	20	.269	.308	26	7	1	0	0	0.0	1	2	4	4	0	12	4	7	10	1	1	2.3	.944	3B-6, OF-1, 2B-1
1977		112	.260	.343	361	94	9	3	5	1.4	41	34	33	29	4	10	3	86	189	17	10	2.8	.942	3B-104, 2B-1
1978	CHI A	24	.292	.323	65	19	0	1	0	0.0	8	4	6	7	1	5	2	12	9	2	2	1.0	.913	DH-12, 3B-6, OF-5
1979		88	.264	.328	201	53	6	2	1	0.5	24	23	12	20	0	25	6	83	5	3	0	1.2	.967	OF-61, DH-10, 2B-2
1980		45	.256	.331	121	31	4	1	1	0.8	9	10	7	11	0	4	2	30	65	7	6	2.5	.931	3B-34, OF-3, DH-2, 1B-1
5 yrs.		289	.264	.335	774	204	20	7	7	0.9	83	73	62	71	5	56	17	218	278	30	19	2.1	.943	3B-150, OF-70, DH-24, 2B-4, 1B-1

Kelvin Moore

MOORE, KELVIN ORLANDO
B. Sept. 26, 1957, LeRoy, Ala.
BR TL 6′ 1″ 195 lbs.

Year	Team	Games	BA	SA	AB	H	2B	3B	HR	HR%	R	RBI	BB	SO	SB	Pinch Hit AB	Pinch Hit H	PO	A	E	DP	TC/G	FA	G by Pos
1981	OAK A	14	.255	.362	47	12	0	1	1	2.1	5	3	5	15	1	1	0	99	7	0	9	8.2	1.000	1B-13
1982		21	.224	.358	67	15	1	1	2	3.0	6	6	3	23	0	1	0	123	9	4	9	6.8	.971	1B-20
1983		41	.210	.363	124	26	4	0	5	4.0	12	16	10	39	2	0	0	293	16	2	38	7.8	.994	1B-40
3 yrs.		76	.223	.361	238	53	5	2	8	3.4	23	25	18	77	3	2	0	515	32	6	56	7.6	.989	1B-73
DIVISIONAL PLAYOFF SERIES																								
1981	OAK A	2	.000	.000	8	0	0	0	0	0.0	0	0	0	2	0	0	0	7	1	0	0	4.0	1.000	1B-2
LEAGUE CHAMPIONSHIP SERIES																								
1981	OAK A	3	.222	.222	9	2	0	0	0	0.0	0	0	0	1	0	0	0	13	3	0	0	5.3	1.000	1B-3

Randy Moore

MOORE, RANDOLPH EDWARD
B. June 21, 1906, Naples, Tex. D. June 12, 1992, Mt. Pleasant, Tex.
BL TR 6′ 185 lbs.

Year	Team	Games	BA	SA	AB	H	2B	3B	HR	HR%	R	RBI	BB	SO	SB	Pinch Hit AB	Pinch Hit H	PO	A	E	DP	TC/G	FA	G by Pos
1927	CHI A	6	.000	.000	15	0	0	0	0	0.0	0	0	0	2	0	2	0	8	1	0	0	2.3	1.000	OF-4
1928		24	.213	.311	61	13	4	1	0	0.0	6	5	3	5	0	6	2	34	1	2	0	2.3	.946	OF-16
1930	BOS N	83	.288	.366	191	55	9	0	2	1.0	24	34	10	13	3	30	6	79	27	6	3	2.4	.946	OF-34, 3B-13
1931		83	.260	.359	192	50	8	1	3	1.6	19	34	13	3	1	32	6	71	39	6	3	2.2	.948	OF-29, 3B-22, 2B-1
1932		107	.293	.390	351	103	21	2	3	0.9	41	43	15	11	1	14	4	258	67	5	34	3.5	.985	OF-41, 3B-31, 1B-22, C-1
1933		135	.302	.425	497	150	23	7	8	1.6	64	70	40	16	3	6	1	355	12	7	5	2.8	.981	OF-122, 1B-10
1934		123	.284	.393	422	120	21	2	7	1.7	55	64	40	16	2	13	5	496	23	12	24	4.9	.977	OF-72, 1B-37
1935		125	.275	.373	407	112	20	4	4	1.0	42	42	26	16	1	23	5	370	20	13	14	4.1	.968	OF-78, 1B-21
1936	BKN N	42	.239	.273	88	21	3	0	0	0.0	4	14	8	1	0	18	7	27	0	1	0	1.3	.964	OF-21
1937	**2 teams**	**BKN N** (13G –.136) **STL N** (8G –.000)																						
″	**total**	21	.103	.138	29	3	1	0	0	0.0	3	2	3	2	0	9	0	27	5	4	0	3.3	.889	C-10, OF-1
10 yrs.		749	.278	.378	2253	627	110	17	27	1.2	258	308	158	85	11	153	36	1725	195	56	83	3.4	.972	OF-418, 1B-90, 3B-66, C-11, 2B-1

Scrappy Moore

MOORE, WILLIAM ALLEN
B. Dec. 16, 1892, St. Louis, Mo. D. Oct. 13, 1964, Little Rock, Ark.
BR TR 5′ 8″ 153 lbs.

Year	Team	Games	BA	SA	AB	H	2B	3B	HR	HR%	R	RBI	BB	SO	SB	Pinch Hit AB	Pinch Hit H	PO	A	E	DP	TC/G	FA	G by Pos
1917	STL A	4	.125	.125	8	1	0	0	0	0.0	1	0	1	0	0	2	1	2	4	2	2	4.0	.750	3B-2

Terry Moore

MOORE, TERRY BLUFORD
B. May 27, 1912, Vernon, Ala. D. Mar. 29, 1995, Collinsville, Ill.
Manager 1954.
BR TR 5′11″ 195 lbs.

Year	Team	Games	BA	SA	AB	H	2B	3B	HR	HR%	R	RBI	BB	SO	SB	Pinch Hit AB	Pinch Hit H	PO	A	E	DP	TC/G	FA	G by Pos
1935	STL N	119	.287	.414	456	131	34	3	6	1.3	63	53	15	40	13	0	0	354	11	6	3	3.2	.984	OF-117
1936		143	.264	.369	590	156	39	4	5	0.8	85	47	37	52	9	7	2	418	14	10	7	3.3	.977	OF-133
1937		115	.267	.349	461	123	17	3	5	1.1	76	43	32	41	13	8	1	307	9	4	2	3.0	.988	OF-106
1938		94	.272	.397	312	85	21	3	4	1.3	49	21	46	19	9	9	1	228	21	6	2	3.1	.976	OF-75, 3B-6
1939		130	.295	.487	417	123	25	2	17	4.1	65	77	43	38	6	7	2	291	17	2	1	2.5	.994	OF-121, P-1
1940		136	.304	.475	537	163	33	4	17	3.2	92	64	42	44	18	3	0	383	11	5	4	3.0	.987	OF-133
1941		122	.294	.400	493	145	26	4	6	1.2	86	68	52	31	3	1	0	293	14	5	3	2.6	.984	OF-121
1942		130	.288	.391	489	141	26	3	6	1.2	80	49	56	26	10	4	2	271	9	5	0	2.2	.982	OF-126, 3B-1
1946		91	.263	.353	278	73	14	1	3	1.1	32	28	18	26	0	25	6	158	5	3	0	2.5	.982	OF-66
1947		127	.283	.370	460	130	17	1	7	1.5	61	45	38	39	1	6	1	292	6	5	2	2.5	.983	OF-120
1948		91	.232	.343	207	48	11	0	4	1.9	30	18	27	12	0	17	4	131	2	1	0	1.9	.993	OF-71
11 yrs.		1298	.280	.399	4700	1318	263	28	80	1.7	719	513	406	368	82	87	19	3126	119	52	24	2.8	.984	OF-1189, 3B-7, P-1

Terry Moore *continued*

WORLD SERIES

Year	Team	Games	BA	SA	AB	H	2B	3B	HR	HR%	R	RBI	BB	SO	SB	Pinch Hit AB	Pinch Hit H	PO	A	E	DP	TC/G	FA	G by Pos
1942	**STL N**	5	.294	.353	17	5	1	0	0	0.0	2	2	2	3	0	0	0	15	0	0	0	3.0	1.000	OF-5
1946		7	.148	.148	27	4	0	0	0	0.0	1	2	2	6	0	0	0	17	1	0	0	2.6	1.000	OF-7
2 yrs.		12	.205	.227	44	9	1	0	0	0.0	3	4	4	9	0	0	0	32	1	0	0	2.8	1.000	OF-12

Andres Mora

MORA, ANDRES BR TR 6′ 180 lbs.
Born Andres Mora (Ibara).
B. May 25, 1955, Rio Bravo, Mexico.

Year	Team	Games	BA	SA	AB	H	2B	3B	HR	HR%	R	RBI	BB	SO	SB	Pinch Hit AB	Pinch Hit H	PO	A	E	DP	TC/G	FA	G by Pos
1976	**BAL A**	73	.218	.350	220	48	11	0	6	2.7	18	25	13	49	1	10	4	55	3	3	0	0.9	.951	DH-34, OF-31
1977		77	.245	.464	233	57	8	2	13	5.6	32	44	5	53	0	16	7	66	2	0	0	1.1	1.000	OF-57, DH-5, 3B-1
1978		76	.214	.354	229	49	8	0	8	3.5	21	14	13	47	0	13	0	129	4	3	0	1.9	.978	OF-69, DH-1
1980	**CLE A**	9	.111	.111	18	2	0	0	0	0.0	0	0	0	0	0	6	1	6	0	0	0	2.0	1.000	OF-3
4 yrs.		235	.223	.383	700	156	27	2	27	3.9	71	83	31	149	1	45	12	256	9	6	0	1.3	.978	OF-160, DH-40, 3B-1

Jerry Morales

MORALES, JULIO RUBEN BR TR 5′10″ 155 lbs.
Born Julio Ruben Morales (Torres).
B. Feb. 18, 1949, Yabucoa, Puerto Rico.

Year	Team	Games	BA	SA	AB	H	2B	3B	HR	HR%	R	RBI	BB	SO	SB	Pinch Hit AB	Pinch Hit H	PO	A	E	DP	TC/G	FA	G by Pos
1969	**SD N**	19	.195	.317	41	8	2	0	1	2.4	5	6	5	7	0	0	0	27	2	0	1	1.5	1.000	OF-19
1970		28	.155	.241	58	9	0	1	1	1.7	6	4	3	11	0	2	0	25	0	2	0	1.0	.926	OF-26
1971		12	.118	.118	17	2	0	0	0	0.0	1	1	2	2	1	2	0	8	0	0	0	1.1	1.000	OF-7
1972		115	.239	.357	347	83	15	7	4	1.2	38	18	35	54	4	19	3	214	8	4	2	2.3	.982	OF-96, 3B-4
1973		122	.281	.420	388	109	23	2	9	2.3	47	34	27	55	6	22	9	214	5	2	1	2.2	.991	OF-100
1974	**CHI N**	151	.273	.423	534	146	21	7	15	2.8	70	82	46	63	2	8	2	266	5	7	2	1.9	.975	OF-143
1975		153	.270	.369	578	156	21	0	12	2.1	62	91	50	65	3	2	2	273	11	6	1	1.9	.979	OF-151
1976		140	.274	.395	537	147	17	0	16	3.0	66	67	41	49	3	5	1	273	12	5	6	2.1	.983	OF-136
1977		136	.290	.447	490	142	34	5	11	2.2	56	69	43	75	0	11	3	247	8	4	3	2.0	.985	OF-128
1978	**STL N**	130	.239	.341	457	109	19	8	4	0.9	44	46	33	44	4	8	1	254	5	6	0	2.1	.977	OF-126
1979	**DET A**	129	.211	.364	440	93	23	1	14	3.2	50	56	30	56	10	7	0	206	6	3	2	1.7	.986	OF-119, DH-7
1980	**NY N**	94	.254	.347	193	49	7	1	3	1.6	19	30	13	31	2	30	7	107	3	3	1	1.8	.973	OF-63
1981	**CHI N**	84	.286	.339	245	70	6	2	1	0.4	27	25	22	29	1	12	3	142	2	2	1	2.0	.986	OF-72
1982		65	.284	.440	116	33	2	2	4	3.4	14	30	9	7	1	30	10	72	5	0	1	1.9	1.000	OF-41
1983		63	.195	.299	87	17	9	0	0	0.0	11	11	7	19	0	41	8	29	1	0	0	1.0	1.000	OF-29
15 yrs.		1441	.259	.382	4528	1173	199	36	95	2.1	516	570	366	567	37	199	49	2357	73	44	21	2.0	.982	OF-1256, DH-7, 3B-4

Jose Morales

MORALES, JOSE MANUEL BR TR 5′11″ 187 lbs.
B. Dec. 30, 1944, Frederiksted, Virgin Islands.

Year	Team	Games	BA	SA	AB	H	2B	3B	HR	HR%	R	RBI	BB	SO	SB	Pinch Hit AB	Pinch Hit H	PO	A	E	DP	TC/G	FA	G by Pos
1973	**2 teams**	**OAK A** (6G –.286) **MON N** (5G –.400)																						
″	**total**	11	.316	.368	19	6	1	0	0	0.0	0	1	1	5	0	7	3	0	0	0	0	0.0	.000	DH-3
1974	**MON N**	25	.269	.538	26	7	4	0	1	3.8	3	5	1	7	0	22	5	3	1	1	0	2.5	.800	C-2
1975		93	.301	.387	163	49	6	1	2	1.2	18	24	14	21	0	51	**15**	234	28	4	19	7.0	.985	1B-27, OF-6, C-5
1976		104	.316	.462	158	50	11	0	4	2.5	12	37	3	20	0	**78**	**25**	137	21	3	9	4.9	.981	1B-21, C-12
1977		65	.203	.324	74	15	4	1	1	1.4	3	9	5	12	0	52	10	52	3	0	4	3.4	1.000	1B-8, C-8
1978	**MIN A**	101	.314	.401	242	76	13	1	2	0.8	22	38	20	35	0	**46**	**14**	1	2	0	0	0.0	1.000	DH-77, 1B-1, OF-1, C-1
1979		92	.267	.335	191	51	5	1	2	1.0	21	27	14	27	0	**42**	9	2	0	0	0	0.0	1.000	DH-77, 1B-1
1980		97	.303	.490	241	73	17	2	8	3.3	36	36	22	19	0	36	**13**	19	0	0	2	0.2	1.000	DH-86, 1B-2, C-2
1981	**BAL A**	38	.244	.349	86	21	3	0	2	2.3	6	14	3	13	0	19	5	13	0	0	1	0.5	1.000	DH-22, 1B-3
1982	**2 teams**	**BAL A** (3G –.000) **LA N** (35G –.300)																						
″	**total**	38	.273	.394	33	9	1	0	1	3.0	1	8	4	10	0	33	9	0	0	0	0	0.0	—	
1983	**LA N**	47	.283	.509	53	15	3	0	3	5.7	4	8	1	11	0	40	12	37	2	2	2	10.3	.951	1B-4
1984		22	.158	.158	19	3	0	0	0	0.0	0	0	1	2	0	19	3	0	0	0	0	0.0	—	
12 yrs.		733	.287	.408	1305	375	68	6	26	2.0	126	207	89	182	0	445	123 **4th**	498	57	10	37	1.5	.982	DH-265, 1B-67, C-30, OF-7

LEAGUE CHAMPIONSHIP SERIES

Year	Team	Games	BA	SA	AB	H	2B	3B	HR	HR%	R	RBI	BB	SO	SB	Pinch Hit AB	Pinch Hit H	PO	A	E	DP	TC/G	FA	G by Pos
1983	**LA N**	2	.000	.000	2	0	0	0	0	0.0	0	0	0	1	0	2	0	0	0	0	0	0.0	—	

Rich Morales

MORALES, RICHARD ANGELO BR TR 5′11″ 170 lbs.
B. Sept. 20, 1943, San Francisco, Calif.

Year	Team	Games	BA	SA	AB	H	2B	3B	HR	HR%	R	RBI	BB	SO	SB	Pinch Hit AB	Pinch Hit H	PO	A	E	DP	TC/G	FA	G by Pos
1967	**CHI A**	8	.000	.000	10	0	0	0	0	0.0	0	0	0	2	0	0	0	6	11	1	1	2.6	.944	SS-7
1968		10	.172	.172	29	5	0	0	0	0.0	2	0	2	5	0	0	0	17	26	1	5	3.7	.977	SS-7, 2B-5
1969		55	.215	.231	121	26	0	1	0	0.0	12	6	7	18	1	3	1	77	118	4	22	3.8	.980	2B-38, SS-13, 3B-1
1970		62	.161	.205	112	18	2	0	1	0.9	6	2	9	16	1	9	1	49	91	7	14	2.6	.952	SS-24, 3B-20, 2B-12
1971		84	.243	.319	185	45	8	0	2	1.1	19	14	22	26	2	12	3	75	159	9	18	3.1	.963	SS-57, 3B-18, 2B-3, OF-1
1972		110	.206	.258	287	59	7	1	2	0.7	24	20	19	49	2	5	1	133	248	11	38	3.4	.972	SS-86, 2B-16, 3B-14
1973	**2 teams**	**CHI A** (7G –.000) **SD N** (90G –.164)																						
″	**total**	97	.161	.194	248	40	6	1	0	0.0	10	17	28	37	0	2	0	194	268	5	49	4.9	.989	2B-81, SS-10, 3B-5
1974	**SD N**	54	.197	.295	61	12	3	0	1	1.6	8	5	8	6	1	2	1	54	61	6	11	2.2	.950	SS-29, 2B-18, 3B-6, 1B-1
8 yrs.		480	.195	.242	1053	205	26	3	6	0.6	81	64	95	159	7	33	7	605	982	44	158	3.5	.973	SS-233, 2B-173, 3B-64, 1B-1, OF-1

Al Moran

MORAN, RICHARD ALAN BR TR 6′ 1½″ 190 lbs.
B. Dec. 5, 1938, Detroit, Mich.

Year	Team	Games	BA	SA	AB	H	2B	3B	HR	HR%	R	RBI	BB	SO	SB	Pinch Hit AB	Pinch Hit H	PO	A	E	DP	TC/G	FA	G by Pos
1963	**NY N**	119	.193	.230	331	64	5	2	1	0.3	26	23	36	60	3	1	0	190	332	27	57	4.7	.951	SS-116, 3B-1
1964		16	.227	.227	22	5	0	0	0	0.0	2	4	2	2	0	0	0	15	31	2	5	3.0	.958	SS-15, 3B-1
2 yrs.		135	.195	.229	353	69	5	2	1	0.3	28	27	38	62	3	1	0	205	363	29	62	4.5	.951	SS-131, 3B-2

Bill Moran

MORAN, WILLIAM L. 175 lbs.
B. Oct. 10, 1869, Joliet, Ill. D. Apr. 8, 1916, Joliet, Ill.

Year	Team	Games	BA	SA	AB	H	2B	3B	HR	HR%	R	RBI	BB	SO	SB	Pinch Hit AB	Pinch Hit H	PO	A	E	DP	TC/G	FA	G by Pos
1892	**STL N**	24	.136	.148	81	11	1	0	0	0.0	2	5	2	12	0	0	0	91	23	14	0	5.8	.891	C-22
1895	**CHI N**	15	.164	.291	55	9	2	1	1	1.8	8	9	3	2	2	0	0	49	18	14	0	5.4	.827	C-15
2 yrs.		39	.147	.206	136	20	3	1	1	0.7	10	14	5	14	2	0	0	140	41	28	0	5.6	.866	C-37

Billy Moran

MORAN, WILLIAM NELSON BR TR 5′11″ 185 lbs.
B. Nov. 27, 1933, Montgomery, Ala.

Year	Team	Games	BA	SA	AB	H	2B	3B	HR	HR%	R	RBI	BB	SO	SB	Pinch Hit AB	Pinch Hit H	PO	A	E	DP	TC/G	FA	G by Pos
1958	**CLE A**	115	.226	.280	257	58	11	0	1	0.4	26	18	13	23	3	4	0	174	210	15	56	3.6	.962	2B-74, SS-38
1959		11	.294	.294	17	5	0	0	0	0.0	1	2	0	1	0	0	0	13	9	1	2	2.1	.957	2B-6, SS-5
1961	**LA A**	54	.260	.347	173	45	7	1	2	1.2	17	22	17	16	0	0	0	109	120	9	31	4.5	.962	2B-51, SS-2
1962		160	.282	.407	659	186	25	3	17	2.6	90	74	39	80	5	0	0	422	477	13	103	5.7	.986	2B-160
1963		153	.275	.375	597	164	29	5	7	1.2	67	65	31	57	1	2	1	352	455	22	98	5.5	.973	2B-151
1964	**2 teams**	**LA A** (50G –.268) **CLE A** (69G –.205)																						
″	**total**	119	.241	.301	349	84	16	1	1	0.3	40	21	31	36	1	12	2	105	177	14	13	2.7	.953	3B-89, 2B-18, 1B-2, SS-1
1965	**CLE A**	22	.125	.125	24	3	0	0	0	0.0	1	0	2	5	0	13	2	6	11	0	2	2.1	1.000	2B-7, SS-1
7 yrs.		634	.263	.355	2076	545	88	10	28	1.3	242	202	133	218	10	31	5	1181	1459	74	305	4.5	.973	2B-467, 3B-89, SS-47, 1B-2

Charley Moran

MORAN, CHARLES BARTHELL (Uncle Charlie) BR TR 5′ 8″ 180 lbs.
B. Feb. 22, 1878, Nashville, Tenn. D. June 14, 1949, Horse Cave, Ky.

Year	Team	Games	BA	SA	AB	H	2B	3B	HR	HR%	R	RBI	BB	SO	SB	Pinch Hit AB	Pinch Hit H	PO	A	E	DP	TC/G	FA	G by Pos
1903	**STL N**	4	.429	.429	14	6	0	0	0	0.0	2	1	0		1	0	0	2	4	0	0	1.5	1.000	P-3, SS-1
1908		21	.175	.254	63	11	1	2	0	0.0	2	2	0		0	5	2	58	26	9	1	5.8	.903	C-16
2 yrs.		25	.221	.286	77	17	1	2	0	0.0	4	3	0		1	5	2	60	30	9	1	4.9	.909	C-16, P-3, SS-1

Charlie Moran

MORAN, CHARLES VINCENT TR
B. Mar. 26, 1879, Washington, D. C. D. Apr. 11, 1934, Washington, D. C.

Year	Team	Games	BA	SA	AB	H	2B	3B	HR	HR%	R	RBI	BB	SO	SB	Pinch Hit AB	Pinch Hit H	PO	A	E	DP	TC/G	FA	G by Pos
1903	**WAS A**	98	.225	.298	373	84	14	5	1	0.3	41	24	33		8	0	0	220	310	32	39	5.7	.943	SS-96, 2B-2
1904	**2 teams**	**WAS A** (62G –.222) **STL A** (82G –.173)																						
″	**total**	144	.196	.225	515	101	13	1	0	0.0	42	21	48		9	0	0	185	343	41	19	4.0	.928	3B-82, SS-61, OF-1
1905	**STL A**	28	.195	.207	82	16	1	0	0	0.0	6	5	10		3	2	1	43	52	9	7	3.7	.913	2B-21, 3B-7
3 yrs.		270	.207	.252	970	201	28	6	1	0.1	89	50	91		20	2	1	448	705	82	65	4.6	.934	SS-157, 3B-89, 2B-23, OF-1

Herbie Moran

MORAN, JOHN HERBERT BL TR 5′ 5″ 150 lbs.
B. Feb. 16, 1884, Costello, Pa. D. Sept. 21, 1954, Clarkson, N. Y.

Year	Team	Games	BA	SA	AB	H	2B	3B	HR	HR%	R	RBI	BB	SO	SB	Pinch Hit AB	Pinch Hit H	PO	A	E	DP	TC/G	FA	G by Pos
1908	**2 teams**	**PHI A** (19G –.153) **BOS N** (8G –.276)																						
″	**total**	27	.193	.193	88	17	0	0	0	0.0	7	6	8		2	0	0	58	3	2	3	2.3	.968	OF-27
1909	**BOS N**	8	.226	.258	31	7	1	0	0	0.0	8	0	5		0	0	0	14	1	0	0	1.9	1.000	OF-8
1910		20	.119	.119	67	8	0	0	0	0.0	11	3	13	14	6	0	0	39	7	2	3	2.4	.958	OF-20
1912	**BKN N**	130	.276	.356	508	140	18	10	1	0.2	77	40	69	38	28	0	0	273	24	12	5	2.4	.961	OF-129
1913		132	.266	.315	515	137	15	5	0	0.0	71	26	45	29	21	3	0	231	15	13	7	2.0	.950	OF-129
1914	**2 teams**	**CIN N** (107G –.235) **BOS N** (41G –.266)																						
″	**total**	148	.244	.295	549	134	13	6	1	0.2	67	39	58	40	30	0	0	234	15	13	4	1.8	.950	OF-148
1915	**BOS N**	130	.200	.255	419	84	13	5	0	0.0	59	21	66	41	16	6	1	168	17	7	3	1.6	.964	OF-123
7 yrs.		595	.242	.296	2177	527	60	26	2	0.1	300	135	264	162	103	9	1	1017	82	49	25	2.0	.957	OF-584
WORLD SERIES																								
1914	**BOS N**	3	.077	.154	13	1	1	0	0	0.0	2	0	1	1	1	0	0	2	0	1	0	1.0	.667	OF-3

Pat Moran

MORAN, PATRICK JOSEPH BR TR 5′10″ 180 lbs.
B. Feb. 7, 1876, Fitchburg, Mass. D. Mar. 7, 1924, Orlando, Fla.
Manager 1915–23.

Year	Team	Games	BA	SA	AB	H	2B	3B	HR	HR%	R	RBI	BB	SO	SB	Pinch Hit AB	Pinch Hit H	PO	A	E	DP	TC/G	FA	G by Pos
1901	**BOS N**	53	.211	.283	180	38	5	1	2	1.1	12	18	3		3	0	0	299	37	14	8	6.7	.960	C-28, 1B-13, 3B-4, SS-3, OF-3, 2B-1
1902		80	.239	.311	251	60	5	5	1	0.4	22	24	17		6	6	1	339	95	8	5	5.9	.982	C-71, 1B-3, OF-1
1903		109	.262	.406	389	102	25	5	7	**1.8**	40	54	29		8	1	0	408	214	24	17	6.0	.963	C-107, 1B-1
1904		113	.226	.299	398	90	11	3	4	1.0	26	34	18		10	2	0	391	200	37	16	5.6	.941	C-72, 3B-39, 1B-2
1905		85	.240	.341	267	64	11	5	2	0.7	22	22	8		3	7	0	389	113	7	5	6.5	.986	C-78
1906	**CHI N**	70	.252	.319	226	57	13	1	0	0.0	22	35	7		6	9	0	335	78	9	6	6.9	.979	C-61
1907		65	.227	.278	198	45	5	1	1	0.5	8	19	10		5	6	2	258	72	9	9	5.7	.973	C-59
1908		50	.260	.307	150	39	5	1	0	0.0	12	12	13		6	4	0	242	56	10	5	6.8	.968	C-45
1909		77	.220	.285	246	54	11	1	1	0.4	18	23	16		2	2	1	181	97	8	3	3.9	.972	C-74
1910	**PHI N**	68	.236	.281	199	47	7	1	0	0.0	13	11	17	16	6	11	1	278	83	4	5	6.5	.989	C-56
1911		34	.184	.214	103	19	3	0	0	0.0	2	8	3	13	0	1	0	148	41	3	4	6.0	.984	C-32
1912		13	.115	.154	26	3	1	0	0	0.0	1	1	1	7	0	4	1	35	7	2	1	3.4	.955	C-13
1913		1	.000	.000	1	0	0	0	0	0.0	0	0	0	0	0	1	0	0	0	0	0	0.0	—	
1914		1	—	—	0	0	0	0	0	—	0	1	0	0	0	0	0	0	0	0	0	0.0	.000	C-1
14 yrs.		819	.235	.312	2634	618	102	24	18	0.7	198	262	142	36	55	54	6	3303	1093	135	84	5.9	.970	C-697, 3B-43, 1B-19, OF-4, SS-3, 2B-1
WORLD SERIES																								
1906	**CHI N**	2	.000	.000	2	0	0	0	0	0.0	0	0	0	0	0	2	0	0	0	0	0	0.0	—	
1907		1	—	—	0	0	0	0	0	—	0	0	0	0	0	0	0	0	0	0	0	0.0	—	
2 yrs.		3	.000	.000	2	0	0	0	0	0.0	0	0	0	0	0	2	0							

Roy Moran

MORAN, ROY ELLIS (Deedle) BR TR 5′ 8″ 155 lbs.
B. Sept. 17, 1884, Vincennes, Ind. D. July 18, 1966, Atlanta, Ga.

Year	Team	Games	BA	SA	AB	H	2B	3B	HR	HR%	R	RBI	BB	SO	SB	Pinch Hit AB	Pinch Hit H	PO	A	E	DP	TC/G	FA	G by Pos
1912	**WAS A**	5	.154	.154	13	2	0	0	0	0.0	1	0	8		3	0	0	7	1	1	0	1.8	.889	OF-5

Mickey Morandini

MORANDINI, MICHAEL ROBERT BL TR 5′11″ 170 lbs.
B. Apr. 22, 1966, Kittanning, Pa.

Year	Team	Games	BA	SA	AB	H	2B	3B	HR	HR%	R	RBI	BB	SO	SB	Pinch Hit AB	Pinch Hit H	PO	A	E	DP	TC/G	FA	G by Pos
1990	**PHI N**	25	.241	.329	79	19	4	0	1	1.3	9	3	6	19	3	1	0	37	61	1	10	4.0	.990	2B-25
1991		98	.249	.317	325	81	11	4	1	0.3	38	20	29	45	13	0	0	183	254	6	45	4.6	.986	2B-97
1992		127	.265	.344	422	112	8	8	3	0.7	47	30	25	64	8	6	3	239	336	6	65	4.6	.990	2B-124, SS-3
1993		120	.247	.355	425	105	19	9	3	0.7	57	33	34	73	13	11	3	208	288	5	48	4.5	.990	2B-111
1994		87	.292	.409	274	80	16	5	2	0.7	40	26	34	33	10	8	3	167	216	6	38	4.9	.985	2B-79
1995		127	.283	.417	494	140	34	7	6	1.2	65	49	42	80	9	9	1	268	336	7	73	5.0	.989	2B-122
6 yrs.		584	.266	.368	2019	537	92	33	16	0.8	256	161	170	314	56	35	10	1102	1491	31	279	4.7	.988	2B-558, SS-3
LEAGUE CHAMPIONSHIP SERIES																								
1993	**PHI N**	4	.250	.375	16	4	0	1	0	0.0	1	2	0	3	1	1	0	8	9	1	2	4.5	.944	2B-4
WORLD SERIES																								
1993	**PHI N**	3	.200	.200	5	1	0	0	0	0.0	1	0	1	2	0	1	0	2	0	0	0	2.0	1.000	2B-1

Mike Mordecai

MORDECAI, MICHAEL HOWARD BB TR 5′11″ 175 lbs.
B. Dec. 13, 1967, Birmingham, Ala.

Year	Team	Games	BA	SA	AB	H	2B	3B	HR	HR%	R	RBI	BB	SO	SB	Pinch Hit AB	Pinch Hit H	PO	A	E	DP	TC/G	FA	G by Pos
1994	ATL N	4	.250	1.000	4	1	0	0	1	25.0	1	3	1	0	0	1	0	1	4	0	0	1.3	1.000	SS-4
1995		69	.280	.480	75	21	6	0	3	4.0	10	11	9	16	0	29	7	39	31	0	12	1.6	1.000	2B-21, 1B-9, SS-6, 3B-6, OF-1
2 yrs.		73	.278	.506	79	22	6	0	4	5.1	11	14	10	16	0	30	7	40	35	0	12	1.6	1.000	2B-21, SS-10, 1B-9, 3B-6, OF-1
DIVISIONAL PLAYOFF SERIES																								
1995	ATL N	2	.667	1.000	3	2	1	0	0	0.0	1	2	0	0	0	2	2	1	0	0	0	1.0	1.000	SS-1
LEAGUE CHAMPIONSHIP SERIES																								
1995	ATL N	2	.000	.000	2	0	0	0	0	0.0	0	0	0	1	0	1	0	0	0	0	0	0.0	.000	SS-1
WORLD SERIES																								
1995	ATL N	3	.333	.333	3	1	0	0	0	0.0	0	0	0	1	0	1	0	0	6	0	0	2.0	1.000	SS-2, DH-1

Ray Morehart

MOREHART, RAYMOND ANDERSON BL TR 5′9″ 157 lbs.
B. Dec. 2, 1899, Abner, Tex. D. Jan. 13, 1989, Dallas, Tex.

Year	Team	Games	BA	SA	AB	H	2B	3B	HR	HR%	R	RBI	BB	SO	SB	Pinch Hit AB	Pinch Hit H	PO	A	E	DP	TC/G	FA	G by Pos
1924	CHI A	31	.200	.280	100	20	4	2	0	0.0	10	8	17	7	3	2	0	39	70	16	12	4.3	.872	SS-27, 2B-2
1926		73	.318	.401	192	61	10	3	0	0.0	27	21	11	15	3	17	6	71	136	11	13	4.5	.950	2B-48
1927	NY A	73	.256	.328	195	50	7	2	1	0.5	45	20	29	18	4	14	2	101	175	16	27	5.5	.945	2B-53
3 yrs.		177	.269	.347	487	131	21	7	1	0.2	82	49	57	40	10	33	8	211	381	43	52	4.9	.932	2B-103, SS-27

Dan Morejon

MOREJON, DANIEL BR TR 6′1″ 175 lbs.
Born Daniel Morejon (Torres).
B. July 21, 1930, Havana, Cuba.

Year	Team	Games	BA	SA	AB	H	2B	3B	HR	HR%	R	RBI	BB	SO	SB	Pinch Hit AB	Pinch Hit H	PO	A	E	DP	TC/G	FA	G by Pos
1958	CIN N	12	.192	.192	26	5	0	0	0	0.0	4	1	9	2	1	1	0	14	0	0	0	1.3	1.000	OF-11

Keith Moreland

MORELAND, BOBBY KEITH BR TR 6′ 190 lbs.
B. May 2, 1954, Dallas, Tex.

Year	Team	Games	BA	SA	AB	H	2B	3B	HR	HR%	R	RBI	BB	SO	SB	Pinch Hit AB	Pinch Hit H	PO	A	E	DP	TC/G	FA	G by Pos
1978	PHI N	1	.000	.000	2	0	0	0	0	0.0	0	0	0	0	0	0	0	4	0	0	0	4.0	1.000	C-1
1979		14	.375	.521	48	18	3	2	0	0.0	3	8	3	5	0	1	0	71	3	0	1	5.7	1.000	C-13
1980		62	.314	.440	159	50	8	0	4	2.5	13	29	8	14	3	17	7	188	24	8	7	4.9	.964	C-39, 3B-4, OF-2
1981		61	.255	.383	196	50	7	0	6	3.1	16	37	15	13	1	5	1	267	31	9	4	5.0	.971	C-50, 3B-7, 1B-2, OF-2
1982	CHI N	138	.261	.399	476	124	17	2	15	3.2	50	68	46	71	0	6	1	384	38	8	2	3.3	.981	OF-86, C-44, 3B-2
1983		154	.302	.460	533	161	30	3	16	3.0	76	70	68	73	0	2	0	244	7	6	1	1.7	.977	OF-151, C-3
1984		140	.279	.422	495	138	17	3	16	3.2	59	80	34	71	1	15	2	393	30	10	19	3.0	.977	OF-103, 1B-29, 3B-8, C-3
1985		161	.307	.440	587	180	30	3	14	2.4	74	106	68	58	12	2	1	313	29	13	7	2.1	.963	OF-148, 1B-12, 3B-11, C-2
1986		156	.271	.384	586	159	30	0	12	2.0	72	79	53	48	3	4	1	340	58	9	16	2.4	.978	OF-121, 3B-24, C-13, 1B-12
1987		153	.266	.465	563	150	29	1	27	4.8	63	88	39	66	3	1	0	99	300	28	27	2.8	.934	3B-150, 1B-1
1988	SD N	143	.256	.331	511	131	23	0	5	1.0	40	64	40	51	2	3	1	747	58	7	55	5.8	.991	1B-73, OF-64, 3B-2
1989	2 teams	DET A (90G –.299) BAL A (33G –.215)																						
″	total	123	.278	.367	425	118	20	0	6	1.4	45	45	31	45	3	17	4	243	32	4	23	2.3	.986	DH-80, 1B-31, 3B-12, C-1
12 yrs.		1306	.279	.411	4581	1279	214	14	121	2.6	511	674	405	515	28	73	18	3293	610	102	162	3.1	.975	OF-677, 3B-220, C-169, 1B-160, DH-80
DIVISIONAL PLAYOFF SERIES																								
1981	PHI N	4	.462	.692	13	6	0	0	1	7.7	2	3	1	1	0	0	0	30	2	1	0	8.3	.970	C-4
LEAGUE CHAMPIONSHIP SERIES																								
1980	PHI N	2	.000	.000	1	0	0	0	0	0.0	0	1	0	0	0	1	0	0	0	0	0	0.0	.000	C-1
1984	CHI N	5	.333	.444	18	6	2	0	0	0.0	3	2	1	1	0	0	0	9	0	0	0	1.8	1.000	OF-5
2 yrs.		7	.316	.421	19	6	2	0	0	0.0	3	3	1	1	0	1	0	9	0	0	0	1.5	1.000	OF-5, C-1
WORLD SERIES																								
1980	PHI N	3	.333	.333	12	4	0	0	0	0.0	1	1	0	1	0	0	0	0	0	0	0	0.0	.000	DH-3

Harry Morelock

MORELOCK, A. HARRY
B. Nov. 1869, Philadelphia, Pa. Deceased.

Year	Team	Games	BA	SA	AB	H	2B	3B	HR	HR%	R	RBI	BB	SO	SB	Pinch Hit AB	Pinch Hit H	PO	A	E	DP	TC/G	FA	G by Pos
1891	PHI N	4	.071	.071	14	1	0	0	0	0.0	1	0	3	3	0	0	0	5	9	3	0	4.3	.824	SS-4
1892		1	.000	.000	3	0	0	0	0	0.0	0	0	1	0	0	0	0	2	1	2	0	5.0	.600	3B-1
2 yrs.		5	.059	.059	17	1	0	0	0	0.0	1	0	4	3	0	0	0	7	10	5	0	4.4	.773	SS-4, 3B-1

Jose Moreno

MORENO, JOSE de los SANTOS BB TR 6′ 175 lbs.
Born Jose de los Santos Mauricio (Moreno).
B. Nov. 1, 1957, Santo Domingo, Dominican Republic.

Year	Team	Games	BA	SA	AB	H	2B	3B	HR	HR%	R	RBI	BB	SO	SB	Pinch Hit AB	Pinch Hit H	PO	A	E	DP	TC/G	FA	G by Pos
1980	NY N	37	.196	.413	46	9	2	1	2	4.3	6	9	3	12	1	26	4	11	11	3	3	3.1	.880	3B-4, 2B-4
1981	SD N	34	.229	.271	48	11	2	0	0	0.0	5	6	1	8	4	23	6	15	2	0	1	1.7	1.000	OF-9, 2B-1
1982	CAL A	11	.000	.000	3	0	0	0	0	0.0	3	0	2	0	0	0	0	2	2	0	0	1.3	1.000	2B-2, DH-1
3 yrs.		82	.206	.330	97	20	4	1	2	2.1	14	15	6	20	5	49	10	28	15	3	4	2.2	.935	OF-9, 2B-7, 3B-4, DH-1

Omar Moreno

MORENO, OMAR RENAN BL TL 6′2″ 180 lbs.
Born Omar Renan Moreno (Quintero).
B. Oct. 24, 1952, Puerto Armuelles, Panama.

Year	Team	Games	BA	SA	AB	H	2B	3B	HR	HR%	R	RBI	BB	SO	SB	Pinch Hit AB	Pinch Hit H	PO	A	E	DP	TC/G	FA	G by Pos
1975	PIT N	6	.167	.167	6	1	0	0	0	0.0	1	0	1	1	1	2	0	0	0	1	0	1.0	.000	OF-1
1976		48	.270	.369	122	33	4	1	2	1.6	24	12	16	24	15	4	2	93	3	4	1	2.4	.960	OF-42
1977		150	.240	.358	492	118	19	9	7	1.4	69	34	38	102	53	6	0	366	10	9	4	2.6	.977	OF-147
1978		155	.235	.303	515	121	15	7	2	0.4	95	33	81	104	**71**	4	1	409	9	7	2	2.8	.984	OF-152
1979		162	.282	.381	**695**	196	21	12	8	1.2	110	69	51	104	**77**	0	0	490	11	13	3	3.2	.975	OF-162
1980		162	.249	.325	**676**	168	20	**13**	2	0.3	87	36	57	101	96	0	0	479	15	5	2	3.1	.990	OF-162
1981		103	.276	.362	434	120	18	8	1	0.2	62	35	26	76	39	0	0	302	6	1	1	3.0	.997	OF-103
1982		158	.245	.315	645	158	18	9	3	0.5	82	44	44	121	60	1	0	396	10	7	3	2.6	.983	OF-157
1983	2 teams	HOU N (97G –.242) NY A (48G –.250)																						
″	total	145	.244	.330	557	136	21	12	1	0.2	65	42	30	103	37	0	0	371	9	7	4	2.7	.982	OF-145
1984	NY A	117	.259	.361	355	92	12	6	4	1.1	37	38	18	48	20	0	0	262	9	4	2	2.5	.985	OF-108, DH-1
1985	2 teams	NY A (34G –.197) KC A (24G –.243)																						
″	total	58	.221	.382	136	30	5	4	3	2.2	21	16	4	24	1	12	0	86	3	0	1	1.9	1.000	OF-47, DH-1
1986	ATL N	118	.234	.351	359	84	18	6	4	1.1	46	27	21	77	17	25	7	151	8	5	3	1.7	.970	OF-97
12 yrs.		1382	.252	.343	4992	1257	171	87	37	0.7	699	386	387	885	487	54	10	3405	93	63	26	2.7	.982	OF-1323, DH-2
LEAGUE CHAMPIONSHIP SERIES																								
1979	PIT N	3	.250	.417	12	3	0	1	0	0.0	3	0	2	2	1	0	0	7	0	0	0	2.3	1.000	OF-3

Omar Moreno *continued*

Year	Team	Lg	Games	BA	SA	AB	H	2B	3B	HR	HR%	R	RBI	BB	SO	SB	Pinch Hit AB	Pinch Hit H	PO	A	E	DP	TC/G	FA	G by Pos
WORLD SERIES																									
1979	**PIT**	**N**	7	.333	.394	33	11	2	0	0	0.0	4	3	1	7	0	0	0	20	1	0	0	3.0	1.000	OF-7

Bill Morgan

MORGAN, HENRY WILLIAM
B. Brooklyn, N. Y. Deceased.

Year	Team	Lg	Games	BA	SA	AB	H	2B	3B	HR	HR%	R	RBI	BB	SO	SB	Pinch Hit AB	Pinch Hit H	PO	A	E	DP	TC/G	FA	G by Pos
1878	**MIL**	**N**	14	.196	.196	56	11	0	0	0	0.0	2	5	3	9		0	0	14	9	7	0	1.8	.767	OF-13, 3B-3, 2B-1
1882	**PIT**	**AA**	17	.258	.318	66	17	2	1	0	0.0	10		4			0	0	38	7	15	1	3.3	.750	OF-11, C-7
1884	**2 teams**	**RIC AA** (11G –.167) **BAL U** (2G –.222)																							
"	**total**		13	.178	.222	45	8	0	1	0	0.0	3		3			0	0	36	18	13	1	4.8	.806	P-5, C-4, OF-3, 2B-2
3 yrs.			44	.216	.251	167	36	2	2	0	0.0	15	5	10	9		0	0	88	34	35	2	3.2	.777	OF-27, C-11, P-5, 3B-3, 2B-3

Bill Morgan

MORGAN, WILLIAM
Deceased.

Year	Team	Lg	Games	BA	SA	AB	H	2B	3B	HR	HR%	R	RBI	BB	SO	SB	Pinch Hit AB	Pinch Hit H	PO	A	E	DP	TC/G	FA	G by Pos
1883	**PIT**	**AA**	32	.158	.193	114	18	2	1	0	0.0	12		7		0	0	0	59	72	25	4	4.6	.840	SS-21, OF-6, C-5, 2B-2
1884	**WAS**	**AA**	45	.173	.191	162	28	1	1	0	0.0	8		8			0	0	117	27	26	2	3.6	.847	OF-31, 2B-14, SS-2
2 yrs.			77	.167	.192	276	46	3	2	0	0.0	20		15		0	0	0	176	99	51	6	4.0	.844	OF-37, SS-23, 2B-16, C-5

Bobby Morgan

MORGAN, ROBERT MORRIS BR TR 5′ 9″ 175 lbs.
B. June 29, 1926, Oklahoma City, Okla.

Year	Team	Lg	Games	BA	SA	AB	H	2B	3B	HR	HR%	R	RBI	BB	SO	SB	Pinch Hit AB	Pinch Hit H	PO	A	E	DP	TC/G	FA	G by Pos
1950	**BKN**	**N**	67	.226	.412	199	45	10	3	7	3.5	38	21	32	43	0	5	1	43	145	8	20	3.2	.959	3B-52, SS-10
1952			67	.236	.387	191	45	8	0	7	3.7	36	16	46	35	2	2	0	61	115	7	11	2.7	.962	3B-60, 2B-5, SS-4
1953			69	.260	.418	196	51	6	2	7	3.6	35	33	33	47	2	9	0	71	105	10	19	3.3	.946	3B-36, SS-21
1954	**PHI**	**N**	135	.262	.418	455	119	25	2	14	3.1	58	50	70	68	3	0	0	251	381	30	73	4.7	.955	SS-129, 3B-8, 2B-5
1955			136	.232	.344	483	112	20	2	10	2.1	61	49	73	72	6	6	2	291	332	18	70	4.7	.972	2B-88, SS-41, 3B-6, 1B-1
1956	**2 teams**	**PHI N** (8G –.200) **STL N** (61G –.195)																							
"	**total**		69	.196	.312	138	27	7	0	3	2.2	15	21	21	28	0	29	5	56	74	9	8	3.7	.935	3B-16, 2B-16, SS-6
1957	**2 teams**	**PHI N** (2G –.000) **CHI N** (125G –.207)																							
"	**total**		127	.207	.299	425	88	20	2	5	1.2	43	27	52	87	5	0	0	236	361	15	59	4.7	.975	2B-118, 3B-12
1958	**CHI**	**N**	1	.000	.000	1	0	0	0	0	0.0	0	0	0	1	0	1	0	0	0	0	0	0.0	—	
8 yrs.			671	.233	.366	2088	487	96	11	53	2.5	286	217	327	381	18	52	8	1009	1513	97	260	4.1	.963	2B-232, SS-211, 3B-190, 1B-1
WORLD SERIES																									
1952	**BKN**	**N**	2	.000	.000	1	0	0	0	0	0.0	0	0	0	0	0	1	0	0	1	0	0	0.5	1.000	3B-2
1953			1	.000	.000	1	0	0	0	0	0.0	0	0	0	0	0	1	0	0	0	0	0	0.0	—	
2 yrs.			3	.000	.000	2	0	0	0	0	0.0	0	0	0	0	0	2	0	0	1	0	0	0.5	1.000	3B-2

Chet Morgan

MORGAN, CHESTER COLLINS (Chick) BL TR 5′ 9″ 160 lbs.
B. June 6, 1910, Cleveland, Miss. D. Sept. 20, 1991, Pasadena, Tex.

Year	Team	Lg	Games	BA	SA	AB	H	2B	3B	HR	HR%	R	RBI	BB	SO	SB	Pinch Hit AB	Pinch Hit H	PO	A	E	DP	TC/G	FA	G by Pos
1935	**DET**	**A**	14	.174	.217	23	4	1	0	0	0.0	2	1	5	0	0	9	1	10	0	1	0	2.8	.909	OF-4
1938			74	.284	.310	306	87	6	1	0	0.0	50	27	20	12	5	0	0	192	6	4	2	2.7	.980	OF-74
2 yrs.			88	.277	.304	329	91	7	1	0	0.0	52	28	25	12	5	9	1	202	6	5	2	2.7	.977	OF-78

Ed Morgan

MORGAN, EDWARD CARRE BR TR 6′½″ 180 lbs.
B. May 22, 1904, Cairo, Ill. D. Apr. 9, 1980, New Orleans, La.

Year	Team	Lg	Games	BA	SA	AB	H	2B	3B	HR	HR%	R	RBI	BB	SO	SB	Pinch Hit AB	Pinch Hit H	PO	A	E	DP	TC/G	FA	G by Pos
1928	**CLE**	**A**	76	.313	.494	265	83	24	6	4	1.5	42	54	21	17	5	1	1	387	69	18	41	6.7	.962	1B-36, OF-21, 3B-14
1929			93	.318	.469	318	101	19	10	3	0.9	60	37	37	23	4	12	4	100	8	11	1	1.5	.908	OF-81
1930			150	.349	.601	584	204	47	11	26	4.5	122	136	62	**66**	8	2	0	1298	80	18	116	8.3	.987	1B-150, OF-19
1931			131	.351	.511	462	162	33	4	11	2.4	87	86	83	46	4	10	2	1117	80	20	102	10.1	.984	1B-117, 3B-3
1932			144	.293	.402	532	156	32	7	4	0.8	96	68	94	44	7	1	0	1430	74	23	100	10.8	.985	1B-142
1933			39	.264	.364	121	32	3	3	1	0.8	10	13	7	9	1	7	2	302	21	1	14	9.8	.997	1B-32, OF-1
1934	**BOS**	**A**	138	.267	.352	528	141	28	4	3	0.6	95	79	81	46	7	1	0	1283	56	16	111	9.9	.988	1B-137
7 yrs.			771	.313	.467	2810	879	186	45	52	1.9	512	473	385	251	36	34	9	5917	388	107	485	8.5	.983	1B-614, OF-122, 3B-17

Eddie Morgan

MORGAN, EDWIN WILLIS (Pepper) BL TL 5′10″ 160 lbs.
B. Nov. 19, 1914, Brady Lake, Ohio D. June 27, 1982, Lakewood, Ohio.

Year	Team	Lg	Games	BA	SA	AB	H	2B	3B	HR	HR%	R	RBI	BB	SO	SB	Pinch Hit AB	Pinch Hit H	PO	A	E	DP	TC/G	FA	G by Pos
1936	**STL**	**N**	8	.278	.444	18	5	0	0	1	5.6	4	3	2	4	0	3	2	8	0	1	0	2.3	.889	OF-4
1937	**BKN**	**N**	31	.188	.250	48	9	3	0	0	0.0	4	5	9	7	0	8	1	68	2	3	4	5.2	.959	OF-7, 1B-7
2 yrs.			39	.212	.303	66	14	3	0	1	1.5	8	8	11	11	0	11	3	76	2	4	4	4.6	.951	OF-11, 1B-7

Joe Morgan

MORGAN, JOE LEONARD BL TR 5′ 7″ 150 lbs.
B. Sept. 19, 1943, Bonham, Tex.
Hall of Fame 1990.

Year	Team	Lg	Games	BA	SA	AB	H	2B	3B	HR	HR%	R	RBI	BB	SO	SB	Pinch Hit AB	Pinch Hit H	PO	A	E	DP	TC/G	FA	G by Pos
1963	**HOU**	**N**	8	.240	.320	25	6	0	1	0	0.0	5	3	5	5	1	1	0	15	15	3	2	4.7	.909	2B-7
1964			10	.189	.189	37	7	0	0	0	0.0	4	0	6	7	0	0	0	31	25	3	4	5.9	.949	2B-10
1965			157	.271	.418	601	163	22	12	14	2.3	100	40	**97**	77	20	0	0	348	492	27	82	5.5	.969	2B-157
1966			122	.285	.391	425	121	14	8	5	1.2	60	42	89	43	11	4	1	256	316	21	61	5.1	.965	2B-117
1967			133	.275	.411	494	136	27	11	6	1.2	73	42	81	51	29	3	0	299	344	14	67	5.0	.979	2B-130, OF-1
1968			10	.250	.350	20	5	0	1	0	0.0	6	0	7	4	3	3	0	10	6	2	2	3.0	.889	2B-5, OF-1
1969			147	.236	.372	535	126	18	5	15	2.8	94	43	110	74	49	2	1	315	328	18	79	4.5	.973	2B-132, OF-14
1970			144	.268	.396	548	147	28	9	8	1.5	102	52	102	55	42	2	1	349	430	17	98	5.6	.979	2B-142
1971			160	.256	.407	583	149	27	**11**	13	2.2	87	56	88	52	40	4	1	336	482	12	93	5.3	.986	2B-157
1972	**CIN**	**N**	149	.292	.435	552	161	23	4	16	2.9	**122**	73	**115**	44	58	1	1	370	436	8	92	5.5	.990	2B-149
1973			157	.290	.493	576	167	35	2	26	4.5	116	82	111	61	67	3	3	417	440	9	106	5.6	.990	2B-154
1974			149	.293	.494	512	150	31	3	22	4.3	107	67	120	69	58	6	2	344	385	13	92	5.2	.982	2B-142
1975			146	.327	.508	498	163	27	6	17	3.4	107	94	**132**	52	67	4	1	356	425	11	96	5.6	.986	2B-142
1976			141	.320	**.576**	472	151	30	5	27	5.7	113	111	114	41	60	6	0	342	335	13	85	5.2	.981	2B-133
1977			153	.288	.478	521	150	21	6	22	4.2	113	78	117	58	49	2	0	351	359	5	100	4.7	.993	2B-151
1978			132	.236	.385	441	104	27	0	13	2.9	68	75	79	40	19	9	2	252	290	11	49	4.5	.980	2B-124
1979			127	.250	.376	436	109	26	1	9	2.1	70	32	93	45	28	3	0	259	329	12	74	5.0	.980	2B-121
1980	**HOU**	**N**	141	.243	.373	461	112	17	5	11	2.4	66	49	**93**	47	24	21	4	244	348	7	68	4.6	.988	2B-130
1981	**SF**	**N**	90	.240	.377	308	74	16	1	8	2.6	47	31	66	37	14	3	1	177	258	4	61	5.0	.991	2B-87
1982			134	.289	.438	463	134	19	4	14	3.0	68	61	85	60	24	12	4	255	366	8	69	5.1	.987	2B-120, 3B-3

Joe Morgan *continued*

Year	Team	Lg	Games	BA	SA	AB	H	2B	3B	HR	HR%	R	RBI	BB	SO	SB	Pinch Hit AB	Pinch Hit H	PO	A	E	DP	TC/G	FA	G by Pos
1983	PHI	N	123	.230	.403	404	93	20	1	16	4.0	72	59	89	54	18	10	3	231	331	17	63	4.9	.971	2B-117
1984	OAK	A	116	.244	.351	365	89	21	0	6	1.6	50	43	66	39	8	12	2	201	229	10	62	4.4	.977	2B-100
22 yrs.			2649	.271	.427	9277	2517	449	96	268	2.9	1650	1133	1865	1015	689	111	27	5758	6969	245	1505	5.1	.981	2B-2527, OF-16, 3B-3
														3rd		**9th**									
LEAGUE CHAMPIONSHIP SERIES																									
1972	CIN	N	5	.263	.579	19	5	0	0	2	10.5	5	3	1	2	1	0	0	11	18	0	3	5.8	1.000	2B-5
1973			5	.100	.150	20	2	1	0	0	0.0	1	1	2	2	0	0	0	12	27	0	3	7.8	1.000	2B-5
1975			3	.273	.545	11	3	3	0	0	0.0	2	1	3	2	4	0	0	2	9	0	1	3.7	1.000	2B-3
1976			3	.000	.000	7	0	0	0	0	0.0	2	0	6	1	2	0	0	9	5	0	2	4.7	1.000	2B-3
1979			3	.000	.000	11	0	0	0	0	0.0	0	0	3	1	1	0	0	12	11	0	2	7.7	1.000	2B-3
1980	HOU	N	4	.154	.385	13	2	1	1	0	0.0	1	0	6	1	0	0	0	9	8	0	3	4.3	1.000	2B-4
1983	PHI	N	4	.067	.067	15	1	0	0	0	0.0	1	0	2	1	0	0	0	8	7	0	0	3.8	1.000	2B-4
7 yrs.			27	.135	.271	96	13	5	1	2	2.1	12	5	23	10	8	0	0	63	85	0	14	5.5	1.000	2B-27
			6th			**5th**								**1st**		**4th**									
WORLD SERIES																									
1972	CIN	N	7	.125	.208	24	3	2	0	0	0.0	4	1	6	3	2	0	0	18	18	1	3	5.3	.973	2B-7
1975			7	.259	.296	27	7	1	0	0	0.0	4	3	5	1	2	0	0	17	28	0	4	6.4	1.000	2B-7
1976			4	.333	.733	15	5	1	1	1	6.7	3	2	2	2	2	0	0	13	10	2	3	6.3	.920	2B-4
1983	PHI	N	5	.263	.684	19	5	0	1	2	10.5	3	2	2	3	1	0	0	8	10	0	3	3.6	1.000	2B-5
4 yrs.			23	.235	.435	85	20	4	2	3	3.5	14	8	15	9	7	0	0	56	66	3	13	5.4	.976	2B-23
																9th									

Joe Morgan

MORGAN, JOSEPH MICHAEL BL TR 5′10″ 170 lbs.
B. Nov. 19, 1930, Walpole, Mass.
Manager 1988–91.

Year	Team	Lg	Games	BA	SA	AB	H	2B	3B	HR	HR%	R	RBI	BB	SO	SB	Pinch Hit AB	Pinch Hit H	PO	A	E	DP	TC/G	FA	G by Pos
1959	2 teams	MIL N (13G –.217) KC A (20G –.190)																							
″	total		33	.205	.273	44	9	1	1	0	0.0	4	4	5	11	0	22	5	10	14	2	1	2.9	.923	2B-7, 3B-2
1960	2 teams	PHI N (26G –.133) CLE A (22G –.298)																							
″	total		48	.192	.300	130	25	4	2	2	1.5	11	6	12	15	0	10	1	35	64	6	4	2.8	.943	3B-36, OF-2
1961	CLE	A	4	.200	.200	10	2	0	0	0	0.0	0	0	1	3	0	2	0	6	0	0	0	3.0	1.000	OF-2
1964	STL	N	3	.000	.000	3	0	0	0	0	0.0	0	0	0	2	0	3	0	0	0	0	0	0.0	—	
4 yrs.			88	.193	.283	187	36	5	3	2	1.1	15	10	18	31	0	37	6	51	78	8	5	2.8	.942	3B-38, 2B-7, OF-4

Ray Morgan

MORGAN, RAYMOND CARYLL BR TR 5′ 8½″ 155 lbs.
B. June 14, 1889, Baltimore, Md. D. Feb. 15, 1940, Baltimore, Md.

Year	Team	Lg	Games	BA	SA	AB	H	2B	3B	HR	HR%	R	RBI	BB	SO	SB	Pinch Hit AB	Pinch Hit H	PO	A	E	DP	TC/G	FA	G by Pos
1911	WAS	A	25	.213	.236	89	19	2	0	0	0.0	11	5	4		2	0	0	29	43	8	1	3.2	.900	3B-25
1912			80	.238	.337	273	65	10	7	1	0.4	40	30	29		11	0	0	157	181	23	23	4.5	.936	2B-75, SS-4, 3B-1
1913			137	.272	.345	481	131	19	8	0	0.0	58	57	68	63	19	0	0	261	372	33	61	4.9	.950	2B-133, SS-4
1914			147	.257	.340	491	126	22	8	1	0.2	50	49	62	34	24	1	0	290	379	37	58	4.8	.948	2B-146
1915			62	.233	.301	193	45	5	4	0	0.0	21	21	30	15	6	1	0	105	179	13	24	4.9	.956	2B-57, SS-2, 3B-2
1916			99	.267	.340	315	84	12	4	1	0.3	41	29	59	29	14	3	0	184	246	22	37	4.8	.951	2B-82, SS-9, 1B-3, 3B-1
1917			101	.266	.308	338	90	9	1	1	0.3	32	33	40	29	7	2	0	210	249	20	45	4.9	.958	2B-95, 3B-3
1918			88	.233	.277	300	70	11	1	0	0.0	25	30	28	14	4	4	1	175	251	18	30	5.4	.959	2B-80, OF-2
8 yrs.			739	.254	.322	2480	630	90	33	4	0.2	278	254	320	184	87	11	1	1411	1900	174	279	4.8	.950	2B-668, 3B-32, SS-19, 1B-3, OF-2

Red Morgan

MORGAN, JAMES EDWARD TR
B. Oct. 6, 1883, Neola, Iowa D. Mar. 25, 1981, New York, N. Y.

Year	Team	Lg	Games	BA	SA	AB	H	2B	3B	HR	HR%	R	RBI	BB	SO	SB	Pinch Hit AB	Pinch Hit H	PO	A	E	DP	TC/G	FA	G by Pos
1906	BOS	A	88	.215	.264	307	66	6	3	1	0.3	20	21	16		7	0	0	126	139	41	8	3.5	.866	3B-88

Vern Morgan

MORGAN, VERNON THOMAS BL TR 6′ 1″ 190 lbs.
B. Aug. 8, 1928, Emporia, Va. D. Nov. 8, 1975, Minneapolis, Minn.

Year	Team	Lg	Games	BA	SA	AB	H	2B	3B	HR	HR%	R	RBI	BB	SO	SB	Pinch Hit AB	Pinch Hit H	PO	A	E	DP	TC/G	FA	G by Pos
1954	CHI	N	24	.234	.266	64	15	2	0	0	0.0	3	2	1	10	0	7	1	8	26	4	1	2.5	.895	3B-15
1955			7	.143	.143	7	1	0	0	0	0.0	1	1	3	4	0	3	0	2	2	2	0	3.0	.667	3B-2
2 yrs.			31	.225	.254	71	16	2	0	0	0.0	4	3	4	14	0	10	1	10	28	6	1	2.6	.864	3B-17

Moe Morhardt

MORHARDT, MEREDITH GOODWIN BL TL 6′ 1″ 185 lbs.
B. Jan. 16, 1937, Manchester, Conn.

Year	Team	Lg	Games	BA	SA	AB	H	2B	3B	HR	HR%	R	RBI	BB	SO	SB	Pinch Hit AB	Pinch Hit H	PO	A	E	DP	TC/G	FA	G by Pos
1961	CHI	N	7	.278	.278	18	5	0	0	0	0.0	3	1	3	5	0	0	0	72	3	3	9	11.1	.962	1B-7
1962			18	.125	.125	16	2	0	0	0	0.0	1	2	2	8	0	16	2	0	0	0	0	0.0	—	
2 yrs.			25	.206	.206	34	7	0	0	0	0.0	4	3	5	13	0	16	2	72	3	3	9	11.1	.962	1B-7

Gene Moriarity

MORIARITY, EUGENE JOHN BL TL 5′ 8″ 190 lbs.
B. Jan. 5, 1865, Holyoke, Mass. Deceased.

Year	Team	Lg	Games	BA	SA	AB	H	2B	3B	HR	HR%	R	RBI	BB	SO	SB	Pinch Hit AB	Pinch Hit H	PO	A	E	DP	TC/G	FA	G by Pos
1884	2 teams	BOS N (4G –.063) IND AA (10G –.216)																							
″	total		14	.170	.245	53	9	0	2	0	0.0	5		0	8		0	0	16	7	6	0	2.1	.793	OF-11, P-2, 3B-1
1885	DET	N	11	.026	.051	39	1	1	0	0	0.0	1	0	0	10		0	0	23	12	9	0	3.7	.795	OF-6, 3B-4, P-1, SS-1
1892	STL	N	47	.175	.260	177	31	4	1	3	1.7	20	19	4	37	7	0	0	96	9	23	0	2.7	.820	OF-47
3 yrs.			72	.152	.227	269	41	5	3	3	1.1	26	19	4	55	7	0	0	135	28	38	0	2.8	.811	OF-64, 3B-5, P-3, SS-1

Bill Moriarty

MORIARTY, WILLIAM JOSEPH BR TR 6′ 2″ 180 lbs.
Brother of George Moriarty.
B. Aug. 1883, Chicago, Ill. D. Dec. 25, 1916, Elgin, Ill.

Year	Team	Lg	Games	BA	SA	AB	H	2B	3B	HR	HR%	R	RBI	BB	SO	SB	Pinch Hit AB	Pinch Hit H	PO	A	E	DP	TC/G	FA	G by Pos
1909	CIN	N	6	.200	.250	20	4	1	0	0	0.0	1	1	0		2	0	0	18	16	2	2	6.0	.944	SS-6

Ed Moriarty

MORIARTY, EDWARD JEROME BR TR 5′10½″ 180 lbs.
B. Oct. 12, 1912, Holyoke, Mass. D. Sept. 29, 1991, Holyoke, Mass.

Year	Team	Lg	Games	BA	SA	AB	H	2B	3B	HR	HR%	R	RBI	BB	SO	SB	Pinch Hit AB	Pinch Hit H	PO	A	E	DP	TC/G	FA	G by Pos
1935	BOS	N	8	.324	.529	34	11	2	1	1	2.9	4	1	0	6	0	0	0	11	25	3	0	4.9	.923	2B-8
1936			6	.167	.167	6	1	0	0	0	0.0	0	0	0	1	0	6	1	0	0	0	0	0.0	—	
2 yrs.			14	.300	.475	40	12	2	1	1	2.5	4	1	0	7	0	6	1	11	25	3	0	4.9	.923	2B-8

George Moriarty

MORIARTY, GEORGE JOSEPH BR TR 6′ 185 lbs.
Brother of Bill Moriarty.
B. July 7, 1884, Chicago, Ill. D. Apr. 8, 1964, Miami, Fla.
Manager 1927–28.

Year	Team		Games	BA	SA	AB	H	2B	3B	HR	HR%	R	RBI	BB	SO	SB	Pinch Hit AB	Pinch Hit H	PO	A	E	DP	TC/G	FA	G by Pos
1903	CHI	N	1	.000	.000	5	0	0	0	0	0.0	1	0	0		0	0	0	3	1	0	0	4.0	1.000	3B-1
1904			4	.000	.000	13	0	0	0	0	0.0	0	0	1		0	0	0	8	3	3	0	3.5	.786	OF-2, 3B-2
1906	NY	A	65	.234	.340	197	46	7	7	0	0.0	22	23	17		8	4	1	129	84	17	5	3.8	.926	3B-39, OF-15, 1B-5, 2B-1
1907			126	.277	.336	437	121	16	5	0	0.0	51	43	25		28	1	0	372	186	43	20	4.6	.928	3B-91, 1B-22, OF-9, 2B-8, SS-1
1908			101	.236	.276	348	82	12	1	0	0.0	25	27	11		22	8	2	609	117	24	30	8.0	.968	1B-52, 3B-28, OF-10, 2B-4
1909	DET	A	133	.273	.338	473	129	20	4	1	0.2	43	39	24		34	3	1	400	265	27	23	5.3	.961	3B-106, 1B-24
1910			136	.251	.324	490	123	24	3	2	0.4	53	60	33		33	1	0	165	302	37	17	3.8	.927	3B-134
1911			130	.243	.308	478	116	20	4	1	0.2	51	60	27		28	0	0	162	274	33	11	3.6	.930	3B-129, 1B-1
1912			105	.248	.315	375	93	23	1	0	0.0	38	54	26		27	1	1	842	97	19	25	9.2	.980	1B-71, 3B-33
1913			102	.239	.265	347	83	5	2	0	0.0	29	30	24	25	33	0	0	136	183	21	9	3.4	.938	3B-93, OF-7
1914			130	.254	.323	465	118	19	5	1	0.2	56	40	39	27	34	0	0	151	313	20	16	3.8	.959	3B-126, 1B-3
1915			31	.211	.237	38	8	1	0	0	0.0	2	0	5	7	1	10	2	11	14	3	1	1.9	.893	3B-12, OF-1, 2B-1, 1B-1
1916	CHI	A	7	.200	.200	5	1	0	0	0	0.0	1	0	2	0	0	3	1	2	2	0	0	2.0	1.000	3B-1, 1B-1
13 yrs.			1071	.251	.312	3671	920	147	32	5	0.1	372	376	234	59	248	31	8	2990	1841	247	157	4.9	.951	3B-795, 1B-180, OF-44, 2B-14, SS-1
WORLD SERIES																									
1909	DET	A	7	.273	.318	22	6	1	0	0	0.0	4	1	3	1	0	0	0	7	14	0	2	3.0	1.000	3B-7

Bill Morley

MORLEY, WILLIAM M. BR TR 5′11″ 170 lbs.
Born William Morley Jennings.
B. Jan. 23, 1890, Holland, Mich. D. May 14, 1985, Lubbock, Tex.

Year	Team		Games	BA	SA	AB	H	2B	3B	HR	HR%	R	RBI	BB	SO	SB	Pinch Hit AB	Pinch Hit H	PO	A	E	DP	TC/G	FA	G by Pos
1913	WAS	A	2	.000	.000	3	0	0	0	0	0.0	0	0	0	0	0	0	0	0	0	0	0	0.0	.000	2B-1

Russ Morman

MORMAN, RUSSELL LEE BR TR 6′ 4″ 215 lbs.
B. Apr. 28, 1962, Independence, Mo.

Year	Team		Games	BA	SA	AB	H	2B	3B	HR	HR%	R	RBI	BB	SO	SB	Pinch Hit AB	Pinch Hit H	PO	A	E	DP	TC/G	FA	G by Pos
1986	CHI	A	49	.252	.358	159	40	5	0	4	2.5	18	17	16	36	1	1	0	342	26	4	31	7.9	.989	1B-47
1988			40	.240	.267	75	18	2	0	0	0.0	8	3	3	17	0	5	2	114	5	2	8	3.5	.983	1B-22, OF-10, DH-3
1989			37	.224	.259	58	13	2	0	0	0.0	5	8	6	16	1	2	2	157	13	2	21	4.8	.988	1B-35, DH-1
1990	KC	A	12	.270	.568	37	10	4	2	1	2.7	5	3	3	3	0	1	0	27	4	0	1	2.6	1.000	OF-8, 1B-3, DH-1
1991			12	.261	.261	23	6	0	0	0	0.0	1	1	1	5	0	4	0	47	3	0	2	4.5	1.000	1B-8, OF-2, DH-1
1994	FLA	N	13	.212	.364	33	7	0	1	1	3.0	2	2	2	9	0	4	0	66	9	1	9	9.5	.987	1B-8
1995			34	.278	.458	72	20	2	1	3	4.2	9	7	3	12	0	13	4	31	1	1	1	1.6	.970	OF-18, 1B-3
7 yrs.			197	.249	.359	457	114	15	4	9	2.0	48	41	34	98	2	30	8	784	61	10	73	5.0	.988	1B-126, OF-38, DH-6

Jeff Moronko

MORONKO, JEFFREY ROBERT BR TR 6′ 2″ 190 lbs.
B. Aug. 17, 1959, Houston, Tex.

Year	Team		Games	BA	SA	AB	H	2B	3B	HR	HR%	R	RBI	BB	SO	SB	Pinch Hit AB	Pinch Hit H	PO	A	E	DP	TC/G	FA	G by Pos
1984	CLE	A	7	.158	.211	19	3	1	0	0	0.0	1	3	3	5	0	1	0	10	7	2	2	2.7	.895	3B-6, DH-1
1987	NY	A	7	.091	.091	11	1	0	0	0	0.0	0	0	0	2	0	0	0	1	9	0	1	1.4	1.000	3B-3, SS-2, OF-2
2 yrs.			14	.133	.167	30	4	1	0	0	0.0	1	3	3	7	0	1	0	11	16	2	3	2.1	.931	3B-9, OF-2, SS-2, DH-1

John Morrill

MORRILL, JOHN FRANCIS (Honest John) BR TR 5′10½″ 155 lbs.
B. Feb. 19, 1855, Boston, Mass. D. Apr. 2, 1932, Boston, Mass.
Manager 1882–89.

Year	Team		Games	BA	SA	AB	H	2B	3B	HR	HR%	R	RBI	BB	SO	SB	Pinch Hit AB	Pinch Hit H	PO	A	E	DP	TC/G	FA	G by Pos
1876	BOS	N	66	.263	.295	278	73	5	2	0	0.0	38	26	3	5		0	0	238	160	78	21	7.0	.836	2B-37, C-23, OF-5, 1B-3
1877			61	.302	.331	242	73	5	1	0	0.0	47	28	6	15		0	0	223	61	38	14	5.2	.882	3B-30, 1B-18, OF-11, 2B-3
1878			60	.240	.270	233	56	5	1	0	0.0	26	23	5	16		0	0	608	25	30	36	10.9	.955	1B-59, OF-1, 3B-1
1879			84	.282	.362	348	98	18	5	0	0.0	56	49	14	32		0	0	383	112	34	25	6.3	.936	3B-51, 1B-33
1880			86	.237	.348	342	81	16	8	2	0.6	51	44	11	37		0	0	479	98	38	30	6.9	.938	1B-46, 3B-40, P-3
1881			81	.289	.379	311	90	19	3	1	0.3	47	39	12	30		0	0	764	61	26	33	10.3	.969	1B-74, 2B-4, P-3, 3B-2
1882			83	.289	.424	349	101	19	11	2	0.6	73	54	18	29		0	0	752	34	34	23	9.8	.959	1B-76, SS-3, 2B-2, P-1, OF-1, 3B-1
1883			97	.319	.525	404	129	33	16	6	1.5	83	68	15	68		0	0	819	44	31	34	8.9	.965	1B-81, OF-7, 3B-6, SS-2, P-2, 2B-2
1884			111	.260	.356	438	114	19	7	3	0.7	80		30	87		0	0	1006	86	41	37	9.6	.964	1B-91, 2B-17, P-7, 3B-2, OF-1
1885			111	.226	.343	394	89	20	7	4	1.0	74	44	64	78		0	0	1010	87	41	61	10.3	.964	1B-92, 2B-17, 3B-2
1886			117	.247	.381	430	106	25	6	7	1.6	86	69	56	81		0	0	535	245	61	44	7.1	.927	SS-55, 1B-42, 2B-20, P-1
1887			127	.280	.438	504	141	32	6	12	2.4	79	81	37	**86**	19	0	0	1231	50	21	76	10.3	.984	1B-127
1888			135	.198	.288	486	96	18	7	4	0.8	60	39	55	68	21	0	0	1401	79	33	67	11.2	.978	1B-133, 2B-2
1889	WAS	N	44	.185	.260	146	27	5	0	2	1.4	20	16	30	23	12	0	0	373	23	13	16	9.1	.968	1B-40, 3B-3, P-1, 2B-1
1890	BOS	P	2	.143	.143	7	1	0	0	0	0.0	1	2	2	1	0	0	0	16	2	1	0	9.5	.947	SS-1, 1B-1
15 yrs.			1265	.260	.367	4912	1275	239	80	43	0.9	821	582	358	656	52	0	0	9838	1167	520	517	9.0	.955	1B-916, 3B-138, 2B-105, SS-61, OF-26, C-23, P-18

Doyt Morris

MORRIS, DOYT THEODORE BR TR 6′ 4″ 195 lbs.
B. July 15, 1916, Stanley, N. C. D. July 4, 1984, Gastonia, N. C.

Year	Team		Games	BA	SA	AB	H	2B	3B	HR	HR%	R	RBI	BB	SO	SB	Pinch Hit AB	Pinch Hit H	PO	A	E	DP	TC/G	FA	G by Pos
1937	PHI	A	6	.154	.154	13	2	0	0	0	0.0	0	0	0	3	0	3	1	7	0	0	0	2.3	1.000	OF-3

E. Morris

MORRIS, E.
B. Trenton, N. J. Deceased.

Year	Team		Games	BA	SA	AB	H	2B	3B	HR	HR%	R	RBI	BB	SO	SB	Pinch Hit AB	Pinch Hit H	PO	A	E	DP	TC/G	FA	G by Pos
1884	BAL	U	1	.000	.000	3	0	0	0	0	0.0	0		0			0	0	0	0	2	0	1.0	.000	P-1, OF-1

Hal Morris

MORRIS, WILLIAM HAROLD BL TL 6′ 3″ 200 lbs.
B. Apr. 9, 1965, Fort Rucker, Ala.

Year	Team		Games	BA	SA	AB	H	2B	3B	HR	HR%	R	RBI	BB	SO	SB	Pinch Hit AB	Pinch Hit H	PO	A	E	DP	TC/G	FA	G by Pos
1988	NY	A	15	.100	.100	20	2	0	0	0	0.0	1	0	0	9	0	10	2	7	0	0	0	1.4	1.000	OF-4, DH-1
1989			15	.278	.278	18	5	0	0	0	0.0	2	4	1	4	0	9	1	12	0	0	2	1.5	1.000	OF-5, 1B-2, DH-1
1990	CIN	N	107	.340	.498	309	105	22	3	7	2.3	50	36	21	32	9	21	7	595	53	4	50	7.6	.994	1B-80, OF-6
1991			136	.318	.479	478	152	33	1	14	2.9	72	59	46	61	10	9	3	979	100	9	87	8.4	.992	1B-128, OF-1
1992			115	.271	.385	395	107	21	3	6	1.5	41	53	45	53	6	8	2	841	86	1	65	8.5	.999	1B-109

Hal Morris *continued*

Year	Team	Games	BA	SA	AB	H	2B	3B	HR	HR%	R	RBI	BB	SO	SB	Pinch Hit AB	Pinch Hit H	PO	A	E	DP	TC/G	FA	G by Pos
1993		101	.317	.420	379	120	18	0	7	1.8	48	49	34	51	2	4	0	746	75	5	61	8.4	.994	1B-98
1994		112	.335	.491	436	146	30	4	10	2.3	60	78	34	62	6	1	0	899	77	6	76	8.8	.994	1B-112
1995		101	.279	.451	359	100	25	2	11	3.1	53	51	29	58	1	5	1	755	72	5	79	8.4	.994	1B-99
8 yrs.		702	.308	.450	2394	737	149	13	55	2.3	327	330	210	330	34	67	16	4834	463	30	420	8.2	.994	1B-628, OF-16, DH-2
DIVISIONAL PLAYOFF SERIES																								
1995	CIN N	3	.500	.600	10	5	1	0	0	0.0	5	2	3	1	1	0	0	22	2	0	1	8.0	1.000	1B-3
LEAGUE CHAMPIONSHIP SERIES																								
1990	CIN N	5	.417	.500	12	5	1	0	0	0.0	3	1	1	0	0	1	1	20	2	0	2	5.5	1.000	1B-4
1995		4	.167	.250	12	2	1	0	0	0.0	0	1	1	1	1	1	0	27	3	0	2	7.5	1.000	1B-4
2 yrs.		9	.292	.375	24	7	2	0	0	0.0	3	2	2	1	1	2	1	47	5	0	4	6.5	1.000	1B-8
WORLD SERIES																								
1990	CIN N	4	.071	.071	14	1	0	0	0	0.0	0	2	1	1	0	0	0	18	1	0	1	4.8	1.000	1B-2, DH-2

John Morris

MORRIS, JOHN DANIEL BL TL 6′ 1″ 185 lbs.
B. Feb. 23, 1961, Freeport, N. Y.

Year	Team	Games	BA	SA	AB	H	2B	3B	HR	HR%	R	RBI	BB	SO	SB	Pinch Hit AB	Pinch Hit H	PO	A	E	DP	TC/G	FA	G by Pos
1986	STL N	39	.240	.290	100	24	0	1	1	1.0	8	14	7	15	6	11	3	68	0	1	0	2.2	.986	OF-31
1987		101	.261	.408	157	41	6	4	3	1.9	22	23	11	22	5	30	10	86	0	1	0	1.2	.989	OF-74
1988		20	.289	.395	38	11	2	1	0	0.0	3	3	1	7	0	6	2	12	0	2	0	0.9	.857	OF-16
1989		96	.239	.342	117	28	4	1	2	1.7	8	14	4	22	1	41	9	45	0	0	0	0.9	1.000	OF-51
1990		18	.111	.111	18	2	0	0	0	0.0	0	0	3	6	0	9	1	4	0	0	0	0.7	1.000	OF-6
1991	PHI N	85	.220	.276	127	28	2	1	1	0.8	15	6	12	25	2	28	6	73	1	2	0	1.3	.974	OF-57
1992	CAL A	43	.193	.263	57	11	1	0	1	1.8	4	3	4	11	1	25	4	13	0	0	0	0.6	1.000	OF-14, DH-6
7 yrs.		402	.236	.326	614	145	15	8	8	1.3	60	63	42	108	15	150	35	301	1	6	0	1.2	.981	OF-249, DH-6
LEAGUE CHAMPIONSHIP SERIES																								
1987	STL N	2	.000	.000	3	0	0	0	0	0.0	0	0	0	0	0	0	0	1	0	0	0	0.5	1.000	OF-2
WORLD SERIES																								
1987	STL N	1	.000	.000	2	0	0	0	0	0.0	0	0	0	0	0	0	0	2	0	0	0	2.0	1.000	OF-1

P. Morris

MORRIS, P.
B. Rockford, Ill. Deceased.

Year	Team	Games	BA	SA	AB	H	2B	3B	HR	HR%	R	RBI	BB	SO	SB	Pinch Hit AB	Pinch Hit H	PO	A	E	DP	TC/G	FA	G by Pos
1884	WAS U	1	.000	.000	3	0	0	0	0	0.0	0		0			0	0	0	3	1	0	4.0	.750	SS-1

Walter Morris

MORRIS, JOHN WALTER BR TR 5′11″
B. Jan. 31, 1880, Rockwall, Tex. D. Aug. 2, 1961, Dallas, Tex.

Year	Team	Games	BA	SA	AB	H	2B	3B	HR	HR%	R	RBI	BB	SO	SB	Pinch Hit AB	Pinch Hit H	PO	A	E	DP	TC/G	FA	G by Pos
1908	STL N	23	.178	.219	73	13	1	1	0	0.0	1	2	0		1	1	0	47	75	8	8	5.7	.938	SS-23

William Morris

Playing record listed under John Fluhrer.

Jim Morrison

MORRISON, JAMES FORREST BR TR 5′11″ 175 lbs.
B. Sept. 23, 1952, Pensacola, Fla.

Year	Team	Games	BA	SA	AB	H	2B	3B	HR	HR%	R	RBI	BB	SO	SB	Pinch Hit AB	Pinch Hit H	PO	A	E	DP	TC/G	FA	G by Pos
1977	PHI N	5	.429	.429	7	3	0	0	0	0.0	3	1	1	1	0	0	0	0	7	1	0	1.6	.875	3B-5
1978		53	.157	.269	108	17	1	1	3	2.8	12	10	10	21	1	12	0	88	97	6	22	5.5	.969	2B-31, 3B-3, OF-1
1979	CHI A	67	.275	.508	240	66	14	0	14	5.8	38	35	15	48	11	4	0	121	185	9	38	4.1	.971	2B-48, 3B-29
1980		162	.283	.424	604	171	40	0	15	2.5	66	57	36	74	9	0	0	422	482	29	117	5.7	.969	2B-161, SS-1, DH-1
1981		90	.234	.372	290	68	8	1	10	3.4	27	34	10	29	3	2	0	64	200	12	15	3.1	.957	3B-87, 2B-1, DH-1
1982	2 teams	CHI A (51G –.223) PIT N (44G –.279)																						
″	total	95	.242	.448	252	61	11	4	11	4.4	27	34	18	29	2	16	3	36	130	12	12	2.2	.933	3B-76, OF-2, 2B-1, SS-1, DH-1
1983	PIT N	66	.304	.487	158	48	7	2	6	3.8	16	25	9	25	2	15	4	55	99	7	21	2.7	.957	2B-28, 3B-25, SS-7
1984		100	.286	.454	304	87	14	2	11	3.6	38	45	20	52	0	13	1	86	166	10	21	2.9	.962	3B-61, 2B-26, SS-2, 1B-1
1985		92	.254	.348	244	62	11	0	4	1.6	17	22	8	44	3	19	4	73	121	5	14	2.7	.975	3B-59, 2B-15, OF-1
1986		154	.274	.482	537	147	35	4	23	4.3	58	88	47	88	9	4	1	92	258	20	12	2.4	.946	3B-151, 2B-1, SS-1
1987	2 teams	PIT N (96G –.264) DET A (34G –.205)																						
″	total	130	.249	.391	465	116	23	2	13	2.8	56	65	29	83	10	11	2	99	251	9	29	2.5	.975	3B-98, SS-20, 2B-12, DH-8, OF-3, 1B-1
1988	2 teams	DET A (24G –.216) ATL N (51G –.152)																						
″	total	75	.181	.259	166	30	7	0	2	1.2	13	19	10	27	0	31	6	57	30	4	3	1.8	.956	3B-24, DH-14, OF-6, 1B-4, P-3, SS-1
12 yrs.		1089	.260	.419	3375	876	171	16	112	3.3	371	435	213	521	50	127	21	1193	2026	124	304	3.3	.963	3B-618, 2B-324, SS-33, DH-25, OF-13, 1B-6, P-3
LEAGUE CHAMPIONSHIP SERIES																								
1978	PHI N	1	.000	.000	1	0	0	0	0	0.0	0	0	0	1	0	1	0	0	0	0	0	0.0	—	
1987	DET A	2	.400	.400	5	2	0	0	0	0.0	1	0	0	1	0	0	0	1	2	0	0	1.5	1.000	3B-1, DH-1
2 yrs.		3	.333	.333	6	2	0	0	0	0.0	1	0	0	2	0	1	0	1	2	0	0	1.5	1.000	3B-1, DH-1

Jon Morrison

MORRISON, JONATHAN W. BL 5′ 9½″ 167 lbs.
B. 1859, London, Ont., Canada Deceased.

Year	Team	Games	BA	SA	AB	H	2B	3B	HR	HR%	R	RBI	BB	SO	SB	Pinch Hit AB	Pinch Hit H	PO	A	E	DP	TC/G	FA	G by Pos
1884	IND AA	44	.264	.401	182	48	6	8	1	0.5	26		7			0	0	78	9	24	4	2.5	.784	OF-44
1887	NY AA	9	.118	.118	34	4	0	0	0	0.0	7		6		0	0	0	12	0	8	0	2.2	.600	OF-9
2 yrs.		53	.241	.356	216	52	6	8	1	0.5	33		13		0	0	0	90	9	32	4	2.5	.756	OF-53

Tom Morrison

MORRISON, THOMAS J. 5′ 3″ 145 lbs.
B. 1875, St. Louis, Mo.

Year	Team	Games	BA	SA	AB	H	2B	3B	HR	HR%	R	RBI	BB	SO	SB	Pinch Hit AB	Pinch Hit H	PO	A	E	DP	TC/G	FA	G by Pos
1895	LOU N	6	.273	.455	22	6	0	2	0	0.0	3	4	1	1	0	0	0	7	9	2	1	3.0	.889	SS-3, 3B-3
1896		8	.148	.185	27	4	1	0	0	0.0	3	0	4	4	0	0	0	7	16	3	1	3.3	.885	3B-5, OF-2, SS-1
2 yrs.		14	.204	.306	49	10	1	2	0	0.0	6	4	5	5	0	0	0	14	25	5	2	3.1	.886	3B-8, SS-4, OF-2

Jack Morrissey

MORRISSEY, JOHN ALBERT (King) BB TR 5′10″ 160 lbs.
B. May 2, 1876, Lansing, Mich. D. Oct. 30, 1936, Lansing, Mich.

Year	Team	Games	BA	SA	AB	H	2B	3B	HR	HR%	R	RBI	BB	SO	SB	Pinch Hit AB	Pinch Hit H	PO	A	E	DP	TC/G	FA	G by Pos
1902	CIN N	12	.282	.359	39	11	1	1	0	0.0	5	3	4		0	0	0	24	26	3	3	4.4	.943	2B-11, OF-1
1903		29	.247	.258	89	22	1	0	0	0.0	14	9	14		3	2	0	48	38	16	7	3.8	.843	2B-17, OF-8, SS-2
2 yrs.		41	.258	.289	128	33	2	1	0	0.0	19	12	18		3	2	0	72	64	19	10	4.0	.877	2B-28, OF-9, SS-2

Jo-Jo Morrissey

MORRISSEY, JOSEPH ANSELM BR TR 6′ 1½″ 178 lbs.
B. Jan. 16, 1904, Warren, R. I. D. May 2, 1950, Worcester, Mass.

Year	Team	Games	BA	SA	AB	H	2B	3B	HR	HR%	R	RBI	BB	SO	SB	Pinch Hit AB	Pinch Hit H	PO	A	E	DP	TC/G	FA	G by Pos
1932	CIN N	89	.242	.286	269	65	10	1	0	0.0	15	13	14	15	2	1	0	144	240	8	38	3.9	.980	SS-45, 2B-42, 3B-12, OF-1
1933		148	.230	.268	534	123	20	0	0	0.0	43	26	20	22	5	1	1	300	461	40	76	4.8	.950	2B-88, SS-63, 3B-15
1936	CHI A	17	.184	.211	38	7	1	0	0	0.0	3	6	2	3	0	4	2	17	22	3	2	3.0	.929	3B-9, SS-4, 2B-1
3 yrs.		254	.232	.271	841	195	31	1	0	0.0	61	45	36	40	7	6	3	461	723	51	116	4.4	.959	2B-131, SS-112, 3B-36, OF-1

John Morrissey

MORRISSEY, JOHN J.
Brother of Tom Morrissey.
B. Dec. 30, 1856, Janesville, Wis. D. Apr. 29, 1884, Janesville, Wis.

Year	Team	Games	BA	SA	AB	H	2B	3B	HR	HR%	R	RBI	BB	SO	SB	Pinch Hit AB	Pinch Hit H	PO	A	E	DP	TC/G	FA	G by Pos
1881	BUF N	12	.213	.255	47	10	2	0	0	0.0	3	3	0	3		0	0	10	22	5	0	3.1	.865	3B-12
1882	DET N	2	.286	.286	7	2	0	0	0	0.0	1	0	0	2		0	0	4	1	2	0	3.5	.714	3B-2
2 yrs.		14	.222	.259	54	12	2	0	0	0.0	4	3	0	5		0	0	14	23	7	0	3.1	.841	3B-14

Tom Morrissey

MORRISSEY, THOMAS J. 5′11″ 180 lbs.
Brother of John Morrissey.
B. 1861, Janesville, Wis. D. Sept. 23, 1941, Janesville, Wis.

Year	Team	Games	BA	SA	AB	H	2B	3B	HR	HR%	R	RBI	BB	SO	SB	Pinch Hit AB	Pinch Hit H	PO	A	E	DP	TC/G	FA	G by Pos
1884	MIL U	12	.170	.213	47	8	2	0	0	0.0	3		0			0	0	7	15	9	1	2.6	.710	3B-12

Bud Morse

MORSE, NEWELL OBEDIAH BR TR 5′ 8″ 160 lbs.
B. Sept. 4, 1904, Berkeley, Calif. D. Apr. 6, 1987, Sparks, Nev.

Year	Team	Games	BA	SA	AB	H	2B	3B	HR	HR%	R	RBI	BB	SO	SB	Pinch Hit AB	Pinch Hit H	PO	A	E	DP	TC/G	FA	G by Pos
1929	PHI A	8	.074	.074	27	2	0	0	0	0.0	1	0	0	2	0	0	0	17	22	1	3	5.0	.975	2B-8

Hap Morse

MORSE, PETER RAYMOND BR TR 5′ 8″ 160 lbs.
B. Dec. 6, 1886, St. Paul, Minn. D. June 19, 1974, St. Paul, Minn.

Year	Team	Games	BA	SA	AB	H	2B	3B	HR	HR%	R	RBI	BB	SO	SB	Pinch Hit AB	Pinch Hit H	PO	A	E	DP	TC/G	FA	G by Pos
1911	STL N	4	.000	.000	8	0	0	0	0	0.0	0	0	1	2	0	1	0	6	5	3	0	4.7	.786	SS-2, OF-1

Bubba Morton

MORTON, WYCLIFFE NATHANIEL BR TR 5′10″ 175 lbs.
B. Dec. 13, 1931, Washington, D. C.

Year	Team	Games	BA	SA	AB	H	2B	3B	HR	HR%	R	RBI	BB	SO	SB	Pinch Hit AB	Pinch Hit H	PO	A	E	DP	TC/G	FA	G by Pos
1961	DET A	77	.287	.407	108	31	5	1	2	1.9	26	19	9	25	3	37	11	39	1	2	1	1.4	.952	OF-30
1962		90	.262	.385	195	51	6	3	4	2.1	30	17	32	32	1	21	5	124	4	1	1	2.0	.992	OF-62, 1B-3
1963	2 teams	DET A (6G –.091) MIL N (15G –.179)																						
″	total	21	.154	.154	39	6	0	0	0	0.0	3	6	4	4	0	10	1	21	0	1	0	1.8	.955	OF-12
1966	CAL A	15	.220	.240	50	11	1	0	0	0.0	4	4	2	6	1	0	0	25	1	0	0	1.9	1.000	OF-14
1967		80	.313	.388	201	63	9	3	0	0.0	23	32	22	29	0	25	8	83	1	0	0	1.4	1.000	OF-61
1968		81	.270	.325	163	44	6	0	1	0.6	13	18	14	18	2	33	10	64	1	1	1	1.3	.985	OF-50, 3B-1
1969		87	.244	.436	172	42	10	1	7	4.1	18	32	28	29	0	34	10	72	5	0	1	1.5	1.000	OF-49, 1B-1
7 yrs.		451	.267	.370	928	248	37	8	14	1.5	117	128	111	143	7	160	45	428	13	5	4	1.6	.989	OF-278, 1B-4, 3B-1

Charlie Morton

MORTON, CHARLES HAZEN BR TR 150 lbs.
B. Oct. 12, 1854, Kingsville, Ohio D. Dec. 9, 1921, Massillon, Ohio.
Manager 1884–85, 1890.

Year	Team	Games	BA	SA	AB	H	2B	3B	HR	HR%	R	RBI	BB	SO	SB	Pinch Hit AB	Pinch Hit H	PO	A	E	DP	TC/G	FA	G by Pos
1882	2 teams	PIT AA (25G –.282) STL AA (9G –.063)																						
″	total	34	.230	.289	135	31	0	4	0	0.0	14		7			0	0	42	25	18	1	2.2	.788	OF-28, 2B-7, 3B-3, SS-1
1884	TOL AA	32	.162	.252	111	18	6	2	0	0.0	11		7			0	0	33	26	8	1	1.9	.881	3B-16, OF-15, P-3, 2B-1
1885	DET N	22	.177	.241	79	14	1	2	0	0.0	9	3	5	10		0	0	23	57	22	4	4.6	.784	3B-18, SS-4
3 yrs.		88	.194	.265	325	63	7	8	0	0.0	34	3	19	10		0	0	98	108	48	6	2.6	.811	OF-43, 3B-37, 2B-8, SS-5, P-3

Guy Morton

MORTON, GUY JR. (Moose) BR TR 6′ 2″ 200 lbs.
Son of Guy Morton.
B. Nov. 4, 1930, Tuscaloosa, Ala.

Year	Team	Games	BA	SA	AB	H	2B	3B	HR	HR%	R	RBI	BB	SO	SB	Pinch Hit AB	Pinch Hit H	PO	A	E	DP	TC/G	FA	G by Pos
1954	BOS A	1	.000	.000	1	0	0	0	0	0.0	0	0	0	1	0	1	0	0	0	0	0	0.0	—	

Walt Moryn

MORYN, WALTER JOSEPH (Moose) BL TR 6′ 2″ 205 lbs.
B. Apr. 12, 1926, St. Paul, Minn.

Year	Team	Games	BA	SA	AB	H	2B	3B	HR	HR%	R	RBI	BB	SO	SB	Pinch Hit AB	Pinch Hit H	PO	A	E	DP	TC/G	FA	G by Pos
1954	BKN N	48	.275	.429	91	25	4	2	2	2.2	16	14	7	11	0	23	5	34	3	5	1	2.0	.881	OF-21
1955		11	.263	.474	19	5	1	0	1	5.3	3	3	5	4	0	4	0	5	0	1	0	0.9	.833	OF-7
1956	CHI N	147	.285	.478	529	151	27	3	23	4.3	69	67	50	67	4	6	0	268	18	5	2	2.1	.983	OF-141
1957		149	.289	.447	568	164	33	0	19	3.3	76	88	50	90	0	4	1	276	13	12	3	2.0	.960	OF-147
1958		143	.264	.494	512	135	26	7	26	5.1	77	77	62	83	1	6	4	265	4	6	1	2.0	.978	OF-141
1959		117	.234	.386	381	89	14	1	14	3.7	41	48	44	66	0	13	5	175	9	2	1	1.8	.989	OF-104
1960	2 teams	CHI N (38G –.294) STL N (75G –.245)																						
″	total	113	.262	.434	309	81	8	3	13	4.2	36	46	30	57	2	22	3	152	6	3	1	1.8	.981	OF-92
1961	2 teams	STL N (17G –.125) PIT N (40G –.200)																						
″	total	57	.175	.299	97	17	3	0	3	3.1	6	11	3	15	0	36	6	25	2	2	1	1.6	.931	OF-18
8 yrs.		785	.266	.446	2506	667	116	16	101	4.0	324	354	251	393	7	114	24	1200	55	36	10	1.9	.972	OF-671

Ross Moschitto

MOSCHITTO, ROSAIRE ALLEN BR TR 6′ 2″ 175 lbs.
B. Feb. 15, 1945, Fresno, Calif.

Year	Team	Games	BA	SA	AB	H	2B	3B	HR	HR%	R	RBI	BB	SO	SB	Pinch Hit AB	Pinch Hit H	PO	A	E	DP	TC/G	FA	G by Pos
1965	NY A	96	.185	.296	27	5	0	0	1	3.7	12	3	0	12	0	1	0	48	0	3	0	0.6	.941	OF-89
1967		14	.111	.111	9	1	0	0	0	0.0	1	0	1	2	0	6	0	2	1	0	0	0.4	1.000	OF-8
2 yrs.		110	.167	.250	36	6	0	0	1	2.8	13	3	1	14	0	7	0	50	1	3	0	0.6	.944	OF-97

Lloyd Moseby

MOSEBY, LLOYD ANTHONY BL TR 6′ 3″ 200 lbs.
B. Nov. 5, 1959, Portland, Ark.

Year	Team	Games	BA	SA	AB	H	2B	3B	HR	HR%	R	RBI	BB	SO	SB	Pinch Hit AB	Pinch Hit H	PO	A	E	DP	TC/G	FA	G by Pos
1980	TOR A	114	.229	.365	389	89	24	1	9	2.3	44	46	25	85	4	2	0	208	12	4	1	2.0	.982	OF-104, DH-6
1981		100	.233	.357	378	88	16	2	9	2.4	36	43	24	86	11	2	0	259	4	3	0	2.7	.989	OF-100
1982		147	.236	.370	487	115	20	9	9	1.8	51	52	33	106	11	7	3	361	4	3	0	2.5	.992	OF-145
1983		151	.315	.499	539	170	31	7	18	3.3	104	81	51	85	27	9	4	399	10	7	1	2.8	.983	OF-147
1984		158	.280	.470	592	166	28	**15**	18	3.0	97	92	78	122	39	3	1	473	8	5	2	3.1	.990	OF-156

Lloyd Moseby *continued*

Year	Team	Lg	Games	BA	SA	AB	H	2B	3B	HR	HR%	R	RBI	BB	SO	SB	Pinch Hit AB	Pinch Hit H	PO	A	E	DP	TC/G	FA	G by Pos
1985			152	.259	.426	584	151	30	7	18	3.1	92	71	76	91	37	1	0	394	7	8	1	2.7	.980	OF-152
1986			152	.253	.418	589	149	24	5	21	3.6	89	86	64	122	32	4	0	371	6	6	1	2.6	.984	OF-147, DH-3
1987			155	.282	.473	592	167	27	4	26	4.4	106	96	70	124	39	0	0	294	7	6	1	2.0	.980	OF-153, DH-2
1988			128	.239	.369	472	113	17	7	10	2.1	77	42	70	93	31	3	0	304	2	5	1	2.5	.984	OF-125, DH-1
1989			135	.221	.349	502	111	25	3	11	2.2	72	43	56	101	24	4	1	288	3	4	1	2.2	.986	OF-120, DH-14
1990	DET	A	122	.248	.406	431	107	16	5	14	3.2	64	51	48	77	17	7	0	288	9	5	5	2.5	.983	OF-116, DH-4
1991			74	.262	.396	260	68	15	1	6	2.3	37	35	21	43	8	11	3	126	1	6	0	1.9	.955	OF-64, DH-7
12 yrs.			1588	.257	.414	5815	1494	273	66	169	2.9	869	738	616	1135	280	53	12	3765	73	62	14	2.5	.984	OF-1529, DH-37
LEAGUE CHAMPIONSHIP SERIES																									
1985	TOR	A	7	.226	.258	31	7	1	0	0	0.0	5	4	2	3	1	0	0	10	0	0	0	1.4	1.000	OF-7
1989			5	.313	.500	16	5	0	0	1	6.3	4	2	5	2	1	0	0	15	0	0	0	3.0	1.000	OF-5
2 yrs.			12	.255	.340	47	12	1	0	1	2.1	9	6	7	5	2	0	0	25	0	0	0	2.1	1.000	OF-12

Arnie Moser

MOSER, ARNOLD ROBERT BR TR 5′11″ 165 lbs.
B. Aug. 9, 1915, Houston, Tex.

Year	Team	Lg	Games	BA	SA	AB	H	2B	3B	HR	HR%	R	RBI	BB	SO	SB	Pinch Hit AB	Pinch Hit H	PO	A	E	DP	TC/G	FA	G by Pos
1937	CIN	N	5	.000	.000	5	0	0	0	0	0.0	0	0	0	2	0	5	0	0	0	0	0	0.0	—	

Gerry Moses

MOSES, GERALD BRAHEEN BR TR 6′ 3″ 210 lbs.
B. Aug. 9, 1946, Yazoo City, Miss.

Year	Team	Lg	Games	BA	SA	AB	H	2B	3B	HR	HR%	R	RBI	BB	SO	SB	Pinch Hit AB	Pinch Hit H	PO	A	E	DP	TC/G	FA	G by Pos
1965	BOS	A	4	.250	1.000	4	1	0	0	1	25.0	1	1	0	2	0	4	1	0	0	0	0	0.0	—	
1968			6	.333	.667	18	6	0	0	2	11.1	2	4	1	4	0	0	0	26	0	1	0	4.5	.963	C-6
1969			53	.304	.474	135	41	9	1	4	3.0	13	17	5	23	0	17	2	191	11	4	1	5.7	.981	C-36
1970			92	.263	.384	315	83	18	1	6	1.9	26	35	21	45	1	5	2	578	45	6	3	7.1	.990	C-88, OF-1
1971	CAL	A	69	.227	.359	181	41	8	2	4	2.2	12	15	10	34	0	8	0	299	38	8	3	5.4	.977	C-63, OF-1
1972	CLE	A	52	.220	.326	141	31	3	0	4	2.8	9	14	11	29	0	10	2	220	17	5	8	5.8	.979	C-39, 1B-3
1973	NY	A	21	.254	.288	59	15	2	0	0	0.0	5	3	2	6	0	3	1	93	9	0	0	5.7	1.000	C-17, DH-1
1974	DET	A	74	.237	.359	198	47	6	3	4	2.0	19	19	11	38	0	1	0	377	26	6	6	5.5	.985	C-74
1975	2 teams		CHI A (2G –.500) SD N (13G –.158)																						
″	total		15	.190	.381	21	4	2	1	0	0.0	2	1	2	3	0	6	1	18	1	2	0	3.0	.905	C-5, 1B-1, DH-1
9 yrs.			386	.251	.381	1072	269	48	8	25	2.3	89	109	63	184	1	54	9	1802	147	32	21	5.9	.984	C-328, 1B-4, DH-2, OF-2

John Moses

MOSES, JOHN WILLIAM BB TL 5′10″ 165 lbs.
B. Aug. 9, 1957, Los Angeles, Calif.

Year	Team	Lg	Games	BA	SA	AB	H	2B	3B	HR	HR%	R	RBI	BB	SO	SB	Pinch Hit AB	Pinch Hit H	PO	A	E	DP	TC/G	FA	G by Pos
1982	SEA	A	22	.318	.545	44	14	5	1	1	2.3	7	3	4	5	5	2	1	16	2	1	0	1.0	.947	OF-19
1983			93	.208	.254	130	27	4	1	0	0.0	19	6	12	20	11	4	1	87	8	2	1	1.2	.979	OF-71, DH-10
1984			19	.343	.429	35	12	1	1	0	0.0	3	2	2	5	1	0	0	26	1	0	0	1.4	1.000	OF-19, DH-1
1985			33	.194	.194	62	12	0	0	0	0.0	4	3	2	8	5	0	0	35	1	0	0	1.2	1.000	OF-29
1986			103	.256	.333	399	102	16	3	3	0.8	56	34	34	65	25	2	0	249	11	5	4	2.5	.981	OF-93, 1B-7, DH-4
1987			116	.246	.331	390	96	16	4	3	0.8	58	38	29	49	23	3	1	271	7	4	3	2.3	.986	OF-100, 1B-16, DH-5
1988	MIN	A	105	.316	.422	206	65	10	3	2	1.0	33	12	15	21	11	21	6	123	1	0	0	1.5	1.000	OF-82, DH-2
1989			129	.281	.368	242	68	12	3	1	0.4	33	31	19	23	14	30	8	168	3	2	0	1.5	.988	OF-108, DH-3, 1B-2, P-1
1990			115	.221	.267	172	38	3	1	1	0.6	26	14	19	19	2	25	7	108	2	0	0	1.1	1.000	OF-85, DH-10, 1B-6, P-2
1991	DET	A	13	.048	.095	21	1	1	0	0	0.0	5	1	2	7	4	1	0	13	0	0	0	1.1	1.000	OF-12
1992	SEA	A	21	.136	.182	22	3	1	0	0	0.0	3	1	5	4	0	1	0	19	0	0	0	1.0	1.000	OF-18, DH-1
11 yrs.			769	.254	.333	1723	438	69	17	11	0.6	247	145	143	226	101	89	24	1115	36	14	8	1.7	.988	OF-636, DH-36, 1B-31, P-3

Wally Moses

MOSES, WALLACE BL TL 5′10″ 160 lbs.
B. Oct. 8, 1910, Uvalda, Ga.

Year	Team	Lg	Games	BA	SA	AB	H	2B	3B	HR	HR%	R	RBI	BB	SO	SB	Pinch Hit AB	Pinch Hit H	PO	A	E	DP	TC/G	FA	G by Pos
1935	PHI	A	85	.325	.446	345	112	21	3	5	1.4	60	35	25	18	3	6	4	157	7	10	1	2.2	.943	OF-80
1936			146	.345	.479	585	202	35	11	7	1.2	98	66	62	32	12	2	0	396	12	11	3	2.9	.974	OF-144
1937			154	.320	.550	649	208	48	13	25	3.9	113	86	54	38	9	0	0	323	16	15	4	2.3	.958	OF-154
1938			142	.307	.424	589	181	29	8	8	1.4	86	49	58	31	15	3	1	304	11	11	3	2.3	.966	OF-139
1939			115	.307	.423	437	134	28	7	3	0.7	68	33	44	23	7	11	2	209	10	8	2	2.2	.965	OF-103
1940			142	.309	.469	537	166	41	9	9	1.7	91	50	75	44	6	8	1	295	10	8	1	2.4	.974	OF-133
1941			116	.301	.418	438	132	31	4	4	0.9	78	35	62	27	3	6	1	263	12	7	5	2.6	.975	OF-109
1942	CHI	A	146	.270	.369	577	156	28	4	7	1.2	73	49	74	27	16	1	0	323	14	7	3	2.4	.980	OF-145
1943			150	.245	.337	599	147	22	**12**	3	0.5	82	48	55	47	56	2	0	370	12	8	2	2.6	.979	OF-148
1944			136	.280	.379	535	150	26	9	3	0.6	82	34	52	22	21	1	0	267	7	7	2	2.1	.975	OF-134
1945			140	.295	.420	569	168	**35**	15	2	0.4	79	50	69	33	11	1	0	329	12	8	1	2.5	.977	OF-139
1946	2 teams		CHI A (56G –.274) BOS A (48G –.206)																						
″	total		104	.239	.373	343	82	20	4	6	1.7	43	33	31	35	4	24	4	176	5	2	1	2.3	.989	OF-80
1947	BOS	A	90	.275	.384	255	70	18	2	2	0.8	32	27	27	16	3	29	5	109	2	3	0	2.0	.974	OF-58
1948			78	.259	.365	189	49	12	1	2	1.1	26	29	21	19	5	27	6	101	2	2	1	2.3	.981	OF-45
1949	PHI	A	110	.276	.367	308	85	19	3	1	0.3	49	25	51	19	1	17	5	169	7	3	3	1.9	.983	OF-92
1950			88	.264	.385	265	70	16	5	2	0.8	47	21	40	17	0	21	4	147	7	2	2	2.5	.987	OF-62
1951			70	.191	.235	136	26	6	0	0	0.0	17	9	21	9	2	34	4	62	1	1	1	2.4	.984	OF-27
17 yrs.			2012	.291	.416	7356	2138	435	110	89	1.2	1124	679	821	457	174	193	37	4000	147	113	35	2.4	.973	OF-1792
WORLD SERIES																									
1946	BOS	A	4	.417	.417	12	5	0	0	0	0.0	1	0	1	2	0	0	0	5	0	0	0	1.3	1.000	OF-4

Doc Moskiman

MOSKIMAN, WILLIAM BANKHEAD BR TR 6′ 170 lbs.
B. Dec. 20, 1879, Oakland, Calif. D. Jan. 11, 1953, San Leandro, Calif.

Year	Team	Lg	Games	BA	SA	AB	H	2B	3B	HR	HR%	R	RBI	BB	SO	SB	Pinch Hit AB	Pinch Hit H	PO	A	E	DP	TC/G	FA	G by Pos
1910	BOS	A	5	.111	.111	9	1	0	0	0	0.0	1	1	2		0	0	0	20	1	0	1	7.0	1.000	1B-2, OF-1

Jim Mosolf

MOSOLF, JAMES FREDERICK BL TR 5′10″ 186 lbs.
B. Aug. 21, 1905, Puyallup, Wash. D. Dec. 28, 1979, Dallas, Ore.

Year	Team	Lg	Games	BA	SA	AB	H	2B	3B	HR	HR%	R	RBI	BB	SO	SB	Pinch Hit AB	Pinch Hit H	PO	A	E	DP	TC/G	FA	G by Pos
1929	PIT	N	8	.462	.692	13	6	1	1	0	0.0	3	2	1	1	0	4	2	7	0	0	0	2.3	1.000	OF-3
1930			40	.333	.412	51	17	2	1	0	0.0	16	9	8	7	0	22	8	12	1	4	0	1.3	.765	OF-12, P-1
1931			39	.250	.341	44	11	1	0	1	2.3	7	8	8	5	0	30	6	5	0	0	0	1.3	1.000	OF-4
1933	CHI	N	31	.268	.390	82	22	5	1	1	1.2	13	9	5	8	0	8	3	51	2	2	0	2.5	.964	OF-22
4 yrs.			118	.295	.405	190	56	9	3	2	1.1	39	28	22	21	0	64	19	75	3	6	0	2.0	.929	OF-41, P-1

Charlie Moss

MOSS, CHARLES CROSBY BR TR 5′10″ 160 lbs.
B. Mar. 20, 1911, Meridian, Miss.

Year	Team	Games	BA	SA	AB	H	2B	3B	HR	HR%	R	RBI	BB	SO	SB	Pinch Hit AB	Pinch Hit H	PO	A	E	DP	TC/G	FA	G by Pos
1934	PHI A	10	.200	.200	10	2	0	0	0	0.0	3	1	0	0	0	4	1	3	1	0	0	0.7	1.000	C-6
1935		4	.333	.333	3	1	0	0	0	0.0	1	1	1	0	0	2	1	0	0	0	0	0.0	.000	C-1
1936		33	.250	.318	44	11	1	1	0	0.0	2	10	6	5	1	14	2	35	4	3	0	2.2	.929	C-19
3 yrs.		47	.246	.298	57	14	1	1	0	0.0	6	12	7	5	1	20	4	38	5	3	0	1.8	.935	C-26

Howie Moss

MOSS, HOWARD GLENN BR TR 5′11½″ 185 lbs.
B. Oct. 17, 1919, Gastonia, N. C. D. May 7, 1989, Baltimore, Md.

Year	Team	Games	BA	SA	AB	H	2B	3B	HR	HR%	R	RBI	BB	SO	SB	Pinch Hit AB	Pinch Hit H	PO	A	E	DP	TC/G	FA	G by Pos
1942	NY N	7	.000	.000	14	0	0	0	0	0.0	0	0	0	4	0	4	0	7	0	0	0	2.3	1.000	OF-3
1946	2 teams	CIN N (7G –.192)	CLE A (8G –.063)																					
″	total	15	.121	.121	58	7	0	0	0	0.0	3	1	3	13	0	1	0	23	19	5	0	3.4	.894	3B-8, OF-6
2 yrs.		22	.097	.097	72	7	0	0	0	0.0	3	1	3	17	0	5	0	30	19	5	0	3.2	.907	OF-9, 3B-8

Les Moss

MOSS, JOHN LESTER BR TR 5′11″ 205 lbs.
B. May 14, 1925, Tulsa, Okla.
Manager 1968, 1979.

Year	Team	Games	BA	SA	AB	H	2B	3B	HR	HR%	R	RBI	BB	SO	SB	Pinch Hit AB	Pinch Hit H	PO	A	E	DP	TC/G	FA	G by Pos
1946	STL A	12	.371	.457	35	13	3	0	0	0.0	4	5	3	5	1	0	0	55	5	2	1	5.2	.968	C-12
1947		96	.157	.255	274	43	5	2	6	2.2	17	27	35	48	0	1	0	362	43	7	6	4.3	.983	C-96
1948		107	.257	.424	335	86	12	1	14	4.2	35	46	39	50	0	5	0	357	52	5	8	4.0	.988	C-103
1949		97	.291	.439	278	81	11	0	10	3.6	28	39	49	32	0	12	2	283	41	10	9	4.0	.970	C-83
1950		84	.266	.401	222	59	6	0	8	3.6	24	34	26	32	0	19	5	204	20	10	4	3.9	.957	C-60
1951	2 teams	STL A (16G –.170)	BOS A (71G –.198)																					
″	total	87	.193	.273	249	48	8	0	4	1.6	23	33	31	42	1	6	0	335	36	7	5	4.7	.981	C-81
1952	STL A	52	.246	.347	118	29	3	0	3	2.5	11	12	15	13	0	13	4	118	17	6	3	3.6	.957	C-39
1953		78	.276	.368	239	66	14	1	2	0.8	21	28	18	31	0	6	0	296	21	7	4	4.6	.978	C-71
1954	BAL A	50	.246	.270	126	31	3	0	0	0.0	7	5	14	16	0	12	2	159	16	5	4	4.7	.972	C-38
1955	2 teams	BAL A (29G –.339)	CHI A (32G –.254)																					
″	total	61	.296	.426	115	34	3	0	4	3.5	10	13	13	14	0	12	2	156	10	1	5	3.5	.994	C-48
1956	CHI A	56	.244	.512	127	31	4	0	10	7.9	20	22	18	15	0	8	1	149	10	1	1	3.3	.994	C-49
1957		42	.270	.348	115	31	3	0	2	1.7	10	12	20	18	0	4	2	138	8	3	2	3.8	.980	C-39
1958		2	.000	.000	1	0	0	0	0	0.0	0	0	1	0	0	1	0	0	0	0	0	0.0	—	
13 yrs.		824	.247	.369	2234	552	75	4	63	2.8	210	276	282	316	2	99	18	2612	279	64	52	4.1	.978	C-719

Johnny Mostil

MOSTIL, JOHN ANTHONY BR TR 5′ 8½″ 168 lbs.
B. June 1, 1896, Chicago, Ill. D. Dec. 10, 1970, Midlothian, Ill.

Year	Team	Games	BA	SA	AB	H	2B	3B	HR	HR%	R	RBI	BB	SO	SB	Pinch Hit AB	Pinch Hit H	PO	A	E	DP	TC/G	FA	G by Pos
1918	CHI A	10	.273	.455	33	9	2	2	0	0.0	4	4	1	6	1	0	0	15	21	3	4	4.3	.923	2B-9
1921		100	.301	.436	326	98	21	7	3	0.9	43	42	28	35	10	5	2	215	14	13	1	2.6	.946	OF-91, 2B-1
1922		132	.303	.472	458	139	28	14	7	1.5	74	70	38	39	14	9	4	333	9	12	2	2.7	.966	OF-132
1923		153	.291	.430	546	159	37	15	3	0.5	91	64	62	51	41	4	0	434	34	15	7	3.2	.969	OF-143, 3B-6, SS-1
1924		118	.325	.439	385	125	22	5	4	1.0	75	49	45	41	7	14	5	281	13	8	2	3.0	.974	OF-102
1925		153	.299	.421	605	181	36	16	2	0.3	**135**	50	**90**	52	**43**	0	0	446	11	7	5	3.0	.985	OF-153
1926		148	.328	.467	600	197	41	15	4	0.7	120	42	79	55	**35**	0	0	440	15	15	4	3.2	.968	OF-147
1927		13	.125	.125	16	2	0	0	0	0.0	3	1	0	1	1	1	0	5	1	1	0	1.2	.857	OF-6
1928		133	.270	.340	503	136	19	8	0	0.0	69	51	66	54	23	2	0	394	18	10	3	3.2	.976	OF-131
1929		12	.229	.314	35	8	3	0	0	0.0	4	3	6	2	1	0	0	25	1	1	1	2.5	.963	OF-11
10 yrs.		972	.301	.427	3507	1054	209	82	23	0.7	618	376	415	336	176	35	11	2588	137	85	29	3.0	.970	OF-916, 2B-10, 3B-6, SS-1

Andy Mota

MOTA, ANDRES ALBERTO BR TR 5′10″ 180 lbs.
Born Andres Alberto Mota (Matos).
Brother of Jose Mota. Son of Manny Mota.
B. Mar. 4, 1966, Santo Domingo, Dominican Republic.

Year	Team	Games	BA	SA	AB	H	2B	3B	HR	HR%	R	RBI	BB	SO	SB	Pinch Hit AB	Pinch Hit H	PO	A	E	DP	TC/G	FA	G by Pos
1991	HOU N	27	.189	.244	90	17	2	0	1	1.1	4	6	1	17	2	0	0	30	66	3	11	3.7	.970	2B-27

Jose Mota

MOTA, JOSE MANUEL BB TR 5′ 9″ 155 lbs.
Born Jose Manuel Mota (Matos).
Brother of Andy Mota. Son of Manny Mota.
B. Mar. 16, 1965, Santo Domingo, Dominican Republic.

Year	Team	Games	BA	SA	AB	H	2B	3B	HR	HR%	R	RBI	BB	SO	SB	Pinch Hit AB	Pinch Hit H	PO	A	E	DP	TC/G	FA	G by Pos
1991	SD N	17	.222	.222	36	8	0	0	0	0.0	4	2	2	7	0	1	0	25	29	3	5	3.6	.947	2B-13, SS-3
1995	KC A	2	.000	.000	2	0	0	0	0	0.0	0	0	0	0	0	0	0	1	3	0	0	2.0	1.000	2B-2
2 yrs.		19	.211	.211	38	8	0	0	0	0.0	4	2	2	7	0	1	0	26	32	3	5	3.4	.951	2B-15, SS-3

Manny Mota

MOTA, MANUEL RAFAEL BR TR 5′10″ 160 lbs.
Born Manuel Rafael Mota (Geronimo).
Father of Jose Mota. Father of Andy Mota.
B. Feb. 18, 1938, Santo Domingo, Dominican Republic.

Year	Team	Games	BA	SA	AB	H	2B	3B	HR	HR%	R	RBI	BB	SO	SB	Pinch Hit AB	Pinch Hit H	PO	A	E	DP	TC/G	FA	G by Pos
1962	SF N	47	.176	.189	74	13	1	0	0	0.0	9	9	7	8	3	15	1	38	18	2	2	1.6	.966	OF-27, 3B-7, 2B-3
1963	PIT N	59	.270	.333	126	34	2	3	0	0.0	20	7	7	18	0	22	6	40	1	2	0	1.1	.953	OF-37, 2B-1
1964		115	.277	.384	271	75	8	3	5	1.8	43	32	10	31	4	21	5	122	5	5	1	1.4	.962	OF-93, 2B-1, C-1
1965		121	.279	.384	294	82	7	6	4	1.4	47	29	22	32	2	32	11	127	5	2	1	1.4	.985	OF-95
1966		116	.332	.472	322	107	16	7	5	1.6	54	46	25	28	7	26	10	152	4	1	0	1.6	.994	OF-96, 3B-4
1967		120	.321	.441	349	112	14	8	4	1.1	53	56	14	46	3	30	5	156	14	2	3	1.7	.988	OF-99, 3B-2
1968		111	.281	.332	331	93	10	2	1	0.3	35	33	20	19	4	21	5	150	8	3	2	1.7	.981	OF-92, 2B-1, 3B-1
1969	2 teams	MON N (31G –.315)	LA N (85G –.323)																					
″	total	116	.321	.389	383	123	7	5	3	0.8	41	30	32	36	6	16	2	157	8	8	2	1.7	.954	OF-102
1970	LA N	124	.305	.384	417	127	12	6	3	0.7	63	37	47	37	11	16	6	172	9	5	3	1.7	.973	OF-111, 3B-1
1971		91	.312	.398	269	84	13	5	0	0.0	24	34	20	20	4	15	5	108	3	4	1	1.4	.965	OF-80
1972		118	.323	.434	371	120	16	5	5	1.3	57	48	27	15	4	25	10	141	3	1	1	1.5	.993	OF-99
1973		89	.314	.365	293	92	11	2	0	0.0	33	23	25	12	1	14	5	96	4	0	0	1.4	1.000	OF-74
1974		66	.281	.316	57	16	2	0	0	0.0	5	16	5	4	0	**53**	15	1	0	0	0	0.3	1.000	OF-3
1975		52	.265	.286	49	13	1	0	0	0.0	3	10	5	1	0	40	10	9	0	0	0	1.8	1.000	OF-5
1976		50	.288	.346	52	15	3	0	0	0.0	1	13	7	5	0	40	12	11	1	0	0	2.0	1.000	OF-6
1977		49	.395	.500	38	15	1	0	1	2.6	5	4	10	0	1	36	14	1	0	0	0	1.0	1.000	OF-1
1978		37	.303	.333	33	10	1	0	0	0.0	2	6	3	4	0	33	10	0	0	0	0	0.0	—	

Manny Mota *continued*

Year	Team	Games	BA	SA	AB	H	2B	3B	HR	HR%	R	RBI	BB	SO	SB	Pinch Hit AB	Pinch Hit H	PO	A	E	DP	TC/G	FA	G by Pos
1979		47	.357	.357	42	15	0	0	0	0.0	1	3	3	4	0	42	15	0	0	0	0	0.0	.000	OF-1
1980		7	.429	.429	7	3	0	0	0	0.0	0	2	0	0	0	7	3	0	0	0	0	0.0	—	
1982		1	.000	.000	1	0	0	0	0	0.0	0	0	0	0	0	1	0	0	0	0	0	0.0	—	
20 yrs.		1536	.304	.389	3779	1149	125	52	31	0.8	496	438	289	320	50	505	150 1st	1481	83	35	16	1.5	.978	OF-1021, 3B-15, 2B-6, C-1
LEAGUE CHAMPIONSHIP SERIES																								
1974	LA N	3	.333	.333	3	1	0	0	0	0.0	0	1	0	0	0	3	1	1	0	0	0	1.0	1.000	OF-1
1977		1	1.000	2.000	1	1	1	0	0	0.0	1	0	0	0	0	1	1	0	0	0	0	0.0	—	
1978		2	1.000	2.000	1	1	1	0	0	0.0	0	0	0	0	0	1	1	0	0	0	0	0.0	—	
3 yrs.		6	.600	1.000	5	3	2	0	0	0.0	1	1	0	0	0	5	3	1	0	0	0	1.0	1.000	OF-1
WORLD SERIES																								
1977	LA N	3	.000	.000	3	0	0	0	0	0.0	0	0	0	1	0	3	0	0	0	0	0	0.0	—	
1978		1	—	—	0	0	0	0	0	—	0	0	1	0	0	0	0	0	0	0	0	0.0	—	
2 yrs.		4	.000	.000	3	0	0	0	0	0.0	0	0	1	1	0	3	0							

Darryl Motley

MOTLEY, DARRYL DeWAYNE BR TR 5′ 9″ 196 lbs.
B. Jan. 21, 1960, Muskogee, Okla.

Year	Team	Games	BA	SA	AB	H	2B	3B	HR	HR%	R	RBI	BB	SO	SB	Pinch Hit AB	Pinch Hit H	PO	A	E	DP	TC/G	FA	G by Pos
1981	KC A	42	.232	.312	125	29	4	0	2	1.6	15	8	7	15	1	3	0	88	3	3	1	2.4	.968	OF-39
1983		19	.235	.441	68	16	1	2	3	4.4	9	11	2	8	2	1	1	42	2	1	0	2.4	.978	OF-18, DH-1
1984		146	.284	.439	522	148	24	6	15	2.9	64	70	28	73	10	9	1	301	7	5	2	2.3	.984	OF-138
1985		123	.222	.413	383	85	20	1	17	4.4	45	49	18	57	6	9	2	198	4	7	1	1.7	.967	OF-114, DH-7
1986	2 teams	KC A (72G –.203) ATL N (5G –.200)																						
″	total	77	.203	.348	227	46	10	1	7	3.1	23	20	12	32	0	12	4	97	2	2	1	1.4	.980	OF-69, DH-2
1987	ATL N	6	.000	.000	8	0	0	0	0	0.0	0	1	0	1	0	4	0	2	0	0	0	1.0	1.000	OF-2
6 yrs.		413	.243	.401	1333	324	59	10	44	3.3	156	159	67	186	19	38	8	728	18	18	5	2.0	.976	OF-380, DH-10
LEAGUE CHAMPIONSHIP SERIES																								
1984	KC A	3	.167	.167	12	2	0	0	0	0.0	0	1	1	3	0	0	0	11	0	0	0	3.7	1.000	OF-3
1985		2	.333	.333	3	1	0	0	0	0.0	1	1	1	2	0	0	0	4	0	0	0	2.0	1.000	OF-2
2 yrs.		5	.200	.200	15	3	0	0	0	0.0	1	2	2	5	0	0	0	15	0	0	0	3.0	1.000	OF-5
WORLD SERIES																								
1985	KC A	5	.364	.636	11	4	0	0	1	9.1	1	3	0	1	0	0	0	4	0	0	0	1.0	1.000	OF-4

Bitsy Mott

MOTT, ELISHA MATTHEW BR TR 5′ 8″ 155 lbs.
B. June 12, 1918, Arcadia, Fla.

Year	Team	Games	BA	SA	AB	H	2B	3B	HR	HR%	R	RBI	BB	SO	SB	Pinch Hit AB	Pinch Hit H	PO	A	E	DP	TC/G	FA	G by Pos
1945	PHI N	90	.221	.249	289	64	8	0	0	0.0	21	22	27	25	2	0	0	184	257	27	53	4.8	.942	SS-63, 2B-27, 3B-7

Curt Motton

MOTTON, CURTELL HOWARD BR TR 5′ 8″ 164 lbs.
B. Sept. 24, 1940, Darnell, La.

Year	Team	Games	BA	SA	AB	H	2B	3B	HR	HR%	R	RBI	BB	SO	SB	Pinch Hit AB	Pinch Hit H	PO	A	E	DP	TC/G	FA	G by Pos
1967	BAL A	27	.200	.323	65	13	2	0	2	3.1	5	9	5	14	0	11	1	36	0	1	0	2.1	.973	OF-18
1968		83	.198	.341	217	43	7	0	8	3.7	27	25	31	43	1	27	5	91	2	1	0	1.7	.989	OF-54
1969		56	.303	.573	89	27	6	0	6	6.7	15	21	13	10	3	25	8	26	0	0	0	1.3	1.000	OF-20
1970		52	.226	.393	84	19	3	1	3	3.6	16	19	18	20	1	26	4	32	1	0	0	1.6	1.000	OF-20
1971		38	.189	.434	53	10	1	0	4	7.5	13	8	10	12	0	15	3	20	1	0	0	1.3	1.000	OF-16
1972	2 teams	MIL A (6G –.167) CAL A (42G –.154)																						
″	total	48	.156	.244	45	7	1	0	1	2.2	7	3	6	14	0	18	1	15	0	0	0	1.3	1.000	OF-12
1973	BAL A	5	.333	.833	6	2	0	0	1	16.7	2	4	1	1	0	2	0	0	0	0	0	0.0		OF-1, DH-1
1974		7	.000	.000	8	0	0	0	0	0.0	0	0	2	2	0	3	0	4	0	0	0	1.3	1.000	OF-2, DH-1
8 yrs.		316	.213	.384	567	121	20	1	25	4.4	85	89	86	116	5	127	22	224	4	2	0	1.6	.991	OF-143, DH-2
LEAGUE CHAMPIONSHIP SERIES																								
1969	BAL A	2	.500	.500	2	1	0	0	0	0.0	0	1	0	0	0	2	1	0	0	0	0	0.0	—	
1971		1	1.000	2.000	1	1	1	0	0	0.0	0	1	0	0	0	1	1	0	0	0	0	0.0	—	
1974		1	.000	.000	1	0	0	0	0	0.0	0	0	0	0	0	1	0	0	0	0	0	0.0	—	
3 yrs.		4	.500	.750	4	2	1	0	0	0.0	0	2	0	0	0	4	2							
WORLD SERIES																								
1969	BAL A	1	.000	.000	1	0	0	0	0	0.0	0	0	0	0	0	1	0	0	0	0	0	0.0	—	

Frank Motz

MOTZ, FRANK H. 6′ 160 lbs.
B. Oct. 1, 1868, Freeburg, Pa. D. Mar. 18, 1944, Akron, Ohio.

Year	Team	Games	BA	SA	AB	H	2B	3B	HR	HR%	R	RBI	BB	SO	SB	Pinch Hit AB	Pinch Hit H	PO	A	E	DP	TC/G	FA	G by Pos
1890	PHI N	1	.000	.000	2	0	0	0	0	0.0	1	3	1	1	1	0	0	8	1	0	2	9.0	1.000	1B-1
1893	CIN N	43	.256	.353	156	40	7	1	2	1.3	16	25	19	10	3	0	0	426	38	9	27	11.0	.981	1B-43
1894		18	.203	.261	69	14	4	0	0	0.0	8	12	9	1	2	0	0	186	18	1	10	11.4	.995	1B-18
3 yrs.		62	.238	.322	227	54	11	1	2	0.9	25	40	29	12	6	0	0	620	57	10	39	11.1	.985	1B-62

Ollie Moulton

MOULTON, ALBERT THEODORE BR TR 5′ 6″ 155 lbs.
B. Jan. 16, 1886, Medway, Mass. D. July 10, 1968, Peabody, Mass.

Year	Team	Games	BA	SA	AB	H	2B	3B	HR	HR%	R	RBI	BB	SO	SB	Pinch Hit AB	Pinch Hit H	PO	A	E	DP	TC/G	FA	G by Pos
1911	STL A	4	.067	.067	15	1	0	0	0	0.0	4	1	4		0	0	0	2	13	1	0	4.0	.938	2B-4

Frank Mountain

MOUNTAIN, FRANK HENRY BR TR 5′11″ 185 lbs.
B. May 17, 1860, Ft. Edward, N. Y. D. Nov. 19, 1939, Schenectady, N. Y.

Year	Team	Games	BA	SA	AB	H	2B	3B	HR	HR%	R	RBI	BB	SO	SB	Pinch Hit AB	Pinch Hit H	PO	A	E	DP	TC/G	FA	G by Pos
1880	TRO N	2	.222	.222	9	2	0	0	0	0.0	1	0	0	4		0	0	0	4	0	0	2.0	1.000	P-2
1881	DET N	7	.160	.280	25	4	1	1	0	0.0	0	4	2	8		0	0	6	6	1	0	1.9	.923	P-7
1882	3 teams	WOR N (5G –.063) PHI AA (9G –.333) WOR N (20G –.271)																						
″	total	34	.262	.385	122	32	5	2	2	1.6	14	6	5	23		0	0	31	54	10	3	2.6	.895	P-26, OF-7, 1B-2, SS-1
1883	COL AA	70	.217	.337	276	60	14	5	3	1.1	36		9			0	0	55	106	26	3	2.6	.861	P-59, OF-12
1884		58	.238	.357	210	50	7	3	4	1.9	26		9			0	0	30	90	10	0	2.2	.923	P-42, OF-17
1885	PIT AA	5	.100	.200	20	2	0	1	0	0.0	1		1			0	0	1	10	2	0	2.6	.846	P-5
1886		18	.145	.200	55	8	1	1	0	0.0	6		13			0	0	160	9	9	6	9.9	.949	1B-16, P-2
7 yrs.		194	.220	.333	717	158	28	13	9	1.3	84	10	39	35		0	0	283	279	58	12	3.1	.906	P-143, OF-36, 1B-18, SS-1

James Mouton

MOUTON, JAMES RALEIGH BR TR 5′ 9″ 175 lbs.
B. Dec. 29, 1968, Denver, Colo.

Year	Team	Games	BA	SA	AB	H	2B	3B	HR	HR%	R	RBI	BB	SO	SB	Pinch Hit AB	Pinch Hit H	PO	A	E	DP	TC/G	FA	G by Pos
1994	**HOU N**	99	.245	.300	310	76	11	0	2	0.6	43	16	27	69	24	3	2	163	5	3	2	1.8	.982	OF-96
1995		104	.262	.376	298	78	18	2	4	1.3	42	27	25	59	25	14	4	134	4	0	0	1.5	1.000	OF-94
2 yrs.		203	.253	.337	608	154	29	2	6	1.0	85	43	52	128	49	17	6	297	9	3	2	1.6	.990	OF-190

Lyle Mouton

MOUTON, LYLE JOSEPH BR TR 6′ 4″ 240 lbs.
B. May 13, 1969, Lafayette, La.

Year	Team	Games	BA	SA	AB	H	2B	3B	HR	HR%	R	RBI	BB	SO	SB	Pinch Hit AB	Pinch Hit H	PO	A	E	DP	TC/G	FA	G by Pos
1995	**CHI A**	58	.302	.475	179	54	16	0	5	2.8	23	27	19	46	1	5	3	94	5	1	1	1.8	.990	OF-53, DH-2

Ray Mowe

MOWE, RAYMOND BENJAMIN BL TR 5′ 7½″ 160 lbs.
B. July 12, 1889, Rochester, Ind. D. Aug. 14, 1968, Sarasota, Fla.

Year	Team	Games	BA	SA	AB	H	2B	3B	HR	HR%	R	RBI	BB	SO	SB	Pinch Hit AB	Pinch Hit H	PO	A	E	DP	TC/G	FA	G by Pos
1913	**BKN N**	5	.111	.111	9	1	0	0	0	0.0	0	0	0	1	0	1	0	7	9	1	1	8.5	.941	SS-2

Mike Mowrey

MOWREY, HARRY HARLAN BR TR 5′10″ 180 lbs.
B. Apr. 20, 1884, Brown's Mill, Pa. D. Mar. 20, 1947, Chambersburg, Pa.

Year	Team	Games	BA	SA	AB	H	2B	3B	HR	HR%	R	RBI	BB	SO	SB	Pinch Hit AB	Pinch Hit H	PO	A	E	DP	TC/G	FA	G by Pos
1905	**CIN N**	7	.267	.300	30	8	1	0	0	0.0	4	6	1		0	0	0	6	16	7	1	4.1	.759	3B-7
1906		21	.321	.377	53	17	3	0	0	0.0	3	6	5		2	4	1	21	37	4	1	3.6	.935	3B-15, SS-1, 2B-1
1907		138	.252	.321	448	113	16	6	1	0.2	43	44	35		10	0	0	178	245	35	14	3.3	.924	3B-127, SS-11
1908		77	.220	.269	227	50	9	1	0	0.0	17	23	12		5	12	2	64	117	15	6	3.2	.923	3B-56, SS-3, OF-3
1909	**2 teams**	**CIN N** (38G –.191) **STL N** (12G –.241)																						
″	**total**	50	.201	.243	144	29	6	0	0	0.0	13	9	24		3	6	1	66	99	15	11	4.1	.917	3B-24, SS-13, 2B-7
1910	**STL N**	143	.282	.368	489	138	24	6	2	0.4	69	70	67	38	21	0	0	171	301	37	30	3.6	.927	3B-141
1911		137	.268	.359	471	126	29	7	0	0.0	59	61	59	46	15	1	0	175	267	26	19	3.5	.944	3B-134, SS-1
1912		114	.255	.341	408	104	13	8	2	0.5	59	50	46	29	19	4	1	131	220	26	22	3.5	.931	3B-108
1913		131	.258	.316	449	116	18	4	0	0.0	61	33	53	40	21	0	0	143	284	21	23	3.4	.953	3B-130
1914	**PIT N**	79	.254	.324	284	72	7	5	1	0.4	24	25	22	20	8	0	0	83	156	10	8	3.2	.960	3B-78
1915	**PIT F**	151	.280	.359	521	146	26	6	1	0.2	56	49	66		40	0	0	174	268	19	15	3.1	.959	3B-151
1916	**BKN N**	144	.244	.313	495	121	22	6	0	0.0	57	60	50	60	16	0	0	154	291	16	17	3.2	.965	3B-144
1917		83	.214	.284	271	58	9	5	0	0.0	20	25	29	25	7	1	0	77	170	12	14	3.2	.954	3B-80, 2B-2
13 yrs.		1275	.256	.329	4290	1098	183	54	7	0.2	485	461	469	258	167	28	5	1443	2471	243	181	3.4	.942	3B-1195, SS-29, 2B-10, OF-3
WORLD SERIES																								
1916	**BKN N**	5	.176	.176	17	3	0	0	0	0.0	2	1	3	2	0	0	0	8	15	2	1	5.0	.920	3B-5

Joe Mowry

MOWRY, JOSEPH ALOYSIUS BB TR 6′ 198 lbs.
B. Apr. 6, 1908, St. Louis, Mo. D. Feb. 9, 1994, St. Louis, Mo.

Year	Team	Games	BA	SA	AB	H	2B	3B	HR	HR%	R	RBI	BB	SO	SB	Pinch Hit AB	Pinch Hit H	PO	A	E	DP	TC/G	FA	G by Pos
1933	**BOS N**	86	.221	.293	249	55	8	5	0	0.0	25	20	15	22	1	20	7	155	2	1	0	2.5	.994	OF-64
1934		25	.215	.291	79	17	3	0	1	1.3	9	4	3	13	0	3	0	45	5	1	2	2.4	.980	OF-20, 2B-1
1935		81	.265	.360	136	36	8	1	1	0.7	17	13	11	13	0	30	**10**	62	3	2	0	1.5	.970	OF-45
3 yrs.		192	.233	.313	464	108	19	6	2	0.4	51	37	29	48	1	53	17	262	10	4	2	2.1	.986	OF-129, 2B-1

Mike Moynahan

MOYNAHAN, MICHAEL BL TR
B. 1856, Chicago, Ill. D. Apr. 9, 1899, Chicago, Ill.

Year	Team	Games	BA	SA	AB	H	2B	3B	HR	HR%	R	RBI	BB	SO	SB	Pinch Hit AB	Pinch Hit H	PO	A	E	DP	TC/G	FA	G by Pos
1880	**BUF N**	27	.330	.400	100	33	5	1	0	0.0	12	14	6	9		0	0	30	70	16	7	4.3	.862	SS-27
1881	**2 teams**	**CLE N** (33G –.230) **DET N** (1G –.250)																						
″	**total**	34	.230	.281	139	32	5	1	0	0.0	13	8	3	15		0	0	68	6	11	2	2.5	.871	OF-32, 3B-2
1883	**PHI AA**	95	.308	.410	400	123	18	10	1	0.3	90		30			0	0	105	268	75	14	4.7	.833	SS-95
1884	**2 teams**	**PHI AA** (1G –.000) **CLE N** (12G –.289)																						
″	**total**	13	.265	.347	49	13	2	1	0	0.0	9	6	7	11		0	0	16	27	11	1	4.2	.796	2B-6, OF-4, SS-3
4 yrs.		169	.292	.378	688	201	30	13	1	0.1	124	28	46	35		0	0	219	371	113	24	4.2	.839	SS-125, OF-36, 2B-6, 3B-2

Bill Mueller

MUELLER, WILLIAM LAWRENCE (Hawk) BR TR 6′ 1½″ 180 lbs.
B. Nov. 9, 1920, Bay City, Mich.

Year	Team	Games	BA	SA	AB	H	2B	3B	HR	HR%	R	RBI	BB	SO	SB	Pinch Hit AB	Pinch Hit H	PO	A	E	DP	TC/G	FA	G by Pos
1942	**CHI A**	26	.165	.176	85	14	1	0	0	0.0	5	5	12	9	2	1	0	81	7	2	1	3.5	.978	OF-26
1945		13	.000	.000	9	0	0	0	0	0.0	3	0	2	1	1	1	0	7	0	2	0	1.3	.778	OF-7
2 yrs.		39	.149	.160	94	14	1	0	0	0.0	8	5	14	10	3	2	0	88	7	4	1	3.0	.960	OF-33

Don Mueller

MUELLER, DONALD FREDERICK (Mandrake the Magician) BL TR 6′ 185 lbs.
Son of Walter Mueller.
B. Apr. 14, 1927, St. Louis, Mo.

Year	Team	Games	BA	SA	AB	H	2B	3B	HR	HR%	R	RBI	BB	SO	SB	Pinch Hit AB	Pinch Hit H	PO	A	E	DP	TC/G	FA	G by Pos
1948	**NY N**	36	.358	.469	81	29	4	1	1	1.2	12	9	0	3	0	14	6	33	3	1	0	1.7	.973	OF-22
1949		51	.232	.304	56	13	4	0	0	0.0	5	1	5	6	0	**42**	7	8	0	0	0	1.3	1.000	OF-6
1950		132	.291	.383	525	153	15	6	7	1.3	60	84	10	26	1	6	2	205	7	3	2	1.7	.986	OF-125
1951		122	.277	.431	469	130	10	7	16	3.4	58	69	19	13	1	7	1	233	5	4	1	2.1	.983	OF-115
1952		126	.281	.421	456	128	14	7	12	2.6	61	49	34	24	2	4	0	221	8	3	4	1.9	.987	OF-120
1953		131	.333	.404	480	160	12	2	6	1.3	56	60	19	13	2	8	4	203	7	6	0	1.8	.972	OF-122
1954		153	.342	.444	619	**212**	35	8	4	0.6	90	71	22	17	2	1	1	263	14	6	5	1.8	.979	OF-153
1955		147	.306	.393	605	185	21	4	8	1.3	67	83	19	12	1	1	1	239	5	6	1	1.7	.976	OF-146
1956		138	.269	.333	453	122	12	1	5	1.1	38	41	15	7	0	21	5	180	4	2	2	1.6	.989	OF-117
1957		135	.258	.318	450	116	7	1	6	1.3	45	37	13	16	2	23	6	174	13	2	4	1.6	.989	OF-115
1958	**CHI A**	70	.253	.283	166	42	5	0	0	0.0	7	16	11	9	0	26	9	57	3	2	1	1.4	.968	OF-43
1959		4	.500	.500	4	2	0	0	0	0.0	0	0	0	0	0	4	2	0	0	0	0	0.0	—	
12 yrs.		1245	.296	.390	4364	1292	139	37	65	1.5	499	520	167	146	11	157	44	1816	69	35	20	1.8	.982	OF-1084
WORLD SERIES																								
1954	**NY N**	4	.389	.389	18	7	0	0	0	0.0	4	1	0	1	0	0	0	3	0	2	0	1.3	.600	OF-4

Emmett Mueller

MUELLER, EMMETT JEROME (Heinie) BB TR 5′ 6″ 167 lbs.
B. July 20, 1912, St. Louis, Mo. D. Oct. 3, 1986, Orlando, Fla.

Year	Team	Games	BA	SA	AB	H	2B	3B	HR	HR%	R	RBI	BB	SO	SB	Pinch Hit AB	Pinch Hit H	PO	A	E	DP	TC/G	FA	G by Pos
1938	**PHI N**	136	.250	.322	444	111	12	4	4	0.9	53	34	64	43	2	7	1	249	306	23	48	4.4	.960	2B-111, 3B-21
1939		115	.279	.437	341	95	19	4	9	2.6	46	43	33	34	4	26	8	163	166	11	38	4.0	.968	2B-51, 3B-17, OF-17, SS-1
1940		97	.247	.346	263	65	13	2	3	1.1	24	28	37	23	2	18	4	146	96	5	13	3.1	.980	2B-34, OF-31, 3B-13, 1B-2
1941		93	.227	.296	233	53	11	1	1	0.4	21	22	22	24	2	24	2	114	107	6	21	3.3	.974	2B-29, OF-21, 3B-19
4 yrs.		441	.253	.353	1281	324	55	11	17	1.3	144	127	156	124	10	75	15	672	675	45	120	3.8	.968	2B-225, 3B-70, OF-69, 1B-2, SS-1

Heinie Mueller

MUELLER, CLARENCE FRANCIS BL TL 5′ 8″ 158 lbs.
Brother of Walter Mueller.
B. Sept. 16, 1899, Creve Coeur, Mo. D. Jan. 23, 1975, De Soto, Mo.

Year	Team	Games	BA	SA	AB	H	2B	3B	HR	HR%	R	RBI	BB	SO	SB	Pinch Hit AB	Pinch Hit H	PO	A	E	DP	TC/G	FA	G by Pos
1920	STL N	4	.318	.364	22	7	1	0	0	0.0	0	1	2	4	1	0	0	12	0	0	0	3.0	1.000	OF-4
1921		55	.352	.494	176	62	10	6	1	0.6	25	34	11	22	2	1	0	117	5	3	1	2.3	.976	OF-54
1922		61	.270	.396	159	43	7	2	3	1.9	20	26	14	18	2	17	5	83	6	5	2	2.1	.947	OF-44
1923		78	.343	.528	265	91	16	9	5	1.9	39	41	18	16	4	4	3	197	9	8	3	2.9	.963	OF-74
1924		92	.264	.365	296	78	12	6	2	0.7	39	37	19	16	8	10	1	335	15	9	17	4.5	.975	OF-53, 1B-27
1925		78	.313	.424	243	76	16	4	1	0.4	33	26	17	11	0	5	2	165	6	8	3	2.5	.955	OF-72
1926	2 teams	STL N (52G –.267) NY N (85G –.249)																						
″	total	137	.256	.353	496	127	13	7	7	1.4	72	57	32	23	15	3	2	300	20	17	5	2.5	.950	OF-133
1927	NY N	84	.289	.379	190	55	6	1	3	1.6	33	19	25	12	2	18	3	117	2	6	3	2.2	.952	OF-56, 1B-1
1928	BOS N	42	.225	.258	151	34	3	1	0	0.0	25	19	17	9	1	1	1	127	6	2	1	3.3	.985	OF-41
1929		46	.204	.247	93	19	2	1	0	0.0	10	11	12	12	2	16	4	45	1	0	0	1.9	1.000	OF-24
1935	STL A	16	.185	.222	27	5	1	0	0	0.0	0	1	1	4	0	11	3	19	3	2	3	4.8	.917	1B-3, OF-2
11 yrs.		693	.282	.389	2118	597	87	37	22	1.0	296	272	168	147	37	86	24	1517	73	60	38	2.8	.964	OF-557, 1B-31

Ray Mueller

MUELLER, RAY COLEMAN (Iron Man) BR TR 5′ 9″ 175 lbs.
B. Mar. 8, 1912, Pittsburg, Kans. D. June 29, 1994, Dauphin County, Pa.

Year	Team	Games	BA	SA	AB	H	2B	3B	HR	HR%	R	RBI	BB	SO	SB	Pinch Hit AB	Pinch Hit H	PO	A	E	DP	TC/G	FA	G by Pos
1935	BOS N	42	.227	.371	97	22	5	0	3	3.1	10	11	3	11	0	2	0	64	27	2	6	2.3	.978	C-40
1936		24	.197	.254	71	14	4	0	0	0.0	5	5	5	17	0	1	0	66	7	1	2	3.2	.986	C-23
1937		64	.251	.353	187	47	9	2	2	1.1	21	26	18	36	1	6	0	169	44	1	6	3.8	.995	C-57
1938		83	.237	.354	274	65	8	6	4	1.5	23	35	16	28	3	8	2	239	47	2	4	3.8	.993	C-75
1939	PIT N	86	.233	.322	180	42	8	1	2	1.1	14	18	14	22	0	3	1	203	32	7	5	3.0	.971	C-81
1940		4	.333	.333	3	1	0	0	0	0.0	1	1	2	0	0	0	0	7	2	0	0	2.3	1.000	C-4
1943	CIN N	141	.260	.379	427	111	19	4	8	1.9	50	52	56	42	1	1	0	579	100	8	17	4.9	.988	C-140
1944		155	.286	.398	555	159	24	4	10	1.8	54	73	53	47	4	0	0	471	65	9	5	3.5	.983	C-155
1946		111	.254	.386	378	96	18	4	8	2.1	35	48	27	37	0	14	0	405	65	3	12	4.7	.994	C-100
1947		71	.250	.401	192	48	11	0	6	3.1	17	33	16	25	1	12	5	221	28	4	2	4.6	.984	C-55
1948		14	.206	.235	34	7	1	0	0	0.0	2	2	4	3	0	4	1	51	5	1	0	5.7	.982	C-10
1949	2 teams	CIN N (32G –.274) NY N (56G –.224)																						
″	total	88	.243	.344	276	67	6	2	6	2.2	24	36	18	27	2	1	0	307	36	4	3	4.0	.988	C-87
1950	2 teams	NY N (4G –.091) PIT N (67G –.269)																						
″	total	71	.257	.413	167	43	8	0	6	3.6	17	24	11	16	2	4	1	228	30	1	3	3.9	.996	C-67
1951	BOS N	28	.157	.229	70	11	2	0	1	1.4	8	9	7	11	0	4	1	85	15	0	3	4.3	1.000	C-23
14 yrs.		982	.252	.368	2911	733	123	23	56	1.9	281	373	250	322	14	60	11	3095	503	43	68	4.0	.988	C-917

Walter Mueller

MUELLER, WALTER JOHN BR TR 5′ 8″ 160 lbs.
Father of Don Mueller. Brother of Heinie Mueller.
B. Dec. 6, 1894, Central, Mo. D. Aug. 16, 1971, St. Louis, Mo.

Year	Team	Games	BA	SA	AB	H	2B	3B	HR	HR%	R	RBI	BB	SO	SB	Pinch Hit AB	Pinch Hit H	PO	A	E	DP	TC/G	FA	G by Pos
1922	PIT N	32	.270	.377	122	33	5	1	2	1.6	21	18	5	7	1	0	0	74	8	2	1	2.7	.976	OF-31
1923		40	.306	.414	111	34	4	4	0	0.0	11	20	4	6	2	14	6	62	2	4	0	2.6	.941	OF-26
1924		30	.260	.320	50	13	1	1	0	0.0	6	8	4	4	1	14	2	20	4	0	0	1.6	1.000	OF-15
1926		19	.242	.274	62	15	0	1	0	0.0	8	3	0	2	0	4	0	29	2	1	0	2.1	.969	OF-15
4 yrs.		121	.275	.362	345	95	10	7	2	0.6	46	49	13	19	4	32	8	185	16	7	1	2.4	.966	OF-87

Mike Muldoon

MULDOON, MICHAEL D. 5′ 8″ 165 lbs.
B. 1858, Ireland Deceased.

Year	Team	Games	BA	SA	AB	H	2B	3B	HR	HR%	R	RBI	BB	SO	SB	Pinch Hit AB	Pinch Hit H	PO	A	E	DP	TC/G	FA	G by Pos
1882	CLE N	84	.246	.378	341	84	17	5	6	1.8	50	45	10	28		0	0	132	137	37	12	3.6	.879	3B-61, OF-23
1883		98	.228	.302	378	86	22	3	0	0.0	54		10	39		0	0	123	170	62	9	3.5	.825	3B-98, OF-2
1884		110	.239	.320	422	101	16	6	2	0.5	46	38	18	67		0	0	130	207	67	16	3.6	.834	3B-109, 2B-1, OF-1
1885	BAL AA	102	.251	.344	410	103	20	6	2	0.5	47		20			0	0	106	184	44	17	3.3	.868	3B-101, 2B-1
1886		101	.199	.276	381	76	13	8	0	0.0	57		34			0	0	177	270	58	22	5.0	.885	2B-57, 3B-44
5 yrs.		495	.233	.323	1932	450	88	28	10	0.5	254	83	92	134		0	0	668	968	268	76	3.8	.859	3B-413, 2B-59, OF-26

Tony Mullane

MULLANE, ANTHONY JOHN (Count, The Apollo of the Box) BB TB 5′10½″ 165 lbs.
B. Jan. 30, 1859, Cork, Ireland D. Apr. 25, 1944, Chicago, Ill. BL 1882

Year	Team	Games	BA	SA	AB	H	2B	3B	HR	HR%	R	RBI	BB	SO	SB	Pinch Hit AB	Pinch Hit H	PO	A	E	DP	TC/G	FA	G by Pos
1881	DET N	5	.263	.263	19	5	0	0	0	0.0	0	1	0	0		0	0	8	7	2	0	3.4	.882	P-5
1882	LOU AA	77	.257	.307	303	78	13	1	0	0.0	46		13			0	0	187	191	24	10	4.9	.940	P-55, 1B-13, OF-12, 2B-2
1883	STL AA	83	.225	.300	307	69	11	6	0	0.0	38		13			0	0	66	108	27	6	2.3	.866	P-53, OF-30, 2B-3, 1B-2
1884	TOL AA	95	.276	.372	352	97	19	3	3	0.9	49		33			0	0	139	161	41	10	3.4	.880	P-68, OF-18, 1B-7, 3B-6, 2B-1, SS-1
1886	CIN AA	91	.225	.293	324	73	12	5	0	0.0	59		25			0	0	114	117	27	10	2.6	.895	P-63, OF-27, 1B-4, 3B-2, SS-1, 2B-1
1887		56	.221	.327	199	44	6	3	3	1.5	35		16		20	0	0	40	73	7	6	2.1	.942	P-48, OF-9
1888		51	.251	.337	175	44	4	4	1	0.6	27	16	8		12	0	0	62	85	14	2	3.0	.913	P-44, 1B-4, OF-3, 2B-2
1889		63	.296	.418	196	58	16	4	0	0.0	53	29	27	21	24	0	0	78	80	22	10	2.7	.878	P-33, 3B-18, OF-12, 1B-4
1890	CIN N	81	.276	.364	286	79	9	8	0	0.0	41	34	39	30	19	0	0	114	116	37	7	3.1	.861	OF-28, P-25, 3B-21, SS-10, 1B-1
1891		64	.148	.172	209	31	1	2	0	0.0	16	10	18	33	4	0	0	33	100	9	3	2.2	.937	P-51, OF-12, 3B-3
1892		39	.169	.212	118	20	3	1	0	0.0	14	9	9	8	4	0	0	38	87	9	6	3.4	.933	P-37, 1B-2
1893	2 teams	CIN N (16G –.288) BAL N (38G –.228)																						
″	total	54	.247	.289	166	41	2	1	1	0.6	26	20	10	17	6	1	0	27	90	8	3	2.4	.936	P-49, OF-2, 1B-1, 3B-1
1894	2 teams	BAL N (21G –.396) CLE N (4G –.077)																						
″	total	25	.333	.379	66	22	3	0	0	0.0	3	9	10	5	3	0	0	10	31	4	2	1.8	.911	P-25
13 yrs.		784	.243	.316	2720	661	99	38	8	0.3	407	128	221	114	92	1	0	916	1246	231	75	2.9	.903	P-556, OF-153, 3B-51, 1B-38, SS-12, 2B-9

Greg Mulleavy

MULLEAVY, GREGORY THOMAS (Moe) BR TR 5′ 9″ 167 lbs.
B. Sept. 25, 1905, Detroit, Mich. D. Feb. 1, 1980, Arcadia, Calif.

Year	Team	Games	BA	SA	AB	H	2B	3B	HR	HR%	R	RBI	BB	SO	SB	Pinch Hit AB	Pinch Hit H	PO	A	E	DP	TC/G	FA	G by Pos
1930	CHI A	77	.263	.346	289	76	14	5	0	0.0	27	28	20	23	5	4	1	137	219	32	41	5.3	.918	SS-73
1932		1	.000	.000	3	0	0	0	0	0.0	0	0	0	0	0	0	0	2	2	0	1	4.0	1.000	2B-1
1933	BOS A	1	—	—	0	0	0	0	0	—	1	0	0	0	0	0	0	0	0	0	0	0.0	—	
3 yrs.		79	.260	.342	292	76	14	5	0	0.0	28	28	20	23	5	4	1	139	221	32	42	5.3	.918	SS-73, 2B-1

Billy Mullen

MULLEN, WILLIAM JOHN BR TR 5′ 8″ 160 lbs.
B. Jan. 23, 1896, St. Louis, Mo. D. May 4, 1971, St. Louis, Mo.

Year	Team	Games	BA	SA	AB	H	2B	3B	HR	HR%	R	RBI	BB	SO	SB	Pinch Hit AB	Pinch Hit H	PO	A	E	DP	TC/G	FA	G by Pos
1920	STL A	1	.000	.000	1	0	0	0	0	0.0	0	0	0	0	0	1	0	0	0	0	0	0.0	—	
1921		4	.000	.000	4	0	0	0	0	0.0	0	0	2	1	0	2	0	2	2	0	0	2.0	1.000	3B-2
1923	BKN N	4	.273	.273	11	3	0	0	0	0.0	1	0	0	0	0	0	0	1	6	1	0	2.0	.875	3B-4
1926	DET A	11	.077	.077	13	1	0	0	0	0.0	2	0	5	1	1	2	0	6	8	2	0	1.8	.875	3B-9
1928	STL A	15	.389	.444	18	7	1	0	0	0.0	2	2	3	4	0	8	3	4	9	2	1	2.5	.867	3B-6
5 yrs.		35	.234	.255	47	11	1	0	0	0.0	5	2	10	6	1	13	3	13	25	5	1	2.0	.884	3B-21

Charlie Mullen

MULLEN, CHARLES GEORGE BR TR 5′10½″ 155 lbs.
B. Mar. 15, 1889, Seattle, Wash. D. June 6, 1963, Seattle, Wash.

Year	Team	Games	BA	SA	AB	H	2B	3B	HR	HR%	R	RBI	BB	SO	SB	Pinch Hit AB	Pinch Hit H	PO	A	E	DP	TC/G	FA	G by Pos
1910	CHI A	41	.195	.228	123	24	2	1	0	0.0	15	13	4		4	1	1	365	23	7	21	10.1	.982	1B-37, OF-2
1911		20	.203	.271	59	12	2	1	0	0.0	7	5	5		1	0	0	176	12	6	2	9.7	.969	1B-20
1914	NY A	93	.260	.285	323	84	8	0	0	0.0	33	44	33	55	11	0	0	898	62	6	54	10.4	.994	1B-93
1915		40	.267	.278	90	24	1	0	0	0.0	11	7	10	12	5	10	3	201	15	4	0	8.1	.982	1B-27
1916		59	.267	.342	146	39	9	1	0	0.0	11	18	9	13	7	14	5	191	46	6	7	5.7	.975	2B-20, 1B-17, OF-6
5 yrs.		253	.247	.285	741	183	22	3	0	0.0	77	87	61	80	28	25	9	1831	158	29	84	9.1	.986	1B-194, 2B-20, OF-8

John Mullen

MULLEN, JOHN BL TL
B. Philadelphia, Pa. Deceased.

Year	Team	Games	BA	SA	AB	H	2B	3B	HR	HR%	R	RBI	BB	SO	SB	Pinch Hit AB	Pinch Hit H	PO	A	E	DP	TC/G	FA	G by Pos
1876	PHI N	1	.000	.000	3	0	0	0	0	0.0	0	0	0	0		0	0	3	2	2	0	7.0	.714	C-1

Moon Mullen

MULLEN, FORD PARKER BL TR 5′ 9″ 165 lbs.
B. Feb. 9, 1917, Olympia, Wash.

Year	Team	Games	BA	SA	AB	H	2B	3B	HR	HR%	R	RBI	BB	SO	SB	Pinch Hit AB	Pinch Hit H	PO	A	E	DP	TC/G	FA	G by Pos
1944	PHI N	118	.267	.304	464	124	9	4	0	0.0	51	31	28	32	4	3	0	295	323	25	53	5.5	.961	2B-114, 3B-1, C-1

Freddie Muller

MULLER, FREDERICK WILLIAM BR TR 5′10″ 170 lbs.
B. Dec. 21, 1907, Newark, Calif. D. Oct. 20, 1976, Davis, Calif.

Year	Team	Games	BA	SA	AB	H	2B	3B	HR	HR%	R	RBI	BB	SO	SB	Pinch Hit AB	Pinch Hit H	PO	A	E	DP	TC/G	FA	G by Pos
1933	BOS A	15	.188	.250	48	9	1	1	0	0.0	6	3	5	5	1	1	0	24	36	5	6	4.6	.923	2B-14
1934		2	.000	.000	1	0	0	0	0	0.0	1	0	1	0	0	0	0	3	1	1	0	2.5	.800	2B-1, 3B-1
2 yrs.		17	.184	.245	49	9	1	1	0	0.0	7	3	6	5	1	1	0	27	37	6	6	4.4	.914	2B-15, 3B-1

Mulligan

MULLIGAN
B. Philadelphia, Pa. Deceased.

Year	Team	Games	BA	SA	AB	H	2B	3B	HR	HR%	R	RBI	BB	SO	SB	Pinch Hit AB	Pinch Hit H	PO	A	E	DP	TC/G	FA	G by Pos
1884	WAS U	1	.250	.250	4	1	0	0	0	0.0	2		0			0	0	4	3	0	0	7.0	1.000	3B-1

Eddie Mulligan

MULLIGAN, EDWARD JOSEPH BR TR 5′ 9″ 152 lbs.
B. Aug. 27, 1894, St. Louis, Mo. D. Mar. 15, 1982, San Rafael, Calif.

Year	Team	Games	BA	SA	AB	H	2B	3B	HR	HR%	R	RBI	BB	SO	SB	Pinch Hit AB	Pinch Hit H	PO	A	E	DP	TC/G	FA	G by Pos
1915	CHI N	11	.364	.409	22	8	1	0	0	0.0	5	2	5	1	2	0	0	23	26	5	9	4.9	.907	SS-10, 3B-1
1916		58	.153	.212	189	29	3	4	0	0.0	13	9	8	30	1	0	0	116	200	40	27	6.1	.888	SS-58
1921	CHI A	152	.251	.330	609	153	21	12	1	0.2	82	45	32	53	13	0	0	162	308	22	28	3.2	.955	3B-152, SS-1
1922		103	.234	.315	372	87	14	8	0	0.0	39	31	22	32	7	10	2	104	216	13	17	3.6	.961	3B-86, SS-7
1928	PIT N	27	.233	.279	43	10	2	0	0	0.0	4	1	3	4	0	9	5	18	18	2	7	3.8	.947	3B-6, 2B-4
5 yrs.		351	.232	.307	1235	287	41	24	1	0.1	143	88	70	120	23	19	7	423	768	82	88	3.9	.936	3B-245, SS-76, 2B-4

George Mullin

MULLIN, GEORGE JOSEPH (Wabash George) BR TR 5′11″ 188 lbs.
B. July 4, 1880, Toledo, Ohio D. Jan. 7, 1944, Wabash, Ind.

Year	Team	Games	BA	SA	AB	H	2B	3B	HR	HR%	R	RBI	BB	SO	SB	Pinch Hit AB	Pinch Hit H	PO	A	E	DP	TC/G	FA	G by Pos
1902	DET A	40	.325	.408	120	39	4	3	0	0.0	20	11	8		1	2	0	30	79	9	3	3.0	.924	P-35, OF-4
1903		46	.278	.389	126	35	9	1	1	0.8	11	12	2		1	4	1	38	108	10	1	3.7	.936	P-41, OF-1
1904		53	.298	.397	151	45	11	2	0	0.0	14	8	10		1	6	**2**	28	163	13	5	4.3	.936	P-45, OF-2
1905		47	.259	.289	135	35	4	0	0	0.0	15	12	12		4	2	0	20	134	6	7	3.6	.963	P-44
1906		50	.225	.324	142	32	6	4	0	0.0	13	6	4		2	8	3	21	113	6	2	3.5	.957	P-40
1907		70	.217	.287	157	34	5	3	0	0.0	16	13	12		2	20	5	15	133	6	1	3.3	.961	P-46
1908		55	.256	.328	125	32	2	2	1	0.8	13	8	7		2	14	3	21	102	5	2	3.3	.961	P-39
1909		53	.214	.270	126	27	7	0	0	0.0	13	17	13		2	10	1	12	99	3	2	2.7	.974	P-40, OF-2
1910		50	.256	.357	129	33	6	2	1	0.8	15	11	8		1	9	0	22	97	8	1	3.2	.937	P-38, OF-2
1911		40	.286	.398	98	28	7	2	0	0.0	4	5	10		1	8	2	9	55	4	2	2.3	.941	P-30
1912		38	.278	.356	90	25	5	1	0	0.0	13	12	17		0	8	1	8	70	6	1	2.8	.929	P-30
1913	2 teams	DET A (12G –.350) WAS A (12G –.190)																						
″	total	24	.268	.268	41	11	0	0	0	0.0	5	1	6	6	1	3	1	2	41	2	1	2.4	.956	P-19
1914	IND F	43	.312	.455	77	24	5	3	0	0.0	11	21	11		0	6	1	9	45	5	1	1.6	.915	P-36
1915	NWK F	6	.100	.100	10	1	0	0	0	0.0	0	0	2		0	1	0	1	5	0	1	1.2	1.000	P-5
14 yrs.		615	.263	.345	1527	401	71	23	3	0.2	163	137	122	6	18	101	20	236	1244	83	30	3.1	.947	P-488, OF-11
WORLD SERIES																								
1907	DET A	2	.000	.000	6	0	0	0	0	0.0	0	0	0	1	0	0	0	1	4	0	0	2.5	1.000	P-2
1908		1	.333	.333	3	1	0	0	0	0.0	1	1	1	0	0	0	0	0	2	0	0	2.0	1.000	P-1
1909		6	.188	.250	16	3	1	0	0	0.0	1	0	1	3	0	2	0	0	12	0	0	3.0	1.000	P-4
3 yrs.		9	.160	.200	25	4	1	0	0	0.0	2	1	2	4	0	2	0	1	18	0	0	2.7	1.000	P-7

Henry Mullin

MULLIN, HENRY J. BR 5′ 9″ 160 lbs.
B. Apr. 1862, St. John, N. B., Canada D. Nov. 8, 1937, Beverly, Mass.

Year	Team	Games	BA	SA	AB	H	2B	3B	HR	HR%	R	RBI	BB	SO	SB	Pinch Hit AB	Pinch Hit H	PO	A	E	DP	TC/G	FA	G by Pos
1884	2 teams	WAS AA (34G –.142) BOS U (2G –.000)																						
″	total	36	.133	.172	128	17	3	1	0	0.0	14		8			0	0	52	10	8	1	1.9	.886	OF-36, 3B-1

Jim Mullin

MULLIN, JAMES HENRY BR TR 5′10″ 173 lbs.
B. Oct. 16, 1883, New York, N. Y. D. Jan. 24, 1925, Philadelphia, Pa.

Year	Team	Games	BA	SA	AB	H	2B	3B	HR	HR%	R	RBI	BB	SO	SB	Pinch Hit AB	Pinch Hit H	PO	A	E	DP	TC/G	FA	G by Pos
1904	2 teams	PHI A (41G –.218) WAS A (27G –.186)																						
″	total	68	.203	.250	212	43	3	2	1	0.5	19	13	9	0	7	6	0	304	114	11	17	7.0	.974	2B-32, 1B-26, SS-2, OF-1
1905	WAS A	50	.190	.307	163	31	7	6	0	0.0	18	13	5		5	4	0	129	101	16	8	5.3	.935	2B-39, 1B-7
2 yrs.		118	.197	.275	375	74	10	8	1	0.3	37	26	14	0	12	10	0	433	215	27	25	6.3	.960	2B-71, 1B-33, SS-2, OF-1

Pat Mullin

MULLIN, PATRICK JOSEPH BL TR 6′ 2″ 190 lbs.
B. Nov. 1, 1917, Trotter, Pa.

Year	Team	Games	BA	SA	AB	H	2B	3B	HR	HR%	R	RBI	BB	SO	SB	Pinch Hit AB	Pinch Hit H	PO	A	E	DP	TC/G	FA	G by Pos
1940	DET A	4	.000	.000	4	0	0	0	0	0.0	0	0	0	0	0	3	0	0	0	0	0	0.0	.000	OF-1
1941		54	.345	.509	220	76	11	5	5	2.3	42	23	18	18	5	2	0	117	2	7	0	2.5	.944	OF-51
1946		93	.246	.355	276	68	13	4	3	1.1	34	35	25	36	3	14	1	121	8	7	1	1.8	.949	OF-75

Pat Mullin *continued*

Year	Team	Games	BA	SA	AB	H	2B	3B	HR	HR%	R	RBI	BB	SO	SB	Pinch Hit AB	Pinch Hit H	PO	A	E	DP	TC/G	FA	G by Pos
1947		116	.256	.470	398	102	28	6	15	3.8	62	62	63	66	3	9	3	229	10	3	2	2.3	.988	OF-106
1948		138	.288	.504	496	143	16	11	23	4.6	91	80	77	57	1	4	0	274	7	8	0	2.2	.972	OF-131
1949		104	.268	.448	310	83	8	6	12	3.9	55	59	42	29	1	26	6	169	4	2	0	2.2	.989	OF-79
1950		69	.218	.380	142	31	5	0	6	4.2	16	23	20	23	1	33	6	62	4	0	1	2.1	1.000	OF-32
1951		110	.281	.481	295	83	11	6	12	4.1	41	51	40	38	2	30	5	151	4	10	1	2.0	.939	OF-83
1952		97	.251	.424	255	64	13	5	7	2.7	29	35	31	30	4	30	6	131	6	3	2	2.2	.979	OF-65
1953		79	.268	.402	97	26	1	0	4	4.1	11	17	14	15	0	57	13	16	1	1	0	1.3	.944	OF-14
10 yrs.		864	.271	.453	2493	676	106	43	87	3.5	381	385	330	312	20	208	40	1270	46	41	7	2.1	.970	OF-637

Rance Mulliniks

MULLINIKS, STEVEN RANCE
B. Jan. 15, 1956, Tulare, Calif.
BL TR 5′11″ 162 lbs.

Year	Team	Games	BA	SA	AB	H	2B	3B	HR	HR%	R	RBI	BB	SO	SB	Pinch Hit AB	Pinch Hit H	PO	A	E	DP	TC/G	FA	G by Pos
1977	**CAL A**	78	.269	.365	271	73	13	2	3	1.1	36	21	23	36	1	1	0	112	229	13	37	4.6	.963	SS-77
1978		50	.185	.252	119	22	3	1	1	0.8	6	6	8	23	2	1	0	68	93	8	22	3.4	.953	SS-47, DH-2
1979		22	.147	.191	68	10	0	0	1	1.5	7	8	4	14	0	0	0	46	43	4	13	4.2	.957	SS-22
1980	**KC A**	36	.259	.315	54	14	3	0	0	0.0	8	6	7	10	0	0	0	30	53	1	9	2.6	.988	SS-18, 2B-14
1981		24	.227	.295	44	10	3	0	0	0.0	6	5	2	7	0	0	0	25	39	5	9	3.1	.928	2B-10, SS-7, 3B-5
1982	**TOR A**	112	.244	.363	311	76	25	0	4	1.3	32	35	37	49	3	22	3	69	154	14	16	2.0	.941	3B-102, SS-16
1983		129	.275	.467	364	100	34	3	10	2.7	54	49	57	43	0	23	10	77	185	7	19	2.0	.974	3B-116, SS-15, 2B-2
1984		125	.324	.440	343	111	21	5	3	0.9	41	42	33	44	2	18	6	67	152	8	10	1.8	.965	3B-119, SS-3, 2B-1
1985		129	.295	.454	366	108	26	1	10	2.7	55	56	55	54	2	19	9	75	162	7	16	2.1	.971	3B-119
1986		117	.259	.417	348	90	22	0	11	3.2	50	45	43	60	1	16	2	60	176	6	13	2.1	.975	3B-110, DH-5, 2B-1
1987		124	.310	.500	332	103	28	1	11	3.3	37	44	34	55	1	24	8	29	137	13	14	1.5	.927	3B-96, DH-22, SS-1
1988		119	.300	.475	337	101	21	1	12	3.6	49	48	56	57	1	17	6	3	5	0	0	0.1	1.000	DH-108, 3B-7
1989		103	.238	.326	273	65	11	2	3	1.1	25	29	34	40	0	18	3	15	50	1	9	0.6	.985	DH-73, 3B-29
1990		57	.289	.392	97	28	4	0	2	2.1	11	16	22	19	2	22	8	23	25	2	5	1.4	.960	3B-22, DH-10, 1B-3
1991		97	.250	.333	240	60	12	1	2	0.8	27	24	44	44	0	19	3	2	3	0	0	0.1	1.000	DH-81, 3B-5
1992		3	.500	.500	2	1	0	0	0	0.0	1	0	1	0	0	2	1	0	0	0	0	0.0	.000	DH-2
16 yrs.		1325	.272	.407	3569	972	226	17	73	2.0	445	434	460	555	15	202	59	701	1506	89	192	1.8	.961	3B-730, DH-303, SS-206, 2B-28, 1B-3
LEAGUE CHAMPIONSHIP SERIES																								
1985	**TOR A**	5	.364	.727	11	4	1	0	1	9.1	1	3	2	2	0	2	2	1	4	0	0	1.0	1.000	3B-5
1989		1	.000	.000	1	0	0	0	0	0.0	0	0	0	1	0	1	0	0	0	0	0	0.0	—	
1991		5	.125	.125	8	1	0	0	0	0.0	1	0	3	0	0	1	0	0	0	0	0	0.0	.000	DH-3
3 yrs.		11	.250	.450	20	5	1	0	1	5.0	2	3	5	3	0	4	2	1	4	0	0	0.6	1.000	3B-5, DH-3

Fran Mullins

MULLINS, FRANCIS JOSEPH
B. May 14, 1957, Oakland, Calif.
BR TR 6′ 180 lbs.

Year	Team	Games	BA	SA	AB	H	2B	3B	HR	HR%	R	RBI	BB	SO	SB	Pinch Hit AB	Pinch Hit H	PO	A	E	DP	TC/G	FA	G by Pos
1980	**CHI A**	21	.194	.258	62	12	4	0	0	0.0	9	3	9	8	0	0	0	15	36	1	7	2.5	.981	3B-21
1984	**SF N**	57	.218	.345	110	24	8	0	2	1.8	8	10	9	29	3	3	2	39	101	5	14	2.4	.966	3B-28, SS-28, 2B-4
1986	**CLE A**	28	.175	.275	40	7	4	0	0	0.0	3	5	2	11	0	3	1	23	46	4	6	2.8	.945	2B-13, SS-11, DH-1, 1B-1
3 yrs.		106	.203	.307	212	43	16	0	2	0.9	20	18	20	48	3	6	3	77	183	10	27	2.5	.963	3B-49, SS-39, 2B-17, DH-1, 1B-1

Joe Mulvey

MULVEY, JOSEPH H.
B. Oct. 27, 1858, Providence, R. I. D. Aug. 21, 1928, Philadelphia, Pa.
BR TR 5′11½″ 178 lbs.

Year	Team	Games	BA	SA	AB	H	2B	3B	HR	HR%	R	RBI	BB	SO	SB	Pinch Hit AB	Pinch Hit H	PO	A	E	DP	TC/G	FA	G by Pos
1883	**2 teams**	**PRO N** (4G –.125) **PHI N** (3G –.500)																						
″	**total**	7	.286	.357	28	8	2	0	0	0.0	3		0	2		0	0	10	11	8	1	4.1	.724	SS-4, 3B-3
1884	**PHI N**	100	.229	.282	401	92	11	2	2	0.5	47		4	49		0	0	151	216	73	20	4.4	.834	3B-100
1885		107	.269	.393	443	119	25	6	6	1.4	74		3	18		0	0	144	201	62	12	3.8	.848	3B-107
1886		107	.267	.365	430	115	16	10	2	0.5	71	53	15	31		0	0	99	191	40	2	3.1	.879	3B-107, OF-1
1887		111	.287	.369	474	136	21	6	2	0.4	93	78	21	14	43	0	0	123	197	50	18	3.3	.865	3B-111
1888		100	.216	.261	398	86	12	3	0	0.0	37	39	9	33	18	0	0	87	174	32	9	2.9	.891	3B-100
1889		129	.289	.393	544	157	21	9	6	1.1	77	77	23	25	23	0	0	165	284	54	20	3.9	.893	3B-129
1890	**PHI P**	120	.287	.430	519	149	26	15	6	1.2	96	87	27	36	20	0	0	144	227	62	15	3.6	.857	3B-120
1891	**PHI AA**	113	.254	.364	453	115	9	13	5	1.1	62	66	17	32	11	0	0	172	241	49	18	4.1	.894	3B-113
1892	**PHI N**	25	.143	.173	98	14	1	1	0	0.0	9	4	6	9	2	0	0	40	58	13	5	4.4	.883	3B-25
1893	**WAS N**	55	.235	.310	226	53	9	4	0	0.0	21	19	7	8	2	0	0	76	140	31	10	4.5	.874	3B-55
1895	**BKN N**	13	.306	.429	49	15	4	1	0	0.0	8	8	2	0	1	0	0	25	30	5	1	4.6	.917	3B-13
12 yrs.		987	.261	.355	4063	1059	157	70	29	0.7	598	431	134	257	120	0	0	1236	1970	479	131	3.7	.870	3B-983, SS-4, OF-1

Jerry Mumphrey

MUMPHREY, JERRY WAYNE
B. Sept. 9, 1952, Tyler, Tex.
BB TR 6′ 2″ 185 lbs.

Year	Team	Games	BA	SA	AB	H	2B	3B	HR	HR%	R	RBI	BB	SO	SB	Pinch Hit AB	Pinch Hit H	PO	A	E	DP	TC/G	FA	G by Pos
1974	**STL N**	5	.000	.000	2	0	0	0	0	0.0	2	0	0	0	0	0	0	0	0	0	0	0.0	.000	OF-1
1975		11	.375	.500	16	6	2	0	0	0.0	2	1	4	3	0	4	2	9	0	0	0	3.0	1.000	OF-3
1976		112	.258	.331	384	99	15	5	1	0.3	51	26	37	53	22	10	3	261	6	2	1	2.9	.993	OF-94
1977		145	.287	.387	463	133	20	10	2	0.4	73	38	47	70	22	16	3	291	8	9	1	2.3	.971	OF-133
1978		125	.262	.335	367	96	13	4	2	0.5	41	37	30	40	14	16	5	178	10	1	1	1.6	.995	OF-116
1979		124	.295	.369	339	100	10	3	3	0.9	53	32	26	39	8	16	5	180	3	3	0	1.6	.984	OF-114
1980	**SD N**	160	.298	.372	564	168	24	3	4	0.7	61	59	49	90	52	6	1	398	10	11	1	2.7	.974	OF-153
1981	**NY A**	80	.307	.429	319	98	11	5	6	1.9	44	32	24	27	14	0	0	219	5	8	0	2.9	.966	OF-79
1982		123	.300	.449	477	143	24	10	9	1.9	76	68	50	66	11	0	0	336	5	5	2	2.8	.986	OF-123
1983	**2 teams**	**NY A** (83G –.262) **HOU N** (44G –.336)																						
″	**total**	127	.288	.427	410	118	21	6	8	2.0	58	53	50	56	7	2	0	330	8	5	1	2.7	.985	OF-126
1984	**HOU N**	151	.290	.391	524	152	20	3	9	1.7	66	83	56	79	15	13	5	317	5	4	2	2.4	.988	OF-137
1985		130	.277	.396	444	123	25	2	8	1.8	52	61	37	57	6	10	4	248	6	8	1	2.1	.969	OF-126
1986	**CHI N**	111	.304	.401	309	94	11	2	5	1.6	37	32	26	45	2	29	10	161	3	3	3	1.8	.982	OF-92
1987		118	.333	.534	309	103	19	2	13	4.2	41	44	35	47	1	35	12	124	5	1	0	1.5	.992	OF-85
1988		63	.136	.167	66	9	2	0	0	0.0	3	9	7	16	0	50	5	5	0	0	0	1.3	1.000	OF-4
15 yrs.		1585	.289	.396	4993	1442	217	55	70	1.4	660	575	478	688	174	207	55	3057	74	60	13	2.3	.981	OF-1386
DIVISIONAL PLAYOFF SERIES																								
1981	**NY A**	5	.095	.095	21	2	0	0	0	0.0	2	0	0	1	1	0	0	15	1	0	0	3.2	1.000	OF-5

Jerry Mumphrey *continued*

Year	Team	Games	BA	SA	AB	H	2B	3B	HR	HR%	R	RBI	BB	SO	SB	Pinch Hit AB	Pinch Hit H	PO	A	E	DP	TC/G	FA	G by Pos
LEAGUE CHAMPIONSHIP SERIES																								
1981	NY A	3	.500	.583	12	6	1	0	0	0.0	2	0	3	2	0	0	0	4	0	0	0	1.3	1.000	OF-3
WORLD SERIES																								
1981	NY A	5	.200	.200	15	3	0	0	0	0.0	2	0	3	2	1	0	0	6	0	0	0	1.2	1.000	OF-5

John Munce

MUNCE, JOHN LEWIS 5′ 8½″ 160 lbs.
B. Nov. 18, 1857, Philadelphia, Pa. D. Mar. 15, 1917, Philadelphia, Pa.

Year	Team	Games	BA	SA	AB	H	2B	3B	HR	HR%	R	RBI	BB	SO	SB	Pinch Hit AB	Pinch Hit H	PO	A	E	DP	TC/G	FA	G by Pos
1884	WIL U	7	.190	.190	21	4	0	0	0	0.0	1		1			0	0	4	2	3	0	1.3	.667	OF-7

Jake Munch

MUNCH, JACOB FERDINAND BL TL 6′ 2½″ 170 lbs.
B. Nov. 16, 1890, Morton, Pa. D. June 8, 1966, Lansdowne, Pa.

Year	Team	Games	BA	SA	AB	H	2B	3B	HR	HR%	R	RBI	BB	SO	SB	Pinch Hit AB	Pinch Hit H	PO	A	E	DP	TC/G	FA	G by Pos
1918	PHI A	22	.267	.333	30	8	0	1	0	0.0	3	0	0	5	0	17	4	19	1	2	1	5.5	.909	OF-2, 1B-2

George Mundinger

MUNDINGER, GEORGE (Mundy) BR TR 6′ 2″ 200 lbs.
B. Nov. 20, 1854, New Orleans, La. D. Oct. 12, 1910, Covington, Ky.

Year	Team	Games	BA	SA	AB	H	2B	3B	HR	HR%	R	RBI	BB	SO	SB	Pinch Hit AB	Pinch Hit H	PO	A	E	DP	TC/G	FA	G by Pos
1884	IND AA	3	.250	.250	8	2	0	0	0	0.0	1		0			0	0	4	2	2	0	2.7	.750	C-3

Bill Mundy

MUNDY, WILLIAM EDWARD BL TL 5′10″ 154 lbs.
B. June 28, 1889, Salineville, Ohio D. Sept. 23, 1958, Kalamazoo, Mich.

Year	Team	Games	BA	SA	AB	H	2B	3B	HR	HR%	R	RBI	BB	SO	SB	Pinch Hit AB	Pinch Hit H	PO	A	E	DP	TC/G	FA	G by Pos
1913	BOS A	15	.255	.255	47	12	0	0	0	0.0	4	4	4	12	0	1	0	134	4	7	4	10.4	.952	1B-14

Noe Munoz

MUNOZ, NOE BR TR 6′ 2″ 180 lbs.
B. Nov. 11, 1967, Escatepec, Mexico.

Year	Team	Games	BA	SA	AB	H	2B	3B	HR	HR%	R	RBI	BB	SO	SB	Pinch Hit AB	Pinch Hit H	PO	A	E	DP	TC/G	FA	G by Pos
1995	LA N	2	.000	.000	1	0	0	0	0	0.0	0	0	0	0	0	0	0	6	0	0	0	3.0	1.000	C-2

Pedro Munoz

MUNOZ, PEDRO JAVIER BR TR 5′11″ 170 lbs.
Born Pedro Javier Munoz (Gonzalez).
B. Sept. 19, 1968, Ponce, Puerto Rico.

Year	Team	Games	BA	SA	AB	H	2B	3B	HR	HR%	R	RBI	BB	SO	SB	Pinch Hit AB	Pinch Hit H	PO	A	E	DP	TC/G	FA	G by Pos
1990	MIN A	22	.271	.341	85	23	4	1	0	0.0	13	5	2	16	3	0	0	34	1	1	1	1.6	.972	OF-21, DH-1
1991		51	.283	.500	138	39	7	1	7	5.1	15	26	9	31	3	6	1	89	3	1	2	2.0	.989	OF-44, DH-2
1992		127	.270	.409	418	113	16	3	12	2.9	44	71	17	90	4	6	1	220	8	3	4	1.8	.987	OF-122, DH-3
1993		104	.233	.393	326	76	11	1	13	4.0	34	38	25	97	1	3	0	172	5	3	2	1.8	.983	OF-102
1994		75	.295	.508	244	72	15	2	11	4.5	35	36	19	67	0	7	1	110	1	4	0	1.6	.965	OF-58, DH-12
1995		104	.301	.489	376	113	17	0	18	4.8	45	58	19	86	0	5	2	29	4	5	1	0.4	.868	DH-77, OF-25, 1B-3
6 yrs.		483	.275	.444	1587	436	70	8	61	3.8	186	234	91	387	11	27	5	654	22	17	10	1.5	.975	OF-372, DH-95, 1B-3

Joe Munson

MUNSON, JOSEPH MARTIN NAPOLEON BL TR 5′ 9″ 184 lbs.
Born Joseph Martin Napoleon Carlson.
B. Nov. 6, 1899, Renovo, Pa. D. Feb. 4, 1991, Drexel Hill, Pa.

Year	Team	Games	BA	SA	AB	H	2B	3B	HR	HR%	R	RBI	BB	SO	SB	Pinch Hit AB	Pinch Hit H	PO	A	E	DP	TC/G	FA	G by Pos
1925	CHI N	9	.371	.514	35	13	3	1	0	0.0	5	3	3	1	1	0	0	17	1	0	1	2.0	1.000	OF-9
1926		33	.257	.406	101	26	2	2	3	3.0	17	15	8	4	0	4	1	51	2	6	1	2.1	.898	OF-28
2 yrs.		42	.287	.434	136	39	5	3	3	2.2	22	18	11	5	1	4	1	68	3	6	2	2.1	.922	OF-37

Red Munson

MUNSON, CLARENCE HANFORD TR
B. July 31, 1883, Cincinnati, Ohio D. Feb. 19, 1957, Mishawaka, Ind.

Year	Team	Games	BA	SA	AB	H	2B	3B	HR	HR%	R	RBI	BB	SO	SB	Pinch Hit AB	Pinch Hit H	PO	A	E	DP	TC/G	FA	G by Pos
1905	PHI N	9	.115	.154	26	3	1	0	0	0.0	1	2	0		0	1	0	32	10	7	0	6.1	.857	C-8

Thurman Munson

MUNSON, THURMAN LEE BR TR 5′11″ 190 lbs.
B. June 7, 1947, Akron, Ohio D. Aug. 2, 1979, Canton, Ohio.

Year	Team	Games	BA	SA	AB	H	2B	3B	HR	HR%	R	RBI	BB	SO	SB	Pinch Hit AB	Pinch Hit H	PO	A	E	DP	TC/G	FA	G by Pos
1969	NY A	26	.256	.349	86	22	1	2	1	1.2	6	9	10	10	0	1	0	119	18	2	0	5.6	.986	C-25
1970		132	.302	.415	453	137	25	4	6	1.3	59	53	57	56	5	9	3	631	80	8	11	5.8	.989	C-125
1971		125	.251	.368	451	113	15	4	10	2.2	71	42	52	65	6	10	3	547	67	1	4	5.2	.998	C-117, OF-1
1972		140	.280	.364	511	143	16	3	7	1.4	54	46	47	58	6	8	2	575	71	15	11	5.0	.977	C-132
1973		147	.301	.487	519	156	29	4	20	3.9	80	74	48	64	4	2	0	673	80	12	11	5.4	.984	C-142
1974		144	.261	.381	517	135	19	2	13	2.5	64	60	44	66	2	2	0	743	75	22	10	6.0	.974	C-137, DH-4
1975		157	.318	.429	597	190	24	3	12	2.0	83	102	45	52	3	1	0	725	95	23	15	5.4	.973	C-130, DH-22, OF-2, 1B-2, 3B-1
1976		152	.302	.432	616	186	27	1	17	2.8	79	105	29	38	14	4	3	546	78	14	8	4.2	.978	C-121, DH-21, OF-11
1977		149	.308	.462	595	183	28	5	18	3.0	85	100	39	55	5	2	0	657	73	12	4	5.1	.984	C-136, DH-10
1978		154	.297	.373	617	183	27	1	6	1.0	73	71	35	70	2	1	1	698	61	11	4	5.1	.986	C-125, DH-14, OF-13
1979		97	.288	.374	382	110	18	3	3	0.8	42	39	32	37	1	1	0	428	44	10	7	5.0	.979	C-88, DH-5, 1B-3
11 yrs.		1423	.292	.410	5344	1558	229	32	113	2.1	696	701	438	571	48	41	12	6342	742	130	85	5.2	.982	C-1278, DH-76, OF-27, 1B-5, 3B-1
LEAGUE CHAMPIONSHIP SERIES																								
1976	NY A	5	.435	.522	23	10	2	0	0	0.0	3	3	0	1	0	0	0	18	6	2	0	5.2	.923	C-5
1977		5	.286	.476	21	6	1	0	1	4.8	3	5	0	2	0	0	0	24	4	0	0	5.6	1.000	C-5
1978		4	.278	.500	18	5	1	0	1	5.6	2	2	0	0	0	0	0	22	4	0	0	6.5	1.000	C-4
3 yrs.		14	.339	.500	62	21	4	0	2	3.2	8	10	0	3	0	0	0	64	14	2	0	5.7	.975	C-14
WORLD SERIES																								
1976	NY A	4	.529	.529	17	9	0	0	0	0.0	2	2	0	1	0	0	0	21	7	0	0	7.0	1.000	C-4
1977		6	.320	.520	25	8	2	0	1	4.0	4	3	2	8	0	0	0	40	5	0	0	7.5	1.000	C-6
1978		6	.320	.440	25	8	3	0	0	0.0	5	7	3	7	1	0	0	33	5	0	1	6.3	1.000	C-6
3 yrs.		16	.373 **5th**	.493	67	25	5	0	1	1.5	11	12	5	16	1	0	0	94	17	0	1	6.9	1.000	C-16

John Munyan

MUNYAN, JOHN B.
B. Nov. 14, 1860, Chester, Pa. D. Feb. 18, 1945, Endicott, N. Y.

Year	Team	Games	BA	SA	AB	H	2B	3B	HR	HR%	R	RBI	BB	SO	SB	Pinch Hit AB	Pinch Hit H	PO	A	E	DP	TC/G	FA	G by Pos
1887	CLE AA	16	.241	.293	58	14	1	1	0	0.0	9		3		4	0	0	30	12	11	2	3.1	.792	OF-12, C-3, 3B-2
1890	2 teams	COL AA (2G –.143) STL AA (96G –.266)																						
″	total	98	.264	.381	349	92	15	7	4	1.1	62		32		11	0	0	477	136	45	10	6.5	.932	C-83, OF-9, 2B-5, 3B-3, SS-1
1891	STL AA	60	.233	.290	176	41	4	3	0	0.0	41	19	41	39	13	0	0	196	53	25	4	4.3	.909	C-43, OF-12, SS-5, 3B-3
3 yrs.		174	.252	.345	583	147	20	11	4	0.7	112	19	76	39	28	0	0	703	201	81	16	5.4	.918	C-129, OF-33, 3B-8, SS-6, 2B-5

Bobby Murcer

MURCER, BOBBY RAY — BL TR 5′11″ 160 lbs.
B. May 20, 1946, Oklahoma City, Okla.

Year	Team		Games	BA	SA	AB	H	2B	3B	HR	HR%	R	RBI	BB	SO	SB	Pinch Hit AB	Pinch Hit H	PO	A	E	DP	TC/G	FA	G by Pos
1965	NY	A	11	.243	.378	37	9	0	1	1	2.7	2	4	5	12	0	0	0	28	41	5	14	6.7	.932	SS-11
1966			21	.174	.217	69	12	1	1	0	0.0	3	5	4	5	2	1	0	31	50	6	4	4.8	.931	SS-18
1969			152	.259	.454	564	146	24	4	26	4.6	82	82	50	103	7	5	0	235	81	22	11	2.3	.935	OF-118, 3B-31
1970			159	.251	.420	581	146	23	3	23	4.0	95	78	87	100	15	2	1	375	15	3	3	2.5	.992	OF-155
1971			146	.331	.543	529	175	25	6	25	4.7	94	94	91	60	14	4	1	317	10	5	1	2.3	.985	OF-143
1972			153	.292	.537	585	171	30	7	33	5.6	**102**	96	63	67	11	3	2	382	11	3	1	2.6	.992	OF-151
1973			160	.304	.464	616	187	29	2	22	3.6	83	95	50	67	6	0	0	380	14	6	2	2.5	.985	OF-160
1974			156	.274	.378	606	166	25	4	10	1.7	69	88	57	59	14	1	0	297	21	7	2	2.1	.978	OF-156
1975	SF	N	147	.298	.432	526	157	29	4	11	2.1	80	91	91	45	9	3	2	201	10	4	3	1.5	.981	OF-144
1976			147	.259	.433	533	138	20	2	23	4.3	73	90	84	78	12	2	0	282	11	12	2	2.1	.961	OF-146
1977	CHI	N	154	.265	.455	554	147	18	3	27	4.9	90	89	80	77	16	5	2	238	11	5	5	1.7	.980	OF-150, 2B-1, SS-1
1978			146	.281	.403	499	140	22	6	9	1.8	66	64	80	57	14	10	4	225	8	5	0	1.7	.979	OF-138
1979	2 teams		CHI N (58G –.258)	NY A (74G –.273)																					
″	total		132	.267	.405	454	121	16	1	15	3.3	64	55	61	52	3	5	1	279	8	3	0	2.3	.990	OF-124
1980	NY	A	100	.269	.438	297	80	9	1	13	4.4	41	57	34	28	2	22	7	82	2	4	0	1.0	.955	OF-59, DH-33
1981			50	.265	.470	117	31	6	0	6	5.1	14	24	12	15	0	22	6	0	0	0	0	0.0	.000	DH-33
1982			65	.227	.418	141	32	6	0	7	5.0	12	30	12	15	2	30	6	0	0	0	0	0.0	.000	DH-47
1983			9	.182	.409	22	4	2	0	1	4.5	2	1	1	1	0	4	0	0	0	0	0	0.0	.000	DH-5
17 yrs.			1908	.277	.445	6730	1862	285	45	252	3.7	972	1043	862	841	127	119	32	3352	293	90	48	2.0	.976	OF-1644, DH-118, 3B-31, SS-30, 2B-1
DIVISIONAL PLAYOFF SERIES																									
1981	NY	A	2	.000	.000	1	0	0	0	0	0.0	0	0	1	0	0	1	0	0	0	0	0	0.0	—	
LEAGUE CHAMPIONSHIP SERIES																									
1980	NY	A	1	.000	.000	4	0	0	0	0	0.0	0	0	0	2	0	0	0	0	0	0	0	0.0	.000	DH-1
1981			1	.333	.333	3	1	0	0	0	0.0	0	0	1	1	0	0	0	0	0	0	0	0.0	.000	DH-1
2 yrs.			2	.143	.143	7	1	0	0	0	0.0	0	0	1	3	0	0	0	0	0	0	0	0.0		DH-2
WORLD SERIES																									
1981	NY	A	4	.000	.000	3	0	0	0	0	0.0	0	0	0	0	0	3	0	0	0	0	0	0.0	—	

Simmy Murch

MURCH, SIMEON AUGUSTUS — BR TR 6′ 4″ 220 lbs.
B. Nov. 21, 1880, Castine, Me. D. June 6, 1939, Exeter, N. H.

Year	Team		Games	BA	SA	AB	H	2B	3B	HR	HR%	R	RBI	BB	SO	SB	Pinch Hit AB	Pinch Hit H	PO	A	E	DP	TC/G	FA	G by Pos
1904	STL	N	13	.137	.157	51	7	1	0	0	0.0	3	1	1		0	0	0	13	27	2	2	3.2	.952	2B-6, 3B-6, SS-1
1905			3	.111	.111	9	1	0	0	0	0.0	0	0	0		0	1	0	6	1	2	0	3.0	.778	2B-2, SS-1
1908	BKN	N	6	.182	.273	11	2	1	0	0	0.0	1	0	1		0	4	0	27	0	1	1	14.0	.964	1B-2
3 yrs.			22	.141	.169	71	10	2	0	0	0.0	4	1	2		0	5	0	46	28	5	3	4.4	.937	2B-8, 3B-6, 1B-2, SS-2

Wilbur Murdoch

MURDOCH, WILBUR EDWIN
B. Mar. 14, 1875, Avon, N. Y. D. Oct. 29, 1941, Los Angeles, Calif.

Year	Team		Games	BA	SA	AB	H	2B	3B	HR	HR%	R	RBI	BB	SO	SB	Pinch Hit AB	Pinch Hit H	PO	A	E	DP	TC/G	FA	G by Pos
1908	STL	N	27	.258	.306	62	16	3	0	0	0.0	5	5	3		4	9	2	21	0	2	0	1.4	.913	OF-16

Tim Murnane

MURNANE, TIMOTHY HAYES — BL TR 5′ 9½″ 172 lbs.
B. June 4, 1852, Naugatuck, Conn. D. Feb. 7, 1917, Boston, Mass.
Manager 1884.

Year	Team		Games	BA	SA	AB	H	2B	3B	HR	HR%	R	RBI	BB	SO	SB	Pinch Hit AB	Pinch Hit H	PO	A	E	DP	TC/G	FA	G by Pos
1876	BOS	N	69	.282	.334	308	87	4	3	2	0.6	60	34	8	12		0	0	697	9	56	30	11.0	.927	1B-65, OF-3, 2B-1
1877			35	.279	.364	140	39	7	1	1	0.7	23	15	6	7		0	0	78	9	13	3	2.9	.870	OF-30, 1B-5
1878	PRO	N	49	.239	.282	188	45	6	1	0	0.0	35	14	8	12		0	0	545	22	38	25	12.3	.937	1B-48, OF-1
1884	BOS	U	76	.235	.264	311	73	5	2	0	0.0	55		22			0	0	603	10	35	8	8.2	.946	1B-63, OF-16
4 yrs.			229	.258	.305	947	244	22	7	3	0.3	173	63	44	31		0	0	1923	50	142	66	9.1	.933	1B-181, OF-50, 2B-1

Murphy

MURPHY
Deceased.

Year	Team		Games	BA	SA	AB	H	2B	3B	HR	HR%	R	RBI	BB	SO	SB	Pinch Hit AB	Pinch Hit H	PO	A	E	DP	TC/G	FA	G by Pos
1884	BOS	U	1	.000	.000	3	0	0	0	0	0.0	0		1			0	0	1	0	2	0	1.5	.333	C-1, OF-1

Billy Murphy

MURPHY, WILLIAM EUGENE — BR TR 6′ 1″ 191 lbs.
B. May 7, 1944, Pineville, La.

Year	Team		Games	BA	SA	AB	H	2B	3B	HR	HR%	R	RBI	BB	SO	SB	Pinch Hit AB	Pinch Hit H	PO	A	E	DP	TC/G	FA	G by Pos
1966	NY	N	84	.230	.341	135	31	4	1	3	2.2	15	13	7	34	1	25	5	57	6	3	1	1.2	.955	OF-57

Buzz Murphy

MURPHY, ROBERT R. — BL TL 5′ 8½″ 155 lbs.
B. Apr. 26, 1895, Denver, Colo. D. May 11, 1938, Denver, Colo.

Year	Team		Games	BA	SA	AB	H	2B	3B	HR	HR%	R	RBI	BB	SO	SB	Pinch Hit AB	Pinch Hit H	PO	A	E	DP	TC/G	FA	G by Pos
1918	BOS	N	9	.375	.719	32	12	2	3	1	3.1	6	9	3	5	0	0	0	13	0	0	0	1.4	1.000	OF-9
1919	WAS	A	79	.262	.321	252	66	7	4	0	0.0	19	28	19	32	5	6	1	177	8	8	2	2.6	.959	OF-73
2 yrs.			88	.275	.366	284	78	9	7	1	0.4	25	37	22	37	5	6	1	190	8	8	2	2.5	.961	OF-82

Clarence Murphy

MURPHY, CLARENCE
Deceased.

Year	Team		Games	BA	SA	AB	H	2B	3B	HR	HR%	R	RBI	BB	SO	SB	Pinch Hit AB	Pinch Hit H	PO	A	E	DP	TC/G	FA	G by Pos
1886	LOU	AA	1	.000	.000	3	0	0	0	0	0.0	0		0			0	0	2	0	0	0	2.0	1.000	OF-1

Connie Murphy

MURPHY, CORNELIUS DAVID — BL TR 5′ 8″ 155 lbs.
B. Nov. 1, 1870, Northfield, Mass. D. Dec. 14, 1945, New Bedford, Mass.

Year	Team		Games	BA	SA	AB	H	2B	3B	HR	HR%	R	RBI	BB	SO	SB	Pinch Hit AB	Pinch Hit H	PO	A	E	DP	TC/G	FA	G by Pos
1893	CIN	N	6	.176	.235	17	3	1	0	0	0.0	3	2	1	2	0	2	0	10	1	1	0	3.0	.917	C-4
1894			1	.000	.000	4	0	0	0	0	0.0	0	0	1	1	0	0	0	0	1	1	0	2.0	.500	C-1
2 yrs.			7	.143	.190	21	3	1	0	0	0.0	3	2	2	3	0	2	0	10	2	2	0	2.8	.857	C-5

Dale Murphy

MURPHY, DALE BRYAN — BR TR 6′ 4″ 210 lbs.
B. Mar. 12, 1956, Portland, Ore.

Year	Team		Games	BA	SA	AB	H	2B	3B	HR	HR%	R	RBI	BB	SO	SB	Pinch Hit AB	Pinch Hit H	PO	A	E	DP	TC/G	FA	G by Pos
1976	ATL	N	19	.262	.354	65	17	6	0	0	0.0	3	9	7	9	0	0	0	100	13	3	0	6.1	.974	C-19
1977			18	.316	.526	76	24	8	1	2	2.6	5	14	0	8	0	0	0	114	11	6	2	7.3	.954	C-18
1978			151	.226	.394	530	120	14	3	23	4.3	66	79	42	**145**	11	7	3	1220	105	23	84	9.0	.983	1B-129, C-21
1979			104	.276	.469	384	106	7	2	21	5.5	53	57	38	67	6	2	0	812	57	20	63	8.6	.978	1B-76, C-27
1980			156	.281	.510	569	160	27	2	33	5.8	98	89	59	**133**	9	1	0	384	15	6	4	2.6	.985	OF-154, 1B-1
1981			104	.247	.390	369	91	12	1	13	3.5	43	50	44	72	14	2	0	264	11	5	5	2.6	.982	OF-103, 1B-3
1982			162	.281	.507	598	168	23	2	36	6.0	113	**109**	93	134	23	1	1	407	6	9	2	2.6	.979	OF-162

Dale Murphy *continued*

Year	Team	Games	BA	SA	AB	H	2B	3B	HR	HR%	R	RBI	BB	SO	SB	Pinch Hit AB	Pinch Hit H	PO	A	E	DP	TC/G	FA	G by Pos
1983		162	.302	**.540**	589	178	24	4	36	6.1	131	**121**	90	110	30	2	0	373	10	6	0	2.4	.985	OF-160
1984		162	.290	**.547**	607	176	32	8	**36**	5.9	94	100	79	134	19	2	0	369	10	5	1	2.4	.987	OF-160
1985		162	.300	.539	616	185	32	2	**37**	6.0	**118**	111	**90**	**141**	10	0	0	334	8	7	4	2.2	.980	OF-161
1986		160	.265	.477	614	163	29	7	29	4.7	89	83	75	141	7	1	1	303	6	6	1	2.0	.981	OF-159
1987		159	.295	.580	566	167	27	1	44	7.8	115	105	115	136	16	0	0	325	14	8	1	2.2	.977	OF-159
1988		156	.226	.421	592	134	35	4	24	4.1	77	77	74	125	3	1	0	340	15	3	4	2.3	.992	OF-156
1989		154	.228	.361	574	131	16	0	20	3.5	60	84	65	142	3	2	0	331	5	5	0	2.3	.985	OF-151
1990	**2 teams**	**ATL N** (97G –.232) **PHI N** (57G –.266)																						
"	**total**	154	.245	.417	563	138	23	1	24	4.3	60	83	61	130	9	4	0	321	7	5	1	2.2	.985	OF-152
1991	**PHI N**	153	.252	.415	544	137	33	1	18	3.3	66	81	48	93	1	9	3	287	6	5	0	2.0	.983	OF-147
1992		18	.161	.274	62	10	1	0	2	3.2	5	7	1	13	0	1	0	19	0	1	0	1.3	.950	OF-16
1993	**CLR N**	26	.143	.167	42	6	1	0	0	0.0	1	7	5	15	0	11	0	16	1	0	0	1.3	1.000	OF-13
18 yrs.		2180	.265	.469	7960	2111	350	39	398	5.0	1197	1266	986	1748	161	46	8	6319	300	123	172	3.1	.982	OF-1853, 1B-209, C-85
														7th										
LEAGUE CHAMPIONSHIP SERIES																								
1982	**ATL N**	3	.273	.273	11	3	0	0	0	0.0	1	0	0	2	1	0	0	8	0	0	0	2.7	1.000	OF-3

Danny Murphy

MURPHY, DANIEL FRANCIS BR TR 5′ 9″ 175 lbs.
B. Aug. 11, 1876, Philadelphia, Pa. D. Nov. 22, 1955, Jersey City, N. J.

Year	Team	Games	BA	SA	AB	H	2B	3B	HR	HR%	R	RBI	BB	SO	SB	Pinch Hit AB	Pinch Hit H	PO	A	E	DP	TC/G	FA	G by Pos
1900	**NY N**	22	.270	.284	74	20	1	0	0	0.0	12	6	8		4	0	0	46	49	12	9	4.9	.888	2B-22
1901		28	.186	.216	102	19	3	0	0	0.0	6	6	4		1	0	0	44	73	20	3	4.9	.854	2B-28
1902	**PHI A**	76	.313	.416	291	91	11	8	1	0.3	48	48	13		12	0	0	167	197	14	22	5.0	.963	2B-76
1903		133	.273	.382	513	140	31	11	1	0.2	65	60	13		17	0	0	241	349	32	34	4.7	.949	2B-133
1904		150	.287	.440	557	160	30	17	7	1.3	78	77	22		22	0	0	280	455	46	35	5.2	.941	2B-150
1905		150	.278	.390	533	148	34	4	6	1.1	71	71	42		23	0	0	287	387	31	29	4.7	.956	2B-150
1906		119	.301	.404	448	135	28	6	2	0.4	48	60	21		17	0	0	239	308	26	38	4.8	.955	2B-119
1907		124	.271	.345	469	127	23	3	2	0.4	51	57	30		11	1	0	271	386	24	28	5.6	.965	2B-122
1908		142	.265	.364	525	139	28	6	4	0.8	51	66	32		16	0	0	308	173	18	18	3.5	.964	OF-84, 2B-56, 1B-2
1909		149	.281	.412	541	152	28	14	5	0.9	61	69	35		19	0	0	191	17	5	5	1.4	.977	OF-149
1910		151	.300	.436	560	168	28	18	4	0.7	70	64	31		18	0	0	209	15	6	5	1.5	.974	OF-151
1911		141	.329	.461	508	167	27	11	6	1.2	104	66	50		22	1	0	164	46	8	8	1.6	.963	OF-136, 2B-4
1912		36	.323	.446	130	42	6	2	2	1.5	27	20	16		8	0	0	39	2	5	2	1.3	.891	OF-36
1913		40	.322	.441	59	19	5	1	0	0.0	3	6	4	8	0	31	8	5	0	0	1	0.6	1.000	OF-9
1914	**BKN F**	52	.304	.435	161	49	9	0	4	2.5	16	32	17		4	6	0	65	8	1	2	1.6	.986	OF-46
1915		5	.167	.167	6	1	0	0	0	0.0	0	0	0		0	3	1	0	1	0	0	0.5	1.000	2B-1, OF-1
16 yrs.		1518	.288	.402	5477	1577	292	101	44	0.8	711	708	338	8	194	42	9	2556	2466	248	239	3.6	.953	2B-861, OF-612, 1B-2
WORLD SERIES																								
1905	**PHI A**	5	.188	.250	16	3	1	0	0	0.0	0	0	0	2	0	0	0	4	10	4	0	3.6	.778	2B-5
1910		5	.350	.650	20	7	3	0	1	5.0	6	8	1	0	1	0	0	6	2	0	2	1.6	1.000	OF-5
1911		6	.304	.435	23	7	3	0	0	0.0	4	2	0	3	0	0	0	8	0	1	0	1.5	.889	OF-6
3 yrs.		16	.288	.458	59	17	7	0	1	1.7	10	10	1	5	1	0	0	18	12	5	2	2.2	.857	OF-11, 2B-5

Danny Murphy

MURPHY, DANIEL FRANCIS BL TR 5′11″ 185 lbs.
B. Aug. 23, 1942, Beverly, Mass.

Year	Team	Games	BA	SA	AB	H	2B	3B	HR	HR%	R	RBI	BB	SO	SB	Pinch Hit AB	Pinch Hit H	PO	A	E	DP	TC/G	FA	G by Pos
1960	**CHI N**	31	.120	.187	75	9	2	0	1	1.3	7	6	4	13	0	7	0	40	1	1	1	2.0	.976	OF-21
1961		4	.385	.846	13	5	0	0	2	15.4	3	3	1	5	0	0	0	5	1	0	0	1.5	1.000	OF-4
1962		14	.200	.343	35	7	3	1	0	0.0	5	3	2	9	0	6	0	5	0	0	0	0.6	1.000	OF-9
1969	**CHI A**	17	.000	.000	1	0	0	0	0	0.0	0	0	2	0	0	0	0	0	4	0	0	0.2	1.000	P-17
1970		51	.333	.833	6	2	0	0	1	16.7	3	1	2	2	0	0	0	4	10	1	1	0.3	.933	P-51
5 yrs.		117	.177	.323	130	23	5	1	4	3.1	18	13	11	29	0	13	0	54	16	2	2	0.7	.972	P-68, OF-34

Danny Murphy

MURPHY, DANIEL JOSEPH (Handsome Dan) 156 lbs.
B. Sept. 10, 1864, Brooklyn, N. Y. D. Dec. 14, 1915, Brooklyn, N. Y.

Year	Team	Games	BA	SA	AB	H	2B	3B	HR	HR%	R	RBI	BB	SO	SB	Pinch Hit AB	Pinch Hit H	PO	A	E	DP	TC/G	FA	G by Pos
1892	**NY N**	8	.115	.115	26	3	0	0	0	0.0	2	0	5	4	0	0	0	39	6	5	1	6.3	.900	C-8

Dave Murphy

MURPHY, DAVID FRANCIS (Dirty Dave) TR
B. May 4, 1876, Adams, Mass. D. Apr. 8, 1940, Adams, Mass.

Year	Team	Games	BA	SA	AB	H	2B	3B	HR	HR%	R	RBI	BB	SO	SB	Pinch Hit AB	Pinch Hit H	PO	A	E	DP	TC/G	FA	G by Pos
1905	**BOS N**	3	.182	.182	11	2	0	0	0	0.0	0	1	0		0	0	0	2	5	2	0	3.0	.778	SS-2, 3B-1

Dick Murphy

MURPHY, RICHARD LEE BL TL 5′11″ 170 lbs.
B. Oct. 25, 1931, Cincinnati, Ohio.

Year	Team	Games	BA	SA	AB	H	2B	3B	HR	HR%	R	RBI	BB	SO	SB	Pinch Hit AB	Pinch Hit H	PO	A	E	DP	TC/G	FA	G by Pos
1954	**CIN N**	6	.000	.000	1	0	0	0	0	0.0	1	0	0	1	0	1	0	0	0	0	0	0.0	—	

Dummy Murphy

MURPHY, HERBERT COURTLAND BR TR 5′10″ 165 lbs.
B. Dec. 18, 1886, Olney, Ill. D. Aug. 10, 1962, Tallahassee, Fla.

Year	Team	Games	BA	SA	AB	H	2B	3B	HR	HR%	R	RBI	BB	SO	SB	Pinch Hit AB	Pinch Hit H	PO	A	E	DP	TC/G	FA	G by Pos
1914	**PHI N**	9	.154	.192	26	4	1	0	0	0.0	1	3	0	4	0	0	0	23	28	8	2	6.6	.864	SS-9

Dwayne Murphy

MURPHY, DWAYNE KEITH BL TR 6′ 1″ 180 lbs.
B. Mar. 18, 1955, Merced, Calif.

Year	Team	Games	BA	SA	AB	H	2B	3B	HR	HR%	R	RBI	BB	SO	SB	Pinch Hit AB	Pinch Hit H	PO	A	E	DP	TC/G	FA	G by Pos
1978	**OAK A**	60	.192	.231	52	10	2	0	0	0.0	15	5	7	14	0	4	1	49	1	0	1	1.0	1.000	OF-45, DH-5
1979		121	.255	.387	388	99	10	4	11	2.8	57	40	84	80	15	2	1	322	10	4	0	2.8	.988	OF-118
1980		159	.274	.380	573	157	18	2	13	2.3	86	68	102	96	26	0	0	507	13	5	0	3.3	.990	OF-158
1981		107	.251	.408	390	98	10	3	15	3.8	58	60	73	91	10	0	0	326	6	5	0	3.1	.985	OF-106, DH-1
1982		151	.238	.418	543	129	15	1	27	5.0	84	94	93	122	26	3	0	452	18	8	3	3.2	.983	OF-147, SS-1, DH-1
1983		130	.227	.380	471	107	17	2	17	3.6	55	75	62	105	7	1	0	365	7	8	0	2.9	.979	OF-124, DH-7
1984		153	.256	.472	559	143	18	2	33	5.9	93	88	74	111	4	0	0	474	14	6	2	3.2	.988	OF-153
1985		152	.233	.400	523	122	21	3	20	3.8	77	59	84	123	4	0	0	432	6	5	1	3.0	.989	OF-150
1986		98	.252	.386	329	83	11	3	9	2.7	50	39	56	80	3	2	2	276	6	2	3	2.9	.993	OF-97, DH-1
1987		82	.233	.374	219	51	7	0	8	3.7	39	35	58	61	4	5	0	187	2	3	0	2.4	.984	OF-79, 2B-1, 1B-1

Dwayne Murphy *continued*

Year	Team	Lg	Games	BA	SA	AB	H	2B	3B	HR	HR%	R	RBI	BB	SO	SB	Pinch Hit AB	Pinch Hit H	PO	A	E	DP	TC/G	FA	G by Pos
1988	DET	A	49	.250	.368	144	36	5	0	4	2.8	14	19	24	26	1	4	1	122	1	0	0	2.7	1.000	OF-43, DH-3
1989	PHI	N	98	.218	.423	156	34	5	0	9	5.8	20	27	29	44	0	43	9	69	1	1	1	1.4	.986	OF-52
12 yrs.			1360	.246	.402	4347	1069	139	20	166	3.8	648	609	746	953	100	64	14	3581	85	47	11	2.9	.987	OF-1272, DH-18, 1B-1, 2B-1, SS-1
DIVISIONAL PLAYOFF SERIES																									
1981	OAK	A	3	.545	.909	11	6	1	0	1	9.1	4	2	1	1	0	0	0	13	0	0	0	4.3	1.000	OF-3
LEAGUE CHAMPIONSHIP SERIES																									
1981	OAK	A	3	.250	.375	8	2	1	0	0	0.0	0	1	2	3	0	0	0	9	0	0	0	3.0	1.000	OF-3

Ed Murphy

MURPHY, EDWARD JOSEPH BR TR 5′11″ 190 lbs.
B. Aug. 23, 1918, Joliet, Ill. D. Dec. 10, 1991, Joliet, Ill.

Year	Team	Lg	Games	BA	SA	AB	H	2B	3B	HR	HR%	R	RBI	BB	SO	SB	Pinch Hit AB	Pinch Hit H	PO	A	E	DP	TC/G	FA	G by Pos
1942	PHI	N	13	.250	.321	28	7	2	0	0	0.0	2	4	2	4	0	5	1	69	3	0	7	9.0	1.000	1B-8

Eddie Murphy

MURPHY, JOHN EDWARD (Honest Eddie) BL TR 5′ 9″ 155 lbs.
B. Oct. 2, 1891, Hancock, N. Y. D. Feb. 21, 1969, Dunmore, Pa.

Year	Team	Lg	Games	BA	SA	AB	H	2B	3B	HR	HR%	R	RBI	BB	SO	SB	Pinch Hit AB	Pinch Hit H	PO	A	E	DP	TC/G	FA	G by Pos
1912	PHI	A	33	.317	.359	142	45	4	1	0	0.0	24	6	11		7	0	0	48	6	3	1	1.7	.947	OF-33
1913			136	.295	.356	508	150	14	7	1	0.2	105	30	70	44	21	1	0	166	14	11	2	1.4	.942	OF-135
1914			148	.272	.340	573	156	12	9	3	0.5	101	43	87	46	36	0	0	194	15	13	4	1.5	.941	OF-148
1915	2 teams		PHI A (68G –.231) CHI A (70G –.315)																						
″	total		138	.274	.334	533	146	14	9	0	0.0	88	43	68	27	33	4	0	177	30	16	0	1.7	.928	OF-128, 3B-6
1916	CHI	A	51	.210	.276	105	22	5	1	0	0.0	14	4	9	5	3	20	4	28	2	1	0	1.2	.968	OF-24, 3B-1
1917			53	.314	.392	51	16	2	1	0	0.0	9	16	5	1	4	32	12	2	0	0	0	0.2	1.000	OF-9
1918			91	.297	.350	286	85	9	3	0	0.0	36	23	22	18	6	18	4	124	18	7	2	2.1	.953	OF-63, 2B-8
1919			30	.486	.600	35	17	4	0	0	0.0	8	5	7	0	0	21	**8**	10	1	1	0	2.0	.917	OF-6
1920			58	.339	.373	118	40	2	1	0	0.0	22	19	12	4	1	33	13	27	13	5	2	2.0	.889	OF-19, 3B-3
1921			6	.200	.200	5	1	0	0	0	0.0	1	0	0	0	0	5	1	0	0	0	0	0.0	—	
1926	PIT	N	16	.118	.118	17	2	0	0	0	0.0	3	6	3	0	0	11	1	5	0	0	0	1.7	1.000	OF-3
11 yrs.			760	.287	.346	2373	680	66	32	4	0.2	411	195	294	145	111	145	43	781	99	57	11	1.6	.939	OF-568, 3B-10, 2B-8
WORLD SERIES																									
1913	PHI	A	5	.227	.227	22	5	0	0	0	0.0	2	0	2	0	0	0	0	15	0	0	0	3.0	1.000	OF-5
1914			4	.188	.313	16	3	2	0	0	0.0	2	0	2	2	0	0	0	4	0	0	0	1.0	1.000	OF-4
1919	CHI	A	3	.000	.000	2	0	0	0	0	0.0	0	0	0	1	0	2	0	0	0	0	0	0.0	—	
3 yrs.			12	.200	.250	40	8	2	0	0	0.0	4	0	4	3	0	2	0	19	0	0	0	2.1	1.000	OF-9

Frank Murphy

MURPHY, FRANCIS PATRICK
B. Apr. 16, 1875, North Tarrytown, N. Y. D. Nov. 4, 1912, Central Islip, N. Y.

Year	Team	Lg	Games	BA	SA	AB	H	2B	3B	HR	HR%	R	RBI	BB	SO	SB	Pinch Hit AB	Pinch Hit H	PO	A	E	DP	TC/G	FA	G by Pos
1901	2 teams		BOS N (45G –.261) NY N (12G –.125)																						
″	total		57	.232	.295	224	52	5	3	1	0.4	17	20	7		7	0	0	114	11	8	1	2.3	.940	OF-57

Howard Murphy

MURPHY, HOWARD BL TR 5′ 8½″ 150 lbs.
B. Jan. 1, 1882, Birmingham, Ala. D. Oct. 5, 1926, Fort Worth, Tex.

Year	Team	Lg	Games	BA	SA	AB	H	2B	3B	HR	HR%	R	RBI	BB	SO	SB	Pinch Hit AB	Pinch Hit H	PO	A	E	DP	TC/G	FA	G by Pos
1909	STL	N	25	.200	.200	60	12	0	0	0	0.0	3	3	4		1	5	1	35	2	3	0	2.1	.925	OF-19

John Murphy

MURPHY, JOHN PATRICK 5′ 7½″ 160 lbs.
B. 1879, New Haven, Conn. D. Apr. 20, 1949, Andover, Mass.

Year	Team	Lg	Games	BA	SA	AB	H	2B	3B	HR	HR%	R	RBI	BB	SO	SB	Pinch Hit AB	Pinch Hit H	PO	A	E	DP	TC/G	FA	G by Pos
1902	STL	N	1	.667	1.000	3	2	1	0	0	0.0	1	1	1		0	0	0	2	0	0	0	2.0	1.000	3B-1
1903	DET	A	5	.182	.227	22	4	1	0	0	0.0	1	1	0	0	0	0	0	7	16	4	1	5.4	.852	SS-5
2 yrs.			6	.240	.320	25	6	2	0	0	0.0	2	2	1	0	0	0	0	9	16	4	1	4.8	.862	SS-5, 3B-1

Larry Murphy

MURPHY, LAWRENCE PATRICK BL
Deceased.

Year	Team	Lg	Games	BA	SA	AB	H	2B	3B	HR	HR%	R	RBI	BB	SO	SB	Pinch Hit AB	Pinch Hit H	PO	A	E	DP	TC/G	FA	G by Pos
1891	WAS	AA	101	.265	.325	400	106	15	3	1	0.3	73	35	63	27	29	0	0	164	10	25	3	2.0	.874	OF-101

Leo Murphy

MURPHY, LEO JOSEPH (Red) BR TR 6′ 1″ 179 lbs.
B. Jan. 7, 1889, Terre Haute, Ind. D. Aug. 12, 1960, Racine, Wis.

Year	Team	Lg	Games	BA	SA	AB	H	2B	3B	HR	HR%	R	RBI	BB	SO	SB	Pinch Hit AB	Pinch Hit H	PO	A	E	DP	TC/G	FA	G by Pos
1915	PIT	N	34	.098	.098	41	4	0	0	0	0.0	4	4	4	12	0	9	1	29	12	3	2	1.3	.932	C-34

Mike Murphy

MURPHY, MICHAEL JEROME BR TR 5′ 9″ 170 lbs.
B. Aug. 19, 1888, Forestville, Pa. D. Oct. 26, 1952, Johnson City, N. Y.

Year	Team	Lg	Games	BA	SA	AB	H	2B	3B	HR	HR%	R	RBI	BB	SO	SB	Pinch Hit AB	Pinch Hit H	PO	A	E	DP	TC/G	FA	G by Pos
1912	STL	N	1	.000	.000	1	0	0	0	0	0.0	0	1	0	0	0	0	0	0	0	0	0	0.0	.000	C-1
1916	PHI	A	14	.111	.111	27	3	0	0	0	0.0	0	1	1	3	0	2	0	29	9	1	0	3.3	.974	C-12
2 yrs.			15	.107	.107	28	3	0	0	0	0.0	0	2	1	3	0	2	0	29	9	1	0	3.0	.974	C-13

Morg Murphy

MURPHY, MORGAN EDWARD BR TR 5′ 8″ 160 lbs.
B. Feb. 12, 1867, E. Providence, R. I. D. Oct. 3, 1938, Providence, R. I.

Year	Team	Lg	Games	BA	SA	AB	H	2B	3B	HR	HR%	R	RBI	BB	SO	SB	Pinch Hit AB	Pinch Hit H	PO	A	E	DP	TC/G	FA	G by Pos
1890	BOS	P	68	.228	.309	246	56	10	2	2	0.8	38	32	24	31	16	0	0	257	62	34	8	5.0	.904	C-67, SS-2, 3B-1, OF-1
1891	BOS	AA	106	.216	.294	402	87	11	4	4	1.0	60	54	36	58	17	0	0	533	118	31	8	6.3	.955	C-104, OF-4
1892	CIN	N	74	.197	.274	234	46	8	2	2	0.9	29	24	25	57	4	0	0	315	67	18	6	5.4	.955	C-74
1893			57	.235	.285	200	47	5	1	1	0.5	25	19	14	35	1	0	0	169	47	15	6	4.1	.935	C-56, 1B-1
1894			75	.275	.322	255	70	9	0	1	0.4	42	37	26	34	6	0	0	196	76	30	5	4.0	.901	C-74, SS-1, 3B-1
1895			25	.268	.293	82	22	2	0	0	0.0	15	16	11	8	6	0	0	70	18	9	1	3.9	.907	C-25
1896	STL	N	49	.257	.309	175	45	5	2	0	0.0	12	11	8	14	1	1	0	178	48	18	5	5.1	.926	C-48
1897			62	.169	.179	207	35	2	0	0	0.0	13	12	6		1	0	0	191	66	11	6	4.4	.959	C-53, 1B-8
1898	2 teams		PIT N (5G –.125) PHI N (25G –.198)																						
″	total		30	.186	.216	102	19	3	0	0	0.0	6	13	7		0	0	0	91	38	5	3	4.5	.963	C-30
1900	PHI	N	11	.278	.333	36	10	0	1	0	0.0	2	3	0		0	0	0	33	15	1	1	4.5	.980	C-11
1901	PHI	A	9	.214	.250	28	6	1	0	0	0.0	5	6	0		1	0	0	39	7	5	1	5.7	.902	C-8, 1B-1
11 yrs.			566	.225	.281	1967	443	56	12	10	0.5	247	227	157	237	53	1	0	2072	562	177	50	4.9	.937	C-550, 1B-10, OF-5, SS-3, 3B-2

Pat Murphy

MURPHY, PATRICK J. TL 5′10″ 160 lbs.
B. Jan. 2, 1857, Auburn, Mass. D. May 16, 1927, Worcester, Mass.

Year	Team	Lg	Games	BA	SA	AB	H	2B	3B	HR	HR%	R	RBI	BB	SO	SB	Pinch Hit AB	Pinch Hit H	PO	A	E	DP	TC/G	FA	G by Pos
1887	**NY**	**N**	17	.214	.250	56	12	2	0	0	0.0	4	4	2	4	1	0	0	79	26	19	3	7.3	.847	C-17
1888			28	.170	.179	106	18	1	0	0	0.0	11	4	6	11	3	0	0	186	56	23	3	9.5	.913	C-28
1889			9	.357	.571	28	10	1	1	1	3.6	5	4	2	0	0	0	0	26	8	5	0	4.3	.872	C-9
1890			32	.235	.294	119	28	5	1	0	0.0	14	9	14	13	3	0	0	157	33	22	2	6.4	.896	C-29, OF-3, SS-1
4 yrs.			86	.220	.272	309	68	9	2	1	0.3	34	21	24	28	7	0	0	448	123	69	8	7.4	.892	C-83, OF-3, SS-1

Tony Murphy

MURPHY, FRANCIS J. 5′ 6½″ 145 lbs.
B. 1863, Brooklyn, N. Y. Deceased.

Year	Team	Lg	Games	BA	SA	AB	H	2B	3B	HR	HR%	R	RBI	BB	SO	SB	Pinch Hit AB	Pinch Hit H	PO	A	E	DP	TC/G	FA	G by Pos
1884	**NY**	**AA**	1	.333	.333	3	1	0	0	0	0.0	1		0			0	0	3	0	0	0	3.0	1.000	C-1

Willie Murphy

MURPHY, WILLIAM H. (Gentle Willie) 5′11″ 198 lbs.
B. Mar. 23, 1864, Springfield, Mass. Deceased.

Year	Team	Lg	Games	BA	SA	AB	H	2B	3B	HR	HR%	R	RBI	BB	SO	SB	Pinch Hit AB	Pinch Hit H	PO	A	E	DP	TC/G	FA	G by Pos
1884	**2 teams**	**CLE N** (42G –.226) **WAS AA** (5G –.476)																							
″	**total**		47	.254	.317	189	48	3	3	1	0.5	21	9	2	23		0	0	69	14	31	0	2.4	.728	OF-46, 3B-1

Yale Murphy

MURPHY, WILLIAM HENRY (Tot Midget) BL TR 5′ 3″ 125 lbs.
B. Nov. 11, 1869, Southville, Mass. D. Feb. 14, 1906, Southville, Mass.

Year	Team	Lg	Games	BA	SA	AB	H	2B	3B	HR	HR%	R	RBI	BB	SO	SB	Pinch Hit AB	Pinch Hit H	PO	A	E	DP	TC/G	FA	G by Pos
1894	**NY**	**N**	74	.271	.307	280	76	6	2	0	0.0	64	28	51	23	28	0	0	150	157	35	15	4.6	.898	SS-49, OF-20, 3B-3, 1B-1, 2B-1
1895			51	.201	.255	184	37	6	2	0	0.0	35	16	27	13	7	0	0	82	39	18	4	2.8	.871	OF-33, SS-8, 3B-8, 2B-1
1897			5	.000	.000	8	0	0	0	0	0.0	1	1	2		0	0	0	3	3	1	0	1.4	.857	SS-3, 2B-2
3 yrs.			130	.239	.282	472	113	12	4	0	0.0	100	45	80	36	35	0	0	235	199	54	19	3.8	.889	SS-60, OF-53, 3B-11, 2B-4, 1B-1

Bill Murray

MURRAY, WILLIAM ALLENWOOD (Dasher) BB TR 5′11″ 165 lbs.
B. Sept. 6, 1893, Vinalhaven, Me. D. Sept. 14, 1943, Boston, Mass.

Year	Team	Lg	Games	BA	SA	AB	H	2B	3B	HR	HR%	R	RBI	BB	SO	SB	Pinch Hit AB	Pinch Hit H	PO	A	E	DP	TC/G	FA	G by Pos
1917	**WAS**	**A**	8	.143	.238	21	3	0	1	0	0.0	2	4	2	2	1	0	0	11	14	3	2	4.0	.893	2B-6, SS-1

Bobby Murray

MURRAY, ROBERT HAYES BL TR 5′ 7″ 155 lbs.
B. July 4, 1898, St. Albans, Vt. D. Jan. 4, 1979, Nashua, N. H.

Year	Team	Lg	Games	BA	SA	AB	H	2B	3B	HR	HR%	R	RBI	BB	SO	SB	Pinch Hit AB	Pinch Hit H	PO	A	E	DP	TC/G	FA	G by Pos
1923	**WAS**	**A**	10	.179	.205	39	7	1	0	0	0.0	2	2	1	4	1	0	0	11	26	0	0	3.7	1.000	3B-10

Ed Murray

MURRAY, EDWARD FRANCIS BR TR 5′ 6″ 145 lbs.
B. May 8, 1895, Mystic, Conn. D. Nov. 8, 1970, Cheyenne, Wyo.

Year	Team	Lg	Games	BA	SA	AB	H	2B	3B	HR	HR%	R	RBI	BB	SO	SB	Pinch Hit AB	Pinch Hit H	PO	A	E	DP	TC/G	FA	G by Pos
1917	**STL**	**A**	1	.000	.000	1	0	0	0	0	0.0	0	0	0	1	0	0	0	0	0	0	0	0.0	.000	SS-1

Eddie Murray

MURRAY, EDDIE CLARENCE BB TR 6′ 2″ 190 lbs.
Brother of Rich Murray.
B. Feb. 24, 1956, Los Angeles, Calif.

Year	Team	Lg	Games	BA	SA	AB	H	2B	3B	HR	HR%	R	RBI	BB	SO	SB	Pinch Hit AB	Pinch Hit H	PO	A	E	DP	TC/G	FA	G by Pos
1977	**BAL**	**A**	160	.283	.470	611	173	29	2	27	4.4	81	88	48	104	0	4	0	375	17	3	34	2.5	.992	DH-111, 1B-42, OF-3
1978			161	.285	.480	610	174	32	3	27	4.4	85	95	70	97	6	0	0	1507	112	6	144	10.1	.996	1B-157, 3B-3, DH-1
1979			159	.295	.475	606	179	30	2	25	4.1	90	99	72	78	10	0	0	1456	107	10	135	9.9	.994	1B-157, DH-2
1980			158	.300	.519	621	186	36	2	32	5.2	100	116	54	71	7	3	1	1369	77	9	158	9.4	.994	1B-154, DH-1
1981			99	.294	.534	378	111	21	2	**22**	5.8	57	**78**	40	43	2	0	0	899	91	1	98	10.0	.999	1B-99
1982			151	.316	.549	550	174	30	1	32	5.8	87	110	70	82	7	0	0	1269	97	4	106	9.1	.997	1B-149, DH-2
1983			156	.306	.538	582	178	30	3	33	5.7	115	111	86	90	5	2	0	1393	114	10	136	9.8	.993	1B-153, DH-2
1984			162	.306	.509	588	180	26	3	29	4.9	97	110	**107**	87	10	0	0	1538	143	13	152	10.5	.992	1B-159, DH-3
1985			156	.297	.523	583	173	37	1	31	5.3	111	124	84	68	5	0	0	1338	152	19	154	9.7	.987	1B-154, DH-2
1986			137	.305	.463	495	151	25	1	17	3.4	61	84	78	49	3	2	0	1045	88	13	100	8.5	.989	1B-119, DH-16
1987			160	.277	.477	618	171	28	3	30	4.9	89	91	73	80	1	0	0	1371	145	10	146	9.5	.993	1B-156, DH-4
1988			161	.284	.474	603	171	27	2	28	4.6	75	84	75	78	5	0	0	867	106	11	101	6.1	.989	1B-103, DH-58
1989	**LA**	**N**	160	.247	.401	594	147	29	1	20	3.4	66	88	87	85	7	1	1	1316	137	6	122	9.1	.996	1B-159, 3B-2
1990			155	.330	.520	558	184	22	3	26	4.7	96	95	82	64	8	4	0	1180	113	10	88	8.7	.992	1B-150
1991			153	.260	.403	576	150	23	1	19	3.3	69	96	55	74	10	3	2	1327	128	7	96	9.7	.995	1B-149, 3B-1
1992	**NY**	**N**	156	.261	.423	551	144	37	2	16	2.9	64	93	66	74	4	3	1	1283	96	12	109	9.0	.991	1B-154
1993			154	.285	.467	610	174	28	1	27	4.4	77	100	40	61	2	0	0	1319	111	18	118	9.4	.988	1B-154
1994	**CLE**	**A**	108	.254	.425	433	110	21	1	17	3.9	57	76	31	53	8	0	0	241	14	3	25	2.4	.988	DH-82, 1B-26
1995			113	.323	.516	436	141	21	0	21	4.8	68	82	39	65	5	1	1	160	22	3	12	1.6	.984	DH-95, 1B-18
19 yrs.			2819	.290	.482	10603 **10th**	3071	532	34	479	4.5	1545	1820	1257	1403	105	23	6	21253	1870	168	2034	8.3	.993	1B-2412, DH-379, 3B-6, OF-3
DIVISIONAL PLAYOFF SERIES																									
1995	**CLE**	**A**	3	.385	.769	13	5	0	1	1	7.7	3	3	2	1	0	0	0	0	0	0	0	0.0	.000	DH-3
LEAGUE CHAMPIONSHIP SERIES																									
1979	**BAL**	**A**	4	.417	.667	12	5	0	0	1	8.3	3	5	5	2	0	0	0	44	3	2	4	12.3	.959	1B-4
1983			4	.267	.467	15	4	0	0	1	6.7	5	3	3	3	1	0	0	36	2	1	2	9.8	.974	1B-4
1995	**CLE**	**A**	6	.250	.417	24	6	1	0	1	4.2	2	3	2	3	0	0	0	0	0	0	0	0.0	.000	DH-6
3 yrs.			14	.294	.490	51	15	1	0	3	5.9	10	11	10	8	1	0	0	80	5	3	6	6.3	.966	1B-8, DH-6
WORLD SERIES																									
1979	**BAL**	**A**	7	.154	.308	26	4	1	0	1	3.8	3	2	4	4	1	0	0	60	7	0	5	9.6	1.000	1B-7
1983			5	.250	.550	20	5	0	0	2	10.0	2	3	1	4	0	0	0	46	1	1	5	9.6	.979	1B-5
1995	**CLE**	**A**	6	.105	.263	19	2	0	0	1	5.3	1	3	5	4	0	0	0	27	0	0	3	4.5	1.000	1B-3, DH-3
3 yrs.			18	.169	.369	65	11	1	0	4	6.2	6	8	10	12	1	0	0	133	8	1	13	7.9	.993	1B-15, DH-3

Jim Murray

MURRAY, JAMES OSCAR BR TL 5′10″ 180 lbs.
B. Jan. 16, 1878, Galveston, Tex. D. Apr. 25, 1945, Galveston, Tex.

Year	Team	Lg	Games	BA	SA	AB	H	2B	3B	HR	HR%	R	RBI	BB	SO	SB	Pinch Hit AB	Pinch Hit H	PO	A	E	DP	TC/G	FA	G by Pos
1902	**CHI**	**N**	12	.170	.170	47	8	0	0	0	0.0	3	1	2		0	0	0	17	1	0	0	1.5	1.000	OF-12
1911	**STL**	**A**	31	.186	.324	102	19	5	0	3	2.9	8	11	5		0	6	1	39	4	3	1	1.8	.935	OF-25
1914	**BOS**	**N**	39	.232	.304	112	26	4	2	0	0.0	10	12	6	24	2	6	2	31	1	2	0	1.1	.941	OF-32
3 yrs.			82	.203	.287	261	53	9	2	3	1.1	21	24	13	24	2	12	3	87	6	5	1	1.4	.949	OF-69

Larry Murray

MURRAY, LARRY BB TR 5′11″ 179 lbs.
B. Mar. 1, 1953, Chicago, Ill.

Year	Team	Lg	Games	BA	SA	AB	H	2B	3B	HR	HR%	R	RBI	BB	SO	SB	Pinch Hit AB	Pinch Hit H	PO	A	E	DP	TC/G	FA	G by Pos
1974	**NY**	**A**	6	.000	.000	1	0	0	0	0	0.0	1	0	0	0	0	0	0	0	0	0	0	0.0	.000	OF-3
1975			6	.000	.000	1	0	0	0	0	0.0	1	0	0	0	0	0	0	1	0	0	0	0.3	1.000	OF-4

Larry Murray *continued*

Year	Team	Games	BA	SA	AB	H	2B	3B	HR	HR%	R	RBI	BB	SO	SB	Pinch Hit AB	Pinch Hit H	PO	A	E	DP	TC/G	FA	G by Pos
1976		8	.100	.100	10	1	0	0	0	0.0	2	2	1	2	2	0	0	9	1	0	0	1.4	1.000	OF-7
1977	OAK A	90	.179	.253	162	29	5	2	1	0.6	19	9	17	36	12	3	1	114	3	1	3	1.4	.992	OF-78, DH-3, SS-1
1978		11	.083	.083	12	1	0	0	0	0.0	1	0	3	2	0	2	0	6	0	0	0	1.0	1.000	OF-6
1979		105	.186	.279	226	42	11	2	2	0.9	25	20	28	34	6	1	0	174	8	7	2	2.0	.963	OF-90, 2B-3
6 yrs.		226	.177	.257	412	73	16	4	3	0.7	49	31	49	74	20	6	1	304	12	8	5	1.7	.975	OF-188, DH-3, 2B-3, SS-1

Miah Murray

MURRAY, JEREMIAH J. BR TR 5′11½″ 170 lbs.
B. Jan. 1, 1865, Boston, Mass. D. Jan. 11, 1922, Boston, Mass.

Year	Team	Games	BA	SA	AB	H	2B	3B	HR	HR%	R	RBI	BB	SO	SB	Pinch Hit AB	Pinch Hit H	PO	A	E	DP	TC/G	FA	G by Pos
1884	PRO N	8	.185	.185	27	5	0	0	0	0.0	1		1	8		0	0	44	4	11	0	6.6	.814	C-7, 1B-1, OF-1
1885	LOU AA	12	.186	.186	43	8	0	0	0	0.0	4		2			0	0	72	19	14	1	7.5	.867	C-12, 1B-2
1888	WAS N	12	.095	.119	42	4	1	0	0	0.0	1	3	1	7	0	0	0	58	14	8	3	6.7	.900	C-10, 1B-2
1891	WAS AA	2	.000	.000	8	0	0	0	0	0.0	0	0	0	1	0	0	0	22	2	0	0	12.0	1.000	C-2
4 yrs.		34	.142	.150	120	17	1	0	0	0.0	6	3	4	16	0	0	0	196	39	33	4	7.2	.877	C-31, 1B-5, OF-1

Ray Murray

MURRAY, RAYMOND LEE (Deacon) BR TR 6′ 3″ 204 lbs.
B. Oct. 12, 1917, Spring Hope, N. C.

Year	Team	Games	BA	SA	AB	H	2B	3B	HR	HR%	R	RBI	BB	SO	SB	Pinch Hit AB	Pinch Hit H	PO	A	E	DP	TC/G	FA	G by Pos
1948	CLE A	4	.000	.000	4	0	0	0	0	0.0	0	0	0	3	0	4	0	0	0	0	0	0.0	—	
1950		55	.273	.381	139	38	8	2	1	0.7	16	13	12	13	1	8	2	156	15	5	2	3.9	.972	C-45
1951	2 teams	CLE A (1G –1.000) PHI A (40G –.213)																						
″	total	41	.220	.268	123	27	6	0	0	0.0	10	14	14	8	0	1	0	111	25	2	5	3.5	.986	C-40
1952	PHI A	44	.206	.265	136	28	5	0	1	0.7	14	10	9	13	0	2	1	175	35	1	3	5.0	.995	C-42
1953		84	.284	.425	268	76	14	3	6	2.2	25	41	18	25	0	6	2	330	45	4	8	4.9	.989	C-78
1954	BAL A	22	.246	.344	61	15	4	1	0	0.0	4	2	2	5	0	0	0	83	9	1	3	4.4	.989	C-21
6 yrs.		250	.252	.352	731	184	37	6	8	1.1	69	80	55	67	1	21	5	855	129	13	21	4.4	.987	C-226

Red Murray

MURRAY, JOHN JOSEPH BR TR 5′10½″ 190 lbs.
B. Mar. 4, 1884, Arnot, Pa. D. Dec. 4, 1958, Sayre, Pa.

Year	Team	Games	BA	SA	AB	H	2B	3B	HR	HR%	R	RBI	BB	SO	SB	Pinch Hit AB	Pinch Hit H	PO	A	E	DP	TC/G	FA	G by Pos
1906	STL N	46	.257	.438	144	37	9	7	1	0.7	18	16	9		5	5	0	73	17	5	2	2.3	.947	OF-34, C-7
1907		132	.262	.367	485	127	10	10	7	1.4	46	46	24		23	1	1	232	25	18	4	2.1	.935	OF-131
1908		154	.282	.400	593	167	19	15	7	1.2	64	62	37		48	0	0	274	22	28	4	2.1	.914	OF-154
1909	NY N	149	.263	.368	570	150	15	12	**7**	**1.2**	74	91	44		48	0	0	222	30	14	1	1.8	.947	OF-148
1910		149	.277	.376	553	153	27	8	4	0.7	78	87	52	51	57	1	1	246	26	15	3	1.9	.948	OF-148
1911		140	.291	.426	488	142	27	15	3	0.6	70	78	43	37	48	6	1	196	12	10	1	1.7	.954	OF-131
1912		143	.277	.413	549	152	26	20	3	0.5	83	92	27	45	38	0	0	255	20	9	7	2.0	.968	OF-143
1913		147	.267	.331	520	139	21	3	2	0.4	70	59	34	28	35	0	0	279	24	11	3	2.1	.965	OF-147
1914		86	.223	.309	139	31	6	3	0	0.0	19	23	9	7	11	26	4	56	2	0	0	1.2	1.000	OF-49
1915	2 teams	NY N (45G –.220) CHI N (51G –.299)																						
″	total	96	.262	.343	271	71	7	3	3	1.1	32	22	15	23	8	17	8	148	12	6	2	2.2	.964	OF-73, 2B-1
1917	NY N	22	.045	.091	22	1	1	0	0	0.0	1	3	4	3	0	8	0	13	0	0	0	1.1	1.000	OF-11, C-1
11 yrs.		1264	.270	.379	4334	1170	168	96	37	0.9	555	579	298	194	321	64	15	1994	190	116	27	2.0	.950	OF-1169, C-8, 2B-1
WORLD SERIES																								
1911	NY N	6	.000	.000	21	0	0	0	0	0.0	0	0	2	5	0	0	0	4	1	3	0	1.3	.625	OF-6
1912		8	.323	.516	31	10	4	1	0	0.0	5	5	2	2	0	0	0	23	1	0	0	3.0	1.000	OF-8
1913		5	.250	.250	16	4	0	0	0	0.0	2	1	2	2	2	0	0	9	0	0	0	1.8	1.000	OF-5
3 yrs.		19	.206	.294	68	14	4	1	0	0.0	7	6	6	9	2	0	0	36	2	3	0	2.2	.927	OF-19

Rich Murray

MURRAY, RICHARD DALE BR TR 6′ 4″ 195 lbs.
Brother of Eddie Murray.
B. July 6, 1957, Los Angeles, Calif.

Year	Team	Games	BA	SA	AB	H	2B	3B	HR	HR%	R	RBI	BB	SO	SB	Pinch Hit AB	Pinch Hit H	PO	A	E	DP	TC/G	FA	G by Pos
1980	SF N	53	.216	.340	194	42	8	2	4	2.1	19	24	11	48	2	0	0	508	35	7	32	10.4	.987	1B-53
1983		4	.200	.200	10	2	0	0	0	0.0	0	1	0	3	0	1	0	20	1	0	1	7.0	1.000	1B-3
2 yrs.		57	.216	.333	204	44	8	2	4	2.0	19	25	11	51	2	1	0	528	36	7	33	10.2	.988	1B-56

Tom Murray

MURRAY, THOMAS W.
B. 1866, Savannah, Ga. Deceased.

Year	Team	Games	BA	SA	AB	H	2B	3B	HR	HR%	R	RBI	BB	SO	SB	Pinch Hit AB	Pinch Hit H	PO	A	E	DP	TC/G	FA	G by Pos
1894	PHI N	1	.000	.000	2	0	0	0	0	0.0	0	0	0	2	0	0	0	4	1	1	0	6.0	.833	SS-1

Tony Murray

MURRAY, ANTHONY JOSEPH BR TR 5′10½″ 154 lbs.
B. Apr. 30, 1904, Chicago, Ill. D. Mar. 19, 1974, Chicago, Ill.

Year	Team	Games	BA	SA	AB	H	2B	3B	HR	HR%	R	RBI	BB	SO	SB	Pinch Hit AB	Pinch Hit H	PO	A	E	DP	TC/G	FA	G by Pos
1923	CHI N	2	.250	.250	4	1	0	0	0	0.0	0	0	0	0	0	0	0	2	0	0	0	1.0	1.000	OF-2

Ivan Murrell

MURRELL, IVAN AUGUSTUS BR TR 6′ 2″ 195 lbs.
Born Ivan Augustus Murrell (Peters).
B. Apr. 24, 1945, Almirante, Panama.

Year	Team	Games	BA	SA	AB	H	2B	3B	HR	HR%	R	RBI	BB	SO	SB	Pinch Hit AB	Pinch Hit H	PO	A	E	DP	TC/G	FA	G by Pos
1963	HOU N	2	.200	.200	5	1	0	0	0	0.0	1	0	0	2	0	0	0	3	0	0	0	1.5	1.000	OF-2
1964		10	.143	.214	14	2	1	0	0	0.0	1	1	0	6	0	3	0	2	0	0	0	0.4	1.000	OF-5
1967		10	.310	.310	29	9	0	0	0	0.0	2	1	1	9	1	4	0	11	0	2	0	2.2	.846	OF-6
1968		32	.102	.153	59	6	1	1	0	0.0	3	3	1	17	0	12	2	24	3	2	2	1.9	.931	OF-15
1969	SD N	111	.255	.381	247	63	10	6	3	1.2	19	25	11	65	3	36	5	152	4	6	3	2.2	.963	OF-72, 1B-2
1970		125	.245	.392	347	85	9	3	12	3.5	43	35	17	93	9	24	4	184	8	6	3	1.9	.970	OF-101, 1B-1
1971		103	.235	.365	255	60	6	3	7	2.7	23	24	7	60	5	33	3	133	2	3	0	1.9	.978	OF-72
1972		5	.143	.143	7	1	0	0	0	0.0	0	1	0	3	0	3	0	2	0	0	0	2.0	1.000	OF-1
1973		93	.229	.429	210	48	13	1	9	4.3	23	21	2	52	2	35	2	249	16	5	14	4.4	.981	OF-37, 1B-24
1974	ATL N	73	.248	.316	133	33	1	1	2	1.5	11	12	5	35	0	30	5	161	9	1	11	3.8	.994	OF-32, 1B-13
10 yrs.		564	.236	.366	1306	308	41	15	33	2.5	126	123	44	342	20	180	21	921	42	25	33	2.6	.975	OF-343, 1B-40

Danny Murtaugh

MURTAUGH, DANIEL EDWARD BR TR 5′ 9″ 165 lbs.
B. Oct. 8, 1917, Chester, Pa. D. Dec. 2, 1976, Chester, Pa.
Manager 1957–64, 1967, 1970–71, 1973–76.

Year	Team	Games	BA	SA	AB	H	2B	3B	HR	HR%	R	RBI	BB	SO	SB	Pinch Hit AB	Pinch Hit H	PO	A	E	DP	TC/G	FA	G by Pos
1941	PHI N	85	.219	.248	347	76	8	1	0	0.0	34	11	26	31	**18**	0	0	234	247	11	49	5.7	.978	2B-85, SS-1
1942		144	.241	.289	506	122	16	4	0	0.0	48	27	49	39	13	2	0	302	377	43	61	5.0	.940	SS-60, 3B-53, 2B-32
1943		113	.273	.335	451	123	17	4	1	0.2	65	35	57	23	4	0	0	321	345	18	76	6.1	.974	2B-113

Danny Murtaugh *continued*

Year	Team	Games	BA	SA	AB	H	2B	3B	HR	HR%	R	RBI	BB	SO	SB	Pinch Hit AB	Pinch Hit H	PO	A	E	DP	TC/G	FA	G by Pos
1946		6	.211	.421	19	4	1	0	1	5.3	1	3	2	2	0	0	0	13	10	1	0	4.0	.958	2B-6
1947	BOS N	3	.125	.125	8	1	0	0	0	0.0	0	0	1	2	0	0	0	7	6	0	1	6.5	1.000	2B-2
1948	PIT N	146	.290	.356	514	149	21	5	1	0.2	56	71	60	40	10	0	0	375	412	17	95	5.5	.979	2B-146
1949		75	.203	.275	236	48	7	2	2	0.8	16	24	29	17	2	1	1	202	182	10	58	5.3	.975	2B-74
1950		118	.294	.392	367	108	20	5	2	0.5	34	37	47	42	2	9	4	273	292	14	84	5.4	.976	2B-108
1951		77	.199	.265	151	30	7	0	1	0.7	9	11	16	19	0	13	3	110	117	8	35	3.5	.966	2B-65, 3B-3
9 yrs.		767	.254	.317	2599	661	97	21	8	0.3	263	219	287	215	49	25	8	1837	1988	122	459	5.3	.969	2B-631, SS-61, 3B-56

Tony Muser

MUSER, ANTHONY JOSEPH BL TL 6′ 2″ 180 lbs.
B. Aug. 1, 1947, Van Nuys, Calif.

Year	Team	Games	BA	SA	AB	H	2B	3B	HR	HR%	R	RBI	BB	SO	SB	Pinch Hit AB	Pinch Hit H	PO	A	E	DP	TC/G	FA	G by Pos
1969	BOS A	2	.111	.111	9	1	0	0	0	0.0	0	1	1	1	0	0	0	17	3	0	3	10.0	1.000	1B-2
1971	CHI A	11	.313	.438	16	5	0	1	0	0.0	2	0	1	1	0	7	2	23	3	1	1	6.8	.963	1B-4
1972		44	.279	.426	61	17	2	2	1	1.6	6	9	2	6	1	12	4	135	7	2	12	4.8	.986	1B-29, OF-1
1973		109	.285	.388	309	88	14	3	4	1.3	38	30	33	36	8	9	4	681	38	6	70	8.0	.992	1B-89, OF-2
1974		103	.291	.340	206	60	5	1	1	0.5	16	18	6	22	1	13	3	419	13	1	46	4.7	.998	1B-80, DH-13
1975	2 teams	CHI A (43G –.243) BAL A (80G –.317)																						
″	total	123	.275	.306	193	53	6	0	0	0.0	22	17	15	17	2	18	6	476	37	3	58	5.0	.994	1B-103
1976	BAL A	136	.227	.264	326	74	7	1	1	0.3	25	30	21	34	1	16	4	693	63	7	65	5.8	.991	1B-109, OF-12, DH-10
1977		120	.229	.280	118	27	6	0	0	0.0	14	7	13	16	1	31	6	232	20	3	36	2.9	.988	1B-77, OF-11, DH-1
1978	MIL A	15	.133	.233	30	4	1	1	0	0.0	0	5	3	5	0	3	0	79	5	1	4	7.1	.988	1B-12
9 yrs.		663	.259	.323	1268	329	41	9	7	0.6	123	117	95	138	14	109	29	2755	189	24	295	5.3	.992	1B-505, OF-26, DH-24

Stan Musial

MUSIAL, STANLEY FRANK (Stan the Man) BL TL 6′ 175 lbs.
B. Nov. 21, 1920, Donora, Pa.
Hall of Fame 1969.

Year	Team	Games	BA	SA	AB	H	2B	3B	HR	HR%	R	RBI	BB	SO	SB	Pinch Hit AB	Pinch Hit H	PO	A	E	DP	TC/G	FA	G by Pos
1941	STL N	12	.426	.574	47	20	4	0	1	2.1	8	7	2	1	1	1	0	20	1	0	0	1.9	1.000	OF-11
1942		140	.315	.490	467	147	32	10	10	2.1	87	72	62	25	6	2	0	296	6	5	0	2.3	.984	OF-135
1943		157	**.357**	**.562**	617	**220**	**48**	**20**	13	2.1	108	81	72	18	9	2	1	376	15	7	4	2.6	.982	OF-155
1944		146	.347	**.549**	568	**197**	**51**	14	12	2.1	112	94	90	28	7	0	0	353	16	5	2	2.6	.987	OF-146
1946		156	**.365**	**.587**	**624**	**228**	**50**	**20**	16	2.6	**124**	103	73	31	7	0	0	1166	69	15	119	8.0	.988	1B-114, OF-42
1947		149	.312	.504	587	183	30	13	19	3.2	113	95	80	24	4	0	0	1360	77	8	138	9.7	.994	1B-149
1948		155	**.376**	**.702**	611	**230**	**46**	**18**	39	6.4	**135**	**131**	79	34	7	0	0	354	11	7	3	2.4	.981	OF-155, 1B-2
1949		157	.338	.624	612	**207**	**41**	**13**	36	5.9	128	123	107	38	3	0	0	337	11	3	5	2.2	.991	OF-156, 1B-1
1950		146	**.346**	**.596**	555	192	41	7	28	5.0	105	109	87	36	5	1	0	760	39	8	67	5.5	.990	OF-77, 1B-69
1951		152	**.355**	.614	578	205	30	**12**	32	5.5	**124**	108	98	40	4	1	1	816	45	10	64	5.8	.989	OF-91, 1B-60
1952		154	**.336**	**.538**	578	**194**	**42**	6	21	3.6	**105**	91	96	29	7	0	0	502	18	5	15	3.3	.990	OF-135, 1B-25, P-1
1953		157	.337	.609	593	200	**53**	9	30	5.1	127	113	**105**	32	3	0	0	294	9	5	1	2.0	.984	OF-157
1954		153	.330	.607	591	195	**41**	9	35	5.9	**120**	126	103	39	1	0	0	307	15	5	8	2.0	.985	OF-152, 1B-10
1955		154	.319	.566	562	179	30	5	33	5.9	97	108	80	39	5	0	0	1000	94	9	93	6.9	.992	1B-110, OF-51
1956		156	.310	.522	594	184	33	6	27	4.5	87	**109**	75	39	2	0	0	954	95	8	96	6.8	.992	1B-103, OF-53
1957		134	**.351**	.612	502	176	38	3	29	5.8	82	102	66	34	1	4	2	1167	99	10	131	9.8	.992	1B-130
1958		135	.337	.528	472	159	35	2	17	3.6	64	62	72	26	0	12	5	1019	100	13	127	9.1	.989	1B-124
1959		115	.255	.428	341	87	13	2	14	4.1	37	44	60	25	0	22	5	624	63	7	72	7.5	.990	1B-90, OF-3
1960		116	.275	.486	331	91	17	1	17	5.1	49	63	41	34	1	28	4	300	19	3	16	3.7	.991	OF-59, 1B-29
1961		123	.288	.489	372	107	22	4	15	4.0	46	70	52	35	0	19	5	149	9	1	0	1.5	.994	OF-103
1962		135	.330	.508	433	143	18	1	19	4.4	57	82	64	46	3	13	8	164	6	4	1	1.5	.977	OF-119
1963		124	.255	.404	337	86	10	2	12	3.6	34	58	35	43	2	21	4	121	1	4	0	1.3	.968	OF-96
22 yrs.		3026	.331	.559	10972	3630	725	177	475	4.3	1949	1951	1599	696	78	126	35	12439	818	142	962	4.6	.989	OF-1896, 1B-1016, P-1
		5th		**9th**	**7th**	**4th**	**3rd**				**6th**	**5th**	**9th**											
WORLD SERIES																								
1942	STL N	5	.222	.278	18	4	1	0	0	0.0	2	2	4	0	0	0	0	13	0	0	0	2.6	1.000	OF-5
1943		5	.278	.278	18	5	0	0	0	0.0	2	0	2	2	0	0	0	7	2	0	0	1.8	1.000	OF-5
1944		6	.304	.522	23	7	2	0	1	4.3	2	2	2	0	0	0	0	11	0	1	0	2.0	.917	OF-6
1946		7	.222	.444	27	6	4	1	0	0.0	3	4	4	2	1	0	0	60	2	0	6	8.9	1.000	1B-7
4 yrs.		23	.256	.395	86	22	7	1	1	1.2	9	8	12	4	1	0	0	91	4	1	6	4.2	.990	OF-16, 1B-7

Danny Musser

MUSSER, WILLIAM DANIEL BL TR 5′ 9½″ 160 lbs.
B. Sept. 5, 1905, Zion, Pa.

Year	Team	Games	BA	SA	AB	H	2B	3B	HR	HR%	R	RBI	BB	SO	SB	Pinch Hit AB	Pinch Hit H	PO	A	E	DP	TC/G	FA	G by Pos
1932	WAS A	1	.500	.500	2	1	0	0	0	0.0	0	0	0	0	0	0	0	0	0	0	0	0.0	.000	3B-1

George Myatt

MYATT, GEORGE EDWARD (Foghorn, Mercury, Stud) BL TR 5′11″ 167 lbs.
B. June 14, 1914, Denver, Colo.
Manager 1968–69.

Year	Team	Games	BA	SA	AB	H	2B	3B	HR	HR%	R	RBI	BB	SO	SB	Pinch Hit AB	Pinch Hit H	PO	A	E	DP	TC/G	FA	G by Pos
1938	NY N	43	.306	.382	170	52	2	1	3	1.8	27	10	14	13	10	0	0	77	128	17	24	5.2	.923	SS-24, 3B-19
1939		22	.189	.226	53	10	2	0	0	0.0	7	3	6	6	2	5	0	10	29	4	3	3.1	.907	3B-14
1943	WAS A	42	.245	.302	53	13	3	0	0	0.0	11	3	13	7	3	12	1	27	35	5	4	4.5	.925	2B-11, SS-2, 3B-2
1944		140	.284	.342	538	153	19	6	0	0.0	86	40	54	44	26	0	0	384	339	41	90	5.5	.946	2B-121, SS-15, OF-3
1945		133	.296	.365	490	145	17	7	1	0.2	81	39	63	43	30	1	0	293	255	18	50	4.3	.968	2B-94, OF-32, 3B-6, SS-1
1946		15	.235	.265	34	8	1	0	0	0.0	7	4	2	3	1	4	1	10	12	2	1	2.7	.917	3B-7, 2B-2
1947		12	.000	.000	7	0	0	0	0	0.0	1	0	4	4	0	6	0	0	1	0	0	1.0	1.000	2B-1
7 yrs.		407	.283	.346	1345	381	44	14	4	0.3	220	99	156	120	72	28	2	801	799	87	172	4.8	.948	2B-229, 3B-48, SS-42, OF-35

Glenn Myatt

MYATT, GLENN CALVIN BL TR 5′11″ 165 lbs.
B. July 9, 1897, Argenta, Ark. D. Aug. 9, 1969, Houston, Tex.

Year	Team	Games	BA	SA	AB	H	2B	3B	HR	HR%	R	RBI	BB	SO	SB	Pinch Hit AB	Pinch Hit H	PO	A	E	DP	TC/G	FA	G by Pos
1920	PHI A	70	.250	.321	196	49	8	3	0	0.0	14	18	12	22	1	8	1	83	22	10	3	2.0	.913	OF-37, C-21
1921		44	.203	.232	69	14	2	0	0	0.0	6	5	6	7	0	7	1	59	18	5	2	3.0	.939	C-27
1923	CLE A	92	.286	.414	220	63	7	6	3	1.4	36	40	16	18	0	18	6	188	37	16	3	3.5	.934	C-69
1924		105	.342	.518	342	117	22	7	8	2.3	55	73	33	12	6	9	2	248	63	7	7	3.3	.978	C-95
1925		106	.271	.455	358	97	15	9	11	3.1	51	54	29	24	2	5	1	273	53	9	2	3.4	.973	C-98, OF-1
1926		56	.248	.325	117	29	5	2	0	0.0	14	13	13	13	1	18	3	94	18	0	0	3.2	1.000	C-35
1927		55	.245	.372	94	23	6	0	2	2.1	15	8	12	7	1	25	5	67	20	2	4	3.4	.978	C-26
1928		58	.288	.400	125	36	7	2	1	0.8	9	15	13	13	0	26	8	72	15	3	2	3.0	.967	C-30

Glenn Myatt *continued*

Year	Team	Games	BA	SA	AB	H	2B	3B	HR	HR%	R	RBI	BB	SO	SB	Pinch Hit AB	Pinch Hit H	PO	A	E	DP	TC/G	FA	G by Pos
1929		59	.233	.302	129	30	4	1	1	0.8	14	17	7	5	0	14	1	99	24	3	3	3.1	.976	C-41
1930		86	.294	.419	265	78	23	2	2	0.8	30	37	18	17	2	13	3	214	43	6	8	3.7	.977	C-71
1931		65	.246	.354	195	48	14	2	1	0.5	21	29	21	13	2	9	3	176	34	2	2	3.7	.991	C-58
1932		82	.246	.397	252	62	12	1	8	3.2	45	46	28	21	2	16	3	211	32	3	3	3.8	.988	C-65
1933		40	.234	.286	77	18	4	0	0	0.0	10	7	15	8	0	12	3	65	17	3	2	3.1	.965	C-27
1934		36	.318	.393	107	34	6	1	0	0.0	18	12	13	5	1	0	0	132	14	3	3	4.4	.980	C-34
1935	**2 teams**	**CLE A** (10G –.083)		**NY N** (13G –.222)																				
"	**total**	23	.130	.241	54	7	1	1	1	1.9	3	8	4	6	0	9	1	48	4	0	0	3.7	1.000	C-14
1936	**DET A**	27	.218	.231	78	17	1	0	0	0.0	5	5	9	4	0	1	1	79	12	0	1	3.4	1.000	C-27
16 yrs.		1004	.270	.391	2678	722	137	37	38	1.4	346	387	249	195	18	190	42	2108	426	72	45	3.4	.972	C-738, OF-38

Buddy Myer

MYER, CHARLES SOLOMON BL TR 5′10½″ 163 lbs.
B. Mar. 16, 1904, Ellisville, Miss. D. Oct. 31, 1974, Baton Rouge, La.

Year	Team	Games	BA	SA	AB	H	2B	3B	HR	HR%	R	RBI	BB	SO	SB	Pinch Hit AB	Pinch Hit H	PO	A	E	DP	TC/G	FA	G by Pos
1925	**WAS A**	4	.250	.250	8	2	0	0	0	0.0	1	0	0	1	0	0	0	1	3	0	0	1.0	1.000	SS-4
1926		132	.304	.380	434	132	18	6	1	0.2	66	62	45	19	10	3	2	226	304	42	47	4.6	.927	SS-117, 3B-8
1927	**2 teams**	**WAS A** (15G –.216)		**BOS A** (133G –.288)																				
"	**total**	148	.281	.379	520	146	23	11	2	0.4	66	54	56	18	12	8	1	305	384	44	78	5.2	.940	SS-116, 3B-14, OF-10, 2B-1
1928	**BOS A**	147	.313	.390	536	168	26	6	1	0.2	78	44	53	28	**30**	1	1	137	306	14	35	3.2	.969	3B-144
1929	**WAS A**	141	.300	.403	563	169	29	10	3	0.5	80	82	63	33	18	1	1	274	363	32	64	4.7	.952	2B-88, 3B-53
1930		138	.303	.377	541	164	18	8	2	0.4	97	61	58	31	14	0	0	330	405	27	89	5.6	.965	2B-134, OF-2
1931		139	.293	.406	591	173	33	11	4	0.7	114	56	58	42	11	0	0	333	398	12	87	5.4	.984	2B-137
1932		143	.279	.426	577	161	38	16	5	0.9	120	52	69	33	12	3	1	352	426	20	97	5.7	.975	2B-139
1933		131	.302	.436	530	160	29	15	4	0.8	95	61	60	29	6	1	0	356	417	17	92	6.1	.978	2B-129
1934		139	.305	.416	524	160	33	8	3	0.6	103	57	102	32	6	4	1	367	420	20	101	6.0	.975	2B-135
1935		151	**.349**	.468	616	215	36	11	5	0.8	115	100	96	40	7	0	0	460	473	20	138	6.3	.979	2B-151
1936		51	.269	.327	156	42	5	2	0	0.0	31	15	42	11	7	7	1	120	143	4	31	6.2	.985	2B-43
1937		125	.293	.384	430	126	16	10	1	0.2	54	65	78	41	2	5	1	308	338	23	90	5.6	.966	2B-119, OF-1
1938		127	.336	.465	437	147	22	8	6	1.4	79	71	93	32	9	5	1	308	355	12	91	5.6	.982	2B-121
1939		83	.302	.376	258	78	10	3	1	0.4	33	32	40	18	4	17	3	175	188	12	48	5.8	.968	2B-65
1940		71	.290	.395	210	61	14	4	0	0.0	28	29	34	10	6	14	1	119	176	10	34	5.6	.967	2B-54
1941		53	.252	.299	107	27	3	1	0	0.0	14	9	18	10	2	25	6	53	54	2	12	4.5	.982	2B-24
17 yrs.		1923	.303	.406	7038	2131	353	130	38	0.5	1174	850	965	428	156	94	20	4224	5153	311	1134	5.4	.968	2B-1340, SS-237, 3B-219, OF-13
WORLD SERIES																								
1925	**WAS A**	3	.250	.250	8	2	0	0	0	0.0	0	0	1	2	0	0	0	1	1	0	0	0.7	1.000	3B-3
1933		5	.300	.350	20	6	1	0	0	0.0	2	2	2	3	0	0	0	15	12	3	3	6.0	.900	2B-5
2 yrs.		8	.286	.321	28	8	1	0	0	0.0	2	2	3	5	0	0	0	16	13	3	3	4.0	.906	2B-5, 3B-3

Al Myers

MYERS, JAMES ALBERT (Cod) BR TR 5′ 8½″ 165 lbs.
B. Oct. 22, 1863, Danville, Ill. D. Dec. 24, 1927, Marshall, Ill.

Year	Team	Games	BA	SA	AB	H	2B	3B	HR	HR%	R	RBI	BB	SO	SB	Pinch Hit AB	Pinch Hit H	PO	A	E	DP	TC/G	FA	G by Pos
1884	**MIL U**	12	.326	.457	46	15	6	0	0	0.0	6		0			0	0	26	30	10	1	5.5	.848	2B-12
1885	**PHI N**	93	.204	.261	357	73	13	2	1	0.3	25		11	41		0	0	201	287	64	31	5.9	.884	2B-93
1886	**KC N**	118	.277	.387	473	131	22	9	4	0.8	69	51	22	42		0	0	298	384	65	50	6.3	.913	2B-118
1887	**WAS N**	105	.232	.301	362	84	9	5	2	0.6	45	36	40	26	18	0	0	244	341	77	29	6.3	.884	2B-78, SS-27
1888		132	.207	.271	502	104	12	7	2	0.4	46	46	37	46	20	0	0	271	399	60	37	5.5	.918	2B-132
1889	**2 teams**	**WAS N** (46G –.261)		**PHI N** (75G –.269)																				
"	**total**	121	.266	.310	481	128	17	2	0	0.0	76	48	58	16	18	0	0	339	409	96	59	7.0	.886	2B-121
1890	**PHI N**	117	.277	.378	487	135	29	7	2	0.4	95	81	57	46	44	0	0	347	352	38	62	6.3	.948	2B-117
1891		135	.230	.302	514	118	27	2	2	0.4	67	69	69	46	8	0	0	354	438	53	67	6.3	.937	2B-135
8 yrs.		833	.245	.320	3222	788	135	34	13	0.4	429	331	294	263	108	0	0	2080	2640	463	336	6.2	.911	2B-806, SS-27

Bert Myers

MYERS, JAMES ALBERT BR TR 5′10″
B. Apr. 8, 1874, Frederick, Md. D. Oct. 12, 1915, Washington, D. C.

Year	Team	Games	BA	SA	AB	H	2B	3B	HR	HR%	R	RBI	BB	SO	SB	Pinch Hit AB	Pinch Hit H	PO	A	E	DP	TC/G	FA	G by Pos
1896	**STL N**	122	.256	.317	454	116	12	8	0	0.0	47	37	40	32	8	0	0	165	243	62	16	3.9	.868	3B-121, SS-1
1898	**WAS N**	31	.264	.345	110	29	1	4	0	0.0	14	13	13		2	0	0	35	61	19	6	3.7	.835	3B-31
1900	**PHI N**	7	.179	.214	28	5	1	0	0	0.0	5	2	3		1	0	0	6	24	3	3	4.7	.909	3B-7
3 yrs.		160	.253	.318	592	150	14	12	0	0.0	66	52	56	32	11	0	0	206	328	84	25	3.9	.864	3B-159, SS-1

Billy Myers

MYERS, WILLIAM HARRISON BR TR 5′ 8″ 168 lbs.
Brother of Lynn Myers.
B. Aug. 14, 1910, Enola, Pa.

Year	Team	Games	BA	SA	AB	H	2B	3B	HR	HR%	R	RBI	BB	SO	SB	Pinch Hit AB	Pinch Hit H	PO	A	E	DP	TC/G	FA	G by Pos
1935	**CIN N**	117	.267	.380	445	119	15	10	5	1.1	60	36	29	81	10	0	0	230	335	37	77	5.4	.939	SS-112
1936		98	.269	.390	323	87	9	6	6	1.9	45	27	28	56	6	0	0	225	304	35	73	5.8	.938	SS-98
1937		124	.251	.370	335	84	13	3	7	2.1	35	43	44	57	0	0	0	198	368	30	68	4.7	.950	SS-121, 2B-6
1938		134	.253	.403	442	112	18	6	12	2.7	57	47	41	80	2	0	0	283	411	47	75	5.5	.937	SS-123, 2B-11
1939		151	.281	.393	509	143	18	6	9	1.8	79	56	71	90	4	0	0	309	512	42	110	5.7	.951	SS-151
1940		90	.202	.319	282	57	14	2	5	1.8	33	30	30	56	0	0	0	155	269	17	62	5.0	.961	SS-88
1941	**CHI N**	24	.222	.286	63	14	1	0	1	1.6	10	4	7	25	1	0	0	37	66	6	13	5.4	.945	SS-19, 2B-1
7 yrs.		738	.257	.377	2399	616	88	33	45	1.9	319	243	250	445	23	0	0	1437	2265	214	478	5.4	.945	SS-712, 2B-18
WORLD SERIES																								
1939	**CIN N**	4	.333	.500	12	4	0	1	0	0.0	2	0	2	3	0	0	0	10	9	2	1	5.3	.905	SS-4
1940		7	.130	.130	23	3	0	0	0	0.0	0	2	2	5	0	0	0	14	18	2	5	4.9	.941	SS-7
2 yrs.		11	.200	.257	35	7	0	1	0	0.0	2	2	4	8	0	0	0	24	27	4	6	5.0	.927	SS-11

George Myers

MYERS, GEORGE D. BR TR 5′ 8″ 170 lbs.
B. Nov. 13, 1860, Buffalo, N. Y. D. Dec. 14, 1926, Buffalo, N. Y.

Year	Team	Games	BA	SA	AB	H	2B	3B	HR	HR%	R	RBI	BB	SO	SB	Pinch Hit AB	Pinch Hit H	PO	A	E	DP	TC/G	FA	G by Pos
1884	**BUF N**	78	.182	.240	325	59	9	2	2	0.6	34		13	33		0	0	320	61	78	5	5.5	.830	C-49, OF-34
1885		89	.206	.239	326	67	7	2	0	0.0	40	19	23	40		0	0	341	96	53	4	5.3	.892	C-69, OF-23
1886	**STL N**	79	.190	.234	295	56	7	3	0	0.0	26	27	18	42		0	0	378	82	38	8	6.3	.924	C-72, OF-6, 3B-1

George Myers *continued*

Year	Team	Games	BA	SA	AB	H	2B	3B	HR	HR%	R	RBI	BB	SO	SB	Pinch Hit AB	Pinch Hit H	PO	A	E	DP	TC/G	FA	G by Pos
1887	**IND N**	69	.217	.272	235	51	8	1	1	0.4	25	20	22	7	26	0	0	236	63	19	13	4.4	.940	C-50, OF-15, 1B-6, 3B-1
1888		66	.238	.298	248	59	9	0	2	0.8	36	16	16	14	28	0	0	235	85	32	6	4.9	.909	C-47, 3B-14, OF-10, 1B-1
1889		43	.195	.215	149	29	3	0	0	0.0	22	12	17	13	12	0	0	106	37	18	1	3.8	.888	OF-23, C-18, 1B-1
6 yrs.		424	.203	.250	1578	321	43	8	5	0.3	183	94	109	149	66	0	0	1616	424	238	37	5.2	.896	C-305, OF-111, 3B-16, 1B-8

Greg Myers

MYERS, GREGORY RICHARD — BL TR 6′ 1″ 200 lbs.
B. Apr. 14, 1966, Riverside, Calif.

Year	Team	Games	BA	SA	AB	H	2B	3B	HR	HR%	R	RBI	BB	SO	SB	Pinch Hit AB	Pinch Hit H	PO	A	E	DP	TC/G	FA	G by Pos
1987	**TOR A**	7	.111	.111	9	1	0	0	0	0.0	1	0	0	3	0	0	0	24	1	0	0	3.6	1.000	C-7
1989		17	.114	.159	44	5	2	0	0	0.0	0	1	2	9	0	1	0	46	6	0	1	3.1	1.000	C-11, DH-6
1990		87	.236	.332	250	59	7	1	5	2.0	33	22	22	33	0	7	2	411	30	3	4	5.1	.993	C-87
1991		107	.262	.411	309	81	22	0	8	2.6	25	36	21	45	0	10	2	484	37	11	5	5.1	.979	C-104
1992	**2 teams**	**TOR A** (22G –.230)	**CAL A** (8G –.235)																					
″	**total**	30	.231	.359	78	18	7	0	1	1.3	4	13	5	11	0	4	1	125	16	1	1	5.3	.993	C-26, DH-1
1993	**CAL A**	108	.255	.362	290	74	10	0	7	2.4	27	40	17	47	3	25	8	369	44	6	5	4.2	.986	C-97, DH-2
1994		45	.246	.341	126	31	6	0	2	1.6	10	8	10	27	0	6	0	194	28	2	0	5.3	.991	C-41, DH-1
1995		85	.260	.418	273	71	12	2	9	3.3	35	38	17	49	0	12	0	340	21	4	5	4.7	.989	C-61, DH-16
8 yrs.		486	.247	.368	1379	340	66	3	32	2.3	135	158	94	224	3	65	13	1993	183	27	21	4.8	.988	C-434, DH-26

Hap Myers

MYERS, RALPH EDWARD — BR TR 6′ 3″ 175 lbs.
B. Apr. 8, 1888, San Francisco, Calif. D. June 30, 1967, San Francisco, Calif.

Year	Team	Games	BA	SA	AB	H	2B	3B	HR	HR%	R	RBI	BB	SO	SB	Pinch Hit AB	Pinch Hit H	PO	A	E	DP	TC/G	FA	G by Pos
1910	**BOS A**	3	.333	.333	6	2	0	0	0	0.0	0	0	0		0	1	0	1	1	0	0	1.0	1.000	OF-2
1911	**2 teams**	**STL A** (11G –.297)	**BOS A** (13G –.368)																					
″	**total**	24	.333	.373	75	25	3	0	0	0.0	7	1	5		4	0	0	223	9	9	10	10.5	.963	1B-23
1913	**BOS N**	140	.273	.326	524	143	20	1	2	0.4	74	50	38	48	57	5	3	1344	85	19	57	10.7	.987	1B-135
1914	**BKN F**	92	.220	.295	305	67	10	5	1	0.3	61	29	44		43	0	0	784	44	9	47	9.5	.989	1B-88
1915		118	.287	.328	341	98	9	1	1	0.3	61	36	32		28	7	1	961	56	10	52	9.6	.990	1B-107
5 yrs.		377	.268	.322	1251	335	42	7	4	0.3	203	116	119	48	132	13	4	3313	195	47	166	10.0	.987	1B-353, OF-2

Henry Myers

MYERS, HENRY C. — BR TR 5′ 9″ 159 lbs.
B. May 1858, Philadelphia, Pa. D. Apr. 18, 1895, Philadelphia, Pa.
Manager 1882.

Year	Team	Games	BA	SA	AB	H	2B	3B	HR	HR%	R	RBI	BB	SO	SB	Pinch Hit AB	Pinch Hit H	PO	A	E	DP	TC/G	FA	G by Pos
1881	**PRO N**	1	.000	.000	4	0	0	0	0	0.0	0	0	0	2		0	0	1	2	0	0	3.0	1.000	SS-1
1882	**BAL AA**	69	.180	.190	294	53	3	0	0	0.0	43		12			0	0	66	264	70	15	5.4	.825	SS-68, P-6
1884	**WIL U**	6	.125	.125	24	3	0	0	0	0.0	3		0			0	0	12	21	3	3	6.0	.917	SS-5, 2B-1
3 yrs.		76	.174	.183	322	56	3	0	0	0.0	46	0	12	2		0	0	79	287	73	18	5.4	.834	SS-74, P-6, 2B-1

Hy Myers

MYERS, HENRY HARRISON — BR TR 5′ 9½″ 175 lbs.
B. Apr. 27, 1889, East Liverpool, Ohio D. May 1, 1965, Minerva, Ohio.

Year	Team	Games	BA	SA	AB	H	2B	3B	HR	HR%	R	RBI	BB	SO	SB	Pinch Hit AB	Pinch Hit H	PO	A	E	DP	TC/G	FA	G by Pos
1909	**BKN N**	6	.227	.273	22	5	1	0	0	0.0	1	6	2		1	0	0	9	0	0	0	1.5	1.000	OF-6
1911		13	.163	.186	43	7	1	0	0	0.0	2	0	2	3	1	0	0	22	2	3	0	2.1	.889	OF-13
1914		70	.286	.379	227	65	3	9	0	0.0	35	17	7	24	2	5	2	102	4	4	0	1.8	.964	OF-60
1915		153	.248	.316	605	150	21	7	2	0.3	69	46	17	51	19	0	0	352	23	14	5	2.5	.964	OF-153
1916		113	.262	.381	412	108	12	14	3	0.7	54	36	21	35	17	6	1	242	11	8	5	2.5	.969	OF-106
1917		120	.268	.348	471	126	15	10	1	0.2	37	41	18	25	5	3	0	410	102	19	15	4.4	.964	OF-66, 1B-22, 2B-19, 3B-15
1918		107	.256	.346	407	104	9	8	4	1.0	36	40	20	26	17	0	0	294	17	8	7	3.0	.975	OF-107
1919		133	.307	**.436**	512	157	23	**14**	5	1.0	62	**73**	23	34	13	0	0	358	13	8	5	2.9	.979	OF-131
1920		154	.304	.462	582	177	36	**22**	4	0.7	83	80	35	54	9	0	0	388	19	9	5	2.7	.978	OF-152, 3B-2
1921		144	.288	.350	549	158	14	4	4	0.7	51	68	22	51	8	0	0	318	78	14	16	2.8	.966	OF-124, 2B-21, 3B-1
1922		153	.317	.408	618	196	20	9	6	1.0	82	89	13	26	9	0	0	399	21	12	2	2.8	.972	OF-153, 2B-1
1923	**STL N**	96	.300	.385	330	99	18	2	2	0.6	29	48	12	19	5	6	1	239	15	6	0	3.0	.977	OF-87
1924		43	.210	.290	124	26	5	1	1	0.8	12	15	3	10	1	5	0	61	25	6	1	2.5	.935	OF-22, 3B-12, 2B-3
1925	**3 teams**	**STL N** (1G –.000)	**CIN N** (3G –.167)	**STL N** (1G –1.000)																				
″	**total**	5	.250	.375	8	2	1	0	0	0.0	2	0	0	0	0	2	1	5	0	0	0	1.7	1.000	OF-3
14 yrs.		1310	.281	.378	4910	1380	179	100	32	0.7	555	559	195	358	107	27	5	3199	330	111	61	2.8	.970	OF-1183, 2B-44, 3B-30, 1B-22
WORLD SERIES																								
1916	**BKN N**	5	.182	.318	22	4	0	0	1	4.5	2	3	0	3	0	0	0	9	1	0	1	2.0	1.000	OF-5
1920		7	.231	.231	26	6	0	0	0	0.0	0	1	0	1	0	0	0	15	1	0	1	2.3	1.000	OF-7
2 yrs.		12	.208	.271	48	10	0	0	1	2.1	2	4	0	4	0	0	0	24	2	0	2	2.2	1.000	OF-12

Lynn Myers

MYERS, LYNNWOOD LINCOLN — BR TR 5′ 6½″ 145 lbs.
Brother of Billy Myers.
B. Feb. 23, 1914, Enola, Pa.

Year	Team	Games	BA	SA	AB	H	2B	3B	HR	HR%	R	RBI	BB	SO	SB	Pinch Hit AB	Pinch Hit H	PO	A	E	DP	TC/G	FA	G by Pos
1938	**STL N**	70	.242	.317	227	55	10	2	1	0.4	18	19	9	25	9	0	0	110	195	18	36	4.7	.944	SS-69
1939		74	.239	.308	117	28	6	1	0	0.0	24	10	12	23	1	5	3	65	94	17	25	3.3	.903	SS-36, 2B-13, 3B-5
2 yrs.		144	.241	.314	344	83	16	3	1	0.3	42	29	21	48	10	5	3	175	289	35	61	4.1	.930	SS-105, 2B-13, 3B-5

Richie Myers

MYERS, RICHARD — BR TR 5′ 6″ 150 lbs.
B. Apr. 7, 1930, Sacramento, Calif.

Year	Team	Games	BA	SA	AB	H	2B	3B	HR	HR%	R	RBI	BB	SO	SB	Pinch Hit AB	Pinch Hit H	PO	A	E	DP	TC/G	FA	G by Pos
1956	**CHI N**	4	.000	.000	1	0	0	0	0	0.0	1	0	0	0	0	1	0	0	0	0	0	0.0	—	

Tim Naehring

NAEHRING, TIMOTHY JAMES — BR TR 6′ 2″ 190 lbs.
B. Feb. 1, 1967, Cincinnati, Ohio.

Year	Team	Games	BA	SA	AB	H	2B	3B	HR	HR%	R	RBI	BB	SO	SB	Pinch Hit AB	Pinch Hit H	PO	A	E	DP	TC/G	FA	G by Pos
1990	**BOS A**	24	.271	.412	85	23	6	0	2	2.4	10	12	8	15	0	0	0	36	66	9	13	4.4	.919	SS-19, 3B-5, 2B-1
1991		20	.109	.127	55	6	1	0	0	0.0	1	3	6	15	0	1	0	17	53	3	9	3.7	.959	SS-17, 3B-2, 2B-1
1992		72	.231	.323	186	43	8	0	3	1.6	12	14	18	31	0	8	0	95	170	3	31	3.9	.989	SS-30, 2B-23, 3B-10, DH-4, OF-1
1993		39	.331	.433	127	42	10	0	1	0.8	14	17	10	26	1	6	2	45	44	2	15	2.4	.978	2B-15, DH-10, 3B-9, SS-4
1994		80	.276	.414	297	82	18	1	7	2.4	41	42	30	56	1	2	1	190	182	6	45	4.5	.984	2B-49, 3B-11, SS-9, 1B-8, DH-7
1995		126	.307	.448	433	133	27	2	10	2.3	61	57	77	66	0	2	1	86	244	16	22	2.8	.954	3B-124, DH-1
6 yrs.		361	.278	.401	1183	329	70	3	23	1.9	139	145	149	209	2	19	4	469	759	39	135	3.5	.969	3B-161, 2B-89, SS-79, DH-22, 1B-8, OF-1

Tim Naehring *continued*

DIVISIONAL PLAYOFF SERIES

Year	Team	Games	BA	SA	AB	H	2B	3B	HR	HR%	R	RBI	BB	SO	SB	Pinch Hit AB	Pinch Hit H	PO	A	E	DP	TC/G	FA	G by Pos
1995	BOS A	3	.308	.538	13	4	0	0	1	7.7	2	1	0	1	0	0	0	5	5	0	0	3.3	1.000	3B-3

Bill Nagel

NAGEL, WILLIAM TAYLOR BR TR 6′ 1″ 190 lbs.
B. Aug. 19, 1915, Memphis, Tenn. D. Oct. 8, 1981, Freehold, N. J.

Year	Team	Games	BA	SA	AB	H	2B	3B	HR	HR%	R	RBI	BB	SO	SB	Pinch Hit AB	Pinch Hit H	PO	A	E	DP	TC/G	FA	G by Pos
1939	PHI A	105	.252	.437	341	86	19	4	12	3.5	39	39	25	86	2	4	0	134	218	21	32	3.7	.944	2B-56, 3B-43, P-1
1941	PHI N	17	.143	.196	56	8	1	1	0	0.0	2	6	3	14	0	2	0	29	38	4	7	4.7	.944	2B-12, OF-2, 3B-1
1945	CHI A	67	.209	.323	220	46	10	3	3	1.4	21	27	15	41	3	9	0	503	35	9	42	9.4	.984	1B-57, 3B-1
3 yrs.		189	.227	.374	617	140	30	8	15	2.4	62	72	43	141	5	15	0	666	291	34	81	5.7	.966	2B-68, 1B-57, 3B-45, OF-2, P-1

Lou Nagelsen

NAGELSEN, LOUIS MARCELLUS BR TR 6′ 2″ 180 lbs.
Born Louis Marcellus Nageleisen.
B. June 29, 1887, Piqua, Ohio D. Oct. 21, 1965, Fort Wayne, Ind.

Year	Team	Games	BA	SA	AB	H	2B	3B	HR	HR%	R	RBI	BB	SO	SB	Pinch Hit AB	Pinch Hit H	PO	A	E	DP	TC/G	FA	G by Pos
1912	CLE A	2	.000	.000	3	0	0	0	0	0.0	0	0	0		0	0	0	2	0	0	0	1.0	1.000	C-2

Russ Nagelson

NAGELSON, RUSSELL CHARLES (Rusty) BL TR 6′ 205 lbs.
B. Sept. 19, 1944, Cincinnati, Ohio.

Year	Team	Games	BA	SA	AB	H	2B	3B	HR	HR%	R	RBI	BB	SO	SB	Pinch Hit AB	Pinch Hit H	PO	A	E	DP	TC/G	FA	G by Pos
1968	CLE A	5	.333	.333	3	1	0	0	0	0.0	0	0	2	2	0	3	1	0	0	0	0	0.0	—	
1969		12	.353	.353	17	6	0	0	0	0.0	1	0	3	3	0	7	1	11	1	0	1	3.0	1.000	OF-3, 1B-1
1970	2 teams	CLE A (17G –.125) DET A (28G –.188)																						
″	total	45	.161	.232	56	9	1	0	1	1.8	8	4	8	15	0	31	6	13	0	0	0	1.4	1.000	OF-8, 1B-1
3 yrs.		62	.211	.263	76	16	1	0	1	1.3	9	4	13	20	0	41	8	24	1	0	1	1.9	1.000	OF-11, 1B-2

Tom Nagle

NAGLE, THOMAS EDWARD BR TR 5′10″ 150 lbs.
B. Oct. 30, 1865, Milwaukee, Wis. D. Mar. 9, 1946, Milwaukee, Wis.

Year	Team	Games	BA	SA	AB	H	2B	3B	HR	HR%	R	RBI	BB	SO	SB	Pinch Hit AB	Pinch Hit H	PO	A	E	DP	TC/G	FA	G by Pos
1890	CHI N	38	.271	.340	144	39	5	1	1	0.7	21	11	7	24	4	0	0	167	25	13	0	5.3	.937	C-33, OF-6
1891		8	.120	.120	25	3	0	0	0	0.0	3	1	1	3	0	0	0	25	4	3	1	4.0	.906	C-7, OF-1
2 yrs.		46	.249	.308	169	42	5	1	1	0.6	24	12	8	27	4	0	0	192	29	16	1	5.0	.932	C-40, OF-7

Bill Nahorodny

NAHORODNY, WILLIAM GERARD BR TR 6′ 2″ 200 lbs.
B. Aug. 31, 1953, Hamtramck, Mich.

Year	Team	Games	BA	SA	AB	H	2B	3B	HR	HR%	R	RBI	BB	SO	SB	Pinch Hit AB	Pinch Hit H	PO	A	E	DP	TC/G	FA	G by Pos
1976	PHI N	3	.200	.400	5	1	1	0	0	0.0	0	0	0	0	0	2	0	7	0	0	0	3.5	1.000	C-2
1977	CHI A	7	.261	.435	23	6	1	0	1	4.3	3	4	2	3	0	0	0	29	6	0	2	5.0	1.000	C-7
1978		107	.236	.349	347	82	11	2	8	2.3	29	35	23	52	1	1	0	509	55	11	6	5.3	.981	C-104, 1B-4, DH-1
1979		65	.257	.413	179	46	10	0	6	3.4	20	29	18	23	0	11	6	223	25	7	3	4.0	.973	C-60, DH-3
1980	ATL N	59	.242	.414	157	38	12	0	5	3.2	14	18	8	21	0	6	1	178	24	2	2	3.7	.990	C-54, 1B-1
1981		14	.231	.308	13	3	1	0	0	0.0	0	2	1	3	0	9	3	7	0	0	0	1.8	1.000	C-3, 1B-1
1982	CLE A	39	.223	.426	94	21	5	1	4	4.3	6	18	2	9	0	7	2	111	11	0	2	3.5	1.000	C-35
1983	DET A	2	.000	.000	1	0	0	0	0	0.0	0	0	1	0	0	1	0	0	0	0	0	0.0	—	
1984	SEA A	12	.240	.360	25	6	0	0	1	4.0	2	3	1	7	0	1	0	41	2	1	2	4.0	.977	C-10, 1B-1
9 yrs.		308	.241	.385	844	203	41	3	25	3.0	74	109	56	118	1	38	12	1105	123	21	17	4.4	.983	C-275, 1B-7, DH-4

Frank Naleway

NALEWAY, FRANK (Chick) BR TR 5′ 9½″ 165 lbs.
B. July 5, 1902, Chicago, Ill. D. Jan. 28, 1949, Chicago, Ill.

Year	Team	Games	BA	SA	AB	H	2B	3B	HR	HR%	R	RBI	BB	SO	SB	Pinch Hit AB	Pinch Hit H	PO	A	E	DP	TC/G	FA	G by Pos
1924	CHI A	1	.000	.000	2	0	0	0	0	0.0	0	0	1	0	0	0	0	1	2	1	0	4.0	.750	SS-1

Doc Nance

NANCE, WILLIAM G. (Kid) BR TR 5′ 7″ 165 lbs.
Born William G. Cooper.
B. Aug. 2, 1876, Fort Worth, Tex. D. May 28, 1958, Fort Worth, Tex.

Year	Team	Games	BA	SA	AB	H	2B	3B	HR	HR%	R	RBI	BB	SO	SB	Pinch Hit AB	Pinch Hit H	PO	A	E	DP	TC/G	FA	G by Pos
1897	LOU N	35	.242	.408	120	29	5	3	3	2.5	25	17	20		3	0	0	60	8	1	4	2.0	.986	OF-35
1898		22	.316	.421	76	24	5	0	1	1.3	13	16	12		2	0	0	28	7	2	2	1.7	.946	OF-22
1901	DET A	132	.280	.373	461	129	24	5	3	0.7	72	66	51		9	0	0	240	20	19	6	2.1	.932	OF-132
1904	STL A	1	.333	.333	3	1	0	0	0	0.0	0		0			0	0	0	0	0	0	0.0	.000	OF-1
4 yrs.		190	.277	.385	660	183	34	8	7	1.1	110	99	83		14	0	0	328	35	22	12	2.0	.943	OF-190

Al Naples

NAPLES, ALOYSIUS FRANCIS BR TR 5′ 9″ 168 lbs.
B. Aug. 29, 1927, St. George, N. Y.

Year	Team	Games	BA	SA	AB	H	2B	3B	HR	HR%	R	RBI	BB	SO	SB	Pinch Hit AB	Pinch Hit H	PO	A	E	DP	TC/G	FA	G by Pos
1949	STL A	2	.143	.286	7	1	1	0	0	0.0	0	0	0	1	0	0	0	1	6	1	0	4.0	.875	SS-2

Danny Napoleon

NAPOLEON, DANIEL BR TR 5′11″ 190 lbs.
B. Jan. 11, 1942, Claysburg, Pa.

Year	Team	Games	BA	SA	AB	H	2B	3B	HR	HR%	R	RBI	BB	SO	SB	Pinch Hit AB	Pinch Hit H	PO	A	E	DP	TC/G	FA	G by Pos
1965	NY N	68	.144	.175	97	14	1	1	0	0.0	5	7	8	23	0	45	9	33	1	2	0	1.6	.944	OF-15, 3B-7
1966		12	.212	.273	33	7	2	0	0	0.0	2	0	1	10	0	1	0	12	1	1	0	1.4	.929	OF-10
2 yrs.		80	.162	.200	130	21	3	1	0	0.0	7	7	9	33	0	46	9	45	2	3	0	1.6	.940	OF-25, 3B-7

Hal Naragon

NARAGON, HAROLD RICHARD BL TR 6′ 160 lbs.
B. Oct. 1, 1928, Zanesville, Ohio.

Year	Team	Games	BA	SA	AB	H	2B	3B	HR	HR%	R	RBI	BB	SO	SB	Pinch Hit AB	Pinch Hit H	PO	A	E	DP	TC/G	FA	G by Pos
1951	CLE A	3	.250	.250	8	2	0	0	0	0.0	0	0	1	0	0	1	1	12	1	1	1	7.0	.929	C-2
1954		46	.238	.297	101	24	2	2	0	0.0	10	12	9	12	0	1	0	132	14	0	1	3.2	1.000	C-45
1955		57	.323	.449	127	41	9	2	1	0.8	12	14	15	8	1	13	3	199	15	2	3	4.2	.991	C-52
1956		53	.287	.402	122	35	3	1	3	2.5	11	18	13	9	0	14	5	162	7	2	0	3.6	.988	C-48
1957		57	.256	.281	121	31	1	1	0	0.0	12	8	12	9	0	24	4	179	14	2	2	5.0	.990	C-39
1958		9	.333	.556	9	3	0	1	0	0.0	2	0	0	0	0	9	3	0	0	0	0	0.0	—	
1959	2 teams	CLE A (14G –.278) WAS A (71G –.241)																						
″	total	85	.247	.303	231	57	7	3	0	0.0	18	16	11	11	0	24	3	313	16	2	1	5.2	.994	C-64
1960	WAS A	33	.207	.228	92	19	2	0	0	0.0	7	5	8	4	0	4	0	119	14	3	1	4.7	.978	C-29
1961	MIN A	57	.302	.374	139	42	2	1	2	1.4	10	11	4	8	0	20	3	168	12	1	4	5.0	.994	C-36
1962		24	.229	.257	35	8	1	0	0	0.0	1	3	3	1	0	15	1	41	0	0	1	4.6	1.000	C-9
10 yrs.		424	.266	.334	985	262	27	11	6	0.6	83	87	76	62	1	125	23	1325	93	13	14	4.4	.991	C-324

WORLD SERIES

Year	Team	Games	BA	SA	AB	H	2B	3B	HR	HR%	R	RBI	BB	SO	SB	Pinch Hit AB	Pinch Hit H	PO	A	E	DP	TC/G	FA	G by Pos
1954	CLE A	1	—	—	0	0	0	0	0	—	0	0	0	0	0	0	0	1	0	0	0	1.0	1.000	C-1

Bill Narleski

NARLESKI, WILLIAM EDWARD (Cap) BR TR 5′ 9″ 160 lbs.
Father of Ray Narleski.
B. June 9, 1899, Perth Amboy, N. J. D. July 22, 1964, Laurel Springs, N. J.

Year	Team	Games	BA	SA	AB	H	2B	3B	HR	HR%	R	RBI	BB	SO	SB	Pinch Hit AB	Pinch Hit H	PO	A	E	DP	TC/G	FA	G by Pos
1929	BOS A	96	.277	.346	260	72	16	1	0	0.0	31	25	21	22	4	3	1	146	200	15	41	4.1	.958	SS-51, 2B-28, 3B-10
1930		39	.235	.327	98	23	9	0	0	0.0	11	7	7	5	0	0	0	50	52	6	10	2.8	.944	SS-19, 3B-14, 2B-5
2 yrs.		135	.265	.341	358	95	25	1	0	0.0	42	32	28	27	4	3	1	196	252	21	51	3.7	.955	SS-70, 2B-33, 3B-24

Jerry Narron

NARRON, JERRY AUSTIN BL TR 6′ 3″ 205 lbs.
B. Jan. 15, 1956, Goldsboro, N. C.

Year	Team	Games	BA	SA	AB	H	2B	3B	HR	HR%	R	RBI	BB	SO	SB	Pinch Hit AB	Pinch Hit H	PO	A	E	DP	TC/G	FA	G by Pos
1979	NY A	61	.171	.309	123	21	3	1	4	3.3	17	18	9	26	0	4	0	167	15	5	2	3.3	.973	C-56, DH-1
1980	SEA A	48	.196	.336	107	21	3	0	4	3.7	7	18	13	18	0	14	3	115	11	1	0	3.2	.992	C-39, DH-1
1981		76	.222	.291	203	45	5	0	3	1.5	13	17	16	35	0	15	3	248	11	1	3	4.0	.996	C-65
1983	CAL A	10	.136	.273	22	3	0	0	1	4.5	1	4	1	3	0	6	0	14	3	2	0	2.7	.895	C-6, DH-1
1984		69	.247	.340	150	37	5	0	3	2.0	9	17	8	12	0	29	7	184	12	1	6	3.7	.995	C-46, 1B-7
1985		67	.220	.364	132	29	4	0	5	3.8	12	14	11	17	0	22	5	146	14	0	4	3.0	1.000	C-45, DH-7, 1B-1
1986		57	.221	.305	95	21	3	1	1	1.1	5	8	9	14	0	11	2	155	14	2	3	3.2	.988	C-51, DH-2
1987	SEA A	4	.000	.000	8	0	0	0	0	0.0	0	0	0	2	0	1	0	9	0	0	0	3.0	1.000	C-3
8 yrs.		392	.211	.318	840	177	23	2	21	2.5	64	96	67	127	0	102	20	1038	80	12	18	3.4	.989	C-311, DH-12, 1B-8
LEAGUE CHAMPIONSHIP SERIES																								
1986	CAL A	4	.500	.500	2	1	0	0	0	0.0	1	0	1	1	0	1	0	0	0	0	0	0.0	.000	C-3

Sam Narron

NARRON, SAMUEL BR TR 5′10″ 180 lbs.
B. Aug. 25, 1913, Middlesex, N. C.

Year	Team	Games	BA	SA	AB	H	2B	3B	HR	HR%	R	RBI	BB	SO	SB	Pinch Hit AB	Pinch Hit H	PO	A	E	DP	TC/G	FA	G by Pos
1935	STL N	4	.429	.429	7	3	0	0	0	0.0	0	0	0	0	0	3	2	5	0	0	0	5.0	1.000	C-1
1942		10	.400	.400	10	4	0	0	0	0.0	0	1	0	2	0	8	3	2	0	0	0	1.0	1.000	C-2
1943		10	.091	.091	11	1	0	0	0	0.0	0	0	1	2	0	7	1	8	1	0	0	3.0	1.000	C-3
3 yrs.		24	.286	.286	28	8	0	0	0	0.0	0	1	1	4	0	18	6	15	1	0	0	2.7	1.000	C-6
WORLD SERIES																								
1943	STL N	1	.000	.000	1	0	0	0	0	0.0	0	0	0	0	0	1	0	0	0	0	0	0.0	—	

Billy Nash

NASH, WILLIAM MITCHELL BR TR 5′ 8½″ 167 lbs.
B. June 24, 1865, Richmond, Va. D. Nov. 15, 1929, East Orange, N. J.
Manager 1896.

Year	Team	Games	BA	SA	AB	H	2B	3B	HR	HR%	R	RBI	BB	SO	SB	Pinch Hit AB	Pinch Hit H	PO	A	E	DP	TC/G	FA	G by Pos
1884	RIC AA	45	.199	.361	166	33	8	8	1	0.6	31		12			0	0	77	87	34	8	4.4	.828	3B-45
1885	BOS N	26	.255	.298	94	24	4	0	0	0.0	9	11	2	9		0	0	34	43	12	6	3.3	.865	3B-19, 2B-8
1886		109	.281	.353	417	117	11	8	1	0.2	61	45	24	28		0	0	160	217	61	14	4.1	.861	3B-90, SS-17
1887		121	.295	.440	475	140	24	12	7	1.5	100	94	60	30	43	0	0	220	243	60	19	4.3	.885	3B-117, OF-5
1888		135	.283	.397	526	149	18	15	4	0.8	71	75	50	46	20	0	0	229	358	58	31	4.7	.910	3B-105, 2B-31
1889		128	.274	.343	481	132	20	2	3	0.6	84	76	79	44	26	0	0	205	274	50	25	4.1	.905	3B-128, P-1
1890	BOS P	129	.266	.379	488	130	28	6	5	1.0	103	90	88	43	26	0	0	198	307	78	37	4.5	.866	3B-129, P-1
1891	BOS N	140	.276	.382	537	148	24	9	5	0.9	92	95	74	50	28	0	0	213	264	53	20	3.8	.900	3B-140
1892		135	.260	.350	526	137	25	5	4	0.8	94	95	59	41	31	0	0	197	351	62	23	4.5	.898	3B-135, OF-1
1893		128	.291	.433	485	141	27	6	10	2.1	115	123	85	29	30	0	0	189	300	41	23	4.1	.923	3B-128
1894		132	.289	.404	512	148	23	6	8	1.6	132	87	91	23	20	0	0	204	267	34	24	3.8	.933	3B-132
1895		132	.289	.417	508	147	23	6	10	2.0	97	108	74	19	18	0	0	193	246	59	26	3.8	.882	3B-132
1896	PHI N	65	.247	.335	227	56	9	1	3	1.3	29	30	34	21	3	0	0	87	148	23	12	4.0	.911	3B-65
1897		104	.258	.329	337	87	20	2	0	0.0	45	39	60		4	1	1	172	206	38	17	4.1	.909	3B-79, SS-19, 2B-4
1898		20	.243	.300	70	17	2	1	0	0.0	9	9	11		0	0	0	35	33	3	6	3.5	.958	3B-20
15 yrs.		1549	.275	.381	5849	1606	266	87	61	1.0	1072	977	803	383	249	1	1	2413	3344	666	291	4.1	.896	3B-1464, 2B-43, SS-36, OF-6, P-2

Cotton Nash

NASH, CHARLES FRANCIS BR TR 6′ 6″ 220 lbs.
B. July 24, 1942, Jersey City, N. J.

Year	Team	Games	BA	SA	AB	H	2B	3B	HR	HR%	R	RBI	BB	SO	SB	Pinch Hit AB	Pinch Hit H	PO	A	E	DP	TC/G	FA	G by Pos
1967	CHI A	3	.000	.000	3	0	0	0	0	0.0	1	0	1	0	0	0	0	10	0	2	3	4.0	.833	1B-3
1969	MIN A	6	.222	.222	9	2	0	0	0	0.0	0	0	1	2	0	0	0	29	5	0	0	4.9	1.000	1B-6, OF-1
1970		4	.250	.250	4	1	0	0	0	0.0	1	2	1	1	0	2	0	11	0	0	2	5.5	1.000	1B-2
3 yrs.		13	.188	.188	16	3	0	0	0	0.0	2	2	3	3	0	2	0	50	5	2	5	4.8	.965	1B-11, OF-1

Ken Nash

NASH, KENNETH LELAND BB TR 5′ 8″ 140 lbs.
Played as J. A. Costello in 1912.
B. July 14, 1888, Weymouth, Mass. D. Feb. 16, 1977, Epsom, N. H.

Year	Team	Games	BA	SA	AB	H	2B	3B	HR	HR%	R	RBI	BB	SO	SB	Pinch Hit AB	Pinch Hit H	PO	A	E	DP	TC/G	FA	G by Pos
1912	CLE A	11	.174	.174	23	4	0	0	0	0.0	2	0	3		0	3	0	6	13	4	1	2.9	.826	SS-8
1914	STL N	24	.275	.373	51	14	3	1	0	0.0	4	6	6	10	0	5	1	15	25	8	2	2.5	.833	3B-10, 2B-6, SS-3
2 yrs.		35	.243	.311	74	18	3	1	0	0.0	6	6	9	10	0	8	1	21	38	12	3	2.6	.831	SS-11, 3B-10, 2B-6

Bob Natal

NATAL, ROBERT MARCEL BR TR 5′11″ 190 lbs.
B. Nov. 13, 1965, Long Beach, Calif.

Year	Team	Games	BA	SA	AB	H	2B	3B	HR	HR%	R	RBI	BB	SO	SB	Pinch Hit AB	Pinch Hit H	PO	A	E	DP	TC/G	FA	G by Pos
1992	MON N	5	.000	.000	6	0	0	0	0	0.0	0	0	1	1	0	1	0	10	0	1	0	2.8	.909	C-4
1993	FLA N	41	.214	.291	117	25	4	1	1	0.9	3	6	6	22	1	2	0	196	18	0	2	5.6	1.000	C-38
1994		10	.276	.345	29	8	2	0	0	0.0	2	2	5	5	1	2	0	50	9	1	0	7.5	.983	C-8
1995		16	.233	.465	43	10	2	1	2	4.7	2	6	1	9	0	3	0	80	3	1	1	6.5	.988	C-13
4 yrs.		72	.221	.328	195	43	8	2	3	1.5	7	14	13	37	2	8	0	336	30	3	3	5.9	.992	C-63

Pete Naton

NATON, PETER ALPHONSUS BR TR 6′ 1″ 200 lbs.
B. Sept. 9, 1931, Flushing, N. Y.

Year	Team	Games	BA	SA	AB	H	2B	3B	HR	HR%	R	RBI	BB	SO	SB	Pinch Hit AB	Pinch Hit H	PO	A	E	DP	TC/G	FA	G by Pos
1953	PIT N	6	.167	.167	12	2	0	0	0	0.0	2	1	2	1	0	1	0	13	0	0	0	3.3	1.000	C-4

Sandy Nava

NAVA, VINCENT P. 5′ 6″ 155 lbs.
Born Irwin Sandy.
B. Apr. 12, 1850, San Francisco, Calif. D. June 15, 1906, Baltimore, Md.

Year	Team	Games	BA	SA	AB	H	2B	3B	HR	HR%	R	RBI	BB	SO	SB	Pinch Hit AB	Pinch Hit H	PO	A	E	DP	TC/G	FA	G by Pos
1882	PRO N	28	.206	.227	97	20	2	0	0	0.0	15		1	13		0	0	112	31	22	6	5.9	.867	C-27, OF-1
1883		29	.240	.320	100	24	4	2	0	0.0	18		3	17		0	0	100	41	32	4	6.0	.815	C-27, OF-2
1884		34	.095	.095	116	11	0	0	0	0.0	10		11	35		0	0	183	54	31	3	7.9	.884	C-27, SS-6, 2B-1

Sandy Nava *continued*

Year	Team	Games	BA	SA	AB	H	2B	3B	HR	HR%	R	RBI	BB	SO	SB	Pinch Hit AB	Pinch Hit H	PO	A	E	DP	TC/G	FA	G by Pos
1885	BAL AA	8	.185	.222	27	5	1	0	0	0.0	2		1			0	0	26	7	7	0	5.0	.825	C-8
1886		2	.200	.200	5	1	0	0	0	0.0	0		0			0	0	5	2	2	0	4.5	.778	SS-1, C-1
5 yrs.		101	.177	.209	345	61	7	2	0	0.0	45		16	65		0	0	426	135	94	13	6.5	.856	C-90, SS-7, OF-3, 2B-1

Tito Navarro

NAVARRO, NORBERTO BB TR 5′10″ 165 lbs.
Born Norberto Navarro (Rodriguez).
B. Sept. 12, 1970, Rio Piedras, Puerto Rico.

Year	Team	Games	BA	SA	AB	H	2B	3B	HR	HR%	R	RBI	BB	SO	SB	Pinch Hit AB	Pinch Hit H	PO	A	E	DP	TC/G	FA	G by Pos
1993	NY N	12	.059	.059	17	1	0	0	0	0.0	1	1	0	4	0	8	1	8	7	0	0	7.5	1.000	SS-2

Earl Naylor

NAYLOR, EARL EUGENE BR TR 6′ 190 lbs.
B. May 19, 1919, Kansas City, Mo. D. Jan. 16, 1990, Winter Haven, Fla.

Year	Team	Games	BA	SA	AB	H	2B	3B	HR	HR%	R	RBI	BB	SO	SB	Pinch Hit AB	Pinch Hit H	PO	A	E	DP	TC/G	FA	G by Pos
1942	PHI N	76	.196	.232	168	33	4	1	0	0.0	9	14	11	18	1	17	5	68	11	1	0	1.5	.988	OF-34, P-20, 1B-1
1943		33	.175	.267	120	21	2	0	3	2.5	12	14	12	16	1	0	0	101	6	4	2	3.4	.964	OF-33
1946	BKN N	3	.000	.000	2	0	0	0	0	0.0	1	0	0	1	0	2	0	0	0	0	0	0.0	—	
3 yrs.		112	.186	.245	290	54	6	1	3	1.0	22	28	23	35	2	19	5	169	17	5	2	2.2	.974	OF-67, P-20, 1B-1

Jack Neagle

NEAGLE, JOHN HENRY BR TR 5′ 6″ 155 lbs.
B. Jan. 2, 1858, Syracuse, N. Y. D. Sept. 20, 1904, Syracuse, N. Y.

Year	Team	Games	BA	SA	AB	H	2B	3B	HR	HR%	R	RBI	BB	SO	SB	Pinch Hit AB	Pinch Hit H	PO	A	E	DP	TC/G	FA	G by Pos
1879	CIN N	3	.167	.167	12	2	0	0	0	0.0	1	2	0	0		0	0	1	2	2	0	1.3	.600	P-2, OF-2
1883	3 teams	PHI N (18G –.164) BAL AA (9G –.286) PIT AA (27G –.188)																						
″	total	54	.196	.230	209	41	5	1	0	0.0	23		8	9		0	0	45	40	19	0	1.7	.817	OF-32, P-30
1884	PIT AA	43	.149	.189	148	22	6	0	0	0.0	13		6			0	0	25	57	29	1	2.5	.739	P-38, OF-6
3 yrs.		100	.176	.211	369	65	11	1	0	0.0	37	2	14	9		0	0	71	99	50	1	2.0	.773	P-70, OF-40

Charlie Neal

NEAL, CHARLES LENARD BR TR 5′10″ 165 lbs.
B. Jan. 30, 1931, Longview, Tex.

Year	Team	Games	BA	SA	AB	H	2B	3B	HR	HR%	R	RBI	BB	SO	SB	Pinch Hit AB	Pinch Hit H	PO	A	E	DP	TC/G	FA	G by Pos
1956	BKN N	62	.287	.382	136	39	5	1	2	1.5	22	14	14	19	2	8	3	70	104	5	24	3.4	.972	2B-51, SS-1
1957		128	.270	.411	448	121	13	7	12	2.7	62	62	53	83	11	1	1	182	340	27	66	4.4	.951	SS-100, 3B-23, 2B-3
1958	LA N	140	.254	.438	473	120	9	6	22	4.7	87	65	61	91	7	2	1	344	361	19	123	5.1	.974	2B-132, 3B-9
1959		151	.287	.464	616	177	30	**11**	19	3.1	103	83	43	86	17	0	0	386	415	9	110	5.3	.989	2B-151, SS-1
1960		139	.256	.363	477	122	23	2	8	1.7	60	40	48	75	5	2	0	251	296	13	79	4.0	.977	2B-136, SS-3
1961		108	.235	.346	341	80	6	1	10	2.9	40	48	30	49	3	4	1	211	246	11	63	4.5	.976	2B-104
1962	NY N	136	.260	.388	508	132	14	9	11	2.2	59	58	56	90	2	0	0	256	389	28	85	4.9	.958	2B-85, SS-39, 3B-12
1963	2 teams	NY N (72G –.225) CIN N (34G –.156)																						
″	total	106	.211	.287	317	67	13	1	3	0.9	28	21	32	64	1	15	3	98	167	12	17	2.9	.957	3B-85, SS-9, 2B-1
8 yrs.		970	.259	.394	3316	858	113	38	87	2.6	461	391	337	557	48	32	9	1798	2318	124	567	4.5	.971	2B-663, SS-153, 3B-129
WORLD SERIES																								
1956	BKN N	1	.000	.000	4	0	0	0	0	0.0	0	0	0	1	0	0	0	2	2	1	1	5.0	.800	2B-1
1959	LA N	6	.370	.667	27	10	2	0	2	7.4	4	6	0	1	1	0	0	18	19	1	7	6.3	.974	2B-6
2 yrs.		7	.323	.581	31	10	2	0	2	6.5	4	6	0	2	1	0	0	20	21	2	8	6.1	.953	2B-7

Offa Neal

NEAL, THEOPHILUS FOUNTAIN BL TR 6′ 185 lbs.
B. June 5, 1876, Logan, Ill. D. Apr. 12, 1950, Mt. Vernon, Ill.

Year	Team	Games	BA	SA	AB	H	2B	3B	HR	HR%	R	RBI	BB	SO	SB	Pinch Hit AB	Pinch Hit H	PO	A	E	DP	TC/G	FA	G by Pos
1905	NY N	4	.000	.000	13	0	0	0	0	0.0	0	0	0		0	0	0	5	4	0	2	2.3	1.000	3B-3, 2B-1

Greasy Neale

NEALE, ALFRED EARLE BL TR 6′ 170 lbs.
B. Nov. 5, 1891, Parkersburg, W. Va. D. Nov. 2, 1973, Lake Worth, Fla.

Year	Team	Games	BA	SA	AB	H	2B	3B	HR	HR%	R	RBI	BB	SO	SB	Pinch Hit AB	Pinch Hit H	PO	A	E	DP	TC/G	FA	G by Pos
1916	CIN N	138	.262	.306	530	139	13	5	0	0.0	53	20	19	79	17	3	0	307	20	9	6	2.5	.973	OF-133
1917		121	.294	.400	385	113	14	9	3	0.8	40	33	24	36	25	2	0	216	13	5	1	2.0	.979	OF-119
1918		107	.270	.367	371	100	11	11	1	0.3	59	32	24	38	23	4	0	249	11	5	2	2.6	.981	OF-102
1919		139	.242	.316	500	121	10	12	1	0.2	57	54	47	51	28	1	0	285	16	13	4	2.3	.959	OF-138
1920		150	.255	.317	530	135	10	7	3	0.6	55	46	45	48	29	0	0	347	19	5	7	2.5	.987	OF-150
1921	2 teams	PHI N (22G –.211) CIN N (63G –.241)																						
″	total	85	.235	.305	298	70	11	5	0	0.0	46	13	36	25	12	3	0	144	7	8	2	1.9	.950	OF-82
1922	CIN N	25	.233	.326	43	10	2	1	0	0.0	11	2	6	3	5	3	1	18	1	3	0	2.2	.864	OF-10
1924		3	.000	.000	4	0	0	0	0	0.0	0	0	0	1	0	0	0	3	0	0	0	1.5	1.000	OF-2
8 yrs.		768	.259	.332	2661	688	71	50	8	0.3	321	200	201	281	139	16	1	1569	87	48	22	2.3	.972	OF-736
WORLD SERIES																								
1919	CIN N	8	.357	.464	28	10	1	1	0	0.0	3	4	2	5	1	0	0	20	0	1	0	2.6	.952	OF-8

Jim Nealon

NEALON, JAMES JOSEPH TR 6′ 1½″
B. Dec. 15, 1884, Sacramento, Calif. D. Apr. 2, 1910, San Francisco, Calif.

Year	Team	Games	BA	SA	AB	H	2B	3B	HR	HR%	R	RBI	BB	SO	SB	Pinch Hit AB	Pinch Hit H	PO	A	E	DP	TC/G	FA	G by Pos
1906	PIT N	154	.255	.353	556	142	21	12	3	0.5	82	**83**	53		15	0	0	1592	102	23	90	11.1	.987	1B-154
1907		105	.257	.325	381	98	10	8	0	0.0	29	47	23		11	1	0	998	68	24	35	10.5	.978	1B-104
2 yrs.		259	.256	.342	937	240	31	20	3	0.3	111	130	76		26	1	0	2590	170	47	125	10.9	.983	1B-258

Tom Needham

NEEDHAM, THOMAS J. (Deerfoot) BR TR 5′10″ 180 lbs.
B. Apr. 7, 1879, Ireland D. Dec. 13, 1926, Steubenville, Ohio.

Year	Team	Games	BA	SA	AB	H	2B	3B	HR	HR%	R	RBI	BB	SO	SB	Pinch Hit AB	Pinch Hit H	PO	A	E	DP	TC/G	FA	G by Pos
1904	BOS N	84	.260	.372	269	70	12	3	4	1.5	18	19	11		3	6	0	326	140	27	8	6.3	.945	C-77, OF-1
1905		83	.218	.269	271	59	6	1	2	0.7	21	17	24		3	1	0	311	135	24	7	5.7	.949	C-77, OF-3, 1B-2
1906		83	.189	.242	285	54	8	2	1	0.4	11	12	13		3	2	0	342	131	20	11	5.8	.959	C-76, 2B-5, 1B-2, OF-1, 3B-1
1907		86	.196	.246	260	51	6	2	1	0.4	19	19	18		4	5	0	288	101	13	9	5.1	.968	C-78, 1B-1
1908	NY N	54	.209	.242	91	19	3	0	0	0.0	8	11	12		0	5	0	168	30	5	2	4.3	.975	C-47
1909	CHI N	13	.143	.143	28	4	0	0	0	0.0	3	0	0		0	6	2	43	5	1	0	7.0	.980	C-7
1910		31	.184	.250	76	14	3	1	0	0.0	9	10	10	10	1	3	0	133	31	3	0	6.0	.982	C-27, 1B-1
1911		27	.194	.226	62	12	2	0	0	0.0	4	5	9	14	2	3	0	94	32	2	2	5.6	.984	C-23
1912		33	.178	.233	90	16	5	0	0	0.0	12	10	7	13	3	1	0	116	39	1	3	4.9	.994	C-32
1913		20	.238	.381	42	10	4	1	0	0.0	5	11	4	8	0	4	0	53	24	3	4	5.3	.962	C-14, 1B-1
1914		9	.118	.176	17	2	1	0	0	0.0	3	3	1	4	1	2	0	22	11	2	0	5.0	.943	C-7
11 yrs.		523	.209	.272	1491	311	50	10	8	0.5	113	117	109	49	20	38	2	1896	679	101	46	5.5	.962	C-465, 1B-7, 2B-5, OF-5, 3B-1
WORLD SERIES																								
1910	CHI N	1	.000	.000	1	0	0	0	0	0.0	0	0	0	0	0	1	0	0	0	0	0	0.0	—	

Troy Neel

NEEL, TROY LEE BL TR 6′ 4″ 210 lbs.
B. Sept. 14, 1965, Freeport, Tex.

Year	Team	Games	BA	SA	AB	H	2B	3B	HR	HR%	R	RBI	BB	SO	SB	Pinch Hit AB	Pinch Hit H	PO	A	E	DP	TC/G	FA	G by Pos
1992	OAK A	24	.264	.491	53	14	3	0	3	5.7	8	9	5	15	0	7	3	16	1	3	0	1.0	.850	OF-9, DH-9, 1B-2
1993		123	.290	.473	427	124	21	0	19	4.4	59	63	49	101	3	7	1	236	22	5	25	2.2	.981	DH-85, 1B-34
1994		83	.266	.475	278	74	13	0	15	5.4	43	48	38	61	2	6	2	295	23	2	34	4.0	.994	1B-45, DH-35
3 yrs.		230	.280	.475	758	212	37	0	37	4.9	110	120	92	177	5	20	6	547	46	10	59	2.8	.983	DH-129, 1B-81, OF-9

Cal Neeman

NEEMAN, CALVIN AMANDUS BR TR 6′ 1″ 192 lbs.
B. Feb. 18, 1929, Valmeyer, Ill.

Year	Team	Games	BA	SA	AB	H	2B	3B	HR	HR%	R	RBI	BB	SO	SB	Pinch Hit AB	Pinch Hit H	PO	A	E	DP	TC/G	FA	G by Pos
1957	CHI N	122	.258	.376	415	107	17	1	10	2.4	37	39	22	87	0	4	0	703	56	8	13	6.5	.990	C-118
1958		76	.259	.473	201	52	7	0	12	6.0	30	29	21	41	0	8	0	340	25	3	6	5.2	.992	C-71
1959		44	.162	.267	105	17	2	0	3	2.9	7	9	11	23	0	5	0	158	9	1	1	4.4	.994	C-38
1960	2 teams	CHI N (9G –.154) PHI N (59G –.181)																						
″	total	68	.179	.312	173	31	7	2	4	2.3	13	13	16	47	0	4	0	286	35	6	3	5.4	.982	C-61
1961	PHI N	19	.226	.258	31	7	1	0	0	0.0	0	2	4	8	1	0	0	63	5	1	0	3.6	.986	C-19
1962	PIT N	24	.180	.300	50	9	1	1	1	2.0	5	5	3	10	0	0	0	103	15	2	1	5.0	.983	C-24
1963	2 teams	CLE A (9G –.000) WAS A (14G –.056)																						
″	total	23	.037	.037	27	1	0	0	0	0.0	1	0	2	5	0	2	0	61	5	1	4	3.2	.985	C-21
7 yrs.		376	.224	.356	1002	224	35	4	30	3.0	93	97	79	221	1	23	0	1714	150	22	28	5.4	.988	C-352

Doug Neff

NEFF, DOUGLAS WILLIAMS BR TR 5′ 9″ 141 lbs.
B. Oct. 8, 1891, Harrisonburg, Va. D. May 23, 1932, Cape Charles, Va.

Year	Team	Games	BA	SA	AB	H	2B	3B	HR	HR%	R	RBI	BB	SO	SB	Pinch Hit AB	Pinch Hit H	PO	A	E	DP	TC/G	FA	G by Pos
1914	WAS A	3	.000	.000	2	0	0	0	0	0.0	0	0	0	0	0	0	0	3	5	1	0	3.0	.889	SS-3
1915		30	.167	.183	60	10	1	0	0	0.0	1	4	4	6	1	0	0	23	41	13	4	2.7	.831	3B-12, 2B-10, SS-7
2 yrs.		33	.161	.177	62	10	1	0	0	0.0	1	4	4	6	1	0	0	26	46	14	4	2.7	.837	3B-12, 2B-10, SS-10

Bob Neighbors

NEIGHBORS, ROBERT OTIS BR TR 5′11″ 165 lbs.
B. Nov. 9, 1917, Talihina, Okla. D. Aug. 8, 1952, North Korea.

Year	Team	Games	BA	SA	AB	H	2B	3B	HR	HR%	R	RBI	BB	SO	SB	Pinch Hit AB	Pinch Hit H	PO	A	E	DP	TC/G	FA	G by Pos
1939	STL A	7	.182	.455	11	2	0	0	1	9.1	3	1	0	1	0	0	0	5	6	1	1	2.4	.917	SS-5

Cy Neighbors

NEIGHBORS, FLEMON CECIL BR
B. Sept. 23, 1880, Fayetteville, Mo. D. May 20, 1964, Tacoma, Wash.

Year	Team	Games	BA	SA	AB	H	2B	3B	HR	HR%	R	RBI	BB	SO	SB	Pinch Hit AB	Pinch Hit H	PO	A	E	DP	TC/G	FA	G by Pos
1908	PIT N	1	—	—	0	0	0	0	0	—	0	0	0		0	0	0	0	0	0	0	0.0	.000	OF-1

Tommy Neill

NEILL, THOMAS WHITE BL TR 6′ 2″ 200 lbs.
B. Nov. 7, 1919, Hartselle, Ala. D. Sept. 22, 1980, Houston, Tex.

Year	Team	Games	BA	SA	AB	H	2B	3B	HR	HR%	R	RBI	BB	SO	SB	Pinch Hit AB	Pinch Hit H	PO	A	E	DP	TC/G	FA	G by Pos
1946	BOS N	13	.267	.311	45	12	2	0	0	0.0	8	7	2	1	0	0	0	19	1	0	0	1.5	1.000	OF-13
1947		7	.200	.400	10	2	0	1	0	0.0	1	0	1	2	0	4	2	2	0	0	0	0.3	1.000	OF-7
2 yrs.		20	.255	.327	55	14	2	1	0	0.0	9	7	3	3	0	4	2	21	1	0	0	1.1	1.000	OF-20

Bernie Neis

NEIS, BERNARD EDMUND BB TR 5′ 7″ 160 lbs.
BR 1920–1921
B. Sept. 26, 1895, Bloomington, Ill. D. Nov. 29, 1972, Inverness, Fla.

Year	Team	Games	BA	SA	AB	H	2B	3B	HR	HR%	R	RBI	BB	SO	SB	Pinch Hit AB	Pinch Hit H	PO	A	E	DP	TC/G	FA	G by Pos
1920	BKN N	95	.253	.337	249	63	11	2	2	0.8	38	22	26	35	9	4	0	145	11	7	4	2.0	.957	OF-83
1921		102	.257	.365	230	59	5	4	4	1.7	34	34	25	41	9	16	6	126	14	8	1	1.9	.946	OF-77, 2B-1
1922		61	.229	.357	70	16	4	1	1	1.4	15	9	13	8	3	9	1	32	3	4	0	1.4	.897	OF-27
1923		126	.274	.364	445	122	17	4	5	1.1	78	37	36	38	8	8	1	268	20	18	3	2.8	.941	OF-111
1924		80	.303	.427	211	64	8	3	4	1.9	43	26	27	17	4	11	2	114	5	8	1	2.0	.937	OF-62
1925	BOS N	106	.285	.394	355	101	20	2	5	1.4	47	45	38	19	8	14	6	282	8	9	1	3.4	.970	OF-87
1926		30	.215	.312	93	20	5	2	0	0.0	16	8	8	10	4	2	0	60	2	5	1	2.9	.925	OF-23
1927	2 teams	CLE A (32G –.302) CHI A (45G –.289)																						
″	total	77	.297	.448	172	51	14	0	4	2.3	26	29	28	18	1	20	5	119	7	5	1	2.6	.962	OF-50
8 yrs.		677	.272	.379	1825	496	84	18	25	1.4	297	210	201	186	46	84	21	1146	70	64	12	2.5	.950	OF-520, 2B-1
WORLD SERIES																								
1920	BKN N	4	.000	.000	5	0	0	0	0	0.0	0	0	1	0	0	1	0	3	0	0	0	1.5	1.000	OF-2

Ernie Neitzke

NEITZKE, ERNEST FREDERICK BR TR 5′10″ 180 lbs.
B. Nov. 13, 1894, Toledo, Ohio D. Apr. 27, 1977, Sylvania, Ohio.

Year	Team	Games	BA	SA	AB	H	2B	3B	HR	HR%	R	RBI	BB	SO	SB	Pinch Hit AB	Pinch Hit H	PO	A	E	DP	TC/G	FA	G by Pos
1921	BOS A	11	.240	.240	25	6	0	0	0	0.0	3	1	4	4	0	0	0	13	4	2	0	1.9	.895	OF-8, P-2

Bob Nelson

NELSON, ROBERT SIDNEY (Babe, Tex) BL TL 6′ 3″ 205 lbs.
B. Aug. 7, 1936, Dallas, Tex.

Year	Team	Games	BA	SA	AB	H	2B	3B	HR	HR%	R	RBI	BB	SO	SB	Pinch Hit AB	Pinch Hit H	PO	A	E	DP	TC/G	FA	G by Pos
1955	BAL A	25	.194	.194	31	6	0	0	0	0.0	4	1	7	13	0	16	3	15	3	3	3	2.6	.857	OF-6, 1B-2
1956		39	.206	.235	68	14	2	0	0	0.0	5	5	7	22	0	15	4	28	3	2	0	1.4	.939	OF-24
1957		15	.217	.391	23	5	0	2	0	0.0	2	5	1	5	0	6	3	6	0	0	0	0.8	1.000	OF-8
3 yrs.		79	.205	.254	122	25	2	2	0	0.0	11	11	15	40	0	37	10	49	6	5	3	1.5	.917	OF-38, 1B-2

Candy Nelson

NELSON, JOHN W. BL TR 5′ 6″ 145 lbs.
B. Mar. 12, 1854, Portland, Me. D. Sept. 4, 1910, Brooklyn, N. Y.

Year	Team	Games	BA	SA	AB	H	2B	3B	HR	HR%	R	RBI	BB	SO	SB	Pinch Hit AB	Pinch Hit H	PO	A	E	DP	TC/G	FA	G by Pos
1878	IND N	19	.131	.143	84	11	1	0	0	0.0	12	5	5	11		0	0	19	50	13	1	4.3	.841	SS-19
1879	TRO N	28	.264	.349	106	28	7	1	0	0.0	17	10	8	4		0	0	42	90	25	8	5.6	.841	SS-24, OF-4
1881	WOR N	24	.282	.320	103	29	1	0	1	1.0	13	15	5	6		0	0	20	94	13	6	5.3	.898	SS-24
1883	NY AA	97	.305	.379	417	127	19	6	0	0.0	75		31			0	0	98	232	47	18	3.9	.875	SS-97
1884		111	.255	.310	432	110	15	3	1	0.2	114		**74**			0	0	120	292	56	16	4.2	.880	SS-110, 2B-1
1885		107	.255	.310	420	107	12	4	1	0.2	98		**61**			0	0	153	370	63	33	5.4	.892	SS-107, 3B-1
1886		109	.225	.252	413	93	7	2	0	0.0	89		64			0	0	159	219	60	19	4.0	.863	SS-73, OF-36
1887	2 teams	NY AA (68G –.245) NY N (1G –.000)																						
″	total	69	.243	.270	259	63	5	1	0	0.0	61	0	48	1	29	0	0	121	111	27	18	3.6	.896	OF-37, SS-32, 3B-1, 2B-1
1890	BKN AA	60	.251	.283	223	56	3	2	0	0.0	44		35		12	0	0	67	198	40	20	5.0	.869	SS-57, OF-4
9 yrs.		624	.254	.302	2457	624	70	19	3	0.1	523	30	331	22	41	0	0	799	1656	344	139	4.5	.877	SS-543, OF-81, 3B-2, 2B-2

Dave Nelson

NELSON, DAVID EARL BR TR 5′10″ 160 lbs.
BB 1968
B. June 20, 1944, Fort Sill, Okla.

Year	Team	Games	BA	SA	AB	H	2B	3B	HR	HR%	R	RBI	BB	SO	SB	Pinch Hit AB	Pinch Hit H	PO	A	E	DP	TC/G	FA	G by Pos
1968	CLE A	88	.233	.307	189	44	4	5	0	0.0	26	19	17	35	23	2	0	124	127	4	27	3.5	.984	2B-59, SS-14
1969		52	.203	.203	123	25	0	0	0	0.0	11	6	9	26	4	5	0	79	94	6	28	5.1	.966	2B-33, OF-2

Dave Nelson *continued*

Year	Team	Games	BA	SA	AB	H	2B	3B	HR	HR%	R	RBI	BB	SO	SB	Pinch Hit AB	Pinch Hit H	PO	A	E	DP	TC/G	FA	G by Pos
1970	WAS A	47	.159	.168	107	17	1	0	0	0.0	5	4	7	24	2	11	2	64	79	2	19	4.4	.986	2B-33
1971		85	.280	.377	329	92	11	3	5	1.5	47	33	23	29	17	3	0	63	150	14	15	2.7	.938	3B-84, 2B-1
1972	TEX A	145	.226	.283	499	113	16	3	2	0.4	68	28	67	81	51	6	0	131	222	22	25	2.8	.941	3B-119, OF-15
1973		142	.286	.378	576	165	24	4	7	1.2	71	48	34	78	43	2	2	327	364	11	98	5.0	.984	2B-140
1974		121	.236	.287	474	112	13	1	3	0.6	71	42	34	72	25	0	0	295	337	20	74	5.4	.969	2B-120, DH-1
1975		28	.212	.300	80	17	1	0	2	2.5	9	10	8	10	6	2	1	56	60	5	16	5.0	.959	2B-23, DH-1
1976	KC A	78	.235	.307	153	36	4	2	1	0.7	24	17	14	26	15	16	0	79	90	4	17	2.4	.977	2B-46, DH-22, 1B-3
1977		27	.188	.292	48	9	3	1	0	0.0	8	4	7	11	1	5	2	11	14	2	3	1.5	.926	2B-11, DH-7
10 yrs.		813	.244	.312	2578	630	77	19	20	0.8	340	211	220	392	187	52	7	1229	1537	90	322	3.9	.968	2B-466, 3B-203, DH-31, OF-17, SS-14, 1B-3
LEAGUE CHAMPIONSHIP SERIES																								
1976	KC A	2	.000	.000	2	0	0	0	0	0.0	0	0	0	1	0	2	0	0	0	0	0	0.0	—	

Jamie Nelson

NELSON, JAMES VICTOR BR TR 5′11″ 180 lbs.
B. Sept. 5, 1959, Clinton, Okla.

Year	Team	Games	BA	SA	AB	H	2B	3B	HR	HR%	R	RBI	BB	SO	SB	Pinch Hit AB	Pinch Hit H	PO	A	E	DP	TC/G	FA	G by Pos
1983	SEA A	40	.219	.281	96	21	3	0	1	1.0	9	5	13	12	4	1	0	202	16	5	2	5.7	.978	C-39

Lynn Nelson

NELSON, LYNN BERNARD (Line Drive) BL TR 5′10½″ 170 lbs.
B. Feb. 24, 1905, Sheldon, N. D. D. Feb. 15, 1955, Kansas City, Mo.

Year	Team	Games	BA	SA	AB	H	2B	3B	HR	HR%	R	RBI	BB	SO	SB	Pinch Hit AB	Pinch Hit H	PO	A	E	DP	TC/G	FA	G by Pos
1930	CHI N	37	.222	.389	18	4	1	1	0	0.0	0	2	0	1	0	0	0	6	22	1	1	0.8	.966	P-37
1933		29	.238	.381	21	5	1	1	0	0.0	5	1	1	3	0	0	0	1	20	0	1	0.9	1.000	P-24
1934		2	—	—	0	0	0	0	0	—	0	0	0	0	0	0	0	0	0	0	0	0.0	.000	P-2
1937	PHI A	74	.354	.549	113	40	6	2	4	3.5	18	29	6	13	1	**38**	**9**	19	15	0	0	0.9	1.000	P-30, OF-6
1938		67	.277	.277	112	31	0	0	0	0.0	12	15	7	12	0	32	6	4	36	2	0	1.3	.952	P-32
1939		40	.188	.212	80	15	2	0	0	0.0	3	5	2	13	0	5	1	11	27	2	6	1.1	.950	P-35
1940	DET A	19	.348	.478	23	8	0	0	1	4.3	4	3	0	6	0	14	5	0	3	0	0	0.5	1.000	P-6
7 yrs.		268	.281	.371	367	103	10	4	5	1.4	42	55	16	48	1	89	21	41	123	5	8	1.0	.970	P-166, OF-6

Ray Nelson

NELSON, RAYMOND (Kell) BR TR 5′ 9″ 150 lbs.
Born Raymond Nelson Kellogg.
B. Aug. 4, 1875, Holyoke, Mass. D. Jan. 8, 1961, Mount Vernon, N. Y.

Year	Team	Games	BA	SA	AB	H	2B	3B	HR	HR%	R	RBI	BB	SO	SB	Pinch Hit AB	Pinch Hit H	PO	A	E	DP	TC/G	FA	G by Pos
1901	NY N	39	.200	.215	130	26	2	0	0	0.0	12	7	10		3	0	0	44	125	22	10	4.9	.885	2B-39

Ricky Nelson

NELSON, RICKY LEE BL TR 6′ 200 lbs.
B. May 8, 1959, Eloy, Ariz.

Year	Team	Games	BA	SA	AB	H	2B	3B	HR	HR%	R	RBI	BB	SO	SB	Pinch Hit AB	Pinch Hit H	PO	A	E	DP	TC/G	FA	G by Pos
1983	SEA A	98	.254	.371	291	74	13	3	5	1.7	32	36	17	50	7	12	5	122	10	4	1	1.5	.971	OF-91, DH-1
1984		9	.200	.400	15	3	0	0	1	6.7	2	2	2	4	0	5	1	2	0	0	0	0.4	1.000	DH-3, OF-2
1985		6	.000	.000	2	0	0	0	0	0.0	2	0	0	1	0	1	0	1	0	0	0	0.3	1.000	OF-3
1986		10	.167	.167	12	2	0	0	0	0.0	2	1	0	4	1	4	1	2	0	1	0	0.6	.667	DH-4, OF-1
4 yrs.		123	.247	.363	320	79	13	3	6	1.9	38	39	19	59	8	22	7	127	10	5	1	1.4	.965	OF-97, DH-8

Rob Nelson

NELSON, ROBERT AUGUSTUS BL TL 6′ 4″ 215 lbs.
B. May 17, 1964, Pasadena, Calif.

Year	Team	Games	BA	SA	AB	H	2B	3B	HR	HR%	R	RBI	BB	SO	SB	Pinch Hit AB	Pinch Hit H	PO	A	E	DP	TC/G	FA	G by Pos
1986	OAK A	5	.222	.333	9	2	1	0	0	0.0	1	0	1	4	0	2	1	3	1	1	1	1.7	.800	1B-2, DH-1
1987	2 teams	OAK A (7G –.167) SD N (10G –.091)																						
"	total	17	.143	.171	35	5	1	0	0	0.0	1	1	1	20	0	7	1	63	11	2	7	8.4	.974	1B-9
1988	SD N	7	.190	.333	21	4	0	0	1	4.8	4	3	2	9	0	2	0	48	5	1	5	10.8	.981	1B-5
1989		42	.195	.329	82	16	0	1	3	3.7	6	7	20	29	1	11	1	201	23	2	17	7.3	.991	1B-31
1990		5	.000	.000	5	0	0	0	0	0.0	0	0	0	4	0	5	0	0	0	0	0	0.0	—	
5 yrs.		76	.178	.283	152	27	2	1	4	2.6	12	11	24	66	1	27	3	315	40	6	30	7.5	.983	1B-47, DH-1

Rocky Nelson

NELSON, GLENN RICHARD BL TL 5′10½″ 175 lbs.
B. Nov. 18, 1924, Portsmouth, Ohio.

Year	Team	Games	BA	SA	AB	H	2B	3B	HR	HR%	R	RBI	BB	SO	SB	Pinch Hit AB	Pinch Hit H	PO	A	E	DP	TC/G	FA	G by Pos
1949	STL N	82	.221	.336	244	54	8	4	4	1.6	28	32	11	12	1	8	2	564	24	0	48	8.4	1.000	1B-70
1950		76	.247	.336	235	58	10	4	1	0.4	27	20	26	9	4	4	1	596	51	5	66	9.3	.992	1B-70
1951	3 teams	STL N (9G –.222) PIT N (71G –.267) CHI A (6G –.000)																						
"	total	86	.257	.344	218	56	8	4	1	0.5	32	15	12	7	0	31	6	326	26	3	37	7.2	.992	1B-36, OF-13
1952	BKN N	37	.256	.282	39	10	1	0	0	0.0	6	3	7	4	0	27	7	16	0	0	2	3.2	1.000	1B-5
1954	CLE A	4	.000	.000	4	0	0	0	0	0.0	0	0	0	1	0	3	0	6	0	0	1	3.0	1.000	1B-2
1956	2 teams	BKN N (31G –.208) STL N (38G –.232)																						
"	total	69	.217	.401	152	33	7	0	7	4.6	13	23	10	16	0	26	3	254	27	2	26	6.0	.993	1B-39, OF-8
1959	PIT N	98	.291	.457	175	51	11	0	6	3.4	31	32	23	19	0	33	13	339	18	3	45	6.2	.992	1B-56, OF-2
1960		93	.300	.470	200	60	11	1	7	3.5	34	35	24	15	1	18	4	463	37	2	48	6.9	.996	1B-73
1961		75	.197	.370	127	25	5	1	5	3.9	15	13	17	11	0	37	5	231	15	1	26	7.1	.996	1B-35
9 yrs.		620	.249	.379	1394	347	61	14	31	2.2	186	173	130	94	6	187	41	2795	198	16	299	7.4	.995	1B-386, OF-23
WORLD SERIES																								
1952	BKN N	4	.000	.000	3	0	0	0	0	0.0	0	0	1	2	0	3	0	0	0	0	0	0.0	—	
1960	PIT N	4	.333	.667	9	3	0	0	1	11.1	2	2	1	1	0	1	0	13	3	0	0	5.3	1.000	1B-3
2 yrs.		8	.250	.500	12	3	0	0	1	8.3	2	2	2	3	0	4	0	13	3	0	0	5.3	1.000	1B-3

Tom Nelson

NELSON, TOM COUSINEAU BR TR 6′ 180 lbs.
B. May 1, 1917, Chicago, Ill. D. Sept. 24, 1973, San Diego, Calif.

Year	Team	Games	BA	SA	AB	H	2B	3B	HR	HR%	R	RBI	BB	SO	SB	Pinch Hit AB	Pinch Hit H	PO	A	E	DP	TC/G	FA	G by Pos
1945	BOS N	40	.165	.182	121	20	2	0	0	0.0	6	6	4	13	1	8	1	39	64	11	9	3.6	.904	3B-20, 2B-12

Dick Nen

NEN, RICHARD LeROY BL TL 6′ 2″ 200 lbs.
Father of Robb Nen.
B. Sept. 24, 1939, South Gate, Calif.

Year	Team	Games	BA	SA	AB	H	2B	3B	HR	HR%	R	RBI	BB	SO	SB	Pinch Hit AB	Pinch Hit H	PO	A	E	DP	TC/G	FA	G by Pos
1963	LA N	7	.125	.500	8	1	0	0	1	12.5	2	1	3	3	0	4	0	22	0	0	0	4.4	1.000	1B-5
1965	WAS A	69	.260	.370	246	64	7	1	6	2.4	18	31	19	47	1	5	1	519	61	4	48	9.0	.993	1B-65
1966		94	.213	.323	235	50	8	0	6	2.6	20	30	28	46	0	20	3	566	38	6	44	8.0	.990	1B-76

Dick Nen *continued*

Year	Team	Games	BA	SA	AB	H	2B	3B	HR	HR%	R	RBI	BB	SO	SB	Pinch Hit AB	Pinch Hit H	PO	A	E	DP	TC/G	FA	G by Pos
1967		110	.218	.332	238	52	7	1	6	2.5	21	29	21	39	0	40	6	516	42	3	49	8.5	.995	1B-65, OF-1
1968	**CHI N**	81	.181	.277	94	17	1	1	2	2.1	8	16	6	17	0	28	4	219	11	3	12	4.5	.987	1B-52
1970	**WAS A**	6	.200	.200	5	1	0	0	0	0.0	1	0	0	0	0	5	1	4	1	0	0	5.0	1.000	1B-1
6 yrs.		367	.224	.335	826	185	23	3	21	2.5	70	107	77	152	1	102	15	1846	153	16	153	7.6	.992	1B-264, OF-1

Jack Ness

NESS, JOHN CHARLES BR TR 6′ 2″ 165 lbs.
B. Nov. 11, 1885, Chicago, Ill. D. Dec. 3, 1957, DeLand, Fla.

Year	Team	Games	BA	SA	AB	H	2B	3B	HR	HR%	R	RBI	BB	SO	SB	Pinch Hit AB	Pinch Hit H	PO	A	E	DP	TC/G	FA	G by Pos
1911	**DET A**	12	.154	.154	39	6	0	0	0	0.0	6	2	2		0	0	0	119	9	3	4	10.9	.977	1B-12
1916	**CHI A**	75	.267	.345	258	69	7	5	1	0.4	32	34	9	32	4	6	3	655	31	15	45	10.2	.979	1B-69
2 yrs.		87	.253	.320	297	75	7	5	1	0.3	38	36	11	32	4	6	3	774	40	18	49	10.3	.978	1B-81

Graig Nettles

NETTLES, GRAIG BL TR 6′ 180 lbs.
Brother of Jim Nettles.
B. Aug. 20, 1944, San Diego, Calif.

Year	Team	Games	BA	SA	AB	H	2B	3B	HR	HR%	R	RBI	BB	SO	SB	Pinch Hit AB	Pinch Hit H	PO	A	E	DP	TC/G	FA	G by Pos
1967	**MIN A**	3	.333	.667	3	1	1	0	0	0.0	0	0	0	0	0	3	1	0	0	0	0	0.0	—	
1968		22	.224	.474	76	17	2	1	5	6.6	13	8	7	20	0	0	0	50	9	2	2	2.5	.967	OF-16, 3B-5, 1B-3
1969		96	.222	.373	225	50	9	2	7	3.1	27	26	32	47	1	28	4	88	44	2	3	1.8	.985	OF-54, 3B-21
1970	**CLE A**	157	.235	.404	549	129	13	1	26	4.7	81	62	81	77	3	5	1	135	358	17	40	3.2	.967	3B-154, OF-3
1971		158	.261	.435	598	156	18	1	28	4.7	78	86	82	56	7	0	0	159	412	16	54	3.7	.973	3B-158
1972		150	.253	.395	557	141	28	0	17	3.1	65	70	57	50	2	0	0	114	358	21	27	3.3	.957	3B-150
1973	**NY A**	160	.234	.386	552	129	18	0	22	4.0	65	81	78	76	0	1	0	117	410	26	39	3.5	.953	3B-157, DH-2
1974		155	.246	.403	566	139	21	1	22	3.9	74	75	59	75	1	1	0	147	377	21	29	3.5	.961	3B-154, SS-1
1975		157	.267	.430	581	155	24	4	21	3.6	71	91	51	88	1	0	0	135	379	19	31	3.4	.964	3B-157
1976		158	.254	.475	583	148	29	2	**32**	**5.5**	88	93	62	94	11	1	0	137	384	19	30	3.4	.965	3B-158, SS-1
1977		158	.255	.496	589	150	23	4	37	6.3	99	107	68	79	2	0	0	132	321	12	31	3.0	.974	3B-156, DH-1
1978		159	.276	.460	587	162	23	2	27	4.6	81	93	59	69	1	0	0	110	326	11	30	2.8	.975	3B-159, SS-2
1979		145	.253	.401	521	132	15	1	20	3.8	71	73	59	53	1	2	0	110	339	16	30	3.2	.966	3B-144
1980		89	.244	.435	324	79	14	0	16	4.9	52	45	42	42	0	3	1	59	182	10	18	2.8	.960	3B-88, SS-1
1981		103	.244	.398	349	85	7	1	15	4.3	46	46	47	49	0	3	1	63	214	8	14	2.8	.972	3B-97, DH-4
1982		122	.232	.402	405	94	11	2	18	4.4	47	55	51	49	1	10	1	73	255	23	23	3.0	.934	3B-113, DH-3
1983		129	.266	.446	462	123	17	3	20	4.3	56	75	51	65	0	6	3	78	273	16	18	2.9	.956	3B-126, DH-1
1984	**SD N**	124	.228	.413	395	90	11	1	20	5.1	56	65	58	55	0	13	3	93	201	20	14	2.6	.936	3B-119
1985		137	.261	.420	440	115	23	1	15	3.4	66	61	72	59	0	9	2	122	229	15	16	2.8	.959	3B-130
1986		126	.218	.379	354	77	9	0	16	4.5	36	55	41	62	0	19	5	83	174	16	14	2.4	.941	3B-114
1987	**ATL N**	112	.209	.350	177	37	8	1	5	2.8	16	33	22	25	1	**72**	13	61	56	3	13	2.6	.975	3B-40, 1B-6
1988	**MON N**	80	.172	.247	93	16	4	0	1	1.1	5	14	9	19	0	54	13	32	14	5	4	3.0	.902	3B-12, 1B-5
22 yrs.		2700	.248	.421	8986	2225	328	28	390	4.3	1193	1314	1088	1209	32	230	48	2098	5315	298	480	3.1	.961	3B-2412, OF-73, 1B-14, DH-11, SS-5
DIVISIONAL PLAYOFF SERIES																								
1981	**NY A**	5	.059	.059	17	1	0	0	0	0.0	1	1	3	1	0	0	0	7	7	0	0	2.8	1.000	3B-5
LEAGUE CHAMPIONSHIP SERIES																								
1969	**MIN A**	1	1.000	1.000	1	1	0	0	0	0.0	0	0	0	0	0	1	1	0	0	0	0	0.0	—	
1976	**NY A**	5	.235	.647	17	4	1	0	2	11.8	2	4	3	3	0	0	0	5	14	0	0	3.8	1.000	3B-5
1977		5	.150	.150	20	3	0	0	0	0.0	1	1	0	3	0	0	0	2	12	0	2	2.8	1.000	3B-5
1978		4	.333	.667	15	5	0	1	1	6.7	3	2	0	1	0	0	0	6	7	0	2	3.3	1.000	3B-4
1980		2	.167	.667	6	1	0	0	1	16.7	1	1	0	1	0	1	0	0	2	0	0	1.0	1.000	3B-2
1981		3	.500	.917	12	6	2	0	1	8.3	2	9	1	0	0	0	0	4	4	1	2	3.0	.889	3B-3
1984	**SD N**	4	.143	.143	14	2	0	0	0	0.0	1	2	1	1	0	0	0	5	7	0	0	3.0	1.000	3B-4
7 yrs.		24	.259	.494	85	22	3	1	5 **4th**	5.9	10	19 **3rd**	5	9	0	2	1	22	46	1	6	3.0	.986	3B-23
WORLD SERIES																								
1976	**NY A**	4	.250	.250	12	3	0	0	0	0.0	0	2	3	1	0	0	0	8	8	0	2	4.0	1.000	3B-4
1977		6	.190	.238	21	4	1	0	0	0.0	1	2	2	3	0	0	0	2	20	1	0	3.8	.957	3B-6
1978		6	.160	.160	25	4	0	0	0	0.0	2	1	0	6	0	0	0	8	18	0	4	4.3	1.000	3B-6
1981		3	.400	.500	10	4	1	0	0	0.0	1	0	1	1	0	0	0	3	10	1	0	4.7	.929	3B-3
1984	**SD N**	5	.250	.250	12	3	0	0	0	0.0	2	2	5	0	0	0	0	7	12	0	1	3.8	1.000	3B-5
5 yrs.		24	.225	.250	80	18	2	0	0	0.0	6	7	11	11	0	0	0	28	68	2	7	4.1	.980	3B-24

Jim Nettles

NETTLES, JAMES WILLIAM BL TL 6′ 186 lbs.
Brother of Graig Nettles.
B. Mar. 2, 1947, San Diego, Calif.

Year	Team	Games	BA	SA	AB	H	2B	3B	HR	HR%	R	RBI	BB	SO	SB	Pinch Hit AB	Pinch Hit H	PO	A	E	DP	TC/G	FA	G by Pos
1970	**MIN A**	13	.250	.250	20	5	0	0	0	0.0	3	0	1	5	0	1	0	8	0	0	0	0.7	1.000	OF-11
1971		70	.250	.399	168	42	5	1	6	3.6	17	24	19	24	3	8	2	139	3	2	1	2.3	.986	OF-62
1972		102	.204	.294	235	48	5	2	4	1.7	28	15	32	52	4	20	7	157	5	3	1	2.1	.982	OF-78, 1B-1
1974	**DET A**	43	.227	.404	141	32	5	1	6	4.3	20	17	15	26	3	1	1	80	1	0	0	2.0	1.000	OF-41
1979	**KC A**	11	.087	.087	23	2	0	0	0	0.0	0	1	3	2	0	2	0	21	0	0	0	2.3	1.000	OF-8, 1B-1
1981	**OAK A**	1	—	—	0	0	0	0	0	—	0	0	0	0	0	0	0	0	0	0	0	0.0	.000	OF-1
6 yrs.		240	.220	.341	587	129	15	4	16	2.7	68	57	70	109	10	32	10	405	9	5	2	2.1	.988	OF-201, 1B-2

Morris Nettles

NETTLES, MORRIS, JR. BL TL 6′ 1″ 170 lbs.
B. Jan. 26, 1952, Los Angeles, Calif.

Year	Team	Games	BA	SA	AB	H	2B	3B	HR	HR%	R	RBI	BB	SO	SB	Pinch Hit AB	Pinch Hit H	PO	A	E	DP	TC/G	FA	G by Pos
1974	**CAL A**	56	.274	.297	175	48	4	0	0	0.0	27	8	17	38	20	2	1	99	0	1	0	1.9	.990	OF-54
1975		112	.231	.269	294	68	11	0	0	0.0	50	23	26	57	22	6	2	186	4	5	0	2.0	.974	OF-90, DH-9
2 yrs.		168	.247	.279	469	116	15	0	0	0.0	77	31	43	95	42	8	3	285	4	6	0	1.9	.980	OF-144, DH-9

Milo Netzel

NETZEL, MILES A. BL TL
B. May 12, 1886, Eldred, Pa. D. Mar. 18, 1938, Oxnard, Calif.

Year	Team	Games	BA	SA	AB	H	2B	3B	HR	HR%	R	RBI	BB	SO	SB	Pinch Hit AB	Pinch Hit H	PO	A	E	DP	TC/G	FA	G by Pos
1909	**CLE A**	10	.189	.216	37	7	1	0	0	0.0	2	3	3		1	1	1	5	9	4	1	2.0	.778	3B-6, OF-3

Otto Neu

NEU, OTTO ADAM (Ott) BR TR 5′11″ 170 lbs.
B. Sept. 24, 1894, Springfield, Ohio D. Sept. 19, 1932, Kenton, Ohio.

Year	Team	Games	BA	SA	AB	H	2B	3B	HR	HR%	R	RBI	BB	SO	SB	Pinch Hit AB	Pinch Hit H	PO	A	E	DP	TC/G	FA	G by Pos
1917	STL A	1	—	—	0	0	0	0	0	—	0	0	0	0	0	0	0	0	0	0	0	0.0	.000	SS-1

Johnny Neun

NEUN, JOHN HENRY BB TL 5′10½″ 175 lbs.
B. Oct. 28, 1900, Baltimore, Md. D. Mar. 28, 1990, Baltimore, Md.
Manager 1946–48.

Year	Team	Games	BA	SA	AB	H	2B	3B	HR	HR%	R	RBI	BB	SO	SB	Pinch Hit AB	Pinch Hit H	PO	A	E	DP	TC/G	FA	G by Pos
1925	DET A	60	.267	.387	75	20	3	3	0	0.0	15	4	9	12	2	33	8	99	4	1	5	8.0	.990	1B-13
1926		97	.298	.388	242	72	14	4	0	0.0	47	15	27	26	4	**42**	**12**	433	22	3	34	9.3	.993	1B-49
1927		79	.324	.407	204	66	9	4	0	0.0	38	27	35	13	22	17	6	548	30	12	45	11.1	.980	1B-53
1928		36	.213	.259	108	23	3	1	0	0.0	15	5	7	10	2	11	3	180	16	5	16	8.0	.975	1B-25
1930	BOS N	81	.325	.429	212	69	12	2	2	0.9	39	23	21	18	9	23	8	431	31	4	46	8.5	.991	1B-55
1931		79	.221	.288	104	23	1	3	0	0.0	17	11	11	14	2	34	4	159	9	1	15	4.7	.994	1B-36
6 yrs.		432	.289	.376	945	273	42	17	2	0.2	171	85	110	93	41	160	41	1850	112	26	161	8.6	.987	1B-231

Phil Nevin

NEVIN, PHILLIP JOSEPH BR TR 6′2″ 180 lbs.
B. Jan. 19, 1971, Fullerton, Calif.

Year	Team	Games	BA	SA	AB	H	2B	3B	HR	HR%	R	RBI	BB	SO	SB	Pinch Hit AB	Pinch Hit H	PO	A	E	DP	TC/G	FA	G by Pos
1995	2 teams	HOU N (18G –.117) DET A (29G –.219)																						
″	total	47	.179	.256	156	28	4	1	2	1.3	13	13	18	40	1	1	0	60	34	5	3	2.2	.949	OF-27, 3B-17, DH-2

Don Newcombe

NEWCOMBE, DONALD (Newk) BL TR 6′4″ 220 lbs.
B. June 14, 1926, Madison, N. J.

Year	Team	Games	BA	SA	AB	H	2B	3B	HR	HR%	R	RBI	BB	SO	SB	Pinch Hit AB	Pinch Hit H	PO	A	E	DP	TC/G	FA	G by Pos
1949	BKN N	39	.229	.271	96	22	4	0	0	0.0	8	10	5	16	0	1	0	17	40	0	2	1.5	1.000	P-38
1950		40	.247	.330	97	24	3	1	1	1.0	8	8	10	19	0	0	0	19	43	2	3	1.6	.969	P-40
1951		40	.223	.272	103	23	3	1	0	0.0	11	8	8	9	0	0	0	24	45	3	3	1.8	.958	P-40
1954		31	.319	.340	47	15	1	0	0	0.0	6	4	4	6	0	1	0	11	16	2	2	1.0	.931	P-29
1955		57	.359	.632	117	42	9	1	7	6.0	18	23	6	18	1	21	8	15	24	4	5	1.3	.907	P-34
1956		52	.234	.342	111	26	6	0	2	1.8	13	16	12	18	1	12	0	25	39	1	5	1.7	.985	P-38
1957		34	.230	.297	74	17	2	0	1	1.4	8	7	11	11	0	3	0	13	41	2	1	2.0	.964	P-28
1958	2 teams	LA N (11G –.417) CIN N (39G –.350)																						
″	total	50	.361	.417	72	26	1	0	1	1.4	11	9	10	12	0	16	6	11	19	0	2	1.0	1.000	P-31
1959	CIN N	61	.305	.410	105	32	2	0	3	2.9	10	21	17	23	0	21	5	14	31	1	4	1.5	.978	P-30
1960	2 teams	CIN N (24G –.139) CLE A (24G –.300)																						
″	total	48	.196	.232	56	11	2	0	0	0.0	1	2	4	15	0	12	1	10	15	3	0	0.8	.893	P-36
10 yrs.		452	.271	.367	878	238	33	3	15	1.7	94	108	87	147	2	87	20	159	313	18	27	1.4	.963	P-344
WORLD SERIES																								
1949	BKN N	2	.000	.000	4	0	0	0	0	0.0	0	0	0	3	0	0	0	1	1	0	0	1.0	1.000	P-2
1955		1	.000	.000	3	0	0	0	0	0.0	0	0	0	0	0	0	0	0	1	0	0	1.0	1.000	P-1
1956		2	.000	.000	1	0	0	0	0	0.0	0	0	0	0	0	0	0	0	2	0	0	1.0	1.000	P-2
3 yrs.		5	.000	.000	8	0	0	0	0	0.0	0	0	0	3	0	0	0	1	4	0	0	1.0	1.000	P-5

John Newell

NEWELL, JOHN A. BR TL
B. Jan. 14, 1868, Wilmington, Del. D. Jan. 28, 1919, Wilmington, Del.

Year	Team	Games	BA	SA	AB	H	2B	3B	HR	HR%	R	RBI	BB	SO	SB	Pinch Hit AB	Pinch Hit H	PO	A	E	DP	TC/G	FA	G by Pos
1891	PIT N	5	.111	.111	18	2	0	0	0	0.0	1	2	0	0	0	0	0	1	10	2	0	2.6	.846	3B-5

T. E. Newell

NEWELL, T. E.
B. St. Louis, Mo. Deceased.

Year	Team	Games	BA	SA	AB	H	2B	3B	HR	HR%	R	RBI	BB	SO	SB	Pinch Hit AB	Pinch Hit H	PO	A	E	DP	TC/G	FA	G by Pos
1877	STL N	1	.000	.000	3	0	0	0	0	0.0	0	0	0	0		0	0	2	3	1	0	6.0	.833	SS-1

Marc Newfield

NEWFIELD, MARC ALEXANDER BR TR 6′4″ 205 lbs.
B. Oct. 19, 1972, Sacramento, Calif.

Year	Team	Games	BA	SA	AB	H	2B	3B	HR	HR%	R	RBI	BB	SO	SB	Pinch Hit AB	Pinch Hit H	PO	A	E	DP	TC/G	FA	G by Pos
1993	SEA A	22	.227	.318	66	15	3	0	1	1.5	5	7	2	8	0	3	0	0	0	0	0	0.0		DH-15, OF-5
1994		12	.184	.289	38	7	1	0	1	2.6	3	4	2	4	0	2	0	2	0	0	0	0.2	1.000	DH-9, OF-3
1995	2 teams	SEA A (24G –.188) SD N (21G –.309)																						
″	total	45	.236	.393	140	33	8	1	4	2.9	13	21	5	24	0	3	2	68	1	0	0	1.6	1.000	OF-43
3 yrs.		79	.225	.357	244	55	12	1	6	2.5	21	32	9	36	0	8	2	70	1	0	0	0.9	1.000	OF-51, DH-24

Al Newman

NEWMAN, ALBERT DWAYNE BB TR 5′9″ 175 lbs.
B. June 30, 1960, Kansas City, Mo.

Year	Team	Games	BA	SA	AB	H	2B	3B	HR	HR%	R	RBI	BB	SO	SB	Pinch Hit AB	Pinch Hit H	PO	A	E	DP	TC/G	FA	G by Pos
1985	MON N	25	.172	.207	29	5	1	0	0	0.0	7	1	3	4	2	2	0	19	36	0	7	3.2	1.000	2B-15, SS-2
1986		95	.200	.232	185	37	3	0	1	0.5	23	8	21	20	11	14	2	98	161	11	35	3.3	.959	2B-59, SS-22
1987	MIN A	110	.221	.303	307	68	15	5	0	0.0	44	29	34	27	15	6	0	120	225	5	44	2.9	.986	SS-55, 2B-47, 3B-12, DH-5, OF-2
1988		105	.223	.250	260	58	7	0	0	0.0	35	19	29	34	12	3	0	97	155	6	33	2.3	.977	3B-60, SS-28, 2B-23
1989		141	.253	.303	446	113	18	2	0	0.0	62	38	59	46	25	9	2	191	282	16	58	3.1	.967	2B-84, 3B-37, SS-31, OF-4, DH-2
1990		144	.242	.278	388	94	14	0	0	0.0	43	30	33	34	13	12	2	190	304	13	81	3.0	.974	2B-89, SS-48, 3B-28, OF-3
1991		118	.191	.211	246	47	5	0	0	0.0	25	19	23	21	4	21	5	130	184	4	39	2.4	.987	SS-55, 3B-35, 2B-35, DH-3, 1B-1, OF-1
1992	TEX A	116	.220	.240	246	54	5	0	0	0.0	25	12	34	26	9	5	2	149	223	8	47	3.1	.979	2B-72, 3B-28, SS-20, OF-1, DH-1
8 yrs.		854	.226	.266	2107	476	68	7	1	0.0	264	156	236	212	91	72	13	994	1570	63	344	2.9	.976	2B-424, SS-261, 3B-200, DH-11, OF-11, 1B-1
LEAGUE CHAMPIONSHIP SERIES																								
1987	MIN A	1	.000	.000	2	0	0	0	0	0.0	0	0	0	0	0	0	0	0	1	0	0	1.0	1.000	2B-1
1991		2	—	—	0	0	0	0	0	—	0	0	0	0	0	0	0	0	0	0	0	0.0		SS-1, 3B-1
2 yrs.		3	.000	.000	2	0	0	0	0	0.0	0	0	0	0	0	0	0	0	1	0	0	0.3	1.000	3B-1, SS-1, 2B-1
WORLD SERIES																								
1987	MIN A	4	.200	.200	5	1	0	0	0	0.0	0	0	1	1	0	1	0	1	2	0	0	1.0	1.000	2B-3
1991		4	.500	1.500	2	1	0	1	0	0.0	0	1	0	0	0	1	0	0	2	0	1	0.5	1.000	3B-2, SS-1, 2B-1
2 yrs.		8	.286	.571	7	2	0	1	0	0.0	0	1	1	1	0	2	0	1	4	0	1	0.7	1.000	2B-4, 3B-2, SS-1

Year	Team	Games	BA	SA	AB	H	2B	3B	HR	HR%	R	RBI	BB	SO	SB	Pinch Hit AB	Pinch Hit H	PO	A	E	DP	TC/G	FA	G by Pos

Charlie Newman

NEWMAN, CHARLES BR TR 5′11″ 160 lbs.
B. Nov. 5, 1868, Juda, Wis. D. Nov. 23, 1947, San Diego, Calif.

1892	**2 teams**	**NY N** (3G –.333) **CHI N** (16G –.164)																						
″	**total**	19	.192	.192	73	14	0	0	0	0.0	5	3	3	6	5	0	0	20	2	2	1	1.3	.917	OF-19

Jeff Newman

NEWMAN, JEFFREY LYNN BR TR 6′ 2″ 215 lbs.
B. Sept. 11, 1948, Ft. Worth, Tex.
Manager 1986.

1976	**OAK A**	43	.195	.247	77	15	4	0	0	0.0	5	4	4	12	0	0	0	140	18	3	1	3.7	.981	C-43
1977		94	.222	.352	162	36	9	0	4	2.5	17	15	4	24	2	1	0	251	36	9	5	3.1	.970	C-94, P-1
1978		105	.239	.373	268	64	7	1	9	3.4	25	32	18	40	0	24	6	399	41	12	20	4.6	.973	C-61, 1B-36, DH-2
1979		143	.231	.399	516	119	17	2	22	4.3	53	71	27	88	2	9	2	730	95	18	38	6.0	.979	C-81, 1B-46, DH-7, 3B-7
1980		127	.233	.384	438	102	19	1	15	3.4	37	56	25	81	3	12	5	675	54	15	28	5.9	.980	1B-60, C-55, DH-9, 3B-2, 2B-1
1981		68	.231	.329	216	50	12	0	3	1.4	17	15	9	28	0	5	0	367	28	2	14	5.9	.995	C-37, 1B-30
1982		72	.199	.315	251	50	11	0	6	2.4	19	30	14	49	0	1	1	347	28	5	6	5.3	.987	C-67, 1B-3, 3B-1, DH-1
1983	**BOS A**	59	.189	.288	132	25	4	0	3	2.3	11	7	10	31	0	4	1	171	19	2	3	3.4	.990	C-51, DH-6
1984		24	.222	.302	63	14	2	0	1	1.6	5	3	5	16	0	0	0	118	8	1	0	5.3	.992	C-24
9 yrs.		735	.224	.357	2123	475	85	4	63	3.0	189	233	116	369	7	56	15	3198	327	67	115	5.0	.981	C-513, 1B-175, DH-25, 3B-10, 2B-1, P-1
DIVISIONAL PLAYOFF SERIES																								
1981	**OAK A**	1	.000	.000	3	0	0	0	0	0.0	0	0	0	1	0	0	0	4	0	0	0	4.0	1.000	C-1
LEAGUE CHAMPIONSHIP SERIES																								
1981	**OAK A**	2	.000	.000	5	0	0	0	0	0.0	0	0	0	2	0	0	0	9	1	0	0	5.0	1.000	C-2

Pat Newnam

NEWNAM, PATRICK HENRY BL TR 6′ 180 lbs.
B. Dec. 10, 1880, Hempstead, Tex. D. June 20, 1938, San Antonio, Tex.

1910	**STL A**	103	.216	.281	384	83	3	8	2	0.5	45	26	29		16	0	0	1041	56	32	53	11.0	.972	1B-103
1911		20	.194	.258	62	12	4	0	0	0.0	11	5	12		4	0	0	200	14	3	11	10.9	.986	1B-20
2 yrs.		123	.213	.278	446	95	7	8	2	0.4	56	31	41		20	0	0	1241	70	35	64	10.9	.974	1B-123

Skeeter Newsome

NEWSOME, LAMAR ASHBY BR TR 5′ 9″ 155 lbs.
B. Oct. 18, 1910, Phenix City, Ala.

1935	**PHI A**	59	.207	.290	145	30	7	1	1	0.7	18	10	5	9	2	7	0	79	110	9	25	4.7	.955	SS-24, 2B-13, 3B-4, OF-1
1936		127	.225	.265	471	106	15	2	0	0.0	41	46	25	27	13	2	0	274	418	31	87	5.7	.957	SS-123, 2B-2, OF-1, 3B-1
1937		122	.253	.315	438	111	22	1	1	0.2	53	30	37	22	11	0	0	256	408	32	76	5.7	.954	SS-122
1938		17	.271	.354	48	13	4	0	0	0.0	7	7	1	4	1	0	0	24	43	2	7	4.6	.971	SS-15
1939		99	.222	.266	248	55	9	1	0	0.0	22	17	19	12	5	1	0	178	221	21	44	4.4	.950	SS-93, 2B-2
1941	**BOS A**	93	.225	.278	227	51	6	0	2	0.9	28	17	22	11	10	0	0	141	204	13	36	3.9	.964	SS-69, 2B-23
1942		29	.274	.337	95	26	6	0	0	0.0	7	9	9	5	2	0	0	56	67	7	13	4.5	.946	3B-12, 2B-10, SS-7
1943		114	.265	.327	449	119	21	2	1	0.2	48	22	21	21	5	0	0	245	346	21	71	5.4	.966	SS-98, 3B-15
1944		136	.242	.309	472	114	26	3	0	0.0	41	41	33	21	4	0	0	270	447	30	87	5.5	.960	SS-126, 2B-8, 3B-1
1945		125	.290	.370	438	127	30	1	1	0.2	45	48	20	15	6	1	0	276	376	22	78	5.3	.967	2B-82, SS-33, 3B-11
1946	**PHI N**	112	.232	.277	375	87	10	2	1	0.3	35	23	30	23	4	3	0	181	321	24	53	4.7	.954	SS-107, 2B-3, 3B-2
1947		95	.229	.287	310	71	8	2	2	0.6	36	22	24	24	4	1	1	136	252	12	60	4.3	.970	SS-85, 2B-6, 3B-1
12 yrs.		1128	.245	.304	3716	910	164	15	9	0.2	381	292	246	194	67	15	1	2116	3213	224	637	5.0	.960	SS-902, 2B-149, 3B-47, OF-2

Warren Newson

NEWSON, WARREN DALE BL TL 5′ 7″ 190 lbs.
B. July 3, 1964, Newnan, Ga.

1991	**CHI A**	71	.295	.424	132	39	5	0	4	3.0	20	25	28	34	2	22	8	48	3	2	0	1.0	.962	OF-50, DH-3
1992		63	.221	.265	136	30	3	0	1	0.7	19	11	37	38	3	15	3	67	5	0	3	1.3	1.000	OF-50, DH-4
1993		26	.300	.450	40	12	0	0	2	5.0	9	6	9	12	0	11	5	5	0	0	0	0.3	1.000	DH-10, OF-5
1994		63	.255	.363	102	26	5	0	2	2.0	16	7	14	23	1	25	7	45	1	1	1	1.3	.979	OF-34, DH-3
1995	**2 teams**	**CHI A** (51G –.235) **SEA A** (33G –.292)																						
″	**total**	84	.261	.395	157	41	2	2	5	3.2	34	15	39	45	2	26	6	77	2	2	0	1.5	.975	OF-47, DH-7
5 yrs.		307	.261	.369	567	148	15	2	14	2.5	98	64	127	152	8	99	29	242	11	5	4	1.2	.981	OF-186, DH-27
DIVISIONAL PLAYOFF SERIES																								
1995	**SEA A**	1	.000	.000	1	0	0	0	0	0.0	0	0	0	1	0	1	0	0	0	0	0	0.0	—	
LEAGUE CHAMPIONSHIP SERIES																								
1993	**CHI A**	2	.200	.800	5	1	0	0	1	20.0	1	1	0	1	0	1	0	0	0	0	0	0.0	.000	DH-1

Gus Niarhos

NIARHOS, CONSTANTINE GREGORY BR TR 6′ 160 lbs.
B. Dec. 6, 1920, Birmingham, Ala.

1946	**NY A**	37	.225	.300	40	9	1	1	0	0.0	11	2	11	2	1	2	0	76	10	1	1	3.0	.989	C-29
1948		83	.268	.338	228	61	12	2	0	0.0	41	19	52	15	1	0	0	376	33	4	7	5.0	.990	C-82
1949		32	.279	.372	43	12	2	1	0	0.0	7	6	13	8	0	2	1	84	7	0	2	3.0	1.000	C-30
1950	**2 teams**	**NY A** (1G –.000) **CHI A** (41G –.324)																						
″	**total**	42	.324	.362	105	34	4	0	0	0.0	17	16	14	6	0	2	0	167	14	4	2	5.1	.978	C-36
1951	**CHI A**	66	.256	.310	168	43	6	0	1	0.6	27	10	47	9	4	4	2	240	31	4	5	4.7	.985	C-59
1952	**BOS A**	29	.103	.103	58	6	0	0	0	0.0	4	4	12	9	0	3	0	107	12	1	2	4.8	.992	C-25
1953		16	.200	.286	35	7	1	1	0	0.0	6	2	4	4	0	0	0	61	5	1	2	4.2	.985	C-16
1954	**PHI N**	3	.200	.200	5	1	0	0	0	0.0	0	0	0	1	0	0	0	9	1	0	0	3.3	1.000	C-3
1955		7	.111	.111	9	1	0	0	0	0.0	1	0	0	2	0	0	0	13	2	0	0	2.1	1.000	C-7
9 yrs.		315	.252	.308	691	174	26	5	1	0.1	114	59	153	56	6	13	3	1133	115	15	21	4.4	.988	C-287
WORLD SERIES																								
1949	**NY A**	1	—	—	0	0	0	0	0	—	0	0	0	0	0	0	0	0	0	0	0	0.0	.000	C-1

Sam Nichol

NICHOL, SAMUEL ANDERSON BR TR 5′10″ 178 lbs.
B. Apr. 20, 1869, Ireland D. Apr. 19, 1937, Steubenville, Ohio.

1888	**PIT N**	8	.045	.045	22	1	0	0	0	0.0	3	0	2	2	0	0	0	19	1	1	0	2.6	.952	OF-8
1890	**COL AA**	14	.161	.161	56	9	0	0	0	0.0	7		2		3	0	0	23	5	3	2	2.2	.903	OF-14
2 yrs.		22	.128	.128	78	10	0	0	0	0.0	10	0	4	2	3	0	0	42	6	4	2	2.4	.923	OF-22

Don Nicholas

NICHOLAS, DONALD LEIGH BL TR 5′7″ 150 lbs.
B. Oct. 30, 1930, Phoenix, Ariz.

Year	Team	Lg	Games	BA	SA	AB	H	2B	3B	HR	HR%	R	RBI	BB	SO	SB	Pinch Hit AB	Pinch Hit H	PO	A	E	DP	TC/G	FA	G by Pos
1952	CHI	A	3	.000	.000	2	0	0	0	0	0.0	0	0	0	0	0	2	0	0	0	0	0	0.0	.000	OF-3
1954			7	—	—	0	0	0	0	0	—	3	0	1	0	0	0	0	0	0	0	0	0.0	.000	OF-7
2 yrs.			10	.000	.000	2	0	0	0	0	0.0	3	0	1	0	0	2	0	0	0	0	0	0.0		OF-10

Simon Nicholls

NICHOLLS, SIMON BURDETTE BL TR 5′11½″ 165 lbs.
B. July 18, 1882, Germantown, Md. D. Mar. 12, 1911, Baltimore, Md.

Year	Team	Lg	Games	BA	SA	AB	H	2B	3B	HR	HR%	R	RBI	BB	SO	SB	Pinch Hit AB	Pinch Hit H	PO	A	E	DP	TC/G	FA	G by Pos
1903	DET	A	2	.375	.375	8	3	0	0	0	0.0	0	0	0		0	0	0	3	3	4	0	5.0	.600	SS-2
1906	PHI	A	12	.182	.205	44	8	1	0	0	0.0	1	1	3		0	0	0	22	33	2	4	4.8	.965	SS-12
1907			126	.302	.337	460	139	12	2	0	0.0	75	23	24		13	2	0	227	337	48	17	5.0	.922	SS-82, 2B-28, 3B-13
1908			150	.216	.280	550	119	17	3	4	0.7	58	31	35		14	0	0	280	434	63	33	5.2	.919	SS-120, 2B-23, 3B-7
1909			21	.211	.268	71	15	2	1	0	0.0	10	3	3		0	1	0	39	49	9	5	4.8	.907	SS-14, 3B-5, 1B-1
1910	CLE	A	3	—	—	0	0	0	0	0	—	0	0	0		0	0	0	0	0	1	0	0.3	.000	SS-3
6 yrs.			314	.251	.300	1133	284	32	6	4	0.4	144	58	65		27	3	0	571	856	127	59	5.0	.918	SS-233, 2B-51, 3B-25, 1B-1

Al Nichols

NICHOLS, ALBERT H. 5′11″ 180 lbs.
B. Brooklyn, N. Y. Deceased.

Year	Team	Lg	Games	BA	SA	AB	H	2B	3B	HR	HR%	R	RBI	BB	SO	SB	Pinch Hit AB	Pinch Hit H	PO	A	E	DP	TC/G	FA	G by Pos
1876	NY	N	57	.179	.198	212	38	4	0	0	0.0	20	9	2	3		0	0	123	135	73	1	5.8	.779	3B-57
1877	LOU	N	6	.211	.316	19	4	0	1	0	0.0	1	0	0	2		0	0	12	22	5	2	6.5	.872	2B-3, SS-1, 3B-1, 1B-1
2 yrs.			63	.182	.208	231	42	4	1	0	0.0	21	9	2	5		0	0	135	157	78	3	5.9	.789	3B-58, 2B-3, SS-1, 1B-1

Art Nichols

NICHOLS, ARTHUR FRANCIS BR TR 5′10″ 175 lbs.
Born Arthur Francis Meikle.
B. July 14, 1871, Manchester, N. H. D. Aug. 9, 1945, Willimantic, Conn.

Year	Team	Lg	Games	BA	SA	AB	H	2B	3B	HR	HR%	R	RBI	BB	SO	SB	Pinch Hit AB	Pinch Hit H	PO	A	E	DP	TC/G	FA	G by Pos
1898	CHI	N	14	.286	.310	42	12	1	0	0	0.0	7	6	4		6	0	0	47	13	2	1	4.4	.968	C-14
1899			17	.255	.362	47	12	2	0	1	2.1	5	11	0		3	2	0	44	10	4	3	3.9	.931	C-15
1900			8	.200	.200	25	5	0	0	0	0.0	1	0	3		1	1	0	21	9	2	0	4.6	.938	C-7
1901	STL	N	93	.244	.308	308	75	11	3	1	0.3	50	33	10		14	6	1	256	60	13	9	3.8	.960	C-47, OF-40
1902			73	.267	.327	251	67	12	0	1	0.4	36	31	21		18	2	0	615	33	13	28	9.3	.980	1B-56, C-11, OF-4
1903			36	.192	.208	120	23	2	0	0	0.0	13	9	12		9	1	0	294	9	10	12	9.2	.968	1B-25, OF-7, C-2
6 yrs.			241	.245	.299	793	194	28	3	3	0.4	112	90	50		51	12	1	1277	134	44	53	6.4	.970	C-96, 1B-81, OF-51

Carl Nichols

NICHOLS, CARL EDWARD BR TR 6′ 184 lbs.
B. Oct. 14, 1962, Los Angeles, Calif.

Year	Team	Lg	Games	BA	SA	AB	H	2B	3B	HR	HR%	R	RBI	BB	SO	SB	Pinch Hit AB	Pinch Hit H	PO	A	E	DP	TC/G	FA	G by Pos
1986	BAL	A	5	.000	.000	5	0	0	0	0	0.0	0	0	1	4	0	0	0	11	0	0	0	2.2	1.000	C-5
1987			13	.381	.429	21	8	1	0	0	0.0	4	3	1	4	0	0	0	39	3	0	1	3.2	1.000	C-13
1988			18	.191	.213	47	9	1	0	0	0.0	2	1	3	10	0	1	0	71	13	1	2	5.3	.988	C-13, OF-3
1989	HOU	N	8	.077	.077	13	1	0	0	0	0.0	0	2	0	3	0	4	0	16	1	0	0	2.8	1.000	C-6
1990			32	.204	.265	49	10	3	0	0	0.0	7	11	8	11	0	11	3	86	10	3	4	5.2	.970	C-15, 1B-3, OF-1
1991			20	.196	.255	51	10	3	0	0	0.0	3	1	5	17	0	4	0	86	14	3	2	6.1	.971	C-17
6 yrs.			96	.204	.247	186	38	8	0	0	0.0	16	18	18	49	0	20	3	309	41	7	9	4.7	.980	C-69, OF-4, 1B-3

Kid Nichols

NICHOLS, CHARLES AUGUSTUS (Nick) BB TR 5′10½″ 175 lbs.
B. Sept. 14, 1869, Madison, Wis. D. Apr. 11, 1953, Kansas City, Mo.
Manager 1904–05.
Hall of Fame 1949.

Year	Team	Lg	Games	BA	SA	AB	H	2B	3B	HR	HR%	R	RBI	BB	SO	SB	Pinch Hit AB	Pinch Hit H	PO	A	E	DP	TC/G	FA	G by Pos
1890	BOS	N	49	.247	.287	174	43	5	1	0	0.0	18	23	11	36	2	0	0	15	85	14	1	2.3	.877	P-48, OF-2
1891			52	.197	.230	183	36	6	0	0	0.0	21	27	12	31	1	0	0	30	100	7	5	2.6	.949	P-52
1892			57	.198	.279	197	39	6	2	2	1.0	21	21	16	51	3	0	0	36	88	5	4	2.2	.961	P-53, OF-5
1893			53	.220	.294	177	39	3	2	2	1.1	25	26	15	22	4	0	0	22	81	7	5	2.1	.936	P-52, OF-1
1894			51	.294	.382	170	50	11	2	0	0.0	39	34	16	24	1	0	0	35	67	7	3	2.1	.936	P-50, OF-1
1895			49	.236	.280	157	37	3	2	0	0.0	23	18	14	28	0	0	0	29	73	4	2	2.2	.962	P-48, OF-1
1896			51	.190	.272	147	28	3	3	1	0.7	27	24	12	18	2	0	0	23	92	1	3	2.3	.991	P-49, OF-2
1897			46	.265	.361	147	39	5	0	3	2.0	20	28	7		4	0	0	29	62	3	1	2.0	.968	P-46
1898			51	.241	.335	158	38	3	3	2	1.3	26	23	4		0	0	0	28	78	5	1	2.2	.955	P-50, 1B-1
1899			42	.191	.235	136	26	3	0	1	0.7	13	12	6		1	0	0	25	71	5	5	2.4	.950	P-42
1900			29	.200	.233	90	18	0	0	1	1.1	14	7	7		1	0	0	19	48	1	1	2.3	.985	P-29
1901			55	.282	.491	163	46	8	7	4	2.5	16	28	8		0	4	2	73	72	10	4	3.1	.935	P-38, OF-7, 1B-5
1904	STL	N	36	.156	.202	109	17	1	2	0	0.0	7	5	7		0	0	0	13	84	5	1	2.8	.951	P-36
1905	2 teams		STL N (8G –.227) PHI N (17G –.189)																						
″	total		25	.200	.213	75	15	1	0	0	0.0	3	2	2		0	0	0	5	32	5	1	1.7	.881	P-24, OF-1
1906	PHI	N	4	.000	.000	3	0	0	0	0	0.0	0	0	0		0	0	0	0	1	0	0	0.3	1.000	P-4
15 yrs.			650	.226	.300	2086	471	58	24	16	0.8	273	278	137	210	19	4	2	382	1034	79	37	2.3	.947	P-621, OF-20, 1B-6

Reid Nichols

NICHOLS, THOMAS REID BR TR 5′11″ 165 lbs.
B. Aug. 5, 1958, Ocala, Fla.

Year	Team	Lg	Games	BA	SA	AB	H	2B	3B	HR	HR%	R	RBI	BB	SO	SB	Pinch Hit AB	Pinch Hit H	PO	A	E	DP	TC/G	FA	G by Pos
1980	BOS	A	12	.222	.278	36	8	0	1	0	0.0	5	3	3	8	0	0	0	24	1	1	0	2.6	.962	OF-9, DH-1
1981			39	.188	.229	48	9	0	1	0	0.0	13	3	2	6	0	1	0	35	4	0	1	1.1	1.000	OF-27, DH-7, 3B-1
1982			92	.302	.461	245	74	16	1	7	2.9	35	33	14	28	5	6	0	169	9	2	4	2.1	.989	OF-82, DH-4
1983			100	.285	.438	274	78	22	1	6	2.2	35	22	26	36	7	19	6	168	5	1	1	1.9	.994	OF-72, DH-18, SS-1
1984			73	.226	.306	124	28	5	1	1	0.8	14	14	12	18	2	20	5	79	3	1	0	1.7	.988	OF-48, DH-1
1985	2 teams		BOS A (21G –.188) CHI A (51G –.297)																						
″	total		72	.273	.380	150	41	8	1	2	1.3	23	18	17	17	6	17	5	85	2	1	1	1.3	.989	OF-58, DH-5, 2B-3
1986	CHI	A	74	.228	.301	136	31	4	0	2	1.5	9	18	11	23	5	16	6	90	4	1	0	1.6	.989	OF-53, DH-3, 2B-2
1987	MON	N	77	.265	.429	147	39	8	2	4	2.7	22	20	14	13	2	16	3	98	5	2	0	1.7	.981	OF-59, 3B-3
8 yrs.			539	.266	.391	1160	308	63	8	22	1.9	156	131	99	149	27	95	25	748	33	9	7	1.7	.989	OF-408, DH-39, 2B-5, 3B-4, SS-1

Roy Nichols

NICHOLS, ROY BR TR 5′11″ 155 lbs.
B. Mar. 3, 1921, Little Rock, Ark.

Year	Team	Lg	Games	BA	SA	AB	H	2B	3B	HR	HR%	R	RBI	BB	SO	SB	Pinch Hit AB	Pinch Hit H	PO	A	E	DP	TC/G	FA	G by Pos
1944	NY	N	11	.222	.333	9	2	1	0	0	0.0	3	0	2	2	0	1	0	3	4	0	0	3.5	1.000	3B-1, 2B-1

Tricky Nichols

NICHOLS, FREDERICK C. BR TR 5′ 7½″ 150 lbs.
B. July 26, 1850, Bridgeport, Conn. D. Aug. 22, 1897, Bridgeport, Conn.

Year	Team		Games	BA	SA	AB	H	2B	3B	HR	HR%	R	RBI	BB	SO	SB	Pinch Hit AB	Pinch Hit H	PO	A	E	DP	TC/G	FA	G by Pos
1876	**BOS**	**N**	1	.000	.000	4	0	0	0	0	0.0	0	0	0	0		0	0	0	2	0	0	2.0	1.000	P-1
1877	**STL**	**N**	51	.167	.210	186	31	4	2	0	0.0	22	9	3	15		0	0	32	62	8	1	1.8	.922	P-42, OF-16
1878	**PRO**	**N**	11	.184	.224	49	9	2	0	0	0.0	2	2	2	10		0	0	6	27	1	2	3.1	.971	P-11
1880	**WOR**	**N**	2	.000	.000	7	0	0	0	0	0.0	0	0	0	0		0	0	0	3	3	0	3.0	.500	P-2
1882	**BAL**	**AA**	26	.158	.168	95	15	1	0	0	0.0	4		7			0	0	26	36	13	0	2.5	.827	P-16, OF-14
5 yrs.			91	.161	.194	341	55	7	2	0	0.0	28	11	12	25		0	0	64	130	25	3	2.1	.886	P-72, OF-30

Bill Nicholson

NICHOLSON, WILLIAM BECK (Swish) BL TR 6′ 205 lbs.
B. Dec. 11, 1914, Chestertown, Md.

Year	Team		Games	BA	SA	AB	H	2B	3B	HR	HR%	R	RBI	BB	SO	SB	Pinch Hit AB	Pinch Hit H	PO	A	E	DP	TC/G	FA	G by Pos
1936	**PHI**	**A**	11	.000	.000	12	0	0	0	0	0.0	2	0	0	5	0	10	0	1	0	0	0	1.0	1.000	OF-1
1939	**CHI**	**N**	58	.295	.464	220	65	12	5	5	2.3	37	38	20	29	0	0	0	123	5	6	0	2.3	.955	OF-58
1940			135	.297	.534	491	146	27	7	25	5.1	78	98	50	67	2	9	2	235	10	13	2	2.1	.950	OF-123
1941			147	.254	.453	532	135	26	1	26	4.9	74	98	82	91	1	4	0	293	10	9	2	2.2	.971	OF-143
1942			152	.294	.476	588	173	22	11	21	3.6	83	78	76	80	8	1	0	327	18	5	2	2.3	.986	OF-151
1943			154	.309	.531	608	188	30	9	**29**	**4.8**	95	**128**	71	78	4	0	0	340	16	8	2	2.4	.978	OF-154
1944			156	.287	.545	582	167	35	8	**33**	5.7	**116**	**122**	93	71	3	0	0	305	18	7	4	2.1	.979	OF-156
1945			151	.243	.377	559	136	28	4	13	2.3	82	88	92	73	4	0	0	300	12	3	4	2.1	.990	OF-151
1946			105	.220	.358	296	65	13	2	8	2.7	36	41	44	44	1	18	6	179	4	5	1	2.3	.973	OF-80
1947			148	.244	.466	487	119	28	1	26	5.3	69	75	87	**83**	1	7	0	281	7	3	1	2.1	.990	OF-140
1948			143	.261	.445	494	129	24	5	19	3.8	68	67	81	60	2	4	3	244	7	5	1	1.9	.980	OF-136
1949	**PHI**	**N**	98	.234	.391	299	70	8	3	11	3.7	42	40	45	53	1	7	0	185	10	1	0	2.2	.995	OF-91
1950			41	.224	.448	58	13	2	1	3	5.2	3	10	8	16	0	24	5	20	0	1	0	1.4	.952	OF-15
1951			85	.241	.459	170	41	9	2	8	4.7	23	30	25	24	0	36	11	75	1	1	0	1.9	.987	OF-41
1952			55	.273	.511	88	24	3	0	6	6.8	17	19	14	26	0	31	8	33	0	0	0	1.7	1.000	OF-19
1953			38	.210	.419	62	13	5	1	2	3.2	12	16	12	20	0	23	2	13	0	0	0	1.1	1.000	OF-12
16 yrs.			1677	.268	.465	5546	1484	272	60	235	4.2	837	948	800	820	27	174	37	2954	118	67	20	2.1	.979	OF-1471
WORLD SERIES																									
1945	**CHI**	**N**	7	.214	.321	28	6	1	1	0	0.0	1	8	2	5	0	0	0	9	0	1	0	1.4	.900	OF-7

Dave Nicholson

NICHOLSON, DAVID LAWRENCE BR TR 6′ 2″ 215 lbs.
B. Aug. 29, 1939, St. Louis, Mo.

Year	Team		Games	BA	SA	AB	H	2B	3B	HR	HR%	R	RBI	BB	SO	SB	Pinch Hit AB	Pinch Hit H	PO	A	E	DP	TC/G	FA	G by Pos
1960	**BAL**	**A**	54	.186	.345	113	21	1	1	5	4.4	17	11	20	55	0	9	0	51	3	1	1	1.3	.982	OF-44
1962			97	.173	.364	173	30	4	1	9	5.2	25	15	27	76	3	4	0	111	4	2	0	1.5	.983	OF-80
1963	**CHI**	**A**	126	.229	.419	449	103	11	4	22	4.9	53	70	63	**175**	2	3	1	213	10	7	1	1.9	.970	OF-123
1964			97	.204	.364	294	60	6	1	13	4.4	40	39	52	126	0	7	1	136	4	4	0	1.6	.972	OF-92
1965			54	.153	.271	85	13	2	1	2	2.4	11	12	9	40	0	12	0	30	0	0	0	0.8	1.000	OF-36
1966	**HOU**	**N**	100	.246	.411	280	69	8	4	10	3.6	36	31	46	92	1	16	2	139	11	5	0	1.7	.968	OF-90
1967	**ATL**	**N**	10	.200	.200	25	5	0	0	0	0.0	2	1	2	9	0	1	0	10	1	0	0	1.6	1.000	OF-7
7 yrs.			538	.212	.381	1419	301	32	12	61	4.3	184	179	219	573	6	52	4	690	33	19	2	1.6	.974	OF-472

Fred Nicholson

NICHOLSON, FRED BR TR 5′10½″ 173 lbs.
B. Sept. 1, 1894, Honey Grove, Tex. D. Jan. 23, 1972, Kilgore, Tex.

Year	Team		Games	BA	SA	AB	H	2B	3B	HR	HR%	R	RBI	BB	SO	SB	Pinch Hit AB	Pinch Hit H	PO	A	E	DP	TC/G	FA	G by Pos
1917	**DET**	**A**	13	.286	.357	14	4	1	0	0	0.0	4	1	1	2	0	4	1	3	0	0	0	1.0	1.000	OF-3
1919	**PIT**	**N**	30	.273	.409	66	18	2	2	1	1.5	8	6	6	11	2	11	2	43	3	2	2	2.7	.958	OF-17, 1B-1
1920			99	.360	.530	247	89	16	7	4	1.6	33	30	18	31	9	**38**	**12**	125	9	6	2	2.4	.957	OF-58
1921	**BOS**	**N**	83	.327	.490	245	80	11	7	5	2.0	36	41	17	29	5	15	3	138	11	6	4	2.4	.961	OF-59, 1B-4, 2B-2
1922			78	.252	.342	222	56	4	5	2	0.9	31	29	23	24	5	12	3	125	5	12	0	2.3	.915	OF-63
5 yrs.			303	.311	.452	794	247	34	21	12	1.5	112	107	65	97	21	80	21	434	28	26	8	2.4	.947	OF-200, 1B-5, 2B-2

Ovid Nicholson

NICHOLSON, OVID EDWARD BL TR 5′ 9½″ 155 lbs.
B. Dec. 30, 1888, Salem, Ind. D. Mar. 24, 1968, Salem, Ind.

Year	Team		Games	BA	SA	AB	H	2B	3B	HR	HR%	R	RBI	BB	SO	SB	Pinch Hit AB	Pinch Hit H	PO	A	E	DP	TC/G	FA	G by Pos
1912	**PIT**	**N**	6	.455	.455	11	5	0	0	0	0.0	2	3	1	2	0	0	0	8	0	0	0	2.0	1.000	OF-4

Parson Nicholson

NICHOLSON, THOMAS C. (Beacon) 6′ 6″ 190 lbs.
B. Apr. 14, 1863, Blaine, Ohio D. Feb. 28, 1917, Bellaire, Ohio.

Year	Team		Games	BA	SA	AB	H	2B	3B	HR	HR%	R	RBI	BB	SO	SB	Pinch Hit AB	Pinch Hit H	PO	A	E	DP	TC/G	FA	G by Pos
1888	**DET**	**N**	24	.259	.388	85	22	2	3	1	1.2	11	9	2	7	6	0	0	44	71	8	5	5.1	.935	2B-24
1890	**TOL**	**AA**	134	.268	.363	523	140	16	11	4	0.8	78		42		46	0	0	294	385	52	45	5.4	.929	2B-134, C-1
1895	**WAS**	**N**	10	.184	.289	38	7	2	1	0	0.0	7	5	7	4	6	0	0	17	34	13	4	6.4	.797	SS-10
3 yrs.			168	.262	.362	646	169	20	15	5	0.8	96	14	51	11	58	0	0	355	490	73	54	5.4	.920	2B-158, SS-10, C-1

George Nicol

NICOL, GEORGE EDWARD TL 5′ 7″ 155 lbs.
B. Oct. 17, 1870, Barry, Ill. D. Aug. 10, 1924, Milwaukee, Wis.

Year	Team		Games	BA	SA	AB	H	2B	3B	HR	HR%	R	RBI	BB	SO	SB	Pinch Hit AB	Pinch Hit H	PO	A	E	DP	TC/G	FA	G by Pos
1890	**STL**	**AA**	3	.286	.429	7	2	1	0	0	0.0	4		4		0	0	0	2	0	0	0	0.7	1.000	P-3
1891	**CHI**	**N**	3	.333	.667	6	2	0	1	0	0.0	0	3	0	1	0	0	0	0	0	3	0	1.0	.000	P-3
1894	**2 teams**		**PIT N** (8G –.450) **LOU N** (27G –.352)																						
″	**total**		35	.367	.484	128	47	7	4	0	0.0	20	22	2	4	4	0	0	32	9	10	1	1.5	.804	OF-26, P-9
3 yrs.			41	.362	.489	141	51	8	5	0	0.0	24	25	6	5	4	0	0	34	9	13	1	1.4	.768	OF-26, P-15

Hugh Nicol

NICOL, HUGH N. BR TR 5′ 4″ 145 lbs.
B. Jan. 1, 1858, Campsie, Scotland D. June 27, 1921, Lafayette, Ind.
Manager 1897.

Year	Team		Games	BA	SA	AB	H	2B	3B	HR	HR%	R	RBI	BB	SO	SB	Pinch Hit AB	Pinch Hit H	PO	A	E	DP	TC/G	FA	G by Pos
1881	**CHI**	**N**	26	.204	.222	108	22	2	0	0	0.0	13	7	4	12		0	0	45	12	5	1	2.3	.919	OF-26, SS-1
1882			47	.199	.274	186	37	9	1	1	0.5	19	16	7	29		0	0	62	35	15	2	2.0	.866	OF-47, SS-8
1883	**STL**	**AA**	94	.288	.340	368	106	13	3	0	0.0	73		18			0	0	162	63	27	7	2.7	.893	OF-84, 2B-11
1884			110	.260	.314	442	115	14	5	0	0.0	79		22			0	0	205	123	45	15	3.3	.879	OF-87, 2B-23, SS-1, 3B-1
1885			112	.207	.238	425	88	11	1	0	0.0	59		34			0	0	214	35	31	2	2.5	.889	OF-111, 3B-1
1886			67	.206	.253	253	52	6	3	0	0.0	44		26			0	0	103	40	19	2	2.3	.883	OF-57, SS-8, 2B-4
1887	**CIN**	**AA**	125	.215	.267	475	102	18	2	1	0.2	122		86		**138**	0	0	194	20	19	1	1.9	.918	OF-125
1888			135	.239	.270	548	131	10	2	1	0.2	112	35	67		103	0	0	217	43	12	9	2.0	.956	OF-125, 2B-12, SS-1
1889			122	.255	.316	474	121	7	8	2	0.4	82	58	54	35	80	0	0	193	39	19	7	2.0	.924	OF-115, 2B-7, 3B-3
1890	**CIN**	**N**	50	.210	.258	186	39	1	4	0	0.0	28	19	19	12	24	0	0	66	15	13	3	1.9	.862	OF-46, SS-3, 2B-1
10 yrs.			888	.235	.282	3465	813	91	29	5	0.1	631	135	337	88	345	0	0	1461	425	205	49	2.3	.902	OF-823, 2B-58, SS-22, 3B-5

Steve Nicosia

NICOSIA, STEVEN RICHARD BR TR 5′10″ 185 lbs.
B. Aug. 6, 1955, Paterson, N. J.

Year	Team	Games	BA	SA	AB	H	2B	3B	HR	HR%	R	RBI	BB	SO	SB	Pinch Hit AB	Pinch Hit H	PO	A	E	DP	TC/G	FA	G by Pos
1978	PIT N	3	.000	.000	5	0	0	0	0	0.0	0	0	1	0	0	1	0	8	1	0	0	9.0	1.000	C-1
1979		70	.288	.435	191	55	16	0	4	2.1	22	13	23	17	0	6	0	320	25	3	4	5.4	.991	C-65
1980		60	.216	.278	176	38	8	0	1	0.6	16	22	19	16	0	2	0	284	25	5	4	5.4	.984	C-58
1981		54	.231	.337	169	39	10	1	2	1.2	21	18	13	10	3	2	0	257	23	5	2	5.5	.982	C-52
1982		39	.280	.340	100	28	3	0	1	1.0	6	7	11	13	0	2	1	183	22	2	1	5.4	.990	C-35, OF-3
1983	2 teams	PIT N (21G –.130) SF N (15G –.333)																						
″	total	36	.215	.278	79	17	2	0	1	1.3	8	7	4	9	0	9	3	131	9	2	0	5.9	.986	C-24
1984	SF N	48	.303	.462	132	40	11	2	2	1.5	9	19	8	14	1	10	4	190	11	3	1	5.0	.985	C-41
1985	2 teams	MON N (42G –.169) TOR A (6G –.267)																						
″	total	48	.186	.209	86	16	2	0	0	0.0	4	2	7	11	1	18	2	109	7	1	2	3.8	.991	C-29, 1B-2
8 yrs.		358	.248	.345	938	233	52	3	11	1.2	86	88	86	90	5	50	10	1482	123	21	14	5.2	.987	C-305, OF-3, 1B-2
WORLD SERIES																								
1979	PIT N	4	.063	.063	16	1	0	0	0	0.0	1	0	0	2	0	0	0	23	2	0	0	6.3	1.000	C-4

Charlie Niebergall

NIEBERGALL, CHARLES ARTHUR (Nig) BR TR 5′10″ 160 lbs.
B. May 23, 1899, New York, N. Y. D. Aug. 29, 1982, Holiday, Fla.

Year	Team	Games	BA	SA	AB	H	2B	3B	HR	HR%	R	RBI	BB	SO	SB	Pinch Hit AB	Pinch Hit H	PO	A	E	DP	TC/G	FA	G by Pos
1921	STL N	5	.167	.167	6	1	0	0	0	0.0	1	0	0	0	0	2	1	2	1	0	0	1.0	1.000	C-3
1923		9	.107	.143	28	3	1	0	0	0.0	2	1	2	2	0	1	0	28	5	0	0	4.7	1.000	C-7
1924		40	.293	.397	58	17	6	0	0	0.0	6	7	3	9	0	6	2	57	20	4	1	2.4	.951	C-34
3 yrs.		54	.228	.304	92	21	7	0	0	0.0	9	8	5	11	0	9	3	87	26	4	1	2.7	.966	C-44

Al Niehaus

NIEHAUS, ALBERT BERNARD BR TR 5′11″ 175 lbs.
B. June 1, 1899, Cincinnati, Ohio D. Oct. 14, 1931, Cincinnati, Ohio.

Year	Team	Games	BA	SA	AB	H	2B	3B	HR	HR%	R	RBI	BB	SO	SB	Pinch Hit AB	Pinch Hit H	PO	A	E	DP	TC/G	FA	G by Pos
1925	2 teams	PIT N (17G –.219) CIN N (51G –.299)																						
″	total	68	.275	.379	211	58	18	2	0	0.0	23	21	14	15	1	8	3	544	33	11	50	9.8	.981	1B-60

Bert Niehoff

NIEHOFF, JOHN ALBERT BR TR 5′10½″ 170 lbs.
B. May 13, 1884, Louisville, Colo. D. Dec. 8, 1974, Inglewood, Calif.

Year	Team	Games	BA	SA	AB	H	2B	3B	HR	HR%	R	RBI	BB	SO	SB	Pinch Hit AB	Pinch Hit H	PO	A	E	DP	TC/G	FA	G by Pos
1913	CIN N	2	.000	.000	8	0	0	0	0	0.0	0	0	0	2	0	0	0	2	9	1	0	6.0	.917	3B-2
1914		142	.242	.337	484	117	16	9	4	0.8	46	49	38	77	20	5	2	157	281	35	15	3.5	.926	3B-134, 2B-3
1915	PHI N	148	.238	.308	529	126	27	2	2	0.4	61	49	30	63	21	0	0	307	411	41	55	5.1	.946	2B-148
1916		146	.243	.356	548	133	**42**	4	4	0.7	65	61	37	57	20	0	0	287	441	50	65	5.3	.936	2B-146, 3B-1
1917		114	.255	.341	361	92	17	4	2	0.6	30	42	23	29	8	7	0	219	345	31	42	5.5	.948	2B-96, 1B-7, 3B-6
1918	2 teams	STL N (22G –.179) NY N (7G –.261)																						
″	total	29	.196	.215	107	21	2	0	0	0.0	8	6	3	14	2	0	0	68	78	7	13	5.3	.954	2B-29
6 yrs.		581	.240	.327	2037	489	104	19	12	0.6	210	207	131	242	71	12	2	1040	1565	165	190	4.8	.940	2B-422, 3B-143, 1B-7
WORLD SERIES																								
1915	PHI N	5	.063	.063	16	1	0	0	0	0.0	1	0	1	5	0	0	0	10	10	0	0	4.0	1.000	2B-5

Milt Nielsen

NIELSEN, MILTON ROBERT BL TL 5′11″ 190 lbs.
B. Feb. 8, 1925, Tyler, Minn.

Year	Team	Games	BA	SA	AB	H	2B	3B	HR	HR%	R	RBI	BB	SO	SB	Pinch Hit AB	Pinch Hit H	PO	A	E	DP	TC/G	FA	G by Pos
1949	CLE A	3	.111	.111	9	1	0	0	0	0.0	1	0	2	4	0	0	0	6	0	0	0	2.0	1.000	OF-3
1951		16	.000	.000	6	0	0	0	0	0.0	1	0	1	1	0	6	0	0	0	0	0	0.0	—	
2 yrs.		19	.067	.067	15	1	0	0	0	0.0	2	0	3	5	0	6	0	6	0	0	0	2.0	1.000	OF-3

Bob Nieman

NIEMAN, ROBERT CHARLES BR TR 5′11″ 195 lbs.
B. Jan. 26, 1927, Cincinnati, Ohio D. Mar. 10, 1985, Corona, Calif.

Year	Team	Games	BA	SA	AB	H	2B	3B	HR	HR%	R	RBI	BB	SO	SB	Pinch Hit AB	Pinch Hit H	PO	A	E	DP	TC/G	FA	G by Pos
1951	STL A	12	.372	.628	43	16	3	1	2	4.7	6	8	3	5	0	1	1	24	1	1	0	2.4	.962	OF-11
1952		131	.289	.456	478	138	22	2	18	3.8	66	74	46	73	0	9	1	230	10	6	5	2.0	.976	OF-125
1953	DET A	142	.281	.453	508	143	32	5	15	3.0	72	69	57	57	0	7	1	271	10	6	1	2.1	.979	OF-135
1954		91	.263	.422	251	66	14	1	8	3.2	24	35	22	32	0	26	8	119	2	2	0	2.0	.984	OF-62
1955	CHI A	99	.283	.460	272	77	11	2	11	4.0	36	53	36	37	1	24	7	118	4	3	2	1.6	.976	OF-78
1956	2 teams	CHI A (14G –.300) BAL A (114G –.322)																						
″	total	128	.320	.495	428	137	21	6	14	3.3	63	68	90	63	1	1	1	267	4	5	1	2.2	.982	OF-124
1957	BAL A	129	.276	.429	445	123	17	6	13	2.9	61	70	63	86	4	9	0	237	6	5	0	2.1	.980	OF-120
1958		105	.325	.522	366	119	20	2	16	4.4	56	60	44	57	2	6	1	145	3	6	0	1.5	.961	OF-100
1959		118	.292	.528	360	105	18	2	21	5.8	49	60	42	55	1	17	4	171	6	5	0	1.9	.973	OF-97
1960	STL N	81	.287	.473	188	54	13	5	4	2.1	19	31	24	31	0	26	4	63	0	4	0	1.2	.940	OF-55
1961	2 teams	STL N (6G –.471) CLE A (39G –.354)																						
″	total	45	.378	.537	82	31	7	0	2	2.4	2	12	7	6	1	27	9	25	1	1	0	1.7	.963	OF-16
1962	2 teams	CLE A (2G –.000) SF N (30G –.300)																						
″	total	32	.290	.452	31	9	2	0	1	3.2	1	4	1	10	0	30	8	2	0	0	0	0.7	1.000	OF-3
12 yrs.		1113	.295	.474	3452	1018	180	32	125	3.6	455	544	435	512	10	183	45	1672	47	44	9	1.9	.975	OF-926
WORLD SERIES																								
1962	SF N	1	—	—	0	0	0	0	0	—	0	0	1	0	0	0	0	0	0	0	0	0.0	—	

Butch Nieman

NIEMAN, ELMER LeROY BL TL 6′2″ 195 lbs.
B. Feb. 8, 1918, Herkimer, Kans. D. Nov. 2, 1993, Topeka, Kans.

Year	Team	Games	BA	SA	AB	H	2B	3B	HR	HR%	R	RBI	BB	SO	SB	Pinch Hit AB	Pinch Hit H	PO	A	E	DP	TC/G	FA	G by Pos
1943	BOS N	101	.251	.406	335	84	15	8	7	2.1	39	46	39	39	4	2	0	195	12	8	1	2.3	.963	OF-93
1944		134	.265	.427	468	124	16	6	16	3.4	65	65	47	47	5	9	2	261	13	7	2	2.2	.975	OF-126
1945		97	.247	.478	247	61	15	0	14	5.7	43	56	43	33	11	36	11	132	4	10	1	2.6	.932	OF-57
3 yrs.		332	.256	.432	1050	269	46	14	37	3.5	147	167	129	119	20	47	13	588	29	25	4	2.3	.961	OF-276

Al Niemiec

NIEMIEC, ALFRED JOSEPH BR TR 5′11″ 158 lbs.
B. May 18, 1911, Meriden, Conn. D. Oct. 29, 1995, Kirkland, Wash.

Year	Team	Games	BA	SA	AB	H	2B	3B	HR	HR%	R	RBI	BB	SO	SB	Pinch Hit AB	Pinch Hit H	PO	A	E	DP	TC/G	FA	G by Pos
1934	BOS A	9	.219	.219	32	7	0	0	0	0.0	2	3	3	4	0	0	0	25	33	0	8	6.4	1.000	2B-9
1936	PHI A	69	.197	.246	203	40	3	2	1	0.5	22	20	26	16	2	10	1	150	196	11	35	6.3	.969	2B-52, SS-5
2 yrs.		78	.200	.243	235	47	3	2	1	0.4	24	23	29	20	2	10	1	175	229	11	43	6.3	.973	2B-61, SS-5

Tom Nieto

NIETO, THOMAS ANDREW BR TR 6′1″ 205 lbs.
B. Oct. 27, 1960, Downey, Calif.

Year	Team	Games	BA	SA	AB	H	2B	3B	HR	HR%	R	RBI	BB	SO	SB	Pinch Hit AB	Pinch Hit H	PO	A	E	DP	TC/G	FA	G by Pos
1984	STL N	33	.279	.430	86	24	4	0	3	3.5	7	12	5	18	0	2	0	135	18	1	0	4.8	.994	C-32
1985		95	.225	.281	253	57	10	2	0	0.0	15	34	26	37	0	1	0	384	28	4	3	4.4	.990	C-95
1986	MON N	30	.200	.323	65	13	3	1	1	1.5	5	7	6	21	0	1	1	123	11	3	1	4.6	.978	C-30

Tom Nieto *continued*

Year	Team	Games	BA	SA	AB	H	2B	3B	HR	HR%	R	RBI	BB	SO	SB	Pinch Hit AB	Pinch Hit H	PO	A	E	DP	TC/G	FA	G by Pos
1987	MIN A	41	.200	.314	105	21	7	1	1	1.0	7	12	8	24	0	1	1	210	17	1	5	5.6	.996	C-40, DH-1
1988		24	.067	.067	60	4	0	0	0	0.0	1	0	1	17	0	0	0	108	6	1	1	4.8	.991	C-24
1989	PHI N	11	.150	.150	20	3	0	0	0	0.0	1	0	6	7	0	0	0	63	2	0	0	5.9	1.000	C-11
1990		17	.167	.167	30	5	0	0	0	0.0	1	4	3	11	0	1	0	57	5	1	1	3.7	.984	C-17
7 yrs.		251	.205	.281	619	127	24	4	5	0.8	37	69	55	135	0	6	2	1080	87	11	11	4.7	.991	C-249, DH-1
LEAGUE CHAMPIONSHIP SERIES																								
1985	STL N	1	.000	.000	3	0	0	0	0	0.0	1	0	1	2	0	0	0	0	0	0	0	0.0	.000	C-1
WORLD SERIES																								
1985	STL N	2	.000	.000	5	0	0	0	0	0.0	0	1	1	2	0	0	0	23	1	0	0	12.0	1.000	C-2

Melvin Nieves

NIEVES, MELVIN BB TR 6′ 2″ 185 lbs.
Born Melvin Nieves (Ramos).
B. Dec. 28, 1971, San Juan, Puerto Rico.

Year	Team	Games	BA	SA	AB	H	2B	3B	HR	HR%	R	RBI	BB	SO	SB	Pinch Hit AB	Pinch Hit H	PO	A	E	DP	TC/G	FA	G by Pos
1992	ATL N	12	.211	.263	19	4	1	0	0	0.0	0	1	2	7	0	6	1	8	0	3	0	1.8	.727	OF-6
1993	SD N	19	.191	.319	47	9	0	0	2	4.3	4	3	3	21	0	6	0	27	0	2	0	1.9	.931	OF-15
1994		10	.263	.474	19	5	1	0	1	5.3	2	4	3	10	0	4	1	11	1	0	0	2.0	1.000	OF-6
1995		98	.205	.419	234	48	6	1	14	6.0	32	38	19	88	2	27	2	106	5	2	2	1.4	.982	OF-79, 1B-2
4 yrs.		139	.207	.398	319	66	8	1	17	5.3	38	46	27	126	2	43	4	152	6	7	2	1.5	.958	OF-106, 1B-2

Tom Niland

NILAND, THOMAS JAMES (Honest Tom) BR TR 5′11″ 160 lbs.
B. Apr. 14, 1870, Brookfield, Mass. D. Apr. 30, 1950, Lynn, Mass.

Year	Team	Games	BA	SA	AB	H	2B	3B	HR	HR%	R	RBI	BB	SO	SB	Pinch Hit AB	Pinch Hit H	PO	A	E	DP	TC/G	FA	G by Pos
1896	STL N	18	.176	.206	68	12	0	1	0	0.0	3	3	5	4	0	0	0	23	16	7	1	2.6	.848	OF-13, SS-5

Billy Niles

NILES, WILLIAM E. 160 lbs.
B. Jan. 11, 1867, Covington, Ky. D. July 3, 1936, Springfield, Ohio.

Year	Team	Games	BA	SA	AB	H	2B	3B	HR	HR%	R	RBI	BB	SO	SB	Pinch Hit AB	Pinch Hit H	PO	A	E	DP	TC/G	FA	G by Pos
1895	PIT N	11	.216	.216	37	8	0	0	0	0.0	2	0	5	2	2	0	0	23	20	4	1	4.3	.915	3B-10, 2B-1

Harry Niles

NILES, HERBERT CLYDE BR TR 5′ 8″ 175 lbs.
B. Sept. 10, 1880, Buchanan, Mich. D. Apr. 18, 1953, Sturgis, Mich.

Year	Team	Games	BA	SA	AB	H	2B	3B	HR	HR%	R	RBI	BB	SO	SB	Pinch Hit AB	Pinch Hit H	PO	A	E	DP	TC/G	FA	G by Pos
1906	STL A	142	.229	.281	541	124	14	4	2	0.4	71	31	46		30	0	0	189	88	15	8	2.1	.949	OF-108, 3B-34
1907		120	.289	.339	492	142	9	5	2	0.4	65	35	28		19	3	2	282	352	34	41	5.7	.949	2B-116, OF-1
1908	2 teams	NY A (96G –.249) BOS A (17G –.273)																						
″	total	113	.251	.355	394	99	14	6	5	1.3	47	27	31		21	5	0	195	249	30	17	4.6	.937	2B-93, OF-7, SS-2
1909	BOS A	145	.245	.291	546	134	12	5	1	0.2	64	38	39		27	1	1	240	87	28	9	2.5	.921	OF-117, 3B-13, SS-9, 2B-5
1910	2 teams	BOS A (18G –.211) CLE A (70G –.212)																						
″	total	88	.212	.290	297	63	9	4	2	0.7	31	21	19		10	8	2	109	38	10	5	1.9	.936	OF-71, SS-7, 3B-5
5 yrs.		608	.248	.310	2270	562	58	24	12	0.5	278	152	163		107	17	5	1015	814	117	80	3.3	.940	OF-304, 2B-214, 3B-52, SS-18

Rabbit Nill

NILL, GEORGE CHARLES BR TR 5′ 7″ 160 lbs.
B. July 14, 1881, Fort Wayne, Ind. D. May 24, 1962, Fort Wayne, Ind.

Year	Team	Games	BA	SA	AB	H	2B	3B	HR	HR%	R	RBI	BB	SO	SB	Pinch Hit AB	Pinch Hit H	PO	A	E	DP	TC/G	FA	G by Pos
1904	WAS A	15	.167	.208	48	8	0	1	0	0.0	4	3	5		0	0	0	29	36	9	3	4.9	.878	2B-15
1905		103	.182	.251	319	58	7	3	3	0.9	46	31	33		12	10	3	146	200	29	15	4.0	.923	3B-54, 2B-33, SS-6
1906		89	.235	.273	315	74	8	2	0	0.0	37	15	47		16	2	0	148	211	36	21	4.6	.909	SS-31, 2B-25, OF-15, 3B-15
1907	2 teams	WAS A (66G –.219) CLE A (12G –.279)																						
″	total	78	.229	.283	258	59	8	3	0	0.0	26	27	18		8	8	2	127	134	16	10	4.0	.942	2B-32, OF-25, 3B-10, SS-2
1908	CLE A	10	.217	.217	23	5	0	0	0	0.0	3	1	0		0	1	0	13	25	6	2	4.9	.864	SS-6, OF-2, 2B-1
5 yrs.		295	.212	.264	963	204	23	9	3	0.3	116	77	103		36	21	5	463	606	96	51	4.3	.918	2B-106, 3B-79, SS-45, OF-42

Dave Nilsson

NILSSON, DAVID WAYNE BL TR 6′ 3″ 185 lbs.
B. Dec. 14, 1969, Brisbane, Australia.

Year	Team	Games	BA	SA	AB	H	2B	3B	HR	HR%	R	RBI	BB	SO	SB	Pinch Hit AB	Pinch Hit H	PO	A	E	DP	TC/G	FA	G by Pos
1992	MIL A	51	.232	.354	164	38	8	0	4	2.4	15	25	17	18	2	1	0	231	16	2	2	4.9	.992	C-46, 1B-3, DH-2
1993		100	.257	.375	296	76	10	2	7	2.4	35	40	37	36	3	4	1	457	33	9	6	5.0	.982	C-91, 1B-4, DH-4
1994		109	.275	.451	397	109	28	3	12	3.0	51	69	34	61	1	5	1	315	15	2	4	3.1	.994	C-60, DH-43, 1B-5
1995		81	.278	.468	263	73	12	1	12	4.6	41	53	24	41	2	14	2	117	7	2	1	1.6	.984	OF-58, DH-14, 1B-7, C-2
4 yrs.		341	.264	.421	1120	296	58	6	35	3.1	142	187	112	156	8	24	4	1120	71	15	13	3.6	.988	C-199, DH-63, OF-58, 1B-19

Al Nixon

NIXON, ALBERT RICHARD BR TL 5′ 7½″ 164 lbs.
B. Apr. 11, 1886, Atlantic City, N. J. D. Nov. 9, 1960, Opelousas, La.

Year	Team	Games	BA	SA	AB	H	2B	3B	HR	HR%	R	RBI	BB	SO	SB	Pinch Hit AB	Pinch Hit H	PO	A	E	DP	TC/G	FA	G by Pos
1915	BKN N	14	.231	.269	26	6	1	0	0	0.0	3	2	2	4	1	2	1	11	1	0	1	0.9	1.000	OF-14
1916		1	1.000	1.000	2	2	0	0	0	0.0	0	0	0	0	0	0	0	0	0	0	0	0.0	.000	OF-1
1918		6	.455	.455	11	5	0	0	0	0.0	1	0	0	0	0	1	1	6	0	0	0	1.5	1.000	OF-4
1921	BOS N	55	.239	.348	138	33	6	3	1	0.7	25	9	7	11	3	6	1	92	4	2	1	2.2	.980	OF-45
1922		86	.264	.352	318	84	14	4	2	0.6	35	22	9	19	6	6	2	189	6	5	0	2.5	.975	OF-79
1923		88	.274	.336	321	88	12	4	0	0.0	53	19	24	14	2	1	0	214	14	3	4	2.9	.987	OF-80
1926	PHI N	93	.293	.402	311	91	18	2	4	1.3	38	41	13	20	5	3	0	206	7	5	3	2.5	.977	OF-88
1927		54	.312	.357	154	48	7	0	0	0.0	18	18	5	5	1	5	1	121	3	4	0	2.9	.969	OF-44
1928		25	.234	.266	64	15	2	0	0	0.0	7	7	6	4	1	3	1	40	1	0	0	2.0	1.000	OF-20
9 yrs.		422	.277	.356	1345	372	60	13	7	0.5	180	118	66	77	19	27	7	879	36	19	9	2.5	.980	OF-375

Donell Nixon

NIXON, ROBERT DONELL BR TR 6′ 1″ 185 lbs.
Brother of Otis Nixon.
B. Dec. 31, 1961, Evergreen, N. C.

Year	Team	Games	BA	SA	AB	H	2B	3B	HR	HR%	R	RBI	BB	SO	SB	Pinch Hit AB	Pinch Hit H	PO	A	E	DP	TC/G	FA	G by Pos
1987	SEA A	46	.250	.348	132	33	4	0	3	2.3	17	12	13	28	21	0	0	76	1	0	0	2.0	1.000	OF-32, DH-6
1988	SF N	59	.346	.385	78	27	3	0	0	0.0	15	6	10	12	11	5	1	59	0	1	0	1.3	.983	OF-46
1989		95	.265	.295	166	44	2	0	1	0.6	23	15	11	30	10	25	5	87	0	3	0	1.4	.967	OF-64
1990	BAL A	8	.250	.350	20	5	2	0	0	0.0	1	2	1	7	5	0	0	5	0	0	0	0.7	1.000	OF-4, DH-3
4 yrs.		208	.275	.333	396	109	11	0	4	1.0	56	35	35	77	47	30	6	227	1	4	0	1.5	.983	OF-146, DH-9
LEAGUE CHAMPIONSHIP SERIES																								
1989	SF N	3	.000	.000	3	0	0	0	0	0.0	0	0	0	1	1	0	0	2	0	1	0	1.5	.667	OF-2
WORLD SERIES																								
1989	SF N	2	.200	.200	5	1	0	0	0	0.0	1	0	1	1	0	1	0	2	0	0	0	1.0	1.000	OF-2

Otis Nixon

NIXON, OTIS JUNIOR BB TR 6′ 2″ 175 lbs.
Brother of Donell Nixon.
B. Jan. 9, 1959, Evergreen, N. C.

Year	Team	Games	BA	SA	AB	H	2B	3B	HR	HR%	R	RBI	BB	SO	SB	Pinch Hit AB	Pinch Hit H	PO	A	E	DP	TC/G	FA	G by Pos
1983	NY A	13	.143	.143	14	2	0	0	0	0.0	2	0	1	5	2	0	0	14	1	1	0	1.8	.938	OF-9
1984	CLE A	49	.154	.154	91	14	0	0	0	0.0	16	1	8	11	12	0	0	81	3	0	0	1.8	1.000	OF-46
1985		104	.235	.315	162	38	4	0	3	1.9	34	9	8	27	20	2	0	129	5	4	1	1.5	.971	OF-80, DH-11
1986		105	.263	.326	95	25	4	1	0	0.0	33	8	13	12	23	3	1	90	3	3	0	1.0	.969	OF-95, DH-5
1987		19	.059	.059	17	1	0	0	0	0.0	2	1	3	4	2	0	0	21	0	0	0	1.2	1.000	OF-17
1988	MON N	90	.244	.288	271	66	8	2	0	0.0	47	15	28	42	46	11	6	176	2	1	1	2.2	.994	OF-82
1989		126	.217	.260	258	56	7	2	0	0.0	41	21	33	36	37	21	2	160	2	2	0	1.7	.988	OF-98
1990		119	.251	.307	231	58	6	2	1	0.4	46	20	28	33	50	28	6	149	6	1	1	1.8	.994	OF-88, SS-1
1991	ATL N	124	.297	.327	401	119	10	1	0	0.0	81	26	47	40	72	8	3	218	6	3	1	2.0	.987	OF-115
1992		120	.294	.346	456	134	14	2	2	0.4	79	22	39	54	41	9	4	333	6	3	1	3.1	.991	OF-111
1993		134	.269	.315	461	124	12	3	1	0.2	77	24	61	63	47	13	2	308	4	3	1	2.7	.990	OF-116
1994	BOS A	103	.274	.317	398	109	15	1	0	0.0	60	25	55	65	42	0	0	254	4	3	1	2.5	.989	OF-103
1995	TEX A	139	.295	.338	589	174	21	2	0	0.0	87	45	58	85	50	0	0	355	4	4	0	2.6	.989	OF-138
13 yrs.		1245	.267	.312	3444	920	101	16	7	0.2	605	217	382	477	444	95	24	2288	46	28	7	2.1	.988	OF-1098, DH-16, SS-1
LEAGUE CHAMPIONSHIP SERIES																								
1992	ATL N	7	.286	.357	28	8	2	0	0	0.0	5	2	4	4	3	0	0	16	0	0	0	2.3	1.000	OF-7
1993		6	.348	.435	23	8	2	0	0	0.0	3	4	5	6	0	0	0	13	0	0	0	2.2	1.000	OF-6
2 yrs.		13	.314	.392	51	16	4	0	0	0.0	8	6	9	10	3	0	0	29	0	0	0	2.2	1.000	OF-13
WORLD SERIES																								
1992	ATL N	6	.296	.333	27	8	1	0	0	0.0	3	1	1	3	5	0	0	18	0	0	0	3.0	1.000	OF-6

Russ Nixon

NIXON, RUSSELL EUGENE BL TR 6′ 1″ 195 lbs.
B. Feb. 19, 1935, Cleves, Ohio.
Manager 1982–83, 1988–90.

Year	Team	Games	BA	SA	AB	H	2B	3B	HR	HR%	R	RBI	BB	SO	SB	Pinch Hit AB	Pinch Hit H	PO	A	E	DP	TC/G	FA	G by Pos
1957	CLE A	62	.281	.362	185	52	7	1	2	1.1	15	18	12	12	0	8	1	268	31	5	5	5.3	.984	C-57
1958		113	.301	.439	376	113	17	4	9	2.4	42	46	13	38	0	18	4	499	31	5	4	5.3	.991	C-101
1959		82	.240	.314	258	62	10	3	1	0.4	23	29	15	28	0	9	2	374	31	6	8	5.6	.985	C-74
1960	2 teams	CLE A (25G –.244) BOS A (80G –.298)																						
″	total	105	.285	.415	354	101	22	3	6	1.7	30	39	19	29	0	11	2	488	34	6	5	5.3	.989	C-99
1961	BOS A	87	.289	.368	242	70	12	2	1	0.4	24	19	13	19	0	18	8	330	24	9	2	5.5	.975	C-66
1962		65	.278	.371	151	42	7	2	1	0.7	11	19	8	14	0	28	10	201	7	0	1	5.5	1.000	C-38
1963		98	.268	.390	287	77	18	1	5	1.7	27	30	22	32	0	25	6	483	22	4	1	6.7	.992	C-76
1964		81	.233	.294	163	38	7	0	1	0.6	10	20	14	29	0	34	9	273	11	3	3	6.4	.990	C-45
1965		59	.270	.321	137	37	5	1	0	0.0	11	11	6	23	0	24	7	200	10	4	0	5.6	.981	C-38
1966	MIN A	51	.260	.302	96	25	2	1	0	0.0	5	7	7	13	0	22	5	137	5	2	0	4.5	.986	C-32
1967		74	.235	.300	170	40	6	1	1	0.6	16	22	18	29	0	19	4	308	26	2	1	4.9	.994	C-69
1968	BOS A	29	.153	.176	85	13	2	0	0	0.0	1	6	7	13	0	2	1	147	6	1	1	5.7	.994	C-27
12 yrs.		906	.268	.361	2504	670	115	19	27	1.1	215	266	154	279	0	218	59	3708	238	47	31	5.5	.988	C-722

Ray Noble

NOBLE, RAFAEL MIGUEL BR TR 5′11″ 210 lbs.
Born Rafael Miguel Noble (Magee).
B. Mar. 15, 1919, Central Hatillo, Cuba.

Year	Team	Games	BA	SA	AB	H	2B	3B	HR	HR%	R	RBI	BB	SO	SB	Pinch Hit AB	Pinch Hit H	PO	A	E	DP	TC/G	FA	G by Pos
1951	NY N	55	.234	.383	141	33	6	0	5	3.5	16	26	6	26	0	18	3	144	8	4	3	3.8	.974	C-41
1952		6	.000	.000	5	0	0	0	0	0.0	0	0	0	1	0	1	0	4	1	0	0	1.0	1.000	C-5
1953		46	.206	.351	97	20	0	1	4	4.1	15	14	19	14	1	4	0	152	13	3	0	4.1	.982	C-41
3 yrs.		107	.218	.362	243	53	6	1	9	3.7	31	40	25	41	1	23	3	300	22	7	3	3.8	.979	C-87
WORLD SERIES																								
1951	NY N	2	.000	.000	2	0	0	0	0	0.0	0	0	0	1	0	2	0	0	1	0	0	0.5	1.000	C-2

Junior Noboa

NOBOA, MILCIADES ARTURO BR TR 5′10″ 155 lbs.
Born Milciades Arturo Noboa (Diaz).
B. Nov. 10, 1964, Azua, Dominican Republic.

Year	Team	Games	BA	SA	AB	H	2B	3B	HR	HR%	R	RBI	BB	SO	SB	Pinch Hit AB	Pinch Hit H	PO	A	E	DP	TC/G	FA	G by Pos
1984	CLE A	23	.364	.364	11	4	0	0	0	0.0	3	0	0	2	1	0	0	7	13	0	4	1.0	1.000	2B-19, DH-1
1987		39	.225	.275	80	18	2	1	0	0.0	7	7	3	6	1	2	0	28	66	3	8	2.9	.969	2B-21, SS-8, 3B-5
1988	CAL A	21	.063	.063	16	1	0	0	0	0.0	4	0	0	1	0	0	0	8	24	1	7	2.4	.970	2B-9, SS-3, 3B-2
1989	MON N	21	.227	.227	44	10	0	0	0	0.0	3	1	1	3	0	5	3	17	45	0	7	3.4	1.000	2B-13, SS-4, 3B-1
1990		81	.266	.335	158	42	7	2	0	0.0	15	14	7	14	4	35	10	47	52	2	10	1.8	.980	2B-31, OF-9, 3B-8, SS-7, P-1
1991		67	.242	.305	95	23	3	0	1	1.1	5	2	1	8	2	46	**14**	20	19	1	4	2.2	.975	OF-7, 2B-6, SS-2, 3B-2, 1B-1
1992	NY N	46	.149	.149	47	7	0	0	0	0.0	7	3	3	8	0	20	2	19	30	3	6	2.5	.942	2B-16, 3B-3, SS-2
1994	2 teams	OAK A (17G –.325) PIT N (2G –.000)																						
″	total	19	.310	.381	42	13	1	1	0	0.0	3	6	2	5	1	3	0	19	33	3	7	3.4	.945	2B-14, SS-2
8 yrs.		317	.239	.288	493	118	13	4	1	0.2	47	33	17	47	9	111	29	165	282	13	53	2.3	.972	2B-129, SS-28, 3B-21, OF-16, P-1, 1B-1, DH-1

Paul Noce

NOCE, PAUL DAVID BR TR 5′10″ 175 lbs.
B. Dec. 16, 1959, San Francisco, Calif.

Year	Team	Games	BA	SA	AB	H	2B	3B	HR	HR%	R	RBI	BB	SO	SB	Pinch Hit AB	Pinch Hit H	PO	A	E	DP	TC/G	FA	G by Pos
1987	CHI N	70	.228	.350	180	41	9	2	3	1.7	17	14	6	49	5	2	0	117	157	5	39	3.8	.982	2B-36, SS-35, 3B-2
1990	CIN N	1	1.000	1.000	1	1	0	0	0	0.0	0	0	0	0	0	1	1	0	0	0	0	0.0	—	
2 yrs.		71	.232	.354	181	42	9	2	3	1.7	17	14	6	49	5	3	1	117	157	5	39	3.8	.982	2B-36, SS-35, 3B-2

George Noftsker

NOFTSKER, GEORGE WASHINGTON BR TR 5′ 8″ 135 lbs.
B. Aug. 24, 1859, Shippensburg, Pa. D. May 8, 1931, Shippensburg, Pa.

Year	Team	Games	BA	SA	AB	H	2B	3B	HR	HR%	R	RBI	BB	SO	SB	Pinch Hit AB	Pinch Hit H	PO	A	E	DP	TC/G	FA	G by Pos
1884	ALT U	7	.040	.040	25	1	0	0	0	0.0	0		0			0	0	21	9	5	1	4.4	.857	OF-5, C-3

Matt Nokes

NOKES, MATTHEW DODGE BL TR 6′ 1″ 180 lbs.
B. Oct. 31, 1963, San Diego, Calif.

Year	Team	Games	BA	SA	AB	H	2B	3B	HR	HR%	R	RBI	BB	SO	SB	Pinch Hit AB	Pinch Hit H	PO	A	E	DP	TC/G	FA	G by Pos
1985	SF N	19	.208	.358	53	11	2	0	2	3.8	3	5	1	9	0	5	0	84	2	2	0	6.3	.977	C-14
1986	DET A	7	.333	.500	24	8	1	0	1	4.2	2	2	1	1	0	0	0	43	2	0	2	6.4	1.000	C-7
1987		135	.289	.536	461	133	14	2	32	6.9	69	87	35	70	2	19	4	600	32	5	2	5.6	.992	C-109, OF-3, 3B-2
1988		122	.251	.424	382	96	18	0	16	4.2	53	53	34	58	0	16	3	574	45	7	8	5.5	.989	C-110, DH-4
1989		87	.250	.388	268	67	10	0	9	3.4	15	39	17	37	1	11	1	235	26	6	3	3.2	.978	C-51, DH-33

Matt Nokes *continued*

Year	Team	Games	BA	SA	AB	H	2B	3B	HR	HR%	R	RBI	BB	SO	SB	Pinch Hit AB	Pinch Hit H	PO	A	E	DP	TC/G	FA	G by Pos
1990	2 teams	DET A (44G –.270) NY A (92G –.237)																						
″	total	136	.248	.373	351	87	9	1	11	3.1	33	40	24	47	2	34	8	237	34	2	6	2.3	.993	C-65, DH-54, OF-2
1991	NY A	135	.268	.469	456	122	20	0	24	5.3	52	77	25	49	3	17	4	690	48	6	7	5.6	.992	C-130, DH-3
1992		121	.224	.424	384	86	9	1	22	5.7	42	59	37	62	0	13	4	552	47	4	6	5.4	.993	C-111
1993		76	.249	.424	217	54	8	0	10	4.6	25	35	16	31	0	9	5	245	19	2	0	4.0	.992	C-56, DH-11
1994		28	.291	.595	79	23	3	0	7	8.9	11	19	5	16	0	6	0	106	6	3	7	4.4	.974	C-17, DH-5, 1B-4
1995	2 teams	BAL A (26G –.122) CLR N (10G –.182)																						
″	total	36	.133	.267	60	8	2	0	2	3.3	5	6	5	15	0	14	1	93	5	2	0	4.8	.980	C-19, DH-2
11 yrs.		902	.254	.441	2735	695	96	4	136	5.0	310	422	200	395	8	144	30	3459	266	39	41	4.6	.990	C-689, DH-112, OF-5, 1B-4, 3B-2
LEAGUE CHAMPIONSHIP SERIES																								
1987	DET A	5	.143	.357	14	2	0	0	1	7.1	2	2	1	4	0	2	0	11	2	0	0	2.6	1.000	C-3, DH-2

Joe Nolan

NOLAN, JOSEPH WILLIAM, JR. BL TR 5′11″ 175 lbs.
B. May 12, 1951, St. Louis, Mo.

Year	Team	Games	BA	SA	AB	H	2B	3B	HR	HR%	R	RBI	BB	SO	SB	Pinch Hit AB	Pinch Hit H	PO	A	E	DP	TC/G	FA	G by Pos
1972	NY N	4	.000	.000	10	0	0	0	0	0.0	0	0	1	3	0	1	0	12	3	1	0	5.3	.938	C-3
1975	ATL N	4	.250	.250	4	1	0	0	0	0.0	0	0	1	0	0	3	0	2	0	0	0	2.0	1.000	C-1
1977		62	.280	.427	82	23	3	0	3	3.7	13	9	13	12	1	39	14	80	7	0	2	4.6	1.000	C-19
1978		95	.230	.347	213	49	7	3	4	1.9	22	22	34	28	3	34	6	295	24	7	3	5.3	.979	C-61
1979		89	.248	.365	230	57	9	3	4	1.7	28	21	27	28	1	14	1	328	27	6	2	4.9	.983	C-74
1980	2 teams	ATL N (17G –.273) CIN N (53G –.312)																						
″	total	70	.307	.403	176	54	8	0	3	1.7	16	26	15	12	0	15	3	271	26	5	7	5.3	.983	C-57
1981	CIN N	81	.309	.407	236	73	18	1	1	0.4	25	26	24	19	1	9	3	393	18	2	2	5.1	.995	C-81
1982	BAL A	77	.233	.356	219	51	7	1	6	2.7	24	35	16	35	1	12	2	292	22	7	2	4.5	.978	C-72
1983		73	.277	.429	184	51	11	1	5	2.7	25	24	16	31	0	12	2	223	16	5	2	3.8	.980	C-65
1984		35	.290	.387	62	18	1	1	1	1.6	2	9	12	10	0	15	4	22	3	1	0	1.5	.962	DH-11, C-6
1985		31	.132	.184	38	5	2	0	0	0.0	1	6	5	5	0	22	2	22	2	0	0	2.7	1.000	C-5, DH-4
11 yrs.		621	.263	.378	1454	382	66	10	27	1.9	156	178	164	183	7	176	37	1940	148	34	20	4.6	.984	C-444, DH-15
LEAGUE CHAMPIONSHIP SERIES																								
1983	BAL A	1	—	—	0	0	0	0	0	—	0	1	0	0	0	0	0	0	0	0	0	0.0	—	
WORLD SERIES																								
1983	BAL A	2	.000	.000	2	0	0	0	0	0.0	0	0	1	0	0	1	0	3	0	0	0	1.5	1.000	C-2

The Only Nolan

NOLAN, EDWARD SYLVESTER BL TR 5′8″ 171 lbs.
B. Nov. 7, 1857, Paterson, N. J. D. May 18, 1913, Paterson, N. J.

Year	Team	Games	BA	SA	AB	H	2B	3B	HR	HR%	R	RBI	BB	SO	SB	Pinch Hit AB	Pinch Hit H	PO	A	E	DP	TC/G	FA	G by Pos
1878	IND N	38	.243	.296	152	37	8	0	0	0.0	11	16	2	10		0	0	19	80	11	5	2.8	.900	P-38, OF-1
1881	CLE N	41	.244	.286	168	41	5	1	0	0.0	12	18	4	13		0	0	32	37	9	2	1.9	.885	P-22, OF-14, 3B-6
1883	PIT AA	7	.308	.346	26	8	1	0	0	0.0	4		1			0	0	2	11	5	0	2.3	.722	P-7, OF-1
1884	WIL U	9	.273	.394	33	9	2	1	0	0.0	5		2			0	0	5	11	1	0	1.9	.941	P-5, OF-4
1885	PHI N	7	.077	.115	26	2	1	0	0	0.0	1		3	8		0	0	1	11	3	0	1.9	.800	P-7, OF-1
5 yrs.		102	.240	.291	405	97	17	2	0	0.0	33	34	12	31		0	0	59	150	29	7	2.2	.878	P-79, OF-21, 3B-6

Red Nonnenkamp

NONNENKAMP, LEO WILLIAM BL TL 5′11″ 165 lbs.
B. July 7, 1911, St. Louis, Mo.

Year	Team	Games	BA	SA	AB	H	2B	3B	HR	HR%	R	RBI	BB	SO	SB	Pinch Hit AB	Pinch Hit H	PO	A	E	DP	TC/G	FA	G by Pos
1933	PIT N	1	.000	.000	1	0	0	0	0	0.0	0	0	0	1	0	1	0	0	0	0	0	0.0	—	
1938	BOS A	87	.283	.317	180	51	4	1	0	0.0	37	18	21	13	6	34	10	101	5	3	2	2.5	.972	OF-39, 1B-5
1939		58	.240	.293	75	18	2	1	0	0.0	12	5	12	6	0	34	9	25	0	1	0	1.7	.962	OF-15
1940		9	.000	.000	7	0	0	0	0	0.0	0	1	1	4	0	7	0	0	0	0	0	0.0	—	
4 yrs.		155	.262	.300	263	69	6	2	0	0.0	49	24	34	24	6	76	19	126	5	4	2	2.3	.970	OF-54, 1B-5

Pete Noonan

NOONAN, PETER JOHN BR TR 6′ 180 lbs.
B. Nov. 24, 1881, W. Stockbridge, Mass. D. Feb. 11, 1965, Great Barrington, Mass.

Year	Team	Games	BA	SA	AB	H	2B	3B	HR	HR%	R	RBI	BB	SO	SB	Pinch Hit AB	Pinch Hit H	PO	A	E	DP	TC/G	FA	G by Pos
1904	PHI A	39	.202	.298	114	23	3	1	2	1.8	13	13	1		1	6	1	205	27	5	6	7.4	.979	C-22, 1B-10
1906	2 teams	CHI N (5G –.333) STL N (44G –.168)																						
″	total	49	.172	.250	128	22	1	3	1	0.8	8	9	11		1	8	2	271	48	14	6	8.3	.958	C-23, 1B-17
1907	STL N	74	.225	.292	236	53	7	3	1	0.4	19	16	9		3	5	1	369	98	24	12	7.0	.951	C-70
3 yrs.		162	.205	.282	478	98	11	7	4	0.8	40	38	21		5	19	4	845	173	43	24	7.5	.959	C-115, 1B-27

Tim Nordbrook

NORDBROOK, TIMOTHY CHARLES BR TR 6′1″ 180 lbs.
B. July 7, 1949, Baltimore, Md.

Year	Team	Games	BA	SA	AB	H	2B	3B	HR	HR%	R	RBI	BB	SO	SB	Pinch Hit AB	Pinch Hit H	PO	A	E	DP	TC/G	FA	G by Pos
1974	BAL A	6	.267	.267	15	4	0	0	0	0.0	4	1	2	2	1	0	0	6	17	0	5	3.8	1.000	SS-5, 2B-1
1975		40	.118	.147	34	4	1	0	0	0.0	6	0	7	7	0	0	0	19	51	2	7	1.8	.972	SS-37, 2B-3
1976	2 teams	BAL A (27G –.227) CAL A (5G –.000)																						
″	total	32	.167	.167	30	5	0	0	0	0.0	5	0	4	8	1	0	0	23	33	1	6	1.8	.982	SS-16, 2B-15, DH-1
1977	2 teams	CHI A (15G –.250) TOR A (24G –.175)																						
″	total	39	.193	.217	83	16	0	1	0	0.0	11	2	11	15	2	12	3	52	74	7	13	3.5	.947	SS-35, DH-2, 3B-1
1978	2 teams	TOR A (7G –.000) MIL A (2G –.000)																						
″	total	9	.000	.000	5	0	0	0	0	0.0	1	0	1	1	0	0	0	2	14	1	0	1.9	.941	SS-9
1979	MIL A	2	.500	.500	2	1	0	0	0	0.0	0	0	0	0	0	0	0	1	0	0	0	0.5	1.000	SS-2
6 yrs.		128	.178	.195	169	30	1	1	0	0.0	27	3	25	33	4	12	3	103	189	11	31	2.4	.964	SS-104, 2B-19, DH-3, 3B-1

Wayne Nordhagen

NORDHAGEN, WAYNE OREN BR TR 6′2″ 205 lbs.
B. July 4, 1948, Thief River Falls, Minn.

Year	Team	Games	BA	SA	AB	H	2B	3B	HR	HR%	R	RBI	BB	SO	SB	Pinch Hit AB	Pinch Hit H	PO	A	E	DP	TC/G	FA	G by Pos
1976	CHI A	22	.189	.226	53	10	2	0	0	0.0	6	5	4	12	0	2	0	35	3	1	0	1.9	.974	OF-10, DH-6, C-5
1977		52	.315	.516	124	39	7	3	4	3.2	16	22	2	12	1	7	2	52	1	5	2	1.1	.914	OF-46, C-3, DH-2
1978		68	.301	.451	206	62	16	0	5	2.4	28	35	5	18	0	15	6	87	12	6	2	1.6	.943	OF-36, DH-16, C-12
1979		78	.280	.466	193	54	15	0	7	3.6	20	25	13	22	0	21	7	28	4	3	0	0.5	.914	DH-47, OF-12, C-5, P-2
1980		123	.277	.458	415	115	22	4	15	3.6	45	59	10	45	0	21	5	120	6	4	1	1.2	.969	OF-74, DH-32

Wayne Nordhagen *continued*

Year	Team	Games	BA	SA	AB	H	2B	3B	HR	HR%	R	RBI	BB	SO	SB	Pinch Hit AB	Pinch Hit H	PO	A	E	DP	TC/G	FA	G by Pos
1981		65	.308	.442	208	64	8	1	6	2.9	19	33	10	25	0	7	1	85	4	5	1	1.6	.947	OF-60
1982	**2 teams**	**TOR A** (72G –.270) **PIT N** (1G –.500)																						
"	**total**	73	.275	.323	189	52	6	0	1	0.5	12	22	10	23	0	26	11	17	1	0	1	0.3	1.000	DH-60, 1B-10, OF-1
1983	**CHI N**	21	.143	.257	35	5	1	0	1	2.9	1	4	0	5	0	15	2	7	0	0	0	1.0	1.000	OF-7
8 yrs.		502	.282	.429	1423	401	77	8	39	2.7	147	205	54	162	1	114	34	431	31	24	7	1.1	.951	OF-246, DH-163, C-25, 1B-10, P-2

Lou Nordyke

NORDYKE, LOUIS ELLIS BR TR 6′ 185 lbs.
B. Aug. 7, 1876, Brighton, Iowa D. Sept. 27, 1945, Los Angeles, Calif.

Year	Team	Games	BA	SA	AB	H	2B	3B	HR	HR%	R	RBI	BB	SO	SB	Pinch Hit AB	Pinch Hit H	PO	A	E	DP	TC/G	FA	G by Pos
1906	**STL A**	25	.245	.264	53	13	1	0	0	0.0	4	7	10		3	12	3	125	4	8	12	11.4	.942	1B-12

Irv Noren

NOREN, IRVING ARNOLD BL TL 6′ 190 lbs.
B. Nov. 29, 1924, Jamestown, N. Y.

Year	Team	Games	BA	SA	AB	H	2B	3B	HR	HR%	R	RBI	BB	SO	SB	Pinch Hit AB	Pinch Hit H	PO	A	E	DP	TC/G	FA	G by Pos
1950	**WAS A**	138	.295	.459	542	160	27	10	14	2.6	80	98	67	77	5	0	0	500	34	13	21	4.0	.976	OF-121, 1B-17
1951		129	.279	.411	509	142	33	5	8	1.6	82	86	51	35	10	3	0	420	15	10	1	3.5	.978	OF-126
1952	**2 teams**	**WAS A** (12G –.245) **NY A** (93G –.235)																						
"	**total**	105	.237	.352	321	76	16	3	5	1.6	40	23	32	37	5	18	3	272	15	2	15	3.2	.993	OF-72, 1B-19
1953	**NY A**	109	.267	.388	345	92	12	6	6	1.7	55	46	42	39	3	15	3	208	11	2	1	2.3	.991	OF-96
1954		125	.319	.481	426	136	21	6	12	2.8	70	66	43	38	4	12	3	243	10	5	2	2.2	.981	OF-116, 1B-1
1955		132	.253	.375	371	94	19	1	8	2.2	49	59	43	33	5	11	1	238	9	5	0	2.0	.980	OF-126
1956		29	.216	.243	37	8	1	0	0	0.0	4	6	12	7	0	13	4	10	2	1	0	1.2	.923	OF-10, 1B-1
1957	**2 teams**	**KC A** (81G –.212) **STL N** (17G –.367)																						
"	**total**	98	.237	.358	190	45	12	1	3	1.6	11	26	15	25	0	54	13	204	13	2	24	5.6	.991	1B-25, OF-14
1958	**STL N**	117	.264	.393	178	47	9	1	4	2.2	24	22	13	21	0	43	8	75	1	2	0	1.0	.974	OF-77
1959	**2 teams**	**STL N** (8G –.125) **CHI N** (65G –.321)																						
"	**total**	73	.311	.451	164	51	7	2	4	2.4	27	19	13	26	2	29	12	85	4	0	2	2.0	1.000	OF-42, 1B-2
1960	**2 teams**	**CHI N** (12G –.091) **LA N** (26G –.200)																						
"	**total**	38	.167	.250	36	6	0	0	1	2.8	1	2	4	12	0	32	5	6	0	1	1	3.5	.857	OF-1, 1B-1
11 yrs.		1093	.275	.410	3119	857	157	35	65	2.1	443	453	335	350	34	230	52	2261	114	43	67	2.8	.982	OF-801, 1B-66
WORLD SERIES																								
1952	**NY A**	4	.300	.300	10	3	0	0	0	0.0	0	1	1	3	0	1	1	2	0	0	0	0.7	1.000	OF-3
1953		2	.000	.000	1	0	0	0	0	0.0	0	0	1	0	0	1	0	0	0	0	0	0.0	—	
1955		5	.063	.063	16	1	0	0	0	0.0	0	1	1	1	0	0	0	13	0	0	0	2.6	1.000	OF-5
3 yrs.		11	.148	.148	27	4	0	0	0	0.0	0	2	3	4	0	2	1	15	0	0	0	1.9	1.000	OF-8

Bill Norman

NORMAN, HENRY WILLIS PATRICK BR TR 6′ 2″ 190 lbs.
B. July 16, 1910, St. Louis, Mo. D. Apr. 21, 1962, Milwaukee, Wis.
Manager 1958–59.

Year	Team	Games	BA	SA	AB	H	2B	3B	HR	HR%	R	RBI	BB	SO	SB	Pinch Hit AB	Pinch Hit H	PO	A	E	DP	TC/G	FA	G by Pos
1931	**CHI A**	24	.182	.218	55	10	2	0	0	0.0	7	6	4	10	0	4	0	41	1	3	0	2.6	.933	OF-17
1932		13	.229	.333	48	11	3	1	0	0.0	6	2	2	3	0	0	0	20	2	2	0	1.8	.917	OF-13
2 yrs.		37	.204	.272	103	21	5	1	0	0.0	13	8	6	13	0	4	0	61	3	5	0	2.3	.928	OF-30

Dan Norman

NORMAN, DANIEL EDMUND BR TR 6′ 2″ 195 lbs.
B. Jan. 11, 1955, Los Angeles, Calif.

Year	Team	Games	BA	SA	AB	H	2B	3B	HR	HR%	R	RBI	BB	SO	SB	Pinch Hit AB	Pinch Hit H	PO	A	E	DP	TC/G	FA	G by Pos
1977	**NY N**	7	.250	.313	16	4	1	0	0	0.0	2	0	4	2	0	1	0	8	0	0	0	1.3	1.000	OF-6
1978		19	.266	.484	64	17	0	1	4	6.3	7	10	2	14	1	1	0	33	1	0	0	1.9	1.000	OF-18
1979		44	.245	.373	110	27	3	1	3	2.7	9	11	10	26	2	13	3	54	4	2	0	1.8	.967	OF-33
1980		69	.185	.283	92	17	1	1	2	2.2	5	9	6	14	5	47	8	19	1	0	0	1.1	1.000	OF-19
1982	**MON N**	53	.212	.348	66	14	3	0	2	3.0	6	7	7	20	0	21	3	30	1	1	0	1.0	.969	OF-31
5 yrs.		192	.227	.362	348	79	8	3	11	3.2	29	37	29	76	8	83	14	144	7	3	0	1.4	.981	OF-107

Les Norman

NORMAN, LESLIE EUGENE BR TR 6′ 1″ 185 lbs.
B. Feb. 25, 1969, Warren, Mich.

Year	Team	Games	BA	SA	AB	H	2B	3B	HR	HR%	R	RBI	BB	SO	SB	Pinch Hit AB	Pinch Hit H	PO	A	E	DP	TC/G	FA	G by Pos
1995	**KC A**	24	.225	.275	40	9	0	1	0	0.0	6	4	6	6	0	5	1	23	1	1	0	1.1	.960	OF-17, DH-5

Nelson Norman

NORMAN, NELSON AUGUSTO (Gus) BB TR 6′ 2″ 160 lbs.
B. May 23, 1958, San Pedro de Macoris, Dominican Republic.

Year	Team	Games	BA	SA	AB	H	2B	3B	HR	HR%	R	RBI	BB	SO	SB	Pinch Hit AB	Pinch Hit H	PO	A	E	DP	TC/G	FA	G by Pos
1978	**TEX A**	23	.265	.324	34	9	2	0	0	0.0	1	1	0	5	0	0	0	16	50	1	2	2.8	.985	SS-18, 3B-6
1979		147	.222	.265	343	76	9	3	0	0.0	36	21	19	41	4	1	0	177	302	24	64	3.5	.952	SS-142, 2B-1
1980		17	.219	.219	32	7	0	0	0	0.0	4	1	1	1	0	0	0	21	45	4	12	4.1	.943	SS-17
1981		7	.231	.308	13	3	1	0	0	0.0	1	2	1	2	0	0	0	5	21	1	5	5.4	.963	SS-5
1982	**PIT N**	3	.000	.000	3	0	0	0	0	0.0	0	0	0	0	0	0	0	1	2	0	0	1.0	1.000	2B-2, SS-1
1987	**MON N**	1	.000	.000	4	0	0	0	0	0.0	0	0	0	1	0	0	0	1	1	1	0	3.0	.667	SS-1
6 yrs.		198	.221	.263	429	95	12	3	0	0.0	42	25	21	50	4	1	0	221	421	31	83	3.5	.954	SS-184, 3B-6, 2B-3

Jim Norris

NORRIS, JAMES FRANCIS BL TL 5′10″ 175 lbs.
B. Dec. 20, 1948, Brooklyn, N. Y.

Year	Team	Games	BA	SA	AB	H	2B	3B	HR	HR%	R	RBI	BB	SO	SB	Pinch Hit AB	Pinch Hit H	PO	A	E	DP	TC/G	FA	G by Pos
1977	**CLE A**	133	.270	.364	440	119	23	6	2	0.5	59	37	64	57	26	10	5	326	9	6	2	2.7	.982	OF-124, 1B-3
1978		113	.283	.378	315	89	14	5	2	0.6	41	27	42	20	12	20	5	196	8	2	6	2.1	.990	OF-78, DH-15, 1B-6
1979		124	.246	.348	353	87	15	6	3	0.8	50	30	44	35	15	18	4	214	2	4	0	2.1	.982	OF-93, DH-13
1980	**TEX A**	119	.247	.276	174	43	5	0	0	0.0	23	16	23	16	6	31	9	96	4	0	1	1.1	1.000	OF-82, 1B-10, DH-1
4 yrs.		489	.264	.351	1282	338	57	17	7	0.5	173	110	173	128	59	79	23	832	23	12	9	2.0	.986	OF-377, DH-29, 1B-19

Leo Norris

NORRIS, LEO JOHN BR TR 5′11″ 165 lbs.
B. May 17, 1908, Bay St. Louis, Miss. D. Feb. 13, 1987, Zachary, La.

Year	Team	Games	BA	SA	AB	H	2B	3B	HR	HR%	R	RBI	BB	SO	SB	Pinch Hit AB	Pinch Hit H	PO	A	E	DP	TC/G	FA	G by Pos
1936	**PHI N**	154	.265	.382	581	154	27	4	11	1.9	64	76	39	79	4	0	0	414	475	53	98	5.9	.944	SS-121, 2B-38
1937		116	.257	.407	381	98	24	3	9	2.4	45	36	21	53	3	5	0	212	264	22	43	4.2	.956	2B-74, 3B-24, SS-20
2 yrs.		270	.262	.392	962	252	51	7	20	2.1	109	112	60	132	7	5	0	626	739	75	141	5.2	.948	SS-141, 2B-112, 3B-24

Billy North

NORTH, WILLIAM ALEX BB TR 5′11″ 185 lbs.
B. May 15, 1948, Seattle, Wash. BR 1971

Year	Team	Games	BA	SA	AB	H	2B	3B	HR	HR%	R	RBI	BB	SO	SB	Pinch Hit AB	Pinch Hit H	PO	A	E	DP	TC/G	FA	G by Pos
1971	**CHI N**	8	.375	.375	16	6	0	0	0	0.0	3	0	4	6	1	0	0	4	0	0	0	0.7	1.000	OF-6
1972		66	.181	.244	127	23	2	3	0	0.0	22	4	13	33	6	13	3	61	3	3	1	1.4	.955	OF-48

Billy North *continued*

Year	Team	Games	BA	SA	AB	H	2B	3B	HR	HR%	R	RBI	BB	SO	SB	Pinch Hit AB	Pinch Hit H	PO	A	E	DP	TC/G	FA	G by Pos
1973	OAK A	146	.285	.348	554	158	10	5	5	0.9	98	34	78	89	53	2	0	429	14	9	5	3.1	.980	OF-138, DH-6
1974		149	.260	.337	543	141	20	5	4	0.7	79	33	69	86	**54**	1	1	437	9	4	2	3.1	.991	OF-138, DH-8
1975		140	.273	.330	524	143	17	5	1	0.2	74	43	81	80	30	1	1	420	10	11	1	3.2	.975	OF-138, DH-1
1976		154	.276	.337	590	163	20	5	2	0.3	91	31	73	95	**75**	1	0	397	8	9	1	2.7	.978	OF-144, DH-8
1977		56	.261	.326	184	48	3	3	1	0.5	32	9	32	25	17	4	0	112	1	2	0	2.2	.983	OF-52, DH-1
1978	2 teams	OAK A (24G –.212)	LA N (110G –.234)																					
"	total	134	.230	.270	356	82	14	0	0	0.0	59	15	74	61	30	9	4	263	3	6	1	2.3	.978	OF-120
1979	SF N	142	.259	.341	460	119	15	4	5	1.1	87	30	96	84	58	11	1	300	8	4	2	2.4	.987	OF-130
1980		128	.251	.292	415	104	12	1	1	0.2	73	19	81	78	45	19	5	313	6	6	1	2.8	.982	OF-115
1981		46	.221	.298	131	29	7	0	1	0.8	22	12	26	28	26	7	1	84	1	3	1	2.4	.966	OF-37
11 yrs.		1169	.261	.323	3900	1016	120	31	20	0.5	640	230	627	665	395	68	16	2820	63	57	15	2.7	.981	OF-1066, DH-24
LEAGUE CHAMPIONSHIP SERIES																								
1974	OAK A	4	.063	.125	16	1	1	0	0	0.0	3	0	2	1	1	0	0	14	0	0	0	3.5	1.000	OF-4
1975		3	.000	.000	10	0	0	0	0	0.0	0	1	2	0	0	0	0	6	1	1	0	2.7	.875	OF-3
1978	LA N	4	.000	.000	8	0	0	0	0	0.0	0	0	0	1	0	0	0	9	0	0	0	2.3	1.000	OF-4
3 yrs.		11	.029	.059	34	1	1	0	0	0.0	3	1	4	2	1	0	0	29	1	1	0	2.8	.968	OF-11
WORLD SERIES																								
1974	OAK A	5	.059	.059	17	1	0	0	0	0.0	3	0	2	5	1	0	0	17	0	1	0	3.6	.944	OF-5
1978	LA N	4	.125	.250	8	1	1	0	0	0.0	2	2	1	0	1	1	1	7	0	0	0	1.8	1.000	OF-4
2 yrs.		9	.080	.120	25	2	1	0	0	0.0	5	2	3	5	2	1	1	24	0	1	0	2.8	.960	OF-9

Hub Northen

NORTHEN, HUBBARD ELWIN BL TL 5′ 8″ 175 lbs.
B. Aug. 16, 1885, Atlanta, Tex. D. Oct. 1, 1947, Shreveport, La.

Year	Team	Games	BA	SA	AB	H	2B	3B	HR	HR%	R	RBI	BB	SO	SB	Pinch Hit AB	Pinch Hit H	PO	A	E	DP	TC/G	FA	G by Pos
1910	STL A	26	.198	.208	96	19	1	0	0	0.0	6	16	5		2	0	0	48	2	4	0	2.1	.926	OF-26
1911	2 teams	CIN N (1G –.000)	BKN N (19G –.316)																					
"	total	20	.316	.395	76	24	2	2	0	0.0	16	1	14	9	4	0	0	46	5	5	0	2.9	.911	OF-19
1912	BKN N	118	.282	.388	412	116	26	6	2	0.5	54	46	41	46	8	15	4	178	11	10	3	2.0	.950	OF-102
3 yrs.		164	.272	.360	584	159	29	8	2	0.3	76	63	60	55	14	15	4	272	18	19	3	2.1	.939	OF-147

Ron Northey

NORTHEY, RONALD JAMES (The Round Man) BL TR 5′10″ 195 lbs.
Father of Scott Northey.
B. Apr. 26, 1920, Mahanoy City, Pa. D. Apr. 16, 1971, Pittsburgh, Pa.

Year	Team	Games	BA	SA	AB	H	2B	3B	HR	HR%	R	RBI	BB	SO	SB	Pinch Hit AB	Pinch Hit H	PO	A	E	DP	TC/G	FA	G by Pos
1942	PHI N	127	.251	.331	402	101	13	2	5	1.2	31	31	28	33	2	17	4	206	12	11	2	2.1	.952	OF-109
1943		147	.278	.430	586	163	31	5	16	2.7	72	68	51	52	2	2	0	292	19	7	6	2.2	.978	OF-145
1944		152	.288	.496	570	164	35	9	22	3.9	72	104	67	51	1	1	0	286	24	6	7	2.1	.981	OF-151
1946		128	.249	.441	438	109	24	6	16	3.7	55	62	39	59	1	14	5	194	7	6	3	1.9	.971	OF-111
1947	2 teams	PHI N (13G –.255)	STL N (110G –.293)																					
"	total	123	.288	.492	358	103	22	3	15	4.2	59	66	54	32	1	13	3	143	16	8	2	1.5	.952	OF-107, 3B-2
1948	STL N	96	.321	.528	246	79	10	1	13	5.3	40	64	38	25	0	25	11	85	2	1	0	1.3	.989	OF-67
1949		90	.260	.423	265	69	18	2	7	2.6	28	50	31	15	0	12	0	93	4	2	2	1.4	.980	OF-73
1950	2 teams	CIN N (27G –.260)	CHI N (53G –.281)																					
"	total	80	.272	.487	191	52	14	0	9	4.7	22	29	25	15	0	27	5	59	3	2	2	1.3	.969	OF-51
1952	CHI N	1	.000	.000	1	0	0	0	0	0.0	0	0	0	0	0	1	0	0	0	0	0	0.0	—	
1955	CHI A	14	.357	.714	14	5	2	0	1	7.1	1	4	3	3	0	10	4	1	0	0	0	0.5	1.000	OF-2
1956		53	.354	.583	48	17	2	0	3	6.3	4	23	8	1	0	39	**15**	4	1	0	0	1.3	1.000	OF-4
1957	2 teams	CHI A (40G –.185)	PHI N (33G –.269)																					
"	total	73	.226	.302	53	12	1	0	1	1.9	1	12	17	11	0	53	12	0	0	0	0	0.0	—	
12 yrs.		1084	.276	.450	3172	874	172	28	108	3.4	385	513	361	297	7	214	59	1363	88	43	24	1.8	.971	OF-820, 3B-2

Scott Northey

NORTHEY, SCOTT RICHARD BR TR 6′ 175 lbs.
Son of Ron Northey.
B. Oct. 15, 1946, Philadelphia, Pa.

Year	Team	Games	BA	SA	AB	H	2B	3B	HR	HR%	R	RBI	BB	SO	SB	Pinch Hit AB	Pinch Hit H	PO	A	E	DP	TC/G	FA	G by Pos
1969	KC A	20	.262	.410	61	16	2	2	1	1.6	11	7	7	19	6	0	0	35	1	1	0	2.1	.973	OF-18

Jim Northrup

NORTHRUP, JAMES THOMAS BL TR 6′ 3″ 190 lbs.
B. Nov. 24, 1939, Breckenridge, Mich.

Year	Team	Games	BA	SA	AB	H	2B	3B	HR	HR%	R	RBI	BB	SO	SB	Pinch Hit AB	Pinch Hit H	PO	A	E	DP	TC/G	FA	G by Pos
1964	DET A	5	.083	.167	12	1	1	0	0	0.0	1	0	0	3	1	3	0	4	0	0	0	2.0	1.000	OF-2
1965		80	.205	.315	219	45	12	3	2	0.9	20	16	12	50	1	24	3	82	0	2	0	1.6	.976	OF-54
1966		123	.265	.465	419	111	24	6	16	3.8	53	58	33	52	4	10	4	241	8	5	1	2.2	.980	OF-113
1967		144	.271	.392	495	134	18	6	10	2.0	63	61	43	83	7	5	1	271	3	8	1	2.0	.972	OF-143
1968		154	.264	.447	580	153	29	7	21	3.6	76	90	50	87	4	4	0	321	7	7	1	2.2	.979	OF-151
1969		148	.295	.508	543	160	31	5	25	4.6	79	66	52	83	4	5	0	323	8	5	2	2.3	.985	OF-143
1970		139	.262	.458	504	132	21	3	24	4.8	71	80	58	68	3	3	1	284	4	2	1	2.1	.993	OF-136
1971		136	.270	.442	459	124	27	2	16	3.5	72	71	60	43	7	14	5	441	20	9	23	3.4	.981	OF-108, 1B-32
1972		134	.261	.362	426	111	15	2	8	1.9	40	42	38	47	4	14	2	224	9	5	2	1.8	.979	OF-127, 1B-2
1973		119	.307	.465	404	124	14	7	12	3.0	55	44	38	41	4	8	2	207	6	4	2	1.9	.982	OF-116
1974	3 teams	DET A (97G –.237)	MON N (21G –.241)	BAL A (8G –.571)																				
"	total	126	.243	.373	437	106	13	1	14	3.2	46	53	43	56	0	10	2	226	6	6	0	2.1	.975	OF-116
1975	BAL A	84	.273	.418	194	53	13	0	5	2.6	27	29	22	22	0	22	8	91	2	2	0	1.6	.979	OF-58, DH-3
12 yrs.		1392	.267	.429	4692	1254	218	42	153	3.3	603	610	449	635	39	122	28	2715	73	55	33	2.2	.981	OF-1267, 1B-34, DH-3
LEAGUE CHAMPIONSHIP SERIES																								
1972	DET A	5	.357	.357	14	5	0	0	0	0.0	0	1	2	3	0	0	0	12	0	0	0	2.4	1.000	OF-5
WORLD SERIES																								
1968	DET A	7	.250	.536	28	7	0	1	2	7.1	4	8	1	5	0	0	0	22	0	2	0	3.4	.917	OF-7

Willie Norwood

NORWOOD, WILLIE BR TR 6′ 185 lbs.
B. Nov. 7, 1950, Green County, Ala.

Year	Team	Games	BA	SA	AB	H	2B	3B	HR	HR%	R	RBI	BB	SO	SB	Pinch Hit AB	Pinch Hit H	PO	A	E	DP	TC/G	FA	G by Pos
1977	MIN A	39	.229	.373	83	19	3	0	3	3.6	15	9	6	17	6	7	1	59	0	3	0	1.9	.952	OF-28, DH-5
1978		125	.255	.376	428	109	22	3	8	1.9	56	46	28	64	25	8	2	227	7	14	1	2.0	.944	OF-115, DH-12

Willie Norwood *continued*

Year	Team	Games	BA	SA	AB	H	2B	3B	HR	HR%	R	RBI	BB	SO	SB	Pinch Hit AB	Pinch Hit H	PO	A	E	DP	TC/G	FA	G by Pos
1979		96	.248	.385	270	67	13	3	6	2.2	32	30	20	51	9	14	5	147	4	4	0	1.8	.974	OF-71, DH-14
1980		34	.164	.233	73	12	2	0	1	1.4	6	8	3	13	1	7	2	42	0	0	0	1.6	1.000	OF-17, DH-9
4 yrs.		294	.242	.367	854	207	40	6	18	2.1	109	93	57	145	41	36	10	475	11	21	1	1.9	.959	OF-231, DH-40

Joe Nossek

NOSSEK, JOSEPH RUDOLPH BR TR 6′ 178 lbs.
B. Nov. 8, 1940, Cleveland, Ohio.

Year	Team	Games	BA	SA	AB	H	2B	3B	HR	HR%	R	RBI	BB	SO	SB	Pinch Hit AB	Pinch Hit H	PO	A	E	DP	TC/G	FA	G by Pos
1964	**MIN A**	7	.000	.000	1	0	0	0	0	0.0	1	0	0	0	0	1	0	0	0	0	0	0.0	.000	OF-2
1965		87	.218	.306	170	37	9	0	2	1.2	19	16	7	22	2	28	7	72	26	4	1	1.8	.961	OF-48, 3B-9
1966	**2 teams**	**MIN A** (4G –.000) **KC A** (87G –.261)																						
″	**total**	91	.261	.343	230	60	10	3	1	0.4	13	27	8	21	4	17	8	161	8	3	1	2.1	.983	OF-80, 3B-1
1967	**KC A**	87	.205	.253	166	34	6	1	0	0.0	12	10	4	26	2	28	1	105	2	2	0	1.7	.982	OF-63
1969	**2 teams**	**OAK A** (13G –.000) **STL N** (9G –.200)																						
″	**total**	22	.091	.091	11	1	0	0	0	0.0	2	0	0	3	0	4	1	9	0	0	0	0.7	1.000	OF-13
1970	**STL N**	1	.000	.000	1	0	0	0	0	0.0	0	0	0	0	0	1	0	0	0	0	0	0.0	—	
6 yrs.		295	.228	.301	579	132	25	4	3	0.5	47	53	19	72	8	79	17	347	36	9	2	1.8	.977	OF-206, 3B-10
WORLD SERIES																								
1965	**MIN A**	6	.200	.200	20	4	0	0	0	0.0	0	0	0	1	0	1	1	13	0	0	0	2.6	1.000	OF-5

Lou Novikoff

NOVIKOFF, LOUIS ALEXANDER (The Mad Russian) BR TR 5′10″ 185 lbs.
B. Oct. 12, 1915, Glendale, Ariz. D. Sept. 30, 1970, South Gate, Calif.

Year	Team	Games	BA	SA	AB	H	2B	3B	HR	HR%	R	RBI	BB	SO	SB	Pinch Hit AB	Pinch Hit H	PO	A	E	DP	TC/G	FA	G by Pos
1941	**CHI N**	62	.241	.355	203	49	8	0	5	2.5	22	24	11	15	0	8	3	92	3	0	0	1.8	1.000	OF-54
1942		128	.300	.416	483	145	25	5	7	1.4	48	64	24	28	3	8	2	232	11	9	2	2.1	.964	OF-120
1943		78	.279	.335	233	65	7	3	0	0.0	22	28	18	15	0	15	6	96	2	2	1	1.6	.980	OF-61
1944		71	.281	.403	139	39	4	2	3	2.2	15	19	10	11	1	39	**12**	39	1	1	0	1.4	.976	OF-29
1946	**PHI N**	17	.304	.348	23	7	1	0	0	0.0	0	3	1	2	0	14	6	9	0	0	0	3.0	1.000	OF-3
5 yrs.		356	.282	.384	1081	305	45	10	15	1.4	107	138	64	71	4	84	29	468	17	12	3	1.9	.976	OF-267

Rube Novotney

NOVOTNEY, RALPH JOSEPH BR TR 6′ 187 lbs.
B. Aug. 5, 1924, Streator, Ill. D. July 16, 1987, Redondo Beach, Calif.

Year	Team	Games	BA	SA	AB	H	2B	3B	HR	HR%	R	RBI	BB	SO	SB	Pinch Hit AB	Pinch Hit H	PO	A	E	DP	TC/G	FA	G by Pos
1949	**CHI N**	22	.269	.328	67	18	2	1	0	0.0	4	6	3	11	0	2	1	82	9	4	3	4.8	.958	C-20

Les Nunamaker

NUNAMAKER, LESLIE GRANT BR TR 6′2″ 190 lbs.
B. Jan. 25, 1889, Malcolm, Neb. D. Nov. 14, 1938, Hastings, Neb.

Year	Team	Games	BA	SA	AB	H	2B	3B	HR	HR%	R	RBI	BB	SO	SB	Pinch Hit AB	Pinch Hit H	PO	A	E	DP	TC/G	FA	G by Pos
1911	**BOS A**	62	.257	.311	183	47	4	3	0	0.0	18	19	12		1	3	0	309	79	11	8	6.8	.972	C-59
1912		35	.252	.340	103	26	5	2	0	0.0	15	6	6		2	0	0	166	33	6	3	5.9	.971	C-35
1913		29	.215	.354	65	14	5	2	0	0.0	9	9	8	8	2	1	0	147	23	4	1	6.4	.977	C-27
1914	**2 teams**	**BOS A** (4G –.200) **NY A** (87G –.265)																						
″	**total**	91	.263	.347	262	69	10	3	2	0.8	19	29	23	34	11	10	3	329	131	15	13	6.1	.968	C-72, 1B-6
1915	**NY A**	87	.225	.273	249	56	6	3	0	0.0	24	17	23	24	3	6	2	350	100	16	9	5.9	.966	C-77, 1B-2
1916		91	.296	.404	260	77	14	7	0	0.0	25	28	34	21	4	11	6	353	102	8	13	5.9	.983	C-79
1917		104	.261	.303	310	81	9	2	0	0.0	22	33	21	25	5	13	7	372	113	12	12	5.5	.976	C-91
1918	**STL A**	85	.259	.307	274	71	9	2	0	0.0	22	22	28	16	6	3	3	322	108	12	10	5.3	.973	C-81, OF-1, 1B-1
1919	**CLE A**	26	.250	.304	56	14	1	1	0	0.0	6	7	2	6	0	10	3	39	12	4	0	3.4	.927	C-16
1920		34	.333	.500	54	18	3	3	0	0.0	10	14	4	5	1	10	1	69	13	4	1	3.7	.953	C-17, 1B-6
1921		46	.359	.443	131	47	7	2	0	0.0	16	24	11	8	1	0	0	166	31	6	3	4.4	.970	C-46
1922		25	.302	.349	43	13	2	0	0	0.0	8	7	4	3	0	11	3	38	5	3	0	3.1	.935	C-15
12 yrs.		715	.268	.339	1990	533	75	30	2	0.1	194	215	176	150	36	78	28	2660	750	101	73	5.6	.971	C-615, 1B-15, OF-1
WORLD SERIES																								
1920	**CLE A**	2	.500	.500	2	1	0	0	0	0.0	0	0	0	0	0	2	1	0	0	0	0	0.0	.000	C-1

Jon Nunnally

NUNNALLY, JONATHAN KEITH BL TR 5′10″ 190 lbs.
B. Nov. 9, 1971, Pelham, N. C.

Year	Team	Games	BA	SA	AB	H	2B	3B	HR	HR%	R	RBI	BB	SO	SB	Pinch Hit AB	Pinch Hit H	PO	A	E	DP	TC/G	FA	G by Pos
1995	**KC A**	119	.244	.472	303	74	15	6	14	4.6	51	42	51	86	6	19	4	196	5	6	1	1.9	.971	OF-107, DH-4

Emory Nusz

NUSZ, EMORY MOBERLY
B. Apr. 2, 1866, Frederick, Md. D. Aug. 3, 1898, Point of Rocks, Md.

Year	Team	Games	BA	SA	AB	H	2B	3B	HR	HR%	R	RBI	BB	SO	SB	Pinch Hit AB	Pinch Hit H	PO	A	E	DP	TC/G	FA	G by Pos
1884	**WAS U**	1	.000	.000	4	0	0	0	0	0.0	1		0			0	0	2	0	2	0	4.0	.500	OF-1

Dizzy Nutter

NUTTER, EVERETT CLARENCE BL TR 5′9″ 160 lbs.
B. Aug. 27, 1893, Roseville, Ohio D. July 25, 1958, Battle Creek, Mich.

Year	Team	Games	BA	SA	AB	H	2B	3B	HR	HR%	R	RBI	BB	SO	SB	Pinch Hit AB	Pinch Hit H	PO	A	E	DP	TC/G	FA	G by Pos
1919	**BOS N**	18	.212	.212	52	11	0	0	0	0.0	4	3	4	5	1	5	0	29	3	0	1	2.7	1.000	OF-12

Joe Nuxhall

NUXHALL, JOSEPH HENRY BL TL 6′3″ 195 lbs.
B. July 30, 1928, Hamilton, Ohio.

Year	Team	Games	BA	SA	AB	H	2B	3B	HR	HR%	R	RBI	BB	SO	SB	Pinch Hit AB	Pinch Hit H	PO	A	E	DP	TC/G	FA	G by Pos
1944	**CIN N**	1	—	—	0	0	0	0	0	—	0	0	0	0	0	0	0	0	0	0	0	0.0	.000	P-1
1952		37	.087	.087	23	2	0	0	0	0.0	0	0	0	8	0	0	0	3	24	1	4	0.8	.964	P-37
1953		30	.327	.551	49	16	2	0	3	6.1	6	8	4	13	0	0	0	6	18	3	0	0.9	.889	P-30
1954		36	.173	.346	52	9	0	0	3	5.8	13	7	8	12	0	0	0	4	29	1	5	1.0	.971	P-35
1955		53	.198	.349	86	17	4	0	3	3.5	10	14	8	24	0	3	0	12	35	3	4	1.0	.940	P-50
1956		44	.186	.356	59	11	2	1	2	3.4	6	7	4	15	0	0	0	6	31	2	3	0.9	.949	P-44
1957		42	.237	.288	59	14	1	1	0	0.0	6	7	5	15	0	1	1	11	20	4	1	0.9	.886	P-39
1958		36	.210	.226	62	13	1	0	0	0.0	4	5	1	13	1	0	0	6	29	3	3	1.1	.921	P-36
1959		28	.250	.318	44	11	3	0	0	0.0	5	2	1	4	0	0	0	6	19	1	1	0.9	.962	P-28
1960		39	.077	.115	26	2	1	0	0	0.0	3	1	1	6	0	0	0	8	26	1	4	0.9	.971	P-38
1961	**KC A**	56	.292	.446	65	19	2	1	2	3.1	5	13	6	18	0	20	5	10	13	3	1	0.7	.885	P-37
1962	**2 teams**	**LA A** (5G –.000) **CIN N** (12G –.269)																						
″	**total**	17	.269	.423	26	7	1	0	1	3.8	3	5	0	3	0	0	0	2	11	0	1	0.8	1.000	P-17
1963	**CIN N**	35	.158	.184	76	12	2	0	0	0.0	6	3	0	25	0	0	0	5	33	5	2	1.2	.884	P-35

Joe Nuxhall *continued*

Year	Team		Games	BA	SA	AB	H	2B	3B	HR	HR%	R	RBI	BB	SO	SB	Pinch Hit AB	Pinch Hit H	PO	A	E	DP	TC/G	FA	G by Pos
1964			34	.130	.185	54	7	0	0	1	1.9	2	1	0	20	1	0	0	5	20	2	1	0.8	.926	P-32
1965			32	.178	.200	45	8	1	0	0	0.0	5	3	2	9	0	0	0	5	13	0	0	0.6	1.000	P-32
1966			35	.100	.125	40	4	1	0	0	0.0	2	2	0	14	0	1	0	6	20	3	1	0.8	.897	P-35
16 yrs.			555	.198	.292	766	152	21	3	15	2.0	76	78	40	199	2	25	6	95	341	32	31	0.9	.932	P-526

Charlie Nyce

NYCE, CHARLES REIFF 5′ 8″ 160 lbs.
Born Charles Reiff Nice.
B. July 1, 1870, Philadelphia, Pa. D. May 9, 1908, Philadelphia, Pa.

Year	Team		Games	BA	SA	AB	H	2B	3B	HR	HR%	R	RBI	BB	SO	SB	Pinch Hit AB	Pinch Hit H	PO	A	E	DP	TC/G	FA	G by Pos
1895	**BOS**	**N**	9	.229	.543	35	8	5	0	2	5.7	7	9	4	2	0	0	0	18	30	6	4	6.0	.889	SS-9

Chris Nyman

NYMAN, CHRISTOPHER CURTIS BR TR 6′ 4″ 200 lbs.
Brother of Nyls Nyman.
B. June 6, 1955, Pomona, Calif.

Year	Team		Games	BA	SA	AB	H	2B	3B	HR	HR%	R	RBI	BB	SO	SB	Pinch Hit AB	Pinch Hit H	PO	A	E	DP	TC/G	FA	G by Pos
1982	**CHI**	**A**	28	.246	.262	65	16	1	0	0	0.0	6	2	3	9	3	5	0	161	12	1	16	6.7	.994	1B-24, OF-2
1983			21	.286	.500	28	8	0	0	2	7.1	12	4	4	7	2	0	0	87	5	0	8	4.6	1.000	1B-10, DH-10
2 yrs.			49	.258	.333	93	24	1	0	2	2.2	18	6	7	16	5	5	0	248	17	1	24	5.8	.996	1B-34, DH-10, OF-2

Nyls Nyman

NYMAN, NYLS WALLACE REX BL TR 6′ 170 lbs.
Brother of Chris Nyman.
B. Mar. 7, 1954, Detroit, Mich.

Year	Team		Games	BA	SA	AB	H	2B	3B	HR	HR%	R	RBI	BB	SO	SB	Pinch Hit AB	Pinch Hit H	PO	A	E	DP	TC/G	FA	G by Pos
1974	**CHI**	**A**	5	.643	.929	14	9	2	1	0	0.0	5	4	0	1	1	1	1	6	1	0	1	2.3	1.000	OF-3
1975			106	.226	.281	327	74	6	3	2	0.6	36	28	11	34	10	3	1	177	6	8	0	1.9	.958	OF-94, DH-4
1976			8	.133	.200	15	2	1	0	0	0.0	2	1	0	3	1	0	0	13	0	0	0	1.9	1.000	OF-7
1977			1	.000	.000	1	0	0	0	0	0.0	0	0	0	0	0	0	0	0	0	0	0	0.0	—	
4 yrs.			120	.238	.303	357	85	9	4	2	0.6	43	33	11	38	12	4	2	196	7	8	1	2.0	.962	OF-104, DH-4

Rebel Oakes

OAKES, ENNIS TELFAIR BL TR 5′ 8″ 170 lbs.
B. Dec. 17, 1886, Homer, La. D. Feb. 29, 1948, Rocky Springs, La.
Manager 1914–15.

Year	Team		Games	BA	SA	AB	H	2B	3B	HR	HR%	R	RBI	BB	SO	SB	Pinch Hit AB	Pinch Hit H	PO	A	E	DP	TC/G	FA	G by Pos
1909	**CIN**	**N**	120	.270	.340	415	112	10	5	3	0.7	55	31	40		23	7	2	218	15	5	3	2.1	.979	OF-113
1910	**STL**	**N**	131	.252	.308	468	118	14	6	0	0.0	50	43	38	38	18	3	1	266	12	18	3	2.3	.939	OF-127
1911			154	.263	.319	551	145	13	6	2	0.4	69	59	41	35	25	2	1	364	26	16	8	2.7	.961	OF-151
1912			136	.281	.358	495	139	19	5	3	0.6	57	58	31	24	26	1	1	324	15	19	5	2.6	.947	OF-136
1913			146	.291	.335	537	156	14	5	0	0.0	59	49	43	32	22	2	1	321	16	11	2	2.4	.968	OF-144
1914	**PIT**	**F**	145	.312	.415	571	178	18	10	7	1.2	82	75	35		28	0	0	313	23	14	2	2.4	.960	OF-145
1915			153	.278	.336	580	161	24	5	0	0.0	55	82	37		21	0	0	348	12	10	2	2.4	.973	OF-153
7 yrs.			985	.279	.346	3617	1009	112	42	15	0.4	427	397	265	129	163	15	6	2154	119	93	25	2.4	.961	OF-969

Prince Oana

OANA, HENRY KAUHANE BR TR 6′ 2″ 193 lbs.
B. Jan. 22, 1908, Waipahu, Hawaii D. June 19, 1976, Austin, Tex.

Year	Team		Games	BA	SA	AB	H	2B	3B	HR	HR%	R	RBI	BB	SO	SB	Pinch Hit AB	Pinch Hit H	PO	A	E	DP	TC/G	FA	G by Pos
1934	**PHI**	**N**	6	.238	.286	21	5	1	0	0	0.0	3	3	0	1	0	2	1	14	0	0	0	3.5	1.000	OF-4
1943	**DET**	**A**	20	.385	.654	26	10	2	1	1	3.8	5	7	1	2	0	9	3	0	6	2	2	0.8	.750	P-10
1945			4	.200	.200	5	1	0	0	0	0.0	0	0	0	0	0	1	0	0	1	0	0	0.3	1.000	P-3
3 yrs.			30	.308	.462	52	16	3	1	1	1.9	8	10	1	3	0	12	4	14	7	2	2	1.4	.913	P-13, OF-4

Johnny Oates

OATES, JOHNNY LANE BL TR 5′11″ 188 lbs.
B. Jan. 21, 1946, Sylva, N. C.
Manager 1991–95.

Year	Team		Games	BA	SA	AB	H	2B	3B	HR	HR%	R	RBI	BB	SO	SB	Pinch Hit AB	Pinch Hit H	PO	A	E	DP	TC/G	FA	G by Pos
1970	**BAL**	**A**	5	.278	.389	18	5	0	1	0	0.0	2	2	2	0	0	1	1	30	1	2	1	8.3	.939	C-4
1972			85	.261	.364	253	66	12	1	4	1.6	20	21	28	31	5	10	1	391	31	2	4	5.2	.995	C-82
1973	**ATL**	**N**	93	.248	.304	322	80	6	0	4	1.2	27	27	22	31	1	6	2	409	57	9	6	5.5	.981	C-86
1974			100	.223	.268	291	65	10	0	1	0.3	22	21	23	24	2	15	4	434	55	4	4	5.4	.992	C-91
1975	**2 teams**	**ATL N** (8G –.222) **PHI N** (90G –.286)																							
″	**total**		98	.282	.345	287	81	15	0	1	0.3	28	25	34	33	1	13	2	450	45	5	10	5.7	.990	C-88
1976	**PHI**	**N**	37	.253	.273	99	25	2	0	0	0.0	10	8	8	12	0	8	2	155	15	1	1	5.2	.994	C-33
1977	**LA**	**N**	60	.269	.353	156	42	4	0	3	1.9	18	11	11	11	1	6	0	258	37	4	3	5.3	.987	C-56
1978			40	.307	.320	75	23	1	0	0	0.0	5	6	5	3	0	14	3	77	10	4	1	3.8	.956	C-24
1979			26	.130	.174	46	6	2	0	0	0.0	4	2	4	1	0	6	1	64	13	2	2	4.0	.975	C-20
1980	**NY**	**A**	39	.188	.281	64	12	3	0	1	1.6	6	3	2	3	1	0	0	99	10	1	1	2.8	.991	C-39
1981			10	.192	.231	26	5	1	0	0	0.0	4	0	2	0	0	0	0	49	3	2	0	5.4	.963	C-10
11 yrs.			593	.250	.313	1637	410	56	2	14	0.9	146	126	141	149	11	79	16	2416	277	36	33	5.1	.987	C-533
LEAGUE CHAMPIONSHIP SERIES																									
1976	**PHI**	**N**	1	.000	.000	1	0	0	0	0	0.0	0	0	0	0	0	0	0	1	0	0	0	1.0	1.000	C-1
WORLD SERIES																									
1977	**LA**	**N**	1	.000	.000	1	0	0	0	0	0.0	0	0	0	0	0	1	0	1	0	0	0	1.0	1.000	C-1
1978			1	1.000	1.000	1	1	0	0	0	0.0	0	0	1	0	0	0	0	3	1	0	0	4.0	1.000	C-1
2 yrs.			2	.500	.500	2	1	0	0	0	0.0	0	0	1	0	0	1	0	4	1	0	0	2.5	1.000	C-2

Sherman Obando

OBANDO, SHERMAN OMAR BR TR 6′ 4″ 215 lbs.
Born Sherman Omar Obando (Gainor).
B. Jan. 23, 1970, Bocas del Toro, Panama.

Year	Team		Games	BA	SA	AB	H	2B	3B	HR	HR%	R	RBI	BB	SO	SB	Pinch Hit AB	Pinch Hit H	PO	A	E	DP	TC/G	FA	G by Pos
1993	**BAL**	**A**	31	.272	.391	92	25	2	0	3	3.3	8	15	4	26	0	3	0	13	0	1	0	0.5	.929	DH-21, OF-8
1995			16	.263	.289	38	10	1	0	0	0.0	0	3	2	12	1	6	2	12	0	1	0	0.9	.923	OF-7, DH-7
2 yrs.			47	.269	.362	130	35	3	0	3	2.3	8	18	6	38	1	9	2	25	0	2	0	0.6	.926	DH-28, OF-15

Henry Oberbeck

OBERBECK, HENRY A.
B. May 17, 1858, St. Louis, Mo. D. Aug. 26, 1921, St. Louis, Mo.

Year	Team	Games	BA	SA	AB	H	2B	3B	HR	HR%	R	RBI	BB	SO	SB	Pinch Hit AB	Pinch Hit H	PO	A	E	DP	TC/G	FA	G by Pos
1883	**2 teams**	**PIT AA** (2G –.222) **STL AA** (4G –.000)																						
″	**total**	6	.087	.130	23	2	1	0	0	0.0	1		0			0	0	28	2	1	3	5.2	.968	OF-4, 1B-2
1884	**2 teams**	**BAL U** (33G –.184) **KC U** (27G –.189)																						
″	**total**	60	.186	.219	215	40	7	0	0	0.0	26		10			0	0	107	59	26	3	2.8	.865	OF-35, 3B-23, P-8, 1B-3
2 yrs.		66	.176	.210	238	42	8	0	0	0.0	27		10			0	0	135	61	27	6	3.0	.879	OF-39, 3B-23, P-8, 1B-5

Ken Oberkfell

OBERKFELL, KENNETH RAY (Obie) BL TR 6′ 175 lbs.
B. May 4, 1956, Highland, Ill.

Year	Team	Games	BA	SA	AB	H	2B	3B	HR	HR%	R	RBI	BB	SO	SB	Pinch Hit AB	Pinch Hit H	PO	A	E	DP	TC/G	FA	G by Pos
1977	**STL N**	9	.111	.111	9	1	0	0	0	0.0	0	1	0	3	0	3	0	3	4	0	1	1.2	1.000	2B-6
1978		24	.120	.140	50	6	1	0	0	0.0	7	0	3	1	0	3	0	30	48	1	8	3.8	.987	2B-17, 3B-4
1979		135	.301	.388	369	111	19	5	1	0.3	53	35	57	35	4	13	3	223	343	9	67	4.2	.984	2B-117, 3B-17, SS-2
1980		116	.303	.417	422	128	27	6	3	0.7	58	46	51	23	4	1	0	227	340	7	64	4.9	.988	2B-101, 3B-16
1981		102	.293	.372	376	110	12	6	2	0.5	43	45	37	28	13	1	0	77	247	15	23	3.3	.956	3B-102, SS-1
1982		137	.289	.370	470	136	22	5	2	0.4	55	34	40	31	11	3	1	80	305	11	23	2.9	.972	3B-135, 2B-1
1983		151	.293	.385	488	143	26	5	3	0.6	62	38	61	27	12	8	3	132	303	18	44	2.8	.960	3B-127, 2B-32, SS-1
1984	**2 teams**	**STL N** (50G –.309) **ATL N** (50G –.233)																						
″	**total**	100	.269	.349	324	87	19	2	1	0.3	38	21	31	27	2	6	1	64	173	8	15	2.5	.967	3B-91, 2B-6, SS-1
1985	**ATL N**	134	.272	.359	412	112	19	4	3	0.7	30	35	51	38	1	10	2	88	257	12	26	2.7	.966	3B-117, 2B-16
1986		151	.270	.360	503	136	24	3	5	1.0	62	48	83	40	7	4	1	116	335	11	39	2.7	.976	3B-130, 2B-41
1987		135	.280	.362	508	142	29	2	3	0.6	59	48	48	29	3	5	0	89	265	7	23	2.6	.981	3B-126, 2B-11
1988	**2 teams**	**ATL N** (120G –.277) **PIT N** (20G –.222)																						
″	**total**	140	.271	.353	476	129	22	4	3	0.6	49	42	37	34	4	15	2	107	237	15	24	2.7	.958	3B-115, 2B-12, SS-3, 1B-1
1989	**2 teams**	**PIT N** (14G –.125) **SF N** (83G –.319)																						
″	**total**	97	.269	.359	156	42	6	1	2	1.3	19	17	10	10	0	50	**18**	131	47	4	11	2.8	.978	3B-38, 1B-16, 2B-10
1990	**HOU N**	77	.207	.280	150	31	6	1	1	0.7	10	12	15	17	1	30	4	93	52	4	16	3.2	.973	3B-24, 2B-11, 1B-11
1991		53	.229	.286	70	16	4	0	0	0.0	7	14	14	8	0	32	6	70	13	2	6	5.0	.976	1B-13, 3B-4
1992	**CAL A**	41	.264	.275	91	24	1	0	0	0.0	6	10	8	5	0	8	1	43	34	1	4	2.8	.987	2B-21, DH-5, 1B-2
16 yrs.		1602	.278	.362	4874	1354	237	44	29	0.6	558	446	546	356	62	192	42	1573	3003	125	394	3.1	.973	3B-1046, 2B-402, 1B-43, SS-8, DH-5
LEAGUE CHAMPIONSHIP SERIES																								
1982	**STL N**	3	.200	.200	15	3	0	0	0	0.0	1	2	0	0	0	0	0	2	4	1	1	2.3	.857	3B-3
1989	**SF N**	3	.000	.000	4	0	0	0	0	0.0	0	0	0	0	0	3	0	0	1	0	0	1.0	1.000	3B-1
2 yrs.		6	.158	.158	19	3	0	0	0	0.0	1	2	0	0	0	3	0	2	5	1	1	2.0	.875	3B-4
WORLD SERIES																								
1982	**STL N**	7	.292	.333	24	7	1	0	0	0.0	4	1	2	1	2	0	0	3	21	1	2	3.6	.960	3B-7
1989	**SF N**	4	.333	.333	6	2	0	0	0	0.0	1	0	3	0	0	1	1	0	5	1	1	1.5	.833	3B-4
2 yrs.		11	.300	.333	30	9	1	0	0	0.0	5	1	5	1	2	1	1	3	26	2	3	2.8	.935	3B-11

Mike O'Berry

O'BERRY, PRESTON MICHAEL BR TR 6′ 2″ 190 lbs.
B. Apr. 20, 1954, Birmingham, Ala.

Year	Team	Games	BA	SA	AB	H	2B	3B	HR	HR%	R	RBI	BB	SO	SB	Pinch Hit AB	Pinch Hit H	PO	A	E	DP	TC/G	FA	G by Pos
1979	**BOS A**	43	.169	.237	59	10	1	0	1	1.7	8	4	5	16	0	0	0	103	7	5	1	2.7	.957	C-43
1980	**CHI N**	19	.208	.229	48	10	1	0	0	0.0	7	5	5	13	0	0	0	94	16	2	2	5.9	.982	C-19
1981	**CIN N**	55	.180	.252	111	20	3	1	1	0.9	6	5	14	19	0	0	0	208	22	4	2	4.3	.983	C-55
1982		21	.222	.267	45	10	2	0	0	0.0	5	3	10	13	0	0	0	84	12	1	2	4.6	.990	C-21
1983	**CAL A**	26	.167	.233	60	10	1	0	1	1.7	7	5	3	11	0	1	0	77	8	0	0	3.3	1.000	C-26
1984	**NY A**	13	.250	.313	32	8	2	0	0	0.0	3	5	2	2	0	1	0	53	5	0	1	4.5	1.000	C-12, 3B-1
1985	**MON N**	20	.190	.190	21	4	0	0	0	0.0	2	0	4	3	1	0	0	53	6	0	2	3.0	1.000	C-20
7 yrs.		197	.191	.247	376	72	10	1	3	0.8	38	27	43	77	1	2	0	672	76	12	10	3.9	.984	C-196, 3B-1

Jim Obradovich

OBRADOVICH, JAMES THOMAS BL TL 6′ 2″ 200 lbs.
B. Sept. 13, 1949, Ft. Campbell, Ky.

Year	Team	Games	BA	SA	AB	H	2B	3B	HR	HR%	R	RBI	BB	SO	SB	Pinch Hit AB	Pinch Hit H	PO	A	E	DP	TC/G	FA	G by Pos
1978	**HOU N**	10	.176	.294	17	3	0	1	0	0.0	3	2	1	3	0	6	0	28	1	0	0	9.7	1.000	1B-3

Billy O'Brien

O'BRIEN, WILLIAM SMITH BR 6′ 185 lbs.
B. Mar. 14, 1860, Albany, N. Y. D. May 26, 1911, Kansas City, Mo.

Year	Team	Games	BA	SA	AB	H	2B	3B	HR	HR%	R	RBI	BB	SO	SB	Pinch Hit AB	Pinch Hit H	PO	A	E	DP	TC/G	FA	G by Pos
1884	**2 teams**	**STP U** (8G –.233) **KC U** (4G –.235)																						
″	**total**	12	.234	.298	47	11	3	0	0	0.0	3		0			0	0	25	28	11	1	4.6	.828	3B-11, P-2, 1B-1
1887	**WAS N**	113	.278	.492	453	126	16	12	**19**	**4.2**	71	73	21	17	11	0	0	1175	39	34	53	10.9	.973	1B-104, 3B-4, OF-4, 2B-2
1888		133	.225	.313	528	119	15	2	9	1.7	42	66	9	70	10	0	0	1273	39	33	55	10.1	.975	1B-132, 3B-1
1889		2	.000	.000	8	0	0	0	0	0.0	1	0	1	1	0	0	0	19	0	0	0	9.5	1.000	1B-2
1890	**BKN AA**	96	.278	.415	388	108	25	8	4	1.0	47		28		5	0	0	1015	35	29	66	11.2	.973	1B-96
5 yrs.		356	.256	.395	1424	364	59	22	32	2.2	164	139	59	88	26	0	0	3507	141	107	175	10.5	.972	1B-335, 3B-16, OF-4, 2B-2, P-2

Charlie O'Brien

O'BRIEN, CHARLES HUGH BR TR 6′ 2″ 195 lbs.
B. May 1, 1960, Tulsa, Okla.

Year	Team	Games	BA	SA	AB	H	2B	3B	HR	HR%	R	RBI	BB	SO	SB	Pinch Hit AB	Pinch Hit H	PO	A	E	DP	TC/G	FA	G by Pos
1985	**OAK A**	16	.273	.364	11	3	1	0	0	0.0	3	1	3	3	0	0	0	23	0	1	0	1.5	.958	C-16
1987	**MIL A**	10	.200	.343	35	7	3	1	0	0.0	2	0	4	4	0	0	0	78	11	0	0	8.9	1.000	C-10
1988		40	.220	.322	118	26	6	0	2	1.7	12	9	5	16	0	0	0	210	20	2	4	5.8	.991	C-40
1989		62	.234	.383	188	44	10	0	6	3.2	22	35	21	11	0	0	0	314	36	5	5	5.7	.986	C-62
1990	**2 teams**	**MIL A** (46G –.186) **NY N** (28G –.162)																						
″	**total**	74	.178	.244	213	38	10	2	0	0.0	17	20	21	34	0	0	0	408	45	5	6	6.2	.989	C-74
1991	**NY N**	69	.185	.256	168	31	6	0	2	1.2	16	14	17	25	0	2	0	396	37	4	7	6.5	.991	C-67
1992		68	.212	.327	156	33	12	0	2	1.3	15	13	16	18	0	4	0	287	44	7	4	5.3	.979	C-64
1993		67	.255	.378	188	48	11	0	4	2.1	15	23	14	14	1	3	1	325	39	5	5	5.7	.986	C-65
1994	**ATL N**	51	.243	.474	152	37	11	0	8	5.3	24	28	15	24	0	3	1	308	26	3	1	7.0	.991	C-48
1995		67	.227	.399	198	45	7	0	9	4.5	18	23	29	40	0	4	1	447	23	4	5	7.4	.992	C-64
10 yrs.		524	.219	.346	1427	312	77	3	33	2.3	144	166	145	189	1	16	3	2796	281	36	37	6.1	.988	C-510
DIVISIONAL PLAYOFF SERIES																								
1995	**ATL N**	2	.200	.200	5	1	0	0	0	0.0	0	0	1	1	0	0	0	8	1	0	0	4.5	1.000	C-2
LEAGUE CHAMPIONSHIP SERIES																								
1995	**ATL N**	2	.400	1.000	5	2	0	0	1	20.0	1	3	0	1	0	1	0	3	1	0	0	4.0	1.000	C-1

Charlie O'Brien *continued*

Year	Team	Games	BA	SA	AB	H	2B	3B	HR	HR%	R	RBI	BB	SO	SB	Pinch Hit AB	Pinch Hit H	PO	A	E	DP	TC/G	FA	G by Pos
WORLD SERIES																								
1995	ATL N	2	.000	.000	3	0	0	0	0	0.0	0	0	0	1	0	0	0	7	2	0	0	4.5	1.000	C-2

Darby O'Brien

O'BRIEN, WILLIAM D. BR TR 6′ 1″ 186 lbs.
B. Sept. 1, 1863, Peoria, Ill. D. June 15, 1893, Peoria, Ill.

Year	Team	Games	BA	SA	AB	H	2B	3B	HR	HR%	R	RBI	BB	SO	SB	Pinch Hit AB	Pinch Hit H	PO	A	E	DP	TC/G	FA	G by Pos
1887	NY AA	127	.301	.437	522	157	30	13	5	1.0	97		40		49	0	0	312	28	31	9	2.7	.916	OF-121, 1B-10, SS-2, 3B-1, P-1
1888	BKN AA	136	.280	.365	532	149	27	6	2	0.4	105	65	30		55	0	0	231	15	18	1	1.9	.932	OF-136
1889		136	.300	.418	567	170	30	11	5	0.9	146	80	61	76	91	0	0	255	14	28	5	2.2	.906	OF-136
1890	BKN N	85	.314	.446	350	110	28	6	2	0.6	78	63	32	43	38	0	0	176	14	8	2	2.3	.960	OF-85
1891		103	.253	.367	395	100	18	6	5	1.3	79	57	39	53	31	0	0	203	11	11	1	2.2	.951	OF-103
1892		122	.243	.298	490	119	14	5	1	0.2	72	56	29	52	57	0	0	222	16	11	3	2.0	.956	OF-122
6 yrs.		709	.282	.387	2856	805	147	47	20	0.7	577	321	231	224	321	0	0	1399	98	107	21	2.2	.933	OF-703, 1B-10, SS-2, 3B-1, P-1

Eddie O'Brien

O'BRIEN, EDWARD JOSEPH BR TR 5′ 9″ 165 lbs.
Brother of Johnny O'Brien.
B. Dec. 11, 1930, South Amboy, N. J.

Year	Team	Games	BA	SA	AB	H	2B	3B	HR	HR%	R	RBI	BB	SO	SB	Pinch Hit AB	Pinch Hit H	PO	A	E	DP	TC/G	FA	G by Pos
1953	PIT N	89	.238	.280	261	62	5	3	0	0.0	21	14	17	30	6	4	0	122	207	23	39	4.3	.935	SS-81
1955		75	.233	.254	236	55	3	1	0	0.0	26	8	18	13	4	3	1	144	19	4	1	2.5	.976	OF-56, 3B-7, SS-4
1956		63	.264	.302	53	14	2	0	0	0.0	17	3	2	2	1	1	0	38	54	2	14	2.6	.979	SS-23, OF-6, 3B-4, 2B-2, P-1
1957		3	.000	.000	4	0	0	0	0	0.0	0	0	0	0	0	0	0	0	2	0	1	0.7	1.000	P-3
1958		1	—	—	0	0	0	0	0	—	0	0	0	0	0	0	0	0	0	0	0	0.0	.000	P-1
5 yrs.		231	.236	.269	554	131	10	4	0	0.0	64	25	37	45	11	8	1	304	282	29	55	3.3	.953	SS-108, OF-62, 3B-11, P-5, 2B-2

George O'Brien

O'BRIEN, GEORGE JOSEPH BR TR 6′ 185 lbs.
B. Nov. 4, 1889, Cleveland, Ohio D. Mar. 24, 1966, Columbus, Ohio.

Year	Team	Games	BA	SA	AB	H	2B	3B	HR	HR%	R	RBI	BB	SO	SB	Pinch Hit AB	Pinch Hit H	PO	A	E	DP	TC/G	FA	G by Pos
1915	STL A	3	.222	.222	9	2	0	0	0	0.0	1	0	1	2	0	0	0	11	3	1	0	5.0	.933	C-3

Jack O'Brien

O'BRIEN, JOHN JOSEPH BL TR 6′ 1″ 165 lbs.
B. Feb. 5, 1873, Watervliet, N. Y. D. June 10, 1933, Watervliet, N. Y.

Year	Team	Games	BA	SA	AB	H	2B	3B	HR	HR%	R	RBI	BB	SO	SB	Pinch Hit AB	Pinch Hit H	PO	A	E	DP	TC/G	FA	G by Pos
1899	WAS N	127	.282	.365	468	132	11	5	6	1.3	68	51	31		17	1	0	271	31	29	6	2.6	.912	OF-121, 3B-4
1901	2 teams	WAS A (11G –.178)	CLE A (92G –.283)																					
″	total	103	.271	.329	420	114	14	5	0	0.0	59	44	25		15	0	0	177	11	12	4	1.9	.940	OF-103, 3B-1
1903	BOS A	96	.210	.302	338	71	14	4	3	0.9	44	38	21		10	9	2	142	31	13	5	2.1	.930	OF-71, 3B-11, 2B-4, SS-1
3 yrs.		326	.259	.335	1226	317	39	14	9	0.7	171	133	77		42	10	2	590	73	54	15	2.3	.925	OF-295, 3B-16, 2B-4, SS-1
WORLD SERIES																								
1903	BOS A	2	.000	.000	2	0	0	0	0	0.0	0	0	0	1	0	2	0	0	0	0	0	0.0	—	

Jack O'Brien

O'BRIEN, JOHN K. BR TR 5′10″ 186 lbs.
Born John K. Byrne.
B. June 12, 1860, Philadelphia, Pa. D. Nov. 2, 1910, Philadelphia, Pa.

Year	Team	Games	BA	SA	AB	H	2B	3B	HR	HR%	R	RBI	BB	SO	SB	Pinch Hit AB	Pinch Hit H	PO	A	E	DP	TC/G	FA	G by Pos
1882	PHI AA	62	.303	.419	241	73	13	3	3	1.2	44		13			0	0	234	81	28	1	5.3	.918	C-45, OF-18, 1B-1, 3B-1
1883		94	.290	.377	390	113	14	10	0	0.0	74		25			0	0	372	89	76	8	5.2	.858	C-58, OF-25, 3B-19, SS-1
1884		36	.283	.362	138	39	6	1	1	0.7	25		9			0	0	195	45	19	8	7.2	.927	C-30, OF-5, 1B-1
1885		62	.267	.342	225	60	9	1	2	0.9	35		20			0	0	276	95	38	10	6.4	.907	C-43, SS-9, 1B-7, OF-3, 3B-2
1886		105	.253	.345	423	107	25	7	0	0.0	65		38			0	0	426	170	70	26	6.2	.895	C-36, 3B-27, 1B-24, SS-10, 2B-7, OF-3
1887	BKN AA	30	.228	.301	123	28	4	1	1	0.8	18		6		8	0	0	98	42	27	4	5.6	.838	C-25, OF-4, 2B-1
1888	BAL AA	57	.224	.332	196	44	11	5	0	0.0	25	18	17		14	0	0	286	43	26	9	6.2	.927	C-37, OF-13, 1B-7
1890	PHI AA	109	.261	.409	433	113	24	14	4	0.9	80		52		31	0	0	1021	54	27	63	9.9	.975	1B-109, OF-1, C-1
8 yrs.		555	.266	.369	2169	577	106	42	11	0.5	366	18	180		53	0	0	2908	619	311	129	6.7	.919	C-275, 1B-149, OF-72, 3B-49, SS-20, 2B-8

Jerry O'Brien

O'BRIEN, JEREMIAH
B. Feb. 2, 1864, New York D. July 4, 1911, Binghamton, N. Y.

Year	Team	Games	BA	SA	AB	H	2B	3B	HR	HR%	R	RBI	BB	SO	SB	Pinch Hit AB	Pinch Hit H	PO	A	E	DP	TC/G	FA	G by Pos
1887	WAS N	1	.000	.000	4	0	0	0	0	0.0	0	0	0	2	0	0	0	0	5	2	0	7.0	.714	2B-1

John O'Brien

O'BRIEN, JOHN E. TR 5′11½″ 187 lbs.
B. Oct. 22, 1851, Columbus, Ohio D. Dec. 31, 1914, Fall River, Mass.

Year	Team	Games	BA	SA	AB	H	2B	3B	HR	HR%	R	RBI	BB	SO	SB	Pinch Hit AB	Pinch Hit H	PO	A	E	DP	TC/G	FA	G by Pos
1884	BAL U	18	.247	.286	77	19	1	1	0	0.0	7		2			0	0	29	3	5	2	2.1	.865	OF-18

John O'Brien

O'BRIEN, JOHN J. (Chewing Gum) BL TR 175 lbs.
B. July 14, 1870, St. John, N. B., Canada D. May 13, 1913, Lewiston, Me.

Year	Team	Games	BA	SA	AB	H	2B	3B	HR	HR%	R	RBI	BB	SO	SB	Pinch Hit AB	Pinch Hit H	PO	A	E	DP	TC/G	FA	G by Pos
1891	BKN N	43	.246	.293	167	41	4	2	0	0.0	22	26	12	17	4	0	0	85	102	32	13	5.1	.854	2B-43
1893	CHI N	4	.357	.500	14	5	0	1	0	0.0	3	1	2	2	0	0	0	10	8	2	1	5.0	.900	2B-4
1895	LOU N	128	.256	.295	539	138	10	4	1	0.2	82	50	45	20	15	0	0	339	397	47	58	6.1	.940	2B-125, 1B-3
1896	2 teams	LOU N (49G –.339)	WAS N (73G –.267)																					
″	total	122	.296	.386	456	135	15	4	6	1.3	62	57	40	19	8	0	0	291	375	44	52	5.8	.938	2B-122
1897	WAS N	86	.244	.322	320	78	12	2	3	0.9	37	45	19		6	0	0	223	260	30	43	6.0	.942	2B-86
1899	2 teams	BAL N (39G –.193)	PIT N (79G –.226)																					
″	total	118	.215	.263	414	89	6	4	2	0.5	40	50	36		12	0	0	309	375	34	53	6.1	.953	2B-118
6 yrs.		501	.254	.316	1910	486	47	17	12	0.6	246	229	154	58	45	0	0	1257	1517	189	220	5.9	.936	2B-498, 1B-3

Johnny O'Brien

O'BRIEN, JOHN THOMAS BR TR 5′ 9″ 170 lbs.
Brother of Eddie O'Brien.
B. Dec. 11, 1930, South Amboy, N. J.

Year	Team	Games	BA	SA	AB	H	2B	3B	HR	HR%	R	RBI	BB	SO	SB	Pinch Hit AB	Pinch Hit H	PO	A	E	DP	TC/G	FA	G by Pos
1953	PIT N	89	.247	.330	279	69	13	2	2	0.7	28	22	21	36	1	5	0	172	210	7	48	5.0	.982	2B-77, SS-1
1955		84	.299	.378	278	83	15	2	1	0.4	22	25	20	19	1	5	0	185	220	13	53	5.4	.969	2B-78
1956		73	.173	.183	104	18	1	0	0	0.0	13	3	5	7	0	8	1	67	99	9	17	2.8	.949	2B-53, P-8, SS-1

Johnny O'Brien *continued*

Year	Team		Games	BA	SA	AB	H	2B	3B	HR	HR%	R	RBI	BB	SO	SB	Pinch Hit AB	Pinch Hit H	PO	A	E	DP	TC/G	FA	G by Pos
1957			34	.314	.429	35	11	2	1	0	0.0	7	1	1	4	0	3	1	14	16	4	2	1.3	.882	P-16, SS-8, 2B-2
1958	**2 teams**	**PIT N** (3G –.000) **STL N** (12G –.000)																							
"	**total**		15	.000	.000	3	0	0	0	0	0.0	4	0	1	1	0	2	0	3	1	0	0	0.6	1.000	SS-5, 2B-1, P-1
1959	**MIL**	**N**	44	.198	.259	116	23	4	0	1	0.9	16	8	11	15	0	0	0	70	83	2	24	4.2	.987	2B-37
6 yrs.			339	.250	.320	815	204	35	5	4	0.5	90	59	59	82	2	23	2	511	629	35	144	4.1	.970	2B-248, P-25, SS-15

Mickey O'Brien

O'BRIEN, FRANK ALOYSIUS BR TR 5′ 8″ 160 lbs.
B. Sept. 13, 1894, San Francisco, Calif. D. Nov. 4, 1971, Monterey Park, Calif.

Year	Team		Games	BA	SA	AB	H	2B	3B	HR	HR%	R	RBI	BB	SO	SB	Pinch Hit AB	Pinch Hit H	PO	A	E	DP	TC/G	FA	G by Pos
1923	**PHI**	**N**	15	.333	.429	21	7	2	0	0	0.0	3	0	2	1	0	6	2	13	7	2	0	2.4	.909	C-9

Pete O'Brien

O'BRIEN, PETER J. BL TR 5′ 7″ 170 lbs.
B. June 17, 1877, Binghamton, N. Y. D. Jan. 31, 1917, Jersey City, N. J.

Year	Team		Games	BA	SA	AB	H	2B	3B	HR	HR%	R	RBI	BB	SO	SB	Pinch Hit AB	Pinch Hit H	PO	A	E	DP	TC/G	FA	G by Pos
1901	**CIN**	**N**	16	.204	.278	54	11	1	0	1	1.9	1	3	2		0	1	0	35	37	9	6	5.4	.889	2B-15
1906	**STL**	**A**	151	.233	.277	524	122	9	4	2	0.4	44	57	42		25	0	0	297	338	42	32	4.5	.938	2B-120, 3B-20, SS-11
1907	**2 teams**	**CLE A** (43G –.228) **WAS A** (39G –.187)																							
"	**total**		82	.208	.258	279	58	8	3	0	0.0	15	18	19		5	4	1	102	199	30	13	4.1	.909	3B-40, SS-22, 2B-18
3 yrs.			249	.223	.271	857	191	18	7	3	0.4	60	78	63		30	5	1	434	574	81	51	4.4	.926	2B-153, 3B-60, SS-33

Pete O'Brien

O'BRIEN, PETER JAMES BR TR 5′ 9½″ 165 lbs.
B. June 16, 1867, Chicago, Ill. D. June 30, 1937, York, Ill.

Year	Team		Games	BA	SA	AB	H	2B	3B	HR	HR%	R	RBI	BB	SO	SB	Pinch Hit AB	Pinch Hit H	PO	A	E	DP	TC/G	FA	G by Pos
1890	**CHI**	**N**	27	.283	.434	106	30	7	0	3	2.8	15	16	5	10	4	0	0	65	80	11	11	5.8	.929	2B-27

Pete O'Brien

O'BRIEN, PETER MICHAEL BL TL 6′ 180 lbs.
B. Feb. 9, 1958, Santa Monica, Calif.

Year	Team		Games	BA	SA	AB	H	2B	3B	HR	HR%	R	RBI	BB	SO	SB	Pinch Hit AB	Pinch Hit H	PO	A	E	DP	TC/G	FA	G by Pos
1982	**TEX**	**A**	20	.239	.507	67	16	4	1	4	6.0	13	13	6	8	1	0	0	39	3	0	5	2.3	1.000	OF-11, DH-4, 1B-3
1983			154	.237	.347	524	124	24	5	8	1.5	53	53	58	62	5	6	2	1191	121	11	105	8.2	.992	1B-133, OF-27, DH-1
1984			142	.287	.448	520	149	26	2	18	3.5	57	80	53	50	3	2	1	1271	105	11	103	9.8	.992	1B-141, OF-1
1985			159	.267	.452	573	153	34	3	22	3.8	69	92	69	53	5	3	0	1457	98	8	125	9.8	.995	1B-159
1986			156	.290	.468	551	160	23	3	23	4.2	86	90	87	66	4	3	1	1224	115	11	123	8.7	.992	1B-155
1987			159	.286	.457	569	163	26	1	23	4.0	84	88	59	61	0	3	0	1233	146	11	118	8.7	.992	1B-158, OF-2
1988			156	.272	.408	547	149	24	1	16	2.9	57	71	72	73	1	5	1	1346	140	8	124	9.6	.995	1B-155, DH-1
1989	**CLE**	**A**	155	.260	.372	554	144	24	1	12	2.2	75	55	83	48	3	4	0	1359	114	9	111	9.6	.994	1B-154, DH-1
1990	**SEA**	**A**	108	.224	.314	366	82	18	0	5	1.4	32	27	44	33	0	6	0	852	76	5	68	8.6	.995	1B-97, OF-6, DH-6
1991			152	.248	.402	560	139	29	3	17	3.0	58	88	44	61	0	3	2	1065	87	5	125	7.1	.996	1B-132, DH-18, OF-13
1992			134	.222	.371	396	88	15	1	14	3.5	40	52	40	27	2	23	4	623	54	3	72	5.9	.996	1B-81, DH-35
1993			72	.257	.390	210	54	7	0	7	3.3	30	27	26	21	0	10	2	77	8	1	10	1.4	.988	DH-52, 1B-9, OF-1
12 yrs.			1567	.261	.409	5437	1421	254	21	169	3.1	654	736	641	563	24	68	13	11737	1067	83	1089	8.3	.994	1B-1377, DH-118, OF-61

Ray O'Brien

O'BRIEN, RAYMOND JOSEPH BL TL 5′ 9″ 175 lbs.
B. Oct. 31, 1892, St. Louis, Mo. D. Mar. 31, 1942, St. Louis, Mo.

Year	Team		Games	BA	SA	AB	H	2B	3B	HR	HR%	R	RBI	BB	SO	SB	Pinch Hit AB	Pinch Hit H	PO	A	E	DP	TC/G	FA	G by Pos
1916	**PIT**	**N**	16	.211	.333	57	12	3	2	0	0.0	5	3	1	14	0	1	0	16	3	3	1	1.6	.864	OF-14

Syd O'Brien

O'BRIEN, SYDNEY LLOYD BR TR 6′ 1″ 185 lbs.
B. Dec. 18, 1944, Compton, Calif.

Year	Team		Games	BA	SA	AB	H	2B	3B	HR	HR%	R	RBI	BB	SO	SB	Pinch Hit AB	Pinch Hit H	PO	A	E	DP	TC/G	FA	G by Pos
1969	**BOS**	**A**	100	.243	.422	263	64	10	5	9	3.4	47	29	15	37	2	18	5	65	143	15	30	2.8	.933	3B-53, SS-15, 2B-12
1970	**CHI**	**A**	121	.247	.340	441	109	13	2	8	1.8	48	44	22	62	3	8	2	158	271	25	50	3.9	.945	3B-68, 2B-43, SS-5
1971	**CAL**	**A**	90	.199	.299	251	50	8	1	5	2.0	25	21	15	33	0	20	6	115	173	11	38	4.5	.963	SS-52, 2B-7, 3B-6, 1B-1, OF-1
1972	**2 teams**	**CAL A** (36G –.179) **MIL A** (31G –.207)																							
"	**total**		67	.196	.299	97	19	4	0	2	2.1	15	6	8	23	0	22	4	21	48	8	8	2.4	.896	3B-17, 2B-10, SS-4, 1B-1
4 yrs.			378	.230	.347	1052	242	35	8	24	2.3	135	100	60	155	5	68	17	359	635	59	126	3.6	.944	3B-144, SS-76, 2B-72, 1B-2, OF-1

Tom O'Brien

O'BRIEN, THOMAS H. BR TR 6′ 1″ 185 lbs.
B. June 22, 1860, Salem, Mass. D. Apr. 21, 1921, Worcester, Mass.

Year	Team		Games	BA	SA	AB	H	2B	3B	HR	HR%	R	RBI	BB	SO	SB	Pinch Hit AB	Pinch Hit H	PO	A	E	DP	TC/G	FA	G by Pos
1882	**WOR**	**N**	22	.202	.236	89	18	1	1	0	0.0	9	7	1	10		0	0	47	9	17	2	3.2	.767	OF-20, 2B-2, 3B-1
1883	**BAL**	**AA**	33	.268	.370	138	37	6	4	0	0.0	16		5			0	0	83	93	36	8	6.4	.830	2B-29, OF-4
1884	**BOS**	**U**	103	.263	.394	449	118	31	8	4	0.9	80		12			0	0	290	267	91	23	6.2	.860	2B-99, OF-3, 1B-2, C-1
1885	**BAL**	**AA**	8	.212	.303	33	7	3	0	0	0.0	4		2			0	0	41	13	4	1	7.3	.931	1B-6, 2B-2
1887	**NY**	**AA**	31	.194	.248	129	25	3	2	0	0.0	13		2		10	0	0	203	10	11	10	6.8	.951	1B-20, OF-8, 2B-2, 3B-2, P-1
1890	**ROC**	**AA**	73	.190	.249	273	52	6	5	0	0.0	36		30		6	0	0	689	41	28	43	10.0	.963	1B-68, 2B-8
6 yrs.			270	.231	.323	1111	257	50	20	4	0.4	158	7	52	10	16	0	0	1353	433	187	87	7.1	.905	2B-142, 1B-96, OF-35, 3B-3, P-1, C-1

Tom O'Brien

O'BRIEN, THOMAS J.
B. Feb. 20, 1873, Verona, Pa. D. Feb. 4, 1901, Phoenix, Ariz.

Year	Team		Games	BA	SA	AB	H	2B	3B	HR	HR%	R	RBI	BB	SO	SB	Pinch Hit AB	Pinch Hit H	PO	A	E	DP	TC/G	FA	G by Pos
1897	**BAL**	**N**	50	.252	.293	147	37	6	0	0	0.0	25	32	20		7	2	1	243	15	9	9	5.4	.966	1B-25, OF-24
1898	**2 teams**	**BAL N** (18G –.217) **PIT N** (107G –.259)																							
"	**total**		125	.254	.315	473	120	10	8	1	0.2	62	59	35		13	2	0	398	66	40	23	4.0	.921	OF-85, 1B-21, 3B-8, 2B-7, SS-4
1899	**NY**	**N**	150	.297	.400	573	170	21	10	6	1.0	100	77	44		23	0	0	269	66	30	12	2.4	.918	OF-127, 3B-21, SS-2, 2B-1, 1B-1
1900	**PIT**	**N**	102	.290	.404	376	109	22	6	3	0.8	60	61	21		12	5	1	726	36	33	39	8.3	.958	1B-65, OF-25, 2B-4, SS-2
4 yrs.			427	.278	.365	1569	436	59	24	10	0.6	247	229	120		55	9	2	1636	183	112	83	4.6	.942	OF-261, 1B-112, 3B-29, 2B-12, SS-8

Tommy O'Brien

O'BRIEN, THOMAS EDWARD (Obie) BR TR 5′11″ 195 lbs.
B. Dec. 19, 1918, Anniston, Ala. D. Nov. 5, 1978, Anniston, Ala.

Year	Team		Games	BA	SA	AB	H	2B	3B	HR	HR%	R	RBI	BB	SO	SB	Pinch Hit AB	Pinch Hit H	PO	A	E	DP	TC/G	FA	G by Pos
1943	**PIT**	**N**	89	.310	.448	232	72	12	7	2	0.9	35	26	15	24	0	27	7	87	23	6	0	2.0	.948	OF-48, 3B-9
1944			85	.250	.372	156	39	6	2	3	1.9	27	20	21	12	1	33	5	50	5	2	1	1.2	.965	OF-48
1945			58	.335	.435	161	54	6	5	0	0.0	23	18	9	13	0	12	3	72	2	3	0	1.7	.961	OF-45

Tommy O'Brien *continued*

Year	Team	Games	BA	SA	AB	H	2B	3B	HR	HR%	R	RBI	BB	SO	SB	Pinch Hit AB	Pinch Hit H	PO	A	E	DP	TC/G	FA	G by Pos
1949	BOS A	49	.224	.336	125	28	5	0	3	2.4	24	10	21	12	1	12	1	58	2	1	0	1.9	.984	OF-32
1950	2 teams	BOS A (9G –.129) WAS A (3G –.111)																						
"	total	12	.125	.150	40	5	1	0	0	0.0	1	4	4	5	0	0	0	21	2	0	0	1.9	1.000	OF-12
5 yrs.		293	.277	.392	714	198	30	14	8	1.1	110	78	70	66	2	84	16	288	34	12	1	1.7	.964	OF-185, 3B-9

Alex Ochoa

OCHOA, ALEX BR TR 6′ 175 lbs.
B. Mar. 29, 1972, Miami Lakes, Fla.

Year	Team	Games	BA	SA	AB	H	2B	3B	HR	HR%	R	RBI	BB	SO	SB	Pinch Hit AB	Pinch Hit H	PO	A	E	DP	TC/G	FA	G by Pos
1995	NY N	11	.297	.324	37	11	1	0	0	0.0	7	0	2	10	1	1	1	20	1	0	0	2.1	1.000	OF-10

Whitey Ock

OCK, HAROLD DAVID BR TR 5′11″ 180 lbs.
B. Mar. 17, 1912, Brooklyn, N. Y. D. Mar. 18, 1975, Mount Kisco, N. Y.

Year	Team	Games	BA	SA	AB	H	2B	3B	HR	HR%	R	RBI	BB	SO	SB	Pinch Hit AB	Pinch Hit H	PO	A	E	DP	TC/G	FA	G by Pos
1935	BKN N	1	.000	.000	3	0	0	0	0	0.0	0	0	1	2	0	0	0	3	0	0	0	3.0	1.000	C-1

Danny O'Connell

O'CONNELL, DANIEL FRANCIS BR TR 5′11″ 168 lbs.
B. Jan. 21, 1927, Paterson, N. J. D. Oct. 2, 1969, Clifton, N. J.

Year	Team	Games	BA	SA	AB	H	2B	3B	HR	HR%	R	RBI	BB	SO	SB	Pinch Hit AB	Pinch Hit H	PO	A	E	DP	TC/G	FA	G by Pos
1950	PIT N	79	.292	.425	315	92	16	1	8	2.5	39	32	24	33	7	2	0	162	267	11	49	5.7	.975	SS-65, 3B-12
1953		149	.294	.401	588	173	26	8	7	1.2	88	55	57	42	3	0	0	226	370	23	43	4.1	.963	3B-104, 2B-47
1954	MIL N	146	.279	.357	541	151	28	4	2	0.4	61	37	38	46	2	4	3	351	386	12	97	5.1	.984	2B-103, 3B-35, 1B-8, SS-1
1955		124	.225	.316	453	102	15	4	6	1.3	47	40	28	43	2	6	1	317	362	14	78	5.7	.980	2B-114, 3B-7, SS-1
1956		139	.239	.321	498	119	17	9	2	0.4	71	42	76	42	3	1	0	299	384	11	99	4.9	.984	2B-138, 3B-4, SS-1
1957	2 teams	MIL N (48G –.235) NY N (95G –.266)																						
"	total	143	.256	.364	547	140	27	4	8	1.5	86	36	52	50	9	1	0	317	408	16	99	5.1	.978	2B-116, 3B-30
1958	SF N	107	.232	.314	306	71	12	2	3	1.0	44	23	51	35	2	0	0	222	278	7	70	4.7	.986	2B-104, 3B-3
1959		34	.190	.241	58	11	3	0	0	0.0	6	0	5	15	0	0	0	31	45	4	4	2.4	.950	3B-26, 2B-8
1961	WAS A	138	.260	.331	493	128	30	1	1	0.2	61	37	77	62	15	5	4	219	343	23	66	4.4	.961	3B-73, 2B-61
1962		84	.263	.335	236	62	7	2	2	0.8	24	18	23	28	5	20	8	70	141	10	21	3.5	.955	3B-41, 2B-22
10 yrs.		1143	.260	.351	4035	1049	181	35	39	1.0	527	320	431	396	48	39	16	2214	2984	131	626	4.7	.975	2B-713, 3B-335, SS-68, 1B-8

Jimmy O'Connell

O'CONNELL, JAMES JOSEPH BL TR 5′10½″ 175 lbs.
B. Feb. 11, 1901, Sacramento, Calif. D. Nov. 11, 1976, Bakersfield, Calif.

Year	Team	Games	BA	SA	AB	H	2B	3B	HR	HR%	R	RBI	BB	SO	SB	Pinch Hit AB	Pinch Hit H	PO	A	E	DP	TC/G	FA	G by Pos
1923	NY N	87	.250	.373	252	63	9	2	6	2.4	42	39	34	32	7	10	0	213	3	4	7	3.1	.982	OF-64, 1B-8
1924		52	.317	.452	104	33	4	2	2	1.9	24	18	11	16	2	15	4	41	6	3	0	1.7	.940	OF-29, 2B-1
2 yrs.		139	.270	.396	356	96	13	4	8	2.2	66	57	45	48	9	25	4	254	9	7	7	2.6	.974	OF-93, 1B-8, 2B-1
WORLD SERIES																								
1923	NY N	2	.000	.000	1	0	0	0	0	0.0	0	0	0	1	0	1	0	0	0	0	0	0.0	—	

John O'Connell

O'CONNELL, JOHN CHARLES BR TR 6′ 170 lbs.
B. June 13, 1904, Berona, Pa. D. Oct. 17, 1992, Canton, Ohio.

Year	Team	Games	BA	SA	AB	H	2B	3B	HR	HR%	R	RBI	BB	SO	SB	Pinch Hit AB	Pinch Hit H	PO	A	E	DP	TC/G	FA	G by Pos
1928	PIT N	1	.000	.000	1	0	0	0	0	0.0	0	0	0	0	0	0	0	1	2	0	0	3.0	1.000	C-1
1929		2	.143	.286	7	1	1	0	0	0.0	1	0	1	1	0	0	0	7	0	0	0	3.5	1.000	C-2
2 yrs.		3	.125	.250	8	1	1	0	0	0.0	1	0	1	1	0	0	0	8	2	0	0	3.3	1.000	C-3

John O'Connell

O'CONNELL, JOHN JOSEPH (Jack)
D. May 14, 1908, Derry, N. H.

Year	Team	Games	BA	SA	AB	H	2B	3B	HR	HR%	R	RBI	BB	SO	SB	Pinch Hit AB	Pinch Hit H	PO	A	E	DP	TC/G	FA	G by Pos
1891	BAL AA	8	.172	.207	29	5	1	0	0	0.0	2	7	3	6	2	0	0	13	15	5	1	4.1	.848	2B-3, SS-3, OF-2
1902	DET A	8	.182	.182	22	4	0	0	0	0.0	1	0	3		0	0	0	37	20	3	3	7.5	.950	2B-6, 1B-2
2 yrs.		16	.176	.196	51	9	1	0	0	0.0	3	7	6	6	2	0	0	50	35	8	4	5.8	.914	2B-9, SS-3, 1B-2, OF-2

Pat O'Connell

O'CONNELL, PATRICK H. BL TR 5′10″ 175 lbs.
B. June 10, 1861, Bangor, Me. D. Jan. 24, 1943, Lewiston, Me.

Year	Team	Games	BA	SA	AB	H	2B	3B	HR	HR%	R	RBI	BB	SO	SB	Pinch Hit AB	Pinch Hit H	PO	A	E	DP	TC/G	FA	G by Pos
1886	BAL AA	42	.181	.223	166	30	3	2	0	0.0	20		11			0	0	65	4	17	0	2.0	.802	OF-41, 1B-1, P-1
1890	BKN AA	11	.225	.325	40	9	2	1	0	0.0	7		7		3	0	0	22	23	8	3	4.8	.849	3B-10, 1B-1
2 yrs.		53	.189	.243	206	39	5	3	0	0.0	27		18		3	0	0	87	27	25	3	2.6	.820	OF-41, 3B-10, 1B-2, P-1

Bucky O'Connor

O'CONNOR, JOHN CHARLES (Okie) BR TR 5′ 9″
B. Dec. 1, 1891, Cahirciveen, Ireland D. May 30, 1982, Bonner Springs, Kans.

Year	Team	Games	BA	SA	AB	H	2B	3B	HR	HR%	R	RBI	BB	SO	SB	Pinch Hit AB	Pinch Hit H	PO	A	E	DP	TC/G	FA	G by Pos
1916	CHI N	1	—	—	0	0	0	0	0	—	0	0	0	0	0	0	0	0	0	0	0	0.0	.000	C-1

Dan O'Connor

O'CONNOR, DANIEL CORNELIUS BL TR 6′ 2″ 185 lbs.
B. Aug. 1868, Guelph, Ont., Canada D. Mar. 3, 1942, Guelph, Ont., Canada.

Year	Team	Games	BA	SA	AB	H	2B	3B	HR	HR%	R	RBI	BB	SO	SB	Pinch Hit AB	Pinch Hit H	PO	A	E	DP	TC/G	FA	G by Pos
1890	LOU AA	6	.462	.577	26	12	1	1	0	0.0	3		1		5	0	0	58	0	0	3	9.7	1.000	1B-6

Jack O'Connor

O'CONNOR, JOHN JOSEPH (Peach Pie) BR TR 5′10″ 170 lbs.
B. June 2, 1869, St. Louis, Mo. D. Nov. 14, 1937, St. Louis, Mo.
Manager 1910.

Year	Team	Games	BA	SA	AB	H	2B	3B	HR	HR%	R	RBI	BB	SO	SB	Pinch Hit AB	Pinch Hit H	PO	A	E	DP	TC/G	FA	G by Pos
1887	CIN AA	12	.100	.100	40	4	0	0	0	0.0	4		2		3	0	0	29	15	7	1	4.3	.863	OF-7, C-5
1888		36	.204	.263	137	28	3	1	1	0.7	14	17	6		12	0	0	68	17	20	0	2.9	.810	OF-34, C-2
1889	COL AA	107	.269	.377	398	107	17	7	4	1.0	69	60	33	37	26	0	0	492	135	35	11	6.0	.947	C-84, OF-19, 2B-4, 1B-3
1890		121	.324	.411	457	148	14	10	2	0.4	89		38		29	0	0	572	164	35	20	6.1	.955	C-106, OF-9, SS-8, 2B-2, 3B-1
1891		56	.266	.345	229	61	12	3	0	0.0	28	37	11	14	10	0	0	135	37	11	5	3.0	.940	OF-40, C-21
1892	CLE N	140	.248	.309	572	142	22	5	1	0.2	71	58	25	48	17	1	0	310	61	19	8	2.8	.951	OF-106, C-34
1893		96	.286	.375	384	110	23	1	3	0.8	72	75	29	12	29	0	0	252	70	19	2	3.4	.944	C-56, OF-44
1894		86	.315	.445	330	104	23	7	2	0.6	67	51	15	7	15	1	0	304	46	21	8	4.4	.943	C-45, OF-33, 1B-7
1895		89	.291	.391	340	99	14	10	0	0.0	51	58	30	22	11	0	0	522	66	16	24	6.8	.974	C-47, 1B-41, 3B-1
1896		68	.297	.359	256	76	11	1	1	0.4	41	43	15	12	15	3	2	242	40	7	13	4.4	.976	C-37, 1B-17, OF-12
1897		103	.290	.378	397	115	21	4	2	0.5	49	69	26		20	4	3	477	23	16	10	5.1	.969	OF-52, 1B-36, C-13
1898		131	.249	.308	478	119	17	4	1	0.2	50	56	26		8	1	0	761	92	20	36	6.6	.977	1B-69, C-48, OF-15
1899	STL N	84	.253	.311	289	73	5	6	0	0.0	33	43	15		7	2	0	427	76	18	20	6.3	.965	C-57, 1B-26
1900	2 teams	STL N (10G –.219) PIT N (43G –.238)																						
"	total	53	.235	.268	179	42	4	1	0	0.0	19	25	5		5	1	0	161	56	11	5	4.4	.952	C-50, 1B-2
1901	PIT N	61	.193	.257	202	39	7	3	0	0.0	16	22	10		2	2	0	256	59	7	5	5.5	.978	C-59
1902		49	.294	.341	170	50	1	2	1	0.6	13	28	3		2	0	0	243	50	6	5	6.1	.980	C-42, 1B-6, OF-1
1903	NY A	64	.203	.231	212	43	4	1	0	0.0	13	12	8		4	0	0	287	56	4	6	5.4	.988	C-63, 1B-1

Jack O'Connor *continued*

Year	Team		Games	BA	SA	AB	H	2B	3B	HR	HR%	R	RBI	BB	SO	SB	Pinch Hit AB	Pinch Hit H	PO	A	E	DP	TC/G	FA	G by Pos
1904	STL	A	14	.213	.234	47	10	1	0	0	0.0	4	2	2		0	0	0	55	11	4	0	5.0	.943	C-14
1906			58	.190	.190	174	33	0	0	0	0.0	8	11	2		4	4	0	248	64	3	2	5.8	.990	C-54
1907			25	.157	.180	89	14	2	0	0	0.0	2	4	0		0	0	0	87	29	1	4	4.7	.991	C-25
1910			1	—	—	0	0	0	0	0	—	0	0	0		0	0	0	1	0	0	0	1.0	1.000	C-1
21 yrs.			1454	.263	.335	5380	1417	201	66	18	0.3	713	671	301	152	219	19	5	5929	1167	280	185	5.1	.962	C-863, OF-372, 1B-208, SS-8, 2B-6, 3B-2

Paddy O'Connor

O'CONNOR, PATRICK FRANCIS BR TR 5′ 8″ 168 lbs.
B. Aug. 4, 1879, County Kerry, Ireland D. Aug. 17, 1950, Springfield, Mass.

Year	Team		Games	BA	SA	AB	H	2B	3B	HR	HR%	R	RBI	BB	SO	SB	Pinch Hit AB	Pinch Hit H	PO	A	E	DP	TC/G	FA	G by Pos
1908	PIT	N	12	.188	.188	16	3	0	0	0	0.0	1	2	0		0	7	2	6	2	1	0	2.3	.889	C-4
1909			9	.313	.375	16	5	1	0	0	0.0	1	3	0		0	5	0	7	2	3	1	3.0	.750	C-3, 3B-1
1910			6	.250	.250	4	1	0	0	0	0.0	0	0	1	1	0	4	1	1	0	0	0	1.0	1.000	C-1
1914	STL	N	10	.000	.000	9	0	0	0	0	0.0	0	0	2	2	0	2	0	9	3	0	0	1.7	1.000	C-7
1915	PIT	F	70	.228	.283	219	50	10	1	0	0.0	15	16	14		4	4	1	275	112	5	4	5.9	.987	C-66
1918	NY	A	1	.333	.333	3	1	0	0	0	0.0	0	0	0	1	0	0	0	2	1	0	0	3.0	1.000	C-1
6 yrs.			108	.225	.273	267	60	11	1	0	0.0	17	21	17	4	4	22	4	300	120	9	5	5.2	.979	C-82, 3B-1
WORLD SERIES																									
1909	PIT	N	1	.000	.000	1	0	0	0	0	0.0	0	0	0	1	0	1	0	0	0	0	0	0.0	—	

Hank O'Day

O'DAY, HENRY FRANCIS (Peep) TR 6′ 180 lbs.
B. July 8, 1862, Chicago, Ill. D. July 2, 1935, Chicago, Ill.
Manager 1912, 1914.

Year	Team		Games	BA	SA	AB	H	2B	3B	HR	HR%	R	RBI	BB	SO	SB	Pinch Hit AB	Pinch Hit H	PO	A	E	DP	TC/G	FA	G by Pos
1884	TOL	AA	64	.211	.256	242	51	9	1	0	0.0	23		10			0	0	61	95	20	5	2.6	.886	P-39, OF-24, 3B-3, 1B-3
1885	PIT	AA	13	.245	.327	49	12	2	1	0	0.0	7		1			0	0	8	19	4	2	2.1	.871	P-12, OF-3
1886	WAS	N	6	.053	.053	19	1	0	0	0	0.0	0	0	0	9		0	0	4	14	2	1	3.3	.900	P-6
1887			36	.198	.224	116	23	3	0	0	0.0	10	7	7	15	1	0	0	15	59	6	4	2.1	.925	P-30, SS-6, OF-2
1888			47	.139	.151	166	23	2	0	0	0.0	6	6	4	41	3	0	0	19	67	8	1	2.0	.915	P-46, SS-2
1889	2 teams	WAS N (13G –.182) NY N (10G –.097)																							
″	total		23	.147	.160	75	11	1	0	0	0.0	6	7	7	17	2	0	0	12	34	3	1	2.1	.939	P-23
1890	NY	P	43	.227	.273	150	34	2	1	1	0.7	24	23	10	27	1	0	0	11	71	7	0	2.1	.921	P-43
7 yrs.			232	.190	.224	817	155	19	3	1	0.1	76	43	39	109	7	0	0	130	359	50	14	2.2	.907	P-199, OF-29, SS-8, 3B-3, 1B-3

Ken O'Dea

O'DEA, JAMES KENNETH BL TR 6′ 180 lbs.
B. Mar. 16, 1913, Lima, N. Y. D. Dec. 17, 1985, Lima, N. Y.

Year	Team		Games	BA	SA	AB	H	2B	3B	HR	HR%	R	RBI	BB	SO	SB	Pinch Hit AB	Pinch Hit H	PO	A	E	DP	TC/G	FA	G by Pos
1935	CHI	N	76	.257	.431	202	52	13	2	6	3.0	30	38	26	18	0	9	1	213	27	9	3	4.0	.964	C-63
1936			80	.307	.423	189	58	10	3	2	1.1	36	38	38	18	0	22	7	211	27	5	1	4.4	.979	C-55
1937			83	.301	.434	219	66	7	5	4	1.8	31	32	24	26	1	13	3	234	29	4	4	4.2	.985	C-64
1938			86	.263	.356	247	65	12	1	3	1.2	22	33	12	18	1	13	2	294	32	10	3	4.7	.970	C-71
1939	NY	N	52	.175	.278	97	17	1	0	3	3.1	7	11	10	16	0	26	3	78	11	5	1	3.1	.947	C-30
1940			48	.240	.302	96	23	4	1	0	0.0	9	12	16	15	0	14	2	89	29	1	1	3.8	.992	C-31
1941			59	.213	.393	89	19	5	1	3	3.4	13	17	8	20	0	**42**	9	62	9	0	0	5.1	1.000	C-14
1942	STL	N	58	.234	.359	192	45	7	1	5	2.6	22	32	17	23	0	9	1	247	37	6	6	5.9	.979	C-49
1943			71	.281	.399	203	57	11	2	3	1.5	15	25	19	25	0	14	4	237	32	3	6	4.9	.989	C-56
1944			85	.249	.374	265	66	11	2	6	2.3	35	37	37	29	1	14	4	326	34	2	4	5.2	.994	C-69
1945			100	.254	.365	307	78	18	2	4	1.3	36	43	50	31	0	8	0	321	50	2	14	4.1	.995	C-91
1946	2 teams	STL N (22G –.123) BOS N (12G –.219)																							
″	total		34	.157	.213	89	14	2	0	1	1.1	6	5	16	12	0	0	0	138	19	1	1	4.6	.994	C-34
12 yrs.			832	.255	.374	2195	560	101	20	40	1.8	262	323	273	251	3	184	36	2450	336	48	44	4.5	.983	C-627
WORLD SERIES																									
1935	CHI	N	1	1.000	1.000	1	1	0	0	0	0.0	0	1	0	0	0	1	1	0	0	0	0	0.0	—	
1938			3	.200	.800	5	1	0	0	1	20.0	1	2	1	0	0	2	0	5	0	0	0	5.0	1.000	C-1
1942	STL	N	1	1.000	1.000	1	1	0	0	0	0.0	0	1	0	0	0	1	1	0	0	0	0	0.0	—	
1943			2	.667	.667	3	2	0	0	0	0.0	0	0	0	0	0	1	0	2	0	0	0	2.0	1.000	C-1
1944			3	.333	.333	3	1	0	0	0	0.0	0	2	0	0	0	3	1	0	0	0	0	0.0	—	
5 yrs.			10	.462	.692	13	6	0	0	1	7.7	1	6	1	0	0	8	3	7	0	0	0	3.5	1.000	C-2

Paul O'Dea

O'DEA, PAUL (Lefty) BL TL 6′ 200 lbs.
B. July 3, 1920, Cleveland, Ohio D. Dec. 11, 1978, Cleveland, Ohio.

Year	Team		Games	BA	SA	AB	H	2B	3B	HR	HR%	R	RBI	BB	SO	SB	Pinch Hit AB	Pinch Hit H	PO	A	E	DP	TC/G	FA	G by Pos
1944	CLE	A	76	.318	.370	173	55	9	0	0	0.0	25	13	23	21	2	25	5	93	3	5	3	2.1	.950	OF-41, 1B-3, P-3
1945			87	.235	.276	221	52	2	2	1	0.5	21	21	20	26	3	30	7	118	5	1	2	2.3	.992	OF-53, P-1
2 yrs.			163	.272	.317	394	107	11	2	1	0.3	46	34	43	47	5	55	12	211	8	6	5	2.2	.973	OF-94, P-4, 1B-3

Heinie Odom

ODOM, HERMAN BOYD BB TR 6′ 170 lbs.
B. Oct. 13, 1900, Rusk, Tex. D. Aug. 31, 1970, Rusk, Tex.

Year	Team		Games	BA	SA	AB	H	2B	3B	HR	HR%	R	RBI	BB	SO	SB	Pinch Hit AB	Pinch Hit H	PO	A	E	DP	TC/G	FA	G by Pos
1925	NY	A	1	1.000	1.000	1	1	0	0	0	0.0	0	0	0	0	0	0	0	0	1	0	0	1.0	1.000	3B-1

Harry O'Donnell

O'DONNELL, HARRY HERMAN BR TR 5′10″ 180 lbs.
B. Apr. 2, 1894, Philadelphia, Pa. D. Jan. 31, 1958, Philadelphia, Pa.

Year	Team		Games	BA	SA	AB	H	2B	3B	HR	HR%	R	RBI	BB	SO	SB	Pinch Hit AB	Pinch Hit H	PO	A	E	DP	TC/G	FA	G by Pos
1927	PHI	N	16	.063	.063	16	1	0	0	0	0.0	1	2	2	2	0	4	0	16	3	0	1	1.6	1.000	C-12

John O'Donnell

O'DONNELL, JOHN
B. Littlestown, Pa. Deceased.

Year	Team		Games	BA	SA	AB	H	2B	3B	HR	HR%	R	RBI	BB	SO	SB	Pinch Hit AB	Pinch Hit H	PO	A	E	DP	TC/G	FA	G by Pos
1884	PHI	U	1	.250	.250	4	1	0	0	0	0.0	0		0			0	0	2	4	5	0	11.0	.545	C-1

Lefty O'Doul

O'DOUL, FRANCIS JOSEPH BL TL 6′ 180 lbs.
B. Mar. 4, 1897, San Francisco, Calif. D. Dec. 7, 1969, San Francisco, Calif.

Year	Team		Games	BA	SA	AB	H	2B	3B	HR	HR%	R	RBI	BB	SO	SB	Pinch Hit AB	Pinch Hit H	PO	A	E	DP	TC/G	FA	G by Pos
1919	NY	A	19	.250	.250	16	4	0	0	0	0.0	2	1	1	2	1	14	4	1	1	0	0	0.5	1.000	P-3, OF-1
1920			13	.167	.250	12	2	1	0	0	0.0	2	1	1	1	0	9	1	0	0	0	0	0.0		P-2, OF-1
1922			8	.333	.444	9	3	1	0	0	0.0	0	4	0	2	0	2	1	1	4	0	1	0.8	1.000	P-6
1923	BOS	A	36	.143	.143	35	5	0	0	0	0.0	2	4	2	3	0	12	2	2	21	1	0	1.0	.958	P-23
1928	NY	N	114	.319	.463	354	113	19	4	8	2.3	67	46	30	8	9	8	4	149	4	6	0	1.7	.962	OF-94

Lefty O'Doul *continued*

Year	Team		Games	BA	SA	AB	H	2B	3B	HR	HR%	R	RBI	BB	SO	SB	Pinch Hit AB	Pinch Hit H	PO	A	E	DP	TC/G	FA	G by Pos
1929	PHI	N	154	**.398**	.622	638	**254**	35	6	32	5.0	152	122	76	19	2	0	0	320	14	10	5	2.2	.971	OF-154
1930			140	.383	.604	528	202	37	7	22	4.2	122	97	63	21	3	8	3	262	3	13	1	2.1	.953	OF-131
1931	BKN	N	134	.336	.482	512	172	32	11	7	1.4	85	75	48	16	5	2	2	285	4	14	0	2.3	.954	OF-132
1932			148	**.368**	.555	595	219	32	8	21	3.5	120	90	50	20	11	0	0	317	4	7	0	2.2	.979	OF-148
1933	2 teams		BKN N (43G –.252) NY N (78G –.306)																						
"	total		121	.284	.438	388	110	14	2	14	3.6	45	56	44	23	3	14	5	197	5	8	0	2.0	.962	OF-104
1934	NY	N	83	.316	.525	177	56	4	3	9	5.1	27	46	18	7	2	37	10	60	1	2	0	1.7	.968	OF-38
11 yrs.			970	.349	.532	3264	1140	175	41	113	3.5	624	542	333	122	36	106	32	1594	61	61	7	2.1	.964	OF-803, P-34
WORLD SERIES																									
1933	NY	N	1	1.000	1.000	1	1	0	0	0	0.0	1	2	0	0	0	1	1	0	0	0	0	0.0	—	

Fred Odwell

ODWELL, FREDERICK WILLIAM (Fritz)
B. Sept. 25, 1872, Downsville, N. Y. D. Aug. 19, 1948, Downsville, N. Y.
BL TR 5′ 9½″ 160 lbs.

Year	Team		Games	BA	SA	AB	H	2B	3B	HR	HR%	R	RBI	BB	SO	SB	Pinch Hit AB	Pinch Hit H	PO	A	E	DP	TC/G	FA	G by Pos
1904	CIN	N	129	.284	.380	468	133	22	10	1	0.2	75	58	26		30	2	1	285	18	14	6	2.5	.956	OF-126, 2B-1
1905			130	.241	.359	468	113	10	9	**9**	**1.9**	79	65	26		21	4	3	216	18	8	5	1.9	.967	OF-126
1906			58	.223	.287	202	45	5	4	0	0.0	20	21	15		11	1	0	94	10	4	0	1.9	.963	OF-57
1907			94	.270	.339	274	74	5	7	0	0.0	24	24	22		10	5	0	187	9	6	2	2.4	.970	OF-84, 2B-1
4 yrs.			411	.258	.352	1412	365	42	30	10	0.7	198	168	89		72	12	4	782	55	32	13	2.2	.963	OF-393, 2B-2

Chuck Oertel

OERTEL, CHARLES FRANK (Ducky, Snuffy)
B. Mar. 12, 1931, Coffeyville, Kans.
BL TR 5′ 8″ 165 lbs.

Year	Team		Games	BA	SA	AB	H	2B	3B	HR	HR%	R	RBI	BB	SO	SB	Pinch Hit AB	Pinch Hit H	PO	A	E	DP	TC/G	FA	G by Pos
1958	BAL	A	14	.167	.417	12	2	0	0	1	8.3	4	1	1	1	0	8	0	1	0	0	0	0.5	1.000	OF-2

Ron Oester

OESTER, RONALD JOHN
B. May 5, 1956, Cincinnati, Ohio.
BB TR 6′ 2″ 185 lbs.

Year	Team		Games	BA	SA	AB	H	2B	3B	HR	HR%	R	RBI	BB	SO	SB	Pinch Hit AB	Pinch Hit H	PO	A	E	DP	TC/G	FA	G by Pos
1978	CIN	N	6	.375	.375	8	3	0	0	0	0.0	1	1	0	2	0	0	0	3	9	0	2	2.0	1.000	SS-6
1979			6	.000	.000	3	0	0	0	0	0.0	0	0	0	1	0	1	0	1	2	0	0	1.5	1.000	SS-2
1980			100	.277	.363	303	84	16	2	2	0.7	40	20	26	44	6	10	3	161	224	10	46	4.0	.975	2B-79, SS-17, 3B-3
1981			105	.271	.398	354	96	16	7	5	1.4	45	42	42	49	2	0	0	213	341	11	64	5.0	.981	2B-103, SS-9
1982			151	.260	.359	549	143	19	4	9	1.6	63	47	35	82	5	6	1	304	403	22	87	4.6	.970	2B-118, SS-29, 3B-13
1983			157	.264	.384	549	145	23	5	11	2.0	63	58	49	106	2	5	2	315	413	17	80	4.8	.977	2B-154
1984			150	.242	.316	553	134	26	3	3	0.5	54	38	41	97	7	6	2	357	388	15	75	5.1	.980	2B-147, SS-1
1985			152	.295	.361	526	155	26	3	1	0.2	59	34	51	65	5	2	0	366	457	9	100	5.6	.989	2B-149
1986			153	.258	.356	523	135	23	2	8	1.5	52	44	52	84	9	4	0	367	475	19	100	5.7	.978	2B-151
1987			69	.253	.367	237	60	9	6	2	0.8	28	23	22	51	2	0	0	183	186	10	37	5.5	.974	2B-69
1988			54	.280	.327	150	42	7	0	0	0.0	20	10	9	24	0	3	1	110	113	1	26	4.1	.996	2B-49, SS-5
1989			109	.246	.305	305	75	15	0	1	0.3	23	14	32	47	1	8	3	215	249	7	44	4.5	.985	2B-102, SS-2
1990			64	.299	.377	154	46	10	1	0	0.0	10	13	10	29	1	13	1	80	90	4	14	3.3	.977	2B-50, 3B-3
13 yrs.			1276	.265	.356	4214	1118	190	33	42	1.0	458	344	369	681	40	58	13	2675	3350	125	675	4.9	.980	2B-1171, SS-71, 3B-19
LEAGUE CHAMPIONSHIP SERIES																									
1990	CIN	N	4	.333	.333	3	1	0	0	0	0.0	1	0	0	1	0	2	0	0	1	0	0	0.5	1.000	2B-2
WORLD SERIES																									
1990	CIN	N	1	1.000	1.000	1	1	0	0	0	0.0	0	1	0	0	0	1	1	0	0	0	0	0.0	—	

Bob O'Farrell

O'FARRELL, ROBERT ARTHUR
B. Oct. 19, 1896, Waukegan, Ill. D. Feb. 20, 1988, Waukegan, Ill.
Manager 1927, 1934.
BR TR 5′ 9½″ 180 lbs.

Year	Team		Games	BA	SA	AB	H	2B	3B	HR	HR%	R	RBI	BB	SO	SB	Pinch Hit AB	Pinch Hit H	PO	A	E	DP	TC/G	FA	G by Pos
1915	CHI	N	2	.333	.333	3	1	0	0	0	0.0	0	0	0	0	0	0	0	1	1	1	0	1.5	.667	C-2
1916			1	—	—	0	0	0	0	0	—	0	0	0	0	0	0	0	0	0	0	0	0.0	.000	C-1
1917			3	.375	.625	8	3	2	0	0	0.0	1	1	1	0	1	0	0	9	1	0	1	3.3	1.000	C-3
1918			52	.283	.425	113	32	7	3	1	0.9	9	14	10	15	0	7	2	115	36	4	3	3.4	.974	C-45
1919			49	.216	.280	125	27	4	2	0	0.0	11	9	7	10	2	9	1	119	48	6	5	4.6	.965	C-38
1920			94	.248	.352	270	67	11	4	3	1.1	29	19	34	23	1	8	0	317	100	19	6	5.1	.956	C-86
1921			96	.250	.396	260	65	12	7	4	1.5	32	32	18	14	2	6	1	269	87	12	8	4.1	.967	C-90
1922			128	.324	.441	392	127	18	8	4	1.0	68	60	79	34	5	2	1	446	143	14	22	4.8	.977	C-125
1923			131	.319	.471	452	144	25	4	12	2.7	73	84	67	38	10	6	3	418	118	13	11	4.4	.976	C-124
1924			71	.240	.344	183	44	6	2	3	1.6	25	28	30	13	2	10	3	204	40	4	5	4.4	.984	C-57
1925	2 teams		CHI N (17G –.182) STL N (94G –.278)																						
"	total		111	.271	.354	339	92	13	3	3	0.9	39	35	48	31	0	14	4	330	67	10	5	4.3	.975	C-95
1926	STL	N	147	.293	.433	492	144	30	9	7	1.4	63	68	61	44	1	1	1	466	117	10	12	4.1	.983	C-146
1927			61	.264	.331	178	47	10	1	0	0.0	19	18	23	22	3	6	2	141	45	4	5	3.6	.979	C-53
1928	2 teams		STL N (16G –.212) NY N (75G –.195)																						
"	total		91	.200	.270	185	37	7	0	2	1.1	29	24	47	25	4	9	1	199	31	3	2	3.0	.987	C-77
1929	NY	N	91	.306	.435	248	76	14	3	4	1.6	35	42	28	30	3	4	2	254	22	6	2	3.4	.979	C-84
1930			94	.301	.446	249	75	16	4	4	1.6	37	54	31	21	1	23	6	259	34	8	0	4.4	.973	C-69
1931			85	.224	.322	174	39	8	3	1	0.6	11	19	21	23	0	5	0	223	27	5	1	3.2	.980	C-80
1932			50	.239	.284	67	16	3	0	0	0.0	7	8	11	10	0	5	1	85	9	3	2	2.4	.969	C-41
1933	STL	N	55	.239	.325	163	39	4	2	2	1.2	16	20	15	25	0	4	1	211	19	7	1	4.7	.970	C-50
1934	2 teams		CIN N (44G –.244) CHI N (22G –.224)																						
"	total		66	.237	.342	190	45	11	3	1	0.5	13	14	14	30	0	2	0	217	35	1	4	4.0	.996	C-64
1935	STL	N	14	.000	.000	10	0	0	0	0	0.0	0	0	2	0	0	4	0	12	0	0	0	1.5	1.000	C-8
21 yrs.			1492	.273	.388	4101	1120	201	58	51	1.2	517	549	547	408	35	125	29	4295	980	130	95	4.0	.976	C-1338
WORLD SERIES																									
1918	CHI	N	3	.000	.000	3	0	0	0	0	0.0	0	0	0	0	0	3	0	0	0	0	0	0.0	.000	C-1
1926	STL	N	7	.304	.348	23	7	1	0	0	0.0	2	2	2	2	0	0	0	35	8	0	0	6.1	1.000	C-7
2 yrs.			10	.269	.308	26	7	1	0	0	0.0	2	2	2	2	0	3	0	35	8	0	0	5.4	1.000	C-8

Jose Offerman

OFFERMAN, JOSE ANTONIO BB TR 6′ 150 lbs.
Born Jose Antonio Oferman (Dono).
B. Nov. 8, 1968, San Pedro de Macoris, Dominican Republic.

Year	Team		Games	BA	SA	AB	H	2B	3B	HR	HR%	R	RBI	BB	SO	SB	Pinch Hit AB	Pinch Hit H	PO	A	E	DP	TC/G	FA	G by Pos
1990	LA	N	29	.155	.207	58	9	0	0	1	1.7	7	7	4	14	1	1	0	30	40	4	5	2.7	.946	SS-27
1991			52	.195	.212	113	22	2	0	0	0.0	10	3	25	32	3	2	0	50	121	10	17	3.6	.945	SS-50
1992			149	.260	.333	534	139	20	8	1	0.2	67	30	57	98	23	1	0	208	398	42	74	4.3	.935	SS-149
1993			158	.269	.331	590	159	21	6	1	0.2	77	62	71	75	30	1	0	250	454	37	95	4.7	.950	SS-158
1994			72	.210	.288	243	51	8	4	1	0.4	27	25	38	38	2	0	0	123	194	11	45	4.6	.966	SS-72
1995			119	.287	.375	429	123	14	6	4	0.9	69	33	69	67	2	3	0	166	312	35	56	4.5	.932	SS-115
6 yrs.			579	.256	.325	1967	503	65	24	8	0.4	257	160	264	324	61	8	0	827	1519	139	292	4.4	.944	SS-571
DIVISIONAL PLAYOFF SERIES																									
1995	LA	N	1	—	—	0	0	0	0	0	—	0	0	0	0	0	0	0	0	0	0	0	0.0	—	

Rowland Office

OFFICE, ROWLAND JOHNIE BL TL 6′ 170 lbs.
B. Oct. 25, 1952, Sacramento, Calif.

Year	Team		Games	BA	SA	AB	H	2B	3B	HR	HR%	R	RBI	BB	SO	SB	Pinch Hit AB	Pinch Hit H	PO	A	E	DP	TC/G	FA	G by Pos
1972	ATL	N	2	.400	.400	5	2	0	0	0	0.0	1	0	1	2	0	1	0	3	0	0	0	3.0	1.000	OF-1
1974			131	.246	.355	248	61	16	1	3	1.2	20	31	16	30	5	11	4	171	0	1	0	1.4	.994	OF-119
1975			126	.290	.361	355	103	14	1	3	0.8	30	30	23	41	2	20	7	229	6	8	0	2.3	.967	OF-107
1976			99	.281	.368	359	101	17	1	4	1.1	51	34	37	49	2	5	2	204	3	3	2	2.3	.986	OF-92
1977			124	.241	.311	428	103	13	1	5	1.2	42	39	23	58	2	20	5	250	8	3	3	2.5	.989	OF-104, 1B-1
1978			146	.250	.354	404	101	13	1	9	2.2	40	40	22	52	8	18	3	291	4	3	2	2.2	.990	OF-136
1979			124	.249	.336	277	69	14	2	2	0.7	35	37	27	33	5	21	5	164	4	2	0	1.8	.988	OF-97
1980	MON	N	116	.267	.401	292	78	13	4	6	2.1	36	30	36	39	3	17	6	150	2	2	1	1.6	.987	OF-97
1981			26	.175	.175	40	7	0	0	0	0.0	4	0	4	6	0	13	3	15	0	1	0	1.1	.938	OF-15
1982			3	.333	.667	3	1	1	0	0	0.0	0	0	0	1	0	2	0	2	0	0	0	2.0	1.000	OF-1
1983	NY	A	2	.000	.000	2	0	0	0	0	0.0	0	1	0	0	0	1	0	2	0	0	0	1.0	1.000	OF-2
11 yrs.			899	.259	.350	2413	626	101	11	32	1.3	259	242	189	311	27	129	35	1481	27	23	8	2.0	.985	OF-771, 1B-1

Jim Oglesby

OGLESBY, JAMES DORN BL TL 6′ 190 lbs.
B. Aug. 10, 1905, Schofield, Mo. D. Sept. 1, 1955, Tulsa, Okla.

Year	Team		Games	BA	SA	AB	H	2B	3B	HR	HR%	R	RBI	BB	SO	SB	Pinch Hit AB	Pinch Hit H	PO	A	E	DP	TC/G	FA	G by Pos
1936	PHI	A	3	.182	.182	11	2	0	0	0	0.0	0	2	2	0	0	0	0	23	2	0	2	8.3	1.000	1B-3

Ben Oglivie

OGLIVIE, BENJAMIN AMBROSIO BL TL 6′ 2″ 160 lbs.
B. Feb. 11, 1949, Colon, Panama

Year	Team		Games	BA	SA	AB	H	2B	3B	HR	HR%	R	RBI	BB	SO	SB	Pinch Hit AB	Pinch Hit H	PO	A	E	DP	TC/G	FA	G by Pos
1971	BOS	A	14	.263	.342	38	10	3	0	0	0.0	2	4	0	5	0	5	0	22	1	1	1	2.2	.958	OF-11
1972			94	.241	.391	253	61	10	2	8	3.2	27	30	18	61	1	24	9	98	5	2	2	1.6	.981	OF-65
1973			58	.218	.333	147	32	9	1	2	1.4	16	9	9	32	1	10	2	56	2	1	0	1.3	.983	OF-32, DH-13
1974	DET	A	92	.270	.385	252	68	11	3	4	1.6	28	29	34	38	12	19	5	162	11	5	13	2.3	.972	OF-63, 1B-10, DH-4
1975			100	.286	.416	332	95	14	1	9	2.7	45	36	16	62	11	3	0	232	8	5	5	2.6	.980	OF-86, 1B-5, DH-2
1976			115	.285	.492	305	87	12	3	15	4.9	36	47	11	44	9	**38**	**9**	234	8	3	13	3.3	.988	OF-64, 1B-9, DH-1
1977			132	.262	.464	450	118	24	2	21	4.7	63	61	40	80	9	12	4	236	10	6	3	2.1	.976	OF-118, DH-2
1978	MIL	A	128	.303	.497	469	142	29	4	18	3.8	71	72	52	69	11	6	1	275	8	6	4	2.3	.979	OF-89, DH-27, 1B-11
1979			139	.282	.525	514	145	30	4	29	5.6	88	81	48	56	12	6	3	320	10	5	3	2.4	.985	OF-120, DH-13, 1B-9
1980			156	.304	.563	592	180	26	2	**41**	6.9	94	118	54	71	11	0	0	384	18	9	3	2.6	.978	OF-152, DH-4
1981			107	.242	.395	400	97	15	2	14	3.5	53	72	37	49	2	1	1	211	3	4	1	2.0	.982	OF-101, DH-6
1982			159	.244	.453	602	147	22	1	34	5.6	92	102	70	81	3	1	0	359	15	7	3	2.4	.982	OF-159
1983			125	.280	.436	411	115	19	3	13	3.2	49	66	60	64	4	10	3	259	8	4	1	2.2	.985	OF-113, DH-8
1984			131	.262	.384	461	121	16	2	12	2.6	49	60	44	56	0	10	3	256	6	8	1	2.1	.970	OF-125, DH-1
1985			101	.290	.440	341	99	17	2	10	2.9	40	61	37	51	0	9	1	190	4	7	0	2.1	.965	OF-91, DH-4
1986			103	.283	.390	346	98	20	1	5	1.4	31	53	30	33	1	8	1	105	4	1	1	1.2	.991	OF-50, DH-42
16 yrs.			1754	.273	.450	5913	1615	277	33	235	4.0	784	901	560	852	87	162	42	3399	121	74	54	2.2	.979	OF-1439, DH-127, 1B-44
DIVISIONAL PLAYOFF SERIES																									
1981	MIL	A	5	.167	.222	18	3	1	0	0	0.0	0	1	0	7	0	0	0	13	1	0	0	2.8	1.000	OF-5
LEAGUE CHAMPIONSHIP SERIES																									
1982	MIL	A	4	.133	.333	15	2	0	0	1	6.7	1	1	0	3	0	0	0	5	0	2	0	1.8	.714	OF-4
WORLD SERIES																									
1982	MIL	A	7	.222	.407	27	6	0	1	1	3.7	4	1	2	4	0	0	0	13	0	1	0	2.0	.929	OF-7

Brusie Ogrodowski

OGRODOWSKI, AMBROSE FRANCIS BR TR 5′11″ 175 lbs.
B. Feb. 17, 1912, Hoytville, Pa. D. Mar. 5, 1956, San Francisco, Calif.

Year	Team		Games	BA	SA	AB	H	2B	3B	HR	HR%	R	RBI	BB	SO	SB	Pinch Hit AB	Pinch Hit H	PO	A	E	DP	TC/G	FA	G by Pos
1936	STL	N	94	.228	.312	237	54	15	1	1	0.4	28	20	10	20	0	9	1	314	32	4	6	4.1	.989	C-85
1937			90	.233	.323	279	65	10	3	3	1.1	37	31	11	17	2	3	2	387	50	7	2	5.1	.984	C-87
2 yrs.			184	.231	.318	516	119	25	4	4	0.8	65	51	21	37	2	12	3	701	82	11	8	4.6	.986	C-172

Hal O'Hagen

O'HAGEN, HARRY P. 6′ 173 lbs.
B. Sept. 30, 1873, Washington, D. C. D. Jan. 14, 1913, Newark, N. J.

Year	Team		Games	BA	SA	AB	H	2B	3B	HR	HR%	R	RBI	BB	SO	SB	Pinch Hit AB	Pinch Hit H	PO	A	E	DP	TC/G	FA	G by Pos
1892	WAS	N	1	.250	.250	4	1	0	0	0	0.0	1	0	0	2	0	0	0	3	3	0	1	6.0	1.000	C-1
1902	3 teams		CHI N (31G –.194) NY N (26G –.143) CLE A (3G –.385)																						
″	total		60	.185	.249	205	38	5	4	0	0.0	17	19	13		13	0	0	533	38	12	30	9.7	.979	1B-52, OF-8
2 yrs.			61	.187	.249	209	39	5	4	0	0.0	18	19	13	2	13	0	0	536	41	12	31	9.7	.980	1B-52, OF-8, C-1

Greg O'Halloran

O'HALLORAN, GREGORY JOSEPH BL TR 6′ 2″ 205 lbs.
B. May 21, 1968, Toronto, Ont., Canada.

Year	Team		Games	BA	SA	AB	H	2B	3B	HR	HR%	R	RBI	BB	SO	SB	Pinch Hit AB	Pinch Hit H	PO	A	E	DP	TC/G	FA	G by Pos
1994	FLA	N	12	.182	.182	11	2	0	0	0	0.0	1	1	0	1	0	11	2	2	0	0	0	2.0	1.000	C-1

Bill O'Hara

O'HARA, WILLIAM ALEXANDER BL TR 5′10″
B. Aug. 14, 1883, Toronto, Ont., Canada D. June 15, 1931, Jersey City, N. J.

Year	Team		Games	BA	SA	AB	H	2B	3B	HR	HR%	R	RBI	BB	SO	SB	Pinch Hit AB	Pinch Hit H	PO	A	E	DP	TC/G	FA	G by Pos
1909	NY	N	115	.236	.286	360	85	9	3	1	0.3	48	30	41		31	0	0	202	19	5	4	2.0	.978	OF-115
1910	STL	N	9	.150	.150	20	3	0	0	0	0.0	1	2	1	3	0	3	0	14	1	0	0	2.5	1.000	OF-4, 1B-1, P-1
2 yrs.			124	.232	.279	380	88	9	3	1	0.3	49	32	42	3	31	3	0	216	20	5	4	2.0	.979	OF-119, 1B-1, P-1

Kid O'Hara

O'HARA, JAMES FRANCIS
B. Dec. 19, 1875, Wilkes-Barre, Pa. D. Dec. 1, 1954, Canton, Ohio.
BB TR 5′ 7½″ 152 lbs.

Year	Team	Games	BA	SA	AB	H	2B	3B	HR	HR%	R	RBI	BB	SO	SB	Pinch Hit AB	Pinch Hit H	PO	A	E	DP	TC/G	FA	G by Pos
1904	BOS N	8	.207	.207	29	6	0	0	0	0.0	3	0	4		1	0	0	10	2	1	0	1.6	.923	OF-8

Tom O'Hara

O'HARA, THOMAS F
B. July 13, 1885, Waverly, N. Y. D. June 8, 1954, Denver, Colo.

Year	Team	Games	BA	SA	AB	H	2B	3B	HR	HR%	R	RBI	BB	SO	SB	Pinch Hit AB	Pinch Hit H	PO	A	E	DP	TC/G	FA	G by Pos
1906	STL N	14	.302	.321	53	16	1	0	0	0.0	8	0	3		3	0	0	24	0	3	0	1.9	.889	OF-14
1907		48	.237	.260	173	41	2	1	0	0.0	11	5	12		1	1	0	78	5	5	2	1.9	.943	OF-47
2 yrs.		62	.252	.274	226	57	3	1	0	0.0	19	5	15		4	1	0	102	5	8	2	1.9	.930	OF-61

Len Okrie

OKRIE, LEONARD JOSEPH
Son of Frank Okrie.
B. July 16, 1923, Detroit, Mich.
BR TR 6′ 185 lbs.

Year	Team	Games	BA	SA	AB	H	2B	3B	HR	HR%	R	RBI	BB	SO	SB	Pinch Hit AB	Pinch Hit H	PO	A	E	DP	TC/G	FA	G by Pos
1948	WAS A	19	.238	.286	42	10	0	1	0	0.0	1	1	1	7	0	2	0	43	10	1	1	3.2	.981	C-17
1950		17	.222	.222	27	6	0	0	0	0.0	1	2	6	7	0	0	0	34	6	0	3	2.4	1.000	C-17
1951		5	.125	.250	8	1	1	0	0	0.0	1	0	2	1	0	0	0	13	4	3	0	4.0	.850	C-5
1952	BOS A	1	.000	.000	1	0	0	0	0	0.0	0	0	0	1	0	0	0	1	0	0	0	1.0	1.000	C-1
4 yrs.		42	.218	.256	78	17	1	1	0	0.0	3	3	9	16	0	2	0	91	20	4	4	2.9	.965	C-40

Jim Olander

OLANDER, JAMES BENTLEY
B. Feb. 21, 1963, Tucson, Ariz.
BR TR 6′ 2″ 185 lbs.

Year	Team	Games	BA	SA	AB	H	2B	3B	HR	HR%	R	RBI	BB	SO	SB	Pinch Hit AB	Pinch Hit H	PO	A	E	DP	TC/G	FA	G by Pos
1991	MIL A	12	.000	.000	9	0	0	0	0	0.0	2	0	2	5	0	0	0	9	0	0	0	0.8	1.000	OF-9, DH-3

Dave Oldfield

OLDFIELD, DAVID
B. Dec. 18, 1864, Philadelphia, Pa. D. Aug. 28, 1939, Philadelphia, Pa.
BB TL 5′ 7″ 175 lbs.

Year	Team	Games	BA	SA	AB	H	2B	3B	HR	HR%	R	RBI	BB	SO	SB	Pinch Hit AB	Pinch Hit H	PO	A	E	DP	TC/G	FA	G by Pos
1883	BAL AA	1	.000	.000	4	0	0	0	0	0.0	0		0			0	0	6	0	3	0	9.0	.667	C-1
1885	BKN AA	10	.320	.360	25	8	1	0	0	0.0	2		3			0	0	47	10	9	0	6.0	.864	C-9, OF-2
1886	2 teams	BKN AA (14G –.236) WAS N (21G –.141)																						
"	total	35	.183	.206	126	23	3	0	0	0.0	9	2	7	15		0	0	141	37	28	1	5.7	.864	C-25, OF-10, SS-1
3 yrs.		46	.200	.226	155	31	4	0	0	0.0	11	2	10	15		0	0	194	47	40	1	5.9	.858	C-35, OF-12, SS-1

John Oldham

OLDHAM, JOHN HARDIN
B. Nov. 6, 1932, Salinas, Calif.
BR TL 6′ 3″ 198 lbs.

Year	Team	Games	BA	SA	AB	H	2B	3B	HR	HR%	R	RBI	BB	SO	SB	Pinch Hit AB	Pinch Hit H	PO	A	E	DP	TC/G	FA	G by Pos
1956	CIN N	1	—	—	0	0	0	0	0	—	0	0	0	0	0	0	0	0	0	0	0	0.0	—	

Bob Oldis

OLDIS, ROBERT CARL
B. Jan. 5, 1928, Preston, Iowa.
BR TR 6′ 1″ 185 lbs.

Year	Team	Games	BA	SA	AB	H	2B	3B	HR	HR%	R	RBI	BB	SO	SB	Pinch Hit AB	Pinch Hit H	PO	A	E	DP	TC/G	FA	G by Pos
1953	WAS A	7	.250	.250	16	4	0	0	0	0.0	0	3	1	2	0	0	0	23	3	0	1	3.7	1.000	C-7
1954		11	.333	.375	24	8	1	0	0	0.0	1	0	1	3	0	1	0	30	2	2	0	3.4	.941	C-8, 3B-2
1955		6	.000	.000	6	0	0	0	0	0.0	1	0	1	0	0	0	0	12	1	0	0	2.2	1.000	C-6
1960	PIT N	22	.200	.250	20	4	1	0	0	0.0	1	1	1	2	0	0	0	42	2	0	0	2.0	1.000	C-22
1961		4	.000	.000	5	0	0	0	0	0.0	0	0	0	0	0	0	0	11	3	0	3	3.5	1.000	C-4
1962	PHI N	38	.263	.313	80	21	1	0	1	1.3	9	10	13	10	0	7	2	134	14	2	4	5.0	.987	C-30
1963		47	.224	.259	85	19	3	0	0	0.0	8	8	3	5	0	11	3	170	15	4	4	4.4	.979	C-43
7 yrs.		135	.237	.275	236	56	6	0	1	0.4	20	22	20	22	0	19	5	422	40	8	12	3.9	.983	C-120, 3B-2
WORLD SERIES																								
1960	PIT N	2	—	—	0	0	0	0	0	—	0	0	0	0	0	0	0	0	0	0	0	0.0	.000	C-2

Rube Oldring

OLDRING, REUBEN HENRY
B. May 30, 1884, New York, N. Y. D. Sept. 9, 1961, Bridgeton, N. J.
BR TR 5′10″ 186 lbs.

Year	Team	Games	BA	SA	AB	H	2B	3B	HR	HR%	R	RBI	BB	SO	SB	Pinch Hit AB	Pinch Hit H	PO	A	E	DP	TC/G	FA	G by Pos
1905	NY A	8	.300	.467	30	9	0	1	1	3.3	2	6	2		4	0	0	24	24	2	4	6.3	.960	SS-8
1906	PHI A	59	.241	.310	174	42	10	1	0	0.0	15	19	2		7	2	0	65	90	17	5	3.1	.901	3B-49, SS-3, 2B-2, 1B-1
1907		117	.286	.395	441	126	27	9	1	0.2	48	40	7		29	0	0	180	10	5	0	1.7	.974	OF-117
1908		116	.221	.270	434	96	14	2	1	0.2	38	39	18		13	0	0	246	9	16	3	2.3	.941	OF-116
1909		90	.230	.328	326	75	13	8	1	0.3	39	28	20		17	0	0	175	7	8	1	2.1	.958	OF-89, 1B-1
1910		134	.308	.430	546	168	27	14	4	0.7	79	57	23		17	0	0	249	14	6	6	2.0	.978	OF-134
1911		121	.297	.394	495	147	11	14	3	0.6	84	59	21		21	1	0	225	13	5	2	2.0	.979	OF-119
1912		98	.301	.370	395	119	14	5	1	0.3	61	24	10		17	1	0	214	8	6	1	2.4	.974	OF-97
1913		136	.283	.394	538	152	27	9	5	0.9	101	71	34	37	40	0	0	248	20	9	3	2.0	.968	OF-136, SS-5
1914		119	.277	.371	466	129	21	7	3	0.6	68	49	18	35	14	2	0	215	7	8	5	2.0	.965	OF-117
1915		107	.248	.363	408	101	23	3	6	1.5	49	42	22	21	11	3	2	224	23	9	6	2.5	.965	OF-96, 3B-8
1916	2 teams	PHI A (40G –.247) NY A (43G –.234)																						
"	total	83	.240	.322	304	73	16	3	1	0.3	27	26	21	22	7	0	0	130	7	11	5	1.8	.926	OF-83
1918	PHI A	49	.233	.263	133	31	2	1	0	0.0	5	11	8	10	0	15	4	39	9	3	3	1.5	.941	OF-30, 3B-2, 2B-2
13 yrs.		1237	.270	.364	4690	1268	205	77	27	0.6	616	471	206	125	197	24	6	2234	241	105	44	2.1	.959	OF-1134, 3B-59, SS-16, 2B-4, 1B-2
WORLD SERIES																								
1911	PHI A	6	.200	.400	25	5	2	0	1	4.0	2	3	0	6	0	0	0	8	0	1	0	1.5	.889	OF-6
1913		5	.273	.364	22	6	0	1	0	0.0	5	0	0	1	1	0	0	10	0	0	0	2.0	1.000	OF-5
1914		4	.067	.067	15	1	0	0	0	0.0	0	0	0	5	0	0	0	6	0	0	0	1.5	1.000	OF-4
3 yrs.		15	.194	.306	62	12	2	1	1	1.6	7	3	0	12	1	0	0	24	0	1	0	1.7	.960	OF-15

Charley O'Leary

O'LEARY, CHARLES TIMOTHY
B. Oct. 15, 1882, Chicago, Ill. D. Jan. 6, 1941, Chicago, Ill.
BR TR 5′ 7″ 165 lbs.

Year	Team	Games	BA	SA	AB	H	2B	3B	HR	HR%	R	RBI	BB	SO	SB	Pinch Hit AB	Pinch Hit H	PO	A	E	DP	TC/G	FA	G by Pos
1904	DET A	135	.213	.254	456	97	10	3	1	0.2	39	16	21		9	0	0	308	439	54	48	5.9	.933	SS-135
1905		148	.213	.248	512	109	13	1	1	0.2	47	33	29		13	0	0	358	411	55	40	5.6	.933	SS-148
1906		128	.219	.271	443	97	13	2	2	0.5	34	34	17		8	1	1	326	398	58	37	6.2	.926	SS-127
1907		139	.241	.286	465	112	19	1	0	0.0	61	34	32		11	1	0	353	448	44	35	6.1	.948	SS-138
1908		65	.251	.322	211	53	9	3	0	0.0	21	17	9		4	0	0	131	179	27	15	5.2	.920	SS-64, 2B-1
1909		76	.203	.241	261	53	10	0	0	0.0	29	13	6		9	0	0	104	162	18	8	3.8	.937	3B-54, 2B-15, SS-4, OF-2
1910		65	.242	.284	211	51	7	1	0	0.0	23	9	9		7	2	0	121	167	16	15	5.1	.947	2B-38, SS-16, 3B-6
1911		74	.266	.313	256	68	8	2	0	0.0	29	25	21		10	0	0	178	212	14	22	5.5	.965	2B-67, 3B-6

Charley O'Leary *continued*

Year	Team	Games	BA	SA	AB	H	2B	3B	HR	HR%	R	RBI	BB	SO	SB	Pinch Hit AB	Pinch Hit H	PO	A	E	DP	TC/G	FA	G by Pos
1912		3	.200	.200	10	2	0	0	0	0.0	1	1	0		0	0	0	5	11	0	0	5.3	1.000	2B-3
1913	**STL N**	120	.218	.280	404	88	15	5	0	0.0	32	31	20	34	3	1	0	218	338	28	33	5.0	.952	SS-102, 2B-15
1934	**STL A**	1	1.000	1.000	1	1	0	0	0	0.0	1	0	0	0	0	1	1	0	0	0	0	0.0	—	
11 yrs.		954	.226	.273	3230	731	104	18	4	0.1	317	213	164	34	74	6	2	2102	2765	314	253	5.5	.939	SS-734, 2B-139, 3B-66, OF-2
WORLD SERIES																								
1907	**DET A**	5	.059	.059	17	1	0	0	0	0.0	0	0	1	3	0	0	0	9	18	2	0	5.8	.931	SS-5
1908		5	.158	.158	19	3	0	0	0	0.0	2	0	0	3	0	0	0	7	12	1	3	4.0	.950	SS-5
1909		1	.000	.000	3	0	0	0	0	0.0	0	0	0	0	0	0	0	1	1	0	0	2.0	1.000	3B-1
3 yrs.		11	.103	.103	39	4	0	0	0	0.0	2	0	1	6	0	0	0	17	31	3	3	4.6	.941	SS-10, 3B-1

Dan O'Leary

O'LEARY, DANIEL (Hustling Dan) BL 5'10" 165 lbs.
B. Oct. 22, 1856, Detroit, Mich. D. June 24, 1922, Chicago, Ill.
Manager 1884.

Year	Team	Games	BA	SA	AB	H	2B	3B	HR	HR%	R	RBI	BB	SO	SB	Pinch Hit AB	Pinch Hit H	PO	A	E	DP	TC/G	FA	G by Pos
1879	**PRO N**	2	.429	.429	7	3	0	0	0	0.0	1	2	0	0		0	0	0	0	0	0	0.0	.000	OF-2
1880	**BOS N**	3	.250	.417	12	3	2	0	0	0.0	1	1	0	3		0	0	1	0	0	0	0.3	1.000	OF-3
1881	**DET N**	2	.000	.000	8	0	0	0	0	0.0	0	0	0	2		0	0	5	0	2	0	3.5	.714	OF-2
1882	**WOR N**	6	.182	.227	22	4	1	0	0	0.0	2	2	5	5		0	0	8	0	2	0	1.7	.800	OF-6
1884	**CIN U**	32	.258	.311	132	34	0	2	1	0.8	14		5			0	0	48	8	9	0	2.0	.862	OF-32
5 yrs.		45	.243	.298	181	44	3	2	1	0.6	18	5	10	10		0	0	62	8	13	0	1.8	.843	OF-45

Troy O'Leary

O'LEARY, TROY FRANKLIN BL TL 6' 175 lbs.
B. Aug. 4, 1969, Compton, Calif.

Year	Team	Games	BA	SA	AB	H	2B	3B	HR	HR%	R	RBI	BB	SO	SB	Pinch Hit AB	Pinch Hit H	PO	A	E	DP	TC/G	FA	G by Pos
1993	**MIL A**	19	.293	.366	41	12	3	0	0	0.0	3	3	5	9	0	2	1	32	1	0	0	1.7	1.000	OF-19
1994		27	.273	.409	66	18	1	1	2	3.0	9	7	5	12	1	4	1	37	2	0	1	1.8	1.000	OF-21, DH-1
1995	**BOS A**	112	.308	.491	399	123	31	6	10	2.5	60	49	29	64	5	12	5	196	6	5	1	1.9	.976	OF-105, DH-3
3 yrs.		158	.302	.470	506	153	35	7	12	2.4	72	59	39	85	6	18	7	265	9	5	2	1.9	.982	OF-145, DH-4

John Olerud

OLERUD, JOHN GARRETT BL TL 6' 5" 205 lbs.
B. Aug. 5, 1968, Seattle, Wash.

Year	Team	Games	BA	SA	AB	H	2B	3B	HR	HR%	R	RBI	BB	SO	SB	Pinch Hit AB	Pinch Hit H	PO	A	E	DP	TC/G	FA	G by Pos
1989	**TOR A**	6	.375	.375	8	3	0	0	0	0.0	2	0	0	1	0	1	0	19	2	0	0	3.5	1.000	1B-5, DH-1
1990		111	.265	.430	358	95	15	1	14	3.9	43	48	57	75	0	7	1	133	10	2	10	1.3	.986	DH-90, 1B-18
1991		139	.256	.438	454	116	30	1	17	3.7	64	68	68	84	0	9	1	1120	78	5	77	8.8	.996	1B-135, DH-1
1992		138	.284	.450	458	130	28	0	16	3.5	68	66	70	61	1	10	4	1057	81	7	72	8.5	.994	1B-133, DH-1
1993		158	**.363**	.599	551	200	**54**	2	24	4.4	109	107	114	65	0	1	0	1160	97	10	107	8.1	.992	1B-137, DH-20
1994		108	.297	.477	384	114	29	2	12	3.1	47	67	61	53	1	3	0	823	68	6	82	8.4	.993	1B-104, DH-3
1995		135	.291	.404	492	143	32	0	8	1.6	72	54	84	54	0	3	1	1098	90	4	102	9.0	.997	1B-133
7 yrs.		795	.296	.471	2705	801	188	6	91	3.4	405	410	454	393	2	34	7	5410	426	34	450	7.5	.994	1B-665, DH-116
LEAGUE CHAMPIONSHIP SERIES																								
1991	**TOR A**	5	.158	.158	19	3	0	0	0	0.0	1	3	3	1	0	0	0	40	3	0	5	8.6	1.000	1B-5
1992		6	.348	.565	23	8	2	0	1	4.3	4	4	2	5	0	0	0	51	1	0	6	8.7	1.000	1B-6
1993		6	.348	.391	23	8	1	0	0	0.0	5	3	4	1	0	0	0	48	9	1	5	9.7	.983	1B-6
3 yrs.		17	.292	.385	65	19	3	0	1	1.5	10	10	9	7	0	0	0	139	13	1	16	9.0	.993	1B-17
WORLD SERIES																								
1992	**TOR A**	4	.308	.308	13	4	0	0	0	0.0	2	0	0	4	0	0	0	25	3	0	2	7.0	1.000	1B-4
1993		5	.235	.471	17	4	1	0	1	5.9	5	2	4	1	0	0	0	36	0	0	3	7.2	1.000	1B-5
2 yrs.		9	.267	.400	30	8	1	0	1	3.3	7	2	4	5	0	0	0	61	3	0	5	7.1	1.000	1B-9

Frank Olin

OLIN, FRANKLIN WALTER BL
B. Jan. 9, 1860, Woodford, Vt. D. May 20, 1951, St. Louis, Mo.

Year	Team	Games	BA	SA	AB	H	2B	3B	HR	HR%	R	RBI	BB	SO	SB	Pinch Hit AB	Pinch Hit H	PO	A	E	DP	TC/G	FA	G by Pos
1884	**3 teams**	**WAS AA** (21G –.386)	**WAS U** (1G –.000)	**TOL AA** (26G –.256)																				
"	**total**	48	.312	.376	173	54	4	2	1	0.6	28		13			0	0	67	33	24	3	2.5	.806	OF-38, 2B-12
1885	**DET N**	1	.500	.500	4	2	0	0	0	0.0	1	0	0	0		0	0	2	2	2	0	6.0	.667	3B-1
2 yrs.		49	.316	.379	177	56	4	2	1	0.6	29	0	13	0		0	0	69	35	26	3	2.5	.800	OF-38, 2B-12, 3B-1

Jose Oliva

OLIVA, JOSE BR TR 6' 3" 215 lbs.
Born Jose Oliva (Galvez).
B. Mar. 3, 1971, San Pedro de Macoris, Dominican Republic.

Year	Team	Games	BA	SA	AB	H	2B	3B	HR	HR%	R	RBI	BB	SO	SB	Pinch Hit AB	Pinch Hit H	PO	A	E	DP	TC/G	FA	G by Pos
1994	**ATL N**	19	.288	.678	59	17	5	0	6	10.2	9	11	7	10	0	3	1	9	32	3	2	2.8	.932	3B-16
1995	**2 teams**	**ATL N** (48G –.156)	**STL N** (22G –.122)																					
"	**total**	70	.142	.284	183	26	5	0	7	3.8	15	20	12	46	0	22	2	41	72	7	9	2.6	.942	3B-43, 1B-3
2 yrs.		89	.178	.380	242	43	10	0	13	5.4	24	31	19	56	0	25	3	50	104	10	11	2.6	.939	3B-59, 1B-3

Tony Oliva

OLIVA, PEDRO BL TR 6' 1" 175 lbs.
Born Pedro Oliva (Lopez).
B. July 20, 1940, Pinar del Rio, Cuba.

Year	Team	Games	BA	SA	AB	H	2B	3B	HR	HR%	R	RBI	BB	SO	SB	Pinch Hit AB	Pinch Hit H	PO	A	E	DP	TC/G	FA	G by Pos
1962	**MIN A**	9	.444	.556	9	4	1	0	0	0.0	3	3	3	2	0	5	2	3	0	0	0	1.5	1.000	OF-2
1963		7	.429	.429	7	3	0	0	0	0.0	0	1	0	2	0	7	3	0	0	0	0	0.0	—	
1964		161	**.323**	.557	672	**217**	**43**	9	32	4.8	**109**	94	34	68	12	2	1	313	5	6	0	2.0	.981	OF-159
1965		149	**.321**	.491	576	**185**	40	5	16	2.8	107	98	55	64	19	1	0	284	10	11	3	2.1	.964	OF-147
1966		159	.307	.502	622	**191**	32	7	25	4.0	99	87	42	72	13	1	1	335	9	10	3	2.2	.972	OF-159
1967		146	.289	.463	557	161	**34**	6	17	3.1	76	83	44	61	11	1	1	286	8	4	2	2.0	.987	OF-146
1968		128	.289	.477	470	136	24	5	18	3.8	54	68	45	61	10	2	0	227	7	4	1	1.9	.983	OF-126
1969		153	.309	.496	637	**197**	**39**	4	24	3.8	97	101	45	66	10	1	0	311	14	6	3	2.2	.982	OF-152
1970		157	.325	.514	628	**204**	**36**	7	23	3.7	96	107	38	67	5	1	1	351	12	12	4	2.4	.968	OF-157
1971		126	**.337**	**.546**	487	164	30	3	22	4.5	73	81	25	44	4	5	0	216	6	7	3	1.9	.969	OF-121
1972		10	.321	.357	28	9	1	0	0	0.0	1	1	2	5	0	1	0	6	0	1	0	0.8	.857	OF-9
1973		146	.291	.410	571	166	20	0	16	2.8	63	92	45	44	2	4	2	0	0	0	0	0.0	.000	DH-142
1974		127	.285	.414	459	131	16	2	13	2.8	43	57	27	31	0	13	7	0	0	0	0	0.0	.000	DH-112
1975		131	.270	.378	455	123	10	0	13	2.9	46	58	41	45	0	10	5	0	0	0	0	0.0	.000	DH-120
1976		67	.211	.260	123	26	3	0	1	0.8	3	16	2	13	0	32	7	0	0	0	0	0.0	.000	DH-32
15 yrs.		1676	.304	.476	6301	1917	329	48	220	3.5	870	947	448	645	86	86	30	2332	71	61	19	1.6	.975	OF-1178, DH-406

Tony Oliva *continued*

Year	Team	Games	BA	SA	AB	H	2B	3B	HR	HR%	R	RBI	BB	SO	SB	Pinch Hit AB	Pinch Hit H	PO	A	E	DP	TC/G	FA	G by Pos
LEAGUE CHAMPIONSHIP SERIES																								
1969	MIN A	3	.385	.769	13	5	2	0	1	7.7	3	2	1	3	1	0	0	6	1	2	0	3.0	.778	OF-3
1970		3	.500	.917	12	6	2	0	1	8.3	2	1	0	1	0	0	0	10	2	0	1	4.0	1.000	OF-3
2 yrs.		6	.440	.840	25	11	4	0	2	8.0	5	3	1	4	1	0	0	16	3	2	1	3.5	.905	OF-6
WORLD SERIES																								
1965	MIN A	7	.192	.346	26	5	1	0	1	3.8	2	2	1	6	0	0	0	20	0	1	0	3.0	.952	OF-7

Ed Olivares

OLIVARES, EDWARD
Born Edward Olivares (Balzac).
Father of Omar Olivares.
B. Nov. 5, 1938, Mayaguez, Puerto Rico.

BR TR 5′11″ 180 lbs.

Year	Team	Games	BA	SA	AB	H	2B	3B	HR	HR%	R	RBI	BB	SO	SB	Pinch Hit AB	Pinch Hit H	PO	A	E	DP	TC/G	FA	G by Pos
1960	STL N	3	.000	.000	5	0	0	0	0	0.0	0	0	0	3	0	2	0	0	1	1	0	2.0	.500	2B-1
1961		21	.167	.167	30	5	0	0	0	0.0	2	1	0	4	1	11	1	8	0	0	0	0.8	1.000	OF-10
2 yrs.		24	.143	.143	35	5	0	0	0	0.0	2	1	0	7	1	13	1	8	1	1	0	0.9	.900	OF-10, 2B-1

Al Oliver

OLIVER, ALBERT (Scoop)
B. Oct. 14, 1946, Portsmouth, Ohio.

BL TL 6′ 195 lbs.

Year	Team	Games	BA	SA	AB	H	2B	3B	HR	HR%	R	RBI	BB	SO	SB	Pinch Hit AB	Pinch Hit H	PO	A	E	DP	TC/G	FA	G by Pos
1968	PIT N	4	.125	.125	8	1	0	0	0	0.0	1	0	0	4	0	3	0	3	0	0	0	3.0	1.000	OF-1
1969		129	.285	.445	463	132	19	2	17	3.7	55	70	21	38	8	7	0	911	50	9	87	7.6	.991	1B-106, OF-21
1970		151	.270	.414	551	149	33	5	12	2.2	63	83	35	35	1	4	2	718	52	9	69	5.0	.988	OF-80, 1B-77
1971		143	.282	.446	529	149	31	7	14	2.6	69	64	27	72	4	6	0	497	15	6	18	3.7	.988	OF-116, 1B-25
1972		140	.312	.437	565	176	27	4	12	2.1	88	89	34	44	2	1	0	353	4	5	4	2.6	.986	OF-138, 1B-3
1973		158	.292	.463	654	191	38	7	20	3.1	90	99	22	52	6	2	0	692	36	13	42	4.7	.982	OF-109, 1B-50
1974		147	.321	.475	617	198	38	12	11	1.8	96	85	33	58	10	2	1	702	26	7	29	5.0	.990	OF-98, 1B-49
1975		155	.280	.454	628	176	39	8	18	2.9	90	84	25	73	4	1	0	409	6	5	6	2.7	.988	OF-153, 1B-4
1976		121	.323	.476	443	143	22	5	12	2.7	62	61	26	29	6	11	3	327	4	5	5	3.1	.985	OF-106, 1B-3
1977		154	.308	.481	568	175	29	6	19	3.3	75	82	40	38	13	6	3	305	6	6	1	2.1	.981	OF-148
1978	TEX A	133	.324	.490	525	170	35	5	14	2.7	65	89	31	41	8	0	0	219	8	3	1	1.7	.987	OF-107, DH-26
1979		136	.323	.470	492	159	28	4	12	2.4	69	76	34	34	4	13	5	260	9	7	2	2.1	.975	OF-119, DH-10
1980		163	.319	.480	656	209	43	3	19	2.9	96	117	39	47	5	2	1	315	9	9	2	2.1	.973	OF-157, DH-4, 1B-1
1981		102	.309	.411	421	130	29	1	4	1.0	53	55	24	28	3	1	1	2	0	0	0	0.0	1.000	DH-101, 1B-1
1982	MON N	160	**.331**	.514	617	**204**	**43**	2	22	3.6	90	**109**	61	59	5	1	1	1286	92	19	96	8.8	.986	1B-159
1983		157	.300	.410	614	184	**38**	3	8	1.3	70	84	44	44	1	4	2	1207	118	13	93	8.7	.990	1B-153, OF-1
1984	2 teams SF N (91G –.298) PHI N (28G –.312)																							
"	total	119	.301	.370	432	130	26	2	0	0.0	36	48	27	36	3	16	4	818	61	13	58	8.4	.985	1B-101, OF-5
1985	2 teams LA N (35G –.253) TOR A (61G –.251)																							
"	total	96	.252	.357	266	67	11	1	5	1.9	21	31	12	24	1	28	6	16	2	2	0	0.3	.900	DH-59, OF-17, 1B-1
18 yrs.		2368	.303	.451	9049	2743	529	77	219	2.4	1189	1326	535	756	84	108	29	9040	498	131	513	4.2	.986	OF-1376, 1B-733, DH-200
LEAGUE CHAMPIONSHIP SERIES																								
1970	PIT N	2	.250	.250	8	2	0	0	0	0.0	0	1	1	0	0	0	0	22	1	0	1	11.5	1.000	1B-2
1971		4	.250	.500	12	3	0	0	1	8.3	2	5	1	3	0	0	0	5	0	0	0	1.3	1.000	OF-4
1972		5	.250	.600	20	5	2	1	1	5.0	3	3	0	4	0	0	0	17	1	0	0	3.6	1.000	OF-5
1974		4	.143	.143	14	2	0	0	0	0.0	1	1	2	2	0	0	0	9	0	0	0	2.3	1.000	OF-4
1975		3	.182	.455	11	2	0	0	1	9.1	1	2	2	0	0	0	0	5	0	0	0	1.7	1.000	OF-3
1985	TOR A	4	.375	.500	8	3	1	0	0	0.0	0	3	0	0	0	2	1	0	0	0	0	0.0	.000	DH-3
6 yrs.		22	.233	.425	73	17	3	1	3	4.1	7	15 **6th**	6	9	0	2	1	58	2	0	1	2.9	1.000	OF-16, DH-3, 1B-2
WORLD SERIES																								
1971	PIT N	5	.211	.316	19	4	2	0	0	0.0	1	2	2	5	0	1	0	11	0	1	0	3.0	.917	OF-4

Bob Oliver

OLIVER, ROBERT LEE
Father of Darren Oliver.
B. Feb. 8, 1943, Shreveport, La.

BR TR 6′ 3″ 205 lbs.

Year	Team	Games	BA	SA	AB	H	2B	3B	HR	HR%	R	RBI	BB	SO	SB	Pinch Hit AB	Pinch Hit H	PO	A	E	DP	TC/G	FA	G by Pos
1965	PIT N	3	.000	.000	2	0	0	0	0	0.0	1	0	0	0	0	0	0	3	0	0	0	1.0	1.000	OF-3
1969	KC A	118	.254	.393	394	100	8	4	13	3.3	43	43	21	74	5	7	2	276	25	8	10	2.6	.974	OF-98, 1B-12, 3B-8
1970		160	.260	.451	612	159	24	6	27	4.4	83	99	42	126	3	2	0	1077	145	14	111	7.7	.989	1B-115, 3B-46
1971		128	.244	.351	373	91	12	2	8	2.1	35	52	14	88	0	22	5	566	37	9	52	5.2	.985	1B-68, OF-48, 3B-2
1972	2 teams CAL A (134G –.269) KC A (16G –.270)																							
"	total	150	.269	.430	572	154	22	5	20	3.5	54	76	29	109	5	1	0	1136	55	10	93	8.0	.992	1B-127, OF-24
1973	CAL A	151	.265	.412	544	144	24	1	18	3.3	51	89	33	100	1	12	2	396	121	11	26	3.8	.979	3B-49, OF-47, 1B-32, DH-12
1974	2 teams CAL A (110G –.248) BAL A (9G –.150)																							
"	total	119	.243	.340	379	92	11	1	8	2.1	23	59	16	56	3	24	4	438	90	14	47	4.8	.974	1B-61, 3B-46, OF-4, DH-2
1975	NY A	18	.132	.158	38	5	1	0	0	0.0	3	1	1	9	0	6	1	39	4	0	9	3.6	1.000	1B-8, DH-3, 3B-1
8 yrs.		847	.256	.400	2914	745	102	19	94	3.2	293	419	156	562	17	74	14	3931	477	66	348	5.5	.985	1B-423, OF-224, 3B-152, DH-17

Dave Oliver

OLIVER, DAVID JACOB
B. Apr. 7, 1951, Stockton, Calif.

BL TR 5′11″ 175 lbs.

Year	Team	Games	BA	SA	AB	H	2B	3B	HR	HR%	R	RBI	BB	SO	SB	Pinch Hit AB	Pinch Hit H	PO	A	E	DP	TC/G	FA	G by Pos
1977	CLE A	7	.318	.409	22	7	0	1	0	0.0	2	3	4	0	0	1	0	20	17	2	7	5.6	.949	2B-7

Gene Oliver

OLIVER, EUGENE GEORGE
B. Mar. 22, 1935, Moline, Ill.

BR TR 6′ 2″ 225 lbs.

Year	Team	Games	BA	SA	AB	H	2B	3B	HR	HR%	R	RBI	BB	SO	SB	Pinch Hit AB	Pinch Hit H	PO	A	E	DP	TC/G	FA	G by Pos
1959	STL N	68	.244	.401	172	42	9	0	6	3.5	14	28	7	41	3	18	4	125	5	4	1	2.4	.970	OF-42, C-9, 1B-5
1961		22	.269	.538	52	14	2	0	4	7.7	8	9	6	10	0	5	1	77	6	1	4	5.3	.988	C-15, OF-1
1962		122	.258	.441	345	89	19	1	14	4.1	42	45	50	59	5	19	6	514	47	5	9	5.2	.991	C-98, OF-8, 1B-3
1963	2 teams STL N (39G –.225) MIL N (95G –.250)																							
"	total	134	.244	.422	398	97	16	2	17	4.3	44	65	40	78	4	16	2	668	33	13	40	5.6	.982	1B-55, C-37, OF-35
1964	MIL N	93	.276	.477	279	77	15	1	13	4.7	45	49	17	41	3	23	3	625	35	12	50	8.7	.982	1B-76, C-1
1965		122	.270	.482	392	106	20	0	21	5.4	56	58	36	61	5	12	3	750	71	17	37	7.2	.980	C-64, 1B-52, OF-1
1966	ATL N	76	.194	.377	191	37	9	1	8	4.2	19	24	16	43	2	24	5	308	26	3	6	6.1	.991	C-48, 1B-5, OF-2

Gene Oliver *continued*

Year	Team	Games	BA	SA	AB	H	2B	3B	HR	HR%	R	RBI	BB	SO	SB	Pinch Hit AB	Pinch Hit H	PO	A	E	DP	TC/G	FA	G by Pos
1967	**2 teams**	**ATL N** (17G –.196) **PHI N** (85G –.224)																						
"	**total**	102	.220	.373	314	69	18	0	10	3.2	37	40	35	64	2	11	0	515	41	9	8	5.9	.984	C-93, 1B-2
1968	**2 teams**	**BOS A** (16G –.143) **CHI N** (8G –.364)																						
"	**total**	24	.196	.196	46	9	0	0	0	0.0	3	2	7	14	0	10	3	83	4	1	0	5.9	.989	C-11, 1B-2, OF-2
1969	**CHI N**	23	.222	.333	27	6	3	0	0	0.0	0	0	1	9	0	14	4	28	2	0	1	5.0	1.000	C-6
10 yrs.		786	.246	.427	2216	546	111	5	93	4.2	268	320	215	420	24	152	31	3693	270	65	156	6.0	.984	C-382, 1B-200, OF-91

Joe Oliver

OLIVER, JOSEPH MELTON BR TR 6′ 3″ 215 lbs.
B. July 24, 1965, Memphis, Tenn.

Year	Team	Games	BA	SA	AB	H	2B	3B	HR	HR%	R	RBI	BB	SO	SB	Pinch Hit AB	Pinch Hit H	PO	A	E	DP	TC/G	FA	G by Pos
1989	**CIN N**	49	.272	.384	151	41	8	0	3	2.0	13	23	6	28	0	7	2	260	21	4	1	6.1	.986	C-47
1990		121	.231	.360	364	84	23	0	8	2.2	34	52	37	75	1	8	4	686	59	6	8	6.4	.992	C-118
1991		94	.216	.379	269	58	11	0	11	4.1	21	41	18	53	0	7	0	496	40	11	6	6.1	.980	C-90
1992		143	.270	.388	485	131	25	1	10	2.1	42	57	35	75	2	2	1	926	64	8	8	7.0	.992	C-141, 1B-1
1993		139	.239	.384	482	115	28	0	14	2.9	40	75	27	91	0	3	1	825	70	7	13	6.2	.992	C-133, 1B-12, OF-1
1994		6	.211	.368	19	4	0	0	1	5.3	1	5	2	3	0	0	0	48	2	1	0	8.5	.980	C-6
1995	**MIL A**	97	.273	.439	337	92	20	0	12	3.6	43	51	27	66	2	1	0	414	40	8	3	4.7	.983	C-91, DH-6, 1B-2
7 yrs.		649	.249	.389	2107	525	115	1	59	2.8	194	304	152	391	5	28	8	3655	296	45	39	6.2	.989	C-626, 1B-15, DH-6, OF-1
LEAGUE CHAMPIONSHIP SERIES																								
1990	**CIN N**	5	.143	.143	14	2	0	0	0	0.0	1	0	0	2	0	0	0	27	1	0	0	5.6	1.000	C-5
WORLD SERIES																								
1990	**CIN N**	4	.333	.500	18	6	3	0	0	0.0	2	2	0	1	0	0	0	27	1	3	0	7.8	.903	C-4

Nate Oliver

OLIVER, NATHANIEL (Pee Wee) BR TR 5′10″ 160 lbs.
B. Dec. 13, 1940, St. Petersburg, Fla.

Year	Team	Games	BA	SA	AB	H	2B	3B	HR	HR%	R	RBI	BB	SO	SB	Pinch Hit AB	Pinch Hit H	PO	A	E	DP	TC/G	FA	G by Pos
1963	**LA N**	65	.239	.307	163	39	2	3	1	0.6	23	9	13	25	3	6	0	111	114	9	26	4.0	.962	2B-57, SS-2
1964		99	.243	.271	321	78	9	0	0	0.0	28	21	31	57	7	1	0	194	247	15	44	4.6	.967	2B-98, SS-1
1965		8	1.000	1.000	1	1	0	0	0	0.0	3	0	0	0	1	0	0	2	1	0	0	1.5	1.000	2B-2
1966		80	.193	.210	119	23	2	0	0	0.0	17	3	13	17	3	3	1	99	114	6	22	3.1	.973	2B-68, SS-2, 3B-1
1967		77	.237	.280	232	55	6	2	0	0.0	18	7	13	50	3	12	3	125	157	12	35	4.1	.959	2B-39, SS-32, OF-1
1968	**SF N**	36	.178	.205	73	13	2	0	0	0.0	3	1	1	13	0	3	0	25	58	10	11	3.3	.892	2B-14, SS-13, 3B-1
1969	**2 teams**	**NY A** (1G –.000) **CHI N** (44G –.159)																						
"	**total**	45	.156	.289	45	7	3	0	1	2.2	15	4	1	10	0	4	0	22	31	0	9	4.1	1.000	2B-13
7 yrs.		410	.226	.268	954	216	24	5	2	0.2	107	45	72	172	17	29	4	578	722	52	147	3.9	.962	2B-291, SS-50, 3B-2, OF-1
WORLD SERIES																								
1966	**LA N**	1	—	—	0	0	0	0	0	—	0	0	0	0	0	0	0	0	0	0	0	0.0	—	

Tom Oliver

OLIVER, THOMAS NOBLE (Rebel) BR TR 6′ 168 lbs.
B. Jan. 15, 1903, Montgomery, Ala. D. Feb. 26, 1988, Montgomery, Ala.

Year	Team	Games	BA	SA	AB	H	2B	3B	HR	HR%	R	RBI	BB	SO	SB	Pinch Hit AB	Pinch Hit H	PO	A	E	DP	TC/G	FA	G by Pos
1930	**BOS A**	154	.293	.351	**646**	189	34	2	0	0.0	86	46	42	25	6	0	0	477	9	9	3	3.2	.982	OF-154
1931		148	.276	.353	586	162	35	5	0	0.0	52	70	25	17	4	0	0	433	15	3	4	3.0	.993	OF-148
1932		122	.264	.327	455	120	23	3	0	0.0	39	37	25	12	1	5	1	328	12	6	4	3.0	.983	OF-116
1933		90	.258	.303	244	63	9	1	0	0.0	25	23	13	7	1	2	1	187	9	3	3	2.3	.985	OF-86
4 yrs.		514	.277	.340	1931	534	101	11	0	0.0	202	176	105	61	12	7	2	1425	45	21	14	3.0	.986	OF-504

Luis Olmo

OLMO, LUIS FRANCISCO (Jibaro) BR TR 5′11½″ 185 lbs.
Born Luis Francisco Rodriguez (Olmo).
B. Aug. 11, 1919, Arecibo, Puerto Rico.

Year	Team	Games	BA	SA	AB	H	2B	3B	HR	HR%	R	RBI	BB	SO	SB	Pinch Hit AB	Pinch Hit H	PO	A	E	DP	TC/G	FA	G by Pos
1943	**BKN N**	57	.303	.412	238	72	6	4	4	1.7	39	37	8	20	3	0	0	128	6	6	0	2.5	.957	OF-57
1944		136	.258	.367	520	134	20	5	9	1.7	65	85	17	37	10	6	3	316	138	27	18	3.5	.944	OF-64, 2B-42, 3B-31
1945		141	.313	.462	556	174	27	**13**	10	1.8	62	110	36	33	15	3	0	253	43	19	7	2.3	.940	OF-106, 3B-31, 2B-1
1949		38	.305	.390	105	32	4	1	1	1.0	15	14	5	11	2	4	2	54	3	3	0	1.8	.950	OF-34
1950	**BOS N**	69	.227	.383	154	35	7	1	5	3.2	23	22	18	23	3	12	0	74	2	2	0	1.4	.974	OF-55, 3B-1
1951		21	.196	.250	56	11	1	1	0	0.0	4	4	4	4	0	3	0	23	2	0	0	1.6	1.000	OF-16
6 yrs.		462	.281	.405	1629	458	65	25	29	1.8	208	272	88	128	33	28	5	848	194	57	25	2.5	.948	OF-332, 3B-63, 2B-43
WORLD SERIES																								
1949	**BKN N**	4	.273	.545	11	3	0	0	1	9.1	2	2	0	2	0	0	0	6	1	0	0	1.8	1.000	OF-4

Barney Olsen

OLSEN, BERNARD CHARLES BR TR 5′11″ 179 lbs.
B. Sept. 11, 1919, Everett, Mass. D. Mar. 30, 1977, Everett, Mass.

Year	Team	Games	BA	SA	AB	H	2B	3B	HR	HR%	R	RBI	BB	SO	SB	Pinch Hit AB	Pinch Hit H	PO	A	E	DP	TC/G	FA	G by Pos
1941	**CHI N**	24	.288	.438	73	21	6	1	1	1.4	13	4	4	11	0	1	1	51	3	3	1	2.5	.947	OF-23

Greg Olson

OLSON, GREGORY WILLIAM BR TR 6′ 200 lbs.
B. Sept. 6, 1960, Marshall, Minn.

Year	Team	Games	BA	SA	AB	H	2B	3B	HR	HR%	R	RBI	BB	SO	SB	Pinch Hit AB	Pinch Hit H	PO	A	E	DP	TC/G	FA	G by Pos
1989	**MIN A**	3	.500	.500	2	1	0	0	0	0.0	0	0	0	0	0	0	0	4	0	0	0	1.3	1.000	C-3
1990	**ATL N**	100	.262	.379	298	78	12	1	7	2.3	36	36	30	51	1	9	1	501	43	7	3	5.6	.987	C-97, 3B-1
1991		133	.241	.345	411	99	25	0	6	1.5	46	44	44	48	1	7	2	721	48	4	7	6.1	.995	C-127
1992		95	.238	.328	302	72	14	2	3	1.0	27	27	34	31	2	1	0	522	43	1	8	6.0	.998	C-94
1993		83	.225	.309	262	59	10	0	4	1.5	23	24	29	27	1	3	0	445	35	6	6	6.0	.988	C-81
5 yrs.		414	.242	.342	1275	309	61	3	20	1.6	132	131	137	157	5	20	3	2193	169	18	24	5.9	.992	C-402, 3B-1
LEAGUE CHAMPIONSHIP SERIES																								
1991	**ATL N**	7	.333	.500	24	8	1	0	1	4.2	3	4	4	3	1	0	0	62	1	0	2	9.0	1.000	C-7
1993		2	.333	.667	3	1	1	0	0	0.0	0	0	0	1	0	0	0	10	0	0	0	5.0	1.000	C-2
2 yrs.		9	.333	.519	27	9	2	0	1	3.7	3	4	4	4	1	0	0	72	1	0	2	8.1	1.000	C-9
WORLD SERIES																								
1991	**ATL N**	7	.222	.296	27	6	2	0	0	0.0	3	1	5	4	1	0	0	47	6	0	1	7.6	1.000	C-7

Ivy Olson

OLSON, IVAN MASSIE BR TR 5′10½″ 175 lbs.
B. Oct. 14, 1885, Kansas City, Mo. D. Sept. 1, 1965, Inglewood, Calif.

Year	Team	Games	BA	SA	AB	H	2B	3B	HR	HR%	R	RBI	BB	SO	SB	Pinch Hit AB	Pinch Hit H	PO	A	E	DP	TC/G	FA	G by Pos
1911	**CLE A**	140	.261	.332	545	142	20	8	1	0.2	89	50	34		20	0	0	293	430	73	51	5.7	.908	SS-139, 3B-1
1912		123	.253	.285	467	118	13	1	0	0.0	68	33	21		16	8	1	230	318	44	18	5.1	.926	SS-56, 3B-35, 2B-21, OF-3
1913		104	.249	.300	370	92	13	3	0	0.0	47	32	22	28	7	7	2	308	158	21	25	5.1	.957	3B-73, 1B-22, 2B-1

Ivy Olson *continued*

Year	Team	Games	BA	SA	AB	H	2B	3B	HR	HR%	R	RBI	BB	SO	SB	Pinch Hit AB	Pinch Hit H	PO	A	E	DP	TC/G	FA	G by Pos
1914		89	.242	.284	310	75	6	2	1	0.3	22	20	13	24	15	6	0	197	197	17	20	5.0	.959	SS-31, 2B-23, 3B-19, OF-6, 1B-3
1915	**2 teams**	**CIN N** (63G –.232) **BKN N** (18G –.077)																						
"	**total**	81	.215	.279	233	50	5	5	0	0.0	20	17	13	13	10	8	0	186	181	22	22	5.0	.943	2B-47, 3B-16, 1B-7, SS-7, OF-1
1916	**BKN N**	108	.254	.322	351	89	13	4	1	0.3	29	38	21	27	14	2	0	243	307	48	28	5.6	.920	SS-103, 2B-3, 1B-1
1917		139	.269	.328	580	156	18	5	2	0.3	64	38	14	34	6	0	0	287	438	51	53	5.6	.934	SS-133, 3B-6
1918		126	.239	.292	506	121	16	4	1	0.2	63	17	27	18	21	0	0	265	388	58	42	5.6	.918	SS-126
1919		140	.278	.337	**590**	**164**	14	9	1	0.2	73	38	30	12	26	0	0	349	445	44	57	6.0	.947	SS-140
1920		143	.254	.314	637	162	13	11	1	0.2	71	46	20	19	4	0	0	326	482	54	68	5.9	.937	SS-125, 2B-21
1921		151	.267	.345	**652**	174	22	10	3	0.5	88	35	28	26	4	0	0	379	530	56	83	6.3	.942	SS-133, 2B-20
1922		136	.272	.347	551	150	26	6	1	0.2	63	47	25	10	8	0	0	332	432	33	82	5.9	.959	2B-85, SS-51
1923		82	.260	.315	292	76	11	1	1	0.3	33	35	14	10	5	2	2	168	245	12	36	5.4	.972	2B-72, 3B-3, SS-2, 1B-1
1924		10	.222	.259	27	6	1	0	0	0.0	0	0	3	1	0	0	0	16	17	2	6	3.5	.943	SS-8, 2B-2
14 yrs.		1572	.258	.318	6111	1575	191	69	13	0.2	730	446	285	222	156	33	5	3579	4568	535	591	5.6	.938	SS-1054, 2B-295, 3B-153, 1B-34, OF-10
WORLD SERIES																								
1916	**BKN N**	5	.250	.375	16	4	0	1	0	0.0	1	2	2	2	0	0	0	9	12	4	0	5.0	.840	SS-5
1920		7	.320	.360	25	8	1	0	0	0.0	2	0	3	1	0	0	0	12	20	0	3	4.6	1.000	SS-7
2 yrs.		12	.293	.366	41	12	1	1	0	0.0	3	2	5	3	0	0	0	21	32	4	3	4.8	.930	SS-12

Karl Olson

OLSON, KARL ARTHUR (Ole)
B. July 6, 1930, Kentfield, Calif.
BR TR 6′ 3″ 205 lbs.

Year	Team	Games	BA	SA	AB	H	2B	3B	HR	HR%	R	RBI	BB	SO	SB	Pinch Hit AB	Pinch Hit H	PO	A	E	DP	TC/G	FA	G by Pos
1951	**BOS A**	5	.100	.100	10	1	0	0	0	0.0	0	0	0	3	0	0	0	8	0	0	0	1.6	1.000	OF-5
1953		25	.123	.211	57	7	2	0	1	1.8	5	6	1	9	0	1	0	31	1	1	0	1.4	.970	OF-24
1954		101	.260	.344	227	59	12	2	1	0.4	25	20	12	23	2	21	3	122	10	6	1	1.8	.957	OF-78
1955		26	.250	.354	48	12	1	2	0	0.0	7	1	1	10	0	3	2	27	1	0	0	1.3	1.000	OF-21
1956	**WAS A**	106	.246	.329	313	77	10	2	4	1.3	34	22	28	41	1	10	2	192	4	2	0	2.0	.990	OF-101
1957	**2 teams**	**WAS A** (8G –.167) **DET A** (8G –.143)																						
"	**total**	16	.154	.154	26	4	0	0	0	0.0	3	1	1	8	0	5	0	16	0	0	0	1.5	1.000	OF-11
6 yrs.		279	.235	.316	681	160	25	6	6	0.9	74	50	43	94	3	40	7	396	16	9	1	1.8	.979	OF-240

Marv Olson

OLSON, MARVIN CLEMENT (Sparky)
B. May 28, 1907, Gayville, S. D.
BR TR 5′ 7″ 160 lbs.

Year	Team	Games	BA	SA	AB	H	2B	3B	HR	HR%	R	RBI	BB	SO	SB	Pinch Hit AB	Pinch Hit H	PO	A	E	DP	TC/G	FA	G by Pos
1931	**BOS A**	15	.189	.208	53	10	1	0	0	0.0	8	5	9	3	0	0	0	49	55	4	9	7.2	.963	2B-15
1932		115	.248	.313	403	100	14	6	0	0.0	58	25	61	26	1	7	2	266	327	28	68	5.8	.955	2B-106, 3B-1
1933		3	.000	.000	1	0	0	0	0	0.0	1	0	0	1	0	0	0	0	0	0	0	0.0	.000	2B-1
3 yrs.		133	.241	.300	457	110	15	6	0	0.0	67	30	70	30	1	7	2	315	382	32	77	5.9	.956	2B-122, 3B-1

Tom O'Malley

O'MALLEY, THOMAS PATRICK
B. Dec. 25, 1960, Orange, N. J.
BL TR 6′ 170 lbs.

Year	Team	Games	BA	SA	AB	H	2B	3B	HR	HR%	R	RBI	BB	SO	SB	Pinch Hit AB	Pinch Hit H	PO	A	E	DP	TC/G	FA	G by Pos
1982	**SF N**	92	.275	.364	291	80	12	4	2	0.7	26	27	33	39	0	9	3	60	161	8	10	2.7	.965	3B-83, SS-1, 2B-1
1983		135	.259	.339	410	106	16	1	5	1.2	40	45	52	47	2	17	5	70	213	18	12	2.6	.940	3B-117
1984	**2 teams**	**SF N** (13G –.120) **CHI A** (12G –.125)																						
"	**total**	25	.122	.122	41	5	0	0	0	0.0	2	3	2	7	0	13	2	7	9	0	1	1.2	1.000	3B-13
1985	**BAL A**	8	.071	.286	14	1	0	0	1	7.1	1	2	0	2	0	5	0	2	3	1	0	2.0	.833	3B-3
1986		56	.254	.320	181	46	9	0	1	0.6	19	18	17	21	0	4	0	37	98	9	8	2.6	.938	3B-55
1987	**TEX A**	45	.274	.368	117	32	8	0	1	0.9	10	12	15	9	0	8	2	21	56	3	3	2.0	.962	3B-40, 2B-1
1988	**MON N**	14	.259	.259	27	7	0	0	0	0.0	3	2	3	4	0	5	1	4	15	2	0	3.0	.905	3B-7
1989	**NY N**	9	.545	.727	11	6	2	0	0	0.0	2	8	0	2	0	7	4	2	1	0	0	1.0	1.000	3B-3
1990		82	.223	.355	121	27	7	0	3	2.5	14	14	11	20	0	40	7	41	33	2	4	1.9	.974	3B-38, 1B-3
9 yrs.		466	.256	.340	1213	310	54	5	13	1.1	117	131	133	151	2	108	24	244	589	43	38	2.4	.951	3B-359, 1B-3, 2B-2, SS-1

Ollie O'Mara

O'MARA, OLIVER EDWARD
B. Mar. 8, 1891, St. Louis, Mo. D. Oct. 24, 1989, Reno, Nev.
BR TR 5′ 9″ 155 lbs.

Year	Team	Games	BA	SA	AB	H	2B	3B	HR	HR%	R	RBI	BB	SO	SB	Pinch Hit AB	Pinch Hit H	PO	A	E	DP	TC/G	FA	G by Pos
1912	**DET A**	1	.000	.000	4	0	0	0	0	0.0	0	0	0		0	0	0	2	4	1	0	7.0	.857	SS-1
1914	**BKN N**	67	.263	.332	247	65	10	2	1	0.4	41	7	16	26	14	0	0	110	183	26	17	5.1	.918	SS-63
1915		149	.244	.300	577	141	26	3	0	0.0	77	31	51	40	11	0	0	319	431	78	44	5.6	.906	SS-149
1916		72	.202	.249	193	39	5	2	0	0.0	18	15	12	20	10	11	1	117	148	30	13	5.8	.898	SS-51
1918		121	.213	.242	450	96	8	1	1	0.2	29	24	7	18	11	0	0	126	262	20	15	3.4	.951	3B-121
1919		2	.000	.000	7	0	0	0	0	0.0	1	0	0	0	0	0	0	4	3	1	0	4.0	.875	3B-2
6 yrs.		412	.231	.279	1478	341	49	8	2	0.1	166	77	86	104	46	11	1	678	1031	156	89	4.8	.916	SS-264, 3B-123
WORLD SERIES																								
1916	**BKN N**	1	.000	.000	1	0	0	0	0	0.0	0	0	0	1	0	1	0	0	0	0	0	0.0	—	

Tom O'Meara

O'MEARA, THOMAS EDWARD
B. Dec. 12, 1872, Chicago, Ill. D. Feb. 16, 1902, Ft. Wayne, Ind.

Year	Team	Games	BA	SA	AB	H	2B	3B	HR	HR%	R	RBI	BB	SO	SB	Pinch Hit AB	Pinch Hit H	PO	A	E	DP	TC/G	FA	G by Pos
1895	**CLE N**	1	.000	.000	1	0	0	0	0	0.0	1	0	1	0	0	0	0	0	1	1	0	2.0	.500	C-1
1896		12	.152	.152	33	5	0	0	0	0.0	5	0	5	7	0	2	0	29	6	3	0	3.8	.921	C-9, 1B-1
2 yrs.		13	.147	.147	34	5	0	0	0	0.0	6	0	6	7	0	2	0	29	7	4	0	3.6	.900	C-10, 1B-1

John O'Neil

O'NEIL, JOHN FRANCIS
B. Apr. 19, 1920, Shelbiana, Ky.
BR TR 5′ 9″ 155 lbs.

Year	Team	Games	BA	SA	AB	H	2B	3B	HR	HR%	R	RBI	BB	SO	SB	Pinch Hit AB	Pinch Hit H	PO	A	E	DP	TC/G	FA	G by Pos
1946	**PHI N**	46	.266	.298	94	25	3	0	0	0.0	12	9	5	12	0	3	0	51	75	8	15	4.2	.940	SS-32

Mickey O'Neil

O'NEIL, GEORGE MICHAEL
B. Apr. 12, 1900, St. Louis, Mo. D. Apr. 8, 1964, St. Louis, Mo.
BR TR 5′10″ 185 lbs.

Year	Team	Games	BA	SA	AB	H	2B	3B	HR	HR%	R	RBI	BB	SO	SB	Pinch Hit AB	Pinch Hit H	PO	A	E	DP	TC/G	FA	G by Pos
1919	**BOS N**	11	.214	.214	28	6	0	0	0	0.0	3	1	1	7	0	0	0	33	19	1	3	4.8	.981	C-11
1920		112	.283	.326	304	86	5	4	0	0.0	19	28	21	20	4	7	3	304	153	18	10	4.5	.962	C-105, 2B-1
1921		98	.249	.332	277	69	9	4	2	0.7	26	29	23	21	2	3	0	276	117	13	8	4.3	.968	C-95
1922		83	.223	.259	251	56	5	2	0	0.0	18	26	14	11	1	3	0	239	70	7	3	4.0	.978	C-79
1923		96	.212	.261	306	65	7	4	0	0.0	29	20	17	14	3	1	0	298	104	11	5	4.3	.973	C-95

Mickey O'Neil *continued*

Year	Team	Games	BA	SA	AB	H	2B	3B	HR	HR%	R	RBI	BB	SO	SB	Pinch Hit AB	Pinch Hit H	PO	A	E	DP	TC/G	FA	G by Pos
1924		106	.246	.262	362	89	4	1	0	0.0	32	22	14	27	4	0	0	362	108	7	8	4.5	.985	C-106
1925		70	.257	.356	222	57	6	5	2	0.9	29	30	21	16	1	1	0	208	31	7	3	3.6	.972	C-69
1926	**BKN N**	75	.209	.264	201	42	5	3	0	0.0	19	20	23	8	3	1	0	247	53	11	5	4.2	.965	C-74
1927	**2 teams**	**WAS A** (5G –.000) **NY N** (16G –.132)																						
"	**total**	21	.114	.114	44	5	0	0	0	0.0	2	3	5	3	0	1	0	53	15	2	2	3.5	.971	C-20
9 yrs.		672	.238	.288	1995	475	41	23	4	0.2	177	179	139	127	18	17	3	2020	670	77	47	4.2	.972	C-654, 2B-1

Bill O'Neill

O'NEILL, WILLIAM JOHN BB TR 5′11″ 175 lbs.
B. Jan. 22, 1880, St. John, N. B., Canada D. July 20, 1920, Woodhaven, N. Y.

Year	Team	Games	BA	SA	AB	H	2B	3B	HR	HR%	R	RBI	BB	SO	SB	Pinch Hit AB	Pinch Hit H	PO	A	E	DP	TC/G	FA	G by Pos
1904	**2 teams**	**BOS A** (17G –.196) **WAS A** (95G –.244)																						
"	**total**	112	.238	.276	416	99	11	1	1	0.2	40	21	24		22	6	**2**	160	25	26	1	2.0	.877	OF-102, 2B-3, SS-2
1906	**CHI A**	94	.248	.276	330	82	4	1	1	0.3	37	21	22		19	1	0	118	12	7	1	1.5	.949	OF-93
2 yrs.		206	.243	.276	746	181	15	2	2	0.3	77	42	46		41	7	2	278	37	33	2	1.7	.905	OF-195, 2B-3, SS-2
WORLD SERIES																								
1906	**CHI A**	1	.000	.000	1	0	0	0	0	0.0	1	0	0	0	0	0	0	1	0	0	0	1.0	1.000	OF-1

Dennie O'Neill

O'NEILL, DENNIS TL 6′ 2½″ 200 lbs.
B. Nov. 22, 1866, Holyoke, Mass. D. Nov. 15, 1912, Rushville, Ind.

Year	Team	Games	BA	SA	AB	H	2B	3B	HR	HR%	R	RBI	BB	SO	SB	Pinch Hit AB	Pinch Hit H	PO	A	E	DP	TC/G	FA	G by Pos
1893	**STL N**	7	.120	.120	25	3	0	0	0	0.0	3	2	4	0	3	0	0	68	0	1	3	9.9	.986	1B-7

Fred O'Neill

O'NEILL, FREDERICK JAMES 5′ 7″ 142 lbs.
B. 1865, London, Ont., Canada D. Mar. 7, 1892, London, Ont., Canada.

Year	Team	Games	BA	SA	AB	H	2B	3B	HR	HR%	R	RBI	BB	SO	SB	Pinch Hit AB	Pinch Hit H	PO	A	E	DP	TC/G	FA	G by Pos
1887	**NY AA**	6	.308	.423	26	8	1	1	0	0.0	4		1		3	0	0	3	1	1	0	0.8	.800	OF-6

Harry O'Neill

O'NEILL, HARRY MINK BR TR 6′ 3″ 205 lbs.
B. May 8, 1917, Philadelphia, Pa. D. Mar. 6, 1945, Iwo Jima, Marianasis.

Year	Team	Games	BA	SA	AB	H	2B	3B	HR	HR%	R	RBI	BB	SO	SB	Pinch Hit AB	Pinch Hit H	PO	A	E	DP	TC/G	FA	G by Pos
1939	**PHI A**	1	—	—	0	0	0	0	0	—	0	0	0	0	0	0	0	0	0	0	0	0.0	.000	C-1

Jack O'Neill

O'NEILL, JOHN JOSEPH BR TR 5′10″ 165 lbs.
Brother of Steve O'Neill. Brother of Mike O'Neill. Brother of Jim O'Neill.
B. Jan. 10, 1873, Galway, Ireland D. June 29, 1935, Scranton, Pa.

Year	Team	Games	BA	SA	AB	H	2B	3B	HR	HR%	R	RBI	BB	SO	SB	Pinch Hit AB	Pinch Hit H	PO	A	E	DP	TC/G	FA	G by Pos
1902	**STL N**	63	.141	.156	192	27	1	1	0	0.0	13	12	13		2	4	0	246	79	9	5	5.7	.973	C-59
1903		75	.236	.280	246	58	9	1	0	0.0	23	27	13		11	1	0	348	135	14	8	6.7	.972	C-74
1904	**CHI N**	51	.214	.262	168	36	5	0	1	0.6	8	19	6		1	2	0	256	62	6	5	6.6	.981	C-49
1905		53	.198	.244	172	34	4	2	0	0.0	16	12	8		6	3	0	276	63	9	8	7.0	.974	C-50
1906	**BOS N**	61	.180	.222	167	30	5	1	0	0.0	14	4	12		0	7	2	279	75	11	7	7.2	.970	C-48, 1B-2, OF-1
5 yrs.		303	.196	.235	945	185	24	5	1	0.1	74	74	52		20	17	2	1405	414	49	33	6.6	.974	C-280, 1B-2, OF-1

Jim O'Neill

O'NEILL, JAMES LEO BR TR 5′10½″ 165 lbs.
Brother of Steve O'Neill. Brother of Mike O'Neill. Brother of Jack O'Neill.
B. Feb. 23, 1893, Minooka, Pa. D. Sept. 5, 1976, Chambersburg, Pa.

Year	Team	Games	BA	SA	AB	H	2B	3B	HR	HR%	R	RBI	BB	SO	SB	Pinch Hit AB	Pinch Hit H	PO	A	E	DP	TC/G	FA	G by Pos
1920	**WAS A**	86	.289	.405	294	85	17	7	1	0.3	27	40	13	30	7	2	0	135	256	23	23	5.0	.944	SS-80, 2B-2
1923		23	.273	.303	33	9	1	0	0	0.0	6	3	1	3	0	2	0	19	29	4	5	3.7	.923	2B-8, 3B-4, SS-1, OF-1
2 yrs.		109	.287	.394	327	94	18	7	1	0.3	33	43	14	33	7	4	0	154	285	27	28	4.9	.942	SS-81, 2B-10, 3B-4, OF-1

John O'Neill

O'NEILL, JOHN J TR
B. New York, N. Y. Deceased.

Year	Team	Games	BA	SA	AB	H	2B	3B	HR	HR%	R	RBI	BB	SO	SB	Pinch Hit AB	Pinch Hit H	PO	A	E	DP	TC/G	FA	G by Pos
1899	**NY N**	2	.000	.000	7	0	0	0	0	0.0	0	0	0		0	0	0	9	4	1	1	7.0	.929	C-2
1902		2	.000	.000	8	0	0	0	0	0.0	0	0	0		0	0	0	10	4	1	0	7.5	.933	C-2
2 yrs.		4	.000	.000	15	0	0	0	0	0.0	0	0	0		0	0	0	19	8	2	1	7.3	.931	C-4

Mike O'Neill

O'NEILL, MICHAEL JOYCE BR TR 5′11″ 185 lbs.
Played as Mike Joyce in 1901.
Brother of Steve O'Neill. Brother of Jack O'Neill. Brother of Jim O'Neill.
B. Sept. 7, 1877, Galway, Ireland D. Aug. 12, 1959, Scranton, Pa.

Year	Team	Games	BA	SA	AB	H	2B	3B	HR	HR%	R	RBI	BB	SO	SB	Pinch Hit AB	Pinch Hit H	PO	A	E	DP	TC/G	FA	G by Pos
1901	**STL N**	6	.400	.400	15	6	0	0	0	0.0	3	2	3		0	1	1	1	6	1	0	1.6	.875	P-5
1902		51	.319	.444	135	43	5	3	2	1.5	21	15	2		0	**12**	1	24	73	8	0	2.7	.924	P-36, OF-3
1903		41	.227	.282	110	25	2	2	0	0.0	12	6	8		3	7	3	28	41	6	3	2.3	.920	P-19, OF-13
1904		30	.231	.352	91	21	7	2	0	0.0	9	16	5		0	2	1	16	69	8	3	3.3	.914	P-25, OF-3
1907	**CIN N**	9	.069	.207	29	2	0	2	0	0.0	5	2	2		1	0	0	18	1	3	0	2.4	.864	OF-9
5 yrs.		137	.255	.355	380	97	14	9	2	0.5	50	41	20		4	22	6	87	190	26	6	2.7	.914	P-85, OF-28

Paul O'Neill

O'NEILL, PAUL ANDREW BL TL 6′ 4″ 200 lbs.
B. Feb. 25, 1963, Columbus, Ohio.

Year	Team	Games	BA	SA	AB	H	2B	3B	HR	HR%	R	RBI	BB	SO	SB	Pinch Hit AB	Pinch Hit H	PO	A	E	DP	TC/G	FA	G by Pos
1985	**CIN N**	5	.333	.417	12	4	1	0	0	0.0	1	1	0	2	0	3	1	3	1	0	0	2.0	1.000	OF-2
1986		3	.000	.000	2	0	0	0	0	0.0	0	0	1	1	0	2	0	0	0	0	0	0.0	—	
1987		84	.256	.487	160	41	14	1	7	4.4	24	28	18	29	2	37	11	90	2	4	2	2.1	.958	OF-42, 1B-2, P-1
1988		145	.252	.414	485	122	25	3	16	3.3	58	73	38	65	8	11	0	410	13	6	14	3.1	.986	OF-118, 1B-21
1989		117	.276	.446	428	118	24	2	15	3.5	49	74	46	64	20	3	3	223	7	4	1	2.0	.983	OF-115
1990		145	.270	.421	503	136	28	0	16	3.2	59	78	53	103	13	8	2	271	12	2	0	2.0	.993	OF-141
1991		152	.256	.481	532	136	36	0	28	5.3	71	91	73	107	12	4	1	301	13	2	2	2.1	.994	OF-150
1992		148	.246	.373	496	122	19	1	14	2.8	59	66	77	85	6	9	3	291	12	1	2	2.1	.997	OF-143
1993	**NY A**	141	.311	.504	498	155	34	1	20	4.0	71	75	44	69	2	12	1	230	7	2	1	1.7	.992	OF-138, DH-2
1994		103	**.359**	.603	368	132	25	1	21	5.7	68	83	72	56	5	9	4	203	7	1	0	2.0	.995	OF-99, DH-4
1995		127	.300	.526	460	138	30	4	22	4.8	82	96	71	76	1	5	2	218	3	3	0	1.8	.987	OF-121, DH-4
11 yrs.		1170	.280	.467	3944	1104	236	13	159	4.0	542	665	493	657	69	103	28	2240	77	25	22	2.1	.989	OF-1069, 1B-23, DH-10, P-1
DIVISIONAL PLAYOFF SERIES																								
1995	**NY A**	5	.333	.833	18	6	0	0	3	16.7	5	6	5	5	0	1	0	13	0	0	0	2.6	1.000	OF-5
LEAGUE CHAMPIONSHIP SERIES																								
1990	**CIN N**	5	.471	.824	17	8	3	0	1	5.9	1	4	1	1	1	0	0	9	2	0	1	2.2	1.000	OF-5
WORLD SERIES																								
1990	**CIN N**	4	.083	.083	12	1	0	0	0	0.0	2	1	5	2	1	0	0	11	0	0	0	2.8	1.000	OF-4

Year	Team		Games	BA	SA	AB	H	2B	3B	HR	HR%	R	RBI	BB	SO	SB	Pinch Hit AB	Pinch Hit H	PO	A	E	DP	TC/G	FA	G by Pos

Peaches O'Neill

O'NEILL, PHILIP BERNARD BR TR 5′11″ 165 lbs.
B. Aug. 30, 1879, Anderson, Ind. D. Aug. 2, 1955, Anderson, Ind.

Year	Team		Games	BA	SA	AB	H	2B	3B	HR	HR%	R	RBI	BB	SO	SB	PH AB	PH H	PO	A	E	DP	TC/G	FA	G by Pos
1904	CIN	N	8	.267	.267	15	4	0	0	0	0.0	0	1	1		0	2	0	7	2	1	0	1.7	.900	C-5, 1B-1

Steve O'Neill

O'NEILL, STEPHEN FRANCIS BR TR 5′10″ 165 lbs.
Brother of Mike O'Neill. Brother of Jack O'Neill. Brother of Jim O'Neill.
B. July 6, 1891, Minooka, Pa. D. Jan. 26, 1962, Cleveland, Ohio.
Manager 1935–37, 1943–48, 1950–54.

Year	Team		Games	BA	SA	AB	H	2B	3B	HR	HR%	R	RBI	BB	SO	SB	PH AB	PH H	PO	A	E	DP	TC/G	FA	G by Pos
1911	CLE	A	9	.148	.185	27	4	1	0	0	0.0	1	1	4		2	0	0	55	17	1	1	8.1	.986	C-9
1912			68	.228	.247	215	49	4	0	0	0.0	17	14	12		2	1	0	316	108	17	9	6.6	.961	C-67
1913			78	.295	.376	234	69	13	3	0	0.0	19	29	10	24	5	0	0	353	119	13	9	6.2	.973	C-78
1914			86	.253	.312	269	68	12	2	0	0.0	28	20	15	35	1	4	1	394	134	24	23	6.7	.957	C-81, 1B-1
1915			121	.236	.298	386	91	14	2	2	0.5	32	34	26	41	2	6	1	556	175	24	17	6.6	.968	C-115
1916			130	.235	.296	378	89	23	0	0	0.0	30	29	24	33	2	2	1	540	154	21	36	5.6	.971	C-128
1917			129	.184	.222	370	68	10	2	0	0.0	21	29	41	55	2	2	0	446	145	12	19	4.7	.980	C-127
1918			114	.242	.312	359	87	8	7	1	0.3	34	35	48	22	5	1	0	409	154	10	10	5.1	.983	C-113
1919			125	.289	.427	398	115	35	7	2	0.5	46	47	48	21	4	2	0	472	125	14	13	5.0	.977	C-123
1920			149	.321	.440	489	157	39	5	3	0.6	63	55	69	39	3	1	0	576	128	17	1	4.9	.976	C-148
1921			106	.322	.403	335	108	22	1	1	0.3	39	50	57	22	0	1	0	393	92	9	8	4.7	.982	C-105
1922			133	.311	.416	392	122	27	4	2	0.5	33	65	73	25	2	2	0	450	116	15	9	4.5	.974	C-130
1923			113	.248	.285	330	82	12	0	0	0.0	31	50	64	34	0	2	0	354	68	14	3	3.9	.968	C-111
1924	BOS	A	106	.238	.293	307	73	15	1	0	0.0	29	38	63	23	0	14	2	342	75	13	2	4.7	.970	C-92
1925	NY	A	35	.286	.374	91	26	5	0	1	1.1	7	13	10	3	0	3	0	113	27	8	8	4.8	.946	C-31
1927	STL	A	74	.230	.283	191	44	7	0	1	0.5	14	22	20	6	0	13	5	180	57	4	8	4.0	.983	C-60
1928			10	.292	.333	24	7	1	0	0	0.0	4	6	8	0	0	0	0	19	4	1	0	2.4	.958	C-10
17 yrs.			1586	.263	.337	4795	1259	248	34	13	0.3	448	537	592	383	30	54	10	5968	1698	217	176	5.2	.972	C-1528, 1B-1
WORLD SERIES																									
1920	CLE	A	7	.333	.476	21	7	3	0	0	0.0	1	2	4	3	0	0	0	23	6	1	2	4.3	.967	C-7

Tip O'Neill

O'NEILL, JAMES EDWARD BR TR 6′ 1½″ 167 lbs.
B. May 25, 1858, Woodstock, Ont., Canada D. Dec. 31, 1915, Montreal, Que., Canada.

Year	Team		Games	BA	SA	AB	H	2B	3B	HR	HR%	R	RBI	BB	SO	SB	PH AB	PH H	PO	A	E	DP	TC/G	FA	G by Pos
1883	NY	N	23	.197	.237	76	15	3	0	0	0.0	8		3	15		0	0	17	24	5	0	1.8	.891	P-19, OF-7
1884	STL	AA	78	.276	.424	297	82	13	11	3	1.0	49		12			0	0	75	37	22	1	1.6	.836	OF-64, P-17, 1B-1
1885			52	.350	.466	206	72	7	4	3	1.5	44		13			0	0	83	6	12	1	1.9	.881	OF-52
1886			138	.328	.440	579	190	28	14	3	0.5	106		47			0	0	279	14	23	4	2.3	.927	OF-138
1887			124	**.435**	**.691**	517	**225**	**52**	**19**	**14**	**2.7**	**167**		50		30	0	0	247	8	30	2	2.3	.895	OF-124
1888			130	**.335**	.446	529	**177**	24	10	5	0.9	96	98	44		26	0	0	231	8	16	1	2.0	.937	OF-130
1889			134	.335	.478	534	179	33	8	9	1.7	123	110	72	37	28	0	0	264	12	19	3	2.2	.936	OF-134
1890	CHI	P	137	.302	.407	577	174	20	16	3	0.5	112	75	65	36	29	0	0	231	8	19	1	1.9	.926	OF-137
1891	STL	AA	127	.323	.451	514	166	28	4	10	1.9	111	95	61	33	25	0	0	195	5	14	0	1.7	.935	OF-127
1892	CIN	N	109	.251	.327	419	105	14	6	2	0.5	63	52	53	25	14	0	0	188	13	17	3	2.0	.922	OF-109
10 yrs.			1052	.326	.458	4248	1385	222	92	52	1.2	879	430	420	146	152	0	0	1810	135	177	16	2.0	.917	OF-1022, P-36, 1B-1

Curly Onis

ONIS, MANUEL DOMINGUEZ (Ralph) BR TR 5′ 9″ 180 lbs.
B. Oct. 24, 1908, Tampa, Fla. D. Jan. 4, 1995, Tampa, Fla.

Year	Team		Games	BA	SA	AB	H	2B	3B	HR	HR%	R	RBI	BB	SO	SB	PH AB	PH H	PO	A	E	DP	TC/G	FA	G by Pos
1935	BKN	N	1	1.000	1.000	1	1	0	0	0	0.0	0	0	0	0	0	0	0	1	0	1	0	2.0	.500	C-1

Eddie Onslow

ONSLOW, EDWARD JOSEPH BL TL 6′ 170 lbs.
Brother of Jack Onslow.
B. Feb. 17, 1893, Meadville, Pa. D. May 8, 1981, Dennison, Ohio.

Year	Team		Games	BA	SA	AB	H	2B	3B	HR	HR%	R	RBI	BB	SO	SB	PH AB	PH H	PO	A	E	DP	TC/G	FA	G by Pos
1912	DET	A	35	.227	.289	128	29	1	2	1	0.8	11	13	3		3	0	0	408	15	12	19	12.4	.972	1B-35
1913			17	.255	.273	55	14	1	0	0	0.0	7	8	5	9	1	0	0	191	7	2	9	11.8	.990	1B-17
1918	CLE	A	2	.167	.167	6	1	0	0	0	0.0	0	0	0	1	0	1	0	0	0	1	0	1.0	.000	OF-1
1927	WAS	A	9	.222	.278	18	4	1	0	0	0.0	1	1	1	0	0	3	0	29	2	0	3	6.2	1.000	1B-5
4 yrs.			63	.232	.280	207	48	3	2	1	0.5	19	22	9	10	4	4	0	628	24	15	31	11.5	.978	1B-57, OF-1

Jack Onslow

ONSLOW, JOHN JAMES BR TR 5′11″ 180 lbs.
Brother of Eddie Onslow.
B. Oct. 13, 1888, Scottdale, Pa. D. Dec. 22, 1960, Concord, Mass.
Manager 1949–50.

Year	Team		Games	BA	SA	AB	H	2B	3B	HR	HR%	R	RBI	BB	SO	SB	PH AB	PH H	PO	A	E	DP	TC/G	FA	G by Pos
1912	DET	A	31	.159	.174	69	11	1	0	0	0.0	7	4	10		1	0	0	109	38	8	4	5.0	.948	C-31
1917	NY	N	9	.250	.375	8	2	1	0	0	0.0	1	0	0	1	0	0	0	11	2	1	0	1.6	.929	C-9
2 yrs.			40	.169	.195	77	13	2	0	0	0.0	8	4	10	1	1	0	0	120	40	9	4	4.2	.947	C-40

Steve Ontiveros

ONTIVEROS, STEVEN ROBERT BB TR 6′ 185 lbs.
B. Oct. 26, 1951, Bakersfield, Calif.

Year	Team		Games	BA	SA	AB	H	2B	3B	HR	HR%	R	RBI	BB	SO	SB	PH AB	PH H	PO	A	E	DP	TC/G	FA	G by Pos
1973	SF	N	24	.242	.333	33	8	0	0	1	3.0	3	5	4	7	0	17	5	36	6	0	2	7.0	1.000	1B-5, OF-1
1974			120	.265	.350	343	91	15	1	4	1.2	45	33	57	41	0	23	4	225	158	19	30	4.2	.953	3B-75, 1B-19, OF-2
1975			108	.289	.366	325	94	16	0	3	0.9	21	31	55	44	2	11	2	80	189	21	15	2.9	.928	3B-89, OF-8, 1B-4
1976			59	.176	.216	74	13	3	0	0	0.0	8	5	6	11	0	44	8	18	8	2	2	1.6	.929	3B-7, OF-7, 1B-4
1977	CHI	N	156	.299	.423	546	163	32	3	10	1.8	54	68	81	69	3	3	1	100	324	20	24	2.9	.955	3B-155
1978			82	.243	.333	276	67	14	4	1	0.4	34	22	34	33	0	4	2	64	194	9	16	3.4	.966	3B-77, 1B-1
1979			152	.285	.370	519	148	28	2	4	0.8	58	57	58	68	0	9	3	105	269	23	28	2.8	.942	3B-142, 1B-1
1980			31	.208	.286	77	16	3	0	1	1.3	7	3	14	17	0	6	0	13	39	4	1	2.3	.929	3B-24
8 yrs.			732	.274	.366	2193	600	111	10	24	1.1	230	224	309	290	5	117	25	641	1187	98	118	3.1	.949	3B-569, 1B-34, OF-18

Jose Oquendo

OQUENDO, JOSE MANUEL BB TR 5′10″ 160 lbs.
BR 1984
Born Jose Manuel Oquendo (Contreras).
B. July 4, 1963, Rio Piedras, Puerto Rico.

Year	Team		Games	BA	SA	AB	H	2B	3B	HR	HR%	R	RBI	BB	SO	SB	PH AB	PH H	PO	A	E	DP	TC/G	FA	G by Pos
1983	NY	N	120	.213	.244	328	70	7	0	1	0.3	29	17	19	60	8	1	0	182	326	21	65	4.6	.960	SS-116
1984			81	.222	.249	189	42	5	0	0	0.0	23	10	15	26	10	3	2	95	152	7	33	3.8	.972	SS-67
1986	STL	N	76	.297	.341	138	41	4	1	0	0.0	20	13	15	20	2	27	6	52	94	8	23	3.0	.948	SS-29, 2B-21, 3B-1, OF-1
1987			116	.286	.335	248	71	9	0	1	0.4	43	24	54	29	4	26	10	149	133	4	31	2.5	.986	OF-46, 2B-32, SS-23, 3B-8, 1B-3, P-1
1988			148	.277	.350	451	125	10	1	7	1.6	36	46	52	40	4	10	2	268	315	11	61	3.6	.981	2B-69, 3B-47, SS-17, 1B-16, OF-15, P-1, C-1

Jose Oquendo *continued*

Year	Team	Games	BA	SA	AB	H	2B	3B	HR	HR%	R	RBI	BB	SO	SB	Pinch Hit AB	Pinch Hit H	PO	A	E	DP	TC/G	FA	G by Pos
1989		163	.291	.372	556	162	28	7	1	0.2	59	48	79	59	3	1	1	356	523	6	108	5.4	.993	2B-156, SS-7, 1B-1
1990		156	.252	.316	469	118	17	5	1	0.2	38	37	74	46	1	3	0	294	403	4	67	4.6	.994	2B-150, SS-4
1991		127	.240	.301	366	88	11	4	1	0.3	37	26	67	48	1	0	0	271	368	9	65	4.5	.986	2B-118, SS-22, 1B-3, P-1
1992		14	.257	.400	35	9	3	1	0	0.0	3	3	5	3	0	2	0	18	30	1	7	3.5	.980	2B-9, SS-5
1993		46	.205	.205	73	15	0	0	0	0.0	7	4	12	8	0	6	1	52	82	1	15	3.6	.993	SS-22, 2B-16
1994		55	.264	.310	129	34	2	2	0	0.0	13	9	21	16	1	12	4	53	98	4	22	3.5	.974	SS-28, 2B-16
1995		88	.209	.300	220	46	8	3	2	0.9	31	17	35	21	1	4	1	134	210	6	46	3.9	.983	2B-62, SS-24, 3B-2, OF-1
12 yrs.		1190	.256	.317	3202	821	104	24	14	0.4	339	254	448	376	35	95	27	1924	2734	82	543	4.1	.983	2B-649, SS-364, OF-63, 3B-58, 1B-23, P-3, C-1
LEAGUE CHAMPIONSHIP SERIES																								
1987	**STL N**	5	.167	.417	12	2	0	0	1	8.3	3	4	3	2	0	1	0	7	0	0	0	1.2	1.000	OF-5, 3B-1
WORLD SERIES																								
1987	**STL N**	7	.250	.250	24	6	0	0	0	0.0	2	2	1	4	0	0	0	8	10	0	0	2.6	1.000	3B-4, OF-3

Ernie Oravetz

ORAVETZ, ERNEST EUGENE BB TL 5′ 4″ 145 lbs.
B. Jan. 24, 1932, Johnstown, Pa.

Year	Team	Games	BA	SA	AB	H	2B	3B	HR	HR%	R	RBI	BB	SO	SB	Pinch Hit AB	Pinch Hit H	PO	A	E	DP	TC/G	FA	G by Pos
1955	**WAS A**	100	.270	.297	263	71	5	1	0	0.0	24	25	26	19	1	35	6	117	1	4	0	2.1	.967	OF-57
1956		88	.248	.299	137	34	3	2	0	0.0	20	11	27	20	1	**49**	11	51	2	3	0	1.8	.946	OF-31
2 yrs.		188	.262	.298	400	105	8	3	0	0.0	44	36	53	39	2	84	17	168	3	7	0	2.0	.961	OF-88

Tony Ordenana

ORDENANA, ANTONIO BR TR 5′ 9″ 158 lbs.
Born Antonio Ordenana (Rodriguez).
B. Oct. 30, 1918, Guanabacoa, Cuba D. Sept. 29, 1988, Miami, Fla.

Year	Team	Games	BA	SA	AB	H	2B	3B	HR	HR%	R	RBI	BB	SO	SB	Pinch Hit AB	Pinch Hit H	PO	A	E	DP	TC/G	FA	G by Pos
1943	**PIT N**	1	.500	.500	4	2	0	0	0	0.0	0	3	0	0	0	0	0	2	5	0	1	7.0	1.000	SS-1

Joe Orengo

ORENGO, JOSEPH CHARLES BR TR 6′ 185 lbs.
B. Nov. 29, 1914, San Francisco, Calif. D. July 24, 1988, San Francisco, Calif.

Year	Team	Games	BA	SA	AB	H	2B	3B	HR	HR%	R	RBI	BB	SO	SB	Pinch Hit AB	Pinch Hit H	PO	A	E	DP	TC/G	FA	G by Pos
1939	**STL N**	7	.000	.000	3	0	0	0	0	0.0	0	0	0	1	0	0	0	3	3	3	0	1.3	.667	SS-7
1940		129	.287	.412	415	119	23	4	7	1.7	58	56	65	90	9	0	0	281	318	29	65	4.8	.954	2B-77, 3B-34, SS-19
1941	**NY N**	77	.214	.321	252	54	11	2	4	1.6	23	25	28	49	1	3	1	117	189	10	22	4.3	.968	3B-59, SS-9, 2B-6
1943	**2 teams**	**NY N** (83G –.218) **BKN N** (7G –.200)																						
″	**total**	90	.217	.331	281	61	10	2	6	2.1	29	30	40	48	1	2	2	734	70	6	49	9.2	.993	1B-82, 3B-6
1944	**DET A**	46	.201	.266	154	31	10	0	0	0.0	14	10	20	29	1	1	0	124	124	20	24	5.7	.925	SS-29, 3B-11, 1B-5, 2B-2
1945	**CHI A**	17	.067	.067	15	1	0	0	0	0.0	5	1	3	2	0	5	0	5	7	1	0	1.6	.923	3B-7, 2B-1
6 yrs.		366	.237	.346	1120	266	54	8	17	1.5	129	122	156	219	12	11	3	1264	711	69	160	5.8	.966	3B-117, 1B-87, 2B-86, SS-64

George Orme

ORME, GEORGE WILLIAM BR TR 5′10″ 160 lbs.
B. Sept. 16, 1891, Lebanon, Ind. D. Mar. 16, 1962, Indianapolis, Ind.

Year	Team	Games	BA	SA	AB	H	2B	3B	HR	HR%	R	RBI	BB	SO	SB	Pinch Hit AB	Pinch Hit H	PO	A	E	DP	TC/G	FA	G by Pos
1920	**BOS A**	4	.333	.333	6	2	0	0	0	0.0	4	1	3	0	0	0	0	8	0	0	0	2.7	1.000	OF-3

Jess Orndorff

ORNDORFF, JESSE WALWORTH THAYER BB TR 6′ 168 lbs.
B. Jan. 15, 1881, Chicago, Ill. D. Sept. 28, 1960, Cardiff-by-the-Sea, Calif.

Year	Team	Games	BA	SA	AB	H	2B	3B	HR	HR%	R	RBI	BB	SO	SB	Pinch Hit AB	Pinch Hit H	PO	A	E	DP	TC/G	FA	G by Pos
1907	**BOS N**	5	.118	.118	17	2	0	0	0	0.0	0	0	0		0	0	0	11	7	2	0	4.0	.900	C-5

Charlie O'Rourke

O'ROURKE, JAMES PATRICK BR TR 6′ 2″ 195 lbs.
B. June 22, 1937, Walla Walla, Wash.

Year	Team	Games	BA	SA	AB	H	2B	3B	HR	HR%	R	RBI	BB	SO	SB	Pinch Hit AB	Pinch Hit H	PO	A	E	DP	TC/G	FA	G by Pos
1959	**STL N**	2	.000	.000	2	0	0	0	0	0.0	0	0	0	0	0	2	0	0	0	0	0	0.0	—	

Frank O'Rourke

O'ROURKE, JAMES FRANCIS (Blackie) BR TR 5′10½″ 165 lbs.
B. Nov. 28, 1894, Hamilton, Ont., Canada D. May 14, 1986, Chatham, N. J.

Year	Team	Games	BA	SA	AB	H	2B	3B	HR	HR%	R	RBI	BB	SO	SB	Pinch Hit AB	Pinch Hit H	PO	A	E	DP	TC/G	FA	G by Pos
1912	**BOS N**	61	.122	.148	196	24	3	1	0	0.0	11	16	11	50	1	0	0	92	167	24	16	4.8	.915	SS-59
1917	**BKN N**	64	.237	.283	198	47	7	1	0	0.0	18	15	14	25	11	4	0	72	134	10	6	3.7	.954	3B-58
1918		4	.167	.167	12	2	0	0	0	0.0	0	2	1	3	0	1	1	3	11	2	1	5.3	.875	2B-2, OF-1
1920	**WAS A**	14	.296	.315	54	16	1	0	0	0.0	8	5	2	5	2	0	0	38	47	4	12	6.4	.955	SS-13, 3B-1
1921		123	.234	.329	444	104	17	8	3	0.7	51	54	26	56	6	0	0	272	378	55	52	5.8	.922	SS-122
1922	**BOS A**	67	.264	.370	216	57	14	3	1	0.5	28	17	20	28	6	0	0	98	170	24	18	4.4	.918	SS-48, 3B-19
1924	**DET A**	47	.276	.359	181	50	11	2	0	0.0	28	19	12	19	7	0	0	127	165	11	28	6.4	.964	2B-40, SS-7
1925		124	.293	.436	482	141	40	7	5	1.0	88	57	32	37	5	0	0	316	391	22	67	5.9	.970	2B-118, 3B-6
1926		111	.242	.300	363	88	16	1	1	0.3	43	41	35	33	8	3	0	191	264	24	43	4.4	.950	3B-58, 2B-41, SS-10
1927	**STL A**	140	.268	.331	538	144	25	3	1	0.2	85	39	64	43	19	2	0	246	299	23	47	4.1	.960	3B-120, 2B-16, 1B-3
1928		99	.263	.348	391	103	24	3	1	0.3	54	62	21	19	10	3	0	150	162	15	13	3.3	.954	3B-96, SS-2
1929		154	.251	.332	585	147	23	9	2	0.3	81	62	41	28	14	0	0	184	255	25	32	3.0	.946	3B-151, 2B-3, SS-2
1930		115	.268	.333	400	107	15	4	1	0.3	52	41	35	30	11	4	1	167	235	19	30	3.8	.955	3B-84, SS-23, 1B-3
1931		8	.222	.222	9	2	0	0	0	0.0	0	0	0	1	1	3	0	15	3	0	0	6.0	1.000	SS-2, 1B-1
14 yrs.		1131	.254	.333	4069	1032	196	42	15	0.4	547	430	314	377	101	20	2	1971	2681	258	365	4.4	.947	3B-593, SS-288, 2B-220, 1B-7, OF-1

Jim O'Rourke

O'ROURKE, JAMES HENRY (Orator Jim) BR TR 5′ 8″ 185 lbs.
Brother of John O'Rourke. Father of Queenie O'Rourke.
B. Sept. 1, 1850, Bridgeport, Conn. D. Jan. 8, 1919, Bridgeport, Conn.
Manager 1881–84, 1893.
Hall of Fame 1945.

Year	Team	Games	BA	SA	AB	H	2B	3B	HR	HR%	R	RBI	BB	SO	SB	Pinch Hit AB	Pinch Hit H	PO	A	E	DP	TC/G	FA	G by Pos
1876	**BOS N**	70	.327	.420	312	102	17	3	2	0.6	61	43	15	17		0	0	170	7	28	1	2.9	.863	OF-68, 1B-2, C-1
1877		61	.362	.445	265	96	14	4	0	0.0	**68**	23	**20**	9		0	0	118	9	23	2	2.5	.847	OF-60, 1B-1
1878		60	.278	.412	255	71	17	7	1	0.4	44	29	5	21		0	0	124	17	22	5	2.7	.865	OF-57, 1B-2, C-2
1879	**PRO N**	81	.348	.459	362	126	19	9	1	0.3	69	46	13	10		0	0	302	29	34	6	4.3	.907	OF-56, 1B-20, C-5, 3B-3
1880	**BOS N**	86	.275	.441	363	100	20	11	**6**	1.7	71	45	21	8		0	0	268	96	43	18	4.4	.894	OF-37, 1B-19, SS-17, 3B-10, C-9
1881	**BUF N**	83	.302	.402	348	105	21	7	0	0.0	71	30	27	18		0	0	148	97	47	8	3.4	.839	3B-56, OF-18, C-8, SS-3, 1B-1
1882		84	.281	.370	370	104	15	6	2	0.5	62		13	13		0	0	149	17	26	3	2.2	.865	OF-81, SS-2, C-2, 3B-1
1883		94	.328	.438	436	143	29	8	1	0.2	102		15	13		0	0	226	61	39	2	3.0	.880	OF-61, C-33, 3B-8, SS-3, P-2
1884		108	.347	.480	467	**162**	33	7	5	1.1	119		35	17		0	0	350	23	30	12	3.4	.926	OF-86, 1B-18, C-10, P-4, 3B-1
1885	**NY N**	112	.300	.442	477	143	21	**16**	5	1.0	119		40	21		0	0	182	13	15	0	1.8	.929	OF-112, C-8

Jim O'Rourke *continued*

Year	Team	Games	BA	SA	AB	H	2B	3B	HR	HR%	R	RBI	BB	SO	SB	Pinch Hit AB	Pinch Hit H	PO	A	E	DP	TC/G	FA	G by Pos
1886		105	.309	.402	440	136	26	6	1	0.2	106	34	39	21		0	0	369	96	28	5	4.4	.943	OF-63, C-47, 1B-2
1887		103	.285	.411	397	113	15	13	3	0.8	73	88	36	11	46	0	0	248	127	48	7	3.9	.887	C-40, 3B-38, OF-28, 2B-2
1888		107	.274	.372	409	112	16	6	4	1.0	50	50	24	30	25	0	0	251	40	14	4	2.8	.954	OF-87, C-15, 1B-4, 3B-2
1889		128	.321	.438	502	161	36	7	3	0.6	89	81	40	34	33	0	0	166	20	22	2	1.6	.894	OF-128, C-1
1890	**NY P**	111	.360	.515	478	172	37	5	9	1.9	112	115	33	20	23	0	0	175	25	15	3	1.9	.930	OF-111
1891	**NY N**	136	.295	.398	555	164	28	7	5	0.9	92	95	26	29	19	0	0	244	44	26	3	2.2	.917	OF-126, C-14
1892		115	.304	.388	448	136	28	5	0	0.0	62	56	30	30	16	0	0	168	17	17	2	1.7	.916	OF-111, C-4, 1B-1
1893	**WAS N**	129	.287	.362	547	157	22	5	3	0.5	75	95	49	26	15	0	0	487	52	27	19	4.4	.952	OF-87, 1B-33, C-9
1904	**NY N**	1	.250	.250	4	1	0	0	0	0.0	1	0	0		0	0	0	4	0	1	0	5.0	.800	C-1
19 yrs.		1774	.310	.422	7435	2304	414	132	51	0.7	1446	830	481	348	177	0	0	4149	790	505	102	3.0	.907	OF-1377, C-209, 3B-119, 1B-103, SS-25, P-6, 2B-2

Joe O'Rourke

O'ROURKE, JOSEPH LEO, JR. BL TR 5′ 7″ 145 lbs.
Son of Patsy O'Rourke.
B. Oct. 28, 1904, Philadelphia, Pa. D. June 27, 1990, Philadelphia, Pa.

Year	Team	Games	BA	SA	AB	H	2B	3B	HR	HR%	R	RBI	BB	SO	SB	Pinch Hit AB	Pinch Hit H	PO	A	E	DP	TC/G	FA	G by Pos
1929	**PHI N**	3	.000	.000	3	0	0	0	0	0.0	0	0	0	1	0	3	0	0	0	0	0	0.0	—	

John O'Rourke

O'ROURKE, JOHN BL TL 6′ 190 lbs.
Brother of Jim O'Rourke.
B. Aug. 23, 1849, Bridgeport, Conn. D. June 23, 1911, Boston, Mass.

Year	Team	Games	BA	SA	AB	H	2B	3B	HR	HR%	R	RBI	BB	SO	SB	Pinch Hit AB	Pinch Hit H	PO	A	E	DP	TC/G	FA	G by Pos
1879	**BOS N**	72	.341	**.521**	317	108	17	11	6	1.9	69	**62**	8	32		0	0	147	10	21	2	2.5	.882	OF-71
1880		81	.275	.425	313	86	22	8	3	1.0	30	36	18	32		0	0	156	19	26	0	2.5	.871	OF-81
1883	**NY AA**	77	.270	.381	315	85	19	5	2	0.6	49		21			0	0	104	12	21	2	1.8	.847	OF-76, 1B-1
3 yrs.		230	.295	.442	945	279	58	24	11	1.2	148	98	47	64		0	0	407	41	68	4	2.3	.868	OF-228, 1B-1

Patsy O'Rourke

O'ROURKE, JOSEPH LEO, SR. BR TR 5′ 7″ 160 lbs.
Father of Joe O'Rourke.
B. Apr. 13, 1881, Philadelphia, Pa. D. Apr. 18, 1956, Philadelphia, Pa.

Year	Team	Games	BA	SA	AB	H	2B	3B	HR	HR%	R	RBI	BB	SO	SB	Pinch Hit AB	Pinch Hit H	PO	A	E	DP	TC/G	FA	G by Pos
1908	**STL N**	53	.195	.244	164	32	4	2	0	0.0	8	16	14		2	0	0	80	171	41	10	5.5	.860	SS-53

Queenie O'Rourke

O'ROURKE, JAMES STEPHEN BR TR 5′ 7″ 150 lbs.
Son of Jim O'Rourke.
B. Dec. 26, 1883, Bridgeport, Conn. D. Dec. 22, 1955, Sparrows Point, Md.

Year	Team	Games	BA	SA	AB	H	2B	3B	HR	HR%	R	RBI	BB	SO	SB	Pinch Hit AB	Pinch Hit H	PO	A	E	DP	TC/G	FA	G by Pos
1908	**NY A**	34	.231	.241	108	25	1	0	0	0.0	5	3	4		4	2	0	46	44	6	4	3.0	.938	OF-14, SS-11, 2B-4, 3B-3

Tim O'Rourke

O'ROURKE, TIMOTHY PATRICK (Voiceless Tim) BL TR 5′10″ 170 lbs.
B. May 18, 1864, Chicago, Ill. D. Apr. 20, 1938, Seattle, Wash.

Year	Team	Games	BA	SA	AB	H	2B	3B	HR	HR%	R	RBI	BB	SO	SB	Pinch Hit AB	Pinch Hit H	PO	A	E	DP	TC/G	FA	G by Pos
1890	**SYR AA**	87	.283	.367	332	94	13	6	1	0.3	48		36		22	0	0	117	168	44	9	3.8	.866	3B-87
1891	**COL AA**	34	.279	.331	136	38	1	3	0	0.0	22	12	15	7	9	0	0	48	76	17	7	4.1	.879	3B-34
1892	**BAL N**	63	.310	.377	239	74	8	4	0	0.0	40	35	24	19	12	0	0	105	181	45	17	5.3	.864	SS-58, OF-4, 3B-1
1893	**2 teams**	**BAL N** (31G –.363) **LOU N** (92G –.281)																						
″	**total**	123	.304	.349	487	148	12	5	0	0.0	102	72	89	19	27	0	0	203	202	55	28	3.7	.880	SS-61, OF-51, 3B-11
1894	**3 teams**	**LOU N** (55G –.277) **STL N** (18G –.282) **WAS N** (7G –.200)																						
″	**total**	80	.272	.332	316	86	9	5	0	0.0	60	39	33	13	11	0	0	369	94	36	39	6.2	.928	1B-30, 3B-21, OF-18, SS-6, 2B-5
5 yrs.		387	.291	.352	1510	440	43	23	1	0.1	272	158	197	58	81	0	0	842	721	197	100	4.5	.888	3B-154, SS-125, OF-73, 1B-30, 2B-5

Tom O'Rourke

O'ROURKE, THOMAS JOSEPH TR 5′ 9″ 158 lbs.
B. Oct. 1865, New York, N. Y. D. July 19, 1929, New York, N. Y.

Year	Team	Games	BA	SA	AB	H	2B	3B	HR	HR%	R	RBI	BB	SO	SB	Pinch Hit AB	Pinch Hit H	PO	A	E	DP	TC/G	FA	G by Pos
1887	**BOS N**	22	.154	.192	78	12	3	0	0	0.0	12	10	7	6	4	0	0	81	29	32	3	6.2	.775	C-21, 3B-1, OF-1
1888		20	.176	.176	74	13	0	0	0	0.0	3	4	1	9	2	0	0	89	37	17	1	6.8	.881	C-20, OF-1
1890	**2 teams**	**NY N** (2G –.000) **SYR AA** (41G –.216)																						
″	**total**	43	.206	.256	160	33	8	0	0	0.0	17	0	13	0	2	0	0	213	54	27	6	6.8	.908	C-42, 1B-1
3 yrs.		85	.186	.221	312	58	11	0	0	0.0	32	14	21	15	8	0	0	383	120	76	10	6.7	.869	C-83, OF-2, 1B-1, 3B-1

Bill Orr

ORR, WILLIAM JOHN BR TR 5′11″ 168 lbs.
B. Apr. 22, 1891, San Francisco, Calif. D. Mar. 10, 1967, Santarium, Calif.

Year	Team	Games	BA	SA	AB	H	2B	3B	HR	HR%	R	RBI	BB	SO	SB	Pinch Hit AB	Pinch Hit H	PO	A	E	DP	TC/G	FA	G by Pos
1913	**PHI A**	27	.194	.239	67	13	1	1	0	0.0	6	7	4	10	1	1	0	57	41	6	3	4.5	.942	SS-16, 1B-3, 3B-2, 2B-2
1914		10	.167	.292	24	4	1	1	0	0.0	3	1	2	5	1	3	1	4	13	5	0	3.1	.773	SS-6, 3B-1
2 yrs.		37	.187	.253	91	17	2	2	0	0.0	9	8	6	15	2	4	1	61	54	11	3	4.2	.913	SS-22, 3B-3, 1B-3, 2B-2

Dave Orr

ORR, DAVID L. BL TR 5′11″ 250 lbs.
B. Sept. 29, 1859, New York, N. Y. D. June 3, 1915, Brooklyn, N. Y.
Manager 1887.

Year	Team	Games	BA	SA	AB	H	2B	3B	HR	HR%	R	RBI	BB	SO	SB	Pinch Hit AB	Pinch Hit H	PO	A	E	DP	TC/G	FA	G by Pos
1883	**2 teams**	**NY AA** (13G –.320) **NY N** (1G –.000)																						
″	**total**	14	.302	.604	53	16	4	3	2	3.8	6		0	1		0	0	148	1	9	4	11.3	.943	1B-13, OF-1
1884	**NY AA**	110	**.354**	.539	458	**162**	32	13	9	2.0	82		5			0	0	1163	24	49	30	10.9	.960	1B-110, OF-3
1885		107	.342	**.543**	444	152	29	**21**	6	1.4	76		8			0	0	1089	20	39	48	10.4	.966	1B-107, P-3
1886		136	.338	**.527**	571	**193**	25	**31**	**7**	1.2	93		17			0	0	1445	34	28	62	11.1	.981	1B-136
1887		84	.368	.516	345	127	25	10	2	0.6	63		22		17	0	0	810	28	28	41	10.3	.968	1B-81, OF-3
1888	**BKN AA**	99	.305	.388	394	120	20	5	1	0.3	57	59	7		11	0	0	976	44	22	41	10.5	.979	1B-99
1889	**COL AA**	134	.327	.446	560	183	31	12	4	0.7	70	87	9	38	12	0	0	1291	61	23	64	10.3	.983	1B-134
1890	**BKN P**	107	.373	.537	464	173	32	13	6	1.3	89	124	30	11	10	0	0	1009	42	30	67	10.1	.972	1B-107
8 yrs.		791	.342	.502	3289	1126	198	108	37	1.1	536	270	98	50	50	0	0	7931	254	228	357	10.6	.973	1B-787, OF-7, P-3

Ernie Orsatti

ORSATTI, ERNEST RALPH BL TL 5′ 7½″ 154 lbs.
B. Sept. 8, 1902, Los Angeles, Calif. D. Sept. 4, 1968, Canoga Park, Calif.

Year	Team	Games	BA	SA	AB	H	2B	3B	HR	HR%	R	RBI	BB	SO	SB	Pinch Hit AB	Pinch Hit H	PO	A	E	DP	TC/G	FA	G by Pos
1927	**STL N**	27	.315	.457	92	29	7	3	0	0.0	15	12	11	12	2	1	0	56	3	5	2	2.5	.922	OF-26
1928		27	.304	.522	69	21	6	0	3	4.3	10	15	10	11	0	3	0	70	3	1	2	3.4	.986	OF-17, 1B-5
1929		113	.332	.460	346	115	21	7	3	0.9	64	39	33	43	7	17	6	259	14	6	9	3.2	.978	OF-77, 1B-10
1930		48	.321	.466	131	42	8	4	1	0.8	24	15	12	18	1	12	3	210	19	3	19	7.0	.987	1B-22, OF-11
1931		78	.291	.468	158	46	16	6	0	0.0	27	19	14	16	1	15	2	94	1	2	0	2.1	.979	OF-45, 1B-1

Ernie Orsatti *continued*

Year	Team	Lg	Games	BA	SA	AB	H	2B	3B	HR	HR%	R	RBI	BB	SO	SB	Pinch Hit AB	Pinch Hit H	PO	A	E	DP	TC/G	FA	G by Pos
1932			101	.336	.456	375	126	27	6	2	0.5	44	44	18	29	5	3	2	207	3	6	1	2.2	.972	OF-96, 1B-1
1933			120	.298	.374	436	130	21	6	0	0.0	55	38	33	33	14	9	3	299	5	5	3	3.0	.984	OF-101, 1B-3
1934			105	.300	.365	337	101	14	4	0	0.0	39	31	27	31	6	10	2	207	5	3	0	2.4	.986	OF-90
1935			90	.240	.321	221	53	9	3	1	0.5	28	24	18	25	10	23	5	115	3	3	2	2.0	.975	OF-60
9 yrs.			709	.306	.416	2165	663	129	39	10	0.5	306	237	176	218	46	93	23	1517	56	34	38	2.8	.979	OF-523, 1B-42
WORLD SERIES																									
1928	STL	N	4	.286	.429	7	2	1	0	0	0.0	1	0	1	3	0	2	0	4	0	0	0	4.0	1.000	OF-1
1930			1	.000	.000	1	0	0	0	0	0.0	0	0	0	0	0	1	0	0	0	0	0	0.0	—	
1931			1	.000	.000	3	0	0	0	0	0.0	0	0	0	3	0	0	0	1	0	0	0	1.0	1.000	OF-1
1934			7	.318	.409	22	7	0	1	0	0.0	3	2	3	1	0	1	0	16	1	2	0	3.2	.895	OF-6
4 yrs.			13	.273	.364	33	9	1	1	0	0.0	4	2	4	7	0	4	0	21	1	2	0	3.0	.917	OF-8

John Orsino

ORSINO, JOHN JOSEPH (Horse) BR TR 6′ 3″ 215 lbs.
B. Apr. 22, 1938, Teaneck, N. J.

Year	Team	Lg	Games	BA	SA	AB	H	2B	3B	HR	HR%	R	RBI	BB	SO	SB	Pinch Hit AB	Pinch Hit H	PO	A	E	DP	TC/G	FA	G by Pos
1961	SF	N	25	.277	.506	83	23	3	2	4	4.8	5	12	3	13	0	3	2	130	9	6	4	5.8	.959	C-25
1962			18	.271	.313	48	13	2	0	0	0.0	4	4	5	11	0	3	1	72	6	3	1	5.1	.963	C-16
1963	BAL	A	116	.272	.475	379	103	18	1	19	5.0	53	56	38	53	2	5	2	656	38	7	10	6.3	.990	C-109, 1B-3
1964			81	.222	.359	248	55	10	0	8	3.2	21	23	23	55	0	12	3	426	32	10	7	6.6	.979	C-66, 1B-5
1965			77	.233	.409	232	54	10	2	9	3.9	30	28	23	51	1	14	4	372	26	6	4	6.0	.985	C-62, 1B-5
1966	WAS	A	14	.174	.217	23	4	1	0	0	0.0	1	0	0	7	0	7	1	28	2	0	3	4.3	1.000	1B-5, C-2
1967			1	.000	.000	1	0	0	0	0	0.0	0	0	0	1	0	1	0	0	0	0	0	0.0	—	
7 yrs.			332	.249	.420	1014	252	44	5	40	3.9	114	123	92	191	3	45	13	1684	113	32	29	6.1	.983	C-280, 1B-18
WORLD SERIES																									
1962	SF	N	1	.000	.000	1	0	0	0	0	0.0	0	0	0	0	0	0	0	0	0	0	0	0.0	.000	C-1

Joe Orsulak

ORSULAK, JOSEPH MICHAEL BL TL 6′ 1″ 185 lbs.
B. May 31, 1962, Glen Ridge, N. J.

Year	Team	Lg	Games	BA	SA	AB	H	2B	3B	HR	HR%	R	RBI	BB	SO	SB	Pinch Hit AB	Pinch Hit H	PO	A	E	DP	TC/G	FA	G by Pos
1983	PIT	N	7	.182	.182	11	2	0	0	0	0.0	0	1	0	2	0	3	0	2	2	0	0	1.0	1.000	OF-4
1984			32	.254	.328	67	17	1	2	0	0.0	12	3	1	7	3	6	1	41	1	0	0	1.7	1.000	OF-25
1985			121	.300	.365	397	119	14	6	0	0.0	54	21	26	27	24	8	4	229	10	6	1	2.1	.976	OF-115
1986			138	.249	.342	401	100	19	6	2	0.5	60	19	28	38	24	22	4	193	11	4	2	1.7	.981	OF-120
1988	BAL	A	125	.288	.422	379	109	21	3	8	2.1	48	27	23	30	9	17	4	228	6	5	2	2.0	.979	OF-117
1989			123	.285	.421	390	111	22	5	7	1.8	59	55	41	35	5	15	6	250	10	4	2	2.3	.985	OF-109, DH-5
1990			124	.269	.397	413	111	14	3	11	2.7	49	57	46	48	6	14	3	267	5	3	2	2.4	.989	OF-109, DH-5
1991			143	.278	.358	486	135	22	1	5	1.0	57	43	28	45	6	14	3	273	22	1	4	2.2	.997	OF-132, DH-2
1992			117	.289	.381	391	113	18	3	4	1.0	45	39	28	34	5	8	1	228	9	4	1	2.2	.983	OF-110, DH-1
1993	NY	N	134	.284	.399	409	116	15	4	8	2.0	59	35	28	25	5	31	10	231	10	5	1	2.1	.980	OF-114, 1B-4
1994			96	.260	.353	292	76	3	0	8	2.7	39	42	16	21	4	13	2	148	9	3	3	1.7	.981	OF-90, 1B-6
1995			108	.283	.372	290	82	19	2	1	0.3	41	37	19	35	1	35	11	111	4	4	0	1.4	.966	OF-86, 1B-1
12 yrs.			1268	.278	.380	3926	1091	168	35	54	1.4	523	379	284	347	92	186	49	2201	99	39	18	2.0	.983	OF-1131, DH-13, 1B-11

Jorge Orta

ORTA, JORGE BL TR 5′10″ 170 lbs.
Born Jorge Orta (Nunez).
B. Nov. 26, 1950, Mazatlan, Mexico.

Year	Team	Lg	Games	BA	SA	AB	H	2B	3B	HR	HR%	R	RBI	BB	SO	SB	Pinch Hit AB	Pinch Hit H	PO	A	E	DP	TC/G	FA	G by Pos
1972	CHI	A	51	.202	.315	124	25	3	1	3	2.4	20	11	6	37	3	11	1	50	85	8	23	3.5	.944	SS-18, 2B-14, 3B-9
1973			128	.266	.376	425	113	9	10	6	1.4	46	40	37	87	8	5	2	255	301	18	75	4.7	.969	2B-122, SS-1
1974			139	.316	.440	525	166	31	2	10	1.9	73	67	40	88	9	7	1	297	313	18	93	4.6	.971	2B-123, DH-10, SS-3
1975			140	.304	.450	542	165	26	10	11	2.0	64	83	48	67	16	3	2	354	354	16	95	5.3	.978	2B-135, DH-2
1976			158	.274	.410	636	174	29	8	14	2.2	74	72	38	77	24	3	0	187	111	15	10	2.0	.952	OF-77, 3B-49, DH-31
1977			144	.282	.417	564	159	27	8	11	2.0	71	84	46	49	4	7	1	287	335	19	64	4.6	.970	2B-139
1978			117	.274	.421	420	115	19	2	13	3.1	45	53	42	39	1	3	1	275	290	9	62	4.9	.984	2B-114, DH-2
1979			113	.262	.437	325	85	18	3	11	3.4	49	46	44	33	1	22	4	57	75	3	17	1.3	.978	DH-62, 2B-41
1980	CLE	A	129	.291	.403	481	140	18	3	10	2.1	78	64	71	44	6	2	0	269	10	5	1	2.2	.982	OF-120, DH-7
1981			88	.272	.376	338	92	14	3	5	1.5	50	34	21	43	4	5	2	150	11	1	2	1.9	.994	OF-86
1982	LA	N	86	.217	.313	115	25	5	0	2	1.7	13	8	12	13	0	60	9	35	1	2	1	2.2	.947	OF-17
1983	TOR	A	103	.237	.408	245	58	6	3	10	4.1	30	38	19	29	1	26	5	16	1	0	1	0.2	1.000	DH-69, OF-17
1984	KC	A	122	.298	.457	403	120	23	7	9	2.2	50	50	28	39	0	13	4	48	0	1	0	0.4	.980	DH-83, OF-26, 2B-1
1985			110	.267	.383	300	80	21	1	4	1.3	32	45	22	28	2	29	8	0	0	0	0	0.0	.000	DH-85
1986			106	.277	.411	336	93	14	2	9	2.7	35	46	23	34	0	21	6	0	0	0	0	0.0	.000	DH-87
1987			21	.180	.380	50	9	4	0	2	4.0	3	4	3	8	0	9	2	0	0	0	0	0.0	.000	DH-12
16 yrs.			1755	.278	.412	5829	1619	267	63	130	2.2	733	745	500	715	79	226	48	2280	1887	115	444	2.7	.973	2B-689, DH-450, OF-343, 3B-58, SS-22
LEAGUE CHAMPIONSHIP SERIES																									
1984	KC	A	3	.100	.300	10	1	0	1	0	0.0	1	1	0	2	0	0	0	0	0	0	0	0.0	.000	DH-3
1985			2	.000	.000	5	0	0	0	0	0.0	0	0	0	1	0	1	0	0	0	0	0	0.0	.000	DH-1
2 yrs.			5	.067	.200	15	1	0	1	0	0.0	1	1	0	3	0	1	0	0	0	0	0	0.0		DH-4
WORLD SERIES																									
1985	KC	A	3	.333	.333	3	1	0	0	0	0.0	0	0	0	0	0	3	1	0	0	0	0	0.0	—	

Frank Ortenzio

ORTENZIO, FRANK JOSEPH, JR. BR TR 6′ 2″ 215 lbs.
B. Feb. 24, 1951, Fresno, Calif.

Year	Team	Lg	Games	BA	SA	AB	H	2B	3B	HR	HR%	R	RBI	BB	SO	SB	Pinch Hit AB	Pinch Hit H	PO	A	E	DP	TC/G	FA	G by Pos
1973	KC	A	9	.280	.480	25	7	2	0	1	4.0	1	6	2	6	0	1	0	51	6	1	4	7.3	.983	1B-7, DH-1

Al Orth

ORTH, ALBERT LEWIS (The Curveless Wonder) BL TR 6′ 200 lbs.
B. Sept. 5, 1872, Tipton, Ind. D. Oct. 8, 1948, Lynchburg, Va.

Year	Team	Lg	Games	BA	SA	AB	H	2B	3B	HR	HR%	R	RBI	BB	SO	SB	Pinch Hit AB	Pinch Hit H	PO	A	E	DP	TC/G	FA	G by Pos
1895	PHI	N	11	.356	.511	45	16	4	0	1	2.2	8	13	1	6	0	0	0	2	14	3	0	1.7	.842	P-11
1896			25	.256	.402	82	21	3	3	1	1.2	12	13	3	11	2	0	0	10	54	7	2	2.8	.901	P-25
1897			53	.329	.447	152	50	7	4	1	0.7	26	17	3		5	11	1	20	70	7	1	2.3	.928	P-36, OF-6
1898			39	.293	.431	123	36	6	4	1	0.8	17	14	3		1	6	2	9	63	3	1	2.3	.960	P-32, OF-1
1899			22	.210	.339	62	13	3	1	1	1.6	5	5	1		2	0	0	5	19	6	0	1.4	.800	P-21, OF-1

Al Orth *continued*

Year	Team	Games	BA	SA	AB	H	2B	3B	HR	HR%	R	RBI	BB	SO	SB	Pinch Hit AB	Pinch Hit H	PO	A	E	DP	TC/G	FA	G by Pos
1900		39	.310	.380	129	40	4	1	1	0.8	6	21	2		2	3	0	23	68	5	3	2.7	.948	P-33, OF-3
1901		41	.281	.352	128	36	6	0	1	0.8	14	15	3		3	2	1	25	83	6	2	2.9	.947	P-35, OF-4
1902	WAS A	56	.217	.291	175	38	3	2	2	1.1	20	10	9		2	3	1	46	97	12	3	2.9	.923	P-38, OF-13, 1B-1, SS-1
1903		55	.302	.444	162	49	9	7	0	0.0	19	11	4		3	6	0	55	98	15	3	3.4	.911	P-36, SS-7, OF-4, 1B-2
1904	2 teams	WAS A (31G –.216) NY A (26G –.297)																						
"	total	57	.247	.295	166	41	4	2	0	0.0	13	18	1		4	4	1	53	74	10	1	2.7	.927	P-30, OF-20
1905	NY A	54	.183	.244	131	24	3	1	1	0.8	13	8	4		2	11	2	31	98	10	1	3.3	.928	P-40, OF-1, 1B-1
1906		47	.274	.341	135	37	2	2	1	0.7	12	17	6		2	1	0	13	103	8	1	2.7	.935	P-45, OF-1
1907		44	.324	.410	105	34	6	0	1	1.0	11	13	4		1	5	0	9	95	9	1	3.1	.920	P-36, OF-1
1908		38	.290	.362	69	20	1	2	0	0.0	4	4	2		0	13	4	6	42	1	2	2.3	.980	P-21
1909		22	.265	.324	34	9	0	1	0	0.0	3	5	5		1	13	5	10	16	0	0	3.7	1.000	2B-6, P-1
15 yrs.		603	.273	.366	1698	464	61	30	12	0.7	183	184	51	17	30	78	17	317	994	102	21	2.8	.928	P-440, OF-55, SS-8, 2B-6, 1B-4

Javier Ortiz

ORTIZ, JAVIER VICTOR
B. Jan. 22, 1963, Boston, Mass.

BR TR 6′ 4″ 220 lbs.

Year	Team	Games	BA	SA	AB	H	2B	3B	HR	HR%	R	RBI	BB	SO	SB	Pinch Hit AB	Pinch Hit H	PO	A	E	DP	TC/G	FA	G by Pos
1990	HOU N	30	.273	.403	77	21	5	1	1	1.3	7	10	12	11	1	6	2	44	1	1	0	1.8	.978	OF-25
1991		47	.277	.386	83	23	4	1	1	1.2	7	5	14	14	0	21	5	27	2	0	1	1.2	1.000	OF-24
2 yrs.		77	.275	.394	160	44	9	2	2	1.3	14	15	26	25	1	27	7	71	3	1	1	1.5	.987	OF-49

Jose Ortiz

ORTIZ, JOSE LUIS
Born Jose Luis Ortiz (Irizarry).
B. June 25, 1947, Ponce, Puerto Rico.

BR TR 5′ 9½″ 155 lbs.

Year	Team	Games	BA	SA	AB	H	2B	3B	HR	HR%	R	RBI	BB	SO	SB	Pinch Hit AB	Pinch Hit H	PO	A	E	DP	TC/G	FA	G by Pos
1969	CHI A	16	.273	.364	11	3	1	0	0	0.0	0	2	1	0	0	1	0	4	1	0	0	0.6	1.000	OF-8
1970		15	.333	.375	24	8	1	0	0	0.0	4	1	2	2	1	1	0	10	3	0	0	1.6	1.000	OF-8
1971	CHI N	36	.295	.398	88	26	7	1	0	0.0	10	3	4	10	2	1	0	53	1	0	1	2.7	1.000	OF-20
3 yrs.		67	.301	.390	123	37	9	1	0	0.0	14	6	7	12	3	3	0	67	5	0	1	2.0	1.000	OF-36

Junior Ortiz

ORTIZ, ADALBERTO
Born Adalberto Ortiz (Colon).
B. Oct. 24, 1959, Humacao, Puerto Rico.

BR TR 5′11″ 174 lbs.

Year	Team	Games	BA	SA	AB	H	2B	3B	HR	HR%	R	RBI	BB	SO	SB	Pinch Hit AB	Pinch Hit H	PO	A	E	DP	TC/G	FA	G by Pos
1982	PIT N	7	.200	.267	15	3	1	0	0	0.0	1	0	1	3	0	0	0	27	3	0	0	4.3	1.000	C-7
1983	2 teams	PIT N (5G –.125) NY N (68G –.254)																						
"	total	73	.249	.275	193	48	5	0	0	0.0	11	12	4	34	1	5	2	293	31	11	2	4.7	.967	C-71
1984	NY N	40	.198	.231	91	18	3	0	0	0.0	6	11	5	15	1	10	1	136	13	3	3	4.8	.980	C-32
1985	PIT N	23	.292	.361	72	21	2	0	1	1.4	4	5	3	17	1	1	0	115	14	2	3	5.7	.985	C-23
1986		49	.336	.391	110	37	6	0	0	0.0	11	14	9	13	0	11	3	165	13	3	2	5.0	.983	C-36
1987		75	.271	.339	192	52	8	1	1	0.5	16	22	15	23	0	8	2	313	39	9	2	5.0	.975	C-72
1988		49	.280	.381	118	33	6	0	2	1.7	8	18	9	9	1	12	3	152	23	3	2	4.4	.983	C-40
1989		91	.217	.265	230	50	6	1	1	0.4	16	22	20	20	2	13	1	334	32	2	2	4.4	.995	C-84
1990	MIN A	71	.335	.388	170	57	7	1	0	0.0	18	18	12	16	0	3	1	247	25	0	6	3.8	1.000	C-68, DH-3
1991		61	.209	.261	134	28	5	1	0	0.0	9	11	15	12	0	1	0	203	17	1	2	3.7	.995	C-60
1992	CLE A	86	.250	.279	244	61	7	0	0	0.0	20	24	12	23	1	3	2	402	38	5	2	5.2	.989	C-86
1993		95	.221	.273	249	55	13	0	0	0.0	19	20	11	26	1	2	0	441	58	5	13	5.3	.990	C-95
1994	TEX A	29	.276	.303	76	21	2	0	0	0.0	3	9	5	11	0	2	0	106	18	1	1	4.5	.992	C-28
13 yrs.		749	.256	.305	1894	484	71	4	5	0.3	142	186	121	222	8	71	15	2934	324	45	40	4.7	.986	C-702, DH-3
LEAGUE CHAMPIONSHIP SERIES																								
1991	MIN A	3	.000	.000	3	0	0	0	0	0.0	0	0	0	0	0	0	0	10	0	0	0	3.3	1.000	C-3
WORLD SERIES																								
1991	MIN A	3	.200	.200	5	1	0	0	0	0.0	0	1	0	1	0	0	0	9	0	0	0	3.0	1.000	C-3

Luis Ortiz

ORTIZ, LUIS ALBERTO
Born Luis Alberto Ortiz (Galarza).
B. May 25, 1970, Santo Domingo, Dominican Republic.

BR TR 6′ 190 lbs.

Year	Team	Games	BA	SA	AB	H	2B	3B	HR	HR%	R	RBI	BB	SO	SB	Pinch Hit AB	Pinch Hit H	PO	A	E	DP	TC/G	FA	G by Pos
1993	BOS A	9	.250	.250	12	3	0	0	0	0.0	0	1	0	2	0	5	1	2	2	0	1	0.6	1.000	3B-5, DH-2
1994		7	.167	.278	18	3	2	0	0	0.0	3	6	1	5	0	1	0	0	0	0	0	0.0	.000	DH-6
1995	TEX A	41	.231	.343	108	25	5	2	1	0.9	10	18	6	18	0	10	1	9	43	8	2	1.6	.867	3B-35, DH-3
3 yrs.		57	.225	.326	138	31	7	2	1	0.7	13	25	7	25	0	16	2	11	45	8	3	1.3	.875	3B-40, DH-11

Roberto Ortiz

ORTIZ, ROBERTO GONZALO
Born Roberto Gonzalo Ortiz (Nunez).
Brother of Baby Ortiz.
B. June 30, 1915, Camaguey, Cuba D. Sept. 15, 1971, Miami, Fla.

BR TR 6′ 4″ 200 lbs.

Year	Team	Games	BA	SA	AB	H	2B	3B	HR	HR%	R	RBI	BB	SO	SB	Pinch Hit AB	Pinch Hit H	PO	A	E	DP	TC/G	FA	G by Pos
1941	WAS A	22	.329	.430	79	26	1	2	1	1.3	10	17	3	10	0	1	0	34	3	6	0	2.0	.860	OF-21
1942		20	.167	.405	42	7	1	3	1	2.4	4	4	5	11	0	7	0	15	1	1	0	1.9	.941	OF-9
1943		1	.250	.250	4	1	0	0	0	0.0	0	0	0	0	0	0	0	3	0	0	0	3.0	1.000	OF-1
1944		85	.253	.361	316	80	11	4	5	1.6	36	35	19	47	4	5	1	165	2	9	1	2.2	.949	OF-80
1949		40	.279	.326	129	36	3	0	1	0.8	12	11	9	12	0	8	4	48	5	3	1	1.8	.946	OF-32
1950	2 teams	WAS A (39G –.227) PHI A (6G –.071)																						
"	total	45	.202	.247	89	18	2	1	0	0.0	5	11	7	15	0	21	2	29	2	0	0	1.4	1.000	OF-22
6 yrs.		213	.255	.349	659	168	18	10	8	1.2	67	78	43	95	4	42	7	294	13	19	2	2.0	.942	OF-165

John Orton

ORTON, JOHN ANDREW
B. Dec. 8, 1965, Santa Cruz, Calif.

BR TR 6′ 1″ 195 lbs.

Year	Team	Games	BA	SA	AB	H	2B	3B	HR	HR%	R	RBI	BB	SO	SB	Pinch Hit AB	Pinch Hit H	PO	A	E	DP	TC/G	FA	G by Pos
1989	CAL A	16	.179	.205	39	7	1	0	0	0.0	4	4	2	17	0	0	0	76	7	1	3	5.3	.988	C-16
1990		31	.190	.286	84	16	5	0	1	1.2	8	6	5	31	0	0	0	139	15	2	1	5.0	.987	C-31
1991		29	.203	.261	69	14	4	0	0	0.0	7	3	10	17	0	0	0	145	23	1	3	5.8	.994	C-28, DH-1
1992		43	.219	.298	114	25	3	0	2	1.8	11	12	7	32	1	0	0	238	23	5	3	6.2	.981	C-43
1993		37	.189	.274	95	18	5	0	1	1.1	5	4	7	24	1	2	0	185	17	4	4	5.7	.981	C-35, OF-1
5 yrs.		156	.200	.274	401	80	18	0	4	1.0	35	29	31	121	2	2	0	783	85	13	14	5.7	.985	C-153, OF-1, DH-1

Ossie Orwoll

ORWOLL, OSWALD CHRISTIAN BL TL 6′ 174 lbs.
B. Nov. 17, 1900, Portland, Ore. D. May 8, 1967, Decorah, Iowa.

Year	Team	Games	BA	SA	AB	H	2B	3B	HR	HR%	R	RBI	BB	SO	SB	Pinch Hit AB	Pinch Hit H	PO	A	E	DP	TC/G	FA	G by Pos
1928	PHI A	64	.306	.406	170	52	13	2	0	0.0	28	22	16	24	3	1	1	328	41	7	32	6.2	.981	1B-34, P-27
1929		30	.255	.333	51	13	2	1	0	0.0	6	6	2	11	0	8	2	18	6	0	1	1.1	1.000	P-12, OF-9
2 yrs.		94	.294	.389	221	65	15	3	0	0.0	34	28	18	35	3	9	3	346	47	7	33	4.9	.983	P-39, 1B-34, OF-9

Fred Osborn

OSBORN, WILFRED PEARL BL TR 5′ 9″ 178 lbs.
B. Nov. 28, 1883, Nevada, Ohio D. Sept. 2, 1954, Upper Sandusky, Ohio.

Year	Team	Games	BA	SA	AB	H	2B	3B	HR	HR%	R	RBI	BB	SO	SB	Pinch Hit AB	Pinch Hit H	PO	A	E	DP	TC/G	FA	G by Pos
1907	PHI N	56	.276	.325	163	45	2	3	0	0.0	22	9	3		4	**19**	**7**	68	2	0	1	1.9	1.000	OF-36, 1B-1
1908		152	.267	.355	555	148	19	12	2	0.4	62	44	30		16	0	0	359	14	12	3	2.5	.969	OF-152
1909		58	.185	.217	189	35	4	1	0	0.0	14	19	12		6	6	1	126	14	3	3	2.6	.979	OF-54
3 yrs.		266	.251	.321	907	228	25	16	2	0.2	98	72	45		26	25	8	553	30	15	7	2.5	.975	OF-242, 1B-1

Bobo Osborne

OSBORNE, LAWRENCE SIDNEY BL TR 6′ 1″ 205 lbs.
Son of Tiny Osborne.
B. Oct. 12, 1935, Chattahoochee, Ga.

Year	Team	Games	BA	SA	AB	H	2B	3B	HR	HR%	R	RBI	BB	SO	SB	Pinch Hit AB	Pinch Hit H	PO	A	E	DP	TC/G	FA	G by Pos
1957	DET A	11	.148	.185	27	4	1	0	0	0.0	4	1	3	7	0	2	0	28	1	0	1	3.2	1.000	OF-5, 1B-4
1958		2	.000	.000	2	0	0	0	0	0.0	0	0	0	0	0	2	0	0	0	0	0	0.0	—	
1959		86	.191	.278	209	40	7	1	3	1.4	27	21	16	41	1	23	0	378	27	8	36	7.2	.981	1B-56, OF-1
1961		71	.215	.355	93	20	7	0	2	2.2	8	13	20	15	1	41	10	60	15	1	6	4.0	.987	1B-11, 3B-8
1962		64	.230	.243	74	17	1	0	0	0.0	12	7	16	25	0	29	6	22	21	5	0	2.3	.896	3B-13, 1B-7, C-1
1963	WAS A	125	.212	.358	358	76	14	1	12	3.4	42	44	49	83	0	22	5	719	81	13	69	8.4	.984	1B-81, 3B-16
6 yrs.		359	.206	.317	763	157	30	2	17	2.2	93	86	104	171	2	119	21	1207	145	27	112	6.8	.980	1B-159, 3B-37, OF-6, C-1

Fred Osborne

OSBORNE, FREDERICK W. TL
B. May 1865 Deceased.

Year	Team	Games	BA	SA	AB	H	2B	3B	HR	HR%	R	RBI	BB	SO	SB	Pinch Hit AB	Pinch Hit H	PO	A	E	DP	TC/G	FA	G by Pos
1890	PIT N	41	.238	.339	168	40	8	3	1	0.6	24	14	6	18	0	0	0	67	19	18	0	2.4	.827	OF-35, P-8

Harry Ostdiek

OSTDIEK, HENRY GIRARD BR TR 5′11″ 185 lbs.
B. Apr. 12, 1881, Ottumwa, Iowa D. May 6, 1956, Minneapolis, Minn.

Year	Team	Games	BA	SA	AB	H	2B	3B	HR	HR%	R	RBI	BB	SO	SB	Pinch Hit AB	Pinch Hit H	PO	A	E	DP	TC/G	FA	G by Pos
1904	CLE A	7	.167	.278	18	3	0	1	0	0.0	1	3	3		1	0	0	29	6	2	1	5.3	.946	C-7
1908	BOS A	1	.000	.000	3	0	0	0	0	0.0	0	0	0		0	0	0	7	1	1	0	9.0	.889	C-1
2 yrs.		8	.143	.238	21	3	0	1	0	0.0	1	3	3		1	0	0	36	7	3	1	5.8	.935	C-8

Champ Osteen

OSTEEN, JAMES CHAMPLIN BL TR 5′ 8″ 150 lbs.
B. Feb. 24, 1877, Hendersonville, N. C. D. Dec. 14, 1962, Greenville, S. C.

Year	Team	Games	BA	SA	AB	H	2B	3B	HR	HR%	R	RBI	BB	SO	SB	Pinch Hit AB	Pinch Hit H	PO	A	E	DP	TC/G	FA	G by Pos
1903	WAS A	10	.200	.300	40	8	0	2	0	0.0	4	4	2		0	0	0	28	32	4	4	6.4	.938	SS-10
1904	NY A	28	.196	.336	107	21	1	4	2	1.9	15	9	1		0	0	0	66	56	8	3	4.5	.938	3B-17, SS-8, 1B-4
1908	STL N	29	.196	.232	112	22	4	0	0	0.0	2	11	0		0	0	0	44	63	14	6	4.2	.884	SS-17, 3B-12
1909		16	.200	.222	45	9	1	0	0	0.0	6	7	7		1	0	0	17	41	8	1	4.1	.879	SS-16
4 yrs.		83	.197	.276	304	60	6	6	2	0.7	27	31	10		1	0	0	155	192	34	14	4.5	.911	SS-51, 3B-29, 1B-4

Red Ostergard

OSTERGARD, ROY LUND BR TR 5′10½″ 175 lbs.
B. May 16, 1896, Denmark, Wis. D. Jan. 13, 1977, Hemet, Calif.

Year	Team	Games	BA	SA	AB	H	2B	3B	HR	HR%	R	RBI	BB	SO	SB	Pinch Hit AB	Pinch Hit H	PO	A	E	DP	TC/G	FA	G by Pos
1921	CHI A	12	.364	.364	11	4	0	0	0	0.0	2	0	0	2	0	11	4	0	0	0	0	0.0	—	

Charlie Osterhout

OSTERHOUT, CHARLES H. (Ostey) TR
B. 1856, Syracuse, N. Y. D. May 21, 1933, Syracuse, N. Y.

Year	Team	Games	BA	SA	AB	H	2B	3B	HR	HR%	R	RBI	BB	SO	SB	Pinch Hit AB	Pinch Hit H	PO	A	E	DP	TC/G	FA	G by Pos
1879	SYR N	2	.000	.000	8	0	0	0	0	0.0	0	0	0	0		0	0	6	2	1	0	4.5	.889	OF-1, C-1

Brian Ostrosser

OSTROSSER, BRIAN LEONARD BL TR 6′ 175 lbs.
B. June 17, 1949, Hamilton, Ont., Canada.

Year	Team	Games	BA	SA	AB	H	2B	3B	HR	HR%	R	RBI	BB	SO	SB	Pinch Hit AB	Pinch Hit H	PO	A	E	DP	TC/G	FA	G by Pos
1973	NY N	4	.000	.000	5	0	0	0	0	0.0	0	0	0	2	0	0	0	1	4	0	0	1.3	1.000	SS-4

John Ostrowski

OSTROWSKI, JOHN THADDEUS BR TR 5′10½″ 170 lbs.
B. Oct. 17, 1917, Chicago, Ill. D. Nov. 13, 1992, Chicago, Ill.

Year	Team	Games	BA	SA	AB	H	2B	3B	HR	HR%	R	RBI	BB	SO	SB	Pinch Hit AB	Pinch Hit H	PO	A	E	DP	TC/G	FA	G by Pos
1943	CHI N	10	.207	.276	29	6	0	1	0	0.0	2	3	3	8	0	0	0	11	5	2	1	2.0	.889	OF-5, 3B-4
1944		8	.154	.231	13	2	1	0	0	0.0	2	2	1	4	0	5	2	1	0	1	0	1.0	.500	OF-2
1945		7	.300	.500	10	3	2	0	0	0.0	4	1	0	0	0	2	0	1	2	1	0	1.0	.750	3B-4
1946		64	.212	.319	160	34	4	2	3	1.9	20	12	20	31	1	10	0	35	82	8	5	2.5	.936	3B-50, 2B-1
1948	BOS A	1	.000	.000	1	0	0	0	0	0.0	0	0	0	1	0	1	0	0	0	0	0	0.0	—	
1949	CHI A	49	.266	.468	158	42	9	4	5	3.2	19	31	15	41	4	6	1	85	12	6	0	2.1	.942	OF-41, 3B-8
1950	2 teams	CHI A (21G –.222) WAS A (55G –.227)																						
″	total	76	.226	.360	186	42	3	2	6	3.2	25	25	28	40	2	16	0	132	4	6	1	2.4	.958	OF-60
7 yrs.		215	.232	.373	557	129	19	9	14	2.5	72	74	67	125	7	40	3	265	105	24	7	2.3	.939	OF-108, 3B-66, 2B-1

Reggie Otero

OTERO, REGINO JOSE BL TR 5′11″ 160 lbs.
Born Regino Jose Otero (Gomez).
B. Sept. 7, 1915, Havana, Cuba D. Oct. 21, 1988, Hialeah, Fla.

Year	Team	Games	BA	SA	AB	H	2B	3B	HR	HR%	R	RBI	BB	SO	SB	Pinch Hit AB	Pinch Hit H	PO	A	E	DP	TC/G	FA	G by Pos
1945	CHI N	14	.391	.391	23	9	0	0	0	0.0	1	5	2	2	0	6	0	54	4	2	4	7.5	.967	1B-8

Ricky Otero

OTERO, RICARDO BB TR 5′ 7″ 150 lbs.
Born Ricardo Otero (Figueroa).
B. Apr. 15, 1972, Vega Baja, Puerto Rico.

Year	Team	Games	BA	SA	AB	H	2B	3B	HR	HR%	R	RBI	BB	SO	SB	Pinch Hit AB	Pinch Hit H	PO	A	E	DP	TC/G	FA	G by Pos
1995	NY N	35	.137	.176	51	7	2	0	0	0.0	5	1	3	10	2	11	3	31	1	0	0	1.4	1.000	OF-23

Amos Otis

OTIS, AMOS JOSEPH BR TR 5′11½″ 165 lbs.
B. Apr. 26, 1947, Mobile, Ala.

Year	Team	Games	BA	SA	AB	H	2B	3B	HR	HR%	R	RBI	BB	SO	SB	Pinch Hit AB	Pinch Hit H	PO	A	E	DP	TC/G	FA	G by Pos
1967	NY N	19	.220	.254	59	13	2	0	0	0.0	6	1	5	13	0	0	0	23	2	0	1	1.5	1.000	OF-16, 3B-1
1969		48	.151	.204	93	14	3	1	0	0.0	6	4	6	27	1	10	1	49	6	1	0	1.5	.982	OF-35, 3B-3
1970	KC A	159	.284	.424	620	176	**36**	9	11	1.8	91	58	68	67	33	1	1	388	15	4	6	2.6	.990	OF-159
1971		147	.301	.443	555	167	26	4	15	2.7	80	79	40	74	**52**	4	0	404	10	4	4	2.9	.990	OF-144
1972		143	.293	.413	540	158	28	2	11	2.0	75	54	50	59	28	5	1	351	6	3	3	2.6	.992	OF-137
1973		148	.300	.484	583	175	21	4	26	4.5	89	93	63	47	13	0	0	330	10	5	4	2.3	.986	OF-135, DH-14
1974		146	.284	.438	552	157	31	9	12	2.2	87	73	58	67	18	3	1	425	8	6	3	3.0	.986	OF-143, DH-2

Amos Otis *continued*

Year	Team	Games	BA	SA	AB	H	2B	3B	HR	HR%	R	RBI	BB	SO	SB	Pinch Hit AB	Pinch Hit H	PO	A	E	DP	TC/G	FA	G by Pos
1975		132	.247	.385	470	116	26	6	9	1.9	87	46	66	48	39	4	0	310	9	4	3	2.5	.988	OF-130
1976		153	.279	.444	592	165	**40**	2	18	3.0	93	86	55	100	26	0	0	373	5	3	1	2.5	.992	OF-152
1977		142	.251	.433	478	120	20	8	17	3.6	85	78	71	88	23	3	1	326	10	3	0	2.4	.991	OF-140
1978		141	.298	.525	486	145	30	7	22	4.5	74	96	66	54	32	3	0	382	9	2	1	2.9	.995	OF-136, DH-1
1979		151	.295	.444	577	170	28	2	18	3.1	100	90	68	92	30	1	1	385	11	3	5	2.7	.992	OF-146, DH-4
1980		107	.251	.383	394	99	16	3	10	2.5	56	53	39	70	16	2	1	310	6	4	1	3.0	.988	OF-105
1981		99	.269	.417	372	100	22	3	9	2.4	49	57	31	59	16	2	1	294	6	2	1	3.1	.993	OF-97, DH-1
1982		125	.286	.421	475	136	25	3	11	2.3	73	88	37	65	9	1	0	308	5	1	1	2.5	.997	OF-125
1983		96	.261	.357	356	93	16	3	4	1.1	35	41	27	63	5	2	1	233	6	1	1	2.5	.996	OF-96, DH-1
1984	PIT N	40	.165	.206	97	16	4	0	0	0.0	6	10	7	15	0	7	2	49	5	2	0	1.8	.964	OF-32
17 yrs.		1996	.277	.425	7299	2020	374	66	193	2.6	1092	1007	757	1008	341	48	11	4940	129	48	35	2.6	.991	OF-1928, DH-23, 3B-4
DIVISIONAL PLAYOFF SERIES																								
1981	KC A	3	.000	.000	12	0	0	0	0	0.0	0	1	0	4	0	0	0	12	0	0	0	4.0	1.000	OF-3
LEAGUE CHAMPIONSHIP SERIES																								
1976	KC A	1	.000	.000	1	0	0	0	0	0.0	0	0	0	0	0	0	0	0	0	0	0	0.0	.000	OF-1
1977		5	.125	.188	16	2	1	0	0	0.0	1	2	2	3	2	1	1	11	1	0	0	2.4	1.000	OF-5
1978		4	.429	.571	14	6	2	0	0	0.0	2	1	3	5	4	0	0	8	0	1	0	2.3	.889	OF-4
1980		3	.333	.417	12	4	1	0	0	0.0	2	0	0	3	2	0	0	11	0	0	0	3.7	1.000	OF-3
4 yrs.		13	.279	.372	43	12	4	0	0	0.0	5	3	5	11	8 **4th**	1	1	30	1	1	0	2.5	.969	OF-13
WORLD SERIES																								
1980	KC A	6	.478	.957	23	11	2	0	3	13.0	4	7	3	3	0	0	0	21	0	0	0	3.5	1.000	OF-6

Bill Otis

OTIS, PAUL FRANKLIN BL TR 5′10½″ 150 lbs.
B. Dec. 24, 1889, Scituate, Mass. D. Dec. 15, 1990, Duluth, Minn.

Year	Team	Games	BA	SA	AB	H	2B	3B	HR	HR%	R	RBI	BB	SO	SB	Pinch Hit AB	Pinch Hit H	PO	A	E	DP	TC/G	FA	G by Pos
1912	NY A	4	.050	.050	20	1	0	0	0	0.0	1	2	3		0	0	0	10	1	1	0	3.0	.917	OF-4

Billy Ott

OTT, WILLIAM JOSEPH BB TR 6′ 1″ 180 lbs.
B. Nov. 23, 1940, New York, N. Y.

Year	Team	Games	BA	SA	AB	H	2B	3B	HR	HR%	R	RBI	BB	SO	SB	Pinch Hit AB	Pinch Hit H	PO	A	E	DP	TC/G	FA	G by Pos
1962	CHI N	12	.143	.250	28	4	0	0	1	3.6	3	2	2	10	0	5	1	9	1	0	0	1.4	1.000	OF-7
1964		20	.179	.256	39	7	3	0	0	0.0	4	1	3	10	0	10	2	12	0	0	0	1.2	1.000	OF-10
2 yrs.		32	.164	.254	67	11	3	0	1	1.5	7	3	5	20	0	15	3	21	1	0	0	1.3	1.000	OF-17

Ed Ott

OTT, NATHAN EDWARD BL TR 5′10″ 190 lbs.
B. July 11, 1951, Muncy, Pa.

Year	Team	Games	BA	SA	AB	H	2B	3B	HR	HR%	R	RBI	BB	SO	SB	Pinch Hit AB	Pinch Hit H	PO	A	E	DP	TC/G	FA	G by Pos
1974	PIT N	7	.000	.000	5	0	0	0	0	0.0	1	0	0	1	0	5	0	1	0	0	0	0.5	1.000	OF-2
1975		5	.200	.200	5	1	0	0	0	0.0	0	0	0	0	0	3	0	2	0	0	0	1.0	1.000	C-2
1976		27	.308	.359	39	12	2	0	0	0.0	2	5	3	5	0	17	6	20	6	0	1	3.3	1.000	C-8
1977		104	.264	.395	311	82	14	3	7	2.3	40	38	32	41	7	18	3	455	49	9	6	5.7	.982	C-90
1978		112	.269	.409	379	102	18	4	9	2.4	49	38	27	56	4	15	5	547	43	16	7	6.0	.974	C-97, OF-4
1979		117	.273	.385	403	110	20	2	7	1.7	49	51	26	62	0	3	1	612	53	4	6	5.8	.994	C-116
1980		120	.260	.357	392	102	14	0	8	2.0	35	41	33	47	1	7	1	571	73	11	5	5.5	.983	C-117, OF-3
1981	CAL A	75	.217	.279	258	56	8	1	2	0.8	20	22	17	42	2	5	0	287	36	7	1	4.6	.979	C-72
8 yrs.		567	.259	.368	1792	465	76	10	33	1.8	196	195	138	254	14	73	16	2495	260	47	26	5.5	.983	C-502, OF-9
LEAGUE CHAMPIONSHIP SERIES																								
1979	PIT N	3	.231	.231	13	3	0	0	0	0.0	0	0	0	2	0	0	0	25	3	0	0	9.3	1.000	C-3
WORLD SERIES																								
1979	PIT N	3	.333	.417	12	4	1	0	0	0.0	2	3	0	2	0	0	0	20	0	0	1	6.7	1.000	C-3

Mel Ott

OTT, MELVIN THOMAS (Master Melvin) BL TR 5′ 9″ 170 lbs.
B. Mar. 2, 1909, Gretna, La. D. Nov. 21, 1958, New Orleans, La.
Manager 1942–48.
Hall of Fame 1951.

Year	Team	Games	BA	SA	AB	H	2B	3B	HR	HR%	R	RBI	BB	SO	SB	Pinch Hit AB	Pinch Hit H	PO	A	E	DP	TC/G	FA	G by Pos
1926	NY N	35	.383	.417	60	23	2	0	0	0.0	7	4	1	9	1	24	9	18	3	2	0	2.3	.913	OF-10
1927		82	.282	.380	163	46	7	3	1	0.6	23	19	13	9	2	**46**	11	52	2	1	1	1.7	.982	OF-32
1928		124	.322	.524	435	140	26	4	18	4.1	69	77	52	36	3	3	0	228	29	8	8	2.2	.970	OF-115, 2B-5, 3B-1
1929		150	.328	.635	545	179	37	2	42	**7.7**	138	152	**113**	38	6	0	0	339	27	11	12	2.5	.971	OF-149, 2B-1
1930		148	.349	.578	521	182	34	5	25	4.8	122	119	103	35	9	1	0	320	23	11	6	2.4	.969	OF-146
1931		138	.292	.545	497	145	23	8	29	**5.8**	104	115	**80**	44	10	1	1	332	20	7	4	2.6	.981	OF-137
1932		154	.318	.601	566	180	30	8	**38**	**6.7**	119	123	**100**	39	6	0	0	347	11	6	5	2.4	.984	OF-154
1933		152	.283	.467	580	164	36	1	23	4.0	98	103	**75**	48	1	0	0	283	12	5	3	2.0	.983	OF-152
1934		153	.326	.591	582	190	29	10	**35**	**6.0**	119	**135**	85	43	0	0	0	286	12	8	1	2.0	.974	OF-153
1935		152	.322	.555	593	191	33	6	31	5.2	113	114	82	58	7	0	0	304	42	6	10	2.3	.983	OF-137, 3B-15
1936		150	.328	**.588**	534	175	28	6	**33**	**6.2**	120	135	111	41	6	1	1	250	20	4	3	1.9	.985	OF-148
1937		151	.294	.523	545	160	28	2	**31**	**5.7**	99	95	**102**	69	7	1	0	198	126	10	6	2.2	.970	OF-91, 3B-60
1938		154	.311	.583	527	164	23	6	**36**	**6.8**	**116**	116	118	47	2	1	0	163	241	15	14	2.8	.964	3B-113, OF-37
1939		125	.308	.581	396	122	23	2	27	**6.8**	85	80	100	50	2	9	2	190	45	11	6	2.1	.955	OF-96, 3B-20
1940		151	.289	.457	536	155	27	3	19	3.5	89	79	100	50	6	0	0	240	92	12	10	2.2	.965	OF-111, 3B-42
1941		148	.286	.495	525	150	29	0	27	5.1	89	90	100	68	5	2	0	256	19	9	3	2.0	.968	OF-145
1942		152	.295	.497	549	162	21	0	**30**	**5.5**	**118**	93	**109**	61	6	0	0	269	15	3	3	1.9	.990	OF-152
1943		125	.234	.418	380	89	12	2	18	4.7	65	47	95	48	7	6	1	219	12	6	1	2.1	.975	OF-111, 3B-1
1944		120	.288	.544	399	115	16	4	26	**6.5**	91	82	90	47	2	10	2	200	19	7	0	2.1	.969	OF-103, 3B-4
1945		135	.308	.499	451	139	23	0	21	4.7	73	79	71	41	1	15	4	217	11	4	1	2.0	.983	OF-118
1946		31	.074	.132	68	5	1	0	1	1.5	2	4	8	15	0	13	1	23	2	0	1	1.6	1.000	OF-16
1947		4	.000	.000	4	0	0	0	0	0.0	0	0	0	0	0	4	0	0	0	0	0	0.0	—	
22 yrs.		2734	.304	.533	9456	2876	488	72	511	5.4	1859 **9th**	1861 **8th**	1708 **6th**	896	89	137	32	4734	783	146	98	2.2	.974	OF-2313, 3B-256, 2B-6

Mel Ott *continued*

WORLD SERIES

Year	Team	Games	BA	SA	AB	H	2B	3B	HR	HR%	R	RBI	BB	SO	SB	Pinch Hit AB	Pinch Hit H	PO	A	E	DP	TC/G	FA	G by Pos
1933	NY N	5	.389	.722	18	7	0	0	2	11.1	3	4	4	4	0	0	0	10	0	0	0	2.0	1.000	OF-5
1936		6	.304	.522	23	7	2	0	1	4.3	4	3	3	1	0	0	0	12	0	1	0	2.2	.923	OF-6
1937		5	.200	.350	20	4	0	0	1	5.0	1	3	1	4	0	0	0	5	9	1	1	3.0	.933	3B-5
3 yrs.		16	.295	.525	61	18	2	0	4	6.6	8	10	8	9	0	0	0	27	9	2	1	2.4	.947	OF-11, 3B-5

Joe Otten

OTTEN, JOSEPH G. TR
B. Murphysboro, Ill. Deceased.

Year	Team	Games	BA	SA	AB	H	2B	3B	HR	HR%	R	RBI	BB	SO	SB	Pinch Hit AB	Pinch Hit H	PO	A	E	DP	TC/G	FA	G by Pos
1895	STL N	26	.241	.241	87	21	0	0	0	0.0	8	8	5	8	2	0	0	75	15	6	3	3.7	.938	C-24, OF-2

Billy Otterson

OTTERSON, WILLIAM JOHN BR TR 5′ 7″ 135 lbs.
B. May 4, 1862, Pittsburgh, Pa. D. Sept. 21, 1940, Pittsburgh, Pa.

Year	Team	Games	BA	SA	AB	H	2B	3B	HR	HR%	R	RBI	BB	SO	SB	Pinch Hit AB	Pinch Hit H	PO	A	E	DP	TC/G	FA	G by Pos
1887	BKN AA	30	.200	.320	100	20	4	1	2	2.0	16		8		8	0	0	41	93	22	11	5.2	.859	SS-30

Phil Ouellette

OUELLETTE, PHILIP ROLAND BB TR 6′ 190 lbs.
B. Nov. 10, 1961, Salem, Ore.

Year	Team	Games	BA	SA	AB	H	2B	3B	HR	HR%	R	RBI	BB	SO	SB	Pinch Hit AB	Pinch Hit H	PO	A	E	DP	TC/G	FA	G by Pos
1986	SF N	10	.174	.174	23	4	0	0	0	0.0	1	0	3	3	0	3	0	42	3	0	0	5.0	1.000	C-9

Johnny Oulliber

OULLIBER, JOHN ANDREW BR TR 5′11″ 165 lbs.
B. Feb. 24, 1911, New Orleans, La. D. Dec. 26, 1980, New Orleans, La.

Year	Team	Games	BA	SA	AB	H	2B	3B	HR	HR%	R	RBI	BB	SO	SB	Pinch Hit AB	Pinch Hit H	PO	A	E	DP	TC/G	FA	G by Pos
1933	CLE A	22	.267	.280	75	20	1	0	0	0.0	9	3	4	5	0	4	0	25	0	0	0	1.4	1.000	OF-18

Chink Outen

OUTEN, WILLIAM AUSTIN BL TR 6′ 200 lbs.
B. June 17, 1905, Mt. Holly, N. C. D. Sept. 11, 1961, Durham, N. C.

Year	Team	Games	BA	SA	AB	H	2B	3B	HR	HR%	R	RBI	BB	SO	SB	Pinch Hit AB	Pinch Hit H	PO	A	E	DP	TC/G	FA	G by Pos
1933	BKN N	93	.248	.392	153	38	10	0	4	2.6	20	17	20	15	1	31	1	98	11	2	1	2.0	.982	C-56

Jimmy Outlaw

OUTLAW, JAMES PAULUS BR TR 5′ 8″ 165 lbs.
B. Jan. 20, 1913, Orme, Tenn.

Year	Team	Games	BA	SA	AB	H	2B	3B	HR	HR%	R	RBI	BB	SO	SB	Pinch Hit AB	Pinch Hit H	PO	A	E	DP	TC/G	FA	G by Pos
1937	CIN N	49	.273	.352	165	45	7	3	0	0.0	18	11	3	31	2	4	0	41	87	12	4	3.4	.914	3B-41
1938		4	—	—	0	0	0	0	0	—	1	0	0	0	0	0	0	0	0	0	0	0.0	—	
1939	BOS N	65	.263	.278	133	35	2	0	0	0.0	15	5	10	14	1	16	4	83	1	3	0	2.1	.966	OF-39, 3B-2
1943	DET A	20	.269	.328	67	18	1	0	1	1.5	8	6	8	4	0	4	1	32	2	0	0	2.1	1.000	OF-16
1944		139	.273	.350	535	146	20	6	3	0.6	69	57	41	40	7	3	0	254	14	10	2	2.0	.964	OF-137
1945		132	.271	.330	446	121	16	5	0	0.0	56	34	45	33	6	7	0	210	55	11	11	2.2	.960	OF-105, 3B-21
1946		92	.261	.341	299	78	14	2	2	0.7	36	31	29	24	5	5	1	101	64	7	4	2.1	.959	OF-43, 3B-38
1947		70	.228	.299	127	29	7	1	0	0.0	20	15	21	14	3	3	0	69	7	2	0	1.7	.974	OF-37, 3B-9
1948		74	.283	.343	198	56	12	0	0	0.0	33	25	31	15	0	11	4	58	88	11	8	2.6	.930	3B-47, OF-13
1949		5	.250	.250	4	1	0	0	0	0.0	1	0	0	1	0	4	1	0	0	0	0	0.0	—	
10 yrs.		650	.268	.334	1974	529	79	17	6	0.3	257	184	188	176	24	57	11	848	318	56	29	2.2	.954	OF-390, 3B-158

WORLD SERIES

Year	Team	Games	BA	SA	AB	H	2B	3B	HR	HR%	R	RBI	BB	SO	SB	Pinch Hit AB	Pinch Hit H	PO	A	E	DP	TC/G	FA	G by Pos
1945	DET A	7	.179	.179	28	5	0	0	0	0.0	1	3	2	1	1	0	0	5	15	0	0	2.9	1.000	3B-7

Dave Owen

OWEN, DAVID BB TR 6′ 1″ 175 lbs.
Brother of Spike Owen.
B. Apr. 25, 1958, Cleburne, Tex.

Year	Team	Games	BA	SA	AB	H	2B	3B	HR	HR%	R	RBI	BB	SO	SB	Pinch Hit AB	Pinch Hit H	PO	A	E	DP	TC/G	FA	G by Pos
1983	CHI N	16	.091	.182	22	2	0	1	0	0.0	1	2	2	7	1	0	0	10	29	0	5	2.3	1.000	SS-14, 3B-3
1984		47	.194	.290	93	18	2	2	1	1.1	8	10	8	15	1	3	2	40	91	7	19	3.1	.949	SS-35, 3B-6, 2B-4
1985		22	.368	.368	19	7	0	0	0	0.0	6	4	1	5	1	3	0	6	14	2	2	1.2	.909	3B-7, SS-7, 2B-4
1988	KC A	7	.000	.000	5	0	0	0	0	0.0	0	0	0	3	0	0	0	7	9	1	6	2.4	.941	SS-7
4 yrs.		92	.194	.273	139	27	2	3	1	0.7	15	16	11	30	3	6	2	63	143	10	32	2.5	.954	SS-63, 3B-16, 2B-8

Larry Owen

OWEN, LAWRENCE THOMAS BR TR 5′11″ 185 lbs.
B. May 31, 1955, Cleveland, Ohio.

Year	Team	Games	BA	SA	AB	H	2B	3B	HR	HR%	R	RBI	BB	SO	SB	Pinch Hit AB	Pinch Hit H	PO	A	E	DP	TC/G	FA	G by Pos
1981	ATL N	13	.000	.000	16	0	0	0	0	0.0	0	0	1	4	0	4	0	23	4	1	2	2.8	.964	C-10
1982		2	.333	.667	3	1	1	0	0	0.0	1	0	0	1	0	0	0	2	1	0	0	1.5	1.000	C-2
1983		17	.118	.118	17	2	0	0	0	0.0	0	1	0	2	0	1	0	30	2	1	1	2.1	.970	C-16
1985		26	.239	.366	71	17	3	0	2	2.8	7	12	8	17	0	2	0	129	11	5	1	5.8	.966	C-25
1987	KC A	76	.189	.317	164	31	6	0	5	3.0	17	14	16	51	0	0	0	370	38	7	4	5.5	.983	C-76
1988		37	.210	.259	81	17	1	0	1	1.2	5	3	9	23	0	0	0	168	13	2	1	4.9	.989	C-37
6 yrs.		171	.193	.293	352	68	11	0	8	2.3	30	30	34	98	0	7	0	722	69	16	9	4.9	.980	C-166

Marv Owen

OWEN, MARVIN JAMES BR TR 6′ 1″ 175 lbs.
B. Mar. 22, 1906, Agnew, Calif. D. June 22, 1991, Mountain View, Calif.

Year	Team	Games	BA	SA	AB	H	2B	3B	HR	HR%	R	RBI	BB	SO	SB	Pinch Hit AB	Pinch Hit H	PO	A	E	DP	TC/G	FA	G by Pos
1931	DET A	105	.223	.308	377	84	11	6	3	0.8	35	39	29	38	2	3	1	308	220	24	46	5.3	.957	3B-37, SS-37, 1B-27, 2B-4
1933		138	.262	.349	550	144	24	9	2	0.4	77	65	44	56	2	1	0	143	226	22	19	2.9	.944	3B-136
1934		154	.317	.451	565	179	34	9	8	1.4	79	96	59	37	3	0	0	202	253	21	33	3.1	.956	3B-154
1935		134	.263	.346	483	127	24	5	2	0.4	52	71	43	37	1	2	1	148	215	16	19	2.9	.958	3B-131
1936		154	.295	.389	583	172	20	4	9	1.5	72	105	53	41	9	0	0	202	281	24	29	3.3	.953	3B-153, 1B-2
1937		107	.288	.376	396	114	22	5	1	0.3	48	45	41	24	3	1	0	108	219	10	17	3.2	.970	3B-106
1938	CHI A	141	.281	.373	577	162	23	6	6	1.0	84	55	45	31	6	1	0	136	305	24	29	3.3	.948	3B-140
1939		58	.237	.284	194	46	9	0	0	0.0	22	15	16	15	4	2	0	63	99	8	11	3.1	.953	3B-55
1940	BOS A	20	.211	.211	57	12	0	0	0	0.0	4	6	8	4	0	3	0	62	24	2	12	5.2	.977	3B-9, 1B-8
9 yrs.		1011	.275	.367	3782	1040	167	44	31	0.8	473	497	338	283	30	13	2	1372	1842	151	215	3.4	.955	3B-921, SS-37, 1B-37, 2B-4

WORLD SERIES

Year	Team	Games	BA	SA	AB	H	2B	3B	HR	HR%	R	RBI	BB	SO	SB	Pinch Hit AB	Pinch Hit H	PO	A	E	DP	TC/G	FA	G by Pos
1934	DET A	7	.069	.069	29	2	0	0	0	0.0	0	1	0	5	1	0	0	9	9	2	1	2.9	.900	3B-7
1935		6	.050	.050	20	1	0	0	0	0.0	2	1	2	3	0	0	0	46	5	1	4	8.7	.981	1B-4, 3B-2
2 yrs.		13	.061	.061	49	3	0	0	0	0.0	2	2	2	8	1	0	0	55	14	3	5	5.5	.958	3B-9, 1B-4

Mickey Owen

OWEN, ARNOLD MALCOLM BR TR 5′10″ 190 lbs.
B. Apr. 4, 1916, Nixa, Mo.

Year	Team	Games	BA	SA	AB	H	2B	3B	HR	HR%	R	RBI	BB	SO	SB	Pinch Hit AB	Pinch Hit H	PO	A	E	DP	TC/G	FA	G by Pos
1937	STL N	80	.231	.265	234	54	4	2	0	0.0	17	20	15	13	1	2	0	287	49	9	6	4.4	.974	C-78
1938		122	.267	.370	397	106	25	2	4	1.0	45	36	32	14	2	5	1	463	67	11	8	4.7	.980	C-116

Mickey Owen *continued*

Year	Team	Games	BA	SA	AB	H	2B	3B	HR	HR%	R	RBI	BB	SO	SB	Pinch Hit AB	Pinch Hit H	PO	A	E	DP	TC/G	FA	G by Pos
1939		131	.259	.349	344	89	18	2	3	0.9	32	35	43	28	6	5	0	452	52	9	7	4.1	.982	C-126
1940		117	.264	.329	307	81	16	2	0	0.0	27	27	34	13	4	4	2	378	56	9	8	3.9	.980	C-113
1941	BKN N	128	.231	.288	386	89	15	2	1	0.3	32	44	34	14	1	0	0	530	64	3	7	4.7	.995	C-128
1942		133	.259	.311	421	109	16	3	0	0.0	53	44	44	17	10	0	0	595	66	9	12	5.0	.987	C-133
1943		106	.260	.301	365	95	11	2	0	0.0	31	54	25	15	4	5	1	421	57	7	11	4.7	.986	C-100, 3B-3, SS-1
1944		130	.273	.336	461	126	20	3	1	0.2	43	42	36	17	4	4	1	507	57	12	8	4.6	.979	C-125, 2B-1
1945		24	.286	.393	84	24	9	0	0	0.0	5	11	10	2	0	0	0	92	13	4	2	4.5	.963	C-24
1949	CHI N	62	.273	.379	198	54	9	3	2	1.0	15	18	12	13	1	3	1	219	35	8	5	4.4	.969	C-59
1950		86	.243	.309	259	63	11	0	2	0.8	22	21	13	16	2	1	0	318	39	8	8	4.2	.978	C-86
1951		58	.184	.232	125	23	6	0	0	0.0	10	15	19	13	1	1	0	188	28	7	6	3.9	.969	C-57
1954	BOS A	32	.235	.324	68	16	3	0	1	1.5	6	11	9	6	0	1	1	85	8	1	4	3.1	.989	C-30
13 yrs.		1209	.255	.322	3649	929	163	21	14	0.4	338	378	326	181	36	31	7	4535	591	97	92	4.4	.981	C-1175, 3B-3, 2B-1, SS-1
WORLD SERIES																								
1941	BKN N	5	.167	.333	12	2	0	1	0	0.0	1	2	3	0	0	0	0	20	4	1	1	5.0	.960	C-5

Spike Owen

OWEN, SPIKE DEE BB TR 5′ 9″ 160 lbs.
Brother of Dave Owen.
B. Apr. 19, 1961, Cleburne, Tex.

Year	Team	Games	BA	SA	AB	H	2B	3B	HR	HR%	R	RBI	BB	SO	SB	Pinch Hit AB	Pinch Hit H	PO	A	E	DP	TC/G	FA	G by Pos
1983	SEA A	80	.196	.271	306	60	11	3	2	0.7	36	21	24	44	10	1	0	122	233	11	45	4.6	.970	SS-80
1984		152	.245	.326	530	130	18	8	3	0.6	67	43	46	63	16	1	1	245	463	17	86	4.8	.977	SS-151
1985		118	.259	.372	352	91	10	6	6	1.7	41	37	34	27	11	0	0	196	361	14	76	4.9	.975	SS-117
1986	2 teams	SEA A (112G –.246)	BOS A (42G –.183)																					
″	total	154	.231	.309	528	122	24	7	1	0.2	67	45	51	51	4	0	0	279	467	21	133	5.0	.973	SS-154
1987	BOS A	132	.259	.343	437	113	17	7	2	0.5	50	48	53	43	11	1	0	176	336	13	69	4.0	.975	SS-130
1988		89	.249	.370	257	64	14	1	5	1.9	40	18	27	27	0	6	1	102	192	10	34	3.7	.967	SS-76, DH-7
1989	MON N	142	.233	.332	437	102	17	4	6	1.4	52	41	76	44	3	1	0	232	388	13	65	4.5	.979	SS-142
1990		149	.234	.342	453	106	24	5	5	1.1	55	35	70	60	8	5	0	216	340	6	52	3.8	.989	SS-148
1991		139	.255	.366	424	108	22	8	3	0.7	39	26	42	61	2	6	2	189	376	8	64	4.3	.986	SS-133
1992		122	.269	.381	386	104	16	3	7	1.8	52	40	50	30	9	5	1	188	300	9	44	4.3	.982	SS-116
1993	NY A	103	.234	.311	334	78	16	2	2	0.6	41	20	29	30	3	4	0	116	312	14	44	4.6	.968	SS-96, DH-1
1994	CAL A	82	.310	.422	268	83	17	2	3	1.1	30	37	49	17	2	1	1	64	137	8	18	2.5	.962	3B-70, SS-5, 1B-4, DH-2, 2B-1
1995		82	.229	.312	218	50	9	3	1	0.5	17	28	18	22	3	38	15	66	95	6	17	2.4	.964	3B-29, SS-25, 2B-16
13 yrs.		1544	.246	.341	4930	1211	215	59	46	0.9	587	439	569	519	82	69	21	2191	4000	150	747	4.2	.976	SS-1373, 3B-99, 2B-17, DH-10, 1B-4
LEAGUE CHAMPIONSHIP SERIES																								
1986	BOS A	7	.429	.524	21	9	0	1	0	0.0	5	3	2	2	1	0	0	12	21	5	2	5.4	.868	SS-7
1988		1	—	—	0	0	0	0	0	—	0	0	1	0	0	0	0	0	0	0	0	0.0	—	
2 yrs.		8	.429	.524	21	9	0	1	0	0.0	5	3	3	2	1	0	0	12	21	5	2	5.4	.868	SS-7
WORLD SERIES																								
1986	BOS A	7	.300	.300	20	6	0	0	0	0.0	2	2	5	6	0	0	0	10	13	0	3	3.3	1.000	SS-7

Eric Owens

OWENS, ERIC BLAKE BR TR 6′ 1″ 185 lbs.
B. Feb. 3, 1971, Danville, Va.

Year	Team	Games	BA	SA	AB	H	2B	3B	HR	HR%	R	RBI	BB	SO	SB	Pinch Hit AB	Pinch Hit H	PO	A	E	DP	TC/G	FA	G by Pos
1995	CIN N	2	1.000	1.000	2	2	0	0	0	0.0	0	1	0	0	0	1	1	0	0	0	0	0.0	.000	3B-2

Frank Owens

OWENS, FRANK WALTER BR TR 6′ 170 lbs.
B. Jan. 26, 1886, Toronto, Ont., Canada D. July 2, 1958, Minneapolis, Minn.

Year	Team	Games	BA	SA	AB	H	2B	3B	HR	HR%	R	RBI	BB	SO	SB	Pinch Hit AB	Pinch Hit H	PO	A	E	DP	TC/G	FA	G by Pos
1905	BOS A	1	.000	.000	2	0	0	0	0	0.0	0	0	0		0	0	0	2	1	0	0	3.0	1.000	C-1
1909	CHI A	64	.201	.236	174	35	4	1	0	0.0	12	17	8		3	6	1	266	62	14	2	6.0	.959	C-57
1914	BKN F	58	.277	.380	184	51	7	3	2	1.1	15	20	9		2	0	0	228	67	10	10	5.3	.967	C-58
1915	BAL F	99	.251	.362	334	84	14	7	3	0.9	32	28	17		4	0	0	462	146	15	19	6.3	.976	C-99
4 yrs.		222	.245	.334	694	170	25	11	5	0.7	59	65	34		9	6	1	958	276	39	31	5.9	.969	C-215

Jack Owens

OWENS, FURMAN LEE BR TR 6′ 1″ 186 lbs.
B. May 6, 1908, Converse, S. C. D. Nov. 14, 1958, Greenville, S. C.

Year	Team	Games	BA	SA	AB	H	2B	3B	HR	HR%	R	RBI	BB	SO	SB	Pinch Hit AB	Pinch Hit H	PO	A	E	DP	TC/G	FA	G by Pos
1935	PHI A	2	.250	.250	8	2	0	0	0	0.0	0	1	0	1	0	0	0	8	1	1	0	5.0	.900	C-2

Jayhawk Owens

OWENS, CLAUDE JAYHAWK BR TR 6′ 1″ 213 lbs.
B. Feb. 10, 1969, Cincinnati, Ohio.

Year	Team	Games	BA	SA	AB	H	2B	3B	HR	HR%	R	RBI	BB	SO	SB	Pinch Hit AB	Pinch Hit H	PO	A	E	DP	TC/G	FA	G by Pos
1993	CLR N	33	.209	.372	86	18	5	0	3	3.5	12	6	6	30	1	2	0	138	19	7	3	5.1	.957	C-32
1994		6	.250	.417	12	3	0	1	0	0.0	4	1	3	3	0	0	0	25	3	0	0	4.7	1.000	C-6
1995		18	.244	.556	45	11	2	0	4	8.9	7	12	2	15	0	2	1	79	6	1	2	5.4	.988	C-16
3 yrs.		57	.224	.434	143	32	7	1	7	4.9	23	19	11	48	1	4	1	242	28	8	5	5.1	.971	C-54
DIVISIONAL PLAYOFF SERIES																								
1995	CLR N	1	.000	.000	1	0	0	0	0	0.0	0	0	0	1	0	0	0	2	1	0	0	3.0	1.000	C-1

Red Owens

OWENS, THOMAS LLEWELLYN BR TR
B. Nov. 1, 1874, Pottsville, Pa. D. Aug. 20, 1952, Harrisburg, Pa.

Year	Team	Games	BA	SA	AB	H	2B	3B	HR	HR%	R	RBI	BB	SO	SB	Pinch Hit AB	Pinch Hit H	PO	A	E	DP	TC/G	FA	G by Pos
1899	PHI N	8	.048	.048	21	1	0	0	0	0.0	0	1	2		0	0	0	13	19	3	2	4.4	.914	2B-8
1905	BKN N	43	.214	.292	168	36	6	2	1	0.6	14	20	6		1	0	0	102	132	18	19	5.9	.929	2B-43
2 yrs.		51	.196	.265	189	37	6	2	1	0.5	14	21	8		1	0	0	115	151	21	21	5.6	.927	2B-51

Henry Oxley

OXLEY, HENRY HAVELOCK 5′11″ 163 lbs.
B. Jan. 4, 1858, Covehead, P. E. I., Canada D. Oct. 12, 1945, Somerville, Mass.

Year	Team	Games	BA	SA	AB	H	2B	3B	HR	HR%	R	RBI	BB	SO	SB	Pinch Hit AB	Pinch Hit H	PO	A	E	DP	TC/G	FA	G by Pos
1884	2 teams	NY N (2G –.000)	NY AA (1G –.000)																					
″	total	3	.000	.000	7	0	0	0	0	0.0	0		1	2		0	0	11	6	2	0	6.3	.895	C-3

Andy Oyler

OYLER, ANDREW PAUL (Pepper) BR TR 5′ 6½″ 138 lbs.
B. May 5, 1880, Newville, Pa. D. Oct. 24, 1970, Cumberland County, Pa.

Year	Team	Games	BA	SA	AB	H	2B	3B	HR	HR%	R	RBI	BB	SO	SB	Pinch Hit AB	Pinch Hit H	PO	A	E	DP	TC/G	FA	G by Pos
1902	BAL A	27	.221	.273	77	17	1	0	1	1.3	9	6	8		3	2	0	34	30	4	2	2.6	.941	3B-20, OF-3, SS-2, 2B-1

Ray Oyler

OYLER, RAYMOND FRANCIS BR TR 5′11″ 165 lbs.
B. Aug. 4, 1938, Indianapolis, Ind. D. Jan. 26, 1981, Redmond, Wash.

Year	Team	Games	BA	SA	AB	H	2B	3B	HR	HR%	R	RBI	BB	SO	SB	Pinch Hit AB	Pinch Hit H	PO	A	E	DP	TC/G	FA	G by Pos
1965	DET A	82	.186	.294	194	36	6	0	5	2.6	22	13	21	61	1	11	3	92	166	11	18	3.8	.959	SS-57, 2B-11, 3B-1, 1B-1
1966		71	.171	.252	210	36	8	3	1	0.5	16	9	23	62	0	1	0	107	194	11	42	4.5	.965	SS-69
1967		148	.207	.264	367	76	14	2	1	0.3	33	29	37	91	0	1	0	185	374	21	61	4.0	.964	SS-146
1968		111	.135	.186	215	29	6	1	1	0.5	13	12	20	59	0	0	0	139	207	8	31	3.2	.977	SS-111
1969	SEA A	106	.165	.267	255	42	5	0	7	2.7	24	22	31	80	1	0	0	143	266	15	47	4.0	.965	SS-106
1970	CAL A	24	.083	.083	24	2	0	0	0	0.0	2	1	3	6	0	7	0	7	12	0	1	1.3	1.000	SS-13, 3B-2
6 yrs.		542	.175	.251	1265	221	39	6	15	1.2	110	86	135	359	2	19	3	673	1219	66	200	3.8	.966	SS-502, 2B-11, 3B-3, 1B-1
WORLD SERIES																								
1968	DET A	4	—	—	0	0	0	0	0	—	0	0	0	0	0	0	0	2	0	0	0	0.5	1.000	SS-4

Ed Pabst

PABST, EDWARD D. A. 5′11″ 170 lbs.
B. 1868, St. Louis, Mo. D. June 19, 1940, St. Louis, Mo.

Year	Team	Games	BA	SA	AB	H	2B	3B	HR	HR%	R	RBI	BB	SO	SB	Pinch Hit AB	Pinch Hit H	PO	A	E	DP	TC/G	FA	G by Pos
1890	2 teams	PHI AA (8G –.400) STL AA (4G –.143)																						
″	total	12	.308	.410	39	12	2	1	0	0.0	8		5		3	0	0	29	6	1	0	3.0	.972	OF-12

Jim Paciorek

PACIOREK, JAMES JOSEPH BR TR 6′ 3″ 205 lbs.
Brother of Tom Paciorek. Brother of John Paciorek.
B. June 7, 1960, Detroit, Mich.

Year	Team	Games	BA	SA	AB	H	2B	3B	HR	HR%	R	RBI	BB	SO	SB	Pinch Hit AB	Pinch Hit H	PO	A	E	DP	TC/G	FA	G by Pos
1987	MIL A	48	.228	.337	101	23	5	0	2	2.0	16	10	12	20	1	8	3	113	22	8	12	3.5	.944	1B-21, 3B-15, OF-5

John Paciorek

PACIOREK, JOHN FRANCIS BR TR 6′ 2″ 200 lbs.
Brother of Jim Paciorek. Brother of Tom Paciorek.
B. Feb. 11, 1945, Detroit, Mich.

Year	Team	Games	BA	SA	AB	H	2B	3B	HR	HR%	R	RBI	BB	SO	SB	Pinch Hit AB	Pinch Hit H	PO	A	E	DP	TC/G	FA	G by Pos
1963	HOU N	1	1.000	1.000	3	3	0	0	0	0.0	4	3	2	0	0	0	0	2	0	0	0	2.0	1.000	OF-1

Tom Paciorek

PACIOREK, THOMAS MARIAN BR TR 6′4″ 215 lbs.
Brother of Jim Paciorek. Brother of John Paciorek.
B. Nov. 2, 1946, Detroit, Mich.

Year	Team	Games	BA	SA	AB	H	2B	3B	HR	HR%	R	RBI	BB	SO	SB	Pinch Hit AB	Pinch Hit H	PO	A	E	DP	TC/G	FA	G by Pos
1970	LA N	8	.222	.333	9	2	1	0	0	0.0	2	0	0	3	0	5	1	1	0	0	0	0.3	1.000	OF-3
1971		2	.500	.500	2	1	0	0	0	0.0	0	1	0	0	0	2	1	1	0	0	0	1.0	1.000	OF-1
1972		11	.255	.404	47	12	4	0	1	2.1	4	6	1	7	1	0	0	53	5	1	4	4.9	.983	OF-6, 1B-6
1973		96	.262	.379	195	51	8	0	5	2.6	26	18	11	35	3	17	4	117	3	2	3	1.5	.984	OF-77, 1B-4
1974		85	.240	.371	175	42	8	6	1	0.6	23	24	10	32	1	18	6	85	1	5	1	1.2	.945	OF-77, 1B-1
1975		62	.193	.269	145	28	8	0	1	0.7	14	5	11	29	4	10	2	69	0	2	0	1.3	.972	OF-54
1976	ATL N	111	.290	.383	324	94	10	4	4	1.2	39	36	19	57	2	20	8	216	10	3	8	2.4	.987	OF-84, 1B-12, 3B-1
1977		72	.239	.348	155	37	8	0	3	1.9	20	15	6	46	1	32	6	248	16	5	20	6.4	.981	1B-32, OF-9, 3B-1
1978	2 teams	ATL N (5G –.333) SEA A (70G –.299)																						
″	total	75	.300	.446	260	78	20	3	4	1.5	34	30	15	40	2	7	2	136	5	2	2	2.0	.986	OF-54, DH-12, 1B-5
1979	SEA A	103	.287	.445	310	89	23	4	6	1.9	38	42	28	62	6	17	4	237	12	1	12	2.8	.996	OF-75, 1B-15
1980		126	.273	.431	418	114	19	1	15	3.6	44	59	17	67	3	14	2	360	22	5	25	3.3	.987	OF-60, 1B-36, DH-23
1981		104	.326	.509	405	132	28	2	14	3.5	50	66	35	50	13	1	1	253	10	7	1	2.6	.974	OF-103
1982	CHI A	104	.312	.490	382	119	27	4	11	2.9	49	55	24	53	3	0	0	835	66	6	85	8.4	.993	1B-102, OF-6
1983		115	.307	.462	420	129	32	3	9	2.1	65	63	25	58	6	9	3	629	38	1	42	5.4	.999	1B-67, OF-55, DH-2
1984		111	.256	.358	363	93	21	2	4	1.1	35	29	25	69	6	18	7	596	25	6	50	5.8	.990	1B-67, OF-41
1985	2 teams	CHI A (46G –.246) NY N (46G –.284)																						
″	total	92	.265	.307	238	63	5	1	1	0.4	28	20	14	36	3	27	5	152	9	1	6	2.1	.994	OF-52, 1B-14, DH-12
1986	TEX A	88	.286	.376	213	61	7	0	4	1.9	17	22	3	41	1	18	5	178	45	4	16	2.9	.982	OF-25, 1B-23, 3B-21, DH-9, SS-1
1987		27	.283	.483	60	17	3	0	3	5.0	6	12	1	19	0	4	1	82	7	1	9	3.3	.989	1B-12, OF-12, DH-3
18 yrs.		1392	.282	.415	4121	1162	232	30	86	2.1	494	503	245	704	55	219	58	4248	274	52	284	3.6	.989	OF-794, 1B-396, DH-61, 3B-23, SS-1
LEAGUE CHAMPIONSHIP SERIES																								
1974	LA N	1	1.000	1.000	1	1	0	0	0	0.0	0	0	0	0	0	1	1	0	0	0	0	0.0	.000	OF-1
1983	CHI A	4	.250	.250	16	4	0	0	0	0.0	1	1	1	2	0	0	0	30	2	0	2	6.4	1.000	1B-3, OF-2
2 yrs.		5	.294	.294	17	5	0	0	0	0.0	1	1	1	2	0	1	1	30	2	0	2	5.3	1.000	1B-3, OF-3
WORLD SERIES																								
1974	LA N	3	.500	1.000	2	1	1	0	0	0.0	1	0	0	0	0	2	1	0	0	0	0	0.0	—	

Frankie Pack

PACK, FRANK BL TR 6′ 190 lbs.
B. Apr. 10, 1928, Morristown, Tenn.

Year	Team	Games	BA	SA	AB	H	2B	3B	HR	HR%	R	RBI	BB	SO	SB	Pinch Hit AB	Pinch Hit H	PO	A	E	DP	TC/G	FA	G by Pos
1949	STL A	1	.000	.000	1	0	0	0	0	0.0	0	0	0	1	0	1	0	0	0	0	0	0.0	—	

Dick Padden

PADDEN, RICHARD JOSEPH (Brains) BR TR 5′10½″ 165 lbs.
B. Sept. 17, 1870, Martins Ferry, Ohio D. Oct. 31, 1922, Martins Ferry, Ohio.

Year	Team	Games	BA	SA	AB	H	2B	3B	HR	HR%	R	RBI	BB	SO	SB	Pinch Hit AB	Pinch Hit H	PO	A	E	DP	TC/G	FA	G by Pos
1896	PIT N	61	.242	.361	219	53	4	8	2	0.9	33	24	14	9	8	0	0	176	149	24	14	5.7	.931	2B-61
1897		134	.282	.364	517	146	16	10	2	0.4	84	58	38		18	0	0	369	402	48	36	6.1	.941	2B-134
1898		128	.257	.311	463	119	7	6	2	0.4	61	43	35		11	0	0	301	407	40	46	5.8	.947	2B-128
1899	WAS N	134	.277	.366	451	125	20	7	2	0.4	66	61	24		27	1	1	341	405	64	45	6.1	.921	SS-85, 2B-48
1901	STL N	123	.256	.332	488	125	17	7	2	0.4	71	62	31		26	0	0	301	360	40	49	5.7	.943	2B-115, SS-8
1902	STL A	117	.264	.349	413	109	26	3	1	0.2	54	40	30		11	0	0	288	363	22	64	5.8	.967	2B-117
1903		29	.202	.234	94	19	3	0	0	0.0	7	6	9		5	0	0	57	93	7	17	5.4	.955	2B-29
1904		132	.238	.298	453	108	19	4	0	0.0	42	36	40		23	0	0	288	373	28	31	5.2	.959	2B-132
1905		16	.172	.224	58	10	1	1	0	0.0	5	4	3		3	0	0	32	44	4	2	5.0	.950	2B-16
9 yrs.		874	.258	.333	3156	814	113	46	11	0.3	423	334	224	9	132	1	1	2153	2596	277	304	5.8	.945	2B-780, SS-93

Tom Padden

PADDEN, THOMAS FRANCIS BR TR 5′11½″ 170 lbs.
B. Oct. 6, 1908, Manchester, N. H. D. June 11, 1973, Manchester, N. H.

Year	Team	Games	BA	SA	AB	H	2B	3B	HR	HR%	R	RBI	BB	SO	SB	Pinch Hit AB	Pinch Hit H	PO	A	E	DP	TC/G	FA	G by Pos
1932	PIT N	47	.263	.331	118	31	6	1	0	0.0	13	10	9	7	0	3	1	111	19	2	1	3.1	.985	C-43
1933		30	.211	.233	90	19	2	0	0	0.0	5	8	2	6	0	3	0	100	22	2	1	4.6	.984	C-27
1934		82	.321	.388	237	76	12	2	0	0.0	27	22	30	23	3	4	1	297	20	7	3	4.3	.978	C-76
1935		97	.272	.318	302	82	9	1	1	0.3	35	30	48	26	1	3	1	425	64	17	2	5.4	.966	C-94
1936		88	.249	.306	281	70	9	2	1	0.4	22	31	22	41	0	1	0	342	62	10	6	4.8	.976	C-87

Tom Padden *continued*

Year	Team	Games	BA	SA	AB	H	2B	3B	HR	HR%	R	RBI	BB	SO	SB	Pinch Hit AB	Pinch Hit H	PO	A	E	DP	TC/G	FA	G by Pos
1937		35	.286	.306	98	28	2	0	0	0.0	14	8	13	11	1	1	0	143	28	3	4	5.1	.983	C-34
1943	2 teams	PHI N (17G –.293) WAS A (3G –.000)																						
"	total	20	.273	.273	44	12	0	0	0	0.0	6	1	3	7	0	2	0	64	7	0	2	3.9	1.000	C-18
7 yrs.		399	.272	.321	1170	318	40	6	2	0.2	122	110	127	121	5	17	3	1482	222	41	19	4.6	.977	C-379

Del Paddock

PADDOCK, DELMAR HAROLD BL TR 5′ 9″ 165 lbs.
B. June 8, 1887, Volga, S. D. D. Feb. 6, 1952, Remer, Minn.

Year	Team	Games	BA	SA	AB	H	2B	3B	HR	HR%	R	RBI	BB	SO	SB	Pinch Hit AB	Pinch Hit H	PO	A	E	DP	TC/G	FA	G by Pos
1912	2 teams	CHI A (1G –.000) NY A (45G –.288)																						
"	total	46	.287	.376	157	45	5	3	1	0.6	26	14	23		9	2	0	55	73	16	4	3.3	.889	3B-41, 2B-2, OF-1

Don Padgett

PADGETT, DON WILSON (Red) BL TR 6′ 190 lbs.
B. Dec. 5, 1911, Caroleen, N. C. D. Dec. 9, 1980, High Point, N. C.

Year	Team	Games	BA	SA	AB	H	2B	3B	HR	HR%	R	RBI	BB	SO	SB	Pinch Hit AB	Pinch Hit H	PO	A	E	DP	TC/G	FA	G by Pos
1937	STL N	123	.314	.457	446	140	22	6	10	2.2	62	74	30	43	4	13	4	225	9	11	5	2.2	.955	OF-109
1938		110	.271	.425	388	105	26	5	8	2.1	59	65	18	28	0	18	6	295	27	9	15	3.6	.973	OF-71, 1B-16, C-6
1939		92	.399	.554	233	93	15	3	5	2.1	38	53	18	11	1	21	4	276	18	7	6	4.6	.977	C-61, 1B-6
1940		93	.242	.388	240	58	15	1	6	2.5	24	41	26	14	1	16	3	244	34	11	5	3.9	.962	C-72, 1B-2
1941		107	.247	.349	324	80	18	0	5	1.5	39	44	21	16	0	22	3	189	7	9	1	2.5	.956	OF-62, C-18, 1B-2
1946	2 teams	BKN N (19G –.167) BOS N (44G –.255)																						
"	total	63	.234	.336	128	30	4	0	3	2.3	8	30	9	11	0	27	4	89	15	5	2	3.0	.954	C-36
1947	PHI N	75	.316	.380	158	50	8	1	0	0.0	14	24	16	5	0	31	8	111	16	5	1	3.4	.962	C-39
1948		36	.230	.270	74	17	3	0	0	0.0	3	7	3	2	0	13	2	64	2	3	0	3.6	.957	C-19
8 yrs.		699	.288	.415	1991	573	111	16	37	1.9	247	338	141	130	6	161	34	1493	128	60	35	3.2	.964	C-251, OF-242, 1B-26

Ernie Padgett

PADGETT, ERNEST KITCHEN (Red) BR TR 5′ 8″ 155 lbs.
B. Mar. 1, 1899, Philadelphia, Pa. D. Apr. 15, 1957, East Orange, N. J.

Year	Team	Games	BA	SA	AB	H	2B	3B	HR	HR%	R	RBI	BB	SO	SB	Pinch Hit AB	Pinch Hit H	PO	A	E	DP	TC/G	FA	G by Pos
1923	BOS N	4	.182	.182	11	2	0	0	0	0.0	3	0	2	0	0	1	0	14	12	1	4	9.0	.963	SS-2, 2B-1
1924		138	.255	.347	502	128	25	9	1	0.2	42	46	37	56	4	0	0	155	288	17	35	3.2	.963	3B-113, 2B-29
1925		86	.305	.395	256	78	9	7	0	0.0	31	29	14	14	3	15	4	127	160	13	30	4.2	.957	2B-47, SS-18, 3B-7
1926	CLE A	36	.210	.242	62	13	0	1	0	0.0	7	6	8	3	1	3	0	13	46	4	4	2.0	.937	3B-29, SS-2
1927		7	.286	.286	7	2	0	0	0	0.0	1	0	0	2	0	3	1	3	2	0	0	1.3	1.000	2B-4
5 yrs.		271	.266	.351	838	223	34	17	1	0.1	84	81	61	75	8	22	5	312	508	35	73	3.4	.959	3B-149, 2B-81, SS-22

Dennis Paepke

PAEPKE, DENNIS RAY BR TR 6′ 202 lbs.
B. Apr. 17, 1945, Long Beach, Calif.

Year	Team	Games	BA	SA	AB	H	2B	3B	HR	HR%	R	RBI	BB	SO	SB	Pinch Hit AB	Pinch Hit H	PO	A	E	DP	TC/G	FA	G by Pos
1969	KC A	12	.111	.148	27	3	1	0	0	0.0	2	0	2	3	0	4	0	56	2	0	0	7.3	1.000	C-8
1971		60	.204	.283	152	31	6	0	2	1.3	11	14	8	29	0	16	3	160	15	3	1	3.6	.983	C-32, OF-17
1972		2	.000	.000	6	0	0	0	0	0.0	0	0	1	2	0	0	0	14	2	3	0	9.5	.842	C-2
1974		6	.167	.167	12	2	0	0	0	0.0	0	0	1	2	0	1	0	10	2	0	1	2.4	1.000	C-4, OF-1
4 yrs.		80	.183	.249	197	36	7	0	2	1.0	13	14	12	36	0	21	3	240	21	6	2	4.2	.978	C-46, OF-18

Andy Pafko

PAFKO, ANDREW (Handy Andy, Pruschka) BR TR 6′ 190 lbs.
B. Feb. 25, 1921, Boyceville, Wis.

Year	Team	Games	BA	SA	AB	H	2B	3B	HR	HR%	R	RBI	BB	SO	SB	Pinch Hit AB	Pinch Hit H	PO	A	E	DP	TC/G	FA	G by Pos
1943	CHI N	13	.379	.431	58	22	3	0	0	0.0	7	10	2	5	1	0	0	25	0	0	0	1.9	1.000	OF-13
1944		128	.269	.350	469	126	16	2	6	1.3	47	62	28	23	2	5	1	333	24	6	4	3.0	.983	OF-123
1945		144	.298	.455	534	159	24	12	12	2.2	64	110	45	36	5	4	1	371	11	2	0	2.7	.995	OF-140
1946		65	.282	.380	234	66	6	4	3	1.3	18	39	27	15	4	1	0	165	13	4	4	2.8	.978	OF-64
1947		129	.302	.454	513	155	25	7	13	2.5	68	66	31	39	4	2	0	327	9	5	3	2.7	.985	OF-127
1948		142	.312	.516	548	171	30	2	26	4.7	82	101	50	50	3	2	1	125	314	29	29	3.4	.938	3B-139
1949		144	.281	.449	519	146	29	2	18	3.5	79	69	63	33	4	1	1	257	109	13	12	2.6	.966	OF-98, 3B-49
1950		146	.304	.591	514	156	24	8	36	7.0	95	92	69	32	4	2	0	342	12	8	1	2.5	.978	OF-144
1951	2 teams	CHI N (49G –.264) BKN N (84G –.249)																						
"	total	133	.255	.501	455	116	16	3	30	6.6	68	93	52	37	2	6	1	263	14	2	3	2.2	.993	OF-126
1952	BKN N	150	.287	.439	551	158	17	5	19	3.4	76	85	64	48	4	4	1	244	37	6	5	1.9	.979	OF-139, 3B-13
1953	MIL N	140	.297	.455	516	153	23	4	17	3.3	70	72	37	33	2	1	0	241	5	6	1	1.8	.976	OF-139
1954		138	.286	.427	510	146	22	4	14	2.7	61	69	37	36	1	0	0	245	9	8	3	1.9	.969	OF-138
1955		86	.266	.377	252	67	3	5	5	2.0	29	34	7	23	1	22	3	105	27	3	1	1.9	.978	OF-58, 3B-12
1956		45	.258	.376	93	24	5	0	2	2.2	15	9	10	13	0	12	3	43	2	1	0	1.2	.978	OF-37
1957		83	.277	.423	220	61	6	1	8	3.6	31	27	10	22	1	22	3	108	1	2	1	1.6	.982	OF-69
1958		95	.238	.348	164	39	7	1	3	1.8	17	23	15	17	0	13	3	107	2	0	0	1.2	1.000	OF-93
1959		71	.218	.324	142	31	8	2	1	0.7	17	15	14	15	0	13	2	87	1	2	0	1.4	.978	OF-64
17 yrs.		1852	.285	.449	6292	1796	264	62	213	3.4	844	976	561	477	38	110	20	3388	590	97	67	2.3	.976	OF-1572, 3B-213
WORLD SERIES																								
1945	CHI N	7	.214	.357	28	6	2	1	0	0.0	5	2	2	5	0	0	0	24	2	1	0	3.9	.963	OF-7
1952	BKN N	7	.190	.190	21	4	0	0	0	0.0	0	2	0	4	0	2	0	12	1	0	0	2.6	1.000	OF-5
1957	MIL N	6	.214	.214	14	3	0	0	0	0.0	1	0	0	1	0	1	0	9	0	0	0	1.8	1.000	OF-5
1958		4	.333	.444	9	3	1	0	0	0.0	0	1	0	0	0	0	0	8	0	0	0	2.0	1.000	OF-4
4 yrs.		24	.222	.292	72	16	3	1	0	0.0	6	5	2	10	0	3	0	53	3	1	0	2.7	.982	OF-21

Jose Pagan

PAGAN, JOSE ANTONIO BR TR 5′ 9″ 160 lbs.
Born Jose Antonio Pagan (Rodriguez).
B. May 5, 1935, Barceloneta, Puerto Rico.

Year	Team	Games	BA	SA	AB	H	2B	3B	HR	HR%	R	RBI	BB	SO	SB	Pinch Hit AB	Pinch Hit H	PO	A	E	DP	TC/G	FA	G by Pos
1959	SF N	31	.174	.196	46	8	1	0	0	0.0	7	1	2	8	1	4	0	17	26	4	3	1.8	.915	3B-18, SS-5, 2B-3
1960		18	.286	.408	49	14	2	2	0	0.0	8	2	1	6	2	6	0	16	17	3	2	3.0	.917	SS-11, 3B-1
1961		134	.253	.332	434	110	15	2	5	1.2	38	46	31	45	8	1	1	230	334	21	55	4.3	.964	SS-132, OF-4
1962		164	.259	.359	580	150	25	6	7	1.2	73	57	47	77	13	0	0	286	461	21	84	4.7	.973	SS-164
1963		148	.234	.300	483	113	12	1	6	1.2	46	39	26	67	10	4	1	262	375	20	69	4.5	.970	SS-143, OF-1, 2B-1
1964		134	.223	.264	367	82	10	1	1	0.3	33	28	35	66	5	0	0	210	303	22	52	3.8	.959	SS-132, OF-8
1965	2 teams	SF N (26G –.205) PIT N (42G –.237)																						
"	total	68	.215	.256	121	26	5	0	0	0.0	16	6	9	16	2	7	1	47	97	12	12	3.3	.923	SS-33, 3B-15
1966	PIT N	109	.264	.370	368	97	15	6	4	1.1	44	54	13	38	0	10	2	86	219	18	26	3.0	.944	3B-83, SS-18, OF-3, 2B-3
1967		81	.289	.351	211	61	6	2	1	0.5	17	19	10	28	1	13	4	73	109	7	14	2.8	.963	3B-25, OF-23, SS-16, 2B-2, C-1
1968		80	.221	.350	163	36	7	1	4	2.5	24	21	11	32	2	22	5	40	65	7	7	1.9	.938	3B-30, OF-19, SS-8, 2B-2, 1B-1

Jose Pagan *continued*

Year	Team	Games	BA	SA	AB	H	2B	3B	HR	HR%	R	RBI	BB	SO	SB	Pinch Hit AB	Pinch Hit H	PO	A	E	DP	TC/G	FA	G by Pos
1969		108	.285	.453	274	78	11	4	9	3.3	29	42	17	46	1	42	**19**	56	78	5	7	2.0	.964	3B-44, OF-23, 2B-1
1970		95	.265	.426	230	61	14	1	7	3.0	21	29	20	24	1	35	9	46	91	6	14	2.4	.958	3B-53, OF-4, 1B-1, 2B-1
1971		57	.241	.342	158	38	1	0	5	3.2	16	15	16	25	0	12	2	53	62	2	9	2.5	.983	3B-41, OF-3, 1B-2
1972		53	.252	.394	127	32	9	0	3	2.4	11	8	5	17	0	22	6	27	37	7	3	2.1	.901	3B-32, OF-2
1973	PHI N	46	.205	.269	78	16	5	0	0	0.0	4	5	1	15	0	29	6	21	18	1	2	1.7	.975	3B-16, 1B-5, OF-2, 2B-1
15 yrs.		1326	.250	.344	3689	922	138	26	52	1.4	387	372	244	510	46	207	56	1470	2292	156	359	3.4	.960	SS-662, 3B-358, OF-92, 2B-14, 1B-9, C-1
LEAGUE CHAMPIONSHIP SERIES																								
1970	PIT N	1	.333	.333	3	1	0	0	0	0.0	0	0	1	1	0	0	0	0	4	0	0	4.0	1.000	3B-1
1971		1	.000	.000	1	0	0	0	0	0.0	0	0	0	0	0	0	0	1	2	0	0	3.0	1.000	3B-1
2 yrs.		2	.250	.250	4	1	0	0	0	0.0	0	0	1	1	0	0	0	1	6	0	0	3.5	1.000	3B-2
WORLD SERIES																								
1962	SF N	7	.368	.526	19	7	0	0	1	5.3	2	2	0	1	0	0	0	8	14	1	2	3.3	.957	SS-7
1971	PIT N	4	.267	.400	15	4	2	0	0	0.0	0	2	0	1	0	0	0	2	8	0	1	2.5	1.000	3B-4
2 yrs.		11	.324	.471	34	11	2	0	1	2.9	2	4	0	2	0	0	0	10	22	1	3	3.0	.970	SS-7, 3B-4

Mike Page

PAGE, MICHAEL RANDY
B. July 12, 1940, Woodruff, S. C.
BL TR 6′ 2½″ 210 lbs.

Year	Team	Games	BA	SA	AB	H	2B	3B	HR	HR%	R	RBI	BB	SO	SB	Pinch Hit AB	Pinch Hit H	PO	A	E	DP	TC/G	FA	G by Pos
1968	ATL N	20	.179	.179	28	5	0	0	0	0.0	1	1	1	9	0	13	1	5	0	0	0	0.8	1.000	OF-6

Mitchell Page

PAGE, MITCHELL OTIS
B. Oct. 15, 1951, Los Angeles, Calif.
BL TR 6′ 2″ 205 lbs.

Year	Team	Games	BA	SA	AB	H	2B	3B	HR	HR%	R	RBI	BB	SO	SB	Pinch Hit AB	Pinch Hit H	PO	A	E	DP	TC/G	FA	G by Pos
1977	OAK A	145	.307	.521	501	154	28	8	21	4.2	85	75	78	95	42	6	2	279	11	14	0	2.2	.954	OF-133, DH-8
1978		147	.285	.459	516	147	25	7	17	3.3	62	70	53	95	23	1	0	211	4	6	0	1.5	.973	OF-114, DH-33
1979		133	.247	.335	478	118	11	2	9	1.9	51	42	52	93	17	1	0	6	0	0	0	0.0	1.000	DH-126, OF-4
1980		110	.244	.443	348	85	10	4	17	4.9	58	51	35	87	14	19	2	0	0	0	0	0.0	.000	DH-101
1981		34	.141	.283	92	13	1	0	4	4.3	9	13	7	29	2	4	1	0	0	0	0	0.0	.000	DH-29
1982		31	.256	.474	78	20	5	0	4	5.1	14	7	7	24	3	3	0	0	0	0	0	0.0	.000	DH-24
1983		57	.241	.278	79	19	3	0	0	0.0	16	1	10	22	3	12	3	12	0	0	0	0.3	1.000	DH-34, OF-10
1984	PIT N	16	.333	.417	12	4	1	0	0	0.0	2	0	3	4	0	12	4	0	0	0	0	0.0	—	
8 yrs.		673	.266	.429	2104	560	84	21	72	3.4	297	259	245	449	104	58	12	508	15	20	0	0.9	.963	DH-355, OF-261

Karl Pagel

PAGEL, KARL DOUGLAS
B. Mar. 29, 1955, Madison, Wis.
BL TL 6′ 2″ 188 lbs.

Year	Team	Games	BA	SA	AB	H	2B	3B	HR	HR%	R	RBI	BB	SO	SB	Pinch Hit AB	Pinch Hit H	PO	A	E	DP	TC/G	FA	G by Pos
1978	CHI N	2	.000	.000	2	0	0	0	0	0.0	0	0	0	2	0	2	0	0	0	0	0	0.0	—	
1979		1	.000	.000	1	0	0	0	0	0.0	0	0	0	1	0	1	0	0	0	0	0	0.0	—	
1981	CLE A	14	.267	.733	15	4	0	2	1	6.7	3	4	4	1	0	5	1	28	6	0	5	4.9	1.000	1B-6, DH-1
1982		23	.167	.167	18	3	0	0	0	0.0	3	2	7	11	0	8	2	30	2	1	2	3.0	.970	1B-10, DH-1
1983		8	.300	.300	20	6	0	0	0	0.0	1	1	0	5	0	3	1	0	0	1	0	0.2	.000	DH-5, OF-1
5 yrs.		48	.232	.357	56	13	0	2	1	1.8	7	7	11	20	0	19	4	58	8	2	7	2.8	.971	1B-16, DH-7, OF-1

Jim Pagliaroni

PAGLIARONI, JAMES VINCENT (Pag)
B. Dec. 8, 1937, Dearborn, Mich.
BR TR 6′ 4″ 210 lbs.

Year	Team	Games	BA	SA	AB	H	2B	3B	HR	HR%	R	RBI	BB	SO	SB	Pinch Hit AB	Pinch Hit H	PO	A	E	DP	TC/G	FA	G by Pos
1955	BOS A	1	—	—	0	0	0	0	0	—	0	1	0	0	0	0	0	0	0	0	0	0.0	.000	C-1
1960		28	.306	.548	62	19	5	2	2	3.2	7	9	13	11	0	7	1	91	5	1	0	5.4	.990	C-18
1961		120	.242	.415	376	91	17	0	16	4.3	50	58	55	74	1	14	3	586	39	10	5	5.9	.984	C-108
1962		90	.258	.438	260	67	14	0	11	4.2	39	37	36	55	2	13	2	411	33	6	4	6.2	.987	C-73
1963	PIT N	92	.230	.381	252	58	5	0	11	4.4	27	26	36	57	0	9	3	435	56	6	4	5.8	.988	C-85
1964		97	.295	.454	302	89	12	3	10	3.3	33	36	41	56	1	1	0	584	42	5	5	6.6	.992	C-96
1965		134	.268	.432	403	108	15	0	17	4.2	42	65	41	84	0	4	1	669	42	4	14	5.5	.994	C-131
1966		123	.235	.377	374	88	20	0	11	2.9	37	49	50	71	0	7	1	613	37	2	6	5.5	.997	C-118
1967		44	.200	.230	100	20	1	1	0	0.0	4	9	16	26	0	7	0	172	13	3	6	4.9	.984	C-38
1968	OAK A	66	.246	.357	199	49	4	0	6	3.0	19	20	24	42	0	3	1	375	16	1	3	6.2	.997	C-63
1969	2 teams	OAK A (14G –.148)	SEA A (40G –.264)																					
″	total	54	.241	.423	137	33	5	1	6	4.4	11	16	18	18	0	16	6	216	19	3	3	6.1	.987	C-36, 1B-2, OF-1
11 yrs.		849	.252	.407	2465	622	98	7	90	3.7	269	326	330	494	4	81	18	4152	302	41	50	5.8	.991	C-767, 1B-2, OF-1

Mike Pagliarulo

PAGLIARULO, MICHAEL TIMOTHY (Pags)
B. Mar. 15, 1960, Medford, Mass.
BL TR 6′ 2″ 195 lbs.

Year	Team	Games	BA	SA	AB	H	2B	3B	HR	HR%	R	RBI	BB	SO	SB	Pinch Hit AB	Pinch Hit H	PO	A	E	DP	TC/G	FA	G by Pos
1984	NY A	67	.239	.448	201	48	15	3	7	3.5	24	34	15	46	0	0	0	44	106	7	16	2.3	.955	3B-67
1985		138	.239	.442	380	91	16	2	19	5.0	55	62	45	86	0	19	6	67	187	13	15	2.0	.951	3B-134
1986		149	.238	.464	504	120	24	3	28	5.6	71	71	54	120	4	9	1	104	283	19	25	2.8	.953	3B-143, SS-2
1987		150	.234	.479	522	122	26	3	32	6.1	76	87	53	111	1	8	0	97	297	17	35	2.8	.959	3B-147, 1B-1
1988		125	.216	.367	444	96	20	1	15	3.4	46	67	37	104	1	9	0	82	232	19	16	2.7	.943	3B-124
1989	2 teams	NY A (74G –.197)	SD N (50G –.196)																					
″	total	124	.197	.299	371	73	17	0	7	1.9	31	30	37	82	3	10	1	44	205	17	9	2.2	.936	3B-118, DH-1
1990	SD N	128	.254	.374	398	101	23	2	7	1.8	29	38	39	66	1	15	3	79	200	13	16	2.5	.955	3B-116
1991	MIN A	121	.279	.384	365	102	20	0	6	1.6	38	36	21	55	1	6	1	56	248	11	30	2.6	.965	3B-118, 2B-1
1992		42	.200	.238	105	21	4	0	0	0.0	10	9	1	17	1	12	2	11	64	3	3	2.1	.962	3B-37, DH-1
1993	2 teams	MIN A (83G –.292)	BAL A (33G –.325)																					
″	total	116	.303	.465	370	112	25	4	9	2.4	55	44	26	49	6	9	2	95	186	8	20	2.6	.972	3B-107, 1B-4
1995	TEX A	86	.232	.349	241	56	16	0	4	1.7	27	27	15	49	0	16	5	111	123	7	17	3.1	.971	3B-68, 1B-11
11 yrs.		1246	.241	.407	3901	942	206	18	134	3.4	462	505	343	785	18	113	21	790	2131	134	202	2.5	.956	3B-1179, 1B-16, DH-2, SS-2, 2B-1
LEAGUE CHAMPIONSHIP SERIES																								
1991	MIN A	5	.333	.600	15	5	1	0	1	6.7	4	3	0	2	0	1	1	4	10	0	1	2.8	1.000	3B-5
WORLD SERIES																								
1991	MIN A	6	.273	.545	11	3	0	0	1	9.1	1	2	1	2	0	4	0	3	3	0	0	1.0	1.000	3B-6

Tom Pagnozzi

PAGNOZZI, THOMAS ALAN
B. July 30, 1962, Tucson, Ariz.
BR TR 6′ 190 lbs.

Year	Team	Games	BA	SA	AB	H	2B	3B	HR	HR%	R	RBI	BB	SO	SB	Pinch Hit AB	Pinch Hit H	PO	A	E	DP	TC/G	FA	G by Pos
1987	STL N	27	.188	.333	48	9	1	0	2	4.2	8	9	4	13	1	7	2	61	5	0	2	2.5	1.000	C-25, 1B-1
1988		81	.282	.328	195	55	9	0	0	0.0	17	15	11	32	0	26	4	340	30	4	11	6.1	.989	1B-28, C-28, 3B-5

Tom Pagnozzi *continued*

Year	Team	Lg	Games	BA	SA	AB	H	2B	3B	HR	HR%	R	RBI	BB	SO	SB	Pinch Hit AB	Pinch Hit H	PO	A	E	DP	TC/G	FA	G by Pos
1989			52	.150	.175	80	12	2	0	0	0.0	3	3	6	19	0	15	2	100	9	2	1	2.7	.982	C-38, 1B-2, 3B-1
1990			69	.277	.373	220	61	15	0	2	0.9	20	23	14	37	1	4	2	345	39	4	4	6.0	.990	C-63, 1B-2
1991			140	.264	.351	459	121	24	5	2	0.4	38	57	36	63	9	0	0	682	81	7	9	5.4	.991	C-139, 1B-3
1992			139	.249	.359	485	121	26	3	7	1.4	33	44	28	64	2	3	0	688	53	1	10	5.4	.999	C-138
1993			92	.258	.373	330	85	15	1	7	2.1	31	41	19	30	1	1	0	421	44	4	4	5.1	.991	C-92
1994			70	.272	.416	243	66	12	1	7	2.9	21	40	21	39	0	0	0	370	41	1	3	5.8	.998	C-70, 1B-1
1995			62	.215	.315	219	47	14	1	2	0.9	17	15	11	31	0	1	0	336	38	2	1	6.2	.995	C-61
9 yrs.			732	.253	.353	2279	577	118	11	29	1.3	188	247	150	328	14	57	10	3343	340	25	45	5.3	.993	C-654, 1B-37, 3B-6
LEAGUE CHAMPIONSHIP SERIES																									
1987	STL	N	1	.000	.000	1	0	0	0	0	0.0	0	0	0	0	0	1	0	0	0	0	0	0.0	—	
WORLD SERIES																									
1987	STL	N	2	.250	.250	4	1	0	0	0	0.0	0	0	0	0	0	1	0	0	0	0	0	0.0	.000	DH-1

Rey Palacios

PALACIOS, ROBERT REY BR TR 5′10″ 190 lbs.
B. Nov. 8, 1962, Brooklyn, N. Y.

Year	Team	Lg	Games	BA	SA	AB	H	2B	3B	HR	HR%	R	RBI	BB	SO	SB	Pinch Hit AB	Pinch Hit H	PO	A	E	DP	TC/G	FA	G by Pos
1988	KC	A	5	.091	.091	11	1	0	0	0	0.0	2	0	0	4	0	1	0	17	1	0	0	4.5	1.000	C-3, 3B-1
1989			55	.170	.277	47	8	2	0	1	2.1	12	8	2	14	0	1	0	96	15	2	8	2.1	.982	3B-21, 1B-18, C-13, DH-2, OF-1
1990			41	.232	.393	56	13	3	0	2	3.6	8	9	5	24	2	1	0	122	7	1	2	3.4	.992	C-27, 1B-7, 3B-3, OF-1
3 yrs.			101	.193	.316	114	22	5	0	3	2.6	22	17	7	42	2	3	0	235	23	3	10	2.7	.989	C-43, 1B-25, 3B-25, DH-2, OF-2

Orlando Palmeiro

PALMEIRO, ORLANDO BL TR 5′11″ 155 lbs.
B. Jan. 19, 1969, Hoboken, N. J.

Year	Team	Lg	Games	BA	SA	AB	H	2B	3B	HR	HR%	R	RBI	BB	SO	SB	Pinch Hit AB	Pinch Hit H	PO	A	E	DP	TC/G	FA	G by Pos
1995	CAL	A	15	.350	.350	20	7	0	0	0	0.0	3	1	1	1	0	9	3	7	0	0	0	0.9	1.000	OF-7, DH-1

Rafael Palmeiro

PALMEIRO, RAFAEL BL TL 6′ 180 lbs.
Born Rafael Palmeiro (Corrales).
B. Sept. 24, 1964, Havana, Cuba.

Year	Team	Lg	Games	BA	SA	AB	H	2B	3B	HR	HR%	R	RBI	BB	SO	SB	Pinch Hit AB	Pinch Hit H	PO	A	E	DP	TC/G	FA	G by Pos
1986	CHI	N	22	.247	.425	73	18	4	0	3	4.1	9	12	4	6	1	2	0	34	2	4	1	2.0	.900	OF-20
1987			84	.276	.543	221	61	15	1	14	6.3	32	30	20	26	2	27	5	176	9	1	16	3.0	.995	OF-45, 1B-18
1988			152	.307	.436	580	178	41	5	8	1.4	75	53	38	34	12	5	0	322	11	5	2	2.2	.985	OF-147, 1B-5
1989	TEX	A	156	.275	.374	559	154	23	4	8	1.4	76	64	63	48	4	3	1	1167	119	12	106	8.5	.991	1B-147, DH-6
1990			154	.319	.468	598	**191**	35	6	14	2.3	72	89	40	59	3	4	0	1215	91	7	123	8.6	.995	1B-146, DH-6
1991			159	.322	.532	631	203	**49**	3	26	4.1	115	88	68	72	4	3	2	1305	96	12	119	8.9	.992	1B-157, DH-2
1992			159	.268	.434	608	163	27	4	22	3.6	84	85	72	83	2	3	0	1251	143	7	131	8.9	.995	1B-156, DH-2
1993			160	.295	.554	597	176	40	2	37	6.2	**124**	105	73	85	22	1	0	1388	147	5	133	9.6	.997	1B-160
1994	BAL	A	111	.319	.550	436	139	32	0	23	5.3	82	76	54	63	7	0	0	958	67	4	86	9.3	.996	1B-111
1995			143	.310	.583	554	172	30	2	39	7.0	89	104	62	65	3	1	0	1178	123	4	120	9.2	.997	1B-142
10 yrs.			1300	.300	.491	4857	1455	296	27	194	4.0	758	706	494	541	60	49	8	8994	808	61	837	7.8	.994	1B-1042, OF-212, DH-16

Dean Palmer

PALMER, DEAN WILLIAM BR TR 6′ 1″ 175 lbs.
B. Dec. 27, 1968, Tallahassee, Fla.

Year	Team	Lg	Games	BA	SA	AB	H	2B	3B	HR	HR%	R	RBI	BB	SO	SB	Pinch Hit AB	Pinch Hit H	PO	A	E	DP	TC/G	FA	G by Pos
1989	TEX	A	16	.105	.211	19	2	2	0	0	0.0	0	1	0	12	0	6	0	3	4	2	0	0.6	.778	3B-6, DH-6, SS-1, OF-1
1991			81	.187	.403	268	50	9	2	15	5.6	38	37	32	98	0	5	2	69	75	9	6	1.8	.941	3B-50, OF-29, DH-5
1992			152	.229	.420	541	124	25	0	26	4.8	74	72	62	**154**	10	4	2	124	254	22	24	2.7	.945	3B-150
1993			148	.245	.503	519	127	31	2	33	6.4	88	96	53	154	11	0	0	86	258	29	21	2.5	.922	3B-148, SS-1
1994			93	.246	.465	342	84	14	2	19	5.6	50	59	26	89	3	3	1	50	181	22	7	2.8	.913	3B-91
1995			36	.336	.613	119	40	6	0	9	7.6	30	24	21	21	1	1	0	19	73	5	7	2.7	.948	3B-36
6 yrs.			526	.236	.460	1808	427	87	6	102	5.6	280	289	194	528	25	19	5	351	845	89	65	2.5	.931	3B-481, OF-30, DH-11, SS-2

Eddie Palmer

PALMER, EDWIN HENRY (Baldy) BR TR 5′ 9½″ 175 lbs.
B. June 1, 1893, Petty, Tex. D. Jan. 9, 1983, Marlow, Okla.

Year	Team	Lg	Games	BA	SA	AB	H	2B	3B	HR	HR%	R	RBI	BB	SO	SB	Pinch Hit AB	Pinch Hit H	PO	A	E	DP	TC/G	FA	G by Pos
1917	PHI	A	16	.212	.231	52	11	1	0	0	0.0	7	5	7	7	1	2	0	16	32	6	1	3.9	.889	3B-13, SS-1

Joe Palmisano

PALMISANO, JOSEPH BR TR 5′ 8″ 160 lbs.
B. Nov. 19, 1902, West Point, Ga. D. Nov. 5, 1971, Albuquerque, N. M.

Year	Team	Lg	Games	BA	SA	AB	H	2B	3B	HR	HR%	R	RBI	BB	SO	SB	Pinch Hit AB	Pinch Hit H	PO	A	E	DP	TC/G	FA	G by Pos
1931	PHI	A	19	.227	.273	44	10	2	0	0	0.0	5	4	6	3	0	2	0	45	4	2	2	3.0	.961	C-16, 2B-1

Stan Palys

PALYS, STANLEY FRANCIS BR TR 6′ 2″ 190 lbs.
B. May 1, 1930, Blakely, Pa.

Year	Team	Lg	Games	BA	SA	AB	H	2B	3B	HR	HR%	R	RBI	BB	SO	SB	Pinch Hit AB	Pinch Hit H	PO	A	E	DP	TC/G	FA	G by Pos
1953	PHI	N	2	.000	.000	2	0	0	0	0	0.0	0	0	1	0	0	0	0	0	0	0	0	0.0	.000	OF-1
1954			2	.250	.250	4	1	0	0	0	0.0	0	0	1	1	0	1	0	2	0	0	0	2.0	1.000	OF-1
1955	2 teams		PHI N (15G –.288) CIN N (79G –.230)																						
″	total		94	.241	.391	274	66	17	0	8	2.9	37	38	18	40	2	22	4	146	4	1	0	2.1	.993	OF-70, 1B-1
1956	CIN	N	40	.226	.340	53	12	0	0	2	3.8	5	5	6	13	0	24	6	13	0	1	0	1.4	.929	OF-10
4 yrs.			138	.237	.378	333	79	17	0	10	3.0	42	43	26	54	2	47	10	161	4	2	0	2.0	.988	OF-82, 1B-1

Jim Pankovits

PANKOVITS, JAMES FRANKLIN BR TR 5′10″ 170 lbs.
B. Aug. 6, 1955, Pennington Gap, Va.

Year	Team	Lg	Games	BA	SA	AB	H	2B	3B	HR	HR%	R	RBI	BB	SO	SB	Pinch Hit AB	Pinch Hit H	PO	A	E	DP	TC/G	FA	G by Pos
1984	HOU	N	53	.284	.407	81	23	7	0	1	1.2	6	14	2	20	2	40	9	22	22	3	7	2.1	.936	2B-15, SS-4, OF-3
1985			75	.244	.331	172	42	3	0	4	2.3	24	14	17	29	1	23	5	81	38	2	8	2.2	.983	OF-33, 2B-21, SS-1, 3B-1
1986			70	.283	.381	113	32	6	1	1	0.9	12	7	11	25	1	38	11	42	58	4	10	3.3	.962	2B-26, OF-5, C-1
1987			50	.230	.311	61	14	2	0	1	1.6	7	8	6	13	2	32	7	19	15	0	3	1.8	1.000	2B-9, OF-6, 3B-4
1988			68	.221	.329	140	31	7	1	2	1.4	13	12	8	28	2	27	2	48	80	11	20	3.2	.921	2B-31, 3B-11, 1B-2
1990	BOS	A	2	—	—	0	0	0	0	0	—	0	0	0	0	0	0	0	0	0	0	0	0.0	.000	2B-2
6 yrs.			318	.250	.349	567	142	25	2	9	1.6	62	55	44	115	8	160	34	212	213	20	48	2.5	.955	2B-104, OF-47, 3B-16, SS-5, 1B-2, C-1
LEAGUE CHAMPIONSHIP SERIES																									
1986	HOU	N	2	.000	.000	2	0	0	0	0	0.0	0	0	0	1	0	2	0	0	0	0	0	0.0	—	

Ken Pape

PAPE, KENNETH WAYNE BR TR 5′11″ 195 lbs.
B. Oct. 1, 1951, San Antonio, Tex.

Year	Team	Lg	Games	BA	SA	AB	H	2B	3B	HR	HR%	R	RBI	BB	SO	SB	Pinch Hit AB	Pinch Hit H	PO	A	E	DP	TC/G	FA	G by Pos
1976	TEX	A	21	.217	.391	23	5	1	0	1	4.3	7	4	3	2	0	1	0	9	23	2	4	2.4	.941	SS-6, 3B-4, DH-3, 2B-1

Stan Papi

PAPI, STANLEY GERARD
B. Feb. 4, 1951, Fresno, Calif.
BR TR 6′ 170 lbs.

Year	Team	Games	BA	SA	AB	H	2B	3B	HR	HR%	R	RBI	BB	SO	SB	Pinch Hit AB	Pinch Hit H	PO	A	E	DP	TC/G	FA	G by Pos
1974	**STL N**	8	.250	.250	4	1	0	0	0	0.0	0	1	0	0	0	1	0	6	3	0	3	1.1	1.000	SS-7, 2B-1
1977	**MON N**	13	.233	.326	43	10	2	1	0	0.0	5	4	1	9	1	0	0	10	15	2	0	2.1	.926	3B-10, SS-2, 2B-1
1978		67	.230	.303	152	35	11	0	0	0.0	15	11	10	28	0	24	3	56	88	6	13	3.6	.960	SS-22, 3B-15, 2B-5
1979	**BOS A**	50	.188	.282	117	22	8	0	1	0.9	9	6	5	20	0	3	0	61	118	3	24	3.8	.984	2B-26, SS-21, DH-1
1980	**2 teams**	**BOS A** (1G –.000) **DET A** (46G –.237)																						
″	**total**	47	.237	.412	114	27	3	4	3	2.6	12	17	5	24	0	4	1	68	80	5	19	3.1	.967	2B-31, 3B-12, SS-5, 1B-1
1981	**DET A**	40	.204	.344	93	19	2	1	3	3.2	8	12	3	18	1	4	1	16	51	4	3	1.9	.944	3B-32, DH-3, OF-1, 2B-1, 1B-1
6 yrs.		225	.218	.331	523	114	26	6	7	1.3	49	51	24	99	2	36	5	217	355	20	62	3.0	.966	3B-69, 2B-65, SS-57, DH-4, 1B-2, OF-1

Erik Pappas

PAPPAS, ERIK DANIEL
B. Apr. 25, 1966, Chicago, Ill.
BR TR 6′ 190 lbs.

Year	Team	Games	BA	SA	AB	H	2B	3B	HR	HR%	R	RBI	BB	SO	SB	Pinch Hit AB	Pinch Hit H	PO	A	E	DP	TC/G	FA	G by Pos
1991	**CHI N**	7	.176	.176	17	3	0	0	0	0.0	1	2	1	5	0	1	1	35	1	0	0	6.0	1.000	C-6
1993	**STL N**	82	.276	.342	228	63	12	0	1	0.4	25	28	35	35	1	3	0	337	32	6	6	4.6	.984	C-63, OF-16, 1B-2
1994		15	.091	.114	44	4	1	0	0	0.0	8	5	10	13	0	0	0	80	4	4	1	5.9	.955	C-15
3 yrs.		104	.242	.298	289	70	13	0	1	0.3	34	35	46	53	1	4	1	452	37	10	7	4.9	.980	C-84, OF-16, 1B-2

Craig Paquette

PAQUETTE, CRAIG HAROLD
B. Mar. 28, 1969, Long Beach, Calif.
BR TR 6′ 190 lbs.

Year	Team	Games	BA	SA	AB	H	2B	3B	HR	HR%	R	RBI	BB	SO	SB	Pinch Hit AB	Pinch Hit H	PO	A	E	DP	TC/G	FA	G by Pos
1993	**OAK A**	105	.219	.382	393	86	20	4	12	3.1	35	46	14	108	4	4	1	82	165	13	17	2.5	.950	3B-104, OF-1, DH-1
1994		14	.143	.184	49	7	2	0	0	0.0	0	0	0	14	1	1	0	14	22	0	3	2.6	1.000	3B-14
1995		105	.226	.417	283	64	13	1	13	4.6	42	49	12	88	5	8	3	72	91	8	18	1.6	.953	3B-75, OF-20, SS-8, 1B-3
3 yrs.		224	.217	.382	725	157	35	5	25	3.4	77	95	26	210	10	13	4	168	278	21	38	2.1	.955	3B-193, OF-21, SS-8, 1B-3, DH-1

Al Pardo

PARDO, ALBERTO JUDAS
B. Sept. 8, 1962, Oviedo, Spain.
BB TR 6′ 2″ 187 lbs.

Year	Team	Games	BA	SA	AB	H	2B	3B	HR	HR%	R	RBI	BB	SO	SB	Pinch Hit AB	Pinch Hit H	PO	A	E	DP	TC/G	FA	G by Pos
1985	**BAL A**	34	.133	.147	75	10	1	0	0	0.0	3	1	3	15	0	7	0	131	7	3	0	4.9	.979	C-29
1986		16	.137	.216	51	7	1	0	1	2.0	3	3	0	14	0	1	0	70	5	1	1	5.1	.987	C-14, DH-1
1988	**PHI N**	2	.000	.000	2	0	0	0	0	0.0	0	0	0	2	0	0	0	2	0	0	0	1.0	1.000	C-2
1989		1	.000	.000	1	0	0	0	0	0.0	0	0	0	0	0	0	0	3	0	0	0	3.0	1.000	C-1
4 yrs.		53	.132	.171	129	17	2	0	1	0.8	6	4	3	31	0	8	0	206	12	4	1	4.7	.982	C-46, DH-1

Johnny Paredes

PAREDES, JHONNY ALFONSO
Born Jhonny Alfonso Paredes (Isambert).
B. Sept. 2, 1962, Maracaibo, Venezuela.
BR TR 5′11″ 165 lbs.

Year	Team	Games	BA	SA	AB	H	2B	3B	HR	HR%	R	RBI	BB	SO	SB	Pinch Hit AB	Pinch Hit H	PO	A	E	DP	TC/G	FA	G by Pos
1988	**MON N**	35	.187	.242	91	17	2	0	1	1.1	6	10	9	17	5	2	2	46	77	3	18	4.3	.976	2B-28, OF-1
1990	**2 teams**	**DET A** (6G –.125) **MON N** (3G –.333)																						
″	**total**	9	.214	.286	14	3	1	0	0	0.0	2	1	2	0	0	1	0	5	14	2	4	3.5	.905	2B-6
1991	**DET A**	16	.333	.333	18	6	0	0	0	0.0	4	0	0	1	1	2	0	11	12	1	5	2.2	.958	2B-7, DH-2, SS-1, 3B-1
3 yrs.		60	.211	.260	123	26	3	0	1	0.8	12	11	11	18	6	5	2	62	103	6	27	3.7	.965	2B-41, DH-2, SS-1, 3B-1, OF-1

Freddy Parent

PARENT, FREDERICK ALFRED
B. Nov. 25, 1875, Biddeford, Me. D. Nov. 2, 1972, Sanford, Me.
BR TR 5′ 7″ 154 lbs.

Year	Team	Games	BA	SA	AB	H	2B	3B	HR	HR%	R	RBI	BB	SO	SB	Pinch Hit AB	Pinch Hit H	PO	A	E	DP	TC/G	FA	G by Pos
1899	**STL N**	2	.125	.125	8	1	0	0	0	0.0	0	1	0		0	0	0	3	5	1	1	4.5	.889	2B-2
1901	**BOS A**	138	.306	.408	517	158	23	9	4	0.8	87	59	41		16	0	0	260	446	63	52	5.6	.918	SS-138
1902		138	.275	.374	**567**	156	31	8	3	0.5	91	62	24		16	0	0	287	496	58	60	6.1	.931	SS-138
1903		139	.304	.441	560	170	31	17	4	0.7	83	80	13		24	0	0	296	456	57	36	5.8	.930	SS-139
1904		155	.291	.389	591	172	22	9	6	1.0	85	77	28		20	0	0	327	493	63	44	5.7	.929	SS-155
1905		153	.234	.277	602	141	16	5	0	0.0	55	33	47		25	0	0	294	461	66	48	5.4	.920	SS-153
1906		149	.235	.297	600	141	14	10	1	0.2	67	49	31		16	0	0	320	480	59	49	5.8	.931	SS-143, 2B-6
1907		114	.276	.355	409	113	19	5	1	0.2	51	26	22		12	12	2	195	191	25	20	4.0	.939	OF-47, SS-43, 3B-7, 2B-5
1908	**CHI A**	119	.207	.251	391	81	7	5	0	0.0	28	35	50		9	0	0	212	442	49	33	6.0	.930	SS-118
1909		136	.261	.303	472	123	10	5	0	0.0	61	30	46		32	0	0	255	363	41	34	4.8	.938	SS-98, OF-37, 2B-1
1910		81	.178	.221	258	46	6	1	1	0.4	23	16	29		14	0	0	119	55	7	5	2.3	.961	OF-62, 2B-11, SS-4, 3B-1
1911		3	.444	.556	9	4	1	0	0	0.0	2	3	2		0	0	0	5	10	0	0	5.0	1.000	2B-3
12 yrs.		1327	.262	.340	4984	1306	180	74	20	0.4	633	471	333		184	12	2	2573	3898	489	382	5.3	.930	SS-1129, OF-146, 2B-28, 3B-8
WORLD SERIES																								
1903	**BOS A**	8	.281	.469	32	9	0	3 **4th**	0	0.0	8	3	1	1	0	0	0	18	30	2	2	6.3	.960	SS-8

Mark Parent

PARENT, MARK ALAN
B. Sept. 16, 1961, Ashland, Ore.
BR TR 6′ 5″ 215 lbs.

Year	Team	Games	BA	SA	AB	H	2B	3B	HR	HR%	R	RBI	BB	SO	SB	Pinch Hit AB	Pinch Hit H	PO	A	E	DP	TC/G	FA	G by Pos
1986	**SD N**	8	.143	.143	14	2	0	0	0	0.0	1	0	1	3	0	4	0	16	0	2	0	6.0	.889	C-3
1987		12	.080	.080	25	2	0	0	0	0.0	0	2	0	9	0	2	0	36	3	0	0	3.9	1.000	C-10
1988		41	.195	.373	118	23	3	0	6	5.1	9	15	6	23	0	3	1	203	15	3	3	6.1	.986	C-36
1989		52	.191	.369	141	27	4	0	7	5.0	12	21	8	34	1	9	2	246	17	0	2	6.3	1.000	C-41, 1B-1
1990		65	.222	.328	189	42	11	0	3	1.6	13	16	16	29	1	5	1	324	31	3	6	6.0	.992	C-60
1991	**TEX A**	3	.000	.000	1	0	0	0	0	0.0	0	0	0	1	0	0	0	5	0	0	0	1.7	1.000	C-3
1992	**BAL A**	17	.235	.441	34	8	1	0	2	5.9	4	4	3	7	0	1	0	73	7	1	1	5.1	.988	C-16
1993		22	.259	.519	54	14	2	0	4	7.4	7	12	3	14	0	2	1	83	5	1	0	4.0	.989	C-21, DH-1
1994	**CHI N**	44	.263	.394	99	26	4	0	3	3.0	8	16	13	24	0	4	2	184	21	5	1	5.7	.976	C-37
1995	**2 teams**	**PIT N** (69G –.232) **CHI N** (12G –.250)																						
″	**total**	81	.234	.479	265	62	11	0	18	6.8	30	38	26	69	0	7	2	431	44	4	1	6.2	.992	C-77
10 yrs.		345	.219	.395	940	206	36	0	43	4.6	84	124	76	213	2	37	9	1601	143	19	14	5.8	.989	C-304, DH-1, 1B-1

Kelly Paris

PARIS, KELLY JAY
B. Oct. 17, 1957, Encino, Calif.
BR TR 6′ 175 lbs.

Year	Team	Games	BA	SA	AB	H	2B	3B	HR	HR%	R	RBI	BB	SO	SB	Pinch Hit AB	Pinch Hit H	PO	A	E	DP	TC/G	FA	G by Pos
1982	**STL N**	12	.103	.103	29	3	0	0	0	0.0	1	1	0	7	0	3	1	9	25	4	4	4.2	.895	3B-5, SS-4
1983	**CIN N**	56	.250	.300	120	30	6	0	0	0.0	13	7	15	22	8	11	1	60	62	6	7	3.6	.953	3B-16, 2B-10, SS-7, 1B-3
1985	**BAL A**	4	.000	.000	8	0	0	0	0	0.0	0	0	0	1	0	1	0	3	3	1	0	1.8	.857	2B-2, DH-2

Kelly Paris *continued*

Year	Team	Games	BA	SA	AB	H	2B	3B	HR	HR%	R	RBI	BB	SO	SB	Pinch Hit AB	Pinch Hit H	PO	A	E	DP	TC/G	FA	G by Pos
1986		5	.200	.200	10	2	0	0	0	0.0	0	0	0	3	0	1	0	0	6	1	1	1.4	.857	3B-3, DH-2
1988	**CHI A**	14	.250	.455	44	11	0	0	3	6.8	6	6	0	6	0	2	0	60	12	1	9	5.6	.986	1B-9, 3B-4
5 yrs.		91	.218	.289	211	46	6	0	3	1.4	20	14	15	39	8	18	2	132	108	13	21	3.8	.949	3B-28, 2B-12, 1B-12, SS-11, DH-4

Tony Parisse

PARISSE, LOUIS PETER BR TR 5′10″ 165 lbs.
B. June 25, 1911, Philadelphia, Pa. D. June 2, 1956, Philadelphia, Pa.

Year	Team	Games	BA	SA	AB	H	2B	3B	HR	HR%	R	RBI	BB	SO	SB	Pinch Hit AB	Pinch Hit H	PO	A	E	DP	TC/G	FA	G by Pos
1943	**PHI A**	6	.176	.176	17	3	0	0	0	0.0	0	1	2	2	0	1	0	16	7	0	0	4.6	1.000	C-5
1944		4	.000	.000	4	0	0	0	0	0.0	0	0	0	1	0	2	0	1	0	1	0	1.0	.500	C-2
2 yrs.		10	.143	.143	21	3	0	0	0	0.0	0	1	2	3	0	3	0	17	7	1	0	3.6	.960	C-7

Ace Parker

PARKER, CLARENCE McKAY BR TR 6′ 180 lbs.
B. May 17, 1912, Portsmouth, Va.

Year	Team	Games	BA	SA	AB	H	2B	3B	HR	HR%	R	RBI	BB	SO	SB	Pinch Hit AB	Pinch Hit H	PO	A	E	DP	TC/G	FA	G by Pos
1937	**PHI A**	38	.117	.202	94	11	0	1	2	2.1	8	13	4	17	0	3	2	54	60	10	12	3.8	.919	SS-19, 2B-9, OF-5
1938		56	.230	.274	113	26	5	0	0	0.0	12	12	10	16	1	4	1	54	75	5	10	3.0	.963	SS-26, 3B-9, 2B-9
2 yrs.		94	.179	.242	207	37	5	1	2	1.0	20	25	14	33	1	7	3	108	135	15	22	3.4	.942	SS-45, 2B-18, 3B-9, OF-5

Billy Parker

PARKER, WILLIAM DAVID BR TR 5′ 8″ 168 lbs.
B. Jan. 14, 1947, Hayneville, Ala.

Year	Team	Games	BA	SA	AB	H	2B	3B	HR	HR%	R	RBI	BB	SO	SB	Pinch Hit AB	Pinch Hit H	PO	A	E	DP	TC/G	FA	G by Pos
1971	**CAL A**	20	.229	.300	70	16	0	1	1	1.4	4	6	2	20	1	0	0	39	52	4	13	4.8	.958	2B-20
1972		36	.212	.313	80	17	2	0	2	2.5	11	8	9	17	0	1	0	29	43	2	8	2.1	.973	3B-21, 2B-9, OF-5, SS-1
1973		38	.225	.265	102	23	2	1	0	0.0	14	7	8	23	0	1	0	82	61	6	15	4.3	.960	2B-32, SS-3
3 yrs.		94	.222	.290	252	56	4	2	3	1.2	29	21	19	60	1	2	0	150	156	12	36	3.5	.962	2B-61, 3B-21, OF-5, SS-4

Dave Parker

PARKER, DAVID GENE (The Cobra) BL TR 6′ 5″ 230 lbs.
B. June 9, 1951, Calhoun, Miss.

Year	Team	Games	BA	SA	AB	H	2B	3B	HR	HR%	R	RBI	BB	SO	SB	Pinch Hit AB	Pinch Hit H	PO	A	E	DP	TC/G	FA	G by Pos
1973	**PIT N**	54	.288	.453	139	40	9	1	4	2.9	17	14	2	27	1	15	4	77	3	3	1	2.1	.964	OF-39
1974		73	.282	.409	220	62	10	3	4	1.8	27	29	10	53	3	21	4	154	8	4	10	3.0	.976	OF-49, 1B-6
1975		148	.308	**.541**	558	172	35	10	25	4.5	75	101	38	89	8	7	4	311	7	9	2	2.3	.972	OF-141
1976		138	.313	.475	537	168	28	10	13	2.4	82	90	30	80	19	4	2	294	12	14	0	2.4	.956	OF-134
1977		159	**.338**	.531	637	**215**	**44**	8	21	3.3	107	88	58	107	17	0	0	389	26	15	0	2.7	.965	OF-158, 2B-1
1978		148	**.334**	**.585**	581	194	32	12	30	5.2	102	117	57	92	20	0	0	302	12	13	3	2.2	.960	OF-147
1979		158	.310	.526	622	193	45	7	25	4.0	109	94	67	101	20	0	0	341	15	15	1	2.3	.960	OF-158
1980		139	.295	.458	518	153	31	1	17	3.3	71	79	25	69	10	7	2	235	14	9	0	2.0	.965	OF-130
1981		67	.258	.454	240	62	14	3	9	3.8	29	48	9	25	6	6	3	110	1	7	0	2.0	.941	OF-60
1982		73	.270	.447	244	66	19	3	6	2.5	41	29	22	45	7	7	2	108	2	5	1	1.8	.957	OF-63
1983		144	.279	.411	552	154	29	4	12	2.2	68	69	28	89	12	2	0	282	3	8	2	2.1	.973	OF-142
1984	**CIN N**	156	.285	.410	607	173	28	0	16	2.6	73	94	41	89	11	6	0	296	6	8	1	2.1	.974	OF-151
1985		160	.312	.551	635	198	**42**	4	34	5.4	88	**125**	52	80	5	2	1	329	12	10	1	2.2	.972	OF-159
1986		162	.273	.477	637	174	31	3	31	4.9	89	116	56	126	1	3	1	278	9	9	2	1.9	.970	OF-159
1987		153	.253	.433	589	149	28	0	26	4.4	77	97	44	104	7	3	0	354	17	11	10	2.5	.971	OF-142, 1B-9
1988	**OAK A**	101	.257	.406	377	97	18	1	12	3.2	43	55	32	70	0	9	4	63	5	3	0	0.7	.958	DH-61, OF-34, 1B-1
1989		144	.264	.432	553	146	27	0	22	4.0	56	97	38	91	0	7	0	2	0	0	0	0.0	1.000	DH-140, OF-1
1990	**MIL A**	157	.289	.451	610	176	30	3	21	3.4	71	92	41	102	4	1	1	24	0	1	4	0.2	.960	DH-153, 1B-3
1991	**2 teams**	**CAL A** (119G –.232)	**TOR A** (13G –.333)																					
″	**total**	132	.239	.365	502	120	26	2	11	2.2	47	59	33	98	3	3	2	0	0	0	0	0.0		DH-130
19 yrs.		2466	.290	.471	9358	2712	526	75	339	3.6	1272	1493	683	1537	154	103	30	3949	152	144	38	1.8	.966	OF-1867, DH-484, 1B-19, 2B-1
LEAGUE CHAMPIONSHIP SERIES																								
1974	**PIT N**	3	.125	.125	8	1	0	0	0	0.0	0	0	0	1	0	1	0	4	1	0	0	2.5	1.000	OF-2
1975		3	.000	.000	10	0	0	0	0	0.0	2	0	1	3	0	0	0	13	1	0	1	4.7	1.000	OF-3
1979		3	.333	.333	12	4	0	0	0	0.0	2	2	2	3	1	0	0	9	0	0	0	3.0	1.000	OF-3
1988	**OAK A**	3	.250	.333	12	3	1	0	0	0.0	1	0	0	4	0	0	0	1	0	1	0	0.7	.500	DH-2, OF-1
1989		4	.188	.563	16	3	0	0	2	12.5	2	3	0	0	0	0	0	0	0	0	0	0.0	.000	DH-4
5 yrs.		16	.190	.310	58	11	1	0	2	3.4	7	5	3	11	1	1	0	27	2	1	1	2.0	.967	OF-9, DH-6
WORLD SERIES																								
1979	**PIT N**	7	.345	.448	29	10	3	0	0	0.0	2	4	2	7	0	0	0	13	1	1	1	2.1	.933	OF-7
1988	**OAK A**	4	.200	.200	15	3	0	0	0	0.0	0	0	2	4	0	0	0	4	0	0	0	1.0	1.000	OF-2, DH-2
1989		3	.222	.667	9	2	1	0	1	11.1	2	2	0	2	0	1	0	0	0	0	0	0.0	.000	DH-2
3 yrs.		14	.283	.415	53	15	4	0	1	1.9	4	6	4	13	0	1	0	17	1	1	1	1.5	.947	OF-9, DH-4

Dixie Parker

PARKER, DOUGLAS WOOLLEY BL TR 5′11″ 160 lbs.
B. Apr. 24, 1895, Forest Home, Ala. D. May 15, 1972, Tuscaloosa, Ala.

Year	Team	Games	BA	SA	AB	H	2B	3B	HR	HR%	R	RBI	BB	SO	SB	Pinch Hit AB	Pinch Hit H	PO	A	E	DP	TC/G	FA	G by Pos
1923	**PHI N**	4	.200	.200	5	1	0	0	0	0.0	0	1	0	1	0	0	0	1	0	1	0	1.0	.500	C-2

Pat Parker

PARKER, CLARENCE PERKINS BR TR 5′ 7″ 160 lbs.
B. May 22, 1893, Somerville, Mass. D. Mar. 21, 1967, Claremont, N. H.

Year	Team	Games	BA	SA	AB	H	2B	3B	HR	HR%	R	RBI	BB	SO	SB	Pinch Hit AB	Pinch Hit H	PO	A	E	DP	TC/G	FA	G by Pos
1915	**STL A**	3	.167	.167	6	1	0	0	0	0.0	0	1	0	3	0	1	0	3	0	0	0	1.5	1.000	OF-2

Rick Parker

PARKER, RICHARD ALAN BR TR 6′ 185 lbs.
B. Mar. 20, 1963, Kansas City, Mo.

Year	Team	Games	BA	SA	AB	H	2B	3B	HR	HR%	R	RBI	BB	SO	SB	Pinch Hit AB	Pinch Hit H	PO	A	E	DP	TC/G	FA	G by Pos
1990	**SF N**	54	.243	.346	107	26	5	0	2	1.9	19	14	10	15	6	19	4	45	3	2	0	1.3	.960	OF-35, 2B-2, SS-1, 3B-1
1991		13	.071	.071	14	1	0	0	0	0.0	0	1	1	5	0	8	0	5	0	0	0	1.3	1.000	OF-4
1993	**HOU N**	45	.333	.400	45	15	3	0	0	0.0	11	4	3	8	1	18	5	18	0	0	0	1.0	1.000	OF-16, 2B-1, SS-1
1994	**NY N**	8	.063	.063	16	1	0	0	0	0.0	1	0	0	2	0	1	0	14	1	0	0	2.5	1.000	OF-6
1995	**LA N**	27	.276	.276	29	8	0	0	0	0.0	3	4	2	4	1	4	0	20	1	0	1	0.8	1.000	OF-21, SS-2, 3B-2
5 yrs.		147	.242	.308	211	51	8	0	2	0.9	34	23	16	34	8	50	9	102	5	2	1	1.2	.982	OF-82, SS-4, 3B-3, 2B-3

Salty Parker

PARKER, FRANCIS JAMES BR TR 6′ 173 lbs.
B. July 8, 1913, East St. Louis, Ill. D. July 27, 1992, Houston, Tex.
Manager 1967, 1972.

Year	Team	Games	BA	SA	AB	H	2B	3B	HR	HR%	R	RBI	BB	SO	SB	Pinch Hit AB	Pinch Hit H	PO	A	E	DP	TC/G	FA	G by Pos
1936	**DET A**	11	.280	.360	25	7	2	0	0	0.0	6	4	2	3	0	0	0	30	21	3	6	6.0	.944	SS-7, 1B-2

Wes Parker

PARKER, MAURICE WESLEY BB TL 6′ 1″ 180 lbs.
B. Nov. 13, 1939, Evanston, Ill.

Year	Team	Games	BA	SA	AB	H	2B	3B	HR	HR%	R	RBI	BB	SO	SB	Pinch Hit AB	Pinch Hit H	PO	A	E	DP	TC/G	FA	G by Pos
1964	LA N	124	.257	.341	214	55	7	1	3	1.4	29	10	14	45	5	30	6	326	26	6	18	3.6	.983	OF-69, 1B-31
1965		154	.238	.352	542	129	24	7	8	1.5	80	51	75	95	13	1	1	1434	95	5	112	9.9	.997	1B-154, OF-1
1966		156	.253	.385	475	120	17	5	12	2.5	67	51	69	83	7	7	1	1149	70	9	74	8.0	.993	1B-140, OF-14
1967		139	.247	.346	413	102	16	5	5	1.2	56	31	65	83	10	13	5	949	70	5	72	7.9	.995	1B-112, OF-18
1968		135	.239	.314	468	112	22	2	3	0.6	42	27	49	87	4	6	0	980	70	2	74	7.4	.998	1B-114, OF-28
1969		132	.278	.427	471	131	23	4	13	2.8	76	68	56	46	4	5	3	1190	79	6	87	9.8	.995	1B-128, OF-2
1970		161	.319	.458	614	196	**47**	4	10	1.6	84	111	79	70	8	0	0	1498	125	7	116	10.1	.996	1B-161
1971		157	.274	.356	533	146	24	1	6	1.1	69	62	63	63	6	1	1	1240	98	5	114	8.1	.996	1B-148, OF-18
1972		130	.279	.354	427	119	14	3	4	0.9	45	59	62	43	3	8	2	1085	68	4	91	9.3	.997	1B-120, OF-5
9 yrs.		1288	.267	.375	4157	1110	194	32	64	1.5	548	470	532	615	60	71	19	9851	701	49	758	8.4	.995	1B-1108, OF-155
WORLD SERIES																								
1965	LA N	7	.304	.522	23	7	0	1	1	4.3	3	2	3	3	2	0	0	55	4	0	6	8.4	1.000	1B-7
1966		4	.231	.385	13	3	2	0	0	0.0	0	0	1	3	0	0	0	31	2	0	4	8.3	1.000	1B-4
2 yrs.		11	.278	.472	36	10	2	1	1	2.8	3	2	4	6	2	0	0	86	6	0	10	8.4	1.000	1B-11

Frank Parkinson

PARKINSON, FRANK JOSEPH BR TR 5′11″ 175 lbs.
B. Mar. 23, 1895, Dickson City, Pa. D. July 4, 1960, Trenton, N. J.

Year	Team	Games	BA	SA	AB	H	2B	3B	HR	HR%	R	RBI	BB	SO	SB	Pinch Hit AB	Pinch Hit H	PO	A	E	DP	TC/G	FA	G by Pos
1921	PHI N	108	.253	.353	391	99	20	2	5	1.3	36	32	13	81	3	1	0	234	405	47	55	6.5	.931	SS-105, 3B-1
1922		141	.275	.413	545	150	18	6	15	2.8	86	70	55	**93**	3	2	0	323	562	34	78	6.6	.963	2B-139
1923		67	.242	.338	219	53	12	0	3	1.4	21	28	13	31	0	5	1	118	175	18	36	4.9	.942	2B-37, SS-15, 3B-11
1924		62	.212	.276	156	33	7	0	1	0.6	14	19	14	28	3	5	1	63	127	7	23	3.3	.964	3B-28, SS-21, 2B-10
4 yrs.		378	.256	.366	1311	335	57	8	24	1.8	157	149	95	233	9	13	2	738	1269	106	192	5.8	.950	2B-186, SS-141, 3B-40

Art Parks

PARKS, ARTIE WILLIAM BL TR 5′ 9″ 170 lbs.
B. Nov. 1, 1911, Paris, Ark. D. Dec. 6, 1989, Little Rock, Ark.

Year	Team	Games	BA	SA	AB	H	2B	3B	HR	HR%	R	RBI	BB	SO	SB	Pinch Hit AB	Pinch Hit H	PO	A	E	DP	TC/G	FA	G by Pos
1937	BKN N	7	.313	.438	16	5	2	0	0	0.0	2	0	2	2	0	3	0	4	1	0	1	1.3	1.000	OF-4
1939		71	.272	.356	239	65	13	2	1	0.4	27	19	28	14	2	4	2	125	2	3	0	2.0	.977	OF-65
2 yrs.		78	.275	.361	255	70	15	2	1	0.4	29	19	30	16	2	7	2	129	3	3	1	2.0	.978	OF-69

Bill Parks

PARKS, WILLIAM ROBERT BR TR 5′ 8″ 150 lbs.
B. June 4, 1849, Easton, Pa. D. Oct. 10, 1911, Easton, Pa.

Year	Team	Games	BA	SA	AB	H	2B	3B	HR	HR%	R	RBI	BB	SO	SB	Pinch Hit AB	Pinch Hit H	PO	A	E	DP	TC/G	FA	G by Pos
1876	BOS N	1	.000	.000	4	0	0	0	0	0.0	0	0	0	0		0	0	3	0	1	0	4.0	.750	OF-1

Derek Parks

PARKS, DEREK GAVIN BR TR 6′ 205 lbs.
B. Sept. 29, 1968, Covina, Calif.

Year	Team	Games	BA	SA	AB	H	2B	3B	HR	HR%	R	RBI	BB	SO	SB	Pinch Hit AB	Pinch Hit H	PO	A	E	DP	TC/G	FA	G by Pos
1992	MIN A	7	.333	.333	6	2	0	0	0	0.0	1	0	1	1	0	0	0	18	1	0	0	2.7	1.000	C-7
1993		7	.200	.200	20	4	0	0	0	0.0	3	1	1	2	0	0	0	28	4	1	1	4.7	.970	C-7
1994		31	.191	.292	89	17	6	0	1	1.1	6	9	4	20	0	3	3	119	16	1	0	4.4	.993	C-31
3 yrs.		45	.200	.278	115	23	6	0	1	0.9	10	10	6	23	0	3	3	165	21	2	1	4.2	.989	C-45

Sam Parrilla

PARRILLA, SAMUEL BR TR 5′11″ 185 lbs.
Born Samuel Parrilla (Monge).
B. June 12, 1943, Santurce, Puerto Rico D. Feb. 9, 1994, Brooklyn, N. Y.

Year	Team	Games	BA	SA	AB	H	2B	3B	HR	HR%	R	RBI	BB	SO	SB	Pinch Hit AB	Pinch Hit H	PO	A	E	DP	TC/G	FA	G by Pos
1970	PHI N	11	.125	.188	16	2	1	0	0	0.0	0	0	1	4	0	7	1	5	0	0	0	1.7	1.000	OF-3

Lance Parrish

PARRISH, LANCE MICHAEL BR TR 6′ 3″ 210 lbs.
B. June 15, 1956, Clairton, Pa.

Year	Team	Games	BA	SA	AB	H	2B	3B	HR	HR%	R	RBI	BB	SO	SB	Pinch Hit AB	Pinch Hit H	PO	A	E	DP	TC/G	FA	G by Pos
1977	DET A	12	.196	.435	46	9	2	0	3	6.5	10	7	5	12	0	0	0	76	6	0	0	6.8	1.000	C-12
1978		85	.219	.424	288	63	11	3	14	4.9	37	41	11	71	0	6	1	353	39	5	5	5.0	.987	C-79
1979		143	.276	.456	493	136	26	3	19	3.9	65	65	49	105	6	3	1	707	79	9	10	5.6	.989	C-142
1980		144	.286	.499	553	158	34	6	24	4.3	79	82	31	109	6	4	1	607	67	7	15	4.6	.990	C-121, DH-16, OF-5, 1B-5
1981		96	.244	.394	348	85	18	2	10	2.9	39	46	34	52	2	0	0	407	40	3	6	4.7	.993	C-90, DH-5
1982		133	.284	.529	486	138	19	2	32	6.6	75	87	40	99	3	2	1	627	76	8	8	5.3	.989	C-132, OF-1
1983		155	.269	.483	605	163	42	3	27	4.5	80	114	44	106	1	2	0	695	73	4	8	4.9	.995	C-131, DH-27
1984		147	.237	.443	578	137	16	2	33	5.7	75	98	41	120	2	3	1	720	67	7	11	5.3	.991	C-127, DH-22
1985		140	.273	.479	549	150	27	1	28	5.1	64	98	41	90	2	1	1	695	53	5	9	5.3	.993	C-120, DH-22
1986		91	.257	.483	327	84	6	1	22	6.7	53	62	38	83	0	4	0	483	48	6	5	5.9	.989	C-85, DH-6
1987	PHI N	130	.245	.399	466	114	21	0	17	3.6	42	67	47	104	0	4	0	724	66	9	1	6.3	.989	C-127
1988		123	.215	.370	424	91	17	2	15	3.5	44	60	47	93	0	3	2	640	73	9	12	6.1	.988	C-117, 1B-1
1989	CAL A	124	.238	.388	433	103	12	1	17	3.9	48	50	42	104	1	2	0	638	63	5	7	5.7	.993	C-122, DH-2
1990		133	.268	.451	470	126	14	0	24	5.1	54	70	46	107	2	1	0	794	90	6	21	6.5	.993	C-131, 1B-4, DH-1
1991		119	.216	.388	402	87	12	0	19	4.7	38	51	35	117	0	5	2	670	57	2	11	6.1	.997	C-111, DH-5, 1B-3
1992	2 teams	CAL A (24G –.229) SEA A (69G –.234)																						
″	total	93	.233	.418	275	64	13	1	12	4.4	26	32	24	70	1	11	0	383	23	6	15	4.7	.985	C-56, 1B-16, DH-16
1993	CLE A	10	.200	.400	20	4	1	0	1	5.0	2	2	4	5	1	1	0	47	10	3	1	6.0	.950	C-10
1994	PIT N	40	.270	.381	126	34	5	0	3	2.4	10	16	18	28	1	2	0	228	15	4	1	6.3	.984	C-38, 1B-1
1995	TOR A	70	.202	.320	178	36	9	0	4	2.2	15	22	15	52	0	1	0	346	41	0	6	5.7	1.000	C-67, DH-1
19 yrs.		1988	.252	.440	7067	1782	305	27	324	4.6	856	1070	612	1527	28	55	10	9840	986	98	152	5.5	.991	C-1818, DH-123, 1B-30, OF-6
LEAGUE CHAMPIONSHIP SERIES																								
1984	DET A	3	.250	.583	12	3	1	0	1	8.3	1	3	0	3	0	0	0	21	2	0	0	7.7	1.000	C-3
WORLD SERIES																								
1984	DET A	5	.278	.500	18	5	1	0	1	5.6	3	2	3	2	1	0	0	30	3	1	1	6.8	.971	C-5

Larry Parrish

PARRISH, LARRY ALTON BR TR 6′ 3″ 190 lbs.
B. Nov. 10, 1953, Winter Haven, Fla.

Year	Team	Games	BA	SA	AB	H	2B	3B	HR	HR%	R	RBI	BB	SO	SB	Pinch Hit AB	Pinch Hit H	PO	A	E	DP	TC/G	FA	G by Pos
1974	MON N	25	.203	.275	69	14	5	0	0	0.0	9	4	6	19	0	1	0	20	51	1	3	3.0	.986	3B-24
1975		145	.274	.410	532	146	32	5	10	1.9	50	65	28	74	4	5	1	105	291	35	33	3.0	.919	3B-143, SS-1, 2B-1
1976		154	.232	.363	543	126	28	5	11	2.0	65	61	41	91	2	1	0	122	310	25	35	3.0	.945	3B-153
1977		123	.246	.386	402	99	19	2	11	2.7	50	46	37	71	2	14	4	81	225	21	11	2.8	.936	3B-115
1978		144	.277	.454	520	144	39	4	15	2.9	68	70	32	103	2	5	3	122	288	23	20	3.1	.947	3B-139
1979		153	.307	.551	544	167	39	2	30	5.5	83	82	41	101	5	0	0	119	290	23	25	2.8	.947	3B-153
1980		126	.254	.427	452	115	27	3	15	3.3	55	72	36	80	2	1	0	106	231	18	15	2.9	.949	3B-124
1981		97	.244	.384	349	85	19	3	8	2.3	41	44	28	73	0	1	0	91	141	16	7	2.6	.935	3B-95

Larry Parrish *continued*

Year	Team	Games	BA	SA	AB	H	2B	3B	HR	HR%	R	RBI	BB	SO	SB	Pinch Hit AB	Pinch Hit H	PO	A	E	DP	TC/G	FA	G by Pos
1982	TEX A	128	.264	.414	440	116	15	0	17	3.9	59	62	30	84	5	5	2	190	12	8	4	1.6	.962	OF-124, 3B-3, DH-2
1983		145	.272	.474	555	151	26	4	26	4.7	76	88	46	91	0	0	0	215	11	9	1	1.6	.962	OF-132, DH-13
1984		156	.285	.465	613	175	42	1	22	3.6	73	101	42	116	2	1	0	155	35	4	6	1.2	.979	OF-81, DH-63, 3B-12
1985		94	.249	.434	346	86	11	1	17	4.9	44	51	33	77	0	1	0	111	7	1	0	1.3	.992	OF-69, DH-22, 3B-2
1986		129	.276	.509	464	128	22	1	28	6.0	67	94	52	114	3	2	0	23	35	4	2	0.5	.935	DH-99, 3B-30
1987		152	.268	.483	557	149	22	1	32	5.7	79	100	49	154	3	5	1	19	26	4	6	0.3	.918	DH-122, 3B-28, OF-1
1988	2 teams	TEX A (68G –.190) BOS A (52G –.259)																						
"	total	120	.217	.360	406	88	14	1	14	3.4	32	52	28	111	0	5	2	221	25	3	18	2.1	.988	DH-81, 1B-36
15 yrs.		1891	.263	.439	6792	1789	360	33	256	3.8	851	992	529	1359	30	47	13	1700	1978	195	186	2.1	.950	3B-1021, OF-407, DH-402, 1B-36, SS-1, 2B-1
DIVISIONAL PLAYOFF SERIES																								
1981	MON N	5	.150	.200	20	3	1	0	0	0.0	3	1	1	3	0	0	0	7	6	0	0	2.6	1.000	3B-5
LEAGUE CHAMPIONSHIP SERIES																								
1981	MON N	5	.263	.368	19	5	2	0	0	0.0	2	2	1	1	0	0	0	3	13	1	3	3.4	.941	3B-5
1988	BOS A	4	.000	.000	6	0	0	0	0	0.0	0	0	0	2	0	3	0	7	0	0	0	2.3	1.000	1B-2, DH-1
2 yrs.		9	.200	.280	25	5	2	0	0	0.0	2	2	1	3	0	3	0	10	13	1	3	3.0	.958	3B-5, 1B-2, DH-1

Jiggs Parrott

PARROTT, WALTER EDWARD 5′11″ 160 lbs.
Brother of Tom Parrott.
B. July 14, 1871, Portland, Ore. D. Apr. 16, 1898, Phoenix, Ariz.

Year	Team	Games	BA	SA	AB	H	2B	3B	HR	HR%	R	RBI	BB	SO	SB	Pinch Hit AB	Pinch Hit H	PO	A	E	DP	TC/G	FA	G by Pos
1892	CHI N	78	.201	.273	333	67	8	5	2	0.6	38	22	8	30	7	0	0	115	164	34	7	4.0	.891	3B-78
1893		110	.244	.312	455	111	10	9	1	0.2	54	65	13	25	25	0	0	163	274	45	23	4.4	.907	3B-99, 2B-7, OF-4
1894		124	.248	.333	517	128	17	9	3	0.6	82	64	16	35	30	0	0	287	380	49	56	5.8	.932	2B-123, 3B-1
1895		3	.250	.250	4	1	0	0	0	0.0	0	0	0	0	0	0	0	2	1	0	0	1.0	1.000	OF-1, SS-1, 1B-1
4 yrs.		315	.235	.310	1309	307	35	23	6	0.5	174	151	37	90	62	0	0	567	819	128	86	4.8	.915	3B-178, 2B-130, OF-5, SS-1, 1B-1

Tom Parrott

PARROTT, THOMAS WILLIAM (Tacky Tom) BR TR 5′10½″ 170 lbs.
Brother of Jiggs Parrott.
B. Apr. 10, 1868, Portland, Ore. D. Jan. 1, 1932, Dundee, Ore.

Year	Team	Games	BA	SA	AB	H	2B	3B	HR	HR%	R	RBI	BB	SO	SB	Pinch Hit AB	Pinch Hit H	PO	A	E	DP	TC/G	FA	G by Pos
1893	2 teams	CHI N (7G –.259) CIN N (24G –.191)																						
"	total	31	.211	.284	95	20	2	1	1	1.1	9	12	2	11	0	1	0	20	47	6	1	2.4	.918	P-26, 3B-2, OF-1, 2B-1
1894	CIN N	68	.323	.480	229	74	12	6	4	1.7	51	40	17	10	4	3	**2**	143	87	22	10	3.7	.913	P-41, OF-13, 1B-12, 3B-1, SS-1, 2B-1
1895		64	.343	.522	201	69	13	7	3	1.5	35	41	11	8	10	0	0	151	70	13	12	3.7	.944	P-41, 1B-14, OF-9
1896	STL N	118	.291	.414	474	138	13	12	7	1.5	62	70	11	24	12	0	0	334	27	18	7	3.1	.953	OF-108, P-7, 1B-6
4 yrs.		281	.301	.438	999	301	40	26	15	1.5	157	163	41	53	26	4	2	648	231	59	30	3.3	.937	OF-131, P-115, 1B-32, 3B-3, 2B-2, SS-1

Casey Parsons

PARSONS, CASEY ROBERT BL TR 6′ 1″ 180 lbs.
B. Apr. 14, 1954, Wenatchee, Wash.

Year	Team	Games	BA	SA	AB	H	2B	3B	HR	HR%	R	RBI	BB	SO	SB	Pinch Hit AB	Pinch Hit H	PO	A	E	DP	TC/G	FA	G by Pos
1981	SEA A	36	.227	.409	22	5	1	0	1	4.5	6	5	1	4	0	8	1	22	2	0	1	1.0	1.000	OF-24, 1B-1
1983	CHI A	8	.200	.200	5	1	0	0	0	0.0	1	0	2	1	0	4	0	3	0	0	0	0.6	1.000	OF-3, DH-2
1984		1	.000	.000	1	0	0	0	0	0.0	0	0	0	1	0	1	0	0	0	0	0	0.0	—	
1987	CLE A	18	.160	.280	25	4	0	0	1	4.0	2	5	0	5	0	14	4	4	0	0	0	0.5	1.000	DH-5, OF-2, 1B-1
4 yrs.		63	.189	.321	53	10	1	0	2	3.8	9	10	3	11	0	27	5	29	2	0	1	0.8	1.000	OF-29, DH-7, 1B-2

Dixie Parsons

PARSONS, EDWARD DIXON BR TR 6′ 2″ 180 lbs.
B. May 12, 1916, Talladega, Ala. D. Oct. 31, 1991, Longview, Tex.

Year	Team	Games	BA	SA	AB	H	2B	3B	HR	HR%	R	RBI	BB	SO	SB	Pinch Hit AB	Pinch Hit H	PO	A	E	DP	TC/G	FA	G by Pos
1939	DET A	5	.000	.000	1	0	0	0	0	0.0	0	0	1	1	0	1	0	2	0	0	0	0.5	1.000	C-4
1942		63	.197	.250	188	37	4	0	2	1.1	8	11	13	22	1	1	0	274	44	6	6	5.2	.981	C-62
1943		40	.142	.170	106	15	3	0	0	0.0	2	4	6	16	0	0	0	167	31	5	2	5.1	.975	C-40
3 yrs.		108	.176	.220	295	52	7	0	2	0.7	10	15	20	39	1	2	0	443	75	11	8	5.0	.979	C-106

John Parsons

PARSONS, JOHN S. 5′ 6″ 138 lbs.
B. Napoleon, Ohio Deceased.

Year	Team	Games	BA	SA	AB	H	2B	3B	HR	HR%	R	RBI	BB	SO	SB	Pinch Hit AB	Pinch Hit H	PO	A	E	DP	TC/G	FA	G by Pos
1884	CIN AA	1	.000	.000	3	0	0	0	0	0.0	0		0			0	0	1	0	0	0	1.0	1.000	OF-1

Roy Partee

PARTEE, ROY ROBERT BR TR 5′10″ 180 lbs.
B. Sept. 7, 1917, Los Angeles, Calif.

Year	Team	Games	BA	SA	AB	H	2B	3B	HR	HR%	R	RBI	BB	SO	SB	Pinch Hit AB	Pinch Hit H	PO	A	E	DP	TC/G	FA	G by Pos
1943	BOS A	96	.281	.341	299	84	14	2	0	0.0	30	31	39	33	0	5	2	349	57	7	11	4.5	.983	C-91
1944		89	.243	.307	280	68	12	0	2	0.7	18	41	37	29	0	5	1	326	40	4	5	4.4	.989	C-85
1946		40	.315	.396	111	35	5	2	0	0.0	13	9	13	14	0	1	1	139	12	4	1	4.1	.974	C-38
1947		60	.231	.243	169	39	2	0	0	0.0	14	16	18	23	0	6	0	207	26	6	4	4.4	.975	C-54
1948	STL A	82	.203	.247	231	47	8	1	0	0.0	14	17	25	21	2	6	0	297	22	6	7	4.3	.982	C-76
5 yrs.		367	.250	.303	1090	273	41	5	2	0.2	89	114	132	120	2	23	4	1318	157	27	28	4.4	.982	C-344
WORLD SERIES																								
1946	BOS A	5	.100	.100	10	1	0	0	0	0.0	1	1	1	2	0	1	0	14	1	0	1	3.0	1.000	C-5

Steve Partenheimer

PARTENHEIMER, HAROLD PHILIP BR TR 5′ 8½″ 145 lbs.
Father of Stan Partenheimer.
B. Aug. 30, 1891, Greenfield, Mass. D. June 16, 1971, Mansfield, Ohio.

Year	Team	Games	BA	SA	AB	H	2B	3B	HR	HR%	R	RBI	BB	SO	SB	Pinch Hit AB	Pinch Hit H	PO	A	E	DP	TC/G	FA	G by Pos
1913	DET A	1	.000	.000	2	0	0	0	0	0.0	0	0	0	0	0	0	0	0	3	1	0	4.0	.750	3B-1

Jay Partridge

PARTRIDGE, JAMES BUGG BL TR 5′11″ 160 lbs.
B. Nov. 15, 1902, Mountville, Ga. D. Jan. 14, 1974, Nashville, Tenn.

Year	Team	Games	BA	SA	AB	H	2B	3B	HR	HR%	R	RBI	BB	SO	SB	Pinch Hit AB	Pinch Hit H	PO	A	E	DP	TC/G	FA	G by Pos
1927	BKN N	146	.260	.348	572	149	17	6	7	1.2	72	40	20	36	9	6	1	330	454	52	63	6.0	.938	2B-140
1928		37	.247	.274	73	18	0	1	0	0.0	18	12	13	6	2	11	4	40	44	9	7	4.7	.903	2B-18, 3B-2
2 yrs.		183	.259	.340	645	167	17	7	7	1.1	90	52	33	42	11	17	5	370	498	61	70	5.8	.934	2B-158, 3B-2

Ben Paschal

PASCHAL, BENJAMIN EDWIN BR TR 5′11″ 185 lbs.
B. Oct. 13, 1895, Enterprise, Ala. D. Nov. 10, 1974, Charlotte, N. C.

Year	Team	Games	BA	SA	AB	H	2B	3B	HR	HR%	R	RBI	BB	SO	SB	Pinch Hit AB	Pinch Hit H	PO	A	E	DP	TC/G	FA	G by Pos
1915	CLE A	9	.111	.111	9	1	0	0	0	0.0	0	0	0	3	0	9	1	0	0	0	0	0.0	—	
1920	BOS A	9	.357	.357	28	10	0	0	0	0.0	5	5	5	2	1	2	1	10	1	0	0	1.6	1.000	OF-7

Ben Paschal *continued*

Year	Team	Games	BA	SA	AB	H	2B	3B	HR	HR%	R	RBI	BB	SO	SB	Pinch Hit AB	Pinch Hit H	PO	A	E	DP	TC/G	FA	G by Pos
1924	**NY A**	4	.250	.333	12	3	1	0	0	0.0	2	3	1	0	0	1	0	4	1	0	1	1.3	1.000	OF-4
1925		89	.360	.611	247	89	16	5	12	4.9	49	56	22	29	14	21	5	117	6	6	0	2.0	.953	OF-66
1926		96	.287	.438	258	74	12	3	7	2.7	46	33	26	35	7	18	6	134	10	10	0	2.1	.935	OF-74
1927		50	.317	.549	82	26	9	2	2	2.4	16	16	4	10	0	22	5	39	1	1	0	1.5	.976	OF-27
1928		65	.316	.456	79	25	6	1	1	1.3	12	15	8	11	1	35	8	26	1	0	0	1.1	1.000	OF-25
1929		42	.208	.333	72	15	3	0	2	2.8	13	11	6	3	1	20	3	37	2	2	0	2.0	.951	OF-20
8 yrs.		364	.309	.488	787	243	47	11	24	3.0	143	139	72	93	24	128	29	367	22	19	1	1.8	.953	OF-223
WORLD SERIES																								
1926	**NY A**	5	.250	.250	4	1	0	0	0	0.0	0	1	1	2	0	4	1	0	0	0	0	0.0	—	
1928		3	.200	.200	10	2	0	0	0	0.0	0	1	1	0	0	1	1	8	0	0	0	2.7	1.000	OF-3
2 yrs.		8	.214	.214	14	3	0	0	0	0.0	0	2	2	2	0	5	2	8	0	0	0	2.7	1.000	OF-3

Johnny Pasek

PASEK, JOHN PAUL BR TR 5′10″ 175 lbs.
B. June 25, 1905, Niagara Falls, N. Y. D. Mar. 13, 1976, Niagara Falls, N. Y.

Year	Team	Games	BA	SA	AB	H	2B	3B	HR	HR%	R	RBI	BB	SO	SB	Pinch Hit AB	Pinch Hit H	PO	A	E	DP	TC/G	FA	G by Pos
1933	**DET A**	28	.246	.311	61	15	4	0	0	0.0	6	4	7	7	2	0	0	75	13	1	3	3.2	.989	C-28
1934	**CHI A**	4	.333	.333	9	3	0	0	0	0.0	1	0	1	1	0	0	0	12	1	0	0	3.3	1.000	C-4
2 yrs.		32	.257	.314	70	18	4	0	0	0.0	7	4	8	8	2	0	0	87	14	1	3	3.2	.990	C-32

Dode Paskert

PASKERT, GEORGE HENRY BR TR 5′11″ 165 lbs.
B. Aug. 28, 1881, Cleveland, Ohio D. Feb. 12, 1959, Cleveland, Ohio.

Year	Team	Games	BA	SA	AB	H	2B	3B	HR	HR%	R	RBI	BB	SO	SB	Pinch Hit AB	Pinch Hit H	PO	A	E	DP	TC/G	FA	G by Pos
1907	**CIN N**	16	.280	.420	50	14	4	0	1	2.0	10	8	2		2	0	0	33	3	1	0	2.3	.973	OF-16
1908		118	.243	.306	395	96	14	4	1	0.3	40	36	27		25	3	1	251	15	13	3	2.4	.953	OF-116
1909		104	.252	.298	322	81	7	4	0	0.0	49	33	34		23	16	3	207	12	6	9	2.6	.973	OF-82, 1B-6
1910		144	.300	.374	506	152	21	5	2	0.4	63	46	70	60	51	2	0	367	25	19	4	2.9	.954	OF-139, 1B-2
1911	**PHI N**	153	.273	.345	560	153	18	5	4	0.7	96	47	70	70	28	0	0	361	20	8	6	2.5	.979	OF-153
1912		145	.315	.413	540	170	37	5	2	0.4	102	43	91	67	36	0	0	342	25	13	4	2.6	.966	OF-141, 2B-2, 3B-1
1913		124	.262	.374	454	119	21	9	4	0.9	83	29	65	69	12	4	0	330	19	10	8	3.0	.972	OF-120
1914		132	.264	.366	451	119	25	6	3	0.7	59	44	56	68	23	3	0	309	26	18	5	2.7	.949	OF-128, SS-4
1915		109	.244	.348	328	80	17	4	3	0.9	51	39	35	38	9	10	3	231	14	7	3	2.3	.972	OF-104, 1B-5
1916		149	.279	.402	555	155	30	7	8	1.4	82	46	54	76	22	2	1	334	16	6	4	2.4	.983	OF-146, SS-1
1917		141	.251	.363	546	137	27	11	4	0.7	78	43	62	63	19	1	1	286	19	5	4	2.2	.984	OF-138
1918	**CHI N**	127	.286	.371	461	132	24	3	3	0.7	69	59	53	**49**	20	0	0	289	26	9	3	2.6	.972	OF-121, 3B-6
1919		87	.196	.281	270	53	11	3	2	0.7	21	29	28	33	7	8	1	146	12	5	1	2.0	.969	OF-80
1920		139	.279	.396	487	136	22	10	5	1.0	57	71	64	58	16	1	0	306	23	15	3	2.5	.956	OF-137
1921	**CIN N**	27	.174	.207	92	16	1	1	0	0.0	8	4	4	8	0	1	0	60	2	1	2	2.6	.984	OF-24
15 yrs.		1715	.268	.361	6017	1613	279	77	42	0.7	868	577	715	659	293	51	10	3852	257	136	59	2.5	.968	OF-1645, 1B-13, 3B-7, SS-5, 2B-2
WORLD SERIES																								
1915	**PHI N**	5	.158	.158	19	3	0	0	0	0.0	2	0	1	2	0	0	0	17	0	0	0	3.4	1.000	OF-5
1918	**CHI N**	6	.190	.238	21	4	1	0	0	0.0	0	2	2	2	0	0	0	17	0	0	0	2.8	1.000	OF-6
2 yrs.		11	.175	.200	40	7	1	0	0	0.0	2	2	3	4	0	0	0	34	0	0	0	3.1	1.000	OF-11

Kevin Pasley

PASLEY, KEVIN PATRICK BR TR 6′ 185 lbs.
B. July 22, 1953, Brooklyln, N. Y.

Year	Team	Games	BA	SA	AB	H	2B	3B	HR	HR%	R	RBI	BB	SO	SB	Pinch Hit AB	Pinch Hit H	PO	A	E	DP	TC/G	FA	G by Pos
1974	**LA N**	1	—	—	0	0	0	0	0	—	0	0	0	0	0	0	0	1	0	0	0	1.0	1.000	C-1
1976		23	.231	.269	52	12	2	0	0	0.0	4	2	3	7	0	0	0	86	15	3	0	4.5	.971	C-23
1977	**2 teams**	**LA N** (2G –.333) **SEA A** (4G –.385)																						
″	**total**	6	.375	.375	16	6	0	0	0	0.0	1	2	1	2	0	0	0	24	1	0	0	4.2	1.000	C-6
1978	**SEA A**	25	.241	.389	54	13	5	0	1	1.9	3	5	2	4	0	0	0	85	4	0	0	3.6	1.000	C-25
4 yrs.		55	.254	.336	122	31	7	0	1	0.8	8	9	6	13	0	0	0	196	20	3	0	4.0	.986	C-55

Dan Pasqua

PASQUA, DANIEL ANTHONY BL TL 6′ 205 lbs.
B. Oct. 17, 1961, Yonkers, N. Y.

Year	Team	Games	BA	SA	AB	H	2B	3B	HR	HR%	R	RBI	BB	SO	SB	Pinch Hit AB	Pinch Hit H	PO	A	E	DP	TC/G	FA	G by Pos
1985	**NY A**	60	.209	.426	148	31	3	1	9	6.1	17	25	16	38	0	15	2	72	2	0	0	1.5	1.000	OF-37, DH-14
1986		102	.293	.525	280	82	17	0	16	5.7	44	45	47	78	2	22	7	172	4	2	6	2.0	.989	OF-81, 1B-5, DH-3
1987		113	.233	.421	318	74	7	1	17	5.3	42	42	40	99	0	22	3	214	10	2	2	2.1	.991	OF-74, DH-20, 1B-12
1988	**CHI A**	129	.227	.417	422	96	16	2	20	4.7	48	50	46	100	1	15	1	316	14	2	13	2.7	.994	OF-112, 1B-7, DH-2
1989		73	.248	.427	246	61	9	1	11	4.5	26	47	25	58	1	3	2	149	3	1	2	2.2	.993	OF-66, DH-5
1990		112	.274	.495	325	89	27	3	13	4.0	43	58	37	66	1	18	4	71	5	3	1	0.8	.962	DH-57, OF-43
1991		134	.259	.465	417	108	22	5	18	4.3	71	66	62	86	0	13	3	587	46	6	47	4.3	.991	1B-83, OF-59, DH-8
1992		93	.211	.347	265	56	16	1	6	2.3	26	33	36	57	0	8	2	185	7	6	4	2.3	.970	OF-81, 1B-5, DH-1
1993		78	.205	.358	176	36	10	1	5	2.8	22	20	26	51	2	7	1	204	12	3	15	2.9	.986	OF-37, 1B-32, DH-6
1994		11	.217	.565	23	5	2	0	2	8.7	2	4	0	9	0	3	0	15	0	4	1	2.4	.789	OF-5, 1B-3
10 yrs.		905	.244	.438	2620	638	129	15	117	4.5	341	390	335	642	7	126	25	1985	103	29	91	2.5	.986	OF-595, 1B-147, DH-116
LEAGUE CHAMPIONSHIP SERIES																								
1993	**CHI A**	2	.000	.000	6	0	0	0	0	0.0	1	0	1	2	0	0	0	13	2	1	2	8.0	.938	1B-2

Mike Pasquella

PASQUELLA, MICHAEL JOHN (Toney) BR TR 5′11″ 167 lbs.
Born Michael John Pasquairello.
B. Nov. 7, 1898, Philadelphia, Pa. D. Apr. 5, 1965, Bridgeport, Conn.

Year	Team	Games	BA	SA	AB	H	2B	3B	HR	HR%	R	RBI	BB	SO	SB	Pinch Hit AB	Pinch Hit H	PO	A	E	DP	TC/G	FA	G by Pos
1919	**2 teams**	**PHI N** (1G –1.000) **STL N** (1G –.000)																						
″	**total**	2	.500	.500	2	1	0	0	0	0.0	1	0	0	1	0	1	0	0	0	0	0	0.0	.000	1B-1

Cliff Pastornicky

PASTORNICKY, CLIFFORD SCOT BR TR 6′ 180 lbs.
B. Nov. 18, 1958, Seattle, Wash.

Year	Team	Games	BA	SA	AB	H	2B	3B	HR	HR%	R	RBI	BB	SO	SB	Pinch Hit AB	Pinch Hit H	PO	A	E	DP	TC/G	FA	G by Pos
1983	**KC A**	10	.125	.313	32	4	0	0	2	6.3	4	5	0	3	0	0	0	5	21	2	0	2.8	.929	3B-10

Bob Pate

PATE, ROBERT WAYNE BR TR 6′3½″ 200 lbs.
B. Dec. 3, 1953, Los Angeles, Calif.

Year	Team	Games	BA	SA	AB	H	2B	3B	HR	HR%	R	RBI	BB	SO	SB	Pinch Hit AB	Pinch Hit H	PO	A	E	DP	TC/G	FA	G by Pos
1980	**MON N**	23	.256	.308	39	10	2	0	0	0.0	3	5	3	6	0	5	1	18	0	0	0	1.0	1.000	OF-18
1981		8	.333	.333	6	2	0	0	0	0.0	0	0	1	0	0	2	0	3	0	0	0	0.6	1.000	OF-5
2 yrs.		31	.267	.311	45	12	2	0	0	0.0	3	5	4	6	0	7	1	21	0	0	0	0.9	1.000	OF-23

Freddie Patek

PATEK, FREDERICK JOSEPH (Moochie, The Flea) BR TR 5′ 5″ 148 lbs.
B. Oct. 9, 1944, Seguin, Tex.

Year	Team	Lg	Games	BA	SA	AB	H	2B	3B	HR	HR%	R	RBI	BB	SO	SB	Pinch Hit AB	Pinch Hit H	PO	A	E	DP	TC/G	FA	G by Pos
1968	PIT	N	61	.255	.322	208	53	4	2	2	1.0	31	18	12	37	18	1	0	90	166	6	23	4.5	.977	SS-52, OF-5, 3B-1
1969			147	.239	.296	460	110	9	1	5	1.1	48	32	53	86	15	0	0	227	399	30	81	4.5	.954	SS-146
1970			84	.245	.342	237	58	10	5	1	0.4	42	19	29	46	8	11	3	122	212	10	42	5.3	.971	SS-65
1971	KC	A	147	.267	.371	591	158	21	**11**	6	1.0	86	36	44	80	49	1	0	301	459	25	107	5.3	.968	SS-147
1972			136	.212	.276	518	110	25	4	0	0.0	59	32	47	64	33	0	0	230	510	22	113	5.6	.971	SS-136
1973			135	.234	.321	501	117	19	5	5	1.0	82	45	54	63	36	0	0	242	503	26	115	5.7	.966	SS-135
1974			149	.225	.298	537	121	18	6	3	0.6	72	38	77	69	33	0	0	250	493	25	108	5.2	.967	SS-149
1975			136	.228	.308	483	110	14	5	5	1.0	58	45	42	65	32	1	0	231	405	27	78	4.8	.959	SS-136, DH-1
1976			144	.241	.306	432	104	19	3	1	0.2	58	43	50	63	51	0	0	233	426	26	87	4.8	.962	SS-143, DH-1
1977			154	.262	.368	497	130	26	6	5	1.0	72	60	41	84	**53**	0	0	252	413	29	70	4.5	.958	SS-154
1978			138	.248	.318	440	109	23	1	2	0.5	54	46	42	56	38	1	1	240	350	32	84	4.5	.949	SS-137
1979			106	.252	.317	306	77	17	0	1	0.3	30	37	16	42	11	0	0	153	249	19	54	4.0	.955	SS-104
1980	CAL	A	86	.264	.392	273	72	10	5	5	1.8	41	34	15	26	7	4	0	129	199	16	42	4.2	.953	SS-81
1981			27	.234	.298	47	11	1	1	0	0.0	3	5	1	6	1	1	1	27	42	2	8	2.7	.972	2B-16, 3B-7, SS-3
14 yrs.			1650	.242	.324	5530	1340	216	55	41	0.7	736	490	523	787	385	20	5	2727	4826	295	1012	4.8	.962	SS-1588, 2B-16, 3B-8, OF-5, DH-2
LEAGUE CHAMPIONSHIP SERIES																									
1970	PIT	N	1	.000	.000	3	0	0	0	0	0.0	0	0	1	2	0	0	0	1	2	0	0	3.0	1.000	SS-1
1976	KC	A	5	.389	.500	18	7	2	0	0	0.0	2	4	0	1	0	0	0	13	18	0	3	6.2	1.000	SS-5
1977			5	.389	.667	18	7	3	1	0	0.0	4	5	1	2	0	0	0	8	18	1	0	5.4	.963	SS-5
1978			4	.077	.308	13	1	0	0	1	7.7	2	2	1	4	0	0	0	9	8	2	2	4.8	.895	SS-4
4 yrs.			15	.288	.481	52	15	5	1	1	1.9	8	11	3	9	0	0	0	31	46	3	5	5.3	.962	SS-15

Bob Patrick

PATRICK, ROBERT LEE BR TR 6′ 2″ 190 lbs.
B. Oct. 27, 1917, Fort Smith, Ark.

Year	Team	Lg	Games	BA	SA	AB	H	2B	3B	HR	HR%	R	RBI	BB	SO	SB	Pinch Hit AB	Pinch Hit H	PO	A	E	DP	TC/G	FA	G by Pos
1941	DET	A	5	.286	.286	7	2	0	0	0	0.0	2	0	0	1	0	2	1	3	0	1	0	1.3	.750	OF-3
1942			4	.250	.750	8	2	1	0	1	12.5	1	3	1	0	0	1	0	5	0	0	0	1.7	1.000	OF-3
2 yrs.			9	.267	.533	15	4	1	0	1	6.7	3	3	1	1	0	3	1	8	0	1	0	1.5	.889	OF-6

Harry Pattee

PATTEE, HARRY ERNEST BL TR 5′ 8″ 149 lbs.
B. Jan. 17, 1882, Charlestown, Mass. D. July 17, 1971, Lynchburg, Va.

Year	Team	Lg	Games	BA	SA	AB	H	2B	3B	HR	HR%	R	RBI	BB	SO	SB	Pinch Hit AB	Pinch Hit H	PO	A	E	DP	TC/G	FA	G by Pos
1908	BKN	N	80	.216	.250	264	57	5	2	0	0.0	19	9	25		24	6	1	158	246	15	15	5.7	.964	2B-74

Claire Patterson

PATTERSON, LORENZO CLAIRE BL TR 6′ 180 lbs.
B. Oct. 5, 1887, Arkansas City, Kans. D. Mar. 28, 1913, Mojave, Calif.

Year	Team	Lg	Games	BA	SA	AB	H	2B	3B	HR	HR%	R	RBI	BB	SO	SB	Pinch Hit AB	Pinch Hit H	PO	A	E	DP	TC/G	FA	G by Pos
1909	CIN	N	4	.125	.125	8	1	0	0	0	0.0	0	1	0		0	2	0	4	0	0	0	2.0	1.000	OF-2

Ham Patterson

PATTERSON, HAMILTON BR TR 6′ 2″ 185 lbs.
Brother of Pat Patterson.
B. Oct. 13, 1877, Belleville, Ill. D. Nov. 25, 1945, E. St. Louis, Ill.

Year	Team	Lg	Games	BA	SA	AB	H	2B	3B	HR	HR%	R	RBI	BB	SO	SB	Pinch Hit AB	Pinch Hit H	PO	A	E	DP	TC/G	FA	G by Pos
1909	2 teams		STL A (17G –.204) CHI A (1G –.000)																						
″	total		18	.192	.212	52	10	1	0	0	0.0	4	5	1		1	5	0	76	4	0	2	6.2	1.000	1B-7, OF-6

Hank Patterson

PATTERSON, HENRY JOSEPH BR TR 5′11½″ 170 lbs.
B. July 17, 1907, San Francisco, Calif. D. Sept. 30, 1970, Panorama City, Calif.

Year	Team	Lg	Games	BA	SA	AB	H	2B	3B	HR	HR%	R	RBI	BB	SO	SB	Pinch Hit AB	Pinch Hit H	PO	A	E	DP	TC/G	FA	G by Pos
1932	BOS	A	1	.000	.000	1	0	0	0	0	0.0	0	0	0	0	0	0	0	0	0	0	0	0.0	.000	C-1

John Patterson

PATTERSON, JOHN ALLEN BB TR 5′ 9″ 160 lbs.
B. Feb. 11, 1967, Key West, Fla.

Year	Team	Lg	Games	BA	SA	AB	H	2B	3B	HR	HR%	R	RBI	BB	SO	SB	Pinch Hit AB	Pinch Hit H	PO	A	E	DP	TC/G	FA	G by Pos
1992	SF	N	32	.184	.214	103	19	1	1	0	0.0	10	4	5	24	5	6	1	66	54	4	16	4.6	.968	2B-22, OF-5
1993			16	.188	.375	16	3	0	0	1	6.3	1	2	0	5	0	16	3	0	0	0	0	0.0	—	
1994			85	.237	.325	240	57	10	1	3	1.3	36	32	16	43	13	23	3	120	163	6	32	4.6	.979	2B-63
1995			95	.205	.273	205	42	5	3	1	0.5	27	14	14	41	4	41	7	114	112	4	30	4.3	.983	2B-53
4 yrs.			228	.215	.287	564	121	16	5	5	0.9	74	52	35	113	22	86	14	300	329	14	78	4.5	.978	2B-138, OF-5

Mike Patterson

PATTERSON, MICHAEL LEE BL TR 5′10″ 170 lbs.
B. Jan. 26, 1958, Santa Monica, Calif.

Year	Team	Lg	Games	BA	SA	AB	H	2B	3B	HR	HR%	R	RBI	BB	SO	SB	Pinch Hit AB	Pinch Hit H	PO	A	E	DP	TC/G	FA	G by Pos
1981	2 teams		OAK A (12G –.348) NY A (4G –.222)																						
″	total		16	.313	.531	32	10	1	3	0	0.0	6	1	2	5	0	5	2	13	0	0	0	1.2	1.000	OF-9, DH-2
1982	NY	A	11	.188	.438	16	3	1	0	1	6.3	3	1	2	6	1	0	0	5	0	0	0	0.5	1.000	OF-9, DH-1
2 yrs.			27	.271	.500	48	13	2	3	1	2.1	9	2	4	11	1	5	2	18	0	0	0	0.9	1.000	OF-18, DH-3

Pat Patterson

PATTERSON, WILLIAM JENNINGS BRYAN BR TR 6′ 175 lbs.
Brother of Ham Patterson.
B. Jan. 29, 1901, Belleville, Ill. D. Oct. 1, 1977, St. Louis, Mo.

Year	Team	Lg	Games	BA	SA	AB	H	2B	3B	HR	HR%	R	RBI	BB	SO	SB	Pinch Hit AB	Pinch Hit H	PO	A	E	DP	TC/G	FA	G by Pos
1921	NY	N	23	.400	.486	35	14	0	0	1	2.9	5	5	2	5	0	2	0	11	29	2	0	2.0	.952	3B-14, SS-7

George Pattison

PATTISON, GEORGE
Deceased.

Year	Team	Lg	Games	BA	SA	AB	H	2B	3B	HR	HR%	R	RBI	BB	SO	SB	Pinch Hit AB	Pinch Hit H	PO	A	E	DP	TC/G	FA	G by Pos
1884	PHI	U	2	.143	.143	7	1	0	0	0	0.0	0		0			0	0	1	1	2	0	2.0	.500	OF-2

Bill Patton

PATTON, GEORGE WILLIAM BR TR 6′ 2″ 180 lbs.
B. Oct. 7, 1912, Cornwall, Pa. D. Mar. 15, 1986, Philadelphia, Pa.

Year	Team	Lg	Games	BA	SA	AB	H	2B	3B	HR	HR%	R	RBI	BB	SO	SB	Pinch Hit AB	Pinch Hit H	PO	A	E	DP	TC/G	FA	G by Pos
1935	PHI	A	9	.300	.400	10	3	1	0	0	0.0	1	2	2	3	0	4	1	4	3	0	1	2.3	1.000	C-3

Gene Patton

PATTON, GENE TUNNEY BL TR 5′10″ 165 lbs.
B. July 8, 1926, Coatesville, Pa.

Year	Team	Lg	Games	BA	SA	AB	H	2B	3B	HR	HR%	R	RBI	BB	SO	SB	Pinch Hit AB	Pinch Hit H	PO	A	E	DP	TC/G	FA	G by Pos
1944	BOS	N	1	—	—	0	0	0	0	0	—	0	0	0	0	0	0	0	0	0	0	0	0.0	—	

Tom Patton

PATTON, THOMAS ALLEN BR TR 5′ 9½″ 185 lbs.
B. Sept. 5, 1935, Honey Brook, Pa.

Year	Team	Lg	Games	BA	SA	AB	H	2B	3B	HR	HR%	R	RBI	BB	SO	SB	Pinch Hit AB	Pinch Hit H	PO	A	E	DP	TC/G	FA	G by Pos
1957	BAL	A	1	.000	.000	2	0	0	0	0	0.0	0	0	0	2	0	0	0	4	2	0	1	6.0	1.000	C-1

Lou Paul

PAUL, LOUIS BR TR
Deceased.

Year	Team	Games	BA	SA	AB	H	2B	3B	HR	HR%	R	RBI	BB	SO	SB	Pinch Hit AB	Pinch Hit H	PO	A	E	DP	TC/G	FA	G by Pos
1876	PHI N	3	.167	.250	12	2	1	0	0	0.0	2	0	0	0		0	0	5	4	5	0	4.7	.643	C-3

Carlos Paula

PAULA, CARLOS BR TR 6′ 3″ 195 lbs.
Born Carlos Paula (Conill).
B. Nov. 28, 1927, Havana, Cuba D. Apr. 25, 1983, Miami, Fla.

Year	Team	Games	BA	SA	AB	H	2B	3B	HR	HR%	R	RBI	BB	SO	SB	Pinch Hit AB	Pinch Hit H	PO	A	E	DP	TC/G	FA	G by Pos
1954	WAS A	9	.167	.208	24	4	1	0	0	0.0	2	2	2	4	0	3	0	14	1	0	0	2.5	1.000	OF-6
1955		115	.299	.447	351	105	20	7	6	1.7	34	45	17	43	2	28	8	154	5	10	3	2.0	.941	OF-85
1956		33	.183	.341	82	15	2	1	3	3.7	8	13	8	15	0	11	3	37	0	1	0	1.9	.974	OF-20
3 yrs.		157	.271	.416	457	124	23	8	9	2.0	44	60	27	62	2	42	11	205	6	11	3	2.0	.950	OF-111

Gene Paulette

PAULETTE, EUGENE EDWARD BR TR 6′ 150 lbs.
B. May 26, 1891, Centralia, Ill. D. Feb. 8, 1966, Little Rock, Ark.

Year	Team	Games	BA	SA	AB	H	2B	3B	HR	HR%	R	RBI	BB	SO	SB	Pinch Hit AB	Pinch Hit H	PO	A	E	DP	TC/G	FA	G by Pos
1911	NY N	10	.167	.167	12	2	0	0	0	0.0	1	1	0	1	0	0	0	29	1	2	0	3.6	.938	1B-7, SS-1, 3B-1
1916	STL A	5	.500	.500	4	2	0	0	0	0.0	1	0	1	1	0	4	2	0	0	0	0	0.0	—	
1917	2 teams	STL A (12G –.182) STL N (95G –.265)																						
″	total	107	.260	.359	354	92	21	7	0	0.0	35	34	19	19	9	6	1	1186	55	12	85	12.3	.990	1B-98, 2B-3, 3B-1
1918	STL N	125	.273	.319	461	126	15	3	0	0.0	33	52	27	16	11	3	0	1171	129	26	77	10.6	.980	1B-97, SS-12, 2B-7, OF-6, 3B-2, P-1
1919	2 teams	STL N (43G –.215) PHI N (67G –.259)																						
″	total	110	.243	.302	387	94	14	3	1	0.3	31	42	28	16	14	3	0	554	209	20	54	7.7	.974	2B-53, 1B-36, OF-10, SS-3
1920	PHI N	143	.288	.343	562	162	16	6	1	0.2	59	36	33	16	9	2	1	1432	103	18	95	11.0	.988	1B-139, SS-2
6 yrs.		500	.269	.330	1780	478	66	19	2	0.1	160	165	108	69	43	18	4	4372	497	78	311	10.3	.984	1B-377, 2B-63, SS-18, OF-16, 3B-4, P-1

Si Pauxtis

PAUXTIS, SIMON FRANCIS BR TR 6′ 175 lbs.
B. July 20, 1885, Pittston, Pa. D. Mar. 13, 1961, Philadelphia, Pa.

Year	Team	Games	BA	SA	AB	H	2B	3B	HR	HR%	R	RBI	BB	SO	SB	Pinch Hit AB	Pinch Hit H	PO	A	E	DP	TC/G	FA	G by Pos
1909	CIN N	4	.125	.125	8	1	0	0	0	0.0	2	0	0		0	0	0	11	1	0	0	3.0	1.000	C-4

Don Pavletich

PAVLETICH, DONALD STEPHEN BR TR 5′11″ 190 lbs.
B. July 13, 1938, Milwaukee, Wis.

Year	Team	Games	BA	SA	AB	H	2B	3B	HR	HR%	R	RBI	BB	SO	SB	Pinch Hit AB	Pinch Hit H	PO	A	E	DP	TC/G	FA	G by Pos
1957	CIN N	1	.000	.000	1	0	0	0	0	0.0	0	0	0	0	0	1	0	0	0	0	0	0.0	—	
1959		1	—	—	0	0	0	0	0	—	1	0	0	0	0	0	0	0	0	0	0	0.0	—	
1962		34	.222	.317	63	14	3	0	1	1.6	7	7	8	18	0	11	3	167	11	0	12	6.6	1.000	1B-25, C-2
1963		71	.208	.350	183	38	11	0	5	2.7	18	18	17	12	0	16	0	409	20	3	21	6.2	.993	1B-57, C-13
1964		34	.242	.451	91	22	4	0	5	5.5	12	11	10	17	0	7	1	168	8	3	2	6.4	.983	C-27, 1B-1
1965		68	.319	.513	191	61	11	1	8	4.2	25	32	23	27	1	11	4	391	18	6	14	6.6	.986	C-54, 1B-9
1966		83	.294	.519	235	69	13	2	12	5.1	29	38	18	37	1	23	6	379	32	9	10	6.5	.979	C-55, 1B-10
1967		74	.238	.403	231	55	14	3	6	2.6	25	34	21	38	2	8	1	414	34	7	8	6.2	.985	C-66, 1B-6, 3B-1
1968		46	.286	.398	98	28	3	1	2	2.0	11	11	8	23	0	20	4	185	13	0	14	7.3	1.000	1B-22, C-5
1969	CHI A	78	.245	.404	188	46	12	0	6	3.2	26	33	28	45	0	19	4	285	28	7	16	5.0	.978	C-51, 1B-13
1970	BOS A	32	.138	.185	65	9	1	1	0	0.0	4	6	10	15	1	7	1	123	12	0	11	5.2	1.000	1B-16, C-10
1971		14	.259	.407	27	7	1	0	1	3.7	5	3	5	5	0	5	1	35	1	1	1	4.6	.973	C-8
12 yrs.		536	.254	.420	1373	349	73	8	46	3.4	163	193	148	237	5	128	25	2556	177	36	109	6.1	.987	C-291, 1B-159, 3B-1

Ted Pawelek

PAWELEK, THEODORE JOHN (Porky) BL TR 5′10½″ 202 lbs.
B. Aug. 15, 1919, Chicago Heights, Ill. D. Feb. 12, 1964, Chicago Heights, Ill.

Year	Team	Games	BA	SA	AB	H	2B	3B	HR	HR%	R	RBI	BB	SO	SB	Pinch Hit AB	Pinch Hit H	PO	A	E	DP	TC/G	FA	G by Pos
1946	CHI N	4	.250	.500	4	1	1	0	0	0.0	0	0	0	0	0	3	1	0	0	0	0	0.0	.000	C-1

Stan Pawloski

PAWLOSKI, STANLEY WALTER BR TR 6′ 1″ 175 lbs.
B. Sept. 6, 1931, Wanamie, Pa.

Year	Team	Games	BA	SA	AB	H	2B	3B	HR	HR%	R	RBI	BB	SO	SB	Pinch Hit AB	Pinch Hit H	PO	A	E	DP	TC/G	FA	G by Pos
1955	CLE A	2	.125	.125	8	1	0	0	0	0.0	0	0	0	2	0	0	0	3	8	0	0	5.5	1.000	2B-2

Fred Payne

PAYNE, FREDERICK THOMAS BR TR 5′10″ 162 lbs.
B. Sept. 2, 1880, Camden, N. Y. D. Jan. 16, 1954, Camden, N. Y.

Year	Team	Games	BA	SA	AB	H	2B	3B	HR	HR%	R	RBI	BB	SO	SB	Pinch Hit AB	Pinch Hit H	PO	A	E	DP	TC/G	FA	G by Pos
1906	DET A	72	.270	.338	222	60	5	5	0	0.0	23	20	13		4	7	3	213	54	9	6	4.3	.967	C-47, OF-17
1907		53	.166	.201	169	28	2	2	0	0.0	17	14	7		4	1	0	213	56	5	5	5.4	.982	C-46, OF-5
1908		20	.067	.067	45	3	0	0	0	0.0	3	2	3		1	2	0	54	10	3	1	3.7	.955	C-16, OF-2
1909	CHI A	32	.244	.268	82	20	2	0	0	0.0	8	12	5		0	2	1	111	38	2	5	5.0	.987	C-27, OF-3
1910		91	.218	.268	257	56	5	4	0	0.0	17	19	11		6	9	2	410	106	14	11	6.6	.974	C-78, OF-2
1911		66	.203	.256	133	27	2	1	1	0.8	14	19	8		6	9	3	213	48	10	10	4.8	.963	C-56
6 yrs.		334	.214	.261	908	194	16	12	1	0.1	82	86	47		21	30	9	1214	312	43	38	5.2	.973	C-270, OF-29
WORLD SERIES																								
1907	DET A	2	.250	.250	4	1	0	0	0	0.0	0	1	0	0	0	0	0	5	1	1	0	7.0	.857	C-1

George Paynter

PAYNTER, GEORGE WASHINGTON BR TR 5′ 9″ 125 lbs.
Born George Washington Paner.
B. July 6, 1871, Cincinnati, Ohio D. Oct. 1, 1950, Cincinnati, Ohio.

Year	Team	Games	BA	SA	AB	H	2B	3B	HR	HR%	R	RBI	BB	SO	SB	Pinch Hit AB	Pinch Hit H	PO	A	E	DP	TC/G	FA	G by Pos
1894	STL N	1	.000	.000	4	0	0	0	0	0.0	0	0	1	0	1	0	0	1	2	0	0	3.0	1.000	OF-1

Johnny Peacock

PEACOCK, JOHN GASTON BL TR 5′11″ 165 lbs.
B. Jan. 10, 1910, Fremont, N. C. D. Oct. 17, 1981, Wilson, N. C.

Year	Team	Games	BA	SA	AB	H	2B	3B	HR	HR%	R	RBI	BB	SO	SB	Pinch Hit AB	Pinch Hit H	PO	A	E	DP	TC/G	FA	G by Pos
1937	BOS A	9	.313	.438	32	10	2	1	0	0.0	3	6	1	0	0	0	0	42	8	1	1	5.7	.980	C-9
1938		72	.303	.364	195	59	7	1	1	0.5	29	39	17	4	4	15	4	187	12	4	4	3.4	.980	C-57, OF-1, 1B-1
1939		92	.277	.347	274	76	11	4	0	0.0	33	36	29	11	1	10	3	314	33	10	6	4.3	.972	C-84
1940		63	.282	.328	131	37	4	1	0	0.0	20	13	23	10	1	12	3	159	13	1	0	3.6	.994	C-48
1941		79	.284	.368	261	74	20	1	0	0.0	28	27	21	3	2	9	3	298	33	4	7	4.8	.988	C-70
1942		88	.266	.311	286	76	7	3	0	0.0	17	25	21	11	1	8	1	280	44	4	8	4.0	.988	C-82
1943		48	.202	.246	114	23	3	1	0	0.0	7	7	10	9	1	14	2	121	18	4	2	4.5	.972	C-32

Johnny Peacock *continued*

Year	Team	Games	BA	SA	AB	H	2B	3B	HR	HR%	R	RBI	BB	SO	SB	Pinch Hit AB	Pinch Hit H	PO	A	E	DP	TC/G	FA	G by Pos
1944	2 teams	BOS A (4G –.000) PHI N (83G –.225)																						
″	total	87	.222	.280	257	57	9	3	0	0.0	21	21	31	5	1	12	4	275	41	3	4	4.2	.991	C-75, 2B-1
1945	2 teams	PHI N (33G –.203) BKN N (48G –.255)																						
″	total	81	.234	.304	184	43	11	1	0	0.0	17	20	30	10	3	19	4	197	20	6	9	3.7	.973	C-61
9 yrs.		619	.262	.325	1734	455	74	16	1	0.1	175	194	183	63	14	99	24	1873	222	37	41	4.1	.983	C-518, OF-1, 2B-1, 1B-1

Elias Peak

PEAK, ELIAS
B. May 23, 1859, Philadelphia, Pa. D. Dec. 17, 1916, Philadelphia, Pa.

Year	Team	Games	BA	SA	AB	H	2B	3B	HR	HR%	R	RBI	BB	SO	SB	Pinch Hit AB	Pinch Hit H	PO	A	E	DP	TC/G	FA	G by Pos
1884	2 teams	BOS U (1G –.667) PHI U (54G –.195)																						
″	total	55	.202	.266	218	44	6	4	0	0.0	37		8			0	0	154	141	70	14	6.6	.808	2B-47, OF-6, SS-2

Dickey Pearce

PEARCE, RICHARD J. BR TR 5′ 3½″ 161 lbs.
B. Feb. 29, 1836, Brooklyn, N. Y. D. Oct. 12, 1908, Onset, Mass.

Year	Team	Games	BA	SA	AB	H	2B	3B	HR	HR%	R	RBI	BB	SO	SB	Pinch Hit AB	Pinch Hit H	PO	A	E	DP	TC/G	FA	G by Pos
1876	STL N	25	.206	.216	102	21	1	0	0	0.0	12	10	3	5		0	0	27	88	14	6	5.2	.891	SS-23, OF-1, 2B-1
1877		8	.172	.172	29	5	0	0	0	0.0	1	4	1	4		0	0	7	31	2	3	5.0	.950	SS-8
2 yrs.		33	.198	.206	131	26	1	0	0	0.0	13	14	4	9		0	0	34	119	16	9	5.1	.905	SS-31, OF-1, 2B-1

Ducky Pearce

PEARCE, WILLIAM C. BR TR 6′ 1″ 185 lbs.
B. Mar. 17, 1885, Corning, Ohio D. May 22, 1933, Brownstown, Ind.

Year	Team	Games	BA	SA	AB	H	2B	3B	HR	HR%	R	RBI	BB	SO	SB	Pinch Hit AB	Pinch Hit H	PO	A	E	DP	TC/G	FA	G by Pos
1908	CIN N	2	.000	.000	2	0	0	0	0	0.0	0	0	0		0	0	0	5	3	0	0	4.0	1.000	C-2
1909		2	.000	.000	2	0	0	0	0	0.0	0	0	0		0	0	0	3	0	0	0	1.5	1.000	C-2
2 yrs.		4	.000	.000	4	0	0	0	0	0.0	0	0	0		0	0	0	8	3	0	0	2.8	1.000	C-4

Harry Pearce

PEARCE, HARRY JAMES BR TR 5′ 9″ 158 lbs.
B. July 12, 1889, Philadelphia, Pa. D. Jan. 8, 1942, Philadelphia, Pa.

Year	Team	Games	BA	SA	AB	H	2B	3B	HR	HR%	R	RBI	BB	SO	SB	Pinch Hit AB	Pinch Hit H	PO	A	E	DP	TC/G	FA	G by Pos
1917	PHI N	7	.250	.438	16	4	3	0	0	0.0	2	2	0	4	0	0	0	7	22	1	1	7.5	.967	SS-4
1918		60	.244	.287	164	40	3	2	0	0.0	16	18	9	31	5	2	0	100	157	17	18	5.5	.938	2B-46, SS-2, 3B-1, 1B-1
1919		68	.180	.217	244	44	3	3	0	0.0	24	9	8	27	6	0	0	130	202	17	30	5.1	.951	2B-43, SS-23, 3B-2
3 yrs.		135	.208	.252	424	88	9	5	0	0.0	42	29	17	62	11	2	0	237	381	35	49	5.4	.946	2B-89, SS-29, 3B-3, 1B-1

Albie Pearson

PEARSON, ALBERT GREGORY BL TL 5′ 5″ 140 lbs.
B. Sept. 12, 1934, Alhambra, Calif.

Year	Team	Games	BA	SA	AB	H	2B	3B	HR	HR%	R	RBI	BB	SO	SB	Pinch Hit AB	Pinch Hit H	PO	A	E	DP	TC/G	FA	G by Pos
1958	WAS A	146	.275	.358	530	146	25	5	3	0.6	63	33	64	31	7	4	2	338	6	7	1	2.5	.980	OF-141
1959	2 teams	WAS A (25G –.188) BAL A (80G –.232)																						
″	total	105	.216	.257	218	47	5	2	0	0.0	31	8	27	8	5	29	6	112	2	2	0	1.6	.983	OF-71
1960	BAL A	48	.244	.305	82	20	2	0	1	1.2	17	6	17	3	4	13	4	38	1	1	0	1.3	.975	OF-32
1961	LA A	144	.288	.400	427	123	21	3	7	1.6	92	41	96	40	11	23	9	233	7	11	2	2.2	.956	OF-113
1962		160	.261	.352	614	160	29	6	5	0.8	**115**	42	95	36	15	0	0	366	8	4	0	2.4	.989	OF-160
1963		154	.304	.398	578	176	26	5	6	1.0	92	47	92	37	17	4	0	340	10	6	5	2.4	.983	OF-148
1964		107	.223	.272	265	59	5	1	2	0.8	34	16	35	22	6	31	7	132	1	3	1	2.1	.978	OF-66
1965	CAL A	122	.278	.369	360	100	17	2	4	1.1	41	21	51	17	12	27	6	166	5	2	1	1.7	.988	OF-101
1966		2	.000	.000	3	0	0	0	0	0.0	0	0	0	1	0	2	0	0	0	0	0	0.0	.000	OF-1
9 yrs.		988	.270	.355	3077	831	130	24	28	0.9	485	214	477	195	77	133	34	1725	40	36	10	2.2	.980	OF-833

Charlie Pechous

PECHOUS, CHARLES EDWARD BR TR 6′ 170 lbs.
B. Oct. 5, 1896, Chicago, Ill. D. Sept. 13, 1980, Kenosha, Wis.

Year	Team	Games	BA	SA	AB	H	2B	3B	HR	HR%	R	RBI	BB	SO	SB	Pinch Hit AB	Pinch Hit H	PO	A	E	DP	TC/G	FA	G by Pos
1915	CHI F	18	.176	.235	51	9	3	0	0	0.0	4	4	4		1	0	0	13	32	3	0	2.7	.938	3B-18
1916	CHI N	22	.145	.188	69	10	1	1	0	0.0	5	4	3	21	1	0	0	22	56	5	2	3.8	.940	3B-22
1917		13	.244	.244	41	10	0	0	0	0.0	2	1	2	9	1	0	0	19	23	4	2	3.8	.913	3B-7, SS-5
3 yrs.		53	.180	.217	161	29	4	1	0	0.0	11	9	9	30	3	0	0	54	111	12	4	3.4	.932	3B-47, SS-5

Hal Peck

PECK, HAROLD ARTHUR BL TL 5′11″ 175 lbs.
B. Apr. 20, 1917, Big Bend, Wis. D. Apr. 13, 1995, Milwaukee, Wis.

Year	Team	Games	BA	SA	AB	H	2B	3B	HR	HR%	R	RBI	BB	SO	SB	Pinch Hit AB	Pinch Hit H	PO	A	E	DP	TC/G	FA	G by Pos
1943	BKN N	1	.000	.000	1	0	0	0	0	0.0	0	0	0	0	0	1	0	0	0	0	0	0.0	—	
1944	PHI A	2	.250	.250	8	2	0	0	0	0.0	0	1	0	2	0	0	0	3	0	0	0	1.5	1.000	OF-2
1945		112	.276	.399	449	124	22	9	5	1.1	51	39	37	28	5	2	0	190	9	12	3	1.9	.943	OF-110
1946		48	.247	.367	150	37	8	2	2	1.3	14	11	16	14	1	12	3	47	4	1	1	1.5	.981	OF-35
1947	CLE A	114	.293	.411	392	115	18	2	8	2.0	58	44	27	31	3	11	4	166	5	3	3	1.8	.983	OF-97
1948		45	.286	.333	63	18	3	0	0	0.0	12	8	4	8	1	30	**8**	13	0	0	0	1.4	1.000	OF-9
1949		33	.310	.345	29	9	1	0	0	0.0	1	9	3	3	0	28	8	1	0	0	0	0.5	1.000	OF-2
7 yrs.		355	.279	.392	1092	305	52	13	15	1.4	136	112	87	86	10	84	23	420	18	16	7	1.8	.965	OF-255
WORLD SERIES																								
1948	CLE A	1	—	—	0	0	0	0	0	—	0	0	0	0	0	0	0	0	0	0	0	0.0	.000	OF-1

Roger Peckinpaugh

PECKINPAUGH, ROGER THORPE BR TR 5′10½″ 165 lbs.
B. Feb. 5, 1891, Wooster, Ohio D. Nov. 17, 1977, Cleveland, Ohio.
Manager 1914, 1928–33, 1941.

Year	Team	Games	BA	SA	AB	H	2B	3B	HR	HR%	R	RBI	BB	SO	SB	Pinch Hit AB	Pinch Hit H	PO	A	E	DP	TC/G	FA	G by Pos
1910	CLE A	15	.200	.200	45	9	0	0	0	0.0	1	6	1		3	1	0	20	38	6	3	4.6	.906	SS-14
1912		69	.212	.250	236	50	4	1	1	0.4	18	22	16		11	2	0	127	188	26	16	5.1	.924	SS-67
1913	2 teams	CLE A (1G –.000) NY A (95G –.268)																						
″	total	96	.268	.347	340	91	10	7	1	0.3	36	32	24	47	19	1	0	184	303	36	30	5.6	.931	SS-94
1914	NY A	157	.223	.284	570	127	14	6	3	0.5	55	51	51	73	38	0	0	356	500	39	45	5.7	.956	SS-157
1915		142	.220	.307	540	119	18	7	5	0.9	67	44	49	72	19	0	0	291	468	47	60	5.7	.942	SS-142
1916		146	.255	.346	552	141	22	8	4	0.7	65	58	62	50	18	0	0	285	468	43	50	5.5	.946	SS-146
1917		148	.260	.330	543	141	24	7	0	0.0	63	41	64	46	17	0	0	292	467	54	84	5.5	.934	SS-148
1918		122	.231	.278	446	103	15	3	0	0.0	59	43	43	41	12	0	0	260	439	28	75	6.0	.961	SS-122
1919		122	.305	.404	453	138	20	2	7	1.5	89	33	59	37	10	1	0	271	434	43	57	6.2	.943	SS-121
1920		139	.270	.386	534	144	26	6	8	1.5	109	54	72	47	8	1	0	263	441	28	56	5.3	.962	SS-137
1921		149	.288	.397	577	166	25	7	8	1.4	128	71	84	44	2	0	0	318	443	42	75	5.4	.948	SS-149
1922	WAS A	147	.254	.308	520	132	14	4	2	0.4	62	48	55	36	11	0	0	265	524	41	93	5.6	.951	SS-147
1923		154	.264	.320	568	150	18	4	2	0.4	73	62	64	30	10	0	0	311	510	45	105	5.6	.948	SS-154
1924		155	.272	.340	523	142	20	5	2	0.4	72	73	72	45	11	0	0	278	487	29	81	5.1	.963	SS-155
1925		126	.294	.379	422	124	16	4	4	0.9	67	64	49	23	13	0	0	219	346	28	71	4.7	.953	SS-124, 1B-1

Roger Peckinpaugh *continued*

Year	Team		Games	BA	SA	AB	H	2B	3B	HR	HR%	R	RBI	BB	SO	SB	Pinch Hit AB	Pinch Hit H	PO	A	E	DP	TC/G	FA	G by Pos
1926			57	.238	.299	147	35	4	1	1	0.7	19	14	28	12	3	9	2	89	109	9	21	4.4	.957	SS-46, 1B-1
1927	CHI	A	68	.295	.350	217	64	6	3	0	0.0	23	23	21	6	2	7	2	101	170	10	30	4.7	.964	SS-60
17 yrs.			2012	.259	.335	7233	1876	256	75	48	0.7	1006	739	814	609	207	22	4	3930	6335	554	952	5.5	.949	SS-1983, 1B-2
WORLD SERIES																									
1921	NY	A	8	.179	.214	28	5	1	0	0	0.0	2	0	4	3	0	0	0	18	28	1	4	5.9	.979	SS-8
1924	WAS	A	4	.417	.583	12	5	2	0	0	0.0	1	2	1	0	1	0	0	7	14	0	3	5.3	1.000	SS-4
1925			7	.250	.417	24	6	1	0	1	4.2	1	2	1	2	1	0	0	10	22	8	3	5.7	.800	SS-7
3 yrs.			19	.250	.359	64	16	4	0	1	1.6	4	4	6	5	2	0	0	35	64	9	10	5.7	.917	SS-19

Bill Pecota

PECOTA, WILLIAM JOSEPH BR TR 6′ 2″ 195 lbs.
B. Feb. 16, 1960, Redwood City, Calif.

Year	Team		Games	BA	SA	AB	H	2B	3B	HR	HR%	R	RBI	BB	SO	SB	Pinch Hit AB	Pinch Hit H	PO	A	E	DP	TC/G	FA	G by Pos
1986	KC	A	12	.207	.276	29	6	2	0	0	0.0	3	2	3	3	0	0	0	7	31	1	1	2.8	.974	3B-12, SS-2
1987			66	.276	.378	156	43	5	1	3	1.9	22	14	15	25	5	7	0	67	135	6	28	3.1	.971	SS-36, 3B-17, 2B-15
1988			90	.208	.275	178	37	3	3	1	0.6	25	15	18	34	7	1	1	98	145	6	25	2.8	.976	SS-41, 3B-21, 1B-11, OF-9, DH-4, 2B-3, C-1
1989			65	.205	.410	83	17	4	2	3	3.6	21	5	7	9	5	0	0	50	79	2	14	1.9	.985	SS-29, OF-15, 2B-12, 3B-7, 1B-4, DH-1
1990			87	.242	.383	240	58	15	2	5	2.1	43	20	33	39	8	2	0	160	195	5	44	3.8	.986	2B-50, SS-21, 3B-11, OF-6, 1B-4, DH-2
1991			125	.286	.399	398	114	23	2	6	1.5	53	45	41	45	16	6	2	163	206	4	28	2.4	.989	3B-102, 2B-34, SS-9, 1B-8, DH-2, OF-1, P-1
1992	NY	N	117	.227	.297	269	61	13	0	2	0.7	28	26	25	40	9	20	6	92	218	12	33	2.5	.963	3B-48, SS-39, 2B-38, 1B-1, P-1
1993	ATL	N	72	.323	.387	62	20	2	1	0	0.0	17	5	2	5	1	30	8	9	13	0	1	0.8	1.000	3B-23, 2B-4, OF-1
1994			64	.214	.313	112	24	5	0	2	1.8	11	16	16	16	1	29	9	16	61	2	4	2.4	.975	3B-31, 2B-1, OF-1
9 yrs.			698	.249	.354	1527	380	72	11	22	1.4	223	148	160	216	52	95	26	662	1083	38	178	2.6	.979	3B-272, SS-177, 2B-157, OF-33, 1B-28, DH-9, P-2, C-1
LEAGUE CHAMPIONSHIP SERIES																									
1993	ATL	N	4	.333	.333	3	1	0	0	0	0.0	1	0	1	1	0	3	1	0	0	0	0	0.0	—	

Les Peden

PEDEN, LESLIE EARL BR TR 6′ 1½″ 212 lbs.
B. Sept. 17, 1923, Azle, Tex.

Year	Team		Games	BA	SA	AB	H	2B	3B	HR	HR%	R	RBI	BB	SO	SB	Pinch Hit AB	Pinch Hit H	PO	A	E	DP	TC/G	FA	G by Pos
1953	WAS	A	9	.250	.393	28	7	1	0	1	3.6	4	1	4	3	0	1	1	26	5	0	1	3.9	1.000	C-8

Stu Pederson

PEDERSON, STUART RUSSELL BL TL 6′ 190 lbs.
B. Jan. 28, 1960, Palo Alto, Calif.

Year	Team		Games	BA	SA	AB	H	2B	3B	HR	HR%	R	RBI	BB	SO	SB	Pinch Hit AB	Pinch Hit H	PO	A	E	DP	TC/G	FA	G by Pos
1985	LA	N	8	.000	.000	4	0	0	0	0	0.0	1	1	0	2	0	3	0	2	0	0	0	0.4	1.000	OF-5

Jorge Pedre

PEDRE, JORGE ENRIQUE BR TR 5′11″ 210 lbs.
B. Oct. 12, 1966, Culver City, Calif.

Year	Team		Games	BA	SA	AB	H	2B	3B	HR	HR%	R	RBI	BB	SO	SB	Pinch Hit AB	Pinch Hit H	PO	A	E	DP	TC/G	FA	G by Pos
1991	KC	A	10	.263	.421	19	5	1	1	0	0.0	2	3	3	5	0	0	0	35	4	1	0	4.0	.975	C-9, 1B-1
1992	CHI	N	4	.000	.000	4	0	0	0	0	0.0	0	0	0	1	0	1	0	3	0	0	0	0.8	1.000	C-4
2 yrs.			14	.217	.348	23	5	1	1	0	0.0	2	3	3	6	0	1	0	38	4	1	0	3.1	.977	C-13, 1B-1

Al Pedrique

PEDRIQUE, ALFREDO JOSE BR TR 6′ 155 lbs.
Born Alfredo Jose Pedrique (Garcia).
B. Aug. 11, 1960, Aragua, Venezuela.

Year	Team		Games	BA	SA	AB	H	2B	3B	HR	HR%	R	RBI	BB	SO	SB	Pinch Hit AB	Pinch Hit H	PO	A	E	DP	TC/G	FA	G by Pos
1987	2 teams		NY N (5G –.000) PIT N (88G –.301)																						
″	total		93	.294	.353	252	74	10	1	1	0.4	24	27	19	29	5	7	0	118	196	11	43	3.8	.966	SS-80, 3B-3, 2B-3
1988	PIT	N	50	.180	.219	128	23	5	0	0	0.0	7	4	8	17	0	1	0	65	124	5	23	3.8	.974	SS-46, 3B-5
1989	DET	A	31	.203	.246	69	14	3	0	0	0.0	1	5	2	15	0	2	0	35	62	3	14	3.1	.970	3B-12, SS-12, 2B-8
3 yrs.			174	.247	.298	449	111	18	1	1	0.2	32	36	29	61	5	10	0	218	382	19	80	3.7	.969	SS-138, 3B-20, 2B-11

Chick Pedroes

PEDROES, CHARLES P.
B. Oct. 27, 1869, Chicago, Ill. D. Aug. 6, 1927, Chicago, Ill.

Year	Team		Games	BA	SA	AB	H	2B	3B	HR	HR%	R	RBI	BB	SO	SB	Pinch Hit AB	Pinch Hit H	PO	A	E	DP	TC/G	FA	G by Pos
1902	CHI	N	2	.000	.000	6	0	0	0	0	0.0	0	0	0		0	0	0	2	0	0	0	1.0	1.000	OF-2

Homer Peel

PEEL, HOMER HEFNER BR TR 5′ 9½″ 170 lbs.
B. Oct. 10, 1902, Fort Sullivan, Tex.

Year	Team		Games	BA	SA	AB	H	2B	3B	HR	HR%	R	RBI	BB	SO	SB	Pinch Hit AB	Pinch Hit H	PO	A	E	DP	TC/G	FA	G by Pos
1927	STL	N	2	.000	.000	2	0	0	0	0	0.0	0	0	0	1	0	1	0	0	0	0	0	0.0	.000	OF-1
1929	PHI	N	53	.269	.359	156	42	12	1	0	0.0	16	19	12	7	1	13	1	100	5	3	2	2.7	.972	OF-39, 1B-1
1930	STL	N	26	.164	.192	73	12	2	0	0	0.0	9	10	3	4	0	4	1	30	0	1	0	1.5	.968	OF-21
1933	NY	N	84	.257	.297	148	38	1	1	1	0.7	16	12	14	10	0	35	9	49	1	2	0	1.2	.962	OF-45
1934			21	.195	.268	41	8	0	0	1	2.4	7	3	1	2	0	10	2	13	0	1	0	1.4	.929	OF-10
5 yrs.			186	.238	.298	420	100	15	2	2	0.5	48	44	30	24	1	63	13	192	6	7	2	1.8	.966	OF-116, 1B-1
WORLD SERIES																									
1933	NY	N	2	.500	.500	2	1	0	0	0	0.0	0	0	0	0	0	1	1	0	0	0	0	0.0	.000	OF-1

Jack Peerson

PEERSON, JACK CHILES BR TR 5′11″ 175 lbs.
B. Aug. 28, 1910, Brunswick, Ga. D. Oct. 23, 1966, Fort Walton Beach, Fla.

Year	Team		Games	BA	SA	AB	H	2B	3B	HR	HR%	R	RBI	BB	SO	SB	Pinch Hit AB	Pinch Hit H	PO	A	E	DP	TC/G	FA	G by Pos
1935	PHI	A	10	.316	.368	19	6	1	0	0	0.0	3	1	1	1	0	4	1	7	13	1	0	5.3	.952	SS-4
1936			8	.324	.412	34	11	1	1	0	0.0	7	5	0	3	0	0	0	19	33	3	5	6.9	.945	SS-7, 2B-1
2 yrs.			18	.321	.396	53	17	2	1	0	0.0	10	6	1	4	0	4	1	26	46	4	5	6.3	.947	SS-11, 2B-1

Charlie Peete

PEETE, CHARLES (Mule) BL TR 5′ 9½″ 190 lbs.
B. Feb. 22, 1929, Franklin, Va. D. Nov. 27, 1956, Caracas, Venezuela.

Year	Team		Games	BA	SA	AB	H	2B	3B	HR	HR%	R	RBI	BB	SO	SB	Pinch Hit AB	Pinch Hit H	PO	A	E	DP	TC/G	FA	G by Pos
1956	STL	N	23	.192	.308	52	10	2	2	0	0.0	3	6	6	10	0	4	1	37	3	0	1	1.9	1.000	OF-21

Julio Peguero

PEGUERO, JULIO CESAR BB TR 6′ 160 lbs.
Born Julio Cesar Peguero (Santana).
B. Sept. 7, 1968, San Isidro, Dominican Republic.

Year	Team		Games	BA	SA	AB	H	2B	3B	HR	HR%	R	RBI	BB	SO	SB	Pinch Hit AB	Pinch Hit H	PO	A	E	DP	TC/G	FA	G by Pos
1992	PHI	N	14	.222	.222	9	2	0	0	0	0.0	3	0	3	3	0	0	0	10	0	0	0	0.7	1.000	OF-14

Steve Pegues

PEGUES, STEVEN ANTONE BR TR 6′ 2″ 190 lbs.
B. May 21, 1968, Pontotoc, Miss.

Year	Team	Games	BA	SA	AB	H	2B	3B	HR	HR%	R	RBI	BB	SO	SB	Pinch Hit AB	Pinch Hit H	PO	A	E	DP	TC/G	FA	G by Pos
1994	2 teams CIN N (11G –.300) PIT N (7G –.385)																							
″	total	18	.361	.417	36	13	2	0	0	0.0	2	2	2	5	1	6	2	13	0	1	0	1.3	.929	OF-11
1995	PIT N	82	.246	.398	171	42	8	0	6	3.5	17	16	4	36	1	34	8	81	2	4	0	1.6	.954	OF-53
2 yrs.		100	.266	.401	207	55	10	0	6	2.9	19	18	6	41	2	40	10	94	2	5	0	1.6	.950	OF-64

Heinie Peitz

PEITZ, HENRY CLEMENT BR TR 5′11″ 165 lbs.
Brother of Joe Peitz.
B. Nov. 28, 1870, St. Louis, Mo. D. Oct. 23, 1943, Cincinnati, Ohio.

Year	Team	Games	BA	SA	AB	H	2B	3B	HR	HR%	R	RBI	BB	SO	SB	Pinch Hit AB	Pinch Hit H	PO	A	E	DP	TC/G	FA	G by Pos
1892	STL N	1	.000	.000	3	0	0	0	0	0.0	0	0	0	0	0	0	0	3	0	0	0	3.0	1.000	C-1
1893		96	.254	.345	362	92	12	9	1	0.3	53	45	54	20	12	0	0	388	116	33	16	5.4	.939	C-74, SS-11, OF-10, 1B-5
1894		99	.263	.399	338	89	19	9	3	0.9	52	49	43	21	14	0	0	320	136	33	18	4.8	.933	3B-47, C-39, 1B-14, P-1
1895		90	.284	.416	334	95	14	12	2	0.6	44	65	29	20	9	0	0	348	93	32	17	5.1	.932	C-71, 1B-11, 3B-10
1896	CIN N	68	.299	.431	211	63	12	5	2	0.9	33	34	30	15	7	1	0	201	42	8	6	3.7	.968	C-67
1897		77	.293	.398	266	78	11	7	1	0.4	35	44	18		3	4	0	261	72	7	8	4.7	.979	C-71, P-2
1898		105	.273	.358	330	90	15	5	1	0.3	49	43	35		9	3	1	323	90	24	12	4.3	.945	C-101
1899		93	.272	.341	290	79	13	2	1	0.3	45	43	45		11	2	0	331	91	10	12	4.7	.977	C-91, P-1
1900		91	.255	.330	294	75	14	1	2	0.7	34	34	20		5	4	0	373	127	20	14	5.9	.962	C-80, 1B-8
1901		82	.305	.401	269	82	13	5	1	0.4	24	24	23		3	6	2	321	127	9	14	5.9	.980	C-49, 2B-21, 3B-6, 1B-2
1902		112	.315	.406	387	122	22	5	1	0.3	54	60	24		7	5	1	376	209	33	40	5.8	.947	2B-48, C-47, 3B-6, 1B-6
1903		105	.260	.318	358	93	15	3	0	0.0	45	42	37		7	2	1	496	129	18	17	6.3	.972	C-78, 1B-11, 3B-9, 2B-4
1904		84	.243	.316	272	66	13	2	1	0.4	32	30	14		1	2	1	425	100	9	17	6.4	.983	C-64, 1B-18, 3B-1
1905	PIT N	88	.223	.259	278	62	10	0	0	0.0	18	27	24		2	2	0	338	105	16	14	5.2	.965	C-87, 2B-1
1906		40	.240	.304	125	30	8	0	0	0.0	13	20	13		1	2	0	186	45	5	2	6.2	.979	C-38
1913	STL N	3	.250	.750	4	1	0	1	0	0.0	1	0	0	0	0	0	0	3	2	3	0	2.7	.625	C-2, OF-1
16 yrs.		1234	.271	.361	4121	1117	191	66	16	0.4	532	560	409	76	91	33	6	4693	1484	260	207	5.3	.960	C-960, 3B-79, 1B-75, 2B-74, SS-11, OF-11, P-4

Joe Peitz

PEITZ, JOSEPH
Brother of Heinie Peitz.
B. Nov. 8, 1869, St. Louis, Mo. D. Dec. 4, 1919, St. Louis, Mo.

Year	Team	Games	BA	SA	AB	H	2B	3B	HR	HR%	R	RBI	BB	SO	SB	Pinch Hit AB	Pinch Hit H	PO	A	E	DP	TC/G	FA	G by Pos
1894	STL N	7	.423	.731	26	11	2	3	0	0.0	10	3	6	1	2	0	0	17	1	4	1	3.1	.818	OF-7

Eddie Pellagrini

PELLAGRINI, EDWARD CHARLES BR TR 5′ 9″ 160 lbs.
B. Mar. 13, 1918, Boston, Mass.

Year	Team	Games	BA	SA	AB	H	2B	3B	HR	HR%	R	RBI	BB	SO	SB	Pinch Hit AB	Pinch Hit H	PO	A	E	DP	TC/G	FA	G by Pos
1946	BOS A	22	.211	.366	71	15	3	1	2	2.8	7	4	3	18	1	0	0	29	40	10	8	3.4	.873	3B-14, SS-9
1947		74	.203	.299	231	47	8	1	4	1.7	29	19	23	35	2	3	0	73	142	14	17	3.4	.939	3B-42, SS-26
1948	STL A	105	.238	.307	290	69	8	3	2	0.7	31	27	34	40	1	2	1	194	292	18	85	5.1	.964	SS-98
1949		79	.238	.306	235	56	8	1	2	0.9	26	15	14	24	2	1	0	164	227	16	52	5.4	.961	SS-76
1951	PHI N	86	.234	.381	197	46	4	5	5	2.5	31	30	23	25	5	12	2	104	132	5	23	3.6	.979	2B-53, SS-8, 3B-6
1952	CIN N	46	.170	.220	100	17	2	0	1	1.0	15	3	8	18	1	6	1	119	67	2	20	5.9	.989	2B-22, 1B-8, SS-1, 3B-1
1953	PIT N	78	.253	.362	174	44	3	2	4	2.3	16	19	14	20	1	32	8	76	98	6	13	3.9	.967	2B-31, 3B-12, SS-3
1954		73	.216	.264	125	27	6	0	0	0.0	12	16	9	21	0	34	7	42	60	2	10	2.7	.981	3B-31, 2B-7, SS-1
8 yrs.		563	.226	.316	1423	321	42	13	20	1.4	167	133	128	201	13	90	19	801	1058	73	228	4.3	.962	SS-222, 2B-113, 3B-106, 1B-8

Lou Pelouze

PELOUZE, LOUIS H. BR TR 5′ 8″ 170 lbs.
Deceased.

Year	Team	Games	BA	SA	AB	H	2B	3B	HR	HR%	R	RBI	BB	SO	SB	Pinch Hit AB	Pinch Hit H	PO	A	E	DP	TC/G	FA	G by Pos
1886	STL N	1	.000	.000	3	0	0	0	0	0.0	0	0	0	2		0	0	4	0	0	0	4.0	1.000	OF-1

Dan Peltier

PELTIER, DANIEL EDWARD BL TL 6′ 1″ 200 lbs.
B. June 30, 1968, Clifton Park, N. Y.

Year	Team	Games	BA	SA	AB	H	2B	3B	HR	HR%	R	RBI	BB	SO	SB	Pinch Hit AB	Pinch Hit H	PO	A	E	DP	TC/G	FA	G by Pos
1992	TEX A	12	.167	.167	24	4	0	0	0	0.0	1	2	0	3	0	3	0	6	0	1	0	0.7	.857	OF-10
1993		65	.269	.344	160	43	7	1	1	0.6	23	17	20	27	0	8	0	80	4	4	2	1.5	.955	OF-55, 1B-5
2 yrs.		77	.255	.321	184	47	7	1	1	0.5	24	19	20	30	0	11	0	86	4	5	2	1.4	.947	OF-65, 1B-5

John Peltz

PELTZ, JOHN BR TR
B. Apr. 23, 1861, New Orleans, La. D. Feb. 27, 1906, New Orleans, La.

Year	Team	Games	BA	SA	AB	H	2B	3B	HR	HR%	R	RBI	BB	SO	SB	Pinch Hit AB	Pinch Hit H	PO	A	E	DP	TC/G	FA	G by Pos
1884	IND AA	106	.219	.361	393	86	13	17	3	0.8	40		7			0	0	155	16	38	1	2.0	.818	OF-106
1888	BAL AA	1	.250	.250	4	1	0	0	0	0.0	1	0	0		1	0	0	1	0	1	0	2.0	.500	OF-1
1890	3 teams BKN AA (98G –.227) SYR AA (5G –.176) TOL AA (20G –.247)																							
″	total	123	.228	.297	474	108	12	9	1	0.2	65		38		17	0	0	239	23	29	8	2.4	.900	OF-123
3 yrs.		230	.224	.326	871	195	25	26	4	0.5	106	0	45		18	0	0	395	39	68	9	2.2	.865	OF-230

Brock Pemberton

PEMBERTON, BROCK BB TL 6′ 3″ 190 lbs.
B. Nov. 5, 1953, Tulsa, Okla.

Year	Team	Games	BA	SA	AB	H	2B	3B	HR	HR%	R	RBI	BB	SO	SB	Pinch Hit AB	Pinch Hit H	PO	A	E	DP	TC/G	FA	G by Pos
1974	NY N	11	.182	.182	22	4	0	0	0	0.0	0	1	0	3	0	7	3	31	4	0	4	8.8	1.000	1B-4
1975		2	.000	.000	2	0	0	0	0	0.0	0	0	0	1	0	2	0	0	0	0	0	0.0	—	
2 yrs.		13	.167	.167	24	4	0	0	0	0.0	0	1	0	4	0	9	3	31	4	0	4	8.8	1.000	1B-4

Rudy Pemberton

PEMBERTON, RUDY HECTOR BR TR 6′ 1″ 185 lbs.
Born Rudy Hector Pemberton (Perez).
B. Dec. 17, 1969, San Pedro de Macoris, Dominican Republic.

Year	Team	Games	BA	SA	AB	H	2B	3B	HR	HR%	R	RBI	BB	SO	SB	Pinch Hit AB	Pinch Hit H	PO	A	E	DP	TC/G	FA	G by Pos
1995	DET A	12	.300	.467	30	9	3	1	0	0.0	3	3	1	5	0	1	0	15	0	0	0	1.4	1.000	OF-8, DH-3

Bert Pena

PENA, ADALBERTO BR TR 5′11″ 165 lbs.
Born Adalberto Pena (Rivera).
B. July 11, 1959, Santurce, Puerto Rico.

Year	Team	Games	BA	SA	AB	H	2B	3B	HR	HR%	R	RBI	BB	SO	SB	Pinch Hit AB	Pinch Hit H	PO	A	E	DP	TC/G	FA	G by Pos
1981	HOU N	4	.500	.500	2	1	0	0	0	0.0	0	0	0	0	0	2	1	1	1	0	1	0.7	1.000	SS-3
1983		4	.125	.125	8	1	0	0	0	0.0	0	0	2	2	0	0	0	1	7	0	2	2.0	1.000	SS-4
1984		24	.205	.308	39	8	1	0	1	2.6	3	4	3	8	0	2	0	26	39	3	5	3.2	.956	SS-21

Bert Pena *continued*

Year	Team	Games	BA	SA	AB	H	2B	3B	HR	HR%	R	RBI	BB	SO	SB	Pinch Hit AB	Pinch Hit H	PO	A	E	DP	TC/G	FA	G by Pos
1985		20	.276	.345	29	8	2	0	0	0.0	7	4	1	6	0	3	2	9	15	1	2	1.7	.960	3B-7, SS-6, 2B-2
1986		15	.207	.241	29	6	1	0	0	0.0	3	2	5	5	1	1	0	20	24	4	2	3.7	.917	SS-10, 3B-2, 2B-1
1987		21	.152	.152	46	7	0	0	0	0.0	5	0	2	7	0	1	0	19	35	1	3	2.8	.982	SS-19, 3B-1
6 yrs.		88	.203	.248	153	31	4	0	1	0.7	18	10	13	28	1	9	3	76	121	9	15	2.7	.956	SS-63, 3B-10, 2B-3

Geronimo Pena

PENA, GERONIMO BB TR 6′ 1″ 170 lbs.
Born Geronimo Pena (Martinez).
B. Mar. 29, 1967, Distrito Nacional, Dominican Republic.

Year	Team	Games	BA	SA	AB	H	2B	3B	HR	HR%	R	RBI	BB	SO	SB	Pinch Hit AB	Pinch Hit H	PO	A	E	DP	TC/G	FA	G by Pos
1990	STL N	18	.244	.289	45	11	2	0	0	0.0	5	2	4	14	1	6	3	24	30	1	7	5.0	.982	2B-11
1991		104	.243	.400	185	45	8	3	5	2.7	38	17	18	45	15	11	3	101	146	6	28	2.9	.976	2B-83, OF-4
1992		62	.305	.478	203	62	12	1	7	3.4	31	31	24	37	13	3	2	125	184	5	40	5.5	.984	2B-57
1993		74	.256	.406	254	65	19	2	5	2.0	34	30	25	71	13	8	0	140	200	12	47	5.5	.966	2B-64
1994		83	.254	.479	213	54	13	1	11	5.2	33	34	24	54	9	17	2	119	170	3	42	4.9	.990	2B-59, 3B-1
1995		32	.267	.376	101	27	6	1	1	1.0	20	8	16	30	3	6	0	50	73	3	18	5.0	.976	2B-25
6 yrs.		373	.264	.427	1001	264	60	8	29	2.9	161	122	111	251	54	51	10	559	803	30	182	4.6	.978	2B-299, OF-4, 3B-1

Roberto Pena

PENA, ROBERTO CESAR BR TR 5′ 8″ 170 lbs.
Born Roberto Cesar Zapata (Pena).
B. Apr. 17, 1937, Santo Domingo, Dominican Republic
D. July 23, 1982, Santiago, Dominican Republic.

Year	Team	Games	BA	SA	AB	H	2B	3B	HR	HR%	R	RBI	BB	SO	SB	Pinch Hit AB	Pinch Hit H	PO	A	E	DP	TC/G	FA	G by Pos
1965	CHI N	51	.218	.294	170	37	5	1	2	1.2	17	12	16	19	1	1	0	74	151	17	29	4.8	.930	SS-50
1966		6	.176	.294	17	3	2	0	0	0.0	0	1	0	4	0	2	0	10	12	1	2	4.6	.957	SS-5
1968	PHI N	138	.260	.300	500	130	13	2	1	0.2	56	38	34	63	3	1	1	230	434	32	93	5.2	.954	SS-133
1969	SD N	139	.250	.322	472	118	16	3	4	0.8	44	30	21	63	0	18	5	289	285	13	54	4.3	.978	SS-65, 2B-33, 3B-27, 1B-12
1970	2 teams	OAK A (19G –.259) MIL A (121G –.238)																						
″	total	140	.241	.306	474	114	20	1	3	0.6	40	45	28	49	4	11	2	222	339	14	68	4.2	.976	SS-111, 2B-15, 1B-7, 3B-5
1971	MIL A	113	.237	.325	274	65	9	3	3	1.1	17	28	15	37	2	29	5	290	112	4	38	3.7	.990	1B-50, 3B-37, SS-23, 2B-1
6 yrs.		587	.245	.310	1907	467	65	10	13	0.7	174	154	114	235	10	62	13	1115	1333	81	284	4.4	.968	SS-387, 1B-69, 3B-69, 2B-49

Tony Pena

PENA, ANTONIO FRANCESCO BR TR 6′ 175 lbs.
Born Antonio Francesco Pena (Padilla).
Brother of Ramon Pena.
B. June 4, 1957, Monte Cristi, Dominican Republic.

Year	Team	Games	BA	SA	AB	H	2B	3B	HR	HR%	R	RBI	BB	SO	SB	Pinch Hit AB	Pinch Hit H	PO	A	E	DP	TC/G	FA	G by Pos
1980	PIT N	8	.429	.571	21	9	1	1	0	0.0	1	1	0	4	0	2	1	38	2	2	0	7.0	.952	C-6
1981		66	.300	.381	210	63	9	1	2	1.0	16	17	8	23	1	2	1	286	41	5	10	5.2	.985	C-64
1982		138	.296	.435	497	147	28	4	11	2.2	53	63	17	57	2	0	0	763	89	16	6	6.3	.982	C-137
1983		151	.301	.435	542	163	22	3	15	2.8	51	70	31	73	6	2	1	976	90	9	9	7.2	.992	C-149
1984		147	.286	.425	546	156	27	2	15	2.7	77	78	36	79	12	1	1	895	95	9	15	6.8	.991	C-146
1985		147	.249	.361	546	136	27	2	10	1.8	53	59	29	67	12	0	0	925	102	12	9	7.1	.988	C-146, 1B-1
1986		144	.288	.406	510	147	26	2	10	2.0	56	52	53	69	9	7	1	824	99	18	13	6.6	.981	C-139, 1B-4
1987	STL N	116	.214	.307	384	82	13	4	5	1.3	40	44	36	54	6	4	1	624	51	8	8	5.8	.988	C-112, 1B-4, OF-2
1988		149	.263	.372	505	133	23	1	10	2.0	55	51	33	60	6	8	1	796	72	6	9	6.0	.993	C-142, 1B-3
1989		141	.259	.337	424	110	17	2	4	0.9	36	37	35	33	5	7	1	675	70	2	13	5.5	.997	C-134, OF-1
1990	BOS A	143	.263	.348	491	129	19	1	7	1.4	62	56	43	71	8	5	2	866	74	5	13	6.6	.995	C-142, 1B-1
1991		141	.231	.321	464	107	23	2	5	1.1	45	48	37	53	8	1	0	864	60	5	15	6.6	.995	C-140
1992		133	.241	.305	410	99	21	1	1	0.2	39	38	24	61	3	1	1	786	57	6	12	6.4	.993	C-132
1993		126	.181	.257	304	55	11	0	4	1.3	20	19	25	46	1	0	0	698	53	4	6	6.0	.995	C-125
1994	CLE A	40	.295	.438	112	33	8	1	2	1.8	18	10	9	11	0	0	0	209	17	1	0	5.7	.996	C-40
1995		91	.262	.376	263	69	15	0	5	1.9	25	28	14	44	1	0	0	508	36	7	2	6.1	.987	C-91
16 yrs.		1881	.263	.369	6229	1638	290	27	106	1.7	647	671	430	805	80	40	11	10733	1008	115	140	6.4	.990	C-1845, 1B-13, OF-3
DIVISIONAL PLAYOFF SERIES																								
1995	CLE A	2	.500	2.000	2	1	0	0	1	50.0	1	1	0	0	0	0	0	5	0	0	0	2.5	1.000	C-2
LEAGUE CHAMPIONSHIP SERIES																								
1987	STL N	7	.381	.476	21	8	0	1	0	0.0	5	0	3	4	1	0	0	55	5	0	0	8.6	1.000	C-7
1990	BOS A	4	.214	.214	14	3	0	0	0	0.0	0	0	0	0	0	0	0	22	4	1	1	6.8	.963	C-4
1995	CLE A	4	.333	.500	6	2	1	0	0	0.0	1	0	1	0	0	0	0	15	1	0	0	4.0	1.000	C-4
3 yrs.		15	.317	.390	41	13	1	1	0	0.0	6	0	4	4	1	0	0	92	10	1	1	6.9	.990	C-15
WORLD SERIES																								
1987	STL N	7	.409	.455	22	9	1	0	0	0.0	2	4	3	2	1	0	0	32	1	1	0	4.9	.971	C-6, DH-1
1995	CLE A	2	.167	.167	6	1	0	0	0	0.0	0	0	0	0	0	0	0	7	1	0	0	4.0	1.000	C-2
2 yrs.		9	.357	.393	28	10	1	0	0	0.0	2	4	3	2	1	0	0	39	2	1	0	4.7	.976	C-8, DH-1

Elmer Pence

PENCE, ELMER CLAIR BR TR 6′ 185 lbs.
B. Aug. 17, 1900, Valley Springs, Calif. D. Sept. 17, 1968, San Francisco, Calif.

Year	Team	Games	BA	SA	AB	H	2B	3B	HR	HR%	R	RBI	BB	SO	SB	Pinch Hit AB	Pinch Hit H	PO	A	E	DP	TC/G	FA	G by Pos
1922	CHI A	1	—	—	0	0	0	0	0	—	0	0	0	0	0	0	0	1	0	0	0	1.0	1.000	OF-1

Jim Pendleton

PENDLETON, JAMES EDWARD BR TR 6′ 185 lbs.
B. Jan. 7, 1924, St. Charles, Mo.

Year	Team	Games	BA	SA	AB	H	2B	3B	HR	HR%	R	RBI	BB	SO	SB	Pinch Hit AB	Pinch Hit H	PO	A	E	DP	TC/G	FA	G by Pos
1953	MIL N	120	.299	.462	251	75	12	4	7	2.8	48	27	7	36	6	5	0	152	35	6	4	1.7	.969	OF-105, SS-7
1954		71	.220	.266	173	38	3	1	1	0.6	20	16	4	21	2	16	3	90	5	5	0	2.0	.950	OF-50
1955		8	.000	.000	10	0	0	0	0	0.0	0	0	0	2	0	5	0	6	0	0	0	2.0	1.000	OF-1, SS-1, 3B-1
1956		14	.000	.000	11	0	0	0	0	0.0	0	0	1	3	0	9	0	3	3	0	0	0.9	1.000	SS-3, 3B-2, 2B-1, 1B-1
1957	PIT N	46	.305	.356	59	18	1	1	0	0.0	9	9	9	14	0	24	6	12	3	2	0	1.4	.882	OF-9, 3B-2, SS-1
1958		3	.333	.333	3	1	0	0	0	0.0	0	0	0	0	0	3	1	0	0	0	0	0.0	—	
1959	CIN N	65	.257	.354	113	29	2	0	3	2.7	13	9	8	18	3	19	6	45	31	3	1	1.8	.962	OF-24, 3B-16, SS-3
1962	HOU N	117	.246	.371	321	79	12	2	8	2.5	30	36	14	57	0	23	7	181	5	7	5	1.9	.964	OF-90, 1B-8, 3B-3, SS-2
8 yrs.		444	.255	.365	941	240	30	8	19	2.0	120	97	43	151	11	104	23	489	82	23	10	1.8	.961	OF-279, 3B-24, SS-17, 1B-9, 2B-1

Year	Team		Games	BA	SA	AB	H	2B	3B	HR	HR%	R	RBI	BB	SO	SB	Pinch Hit AB	Pinch Hit H	PO	A	E	DP	TC/G	FA	G by Pos

Terry Pendleton

PENDLETON, TERRY LEE BB TR 5′ 9″ 180 lbs.
B. July 16, 1960, Los Angeles, Calif.

Year	Team		Games	BA	SA	AB	H	2B	3B	HR	HR%	R	RBI	BB	SO	SB	Pinch Hit AB	Pinch Hit H	PO	A	E	DP	TC/G	FA	G by Pos
1984	**STL**	**N**	67	.324	.420	262	85	16	3	1	0.4	37	33	16	32	20	1	0	59	155	13	10	3.4	.943	3B-66
1985			149	.240	.306	559	134	16	3	5	0.9	56	69	37	75	17	2	1	129	361	18	26	3.4	.965	3B-149
1986			159	.239	.306	578	138	26	5	1	0.2	56	59	34	59	24	3	0	133	371	20	36	3.3	.962	3B-156, OF-1
1987			159	.286	.412	583	167	29	4	12	2.1	82	96	70	74	19	1	1	117	369	26	27	3.2	.949	3B-158
1988			110	.253	.361	391	99	20	2	6	1.5	44	53	21	51	3	11	4	75	239	12	13	3.2	.963	3B-101
1989			162	.264	.390	613	162	28	5	13	2.1	83	74	44	81	9	3	0	113	392	15	25	3.2	.971	3B-161
1990			121	.230	.324	447	103	20	2	6	1.3	46	58	30	58	7	5	3	91	248	19	18	3.1	.947	3B-117
1991	**ATL**	**N**	153	**.319**	.517	586	**187**	34	8	22	3.8	94	86	43	70	10	4	1	108	349	24	31	3.3	.950	3B-148
1992			160	.311	.473	640	**199**	39	1	21	3.3	98	105	37	67	5	2	0	133	325	19	27	3.0	.960	3B-158
1993			161	.272	.408	633	172	33	1	17	2.7	81	84	36	97	5	2	0	128	319	19	32	2.9	.959	3B-161
1994			77	.252	.398	309	78	18	3	7	2.3	25	30	12	57	2	0	0	60	147	11	12	2.8	.950	3B-77
1995	**FLA**	**N**	133	.290	.439	513	149	32	1	14	2.7	70	78	38	84	1	4	1	104	249	18	21	2.9	.951	3B-130
12 yrs.			1611	.274	.398	6114	1673	311	38	125	2.0	772	825	418	805	122	38	11	1250	3524	214	278	3.2	.957	3B-1582, OF-1
LEAGUE CHAMPIONSHIP SERIES																									
1985	**STL**	**N**	6	.208	.250	24	5	1	0	0	0.0	2	4	1	2	0	0	0	6	18	1	2	4.2	.960	3B-6
1987			6	.211	.316	19	4	0	1	0	0.0	3	1	0	6	0	0	0	3	11	0	1	2.3	1.000	3B-6
1991	**ATL**	**N**	7	.167	.267	30	5	1	1	0	0.0	1	1	1	3	0	0	0	5	11	0	1	2.3	1.000	3B-7
1992			7	.233	.300	30	7	2	0	0	0.0	2	3	0	2	0	0	0	4	18	0	2	3.1	1.000	3B-7
1993			6	.346	.500	26	9	1	0	1	3.8	4	5	0	2	0	0	0	7	5	0	1	2.0	1.000	3B-6
5 yrs.			32 **2nd**	.233	.326	129 **2nd**	30 **5th**	5	2 **4th**	1	0.8	12	14 **7th**	2	15	0	0	0	25	63	1	7	2.8	.989	3B-32
WORLD SERIES																									
1985	**STL**	**N**	7	.261	.391	23	6	1	1	0	0.0	3	3	3	2	0	0	0	6	14	1	3	3.0	.952	3B-7
1987			3	.429	.429	7	3	0	0	0	0.0	2	1	1	1	2	0	0	0	0	0	0	0.0	.000	DH-2
1991	**ATL**	**N**	7	.367	.667	30	11	3	0	2	6.7	6	3	3	1	0	0	0	3	20	2	2	3.6	.920	3B-7
1992			6	.240	.320	25	6	2	0	0	0.0	2	2	1	5	0	0	0	4	19	0	1	3.8	1.000	3B-6
4 yrs.			23	.306	.471	85	26	6	1	2	2.4	13	9	8	9	2	0	0	13	53	3	6	3.1	.957	3B-20, DH-2

Shannon Penn

PENN, SHANNON DION BB TR 5′10″ 163 lbs.
B. Sept. 11, 1969, Cincinnati, Ohio.

Year	Team		Games	BA	SA	AB	H	2B	3B	HR	HR%	R	RBI	BB	SO	SB	Pinch Hit AB	Pinch Hit H	PO	A	E	DP	TC/G	FA	G by Pos
1995	**DET**	**A**	3	.333	.333	9	3	0	0	0	0.0	0	0	1	2	0	0	0	10	9	3	4	7.3	.864	2B-3

William Pennyfeather

PENNYFEATHER, WILLIAM NATHANIEL BR TR 6′ 2″ 195 lbs.
B. May 25, 1968, Perth Amboy, N. J.

Year	Team		Games	BA	SA	AB	H	2B	3B	HR	HR%	R	RBI	BB	SO	SB	Pinch Hit AB	Pinch Hit H	PO	A	E	DP	TC/G	FA	G by Pos
1992	**PIT**	**N**	15	.222	.222	9	2	0	0	0	0.0	2	0	0	0	0	1	0	8	0	0	0	0.8	1.000	OF-10
1993			21	.206	.235	34	7	1	0	0	0.0	4	2	0	6	0	5	0	21	0	0	0	1.2	1.000	OF-17
1994			4	.000	.000	3	0	0	0	0	0.0	0	0	0	0	0	3	0	0	0	0	0	0.0	.000	OF-1
3 yrs.			40	.196	.217	46	9	1	0	0	0.0	6	2	0	6	0	9	0	29	0	0	0	1.0	1.000	OF-28

Jimmy Peoples

PEOPLES, JAMES ELSWORTH TR 5′ 8″ 200 lbs.
B. Oct. 8, 1863, Big Beaver, Mich. D. Aug. 29, 1920, Detroit, Mich.

Year	Team		Games	BA	SA	AB	H	2B	3B	HR	HR%	R	RBI	BB	SO	SB	Pinch Hit AB	Pinch Hit H	PO	A	E	DP	TC/G	FA	G by Pos
1884	**CIN**	**AA**	69	.169	.199	267	45	2	3	0	0.0	28		6			0	0	142	168	46	21	4.9	.871	SS-47, C-14, OF-10, 1B-1, 3B-1
1885	**2 teams**		**CIN AA** (7G –.182) **BKN AA** (41G –.199)																						
″	**total**		48	.197	.249	173	34	4	1	1	0.6	22		6			0	0	200	78	32	7	6.2	.897	C-42, OF-2, SS-2, P-2, 3B-1, 1B-1
1886	**BKN**	**AA**	93	.218	.282	340	74	7	3	3	0.9	43		20			0	0	419	190	87	14	7.0	.875	C-76, SS-14, OF-8, 3B-1
1887			73	.254	.332	268	68	14	2	1	0.4	36		16		22	0	0	265	122	66	5	6.1	.854	C-57, OF-8, 1B-4, SS-4, 2B-1
1888			32	.194	.301	103	20	5	3	0	0.0	15	17	8		10	0	0	181	56	29	7	8.3	.891	C-25, SS-5, OF-2
1889	**COL**	**AA**	29	.230	.360	100	23	6	2	1	1.0	13	16	6	8	3	0	0	120	37	16	1	5.8	.908	C-22, OF-5, 2B-2, SS-1
6 yrs.			344	.211	.278	1251	264	38	14	6	0.5	157	33	62	8	35	0	0	1327	651	276	55	6.3	.878	C-236, SS-73, OF-35, 1B-6, 2B-3, 3B-3, P-2

Joe Pepitone

PEPITONE, JOSEPH ANTHONY (Pepi) BL TL 6′ 2″ 185 lbs.
B. Oct. 9, 1940, Brooklyn, N. Y.

Year	Team		Games	BA	SA	AB	H	2B	3B	HR	HR%	R	RBI	BB	SO	SB	Pinch Hit AB	Pinch Hit H	PO	A	E	DP	TC/G	FA	G by Pos
1962	**NY**	**A**	63	.239	.442	138	33	3	2	7	5.1	14	17	3	21	1	19	5	126	11	2	9	2.9	.986	OF-32, 1B-16
1963			157	.271	.448	580	157	16	3	27	4.7	79	89	23	63	3	9	1	1166	104	8	111	8.0	.994	1B-143, OF-16
1964			160	.251	.418	613	154	12	3	28	4.6	71	100	24	63	2	3	1	1346	121	18	128	8.0	.988	1B-155, OF-30
1965			143	.247	.394	531	131	18	3	18	3.4	51	62	43	59	4	2	0	1081	75	4	104	7.4	.997	1B-115, OF-41
1966			152	.255	.463	585	149	21	4	31	5.3	85	83	29	58	4	1	0	1126	97	9	94	7.1	.993	1B-119, OF-55
1967			133	.251	.377	501	126	18	3	13	2.6	45	64	34	62	1	4	1	321	13	8	6	2.7	.977	OF-123, 1B-6
1968			108	.245	.403	380	93	9	3	15	3.9	41	56	37	45	8	4	0	318	8	4	11	3.2	.988	OF-92, 1B-12
1969			135	.242	.442	513	124	16	3	27	5.3	49	70	30	42	8	4	2	1254	74	7	118	10.1	.995	1B-132
1970	**2 teams**		**HOU N** (75G –.251) **CHI N** (56G –.268)																						
″	**total**		131	.258	.482	492	127	18	7	26	5.3	82	79	33	43	5	2	0	576	33	4	45	4.2	.993	OF-84, 1B-63
1971	**CHI**	**N**	115	.307	.482	427	131	19	4	16	3.7	50	61	24	41	1	2	1	904	64	10	75	8.3	.990	1B-95, OF-23
1972			66	.262	.397	214	56	5	0	8	3.7	23	21	13	22	1	5	1	552	31	2	51	8.9	.997	1B-66
1973	**2 teams**		**CHI N** (31G –.268) **ATL N** (3G –.364)																						
″	**total**		34	.276	.374	123	34	3	0	3	2.4	16	19	9	7	3	3	1	266	19	5	33	9.4	.983	1B-31
12 yrs.			1397	.258	.432	5097	1315	158	35	219	4.3	606	721	302	526	41	58	13	9036	650	81	785	6.7	.992	1B-953, OF-496
WORLD SERIES																									
1963	**NY**	**A**	4	.154	.154	13	2	0	0	0	0.0	0	0	1	3	0	0	0	37	6	1	8	11.0	.977	1B-4
1964			7	.154	.308	26	4	1	0	1	3.8	1	5	2	3	0	0	0	64	5	0	6	9.9	1.000	1B-7
2 yrs.			11	.154	.256	39	6	1	0	1	2.6	1	5	3	6	0	0	0	101	11	1	14	10.3	.991	1B-11

Henry Peploski

PEPLOSKI, HENRY STEPHEN (Pep) BL TR 5′ 9″ 155 lbs.
Brother of Pepper Peploski.
B. Sept. 15, 1905, Garlin, Poland D. Jan. 28, 1982, Dover, N. J.

Year	Team		Games	BA	SA	AB	H	2B	3B	HR	HR%	R	RBI	BB	SO	SB	Pinch Hit AB	Pinch Hit H	PO	A	E	DP	TC/G	FA	G by Pos
1929	**BOS**	**N**	6	.200	.200	10	2	0	0	0	0.0	1	1	1	3	0	4	1	2	3	0	2	2.5	1.000	3B-2

Pepper Peploski

PEPLOSKI, JOSEPH ALOYSIUS BR TR 5′ 8″ 155 lbs.
Brother of Henry Peploski.
B. Sept. 12, 1891, Brooklyn, N. Y. D. July 13, 1972, New York, N. Y.

Year	Team	Games	BA	SA	AB	H	2B	3B	HR	HR%	R	RBI	BB	SO	SB	Pinch Hit AB	Pinch Hit H	PO	A	E	DP	TC/G	FA	G by Pos
1913	DET A	2	.500	.500	4	2	0	0	0	0.0	1	0	0	0	0	0	0	0	1	0	0	0.5	1.000	3B-2

Don Pepper

PEPPER, DONALD HOYTE BL TL 6′ 4½″ 215 lbs.
B. Oct. 8, 1943, Saratoga Springs, N. Y.

Year	Team	Games	BA	SA	AB	H	2B	3B	HR	HR%	R	RBI	BB	SO	SB	Pinch Hit AB	Pinch Hit H	PO	A	E	DP	TC/G	FA	G by Pos
1966	DET A	4	.000	.000	3	0	0	0	0	0.0	0	0	0	1	0	3	0	2	0	0	0	2.0	1.000	1B-1

Ray Pepper

PEPPER, RAYMOND WATSON BR TR 6′ 2″ 195 lbs.
B. Aug. 5, 1905, Decatur, Ala.

Year	Team	Games	BA	SA	AB	H	2B	3B	HR	HR%	R	RBI	BB	SO	SB	Pinch Hit AB	Pinch Hit H	PO	A	E	DP	TC/G	FA	G by Pos
1932	STL N	21	.246	.316	57	14	2	1	0	0.0	3	7	5	13	1	4	0	33	1	1	0	2.1	.971	OF-17
1933		3	.222	.556	9	2	0	0	1	11.1	2	2	0	1	0	1	0	3	0	0	0	1.5	1.000	OF-2
1934	STL A	148	.298	.399	564	168	24	6	7	1.2	71	101	29	67	1	12	2	299	15	12	4	2.4	.963	OF-136
1935		92	.253	.379	261	66	15	3	4	1.5	20	37	20	32	0	34	7	103	5	2	1	1.9	.982	OF-57
1936		75	.282	.371	124	35	5	0	2	1.6	13	23	5	23	0	54	18	31	1	2	0	1.9	.941	OF-18
5 yrs.		339	.281	.387	1015	285	46	10	14	1.4	109	170	59	136	2	105	27	469	22	17	5	2.2	.967	OF-230

Jack Perconte

PERCONTE, JOHN PATRICK BL TR 5′10″ 160 lbs.
B. Aug. 31, 1954, Joliet, Ill.

Year	Team	Games	BA	SA	AB	H	2B	3B	HR	HR%	R	RBI	BB	SO	SB	Pinch Hit AB	Pinch Hit H	PO	A	E	DP	TC/G	FA	G by Pos
1980	LA N	14	.235	.235	17	4	0	0	0	0.0	2	2	2	1	3	3	0	13	18	0	3	3.4	1.000	2B-9
1981		8	.222	.444	9	2	0	1	0	0.0	2	1	2	2	1	5	2	4	13	0	3	8.5	1.000	2B-2
1982	CLE A	93	.237	.292	219	52	4	4	0	0.0	27	15	22	25	9	7	1	131	199	8	23	4.0	.976	2B-82, DH-2
1983		14	.269	.308	26	7	1	0	0	0.0	1	0	5	2	3	2	1	20	37	3	12	4.6	.950	2B-13
1984	SEA A	155	.294	.346	612	180	24	4	0	0.0	93	31	57	47	29	4	1	303	438	14	90	5.0	.981	2B-150
1985		125	.264	.340	485	128	17	7	2	0.4	60	23	50	36	31	2	1	244	381	9	91	5.1	.986	2B-125
1986	CHI A	24	.219	.233	73	16	1	0	0	0.0	6	4	11	10	2	0	0	46	54	1	12	4.2	.990	2B-24
7 yrs.		433	.270	.329	1441	389	47	16	2	0.1	191	76	149	123	78	23	6	761	1140	35	234	4.8	.982	2B-405, DH-2

Eddie Perez

PEREZ, EDUARDO BR TR 6′ 1″ 175 lbs.
B. May 4, 1968, Ciudad Ojeda, Venezuela.

Year	Team	Games	BA	SA	AB	H	2B	3B	HR	HR%	R	RBI	BB	SO	SB	Pinch Hit AB	Pinch Hit H	PO	A	E	DP	TC/G	FA	G by Pos
1995	ATL N	7	.308	.615	13	4	1	0	1	7.7	1	4	0	2	0	1	0	34	2	0	3	6.0	1.000	C-5, 1B-1

Eduardo Perez

PEREZ, EDUARDO ATANACIO BR TR 6′ 4″ 215 lbs.
Son of Tony Perez.
B. Sept. 11, 1969, Cincinnati, Ohio.

Year	Team	Games	BA	SA	AB	H	2B	3B	HR	HR%	R	RBI	BB	SO	SB	Pinch Hit AB	Pinch Hit H	PO	A	E	DP	TC/G	FA	G by Pos
1993	CAL A	52	.250	.372	180	45	6	2	4	2.2	16	30	9	39	5	4	0	24	101	5	7	2.7	.962	3B-45, DH-3
1994		38	.209	.380	129	27	7	0	5	3.9	10	16	12	29	3	1	0	305	15	1	29	8.4	.997	1B-38
1995		29	.169	.296	71	12	4	1	1	1.4	9	7	12	9	0	4	1	16	37	7	3	2.5	.883	3B-23, DH-1
3 yrs.		119	.221	.361	380	84	17	3	10	2.6	35	53	33	77	8	9	1	345	153	13	39	4.6	.975	3B-68, 1B-38, DH-4

Marty Perez

PEREZ, MARTIN ROMAN BR TR 5′11″ 160 lbs.
B. Feb. 28, 1947, Visalia, Calif.

Year	Team	Games	BA	SA	AB	H	2B	3B	HR	HR%	R	RBI	BB	SO	SB	Pinch Hit AB	Pinch Hit H	PO	A	E	DP	TC/G	FA	G by Pos
1969	CAL A	13	.231	.231	13	3	0	0	0	0.0	3	0	2	1	0	0	0	12	19	0	6	2.8	1.000	SS-7, 3B-2, 2B-2
1970		3	.000	.000	3	0	0	0	0	0.0	0	1	0	0	0	0	0	3	2	1	1	3.0	.833	SS-2
1971	ATL N	130	.227	.307	410	93	15	3	4	1.0	28	32	25	44	1	2	0	195	382	28	91	4.8	.954	SS-126, 2B-1
1972		141	.228	.265	479	109	13	1	1	0.2	33	28	30	55	0	1	0	220	378	27	73	4.4	.957	SS-141
1973		141	.250	.347	501	125	15	5	8	1.6	66	57	49	66	2	5	2	215	416	25	78	4.7	.962	SS-139
1974		127	.260	.340	447	116	20	5	2	0.4	51	34	35	51	2	8	1	236	333	10	69	4.7	.983	2B-102, SS-14, 3B-6
1975		120	.275	.328	461	127	14	2	2	0.4	50	34	37	44	2	0	0	262	349	10	75	5.0	.984	2B-116, SS-7
1976	2 teams	ATL N (31G –.250) SF N (93G –.259)																						
″	total	124	.257	.322	428	110	17	1	3	0.7	49	32	38	37	3	5	1	256	357	14	71	4.8	.978	2B-107, SS-22, 3B-2
1977	2 teams	NY A (1G –.500) OAK A (115G –.231)																						
″	total	116	.233	.313	377	88	14	5	2	0.5	32	23	29	66	1	3	1	207	318	16	54	4.4	.970	2B-105, 3B-13, SS-4
1978	OAK A	16	.000	.000	12	0	0	0	0	0.0	1	0	0	5	0	0	0	4	12	1	1	1.1	.941	3B-11, SS-3, 2B-1
10 yrs.		931	.246	.316	3131	771	108	22	22	0.7	313	241	245	369	11	24	5	1610	2566	132	519	4.6	.969	SS-465, 2B-434, 3B-34

Robert Perez

PEREZ, ROBERT ALEXANDER BR TR 6′ 3″ 205 lbs.
Born Robert Alexander Perez (Jimenez).
B. June 4, 1969, Bolivar, Venezuela.

Year	Team	Games	BA	SA	AB	H	2B	3B	HR	HR%	R	RBI	BB	SO	SB	Pinch Hit AB	Pinch Hit H	PO	A	E	DP	TC/G	FA	G by Pos
1994	TOR A	4	.125	.125	8	1	0	0	0	0.0	0	0	0	1	0	0	0	3	1	0	0	1.0	1.000	OF-4
1995		17	.188	.292	48	9	2	0	1	2.1	2	3	0	5	0	4	2	30	0	0	0	2.0	1.000	OF-15
2 yrs.		21	.179	.268	56	10	2	0	1	1.8	2	3	0	6	0	4	2	33	1	0	0	1.8	1.000	OF-19

Tomas Perez

PEREZ, TOMAS ORLANDO BB TR 5′11″ 165 lbs.
B. Dec. 29, 1973, Barquisimeto, Venezuela.

Year	Team	Games	BA	SA	AB	H	2B	3B	HR	HR%	R	RBI	BB	SO	SB	Pinch Hit AB	Pinch Hit H	PO	A	E	DP	TC/G	FA	G by Pos
1995	TOR A	41	.245	.327	98	24	3	1	1	1.0	12	8	7	18	0	2	1	49	78	5	17	3.4	.962	SS-31, 2B-7, 3B-1

Tony Perez

PEREZ, ATANASIO BR TR 6′ 2″ 175 lbs.
Father of Eduardo Perez.
B. May 14, 1942, Camaguey, Cuba.
Manager 1993.

Year	Team	Games	BA	SA	AB	H	2B	3B	HR	HR%	R	RBI	BB	SO	SB	Pinch Hit AB	Pinch Hit H	PO	A	E	DP	TC/G	FA	G by Pos
1964	CIN N	12	.080	.120	25	2	1	0	0	0.0	1	1	3	9	0	6	0	51	0	1	2	8.7	.981	1B-6
1965		104	.260	.466	281	73	14	4	12	4.3	40	47	21	67	0	25	6	525	40	6	55	6.1	.989	1B-93
1966		99	.265	.381	257	68	10	4	4	1.6	25	39	14	44	1	28	5	530	23	6	46	7.5	.989	1B-75
1967		156	.290	.490	600	174	28	7	26	4.3	78	102	33	102	0	0	0	249	234	13	26	3.1	.974	3B-139, 1B-18, 2B-1
1968		160	.282	.430	625	176	25	7	18	2.9	93	92	51	92	3	0	0	151	343	25	33	3.2	.952	3B-160
1969		160	.294	.526	629	185	31	2	37	5.9	103	122	63	131	4	0	0	136	342	32	35	3.2	.937	3B-160
1970		158	.317	.589	587	186	28	6	40	6.8	107	129	83	134	8	1	0	167	292	35	38	3.1	.929	3B-153, 1B-8
1971		158	.269	.438	609	164	22	3	25	4.1	72	91	51	120	4	1	0	281	308	20	42	3.2	.967	3B-148, 1B-44
1972		136	.283	.497	515	146	33	7	21	4.1	64	90	55	121	4	2	0	1207	68	9	111	9.4	.993	1B-136
1973		151	.314	.527	564	177	33	3	27	4.8	73	101	74	117	3	1	0	1318	85	13	131	9.4	.991	1B-151
1974		158	.265	.460	596	158	28	2	28	4.7	81	101	61	112	1	1	0	1292	75	6	111	8.7	.996	1B-157
1975		137	.282	.466	511	144	28	3	20	3.9	74	109	54	101	1	4	0	1192	72	9	113	9.6	.993	1B-132
1976		139	.260	.452	527	137	32	6	19	3.6	77	91	50	88	10	8	3	1158	73	5	110	9.1	.996	1B-136

Tony Perez *continued*

Year	Team	Games	BA	SA	AB	H	2B	3B	HR	HR%	R	RBI	BB	SO	SB	Pinch Hit AB	Pinch Hit H	PO	A	E	DP	TC/G	FA	G by Pos
1977	MON N	154	.283	.463	559	158	32	6	19	3.4	71	91	63	111	4	6	1	1312	110	11	88	9.7	.992	1B-148
1978		148	.290	.449	544	158	38	3	14	2.6	63	78	38	104	2	2	0	1181	82	11	116	8.8	.991	1B-145
1979		132	.270	.425	489	132	29	4	13	2.7	58	73	38	82	2	3	1	1114	65	11	81	9.2	.991	1B-129
1980	BOS A	151	.275	.467	585	161	31	3	25	4.3	73	105	41	93	1	1	0	1301	87	10	150	9.3	.993	1B-137, DH-13
1981		84	.252	.395	306	77	11	3	9	2.9	35	39	27	66	0	5	2	519	37	4	63	7.1	.993	1B-56, DH-23
1982		69	.260	.444	196	51	14	2	6	3.1	18	31	19	48	0	21	5	5	1	1	0	0.1	.857	DH-46, 1B-2
1983	PHI N	91	.241	.372	253	61	11	2	6	2.4	18	43	28	57	1	19	4	514	40	1	36	8.0	.998	1B-69
1984	CIN N	71	.241	.343	137	33	6	1	2	1.5	9	15	11	21	0	38	11	186	12	2	17	6.5	.990	1B-31
1985		72	.328	.470	183	60	8	0	6	3.3	25	33	22	22	0	20	4	340	22	2	34	7.3	.995	1B-50
1986		77	.255	.355	200	51	12	1	2	1.0	14	29	25	25	0	22	5	398	29	7	46	7.9	.984	1B-55
23 yrs.		2777	.279	.463	9778	2732	505	79	379	3.9	1272	1652	925	1867	49	214	47	15127	2440	240	1484	6.8	.987	1B-1778, 3B-760, DH-82, 2B-1
														4th										

LEAGUE CHAMPIONSHIP SERIES

Year	Team	Games	BA	SA	AB	H	2B	3B	HR	HR%	R	RBI	BB	SO	SB	Pinch Hit AB	Pinch Hit H	PO	A	E	DP	TC/G	FA	G by Pos
1970	CIN N	3	.333	.750	12	4	2	0	1	8.3	1	2	1	1	0	0	0	1	0	0	0	0.3	1.000	3B-3, 1B-1
1972		5	.200	.250	20	4	1	0	0	0.0	0	2	0	7	0	0	0	45	3	0	2	9.6	1.000	1B-5
1973		5	.091	.227	22	2	0	0	1	4.5	1	2	0	4	0	0	0	47	4	0	3	10.2	1.000	1B-5
1975		3	.417	.667	12	5	0	0	1	8.3	3	4	1	2	0	0	0	27	5	0	2	10.7	1.000	1B-3
1976		3	.200	.200	10	2	0	0	0	0.0	1	3	1	2	0	0	0	27	2	1	2	10.0	.967	1B-3
1983	PHI N	1	1.000	1.000	1	1	0	0	0	0.0	0	0	0	0	0	1	1	0	0	0	0	0.0	—	
6 yrs.		20	.234	.390	77	18	3	0	3	3.9	6	13	3	16	0	1	1	147	14	1	9	8.1	.994	1B-17, 3B-3
												9th												

WORLD SERIES

Year	Team	Games	BA	SA	AB	H	2B	3B	HR	HR%	R	RBI	BB	SO	SB	Pinch Hit AB	Pinch Hit H	PO	A	E	DP	TC/G	FA	G by Pos
1970	CIN N	5	.056	.056	18	1	0	0	0	0.0	2	0	3	4	0	0	0	3	13	1	0	3.4	.941	3B-5
1972		7	.435	.522	23	10	2	0	0	0.0	3	2	4	4	0	0	0	73	3	1	3	11.0	.987	1B-7
1975		7	.179	.500	28	5	0	0	3	10.7	4	7	3	9	1	0	0	66	5	1	5	10.3	.986	1B-7
1976		4	.313	.375	16	5	1	0	0	0.0	1	2	1	2	0	0	0	32	4	0	4	9.0	1.000	1B-4
1983	PHI N	4	.200	.200	10	2	0	0	0	0.0	0	0	0	2	0	2	1	13	1	0	2	7.0	1.000	1B-2
5 yrs.		27	.242	.368	95	23	3	0	3	3.2	10	11	11	21	1	2	1	187	26	3	14	8.6	.986	1B-20, 3B-5

Tony Perezchica

PEREZCHICA, ANTONIO LLAMAS BR TR 5′11″ 165 lbs.
Born Antonio Llamas Perezchica (Gonzales).
B. Apr. 20, 1966, Mexicali, Mexico.

Year	Team	Games	BA	SA	AB	H	2B	3B	HR	HR%	R	RBI	BB	SO	SB	Pinch Hit AB	Pinch Hit H	PO	A	E	DP	TC/G	FA	G by Pos
1988	SF N	7	.125	.125	8	1	0	0	0	0.0	1	1	2	1	0	0	0	5	5	0	0	1.7	1.000	2B-6
1990		4	.333	.333	3	1	0	0	0	0.0	1	0	1	2	0	1	0	2	0	0	0	0.5	1.000	2B-2, SS-2
1991	2 teams	SF N (23G –.229) CLE A (17G –.364)																						
″	total	40	.271	.386	70	19	6	1	0	0.0	6	3	5	17	0	9	2	23	40	2	7	2.1	.969	SS-19, 2B-8, 3B-3, DH-1
1992	CLE A	18	.100	.150	20	2	1	0	0	0.0	2	1	2	6	0	1	1	8	11	2	0	1.2	.905	3B-9, SS-4, 2B-4, DH-1
4 yrs.		69	.228	.317	101	23	7	1	0	0.0	10	5	10	26	0	11	3	38	56	4	7	1.7	.959	SS-25, 2B-20, 3B-12, DH-2

Broderick Perkins

PERKINS, BRODERICK PHILLIP BL TL 5′10″ 180 lbs.
B. Nov. 23, 1954, Pittsburg, Calif.

Year	Team	Games	BA	SA	AB	H	2B	3B	HR	HR%	R	RBI	BB	SO	SB	Pinch Hit AB	Pinch Hit H	PO	A	E	DP	TC/G	FA	G by Pos
1978	SD N	62	.240	.341	217	52	14	1	2	0.9	14	33	5	29	4	5	0	538	41	4	56	9.9	.993	1B-59
1979		57	.264	.264	87	23	0	0	0	0.0	8	8	8	12	0	26	4	155	10	3	16	6.0	.982	1B-28
1980		43	.370	.520	100	37	9	0	2	2.0	18	14	11	10	2	12	4	159	9	3	14	5.7	.982	1B-20, OF-10
1981		92	.280	.398	254	71	18	3	2	0.8	27	40	14	16	0	14	4	602	38	3	56	7.7	.995	1B-80, OF-3
1982		125	.271	.340	347	94	10	4	2	0.6	32	34	26	20	2	29	11	831	64	6	61	8.3	.993	1B-98, OF-11
1983	CLE A	79	.272	.326	184	50	10	0	0	0.0	23	24	9	19	1	28	5	148	6	2	12	3.0	.987	1B-19, OF-17, DH-16
1984		58	.197	.212	66	13	1	0	0	0.0	5	4	7	10	0	41	6	8	0	0	2	0.7	1.000	DH-10, 1B-2
7 yrs.		516	.271	.352	1255	340	62	8	8	0.6	127	157	80	116	9	155	34	2441	168	21	217	7.1	.992	1B-306, OF-41, DH-26

Cy Perkins

PERKINS, RALPH FOSTER BR TR 5′10½″ 158 lbs.
B. Feb. 27, 1896, Gloucester, Mass. D. Oct. 2, 1963, Philadelphia, Pa.

Year	Team	Games	BA	SA	AB	H	2B	3B	HR	HR%	R	RBI	BB	SO	SB	Pinch Hit AB	Pinch Hit H	PO	A	E	DP	TC/G	FA	G by Pos
1915	PHI A	7	.200	.250	20	4	1	0	0	0.0	2	0	3	3	0	1	0	38	8	4	0	8.3	.920	C-6
1917		6	.167	.167	18	3	0	0	0	0.0	1	2	2	1	0	0	0	31	14	1	1	7.7	.978	C-6
1918		68	.188	.229	218	41	4	1	1	0.5	9	14	8	15	1	7	1	201	103	3	11	5.1	.990	C-60
1919		101	.252	.357	305	77	12	7	2	0.7	22	29	27	22	2	6	1	357	153	16	16	5.5	.970	C-87, SS-8
1920		148	.260	.363	493	128	24	6	5	1.0	40	52	28	35	5	1	0	528	182	15	16	4.9	.979	C-146, 2B-1
1921		141	.288	.428	538	155	31	4	12	2.2	58	73	32	32	5	0	0	540	137	20	16	4.9	.971	C-141
1922		148	.267	.366	505	135	20	6	6	1.2	58	69	40	30	1	7	1	432	130	9	10	4.0	.984	C-141
1923		143	.270	.370	500	135	34	5	2	0.4	53	65	65	30	1	4	1	475	102	17	12	4.3	.971	C-137
1924		128	.242	.311	392	95	19	4	0	0.0	31	32	31	20	3	0	0	415	102	9	9	4.1	.983	C-128
1925		65	.307	.400	140	43	10	0	1	0.7	21	18	26	6	0	4	1	213	36	5	3	4.3	.980	C-58, 3B-1
1926		63	.291	.331	148	43	6	0	0	0.0	14	19	18	7	0	7	4	205	38	4	5	4.5	.984	C-55
1927		59	.255	.358	137	35	7	2	1	0.7	11	15	12	8	0	2	0	162	29	4	2	3.5	.979	C-54, 1B-1
1928		19	.172	.172	29	5	0	0	0	0.0	1	1	1	1	0	0	0	47	7	1	0	2.9	.982	C-19
1929		38	.211	.263	76	16	4	0	0	0.0	4	9	5	4	0	0	0	85	15	1	1	2.7	.990	C-38
1930		20	.158	.211	38	6	2	0	0	0.0	1	4	2	3	0	0	0	52	3	2	1	2.8	.965	C-19, 1B-1
1931	NY A	16	.255	.277	47	12	1	0	0	0.0	3	7	1	4	0	0	0	51	7	0	0	3.6	1.000	C-16
1934	DET A	1	.000	.000	1	0	0	0	0	0.0	0	0	0	0	0	1	0	0	0	0	0	0.0	—	
17 yrs.		1171	.259	.352	3605	933	175	35	30	0.8	329	409	301	221	18	40	9	3832	1066	111	103	4.5	.978	C-1111, SS-8, 1B-2, 3B-1, 2B-1

Sam Perlozzo

PERLOZZO, SAMUEL BENEDICT BR TR 5′ 9″ 170 lbs.
B. Mar. 4, 1951, Cumberland, Md.

Year	Team	Games	BA	SA	AB	H	2B	3B	HR	HR%	R	RBI	BB	SO	SB	Pinch Hit AB	Pinch Hit H	PO	A	E	DP	TC/G	FA	G by Pos
1977	MIN A	10	.292	.458	24	7	0	2	0	0.0	6	0	2	3	0	2	0	12	17	0	2	2.6	1.000	2B-10, 3B-1
1979	SD N	2	.000	.000	2	0	0	0	0	0.0	0	0	1	0	0	0	0	1	0	1	0	1.0	.500	2B-2
2 yrs.		12	.269	.423	26	7	0	2	0	0.0	6	0	3	3	0	2	0	13	17	1	2	2.4	.968	2B-12, 3B-1

Jack Perrin

PERRIN, JOHN STEPHENSON BL TR 5′ 9″ 160 lbs.
B. Feb. 4, 1898, Escanaba, Mich. D. June 24, 1969, Detroit, Mich.

Year	Team	Games	BA	SA	AB	H	2B	3B	HR	HR%	R	RBI	BB	SO	SB	Pinch Hit AB	Pinch Hit H	PO	A	E	DP	TC/G	FA	G by Pos
1921	BOS A	4	.231	.231	13	3	0	0	0	0.0	3	1	0	3	0	0	0	1	0	0	0	0.3	1.000	OF-4

Nig Perrine

PERRINE, JOHN GROVER BR TR 5′ 9″ 160 lbs.
B. Jan. 14, 1885, Clinton, Wis. D. Aug. 13, 1948, Kansas City, Mo.

Year	Team	Lg	Games	BA	SA	AB	H	2B	3B	HR	HR%	R	RBI	BB	SO	SB	Pinch Hit AB	Pinch Hit H	PO	A	E	DP	TC/G	FA	G by Pos
1907	**WAS**	**A**	44	.171	.212	146	25	4	1	0	0.0	13	15	13		10	0	0	90	117	14	13	5.0	.937	2B-24, SS-18, 3B-2

George Perring

PERRING, GEORGE WILSON BR TR 6′ 190 lbs.
B. Aug. 13, 1884, Sharon, Wis. D. Aug. 20, 1960, Beloit, Wis.

Year	Team	Lg	Games	BA	SA	AB	H	2B	3B	HR	HR%	R	RBI	BB	SO	SB	Pinch Hit AB	Pinch Hit H	PO	A	E	DP	TC/G	FA	G by Pos
1908	**CLE**	**A**	89	.216	.274	310	67	8	5	0	0.0	23	19	16		0	0	0	133	236	29	16	4.5	.927	SS-48, 3B-41
1909			88	.223	.322	283	63	10	9	0	0.0	26	20	19		6	0	0	105	188	22	11	3.7	.930	3B-66, SS-11, 2B-8
1910			39	.221	.320	122	27	6	3	0	0.0	14	8	3		3	2	0	87	69	9	7	4.5	.945	3B-33, 1B-4
1914	**KC**	**F**	144	.278	.387	496	138	28	10	2	0.4	68	69	59		7	6	3	486	242	28	46	5.3	.963	3B-101, 1B-41, P-1, SS-1
1915			153	.259	.358	553	143	23	7	6	1.1	67	67	55		10	0	0	454	334	24	38	4.9	.970	3B-102, 2B-31, 1B-31, SS-1
5 yrs.			513	.248	.343	1764	438	75	34	8	0.5	198	183	152		26	8	3	1265	1069	112	118	4.7	.954	3B-343, 1B-76, SS-61, 2B-39, P-1

Bob Perry

PERRY, MELVIN GRAY BR TR 6′ 2″ 180 lbs.
B. Sept. 14, 1934, New Bern, N. C.

Year	Team	Lg	Games	BA	SA	AB	H	2B	3B	HR	HR%	R	RBI	BB	SO	SB	Pinch Hit AB	Pinch Hit H	PO	A	E	DP	TC/G	FA	G by Pos
1963	**LA**	**A**	61	.253	.361	166	42	9	0	3	1.8	16	14	9	31	1	4	2	86	1	5	0	1.7	.946	OF-55
1964			70	.276	.362	221	61	8	1	3	1.4	19	16	14	52	1	7	0	115	2	3	0	1.9	.975	OF-62
2 yrs.			131	.266	.362	387	103	17	1	6	1.6	35	30	23	83	2	11	2	201	3	8	0	1.8	.962	OF-117

Boyd Perry

PERRY, BOYD GLENN BR TR 5′10″ 158 lbs.
B. Mar. 21, 1914, Snow Camp, N. C. D. July 29, 1990, Burlington, N. C.

Year	Team	Lg	Games	BA	SA	AB	H	2B	3B	HR	HR%	R	RBI	BB	SO	SB	Pinch Hit AB	Pinch Hit H	PO	A	E	DP	TC/G	FA	G by Pos
1941	**DET**	**A**	36	.181	.241	83	15	5	0	0	0.0	9	11	10	9	1	0	0	46	62	4	12	3.1	.964	SS-25, 2B-11

Clay Perry

PERRY, CLAYTON SHIELDS BR TR 5′10½″ 175 lbs.
B. Dec. 18, 1881, Rice Lake, Wis. D. Jan. 16, 1954, Rice Lake, Wis.

Year	Team	Lg	Games	BA	SA	AB	H	2B	3B	HR	HR%	R	RBI	BB	SO	SB	Pinch Hit AB	Pinch Hit H	PO	A	E	DP	TC/G	FA	G by Pos
1908	**DET**	**A**	5	.182	.182	11	2	0	0	0	0.0	0	0	0		0	0	0	4	7	1	1	2.4	.917	3B-5

Gerald Perry

PERRY, GERALD JUNE BL TR 5′11″ 172 lbs.
B. Oct. 30, 1960, Savannah, Ga.

Year	Team	Lg	Games	BA	SA	AB	H	2B	3B	HR	HR%	R	RBI	BB	SO	SB	Pinch Hit AB	Pinch Hit H	PO	A	E	DP	TC/G	FA	G by Pos
1983	**ATL**	**N**	27	.359	.487	39	14	2	0	1	2.6	5	6	5	4	0	16	7	55	0	1	5	7.0	.982	1B-7, OF-1
1984			122	.265	.372	347	92	12	2	7	2.0	52	47	61	38	15	16	8	550	28	12	41	5.0	.980	1B-64, OF-53
1985			110	.214	.273	238	51	5	0	3	1.3	22	13	23	28	9	44	6	541	37	9	48	10.5	.985	1B-55, OF-1
1986			29	.271	.386	70	19	2	0	2	2.9	6	11	8	4	0	11	3	24	1	2	2	1.2	.926	OF-21, 1B-1
1987			142	.270	.411	533	144	35	2	12	2.3	77	74	48	63	42	5	1	1297	72	14	118	9.7	.990	1B-136, OF-7
1988			141	.300	.400	547	164	29	1	8	1.5	61	74	36	49	29	0	0	1282	106	17	102	10.0	.988	1B-141
1989			72	.252	.338	266	67	11	0	4	1.5	24	21	32	28	10	0	0	618	51	9	49	9.4	.987	1B-72
1990	**KC**	**A**	133	.254	.361	465	118	22	2	8	1.7	57	57	39	56	17	12	0	394	40	6	41	3.7	.986	DH-68, 1B-51
1991	**STL**	**N**	109	.240	.380	242	58	8	4	6	2.5	29	36	22	34	15	41	11	413	29	5	30	6.8	.989	1B-61, OF-5
1992			87	.238	.315	143	34	8	0	1	0.7	13	18	15	23	3	54	12	221	11	3	23	8.1	.987	1B-29
1993			96	.337	.510	98	33	5	0	4	4.1	21	16	18	23	1	**70**	**24**	79	3	2	5	5.3	.976	1B-15, OF-1
1994			60	.325	.532	77	25	7	0	3	3.9	12	18	15	12	1	40	12	96	4	1	9	7.8	.990	1B-13
1995			65	.165	.215	79	13	4	0	0	0.0	4	5	6	12	0	50	11	70	3	0	3	6.6	1.000	1B-11
13 yrs.			1193	.265	.376	3144	832	150	11	59	1.9	383	396	328	374	142	359	95	5640	385	81	476	7.5	.987	1B-656, OF-89, DH-68

Hank Perry

PERRY, WILLIAM HENRY (Socks) BL TR 5′11″ 190 lbs.
B. July 28, 1886, Howell, Mich. D. July 18, 1956, Pontiac, Mich.

Year	Team	Lg	Games	BA	SA	AB	H	2B	3B	HR	HR%	R	RBI	BB	SO	SB	Pinch Hit AB	Pinch Hit H	PO	A	E	DP	TC/G	FA	G by Pos
1912	**DET**	**A**	13	.167	.194	36	6	1	0	0	0.0	3	0	3		0	6	3	20	2	0	0	3.1	1.000	OF-7

Herbert Perry

PERRY, HERBERT EDWARD, JR. BR TR 6′ 2″ 210 lbs.
B. Sept. 15, 1969, Live Oak, Fla.

Year	Team	Lg	Games	BA	SA	AB	H	2B	3B	HR	HR%	R	RBI	BB	SO	SB	Pinch Hit AB	Pinch Hit H	PO	A	E	DP	TC/G	FA	G by Pos
1994	**CLE**	**A**	4	.111	.111	9	1	0	0	0	0.0	1	1	3	1	0	0	0	25	5	1	1	7.8	.968	3B-2, 1B-2
1995			52	.315	.463	162	51	13	1	3	1.9	23	23	13	28	1	3	0	391	30	0	30	8.3	1.000	1B-45, DH-5, 3B-1
2 yrs.			56	.304	.444	171	52	13	1	3	1.8	24	24	16	29	1	3	0	416	35	1	31	8.2	.998	1B-47, DH-5, 3B-3
DIVISIONAL PLAYOFF SERIES																									
1995	**CLE**	**A**	1	.000	.000	1	0	0	0	0	0.0	0	0	0	0	0	1	0	0	0	0	0	0.0	—	
LEAGUE CHAMPIONSHIP SERIES																									
1995	**CLE**	**A**	3	.000	.000	8	0	0	0	0	0.0	0	0	1	3	0	0	0	30	0	0	2	10.0	1.000	1B-3
WORLD SERIES																									
1995	**CLE**	**A**	3	.000	.000	5	0	0	0	0	0.0	0	0	0	2	0	0	0	13	2	0	2	5.0	1.000	1B-3

Johnny Pesky

PESKY, JOHN MICHAEL BL TR 5′ 9″ 168 lbs.
Born John Michael Paveskovich.
B. Sept. 27, 1919, Portland, Ore.
Manager 1963–64, 1980.

Year	Team	Lg	Games	BA	SA	AB	H	2B	3B	HR	HR%	R	RBI	BB	SO	SB	Pinch Hit AB	Pinch Hit H	PO	A	E	DP	TC/G	FA	G by Pos
1942	**BOS**	**A**	147	.331	.416	620	**205**	29	9	2	0.3	105	51	42	36	12	0	0	320	465	37	94	5.6	.955	SS-147
1946			153	.335	.427	**621**	**208**	43	4	2	0.3	115	55	65	29	9	0	0	296	479	25	96	5.2	.969	SS-153
1947			155	.324	.392	**638**	**207**	27	8	0	0.0	106	39	72	22	12	0	0	276	429	17	97	4.7	.976	SS-133, 3B-22
1948			143	.281	.365	565	159	26	6	3	0.5	124	55	99	32	3	2	1	121	303	22	35	3.2	.951	3B-141
1949			148	.306	.384	604	185	27	7	2	0.3	111	69	100	19	8	0	0	184	333	16	48	3.6	.970	3B-148
1950			127	.312	.388	490	153	22	6	1	0.2	112	49	104	31	2	2	0	183	289	13	36	3.9	.973	3B-116, SS-8
1951			131	.313	.398	480	150	20	6	3	0.6	93	41	84	15	2	9	3	223	370	26	79	5.1	.958	SS-106, 3B-11, 2B-5
1952	**2 teams**	**BOS A** (25G –.149) **DET A** (69G –.254)																							
″	**total**		94	.225	.262	244	55	6	0	1	0.4	36	11	57	16	1	14	1	126	172	15	38	3.6	.952	SS-43, 2B-22, 3B-22
1953	**DET**	**A**	103	.292	.390	308	90	22	1	2	0.6	43	24	27	10	3	30	12	166	183	3	49	4.8	.991	2B-73
1954	**2 teams**	**DET A** (20G –.176) **WAS A** (49G –.253)																							
″	**total**		69	.246	.320	175	43	4	3	1	0.6	22	10	13	8	1	29	4	92	91	4	22	4.9	.979	2B-37, SS-1
10 yrs.			1270	.307	.386	4745	1455	226	50	17	0.4	867	404	663	218	53	86	21	1987	3114	178	594	4.4	.966	SS-591, 3B-460, 2B-137
WORLD SERIES																									
1946	**BOS**	**A**	7	.233	.233	30	7	0	0	0	0.0	2	0	1	3	1	0	0	13	16	4	5	4.7	.879	SS-7

Roberto Petagine

PETAGINE, ROBERTO ANTONIO BL TL 6′ 1″ 172 lbs.
Born Roberto Antonio Petagine (Guerra).
B. June 7, 1971, Nueva Esparita, Venezuela.

Year	Team	Games	BA	SA	AB	H	2B	3B	HR	HR%	R	RBI	BB	SO	SB	Pinch Hit AB	Pinch Hit H	PO	A	E	DP	TC/G	FA	G by Pos
1994	HOU N	8	.000	.000	7	0	0	0	0	0.0	0	0	1	3	0	6	0	3	0	0	0	1.5	1.000	1B-2
1995	SD N	89	.234	.371	124	29	8	0	3	2.4	15	17	26	41	0	30	8	264	22	1	21	5.4	.997	1B-51, OF-2
2 yrs.		97	.221	.351	131	29	8	0	3	2.3	15	17	27	44	0	36	8	267	22	1	21	5.3	.997	1B-53, OF-2

Bill Peterman

PETERMAN, WILLIAM DAVID BR TR 6′ 2″ 185 lbs.
B. Apr. 20, 1921, Philadelphia, Pa.

Year	Team	Games	BA	SA	AB	H	2B	3B	HR	HR%	R	RBI	BB	SO	SB	Pinch Hit AB	Pinch Hit H	PO	A	E	DP	TC/G	FA	G by Pos
1942	PHI N	1	1.000	1.000	1	1	0	0	0	0.0	0	0	0	0	0	0	0	0	0	0	0	0.0	.000	C-1

Gary Peters

PETERS, GARY CHARLES BL TL 6′ 2″ 200 lbs.
B. Apr. 21, 1937, Grove City, Pa.

Year	Team	Games	BA	SA	AB	H	2B	3B	HR	HR%	R	RBI	BB	SO	SB	Pinch Hit AB	Pinch Hit H	PO	A	E	DP	TC/G	FA	G by Pos
1959	CHI A	2	—	—	0	0	0	0	0	—	0	0	0	0	0	0	0	0	0	0	0	0.0	.000	P-2
1960		2	—	—	0	0	0	0	0	—	0	0	0	0	0	0	0	0	0	0	0	0.0	.000	P-2
1961		3	.333	.333	3	1	0	0	0	0.0	1	0	0	1	0	0	0	3	6	0	1	3.0	1.000	P-3
1962		5	—	—	0	0	0	0	0	—	0	0	0	0	0	0	0	0	2	0	0	0.4	1.000	P-5
1963		50	.259	.444	81	21	4	1	3	3.7	12	12	3	19	0	1	0	17	30	2	4	1.2	.959	P-41
1964		54	.208	.367	120	25	7	0	4	3.3	9	19	2	29	0	15	4	16	41	3	4	1.6	.950	P-37
1965		42	.181	.236	72	13	1	0	1	1.4	2	6	2	15	0	7	3	12	32	1	0	1.4	.978	P-33
1966		38	.235	.358	81	19	3	2	1	1.2	12	9	0	19	0	5	1	7	41	1	4	1.6	.980	P-30
1967		48	.212	.313	99	21	0	2	2	2.0	10	13	2	23	0	6	1	15	50	2	5	1.8	.970	P-38
1968		46	.208	.361	72	15	3	1	2	2.8	10	8	6	13	0	14	2	12	21	0	3	1.1	1.000	P-31
1969		37	.169	.310	71	12	4	0	2	2.8	9	4	2	15	0	0	0	6	25	1	1	0.9	.969	P-36
1970	BOS A	37	.244	.341	82	20	3	1	1	1.2	12	11	8	11	0	0	0	7	27	3	3	1.1	.919	P-34
1971		53	.271	.406	96	26	4	0	3	3.1	7	19	3	20	0	18	5	13	27	2	2	1.2	.952	P-34
1972		33	.200	.267	30	6	2	0	0	0.0	2	1	1	7	0	0	0	3	10	0	0	0.4	1.000	P-33
14 yrs.		450	.222	.348	807	179	31	7	19	2.4	86	102	29	172	0	66	16	111	312	15	27	1.2	.966	P-359

John Peters

PETERS, JOHN WILLIAM (Big Pete, Shotgun) BR TR 6′ 192 lbs.
B. July 14, 1893, Kansas City, Kans. D. Feb. 21, 1932, Kansas City, Mo.

Year	Team	Games	BA	SA	AB	H	2B	3B	HR	HR%	R	RBI	BB	SO	SB	Pinch Hit AB	Pinch Hit H	PO	A	E	DP	TC/G	FA	G by Pos
1915	DET A	1	.000	.000	3	0	0	0	0	0.0	0	0	0	1	0	0	0	6	3	0	0	9.0	1.000	C-1
1918	CLE A	1	.000	.000	1	0	0	0	0	0.0	0	0	1	1	0	0	0	3	1	4	0	8.0	.500	C-1
1921	PHI N	55	.290	.374	155	45	4	0	3	1.9	7	23	6	13	1	10	5	116	24	10	0	3.4	.933	C-44
1922		55	.245	.406	143	35	9	1	4	2.8	15	24	9	18	0	15	3	118	24	7	3	3.8	.953	C-39
4 yrs.		112	.265	.384	302	80	13	1	7	2.3	22	47	16	33	1	25	8	243	52	21	3	3.7	.934	C-85

Johnny Peters

PETERS, JOHN PAUL BR TR 180 lbs.
B. Apr. 8, 1850, Louisiana, Mo. D. Jan. 4, 1924, St. Louis, Mo.

Year	Team	Games	BA	SA	AB	H	2B	3B	HR	HR%	R	RBI	BB	SO	SB	Pinch Hit AB	Pinch Hit H	PO	A	E	DP	TC/G	FA	G by Pos
1876	CHI N	66	.351	.418	316	111	14	2	1	0.3	70	47	3	2		0	0	95	193	21	16	4.6	.932	SS-66, P-1
1877		60	.317	.377	265	84	10	3	0	0.0	45	41	1	7		0	0	124	215	45	23	6.4	.883	SS-60
1878	MIL N	55	.309	.341	246	76	6	1	0	0.0	33	22	5	8		0	0	130	205	53	18	6.9	.863	2B-34, SS-22
1879	CHI N	83	.245	.298	379	93	13	2	1	0.3	45	31	1	19		0	0	94	271	71	14	5.3	.837	SS-83
1880	PRO N	86	.228	.242	359	82	5	0	0	0.0	30	24	5	15		0	0	111	268	42	26	4.9	.900	SS-86
1881	BUF N	54	.214	.258	229	49	8	1	0	0.0	21	25	3	12		0	0	105	185	47	17	6.2	.861	SS-53, OF-1
1882	PIT AA	78	.288	.324	333	96	10	1	0	0.0	46		4			0	0	92	282	51	21	5.4	.880	SS-77, 2B-1
1883		8	.107	.107	28	3	0	0	0	0.0	3		0			0	0	9	27	8	3	5.5	.818	SS-8
1884		1	.000	.000	4	0	0	0	0	0.0	0		0			0	0	1	1	1	0	3.0	.667	SS-1
9 yrs.		491	.275	.318	2159	594	66	10	2	0.1	293	190	22	63		0	0	761	1647	339	138	5.6	.877	SS-456, 2B-35, OF-1, P-1

Ricky Peters

PETERS, RICHARD DEVIN BB TR 5′ 9″ 170 lbs.
B. Nov. 21, 1955, Lynwood, Calif.

Year	Team	Games	BA	SA	AB	H	2B	3B	HR	HR%	R	RBI	BB	SO	SB	Pinch Hit AB	Pinch Hit H	PO	A	E	DP	TC/G	FA	G by Pos
1979	DET A	12	.263	.263	19	5	0	0	0	0.0	3	2	5	3	0	1	0	4	0	2	0	0.7	.667	3B-3, DH-3, 2B-2, OF-1
1980		133	.291	.373	477	139	19	7	2	0.4	79	42	54	48	13	13	3	296	1	7	1	2.5	.977	OF-109, DH-11
1981		63	.256	.319	207	53	7	3	0	0.0	26	15	29	28	1	5	1	103	3	1	1	1.9	.991	OF-38, DH-19
1983	OAK A	55	.287	.326	178	51	7	0	0	0.0	20	20	12	21	4	2	1	141	3	2	1	2.7	.986	OF-47, DH-8
1986		44	.184	.211	38	7	1	0	0	0.0	7	1	7	7	2	9	3	29	1	0	1	0.9	1.000	OF-27, DH-4, 2B-1
5 yrs.		307	.277	.343	919	255	34	10	2	0.2	135	80	107	107	20	30	8	573	8	12	4	2.2	.980	OF-222, DH-45, 3B-3, 2B-3

Rusty Peters

PETERS, RUSSELL DIXON BR TR 5′11″ 170 lbs.
B. Dec. 14, 1914, Roanoke, Va.

Year	Team	Games	BA	SA	AB	H	2B	3B	HR	HR%	R	RBI	BB	SO	SB	Pinch Hit AB	Pinch Hit H	PO	A	E	DP	TC/G	FA	G by Pos
1936	PHI A	45	.218	.353	119	26	3	2	3	2.5	12	16	4	28	1	7	0	51	82	14	15	3.9	.905	SS-25, 3B-10, OF-2, 2B-1
1937		116	.260	.372	339	88	17	6	3	0.9	39	43	41	59	4	6	3	191	266	29	39	4.3	.940	2B-70, 3B-31, SS-13
1938		2	.000	.000	7	0	0	0	0	0.0	0	0	0	1	0	0	0	3	2	2	0	3.5	.714	SS-2
1940	CLE A	30	.239	.338	71	17	3	2	0	0.0	5	7	4	14	1	9	3	32	44	8	8	3.8	.905	2B-9, 3B-6, SS-6, 1B-1
1941		29	.206	.238	63	13	2	0	0	0.0	6	2	7	10	0	1	0	26	45	10	9	3.5	.877	SS-11, 3B-9, 2B-3
1942		34	.224	.345	58	13	5	1	0	0.0	6	2	2	14	0	5	1	21	46	4	8	2.7	.944	SS-24, 3B-1, 2B-1
1943		79	.219	.279	215	47	6	2	1	0.5	22	19	18	29	1	11	2	66	98	11	17	2.6	.937	3B-46, SS-14, 2B-6, OF-2
1944		88	.223	.301	282	63	13	3	1	0.4	23	24	15	35	2	5	1	180	209	9	52	4.7	.977	2B-63, SS-13, 3B-8
1946		9	.286	.286	21	6	0	0	0	0.0	0	2	1	1	0	2	1	11	13	0	3	3.4	1.000	SS-7
1947	STL A	39	.340	.426	47	16	4	0	0	0.0	10	2	6	8	0	11	6	34	31	3	9	4.5	.956	2B-13, SS-2
10 yrs.		471	.236	.326	1222	289	53	16	8	0.7	123	117	98	199	9	57	17	615	836	90	160	3.9	.942	2B-166, SS-117, 3B-111, OF-4, 1B-1

Bob Peterson

PETERSON, ROBERT A. BR TR 6′ 1″ 160 lbs.
B. July 16, 1884, Philadelphia, Pa. D. Nov. 27, 1962, Evesham, N. J.

Year	Team	Games	BA	SA	AB	H	2B	3B	HR	HR%	R	RBI	BB	SO	SB	Pinch Hit AB	Pinch Hit H	PO	A	E	DP	TC/G	FA	G by Pos
1906	BOS A	39	.203	.254	118	24	1	1	1	0.8	10	9	11		1	2	0	136	52	21	2	5.8	.900	C-30, 2B-3, 1B-2, OF-1
1907		4	.077	.077	13	1	0	0	0	0.0	1	0	0		0	0	0	18	5	0	0	5.8	1.000	C-4
2 yrs.		43	.191	.237	131	25	1	1	1	0.8	11	9	11		1	2	0	154	57	21	2	5.8	.909	C-34, 2B-3, 1B-2, OF-1

Buddy Peterson

PETERSON, CARL FRANCIS BR TR 5′ 9½″ 170 lbs.
B. Apr. 23, 1925, Portland, Ore.

Year	Team	Games	BA	SA	AB	H	2B	3B	HR	HR%	R	RBI	BB	SO	SB	Pinch Hit AB	Pinch Hit H	PO	A	E	DP	TC/G	FA	G by Pos
1955	CHI A	6	.286	.333	21	6	1	0	0	0.0	7	2	3	2	0	1	1	10	15	1	4	4.3	.962	SS-6
1957	BAL A	7	.176	.294	17	3	2	0	0	0.0	1	0	2	2	0	1	0	12	14	1	3	3.9	.963	SS-7
2 yrs.		13	.237	.316	38	9	3	0	0	0.0	8	2	5	4	0	2	1	22	29	2	7	4.1	.962	SS-13

Cap Peterson

PETERSON, CHARLES ANDREW BR TR 6′ 2″ 195 lbs.
B. Aug. 15, 1942, Tacoma, Wash. D. May 16, 1980, Tacoma, Wash.

Year	Team	Games	BA	SA	AB	H	2B	3B	HR	HR%	R	RBI	BB	SO	SB	Pinch Hit AB	Pinch Hit H	PO	A	E	DP	TC/G	FA	G by Pos
1962	SF N	4	.167	.167	6	1	0	0	0	0.0	1	0	1	4	0	3	0	1	2	0	1	1.5	1.000	SS-2
1963		22	.259	.352	54	14	2	0	1	1.9	7	2	2	13	0	8	1	16	24	5	0	2.6	.889	2B-8, 3B-5, OF-3, SS-1
1964		66	.203	.284	74	15	1	1	1	1.4	8	8	3	20	0	**55**	12	11	1	0	0	0.9	1.000	OF-10, 1B-2, 3B-1, 2B-1
1965		63	.248	.400	105	26	7	0	3	2.9	14	15	10	16	0	38	5	22	1	0	0	0.9	1.000	OF-27
1966		89	.237	.311	190	45	6	1	2	1.1	13	19	11	32	2	37	5	73	4	1	3	1.5	.987	OF-51, 1B-2
1967	WAS A	122	.240	.351	405	97	17	2	8	2.0	35	46	32	61	0	21	3	190	5	6	1	2.0	.970	OF-101
1968		94	.204	.288	226	46	8	1	3	1.3	20	18	18	31	2	39	11	82	2	0	0	1.6	1.000	OF-52
1969	CLE A	76	.227	.282	110	25	3	0	1	0.9	8	14	24	18	0	39	9	40	2	1	1	1.3	.977	OF-30, 3B-4
8 yrs.		536	.230	.325	1170	269	44	5	19	1.6	106	122	101	195	4	240	46	435	41	13	6	1.6	.973	OF-274, 3B-10, 2B-9, 1B-4, SS-3

Hardy Peterson

PETERSON, HARDING WILLIAM BR TR 6′ 205 lbs.
B. Oct. 17, 1929, Perth Amboy, N. J.

Year	Team	Games	BA	SA	AB	H	2B	3B	HR	HR%	R	RBI	BB	SO	SB	Pinch Hit AB	Pinch Hit H	PO	A	E	DP	TC/G	FA	G by Pos
1955	PIT N	32	.247	.358	81	20	6	0	1	1.2	7	10	7	7	0	2	0	117	21	5	4	4.6	.965	C-31
1957		30	.301	.438	73	22	2	1	2	2.7	10	11	9	10	0	0	0	116	14	2	3	4.4	.985	C-30
1958		2	.333	.333	6	2	0	0	0	0.0	0	0	1	0	0	0	0	7	1	0	0	4.0	1.000	C-2
1959		2	.000	.000	1	0	0	0	0	0.0	0	0	0	0	0	0	0	4	0	0	0	2.0	1.000	C-2
4 yrs.		66	.273	.391	161	44	8	1	3	1.9	17	21	17	17	0	2	0	244	36	7	7	4.4	.976	C-65

Ted Petoskey

PETOSKEY, FREDERICK LEE BR TR 5′11½″ 183 lbs.
B. Jan. 5, 1911, St. Charles, Mich.

Year	Team	Games	BA	SA	AB	H	2B	3B	HR	HR%	R	RBI	BB	SO	SB	Pinch Hit AB	Pinch Hit H	PO	A	E	DP	TC/G	FA	G by Pos
1934	CIN N	6	.000	.000	7	0	0	0	0	0.0	0	1	0	5	0	4	0	6	1	0	1	3.5	1.000	OF-2
1935		4	.400	.400	5	2	0	0	0	0.0	0	0	0	1	1	1	1	1	0	0	0	0.5	1.000	OF-2
2 yrs.		10	.167	.167	12	2	0	0	0	0.0	0	1	0	6	1	5	1	7	1	0	1	2.0	1.000	OF-4

Geno Petralli

PETRALLI, EUGENE JAMES BL TR 6′ 2″ 185 lbs.
B. Sept. 25, 1959, Sacramento, Calif. BB 1982–1987

Year	Team	Games	BA	SA	AB	H	2B	3B	HR	HR%	R	RBI	BB	SO	SB	Pinch Hit AB	Pinch Hit H	PO	A	E	DP	TC/G	FA	G by Pos
1982	TOR A	16	.364	.409	44	16	2	0	0	0.0	3	1	4	6	0	3	1	51	4	1	0	3.7	.982	C-12, 3B-3
1983		6	.000	.000	4	0	0	0	0	0.0	0	0	1	1	1	1	0	7	0	0	0	1.2	1.000	C-5, DH-1
1984		3	.000	.000	3	0	0	0	0	0.0	0	0	0	0	0	2	0	1	1	0	0	1.0	1.000	C-1, DH-1
1985	TEX A	42	.270	.290	100	27	2	0	0	0.0	7	11	8	12	1	3	0	179	16	2	6	4.8	.990	C-41
1986		69	.255	.409	137	35	9	3	2	1.5	17	18	5	14	3	22	4	163	14	4	2	3.0	.978	C-41, 3B-15, DH-2, 2B-2
1987		101	.302	.480	202	61	11	2	7	3.5	28	31	27	29	0	26	5	370	34	5	4	4.4	.988	C-63, 3B-17, 1B-5, 2B-4, OF-3, DH-2
1988		129	.282	.393	351	99	14	2	7	2.0	35	36	41	52	0	23	6	421	54	10	8	4.0	.979	C-85, DH-23, 3B-9, 2B-2, 1B-2
1989		70	.304	.408	184	56	7	0	4	2.2	18	23	17	24	0	15	4	258	15	3	3	4.2	.989	C-49, DH-16
1990		133	.255	.302	325	83	13	1	0	0.0	28	21	50	49	0	24	5	602	46	6	7	5.1	.991	C-118, 3B-7, 2B-3
1991		87	.271	.352	199	54	8	1	2	1.0	21	20	21	25	2	22	3	294	25	11	5	4.2	.967	C-66, 3B-7, DH-5
1992		94	.198	.276	192	38	12	0	1	0.5	11	18	20	34	0	32	8	264	24	4	6	3.9	.986	C-54, DH-14, 3B-4, 2B-2
1993		59	.241	.301	133	32	5	0	1	0.8	16	13	22	17	2	13	1	179	11	2	4	4.5	.990	C-39, DH-2, 2B-1, 3B-1
12 yrs.		809	.267	.360	1874	501	83	9	24	1.3	184	192	216	263	9	186	37	2789	244	48	45	4.2	.984	C-574, DH-66, 3B-63, 2B-14, 1B-7, OF-3

Rico Petrocelli

PETROCELLI, AMERICO PETER BR TR 6′ 175 lbs.
B. June 27, 1943, Brooklyn, N. Y.

Year	Team	Games	BA	SA	AB	H	2B	3B	HR	HR%	R	RBI	BB	SO	SB	Pinch Hit AB	Pinch Hit H	PO	A	E	DP	TC/G	FA	G by Pos
1963	BOS A	1	.250	.500	4	1	1	0	0	0.0	0	1	0	1	0	0	0	3	2	1	0	6.0	.833	SS-1
1965		103	.232	.412	323	75	15	2	13	4.0	38	33	36	71	0	8	0	151	278	19	45	4.8	.958	SS-93
1966		139	.238	.383	522	124	20	1	18	3.4	58	59	41	99	1	6	0	211	390	28	72	4.8	.955	SS-127, 3B-5
1967		142	.259	.420	491	127	24	2	17	3.5	53	66	49	93	2	1	0	223	432	19	73	4.8	.972	SS-141
1968		123	.234	.374	406	95	17	2	12	3.0	41	46	31	73	0	4	1	178	361	12	68	4.7	.978	SS-117, 1B-1
1969		154	.297	.589	535	159	32	2	40	7.5	92	97	98	68	3	0	0	269	469	15	103	4.9	.980	SS-153, 3B-1
1970		157	.261	.473	583	152	31	3	29	5.0	82	103	67	82	1	1	0	276	430	21	80	4.6	.971	SS-141, 3B-18
1971		158	.251	.461	553	139	24	4	28	5.1	82	89	91	108	2	2	1	118	334	11	37	3.0	.976	3B-156
1972		147	.240	.363	521	125	15	2	15	2.9	62	75	78	91	0	1	1	146	278	13	38	3.0	.970	3B-146
1973		100	.244	.396	356	87	13	1	13	3.7	44	45	47	64	0	1	0	73	224	6	22	3.1	.980	3B-99
1974		129	.267	.421	454	121	23	1	15	3.3	53	76	48	74	1	5	1	83	219	12	23	2.5	.962	3B-116, DH-9
1975		115	.239	.333	402	96	15	1	7	1.7	31	59	41	66	0	1	0	85	229	13	13	2.9	.960	3B-113, DH-1
1976		85	.212	.287	240	51	7	1	3	1.3	17	24	34	36	0	2	0	70	134	6	15	2.5	.971	3B-73, 2B-5, DH-4, SS-1, 1B-1
13 yrs.		1553	.251	.420	5390	1352	237	22	210	3.9	653	773	661	926	10	32	4	1886	3780	176	589	3.8	.970	SS-774, 3B-727, DH-14, 2B-5, 1B-2
LEAGUE CHAMPIONSHIP SERIES																								
1975	BOS A	3	.167	.417	12	2	0	0	1	8.3	1	2	0	3	0	0	0	4	3	0	1	2.3	1.000	3B-3
WORLD SERIES																								
1967	BOS A	7	.200	.550	20	4	1	0	2	10.0	3	3	3	8	0	0	0	11	21	2	1	4.9	.941	SS-7
1975		7	.308	.346	26	8	1	0	0	0.0	3	4	3	6	0	0	0	7	15	0	1	3.1	1.000	3B-7
2 yrs.		14	.261	.435	46	12	2	0	2	4.3	6	7	6	14	0	0	0	18	36	2	2	4.0	.964	3B-7, SS-7

Pat Pettee

PETTEE, PATRICK E. BR TR 5′10″ 170 lbs.
B. Jan. 10, 1863, Natick, Mass. D. Oct. 9, 1934, Natick, Mass.

Year	Team	Games	BA	SA	AB	H	2B	3B	HR	HR%	R	RBI	BB	SO	SB	Pinch Hit AB	Pinch Hit H	PO	A	E	DP	TC/G	FA	G by Pos
1891	LOU AA	2	.000	.000	5	0	0	0	0	0.0	1	0	3	1	1	0	0	3	6	2	1	5.5	.818	2B-2

Ned Pettigrew

PETTIGREW, JIM NED BR TR 5′11″ 175 lbs.
B. Aug. 25, 1881, Honey Grove, Tex. D. Aug. 20, 1952, Duncan, Okla.

Year	Team	Games	BA	SA	AB	H	2B	3B	HR	HR%	R	RBI	BB	SO	SB	Pinch Hit AB	Pinch Hit H	PO	A	E	DP	TC/G	FA	G by Pos
1914	BUF F	2	.000	.000	2	0	0	0	0	0.0	0	0	0		0	2	0	0	0	0	0	0.0	—	

Joe Pettini

PETTINI, JOSEPH PAUL BR TR 5′ 9″ 165 lbs.
B. Jan. 26, 1955, Wheeling, W. Va.

Year	Team	Games	BA	SA	AB	H	2B	3B	HR	HR%	R	RBI	BB	SO	SB	Pinch Hit AB	Pinch Hit H	PO	A	E	DP	TC/G	FA	G by Pos
1980	SF N	63	.232	.274	190	44	3	1	1	0.5	19	9	17	33	5	2	1	66	147	8	24	3.3	.964	SS-42, 3B-18, 2B-8
1981		35	.069	.103	29	2	1	0	0	0.0	3	2	4	5	1	1	0	13	37	6	4	1.7	.893	2B-12, SS-12, 3B-9
1982		29	.205	.231	39	8	1	0	0	0.0	5	2	3	4	0	2	0	24	33	4	5	2.3	.934	SS-26, 3B-1
1983		61	.186	.209	86	16	0	1	0	0.0	11	7	9	11	4	3	0	44	82	6	16	2.5	.955	SS-26, 2B-14, 3B-12
4 yrs.		188	.203	.238	344	70	5	2	1	0.3	38	20	33	53	10	8	1	147	299	24	49	2.6	.949	SS-106, 3B-40, 2B-34

Gary Pettis

PETTIS, GARY GEORGE BB TR 6′ 1″ 165 lbs.
B. Apr. 3, 1958, Oakland, Calif.

Year	Team	Games	BA	SA	AB	H	2B	3B	HR	HR%	R	RBI	BB	SO	SB	Pinch Hit AB	Pinch Hit H	PO	A	E	DP	TC/G	FA	G by Pos
1982	CAL A	10	.200	.800	5	1	0	0	1	20.0	5	1	0	2	0	0	0	5	1	0	0	0.8	1.000	OF-8
1983		22	.294	.494	85	25	2	3	3	3.5	19	6	7	15	8	0	0	49	5	1	2	2.6	.982	OF-21
1984		140	.227	.300	397	90	11	6	2	0.5	63	29	60	115	48	2	0	337	11	6	4	2.6	.983	OF-134
1985		125	.257	.323	443	114	10	8	1	0.2	67	32	62	125	56	0	0	368	13	4	5	3.2	.990	OF-122
1986		154	.258	.343	539	139	23	4	5	0.9	93	58	69	132	50	0	0	462	9	7	3	3.1	.985	OF-153, DH-1
1987		133	.208	.259	394	82	13	2	1	0.3	49	17	52	124	24	0	0	344	2	7	2	2.7	.980	OF-131
1988	DET A	129	.210	.277	458	96	14	4	3	0.7	65	36	47	85	44	2	0	361	5	5	0	2.9	.987	OF-126, DH-2
1989		119	.257	.309	444	114	8	6	1	0.2	77	18	84	106	43	1	0	325	1	4	0	2.8	.988	OF-119
1990	TEX A	136	.239	.336	423	101	16	8	3	0.7	66	31	57	118	38	5	1	285	10	2	4	2.3	.993	OF-128, DH-2
1991		137	.216	.277	282	61	7	5	0	0.0	37	19	54	91	29	10	0	248	4	6	1	2.0	.977	OF-126, DH-3
1992	2 teams	SD N (30G –.200) DET A (48G –.202)																						
″	total	78	.201	.289	159	32	5	3	1	0.6	27	12	29	45	14	14	3	164	2	2	0	2.8	.988	OF-60
11 yrs.		1183	.236	.310	3629	855	109	49	21	0.6	568	259	521	958	354	34	4	2948	63	44	21	2.7	.986	OF-1128, DH-8
LEAGUE CHAMPIONSHIP SERIES																								
1986	CAL A	7	.346	.500	26	9	1	0	1	3.8	4	4	3	5	0	0	0	24	0	1	0	3.6	.960	OF-7

Bob Pettit

PETTIT, ROBERT HENRY BL TR 5′ 9″ 160 lbs.
B. July 19, 1861, Williamstown, Mass. D. Nov. 1, 1910, Derby, Conn.

Year	Team	Games	BA	SA	AB	H	2B	3B	HR	HR%	R	RBI	BB	SO	SB	Pinch Hit AB	Pinch Hit H	PO	A	E	DP	TC/G	FA	G by Pos
1887	CHI N	32	.261	.370	138	36	3	3	2	1.4	29	12	8	15	16	0	0	35	8	6	0	1.4	.878	OF-32, C-1, P-1
1888		43	.254	.379	169	43	1	4	4	2.4	23	23	7	9	7	0	0	46	8	4	3	1.3	.931	OF-43
1891	MIL AA	21	.175	.263	80	14	4	0	1	1.3	10	5	7	7	2	0	0	22	35	6	1	2.9	.905	2B-9, OF-7, 3B-6
3 yrs.		96	.240	.351	387	93	8	7	7	1.8	62	40	22	31	25	0	0	103	51	16	4	1.7	.906	OF-82, 2B-9, 3B-6, C-1, P-1

Marty Pevey

PEVEY, MARTY ASHLEY BL TR 6′ 1″ 185 lbs.
B. Dec. 25, 1962, Savannah, Ga.

Year	Team	Games	BA	SA	AB	H	2B	3B	HR	HR%	R	RBI	BB	SO	SB	Pinch Hit AB	Pinch Hit H	PO	A	E	DP	TC/G	FA	G by Pos
1989	MON N	13	.220	.293	41	9	1	1	0	0.0	2	3	0	8	0	2	0	58	7	1	0	5.5	.985	C-11, OF-1

Larry Pezold

PEZOLD, LORENZ JOHANNES BR TR 5′ 9½″ 175 lbs.
B. June 22, 1893, New Orleans, La. D. Oct. 22, 1957, Baton Rouge, La.

Year	Team	Games	BA	SA	AB	H	2B	3B	HR	HR%	R	RBI	BB	SO	SB	Pinch Hit AB	Pinch Hit H	PO	A	E	DP	TC/G	FA	G by Pos
1914	CLE A	23	.225	.254	71	16	0	1	0	0.0	4	5	9	6	2	2	0	21	41	13	2	3.6	.827	3B-20, OF-1

Big Jeff Pfeffer

PFEFFER, FRANCIS XAVIER BR TR 6′ 1″ 185 lbs.
Brother of Jeff Pfeffer.
B. Mar. 31, 1882, Champaign, Ill. D. Dec. 19, 1954, Kankakee, Ill.

Year	Team	Games	BA	SA	AB	H	2B	3B	HR	HR%	R	RBI	BB	SO	SB	Pinch Hit AB	Pinch Hit H	PO	A	E	DP	TC/G	FA	G by Pos
1905	CHI N	15	.200	.275	40	8	3	0	0	0.0	4	3	0		2	0	0	4	24	0	0	1.9	1.000	P-15
1906	BOS N	60	.196	.272	158	31	3	3	1	0.6	10	11	5		2	8	0	32	93	5	1	2.7	.962	P-35, OF-14
1907		21	.250	.300	60	15	3	0	0	0.0	1	6	2		0	2	0	4	38	2	0	2.3	.955	P-19
1908		4	.000	.000	2	0	0	0	0	0.0	0	0	0		0	0	0	0	1	0	0	0.3	1.000	P-4
1910	CHI N	14	.176	.353	17	3	1	1	0	0.0	1	2	1	1	0	0	0	1	10	0	0	0.8	1.000	P-13, OF-1
1911	BOS N	33	.196	.304	46	9	2	0	1	2.2	4	6	5	7	0	3	0	10	25	0	0	1.2	1.000	P-26, OF-3, 1B-1
6 yrs.		147	.204	.285	323	66	12	4	2	0.6	20	28	13	8	4	13	0	51	191	7	1	1.9	.972	P-112, OF-18, 1B-1

Fred Pfeffer

PFEFFER, NATHANIEL FREDERICK (Dandelion, Fritz) BR TR 5′10½″ 184 lbs.
B. Mar. 17, 1860, Louisville, Ky. D. Apr. 10, 1932, Chicago, Ill.
Manager 1892.

Year	Team	Games	BA	SA	AB	H	2B	3B	HR	HR%	R	RBI	BB	SO	SB	Pinch Hit AB	Pinch Hit H	PO	A	E	DP	TC/G	FA	G by Pos
1882	TRO N	85	.218	.273	330	72	7	4	1	0.3	26	31	1	24		0	0	169	282	76	35	6.2	.856	SS-83, 2B-2
1883	CHI N	96	.235	.340	371	87	22	7	1	0.3	41		8	50		0	0	281	328	86	56	7.0	.876	2B-79, SS-18, 3B-1, 1B-1
1884		112	.289	.514	467	135	10	10	25	5.4	105		25	47		0	0	395	422	88	85	8.0	.903	2B-112, P-1
1885		112	.241	.330	469	113	12	6	6	1.3	90	71	26	47		0	0	328	397	86	66	7.1	.894	2B-109, P-5, OF-1
1886		118	.264	.378	474	125	17	8	7	1.5	88	95	36	46		0	0	344	340	73	66	6.4	.904	2B-118, 1B-1
1887		123	.278	.447	479	133	21	6	16	3.3	95	89	34	20	57	0	0	394	402	72	68	6.9	.917	2B-123, OF-2
1888		135	.250	.377	517	129	22	10	8	1.5	90	57	32	38	64	0	0	421	457	65	78	7.0	.931	2B-135
1889		134	.228	.322	531	121	15	7	7	1.3	85	77	53	51	45	0	0	452	483	56	69	7.4	.943	2B-134
1890	CHI P	124	.257	.361	499	128	21	8	5	1.0	86	80	44	23	27	0	0	441	387	76	73	7.3	.916	2B-124
1891	CHI N	137	.247	.349	498	123	12	9	7	1.4	93	77	79	60	40	0	0	429	474	77	78	7.2	.921	2B-137
1892	LOU N	124	.257	.338	470	121	14	9	2	0.4	78	76	67	36	27	0	0	401	384	58	75	6.6	.931	2B-116, 1B-10, OF-1, P-1
1893		125	.254	.376	508	129	29	12	3	0.6	85	75	51	18	32	0	0	355	398	49	74	6.4	.939	2B-125
1894		104	.308	.443	409	126	12	14	5	1.2	68	59	30	14	31	0	0	282	340	48	67	6.3	.928	2B-90, SS-15, P-1
1895		11	.289	.311	45	13	1	0	0	0.0	8	5	5	3	2	0	0	53	22	12	6	7.9	.862	SS-5, 2B-3, 1B-3
1896	2 teams	NY N (4G –.143) CHI N (94G –.244)																						
″	total	98	.241	.337	374	90	16	7	2	0.5	46	56	24	21	22	0	0	236	317	36	43	6.0	.939	2B-98
1897	CHI N	32	.228	.246	114	26	0	1	0	0.0	10	11	12		5	0	0	73	93	22	12	5.9	.883	2B-32
16 yrs.		1670	.255	.370	6555	1671	231	118	95	1.4	1094	859	527	498	352	0	0	5054	5526	980	951	6.9	.915	2B-1537, SS-121, 1B-15, P-8, OF-4, 3B-1

Monte Pfeffer

PFEFFER, MONTE BR TR 5′ 4½″ 147 lbs.
Born Monte Pfeiffer.
B. Oct. 8, 1891, New York, N. Y. D. Sept. 27, 1941, New York, N. Y.

Year	Team	Games	BA	SA	AB	H	2B	3B	HR	HR%	R	RBI	BB	SO	SB	Pinch Hit AB	Pinch Hit H	PO	A	E	DP	TC/G	FA	G by Pos
1913	PHI A	1	.000	.000	3	0	0	0	0	0.0	0	0	0	1	0	1	0	0	4	1	0	5.0	.800	SS-1

Bobby Pfeil

PFEIL, ROBERT RAYMOND BR TR 6′ 1″ 180 lbs.
B. Nov. 13, 1943, Passaic, N. J.

Year	Team	Games	BA	SA	AB	H	2B	3B	HR	HR%	R	RBI	BB	SO	SB	Pinch Hit AB	Pinch Hit H	PO	A	E	DP	TC/G	FA	G by Pos
1969	NY N	62	.232	.275	211	49	9	0	0	0.0	20	10	7	27	0	9	5	53	105	4	12	2.6	.975	3B-49, 2B-11, OF-2
1971	PHI N	44	.271	.400	70	19	3	0	2	2.9	5	9	6	9	1	17	3	15	27	1	7	1.7	.977	3B-15, C-4, OF-3, 2B-1, 1B-1, SS-1
2 yrs.		106	.242	.306	281	68	12	0	2	0.7	25	19	13	36	1	26	8	68	132	5	19	2.4	.976	3B-64, 2B-12, OF-5, C-4, 1B-1, SS-1

George Pfister

PFISTER, GEORGE EDWARD BR TR 6′ 200 lbs.
B. Sept. 4, 1918, Bound Brook, N. J.

Year	Team	Games	BA	SA	AB	H	2B	3B	HR	HR%	R	RBI	BB	SO	SB	Pinch Hit AB	Pinch Hit H	PO	A	E	DP	TC/G	FA	G by Pos
1941	BKN N	1	.000	.000	2	0	0	0	0	0.0	0	0	0	0	0	0	0	3	2	0	1	5.0	1.000	C-1

Monte Pfyl

PFYL, MEINHARD CHARLES — BL TL 6' 3" 190 lbs.
B. May 11, 1884, St. Louis, Mo. D. Oct. 18, 1945, San Francisco, Calif.

Year	Team	Games	BA	SA	AB	H	2B	3B	HR	HR%	R	RBI	BB	SO	SB	Pinch Hit AB	Pinch Hit H	PO	A	E	DP	TC/G	FA	G by Pos
1907	NY N	1	—	—	0	0	0	0	0	—	0	0	0		0	0	0	0	0	0	0	0.0	.000	1B-1

Art Phelan

PHELAN, ARTHUR THOMAS (Dugan) — BR TR 5' 8" 160 lbs.
B. Aug. 14, 1887, Niantic, Ill. D. Dec. 27, 1964, Fort Worth, Tex.

Year	Team	Games	BA	SA	AB	H	2B	3B	HR	HR%	R	RBI	BB	SO	SB	Pinch Hit AB	Pinch Hit H	PO	A	E	DP	TC/G	FA	G by Pos
1910	CIN N	23	.214	.214	42	9	0	0	0	0.0	7	4	7	6	5	2	0	19	20	0	1	2.3	1.000	3B-8, 2B-5, OF-3, SS-1
1912		130	.243	.330	461	112	9	11	3	0.7	56	54	46	37	25	0	0	155	255	33	18	3.4	.926	3B-127, 2B-3
1913	CHI N	90	.251	.363	259	65	11	6	2	0.8	41	35	29	25	8	7	3	102	148	19	12	3.2	.929	2B-46, 3B-38, SS-1
1914		25	.283	.370	46	13	2	1	0	0.0	5	3	4	3	0	13	6	12	21	3	1	3.0	.917	3B-7, 2B-3, SS-2
1915		133	.219	.306	448	98	16	7	3	0.7	41	35	55	42	12	0	0	197	267	28	19	3.7	.943	3B-110, 2B-24
5 yrs.		401	.236	.326	1256	297	38	25	8	0.6	150	131	141	113	50	22	9	485	711	83	51	3.4	.935	3B-290, 2B-81, SS-4, OF-3

Dan Phelan

PHELAN, DANIEL T.
B. July 23, 1864, Thomaston, Conn. D. Dec. 7, 1945, West Haven, Conn.

Year	Team	Games	BA	SA	AB	H	2B	3B	HR	HR%	R	RBI	BB	SO	SB	Pinch Hit AB	Pinch Hit H	PO	A	E	DP	TC/G	FA	G by Pos
1890	LOU AA	8	.250	.344	32	8	1	1	0	0.0	4		0		1	0	0	76	3	2	0	10.1	.975	1B-8

Dick Phelan

PHELAN, JAMES DICKSON — BR
B. Dec. 10, 1854, Towanda, Pa. D. Feb. 13, 1931, San Antonio, Tex.

Year	Team	Games	BA	SA	AB	H	2B	3B	HR	HR%	R	RBI	BB	SO	SB	Pinch Hit AB	Pinch Hit H	PO	A	E	DP	TC/G	FA	G by Pos
1884	BAL U	101	.246	.316	402	99	13	3	3	0.7	63		12			0	0	277	256	80	34	5.8	.869	2B-100, 3B-5, OF-1
1885	2 teams	BUF N (4G –.125) STL N (2G –.250)																						
"	total	6	.150	.350	20	3	1	0	1	5.0	3	4	0	5		0	0	8	15	5	2	4.7	.821	2B-4, 3B-2
2 yrs.		107	.242	.318	422	102	14	3	4	0.9	66	4	12	5		0	0	285	271	85	36	5.7	.867	2B-104, 3B-7, OF-1

Babe Phelps

PHELPS, ERNEST GORDON (Blimp) — BL TR 6' 2" 225 lbs.
B. Apr. 19, 1908, Odenton, Md. D. Dec. 10, 1992, Odenton, Md.

Year	Team	Games	BA	SA	AB	H	2B	3B	HR	HR%	R	RBI	BB	SO	SB	Pinch Hit AB	Pinch Hit H	PO	A	E	DP	TC/G	FA	G by Pos
1931	WAS A	3	.333	.333	3	1	0	0	0	0.0	0	0	0	0	0	3	1	0	0	0	0	0.0	—	
1933	CHI N	3	.286	.286	7	2	0	0	0	0.0	0	2	0	1	0	1	0	6	2	0	1	4.0	1.000	C-2
1934		44	.286	.500	70	20	5	2	2	2.9	7	12	1	8	0	26	9	44	7	1	0	2.9	.981	C-18
1935	BKN N	47	.364	.579	121	44	7	2	5	4.1	17	22	9	10	0	12	6	118	16	6	4	4.1	.957	C-34
1936		115	.367	.498	319	117	23	2	5	1.6	36	57	27	18	1	15	5	337	49	9	6	4.0	.977	C-98, OF-1
1937		121	.313	.469	409	128	37	3	7	1.7	42	58	25	28	2	8	1	465	76	16	10	5.0	.971	C-111
1938		66	.308	.457	208	64	12	2	5	2.4	33	46	23	15	2	9	1	218	25	5	5	4.5	.980	C-55
1939		98	.285	.418	323	92	21	2	6	1.9	33	42	24	24	0	6	1	361	40	8	6	4.4	.980	C-92
1940		118	.295	.492	370	109	24	5	13	3.5	47	61	30	27	2	16	2	436	35	11	4	4.8	.977	C-99, 1B-1
1941		16	.233	.533	30	7	3	0	2	6.7	3	4	1	2	0	5	1	33	1	1	0	3.2	.971	C-11
1942	PIT N	95	.284	.440	257	73	11	1	9	3.5	21	41	20	21	2	22	7	244	40	12	5	4.1	.959	C-72
11 yrs.		726	.310	.472	2117	657	143	19	54	2.6	239	345	160	154	9	123	34	2262	291	69	41	4.4	.974	C-592, 1B-1, OF-1

Ed Phelps

PHELPS, EDWARD JAYKILL — BR TR 5'11" 185 lbs.
B. Mar. 3, 1879, Albany, N. Y. D. Jan. 31, 1942, East Greenbush, N. Y.

Year	Team	Games	BA	SA	AB	H	2B	3B	HR	HR%	R	RBI	BB	SO	SB	Pinch Hit AB	Pinch Hit H	PO	A	E	DP	TC/G	FA	G by Pos
1902	PIT N	18	.213	.230	61	13	1	0	0	0.0	5	6	4		2	0	0	89	11	3	3	5.7	.971	C-13, 1B-5
1903		81	.282	.352	273	77	7	3	2	0.7	32	31	17		2	1	0	345	83	8	7	5.5	.982	C-76, 1B-3
1904		94	.242	.278	302	73	5	3	0	0.0	29	28	15		2	1	0	372	97	17	8	5.3	.965	C-91, 1B-1
1905	CIN N	44	.231	.301	156	36	5	3	0	0.0	18	18	12		4	0	0	189	55	13	5	5.8	.949	C-44
1906	2 teams	CIN N (12G –.275) PIT N (43G –.237)																						
"	total	55	.247	.323	158	39	3	3	1	0.6	12	17	12		3	2	0	231	45	7	4	5.2	.975	C-54
1907	PIT N	43	.212	.221	113	24	1	0	0	0.0	11	12	9		1	6	0	156	39	4	3	5.5	.980	C-35, 1B-1
1908		34	.234	.328	64	15	2	2	0	0.0	3	11	2		0	12	**7**	69	15	2	0	4.3	.977	C-20
1909	STL N	100	.248	.297	306	76	13	1	0	0.0	43	22	39		7	19	3	330	87	20	11	5.3	.954	C-82
1910		93	.263	.293	270	71	4	2	0	0.0	25	37	36	29	9	13	3	320	84	10	10	5.2	.976	C-80
1912	BKN N	52	.288	.378	111	32	4	3	0	0.0	8	23	16	15	1	20	4	130	35	4	4	5.3	.976	C-32
1913		15	.222	.222	18	4	0	0	0	0.0	0	0	1	2	0	10	2	6	1	1	0	2.0	.875	C-4
11 yrs.		629	.251	.302	1832	460	45	20	3	0.2	186	205	163	46	31	84	19	2237	552	89	55	5.3	.969	C-531, 1B-10
WORLD SERIES																								
1903	PIT N	8	.231	.308	26	6	2	0	0	0.0	1	2	1	6	0	1	0	36	4	2	0	6.0	.952	C-7

Ken Phelps

PHELPS, KENNETH ALLEN — BL TL 6' 1" 209 lbs.
B. Aug. 6, 1954, Seattle, Wash.

Year	Team	Games	BA	SA	AB	H	2B	3B	HR	HR%	R	RBI	BB	SO	SB	Pinch Hit AB	Pinch Hit H	PO	A	E	DP	TC/G	FA	G by Pos
1980	KC A	3	.000	.000	4	0	0	0	0	0.0	0	0	0	2	0	1	0	14	0	0	2	7.0	1.000	1B-2
1981		21	.136	.227	22	3	0	1	0	0.0	1	1	1	13	0	15	2	4	1	0	0	0.8	1.000	DH-4, 1B-2
1982	MON N	10	.250	.250	8	2	0	0	0	0.0	0	0	0	3	0	8	2	0	0	0	0	0.0	—	
1983	SEA A	50	.236	.449	127	30	4	1	7	5.5	10	16	13	25	0	11	3	164	16	0	11	4.4	1.000	1B-22, DH-19
1984		101	.241	.521	290	70	9	0	24	8.3	52	51	61	73	3	15	2	72	4	1	7	0.8	.987	DH-84, 1B-9
1985		61	.207	.466	116	24	3	0	9	7.8	18	24	24	33	2	25	5	31	2	0	5	1.0	1.000	DH-25, 1B-8
1986		125	.247	.526	344	85	16	4	24	7.0	69	64	88	96	2	16	3	487	34	9	58	5.0	.983	1B-55, DH-52
1987		120	.259	.548	332	86	13	1	27	8.1	68	68	80	75	1	12	2	8	0	0	0	0.1	1.000	DH-114, 1B-1
1988	2 teams	SEA A (72G –.284) NY A (45G –.224)																						
"	total	117	.263	.549	297	78	13	0	24	8.1	54	54	70	61	1	17	2	18	2	1	2	0.2	.952	DH-92, 1B-4
1989	2 teams	NY A (86G –.249) OAK A (11G –.111)																						
"	total	97	.242	.371	194	47	4	0	7	3.6	26	29	31	47	0	**38**	**11**	56	2	1	5	0.9	.983	DH-56, 1B-9
1990	2 teams	OAK A (32G –.186) CLE A (24G –.115)																						
"	total	56	.150	.192	120	18	2	0	1	0.8	10	6	22	21	1	17	4	111	10	1	7	3.0	.992	DH-21, 1B-19
11 yrs.		761	.239	.480	1854	443	64	7	123	6.6	308	313	390	449	10	175	36	965	71	13	97	1.8	.988	DH-467, 1B-131
LEAGUE CHAMPIONSHIP SERIES																								
1989	OAK A	1	1.000	2.000	1	1	1	0	0	0.0	0	0	0	0	0	1	1	0	0	0	0	0.0	—	
WORLD SERIES																								
1989	OAK A	1	.000	.000	1	0	0	0	0	0.0	0	0	0	0	0	1	0	0	0	0	0	0.0	—	

Neal Phelps

PHELPS, CORNELIUS CARMAN
B. Nov. 19, 1840, New York, N. Y. D. Feb. 12, 1885, New York, N. Y.

Year	Team	Games	BA	SA	AB	H	2B	3B	HR	HR%	R	RBI	BB	SO	SB	Pinch Hit AB	Pinch Hit H	PO	A	E	DP	TC/G	FA	G by Pos
1876	2 teams	NY N (1G –.000) PHI N (1G –.000)																						
"	total	2	.000	.000	7	0	0	0	0	0.0	0	0	0	1		0	0	5	1	4	0	5.0	.600	C-1, OF-1

Year	Team	Games	BA	SA	AB	H	2B	3B	HR	HR%	R	RBI	BB	SO	SB	Pinch Hit AB	Pinch Hit H	PO	A	E	DP	TC/G	FA	G by Pos

Dave Philley

PHILLEY, DAVID EARL BB TR 6′ 188 lbs.
B. May 16, 1920, Paris, Tex.

Year	Team	Games	BA	SA	AB	H	2B	3B	HR	HR%	R	RBI	BB	SO	SB	Pinch Hit AB	Pinch Hit H	PO	A	E	DP	TC/G	FA	G by Pos
1941	**CHI A**	7	.222	.333	9	2	1	0	0	0.0	4	0	3	3	0	4	0	0	0	0	0	0.0	.000	OF-2
1946		17	.353	.471	68	24	2	3	0	0.0	10	17	4	4	5	0	0	55	3	1	0	3.5	.983	OF-17
1947		143	.258	.354	551	142	25	11	2	0.4	55	45	35	39	21	6	2	356	15	5	3	2.7	.987	OF-133, 3B-4
1948		137	.287	.387	488	140	28	3	5	1.0	51	42	50	33	8	8	1	381	22	9	6	3.2	.978	OF-128
1949		146	.286	.346	598	171	20	8	0	0.0	84	44	54	51	13	1	0	282	16	7	3	2.1	.977	OF-145
1950		156	.242	.360	619	150	21	5	14	2.3	69	80	52	57	6	1	0	367	19	8	8	2.6	.980	OF-154
1951	**2 teams**	**CHI A** (7G –.240) **PHI A** (125G –.263)																						
″	**total**	132	.262	.373	493	129	20	7	7	1.4	71	61	65	41	10	5	1	314	15	8	4	2.7	.976	OF-126
1952	**PHI A**	151	.263	.355	586	154	25	4	7	1.2	80	71	59	35	11	0	0	445	16	4	3	3.1	.991	OF-149, 3B-2
1953		157	.303	.424	620	188	30	9	9	1.5	80	59	51	35	13	1	0	296	18	6	0	2.0	.981	OF-157, 3B-1
1954	**CLE A**	133	.226	.347	452	102	13	3	12	2.7	48	60	57	48	2	4	1	237	6	4	0	1.9	.984	OF-129
1955	**2 teams**	**CLE A** (43G –.298) **BAL A** (83G –.299)																						
″	**total**	126	.299	.422	415	124	17	5	8	1.9	65	50	46	48	1	10	4	198	7	6	4	1.8	.972	OF-116, 3B-2
1956	**2 teams**	**BAL A** (32G –.205) **CHI A** (86G –.265)																						
″	**total**	118	.247	.351	396	98	18	4	5	1.3	57	64	48	40	4	12	0	407	25	12	34	3.8	.973	OF-61, 1B-51, 3B-5
1957	**2 teams**	**CHI A** (22G –.324) **DET A** (65G –.283)																						
″	**total**	87	.295	.377	244	72	12	1	2	0.8	24	25	11	26	4	29	12	273	25	3	21	5.1	.990	OF-29, 1B-29, 3B-1
1958	**PHI N**	91	.309	.444	207	64	11	4	3	1.4	30	31	15	20	1	44	**18**	183	12	1	12	4.7	.995	OF-24, 1B-18
1959		99	.291	.461	254	74	18	2	7	2.8	32	37	18	27	0	38	15	238	15	4	18	4.4	.984	OF-34, 1B-24
1960	**3 teams**	**PHI N** (14G –.333) **SF N** (39G –.164) **BAL A** (14G –.265)																						
″	**total**	67	.218	.327	110	24	4	1	2	1.8	13	16	13	21	1	48	11	32	0	1	1	1.2	.970	OF-21, 3B-4, 1B-2
1961	**BAL A**	99	.250	.361	144	36	9	2	1	0.7	13	23	10	20	2	**72**	**24**	24	0	0	0	0.9	1.000	OF-25, 1B-1
1962	**BOS A**	38	.143	.190	42	6	2	0	0	0.0	3	4	5	3	0	28	4	6	0	0	0	1.5	1.000	OF-4
18 yrs.		1904	.270	.377	6296	1700	276	72	84	1.3	789	729	596	551	102	311	93	4094	214	79	117	2.7	.982	OF-1454, 1B-125, 3B-19
WORLD SERIES																								
1954	**CLE A**	4	.125	.125	8	1	0	0	0	0.0	0	0	1	3	0	2	0	1	0	0	0	0.5	1.000	OF-2

Adolfo Phillips

PHILLIPS, ADOLFO EMILIO BR TR 6′ 1″ 175 lbs.
Born Adolfo Emilio Phillips (Lopez).
B. Dec. 16, 1941, Bethania, Panama.

Year	Team	Games	BA	SA	AB	H	2B	3B	HR	HR%	R	RBI	BB	SO	SB	Pinch Hit AB	Pinch Hit H	PO	A	E	DP	TC/G	FA	G by Pos
1964	**PHI N**	13	.231	.231	13	3	0	0	0	0.0	4	0	3	3	0	6	2	5	1	0	0	1.5	1.000	OF-4
1965		41	.230	.379	87	20	4	0	3	3.4	14	5	5	34	3	6	1	46	0	0	0	1.4	1.000	OF-32
1966	**2 teams**	**PHI N** (2G –.000) **CHI N** (116G –.262)																						
″	**total**	118	.260	.449	419	109	29	1	16	3.8	69	36	43	135	32	4	1	260	14	6	2	2.5	.979	OF-112
1967	**CHI N**	144	.268	.458	448	120	20	7	17	3.8	66	70	80	93	24	2	0	340	13	7	0	2.6	.981	OF-141
1968		143	.241	.399	439	106	20	5	13	3.0	49	33	47	90	9	2	0	311	11	7	3	2.3	.979	OF-141
1969	**2 teams**	**CHI N** (28G –.224) **MON N** (58G –.216)																						
″	**total**	86	.218	.335	248	54	7	5	4	1.6	30	8	35	77	7	4	0	142	3	4	0	1.9	.973	OF-78
1970	**MON N**	92	.238	.379	214	51	6	3	6	2.8	36	21	36	51	7	18	3	130	1	2	0	1.8	.985	OF-75
1972	**CLE A**	12	.000	.000	7	0	0	0	0	0.0	2	0	2	2	0	3	0	7	0	0	0	0.7	1.000	OF-10
8 yrs.		649	.247	.410	1875	463	86	21	59	3.1	270	173	251	485	82	45	7	1241	43	26	5	2.2	.980	OF-593

Bill Phillips

PHILLIPS, WILLIAM B. BR TR 202 lbs.
B. 1857, St. John, N. B., Canada D. Oct. 7, 1900, Chicago, Ill.

Year	Team	Games	BA	SA	AB	H	2B	3B	HR	HR%	R	RBI	BB	SO	SB	Pinch Hit AB	Pinch Hit H	PO	A	E	DP	TC/G	FA	G by Pos
1879	**CLE N**	81	.271	.334	365	99	15	4	0	0.0	58	29	2	20		0	0	775	32	54	25	9.8	.937	1B-75, C-11, OF-2
1880		85	.254	.365	334	85	14	10	1	0.3	41	36	6	29		0	0	842	25	33	37	10.6	.963	1B-85
1881		85	.272	.387	357	97	18	10	1	0.3	51	44	5	19		0	0	806	24	29	51	10.1	.966	1B-85
1882		78	.260	.388	335	87	17	7	4	1.2	40	47	7	18		0	0	830	25	25	55	11.1	.972	1B-78, C-1
1883		97	.246	.380	382	94	29	8	2	0.5	42		8	49		0	0	953	22	33	53	10.4	.967	1B-97
1884		111	.276	.401	464	128	25	12	3	0.6	58	**46**	18	80		0	0	1107	30	48	59	10.7	.959	1B-111
1885	**BKN AA**	99	.302	.422	391	118	16	11	3	0.8	65		27			0	0	1109	24	32	40	11.8	.973	1B-99
1886		141	.274	.369	585	160	26	15	0	0.0	68		33			0	0	1395	33	32	65	10.4	.978	1B-141
1887		132	.266	.383	533	142	34	11	2	0.4	82		45		16	0	0	1299	46	24	62	10.4	.982	1B-132
1888	**KC AA**	129	.236	.320	509	120	20	10	1	0.2	57	56	27		10	0	0	1476	55	32	66	12.1	.980	1B-129
10 yrs.		1038	.266	.374	4255	1130	214	98	17	0.4	562	258	178	215	26	0	0	10592	316	342	513	10.8	.970	1B-1032, C-12, OF-2

Bubba Phillips

PHILLIPS, JOHN MELVIN BR TR 5′ 9″ 180 lbs.
B. Feb. 24, 1928, West Point, Miss. D. June 22, 1993, Hattiesburg, Miss.

Year	Team	Games	BA	SA	AB	H	2B	3B	HR	HR%	R	RBI	BB	SO	SB	Pinch Hit AB	Pinch Hit H	PO	A	E	DP	TC/G	FA	G by Pos
1955	**DET A**	95	.234	.304	184	43	4	0	3	1.6	18	23	14	20	2	17	1	131	11	3	1	2.1	.979	OF-65, 3B-4
1956	**CHI A**	67	.273	.394	99	27	6	0	2	2.0	16	11	6	12	1	13	4	61	4	0	2	1.8	1.000	OF-35, 3B-2
1957		121	.270	.372	393	106	13	3	7	1.8	38	42	28	32	5	3	0	147	230	14	17	3.3	.964	3B-97, OF-20
1958		84	.273	.369	260	71	10	0	5	1.9	26	30	15	14	3	4	0	122	87	8	13	2.6	.963	3B-47, OF-37
1959		117	.264	.380	379	100	27	1	5	1.3	43	40	27	28	1	1	0	127	202	15	13	2.8	.956	3B-100, OF-23
1960	**CLE A**	113	.207	.299	304	63	14	1	4	1.3	34	33	14	37	1	5	0	109	135	13	18	2.3	.949	3B-85, OF-25, SS-1
1961		143	.264	.408	546	144	23	1	18	3.3	64	72	29	61	1	0	0	188	246	19	23	3.2	.958	3B-143
1962		148	.258	.358	562	145	26	0	10	1.8	53	54	20	55	4	1	0	183	243	11	16	2.9	.975	3B-145, OF-3, 2B-1
1963	**DET A**	128	.246	.310	464	114	11	2	5	1.1	42	45	19	42	6	6	2	125	226	15	26	3.0	.959	3B-117, OF-5
1964		46	.253	.368	87	22	1	0	3	3.4	14	6	10	13	1	17	4	18	40	1	5	2.6	.983	3B-22, OF-1
10 yrs.		1062	.255	.358	3278	835	135	8	62	1.9	348	356	182	314	25	67	11	1211	1424	99	134	2.8	.964	3B-762, OF-214, 2B-1, SS-1
WORLD SERIES																								
1959	**CHI A**	3	.300	.400	10	3	1	0	0	0.0	0	0	0	0	0	0	0	6	3	0	0	2.3	1.000	3B-3, OF-1

Damon Phillips

PHILLIPS, DAMON ROSWELL (Dee) BR TR 6′ 176 lbs.
B. June 8, 1919, Corsicana, Tex.

Year	Team	Games	BA	SA	AB	H	2B	3B	HR	HR%	R	RBI	BB	SO	SB	Pinch Hit AB	Pinch Hit H	PO	A	E	DP	TC/G	FA	G by Pos
1942	**CIN N**	28	.202	.226	84	17	2	0	0	0.0	4	6	7	5	0	1	0	49	84	5	17	5.1	.964	SS-27
1944	**BOS N**	140	.258	.329	489	126	30	1	1	0.2	35	53	28	34	1	0	0	206	336	33	55	3.8	.943	3B-90, SS-60
1946		2	.500	.500	2	1	0	0	0	0.0	0	0	0	0	0	2	1	0	0	0	0	0.0	—	
3 yrs.		170	.250	.315	575	144	32	1	1	0.2	39	59	35	39	1	3	1	255	420	38	72	4.0	.947	3B-90, SS-87

Dick Phillips

PHILLIPS, RICHARD EUGENE BL TR 6′ 180 lbs.
B. Nov. 24, 1931, Racine, Wis.

Year	Team	Games	BA	SA	AB	H	2B	3B	HR	HR%	R	RBI	BB	SO	SB	Pinch Hit AB	Pinch Hit H	PO	A	E	DP	TC/G	FA	G by Pos
1962	**SF N**	5	.000	.000	3	0	0	0	0	0.0	1	1	1	1	0	3	0	1	0	0	0	1.0	1.000	1B-1
1963	**WAS A**	124	.237	.355	321	76	8	0	10	3.1	33	32	29	35	1	39	8	657	64	4	73	9.4	.994	1B-68, 2B-5, 3B-4

Dick Phillips *continued*

Year	Team	Games	BA	SA	AB	H	2B	3B	HR	HR%	R	RBI	BB	SO	SB	Pinch Hit AB	Pinch Hit H	PO	A	E	DP	TC/G	FA	G by Pos
1964		109	.231	.291	234	54	6	1	2	0.9	17	23	27	22	1	39	5	475	43	3	50	8.0	.994	1B-61, 3B-4
1966		25	.162	.162	37	6	0	0	0	0.0	3	4	2	5	0	18	2	46	2	0	2	9.6	1.000	1B-5
4 yrs.		263	.229	.316	595	136	14	1	12	2.0	54	60	59	63	2	99	15	1179	109	7	125	8.8	.995	1B-135, 3B-8, 2B-5

Ed Phillips

PHILLIPS, HOWARD EDWARD
B. July 8, 1931, St. Louis, Mo.
BB TR 6′ 1″ 180 lbs.

Year	Team	Games	BA	SA	AB	H	2B	3B	HR	HR%	R	RBI	BB	SO	SB	Pinch Hit AB	Pinch Hit H	PO	A	E	DP	TC/G	FA	G by Pos
1953	STL N	9	—	—	0	0	0	0	0	—	4	0	0	0	0	0	0	0	0	0	0	0.0	—	

Eddie Phillips

PHILLIPS, EDWARD DAVID
B. Feb. 17, 1901, Worcester, Mass. D. Jan. 26, 1968, Buffalo, N. Y.
BR TR 6′ 178 lbs.

Year	Team	Games	BA	SA	AB	H	2B	3B	HR	HR%	R	RBI	BB	SO	SB	Pinch Hit AB	Pinch Hit H	PO	A	E	DP	TC/G	FA	G by Pos
1924	BOS N	3	.000	.000	3	0	0	0	0	0.0	0	0	0	2	0	2	0	0	1	0	0	1.0	1.000	C-1
1929	DET A	68	.235	.330	221	52	13	1	2	0.9	24	21	20	16	0	4	1	255	34	10	4	4.7	.967	C-63
1931	PIT N	106	.232	.360	353	82	18	3	7	2.0	30	44	41	49	1	1	0	293	49	5	12	3.4	.986	C-103
1932	NY A	9	.290	.516	31	9	1	0	2	6.5	4	4	2	3	1	0	0	46	6	0	0	5.8	1.000	C-9
1934	WAS A	56	.195	.278	169	33	6	1	2	1.2	6	16	26	24	1	3	0	162	21	3	4	3.5	.984	C-53
1935	CLE A	70	.273	.368	220	60	16	1	1	0.5	18	41	15	21	0	1	0	233	18	5	3	3.7	.980	C-69
6 yrs.		312	.237	.345	997	236	54	6	14	1.4	82	126	104	115	3	11	1	989	129	23	23	3.8	.980	C-298

J. R. Phillips

PHILLIPS, CHARLES GENE
B. Apr. 29, 1970, West Covina, Calif.
BL TL 6′ 2″ 205 lbs.

Year	Team	Games	BA	SA	AB	H	2B	3B	HR	HR%	R	RBI	BB	SO	SB	Pinch Hit AB	Pinch Hit H	PO	A	E	DP	TC/G	FA	G by Pos
1993	SF N	11	.313	.688	16	5	1	1	1	6.3	1	4	0	5	0	6	1	32	2	1	1	7.0	.971	1B-5
1994		15	.132	.211	38	5	0	0	1	2.6	1	3	1	13	1	5	0	79	10	1	7	9.0	.989	1B-10
1995		92	.195	.351	231	45	9	0	9	3.9	27	28	19	69	1	14	3	536	36	4	45	7.2	.993	1B-79, OF-1
3 yrs.		118	.193	.351	285	55	10	1	11	3.9	29	35	20	87	2	25	4	647	48	6	53	7.4	.991	1B-94, OF-1

Jack Phillips

PHILLIPS, JACK DORN (Stretch)
B. Sept. 6, 1921, Clarence, N. Y.
BR TR 6′ 4″ 193 lbs.

Year	Team	Games	BA	SA	AB	H	2B	3B	HR	HR%	R	RBI	BB	SO	SB	Pinch Hit AB	Pinch Hit H	PO	A	E	DP	TC/G	FA	G by Pos
1947	NY A	16	.278	.417	36	10	0	1	1	2.8	5	2	3	5	0	4	0	71	1	1	8	7.3	.986	1B-10
1948		1	.000	.000	2	0	0	0	0	0.0	0	0	0	1	0	0	0	8	0	1	0	9.0	.889	1B-1
1949	2 teams	NY A (45G –.308) PIT N (18G –.232)																						
″	total	63	.279	.374	147	41	7	2	1	0.7	22	13	16	15	2	7	2	380	22	6	42	7.4	.985	1B-54, 3B-1
1950	PIT N	69	.293	.457	208	61	7	6	5	2.4	25	34	20	17	1	11	3	455	47	9	47	8.8	.982	1B-54, 3B-3, P-1
1951		70	.237	.321	156	37	7	3	0	0.0	12	12	15	17	1	12	2	324	28	4	38	6.2	.989	1B-53, 3B-4
1952		1	.000	.000	1	0	0	0	0	0.0	0	0	0	0	0	0	0	2	0	0	1	2.0	1.000	1B-1
1955	DET A	55	.316	.444	117	37	8	2	1	0.9	15	20	10	12	0	17	8	239	15	2	16	6.7	.992	1B-35, 3B-3
1956		67	.295	.384	224	66	13	2	1	0.4	31	20	21	19	1	9	3	425	32	10	49	8.1	.979	1B-56, OF-1, 2B-1
1957		1	.000	.000	1	0	0	0	0	0.0	1	0	0	0	0	1	0	0	0	0	0	0.0	—	
9 yrs.		343	.283	.396	892	252	42	16	9	1.0	111	101	85	86	5	61	18	1904	145	33	201	7.5	.984	1B-264, 3B-11, 2B-1, OF-1, P-1
WORLD SERIES																								
1947	NY A	2	.000	.000	2	0	0	0	0	0.0	0	0	0	0	0	1	0	4	0	0	1	4.0	1.000	1B-1

John Phillips

PHILLIPS, JOHN STEPHEN
B. May 24, 1919, St. Louis, Mo. D. June 16, 1958, St. Louis, Mo.
BR TR 6′ 1″ 185 lbs.

Year	Team	Games	BA	SA	AB	H	2B	3B	HR	HR%	R	RBI	BB	SO	SB	Pinch Hit AB	Pinch Hit H	PO	A	E	DP	TC/G	FA	G by Pos
1945	NY N	2	.500	.500	2	1	0	0	0	0.0	1	0	0	0	0	0	0	1	0	0	0	1.0	1.000	P-1

Marr Phillips

PHILLIPS, MARR B.
B. June 16, 1857, Pittsburgh, Pa. D. Apr. 1, 1928, Pittsburgh, Pa.
BR 5′ 6½″ 164 lbs.

Year	Team	Games	BA	SA	AB	H	2B	3B	HR	HR%	R	RBI	BB	SO	SB	Pinch Hit AB	Pinch Hit H	PO	A	E	DP	TC/G	FA	G by Pos
1884	IND AA	97	.269	.351	413	111	18	8	0	0.0	41		5			0	0	108	335	71	16	5.3	.862	SS-97
1885	2 teams	DET N (33G –.209) PIT AA (4G –.267)																						
″	total	37	.214	.247	154	33	5	0	0	0.0	14	17	2	13		0	0	37	132	23	8	5.2	.880	SS-37
1890	ROC AA	64	.206	.237	257	53	8	0	0	0.0	18		16		10	0	0	101	222	29	24	5.5	.918	SS-64
3 yrs.		198	.239	.296	824	197	31	8	0	0.0	73	17	23	13	10	0	0	246	689	123	48	5.3	.884	SS-198

Mike Phillips

PHILLIPS, MICHAEL DWAINE
B. Aug. 19, 1950, Beaumont, Tex.
BL TR 6′ 170 lbs.

Year	Team	Games	BA	SA	AB	H	2B	3B	HR	HR%	R	RBI	BB	SO	SB	Pinch Hit AB	Pinch Hit H	PO	A	E	DP	TC/G	FA	G by Pos
1973	SF N	63	.240	.375	104	25	3	4	1	1.0	18	9	6	17	0	5	1	42	69	6	9	2.1	.949	3B-28, SS-20, 2B-7
1974		100	.219	.269	283	62	6	1	2	0.7	19	20	14	37	4	13	2	125	195	19	33	3.9	.944	3B-34, 2B-30, SS-23
1975	2 teams	SF N (10G –.194) NY N (116G –.256)																						
″	total	126	.251	.316	414	104	10	7	1	0.2	34	29	31	51	4	3	0	203	364	32	56	4.7	.947	SS-115, 2B-7, 3B-6
1976	NY N	87	.256	.363	262	67	4	6	4	1.5	30	29	25	29	2	13	3	115	191	11	26	3.9	.965	SS-53, 2B-19, 3B-10
1977	2 teams	NY N (38G –.209) STL N (48G –.241)																						
″	total	86	.225	.306	173	39	5	3	1	0.6	22	12	20	36	1	24	0	90	126	7	31	2.9	.969	2B-35, SS-29, 3B-14
1978	STL N	76	.268	.348	164	44	8	1	1	0.6	14	28	13	25	0	19	1	107	135	7	31	3.8	.972	2B-55, SS-10, 3B-1
1979		44	.227	.309	97	22	3	1	1	1.0	10	6	10	9	0	1	0	54	107	4	16	3.9	.976	SS-25, 2B-16, 3B-1
1980		63	.234	.273	128	30	5	0	0	0.0	13	7	9	17	0	9	2	63	130	9	27	3.7	.955	SS-37, 2B-9, 3B-8
1981	2 teams	SD N (14G –.207) MON N (34G –.218)																						
″	total	48	.214	.262	84	18	2	1	0	0.0	6	4	5	18	1	5	1	57	74	3	16	3.2	.978	SS-27, 2B-15
1982	MON N	14	.125	.125	8	1	0	0	0	0.0	0	1	0	3	0	1	0	8	10	0	1	1.5	1.000	2B-10, SS-2
1983		5	.000	.000	2	0	0	0	0	0.0	0	0	0	0	0	0	0	0	0	1	0	0.2	.000	SS-3, 3B-2
11 yrs.		712	.240	.314	1719	412	46	24	11	0.6	166	145	133	242	12	93	10	864	1401	99	246	3.6	.958	SS-344, 2B-203, 3B-104
DIVISIONAL PLAYOFF SERIES																								
1981	MON N	1	.000	.000	1	0	0	0	0	0.0	0	0	0	0	0	0	0	1	1	0	0	2.0	1.000	2B-1

Tony Phillips

PHILLIPS, KEITH ANTHONY
B. Apr. 25, 1959, Atlanta, Ga.
BB TR 5′ 9″ 155 lbs.

Year	Team	Games	BA	SA	AB	H	2B	3B	HR	HR%	R	RBI	BB	SO	SB	Pinch Hit AB	Pinch Hit H	PO	A	E	DP	TC/G	FA	G by Pos
1982	OAK A	40	.210	.284	81	17	2	2	0	0.0	11	8	12	26	2	0	0	46	95	7	17	3.8	.953	SS-39
1983		148	.248	.320	412	102	12	3	4	1.0	54	35	48	70	16	1	1	218	383	30	85	3.7	.952	SS-101, 2B-63, 3B-4, DH-1
1984		154	.266	.359	451	120	24	3	4	0.9	62	37	42	86	10	2	0	255	391	28	90	3.7	.958	SS-91, 2B-90, OF-1
1985		42	.280	.453	161	45	12	2	4	2.5	23	17	13	34	3	1	0	54	103	3	13	2.9	.981	3B-31, 2B-24
1986		118	.256	.345	441	113	14	5	5	1.1	76	52	76	82	15	0	0	191	326	13	43	4.2	.975	2B-88, 3B-30, OF-4, DH-2, SS-1

Tony Phillips *continued*

Year	Team	Games	BA	SA	AB	H	2B	3B	HR	HR%	R	RBI	BB	SO	SB	Pinch Hit AB	Pinch Hit H	PO	A	E	DP	TC/G	FA	G by Pos
1987		111	.240	.372	379	91	20	0	10	2.6	48	46	57	76	7	6	1	179	299	14	47	4.5	.972	2B-87, 3B-11, SS-9, OF-2
1988		79	.203	.307	212	43	8	4	2	0.9	32	17	36	50	0	5	1	84	80	10	18	1.7	.943	3B-32, OF-31, 2B-27, SS-10, 1B-3
1989		143	.262	.348	451	118	15	6	4	0.9	48	47	58	66	3	10	3	184	321	15	54	3.1	.971	2B-84, 3B-49, SS-17, OF-16, 1B-1
1990	**DET A**	152	.251	.351	573	144	23	5	8	1.4	97	55	99	85	19	1	0	180	368	23	62	3.3	.960	3B-104, 2B-47, SS-11, OF-8, DH-4
1991		146	.284	.438	564	160	28	4	17	3.0	87	72	79	95	10	6	2	269	237	8	51	3.0	.984	OF-56, 3B-46, 2B-36, DH-18, SS-13
1992		159	.276	.388	606	167	32	3	10	1.7	**114**	64	114	93	12	1	0	301	195	11	45	2.8	.978	OF-69, 2B-57, DH-34, 3B-20, SS-1
1993		151	.313	.398	566	177	27	0	7	1.2	113	57	**132**	102	16	3	2	321	165	13	34	3.0	.974	OF-108, 2B-51, DH-4, 3B-1
1994		114	.281	.468	438	123	19	3	19	4.3	91	61	95	105	13	1	1	254	42	6	7	2.5	.980	OF-104, 2B-12, DH-6
1995	**CAL A**	139	.261	.459	525	137	21	1	27	5.1	119	61	113	135	13	2	0	166	179	20	17	2.6	.945	3B-88, OF-48, DH-2
14 yrs.		1696	.266	.385	5860	1557	257	41	121	2.1	975	629	974	1105	139	39	11	2702	3184	201	583	3.2	.967	2B-666, OF-447, 3B-416, SS-293, DH-71, 1B-4
LEAGUE CHAMPIONSHIP SERIES																								
1988	**OAK A**	2	.286	.429	7	2	1	0	0	0.0	0	0	1	3	0	0	0	10	0	0	1	3.3	1.000	OF-2, 2B-1
1989		5	.167	.222	18	3	1	0	0	0.0	1	1	2	4	2	0	0	4	14	0	2	3.0	1.000	3B-3, 2B-3
2 yrs.		7	.200	.280	25	5	2	0	0	0.0	1	1	3	7	2	0	0	14	14	0	3	3.1	1.000	2B-4, 3B-3, OF-2
WORLD SERIES																								
1988	**OAK A**	2	.250	.250	4	1	0	0	0	0.0	1	0	1	2	0	0	0	3	5	0	1	4.0	1.000	2B-1, OF-1
1989		4	.235	.471	17	4	1	0	1	5.9	2	3	0	3	0	0	0	8	15	0	1	3.3	1.000	2B-4, 3B-2, OF-1
2 yrs.		6	.238	.429	21	5	1	0	1	4.8	3	3	1	5	0	0	0	11	20	0	2	3.4	1.000	2B-5, 3B-2, OF-2

Mike Piazza

PIAZZA, MICHAEL JOSEPH
B. Sept. 4, 1968, Norristown, Pa.

BR TR 6′ 3″ 200 lbs.

Year	Team	Games	BA	SA	AB	H	2B	3B	HR	HR%	R	RBI	BB	SO	SB	Pinch Hit AB	Pinch Hit H	PO	A	E	DP	TC/G	FA	G by Pos
1992	**LA N**	21	.232	.319	69	16	3	0	1	1.4	5	7	4	12	0	5	2	94	7	1	1	6.4	.990	C-16
1993		149	.318	.561	547	174	24	2	35	6.4	81	112	46	86	3	5	0	901	98	11	11	6.9	.989	C-146, 1B-1
1994		107	.319	.541	405	129	18	0	24	5.9	64	92	33	65	1	8	3	640	38	10	3	6.6	.985	C-104
1995		112	.346	.606	434	150	17	0	32	**7.4**	82	93	39	80	1	2	1	805	51	9	5	7.7	.990	C-112
4 yrs.		389	.322	.557	1455	469	62	2	92	6.3	232	304	122	243	5	20	6	2440	194	31	20	7.0	.988	C-378, 1B-1
DIVISIONAL PLAYOFF SERIES																								
1995	**LA N**	3	.214	.500	14	3	1	0	1	7.1	1	1	0	2	0	0	0	31	0	0	0	10.3	1.000	C-3

Rob Picciolo

PICCIOLO, ROBERT MICHAEL
B. Feb. 4, 1953, Santa Monica, Calif.

BR TR 6′ 2″ 185 lbs.

Year	Team	Games	BA	SA	AB	H	2B	3B	HR	HR%	R	RBI	BB	SO	SB	Pinch Hit AB	Pinch Hit H	PO	A	E	DP	TC/G	FA	G by Pos
1977	**OAK A**	148	.200	.258	419	84	12	3	2	0.5	35	22	9	55	1	0	0	213	381	21	70	4.2	.966	SS-148
1978		78	.226	.301	93	21	1	0	2	2.2	16	7	2	13	1	0	0	74	90	7	19	2.3	.959	SS-41, 2B-19, 3B-13
1979		115	.253	.328	348	88	16	2	2	0.6	37	27	3	45	2	1	1	203	288	17	55	4.4	.967	SS-105, 2B-6, 3B-4, OF-1
1980		95	.240	.343	271	65	9	2	5	1.8	32	18	2	63	1	1	0	164	208	6	39	3.9	.984	SS-49, 2B-47, OF-1
1981		82	.268	.397	179	48	5	3	4	2.2	23	13	5	22	0	0	0	99	157	5	30	3.2	.981	SS-82
1982	**2 teams**	**OAK A** (18G –.224) **MIL A** (22G –.286)																						
″	**total**	40	.243	.271	70	17	2	0	0	0.0	10	4	2	14	1	5	2	47	72	3	14	3.4	.975	SS-24, 2B-11, DH-1
1983	**MIL A**	14	.222	.333	27	6	3	0	0	0.0	2	1	0	4	0	3	0	27	20	1	7	3.7	.979	SS-7, 2B-2, 3B-2, DH-1, 1B-1
1984	**CAL A**	87	.202	.277	119	24	6	0	1	0.8	18	9	0	21	0	1	0	69	135	6	22	2.4	.971	SS-66, 3B-13, 2B-9, OF-1
1985	**OAK A**	71	.275	.324	102	28	2	0	1	1.0	19	8	2	17	3	9	3	56	66	5	12	1.8	.961	3B-19, 2B-17, 1B-13, DH-10, SS-9, OF-2
9 yrs.		730	.234	.312	1628	381	56	10	17	1.0	192	109	25	254	9	20	6	952	1417	71	268	3.4	.971	SS-531, 2B-111, 3B-51, 1B-14, DH-12, OF-5
DIVISIONAL PLAYOFF SERIES																								
1981	**OAK A**	1	.333	.333	3	1	0	0	0	0.0	0	0	0	0	0	0	0	1	2	0	0	3.0	1.000	SS-1
LEAGUE CHAMPIONSHIP SERIES																								
1981	**OAK A**	2	.200	.200	5	1	0	0	0	0.0	1	0	0	2	0	0	0	5	5	1	1	5.5	.909	SS-2

Nick Picciuto

PICCIUTO, NICHOLAS THOMAS
B. Aug. 27, 1921, Newark, N. J.

BR TR 5′ 8½″ 165 lbs.

Year	Team	Games	BA	SA	AB	H	2B	3B	HR	HR%	R	RBI	BB	SO	SB	Pinch Hit AB	Pinch Hit H	PO	A	E	DP	TC/G	FA	G by Pos
1945	**PHI N**	36	.135	.202	89	12	6	0	0	0.0	7	6	6	17	0	2	0	32	38	10	2	2.4	.875	3B-30, 2B-4

Val Picinich

PICINICH, VALENTINE JOHN
B. Sept. 8, 1896, New York, N. Y. D. Dec. 5, 1942, Nobleboro, Me.

BR TR 5′ 9″ 165 lbs.

Year	Team	Games	BA	SA	AB	H	2B	3B	HR	HR%	R	RBI	BB	SO	SB	Pinch Hit AB	Pinch Hit H	PO	A	E	DP	TC/G	FA	G by Pos
1916	**PHI A**	40	.195	.237	118	23	3	1	0	0.0	8	5	6	33	1	3	2	179	52	8	6	6.5	.967	C-37
1917		2	.333	.333	6	2	0	0	0	0.0	0	0	1	2	0	0	0	10	1	3	0	7.0	.786	C-2
1918	**WAS A**	47	.230	.297	148	34	3	2	1	0.7	13	12	9	25	0	1	0	216	48	11	5	6.0	.960	C-46
1919		80	.274	.401	212	58	12	3	3	1.4	18	22	17	43	6	11	2	303	92	9	5	5.9	.978	C-69
1920		48	.203	.346	133	27	6	2	3	2.3	14	14	9	33	0	2	0	185	41	5	6	5.1	.978	C-45
1921		45	.277	.340	141	39	9	0	0	0.0	10	12	16	21	0	0	0	197	29	8	1	5.2	.966	C-45
1922		76	.229	.305	210	48	12	2	0	0.0	16	19	23	33	1	0	0	273	55	8	4	4.4	.976	C-76
1923	**BOS A**	87	.276	.384	268	74	21	1	2	0.7	33	31	46	32	3	6	0	247	89	15	7	4.3	.957	C-81
1924		68	.266	.354	158	42	5	3	1	0.6	24	24	28	19	5	16	3	155	36	10	2	3.9	.950	C-51
1925		90	.255	.351	251	64	21	0	1	0.4	31	25	33	21	2	11	3	242	54	10	4	4.0	.967	C-74, 1B-2
1926	**CIN N**	89	.263	.362	240	63	16	1	2	0.8	33	31	29	22	4	2	2	240	52	10	6	3.5	.967	C-86
1927		65	.254	.335	173	44	8	3	0	0.0	16	12	24	15	3	4	0	218	31	5	8	4.2	.980	C-61
1928		96	.302	.420	324	98	15	1	7	2.2	29	35	20	25	1	2	0	279	65	6	6	3.8	.983	C-93
1929	**BKN N**	93	.260	.407	273	71	16	6	4	1.5	28	31	34	24	3	6	1	311	62	8	8	4.5	.979	C-85
1930		35	.217	.283	46	10	3	0	0	0.0	4	3	5	6	1	1	0	43	8	3	0	2.5	.944	C-22
1931		24	.267	.422	45	12	4	0	1	2.2	5	4	4	9	1	5	2	55	4	2	1	2.5	.967	C-24
1932		41	.257	.386	70	18	6	0	1	1.4	8	11	4	8	0	16	3	59	6	1	1	2.8	.985	C-24
1933	**2 teams**	**BKN N** (6G –.167) **PIT N** (16G –.250)																						
″	**total**	22	.241	.379	58	14	5	0	1	1.7	7	7	5	11	0	0	0	54	8	2	0	2.9	.969	C-22
18 yrs.		1048	.258	.361	2874	741	165	25	27	0.9	297	298	313	382	31	86	18	3266	733	124	70	4.4	.970	C-943, 1B-2

Charlie Pick

PICK, CHARLES THOMAS BL TR 5′10″ 160 lbs.
B. Apr. 10, 1888, Brookneal, Va. D. June 26, 1954, Lynchburg, Va.

Year	Team	Games	BA	SA	AB	H	2B	3B	HR	HR%	R	RBI	BB	SO	SB	Pinch Hit AB	Pinch Hit H	PO	A	E	DP	TC/G	FA	G by Pos
1914	WAS A	10	.391	.391	23	9	0	0	0	0.0	0	1	4	4	1	2	1	8	2	2	0	1.7	.833	OF-7
1915		3	.000	.000	2	0	0	0	0	0.0	0	0	0	0	0	2	0	0	0	0	0	0.0	—	
1916	PHI A	121	.241	.281	398	96	10	3	0	0.0	29	20	40	24	25	5	1	156	232	44	25	3.7	.898	3B-108, OF-8
1918	CHI N	29	.326	.393	89	29	4	1	0	0.0	13	12	14	4	7	0	0	45	77	7	6	4.6	.946	2B-20, 3B-8
1919	2 teams	CHI N (75G –.242) BOS N (34G –.254)																						
″	total	109	.245	.313	383	94	9	7	1	0.3	39	25	21	17	21	3	1	209	324	33	42	5.4	.942	2B-92, 3B-8, OF-3, 1B-2
1920	BOS N	95	.274	.363	383	105	16	6	2	0.5	34	28	23	11	10	1	1	219	333	28	45	6.2	.952	2B-94
6 yrs.		367	.261	.325	1278	333	39	17	3	0.2	115	86	102	60	64	13	4	637	968	114	118	4.9	.934	2B-206, 3B-124, OF-18, 1B-2
WORLD SERIES																								
1918	CHI N	6	.389	.444	18	7	1	0	0	0.0	2	0	1	1	0	0	0	12	11	0	3	3.8	1.000	2B-6

Eddie Pick

PICK, EDGAR EVERETT BB TR 6′ 185 lbs.
B. May 7, 1899, Attleboro, Mass. D. May 13, 1967, Santa Monica, Calif.

Year	Team	Games	BA	SA	AB	H	2B	3B	HR	HR%	R	RBI	BB	SO	SB	Pinch Hit AB	Pinch Hit H	PO	A	E	DP	TC/G	FA	G by Pos
1923	CIN N	9	.375	.375	8	3	0	0	0	0.0	2	2	3	3	0	2	0	2	0	0	0	0.5	1.000	OF-4
1924		3	.000	.000	2	0	0	0	0	0.0	0	0	0	1	0	1	0	1	0	0	0	1.0	1.000	OF-1
1927	CHI N	54	.171	.254	181	31	5	2	2	1.1	23	15	20	26	0	0	0	61	73	13	9	2.9	.912	3B-49, 2B-1, OF-1
3 yrs.		66	.178	.257	191	34	5	2	2	1.0	25	17	23	30	0	3	0	64	73	13	9	2.7	.913	3B-49, OF-6, 2B-1

Ollie Pickering

PICKERING, OLIVER DANIEL (Pick, Von Der Ahe) BL TR 5′11″ 170 lbs.
B. Apr. 9, 1870, Olney, Ill. D. Jan. 20, 1952, Vincennes, Ind.

Year	Team	Games	BA	SA	AB	H	2B	3B	HR	HR%	R	RBI	BB	SO	SB	Pinch Hit AB	Pinch Hit H	PO	A	E	DP	TC/G	FA	G by Pos
1896	LOU N	45	.303	.406	165	50	6	4	1	0.6	28	22	12	11	13	0	0	97	12	12	4	2.7	.901	OF-45
1897	2 teams	LOU N (63G –.252) CLE N (46G –.352)																						
″	total	109	.294	.350	428	126	10	4	2	0.5	67	43	36		38	1	0	244	20	16	3	2.6	.943	OF-108, 2B-1
1901	CLE A	137	.309	.377	547	169	25	6	0	0.0	102	40	58		36	0	0	315	22	18	9	2.6	.949	OF-137
1902		69	.256	.317	293	75	5	2	3	1.0	46	26	19		22	2	2	155	5	4	2	2.5	.976	OF-64, 1B-2
1903	PHI A	137	.281	.346	512	144	18	6	1	0.2	93	36	53		40	2	0	272	17	9	5	2.2	.970	OF-135
1904		124	.226	.262	455	103	10	3	0	0.0	56	30	45		17	2	0	217	13	15	2	2.0	.939	OF-121
1907	STL A	151	.276	.337	576	159	15	10	0	0.0	63	60	35		15	1	0	210	14	12	5	1.6	.949	OF-151
1908	WAS A	113	.225	.282	373	84	7	4	2	0.5	45	30	28		13	14	3	135	6	9	1	1.5	.940	OF-98
8 yrs.		885	.272	.332	3349	910	96	39	9	0.3	500	287	286	11	194	22	5	1645	109	95	31	2.1	.949	OF-859, 1B-2, 2B-1

Urbane Pickering

PICKERING, URBANE HENRY (Dick) BR TR 5′10″ 180 lbs.
B. June 3, 1899, Hoxie, Kans. D. May 13, 1970, Modesto, Calif.

Year	Team	Games	BA	SA	AB	H	2B	3B	HR	HR%	R	RBI	BB	SO	SB	Pinch Hit AB	Pinch Hit H	PO	A	E	DP	TC/G	FA	G by Pos
1931	BOS A	103	.252	.393	341	86	13	4	9	2.6	48	52	33	53	3	12	3	129	189	16	12	3.7	.952	3B-74, 2B-16
1932		132	.260	.357	457	119	28	5	2	0.4	47	40	39	71	3	5	2	111	222	22	22	2.8	.938	3B-126, C-1
2 yrs.		235	.257	.372	798	205	41	9	11	1.4	95	92	72	124	6	17	5	240	411	38	34	3.2	.945	3B-200, 2B-16, C-1

Dave Pickett

PICKETT, DAVID T. 5′7½″ 170 lbs.
B. May 26, 1874, Brookline, Mass. D. Apr. 22, 1950, Easton, Mass.

Year	Team	Games	BA	SA	AB	H	2B	3B	HR	HR%	R	RBI	BB	SO	SB	Pinch Hit AB	Pinch Hit H	PO	A	E	DP	TC/G	FA	G by Pos
1898	BOS N	14	.279	.302	43	12	1	0	0	0.0	3	3	6		2	0	0	20	1	1	0	1.6	.955	OF-14

John Pickett

PICKETT, JOHN THOMAS BR TR
B. Feb. 20, 1866, Chicago, Ill. D. July 4, 1922, Chicago, Ill.

Year	Team	Games	BA	SA	AB	H	2B	3B	HR	HR%	R	RBI	BB	SO	SB	Pinch Hit AB	Pinch Hit H	PO	A	E	DP	TC/G	FA	G by Pos
1889	KC AA	53	.224	.259	201	45	7	0	0	0.0	20	12	11	21	7	0	0	77	44	23	4	2.7	.840	OF-28, 3B-14, 2B-11
1890	PHI P	100	.280	.371	407	114	7	9	4	1.0	82	64	40	17	12	0	0	236	284	62	46	5.8	.893	2B-100
1892	BAL N	36	.213	.291	141	30	2	3	1	0.7	13	12	7	10	2	0	0	86	109	18	9	5.9	.915	2B-36
3 yrs.		189	.252	.326	749	189	16	12	5	0.7	115	88	58	48	21	0	0	399	437	103	59	5.0	.890	2B-147, OF-28, 3B-14

Ty Pickup

PICKUP, CLARENCE WILLIAM BR TR 6′ 180 lbs.
B. Oct. 29, 1897, Philadelphia, Pa. D. Aug. 2, 1974, Philadelphia, Pa.

Year	Team	Games	BA	SA	AB	H	2B	3B	HR	HR%	R	RBI	BB	SO	SB	Pinch Hit AB	Pinch Hit H	PO	A	E	DP	TC/G	FA	G by Pos
1918	PHI N	1	1.000	1.000	1	1	0	0	0	0.0	0	0	0	0	0	0	0	1	0	0	0	1.0	1.000	OF-1

Gracie Pierce

PIERCE, GRAYSON S. BL TR 5′11″ 176 lbs.
B. New York, N. Y. D. Aug. 29, 1894, New York, N. Y.

Year	Team	Games	BA	SA	AB	H	2B	3B	HR	HR%	R	RBI	BB	SO	SB	Pinch Hit AB	Pinch Hit H	PO	A	E	DP	TC/G	FA	G by Pos
1882	2 teams	LOU AA (9G –.303) BAL AA (41G –.199)																						
″	total	50	.217	.245	184	40	3	1	0	0.0	11		4			0	0	154	127	65	21	6.8	.812	2B-47, OF-3, SS-1
1883	2 teams	COL AA (11G –.171) NY N (18G –.081)																						
″	total	29	.117	.136	103	12	0	1	0	0.0	8		1	9		0	0	67	13	17	4	3.2	.825	OF-23, 2B-7
1884	NY AA	5	.250	.300	20	5	1	0	0	0.0	2		0			0	0	10	2	7	0	3.2	.632	OF-3, 2B-3
3 yrs.		84	.186	.212	307	57	4	2	0	0.0	21		5	9		0	0	231	142	89	25	5.3	.807	2B-57, OF-29, SS-1

Jack Pierce

PIERCE, LAVERN JACK BL TR 6′ 210 lbs.
B. June 2, 1948, Laurel, Miss.

Year	Team	Games	BA	SA	AB	H	2B	3B	HR	HR%	R	RBI	BB	SO	SB	Pinch Hit AB	Pinch Hit H	PO	A	E	DP	TC/G	FA	G by Pos
1973	ATL N	11	.050	.050	20	1	0	0	0	0.0	0	0	1	8	0	5	0	42	4	0	1	7.7	1.000	1B-6
1974		6	.111	.111	9	1	0	0	0	0.0	1	0	1	0	0	3	1	21	2	1	1	12.0	.958	1B-2
1975	DET A	53	.235	.424	170	40	6	1	8	4.7	19	22	20	40	0	4	0	407	26	13	38	9.1	.971	1B-49
3 yrs.		70	.211	.372	199	42	6	1	8	4.0	20	22	22	48	0	12	1	470	32	14	40	9.1	.973	1B-57

Maury Pierce

PIERCE, MAURICE
B. Baltimore, Md. Deceased.

Year	Team	Games	BA	SA	AB	H	2B	3B	HR	HR%	R	RBI	BB	SO	SB	Pinch Hit AB	Pinch Hit H	PO	A	E	DP	TC/G	FA	G by Pos
1884	WAS U	2	.143	.143	7	1	0	0	0	0.0	0		0			0	0	5	2	2	0	4.5	.778	3B-2

Andy Piercy

PIERCY, ANDREW J. TR
B. Aug. 1856, San Jose, Calif. D. Dec. 27, 1932, San Jose, Calif.

Year	Team	Games	BA	SA	AB	H	2B	3B	HR	HR%	R	RBI	BB	SO	SB	Pinch Hit AB	Pinch Hit H	PO	A	E	DP	TC/G	FA	G by Pos
1881	CHI N	2	.250	.250	8	2	0	0	0	0.0	1	0	0	1		0	0	6	3	3	0	6.0	.750	3B-1, 2B-1

Jimmy Piersall

PIERSALL, JAMES ANTHONY BR TR 6′ 175 lbs.
B. Nov. 14, 1929, Waterbury, Conn.

Year	Team	Games	BA	SA	AB	H	2B	3B	HR	HR%	R	RBI	BB	SO	SB	Pinch Hit AB	Pinch Hit H	PO	A	E	DP	TC/G	FA	G by Pos
1950	BOS A	6	.286	.286	7	2	0	0	0	0.0	4	0	4	0	0	1	1	9	0	0	0	4.5	1.000	OF-2
1952		56	.267	.335	161	43	8	0	1	0.6	28	16	28	26	3	0	0	79	79	10	13	3.2	.940	SS-30, OF-22, 3B-1
1953		151	.272	.354	585	159	21	9	3	0.5	76	52	41	52	11	0	0	352	15	5	7	2.5	.987	OF-151
1954		133	.285	.395	474	135	24	2	8	1.7	77	38	36	42	5	6	0	249	10	4	2	2.1	.985	OF-126
1955		149	.283	.427	515	146	25	5	13	2.5	68	62	67	52	6	2	1	425	7	3	2	3.0	.993	OF-147

Jimmy Piersall *continued*

Year	Team	Games	BA	SA	AB	H	2B	3B	HR	HR%	R	RBI	BB	SO	SB	Pinch Hit AB	Pinch Hit H	PO	A	E	DP	TC/G	FA	G by Pos
1956		155	.293	.449	601	176	**40**	6	14	2.3	91	87	58	48	7	0	0	455	10	4	1	3.0	.991	OF-155
1957		151	.261	.415	609	159	27	5	19	3.1	103	63	62	54	14	0	0	397	12	4	0	2.7	.990	OF-151
1958		130	.237	.350	417	99	13	5	8	1.9	55	48	42	43	12	5	1	314	8	5	2	2.6	.985	OF-125
1959	**CLE A**	100	.246	.338	317	78	13	2	4	1.3	42	30	24	31	6	6	1	216	4	4	2	2.4	.982	OF-91, 3B-1
1960		138	.282	.434	486	137	12	4	18	3.7	70	66	24	38	18	7	1	355	5	3	0	2.7	.992	OF-134
1961		121	.322	.442	484	156	26	7	6	1.2	81	40	43	46	8	1	1	328	9	3	3	2.8	.991	OF-120
1962	**WAS A**	135	.244	.329	471	115	20	4	4	0.8	38	31	39	53	12	5	1	308	5	1	0	2.4	.997	OF-132
1963	**3 teams**	**WAS A** (29G –.245) **NY N** (40G –.194) **LA A** (20G –.308)																						
"	**total**	89	.233	.285	270	63	6	1	2	0.7	26	19	21	30	5	7	2	158	3	0	0	2.1	1.000	OF-77
1964	**LA A**	87	.314	.380	255	80	11	0	2	0.8	28	13	16	32	5	13	2	115	2	0	2	1.6	1.000	OF-72
1965	**CAL A**	53	.268	.402	112	30	5	2	2	1.8	10	12	5	15	2	14	3	62	0	1	0	1.5	.984	OF-41
1966		75	.211	.252	123	26	5	0	0	0.0	14	14	13	19	1	15	4	69	3	2	0	1.2	.973	OF-63
1967		5	.000	.000	3	0	0	0	0	0.0	0	0	0	2	0	3	0	1	0	0	0	1.0	1.000	OF-1
17 yrs.		1734	.272	.386	5890	1604	256	52	104	1.8	811	591	523	583	115	85	18	3892	172	49	34	2.5	.988	OF-1610, SS-30, 3B-2

Dave Pierson

PIERSON, DAVID P. BR TR 5′ 7″ 142 lbs.
Brother of Dick Pierson.
B. Aug. 20, 1855, Wilkes-Barre, Pa. D. Nov. 11, 1922, Trenton, N. J.

Year	Team	Games	BA	SA	AB	H	2B	3B	HR	HR%	R	RBI	BB	SO	SB	Pinch Hit AB	Pinch Hit H	PO	A	E	DP	TC/G	FA	G by Pos
1876	**CIN N**	57	.236	.262	233	55	4	1	0	0.0	33	13	1	9		0	0	159	58	59	6	4.2	.786	C-31, OF-30, 3B-1, 2B-1, SS-1, P-1

Dick Pierson

PIERSON, EDMUND DANA TR
Brother of Dave Pierson.
B. Oct. 24, 1857, Wilkes-Barre, Pa. D. July 20, 1922, Newark, N. J.

Year	Team	Games	BA	SA	AB	H	2B	3B	HR	HR%	R	RBI	BB	SO	SB	Pinch Hit AB	Pinch Hit H	PO	A	E	DP	TC/G	FA	G by Pos
1885	**NY AA**	3	.111	.111	9	1	0	0	0	0.0	1		2			0	0	9	6	7	1	7.3	.682	2B-3

Tony Piet

PIET, ANTHONY FRANCIS BR TR 6′ 175 lbs.
Born Anthony Francis Pietruszka.
B. Dec. 7, 1906, Berwick, Pa. D. Dec. 1, 1981, Hinsdale, Ill.

Year	Team	Games	BA	SA	AB	H	2B	3B	HR	HR%	R	RBI	BB	SO	SB	Pinch Hit AB	Pinch Hit H	PO	A	E	DP	TC/G	FA	G by Pos
1931	**PIT N**	44	.299	.419	167	50	12	4	0	0.0	22	24	13	24	10	0	0	103	134	3	17	5.3	.988	2B-44, SS-1
1932		154	.282	.390	574	162	25	8	7	1.2	66	85	46	56	19	0	0	378	454	26	80	5.6	.970	2B-154
1933		107	.323	.417	362	117	21	5	1	0.3	45	42	19	28	12	9	2	241	305	26	61	5.9	.955	2B-97
1934	**CIN N**	106	.259	.337	421	109	20	5	1	0.2	58	38	23	44	6	4	2	171	245	25	34	4.4	.943	3B-51, 2B-49
1935	**2 teams**	**CIN N** (6G –.200) **CHI A** (77G –.298)																						
"	**total**	83	.296	.421	297	88	18	5	3	1.0	49	29	33	27	2	1	0	151	245	12	33	5.3	.971	2B-59, 3B-17, OF-1
1936	**CHI A**	109	.273	.386	352	96	15	2	7	2.0	69	42	66	48	15	7	1	167	317	18	49	5.0	.964	2B-68, 3B-32
1937		100	.235	.322	332	78	15	1	4	1.2	34	38	32	36	14	1	1	119	207	16	24	3.5	.953	3B-86, 2B-13
1938	**DET A**	41	.212	.287	80	17	6	0	0	0.0	9	14	15	11	2	17	5	12	45	5	3	3.3	.919	3B-18, 2B-1
8 yrs.		744	.277	.378	2585	717	132	30	23	0.9	352	312	247	274	80	39	11	1342	1952	131	301	5.0	.962	2B-485, 3B-204, OF-1, SS-1

Sandy Piez

PIEZ, CHARLES WILLIAM BR TR 5′10″ 170 lbs.
B. Oct. 13, 1892, New York, N. Y. D. Dec. 29, 1930, Atlantic City, N. J.

Year	Team	Games	BA	SA	AB	H	2B	3B	HR	HR%	R	RBI	BB	SO	SB	Pinch Hit AB	Pinch Hit H	PO	A	E	DP	TC/G	FA	G by Pos
1914	**NY N**	35	.375	.625	8	3	0	1	0	0.0	9	3	0	1	4	0	0	8	0	0	0	2.0	1.000	OF-4

Joe Pignatano

PIGNATANO, JOSEPH BENJAMIN BR TR 5′10″ 180 lbs.
B. Aug. 4, 1929, Brooklyn, N. Y.

Year	Team	Games	BA	SA	AB	H	2B	3B	HR	HR%	R	RBI	BB	SO	SB	Pinch Hit AB	Pinch Hit H	PO	A	E	DP	TC/G	FA	G by Pos
1957	**BKN N**	8	.214	.286	14	3	1	0	0	0.0	0	1	0	5	0	0	0	36	1	0	0	6.2	1.000	C-6
1958	**LA N**	63	.218	.437	142	31	4	0	9	6.3	18	17	16	26	4	3	0	286	18	0	3	5.3	1.000	C-57
1959		52	.237	.302	139	33	4	1	1	0.7	17	11	21	15	1	0	0	322	17	1	8	6.9	.997	C-49
1960		58	.233	.344	90	21	4	0	2	2.2	11	9	15	17	1	5	3	231	21	4	2	6.4	.984	C-40
1961	**KC A**	92	.243	.358	243	59	10	3	4	1.6	31	22	36	42	2	7	1	380	35	9	7	5.0	.979	C-83, 3B-2
1962	**2 teams**	**SF N** (7G –.200) **NY N** (27G –.232)																						
"	**total**	34	.230	.262	61	14	2	0	0	0.0	4	2	6	11	0	5	0	107	13	1	2	3.8	.992	C-32
6 yrs.		307	.234	.351	689	161	25	4	16	2.3	81	62	94	116	8	20	4	1362	105	15	22	5.5	.990	C-267, 3B-2
WORLD SERIES																								
1959	**LA N**	1	—	—	0	0	0	0	0	—	0	0	0	0	0	0	0	1	0	0	0	1.0	1.000	C-1

Jay Pike

PIKE, JACOB EMANUEL
Brother of Lip Pike.
B. Brooklyn, N. Y. Deceased.

Year	Team	Games	BA	SA	AB	H	2B	3B	HR	HR%	R	RBI	BB	SO	SB	Pinch Hit AB	Pinch Hit H	PO	A	E	DP	TC/G	FA	G by Pos
1877	**HAR N**	1	.250	.250	4	1	0	0	0	0.0	0	0	0	0		0	0	0	0	1	0	1.0	.000	OF-1

Jess Pike

PIKE, JESS WILLARD BL TL 6′ 3″ 175 lbs.
B. July 31, 1915, Dustin, Okla. D. Mar. 28, 1984, San Diego, Calif.

Year	Team	Games	BA	SA	AB	H	2B	3B	HR	HR%	R	RBI	BB	SO	SB	Pinch Hit AB	Pinch Hit H	PO	A	E	DP	TC/G	FA	G by Pos
1946	**NY N**	16	.171	.317	41	7	1	1	1	2.4	4	6	6	9	0	4	0	13	0	1	0	1.4	.929	OF-10

Lip Pike

PIKE, LIPMAN EMANUEL (The Iron Batter) BL TL 5′ 8″ 158 lbs.
Brother of Jay Pike.
B. May 25, 1845, New York, N. Y. D. Oct. 10, 1893, Brooklyn, N. Y.
Manager 1877.

Year	Team	Games	BA	SA	AB	H	2B	3B	HR	HR%	R	RBI	BB	SO	SB	Pinch Hit AB	Pinch Hit H	PO	A	E	DP	TC/G	FA	G by Pos
1876	**STL N**	63	.323	.472	282	91	19	10	1	0.4	55	50	8	9		0	0	90	16	13	7	1.9	.891	OF-62, 2B-2
1877	**CIN N**	58	.298	.420	262	78	12	4	**4**	**1.5**	45	23	9	7		0	0	144	75	51	7	4.4	.811	OF-38, 2B-22, SS-2
1878	**2 teams**	**CIN N** (31G –.324) **PRO N** (5G –.227)																						
"	**total**	36	.311	.365	167	52	5	2	0	0.0	32	15	5	10		0	0	51	17	16	1	2.3	.810	OF-31, 2B-5
1881	**WOR N**	5	.111	.111	18	2	0	0	0	0.0	1	0	4	3		0	0	10	1	6	1	3.4	.647	OF-5
1887	**NY AA**	1	.000	.000	4	0	0	0	0	0.0	0		0		0	0	0	2	0	0	0	2.0	1.000	OF-1
5 yrs.		163	.304	.417	733	223	36	16	5	0.7	133	88	26	29	0	0	0	297	109	86	16	2.9	.825	OF-137, 2B-29, SS-2

Al Pilarcik

PILARCIK, ALFRED JAMES BL TL 5′10″ 180 lbs.
B. July 3, 1930, Whiting, Ind.

Year	Team	Games	BA	SA	AB	H	2B	3B	HR	HR%	R	RBI	BB	SO	SB	Pinch Hit AB	Pinch Hit H	PO	A	E	DP	TC/G	FA	G by Pos
1956	**KC A**	69	.251	.351	239	60	10	1	4	1.7	28	22	30	32	9	4	1	154	9	4	1	2.5	.976	OF-67
1957	**BAL A**	142	.278	.398	407	113	16	3	9	2.2	52	49	53	28	14	15	3	234	15	1	2	2.0	.996	OF-126
1958		141	.243	.306	379	92	21	0	1	0.3	40	24	42	37	7	24	7	213	5	3	0	1.9	.986	OF-118

Al Pilarcik *continued*

Year	Team	Games	BA	SA	AB	H	2B	3B	HR	HR%	R	RBI	BB	SO	SB	Pinch Hit AB	Pinch Hit H	PO	A	E	DP	TC/G	FA	G by Pos
1959		130	.282	.366	273	77	12	1	3	1.1	37	16	30	25	9	21	7	133	3	3	1	1.3	.978	OF-106
1960		104	.247	.345	194	48	5	1	4	2.1	30	17	15	16	0	23	6	75	4	0	0	1.1	1.000	OF-75
1961	**2 teams**	**KC A** (35G –.200) **CHI A** (47G –.177)																						
″	**total**	82	.189	.246	122	23	2	1	1	0.8	18	15	15	12	2	28	6	63	4	2	1	1.8	.971	OF-38
6 yrs.		668	.256	.346	1614	413	66	7	22	1.4	205	143	185	150	41	115	30	872	40	13	5	1.7	.986	OF-530

Andy Pilney

PILNEY, ANTONE JAMES BR TR 5′11″ 174 lbs.
B. Jan. 19, 1913, Frontenac, Kans.

Year	Team	Games	BA	SA	AB	H	2B	3B	HR	HR%	R	RBI	BB	SO	SB	Pinch Hit AB	Pinch Hit H	PO	A	E	DP	TC/G	FA	G by Pos
1936	**BOS N**	3	.000	.000	2	0	0	0	0	0.0	0	0	0	1	0	2	0	0	0	0	0	0.0	—	

George Pinckney

PINCKNEY, GEORGE BURTON BR TR 5′7″ 160 lbs.
B. Jan. 11, 1862, Orange Prairie, Ill. D. Nov. 10, 1926, Peoria, Ill.

Year	Team	Games	BA	SA	AB	H	2B	3B	HR	HR%	R	RBI	BB	SO	SB	Pinch Hit AB	Pinch Hit H	PO	A	E	DP	TC/G	FA	G by Pos
1884	**CLE N**	36	.313	.375	144	45	9	0	0	0.0	18	16	10	7		0	0	73	110	32	11	6.0	.851	2B-25, SS-11
1885	**BKN AA**	110	.277	.336	447	124	16	5	0	0.0	77		27			0	0	207	267	56	20	4.8	.894	2B-57, 3B-51, SS-3
1886		141	.261	.322	**597**	156	22	7	0	0.0	119		**70**			0	0	184	234	69	17	3.4	.858	3B-141, P-1
1887		138	.267	.348	580	155	26	6	3	0.5	133		61		59	0	0	197	294	60	26	4.0	.891	3B-136, SS-2
1888		143	.271	.351	575	156	18	8	4	0.7	**134**	52	66		51	0	0	189	234	48	14	3.3	.898	3B-143
1889		138	.246	.339	545	134	25	7	4	0.7	103	82	59	43	47	0	0	183	278	53	19	3.7	.897	3B-138
1890	**BKN N**	126	.309	.431	485	150	20	9	7	1.4	115	83	80	19	47	0	0	179	222	29	15	3.4	.933	3B-126
1891		135	.273	.347	501	137	19	6	2	0.4	80	71	66	32	44	0	0	152	276	46	10	3.5	.903	3B-130, SS-5
1892	**STL N**	78	.172	.197	290	50	3	2	0	0.0	31	25	36	26	4	0	0	84	161	31	12	3.5	.888	3B-78
1893	**LOU N**	118	.235	.296	446	105	12	6	1	0.2	64	62	50	8	12	0	0	126	279	34	26	3.7	.923	3B-118
10 yrs.		1163	.263	.338	4610	1212	170	56	21	0.5	874	391	525	135	264	0	0	1574	2355	458	170	3.8	.896	3B-1061, 2B-82, SS-21, P-1

Babe Pinelli

PINELLI, RALPH ARTHUR BR TR 5′9″ 165 lbs.
Born Rinaldo Angelo Paolinelli.
B. Oct. 18, 1895, San Francisco, Calif. D. Oct. 22, 1984, Daly City, Calif.

Year	Team	Games	BA	SA	AB	H	2B	3B	HR	HR%	R	RBI	BB	SO	SB	Pinch Hit AB	Pinch Hit H	PO	A	E	DP	TC/G	FA	G by Pos
1918	**CHI A**	24	.231	.308	78	18	1	1	1	1.3	7	7	7	8	3	0	0	28	33	11	4	3.0	.847	3B-24
1920	**DET A**	102	.229	.282	284	65	9	3	0	0.0	33	21	25	16	6	4	0	144	226	23	20	4.2	.941	3B-74, SS-18, 2B-1
1922	**CIN N**	156	.305	.371	547	167	19	7	1	0.2	77	72	48	37	17	0	0	204	350	32	19	3.8	.945	3B-156
1923		117	.277	.333	423	117	14	5	0	0.0	44	51	27	29	10	0	0	131	250	25	17	3.5	.938	3B-116
1924		144	.306	.365	510	156	16	7	0	0.0	61	70	32	32	23	1	1	182	318	23	21	3.7	.956	3B-143
1925		130	.283	.386	492	139	33	6	2	0.4	68	49	22	28	8	6	2	151	321	30	36	4.0	.940	3B-109, SS-17
1926		71	.222	.295	207	46	7	4	0	0.0	26	24	15	5	2	3	1	58	150	12	9	3.1	.945	3B-40, SS-27, 2B-3
1927		30	.197	.263	76	15	2	0	1	1.3	11	4	6	7	2	0	0	33	54	2	5	3.1	.978	3B-15, SS-9, 2B-5
8 yrs.		774	.276	.346	2617	723	101	33	5	0.2	327	298	182	162	71	14	4	931	1702	158	131	3.7	.943	3B-677, SS-71, 2B-9

Lou Piniella

PINIELLA, LOUIS VICTOR (Sweet Lou) BR TR 6′ 182 lbs.
B. Aug. 28, 1943, Tampa, Fla.
Manager 1986–88, 1990–95.

Year	Team	Games	BA	SA	AB	H	2B	3B	HR	HR%	R	RBI	BB	SO	SB	Pinch Hit AB	Pinch Hit H	PO	A	E	DP	TC/G	FA	G by Pos
1964	**BAL A**	4	.000	.000	1	0	0	0	0	0.0	0	0	0	0	0	1	0	0	0	0	0	0.0	—	
1968	**CLE A**	6	.000	.000	5	0	0	0	0	0.0	1	1	0	0	0	2	0	1	0	0	0	0.5	1.000	OF-2
1969	**KC A**	135	.282	.416	493	139	21	6	11	2.2	43	68	33	56	2	9	3	278	13	7	1	2.3	.977	OF-129
1970		144	.301	.424	542	163	24	5	11	2.0	54	88	35	42	3	4	1	250	6	4	2	1.9	.985	OF-139, 1B-1
1971		126	.279	.368	448	125	21	5	3	0.7	43	51	21	43	5	13	3	201	6	3	2	1.8	.986	OF-115
1972		151	.312	.441	574	179	**33**	4	11	1.9	65	72	34	59	7	1	0	275	8	7	2	1.9	.976	OF-150
1973		144	.250	.361	513	128	28	1	9	1.8	53	69	30	65	5	7	1	196	9	3	3	1.5	.986	OF-128, DH-9
1974	**NY A**	140	.305	.407	518	158	26	0	9	1.7	71	70	32	58	1	2	1	270	16	3	0	2.1	.990	OF-130, DH-6, 1B-1
1975		74	.196	.226	199	39	4	1	0	0.0	7	22	16	22	0	19	4	65	5	1	0	1.2	.986	OF-46, DH-12
1976		100	.281	.394	327	92	16	6	3	0.9	36	38	18	34	0	14	4	106	4	2	0	1.3	.982	OF-49, DH-38
1977		103	.330	.510	339	112	19	3	12	3.5	47	45	20	31	2	11	2	86	3	2	1	1.0	.978	OF-51, DH-43, 1B-1
1978		130	.314	.445	472	148	34	5	6	1.3	67	69	34	36	3	9	4	213	4	7	0	1.8	.969	OF-103, DH-23
1979		130	.297	.425	461	137	22	2	11	2.4	49	69	17	31	3	12	6	204	13	4	1	1.7	.982	OF-112, DH-16
1980		116	.287	.361	321	92	18	0	2	0.6	39	27	29	20	0	24	4	157	8	5	1	1.5	.971	OF-104, DH-7
1981		60	.277	.428	159	44	9	0	5	3.1	16	18	13	9	0	9	1	69	2	1	1	1.3	.986	OF-36, DH-19
1982		102	.307	.448	261	80	17	1	6	2.3	33	37	18	18	0	25	9	68	2	0	1	0.7	1.000	DH-55, OF-40
1983		53	.291	.405	148	43	9	1	2	1.4	19	16	11	12	1	10	3	67	4	3	2	1.7	.959	OF-43, DH-1
1984		29	.302	.407	86	26	4	1	1	1.2	8	6	7	5	0	3	0	40	3	0	0	1.7	1.000	OF-24, DH-2
18 yrs.		1747	.291	.409	5867	1705	305	41	102	1.7	651	766	368	541	32	175	46	2546	106	52	17	1.7	.981	OF-1401, DH-231, 1B-3
DIVISIONAL PLAYOFF SERIES																								
1981	**NY A**	4	.200	.600	10	2	1	0	1	10.0	1	3	0	0	0	2	1	0	0	0	0	0.0	.000	DH-4
LEAGUE CHAMPIONSHIP SERIES																								
1976	**NY A**	4	.273	.364	11	3	1	0	0	0.0	1	0	0	1	0	1	0	0	0	0	0	0.0	.000	DH-3
1977		5	.333	.476	21	7	3	0	0	0.0	1	2	0	1	0	0	0	9	1	0	0	2.0	1.000	OF-4, DH-1
1978		4	.235	.235	17	4	0	0	0	0.0	2	0	0	3	0	0	0	13	0	0	0	3.3	1.000	OF-4
1980		2	.200	.800	5	1	0	0	1	20.0	1	1	2	1	0	0	0	5	0	0	0	2.5	1.000	OF-2
1981		3	.600	1.200	5	3	0	0	1	20.0	2	3	0	0	0	2	2	0	0	0	0	0.0		DH-2, OF-1
5 yrs.		18	.305	.475	59	18	4	0	2	3.4	7	6	2	6	0	3	2	27	1	0	0	1.6	1.000	OF-11, DH-6
WORLD SERIES																								
1976	**NY A**	4	.333	.444	9	3	1	0	0	0.0	1	0	0	0	0	2	0	1	0	0	0	0.2	1.000	DH-3, OF-2
1977		6	.273	.273	22	6	0	0	0	0.0	1	3	0	3	0	0	0	16	1	1	0	3.0	.944	OF-6
1978		6	.280	.280	25	7	0	0	0	0.0	3	4	0	0	1	0	0	14	1	0	1	2.5	1.000	OF-6
1981		6	.438	.500	16	7	1	0	0	0.0	2	3	0	1	1	3	2	7	0	0	0	2.3	1.000	OF-3
4 yrs.		22	.319	.347	72	23	2	0	0	0.0	7	10	0	4	2	5	2	38	2	1	1	2.0	.976	OF-17, DH-3

Vada Pinson

PINSON, VADA EDWARD BL TL 5′11″ 170 lbs.
B. Aug. 11, 1938, Memphis, Tenn. D. Oct. 21, 1995, Oakland, Calif.

Year	Team	Games	BA	SA	AB	H	2B	3B	HR	HR%	R	RBI	BB	SO	SB	Pinch Hit AB	Pinch Hit H	PO	A	E	DP	TC/G	FA	G by Pos
1958	**CIN N**	27	.271	.375	96	26	7	0	1	1.0	20	8	11	18	2	0	0	50	4	0	1	2.0	1.000	OF-27
1959		154	.316	.509	**648**	205	**47**	9	20	3.1	**131**	84	55	98	21	0	0	423	11	7	4	2.9	.984	OF-154
1960		154	.287	.472	**652**	187	**37**	12	20	3.1	107	61	47	96	32	0	0	401	11	8	1	2.7	.981	OF-154
1961		154	.343	.504	607	**208**	34	8	16	2.6	101	87	39	63	23	1	1	391	19	10	4	2.7	.976	OF-153
1962		155	.292	.477	619	181	31	7	23	3.7	107	100	45	68	26	3	1	344	13	4	1	2.4	.989	OF-152

Vada Pinson *continued*

Year	Team		Games	BA	SA	AB	H	2B	3B	HR	HR%	R	RBI	BB	SO	SB	Pinch Hit AB	Pinch Hit H	PO	A	E	DP	TC/G	FA	G by Pos
1963			162	.313	.514	652	**204**	37	**14**	22	3.4	96	106	36	80	27	0	0	357	9	8	0	2.3	.979	OF-162
1964			156	.266	.448	625	166	23	11	23	3.7	99	84	42	99	8	1	0	299	14	9	1	2.1	.972	OF-156
1965			159	.305	.484	669	204	34	10	22	3.3	97	94	43	81	21	0	0	354	9	3	1	2.3	.992	OF-159
1966			156	.288	.442	618	178	35	6	16	2.6	70	76	33	83	18	3	2	344	9	13	1	2.4	.964	OF-154
1967			158	.288	.454	650	187	28	**13**	18	2.8	90	66	26	86	26	2	0	341	4	5	1	2.2	.986	OF-157
1968			130	.271	.383	499	135	29	6	5	1.0	60	48	32	59	17	10	2	258	7	6	0	2.2	.978	OF-123
1969	**STL**	**N**	132	.255	.384	495	126	22	6	10	2.0	58	70	35	63	4	8	1	218	6	1	2	1.8	.996	OF-124
1970	**CLE**	**A**	148	.286	.481	574	164	28	6	24	4.2	74	82	28	69	7	8	1	284	9	5	5	2.0	.983	OF-141, 1B-7
1971			146	.263	.376	566	149	23	4	11	1.9	60	35	21	58	25	7	2	315	11	7	4	2.3	.979	OF-141, 1B-3
1972	**CAL**	**A**	136	.275	.376	484	133	24	2	7	1.4	56	49	30	54	17	7	1	207	11	2	3	1.6	.991	OF-134, 1B-1
1973			124	.260	.367	466	121	14	6	8	1.7	56	57	20	55	5	4	1	210	11	8	2	1.9	.965	OF-120
1974	**KC**	**A**	115	.276	.374	406	112	18	2	6	1.5	46	41	21	45	21	9	3	198	9	4	2	1.9	.981	OF-110, DH-2, 1B-1
1975			103	.223	.335	319	71	14	5	4	1.3	38	22	10	21	5	17	2	151	6	1	0	1.7	.994	OF-82, DH-5, 1B-4
18 yrs.			2469	.286	.442	9645	2757	485	127	256	2.7	1366	1170	574	1196	305	80	17	5145	173	101	33	2.2	.981	OF-2403, 1B-16, DH-7
WORLD SERIES																									
1961	**CIN**	**N**	5	.091	.136	22	2	1	0	0	0.0	0	0	0	1	0	0	0	18	1	1	0	4.0	.950	OF-5

Wally Pipp

PIPP, WALTER CLEMENT BL TL 6′ 1″ 180 lbs.
B. Feb. 17, 1893, Chicago, Ill. D. Jan. 11, 1965, Grand Rapids, Mich.

Year	Team		Games	BA	SA	AB	H	2B	3B	HR	HR%	R	RBI	BB	SO	SB	Pinch Hit AB	Pinch Hit H	PO	A	E	DP	TC/G	FA	G by Pos
1913	**DET**	**A**	12	.161	.355	31	5	0	3	0	0.0	3	5	2	6	0	2	0	80	4	2	6	8.6	.977	1B-10
1915	**NY**	**A**	136	.246	.367	479	118	20	13	4	0.8	59	60	66	81	18	2	2	1396	85	12	85	11.1	.992	1B-134
1916			151	.262	.417	545	143	20	14	**12**	2.2	70	93	54	**82**	16	1	1	1513	99	13	89	11.0	.992	1B-148
1917			155	.244	.380	587	143	29	12	**9**	**1.5**	82	70	60	66	11	0	0	1609	109	17	97	11.2	.990	1B-155
1918			91	.304	.415	349	106	15	9	2	0.6	48	44	22	34	11	0	0	918	61	12	75	10.9	.988	1B-91
1919			138	.275	.398	523	144	23	10	7	1.3	74	50	39	42	9	0	0	1488	94	15	77	11.6	.991	1B-138
1920			153	.280	.430	610	171	30	14	11	1.8	109	76	48	54	4	0	0	1649	100	15	101	11.5	.991	1B-153
1921			153	.296	.427	588	174	35	9	8	1.4	96	97	45	28	17	0	0	1624	89	16	116	11.3	.991	1B-153
1922			152	.329	.466	577	190	32	10	9	1.6	96	90	56	32	7	0	0	1667	88	13	106	11.6	.993	1B-152
1923			144	.304	.397	569	173	19	8	6	1.1	79	108	36	28	6	0	0	1461	81	12	97	10.8	.992	1B-144
1924			153	.295	.457	589	174	30	**19**	9	1.5	88	113	51	36	12	0	0	1447	106	9	106	10.2	.994	1B-153
1925			62	.230	.348	178	41	6	3	3	1.7	19	24	13	12	3	9	0	399	38	4	40	9.4	.991	1B-47
1926	**CIN**	**N**	155	.291	.413	574	167	22	15	6	1.0	72	99	49	26	8	0	0	1710	92	15	140	11.7	.992	1B-155
1927			122	.260	.343	443	115	19	6	2	0.5	49	41	32	11	2	7	3	1145	66	5	86	10.7	.996	1B-114
1928			95	.283	.368	272	77	11	3	2	0.7	30	26	23	13	1	20	6	673	40	8	69	10.0	.989	1B-72
15 yrs.			1872	.281	.408	6914	1941	311	148	90	1.3	974	996	596	551	125	41	12	18779	1152	168	1290	11.0	.992	1B-1819
WORLD SERIES																									
1921	**NY**	**A**	8	.154	.192	26	4	1	0	0	0.0	1	2	2	3	1	0	0	91	1	0	5	11.5	1.000	1B-8
1922			5	.286	.333	21	6	1	0	0	0.0	0	3	0	2	1	0	0	51	4	0	7	11.0	1.000	1B-5
1923			6	.250	.250	20	5	0	0	0	0.0	2	2	4	1	0	0	0	63	3	0	6	11.0	1.000	1B-6
3 yrs.			19	.224	.254	67	15	2	0	0	0.0	3	7	6	6	2	0	0	205	8	0	18	11.2	1.000	1B-19

Jim Pirie

PIRIE, JAMES MOIR 5′ 8″ 169 lbs.
B. Mar. 31, 1853, Ont., Canada D. June 2, 1934, Dundas, Ont., Canada.

Year	Team		Games	BA	SA	AB	H	2B	3B	HR	HR%	R	RBI	BB	SO	SB	Pinch Hit AB	Pinch Hit H	PO	A	E	DP	TC/G	FA	G by Pos
1883	**PHI**	**N**	5	.158	.158	19	3	0	0	0	0.0	1		0	2		0	0	6	9	11	1	5.2	.577	SS-5

Greg Pirkl

PIRKL, GREGORY DANIEL BR TR 6′ 5″ 225 lbs.
B. Aug. 7, 1970, Long Beach, Calif.

Year	Team		Games	BA	SA	AB	H	2B	3B	HR	HR%	R	RBI	BB	SO	SB	Pinch Hit AB	Pinch Hit H	PO	A	E	DP	TC/G	FA	G by Pos
1993	**SEA**	**A**	7	.174	.304	23	4	0	0	1	4.3	1	4	0	4	0	0	0	42	5	0	8	6.7	1.000	1B-5, DH-2
1994			19	.264	.660	53	14	3	0	6	11.3	7	11	1	12	0	4	3	56	1	1	3	3.4	.983	DH-10, 1B-7
1995			10	.235	.235	17	4	0	0	0	0.0	2	0	1	7	0	5	0	32	3	0	1	5.0	1.000	1B-6, DH-1
3 yrs.			36	.237	.495	93	22	3	0	7	7.5	10	15	2	23	0	9	3	130	9	1	12	4.5	.993	1B-18, DH-13

Jim Pisoni

PISONI, JAMES PETE BR TR 5′10″ 169 lbs.
B. Aug. 14, 1929, St. Louis, Mo.

Year	Team		Games	BA	SA	AB	H	2B	3B	HR	HR%	R	RBI	BB	SO	SB	Pinch Hit AB	Pinch Hit H	PO	A	E	DP	TC/G	FA	G by Pos
1953	**STL**	**A**	3	.083	.333	12	1	0	0	1	8.3	1	1	0	5	0	0	0	7	0	0	0	2.3	1.000	OF-3
1956	**KC**	**A**	10	.267	.467	30	8	0	0	2	6.7	4	5	2	8	0	1	0	24	4	1	1	3.2	.966	OF-9
1957			44	.237	.392	97	23	2	2	3	3.1	14	12	10	17	0	0	0	88	3	1	1	2.1	.989	OF-44
1959	**2 teams**		**MIL N** (9G –.167) **NY A** (17G –.176)																						
″	**total**		26	.171	.244	41	7	1	1	0	0.0	6	1	3	15	0	1	0	32	1	1	0	1.4	.971	OF-24
1960	**NY**	**A**	20	.111	.111	9	1	0	0	0	0.0	1	1	1	2	0	0	0	15	0	1	0	0.9	.938	OF-18
5 yrs.			103	.212	.354	189	40	3	3	6	3.2	26	20	16	47	0	2	0	166	8	4	2	1.8	.978	OF-98

Alex Pitko

PITKO, ALEXANDER (Spunk) BR TR 5′10″ 180 lbs.
B. Nov. 22, 1914, Burlington, N. J.

Year	Team		Games	BA	SA	AB	H	2B	3B	HR	HR%	R	RBI	BB	SO	SB	Pinch Hit AB	Pinch Hit H	PO	A	E	DP	TC/G	FA	G by Pos
1938	**PHI**	**N**	7	.316	.368	19	6	1	0	0	0.0	2	2	3	3	1	0	0	8	0	1	0	1.3	.889	OF-7
1939	**WAS**	**A**	4	.125	.125	8	1	0	0	0	0.0	0	1	1	3	0	1	0	3	0	0	0	1.0	1.000	OF-3
2 yrs.			11	.259	.296	27	7	1	0	0	0.0	2	3	4	6	1	1	0	11	0	1	0	1.2	.917	OF-10

Jake Pitler

PITLER, JACOB ALBERT BR TR 5′ 8″ 150 lbs.
B. Apr. 22, 1894, New York, N. Y. D. Feb. 3, 1968, Binghamton, N. Y.

Year	Team		Games	BA	SA	AB	H	2B	3B	HR	HR%	R	RBI	BB	SO	SB	Pinch Hit AB	Pinch Hit H	PO	A	E	DP	TC/G	FA	G by Pos
1917	**PIT**	**N**	109	.233	.280	382	89	8	5	0	0.0	39	23	30	24	6	0	0	286	277	20	46	5.3	.966	2B-106, OF-3
1918			2	.000	.000	1	0	0	0	0	0.0	1	0	1	0	2	0	0	2	2	2	0	6.0	.667	2B-1
2 yrs.			111	.232	.279	383	89	8	5	0	0.0	40	23	31	24	8	0	0	288	279	22	46	5.4	.963	2B-107, OF-3

Chris Pittaro

PITTARO, CHRISTOPHER FRANCIS BB TR 5′11″ 170 lbs.
B. Sept. 16, 1961, Trenton, N. J.

Year	Team		Games	BA	SA	AB	H	2B	3B	HR	HR%	R	RBI	BB	SO	SB	Pinch Hit AB	Pinch Hit H	PO	A	E	DP	TC/G	FA	G by Pos
1985	**DET**	**A**	27	.242	.323	62	15	3	1	0	0.0	10	7	5	13	1	1	0	15	36	6	5	2.1	.895	3B-22, 2B-4, DH-1
1986	**MIN**	**A**	11	.095	.095	21	2	0	0	0	0.0	0	0	0	8	0	0	0	15	19	1	8	2.9	.971	2B-8, SS-4
1987			14	.333	.333	12	4	0	0	0	0.0	6	0	1	0	1	0	0	10	6	0	3	2.0	1.000	2B-8
3 yrs.			52	.221	.274	95	21	3	1	0	0.0	16	7	6	21	2	1	0	40	61	7	16	2.3	.935	3B-22, 2B-20, SS-4, DH-1

Pinky Pittenger

PITTENGER, CLARKE ALONZO BR TR 5′10″ 160 lbs.
B. Feb. 24, 1899, Hudson, Mich. D. Nov. 4, 1977, Ft. Lauderdale, Fla.

Year	Team	Games	BA	SA	AB	H	2B	3B	HR	HR%	R	RBI	BB	SO	SB	Pinch Hit AB	Pinch Hit H	PO	A	E	DP	TC/G	FA	G by Pos
1921	BOS A	40	.198	.209	91	18	1	0	0	0.0	6	5	4	13	3	6	1	66	13	1	1	2.4	.988	OF-27, 3B-3, SS-2, 2B-1
1922		66	.258	.274	186	48	3	0	0	0.0	16	7	9	10	2	1	0	88	148	22	19	4.3	.915	3B-31, SS-29
1923		60	.215	.243	177	38	5	0	0	0.0	15	15	5	10	3	2	0	97	112	8	13	3.9	.963	2B-42, SS-10, 3B-3
1925	CHI N	59	.312	.376	173	54	7	2	0	0.0	21	15	12	7	5	6	1	71	127	11	13	4.4	.947	SS-24, 3B-24
1927	CIN N	31	.274	.369	84	23	5	0	1	1.2	17	10	2	5	4	0	0	55	83	8	19	4.7	.945	2B-20, SS-9, 3B-2
1928		40	.237	.289	38	9	0	1	0	0.0	12	4	0	1	2	3	0	15	33	4	7	2.6	.923	SS-12, 3B-4, 2B-4
1929		77	.295	.348	210	62	11	0	0	0.0	31	27	5	4	8	0	0	117	179	14	40	5.0	.955	SS-50, 3B-8, 2B-4
7 yrs.		373	.263	.306	959	252	32	3	1	0.1	118	83	37	50	27	18	2	509	695	68	112	4.1	.947	SS-136, 3B-75, 2B-71, OF-27

Joe Pittman

PITTMAN, JOSEPH WAYNE BR TR 6′ 1″ 180 lbs.
B. Jan. 1, 1954, Houston, Tex.

Year	Team	Games	BA	SA	AB	H	2B	3B	HR	HR%	R	RBI	BB	SO	SB	Pinch Hit AB	Pinch Hit H	PO	A	E	DP	TC/G	FA	G by Pos
1981	HOU N	52	.281	.341	135	38	4	2	0	0.0	11	7	11	16	4	16	4	59	92	3	14	3.9	.981	2B-35, 3B-4
1982	2 teams	HOU N (15G –.200) SD N (55G –.254)																						
″	total	70	.250	.273	128	32	3	0	0	0.0	16	7	9	15	8	15	2	52	97	6	18	3.3	.961	2B-30, SS-13, 3B-3, OF-1
1984	SF N	17	.227	.227	22	5	0	0	0	0.0	2	2	0	6	1	3	0	5	13	1	1	1.5	.947	SS-6, 2B-5, 3B-2
3 yrs.		139	.263	.302	285	75	7	2	0	0.0	29	16	20	37	13	34	6	116	202	10	33	3.3	.970	2B-70, SS-19, 3B-9, OF-1
DIVISIONAL PLAYOFF SERIES																								
1981	HOU N	2	.000	.000	2	0	0	0	0	0.0	0	0	0	0	0	2	0	0	0	0	0	0.0	—	

Gaylen Pitts

PITTS, GAYLEN RICHARD BR TR 6′ 1″ 175 lbs.
B. June 6, 1946, Wichita, Kans.

Year	Team	Games	BA	SA	AB	H	2B	3B	HR	HR%	R	RBI	BB	SO	SB	Pinch Hit AB	Pinch Hit H	PO	A	E	DP	TC/G	FA	G by Pos
1974	OAK A	18	.244	.317	41	10	3	0	0	0.0	4	3	5	4	0	1	1	22	28	4	3	3.0	.926	3B-11, 2B-6, 1B-1
1975		10	.333	.667	3	1	1	0	0	0.0	1	1	0	0	0	0	0	4	6	1	1	1.2	.909	3B-6, SS-2, 2B-1
2 yrs.		28	.250	.341	44	11	4	0	0	0.0	5	4	5	4	0	1	1	26	34	5	4	2.4	.923	3B-17, 2B-7, SS-2, 1B-1

Herman Pitz

PITZ, HERMAN 5′ 6″ 140 lbs.
B. July 18, 1865, Brooklyn, N. Y. D. Sept. 3, 1924, Far Rockaway, N. Y.

Year	Team	Games	BA	SA	AB	H	2B	3B	HR	HR%	R	RBI	BB	SO	SB	Pinch Hit AB	Pinch Hit H	PO	A	E	DP	TC/G	FA	G by Pos
1890	2 teams	BKN AA (61G –.138) SYR AA (29G –.221)																						
″	total	90	.165	.165	284	47	0	0	0	0.0	43		58		39	0	0	268	134	55	8	5.2	.880	C-61, 3B-16, OF-10, SS-1

Phil Plantier

PLANTIER, PHILLIP ALAN BL TR 6′ 175 lbs.
B. Jan. 27, 1969, Manchester, N. H.

Year	Team	Games	BA	SA	AB	H	2B	3B	HR	HR%	R	RBI	BB	SO	SB	Pinch Hit AB	Pinch Hit H	PO	A	E	DP	TC/G	FA	G by Pos
1990	BOS A	14	.133	.200	15	2	1	0	0	0.0	1	3	4	6	0	6	1	0	0	0	0	0.0		DH-4, OF-1
1991		53	.331	.615	148	49	7	1	11	7.4	27	35	23	38	1	8	3	80	1	2	0	1.8	.976	OF-40, DH-5
1992		108	.246	.361	349	86	19	0	7	2.0	46	30	44	83	2	12	4	148	6	4	0	1.6	.975	OF-76, DH-23
1993	SD N	138	.240	.509	462	111	20	1	34	7.4	67	100	61	124	4	5	0	272	14	3	3	2.2	.990	OF-134
1994		96	.220	.440	341	75	21	0	18	5.3	44	41	36	91	3	6	0	159	5	2	0	1.8	.988	OF-91
1995	2 teams	HOU N (22G –.250) SD N (54G –.257)																						
″	total	76	.255	.407	216	55	6	0	9	4.2	33	34	28	48	1	12	2	89	5	4	1	1.7	.959	OF-59
6 yrs.		485	.247	.453	1531	378	74	2	79	5.2	218	243	196	390	11	49	10	748	31	15	4	1.8	.981	OF-401, DH-32

Don Plarski

PLARSKI, DONALD JOSEPH BR TR 5′ 6″ 160 lbs.
B. Nov. 9, 1929, Chicago, Ill. D. Dec. 29, 1981, St. Louis, Mo.

Year	Team	Games	BA	SA	AB	H	2B	3B	HR	HR%	R	RBI	BB	SO	SB	Pinch Hit AB	Pinch Hit H	PO	A	E	DP	TC/G	FA	G by Pos
1955	KC A	8	.091	.091	11	1	0	0	0	0.0	0	0	0	2	1	1	0	7	0	0	0	1.2	1.000	OF-6

Elmo Plaskett

PLASKETT, ELMO ALEXANDER BR TR 5′10″ 195 lbs.
B. June 27, 1938, Frederiksted, Virgin Islands.

Year	Team	Games	BA	SA	AB	H	2B	3B	HR	HR%	R	RBI	BB	SO	SB	Pinch Hit AB	Pinch Hit H	PO	A	E	DP	TC/G	FA	G by Pos
1962	PIT N	7	.286	.500	14	4	0	0	1	7.1	2	3	1	3	0	4	0	13	1	0	0	3.5	1.000	C-4
1963		10	.143	.143	21	3	0	0	0	0.0	1	2	0	5	0	5	1	18	2	0	0	3.3	1.000	C-5, 3B-1
2 yrs.		17	.200	.286	35	7	0	0	1	2.9	3	5	1	8	0	9	1	31	3	0	0	3.4	1.000	C-9, 3B-1

Whitey Platt

PLATT, MIZELL GEORGE BR TR 6′ 1½″ 190 lbs.
B. Aug. 21, 1920, West Palm Beach, Fla. D. July 27, 1970, West Palm Beach, Fla.

Year	Team	Games	BA	SA	AB	H	2B	3B	HR	HR%	R	RBI	BB	SO	SB	Pinch Hit AB	Pinch Hit H	PO	A	E	DP	TC/G	FA	G by Pos
1942	CHI N	4	.063	.063	16	1	0	0	0	0.0	1	2	0	3	0	0	0	7	1	0	0	2.0	1.000	OF-4
1943		20	.171	.244	41	7	3	0	0	0.0	2	2	1	7	0	4	1	20	0	1	0	1.5	.952	OF-14
1946	CHI A	84	.251	.360	247	62	8	5	3	1.2	28	32	17	34	1	24	6	130	4	4	1	2.3	.971	OF-61
1948	STL A	123	.271	.410	454	123	22	10	7	1.5	57	82	39	51	1	8	2	230	5	13	2	2.2	.948	OF-114
1949		102	.258	.344	244	63	8	2	3	1.2	29	29	24	27	0	**34**	7	156	5	3	1	2.7	.982	OF-59, 1B-2
5 yrs.		333	.255	.369	1002	256	41	17	13	1.3	117	147	81	122	2	70	16	543	15	21	4	2.3	.964	OF-252, 1B-2

Al Platte

PLATTE, ALFRED FREDERICK JOSEPH BL TL 5′ 7″ 160 lbs.
B. Apr. 13, 1890, Grand Rapids, Mich. D. Aug. 29, 1976, Grand Rapids, Mich.

Year	Team	Games	BA	SA	AB	H	2B	3B	HR	HR%	R	RBI	BB	SO	SB	Pinch Hit AB	Pinch Hit H	PO	A	E	DP	TC/G	FA	G by Pos
1913	DET A	7	.111	.167	18	2	1	0	0	0.0	1	0	1	1	0	2	0	8	0	2	0	2.0	.800	OF-5

Rance Pless

PLESS, RANCE BR TR 6′ 195 lbs.
B. Dec. 6, 1925, Greeneville, Tenn.

Year	Team	Games	BA	SA	AB	H	2B	3B	HR	HR%	R	RBI	BB	SO	SB	Pinch Hit AB	Pinch Hit H	PO	A	E	DP	TC/G	FA	G by Pos
1956	KC A	48	.271	.329	85	23	3	1	0	0.0	4	9	10	13	0	26	7	142	20	0	20	8.1	1.000	1B-15, 3B-5

Herb Plews

PLEWS, HERBERT EUGENE BL TR 5′11″ 160 lbs.
B. June 14, 1928, Helena, Mont.

Year	Team	Games	BA	SA	AB	H	2B	3B	HR	HR%	R	RBI	BB	SO	SB	Pinch Hit AB	Pinch Hit H	PO	A	E	DP	TC/G	FA	G by Pos
1956	WAS A	91	.270	.375	256	69	10	7	1	0.4	24	25	26	40	1	24	4	140	175	18	39	4.6	.946	2B-66, SS-5, 3B-2
1957		104	.271	.362	329	89	19	4	1	0.3	51	26	28	39	0	25	5	203	188	11	43	4.3	.973	2B-79, 3B-11, SS-4
1958		111	.258	.337	380	98	12	6	2	0.5	46	29	17	45	2	22	4	156	208	16	45	3.8	.958	2B-64, 3B-36
1959	2 teams	WAS A (27G –.225) BOS A (13G –.083)																						
″	total	40	.192	.212	52	10	1	0	0	0.0	4	2	3	9	0	32	7	21	18	2	3	5.1	.951	2B-8
4 yrs.		346	.262	.348	1017	266	42	17	4	0.4	125	82	74	133	3	103	20	520	589	47	130	4.2	.959	2B-217, 3B-49, SS-9

Walter Plock

PLOCK, WALTER S. 6′ 3″ 180 lbs.
B. July 2, 1869, Philadelphia, Pa. D. Apr. 28, 1900, Richmond, Va.

Year	Team	Games	BA	SA	AB	H	2B	3B	HR	HR%	R	RBI	BB	SO	SB	Pinch Hit AB	Pinch Hit H	PO	A	E	DP	TC/G	FA	G by Pos
1891	PHI N	2	.400	.400	5	2	0	0	0	0.0	2	0	0	1	0	0	0	0	0	1	0	0.5	.000	OF-2

Bill Plummer

PLUMMER, WILLIAM FRANCIS
B. Mar. 21, 1947, Oakland, Calif.
Manager 1992.

BR TR 6′ 1″ 190 lbs.

Year	Team	Lg	Games	BA	SA	AB	H	2B	3B	HR	HR%	R	RBI	BB	SO	SB	Pinch Hit AB	Pinch Hit H	PO	A	E	DP	TC/G	FA	G by Pos
1968	CHI	N	2	.000	.000	2	0	0	0	0	0.0	0	0	0	1	0	1	0	2	0	0	0	2.0	1.000	C-1
1970	CIN	N	4	.125	.125	8	1	0	0	0	0.0	0	0	0	2	0	0	0	6	0	1	0	1.8	.857	C-4
1971			10	.000	.000	19	0	0	0	0	0.0	0	0	0	4	0	3	0	8	6	0	0	2.3	1.000	C-4, 3B-2
1972			38	.186	.284	102	19	4	0	2	2.0	8	9	4	20	0	0	0	156	9	1	3	4.4	.994	C-36, 1B-1, 3B-1
1973			50	.151	.227	119	18	3	0	2	1.7	8	11	18	26	1	2	0	172	10	2	3	3.9	.989	C-42, 3B-5
1974			50	.225	.333	120	27	7	0	2	1.7	7	10	6	21	1	1	0	208	14	6	1	4.6	.974	C-49, 3B-1
1975			65	.182	.245	159	29	7	0	1	0.6	17	19	24	28	1	4	1	186	14	2	5	3.2	.990	C-63
1976			56	.248	.379	153	38	6	1	4	2.6	16	19	14	36	0	3	2	235	21	6	1	4.9	.977	C-54
1977			51	.137	.205	117	16	5	0	1	0.9	10	7	17	34	1	2	0	194	15	3	3	4.2	.986	C-50
1978	SEA	A	41	.215	.333	93	20	5	0	2	2.2	6	7	12	19	0	1	0	127	9	3	1	3.5	.978	C-40
10 yrs.			367	.188	.279	892	168	37	1	14	1.6	72	82	95	191	4	17	3	1294	98	24	17	4.0	.983	C-343, 3B-9, 1B-1

Biff Pocoroba

POCOROBA, BIFF BENEDICT
B. July 25, 1953, Burbank, Calif.

BB TR 5′10″ 175 lbs.
BL 1981–1984

Year	Team	Lg	Games	BA	SA	AB	H	2B	3B	HR	HR%	R	RBI	BB	SO	SB	Pinch Hit AB	Pinch Hit H	PO	A	E	DP	TC/G	FA	G by Pos
1975	ATL	N	67	.255	.319	188	48	7	1	1	0.5	15	22	20	11	0	8	3	237	25	8	2	4.4	.970	C-62
1976			54	.241	.282	174	42	7	0	0	0.0	16	14	19	12	1	2	0	273	39	7	5	5.9	.978	C-54
1977			113	.290	.445	321	93	24	1	8	2.5	46	44	57	27	3	20	3	542	78	7	8	6.3	.989	C-100
1978			92	.242	.332	289	70	8	0	6	2.1	21	34	29	14	0	13	2	454	43	5	1	6.4	.990	C-79
1979			28	.316	.421	38	12	4	0	0	0.0	6	4	7	0	1	16	6	39	3	3	0	6.4	.933	C-7
1980			70	.265	.386	83	22	4	0	2	2.4	7	8	11	11	1	53	15	56	1	4	0	6.1	.934	C-10
1981			57	.180	.213	122	22	4	0	0	0.0	4	8	12	15	0	26	4	43	34	3	6	2.7	.962	3B-21, C-9
1982			56	.275	.383	120	33	7	0	2	1.7	5	22	13	12	0	17	4	144	16	2	2	4.3	.988	C-36, 3B-2
1983			55	.267	.367	120	32	6	0	2	1.7	11	16	12	7	0	20	1	166	12	3	1	5.3	.983	C-34
1984			4	.000	.000	2	0	0	0	0	0.0	1	0	2	0	0	2	0	0	0	0	0	0.0	—	
10 yrs.			596	.257	.351	1457	374	71	2	21	1.4	132	172	182	109	6	177	38	1954	251	42	25	5.4	.981	C-391, 3B-23
LEAGUE CHAMPIONSHIP SERIES																									
1982	ATL	N	1	.000	.000	1	0	0	0	0	0.0	0	0	0	0	0	1	0	0	0	0	0	0.0	—	

Mike Poepping

POEPPING, MICHAEL HAROLD
B. Aug. 7, 1950, Little Falls, Minn.

BR TR 6′ 6″ 230 lbs.

Year	Team	Lg	Games	BA	SA	AB	H	2B	3B	HR	HR%	R	RBI	BB	SO	SB	Pinch Hit AB	Pinch Hit H	PO	A	E	DP	TC/G	FA	G by Pos
1975	MIN	A	14	.135	.162	37	5	1	0	0	0.0	0	1	5	7	0	1	0	18	1	1	0	1.5	.950	OF-13

Jimmy Pofahl

POFAHL, JAMES WILLARD
B. June 18, 1917, Faribault, Minn. D. Sept. 14, 1984, Owatonna, Minn.

BR TR 5′11″ 185 lbs.

Year	Team	Lg	Games	BA	SA	AB	H	2B	3B	HR	HR%	R	RBI	BB	SO	SB	Pinch Hit AB	Pinch Hit H	PO	A	E	DP	TC/G	FA	G by Pos
1940	WAS	A	119	.234	.330	406	95	23	5	2	0.5	34	36	37	55	2	2	0	200	317	25	73	4.7	.954	SS-112, 2B-4
1941			22	.187	.280	75	14	3	2	0	0.0	9	6	10	11	1	0	0	30	55	6	8	4.3	.934	SS-21
1942			84	.208	.247	283	59	7	2	0	0.0	22	28	29	30	4	6	2	166	204	18	45	5.0	.954	SS-49, 2B-15, 3B-14
3 yrs.			225	.220	.295	764	168	33	9	2	0.3	65	70	76	96	7	8	2	396	576	49	126	4.7	.952	SS-182, 2B-19, 3B-14

John Poff

POFF, JOHN WILLIAM
B. Oct. 23, 1952, Chillicothe, Ohio.

BL TL 6′ 2″ 190 lbs.

Year	Team	Lg	Games	BA	SA	AB	H	2B	3B	HR	HR%	R	RBI	BB	SO	SB	Pinch Hit AB	Pinch Hit H	PO	A	E	DP	TC/G	FA	G by Pos
1979	PHI	N	12	.105	.158	19	2	1	0	0	0.0	2	1	1	4	0	6	0	8	0	1	0	1.8	.889	OF-4, 1B-1
1980	MIL	A	19	.250	.368	68	17	1	2	1	1.5	7	7	3	7	0	2	1	38	0	1	0	2.3	.974	OF-7, DH-7, 1B-3
2 yrs.			31	.218	.322	87	19	2	2	1	1.1	9	8	4	11	0	8	1	46	0	2	0	2.2	.958	OF-11, DH-7, 1B-4

Aaron Pointer

POINTER, AARON ELTON (Hawk)
B. Apr. 19, 1942, Little Rock, Ark.

BR TR 6′ 2″ 185 lbs.

Year	Team	Lg	Games	BA	SA	AB	H	2B	3B	HR	HR%	R	RBI	BB	SO	SB	Pinch Hit AB	Pinch Hit H	PO	A	E	DP	TC/G	FA	G by Pos
1963	HOU	N	2	.200	.200	5	1	0	0	0	0.0	0	0	0	1	0	0	0	1	0	0	0	1.0	1.000	OF-1
1966			11	.346	.500	26	9	1	0	1	3.8	5	5	5	6	1	1	0	13	3	0	1	1.5	1.000	OF-11
1967			27	.157	.257	70	11	4	0	1	1.4	6	10	13	26	1	3	0	37	2	2	0	1.9	.951	OF-22
3 yrs.			40	.208	.317	101	21	5	0	2	2.0	11	15	18	33	2	4	0	51	5	2	1	1.7	.966	OF-34

Hugh Poland

POLAND, HUGH REID
B. Jan. 19, 1913, Tompkinsville, Ky. D. Mar. 30, 1984, Guthrie, Ky.

BL TR 5′11½″ 185 lbs.

Year	Team	Lg	Games	BA	SA	AB	H	2B	3B	HR	HR%	R	RBI	BB	SO	SB	Pinch Hit AB	Pinch Hit H	PO	A	E	DP	TC/G	FA	G by Pos
1943	2 teams		NY N (4G –.083) BOS N (44G –.191)																						
"	total		48	.183	.242	153	28	7	1	0	0.0	5	15	5	11	0	5	1	143	11	5	3	3.8	.969	C-42
1944	BOS	N	8	.130	.174	23	3	1	0	0	0.0	1	2	0	1	0	2	0	31	0	2	0	5.5	.939	C-6
1946			4	.167	.333	6	1	1	0	0	0.0	0	0	0	0	0	2	1	6	0	0	0	3.0	1.000	C-2
1947	2 teams		PHI N (4G –.000) CIN N (16G –.333)																						
"	total		20	.231	.269	26	6	1	0	0	0.0	1	2	1	4	0	14	4	11	2	2	0	3.0	.867	C-5
1948	CIN	N	3	.333	.333	3	1	0	0	0	0.0	0	0	0	0	0	3	1	0	0	0	0	0.0	—	
5 yrs.			83	.185	.242	211	39	10	1	0	0.0	7	19	6	16	0	26	7	191	13	9	3	3.9	.958	C-55

Mark Polhemus

POLHEMUS, MARK S. (Humpty Dumpty)
B. Oct. 4, 1862, Brooklyn, N.Y. D. Nov. 12, 1923, Lynn, Mass.

5′ 6½″ 185 lbs.

Year	Team	Lg	Games	BA	SA	AB	H	2B	3B	HR	HR%	R	RBI	BB	SO	SB	Pinch Hit AB	Pinch Hit H	PO	A	E	DP	TC/G	FA	G by Pos
1887	IND	N	20	.240	.253	75	18	1	0	0	0.0	6	8	2	9	4	0	0	21	8	10	0	2.0	.744	OF-20

Gus Polidor

POLIDOR, GUSTAVO ADOLFO
Born Gustavo Adolfo Polidor (Gonzalez).
B. Oct. 26, 1961, Caracas, Venezuela D. Apr. 28, 1995, Caracas, Venezuela.

BR TR 6′ 170 lbs.

Year	Team	Lg	Games	BA	SA	AB	H	2B	3B	HR	HR%	R	RBI	BB	SO	SB	Pinch Hit AB	Pinch Hit H	PO	A	E	DP	TC/G	FA	G by Pos
1985	CAL	A	2	1.000	1.000	1	1	0	0	0	0.0	1	0	0	0	0	0	0	0	2	0	0	1.0	1.000	SS-1, OF-1
1986			6	.263	.316	19	5	1	0	0	0.0	1	1	1	0	0	0	0	10	13	0	2	3.8	1.000	2B-4, SS-1, 3B-1
1987			63	.263	.328	137	36	3	0	2	1.5	12	15	2	15	0	3	1	46	92	2	14	2.3	.986	SS-46, 3B-11, 2B-3
1988			54	.148	.185	81	12	3	0	0	0.0	4	4	3	11	0	8	2	31	54	1	9	1.7	.988	SS-25, 3B-22, 2B-3
1989	MIL	A	79	.194	.234	175	34	7	0	0	0.0	15	14	6	18	3	3	0	78	123	12	20	2.6	.944	3B-30, 2B-29, SS-21, DH-2
1990			18	.067	.067	15	1	0	0	0	0.0	0	1	0	1	0	0	0	2	13	0	0	0.8	1.000	3B-14, SS-2, 2B-2
1993	FLA	N	7	.167	.333	6	1	1	0	0	0.0	0	0	0	2	0	5	1	1	0	0	0	0.5	1.000	3B-1, 2B-1
7 yrs.			229	.207	.256	434	90	15	0	2	0.5	33	35	12	47	3	19	4	168	297	15	45	2.2	.969	SS-96, 3B-79, 2B-42, DH-2, OF-1

Nick Polly

POLLY, NICHOLAS BR TR 5′11″ 190 lbs.
Born Nicholas Polachanin.
B. Apr. 18, 1917, Chicago, Ill. D. Jan. 17, 1993, Chicago, Ill.

Year	Team	Games	BA	SA	AB	H	2B	3B	HR	HR%	R	RBI	BB	SO	SB	Pinch Hit AB	Pinch Hit H	PO	A	E	DP	TC/G	FA	G by Pos
1937	BKN N	10	.222	.222	18	4	0	0	0	0.0	2	2	0	1	0	3	1	4	13	3	0	2.9	.850	3B-7
1945	BOS A	4	.143	.143	7	1	0	0	0	0.0	0	1	0	1	0	2	0	1	2	0	0	1.5	1.000	3B-2
2 yrs.		14	.200	.200	25	5	0	0	0	0.0	2	3	0	2	0	5	1	5	15	3	0	2.6	.870	3B-9

Luis Polonia

POLONIA, LUIS ANDREW BL TL 5′8″ 155 lbs.
Born Luis Andrew Polonia (Almonte). BB 1987
B. Oct. 12, 1964, Santiago City, Dominican Republic.

Year	Team	Games	BA	SA	AB	H	2B	3B	HR	HR%	R	RBI	BB	SO	SB	Pinch Hit AB	Pinch Hit H	PO	A	E	DP	TC/G	FA	G by Pos
1987	OAK A	125	.287	.398	435	125	16	10	4	0.9	78	49	32	64	29	8	3	235	2	5	1	2.0	.979	OF-104, DH-18
1988		84	.292	.378	288	84	11	4	2	0.7	51	27	21	40	24	9	2	155	3	2	1	2.1	.988	OF-76, DH-2
1989	2 teams	OAK A (59G –.286) NY A (66G –.313)																						
″	total	125	.300	.388	433	130	17	6	3	0.7	70	46	25	44	22	14	6	231	9	4	2	2.1	.984	OF-108, DH-9
1990	2 teams	NY A (11G –.318) CAL A (109G –.336)																						
″	total	120	.335	.412	403	135	7	9	2	0.5	52	35	25	43	21	19	6	142	3	3	2	1.5	.980	OF-85, DH-15
1991	CAL A	150	.296	.379	604	179	28	8	2	0.3	92	50	52	74	48	5	1	246	9	5	1	1.8	.981	OF-143, DH-4
1992		149	.286	.329	577	165	17	4	0	0.0	83	35	45	64	51	4	1	192	8	4	1	1.4	.980	OF-99, DH-47
1993		152	.271	.326	576	156	17	6	1	0.2	75	32	48	53	55	8	2	286	12	5	3	2.1	.983	OF-141, DH-3
1994	NY A	95	.311	.414	350	109	21	6	1	0.3	62	36	37	36	20	10	4	154	9	4	2	1.9	.976	OF-84, DH-2
1995	2 teams	NY A (67G –.261) ATL N (28G –.264)																						
″	total	95	.261	.357	291	76	16	3	2	0.7	43	17	28	38	13	24	9	143	5	0	1	1.9	1.000	OF-79
9 yrs.		1095	.293	.372	3957	1159	150	56	17	0.4	606	327	313	456	283	101	34	1784	60	32	14	1.8	.983	OF-919, DH-100
DIVISIONAL PLAYOFF SERIES																								
1995	ATL N	3	.333	.333	3	1	0	0	0	0.0	0	2	0	1	1	3	1	0	0	0	0	0.0	—	
LEAGUE CHAMPIONSHIP SERIES																								
1988	OAK A	3	.400	.400	5	2	0	0	0	0.0	0	0	1	2	0	0	0	2	0	0	0	2.0	1.000	OF-1
1995	ATL N	3	.500	.500	2	1	0	0	0	0.0	0	1	0	0	0	2	1	0	0	0	0	0.0	.000	OF-1
2 yrs.		6	.429	.429	7	3	0	0	0	0.0	0	1	1	2	0	2	1	2	0	0	0	1.0	1.000	OF-2
WORLD SERIES																								
1988	OAK A	3	.111	.111	9	1	0	0	0	0.0	1	0	0	2	0	2	0	2	0	0	0	1.0	1.000	OF-2
1995	ATL N	6	.286	.571	14	4	1	0	1	7.1	3	4	1	3	1	2	0	3	0	0	0	0.8	1.000	OF-4
2 yrs.		9	.217	.391	23	5	1	0	1	4.3	4	4	1	5	1	4	0	5	0	0	0	0.8	1.000	OF-6

Carlos Ponce

PONCE, CARLOS ANTONIO BR TR 5′10″ 170 lbs.
Born Carlos Antonio Ponce (Diaz).
B. Feb. 7, 1959, Rio Piedras, Puerto Rico.

Year	Team	Games	BA	SA	AB	H	2B	3B	HR	HR%	R	RBI	BB	SO	SB	Pinch Hit AB	Pinch Hit H	PO	A	E	DP	TC/G	FA	G by Pos
1985	MIL A	21	.161	.242	62	10	2	0	1	1.6	4	5	1	9	0	3	0	67	3	0	7	2.9	1.000	1B-15, OF-6, DH-3

Ralph Pond

POND, RALPH BENJAMIN
B. May 4, 1888, Eau Claire, Wis. D. Sept. 8, 1947, Cleveland, Ohio.

Year	Team	Games	BA	SA	AB	H	2B	3B	HR	HR%	R	RBI	BB	SO	SB	Pinch Hit AB	Pinch Hit H	PO	A	E	DP	TC/G	FA	G by Pos
1910	BOS A	1	.250	.250	4	1	0	0	0	0.0	0	0	0		1	0	0	0	0	1	0	1.0	.000	OF-1

Harlin Pool

POOL, HARLON WELTY (Samson) BL TR 5′10″ 195 lbs.
B. Mar. 12, 1908, Lakeport, Calif. D. Feb. 15, 1963, Rodeo, Calif.

Year	Team	Games	BA	SA	AB	H	2B	3B	HR	HR%	R	RBI	BB	SO	SB	Pinch Hit AB	Pinch Hit H	PO	A	E	DP	TC/G	FA	G by Pos
1934	CIN N	99	.327	.433	358	117	22	5	2	0.6	38	50	17	18	3	6	3	196	8	10	1	2.3	.953	OF-94
1935		28	.176	.324	68	12	6	2	0	0.0	8	11	2	2	0	9	1	24	1	1	0	1.4	.962	OF-18
2 yrs.		127	.303	.415	426	129	28	7	2	0.5	46	61	19	20	3	15	4	220	9	11	1	2.1	.954	OF-112

Jim Poole

POOLE, JAMES ROBERT (Easy) BL TR 6′ 175 lbs.
B. May 12, 1895, Taylorsville, N. C. D. Jan. 2, 1975, Hickory, N. C.

Year	Team	Games	BA	SA	AB	H	2B	3B	HR	HR%	R	RBI	BB	SO	SB	Pinch Hit AB	Pinch Hit H	PO	A	E	DP	TC/G	FA	G by Pos
1925	PHI A	133	.298	.423	480	143	29	8	5	1.0	65	67	27	37	5	6	2	1166	65	23	102	10.2	.982	1B-123
1926		112	.294	.452	361	106	23	5	8	2.2	49	63	23	25	4	9	2	888	55	8	71	9.3	.992	1B-101, OF-1
1927		38	.222	.242	99	22	2	0	0	0.0	4	10	9	6	0	8	0	264	17	2	14	9.1	.993	1B-31
3 yrs.		283	.288	.415	940	271	54	13	13	1.4	118	140	59	68	9	23	4	2318	137	33	187	9.7	.987	1B-255, OF-1

Ray Poole

POOLE, RAYMOND HERMAN BL TR 6′ 180 lbs.
B. Jan. 16, 1920, Salisbury, N. C.

Year	Team	Games	BA	SA	AB	H	2B	3B	HR	HR%	R	RBI	BB	SO	SB	Pinch Hit AB	Pinch Hit H	PO	A	E	DP	TC/G	FA	G by Pos
1941	PHI A	2	.000	.000	2	0	0	0	0	0.0	0	0	0	1	0	2	0	0	0	0	0	0.0	—	
1947		13	.231	.231	13	3	0	0	0	0.0	1	1	1	4	0	13	3	0	0	0	0	0.0	—	
2 yrs.		15	.200	.200	15	3	0	0	0	0.0	1	1	1	5	0	15	3							

Tom Poorman

POORMAN, THOMAS IVERSON BL TR 5′10½″ 170 lbs.
B. Oct. 14, 1857, Lock Haven, Pa. D. Feb. 18, 1905, Lock Haven, Pa.

Year	Team	Games	BA	SA	AB	H	2B	3B	HR	HR%	R	RBI	BB	SO	SB	Pinch Hit AB	Pinch Hit H	PO	A	E	DP	TC/G	FA	G by Pos
1880	2 teams	BUF N (19G –.157) CHI N (7G –.200)																						
″	total	26	.168	.232	95	16	2	2	0	0.0	8	1	0	15		0	0	19	25	9	0	1.8	.830	OF-17, P-13
1884	TOL AA	94	.233	.291	382	89	8	7	0	0.0	56		10			0	0	130	31	30	5	2.0	.843	OF-93, P-1
1885	BOS N	56	.238	.326	227	54	5	3	3	1.3	44	25	7	32		0	0	82	9	14	1	1.9	.867	OF-56
1886		96	.261	.361	371	97	16	6	3	0.8	72	41	19	52		0	0	145	21	18	6	1.9	.902	OF-96
1887	PHI AA	135	.265	.381	585	155	18	**19**	4	0.7	140		35		88	0	0	237	18	25	6	2.0	.911	OF-135, 2B-2, P-1
1888		97	.227	.316	383	87	16	6	2	0.5	76	44	31		46	0	0	115	8	14	1	1.4	.898	OF-97
6 yrs.		504	.244	.335	2043	498	65	43	12	0.6	396	111	102	99	134	0	0	728	112	110	19	1.9	.884	OF-494, P-15, 2B-2

Dave Pope

POPE, DAVID BL TR 5′10½″ 170 lbs.
B. June 17, 1925, Talladega, Ala.

Year	Team	Games	BA	SA	AB	H	2B	3B	HR	HR%	R	RBI	BB	SO	SB	Pinch Hit AB	Pinch Hit H	PO	A	E	DP	TC/G	FA	G by Pos
1952	CLE A	12	.294	.471	34	10	1	1	1	2.9	9	4	1	7	0	3	0	13	0	0	0	1.3	1.000	OF-10
1954		60	.294	.451	102	30	2	1	4	3.9	21	13	10	22	2	19	5	45	1	0	0	1.6	1.000	OF-29
1955	2 teams	CLE A (35G –.298) BAL A (86G –.248)																						
″	total	121	.264	.393	326	86	13	4	7	2.1	38	52	28	65	5	31	12	214	3	3	1	2.1	.986	OF-104
1956	2 teams	BAL A (12G –.158) CLE A (25G –.243)																						
″	total	37	.225	.281	89	20	3	1	0	0.0	7	4	1	19	0	13	2	37	1	0	0	1.7	1.000	OF-22
4 yrs.		230	.265	.390	551	146	19	7	12	2.2	75	73	40	113	7	66	19	309	5	3	1	1.9	.991	OF-165
WORLD SERIES																								
1954	CLE A	3	.000	.000	3	0	0	0	0	0.0	0	0	1	1	0	3	0	0	0	0	0	0.0	.000	OF-2

Paul Popovich

POPOVICH, PAUL EDWARD
B. Aug. 18, 1940, Flemington, W. Va.
BB TR 6′ 175 lbs.
BR 1964, 1966–1967

Year	Team	Games	BA	SA	AB	H	2B	3B	HR	HR%	R	RBI	BB	SO	SB	Pinch Hit AB	Pinch Hit H	PO	A	E	DP	TC/G	FA	G by Pos
1964	CHI N	1	1.000	1.000	1	1	0	0	0	0.0	0	0	0	0	0	1	1	0	0	0	0	0.0	—	
1966		2	.000	.000	6	0	0	0	0	0.0	0	0	0	2	0	0	0	5	3	1	1	4.5	.889	2B-2
1967		49	.214	.239	159	34	4	0	0	0.0	18	2	9	12	0	5	0	66	116	5	23	3.7	.973	SS-31, 2B-17, 3B-2
1968	LA N	134	.232	.270	418	97	8	1	2	0.5	35	25	29	37	1	4	0	232	349	11	68	4.2	.981	2B-89, SS-45, 3B-7
1969	2 teams	LA N (28G –.200) CHI N (60G –.312)																						
″	total	88	.284	.328	204	58	6	0	1	0.5	31	18	19	18	0	25	8	93	136	6	30	3.6	.974	2B-48, SS-10, 3B-6, OF-1
1970	CHI N	78	.253	.355	186	47	5	1	4	2.2	22	20	18	18	0	26	2	75	97	4	26	3.2	.977	2B-22, SS-17, 3B-16
1971		89	.217	.310	226	49	7	1	4	1.8	24	28	14	17	0	30	2	78	146	4	27	4.0	.982	2B-40, 3B-16, SS-1
1972		58	.194	.271	129	25	3	2	1	0.8	8	11	12	8	0	12	2	77	127	4	30	4.6	.981	2B-36, SS-8, 3B-1
1973		99	.236	.300	280	66	6	3	2	0.7	24	24	18	27	3	9	1	179	262	8	58	4.8	.982	2B-84, SS-9, 3B-1
1974	PIT N	59	.217	.265	83	18	2	1	0	0.0	9	5	5	10	0	38	9	24	38	2	9	2.9	.969	2B-12, SS-10
1975		25	.200	.225	40	8	1	0	0	0.0	5	1	3	2	0	15	3	17	21	1	3	2.4	.974	SS-8, 2B-8
11 yrs.		682	.233	.292	1732	403	42	9	14	0.8	176	134	127	151	4	165	28	846	1295	46	275	4.0	.979	2B-358, SS-139, 3B-49, OF-1
LEAGUE CHAMPIONSHIP SERIES																								
1974	PIT N	3	.600	.600	5	3	0	0	0	0.0	1	0	0	0	0	3	3	2	0	0	0	0.7	1.000	SS-3

Tom Poquette

POQUETTE, THOMAS ARTHUR
B. Oct. 30, 1951, Eau Claire, Wis.
BL TR 5′10″ 175 lbs.

Year	Team	Games	BA	SA	AB	H	2B	3B	HR	HR%	R	RBI	BB	SO	SB	Pinch Hit AB	Pinch Hit H	PO	A	E	DP	TC/G	FA	G by Pos
1973	KC A	21	.214	.250	28	6	1	0	0	0.0	4	3	1	4	1	0	0	19	1	3	0	1.1	.870	OF-20
1976		104	.302	.430	344	104	18	10	2	0.6	43	34	29	31	6	7	1	188	1	4	0	1.9	.979	OF-98, DH-2
1977		106	.292	.412	342	100	23	6	2	0.6	43	33	19	21	1	12	1	177	4	0	1	1.9	1.000	OF-96
1978		80	.216	.338	204	44	9	2	4	2.0	16	30	14	9	2	21	6	144	5	7	0	2.4	.955	OF-63, DH-1
1979	2 teams	KC A (21G –.192) BOS A (63G –.331)																						
″	total	84	.311	.394	180	56	9	0	2	1.1	15	26	9	11	2	28	4	80	3	4	2	1.5	.954	OF-53, DH-4
1981	2 teams	BOS A (3G –.000) TEX A (30G –.156)																						
″	total	33	.152	.167	66	10	1	0	0	0.0	2	7	5	1	0	12	3	26	0	1	0	1.4	.963	OF-20
1982	KC A	24	.145	.161	62	9	1	0	0	0.0	4	3	4	5	1	3	0	44	1	2	0	2.0	.957	OF-23
7 yrs.		452	.268	.373	1226	329	62	18	10	0.8	127	136	81	82	13	83	15	678	15	21	3	1.9	.971	OF-373, DH-7
LEAGUE CHAMPIONSHIP SERIES																								
1976	KC A	5	.188	.313	16	3	2	0	0	0.0	1	4	2	3	0	0	0	13	0	0	0	2.6	1.000	OF-5
1977		2	.167	.167	6	1	0	0	0	0.0	0	0	0	0	0	0	0	3	0	0	0	1.5	1.000	OF-2
1978		1	.000	.000	1	0	0	0	0	0.0	0	0	0	0	0	1	0	0	0	0	0	0.0	—	
3 yrs.		8	.174	.261	23	4	2	0	0	0.0	1	4	2	3	0	1	0	16	0	0	0	2.3	1.000	OF-7

Bob Porter

PORTER, ROBERT LEE, JR.
B. July 22, 1959, Yuma, Ariz.
BL TL 5′10″ 180 lbs.

Year	Team	Games	BA	SA	AB	H	2B	3B	HR	HR%	R	RBI	BB	SO	SB	Pinch Hit AB	Pinch Hit H	PO	A	E	DP	TC/G	FA	G by Pos
1981	ATL N	17	.286	.357	14	4	1	0	0	0.0	2	4	2	1	0	14	4	0	0	0	0	0.0	—	
1982		24	.111	.111	27	3	0	0	0	0.0	1	0	1	9	0	16	1	7	0	0	1	1.4	1.000	OF-4, 1B-1
2 yrs.		41	.171	.195	41	7	1	0	0	0.0	3	4	3	10	0	30	5	7	0	0	1	1.4	1.000	OF-4, 1B-1

Dan Porter

PORTER, DANIEL EDWARD
B. Oct. 17, 1931, Decatur, Ill.
BL TL 6′ 164 lbs.

Year	Team	Games	BA	SA	AB	H	2B	3B	HR	HR%	R	RBI	BB	SO	SB	Pinch Hit AB	Pinch Hit H	PO	A	E	DP	TC/G	FA	G by Pos
1951	WAS A	13	.211	.211	19	4	0	0	0	0.0	2	0	2	4	0	9	2	4	0	0	0	1.3	1.000	OF-3

Darrell Porter

PORTER, DARRELL RAY
B. Jan. 17, 1952, Joplin, Mo.
BL TR 6′ 193 lbs.

Year	Team	Games	BA	SA	AB	H	2B	3B	HR	HR%	R	RBI	BB	SO	SB	Pinch Hit AB	Pinch Hit H	PO	A	E	DP	TC/G	FA	G by Pos
1971	MIL A	22	.214	.329	70	15	2	0	2	2.9	4	9	9	20	2	1	0	108	18	3	2	5.9	.977	C-22
1972		18	.125	.196	56	7	1	0	1	1.8	2	2	5	21	0	0	0	113	8	3	3	6.9	.976	C-18
1973		117	.254	.457	350	89	19	2	16	4.6	50	67	57	85	5	9	4	372	47	10	9	3.9	.977	C-90, DH-19
1974		131	.241	.377	432	104	15	4	12	2.8	59	56	50	88	8	5	1	484	60	12	8	4.4	.978	C-117, DH-9
1975		130	.232	.418	409	95	12	5	18	4.4	66	60	89	77	2	2	0	532	82	13	10	5.0	.979	C-124, DH-2
1976		119	.208	.288	389	81	14	1	5	1.3	43	32	51	61	2	7	1	491	52	14	7	4.9	.975	C-111, DH-2
1977	KC A	130	.275	.452	425	117	21	3	16	3.8	61	60	53	70	1	5	2	663	61	13	4	5.8	.982	C-125, DH-1
1978		150	.265	.444	520	138	27	6	18	3.5	77	78	75	75	0	5	2	608	62	8	10	4.6	.988	C-145, DH-4
1979		157	.291	.484	533	155	23	10	20	3.8	101	112	**121**	65	3	0	0	628	68	13	15	4.5	.982	C-141, DH-15
1980		118	.249	.342	418	104	14	2	7	1.7	51	51	69	50	1	4	0	322	37	8	6	3.2	.978	C-81, DH-34
1981	STL N	61	.224	.408	174	39	10	2	6	3.4	22	31	39	32	1	6	0	206	31	5	2	4.7	.979	C-52
1982		120	.231	.402	373	86	18	5	12	3.2	46	48	66	66	1	8	1	469	64	9	8	4.9	.983	C-111
1983		145	.262	.431	443	116	24	3	15	3.4	57	66	68	94	1	19	6	578	70	7	8	4.9	.989	C-133
1984		127	.232	.363	422	98	16	3	11	2.6	56	68	60	79	5	11	2	620	58	11	6	5.6	.984	C-122
1985		84	.221	.412	240	53	12	2	10	4.2	30	36	41	48	6	6	2	386	26	4	4	5.1	.990	C-82
1986	TEX A	68	.265	.535	155	41	6	0	12	7.7	21	29	22	51	1	18	5	165	9	1	2	4.0	.994	C-25, DH-19
1987		85	.238	.423	130	31	3	0	7	5.4	19	21	30	43	0	36	7	21	2	0	2	0.5	1.000	DH-35, C-7, 1B-5
17 yrs.		1782	.247	.409	5539	1369	237	48	188	3.4	765	826	905	1025	39	142	33	6766	755	134	106	4.6	.982	C-1506, DH-140, 1B-5
LEAGUE CHAMPIONSHIP SERIES																								
1977	KC A	5	.333	.333	15	5	0	0	0	0.0	3	0	3	0	0	0	0	18	0	0	0	3.6	1.000	C-5
1978		4	.357	.429	14	5	1	0	0	0.0	1	3	2	0	0	0	0	21	1	0	1	5.5	1.000	C-4
1980		3	.100	.100	10	1	0	0	0	0.0	2	0	1	0	0	0	0	17	1	0	0	6.0	1.000	C-3
1982	STL N	3	.556	.889	9	5	3	0	0	0.0	3	1	5	2	0	0	0	15	3	0	0	6.0	1.000	C-3
1985		5	.267	.333	15	4	1	0	0	0.0	1	0	5	4	0	0	0	25	2	1	1	5.6	.964	C-5
5 yrs.		20	.317	.397	63	20	5	0	0	0.0	10	4	16 4th	6	0	0	0	96	7	1	2	5.2	.990	C-20
WORLD SERIES																								
1980	KC A	5	.143	.143	14	2	0	0	0	0.0	1	0	3	4	0	1	0	13	2	0	0	3.8	1.000	C-4
1982	STL N	7	.286	.464	28	8	2	0	1	3.6	1	5	1	4	0	0	0	33	2	0	1	5.0	1.000	C-7
1985		5	.133	.133	15	2	0	0	0	0.0	0	0	2	5	0	0	0	36	4	0	1	8.0	1.000	C-5
3 yrs.		17	.211	.298	57	12	2	0	1	1.8	2	5	6	13	0	1	0	82	8	0	2	5.6	1.000	C-16

Dick Porter

PORTER, RICHARD TWILLEY (Twitchy)
B. Dec. 30, 1901, Princess Anne, Md. D. Sept. 24, 1974, Philadelphia, Pa.
BL TR 5′10″ 170 lbs.

Year	Team	Games	BA	SA	AB	H	2B	3B	HR	HR%	R	RBI	BB	SO	SB	Pinch Hit AB	Pinch Hit H	PO	A	E	DP	TC/G	FA	G by Pos
1929	CLE A	71	.328	.479	192	63	16	5	1	0.5	26	24	17	14	3	20	9	95	63	8	8	3.2	.952	OF-30, 2B-22
1930		119	.350	.498	480	168	43	8	4	0.8	100	57	55	31	3	1	1	189	12	8	4	1.8	.962	OF-118

Dick Porter *continued*

Year	Team	Games	BA	SA	AB	H	2B	3B	HR	HR%	R	RBI	BB	SO	SB	Pinch Hit AB	Pinch Hit H	PO	A	E	DP	TC/G	FA	G by Pos
1931		114	.312	.391	414	129	24	3	1	0.2	82	38	56	36	6	4	1	187	12	6	0	1.9	.971	OF-109, 2B-1
1932		146	.308	.420	621	191	42	8	4	0.6	106	62	64	43	2	1	0	269	2	5	0	1.9	.982	OF-145
1933		132	.267	.329	499	133	19	6	0	0.0	73	41	51	42	4	6	2	236	9	1	3	2.0	.996	OF-124
1934	**2 teams**	**CLE A** (13G –.227) **BOS A** (80G –.302)																						
"	**total**	93	.291	.395	309	90	15	7	1	0.3	40	62	25	20	5	16	2	123	1	7	1	1.5	.947	OF-85
6 yrs.		675	.308	.414	2515	774	159	37	11	0.4	427	284	268	186	23	48	15	1099	99	35	16	1.9	.972	OF-611, 2B-23

Irv Porter

PORTER, IRVING MARBLE BB TR 5′9″ 155 lbs.
B. May 17, 1888, Lynn, Mass. D. Feb. 20, 1971, Lynn, Mass.

Year	Team	Games	BA	SA	AB	H	2B	3B	HR	HR%	R	RBI	BB	SO	SB	Pinch Hit AB	Pinch Hit H	PO	A	E	DP	TC/G	FA	G by Pos
1914	**CHI A**	1	.250	.250	4	1	0	0	0	0.0	1	0	0	1	0	0	0	1	0	0	0	1.0	1.000	OF-1

J. W. Porter

PORTER, J. W. (Jay) BR TR 6′2″ 180 lbs.
B. Jan. 17, 1933, Shawnee, Okla.

Year	Team	Games	BA	SA	AB	H	2B	3B	HR	HR%	R	RBI	BB	SO	SB	Pinch Hit AB	Pinch Hit H	PO	A	E	DP	TC/G	FA	G by Pos
1952	**STL A**	33	.250	.308	104	26	4	1	0	0.0	12	7	10	10	4	1	0	74	4	3	0	2.6	.963	OF-29, 3B-2
1955	**DET A**	24	.236	.273	55	13	2	0	0	0.0	6	3	8	15	0	8	2	72	2	0	5	5.3	1.000	1B-6, OF-4, C-4
1956		14	.095	.095	21	2	0	0	0	0.0	0	3	0	8	0	10	0	9	0	1	1	2.5	.900	OF-2, C-2
1957		58	.250	.350	140	35	8	0	2	1.4	14	18	14	20	0	17	4	118	11	6	5	3.2	.956	OF-27, C-12, 1B-3
1958	**CLE A**	40	.200	.353	85	17	1	0	4	4.7	13	19	9	23	0	17	3	108	10	0	1	4.7	1.000	C-20, 1B-4, 3B-1
1959	**2 teams**	**WAS A** (37G –.226) **STL N** (23G –.212)																						
"	**total**	60	.223	.317	139	31	7	0	2	1.4	13	12	12	20	0	6	2	198	25	1	4	4.0	.996	C-53, 1B-3
6 yrs.		229	.228	.316	544	124	22	1	8	1.5	58	62	53	96	4	59	11	579	52	11	16	3.7	.983	C-91, OF-62, 1B-16, 3B-3

Matt Porter

PORTER, MATTHEW SHELDON
B. 1859, N. Y. Deceased.
Manager 1884.

Year	Team	Games	BA	SA	AB	H	2B	3B	HR	HR%	R	RBI	BB	SO	SB	Pinch Hit AB	Pinch Hit H	PO	A	E	DP	TC/G	FA	G by Pos
1884	**KC U**	3	.083	.167	12	1	1	0	0	0.0	1		0	0		0	0	4	3	2	1	3.0	.778	OF-3

Jorge Posada

POSADA, JORGE RAFAEL BB TR 6′2″ 190 lbs.
Born Jorge Rafael Posada (Villeta).
B. Aug. 17, 1971, Santurce, Puerto Rico.

Year	Team	Games	BA	SA	AB	H	2B	3B	HR	HR%	R	RBI	BB	SO	SB	Pinch Hit AB	Pinch Hit H	PO	A	E	DP	TC/G	FA	G by Pos
1995	**NY A**	1	—	—	0	0	0	0	0	—	0	0	0	0	0	0	0	1	0	0	0	1.0	1.000	C-1
DIVISIONAL PLAYOFF SERIES																								
1995	**NY A**	1	—	—	0	0	0	0	0	—	1	0	0	0	0	0	0	0	0	0	0	0.0	—	

Leo Posada

POSADA, LEOPOLDO JESUS (Popy) BR TR 5′11″ 175 lbs.
Born Leopoldo Jesus Posada (Hernandez).
B. Apr. 15, 1936, Havana, Cuba.

Year	Team	Games	BA	SA	AB	H	2B	3B	HR	HR%	R	RBI	BB	SO	SB	Pinch Hit AB	Pinch Hit H	PO	A	E	DP	TC/G	FA	G by Pos
1960	**KC A**	10	.361	.556	36	13	0	2	1	2.8	8	2	3	7	1	1	0	11	1	0	0	1.3	1.000	OF-9
1961		116	.253	.366	344	87	10	4	7	2.0	37	53	36	84	0	12	5	205	8	6	0	2.1	.973	OF-102
1962		29	.196	.261	46	9	1	1	0	0.0	6	3	7	14	0	16	3	15	1	0	1	1.5	1.000	OF-11
3 yrs.		155	.256	.371	426	109	11	7	8	1.9	51	58	46	105	1	29	8	231	10	6	1	2.0	.976	OF-122

Scott Pose

POSE, SCOTT VERNON BL TR 5′11″ 165 lbs.
B. Feb. 11, 1967, Davenport, Iowa.

Year	Team	Games	BA	SA	AB	H	2B	3B	HR	HR%	R	RBI	BB	SO	SB	Pinch Hit AB	Pinch Hit H	PO	A	E	DP	TC/G	FA	G by Pos
1993	**FLA N**	15	.195	.244	41	8	2	0	0	0.0	0	3	2	4	0	5	0	14	0	0	0	1.4	1.000	OF-10

Lew Post

POST, LEWIS G.
B. Apr. 12, 1875, Woodland, Mich. D. Aug. 21, 1944, Chicago, Ill.

Year	Team	Games	BA	SA	AB	H	2B	3B	HR	HR%	R	RBI	BB	SO	SB	Pinch Hit AB	Pinch Hit H	PO	A	E	DP	TC/G	FA	G by Pos
1902	**DET A**	3	.083	.083	12	1	0	0	0	0.0	2	2	0		0	0	0	4	0	1	0	1.7	.800	OF-3

Sam Post

POST, SAMUEL GILBERT BL TL 6′1½″ 170 lbs.
B. Nov. 17, 1896, Richmond, Va. D. Mar. 31, 1971, Portsmouth, Va.

Year	Team	Games	BA	SA	AB	H	2B	3B	HR	HR%	R	RBI	BB	SO	SB	Pinch Hit AB	Pinch Hit H	PO	A	E	DP	TC/G	FA	G by Pos
1922	**BKN N**	9	.280	.280	25	7	0	0	0	0.0	3	4	1	4	1	1	1	54	1	1	1	7.0	.982	1B-8

Wally Post

POST, WALTER CHARLES BR TR 6′1″ 190 lbs.
B. July 9, 1929, St. Wendelin, Ohio D. Jan. 6, 1982, St. Henry, Ohio.

Year	Team	Games	BA	SA	AB	H	2B	3B	HR	HR%	R	RBI	BB	SO	SB	Pinch Hit AB	Pinch Hit H	PO	A	E	DP	TC/G	FA	G by Pos
1949	**CIN N**	6	.250	.250	8	2	0	0	0	0.0	1	1	0	3	0	2	2	3	0	1	0	1.3	.750	OF-3
1951		15	.220	.366	41	9	3	0	1	2.4	6	7	3	4	0	2	1	25	1	1	0	3.0	.963	OF-9
1952		19	.155	.276	58	9	1	0	2	3.4	5	7	4	20	0	3	0	38	1	0	0	2.4	1.000	OF-16
1953		11	.242	.364	33	8	1	0	1	3.0	3	4	4	6	1	0	0	22	2	1	0	2.3	.960	OF-11
1954		130	.255	.435	451	115	21	3	18	4.0	46	83	26	70	2	13	3	231	13	11	2	2.2	.957	OF-116
1955		154	.309	.574	601	186	33	3	40	6.7	116	109	60	**102**	7	0	0	298	13	7	2	2.1	.978	OF-154
1956		143	.249	.506	539	134	25	3	36	6.7	94	83	37	**124**	6	6	0	292	16	10	1	2.3	.969	OF-136
1957		134	.244	.437	467	114	26	2	20	4.3	68	74	33	84	2	10	2	252	12	4	4	2.2	.985	OF-124
1958	**PHI N**	110	.282	.449	379	107	21	3	12	3.2	51	62	32	74	0	20	5	185	12	10	0	2.3	.952	OF-91
1959		132	.254	.457	468	119	17	6	22	4.7	62	94	36	**101**	0	12	3	226	12	2	3	2.0	.992	OF-120
1960	**2 teams**	**PHI N** (34G –.286) **CIN N** (77G –.281)																						
"	**total**	111	.282	.520	333	94	20	1	19	5.7	47	50	37	75	0	24	2	168	9	2	0	2.0	.989	OF-89
1961	**CIN N**	99	.294	.585	282	83	16	3	20	7.1	44	57	22	61	0	25	7	133	7	6	3	1.8	.959	OF-81
1962		109	.263	.498	285	75	10	3	17	6.0	43	62	32	67	1	27	9	110	5	8	0	1.4	.935	OF-90
1963	**2 teams**	**CIN N** (5G –.000) **MIN A** (21G –.191)																						
"	**total**	26	.167	.315	54	9	0	1	2	3.7	7	6	2	18	0	12	0	17	0	0	0	1.3	1.000	OF-13
1964	**CLE A**	5	.000	.000	8	0	0	0	0	0.0	1	0	3	4	0	3	0	2	0	1	0	1.5	.667	OF-2
15 yrs.		1204	.266	.485	4007	1064	194	28	210	5.2	594	699	331	813	19	159	34	2002	103	64	15	2.1	.970	OF-1055
WORLD SERIES																								
1961	**CIN N**	5	.333	.556	18	6	1	0	1	5.6	3	2	0	1	0	0	0	8	0	0	0	1.6	1.000	OF-5

Mike Potter

POTTER, MICHAEL GARY BR TR 6′1″ 190 lbs.
B. May 16, 1951, Montebello, Calif.

Year	Team	Games	BA	SA	AB	H	2B	3B	HR	HR%	R	RBI	BB	SO	SB	Pinch Hit AB	Pinch Hit H	PO	A	E	DP	TC/G	FA	G by Pos
1976	**STL N**	9	.000	.000	16	0	0	0	0	0.0	0	0	1	6	0	5	0	9	0	0	0	2.3	1.000	OF-4
1977		5	.000	.000	7	0	0	0	0	0.0	0	0	0	2	0	5	0	0	0	0	0	0.0	.000	OF-1
2 yrs.		14	.000	.000	23	0	0	0	0	0.0	0	0	1	8	0	10	0	9	0	0	0	1.8	1.000	OF-5

Dan Potts

POTTS, VIVIAN
B. Jan. 1869, Bristol, Pa. Deceased.

Year	Team	Games	BA	SA	AB	H	2B	3B	HR	HR%	R	RBI	BB	SO	SB	Pinch Hit AB	Pinch Hit H	PO	A	E	DP	TC/G	FA	G by Pos
1892	**WAS N**	1	.250	.250	4	1	0	0	0	0.0	0	0	0	1	0	0	0	4	3	0	0	7.0	1.000	C-1

John Potts

POTTS, JOHN FREDERICK (Fred) BL TR 5′ 7″ 165 lbs.
B. Feb. 6, 1887, Tipp City, Ohio D. Sept. 5, 1962, Cleveland, Ohio.

Year	Team	Games	BA	SA	AB	H	2B	3B	HR	HR%	R	RBI	BB	SO	SB	Pinch Hit AB	Pinch Hit H	PO	A	E	DP	TC/G	FA	G by Pos
1914	**KC F**	41	.265	.333	102	27	4	0	1	1.0	14	9	25		7	8	1	40	2	3	2	1.5	.933	OF-31

Ken Poulsen

POULSEN, KEN STERLING BL TR 6′ 1″ 190 lbs.
B. Aug. 4, 1947, Van Nuys, Calif.

Year	Team	Games	BA	SA	AB	H	2B	3B	HR	HR%	R	RBI	BB	SO	SB	Pinch Hit AB	Pinch Hit H	PO	A	E	DP	TC/G	FA	G by Pos
1967	**BOS A**	5	.200	.400	5	1	1	0	0	0.0	0	0	0	2	0	2	0	0	2	1	0	1.0	.667	3B-2, SS-1

Abner Powell

POWELL, CHARLES ABNER BL TR 5′ 7″ 160 lbs.
B. Dec. 15, 1860, Shenandoah, Pa. D. Aug. 7, 1953, New Orleans, La.

Year	Team	Games	BA	SA	AB	H	2B	3B	HR	HR%	R	RBI	BB	SO	SB	Pinch Hit AB	Pinch Hit H	PO	A	E	DP	TC/G	FA	G by Pos
1884	**WAS U**	48	.283	.387	191	54	10	5	0	0.0	36		3			0	0	55	46	18	0	2.3	.849	OF-30, P-18, 3B-2, SS-1, 2B-1
1886	**2 teams**	**BAL AA** (11G –.179) **CIN AA** (19G –.230)																						
″	**total**	30	.212	.274	113	24	3	2	0	0.0	17		5			0	0	30	48	17	4	2.8	.821	OF-17, P-11, SS-6
2 yrs.		78	.257	.345	304	78	13	7	0	0.0	53		8			0	0	85	94	35	4	2.5	.836	OF-47, P-29, SS-7, 3B-2, 2B-1

Alonzo Powell

POWELL, ALONZO SIDNEY BR TR 6′ 2″ 190 lbs.
B. Dec. 12, 1964, San Francisco, Calif.

Year	Team	Games	BA	SA	AB	H	2B	3B	HR	HR%	R	RBI	BB	SO	SB	Pinch Hit AB	Pinch Hit H	PO	A	E	DP	TC/G	FA	G by Pos
1987	**MON N**	14	.195	.268	41	8	3	0	0	0.0	3	4	5	17	0	4	0	13	0	0	0	1.2	1.000	OF-11
1991	**SEA A**	57	.216	.369	111	24	6	1	3	2.7	16	12	11	24	0	13	2	66	2	2	4	1.3	.971	OF-40, 1B-7, DH-7
2 yrs.		71	.211	.342	152	32	9	1	3	2.0	19	16	16	41	0	17	2	79	2	2	4	1.3	.976	OF-51, 1B-7, DH-7

Bob Powell

POWELL, ROBERT LEROY BR TR 6′ 1″ 190 lbs.
B. Oct. 17, 1933, Flint, Mich.

Year	Team	Games	BA	SA	AB	H	2B	3B	HR	HR%	R	RBI	BB	SO	SB	Pinch Hit AB	Pinch Hit H	PO	A	E	DP	TC/G	FA	G by Pos
1955	**CHI A**	1	—	—	0	0	0	0	0	—	0	0	0	0	0	0	0	0	0	0	0	0.0	—	
1957		1	—	—	0	0	0	0	0	—	1	0	0	0	0	0	0	0	0	0	0	0.0	—	
2 yrs.		2	—	—	0	0	0	0	0	—	1	0	0	0	0	0	0	0	0	0	0	0.0	—	

Boog Powell

POWELL, JOHN WESLEY BL TR 6′ 4½″ 230 lbs.
B. Aug. 17, 1941, Lakeland, Fla.

Year	Team	Games	BA	SA	AB	H	2B	3B	HR	HR%	R	RBI	BB	SO	SB	Pinch Hit AB	Pinch Hit H	PO	A	E	DP	TC/G	FA	G by Pos
1961	**BAL A**	4	.077	.077	13	1	0	0	0	0.0	0	1	0	2	0	1	0	3	0	0	0	1.0	1.000	OF-3
1962		124	.242	.398	400	97	13	2	15	3.8	44	53	38	79	1	10	2	194	1	6	0	1.8	.970	OF-112, 1B-1
1963		140	.265	.470	491	130	22	2	25	5.1	67	82	49	87	1	3	1	316	18	9	11	2.4	.974	OF-121, 1B-23
1964		134	.290	**.606**	424	123	17	0	39	**9.2**	74	99	76	91	0	12	2	223	19	5	6	1.9	.980	OF-124, 1B-5
1965		144	.248	.407	472	117	20	2	17	3.6	54	72	71	93	1	8	1	658	53	5	50	4.8	.993	1B-78, OF-71
1966		140	.287	.532	491	141	18	0	34	6.9	78	109	67	125	0	4	2	1094	68	13	96	8.6	.989	1B-136
1967		125	.234	.366	415	97	14	1	13	3.1	53	55	55	94	1	13	4	903	64	14	82	8.6	.986	1B-114
1968		154	.249	.411	550	137	21	1	22	4.0	60	85	73	97	7	4	1	1293	79	14	102	9.3	.990	1B-149
1969		152	.304	.559	533	162	25	0	37	6.9	83	121	72	76	1	7	1	1192	84	7	105	8.9	.995	1B-144
1970		154	.297	.549	526	156	28	0	35	6.7	82	114	104	80	1	8	2	1209	89	10	107	9.0	.992	1B-145
1971		128	.256	.459	418	107	19	0	22	5.3	59	92	82	64	1	4	1	1031	67	5	97	8.9	.995	1B-124
1972		140	.252	.434	465	117	20	1	21	4.5	53	81	65	92	4	7	1	1116	70	15	111	9.0	.988	1B-133
1973		114	.265	.395	370	98	13	1	11	3.0	52	54	85	64	0	6	3	988	77	12	95	9.7	.989	1B-111
1974		110	.265	.413	344	91	13	1	12	3.5	37	45	52	58	0	8	1	866	61	4	102	9.0	.996	1B-102, DH-1
1975	**CLE A**	134	.297	.524	435	129	18	0	27	**6.2**	64	86	59	72	1	11	4	997	69	3	92	8.5	.997	1B-121, DH-5
1976		95	.215	.338	293	63	9	0	9	3.1	29	33	41	43	1	10	3	698	61	10	76	8.6	.987	1B-89
1977	**LA N**	50	.244	.244	41	10	0	0	0	0.0	0	5	12	9	0	36	8	15	0	1	1	4.0	.938	1B-4
17 yrs.		2042	.266	.462	6681	1776	270	11	339	5.1	889	1187	1001	1226	20	152	37	12796	880	133	1133	7.2	.990	1B-1479, OF-431, DH-6
LEAGUE CHAMPIONSHIP SERIES																								
1969	**BAL A**	3	.385	.615	13	5	0	0	1	7.7	2	1	2	0	0	0	0	34	0	0	2	11.3	1.000	1B-3
1970		3	.429	.786	14	6	2	0	1	7.1	2	6	0	3	0	0	0	24	1	0	3	8.3	1.000	1B-3
1971		3	.300	.900	10	3	0	0	2	20.0	4	3	3	3	0	0	0	28	2	0	3	10.0	1.000	1B-3
1973		1	.000	.000	4	0	0	0	0	0.0	1	0	0	1	0	0	0	7	0	0	0	7.0	1.000	1B-1
1974		2	.125	.125	8	1	0	0	0	0.0	0	1	0	0	0	0	0	22	1	0	1	11.5	1.000	1B-2
5 yrs.		12	.306	.592	49	15	2	0	4	8.2	9	11	5	7	0	0	0	115	4	0	9	9.9	1.000	1B-12
				6th						**3rd**														
WORLD SERIES																								
1966	**BAL A**	4	.357	.429	14	5	1	0	0	0.0	1	1	0	1	0	0	0	27	1	0	3	7.0	1.000	1B-4
1969		5	.263	.263	19	5	0	0	0	0.0	0	0	1	4	0	0	0	46	2	1	3	9.8	.980	1B-5
1970		5	.294	.706	17	5	1	0	2	11.8	6	5	5	2	0	0	0	38	2	0	3	8.0	1.000	1B-5
1971		7	.111	.111	27	3	0	0	0	0.0	1	1	1	3	0	0	0	52	4	1	1	8.1	.982	1B-7
4 yrs.		21	.234	.338	77	18	2	0	2	2.6	8	7	7	10	0	0	0	163	9	2	10	8.3	.989	1B-21

Hosken Powell

POWELL, HOSKEN BL TL 6′ 1″ 175 lbs.
B. May 14, 1955, Selma, Ala.

Year	Team	Games	BA	SA	AB	H	2B	3B	HR	HR%	R	RBI	BB	SO	SB	Pinch Hit AB	Pinch Hit H	PO	A	E	DP	TC/G	FA	G by Pos
1978	**MIN A**	121	.247	.333	381	94	20	2	3	0.8	55	31	45	31	11	7	2	219	9	4	2	2.0	.983	OF-117
1979		104	.293	.379	338	99	17	3	2	0.6	49	36	33	25	5	15	2	165	6	4	3	1.8	.977	OF-93, DH-5
1980		137	.262	.355	485	127	17	5	6	1.2	58	35	32	46	14	14	2	265	11	9	1	2.2	.968	OF-129
1981		80	.239	.326	264	63	11	3	2	0.8	30	25	17	31	7	11	3	122	6	4	1	1.8	.970	OF-64, DH-8
1982	**TOR A**	112	.275	.389	265	73	13	4	3	1.1	43	26	12	23	4	30	10	111	2	3	0	1.2	.974	OF-75, DH-19
1983		40	.169	.205	83	14	0	0	1	1.2	6	7	5	8	2	12	2	52	1	1	1	1.5	.981	OF-33, 1B-1, DH-1
6 yrs.		594	.259	.349	1816	470	78	17	17	0.9	241	160	144	164	43	89	21	934	35	25	8	1.8	.975	OF-511, DH-33, 1B-1

Jake Powell

POWELL, ALVIN JACOB BR TR 5′11½″ 180 lbs.
B. July 15, 1908, Silver Spring, Md. D. Nov. 4, 1948, Washington, D. C.

Year	Team	Games	BA	SA	AB	H	2B	3B	HR	HR%	R	RBI	BB	SO	SB	Pinch Hit AB	Pinch Hit H	PO	A	E	DP	TC/G	FA	G by Pos
1930	**WAS A**	3	.000	.000	4	0	0	0	0	0.0	1	0	0	1	0	1	0	3	0	0	0	1.5	1.000	OF-2
1934		9	.286	.343	35	10	2	0	0	0.0	6	1	4	2	1	0	0	18	3	1	0	2.4	.955	OF-9
1935		139	.312	.428	551	172	26	10	6	1.1	88	98	37	37	15	2	0	361	12	9	4	2.8	.976	OF-136, 2B-2
1936	**2 teams**	**WAS A** (53G –.290) **NY A** (87G –.306)																						
″	**total**	140	.299	.418	538	161	24	8	8	1.5	102	78	52	51	26	4	3	311	8	11	3	2.4	.967	OF-137
1937	**NY A**	97	.263	.364	365	96	22	3	3	0.8	54	45	25	36	7	3	0	201	5	4	2	2.2	.981	OF-94

Jake Powell *continued*

Year	Team	Games	BA	SA	AB	H	2B	3B	HR	HR%	R	RBI	BB	SO	SB	Pinch Hit AB	Pinch Hit H	PO	A	E	DP	TC/G	FA	G by Pos
1938		45	.256	.378	164	42	12	1	2	1.2	27	20	15	20	3	1	0	86	1	2	0	2.1	.978	OF-43
1939		31	.244	.349	86	21	4	1	1	1.2	12	9	3	8	1	4	1	56	1	1	0	2.5	.983	OF-23
1940		12	.185	.185	27	5	0	0	0	0.0	3	2	1	4	0	2	0	15	1	0	0	2.3	1.000	OF-7
1943	**WAS A**	37	.265	.371	132	35	10	2	0	0.0	14	20	5	13	3	3	1	83	4	2	0	2.7	.978	OF-33
1944		96	.240	.278	367	88	9	1	1	0.3	29	37	16	26	7	5	0	196	5	4	0	2.3	.980	OF-90, 3B-1
1945	**2 teams**	**WAS A** (31G –.194) **PHI N** (48G –.231)																						
"	**total**	79	.218	.255	271	59	7	0	1	0.4	17	17	16	21	2	4	1	123	6	4	3	1.9	.970	OF-71
11 yrs.		688	.271	.363	2540	689	116	26	22	0.9	353	327	174	219	65	29	6	1453	46	38	12	2.4	.975	OF-645, 2B-2, 3B-1
WORLD SERIES																								
1936	**NY A**	6	.455	.636	22	10	1	0	1	4.5	8	5	4	4	1	0	0	12	0	0	0	2.0	1.000	OF-6
1937		1	.000	.000	1	0	0	0	0	0.0	0	0	0	1	0	1	0	0	0	0	0	0.0	—	
1938		1	—	—	0	0	0	0	0	—	0	0	0	0	0	0	0	0	0	0	0	0.0	.000	OF-1
3 yrs.		8	.435	.609	23	10	1	0	1	4.3	8	5	4	5	1	1	0	12	0	0	0	1.7	1.000	OF-7

Jim Powell

POWELL, JAMES EDWIN 5′10″ 170 lbs.
B. Aug. 30, 1859, Richmond, Va. D. Nov. 20, 1929, Butte, Mont.

Year	Team	Games	BA	SA	AB	H	2B	3B	HR	HR%	R	RBI	BB	SO	SB	Pinch Hit AB	Pinch Hit H	PO	A	E	DP	TC/G	FA	G by Pos
1884	**RIC AA**	41	.245	.351	151	37	8	4	0	0.0	23		7			0	0	380	18	24	15	10.3	.943	1B-41

Martin Powell

POWELL, MARTIN J. BL TL 6′ 170 lbs.
B. Mar. 25, 1856, Fitchburg, Mass. D. Feb. 5, 1888, Fitchburg, Mass.

Year	Team	Games	BA	SA	AB	H	2B	3B	HR	HR%	R	RBI	BB	SO	SB	Pinch Hit AB	Pinch Hit H	PO	A	E	DP	TC/G	FA	G by Pos
1881	**DET N**	55	.338	.429	219	74	9	4	1	0.5	47	38	15	9		0	0	513	17	31	47	10.0	.945	1B-55, C-1
1882		80	.240	.287	338	81	13	0	1	0.3	44	29	19	27		0	0	680	14	44	27	9.2	.940	1B-80
1883		101	.273	.344	421	115	17	5	1	0.2	76		28	23		0	0	995	32	54	62	10.7	.950	1B-101
1884	**CIN U**	43	.319	.378	185	59	4	2	1	0.5	46		13			0	0	463	11	30	19	11.7	.940	1B-43
1885	**PHI AA**	19	.160	.240	75	12	0	3	0	0.0	5		1			0	0	178	3	5	6	9.8	.973	1B-19
5 yrs.		298	.275	.342	1238	341	43	14	4	0.3	218	67	76	59		0	0	2829	77	164	161	10.3	.947	1B-298, C-1

Paul Ray Powell

POWELL, PAUL RAY BR TR 5′11″ 185 lbs.
B. Mar. 19, 1948, San Angelo, Tex.

Year	Team	Games	BA	SA	AB	H	2B	3B	HR	HR%	R	RBI	BB	SO	SB	Pinch Hit AB	Pinch Hit H	PO	A	E	DP	TC/G	FA	G by Pos
1971	**MIN A**	20	.161	.258	31	5	0	0	1	3.2	7	2	3	12	0	2	0	24	0	0	0	1.6	1.000	OF-15
1973	**LA N**	2	.000	.000	1	0	0	0	0	0.0	0	0	0	1	0	1	0	0	0	0	0	0.0	.000	OF-1
1975		8	.200	.300	10	2	1	0	0	0.0	2	0	1	2	0	0	0	18	3	1	1	2.8	.955	C-7, OF-1
3 yrs.		30	.167	.262	42	7	1	0	1	2.4	9	2	4	15	0	3	0	42	3	1	1	1.9	.978	OF-17, C-7

Ray Powell

POWELL, RAYMOND RAETH (Rabbit) BL TR 5′ 9″ 160 lbs.
B. Nov. 20, 1888, Siloam Springs, Ark. D. Oct. 16, 1962, Chillicothe, Mo.

Year	Team	Games	BA	SA	AB	H	2B	3B	HR	HR%	R	RBI	BB	SO	SB	Pinch Hit AB	Pinch Hit H	PO	A	E	DP	TC/G	FA	G by Pos
1913	**DET A**	2	—	—	0	0	0	0	0	—	0	0	0	0	0	0	0	0	0	0	0	0.0	.000	OF-1
1917	**BOS N**	88	.272	.356	357	97	10	4	4	1.1	42	30	24	54	12	0	0	231	14	6	2	2.9	.976	OF-88
1918		53	.213	.303	188	40	7	5	0	0.0	31	20	29	30	2	0	0	121	8	7	2	2.6	.949	OF-53
1919		123	.236	.326	470	111	12	12	2	0.4	51	33	41	**79**	16	1	0	213	21	12	7	2.0	.951	OF-122
1920		147	.225	.314	609	137	12	12	6	1.0	69	29	44	83	10	0	0	370	25	18	5	2.8	.956	OF-147
1921		149	.306	.462	624	191	25	**18**	12	1.9	114	74	58	**85**	6	0	0	377	21	19	3	2.8	.954	OF-149
1922		142	.296	.409	550	163	22	11	6	1.1	82	37	59	66	3	5	0	377	18	8	2	3.0	.980	OF-136
1923		97	.302	.420	338	102	20	4	4	1.2	57	38	45	36	1	8	3	214	8	14	0	2.8	.941	OF-84
1924		74	.261	.335	188	49	9	1	1	0.5	21	15	21	28	1	23	6	117	9	7	3	2.9	.947	OF-46
9 yrs.		875	.268	.375	3324	890	117	67	35	1.1	467	276	321	461	51	37	9	2020	124	91	24	2.7	.959	OF-826

Tom Power

POWER, THOMAS E. 5′11″ 164 lbs.
B. San Francisco, Calif. D. Feb. 25, 1898, San Francisco, Calif.

Year	Team	Games	BA	SA	AB	H	2B	3B	HR	HR%	R	RBI	BB	SO	SB	Pinch Hit AB	Pinch Hit H	PO	A	E	DP	TC/G	FA	G by Pos
1890	**BAL AA**	38	.208	.248	125	26	3	1	0	0.0	11		13		6	0	0	289	39	20	12	9.2	.943	1B-26, 2B-12

Vic Power

POWER, VICTOR FELIPE BR TR 6′ 186 lbs.
Born Victor Felipe Pellot (Power).
B. Nov. 1, 1927, Arecibo, Puerto Rico.

Year	Team	Games	BA	SA	AB	H	2B	3B	HR	HR%	R	RBI	BB	SO	SB	Pinch Hit AB	Pinch Hit H	PO	A	E	DP	TC/G	FA	G by Pos
1954	**PHI A**	127	.255	.366	462	118	17	5	8	1.7	36	38	19	19	2	7	3	406	26	6	20	3.5	.986	OF-101, 1B-21, 3B-1, SS-1
1955	**KC A**	147	.319	.505	596	190	34	10	19	3.2	91	76	35	27	0	3	1	1281	130	10	140	9.9	.993	1B-144
1956		127	.309	.447	530	164	21	5	14	2.6	77	63	24	16	2	4	2	807	200	12	113	7.8	.988	1B-76, 2B-47, OF-7
1957		129	.259	.385	467	121	15	1	14	3.0	48	42	19	21	3	10	2	992	106	3	95	9.0	.997	1B-113, OF-6, 2B-4
1958	**2 teams**	**KC A** (52G –.302) **CLE A** (93G –.317)																						
"	**total**	145	.312	.490	590	184	37	**10**	16	2.7	98	80	20	14	3	3	0	806	220	12	122	6.3	.988	1B-91, 3B-42, 2B-28, SS-2, OF-1
1959	**CLE A**	147	.289	.412	595	172	31	6	10	1.7	102	60	40	22	9	0	0	1094	174	10	105	8.6	.992	1B-121, 2B-21, 3B-7
1960		147	.288	.395	580	167	26	3	10	1.7	69	84	24	20	9	0	0	1184	151	5	146	8.6	.996	1B-147, SS-5, 3B-4
1961		147	.268	.369	563	151	34	4	5	0.9	64	63	38	16	4	0	0	1174	164	10	108	9.1	.993	1B-141, 2B-7
1962	**MIN A**	144	.290	.421	611	177	28	2	16	2.6	80	63	22	35	7	3	2	1195	134	10	133	9.3	.993	1B-142, 2B-2
1963		138	.270	.384	541	146	28	2	10	1.8	65	52	22	24	3	7	2	947	129	12	95	7.4	.989	1B-124, 2B-18, 3B-5
1964	**3 teams**	**MIN A** (19G –.222) **LA A** (68G –.249) **PHI N** (18G –.208)																						
"	**total**	105	.239	.306	314	75	12	0	3	1.0	24	17	11	20	1	14	2	517	104	5	43	5.6	.992	1B-77, 3B-28, 2B-6
1965	**CAL A**	124	.259	.320	197	51	7	1	1	0.5	11	20	5	13	2	15	2	430	54	2	38	4.2	.996	1B-107, 2B-6, 3B-2
12 yrs.		1627	.284	.411	6046	1716	290	49	126	2.1	765	658	279	247	45	66	16	10833	1592	97	1158	7.6	.992	1B-1304, 2B-139, OF-115, 3B-89, SS-8

Johnny Powers

POWERS, JOHN CALVIN BL TR 6′ 1″ 185 lbs.
B. July 8, 1929, Birmingham, Ala.

Year	Team	Games	BA	SA	AB	H	2B	3B	HR	HR%	R	RBI	BB	SO	SB	Pinch Hit AB	Pinch Hit H	PO	A	E	DP	TC/G	FA	G by Pos
1955	**PIT N**	2	.250	.250	4	1	0	0	0	0.0	0	0	0	0	0	0	0	4	0	0	0	2.0	1.000	OF-2
1956		11	.048	.048	21	1	0	0	0	0.0	0	0	1	4	0	6	0	9	0	0	0	1.8	1.000	OF-5
1957		20	.286	.543	35	10	3	0	2	5.7	7	8	5	9	0	9	3	14	1	0	0	1.7	1.000	OF-8, 2B-1
1958		57	.183	.268	82	15	1	0	2	2.4	6	2	8	19	0	38	8	27	1	0	0	2.0	1.000	OF-14
1959	**CIN N**	43	.256	.488	43	11	2	1	2	4.7	8	4	3	13	0	36	8	4	0	0	0	0.8	1.000	OF-5
1960	**2 teams**	**BAL A** (10G –.111) **CLE A** (8G –.167)																						
"	**total**	18	.133	.233	30	4	1	1	0	0.0	5	0	5	3	0	9	0	13	0	1	0	1.6	.929	OF-9
6 yrs.		151	.195	.330	215	42	7	2	6	2.8	26	14	22	48	0	98	19	71	2	1	0	1.7	.986	OF-43, 2B-1

Les Powers

POWERS, LESLIE EDWIN BL TL 6′ 175 lbs.
B. Nov. 5, 1909, Seattle, Wash. D. Nov. 13, 1978, Santa Monica, Calif.

Year	Team	Games	BA	SA	AB	H	2B	3B	HR	HR%	R	RBI	BB	SO	SB	Pinch Hit AB	Pinch Hit H	PO	A	E	DP	TC/G	FA	G by Pos
1938	NY N	3	.000	.000	3	0	0	0	0	0.0	0	0	0	1	0	3	0	0	0	0	0	0.0	—	
1939	PHI N	19	.346	.404	52	18	1	1	0	0.0	7	2	4	6	0	4	1	112	4	2	10	9.1	.983	1B-13
2 yrs.		22	.327	.382	55	18	1	1	0	0.0	7	2	4	7	0	7	1	112	4	2	10	9.1	.983	1B-13

Mike Powers

POWERS, ELLIS FOREE BL TL 6′ 1″ 185 lbs.
B. Mar. 2, 1906, Toddspoint, Ky. D. Dec. 2, 1983, Louisville, Ky.

Year	Team	Games	BA	SA	AB	H	2B	3B	HR	HR%	R	RBI	BB	SO	SB	Pinch Hit AB	Pinch Hit H	PO	A	E	DP	TC/G	FA	G by Pos
1932	CLE A	14	.182	.303	33	6	4	0	0	0.0	4	5	2	2	0	5	0	11	0	1	0	1.5	.917	OF-8
1933		24	.277	.362	47	13	2	1	0	0.0	6	2	6	6	2	11	3	20	0	1	0	1.9	.952	OF-11
2 yrs.		38	.237	.338	80	19	6	1	0	0.0	10	7	8	8	2	16	3	31	0	2	0	1.7	.939	OF-19

Mike Powers

POWERS, MICHAEL RILEY BR TR
B. Sept. 22, 1870, Pittsfield, Mass. D. Apr. 26, 1909, Philadelphia, Pa.

Year	Team	Games	BA	SA	AB	H	2B	3B	HR	HR%	R	RBI	BB	SO	SB	Pinch Hit AB	Pinch Hit H	PO	A	E	DP	TC/G	FA	G by Pos
1898	LOU N	34	.273	.404	99	27	4	3	1	1.0	13	19	5		1	5	0	112	21	4	3	4.7	.971	C-22, 1B-6, OF-1
1899	2 teams	LOU N (49G –.207) WAS N (14G –.263)																						
″	total	63	.217	.285	207	45	10	2	0	0.0	18	25	7		1	5	0	208	41	16	6	4.6	.940	C-50, 1B-8
1901	PHI A	116	.251	.341	431	108	26	5	1	0.2	53	47	18		10	2	1	430	137	29	7	5.2	.951	C-111, 1B-3
1902		71	.264	.325	246	65	7	1	2	0.8	35	39	14		3	1	0	250	112	18	6	5.4	.953	C-68, 1B-3
1903		75	.227	.279	247	56	11	1	0	0.0	19	23	5		1	2	0	398	88	9	6	6.8	.982	C-66, 1B-7
1904		57	.190	.207	184	35	3	0	0	0.0	11	11	6		3	0	0	339	52	14	6	7.1	.965	C-56, OF-1
1905	3 teams	PHI A (19G –.131) NY A (11G –.182) PHI A (21G –.183)																						
″	total	51	.162	.169	154	25	1	0	0	0.0	11	12	4	0	4	0	0	290	54	14	6	7.0	.961	C-44, 1B-7
1906	PHI A	58	.157	.162	185	29	1	0	0	0.0	5	7	1		2	0	0	299	79	10	2	6.7	.974	C-57, 1B-1
1907		59	.182	.201	159	29	3	0	0	0.0	9	9	7		1	0	0	313	80	7	8	6.8	.983	C-59
1908		62	.180	.227	172	31	6	1	0	0.0	8	7	5		1	0	0	309	76	13	3	6.4	.967	C-60, 1B-2
1909		1	.250	.250	4	1	0	0	0	0.0	1	0	0		0	0	0	9	1	0	0	10.0	1.000	C-1
11 yrs.		647	.216	.269	2088	451	72	13	4	0.2	183	199	72	0	27	15	1	2957	741	134	53	6.1	.965	C-594, 1B-37, OF-2
WORLD SERIES																								
1905	PHI A	3	.143	.286	7	1	1	0	0	0.0	0	0	0	0	0	0	0	13	4	0	0	5.7	1.000	C-3

Phil Powers

POWERS, PHILLIP B. (Grandmother) BR TR 5′ 7″ 166 lbs.
B. July 26, 1854, New York, N. Y. D. Dec. 22, 1914, New York, N. Y.

Year	Team	Games	BA	SA	AB	H	2B	3B	HR	HR%	R	RBI	BB	SO	SB	Pinch Hit AB	Pinch Hit H	PO	A	E	DP	TC/G	FA	G by Pos
1878	CHI N	8	.161	.258	31	5	1	1	0	0.0	2	2	1	5		0	0	47	19	5	0	8.9	.930	C-8
1880	BOS N	37	.143	.183	126	18	5	0	0	0.0	11	10	5	15		0	0	152	59	37	6	6.4	.851	C-37, OF-2
1881	CLE N	5	.067	.067	15	1	0	0	0	0.0	1	0	1	2		0	0	17	5	1	1	4.6	.957	C-4, 3B-1
1882	CIN AA	16	.217	.267	60	13	1	1	0	0.0	4		3			0	0	89	13	7	3	6.8	.936	C-10, 1B-5, OF-1
1883		30	.246	.325	114	28	1	4	0	0.0	16		3			0	0	74	20	12	0	3.5	.887	C-17, OF-13
1884		34	.138	.146	130	18	1	0	0	0.0	10		5			0	0	160	56	26	5	6.9	.893	C-31, OF-2, 1B-2
1885	2 teams	CIN AA (15G –.267) BAL AA (9G –.118)																						
″	total	24	.213	.245	94	20	3	0	0	0.0	12		1			0	0	101	30	25	1	6.5	.840	C-23, OF-1
7 yrs.		154	.181	.223	570	103	12	6	0	0.0	56	12	19	22		0	0	640	202	113	16	6.1	.882	C-130, OF-19, 1B-7, 3B-1

Carl Powis

POWIS, CARL EDGAR (Jug) BR TR 6′ 185 lbs.
B. Jan. 11, 1928, Philadelphia, Pa.

Year	Team	Games	BA	SA	AB	H	2B	3B	HR	HR%	R	RBI	BB	SO	SB	Pinch Hit AB	Pinch Hit H	PO	A	E	DP	TC/G	FA	G by Pos
1957	BAL A	15	.195	.317	41	8	3	1	0	0.0	4	2	7	9	2	2	0	19	1	2	0	1.7	.909	OF-13

Arquimedez Pozo

POZO, ARQUIMEDEZ BR TR 5′10″ 160 lbs.
Born Arquimedez Pozo (Ortiz).
B. Aug. 24, 1973, Santo Domingo, Dominican Republic.

Year	Team	Games	BA	SA	AB	H	2B	3B	HR	HR%	R	RBI	BB	SO	SB	Pinch Hit AB	Pinch Hit H	PO	A	E	DP	TC/G	FA	G by Pos
1995	SEA A	1	.000	.000	1	0	0	0	0	0.0	0	0	0	0	0	1	0	0	1	0	0	1.0	1.000	2B-1

Johnny Pramesa

PRAMESA, JOHN STEVEN BR TR 6′ 2″ 210 lbs.
B. Aug. 28, 1925, Barton, Ohio.

Year	Team	Games	BA	SA	AB	H	2B	3B	HR	HR%	R	RBI	BB	SO	SB	Pinch Hit AB	Pinch Hit H	PO	A	E	DP	TC/G	FA	G by Pos
1949	CIN N	17	.240	.400	25	6	1	0	1	4.0	2	2	3	5	0	4	1	27	1	1	0	2.2	.966	C-13
1950		74	.307	.425	228	70	10	1	5	2.2	14	30	19	15	0	1	0	328	37	7	2	5.1	.981	C-73
1951		72	.229	.348	227	52	5	2	6	2.6	12	22	5	17	0	9	2	241	27	9	4	4.4	.968	C-63
1952	CHI N	22	.283	.370	46	13	1	0	1	2.2	1	5	4	4	0	5	2	62	6	3	3	4.2	.958	C-17
4 yrs.		185	.268	.386	526	141	17	3	13	2.5	29	59	31	41	0	19	5	658	71	20	9	4.5	.973	C-166

Del Pratt

PRATT, DERRILL BURNHAM BR TR 5′11″ 175 lbs.
B. Jan. 10, 1888, Walhalla, S. C. D. Sept. 30, 1977, Texas City, Tex.

Year	Team	Games	BA	SA	AB	H	2B	3B	HR	HR%	R	RBI	BB	SO	SB	Pinch Hit AB	Pinch Hit H	PO	A	E	DP	TC/G	FA	G by Pos
1912	STL A	151	.302	.426	570	172	26	15	5	0.9	76	69	36		24	0	0	339	407	51	61	5.3	.936	2B-121, SS-21, OF-8, 3B-1
1913		155	.296	.402	592	175	31	13	2	0.3	60	87	40	57	37	0	0	440	431	42	60	5.9	.954	2B-146, 1B-9
1914		158	.283	.411	584	165	34	13	5	0.9	85	65	50	45	37	0	0	372	425	46	48	5.3	.945	2B-152, OF-5, SS-1
1915		159	.291	.394	602	175	31	11	3	0.5	61	78	26	43	32	0	0	417	441	31	82	5.6	.965	2B-158
1916		158	.267	.391	596	159	35	12	5	0.8	64	**103**	54	56	26	0	0	438	491	33	74	6.1	.966	2B-158
1917		123	.247	.338	450	111	22	8	1	0.2	40	53	33	36	18	0	0	346	355	29	64	5.9	.960	2B-119, 1B-4
1918	NY A	126	.275	.356	477	131	19	7	2	0.4	65	55	35	26	12	0	0	340	386	23	82	5.9	.969	2B-126
1919		140	.292	.393	527	154	27	7	4	0.8	69	56	36	24	22	0	0	315	491	26	64	5.9	.969	2B-140
1920		154	.314	.427	574	180	37	8	4	0.7	84	97	50	24	12	0	0	354	515	26	77	5.8	.971	2B-154
1921	BOS A	135	.324	.461	521	169	36	10	5	1.0	80	100	44	10	8	1	0	283	408	28	90	5.4	.961	2B-134
1922		154	.301	.427	607	183	44	7	6	1.0	73	86	53	20	7	0	0	362	484	30	80	5.7	.966	2B-154
1923	DET A	101	.310	.391	297	92	18	3	0	0.0	43	40	25	9	5	8	4	281	179	18	32	5.4	.962	2B-60, 1B-17, 3B-12
1924		121	.303	.399	429	130	32	3	1	0.2	56	77	31	10	6	1	0	621	225	23	73	7.4	.974	2B-63, 1B-51, 3B-4
13 yrs.		1835	.292	.403	6826	1996	392	117	43	0.6	856	966	513	360	246	10	4	4908	5238	406	887	5.8	.962	2B-1685, 1B-81, SS-22, 3B-17, OF-13

Frank Pratt

PRATT, FRANCIS BRUCE (Truckhorse) BL TR 5′ 9½″ 155 lbs.
B. Aug. 24, 1897, Blocton, Ala. D. Mar. 8, 1974, Centreville, Ala.

Year	Team	Games	BA	SA	AB	H	2B	3B	HR	HR%	R	RBI	BB	SO	SB	Pinch Hit AB	Pinch Hit H	PO	A	E	DP	TC/G	FA	G by Pos
1921	CHI A	1	.000	.000	1	0	0	0	0	0.0	0	0	0	0	0	1	0	0	0	0	0	0.0	—	

Larry Pratt

PRATT, LESTER JOHN BR TR 6′ 183 lbs.
B. Oct. 8, 1886, Gibson City, Ill. D. Jan. 8, 1969, Peoria, Ill.

Year	Team		Games	BA	SA	AB	H	2B	3B	HR	HR%	R	RBI	BB	SO	SB	Pinch Hit AB	Pinch Hit H	PO	A	E	DP	TC/G	FA	G by Pos
1914	BOS	A	5	.000	.000	4	0	0	0	0	0.0	0	0	0	4	0	0	0	7	5	1	0	2.6	.923	C-5
1915	2 teams	BKN F (20G –.184) NWK F (5G –.500)																							
″	total		25	.208	.321	53	11	3	0	1	1.9	7	2	5		4	4	0	59	22	4	0	4.3	.953	C-20
2 yrs.			30	.193	.298	57	11	3	0	1	1.8	7	2	5	4	4	4	0	66	27	5	0	3.9	.949	C-25

Todd Pratt

PRATT, TODD ALAN BR TR 6′ 3″ 195 lbs.
B. Feb. 9, 1967, Bellevue, Neb.

Year	Team		Games	BA	SA	AB	H	2B	3B	HR	HR%	R	RBI	BB	SO	SB	Pinch Hit AB	Pinch Hit H	PO	A	E	DP	TC/G	FA	G by Pos
1992	PHI	N	16	.283	.435	46	13	1	0	2	4.3	6	10	4	12	0	4	0	65	4	2	1	6.5	.972	C-11
1993			33	.287	.529	87	25	6	0	5	5.7	8	13	5	19	0	6	1	169	7	2	3	6.8	.989	C-26
1994			28	.196	.333	102	20	6	1	2	2.0	10	9	12	29	0	0	0	172	9	0	1	6.5	1.000	C-28
1995	CHI	N	25	.133	.167	60	8	2	0	0	0.0	3	4	6	21	0	0	0	149	9	3	0	6.4	.981	C-25
4 yrs.			102	.224	.373	295	66	15	1	9	3.1	27	36	27	81	0	10	1	555	29	7	5	6.6	.988	C-90
LEAGUE CHAMPIONSHIP SERIES																									
1993	PHI	N	1	.000	.000	1	0	0	0	0	0.0	0	0	0	1	0	0	0	1	0	0	0	1.0	1.000	C-1

Mel Preibisch

PREIBISCH, MELVIN ALOYSIUS (Primo) BR TR 5′11″ 185 lbs.
B. Nov. 23, 1914, Sealy, Tex. D. Apr. 12, 1980, Sealy, Tex.

Year	Team		Games	BA	SA	AB	H	2B	3B	HR	HR%	R	RBI	BB	SO	SB	Pinch Hit AB	Pinch Hit H	PO	A	E	DP	TC/G	FA	G by Pos
1940	BOS	N	11	.225	.275	40	9	2	0	0	0.0	3	5	2	4	0	0	0	29	1	0	0	2.7	1.000	OF-11
1941			5	.000	.000	4	0	0	0	0	0.0	0	0	1	2	0	2	0	1	0	0	0	0.5	1.000	OF-2
2 yrs.			16	.205	.250	44	9	2	0	0	0.0	3	5	3	6	0	2	0	30	1	0	0	2.4	1.000	OF-13

Bobby Prescott

PRESCOTT, GEORGE BERTRAND BR TR 5′11″ 180 lbs.
B. Mar. 27, 1931, Colon, Panama.

Year	Team		Games	BA	SA	AB	H	2B	3B	HR	HR%	R	RBI	BB	SO	SB	Pinch Hit AB	Pinch Hit H	PO	A	E	DP	TC/G	FA	G by Pos
1961	KC	A	10	.083	.083	12	1	0	0	0	0.0	0	0	2	5	0	7	1	0	0	0	0	0.0	.000	OF-2

Jim Presley

PRESLEY, JAMES ARTHUR BR TR 6′ 1″ 176 lbs.
B. Oct. 23, 1961, Pensacola, Fla.

Year	Team		Games	BA	SA	AB	H	2B	3B	HR	HR%	R	RBI	BB	SO	SB	Pinch Hit AB	Pinch Hit H	PO	A	E	DP	TC/G	FA	G by Pos
1984	SEA	A	70	.227	.402	251	57	12	1	10	4.0	27	36	6	63	1	1	0	48	113	7	12	2.4	.958	3B-69, DH-1
1985			155	.275	.484	570	157	33	1	28	4.9	71	84	44	100	2	1	0	82	335	17	24	2.8	.961	3B-154
1986			155	.265	.463	616	163	33	4	27	4.4	83	107	32	172	0	0	0	110	308	15	31	2.8	.965	3B-155
1987			152	.247	.433	575	142	23	6	24	4.2	78	88	38	157	2	1	1	113	315	21	29	2.9	.953	3B-148, SS-4, DH-1
1988			150	.230	.355	544	125	26	0	14	2.6	50	62	36	114	3	0	0	112	234	22	25	2.5	.940	3B-146, DH-4
1989			117	.236	.385	390	92	20	1	12	3.1	42	41	21	107	0	6	1	222	169	18	29	3.4	.956	3B-90, 1B-30, DH-1
1990	ATL	N	140	.242	.414	541	131	34	1	19	3.5	59	72	29	130	1	1	0	178	242	26	29	3.0	.942	3B-133, 1B-17
1991	SD	N	20	.136	.186	59	8	0	0	1	1.7	3	5	4	16	0	4	1	13	23	3	0	2.4	.923	3B-16
8 yrs.			959	.247	.420	3546	875	181	14	135	3.8	413	495	210	859	9	14	3	878	1739	129	179	2.8	.953	3B-911, 1B-47, DH-7, SS-4

Walt Preston

PRESTON, WALTER B. BL TR 6′ 175 lbs.
B. 1870, Richmond, Va. Deceased.

Year	Team		Games	BA	SA	AB	H	2B	3B	HR	HR%	R	RBI	BB	SO	SB	Pinch Hit AB	Pinch Hit H	PO	A	E	DP	TC/G	FA	G by Pos
1895	LOU	N	50	.279	.365	197	55	6	4	1	0.5	42	24	17	17	11	0	0	71	54	33	5	3.1	.791	OF-26, 3B-25

Jackie Price

PRICE, JOHN THOMAS REID BL TR 5′10½″ 150 lbs.
B. Nov. 13, 1912, Winborn, Miss. D. Oct. 2, 1967, San Francisco, Calif.

Year	Team		Games	BA	SA	AB	H	2B	3B	HR	HR%	R	RBI	BB	SO	SB	Pinch Hit AB	Pinch Hit H	PO	A	E	DP	TC/G	FA	G by Pos
1946	CLE	A	7	.231	.231	13	3	0	0	0	0.0	1	0	0	0	0	2	1	7	11	1	1	4.8	.947	SS-4

Jim Price

PRICE, JIMMIE WILLIAM BR TR 6′ 192 lbs.
B. Oct. 13, 1941, Harrisburg, Pa.

Year	Team		Games	BA	SA	AB	H	2B	3B	HR	HR%	R	RBI	BB	SO	SB	Pinch Hit AB	Pinch Hit H	PO	A	E	DP	TC/G	FA	G by Pos
1967	DET	A	44	.261	.304	92	24	4	0	0	0.0	9	8	4	10	0	20	5	139	8	4	1	6.3	.974	C-24
1968			64	.174	.273	132	23	4	0	3	2.3	12	13	13	14	0	22	5	223	14	1	1	5.7	.996	C-42
1969			72	.234	.417	192	45	8	0	9	4.7	21	28	18	20	0	21	2	337	18	4	4	7.0	.989	C-51
1970			52	.182	.326	132	24	4	0	5	3.8	12	15	21	23	0	12	1	266	8	6	2	7.4	.979	C-38
1971			29	.241	.333	54	13	2	0	1	1.9	4	7	6	3	0	2	0	99	7	2	2	4.3	.981	C-25
5 yrs.			261	.214	.341	602	129	22	0	18	3.0	58	71	62	70	0	77	13	1064	55	17	10	6.3	.985	C-180
WORLD SERIES																									
1968	DET	A	2	.000	.000	2	0	0	0	0	0.0	0	0	0	1	0	2	0	0	0	0	0	0.0	—	

Joe Price

PRICE, JOSEPH PRESTON (Lumber) BR TR 6′ 1½″ 187 lbs.
B. Apr. 10, 1897, Milligan College, Tenn. D. Jan. 15, 1961, Washington, D. C.

Year	Team		Games	BA	SA	AB	H	2B	3B	HR	HR%	R	RBI	BB	SO	SB	Pinch Hit AB	Pinch Hit H	PO	A	E	DP	TC/G	FA	G by Pos
1928	NY	N	1	.000	.000	1	0	0	0	0	0.0	0	0	0	1	0	0	0	0	0	0	0	0.0	.000	OF-1

Bob Prichard

PRICHARD, ROBERT ALEXANDER BL TL 6′ 1″ 195 lbs.
B. Oct. 21, 1917, Paris, Tex. D. Sept. 25, 1991, Abilene, Tex.

Year	Team		Games	BA	SA	AB	H	2B	3B	HR	HR%	R	RBI	BB	SO	SB	Pinch Hit AB	Pinch Hit H	PO	A	E	DP	TC/G	FA	G by Pos
1939	WAS	A	26	.235	.294	85	20	5	0	0	0.0	8	8	19	16	0	0	0	251	13	2	30	10.2	.992	1B-26

Gerry Priddy

PRIDDY, GERALD EDWARD BR TR 5′11½″ 180 lbs.
B. Nov. 9, 1919, Los Angeles, Calif. D. Mar. 3, 1980, North Hollywood, Calif.

Year	Team		Games	BA	SA	AB	H	2B	3B	HR	HR%	R	RBI	BB	SO	SB	Pinch Hit AB	Pinch Hit H	PO	A	E	DP	TC/G	FA	G by Pos
1941	NY	A	56	.213	.270	174	37	7	0	1	0.6	18	26	18	16	4	2	1	167	119	8	46	5.3	.973	2B-31, 3B-14, 1B-10
1942			59	.280	.381	189	53	9	2	2	1.1	23	28	31	27	0	3	1	146	114	9	26	4.7	.967	3B-35, 1B-11, 2B-8, SS-3
1943	WAS	A	149	.271	.359	560	152	31	3	4	0.7	68	62	67	76	5	0	0	398	451	27	111	5.8	.969	2B-134, SS-15, 3B-1
1946			138	.254	.364	511	130	22	8	6	1.2	54	58	57	73	9	0	0	378	428	32	105	6.1	.962	2B-138
1947			147	.214	.283	505	108	20	3	3	0.6	42	49	62	79	7	1	0	382	405	16	89	5.5	.980	2B-146
1948	STL	A	151	.296	.443	560	166	40	9	8	1.4	96	79	86	71	6	3	0	407	471	29	132	6.2	.968	2B-146
1949			145	.290	.414	544	158	26	4	11	2.0	83	63	80	81	5	0	0	407	415	27	96	5.9	.968	2B-145
1950	DET	A	157	.277	.401	618	171	26	6	13	2.1	104	75	95	95	2	0	0	440	542	19	150	6.4	.981	2B-157
1951			154	.260	.360	584	152	22	6	8	1.4	73	57	69	73	4	0	0	438	464	18	118	5.9	.980	2B-154, SS-1
1952			75	.283	.430	279	79	23	3	4	1.4	37	20	42	29	1	0	0	211	209	14	48	5.8	.968	2B-75
1953			65	.235	.301	196	46	6	2	1	0.5	14	24	17	19	1	9	2	203	118	5	35	5.6	.985	2B-45, 1B-11, 3B-2
11 yrs.			1296	.265	.373	4720	1252	232	46	61	1.3	612	541	624	639	44	18	4	3577	3736	204	956	5.9	.973	2B-1179, 3B-52, 1B-32, SS-19
WORLD SERIES																									
1942	NY	A	3	.100	.200	10	1	1	0	0	0.0	0	1	1	0	0	0	0	22	4	1	1	6.8	.963	1B-3, 3B-1

Curtis Pride

PRIDE, CURTIS JOHN
B. Dec. 17, 1968, Washington, D. C.
BL TR 6′ 205 lbs.

Year	Team	Games	BA	SA	AB	H	2B	3B	HR	HR%	R	RBI	BB	SO	SB	Pinch Hit AB	Pinch Hit H	PO	A	E	DP	TC/G	FA	G by Pos
1993	MON N	10	.444	1.111	9	4	1	1	1	11.1	3	5	0	3	1	8	4	2	0	0	0	1.0	1.000	OF-2
1995		48	.175	.190	63	11	1	0	0	0.0	10	2	5	16	3	18	2	23	0	2	0	1.0	.920	OF-24
2 yrs.		58	.208	.306	72	15	2	1	1	1.4	13	7	5	19	4	26	6	25	0	2	0	1.0	.926	OF-26

Johnnie Priest

PRIEST, JOHN GOODING
B. June 23, 1886, St. Joseph, Mo. D. Nov. 4, 1979, Washington, D. C.
BR TR 5′11″ 170 lbs.

Year	Team	Games	BA	SA	AB	H	2B	3B	HR	HR%	R	RBI	BB	SO	SB	Pinch Hit AB	Pinch Hit H	PO	A	E	DP	TC/G	FA	G by Pos
1911	NY A	7	.143	.143	21	3	0	0	0	0.0	2	2	2		3	0	0	8	10	3	0	3.0	.857	2B-5, 3B-2
1912		2	.500	.500	2	1	0	0	0	0.0	1	1	0		0	2	1	0	0	0	0	0.0	—	
2 yrs.		9	.174	.174	23	4	0	0	0	0.0	3	3	2		3	2	1	8	10	3	0	3.0	.857	2B-5, 3B-2

Tom Prince

PRINCE, THOMAS ALBERT
B. Aug. 13, 1964, Kankakee, Ill.
BR TR 5′11″ 185 lbs.

Year	Team	Games	BA	SA	AB	H	2B	3B	HR	HR%	R	RBI	BB	SO	SB	Pinch Hit AB	Pinch Hit H	PO	A	E	DP	TC/G	FA	G by Pos
1987	PIT N	4	.222	.667	9	2	1	0	1	11.1	1	2	0	2	0	0	0	14	3	0	0	4.3	1.000	C-4
1988		29	.176	.203	74	13	2	0	0	0.0	3	6	4	15	0	2	0	108	8	2	1	4.2	.983	C-28
1989		21	.135	.212	52	7	4	0	0	0.0	1	5	6	12	1	0	0	85	11	4	1	4.8	.960	C-21
1990		4	.100	.100	10	1	0	0	0	0.0	1	0	1	2	0	1	0	16	1	0	0	5.7	1.000	C-3
1991		26	.265	.441	34	9	3	0	1	2.9	4	2	7	3	0	5	0	53	9	1	0	3.2	.984	C-19, 1B-1
1992		27	.091	.136	44	4	2	0	0	0.0	1	5	6	9	1	6	0	76	8	2	0	4.3	.977	C-19, 3B-1
1993		66	.196	.307	179	35	14	0	2	1.1	14	24	13	38	1	8	3	271	31	5	6	5.2	.984	C-59
1994	LA N	3	.333	.333	6	2	0	0	0	0.0	2	1	1	3	0	0	0	11	1	0	0	4.0	1.000	C-3
1995		18	.200	.375	40	8	2	1	1	2.5	3	4	4	10	0	2	0	71	8	1	1	4.7	.988	C-17
9 yrs.		198	.181	.281	448	81	28	1	5	1.1	30	49	42	94	3	24	3	705	80	15	9	4.6	.981	C-173, 3B-1, 1B-1

Walter Prince

PRINCE, WALTER FARR
B. May 9, 1861, Amherst, N. H. D. Mar. 2, 1938, Bristol, N. H.
BL TR 5′ 9″ 150 lbs.

Year	Team	Games	BA	SA	AB	H	2B	3B	HR	HR%	R	RBI	BB	SO	SB	Pinch Hit AB	Pinch Hit H	PO	A	E	DP	TC/G	FA	G by Pos
1883	LOU AA	4	.182	.182	11	2	0	0	0	0.0	1		0			0	0	14	2	6	0	4.4	.727	1B-2, OF-2, SS-1
1884	3 teams	DET N (7G –.143) WAS AA (43G –.217) WAS U (1G –.250)																						
″	total	51	.209	.246	191	40	3	2	0	0.0	22		16	4		0	0	417	4	33	19	8.9	.927	1B-44, OF-7
2 yrs.		55	.208	.243	202	42	3	2	0	0.0	23		16	4		0	0	431	6	39	19	8.5	.918	1B-46, OF-9, SS-1

Buddy Pritchard

PRITCHARD, HAROLD WILLIAM
B. Jan. 25, 1936, South Gate, Calif.
BR TR 6′ 1″ 195 lbs.

Year	Team	Games	BA	SA	AB	H	2B	3B	HR	HR%	R	RBI	BB	SO	SB	Pinch Hit AB	Pinch Hit H	PO	A	E	DP	TC/G	FA	G by Pos
1957	PIT N	23	.091	.091	11	1	0	0	0	0.0	1	0	0	4	0	5	0	11	8	1	3	1.5	.950	SS-10, 2B-3

George Proeser

PROESER, GEORGE (White Wings)
B. May 30, 1864, Cincinnati, Ohio D. Oct. 14, 1941, New Burlington, Ohio.
BL TL 5′10″ 190 lbs.

Year	Team	Games	BA	SA	AB	H	2B	3B	HR	HR%	R	RBI	BB	SO	SB	Pinch Hit AB	Pinch Hit H	PO	A	E	DP	TC/G	FA	G by Pos
1888	CLE AA	7	.304	.391	23	7	2	0	0	0.0	5	1	1		0	0	0	0	11	2	0	1.9	.846	P-7
1890	SYR AA	13	.245	.358	53	13	1	1	1	1.9	11		10		1	0	0	16	1	2	0	1.5	.895	OF-13
2 yrs.		20	.263	.368	76	20	3	1	1	1.3	16	1	11		1	0	0	16	12	4	0	1.6	.875	OF-13, P-7

Jake Propst

PROPST, WILLIAM JACOB
B. Mar. 10, 1895, Kennedy, Ala. D. Feb. 24, 1967, Columbus, Miss.
BL TR 5′10″ 165 lbs.

Year	Team	Games	BA	SA	AB	H	2B	3B	HR	HR%	R	RBI	BB	SO	SB	Pinch Hit AB	Pinch Hit H	PO	A	E	DP	TC/G	FA	G by Pos
1923	WAS A	1	.000	.000	1	0	0	0	0	0.0	0	0	0	0	0	1	0	0	0	0	0	0.0	—	

Doc Prothro

PROTHRO, JAMES THOMPSON
B. July 16, 1893, Memphis, Tenn. D. Oct. 14, 1971, Memphis, Tenn.
Manager 1939–41.
BR TR 5′10½″ 170 lbs.

Year	Team	Games	BA	SA	AB	H	2B	3B	HR	HR%	R	RBI	BB	SO	SB	Pinch Hit AB	Pinch Hit H	PO	A	E	DP	TC/G	FA	G by Pos
1920	WAS A	6	.385	.385	13	5	0	0	0	0.0	2	2	0	4	0	2	1	4	5	0	4	2.3	1.000	SS-2, 3B-2
1923		6	.250	.500	8	2	0	1	0	0.0	2	3	1	3	0	0	0	5	11	0	0	2.7	1.000	3B-6
1924		46	.333	.465	159	53	11	5	0	0.0	17	24	15	11	4	0	0	40	68	10	6	2.6	.915	3B-45
1925	BOS A	119	.313	.383	415	130	23	3	0	0.0	44	51	52	21	9	7	0	122	216	20	17	3.2	.944	3B-108, SS-3
1926	CIN N	3	.200	.600	5	1	0	1	0	0.0	1	1	1	1	0	1	0	0	2	0	0	1.0	1.000	3B-2
5 yrs.		180	.318	.408	600	191	34	10	0	0.0	66	81	69	40	13	10	1	171	302	30	27	3.0	.940	3B-163, SS-5

Gibby Pruess

PRUESS, EARL HENRY
B. Apr. 2, 1895, Chicago, Ill. D. Aug. 28, 1979, Branson, Mo.
BR TR 5′10½″ 170 lbs.

Year	Team	Games	BA	SA	AB	H	2B	3B	HR	HR%	R	RBI	BB	SO	SB	Pinch Hit AB	Pinch Hit H	PO	A	E	DP	TC/G	FA	G by Pos
1920	STL A	1	—	—	0	0	0	0	0	—	1	0	1	0	1	0	0	2	0	0	0	2.0	1.000	OF-1

Jim Pruett

PRUETT, JAMES CALVIN
B. Dec. 16, 1917, Nashville, Tenn.
BR TR 5′10″ 178 lbs.

Year	Team	Games	BA	SA	AB	H	2B	3B	HR	HR%	R	RBI	BB	SO	SB	Pinch Hit AB	Pinch Hit H	PO	A	E	DP	TC/G	FA	G by Pos
1944	PHI A	3	.250	.250	4	1	0	0	0	0.0	1	0	1	0	0	1	0	7	1	0	1	4.0	1.000	C-2
1945		6	.222	.222	9	2	0	0	0	0.0	1	0	1	2	0	2	0	12	1	0	0	3.3	1.000	C-4
2 yrs.		9	.231	.231	13	3	0	0	0	0.0	2	0	2	2	0	3	0	19	2	0	1	3.5	1.000	C-6

Ron Pruitt

PRUITT, RONALD RALPH (Do-It)
B. Oct. 21, 1951, Flint, Mich.
BR TR 6′ 185 lbs.

Year	Team	Games	BA	SA	AB	H	2B	3B	HR	HR%	R	RBI	BB	SO	SB	Pinch Hit AB	Pinch Hit H	PO	A	E	DP	TC/G	FA	G by Pos
1975	TEX A	14	.176	.176	17	3	0	0	0	0.0	2	0	1	3	0	0	0	21	5	0	0	1.9	1.000	C-13, OF-1
1976	CLE A	47	.267	.302	86	23	1	1	0	0.0	7	5	16	8	2	7	3	73	16	1	2	2.1	.989	OF-26, 3B-6, C-6, DH-4, 1B-1
1977		78	.288	.379	219	63	10	2	2	0.9	29	32	28	22	2	8	1	113	6	3	0	1.6	.975	OF-69, C-4, DH-4, 3B-1
1978		71	.235	.374	187	44	6	1	6	3.2	17	17	16	20	2	10	3	199	15	4	4	3.1	.982	C-48, OF-16, DH-5, 3B-2
1979		64	.283	.361	166	47	7	0	2	1.2	23	21	19	21	2	18	6	66	5	2	1	1.3	.973	OF-29, DH-14, C-11, 3B-3
1980	2 teams	CLE A (23G –.306) CHI A (33G –.300)																						
″	total	56	.302	.387	106	32	3	0	2	1.9	9	15	12	13	0	20	5	34	2	1	1	1.0	.973	OF-17, DH-9, C-5, 3B-5, 1B-1
1981	CLE A	5	.000	.000	9	0	0	0	0	0.0	0	0	1	2	0	2	0	3	0	0	0	0.6	1.000	OF-3, DH-1, C-1
1982	SF N	5	.500	.750	4	2	1	0	0	0.0	1	2	1	1	0	2	1	5	0	0	0	2.5	1.000	C-1, OF-1
1983		1	.000	.000	1	0	0	0	0	0.0	0	0	0	0	0	1	0	0	0	0	0	0.0	—	
9 yrs.		341	.269	.360	795	214	28	4	12	1.5	88	92	94	90	8	68	19	514	49	11	8	1.9	.981	OF-162, C-89, DH-37, 3B-17, 1B-2

Greg Pryor

PRYOR, GREGORY RUSSELL
B. Oct. 2, 1949, Marietta, Ohio.
BR TR 6′ 180 lbs.

Year	Team	Games	BA	SA	AB	H	2B	3B	HR	HR%	R	RBI	BB	SO	SB	Pinch Hit AB	Pinch Hit H	PO	A	E	DP	TC/G	FA	G by Pos
1976	TEX A	5	.375	.375	8	3	0	0	0	0.0	2	1	0	1	0	0	0	4	8	0	1	2.4	1.000	2B-3, 3B-1, SS-1
1978	CHI A	82	.261	.338	222	58	11	0	2	0.9	27	15	11	18	3	0	0	100	202	11	31	3.8	.965	2B-35, SS-28, 3B-20
1979		143	.275	.355	476	131	23	3	3	0.6	60	34	35	41	3	1	0	218	447	26	69	4.2	.962	SS-119, 2B-25, 3B-22

Greg Pryor *continued*

Year	Team	Lg	Games	BA	SA	AB	H	2B	3B	HR	HR%	R	RBI	BB	SO	SB	Pinch Hit AB	Pinch Hit H	PO	A	E	DP	TC/G	FA	G by Pos
1980			122	.240	.325	338	81	18	4	1	0.3	32	29	12	35	2	5	1	130	344	16	55	4.0	.967	SS-76, 3B-41, 2B-5, DH-1
1981			47	.224	.237	76	17	1	0	0	0.0	4	6	6	8	0	1	0	27	65	6	8	2.2	.939	3B-27, SS-13, 2B-5
1982	**KC**	**A**	73	.270	.388	152	41	10	1	2	1.3	23	12	10	20	2	3	0	78	112	5	18	2.6	.974	3B-40, 2B-15, 1B-14, SS-7
1983			68	.217	.278	115	25	4	0	1	0.9	9	14	7	8	0	1	0	38	100	5	10	2.1	.965	3B-60, 1B-6, 2B-3
1984			123	.263	.356	270	71	11	1	4	1.5	32	25	12	28	0	3	1	87	190	8	27	2.2	.972	3B-105, 2B-22, SS-2, DH-1, 1B-1
1985			63	.219	.272	114	25	3	0	1	0.9	8	3	8	12	0	6	0	47	87	5	16	2.3	.964	3B-26, 2B-20, SS-13, DH-1, 1B-1
1986			63	.170	.205	112	19	4	0	0	0.0	7	7	3	14	1	4	1	30	88	6	15	1.9	.952	3B-35, SS-17, 2B-12, 1B-1
10 yrs.			789	.250	.327	1883	471	85	9	14	0.7	204	146	104	185	11	24	3	759	1643	88	250	3.0	.965	3B-377, SS-276, 2B-145, 1B-23, DH-3
LEAGUE CHAMPIONSHIP SERIES																									
1984	**KC**	**A**	1	—	—	0	0	0	0	0	—	0	0	0	0	0	0	0	1	0	0	0	1.0	1.000	3B-1
WORLD SERIES																									
1985	**KC**	**A**	1	—	—	0	0	0	0	0	—	0	0	0	0	0	0	0	0	1	0	0	1.0	1.000	3B-1

George Puccinelli

PUCCINELLI, GEORGE LAWRENCE (Count)
B. June 22, 1907, San Francisco, Calif. D. Apr. 16, 1956, San Francisco, Calif.
BR TR 6′½″ 190 lbs.

Year	Team	Lg	Games	BA	SA	AB	H	2B	3B	HR	HR%	R	RBI	BB	SO	SB	Pinch Hit AB	Pinch Hit H	PO	A	E	DP	TC/G	FA	G by Pos
1930	**STL**	**N**	11	.563	1.188	16	9	1	0	3	18.8	5	8	0	1	0	8	4	2	0	0	0	0.7	1.000	OF-3
1932			31	.278	.435	108	30	8	0	3	2.8	17	11	12	13	1	1	0	59	6	4	1	2.3	.942	OF-30
1934	**STL**	**A**	10	.231	.500	26	6	1	0	2	7.7	4	5	1	8	0	4	0	15	1	1	0	2.8	.941	OF-6
1936	**PHI**	**A**	135	.278	.429	457	127	30	3	11	2.4	83	78	65	70	2	17	3	245	11	14	1	2.3	.948	OF-117
4 yrs.			187	.283	.453	607	172	40	3	19	3.1	109	102	78	92	3	30	7	321	18	19	2	2.3	.947	OF-156
WORLD SERIES																									
1930	**STL**	**N**	1	.000	.000	1	0	0	0	0	0.0	0	0	0	0	0	1	0	0	0	0	0	0.0	—	

Kirby Puckett

PUCKETT, KIRBY
B. Mar. 14, 1961, Chicago, Ill.
BR TR 5′ 8″ 215 lbs.

Year	Team	Lg	Games	BA	SA	AB	H	2B	3B	HR	HR%	R	RBI	BB	SO	SB	Pinch Hit AB	Pinch Hit H	PO	A	E	DP	TC/G	FA	G by Pos
1984	**MIN**	**A**	128	.296	.336	557	165	12	5	0	0.0	63	31	16	69	14	0	0	438	16	3	4	3.6	.993	OF-128
1985			161	.288	.385	**691**	199	29	13	4	0.6	80	74	41	87	21	1	0	465	19	8	5	3.1	.984	OF-161
1986			161	.328	.537	680	223	37	6	31	4.6	119	96	34	99	20	4	1	429	8	6	3	2.8	.986	OF-160
1987			157	.332	.534	624	**207**	32	5	28	4.5	96	99	32	91	12	2	0	341	8	5	2	2.3	.986	OF-147, DH-8
1988			158	.356	.545	**657**	**234**	42	5	24	3.7	109	121	23	83	6	1	0	450	12	3	4	2.9	.994	OF-158
1989			159	**.339**	.465	635	**215**	45	4	9	1.4	75	85	41	59	11	2	1	438	13	4	3	2.9	.991	OF-157, DH-2
1990			146	.298	.446	551	164	40	3	12	2.2	82	80	57	73	5	1	1	354	9	4	3	2.5	.989	OF-141, DH-4, SS-1, 3B-1, 2B-1
1991			152	.319	.460	611	195	29	6	15	2.5	92	89	31	78	11	0	0	373	13	6	5	2.6	.985	OF-152
1992			160	.329	.490	639	**210**	38	4	19	3.0	104	110	44	97	17	2	1	394	9	3	3	2.5	.993	OF-149, DH-9, 3B-2, 2B-2, SS-1
1993			156	.296	.474	622	184	39	3	22	3.5	89	89	47	93	8	0	0	312	13	2	2	2.1	.994	OF-139, DH-17
1994			108	.317	.540	439	139	32	3	20	4.6	79	**112**	28	47	6	0	0	204	13	3	1	2.0	.986	OF-95, DH-13
1995			137	.314	.515	538	169	39	0	23	4.3	83	99	56	89	3	1	0	194	10	4	0	1.5	.981	OF-109, DH-28, 2B-1, SS-1, 3B-1
12 yrs.			1783	.318	.477	7244	2304	414	57	207	2.9	1071	1085	450	965	134	14	4	4392	143	51	35	2.6	.989	OF-1696, DH-81, 3B-4, 2B-4, SS-3
LEAGUE CHAMPIONSHIP SERIES																									
1987	**MIN**	**A**	5	.208	.375	24	5	1	0	1	4.2	3	3	0	5	1	0	0	7	0	0	0	1.4	1.000	OF-5
1991			5	.429	.762	21	9	1	0	2	9.5	4	6	1	4	0	0	0	13	1	0	0	2.8	1.000	OF-5
2 yrs.			10	.311	.556 8th	45	14	2	0	3	6.7 7th	7	9	1	9	1	0	0	20	1	0	0	2.1	1.000	OF-10
WORLD SERIES																									
1987	**MIN**	**A**	7	.357	.464	28	10	1	1	0	0.0	5	3	2	1	1	0	0	15	1	1	0	2.4	.941	OF-7
1991			7	.250	.583	24	6	0	1	2	8.3	4	4	5	7	1	0	0	16	1	0	0	2.4	1.000	OF-7
2 yrs.			14	.308	.519	52	16	1	2	2	3.8	9	7	7	8	2	0	0	31	2	1	0	2.4	.971	OF-14

John Puhl

PUHL, JOHN
B. July 10, 1876, Brooklyn, N. Y. D. Aug. 24, 1900, Bayonne, N. J.

Year	Team	Lg	Games	BA	SA	AB	H	2B	3B	HR	HR%	R	RBI	BB	SO	SB	Pinch Hit AB	Pinch Hit H	PO	A	E	DP	TC/G	FA	G by Pos
1898	**NY**	**N**	2	.222	.222	9	2	0	0	0	0.0	1	1	0		0	0	0	1	5	3	1	4.5	.667	3B-2
1899			1	.000	.000	2	0	0	0	0	0.0	0	0	0		0	0	0	0	2	1	0	3.0	.667	3B-1
2 yrs.			3	.182	.182	11	2	0	0	0	0.0	1	1	0		0	0	0	1	7	4	1	4.0	.667	3B-3

Terry Puhl

PUHL, TERRY STEPHEN
B. July 8, 1956, Melville, Sask., Canada.
BL TR 6′ 2″ 195 lbs.

Year	Team	Lg	Games	BA	SA	AB	H	2B	3B	HR	HR%	R	RBI	BB	SO	SB	Pinch Hit AB	Pinch Hit H	PO	A	E	DP	TC/G	FA	G by Pos
1977	**HOU**	**N**	60	.301	.402	229	69	13	5	0	0.0	40	10	30	31	10	0	0	119	3	1	0	2.1	.992	OF-59
1978			149	.289	.368	585	169	25	6	3	0.5	87	35	48	46	32	1	1	386	6	3	2	2.7	.992	OF-148
1979			157	.287	.377	600	172	22	4	8	1.3	87	49	58	46	30	5	1	352	7	0	3	2.4	1.000	OF-152
1980			141	.282	.419	535	151	24	5	13	2.4	75	55	60	52	27	6	0	311	14	3	3	2.4	.991	OF-135
1981			96	.251	.354	350	88	19	4	3	0.9	43	28	31	49	22	8	1	185	5	0	1	2.2	1.000	OF-88
1982			145	.262	.379	507	133	17	9	8	1.6	64	50	51	49	17	7	3	257	4	3	3	1.9	.989	OF-138
1983			137	.292	.428	465	136	25	7	8	1.7	66	44	36	48	24	15	4	220	4	2	1	1.8	.991	OF-124
1984			132	.301	.434	449	135	19	7	9	2.0	66	55	59	45	13	5	2	213	6	3	4	1.8	.986	OF-126
1985			57	.284	.418	194	55	14	3	2	1.0	34	23	18	23	6	3	1	92	3	0	1	1.8	1.000	OF-53
1986			81	.244	.355	172	42	10	0	3	1.7	17	14	15	24	3	28	8	65	0	0	0	1.4	1.000	OF-47
1987			90	.230	.320	122	28	5	0	2	1.6	9	15	11	16	1	52	15	48	0	1	0	1.2	.980	OF-40
1988			113	.303	.389	234	71	7	2	3	1.3	42	19	35	30	22	36	11	116	2	2	0	1.5	.983	OF-78
1989			121	.271	.364	354	96	25	4	0	0.0	41	27	45	39	9	15	4	212	3	0	1	2.0	1.000	OF-103, 1B-3
1990			37	.293	.317	41	12	1	0	0	0.0	5	8	5	7	1	20	8	9	0	0	0	1.0	1.000	OF-8, 1B-1
1991	**KC**	**A**	15	.222	.222	18	4	0	0	0	0.0	0	3	3	2	0	10	2	0	0	0	0	0.0		DH-2, OF-1
15 yrs.			1531	.280	.388	4855	1361	226	56	62	1.3	676	435	505	507	217	211	61	2585	57	18	19	2.0	.993	OF-1300, 1B-4, DH-2
DIVISIONAL PLAYOFF SERIES																									
1981	**HOU**	**N**	5	.190	.238	21	4	1	0	0	0.0	2	0	0	1	1	0	0	7	1	0	0	1.6	1.000	OF-5

Terry Puhl *continued*

LEAGUE CHAMPIONSHIP SERIES

Year	Team	Games	BA	SA	AB	H	2B	3B	HR	HR%	R	RBI	BB	SO	SB	Pinch Hit AB	Pinch Hit H	PO	A	E	DP	TC/G	FA	G by Pos
1980	HOU N	5	.526	.632	19	10	2	0	0	0.0	4	3	3	2	2	1	0	13	0	0	0	3.3	1.000	OF-4
1986		3	.667	.667	3	2	0	0	0	0.0	0	0	0	0	1	3	2	0	0	0	0	0.0	—	
2 yrs.		8	.545	.636	22	12	2	0	0	0.0	4	3	3	2	3	4	2	13	0	0	0	3.3	1.000	OF-4

Rich Puig

PUIG, RICHARD GERALD
B. Mar. 16, 1953, Tampa, Fla.

BL TR 5′10″ 165 lbs.

Year	Team	Games	BA	SA	AB	H	2B	3B	HR	HR%	R	RBI	BB	SO	SB	Pinch Hit AB	Pinch Hit H	PO	A	E	DP	TC/G	FA	G by Pos
1974	NY N	4	.000	.000	10	0	0	0	0	0.0	0	0	1	2	0	0	0	7	6	1	2	3.5	.929	2B-3, 3B-1

Luis Pujols

PUJOLS, LUIS BIENVENIDO
Born Luis Bienvenido Pujols (Toribio).
B. Nov. 18, 1955, Santiago, Dominican Republic.

BR TR 6′ 2″ 175 lbs.

Year	Team	Games	BA	SA	AB	H	2B	3B	HR	HR%	R	RBI	BB	SO	SB	Pinch Hit AB	Pinch Hit H	PO	A	E	DP	TC/G	FA	G by Pos
1977	HOU N	6	.067	.067	15	1	0	0	0	0.0	0	0	0	5	0	0	0	18	4	0	0	3.7	1.000	C-6
1978		56	.131	.216	153	20	8	1	1	0.7	11	11	12	45	0	0	0	272	33	6	2	5.6	.981	C-55, 1B-1
1979		26	.227	.280	75	17	2	1	0	0.0	7	8	2	14	0	0	0	136	6	1	0	5.5	.993	C-26
1980		78	.199	.235	221	44	6	1	0	0.0	15	20	13	29	0	7	0	349	35	4	5	5.1	.990	C-75, 3B-1
1981		40	.239	.308	117	28	3	1	1	0.9	5	14	10	17	1	3	1	192	14	1	1	5.3	.995	C-39
1982		65	.199	.324	176	35	6	2	4	2.3	8	15	10	40	0	1	0	295	39	3	3	5.3	.991	C-64
1983		40	.195	.218	87	17	2	0	0	0.0	4	12	5	14	0	0	0	180	20	6	0	5.3	.971	C-39
1984	KC A	4	.200	.200	5	1	0	0	0	0.0	0	1	0	0	0	1	0	9	0	0	0	2.3	1.000	C-4
1985	TEX A	1	1.000	1.000	1	1	0	0	0	0.0	0	0	0	0	0	0	0	1	0	0	0	1.0	1.000	C-1
9 yrs.		316	.193	.260	850	164	27	6	6	0.7	50	81	52	164	1	12	1	1452	151	21	11	5.2	.987	C-309, 3B-1, 1B-1
DIVISIONAL PLAYOFF SERIES																								
1981	HOU N	2	.000	.000	6	0	0	0	0	0.0	0	0	0	1	0	0	0	12	1	0	0	6.5	1.000	C-2
LEAGUE CHAMPIONSHIP SERIES																								
1980	HOU N	4	.100	.300	10	1	0	1	0	0.0	1	0	3	0	0	0	0	21	2	0	0	5.8	1.000	C-4

Harvey Pulliam

PULLIAM, HARVEY JEROME
B. Oct. 20, 1967, San Francisco, Calif.

BR TR 6′ 210 lbs.

Year	Team	Games	BA	SA	AB	H	2B	3B	HR	HR%	R	RBI	BB	SO	SB	Pinch Hit AB	Pinch Hit H	PO	A	E	DP	TC/G	FA	G by Pos
1991	KC A	18	.273	.576	33	9	1	0	3	9.1	4	4	3	9	0	3	0	21	1	2	0	1.6	.917	OF-15
1992		4	.200	.400	5	1	1	0	0	0.0	2	0	1	3	0	0	0	3	0	0	0	1.0	1.000	DH-2, OF-1
1993		27	.258	.387	62	16	5	0	1	1.6	7	6	2	14	0	6	1	33	0	1	0	1.3	.971	OF-26
1995	CLR N	5	.400	1.200	5	2	1	0	1	20.0	1	3	0	2	0	4	2	0	0	0	0	0.0	.000	OF-1
4 yrs.		54	.267	.486	105	28	8	0	5	4.8	14	13	6	28	0	13	3	57	1	3	0	1.4	.951	OF-43, DH-2

Blondie Purcell

PURCELL, WILLIAM ALOYSIUS
B. Mar. 16, 1854, Paterson, N. J. D. Feb. 20, 1912, Trenton, N. J.
Manager 1883.

BR TR 5′ 9½″ 159 lbs.

Year	Team	Games	BA	SA	AB	H	2B	3B	HR	HR%	R	RBI	BB	SO	SB	Pinch Hit AB	Pinch Hit H	PO	A	E	DP	TC/G	FA	G by Pos
1879	2 teams	SYR N (63G –.260) CIN N (12G –.220)																						
″	total	75	.254	.291	327	83	6	3	0	0.0	42	29	3	16		0	0	98	41	33	0	2.1	.808	OF-57, P-24, C-1
1880	CIN N	77	.292	.378	325	95	13	6	1	0.3	48	24	5	13		0	0	88	54	25	1	2.1	.850	OF-55, P-25, SS-1
1881	2 teams	CLE N (20G –.175) BUF N (30G –.292)																						
″	total	50	.244	.321	193	47	9	3	0	0.0	18	21	14	16		0	0	74	24	29	0	2.4	.772	OF-45, P-9
1882	BUF N	84	.276	.371	380	105	18	6	2	0.5	79		14	27		0	0	144	21	35	0	2.3	.825	OF-82, P-6
1883	PHI N	97	.268	.346	425	114	20	5	1	0.2	70		13	26		0	0	130	146	66	9	3.4	.807	3B-46, OF-44, P-11
1884		103	.252	.318	428	108	11	7	1	0.2	67		29	30		0	0	182	12	28	1	2.1	.874	OF-103, P-1
1885	2 teams	PHI AA (66G –.296) BOS N (21G –.218)																						
″	total	87	.279	.350	391	109	16	6	0	0.0	80	3	19	15		0	0	97	16	19	1	1.5	.856	OF-87, P-1
1886	BAL AA	26	.224	.247	85	19	0	1	0	0.0	17		17			0	0	35	4	6	0	1.6	.867	OF-26, SS-1, P-1
1887		140	.250	.344	567	142	25	8	4	0.7	101		46		88	0	0	203	18	18	5	1.7	.925	OF-140, P-1
1888	2 teams	BAL AA (101G –.236) PHI AA (18G – 167)																						
″	total	119	.227	.286	472	107	12	5	2	0.4	63	45	32		26	0	0	172	14	20	4	1.7	.903	OF-117, SS-2, 3B-1, 1B-1
1889	PHI AA	129	.316	.381	507	160	19	7	0	0.0	72	85	50	27	22	0	0	172	15	20	3	1.6	.903	OF-129
1890		110	.276	.363	463	128	28	3	2	0.4	110		43		48	0	0	170	17	10	3	1.8	.949	OF-110
12 yrs.		1097	.267	.340	4563	1217	177	60	13	0.3	767	207	285	170	184	0	0	1565	382	309	27	2.0	.863	OF-995, P-79, 3B-47, SS-4, 1B-1, C-1

Pid Purdy

PURDY, EVERETT VIRGIL
B. June 15, 1904, Beatrice, Neb. D. Jan. 16, 1951, Beatrice, Neb.

BL TR 5′ 6″ 150 lbs.

Year	Team	Games	BA	SA	AB	H	2B	3B	HR	HR%	R	RBI	BB	SO	SB	Pinch Hit AB	Pinch Hit H	PO	A	E	DP	TC/G	FA	G by Pos
1926	CHI A	11	.182	.303	33	6	2	1	0	0.0	5	6	2	1	0	2	0	17	1	0	0	2.0	1.000	OF-9
1927	CIN N	18	.355	.565	62	22	2	4	1	1.6	15	12	4	3	0	2	1	35	0	2	0	2.3	.946	OF-16
1928		70	.309	.368	223	69	11	1	0	0.0	32	25	23	13	1	8	6	137	3	5	1	2.4	.966	OF-61
1929		82	.271	.381	181	49	7	5	1	0.6	22	16	19	8	2	33	8	84	3	2	0	2.1	.978	OF-42
4 yrs.		181	.293	.393	499	146	22	11	2	0.4	74	59	48	25	3	45	15	273	7	9	1	2.3	.969	OF-128

Jesse Purnell

PURNELL, JESSE RHOADES (Scrappy)
B. May 11, 1881, Glenside, Pa. D. July 4, 1966, Philadelphia, Pa.

BL TR 5′ 5½″ 140 lbs.

Year	Team	Games	BA	SA	AB	H	2B	3B	HR	HR%	R	RBI	BB	SO	SB	Pinch Hit AB	Pinch Hit H	PO	A	E	DP	TC/G	FA	G by Pos
1904	PHI N	7	.105	.105	19	2	0	0	0	0.0	2	1	4		1	0	0	7	12	3	0	3.1	.864	3B-7

Billy Purtell

PURTELL, WILLIAM PATRICK
B. Jan. 6, 1886, Columbus, Ohio D. Mar. 17, 1962, Bradenton, Fla.

BR TR 5′ 9″ 170 lbs.

Year	Team	Games	BA	SA	AB	H	2B	3B	HR	HR%	R	RBI	BB	SO	SB	Pinch Hit AB	Pinch Hit H	PO	A	E	DP	TC/G	FA	G by Pos
1908	CHI A	26	.130	.159	69	9	2	0	0	0.0	3	3	2		2	1	0	18	60	5	5	3.3	.940	3B-25
1909		103	.258	.299	361	93	9	3	0	0.0	34	40	19		14	0	0	162	248	24	24	4.2	.945	3B-71, 2B-32
1910	2 teams	CHI A (102G –.234) BOS A (49G –.208)																						
″	total	151	.226	.267	536	121	6	5	2	0.4	36	51	39		7	0	0	166	341	52	20	3.7	.907	3B-143, SS-8
1911	BOS A	27	.280	.415	82	23	5	3	0	0.0	5	7	1		1	5	1	29	35	10	1	3.2	.865	3B-16, SS-3, 2B-3, OF-1
1914	DET A	26	.171	.224	76	13	4	0	0	0.0	4	3	2	7	0	8	1	21	36	4	2	3.4	.934	3B-16, SS-1, 2B-1
5 yrs.		333	.230	.278	1124	259	26	11	2	0.2	82	104	63	7	24	14	2	396	720	95	52	3.8	.922	3B-271, 2B-36, SS-12, OF-1

Ed Putman

PUTMAN, EDDY WILLIAM BR TR 6′ 1″ 190 lbs.
B. Sept. 25, 1953, Los Angeles, Calif.

Year	Team	Games	BA	SA	AB	H	2B	3B	HR	HR%	R	RBI	BB	SO	SB	Pinch Hit AB	Pinch Hit H	PO	A	E	DP	TC/G	FA	G by Pos
1976	CHI N	5	.429	.429	7	3	0	0	0	0.0	0	0	0	0	0	2	1	16	0	0	0	4.0	1.000	C-3, 1B-1
1978		17	.200	.200	25	5	0	0	0	0.0	2	3	4	6	0	5	2	15	13	2	1	2.3	.933	3B-8, 1B-3, C-2
1979	DET A	21	.231	.462	39	9	3	0	2	5.1	4	4	4	12	0	3	0	75	7	1	5	4.0	.988	C-16, 1B-5
3 yrs.		43	.239	.366	71	17	3	0	2	2.8	6	7	8	18	0	10	3	106	20	3	6	3.4	.977	C-21, 1B-9, 3B-8

Pat Putnam

PUTNAM, PATRICK EDWARD BL TR 6′ 205 lbs.
B. Dec. 3, 1953, Bethel, Vt.

Year	Team	Games	BA	SA	AB	H	2B	3B	HR	HR%	R	RBI	BB	SO	SB	Pinch Hit AB	Pinch Hit H	PO	A	E	DP	TC/G	FA	G by Pos
1977	TEX A	11	.308	.462	26	8	4	0	0	0.0	3	3	1	4	0	2	1	35	1	0	3	3.6	1.000	1B-7, DH-3
1978		20	.152	.239	46	7	1	0	1	2.2	4	2	2	5	0	5	1	15	1	0	1	1.0	1.000	DH-12, 1B-4
1979		139	.277	.458	426	118	19	2	18	4.2	57	64	23	50	1	21	8	832	62	5	65	7.0	.994	1B-96, DH-32
1980		147	.263	.407	410	108	16	2	13	3.2	42	55	36	49	0	18	8	979	80	9	107	7.7	.992	1B-137, DH-1, 3B-1
1981		95	.266	.418	297	79	17	2	8	2.7	33	35	17	38	4	2	0	771	64	7	65	8.7	.992	1B-94, OF-3
1982		43	.230	.344	122	28	8	0	2	1.6	14	9	10	18	0	6	1	287	24	3	26	7.7	.990	1B-39, OF-1, 3B-1
1983	SEA A	144	.269	.448	469	126	23	2	19	4.1	58	67	39	57	2	12	4	1067	85	7	105	8.5	.994	1B-125, DH-11
1984	2 teams	SEA A (64G –.200) MIN A (14G –.079)																						
″	total	78	.176	.244	193	34	7	0	2	1.0	12	20	16	39	3	25	4	46	6	1	7	1.6	.981	DH-14, OF-13, 1B-6
8 yrs.		677	.255	.406	1989	508	95	8	63	3.2	223	255	144	260	10	91	27	4032	323	32	379	7.3	.993	1B-508, DH-73, OF-17, 3B-2

Jim Pyburn

PYBURN, JAMES EDWARD BR TR 6′ 190 lbs.
B. Nov. 1, 1932, Fairfield, Ala.

Year	Team	Games	BA	SA	AB	H	2B	3B	HR	HR%	R	RBI	BB	SO	SB	Pinch Hit AB	Pinch Hit H	PO	A	E	DP	TC/G	FA	G by Pos
1955	BAL A	39	.204	.265	98	20	2	2	0	0.0	5	7	8	24	1	6	1	27	36	0	1	1.9	1.000	3B-33, OF-1
1956		84	.173	.269	156	27	3	3	2	1.3	23	11	17	26	4	7	2	114	5	3	3	1.6	.975	OF-77
1957		35	.225	.300	40	9	0	0	1	2.5	8	2	9	6	1	5	1	41	3	0	0	1.5	1.000	OF-28, C-1
3 yrs.		158	.190	.272	294	56	5	5	3	1.0	36	20	34	56	6	18	4	182	44	3	4	1.6	.987	OF-106, 3B-33, C-1

Eddie Pye

PYE, ROBERT EDWARD BR TR 5′10″ 175 lbs.
B. Feb. 13, 1967, Columbia, Tenn.

Year	Team	Games	BA	SA	AB	H	2B	3B	HR	HR%	R	RBI	BB	SO	SB	Pinch Hit AB	Pinch Hit H	PO	A	E	DP	TC/G	FA	G by Pos
1994	LA N	7	.100	.100	10	1	0	0	0	0.0	2	0	1	4	0	2	1	4	13	0	4	2.8	1.000	SS-3, 2B-3
1995		7	.000	.000	8	0	0	0	0	0.0	0	0	0	4	0	5	0	0	0	0	0	0.0	.000	3B-2
2 yrs.		14	.056	.056	18	1	0	0	0	0.0	2	0	1	8	0	7	1	4	13	0	4	2.1	1.000	SS-3, 2B-3, 3B-2

Frankie Pytlak

PYTLAK, FRANK ANTHONY BR TR 5′ 7½″ 160 lbs.
B. July 30, 1908, Buffalo, N. Y. D. May 8, 1977, Buffalo, N. Y.

Year	Team	Games	BA	SA	AB	H	2B	3B	HR	HR%	R	RBI	BB	SO	SB	Pinch Hit AB	Pinch Hit H	PO	A	E	DP	TC/G	FA	G by Pos
1932	CLE A	12	.241	.345	29	7	1	1	0	0.0	5	4	3	2	0	0	0	40	7	0	0	3.9	1.000	C-12
1933		80	.310	.423	248	77	10	6	2	0.8	36	33	17	10	3	6	3	246	57	0	11	4.4	1.000	C-69
1934		91	.260	.329	289	75	12	4	0	0.0	46	35	36	11	11	3	1	325	38	4	4	4.2	.989	C-88
1935		55	.295	.369	149	44	6	1	1	0.7	14	12	11	4	3	7	3	166	20	3	2	3.9	.984	C-48
1936		75	.321	.424	224	72	15	4	0	0.0	35	31	24	11	5	15	3	224	35	1	6	4.5	.996	C-58
1937		125	.315	.390	397	125	15	6	1	0.3	60	44	52	15	16	9	4	559	80	9	13	5.6	.986	C-115
1938		113	.308	.393	364	112	14	7	1	0.3	46	43	36	15	9	15	2	475	56	7	11	5.4	.987	C-99
1939		63	.268	.333	183	49	2	5	0	0.0	20	14	20	5	4	5	3	227	24	0	5	4.9	1.000	C-51
1940		62	.141	.168	149	21	2	1	0	0.0	16	16	17	5	0	3	1	235	30	1	5	4.5	.996	C-58, OF-1
1941	BOS A	106	.271	.363	336	91	23	1	2	0.6	36	39	28	19	5	11	4	416	41	4	7	5.1	.991	C-91
1945		9	.118	.118	17	2	0	0	0	0.0	1	0	3	0	0	2	0	17	6	0	0	3.8	1.000	C-6
1946		4	.143	.143	14	2	0	0	0	0.0	1	1	0	0	0	0	0	28	1	0	0	7.3	1.000	C-4
12 yrs.		795	.282	.363	2399	677	100	36	7	0.3	316	272	247	97	56	76	24	2958	395	29	64	4.8	.991	C-699, OF-1

Tim Pyznarski

PYZNARSKI, TIMOTHY MATTHEW BR TR 6′ 2″ 195 lbs.
B. Feb. 4, 1960, Chicago, Ill.

Year	Team	Games	BA	SA	AB	H	2B	3B	HR	HR%	R	RBI	BB	SO	SB	Pinch Hit AB	Pinch Hit H	PO	A	E	DP	TC/G	FA	G by Pos
1986	SD N	15	.238	.262	42	10	1	0	0	0.0	3	0	4	11	2	1	0	118	8	3	11	9.9	.977	1B-13

Jimmy Qualls

QUALLS, JAMES ROBERT BB TR 5′10″ 158 lbs.
B. Oct. 9, 1946, Exeter, Calif.

Year	Team	Games	BA	SA	AB	H	2B	3B	HR	HR%	R	RBI	BB	SO	SB	Pinch Hit AB	Pinch Hit H	PO	A	E	DP	TC/G	FA	G by Pos
1969	CHI N	43	.250	.342	120	30	5	3	0	0.0	12	9	2	14	2	4	2	62	5	0	2	1.7	1.000	OF-35, 2B-4
1970	MON N	9	.111	.111	9	1	0	0	0	0.0	1	1	0	0	0	5	1	2	2	0	0	1.0	1.000	2B-2, OF-2
1972	CHI A	11	.000	.000	10	0	0	0	0	0.0	0	0	0	2	0	7	0	3	0	0	0	3.0	1.000	OF-1
3 yrs.		63	.223	.302	139	31	5	3	0	0.0	13	10	2	16	2	16	3	67	7	0	2	1.7	1.000	OF-38, 2B-6

Billy Queen

QUEEN, WILLIAM EDDLEMAN (Doc) BR TR 6′ 1″ 185 lbs.
B. Nov. 28, 1928, Gastonia, N. C.

Year	Team	Games	BA	SA	AB	H	2B	3B	HR	HR%	R	RBI	BB	SO	SB	Pinch Hit AB	Pinch Hit H	PO	A	E	DP	TC/G	FA	G by Pos
1954	MIL N	3	.000	.000	2	0	0	0	0	0.0	0	0	0	2	0	2	0	1	0	0	0	1.0	1.000	OF-1

Mel Queen

QUEEN, MELVIN DOUGLAS BL TR 6′ 1″ 189 lbs.
Son of Mel Queen.
B. Mar. 26, 1942, Johnson City, N. Y.

Year	Team	Games	BA	SA	AB	H	2B	3B	HR	HR%	R	RBI	BB	SO	SB	Pinch Hit AB	Pinch Hit H	PO	A	E	DP	TC/G	FA	G by Pos
1964	CIN N	48	.200	.284	95	19	2	0	2	2.1	7	12	4	19	0	26	5	42	0	1	0	2.2	.977	OF-20
1965		5	.000	.000	3	0	0	0	0	0.0	0	0	0	1	0	3	0	1	0	0	0	1.0	1.000	OF-1
1966		56	.127	.145	55	7	1	0	0	0.0	4	5	10	12	0	17	3	35	2	0	0	0.9	1.000	OF-32, P-7
1967		49	.210	.259	81	17	4	0	0	0.0	6	5	4	10	2	13	1	15	17	2	2	1.1	.941	P-31
1968		10	.125	.125	8	1	0	0	0	0.0	2	0	1	3	0	3	0	0	4	0	0	0.8	1.000	P-5
1969		2	.167	.167	6	1	0	0	0	0.0	0	1	0	2	0	0	0	0	1	0	0	0.5	1.000	P-2
1970	CAL A	37	.250	.250	16	4	0	0	0	0.0	1	1	0	2	0	4	3	1	5	0	0	0.2	1.000	P-34
1971		45	.000	.000	8	0	0	0	0	0.0	0	1	1	0	0	2	0	1	8	1	0	0.2	.900	P-44
1972		17	.000	.000	2	0	0	0	0	0.0	0	0	1	1	0	0	0	1	4	0	0	0.3	1.000	P-17
9 yrs.		269	.179	.226	274	49	7	0	2	0.7	20	25	21	50	2	68	12	96	41	4	2	0.7	.972	P-140, OF-53

George Quellich

QUELLICH, GEORGE WILLIAM BR TR 6′ 1″ 180 lbs.
B. Feb. 10, 1903, Johnsville, Calif. D. Aug. 31, 1958, Johnsville, Calif.

Year	Team	Games	BA	SA	AB	H	2B	3B	HR	HR%	R	RBI	BB	SO	SB	Pinch Hit AB	Pinch Hit H	PO	A	E	DP	TC/G	FA	G by Pos
1931	DET A	13	.222	.370	54	12	5	0	1	1.9	6	11	3	4	1	0	0	27	2	0	0	2.2	1.000	OF-13

Joe Quest

QUEST, JOSEPH L. BR TR 5′ 6″ 150 lbs.
B. Nov. 16, 1852, New Castle, Pa. D. Nov. 14, 1924, San Diego, Calif.

Year	Team	Games	BA	SA	AB	H	2B	3B	HR	HR%	R	RBI	BB	SO	SB	Pinch Hit AB	Pinch Hit H	PO	A	E	DP	TC/G	FA	G by Pos
1878	IND N	62	.205	.230	278	57	3	2	0	0.0	45	13	12	24		0	0	228	196	60	27	7.8	.876	2B-62
1879	CHI N	83	.207	.260	334	69	16	1	0	0.0	38	22	9	33		0	0	263	331	48	30	7.7	.925	2B-83
1880		82	.237	.283	300	71	12	1	0	0.0	37	27	8	16		0	0	226	278	60	26	6.8	.894	2B-80, SS-2, 3B-1
1881		78	.246	.276	293	72	6	0	1	0.3	35	26	2	29		0	0	242	252	37	28	6.8	.930	2B-77, SS-1
1882		42	.201	.258	159	32	5	2	0	0.0	24	15	8	16		0	0	113	128	35	18	6.6	.873	2B-41, SS-1
1883	2 teams	DET N (37G –.234) STL AA (19G –.256)																						
″	total	56	.242	.321	215	52	11	3	0	0.0	34		11	18		0	0	162	161	38	29	6.4	.895	2B-56
1884	2 teams	STL AA (81G –.206) PIT AA (12G –.209)																						
″	total	93	.207	.269	353	73	12	5	0	0.0	48		19			0	0	261	286	64	45	6.6	.895	2B-87, SS-5, OF-1
1885	DET N	55	.195	.255	200	39	8	2	0	0.0	24	21	14	25		0	0	117	169	37	13	5.9	.885	2B-39, SS-15, OF-1
1886	PHI AA	42	.207	.247	150	31	4	1	0	0.0	14		20			0	0	63	146	39	16	5.8	.843	SS-41, 2B-2
9 yrs.		593	.217	.267	2282	496	77	17	1	0.0	299	124	103	161		0	0	1675	1947	418	232	6.8	.897	2B-527, SS-65, OF-2, 3B-1

Hal Quick

QUICK, JAMES HAROLD (Blondie) BR TR 5′10″ 165 lbs.
B. Oct. 4, 1917, Rome, Ga. D. Mar. 9, 1974, Swansea, Ill.

Year	Team	Games	BA	SA	AB	H	2B	3B	HR	HR%	R	RBI	BB	SO	SB	Pinch Hit AB	Pinch Hit H	PO	A	E	DP	TC/G	FA	G by Pos
1939	WAS A	12	.244	.268	41	10	1	0	0	0.0	3	2	1	1	1	1	0	18	33	4	6	5.5	.927	SS-10

Frank Quilici

QUILICI, FRANCIS RALPH (Guido) BR TR 6′ 1″ 170 lbs.
B. May 11, 1939, Chicago, Ill.
Manager 1972–75.

Year	Team	Games	BA	SA	AB	H	2B	3B	HR	HR%	R	RBI	BB	SO	SB	Pinch Hit AB	Pinch Hit H	PO	A	E	DP	TC/G	FA	G by Pos
1965	MIN A	56	.208	.255	149	31	5	1	0	0.0	16	7	15	33	1	2	0	96	120	2	34	3.9	.991	2B-52, SS-4
1967		23	.105	.158	19	2	1	0	0	0.0	2	0	3	4	0	2	0	10	13	1	4	1.1	.958	2B-13, 3B-8, SS-1
1968		97	.245	.341	229	56	11	4	1	0.4	22	22	21	45	0	6	1	130	176	5	34	3.3	.984	2B-48, 3B-40, SS-6, 1B-1
1969		118	.174	.250	144	25	3	1	2	1.4	19	12	12	22	2	7	2	99	139	6	17	2.0	.975	3B-84, 2B-36, SS-1
1970		111	.227	.291	141	32	3	0	2	1.4	19	12	15	16	0	3	1	114	133	6	26	2.5	.976	2B-73, 3B-27, SS-1
5 yrs.		405	.214	.287	682	146	23	6	5	0.7	78	53	66	120	3	20	4	449	581	20	115	2.7	.981	2B-222, 3B-159, SS-13, 1B-1
LEAGUE CHAMPIONSHIP SERIES																								
1970	MIN A	3	.000	.000	2	0	0	0	0	0.0	0	0	0	1	0	1	0	1	1	0	1	1.0	1.000	2B-2
WORLD SERIES																								
1965	MIN A	7	.200	.300	20	4	2	0	0	0.0	2	1	4	3	0	0	0	14	19	2	0	5.0	.943	2B-7

Lee Quillen

QUILLEN, LEON ABNER BR TR 5′10″ 165 lbs.
B. May 5, 1882, North Branch, Minn. D. Mar. 14, 1965, White Bear Lake, Minn.

Year	Team	Games	BA	SA	AB	H	2B	3B	HR	HR%	R	RBI	BB	SO	SB	Pinch Hit AB	Pinch Hit H	PO	A	E	DP	TC/G	FA	G by Pos
1906	CHI A	4	.333	.333	9	3	0	0	0	0.0	1	0	0		1	1	0	4	5	6	1	5.0	.600	SS-3
1907		49	.192	.225	151	29	5	0	0	0.0	17	14	10		8	0	0	45	103	22	4	3.5	.871	3B-48
2 yrs.		53	.200	.231	160	32	5	0	0	0.0	18	14	10		9	1	0	49	108	28	5	3.6	.849	3B-48, SS-3

Finners Quinlan

QUINLAN, THOMAS FINNERS BL TL 5′ 8″ 154 lbs.
B. Oct. 21, 1887, Scranton, Pa. D. Feb. 17, 1966, Scranton, Pa.

Year	Team	Games	BA	SA	AB	H	2B	3B	HR	HR%	R	RBI	BB	SO	SB	Pinch Hit AB	Pinch Hit H	PO	A	E	DP	TC/G	FA	G by Pos
1913	STL N	13	.160	.160	50	8	0	0	0	0.0	1	1	1	9	0	1	0	23	3	3	2	2.4	.897	OF-12
1915	CHI A	42	.193	.219	114	22	3	0	0	0.0	11	7	4	11	3	4	0	43	5	0	2	1.5	1.000	OF-32
2 yrs.		55	.183	.201	164	30	3	0	0	0.0	12	8	5	20	3	5	0	66	8	3	4	1.8	.961	OF-44

Frank Quinlan

QUINLAN, FRANCIS PATRICK
B. Mar. 9, 1869, Marlboro, Mass. D. May 4, 1904, Brockton, Mass.

Year	Team	Games	BA	SA	AB	H	2B	3B	HR	HR%	R	RBI	BB	SO	SB	Pinch Hit AB	Pinch Hit H	PO	A	E	DP	TC/G	FA	G by Pos
1891	BOS AA	2	.000	.000	5	0	0	0	0	0.0	0	0	0	2	0	0	0	5	1	0	0	3.0	1.000	C-1, OF-1

Tom Quinlan

QUINLAN, THOMAS RAYMOND BR TR 6′ 3″ 200 lbs.
B. Mar. 27, 1968, St. Paul, Minn.

Year	Team	Games	BA	SA	AB	H	2B	3B	HR	HR%	R	RBI	BB	SO	SB	Pinch Hit AB	Pinch Hit H	PO	A	E	DP	TC/G	FA	G by Pos
1990	TOR A	1	.500	.500	2	1	0	0	0	0.0	0	0	0	1	0	0	0	0	1	0	0	1.0	1.000	3B-1
1992		13	.067	.133	15	1	1	0	0	0.0	2	2	2	9	0	1	0	4	6	1	0	0.8	.909	3B-13
1994	PHI N	24	.200	.343	35	7	2	0	1	2.9	6	3	3	13	0	4	0	9	19	1	1	1.5	.966	3B-20
3 yrs.		38	.173	.288	52	9	3	0	1	1.9	8	5	5	23	0	5	0	13	26	2	1	1.2	.951	3B-34

Frank Quinn

QUINN, FRANK J. 5′ 8″
B. 1876, Grand Rapids, Mich. D. Feb. 17, 1920, Camden, Ind.

Year	Team	Games	BA	SA	AB	H	2B	3B	HR	HR%	R	RBI	BB	SO	SB	Pinch Hit AB	Pinch Hit H	PO	A	E	DP	TC/G	FA	G by Pos
1899	CHI N	12	.176	.235	34	6	0	1	0	0.0	6	1	6		1	1	0	10	1	1	0	1.1	.917	OF-10, 2B-1

Joe Quinn

QUINN, JOSEPH C. 5′ 8½″ 148 lbs.
B. 1849, Chicago, Ill. D. Jan. 2, 1909, Chicago, Ill.

Year	Team	Games	BA	SA	AB	H	2B	3B	HR	HR%	R	RBI	BB	SO	SB	Pinch Hit AB	Pinch Hit H	PO	A	E	DP	TC/G	FA	G by Pos
1877	CHI N	4	.071	.071	14	1	0	0	0	0.0	1	0	1	0		0	0	7	1	4	0	3.0	.667	OF-4

Joe Quinn

QUINN, JOSEPH J. (Ol' Reliable, Uncle Joe) BR TR 5′ 7″ 158 lbs.
B. Dec. 25, 1864, Sydney, Australia D. Nov. 12, 1940, St. Louis, Mo.
Manager 1895, 1899.

Year	Team	Games	BA	SA	AB	H	2B	3B	HR	HR%	R	RBI	BB	SO	SB	Pinch Hit AB	Pinch Hit H	PO	A	E	DP	TC/G	FA	G by Pos
1884	STL U	103	.270	.324	429	116	21	1	0	0.0	74		9			0	0	1039	36	64	55	11.0	.944	1B-100, OF-3, SS-1
1885	STL N	97	.213	.248	343	73	8	2	0	0.0	27	15	9	38		0	0	229	76	35	4	3.4	.897	OF-57, 3B-31, 1B-11
1886		75	.232	.306	271	63	11	3	1	0.4	33	21	8	31		0	0	199	55	34	13	3.8	.882	OF-48, 2B-15, 1B-7, 3B-4, SS-2
1888	BOS N	38	.301	.468	156	47	8	3	4	2.6	19	29	2	5	12	0	0	97	115	20	11	6.1	.914	2B-38
1889		112	.261	.327	444	116	13	5	2	0.5	57	69	25	21	24	0	0	174	314	59	36	4.9	.892	SS-63, 2B-47, 3B-2
1890	BOS P	130	.301	.411	509	153	19	8	7	1.4	87	82	44	24	29	0	0	431	395	51	70	6.7	.942	2B-130
1891	BOS N	124	.240	.313	508	122	8	10	3	0.6	70	63	28	28	24	0	0	275	364	42	44	5.5	.938	2B-124
1892		143	.218	.254	532	116	14	1	1	0.2	63	59	35	40	17	0	0	356	426	40	75	5.7	.951	2B-143
1893	STL N	135	.230	.285	547	126	18	6	0	0.0	68	71	33	7	24	0	0	354	366	44	63	5.7	.942	2B-135
1894		106	.286	.365	405	116	18	1	4	1.0	59	61	24	8	25	0	0	341	339	34	74	6.7	.952	2B-106
1895		134	.311	.390	543	169	19	9	2	0.4	84	74	36	6	22	0	0	359	390	43	63	5.9	.946	2B-134
1896	2 teams	STL N (48G –.209) BAL N (24G –.329)																						
″	total	72	.245	.297	273	67	7	2	1	0.4	41	22	15	6	14	2	0	123	206	16	10	4.9	.954	2B-56, OF-8, 3B-5, SS-1
1897	BAL N	75	.260	.337	285	74	11	4	1	0.4	33	45	13		12	2	0	142	176	16	22	4.3	.952	3B-37, SS-21, 2B-11, OF-6, 1B-2
1898	2 teams	BAL N (12G –.250) STL N (103G –.251)																						
″	total	115	.251	.302	407	102	11	5	0	0.0	40	41	25		13	1	0	235	356	35	31	5.5	.944	2B-63, SS-41, 3B-8, OF-2
1899	CLE N	147	.286	.345	615	176	24	6	0	0.0	73	72	21		22	0	0	350	440	31	61	5.6	.962	2B-147

Joe Quinn *continued*

Year	Team	Games	BA	SA	AB	H	2B	3B	HR	HR%	R	RBI	BB	SO	SB	Pinch Hit AB	Pinch Hit H	PO	A	E	DP	TC/G	FA	G by Pos
1900	2 teams	STL N (22G –.263) CIN N (74G –.274)																						
″	total	96	.272	.312	346	94	7	2	1	0.3	30	36	26		11	1	1	198	215	24	28	4.6	.945	2B-88, SS-6, 3B-1
1901	WAS A	66	.252	.342	266	67	11	2	3	1.1	33	36	11		7	0	0	158	177	16	17	5.3	.954	2B-66
17 yrs.		1768	.261	.328	6879	1797	228	70	30	0.4	891	796	364	214	256	6	1	5060	4446	604	677	5.7	.940	2B-1303, SS-135, OF-124, 1B-120, 3B-88

John Quinn

QUINN, JOHN EDWARD (Pit) BR TR 5′11″ 150 lbs.
B. Sept. 12, 1885, Framingham, Mass. D. Apr. 9, 1956, Marlboro, Mass.

Year	Team	Games	BA	SA	AB	H	2B	3B	HR	HR%	R	RBI	BB	SO	SB	Pinch Hit AB	Pinch Hit H	PO	A	E	DP	TC/G	FA	G by Pos
1911	PHI N	1	.000	.000	2	0	0	0	0	0.0	0	0	0	0	0	0	0	3	1	0	0	4.0	1.000	C-1

Paddy Quinn

QUINN, PATRICK 5′8″ 162 lbs.
B. Boston, Mass. D. Mar. 1893

Year	Team	Games	BA	SA	AB	H	2B	3B	HR	HR%	R	RBI	BB	SO	SB	Pinch Hit AB	Pinch Hit H	PO	A	E	DP	TC/G	FA	G by Pos
1881	2 teams	BOS N (1G –.000) WOR N (2G –.143)																						
″	total	3	.091	.091	11	1	0	0	0	0.0	0	1	1	2		0	0	15	1	2	0	6.0	.889	C-2, 1B-1

Tom Quinn

QUINN, THOMAS OSCAR BR TR 5′8″ 180 lbs.
B. Apr. 25, 1864, Annapolis, Md. D. July 24, 1932, Pittsburgh, Pa.

Year	Team	Games	BA	SA	AB	H	2B	3B	HR	HR%	R	RBI	BB	SO	SB	Pinch Hit AB	Pinch Hit H	PO	A	E	DP	TC/G	FA	G by Pos
1886	PIT AA	3	.000	.000	11	0	0	0	0	0.0	1		0			0	0	10	3	1	0	4.7	.929	C-3
1889	BAL AA	55	.175	.211	194	34	2	1	1	0.5	18	15	19	22	6	0	0	290	81	30	10	7.3	.925	C-55
1890	PIT P	55	.213	.275	207	44	4	3	1	0.5	23	15	17	8	1	0	0	203	58	33	3	5.3	.888	C-55
3 yrs.		113	.189	.238	412	78	6	4	2	0.5	42	30	36	30	7	0	0	503	142	64	13	6.3	.910	C-113

Luis Quinones

QUINONES, LUIS RAUL BB TR 5′11″ 165 lbs.
Born Luis Raul Quinones (Torruellas).
B. Apr. 28, 1962, Ponce, Puerto Rico.

Year	Team	Games	BA	SA	AB	H	2B	3B	HR	HR%	R	RBI	BB	SO	SB	Pinch Hit AB	Pinch Hit H	PO	A	E	DP	TC/G	FA	G by Pos
1983	OAK A	19	.190	.286	42	8	2	1	0	0.0	5	4	1	4	1	1	1	22	24	1	7	2.2	.979	2B-6, 3B-4, DH-4, OF-4, SS-3
1986	SF N	71	.179	.245	106	19	1	3	0	0.0	13	11	3	17	3	7	0	28	66	8	10	1.4	.922	SS-33, 3B-31, 2B-8
1987	CHI N	49	.218	.277	101	22	6	0	0	0.0	12	8	10	16	0	23	4	35	58	3	10	2.9	.969	SS-28, 2B-4, 3B-1
1988	CIN N	23	.231	.346	52	12	3	0	1	1.9	4	11	2	11	1	6	1	15	37	2	5	3.0	.963	SS-10, 3B-4, 2B-4
1989		97	.244	.412	340	83	13	4	12	3.5	43	34	25	46	2	5	1	112	213	10	25	3.1	.970	2B-53, 3B-50, SS-5
1990		83	.241	.331	145	35	7	0	2	1.4	10	17	13	29	1	36	13	44	85	6	15	3.0	.956	3B-22, 2B-13, SS-9, 1B-1
1991		97	.222	.325	212	47	4	3	4	1.9	15	20	21	31	1	36	6	68	106	7	23	3.2	.961	2B-33, 3B-19, SS-5
1992	MIN A	3	.200	.200	5	1	0	0	0	0.0	0	1	0	0	0	1	0	3	2	2	0	2.3	.714	SS-1, 3B-1, DH-1
8 yrs.		442	.226	.341	1003	227	36	11	19	1.9	102	106	75	154	9	115	26	327	591	39	95	2.7	.959	3B-132, 2B-121, SS-94, DH-5, OF-4, 1B-1
LEAGUE CHAMPIONSHIP SERIES																								
1990	CIN N	3	.500	.500	2	1	0	0	0	0.0	1	2	0	0	1	2	1	0	0	0	0	0.0	—	

Rey Quinones

QUINONES, REY FRANCISCO BR TR 5′11″ 160 lbs.
Born Rey Francisco Quinones (Santiago).
B. Nov. 11, 1963, Rio Piedras, Puerto Rico.

Year	Team	Games	BA	SA	AB	H	2B	3B	HR	HR%	R	RBI	BB	SO	SB	Pinch Hit AB	Pinch Hit H	PO	A	E	DP	TC/G	FA	G by Pos
1986	2 teams	BOS A (62G –.237) SEA A (36G –.189)																						
″	total	98	.218	.295	312	68	16	1	2	0.6	32	22	24	57	4	0	0	143	247	24	54	4.2	.942	SS-98
1987	SEA A	135	.276	.397	478	132	18	2	12	2.5	55	56	26	71	1	0	0	204	384	25	76	4.5	.959	SS-135
1988		140	.248	.393	499	124	30	3	12	2.4	63	52	23	71	0	2	0	202	396	23	103	4.5	.963	SS-135, DH-4
1989	2 teams	SEA A (7G –.105) PIT N (71G –.209)																						
″	total	78	.201	.283	244	49	11	0	3	1.2	23	29	16	41	0	2	0	99	193	22	27	4.1	.930	SS-76
4 yrs.		451	.243	.357	1533	373	75	6	29	1.9	173	159	89	240	5	4	0	648	1220	94	260	4.4	.952	SS-444, DH-4

Carlos Quintana

QUINTANA, CARLOS NARCIS BR TR 6′ 175 lbs.
Born Carlos Narcis Quintana (Hernandez).
B. Aug. 26, 1965, Estado Miranda, Venezuela.

Year	Team	Games	BA	SA	AB	H	2B	3B	HR	HR%	R	RBI	BB	SO	SB	Pinch Hit AB	Pinch Hit H	PO	A	E	DP	TC/G	FA	G by Pos
1988	BOS A	5	.333	.333	6	2	0	0	0	0.0	1	2	2	3	0	0	0	4	0	0	0	1.0	1.000	OF-3, DH-1
1989		34	.208	.273	77	16	5	0	0	0.0	6	6	7	12	0	7	2	31	0	2	0	1.1	.939	OF-21, DH-7, 1B-1
1990		149	.287	.383	512	147	28	0	7	1.4	56	67	52	74	1	7	3	1190	137	17	116	8.9	.987	1B-148, OF-3
1991		149	.295	.412	478	141	21	1	11	2.3	69	71	61	66	1	17	5	1041	102	9	101	7.6	.992	1B-138, OF-13, DH-1
1993		101	.244	.271	303	74	5	0	1	0.3	31	19	31	52	1	11	2	412	25	3	31	4.2	.993	1B-53, OF-51
5 yrs.		438	.276	.362	1376	380	59	1	19	1.4	163	165	153	207	3	42	12	2678	264	31	248	6.8	.990	1B-340, OF-91, DH-9
LEAGUE CHAMPIONSHIP SERIES																								
1990	BOS A	4	.000	.000	13	0	0	0	0	0.0	0	1	1	0	0	0	0	29	2	0	5	7.8	1.000	1B-4

Marshall Quinton

QUINTON, MARSHALL J. 5′11″ 190 lbs.
B. Philadelphia, Pa. Deceased.

Year	Team	Games	BA	SA	AB	H	2B	3B	HR	HR%	R	RBI	BB	SO	SB	Pinch Hit AB	Pinch Hit H	PO	A	E	DP	TC/G	FA	G by Pos
1884	RIC AA	26	.234	.287	94	22	5	0	0	0.0	12		0			0	0	64	26	12	3	3.9	.882	C-14, OF-10, SS-2
1885	PHI AA	7	.207	.241	29	6	1	0	0	0.0	6		1			0	0	40	13	8	0	8.7	.869	C-7
2 yrs.		33	.228	.276	123	28	6	0	0	0.0	18		1			0	0	104	39	20	3	4.9	.877	C-21, OF-10, SS-2

Jamie Quirk

QUIRK, JAMES PATRICK BL TR 6′4″ 190 lbs.
B. Oct. 22, 1954, Whittier, Calif.

Year	Team	Games	BA	SA	AB	H	2B	3B	HR	HR%	R	RBI	BB	SO	SB	Pinch Hit AB	Pinch Hit H	PO	A	E	DP	TC/G	FA	G by Pos
1975	KC A	14	.256	.333	39	10	0	0	1	2.6	2	5	2	7	0	1	1	19	3	2	0	1.8	.917	OF-10, 3B-2, DH-1
1976		64	.246	.325	114	28	6	0	1	0.9	11	15	2	22	0	32	7	9	14	2	2	0.6	.920	DH-19, SS-12, 3B-11, 1B-2
1977	MIL A	93	.217	.330	221	48	14	1	3	1.4	16	13	8	47	0	29	5	19	4	2	2	0.4	.920	DH-53, OF-10, 3B-8
1978	KC A	17	.207	.276	29	6	2	0	0	0.0	3	2	5	4	0	4	2	11	16	2	1	2.2	.931	3B-10, SS-2, DH-1
1979		51	.304	.443	79	24	6	1	1	1.3	8	11	5	13	0	30	8	16	9	1	0	1.0	.962	DH-9, C-9, SS-5, 3B-3
1980		62	.276	.399	163	45	5	0	5	3.1	13	21	7	24	3	12	1	72	66	8	3	3.2	.945	3B-28, C-15, 1B-1, DH-1
1981		46	.250	.320	100	25	7	0	0	0.0	8	10	6	17	0	18	4	63	23	4	2	2.8	.956	C-22, 3B-8, DH-1, 2B-1
1982		36	.231	.308	78	18	3	0	1	1.3	8	5	3	15	0	7	1	110	12	0	1	3.3	1.000	C-29, 1B-6, OF-1, 3B-1
1983	STL N	48	.209	.326	86	18	2	1	2	2.3	3	11	6	27	0	17	1	68	13	6	1	2.9	.931	C-22, 3B-7, SS-1
1984	2 teams	CHI A (3G –.000) CLE A (1G –1.000)																						
″	total	4	.333	1.333	3	1	0	0	1	33.3	1	2	0	2	0	2	0	1	0	0	0	0.5	1.000	C-1, 3B-1
1985	KC A	19	.281	.368	57	16	3	1	0	0.0	3	4	2	9	0	4	0	66	8	1	1	4.2	.987	C-17, 1B-1
1986		80	.215	.370	219	47	10	0	8	3.7	24	26	17	41	0	20	4	303	64	4	13	5.2	.989	C-41, SS-24, 1B-6, OF-1

Jamie Quirk *continued*

Year	Team	Games	BA	SA	AB	H	2B	3B	HR	HR%	R	RBI	BB	SO	SB	Pinch Hit AB	Pinch Hit H	PO	A	E	DP	TC/G	FA	G by Pos
1987		109	.236	.345	296	70	17	0	5	1.7	24	33	28	56	1	5	2	532	40	8	3	5.3	.986	C-108, SS-1
1988		84	.240	.408	196	47	7	1	8	4.1	22	25	28	41	1	7	0	412	34	8	5	5.6	.982	C-79, 3B-1, 1B-1
1989	**3 teams**	**NY A** (13G –.083) **OAK A** (9G –.200) **BAL A** (25G –.216)																						
"	**total**	47	.176	.235	85	15	2	0	1	1.2	6	10	12	20	0	11	1	129	15	1	3	3.7	.993	C-32, 3B-3, 1B-1, SS-1, OF-1, DH-1
1990	**OAK A**	56	.281	.413	121	34	5	1	3	2.5	12	26	14	34	0	11	4	168	18	5	4	3.5	.974	C-37, 1B-8, 3B-8, OF-1, DH-1
1991		76	.261	.296	203	53	4	0	1	0.5	16	17	16	28	0	17	5	337	38	6	6	6.0	.984	C-54, 1B-8, DH-1, 3B-1
1992		78	.220	.305	177	39	7	1	2	1.1	13	11	16	28	0	17	6	287	28	8	6	4.5	.975	C-59, 1B-9, 3B-2, DH-1
18 yrs.		984	.240	.347	2266	544	100	7	43	1.9	193	247	177	435	5	244	52	2622	405	68	53	3.8	.978	C-525, 3B-94, DH-89, SS-46, 1B-43, OF-24, 2B-1
LEAGUE CHAMPIONSHIP SERIES																								
1976	**KC A**	4	.143	.429	7	1	0	1	0	0.0	1	2	0	2	0	1	0	0	0	0	0	0.0	.000	DH-2
1985		1	.000	.000	1	0	0	0	0	0.0	0	0	0	0	0	1	0	0	0	0	0	0.0	—	
1990	**OAK A**	1	1.000	1.000	1	1	0	0	0	0.0	0	0	0	0	0	1	1	0	0	0	0	0.0	—	
1992		1	.000	.000	1	0	0	0	0	0.0	0	0	0	0	0	1	0	0	0	0	0	0.0	—	
4 yrs.		7	.200	.400	10	2	0	1	0	0.0	1	2	0	2	0	4	1	0	0	0	0	0.0		DH-2
WORLD SERIES																								
1990	**OAK A**	1	.000	.000	3	0	0	0	0	0.0	0	0	0	2	0	0	0	2	2	0	0	4.0	1.000	C-1

Brian Raabe

RAABE, BRIAN CHARLES — BR TR 5′ 9″ 170 lbs.
B. Nov. 5, 1967, New Ulm, Minn.

Year	Team	Games	BA	SA	AB	H	2B	3B	HR	HR%	R	RBI	BB	SO	SB	Pinch Hit AB	Pinch Hit H	PO	A	E	DP	TC/G	FA	G by Pos
1995	**MIN A**	6	.214	.214	14	3	0	0	0	0.0	4	1	1	0	0	1	1	5	7	0	3	2.0	1.000	2B-4, 3B-2

Johnny Rabb

RABB, JOHN ANDREW — BR TR 6′ 1″ 179 lbs.
B. June 23, 1960, Los Angeles, Calif.

Year	Team	Games	BA	SA	AB	H	2B	3B	HR	HR%	R	RBI	BB	SO	SB	Pinch Hit AB	Pinch Hit H	PO	A	E	DP	TC/G	FA	G by Pos
1982	**SF N**	2	.500	1.500	2	1	0	1	0	0.0	0	0	0	1	0	1	0	1	0	0	0	1.0	1.000	OF-1
1983		40	.231	.346	104	24	9	0	1	1.0	10	14	9	17	1	6	2	176	13	5	2	5.9	.974	C-31, OF-2
1984		54	.195	.317	82	16	1	0	3	3.7	10	9	10	33	1	28	2	107	7	3	3	4.3	.974	1B-13, OF-8, C-6
1985	**ATL N**	3	.000	.000	2	0	0	0	0	0.0	0	0	0	1	0	2	0	0	0	0	0	0.0	.000	OF-1
1988	**SEA A**	9	.357	.500	14	5	2	0	0	0.0	2	4	0	1	0	3	0	5	0	0	0	0.6	1.000	DH-5, OF-2, 1B-1
5 yrs.		108	.225	.353	204	46	12	1	4	2.0	22	27	19	53	2	40	4	289	20	8	5	4.5	.975	C-37, 1B-14, OF-14, DH-5

Joe Rabbitt

RABBITT, JOSEPH PATRICK — BL TR 5′10″ 165 lbs.
B. Jan. 15, 1900, Frontenac, Kans. D. Dec. 5, 1969, Norwalk, Conn.

Year	Team	Games	BA	SA	AB	H	2B	3B	HR	HR%	R	RBI	BB	SO	SB	Pinch Hit AB	Pinch Hit H	PO	A	E	DP	TC/G	FA	G by Pos
1922	**CLE A**	2	.333	.333	3	1	0	0	0	0.0	1	0	0	0	0	0	0	1	0	0	0	1.0	1.000	OF-1

Marv Rackley

RACKLEY, MARVIN EUGENE — BL TL 5′10″ 170 lbs.
B. July 25, 1921, Seneca, S. C.

Year	Team	Games	BA	SA	AB	H	2B	3B	HR	HR%	R	RBI	BB	SO	SB	Pinch Hit AB	Pinch Hit H	PO	A	E	DP	TC/G	FA	G by Pos
1947	**BKN N**	18	.222	.222	9	2	0	0	0	0.0	2	2	1	0	0	5	1	7	0	0	0	3.5	1.000	OF-2
1948		88	.327	.409	281	92	13	5	0	0.0	55	15	19	25	8	11	3	143	7	8	1	2.1	.949	OF-74
1949	**3 teams**	**BKN N** (9G –.444) **PIT N** (11G –.314) **BKN N** (54G –.291)																						
"	**total**	74	.303	.368	185	56	7	1	1	0.5	30	17	16	11	2	17	6	96	0	1	0	1.8	.990	OF-55
1950	**CIN N**	5	.500	.500	2	1	0	0	0	0.0	0	1	0	0	0	2	1	0	0	0	0	0.0	—	
4 yrs.		185	.317	.390	477	151	20	6	1	0.2	87	35	36	36	10	35	11	246	7	9	1	2.0	.966	OF-131
WORLD SERIES																								
1949	**BKN N**	2	.000	.000	5	0	0	0	0	0.0	0	0	0	2	0	0	0	2	0	0	0	1.0	1.000	OF-2

Old Hoss Radbourn

RADBOURN, CHARLES GARDNER — BR TR 5′ 9″ 168 lbs. BB 1886
B. Dec. 11, 1854, Rochester, N. Y. D. Feb. 5, 1897, Bloomington, Ill.
Hall of Fame 1939.

Year	Team	Games	BA	SA	AB	H	2B	3B	HR	HR%	R	RBI	BB	SO	SB	Pinch Hit AB	Pinch Hit H	PO	A	E	DP	TC/G	FA	G by Pos
1880	**BUF N**	6	.143	.143	21	3	0	0	0	0.0	1	1	0	1		0	0	15	16	3	2	5.7	.912	OF-3, 2B-3
1881	**PRO N**	72	.219	.252	270	59	9	0	0	0.0	27	28	10	15		0	0	57	121	30	8	2.6	.856	P-41, OF-25, SS-13
1882		83	.239	.282	326	78	11	0	1	0.3	30		12	22		0	0	71	105	16	5	2.2	.917	P-55, OF-31, SS-1
1883		89	.283	.352	381	108	11	3	3	0.8	59		14	16		0	0	74	142	22	8	2.4	.908	P-76, OF-20, 1B-2
1884		87	.230	.263	361	83	7	1	1	0.3	48		26	42		0	0	69	131	25	4	2.5	.889	P-75, OF-7, 1B-5, SS-2, 2B-1
1885		66	.233	.285	249	58	9	2	0	0.0	34	22	36	27		0	0	40	122	22	9	2.7	.880	P-49, OF-16, 2B-2
1886	**BOS N**	66	.237	.289	253	60	5	1	2	0.8	30	22	17	36		0	0	39	107	12	8	2.7	.924	P-58
1887		51	.229	.280	175	40	2	2	1	0.6	25	24	18	21	6	0	0	15	69	16	3	1.9	.840	P-50, OF-2
1888		24	.215	.228	79	17	1	0	0	0.0	6	6	3	14	4	0	0	14	37	6	1	2.4	.895	P-24
1889		35	.189	.221	122	23	1	0	1	0.8	17	13	9	19	3	0	0	19	58	2	6	2.2	.975	P-33, OF-2, 3B-1
1890	**BOS P**	45	.253	.292	154	39	6	0	0	0.0	20	16	9	20	7	0	0	16	99	8	4	2.7	.935	P-41, OF-4, 1B-1
1891	**CIN N**	29	.177	.240	96	17	2	2	0	0.0	11	10	4	11	1	0	0	9	40	7	1	1.9	.875	P-26, OF-2, 3B-1
12 yrs.		653	.235	.281	2487	585	64	11	9	0.4	308	142	158	244	21	0	0	438	1047	169	59	2.5	.898	P-528, OF-112, SS-16, 1B-8, 2B-6, 3B-2

Rip Radcliff

RADCLIFF, RAYMOND ALLEN — BL TL 5′10″ 170 lbs.
B. Jan. 19, 1906, Kiowa, Okla. D. May 23, 1962, Enid, Okla.

Year	Team	Games	BA	SA	AB	H	2B	3B	HR	HR%	R	RBI	BB	SO	SB	Pinch Hit AB	Pinch Hit H	PO	A	E	DP	TC/G	FA	G by Pos
1934	**CHI A**	14	.268	.339	56	15	2	1	0	0.0	7	5	0	2	1	0	0	35	0	2	0	2.6	.946	OF-14
1935		146	.286	.404	623	178	28	8	10	1.6	95	68	53	21	4	2	0	231	8	8	1	1.7	.968	OF-142
1936		138	.335	.447	618	207	31	7	8	1.3	120	82	44	12	6	6	3	213	6	15	2	1.8	.936	OF-132
1937		144	.325	.445	584	190	38	10	4	0.7	105	79	53	25	6	5	3	273	9	10	5	2.1	.966	OF-139
1938		129	.330	.429	503	166	23	6	5	1.0	64	81	36	17	5	7	2	466	15	10	25	4.0	.980	OF-99, 1B-23
1939		113	.264	.353	397	105	25	2	2	0.5	49	53	26	21	6	13	1	300	12	6	11	3.2	.981	OF-78, 1B-20
1940	**STL A**	150	.342	.466	584	**200**	33	9	7	1.2	83	81	47	20	6	5	1	307	10	9	4	2.3	.972	OF-139, 1B-4
1941	**2 teams**	**STL A** (19G –.282) **DET A** (96G –.317)																						
"	**total**	115	.311	.411	450	140	16	7	5	1.1	59	53	29	14	5	8	0	205	7	5	3	2.1	.977	OF-101, 1B-3
1942	**DET A**	62	.250	.306	144	36	5	0	1	0.7	13	20	9	6	0	29	3	83	6	1	1	3.2	.989	OF-24, 1B-4
1943		70	.261	.296	115	30	4	0	0	0.0	3	10	13	3	1	**44**	11	39	3	0	1	2.1	1.000	OF-19, 1B-1
10 yrs.		1081	.311	.417	4074	1267	205	50	42	1.0	598	532	310	141	40	119	24	2152	76	66	53	2.4	.971	OF-887, 1B-55

Dave Rader

RADER, DAVID MARTIN BL TR 5′11″ 165 lbs.
B. Dec. 26, 1948, Claremore, Okla.

Year	Team	Games	BA	SA	AB	H	2B	3B	HR	HR%	R	RBI	BB	SO	SB	Pinch Hit AB	Pinch Hit H	PO	A	E	DP	TC/G	FA	G by Pos
1971	SF N	3	.000	.000	4	0	0	0	0	0.0	0	0	0	0	0	3	0	1	0	0	0	1.0	1.000	C-1
1972		133	.259	.333	459	119	14	1	6	1.3	44	41	29	31	1	9	2	661	45	11	7	5.6	.985	C-127
1973		148	.229	.338	462	106	15	4	9	1.9	59	41	63	22	0	4	3	701	48	7	5	5.1	.991	C-148
1974		113	.291	.362	323	94	16	2	1	0.3	26	26	31	21	1	13	4	461	38	8	4	4.7	.984	C-109
1975		98	.291	.394	292	85	15	0	5	1.7	39	31	32	30	1	7	1	457	37	8	7	5.3	.984	C-94
1976		88	.263	.333	255	67	15	0	1	0.4	25	22	27	21	2	12	2	349	32	6	4	4.8	.984	C-81
1977	STL N	66	.263	.368	114	30	7	1	1	0.9	15	16	9	10	3	28	9	147	13	4	2	4.3	.976	C-38
1978	CHI N	116	.203	.295	305	62	13	3	3	1.0	29	36	34	26	1	13	4	412	51	11	7	4.2	.977	C-114
1979	PHI N	31	.204	.315	54	11	1	1	1	1.9	3	5	6	7	0	7	1	62	6	5	1	2.9	.932	C-25
1980	BOS A	50	.328	.474	137	45	11	0	3	2.2	14	17	14	12	1	9	2	140	15	3	4	3.7	.981	C-34, DH-9
10 yrs.		846	.257	.349	2405	619	107	12	30	1.2	254	235	245	180	10	105	28	3391	285	63	41	4.8	.983	C-771, DH-9

Don Rader

RADER, DONALD RUSSELL BL TR 5′10″ 164 lbs.
B. Sept. 5, 1893, Wolcott, Ind. D. June 26, 1983, Walla Walla, Wash.

Year	Team	Games	BA	SA	AB	H	2B	3B	HR	HR%	R	RBI	BB	SO	SB	Pinch Hit AB	Pinch Hit H	PO	A	E	DP	TC/G	FA	G by Pos
1913	CHI A	2	.333	.667	3	1	1	0	0	0.0	1	0	0	0	0	0	0	2	0	1	0	1.5	.667	OF-1, 3B-1
1921	PHI N	9	.281	.344	32	9	2	0	0	0.0	4	3	3	5	0	0	0	15	22	0	3	4.1	1.000	SS-9
2 yrs.		11	.286	.371	35	10	3	0	0	0.0	5	3	3	5	0	0	0	17	22	1	3	3.6	.975	SS-9, OF-1, 3B-1

Doug Rader

RADER, DOUGLAS LEE (Rojo, The Red Rooster) BR TR 6′ 2″ 208 lbs.
B. July 30, 1944, Chicago, Ill.
Manager 1983–86, 1989–91.

Year	Team	Games	BA	SA	AB	H	2B	3B	HR	HR%	R	RBI	BB	SO	SB	Pinch Hit AB	Pinch Hit H	PO	A	E	DP	TC/G	FA	G by Pos
1967	HOU N	47	.333	.481	162	54	10	4	2	1.2	24	26	7	31	0	6	1	270	33	8	27	7.2	.974	1B-36, 3B-7
1968		98	.267	.393	333	89	16	4	6	1.8	42	43	31	51	2	7	3	130	171	22	18	3.5	.932	3B-86, 1B-5
1969		155	.246	.359	569	140	25	3	11	1.9	62	83	62	103	1	0	0	140	307	26	36	3.0	.945	3B-154, 1B-4
1970		156	.252	.436	576	145	25	3	25	4.3	90	87	57	102	3	1	0	149	357	18	39	3.4	.966	3B-154, 1B-1
1971		135	.244	.378	484	118	21	4	12	2.5	51	56	40	112	5	1	0	93	275	21	28	2.9	.946	3B-135
1972		152	.237	.425	553	131	24	7	22	4.0	70	90	57	120	5	0	0	119	340	20	31	3.2	.958	3B-152
1973		154	.254	.409	574	146	26	0	21	3.7	79	89	46	97	4	2	0	134	296	25	24	3.0	.945	3B-152
1974		152	.257	.415	533	137	27	3	17	3.2	61	78	60	131	7	0	0	128	347	17	28	3.2	.965	3B-152
1975		129	.223	.364	448	100	23	2	12	2.7	41	48	42	101	5	4	2	114	259	11	25	3.0	.971	3B-124, SS-2
1976	SD N	139	.257	.378	471	121	22	4	9	1.9	45	55	55	102	3	2	0	109	318	20	22	3.3	.955	3B-137
1977	2 teams	SD N (52G –.271) TOR A (96G –.240)																						
″	total	148	.251	.437	483	121	26	5	18	3.7	66	67	71	105	2	11	1	140	210	13	12	2.6	.964	3B-96, DH-34, 1B-7, OF-1
11 yrs.		1465	.251	.403	5186	1302	245	39	155	3.0	631	722	528	1055	37	34	7	1526	2913	201	290	3.2	.957	3B-1349, 1B-53, DH-34, SS-2, OF-1

Paul Radford

RADFORD, PAUL REVERE BR TR 5′ 6″ 148 lbs.
B. Oct. 14, 1861, Roxbury, Mass. D. Feb. 21, 1945, Boston, Mass.

Year	Team	Games	BA	SA	AB	H	2B	3B	HR	HR%	R	RBI	BB	SO	SB	Pinch Hit AB	Pinch Hit H	PO	A	E	DP	TC/G	FA	G by Pos
1883	BOS N	72	.205	.252	258	53	6	3	0	0.0	46	14	9	26		0	0	86	16	20	2	1.7	.836	OF-72
1884	PRO N	97	.197	.248	355	70	11	2	1	0.3	56		25	43		0	0	146	29	24	4	2.0	.879	OF-96, P-2
1885		105	.243	.302	371	90	12	5	0	0.0	55	32	33	43		0	0	156	73	40	7	2.5	.851	OF-88, SS-16, P-3, 2B-1
1886	KC N	122	.229	.284	493	113	17	5	0	0.0	78	20	58	48		0	0	179	136	46	13	2.9	.873	OF-92, SS-30, 2B-1
1887	NY AA	128	.265	.342	486	129	15	5	4	0.8	127		**106**		73	0	0	226	294	89	36	4.6	.854	SS-76, OF-37, 2B-18, P-2
1888	BKN AA	90	.218	.286	308	67	9	3	2	0.6	48	29	35		33	0	0	186	28	12	3	2.5	.947	OF-88, 2B-2
1889	CLE N	136	.238	.308	487	116	21	5	1	0.2	94	46	91	37	30	0	0	205	24	14	6	1.8	.942	OF-136, 3B-1
1890	CLE P	122	.292	.408	466	136	24	12	2	0.4	98	62	82	28	25	0	0	228	176	42	19	3.5	.906	OF-80, SS-36, 3B-7, 2B-4, P-1
1891	BOS AA	133	.259	.305	456	118	11	5	0	0.0	102	65	96	36	55	0	0	239	455	71	52	5.6	.907	SS-131, OF-4, P-1
1892	WAS N	137	.255	.314	510	130	19	4	1	0.2	93	37	86	47	35	0	0	186	198	66	22	3.3	.853	OF-62, 3B-54, SS-20, 2B-2
1893		124	.228	.293	464	106	18	3	2	0.4	87	34	105	42	32	0	0	198	33	25	4	2.0	.902	OF-123, 2B-1, P-1
1894		95	.240	.311	325	78	13	5	0	0.0	61	49	65	23	24	0	0	219	247	73	23	5.6	.865	SS-47, 2B-25, OF-24
12 yrs.		1361	.242	.308	4979	1206	176	57	13	0.3	945	388	791	373	307	0	0	2254	1709	522	191	3.2	.884	OF-902, SS-356, 3B-62, 2B-54, P-10

Jack Radtke

RADTKE, JACK WILLIAM BB TR 5′ 8″ 155 lbs.
B. Apr. 14, 1913, Denver, Colo.

Year	Team	Games	BA	SA	AB	H	2B	3B	HR	HR%	R	RBI	BB	SO	SB	Pinch Hit AB	Pinch Hit H	PO	A	E	DP	TC/G	FA	G by Pos
1936	BKN N	33	.097	.097	31	3	0	0	0	0.0	8	2	4	9	3	1	0	18	28	4	3	2.2	.920	2B-14, 3B-5, SS-4

Jack Rafter

RAFTER, JOHN CORNELIUS BR TR 5′ 8″ 165 lbs.
B. Feb. 20, 1875, Troy, N. Y. D. Jan. 5, 1943, Troy, N. Y.

Year	Team	Games	BA	SA	AB	H	2B	3B	HR	HR%	R	RBI	BB	SO	SB	Pinch Hit AB	Pinch Hit H	PO	A	E	DP	TC/G	FA	G by Pos
1904	PIT N	1	.000	.000	3	0	0	0	0	0.0	0	0	0		0	0	0	3	1	0	0	4.0	1.000	C-1

Tom Raftery

RAFTERY, THOMAS FRANCIS BR TR 5′10½″ 175 lbs.
B. Oct. 5, 1881, Boston, Mass. D. Dec. 31, 1954, Boston, Mass.

Year	Team	Games	BA	SA	AB	H	2B	3B	HR	HR%	R	RBI	BB	SO	SB	Pinch Hit AB	Pinch Hit H	PO	A	E	DP	TC/G	FA	G by Pos
1909	CLE A	8	.219	.344	32	7	2	1	0	0.0	6	0	4		1	0	0	12	0	0	0	1.5	1.000	OF-8

Tom Ragland

RAGLAND, THOMAS BR TR 5′10″ 155 lbs.
B. June 16, 1946, Talladega, Ala.

Year	Team	Games	BA	SA	AB	H	2B	3B	HR	HR%	R	RBI	BB	SO	SB	Pinch Hit AB	Pinch Hit H	PO	A	E	DP	TC/G	FA	G by Pos
1971	WAS A	10	.174	.174	23	4	0	0	0	0.0	1	0	0	5	0	0	0	18	15	0	3	3.3	1.000	2B-10
1972	TEX A	25	.172	.207	58	10	2	0	0	0.0	3	2	5	11	0	4	0	30	34	1	6	3.1	.985	2B-13, 3B-5, SS-3
1973	CLE A	67	.257	.306	183	47	7	1	0	0.0	16	12	8	31	2	2	0	136	166	5	43	4.6	.984	2B-65, SS-2
3 yrs.		102	.231	.273	264	61	9	1	0	0.0	20	14	13	47	2	6	0	184	215	6	52	4.1	.985	2B-88, 3B-5, SS-5

Larry Raines

RAINES, LAWRENCE GLENN HOPE BR TR 5′10″ 165 lbs.
B. Mar. 9, 1930, St. Albans, W. Va. D. Jan. 28, 1978, Lansing, Mich.

Year	Team	Games	BA	SA	AB	H	2B	3B	HR	HR%	R	RBI	BB	SO	SB	Pinch Hit AB	Pinch Hit H	PO	A	E	DP	TC/G	FA	G by Pos
1957	CLE A	96	.262	.344	244	64	14	0	2	0.8	39	16	19	40	5	21	5	84	109	13	15	2.9	.937	3B-27, SS-25, 2B-10, OF-8
1958		7	.000	.000	9	0	0	0	0	0.0	0	0	0	5	0	2	0	6	8	1	4	7.5	.933	2B-2
2 yrs.		103	.253	.332	253	64	14	0	2	0.8	39	16	19	45	5	23	5	90	117	14	19	3.1	.937	3B-27, SS-25, 2B-12, OF-8

Tim Raines

RAINES, TIMOTHY (Rock) BB TR 5′ 8″ 160 lbs.
B. Sept. 16, 1959, Sanford, Fla.

Year	Team	Games	BA	SA	AB	H	2B	3B	HR	HR%	R	RBI	BB	SO	SB	Pinch Hit AB	Pinch Hit H	PO	A	E	DP	TC/G	FA	G by Pos
1979	MON N	6	—	—	0	0	0	0	0	—	3	0	0	0	2	0	0	0	0	0	0	0.0	—	
1980		15	.050	.050	20	1	0	0	0	0.0	5	0	6	3	5	0	0	15	16	0	2	3.9	1.000	2B-7, OF-1
1981		88	.304	.438	313	95	13	7	5	1.6	61	37	45	31	**71**	0	0	162	8	4	0	2.1	.977	OF-81, 2B-1

Tim Raines *continued*

Year	Team	Games	BA	SA	AB	H	2B	3B	HR	HR%	R	RBI	BB	SO	SB	Pinch Hit AB	Pinch Hit H	PO	A	E	DP	TC/G	FA	G by Pos
1982		156	.277	.369	647	179	32	8	4	0.6	90	43	75	83	**78**	0	0	293	126	8	12	2.7	.981	OF-120, 2B-36
1983		156	.298	.429	615	183	32	8	11	1.8	**133**	71	97	70	**90**	1	1	314	23	4	3	2.1	.988	OF-154, 2B-7
1984		160	.309	.437	622	192	**38**	9	8	1.3	106	60	87	69	**75**	0	0	420	8	6	1	2.7	.986	OF-160, 2B-2
1985		150	.320	.475	575	184	30	13	11	1.9	115	41	81	60	70	7	0	284	8	2	4	2.0	.993	OF-145
1986		151	**.334**	.476	580	194	35	10	9	1.6	91	62	78	60	70	4	1	270	13	6	1	2.0	.979	OF-147
1987		139	.330	.526	530	175	34	8	18	3.4	**123**	68	90	52	50	0	0	297	9	4	1	2.2	.987	OF-139
1988		109	.270	.431	429	116	19	7	12	2.8	66	48	53	44	33	1	0	235	5	3	1	2.3	.988	OF-108
1989		145	.286	.418	517	148	29	6	9	1.7	76	60	93	48	41	4	3	253	7	1	0	1.9	.996	OF-139
1990		130	.287	.392	457	131	11	5	9	2.0	65	62	70	43	49	8	2	239	3	6	1	2.0	.976	OF-123
1991	**CHI A**	155	.268	.345	609	163	20	6	5	0.8	102	50	83	68	51	5	0	273	12	3	3	1.9	.990	OF-133, DH-19
1992		144	.294	.405	551	162	22	9	7	1.3	102	54	81	48	45	4	3	312	12	2	0	2.3	.994	OF-129, DH-14
1993		115	.306	.480	415	127	16	4	16	3.9	75	54	64	35	21	4	1	200	5	0	1	1.8	1.000	OF-112
1994		101	.266	.409	384	102	15	5	10	2.6	80	52	61	43	13	6	0	203	3	4	1	2.2	.981	OF-97
1995		133	.285	.422	502	143	25	4	12	2.4	81	67	70	52	13	9	1	193	7	4	1	1.6	.980	OF-108, DH-22
17 yrs.		2053	.296	.428	7766	2295	371	109	146	1.9	1374	829	1134	809	777 **4th**	53	12	3963	265	57	32	2.1	.987	OF-1896, DH-55, 2B-53
LEAGUE CHAMPIONSHIP SERIES																								
1981	**MON N**	5	.238	.333	21	5	2	0	0	0.0	1	1	0	3	0	0	0	9	0	0	0	1.8	1.000	OF-5
1993	**CHI A**	6	.444	.519	27	12	2	0	0	0.0	5	1	2	2	1	0	0	12	2	0	0	2.3	1.000	OF-6
2 yrs.		11	.354 **8th**	.438	48	17	4	0	0	0.0	6	2	2	5	1	0	0	21	2	0	0	2.1	1.000	OF-11

John Rainey

RAINEY, JOHN PAUL BL TR 5′10″ 164 lbs.
B. July 26, 1864, Birmingham, Mich. D. Nov. 11, 1912, Detroit, Mich.

Year	Team	Games	BA	SA	AB	H	2B	3B	HR	HR%	R	RBI	BB	SO	SB	Pinch Hit AB	Pinch Hit H	PO	A	E	DP	TC/G	FA	G by Pos
1887	**NY N**	17	.293	.345	58	17	3	0	0	0.0	6	12	5	6	0	0	0	19	26	10	3	3.2	.818	3B-17
1890	**BUF P**	42	.235	.295	166	39	5	1	1	0.6	29	20	24	15	12	0	0	72	42	17	8	3.0	.870	OF-28, SS-7, 3B-6, 2B-2
2 yrs.		59	.250	.308	224	56	8	1	1	0.4	35	32	29	21	12	0	0	91	68	27	11	3.1	.855	OF-28, 3B-23, SS-7, 2B-2

Gary Rajsich

RAJSICH, GARY LOUIS BL TL 6′ 2″ 190 lbs.
Brother of Dave Rajsich.
B. Oct. 28, 1954, Youngstown, Ohio.

Year	Team	Games	BA	SA	AB	H	2B	3B	HR	HR%	R	RBI	BB	SO	SB	Pinch Hit AB	Pinch Hit H	PO	A	E	DP	TC/G	FA	G by Pos
1982	**NY N**	80	.259	.383	162	42	8	3	2	1.2	17	12	17	40	1	35	2	70	1	0	1	1.9	1.000	OF-35, 1B-2
1983		11	.333	.500	36	12	3	0	1	2.8	5	3	3	1	0	1	0	94	6	0	9	10.0	1.000	1B-10
1984	**STL N**	7	.143	.143	7	1	0	0	0	0.0	1	2	2	1	0	4	1	13	0	0	2	4.3	1.000	1B-3
1985	**SF N**	51	.165	.231	91	15	6	0	0	0.0	5	10	17	22	0	23	1	185	11	2	17	8.6	.990	1B-23
4 yrs.		149	.236	.345	296	70	17	3	3	1.0	28	27	39	64	1	63	4	362	18	2	29	5.2	.995	1B-38, OF-35

Doc Ralston

RALSTON, SAMUEL BERYL BR TR 6′ 185 lbs.
B. Aug. 3, 1885, Pierpont, Ohio D. Aug. 29, 1950, Lancaster, Pa.

Year	Team	Games	BA	SA	AB	H	2B	3B	HR	HR%	R	RBI	BB	SO	SB	Pinch Hit AB	Pinch Hit H	PO	A	E	DP	TC/G	FA	G by Pos
1910	**WAS A**	22	.205	.219	73	15	1	0	0	0.0	4	3	3		2	0	0	38	3	1	1	1.9	.976	OF-22

Bob Ramazzotti

RAMAZZOTTI, ROBERT LOUIS BR TR 5′ 8½″ 175 lbs.
B. Jan. 16, 1917, Elmora, Pa.

Year	Team	Games	BA	SA	AB	H	2B	3B	HR	HR%	R	RBI	BB	SO	SB	Pinch Hit AB	Pinch Hit H	PO	A	E	DP	TC/G	FA	G by Pos
1946	**BKN N**	62	.208	.242	120	25	4	0	0	0.0	10	7	9	13	0	15	1	52	64	4	9	2.6	.967	3B-30, 2B-16
1948		4	.000	.000	3	0	0	0	0	0.0	0	0	0	1	0	2	0	2	1	0	0	1.0	1.000	3B-2, 2B-1
1949	**2 teams**	**BKN N** (5G –.154) **CHI N** (65G –.179)																						
″	**total**	70	.177	.217	203	36	3	1	1	0.5	15	9	5	36	9	11	2	61	130	7	20	3.6	.965	3B-39, SS-12, 2B-4
1950	**CHI N**	61	.262	.345	145	38	3	3	1	0.7	19	6	4	16	3	6	2	73	92	9	19	4.0	.948	2B-31, 3B-10, SS-3
1951		73	.247	.323	158	39	5	2	1	0.6	13	15	10	23	0	9	2	83	152	11	35	4.2	.955	SS-51, 2B-6, 3B-1
1952		50	.284	.361	183	52	5	3	1	0.5	26	12	14	14	3	0	0	90	143	5	28	4.8	.979	2B-50
1953		26	.154	.205	39	6	2	0	0	0.0	3	4	3	4	0	3	0	28	23	5	6	3.1	.911	2B-18
7 yrs.		346	.230	.291	851	196	22	9	4	0.5	86	53	45	107	15	46	7	389	605	41	117	3.8	.960	2B-126, 3B-82, SS-66

Manny Ramirez

RAMIREZ, MANUEL ARISTIDES BR TR 6′ 190 lbs.
Born Manuel Aristides Ramirez (Onelcida).
B. May 30, 1972, Santo Domingo, Dominican Republic.

Year	Team	Games	BA	SA	AB	H	2B	3B	HR	HR%	R	RBI	BB	SO	SB	Pinch Hit AB	Pinch Hit H	PO	A	E	DP	TC/G	FA	G by Pos
1993	**CLE A**	22	.170	.302	53	9	1	0	2	3.8	5	5	2	8	0	4	1	3	0	0	0	0.1	1.000	DH-20, OF-1
1994		91	.269	.521	290	78	22	0	17	5.9	51	60	42	72	4	5	0	150	7	1	2	1.8	.994	OF-84, DH-5
1995		137	.308	.558	484	149	26	1	31	6.4	85	107	75	112	6	3	0	219	3	5	2	1.7	.978	OF-131, DH-5
3 yrs.		250	.285	.528	827	236	49	1	50	6.0	141	172	119	192	10	12	1	372	10	6	4	1.6	.985	OF-216, DH-30
DIVISIONAL PLAYOFF SERIES																								
1995	**CLE A**	3	.000	.000	12	0	0	0	0	0.0	1	0	1	2	0	0	0	3	0	0	0	1.0	1.000	OF-3
LEAGUE CHAMPIONSHIP SERIES																								
1995	**CLE A**	6	.286	.571	21	6	0	0	2	9.5	2	2	2	5	0	0	0	9	0	0	0	1.5	1.000	OF-6
WORLD SERIES																								
1995	**CLE A**	6	.222	.389	18	4	0	0	1	5.6	2	2	4	5	1	0	0	8	0	0	0	1.3	1.000	OF-6

Mario Ramirez

RAMIREZ, MARIO BR TR 5′ 9″ 155 lbs.
Born Mario Ramirez (Torres).
B. Sept. 12, 1957, Yauco, Puerto Rico.

Year	Team	Games	BA	SA	AB	H	2B	3B	HR	HR%	R	RBI	BB	SO	SB	Pinch Hit AB	Pinch Hit H	PO	A	E	DP	TC/G	FA	G by Pos
1980	**NY N**	18	.208	.208	24	5	0	0	0	0.0	2	0	1	7	0	0	0	13	21	0	6	2.4	1.000	SS-7, 2B-4, 3B-3
1981	**SD N**	13	.077	.077	13	1	0	0	0	0.0	1	1	2	5	0	3	1	5	11	0	1	4.0	1.000	SS-2, 3B-2
1982		13	.174	.217	23	4	1	0	0	0.0	1	1	2	4	0	5	1	10	21	1	3	3.2	.969	SS-8, 3B-1, 2B-1
1983		55	.196	.308	107	21	6	3	0	0.0	11	12	20	23	0	15	0	50	86	2	14	3.5	.986	SS-38, 3B-1
1984		48	.119	.237	59	7	1	0	2	3.4	12	9	13	14	0	3	0	34	45	3	12	2.0	.963	SS-33, 3B-6, 2B-2
1985		37	.283	.383	60	17	0	0	2	3.3	6	5	3	11	0	5	3	25	38	5	9	2.0	.926	SS-27, 2B-7
6 yrs.		184	.192	.283	286	55	8	3	4	1.4	33	28	41	64	0	31	5	137	222	11	45	2.6	.970	SS-115, 2B-14, 3B-13
LEAGUE CHAMPIONSHIP SERIES																								
1984	**SD N**	2	.000	.000	2	0	0	0	0	0.0	0	0	0		0	2	0	0	0	0	0	0.0	—	

Milt Ramirez

RAMIREZ, MILTON BR TR 5′9″ 150 lbs.
Born Milton Ramirez (Barboza).
B. Apr. 2, 1950, Mayaguez, Puerto Rico.

Year	Team	Lg	Games	BA	SA	AB	H	2B	3B	HR	HR%	R	RBI	BB	SO	SB	Pinch Hit AB	Pinch Hit H	PO	A	E	DP	TC/G	FA	G by Pos
1970	STL	N	62	.190	.241	79	15	2	1	0	0.0	8	3	8	9	0	1	0	63	92	14	25	2.8	.917	SS-59, 3B-1
1971			4	.273	.273	11	3	0	0	0	0.0	2	0	2	1	0	0	0	11	7	1	1	4.8	.947	SS-4
1979	OAK	A	28	.161	.210	62	10	1	1	0	0.0	4	3	3	8	0	0	0	25	43	5	5	2.4	.932	3B-12, 2B-11, SS-8
3 yrs.			94	.184	.230	152	28	3	2	0	0.0	14	6	13	18	0	1	0	99	142	20	31	2.7	.923	SS-71, 3B-13, 2B-11

Orlando Ramirez

RAMIREZ, ORLANDO BR TR 5′10″ 175 lbs.
Born Orlando Ramirez (Leal).
B. Dec. 18, 1951, Cartagena, Colombia.

Year	Team	Lg	Games	BA	SA	AB	H	2B	3B	HR	HR%	R	RBI	BB	SO	SB	Pinch Hit AB	Pinch Hit H	PO	A	E	DP	TC/G	FA	G by Pos
1974	CAL	A	31	.163	.163	86	14	0	0	0	0.0	4	7	6	23	2	0	0	41	90	6	20	4.4	.956	SS-31
1975			44	.240	.300	100	24	4	1	0	0.0	10	4	11	22	9	1	0	62	90	16	27	4.2	.905	SS-40
1976			30	.200	.214	70	14	1	0	0	0.0	3	5	6	11	3	0	0	30	82	4	11	3.9	.966	SS-30
1977			25	.077	.077	13	1	0	0	0	0.0	6	0	0	3	1	0	0	6	17	1	2	2.7	.958	2B-5, SS-3, DH-1
1979			13	.000	.000	12	0	0	0	0	0.0	1	0	1	6	1	0	0	7	20	5	3	2.9	.844	SS-10, DH-1
5 yrs.			143	.189	.214	281	53	5	1	0	0.0	24	16	24	65	16	1	0	146	299	32	63	3.9	.933	SS-114, 2B-5, DH-2

Rafael Ramirez

RAMIREZ, RAFAEL EMILIO BR TR 6′ 170 lbs.
Born Rafael Emilio Ramirez (Peguero).
B. Feb. 18, 1958, San Pedro de Macoris, Dominican Republic.

Year	Team	Lg	Games	BA	SA	AB	H	2B	3B	HR	HR%	R	RBI	BB	SO	SB	Pinch Hit AB	Pinch Hit H	PO	A	E	DP	TC/G	FA	G by Pos
1980	ATL	N	50	.267	.352	165	44	6	1	2	1.2	17	11	2	33	2	0	0	63	140	11	25	4.7	.949	SS-46
1981			95	.218	.303	307	67	16	2	2	0.7	30	20	24	47	7	0	0	181	306	30	55	5.4	.942	SS-95
1982			157	.278	.379	609	169	24	4	10	1.6	74	52	36	49	27	0	0	300	528	38	130	5.5	.956	SS-157
1983			152	.297	.368	622	185	13	5	7	1.1	82	58	36	48	16	1	0	232	490	39	116	5.0	.949	SS-152
1984			145	.266	.327	591	157	22	4	2	0.3	51	48	26	70	14	0	0	251	443	30	94	5.0	.959	SS-145
1985			138	.248	.333	568	141	25	4	5	0.9	54	58	20	63	2	3	2	214	451	32	115	5.2	.954	SS-133
1986			134	.240	.335	496	119	21	1	8	1.6	57	33	21	60	19	5	1	156	371	29	68	3.8	.948	SS-86, 3B-57, OF-3
1987			56	.263	.346	179	47	12	0	1	0.6	22	21	8	16	6	8	2	66	110	10	33	3.7	.946	SS-38, 3B-12
1988	HOU	N	155	.276	.378	566	156	30	5	6	1.1	51	59	18	61	3	4	3	232	408	23	68	4.3	.965	SS-154
1989			151	.246	.324	537	132	20	2	6	1.1	46	54	29	64	3	5	1	189	326	30	60	3.7	.945	SS-149
1990			132	.261	.330	445	116	19	3	2	0.4	44	37	24	46	10	5	0	190	321	25	57	4.2	.953	SS-129
1991			101	.236	.292	233	55	10	0	1	0.4	17	20	13	40	3	39	9	86	124	8	22	2.9	.963	SS-45, 2B-27, 3B-2
1992			73	.250	.301	176	44	6	0	1	0.6	17	13	7	24	0	17	2	60	114	7	17	3.1	.961	SS-57, 3B-1
13 yrs.			1539	.261	.342	5494	1432	224	31	53	1.0	562	484	264	621	112	87	20	2220	4132	312	860	4.5	.953	SS-1386, 3B-72, 2B-27, OF-3
LEAGUE CHAMPIONSHIP SERIES																									
1982	ATL	N	3	.182	.182	11	2	0	0	0	0.0	1	1	1	1	0	0	0	5	11	1	0	5.7	.941	SS-3

Bobby Ramos

RAMOS, ROBERTO BR TR 5′11″ 190 lbs.
B. Nov. 5, 1955, Calabazar de Sagua, Cuba.

Year	Team	Lg	Games	BA	SA	AB	H	2B	3B	HR	HR%	R	RBI	BB	SO	SB	Pinch Hit AB	Pinch Hit H	PO	A	E	DP	TC/G	FA	G by Pos
1978	MON	N	2	.000	.000	4	0	0	0	0	0.0	0	0	0	1	0	1	0	3	1	0	0	4.0	1.000	C-1
1980			13	.156	.219	32	5	2	0	0	0.0	5	2	5	5	0	1	1	47	7	2	0	4.7	.964	C-12
1981			26	.195	.293	41	8	1	0	1	2.4	4	3	3	5	0	3	2	70	5	2	2	3.3	.974	C-23
1982	NY	A	4	.091	.364	11	1	0	0	1	9.1	1	2	0	3	0	0	0	21	1	0	0	5.5	1.000	C-4
1983	MON	N	27	.230	.311	61	14	3	1	0	0.0	2	5	8	11	0	0	0	111	14	2	0	5.1	.984	C-25
1984			31	.193	.277	83	16	1	0	2	2.4	8	5	6	13	0	0	0	138	22	3	1	5.3	.982	C-31
6 yrs.			103	.190	.280	232	44	7	1	4	1.7	20	17	22	38	0	5	3	390	50	9	3	4.7	.980	C-96

Chucho Ramos

RAMOS, JESUS MANUEL BR TL 5′10½″ 167 lbs.
Born Jesus Manuel Ramos (Garcia).
B. Apr. 12, 1918, Maturin, Venezuela D. Sept. 2, 1977, Caracas, Venezuela.

Year	Team	Lg	Games	BA	SA	AB	H	2B	3B	HR	HR%	R	RBI	BB	SO	SB	Pinch Hit AB	Pinch Hit H	PO	A	E	DP	TC/G	FA	G by Pos
1944	CIN	N	4	.500	.600	10	5	1	0	0	0.0	1	0	0	0	0	0	0	5	0	0	0	1.7	1.000	OF-3

Domingo Ramos

RAMOS, DOMINGO ANTONIO BR TR 5′10″ 154 lbs.
Born Domingo Antonio Ramos (DeRamos).
B. Mar. 29, 1958, Santiago, Dominican Republic.

Year	Team	Lg	Games	BA	SA	AB	H	2B	3B	HR	HR%	R	RBI	BB	SO	SB	Pinch Hit AB	Pinch Hit H	PO	A	E	DP	TC/G	FA	G by Pos
1978	NY	A	1	—	—	0	0	0	0	0	—	0	0	0	0	0	0	0	0	0	0	0	0.0	.000	SS-1
1980	TOR	A	5	.125	.125	16	2	0	0	0	0.0	0	0	2	5	0	0	0	5	10	0	3	3.0	1.000	2B-2, SS-2, DH-1
1982	SEA	A	8	.154	.231	26	4	2	0	0	0.0	3	1	3	2	0	0	0	9	14	2	0	3.1	.920	SS-8
1983			53	.283	.362	127	36	4	0	2	1.6	14	10	7	12	3	9	1	51	109	8	22	3.7	.952	SS-28, 3B-8, 2B-8, DH-2
1984			59	.185	.210	81	15	2	0	0	0.0	6	2	5	12	2	2	0	51	49	5	10	1.8	.952	3B-38, SS-13, 1B-5, 2B-3
1985			75	.196	.250	168	33	6	0	1	0.6	19	15	17	23	0	2	0	87	119	10	26	2.8	.954	SS-36, 2B-20, 1B-14, 3B-7
1986			49	.182	.202	99	18	2	0	0	0.0	8	5	8	13	0	0	0	55	93	6	16	3.3	.961	SS-21, 2B-16, 3B-8, DH-2
1987			42	.311	.427	103	32	6	0	2	1.9	9	11	3	12	0	1	0	47	88	5	19	3.7	.964	SS-25, 3B-7, 2B-6
1988	2 teams		CLE A (22G –.261)	CAL A (10G –.133)																					
″	total		32	.230	.246	61	14	1	0	0	0.0	10	5	3	7	0	4	1	37	43	1	8	2.6	.988	2B-11, 3B-10, 1B-5, SS-4, OF-1
1989	CHI	N	85	.263	.335	179	47	6	2	1	0.6	18	19	17	23	1	14	6	49	142	11	20	2.8	.946	SS-42, 3B-30
1990			98	.265	.314	226	60	5	0	2	0.9	22	17	27	29	0	18	2	62	100	10	19	2.0	.942	3B-66, SS-21, 2B-1
11 yrs.			507	.240	.297	1086	261	34	2	8	0.7	109	85	92	138	6	50	10	453	767	58	143	2.7	.955	SS-201, 3B-174, 2B-67, 1B-24, DH-5, OF-1
LEAGUE CHAMPIONSHIP SERIES																									
1989	CHI	N	1	.000	.000	1	0	0	0	0	0.0	0	0	0	0	0	1	0	0	0	0	0	0.0	—	

John Ramos

RAMOS, JOHN JOSEPH BR TR 6′ 190 lbs.
B. Aug. 6, 1965, Tampa, Fla.

Year	Team	Lg	Games	BA	SA	AB	H	2B	3B	HR	HR%	R	RBI	BB	SO	SB	Pinch Hit AB	Pinch Hit H	PO	A	E	DP	TC/G	FA	G by Pos
1991	NY	A	10	.308	.346	26	8	1	0	0	0.0	4	3	1	3	0	1	0	23	1	0	0	2.7	1.000	C-5, DH-4

Bill Ramsey

RAMSEY, WILLIAM THRACE (Square Jaw) BR TR 6′ 175 lbs.
B. Oct. 20, 1920, Osceola, Ark.

Year	Team	Lg	Games	BA	SA	AB	H	2B	3B	HR	HR%	R	RBI	BB	SO	SB	Pinch Hit AB	Pinch Hit H	PO	A	E	DP	TC/G	FA	G by Pos
1945	BOS	N	78	.292	.372	137	40	8	0	1	0.7	16	12	4	22	1	29	5	78	1	3	0	1.9	.963	OF-43

Fernando Ramsey

RAMSEY, FERNANDO DAVID BR TR 6′ 1″ 175 lbs.
Born Fernando David Ramsey (Ramsey).
B. Dec. 20, 1965, Rainbow, Panama.

Year	Team	Games	BA	SA	AB	H	2B	3B	HR	HR%	R	RBI	BB	SO	SB	Pinch Hit AB	Pinch Hit H	PO	A	E	DP	TC/G	FA	G by Pos
1992	CHI N	18	.120	.120	25	3	0	0	0	0.0	0	2	0	6	0	1	0	17	0	0	0	1.1	1.000	OF-15

Mike Ramsey

RAMSEY, MICHAEL JAMES BB TL 6′ 170 lbs.
B. July 8, 1960, Thomson, Ga.

Year	Team	Games	BA	SA	AB	H	2B	3B	HR	HR%	R	RBI	BB	SO	SB	Pinch Hit AB	Pinch Hit H	PO	A	E	DP	TC/G	FA	G by Pos
1987	LA N	48	.232	.296	125	29	4	2	0	0.0	18	12	10	32	2	0	0	70	1	2	0	1.7	.973	OF-43

Mike Ramsey

RAMSEY, MICHAEL JEFFREY BB TR 6′ 1″ 170 lbs.
B. May 29, 1954, Roanoke, Va.

Year	Team	Games	BA	SA	AB	H	2B	3B	HR	HR%	R	RBI	BB	SO	SB	Pinch Hit AB	Pinch Hit H	PO	A	E	DP	TC/G	FA	G by Pos
1978	STL N	12	.200	.200	5	1	0	0	0	0.0	4	0	0	1	0	1	0	4	6	1	3	2.8	.909	SS-4
1980		59	.262	.341	126	33	8	1	0	0.0	11	8	3	17	0	18	6	62	94	9	19	3.2	.945	2B-24, SS-20, 3B-8
1981		47	.258	.282	124	32	3	0	0	0.0	19	9	8	16	4	7	1	56	126	6	21	4.5	.968	SS-35, 3B-5, OF-1, 2B-1
1982		112	.230	.289	256	59	8	2	1	0.4	18	21	22	34	6	16	4	135	219	10	42	3.8	.973	2B-43, 3B-28, SS-22, OF-2
1983		97	.263	.337	175	46	4	3	1	0.6	25	16	12	23	4	6	1	94	149	8	34	2.6	.968	2B-66, SS-20, 3B-8, OF-1
1984	2 teams	STL N (21G –.067) MON N (37G –.214)																						
″	total	58	.188	.212	85	16	2	0	0	0.0	3	3	1	16	0	2	0	44	79	3	19	2.4	.976	SS-33, 2B-19, 3B-1
1985	LA N	9	.133	.200	15	2	1	0	0	0.0	1	0	2	4	0	5	1	5	11	2	1	3.0	.889	SS-4, 2B-2
7 yrs.		394	.240	.296	786	189	26	6	2	0.3	81	57	48	111	14	55	13	400	684	39	139	3.2	.965	2B-155, SS-138, 3B-50, OF-4
WORLD SERIES																								
1982	STL N	3	.000	.000	1	0	0	0	0	0.0	1	0	0	1	0	0	0	0	0	0	0	0.0	.000	3B-2

Dick Rand

RAND, RICHARD HILTON BR TR 6′ 2″ 185 lbs.
B. Mar. 7, 1931, South Gate, Calif.

Year	Team	Games	BA	SA	AB	H	2B	3B	HR	HR%	R	RBI	BB	SO	SB	Pinch Hit AB	Pinch Hit H	PO	A	E	DP	TC/G	FA	G by Pos
1953	STL N	9	.290	.323	31	9	1	0	0	0.0	3	1	2	6	0	0	0	56	7	1	0	7.1	.984	C-9
1955		3	.300	.600	10	3	0	0	1	10.0	1	3	1	1	0	0	0	9	1	0	0	3.3	1.000	C-3
1957	PIT N	60	.219	.286	105	23	2	1	1	1.0	7	9	11	24	0	3	1	172	11	5	5	3.3	.973	C-57
3 yrs.		72	.240	.315	146	35	3	1	2	1.4	11	13	14	31	0	3	1	237	19	6	5	3.8	.977	C-69

Joe Randa

RANDA, JOSEPH GREGORY BR TR 5′11″ 190 lbs.
B. Dec. 18, 1969, Milwaukee, Wis.

Year	Team	Games	BA	SA	AB	H	2B	3B	HR	HR%	R	RBI	BB	SO	SB	Pinch Hit AB	Pinch Hit H	PO	A	E	DP	TC/G	FA	G by Pos
1995	KC A	34	.171	.243	70	12	2	0	1	1.4	6	5	6	17	0	5	0	15	44	3	4	1.9	.952	3B-22, 2B-9, DH-2

Bob Randall

RANDALL, ROBERT LEE BR TR 6′ 2″ 175 lbs.
B. June 6, 1949, Norton, Kans.

Year	Team	Games	BA	SA	AB	H	2B	3B	HR	HR%	R	RBI	BB	SO	SB	Pinch Hit AB	Pinch Hit H	PO	A	E	DP	TC/G	FA	G by Pos
1976	MIN A	153	.267	.328	475	127	18	4	1	0.2	55	34	28	38	3	0	0	327	423	24	124	5.1	.969	2B-153
1977		103	.239	.294	306	73	13	2	0	0.0	36	22	15	25	1	5	1	222	297	8	74	4.9	.985	2B-101, DH-4, 3B-1, 1B-1
1978		119	.270	.321	330	89	11	3	0	0.0	36	21	24	22	5	11	2	231	345	10	81	4.9	.983	2B-116, 3B-2, DH-1
1979		80	.246	.281	199	49	7	0	0	0.0	25	14	15	17	2	13	2	130	169	5	48	3.8	.984	2B-71, 3B-7, OF-1, SS-1
1980		5	.200	.267	15	3	1	0	0	0.0	2	0	1	0	1	1	0	1	10	1	1	2.4	.917	3B-4, 2B-1
5 yrs.		460	.257	.311	1325	341	50	9	1	0.1	154	91	83	102	11	30	5	911	1244	48	328	4.7	.978	2B-442, 3B-14, DH-5, SS-1, OF-1, 1B-1

Jim Randall

RANDALL, JAMES ODELL BB TR 5′11″ 195 lbs.
B. Aug. 19, 1960, Mobile, Ala.

Year	Team	Games	BA	SA	AB	H	2B	3B	HR	HR%	R	RBI	BB	SO	SB	Pinch Hit AB	Pinch Hit H	PO	A	E	DP	TC/G	FA	G by Pos
1988	CHI A	4	.000	.000	12	0	0	0	0	0.0	1	1	2	3	0	0	0	15	2	0	2	4.3	1.000	1B-2, OF-1, DH-1

Newt Randall

RANDALL, NEWTON J. BR TR 5′10″
B. Feb. 3, 1880, New Lowell, Ont., Canada D. May 3, 1955, Duluth, Minn.

Year	Team	Games	BA	SA	AB	H	2B	3B	HR	HR%	R	RBI	BB	SO	SB	Pinch Hit AB	Pinch Hit H	PO	A	E	DP	TC/G	FA	G by Pos
1907	2 teams	CHI N (22G –.205) BOS N (75G –.213)																						
″	total	97	.211	.271	336	71	10	5	0	0.0	22	19	27		6	3	0	150	12	15	2	1.9	.915	OF-94

Lenny Randle

RANDLE, LEONARD SHENOFF BB TR 5′10″ 169 lbs.
BR 1971
B. Feb. 12, 1949, Long Beach, Calif.

Year	Team	Games	BA	SA	AB	H	2B	3B	HR	HR%	R	RBI	BB	SO	SB	Pinch Hit AB	Pinch Hit H	PO	A	E	DP	TC/G	FA	G by Pos
1971	WAS A	75	.219	.298	215	47	11	0	2	0.9	27	13	24	56	1	6	0	178	178	12	50	5.6	.967	2B-66
1972	TEX A	74	.193	.269	249	48	13	0	2	0.8	23	21	13	51	4	4	0	161	177	20	39	5.0	.944	2B-65, SS-4, OF-2
1973		10	.207	.414	29	6	1	1	1	3.4	3	1	0	2	0	0	0	19	9	2	3	4.3	.933	2B-5, OF-2
1974		151	.302	.356	520	157	17	4	1	0.2	65	49	29	43	26	2	2	218	285	23	53	3.4	.956	3B-89, 2B-40, OF-21, DH-2, SS-1
1975		156	.276	.359	601	166	24	7	4	0.7	85	57	57	80	16	4	1	376	270	16	68	4.0	.976	2B-79, OF-66, 3B-17, DH-3, C-1, SS-1
1976		142	.224	.273	539	121	11	6	1	0.2	53	51	46	63	30	2	0	354	324	20	63	4.8	.971	2B-113, OF-30, 3B-2, DH-1
1977	NY N	136	.304	.404	513	156	22	7	5	1.0	78	27	65	70	33	5	0	152	261	15	33	3.1	.965	3B-110, 2B-20, OF-6, SS-1
1978		132	.233	.320	437	102	16	8	2	0.5	53	35	64	57	14	15	5	111	215	11	21	2.6	.967	3B-124, 2B-5
1979	NY A	20	.179	.179	39	7	0	0	0	0.0	2	3	3	2	0	5	1	19	2	0	0	1.6	1.000	OF-11, DH-2
1980	CHI N	130	.276	.370	489	135	19	6	5	1.0	67	39	50	55	19	8	4	119	273	25	12	3.1	.940	3B-111, 2B-17, OF-6
1981	SEA A	82	.231	.315	273	63	9	1	4	1.5	22	25	17	22	11	5	0	89	178	5	23	3.1	.982	3B-59, 2B-21, OF-5, SS-3
1982		30	.174	.217	46	8	2	0	0	0.0	10	1	4	4	2	1	1	10	27	3	3	1.4	.925	DH-13, 3B-9, 2B-6
12 yrs.		1138	.257	.335	3950	1016	145	40	27	0.7	488	322	372	505	156	57	14	1806	2199	152	368	3.6	.963	3B-521, 2B-437, OF-149, DH-21, SS-10, C-1

Willie Randolph

RANDOLPH, WILLIE LARRY BR TR 5′11″ 165 lbs.
B. July 6, 1954, Holly Hill, S. C.

Year	Team	Games	BA	SA	AB	H	2B	3B	HR	HR%	R	RBI	BB	SO	SB	Pinch Hit AB	Pinch Hit H	PO	A	E	DP	TC/G	FA	G by Pos
1975	PIT N	30	.164	.180	61	10	1	0	0	0.0	9	3	7	6	1	8	2	34	45	6	8	5.7	.929	2B-14, 3B-1
1976	NY A	125	.267	.328	430	115	15	4	1	0.2	59	40	58	39	37	1	0	307	415	19	87	6.0	.974	2B-124
1977		147	.274	.387	551	151	28	11	4	0.7	91	40	64	53	13	0	0	350	454	16	108	5.6	.980	2B-147
1978		134	.279	.357	499	139	18	6	3	0.6	87	42	82	51	36	0	0	296	400	16	80	5.3	.978	2B-134
1979		153	.270	.368	574	155	15	13	5	0.9	98	61	95	39	33	0	0	355	478	13	128	5.5	.985	2B-153
1980		138	.294	.407	513	151	23	7	7	1.4	99	46	**119**	45	30	0	0	361	401	19	97	5.7	.976	2B-138
1981		93	.232	.305	357	83	14	3	2	0.6	59	24	57	24	14	0	0	205	268	11	74	5.2	.977	2B-93
1982		144	.280	.349	553	155	21	4	3	0.5	85	36	75	35	16	0	0	352	380	14	100	5.2	.981	2B-142, DH-1
1983		104	.279	.348	420	117	21	1	2	0.5	73	38	53	32	12	0	0	265	298	12	77	5.5	.979	2B-104
1984		142	.287	.348	564	162	24	2	2	0.4	86	31	86	42	10	0	0	334	419	13	112	5.4	.983	2B-142

Willie Randolph *continued*

Year	Team	Games	BA	SA	AB	H	2B	3B	HR	HR%	R	RBI	BB	SO	SB	Pinch Hit AB	Pinch Hit H	PO	A	E	DP	TC/G	FA	G by Pos
1985		143	.276	.356	497	137	21	2	5	1.0	75	40	85	39	16	0	0	303	425	11	104	5.2	.985	2B-143
1986		141	.276	.346	492	136	15	2	5	1.0	76	50	94	49	15	2	1	313	381	20	94	5.1	.972	2B-139, DH-1
1987		120	.305	.414	449	137	24	2	7	1.6	96	67	82	25	11	0	0	286	338	12	89	5.3	.981	2B-119, DH-1
1988		110	.230	.300	404	93	20	1	2	0.5	43	34	55	39	8	0	0	254	339	7	83	5.5	.988	2B-110
1989	LA N	145	.282	.326	549	155	18	0	2	0.4	62	36	71	51	7	3	0	260	412	9	85	4.9	.987	2B-140
1990	2 teams	LA N (26G –.271) OAK A (93G –.257)																						
"	total	119	.260	.325	388	101	13	3	2	0.5	52	30	45	34	7	2	1	198	313	11	72	4.5	.979	2B-110, DH-6
1991	MIL A	124	.327	.374	431	141	14	3	0	0.0	60	54	75	38	4	8	4	237	378	20	96	5.2	.969	2B-121, DH-2
1992	NY N	90	.252	.318	286	72	11	1	2	0.7	29	15	40	34	1	7	1	149	195	8	53	4.5	.977	2B-79
18 yrs.		2202	.276	.351	8018	2210	316	65	54	0.7	1239	687	1243	675	271	31	9	4859	6339	237	1547	5.3	.979	2B-2152, DH-11, 3B-1
DIVISIONAL PLAYOFF SERIES																								
1981	NY A	5	.200	.200	20	4	0	0	0	0.0	0	1	1	4	0	0	0	7	10	0	0	3.4	1.000	2B-5
LEAGUE CHAMPIONSHIP SERIES																								
1975	PIT N	2	.000	.000	2	0	0	0	0	0.0	1	0	0	1	0	1	0	0	1	0	0	1.0	1.000	2B-1
1976	NY A	5	.118	.118	17	2	0	0	0	0.0	0	1	3	1	1	0	0	8	14	0	2	4.4	1.000	2B-5
1977		5	.278	.333	18	5	1	0	0	0.0	4	2	1	0	0	0	0	13	9	0	2	4.4	1.000	2B-5
1980		3	.385	.538	13	5	2	0	0	0.0	0	1	1	3	0	0	0	2	9	0	2	3.7	1.000	2B-3
1981		3	.333	.583	12	4	0	0	1	8.3	2	2	0	1	0	0	0	12	12	0	4	8.0	1.000	2B-3
1990	OAK A	4	.375	.375	8	3	0	0	0	0.0	1	3	1	0	0	0	0	5	9	0	1	3.5	1.000	2B-4
6 yrs.		22	.271	.357	70	19	3	0	1	1.4	8	9	6	6	1	1	0	40	54	0	11	4.5	1.000	2B-21
WORLD SERIES																								
1976	NY A	4	.071	.071	14	1	0	0	0	0.0	1	0	1	3	0	0	0	13	8	0	5	5.3	1.000	2B-4
1977		6	.160	.360	25	4	2	0	1	4.0	5	1	2	2	0	0	0	13	14	0	1	4.5	1.000	2B-6
1981		6	.222	.722	18	4	1	1	2	11.1	5	3	9	0	1	0	0	13	11	0	2	4.0	1.000	2B-6
1990	OAK A	4	.267	.267	15	4	0	0	0	0.0	0	0	1	0	1	0	0	14	12	0	5	6.5	1.000	2B-4
4 yrs.		20	.181	.375	72	13	3	1	3	4.2	11	4	13	5	2	0	0	53	45	0	13	4.9	1.000	2B-20

Merritt Ranew

RANEW, MERRITT THOMAS
B. May 10, 1938, Albany, Ga.
BL TR 5′11″ 170 lbs.

Year	Team	Games	BA	SA	AB	H	2B	3B	HR	HR%	R	RBI	BB	SO	SB	Pinch Hit AB	Pinch Hit H	PO	A	E	DP	TC/G	FA	G by Pos
1962	HOU N	71	.234	.390	218	51	6	8	4	1.8	26	24	14	43	2	15	1	357	35	8	1	6.9	.980	C-58
1963	CHI N	78	.338	.461	154	52	8	1	3	1.9	18	15	9	32	1	41	**17**	213	19	3	14	5.3	.987	C-37, 1B-7
1964	2 teams	CHI N (16G –.091) MIL N (9G –.118)																						
"	total	25	.100	.100	50	5	0	0	0	0.0	1	1	2	9	0	11	2	53	10	0	0	5.3	1.000	C-12
1965	CAL A	41	.209	.286	91	19	4	0	1	1.1	12	10	7	22	0	17	2	78	7	1	1	3.6	.988	C-24
1969	SEA A	54	.247	.272	81	20	2	0	0	0.0	11	4	10	14	0	31	6	62	4	2	2	4.0	.971	C-13, OF-3, 3B-1
5 yrs.		269	.247	.352	594	147	20	9	8	1.3	68	54	42	120	3	115	28	763	75	14	18	5.5	.984	C-144, 1B-7, OF-3, 3B-1

Jeff Ransom

RANSOM, JEFFREY DEAN
B. Nov. 11, 1960, Fresno, Calif.
BR TR 5′11″ 185 lbs.

Year	Team	Games	BA	SA	AB	H	2B	3B	HR	HR%	R	RBI	BB	SO	SB	Pinch Hit AB	Pinch Hit H	PO	A	E	DP	TC/G	FA	G by Pos
1981	SF N	5	.267	.333	15	4	1	0	0	0.0	2	0	1	1	0	0	0	28	5	0	0	6.6	1.000	C-5
1982		15	.159	.159	44	7	0	0	0	0.0	5	3	6	7	0	1	0	71	8	1	1	5.7	.988	C-14
1983		6	.200	.350	20	4	0	0	1	5.0	3	3	4	7	0	0	0	32	3	2	0	6.2	.946	C-6
3 yrs.		26	.190	.241	79	15	1	0	1	1.3	10	6	11	15	0	1	0	131	16	3	1	6.0	.980	C-25

Earl Rapp

RAPP, EARL WELLINGTON
B. May 20, 1921, Corunna, Mich. D. Feb. 13, 1992, Swedesboro, N. J.
BL TR 6′ 2″ 185 lbs.

Year	Team	Games	BA	SA	AB	H	2B	3B	HR	HR%	R	RBI	BB	SO	SB	Pinch Hit AB	Pinch Hit H	PO	A	E	DP	TC/G	FA	G by Pos
1949	2 teams	DET A (1G –.000) CHI A (19G –.259)																						
"	total	20	.259	.315	54	14	1	1	0	0.0	3	11	6	6	1	5	1	36	2	1	0	3.0	.974	OF-13
1951	2 teams	NY N (13G –.091) STL A (26G –.327)																						
"	total	39	.303	.459	109	33	5	3	2	1.8	14	15	13	14	1	12	1	45	2	1	0	1.9	.979	OF-25
1952	2 teams	STL A (30G –.143) WAS A (46G –.284)																						
"	total	76	.224	.310	116	26	10	0	0	0.0	10	13	6	21	0	**54**	**10**	23	0	1	0	1.4	.958	OF-17
3 yrs.		135	.262	.369	279	73	16	4	2	0.7	27	39	25	41	2	71	12	104	4	3	0	2.0	.973	OF-55

Goldie Rapp

RAPP, JOSEPH ALOYSIUS
B. Feb. 6, 1892, Cincinnati, Ohio D. July 1, 1966, La Mesa, Calif.
BB TR 5′10″ 165 lbs.

Year	Team	Games	BA	SA	AB	H	2B	3B	HR	HR%	R	RBI	BB	SO	SB	Pinch Hit AB	Pinch Hit H	PO	A	E	DP	TC/G	FA	G by Pos
1921	2 teams	NY N (58G –.215) PHI N (52G –.277)																						
"	total	110	.248	.308	383	95	16	2	1	0.3	49	25	29	21	9	1	0	117	226	20	19	3.4	.945	3B-106, 2B-1
1922	PHI N	119	.253	.317	502	127	26	3	0	0.0	58	38	32	29	6	0	0	123	254	22	20	3.4	.945	3B-117, SS-2
1923		47	.263	.307	179	47	5	0	1	0.6	27	10	14	14	1	2	1	58	84	8	9	3.3	.947	3B-45
3 yrs.		276	.253	.312	1064	269	47	5	2	0.2	134	73	75	64	16	3	1	298	564	50	48	3.4	.945	3B-268, SS-2, 2B-1

Bill Rariden

RARIDEN, WILLIAM ANGEL (Bedford Bill)
B. Feb. 4, 1888, Bedford, Ind. D. Aug. 28, 1942, Bedford, Ind.
BR TR 5′10″ 168 lbs.

Year	Team	Games	BA	SA	AB	H	2B	3B	HR	HR%	R	RBI	BB	SO	SB	Pinch Hit AB	Pinch Hit H	PO	A	E	DP	TC/G	FA	G by Pos
1909	BOS N	13	.143	.167	42	6	1	0	0	0.0	1	1	4		1	0	0	47	15	6	2	5.2	.912	C-13
1910		49	.226	.299	137	31	5	1	1	0.7	15	14	12	22	1	0	0	177	75	10	6	5.3	.962	C-49
1911		70	.228	.264	246	56	9	0	0	0.0	22	21	21	18	3	1	0	293	120	22	12	6.3	.949	C-65, 3B-3, 2B-1
1912		79	.223	.255	247	55	3	1	1	0.4	27	14	18	35	3	6	2	297	103	15	6	5.7	.964	C-73
1913		95	.236	.325	246	58	9	2	3	1.2	31	30	30	21	5	5	1	377	111	12	6	5.7	.976	C-87
1914	IND F	131	.235	.298	396	93	15	5	0	0.0	44	47	61		12	1	0	714	215	18	14	7.3	.981	C-130
1915	NWK F	142	.270	.369	444	120	30	7	0	0.0	49	40	60		8	0	0	709	238	21	18	6.8	.978	C-142
1916	NY N	120	.222	.274	351	78	9	3	1	0.3	23	29	55	32	4	1	1	576	144	21	10	6.2	.972	C-119
1917		104	.271	.316	266	72	10	1	0	0.0	20	25	42	17	3	0	0	354	74	13	7	4.4	.971	C-100
1918		69	.224	.262	183	41	5	1	0	0.0	15	17	15	15	1	4	0	195	45	4	3	3.9	.984	C-63
1919	CIN N	75	.216	.284	218	47	6	3	1	0.5	16	24	17	19	4	4	2	283	67	6	5	5.1	.983	C-70
1920		39	.248	.277	101	25	3	0	0	0.0	9	10	5	0	2	2	0	107	34	4	3	3.9	.972	C-37
12 yrs.		986	.237	.298	2877	682	105	24	7	0.2	272	272	340	179	47	24	6	4129	1241	152	92	5.8	.972	C-948, 3B-3, 2B-1
WORLD SERIES																								
1917	NY N	5	.385	.385	13	5	0	0	0	0.0	2	2	2	1	0	0	0	25	10	0	1	7.0	1.000	C-5
1919	CIN N	5	.211	.211	19	4	0	0	0	0.0	0	2	0	0	1	0	0	25	3	1	0	5.8	.966	C-5
2 yrs.		10	.281	.281	32	9	0	0	0	0.0	2	4	2	1	1	0	0	50	13	1	1	6.4	.984	C-10

Morrie Rath

RATH, MORRIS CHARLES BL TR 5′ 8½″ 160 lbs.
B. Dec. 25, 1886, Mobeetie, Tex. D. Nov. 18, 1945, Upper Darby, Pa.

Year	Team	Games	BA	SA	AB	H	2B	3B	HR	HR%	R	RBI	BB	SO	SB	Pinch Hit AB	Pinch Hit H	PO	A	E	DP	TC/G	FA	G by Pos
1909	PHI A	7	.269	.308	26	7	1	0	0	0.0	4	3	2		1	0	0	20	18	7	2	7.5	.844	SS-4, 3B-2
1910	2 teams	PHI A (18G –.154) CLE A (24G –.194)																						
″	total	42	.183	.215	93	17	3	0	0	0.0	8	1	15		2	3	0	36	60	5	5	2.7	.950	3B-33, 2B-3, SS-1
1912	CHI A	157	.272	.301	591	161	10	2	1	0.2	104	19	95		30	0	0	353	463	31	46	5.4	.963	2B-157
1913		90	.200	.207	295	59	2	0	0	0.0	37	12	46	22	22	2	1	159	251	16	32	5.0	.962	2B-86
1919	CIN N	138	.264	.298	537	142	13	1	1	0.2	77	29	64	24	17	0	0	345	452	21	59	5.9	.974	2B-138
1920		129	.267	.308	506	135	7	4	2	0.4	61	28	36	24	10	1	0	312	400	17	60	5.7	.977	2B-126, 3B-1, OF-1
6 yrs.		563	.254	.285	2048	521	36	7	4	0.2	291	92	258	70	82	6	1	1225	1644	97	204	5.4	.967	2B-510, 3B-36, SS-5, OF-1
WORLD SERIES																								
1919	CIN N	8	.226	.258	31	7	1	0	0	0.0	5	2	4	1	2	0	0	22	17	2	3	5.1	.951	2B-8

Gene Ratliff

RATLIFF, KELLY EUGENE BR TR 6′ 5″ 185 lbs.
B. Sept. 28, 1945, Macon, Ga.

Year	Team	Games	BA	SA	AB	H	2B	3B	HR	HR%	R	RBI	BB	SO	SB	Pinch Hit AB	Pinch Hit H	PO	A	E	DP	TC/G	FA	G by Pos
1965	HOU N	4	.000	.000	4	0	0	0	0	0.0	0	0	0	4	0	4	0	0	0	0	0	0.0	—	

Paul Ratliff

RATLIFF, PAUL HAWTHORNE BL TR 6′ 2″ 190 lbs.
B. Jan. 23, 1944, San Diego, Calif.

Year	Team	Games	BA	SA	AB	H	2B	3B	HR	HR%	R	RBI	BB	SO	SB	Pinch Hit AB	Pinch Hit H	PO	A	E	DP	TC/G	FA	G by Pos
1963	MIN A	10	.190	.381	21	4	1	0	1	4.8	2	3	2	7	0	4	2	37	4	1	1	6.0	.976	C-7
1970		69	.268	.443	149	40	7	2	5	3.4	19	22	15	51	0	22	4	183	11	4	4	3.7	.980	C-53
1971	2 teams	MIN A (21G –.159) MIL A (23G –.171)																						
″	total	44	.165	.365	85	14	2	0	5	5.9	6	13	9	38	0	16	1	126	9	2	1	4.9	.985	C-28
1972	MIL A	22	.071	.143	42	3	0	0	1	2.4	1	4	2	23	0	10	0	38	5	0	0	3.3	1.000	C-13
4 yrs.		145	.205	.374	297	61	10	2	12	4.0	28	42	28	119	0	52	7	384	29	7	6	4.2	.983	C-101
LEAGUE CHAMPIONSHIP SERIES																								
1970	MIN A	1	.250	.250	4	1	0	0	0	0.0	0	0	0	1	0	0	0	7	0	1	0	8.0	.875	C-1

Tommy Raub

RAUB, THOMAS JEFFERSON BR TR 5′10″ 155 lbs.
B. Dec. 1, 1870, Raubsville, Pa. D. Feb. 16, 1949, Phillipsburg, N. J.

Year	Team	Games	BA	SA	AB	H	2B	3B	HR	HR%	R	RBI	BB	SO	SB	Pinch Hit AB	Pinch Hit H	PO	A	E	DP	TC/G	FA	G by Pos
1903	CHI N	36	.226	.310	84	19	3	2	0	0.0	6	7	5		3	8	3	90	20	15	3	4.6	.880	C-12, 1B-6, OF-5, 3B-4
1906	STL N	24	.282	.410	78	22	2	4	0	0.0	9	2	4		2	0	0	81	30	5	1	5.3	.957	C-22
2 yrs.		60	.253	.358	162	41	5	6	0	0.0	15	9	9		5	8	3	171	50	20	4	4.9	.917	C-34, 1B-6, OF-5, 3B-4

Bob Raudman

RAUDMAN, ROBERT JOYCE (Shorty) BL TL 5′ 9½″ 185 lbs.
B. Mar. 14, 1942, Erie, Pa.

Year	Team	Games	BA	SA	AB	H	2B	3B	HR	HR%	R	RBI	BB	SO	SB	Pinch Hit AB	Pinch Hit H	PO	A	E	DP	TC/G	FA	G by Pos
1966	CHI N	8	.241	.310	29	7	2	0	0	0.0	1	2	1	4	0	0	0	8	2	1	0	1.4	.909	OF-8
1967		8	.154	.154	26	4	0	0	0	0.0	0	1	1	4	0	0	0	13	1	2	1	2.0	.875	OF-8
2 yrs.		16	.200	.236	55	11	2	0	0	0.0	1	3	2	8	0	0	0	21	3	3	1	1.7	.889	OF-16

Johnny Rawlings

RAWLINGS, JOHN WILLIAM BR TR 5′ 8″ 158 lbs.
B. Aug. 17, 1892, Bloomfield, Iowa D. Oct. 16, 1972, Inglewood, Calif.

Year	Team	Games	BA	SA	AB	H	2B	3B	HR	HR%	R	RBI	BB	SO	SB	Pinch Hit AB	Pinch Hit H	PO	A	E	DP	TC/G	FA	G by Pos
1914	2 teams	CIN N (33G –.217) KC F (61G –.212)																						
″	total	94	.213	.229	253	54	4	0	0	0.0	28	23	28	8	7	7	1	138	264	30	27	5.2	.931	SS-66, 3B-10, 2B-7
1915	KC F	120	.216	.263	399	86	9	2	2	0.5	40	24	27		17	0	0	209	366	46	36	5.2	.926	SS-120
1917	BOS N	122	.256	.318	371	95	9	4	2	0.5	37	31	38	32	12	5	1	207	347	15	46	4.9	.974	2B-96, SS-17, OF-1, 3B-1
1918		111	.207	.239	410	85	7	3	0	0.0	32	21	30	31	10	1	0	208	309	19	34	4.9	.965	SS-71, 2B-20, OF-18
1919		77	.255	.309	275	70	8	2	1	0.4	30	16	16	20	10	3	0	127	185	12	22	4.3	.963	2B-58, OF-12, SS-5
1920	2 teams	BOS N (5G –.000) PHI N (98G –.234)																						
″	total	103	.233	.315	387	90	19	2	3	0.8	39	32	22	26	9	2	0	222	322	17	53	5.7	.970	2B-98
1921	2 teams	PHI N (60G –.291) NY N (86G –.267)																						
″	total	146	.278	.339	561	156	22	3	2	0.4	60	46	26	31	8	0	0	344	495	32	93	5.9	.963	2B-146, SS-1
1922	NY N	88	.282	.386	308	87	13	8	1	0.3	46	30	23	15	7	5	1	169	253	7	45	5.2	.984	2B-77, 3B-5
1923	PIT N	119	.284	.347	461	131	18	4	1	0.2	53	45	25	29	9	0	0	294	388	30	68	6.0	.958	2B-119
1924		3	.333	.333	3	1	0	0	0	0.0	0	2	0	0	0	3	1	0	0	0	0	0.0	—	
1925		36	.282	.400	110	31	7	0	2	1.8	17	13	8	8	0	3	0	60	91	3	12	5.3	.981	2B-29
1926		61	.232	.265	181	42	6	0	0	0.0	27	20	14	10	3	2	1	126	164	9	25	5.1	.970	2B-59
12 yrs.		1080	.250	.309	3719	928	122	28	14	0.4	409	303	257	210	92	31	5	2104	3184	220	461	5.3	.960	2B-709, SS-280, OF-31, 3B-16
WORLD SERIES																								
1921	NY N	8	.333	.433	30	10	3	0	0	0.0	2	4	0	3	0	0	0	20	27	0	5	5.9	1.000	2B-8

Irv Ray

RAY, IRVING BURTON (Stubby) BL TR 5′ 6″ 165 lbs.
B. Jan. 22, 1864, Harrington, Me. D. Feb. 21, 1948, Harrington, Me.

Year	Team	Games	BA	SA	AB	H	2B	3B	HR	HR%	R	RBI	BB	SO	SB	Pinch Hit AB	Pinch Hit H	PO	A	E	DP	TC/G	FA	G by Pos
1888	BOS N	50	.248	.316	206	51	2	3	2	1.0	26	26	6	11	7	0	0	61	133	30	6	4.4	.866	SS-48, 2B-3
1889	2 teams	BOS N (9G –.303) BAL AA (26G –.340)																						
″	total	35	.331	.381	139	46	5	1	0	0.0	28	19	11	6	13	0	0	45	72	28	10	4.1	.807	SS-25, OF-6, 3B-4
1890	BAL AA	38	.360	.453	139	50	6	2	1	0.7	28		15		11	0	0	40	104	17	7	4.2	.894	SS-38
1891		103	.278	.342	418	116	17	5	0	0.0	72	58	54	18	28	0	0	168	114	42	10	3.1	.870	OF-64, SS-40
4 yrs.		226	.292	.359	902	263	30	11	3	0.3	154	103	86	35	59	0	0	314	423	117	33	3.7	.863	SS-151, OF-70, 3B-4, 2B-3

Johnny Ray

RAY, JOHNNY CORNELIUS BB TR 5′11″ 170 lbs.
B. Mar. 1, 1957, Chouteau, Okla.

Year	Team	Games	BA	SA	AB	H	2B	3B	HR	HR%	R	RBI	BB	SO	SB	Pinch Hit AB	Pinch Hit H	PO	A	E	DP	TC/G	FA	G by Pos
1981	PIT N	31	.245	.353	102	25	11	0	0	0.0	10	6	6	9	0	2	1	52	96	2	22	4.8	.987	2B-31
1982		162	.281	.382	647	182	30	7	7	1.1	79	63	36	34	16	0	0	381	512	21	89	5.6	.977	2B-162
1983		151	.283	.399	576	163	**38**	7	5	0.9	68	53	35	26	18	5	1	320	452	13	102	5.2	.983	2B-151, 3B-1
1984		155	.312	.434	555	173	**38**	6	6	1.1	75	67	37	31	11	9	3	331	400	12	90	5.0	.984	2B-149
1985		154	.274	.375	594	163	33	3	7	1.2	67	70	46	24	13	4	1	305	423	18	89	4.9	.976	2B-151
1986		155	.301	.394	579	174	33	0	7	1.2	67	78	58	47	6	8	2	280	479	5	89	5.1	.993	2B-151
1987	2 teams	PIT N (123G –.273) CAL A (30G –.346)																						
″	total	153	.289	.374	599	173	30	3	5	0.8	64	69	44	46	4	6	1	300	448	14	103	5.1	.982	2B-148, DH-1
1988	CAL A	153	.306	.429	602	184	42	7	6	1.0	75	83	36	38	4	4	2	269	328	20	64	4.1	.968	2B-104, OF-40, DH-6
1989		134	.289	.358	530	153	16	3	5	0.9	52	62	36	30	6	4	2	279	403	11	98	5.3	.984	2B-130
1990		105	.277	.371	404	112	23	0	5	1.2	47	43	19	44	2	5	0	241	295	7	82	5.4	.987	2B-100, DH-1
10 yrs.		1353	.290	.391	5188	1502	294	36	53	1.0	604	594	353	329	80	47	13	2758	3836	123	828	5.1	.982	2B-1277, OF-40, DH-8, 3B-1

Larry Ray

RAY, LARRY DALE BL TR 6′ 1″ 195 lbs.
B. Mar. 11, 1958, Madison, Ind.

Year	Team	Games	BA	SA	AB	H	2B	3B	HR	HR%	R	RBI	BB	SO	SB	Pinch Hit AB	Pinch Hit H	PO	A	E	DP	TC/G	FA	G by Pos
1982	HOU N	5	.167	.167	6	1	0	0	0	0.0	0	1	0	4	0	4	1	1	0	0	0	1.0	1.000	OF-1

Floyd Rayford

RAYFORD, FLOYD KINNARD BR TR 5′10″ 190 lbs.
B. July 27, 1957, Memphis, Tenn.

Year	Team	Games	BA	SA	AB	H	2B	3B	HR	HR%	R	RBI	BB	SO	SB	Pinch Hit AB	Pinch Hit H	PO	A	E	DP	TC/G	FA	G by Pos
1980	BAL A	8	.222	.222	18	4	0	0	0	0.0	1	1	0	5	0	2	1	3	11	2	0	2.7	.875	3B-4, 2B-1, DH-1
1982		34	.132	.302	53	7	0	0	3	5.7	7	5	6	14	0	1	1	11	43	6	2	1.9	.900	3B-27, C-2, DH-2
1983	STL N	56	.212	.337	104	22	4	0	3	2.9	5	14	10	27	1	26	5	13	40	7	3	1.8	.883	3B-33
1984	BAL A	86	.256	.360	250	64	14	0	4	1.6	24	27	12	51	0	4	1	310	67	6	5	4.3	.984	C-66, 3B-22, 1B-1
1985		105	.306	.521	359	110	21	1	18	5.0	55	48	10	69	3	9	2	176	152	7	13	3.1	.979	3B-78, C-29, DH-1
1986		81	.176	.310	210	37	4	0	8	3.8	15	19	15	50	0	3	0	72	117	16	15	2.5	.922	3B-72, C-10, DH-1
1987		20	.220	.340	50	11	0	0	2	4.0	5	3	2	9	0	2	1	94	10	3	4	5.6	.972	C-17, 3B-1, DH-1
7 yrs.		390	.244	.397	1044	255	43	1	38	3.6	112	117	55	225	4	47	11	679	440	47	42	3.2	.960	3B-237, C-124, DH-6, 1B-1, 2B-1

Fred Raymer

RAYMER, FREDERICK CHARLES BR TR 5′11″ 185 lbs.
B. Nov. 12, 1875, Leavenworth, Kans. D. June 11, 1957, Los Angeles, Calif.

Year	Team	Games	BA	SA	AB	H	2B	3B	HR	HR%	R	RBI	BB	SO	SB	Pinch Hit AB	Pinch Hit H	PO	A	E	DP	TC/G	FA	G by Pos
1901	CHI N	120	.233	.272	463	108	14	2	0	0.0	41	43	11		18	1	1	186	235	42	15	3.9	.909	3B-82, SS-29, 1B-5, 2B-3
1904	BOS N	114	.210	.260	419	88	12	3	1	0.2	28	27	13		17	0	0	272	351	27	38	5.7	.958	2B-114
1905		137	.211	.247	498	105	14	2	0	0.0	26	31	8		15	1	0	270	381	34	33	5.0	.950	2B-134, OF-1, 1B-1
3 yrs.		371	.218	.259	1380	301	40	7	1	0.1	95	101	32		50	2	1	728	967	103	86	4.9	.943	2B-251, 3B-82, SS-29, 1B-6, OF-1

Harry Raymond

RAYMOND, HARRY H. 5′ 9″ 179 lbs.
B. Feb. 20, 1862, Utica, N. Y. D. Mar. 21, 1925, San Diego, Calif.

Year	Team	Games	BA	SA	AB	H	2B	3B	HR	HR%	R	RBI	BB	SO	SB	Pinch Hit AB	Pinch Hit H	PO	A	E	DP	TC/G	FA	G by Pos
1888	LOU AA	32	.211	.228	123	26	2	0	0	0.0	8	13	1		7	0	0	59	55	15	1	4.0	.884	3B-31, OF-1
1889		130	.239	.297	515	123	12	9	0	0.0	58	47	19	45	19	0	0	207	261	60	23	4.0	.886	3B-129, OF-1, P-1
1890		123	.259	.299	521	135	7	4	2	0.4	91		22		18	0	0	195	267	62	22	4.3	.882	3B-119, SS-4
1891		14	.203	.237	59	12	2	0	0	0.0	4	2	5	6	3	0	0	37	51	10	9	7.0	.898	SS-14
1892	2 teams PIT N (12G –.082) WAS N (4G –.067)																							
″	total	16	.078	.109	64	5	0	1	0	0.0	6	2	7	10	2	0	0	18	39	11	1	4.3	.838	3B-16
5 yrs.		315	.235	.279	1282	301	23	14	2	0.2	167	64	54	61	49	0	0	516	673	158	56	4.3	.883	3B-295, SS-18, OF-2, P-1

Lou Raymond

RAYMOND, LOUIS ANTHONY BR TR 5′10½″ 187 lbs.
Born Louis Anthony Raymondjack.
B. Dec. 11, 1894, Buffalo, N. Y. D. May 2, 1979, Rochester, N. Y.

Year	Team	Games	BA	SA	AB	H	2B	3B	HR	HR%	R	RBI	BB	SO	SB	Pinch Hit AB	Pinch Hit H	PO	A	E	DP	TC/G	FA	G by Pos
1919	PHI N	1	.500	.500	2	1	0	0	0	0.0	0	0	0	0	0	0	0	0	0	0	0	0.0	.000	2B-1

Randy Ready

READY, RANDY MAX BR TR 5′11″ 175 lbs.
B. Jan. 8, 1960, San Mateo, Calif.

Year	Team	Games	BA	SA	AB	H	2B	3B	HR	HR%	R	RBI	BB	SO	SB	Pinch Hit AB	Pinch Hit H	PO	A	E	DP	TC/G	FA	G by Pos
1983	MIL A	12	.405	.676	37	15	3	2	1	2.7	8	6	6	3	0	1	0	5	8	0	1	1.3	1.000	DH-6, 3B-4
1984		37	.187	.325	123	23	6	1	3	2.4	13	13	14	18	0	1	0	29	76	6	4	3.1	.946	3B-36
1985		48	.265	.387	181	48	9	5	1	0.6	29	21	14	23	0	2	0	93	14	1	1	2.2	.991	OF-37, 3B-7, 2B-3, DH-2
1986	2 teams MIL A (23G –.190) SD N (1G –.000)																							
″	total	24	.183	.268	82	15	4	0	1	1.2	8	4	9	10	2	2	0	35	23	4	4	2.7	.935	OF-11, 2B-7, 3B-4, DH-1
1987	SD N	124	.309	.520	350	108	26	6	12	3.4	69	54	67	44	7	25	6	124	220	15	35	3.0	.958	3B-52, 2B-51, OF-16
1988		114	.266	.390	331	88	16	2	7	2.1	43	39	39	38	6	24	5	112	153	11	22	2.8	.960	3B-57, 2B-26, OF-16
1989	2 teams SD N (28G –.254) PHI N (72G –.267)																							
″	total	100	.264	.425	254	67	13	2	8	3.1	37	26	42	37	4	28	6	80	72	9	13	2.1	.944	OF-37, 3B-32, 2B-9
1990	PHI N	101	.244	.309	217	53	9	1	1	0.5	26	26	29	35	3	45	12	78	86	2	18	2.9	.988	OF-30, 2B-28
1991		76	.249	.322	205	51	10	1	1	0.5	32	20	47	25	2	12	2	127	145	3	22	4.2	.989	2B-66
1992	OAK A	61	.200	.288	125	25	2	0	3	2.4	17	17	25	23	1	16	6	53	19	5	5	1.2	.935	OF-24, DH-24, 3B-7, 2B-4, 1B-4
1993	MON N	40	.254	.351	134	34	8	1	1	0.7	22	10	23	8	2	1	0	135	92	8	22	5.3	.966	2B-28, 1B-13, 3B-3
1994	PHI N	17	.381	.476	42	16	1	0	1	2.4	5	3	8	6	0	3	1	18	27	0	3	3.8	1.000	2B-11, 3B-1
1995		23	.138	.138	29	4	0	0	0	0.0	3	0	3	6	0	16	2	29	2	1	3	8.0	.969	1B-3, 2B-1
13 yrs.		777	.259	.387	2110	547	107	21	40	1.9	312	239	326	276	27	176	40	918	937	65	153	2.9	.966	2B-234, 3B-203, OF-171, DH-33, 1B-20
LEAGUE CHAMPIONSHIP SERIES																								
1992	OAK A	1	.000	.000	1	0	0	0	0	0.0	0	0	0	1	0	1	0	0	0	0	0	0.0	—	

Leroy Reams

REAMS, LEROY BL TR 6′ 2″ 175 lbs.
B. Aug. 11, 1943, Pine Bluff, Ark.

Year	Team	Games	BA	SA	AB	H	2B	3B	HR	HR%	R	RBI	BB	SO	SB	Pinch Hit AB	Pinch Hit H	PO	A	E	DP	TC/G	FA	G by Pos
1969	PHI N	1	.000	.000	1	0	0	0	0	0.0	0	0	0	1	0	1	0	0	0	0	0	0.0	—	

Phil Reardon

REARDON, PHILIP MICHAEL BR TR
B. Oct. 3, 1883, Brooklyn, N. Y. D. Sept. 28, 1920, Brooklyn, N. Y.

Year	Team	Games	BA	SA	AB	H	2B	3B	HR	HR%	R	RBI	BB	SO	SB	Pinch Hit AB	Pinch Hit H	PO	A	E	DP	TC/G	FA	G by Pos
1906	BKN N	5	.071	.071	14	1	0	0	0	0.0	0	0	0		0	1	0	10	1	1	1	3.0	.917	OF-4

Art Rebel

REBEL, ARTHUR ANTHONY BL TL 5′ 8″ 180 lbs.
B. Mar. 4, 1915, Cincinnati, Ohio.

Year	Team	Games	BA	SA	AB	H	2B	3B	HR	HR%	R	RBI	BB	SO	SB	Pinch Hit AB	Pinch Hit H	PO	A	E	DP	TC/G	FA	G by Pos
1938	PHI N	7	.222	.222	9	2	0	0	0	0.0	2	1	1	1	0	4	0	3	0	0	0	1.0	1.000	OF-3
1945	STL N	26	.347	.403	72	25	4	0	0	0.0	12	5	6	4	1	8	1	37	4	1	0	2.3	.976	OF-18
2 yrs.		33	.333	.383	81	27	4	0	0	0.0	14	6	7	5	1	12	1	40	4	1	0	2.1	.978	OF-21

Jeff Reboulet

REBOULET, JEFFREY ALLEN BR TR 6′ 167 lbs.
B. Apr. 30, 1967, Dayton, Ohio.

Year	Team	Games	BA	SA	AB	H	2B	3B	HR	HR%	R	RBI	BB	SO	SB	Pinch Hit AB	Pinch Hit H	PO	A	E	DP	TC/G	FA	G by Pos
1992	MIN A	73	.190	.277	137	26	7	1	1	0.7	15	16	23	26	3	2	0	71	163	5	31	3.0	.979	SS-36, 3B-22, 2B-13, OF-7, DH-1
1993		109	.258	.304	240	62	8	0	1	0.4	33	15	35	37	5	5	1	122	215	6	40	3.1	.983	SS-62, 3B-35, 2B-11, OF-3, DH-1

Jeff Reboulet *continued*

Year	Team	Games	BA	SA	AB	H	2B	3B	HR	HR%	R	RBI	BB	SO	SB	Pinch Hit AB	Pinch Hit H	PO	A	E	DP	TC/G	FA	G by Pos
1994		74	.259	.376	189	49	11	1	3	1.6	28	23	18	23	0	3	2	150	131	7	29	3.7	.976	SS-42, 2B-14, 1B-10, 3B-6, OF-4, DH-1
1995		87	.292	.398	216	63	11	0	4	1.9	39	23	27	34	1	10	3	164	159	4	36	3.5	.988	SS-39, 3B-22, 1B-17, 2B-15, C-1
4 yrs.		343	.256	.343	782	200	37	2	9	1.2	115	77	103	120	9	20	6	507	668	22	136	3.3	.982	SS-179, 3B-85, 2B-53, 1B-27, OF-14, DH-3, C-1

John Reccius

RECCIUS, JOHN 5′ 6½″
Brother of Phil Reccius.
B. Oct. 29, 1859, Louisville, Ky. D. Sept. 1, 1930, Louisville, Ky.

Year	Team	Games	BA	SA	AB	H	2B	3B	HR	HR%	R	RBI	BB	SO	SB	Pinch Hit AB	Pinch Hit H	PO	A	E	DP	TC/G	FA	G by Pos
1882	LOU AA	74	.237	.316	266	63	12	3	1	0.4	46		23			0	0	91	40	23	3	2.0	.851	OF-65, P-13
1883		18	.143	.175	63	9	2	0	0	0.0	10		7			0	0	35	3	7	1	2.4	.844	OF-18, P-1
2 yrs.		92	.219	.289	329	72	14	3	1	0.3	56		30			0	0	126	43	30	4	2.1	.849	OF-83, P-14

Phil Reccius

RECCIUS, PHILIP 5′ 9″ 163 lbs.
Brother of John Reccius.
B. June 7, 1862, Louisville, Ky. D. Feb. 15, 1903, Louisville, Ky.

Year	Team	Games	BA	SA	AB	H	2B	3B	HR	HR%	R	RBI	BB	SO	SB	Pinch Hit AB	Pinch Hit H	PO	A	E	DP	TC/G	FA	G by Pos
1882	LOU AA	4	.133	.133	15	2	0	0	0	0.0	0		0			0	0	6	1	2	0	2.3	.778	OF-4
1883		1	.333	.667	3	1	1	0	0	0.0	1		0			0	0	1	0	0	0	1.0	1.000	OF-1
1884		73	.240	.323	263	63	9	2	3	1.1	23		5			0	0	56	147	31	7	3.0	.868	3B-51, P-18, SS-10
1885		102	.241	.318	402	97	8	10	1	0.2	57		13			0	0	107	193	59	18	3.5	.836	3B-97, P-7
1886		5	.308	.538	13	4	1	1	0	0.0	4		3			0	0	6	2	1	0	1.5	.889	OF-5, P-1
1887	2 teams	LOU AA (11G –.243) CLE AA (62G –.205)																						
″	total	73	.211	.263	266	56	8	3	0	0.0	32		32		12	0	0	109	144	34	18	3.9	.882	3B-62, OF-10, P-1, SS-1
1888	LOU AA	2	.222	.333	9	2	1	0	0	0.0	0	4	1		0	0	0	0	3	1	0	2.0	.750	3B-2
1890	ROC AA	1	.000	.000	4	0	0	0	0	0.0	0		0		0	0	0	0	0	0	0	0.0	.000	OF-1
8 yrs.		261	.231	.305	975	225	28	16	4	0.4	117	4	54		12	0	0	285	490	128	43	3.3	.858	3B-212, P-27, OF-21, SS-11

Johnny Reder

REDER, JOHN ANTHONY BR TR 6′ 184 lbs.
B. Sept. 24, 1909, Lublin, Poland D. Apr. 12, 1990, Fall River, Mass.

Year	Team	Games	BA	SA	AB	H	2B	3B	HR	HR%	R	RBI	BB	SO	SB	Pinch Hit AB	Pinch Hit H	PO	A	E	DP	TC/G	FA	G by Pos
1932	BOS A	17	.135	.162	37	5	1	0	0	0.0	4	3	6	6	0	4	0	89	8	2	11	9.0	.980	1B-10, 3B-1

Buck Redfern

REDFERN, GEORGE HOWARD BR TR 5′11″ 165 lbs.
B. Apr. 7, 1902, Asheville, N. C. D. Sept. 8, 1964, Asheville, N. C.

Year	Team	Games	BA	SA	AB	H	2B	3B	HR	HR%	R	RBI	BB	SO	SB	Pinch Hit AB	Pinch Hit H	PO	A	E	DP	TC/G	FA	G by Pos
1928	CHI A	86	.234	.280	261	61	6	3	0	0.0	22	35	12	19	8	1	0	167	223	24	39	5.2	.942	2B-45, SS-33, 3B-1
1929		21	.136	.136	44	6	0	0	0	0.0	0	3	3	3	1	1	0	23	22	2	2	2.3	.957	2B-11, 3B-5, SS-4
2 yrs.		107	.220	.259	305	67	6	3	0	0.0	22	38	15	22	9	2	0	190	245	26	41	4.7	.944	2B-56, SS-37, 3B-6

Joe Redfield

REDFIELD, JOSEPH RANDALL BR TR 6′ 2″ 190 lbs.
B. Jan. 14, 1961, Doylestown, Pa.

Year	Team	Games	BA	SA	AB	H	2B	3B	HR	HR%	R	RBI	BB	SO	SB	Pinch Hit AB	Pinch Hit H	PO	A	E	DP	TC/G	FA	G by Pos
1988	CAL A	1	.000	.000	2	0	0	0	0	0.0	0	0	0	0	0	0	0	0	1	0	1	1.0	1.000	3B-1
1991	PIT N	11	.111	.111	18	2	0	0	0	0.0	1	0	4	1	0	3	0	4	7	1	3	1.3	.917	3B-9
2 yrs.		12	.100	.100	20	2	0	0	0	0.0	1	0	4	1	0	3	0	4	8	1	4	1.3	.923	3B-10

Glenn Redmon

REDMON, GLENN VINCENT BR TR 5′11″ 180 lbs.
B. Jan. 11, 1948, Detroit, Mich.

Year	Team	Games	BA	SA	AB	H	2B	3B	HR	HR%	R	RBI	BB	SO	SB	Pinch Hit AB	Pinch Hit H	PO	A	E	DP	TC/G	FA	G by Pos
1974	SF N	7	.235	.412	17	4	3	0	0	0.0	0	4	1	3	0	2	0	12	9	1	2	5.5	.955	2B-4

Billy Redmond

REDMOND, WILLIAM T. BL TL
B. Brooklyn, N. Y. Deceased.

Year	Team	Games	BA	SA	AB	H	2B	3B	HR	HR%	R	RBI	BB	SO	SB	Pinch Hit AB	Pinch Hit H	PO	A	E	DP	TC/G	FA	G by Pos
1877	CIN N	3	.250	.333	12	3	1	0	0	0.0	1	3	1	1		0	0	6	14	4	0	8.0	.833	SS-3
1878	MIL N	48	.230	.273	187	43	8	0	0	0.0	16	21	8	13		0	0	45	106	41	5	3.8	.786	SS-39, OF-7, 3B-3, C-1
2 yrs.		51	.231	.276	199	46	9	0	0	0.0	17	24	9	14		0	0	51	120	45	5	4.1	.792	SS-42, OF-7, 3B-3, C-1

Harry Redmond

REDMOND, HARRY JOHN BR TR 5′ 8″ 170 lbs.
B. Sept. 13, 1887, Cleveland, Ohio D. July 10, 1960, Cleveland, Ohio.

Year	Team	Games	BA	SA	AB	H	2B	3B	HR	HR%	R	RBI	BB	SO	SB	Pinch Hit AB	Pinch Hit H	PO	A	E	DP	TC/G	FA	G by Pos
1909	BKN N	6	.000	.000	19	0	0	0	0	0.0	3	1	0		0	1	0	12	21	4	2	7.4	.892	2B-5

Jack Redmond

REDMOND, JOHN McKITTRICK, JR. (Red) BL TR 5′11″ 185 lbs.
B. Sept. 3, 1910, Florence, Ariz. D. July 27, 1968, Garland, Tex.

Year	Team	Games	BA	SA	AB	H	2B	3B	HR	HR%	R	RBI	BB	SO	SB	Pinch Hit AB	Pinch Hit H	PO	A	E	DP	TC/G	FA	G by Pos
1935	WAS A	22	.176	.294	34	6	1	0	1	2.9	8	7	3	1	0	8	1	39	5	1	3	3.0	.978	C-15

Wayne Redmond

REDMOND, HOWARD WAYNE BR TR 5′10″ 165 lbs.
B. Nov. 25, 1945, Athens, Ala.

Year	Team	Games	BA	SA	AB	H	2B	3B	HR	HR%	R	RBI	BB	SO	SB	Pinch Hit AB	Pinch Hit H	PO	A	E	DP	TC/G	FA	G by Pos
1965	DET A	4	.000	.000	4	0	0	0	0	0.0	1	0	1	1	0	0	0	3	0	0	0	1.5	1.000	OF-2
1969		5	.000	.000	3	0	0	0	0	0.0	0	0	0	2	0	3	0	0	0	0	0	0.0	—	
2 yrs.		9	.000	.000	7	0	0	0	0	0.0	1	0	1	3	0	3	0	3	0	0	0	1.5	1.000	OF-2

Gary Redus

REDUS, GARY EUGENE BR TR 6′ 1″ 180 lbs.
B. Nov. 1, 1956, Tanner, Ala.

Year	Team	Games	BA	SA	AB	H	2B	3B	HR	HR%	R	RBI	BB	SO	SB	Pinch Hit AB	Pinch Hit H	PO	A	E	DP	TC/G	FA	G by Pos
1982	CIN N	20	.217	.337	83	18	3	2	1	1.2	12	7	5	21	11	0	0	29	3	1	0	1.6	.970	OF-20
1983		125	.247	.444	453	112	20	9	17	3.8	90	51	71	111	39	4	2	235	11	7	0	2.1	.972	OF-120
1984		123	.254	.376	394	100	21	3	7	1.8	69	22	52	71	48	10	3	200	6	7	3	1.9	.967	OF-114
1985		101	.252	.415	246	62	14	4	6	2.4	51	28	44	52	48	17	6	140	3	2	0	1.7	.986	OF-85
1986	PHI N	90	.247	.432	340	84	22	4	11	3.2	62	33	47	78	25	2	0	185	8	4	2	2.2	.980	OF-89
1987	CHI A	130	.236	.392	475	112	26	6	12	2.5	78	48	69	90	52	0	0	262	13	6	4	2.2	.979	OF-123, DH-4
1988	2 teams	CHI A (77G –.263) PIT N (30G –.197)																						
″	total	107	.249	.381	333	83	12	4	8	2.4	54	38	48	71	31	16	4	182	9	4	1	2.2	.979	OF-87, DH-2
1989	PIT N	98	.283	.462	279	79	18	7	6	2.2	42	33	40	51	25	12	3	583	55	9	43	7.4	.986	1B-72, OF-16
1990		96	.247	.419	227	56	15	3	6	2.6	32	23	33	38	11	19	3	461	36	8	29	6.4	.984	1B-72, OF-7
1991		98	.246	.393	252	62	12	2	7	2.8	45	24	28	39	17	31	9	403	26	6	35	5.4	.986	1B-47, OF-33

Gary Redus *continued*

Year	Team	Games	BA	SA	AB	H	2B	3B	HR	HR%	R	RBI	BB	SO	SB	Pinch Hit AB	Pinch Hit H	PO	A	E	DP	TC/G	FA	G by Pos
1992		76	.256	.381	176	45	7	3	3	1.7	26	12	17	25	11	16	3	301	16	1	14	6.2	.997	1B-36, OF-15
1993	TEX A	77	.288	.459	222	64	12	4	6	2.7	28	31	23	35	4	21	5	124	4	3	5	1.9	.977	OF-61, 1B-5, DH-1, 2B-1
1994		18	.273	.303	33	9	1	0	0	0.0	2	2	4	6	0	9	2	41	2	0	3	3.6	1.000	OF-7, 1B-5
13 yrs.		1159	.252	.410	3513	886	183	51	90	2.6	591	352	481	688	322	157	40	3146	192	58	139	3.3	.983	OF-777, 1B-237, DH-7, 2B-1
LEAGUE CHAMPIONSHIP SERIES																								
1990	PIT N	5	.250	.250	8	2	0	0	0	0.0	1	0	1	3	1	3	1	16	0	0	0	8.0	1.000	1B-2
1991		5	.158	.158	19	3	0	0	0	0.0	1	0	1	4	2	0	0	51	0	2	2	10.6	.962	1B-5
1992		5	.438	.813	16	7	4	1	0	0.0	4	3	2	3	0	1	0	31	4	0	1	7.0	1.000	1B-5
3 yrs.		15	.279	.419	43	12	4	1	0	0.0	6	3	4	10	3	4	1	98	4	2	3	8.7	.981	1B-12

Bob Reece

REECE, ROBERT SCOTT
B. Jan. 5, 1951, Sacramento, Calif.
BR TR 6′ 1″ 190 lbs.

Year	Team	Games	BA	SA	AB	H	2B	3B	HR	HR%	R	RBI	BB	SO	SB	Pinch Hit AB	Pinch Hit H	PO	A	E	DP	TC/G	FA	G by Pos
1978	MON N	9	.182	.273	11	2	1	0	0	0.0	2	3	0	4	0	0	0	16	2	1	1	2.1	.947	C-9

Bill Reed

REED, WILLIAM JOSEPH
B. Nov. 12, 1922, Shawano, Wis.
BL TR 5′10½″ 175 lbs.

Year	Team	Games	BA	SA	AB	H	2B	3B	HR	HR%	R	RBI	BB	SO	SB	Pinch Hit AB	Pinch Hit H	PO	A	E	DP	TC/G	FA	G by Pos
1952	BOS N	15	.250	.250	52	13	0	0	0	0.0	4	0	0	5	0	1	0	22	32	4	6	4.1	.931	2B-14

Darren Reed

REED, DARREN DOUGLAS
B. Oct. 16, 1965, Ojai, Calif.
BR TR 6′ 1″ 190 lbs.

Year	Team	Games	BA	SA	AB	H	2B	3B	HR	HR%	R	RBI	BB	SO	SB	Pinch Hit AB	Pinch Hit H	PO	A	E	DP	TC/G	FA	G by Pos
1990	NY N	26	.205	.436	39	8	4	1	1	2.6	5	2	3	11	1	8	0	20	1	1	0	1.6	.955	OF-14
1992	2 teams	MON N (42G –.173)	MIN A (14G –.182)																					
″	total	56	.175	.342	114	20	4	0	5	4.4	12	14	8	34	0	14	1	51	2	0	0	1.2	1.000	OF-42, DH-1
2 yrs.		82	.183	.366	153	28	8	1	6	3.9	17	16	11	45	1	22	1	71	3	1	0	1.3	.987	OF-56, DH-1

Jack Reed

REED, JOHN BURWELL
B. Feb. 2, 1933, Silver City, Miss.
BR TR 6′ 185 lbs.

Year	Team	Games	BA	SA	AB	H	2B	3B	HR	HR%	R	RBI	BB	SO	SB	Pinch Hit AB	Pinch Hit H	PO	A	E	DP	TC/G	FA	G by Pos
1961	NY A	28	.154	.154	13	2	0	0	0	0.0	4	1	1	1	0	0	0	14	0	1	0	0.6	.933	OF-27
1962		88	.302	.465	43	13	2	1	1	2.3	17	4	4	7	2	2	0	48	0	3	0	0.7	.941	OF-75
1963		106	.205	.274	73	15	3	1	0	0.0	18	1	9	14	5	6	0	73	2	0	0	0.8	1.000	OF-89
3 yrs.		222	.233	.326	129	30	5	2	1	0.8	39	6	14	22	7	8	0	135	2	4	0	0.7	.972	OF-191
WORLD SERIES																								
1961	NY A	3	—	—	0	0	0	0	0	—	0	0	0	0	0	0	0	0	0	0	0	0.0	.000	OF-3

Jeff Reed

REED, JEFFREY SCOTT
B. Nov. 12, 1962, Joliet, Ill.
BL TR 6′ 2″ 190 lbs.

Year	Team	Games	BA	SA	AB	H	2B	3B	HR	HR%	R	RBI	BB	SO	SB	Pinch Hit AB	Pinch Hit H	PO	A	E	DP	TC/G	FA	G by Pos
1984	MIN A	18	.143	.286	21	3	3	0	0	0.0	3	1	2	6	0	0	0	41	2	1	1	2.4	.977	C-18
1985		7	.200	.200	10	2	0	0	0	0.0	2	0	0	3	0	1	0	9	3	0	0	1.7	1.000	C-7
1986		68	.236	.321	165	39	6	1	2	1.2	13	9	16	19	1	7	3	332	19	2	5	5.5	.994	C-64
1987	MON N	75	.213	.280	207	44	11	0	1	0.5	15	21	12	20	0	5	1	357	36	12	6	5.5	.970	C-74
1988	2 teams	MON N (43G –.220)	CIN N (49G –.232)																					
″	total	92	.226	.287	265	60	9	2	1	0.4	20	16	28	41	1	6	1	468	38	3	3	5.8	.994	C-88
1989	CIN N	102	.223	.293	287	64	11	0	3	1.0	16	23	34	46	0	5	0	504	50	7	2	5.7	.988	C-99
1990		72	.251	.360	175	44	8	1	3	1.7	12	16	24	26	0	3	0	358	26	5	1	5.6	.987	C-70
1991		91	.267	.370	270	72	15	2	3	1.1	20	31	23	38	0	4	1	527	29	5	7	6.3	.991	C-89
1992		15	.160	.160	25	4	0	0	0	0.0	2	2	1	4	0	9	0	29	2	0	0	5.2	1.000	C-6
1993	SF N	66	.261	.437	119	31	3	0	6	5.0	10	12	16	22	0	33	6	180	14	0	4	5.2	1.000	C-37
1994		50	.175	.233	103	18	3	0	1	1.0	11	7	11	21	0	19	4	138	9	1	1	4.5	.993	C-33
1995		66	.265	.283	113	30	2	0	0	0.0	12	9	20	17	0	25	4	175	21	1	2	4.7	.995	C-42
12 yrs.		722	.234	.315	1760	411	71	6	20	1.1	136	147	187	263	2	117	20	3118	249	37	32	5.4	.989	C-627
LEAGUE CHAMPIONSHIP SERIES																								
1990	CIN N	4	.000	.000	7	0	0	0	0	0.0	0	0	0	2	0	0	0	24	1	0	0	6.3	1.000	C-4

Jody Reed

REED, JODY ERIC
B. July 26, 1962, Tampa, Fla.
BR TR 5′ 9″ 170 lbs.

Year	Team	Games	BA	SA	AB	H	2B	3B	HR	HR%	R	RBI	BB	SO	SB	Pinch Hit AB	Pinch Hit H	PO	A	E	DP	TC/G	FA	G by Pos
1987	BOS A	9	.300	.400	30	9	1	1	0	0.0	4	8	4	0	1	0	0	11	26	0	9	4.1	1.000	SS-6, 2B-2, 3B-1
1988		109	.293	.376	338	99	23	1	1	0.3	60	28	45	21	1	0	0	147	282	11	57	4.0	.975	SS-94, 2B-11, 3B-4
1989		146	.288	.393	524	151	42	2	3	0.6	76	40	73	44	4	3	1	255	423	19	88	4.6	.973	SS-77, 2B-70, 3B-4, OF-1, DH-1
1990		155	.289	.390	598	173	**45**	0	5	0.8	70	51	75	65	4	1	0	278	478	16	103	4.5	.979	2B-119, SS-50, DH-1
1991		153	.283	.382	618	175	42	2	5	0.8	87	60	60	53	6	0	0	314	449	14	110	4.9	.982	2B-152, SS-6
1992		143	.247	.316	550	136	27	1	3	0.5	64	40	62	44	7	0	0	304	472	14	113	5.5	.982	2B-142, DH-1
1993	LA N	132	.276	.346	445	123	21	2	2	0.4	48	31	38	40	1	1	1	280	413	5	76	5.3	.993	2B-132
1994	MIL A	108	.271	.341	399	108	22	0	2	0.5	48	37	57	34	5	2	0	231	351	3	72	5.5	.995	2B-106
1995	SD N	131	.256	.328	445	114	18	1	4	0.9	58	40	59	38	6	0	0	305	366	4	78	5.0	.994	2B-130, SS-5
9 yrs.		1086	.276	.361	3947	1088	241	10	25	0.6	515	335	473	339	35	7	2	2125	3260	86	706	4.9	.984	2B-864, SS-238, 3B-9, DH-3, OF-1
LEAGUE CHAMPIONSHIP SERIES																								
1988	BOS A	4	.273	.364	11	3	1	0	0	0.0	0	0	2	1	0	0	0	3	10	0	2	3.3	1.000	SS-4
1990		4	.133	.133	15	2	0	0	0	0.0	0	1	0	2	0	0	0	11	11	0	4	3.1	1.000	2B-4, SS-3
2 yrs.		8	.192	.231	26	5	1	0	0	0.0	0	1	2	3	0	0	0	14	21	0	6	3.2	1.000	SS-7, 2B-4

Milt Reed

REED, MILTON D.
B. July 4, 1890, Atlanta, Ga. D. July 27, 1938, Atlanta, Ga.
BL TR 5′ 9½″ 150 lbs.

Year	Team	Games	BA	SA	AB	H	2B	3B	HR	HR%	R	RBI	BB	SO	SB	Pinch Hit AB	Pinch Hit H	PO	A	E	DP	TC/G	FA	G by Pos
1911	STL N	1	.000	.000	1	0	0	0	0	0.0	0	0	0	0	0	1	0	0	0	0	0	0.0	—	
1913	PHI N	13	.250	.292	24	6	1	0	0	0.0	4	0	1	5	1	1	1	7	14	3	0	2.0	.875	SS-9, 2B-3
1914		44	.206	.243	107	22	2	1	0	0.0	10	2	10	13	4	6	2	41	54	11	4	3.1	.896	SS-22, 2B-11, 3B-1
1915	BKN F	10	.290	.387	31	9	1	1	0	0.0	2	8	2		2	0	0	18	20	6	2	4.4	.864	SS-10
4 yrs.		68	.227	.276	163	37	4	2	0	0.0	16	10	13	18	7	8	3	66	88	20	6	3.1	.885	SS-41, 2B-14, 3B-1

Ted Reed

REED, RALPH EDWIN
B. Oct. 18, 1890, Beaver, Pa. D. Feb. 16, 1959, Beaver, Pa.
BR TR 5′11″ 190 lbs.

Year	Team	Games	BA	SA	AB	H	2B	3B	HR	HR%	R	RBI	BB	SO	SB	Pinch Hit AB	Pinch Hit H	PO	A	E	DP	TC/G	FA	G by Pos
1915	NWK F	20	.260	.325	77	20	1	2	0	0.0	5	4	2		1	0	0	36	33	11	4	4.0	.863	3B-20

Year	Team	Games	BA	SA	AB	H	2B	3B	HR	HR%	R	RBI	BB	SO	SB	Pinch Hit AB	Pinch Hit H	PO	A	E	DP	TC/G	FA	G by Pos

Icicle Reeder

REEDER, EDWARD JAMES BR 6′
B. May 1859, Cincinnati, Ohio Deceased.

Year	Team	Games	BA	SA	AB	H	2B	3B	HR	HR%	R	RBI	BB	SO	SB	Pinch Hit AB	Pinch Hit H	PO	A	E	DP	TC/G	FA	G by Pos
1884	**2 teams**	**CIN AA** (3G –.143) **WAS U** (3G –.167)																						
″	**total**	6	.154	.154	26	4	0	0	0	0.0	0		0			0	0	5	0	2	0	1.2	.714	OF-6

Nick Reeder

REEDER, NICHOLAS (Old Emergency No. 2) BR TR 5′ 9″ 189 lbs.
Born Nicholas Herchenroeder.
B. Mar. 22, 1867, Louisville, Ky. D. Sept. 26, 1894, Louisville, Ky.

Year	Team	Games	BA	SA	AB	H	2B	3B	HR	HR%	R	RBI	BB	SO	SB	Pinch Hit AB	Pinch Hit H	PO	A	E	DP	TC/G	FA	G by Pos
1891	**LOU AA**	1	.000	.000	2	0	0	0	0	0.0	0	0	0	1	0	0	0	0	1	0	0	1.0	1.000	3B-1

Andy Reese

REESE, ANDREW JACKSON BR TR 5′11″ 180 lbs.
B. Feb. 7, 1904, Tupelo, Miss. D. Jan. 10, 1966, Tupelo, Miss.

Year	Team	Games	BA	SA	AB	H	2B	3B	HR	HR%	R	RBI	BB	SO	SB	Pinch Hit AB	Pinch Hit H	PO	A	E	DP	TC/G	FA	G by Pos
1927	**NY N**	97	.265	.349	355	94	14	2	4	1.1	43	21	13	52	5	12	2	92	128	18	15	2.9	.924	3B-64, OF-16, 1B-1
1928		109	.308	.416	406	125	18	4	6	1.5	61	44	13	24	7	4	0	232	136	16	21	3.6	.958	OF-64, 2B-26, SS-6, 3B-6, 1B-6
1929		58	.263	.344	209	55	11	3	0	0.0	36	21	15	19	8	2	0	117	168	11	24	5.3	.963	2B-44, OF-8, 3B-4
1930		67	.273	.390	172	47	4	2	4	2.3	26	25	10	12	1	17	3	70	13	5	1	2.1	.943	OF-32, 3B-10
4 yrs.		331	.281	.378	1142	321	47	11	14	1.2	166	111	51	107	21	35	5	511	445	50	61	3.5	.950	OF-120, 3B-84, 2B-70, 1B-7, SS-6

Jimmy Reese

REESE, JAMES HERMAN BL TR 5′11½″ 165 lbs.
Born James Harrison Solomon.
B. Oct. 1, 1901, New York, N. Y. D. June 13, 1994, Santa Ana, Calif.

Year	Team	Games	BA	SA	AB	H	2B	3B	HR	HR%	R	RBI	BB	SO	SB	Pinch Hit AB	Pinch Hit H	PO	A	E	DP	TC/G	FA	G by Pos
1930	**NY A**	77	.346	.489	188	65	14	2	3	1.6	44	18	11	8	1	20	10	93	105	5	26	3.8	.975	2B-48, 3B-5
1931		65	.241	.335	245	59	10	2	3	1.2	41	26	17	10	2	3	1	173	168	10	44	5.8	.972	2B-61
1932	**STL N**	90	.265	.333	309	82	15	0	2	0.6	38	26	20	19	4	10	4	209	220	9	48	5.7	.979	2B-77
3 yrs.		232	.278	.373	742	206	39	4	8	1.1	123	70	48	37	7	33	15	475	493	24	118	5.2	.976	2B-186, 3B-5

Pee Wee Reese

REESE, HAROLD HENRY (The Little Colonel) BR TR 5′10″ 160 lbs.
B. July 23, 1918, Ekron, Ky.
Hall of Fame 1984.

Year	Team	Games	BA	SA	AB	H	2B	3B	HR	HR%	R	RBI	BB	SO	SB	Pinch Hit AB	Pinch Hit H	PO	A	E	DP	TC/G	FA	G by Pos
1940	**BKN N**	84	.272	.372	312	85	8	4	5	1.6	58	28	45	42	15	0	0	190	238	18	41	5.4	.960	SS-83
1941		152	.229	.294	595	136	23	5	2	0.3	76	46	68	56	10	1	0	346	473	47	76	5.7	.946	SS-151
1942		151	.255	.332	564	144	24	5	3	0.5	87	53	82	55	15	0	0	337	482	35	99	5.7	.959	SS-151
1946		152	.284	.378	542	154	16	10	5	0.9	79	60	87	71	10	0	0	285	463	26	104	5.1	.966	SS-152
1947		142	.284	.426	476	135	24	4	12	2.5	81	73	**104**	67	7	0	0	266	441	25	99	5.2	.966	SS-142
1948		151	.274	.390	566	155	31	4	9	1.6	96	75	79	63	25	2	0	335	453	31	93	5.5	.962	SS-149
1949		155	.279	.410	617	172	27	3	16	2.6	**132**	73	116	59	26	0	0	316	454	18	93	5.1	.977	SS-155
1950		141	.260	.380	531	138	21	5	11	2.1	97	52	91	62	17	0	0	291	414	26	95	5.2	.964	SS-134, 3B-7
1951		154	.286	.393	616	176	20	8	10	1.6	94	84	81	57	20	0	0	292	422	35	106	4.9	.953	SS-154
1952		149	.272	.365	559	152	18	8	6	1.1	94	58	86	59	**30**	4	1	282	376	21	89	4.7	.969	SS-145
1953		140	.271	.420	524	142	25	7	13	2.5	108	61	82	61	22	3	0	265	380	23	83	4.9	.966	SS-135
1954		141	.309	.455	554	171	35	8	10	1.8	98	69	90	62	8	1	1	270	426	25	74	5.2	.965	SS-140
1955		145	.282	.403	553	156	29	4	10	1.8	99	61	78	60	8	3	0	239	404	23	86	4.7	.965	SS-142
1956		147	.257	.344	572	147	19	2	9	1.6	85	46	56	69	13	1	0	269	388	25	80	4.6	.963	SS-136, 3B-12
1957		103	.224	.248	330	74	3	1	1	0.3	33	29	39	32	5	4	1	97	228	19	21	3.5	.945	3B-75, SS-23
1958	**LA N**	59	.224	.381	147	33	7	2	4	2.7	21	17	26	15	1	15	1	44	89	10	16	3.3	.930	SS-22, 3B-21
16 yrs.		2166	.269	.377	8058	2170	330	80	126	1.6	1338	885	1210	890	232	34	4	4124	6131	407	1255	5.0	.962	SS-2014, 3B-115
WORLD SERIES																								
1941	**BKN N**	5	.200	.200	20	4	0	0	0	0.0	1	2	0	0	0	0	0	13	14	3	4	6.0	.900	SS-5
1947		7	.304	.348	23	7	1	0	0	0.0	5	4	6	3	3	0	0	8	15	1	5	3.4	.958	SS-7
1949		5	.316	.526	19	6	1	0	1	5.3	2	2	1	0	1	0	0	5	9	1	0	3.0	.933	SS-5
1952		7	.345	.448	29	10	0	0	1	3.4	4	4	2	2	1	0	0	15	18	2	3	5.0	.943	SS-7
1953		6	.208	.292	24	5	0	1	0	0.0	0	0	4	1	0	0	0	7	14	0	0	3.5	1.000	SS-6
1955		7	.296	.333	27	8	1	0	0	0.0	5	2	3	5	0	0	0	15	23	1	7	5.6	.974	SS-7
1956		7	.222	.296	27	6	0	1	0	0.0	3	2	2	6	0	0	0	14	21	1	7	5.1	.972	SS-7
7 yrs.		44 **9th**	.272	.349	169 **9th**	46 **5th**	3	2	2	1.2	20	16	18	17	5	0	0	77	114	9	26	4.5	.955	SS-44

Rich Reese

REESE, RICHARD BENJAMIN BL TL 6′ 3″ 185 lbs.
B. Sept. 29, 1941, Leipsic, Ohio.

Year	Team	Games	BA	SA	AB	H	2B	3B	HR	HR%	R	RBI	BB	SO	SB	Pinch Hit AB	Pinch Hit H	PO	A	E	DP	TC/G	FA	G by Pos
1964	**MIN A**	10	.000	.000	7	0	0	0	0	0.0	0	0	0	1	0	7	0	3	0	0	0	3.0	1.000	1B-1
1965		14	.286	.429	7	2	1	0	0	0.0	0	0	2	2	0	4	1	14	1	0	0	2.1	1.000	1B-6, OF-1
1966		3	.000	.000	2	0	0	0	0	0.0	0	0	1	2	0	2	0	0	0	0	0	0.0	—	
1967		95	.248	.416	101	25	5	0	4	4.0	13	20	8	17	0	41	**13**	107	4	1	5	2.4	.991	1B-36, OF-10
1968		126	.259	.352	332	86	15	2	4	1.2	40	28	18	36	3	30	6	642	38	6	36	6.7	.991	1B-87, OF-15
1969		132	.322	.513	419	135	24	4	16	3.8	52	69	23	57	1	17	4	929	57	7	97	8.1	.993	1B-117, OF-5
1970		153	.261	.371	501	131	15	5	10	2.0	63	56	48	70	5	12	4	1118	82	10	94	8.3	.992	1B-146
1971		120	.219	.353	329	72	8	3	10	3.0	40	39	20	35	7	20	6	679	44	4	71	7.0	.994	1B-95, OF-9
1972		132	.218	.330	197	43	3	2	5	2.5	23	26	25	27	0	26	7	419	30	7	55	4.1	.985	1B-98, OF-13
1973	**2 teams**	**DET A** (59G –.137) **MIN A** (22G –.174)																						
″	**total**	81	.144	.248	125	18	2	1	3	2.4	17	7	13	23	0	15	3	198	13	1	15	2.8	.995	1B-54, OF-21
10 yrs.		866	.253	.384	2020	512	73	17	52	2.6	248	245	158	270	16	174	44	4109	269	36	373	6.2	.992	1B-640, OF-74
LEAGUE CHAMPIONSHIP SERIES																								
1969	**MIN A**	3	.167	.167	12	2	0	0	0	0.0	0	2	1	1	0	0	0	26	5	0	3	10.3	1.000	1B-3
1970		2	.143	.143	7	1	0	0	0	0.0	0	0	1	1	0	0	0	16	2	0	3	9.0	1.000	1B-2
2 yrs.		5	.158	.158	19	3	0	0	0	0.0	0	2	2	2	0	0	0	42	7	0	6	9.8	1.000	1B-5

Bobby Reeves

REEVES, ROBERT EDWIN (Gunner) BR TR 5′11″ 170 lbs.
B. June 24, 1904, Hill City, Tenn. D. June 4, 1993, Chattanooga, Tenn.

Year	Team	Games	BA	SA	AB	H	2B	3B	HR	HR%	R	RBI	BB	SO	SB	Pinch Hit AB	Pinch Hit H	PO	A	E	DP	TC/G	FA	G by Pos
1926	**WAS A**	20	.224	.265	49	11	0	1	0	0.0	4	7	6	9	1	1	0	23	29	3	4	3.1	.945	3B-16, SS-1, 2B-1
1927		112	.255	.318	380	97	11	5	1	0.3	37	39	21	53	3	0	0	207	315	46	37	5.2	.919	SS-96, 3B-12, 2B-2
1928		102	.303	.419	353	107	16	8	3	0.8	44	42	24	47	4	2	1	231	265	45	40	5.6	.917	SS-66, 2B-22, 3B-8, OF-1

Bobby Reeves *continued*

Year	Team	Games	BA	SA	AB	H	2B	3B	HR	HR%	R	RBI	BB	SO	SB	Pinch Hit AB	Pinch Hit H	PO	A	E	DP	TC/G	FA	G by Pos
1929	BOS A	140	.248	.311	460	114	19	2	2	0.4	66	28	60	57	7	1	0	152	242	38	27	3.2	.912	3B-132, 2B-2, 1B-1
1930		92	.217	.294	272	59	7	4	2	0.7	41	18	50	36	6	4	1	123	183	27	32	3.8	.919	3B-62, SS-15, 2B-11
1931		36	.167	.238	84	14	2	2	0	0.0	11	1	14	16	0	2	0	64	64	12	11	4.7	.914	2B-29, P-1
6 yrs.		502	.252	.329	1598	402	55	22	8	0.5	203	135	175	218	21	10	2	800	1098	171	151	4.3	.917	3B-230, SS-178, 2B-67, 1B-1, P-1, OF-1

Rudy Regalado

REGALADO, RUDOLPH VALENTINO
B. May 21, 1930, Los Angeles, Calif.
BR TR 6′ 1″ 185 lbs.

Year	Team	Games	BA	SA	AB	H	2B	3B	HR	HR%	R	RBI	BB	SO	SB	Pinch Hit AB	Pinch Hit H	PO	A	E	DP	TC/G	FA	G by Pos
1954	CLE A	65	.250	.311	180	45	5	0	2	1.1	21	24	19	16	0	8	1	62	86	5	7	2.9	.967	3B-50, 2B-2
1955		10	.269	.346	26	7	2	0	0	0.0	2	5	2	4	0	1	0	8	15	1	2	2.7	.958	3B-8, 2B-1
1956		16	.234	.255	47	11	1	0	0	0.0	4	2	4	1	0	1	0	10	10	5	3	1.7	.800	3B-14, 1B-1
3 yrs.		91	.249	.304	253	63	8	0	2	0.8	27	31	25	21	0	10	1	80	111	11	12	2.7	.946	3B-72, 2B-3, 1B-1
WORLD SERIES																								
1954	CLE A	4	.333	.333	3	1	0	0	0	0.0	0	1	0	0	0	2	1	0	0	0	0	0.0	.000	3B-1

Bill Regan

REGAN, WILLIAM WRIGHT
B. Jan. 23, 1899, Pittsburgh, Pa. D. June 11, 1968, Pittsburgh, Pa.
BR TR 5′10″ 155 lbs.

Year	Team	Games	BA	SA	AB	H	2B	3B	HR	HR%	R	RBI	BB	SO	SB	Pinch Hit AB	Pinch Hit H	PO	A	E	DP	TC/G	FA	G by Pos
1926	BOS A	108	.263	.360	403	106	21	3	4	1.0	40	34	23	37	6	2	0	264	392	24	66	6.4	.965	2B-106
1927		129	.274	.408	468	128	37	10	2	0.4	43	66	26	51	10	7	1	283	397	28	76	5.9	.960	2B-121
1928		138	.264	.387	511	135	30	6	7	1.4	53	75	21	40	9	0	0	294	467	29	87	5.7	.963	2B-137, OF-1
1929		104	.288	.407	371	107	27	7	1	0.3	38	54	22	38	7	2	1	203	296	21	68	5.1	.960	2B-91, 3B-10, 1B-1
1930		134	.266	.393	507	135	35	10	3	0.6	54	53	25	60	4	5	2	309	440	29	92	6.0	.963	2B-127, 3B-2
1931	PIT N	28	.202	.308	104	21	8	0	1	1.0	8	10	5	19	2	0	0	63	90	9	14	5.8	.944	2B-28
6 yrs.		641	.267	.387	2364	632	158	36	18	0.8	236	292	122	245	38	16	4	1416	2082	140	403	5.8	.962	2B-610, 3B-12, 1B-1, OF-1

Joe Regan

REGAN, JOSEPH CHARLES
B. July 12, 1872, Seymour, Conn. D. Nov. 18, 1948, Hartford, Conn.
BR TR 6′ 1″

Year	Team	Games	BA	SA	AB	H	2B	3B	HR	HR%	R	RBI	BB	SO	SB	Pinch Hit AB	Pinch Hit H	PO	A	E	DP	TC/G	FA	G by Pos
1898	NY N	2	.200	.200	5	1	0	0	0	0.0	1	2	0		0	0	0	1	0	0	0	0.5	1.000	OF-2

Tony Rego

REGO, ANTONE (Mighty Midget)
Born Antone DoRego.
B. Oct. 31, 1897, Wailuku, Hawaii D. Jan. 6, 1978, Tulsa, Okla.
BR TR 5′ 4″ 140 lbs.

Year	Team	Games	BA	SA	AB	H	2B	3B	HR	HR%	R	RBI	BB	SO	SB	Pinch Hit AB	Pinch Hit H	PO	A	E	DP	TC/G	FA	G by Pos
1924	STL A	23	.224	.241	58	13	1	0	0	0.0	5	5	1	3	0	1	1	57	12	2	2	3.2	.972	C-22
1925		20	.406	.531	32	13	2	1	0	0.0	5	3	3	2	0	1	0	35	12	1	1	2.5	.979	C-19
2 yrs.		43	.289	.344	90	26	3	1	0	0.0	10	8	4	5	0	2	1	92	24	3	3	2.9	.975	C-41

Wally Rehg

REHG, WALTER PHILLIP
B. Aug. 31, 1888, Summerfield, Ill. D. Apr. 5, 1946, Burbank, Calif.
BR TR 5′ 8″ 160 lbs.

Year	Team	Games	BA	SA	AB	H	2B	3B	HR	HR%	R	RBI	BB	SO	SB	Pinch Hit AB	Pinch Hit H	PO	A	E	DP	TC/G	FA	G by Pos
1912	PIT N	8	.000	.000	9	0	0	0	0	0.0	1	0	2	1	0	4	0	2	0	0	0	1.0	1.000	OF-2
1913	BOS A	30	.277	.347	101	28	3	2	0	0.0	14	9	2	7	4	2	1	30	3	2	0	1.3	.943	OF-27
1914		84	.219	.272	151	33	4	2	0	0.0	14	11	18	11	5	**36**	**10**	45	4	1	3	1.2	.980	OF-42
1915		5	.200	.200	5	1	0	0	0	0.0	2	0	0	1	1	3	1	1	0	0	0	1.0	1.000	OF-1
1917	BOS N	86	.270	.349	341	92	12	6	1	0.3	48	31	24	32	13	0	0	122	9	6	2	1.6	.956	OF-86
1918		40	.241	.316	133	32	5	1	1	0.8	6	12	5	14	3	2	0	75	6	1	1	2.2	.988	OF-38
1919	CIN N	5	.167	.167	12	2	0	0	0	0.0	1	3	1	0	0	0	0	5	2	1	0	1.6	.875	OF-5
7 yrs.		258	.250	.319	752	188	24	11	2	0.3	86	66	52	66	26	47	12	280	24	11	6	1.6	.965	OF-201

Frank Reiber

REIBER, FRANK BERNARD (Tubby)
B. Sept. 19, 1909, Huntington, W. Va.
BR TR 5′ 8½″ 169 lbs.

Year	Team	Games	BA	SA	AB	H	2B	3B	HR	HR%	R	RBI	BB	SO	SB	Pinch Hit AB	Pinch Hit H	PO	A	E	DP	TC/G	FA	G by Pos
1933	DET A	13	.278	.556	18	5	0	1	1	5.6	3	3	2	3	0	6	1	13	0	1	0	2.3	.929	C-6
1934		3	.000	.000	1	0	0	0	0	0.0	0	0	2	0	0	1	0	0	0	0	0	0.0	—	
1935		8	.273	.273	11	3	0	0	0	0.0	3	1	3	3	0	2	0	10	0	0	1	2.0	1.000	C-5
1936		20	.273	.364	55	15	2	0	1	1.8	7	5	5	7	0	2	0	47	7	1	0	3.1	.982	C-17, OF-1
4 yrs.		44	.271	.388	85	23	2	1	2	2.4	13	9	12	13	0	11	1	70	7	2	1	2.7	.975	C-28, OF-1

Herm Reich

REICH, HERMAN CHARLES
B. Nov. 23, 1917, Bell, Calif.
BR TL 6′ 2″ 200 lbs.

Year	Team	Games	BA	SA	AB	H	2B	3B	HR	HR%	R	RBI	BB	SO	SB	Pinch Hit AB	Pinch Hit H	PO	A	E	DP	TC/G	FA	G by Pos
1949	3 teams	WAS A (2G –.000) CLE A (1G –.500) CHI N (108G –.280)																						
″	total	111	.279	.359	390	109	18	2	3	0.8	43	34	14	33	4	10	1	786	87	10	58	8.7	.989	1B-85, OF-17

Rick Reichardt

REICHARDT, FREDERIC CARL
B. Mar. 16, 1943, Madison, Wis.
BR TR 6′ 3″ 210 lbs.

Year	Team	Games	BA	SA	AB	H	2B	3B	HR	HR%	R	RBI	BB	SO	SB	Pinch Hit AB	Pinch Hit H	PO	A	E	DP	TC/G	FA	G by Pos
1964	LA A	11	.162	.162	37	6	0	0	0	0.0	0	0	1	12	1	0	0	26	0	0	0	2.4	1.000	OF-11
1965	CAL A	20	.267	.360	75	20	4	0	1	1.3	8	6	5	12	4	0	0	38	1	1	1	2.0	.975	OF-20
1966		89	.288	.480	319	92	5	4	16	5.0	48	44	27	61	8	2	1	153	8	4	1	1.9	.976	OF-87
1967		146	.265	.404	498	132	14	2	17	3.4	56	69	35	90	5	9	2	254	10	7	4	2.0	.974	OF-138
1968		151	.255	.421	534	136	20	3	21	3.9	62	73	42	118	8	5	1	267	9	3	2	1.9	.989	OF-148
1969		137	.254	.371	493	125	11	4	13	2.6	60	68	43	100	3	0	0	270	16	5	5	2.1	.983	OF-136, 1B-3
1970	2 teams	CAL A (9G –.167) WAS A (107G –.253)																						
″	total	116	.251	.473	283	71	14	2	15	5.3	43	47	26	69	2	41	8	135	0	2	0	1.7	.985	OF-80, 3B-1
1971	CHI A	138	.278	.429	496	138	14	2	19	3.8	53	62	37	90	5	7	2	333	7	5	2	2.5	.986	OF-128, 1B-9
1972		101	.251	.409	291	73	14	4	8	2.7	31	43	28	63	2	10	1	157	2	3	1	1.8	.981	OF-90
1973	2 teams	CHI A (46G –.275) KC A (41G –.220)																						
″	total	87	.250	.382	280	70	13	3	6	2.1	30	33	19	57	2	9	3	68	2	0	1	0.9	1.000	OF-44, DH-37
1974	KC A	1	1.000	1.000	1	1	0	0	0	0.0	0	0	0	0	0	1	1	0	0	0	0	0.0	—	
11 yrs.		997	.261	.414	3307	864	109	24	116	3.5	391	445	263	672	40	84	19	1701	55	30	17	1.9	.983	OF-882, DH-37, 1B-12, 3B-1

Dick Reichle

REICHLE, RICHARD WENDELL — BL TR 6′ 185 lbs.
B. Nov. 23, 1896, Lincoln, Ill. D. June 13, 1967, St. Louis, Mo.

Year	Team		Games	BA	SA	AB	H	2B	3B	HR	HR%	R	RBI	BB	SO	SB	Pinch Hit AB	Pinch Hit H	PO	A	E	DP	TC/G	FA	G by Pos
1922	BOS	A	6	.250	.292	24	6	1	0	0	0.0	3	0	0	2	0	0	0	15	0	0	0	2.5	1.000	OF-6
1923			122	.258	.330	361	93	17	3	1	0.3	40	39	22	34	3	19	5	190	10	5	2	2.2	.976	OF-93
2 yrs.			128	.257	.327	385	99	18	3	1	0.3	43	39	22	36	3	19	5	205	10	5	2	2.2	.977	OF-99

Billy Reid

REID, WILLIAM ALEXANDER — BL TR 6′ 170 lbs.
B. May 17, 1857, London, Ont., Canada D. June 26, 1940, London, Ont., Canada.

Year	Team		Games	BA	SA	AB	H	2B	3B	HR	HR%	R	RBI	BB	SO	SB	Pinch Hit AB	Pinch Hit H	PO	A	E	DP	TC/G	FA	G by Pos
1883	BAL	AA	24	.278	.309	97	27	3	0	0	0.0	14		4			0	0	61	65	24	7	6.3	.840	2B-23, SS-1
1884	PIT	AA	19	.243	.271	70	17	2	0	0	0.0	11		4			0	0	24	2	11	0	1.9	.703	OF-17, 3B-1, 1B-1, 2B-1
2 yrs.			43	.263	.293	167	44	5	0	0	0.0	25		8			0	0	85	67	35	7	4.3	.813	2B-24, OF-17, 3B-1, 1B-1, SS-1

Jessie Reid

REID, JESSIE THOMAS — BL TL 6′ 1″ 200 lbs.
B. June 1, 1962, Honolulu, Hawaii

Year	Team		Games	BA	SA	AB	H	2B	3B	HR	HR%	R	RBI	BB	SO	SB	Pinch Hit AB	Pinch Hit H	PO	A	E	DP	TC/G	FA	G by Pos
1987	SF	N	6	.125	.500	8	1	0	0	1	12.5	1	1	1	5	0	5	0	3	0	0	0	1.0	1.000	OF-3
1988			2	.000	.000	2	0	0	0	0	0.0	0	0	0	1	0	2	0	0	0	0	0	0.0	—	
2 yrs.			8	.100	.400	10	1	0	0	1	10.0	1	1	1	6	0	7	0	3	0	0	0	1.0	1.000	OF-3

Scott Reid

REID, SCOTT DONALD — BL TR 6′ 1″ 195 lbs.
B. Jan. 7, 1947, Chicago, Ill.

Year	Team		Games	BA	SA	AB	H	2B	3B	HR	HR%	R	RBI	BB	SO	SB	Pinch Hit AB	Pinch Hit H	PO	A	E	DP	TC/G	FA	G by Pos
1969	PHI	N	13	.211	.211	19	4	0	0	0	0.0	5	0	7	5	0	5	1	7	0	0	0	1.4	1.000	OF-5
1970			25	.122	.143	49	6	1	0	0	0.0	5	1	11	22	0	4	0	28	6	0	1	1.9	1.000	OF-18
2 yrs.			38	.147	.162	68	10	1	0	0	0.0	10	1	18	27	0	9	1	35	6	0	1	1.8	1.000	OF-23

Charlie Reilley

REILLEY, CHARLES E. — BR TR 5′ 8″ 160 lbs.
B. 1856, Hartford, Conn. Deceased.

Year	Team		Games	BA	SA	AB	H	2B	3B	HR	HR%	R	RBI	BB	SO	SB	Pinch Hit AB	Pinch Hit H	PO	A	E	DP	TC/G	FA	G by Pos
1879	TRO	N	62	.229	.258	236	54	5	1	0	0.0	17	19	1	20		0	0	354	51	53	6	7.4	.884	C-49, 1B-11, OF-2
1880	CIN	N	30	.204	.214	103	21	1	0	0	0.0	8	9	0	5		0	0	68	16	14	0	3.0	.857	OF-16, C-13, 3B-4
1881	2 teams		DET N (19G –.171)			WOR N (2G –.375)																			
″	total		21	.192	.218	78	15	2	0	0	0.0	10	4	0	11		0	0	65	29	19	2	4.9	.832	C-12, OF-4, SS-3, 3B-3, 1B-1
1882	PRO	N	3	.182	.182	11	2	0	0	0	0.0	0		1	2		0	0	14	1	6	0	7.0	.714	C-3
1884	BOS	U	3	.000	.000	11	0	0	0	0	0.0	1		1			0	0	3	0	1	0	1.3	.750	OF-2, 3B-1
5 yrs.			119	.210	.232	439	92	8	1	0	0.0	36	32	3	38		0	0	504	97	93	8	5.6	.866	C-77, OF-24, 1B-12, 3B-8, SS-3

Duke Reilley

REILLEY, ALEXANDER ALOYSIUS (Midget) — BB TR 5′ 4½″ 148 lbs.
B. Aug. 25, 1884, Chicago, Ill. D. Mar. 4, 1968, Indianapolis, Ind.

Year	Team		Games	BA	SA	AB	H	2B	3B	HR	HR%	R	RBI	BB	SO	SB	Pinch Hit AB	Pinch Hit H	PO	A	E	DP	TC/G	FA	G by Pos
1909	CLE	A	20	.210	.210	62	13	0	0	0	0.0	10	0	4		5	0	0	46	1	1	1	2.7	.979	OF-18

Arch Reilly

REILLY, ARCHER EDWIN — BR TR 5′10″ 163 lbs.
B. Aug. 17, 1891, Alton, Ill. D. Nov. 29, 1963, Columbus, Ohio.

Year	Team		Games	BA	SA	AB	H	2B	3B	HR	HR%	R	RBI	BB	SO	SB	Pinch Hit AB	Pinch Hit H	PO	A	E	DP	TC/G	FA	G by Pos
1917	PIT	N	1	—	—	0	0	0	0	0	—	0	0	0	0	0	0	0	1	0	0	0	1.0	1.000	3B-1

Barney Reilly

REILLY, BERNARD EUGENE — BR TR 6′ 175 lbs.
B. Feb. 7, 1884, Brockton, Mass. D. Nov. 15, 1934, St. Joseph, Mo.

Year	Team		Games	BA	SA	AB	H	2B	3B	HR	HR%	R	RBI	BB	SO	SB	Pinch Hit AB	Pinch Hit H	PO	A	E	DP	TC/G	FA	G by Pos
1909	CHI	A	12	.200	.200	25	5	0	0	0	0.0	3	3	3		2	0	0	18	33	2	0	4.4	.962	2B-11, OF-1

Charlie Reilly

REILLY, CHARLES THOMAS (Princeton Charlie) — BB TR 5′11″ 190 lbs.
Born Charles Thomas O'Reilly.
B. June 24, 1855, Princeton, N. J. D. Dec. 16, 1937, Los Angeles, Calif.

Year	Team		Games	BA	SA	AB	H	2B	3B	HR	HR%	R	RBI	BB	SO	SB	Pinch Hit AB	Pinch Hit H	PO	A	E	DP	TC/G	FA	G by Pos
1889	COL	AA	6	.478	.913	23	11	1	0	3	13.0	5	6	2	2	9	0	0	7	17	2	0	4.3	.923	3B-6
1890			137	.266	.343	530	141	23	3	4	0.8	75		35		43	0	0	206	354	67	26	4.6	.893	3B-136, 2B-1
1891	PIT	N	114	.219	.284	415	91	8	5	3	0.7	43	44	29	58	20	0	0	156	261	67	10	4.2	.862	3B-99, SS-11, OF-4
1892	PHI	N	91	.196	.245	331	65	7	3	1	0.3	42	24	18	43	13	2	**1**	136	178	31	13	3.9	.910	3B-70, OF-15, 2B-4
1893			104	.245	.346	416	102	16	7	4	1.0	64	56	33	36	13	0	0	164	235	47	21	4.3	.895	3B-104
1894			39	.296	.333	135	40	1	2	0	0.0	21	19	16	10	9	0	0	53	71	16	4	3.6	.886	3B-28, OF-5, 2B-4, 1B-1, SS-1
1895			49	.268	.313	179	48	6	1	0	0.0	28	25	13	12	7	0	0	82	133	23	15	4.9	.903	SS-34, 3B-11, 2B-3, OF-1
1897	WAS	N	101	.276	.362	351	97	18	3	2	0.6	64	60	34		18	0	0	149	224	39	17	4.1	.905	3B-101
8 yrs.			641	.250	.325	2380	595	80	24	17	0.7	342	234	180	161	132	2	1	953	1473	292	106	4.3	.893	3B-555, SS-46, OF-25, 2B-12, 1B-1

Hal Reilly

REILLY, HAROLD JOHN (Turk) — BL TL 6′ 180 lbs.
B. Apr. 1, 1894, Oshkosh, Wis. D. Dec. 24, 1957, Chicago, Ill.

Year	Team		Games	BA	SA	AB	H	2B	3B	HR	HR%	R	RBI	BB	SO	SB	Pinch Hit AB	Pinch Hit H	PO	A	E	DP	TC/G	FA	G by Pos
1919	CHI	N	1	.000	.000	3	0	0	0	0	0.0	0	0	0	1	0	0	0	0	0	0	0	0.0	.000	OF-1

Joe Reilly

REILLY, JOSEPH J. — 5′10″ 140 lbs.
B. 1861, New York, N. Y. Deceased.

Year	Team		Games	BA	SA	AB	H	2B	3B	HR	HR%	R	RBI	BB	SO	SB	Pinch Hit AB	Pinch Hit H	PO	A	E	DP	TC/G	FA	G by Pos
1885	NY	AA	10	.175	.250	40	7	3	0	0	0.0	6		2			0	0	33	29	11	3	7.3	.849	2B-8, 3B-2

Josh Reilly

REILLY, CHARLES
B. 1868, San Francisco, Calif. D. June 13, 1938, San Francisco, Calif.

Year	Team		Games	BA	SA	AB	H	2B	3B	HR	HR%	R	RBI	BB	SO	SB	Pinch Hit AB	Pinch Hit H	PO	A	E	DP	TC/G	FA	G by Pos
1896	CHI	N	9	.214	.238	42	9	1	0	0	0.0	6	2	1	1	2	0	0	21	32	11	1	7.1	.828	2B-8, SS-1

Long John Reilly

REILLY, JOHN GOOD — BR TR 6′ 3″ 178 lbs.
B. Oct. 5, 1858, Cincinnati, Ohio D. May 31, 1937, Cincinnati, Ohio.

Year	Team		Games	BA	SA	AB	H	2B	3B	HR	HR%	R	RBI	BB	SO	SB	Pinch Hit AB	Pinch Hit H	PO	A	E	DP	TC/G	FA	G by Pos
1880	CIN	N	73	.206	.265	272	56	8	4	0	0.0	21	16	3	36		0	0	616	13	36	36	8.9	.946	1B-72, OF-3
1883	CIN	AA	98	.311	.485	437	136	21	14	9	2.1	103		9			0	0	960	19	40	50	10.3	.961	1B-98, OF-1
1884			105	.339	**.551**	448	152	24	19	**11**	**2.5**	114		5			0	0	979	26	30	60	9.7	.971	1B-103, OF-3, SS-1
1885			111	.297	.411	482	143	18	11	5	1.0	92		11			0	0	1042	22	42	59	9.7	.962	1B-107, OF-7
1886			115	.265	.370	441	117	12	11	4	0.9	92		31			0	0	1126	38	42	80	10.4	.965	1B-110, OF-6
1887			134	.309	.477	551	170	35	14	10	1.8	106		22		50	0	0	1291	34	26	84	9.9	.981	1B-127, OF-9
1888			127	.321	**.501**	527	169	28	14	**13**	**2.5**	112	**103**	17		82	0	0	1275	45	31	73	10.6	.977	1B-117, OF-10
1889			111	.260	.412	427	111	24	13	5	1.2	84	66	34	37	43	0	0	1145	30	19	76	10.8	.984	1B-109, OF-2
1890	CIN	N	133	.300	.472	553	166	25	**26**	6	1.1	114	86	16	41	29	0	0	1393	38	33	77	11.0	.977	1B-132, OF-1
1891			135	.242	.348	546	132	20	13	4	0.7	60	64	9	42	22	0	0	1161	34	27	61	9.0	.978	1B-100, OF-36
10 yrs.			1142	.289	.437	4684	1352	215	139	67	1.4	898	335	157	156	226	0	0	10988	299	326	656	10.1	.972	1B-1075, OF-78, SS-1

Tom Reilly

REILLY, THOMAS HENRY BR TR 5'10"
B. Aug. 3, 1884, St. Louis, Mo. D. Oct. 18, 1918, New Orleans, La.

Year	Team	Lg	Games	BA	SA	AB	H	2B	3B	HR	HR%	R	RBI	BB	SO	SB	Pinch Hit AB	Pinch Hit H	PO	A	E	DP	TC/G	FA	G by Pos
1908	STL	N	29	.173	.222	81	14	1	0	1	1.2	5	3	2		4	0	0	34	69	16	10	4.1	.866	SS-29
1909			5	.286	.571	7	2	0	1	0	0.0	0	2	0	0	0	0	0	2	7	0	0	1.8	1.000	SS-5
1914	CLE	A	1	.000	.000	1	0	0	0	0	0.0	0	0	0	0	0	1	0	0	0	0	0	0.0	—	
3 yrs.			35	.180	.247	89	16	1	1	1	1.1	5	5	2	0	4	1	0	36	76	16	10	3.8	.875	SS-34

Kevin Reimer

REIMER, KEVIN MICHAEL BL TR 6' 2" 215 lbs.
B. June 28, 1964, Macon, Ga.

Year	Team	Lg	Games	BA	SA	AB	H	2B	3B	HR	HR%	R	RBI	BB	SO	SB	Pinch Hit AB	Pinch Hit H	PO	A	E	DP	TC/G	FA	G by Pos
1988	TEX	A	12	.120	.240	25	3	0	0	1	4.0	2	2	0	6	0	5	0	0	0	0	0	0.0		DH-7, OF-1
1989			3	.000	.000	5	0	0	0	0	0.0	0	0	0	1	0	2	0	0	0	0	0	0.0	.000	DH-1
1990			64	.260	.430	100	26	9	1	2	2.0	5	15	10	22	0	40	**12**	12	0	2	0	0.5	.857	DH-21, OF-9
1991			136	.269	.477	394	106	22	0	20	5.1	46	69	33	93	0	28	8	110	0	6	0	1.0	.948	OF-66, DH-56
1992			148	.267	.437	494	132	32	2	16	3.2	56	58	42	103	2	15	5	198	7	11	1	1.5	.949	OF-110, DH-32
1993	MIL	A	125	.249	.394	437	109	22	1	13	3.0	53	60	30	72	5	11	2	75	1	3	0	0.7	.962	DH-83, OF-37
6 yrs.			488	.258	.430	1455	376	85	4	52	3.6	162	204	115	297	7	101	27	395	8	22	1	1.0	.948	OF-223, DH-200

Mike Reinbach

REINBACH, MICHAEL WAYNE BL TR 6' 2" 195 lbs.
B. Aug. 6, 1949, San Diego, Calif.

Year	Team	Lg	Games	BA	SA	AB	H	2B	3B	HR	HR%	R	RBI	BB	SO	SB	Pinch Hit AB	Pinch Hit H	PO	A	E	DP	TC/G	FA	G by Pos
1974	BAL	A	12	.250	.300	20	5	1	0	0	0.0	2	2	2	5	0	7	1	3	0	0	0	0.5	1.000	OF-3, DH-3

Wally Reinecker

REINECKER, WALTER JOSEPH BR TR 5' 6" 150 lbs.
Born Walter Joseph Smith.
B. Apr. 21, 1890, Pittsburgh, Pa. D. Apr. 18, 1957, Pittsburgh, Pa.

Year	Team	Lg	Games	BA	SA	AB	H	2B	3B	HR	HR%	R	RBI	BB	SO	SB	Pinch Hit AB	Pinch Hit H	PO	A	E	DP	TC/G	FA	G by Pos
1915	BAL	F	3	.125	.125	8	1	0	0	0	0.0	0	0	0		0	0	0	3	1	3	0	2.3	.571	3B-3

Art Reinholz

REINHOLZ, ARTHUR AUGUST BR TR 5'10½" 175 lbs.
B. Jan. 27, 1903, Detroit, Mich. D. Dec. 29, 1980, New Port Richey, Fla.

Year	Team	Lg	Games	BA	SA	AB	H	2B	3B	HR	HR%	R	RBI	BB	SO	SB	Pinch Hit AB	Pinch Hit H	PO	A	E	DP	TC/G	FA	G by Pos
1928	CLE	A	2	.333	.333	3	1	0	0	0	0.0	0	0	1	0	0	0	0	1	4	1	0	3.0	.833	3B-2

Charlie Reipschlager

REIPSCHLAGER, CHARLES W. BR TR 5' 6½" 160 lbs.
Deceased.

Year	Team	Lg	Games	BA	SA	AB	H	2B	3B	HR	HR%	R	RBI	BB	SO	SB	Pinch Hit AB	Pinch Hit H	PO	A	E	DP	TC/G	FA	G by Pos
1883	NY	AA	37	.186	.241	145	27	4	2	0	0.0	8		4			0	0	212	46	17	1	7.4	.938	C-29, OF-8
1884			59	.240	.313	233	56	13	2	0	0.0	21		1			0	0	378	111	42	4	9.0	.921	C-51, OF-8
1885			72	.243	.291	268	65	11	1	0	0.0	29		9			0	0	277	135	57	8	6.4	.878	C-59, OF-6, 3B-6, SS-1, 2B-1
1886			65	.211	.280	232	49	4	6	0	0.0	21		9			0	0	280	107	52	5	6.7	.882	C-57, OF-9
1887	CLE	AA	63	.212	.273	231	49	8	3	0	0.0	20		11		7	0	0	314	106	45	13	7.3	.903	C-48, 1B-16
5 yrs.			296	.222	.283	1109	246	40	14	0	0.0	99		34		7	0	0	1461	505	213	31	7.3	.902	C-244, OF-31, 1B-16, 3B-6, SS-1, 2B-1

Bobby Reis

REIS, ROBERT JOSEPH THOMAS BR TR 6' 1" 175 lbs.
B. Jan. 2, 1909, Woodside, N. Y. D. May 1, 1973, St. Paul, Minn.

Year	Team	Lg	Games	BA	SA	AB	H	2B	3B	HR	HR%	R	RBI	BB	SO	SB	Pinch Hit AB	Pinch Hit H	PO	A	E	DP	TC/G	FA	G by Pos
1931	BKN	N	6	.294	.294	17	5	0	0	0	0.0	3	2	2	0	0	0	0	7	7	1	0	2.5	.933	3B-6
1932			1	.250	.250	4	1	0	0	0	0.0	0	0	0	1	0	0	0	0	1	1	0	2.0	.500	3B-1
1935			52	.247	.329	85	21	3	2	0	0.0	10	4	6	13	2	9	3	42	28	2	6	1.8	.972	OF-21, P-14, 2B-4, 3B-1, 1B-1
1936	BOS	N	37	.217	.250	60	13	2	0	0	0.0	3	5	3	6	0	0	0	14	47	0	2	1.6	1.000	P-35, OF-2
1937			45	.244	.302	86	21	5	0	0	0.0	10	6	13	12	2	13	4	74	2	1	1	3.0	.987	OF-18, 1B-4, P-4
1938			34	.184	.184	49	9	0	0	0	0.0	6	4	1	3	1	2	0	17	17	1	0	1.1	.971	P-16, OF-10, SS-3, C-1, 2B-1
6 yrs.			175	.233	.279	301	70	10	2	0	0.0	32	21	25	35	5	24	7	154	102	6	9	1.8	.977	P-69, OF-51, 3B-8, 2B-5, 1B-5, SS-3, C-1

Pete Reiser

REISER, HAROLD PATRICK (Pistol Pete) BL TR 5'11" 185 lbs.
B. Mar. 17, 1919, St. Louis, Mo. D. Oct. 25, 1981, Palm Springs, Calif. BB 1948–1952

Year	Team	Lg	Games	BA	SA	AB	H	2B	3B	HR	HR%	R	RBI	BB	SO	SB	Pinch Hit AB	Pinch Hit H	PO	A	E	DP	TC/G	FA	G by Pos
1940	BKN	N	58	.293	.418	225	66	11	4	3	1.3	34	20	15	33	2	6	0	72	70	7	8	2.9	.953	3B-30, OF-17, SS-5
1941			137	**.343**	**.558**	536	184	**39**	**17**	14	2.6	**117**	76	46	71	4	1	0	356	14	7	0	2.8	.981	OF-133
1942			125	.310	.463	480	149	33	5	10	2.1	89	64	48	45	**20**	0	0	277	9	9	2	2.4	.969	OF-125
1946			122	.277	.428	423	117	21	5	11	2.6	75	73	55	58	**34**	10	3	221	50	7	4	2.5	.975	OF-97, 3B-15
1947			110	.309	.418	388	120	23	2	5	1.3	68	46	68	41	14	2	0	240	3	3	0	2.3	.988	OF-108
1948			64	.236	.354	127	30	8	2	1	0.8	17	19	29	21	4	21	10	56	8	2	1	1.9	.970	OF-30, 3B-4
1949	BOS	N	84	.271	.443	221	60	8	3	8	3.6	32	40	33	42	3	10	4	142	10	4	4	2.3	.974	OF-63, 3B-4
1950			53	.205	.269	78	16	2	0	1	1.3	12	10	18	22	1	24	3	46	0	1	0	1.9	.979	OF-24, 3B-1
1951	PIT	N	74	.271	.421	140	38	9	3	2	1.4	22	13	27	20	4	33	11	56	8	2	1	2.1	.970	OF-27, 3B-5
1952	CLE	A	34	.136	.364	44	6	1	0	3	6.8	7	7	4	16	1	15	1	20	0	0	0	2.0	1.000	OF-10
10 yrs.			861	.295	.450	2662	786	155	41	58	2.2	473	368	343	369	87	122	32	1486	172	42	20	2.4	.975	OF-634, 3B-59, SS-5
WORLD SERIES																									
1941	BKN	N	5	.200	.500	20	4	1	1	1	5.0	1	3	1	6	0	0	0	14	1	0	0	3.0	1.000	OF-5
1947			5	.250	.250	8	2	0	0	0	0.0	1	0	3	1	0	0	0	7	0	1	0	2.7	.875	OF-3
2 yrs.			10	.214	.429	28	6	1	1	1	3.6	2	3	4	7	0	0	0	21	1	1	0	2.9	.957	OF-8

Charlie Reising

REISING, CHARLES (Pop)
B. Aug. 28, 1861, Lanesville, Ind. D. July 26, 1915, Louisville, Ky.

Year	Team	Lg	Games	BA	SA	AB	H	2B	3B	HR	HR%	R	RBI	BB	SO	SB	Pinch Hit AB	Pinch Hit H	PO	A	E	DP	TC/G	FA	G by Pos
1884	IND	AA	2	.000	.000	8	0	0	0	0	0.0	0		1			0	0	2	0	3	0	2.5	.400	OF-2

Al Reiss

REISS, ALBERT ALLEN BB TR 5'10½" 165 lbs.
B. Jan. 8, 1909, Elizabeth, N. J. D. May 13, 1989, Red Bank, N. J.

Year	Team	Lg	Games	BA	SA	AB	H	2B	3B	HR	HR%	R	RBI	BB	SO	SB	Pinch Hit AB	Pinch Hit H	PO	A	E	DP	TC/G	FA	G by Pos
1932	PHI	A	9	.200	.200	5	1	0	0	0	0.0	0	1	1	1	0	2	0	2	3	0	0	0.8	1.000	SS-6

Heinie Reitz

REITZ, HENRY P. BL TR 5' 7½" 160 lbs.
B. June 29, 1867, Chicago, Ill. D. Nov. 10, 1914, San Francisco, Calif.

Year	Team	Lg	Games	BA	SA	AB	H	2B	3B	HR	HR%	R	RBI	BB	SO	SB	Pinch Hit AB	Pinch Hit H	PO	A	E	DP	TC/G	FA	G by Pos
1893	BAL	N	130	.286	.380	490	140	17	13	1	0.2	90	76	65	32	24	0	0	315	421	48	62	6.0	.939	2B-130
1894			108	.303	.504	446	135	22	**31**	2	0.4	86	105	42	24	18	0	0	278	373	25	53	6.2	.963	2B-97, 3B-12
1895			71	.294	.396	245	72	15	5	0	0.0	45	29	18	11	15	3	0	138	162	21	26	4.8	.935	2B-48, 3B-18, SS-1
1896			120	.287	.371	464	133	15	6	4	0.9	76	106	49	32	28	0	0	259	342	31	54	5.2	.951	2B-118, SS-3
1897			128	.289	.358	477	138	15	6	2	0.4	76	84	50		23	0	0	280	449	29	62	5.9	.962	2B-128

Heinie Reitz *continued*

Year	Team	Games	BA	SA	AB	H	2B	3B	HR	HR%	R	RBI	BB	SO	SB	Pinch Hit AB	Pinch Hit H	PO	A	E	DP	TC/G	FA	G by Pos
1898	**WAS N**	132	.303	.364	489	148	20	2	2	0.4	62	47	32		11	0	0	323	401	31	56	5.7	.959	2B-132
1899	**PIT N**	34	.262	.323	130	34	4	2	0	0.0	11	15	10		3	0	0	86	110	5	8	5.9	.975	2B-34
7 yrs.		723	.292	.391	2741	800	108	65	11	0.4	446	462	266	99	122	3	0	1679	2258	190	321	5.7	.954	2B-687, 3B-30, SS-4

Ken Reitz

REITZ, KENNETH JOHN BR TR 6′ 180 lbs.
B. June 24, 1951, San Francisco, Calif.

Year	Team	Games	BA	SA	AB	H	2B	3B	HR	HR%	R	RBI	BB	SO	SB	Pinch Hit AB	Pinch Hit H	PO	A	E	DP	TC/G	FA	G by Pos
1972	**STL N**	21	.359	.410	78	28	4	0	0	0.0	5	10	2	4	0	1	0	17	26	2	3	2.3	.956	3B-20
1973		147	.235	.333	426	100	20	2	6	1.4	40	42	9	25	0	12	2	88	213	8	20	2.3	.974	3B-135, SS-1
1974		154	.271	.363	579	157	28	2	7	1.2	48	54	23	63	0	3	1	131	281	12	29	2.8	.972	3B-151, SS-2
1975		161	.269	.340	592	159	25	1	5	0.8	43	63	22	54	1	1	0	124	279	23	21	2.7	.946	3B-160
1976	**SF N**	155	.267	.333	577	154	21	1	5	0.9	40	66	24	48	5	0	0	141	304	19	33	3.0	.959	3B-155, SS-1
1977	**STL N**	157	.261	.412	587	153	36	1	17	2.9	58	79	19	74	2	0	0	121	320	9	35	2.9	.980	3B-157
1978		150	.246	.357	540	133	26	2	10	1.9	41	75	23	61	1	4	4	111	314	12	18	2.9	.973	3B-150
1979		159	.268	.382	605	162	41	2	8	1.3	42	73	25	85	1	2	0	124	290	12	26	2.7	.972	3B-158
1980		151	.270	.379	523	141	33	0	8	1.5	39	58	22	44	0	1	0	86	293	8	25	2.6	.979	3B-150
1981	**CHI N**	82	.215	.281	260	56	9	1	2	0.8	10	28	15	56	0	1	0	57	157	5	11	2.7	.977	3B-81
1982	**PIT N**	7	.000	.000	10	0	0	0	0	0.0	0	0	0	4	0	3	0	0	6	0	0	1.5	1.000	3B-4
11 yrs.		1344	.260	.359	4777	1243	243	12	68	1.4	366	548	184	518	10	28	7	1000	2483	110	221	2.7	.969	3B-1321, SS-4

Butch Rementer

REMENTER, WILLIS J. TR
B. Mar. 14, 1878, Philadelphia, Pa. D. Sept. 23, 1922, Philadelphia, Pa.

Year	Team	Games	BA	SA	AB	H	2B	3B	HR	HR%	R	RBI	BB	SO	SB	Pinch Hit AB	Pinch Hit H	PO	A	E	DP	TC/G	FA	G by Pos
1904	**PHI N**	1	.000	.000	2	0	0	0	0	0.0	0	0	0		0	0	0	3	0	0	0	3.0	1.000	C-1

Jack Remsen

REMSEN, JOHN JAY BR TR 5′11″ 170 lbs.
B. Apr. 1851, Brooklyn, N. Y. Deceased.

Year	Team	Games	BA	SA	AB	H	2B	3B	HR	HR%	R	RBI	BB	SO	SB	Pinch Hit AB	Pinch Hit H	PO	A	E	DP	TC/G	FA	G by Pos
1876	**HAR N**	69	.275	.352	324	89	12	5	1	0.3	62	30	1	15		0	0	177	12	24	5	3.1	.887	OF-69
1877	**STL N**	33	.260	.350	123	32	3	4	0	0.0	14	13	4	3		0	0	73	4	8	0	2.6	.906	OF-33
1878	**CHI N**	56	.232	.304	224	52	11	1	1	0.4	32	19	**17**	33		0	0	103	14	7	5	2.2	.944	OF-56
1879		42	.217	.270	152	33	4	2	0	0.0	14	8	2	23		0	0	187	9	22	3	5.2	.899	OF-31, 1B-11
1881	**CLE N**	48	.174	.233	172	30	4	3	0	0.0	14	13	9	31		0	0	117	7	18	1	3.0	.873	OF-48
1884	**2 teams**	**PHI N** (12G –.209) **BKN AA** (81G –.223)																						
″	**total**	93	.221	.305	344	76	8	6	3	0.9	54		29	9		0	0	169	10	16	2	2.1	.918	OF-93
6 yrs.		341	.233	.307	1339	312	42	21	5	0.4	190	83	62	114		0	0	826	56	95	16	2.9	.903	OF-330, 1B-11

Jerry Remy

REMY, GERALD PETER BL TR 5′9″ 165 lbs.
B. Nov. 8, 1952, Fall River, Mass.

Year	Team	Games	BA	SA	AB	H	2B	3B	HR	HR%	R	RBI	BB	SO	SB	Pinch Hit AB	Pinch Hit H	PO	A	E	DP	TC/G	FA	G by Pos
1975	**CAL A**	147	.258	.311	569	147	17	5	1	0.2	82	46	45	55	34	0	0	336	427	14	111	5.3	.982	2B-147
1976		143	.263	.303	502	132	14	3	0	0.0	64	28	38	43	35	1	1	279	406	16	77	5.1	.977	2B-133, DH-5
1977		154	.252	.341	575	145	19	10	4	0.7	74	44	59	59	41	1	0	307	420	19	90	4.9	.975	2B-152, 3B-1
1978	**BOS A**	148	.278	.350	583	162	24	6	2	0.3	87	44	40	55	30	1	0	328	446	13	114	5.4	.983	2B-140, DH-4, SS-1
1979		80	.297	.346	306	91	11	2	0	0.0	49	29	26	25	14	1	0	147	205	11	43	4.8	.970	2B-76
1980		63	.313	.361	230	72	7	2	0	0.0	24	9	10	14	14	4	1	109	189	7	30	5.0	.977	2B-60, OF-1
1981		88	.307	.338	358	110	9	1	0	0.0	55	31	36	30	9	1	0	162	272	7	58	5.1	.984	2B-87
1982		155	.280	.324	636	178	22	3	0	0.0	89	47	55	77	16	1	0	290	432	13	104	4.8	.982	2B-154
1983		146	.275	.319	592	163	16	5	0	0.0	73	43	40	35	11	2	0	295	376	7	104	4.7	.990	2B-144
1984		30	.250	.279	104	26	1	1	0	0.0	8	8	7	11	4	5	0	40	70	3	13	4.7	.973	2B-24
10 yrs.		1154	.275	.328	4455	1226	140	38	7	0.2	605	329	356	404	208	16	2	2293	3243	110	744	5.0	.981	2B-1117, DH-9, SS-1, OF-1, 3B-1

Rick Renick

RENICK, WARREN RICHARD BR TR 6′ 188 lbs.
B. Mar. 16, 1944, London, Ohio.

Year	Team	Games	BA	SA	AB	H	2B	3B	HR	HR%	R	RBI	BB	SO	SB	Pinch Hit AB	Pinch Hit H	PO	A	E	DP	TC/G	FA	G by Pos
1968	**MIN A**	42	.216	.402	97	21	5	2	3	3.1	16	13	9	42	0	1	0	50	91	8	13	3.7	.946	SS-40
1969		71	.245	.374	139	34	3	0	5	3.6	21	17	12	32	0	25	8	34	59	10	7	2.2	.903	3B-30, OF-10, SS-6
1970		81	.229	.391	179	41	8	0	7	3.9	20	25	22	29	0	26	7	52	54	2	5	1.9	.981	3B-30, OF-25, SS-1
1971		27	.222	.333	45	10	2	0	1	2.2	4	8	5	14	0	13	1	11	8	2	0	1.5	.905	OF-7, 3B-7
1972		55	.172	.323	93	16	2	0	4	4.3	10	8	15	25	0	24	2	39	10	1	9	1.6	.980	OF-21, 1B-6, 3B-4, SS-1
5 yrs.		276	.221	.373	553	122	20	2	20	3.6	71	71	63	142	0	89	18	186	222	23	34	2.3	.947	3B-71, OF-63, SS-48, 1B-6
LEAGUE CHAMPIONSHIP SERIES																								
1969	**MIN A**	1	.000	.000	1	0	0	0	0	0.0	0	0	0	0	0	1	0	0	0	0	0	0.0	—	
1970		2	.200	.200	5	1	0	0	0	0.0	0	0	0	1	0	1	0	1	3	0	0	4.0	1.000	3B-1
2 yrs.		3	.167	.167	6	1	0	0	0	0.0	0	0	0	1	0	2	0	1	3	0	0	4.0	1.000	3B-1

Bill Renna

RENNA, WILLIAM BENEDITTO (Big Bill) BR TR 6′3″ 218 lbs.
B. Oct. 14, 1924, Hanford, Calif.

Year	Team	Games	BA	SA	AB	H	2B	3B	HR	HR%	R	RBI	BB	SO	SB	Pinch Hit AB	Pinch Hit H	PO	A	E	DP	TC/G	FA	G by Pos
1953	**NY A**	61	.314	.463	121	38	6	3	2	1.7	19	13	13	31	0	17	5	57	0	1	0	1.5	.983	OF-40
1954	**PHI A**	123	.232	.379	422	98	15	4	13	3.1	52	53	41	60	1	9	3	226	13	7	5	2.1	.972	OF-115
1955	**KC A**	100	.213	.349	249	53	7	3	7	2.8	33	28	31	42	0	23	4	118	5	1	2	1.6	.992	OF-79
1956		33	.271	.458	48	13	3	0	2	4.2	12	5	3	10	1	9	2	18	1	1	0	0.8	.950	OF-25
1958	**BOS A**	39	.268	.571	56	15	5	0	4	7.1	5	18	6	14	0	25	7	17	0	0	0	1.5	1.000	OF-11
1959		14	.091	.091	22	2	0	0	0	0.0	2	2	5	9	0	8	1	5	0	0	0	0.7	1.000	OF-7
6 yrs.		370	.239	.391	918	219	36	10	28	3.1	123	119	99	166	2	91	22	441	19	10	7	1.7	.979	OF-277

Tony Rensa

RENSA, GEORGE ANTHONY (Pug) BR TR 5′10″ 180 lbs.
B. Sept. 29, 1901, Parsons, Pa. D. Jan. 4, 1987, Wilkes-Barre, Pa.

Year	Team	Games	BA	SA	AB	H	2B	3B	HR	HR%	R	RBI	BB	SO	SB	Pinch Hit AB	Pinch Hit H	PO	A	E	DP	TC/G	FA	G by Pos
1930	**2 teams**	**DET A** (20G –.270) **PHI N** (54G –.285)																						
″	**total**	74	.282	.431	209	59	13	3	4	1.9	37	34	16	25	1	6	1	177	27	13	6	3.2	.940	C-67
1931	**PHI N**	19	.103	.138	29	3	1	0	0	0.0	2	2	6	2	0	2	0	35	11	2	2	2.8	.958	C-17
1933	**NY A**	8	.310	.448	29	9	2	1	0	0.0	4	3	1	3	0	0	0	39	4	1	1	5.5	.977	C-8
1937	**CHI A**	26	.298	.421	57	17	5	1	0	0.0	10	5	8	6	3	2	1	70	9	2	3	3.5	.975	C-23
1938		59	.248	.333	165	41	5	0	3	1.8	15	19	25	16	1	2	0	185	36	4	4	3.9	.982	C-57
1939		14	.200	.200	25	5	0	0	0	0.0	3	2	1	2	0	1	1	29	6	1	0	2.8	.972	C-13
6 yrs.		200	.261	.372	514	134	26	5	7	1.4	71	65	57	54	5	13	3	535	93	23	16	3.5	.965	C-185

Rick Renteria

RENTERIA, RICHARD AVINA — BR TR 5′ 9″ 172 lbs.
B. Dec. 25, 1961, Harbor City, Calif.

Year	Team	Games	BA	SA	AB	H	2B	3B	HR	HR%	R	RBI	BB	SO	SB	Pinch Hit AB	Pinch Hit H	PO	A	E	DP	TC/G	FA	G by Pos
1986	PIT N	10	.250	.333	12	3	1	0	0	0.0	2	1	0	4	0	9	2	1	2	2	0	5.0	.600	3B-1
1987	SEA A	12	.100	.200	10	1	1	0	0	0.0	2	0	1	2	1	3	0	3	4	1	1	0.9	.875	2B-4, DH-4, SS-1
1988		31	.205	.307	88	18	9	0	0	0.0	6	6	2	8	1	7	1	33	44	3	10	4.0	.962	SS-11, 3B-5, 2B-4
1993	FLA N	103	.255	.327	263	67	9	2	2	0.8	27	30	21	31	0	31	5	84	151	2	20	3.3	.992	2B-45, 3B-25, OF-1
1994		28	.224	.347	49	11	0	0	2	4.1	5	4	1	4	0	11	1	10	22	1	7	1.5	.970	3B-14, 2B-6, OF-2
5 yrs.		184	.237	.322	422	100	20	2	4	0.9	42	41	25	49	2	61	9	131	223	9	38	3.0	.975	2B-59, 3B-45, SS-12, DH-4, OF-3

Bob Repass

REPASS, ROBERT WILLIS — BR TR 6′ 1″ 185 lbs.
B. Nov. 6, 1917, West Pittston, Pa.

Year	Team	Games	BA	SA	AB	H	2B	3B	HR	HR%	R	RBI	BB	SO	SB	Pinch Hit AB	Pinch Hit H	PO	A	E	DP	TC/G	FA	G by Pos
1939	STL N	3	.333	.500	6	2	1	0	0	0.0	0	1	0	2	0	1	1	1	5	0	1	3.0	1.000	2B-2
1942	WAS A	81	.239	.313	259	62	11	1	2	0.8	30	23	33	30	6	6	1	142	178	12	21	4.5	.964	2B-33, 3B-29, SS-11
2 yrs.		84	.242	.317	265	64	12	1	2	0.8	30	24	33	32	6	7	2	143	183	12	22	4.5	.964	2B-35, 3B-29, SS-11

Roger Repoz

REPOZ, ROGER ALLEN — BL TL 6′ 3″ 190 lbs.
B. Aug. 3, 1940, Bellingham, Wash.

Year	Team	Games	BA	SA	AB	H	2B	3B	HR	HR%	R	RBI	BB	SO	SB	Pinch Hit AB	Pinch Hit H	PO	A	E	DP	TC/G	FA	G by Pos
1964	NY A	11	.000	.000	1	0	0	0	0	0.0	1	0	1	1	0	1	0	1	0	0	0	0.1	1.000	OF-9
1965		79	.220	.454	218	48	7	4	12	5.5	34	28	25	57	1	11	0	133	1	1	0	2.0	.993	OF-69
1966	2 teams	NY A (37G –.349) KC A (101G –.216)																						
″	total	138	.232	.384	362	84	14	4	11	3.0	44	43	48	88	3	16	2	466	22	5	27	3.9	.990	OF-82, 1B-45
1967	2 teams	KC A (40G –.241) CAL A (74G –.250)																						
″	total	114	.247	.399	263	65	15	2	7	2.7	34	28	31	57	6	23	4	167	6	5	0	1.9	.972	OF-94
1968	CAL A	133	.240	.371	375	90	8	1	13	3.5	30	54	38	83	8	25	6	226	4	3	1	2.0	.987	OF-114
1969		103	.164	.288	219	36	1	1	8	3.7	25	19	32	52	1	24	2	296	22	2	26	4.1	.994	OF-48, 1B-31
1970		137	.238	.442	407	97	17	6	18	4.4	50	47	45	90	4	20	3	330	9	2	11	2.7	.994	OF-110, 1B-18
1971		113	.199	.374	297	59	11	1	13	4.4	39	42	60	69	3	8	1	227	9	0	5	2.1	1.000	OF-97, 1B-13
1972		3	.333	.333	3	1	0	0	0	0.0	0	0	0	2	0	3	1	0	0	0	0	0.0	—	
9 yrs.		831	.224	.390	2145	480	73	19	82	3.8	257	261	280	499	26	131	19	1846	73	18	70	2.7	.991	OF-623, 1B-107

Rip Repulski

REPULSKI, ELDON JOHN — BR TR 6′ 195 lbs.
B. Oct. 4, 1927, Sauk Rapids, Minn. D. Feb. 10, 1993, Waite Park, Minn.

Year	Team	Games	BA	SA	AB	H	2B	3B	HR	HR%	R	RBI	BB	SO	SB	Pinch Hit AB	Pinch Hit H	PO	A	E	DP	TC/G	FA	G by Pos
1953	STL N	153	.275	.413	567	156	25	4	15	2.6	75	66	33	71	3	0	0	361	7	5	1	2.4	.987	OF-153
1954		152	.283	.454	619	175	39	5	19	3.1	99	79	43	75	8	0	0	302	4	8	0	2.1	.975	OF-152
1955		147	.270	.467	512	138	28	2	23	4.5	64	73	49	66	5	10	3	260	5	7	1	1.9	.974	OF-141
1956		112	.277	.428	376	104	18	3	11	2.9	44	55	24	46	2	17	7	187	3	5	0	2.0	.974	OF-100
1957	PHI N	134	.260	.436	516	134	23	4	20	3.9	65	68	19	74	7	3	0	264	6	9	2	2.1	.968	OF-130
1958		85	.244	.479	238	58	9	4	13	5.5	33	40	15	47	0	30	8	90	3	5	0	1.8	.949	OF-56
1959	LA N	53	.255	.362	94	24	4	0	2	2.1	11	14	13	23	0	25	8	30	0	0	0	1.0	1.000	OF-31
1960	2 teams	LA N (4G –.200) BOS A (73G –.243)																						
″	total	77	.241	.362	141	34	6	1	3	2.1	14	20	10	26	0	39	9	57	0	0	0	1.6	1.000	OF-35
1961	BOS A	15	.280	.320	25	7	1	0	0	0.0	2	1	1	5	0	10	3	4	0	0	0	1.0	1.000	OF-4
9 yrs.		928	.269	.436	3088	830	153	23	106	3.4	407	416	207	433	25	134	38	1555	28	39	4	2.0	.976	OF-802
WORLD SERIES																								
1959	LA N	1	—	—	0	0	0	0	0	—	0	0	1	0	0	0	0	0	0	0	0	0.0	.000	OF-1

Dino Restelli

RESTELLI, DINO PAUL (Dingo) — BR TR 6′ 1½″ 191 lbs.
B. Sept. 23, 1924, St. Louis, Mo.

Year	Team	Games	BA	SA	AB	H	2B	3B	HR	HR%	R	RBI	BB	SO	SB	Pinch Hit AB	Pinch Hit H	PO	A	E	DP	TC/G	FA	G by Pos
1949	PIT N	72	.250	.453	232	58	11	0	12	5.2	41	40	35	26	3	8	2	169	5	7	2	2.9	.961	OF-61, 1B-1
1951		21	.184	.289	38	7	1	0	1	2.6	1	3	2	4	0	8	1	22	1	2	1	2.3	.920	OF-11
2 yrs.		93	.241	.430	270	65	12	0	13	4.8	42	43	37	30	3	16	3	191	6	9	3	2.8	.956	OF-72, 1B-1

Merv Rettenmund

RETTENMUND, MERVIN WELDON — BR TR 5′10″ 190 lbs.
B. June 6, 1943, Flint, Mich.

Year	Team	Games	BA	SA	AB	H	2B	3B	HR	HR%	R	RBI	BB	SO	SB	Pinch Hit AB	Pinch Hit H	PO	A	E	DP	TC/G	FA	G by Pos
1968	BAL A	31	.297	.469	64	19	5	0	2	3.1	10	7	18	20	1	6	3	29	1	0	0	1.3	1.000	OF-23
1969		95	.247	.395	190	47	10	3	4	2.1	27	25	28	28	6	17	2	107	3	1	0	1.4	.991	OF-78
1970		106	.322	.544	338	109	17	2	18	5.3	60	58	38	59	13	17	5	201	6	5	1	2.3	.976	OF-93
1971		141	.318	.448	491	156	23	4	11	2.2	81	75	87	60	15	3	0	292	7	7	4	2.3	.977	OF-134
1972		102	.233	.339	301	70	10	2	6	2.0	40	21	41	37	6	10	3	174	6	2	2	1.9	.989	OF-98
1973		95	.262	.411	321	84	17	2	9	2.8	59	44	57	38	11	11	5	196	4	3	1	2.3	.985	OF-90
1974	CIN N	80	.216	.332	208	45	6	0	6	2.9	30	28	37	39	5	14	3	103	3	0	0	1.5	1.000	OF-69
1975		93	.239	.314	188	45	6	1	2	1.1	24	19	35	22	5	30	6	99	2	0	1	1.6	1.000	OF-61, 3B-1
1976	SD N	86	.229	.321	140	32	7	0	2	1.4	16	11	29	23	4	40	12	79	6	2	1	2.0	.977	OF-43
1977		107	.286	.444	126	36	6	1	4	3.2	23	17	33	28	1	**67**	**21**	30	0	0	0	1.1	1.000	OF-27, 3B-1
1978	CAL A	50	.269	.361	108	29	5	1	1	0.9	16	14	30	13	0	15	2	30	0	1	0	0.8	.968	OF-22, DH-18
1979		35	.263	.329	76	20	2	0	1	1.3	7	10	11	14	1	10	4	6	0	0	0	0.2	1.000	DH-17, OF-9
1980		2	.250	.250	4	1	0	0	0	0.0	0	0	1	1	0	1	0	0	0	0	0	0.0	.000	DH-1
13 yrs.		1023	.271	.406	2555	693	114	16	66	2.6	393	329	445	382	68	241	66	1346	38	21	10	1.8	.985	OF-747, DH-36, 3B-2
LEAGUE CHAMPIONSHIP SERIES																								
1969	BAL A	1	—	—	0	0	0	0	0	—	0	0	0	0	0	0	0	0	0	0	0	0.0	—	
1970		1	.333	.333	3	1	0	0	0	0.0	1	1	2	1	1	0	0	3	1	0	0	4.0	1.000	OF-1
1971		3	.250	.375	8	2	1	0	0	0.0	0	1	0	3	0	0	0	7	0	0	0	2.3	1.000	OF-3
1973		3	.091	.091	11	1	0	0	0	0.0	1	0	3	2	0	0	0	3	0	0	0	1.0	1.000	OF-3
1975	CIN N	2	.000	.000	1	0	0	0	0	0.0	0	0	1	0	0	1	0	0	0	0	0	0.0	—	
1979	CAL A	2	.000	.000	2	0	0	0	0	0.0	0	0	2	1	0	0	0	0	0	0	0	0.0	.000	DH-2
6 yrs.		12	.160	.200	25	4	1	0	0	0.0	2	2	8	7	1	1	0	13	1	0	0	1.6	1.000	OF-7, DH-2
WORLD SERIES																								
1969	BAL A	1	—	—	0	0	0	0	0	—	0	0	0	0	0	0	0	0	0	0	0	0.0	—	
1970		2	.400	1.000	5	2	0	0	1	20.0	2	2	1	0	0	1	0	3	0	0	0	3.0	1.000	OF-1
1971		7	.185	.296	27	5	0	0	1	3.7	3	4	0	4	0	1	0	17	0	0	0	2.8	1.000	OF-6
1975	CIN N	3	.000	.000	3	0	0	0	0	0.0	0	0	0	1	0	3	0	0	0	0	0	0.0	—	
4 yrs.		13	.200	.371	35	7	0	0	2	5.7	5	6	1	5	0	5	0	20	0	0	0	2.9	1.000	OF-7

Ken Retzer

RETZER, KENNETH LEO BL TR 6′ 185 lbs.
B. Apr. 30, 1934, Wood River, Ill.

Year	Team	Games	BA	SA	AB	H	2B	3B	HR	HR%	R	RBI	BB	SO	SB	Pinch Hit AB	Pinch Hit H	PO	A	E	DP	TC/G	FA	G by Pos
1961	WAS A	16	.340	.472	53	18	4	0	1	1.9	7	3	4	5	1	0	0	71	8	1	2	5.0	.988	C-16
1962		109	.285	.400	340	97	11	2	8	2.4	36	37	26	21	2	11	2	488	44	8	5	5.5	.985	C-99
1963		95	.242	.336	265	64	10	0	5	1.9	21	31	17	20	2	15	2	320	35	7	5	4.5	.981	C-81
1964		17	.094	.094	32	3	0	0	0	0.0	1	1	5	4	0	4	2	56	10	2	1	5.2	.971	C-13
4 yrs.		237	.264	.367	690	182	25	2	14	2.0	65	72	52	50	5	30	6	935	97	18	13	5.0	.983	C-209

Dave Revering

REVERING, DAVID ALLEN BL TR 6′ 4″ 210 lbs.
B. Feb. 12, 1953, Roseville, Calif.

Year	Team	Games	BA	SA	AB	H	2B	3B	HR	HR%	R	RBI	BB	SO	SB	Pinch Hit AB	Pinch Hit H	PO	A	E	DP	TC/G	FA	G by Pos
1978	OAK A	152	.271	.415	521	141	21	3	16	3.1	49	46	26	55	0	12	3	1013	110	13	98	8.1	.989	1B-138, DH-3
1979		125	.288	.483	472	136	25	5	19	4.0	63	77	34	65	1	3	2	828	80	13	77	7.5	.986	1B-104, DH-18
1980		106	.290	.492	376	109	21	5	15	4.0	48	62	32	37	1	11	4	724	67	9	56	8.0	.989	1B-95, DH-5
1981	2 teams	OAK A (31G –.230) NY A (45G –.235)																						
″	total	76	.233	.335	206	48	5	2	4	1.9	20	17	22	32	0	11	1	464	43	3	36	6.8	.994	1B-73, DH-2
1982	3 teams	NY A (14G –.150) TOR A (55G –.215) SEA A (29G –.207)																						
″	total	98	.202	.346	257	52	11	1	8	3.1	25	32	34	51	0	20	2	351	15	3	33	3.9	.992	DH-50, 1B-44
5 yrs.		557	.265	.430	1832	486	83	16	62	3.4	205	234	148	240	2	57	12	3380	315	41	300	7.0	.989	1B-454, DH-78
DIVISIONAL PLAYOFF SERIES																								
1981	NY A	2	—	—	0	0	0	0	0	—	0	0	0	0	0	0	0	3	0	0	0	1.5	1.000	1B-2
LEAGUE CHAMPIONSHIP SERIES																								
1981	NY A	2	.500	.500	2	1	0	0	0	0.0	0	0	0	0	0	0	0	6	1	0	2	3.5	1.000	1B-2

Gilberto Reyes

REYES, GILBERTO ROLANDO BR TR 6′ 3″ 195 lbs.
Born Gilberto Rolando Reyes (Polanco).
B. Dec. 10, 1963, Santo Domingo, Dominican Republic.

Year	Team	Games	BA	SA	AB	H	2B	3B	HR	HR%	R	RBI	BB	SO	SB	Pinch Hit AB	Pinch Hit H	PO	A	E	DP	TC/G	FA	G by Pos
1983	LA N	19	.161	.226	31	5	2	0	0	0.0	1	0	0	5	0	0	0	59	9	4	2	3.8	.944	C-19
1984		4	.000	.000	5	0	0	0	0	0.0	0	0	0	3	0	2	0	5	0	0	0	2.5	1.000	C-2
1985		6	.000	.000	1	0	0	0	0	0.0	0	0	1	1	0	1	0	6	4	0	0	1.7	1.000	C-6
1987		1	—	—	0	0	0	0	0	—	0	0	0	0	0	0	0	2	0	0	0	2.0	1.000	C-1
1988		5	.111	.111	9	1	0	0	0	0.0	1	0	0	3	0	1	0	16	0	0	1	3.2	1.000	C-5
1989	MON N	4	.200	.200	5	1	0	0	0	0.0	0	1	0	1	0	0	0	10	1	0	0	2.8	1.000	C-4
1991		83	.217	.261	207	45	9	0	0	0.0	11	13	19	51	2	2	1	375	61	11	4	5.6	.975	C-80
7 yrs.		122	.202	.244	258	52	11	0	0	0.0	13	14	20	64	2	6	1	473	75	15	7	4.8	.973	C-117

Nap Reyes

REYES, NAPOLEON BR TR 6′ 195 lbs.
Born Napoleon Reyes (Aguilera).
B. Nov. 24, 1919, Santiago, Cuba D. Sept. 15, 1995, Miami, Fla.

Year	Team	Games	BA	SA	AB	H	2B	3B	HR	HR%	R	RBI	BB	SO	SB	Pinch Hit AB	Pinch Hit H	PO	A	E	DP	TC/G	FA	G by Pos
1943	NY N	40	.256	.320	125	32	4	2	0	0.0	13	13	4	12	2	1	0	340	9	2	25	9.0	.994	1B-38, 3B-1
1944		116	.289	.422	374	108	16	5	8	2.1	38	53	15	24	2	11	4	585	120	12	49	7.0	.983	1B-63, 3B-37, OF-3
1945		122	.288	.376	431	124	15	4	5	1.2	39	44	25	26	1	3	0	170	233	14	13	3.5	.966	3B-115, 1B-5
1950		1	.000	.000	1	0	0	0	0	0.0	0	0	0	0	0	0	0	2	0	1	0	3.0	.667	1B-1
4 yrs.		279	.284	.387	931	264	35	11	13	1.4	90	110	44	62	5	15	4	1097	362	29	87	5.7	.981	3B-153, 1B-107, OF-3

Bill Reynolds

REYNOLDS, WILLIAM DEE BR TR 6′ 185 lbs.
B. Aug. 14, 1884, Eastland, Tex. D. June 5, 1924, Carnegie, Okla.

Year	Team	Games	BA	SA	AB	H	2B	3B	HR	HR%	R	RBI	BB	SO	SB	Pinch Hit AB	Pinch Hit H	PO	A	E	DP	TC/G	FA	G by Pos
1913	NY A	5	.000	.000	5	0	0	0	0	0.0	0	0	0	1	0	0	0	10	1	1	0	2.4	.917	C-5
1914		4	.400	.400	5	2	0	0	0	0.0	0	0	0	3	0	3	1	4	1	0	0	5.0	1.000	C-1
2 yrs.		9	.200	.200	10	2	0	0	0	0.0	0	0	0	4	0	3	1	14	2	1	0	2.8	.941	C-6

Carl Reynolds

REYNOLDS, CARL NETTLES BR TR 6′ 194 lbs.
B. Feb. 1, 1903, LaRue, Tex. D. May 29, 1978, Houston, Tex.

Year	Team	Games	BA	SA	AB	H	2B	3B	HR	HR%	R	RBI	BB	SO	SB	Pinch Hit AB	Pinch Hit H	PO	A	E	DP	TC/G	FA	G by Pos
1927	CHI A	14	.214	.357	42	9	3	0	1	2.4	5	7	5	7	1	0	0	37	1	0	0	2.9	1.000	OF-13
1928		84	.323	.491	291	94	21	11	2	0.7	51	36	17	13	15	10	6	135	6	3	2	1.9	.979	OF-74
1929		131	.317	.474	517	164	24	12	11	2.1	81	67	20	37	19	0	0	268	13	15	5	2.3	.949	OF-131
1930		138	.359	.584	563	202	25	18	22	3.9	103	100	20	39	16	5	0	336	11	9	1	2.7	.975	OF-132
1931		118	.290	.442	462	134	24	14	6	1.3	71	77	24	26	17	9	3	233	10	13	3	2.3	.949	OF-109
1932	WAS A	102	.305	.475	406	124	28	7	9	2.2	53	63	14	19	8	5	1	229	3	4	0	2.5	.983	OF-95
1933	STL A	135	.286	.451	475	136	26	14	8	1.7	81	71	50	25	5	13	3	269	8	10	3	2.3	.965	OF-124
1934	BOS A	113	.303	.438	413	125	26	9	4	1.0	61	86	27	28	5	14	3	244	6	6	3	2.6	.977	OF-100
1935		78	.270	.430	244	66	13	4	6	2.5	33	35	24	20	4	11	2	146	7	4	0	2.5	.975	OF-64
1936	WAS A	89	.276	.392	293	81	18	2	4	1.4	41	41	21	22	8	15	3	142	8	5	0	2.2	.968	OF-72
1937	CHI N	7	.273	.364	11	3	1	0	0	0.0	0	1	2	2	0	4	1	4	0	1	0	2.5	.800	OF-2
1938		125	.302	.416	497	150	28	10	3	0.6	59	67	22	32	9	0	0	328	10	6	4	2.8	.983	OF-125
1939		88	.246	.367	281	69	10	6	4	1.4	33	44	16	38	5	14	3	168	5	5	1	2.5	.972	OF-72
13 yrs.		1222	.302	.458	4495	1357	247	107	80	1.8	672	695	262	308	112	100	25	2539	88	81	22	2.4	.970	OF-1113
WORLD SERIES																								
1938	CHI N	4	.000	.000	12	0	0	0	0	0.0	0	0	1	3	0	1	0	7	0	0	0	2.3	1.000	OF-3

Charlie Reynolds

REYNOLDS, CHARLES LAWRENCE 5′ 9″ 175 lbs.
B. May 1, 1865, Williamsburg, Ind. D. July 3, 1944, Denver, Colo.

Year	Team	Games	BA	SA	AB	H	2B	3B	HR	HR%	R	RBI	BB	SO	SB	Pinch Hit AB	Pinch Hit H	PO	A	E	DP	TC/G	FA	G by Pos
1889	2 teams	KC AA (1G –.250) BKN AA (12G –.214)																						
″	total	13	.217	.283	46	10	1	1	0	0.0	6	4	1	7	2	0	0	49	18	8	0	5.8	.893	C-13

Craig Reynolds

REYNOLDS, GORDON CRAIG BL TR 6′ 1″ 175 lbs.
B. Dec. 27, 1952, Houston, Tex.

Year	Team	Games	BA	SA	AB	H	2B	3B	HR	HR%	R	RBI	BB	SO	SB	Pinch Hit AB	Pinch Hit H	PO	A	E	DP	TC/G	FA	G by Pos
1975	PIT N	31	.224	.263	76	17	3	0	0	0.0	8	4	3	5	0	1	1	43	82	4	12	4.3	.969	SS-30
1976		7	.250	1.000	4	1	0	0	1	25.0	1	1	0	0	0	0	0	2	6	1	1	1.8	.889	SS-4, 2B-1
1977	SEA A	135	.248	.319	420	104	12	3	4	1.0	41	28	15	23	6	2	1	197	397	28	86	4.6	.955	SS-134
1978		148	.292	.374	548	160	16	7	5	0.9	57	44	36	41	9	1	0	243	461	29	102	5.0	.960	SS-146
1979	HOU N	146	.265	.333	555	147	20	9	0	0.0	63	39	21	49	12	5	1	208	428	23	88	4.6	.965	SS-143
1980		137	.226	.304	381	86	9	6	3	0.8	34	28	20	39	2	2	0	162	362	17	59	4.0	.969	SS-135
1981		87	.260	.402	323	84	10	**12**	4	1.2	43	31	12	31	3	2	1	139	261	11	36	4.8	.973	SS-85
1982		54	.254	.347	118	30	2	3	1	0.8	16	7	11	9	3	5	0	45	98	6	15	3.5	.960	SS-35, 3B-7

Craig Reynolds *continued*

Year	Team	Lg	Games	BA	SA	AB	H	2B	3B	HR	HR%	R	RBI	BB	SO	SB	Pinch Hit AB	Pinch Hit H	PO	A	E	DP	TC/G	FA	G by Pos
1983			65	.214	.276	98	21	3	0	1	1.0	10	6	6	10	0	12	2	37	57	3	15	1.9	.969	2B-26, 3B-15, SS-8, OF-1
1984			146	.260	.364	527	137	15	11	6	1.1	61	60	22	53	7	4	2	212	473	25	91	4.9	.965	SS-143, 3B-1
1985			107	.272	.393	379	103	18	8	4	1.1	43	32	12	30	4	10	3	159	319	11	65	4.7	.978	SS-102, 2B-1
1986			114	.249	.348	313	78	7	3	6	1.9	32	41	12	31	3	22	9	124	209	7	38	3.1	.979	SS-98, 1B-5, 3B-4, OF-2, P-1
1987			135	.254	.348	374	95	17	3	4	1.1	35	28	30	44	5	12	3	160	292	14	43	3.6	.970	SS-129, 3B-2
1988			78	.255	.317	161	41	7	0	1	0.6	20	14	8	23	3	22	4	88	81	9	20	2.9	.949	SS-22, 3B-19, 2B-11, 1B-10
1989			101	.201	.254	189	38	4	0	2	1.1	16	14	19	18	1	37	5	86	136	8	24	3.2	.965	2B-29, SS-26, 3B-10, 1B-5, OF-1, P-1
15 yrs.			1491	.256	.345	4466	1142	143	65	42	0.9	480	377	227	406	58	137	32	1905	3662	196	695	4.1	.966	SS-1240, 2B-68, 3B-58, 1B-20, OF-4, P-2
DIVISIONAL PLAYOFF SERIES																									
1981	**HOU**	**N**	2	.333	.333	3	1	0	0	0	0.0	1	0	0	1	0	1	1	1	0	0	0	1.0	1.000	SS-1
LEAGUE CHAMPIONSHIP SERIES																									
1975	**PIT**	**N**	2	.000	.000	1	0	0	0	0	0.0	0	0	0	0	0	0	0	0	0	1	0	1.0	.000	SS-1
1980	**HOU**	**N**	4	.154	.231	13	2	1	0	0	0.0	2	0	3	1	0	0	0	8	12	1	1	5.3	.952	SS-4
1986			4	.333	.333	12	4	0	0	0	0.0	1	0	1	3	0	1	0	7	8	2	0	4.3	.882	SS-4
3 yrs.			10	.231	.269	26	6	1	0	0	0.0	3	0	4	4	0	1	0	15	20	4	1	4.3	.897	SS-9

Danny Reynolds

REYNOLDS, DANIEL VANCE (Squirrel)
B. Nov. 27, 1919, Stony Point, N. C.
BR TR 5′11″ 158 lbs.

Year	Team	Lg	Games	BA	SA	AB	H	2B	3B	HR	HR%	R	RBI	BB	SO	SB	Pinch Hit AB	Pinch Hit H	PO	A	E	DP	TC/G	FA	G by Pos
1945	**CHI**	**A**	29	.167	.222	72	12	2	1	0	0.0	6	4	3	8	1	4	0	39	62	4	13	4.2	.962	SS-14, 2B-11

Don Reynolds

REYNOLDS, DONALD EDWARD
Brother of Harold Reynolds.
B. Apr. 16, 1953, Arkadelphia, Ark.
BR TR 5′ 8″ 178 lbs.

Year	Team	Lg	Games	BA	SA	AB	H	2B	3B	HR	HR%	R	RBI	BB	SO	SB	Pinch Hit AB	Pinch Hit H	PO	A	E	DP	TC/G	FA	G by Pos
1978	**SD**	**N**	57	.253	.276	87	22	2	0	0	0.0	8	10	15	14	1	30	7	22	2	2	0	1.0	.923	OF-25
1979			30	.222	.333	45	10	1	2	0	0.0	6	6	7	6	0	12	0	17	2	1	1	1.4	.950	OF-14
2 yrs.			87	.242	.295	132	32	3	2	0	0.0	14	16	22	20	1	42	7	39	4	3	1	1.2	.935	OF-39

Harold Reynolds

REYNOLDS, HAROLD CRAIG
Brother of Don Reynolds.
B. Nov. 26, 1960, Eugene, Ore.
BB TR 5′11″ 165 lbs.

Year	Team	Lg	Games	BA	SA	AB	H	2B	3B	HR	HR%	R	RBI	BB	SO	SB	Pinch Hit AB	Pinch Hit H	PO	A	E	DP	TC/G	FA	G by Pos
1983	**SEA**	**A**	20	.203	.305	59	12	4	1	0	0.0	8	1	2	9	0	0	0	30	48	2	14	4.4	.975	2B-18
1984			10	.300	.300	10	3	0	0	0	0.0	3	0	0	1	1	0	0	8	12	0	3	3.3	1.000	2B-6
1985			66	.144	.192	104	15	3	1	0	0.0	15	6	17	14	3	2	0	69	123	8	22	3.3	.960	2B-61
1986			126	.222	.290	445	99	19	4	1	0.2	46	24	29	42	30	0	0	278	415	16	111	5.6	.977	2B-126
1987			160	.275	.370	530	146	31	8	1	0.2	73	35	39	34	**60**	0	0	347	507	20	111	5.5	.977	2B-160
1988			158	.283	.383	598	169	26	**11**	4	0.7	61	41	51	51	35	0	0	303	471	18	111	5.0	.977	2B-158
1989			153	.300	.369	613	184	24	9	0	0.0	87	43	55	45	25	2	0	311	506	17	109	5.5	.980	2B-151, DH-1
1990			160	.252	.347	**642**	162	36	5	5	0.8	100	55	81	52	31	0	0	330	499	19	110	5.3	.978	2B-160
1991			161	.254	.341	631	160	34	6	3	0.5	95	57	72	63	28	2	0	348	463	18	133	5.2	.978	2B-159, DH-1
1992			140	.247	.330	458	113	23	3	3	0.7	55	33	45	41	15	11	2	303	362	12	88	5.0	.982	2B-134, OF-1, DH-1
1993	**BAL**	**A**	145	.252	.334	485	122	20	4	4	0.8	64	47	66	47	12	3	1	306	396	10	110	5.0	.986	2B-141, DH-1
1994	**CAL**	**A**	74	.232	.290	207	48	10	1	0	0.0	33	11	23	18	10	12	5	116	130	1	24	3.7	.996	2B-65, DH-1
12 yrs.			1373	.258	.341	4782	1233	230	53	21	0.4	640	353	480	417	250	32	8	2749	3932	141	946	5.1	.979	2B-1339, DH-5, OF-1

R. J. Reynolds

REYNOLDS, ROBERT JAMES
B. Apr. 19, 1959, Sacramento, Calif.
BB TR 6′ 180 lbs.

Year	Team	Lg	Games	BA	SA	AB	H	2B	3B	HR	HR%	R	RBI	BB	SO	SB	Pinch Hit AB	Pinch Hit H	PO	A	E	DP	TC/G	FA	G by Pos
1983	**LA**	**N**	24	.236	.345	55	13	0	0	2	3.6	5	11	3	11	5	7	2	25	2	2	1	1.6	.931	OF-18
1984			73	.258	.350	240	62	12	2	2	0.8	23	24	14	38	7	13	5	104	4	3	1	1.8	.973	OF-63
1985	**2 teams**		**LA N** (73G –.266) **PIT N** (31G –.308)																						
″	**total**		104	.282	.395	337	95	15	7	3	0.9	44	42	22	49	18	19	3	159	6	6	0	2.0	.965	OF-85
1986	**PIT**	**N**	118	.269	.420	402	108	30	2	9	2.2	63	48	40	78	16	11	2	190	2	9	0	1.8	.955	OF-112
1987			117	.260	.400	335	87	24	1	7	2.1	47	51	34	80	14	23	6	134	7	1	2	1.4	.993	OF-99
1988			130	.248	.359	323	80	14	2	6	1.9	35	51	20	62	15	42	9	142	7	4	2	1.6	.974	OF-95
1989			125	.270	.375	363	98	16	2	6	1.7	45	48	34	66	22	31	9	200	6	2	3	2.1	.990	OF-98
1990			95	.288	.344	215	62	10	1	0	0.0	25	19	23	35	12	38	8	102	3	3	0	1.8	.972	OF-59
8 yrs.			786	.267	.381	2270	605	121	17	35	1.5	287	294	190	419	109	184	44	1056	37	30	9	1.8	.973	OF-629
LEAGUE CHAMPIONSHIP SERIES																									
1990	**PIT**	**N**	6	.200	.200	10	2	0	0	0	0.0	0	0	2	2	1	3	0	2	0	1	0	1.0	.667	OF-3

Ronn Reynolds

REYNOLDS, RONN DWAYNE
B. Sept. 28, 1958, Wichita, Kans.
BR TR 6′ 200 lbs.

Year	Team	Lg	Games	BA	SA	AB	H	2B	3B	HR	HR%	R	RBI	BB	SO	SB	Pinch Hit AB	Pinch Hit H	PO	A	E	DP	TC/G	FA	G by Pos
1982	**NY**	**N**	2	.000	.000	4	0	0	0	0	0.0	0	0	1	1	0	0	0	3	0	0	0	1.5	1.000	C-2
1983			24	.197	.212	66	13	1	0	0	0.0	4	2	8	12	0	0	0	99	14	7	2	5.0	.942	C-24
1985			28	.209	.256	43	9	2	0	0	0.0	4	1	0	18	0	2	0	86	9	1	2	3.8	.990	C-25
1986	**PHI**	**N**	43	.214	.317	126	27	4	0	3	2.4	8	10	5	30	0	1	1	198	16	2	3	5.1	.991	C-42
1987	**HOU**	**N**	38	.167	.235	102	17	4	0	1	1.0	5	7	3	29	0	0	0	216	16	6	1	6.3	.975	C-38
1990	**SD**	**N**	8	.067	.133	15	1	1	0	0	0.0	1	1	1	6	0	0	0	26	2	0	0	3.5	1.000	C-8
6 yrs.			143	.188	.256	356	67	12	0	4	1.1	22	21	18	96	0	3	1	628	57	16	8	5.0	.977	C-139

Tommie Reynolds

REYNOLDS, TOMMIE D
B. Aug. 15, 1941, Arizona, La.
BR TR 6′ 2″ 190 lbs.
BB 1967

Year	Team	Lg	Games	BA	SA	AB	H	2B	3B	HR	HR%	R	RBI	BB	SO	SB	Pinch Hit AB	Pinch Hit H	PO	A	E	DP	TC/G	FA	G by Pos
1963	**KC**	**A**	8	.053	.105	19	1	1	0	0	0.0	1	0	1	7	0	3	0	8	0	2	0	2.0	.800	OF-5
1964			31	.202	.277	94	19	1	0	2	2.1	11	9	10	22	0	5	2	39	5	3	0	1.7	.936	OF-25, 3B-3
1965			90	.237	.311	270	64	11	3	1	0.4	34	22	36	41	9	7	1	154	8	3	2	2.0	.982	OF-83, 3B-1
1967	**NY**	**N**	101	.206	.257	136	28	1	0	2	1.5	16	9	11	26	1	22	5	69	6	2	1	1.0	.974	OF-72, 3B-5, C-1
1969	**OAK**	**A**	107	.257	.308	315	81	10	0	2	0.6	51	20	34	29	1	20	6	184	5	4	2	2.2	.979	OF-89

Tommie Reynolds *continued*

Year	Team	Games	BA	SA	AB	H	2B	3B	HR	HR%	R	RBI	BB	SO	SB	Pinch Hit AB	Pinch Hit H	PO	A	E	DP	TC/G	FA	G by Pos
1970	CAL A	59	.250	.317	120	30	3	1	1	0.8	11	6	6	10	1	24	4	63	1	2	0	2.0	.970	OF-32, 3B-1
1971		45	.186	.291	86	16	3	0	2	2.3	4	8	9	6	0	21	4	44	3	1	1	1.8	.979	OF-26, 3B-1
1972	MIL A	72	.200	.300	130	26	5	1	2	1.5	13	13	10	25	0	32	7	77	2	3	0	1.9	.963	OF-41, 3B-1, 1B-1
8 yrs.		513	.226	.296	1170	265	35	5	12	1.0	141	87	117	166	12	134	29	638	30	20	6	1.8	.971	OF-373, 3B-12, 1B-1, C-1

Bobby Rhawn

RHAWN, ROBERT JOHN (Rocky) BR TR 5′8″ 180 lbs.
B. Feb. 13, 1919, Catawissa, Pa. D. June 9, 1984, Danville, Pa.

Year	Team	Games	BA	SA	AB	H	2B	3B	HR	HR%	R	RBI	BB	SO	SB	Pinch Hit AB	Pinch Hit H	PO	A	E	DP	TC/G	FA	G by Pos
1947	NY N	13	.311	.444	45	14	3	0	1	2.2	7	3	8	1	0	0	0	19	37	4	6	4.6	.933	2B-8, 3B-5
1948		36	.273	.432	44	12	2	1	1	2.3	11	8	8	6	3	4	2	17	28	5	4	2.4	.900	SS-14, 3B-7
1949	3 teams	NY N (14G –.172) PIT N (3G –.143) CHI A (24G –.205)																						
″	total	41	.193	.248	109	21	4	1	0	0.0	20	7	19	10	1	3	1	52	82	7	12	4.4	.950	3B-21, 2B-8, SS-3
3 yrs.		90	.237	.333	198	47	9	2	2	1.0	38	18	35	17	4	7	3	88	147	16	22	3.8	.936	3B-33, SS-17, 2B-16

Cy Rheam

RHEAM, KENNETH JOHNSTON BR TR 6′ 175 lbs.
B. Sept. 28, 1893, Pittsburgh, Pa. D. Oct. 23, 1947, Pittsburgh, Pa.

Year	Team	Games	BA	SA	AB	H	2B	3B	HR	HR%	R	RBI	BB	SO	SB	Pinch Hit AB	Pinch Hit H	PO	A	E	DP	TC/G	FA	G by Pos
1914	PIT F	73	.210	.262	214	45	5	3	0	0.0	15	20	9		6	5	1	431	55	16	16	7.4	.968	1B-43, 3B-13, 2B-11, OF-1
1915		34	.174	.217	69	12	0	0	1	1.4	10	5	1		4	4	1	51	2	2	0	2.4	.964	OF-22, 1B-1
2 yrs.		107	.201	.251	283	57	5	3	1	0.4	25	25	10		10	9	2	482	57	18	16	6.1	.968	1B-44, OF-23, 3B-13, 2B-11

Billy Rhiel

RHIEL, WILLIAM JOSEPH BR TR 5′11″ 175 lbs.
B. Aug. 16, 1900, Youngstown, Ohio D. Aug. 16, 1946, Youngstown, Ohio.

Year	Team	Games	BA	SA	AB	H	2B	3B	HR	HR%	R	RBI	BB	SO	SB	Pinch Hit AB	Pinch Hit H	PO	A	E	DP	TC/G	FA	G by Pos
1929	BKN N	76	.278	.420	205	57	9	4	4	2.0	27	25	19	25	0	14	2	105	159	7	18	4.8	.974	2B-47, 3B-7, SS-2
1930	BOS N	20	.170	.255	47	8	4	0	0	0.0	3	4	2	5	0	3	0	8	13	1	2	1.5	.955	3B-13, 2B-2
1932	DET A	84	.280	.392	250	70	13	3	3	1.2	30	38	17	23	2	27	13	150	65	5	21	3.9	.977	3B-36, 1B-12, OF-8, 2B-1
1933		19	.176	.294	17	3	0	1	0	0.0	1	1	5	4	0	13	3	4	0	0	0	4.0	1.000	OF-1
4 yrs.		199	.266	.387	519	138	26	8	7	1.3	61	68	43	57	2	57	18	267	237	13	41	4.0	.975	3B-56, 2B-50, 1B-12, OF-9, SS-2

Dusty Rhodes

RHODES, JAMES LAMAR BL TR 6′ 178 lbs.
B. May 13, 1927, Mathews, Ala.

Year	Team	Games	BA	SA	AB	H	2B	3B	HR	HR%	R	RBI	BB	SO	SB	Pinch Hit AB	Pinch Hit H	PO	A	E	DP	TC/G	FA	G by Pos
1952	NY N	67	.250	.477	176	44	8	1	10	5.7	34	36	23	33	1	9	1	97	3	9	0	1.9	.917	OF-56
1953		76	.233	.479	163	38	7	0	11	6.7	18	30	10	28	0	29	5	76	6	3	4	1.8	.965	OF-47
1954		82	.341	.695	164	56	7	3	15	9.1	31	50	18	25	1	45	15	62	1	1	0	1.7	.984	OF-37
1955		94	.305	.449	187	57	5	2	6	3.2	22	32	27	26	1	44	11	68	2	1	0	1.6	.986	OF-45
1956		111	.217	.381	244	53	10	3	8	3.3	20	33	30	41	0	39	7	85	6	4	1	1.4	.958	OF-68
1957		92	.205	.305	190	39	5	1	4	2.1	20	19	18	34	0	46	7	63	0	0	0	1.4	1.000	OF-44
1959	SF N	54	.188	.229	48	9	2	0	0	0.0	1	7	5	9	0	48	9	0	0	0	0	0.0	—	
7 yrs.		576	.253	.445	1172	296	44	10	54	4.6	146	207	131	196	3	260	55	451	18	18	5	1.6	.963	OF-297
WORLD SERIES																								
1954	NY N	3	.667	1.667	6	4	0	0	2	33.3	2	7	1	2	0	3	3	4	0	0	0	2.0	1.000	OF-2

Karl Rhodes

RHODES, KARL DERRICK (Tuffy) BL TL 6′ 175 lbs.
B. Aug. 21, 1968, Cincinnati, Ohio.

Year	Team	Games	BA	SA	AB	H	2B	3B	HR	HR%	R	RBI	BB	SO	SB	Pinch Hit AB	Pinch Hit H	PO	A	E	DP	TC/G	FA	G by Pos
1990	HOU N	38	.244	.372	86	21	6	1	1	1.2	12	3	13	12	4	6	3	61	2	3	0	2.2	.955	OF-30
1991		44	.213	.272	136	29	3	1	1	0.7	7	12	14	26	2	3	0	87	4	4	1	2.2	.958	OF-44
1992		5	.000	.000	4	0	0	0	0	0.0	0	0	0	2	0	4	0	0	0	0	0	0.0	.000	OF-1
1993	2 teams	HOU N (5G –.000) CHI N (15G –.288)																						
″	total	20	.278	.519	54	15	2	1	3	5.6	12	7	11	9	2	3	0	33	1	1	0	1.9	.971	OF-18
1994	CHI N	95	.234	.387	269	63	17	0	8	3.0	39	19	33	64	6	21	7	142	4	5	1	2.0	.967	OF-76
1995	2 teams	CHI N (13G –.125) BOS A (10G –.080)																						
″	total	23	.098	.122	41	4	1	0	0	0.0	4	3	3	8	0	9	1	26	0	2	0	1.4	.929	OF-20
6 yrs.		225	.224	.349	590	132	29	3	13	2.2	74	44	74	121	14	46	11	349	11	15	2	2.0	.960	OF-189

Kevin Rhomberg

RHOMBERG, KEVIN JAY BR TR 6′ 175 lbs.
B. Nov. 22, 1955, Dubuque, Iowa.

Year	Team	Games	BA	SA	AB	H	2B	3B	HR	HR%	R	RBI	BB	SO	SB	Pinch Hit AB	Pinch Hit H	PO	A	E	DP	TC/G	FA	G by Pos
1982	CLE A	16	.333	.500	18	6	0	0	1	5.6	3	1	2	4	0	2	0	9	2	1	1	1.0	.917	OF-7, DH-4, 3B-1
1983		12	.476	.476	21	10	0	0	0	0.0	2	2	2	4	1	1	0	10	0	0	0	1.0	1.000	OF-9, DH-1
1984		13	.250	.250	8	2	0	0	0	0.0	0	0	0	3	0	3	0	7	1	0	0	0.8	1.000	OF-7, 2B-1, DH-1, 1B-1
3 yrs.		41	.383	.447	47	18	0	0	1	2.1	5	3	4	11	1	6	0	26	3	1	1	0.9	.967	OF-23, DH-6, 1B-1, 2B-1, 3B-1

Hal Rhyne

RHYNE, HAROLD J. BR TR 5′8½″ 163 lbs.
B. Mar. 30, 1899, Paso Robles, Calif. D. Jan. 7, 1971, Orangevale, Calif.

Year	Team	Games	BA	SA	AB	H	2B	3B	HR	HR%	R	RBI	BB	SO	SB	Pinch Hit AB	Pinch Hit H	PO	A	E	DP	TC/G	FA	G by Pos
1926	PIT N	109	.251	.322	366	92	14	3	2	0.5	46	39	35	21	1	0	0	271	346	26	80	5.8	.960	2B-66, SS-44, 3B-1
1927		62	.274	.304	168	46	5	0	0	0.0	21	17	14	9	0	1	0	118	122	11	22	4.0	.956	2B-45, 3B-10, SS-7
1929	BOS A	120	.251	.350	346	87	24	5	0	0.0	41	38	25	14	4	1	0	220	298	36	71	4.8	.935	SS-114, 3B-1, OF-1
1930		107	.203	.264	296	60	8	5	0	0.0	34	23	25	19	1	0	0	188	284	28	63	4.7	.944	SS-107
1931		147	.273	.343	565	154	34	3	0	0.0	75	51	57	41	3	0	0	295	502	31	74	5.6	.963	SS-147
1932		71	.227	.333	207	47	12	5	0	0.0	26	14	23	14	3	10	3	99	168	10	31	4.6	.964	SS-55, 3B-4, 2B-1
1933	CHI A	39	.265	.301	83	22	1	1	0	0.0	9	10	5	9	1	6	1	48	72	7	13	3.7	.945	2B-19, 3B-13, SS-2
7 yrs.		655	.250	.323	2031	508	98	22	2	0.1	252	192	184	127	13	18	4	1239	1792	149	354	5.0	.953	SS-476, 2B-131, 3B-29, OF-1
WORLD SERIES																								
1927	PIT N	1	.000	.000	4	0	0	0	0	0.0	0	0	0	0	0	0	0	0	6	0	0	6.0	1.000	2B-1

Bob Rice

RICE, ROBERT TURNBULL BR TR 5′10″ 170 lbs.
B. May 28, 1899, Philadelphia, Pa. D. Feb. 20, 1986, Elizabethtown, Pa.

Year	Team	Games	BA	SA	AB	H	2B	3B	HR	HR%	R	RBI	BB	SO	SB	Pinch Hit AB	Pinch Hit H	PO	A	E	DP	TC/G	FA	G by Pos
1926	PHI N	19	.148	.185	54	8	0	1	0	0.0	3	10	3	4	0	0	0	17	33	6	8	2.9	.893	3B-15, SS-2, 2B-2

Del Rice

RICE, DELBERT W. BR TR 6′2″ 190 lbs.
B. Oct. 27, 1922, Portsmouth, Ohio D. Jan. 26, 1983, Buena Park, Calif.
Manager 1972.

Year	Team	Games	BA	SA	AB	H	2B	3B	HR	HR%	R	RBI	BB	SO	SB	Pinch Hit AB	Pinch Hit H	PO	A	E	DP	TC/G	FA	G by Pos
1945	STL N	83	.261	.364	253	66	17	3	1	0.4	27	28	16	33	0	6	1	284	39	2	6	4.2	.994	C-77
1946		55	.273	.367	139	38	8	1	1	0.7	10	12	8	16	0	2	0	196	12	5	0	4.0	.977	C-53
1947		97	.218	.406	261	57	7	3	12	4.6	28	44	36	40	1	3	0	380	33	8	7	4.5	.981	C-94

Del Rice *continued*

Year	Team	Games	BA	SA	AB	H	2B	3B	HR	HR%	R	RBI	BB	SO	SB	Pinch Hit AB	Pinch Hit H	PO	A	E	DP	TC/G	FA	G by Pos
1948		100	.197	.279	290	57	10	1	4	1.4	24	34	37	46	1	0	0	447	46	2	5	5.0	.996	C-99
1949		92	.236	.342	284	67	16	1	4	1.4	25	29	30	40	0	0	0	355	29	3	4	4.2	.992	C-92
1950		130	.244	.372	414	101	20	3	9	2.2	39	54	43	65	0	0	0	572	63	10	12	5.0	.984	C-130
1951		122	.251	.364	374	94	13	1	9	2.4	34	47	34	26	0	3	0	447	66	8	12	4.3	.985	C-120
1952		147	.259	.388	495	128	27	2	11	2.2	43	65	33	38	0	1	0	677	81	6	8	5.2	.992	C-147
1953		135	.236	.337	419	99	22	1	6	1.4	32	37	48	49	0	0	0	627	60	8	6	5.1	.988	C-135
1954		56	.252	.374	147	37	10	1	2	1.4	13	16	16	21	0	4	2	248	20	4	2	5.2	.985	C-52
1955	2 teams	STL N (20G –.203) MIL N (27G –.197)																						
"	total	47	.200	.308	130	26	3	1	3	2.3	11	14	13	18	0	7	0	164	18	5	3	4.7	.973	C-40
1956	MIL N	71	.213	.319	188	40	9	1	3	1.6	15	17	18	34	0	5	1	271	21	5	2	4.6	.983	C-65
1957		54	.229	.438	144	33	1	1	9	6.3	15	20	17	37	0	6	1	235	14	2	3	5.2	.992	C-48
1958		43	.223	.306	121	27	7	0	1	0.8	10	8	8	30	0	6	2	174	13	1	1	4.9	.995	C-38
1959		13	.207	.207	29	6	0	0	0	0.0	3	1	2	3	0	4	1	42	1	2	1	5.0	.956	C-9
1960	3 teams	CHI N (18G –.231) STL N (1G –.000) BAL A (1G –.000)																						
"	total	20	.218	.273	55	12	3	0	0	0.0	2	4	3	7	0	0	0	90	7	3	0	5.0	.970	C-20
1961	LA A	44	.241	.434	83	20	4	0	4	4.8	11	11	20	19	0	15	4	144	14	1	0	5.3	.994	C-30
17 yrs.		1309	.237	.356	3826	908	177	20	79	2.1	342	441	382	522	2	62	12	5353	537	75	72	4.8	.987	C-1249
WORLD SERIES																								
1946	STL N	3	.500	.667	6	3	1	0	0	0.0	2	0	2	0	0	0	0	9	1	0	0	3.3	1.000	C-3
1957	MIL N	2	.167	.167	6	1	0	0	0	0.0	0	0	1	2	0	0	0	15	2	0	2	8.5	1.000	C-2
2 yrs.		5	.333	.417	12	4	1	0	0	0.0	2	0	3	2	0	0	0	24	3	0	2	5.4	1.000	C-5

Hal Rice

RICE, HAROLD HOUSTEN (Hoot) BL TR 6′ 1″ 195 lbs.
B. Feb. 11, 1924, Morganette, W. Va.

Year	Team	Games	BA	SA	AB	H	2B	3B	HR	HR%	R	RBI	BB	SO	SB	Pinch Hit AB	Pinch Hit H	PO	A	E	DP	TC/G	FA	G by Pos
1948	STL N	8	.323	.484	31	10	1	2	0	0.0	3	3	2	4	0	0	0	16	0	0	0	2.0	1.000	OF-8
1949		40	.196	.348	46	9	2	1	1	2.2	3	9	3	7	0	27	6	8	1	0	0	0.9	1.000	OF-10
1950		44	.211	.297	128	27	3	1	2	1.6	12	11	10	10	0	6	1	67	3	2	0	1.9	.972	OF-37
1951		69	.254	.364	236	60	12	1	4	1.7	20	38	24	22	0	5	1	116	6	6	0	2.0	.953	OF-63
1952		98	.288	.441	295	85	14	5	7	2.4	37	45	16	26	1	19	3	132	5	4	0	1.7	.972	OF-81
1953	2 teams	STL N (8G –.250) PIT N (78G –.311)																						
"	total	86	.310	.412	294	91	16	1	4	1.4	39	42	17	25	0	17	3	167	14	5	2	2.7	.973	OF-70
1954	2 teams	PIT N (28G –.173) CHI N (51G –.153)																						
"	total	79	.163	.222	153	25	4	1	1	0.7	15	14	22	39	0	29	2	79	5	3	2	1.8	.966	OF-48
7 yrs.		424	.260	.372	1183	307	52	12	19	1.6	129	162	94	133	1	103	16	585	34	20	4	2.0	.969	OF-317

Harry Rice

RICE, HARRY FRANCIS BL TR 5′ 9″ 185 lbs.
B. Nov. 22, 1901, Ware Station, Ill. D. Jan. 1, 1971, Portland, Ore.

Year	Team	Games	BA	SA	AB	H	2B	3B	HR	HR%	R	RBI	BB	SO	SB	Pinch Hit AB	Pinch Hit H	PO	A	E	DP	TC/G	FA	G by Pos
1923	STL A	4	.000	.000	3	0	0	0	0	0.0	0	0	0	0	0	3	0	0	0	0	0	0.0	—	
1924		54	.280	.355	93	26	7	0	0	0.0	19	15	7	5	1	22	7	26	38	7	6	2.8	.901	3B-15, 2B-4, OF-2, SS-2, 1B-2
1925		103	.359	.568	354	127	25	8	11	3.1	87	47	54	15	8	14	6	207	18	7	4	2.5	.970	OF-85, 1B-3, 3B-1, 2B-1, C-1
1926		148	.313	.441	578	181	27	10	9	1.6	86	59	63	40	10	4	2	322	49	16	7	2.7	.959	OF-133, 3B-7, 2B-4, SS-2
1927		137	.287	.412	520	149	26	9	7	1.3	90	68	50	21	6	0	0	281	36	23	9	2.5	.932	OF-130, 3B-7
1928	DET A	131	.302	.425	510	154	21	12	6	1.2	87	81	44	27	20	2	0	347	10	14	0	2.8	.962	OF-129, 3B-2
1929		130	.304	.425	536	163	33	7	6	1.1	97	69	61	23	6	1	0	347	20	15	6	2.9	.961	OF-127, 3B-3
1930	2 teams	DET A (37G –.305) NY A (100G –.298)																						
"	total	137	.300	.426	474	142	23	5	9	1.9	78	98	50	29	3	8	1	326	12	13	5	2.7	.963	OF-122, 1B-6, 3B-1
1931	WAS A	47	.265	.370	162	43	5	6	0	0.0	32	15	12	10	2	5	3	89	3	3	0	2.3	.968	OF-42
1933	CIN N	143	.261	.322	510	133	19	6	0	0.0	44	54	35	24	4	1	0	315	14	3	3	2.3	.991	OF-141, 3B-1
10 yrs.		1034	.299	.421	3740	1118	186	63	48	1.3	620	506	376	194	60	60	19	2260	200	101	40	2.6	.961	OF-911, 3B-37, 1B-11, 2B-9, SS-4, C-1

Jim Rice

RICE, JAMES EDWARD BR TR 6′ 2″ 200 lbs.
B. Mar. 8, 1953, Anderson, S. C.

Year	Team	Games	BA	SA	AB	H	2B	3B	HR	HR%	R	RBI	BB	SO	SB	Pinch Hit AB	Pinch Hit H	PO	A	E	DP	TC/G	FA	G by Pos
1974	BOS A	24	.269	.373	67	18	2	1	1	1.5	6	13	4	12	0	6	0	4	0	1	0	0.3	.800	DH-16, OF-3
1975		144	.309	.491	564	174	29	4	22	3.9	92	102	36	122	10	0	0	162	6	0	0	1.2	1.000	OF-90, DH-54
1976		153	.282	.482	581	164	25	8	25	4.3	75	85	28	**123**	8	3	1	199	8	7	0	1.4	.967	OF-98, DH-54
1977		160	.320	**.593**	644	206	29	**15**	**39**	6.1	104	114	53	120	5	0	0	83	4	4	1	0.6	.956	DH-116, OF-44
1978		163	.315	**.600**	**677**	**213**	25	**15**	**46**	6.8	121	**139**	58	126	7	0	0	245	13	3	1	1.6	.989	OF-114, DH-49
1979		158	.325	.596	619	201	39	6	39	6.3	117	130	57	97	9	1	0	241	8	4	1	1.6	.984	OF-125, DH-33
1980		124	.294	.504	504	148	22	6	24	4.8	81	86	30	87	8	0	0	233	10	3	2	2.0	.988	OF-109, DH-15
1981		108	.284	.441	**451**	128	18	1	17	3.8	51	62	34	76	2	0	0	237	9	3	0	2.3	.988	OF-108
1982		145	.309	.494	573	177	24	5	24	4.2	86	97	55	98	0	0	0	273	10	9	3	2.0	.969	OF-145
1983		155	.305	.550	626	191	34	1	**39**	6.2	90	**126**	52	102	0	0	0	339	21	6	5	2.4	.984	OF-151, DH-4
1984		159	.280	.467	657	184	25	7	28	4.3	98	122	44	102	4	0	0	336	12	4	3	2.2	.989	OF-157, DH-2
1985		140	.291	.487	546	159	20	3	27	4.9	85	103	51	75	2	2	0	236	8	9	1	1.8	.964	OF-130, DH-7
1986		157	.324	.490	618	200	39	2	20	3.2	98	110	62	78	0	0	0	330	16	8	0	2.3	.977	OF-156, DH-1
1987		108	.277	.408	404	112	14	0	13	3.2	66	62	45	77	1	2	1	155	12	4	2	1.6	.977	OF-94, DH-12
1988		135	.264	.406	485	128	18	3	15	3.1	57	72	48	89	1	5	2	30	0	1	0	0.2	.968	DH-112, OF-19
1989		56	.234	.344	209	49	10	2	3	1.4	22	28	13	39	1	3	1	0	0	0	0	0.0	.000	DH-55
16 yrs.		2089	.298	.502	8225	2452	373	79	382	4.6	1249	1451	670	1423	58	22	5	3103	137	66	19	1.6	.980	OF-1543, DH-530
LEAGUE CHAMPIONSHIP SERIES																								
1986	BOS A	7	.161	.387	31	5	1	0	2	6.5	8	6	1	8	0	0	0	13	1	0	0	2.0	1.000	OF-7
1988		4	.154	.154	13	2	0	0	0	0.0	0	1	2	4	0	0	0	0	0	0	0	0.0	.000	DH-4
2 yrs.		11	.159	.318	44	7	1	0	2	4.5	8	7	3	12	0	0	0	13	1	0	0	1.3	1.000	OF-7, DH-4
WORLD SERIES																								
1986	BOS A	7	.333	.444	27	9	1	1	0	0.0	6	0	6	9	0	0	0	16	2	0	1	2.6	1.000	OF-7

Len Rice

RICE, LEONARD OLIVER BR TR 6′ 180 lbs.
B. Sept. 2, 1918, Lead, S. D. D. June 13, 1992, Sonora, Calif.

Year	Team	Games	BA	SA	AB	H	2B	3B	HR	HR%	R	RBI	BB	SO	SB	Pinch Hit AB	Pinch Hit H	PO	A	E	DP	TC/G	FA	G by Pos
1944	CIN N	10	.000	.000	4	0	0	0	0	0.0	1	0	0	0	0	1	0	4	0	0	0	0.8	1.000	C-5
1945	CHI N	32	.232	.263	99	23	3	0	0	0.0	10	7	5	8	2	2	0	115	8	3	1	4.3	.976	C-29
2 yrs.		42	.223	.252	103	23	3	0	0	0.0	11	7	5	8	2	3	0	119	8	3	1	3.8	.977	C-34

Sam Rice

RICE, EDGAR CHARLES — BL TR 5′ 9″ 150 lbs.
B. Feb. 20, 1890, Morocco, Ind. D. Oct. 13, 1974, Rossmor, Md.
Hall of Fame 1963.

Year	Team	Games	BA	SA	AB	H	2B	3B	HR	HR%	R	RBI	BB	SO	SB	Pinch Hit AB	Pinch Hit H	PO	A	E	DP	TC/G	FA	G by Pos
1915	WAS A	4	.375	.375	8	3	0	0	0	0.0	1	0	0	1	0	0	0	1	7	1	1	2.3	.889	P-4
1916		58	.299	.386	197	59	8	3	1	0.5	26	17	15	13	4	6	2	83	11	4	1	1.9	.959	OF-46, P-5
1917		155	.302	.369	586	177	25	7	0	0.0	77	69	50	41	35	0	0	265	26	12	5	2.0	.960	OF-155
1918		7	.348	.391	23	8	1	0	0	0.0	3	3	2	0	1	1	0	11	4	0	1	2.5	1.000	OF-6
1919		141	.321	.411	557	179	23	9	3	0.5	80	71	42	26	26	0	0	285	18	12	3	2.2	.962	OF-141
1920		153	.338	.428	624	211	29	9	3	0.5	83	80	39	23	**63**	0	0	454	24	20	5	3.3	.960	OF-153
1921		143	.330	.467	561	185	39	13	4	0.7	83	79	38	10	25	1	0	380	18	15	3	2.9	.964	OF-141
1922		154	.295	.423	**633**	187	37	13	6	0.9	91	69	48	13	20	0	0	385	23	21	3	2.8	.951	OF-154
1923		148	.316	.450	595	188	35	**18**	3	0.5	117	75	57	12	20	1	0	307	21	10	8	2.3	.970	OF-147
1924		154	.334	.441	**646**	**216**	38	14	1	0.2	106	76	46	24	24	0	0	331	18	12	4	2.3	.967	OF-154
1925		152	.350	.442	649	227	31	13	1	0.2	111	87	37	10	26	0	0	339	20	12	7	2.4	.968	OF-152
1926		152	.337	.445	**641**	**216**	32	14	3	0.5	98	76	42	20	25	0	0	342	25	15	5	2.5	.961	OF-152
1927		142	.297	.408	603	179	33	14	2	0.3	98	65	36	11	19	3	0	258	12	7	2	2.0	.975	OF-139
1928		148	.328	.438	616	202	32	15	2	0.3	95	55	49	15	16	0	0	240	11	7	5	1.8	.973	OF-147
1929		150	.323	.424	616	199	39	10	1	0.2	119	62	55	9	16	2	0	272	20	9	5	2.0	.970	OF-147
1930		147	.349	.457	593	207	35	13	1	0.2	121	73	55	14	13	0	0	297	13	12	4	2.2	.963	OF-145
1931		120	.310	.400	413	128	21	8	0	0.0	81	42	35	11	6	7	1	221	7	7	2	2.2	.970	OF-105
1932		106	.323	.438	288	93	16	7	1	0.3	58	34	32	6	7	33	5	132	7	4	2	2.1	.972	OF-69
1933		73	.294	.447	85	25	4	3	1	1.2	19	12	3	7	0	28	7	41	4	0	2	1.2	1.000	OF-39
1934	CLE A	97	.293	.364	335	98	19	1	1	0.3	48	33	28	9	5	23	5	129	2	5	0	1.7	.963	OF-78
20 yrs.		2404	.322	.427	9269	2987	497	184	34	0.4	1515	1078	709	275	351	105	20	4773	291	185	68	2.3	.965	OF-2270, P-9
WORLD SERIES																								
1924	WAS A	7	.207	.207	29	6	0	0	0	0.0	2	1	3	2	2	0	0	13	4	1	1	2.6	.944	OF-7
1925		7	.364	.364	33	12	0	0	0	0.0	5	3	0	1	0	0	0	17	0	0	0	2.4	1.000	OF-7
1933		1	1.000	1.000	1	1	0	0	0	0.0	0	0	0	0	0	1	1	0	0	0	0	0.0	—	
3 yrs.		15	.302	.302	63	19	0	0	0	0.0	7	4	3	3	2	1	1	30	4	1	1	2.5	.971	OF-14

Lee Richard

RICHARD, LEE EDWARD (Bee Bee) — BR TR 5′11″ 165 lbs. BB 1975
B. Sept. 18, 1948, Lafayette, La.

Year	Team	Games	BA	SA	AB	H	2B	3B	HR	HR%	R	RBI	BB	SO	SB	Pinch Hit AB	Pinch Hit H	PO	A	E	DP	TC/G	FA	G by Pos
1971	CHI A	87	.231	.304	260	60	7	3	2	0.8	38	17	20	46	8	6	0	107	213	27	31	4.1	.922	SS-68, OF-16
1972		11	.241	.241	29	7	0	0	0	0.0	5	1	0	7	1	1	1	8	2	0	1	1.4	1.000	OF-6, SS-1
1974		32	.164	.179	67	11	1	0	0	0.0	5	1	5	8	0	0	0	14	40	5	11	2.2	.915	3B-12, SS-6, DH-5, 2B-3, OF-1
1975		43	.200	.244	45	9	0	1	0	0.0	11	5	4	7	2	0	0	20	33	3	3	1.8	.946	3B-12, SS-9, DH-5, 2B-5
1976	STL N	66	.176	.264	91	16	4	2	0	0.0	12	5	4	9	1	3	0	71	71	7	18	3.8	.953	2B-26, SS-12, 3B-1
5 yrs.		239	.209	.270	492	103	12	6	2	0.4	71	29	33	77	12	10	1	220	359	42	64	3.3	.932	SS-96, 2B-34, 3B-25, OF-23, DH-10

Fred Richards

RICHARDS, FRED CHARLES (Fuzzy) — BL TL 6′ 1½″ 185 lbs.
B. Nov. 3, 1927, Warren, Ohio.

Year	Team	Games	BA	SA	AB	H	2B	3B	HR	HR%	R	RBI	BB	SO	SB	Pinch Hit AB	Pinch Hit H	PO	A	E	DP	TC/G	FA	G by Pos
1951	CHI N	10	.296	.370	27	8	2	0	0	0.0	1	4	2	3	0	1	0	62	8	0	3	7.8	1.000	1B-9

Gene Richards

RICHARDS, EUGENE — BL TL 6′ 175 lbs.
B. Sept. 29, 1953, Monticello, S. C.

Year	Team	Games	BA	SA	AB	H	2B	3B	HR	HR%	R	RBI	BB	SO	SB	Pinch Hit AB	Pinch Hit H	PO	A	E	DP	TC/G	FA	G by Pos
1977	SD N	146	.290	.390	525	152	16	11	5	1.0	79	32	60	80	56	14	4	416	35	13	23	3.3	.972	OF-109, 1B-32
1978		154	.308	.420	555	171	26	12	4	0.7	90	45	64	80	37	9	1	421	20	17	23	3.1	.963	OF-124, 1B-26
1979		150	.279	.365	545	152	17	9	4	0.7	77	41	47	62	24	20	3	320	7	9	2	2.5	.973	OF-132
1980		158	.301	.385	642	193	26	8	4	0.6	91	41	61	73	61	2	1	307	21	7	4	2.1	.979	OF-156
1981		104	.288	.407	393	113	14	**12**	3	0.8	47	42	53	44	20	2	1	178	14	5	1	1.9	.975	OF-102
1982		132	.286	.359	521	149	13	8	3	0.6	63	28	36	52	30	3	0	423	20	11	18	3.5	.976	OF-103, 1B-25
1983		95	.275	.386	233	64	11	3	3	1.3	37	22	17	17	14	36	6	96	2	2	0	1.9	.980	OF-54
1984	SF N	87	.252	.281	135	34	4	0	0	0.0	18	4	18	28	5	48	10	46	1	3	0	1.9	.940	OF-26
8 yrs.		1026	.290	.383	3549	1028	127	63	26	0.7	502	255	356	436	247	134	26	2207	120	67	71	2.7	.972	OF-806, 1B-83

Paul Richards

RICHARDS, PAUL RAPIER — BR TR 6′ 1½″ 180 lbs.
B. Nov. 21, 1908, Waxahachie, Tex. D. May 4, 1986, Waxahachie, Tex.
Manager 1951–61, 1976.

Year	Team	Games	BA	SA	AB	H	2B	3B	HR	HR%	R	RBI	BB	SO	SB	Pinch Hit AB	Pinch Hit H	PO	A	E	DP	TC/G	FA	G by Pos
1932	BKN N	3	.000	.000	8	0	0	0	0	0.0	0	0	0	2	0	0	0	21	3	0	0	8.0	1.000	C-3
1933	NY N	51	.195	.230	87	17	3	0	0	0.0	4	10	3	12	0	14	2	74	17	1	2	2.6	.989	C-36
1934		42	.160	.173	75	12	1	0	0	0.0	10	3	13	8	0	3	2	86	15	0	3	2.7	1.000	C-37
1935	2 teams	NY N (7G –.250) PHI A (85G –.245)																						
″	total	92	.245	.337	261	64	10	1	4	1.5	31	29	26	13	0	6	2	300	42	8	5	4.2	.977	C-83
1943	DET A	100	.220	.297	313	69	7	1	5	1.6	32	33	38	35	1	0	0	537	86	9	12	6.3	.986	C-100
1944		95	.237	.310	300	71	13	0	3	1.0	24	37	35	30	8	3	0	413	60	10	13	5.4	.979	C-90
1945		83	.256	.355	234	60	12	1	3	1.3	26	32	19	31	4	0	0	361	44	2	7	4.9	.995	C-83
1946		57	.201	.266	139	28	5	2	0	0.0	13	11	23	18	2	3	2	311	35	1	6	6.4	.997	C-54
8 yrs.		523	.227	.301	1417	321	51	5	15	1.1	140	155	157	149	15	29	8	2103	302	31	48	5.0	.987	C-486
WORLD SERIES																								
1945	DET A	7	.211	.316	19	4	2	0	0	0.0	0	6	4	3	0	0	0	46	5	1	1	7.4	.981	C-7

Richardson

RICHARDSON — 5′ 4″ 136 lbs.
B. Boston, Ma. Deceased.

Year	Team	Games	BA	SA	AB	H	2B	3B	HR	HR%	R	RBI	BB	SO	SB	Pinch Hit AB	Pinch Hit H	PO	A	E	DP	TC/G	FA	G by Pos
1884	CHI U	1	.000	.000	4	0	0	0	0	0.0	0		0			0	0	1	1	1	0	3.0	.667	2B-1

Bill Richardson

RICHARDSON, WILLIAM HENRY — BR TR 5′11″ 200 lbs.
B. Sept. 24, 1878, Salem, Ind. D. Nov. 6, 1949, Sullivan, Ind.

Year	Team	Games	BA	SA	AB	H	2B	3B	HR	HR%	R	RBI	BB	SO	SB	Pinch Hit AB	Pinch Hit H	PO	A	E	DP	TC/G	FA	G by Pos
1901	STL N	15	.212	.365	52	11	2	0	2	3.8	7	7	6		1	0	0	154	5	3	7	10.8	.981	1B-15

Bobby Richardson

RICHARDSON, ROBERT CLINTON — BR TR 5′ 9″ 170 lbs.
B. Aug. 19, 1935, Sumter, S. C.

Year	Team	Games	BA	SA	AB	H	2B	3B	HR	HR%	R	RBI	BB	SO	SB	Pinch Hit AB	Pinch Hit H	PO	A	E	DP	TC/G	FA	G by Pos
1955	NY A	11	.154	.154	26	4	0	0	0	0.0	2	3	2	0	1	0	0	14	9	3	2	2.6	.885	2B-6, SS-4
1956		5	.143	.143	7	1	0	0	0	0.0	1	0	0	1	0	0	0	15	4	0	2	3.8	1.000	2B-5

Bobby Richardson *continued*

Year	Team	Games	BA	SA	AB	H	2B	3B	HR	HR%	R	RBI	BB	SO	SB	Pinch Hit AB	Pinch Hit H	PO	A	E	DP	TC/G	FA	G by Pos
1957		97	.256	.298	305	78	11	1	0	0.0	36	19	9	26	1	1	0	206	223	9	60	4.7	.979	2B-93
1958		73	.247	.302	182	45	6	2	0	0.0	18	14	8	5	1	0	0	115	141	8	38	4.0	.970	2B-51, 3B-13, SS-2
1959		134	.301	.377	469	141	18	6	2	0.4	53	33	26	20	5	0	0	269	336	22	94	4.6	.965	2B-109, SS-14, 3B-12
1960		150	.252	.298	460	116	12	3	1	0.2	45	26	35	19	6	1	0	318	350	18	103	4.5	.974	2B-141, 3B-11
1961		162	.261	.316	662	173	17	5	3	0.5	80	49	30	23	9	1	0	413	376	18	136	5.0	.978	2B-161
1962		161	.302	.406	**692**	**209**	38	5	8	1.2	99	59	37	24	11	0	0	378	452	15	116	5.2	.982	2B-161
1963		151	.265	.330	**630**	167	20	6	3	0.5	72	48	25	22	15	1	0	335	424	12	105	5.1	.984	2B-150
1964		159	.267	.333	**679**	181	25	4	4	0.6	90	50	28	36	11	2	1	402	413	15	109	5.3	.982	2B-157, SS-1
1965		160	.247	.322	664	164	28	2	6	0.9	76	47	37	39	7	3	0	372	403	15	121	5.0	.981	2B-158
1966		149	.251	.330	610	153	21	3	7	1.1	71	42	25	28	6	2	0	322	410	15	91	5.0	.980	2B-147, 3B-2
12 yrs.		1412	.266	.335	5386	1432	196	37	34	0.6	643	390	262	243	73	11	1	3159	3541	150	977	4.9	.978	2B-1339, 3B-38, SS-21
WORLD SERIES																								
1957	NY A	2	—	—	0	0	0	0	0	—	0	0	0	0	0	0	0	0	0	0	0	0.0	.000	2B-1
1958		4	.000	.000	5	0	0	0	0	0.0	0	0	0	0	0	0	0	0	1	0	0	0.3	1.000	3B-4
1960		7	.367	.667	30	11	2	2	1	3.3	8	12	1	1	0	0	0	21	28	2	7	7.3	.961	2B-7
1961		5	.391	.435	23	9	1	0	0	0.0	2	0	0	0	1	0	0	10	16	0	1	5.2	1.000	2B-5
1962		7	.148	.148	27	4	0	0	0	0.0	3	0	3	1	0	0	0	19	19	1	4	5.6	.974	2B-7
1963		4	.214	.286	14	3	1	0	0	0.0	0	0	1	3	0	0	0	7	14	0	5	5.3	1.000	2B-4
1964		7	.406	.469	32	13	2	0	0	0.0	3	3	0	2	1	0	0	19	19	2	5	5.7	.950	2B-7
7 yrs.		36	.305	.405	131	40	6	2	1	0.8	16	15	5	7	2	0	0	76	97	5	22	5.1	.972	2B-31, 3B-4

Danny Richardson

RICHARDSON, DANIEL BR TR 5′ 8″ 165 lbs.
B. Jan. 25, 1863, Elmira, N. Y. D. Sept. 12, 1926, New York, N. Y.
Manager 1892.

Year	Team	Games	BA	SA	AB	H	2B	3B	HR	HR%	R	RBI	BB	SO	SB	Pinch Hit AB	Pinch Hit H	PO	A	E	DP	TC/G	FA	G by Pos
1884	NY N	74	.253	.300	277	70	8	1	1	0.4	36		16	17		0	0	110	54	24	9	2.5	.872	OF-55, SS-19
1885		49	.263	.338	198	52	9	3	0	0.0	26		10	14		0	0	52	58	5	1	2.2	.957	OF-22, 3B-21, P-9
1886		68	.232	.291	237	55	9	1	1	0.4	43	27	17	21		0	0	103	26	6	3	1.9	.956	OF-64, P-5, SS-1, 3B-1, 2B-1
1887		122	.278	.384	450	125	19	10	3	0.7	79	62	36	25	41	0	0	273	413	59	47	6.1	.921	2B-108, 3B-14, P-1
1888		135	.226	.323	561	127	16	7	8	1.4	82	61	15	35	35	0	0	321	423	46	43	5.9	.942	2B-135
1889		125	.280	.398	497	139	22	8	7	1.4	88	100	46	37	32	0	0	332	416	53	60	6.4	.934	2B-125
1890	NY P	123	.256	.335	528	135	12	9	4	0.8	102	80	37	19	37	0	0	301	430	72	54	6.5	.910	SS-68, 2B-56
1891	NY N	123	.269	.353	516	139	18	5	5	1.0	85	51	33	27	28	0	0	358	461	46	64	7.0	.947	2B-114, SS-9
1892	WAS N	142	.240	.294	551	132	13	4	3	0.5	48	58	25	45	25	0	0	389	541	60	69	6.9	.939	SS-93, 2B-49, 3B-1
1893	BKN N	54	.223	.272	206	46	6	2	0	0.0	36	27	13	18	7	0	0	130	129	14	21	5.1	.949	2B-46, 3B-5, SS-3
1894	LOU N	116	.253	.309	430	109	17	2	1	0.2	51	40	35	31	8	0	0	267	388	57	64	6.1	.920	SS-107, 2B-10
11 yrs.		1131	.254	.333	4451	1129	149	52	33	0.7	676	506	283	289	213	0	0	2636	3339	442	435	5.6	.931	2B-644, SS-300, OF-141, 3B-42, P-15

Hardy Richardson

RICHARDSON, ABRAM HARDING (Old True Blue) BR TR 5′ 9½″ 170 lbs.
B. Apr. 21, 1855, Clarksboro, N. J. D. Jan. 14, 1931, Utica, N. Y.

Year	Team	Games	BA	SA	AB	H	2B	3B	HR	HR%	R	RBI	BB	SO	SB	Pinch Hit AB	Pinch Hit H	PO	A	E	DP	TC/G	FA	G by Pos
1879	BUF N	79	.283	.396	336	95	18	10	0	0.0	54	37	16	30		0	0	94	153	44	13	3.7	.849	3B-78, C-1
1880		83	.259	.359	343	89	18	8	0	0.0	48	17	14	37		0	0	123	163	52	6	3.9	.846	3B-81, C-5
1881		83	.291	.413	344	100	18	9	2	0.6	62	53	12	27		0	0	195	62	24	6	3.3	.915	OF-79, 2B-5, 3B-1, SS-1
1882		83	.271	.390	354	96	20	8	2	0.6	61		11	33		0	0	275	280	63	28	7.4	.898	2B-83
1883		92	.311	.439	399	124	34	7	1	0.3	73		22	20		0	0	289	344	68	33	7.6	.903	2B-92
1884		102	.301	.444	439	132	27	9	6	1.4	85		22	41		0	0	275	258	57	21	5.7	.903	2B-71, OF-24, 3B-5, 1B-3
1885		96	.319	.458	426	136	19	11	6	1.4	90	44	20	22		0	0	284	179	49	19	5.1	.904	2B-50, OF-48, SS-1, P-1
1886	DET N	125	.351	.504	**538**	**189**	27	11	**11**	2.0	125	61	46	27		0	0	242	153	32	17	3.3	.925	OF-80, 2B-42, P-4, SS-3, 3B-2
1887		120	.328	.501	543	178	25	18	11	2.0	131	94	31	40	29	0	0	328	223	37	28	4.8	.937	2B-64, OF-59
1888		58	.289	.444	266	77	18	1	7	2.6	60	32	17	23	13	0	0	173	185	29	21	6.7	.925	2B-58
1889	BOS N	132	.304	.438	536	163	33	9	7	1.3	122	79	48	44	47	0	0	320	316	51	45	5.2	.926	2B-86, OF-46
1890	BOS P	130	.326	.494	555	181	26	14	13	2.3	126	**146**	52	46	42	0	0	260	37	13	8	2.4	.958	OF-124, SS-6, 1B-1
1891	BOS AA	74	.255	.392	278	71	9	4	7	2.5	45	52	40	26	16	0	0	141	36	10	5	2.5	.947	OF-60, 3B-9, SS-4, 1B-3
1892	**2 teams**	**WAS N** (10G –.108) **NY N** (64G –.214)																						
″	**total**	74	.200	.295	285	57	11	5	2	0.7	38	34	26	29	16	0	0	237	140	25	16	5.4	.938	2B-34, OF-24, 1B-9, SS-6, 3B-2
14 yrs.		1331	.299	.437	5642	1688	303	124	75	1.3	1120	649	377	445	163	0	0	3236	2529	554	266	4.7	.912	2B-585, OF-544, 3B-178, SS-21, 1B-16, C-6, P-5

Jeff Richardson

RICHARDSON, JEFFREY SCOTT BR TR 6′ 2″ 180 lbs.
B. Aug. 26, 1965, Grand Island, Neb.

Year	Team	Games	BA	SA	AB	H	2B	3B	HR	HR%	R	RBI	BB	SO	SB	Pinch Hit AB	Pinch Hit H	PO	A	E	DP	TC/G	FA	G by Pos
1989	CIN N	53	.168	.248	125	21	4	0	2	1.6	10	11	10	23	1	5	2	50	81	4	16	2.9	.970	SS-39, 3B-8
1991	PIT N	6	.250	.250	4	1	0	0	0	0.0	0	0	0	3	0	1	0	0	1	0	0	0.2	1.000	3B-3, SS-2
1993	BOS A	15	.208	.292	24	5	2	0	0	0.0	3	2	1	3	0	2	0	12	30	0	5	2.8	1.000	2B-8, SS-5, 3B-1, DH-1
3 yrs.		74	.176	.255	153	27	6	0	2	1.3	13	13	11	29	1	8	2	62	112	4	21	2.7	.978	SS-46, 3B-12, 2B-8, DH-1

Ken Richardson

RICHARDSON, KENNETH FRANKLIN BR TR 5′10½″ 187 lbs.
B. May 2, 1915, Orleans, Ind. D. Dec. 7, 1987, Woodland Hills, Calif.

Year	Team	Games	BA	SA	AB	H	2B	3B	HR	HR%	R	RBI	BB	SO	SB	Pinch Hit AB	Pinch Hit H	PO	A	E	DP	TC/G	FA	G by Pos
1942	PHI A	6	.067	.067	15	1	0	0	0	0.0	1	0	2	0	0	1	0	18	2	1	1	4.2	.952	OF-3, 3B-1, 1B-1
1946	PHI N	6	.150	.200	20	3	1	0	0	0.0	1	2	0	2	0	0	0	16	15	2	0	5.5	.939	2B-6
2 yrs.		12	.114	.143	35	4	1	0	0	0.0	2	2	2	2	0	1	0	34	17	3	1	4.9	.944	2B-6, OF-3, 3B-1, 1B-1

Nolen Richardson

RICHARDSON, CLIFFORD NOLEN BR TR 6′ 1½″ 170 lbs.
B. Jan. 18, 1903, Chattanooga, Tenn. D. Sept. 25, 1951, Athens, Ga.

Year	Team	Games	BA	SA	AB	H	2B	3B	HR	HR%	R	RBI	BB	SO	SB	Pinch Hit AB	Pinch Hit H	PO	A	E	DP	TC/G	FA	G by Pos
1929	DET A	13	.190	.190	21	4	0	0	0	0.0	2	2	2	1	1	0	0	15	11	5	2	2.4	.839	SS-13
1931		38	.270	.358	148	40	9	2	0	0.0	13	16	6	3	2	0	0	31	75	6	2	2.9	.946	3B-38
1932		69	.219	.277	155	34	5	2	0	0.0	13	12	9	13	5	0	0	56	102	3	9	2.3	.981	3B-65, SS-4
1935	NY A	12	.217	.283	46	10	1	1	0	0.0	3	5	3	1	0	0	0	23	24	4	4	4.3	.922	SS-12
1938	CIN N	35	.290	.330	100	29	4	0	0	0.0	8	10	3	4	0	0	0	56	87	5	13	4.2	.966	SS-35
1939		1	.000	.000	3	0	0	0	0	0.0	0	0	0	0	0	0	0	4	3	0	1	7.0	1.000	SS-1
6 yrs.		168	.247	.309	473	117	19	5	0	0.0	39	45	23	22	8	0	0	185	302	23	31	3.0	.955	3B-103, SS-65

Tom Richardson

RICHARDSON, THOMAS MITCHELL BR TR 6′ 190 lbs.
B. Aug. 7, 1883, Louisville, Ill. D. Nov. 15, 1939, Onawa, Iowa.

Year	Team	Games	BA	SA	AB	H	2B	3B	HR	HR%	R	RBI	BB	SO	SB	Pinch Hit AB	Pinch Hit H	PO	A	E	DP	TC/G	FA	G by Pos
1917	STL A	1	.000	.000	1	0	0	0	0	0.0	0	0	0	0	0	1	0	0	0	0	0	0.0	—	

Mike Richardt

RICHARDT, MICHAEL ANTHONY BR TR 6′ 170 lbs.
B. May 24, 1958, North Hollywood, Calif.

Year	Team	Games	BA	SA	AB	H	2B	3B	HR	HR%	R	RBI	BB	SO	SB	Pinch Hit AB	Pinch Hit H	PO	A	E	DP	TC/G	FA	G by Pos
1980	TEX A	22	.225	.254	71	16	2	0	0	0.0	2	8	1	7	0	0	0	32	55	2	11	4.2	.978	2B-20, DH-1
1982		119	.241	.289	402	97	10	0	3	0.7	34	43	23	42	9	1	0	253	279	6	68	4.5	.989	2B-98, DH-15, OF-6
1983		22	.157	.241	83	13	2	1	1	1.2	9	7	2	11	2	2	0	56	61	1	16	5.9	.992	2B-20
1984	2 teams	TEX A (7G –.111) HOU N (16G –.267)																						
″	total	23	.208	.250	24	5	1	0	0	0.0	1	2	1	2	0	17	4	5	6	0	4	2.8	1.000	2B-4
4 yrs.		186	.226	.276	580	131	15	1	4	0.7	46	60	27	62	11	20	4	346	401	9	99	4.6	.988	2B-142, DH-16, OF-6

Lance Richbourg

RICHBOURG, LANCE CLAYTON BL TR 5′10½″ 160 lbs.
B. Dec. 18, 1897, DeFuniak Springs, Fla. D. Sept. 10, 1975, Crestview, Fla.

Year	Team	Games	BA	SA	AB	H	2B	3B	HR	HR%	R	RBI	BB	SO	SB	Pinch Hit AB	Pinch Hit H	PO	A	E	DP	TC/G	FA	G by Pos
1921	PHI N	10	.200	.400	5	1	1	0	0	0.0	2	0	0	3	1	2	0	3	4	0	0	1.8	1.000	2B-4
1924	WAS A	15	.281	.406	32	9	2	1	0	0.0	3	1	2	6	0	6	4	11	2	0	1	1.9	1.000	OF-7
1927	BOS N	115	.309	.389	450	139	12	9	2	0.4	57	34	22	30	24	4	1	233	10	12	0	2.3	.953	OF-110
1928		148	.337	.428	612	206	26	12	2	0.3	105	52	62	39	11	0	0	367	8	11	1	2.6	.972	OF-148
1929		139	.305	.411	557	170	24	13	3	0.5	76	56	42	26	7	3	0	323	14	10	2	2.6	.971	OF-134
1930		130	.304	.395	529	161	23	8	3	0.6	81	54	19	31	13	2	1	294	9	9	4	2.4	.971	OF-128
1931		97	.287	.388	286	82	11	6	2	0.7	32	29	19	14	9	22	5	154	3	3	2	2.3	.981	OF-71
1932	CHI N	44	.257	.318	148	38	2	2	1	0.7	22	21	8	4	0	10	3	70	2	1	1	2.2	.986	OF-33
8 yrs.		698	.308	.400	2619	806	101	51	13	0.5	378	247	174	153	65	49	14	1455	52	46	11	2.4	.970	OF-631, 2B-4

Rob Richie

RICHIE, ROBERT EUGENE BL TR 6′ 2″ 190 lbs.
B. Sept. 5, 1965, Reno, Nev.

Year	Team	Games	BA	SA	AB	H	2B	3B	HR	HR%	R	RBI	BB	SO	SB	Pinch Hit AB	Pinch Hit H	PO	A	E	DP	TC/G	FA	G by Pos
1989	DET A	19	.265	.490	49	13	4	2	1	2.0	6	10	5	10	0	4	0	21	1	2	0	1.4	.917	OF-13, DH-4

Don Richmond

RICHMOND, DONALD LESTER BL TR 6′ 1″ 175 lbs.
B. Oct. 27, 1919, Gillett, Pa. D. May 24, 1981, Elmira, N. Y.

Year	Team	Games	BA	SA	AB	H	2B	3B	HR	HR%	R	RBI	BB	SO	SB	Pinch Hit AB	Pinch Hit H	PO	A	E	DP	TC/G	FA	G by Pos
1941	PHI A	9	.200	.286	35	7	1	1	0	0.0	3	5	0	1	0	0	0	6	16	1	3	2.6	.957	3B-9
1946		16	.290	.387	62	18	3	0	1	1.6	3	9	0	10	1	0	0	19	28	3	1	3.1	.940	3B-16
1947		19	.190	.333	21	4	1	1	0	0.0	2	4	3	3	0	11	2	1	3	2	0	1.2	.667	3B-4, 2B-1
1951	STL N	12	.088	.206	34	3	1	0	1	2.9	3	4	3	3	0	0	0	14	28	0	3	3.8	1.000	3B-11
4 yrs.		56	.211	.316	152	32	6	2	2	1.3	11	22	6	17	1	11	2	40	75	6	7	3.0	.950	3B-40, 2B-1

John Richmond

RICHMOND, JOHN H. TR 5′ 9″ 170 lbs.
B. 1854, Pennsylvania Deceased.

Year	Team	Games	BA	SA	AB	H	2B	3B	HR	HR%	R	RBI	BB	SO	SB	Pinch Hit AB	Pinch Hit H	PO	A	E	DP	TC/G	FA	G by Pos
1879	SYR N	62	.213	.287	254	54	8	4	1	0.4	31	23	4	24		0	0	132	75	30	5	3.6	.873	OF-35, SS-28, C-2
1880	BOS N	32	.248	.287	129	32	3	1	0	0.0	12	9	2	18		0	0	31	73	19	14	3.8	.846	SS-31, OF-1
1881		27	.276	.367	98	27	2	2	1	1.0	13	12	6	7		0	0	62	10	5	1	2.9	.935	OF-25, SS-2
1882	2 teams	CLE N (41G –.171) PHI AA (18G –.185)																						
″	total	59	.176	.254	205	36	8	4	0	0.0	20	11	22	27		0	0	94	16	11	0	2.1	.909	OF-59
1883	COL AA	92	.283	.343	385	109	7	8	0	0.0	63		25			0	0	122	306	60	19	5.2	.877	SS-91, OF-2
1884		105	.251	.342	398	100	13	7	3	0.8	57		35			0	0	96	306	62	26	4.4	.866	SS-105
1885	PIT AA	34	.206	.252	131	27	2	2	0	0.0	14		8			0	0	27	66	17	6	3.2	.845	SS-23, OF-11
7 yrs.		411	.241	.312	1600	385	43	28	5	0.3	210	55	102	76		0	0	564	852	204	71	3.9	.874	SS-280, OF-133, C-2

Lee Richmond

RICHMOND, J. LEE TL 5′10″ 155 lbs.
B. May 5, 1857, Sheffield, Ohio D. Oct. 1, 1929, Toledo, Ohio.

Year	Team	Games	BA	SA	AB	H	2B	3B	HR	HR%	R	RBI	BB	SO	SB	Pinch Hit AB	Pinch Hit H	PO	A	E	DP	TC/G	FA	G by Pos
1879	BOS N	1	.333	.333	6	2	0	0	0	0.0	0	1	0	1		0	0	0	2	0	0	2.0	1.000	P-1
1880	WOR N	77	.227	.278	309	70	8	4	0	0.0	44	34	9	32		0	0	17	99	26	1	1.5	.817	P-74, OF-20
1881		61	.250	.278	252	63	5	1	0	0.0	31	28	10	10		0	0	26	101	13	4	2.2	.907	P-53, OF-11
1882		55	.281	.421	228	64	8	9	2	0.9	50	28	9	11		0	0	23	101	19	2	2.4	.867	P-48, OF-11
1883	PRO N	49	.284	.402	194	55	8	6	1	0.5	41		15	19		0	0	49	22	22	0	1.8	.763	OF-41, P-12
1886	CIN AA	8	.276	.276	29	8	0	0	0	0.0	3		3			0	0	6	2	6	0	1.4	.571	OF-7, P-3
6 yrs.		251	.257	.334	1018	262	29	20	3	0.3	169	91	46	73		0	0	121	327	86	7	1.9	.839	P-191, OF-90

Al Richter

RICHTER, ALLEN GORDON BR TR 6′ 175 lbs.
B. Feb. 7, 1927, Norfolk, Va.

Year	Team	Games	BA	SA	AB	H	2B	3B	HR	HR%	R	RBI	BB	SO	SB	Pinch Hit AB	Pinch Hit H	PO	A	E	DP	TC/G	FA	G by Pos
1951	BOS A	5	.091	.091	11	1	0	0	0	0.0	1	0	3	0	0	2	0	8	10	0	5	6.0	1.000	SS-3
1953		1	—	—	0	0	0	0	0	—	0	0	0	0	0	0	0	1	1	0	1	2.0	1.000	SS-1
2 yrs.		6	.091	.091	11	1	0	0	0	0.0	1	0	3	0	0	2	0	9	11	0	6	5.0	1.000	SS-4

John Richter

RICHTER, JOHN M. 6′ 178 lbs.
B. Feb. 8, 1873, Louisville, Ky. D. Oct. 4, 1927, Louisville, Ky.

Year	Team	Games	BA	SA	AB	H	2B	3B	HR	HR%	R	RBI	BB	SO	SB	Pinch Hit AB	Pinch Hit H	PO	A	E	DP	TC/G	FA	G by Pos
1898	LOU N	3	.154	.154	13	2	0	0	0	0.0	1	0	0		0	0	0	5	8	1	1	4.7	.929	3B-3

Joe Rickert

RICKERT, JOSEPH FRANCIS (Diamond Joe) BR TR 5′10½″ 165 lbs.
B. Dec. 12, 1876, London, Ohio D. Oct. 15, 1943, Springfield, Ohio.

Year	Team	Games	BA	SA	AB	H	2B	3B	HR	HR%	R	RBI	BB	SO	SB	Pinch Hit AB	Pinch Hit H	PO	A	E	DP	TC/G	FA	G by Pos
1898	PIT N	2	.167	.167	6	1	0	0	0	0.0	0	0	0		0	0	0	10	0	0	0	5.0	1.000	OF-2
1901	BOS N	13	.167	.250	60	10	1	2	0	0.0	6	1	3		1	0	0	35	2	1	1	2.9	.974	OF-13
2 yrs.		15	.167	.242	66	11	1	2	0	0.0	6	1	3		1	0	0	45	2	1	1	3.2	.979	OF-15

Marv Rickert

RICKERT, MARVIN AUGUST (Twitch) BL TR 6′ 2″ 195 lbs.
B. Jan. 8, 1921, Longbranch, Wash. D. June 3, 1978, Oakville, Wash.

Year	Team	Games	BA	SA	AB	H	2B	3B	HR	HR%	R	RBI	BB	SO	SB	Pinch Hit AB	Pinch Hit H	PO	A	E	DP	TC/G	FA	G by Pos
1942	CHI N	8	.269	.269	26	7	0	0	0	0.0	5	1	1	5	0	1	0	18	1	0	0	3.2	1.000	OF-6
1946		111	.263	.378	392	103	18	3	7	1.8	44	47	28	54	3	6	0	200	5	6	1	2.0	.972	OF-104
1947		71	.146	.190	137	20	0	0	2	1.5	7	15	15	17	0	27	6	123	8	1	8	3.6	.992	OF-30, 1B-7

Marv Rickert *continued*

Year	Team	Games	BA	SA	AB	H	2B	3B	HR	HR%	R	RBI	BB	SO	SB	Pinch Hit AB	Pinch Hit H	PO	A	E	DP	TC/G	FA	G by Pos
1948	2 teams	CIN N (8G –.167) BOS N (3G –.231)																						
″	total	11	.211	.316	19	4	0	1	0	0.0	1	2	0	1	0	6	1	9	1	0	0	3.3	1.000	OF-3
1949	BOS N	100	.292	.444	277	81	18	3	6	2.2	44	49	23	38	1	12	3	223	14	6	8	2.8	.975	OF-75, 1B-12
1950	2 teams	PIT N (17G –.150) CHI A (84G –.237)																						
″	total	101	.232	.315	298	69	9	2	4	1.3	38	31	21	46	0	20	1	154	3	5	1	2.0	.969	OF-81, 1B-1
6 yrs.		402	.247	.352	1149	284	45	9	19	1.7	139	145	88	161	4	72	11	727	32	18	18	2.4	.977	OF-299, 1B-20
WORLD SERIES																								
1948	BOS N	5	.211	.368	19	4	0	0	1	5.3	2	2	0	4	0	0	0	20	0	0	0	4.0	1.000	OF-5

Dave Ricketts

RICKETTS, DAVID WILLIAM BB TR 6′ 190 lbs.
Brother of Dick Ricketts.
B. July 12, 1935, Pottstown, Pa.

Year	Team	Games	BA	SA	AB	H	2B	3B	HR	HR%	R	RBI	BB	SO	SB	Pinch Hit AB	Pinch Hit H	PO	A	E	DP	TC/G	FA	G by Pos
1963	STL N	3	.250	.250	8	2	0	0	0	0.0	0	0	0	2	0	0	0	14	0	0	0	4.7	1.000	C-3
1965		11	.241	.241	29	7	0	0	0	0.0	1	0	1	3	0	1	0	41	2	1	0	4.0	.977	C-11
1967		52	.273	.384	99	27	8	0	1	1.0	11	14	4	7	0	32	7	111	10	0	0	5.8	1.000	C-21
1968		20	.136	.136	22	3	0	0	0	0.0	1	1	0	3	0	19	2	5	0	0	0	5.0	1.000	C-1
1969		30	.273	.295	44	12	1	0	0	0.0	2	5	4	5	0	18	5	57	1	1	0	7.4	.983	C-8
1970	PIT N	14	.182	.182	11	2	0	0	0	0.0	0	0	1	3	0	7	1	8	2	1	0	1.6	.909	C-7
6 yrs.		130	.249	.305	213	53	9	0	1	0.5	15	20	10	23	0	77	15	236	15	3	0	5.0	.988	C-51
WORLD SERIES																								
1967	STL N	3	.000	.000	3	0	0	0	0	0.0	0	0	0	0	0	3	0	0	0	0	0	0.0	—	
1968		1	1.000	1.000	1	1	0	0	0	0.0	0	0	0	0	0	1	1	0	0	0	0	0.0	—	
2 yrs.		4	.250	.250	4	1	0	0	0	0.0	0	0	0	0	0	4	1							

Branch Rickey

RICKEY, WESLEY BRANCH (The Mahatma) BL TR 5′ 9″ 175 lbs.
B. Dec. 20, 1881, Flat, Ohio D. Dec. 9, 1965, Columbia, Mo.
Manager 1913–15, 1919–25.
Hall of Fame 1967.

Year	Team	Games	BA	SA	AB	H	2B	3B	HR	HR%	R	RBI	BB	SO	SB	Pinch Hit AB	Pinch Hit H	PO	A	E	DP	TC/G	FA	G by Pos
1905	STL A	1	.000	.000	3	0	0	0	0	0.0	0	0	0		0	0	0	2	1	0	0	3.0	1.000	C-1
1906		64	.284	.393	201	57	7	3	3	1.5	22	24	16		4	7	2	234	58	14	2	5.6	.954	C-54, OF-1
1907	NY A	52	.182	.241	137	25	2	3	0	0.0	16	15	11		4	12	1	159	16	17	5	4.6	.911	OF-24, C-11, 1B-7
1914	STL A	2	.000	.000	2	0	0	0	0	0.0	0	0	0	1	0	2	0	0	0	0	0	0.0	—	
4 yrs.		119	.239	.327	343	82	9	6	3	0.9	38	39	27	1	8	21	3	395	75	31	7	5.1	.938	C-66, OF-25, 1B-7

Chris Rickley

RICKLEY, CHRISTIAN 5′ 8″ 160 lbs.
B. Oct. 7, 1859, Philadelphia, Pa. D. Oct. 25, 1911, Philadelphia, Pa.

Year	Team	Games	BA	SA	AB	H	2B	3B	HR	HR%	R	RBI	BB	SO	SB	Pinch Hit AB	Pinch Hit H	PO	A	E	DP	TC/G	FA	G by Pos
1884	PHI U	6	.200	.280	25	5	2	0	0	0.0	5		2			0	0	7	21	9	2	6.2	.757	SS-6

John Ricks

RICKS, JOHN
Deceased.

Year	Team	Games	BA	SA	AB	H	2B	3B	HR	HR%	R	RBI	BB	SO	SB	Pinch Hit AB	Pinch Hit H	PO	A	E	DP	TC/G	FA	G by Pos
1891	STL AA	5	.167	.167	18	3	0	0	0	0.0	3	0	0	2	0	0	0	11	6	4	0	4.2	.810	3B-5
1894	STL N	1	.000	.000	1	0	0	0	0	0.0	0	0	0	0	0	0	0	1	0	3	0	4.0	.250	3B-1
2 yrs.		6	.158	.158	19	3	0	0	0	0.0	3	0	0	2	0	0	0	12	6	7	0	4.2	.720	3B-6

Art Rico

RICO, ARTHUR RAYMOND BR TR 5′ 9½″ 185 lbs.
B. July 23, 1896, Roxbury, Mass. D. Jan. 3, 1919, Boston, Mass.

Year	Team	Games	BA	SA	AB	H	2B	3B	HR	HR%	R	RBI	BB	SO	SB	Pinch Hit AB	Pinch Hit H	PO	A	E	DP	TC/G	FA	G by Pos
1916	BOS N	4	.000	.000	4	0	0	0	0	0.0	0	0	0	0	0	0	0	5	1	0	0	1.5	1.000	C-4
1917		13	.286	.357	14	4	1	0	0	0.0	1	2	0	2	0	0	0	15	4	1	1	1.7	.950	C-11, OF-1
2 yrs.		17	.222	.278	18	4	1	0	0	0.0	1	2	0	2	0	0	0	20	5	1	1	1.6	.962	C-15, OF-1

Fred Rico

RICO, ALFREDO CRUZ BR TR 5′10″ 180 lbs.
B. July 4, 1944, Jerome, Ariz.

Year	Team	Games	BA	SA	AB	H	2B	3B	HR	HR%	R	RBI	BB	SO	SB	Pinch Hit AB	Pinch Hit H	PO	A	E	DP	TC/G	FA	G by Pos
1969	KC A	12	.231	.308	26	6	2	0	0	0.0	2	2	9	10	0	1	0	27	4	0	0	3.1	1.000	OF-9, 3B-1

Harry Riconda

RICONDA, HENRY PAUL BR TR 5′10″ 175 lbs.
B. Mar. 17, 1897, New York, N. Y. D. Nov. 15, 1958, Mahopac, N. Y.

Year	Team	Games	BA	SA	AB	H	2B	3B	HR	HR%	R	RBI	BB	SO	SB	Pinch Hit AB	Pinch Hit H	PO	A	E	DP	TC/G	FA	G by Pos
1923	PHI A	55	.263	.371	175	46	11	4	0	0.0	23	12	12	18	4	4	0	46	118	16	9	3.7	.911	3B-47, SS-2
1924		83	.253	.342	281	71	16	3	1	0.4	34	21	27	43	3	4	0	97	148	19	14	3.5	.928	3B-73, SS-2, C-1
1926	BOS N	4	.167	.167	12	2	0	0	0	0.0	1	0	2	2	0	0	0	6	3	2	0	2.8	.818	3B-4
1928	BKN N	92	.224	.338	281	63	15	4	3	1.1	22	35	20	28	6	1	0	181	222	20	25	4.7	.953	2B-53, 3B-21, SS-16
1929	PIT N	8	.467	.600	15	7	2	0	0	0.0	3	2	0	0	0	3	1	12	9	4	3	6.3	.840	SS-4
1930	CIN N	1	.000	.000	1	0	0	0	0	0.0	0	0	0	0	0	1	0	0	0	0	0	0.0	—	
6 yrs.		243	.247	.349	765	189	44	11	4	0.5	83	70	61	91	13	13	1	342	500	61	51	4.0	.932	3B-145, 2B-53, SS-24, C-1

John Riddle

RIDDLE, JOHN H. BR TR
B. Feb. 1864, Philadelphia, Pa. Deceased.

Year	Team	Games	BA	SA	AB	H	2B	3B	HR	HR%	R	RBI	BB	SO	SB	Pinch Hit AB	Pinch Hit H	PO	A	E	DP	TC/G	FA	G by Pos
1889	WAS N	11	.216	.297	37	8	3	0	0	0.0	3	3	2	8	0	0	0	40	15	11	1	6.0	.833	C-9, OF-2
1890	PHI AA	27	.082	.106	85	7	0	1	0	0.0	7		17		4	0	0	76	25	15	2	4.1	.871	C-13, OF-12, 2B-2, 3B-1
2 yrs.		38	.123	.164	122	15	3	1	0	0.0	10	3	19	8	4	0	0	116	40	26	3	4.7	.857	C-22, OF-14, 2B-2, 3B-1

Johnny Riddle

RIDDLE, JOHN LUDY (Mutt) BR TR 5′11″ 190 lbs.
Brother of Elmer Riddle.
B. Oct. 3, 1905, Clinton, S. C.

Year	Team	Games	BA	SA	AB	H	2B	3B	HR	HR%	R	RBI	BB	SO	SB	Pinch Hit AB	Pinch Hit H	PO	A	E	DP	TC/G	FA	G by Pos
1930	CHI A	25	.241	.328	58	14	3	1	0	0.0	7	4	3	6	0	0	0	48	13	0	3	2.4	1.000	C-25
1937	2 teams	WAS A (8G –.269) BOS N (2G –.000)																						
″	total	10	.241	.241	29	7	0	0	0	0.0	2	3	1	2	0	0	0	32	8	1	1	4.1	.976	C-10
1938	BOS N	19	.281	.298	57	16	1	0	0	0.0	6	2	4	2	0	0	0	63	15	4	4	4.3	.951	C-19
1941	CIN N	10	.300	.300	10	3	0	0	0	0.0	2	0	0	1	0	0	0	18	1	0	0	1.9	1.000	C-10
1944		1	—	—	0	0	0	0	0	—	0	0	0	0	0	0	0	0	0	0	0	0.0	.000	C-1
1945		23	.178	.178	45	8	0	0	0	0.0	0	2	4	6	0	1	0	51	11	0	3	2.7	1.000	C-23
1948	PIT N	10	.200	.200	15	3	0	0	0	0.0	1	0	1	2	0	0	0	18	3	0	1	2.1	1.000	C-10
7 yrs.		98	.238	.266	214	51	4	1	0	0.0	18	11	13	19	0	1	0	230	51	5	12	2.9	.983	C-98

Hank Riebe

RIEBE, HARVEY DONALD BR TR 5′ 9½″ 175 lbs.
B. Oct. 10, 1921, Cleveland, Ohio.

Year	Team	Games	BA	SA	AB	H	2B	3B	HR	HR%	R	RBI	BB	SO	SB	Pinch Hit AB	Pinch Hit H	PO	A	E	DP	TC/G	FA	G by Pos
1942	DET A	11	.314	.371	35	11	2	0	0	0.0	1	2	0	6	0	0	0	42	5	0	1	4.3	1.000	C-11
1947		8	.000	.000	7	0	0	0	0	0.0	0	2	0	2	0	5	0	2	0	0	0	0.7	1.000	C-3
1948		25	.194	.194	62	12	0	0	0	0.0	0	5	3	5	0	1	0	90	6	0	1	4.0	1.000	C-24
1949		17	.182	.242	33	6	2	0	0	0.0	1	2	0	5	1	6	1	21	3	1	1	2.3	.960	C-11
4 yrs.		61	.212	.241	137	29	4	0	0	0.0	2	11	3	18	1	12	1	155	14	1	3	3.5	.994	C-49

Nikco Riesgo

RIESGO, DAMON NIKCO BR TR 6′ 2″ 185 lbs.
B. Jan. 11, 1967, Long Beach, Calif.

Year	Team	Games	BA	SA	AB	H	2B	3B	HR	HR%	R	RBI	BB	SO	SB	Pinch Hit AB	Pinch Hit H	PO	A	E	DP	TC/G	FA	G by Pos
1991	MON N	4	.143	.143	7	1	0	0	0	0.0	1	0	3	1	0	2	0	0	1	1	0	1.0	.500	OF-2

Joe Riggert

RIGGERT, JOSEPH ALOYSIUS BR TR 5′ 9½″ 170 lbs.
B. Dec. 11, 1886, Janesville, Wis. D. Dec. 10, 1973, Kansas City, Mo.

Year	Team	Games	BA	SA	AB	H	2B	3B	HR	HR%	R	RBI	BB	SO	SB	Pinch Hit AB	Pinch Hit H	PO	A	E	DP	TC/G	FA	G by Pos
1911	BOS A	50	.212	.336	146	31	4	4	2	1.4	19	13	12		5	8	3	63	2	5	1	1.8	.929	OF-38
1914	2 teams	BKN N (27G –.193)	STL N (34G –.213)																					
″	total	61	.203	.331	172	35	6	5	2	1.2	15	14	9	34	6	8	0	78	6	3	1	1.7	.966	OF-50
1919	BOS N	63	.283	.408	240	68	8	5	4	1.7	34	17	25	30	9	0	0	165	6	9	2	3.0	.950	OF-61
3 yrs.		174	.240	.366	558	134	18	14	8	1.4	68	44	46	64	20	16	3	306	14	17	4	2.3	.950	OF-149

Lew Riggs

RIGGS, LEWIS SIDNEY BL TR 6′ 175 lbs.
B. Apr. 22, 1910, Mebane, N. C. D. Aug. 12, 1975, Durham, N. C.

Year	Team	Games	BA	SA	AB	H	2B	3B	HR	HR%	R	RBI	BB	SO	SB	Pinch Hit AB	Pinch Hit H	PO	A	E	DP	TC/G	FA	G by Pos
1934	STL N	2	.000	.000	1	0	0	0	0	0.0	0	0	0	1	0	1	0	0	0	0	0	0.0	—	
1935	CIN N	142	.278	.385	532	148	26	8	5	0.9	73	46	43	32	8	2	0	132	269	31	21	3.2	.928	3B-135
1936		141	.257	.372	538	138	20	12	6	1.1	69	57	38	33	5	1	1	122	267	13	19	2.9	.968	3B-140
1937		122	.242	.359	384	93	17	5	6	1.6	43	45	24	17	4	17	4	112	226	21	16	3.4	.942	3B-100, 2B-4, SS-1
1938		142	.252	.352	531	134	21	13	2	0.4	53	55	40	28	3	2	0	146	280	24	18	3.2	.947	3B-142
1939		22	.158	.184	38	6	1	0	0	0.0	5	1	5	4	1	6	1	6	16	1	1	2.1	.957	3B-11
1940		41	.292	.458	72	21	7	1	1	1.4	8	9	2	4	0	27	8	10	23	2	2	3.2	.943	3B-11
1941	BKN N	77	.305	.487	197	60	13	4	5	2.5	27	36	16	12	1	29	**10**	55	78	10	6	3.2	.930	3B-43, 2B-1, 1B-1
1942		70	.278	.356	180	50	5	0	3	1.7	20	22	13	9	0	21	8	37	65	6	7	2.3	.944	3B-46, 1B-1
1946		1	.000	.000	4	0	0	0	0	0.0	0	0	0	0	0	0	0	2	2	0	0	4.0	1.000	3B-1
10 yrs.		760	.262	.375	2477	650	110	43	28	1.1	298	271	181	140	22	106	32	622	1226	108	90	3.1	.945	3B-629, 2B-5, 1B-2, SS-1
WORLD SERIES																								
1940	CIN N	3	.000	.000	3	0	0	0	0	0.0	1	0	0	2	0	3	0	0	0	0	0	0.0	—	
1941	BKN N	3	.250	.250	8	2	0	0	0	0.0	0	1	1	1	0	1	1	1	5	0	1	3.0	1.000	3B-2
2 yrs.		6	.182	.182	11	2	0	0	0	0.0	1	1	1	3	0	4	1	1	5	0	1	3.0	1.000	3B-2

Bill Rigney

RIGNEY, WILLIAM JOSEPH (Specs, The Cricket) BR TR 6′ 1″ 178 lbs.
B. Jan. 29, 1918, Alameda, Calif.
Manager 1956–72, 1976.

Year	Team	Games	BA	SA	AB	H	2B	3B	HR	HR%	R	RBI	BB	SO	SB	Pinch Hit AB	Pinch Hit H	PO	A	E	DP	TC/G	FA	G by Pos
1946	NY N	110	.236	.292	360	85	9	1	3	0.8	38	31	36	29	9	3	0	130	224	17	22	3.5	.954	3B-73, SS-33
1947		130	.267	.420	531	142	24	3	17	3.2	84	59	51	54	7	1	1	264	358	25	56	4.7	.961	2B-72, 3B-41, SS-24
1948		113	.264	.389	424	112	17	3	10	2.4	72	43	47	54	4	2	0	265	287	20	49	5.1	.965	2B-105, SS-7
1949		122	.278	.404	389	108	19	6	6	1.5	53	47	47	38	3	4	0	185	317	32	46	4.4	.940	SS-81, 2B-26, 3B-14
1950		56	.181	.205	83	15	2	0	0	0.0	8	8	8	13	0	20	3	44	47	3	10	2.8	.968	2B-23, 3B-11
1951		44	.232	.435	69	16	2	0	4	5.8	9	9	8	7	0	16	4	25	39	3	10	3.2	.955	3B-12, 2B-9
1952		60	.300	.411	90	27	5	1	1	1.1	15	14	11	6	2	31	10	32	37	6	9	3.1	.920	3B-10, 2B-9, SS-4, 1B-1
1953		19	.250	.250	20	5	0	0	0	0.0	2	1	0	5	0	15	3	5	1	0	0	2.0	1.000	3B-2, 2B-1
8 yrs.		654	.259	.376	1966	510	78	14	41	2.1	281	212	208	206	25	92	21	950	1310	106	202	4.2	.955	2B-245, 3B-163, SS-149, 1B-1
WORLD SERIES																								
1951	NY N	4	.250	.250	4	1	0	0	0	0.0	0	1	0	1	0	4	1	0	0	0	0	0.0	—	

Topper Rigney

RIGNEY, EMORY ELMO BR TR 5′ 9″ 150 lbs.
B. Jan. 7, 1897, Groveton, Tex. D. June 6, 1972, San Antonio, Tex.

Year	Team	Games	BA	SA	AB	H	2B	3B	HR	HR%	R	RBI	BB	SO	SB	Pinch Hit AB	Pinch Hit H	PO	A	E	DP	TC/G	FA	G by Pos
1922	DET A	155	.300	.369	536	161	17	7	2	0.4	68	63	68	44	17	0	0	262	493	50	74	5.2	.938	SS-155
1923		129	.315	.419	470	148	24	11	1	0.2	63	74	55	35	7	0	0	209	383	35	46	4.9	.944	SS-129
1924		147	.289	.407	499	144	29	9	4	0.8	81	93	102	39	11	1	0	273	463	25	72	5.2	.967	SS-146
1925		62	.247	.349	146	36	5	2	2	1.4	21	18	21	15	2	6	0	56	95	10	8	2.9	.938	SS-51, 3B-4
1926	BOS A	148	.270	.377	525	142	32	6	4	0.8	71	53	108	31	6	2	0	286	492	25	80	5.5	.969	SS-146
1927	2 teams	BOS A (8G –.111)	WAS A (45G –.273)																					
″	total	53	.253	.347	150	38	6	4	0	0.0	20	13	23	12	1	10	4	77	107	13	24	4.6	.934	SS-33, 3B-10
6 yrs.		694	.288	.387	2326	669	113	39	13	0.6	324	314	377	176	44	19	4	1163	2033	158	304	5.0	.953	SS-660, 3B-14

Cully Rikard

RIKARD, CULLY BL TR 6′ 183 lbs.
B. May 9, 1914, Oxford, Miss.

Year	Team	Games	BA	SA	AB	H	2B	3B	HR	HR%	R	RBI	BB	SO	SB	Pinch Hit AB	Pinch Hit H	PO	A	E	DP	TC/G	FA	G by Pos
1941	PIT N	6	.200	.250	20	4	1	0	0	0.0	1	0	1	1	0	1	0	18	0	0	0	3.6	1.000	OF-5
1942		38	.192	.269	52	10	2	1	0	0.0	6	5	7	8	0	15	4	23	0	1	0	1.5	.958	OF-16
1947		109	.287	.398	324	93	16	4	4	1.2	57	32	50	39	1	29	6	177	2	4	0	2.3	.978	OF-79
3 yrs.		153	.270	.374	396	107	19	5	4	1.0	64	37	58	48	1	45	10	218	2	5	0	2.3	.978	OF-100

Ernest Riles

RILES, ERNEST BL TR 6′ 1″ 180 lbs.
B. Oct. 2, 1960, Cairo, Ga.

Year	Team	Games	BA	SA	AB	H	2B	3B	HR	HR%	R	RBI	BB	SO	SB	Pinch Hit AB	Pinch Hit H	PO	A	E	DP	TC/G	FA	G by Pos
1985	MIL A	116	.286	.377	448	128	12	7	5	1.1	54	45	36	54	2	1	0	183	310	22	62	4.4	.957	SS-115, DH-1
1986		145	.252	.357	524	132	24	2	9	1.7	69	47	54	80	7	4	0	212	327	20	76	3.9	.964	SS-142
1987		83	.261	.351	276	72	11	1	4	1.4	38	38	30	47	3	4	0	76	152	13	25	2.8	.946	3B-65, SS-21
1988	2 teams	MIL A (41G –.252)	SF N (79G –.294)																					
″	total	120	.277	.376	314	87	13	3	4	1.3	33	37	17	59	3	26	6	82	197	7	25	2.7	.976	3B-58, SS-25, 2B-17, DH-5
1989	SF N	122	.278	.404	302	84	13	2	7	2.3	43	40	28	50	0	38	9	69	144	9	16	2.0	.959	3B-83, 2B-18, SS-7, OF-5
1990		92	.200	.381	155	31	2	1	8	5.2	22	21	26	26	0	42	12	53	105	3	14	2.7	.981	SS-26, 2B-24, 3B-10
1991	OAK A	108	.214	.324	281	60	8	4	5	1.8	30	32	31	42	3	27	4	113	143	11	26	2.6	.959	3B-69, SS-20, 2B-7, 1B-5
1992	HOU N	39	.262	.328	61	16	1	0	1	1.6	5	4	2	11	1	20	4	29	15	1	2	2.6	.978	SS-6, 3B-5, 1B-4, 2B-2
1993	BOS A	94	.189	.350	143	27	8	0	5	3.5	15	20	20	40	1	**47**	8	26	53	0	8	1.7	1.000	2B-20, DH-15, 3B-11, 1B-1
9 yrs.		919	.254	.365	2504	637	92	20	48	1.9	309	284	244	409	20	209	43	843	1446	86	254	3.0	.964	SS-362, 3B-301, 2B-88, DH-21, 1B-10, OF-5

Ernest Riles *continued*

Year	Team	Lg	Games	BA	SA	AB	H	2B	3B	HR	HR%	R	RBI	BB	SO	SB	Pinch Hit AB	Pinch Hit H	PO	A	E	DP	TC/G	FA	G by Pos
LEAGUE CHAMPIONSHIP SERIES																									
1989	**SF**	**N**	1	.000	.000	1	0	0	0	0	0.0	0	0	0	0	0	1	0	0	0	0	0	0.0	—	
WORLD SERIES																									
1989	**SF**	**N**	4	.000	.000	8	0	0	0	0	0.0	0	0	0	1	0	1	0	0	0	0	0	0.0	.000	DH-2

Billy Riley

RILEY, WILLIAM JAMES (Pigtail Billy) BR TR 5′10″ 160 lbs.
B. 1855, Cincinnati, Ohio D. Nov. 9, 1887, Cincinnati, Ohio.

Year	Team	Lg	Games	BA	SA	AB	H	2B	3B	HR	HR%	R	RBI	BB	SO	SB	Pinch Hit AB	Pinch Hit H	PO	A	E	DP	TC/G	FA	G by Pos
1879	**CLE**	**N**	44	.145	.158	165	24	2	0	0	0.0	14	9	2	26		0	0	90	12	19	1	2.7	.843	OF-43, 1B-1, C-1

Jim Riley

RILEY, JAMES NORMAN BL TR 5′10½″ 185 lbs.
B. May 25, 1895, Bayfield, N. B., Canada D. May 25, 1969, Seguin, Tex.

Year	Team	Lg	Games	BA	SA	AB	H	2B	3B	HR	HR%	R	RBI	BB	SO	SB	Pinch Hit AB	Pinch Hit H	PO	A	E	DP	TC/G	FA	G by Pos
1921	**STL**	**A**	4	.000	.000	11	0	0	0	0	0.0	0	0	1	3	0	0	0	4	5	2	0	2.8	.818	2B-4
1923	**WAS**	**A**	2	.000	.000	3	0	0	0	0	0.0	1	0	2	0	0	0	0	15	0	2	2	8.5	.882	1B-2
2 yrs.			6	.000	.000	14	0	0	0	0	0.0	1	0	3	3	0	0	0	19	5	4	2	4.7	.857	2B-4, 1B-2

Jimmy Riley

RILEY, JAMES JOSEPH BR TR 6′ 165 lbs.
B. Nov. 10, 1886, Buffalo, N. Y. D. Mar. 25, 1949, Buffalo, N. Y.

Year	Team	Lg	Games	BA	SA	AB	H	2B	3B	HR	HR%	R	RBI	BB	SO	SB	Pinch Hit AB	Pinch Hit H	PO	A	E	DP	TC/G	FA	G by Pos
1910	**BOS**	**N**	1	.000	.000	1	0	0	0	0	0.0	0	0	1	1	0	0	0	3	0	2	0	5.0	.600	OF-1

Lee Riley

RILEY, LEON FRANCIS BL TR 6′ 1″ 185 lbs.
B. Aug. 20, 1906, Princeton, Neb. D. Sept. 13, 1970, Schenectady, N. Y.

Year	Team	Lg	Games	BA	SA	AB	H	2B	3B	HR	HR%	R	RBI	BB	SO	SB	Pinch Hit AB	Pinch Hit H	PO	A	E	DP	TC/G	FA	G by Pos
1944	**PHI**	**N**	4	.083	.167	12	1	1	0	0	0.0	1	1	0	0	0	1	0	2	0	0	0	0.7	1.000	OF-3

Frank Ringo

RINGO, FRANK C. BR 5′11″ 175 lbs.
B. Oct. 12, 1860, Parksville, Mo. D. Apr. 12, 1889, Kansas City, Mo.

Year	Team	Lg	Games	BA	SA	AB	H	2B	3B	HR	HR%	R	RBI	BB	SO	SB	Pinch Hit AB	Pinch Hit H	PO	A	E	DP	TC/G	FA	G by Pos
1883	**PHI**	**N**	60	.190	.244	221	42	10	1	0	0.0	24		6	34		0	0	197	98	64	9	5.7	.822	C-39, OF-11, SS-6, 3B-5, 2B-2
1884	**2 teams**		**PHI N** (26G –.132) **PHI AA** (2G –.000)																						
″	**total**		28	.124	.144	97	12	2	0	0	0.0	4		3	19		0	0	120	19	39	2	6.4	.781	C-28
1885	**2 teams**		**DET N** (17G –.246) **PIT AA** (3G –.182)																						
″	**total**		20	.237	.276	76	18	3	0	0	0.0	12	2	0	7		0	0	71	44	18	4	6.7	.865	C-11, 3B-8, OF-1
1886	**2 teams**		**PIT AA** (15G –.214) **KC N** (16G –.232)																						
″	**total**		31	.223	.339	112	25	9	2	0	0.0	9	7	6	10		0	0	148	38	19	8	6.6	.907	C-19, 1B-9, OF-2, 3B-1
4 yrs.			139	.192	.251	506	97	24	3	0	0.0	49	9	15	70		0	0	536	199	140	23	6.2	.840	C-97, OF-14, 3B-14, 1B-9, SS-6, 2B-2

Bob Rinker

RINKER, ROBERT JOHN BR TR 6′ 190 lbs.
B. Apr. 21, 1921, Audenried, Pa.

Year	Team	Lg	Games	BA	SA	AB	H	2B	3B	HR	HR%	R	RBI	BB	SO	SB	Pinch Hit AB	Pinch Hit H	PO	A	E	DP	TC/G	FA	G by Pos
1950	**PHI**	**A**	3	.333	.333	3	1	0	0	0	0.0	0	0	0	0	0	2	1	0	0	0	0	0.0	.000	C-1

Juan Rios

RIOS, JUAN ONOFRE BR TR 6′ 3″ 185 lbs.
Born Juan Onofre Velez (Rios).
B. July 14, 1942, Mayaguez, Puerto Rico.

Year	Team	Lg	Games	BA	SA	AB	H	2B	3B	HR	HR%	R	RBI	BB	SO	SB	Pinch Hit AB	Pinch Hit H	PO	A	E	DP	TC/G	FA	G by Pos
1969	**KC**	**A**	87	.224	.276	196	44	5	1	1	0.5	20	5	7	19	1	12	3	103	109	9	23	2.7	.959	2B-46, SS-32, 3B-4

Billy Ripken

RIPKEN, WILLIAM OLIVER BR TR 6′ 1″ 180 lbs.
Son of Cal Ripken. Brother of Cal Ripken.
B. Dec. 16, 1964, Havre de Grace, Md.

Year	Team	Lg	Games	BA	SA	AB	H	2B	3B	HR	HR%	R	RBI	BB	SO	SB	Pinch Hit AB	Pinch Hit H	PO	A	E	DP	TC/G	FA	G by Pos
1987	**BAL**	**A**	58	.308	.372	234	72	9	0	2	0.9	27	20	21	23	4	0	0	133	162	3	53	5.1	.990	2B-58
1988			150	.207	.258	512	106	18	1	2	0.4	52	34	33	63	8	0	0	310	440	12	110	5.0	.984	2B-149, 3B-2
1989			115	.239	.305	318	76	11	2	2	0.6	31	26	22	53	1	0	0	255	335	9	81	5.2	.985	2B-114, DH-1
1990			129	.291	.387	406	118	28	1	3	0.7	48	38	28	43	5	1	1	250	366	8	84	4.9	.987	2B-127
1991			104	.216	.261	287	62	11	1	0	0.0	24	14	15	31	0	0	0	201	284	7	75	4.8	.986	2B-103
1992			111	.230	.312	330	76	15	0	4	1.2	35	36	18	26	2	0	0	217	317	4	66	4.9	.993	2B-108, DH-2
1993	**TEX**	**A**	50	.189	.220	132	25	4	0	0	0.0	12	11	11	19	0	0	0	80	123	2	28	3.9	.990	2B-34, SS-18, 3B-1
1994			32	.309	.370	81	25	5	0	0	0.0	9	6	3	11	2	4	1	29	50	2	10	2.5	.975	3B-18, 2B-12, SS-2, 1B-1
1995	**CLE**	**A**	8	.412	.765	17	7	0	0	2	11.8	4	3	0	3	0	0	0	7	6	0	1	1.6	1.000	2B-7, 3B-1
9 yrs.			757	.245	.312	2317	567	101	5	15	0.6	242	188	151	272	22	5	2	1482	2083	47	508	4.8	.987	2B-712, 3B-22, SS-20, DH-3, 1B-1

Cal Ripken

RIPKEN, CALVIN EDWIN, JR. BR TR 6′ 4″ 200 lbs.
Brother of Billy Ripken. Son of Cal Ripken.
B. Aug. 24, 1960, Havre de Grace, Md.

Year	Team	Lg	Games	BA	SA	AB	H	2B	3B	HR	HR%	R	RBI	BB	SO	SB	Pinch Hit AB	Pinch Hit H	PO	A	E	DP	TC/G	FA	G by Pos
1981	**BAL**	**A**	23	.128	.128	39	5	0	0	0	0.0	1	0	1	8	0	4	0	13	30	3	6	2.6	.935	SS-12, 3B-6
1982			160	.264	.475	598	158	32	5	28	4.7	90	93	46	95	3	0	0	221	440	19	64	4.1	.972	SS-94, 3B-71
1983			162	.318	.517	**663**	**211**	**47**	2	27	4.1	**121**	102	58	97	0	0	0	272	534	25	113	5.1	.970	SS-162
1984			162	.304	.510	641	195	37	7	27	4.2	103	86	71	89	2	0	0	297	583	26	122	5.6	.971	SS-162
1985			161	.282	.469	642	181	32	5	26	4.0	116	110	67	68	2	0	0	286	474	26	123	4.9	.967	SS-161
1986			162	.282	.461	627	177	35	1	25	4.0	98	81	70	60	4	0	0	240	482	13	105	4.5	.982	SS-162
1987			162	.252	.436	624	157	28	3	27	4.3	97	98	81	77	3	0	0	240	480	20	103	4.6	.973	SS-162
1988			161	.264	.431	575	152	25	1	23	4.0	87	81	102	69	2	0	0	284	480	21	119	4.9	.973	SS-161
1989			162	.257	.401	646	166	30	0	21	3.3	80	93	57	72	3	0	0	276	531	8	119	5.0	.990	SS-162
1990			161	.250	.415	600	150	28	4	21	3.5	78	84	82	66	3	0	0	242	435	3	94	4.2	.996	SS-161
1991			162	.323	.566	650	210	46	5	34	5.2	99	114	53	46	6	0	0	267	528	11	114	5.0	.986	SS-162
1992			162	.251	.366	637	160	29	1	14	2.2	73	72	64	50	4	0	0	287	445	12	119	4.6	.984	SS-162
1993			162	.257	.420	**641**	165	26	3	24	3.7	87	90	65	58	1	0	0	226	495	17	101	4.6	.977	SS-162
1994			112	.315	.459	444	140	19	3	13	2.9	71	75	32	41	1	0	0	130	321	7	70	4.1	.985	SS-112
1995			144	.262	.422	550	144	33	2	17	3.1	71	88	52	59	0	0	0	205	409	7	99	4.3	.989	SS-144
15 yrs.			2218	.276	.453	8577	2371	447	42	327	3.8	1272	1267	901	955	34	4	0	3486	6667	218	1471	4.7	.979	SS-2141, 3B-77
LEAGUE CHAMPIONSHIP SERIES																									
1983	**BAL**	**A**	4	.400	.533	15	6	2	0	0	0.0	5	1	2	3	0	0	0	7	11	0	2	4.5	1.000	SS-4
WORLD SERIES																									
1983	**BAL**	**A**	5	.167	.167	18	3	0	0	0	0.0	2	1	3	4	0	0	0	6	14	0	3	4.0	1.000	SS-5

Jimmy Ripple

RIPPLE, JAMES ALBERT — B. Oct. 14, 1909, Export, Pa. D. July 16, 1959, Greensburg, Pa. — BL TR 5′10″ 170 lbs. BB 1936

Year	Team		Games	BA	SA	AB	H	2B	3B	HR	HR%	R	RBI	BB	SO	SB	Pinch Hit AB	Pinch Hit H	PO	A	E	DP	TC/G	FA	G by Pos
1936	NY	N	96	.305	.441	311	95	17	2	7	2.3	42	47	28	15	1	19	9	190	5	4	10	2.6	.980	OF-76
1937			121	.317	.420	426	135	23	3	5	1.2	70	66	29	20	3	11	4	193	6	4	1	1.8	.980	OF-111
1938			134	.261	.375	501	131	21	3	10	2.0	68	60	49	21	2	3	0	236	13	6	2	1.9	.976	OF-131
1939	2 teams	NY N (66G –.228) BKN N (28G –.330)																							
″	total		94	.275	.376	229	63	12	4	1	0.4	28	40	19	15	0	**38**	9	91	2	0	0	1.8	1.000	OF-51
1940	2 teams	BKN N (7G –.231) CIN N (32G –.307)																							
″	total		39	.298	.491	114	34	10	0	4	3.5	15	20	15	7	1	5	1	55	0	0	0	1.7	1.000	OF-33
1941	CIN	N	38	.216	.324	102	22	6	1	1	1.0	10	9	9	4	0	11	2	36	1	0	0	1.5	1.000	OF-25
1943	PHI	A	32	.238	.278	126	30	3	1	0	0.0	8	15	7	7	0	1	0	55	0	0	0	1.8	1.000	OF-31
7 yrs.			554	.282	.395	1809	510	92	14	28	1.5	241	257	156	89	7	88	25	856	27	14	13	2.0	.984	OF-458
WORLD SERIES																									
1936	NY	N	5	.333	.583	12	4	0	0	1	8.3	2	3	3	3	0	0	0	8	0	0	0	1.6	1.000	OF-5
1937			5	.294	.294	17	5	0	0	0	0.0	2	0	3	1	0	0	0	11	0	0	0	2.2	1.000	OF-5
1940	CIN	N	7	.333	.571	21	7	2	0	1	4.8	3	6	4	2	0	0	0	14	0	0	0	2.0	1.000	OF-7
3 yrs.			17	.320	.480	50	16	2	0	2	4.0	7	9	10	6	0	0	0	33	0	0	0	1.9	1.000	OF-17

Swede Risberg

RISBERG, CHARLES AUGUST — B. Oct. 13, 1894, San Francisco, Calif. D. Oct. 13, 1975, Red Bluff, Calif. — BR TR 6′ 165 lbs.

Year	Team		Games	BA	SA	AB	H	2B	3B	HR	HR%	R	RBI	BB	SO	SB	Pinch Hit AB	Pinch Hit H	PO	A	E	DP	TC/G	FA	G by Pos
1917	CHI	A	149	.203	.285	474	96	20	8	1	0.2	59	45	59	65	16	2	1	291	352	61	57	4.8	.913	SS-146
1918			82	.256	.333	273	70	12	3	1	0.4	36	27	23	32	5	4	1	168	160	21	27	4.6	.940	SS-30, 3B-24, 2B-12, 1B-7, OF-3
1919			119	.256	.345	414	106	19	6	2	0.5	48	38	35	38	19	0	0	379	291	34	49	5.9	.952	SS-97, 1B-22
1920			126	.266	.369	458	122	21	10	2	0.4	53	65	31	45	12	2	0	238	400	45	59	5.5	.934	SS-124
4 yrs.			476	.243	.332	1619	394	72	27	6	0.4	196	175	148	180	52	8	2	1076	1203	161	192	5.2	.934	SS-397, 1B-29, 3B-24, 2B-12, OF-3
WORLD SERIES																									
1917	CHI	A	2	.500	.500	2	1	0	0	0	0.0	0	1	0	0	0	2	1	0	0	0	0	0.0	—	
1919			8	.080	.160	25	2	0	1	0	0.0	3	0	5	3	1	0	0	23	30	4	6	7.1	.930	SS-8
2 yrs.			10	.111	.185	27	3	0	1	0	0.0	3	1	5	3	1	2	1	23	30	4	6	7.1	.930	SS-8

Pop Rising

RISING, PERCIVAL SUMNER — B. Jan. 2, 1872, Industry, Pa. D. Jan. 28, 1938, Rochester, Pa.

Year	Team		Games	BA	SA	AB	H	2B	3B	HR	HR%	R	RBI	BB	SO	SB	Pinch Hit AB	Pinch Hit H	PO	A	E	DP	TC/G	FA	G by Pos
1905	BOS	A	8	.111	.278	18	2	1	1	0	0.0	2	2	2		0	4	0	4	2	0	0	1.5	1.000	OF-3, 3B-1

Claude Ritchey

RITCHEY, CLAUDE CASSIUS (Little All Right) — B. Oct. 5, 1873, Emlenton, Pa. D. Nov. 8, 1951, Emlenton, Pa. — BB TR 5′ 6½″ 167 lbs.

Year	Team		Games	BA	SA	AB	H	2B	3B	HR	HR%	R	RBI	BB	SO	SB	Pinch Hit AB	Pinch Hit H	PO	A	E	DP	TC/G	FA	G by Pos
1897	CIN	N	101	.282	.341	337	95	12	4	0	0.0	58	41	42		11	0	0	192	229	50	24	4.7	.894	SS-70, OF-22, 2B-8
1898	LOU	N	151	.254	.314	551	140	10	4	5	0.9	65	51	46		19	0	0	402	440	58	62	6.0	.936	SS-80, 2B-71
1899			147	.300	.377	536	161	15	7	4	0.7	65	71	49		21	0	0	375	449	54	56	5.9	.938	2B-137, SS-11
1900	PIT	N	123	.292	.368	476	139	17	8	1	0.2	62	67	29		18	0	0	303	357	33	51	5.6	.952	2B-123
1901			140	.296	.354	540	160	20	4	1	0.2	66	74	47		15	0	0	340	396	46	54	5.6	.941	2B-139, SS-1
1902			115	.277	.328	405	112	13	1	2	0.5	54	55	53		10	0	0	275	341	22	48	5.5	.966	2B-114, OF-1
1903			138	.287	.381	506	145	28	10	0	0.0	66	59	55		15	0	0	281	460	30	45	5.6	.961	2B-137
1904			156	.263	.347	544	143	22	12	0	0.0	79	51	59		12	0	0	332	484	36	48	5.4	.958	2B-156, SS-2
1905			153	.255	.332	533	136	29	6	0	0.0	54	52	51		12	0	0	281	478	31	59	5.1	.961	2B-153, SS-2
1906			152	.269	.339	484	130	21	5	1	0.2	46	62	68		6	1	1	326	439	27	59	5.2	.966	2B-151
1907	BOS	N	144	.255	.317	499	127	17	4	2	0.4	45	51	50		8	0	0	340	460	24	55	5.7	.971	2B-144
1908			121	.273	.325	421	115	10	3	2	0.5	44	36	50		7	1	0	325	368	24	46	6.0	.967	2B-120
1909			30	.172	.184	87	15	1	0	0	0.0	4	3	8		1	4	1	65	52	5	10	4.9	.959	2B-25
13 yrs.			1671	.273	.342	5919	1618	215	68	18	0.3	708	673	607		155	6	2	3837	4953	440	617	5.5	.952	2B-1478, SS-166, OF-23
WORLD SERIES																									
1903	PIT	N	8	.111	.148	27	3	1	0	0	0.0	2	2	4	7	1	0	0	20	28	0	5	6.0	1.000	2B-8

Charles Ritter

RITTER, CHARLES J. — Deceased.

Year	Team		Games	BA	SA	AB	H	2B	3B	HR	HR%	R	RBI	BB	SO	SB	Pinch Hit AB	Pinch Hit H	PO	A	E	DP	TC/G	FA	G by Pos
1885	BUF	N	2	.167	.167	6	1	0	0	0	0.0	0	0	0	2		0	0	8	5	3	1	8.0	.813	2B-2

Floyd Ritter

RITTER, FLOYD ALEXANDER — B. June 1, 1870, Dorset, Ohio D. Feb. 7, 1943, Stevenson, Wash. — BR TR 5′ 8″ 155 lbs.

Year	Team		Games	BA	SA	AB	H	2B	3B	HR	HR%	R	RBI	BB	SO	SB	Pinch Hit AB	Pinch Hit H	PO	A	E	DP	TC/G	FA	G by Pos
1890	TOL	AA	1	.000	.000	3	0	0	0	0	0.0	0		0		0	0	0	4	3	2	0	9.0	.778	C-1

Lew Ritter

RITTER, LEWIS ELMER (Old Dog) — B. Sept. 7, 1875, Liverpool, Pa. D. May 27, 1952, Harrisburg, Pa. — BR TR 5′ 9″ 150 lbs.

Year	Team		Games	BA	SA	AB	H	2B	3B	HR	HR%	R	RBI	BB	SO	SB	Pinch Hit AB	Pinch Hit H	PO	A	E	DP	TC/G	FA	G by Pos
1902	BKN	N	16	.211	.246	57	12	2	0	0	0.0	5	2	1		2	0	0	91	18	3	2	7.0	.973	C-16
1903			78	.236	.317	259	61	9	6	0	0.0	26	37	19		9	2	1	309	80	25	6	5.4	.940	C-74, OF-2
1904			72	.248	.276	214	53	4	1	0	0.0	23	19	20		17	7	2	258	100	13	13	5.9	.965	C-57, 2B-5, 3B-1
1905			92	.219	.293	311	68	10	5	1	0.3	32	28	15		16	2	0	406	109	26	4	6.0	.952	C-84, OF-4, 3B-2
1906			73	.208	.239	226	47	1	3	0	0.0	22	15	16		6	6	1	257	68	10	5	5.0	.970	C-53, OF-9, 1B-3, 3B-2
1907			93	.203	.232	271	55	6	1	0	0.0	15	17	18		5	3	0	391	103	16	11	5.7	.969	C-89
1908			38	.192	.232	99	19	2	1	0	0.0	6	2	7		0	1	0	132	44	7	0	4.9	.962	C-37
7 yrs.			462	.219	.269	1437	315	34	17	1	0.1	129	120	96		55	21	4	1844	522	100	41	5.6	.959	C-410, OF-15, 2B-5, 3B-5, 1B-3

Ed Ritterson

RITTERSON, EDWARD WEST — B. Apr. 26, 1855, Philadelphia, Pa. D. July 28, 1917, Bucks County, Pa. — BR TR 5′ 8″

Year	Team		Games	BA	SA	AB	H	2B	3B	HR	HR%	R	RBI	BB	SO	SB	Pinch Hit AB	Pinch Hit H	PO	A	E	DP	TC/G	FA	G by Pos
1876	PHI	N	16	.250	.308	52	13	3	0	0	0.0	8	4	0	2		0	0	43	8	23	1	3.9	.689	C-14, OF-4, 3B-1

Jim Ritz

RITZ, JAMES L. — B. 1874, Pittsburgh, Pa. D. Nov. 10, 1896, Pittsburgh, Pa.

Year	Team		Games	BA	SA	AB	H	2B	3B	HR	HR%	R	RBI	BB	SO	SB	Pinch Hit AB	Pinch Hit H	PO	A	E	DP	TC/G	FA	G by Pos
1894	PIT	N	1	.000	.000	4	0	0	0	0	0.0	1	0	0	0	1	0	0	1	2	1	1	4.0	.750	3B-1

Bombo Rivera

RIVERA, JESUS MANUEL BR TR 5′10″ 187 lbs.
Born Jesus Manuel Rivera (Torres).
B. Aug. 2, 1952, Ponce, Puerto Rico.

Year	Team	Games	BA	SA	AB	H	2B	3B	HR	HR%	R	RBI	BB	SO	SB	Pinch Hit AB	Pinch Hit H	PO	A	E	DP	TC/G	FA	G by Pos
1975	**MON N**	5	.111	.111	9	1	0	0	0	0.0	1	0	2	3	0	1	0	8	0	1	0	1.8	.889	OF-5
1976		68	.276	.411	185	51	11	4	2	1.1	22	19	13	32	1	15	5	89	7	5	3	1.8	.950	OF-56
1978	**MIN A**	101	.271	.355	251	68	8	2	3	1.2	35	23	35	47	5	19	4	162	5	3	0	1.8	.982	OF-94, DH-1
1979		112	.281	.392	263	74	13	5	2	0.8	37	31	17	40	5	26	6	169	12	2	0	1.7	.989	OF-105, DH-2
1980		44	.221	.363	113	25	7	0	3	2.7	13	10	4	20	0	6	1	58	1	5	1	1.7	.922	OF-37, DH-1
1982	**KC A**	5	.100	.100	10	1	0	0	0	0.0	1	0	0	2	0	1	0	4	0	0	0	1.3	1.000	OF-3
6 yrs.		335	.265	.374	831	220	39	11	10	1.2	109	83	71	144	11	68	16	490	25	16	4	1.7	.970	OF-300, DH-4

German Rivera

RIVERA, GERMAN BR TR 6′ 2″ 170 lbs.
Born German Rivera (Diaz).
B. July 6, 1960, Santurce, Puerto Rico.

Year	Team	Games	BA	SA	AB	H	2B	3B	HR	HR%	R	RBI	BB	SO	SB	Pinch Hit AB	Pinch Hit H	PO	A	E	DP	TC/G	FA	G by Pos
1983	**LA N**	13	.353	.412	17	6	1	0	0	0.0	1	0	2	2	0	5	1	2	11	1	0	1.8	.929	3B-8
1984		94	.260	.357	227	59	12	2	2	0.9	20	17	21	30	1	5	1	55	167	15	12	2.6	.937	3B-90
1985	**HOU N**	13	.194	.306	36	7	2	1	0	0.0	3	2	4	8	0	3	0	7	25	2	3	3.1	.941	3B-11
3 yrs.		120	.257	.354	280	72	15	3	2	0.7	24	19	27	40	1	13	2	64	203	18	15	2.6	.937	3B-109

Jim Rivera

RIVERA, MANUEL JOSEPH (Jungle Jim) BL TL 6′ 196 lbs.
B. July 22, 1922, New York, N. Y.

Year	Team	Games	BA	SA	AB	H	2B	3B	HR	HR%	R	RBI	BB	SO	SB	Pinch Hit AB	Pinch Hit H	PO	A	E	DP	TC/G	FA	G by Pos
1952	**2 teams**	**STL A** (97G –.256) **CHI A** (53G –.249)																						
″	**total**	150	.253	.363	537	136	20	9	7	1.3	72	48	50	86	21	6	2	430	9	9	2	3.2	.980	OF-141
1953	**CHI A**	156	.259	.420	567	147	26	**16**	11	1.9	79	78	53	70	22	0	0	385	15	10	5	2.6	.976	OF-156
1954		145	.286	.431	490	140	16	8	13	2.7	62	61	49	68	18	3	0	255	5	11	0	1.9	.959	OF-143
1955		147	.264	.401	454	120	24	4	10	2.2	71	52	62	59	**25**	7	2	288	22	6	7	2.2	.981	OF-143
1956		139	.255	.395	491	125	23	5	12	2.4	76	66	49	75	20	9	2	271	9	7	4	2.1	.976	OF-134
1957		125	.256	.443	402	103	21	6	14	3.5	51	52	40	80	18	11	3	374	14	7	22	3.5	.982	OF-82, 1B-31
1958		116	.225	.380	276	62	8	4	9	3.3	37	35	24	49	21	9	0	153	7	1	3	1.6	.994	OF-99
1959		80	.220	.384	177	39	9	4	4	2.3	18	19	11	19	5	4	0	75	5	2	3	1.2	.976	OF-69
1960		48	.294	.471	17	5	0	0	1	5.9	17	1	3	3	4	2	0	16	0	0	0	0.7	1.000	OF-24
1961	**2 teams**	**CHI A** (1G –.000) **KC A** (64G –.241)																						
″	**total**	65	.241	.340	141	34	8	0	2	1.4	20	10	24	14	6	23	4	51	0	1	0	1.2	.981	OF-43
10 yrs.		1171	.256	.402	3552	911	155	56	83	2.3	503	422	365	523	160	74	13	2298	86	54	46	2.3	.978	OF-1034, 1B-31
WORLD SERIES																								
1959	**CHI A**	5	.000	.000	11	0	0	0	0	0.0	1	0	3	1	0	0	0	10	1	0	0	2.2	1.000	OF-5

Luis Rivera

RIVERA, LUIS ANTONIO BR TR 5′ 9″ 170 lbs.
Born Luis Antonio Rivera (Pedraza).
B. Jan. 3, 1964, Cidra, Puerto Rico.

Year	Team	Games	BA	SA	AB	H	2B	3B	HR	HR%	R	RBI	BB	SO	SB	Pinch Hit AB	Pinch Hit H	PO	A	E	DP	TC/G	FA	G by Pos
1986	**MON N**	55	.205	.283	166	34	11	1	0	0.0	20	13	17	33	1	2	0	64	119	9	24	3.5	.953	SS-55
1987		18	.156	.219	32	5	2	0	0	0.0	0	1	1	8	0	3	1	9	27	3	4	2.6	.923	SS-15
1988		123	.224	.318	371	83	17	3	4	1.1	35	30	24	69	3	8	2	160	301	18	69	4.1	.962	SS-116
1989	**BOS A**	93	.257	.362	323	83	17	1	5	1.5	35	29	20	60	2	1	0	127	240	16	59	4.2	.958	SS-90, 2B-1, DH-1
1990		118	.225	.344	346	78	20	0	7	2.0	38	45	25	58	4	2	1	187	310	18	69	4.4	.965	SS-112, 2B-3, 3B-1
1991		129	.258	.384	414	107	22	3	8	1.9	64	40	35	86	4	0	0	180	386	24	87	4.6	.959	SS-129
1992		102	.215	.260	288	62	11	1	0	0.0	17	29	26	56	4	6	0	120	287	14	57	4.3	.967	SS-93, 2B-1, 3B-1, OF-1, DH-1
1993		62	.208	.308	130	27	8	1	1	0.8	13	7	11	36	1	4	1	65	111	6	28	3.0	.967	SS-27, 2B-27, DH-5, 3B-2
1994	**NY N**	32	.279	.581	43	12	2	1	3	7.0	11	5	4	14	0	17	6	19	29	2	9	3.1	.960	SS-11, 2B-5
9 yrs.		732	.232	.335	2113	491	110	11	28	1.3	233	199	163	420	19	43	11	931	1810	110	406	4.1	.961	SS-648, 2B-37, DH-7, 3B-4, OF-1
LEAGUE CHAMPIONSHIP SERIES																								
1990	**BOS A**	4	.222	.333	9	2	1	0	0	0.0	1	0	0	2	0	0	0	6	16	1	3	5.8	.957	SS-4

Ruben Rivera

RIVERA, RUBEN BR TR 6′ 3″ 200 lbs.
Born Ruben Rivera (Moreno).
B. Nov. 14, 1973, Chorrera, Panama.

Year	Team	Games	BA	SA	AB	H	2B	3B	HR	HR%	R	RBI	BB	SO	SB	Pinch Hit AB	Pinch Hit H	PO	A	E	DP	TC/G	FA	G by Pos
1995	**NY A**	5	.000	.000	1	0	0	0	0	0.0	0	0	0	1	0	0	0	2	0	0	0	0.5	1.000	OF-4

Mickey Rivers

RIVERS, JOHN MILTON (Mick the Quick) BL TL 5′10″ 165 lbs.
B. Oct. 31, 1948, Miami, Fla.

Year	Team	Games	BA	SA	AB	H	2B	3B	HR	HR%	R	RBI	BB	SO	SB	Pinch Hit AB	Pinch Hit H	PO	A	E	DP	TC/G	FA	G by Pos
1970	**CAL A**	17	.320	.400	25	8	2	0	0	0.0	6	3	3	5	1	9	1	10	0	0	0	2.0	1.000	OF-5
1971		78	.265	.336	268	71	12	2	1	0.4	31	12	19	38	13	7	2	159	5	4	2	2.2	.976	OF-75
1972		58	.214	.277	159	34	6	2	0	0.0	18	7	8	26	4	7	2	105	0	2	0	2.2	.981	OF-48
1973		30	.349	.457	129	45	6	4	0	0.0	26	16	8	11	8	0	0	60	0	6	0	2.3	.909	OF-29
1974		118	.285	.393	466	133	19	**11**	3	0.6	69	31	39	47	30	1	0	309	9	2	3	2.8	.994	OF-116
1975		155	.284	.359	616	175	17	**13**	1	0.2	70	53	43	42	**70**	2	0	371	13	9	3	2.6	.977	OF-152, DH-1
1976	**NY A**	137	.312	.432	590	184	31	8	8	1.4	95	67	13	51	43	1	1	407	6	6	0	3.1	.986	OF-136
1977		138	.326	.439	565	184	18	5	12	2.1	79	69	18	45	22	4	0	380	11	7	1	2.9	.982	OF-136, DH-1
1978		141	.265	.397	559	148	25	8	11	2.0	78	48	29	51	25	3	2	384	8	8	2	2.9	.980	OF-138
1979	**2 teams**	**NY A** (74G –.287) **TEX A** (58G –.300)																						
″	**total**	132	.293	.424	533	156	27	8	9	1.7	72	50	22	39	10	6	2	300	8	7	1	2.5	.978	OF-126, DH-1
1980	**TEX A**	147	.333	.437	630	210	32	6	7	1.1	96	60	20	34	18	4	1	342	19	8	4	2.5	.978	OF-141, DH-4
1981		99	.286	.371	399	114	21	2	3	0.8	62	26	24	31	9	5	0	225	12	1	3	2.5	.996	OF-97
1982		19	.235	.324	68	16	1	1	1	1.5	6	4	0	7	0	3	1	0	0	0	0	0.0	.000	DH-16
1983		96	.285	.350	309	88	17	0	1	0.3	37	20	11	21	9	20	8	48	1	1	0	0.7	.980	DH-53, OF-23
1984		102	.300	.387	313	94	13	1	4	1.3	40	33	9	23	5	31	8	49	3	0	2	0.7	1.000	DH-48, OF-30
15 yrs.		1467	.295	.397	5629	1660	247	71	61	1.1	785	499	266	471	267	103	28	3149	95	61	21	2.4	.982	OF-1252, DH-124
LEAGUE CHAMPIONSHIP SERIES																								
1976	**NY A**	5	.348	.435	23	8	0	1	0	0.0	5	0	1	1	0	0	0	11	0	0	0	2.2	1.000	OF-5
1977		5	.391	.478	23	9	2	0	0	0.0	5	2	0	2	1	0	0	19	0	0	0	3.8	1.000	OF-5
1978		4	.455	.455	11	5	0	0	0	0.0	0	0	2	0	0	0	0	8	1	0	1	2.3	1.000	OF-4
3 yrs.		14	.386 **4th**	.456	57	22	2	1	0	0.0	10	2	3	3	1	0	0	38	1	0	1	2.8	1.000	OF-14

Mickey Rivers *continued*

Year	Team		Games	BA	SA	AB	H	2B	3B	HR	HR%	R	RBI	BB	SO	SB	Pinch Hit AB	Pinch Hit H	PO	A	E	DP	TC/G	FA	G by Pos
WORLD SERIES																									
1976	NY	A	4	.167	.167	18	3	0	0	0	0.0	1	0	1	2	1	0	0	14	0	0	0	3.5	1.000	OF-4
1977			6	.222	.296	27	6	2	0	0	0.0	1	1	0	2	1	0	0	24	1	0	0	4.2	1.000	OF-6
1978			5	.333	.333	18	6	0	0	0	0.0	2	1	0	2	1	1	0	7	0	0	0	1.8	1.000	OF-4
3 yrs.			15	.238	.270	63	15	2	0	0	0.0	4	2	1	6	3	1	0	45	1	0	0	3.3	1.000	OF-14

Johnny Rizzo

RIZZO, JOHN COSTA
B. July 30, 1912, Houston, Tex. D. Dec. 4, 1977, Houston, Tex.
BR TR 6′ 190 lbs.

Year	Team		Games	BA	SA	AB	H	2B	3B	HR	HR%	R	RBI	BB	SO	SB	Pinch Hit AB	Pinch Hit H	PO	A	E	DP	TC/G	FA	G by Pos
1938	PIT	N	143	.301	.514	555	167	31	9	23	4.1	97	111	54	61	1	1	0	284	5	15	1	2.2	.951	OF-140
1939			94	.261	.403	330	86	23	3	6	1.8	49	55	42	27	0	5	1	186	2	5	0	2.2	.974	OF-86
1940	3 teams		PIT N (9G –.179) CIN N (31G –.282) PHI N (103G –.292)																						
"	total		143	.283	.471	505	143	19	2	24	4.8	71	72	56	50	3	6	1	290	38	14	6	2.5	.959	OF-128, 3B-7
1941	PHI	N	99	.217	.323	235	51	9	2	4	1.7	20	24	24	34	1	30	5	115	10	6	2	2.0	.954	OF-62, 3B-2
1942	BKN	N	78	.230	.323	217	50	8	0	4	1.8	31	27	24	25	2	6	0	124	6	3	1	1.9	.977	OF-70
5 yrs.			557	.270	.435	1842	497	90	16	61	3.3	268	289	200	197	7	48	7	999	61	43	10	2.2	.961	OF-486, 3B-9

Phil Rizzuto

RIZZUTO, PHILIP FRANCIS (Scooter)
Born Fiero Francis Rizzuto.
B. Sept. 25, 1917, New York, N. Y.
Hall of Fame 1994.
BR TR 5′ 6″ 150 lbs.

Year	Team		Games	BA	SA	AB	H	2B	3B	HR	HR%	R	RBI	BB	SO	SB	Pinch Hit AB	Pinch Hit H	PO	A	E	DP	TC/G	FA	G by Pos
1941	NY	A	133	.307	.398	515	158	20	9	3	0.6	65	46	27	36	14	3	0	252	399	29	109	5.3	.957	SS-128
1942			144	.284	.374	553	157	24	7	4	0.7	79	68	44	40	22	0	0	324	445	30	114	5.5	.962	SS-144
1946			126	.257	.310	471	121	17	1	2	0.4	53	38	34	39	14	0	0	267	378	26	97	5.4	.961	SS-125
1947			153	.273	.364	549	150	26	9	2	0.4	78	60	57	31	11	1	1	340	450	25	111	5.4	.969	SS-151
1948			128	.252	.328	464	117	13	2	6	1.3	65	50	60	24	6	0	0	259	348	17	85	4.9	.973	SS-128
1949			153	.275	.358	614	169	22	7	5	0.8	110	64	72	34	18	0	0	329	440	23	118	5.2	.971	SS-152
1950			155	.324	.439	617	200	36	7	7	1.1	125	66	92	38	12	0	0	301	452	14	123	4.9	.982	SS-155
1951			144	.274	.346	540	148	21	6	2	0.4	87	43	58	27	18	0	0	317	407	24	113	5.2	.968	SS-144
1952			152	.254	.341	578	147	24	10	2	0.3	89	43	67	42	17	0	0	308	458	19	116	5.2	.976	SS-152
1953			134	.271	.351	413	112	21	3	2	0.5	54	54	71	39	4	0	0	214	409	24	100	4.9	.963	SS-133
1954			127	.195	.251	307	60	11	0	2	0.7	47	15	41	23	3	1	1	185	294	16	84	3.9	.968	SS-126, 2B-1
1955			81	.259	.322	143	37	4	1	1	0.7	19	9	22	18	7	0	0	93	132	10	30	2.9	.957	SS-79, 2B-1
1956			31	.231	.231	52	12	0	0	0	0.0	6	6	6	6	3	0	0	31	54	6	17	3.0	.934	SS-30
13 yrs.			1661	.273	.355	5816	1588	239	62	38	0.7	877	562	651	397	149	5	2	3220	4666	263	1217	4.9	.968	SS-1647, 2B-2
WORLD SERIES																									
1941	NY	A	5	.111	.111	18	2	0	0	0	0.0	0	0	3	1	1	0	0	12	18	1	6	6.2	.968	SS-5
1942			5	.381	.524	21	8	0	0	1	4.8	2	1	2	1	2	0	0	15	14	1	1	6.0	.967	SS-5
1947			7	.308	.346	26	8	1	0	0	0.0	3	2	4	0	2	0	0	19	15	0	3	4.9	1.000	SS-7
1949			5	.167	.167	18	3	0	0	0	0.0	2	1	3	1	1	0	0	5	15	0	3	4.0	1.000	SS-5
1950			4	.143	.143	14	2	0	0	0	0.0	1	0	3	0	1	0	0	5	8	0	2	3.3	1.000	SS-4
1951			6	.320	.440	25	8	0	0	1	4.0	5	3	2	3	0	0	0	15	24	1	9	6.7	.975	SS-6
1952			7	.148	.185	27	4	1	0	0	0.0	2	0	5	2	0	0	0	13	17	1	4	4.4	.968	SS-7
1953			6	.316	.368	19	6	1	0	0	0.0	4	0	3	2	1	0	0	11	19	1	4	5.2	.968	SS-6
1955			7	.267	.267	15	4	0	0	0	0.0	2	1	5	1	2	0	0	13	14	0	1	3.9	1.000	SS-7
9 yrs.			52	.246	.295	183	45	3	0	2	1.1	21	8	30	11	10	0	0	108	144	5	33	4.9	.981	SS-52
			6th			**7th**	**7th**					**10th**		**4th**		**3rd**									

Mel Roach

ROACH, MELVIN EARL
B. Jan. 25, 1933, Richmond, Va.
BR TR 6′ 1″ 190 lbs.

Year	Team		Games	BA	SA	AB	H	2B	3B	HR	HR%	R	RBI	BB	SO	SB	Pinch Hit AB	Pinch Hit H	PO	A	E	DP	TC/G	FA	G by Pos
1953	MIL	N	5	.000	.000	2	0	0	0	0	0.0	1	0	0	1	0	1	0	0	0	0	0	0.0	.000	2B-1
1954			3	.000	.000	4	0	0	0	0	0.0	0	0	0	1	0	2	0	3	0	0	2	3.0	1.000	1B-1
1957			7	.167	.167	6	1	0	0	0	0.0	1	0	0	3	0	3	0	4	3	0	0	1.4	1.000	2B-5
1958			44	.309	.426	136	42	7	0	3	2.2	14	10	6	15	0	12	3	65	82	3	13	4.3	.980	2B-27, OF-7, 1B-1
1959			19	.097	.097	31	3	0	0	0	0.0	1	0	2	4	0	5	0	12	16	5	2	2.5	.848	2B-8, OF-4, 3B-1
1960			48	.300	.450	140	42	12	0	3	2.1	12	18	6	19	0	10	3	70	29	4	5	2.4	.961	OF-21, 2B-20, 3B-1, 1B-1
1961	2 teams		MIL N (13G –.167) CHI N (23G –.128)																						
"	total		36	.147	.213	75	11	2	0	1	1.3	4	7	5	13	1	13	3	83	8	2	8	3.7	.978	OF-9, 1B-9, 2B-7
1962	PHI	N	65	.190	.229	105	20	4	0	0	0.0	9	8	5	19	0	28	4	42	36	3	5	1.9	.963	3B-26, 2B-9, 1B-4, OF-3
8 yrs.			227	.238	.331	499	119	25	0	7	1.4	42	43	24	75	1	74	13	279	174	17	35	2.8	.964	2B-77, OF-44, 3B-28, 1B-16

Mike Roach

ROACH, MICHAEL STEPHEN
B. Dec. 23, 1873, New York, N. Y. D. Nov. 12, 1916, New York, N. Y.

Year	Team		Games	BA	SA	AB	H	2B	3B	HR	HR%	R	RBI	BB	SO	SB	Pinch Hit AB	Pinch Hit H	PO	A	E	DP	TC/G	FA	G by Pos
1899	WAS	N	24	.218	.231	78	17	1	0	0	0.0	7	7	3		3	2	1	82	17	4	3	4.5	.961	C-20, 1B-3

Roxy Roach

ROACH, WILBUR CHARLES
B. Nov. 28, 1882, Anita, Pa. D. Dec. 25, 1947, Bay City, Mich.
BR TR 5′11″ 160 lbs.

Year	Team		Games	BA	SA	AB	H	2B	3B	HR	HR%	R	RBI	BB	SO	SB	Pinch Hit AB	Pinch Hit H	PO	A	E	DP	TC/G	FA	G by Pos
1910	NY	A	70	.214	.273	220	47	9	2	0	0.0	27	20	29		15	3	0	120	173	28	27	4.8	.913	SS-58, OF-9
1911			13	.250	.350	40	10	2	1	0	0.0	4	2	6		0	0	0	26	37	8	5	5.5	.887	SS-8, 2B-5
1912	WAS	A	2	.500	2.000	2	1	0	0	1	50.0	1	1	0		0	0	0	0	1	1	0	1.0	.500	SS-2
1915	BUF	F	92	.269	.361	346	93	20	3	2	0.6	35	31	17		11	0	0	212	297	22	38	5.8	.959	SS-92
4 yrs.			177	.248	.334	608	151	31	6	3	0.5	67	54	52		26	3	0	358	508	59	70	5.3	.936	SS-160, OF-9, 2B-5

Mike Roarke

ROARKE, MICHAEL THOMAS
B. Nov. 8, 1930, West Warwick, R. I.
BR TR 6′ 2″ 195 lbs.

Year	Team		Games	BA	SA	AB	H	2B	3B	HR	HR%	R	RBI	BB	SO	SB	Pinch Hit AB	Pinch Hit H	PO	A	E	DP	TC/G	FA	G by Pos
1961	DET	A	86	.223	.284	229	51	6	1	2	0.9	21	22	20	31	0	1	0	383	22	5	5	4.8	.988	C-85
1962			56	.213	.346	136	29	4	1	4	2.9	11	14	13	17	0	3	1	247	24	5	1	5.2	.982	C-53
1963			23	.318	.318	44	14	0	0	0	0.0	5	1	2	3	0	7	1	67	5	1	1	4.6	.986	C-16
1964			29	.232	.244	82	19	1	0	0	0.0	4	7	10	10	0	2	1	165	11	1	0	6.6	.994	C-27
4 yrs.			194	.230	.297	491	113	11	2	6	1.2	41	44	45	61	0	13	3	862	62	12	7	5.2	.987	C-181

Fred Roat

ROAT, FREDERICK R. TR
B. Nov. 10, 1867, Oregon, Ill. D. Sept. 24, 1913, Oregon, Ill.

Year	Team	Games	BA	SA	AB	H	2B	3B	HR	HR%	R	RBI	BB	SO	SB	Pinch Hit AB	Pinch Hit H	PO	A	E	DP	TC/G	FA	G by Pos
1890	PIT N	57	.223	.260	215	48	2	0	2	0.9	18	17	16	22	7	0	0	154	102	35	12	5.1	.880	3B-44, 1B-9, OF-4
1892	CHI N	8	.194	.258	31	6	0	1	0	0.0	4	2	2	3	2	0	0	11	24	4	1	4.9	.897	2B-8
2 yrs.		65	.220	.260	246	54	2	1	2	0.8	22	19	18	25	9	0	0	165	126	39	13	5.1	.882	3B-44, 1B-9, 2B-8, OF-4

Tommy Robello

ROBELLO, THOMAS VARDASCO (Tony) BR TR 5′10½″ 175 lbs.
B. Feb. 9, 1913, San Leandro, Calif. D. Dec. 25, 1994, Fort Worth, Tex.

Year	Team	Games	BA	SA	AB	H	2B	3B	HR	HR%	R	RBI	BB	SO	SB	Pinch Hit AB	Pinch Hit H	PO	A	E	DP	TC/G	FA	G by Pos
1933	CIN N	14	.233	.333	30	7	3	0	0	0.0	1	3	1	5	0	1	0	15	27	2	3	3.4	.955	2B-11, 3B-2
1934		2	.000	.000	2	0	0	0	0	0.0	0	0	0	1	0	2	0	0	0	0	0	0.0	—	
2 yrs.		16	.219	.313	32	7	3	0	0	0.0	1	3	1	6	0	3	0	15	27	2	3	3.4	.955	2B-11, 3B-2

Skippy Roberge

ROBERGE, JOSEPH ALBERT ARMAND BR TR 5′11″ 185 lbs.
B. May 19, 1917, Lowell, Mass. D. June 7, 1993, Lowell, Mass.

Year	Team	Games	BA	SA	AB	H	2B	3B	HR	HR%	R	RBI	BB	SO	SB	Pinch Hit AB	Pinch Hit H	PO	A	E	DP	TC/G	FA	G by Pos
1941	BOS N	55	.216	.251	167	36	6	0	0	0.0	12	15	9	18	0	2	1	98	138	6	32	4.6	.975	2B-46, 3B-5, SS-2
1942		74	.215	.273	172	37	7	0	1	0.6	10	12	9	19	1	2	0	92	129	7	21	3.7	.969	2B-29, 3B-27, SS-6
1946		48	.231	.325	169	39	6	2	2	1.2	13	20	7	12	1	0	0	63	80	4	11	3.1	.973	3B-48
3 yrs.		177	.220	.283	508	112	19	2	3	0.6	35	47	25	49	2	4	1	253	347	17	64	3.8	.972	3B-80, 2B-75, SS-8

Kevin Roberson

ROBERSON, KEVIN LYNN BB TR 6′4″ 210 lbs.
B. Jan. 29, 1968, Decatur, Ill.

Year	Team	Games	BA	SA	AB	H	2B	3B	HR	HR%	R	RBI	BB	SO	SB	Pinch Hit AB	Pinch Hit H	PO	A	E	DP	TC/G	FA	G by Pos
1993	CHI N	62	.189	.372	180	34	4	1	9	5.0	23	27	12	48	0	14	2	77	2	3	0	1.6	.963	OF-51
1994		44	.218	.509	55	12	4	0	4	7.3	8	9	2	14	0	35	9	7	1	2	0	1.1	.800	OF-9
1995		32	.184	.526	38	7	1	0	4	10.5	5	6	6	14	0	20	4	8	0	0	0	0.7	1.000	OF-11
3 yrs.		138	.194	.421	273	53	9	1	17	6.2	36	42	20	76	0	69	15	92	3	5	0	1.4	.950	OF-71

Bip Roberts

ROBERTS, LEON JOSEPH BB TR 5′7″ 150 lbs.
B. Oct. 27, 1963, Berkeley, Calif.

Year	Team	Games	BA	SA	AB	H	2B	3B	HR	HR%	R	RBI	BB	SO	SB	Pinch Hit AB	Pinch Hit H	PO	A	E	DP	TC/G	FA	G by Pos
1986	SD N	101	.253	.303	241	61	5	2	1	0.4	34	12	14	29	14	3	1	166	172	10	33	4.0	.971	2B-87
1988		5	.333	.333	9	3	0	0	0	0.0	1	0	1	2	0	2	0	2	3	1	1	2.0	.833	3B-2, 2B-1
1989		117	.301	.422	329	99	15	8	3	0.9	81	25	49	45	21	17	6	134	113	9	17	2.2	.965	OF-54, 3B-37, SS-14, 2B-9
1990		149	.309	.433	556	172	36	3	9	1.6	104	44	55	65	46	5	0	227	160	13	22	2.5	.967	OF-75, 3B-56, SS-18, 2B-8
1991		117	.281	.347	424	119	13	3	3	0.7	66	32	37	71	26	7	1	239	185	10	35	3.8	.977	2B-68, OF-46
1992	CIN N	147	.323	.432	532	172	34	6	4	0.8	92	45	62	54	44	12	4	209	152	7	13	2.3	.981	OF-79, 2B-42, 3B-36
1993		83	.240	.295	292	70	13	0	1	0.3	46	18	38	46	26	3	0	152	176	6	31	4.2	.982	2B-64, OF-11, 3B-3, SS-1
1994	SD N	105	.320	.397	403	129	15	5	2	0.5	52	31	39	57	21	2	2	177	221	9	41	3.7	.978	2B-90, OF-20
1995		73	.304	.372	296	90	14	0	2	0.7	40	25	17	36	20	2	1	133	88	4	15	2.7	.982	OF-50, 2B-25, SS-7
9 yrs.		897	.297	.386	3082	915	145	27	25	0.8	516	232	312	405	218	53	15	1439	1270	69	208	3.1	.975	2B-394, OF-335, 3B-134, SS-40

Curt Roberts

ROBERTS, CURTIS BENJAMIN BR TR 5′8″ 165 lbs.
B. Aug. 16, 1929, Pineland, Tex. D. Nov. 14, 1969, Oakland, Calif.

Year	Team	Games	BA	SA	AB	H	2B	3B	HR	HR%	R	RBI	BB	SO	SB	Pinch Hit AB	Pinch Hit H	PO	A	E	DP	TC/G	FA	G by Pos
1954	PIT N	134	.232	.302	496	115	18	7	1	0.2	47	36	55	49	6	2	1	357	394	24	82	5.9	.969	2B-131
1955		6	.118	.176	17	2	1	0	0	0.0	1	0	2	1	0	0	0	7	14	2	4	3.8	.913	2B-6
1956		31	.177	.323	62	11	5	2	0	0.0	6	4	5	12	1	4	1	39	45	1	12	3.1	.988	2B-27
3 yrs.		171	.223	.301	575	128	24	9	1	0.2	54	40	62	62	7	6	2	403	453	27	98	5.4	.969	2B-164

Dave Roberts

ROBERTS, DAVID LEONARD BL TL 6′ 172 lbs.
B. June 30, 1933, Panama City, Panama.

Year	Team	Games	BA	SA	AB	H	2B	3B	HR	HR%	R	RBI	BB	SO	SB	Pinch Hit AB	Pinch Hit H	PO	A	E	DP	TC/G	FA	G by Pos
1962	HOU N	16	.245	.358	53	13	3	0	1	1.9	3	10	8	8	0	4	1	47	1	0	1	2.7	1.000	OF-12, 1B-6
1964		61	.184	.256	125	23	4	1	1	0.8	9	7	14	28	0	22	4	274	27	6	18	8.1	.980	1B-34, OF-4
1966	PIT N	14	.125	.188	16	2	1	0	0	0.0	3	0	0	7	0	9	2	17	2	1	2	10.0	.950	1B-2
3 yrs.		91	.196	.278	194	38	8	1	2	1.0	15	17	22	43	0	35	7	338	30	7	21	6.5	.981	1B-42, OF-16

Dave Roberts

ROBERTS, DAVID WAYNE BR TR 6′3″ 215 lbs.
B. Feb. 17, 1951, Lebanon, Ore.

Year	Team	Games	BA	SA	AB	H	2B	3B	HR	HR%	R	RBI	BB	SO	SB	Pinch Hit AB	Pinch Hit H	PO	A	E	DP	TC/G	FA	G by Pos
1972	SD N	100	.244	.321	418	102	17	0	5	1.2	38	33	18	64	7	0	0	92	198	21	27	2.9	.932	3B-84, 2B-20, SS-3, C-1
1973		127	.286	.472	479	137	20	3	21	4.4	56	64	17	83	11	8	1	92	276	24	31	3.2	.939	3B-111, 2B-12
1974		113	.167	.252	318	53	10	1	5	1.6	26	18	32	69	2	4	1	88	180	13	17	2.6	.954	3B-103, SS-3, OF-1
1975		33	.283	.354	113	32	2	0	2	1.8	7	12	13	19	3	0	0	37	68	8	7	3.2	.929	3B-30, 2B-5
1977		82	.220	.323	186	41	14	1	1	0.5	15	23	11	32	2	16	3	256	30	7	4	4.3	.976	C-63, 3B-2, 2B-2, SS-1
1978		54	.216	.309	97	21	4	1	1	1.0	7	7	12	25	0	4	0	150	14	3	0	3.3	.982	C-41, 1B-8, OF-2
1979	TEX A	44	.262	.417	84	22	2	1	3	3.6	12	14	7	17	1	4	2	82	30	1	10	2.6	.991	C-14, OF-11, 2B-8, 1B-6, DH-4, 3B-1
1980		101	.238	.383	235	56	4	0	10	4.3	27	30	13	38	0	13	4	138	100	11	11	2.4	.956	3B-37, SS-33, C-22, OF-5, 2B-4, 1B-4
1981	HOU N	27	.241	.352	54	13	3	0	1	1.9	4	5	3	6	1	11	2	88	16	5	7	5.2	.954	1B-10, 3B-7, 2B-3, C-1
1982	PHI N	28	.182	.212	33	6	1	0	0	0.0	2	2	2	8	0	2	0	23	20	3	4	1.6	.935	3B-11, C-10, 2B-7
10 yrs.		709	.239	.357	2017	483	77	7	49	2.4	194	208	128	361	27	62	13	1046	932	96	118	3.0	.954	3B-386, C-152, 2B-61, SS-40, 1B-28, OF-19, DH-4
DIVISIONAL PLAYOFF SERIES																								
1981	HOU N	1	.000	.000	1	0	0	0	0	0.0	0	0	0	1	0	1	0	0	0	0	0	0.0	—	

Leon Roberts

ROBERTS, LEON KAUFFMAN BR TR 6′3″ 200 lbs.
B. Jan. 22, 1951, Vicksburg, Mich.

Year	Team	Games	BA	SA	AB	H	2B	3B	HR	HR%	R	RBI	BB	SO	SB	Pinch Hit AB	Pinch Hit H	PO	A	E	DP	TC/G	FA	G by Pos
1974	DET A	17	.270	.381	63	17	3	2	0	0.0	5	7	3	10	0	1	0	25	0	2	0	1.6	.926	OF-17
1975		129	.257	.385	447	115	17	5	10	2.2	51	38	36	94	3	3	1	268	10	5	2	2.2	.982	OF-127, DH-1
1976	HOU N	87	.289	.443	235	68	11	2	7	3.0	31	33	19	43	1	27	7	99	1	2	0	1.7	.980	OF-60
1977		19	.074	.074	27	2	0	0	0	0.0	1	2	1	8	0	10	2	3	2	0	0	0.6	1.000	OF-9
1978	SEA A	134	.301	.515	472	142	21	7	22	4.7	78	92	41	52	6	8	4	296	10	8	4	2.4	.975	OF-128, DH-2
1979		140	.271	.451	450	122	24	6	15	3.3	61	54	56	64	3	12	4	286	6	5	2	2.2	.983	OF-136, DH-1
1980		119	.251	.396	374	94	18	3	10	2.7	48	33	43	59	8	12	2	238	6	4	1	2.3	.984	OF-104, DH-4
1981	TEX A	72	.279	.421	233	65	17	2	4	1.7	26	31	25	38	3	4	0	130	2	1	0	1.9	.992	OF-71

Leon Roberts *continued*

Year	Team	Games	BA	SA	AB	H	2B	3B	HR	HR%	R	RBI	BB	SO	SB	Pinch Hit AB	Pinch Hit H	PO	A	E	DP	TC/G	FA	G by Pos
1982	**2 teams**	**TEX A** (31G –.233) **TOR A** (40G –.229)																						
″	**total**	71	.230	.303	178	41	7	0	2	1.1	13	11	11	30	1	16	4	66	0	0	0	1.0	1.000	OF-44, DH-22
1983	**KC A**	84	.258	.404	213	55	7	0	8	3.8	24	24	17	27	1	13	4	139	3	3	0	1.9	.979	OF-76, DH-1
1984		29	.222	.289	45	10	1	1	0	0.0	4	3	4	3	0	13	3	24	0	0	0	1.2	1.000	OF-16, DH-3, P-1
11 yrs.		901	.267	.419	2737	731	126	28	78	2.8	342	328	256	428	26	119	31	1574	40	30	9	2.0	.982	OF-788, DH-34, P-1

Red Roberts

ROBERTS, CHARLES EMORY BR TR 6′ 170 lbs.
B. Aug. 8, 1918, Carrollton, Ga.

Year	Team	Games	BA	SA	AB	H	2B	3B	HR	HR%	R	RBI	BB	SO	SB	Pinch Hit AB	Pinch Hit H	PO	A	E	DP	TC/G	FA	G by Pos
1943	**WAS A**	9	.261	.435	23	6	1	0	1	4.3	1	3	4	2	0	1	0	8	9	5	1	3.1	.773	SS-6, 3B-1

Skipper Roberts

ROBERTS, CLARENCE ASHLEY BL TR 5′10½″ 175 lbs.
B. Jan. 11, 1888, Wardner, Ida. D. Dec. 24, 1963, Long Beach, Calif.

Year	Team	Games	BA	SA	AB	H	2B	3B	HR	HR%	R	RBI	BB	SO	SB	Pinch Hit AB	Pinch Hit H	PO	A	E	DP	TC/G	FA	G by Pos
1913	**STL N**	26	.146	.195	41	6	2	0	0	0.0	4	3	3	13	1	7	0	44	11	9	2	4.0	.859	C-16
1914	**2 teams**	**PIT F** (52G –.234) **CHI F** (4G –.333)																						
″	**total**	56	.237	.351	97	23	4	2	1	1.0	12	9	3		3	29	**8**	77	24	7	3	4.5	.935	C-23, OF-1
2 yrs.		82	.210	.304	138	29	6	2	1	0.7	16	12	6	13	4	36	8	121	35	16	5	4.3	.907	C-39, OF-1

Andre Robertson

ROBERTSON, ANDRE LEVETT BR TR 5′10″ 155 lbs.
B. Oct. 2, 1957, Orange, Tex.

Year	Team	Games	BA	SA	AB	H	2B	3B	HR	HR%	R	RBI	BB	SO	SB	Pinch Hit AB	Pinch Hit H	PO	A	E	DP	TC/G	FA	G by Pos
1981	**NY A**	10	.263	.316	19	5	1	0	0	0.0	1	0	0	3	1	0	0	9	24	0	3	3.0	1.000	SS-8, 2B-3
1982		44	.220	.314	118	26	5	0	2	1.7	16	9	8	19	0	3	0	84	98	6	27	4.3	.968	SS-27, 2B-15, 3B-2
1983		98	.248	.326	322	80	16	3	1	0.3	37	22	8	54	2	0	0	163	302	15	64	4.5	.969	SS-78, 2B-29
1984		52	.214	.264	140	30	5	1	0	0.0	10	6	4	20	0	0	0	68	142	16	36	4.1	.929	SS-49, 2B-6
1985		50	.328	.416	125	41	5	0	2	1.6	16	17	6	24	1	2	0	32	67	10	16	2.2	.908	3B-33, SS-14, 2B-2
5 yrs.		254	.251	.327	724	182	32	4	5	0.7	80	54	26	120	4	5	0	356	633	47	146	3.9	.955	SS-176, 2B-55, 3B-35
LEAGUE CHAMPIONSHIP SERIES																								
1981	**NY A**	1	.000	.000	1	0	0	0	0	0.0	0	0	0	0	0	0	0	2	1	0	1	3.0	1.000	SS-1
WORLD SERIES																								
1981	**NY A**	1	—	—	0	0	0	0	0	—	0	0	0	0	0	0	0	0	0	0	0	0.0	—	

Bob Robertson

ROBERTSON, ROBERT EUGENE BR TR 6′ 1″ 195 lbs.
B. Oct. 2, 1946, Frostburg, Md.

Year	Team	Games	BA	SA	AB	H	2B	3B	HR	HR%	R	RBI	BB	SO	SB	Pinch Hit AB	Pinch Hit H	PO	A	E	DP	TC/G	FA	G by Pos
1967	**PIT N**	9	.171	.343	35	6	0	0	2	5.7	4	4	3	12	0	0	0	91	5	1	9	10.8	.990	1B-9
1969		32	.208	.302	96	20	4	1	1	1.0	7	9	8	30	1	5	2	214	16	1	19	8.9	.996	1B-26
1970		117	.287	.564	390	112	19	4	27	6.9	69	82	51	98	4	8	2	915	81	8	108	9.4	.992	1B-99, 3B-5, OF-3
1971		131	.271	.484	469	127	18	2	26	5.5	65	72	60	101	1	5	0	1089	128	9	107	9.7	.993	1B-126
1972		115	.193	.346	306	59	11	0	12	3.9	25	41	41	84	1	4	0	543	82	7	59	5.1	.989	1B-89, OF-23, 3B-11
1973		119	.239	.385	397	95	16	0	14	3.5	43	40	55	77	0	10	1	957	79	5	91	9.7	.995	1B-107
1974		91	.229	.479	236	54	11	0	16	6.8	25	48	33	48	0	28	8	494	37	5	44	8.5	.991	1B-63
1975		75	.274	.452	124	34	4	0	6	4.8	17	18	23	25	0	40	6	209	18	1	10	8.4	.996	1B-27
1976		61	.217	.318	129	28	5	1	2	1.6	10	25	16	23	0	25	3	257	17	1	28	9.5	.996	1B-29
1978	**SEA A**	64	.230	.420	174	40	5	2	8	4.6	17	28	24	39	0	16	4	141	8	0	16	3.2	1.000	DH-29, 1B-18
1979	**TOR A**	15	.103	.207	29	3	0	0	1	3.4	1	1	3	9	0	3	0	54	7	0	6	4.7	1.000	1B-9, DH-4
11 yrs.		829	.242	.434	2385	578	93	10	115	4.8	283	368	317	546	7	144	26	4964	478	38	497	8.1	.993	1B-602, DH-33, OF-26, 3B-16
LEAGUE CHAMPIONSHIP SERIES																								
1970	**PIT N**	2	.200	.400	5	1	1	0	0	0.0	0	0	0	0	0	1	0	11	1	0	1	12.0	1.000	1B-1
1971		4	.438	1.250	16	7	1	0	4	25.0	5	6	0	2	0	0	0	25	2	0	3	6.8	1.000	1B-4
1972		4	—	—	0	0	0	0	0	—	0	0	1	0	0	0	0	2	1	0	0	0.8	1.000	1B-4
1974		1	.000	.000	5	0	0	0	0	0.0	1	0	0	0	0	0	0	11	0	0	0	11.0	1.000	1B-1
1975		3	.500	.500	2	1	0	0	0	0.0	0	1	1	0	0	2	1	1	0	0	0	1.0	1.000	1B-1
5 yrs.		14	.321	.821	28	9	2	0	4	14.3	6	7	2	2	0	3	1	50	4	0	4	4.9	1.000	1B-11
WORLD SERIES																								
1971	**PIT N**	7	.240	.480	25	6	0	0	2	8.0	4	5	4	8	0	0	0	64	4	1	5	9.9	.986	1B-7

Daryl Robertson

ROBERTSON, DARYL BERDINE BR TR 6′ 184 lbs.
B. Jan. 5, 1936, Cripple Creek, Colo.

Year	Team	Games	BA	SA	AB	H	2B	3B	HR	HR%	R	RBI	BB	SO	SB	Pinch Hit AB	Pinch Hit H	PO	A	E	DP	TC/G	FA	G by Pos
1962	**CHI N**	9	.105	.105	19	2	0	0	0	0.0	0	2	2	10	0	2	0	8	14	0	1	3.1	1.000	SS-6, 3B-1

Dave Robertson

ROBERTSON, DAVIS AYDELOTTE BL TL 6′ 186 lbs.
B. Sept. 25, 1889, Portsmouth, Va. D. Nov. 5, 1970, Virginia Beach, Va.

Year	Team	Games	BA	SA	AB	H	2B	3B	HR	HR%	R	RBI	BB	SO	SB	Pinch Hit AB	Pinch Hit H	PO	A	E	DP	TC/G	FA	G by Pos
1912	**NY N**	3	.500	.500	2	1	0	0	0	0.0	0	1	0	1	1	0	0	2	0	0	0	2.0	1.000	1B-1
1914		82	.266	.359	256	68	12	3	2	0.8	25	32	10	26	9	10	0	101	13	6	2	1.7	.950	OF-71
1915		138	.294	.379	544	160	17	10	3	0.6	72	58	22	52	22	3	0	225	13	11	4	1.8	.956	OF-138
1916		150	.307	.426	587	180	18	8	**12**	2.0	88	69	14	56	21	5	2	248	17	11	5	1.9	.960	OF-144
1917		142	.259	.391	532	138	16	9	**12**	2.3	64	54	10	47	17	1	1	266	12	17	1	2.1	.942	OF-140
1919	**2 teams**	**NY N** (1G –.000) **CHI N** (27G –.208)																						
″	**total**	28	.208	.260	96	20	2	0	1	1.0	8	10	1	10	3	2	0	53	2	4	0	2.4	.932	OF-25
1920	**CHI N**	134	.300	.462	500	150	29	11	10	2.0	68	75	40	44	17	0	0	230	10	8	1	1.9	.968	OF-134
1921	**2 teams**	**CHI N** (22G –.222) **PIT N** (60G –.322)																						
″	**total**	82	.308	.477	266	82	21	3	6	2.3	36	62	13	19	4	15	4	126	2	5	0	2.0	.962	OF-65
1922	**NY N**	42	.277	.383	47	13	2	0	1	2.1	5	3	3	7	0	30	7	9	1	1	1	1.4	.909	OF-8
9 yrs.		801	.287	.409	2830	812	117	44	47	1.7	366	364	113	262	94	66	14	1260	70	63	14	1.9	.955	OF-725, 1B-1
WORLD SERIES																								
1917	**NY N**	6	.500	.636	22	11	1	1	0	0.0	3	1	0	0	2	0	0	6	2	1	0	1.5	.889	OF-6

Don Robertson

ROBERTSON, DONALD ALEXANDER BL TL 5′10″ 180 lbs.
B. Oct. 15, 1930, Harvey, Ill.

Year	Team	Games	BA	SA	AB	H	2B	3B	HR	HR%	R	RBI	BB	SO	SB	Pinch Hit AB	Pinch Hit H	PO	A	E	DP	TC/G	FA	G by Pos
1954	**CHI N**	14	.000	.000	6	0	0	0	0	0.0	2	0	0	2	0	4	0	1	0	0	0	0.2	1.000	OF-6

Gene Robertson

ROBERTSON, EUGENE EDWARD BL TR 5′ 7″ 152 lbs.
B. Dec. 25, 1899, St. Louis, Mo. D. Oct. 21, 1981, Fallon, Nev.

Year	Team	Games	BA	SA	AB	H	2B	3B	HR	HR%	R	RBI	BB	SO	SB	Pinch Hit AB	Pinch Hit H	PO	A	E	DP	TC/G	FA	G by Pos
1919	STL A	5	.143	.143	7	1	0	0	0	0.0	1	0	1	2	0	2	0	2	1	1	0	2.0	.750	SS-2
1922		18	.296	.444	27	8	2	1	0	0.0	2	1	0	1	1	3	2	8	18	2	1	2.0	.929	3B-7, SS-6, 2B-1
1923		78	.247	.295	251	62	10	1	0	0.0	36	17	21	7	4	0	0	87	118	14	7	2.9	.936	3B-74, 2B-1
1924		121	.319	.421	439	140	25	4	4	0.9	70	52	35	14	3	5	2	114	207	14	22	3.0	.958	3B-110, 2B-2
1925		154	.271	.405	582	158	26	5	14	2.4	97	76	81	30	10	0	0	202	288	32	42	3.4	.939	3B-154, SS-1
1926		78	.251	.360	247	62	12	6	1	0.4	23	19	17	10	5	10	4	75	149	19	13	3.6	.922	3B-55, SS-10, 2B-3
1928	NY A	83	.291	.339	251	73	9	0	1	0.4	29	36	14	6	2	9	0	78	120	15	7	2.9	.930	3B-70, 2B-3
1929	2 teams	NY A (9G –.298) BOS N (8G –.286)																						
″	total	98	.297	.377	337	100	15	6	0	0.0	46	41	29	6	4	12	2	87	128	9	6	2.7	.960	3B-83, SS-1
1930	BOS N	21	.186	.203	59	11	1	0	0	0.0	7	7	5	3	0	2	0	15	22	2	3	2.3	.949	3B-17
9 yrs.		656	.280	.373	2200	615	100	23	20	0.9	311	249	203	79	29	43	10	668	1051	108	101	3.0	.941	3B-570, SS-20, 2B-10
WORLD SERIES																								
1928	NY A	3	.125	.125	8	1	0	0	0	0.0	1	2	1	0	0	1	0	1	1	1	0	1.0	.667	3B-3

Jim Robertson

ROBERTSON, ALFRED JAMES BR TR 5′ 9″ 183 lbs.
B. Jan. 29, 1928, Chicago, Ill.

Year	Team	Games	BA	SA	AB	H	2B	3B	HR	HR%	R	RBI	BB	SO	SB	Pinch Hit AB	Pinch Hit H	PO	A	E	DP	TC/G	FA	G by Pos
1954	PHI A	63	.184	.238	147	27	8	0	0	0.0	9	8	23	25	0	9	1	207	18	6	6	4.6	.974	C-50
1955	KC A	6	.250	.250	8	2	0	0	0	0.0	1	0	1	2	0	2	0	8	2	0	0	2.5	1.000	C-4
2 yrs.		69	.187	.239	155	29	8	0	0	0.0	10	8	24	27	0	11	1	215	20	6	6	4.5	.975	C-54

Sherry Robertson

ROBERTSON, SHERRARD ALEXANDER BL TR 6′ 180 lbs.
B. Jan. 1, 1919, Montreal, Que., Canada D. Oct. 23, 1970, Houghton, S. D.

Year	Team	Games	BA	SA	AB	H	2B	3B	HR	HR%	R	RBI	BB	SO	SB	Pinch Hit AB	Pinch Hit H	PO	A	E	DP	TC/G	FA	G by Pos
1940	WAS A	10	.212	.273	33	7	0	1	0	0.0	4	0	5	6	0	0	0	17	30	3	9	5.0	.940	SS-10
1941		1	.000	.000	3	0	0	0	0	0.0	0	0	0	3	0	0	0	1	2	1	0	4.0	.750	3B-1
1943		59	.217	.342	120	26	4	1	3	2.5	22	14	17	19	0	26	5	27	45	8	1	2.9	.900	3B-27, SS-1
1946		74	.200	.330	230	46	6	3	6	2.6	30	19	30	42	6	13	0	88	132	19	22	3.7	.921	3B-38, 2B-14, SS-12, OF-1
1947		95	.233	.301	266	62	9	3	1	0.4	25	23	32	52	4	23	3	144	27	8	2	2.6	.955	OF-55, 3B-10, 2B-4
1948		71	.246	.369	187	46	11	3	2	1.1	19	22	24	26	8	17	7	105	3	7	0	2.3	.939	OF-51
1949		110	.251	.401	374	94	17	3	11	2.9	59	42	42	35	10	9	2	185	253	25	43	4.5	.946	2B-71, 3B-19, OF-13
1950		71	.260	.382	123	32	3	3	2	1.6	19	16	22	18	1	32	7	49	28	4	5	3.0	.951	OF-14, 2B-12, 3B-1
1951		62	.189	.252	111	21	2	1	1	0.9	14	10	9	22	2	34	6	54	2	3	1	2.7	.949	OF-22
1952	2 teams	WAS A (1G –.000) PHI A (43G –.200)																						
″	total	44	.200	.250	60	12	3	0	0	0.0	8	5	21	15	1	19	5	26	12	2	2	2.4	.950	2B-8, OF-7, 3B-2
10 yrs.		597	.230	.342	1507	346	55	18	26	1.7	200	151	202	238	32	173	35	696	534	80	85	3.3	.939	OF-163, 2B-109, 3B-98, SS-23

Billy Jo Robidoux

ROBIDOUX, WILLIAM JOSEPH BL TR 6′ 1″ 200 lbs.
B. Jan. 13, 1964, Ware, Mass.

Year	Team	Games	BA	SA	AB	H	2B	3B	HR	HR%	R	RBI	BB	SO	SB	Pinch Hit AB	Pinch Hit H	PO	A	E	DP	TC/G	FA	G by Pos
1985	MIL A	18	.176	.392	51	9	2	0	3	5.9	5	8	12	16	0	4	0	64	6	0	6	3.9	1.000	OF-11, 1B-6, DH-1
1986		56	.227	.287	181	41	8	0	1	0.6	15	21	33	36	0	2	0	326	29	5	35	6.8	.986	1B-43, DH-10
1987		23	.194	.194	62	12	0	0	0	0.0	9	4	8	17	0	4	0	53	4	1	9	2.9	.983	1B-10, DH-10
1988		33	.253	.308	91	23	5	0	0	0.0	9	5	8	14	1	3	1	212	25	4	21	7.8	.983	1B-30, DH-1
1989	CHI A	16	.128	.179	39	5	2	0	0	0.0	2	1	4	9	0	1	0	93	7	1	17	6.3	.990	1B-15, OF-1
1990	BOS A	27	.182	.341	44	8	4	0	1	2.3	3	4	6	14	0	11	1	49	4	1	4	3.6	.981	1B-11, DH-4
6 yrs.		173	.209	.286	468	98	21	0	5	1.1	43	43	71	106	1	25	2	797	75	12	92	5.8	.986	1B-115, DH-26, OF-12

Aaron Robinson

ROBINSON, AARON ANDREW BL TR 6′ 2″ 205 lbs.
B. June 23, 1915, Lancaster, S. C. D. Mar. 9, 1966, Lancaster, S. C.

Year	Team	Games	BA	SA	AB	H	2B	3B	HR	HR%	R	RBI	BB	SO	SB	Pinch Hit AB	Pinch Hit H	PO	A	E	DP	TC/G	FA	G by Pos
1943	NY A	1	.000	.000	1	0	0	0	0	0.0	0	0	0	1	0	1	0	0	0	0	0	0.0	—	
1945		50	.281	.481	160	45	6	1	8	5.0	19	24	21	23	0	4	3	186	16	0	3	4.5	1.000	C-45
1946		100	.297	.506	330	98	17	2	16	4.8	32	64	48	39	0	4	1	410	50	8	5	4.9	.983	C-95
1947		82	.270	.413	252	68	11	5	5	2.0	23	36	40	26	0	7	1	346	38	1	3	5.2	.997	C-74
1948	CHI A	98	.252	.380	326	82	14	2	8	2.5	47	39	46	30	0	6	1	303	50	4	4	3.9	.989	C-92
1949	DET A	110	.269	.423	331	89	12	0	13	3.9	38	56	73	21	0	2	0	458	44	7	9	4.7	.986	C-108
1950		107	.226	.346	283	64	7	0	9	3.2	37	37	75	35	0	3	3	355	42	3	4	3.9	.993	C-103
1951	2 teams	DET A (36G –.207) BOS A (26G –.203)																						
″	total	62	.205	.301	156	32	7	1	2	1.3	12	16	34	19	0	2	1	201	31	2	3	3.9	.991	C-60
8 yrs.		610	.260	.412	1839	478	74	11	61	3.3	208	272	337	194	0	29	10	2259	271	25	31	4.4	.990	C-577
WORLD SERIES																								
1947	NY A	3	.200	.200	10	2	0	0	0	0.0	2	1	2	1	0	0	0	13	2	1	0	5.3	.938	C-3

Bill Robinson

ROBINSON, WILLIAM HENRY BR TR 6′ 2″ 189 lbs.
B. June 26, 1943, McKeesport, Pa.

Year	Team	Games	BA	SA	AB	H	2B	3B	HR	HR%	R	RBI	BB	SO	SB	Pinch Hit AB	Pinch Hit H	PO	A	E	DP	TC/G	FA	G by Pos
1966	ATL N	6	.273	.455	11	3	0	1	0	0.0	1	3	0	1	0	1	0	4	0	1	0	1.0	.800	OF-5
1967	NY A	116	.196	.281	342	67	6	1	7	2.0	31	29	28	56	2	15	0	169	10	6	1	1.8	.968	OF-102
1968		107	.240	.380	342	82	16	7	6	1.8	34	40	26	54	7	9	1	195	3	3	1	2.1	.985	OF-98
1969		87	.171	.279	222	38	11	2	3	1.4	23	21	16	39	3	29	4	103	5	4	0	1.8	.964	OF-62, 1B-1
1972	PHI N	82	.239	.426	188	45	9	1	8	4.3	19	21	5	30	2	9	1	109	2	2	1	1.6	.982	OF-72
1973		124	.288	.529	452	130	32	1	25	5.5	62	65	27	91	5	12	4	234	18	8	1	2.0	.969	OF-113, 3B-14
1974		100	.236	.346	280	66	14	1	5	1.8	32	29	17	61	5	19	5	162	8	5	0	2.0	.971	OF-87
1975	PIT N	92	.280	.450	200	56	12	2	6	3.0	26	33	11	36	3	33	5	107	3	1	1	1.9	.991	OF-57
1976		122	.303	.534	393	119	22	3	21	5.3	55	64	16	73	2	11	5	186	53	8	11	2.1	.968	OF-78, 3B-37, 1B-3
1977		137	.304	.525	507	154	32	1	26	5.1	74	104	25	92	12	8	0	758	59	13	63	5.7	.984	1B-86, OF-43, 3B-17
1978		136	.246	.411	499	123	36	2	14	2.8	70	80	35	105	14	0	0	268	51	8	8	2.1	.976	OF-127, 3B-29, 1B-3
1979		148	.264	.504	421	111	17	6	24	5.7	59	75	24	81	13	12	3	394	19	3	18	2.7	.993	OF-125, 1B-28, 3B-3
1980		100	.287	.463	272	78	10	1	12	4.4	28	36	15	45	1	16	5	427	22	7	30	5.1	.985	1B-49, OF-41
1981		39	.216	.318	88	19	3	0	2	2.3	8	8	5	18	1	15	1	148	10	2	9	5.2	.988	1B-23, OF-7, 3B-1
1982	2 teams	PIT N (31G –.239) PHI N (35G –.261)																						
″	total	66	.250	.464	140	35	9	0	7	5.0	14	31	12	34	1	26	5	69	4	1	5	1.6	.986	OF-41, 1B-5
1983	PHI N	10	.143	.143	7	1	0	0	0	0.0	0	2	1	4	0	7	1	3	0	1	0	0.7	.750	1B-3, 3B-2, OF-1
16 yrs.		1472	.258	.438	4364	1127	229	29	166	3.8	536	641	263	820	71	222	40	3336	267	73	149	2.7	.980	OF-1059, 1B-201, 3B-103

Bill Robinson *continued*

Year	Team	Games	BA	SA	AB	H	2B	3B	HR	HR%	R	RBI	BB	SO	SB	Pinch Hit AB	Pinch Hit H	PO	A	E	DP	TC/G	FA	G by Pos
LEAGUE CHAMPIONSHIP SERIES																								
1975	PIT N	2	.000	.000	2	0	0	0	0	0.0	0	0	0	1	0	2	0	0	0	0	0	0.0	—	
1979		3	.000	.000	3	0	0	0	0	0.0	0	0	0	0	0	0	0	3	0	0	0	1.0	1.000	OF-3
2 yrs.		5	.000	.000	5	0	0	0	0	0.0	0	0	0	1	0	2	0	3	0	0	0	1.0	1.000	OF-3
WORLD SERIES																								
1979	PIT N	7	.263	.316	19	5	1	0	0	0.0	2	2	0	4	0	1	1	11	1	0	0	2.0	1.000	OF-6

Brooks Robinson

ROBINSON, BROOKS CALBERT BR TR 6′ 1″ 180 lbs.
B. May 18, 1937, Little Rock, Ark.
Hall of Fame 1983.

Year	Team	Games	BA	SA	AB	H	2B	3B	HR	HR%	R	RBI	BB	SO	SB	Pinch Hit AB	Pinch Hit H	PO	A	E	DP	TC/G	FA	G by Pos
1955	BAL A	6	.091	.091	22	2	0	0	0	0.0	0	1	0	10	0	0	0	2	8	2	1	2.0	.833	3B-6
1956		15	.227	.386	44	10	4	0	1	2.3	5	1	1	5	0	1	0	9	25	2	3	2.4	.944	3B-14, 2B-1
1957		50	.239	.359	117	28	6	1	2	1.7	13	14	7	10	1	5	0	34	66	3	5	2.2	.971	3B-47
1958		145	.238	.305	463	110	16	3	3	0.6	31	32	31	51	1	4	1	157	283	22	32	3.0	.952	3B-140, 2B-16
1959		88	.284	.383	313	89	15	2	4	1.3	29	24	17	37	2	1	1	92	187	13	25	3.3	.955	3B-87, 2B-1
1960		152	.294	.440	595	175	27	9	14	2.4	74	88	35	49	2	0	0	174	330	12	35	3.3	.977	3B-152, 2B-3
1961		163	.287	.397	**668**	192	38	7	7	1.0	89	61	47	57	1	0	0	155	334	14	34	3.0	.972	3B-163, 2B-2, SS-1
1962		162	.303	.486	634	192	29	9	23	3.6	77	86	42	70	3	0	0	165	340	11	32	3.1	.979	3B-162, SS-3, 2B-2
1963		161	.251	.365	589	148	26	4	11	1.9	67	67	46	84	2	1	0	153	331	12	43	3.1	.976	3B-160, SS-1
1964		163	.317	.521	612	194	35	3	28	4.6	82	**118**	51	64	1	0	0	153	327	14	40	3.0	.972	3B-163
1965		144	.297	.445	559	166	25	2	18	3.2	81	80	47	47	3	1	1	144	296	15	36	3.2	.967	3B-143
1966		157	.269	.444	620	167	35	2	23	3.7	91	100	56	36	2	0	0	174	313	12	26	3.2	.976	3B-157
1967		158	.269	.434	610	164	25	5	22	3.6	88	77	54	54	1	0	0	147	405	11	37	3.6	.980	3B-158
1968		162	.253	.416	608	154	36	6	17	2.8	65	75	44	55	1	0	0	168	353	16	31	3.3	.970	3B-162
1969		156	.234	.395	598	140	21	3	23	3.8	73	84	56	55	2	0	0	163	370	13	37	3.5	.976	3B-156
1970		158	.276	.429	608	168	31	4	18	3.0	84	94	53	53	1	2	0	157	321	17	30	3.2	.966	3B-156
1971		156	.272	.413	589	160	21	1	20	3.4	67	92	63	50	0	0	0	131	354	16	35	3.2	.968	3B-156
1972		153	.250	.342	556	139	23	2	8	1.4	48	64	43	45	1	3	0	129	333	11	27	3.1	.977	3B-152
1973		155	.257	.344	549	141	17	2	9	1.6	53	72	55	50	2	1	0	129	354	15	25	3.2	.970	3B-154
1974		153	.288	.374	553	159	27	0	7	1.3	46	59	56	47	2	0	0	115	410	18	44	3.5	.967	3B-153
1975		144	.201	.274	482	97	15	1	6	1.2	50	53	44	33	0	2	0	96	326	9	30	3.0	.979	3B-143
1976		71	.211	.307	218	46	8	2	3	1.4	16	11	8	24	0	2	0	59	126	6	11	2.7	.969	3B-71
1977		24	.149	.255	47	7	2	0	1	2.1	3	4	4	4	0	8	1	6	28	0	2	2.3	1.000	3B-15
23 yrs.		2896 **9th**	.267	.401	10654 **9th**	2848	482	68	268	2.5	1232	1357	860	990	28	31	4	2712	6220	264	621	3.2	.971	3B-2870, 2B-25, SS-5
LEAGUE CHAMPIONSHIP SERIES																								
1969	BAL A	3	.500	.571	14	7	1	0	0	0.0	1	0	0	0	0	0	0	5	10	0	0	5.0	1.000	3B-3
1970		3	.583	.750	12	7	2	0	0	0.0	4	1	0	1	0	0	0	3	5	0	0	2.7	1.000	3B-3
1971		3	.364	.727	11	4	1	0	1	9.1	2	3	0	1	0	0	0	4	7	0	0	3.7	1.000	3B-3
1973		5	.250	.350	20	5	2	0	0	0.0	1	2	1	1	0	0	0	2	14	1	0	3.4	.941	3B-5
1974		4	.083	.333	12	1	0	0	1	8.3	1	1	1	0	0	0	0	4	13	0	1	4.3	1.000	3B-4
5 yrs.		18	.348 10th	.522	69	24	6 **7th**	0	2	2.9	9	7	2	3	0	0	0	18	49	1	1	3.8	.985	3B-18
WORLD SERIES																								
1966	BAL A	4	.214	.429	14	3	0	0	1	7.1	2	1	1	0	0	0	0	4	6	0	1	2.5	1.000	3B-4
1969		5	.053	.053	19	1	0	0	0	0.0	0	2	0	3	0	0	0	1	16	0	0	3.4	1.000	3B-5
1970		5	.429	.810	21	9	2	0	2	9.5	5	6	0	2	0	0	0	9	14	1	2	4.8	.958	3B-5
1971		7	.318	.318	22	7	0	0	0	0.0	2	5	3	1	0	0	0	6	17	2	1	3.6	.920	3B-7
4 yrs.		21	.263	.408	76	20	2	0	3	3.9	9	14	4	6	0	0	0	20	53	3	4	3.6	.961	3B-21

Bruce Robinson

ROBINSON, BRUCE PHILIP BL TR 6′ 1″ 185 lbs.
Brother of Dave Robinson.
B. Apr. 16, 1954, La Jolla, Calif.

Year	Team	Games	BA	SA	AB	H	2B	3B	HR	HR%	R	RBI	BB	SO	SB	Pinch Hit AB	Pinch Hit H	PO	A	E	DP	TC/G	FA	G by Pos
1978	OAK A	28	.250	.310	84	21	3	1	0	0.0	5	8	3	8	0	1	0	150	16	6	2	6.1	.965	C-28
1979	NY A	6	.167	.167	12	2	0	0	0	0.0	0	2	1	0	0	0	0	33	0	2	1	5.8	.943	C-6
1980		4	.000	.000	5	0	0	0	0	0.0	0	0	0	4	0	1	0	5	0	0	0	1.7	1.000	C-3
3 yrs.		38	.228	.277	101	23	3	1	0	0.0	5	10	4	12	0	2	0	188	16	8	3	5.7	.962	C-37

Charlie Robinson

ROBINSON, CHARLES HENRY BL TR
B. July 27, 1856, Westerly, R. I. D. May 18, 1913, Providence, R. I.

Year	Team	Games	BA	SA	AB	H	2B	3B	HR	HR%	R	RBI	BB	SO	SB	Pinch Hit AB	Pinch Hit H	PO	A	E	DP	TC/G	FA	G by Pos
1884	IND AA	20	.287	.313	80	23	2	0	0	0.0	11		3			0	0	98	31	5	3	6.4	.963	C-17, SS-3, OF-1
1885	BKN AA	11	.150	.250	40	6	2	1	0	0.0	5		3			0	0	47	16	12	1	6.8	.840	C-11
2 yrs.		31	.242	.292	120	29	4	1	0	0.0	16		6			0	0	145	47	17	4	6.5	.919	C-28, SS-3, OF-1

Craig Robinson

ROBINSON, CRAIG GEORGE BR TR 5′10″ 165 lbs.
B. Aug. 21, 1948, Abington, Pa.

Year	Team	Games	BA	SA	AB	H	2B	3B	HR	HR%	R	RBI	BB	SO	SB	Pinch Hit AB	Pinch Hit H	PO	A	E	DP	TC/G	FA	G by Pos
1972	PHI N	5	.200	.267	15	3	1	0	0	0.0	0	0	1	2	0	0	0	4	16	0	4	5.0	1.000	SS-4
1973		46	.226	.274	146	33	7	0	0	0.0	11	7	0	25	1	2	0	70	112	10	26	4.2	.948	SS-42, 2B-4
1974	ATL N	145	.230	.265	452	104	4	6	0	0.0	52	29	30	57	11	1	1	238	395	29	73	4.7	.956	SS-142
1975	**2 teams**	**ATL N** (11G –.059) **SF N** (29G –.069)																						
″	**total**	40	.065	.087	46	3	1	0	0	0.0	5	0	2	11	0	2	0	34	37	4	9	2.7	.947	SS-19, 2B-9
1976	**2 teams**	**SF N** (15G –.308) **ATL N** (15G –.235)																						
″	**total**	30	.267	.300	30	8	1	0	0	0.0	8	5	8	6	0	3	2	12	36	5	4	2.9	.906	2B-12, 3B-3, SS-3
1977	ATL N	27	.207	.241	29	6	1	0	0	0.0	4	1	1	6	0	4	0	26	27	0	6	2.3	1.000	SS-23
6 yrs.		293	.219	.256	718	157	15	6	0	0.0	80	42	42	107	12	12	3	384	623	48	122	4.0	.955	SS-233, 2B-25, 3B-3

Dave Robinson

ROBINSON, DAVID TANNER BB TL 6′ 1″ 186 lbs.
Brother of Bruce Robinson.
B. May 22, 1946, Minneapolis, Minn.

Year	Team	Games	BA	SA	AB	H	2B	3B	HR	HR%	R	RBI	BB	SO	SB	Pinch Hit AB	Pinch Hit H	PO	A	E	DP	TC/G	FA	G by Pos
1970	SD N	15	.316	.526	38	12	2	0	2	5.3	5	6	5	4	2	2	0	22	1	0	1	1.8	1.000	OF-13
1971		7	.000	.000	6	0	0	0	0	0.0	0	0	1	3	0	6	0	0	0	0	0	0.0	—	
2 yrs.		22	.273	.455	44	12	2	0	2	4.5	5	6	6	7	2	8	0	22	1	0	1	1.8	1.000	OF-13

Earl Robinson

ROBINSON, EARL JOHN — BR TR 6′ 1″ 190 lbs.
B. Nov. 3, 1936, New Orleans, La.

Year	Team	Games	BA	SA	AB	H	2B	3B	HR	HR%	R	RBI	BB	SO	SB	Pinch Hit AB	Pinch Hit H	PO	A	E	DP	TC/G	FA	G by Pos
1958	LA N	8	.200	.200	15	3	0	0	0	0.0	3	0	1	4	0	0	0	4	10	0	0	2.3	1.000	3B-6
1961	BAL A	96	.266	.455	222	59	12	3	8	3.6	37	30	31	54	4	20	5	136	6	4	3	1.8	.973	OF-82
1962		29	.286	.413	63	18	3	1	1	1.6	12	4	8	10	2	6	3	35	0	0	0	2.1	1.000	OF-17
1964		37	.273	.405	121	33	5	1	3	2.5	11	10	7	24	1	2	1	67	3	1	0	2.1	.986	OF-34
4 yrs.		170	.268	.425	421	113	20	5	12	2.9	63	44	47	92	7	28	9	242	19	5	3	1.9	.981	OF-133, 3B-6

Eddie Robinson

ROBINSON, WILLIAM EDWARD — BL TR 6′ 2½″ 210 lbs.
B. Dec. 15, 1920, Paris, Tex.

Year	Team	Games	BA	SA	AB	H	2B	3B	HR	HR%	R	RBI	BB	SO	SB	Pinch Hit AB	Pinch Hit H	PO	A	E	DP	TC/G	FA	G by Pos
1942	CLE A	8	.125	.125	8	1	0	0	0	0.0	1	2	1	0	0	6	1	7	0	0	0	7.0	1.000	1B-1
1946		8	.400	.733	30	12	1	0	3	10.0	6	4	2	4	0	0	0	71	1	1	4	10.4	.986	1B-7
1947		95	.245	.415	318	78	10	1	14	4.4	52	52	30	18	1	5	1	800	55	5	79	9.9	.994	1B-87
1948		134	.254	.408	493	125	18	5	16	3.2	53	83	36	42	1	4	1	1213	79	7	123	9.9	.995	1B-131
1949	WAS A	143	.294	.459	527	155	27	3	18	3.4	66	78	67	30	3	0	0	1299	100	18	133	9.9	.987	1B-143
1950	2 teams	WAS A (36G –.233) CHI A (119G –.314)																						
″	total	155	.295	.450	553	163	15	4	21	3.8	83	86	85	32	0	0	0	1300	82	14	141	9.0	.990	1B-155
1951	CHI A	151	.282	.495	564	159	23	5	29	5.1	85	117	77	54	2	2	0	1296	91	17	143	9.6	.988	1B-147
1952		155	.296	.466	594	176	33	1	22	3.7	79	104	70	49	2	0	0	1329	89	14	145	9.2	.990	1B-155
1953	PHI A	156	.247	.413	615	152	28	4	22	3.6	64	102	63	56	1	1	0	1366	71	17	135	9.4	.988	1B-155
1954	NY A	85	.261	.387	142	37	9	0	3	2.1	11	27	19	21	0	**49**	**15**	227	19	5	21	8.7	.980	1B-29
1955		88	.208	.491	173	36	1	0	16	9.2	25	42	36	26	0	34	5	390	20	2	35	9.0	.995	1B-46
1956	2 teams	NY A (26G –.222) KC A (75G –.198)																						
″	total	101	.204	.332	226	46	6	1	7	3.1	20	23	31	23	0	34	6	481	25	9	56	8.4	.983	1B-61
1957	3 teams	DET A (13G –.000) CLE A (19G –.222) BAL A (4G –.000)																						
″	total	36	.154	.256	39	6	1	0	1	2.6	1	3	4	4	0	21	1	44	4	0	3	6.0	1.000	1B-8
13 yrs.		1315	.268	.440	4282	1146	172	24	172	4.0	546	723	521	359	10	156	30	9823	636	109	1018	9.4	.990	1B-1125
WORLD SERIES																								
1948	CLE A	6	.300	.300	20	6	0	0	0	0.0	0	1	1	0	0	0	0	60	7	0	8	11.2	1.000	1B-6
1955	NY A	4	.667	.667	3	2	0	0	0	0.0	0	1	2	1	0	1	1	6	0	0	2	6.0	1.000	1B-1
2 yrs.		10	.348	.348	23	8	0	0	0	0.0	0	2	3	1	0	1	1	66	7	0	10	10.4	1.000	1B-7

Floyd Robinson

ROBINSON, FLOYD ANDREW — BL TR 5′ 9″ 175 lbs.
B. May 9, 1936, Prescott, Ark.

Year	Team	Games	BA	SA	AB	H	2B	3B	HR	HR%	R	RBI	BB	SO	SB	Pinch Hit AB	Pinch Hit H	PO	A	E	DP	TC/G	FA	G by Pos
1960	CHI A	22	.283	.283	46	13	0	0	0	0.0	7	1	11	8	2	4	0	24	0	1	0	1.5	.960	OF-17
1961		132	.310	.465	432	134	20	7	11	2.5	69	59	52	32	7	23	6	218	7	2	0	2.1	.991	OF-106
1962		156	.312	.475	600	187	**45**	10	11	1.8	89	109	72	47	4	1	0	278	13	8	2	1.9	.973	OF-155
1963		146	.283	.419	527	149	21	6	13	2.5	71	71	62	43	4	9	2	245	8	4	4	1.9	.984	OF-137
1964		141	.301	.408	525	158	17	3	11	2.1	83	59	70	41	9	6	2	225	5	3	0	1.7	.987	OF-138
1965		156	.265	.385	577	153	15	6	14	2.4	70	66	76	51	4	9	2	254	6	4	0	1.7	.985	OF-153
1966		127	.237	.325	342	81	11	2	5	1.5	44	35	44	32	8	17	0	148	2	6	0	1.4	.962	OF-113
1967	CIN N	55	.238	.338	130	31	6	2	1	0.8	19	10	14	14	3	15	2	53	0	1	0	1.4	.981	OF-39
1968	2 teams	OAK A (53G –.247) BOS A (24G –.125)																						
″	total	77	.219	.295	105	23	5	0	1	1.0	6	16	7	14	1	42	9	25	1	1	0	0.9	.963	OF-29
9 yrs.		1012	.283	.409	3284	929	140	36	67	2.0	458	426	408	282	42	126	23	1470	42	30	6	1.7	.981	OF-887

Frank Robinson

ROBINSON, FRANK — BR TR 6′ 1″ 183 lbs.
B. Aug. 31, 1935, Beaumont, Tex.
Manager 1975–77, 1981–84, 1988–91.
Hall of Fame 1982.

Year	Team	Games	BA	SA	AB	H	2B	3B	HR	HR%	R	RBI	BB	SO	SB	Pinch Hit AB	Pinch Hit H	PO	A	E	DP	TC/G	FA	G by Pos
1956	CIN N	152	.290	.558	572	166	27	6	38	6.6	**122**	83	64	95	8	0	0	323	5	8	1	2.2	.976	OF-152
1957		150	.322	.529	611	197	29	5	29	4.7	97	75	44	92	10	0	0	487	36	6	19	3.3	.989	OF-136, 1B-24
1958		148	.269	.504	554	149	25	6	31	5.6	90	83	62	80	10	5	0	314	24	6	1	2.3	.983	OF-138, 3B-11
1959		146	.311	.583	540	168	31	4	36	6.7	106	125	69	93	18	0	0	1049	78	18	111	6.9	.984	1B-125, OF-40
1960		139	.297	**.595**	464	138	33	6	31	6.7	86	83	82	67	13	10	5	775	62	10	61	6.5	.988	1B-78, OF-51, 3B-1
1961		153	.323	**.611**	545	176	32	7	37	6.8	117	124	71	64	22	4	2	284	15	3	3	2.0	.990	OF-150, 3B-1
1962		162	.342	**.624**	609	208	**51**	2	39	6.4	**134**	136	76	62	18	0	0	315	10	2	2	2.0	.994	OF-161
1963		140	.259	.442	482	125	19	3	21	4.4	79	91	81	69	26	2	2	238	13	4	1	1.8	.984	OF-139, 1B-1
1964		156	.306	.548	568	174	38	6	29	5.1	103	96	79	67	23	0	0	279	7	4	3	1.9	.986	OF-156
1965		156	.296	.540	582	172	33	5	33	5.7	109	113	70	100	13	1	1	282	5	3	1	1.9	.990	OF-155
1966	BAL A	155	**.316**	**.637**	576	182	34	2	**49**	**8.5**	**122**	**122**	87	90	8	1	1	282	6	5	3	1.9	.983	OF-151, 1B-3
1967		129	.311	.576	479	149	23	7	30	6.3	83	94	71	84	2	0	0	207	8	2	3	1.7	.991	OF-126, 1B-2
1968		130	.268	.444	421	113	27	1	15	3.6	69	52	73	84	11	12	4	193	5	7	0	1.7	.966	OF-117, 1B-3
1969		148	.308	.540	539	166	19	5	32	5.9	111	100	88	62	9	3	2	367	19	5	18	2.6	.987	OF-134, 1B-19
1970		132	.306	.520	471	144	24	1	25	5.3	88	78	69	70	2	6	3	262	11	4	6	2.2	.986	OF-120, 1B-7
1971		133	.281	.510	455	128	16	2	28	6.2	82	99	72	62	3	8	0	449	20	11	25	3.7	.977	OF-92, 1B-37
1972	LA N	103	.251	.442	342	86	6	1	19	5.6	41	59	55	76	2	5	0	168	6	6	2	1.9	.967	OF-95
1973	CAL A	147	.266	.489	534	142	29	0	30	5.6	85	97	82	93	1	2	1	38	3	1	1	0.3	.976	DH-127, OF-17
1974	2 teams	CAL A (129G –.251) CLE A (15G –.200)																						
″	total	144	.245	.453	477	117	27	3	22	4.6	81	68	85	95	5	6	0	23	0	1	1	0.2	.958	DH-134, 1B-4, OF-1
1975	CLE A	49	.237	.508	118	28	5	0	9	7.6	19	24	29	15	0	6	2	0	0	0	0	0.0	.000	DH-42
1976		36	.224	.358	67	15	0	0	3	4.5	5	10	11	12	0	16	5	11	0	0	1	0.5	1.000	DH-18, 1B-2, OF-1
21 yrs.		2808	.294	.537	10006	2943	528	72	586	5.9	1829	1812	1420	1532	204	87	28	6346	333	106	263	2.4	.984	OF-2132, DH-321, 1B-305, 3B-13
									4th		**10th**													
LEAGUE CHAMPIONSHIP SERIES																								
1969	BAL A	3	.333	.750	12	4	2	0	1	8.3	1	2	3	3	0	0	0	2	0	1	0	1.0	.667	OF-3
1970		3	.200	.500	10	2	0	0	1	10.0	3	2	5	2	0	0	0	2	0	0	0	0.7	1.000	OF-3
1971		3	.083	.167	12	1	1	0	0	0.0	2	1	1	4	0	0	0	7	0	0	0	2.3	1.000	OF-3
3 yrs.		9	.206	.471	34	7	3	0	2	5.9	6	5	9	9	0	0	0	11	0	1	0	1.3	.917	OF-9
WORLD SERIES																								
1961	CIN N	5	.200	.533	15	3	2	0	1	6.7	3	4	3	4	0	0	0	5	0	0	0	1.0	1.000	OF-5
1966	BAL A	4	.286	.857	14	4	0	1	2	14.3	4	3	2	3	0	0	0	6	0	0	0	1.5	1.000	OF-4
1969		5	.188	.375	16	3	0	0	1	6.3	2	1	4	3	0	0	0	13	0	0	0	2.6	1.000	OF-5

Frank Robinson *continued*

Year	Team	Games	BA	SA	AB	H	2B	3B	HR	HR%	R	RBI	BB	SO	SB	Pinch Hit AB	Pinch Hit H	PO	A	E	DP	TC/G	FA	G by Pos
1970		5	.273	.545	22	6	0	0	2	9.1	5	4	0	5	0	0	0	7	0	0	0	1.4	1.000	OF-5
1971		7	.280	.520	25	7	0	0	2	8.0	5	2	2	8	0	0	0	12	0	0	0	1.7	1.000	OF-7
5 yrs.		26	.250	.554	92	23	2	1	8	8.7	19	14	11	23	0	0	0	43	0	0	0	1.7	1.000	OF-26
									7th	**4th**				**10th**										

Fred Robinson

ROBINSON, FREDERIC HENRY BR TR
Brother of Wilbert Robinson.
B. July 6, 1856, South Acton, Mass. D. Dec. 18, 1933, Hudson, Mass.

Year	Team	Games	BA	SA	AB	H	2B	3B	HR	HR%	R	RBI	BB	SO	SB	Pinch Hit AB	Pinch Hit H	PO	A	E	DP	TC/G	FA	G by Pos
1884	CIN U	3	.231	.231	13	3	0	0	0	0.0	1		0			0	0	2	6	3	0	3.7	.727	2B-3

Jack Robinson

ROBINSON, JOHN W. TR
B. July 15, 1880, Portland, Me. D. July 22, 1921, Macon, Ga.

Year	Team	Games	BA	SA	AB	H	2B	3B	HR	HR%	R	RBI	BB	SO	SB	Pinch Hit AB	Pinch Hit H	PO	A	E	DP	TC/G	FA	G by Pos
1902	NY N	4	.000	.000	9	0	0	0	0	0.0	0	0	0		0	1	0	13	3	0	0	5.3	1.000	C-3

Jackie Robinson

ROBINSON, JOHN ROOSEVELT BR TR 5′11½″ 195 lbs.
B. Jan. 31, 1919, Cairo, Ga. D. Oct. 24, 1972, Stamford, Conn.
Hall of Fame 1962.

Year	Team	Games	BA	SA	AB	H	2B	3B	HR	HR%	R	RBI	BB	SO	SB	Pinch Hit AB	Pinch Hit H	PO	A	E	DP	TC/G	FA	G by Pos
1947	BKN N	151	.297	.427	590	175	31	5	12	2.0	125	48	74	36	**29**	0	0	1323	92	16	144	9.5	.989	1B-151
1948		147	.296	.453	574	170	38	8	12	2.1	108	85	57	37	22	2	1	514	342	15	97	5.7	.983	2B-116, 1B-30, 3B-6
1949		156	**.342**	.528	593	203	38	12	16	2.7	122	124	86	27	**37**	0	0	395	421	16	119	5.3	.981	2B-156
1950		144	.328	.500	518	170	39	4	14	2.7	99	81	80	24	12	2	1	359	390	11	133	5.3	.986	2B-144
1951		153	.338	.527	548	185	33	7	19	3.5	106	88	79	27	25	3	1	390	435	7	137	5.4	.992	2B-153
1952		149	.308	.465	510	157	17	3	19	3.7	104	75	106	40	24	2	0	353	400	20	113	5.3	.974	2B-146
1953		136	.329	.502	484	159	34	7	12	2.5	109	95	74	30	17	5	1	238	126	6	25	2.7	.984	OF-76, 3B-44, 2B-9, 1B-6, SS-1
1954		124	.311	.505	386	120	22	4	15	3.9	62	59	63	20	7	7	1	166	109	7	6	2.4	.975	OF-64, 3B-50, 2B-4
1955		105	.256	.363	317	81	6	2	8	2.5	51	36	61	18	12	9	1	100	183	10	19	3.1	.966	3B-84, OF-10, 2B-1, 1B-1
1956		117	.275	.412	357	98	15	2	10	2.8	61	43	60	32	12	10	1	169	230	9	37	3.9	.978	3B-72, 2B-22, 1B-9, OF-2
10 yrs.		1382	.311	.474	4877	1518	273	54	137	2.8	947	734	740	291	197	40	7	4007	2728	117	830	5.0	.983	2B-751, 3B-256, 1B-197, OF-152, SS-1
WORLD SERIES																								
1947	BKN N	7	.259	.333	27	7	2	0	0	0.0	3	3	2	4	2	0	0	49	6	0	8	7.9	1.000	1B-7
1949		5	.188	.250	16	3	1	0	0	0.0	2	2	4	2	0	0	0	12	9	1	1	4.4	.955	2B-5
1952		7	.174	.304	23	4	0	0	1	4.3	4	2	7	5	2	0	0	10	20	0	4	4.3	1.000	2B-7
1953		6	.320	.400	25	8	2	0	0	0.0	3	2	1	0	1	0	0	8	0	0	0	1.3	1.000	OF-6
1955		6	.182	.318	22	4	1	1	0	0.0	5	1	2	1	1	0	0	4	18	2	3	4.0	.917	3B-6
1956		7	.250	.417	24	6	1	0	1	4.2	5	2	5	2	0	0	0	5	12	0	1	2.4	1.000	3B-7
6 yrs.		38	.234	.343	137	32	7	1	2	1.5	22	12	21	14	6	0	0	88	65	3	17	4.1	.981	3B-13, 2B-12, 1B-7, OF-6
											9th		**8th**											

Rabbit Robinson

ROBINSON, WILLIAM CLYDE (Tug) BR TR 5′6″ 148 lbs.
B. Mar. 5, 1882, Wellsburg, W. Va. D. Apr. 9, 1915, Waterbury, Conn.

Year	Team	Games	BA	SA	AB	H	2B	3B	HR	HR%	R	RBI	BB	SO	SB	Pinch Hit AB	Pinch Hit H	PO	A	E	DP	TC/G	FA	G by Pos
1903	WAS A	103	.212	.290	373	79	10	8	1	0.3	41	20	33		16	0	0	185	248	43	27	4.6	.910	2B-45, OF-30, SS-24, 3B-5
1904	DET A	101	.241	.319	320	77	13	6	0	0.0	30	37	29		14	5	1	151	216	22	17	4.1	.943	SS-30, 3B-26, OF-20, 2B-19
1910	CIN N	2	.000	.000	7	0	0	0	0	0.0	0	1	1	0	0	0	0	1	2	0	0	1.5	1.000	3B-2
3 yrs.		206	.223	.300	700	156	23	14	1	0.1	71	58	63	0	30	5	1	337	466	65	44	4.3	.925	2B-64, SS-54, OF-50, 3B-33

Wilbert Robinson

ROBINSON, WILBERT (Uncle Robbie) BR TR 5′8½″ 215 lbs.
Brother of Fred Robinson.
B. June 29, 1863, Bolton, Mass. D. Aug. 8, 1934, Atlanta, Ga.
Manager 1902, 1914–31.
Hall of Fame 1945.

Year	Team	Games	BA	SA	AB	H	2B	3B	HR	HR%	R	RBI	BB	SO	SB	Pinch Hit AB	Pinch Hit H	PO	A	E	DP	TC/G	FA	G by Pos
1886	PHI AA	87	.202	.260	342	69	11	3	1	0.3	57		21			0	0	442	118	58	26	7.0	.906	C-61, 1B-22, OF-5
1887		68	.227	.277	264	60	6	2	1	0.4	28		14		15	0	0	291	138	50	9	6.7	.896	C-67, 1B-3, OF-1
1888		66	.244	.299	254	62	7	2	1	0.4	32	31	9		11	0	0	437	143	39	7	9.4	.937	C-65, 1B-1
1889		69	.231	.295	264	61	13	2	0	0.0	31	28	6	34	9	0	0	290	106	24	8	6.1	.943	C-69
1890	2 teams	PHI AA (82G –.237)	BAL AA (14G –.271)																					
″	total	96	.241	.332	377	91	14	4	4	1.1	39		19		21	0	0	515	115	41	14	7.0	.939	C-93, 1B-3
1891	BAL AA	93	.216	.287	334	72	8	5	2	0.6	25	46	16	37	18	0	0	415	80	25	11	5.6	.952	C-92, OF-1
1892	BAL N	90	.267	.352	330	88	14	4	2	0.6	36	57	15	35	5	0	0	349	86	38	11	5.3	.920	C-87, 1B-2, OF-1
1893		95	.334	.435	359	120	21	3	3	0.8	49	57	26	22	17	1	0	350	72	26	8	4.8	.942	C-93, 1B-1
1894		109	.353	.430	414	146	21	4	1	0.2	69	98	46	18	12	0	0	370	84	27	8	4.4	.944	C-109
1895		77	.262	.337	282	74	19	1	0	0.0	38	48	12	19	11	2	1	243	78	7	6	4.4	.979	C-75
1896		67	.347	.457	245	85	9	6	2	0.8	43	38	14	13	9	0	0	260	48	17	5	4.9	.948	C-67
1897		48	.315	.365	181	57	9	0	0	0.0	25	23	8		0	0	0	184	36	8	2	4.8	.965	C-48
1898		79	.277	.332	289	80	12	2	0	0.0	29	38	16		3	1	1	288	72	13	4	4.8	.965	C-77
1899		108	.284	.337	356	101	15	2	0	0.0	40	47	31		5	3	2	286	83	20	2	3.7	.949	C-105
1900	STL N	60	.248	.281	210	52	5	1	0	0.0	26	28	11		7	5	1	189	72	7	3	5.0	.974	C-54
1901	BAL A	68	.301	.377	239	72	12	3	0	0.0	32	26	10		9	1	0	235	61	16	4	4.7	.949	C-67
1902		91	.293	.391	335	98	16	7	1	0.3	39	57	12		11	4	2	262	75	18	4	4.1	.949	C-87
17 yrs.		1371	.273	.346	5075	1388	212	51	18	0.4	638	622	286	178	163	17	7	5406	1467	434	132	5.4	.941	C-1316, 1B-32, OF-8

Yank Robinson

ROBINSON, WILLIAM H. BR TR 5′6½″ 170 lbs.
B. Sept. 19, 1859, Philadelphia, Pa. D. Aug. 25, 1894, St. Louis, Mo.

Year	Team	Games	BA	SA	AB	H	2B	3B	HR	HR%	R	RBI	BB	SO	SB	Pinch Hit AB	Pinch Hit H	PO	A	E	DP	TC/G	FA	G by Pos
1882	DET N	11	.179	.205	39	7	1	0	0	0.0	1	2	1	13		0	0	11	23	8	2	3.5	.810	SS-10, OF-1, P-1
1884	BAL U	102	.267	.359	415	111	24	4	2	0.5	101		**37**			0	0	219	238	90	14	5.0	.835	3B-71, SS-14, P-11, C-11, 2B-3
1885	STL AA	78	.261	.345	287	75	8	8	0	0.0	63		29			0	0	155	76	32	7	3.3	.878	OF-52, 2B-19, C-5, 3B-2, 1B-1
1886		133	.274	.385	481	132	26	9	3	0.6	89		64			0	0	362	418	103	69	6.6	.883	2B-125, 3B-6, P-1, SS-1, OF-1
1887		125	.305	.405	430	131	32	4	1	0.2	102		92		75	0	0	332	368	83	52	6.1	.894	2B-117, 3B-6, SS-2, OF-2, C-1, P-1
1888		134	.231	.314	455	105	17	6	3	0.7	111	53	**116**		56	0	0	251	350	72	24	4.9	.893	2B-102, SS-34
1889		132	.208	.292	452	94	17	3	5	1.1	97	70	**118**	55	39	0	0	305	333	81	53	5.4	.887	2B-132
1890	PIT P	98	.229	.281	306	70	10	3	0	0.0	59	38	101	33	17	0	0	226	286	65	46	5.9	.887	2B-98

Yank Robinson *continued*

Year	Team		Games	BA	SA	AB	H	2B	3B	HR	HR%	R	RBI	BB	SO	SB	Pinch Hit AB	Pinch Hit H	PO	A	E	DP	TC/G	FA	G by Pos
1891	**2 teams**		**CIN AA** (97G –.178)		**STL AA** (1G –.000)																				
"	**total**		98	.177	.235	345	61	9	4	1	0.3	48	37	68	51	23	0	0	225	287	79	33	6.0	.866	2B-98
1892	**WAS**	**N**	67	.179	.225	218	39	4	3	0	0.0	26	19	38	28	11	0	0	86	146	42	13	4.1	.847	3B-58, SS-5, 2B-4
10 yrs.			978	.241	.323	3428	825	148	44	15	0.4	697	219	664	180	221	0	0	2172	2525	655	313	5.4	.878	2B-698, 3B-143, SS-66, OF-56, C-17, P-14, 1B-1

Rafael Robles

ROBLES, RAFAEL ORLANDO BR TR 6′ 170 lbs.
Born Rafael Orlando Robles (Natera).
B. Oct. 20, 1947, San Pedro de Macoris, Dominican Republic.

Year	Team		Games	BA	SA	AB	H	2B	3B	HR	HR%	R	RBI	BB	SO	SB	Pinch Hit AB	Pinch Hit H	PO	A	E	DP	TC/G	FA	G by Pos
1969	**SD**	**N**	6	.100	.100	20	2	0	0	0	0.0	1	0	1	3	1	0	0	7	10	2	1	3.2	.895	SS-6
1970			23	.213	.225	89	19	1	0	0	0.0	5	3	5	11	3	0	0	38	83	4	14	5.4	.968	SS-23
1972			18	.167	.167	24	4	0	0	0	0.0	1	0	0	3	0	8	1	5	16	1	0	1.4	.955	SS-15, 3B-1
3 yrs.			47	.188	.195	133	25	1	0	0	0.0	7	3	6	17	4	8	1	50	109	7	15	3.7	.958	SS-44, 3B-1

Sergio Robles

ROBLES, SERGIO BR TR 6′ 2″ 190 lbs.
Born Sergio Robles (Valenzuela).
B. Apr. 16, 1946, Magdalena, Mexico.

Year	Team		Games	BA	SA	AB	H	2B	3B	HR	HR%	R	RBI	BB	SO	SB	Pinch Hit AB	Pinch Hit H	PO	A	E	DP	TC/G	FA	G by Pos
1972	**BAL**	**A**	2	.200	.200	5	1	0	0	0	0.0	0	0	0	0	0	1	1	2	0	0	0	2.0	1.000	C-1
1973			8	.077	.077	13	1	0	0	0	0.0	0	0	3	1	0	0	0	32	1	0	0	4.1	1.000	C-8
1976	**LA**	**N**	6	.000	.000	3	0	0	0	0	0.0	0	0	0	2	0	0	0	9	0	0	0	1.5	1.000	C-6
3 yrs.			16	.095	.095	21	2	0	0	0	0.0	0	0	3	3	0	1	1	43	1	0	0	2.9	1.000	C-15

Tom Robson

ROBSON, THOMAS JAMES BR TR 6′ 3″ 215 lbs.
B. Jan. 15, 1946, Rochester, N. Y.

Year	Team		Games	BA	SA	AB	H	2B	3B	HR	HR%	R	RBI	BB	SO	SB	Pinch Hit AB	Pinch Hit H	PO	A	E	DP	TC/G	FA	G by Pos
1974	**TEX**	**A**	6	.231	.308	13	3	1	0	0	0.0	2	2	4	3	0	0	0	2	0	0	1	0.3	1.000	DH-5, 1B-1
1975			17	.200	.200	35	7	0	0	0	0.0	3	2	1	3	0	8	2	38	2	0	6	4.4	1.000	1B-5, DH-4
2 yrs.			23	.208	.229	48	10	1	0	0	0.0	5	4	5	6	0	8	2	40	2	0	7	2.8	1.000	DH-9, 1B-6

Mickey Rocco

ROCCO, MICHAEL DOMINICK BL TL 5′11″ 188 lbs.
B. Mar. 2, 1916, St. Paul, Minn.

Year	Team		Games	BA	SA	AB	H	2B	3B	HR	HR%	R	RBI	BB	SO	SB	Pinch Hit AB	Pinch Hit H	PO	A	E	DP	TC/G	FA	G by Pos
1943	**CLE**	**A**	108	.240	.331	405	97	14	4	5	1.2	43	46	51	40	1	0	0	1012	61	5	111	10.0	.995	1B-108
1944			155	.266	.392	**653**	174	29	7	13	2.0	87	70	56	51	4	0	0	1467	138	11	158	10.4	.993	1B-155
1945			143	.264	.388	565	149	28	6	10	1.8	81	56	52	40	0	2	0	1203	115	10	112	9.4	.992	1B-141
1946			34	.245	.327	98	24	2	0	2	2.0	8	14	15	15	1	6	1	201	28	1	18	8.5	.996	1B-27
4 yrs.			440	.258	.372	1721	444	73	17	30	1.7	219	186	174	146	6	8	1	3883	342	27	399	9.9	.994	1B-431

Jack Roche

ROCHE, JOHN JOSEPH (Red) BR TR 6′ 1″ 178 lbs.
B. Nov. 22, 1890, Los Angeles, Calif. D. Mar. 30, 1983, Peoria, Ariz.

Year	Team		Games	BA	SA	AB	H	2B	3B	HR	HR%	R	RBI	BB	SO	SB	Pinch Hit AB	Pinch Hit H	PO	A	E	DP	TC/G	FA	G by Pos
1914	**STL**	**N**	12	.667	1.111	9	6	2	1	0	0.0	1	3	0	1	1	6	5	2	0	1	1	0.6	.667	C-5
1915			46	.205	.256	39	8	0	1	0	0.0	2	6	4	8	1	37	8	1	3	0	1	1.0	1.000	C-4
1917			1	.000	.000	1	0	0	0	0	0.0	0	0	0	0	0	0	0	0	0	1	0	1.0	.000	C-1
3 yrs.			59	.286	.408	49	14	2	2	0	0.0	3	9	4	9	2	43	13	3	3	2	2	0.8	.750	C-10

Ben Rochefort

ROCHEFORT, BENNETT HAROLD BL TR 6′ 2″ 185 lbs.
Born Bennett Harold Rochefort Gilbert.
B. Aug. 15, 1896, Camden, N. J. D. Apr. 2, 1981, Red Bank, N. J.

Year	Team		Games	BA	SA	AB	H	2B	3B	HR	HR%	R	RBI	BB	SO	SB	Pinch Hit AB	Pinch Hit H	PO	A	E	DP	TC/G	FA	G by Pos
1914	**PHI**	**A**	1	.500	.500	2	1	0	0	0	0.0	0	0	0	1	0	0	0	4	1	0	0	5.0	1.000	1B-1

Lou Rochelli

ROCHELLI, LOUIS JOSEPH BR TR 6′ 1″ 175 lbs.
B. Jan. 11, 1919, Staunton, Ill. D. Oct. 23, 1992, Victoria, Tex.

Year	Team		Games	BA	SA	AB	H	2B	3B	HR	HR%	R	RBI	BB	SO	SB	Pinch Hit AB	Pinch Hit H	PO	A	E	DP	TC/G	FA	G by Pos
1944	**BKN**	**N**	5	.176	.294	17	3	0	1	0	0.0	0	2	2	6	0	0	0	12	15	1	1	5.6	.964	SS-5

Les Rock

ROCK, LESTER HENRY BL TR 6′ 2″ 184 lbs.
Born Lester Henry Schwarzrock.
B. Aug. 19, 1912, Springfield, Minn. D. Sept. 9, 1991, Davis, Calif.

Year	Team		Games	BA	SA	AB	H	2B	3B	HR	HR%	R	RBI	BB	SO	SB	Pinch Hit AB	Pinch Hit H	PO	A	E	DP	TC/G	FA	G by Pos
1936	**CHI**	**A**	2	.000	.000	1	0	0	0	0	0.0	0	1	0	0	0	0	0	0	0	0	0	0.0	.000	1B-2

Ike Rockenfield

ROCKENFIELD, ISAAC BROC BR TR 5′ 7″ 150 lbs.
B. Nov. 3, 1876, Omaha, Neb. D. Feb. 21, 1927, San Diego, Calif.

Year	Team		Games	BA	SA	AB	H	2B	3B	HR	HR%	R	RBI	BB	SO	SB	Pinch Hit AB	Pinch Hit H	PO	A	E	DP	TC/G	FA	G by Pos
1905	**STL**	**A**	95	.217	.255	322	70	12	0	0	0.0	40	16	46		11	0	0	210	255	37	19	5.3	.926	2B-95
1906			27	.236	.281	89	21	4	0	0	0.0	3	8	1		0	1	1	67	63	6	5	5.2	.956	2B-26
2 yrs.			122	.221	.260	411	91	16	0	0	0.0	43	24	47		11	1	1	277	318	43	24	5.3	.933	2B-121

Pat Rockett

ROCKETT, PATRICK EDWARD BR TR 5′11″ 170 lbs.
B. Jan. 9, 1955, San Antonio, Tex.

Year	Team		Games	BA	SA	AB	H	2B	3B	HR	HR%	R	RBI	BB	SO	SB	Pinch Hit AB	Pinch Hit H	PO	A	E	DP	TC/G	FA	G by Pos
1976	**ATL**	**N**	4	.200	.200	5	1	0	0	0	0.0	0	0	0	1	0	3	0	0	1	0	0	0.5	1.000	SS-2
1977			93	.254	.303	264	67	10	0	1	0.4	27	24	27	32	1	4	2	152	209	23	38	4.6	.940	SS-84
1978			55	.141	.155	142	20	2	0	0	0.0	6	4	13	12	1	1	0	64	97	5	16	3.3	.970	SS-51
3 yrs.			152	.214	.251	411	88	12	0	1	0.2	33	28	40	45	2	8	2	216	307	28	54	4.0	.949	SS-137

Andre Rodgers

RODGERS, KENNETH ANDRE IAN (Andy) BR TR 6′ 3″ 200 lbs.
B. Dec. 2, 1934, Nassau, Bahamas.

Year	Team		Games	BA	SA	AB	H	2B	3B	HR	HR%	R	RBI	BB	SO	SB	Pinch Hit AB	Pinch Hit H	PO	A	E	DP	TC/G	FA	G by Pos
1957	**NY**	**N**	32	.244	.395	86	21	2	1	3	3.5	8	9	9	21	0	2	0	44	75	8	14	4.5	.937	SS-20, 3B-8
1958	**SF**	**N**	22	.206	.381	63	13	3	1	2	3.2	7	11	4	14	0	4	1	26	43	2	8	3.9	.972	SS-18
1959			71	.250	.390	228	57	12	1	6	2.6	32	24	32	50	2	2	1	110	197	22	35	5.0	.933	SS-66
1960			81	.244	.355	217	53	8	5	2	0.9	22	22	24	44	1	16	7	112	129	12	26	3.6	.953	SS-41, 3B-21, 1B-6, OF-2
1961	**CHI**	**N**	73	.266	.430	214	57	17	0	6	2.8	27	23	25	54	1	7	1	408	83	9	44	7.2	.982	1B-42, SS-24, OF-2, 2B-1
1962			138	.278	.388	461	128	20	8	5	1.1	40	44	44	93	5	6	0	250	434	28	92	5.3	.961	SS-133, 1B-1
1963			150	.229	.306	516	118	17	4	5	1.0	51	33	65	90	5	0	0	271	454	35	100	5.1	.954	SS-150
1964			129	.239	.371	448	107	17	3	12	2.7	50	46	53	88	5	3	0	232	428	24	68	5.4	.965	SS-126

Andre Rodgers *continued*

Year	Team		Games	BA	SA	AB	H	2B	3B	HR	HR%	R	RBI	BB	SO	SB	Pinch Hit AB	Pinch Hit H	PO	A	E	DP	TC/G	FA	G by Pos
1965	PIT	N	75	.287	.388	178	51	12	0	2	1.1	17	25	18	28	2	26	8	88	110	8	27	3.7	.961	SS-33, 3B-15, 1B-6, 2B-1
1966			36	.184	.204	49	9	1	0	0	0.0	6	4	8	7	0	23	6	19	14	2	6	2.7	.943	SS-5, 3B-3, OF-3, 1B-?
1967			47	.230	.377	61	14	3	0	2	3.3	8	4	8	18	1	22	4	47	26	2	5	3.9	.973	1B-9, 3B-5, SS-3, 2B-2
11 yrs.			854	.249	.365	2521	628	112	23	45	1.8	268	245	290	507	22	111	28	1607	1993	152	425	5.0	.959	SS-619, 1B-66, 3B-52, OF-7, 2B-4

Bill Rodgers

RODGERS, WILBUR KINCAID (Raw Meat Bill) BL TR 5′ 8½″ 170 lbs.
B. Apr. 18, 1887, Pleasant Ridge, Ohio D. Dec. 24, 1978, Goliad, Tex.

Year	Team		Games	BA	SA	AB	H	2B	3B	HR	HR%	R	RBI	BB	SO	SB	Pinch Hit AB	Pinch Hit H	PO	A	E	DP	TC/G	FA	G by Pos
1915	3 teams	CLE A (16G –.311) BOS A (11G –.000) CIN N (72G –.239)																							
″	total		99	.246	.333	264	65	15	4	0	0.0	30	19	22	38	11	8	2	129	225	20	32	4.4	.947	2B-75, SS-8, 3B-1, OF-1
1916	CIN	N	3	.000	.000	4	0	0	0	0	0.0	0	0	0	2	0	1	0	1	1	0	0	2.0	1.000	SS-1
2 yrs.			102	.243	.328	268	65	15	4	0	0.0	30	19	22	40	11	9	2	130	226	20	32	4.4	.947	2B-75, SS-9, 3B-1, OF-1

Bill Rodgers

RODGERS, WILLIAM SHERMAN BL TL 6′ 162 lbs.
B. Dec. 5, 1922, Harrisburg, Pa.

Year	Team		Games	BA	SA	AB	H	2B	3B	HR	HR%	R	RBI	BB	SO	SB	Pinch Hit AB	Pinch Hit H	PO	A	E	DP	TC/G	FA	G by Pos
1944	PIT	N	2	.250	.250	4	1	0	0	0	0.0	1	0	0	1	0	0	0	0	0	0	0	0.0	.000	OF-1
1945			1	1.000	1.000	1	1	0	0	0	0.0	0	0	0	0	0	1	1	0	0	0	0	0.0	—	
2 yrs.			3	.400	.400	5	2	0	0	0	0.0	1	0	0	1	0	1	1	0	0	0	0	0.0		OF-1

Buck Rodgers

RODGERS, ROBERT LEROY BB TR 6′ 2″ 190 lbs.
B. Aug. 16, 1938, Delaware, Ohio.
Manager 1980–82, 1985–94.

Year	Team		Games	BA	SA	AB	H	2B	3B	HR	HR%	R	RBI	BB	SO	SB	Pinch Hit AB	Pinch Hit H	PO	A	E	DP	TC/G	FA	G by Pos
1961	LA	A	16	.321	.464	56	18	2	0	2	3.6	8	13	1	6	0	3	2	71	11	3	2	6.1	.965	C-14
1962			155	.258	.372	565	146	34	6	6	1.1	65	61	45	68	1	11	1	826	73	10	14	6.1	.989	C-150
1963			100	.233	.293	300	70	6	0	4	1.3	24	23	29	35	2	15	5	416	48	10	5	5.6	.979	C-85
1964			148	.243	.313	514	125	18	3	4	0.8	38	54	40	71	4	5	2	884	87	13	14	6.7	.987	C-146
1965	CAL	A	132	.209	.265	411	86	14	3	1	0.2	33	32	35	61	4	8	2	682	52	7	7	5.8	.991	C-128
1966			133	.236	.339	454	107	20	3	7	1.5	45	48	29	57	3	7	3	662	69	6	7	5.5	.992	C-133
1967			139	.219	.305	429	94	13	3	6	1.4	29	41	34	55	1	6	0	728	73	7	11	6.0	.991	C-134, OF-1
1968			91	.190	.225	258	49	6	0	1	0.4	13	14	16	48	2	7	0	407	50	7	11	5.3	.985	C-87
1969			18	.196	.217	46	9	1	0	0	0.0	4	2	5	8	0	0	0	74	9	0	3	4.6	1.000	C-18
9 yrs.			932	.232	.312	3033	704	114	18	31	1.0	259	288	234	409	17	62	15	4750	472	63	74	5.9	.988	C-895, OF-1

Eric Rodin

RODIN, ERIC CHAPMAN BR TR 6′ 2″ 215 lbs.
B. Feb. 5, 1930, Orange, N. J. D. Jan. 4, 1991, Somerville, N. J.

Year	Team		Games	BA	SA	AB	H	2B	3B	HR	HR%	R	RBI	BB	SO	SB	Pinch Hit AB	Pinch Hit H	PO	A	E	DP	TC/G	FA	G by Pos
1954	NY	N	5	.000	.000	6	0	0	0	0	0.0	0	0	0	2	0	3	0	3	0	0	0	1.0	1.000	OF-3

Alex Rodriguez

RODRIGUEZ, ALEXANDER EMMANUEL BR TR 6′ 3″ 190 lbs.
B. July 27, 1975, New York, N. Y.

Year	Team		Games	BA	SA	AB	H	2B	3B	HR	HR%	R	RBI	BB	SO	SB	Pinch Hit AB	Pinch Hit H	PO	A	E	DP	TC/G	FA	G by Pos
1994	SEA	A	17	.204	.204	54	11	0	0	0	0.0	4	2	3	20	3	0	0	20	45	6	9	4.2	.915	SS-17
1995			48	.232	.408	142	33	6	2	5	3.5	15	19	6	42	4	0	0	55	106	8	14	3.6	.953	SS-46, DH-1
2 yrs.			65	.224	.352	196	44	6	2	5	2.6	19	21	9	62	7	0	0	75	151	14	23	3.8	.942	SS-63, DH-1
DIVISIONAL PLAYOFF SERIES																									
1995	SEA	A	1	.000	.000	1	0	0	0	0	0.0	1	0	0	0	0	0	0	0	0	0	0	0.0	.000	SS-1
LEAGUE CHAMPIONSHIP SERIES																									
1995	SEA	A	1	.000	.000	1	0	0	0	0	0.0	0	0	0	1	0	1	0	0	0	0	0	0.0	—	

Aurelio Rodriguez

RODRIGUEZ, AURELIO (Leo) BR TR 5′10″ 180 lbs.
Born Aurelio Rodriguez (Ituarte).
B. Dec. 28, 1947, Cananea, Mexico.

Year	Team		Games	BA	SA	AB	H	2B	3B	HR	HR%	R	RBI	BB	SO	SB	Pinch Hit AB	Pinch Hit H	PO	A	E	DP	TC/G	FA	G by Pos
1967	CAL	A	29	.238	.300	130	31	3	1	1	0.8	14	8	2	21	1	0	0	19	75	1	11	3.3	.989	3B-29
1968			76	.242	.309	223	54	10	1	1	0.4	14	16	17	35	0	3	2	65	116	15	18	2.7	.923	3B-70, 2B-2
1969			159	.232	.307	561	130	17	2	7	1.2	47	49	32	88	5	0	0	145	352	24	42	3.3	.954	3B-159
1970	2 teams	CAL A (17G –.270) WAS A (142G –.247)																							
″	total		159	.249	.420	610	152	33	7	19	3.1	70	83	40	87	15	0	0	127	398	18	42	3.4	.967	3B-153, SS-7
1971	DET	A	154	.253	.401	604	153	30	7	15	2.5	68	39	27	93	4	3	1	128	344	23	35	3.2	.954	3B-153, SS-1
1972			153	.236	.356	601	142	23	5	13	2.2	65	56	28	104	2	1	0	150	350	17	34	3.3	.967	3B-153, SS-2
1973			160	.222	.330	555	123	27	3	9	1.6	46	58	31	85	3	0	0	137	338	14	31	3.0	.971	3B-160, SS-1
1974			159	.222	.306	571	127	23	5	5	0.9	54	49	26	70	2	0	0	132	389	21	40	3.4	.961	3B-159
1975			151	.245	.385	507	124	20	6	13	2.6	47	60	30	63	1	0	0	136	375	25	33	3.5	.953	3B-151
1976			128	.240	.325	480	115	13	2	8	1.7	40	50	19	61	0	0	0	120	280	9	21	3.2	.978	3B-128
1977			96	.219	.369	306	67	14	1	10	3.3	30	32	16	36	1	10	1	60	222	8	19	3.0	.972	3B-95, SS-1
1978			134	.265	.395	385	102	25	2	7	1.8	40	43	19	37	0	20	7	79	228	4	20	2.4	.987	3B-131
1979			106	.254	.350	343	87	18	0	5	1.5	27	36	11	40	0	3	0	72	211	13	23	2.8	.956	3B-106, 1B-1
1980	2 teams	SD N (89G –.200) NY A (52G –.220)																							
″	total		141	.209	.310	339	71	13	3	5	1.5	21	27	13	61	1	6	0	71	219	13	21	2.1	.957	3B-137, 2B-6, SS-2
1981	NY	A	27	.346	.500	52	18	2	0	2	3.8	4	8	2	10	0	1	1	20	34	2	4	2.2	.964	3B-20, 2B-3, DH-2, 1B-1
1982	CHI	A	118	.241	.342	257	62	15	1	3	1.2	24	31	11	35	0	1	0	79	209	9	20	2.5	.970	3B-112, 2B-3, SS-2
1983	2 teams	BAL A (45G –.119) CHI A (22G –.200)																							
″	total		67	.138	.184	87	12	1	0	1	1.1	1	3	0	16	0	0	0	22	67	2	7	1.4	.978	3B-67
17 yrs.			2017	.237	.351	6611	1570	287	46	124	1.9	612	648	324	942	35	48	12	1562	4207	218	421	3.0	.964	3B-1983, SS-16, 2B-14, DH-2, 1B-2
LEAGUE CHAMPIONSHIP SERIES																									
1972	DET	A	5	.000	.000	16	0	0	0	0	0.0	0	0	2	2	0	0	0	2	14	1	2	3.4	.941	3B-5
1980	NY	A	2	.333	.500	6	2	1	0	0	0.0	0	0	0	0	0	0	0	2	2	0	0	2.0	1.000	3B-2
1981			1	—	—	0	0	0	0	0	—	0	0	0	0	0	0	0	0	0	0	0	0.0	.000	3B-1
1983	CHI	A	2	—	—	0	0	0	0	0	—	0	0	0	0	0	0	0	0	0	1	0	0.5	.000	3B-2
4 yrs.			10	.091	.136	22	2	1	0	0	0.0	0	0	2	2	0	0	0	4	16	2	2	2.2	.909	3B-10
WORLD SERIES																									
1981	NY	A	4	.417	.417	12	5	0	0	0	0.0	1	0	1	2	0	0	0	3	9	0	0	4.0	1.000	3B-3

Carlos Rodriguez

RODRIGUEZ, CARLOS BB TR 5′ 9″ 160 lbs.
Born Carlos Rodriguez (Marquez).
B. Nov. 1, 1967, Mexico City, Mexico.

Year	Team	Games	BA	SA	AB	H	2B	3B	HR	HR%	R	RBI	BB	SO	SB	Pinch Hit AB	Pinch Hit H	PO	A	E	DP	TC/G	FA	G by Pos
1991	NY A	15	.189	.189	37	7	0	0	0	0.0	1	2	1	2	0	2	0	11	34	2	9	3.4	.957	SS-11, 2B-3
1994	BOS A	57	.287	.397	174	50	14	1	1	0.6	15	13	11	13	1	3	2	87	132	6	36	4.0	.973	SS-32, 2B-20, 3B-4
1995		13	.333	.400	30	10	2	0	0	0.0	5	5	2	2	0	2	2	16	27	1	6	3.1	.977	2B-7, SS-6, 3B-1
3 yrs.		85	.278	.365	241	67	16	1	1	0.4	21	20	14	17	1	7	4	114	193	9	51	3.8	.972	SS-49, 2B-30, 3B-5

Edwin Rodriguez

RODRIGUEZ, EDWIN BR TR 5′11″ 172 lbs.
Born Edwin Rodriguez (Morales).
B. Aug. 14, 1960, Ponce, Puerto Rico.

Year	Team	Games	BA	SA	AB	H	2B	3B	HR	HR%	R	RBI	BB	SO	SB	Pinch Hit AB	Pinch Hit H	PO	A	E	DP	TC/G	FA	G by Pos
1982	NY A	3	.333	.333	9	3	0	0	0	0.0	2	1	1	1	0	0	0	2	12	2	1	5.3	.875	2B-3
1983	SD N	7	.167	.250	12	2	1	0	0	0.0	1	0	1	3	0	0	0	8	8	0	2	2.0	1.000	2B-5, SS-2, 3B-1
1985		1	.000	.000	1	0	0	0	0	0.0	0	0	0	0	0	1	0	0	0	0	0	0.0	—	
3 yrs.		11	.227	.273	22	5	1	0	0	0.0	3	1	2	4	0	1	0	10	20	2	3	2.9	.938	2B-8, SS-2, 3B-1

Ellie Rodriguez

RODRIGUEZ, ELISEO BR TR 5′11″ 185 lbs.
Born Eliseo Rodriguez (Delgado).
B. May 24, 1946, Fajardo, Puerto Rico.

Year	Team	Games	BA	SA	AB	H	2B	3B	HR	HR%	R	RBI	BB	SO	SB	Pinch Hit AB	Pinch Hit H	PO	A	E	DP	TC/G	FA	G by Pos
1968	NY A	9	.208	.208	24	5	0	0	0	0.0	1	1	3	3	0	0	0	41	3	0	0	4.9	1.000	C-9
1969	KC A	95	.236	.296	267	63	10	0	2	0.7	27	20	31	26	3	6	1	433	39	5	2	5.3	.990	C-90
1970		80	.225	.290	231	52	8	2	1	0.4	25	15	27	35	2	5	2	451	32	6	5	6.5	.988	C-75
1971	MIL A	115	.210	.257	319	67	10	1	1	0.3	28	30	41	51	1	6	1	520	67	5	8	5.2	.992	C-114
1972		116	.285	.352	355	101	14	2	2	0.6	31	35	52	43	1	3	1	542	54	10	6	5.3	.983	C-114
1973		94	.269	.303	290	78	8	1	0	0.0	30	30	41	28	4	6	1	324	40	5	5	4.1	.986	C-75, DH-14
1974	CAL A	140	.253	.357	395	100	20	0	7	1.8	48	36	69	56	4	4	3	782	75	7	7	6.3	.992	C-137, DH-1
1975		90	.235	.301	226	53	6	0	3	1.3	20	27	49	37	2	0	0	492	33	5	2	5.9	.991	C-90
1976	LA N	36	.212	.212	66	14	0	0	0	0.0	10	9	19	12	0	1	1	128	17	2	2	4.5	.986	C-33
9 yrs.		775	.245	.308	2173	533	76	6	16	0.7	220	203	332	291	17	31	10	3713	360	45	37	5.5	.989	C-737, DH-15

Hec Rodriguez

RODRIGUEZ, HECTOR ANTONIO BR TR 5′ 8″ 165 lbs.
Born Hector Antonio Rodriguez (Ordenana).
B. June 13, 1920, Alquizar, Cuba.

Year	Team	Games	BA	SA	AB	H	2B	3B	HR	HR%	R	RBI	BB	SO	SB	Pinch Hit AB	Pinch Hit H	PO	A	E	DP	TC/G	FA	G by Pos
1952	CHI A	124	.265	.307	407	108	14	0	1	0.2	55	40	47	22	7	8	2	145	232	16	26	3.5	.959	3B-113

Henry Rodriguez

RODRIGUEZ, HENRY ANDERSON BL TL 6′ 1″ 180 lbs.
Born Henry Anderson Rodriguez (Lorenzo).
B. Nov. 8, 1967, Santo Domingo, Dominican Republic.

Year	Team	Games	BA	SA	AB	H	2B	3B	HR	HR%	R	RBI	BB	SO	SB	Pinch Hit AB	Pinch Hit H	PO	A	E	DP	TC/G	FA	G by Pos
1992	LA N	53	.219	.329	146	32	7	0	3	2.1	11	14	8	30	0	5	0	68	8	3	2	1.6	.962	OF-48, 1B-1
1993		76	.222	.415	176	39	10	0	8	4.5	20	23	11	39	1	15	4	127	9	1	2	2.2	.993	OF-48, 1B-13
1994		104	.268	.405	306	82	14	2	8	2.6	33	49	17	58	0	15	4	198	9	2	3	2.0	.990	OF-86, 1B-17
1995	2 teams	LA N (21G –.263) MON N (24G –.207)																						
″	total	45	.239	.326	138	33	4	1	2	1.4	13	15	11	28	0	8	0	126	7	1	8	3.4	.993	OF-28, 1B-11
4 yrs.		278	.243	.379	766	186	35	3	21	2.7	77	101	47	155	1	43	8	519	33	7	15	2.2	.987	OF-210, 1B-42

Ivan Rodriguez

RODRIGUEZ, IVAN (Pudge) BR TR 5′ 9″ 165 lbs.
Born Ivan Rodriguez (Torres).
B. Nov. 27, 1971, Manati, Puerto Rico.

Year	Team	Games	BA	SA	AB	H	2B	3B	HR	HR%	R	RBI	BB	SO	SB	Pinch Hit AB	Pinch Hit H	PO	A	E	DP	TC/G	FA	G by Pos
1991	TEX A	88	.264	.354	280	74	16	0	3	1.1	24	27	5	42	0	2	0	517	62	10	6	6.7	.983	C-88
1992		123	.260	.360	420	109	16	1	8	1.9	39	37	24	73	0	9	1	763	85	15	10	7.3	.983	C-116, DH-2
1993		137	.273	.412	473	129	28	4	10	2.1	56	66	29	70	8	5	3	801	76	8	6	6.6	.991	C-134, DH-1
1994		99	.298	.488	363	108	19	1	16	4.4	56	57	31	42	6	1	0	600	44	5	2	6.6	.992	C-99
1995		130	.303	.449	492	149	32	2	12	2.4	56	67	16	48	0	6	4	707	67	8	3	6.1	.990	C-127, DH-1
5 yrs.		577	.281	.416	2028	569	111	8	49	2.4	231	254	105	275	14	23	8	3388	334	46	27	6.6	.988	C-564, DH-4

Jose Rodriguez

RODRIGUEZ, JOSE BR TR 6′ 170 lbs.
B. Feb. 23, 1894, Havana, Cuba D. Jan. 21, 1953, Havana, Cuba.

Year	Team	Games	BA	SA	AB	H	2B	3B	HR	HR%	R	RBI	BB	SO	SB	Pinch Hit AB	Pinch Hit H	PO	A	E	DP	TC/G	FA	G by Pos
1916	NY N	1	—	—	0	0	0	0	0	—	0	0	0	0	0	0	0	0	0	0	0	0.0	—	
1917		7	.200	.300	20	4	0	1	0	0.0	2	2	2	1	2	0	0	45	1	0	2	6.6	1.000	1B-7
1918		50	.160	.192	125	20	0	2	0	0.0	15	15	12	3	6	2	0	122	102	5	16	4.4	.978	2B-42, 1B-8, 3B-2
3 yrs.		58	.166	.207	145	24	0	3	0	0.0	17	17	14	4	8	2	0	167	103	5	18	4.7	.982	2B-42, 1B-15, 3B-2

Ruben Rodriguez

RODRIGUEZ, RUBEN DARIO BR TR 6′ 170 lbs.
Born Ruben Dario Rodriguez (Martinez).
B. Aug. 4, 1964, Cabrera, Dominican Republic.

Year	Team	Games	BA	SA	AB	H	2B	3B	HR	HR%	R	RBI	BB	SO	SB	Pinch Hit AB	Pinch Hit H	PO	A	E	DP	TC/G	FA	G by Pos
1986	PIT N	2	.000	.000	3	0	0	0	0	0.0	0	0	0	1	0	0	0	6	1	0	0	3.5	1.000	C-2
1988		2	.200	.600	5	1	0	1	0	0.0	1	1	0	2	0	0	0	9	0	0	0	4.5	1.000	C-2
2 yrs.		4	.125	.375	8	1	0	1	0	0.0	1	1	0	3	0	0	0	15	1	0	0	4.0	1.000	C-4

Steve Rodriguez

RODRIGUEZ, STEVEN JAMES BR TR 5′ 8″ 170 lbs.
B. Nov. 29, 1970, Las Vegas, Nev.

Year	Team	Games	BA	SA	AB	H	2B	3B	HR	HR%	R	RBI	BB	SO	SB	Pinch Hit AB	Pinch Hit H	PO	A	E	DP	TC/G	FA	G by Pos
1995	2 teams	BOS A (6G –.125) DET A (12G –.194)																						
″	total	18	.179	.205	39	7	1	0	0	0.0	5	0	6	10	2	3	0	22	38	2	6	3.3	.968	2B-13, SS-5, DH-1

Vic Rodriguez

RODRIGUEZ, VICTOR MANUEL BR TR 5′11″ 160 lbs.
Born Victor Manuel Rodriguez (Rivera).
B. July 14, 1961, New York, N. Y.

Year	Team	Games	BA	SA	AB	H	2B	3B	HR	HR%	R	RBI	BB	SO	SB	Pinch Hit AB	Pinch Hit H	PO	A	E	DP	TC/G	FA	G by Pos
1984	BAL A	11	.412	.588	17	7	3	0	0	0.0	4	2	0	2	0	0	0	8	15	1	1	2.4	.958	2B-7, DH-3
1989	MIN A	6	.455	.636	11	5	2	0	0	0.0	2	0	0	1	0	0	0	3	6	1	1	1.7	.900	3B-5, DH-1
2 yrs.		17	.429	.607	28	12	5	0	0	0.0	6	2	0	3	0	0	0	11	21	2	2	2.1	.941	2B-7, 3B-5, DH-4

Gary Roenicke

ROENICKE, GARY STEVEN BR TR 6′ 3″ 205 lbs.
Brother of Ron Roenicke.
B. Dec. 5, 1954, Covina, Calif.

Year	Team	Games	BA	SA	AB	H	2B	3B	HR	HR%	R	RBI	BB	SO	SB	Pinch Hit AB	Pinch Hit H	PO	A	E	DP	TC/G	FA	G by Pos
1976	MON N	29	.222	.344	90	20	3	1	2	2.2	9	5	4	18	0	4	1	39	3	2	0	1.8	.955	OF-25
1978	BAL A	27	.259	.466	58	15	3	0	3	5.2	5	15	8	3	0	6	1	22	1	0	0	1.1	1.000	OF-20

Gary Roenicke *continued*

Year	Team	Games	BA	SA	AB	H	2B	3B	HR	HR%	R	RBI	BB	SO	SB	Pinch Hit AB	Pinch Hit H	PO	A	E	DP	TC/G	FA	G by Pos
1979		133	.261	.508	376	98	16	1	25	6.6	60	64	61	74	1	2	0	246	10	5	1	2.0	.981	OF-130, DH-2
1980		118	.239	.384	297	71	13	0	10	3.4	40	28	41	49	2	12	6	197	8	0	1	1.8	1.000	OF-113
1981		85	.269	.384	219	59	16	0	3	1.4	31	20	23	29	1	16	3	175	2	3	1	2.2	.983	OF-83
1982		137	.270	.499	393	106	25	1	21	5.3	58	74	70	73	6	18	5	363	13	3	7	2.8	.992	OF-125, 1B-10
1983		115	.260	.477	323	84	13	0	19	5.9	45	64	30	35	2	38	8	219	9	3	5	2.1	.987	OF-100, 1B-7, DH-2, 3B-2
1984		121	.224	.380	326	73	19	1	10	3.1	36	44	58	43	1	21	5	197	6	1	0	1.7	.995	OF-117
1985		113	.218	.458	225	49	9	0	15	6.7	36	43	44	36	2	29	3	134	6	1	0	1.3	.993	OF-88, DH-17
1986	NY A	69	.265	.368	136	36	5	0	3	2.2	11	18	27	30	1	18	6	46	6	0	0	0.9	1.000	OF-37, DH-15, 3B-3, 1B-2
1987	ATL N	67	.219	.450	151	33	8	0	9	6.0	25	28	32	23	0	15	3	110	7	2	8	2.2	.983	OF-44, 1B-9
1988		49	.228	.298	114	26	5	0	1	0.9	11	7	8	15	0	16	1	53	0	0	0	1.5	1.000	OF-35, 1B-1
12 yrs.		1063	.247	.434	2708	670	135	4	121	4.5	367	410	406	428	16	195	42	1801	71	20	23	1.9	.989	OF-917, DH-36, 1B-29, 3B-5
LEAGUE CHAMPIONSHIP SERIES																								
1979	BAL A	2	.200	.200	5	1	0	0	0	0.0	1	1	0	0	0	1	0	3	1	0	1	2.0	1.000	OF-2
1983		3	.750	1.750	4	3	1	0	1	25.0	4	4	5	0	0	0	0	4	1	0	0	1.7	1.000	OF-3
2 yrs.		5	.444	.889	9	4	1	0	1	11.1	5	5	5	0	0	1	0	7	2	0	1	1.8	1.000	OF-5
WORLD SERIES																								
1979	BAL A	6	.125	.188	16	2	1	0	0	0.0	1	0	0	6	0	1	0	14	1	0	0	3.0	1.000	OF-5
1983		3	.000	.000	7	0	0	0	0	0.0	0	0	0	2	0	2	0	2	1	0	0	1.5	1.000	OF-2
2 yrs.		9	.087	.130	23	2	1	0	0	0.0	1	0	0	8	0	3	0	16	2	0	0	2.6	1.000	OF-7

Ron Roenicke

ROENICKE, RONALD JON
Brother of Gary Roenicke.
B. Aug. 19, 1956, Covina, Calif.

BB TL 6′ 180 lbs.

Year	Team	Games	BA	SA	AB	H	2B	3B	HR	HR%	R	RBI	BB	SO	SB	Pinch Hit AB	Pinch Hit H	PO	A	E	DP	TC/G	FA	G by Pos
1981	LA N	22	.234	.234	47	11	0	0	0	0.0	6	0	6	8	1	4	0	38	1	0	1	2.0	1.000	OF-20
1982		109	.259	.336	143	37	8	0	1	0.7	18	12	21	32	5	44	13	59	1	1	0	0.8	.984	OF-72
1983	2 teams	LA N (81G –.221) SEA A (59G –.253)																						
"	total	140	.239	.338	343	82	16	0	6	1.7	35	35	47	48	9	24	5	243	14	3	7	2.1	.988	OF-116, 1B-6, DH-1
1984	SD N	12	.300	.500	20	6	1	0	1	5.0	4	2	2	5	0	2	0	10	0	0	0	1.0	1.000	OF-10
1985	SF N	65	.256	.406	133	34	9	1	3	2.3	23	13	35	27	6	23	4	63	0	1	0	1.8	.984	OF-35
1986	PHI N	102	.247	.356	275	68	13	1	5	1.8	42	42	61	52	2	21	4	181	3	2	0	2.2	.989	OF-83
1987		63	.167	.269	78	13	3	1	1	1.3	9	4	14	15	1	38	5	26	1	1	0	1.1	.964	OF-26
1988	CIN N	14	.135	.162	37	5	1	0	0	0.0	4	5	4	8	0	2	1	18	0	0	0	1.3	1.000	OF-14
8 yrs.		527	.238	.338	1076	256	51	3	17	1.6	141	113	190	195	24	158	32	638	20	8	8	1.7	.988	OF-376, 1B-6, DH-1
WORLD SERIES																								
1984	SD N	2	—	—	0	0	0	0	0	—	0	0	0	0	0	0	0	0	0	0	0	0.0	.000	OF-1

Oscar Roettger

ROETTGER, OSCAR FREDERICK LOUIS
Brother of Wally Roettger.
B. Feb. 19, 1900, St. Louis, Mo. D. July 4, 1986, St. Louis, Mo.

BR TR 6′ 170 lbs.

Year	Team	Games	BA	SA	AB	H	2B	3B	HR	HR%	R	RBI	BB	SO	SB	Pinch Hit AB	Pinch Hit H	PO	A	E	DP	TC/G	FA	G by Pos
1923	NY A	5	.000	.000	2	0	0	0	0	0.0	0	0	0	0	0	0	0	3	2	0	0	1.0	1.000	P-5
1924		1	—	—	0	0	0	0	0	—	0	0	0	0	0	0	0	0	0	0	0	0.0	.000	P-1
1927	BKN N	5	.000	.000	4	0	0	0	0	0.0	0	0	1	1	0	2	0	0	0	0	0	0.0	.000	OF-1
1932	PHI A	26	.233	.250	60	14	1	0	0	0.0	7	6	5	4	0	10	0	130	5	3	6	9.2	.978	1B-15
4 yrs.		37	.212	.227	66	14	1	0	0	0.0	7	6	6	5	0	12	0	133	7	3	6	6.5	.979	1B-15, P-6, OF-1

Wally Roettger

ROETTGER, WALTER HENRY
Brother of Oscar Roettger.
B. Aug. 28, 1902, St. Louis, Mo. D. Sept. 14, 1951, Champaign, Ill.

BR TR 6′ 1½″ 190 lbs.

Year	Team	Games	BA	SA	AB	H	2B	3B	HR	HR%	R	RBI	BB	SO	SB	Pinch Hit AB	Pinch Hit H	PO	A	E	DP	TC/G	FA	G by Pos
1927	STL N	5	.000	.000	1	0	0	0	0	0.0	0	0	1	0	0	0	0	2	0	2	0	1.3	.500	OF-3
1928		68	.341	.506	261	89	17	4	6	2.3	27	44	10	22	2	2	0	152	2	3	1	2.4	.981	OF-66
1929		79	.253	.349	269	68	11	3	3	1.1	27	42	13	27	0	10	1	137	4	1	0	2.1	.993	OF-69
1930	NY N	121	.283	.379	420	119	15	5	5	1.2	51	51	25	29	1	7	3	233	9	2	1	2.1	.992	OF-114
1931	2 teams	CIN N (44G –.351) STL N (45G –.285)																						
"	total	89	.321	.435	336	108	23	6	1	0.3	41	37	16	23	1	3	1	168	4	3	1	2.0	.983	OF-86
1932	CIN N	106	.277	.372	347	96	18	3	3	0.9	26	43	23	24	0	10	3	214	3	2	2	2.3	.991	OF-94
1933		84	.239	.297	209	50	7	1	1	0.5	13	17	8	10	0	28	8	124	4	3	2	2.4	.977	OF-55
1934	PIT N	47	.245	.311	106	26	5	1	0	0.0	7	11	3	8	0	23	7	51	1	0	0	2.3	1.000	OF-23
8 yrs.		599	.285	.387	1949	556	96	23	19	1.0	192	245	99	143	4	83	23	1081	27	16	7	2.2	.986	OF-510
WORLD SERIES																								
1931	STL N	3	.286	.357	14	4	1	0	0	0.0	1	0	0	3	0	0	0	4	0	0	0	1.3	1.000	OF-3

Ed Roetz

ROETZ, EDWARD BERNARD
B. Aug. 6, 1905, Philadelphia, Pa. D. Mar. 16, 1965, Philadelphia, Pa.

BR TR 5′10″ 160 lbs.

Year	Team	Games	BA	SA	AB	H	2B	3B	HR	HR%	R	RBI	BB	SO	SB	Pinch Hit AB	Pinch Hit H	PO	A	E	DP	TC/G	FA	G by Pos
1929	STL A	16	.244	.378	45	11	4	1	0	0.0	7	5	4	6	0	0	0	64	25	7	11	6.0	.927	SS-8, 1B-5, 2B-2, 3B-1

Billy Rogell

ROGELL, WILLIAM GEORGE
B. Nov. 24, 1904, Springfield, Ill.

BB TR 5′10½″ 163 lbs.

Year	Team	Games	BA	SA	AB	H	2B	3B	HR	HR%	R	RBI	BB	SO	SB	Pinch Hit AB	Pinch Hit H	PO	A	E	DP	TC/G	FA	G by Pos
1925	BOS A	58	.195	.237	169	33	5	1	0	0.0	12	17	11	17	0	2	0	107	161	19	34	5.2	.934	2B-49, SS-6
1927		82	.266	.420	207	55	14	6	2	1.0	35	28	24	28	3	15	3	52	127	6	10	3.2	.968	3B-53, OF-2, 2B-2
1928		102	.233	.294	296	69	10	4	0	0.0	33	29	22	47	2	7	1	158	233	23	34	4.2	.944	SS-67, 2B-22, OF-6, 3B-3
1930	DET A	54	.167	.222	144	24	4	2	0	0.0	20	9	15	23	1	2	0	62	114	10	20	4.0	.946	SS-33, 3B-13, OF-1
1931		48	.303	.432	185	56	12	3	2	1.1	21	24	24	17	8	0	0	91	182	12	26	5.9	.958	SS-48
1932		143	.271	.394	554	150	29	6	9	1.6	88	61	50	38	14	0	0	276	437	42	88	5.3	.944	SS-139, 3B-4
1933		155	.295	.404	587	173	42	11	0	0.0	67	57	79	33	6	0	0	326	526	51	116	5.8	.944	SS-155
1934		154	.296	.392	592	175	32	8	3	0.5	114	100	74	36	13	0	0	259	518	31	99	5.2	.962	SS-154
1935		150	.275	.388	560	154	23	11	6	1.1	88	71	80	29	3	0	0	280	512	24	104	5.4	.971	SS-150
1936		146	.274	.368	585	160	27	5	6	1.0	85	68	73	41	14	1	0	287	464	27	99	5.3	.965	SS-146, 3B-1
1937		146	.276	.403	536	148	30	7	8	1.5	85	64	83	48	5	0	0	323	451	26	103	5.5	.968	SS-146
1938		136	.259	.353	501	130	22	8	3	0.6	76	55	86	37	9	2	0	291	431	31	101	5.6	.959	SS-134

Billy Rogell *continued*

Year	Team	Games	BA	SA	AB	H	2B	3B	HR	HR%	R	RBI	BB	SO	SB	Pinch Hit AB	Pinch Hit H	PO	A	E	DP	TC/G	FA	G by Pos
1939		74	.230	.333	174	40	6	3	2	1.1	24	23	26	14	3	3	0	84	135	16	26	3.6	.932	SS-43, 3B-21, 2B-2
1940	CHI N	33	.136	.186	59	8	0	0	1	1.7	7	3	2	8	1	6	1	19	24	6	2	1.9	.878	SS-14, 3B-9, 2B-3
14 yrs.		1481	.267	.370	5149	1375	256	75	42	0.8	755	609	649	416	82	38	5	2615	4315	324	862	5.1	.955	SS-1235, 3B-104, 2B-78, OF-9
WORLD SERIES																								
1934	DET A	7	.276	.310	29	8	1	0	0	0.0	3	4	1	4	0	0	0	11	17	3	4	4.4	.903	SS-7
1935		6	.292	.375	24	7	2	0	0	0.0	1	1	2	5	0	0	0	13	12	0	6	4.2	1.000	SS-6
2 yrs.		13	.283	.340	53	15	3	0	0	0.0	4	5	3	9	0	0	0	24	29	3	10	4.3	.946	SS-13

Emmett Rogers

ROGERS, EMMETT BB 5′10″ 165 lbs.
B. 1865, Rome, N. Y. Deceased.

Year	Team	Games	BA	SA	AB	H	2B	3B	HR	HR%	R	RBI	BB	SO	SB	Pinch Hit AB	Pinch Hit H	PO	A	E	DP	TC/G	FA	G by Pos
1890	TOL AA	35	.173	.255	110	19	3	3	0	0.0	18		14		2	0	0	190	52	20	3	7.5	.924	C-34, OF-1

Jay Rogers

ROGERS, JAY LEWIS BR TR 5′11½″ 178 lbs.
B. Aug. 3, 1888, Sandusky, N. Y. D. July 1, 1964, Carlisle, Pa.

Year	Team	Games	BA	SA	AB	H	2B	3B	HR	HR%	R	RBI	BB	SO	SB	Pinch Hit AB	Pinch Hit H	PO	A	E	DP	TC/G	FA	G by Pos
1914	NY A	5	.000	.000	8	0	0	0	0	0.0	0	0	0	4	0	1	0	10	2	1	0	3.3	.923	C-4

Jim Rogers

ROGERS, JAMES F. 5′ 7½″ 180 lbs.
B. Apr. 9, 1872, Hartford, Conn. D. Jan. 21, 1900, Bridgeport, Conn.
Manager 1897.

Year	Team	Games	BA	SA	AB	H	2B	3B	HR	HR%	R	RBI	BB	SO	SB	Pinch Hit AB	Pinch Hit H	PO	A	E	DP	TC/G	FA	G by Pos
1896	2 teams	WAS N (38G –.279) LOU N (72G –.259)																						
″	total	110	.266	.349	444	118	14	10	1	0.2	60	68	25	23	16	0	0	665	154	41	51	7.7	.952	1B-60, 3B-32, SS-12, 2B-6, OF-1
1897	LOU N	41	.147	.233	150	22	3	2	2	1.3	22	22	22		4	0	0	108	121	16	12	5.8	.935	2B-39, 1B-3
2 yrs.		151	.236	.320	594	140	17	12	3	0.5	82	90	47	23	20	0	0	773	275	57	63	7.2	.948	1B-63, 2B-45, 3B-32, SS-12, OF-1

Packy Rogers

ROGERS, STANLEY FRANK BR TR 5′ 8″ 175 lbs.
Born Stanley Frank Hazinski.
B. Apr. 26, 1913, Swoyersville, Pa.

Year	Team	Games	BA	SA	AB	H	2B	3B	HR	HR%	R	RBI	BB	SO	SB	Pinch Hit AB	Pinch Hit H	PO	A	E	DP	TC/G	FA	G by Pos
1938	BKN N	23	.189	.270	37	7	1	1	0	0.0	3	5	6	6	0	2	0	25	22	2	3	2.3	.959	SS-9, 3B-8, 2B-3, OF-1

Mike Rogodzinski

ROGODZINSKI, MICHAEL GEORGE BL TR 6′ 185 lbs.
B. Feb. 22, 1948, Evanston, Ill.

Year	Team	Games	BA	SA	AB	H	2B	3B	HR	HR%	R	RBI	BB	SO	SB	Pinch Hit AB	Pinch Hit H	PO	A	E	DP	TC/G	FA	G by Pos
1973	PHI N	66	.237	.350	80	19	3	0	2	2.5	13	7	12	19	0	47	**16**	16	2	1	0	1.2	.947	OF-16
1974		17	.067	.067	15	1	0	0	0	0.0	1	1	2	3	0	15	1	0	0	0	0	0.0	.000	OF-1
1975		16	.263	.316	19	5	1	0	0	0.0	3	4	3	2	0	11	4	2	0	1	0	1.5	.667	OF-2
3 yrs.		99	.219	.307	114	25	4	0	2	1.8	17	12	17	24	0	73	21	18	2	2	0	1.2	.909	OF-19

Dave Rohde

ROHDE, DAVID GRANT BB TR 6′ 2″ 180 lbs.
B. May 8, 1964, Los Altos, Calif.

Year	Team	Games	BA	SA	AB	H	2B	3B	HR	HR%	R	RBI	BB	SO	SB	Pinch Hit AB	Pinch Hit H	PO	A	E	DP	TC/G	FA	G by Pos
1990	HOU N	59	.184	.224	98	18	4	0	0	0.0	8	5	9	20	0	22	3	28	70	0	11	2.6	1.000	2B-32, 3B-4, SS-2
1991		29	.122	.122	41	5	0	0	0	0.0	3	0	5	8	0	17	2	13	23	0	2	3.3	1.000	2B-4, SS-3, 3B-3, 1B-1
1992	CLE A	5	.000	.000	7	0	0	0	0	0.0	0	0	2	3	0	2	0	3	6	1	1	2.0	.900	3B-5
3 yrs.		93	.158	.185	146	23	4	0	0	0.0	11	5	16	31	0	41	5	44	99	1	14	2.7	.993	2B-36, 3B-12, SS-5, 1B-1

George Rohe

ROHE, GEORGE ANTHONY (Whitey) BR TR 5′ 9″ 165 lbs.
B. Sept. 15, 1875, Cincinnati, Ohio D. June 10, 1957, Cincinnati, Ohio.

Year	Team	Games	BA	SA	AB	H	2B	3B	HR	HR%	R	RBI	BB	SO	SB	Pinch Hit AB	Pinch Hit H	PO	A	E	DP	TC/G	FA	G by Pos
1901	BAL A	14	.278	.333	36	10	2	0	0	0.0	7	4	5		1	1	0	67	3	7	6	5.5	.909	1B-8, 3B-6
1905	CHI A	34	.212	.248	113	24	1	0	1	0.9	14	12	12		2	1	0	47	72	6	10	3.8	.952	3B-17, 2B-16
1906		75	.258	.289	225	58	5	1	0	0.0	14	25	16		8	12	2	76	137	17	8	3.7	.926	3B-57, 2B-5, OF-1
1907		144	.213	.255	494	105	11	2	2	0.4	46	51	39		16	2	0	183	372	56	38	4.2	.908	3B-76, 2B-39, SS-30
4 yrs.		267	.227	.266	868	197	19	3	3	0.3	81	92	72		27	16	2	373	584	86	62	4.1	.918	3B-156, 2B-60, SS-30, 1B-8, OF-1
WORLD SERIES																								
1906	CHI A	6	.333	.571	21	7	1	2	0	0.0	2	4	3	1	2	0	0	4	16	3	0	3.8	.870	3B-6

Dan Rohn

ROHN, DANIEL JAY BL TR 5′ 8″ 165 lbs.
B. Jan. 10, 1956, Alpena, Mich.

Year	Team	Games	BA	SA	AB	H	2B	3B	HR	HR%	R	RBI	BB	SO	SB	Pinch Hit AB	Pinch Hit H	PO	A	E	DP	TC/G	FA	G by Pos
1983	CHI N	23	.387	.613	31	12	3	2	0	0.0	3	6	2	2	1	17	6	12	12	2	2	3.7	.923	2B-6, SS-1
1984		25	.129	.226	31	4	0	0	1	3.2	1	3	1	6	0	13	2	5	15	0	1	1.2	1.000	3B-7, SS-5, 2B-5
1986	CLE A	6	.200	.200	10	2	0	0	0	0.0	1	2	1	1	0	1	0	4	10	2	1	3.2	.875	2B-2, 3B-2, SS-1
3 yrs.		54	.250	.389	72	18	3	2	1	1.4	5	11	4	9	1	31	8	21	37	4	4	2.1	.935	2B-13, 3B-9, SS-7

Ray Rohwer

ROHWER, RAY BL TL 5′10″ 155 lbs.
B. June 5, 1895, Dixon, Calif. D. Jan. 24, 1988, Davis, Calif.

Year	Team	Games	BA	SA	AB	H	2B	3B	HR	HR%	R	RBI	BB	SO	SB	Pinch Hit AB	Pinch Hit H	PO	A	E	DP	TC/G	FA	G by Pos
1921	PIT N	30	.250	.425	40	10	3	2	0	0.0	6	6	4	8	0	18	2	14	2	3	0	1.9	.842	OF-10
1922		53	.295	.457	129	38	6	3	3	2.3	19	22	10	17	1	19	5	56	5	4	1	2.2	.938	OF-30
2 yrs.		83	.284	.450	169	48	9	5	3	1.8	25	28	14	25	1	37	7	70	7	7	1	2.1	.917	OF-40

Tony Roig

ROIG, ANTON AMBROSE BR TR 6′ 1″ 180 lbs.
B. Dec. 23, 1927, New Orleans, La.

Year	Team	Games	BA	SA	AB	H	2B	3B	HR	HR%	R	RBI	BB	SO	SB	Pinch Hit AB	Pinch Hit H	PO	A	E	DP	TC/G	FA	G by Pos
1953	WAS A	3	.125	.250	8	1	1	0	0	0.0	0	0	0	1	0	1	1	7	7	0	2	7.0	1.000	2B-2
1955		29	.228	.281	57	13	1	1	0	0.0	3	4	2	15	0	3	1	21	52	7	11	2.7	.913	SS-21, 3B-8, 2B-1
1956		44	.210	.286	119	25	5	2	0	0.0	11	7	20	29	2	3	1	83	110	8	30	4.4	.960	2B-27, SS-19
3 yrs.		76	.212	.283	184	39	7	3	0	0.0	14	11	22	45	2	7	3	111	169	15	43	3.8	.949	SS-40, 2B-30, 3B-8

Cookie Rojas

ROJAS, OCTAVIO VICTOR BR TR 5′10″ 160 lbs.
Born Octavio Victor Rojas (Rivas).
B. Mar. 6, 1939, Havana, Cuba.
Manager 1988.

Year	Team	Games	BA	SA	AB	H	2B	3B	HR	HR%	R	RBI	BB	SO	SB	Pinch Hit AB	Pinch Hit H	PO	A	E	DP	TC/G	FA	G by Pos
1962	CIN N	39	.221	.244	86	19	2	0	0	0.0	9	6	9	4	1	2	0	60	52	6	13	3.8	.949	2B-30, 3B-1
1963	PHI N	64	.221	.286	77	17	0	1	1	1.3	18	2	3	8	4	8	3	43	68	1	13	4.3	.991	2B-25, OF-1
1964		109	.291	.394	340	99	19	5	2	0.6	58	31	22	17	1	16	1	164	76	7	11	2.2	.972	OF-70, 2B-20, SS-18, 3B-1, C-1
1965		142	.303	.380	521	158	25	3	3	0.6	78	42	42	33	5	11	2	274	255	9	59	3.5	.983	2B-84, OF-55, SS-11, C-2, 1B-1
1966		156	.268	.329	626	168	18	1	6	1.0	77	55	35	46	4	1	0	319	295	13	69	3.8	.979	2B-106, OF-56, SS-2

Cookie Rojas *continued*

Year	Team	Games	BA	SA	AB	H	2B	3B	HR	HR%	R	RBI	BB	SO	SB	Pinch Hit AB	Pinch Hit H	PO	A	E	DP	TC/G	FA	G by Pos
1967		147	.259	.330	528	137	21	2	4	0.8	60	45	30	58	8	5	2	297	360	15	92	4.4	.978	2B-137, OF-9, C-3, SS-2, 3B-1, P-1
1968		152	.232	.306	621	144	19	0	9	1.4	53	48	16	55	4	2	0	365	424	10	110	5.3	.987	2B-150, C-1
1969		110	.228	.292	391	89	11	1	4	1.0	35	30	23	28	1	11	1	260	229	11	68	5.2	.978	2B-95, OF-2
1970	**2 teams**	**STL N** (23G –.106) **KC A** (98G –.260)																						
"	**total**	121	.244	.302	431	105	13	3	2	0.5	38	30	23	33	3	12	2	242	313	9	78	4.9	.984	2B-107, OF-6, SS-2
1971	**KC A**	115	.300	.406	414	124	22	2	6	1.4	56	59	39	35	8	2	0	254	293	5	76	4.8	.991	2B-111, SS-2, OF-1
1972		137	.261	.331	487	127	25	0	3	0.6	49	53	41	35	2	2	0	265	368	9	83	4.6	.986	2B-133, 3B-6, SS-2
1973		139	.276	.372	551	152	29	3	6	1.1	78	69	37	38	18	3	2	302	424	13	114	5.4	.982	2B-137
1974		144	.271	.339	542	147	17	1	6	1.1	52	60	30	43	8	8	1	292	368	9	94	4.7	.987	2B-141
1975		120	.254	.323	406	103	18	2	2	0.5	34	37	30	24	4	8	3	233	303	11	65	4.6	.980	2B-117, DH-1
1976		63	.242	.288	132	32	6	0	0	0.0	11	16	8	15	2	28	7	53	52	1	13	1.9	.991	2B-40, DH-9, 3B-6, 1B-1
1977		64	.250	.321	156	39	9	1	0	0.0	8	10	8	17	1	17	3	49	80	5	13	2.5	.963	3B-31, 2B-16, DH-6
16 yrs.		1822	.263	.337	6309	1660	254	25	54	0.9	714	593	396	489	74	136	27	3472	3960	134	971	4.3	.982	2B-1449, OF-200, 3B-46, SS-39, DH-16, C-7, 1B-2, P-1
LEAGUE CHAMPIONSHIP SERIES																								
1976	**KC A**	4	.333	.333	9	3	0	0	0	0.0	2	1	0	0	1	2	0	4	6	0	1	2.5	1.000	2B-4
1977		1	.250	.250	4	1	0	0	0	0.0	0	0	0	1	1	0	0	0	0	0	0	0.0	.000	DH-1
2 yrs.		5	.308	.308	13	4	0	0	0	0.0	2	1	0	1	2	2	0	4	6	0	1	2.0	1.000	2B-4, DH-1

Stan Rojek

ROJEK, STANLEY ANDREW
B. Apr. 21, 1919, North Tonawanda, N.Y.

BR TR 5′10″ 170 lbs.

Year	Team	Games	BA	SA	AB	H	2B	3B	HR	HR%	R	RBI	BB	SO	SB	Pinch Hit AB	Pinch Hit H	PO	A	E	DP	TC/G	FA	G by Pos
1942	**BKN N**	1	—	—	0	0	0	0	0	—	1	0	0	0	0	0	0	0	0	0	0	0.0	—	
1946		45	.277	.362	47	13	2	1	0	0.0	11	2	4	1	1	10	3	20	32	1	4	2.1	.981	SS-15, 2B-6, 3B-4
1947		32	.263	.287	80	21	0	1	0	0.0	7	7	7	3	1	1	0	41	73	2	17	3.5	.983	SS-17, 3B-9, 2B-7
1948	**PIT N**	156	.290	.367	**641**	186	27	5	4	0.6	85	51	61	41	24	0	0	262	475	29	91	4.9	.962	SS-156
1949		144	.244	.285	557	136	19	2	0	0.0	72	31	50	31	4	0	0	240	461	25	92	5.0	.966	SS-144
1950		76	.257	.317	230	59	12	1	0	0.0	28	17	18	13	2	4	0	110	161	9	39	3.9	.968	SS-68, 2B-3
1951	**2 teams**	**PIT N** (8G –.188) **STL N** (51G –.274)																						
"	**total**	59	.267	.332	202	54	7	3	0	0.0	21	14	10	11	0	0	0	100	144	8	36	4.3	.968	SS-59
1952	**STL A**	9	.143	.143	7	1	0	0	0	0.0	0	0	2	0	0	2	0	5	8	0	1	2.6	1.000	SS-4, 2B-1
8 yrs.		522	.266	.326	1764	470	67	13	4	0.2	225	122	152	100	32	17	3	778	1354	74	280	4.5	.966	SS-463, 2B-17, 3B-13

Red Rolfe

ROLFE, ROBERT ABIAL
B. Oct. 17, 1908, Penacook, N. H. D. July 8, 1969, Gifford, N. H.
Manager 1949–52.

BL TR 5′11½″ 170 lbs.

Year	Team	Games	BA	SA	AB	H	2B	3B	HR	HR%	R	RBI	BB	SO	SB	Pinch Hit AB	Pinch Hit H	PO	A	E	DP	TC/G	FA	G by Pos
1931	**NY A**	1	—	—	0	0	0	0	0	—	0	0	0	0	0	0	0	1	0	0	0	1.0	1.000	SS-1
1934		89	.287	.348	279	80	13	2	0	0.0	54	18	26	16	2	15	5	121	159	19	31	4.2	.936	SS-46, 3B-26
1935		149	.300	.404	639	192	33	9	5	0.8	108	67	57	39	7	0	0	197	283	19	22	3.3	.962	3B-136, SS-17
1936		135	.319	.493	568	181	39	**15**	10	1.8	116	70	68	38	3	0	0	162	265	19	20	3.4	.957	3B-133
1937		154	.276	.378	648	179	34	10	4	0.6	143	62	90	53	4	0	0	195	309	20	27	3.4	.962	3B-154
1938		151	.311	.441	631	196	36	8	10	1.6	132	80	74	44	13	0	0	151	294	19	26	3.1	.959	3B-151
1939		152	.329	.495	648	**213**	**46**	10	14	2.2	**139**	80	81	41	7	0	0	151	282	19	22	3.0	.958	3B-152
1940		139	.250	.366	588	147	26	6	10	1.7	102	53	50	48	4	1	0	161	288	24	24	3.4	.949	3B-138
1941		136	.264	.364	561	148	22	5	8	1.4	106	42	57	38	3	2	0	140	263	23	28	3.2	.946	3B-134
1942		69	.219	.355	265	58	8	2	8	3.0	42	25	23	18	1	8	1	57	132	8	16	3.3	.959	3B-60
10 yrs.		1175	.289	.413	4827	1394	257	67	69	1.4	942	497	526	335	44	26	6	1336	2275	170	216	3.3	.955	3B-1084, SS-64
WORLD SERIES																								
1936	**NY A**	6	.400	.400	25	10	0	0	0	0.0	5	4	3	1	0	0	0	14	7	1	0	3.7	.955	3B-6
1937		5	.300	.500	20	6	2	1	0	0.0	3	1	3	2	0	0	0	2	6	0	0	1.6	1.000	3B-5
1938		4	.167	.167	18	3	0	0	0	0.0	0	1	0	3	1	0	0	0	4	2	0	1.5	.667	3B-4
1939		4	.125	.125	16	2	0	0	0	0.0	2	0	0	0	0	0	0	3	8	1	2	3.0	.917	3B-4
1941		5	.300	.300	20	6	0	0	0	0.0	2	0	2	1	0	0	0	7	8	0	1	3.0	1.000	3B-5
1942		4	.353	.471	17	6	2	0	0	0.0	5	0	1	2	0	0	0	3	5	0	1	2.0	1.000	3B-4
6 yrs.		28	.284	.336	116	33	4	1	0	0.0	17	6	9	9	1	0	0	29	38	4	4	2.5	.944	3B-28

Ray Rolling

ROLLING, RAYMOND COPELAND
B. Sept. 8, 1886, Martinsburg, Mo. D. Aug. 25, 1966, St. Paul, Minn.

BR TR 5′10½″ 160 lbs.

Year	Team	Games	BA	SA	AB	H	2B	3B	HR	HR%	R	RBI	BB	SO	SB	Pinch Hit AB	Pinch Hit H	PO	A	E	DP	TC/G	FA	G by Pos
1912	**STL N**	5	.200	.200	15	3	0	0	0	0.0	0	0	0	5	0	0	0	9	9	1	0	4.8	.947	2B-4

Red Rollings

ROLLINGS, WILLIAM RUSSELL
B. Mar. 31, 1904, Mobile, Ala. D. Dec. 31, 1964, Mobile, Ala.

BL TR 5′11″ 167 lbs.

Year	Team	Games	BA	SA	AB	H	2B	3B	HR	HR%	R	RBI	BB	SO	SB	Pinch Hit AB	Pinch Hit H	PO	A	E	DP	TC/G	FA	G by Pos
1927	**BOS A**	82	.266	.299	184	49	4	1	0	0.0	19	9	12	10	3	14	6	105	75	7	13	3.3	.963	3B-44, 1B-10, 2B-2
1928		50	.229	.333	48	11	3	1	0	0.0	7	9	6	8	0	29	7	20	1	2	2	1.6	.913	1B-5, OF-4, 2B-4, 3B-1
1930	**BOS N**	52	.236	.285	123	29	6	0	0	0.0	10	10	9	5	2	12	4	42	73	6	9	3.2	.950	3B-28, 2B-10
3 yrs.		184	.251	.299	355	89	13	2	0	0.0	36	28	27	23	5	55	17	167	149	15	24	3.1	.955	3B-73, 2B-16, 1B-15, OF-4

Rich Rollins

ROLLINS, RICHARD JOHN (Red)
B. Apr. 16, 1938, Mt. Pleasant, Pa.

BR TR 5′10″ 185 lbs.

Year	Team	Games	BA	SA	AB	H	2B	3B	HR	HR%	R	RBI	BB	SO	SB	Pinch Hit AB	Pinch Hit H	PO	A	E	DP	TC/G	FA	G by Pos
1961	**MIN A**	13	.294	.353	17	5	1	0	0	0.0	3	3	2	2	0	3	2	5	10	0	2	1.7	1.000	2B-5, 3B-4
1962		159	.298	.428	624	186	23	5	16	2.6	96	96	75	62	3	0	0	137	324	28	33	3.1	.943	3B-159, SS-1
1963		136	.307	.444	531	163	23	1	16	3.0	75	61	36	59	2	4	0	122	225	26	22	2.8	.930	3B-132, 2B-1
1964		148	.270	.406	596	161	25	**10**	12	2.0	87	68	53	80	2	1	0	134	297	24	17	3.1	.947	3B-146
1965		140	.249	.333	469	117	22	1	5	1.1	59	32	37	54	4	13	2	144	264	20	25	3.3	.953	3B-112, 2B-16
1966		90	.245	.390	269	66	7	1	10	3.7	30	40	13	34	0	21	8	57	109	8	13	2.6	.954	3B-65, 2B-2, OF-1
1967		109	.245	.342	339	83	11	2	6	1.8	31	39	27	58	1	14	4	83	153	9	13	2.5	.963	3B-97
1968		93	.241	.355	203	49	5	0	6	3.0	14	30	10	34	3	41	8	28	93	9	4	2.3	.931	3B-56
1969	**SEA A**	58	.225	.326	187	42	7	0	4	2.1	15	21	7	19	2	14	4	42	104	8	7	3.2	.948	3B-47, SS-1
1970	**2 teams**	**MIL A** (14G –.200) **CLE A** (42G –.233)																						
"	**total**	56	.221	.324	68	15	1	0	2	2.9	9	9	6	9	0	42	8	3	15	2	3	1.7	.900	3B-12
10 yrs.		1002	.269	.388	3303	887	125	20	77	2.3	419	399	266	411	17	153	36	755	1594	134	139	2.9	.946	3B-830, 2B-24, SS-2, OF-1

Rich Rollins *continued*

Year	Team	Games	BA	SA	AB	H	2B	3B	HR	HR%	R	RBI	BB	SO	SB	Pinch Hit AB	Pinch Hit H	PO	A	E	DP	TC/G	FA	G by Pos
WORLD SERIES																								
1965	MIN A	3	.000	.000	2	0	0	0	0	0.0	0	0	1	0	0	2	0	0	0	0	0	0.0	—	

William Rollinson

ROLLINSON, WILLIAM
Born William Henry Winslow.
B. June 10, 1856, Fairfield, Me. D. Sept. 28, 1938, Bristow, Va.

Year	Team	Games	BA	SA	AB	H	2B	3B	HR	HR%	R	RBI	BB	SO	SB	Pinch Hit AB	Pinch Hit H	PO	A	E	DP	TC/G	FA	G by Pos
1884	WAS U	1	.000	.000	3	0	0	0	0	0.0	0		0			0	0	6	4	4	0	14.0	.714	C-1

Bill Roman

ROMAN, WILLIAM ANTHONY BL TL 6′ 4″ 190 lbs.
B. Oct. 11, 1938, Detroit, Mich.

Year	Team	Games	BA	SA	AB	H	2B	3B	HR	HR%	R	RBI	BB	SO	SB	Pinch Hit AB	Pinch Hit H	PO	A	E	DP	TC/G	FA	G by Pos
1964	DET A	3	.375	.750	8	3	0	0	1	12.5	2	1	0	2	0	2	1	13	1	0	2	7.0	1.000	1B-2
1965		21	.074	.074	27	2	0	0	0	0.0	0	0	2	7	0	13	2	38	1	0	2	6.5	1.000	1B-6
2 yrs.		24	.143	.229	35	5	0	0	1	2.9	2	1	2	9	0	15	3	51	2	0	4	6.6	1.000	1B-8

Johnny Romano

ROMANO, JOHN ANTHONY (Honey) BR TR 5′11″ 205 lbs.
B. Aug. 23, 1934, Hoboken, N. J.

Year	Team	Games	BA	SA	AB	H	2B	3B	HR	HR%	R	RBI	BB	SO	SB	Pinch Hit AB	Pinch Hit H	PO	A	E	DP	TC/G	FA	G by Pos
1958	CHI A	4	.286	.286	7	2	0	0	0	0.0	1	1	1	0	0	2	0	13	0	0	0	6.5	1.000	C-2
1959		53	.294	.468	126	37	5	1	5	4.0	20	25	23	18	0	13	8	169	16	4	5	5.0	.979	C-38
1960	CLE A	108	.272	.475	316	86	12	2	16	5.1	40	52	37	50	0	11	0	470	30	6	6	5.1	.988	C-99
1961		142	.299	.483	509	152	29	1	21	4.1	76	80	61	60	0	2	0	752	58	9	8	5.8	.989	C-141
1962		135	.261	.479	459	120	19	3	25	5.4	71	81	73	64	0	4	3	657	63	7	6	5.6	.990	C-130
1963		89	.216	.369	255	55	5	2	10	3.9	28	34	38	49	4	16	4	413	28	4	5	5.9	.991	C-71, OF-4
1964		106	.241	.460	352	85	18	1	19	5.4	46	47	51	83	2	10	2	723	38	7	3	7.9	.991	C-96, 1B-1
1965	CHI A	122	.242	.424	356	86	11	0	18	5.1	39	48	59	74	0	8	1	575	62	5	10	5.5	.992	C-111, OF-4, 1B-2
1966		122	.231	.404	329	76	12	0	15	4.6	33	47	58	72	0	16	4	622	46	4	7	6.6	.994	C-102
1967	STL N	24	.121	.138	58	7	1	0	0	0.0	1	2	13	15	1	4	0	111	3	2	1	5.8	.983	C-20
10 yrs.		905	.255	.443	2767	706	112	10	129	4.7	355	417	414	485	7	86	22	4505	344	48	51	6.0	.990	C-810, OF-8, 1B-3
WORLD SERIES																								
1959	CHI A	2	.000	.000	1	0	0	0	0	0.0	0	0	0	0	0	1	0	0	0	0	0	0.0	—	

Tom Romano

ROMANO, THOMAS MICHAEL BR TR 5′10″ 170 lbs.
B. Oct. 25, 1958, Syracuse, N. Y.

Year	Team	Games	BA	SA	AB	H	2B	3B	HR	HR%	R	RBI	BB	SO	SB	Pinch Hit AB	Pinch Hit H	PO	A	E	DP	TC/G	FA	G by Pos
1987	MON N	7	.000	.000	3	0	0	0	0	0.0	1	0	0	1	0	2	0	0	0	0	0	0.0	.000	OF-3

Ed Romero

ROMERO, EDGARDO RALPH BR TR 5′11″ 160 lbs.
Born Edgardo Ralph Romero (Rivera).
B. Dec. 9, 1957, Santurce, Puerto Rico.

Year	Team	Games	BA	SA	AB	H	2B	3B	HR	HR%	R	RBI	BB	SO	SB	Pinch Hit AB	Pinch Hit H	PO	A	E	DP	TC/G	FA	G by Pos
1977	MIL A	10	.280	.320	25	7	1	0	0	0.0	4	2	4	3	0	0	0	9	24	1	3	3.4	.971	SS-10
1980		42	.260	.356	104	27	7	0	1	1.0	20	10	9	11	2	1	0	60	102	12	20	4.3	.931	SS-22, 2B-15, 3B-3
1981		44	.198	.264	91	18	3	0	1	1.1	6	10	4	9	0	0	0	61	102	6	29	3.9	.964	SS-22, 2B-18, 3B-3
1982		52	.250	.326	144	36	8	0	1	0.7	18	7	8	16	0	2	1	103	113	7	34	4.3	.969	2B-39, SS-10, 3B-2, OF-1
1983		59	.317	.386	145	46	7	0	1	0.7	17	18	8	8	1	14	6	59	58	5	14	2.4	.959	SS-22, OF-15, DH-5, 3B-5, 2B-3
1984		116	.252	.294	357	90	12	0	1	0.3	36	31	29	25	3	1	0	141	256	18	35	3.6	.957	3B-59, SS-39, 2B-11, 1B-4, DH-2, OF-1
1985		88	.251	.303	251	63	11	1	0	0.0	24	21	26	20	1	0	0	157	219	8	53	4.3	.979	SS-43, 2B-31, OF-14, 3B-1
1986	BOS A	100	.210	.283	233	49	11	0	2	0.9	41	23	18	16	2	0	0	111	159	12	32	2.9	.957	SS-75, 3B-18, 2B-4, OF-1
1987		88	.272	.294	235	64	5	0	0	0.0	23	14	18	22	0	6	1	122	151	6	28	3.3	.978	2B-29, 3B-24, SS-24, 1B-8
1988		31	.240	.280	75	18	3	0	0	0.0	3	5	3	8	0	2	0	21	42	0	5	2.1	1.000	3B-15, SS-8, 2B-5, DH-1, 1B-1
1989	3 teams BOS A (46G –.212) ATL N (7G –.263) MIL A (15G –.200)																							
″	total	68	.214	.275	182	39	8	0	1	0.5	18	10	7	17	0	2	0	89	152	5	32	3.5	.980	2B-37, 3B-19, SS-13, DH-2
1990	DET A	32	.229	.271	70	16	3	0	0	0.0	8	4	6	4	0	5	1	15	41	1	9	1.9	.982	3B-27, DH-3
12 yrs.		730	.247	.302	1912	473	79	1	8	0.4	218	155	140	159	9	33	9	948	1419	81	294	3.4	.967	SS-288, 2B-192, 3B-176, OF-32, 1B-13, DH-13
DIVISIONAL PLAYOFF SERIES																								
1981	MIL A	1	.500	.500	2	1	0	0	0	0.0	1	0	0	1	0	0	0	2	2	0	0	4.0	1.000	2B-1
LEAGUE CHAMPIONSHIP SERIES																								
1986	BOS A	1	.000	.000	2	0	0	0	0	0.0	0	0	0	0	0	0	0	0	0	0	0	0.0	.000	SS-1
1988		1	—	—	0	0	0	0	0	—	0	0	0	0	0	0	0	0	0	0	0	0.0	—	
2 yrs.		2	.000	.000	2	0	0	0	0	0.0	0	0	0	0	0	0	0	0	0	0	0	0.0		SS-1
WORLD SERIES																								
1986	BOS A	3	.000	.000	1	0	0	0	0	0.0	0	0	0	0	0	0	0	0	1	0	0	0.3	1.000	SS-3

Kevin Romine

ROMINE, KEVIN ANDREW BR TR 5′11″ 185 lbs.
B. May 23, 1961, Exeter, N. H.

Year	Team	Games	BA	SA	AB	H	2B	3B	HR	HR%	R	RBI	BB	SO	SB	Pinch Hit AB	Pinch Hit H	PO	A	E	DP	TC/G	FA	G by Pos
1985	BOS A	24	.214	.286	28	6	2	0	0	0.0	3	1	1	4	1	1	1	20	1	0	0	0.9	1.000	OF-23, DH-1
1986		35	.257	.314	35	9	2	0	0	0.0	6	2	3	9	2	1	0	45	1	0	1	1.4	1.000	OF-33
1987		9	.292	.375	24	7	2	0	0	0.0	5	2	2	6	0	1	0	10	1	0	1	1.2	1.000	OF-7, DH-2
1988		57	.192	.282	78	15	2	1	1	1.3	17	6	7	15	2	3	0	44	0	2	0	0.9	.957	OF-45, DH-5
1989		92	.274	.332	274	75	13	0	1	0.4	30	23	21	53	1	8	3	157	9	3	4	1.9	.982	OF-89, DH-2
1990		70	.272	.368	136	37	7	0	2	1.5	21	14	12	27	4	5	2	81	0	2	0	1.3	.976	OF-64, DH-1
1991		44	.164	.255	55	9	2	0	1	1.8	7	7	3	10	1	7	2	27	0	1	0	0.8	.964	OF-23, DH-14
7 yrs.		331	.251	.325	630	158	30	1	5	0.8	89	55	49	124	11	26	8	384	12	8	6	1.3	.980	OF-284, DH-25
LEAGUE CHAMPIONSHIP SERIES																								
1988	BOS A	2	—	—	0	0	0	0	0	—	1	0	0	0	0	0	0	0	0	0	0	0.0	—	

Marc Ronan

RONAN, EDWARD MARCUS BL TR 6′ 2″ 190 lbs.
B. Sept. 19, 1969, Ozark, Ala.

Year	Team	Games	BA	SA	AB	H	2B	3B	HR	HR%	R	RBI	BB	SO	SB	Pinch Hit AB	Pinch Hit H	PO	A	E	DP	TC/G	FA	G by Pos
1993	STL N	6	.083	.083	12	1	0	0	0	0.0	0	0	0	5	0	0	0	29	0	0	0	4.8	1.000	C-6

Henri Rondeau

RONDEAU, HENRI JOSEPH
B. May 5, 1887, Danielson, Conn. D. May 28, 1943, Woonsocket, R. I.
BR TR 5′10½″ 175 lbs.

Year	Team	Games	BA	SA	AB	H	2B	3B	HR	HR%	R	RBI	BB	SO	SB	Pinch Hit AB	Pinch Hit H	PO	A	E	DP	TC/G	FA	G by Pos
1913	DET A	35	.186	.214	70	13	2	0	0	0.0	5	5	14	16	1	13	2	100	26	4	2	6.5	.969	C-14, 1B-6
1915	WAS A	14	.175	.175	40	7	0	0	0	0.0	3	4	4	3	1	3	0	29	2	0	0	2.8	1.000	OF-11
1916		50	.222	.309	162	36	5	3	1	0.6	20	28	18	18	7	0	0	110	4	5	0	2.5	.958	OF-48
3 yrs.		99	.206	.265	272	56	7	3	1	0.4	28	37	36	37	9	16	2	239	32	9	2	3.5	.968	OF-59, C-14, 1B-6

Gene Roof

ROOF, EUGENE LAWRENCE
Brother of Phil Roof.
B. Jan. 13, 1958, Paducah, Ky.
BB TR 6′ 2″ 180 lbs.

Year	Team	Games	BA	SA	AB	H	2B	3B	HR	HR%	R	RBI	BB	SO	SB	Pinch Hit AB	Pinch Hit H	PO	A	E	DP	TC/G	FA	G by Pos
1981	STL N	23	.300	.400	60	18	6	0	0	0.0	11	3	12	16	5	2	0	38	0	2	0	2.0	.950	OF-20
1982		11	.267	.267	15	4	0	0	0	0.0	3	2	1	4	2	7	2	5	0	0	0	1.0	1.000	OF-5
1983	2 teams	STL N (6G –.000) MON N (8G –.167)																						
″	total	14	.133	.267	15	2	2	0	0	0.0	3	1	1	3	0	7	1	3	0	0	0	0.5	1.000	OF-6
3 yrs.		48	.267	.356	90	24	8	0	0	0.0	17	6	14	23	7	16	3	46	0	2	0	1.5	.958	OF-31

Phil Roof

ROOF, PHILLIP ANTHONY
Brother of Gene Roof.
B. Mar. 5, 1941, Paducah, Ky.
BR TR 6′ 2″ 190 lbs.

Year	Team	Games	BA	SA	AB	H	2B	3B	HR	HR%	R	RBI	BB	SO	SB	Pinch Hit AB	Pinch Hit H	PO	A	E	DP	TC/G	FA	G by Pos
1961	MIL N	1	—	—	0	0	0	0	0	—	0	0	0	0	0	0	0	2	0	0	0	2.0	1.000	C-1
1964		1	.000	.000	2	0	0	0	0	0.0	0	0	0	1	0	0	0	8	0	0	0	8.0	1.000	C-1
1965	2 teams	CAL A (9G –.136) CLE A (43G –.173)																						
″	total	52	.162	.176	74	12	1	0	0	0.0	4	3	5	19	0	4	0	214	23	2	3	4.8	.992	C-50
1966	KC A	127	.209	.320	369	77	14	3	7	1.9	33	44	37	95	2	4	0	684	52	11	8	6.0	.985	C-123, 1B-2
1967		114	.205	.333	327	67	14	5	6	1.8	23	24	23	85	4	1	0	677	55	7	6	6.5	.991	C-113
1968	OAK A	34	.188	.234	64	12	0	0	1	1.6	5	2	2	15	1	2	0	116	6	4	2	3.9	.968	C-32
1969		106	.235	.291	247	58	6	1	2	0.8	19	19	33	55	1	1	0	493	40	9	4	5.1	.983	C-106
1970	MIL A	110	.227	.377	321	73	7	1	13	4.0	39	37	32	72	3	3	1	596	47	8	6	6.0	.988	C-107, 1B-1
1971	2 teams	MIL A (41G –.193) MIN A (31G –.241)																						
″	total	72	.214	.269	201	43	6	1	1	0.5	12	16	16	46	0	5	0	359	38	8	5	6.0	.980	C-68
1972	MIN A	61	.205	.356	146	30	11	1	3	2.1	16	12	6	27	0	0	0	257	11	6	0	4.5	.978	C-61
1973		47	.197	.274	117	23	4	1	1	0.9	10	15	13	27	0	0	0	218	17	2	4	5.0	.992	C-47
1974		44	.196	.268	97	19	1	0	2	2.1	10	13	6	24	0	0	0	200	24	0	3	5.1	1.000	C-44
1975		63	.302	.484	126	38	2	0	7	5.6	18	21	9	28	0	0	0	245	30	3	4	4.4	.989	C-63
1976	2 teams	MIN A (18G –.217) CHI A (4G –.111)																						
″	total	22	.200	.255	55	11	3	0	0	0.0	1	4	2	9	0	5	1	76	12	3	3	5.4	.967	C-16, DH-1
1977	TOR A	3	.000	.000	5	0	0	0	0	0.0	0	0	0	1	0	0	0	10	1	0	1	3.7	1.000	C-3
15 yrs.		857	.215	.319	2151	463	69	13	43	2.0	190	210	184	504	11	25	2	4155	356	63	49	5.5	.986	C-835, 1B-3, DH-1

George Rooks

ROOKS, GEORGE BRINTON McCLELLAN
Born George Brinton McClellan Ruckser.
B. Oct. 21, 1863, Chicago, Ill. D. Mar. 11, 1935, Chicago, Ill.
BR TR 5′11″ 170 lbs.

Year	Team	Games	BA	SA	AB	H	2B	3B	HR	HR%	R	RBI	BB	SO	SB	Pinch Hit AB	Pinch Hit H	PO	A	E	DP	TC/G	FA	G by Pos
1891	BOS N	5	.125	.125	16	2	0	0	0	0.0	1	0	4	1	0	0	0	11	1	0	0	2.4	1.000	OF-5

Rolando Roomes

ROOMES, ROLANDO AUDLEY
B. Feb. 15, 1962, Kingston, Jamaica.
BR TR 6′ 3″ 180 lbs.

Year	Team	Games	BA	SA	AB	H	2B	3B	HR	HR%	R	RBI	BB	SO	SB	Pinch Hit AB	Pinch Hit H	PO	A	E	DP	TC/G	FA	G by Pos
1988	CHI N	17	.188	.188	16	3	0	0	0	0.0	3	0	0	4	0	4	0	5	0	1	0	1.2	.833	OF-5
1989	CIN N	107	.263	.419	315	83	18	5	7	2.2	36	34	13	100	12	11	4	201	4	4	0	2.1	.981	OF-100
1990	2 teams	CIN N (30G –.213) MON N (16G –.286)																						
″	total	46	.227	.333	75	17	0	1	2	2.7	6	8	1	26	0	14	4	39	1	0	0	1.6	1.000	OF-25
3 yrs.		170	.254	.394	406	103	18	6	9	2.2	45	42	14	130	12	29	8	245	5	5	0	2.0	.980	OF-130

Frank Rooney

ROONEY, FRANK L.
Born Frank Rovny.
B. Oct. 12, 1884, Podebrady, Austria-Hungary D. Apr. 6, 1977, Bessemer, Mich.

Year	Team	Games	BA	SA	AB	H	2B	3B	HR	HR%	R	RBI	BB	SO	SB	Pinch Hit AB	Pinch Hit H	PO	A	E	DP	TC/G	FA	G by Pos
1914	IND F	12	.200	.343	35	7	0	1	1	2.9	1	8	1		2	3	0	98	2	2	6	11.3	.980	1B-9

Pat Rooney

ROONEY, PATRICK EUGENE
B. Nov. 28, 1957, Chicago, Ill.
BR TR 6′ 1″ 190 lbs.

Year	Team	Games	BA	SA	AB	H	2B	3B	HR	HR%	R	RBI	BB	SO	SB	Pinch Hit AB	Pinch Hit H	PO	A	E	DP	TC/G	FA	G by Pos
1981	MON N	4	.000	.000	5	0	0	0	0	0.0	0	0	0	3	0	2	0	1	0	0	0	0.5	1.000	OF-2

Jorge Roque

ROQUE, JORGE
Born Jorge Roque (Vargas).
B. Apr. 28, 1950, Ponce, Puerto Rico.
BR TR 5′10″ 158 lbs.

Year	Team	Games	BA	SA	AB	H	2B	3B	HR	HR%	R	RBI	BB	SO	SB	Pinch Hit AB	Pinch Hit H	PO	A	E	DP	TC/G	FA	G by Pos
1970	STL N	5	.000	.000	1	0	0	0	0	0.0	2	0	0	1	0	1	0	0	0	0	0	0.0	.000	OF-1
1971		3	.300	.300	10	3	0	0	0	0.0	2	1	0	3	1	0	0	6	0	0	0	2.0	1.000	OF-3
1972		32	.104	.209	67	7	2	1	1	1.5	3	5	6	19	1	6	1	50	0	1	0	2.1	.980	OF-24
1973	MON N	25	.148	.230	61	9	2	0	1	1.6	7	6	4	17	2	0	0	41	2	6	0	2.0	.878	OF-24
4 yrs.		65	.137	.223	139	19	4	1	2	1.4	14	12	10	40	4	7	1	97	2	7	0	2.0	.934	OF-52

Luis Rosado

ROSADO, LUIS (Papo)
Born Luis Rosado (Robles).
B. Dec. 6, 1955, Santurce, Puerto Rico.
BR TR 6′ 180 lbs.

Year	Team	Games	BA	SA	AB	H	2B	3B	HR	HR%	R	RBI	BB	SO	SB	Pinch Hit AB	Pinch Hit H	PO	A	E	DP	TC/G	FA	G by Pos
1977	NY N	9	.208	.250	24	5	1	0	0	0.0	1	3	1	3	0	1	0	46	4	2	4	6.5	.962	1B-7, C-1
1980		2	.000	.000	4	0	0	0	0	0.0	0	0	0	1	0	1	0	11	0	0	1	11.0	1.000	1B-1
2 yrs.		11	.179	.214	28	5	1	0	0	0.0	1	3	1	4	0	2	0	57	4	2	5	7.0	.968	1B-8, C-1

Buddy Rosar

ROSAR, WARREN VINCENT
B. July 3, 1914, Buffalo, N. Y. D. Mar. 13, 1994, Rochester, N. Y.
BR TR 5′ 9″ 190 lbs.

Year	Team	Games	BA	SA	AB	H	2B	3B	HR	HR%	R	RBI	BB	SO	SB	Pinch Hit AB	Pinch Hit H	PO	A	E	DP	TC/G	FA	G by Pos
1939	NY A	43	.276	.343	105	29	5	1	0	0.0	18	12	13	10	4	4	3	137	10	3	1	4.3	.980	C-35
1940		73	.298	.425	228	68	11	3	4	1.8	34	37	19	11	7	10	4	258	30	5	8	4.7	.983	C-63
1941		67	.287	.402	209	60	17	2	1	0.5	25	36	22	10	0	6	0	246	24	1	6	4.5	.996	C-60
1942		69	.230	.306	209	48	10	0	2	1.0	18	34	17	20	1	12	3	249	26	1	7	4.8	.996	C-58
1943	CLE A	115	.283	.340	382	108	17	1	1	0.3	53	41	33	12	0	6	1	480	91	10	11	5.1	.983	C-114

Buddy Rosar *continued*

Year	Team	Games	BA	SA	AB	H	2B	3B	HR	HR%	R	RBI	BB	SO	SB	Pinch Hit AB	Pinch Hit H	PO	A	E	DP	TC/G	FA	G by Pos
1944		99	.263	.308	331	87	9	3	0	0.0	29	30	34	17	1	1	0	409	59	5	13	4.8	.989	C-98
1945	PHI A	92	.210	.267	300	63	12	1	1	0.3	23	25	20	16	2	5	1	338	54	5	6	4.7	.987	C-85
1946		121	.283	.358	424	120	22	2	2	0.5	34	47	36	17	1	4	1	532	73	0	9	5.2	1.000	C-117
1947		102	.259	.334	359	93	20	2	1	0.3	40	33	40	13	1	1	0	406	70	2	12	4.7	.996	C-102
1948		90	.255	.338	302	77	13	0	4	1.3	30	41	39	12	0	0	0	335	39	1	10	4.2	.997	C-90
1949		32	.200	.221	95	19	2	0	0	0.0	7	6	16	5	0	1	0	112	9	1	2	3.9	.992	C-31
1950	BOS A	27	.298	.357	84	25	2	0	1	1.2	13	12	7	4	0	2	1	108	6	1	1	4.6	.991	C-25
1951		58	.229	.288	170	39	7	0	1	0.6	11	13	19	14	0	2	0	235	20	1	6	4.6	.996	C-56
13 yrs.		988	.261	.334	3198	836	147	15	18	0.6	335	367	315	161	17	54	14	3845	511	36	92	4.7	.992	C-934
WORLD SERIES																								
1941	NY A	1	—	—	0	0	0	0	0	—	0	0	0	0	0	0	0	0	0	0	0	0.0	.000	C-1
1942		1	1.000	1.000	1	1	0	0	0	0.0	0	0	0	0	0	1	1	0	0	0	0	0.0	—	
2 yrs.		2	1.000	1.000	1	1	0	0	0	0.0	0	0	0	0	0	1	1	0	0	0	0	0.0		C-1

Jimmy Rosario

ROSARIO, ANGEL RAMON BB TR 5′10″ 155 lbs.
Born Angel Ramon Rosario (Ferrer).
B. May 5, 1945, Bayamon, Puerto Rico.

Year	Team	Games	BA	SA	AB	H	2B	3B	HR	HR%	R	RBI	BB	SO	SB	Pinch Hit AB	Pinch Hit H	PO	A	E	DP	TC/G	FA	G by Pos
1971	SF N	92	.224	.266	192	43	6	1	0	0.0	26	13	33	35	7	11	1	151	1	0	0	2.3	1.000	OF-67
1972		7	.000	.000	2	0	0	0	0	0.0	1	0	0	0	0	2	0	0	0	0	0	0.0	.000	OF-1
1976	MIL A	15	.189	.270	37	7	0	0	1	2.7	4	5	3	8	1	1	0	20	0	0	0	1.4	1.000	OF-12, DH-2
3 yrs.		114	.216	.264	231	50	6	1	1	0.4	31	18	36	43	8	14	1	171	1	0	0	2.1	1.000	OF-80, DH-2
LEAGUE CHAMPIONSHIP SERIES																								
1971	SF N	1	—	—	0	0	0	0	0	—	0	0	0	0	0	0	0	0	0	0	0	0.0	—	

Santiago Rosario

ROSARIO, SANTIAGO BL TL 5′11″ 165 lbs.
B. July 25, 1939, Guayanilla, Puerto Rico.

Year	Team	Games	BA	SA	AB	H	2B	3B	HR	HR%	R	RBI	BB	SO	SB	Pinch Hit AB	Pinch Hit H	PO	A	E	DP	TC/G	FA	G by Pos
1965	KC A	81	.235	.341	85	20	3	0	2	2.4	8	8	6	16	0	46	11	99	7	1	5	3.1	.991	1B-31, OF-3

Victor Rosario

ROSARIO, VICTOR MANUEL BR TR 5′11″ 155 lbs.
Born Victor Manuel Rosario (Rivera).
B. Aug. 26, 1966, Hato Mayor del Rey, Puerto Rico.

Year	Team	Games	BA	SA	AB	H	2B	3B	HR	HR%	R	RBI	BB	SO	SB	Pinch Hit AB	Pinch Hit H	PO	A	E	DP	TC/G	FA	G by Pos
1990	ATL N	9	.143	.143	7	1	0	0	0	0.0	3	0	1	1	0	1	0	3	4	0	0	1.8	1.000	SS-3, 2B-1

Bobby Rose

ROSE, ROBERT RICHARD BR TR 5′11″ 170 lbs.
B. Mar. 15, 1967, Covina, Calif.

Year	Team	Games	BA	SA	AB	H	2B	3B	HR	HR%	R	RBI	BB	SO	SB	Pinch Hit AB	Pinch Hit H	PO	A	E	DP	TC/G	FA	G by Pos
1989	CAL A	14	.211	.421	38	8	1	2	1	2.6	4	3	2	10	0	1	0	10	21	2	1	2.5	.939	3B-10, 2B-3
1990		7	.385	.615	13	5	0	0	1	7.7	5	2	2	1	0	2	1	3	7	0	1	1.4	1.000	2B-4, 3B-3
1991		22	.277	.431	65	18	5	1	1	1.5	5	8	3	13	0	3	2	44	31	0	7	3.4	1.000	2B-8, OF-7, 3B-4, 1B-3
1992		30	.214	.345	84	18	5	0	2	2.4	10	10	8	9	1	2	1	58	94	7	19	5.3	.956	2B-28, 1B-2
4 yrs.		73	.245	.405	200	49	11	3	5	2.5	24	23	15	33	1	8	4	115	153	9	28	3.8	.968	2B-43, 3B-17, OF-7, 1B-5

Pete Rose

ROSE, PETER EDWARD (Charlie Hustle) BB TR 5′11″ 192 lbs.
B. Apr. 14, 1941, Cincinnati, Ohio.
Manager 1984–89.

Year	Team	Games	BA	SA	AB	H	2B	3B	HR	HR%	R	RBI	BB	SO	SB	Pinch Hit AB	Pinch Hit H	PO	A	E	DP	TC/G	FA	G by Pos
1963	CIN N	157	.273	.371	623	170	25	9	6	1.0	101	41	55	72	13	0	0	360	366	22	78	4.7	.971	2B-157, OF-1
1964		136	.269	.326	516	139	13	2	4	0.8	64	34	36	51	4	11	2	263	301	12	63	4.5	.979	2B-128
1965		162	.312	.446	**670**	**209**	35	11	11	1.6	117	81	69	76	8	0	0	382	403	20	93	5.0	.975	2B-162
1966		156	.313	.460	654	205	38	5	16	2.4	97	70	37	61	4	0	0	409	374	18	83	5.1	.978	2B-140, 3B-16
1967		148	.301	.444	585	176	32	8	12	2.1	86	76	56	66	11	0	0	287	93	11	15	2.5	.972	OF-123, 2B-35
1968		149	**.335**	.470	626	**210**	42	6	10	1.6	94	49	56	76	3	0	0	270	20	3	4	1.9	.990	OF-148, 2B-3, 1B-1
1969		156	**.348**	.512	627	218	33	11	16	2.6	**120**	82	88	65	7	0	0	317	10	4	3	2.1	.988	OF-156, 2B-2
1970		159	.316	.470	649	**205**	37	9	15	2.3	120	52	73	64	12	1	0	309	8	1	2	2.0	.997	OF-159
1971		160	.304	.421	632	192	27	4	13	2.1	86	44	68	50	13	2	0	306	13	2	1	2.0	.994	OF-158
1972		154	.307	.417	**645**	**198**	31	11	6	0.9	107	57	73	46	10	0	0	330	15	2	2	2.3	.994	OF-154
1973		160	**.338**	.437	**680**	**230**	36	8	5	0.7	115	64	65	42	10	0	0	343	15	3	0	2.3	.992	OF-159
1974		163	.284	.388	652	185	**45**	7	3	0.5	**110**	51	106	54	2	0	0	346	11	1	3	2.2	.997	OF-163
1975		162	.317	.432	662	210	**47**	4	7	1.1	**112**	74	89	50	0	0	0	161	230	14	21	2.4	.965	3B-137, OF-35
1976		162	.323	.450	665	**215**	**42**	6	10	1.5	**130**	63	86	54	9	3	2	115	293	13	25	2.6	.969	3B-159, OF-1
1977		162	.311	.432	**655**	204	38	7	9	1.4	95	64	66	42	16	1	0	98	268	16	18	2.4	.958	3B-161
1978		159	.302	.421	655	198	**51**	3	7	1.1	103	52	62	30	13	0	0	135	256	15	25	2.5	.963	3B-156, OF-7, 1B-2
1979	PHI N	163	.331	.430	628	208	40	5	4	0.6	90	59	95	32	20	0	0	1429	93	10	124	9.3	.993	1B-159, 3B-5, 2B-1
1980		162	.282	.354	655	185	**42**	1	1	0.2	95	64	66	33	12	1	0	1427	123	5	113	9.6	.997	1B-162
1981		107	.325	.390	431	**140**	18	5	0	0.0	73	33	46	26	4	0	0	929	91	4	69	9.6	.996	1B-107
1982		162	.271	.338	634	172	25	4	3	0.5	80	54	66	32	8	0	0	1428	123	8	114	9.6	.995	1B-162
1983		151	.245	.286	493	121	14	3	0	0.0	52	45	52	28	7	22	8	827	74	10	57	6.2	.989	1B-112, OF-35
1984	2 teams	MON N (95G –.259) CIN N (26G –.365)																						
″	total	121	.286	.337	374	107	15	2	0	0.0	43	34	40	27	1	27	7	530	53	8	36	6.5	.986	1B-63, OF-28
1985	CIN N	119	.264	.319	405	107	12	2	2	0.5	60	46	86	35	8	8	1	870	73	5	80	8.6	.995	1B-110
1986		72	.219	.270	237	52	8	2	0	0.0	15	25	30	31	3	8	1	523	43	6	54	9.4	.990	1B-61
24 yrs.		3562	.303	.409	14053	4256	746	135	160	1.1	2165	1314	1566	1143	198	84	21	12394	3349	213	1083	4.5	.987	OF-1327, 1B-939, 3B-634,
		1st			**1st**	**1st**	**2nd**				**4th**		**10th**											2B-628
DIVISIONAL PLAYOFF SERIES																								
1981	PHI N	5	.300	.350	20	6	1	0	0	0.0	1	2	2	0	0	0	0	29	8	0	0	7.4	1.000	1B-5
LEAGUE CHAMPIONSHIP SERIES																								
1970	CIN N	3	.231	.231	13	3	0	0	0	0.0	1	1	0	0	0	0	0	3	0	0	0	1.0	1.000	OF-3
1972		5	.450	.650	20	9	4	0	0	0.0	1	2	1	2	0	0	0	10	0	0	0	2.0	1.000	OF-5
1973		5	.381	.714	21	8	1	0	2	9.5	3	2	2	2	0	0	0	10	1	0	0	2.2	1.000	OF-5
1975		3	.357	.571	14	5	0	0	1	7.1	3	2	0	2	0	0	0	2	1	0	0	1.0	1.000	3B-3
1976		3	.429	.714	14	6	2	1	0	0.0	3	2	1	0	0	0	0	2	5	1	1	2.7	.875	3B-3

Pete Rose *continued*

Year	Team	Games	BA	SA	AB	H	2B	3B	HR	HR%	R	RBI	BB	SO	SB	Pinch Hit AB	Pinch Hit H	PO	A	E	DP	TC/G	FA	G by Pos
1980	PHI N	5	.400	.400	20	8	0	0	0	0.0	3	2	5	3	0	0	0	53	7	0	5	12.0	1.000	1B-5
1983		4	.375	.375	16	6	0	0	0	0.0	3	0	1	1	1	0	0	29	2	0	0	7.8	1.000	1B-4
7 yrs.		28	.381	.534	118	45	7	1	3	2.5	17	11	10	10	1	0	0	109	16	1	6	4.5	.992	OF-13, 1B-9, 3B-6
		3rd	**5th**	**9th**	**3rd**	**1st**	**1st**				**3rd**													
WORLD SERIES																								
1970	CIN N	5	.250	.450	20	5	1	0	1	5.0	2	2	2	0	0	0	0	14	1	1	0	3.2	.938	OF-5
1972		7	.214	.321	28	6	0	0	1	3.6	3	2	4	4	1	0	0	14	1	0	0	2.1	1.000	OF-7
1975		7	.370	.481	27	10	1	1	0	0.0	3	2	5	1	0	0	0	7	8	0	2	2.1	1.000	3B-7
1976		4	.188	.250	16	3	1	0	0	0.0	1	1	2	2	0	0	0	6	3	0	0	2.3	1.000	3B-4
1980	PHI N	6	.261	.304	23	6	1	0	0	0.0	2	1	2	2	0	0	0	49	6	0	8	9.2	1.000	1B-6
1983		5	.313	.375	16	5	1	0	0	0.0	1	1	1	3	0	1	0	26	4	0	0	7.5	1.000	1B-3, OF-1
6 yrs.		34	.269	.369	130	35	5	1	2	1.5	12	9	16	12	1	1	0	116	23	1	10	4.2	.993	OF-13, 3B-11, 1B-9

Johnny Roseboro

ROSEBORO, JOHN JUNIOR
B. May 13, 1933, Ashland, Ohio.

BL TR 5′11½″ 190 lbs.

Year	Team	Games	BA	SA	AB	H	2B	3B	HR	HR%	R	RBI	BB	SO	SB	Pinch Hit AB	Pinch Hit H	PO	A	E	DP	TC/G	FA	G by Pos
1957	BKN N	35	.145	.261	69	10	2	0	2	2.9	6	6	10	20	0	3	0	136	7	3	4	6.1	.979	C-19, 1B-5
1958	LA N	114	.271	.456	384	104	11	9	14	3.6	52	43	36	56	11	7	1	598	36	8	5	5.9	.988	C-104, OF-5
1959		118	.232	.378	397	92	14	7	10	2.5	39	38	52	69	7	2	0	848	54	8	10	7.8	.991	C-117
1960		103	.213	.369	287	61	15	3	8	2.8	22	42	44	53	7	14	4	640	48	5	10	7.8	.993	C-87, 3B-1, 1B-1
1961		128	.251	.459	394	99	16	6	18	4.6	59	59	56	62	6	7	3	877	56	13	16	7.6	.986	C-125
1962		128	.249	.380	389	97	16	7	7	1.8	45	55	50	60	12	4	0	842	57	14	10	7.1	.985	C-128
1963		135	.236	.351	470	111	13	7	9	1.9	50	49	36	50	7	3	1	908	66	8	6	7.3	.992	C-134
1964		134	.287	.372	414	119	24	1	3	0.7	42	45	44	61	3	12	4	809	64	6	8	6.9	.993	C-128
1965		136	.233	.311	437	102	10	0	8	1.8	42	57	34	51	1	9	4	824	55	5	7	6.7	.994	C-131, 3B-1
1966		142	.276	.398	445	123	23	2	9	2.0	47	53	44	51	3	8	1	904	65	7	11	7.1	.993	C-138
1967		116	.272	.374	334	91	18	2	4	1.2	37	24	38	33	2	17	5	550	60	10	6	5.8	.984	C-107
1968	MIN A	135	.216	.311	380	82	12	0	8	2.1	31	39	46	57	2	22	3	689	52	7	5	6.4	.991	C-117
1969		115	.263	.321	361	95	12	0	3	0.8	33	32	39	44	5	3	0	585	52	13	16	5.9	.980	C-111
1970	WAS A	46	.233	.314	86	20	4	0	1	1.2	7	6	18	10	1	17	3	122	6	0	1	4.3	1.000	C-30
14 yrs.		1585	.249	.371	4847	1206	190	44	104	2.1	512	548	547	677	67	128	29	9332	678	107	115	6.8	.989	C-1476, 1B-6, OF-5, 3B-2
LEAGUE CHAMPIONSHIP SERIES																								
1969	MIN A	2	.200	.200	5	1	0	0	0	0.0	0	0	0	0	0	0	0	6	1	0	0	3.5	1.000	C-2
WORLD SERIES																								
1959	LA N	6	.095	.095	21	2	0	0	0	0.0	0	1	0	2	0	0	0	35	4	0	1	6.5	1.000	C-6
1963		4	.143	.357	14	2	0	0	1	7.1	1	3	0	4	0	0	0	43	0	0	0	10.8	1.000	C-4
1965		7	.286	.333	21	6	1	0	0	0.0	1	3	5	3	1	0	0	57	4	0	0	8.7	1.000	C-7
1966		4	.071	.071	14	1	0	0	0	0.0	0	0	0	3	0	0	0	22	2	0	1	6.0	1.000	C-4
4 yrs.		21	.157	.214	70	11	1	0	1	1.4	2	7	5	12	1	0	0	157	10	0	2	8.0	1.000	C-21

Bob Roselli

ROSELLI, ROBERT EDWARD
B. Dec. 10, 1931, San Francisco, Calif.

BR TR 5′11″ 185 lbs.

Year	Team	Games	BA	SA	AB	H	2B	3B	HR	HR%	R	RBI	BB	SO	SB	Pinch Hit AB	Pinch Hit H	PO	A	E	DP	TC/G	FA	G by Pos
1955	MIL N	6	.222	.333	9	2	1	0	0	0.0	1	0	1	4	0	3	0	9	2	1	0	6.0	.917	C-2
1956		4	.500	2.000	2	1	0	0	1	50.0	1	1	0	1	0	1	1	8	1	0	1	3.0	1.000	C-3
1958		1	.000	.000	1	0	0	0	0	0.0	0	0	0	0	0	1	0	0	0	0	0	0.0	—	
1961	CHI A	22	.263	.342	38	10	3	0	0	0.0	2	4	0	11	0	12	4	32	3	0	0	3.5	1.000	C-10
1962		35	.188	.313	64	12	3	1	1	1.6	4	5	11	15	1	15	2	80	5	1	2	4.3	.988	C-20
5 yrs.		68	.219	.351	114	25	7	1	2	1.8	8	10	12	31	1	32	7	129	11	2	3	4.1	.986	C-35

Dave Rosello

ROSELLO, DAVID
Born David Rosello (Rodriguez).
B. June 25, 1950, Mayaguez, Puerto Rico.

BR TR 5′11″ 160 lbs.

Year	Team	Games	BA	SA	AB	H	2B	3B	HR	HR%	R	RBI	BB	SO	SB	Pinch Hit AB	Pinch Hit H	PO	A	E	DP	TC/G	FA	G by Pos
1972	CHI N	5	.250	.500	12	3	0	0	1	8.3	2	3	3	2	0	0	0	11	11	4	4	5.2	.846	SS-5
1973		16	.263	.316	38	10	2	0	0	0.0	4	2	2	4	2	1	0	30	29	3	7	4.4	.952	2B-13, SS-1
1974		62	.203	.250	148	30	7	0	0	0.0	9	10	10	28	1	2	1	97	114	8	37	3.6	.963	2B-49, SS-12
1975		19	.259	.345	58	15	2	0	1	1.7	7	8	9	8	0	0	0	27	53	4	7	4.4	.952	SS-19
1976		91	.242	.286	227	55	5	1	1	0.4	27	11	41	33	1	1	0	129	217	12	45	4.1	.966	SS-86, 2B-1
1977		56	.220	.305	82	18	2	1	1	1.2	18	9	12	12	0	22	7	8	42	6	2	1.6	.893	3B-21, SS-10, 2B-3
1979	CLE A	59	.243	.402	107	26	6	1	3	2.8	20	14	15	27	1	3	1	43	98	5	16	2.5	.966	2B-33, 3B-14, SS-11
1980		71	.248	.325	117	29	3	0	2	1.7	16	12	9	19	0	1	0	76	91	4	18	2.5	.977	2B-43, 3B-22, SS-3, DH-1
1981		43	.238	.321	84	20	4	0	1	1.2	11	7	7	12	0	10	1	55	63	3	15	2.9	.975	2B-26, 3B-8, DH-4, SS-4
9 yrs.		422	.236	.313	873	206	31	3	10	1.1	114	76	108	145	5	40	10	476	718	49	151	3.2	.961	2B-168, SS-151, 3B-65, DH-5

Chief Roseman

ROSEMAN, JAMES JOHN
B. July 4, 1856, Brooklyn, N. Y. D. July 4, 1938, Brooklyn, N. Y.
Manager 1890.

BR TR 5′ 7″ 167 lbs.

Year	Team	Games	BA	SA	AB	H	2B	3B	HR	HR%	R	RBI	BB	SO	SB	Pinch Hit AB	Pinch Hit H	PO	A	E	DP	TC/G	FA	G by Pos
1882	TRO N	82	.236	.344	331	78	21	6	1	0.3	41	43	3	41		0	0	107	21	22	6	1.8	.853	OF-82
1883	NY AA	93	.251	.314	398	100	13	6	0	0.0	48		11			0	0	123	19	22	5	1.8	.866	OF-91, 1B-2
1884		107	.298	.413	436	130	16	11	4	0.9	97		21			0	0	157	12	22	0	1.8	.885	OF-107
1885		101	.278	.405	410	114	13	15	3	0.7	72		25			0	0	177	9	29	1	2.1	.865	OF-101, P-1
1886		134	.227	.324	559	127	19	10	5	0.9	90		24			0	0	203	20	27	6	1.9	.892	OF-134, P-1
1887	**3 teams**	**PHI AA** (21G –.219) **NY AA** (60G –.228) **BKN AA** (1G –.333)																						
″	**total**	82	.227	.278	317	72	12	2	0	0.0	48		19		6	0	0	166	11	27	4	2.4	.868	OF-81, 1B-3, P-2
1890	**2 teams**	**STL AA** (80G –.341) **LOU AA** (2G –.250)																						
″	**total**	82	.339	.442	310	105	26	0	2	0.6	47		30		7	0	0	296	17	24	17	4.1	.929	OF-58, 1B-24
7 yrs.		681	.263	.359	2761	726	120	50	15	0.5	443	43	133	41	13	0	0	1229	109	173	39	2.2	.886	OF-654, 1B-29, P-4

Al Rosen

ROSEN, ALBERT LEONARD (Flip)
B. Feb. 29, 1924, Spartanburg, S. C.

BR TR 5′10½″ 180 lbs.

Year	Team	Games	BA	SA	AB	H	2B	3B	HR	HR%	R	RBI	BB	SO	SB	Pinch Hit AB	Pinch Hit H	PO	A	E	DP	TC/G	FA	G by Pos
1947	CLE A	7	.111	.111	9	1	0	0	0	0.0	1	0	0	3	0	4	1	1	1	0	1	0.7	1.000	3B-2, OF-1
1948		5	.200	.200	5	1	0	0	0	0.0	0	0	0	2	0	3	1	1	1	0	0	1.0	1.000	3B-2
1949		23	.159	.205	44	7	2	0	0	0.0	3	5	7	4	0	13	2	10	16	0	1	2.6	1.000	3B-10
1950		155	.287	.543	554	159	23	4	**37**	**6.7**	100	116	100	72	5	1	0	151	322	15	24	3.2	.969	3B-154
1951		154	.265	.447	573	152	30	1	24	4.2	82	102	85	71	7	0	0	157	277	19	20	2.9	.958	3B-154

Al Rosen *continued*

Year	Team	Games	BA	SA	AB	H	2B	3B	HR	HR%	R	RBI	BB	SO	SB	Pinch Hit AB	Pinch Hit H	PO	A	E	DP	TC/G	FA	G by Pos
1952		148	.302	.524	567	171	32	5	28	4.9	101	**105**	75	54	8	0	0	177	265	20	29	3.0	.957	3B-147, 1B-4, SS-3
1953		155	.336	**.613**	599	201	27	5	**43**	7.2	**115**	**145**	85	48	8	1	0	178	338	19	39	3.4	.964	3B-154, 1B-1, SS-1
1954		137	.300	.506	466	140	20	2	24	5.2	76	102	85	43	6	5	2	502	188	18	48	5.2	.975	3B-87, 1B-46, SS-1, 2B-1
1955		139	.244	.402	492	120	13	1	21	4.3	61	81	92	44	4	2	0	396	221	18	48	4.3	.972	3B-106, 1B-41
1956		121	.267	.428	416	111	18	2	15	3.6	64	61	58	44	1	4	0	89	219	18	20	2.8	.945	3B-116
10 yrs.		1044	.285	.495	3725	1063	165	20	192	5.2	603	717	587	385	39	33	6	1662	1848	127	230	3.5	.965	3B-932, 1B-92, SS-5, 2B-1, OF-1
WORLD SERIES																								
1948	CLE A	1	.000	.000	1	0	0	0	0	0.0	0	0	0	0	0	1	0	0	0	0	0	0.0	—	
1954		3	.250	.250	12	3	0	0	0	0.0	0	0	1	0	0	0	0	2	3	0	0	1.7	1.000	3B-3
2 yrs.		4	.231	.231	13	3	0	0	0	0.0	0	0	1	0	0	1	0	2	3	0	0	1.7	1.000	3B-3

Goody Rosen

ROSEN, GOODWIN GEORGE BL TL 5′9½″ 160 lbs.
B. Aug. 28, 1912, Toronto, Ont., Canada D. Apr. 6, 1994, Toronto, Ont., Canada.

Year	Team	Games	BA	SA	AB	H	2B	3B	HR	HR%	R	RBI	BB	SO	SB	Pinch Hit AB	Pinch Hit H	PO	A	E	DP	TC/G	FA	G by Pos
1937	BKN N	22	.312	.403	77	24	5	1	0	0.0	10	6	6	6	2	0	0	50	1	1	1	2.5	.981	OF-21
1938		138	.281	.389	473	133	17	11	4	0.8	75	51	65	43	0	19	2	263	19	3	4	2.5	.989	OF-113
1939		54	.251	.344	183	46	6	4	1	0.5	22	12	23	21	4	4	0	106	0	0	0	2.3	1.000	OF-47
1944		89	.261	.314	264	69	8	3	0	0.0	38	23	26	27	0	21	5	199	12	2	0	3.3	.991	OF-65
1945		145	.325	.460	606	197	24	11	12	2.0	126	75	50	36	4	3	0	392	7	3	1	2.9	.993	OF-141
1946	2 teams	BKN N (3G –.333) NY N (100G –.281)																						
″	total	103	.281	.390	313	88	11	4	5	1.6	39	30	48	33	2	15	3	200	3	5	0	2.4	.976	OF-85
6 yrs.		551	.291	.398	1916	557	71	34	22	1.1	310	197	218	166	12	62	10	1210	42	14	6	2.7	.989	OF-472

Harry Rosenberg

ROSENBERG, HARRY BR TR 5′10″ 180 lbs.
Brother of Lou Rosenberg.
B. June 22, 1909, San Francisco, Calif.

Year	Team	Games	BA	SA	AB	H	2B	3B	HR	HR%	R	RBI	BB	SO	SB	Pinch Hit AB	Pinch Hit H	PO	A	E	DP	TC/G	FA	G by Pos
1930	NY N	9	.000	.000	5	0	0	0	0	0.0	1	0	1	4	0	4	0	2	0	0	0	0.7	1.000	OF-3

Lou Rosenberg

ROSENBERG, LOUIS BR TR 5′7″ 155 lbs.
Brother of Harry Rosenberg.
B. Mar. 5, 1904, San Francisco, Calif. D. Sept. 8, 1991, Daly City, Calif.

Year	Team	Games	BA	SA	AB	H	2B	3B	HR	HR%	R	RBI	BB	SO	SB	Pinch Hit AB	Pinch Hit H	PO	A	E	DP	TC/G	FA	G by Pos
1923	CHI A	3	.250	.250	4	1	0	0	0	0.0	0	0	0	1	0	1	0	1	0	0	0	0.5	1.000	2B-2

Max Rosenfeld

ROSENFELD, MAX BR TR 5′8″ 175 lbs.
B. Dec. 23, 1902, New York, N. Y. D. Mar. 10, 1969, Miami, Fla.

Year	Team	Games	BA	SA	AB	H	2B	3B	HR	HR%	R	RBI	BB	SO	SB	Pinch Hit AB	Pinch Hit H	PO	A	E	DP	TC/G	FA	G by Pos
1931	BKN N	3	.222	.333	9	2	1	0	0	0.0	0	0	1	1	0	0	0	6	0	0	0	2.0	1.000	OF-3
1932		34	.359	.590	39	14	3	0	2	5.1	8	7	0	10	2	3	0	31	1	1	1	1.1	.970	OF-30
1933		5	.111	.111	9	1	0	0	0	0.0	0	0	1	1	0	1	0	7	0	0	0	3.5	1.000	OF-2
3 yrs.		42	.298	.474	57	17	4	0	2	3.5	8	7	2	12	2	4	0	44	1	1	1	1.3	.978	OF-35

Larry Rosenthal

ROSENTHAL, LAWRENCE JOHN BL TL 6′½″ 190 lbs.
B. May 21, 1910, St. Paul, Minn. D. Mar. 4, 1992, Woodbury, Minn.

Year	Team	Games	BA	SA	AB	H	2B	3B	HR	HR%	R	RBI	BB	SO	SB	Pinch Hit AB	Pinch Hit H	PO	A	E	DP	TC/G	FA	G by Pos
1936	CHI A	85	.281	.407	317	89	15	8	3	0.9	71	47	59	37	2	4	3	243	7	6	3	3.2	.977	OF-80
1937		58	.289	.402	97	28	5	3	0	0.0	20	9	9	20	1	29	**9**	46	3	1	1	2.0	.980	OF-25
1938		61	.286	.381	105	30	5	1	1	1.0	14	12	12	13	0	30	6	44	3	2	1	2.2	.959	OF-22
1939		107	.265	.454	324	86	21	5	10	3.1	50	51	53	46	6	12	1	193	5	2	1	2.2	.990	OF-93
1940		107	.301	.453	276	83	14	5	6	2.2	46	42	64	32	2	11	2	208	4	5	0	2.4	.977	OF-91
1941	2 teams	CHI A (20G –.237) CLE A (45G –.187)																						
″	total	65	.209	.299	134	28	7	1	1	0.7	19	9	21	15	1	30	6	63	4	2	0	2.1	.971	OF-32, 1B-1
1944	2 teams	NY A (36G –.198) PHI A (32G –.204)																						
″	total	68	.200	.252	155	31	5	0	1	0.6	14	15	24	24	1	19	4	92	2	2	1	2.1	.979	OF-45
1945	PHI A	28	.200	.293	75	15	3	2	0	0.0	6	5	9	8	0	4	0	35	1	0	0	1.7	1.000	OF-21
8 yrs.		579	.263	.392	1483	390	75	25	22	1.5	240	190	251	195	13	139	31	924	29	20	7	2.4	.979	OF-409, 1B-1

Si Rosenthal

ROSENTHAL, SIMON BL TL 5′9″ 165 lbs.
B. Nov. 13, 1903, Boston, Mass. D. Apr. 7, 1969, Boston, Mass.

Year	Team	Games	BA	SA	AB	H	2B	3B	HR	HR%	R	RBI	BB	SO	SB	Pinch Hit AB	Pinch Hit H	PO	A	E	DP	TC/G	FA	G by Pos
1925	BOS A	19	.264	.389	72	19	5	2	0	0.0	6	8	7	3	1	2	0	31	3	3	0	2.2	.919	OF-17
1926		104	.267	.372	285	76	12	3	4	1.4	34	34	19	18	4	35	9	100	0	4	0	1.6	.962	OF-67
2 yrs.		123	.266	.375	357	95	17	5	4	1.1	40	42	26	21	5	37	9	131	3	7	0	1.7	.950	OF-84

Jack Roser

ROSER, JOHN WILLIAM JOSEPH (Bunny) BL TL 5′11″ 175 lbs.
B. Nov. 15, 1901, St. Louis, Mo. D. May 6, 1979, Rocky Hill, Conn.

Year	Team	Games	BA	SA	AB	H	2B	3B	HR	HR%	R	RBI	BB	SO	SB	Pinch Hit AB	Pinch Hit H	PO	A	E	DP	TC/G	FA	G by Pos
1922	BOS N	32	.239	.336	113	27	3	4	0	0.0	13	16	10	19	2	0	0	63	2	6	0	2.2	.915	OF-32

Chet Ross

ROSS, CHESTER JAMES BR TR 6′1″ 195 lbs.
B. Apr. 1, 1917, Buffalo, N. Y. D. Feb. 21, 1989, Buffalo, N. Y.

Year	Team	Games	BA	SA	AB	H	2B	3B	HR	HR%	R	RBI	BB	SO	SB	Pinch Hit AB	Pinch Hit H	PO	A	E	DP	TC/G	FA	G by Pos
1939	BOS N	11	.323	.419	31	10	1	1	0	0.0	4	0	2	10	0	3	0	19	1	0	0	2.5	1.000	OF-8
1940		149	.281	.460	569	160	23	14	17	3.0	84	89	59	**127**	4	0	0	347	12	14	2	2.5	.962	OF-149
1941		29	.120	.140	50	6	1	0	0	0.0	1	4	9	17	0	17	2	21	1	0	0	1.8	1.000	OF-12
1942		76	.195	.314	220	43	7	2	5	2.3	20	19	16	37	0	18	4	123	2	1	0	2.2	.992	OF-57
1943		94	.218	.347	285	62	12	2	7	2.5	27	32	26	67	1	19	5	165	8	4	1	2.3	.977	OF-78
1944		54	.227	.409	154	35	9	2	5	3.2	20	26	12	23	1	15	2	75	8	0	2	2.2	1.000	OF-38
6 yrs.		413	.241	.392	1309	316	53	21	34	2.6	156	170	124	281	6	72	13	750	32	19	5	2.3	.976	OF-342

Don Ross

ROSS, DONALD RAYMOND BR TR 6′1″ 185 lbs.
B. July 16, 1914, Pasadena, Calif.

Year	Team	Games	BA	SA	AB	H	2B	3B	HR	HR%	R	RBI	BB	SO	SB	Pinch Hit AB	Pinch Hit H	PO	A	E	DP	TC/G	FA	G by Pos
1938	DET A	77	.260	.306	265	69	7	1	1	0.4	22	30	28	11	1	2	0	90	157	14	15	3.5	.946	3B-75
1940	BKN N	10	.289	.421	38	11	2	0	1	2.6	4	8	3	3	1	0	0	10	19	4	0	3.3	.879	3B-10
1942	DET A	87	.274	.376	226	62	10	2	3	1.3	29	30	36	16	2	22	8	94	30	7	4	2.3	.947	OF-38, 3B-20
1943		89	.267	.320	247	66	13	0	0	0.0	19	18	20	3	2	24	5	106	65	9	10	2.8	.950	OF-38, SS-18, 2B-7, 3B-1
1944		66	.210	.275	167	35	5	0	2	1.2	14	15	14	9	2	24	8	85	7	3	1	2.4	.968	OF-37, SS-2, 1B-1

Don Ross *continued*

Year	Team	Games	BA	SA	AB	H	2B	3B	HR	HR%	R	RBI	BB	SO	SB	Pinch Hit AB	Pinch Hit H	PO	A	E	DP	TC/G	FA	G by Pos
1945	**2 teams**	**DET A** (8G –.379)	**CLE A** (106G –.262)																					
"	**total**	114	.270	.339	392	106	19	1	2	0.5	29	47	47	16	2	1	1	125	193	14	14	2.9	.958	3B-114
1946	**CLE A**	55	.268	.373	153	41	7	0	3	2.0	12	14	17	12	0	12	1	36	50	5	5	2.1	.945	3B-41, OF-2
7 yrs.		498	.262	.334	1488	390	63	4	12	0.8	129	162	165	70	10	85	23	546	521	56	49	2.8	.950	3B-261, OF-115, SS-20, 2B-7, 1B-1

Joe Rossi

ROSSI, JOSEPH ANTHONY BR TR 6′ 1″ 205 lbs.
B. Mar. 13, 1923, Oakland, Calif.

Year	Team	Games	BA	SA	AB	H	2B	3B	HR	HR%	R	RBI	BB	SO	SB	Pinch Hit AB	Pinch Hit H	PO	A	E	DP	TC/G	FA	G by Pos
1952	**CIN N**	55	.221	.255	145	32	0	1	1	0.7	14	6	20	20	1	8	2	192	21	4	3	4.7	.982	C-46

Claude Rossman

ROSSMAN, CLAUDE R. BL TL 6′ 188 lbs.
B. June 17, 1881, Philmont, N. Y. D. Jan. 16, 1928, Poughkeepsie, N. Y.

Year	Team	Games	BA	SA	AB	H	2B	3B	HR	HR%	R	RBI	BB	SO	SB	Pinch Hit AB	Pinch Hit H	PO	A	E	DP	TC/G	FA	G by Pos
1904	**CLE A**	18	.210	.290	62	13	5	0	0	0.0	5	6	0		0	1	1	14	0	1	0	0.9	.933	OF-17
1906		118	.308	.359	396	122	13	2	1	0.3	49	53	17		11	11	4	1150	45	19	47	11.5	.984	1B-105, OF-1
1907	**DET A**	153	.277	.342	571	158	21	8	0	0.0	60	69	33		20	0	0	1478	62	30	57	10.3	.981	1B-153
1908		138	.294	.418	524	154	33	13	2	0.4	45	71	27		8	0	0	1429	102	29	70	11.3	.981	1B-138
1909	**2 teams**	**DET A** (82G –.261)	**STL A** (2G –.125)																					
"	**total**	84	.258	.305	295	76	8	3	0	0.0	16	39	13		10	5	0	915	36	18	30	12.6	.981	1B-75, OF-2
5 yrs.		511	.283	.359	1848	523	80	26	3	0.2	175	238	90		49	17	5	4986	245	97	204	10.9	.982	1B-471, OF-20
WORLD SERIES																								
1907	**DET A**	5	.400	.500	20	8	0	1	0	0.0	1	2	1	0	2	0	0	52	4	1	0	11.4	.982	1B-5
1908		5	.211	.211	19	4	0	0	0	0.0	3	3	1	4	0	0	0	48	5	2	4	11.0	.964	1B-5
2 yrs.		10	.308	.359	39	12	0	1	0	0.0	4	5	2	4	2	0	0	100	9	3	4	11.2	.973	1B-10

Rico Rossy

ROSSY, ELAM JOSE BR TR 5′10″ 175 lbs.
Born Elam Jose Rossy (Ramos).
B. Feb. 16, 1964, San Juan, Puerto Rico.

Year	Team	Games	BA	SA	AB	H	2B	3B	HR	HR%	R	RBI	BB	SO	SB	Pinch Hit AB	Pinch Hit H	PO	A	E	DP	TC/G	FA	G by Pos
1991	**ATL N**	5	.000	.000	1	0	0	0	0	0.0	0	0	0	1	0	1	0	0	0	0	0	0.0	.000	SS-1
1992	**KC A**	59	.215	.302	149	32	8	1	1	0.7	21	12	20	20	0	0	0	73	156	10	40	3.8	.958	SS-51, 3B-9, 2B-3
1993		46	.221	.337	86	19	4	0	2	2.3	10	12	9	11	0	2	1	42	76	1	18	2.3	.992	2B-24, 3B-16, SS-11
3 yrs.		110	.216	.314	236	51	12	1	3	1.3	31	24	29	32	0	3	1	115	232	11	58	3.1	.969	SS-63, 2B-27, 3B-25

Braggo Roth

ROTH, ROBERT FRANK BR TR 5′ 7½″ 170 lbs.
Brother of Frank Roth.
B. Aug. 28, 1892, Burlington, Wis. D. Sept. 11, 1936, Chicago, Ill.

Year	Team	Games	BA	SA	AB	H	2B	3B	HR	HR%	R	RBI	BB	SO	SB	Pinch Hit AB	Pinch Hit H	PO	A	E	DP	TC/G	FA	G by Pos
1914	**CHI A**	34	.294	.444	126	37	4	6	1	0.8	14	10	8	25	3	0	0	54	7	5	1	1.9	.924	OF-34
1915	**2 teams**	**CHI A** (70G –.250)	**CLE A** (39G –.299)																					
"	**total**	109	.268	.438	384	103	10	17	**7**	**1.8**	67	55	51	72	26	4	0	139	53	27	2	2.1	.877	OF-69, 3B-35
1916	**CLE A**	125	.286	.396	409	117	19	7	4	1.0	50	72	38	48	29	12	6	166	20	9	6	1.7	.954	OF-112
1917		145	.285	.388	495	141	30	9	1	0.2	69	72	52	**73**	51	10	3	228	18	11	6	1.9	.957	OF-135
1918		106	.283	.411	375	106	21	12	1	0.3	53	59	53	41	35	0	0	175	16	13	3	1.9	.936	OF-106
1919	**2 teams**	**PHI A** (48G –.323)	**BOS A** (63G –.256)																					
"	**total**	111	.287	.431	422	121	22	12	5	1.2	65	52	39	53	20	5	1	203	8	10	3	2.1	.955	OF-103
1920	**WAS A**	138	.291	.432	468	136	23	8	9	1.9	80	92	75	57	24	8	3	184	15	10	3	1.6	.952	OF-128
1921	**NY A**	43	.283	.408	152	43	9	2	2	1.3	29	10	19	20	1	6	2	69	3	6	0	2.1	.923	OF-37
8 yrs.		811	.284	.416	2831	804	138	73	30	1.1	427	422	335	389	189	45	15	1218	140	91	21	1.9	.937	OF-724, 3B-35

Frank Roth

ROTH, FRANCIS CHARLES BR TR 5′10″ 160 lbs.
Brother of Braggo Roth.
B. Oct. 11, 1878, Chicago, Ill. D. Mar. 27, 1955, Burlington, Wis.

Year	Team	Games	BA	SA	AB	H	2B	3B	HR	HR%	R	RBI	BB	SO	SB	Pinch Hit AB	Pinch Hit H	PO	A	E	DP	TC/G	FA	G by Pos
1903	**PHI N**	68	.273	.359	220	60	11	4	0	0.0	27	22	9		3	7	3	235	82	22	9	5.6	.935	C-60, 3B-1
1904		81	.258	.314	229	59	8	1	1	0.4	28	20	12		8	**12**	**4**	250	76	17	8	5.0	.950	C-67, 2B-1, 1B-1
1905	**STL A**	35	.234	.262	107	25	3	0	0	0.0	9	7	6		1	5	0	114	36	6	3	5.4	.962	C-29
1906	**CHI A**	16	.196	.255	51	10	1	1	0	0.0	4	7	3		1	1	0	76	19	1	1	6.4	.990	C-15
1909	**CIN N**	56	.238	.313	147	35	7	2	0	0.0	12	16	6		5	2	0	188	46	8	4	4.5	.967	C-54
1910		26	.241	.310	29	7	2	0	0	0.0	3	3	0	2	1	19	4	11	4	1	0	3.2	.938	C-4, OF-1
6 yrs.		282	.250	.315	783	196	32	8	1	0.1	83	75	36	2	19	46	11	874	263	55	25	5.1	.954	C-229, 1B-1, 2B-1, OF-1, 3B-1

Bob Rothel

ROTHEL, ROBERT BURTON BR TR 5′10½″ 170 lbs.
B. Sept. 17, 1923, Columbia Station, Ohio D. Mar. 21, 1984, Huron, Ohio.

Year	Team	Games	BA	SA	AB	H	2B	3B	HR	HR%	R	RBI	BB	SO	SB	Pinch Hit AB	Pinch Hit H	PO	A	E	DP	TC/G	FA	G by Pos
1945	**CLE A**	4	.200	.200	10	2	0	0	0	0.0	0	0	3	1	0	0	0	2	5	1	0	2.0	.875	3B-4

Bobby Rothermel

ROTHERMEL, EDWARD HILL
B. Dec. 18, 1870, Fleetwood, Pa. D. Feb. 11, 1927, Detroit, Mich.

Year	Team	Games	BA	SA	AB	H	2B	3B	HR	HR%	R	RBI	BB	SO	SB	Pinch Hit AB	Pinch Hit H	PO	A	E	DP	TC/G	FA	G by Pos
1899	**BAL N**	10	.095	.095	21	2	0	0	0	0.0	1	3	1		0	2	1	11	15	4	0	3.8	.867	2B-5, 3B-2, SS-1

Jack Rothfuss

ROTHFUSS, JOHN ALBERT BR TR 5′11½″ 195 lbs.
B. Apr. 18, 1872, Newark, N. J. D. Apr. 20, 1947, Basking Ridge, N. J.

Year	Team	Games	BA	SA	AB	H	2B	3B	HR	HR%	R	RBI	BB	SO	SB	Pinch Hit AB	Pinch Hit H	PO	A	E	DP	TC/G	FA	G by Pos
1897	**PIT N**	35	.313	.409	115	36	3	1	2	1.7	20	18	5		3	2	0	231	12	4	8	7.7	.984	1B-32

Claude Rothgeb

ROTHGEB, CLAUDE JAMES BB 6′½″ 200 lbs.
B. Jan. 1, 1880, Milford, Ill. D. July 6, 1944, Manitowoc, Wis.

Year	Team	Games	BA	SA	AB	H	2B	3B	HR	HR%	R	RBI	BB	SO	SB	Pinch Hit AB	Pinch Hit H	PO	A	E	DP	TC/G	FA	G by Pos
1905	**WAS A**	6	.154	.154	13	2	0	0	0	0.0	2	0	0		1	3	0	4	1	0	0	1.7	1.000	OF-3

Jack Rothrock

ROTHROCK, JOHN HOUSTON BB TR 5′11½″ 165 lbs.
B. Mar. 14, 1905, Long Beach, Calif. D. Feb. 2, 1980, San Bernardino, Calif.

Year	Team	Games	BA	SA	AB	H	2B	3B	HR	HR%	R	RBI	BB	SO	SB	Pinch Hit AB	Pinch Hit H	PO	A	E	DP	TC/G	FA	G by Pos
1925	**BOS A**	22	.345	.509	55	19	3	3	0	0.0	6	7	3	7	0	0	0	37	38	9	6	3.8	.893	SS-22
1926		15	.294	.353	17	5	1	0	0	0.0	3	2	3	1	0	10	4	3	6	4	0	6.5	.692	SS-2
1927		117	.259	.360	428	111	24	8	1	0.2	61	36	24	46	5	6	1	323	284	26	63	5.8	.959	SS-40, 2B-36, 3B-20, 1B-13
1928		117	.267	.343	344	92	9	4	3	0.9	52	22	33	40	12	9	2	242	61	12	14	3.1	.962	OF-53, 3B-17, 1B-16, SS-13, 2B-2, P-1, C-1
1929		143	.300	.408	473	142	19	7	6	1.3	70	59	43	47	23	10	2	342	12	11	3	2.9	.970	OF-128

Jack Rothrock *continued*

Year	Team	Games	BA	SA	AB	H	2B	3B	HR	HR%	R	RBI	BB	SO	SB	Pinch Hit AB	Pinch Hit H	PO	A	E	DP	TC/G	FA	G by Pos
1930		45	.277	.354	65	18	3	1	0	0.0	4	4	2	9	0	32	9	17	3	1	1	2.1	.952	OF-9, 3B-1
1931		133	.278	.383	475	132	32	3	4	0.8	81	42	47	48	13	20	9	294	97	11	15	3.6	.973	OF-79, 2B-23, 1B-8, 3B-2, SS-1
1932	2 teams	BOS A (12G –.208)	CHI A (39G –.188)																					
″	total	51	.196	.241	112	22	3	1	0	0.0	11	6	10	14	4	7	1	58	14	8	1	2.0	.900	OF-31, 3B-8, 1B-1
1934	STL N	154	.284	.399	**647**	184	35	3	11	1.7	106	72	49	56	10	0	0	343	12	9	4	2.3	.975	OF-154, 2B-1
1935		129	.273	.347	502	137	18	5	3	0.6	76	56	57	29	7	1	0	283	5	6	1	2.3	.980	OF-127
1937	PHI A	88	.267	.332	232	62	15	0	0	0.0	28	21	28	15	1	29	8	132	3	1	0	2.3	.993	OF-58, 2B-1
11 yrs.		1014	.276	.370	3350	924	162	35	28	0.8	498	327	299	312	75	124	36	2074	535	98	108	3.1	.964	OF-639, SS-78, 2B-63, 3B-48, 1B-38, P-1, C-1
WORLD SERIES																								
1934	STL N	7	.233	.400	30	7	3	1	0	0.0	3	6	1	2	0	0	0	19	0	1	0	2.9	.950	OF-7

Edd Roush

ROUSH, EDD J. (Eddie) BL TL 5′11″ 170 lbs.
B. May 8, 1893, Oakland City, Ind. D. Mar. 21, 1988, Bradenton, Fla.
Hall of Fame 1962.

Year	Team	Games	BA	SA	AB	H	2B	3B	HR	HR%	R	RBI	BB	SO	SB	Pinch Hit AB	Pinch Hit H	PO	A	E	DP	TC/G	FA	G by Pos
1913	CHI A	9	.100	.100	10	1	0	0	0	0.0	2	0	0	2	0	4	1	3	0	0	0	1.5	1.000	OF-2
1914	IND F	74	.325	.440	166	54	8	4	1	0.6	26	30	6		12	27	7	102	6	2	2	2.4	.982	OF-43, 1B-2
1915	NWK F	145	.298	.390	551	164	20	11	3	0.5	73	60	38		28	1	1	331	20	10	3	2.5	.972	OF-144
1916	2 teams	NY N (39G –.188)	CIN N (69G –.287)																					
″	total	108	.267	.375	341	91	7	15	0	0.0	38	20	14	23	19	23	2	210	9	7	2	2.7	.969	OF-84
1917	CIN N	136	**.341**	.454	522	178	19	14	4	0.8	82	67	27	24	21	1	0	335	15	14	0	2.7	.962	OF-134
1918		113	.333	**.455**	435	145	18	10	5	1.1	61	62	22	10	24	0	0	320	13	14	2	3.1	.960	OF-113
1919		133	**.321**	.431	504	162	19	12	4	0.8	73	71	42	19	20	0	0	335	22	4	5	2.7	.989	OF-133
1920		149	.339	.453	579	196	22	16	4	0.7	81	90	42	22	36	0	0	537	25	13	13	3.8	.977	OF-139, 1B-11, 2B-1
1921		112	.352	.502	418	147	27	12	4	1.0	68	71	31	8	19	2	1	286	9	6	0	2.8	.980	OF-108
1922		49	.352	.461	165	58	7	4	1	0.6	29	24	19	5	5	6	1	96	8	1	0	2.4	.990	OF-43
1923		138	.351	.531	527	185	**41**	18	6	1.1	88	88	46	16	10	1	0	337	14	11	3	2.6	.970	OF-137
1924		121	.348	.501	483	168	23	**21**	3	0.6	67	72	22	11	17	2	2	270	10	12	4	2.5	.959	OF-119
1925		134	.339	.494	540	183	28	16	8	1.5	91	83	35	14	22	0	0	343	15	8	3	2.7	.978	OF-134
1926		144	.323	.462	563	182	37	10	7	1.2	95	79	38	17	8	0	0	306	12	15	2	2.3	.955	OF-144, 1B-1
1927	NY N	140	.304	.402	570	173	27	4	7	1.2	83	58	26	15	18	2	0	327	19	9	4	2.6	.975	OF-138
1928		46	.252	.356	163	41	5	3	2	1.2	20	13	14	8	1	6	3	100	7	5	0	2.9	.955	OF-39
1929		115	.324	.451	450	146	19	7	8	1.8	76	52	45	16	6	6	3	248	18	5	5	2.5	.982	OF-107
1931	CIN N	101	.271	.338	376	102	12	5	1	0.3	46	41	17	5	2	13	3	197	5	4	1	2.3	.981	OF-88
18 yrs.		1967	.323	.446	7363	2376	339	182	68	0.9	1099	981	484	215	268	94	24	4683	227	140	49	2.7	.972	OF-1849, 1B-14, 2B-1
WORLD SERIES																								
1919	CIN N	8	.214	.357	28	6	2	1	0	0.0	6	7	3	0	2	0	0	30	3	2	2	4.4	.943	OF-8

Phil Routcliffe

ROUTCLIFFE, PHILIP JOHN BR TR 6′ 175 lbs.
B. Oct. 24, 1870, Oswego, N. Y. D. Oct. 4, 1918, Oswego, N. Y.

Year	Team	Games	BA	SA	AB	H	2B	3B	HR	HR%	R	RBI	BB	SO	SB	Pinch Hit AB	Pinch Hit H	PO	A	E	DP	TC/G	FA	G by Pos
1890	PIT N	1	.250	.250	4	1	0	0	0	0.0	1	1	0	0	1	0	0	3	0	0	0	3.0	1.000	OF-1

Dave Rowan

ROWAN, DAVID BL TL 5′11″ 175 lbs.
Born David Drohan.
B. Dec. 6, 1882, Elora, Ont., Canada D. July 30, 1955, Toronto, Ont., Canada.

Year	Team	Games	BA	SA	AB	H	2B	3B	HR	HR%	R	RBI	BB	SO	SB	Pinch Hit AB	Pinch Hit H	PO	A	E	DP	TC/G	FA	G by Pos
1911	STL A	18	.385	.431	65	25	1	1	0	0.0	7	11	4		0	0	0	161	11	10	5	10.1	.945	1B-18

Wade Rowdon

ROWDON, WADE LEE BR TR 6′ 2″ 170 lbs.
B. Sept. 7, 1960, Riverhead, N. Y.

Year	Team	Games	BA	SA	AB	H	2B	3B	HR	HR%	R	RBI	BB	SO	SB	Pinch Hit AB	Pinch Hit H	PO	A	E	DP	TC/G	FA	G by Pos
1984	CIN N	4	.286	.286	7	2	0	0	0	0.0	0	0	0	1	0	0	0	3	5	0	1	4.0	1.000	SS-1, 3B-1
1985		5	.222	.222	9	2	0	0	0	0.0	2	2	2	1	0	0	0	1	3	2	0	1.5	.667	3B-4
1986		38	.250	.338	80	20	5	1	0	0.0	9	10	9	17	2	15	2	22	34	6	7	3.0	.903	3B-7, SS-6, OF-5, 2B-3
1987	CHI N	11	.226	.419	31	7	1	1	1	3.2	2	4	3	10	0	2	0	3	15	4	0	2.4	.818	3B-9
1988	BAL A	20	.100	.100	30	3	0	0	0	0.0	1	0	0	6	1	4	2	7	14	1	1	1.2	.955	3B-8, OF-5, DH-5
5 yrs.		78	.217	.299	157	34	6	2	1	0.6	14	16	14	35	3	21	4	36	71	13	9	2.2	.892	3B-29, OF-10, SS-7, DH-5, 2B-3

Dave Rowe

ROWE, DAVID ELWOOD (Eli) BR TR 5′ 9″ 180 lbs.
Brother of Jack Rowe.
B. Oct. 9, 1854, Harrisburg, Pa. D. Dec. 9, 1930, Glendale, Calif.
Manager 1886, 1888.

Year	Team	Games	BA	SA	AB	H	2B	3B	HR	HR%	R	RBI	BB	SO	SB	Pinch Hit AB	Pinch Hit H	PO	A	E	DP	TC/G	FA	G by Pos
1877	CHI N	2	.286	.286	7	2	0	0	0	0.0	0	0	0	3		0	0	2	0	1	0	1.0	.667	OF-2, P-1
1882	CLE N	24	.258	.392	97	25	4	3	1	1.0	13	17	4	9		0	0	33	4	7	1	1.8	.841	OF-23, P-1
1883	BAL AA	59	.313	.402	256	80	11	6	0	0.0	40		2			0	0	98	21	23	2	2.3	.838	OF-50, SS-7, 1B-3, P-1
1884	STL U	109	.293	.423	**485**	142	32	11	3	0.6	95		10			0	0	174	62	30	6	2.4	.887	OF-92, SS-14, 2B-2, 1B-2, P-1
1885	STL N	16	.161	.210	62	10	3	0	0	0.0	8	3	5	8		0	0	28	1	3	1	2.0	.906	OF-16
1886	KC N	105	.240	.354	429	103	24	8	3	0.7	53	57	15	43		0	0	185	62	44	11	2.8	.849	OF-90, SS-11, 2B-4
1888	KC AA	32	.172	.262	122	21	3	4	0	0.0	14	13	6		2	0	0	54	10	6	1	2.2	.914	OF-32
7 yrs.		347	.263	.374	1458	383	77	32	7	0.5	223	90	42	63	2	0	0	574	160	114	22	2.4	.866	OF-305, SS-32, 2B-6, 1B-5, P-4

Harland Rowe

ROWE, HARLAND STIMSON (Hypie) BL TR 6′ 1″ 170 lbs.
B. Apr. 20, 1896, Springvale, Me. D. May 26, 1969, Springvale, Me.

Year	Team	Games	BA	SA	AB	H	2B	3B	HR	HR%	R	RBI	BB	SO	SB	Pinch Hit AB	Pinch Hit H	PO	A	E	DP	TC/G	FA	G by Pos
1916	PHI A	17	.139	.167	36	5	1	0	0	0.0	2	3	2	8	0	6	1	5	12	3	0	2.5	.850	3B-7, OF-1

Jack Rowe

ROWE, JOHN CHARLES BL TR 5′ 8″ 170 lbs.
Brother of Dave Rowe.
B. Dec. 18, 1857, Harrisburg, Pa. D. Apr. 25, 1911, St. Louis, Mo.
Manager 1890.

Year	Team	Games	BA	SA	AB	H	2B	3B	HR	HR%	R	RBI	BB	SO	SB	Pinch Hit AB	Pinch Hit H	PO	A	E	DP	TC/G	FA	G by Pos
1879	BUF N	8	.353	.382	34	12	1	0	0	0.0	8	8	0	1		0	0	36	9	6	0	6.4	.882	C-6, OF-2
1880		79	.252	.328	326	82	10	6	1	0.3	43	36	6	17		0	0	267	68	46	3	4.3	.879	C-60, OF-25, 3B-3
1881		64	.333	.480	246	82	11	**11**	1	0.4	30	43	1	12		0	0	219	73	36	7	5.0	.890	C-46, SS-7, 3B-7, OF-5
1882		75	.266	.354	308	82	14	5	1	0.3	43		12	0		0	0	260	117	31	8	5.4	.924	C-46, SS-22, 3B-7, OF-1
1883		87	.278	.372	374	104	18	7	1	0.3	65		15	14		0	0	280	98	63	6	4.5	.857	C-49, OF-28, SS-18, 3B-3

Jack Rowe *continued*

Year	Team		Games	BA	SA	AB	H	2B	3B	HR	HR%	R	RBI	BB	SO	SB	Pinch Hit AB	Pinch Hit H	PO	A	E	DP	TC/G	FA	G by Pos
1884			93	.315	.450	400	126	14	14	4	1.0	85		23	14		0	0	414	75	36	4	5.2	.931	C-65, OF-30, SS-6
1885			98	.290	.409	421	122	28	8	2	0.5	62	51	13	19		0	0	219	216	67	26	5.0	.867	SS-65, C-23, OF-12
1886	DET	N	111	.303	.425	468	142	21	9	6	1.3	97	87	26	27		0	0	97	311	54	26	4.1	.883	SS-110, C-3
1887			124	.318	.445	537	171	30	10	6	1.1	135	96	39	11	22	0	0	119	378	51	36	4.4	.907	SS-124
1888			105	.277	.368	451	125	19	8	2	0.4	62	74	19	28	10	0	0	133	312	72	24	4.9	.861	SS-105
1889	PIT	N	75	.259	.341	317	82	14	3	2	0.6	57	32	22	16	5	0	0	108	228	39	26	5.0	.896	SS-75
1890	BUF	P	125	.250	.333	504	126	22	7	2	0.4	77	76	48	18	10	0	0	228	381	67	56	5.4	.901	SS-125
12 yrs.			1044	.286	.392	4386	1256	202	88	28	0.6	764	503	224	177	47	0	0	2380	2266	568	222	4.8	.891	SS-657, C-298, OF-103, 3B-20

Schoolboy Rowe

ROWE, LYNWOOD THOMAS BR TR 6′ 4½″ 210 lbs.
B. Jan. 11, 1910, Waco, Tex. D. Jan. 8, 1961, El Dorado, Ark.

Year	Team		Games	BA	SA	AB	H	2B	3B	HR	HR%	R	RBI	BB	SO	SB	Pinch Hit AB	Pinch Hit H	PO	A	E	DP	TC/G	FA	G by Pos
1933	DET	A	21	.220	.240	50	11	1	0	0	0.0	6	6	1	4	0	1	0	1	33	0	1	1.8	1.000	P-19
1934			51	.303	.450	109	33	8	1	2	1.8	15	22	6	20	0	6	1	9	46	0	3	1.2	1.000	P-45
1935			45	.312	.459	109	34	3	2	3	2.8	19	28	12	12	0	3	1	11	42	1	1	1.3	.981	P-42
1936			45	.256	.333	90	23	2	1	1	1.1	16	12	13	15	0	4	2	10	50	1	3	1.5	.984	P-41
1937			10	.200	.200	10	2	0	0	0	0.0	2	1	1	4	0	0	0	6	6	0	0	1.2	1.000	P-10
1938			4	.167	.333	6	1	1	0	0	0.0	1	0	0	1	0	0	0	0	8	1	0	2.3	.889	P-4
1939			31	.246	.328	61	15	0	1	1	1.6	7	12	5	7	1	3	1	9	27	2	5	1.4	.947	P-28
1940			27	.269	.433	67	18	6	1	1	1.5	7	18	5	13	1	0	0	10	28	0	2	1.4	1.000	P-27
1941			32	.273	.436	55	15	0	3	1	1.8	10	12	5	8	0	5	3	9	29	3	2	1.5	.927	P-27
1942	**2 teams**		**DET A** (2G –.000)	**BKN N** (14G –.211)																					
″	**total**		16	.174	.174	23	4	0	0	0	0.0	2	2	1	4	0	5	1	2	11	0	0	1.2	1.000	P-11
1943	PHI	N	82	.300	.458	120	36	7	0	4	3.3	14	18	15	21	0	**49**	**15**	9	42	1	4	1.9	.981	P-27
1946			30	.180	.311	61	11	5	0	1	1.6	4	6	3	16	0	12	2	2	20	0	0	1.3	1.000	P-17
1947			43	.278	.380	79	22	2	0	2	2.5	9	11	13	18	0	12	2	6	32	1	0	1.3	.974	P-31
1948			31	.192	.250	52	10	0	0	1	1.9	3	4	4	10	1	1	0	9	31	1	0	1.4	.976	P-30
1949			23	.235	.471	17	4	1	0	1	5.9	1	1	2	4	0	0	0	4	16	3	1	1.0	.870	P-23
15 yrs.			491	.263	.382	909	239	36	9	18	2.0	116	153	86	157	3	101	28	97	421	14	22	1.4	.974	P-382
WORLD SERIES																									
1934	DET	A	3	.000	.000	7	0	0	0	0	0.0	0	0	0	5	0	0	0	1	1	0	0	0.7	1.000	P-3
1935			3	.250	.375	8	2	1	0	0	0.0	0	0	0	1	0	0	0	3	5	1	0	3.0	.889	P-3
1940			2	.000	.000	1	0	0	0	0	0.0	0	0	0	1	0	0	0	0	1	0	0	0.5	1.000	P-2
3 yrs.			8	.125	.188	16	2	1	0	0	0.0	0	0	0	7	0	0	0	4	7	1	0	1.5	.917	P-8

Bama Rowell

ROWELL, CARVEL WILLIAM BL TR 5′11″ 185 lbs.
B. Jan. 13, 1916, Citronelle, Ala. D. Aug. 16, 1993, Citronelle, Ala.

Year	Team		Games	BA	SA	AB	H	2B	3B	HR	HR%	R	RBI	BB	SO	SB	Pinch Hit AB	Pinch Hit H	PO	A	E	DP	TC/G	FA	G by Pos
1939	BOS	N	21	.186	.288	59	11	2	2	0	0.0	5	6	1	4	0	5	0	27	2	5	0	2.1	.853	OF-16
1940			130	.305	.395	486	148	19	8	3	0.6	46	58	18	22	12	8	2	258	360	32	81	5.3	.951	2B-115, OF-7
1941			138	.267	.383	483	129	23	6	7	1.4	49	60	39	36	11	6	1	296	317	41	83	5.1	.937	2B-112, OF-14, 3B-2
1946			95	.280	.392	293	82	12	6	3	1.0	37	31	29	15	5	9	4	168	8	4	2	2.1	.978	OF-85
1947			113	.276	.385	384	106	23	2	5	1.3	48	40	18	14	7	4	1	216	21	15	1	2.3	.940	OF-100, 2B-7, 3B-4
1948	PHI	N	77	.240	.357	196	47	16	2	1	0.5	15	22	8	14	2	28	7	76	42	12	7	2.8	.908	3B-18, OF-17, 2B-12
6 yrs.			574	.275	.382	1901	523	95	26	19	1.0	200	217	113	105	37	60	15	1041	750	109	174	3.7	.943	2B-246, OF-239, 3B-24

Ed Rowen

ROWEN, W. EDWARD 5′ 6″ 155 lbs.
B. Oct. 22, 1857, Bridgeport, Conn. D. Feb. 22, 1892, Bridgeport, Conn.

Year	Team		Games	BA	SA	AB	H	2B	3B	HR	HR%	R	RBI	BB	SO	SB	Pinch Hit AB	Pinch Hit H	PO	A	E	DP	TC/G	FA	G by Pos
1882	BOS	N	83	.248	.303	327	81	7	4	1	0.3	36	43	19	18		0	0	258	72	44	5	4.2	.882	OF-48, C-34, SS-6, 3B-1
1883	PHI	AA	49	.219	.281	196	43	10	1	0	0.0	28		10			0	0	276	57	60	2	7.3	.847	C-44, OF-8, 3B-1, 2B-1
1884			4	.400	.467	15	6	1	0	0	0.0	4		1			0	0	21	4	6	1	7.8	.806	C-4
3 yrs.			136	.242	.299	538	130	18	5	1	0.2	68	43	30	18		0	0	555	133	110	8	5.4	.862	C-82, OF-56, SS-6, 3B-2, 2B-1

Chuck Rowland

ROWLAND, CHARLIE LELAND BR TR 6′ 1″ 185 lbs.
B. July 23, 1899, Warrenton, N. C. D. Jan. 21, 1992, Raleigh, N. C.

Year	Team		Games	BA	SA	AB	H	2B	3B	HR	HR%	R	RBI	BB	SO	SB	Pinch Hit AB	Pinch Hit H	PO	A	E	DP	TC/G	FA	G by Pos
1923	PHI	A	5	.000	.000	6	0	0	0	0	0.0	0	0	0	2	0	1	0	5	1	0	0	1.5	1.000	C-4

Rich Rowland

ROWLAND, RICHARD GARNET BR TR 6′ 1″ 210 lbs.
B. Feb. 25, 1964, Cloverdale, Calif.

Year	Team		Games	BA	SA	AB	H	2B	3B	HR	HR%	R	RBI	BB	SO	SB	Pinch Hit AB	Pinch Hit H	PO	A	E	DP	TC/G	FA	G by Pos
1990	DET	A	7	.158	.211	19	3	1	0	0	0.0	3	0	2	4	0	1	0	29	0	1	0	4.3	.967	C-5, DH-2
1991			4	.250	.250	4	1	0	0	0	0.0	0	1	1	2	0	1	0	2	1	0	0	1.0	1.000	C-2, DH-1
1992			6	.214	.214	14	3	0	0	0	0.0	2	0	3	3	0	0	0	12	1	0	1	1.9	1.000	C-3, DH-2, 3B-1, 1B-1
1993			21	.217	.283	46	10	3	0	0	0.0	2	4	5	16	0	3	2	75	7	1	1	4.2	.988	C-17, DH-3
1994	BOS	A	46	.229	.483	118	27	3	0	9	7.6	14	20	11	35	0	5	0	196	12	6	0	4.9	.972	C-39, DH-4, 1B-1
1995			14	.172	.207	29	5	1	0	0	0.0	1	1	0	11	0	4	1	39	3	1	2	3.1	.977	C-11, DH-3
6 yrs.			98	.213	.365	230	49	8	0	9	3.9	22	26	22	71	0	14	3	353	24	9	4	4.1	.977	C-77, DH-15, 1B-2, 3B-1

Jim Roxburgh

ROXBURGH, JAMES A. BR TR 5′10″ 170 lbs.
B. Jan. 17, 1858, San Francisco, Calif. D. Feb. 21, 1934, San Francisco, Calif.

Year	Team		Games	BA	SA	AB	H	2B	3B	HR	HR%	R	RBI	BB	SO	SB	Pinch Hit AB	Pinch Hit H	PO	A	E	DP	TC/G	FA	G by Pos
1884	BAL	AA	2	.500	.500	4	2	0	0	0	0.0	1		1			0	0	12	2	3	0	8.5	.824	C-2
1887	PHI	AA	2	.125	.125	8	1	0	0	0	0.0	0		0		0	0	0	6	3	2	0	3.7	.818	C-2, 2B-1
2 yrs.			4	.250	.250	12	3	0	0	0	0.0	1		1		0	0	0	18	5	5	0	5.6	.821	C-4, 2B-1

Stan Royer

ROYER, STANLEY DEAN BR TR 6′ 3″ 195 lbs.
B. Aug. 31, 1967, Olney, Ill.

Year	Team		Games	BA	SA	AB	H	2B	3B	HR	HR%	R	RBI	BB	SO	SB	Pinch Hit AB	Pinch Hit H	PO	A	E	DP	TC/G	FA	G by Pos
1991	STL	N	9	.286	.333	21	6	1	0	0	0.0	1	1	1	2	0	3	1	5	4	0	0	1.8	1.000	3B-5
1992			13	.323	.581	31	10	2	0	2	6.5	6	9	1	4	0	3	1	34	11	3	9	5.3	.938	3B-5, 1B-4
1993			24	.304	.413	46	14	2	0	1	2.2	4	8	2	14	0	12	4	22	16	3	1	3.4	.927	3B-10, 1B-2
1994	**2 teams**		**STL N** (39G –.175)	**BOS A** (4G –.111)																					
″	**total**		43	.167	.288	66	11	5	0	1	1.5	3	3	0	21	0	27	3	41	14	3	2	2.9	.948	1B-12, 3B-8
4 yrs.			89	.250	.384	164	41	10	0	4	2.4	14	21	4	41	0	45	9	102	45	9	12	3.4	.942	3B-28, 1B-18

Jerry Royster

ROYSTER, JERON KENNIS BR TR 6′ 165 lbs.
B. Oct. 18, 1952, Sacramento, Calif.

Year	Team	Games	BA	SA	AB	H	2B	3B	HR	HR%	R	RBI	BB	SO	SB	Pinch Hit AB	Pinch Hit H	PO	A	E	DP	TC/G	FA	G by Pos
1973	LA N	10	.211	.211	19	4	0	0	0	0.0	1	2	0	5	1	0	0	3	14	3	1	2.9	.850	3B-6, 2B-1
1974		6	—	—	0	0	0	0	0	—	2	0	0	0	1	0	0	0	3	0	0	1.0	1.000	2B-1, OF-1, 3B-1
1975		13	.250	.361	36	9	2	1	0	0.0	2	1	1	3	1	2	0	12	15	2	4	1.9	.931	OF-7, 2B-4, 3B-3, SS-1
1976	ATL N	149	.248	.304	533	132	13	1	5	0.9	65	45	52	53	24	1	0	158	310	19	35	3.2	.961	3B-148, SS-2
1977		140	.216	.288	445	96	10	2	6	1.3	64	28	38	67	28	4	0	182	267	28	40	3.3	.941	3B-56, SS-51, 2B-38
1978		140	.259	.333	529	137	17	8	2	0.4	67	35	56	49	27	4	2	284	376	23	66	5.0	.966	2B-75, SS-60, 3B-1
1979		154	.273	.349	601	164	25	6	3	0.5	103	51	62	59	35	3	0	261	405	22	62	4.4	.968	3B-80, 2B-77
1980		123	.242	.319	392	95	17	5	1	0.3	42	20	37	48	22	4	1	195	166	18	32	2.7	.953	2B-49, 3B-48, OF-41
1981		64	.204	.269	93	19	4	1	0	0.0	13	9	7	14	7	17	4	35	51	4	9	2.4	.956	3B-24, 2B-13
1982		108	.295	.383	261	77	13	2	2	0.8	43	25	22	36	14	6	1	105	112	11	20	2.0	.952	3B-62, OF-25, 2B-16, SS-10
1983		91	.235	.328	268	63	10	3	3	1.1	32	30	28	35	11	4	1	112	156	10	29	2.7	.964	3B-47, 2B-26, OF-18, SS-13
1984		81	.207	.295	227	47	13	2	1	0.4	22	21	15	41	6	15	1	99	162	9	23	3.7	.967	2B-29, 3B-17, SS-16, OF-11
1985	SD N	90	.281	.410	249	70	13	2	5	2.0	31	31	32	31	6	10	1	130	214	8	37	3.7	.977	2B-58, 3B-29, SS-7, OF-2
1986		118	.257	.362	257	66	12	0	5	1.9	31	26	32	45	3	32	8	87	166	14	23	2.4	.948	3B-59, SS-24, 2B-21, OF-7
1987	2 teams	CHI A (55G –.240) NY A (18G –.357)																						
″	total	73	.265	.439	196	52	13	0	7	3.6	26	27	23	32	4	9	2	66	75	4	9	2.3	.972	3B-43, OF-14, 2B-6, SS-1
1988	ATL N	68	.176	.206	102	18	3	0	0	0.0	8	1	6	16	0	31	7	49	11	1	1	1.5	.984	OF-26, 3B-10, SS-2, 2B-2
16 yrs.		1428	.249	.333	4208	1049	165	33	40	1.0	552	352	411	534	189	142	28	1778	2503	176	391	3.2	.961	3B-634, 2B-416, SS-187, OF-152
LEAGUE CHAMPIONSHIP SERIES																								
1982	ATL N	3	.182	.182	11	2	0	0	0	0.0	0	0	0	2	0	0	0	4	0	0	0	1.0	1.000	OF-3, 3B-1

Willie Royster

ROYSTER, WILLIE ARTHUR BR TR 5′11″ 180 lbs.
B. Apr. 11, 1954, Clarksville, Va.

Year	Team	Games	BA	SA	AB	H	2B	3B	HR	HR%	R	RBI	BB	SO	SB	Pinch Hit AB	Pinch Hit H	PO	A	E	DP	TC/G	FA	G by Pos
1981	BAL A	4	.000	.000	4	0	0	0	0	0.0	0	0	0	2	0	1	0	5	0	0	0	1.3	1.000	C-4

Vic Roznovsky

ROZNOVSKY, VICTOR JOSEPH BL TR 6′ 170 lbs.
B. Oct. 19, 1938, Shiner, Tex.

Year	Team	Games	BA	SA	AB	H	2B	3B	HR	HR%	R	RBI	BB	SO	SB	Pinch Hit AB	Pinch Hit H	PO	A	E	DP	TC/G	FA	G by Pos
1964	CHI N	35	.197	.211	76	15	1	0	0	0.0	2	2	5	18	0	16	1	67	14	2	2	3.2	.976	C-26
1965		71	.221	.308	172	38	4	1	3	1.7	9	15	16	30	1	11	4	270	30	5	6	4.8	.984	C-63
1966	BAL A	41	.237	.320	97	23	5	0	1	1.0	4	10	9	11	0	5	2	176	13	1	1	5.6	.995	C-34
1967		45	.206	.258	97	20	5	0	0	0.0	7	10	1	20	0	20	6	133	10	1	2	6.3	.993	C-23
1969	PHI N	13	.231	.231	13	3	0	0	0	0.0	0	1	1	4	0	12	3	6	0	0	0	3.0	1.000	C-2
5 yrs.		205	.218	.281	455	99	15	1	4	0.9	22	38	32	83	1	64	16	652	67	9	11	4.9	.988	C-148

Al Rubeling

RUBELING, ALBERT WILLIAM BR TR 6′ 185 lbs.
B. May 10, 1913, Baltimore, Md. D. Jan. 28, 1988, Baltimore, Md.

Year	Team	Games	BA	SA	AB	H	2B	3B	HR	HR%	R	RBI	BB	SO	SB	Pinch Hit AB	Pinch Hit H	PO	A	E	DP	TC/G	FA	G by Pos
1940	PHI A	108	.245	.351	376	92	16	6	4	1.1	49	38	48	58	4	0	0	120	211	22	19	3.3	.938	3B-98, 2B-10
1941		6	.263	.263	19	5	0	0	0	0.0	0	2	2	1	0	0	0	7	8	3	1	3.0	.833	3B-6
1943	PIT N	47	.262	.357	168	44	8	4	0	0.0	23	9	8	17	0	2	1	89	140	6	27	5.2	.974	2B-44, 3B-1
1944		92	.245	.370	184	45	7	2	4	2.2	22	30	19	19	4	**41**	9	70	56	2	7	2.5	.984	OF-18, 2B-17, 3B-16
4 yrs.		253	.249	.355	747	186	31	12	8	1.1	94	79	77	95	8	43	10	286	415	33	54	3.5	.955	3B-121, 2B-71, OF-18

Sonny Ruberto

RUBERTO, JOHN EDWARD BR TR 5′11″ 175 lbs.
B. Jan. 2, 1946, Staten Island, N. Y.

Year	Team	Games	BA	SA	AB	H	2B	3B	HR	HR%	R	RBI	BB	SO	SB	Pinch Hit AB	Pinch Hit H	PO	A	E	DP	TC/G	FA	G by Pos
1969	SD N	19	.143	.143	21	3	0	0	0	0.0	3	0	1	7	0	1	0	38	6	0	0	2.9	1.000	C-15
1972	CIN N	2	.000	.000	3	0	0	0	0	0.0	0	0	0	1	0	0	0	5	0	0	0	2.5	1.000	C-2
2 yrs.		21	.125	.125	24	3	0	0	0	0.0	3	0	1	8	0	1	0	43	6	0	0	2.9	1.000	C-17

Art Ruble

RUBLE, WILLIAM ARTHUR (Speedy) BL TR 5′10½″ 168 lbs.
B. Mar. 11, 1903, Knoxville, Tenn. D. Nov. 1, 1983, Maryville, Tenn.

Year	Team	Games	BA	SA	AB	H	2B	3B	HR	HR%	R	RBI	BB	SO	SB	Pinch Hit AB	Pinch Hit H	PO	A	E	DP	TC/G	FA	G by Pos
1927	DET A	56	.165	.253	91	15	4	2	0	0.0	16	11	14	15	2	3	0	62	3	2	2	1.6	.970	OF-43
1934	PHI N	19	.278	.352	54	15	4	0	0	0.0	7	8	7	3	0	4	0	24	2	5	1	2.2	.839	OF-14
2 yrs.		75	.207	.290	145	30	8	2	0	0.0	23	19	21	18	2	7	0	86	5	7	3	1.7	.929	OF-57

Johnny Rucker

RUCKER, JOHN JOEL (The Crabapple Comet) BL TR 6′2″ 175 lbs.
B. Jan. 15, 1917, Crabapple, Ga. D. Aug. 7, 1985, Moultrie, Ga.

Year	Team	Games	BA	SA	AB	H	2B	3B	HR	HR%	R	RBI	BB	SO	SB	Pinch Hit AB	Pinch Hit H	PO	A	E	DP	TC/G	FA	G by Pos
1940	NY N	86	.296	.401	277	82	7	5	4	1.4	38	23	7	32	4	20	8	121	3	6	0	2.3	.954	OF-57
1941		143	.288	.383	**622**	179	38	9	1	0.2	95	42	29	61	8	1	1	344	13	12	5	2.6	.967	OF-142
1943		132	.273	.339	505	138	19	4	2	0.4	56	46	22	44	4	13	3	300	9	10	3	2.7	.969	OF-117
1944		144	.244	.325	587	143	14	8	6	1.0	79	39	24	48	8	2	0	310	14	5	0	2.4	.985	OF-139
1945		105	.273	.417	429	117	19	11	7	1.6	58	51	20	36	7	4	1	256	6	6	2	2.7	.978	OF-98
1946		95	.264	.340	197	52	8	2	1	0.5	28	13	7	27	4	12	3	91	1	5	0	1.8	.948	OF-54
6 yrs.		705	.272	.366	2617	711	105	39	21	0.8	354	214	109	248	35	52	16	1422	46	44	10	2.5	.971	OF-607

John Rudderham

RUDDERHAM, JOHN EDMUND BR TR 5′8″ 170 lbs.
B. Aug. 30, 1863, Quincy, Mass. D. Apr. 3, 1942, Randolph, Mass.

Year	Team	Games	BA	SA	AB	H	2B	3B	HR	HR%	R	RBI	BB	SO	SB	Pinch Hit AB	Pinch Hit H	PO	A	E	DP	TC/G	FA	G by Pos
1884	BOS U	1	.250	.250	4	1	0	0	0	0.0	0		0			0	0	0	0	2	0	2.0	.000	OF-1

Joe Rudi

RUDI, JOSEPH ODEN BR TR 6′2″ 200 lbs.
B. Sept. 7, 1946, Modesto, Calif.

Year	Team	Games	BA	SA	AB	H	2B	3B	HR	HR%	R	RBI	BB	SO	SB	Pinch Hit AB	Pinch Hit H	PO	A	E	DP	TC/G	FA	G by Pos
1967	KC A	19	.186	.233	43	8	2	0	0	0.0	4	1	3	7	0	4	0	69	1	1	1	4.7	.986	1B-9, OF-6
1968	OAK A	68	.177	.232	181	32	5	1	1	0.6	10	12	12	32	1	17	2	77	1	1	0	1.4	.987	OF-56
1969		35	.189	.279	122	23	3	1	2	1.6	10	6	5	16	1	5	1	134	9	3	10	5.0	.979	OF-18, 1B-11
1970		106	.309	.480	350	108	23	2	11	3.1	40	42	16	61	3	18	2	302	18	4	17	3.6	.988	OF-63, 1B-28
1971		127	.267	.386	513	137	23	4	10	1.9	62	52	28	62	3	3	0	280	7	2	1	2.3	.993	OF-121, 1B-5
1972		147	.305	.486	593	**181**	32	**9**	19	3.2	94	75	37	62	3	0	0	247	9	2	1	1.7	.992	OF-147, 3B-1
1973		120	.270	.414	437	118	25	1	12	2.7	53	66	30	72	0	2	0	231	6	2	2	2.0	.992	OF-117, DH-1, 1B-1
1974		158	.293	.484	593	174	**39**	4	22	3.7	73	99	34	92	2	1	0	416	18	5	21	2.6	.989	OF-140, 1B-27, DH-2
1975		126	.278	.494	468	130	26	6	21	4.5	66	75	40	56	2	2	1	804	37	7	65	6.2	.992	1B-91, OF-44, DH-2
1976		130	.270	.424	500	135	32	3	13	2.6	54	94	41	71	6	2	1	270	7	3	4	2.2	.989	OF-126, 1B-2, DH-2

Joe Rudi *continued*

Year	Team	Games	BA	SA	AB	H	2B	3B	HR	HR%	R	RBI	BB	SO	SB	Pinch Hit AB	Pinch Hit H	PO	A	E	DP	TC/G	FA	G by Pos
1977	**CAL A**	64	.264	.496	242	64	13	2	13	5.4	48	53	22	48	1	0	0	131	3	0	0	2.1	1.000	OF-61, DH-3
1978		133	.256	.416	497	127	27	1	17	3.4	58	79	28	82	2	4	1	292	10	2	9	2.3	.993	OF-111, DH-11, 1B-10
1979		90	.242	.394	330	80	11	3	11	3.3	35	61	24	61	0	4	2	207	7	2	5	2.5	.991	OF-80, 1B-5, DH-3
1980		104	.237	.417	372	88	17	1	16	4.3	42	53	17	84	1	7	2	244	5	2	5	2.5	.992	OF-90, 1B-6, DH-3
1981	**BOS A**	49	.180	.352	122	22	3	0	6	4.9	14	24	8	29	0	22	5	47	1	0	2	1.8	1.000	DH-21, 1B-5, OF-1
1982	**OAK A**	71	.212	.332	193	41	6	1	5	2.6	21	18	24	35	0	10	0	416	20	5	37	6.7	.989	1B-49, OF-14, DH-3
16 yrs.		1547	.264	.427	5556	1468	287	39	179	3.2	684	810	369	870	25	101	17	4167	159	41	180	2.9	.991	OF-1195, 1B-249, DH-51, 3B-1
LEAGUE CHAMPIONSHIP SERIES																								
1971	**OAK A**	2	.143	.286	7	1	1	0	0	0.0	0	0	1	0	0	0	0	4	0	0	0	2.0	1.000	OF-2
1972		5	.250	.300	20	5	1	0	0	0.0	1	2	1	4	0	0	0	11	0	0	0	2.2	1.000	OF-5
1973		5	.222	.389	18	4	0	0	1	5.6	1	3	3	1	0	0	0	11	0	0	0	2.2	1.000	OF-5
1974		4	.154	.308	13	2	0	1	0	0.0	0	1	3	2	0	0	0	5	0	0	0	1.3	1.000	OF-4
1975		3	.250	.417	12	3	2	0	0	0.0	1	0	0	1	0	0	0	22	2	0	0	8.0	1.000	1B-2, OF-1
5 yrs.		19	.214	.343	70	15	4	1	1	1.4	3	6	8	8	0	0	0	53	2	0	0	2.9	1.000	OF-17, 1B-2
WORLD SERIES																								
1972	**OAK A**	7	.240	.360	25	6	0	0	1	4.0	1	1	2	5	0	0	0	20	0	0	0	2.9	1.000	OF-7
1973		7	.333	.407	27	9	2	0	0	0.0	3	4	3	4	0	0	0	20	2	0	1	3.1	1.000	OF-7
1974		5	.333	.500	18	6	0	0	1	5.6	1	4	0	3	0	0	0	28	0	0	1	4.0	1.000	OF-5, 1B-2
3 yrs.		19	.300	.414	70	21	2	0	2	2.9	5	9	5	12	0	0	0	68	2	0	2	3.3	1.000	OF-19, 1B-2

Dutch Rudolph

RUDOLPH, JOHN HERMAN BL TL 5′10″ 160 lbs.
B. July 10, 1882, Natrona, Pa. D. Apr. 17, 1967, Natrona, Pa.

Year	Team	Games	BA	SA	AB	H	2B	3B	HR	HR%	R	RBI	BB	SO	SB	Pinch Hit AB	Pinch Hit H	PO	A	E	DP	TC/G	FA	G by Pos
1903	**PHI N**	1	.000	.000	1	0	0	0	0	0.0	0	0	0		0	1	0	0	0	0	0	0.0	—	
1904	**CHI N**	2	.333	.333	3	1	0	0	0	0.0	0	0	0		0	0	0	1	0	0	0	0.5	1.000	OF-2
2 yrs.		3	.250	.250	4	1	0	0	0	0.0	0	0	0		0	1	0	1	0	0	0	0.5	1.000	OF-2

Ken Rudolph

RUDOLPH, KENNETH VICTOR BR TR 6′ 1″ 180 lbs.
B. Dec. 29, 1946, Rockford, Ill.

Year	Team	Games	BA	SA	AB	H	2B	3B	HR	HR%	R	RBI	BB	SO	SB	Pinch Hit AB	Pinch Hit H	PO	A	E	DP	TC/G	FA	G by Pos
1969	**CHI N**	27	.206	.324	34	7	1	0	1	2.9	7	6	6	11	0	10	3	41	3	1	0	3.2	.978	C-11, OF-3
1970		20	.100	.125	40	4	1	0	0	0.0	1	2	1	12	0	3	0	67	6	0	1	4.6	1.000	C-16
1971		25	.197	.237	76	15	3	0	0	0.0	5	7	6	20	0	0	0	153	16	0	1	6.8	1.000	C-25
1972		42	.236	.321	106	25	1	1	2	1.9	10	9	6	14	1	1	0	178	23	7	2	5.1	.966	C-41
1973		64	.206	.300	170	35	8	1	2	1.2	12	17	7	25	1	0	0	259	28	9	4	4.6	.970	C-64
1974	**SF N**	57	.259	.278	158	41	3	0	0	0.0	11	10	21	15	0	0	0	253	25	1	4	5.0	.996	C-56
1975	**STL N**	44	.200	.263	80	16	2	0	1	1.3	5	6	3	10	0	14	1	93	11	3	1	3.5	.972	C-31
1976		27	.160	.220	50	8	3	0	0	0.0	1	5	1	7	0	13	4	61	2	4	1	4.8	.940	C-14
1977	**2 teams**	**SF N** (11G –.200)	**BAL A** (11G –.286)																					
″	**total**	22	.241	.276	29	7	1	0	0	0.0	3	2	1	7	0	5	0	66	10	2	4	3.5	.974	C-22
9 yrs.		328	.213	.273	743	158	23	2	6	0.8	55	64	52	121	2	46	8	1171	124	27	18	4.7	.980	C-280, OF-3

Muddy Ruel

RUEL, HEROLD DOMINIC BR TR 5′ 9″ 150 lbs.
B. Feb. 20, 1896, St. Louis, Mo. D. Nov. 13, 1963, Palo Alto, Calif.
Manager 1947.

Year	Team	Games	BA	SA	AB	H	2B	3B	HR	HR%	R	RBI	BB	SO	SB	Pinch Hit AB	Pinch Hit H	PO	A	E	DP	TC/G	FA	G by Pos
1915	**STL A**	10	.000	.000	14	0	0	0	0	0.0	0	1	5	5	0	2	0	20	3	1	0	4.0	.958	C-6
1917	**NY A**	6	.118	.118	17	2	0	0	0	0.0	1	1	2	2	1	0	0	23	6	0	0	4.8	1.000	C-6
1918		3	.333	.333	6	2	0	0	0	0.0	0	0	2	1	1	0	0	8	2	0	0	5.0	1.000	C-2
1919		81	.240	.266	233	56	6	0	0	0.0	18	31	34	26	4	0	0	340	90	11	6	5.4	.975	C-81
1920		82	.268	.341	261	70	14	1	1	0.4	30	15	15	18	4	1	0	317	62	6	2	4.8	.984	C-80
1921	**BOS A**	113	.277	.349	358	99	21	1	1	0.3	41	43	41	15	2	2	0	375	86	11	7	4.3	.977	C-109
1922		116	.255	.302	361	92	15	1	0	0.0	34	28	41	26	4	4	1	359	96	10	17	4.2	.978	C-112
1923	**WAS A**	136	.316	.383	449	142	24	3	0	0.0	63	54	55	21	4	3	2	528	146	14	14	5.2	.980	C-133
1924		149	.283	.331	501	142	20	2	0	0.0	50	57	62	20	7	2	1	612	112	15	23	5.0	.980	C-147
1925		127	.310	.344	393	122	9	2	0	0.0	55	54	63	16	4	0	0	493	103	11	19	4.8	.982	C-126, 1B-1
1926		117	.299	.389	368	110	22	4	1	0.3	42	53	61	14	7	0	0	452	81	6	13	4.6	.989	C-117
1927		131	.308	.376	428	132	16	5	1	0.2	61	52	63	18	9	2	0	495	100	7	8	4.7	.988	C-128
1928		108	.257	.320	350	90	18	2	0	0.0	31	55	44	14	12	4	2	416	75	6	6	4.8	.988	C-101, 1B-2
1929		69	.245	.287	188	46	4	2	0	0.0	16	20	31	7	0	6	0	247	52	3	6	4.8	.990	C-63
1930		66	.253	.308	198	50	3	4	0	0.0	18	26	24	13	1	4	2	243	32	4	5	4.7	.986	C-60
1931	**2 teams**	**BOS A** (33G –.301)	**DET A** (14G –.120)																					
″	**total**	47	.233	.278	133	31	6	0	0	0.0	7	9	14	7	0	2	0	143	38	8	4	4.3	.958	C-44
1932	**DET A**	50	.235	.294	136	32	4	2	0	0.0	10	18	17	6	1	3	1	150	25	2	3	3.6	.989	C-49
1933	**STL A**	28	.190	.222	63	12	2	0	0	0.0	13	8	24	4	0	5	0	72	21	0	3	3.3	1.000	C-28
1934	**CHI A**	22	.211	.263	57	12	3	0	0	0.0	4	7	8	5	0	1	0	75	8	2	1	4.0	.976	C-21
19 yrs.		1461	.275	.332	4514	1242	187	29	4	0.1	494	532	606	238	61	41	9	5368	1138	117	137	4.7	.982	C-1413, 1B-3
WORLD SERIES																								
1924	**WAS A**	7	.095	.143	21	2	1	0	0	0.0	2	0	6	1	0	0	0	51	5	0	1	8.0	1.000	C-7
1925		7	.316	.368	19	6	1	0	0	0.0	0	1	3	2	0	0	0	35	6	0	0	5.9	1.000	C-7
2 yrs.		14	.200	.250	40	8	2	0	0	0.0	2	1	9	3	0	0	0	86	11	0	1	6.9	1.000	C-14

Dutch Ruether

RUETHER, WALTER HENRY BL TL 6′ 1½″ 180 lbs.
B. Sept. 13, 1893, Alameda, Calif. D. May 16, 1970, Phoenix, Ariz.

Year	Team	Games	BA	SA	AB	H	2B	3B	HR	HR%	R	RBI	BB	SO	SB	Pinch Hit AB	Pinch Hit H	PO	A	E	DP	TC/G	FA	G by Pos
1917	**2 teams**	**CHI N** (31G –.273)	**CIN N** (19G –.208)																					
″	**total**	50	.250	.382	68	17	3	3	0	0.0	4	12	11	17	1	22	6	43	23	2	3	3.1	.971	P-17, 1B-5
1918	**CIN N**	2	.000	.000	3	0	0	0	0	0.0	0	0	0	2	0	0	0	0	2	0	0	1.0	1.000	P-2
1919		42	.261	.348	92	24	2	3	0	0.0	8	6	4	18	1	7	2	10	57	2	1	2.1	.971	P-33
1920		45	.192	.231	104	20	4	0	0	0.0	3	10	5	24	0	7	0	10	74	4	6	2.3	.955	P-37, 1B-1
1921	**BKN N**	49	.351	.505	97	34	5	2	2	2.1	12	13	4	9	1	11	3	6	51	2	3	1.6	.966	P-36
1922		67	.208	.320	125	26	6	1	2	1.6	12	20	12	11	0	27	6	9	56	0	6	1.9	1.000	P-35
1923		49	.274	.282	117	32	1	0	0	0.0	6	10	12	12	0	12	3	9	53	2	7	1.8	.969	P-34, 1B-1
1924		34	.242	.290	62	15	1	1	0	0.0	5	4	5	2	0	4	0	5	46	1	3	1.7	.981	P-30

Dutch Ruether *continued*

Year	Team	Games	BA	SA	AB	H	2B	3B	HR	HR%	R	RBI	BB	SO	SB	Pinch Hit AB	Pinch Hit H	PO	A	E	DP	TC/G	FA	G by Pos
1925	WAS A	55	.333	.426	108	36	3	2	1	0.9	18	15	10	8	0	19	6	7	46	2	2	1.8	.964	P-30, 1B-1
1926	2 teams	WAS A (47G –.250)	NY A (13G –.095)																					
"	total	60	.221	.265	113	25	2	0	1	0.9	8	11	6	11	0	30	6	4	41	2	2	1.7	.957	P-28
1927	NY A	35	.263	.338	80	21	3	0	1	1.3	7	10	8	15	0	6	2	7	47	0	2	2.0	1.000	P-27
11 yrs.		488	.258	.335	969	250	30	12	7	0.7	83	111	77	129	3	145	34	110	496	17	35	2.0	.973	P-309, 1B-8
WORLD SERIES																								
1919	CIN N	3	.667	1.500	6	4	1	2	0	0.0	2	4	1	0	0	1	0	0	2	0	0	1.0	1.000	P-2
1925	WAS A	1	.000	.000	1	0	0	0	0	0.0	0	0	0	0	0	1	0	0	0	0	0	0.0	—	
1926	NY A	3	.000	.000	4	0	0	0	0	0.0	0	0	0	0	0	2	0	0	2	0	0	2.0	1.000	P-1
3 yrs.		7	.364	.818	11	4	1	2	0	0.0	2	4	1	0	0	4	0	0	4	0	0	1.3	1.000	P-3

Rudy Rufer

RUFER, RUDOLPH JOSEPH BR TR 6'½" 165 lbs.
B. Oct. 28, 1926, Ridgewood, N. Y.

Year	Team	Games	BA	SA	AB	H	2B	3B	HR	HR%	R	RBI	BB	SO	SB	Pinch Hit AB	Pinch Hit H	PO	A	E	DP	TC/G	FA	G by Pos
1949	NY N	7	.067	.067	15	1	0	0	0	0.0	1	2	2	0	0	0	0	9	13	1	2	3.3	.957	SS-7
1950		15	.091	.091	11	1	0	0	0	0.0	1	0	0	1	1	3	0	1	7	1	1	1.1	.889	SS-8
2 yrs.		22	.077	.077	26	2	0	0	0	0.0	2	2	2	1	1	3	0	10	20	2	3	2.1	.938	SS-15

Red Ruffing

RUFFING, CHARLES HERBERT BR TR 6' 1½" 205 lbs.
B. May 3, 1904, Granville, Ill. D. Feb. 17, 1986, Mayfield Heights, Ohio.
Hall of Fame 1967.

Year	Team	Games	BA	SA	AB	H	2B	3B	HR	HR%	R	RBI	BB	SO	SB	Pinch Hit AB	Pinch Hit H	PO	A	E	DP	TC/G	FA	G by Pos
1924	BOS A	8	.143	.429	7	1	0	1	0	0.0	0	0	0	1	0	0	0	0	3	0	0	0.4	1.000	P-8
1925		37	.215	.316	79	17	4	2	0	0.0	6	11	1	22	0	0	0	7	50	1	3	1.6	.983	P-37
1926		37	.196	.275	51	10	1	0	1	2.0	8	5	2	12	0	0	0	8	42	0	3	1.4	1.000	P-37
1927		29	.255	.345	55	14	3	1	0	0.0	5	4	0	6	0	2	0	8	36	1	1	1.7	.978	P-26
1928		60	.314	.488	121	38	13	1	2	1.7	12	19	3	12	0	17	5	7	51	3	4	1.5	.951	P-42
1929		60	.307	.439	114	35	9	0	2	1.8	9	17	2	13	0	22	6	7	46	3	1	1.5	.946	P-35, OF-2
1930	2 teams	BOS A (6G –.273)	NY A (52G –.374)																					
"	total	58	.364	.582	110	40	8	2	4	3.6	17	22	7	8	0	17	6	3	29	3	0	0.9	.914	P-38
1931	NY A	48	.330	.505	109	36	8	1	3	2.8	14	12	1	13	0	10	3	5	32	0	1	1.0	1.000	P-37, OF-1
1932		55	.306	.444	124	38	6	1	3	2.4	20	19	6	10	0	18	4	4	38	2	4	1.3	.955	P-35
1933		55	.252	.348	115	29	3	1	2	1.7	10	13	7	15	0	19	2	8	45	2	5	1.6	.964	P-35
1934		45	.248	.327	113	28	3	0	2	1.8	11	13	3	17	0	8	0	10	32	3	2	1.3	.933	P-36
1935		50	.339	.486	109	37	10	0	2	1.8	13	18	3	9	0	18	8	17	26	0	3	1.4	1.000	P-30
1936		53	.291	.449	127	37	5	0	5	3.9	14	22	11	12	0	17	6	13	56	1	6	2.1	.986	P-33
1937		54	.202	.248	129	26	3	0	1	0.8	11	10	13	24	0	21	6	9	28	1	2	1.2	.974	P-31
1938		45	.224	.364	107	24	4	1	3	2.8	12	17	17	21	0	12	2	11	34	0	2	1.5	1.000	P-31
1939		44	.307	.342	114	35	1	0	1	0.9	12	20	7	18	1	11	1	8	32	2	2	1.5	.952	P-28
1940		33	.124	.202	89	11	4	0	1	1.1	8	7	3	9	0	1	0	6	30	2	2	1.3	.947	P-30
1941		38	.303	.483	89	27	8	1	2	2.2	10	22	4	12	0	15	6	7	21	0	3	1.2	1.000	P-23
1942		30	.250	.338	80	20	4	0	1	1.3	8	13	5	13	0	6	1	8	30	1	5	1.6	.974	P-24
1945		21	.217	.326	46	10	0	1	1	2.2	4	5	0	8	0	10	1	2	11	1	1	1.3	.929	P-11
1946		8	.120	.160	25	3	1	0	0	0.0	1	1	1	8	0	0	0	2	5	0	0	0.9	1.000	P-8
1947	CHI A	14	.208	.208	24	5	0	0	0	0.0	2	3	1	3	0	4	1	2	7	0	1	1.0	1.000	P-9
22 yrs.		882	.269	.389	1937	521	98	13	36	1.9	207	273	97	266	1	228	58	152	684	26	51	1.4	.970	P-624, OF-3
WORLD SERIES																								
1932	NY A	2	.000	.000	4	0	0	0	0	0.0	0	0	1	1	0	0	0	1	3	0	0	4.0	1.000	P-1
1936		3	.000	.000	5	0	0	0	0	0.0	0	0	1	2	0	1	0	1	3	0	0	2.0	1.000	P-2
1937		1	.500	.750	4	2	1	0	0	0.0	0	3	0	0	0	0	0	0	0	0	0	0.0	.000	P-1
1938		2	.167	.167	6	1	0	0	0	0.0	1	1	1	0	0	0	0	2	4	0	0	3.0	1.000	P-2
1939		1	.333	.333	3	1	0	0	0	0.0	0	0	0	1	0	0	0	0	3	0	1	3.0	1.000	P-1
1941		1	.000	.000	3	0	0	0	0	0.0	0	0	0	0	0	0	0	0	0	0	0	0.0	.000	P-1
1942		4	.222	.222	9	2	0	0	0	0.0	0	0	0	2	0	2	0	0	1	0	0	0.5	1.000	P-2
7 yrs.		14	.176	.206	34	6	1	0	0	0.0	1	4	3	6	0	3	0	4	14	0	1	1.8	1.000	P-10

Chico Ruiz

RUIZ, HIRALDO BB TR 6' 169 lbs.
Born Hiraldo Ruiz (Sablon).
B. Dec. 5, 1938, Santo Domingo, Cuba D. Feb. 9, 1972, San Diego, Calif.

Year	Team	Games	BA	SA	AB	H	2B	3B	HR	HR%	R	RBI	BB	SO	SB	Pinch Hit AB	Pinch Hit H	PO	A	E	DP	TC/G	FA	G by Pos
1964	CIN N	77	.244	.318	311	76	13	2	2	0.6	33	16	7	41	11	3	0	95	149	11	28	3.2	.957	3B-49, 2B-30
1965		29	.111	.167	18	2	1	0	0	0.0	7	1	0	5	1	7	2	3	5	1	0	1.3	.889	3B-4, SS-3
1966		82	.255	.291	110	28	2	1	0	0.0	13	5	5	14	1	35	13	23	35	4	3	1.5	.935	3B-27, OF-8, SS-6
1967		105	.220	.300	250	55	12	4	0	0.0	32	13	11	35	9	17	3	131	168	10	33	3.6	.968	2B-56, 3B-13, SS-11, OF-5
1968		85	.259	.288	139	36	2	1	0	0.0	15	9	12	18	4	31	7	96	99	5	21	3.4	.975	2B-34, 1B-16, 3B-5, SS-3
1969		88	.245	.276	196	48	4	1	0	0.0	19	13	14	28	4	11	2	120	147	12	36	3.6	.957	2B-39, SS-29, 3B-7, 1B-2, OF-1
1970	CAL A	68	.243	.290	107	26	3	1	0	0.0	10	12	7	16	3	30	3	26	46	2	4	2.1	.973	3B-27, SS-3, 2B-3, 1B-2, C-1
1971		31	.263	.263	19	5	0	0	0	0.0	4	0	2	7	1	11	3	2	4	0	0	1.2	1.000	3B-3, 2B-2
8 yrs.		565	.240	.295	1150	276	37	10	2	0.2	133	69	58	164	34	145	33	496	653	45	125	3.1	.962	2B-164, 3B-135, SS-55, 1B-20, OF-14, C-1

Chico Ruiz

RUIZ, MANUEL (Manny) BR TR 5'11½" 170 lbs.
Born Manuel Ruiz (Cruz).
B. Nov. 1, 1951, Santurce, Puerto Rico

Year	Team	Games	BA	SA	AB	H	2B	3B	HR	HR%	R	RBI	BB	SO	SB	Pinch Hit AB	Pinch Hit H	PO	A	E	DP	TC/G	FA	G by Pos
1978	ATL N	18	.283	.348	46	13	3	0	0	0.0	3	2	2	4	0	1	0	31	32	1	5	4.3	.984	2B-14, 3B-1
1980		25	.308	.462	26	8	2	1	0	0.0	3	2	3	7	0	5	0	9	17	3	1	1.3	.897	3B-16, SS-4, 2B-2
2 yrs.		43	.292	.389	72	21	5	1	0	0.0	6	4	5	11	0	6	0	40	49	4	6	2.5	.957	3B-17, 2B-16, SS-4

Joe Rullo

RULLO, JOSEPH VINCENT BR TR 5'11" 168 lbs.
B. June 16, 1916, New York, N. Y. D. Oct. 28, 1969, Philadelphia, Pa.

Year	Team	Games	BA	SA	AB	H	2B	3B	HR	HR%	R	RBI	BB	SO	SB	Pinch Hit AB	Pinch Hit H	PO	A	E	DP	TC/G	FA	G by Pos
1943	PHI A	16	.291	.345	55	16	3	0	0	0.0	2	6	8	7	0	0	0	27	51	3	10	5.1	.963	2B-16
1944		35	.167	.167	96	16	0	0	0	0.0	5	5	6	19	1	0	0	78	88	9	22	5.1	.949	2B-33, 1B-1
2 yrs.		51	.212	.232	151	32	3	0	0	0.0	7	11	14	26	1	0	0	105	139	12	32	5.1	.953	2B-49, 1B-1

Bill Rumler

RUMLER, WILLIAM GEORGE BR TR 6′ 1″ 190 lbs.
B. Mar. 27, 1891, Milford, Neb. D. May 26, 1966, Lincoln, Neb.

Year	Team		Games	BA	SA	AB	H	2B	3B	HR	HR%	R	RBI	BB	SO	SB	Pinch Hit AB	Pinch Hit H	PO	A	E	DP	TC/G	FA	G by Pos
1914	STL	A	33	.174	.196	46	8	1	0	0	0.0	2	6	3	12	2	13	2	26	12	1	1	2.6	.974	C-9, OF-6
1916			27	.324	.405	37	12	3	0	0	0.0	6	10	3	7	0	15	6	23	11	1	1	3.9	.971	C-9
1917			78	.261	.420	88	23	3	4	1	1.1	7	16	8	9	2	**71**	**16**	13	2	1	0	1.8	.938	OF-9
3 yrs.			138	.251	.357	171	43	7	4	1	0.6	15	32	14	28	4	99	24	62	25	3	2	2.7	.967	C-18, OF-15

Paul Runge

RUNGE, PAUL WILLIAM BR TR 6′ 165 lbs.
B. May 21, 1958, Kingston, N. Y.

Year	Team		Games	BA	SA	AB	H	2B	3B	HR	HR%	R	RBI	BB	SO	SB	Pinch Hit AB	Pinch Hit H	PO	A	E	DP	TC/G	FA	G by Pos
1981	ATL	N	10	.259	.296	27	7	1	0	0	0.0	2	2	4	4	0	0	0	14	27	4	5	4.5	.911	SS-10
1982			4	.000	.000	2	0	0	0	0	0.0	0	0	0	0	0	2	0	0	0	0	0	0.0	—	
1983			5	.250	.250	8	2	0	0	0	0.0	0	1	1	4	0	1	0	4	3	0	1	3.5	1.000	2B-2
1984			28	.267	.322	90	24	3	1	0	0.0	5	3	10	14	5	0	0	53	101	5	18	5.0	.969	2B-22, SS-7, 3B-3
1985			50	.218	.287	87	19	3	0	1	1.1	15	5	18	18	0	12	2	15	66	7	5	2.5	.920	3B-28, SS-5, 2B-2
1986			7	.250	.250	8	2	0	0	0	0.0	1	0	2	4	0	0	0	5	12	0	0	3.4	1.000	2B-5
1987			27	.213	.426	47	10	1	0	3	6.4	9	8	5	10	0	3	0	15	27	2	5	2.1	.955	3B-10, SS-9, 2B-2
1988			52	.211	.276	76	16	5	0	0	0.0	11	7	14	21	0	21	4	22	32	1	3	1.7	.982	3B-19, 2B-7, SS-6
8 yrs.			183	.232	.310	345	80	13	1	4	1.2	43	26	54	75	5	39	6	128	268	19	37	3.0	.954	3B-60, 2B-40, SS-37

Tom Runnells

RUNNELLS, THOMAS WILLIAM BB TR 6′ 175 lbs.
B. Apr. 17, 1955, Greeley, Colo.
Manager 1991–92.

Year	Team		Games	BA	SA	AB	H	2B	3B	HR	HR%	R	RBI	BB	SO	SB	Pinch Hit AB	Pinch Hit H	PO	A	E	DP	TC/G	FA	G by Pos
1985	CIN	N	28	.200	.229	35	7	1	0	0	0.0	3	0	3	4	0	9	3	10	22	0	4	2.7	1.000	SS-11, 2B-1
1986			12	.091	.182	11	1	1	0	0	0.0	1	0	0	2	0	5	0	4	5	0	1	1.3	1.000	2B-4, 3B-3
2 yrs.			40	.174	.217	46	8	2	0	0	0.0	4	0	3	6	0	14	3	14	27	0	5	2.2	1.000	SS-11, 2B-5, 3B-3

Pete Runnels

RUNNELS, JAMES EDWARD BL TR 6′ 170 lbs.
Born James Edward Runnells.
B. Jan. 28, 1928, Lufkin, Tex. D. May 20, 1991, Pasadena, Tex.
Manager 1966.

Year	Team		Games	BA	SA	AB	H	2B	3B	HR	HR%	R	RBI	BB	SO	SB	Pinch Hit AB	Pinch Hit H	PO	A	E	DP	TC/G	FA	G by Pos
1951	WAS	A	78	.278	.337	273	76	12	2	0	0.0	31	25	31	24	0	5	0	159	176	18	41	4.8	.949	SS-73
1952			152	.285	.333	555	158	18	3	1	0.2	70	64	72	55	0	4	1	319	410	25	99	5.1	.967	SS-147, 2B-1
1953			137	.257	.321	486	125	15	5	2	0.4	64	50	64	36	3	8	3	219	351	26	94	4.5	.956	SS-121, 2B-11
1954			139	.268	.383	488	131	17	15	3	0.6	75	56	78	60	2	5	2	264	372	29	92	4.9	.956	SS-107, 2B-27, OF-1
1955			134	.284	.346	503	143	17	4	2	0.4	66	49	55	51	3	4	0	349	340	18	107	5.3	.975	2B-132, SS-2
1956			147	.310	.433	578	179	29	9	8	1.4	72	76	58	64	5	2	1	875	229	14	131	7.3	.987	1B-81, 2B-69, SS-3
1957			134	.230	.298	473	109	18	4	2	0.4	53	35	55	51	2	12	2	699	160	8	84	6.8	.991	1B-72, 3B-32, 2B-23
1958	BOS	A	147	.322	.438	568	183	32	5	8	1.4	103	59	87	49	1	0	0	631	335	11	129	6.6	.989	2B-106, 1B-42
1959			147	.314	.427	560	176	33	6	6	1.1	95	57	95	48	6	2	1	663	307	10	131	6.4	.990	2B-101, 1B-44, SS-9
1960			143	**.320**	.394	528	169	29	2	2	0.4	80	35	71	51	5	2	1	420	377	11	114	4.3	.986	2B-129, 1B-57, 3B-3
1961			143	.317	.414	360	114	20	3	3	0.8	49	38	46	32	5	23	5	715	90	6	97	6.1	.993	1B-113, 3B-11, 2B-7, SS-1
1962			152	**.326**	.456	562	183	33	5	10	1.8	80	60	79	57	3	1	0	1309	104	10	125	9.4	.993	1B-151
1963	HOU	N	124	.253	.296	388	98	9	1	2	0.5	35	23	45	42	2	16	4	593	111	6	50	6.5	.992	1B-70, 2B-36, 3B-3
1964			22	.196	.216	51	10	1	0	0	0.0	3	3	8	7	0	6	0	138	5	2	8	10.4	.986	1B-14
14 yrs.			1799	.291	.378	6373	1854	283	64	49	0.8	876	630	844	627	37	90	20	7353	3367	194	1302	6.1	.982	1B-644, 2B-642, SS-463, 3B-49, OF-1

Amos Rusie

RUSIE, AMOS WILSON (The Hoosier Thunderbolt) BR TR 6′ 1″ 210 lbs.
B. May 30, 1871, Mooresville, Ind. D. Dec. 6, 1942, Seattle, Wash.
Hall of Fame 1977.

Year	Team		Games	BA	SA	AB	H	2B	3B	HR	HR%	R	RBI	BB	SO	SB	Pinch Hit AB	Pinch Hit H	PO	A	E	DP	TC/G	FA	G by Pos
1889	IND	N	33	.175	.223	103	18	3	1	0	0.0	15	4	2	19	3	0	0	9	32	6	2	1.4	.872	P-33
1890	NY	N	73	.278	.366	284	79	13	6	0	0.0	31	28	7	26	6	0	0	39	131	23	5	2.4	.881	P-67, OF-14
1891			62	.245	.286	220	54	5	2	0	0.0	30	15	3	25	2	**1**	0	10	106	14	4	2.1	.892	P-61, OF-1
1892			69	.210	.278	252	53	6	4	1	0.4	18	26	3	29	4	1	0	30	133	22	5	2.7	.881	P-64, OF-4
1893			56	.269	.363	212	57	3	4	3	1.4	32	27	3	19	0	0	0	23	114	15	5	2.7	.901	P-56
1894			56	.280	.398	186	52	5	4	3	1.6	20	26	5	24	5	2	1	28	113	14	4	2.9	.910	P-54
1895			53	.246	.291	179	44	3	1	1	0.6	14	19	0	28	2	3	0	22	93	11	4	2.5	.913	P-49, OF-1
1897			40	.278	.326	144	40	1	3	0	0.0	25	22	3		1	2	0	19	77	8	3	2.7	.923	P-38
1898			41	.210	.283	138	29	2	4	0	0.0	23	8	1		2	2	1	20	68	12	3	2.6	.880	P-37, 1B-1, OF-1
1901	CIN	N	3	.125	.125	8	1	0	0	0	0.0	0	1	0		0	0	0	1	8	1	0	3.3	.900	P-3
10 yrs.			486	.247	.319	1726	427	41	29	8	0.5	208	176	27	170	25	11	2	201	875	126	35	2.5	.895	P-462, OF-21, 1B-1

John Russ

RUSS, JOHN
B. Apr. 1, 1858, Cannelton, Ind. D. Jan. 18, 1912, Louisville, Ky.

Year	Team		Games	BA	SA	AB	H	2B	3B	HR	HR%	R	RBI	BB	SO	SB	Pinch Hit AB	Pinch Hit H	PO	A	E	DP	TC/G	FA	G by Pos
1882	BAL	AA	1	.333	.333	3	1	0	0	0	0.0	0		0			0	0	0	1	0	0	0.5	1.000	P-1, OF-1

Bill Russell

RUSSELL, WILLIAM ELLIS BR TR 6′ 175 lbs.
B. Oct. 21, 1948, Pittsburg, Kans. BB 1971

Year	Team		Games	BA	SA	AB	H	2B	3B	HR	HR%	R	RBI	BB	SO	SB	Pinch Hit AB	Pinch Hit H	PO	A	E	DP	TC/G	FA	G by Pos
1969	LA	N	98	.226	.344	212	48	6	2	5	2.4	35	15	22	45	4	22	6	132	4	3	1	1.6	.978	OF-86
1970			81	.259	.363	278	72	11	9	0	0.0	30	28	16	28	9	7	1	167	10	3	1	2.3	.983	OF-79, SS-1
1971			91	.227	.327	211	48	7	4	2	0.9	29	15	11	39	6	3	0	131	114	8	23	2.9	.968	2B-41, OF-40, SS-6
1972			129	.272	.366	434	118	19	5	4	0.9	47	34	34	64	14	5	2	202	439	34	69	5.3	.950	SS-121, OF-6
1973			162	.265	.337	615	163	26	3	4	0.7	55	56	34	63	15	0	0	243	560	31	106	5.1	.963	SS-162
1974			160	.269	.351	553	149	18	6	5	0.9	61	65	53	53	14	1	0	194	491	39	68	4.5	.946	SS-160, OF-1
1975			84	.206	.258	252	52	9	2	0	0.0	24	14	23	28	5	0	0	94	230	11	27	4.0	.967	SS-83
1976			149	.274	.343	554	152	17	3	5	0.9	53	65	21	46	15	0	0	251	476	28	90	5.1	.963	SS-149
1977			153	.278	.360	634	176	28	6	4	0.6	84	51	24	43	16	0	0	234	523	29	102	5.1	.963	SS-153
1978			155	.286	.365	625	179	32	4	3	0.5	72	46	30	34	10	1	0	245	533	31	91	5.2	.962	SS-155
1979			153	.271	.359	627	170	26	4	7	1.1	72	56	24	43	6	3	1	218	452	30	70	4.7	.957	SS-150
1980			130	.264	.341	466	123	23	2	3	0.6	38	34	18	44	13	1	0	179	387	19	57	4.5	.968	SS-129
1981			82	.233	.282	262	61	9	2	0	0.0	20	22	19	20	2	0	0	128	261	14	49	5.0	.965	SS-80
1982			153	.274	.340	497	136	20	2	3	0.6	64	46	63	30	10	2	2	216	502	29	64	5.0	.961	SS-150
1983			131	.246	.286	451	111	13	1	1	0.2	47	30	33	31	13	5	0	192	392	22	61	4.8	.964	SS-127

Bill Russell *continued*

Year	Team	Games	BA	SA	AB	H	2B	3B	HR	HR%	R	RBI	BB	SO	SB	Pinch Hit AB	Pinch Hit H	PO	A	E	DP	TC/G	FA	G by Pos
1984		89	.267	.321	262	70	12	1	0	0.0	25	19	25	24	4	6	1	115	173	9	29	3.4	.970	SS-65, OF-18, 2B-5
1985		76	.260	.308	169	44	6	1	0	0.0	19	13	18	9	4	20	5	60	82	10	11	2.7	.934	SS-23, OF-21, 2B-8, 3B-5
1986		105	.250	.301	216	54	11	0	0	0.0	21	18	15	23	7	31	10	103	84	5	17	2.2	.974	OF-48, SS-32, 2B-8, 3B-1
18 yrs.		2181	.263	.338	7318	1926	293	57	46	0.6	796	627	483	667	167	107	28	3104	5713	355	936	4.3	.961	SS-1746, OF-299, 2B-62, 3B-6
DIVISIONAL PLAYOFF SERIES																								
1981	LA N	5	.250	.313	16	4	1	0	0	0.0	1	2	3	1	0	0	0	10	15	2	0	5.4	.926	SS-5
LEAGUE CHAMPIONSHIP SERIES																								
1974	LA N	4	.389	.389	18	7	0	0	0	0.0	1	3	1	0	0	0	0	13	16	0	4	7.3	1.000	SS-4
1977		4	.278	.333	18	5	1	0	0	0.0	3	2	0	0	0	0	0	11	12	2	3	6.3	.920	SS-4
1978		4	.412	.471	17	7	1	0	0	0.0	1	2	1	1	0	0	0	4	14	0	3	4.5	1.000	SS-4
1981		5	.313	.438	16	5	0	1	0	0.0	2	1	1	1	0	0	0	10	13	0	3	4.6	1.000	SS-5
1983		4	.286	.286	14	4	0	0	0	0.0	1	0	2	4	1	0	0	4	10	1	2	3.8	.933	SS-4
5 yrs.		21	.337	.386	83	28 **7th**	2	1	0	0.0	8	8	5	6	1	0	0	42	65	3	15	5.2	.973	SS-21
WORLD SERIES																								
1974	LA N	5	.222	.333	18	4	0	1	0	0.0	0	2	0	2	0	0	0	4	11	1	2	3.2	.938	SS-5
1977		6	.154	.231	26	4	0	1	0	0.0	3	2	1	3	0	0	0	9	21	0	4	5.0	1.000	SS-6
1978		6	.423	.500	26	11	2	0	0	0.0	1	2	2	2	1	0	0	11	20	3	3	5.7	.912	SS-6
1981		6	.240	.240	25	6	0	0	0	0.0	1	2	0	1	1	0	0	4	26	1	3	5.2	.968	SS-6
4 yrs.		23	.263	.326	95	25	2	2	0	0.0	5	8	3	8	2	0	0	28	78	5	12	4.8	.955	SS-23

Harvey Russell

RUSSELL, HARVEY HOLMES BL TR 5′ 9½″ 163 lbs.
B. Jan. 10, 1887, Marshall, Va. D. Jan. 8, 1980, Alexandria, Va.

Year	Team	Games	BA	SA	AB	H	2B	3B	HR	HR%	R	RBI	BB	SO	SB	Pinch Hit AB	Pinch Hit H	PO	A	E	DP	TC/G	FA	G by Pos
1914	BAL F	81	.232	.274	168	39	3	2	0	0.0	18	13	18		2	29	7	193	46	13	2	5.1	.948	C-47, SS-1, OF-1
1915		53	.260	.329	73	19	1	2	0	0.0	5	11	14		1	24	5	72	20	1	4	4.4	.989	C-21
2 yrs.		134	.241	.290	241	58	4	4	0	0.0	23	24	32		3	53	12	265	66	14	6	4.9	.959	C-68, SS-1, OF-1

Jim Russell

RUSSELL, JAMES WILLIAM BB TR 6′ 1″ 181 lbs.
B. Oct. 1, 1918, Fayette City, Pa. D. Nov. 24, 1987, Pittsburgh, Pa.

Year	Team	Games	BA	SA	AB	H	2B	3B	HR	HR%	R	RBI	BB	SO	SB	Pinch Hit AB	Pinch Hit H	PO	A	E	DP	TC/G	FA	G by Pos
1942	PIT N	3	.071	.071	14	1	0	0	0	0.0	2	0	1	4	0	1	0	12	0	0	0	4.0	1.000	OF-3
1943		146	.259	.358	533	138	19	11	4	0.8	79	44	77	67	12	7	2	323	16	3	6	2.4	.991	OF-134, 1B-6
1944		152	.312	.460	580	181	34	14	8	1.4	109	66	79	63	6	2	0	345	20	5	7	2.5	.986	OF-149
1945		146	.284	.433	510	145	24	8	12	2.4	88	77	71	40	15	6	0	313	9	9	1	2.4	.973	OF-140
1946		146	.277	.403	516	143	29	6	8	1.6	68	50	67	54	11	5	1	351	9	12	7	2.7	.968	OF-134, 1B-5
1947		128	.253	.381	478	121	21	8	8	1.7	68	51	63	58	7	9	3	343	6	7	3	3.0	.980	OF-119
1948	BOS N	89	.264	.410	322	85	18	1	9	2.8	44	54	46	31	4	4	0	246	3	2	0	3.0	.992	OF-84
1949		130	.231	.347	415	96	22	1	8	1.9	57	54	64	68	3	6	0	269	3	7	3	2.3	.975	OF-120
1950	BKN N	78	.229	.425	214	49	8	2	10	4.7	37	32	31	36	1	18	3	131	3	1	0	2.5	.993	OF-55
1951		16	.000	.000	13	0	0	0	0	0.0	2	0	4	6	0	10	0	3	0	0	0	0.8	1.000	OF-4
10 yrs.		1034	.267	.400	3595	959	175	51	67	1.9	554	428	503	427	59	68	9	2336	69	46	27	2.6	.981	OF-942, 1B-11

John Russell

RUSSELL, JOHN WILLIAM BR TR 6′ 195 lbs.
B. Jan. 5, 1961, Oklahoma City, Okla.

Year	Team	Games	BA	SA	AB	H	2B	3B	HR	HR%	R	RBI	BB	SO	SB	Pinch Hit AB	Pinch Hit H	PO	A	E	DP	TC/G	FA	G by Pos
1984	PHI N	39	.283	.444	99	28	8	1	2	2.0	11	11	12	33	0	9	4	51	1	0	0	1.7	1.000	OF-29, C-2
1985		81	.218	.398	216	47	12	0	9	4.2	22	23	18	72	2	15	4	170	9	4	7	2.7	.978	OF-49, 1B-18
1986		93	.241	.444	315	76	21	2	13	4.1	35	60	25	103	0	4	1	498	39	13	10	6.2	.976	C-89
1987		24	.145	.306	62	9	1	0	3	4.8	5	8	3	17	0	6	2	48	1	1	0	2.9	.980	OF-10, C-7
1988		22	.245	.388	49	12	1	0	2	4.1	5	4	3	15	0	7	0	77	9	5	3	6.1	.945	C-15
1989	ATL N	74	.182	.233	159	29	2	0	2	1.3	14	9	8	53	0	17	1	196	28	4	1	3.6	.982	C-45, OF-14, 3B-2, 1B-2, P-1
1990	TEX A	68	.273	.352	128	35	4	0	2	1.6	16	8	11	41	1	17	4	148	11	3	0	2.7	.981	C-31, DH-19, OF-6, 1B-3, 3B-1
1991		22	.111	.111	27	3	0	0	0	0.0	3	1	1	7	0	9	1	24	0	0	0	1.3	1.000	OF-8, C-5, DH-5
1992		7	.100	.100	10	1	0	0	0	0.0	1	2	1	4	0	4	0	14	2	1	0	2.4	.941	C-4, OF-2, DH-1
1993		18	.227	.409	22	5	1	0	1	4.5	1	3	2	10	0	5	2	31	0	0	0	2.2	1.000	C-11, 1B-1, OF-1, 3B-1
10 yrs.		448	.225	.371	1087	245	50	3	34	3.1	113	129	84	355	3	93	19	1257	100	31	21	3.6	.978	C-209, OF-119, DH-25, 1B-24, 3B-4, P-1

Lloyd Russell

RUSSELL, LLOYD OPAL (Tex) BR TR 5′11″ 166 lbs.
B. Apr. 10, 1913, Atoka, Okla. D. May 24, 1968, Waco, Tex.

Year	Team	Games	BA	SA	AB	H	2B	3B	HR	HR%	R	RBI	BB	SO	SB	Pinch Hit AB	Pinch Hit H	PO	A	E	DP	TC/G	FA	G by Pos
1938	CLE A	2	—	—	0	0	0	0	0	—	0	0	0	0	0	0	0	0	0	0	0	0.0	—	

Paul Russell

RUSSELL, PAUL A.
B. 1870, Reading, Pa. D. Pottstown, Pa.

Year	Team	Games	BA	SA	AB	H	2B	3B	HR	HR%	R	RBI	BB	SO	SB	Pinch Hit AB	Pinch Hit H	PO	A	E	DP	TC/G	FA	G by Pos
1894	STL N	3	.100	.100	10	1	0	0	0	0.0	1	0	0	2	0	0	0	5	6	2	0	4.3	.846	3B-1, OF-1, 2B-1

Reb Russell

RUSSELL, EWELL ALBERT BL TL 5′11″ 185 lbs.
B. Apr. 12, 1889, Jackson, Miss. D. Sept. 30, 1973, Indianapolis, Ind.

Year	Team	Games	BA	SA	AB	H	2B	3B	HR	HR%	R	RBI	BB	SO	SB	Pinch Hit AB	Pinch Hit H	PO	A	E	DP	TC/G	FA	G by Pos
1913	CHI A	52	.189	.292	106	20	5	3	0	0.0	9	7	1	29	0	1	1	10	71	4	3	1.7	.953	P-51
1914		43	.266	.313	64	17	1	1	0	0.0	6	7	1	14	0	5	2	3	50	3	0	1.5	.946	P-38
1915		45	.244	.337	86	21	2	3	0	0.0	11	7	4	14	1	3	0	11	56	2	1	1.7	.971	P-41
1916		56	.143	.165	91	13	2	0	0	0.0	9	6	0	18	1	0	0	4	71	2	2	1.4	.974	P-56
1917		39	.279	.412	68	19	3	3	0	0.0	5	9	2	10	0	3	0	14	51	1	2	1.8	.985	P-35, OF-1
1918		27	.140	.200	50	7	3	0	0	0.0	2	3	0	6	0	6	0	4	28	0	1	1.6	1.000	P-19, OF-1
1919		1	—	—	0	0	0	0	0	—	0	0	0	0	0	0	0	0	0	0	0	0.0	.000	P-1
1922	PIT N	60	.368	.668	220	81	14	8	12	5.5	51	75	14	18	4	0	0	115	5	4	2	2.1	.968	OF-60
1923		94	.289	.491	291	84	18	7	9	3.1	49	58	20	21	3	17	5	156	4	5	0	2.2	.970	OF-76
9 yrs.		417	.268	.433	976	262	48	25	21	2.2	142	172	42	130	9	35	8	317	336	21	11	1.8	.969	P-241, OF-138
WORLD SERIES																								
1917	CHI A	1	—	—	0	0	0	0	0	—	0	0	0	0	0	0	0	0	0	0	0	0.0	.000	P-1

Rip Russell

RUSSELL, GLEN DAVID BR TR 6′ 1″ 180 lbs.
B. Jan. 26, 1915, Los Angeles, Calif. D. Sept. 26, 1976, Los Alamitos, Calif.

Year	Team	Games	BA	SA	AB	H	2B	3B	HR	HR%	R	RBI	BB	SO	SB	Pinch Hit AB	Pinch Hit H	PO	A	E	DP	TC/G	FA	G by Pos
1939	CHI N	143	.273	.386	542	148	24	5	9	1.7	55	79	36	56	2	0	0	1383	83	18	109	10.4	.988	1B-143
1940		68	.247	.367	215	53	7	2	5	2.3	15	33	8	23	1	15	5	519	22	10	22	10.2	.982	1B-51, 3B-3

Rip Russell *continued*

Year	Team	Lg	Games	BA	SA	AB	H	2B	3B	HR	HR%	R	RBI	BB	SO	SB	Pinch Hit AB	Pinch Hit H	PO	A	E	DP	TC/G	FA	G by Pos
1941			6	.294	.353	17	5	1	0	0	0.0	1	1	1	5	0	0	0	36	3	1	4	8.0	.975	1B-5
1942			102	.242	.351	302	73	9	0	8	2.6	32	41	17	21	0	**31**	5	392	90	14	40	6.9	.972	1B-35, 2B-24, 3B-10, OF-3
1946	BOS	A	80	.208	.318	274	57	10	1	6	2.2	22	35	13	30	1	9	2	61	140	12	25	2.9	.944	3B-70, 2B-3
1947			26	.154	.231	52	8	1	0	1	1.9	8	3	8	7	0	12	1	7	29	3	2	3.0	.923	3B-13
6 yrs.			425	.245	.356	1402	344	52	8	29	2.1	133	192	83	142	4	67	13	2398	367	58	202	7.8	.979	1B-234, 3B-96, 2B-27, OF-3
WORLD SERIES																									
1946	BOS	A	2	1.000	1.000	2	2	0	0	0	0.0	1	0	0	0	0	2	2	0	0	0	0	0.0	.000	3B-1

Hank Ruszkowski

RUSZKOWSKI, HENRY ALEXANDER BR TR 6′ 190 lbs.
B. Nov. 10, 1925, Cleveland, Ohio.

Year	Team	Lg	Games	BA	SA	AB	H	2B	3B	HR	HR%	R	RBI	BB	SO	SB	Pinch Hit AB	Pinch Hit H	PO	A	E	DP	TC/G	FA	G by Pos
1944	CLE	A	3	.375	.375	8	3	0	0	0	0.0	1	1	0	1	0	1	0	5	2	0	0	3.5	1.000	C-2
1945			14	.204	.204	49	10	0	0	0	0.0	2	5	4	9	0	0	0	63	14	2	2	5.6	.975	C-14
1947			23	.259	.667	27	7	2	0	3	11.1	5	4	2	6	0	7	2	14	6	0	0	1.3	1.000	C-16
3 yrs.			40	.238	.369	84	20	2	0	3	3.6	8	10	6	16	0	8	2	82	22	2	2	3.3	.981	C-32

Babe Ruth

RUTH, GEORGE HERMAN (The Bambino, The Sultan of Swat) BL TL 6′ 2″ 215 lbs.
B. Feb. 6, 1895, Baltimore, Md. D. Aug. 16, 1948, New York, N. Y.
Hall of Fame 1936.

Year	Team	Lg	Games	BA	SA	AB	H	2B	3B	HR	HR%	R	RBI	BB	SO	SB	Pinch Hit AB	Pinch Hit H	PO	A	E	DP	TC/G	FA	G by Pos
1914	BOS	A	5	.200	.300	10	2	1	0	0	0.0	1	0	0	4	0	1	0	0	7	0	0	1.8	1.000	P-4
1915			42	.315	.576	92	29	10	1	4	4.3	16	21	9	23	0	10	1	17	63	2	3	2.6	.976	P-32
1916			67	.272	.419	136	37	5	3	3	2.2	18	16	10	23	0	19	4	24	83	3	6	2.5	.973	P-44
1917			52	.325	.472	123	40	6	3	2	1.6	14	12	12	18	0	7	1	19	101	2	4	3.0	.984	P-41
1918			95	.300	**.555**	317	95	26	11	**11**	**3.5**	50	66	57	**58**	6	3	1	270	72	18	16	3.9	.950	OF-59, P-20, 1B-13
1919			130	.322	**.657**	432	139	34	12	**29**	**6.7**	**103**	**114**	101	58	7	1	0	270	53	4	11	2.5	.988	OF-111, P-17, 1B-4
1920	NY	A	142	.376	**.847**[1]	458	172	36	9	**54**	**11.8**[1]	**158**	**137**	**148**	80	14	1	0	270	21	20	4	2.2	.936	OF-139, 1B-2, P-1
1921			152	.378	**.846**	540	204	44	16	**59**	**10.9**	**177**	**171**	**144**	81	17	0	0	357	19	13	6	2.5	.967	OF-152, 1B-2, P-2
1922			110	.315	**.672**	406	128	24	8	35	**8.6**	94	99	84	80	2	0	0	226	14	9	4	2.2	.964	OF-110, 1B-1
1923			152	.393	**.764**	522	205	45	13	**41**	**7.9**	**151**	**131**	**170**[1]	**93**	17	0	0	419	21	12	4	3.0	.973	OF-148, 1B-4
1924			153	**.378**	**.739**	529	200	39	7	**46**	**8.7**	**143**	121	**142**	**81**	9	1	1	340	18	14	4	2.4	.962	OF-152
1925			98	.290	.543	359	104	12	2	25	7.0	61	66	59	68	2	0	0	207	15	6	3	2.3	.974	OF-98
1926			152	.372	**.737**	495	184	30	5	**47**	**9.5**	**139**	**145**	**144**	76	11	3	0	318	11	7	7	2.2	.979	OF-149, 1B-2
1927			151	.356	**.772**	540	192	29	8	**60**	**11.1**	**158**	164	**138**	**89**	7	0	0	328	14	13	4	2.4	.963	OF-151
1928			154	.323	**.709**	536	173	29	8	**54**	**10.1**	**163**	**142**	**135**	**87**	4	0	0	304	9	8	0	2.1	.975	OF-154
1929			135	.345	**.697**	499	172	26	6	**46**	**9.2**	121	154	72	60	5	2	1	240	5	4	2	1.9	.984	OF-133
1930			145	.359	**.732**	518	186	28	9	**49**	**9.5**	150	153	**136**	61	10	0	0	266	14	10	0	2.0	.966	OF-144, P-1
1931			145	.373	**.700**	534	199	31	3	**46**	**8.6**	149	163	**128**	51	5	2	0	242	5	7	2	1.8	.972	OF-142, 1B-1
1932			133	.341	.661	457	156	13	5	41	9.0	120	137	**130**	62	2	1	1	212	10	9	1	1.8	.961	OF-127, 1B-1
1933			137	.301	.582	459	138	21	3	34	7.4	97	103	**114**	90	4	4	1	222	10	8	4	1.8	.967	OF-132, 1B-1, P-1
1934			125	.288	.537	365	105	17	4	22	6.0	78	84	103	63	1	11	2	197	3	8	0	1.9	.962	OF-111
1935	BOS	N	28	.181	.431	72	13	0	0	6	8.3	13	12	20	24	0	1	0	39	1	2	0	1.6	.952	OF-26
22 yrs.			2503	.342	.690	8399	2873	506	136	714	8.5	2174	2211	2056	1330	123	67	13	4787	569	179	85	2.3	.968	OF-2238, P-163, 1B-31
				10th	**1st**					**2nd**	**1st**	**2nd**	**2nd**	**1st**											
WORLD SERIES																									
1915	BOS	A	1	.000	.000	1	0	0	0	0	0.0	0	0	0	0	0	1	0	0	0	0	0	0.0	—	
1916			1	.000	.000	5	0	0	0	0	0.0	0	1	0	2	0	0	0	2	4	0	0	6.0	1.000	P-1
1918			3	.200	.600	5	1	0	1	0	0.0	0	2	0	2	0	0	0	1	5	0	1	1.5	1.000	OF-2, P-2
1921	NY	A	6	.313	.500	16	5	0	0	1	6.3	3	4	5	8	2	1	0	9	0	0	0	1.8	1.000	OF-5
1922			5	.118	.176	17	2	1	0	0	0.0	1	1	2	3	0	0	0	9	0	0	0	1.8	1.000	OF-5
1923			6	.368	1.000	19	7	1	1	3	15.8	8	3	8	6	0	0	0	17	0	1	0	2.6	.944	OF-6, 1B-1
1926			7	.300	.900	20	6	0	0	4	20.0	6	5	11	2	1	0	0	8	2	0	0	1.4	1.000	OF-7
1927			4	.400	.800	15	6	0	0	2	13.3	4	7	2	2	1	0	0	10	0	0	0	2.5	1.000	OF-4
1928			4	.625	1.375	16	10	3	0	3	18.8	9	4	1	2	0	0	0	9	1	0	0	2.5	1.000	OF-4
1932			4	.333	.733	15	5	0	0	2	13.3	6	6	4	3	0	0	0	8	0	1	0	2.3	.889	OF-4
10 yrs.			41	.326	.744	129	42	5	2	15	11.6	37	33	33	30	4	2	0	73	12	2	1	2.1	.977	OF-37, P-3, 1B-1
			10th		**2nd**		**10th**			**2nd**	**2nd**	**3rd**	**4th**	**2nd**	**4th**										

Jim Rutherford

RUTHERFORD, JAMES HOLLIS BL TR 6′ 1″ 180 lbs.
B. Sept. 26, 1886, Stillwater, Minn. D. Sept. 18, 1956, Cleveland, Ohio.

Year	Team	Lg	Games	BA	SA	AB	H	2B	3B	HR	HR%	R	RBI	BB	SO	SB	Pinch Hit AB	Pinch Hit H	PO	A	E	DP	TC/G	FA	G by Pos
1910	CLE	A	1	.500	.500	2	1	0	0	0	0.0	0	0	0		0	0	0	1	0	0	0	1.0	1.000	OF-1

Mickey Rutner

RUTNER, MILTON BR TR 5′11″ 190 lbs.
B. Mar. 18, 1920, Hempstead, N. Y.

Year	Team	Lg	Games	BA	SA	AB	H	2B	3B	HR	HR%	R	RBI	BB	SO	SB	Pinch Hit AB	Pinch Hit H	PO	A	E	DP	TC/G	FA	G by Pos
1947	PHI	A	12	.250	.333	48	12	1	0	1	2.1	4	4	3	2	0	1	0	5	18	3	2	2.4	.885	3B-11

Mark Ryal

RYAL, MARK DWAYNE BL TL 6′ 1″ 180 lbs.
B. Apr. 28, 1960, Henryetta, Okla.

Year	Team	Lg	Games	BA	SA	AB	H	2B	3B	HR	HR%	R	RBI	BB	SO	SB	Pinch Hit AB	Pinch Hit H	PO	A	E	DP	TC/G	FA	G by Pos
1982	KC	A	6	.077	.077	13	1	0	0	0	0.0	0	0	1	3	0	1	0	9	0	1	0	2.0	.900	OF-5
1985	CHI	A	12	.152	.242	33	5	3	0	0	0.0	4	3	3	3	0	0	0	21	0	0	0	1.8	1.000	OF-12
1986	CAL	A	13	.375	.563	32	12	0	0	2	6.3	6	5	2	4	1	5	2	32	2	1	1	2.9	.971	OF-6, 1B-4, DH-2
1987			58	.200	.410	100	20	6	0	5	5.0	7	18	3	15	0	31	10	50	1	3	1	1.8	.944	OF-21, DH-5, 1B-4
1989	PHI	N	29	.242	.303	33	8	2	0	0	0.0	2	5	1	6	0	19	4	17	0	0	0	2.1	1.000	OF-4, 1B-4
1990	PIT	N	9	.083	.083	12	1	0	0	0	0.0	0	0	0	3	0	7	0	4	0	0	0	1.0	1.000	OF-4
6 yrs.			127	.211	.354	223	47	11	0	7	3.1	19	31	10	34	1	63	16	133	3	5	2	2.0	.965	OF-52, 1B-12, DH-7

Blondy Ryan

RYAN, JOHN COLLINS BR TR 6′ 1″ 178 lbs.
B. Jan. 4, 1906, Lynn, Mass. D. Nov. 28, 1959, Swampscott, Mass.

Year	Team	Lg	Games	BA	SA	AB	H	2B	3B	HR	HR%	R	RBI	BB	SO	SB	Pinch Hit AB	Pinch Hit H	PO	A	E	DP	TC/G	FA	G by Pos
1930	CHI	A	28	.207	.333	87	18	0	4	1	1.1	9	10	6	13	2	0	0	30	44	10	6	3.2	.881	3B-23, SS-2, 2B-1
1933	NY	N	146	.238	.293	525	125	10	5	3	0.6	47	48	15	62	0	0	0	296	494	42	95	5.7	.950	SS-146
1934			110	.242	.306	385	93	19	0	2	0.5	35	41	19	68	3	1	0	159	283	26	33	3.9	.944	3B-65, SS-30, 2B-25

Blondy Ryan *continued*

Year	Team	Games	BA	SA	AB	H	2B	3B	HR	HR%	R	RBI	BB	SO	SB	Pinch Hit AB	Pinch Hit H	PO	A	E	DP	TC/G	FA	G by Pos
1935	2 teams	PHI N (39G –.264) NY A (30G –.238)																						
″	total	69	.252	.308	234	59	4	3	1	0.4	25	21	10	30	1	2	1	135	191	32	36	5.3	.911	SS-65, 3B-1, 2B-1
1937	NY N	21	.240	.347	75	18	3	1	1	1.3	10	13	6	8	0	1	1	41	57	6	13	5.0	.942	SS-19, 3B-1, 2B-1
1938		12	.208	.208	24	5	0	0	0	0.0	1	0	1	3	0	2	1	6	16	2	2	2.4	.917	2B-5, 3B-3, SS-2
6 yrs.		386	.239	.304	1330	318	36	13	8	0.6	127	133	57	184	6	6	3	667	1085	118	185	4.8	.937	SS-264, 3B-93, 2B-33
WORLD SERIES																								
1933	NY N	5	.278	.278	18	5	0	0	0	0.0	0	1	1	5	0	0	0	10	20	1	2	6.2	.968	SS-5
1937		1	.000	.000	1	0	0	0	0	0.0	0	0	0	1	0	1	0	0	0	0	0	0.0	—	
2 yrs.		6	.263	.263	19	5	0	0	0	0.0	0	1	1	6	0	1	0	10	20	1	2	6.2	.968	SS-5

Bud Ryan

RYAN, JOHN BUDD BL TR 5′ 9½″ 172 lbs.
B. Oct. 6, 1885, Denver, Colo. D. July 9, 1956, Sacramento, Calif.

Year	Team	Games	BA	SA	AB	H	2B	3B	HR	HR%	R	RBI	BB	SO	SB	Pinch Hit AB	Pinch Hit H	PO	A	E	DP	TC/G	FA	G by Pos
1912	CLE A	93	.271	.372	328	89	12	9	1	0.3	53	31	30		12	3	1	167	11	7	2	2.1	.962	OF-90
1913		73	.296	.329	243	72	6	1	0	0.0	26	32	11	13	9	4	2	144	8	2	2	2.3	.987	OF-67, 1B-1
2 yrs.		166	.282	.354	571	161	18	10	1	0.2	79	63	41	13	21	7	3	311	19	9	4	2.1	.973	OF-157, 1B-1

Connie Ryan

RYAN, CORNELIUS JOSEPH BR TR 5′11″ 175 lbs.
B. Feb. 27, 1920, New Orleans, La. D. Jan. 3, 1996, Metairie, La.
Manager 1975, 1977.

Year	Team	Games	BA	SA	AB	H	2B	3B	HR	HR%	R	RBI	BB	SO	SB	Pinch Hit AB	Pinch Hit H	PO	A	E	DP	TC/G	FA	G by Pos
1942	NY N	11	.185	.185	27	5	0	0	0	0.0	4	2	4	3	1	0	0	31	36	4	6	6.5	.944	2B-11
1943	BOS N	132	.212	.249	457	97	10	2	1	0.2	52	24	58	56	7	1	0	257	374	24	47	5.0	.963	2B-100, 3B-30
1944		88	.295	.416	332	98	18	5	4	1.2	56	25	36	40	13	0	0	233	296	14	58	5.8	.974	2B-80, 3B-14
1946		143	.241	.335	502	121	28	8	1	0.2	55	48	55	63	7	1	0	300	367	22	58	4.8	.968	2B-120, 3B-24
1947		150	.265	.371	544	144	33	5	5	0.9	60	69	71	60	5	0	0	394	433	23	88	5.6	.973	2B-150, SS-1
1948		51	.213	.238	122	26	3	0	0	0.0	14	10	21	16	0	7	1	91	114	7	19	4.8	.967	2B-40, 3B-4
1949		85	.250	.409	208	52	13	1	6	2.9	28	20	21	30	1	23	5	118	131	8	24	4.1	.969	3B-25, SS-18, 2B-16, 1B-3
1950	2 teams	BOS N (20G –.194) CIN N (106G –.259)																						
″	total	126	.248	.358	439	109	20	5	6	1.4	57	49	64	55	4	1	0	361	342	16	29	5.8	.978	2B-123
1951	CIN N	136	.237	.391	473	112	17	4	16	3.4	75	53	79	72	11	7	3	348	353	22	75	5.7	.970	2B-121, 3B-3, 1B-2, OF-1
1952	PHI N	154	.241	.366	577	139	24	6	12	2.1	81	49	69	72	13	0	0	348	462	23	95	5.4	.972	2B-154
1953	2 teams	PHI N (90G –.296) CHI A (17G –.222)																						
″	total	107	.282	.422	301	85	15	6	5	1.7	53	32	39	47	7	22	8	158	199	17	40	4.5	.955	2B-65, 3B-16, 1B-2
1954	CIN N	1	—	—	0	0	0	0	0	—	0	0	1	0	0	0	0	0	0	0	0	0.0	—	
12 yrs.		1184	.248	.357	3982	988	181	42	56	1.4	535	381	518	514	69	62	17	2639	3107	180	539	5.3	.970	2B-980, 3B-116, SS-19, 1B-7, OF-1
WORLD SERIES																								
1948	BOS N	2	.000	.000	1	0	0	0	0	0.0	0	0	0	1	0	1	0	0	0	0	0	0.0	—	

Cyclone Ryan

RYAN, DANIEL R. TR 6′ 200 lbs.
B. 1866, Capperwhite, Ireland D. Jan. 30, 1917, Medfield, Mass.

Year	Team	Games	BA	SA	AB	H	2B	3B	HR	HR%	R	RBI	BB	SO	SB	Pinch Hit AB	Pinch Hit H	PO	A	E	DP	TC/G	FA	G by Pos
1887	NY AA	8	.219	.250	32	7	1	0	0	0.0	4		3		1	0	0	72	4	5	7	8.1	.938	1B-8, P-2
1891	BOS N	1	.000	.000	1	0	0	0	0	0.0	0	0	0	0	0	0	0	0	1	0	0	1.0	1.000	P-1
2 yrs.		9	.212	.242	33	7	1	0	0	0.0	4	0	3	0	1	0	0	72	5	5	7	7.5	.939	1B-8, P-3

Jack Ryan

RYAN, JOHN FRANCIS BR TR 6′ 185 lbs.
B. May 5, 1905, West Mineral, Kans. D. Sept. 2, 1967, Rochester, Minn.

Year	Team	Games	BA	SA	AB	H	2B	3B	HR	HR%	R	RBI	BB	SO	SB	Pinch Hit AB	Pinch Hit H	PO	A	E	DP	TC/G	FA	G by Pos
1929	BOS A	2	.000	.000	3	0	0	0	0	0.0	0	0	0	0	0	0	0	1	0	0	0	0.5	1.000	OF-2

Jimmy Ryan

RYAN, JAMES EDWARD (Pony) BR TL 5′ 9″ 162 lbs.
B. Feb. 11, 1863, Clinton, Mass. D. Oct. 26, 1923, Chicago, Ill.

Year	Team	Games	BA	SA	AB	H	2B	3B	HR	HR%	R	RBI	BB	SO	SB	Pinch Hit AB	Pinch Hit H	PO	A	E	DP	TC/G	FA	G by Pos
1885	CHI N	3	.462	.538	13	6	1	0	0	0.0	2	2	1	1		0	0	6	11	7	0	8.0	.708	SS-2, OF-1
1886		84	.306	.431	327	100	17	6	4	1.2	58	53	12	28		0	0	115	55	30	4	2.2	.850	OF-70, SS-6, 3B-6, P-5, 2B-5
1887		126	.285	.435	508	145	23	10	11	2.2	117	74	53	19	50	0	0	172	54	39	8	2.0	.853	OF-122, P-8, 2B-3
1888		129	.332	**.515**	549	**182**	**33**	10	**16**	**2.9**	115	64	35	50	60	0	0	219	43	38	6	2.2	.873	OF-128, P-8
1889		135	.307	.498	576	177	31	14	17	3.0	140	72	70	62	45	0	0	286	133	57	19	3.5	.880	OF-106, SS-29
1890	CHI P	118	.340	.463	486	165	32	5	6	1.2	99	89	60	36	30	0	0	257	25	25	5	2.6	.919	OF-118
1891	CHI N	118	.277	.434	505	140	22	15	9	1.8	110	66	53	38	27	0	0	235	29	28	3	2.4	.904	OF-117, SS-2, P-2
1892		128	.293	.438	505	148	21	11	10	2.0	105	65	61	41	27	0	0	258	50	30	7	2.6	.911	OF-120, SS-9
1893		83	.299	.428	341	102	21	7	3	0.9	82	30	59	25	8	0	0	182	41	25	4	3.0	.899	OF-73, SS-10, P-1
1894		108	.361	.487	474	171	37	7	3	0.6	132	62	50	23	11	0	0	221	22	24	3	2.5	.910	OF-108
1895		108	.317	.445	438	139	22	8	6	1.4	83	49	48	22	18	0	0	161	18	12	6	1.8	.937	OF-108
1896		128	.305	.413	489	149	24	10	3	0.6	83	86	46	16	29	0	0	207	21	22	4	2.0	.912	OF-128
1897		136	.300	.458	520	156	33	17	5	1.0	103	85	50		27	0	0	211	28	14	7	1.9	.945	OF-136
1898		144	.323	.446	572	185	32	13	4	0.7	122	79	73		29	0	0	267	20	27	2	2.2	.914	OF-144
1899		125	.301	.394	525	158	20	10	3	0.6	91	68	43		9	0	0	266	18	13	6	2.4	.956	OF-125
1900		105	.277	.393	415	115	25	4	5	1.2	66	59	29		19	0	0	177	12	18	3	2.0	.913	OF-105
1902	WAS A	120	.320	.448	484	155	32	6	6	1.2	92	44	43		10	0	0	280	16	16	0	2.6	.949	OF-120
1903		114	.245	.368	437	107	25	4	7	1.6	42	46	17		9	0	0	288	7	9	1	2.7	.970	OF-114
18 yrs.		2012	.306	.443	8164	2500	451	157	118	1.4	1642	1093	803	361	408	0	0	3808	603	434	88	2.4	.910	OF-1943, SS-58, P-24, 2B-8, 3B-6

John Ryan

RYAN, JOHN BERNARD (Jack) BR TR 5′10½″ 165 lbs.
B. Nov. 12, 1868, Haverhill, Mass. D. Aug. 21, 1952, Boston, Mass.

Year	Team	Games	BA	SA	AB	H	2B	3B	HR	HR%	R	RBI	BB	SO	SB	Pinch Hit AB	Pinch Hit H	PO	A	E	DP	TC/G	FA	G by Pos
1889	LOU AA	21	.177	.190	79	14	1	0	0	0.0	8	2	3	17	2	0	0	63	26	14	1	4.9	.864	C-15, OF-4, 3B-2
1890		93	.217	.288	337	73	16	4	0	0.0	43		12		6	0	0	420	148	43	5	6.5	.930	C-89, OF-3, SS-1, 1B-1
1891		75	.225	.300	253	57	5	4	2	0.8	24	25	15	40	3	0	0	333	99	38	15	5.9	.919	C-56, 1B-11, 3B-6, OF-4, 2B-3
1894	BOS N	53	.269	.413	201	54	12	7	1	0.5	39	29	13	16	3	0	0	173	47	21	8	4.5	.913	C-51, 1B-2
1895		49	.291	.328	189	55	7	0	0	0.0	22	18	6	6	3	0	0	183	63	14	6	5.3	.946	C-43, 2B-5, OF-1
1896		8	.094	.125	32	3	1	0	0	0.0	2	0	0	1	0	0	0	32	9	4	1	5.6	.911	C-8
1898	BKN N	87	.189	.252	301	57	11	4	0	0.0	39	24	15		5	0	0	297	97	17	14	4.6	.959	C-84, 3B-4, 1B-1
1899	BAL N	2	.500	.750	4	2	1	0	0	0.0	0	1	0		1	0	0	4	4	0	1	4.0	1.000	C-2

John Ryan *continued*

Year	Team	Games	BA	SA	AB	H	2B	3B	HR	HR%	R	RBI	BB	SO	SB	Pinch Hit AB	Pinch Hit H	PO	A	E	DP	TC/G	FA	G by Pos
1901	STL N	83	.197	.250	300	59	6	5	0	0.0	27	31	7		5	1	0	362	118	14	17	6.0	.972	C-65, 2B-9, 1B-5, OF-3
1902		76	.180	.225	267	48	4	4	0	0.0	23	14	4		2	0	0	303	103	12	12	5.4	.971	C-66, 3B-4, 1B-4, 2B-2, SS-1
1903		67	.238	.282	227	54	5	1	1	0.4	18	10	10		2	0	0	343	81	10	21	6.5	.977	C-47, 1B-18, SS-2
1912	WAS A	1	.000	.000	1	0	0	0	0	0.0	0	0	0		0	0	0	1	1	0	0	2.0	1.000	3B-1
1913		1	.000	.000	1	0	0	0	0	0.0	0	0	0	0	0	0	0	1	1	0	0	2.0	1.000	C-1
13 yrs.		616	.217	.281	2192	476	69	29	4	0.2	245	154	85	80	32	1	0	2515	797	187	101	5.6	.947	C-527, 1B-42, 2B-19, 3B-17, OF-15, SS-4

John Ryan

RYAN, JOHN J.
B. St. Louis, Mo. Deceased.

Year	Team	Games	BA	SA	AB	H	2B	3B	HR	HR%	R	RBI	BB	SO	SB	Pinch Hit AB	Pinch Hit H	PO	A	E	DP	TC/G	FA	G by Pos
1895	STL N	2	.000	.000	2	0	0	0	0	0.0	0	0	0	0	0	0	0	0	0	1	0	0.5	.000	3B-2

Johnny Ryan

RYAN, JOHN JOSEPH 5′ 7½″ 150 lbs.
B. Oct. 1853, Philadelphia, Pa. D. Mar. 22, 1902, Philadelphia, Pa.

Year	Team	Games	BA	SA	AB	H	2B	3B	HR	HR%	R	RBI	BB	SO	SB	Pinch Hit AB	Pinch Hit H	PO	A	E	DP	TC/G	FA	G by Pos
1876	LOU N	64	.253	.295	241	61	5	1	1	0.4	32	18	6	**23**		0	0	132	2	17	1	2.3	.887	OF-64, P-1
1877	CIN N	6	.154	.231	26	4	0	1	0	0.0	2	2	1	5		0	0	10	0	3	0	2.2	.769	OF-6
2 yrs.		70	.243	.288	267	65	5	2	1	0.4	34	20	7	28		0	0	142	2	20	1	2.3	.878	OF-70, P-1

Lew Ryan

Playing record listed under Lew Malone.

Mike Ryan

RYAN, MICHAEL JAMES BR TR 6′ 2″ 205 lbs.
B. Nov. 25, 1941, Haverhill, Mass.

Year	Team	Games	BA	SA	AB	H	2B	3B	HR	HR%	R	RBI	BB	SO	SB	Pinch Hit AB	Pinch Hit H	PO	A	E	DP	TC/G	FA	G by Pos
1964	BOS A	1	.333	.333	3	1	0	0	0	0.0	0	2	1	0	0	0	0	5	0	0	0	5.0	1.000	C-1
1965		33	.159	.262	107	17	0	1	3	2.8	7	9	5	19	0	0	0	194	18	4	0	6.5	.981	C-33
1966		116	.214	.287	369	79	15	3	2	0.5	27	32	29	68	1	3	1	685	50	6	7	6.5	.992	C-114
1967		79	.199	.261	226	45	4	2	2	0.9	21	27	26	42	2	0	0	473	34	6	11	6.5	.988	C-79
1968	PHI N	96	.179	.216	296	53	6	1	1	0.3	12	15	15	59	0	1	0	501	62	5	7	5.9	.991	C-96
1969		133	.204	.332	446	91	17	2	12	2.7	41	44	30	66	1	1	0	769	79	8	13	6.5	.991	C-132
1970		46	.179	.284	134	24	8	0	2	1.5	14	11	16	24	0	0	0	238	15	2	1	5.5	.992	C-46
1971		43	.164	.284	134	22	5	1	3	2.2	9	6	10	32	0	0	0	222	30	0	2	5.9	1.000	C-43
1972		46	.179	.274	106	19	4	0	2	1.9	6	10	10	25	0	0	0	216	21	2	3	5.2	.992	C-46
1973		28	.232	.348	69	16	1	2	1	1.4	7	5	6	19	0	1	0	121	9	1	0	4.9	.992	C-27
1974	PIT N	15	.100	.100	30	3	0	0	0	0.0	2	0	4	16	0	0	0	49	7	0	1	3.7	1.000	C-15
11 yrs.		636	.193	.280	1920	370	60	12	28	1.5	146	161	152	370	4	6	1	3473	325	34	45	6.1	.991	C-632
WORLD SERIES																								
1967	BOS A	1	.000	.000	2	0	0	0	0	0.0	0	0	0	1	0	0	0	4	0	0	0	4.0	1.000	C-1

Tom Ryder

RYDER, THOMAS BL
Deceased.

Year	Team	Games	BA	SA	AB	H	2B	3B	HR	HR%	R	RBI	BB	SO	SB	Pinch Hit AB	Pinch Hit H	PO	A	E	DP	TC/G	FA	G by Pos
1884	STL U	8	.250	.286	28	7	1	0	0	0.0	4		2			0	0	10	3	7	0	2.5	.650	OF-8

Gene Rye

RYE, EUGENE RUDOLPH (Half-Pint) BL TR 5′ 6″ 165 lbs.
Born Eugene Rudolph Mercantelli.
B. Nov. 15, 1906, Chicago, Ill. D. Jan. 21, 1980, Park Ridge, Ill.

Year	Team	Games	BA	SA	AB	H	2B	3B	HR	HR%	R	RBI	BB	SO	SB	Pinch Hit AB	Pinch Hit H	PO	A	E	DP	TC/G	FA	G by Pos
1931	BOS A	17	.179	.179	39	7	0	0	0	0.0	3	1	2	5	0	7	1	17	0	1	0	1.8	.944	OF-10

Alex Sabo

SABO, ALEXANDER (Giz) BR TR 6′ 192 lbs.
Born Alexander Szabo.
B. Feb. 14, 1910, New Brunswick, N. J.

Year	Team	Games	BA	SA	AB	H	2B	3B	HR	HR%	R	RBI	BB	SO	SB	Pinch Hit AB	Pinch Hit H	PO	A	E	DP	TC/G	FA	G by Pos
1936	WAS A	4	.375	.375	8	3	0	0	0	0.0	1	1	0	2	0	1	1	10	2	1	0	3.3	.923	C-4
1937		1	—	—	0	0	0	0	0	—	0	0	0	0	0	0	0	1	0	0	0	1.0	1.000	C-1
2 yrs.		5	.375	.375	8	3	0	0	0	0.0	1	1	0	2	0	1	1	11	2	1	0	2.8	.929	C-5

Chris Sabo

SABO, CHRISTOPHER ANDREW (Spuds) BR TR 5′11″ 185 lbs.
B. Jan. 19, 1962, Detroit, Mich.

Year	Team	Games	BA	SA	AB	H	2B	3B	HR	HR%	R	RBI	BB	SO	SB	Pinch Hit AB	Pinch Hit H	PO	A	E	DP	TC/G	FA	G by Pos
1988	CIN N	137	.271	.414	538	146	40	2	11	2.0	74	44	29	52	46	2	0	75	318	14	31	3.0	.966	3B-135, SS-2
1989		82	.260	.395	304	79	21	1	6	2.0	40	29	25	33	14	5	0	36	145	11	12	2.5	.943	3B-76
1990		148	.270	.476	567	153	38	2	25	4.4	95	71	61	58	25	1	0	70	273	12	17	2.4	.966	3B-146
1991		153	.301	.505	582	175	35	3	26	4.5	91	88	44	79	19	2	1	86	255	12	24	2.3	.966	3B-151
1992		96	.244	.422	344	84	19	3	12	3.5	42	43	30	54	4	2	0	60	159	9	13	2.5	.961	3B-93
1993		148	.259	.440	552	143	33	2	21	3.8	86	82	43	105	6	0	0	79	242	11	16	2.2	.967	3B-148
1994	BAL A	68	.256	.465	258	66	15	3	11	4.3	41	42	20	38	1	2	0	52	49	4	5	1.5	.962	3B-37, OF-22, DH-10
1995	2 teams	CHI A (20G –.254) STL N (5G –.154)																						
″	total	25	.238	.345	84	20	6	0	1	1.2	10	11	4	14	3	4	1	21	4	2	2	1.4	.926	DH-15, 1B-3, 3B-2
8 yrs.		857	.268	.447	3229	866	207	16	113	3.5	479	410	256	433	118	18	2	479	1445	75	120	2.4	.962	3B-788, DH-25, OF-22, 1B-3, SS-2
LEAGUE CHAMPIONSHIP SERIES																								
1990	CIN N	6	.227	.364	22	5	0	0	1	4.5	1	3	1	4	0	0	0	7	7	0	1	2.3	1.000	3B-6
WORLD SERIES																								
1990	CIN N	4	.563	1.000	16	9	1	0	2	12.5	2	5	2	2	0	0	0	3	14	0	0	4.3	1.000	3B-4

Frank Sacka

SACKA, FRANK BR TR 6′ 195 lbs.
B. Aug. 30, 1924, Romulus, Mich. D. Dec. 7, 1994, Dearborn, Mich.

Year	Team	Games	BA	SA	AB	H	2B	3B	HR	HR%	R	RBI	BB	SO	SB	Pinch Hit AB	Pinch Hit H	PO	A	E	DP	TC/G	FA	G by Pos
1951	WAS A	7	.250	.250	16	4	0	0	0	0.0	1	3	0	5	0	1	0	21	4	1	0	4.3	.962	C-6
1953		7	.278	.278	18	5	0	0	0	0.0	2	3	3	1	0	1	0	25	5	0	0	5.0	1.000	C-6
2 yrs.		14	.265	.265	34	9	0	0	0	0.0	3	6	3	6	0	2	0	46	9	1	0	4.7	.982	C-12

Mike Sadek

SADEK, MICHAEL GEORGE
B. May 30, 1946, Minneapolis, Minn.
BR TR 5′9″ 165 lbs.
BB 1979

Year	Team	Games	BA	SA	AB	H	2B	3B	HR	HR%	R	RBI	BB	SO	SB	Pinch Hit AB	Pinch Hit H	PO	A	E	DP	TC/G	FA	G by Pos
1973	SF N	39	.167	.212	66	11	1	1	0	0.0	6	4	11	8	1	0	0	146	7	3	1	4.5	.981	C-35
1975		42	.236	.321	106	25	5	2	0	0.0	14	9	14	14	1	4	3	207	10	1	3	5.7	.995	C-38
1976		55	.204	.226	93	19	2	0	0	0.0	8	7	11	10	0	2	1	191	11	3	0	4.0	.985	C-51
1977		61	.230	.310	126	29	7	0	1	0.8	12	15	12	5	2	4	2	227	32	2	3	4.6	.992	C-57
1978		40	.239	.321	109	26	3	0	2	1.8	15	9	10	11	1	0	0	182	15	5	2	5.5	.975	C-37
1979		63	.238	.302	126	30	5	0	1	0.8	14	11	15	24	1	3	0	246	21	2	2	4.4	.993	C-60, OF-1
1980		64	.252	.311	151	38	4	1	1	0.7	14	16	27	18	0	3	0	266	29	8	1	5.1	.974	C-59
1981		19	.167	.250	36	6	3	0	0	0.0	5	3	8	7	0	0	0	79	15	2	2	5.1	.979	C-19
8 yrs.		383	.226	.292	813	184	30	4	5	0.6	88	74	108	97	6	16	6	1544	140	26	14	4.8	.985	C-356, OF-1

Bob Sadowski

SADOWSKI, ROBERT FRANK (Sid)
B. Jan. 15, 1937, St. Louis, Mo.
BL TR 6′ 175 lbs.

Year	Team	Games	BA	SA	AB	H	2B	3B	HR	HR%	R	RBI	BB	SO	SB	Pinch Hit AB	Pinch Hit H	PO	A	E	DP	TC/G	FA	G by Pos
1960	STL N	1	.000	.000	1	0	0	0	0	0.0	0	0	1	0	0	0	0	0	0	1	0	1.0	.000	2B-1
1961	PHI N	16	.130	.130	54	7	0	0	0	0.0	4	0	4	7	1	3	0	10	23	1	3	2.4	.971	3B-14
1962	CHI A	79	.231	.438	130	30	3	3	6	4.6	22	24	13	22	0	44	10	33	62	2	9	3.5	.979	3B-16, 2B-12
1963	LA A	88	.250	.313	144	36	6	0	1	0.7	12	22	15	34	2	**50**	12	49	13	2	1	1.8	.969	OF-25, 3B-6, 2B-4
4 yrs.		184	.222	.331	329	73	9	3	7	2.1	38	46	33	63	3	97	22	92	98	6	13	2.5	.969	3B-36, OF-25, 2B-17

Eddie Sadowski

SADOWSKI, EDWARD ROMAN
Brother of Ted Sadowski. Brother of Bob Sadowski.
B. Jan. 19, 1931, Pittsburgh, Pa. D. Nov. 6, 1993, Garden Grove, Calif.
BR TR 5′11″ 175 lbs.

Year	Team	Games	BA	SA	AB	H	2B	3B	HR	HR%	R	RBI	BB	SO	SB	Pinch Hit AB	Pinch Hit H	PO	A	E	DP	TC/G	FA	G by Pos
1960	BOS A	38	.215	.333	93	20	2	0	3	3.2	10	8	8	13	0	0	0	178	11	1	0	5.3	.995	C-36
1961	LA A	69	.232	.384	164	38	13	0	4	2.4	16	12	11	33	2	9	1	295	17	4	4	5.6	.987	C-56
1962		27	.200	.327	55	11	4	0	1	1.8	4	3	2	14	1	7	1	86	4	3	0	5.2	.968	C-18
1963		80	.172	.259	174	30	1	1	4	2.3	24	15	17	33	2	6	1	340	38	1	7	5.6	.997	C-68
1966	ATL N	3	.111	.111	9	1	0	0	0	0.0	1	1	1	1	0	0	0	15	2	0	0	5.7	1.000	C-3
5 yrs.		217	.202	.319	495	100	20	1	12	2.4	55	39	39	94	5	22	3	914	72	9	11	5.5	.991	C-181

Olmedo Saenz

SAENZ, OLMEDO
Born Olmedo Saenz (Sanchez).
B. Oct. 8, 1970, Chitre Herrera, Panama.
BR TR 6′2″ 185 lbs.

Year	Team	Games	BA	SA	AB	H	2B	3B	HR	HR%	R	RBI	BB	SO	SB	Pinch Hit AB	Pinch Hit H	PO	A	E	DP	TC/G	FA	G by Pos
1994	CHI A	5	.143	.286	14	2	0	1	0	0.0	2	0	0	5	0	0	0	3	6	0	0	1.8	1.000	3B-5

Tom Saffell

SAFFELL, THOMAS JUDSON
B. July 26, 1921, Etowah, Tenn.
BL TR 5′11″ 170 lbs.

Year	Team	Games	BA	SA	AB	H	2B	3B	HR	HR%	R	RBI	BB	SO	SB	Pinch Hit AB	Pinch Hit H	PO	A	E	DP	TC/G	FA	G by Pos
1949	PIT N	73	.322	.395	205	66	7	1	2	1.0	36	25	21	27	5	18	6	122	2	1	1	2.4	.992	OF-53
1950		67	.203	.275	182	37	7	0	2	1.1	18	6	14	34	1	21	4	128	5	1	0	3.1	.993	OF-43
1951		49	.200	.246	65	13	0	0	1	1.5	11	5	5	18	1	24	3	25	1	2	0	1.6	.929	OF-17
1955	2 teams PIT N (73G –.168) KC A (9G –.216)																							
″	total	82	.180	.207	150	27	1	0	1	0.7	26	4	19	29	2	17	4	103	2	4	0	1.9	.963	OF-56
4 yrs.		271	.238	.296	602	143	15	1	6	1.0	91	40	59	108	9	80	17	378	10	8	1	2.3	.980	OF-169

Harry Sage

SAGE, HARRY (Doc)
B. Mar. 16, 1864, Rock Island, Ill. D. May 27, 1947, Rock Island, Ill.
BR TR 5′10″ 185 lbs.

Year	Team	Games	BA	SA	AB	H	2B	3B	HR	HR%	R	RBI	BB	SO	SB	Pinch Hit AB	Pinch Hit H	PO	A	E	DP	TC/G	FA	G by Pos
1890	TOL AA	81	.149	.229	275	41	8	4	2	0.7	40		29		10	0	0	336	154	27	3	6.4	.948	C-80, OF-1

Vic Saier

SAIER, VICTOR SYLVESTER
B. May 4, 1891, Lansing, Mich. D. May 14, 1967, East Lansing, Mich.
BL TR 5′11″ 185 lbs.

Year	Team	Games	BA	SA	AB	H	2B	3B	HR	HR%	R	RBI	BB	SO	SB	Pinch Hit AB	Pinch Hit H	PO	A	E	DP	TC/G	FA	G by Pos
1911	CHI N	86	.259	.336	259	67	15	1	1	0.4	42	37	25	37	11	12	4	715	33	15	44	10.5	.980	1B-73
1912		122	.288	.419	451	130	25	14	2	0.4	74	61	34	65	11	1	0	1165	52	10	67	10.2	.992	1B-120
1913		148	.288	.477	518	149	14	**21**	14	2.7	93	92	62	62	26	1	0	1469	71	26	79	10.6	.983	1B-148
1914		153	.240	.415	537	129	24	8	18	3.4	87	72	94	61	19	0	0	1521	59	22	62	10.5	.986	1B-153
1915		144	.264	.445	497	131	35	11	11	2.2	74	64	64	62	29	4	1	1348	65	21	71	10.3	.985	1B-139
1916		147	.253	.357	498	126	25	3	7	1.4	60	50	79	68	20	0	0	1622	74	27	78	11.7	.984	1B-147
1917		6	.238	.286	21	5	1	0	0	0.0	5	2	2	1	0	0	0	56	7	0	3	10.5	1.000	1B-6
1919	PIT N	58	.223	.313	166	37	3	3	2	1.2	19	17	18	13	5	7	3	493	17	8	18	10.2	.985	1B-51
8 yrs.		864	.263	.408	2947	774	142	61	55	1.9	454	395	378	369	121	25	8	8389	378	129	422	10.6	.985	1B-837

Lenn Sakata

SAKATA, LENN HARUKI
B. June 8, 1954, Honolulu, Hawaii.
BR TR 5′9″ 160 lbs.

Year	Team	Games	BA	SA	AB	H	2B	3B	HR	HR%	R	RBI	BB	SO	SB	Pinch Hit AB	Pinch Hit H	PO	A	E	DP	TC/G	FA	G by Pos
1977	MIL A	53	.162	.214	154	25	2	0	2	1.3	13	12	9	22	1	0	0	102	159	4	43	5.0	.985	2B-53
1978		30	.192	.244	78	15	4	0	0	0.0	8	3	8	11	1	0	0	50	66	3	12	4.1	.975	2B-29
1979		4	.500	.643	14	7	2	0	0	0.0	1	1	0	1	0	0	0	10	13	0	5	5.8	1.000	2B-4
1980	BAL A	43	.193	.313	83	16	3	2	1	1.2	12	9	6	10	2	5	4	55	73	2	18	3.3	.985	2B-34, SS-4, DH-1
1981		61	.227	.353	150	34	4	0	5	3.3	19	15	11	18	4	1	0	82	148	7	33	3.8	.970	SS-42, 2B-20
1982		136	.259	.370	343	89	18	1	6	1.7	40	31	30	39	7	9	3	182	299	16	61	3.6	.968	2B-83, SS-56
1983		66	.254	.373	134	34	7	0	3	2.2	23	12	16	17	8	3	0	84	117	2	36	3.3	.990	2B-60, DH-1, C-1
1984		81	.191	.255	157	30	1	0	3	1.9	23	11	6	15	4	5	1	80	161	3	33	3.2	.988	2B-76, OF-1
1985		55	.227	.351	97	22	3	0	3	3.1	15	6	6	15	3	1	0	58	87	6	18	3.0	.960	2B-50, DH-1
1986	OAK A	17	.353	.412	34	12	2	0	0	0.0	4	5	3	6	0	0	0	21	39	1	4	3.6	.984	2B-16, DH-1
1987	NY A	19	.267	.444	45	12	0	1	2	4.4	5	4	2	4	0	0	0	8	30	2	4	2.2	.950	3B-12, 2B-6
11 yrs.		565	.230	.330	1289	296	46	4	25	1.9	163	109	97	158	30	24	8	732	1192	46	267	3.6	.977	2B-431, SS-102, 3B-12, DH-4, OF-1, C-1
WORLD SERIES																								
1983	BAL A	1	.000	.000	1	0	0	0	0	0.0	0	0	0	0	0	0	0	2	2	0	1	4.0	1.000	2B-1

Mark Salas

SALAS, MARK BRUCE (Chief)
B. Mar. 8, 1961, Montebello, Calif.
BL TR 6′ 180 lbs.

Year	Team	Games	BA	SA	AB	H	2B	3B	HR	HR%	R	RBI	BB	SO	SB	Pinch Hit AB	Pinch Hit H	PO	A	E	DP	TC/G	FA	G by Pos
1984	STL N	14	.100	.150	20	2	1	0	0	0.0	1	1	0	3	0	8	1	13	2	0	0	2.1	1.000	C-4, OF-3
1985	MIN A	120	.300	.458	360	108	20	5	9	2.5	51	41	18	37	0	12	1	529	39	5	10	4.9	.991	C-115, DH-3
1986		91	.233	.384	258	60	7	4	8	3.1	28	33	18	32	3	25	5	358	32	8	5	5.2	.980	C-69, DH-8
1987	2 teams MIN A (22G –.378) NY A (50G –.200)																							
″	total	72	.250	.400	160	40	6	0	6	3.8	21	21	15	23	0	19	4	258	16	1	0	4.6	.996	C-55, DH-4, OF-1
1988	CHI A	75	.250	.332	196	49	7	0	3	1.5	17	9	12	17	0	7	1	251	35	6	5	4.2	.979	C-69, DH-1

Mark Salas *continued*

Year	Team		Games	BA	SA	AB	H	2B	3B	HR	HR%	R	RBI	BB	SO	SB	Pinch Hit AB	Pinch Hit H	PO	A	E	DP	TC/G	FA	G by Pos
1989	**CLE**	**A**	30	.221	.377	77	17	4	1	2	2.6	4	7	5	13	0	11	0	3	1	0	0	0.2	1.000	DH-20, C-5
1990	**DET**	**A**	74	.232	.415	164	38	3	0	9	5.5	18	24	21	28	0	17	2	227	23	3	3	4.1	.988	C-57, DH-3, 3B-1
1991			33	.088	.158	57	5	1	0	1	1.8	2	7	0	10	0	15	1	28	2	0	0	1.3	1.000	C-11, DH-8, 1B-5
8 yrs.			509	.247	.389	1292	319	49	10	38	2.9	142	143	89	163	3	114	15	1667	150	23	23	4.2	.988	C-385, DH-47, 1B-5, OF-4, 3B-1

Angel Salazar

SALAZAR, ARGENIS ANTONIO BR TR 5′11″ 180 lbs.
Born Argenis Antonio Salazar (Yepez).
B. Nov. 4, 1961, Anaco, Venezuela.

Year	Team		Games	BA	SA	AB	H	2B	3B	HR	HR%	R	RBI	BB	SO	SB	Pinch Hit AB	Pinch Hit H	PO	A	E	DP	TC/G	FA	G by Pos
1983	**MON**	**N**	36	.216	.297	37	8	1	1	0	0.0	5	1	1	8	0	2	0	28	28	2	9	1.7	.966	SS-34
1984			80	.155	.201	174	27	4	2	0	0.0	12	12	4	38	1	0	0	88	155	10	35	3.2	.960	SS-80
1986	**KC**	**A**	117	.245	.326	298	73	20	2	0	0.0	24	24	7	47	1	1	0	121	284	9	50	3.6	.978	SS-115, 2B-1
1987			116	.205	.246	317	65	7	0	2	0.6	24	21	6	46	4	0	0	134	332	9	56	4.1	.981	SS-116
1988	**CHI**	**N**	34	.250	.300	60	15	1	1	0	0.0	4	1	1	11	0	3	0	38	53	3	11	2.9	.968	SS-29, 2B-2, 3B-1
5 yrs.			383	.212	.270	886	188	33	6	2	0.2	69	59	19	150	6	6	0	409	852	33	161	3.4	.974	SS-374, 2B-3, 3B-1

Luis Salazar

SALAZAR, LUIS ERNESTO BR TR 5′ 9″ 185 lbs.
Born Luis Ernesto Salazar (Garacia).
B. May 19, 1956, Barcelona, Venezuela.

Year	Team		Games	BA	SA	AB	H	2B	3B	HR	HR%	R	RBI	BB	SO	SB	Pinch Hit AB	Pinch Hit H	PO	A	E	DP	TC/G	FA	G by Pos
1980	**SD**	**N**	44	.337	.462	169	57	4	7	1	0.6	28	25	9	25	11	0	0	39	88	7	7	2.9	.948	3B-42, OF-4
1981			109	.302	.403	400	121	19	6	3	0.8	37	38	16	72	11	2	0	108	191	14	17	2.7	.955	3B-94, OF-23
1982			145	.242	.336	524	127	15	5	8	1.5	55	62	23	80	32	2	0	133	326	29	32	3.3	.941	3B-129, SS-18, OF-1
1983			134	.258	.387	481	124	16	2	14	2.9	52	45	17	80	24	6	2	122	274	21	22	3.0	.950	3B-118, SS-19
1984			93	.241	.329	228	55	7	2	3	1.3	20	17	6	38	11	14	4	87	97	6	5	2.2	.968	3B-58, OF-24, SS-4
1985	**CHI**	**A**	122	.245	.404	327	80	18	2	10	3.1	39	45	12	60	14	15	6	180	57	10	13	1.8	.960	OF-84, 3B-39, DH-8, 1B-6
1986			4	.143	.143	7	1	0	0	0	0.0	1	0	1	3	0	2	0	0	0	0	0	0.0	.000	DH-2
1987	**SD**	**N**	84	.254	.328	189	48	5	0	3	1.6	13	17	14	30	3	18	3	56	95	9	11	2.2	.944	3B-38, SS-22, OF-10, P-2, 1B-1
1988	**DET**	**A**	130	.270	.385	452	122	14	1	12	2.7	61	62	21	70	6	9	5	199	151	10	22	2.5	.972	OF-68, SS-37, 3B-31, 2B-5, 1B-4
1989	**2 teams**		**SD N** (95G –.268) **CHI N** (26G –.325)																						
″	**total**		121	.282	.414	326	92	12	2	9	2.8	34	34	15	57	1	15	6	79	154	10	19	2.0	.959	3B-97, OF-16, SS-9, 1B-2
1990	**CHI**	**N**	115	.254	.388	410	104	13	3	12	2.9	44	47	19	59	3	5	1	96	137	12	12	2.1	.951	3B-91, OF-28
1991			103	.258	.432	333	86	14	1	14	4.2	34	38	15	45	0	13	2	76	152	10	7	2.5	.958	3B-86, 1B-7, OF-1
1992			98	.208	.310	255	53	7	2	5	2.0	20	25	11	34	1	17	4	114	98	6	16	2.4	.972	3B-40, OF-34, SS-12, 1B-5
13 yrs.			1302	.261	.381	4101	1070	144	33	94	2.3	438	455	179	653	117	118	33	1289	1820	144	183	2.5	.956	3B-863, OF-293, SS-121, 1B-25, DH-10, 2B-5, P-2
LEAGUE CHAMPIONSHIP SERIES																									
1984	**SD**	**N**	3	.200	.600	5	1	0	1	0	0.0	0	0	0	1	0	1	0	0	3	0	0	1.0	1.000	OF-2, 3B-1
1989	**CHI**	**N**	5	.368	.632	19	7	0	1	1	5.3	2	2	0	0	0	0	0	4	5	1	0	2.0	.900	3B-5
2 yrs.			8	.333	.625	24	8	0	2	1	4.2	2	2	0	1	0	1	0	4	8	1	0	1.6	.923	3B-6, OF-2
									4th																
WORLD SERIES																									
1984	**SD**	**N**	4	.333	.333	3	1	0	0	0	0.0	0	0	0	0	0	1	1	1	0	0	0	0.3	1.000	OF-2, 3B-1

Ed Sales

SALES, EDWARD A. BL TR
B. 1861, Harrisburg, Pa. D. Aug. 10, 1912, New Haven, Conn.

Year	Team		Games	BA	SA	AB	H	2B	3B	HR	HR%	R	RBI	BB	SO	SB	Pinch Hit AB	Pinch Hit H	PO	A	E	DP	TC/G	FA	G by Pos
1890	**PIT**	**N**	51	.228	.312	189	43	7	3	1	0.5	19	23	16	15	3	0	0	85	151	35	10	5.3	.871	SS-51

Bill Salkeld

SALKELD, WILLIAM FRANKLIN BL TR 5′10″ 190 lbs.
B. Mar. 8, 1917, Pocatello, Ida. D. Apr. 22, 1967, Los Angeles, Calif.

Year	Team		Games	BA	SA	AB	H	2B	3B	HR	HR%	R	RBI	BB	SO	SB	Pinch Hit AB	Pinch Hit H	PO	A	E	DP	TC/G	FA	G by Pos
1945	**PIT**	**N**	95	.311	.547	267	83	16	1	15	5.6	45	52	50	16	2	8	2	279	40	9	8	3.8	.973	C-86
1946			69	.294	.400	160	47	8	0	3	1.9	18	19	39	16	2	17	3	176	31	6	3	4.2	.972	C-51
1947			47	.213	.246	61	13	2	0	0	0.0	5	8	6	8	0	29	9	29	4	1	0	2.3	.971	C-15
1948	**BOS**	**N**	78	.242	.414	198	48	8	1	8	4.0	26	28	42	37	1	12	1	254	32	3	5	4.9	.990	C-59
1949			66	.255	.379	161	41	5	0	5	3.1	17	25	44	24	1	4	0	230	21	5	3	4.1	.980	C-63
1950	**CHI**	**A**	1	.000	.000	3	0	0	0	0	0.0	0	0	1	0	0	0	0	4	0	0	0	4.0	1.000	C-1
6 yrs.			356	.273	.433	850	232	39	2	31	3.6	111	132	182	101	6	70	15	972	128	24	19	4.1	.979	C-275
WORLD SERIES																									
1948	**BOS**	**N**	5	.222	.556	9	2	0	0	1	11.1	2	1	5	1	0	1	0	19	2	0	0	4.2	1.000	C-5

Chico Salmon

SALMON, RUTHFORD EDUARDO BR TR 5′10″ 160 lbs.
B. Dec. 3, 1940, Colon, Panama.

Year	Team		Games	BA	SA	AB	H	2B	3B	HR	HR%	R	RBI	BB	SO	SB	Pinch Hit AB	Pinch Hit H	PO	A	E	DP	TC/G	FA	G by Pos
1964	**CLE**	**A**	86	.307	.424	283	87	17	2	4	1.4	43	25	13	37	10	6	2	191	67	2	14	2.7	.992	OF-53, 2B-32, 1B-13
1965			79	.242	.383	120	29	8	0	3	2.5	20	12	5	19	7	19	5	151	16	3	14	3.1	.982	1B-28, OF-17, 3B-5, 2B-5
1966			126	.256	.346	422	108	13	2	7	1.7	46	40	21	41	10	10	2	315	225	19	53	4.3	.966	SS-61, 2B-28, 1B-24, OF-10, 3B-6
1967			90	.227	.330	203	46	13	1	2	1.0	19	19	17	29	10	5	3	199	103	5	26	3.3	.984	OF-28, 2B-24, 1B-24, SS-14, 3B-4
1968			103	.214	.283	276	59	8	1	3	1.1	24	12	12	30	7	9	0	152	145	8	29	3.0	.974	2B-45, 3B-18, SS-15, OF-13, 1B-11
1969	**BAL**	**A**	52	.297	.451	91	27	5	0	3	3.3	18	12	10	22	0	14	3	90	42	8	9	3.6	.943	1B-17, SS-9, 2B-9, 3B-3, OF-1
1970			63	.250	.395	172	43	4	0	7	4.1	19	22	8	30	2	13	2	61	87	9	12	2.7	.943	SS-33, 2B-12, 3B-11, 1B-2
1971			42	.179	.262	84	15	1	0	2	2.4	11	7	3	21	0	19	3	75	30	6	12	3.8	.946	1B-9, 2B-9, 3B-6, SS-5
1972			17	.063	.125	16	1	1	0	0	0.0	2	0	0	4	0	14	1	1	2	0	1	1.0	1.000	1B-2, 3B-1
9 yrs.			658	.249	.354	1667	415	70	6	31	1.9	202	149	89	233	46	109	21	1235	717	60	170	3.3	.970	2B-164, SS-137, 1B-130, OF-122, 3B-54
LEAGUE CHAMPIONSHIP SERIES																									
1969	**BAL**	**A**	1	.000	.000	1	0	0	0	0	0.0	0	0	0	0	0	1	0	0	0	0	0	0.0	—	
WORLD SERIES																									
1969	**BAL**	**A**	2	—	—	0	0	0	0	0	—	0	0	0	0	0	0	0	0	0	0	0	0.0	—	
1970			1	1.000	1.000	1	1	0	0	0	0.0	1	0	0	0	0	1	1	0	0	0	0	0.0	—	
2 yrs.			3	1.000	1.000	1	1	0	0	0	0.0	1	0	0	0	0	1	1							

Year	Team	Games	BA	SA	AB	H	2B	3B	HR	HR%	R	RBI	BB	SO	SB	Pinch Hit AB	Pinch Hit H	PO	A	E	DP	TC/G	FA	G by Pos

Tim Salmon

SALMON, TIMOTHY JAMES BR TR 6′ 3″ 200 lbs.
B. Aug. 24, 1968, Long Beach, Calif.

Year	Team	Games	BA	SA	AB	H	2B	3B	HR	HR%	R	RBI	BB	SO	SB	Pinch Hit AB	Pinch Hit H	PO	A	E	DP	TC/G	FA	G by Pos
1992	CAL A	23	.177	.266	79	14	1	0	2	2.5	8	6	11	23	1	0	0	40	1	2	1	2.0	.953	OF-21
1993		142	.283	.536	515	146	35	1	31	6.0	93	95	82	135	5	0	0	335	12	7	2	2.5	.980	OF-140, DH-1
1994		100	.287	.531	373	107	18	2	23	6.2	67	70	54	102	1	1	1	219	9	8	1	2.4	.966	OF-99
1995		143	.330	.594	537	177	34	3	34	6.3	111	105	91	111	5	0	0	319	7	4	0	2.3	.988	OF-142, DH-1
4 yrs.		408	.295	.541	1504	444	88	6	90	6.0	279	276	238	371	12	1	1	913	29	21	4	2.4	.978	OF-402, DH-2

Jack Saltzgaver

SALTZGAVER, OTTO HAMLIN BL TR 5′11″ 165 lbs.
B. Jan. 23, 1903, Croton, Iowa D. Feb. 1, 1978, Keokuk, Iowa.

Year	Team	Games	BA	SA	AB	H	2B	3B	HR	HR%	R	RBI	BB	SO	SB	Pinch Hit AB	Pinch Hit H	PO	A	E	DP	TC/G	FA	G by Pos
1932	NY A	20	.128	.213	47	6	2	1	0	0.0	10	5	10	10	1	2	0	38	30	3	5	4.4	.958	2B-16
1934		94	.271	.351	350	95	8	1	6	1.7	64	36	48	28	8	6	2	93	132	12	13	2.7	.949	3B-84, 1B-4
1935		61	.262	.362	149	39	6	0	3	2.0	17	18	23	12	0	12	2	70	82	8	11	3.3	.950	2B-25, 3B-18, 1B-6
1936		34	.211	.300	90	19	5	0	1	1.1	14	13	13	18	0	2	0	44	34	2	5	3.1	.975	3B-16, 2B-6, 1B-4
1937		17	.182	.182	11	2	0	0	0	0.0	6	0	3	4	0	2	1	34	1	0	4	8.8	1.000	1B-4
1945	PIT N	52	.325	.419	117	38	5	3	0	0.0	20	10	8	8	0	20	3	63	66	5	11	4.2	.963	2B-31, 3B-1
6 yrs.		278	.260	.347	764	199	26	5	10	1.3	131	82	105	80	9	44	8	342	345	30	49	3.3	.958	3B-119, 2B-78, 1B-18

Ed Samcoff

SAMCOFF, EDWARD WILLIAM BR TR 5′10″ 165 lbs.
B. Sept. 1, 1924, Sacramento, Calif.

Year	Team	Games	BA	SA	AB	H	2B	3B	HR	HR%	R	RBI	BB	SO	SB	Pinch Hit AB	Pinch Hit H	PO	A	E	DP	TC/G	FA	G by Pos
1951	PHI A	4	.000	.000	11	0	0	0	0	0.0	0	0	1	2	0	1	0	5	5	0	3	3.3	1.000	2B-3

Ron Samford

SAMFORD, RONALD EDWARD BR TR 5′11″ 156 lbs.
B. Feb. 28, 1930, Dallas, Tex.

Year	Team	Games	BA	SA	AB	H	2B	3B	HR	HR%	R	RBI	BB	SO	SB	Pinch Hit AB	Pinch Hit H	PO	A	E	DP	TC/G	FA	G by Pos
1954	NY N	12	.000	.000	5	0	0	0	0	0.0	2	0	0	1	0	1	0	3	2	0	0	1.7	1.000	2B-3
1955	DET A	1	.000	.000	1	0	0	0	0	0.0	0	0	0	1	0	0	0	0	2	0	0	2.0	1.000	SS-1
1957		54	.220	.275	91	20	1	2	0	0.0	6	5	6	15	1	0	0	53	95	6	23	3.1	.961	SS-35, 2B-11, 3B-4
1959	WAS A	91	.224	.342	237	53	13	0	5	2.1	23	22	11	29	1	3	0	130	214	18	39	4.2	.950	SS-64, 2B-23
4 yrs.		158	.219	.317	334	73	14	2	5	1.5	31	27	17	46	2	4	0	186	313	24	62	3.7	.954	SS-100, 2B-37, 3B-4

Billy Sample

SAMPLE, WILLIAM AMOS BR TR 5′ 9″ 175 lbs.
B. Apr. 2, 1955, Roanoke, Va.

Year	Team	Games	BA	SA	AB	H	2B	3B	HR	HR%	R	RBI	BB	SO	SB	Pinch Hit AB	Pinch Hit H	PO	A	E	DP	TC/G	FA	G by Pos
1978	TEX A	8	.467	.600	15	7	2	0	0	0.0	2	3	0	3	0	2	1	0	0	0	0	0.0		DH-3, OF-2
1979		128	.292	.415	325	95	21	2	5	1.5	60	35	37	28	8	18	5	173	7	0	1	1.6	1.000	OF-103, DH-9
1980		99	.260	.368	204	53	10	0	4	2.0	29	19	18	15	8	23	5	105	2	3	0	1.4	.973	OF-72, DH-4
1981		66	.283	.391	230	65	16	0	3	1.3	36	25	17	21	4	3	0	132	4	1	1	2.1	.993	OF-64
1982		97	.261	.394	360	94	14	2	10	2.8	56	29	27	35	10	1	0	196	6	4	1	2.2	.981	OF-91, DH-1
1983		147	.274	.401	554	152	28	3	12	2.2	80	57	44	46	44	2	0	329	8	4	0	2.3	.988	OF-146
1984		130	.247	.327	489	121	20	2	5	1.0	67	33	29	46	18	11	4	285	3	4	2	2.4	.986	OF-122, DH-2
1985	NY A	59	.288	.345	139	40	5	0	1	0.7	18	15	9	10	2	5	2	89	1	1	0	1.7	.989	OF-55
1986	ATL N	92	.285	.430	200	57	11	0	6	3.0	23	14	14	26	4	33	9	69	1	1	1	1.2	.986	OF-56, 2B-1
9 yrs.		826	.272	.384	2516	684	127	9	46	1.8	371	230	195	230	98	98	26	1378	32	18	6	2.0	.987	OF-711, DH-19, 2B-1

Amado Samuel

SAMUEL, AMADO RUPERTO BR TR 6′ 1″ 170 lbs.
B. Dec. 6, 1938, San Pedro de Macoris, Dominican Republic.

Year	Team	Games	BA	SA	AB	H	2B	3B	HR	HR%	R	RBI	BB	SO	SB	Pinch Hit AB	Pinch Hit H	PO	A	E	DP	TC/G	FA	G by Pos
1962	MIL N	76	.206	.297	209	43	10	0	3	1.4	16	20	12	54	0	5	1	85	160	11	29	3.8	.957	SS-36, 2B-28, 3B-3
1963		15	.176	.235	17	3	1	0	0	0.0	0	0	0	4	0	0	0	12	14	4	3	2.7	.867	SS-7, 2B-4
1964	NY N	53	.232	.282	142	33	7	0	0	0.0	7	5	4	24	0	2	1	52	124	11	24	3.5	.941	SS-34, 3B-17, 2B-3
3 yrs.		144	.215	.288	368	79	18	0	3	0.8	23	25	16	82	0	7	2	149	298	26	56	3.6	.945	SS-77, 2B-35, 3B-20

Juan Samuel

SAMUEL, JUAN MILTON (Sammy) BR TR 5′11″ 170 lbs.
Born Juan Milton Romero (Samuel).
B. Dec. 9, 1960, San Pedro de Macoris, Dominican Republic.

Year	Team	Games	BA	SA	AB	H	2B	3B	HR	HR%	R	RBI	BB	SO	SB	Pinch Hit AB	Pinch Hit H	PO	A	E	DP	TC/G	FA	G by Pos
1983	PHI N	18	.277	.446	65	18	1	2	2	3.1	14	5	4	16	3	0	0	44	54	9	9	5.9	.916	2B-18
1984		160	.272	.442	**701**	191	36	**19**	15	2.1	105	69	28	**168**	72	2	1	388	438	33	77	5.4	.962	2B-160
1985		161	.264	.436	**663**	175	31	13	19	2.9	101	74	33	**141**	53	1	0	389	463	15	88	5.5	.983	2B-159
1986		145	.266	.448	591	157	36	12	16	2.7	90	78	26	**142**	42	2	2	290	440	25	83	5.3	.967	2B-143
1987		160	.272	.502	**655**	178	37	**15**	28	4.3	113	100	60	**162**	35	0	0	374	434	18	99	5.2	.978	2B-160
1988		157	.243	.380	629	153	32	9	12	1.9	68	67	39	151	33	1	1	351	387	16	92	4.8	.979	2B-152, OF-3, 3B-1
1989	2 teams	PHI N (51G –.246) NY N (86G –.228)																						
"	total	137	.235	.335	532	125	16	2	11	2.1	69	48	42	120	42	2	1	339	6	4	3	2.6	.989	OF-134
1990	LA N	143	.242	.382	492	119	24	3	13	2.6	62	52	51	126	38	6	1	273	262	16	47	4.0	.971	2B-108, OF-31
1991		153	.271	.389	594	161	22	6	12	2.0	74	58	49	133	23	2	1	300	442	17	73	5.0	.978	2B-152
1992	2 teams	LA N (47G –.262) KC A (29G –.284)																						
"	total	76	.272	.344	224	61	8	4	0	0.0	22	23	14	49	8	15	4	121	106	11	22	3.6	.954	2B-48, OF-19
1993	CIN N	103	.230	.345	261	60	10	4	4	1.5	31	26	23	53	9	18	3	151	172	10	33	4.0	.970	2B-70, 1B-6, 3B-4, OF-3
1994	DET A	59	.309	.559	136	42	9	5	5	3.7	32	21	10	26	5	5	2	82	28	1	4	2.4	.991	OF-27, DH-10, 2B-8, 1B-2
1995	2 teams	DET A (76G –.281) KC A (15G –.176)																						
"	total	91	.263	.498	205	54	10	1	12	5.9	31	39	29	49	6	29	7	300	35	9	29	4.2	.974	1B-38, DH-23, OF-14, 2B-6
13 yrs.		1563	.260	.418	5748	1494	272	95	149	2.6	812	660	408	1336	369	83	23	3402	3267	184	659	4.6	.973	2B-1184, OF-231, 1B-46, DH-33, 3B-5
LEAGUE CHAMPIONSHIP SERIES																								
1983	PHI N	1	—	—	0	0	0	0	0	—	0	0	0	0	0	0	0	0	0	0	0	0.0	—	
WORLD SERIES																								
1983	PHI N	3	.000	.000	1	0	0	0	0	0.0	0	0	0	0	0	1	0	0	0	0	0	0.0	—	

Ike Samuls

SAMULS, SAMUEL EARL BR TR
B. Feb. 20, 1876, Austria-Hungary D. Jan. 1, 1942, Los Angeles, Calif.

Year	Team	Games	BA	SA	AB	H	2B	3B	HR	HR%	R	RBI	BB	SO	SB	Pinch Hit AB	Pinch Hit H	PO	A	E	DP	TC/G	FA	G by Pos
1895	STL N	24	.230	.257	74	17	2	0	0	0.0	5	5	5	7	5	0	0	22	45	24	1	3.8	.736	3B-21, SS-3

Gus Sanberg

SANBERG, GUSTAVE E. BR TR 6′ 1″ 189 lbs.
B. Feb. 23, 1896, Long Island City, N. Y. D. Feb. 3, 1930, Los Angeles, Calif.

Year	Team	Games	BA	SA	AB	H	2B	3B	HR	HR%	R	RBI	BB	SO	SB	Pinch Hit AB	Pinch Hit H	PO	A	E	DP	TC/G	FA	G by Pos
1923	CIN N	7	.176	.235	17	3	1	0	0	0.0	1	1	1	1	0	2	1	11	3	0	0	2.8	1.000	C-5
1924		24	.173	.173	52	9	0	0	0	0.0	1	3	2	7	0	0	0	56	11	0	1	2.8	1.000	C-24
2 yrs.		31	.174	.188	69	12	1	0	0	0.0	2	4	3	8	0	2	1	67	14	0	1	2.8	1.000	C-29

Alejandro Sanchez

SANCHEZ, ALEJANDRO BR TR 6′ 175 lbs.
Born Alejandro Sanchez (Pimentel).
B. Feb. 14, 1959, San Pedro de Macoris, Dominican Republic.

Year	Team	Games	BA	SA	AB	H	2B	3B	HR	HR%	R	RBI	BB	SO	SB	Pinch Hit AB	Pinch Hit H	PO	A	E	DP	TC/G	FA	G by Pos
1982	PHI N	7	.286	.786	14	4	1	0	2	14.3	3	4	0	4	0	1	1	7	0	0	0	1.8	1.000	OF-4
1983		8	.286	.286	7	2	0	0	0	0.0	2	2	0	2	0	4	2	1	0	1	0	1.0	.500	OF-2
1984	SF N	13	.195	.244	41	8	0	1	0	0.0	3	2	0	12	2	2	0	18	2	1	0	1.9	.952	OF-11
1985	DET A	71	.248	.459	133	33	6	2	6	4.5	19	12	0	39	2	18	6	35	1	3	0	0.7	.923	OF-31, DH-28
1986	MIN A	8	.125	.125	16	2	0	0	0	0.0	1	1	1	8	0	4	0	0	0	0	0	0.0		DH-3, OF-1
1987	OAK A	2	.000	.000	3	0	0	0	0	0.0	0	0	0	1	0	1	0	1	0	0	0	0.5	1.000	OF-1, DH-1
6 yrs.		109	.229	.402	214	49	7	3	8	3.7	28	21	1	66	4	30	9	62	3	5	0	0.9	.929	OF-50, DH-32

Celerino Sanchez

SANCHEZ, CELERINO BR TR 5′11″ 160 lbs.
Born Celerino Sanchez (Perez).
B. Feb. 3, 1944, Veracruz, Mexico D. May 1, 1992, Leon, Mexico.

Year	Team	Games	BA	SA	AB	H	2B	3B	HR	HR%	R	RBI	BB	SO	SB	Pinch Hit AB	Pinch Hit H	PO	A	E	DP	TC/G	FA	G by Pos
1972	NY A	71	.248	.304	250	62	8	3	0	0.0	18	22	12	30	0	1	0	47	167	14	13	3.4	.939	3B-68
1973		34	.219	.313	64	14	3	0	1	1.6	12	9	2	12	1	7	0	8	16	1	2	1.0	.960	3B-11, DH-11, SS-2, OF-2
2 yrs.		105	.242	.306	314	76	11	3	1	0.3	30	31	14	42	1	8	0	55	183	15	15	2.7	.941	3B-79, DH-11, SS-2, OF-2

Orlando Sanchez

SANCHEZ, ORLANDO BL TR 6′ 1″ 195 lbs.
Born Orlando Sanchez (Marquez).
B. Sept. 7, 1956, Canovanas, Puerto Rico.

Year	Team	Games	BA	SA	AB	H	2B	3B	HR	HR%	R	RBI	BB	SO	SB	Pinch Hit AB	Pinch Hit H	PO	A	E	DP	TC/G	FA	G by Pos
1981	STL N	27	.286	.367	49	14	2	1	0	0.0	5	6	2	6	1	11	3	50	0	4	1	3.0	.926	C-18
1982		26	.189	.243	37	7	0	1	0	0.0	6	3	5	5	0	9	2	34	4	0	1	2.5	1.000	C-15
1983		6	.000	.000	6	0	0	0	0	0.0	0	0	0	4	0	5	0	1	0	0	0	1.0	1.000	C-1
1984	2 teams KC A (10G –.100) BAL A (4G –.250)																							
″	total	14	.167	.222	18	3	1	0	0	0.0	0	3	0	4	0	10	2	10	1	0	0	2.2	1.000	C-5
4 yrs.		73	.218	.282	110	24	3	2	0	0.0	11	12	7	19	1	35	7	95	5	4	2	2.7	.962	C-39

Rey Sanchez

SANCHEZ, REY FRANCISCO BR TR 5′10″ 180 lbs.
Born Rey Francisco Sanchez (Guadalupe).
B. Oct. 5, 1967, Rio Piedras, Puerto Rico.

Year	Team	Games	BA	SA	AB	H	2B	3B	HR	HR%	R	RBI	BB	SO	SB	Pinch Hit AB	Pinch Hit H	PO	A	E	DP	TC/G	FA	G by Pos
1991	CHI N	13	.261	.261	23	6	0	0	0	0.0	1	2	4	3	0	0	0	11	25	0	1	3.0	1.000	SS-10, 2B-2
1992		74	.251	.341	255	64	14	3	1	0.4	24	19	10	17	2	3	1	148	202	9	52	5.0	.975	SS-68, 2B-4
1993		105	.282	.326	344	97	11	2	0	0.0	35	28	15	22	1	10	4	158	316	15	60	5.0	.969	SS-98
1994		96	.285	.337	291	83	13	1	0	0.0	26	24	20	29	2	7	1	152	275	9	52	4.5	.979	2B-50, SS-30, 3B-17
1995		114	.278	.360	428	119	22	2	3	0.7	57	27	14	48	6	1	0	195	351	7	59	4.8	.987	2B-111, SS-4
5 yrs.		402	.275	.341	1341	369	60	8	4	0.3	143	100	63	119	11	21	6	664	1169	40	224	4.8	.979	SS-210, 2B-167, 3B-17

Heinie Sand

SAND, JOHN HENRY BR TR 5′ 8″ 160 lbs.
B. July 3, 1897, San Francisco, Calif. D. Nov. 3, 1958, San Francisco, Calif.

Year	Team	Games	BA	SA	AB	H	2B	3B	HR	HR%	R	RBI	BB	SO	SB	Pinch Hit AB	Pinch Hit H	PO	A	E	DP	TC/G	FA	G by Pos
1923	PHI N	132	.228	.309	470	107	16	5	4	0.9	85	32	82	56	7	1	0	296	424	50	92	5.9	.935	SS-120, 3B-11
1924		137	.245	.340	539	132	21	6	6	1.1	79	40	52	57	5	0	0	333	460	34	95	6.0	.959	SS-137
1925		148	.278	.385	496	138	30	7	3	0.6	69	55	64	65	1	4	0	352	420	60	91	5.8	.928	SS-143
1926		149	.272	.363	567	154	30	5	4	0.7	99	37	66	56	2	0	0	358	495	55	88	6.1	.939	SS-149
1927		141	.299	.376	535	160	22	8	1	0.2	87	49	58	59	5	2	1	244	352	29	46	4.3	.954	SS-86, 3B-58
1928		141	.211	.277	426	90	26	1	0	0.0	38	38	60	47	1	4	1	290	410	36	94	5.4	.951	SS-137
6 yrs.		848	.258	.344	3033	781	145	32	18	0.6	457	251	382	340	21	11	2	1873	2561	264	506	5.6	.944	SS-772, 3B-69

Ryne Sandberg

SANDBERG, RYNE DEE (Ryno) BR TR 6′ 1″ 175 lbs.
B. Sept. 18, 1959, Spokane, Wash.

Year	Team	Games	BA	SA	AB	H	2B	3B	HR	HR%	R	RBI	BB	SO	SB	Pinch Hit AB	Pinch Hit H	PO	A	E	DP	TC/G	FA	G by Pos
1981	PHI N	13	.167	.167	6	1	0	0	0	0.0	2	0	0	1	0	0	0	7	7	0	1	2.3	1.000	SS-5, 2B-1
1982	CHI N	156	.271	.372	635	172	33	5	7	1.1	103	54	36	90	32	1	0	136	373	12	28	3.3	.977	3B-133, 2B-24
1983		158	.261	.351	633	165	25	4	8	1.3	94	48	51	79	37	4	2	330	571	13	126	5.8	.986	2B-157, SS-1
1984		156	.314	.520	636	200	36	**19**	19	3.0	**114**	84	52	101	32	0	0	314	550	6	102	5.6	.993	2B-156
1985		153	.305	.504	609	186	31	6	26	4.3	113	83	57	97	54	1	0	353	501	12	99	5.6	.986	2B-153, SS-1
1986		154	.284	.411	627	178	28	5	14	2.2	68	76	46	79	34	1	1	309	492	5	86	5.3	.994	2B-153
1987		132	.294	.442	523	154	25	2	16	3.1	81	59	59	79	21	2	1	294	375	10	84	5.2	.985	2B-131
1988		155	.264	.419	618	163	23	8	19	3.1	77	69	54	91	25	2	0	291	522	11	79	5.4	.987	2B-153
1989		157	.290	.497	606	176	25	5	30	5.0	**104**	76	59	85	15	2	0	294	466	6	80	4.9	.992	2B-155
1990		155	.306	.559	615	188	30	3	**40**	6.5	**116**	100	50	84	25	2	0	278	469	8	81	4.9	.989	2B-154
1991		158	.291	.485	585	170	32	2	26	4.4	104	100	87	89	22	3	1	267	515	4	66	5.0	.995	2B-157
1992		158	.304	.510	612	186	32	8	26	4.2	100	87	68	73	17	1	0	283	539	8	94	5.3	.990	2B-157
1993		117	.309	.412	456	141	20	0	9	2.0	67	45	37	62	9	3	1	209	347	7	76	4.9	.988	2B-115
1994		57	.238	.390	223	53	9	5	5	2.2	36	24	23	40	2	0	0	96	202	4	35	5.3	.987	2B-57
14 yrs.		1879	.289	.455	7384	2133	349	72	245	3.3	1179	905	679	1050	325	22	6	3461	5929	106	1037	5.1	.989	2B-1723, 3B-133, SS-7
LEAGUE CHAMPIONSHIP SERIES																								
1984	CHI N	5	.368	.474	19	7	2	0	0	0.0	3	2	3	2	3	0	0	12	18	1	6	6.2	.968	2B-5
1989		5	.400	.800	20	8	3	1	1	5.0	6	4	3	4	0	0	0	7	11	0	1	3.6	1.000	2B-5
2 yrs.		10	.385	.641	39	15	5	1	1	2.6	9	6	6	6	3	0	0	19	29	1	7	4.9	.980	2B-10

Ben Sanders

SANDERS, ALEXANDER BENNETT BR TR 6′ 210 lbs.
B. Feb. 16, 1865, Catharpin, Va. D. Aug. 29, 1930, Memphis, Tenn.

Year	Team	Games	BA	SA	AB	H	2B	3B	HR	HR%	R	RBI	BB	SO	SB	Pinch Hit AB	Pinch Hit H	PO	A	E	DP	TC/G	FA	G by Pos
1888	PHI N	57	.246	.322	236	58	11	2	1	0.4	26	25	8	12	13	0	0	55	79	10	1	2.5	.931	P-31, OF-25, 3B-1
1889		44	.278	.349	169	47	8	2	0	0.0	21	21	6	11	4	0	0	24	58	11	1	2.0	.882	P-44, OF-3
1890	PHI P	52	.312	.407	189	59	6	6	0	0.0	31	30	10	10	2	0	0	30	95	11	6	2.6	.919	P-43, OF-10
1891	PHI AA	40	.250	.359	156	39	6	4	1	0.6	24	19	7	12	2	1	0	32	31	8	1	1.7	.887	OF-22, P-19
1892	LOU N	54	.273	.399	198	54	12	2	3	1.5	30	18	16	17	6	0	0	172	61	12	7	4.5	.951	P-31, 1B-15, OF-9
5 yrs.		247	.271	.366	948	257	43	16	5	0.5	132	113	47	62	27	1	0	313	324	52	16	2.7	.925	P-168, OF-69, 1B-15, 3B-1

Deion Sanders

SANDERS, DEION LUWYNN (Neon, Prime Time) BL TL 6′ 1″ 195 lbs.
B. Aug. 9, 1967, Fort Myers, Fla.

Year	Team	Games	BA	SA	AB	H	2B	3B	HR	HR%	R	RBI	BB	SO	SB	Pinch Hit AB	Pinch Hit H	PO	A	E	DP	TC/G	FA	G by Pos
1989	NY A	14	.234	.404	47	11	2	0	2	4.3	7	7	3	8	1	1	0	30	1	1	0	2.3	.969	OF-14
1990		57	.158	.271	133	21	2	2	3	2.3	24	9	13	27	8	4	0	69	2	2	1	1.6	.973	OF-42, DH-4
1991	ATL N	54	.191	.345	110	21	1	2	4	3.6	16	13	12	23	11	4	0	57	3	3	0	1.4	.952	OF-44
1992		97	.304	.495	303	92	6	**14**	8	2.6	54	28	18	52	26	14	5	174	4	3	0	2.4	.983	OF-75
1993		95	.276	.452	272	75	18	6	6	2.2	42	28	16	42	19	29	12	137	1	2	1	2.3	.986	OF-60
1994	2 teams	ATL N (46G –.288) CIN N (46G –.277)																						
″	total	92	.283	.381	375	106	17	4	4	1.1	58	28	32	63	38	3	1	209	2	2	0	2.3	.991	OF-91
1995	2 teams	CIN N (33G –.240) SF N (52G –.285)																						
″	total	85	.268	.399	343	92	11	8	6	1.7	48	28	27	60	24	1	1	215	2	5	1	2.6	.977	OF-85
7 yrs.		494	.264	.408	1583	418	57	36	33	2.1	249	141	121	275	127	56	19	891	15	18	3	2.2	.981	OF-411, DH-4
LEAGUE CHAMPIONSHIP SERIES																								
1992	ATL N	4	.000	.000	5	0	0	0	0	0.0	0	0	0	3	0	3	0	1	0	0	0	0.3	1.000	OF-3
1993		5	.000	.000	3	0	0	0	0	0.0	0	0	0	1	0	3	0	0	0	0	0	0.0	.000	OF-1
2 yrs.		9	.000	.000	8	0	0	0	0	0.0	0	0	0	4	0	6	0	1	0	0	0	0.3	1.000	OF-4
WORLD SERIES																								
1992	ATL N	4	.533	.667	15	8	2	0	0	0.0	4	1	2	1	5	0	0	5	1	0	0	1.5	1.000	OF-4

John Sanders

SANDERS, JOHN FRANK BR TR 6′ 2″ 200 lbs.
B. Nov. 20, 1945, Grand Island, Neb.

Year	Team	Games	BA	SA	AB	H	2B	3B	HR	HR%	R	RBI	BB	SO	SB	Pinch Hit AB	Pinch Hit H	PO	A	E	DP	TC/G	FA	G by Pos
1965	KC A	1	—	—	0	0	0	0	0	—	0	0	0	0	0	0	0	0	0	0	0	0.0	—	

Ray Sanders

SANDERS, RAYMOND FLOYD BL TR 6′ 2″ 185 lbs.
B. Dec. 4, 1916, Bonne Terre, Mo. D. Oct. 28, 1983, Washington, Mo.

Year	Team	Games	BA	SA	AB	H	2B	3B	HR	HR%	R	RBI	BB	SO	SB	Pinch Hit AB	Pinch Hit H	PO	A	E	DP	TC/G	FA	G by Pos
1942	STL N	95	.252	.379	282	71	17	2	5	1.8	37	39	42	31	2	15	2	626	35	6	54	8.7	.991	1B-77
1943		144	.280	.414	478	134	21	5	11	2.3	69	73	77	33	1	3	0	1302	71	7	142	9.8	.995	1B-141
1944		154	.295	.441	601	177	34	9	12	2.0	87	102	71	50	2	3	1	1370	64	8	142	9.5	.994	1B-152
1945		143	.276	.385	537	148	29	3	8	1.5	85	78	83	55	3	1	0	1259	90	19	113	9.6	.986	1B-142
1946	BOS N	80	.243	.359	259	63	12	0	6	2.3	43	35	50	38	0	2	1	659	61	9	57	9.5	.988	1B-77
1948		5	.250	.250	4	1	0	0	0	0.0	0	2	1	0	0	4	1	0	0	0	0	0.0	—	
1949		9	.143	.190	21	3	1	0	0	0.0	0	0	4	9	0	1	0	52	9	1	2	8.9	.984	1B-7
7 yrs.		630	.274	.401	2182	597	114	19	42	1.9	321	329	328	216	8	29	5	5268	330	50	510	9.5	.991	1B-596
WORLD SERIES																								
1942	STL N	2	.000	.000	1	0	0	0	0	0.0	1	0	1	0	0	1	0	0	0	0	0	0.0	—	
1943		5	.294	.471	17	5	0	0	1	5.9	3	2	3	4	0	0	0	41	5	0	4	9.2	1.000	1B-5
1944		6	.286	.429	21	6	0	0	1	4.8	5	1	5	8	0	0	0	52	2	0	3	9.0	1.000	1B-6
1948	BOS N	1	.000	.000	1	0	0	0	0	0.0	0	0	0	0	0	1	0	0	0	0	0	0.0	—	
4 yrs.		14	.275	.425	40	11	0	0	2	5.0	9	3	9	12	0	2	0	93	7	0	7	9.1	1.000	1B-11

Reggie Sanders

SANDERS, REGINALD JEROME BR TR 6′ 2″ 205 lbs.
B. Sept. 9, 1949, Birmingham, Ala.

Year	Team	Games	BA	SA	AB	H	2B	3B	HR	HR%	R	RBI	BB	SO	SB	Pinch Hit AB	Pinch Hit H	PO	A	E	DP	TC/G	FA	G by Pos
1974	DET A	26	.273	.434	99	27	7	0	3	3.0	12	10	5	20	1	0	0	218	17	3	19	9.2	.987	1B-25, DH-1

Reggie Sanders

SANDERS, REGINALD LAVERNE BR TR 6′ 180 lbs.
B. Dec. 1, 1967, Florence, S. C.

Year	Team	Games	BA	SA	AB	H	2B	3B	HR	HR%	R	RBI	BB	SO	SB	Pinch Hit AB	Pinch Hit H	PO	A	E	DP	TC/G	FA	G by Pos
1991	CIN N	9	.200	.275	40	8	0	0	1	2.5	6	3	0	9	1	0	0	22	0	0	0	2.4	1.000	OF-9
1992		116	.270	.462	385	104	26	6	12	3.1	62	36	48	98	16	11	3	262	11	6	4	2.5	.978	OF-110
1993		138	.274	.444	496	136	16	4	20	4.0	90	83	51	118	27	1	0	312	3	8	0	2.4	.975	OF-137
1994		107	.263	.480	400	105	20	8	17	4.3	66	62	41	**114**	21	3	0	217	12	6	2	2.3	.974	OF-104
1995		133	.306	.579	484	148	36	6	28	5.8	91	99	69	122	36	3	0	268	12	5	2	2.2	.982	OF-130
5 yrs.		503	.278	.488	1805	501	98	24	78	4.3	315	283	209	461	101	18	3	1081	38	25	8	2.3	.978	OF-490
DIVISIONAL PLAYOFF SERIES																								
1995	CIN N	3	.154	.462	13	2	1	0	1	7.7	3	2	1	9	2	0	0	7	0	1	0	2.7	.875	OF-3
LEAGUE CHAMPIONSHIP SERIES																								
1995	CIN N	4	.125	.125	16	2	0	0	0	0.0	0	0	2	10	0	0	0	7	0	1	0	2.0	.875	OF-4

Mike Sandlock

SANDLOCK, MICHAEL JOSEPH BB TR 6′ 1″ 180 lbs.
B. Oct. 17, 1915, Old Greenwich, Conn. BL 1944

Year	Team	Games	BA	SA	AB	H	2B	3B	HR	HR%	R	RBI	BB	SO	SB	Pinch Hit AB	Pinch Hit H	PO	A	E	DP	TC/G	FA	G by Pos
1942	BOS N	2	1.000	1.000	1	1	0	0	0	0.0	1	0	0	0	0	0	0	0	0	0	0	0.0	.000	SS-2
1944		30	.100	.100	30	3	0	0	0	0.0	1	2	5	3	0	0	0	17	35	3	3	1.9	.945	3B-22, SS-7
1945	BKN N	80	.282	.405	195	55	14	2	2	1.0	21	17	18	19	2	4	2	224	53	6	5	3.8	.979	C-47, SS-22, 2B-4, 3B-2
1946		19	.147	.147	34	5	0	0	0	0.0	1	0	3	4	0	1	1	61	13	2	1	4.2	.974	C-17, 3B-1
1953	PIT N	64	.231	.258	186	43	5	0	0	0.0	10	12	12	19	0	0	0	290	49	3	4	5.3	.991	C-64
5 yrs.		195	.240	.305	446	107	19	2	2	0.4	34	31	38	45	2	5	3	592	150	14	13	4.0	.981	C-128, SS-31, 3B-25, 2B-4

Charlie Sands

SANDS, CHARLES DUANE BL TR 6′ 2″ 200 lbs.
B. Dec. 17, 1947, Newport News, Va.

Year	Team	Games	BA	SA	AB	H	2B	3B	HR	HR%	R	RBI	BB	SO	SB	Pinch Hit AB	Pinch Hit H	PO	A	E	DP	TC/G	FA	G by Pos
1967	NY A	1	.000	.000	1	0	0	0	0	0.0	0	0	0	1	0	1	0	0	0	0	0	0.0	—	
1971	PIT N	28	.200	.400	25	5	2	0	1	4.0	4	5	7	6	0	18	5	9	1	0	1	3.3	1.000	C-3
1972		1	.000	.000	1	0	0	0	0	0.0	0	0	0	0	0	1	0	0	0	0	0	0.0	—	
1973	CAL A	17	.273	.485	33	9	2	1	1	3.0	5	5	5	10	0	6	0	32	1	3	2	3.6	.917	C-10
1974		43	.193	.361	83	16	2	0	4	4.8	6	13	23	17	0	12	1	20	0	0	0	0.8	1.000	DH-21, C-5
1975	OAK A	3	.500	.500	2	1	0	0	0	0.0	0	0	1	1	0	2	1	0	0	0	0	0.0	.000	DH-1
6 yrs.		93	.214	.393	145	31	6	1	6	4.1	15	23	36	35	0	40	7	61	2	3	3	1.6	.955	DH-22, C-18
WORLD SERIES																								
1971	PIT N	1	.000	.000	1	0	0	0	0	0.0	0	0	0	1	0	1	0	0	0	0	0	0.0	—	

Tom Sandt

SANDT, THOMAS JAMES BR TR 5′11″ 175 lbs.
B. Dec. 22, 1950, Brooklyn, N. Y.

Year	Team	Games	BA	SA	AB	H	2B	3B	HR	HR%	R	RBI	BB	SO	SB	Pinch Hit AB	Pinch Hit H	PO	A	E	DP	TC/G	FA	G by Pos
1975	OAK A	1	—	—	0	0	0	0	0	—	0	0	0	0	0	0	0	0	0	0	0	0.0	.000	2B-1
1976		41	.209	.224	67	14	1	0	0	0.0	6	3	7	9	0	2	0	44	60	3	11	2.7	.972	SS-29, 2B-9, 3B-2
2 yrs.		42	.209	.224	67	14	1	0	0	0.0	6	3	7	9	0	2	0	44	60	3	11	2.6	.972	SS-29, 2B-10, 3B-2

Jack Sanford

SANFORD, JOHN HOWARD BR TR 6' 3" 195 lbs.
B. June 23, 1917, Chatham, Va.

Year	Team	Games	BA	SA	AB	H	2B	3B	HR	HR%	R	RBI	BB	SO	SB	Pinch Hit AB	Pinch Hit H	PO	A	E	DP	TC/G	FA	G by Pos
1940	WAS A	34	.197	.262	122	24	4	2	0	0.0	5	10	6	17	0	0	0	282	15	2	38	8.8	.993	1B-34
1941		3	.400	.800	5	2	0	1	0	0.0	1	0	1	1	0	1	1	12	0	0	1	12.0	1.000	1B-1
1946		10	.231	.308	26	6	0	1	0	0.0	7	1	2	6	0	4	0	66	1	2	7	11.5	.971	1B-6
3 yrs.		47	.209	.288	153	32	4	4	0	0.0	13	11	9	24	0	5	1	360	16	4	46	9.3	.989	1B-41

Manny Sanguillen

SANGUILLEN, MANUEL DE JESUS BR TR 6' 193 lbs.
Born Manuel de Jesus Sanguillen (Magan).
B. Mar. 21, 1944, Colon, Panama.

Year	Team	Games	BA	SA	AB	H	2B	3B	HR	HR%	R	RBI	BB	SO	SB	Pinch Hit AB	Pinch Hit H	PO	A	E	DP	TC/G	FA	G by Pos
1967	PIT N	30	.271	.313	96	26	4	0	0	0.0	6	8	4	12	0	1	0	133	11	2	4	5.2	.986	C-28
1969		129	.303	.407	459	139	21	6	5	1.1	62	57	12	48	8	18	7	825	71	17	11	8.1	.981	C-113
1970		128	.325	.444	486	158	19	9	7	1.4	63	61	17	45	2	3	1	775	66	10	12	6.8	.988	C-125
1971		138	.319	.426	533	170	26	5	7	1.3	60	81	19	32	6	4	2	712	72	5	12	5.8	.994	C-135
1972		136	.298	.404	520	155	18	8	7	1.3	55	71	21	38	1	10	4	724	50	9	4	6.1	.989	C-127, OF-2
1973		149	.282	.411	589	166	26	7	12	2.0	64	65	17	29	2	4	1	632	41	17	11	4.7	.975	C-89, OF-59
1974		151	.287	.371	596	171	21	4	7	1.2	77	68	21	27	2	4	1	713	76	12	8	5.3	.985	C-151
1975		133	.328	.451	481	158	24	4	9	1.9	60	58	48	31	5	2	0	650	53	9	4	5.4	.987	C-132
1976		114	.290	.378	389	113	16	6	2	0.5	52	36	28	18	2	5	2	518	52	13	7	5.3	.978	C-111
1977	OAK A	152	.275	.354	571	157	17	5	6	1.1	42	58	22	35	2	3	2	419	54	7	7	3.2	.985	C-77, DH-58, OF-9, 1B-7
1978	PIT N	85	.264	.336	220	58	5	1	3	1.4	15	16	9	10	2	27	5	438	20	0	26	7.9	1.000	1B-40, C-18
1979		56	.230	.351	74	17	5	2	0	0.0	8	4	2	5	0	42	9	67	6	2	3	5.8	.973	C-8, 1B-5
1980		47	.250	.313	48	12	3	0	0	0.0	2	2	3	1	3	37	12	40	3	2	3	9.0	.956	1B-5
13 yrs.		1448	.296	.398	5062	1500	205	57	65	1.3	566	585	223	331	35	160	46	6646	575	105	112	5.6	.986	C-1114, OF-70, DH-58, 1B-57
LEAGUE CHAMPIONSHIP SERIES																								
1970	PIT N	3	.167	.167	12	2	0	0	0	0.0	0	0	0	1	0	0	0	13	1	1	0	5.0	.933	C-3
1971		4	.267	.267	15	4	0	0	0	0.0	1	1	1	1	1	0	0	30	1	0	0	7.8	1.000	C-4
1972		5	.313	.563	16	5	1	0	1	6.3	4	2	0	0	0	1	1	22	0	1	1	4.6	.957	C-5
1974		4	.250	.313	16	4	1	0	0	0.0	0	0	0	0	0	1	0	19	2	2	1	5.8	.913	C-4
1975		3	.167	.167	12	2	0	0	0	0.0	0	0	0	0	0	0	0	29	1	1	1	10.3	.968	C-3
5 yrs.		19	.239	.310	71	17	2	0	1	1.4	5	3	1	2	1	1	1	113	5	5	3	6.5	.959	C-19
WORLD SERIES																								
1971	PIT N	7	.379	.414	29	11	1	0	0	0.0	3	0	0	3	2	0	0	37	0	0	1	5.3	1.000	C-7
1979		3	.333	.333	3	1	0	0	0	0.0	0	1	0	0	0	3	1	0	0	0	0	0.0	—	
2 yrs.		10	.375	.406	32	12	1	0	0	0.0	3	1	0	3	2	3	1	37	0	0	1	5.3	1.000	C-7

Ed Sanicki

SANICKI, EDWARD ROBERT (Butch) BR TR 5' 9½" 175 lbs.
B. July 7, 1923, Wallington, N. J.

Year	Team	Games	BA	SA	AB	H	2B	3B	HR	HR%	R	RBI	BB	SO	SB	Pinch Hit AB	Pinch Hit H	PO	A	E	DP	TC/G	FA	G by Pos
1949	PHI N	7	.231	.923	13	3	0	0	3	23.1	4	7	1	4	0	1	0	12	0	0	0	2.0	1.000	OF-6
1951		13	.500	.750	4	2	1	0	0	0.0	1	1	1	1	1	1	0	1	0	0	0	0.1	1.000	OF-10
2 yrs.		20	.294	.882	17	5	1	0	3	17.6	5	8	2	5	1	2	0	13	0	0	0	0.8	1.000	OF-16

Ben Sankey

SANKEY, BENJAMIN TURNER BR TR 5'10" 155 lbs.
B. Sept. 2, 1907, Nauvoo, Ala.

Year	Team	Games	BA	SA	AB	H	2B	3B	HR	HR%	R	RBI	BB	SO	SB	Pinch Hit AB	Pinch Hit H	PO	A	E	DP	TC/G	FA	G by Pos
1929	PIT N	2	.143	.143	7	1	0	0	0	0.0	1	0	0	1	0	0	0	3	7	1	1	5.5	.909	SS-2
1930		13	.167	.167	30	5	0	0	0	0.0	6	0	2	3	0	0	0	17	26	5	3	4.8	.896	SS-6, 2B-4
1931		57	.227	.318	132	30	2	5	0	0.0	14	14	14	10	0	4	0	73	127	18	24	4.1	.917	SS-49, 3B-2, 2B-2
3 yrs.		72	.213	.284	169	36	2	5	0	0.0	21	14	16	14	0	4	0	93	160	24	28	4.3	.913	SS-57, 2B-6, 3B-2

Andres Santana

SANTANA, ANDRES CONFESOR BB TR 5'11" 160 lbs.
Born Andres Confesor Sanchez (Belonis).
B. Feb. 5, 1968, San Pedro de Macoris, Dominican Republic.

Year	Team	Games	BA	SA	AB	H	2B	3B	HR	HR%	R	RBI	BB	SO	SB	Pinch Hit AB	Pinch Hit H	PO	A	E	DP	TC/G	FA	G by Pos
1990	SF N	6	.000	.000	2	0	0	0	0	0.0	0	1	0	0	0	0	0	2	1	0	1	1.0	1.000	SS-3

Rafael Santana

SANTANA, RAFAEL FRANCISCO (Ralph) BR TR 6' 1" 156 lbs.
Born Rafael Francisco Santana (de la Cruz).
B. Jan. 31, 1958, La Romana, Dominican Republic.

Year	Team	Games	BA	SA	AB	H	2B	3B	HR	HR%	R	RBI	BB	SO	SB	Pinch Hit AB	Pinch Hit H	PO	A	E	DP	TC/G	FA	G by Pos
1983	STL N	30	.214	.214	14	3	0	0	0	0.0	1	2	2	2	0	4	0	3	8	4	3	0.8	.733	2B-9, SS-6, 3B-4
1984	NY N	51	.276	.382	152	42	11	1	1	0.7	14	12	9	17	0	1	0	92	104	6	34	4.0	.970	SS-50
1985		154	.257	.302	529	136	19	1	1	0.2	41	29	29	54	1	1	0	301	396	25	81	4.7	.965	SS-153
1986		139	.218	.254	394	86	11	0	1	0.3	38	28	36	43	0	2	0	203	369	16	68	4.3	.973	SS-137, 2B-1
1987		139	.255	.346	439	112	21	2	5	1.1	41	44	29	57	1	1	0	213	396	17	82	4.5	.973	SS-138
1988	NY A	148	.240	.294	480	115	12	1	4	0.8	50	38	33	61	1	0	0	202	421	22	96	4.4	.966	SS-148
1990	CLE A	7	.231	.462	13	3	0	0	1	7.7	3	3	0	0	0	0	0	2	9	0	2	1.6	1.000	SS-7
7 yrs.		668	.246	.307	2021	497	74	5	13	0.6	188	156	138	234	3	9	0	1016	1703	90	366	4.3	.968	SS-639, 2B-10, 3B-4
LEAGUE CHAMPIONSHIP SERIES																								
1986	NY N	6	.176	.176	17	3	0	0	0	0.0	0	0	0	3	0	0	0	13	18	0	5	5.2	1.000	SS-6
WORLD SERIES																								
1986	NY N	7	.250	.250	20	5	0	0	0	0.0	3	2	2	5	0	0	0	11	17	1	4	4.1	.966	SS-7

F. P. Santangelo

SANTANGELO, FRANK-PAUL BB TR 5'10" 165 lbs.
B. Oct. 24, 1967, Livonia, Mich.

Year	Team	Games	BA	SA	AB	H	2B	3B	HR	HR%	R	RBI	BB	SO	SB	Pinch Hit AB	Pinch Hit H	PO	A	E	DP	TC/G	FA	G by Pos
1995	MON N	35	.296	.398	98	29	5	1	1	1.0	11	9	12	9	1	9	3	47	0	1	0	1.6	.979	OF-25, 2B-5

Benito Santiago

SANTIAGO, BENITO BR TR 6' 1" 180 lbs.
Born Benito Santiago (Rivera).
B. Mar. 9, 1965, Ponce, Puerto Rico.

Year	Team	Games	BA	SA	AB	H	2B	3B	HR	HR%	R	RBI	BB	SO	SB	Pinch Hit AB	Pinch Hit H	PO	A	E	DP	TC/G	FA	G by Pos
1986	SD N	17	.290	.468	62	18	2	0	3	4.8	10	6	2	12	0	0	0	80	7	5	2	5.4	.946	C-17
1987		146	.300	.467	546	164	33	2	18	3.3	64	79	16	112	21	0	0	817	80	22	12	6.3	.976	C-146
1988		139	.248	.362	492	122	22	2	10	2.0	49	46	24	82	15	7	2	725	75	12	11	6.0	.985	C-136
1989		129	.236	.387	462	109	16	3	16	3.5	50	62	26	89	11	2	0	685	81	20	10	6.2	.975	C-127
1990		100	.270	.419	344	93	8	5	11	3.2	42	53	27	55	5	4	1	538	51	12	6	6.1	.980	C-98
1991		152	.267	.403	580	155	22	3	17	2.9	60	87	23	114	8	2	2	830	100	14	14	6.2	.985	C-151, OF-1
1992		106	.251	.383	386	97	21	0	10	2.6	37	42	21	52	2	4	1	584	53	12	6	6.3	.982	C-103

Benito Santiago *continued*

Year	Team	Lg	Games	BA	SA	AB	H	2B	3B	HR	HR%	R	RBI	BB	SO	SB	Pinch Hit AB	Pinch Hit H	PO	A	E	DP	TC/G	FA	G by Pos
1993	**FLA**	**N**	139	.230	.380	469	108	19	6	13	2.8	49	50	37	88	10	5	1	740	64	11	4	5.9	.987	C-136, OF-1
1994			101	.273	.424	337	92	14	2	11	3.3	35	41	25	57	1	8	2	511	64	5	3	6.0	.991	C-97
1995	**CIN**	**N**	81	.286	.485	266	76	20	0	11	4.1	40	44	24	48	2	7	3	481	33	2	6	6.2	.996	C-75, 1B-8
10 yrs.			1110	.262	.410	3944	1034	177	23	120	3.0	436	510	225	709	75	39	12	5991	608	115	74	6.1	.983	C-1086, 1B-8, OF-2
DIVISIONAL PLAYOFF SERIES																									
1995	**CIN**	**N**	3	.333	.667	9	3	0	0	1	11.1	2	3	3	3	0	0	0	20	0	0	0	6.7	1.000	C-3
LEAGUE CHAMPIONSHIP SERIES																									
1995	**CIN**	**N**	4	.231	.231	13	3	0	0	0	0.0	0	0	2	3	0	0	0	23	1	0	1	6.0	1.000	C-4

Ron Santo

SANTO, RONALD EDWARD BR TR 6′ 190 lbs.
B. Feb. 25, 1940, Seattle, Wash.

Year	Team	Lg	Games	BA	SA	AB	H	2B	3B	HR	HR%	R	RBI	BB	SO	SB	Pinch Hit AB	Pinch Hit H	PO	A	E	DP	TC/G	FA	G by Pos
1960	**CHI**	**N**	95	.251	.409	347	87	24	2	9	2.6	44	44	31	44	0	1	0	78	144	13	6	2.5	.945	3B-94
1961			154	.284	.479	578	164	32	6	23	4.0	84	83	73	77	2	1	1	157	307	31	41	3.2	.937	3B-153
1962			162	.227	.358	604	137	20	4	17	2.8	44	83	65	94	4	2	0	167	343	24	35	3.2	.955	3B-157, SS-8
1963			162	.297	.481	630	187	29	6	25	4.0	79	99	42	92	6	0	0	136	374	26	25	3.3	.951	3B-162
1964			161	.313	.564	592	185	33	**13**	30	5.1	94	114	**86**	96	3	0	0	156	367	20	31	3.4	.963	3B-161
1965			164	.285	.510	608	173	30	4	33	5.4	88	101	88	109	3	0	0	155	373	24	27	3.4	.957	3B-164
1966			155	.312	.538	561	175	21	8	30	5.3	93	94	**95**	78	4	0	0	157	408	26	41	3.7	.956	3B-152, SS-8
1967			161	.300	.512	586	176	23	4	31	5.3	107	98	**96**	103	1	0	0	187	393	26	33	3.8	.957	3B-161
1968			162	.246	.421	577	142	17	3	26	4.5	86	98	**96**	106	3	0	0	130	378	15	33	3.2	.971	3B-162
1969			160	.289	.485	575	166	18	4	29	5.0	97	123	96	97	1	1	0	144	334	27	23	3.2	.947	3B-160
1970			154	.267	.476	555	148	30	4	26	4.7	83	114	92	108	2	2	1	144	320	27	36	3.2	.945	3B-152, OF-1
1971			154	.267	.423	555	148	22	1	21	3.8	77	88	79	95	4	1	0	128	275	18	29	2.7	.957	3B-149, OF-6
1972			133	.302	.487	464	140	25	5	17	3.7	68	74	69	75	1	1	1	119	282	22	23	3.2	.948	3B-129, 2B-3, SS-1, OF-1
1973			149	.267	.440	536	143	29	2	20	3.7	65	77	63	97	1	2	0	107	271	20	17	2.7	.950	3B-146
1974	**CHI**	**A**	117	.221	.299	375	83	12	1	5	1.3	29	41	37	72	0	5	3	135	148	8	49	2.5	.973	DH-47, 2B-39, 3B-28, 1B-3, SS-1
15 yrs.			2243	.277	.464	8143	2254	365	67	342	4.2	1138	1331	1108	1343	35	16	6	2100	4717	327	449	3.2	.954	3B-2130, DH-47, 2B-42, SS-18, OF-8, 1B-3

Rafael Santo Domingo

SANTO DOMINGO, RAFAEL BB TR 6′ 160 lbs.
Born Rafael Santo Domingo (Molina).
B. Nov. 24, 1955, Orocovis, Puerto Rico.

Year	Team	Lg	Games	BA	SA	AB	H	2B	3B	HR	HR%	R	RBI	BB	SO	SB	Pinch Hit AB	Pinch Hit H	PO	A	E	DP	TC/G	FA	G by Pos
1979	**CIN**	**N**	7	.167	.167	6	1	0	0	0	0.0	0	0	1	3	0	6	1	0	0	0	0	0.0	—	

Nelson Santovenia

SANTOVENIA, NELSON GIL BR TR 6′ 3″ 195 lbs.
Born Nelson Gil Santovenia (Mayol).
B. July 27, 1961, Pina del Rio, Cuba.

Year	Team	Lg	Games	BA	SA	AB	H	2B	3B	HR	HR%	R	RBI	BB	SO	SB	Pinch Hit AB	Pinch Hit H	PO	A	E	DP	TC/G	FA	G by Pos
1987	**MON**	**N**	2	.000	.000	1	0	0	0	0	0.0	0	0	0	0	0	1	0	1	0	0	0	1.0	1.000	C-1
1988			92	.236	.392	309	73	20	2	8	2.6	26	41	24	77	2	1	1	465	63	9	7	6.2	.983	C-86, 1B-1
1989			97	.250	.352	304	76	14	1	5	1.6	30	31	24	37	2	7	1	564	66	12	8	7.1	.981	C-89, 1B-1
1990			59	.190	.331	163	31	3	1	6	3.7	13	28	8	31	0	10	4	264	24	6	7	5.8	.980	C-51
1991			41	.250	.365	96	24	5	0	2	2.1	7	14	2	18	0	7	3	140	16	3	7	4.3	.981	C-30, 1B-7
1992	**CHI**	**A**	2	.333	1.333	3	1	0	0	1	33.3	1	2	0	0	0	0	0	3	0	0	0	1.5	1.000	C-2
1993	**KC**	**A**	4	.125	.125	8	1	0	0	0	0.0	0	0	1	2	0	1	0	14	1	0	0	3.8	1.000	C-4
7 yrs.			297	.233	.364	884	206	42	4	22	2.5	77	116	59	165	4	27	9	1451	170	30	29	6.1	.982	C-263, 1B-9

Ed Santry

SANTRY, EDWARD
B. 1861, Chicago, Ill. D. Mar. 6, 1899, Chicago, Ill.

Year	Team	Lg	Games	BA	SA	AB	H	2B	3B	HR	HR%	R	RBI	BB	SO	SB	Pinch Hit AB	Pinch Hit H	PO	A	E	DP	TC/G	FA	G by Pos
1884	**DET**	**N**	6	.182	.182	22	4	0	0	0	0.0	1		1	2		0	0	14	16	5	1	5.8	.857	SS-5, 2B-1

Joe Sargent

SARGENT, JOSEPH ALEXANDER (Horse Belly) BR TR 5′10″ 165 lbs.
B. Sept. 24, 1893, Rochester, N. Y. D. July 5, 1950, Rochester, N. Y.

Year	Team	Lg	Games	BA	SA	AB	H	2B	3B	HR	HR%	R	RBI	BB	SO	SB	Pinch Hit AB	Pinch Hit H	PO	A	E	DP	TC/G	FA	G by Pos
1921	**DET**	**A**	66	.253	.388	178	45	8	5	2	1.1	21	22	24	26	2	1	0	112	134	21	21	4.0	.921	2B-24, 3B-23, SS-19

Bill Sarni

SARNI, WILLIAM FLORINE BR TR 5′11″ 180 lbs.
B. Sept. 19, 1927, Los Angeles, Calif. D. Apr. 15, 1983, Creve Coeur, Mo.

Year	Team	Lg	Games	BA	SA	AB	H	2B	3B	HR	HR%	R	RBI	BB	SO	SB	Pinch Hit AB	Pinch Hit H	PO	A	E	DP	TC/G	FA	G by Pos
1951	**STL**	**N**	36	.174	.186	86	15	1	0	0	0.0	7	2	9	13	1	1	0	107	13	2	3	3.5	.984	C-35
1952			3	.200	.200	5	1	0	0	0	0.0	0	0	0	1	0	0	0	19	0	0	0	6.3	1.000	C-3
1954			123	.300	.439	380	114	18	4	9	2.4	40	70	25	42	3	6	3	486	41	2	12	4.5	.996	C-118
1955			107	.255	.342	325	83	15	2	3	0.9	32	34	27	33	1	11	3	482	39	7	8	5.3	.987	C-99
1956	**2 teams**		**STL N** (43G –.291) **NY N** (78G –.231)																						
″	**total**		121	.254	.399	386	98	16	5	10	2.6	28	45	28	46	1	6	1	586	61	5	10	5.6	.992	C-116
5 yrs.			390	.263	.380	1182	311	50	11	22	1.9	107	151	89	135	6	24	7	1680	154	16	33	5.0	.991	C-371

Mackey Sasser

SASSER, MACK DANIEL BL TR 6′ 1″ 190 lbs.
B. Aug. 3, 1962, Fort Gaines, Ga.

Year	Team	Lg	Games	BA	SA	AB	H	2B	3B	HR	HR%	R	RBI	BB	SO	SB	Pinch Hit AB	Pinch Hit H	PO	A	E	DP	TC/G	FA	G by Pos
1987	**2 teams**		**SF N** (2G –.000) **PIT N** (12G –.217)																						
″	**total**		14	.185	.185	27	5	0	0	0	0.0	2	2	0	2	0	9	4	29	0	0	0	4.8	1.000	C-6
1988	**NY**	**N**	60	.285	.407	123	35	10	1	1	0.8	9	17	6	9	0	19	3	235	17	6	2	5.9	.977	C-42, OF-1, 3B-1
1989			72	.291	.407	182	53	14	2	1	0.5	17	22	7	15	0	17	5	335	19	3	3	5.7	.992	C-62, 3B-1
1990			100	.307	.426	270	83	14	0	6	2.2	31	41	15	19	0	25	6	501	43	14	4	6.3	.975	C-87, 1B-1
1991			96	.272	.417	228	62	14	2	5	2.2	18	35	9	19	0	38	10	271	21	3	6	4.0	.990	C-43, OF-21, 1B-10
1992			92	.241	.326	141	34	6	0	2	1.4	7	18	3	10	0	55	8	131	5	1	4	2.9	.993	C-27, 1B-12, OF-9
1993	**SEA**	**A**	83	.218	.309	188	41	10	2	1	0.5	18	21	15	30	1	23	6	60	4	3	0	1.1	.955	OF-37, DH-19, C-4, 1B-1
1994			3	.000	.000	4	0	0	0	0	0.0	0	0	0	0	0	2	0	0	0	0	0	0.0		OF-1, C-1
1995	**PIT**	**N**	14	.154	.192	26	4	1	0	0	0.0	1	0	0	0	0	7	2	35	3	0	0	3.5	1.000	C-11
9 yrs.			534	.267	.377	1189	317	69	7	16	1.3	103	156	55	104	1	195	44	1597	112	30	19	4.4	.983	C-283, OF-69, 1B-24, DH-19, 3B-2
LEAGUE CHAMPIONSHIP SERIES																									
1988	**NY**	**N**	4	.200	.200	5	1	0	0	0	0.0	0	0	0	1	0	2	0	2	0	0	0	1.0	1.000	C-2

Tom Satriano

SATRIANO, THOMAS VICTOR NICHOLAS (Satch) BL TR 6′ 1″ 185 lbs.
B. Aug. 28, 1940, Pittsburgh, Pa.

Year	Team	Games	BA	SA	AB	H	2B	3B	HR	HR%	R	RBI	BB	SO	SB	Pinch Hit AB	Pinch Hit H	PO	A	E	DP	TC/G	FA	G by Pos
1961	LA A	35	.198	.302	96	19	5	1	1	1.0	15	8	12	16	2	3	0	29	61	8	7	2.9	.918	3B-23, 2B-10, SS-1
1962		10	.421	.842	19	8	2	0	2	10.5	4	6	0	1	0	7	3	2	8	2	1	2.4	.833	3B-5
1963		23	.180	.200	50	9	1	0	0	0.0	1	2	9	10	0	9	0	17	33	3	2	3.3	.943	3B-13, C-2, 1B-1
1964		108	.200	.247	255	51	9	0	1	0.4	18	17	30	37	0	19	4	383	72	8	32	4.7	.983	3B-38, 1B-32, C-25, SS-2, 2B-1
1965	CAL A	47	.165	.228	79	13	2	0	1	1.3	8	4	10	10	1	11	1	83	33	1	4	2.8	.991	3B-15, 2B-12, C-12, 1B-3
1966		103	.239	.288	226	54	5	3	0	0.0	16	24	27	32	3	8	1	283	58	6	13	3.2	.983	C-43, 1B-36, 3B-25, 2B-4
1967		90	.224	.318	201	45	7	0	4	2.0	13	21	28	25	1	22	4	150	85	7	10	3.0	.971	3B-38, C-23, 2B-15, 1B-5
1968		111	.253	.364	297	75	9	0	8	2.7	20	35	37	44	0	17	4	433	67	8	11	4.6	.984	C-85, 2B-14, 3B-11, 1B-1
1969	2 teams	CAL A (41G –.259) BOS A (47G –.189)																						
"	total	88	.221	.251	235	52	4	0	1	0.4	14	27	40	27	0	9	3	463	36	6	8	5.8	.988	C-80, 1B-5, 2B-2
1970	BOS A	59	.236	.358	165	39	9	1	3	1.8	21	13	21	23	0	7	1	318	19	5	5	6.7	.985	C-51
10 yrs.		674	.225	.303	1623	365	53	5	21	1.3	130	157	214	225	7	112	21	2161	472	54	93	4.2	.980	C-321, 3B-168, 1B-83, 2B-58, SS-3

Frank Saucier

SAUCIER, FRANCIS FIELD BL TR 6′ 1″ 180 lbs.
B. May 28, 1926, Leslie, Mo.

Year	Team	Games	BA	SA	AB	H	2B	3B	HR	HR%	R	RBI	BB	SO	SB	Pinch Hit AB	Pinch Hit H	PO	A	E	DP	TC/G	FA	G by Pos
1951	STL A	18	.071	.143	14	1	1	0	0	0.0	4	1	3	4	0	7	1	5	0	2	0	2.3	.714	OF-3

Ed Sauer

SAUER, EDWARD (Horn) BR TR 6′ 1″ 188 lbs.
Brother of Hank Sauer.
B. Jan. 3, 1919, Pittsburgh, Pa. D. July 1, 1988, Thousand Oaks, Calif.

Year	Team	Games	BA	SA	AB	H	2B	3B	HR	HR%	R	RBI	BB	SO	SB	Pinch Hit AB	Pinch Hit H	PO	A	E	DP	TC/G	FA	G by Pos
1943	CHI N	14	.273	.327	55	15	3	0	0	0.0	3	9	3	6	1	0	0	40	1	1	0	3.0	.976	OF-13, 3B-1
1944		23	.220	.300	50	11	4	0	0	0.0	3	5	2	6	0	9	2	23	1	1	0	2.1	.960	OF-12
1945		49	.258	.387	93	24	4	1	2	2.2	8	11	8	23	2	15	3	44	1	0	1	1.7	1.000	OF-26
1949	2 teams	STL N (24G –.222) BOS N (79G –.266)																						
"	total	103	.259	.355	259	67	14	1	3	1.2	31	32	20	42	0	19	4	146	5	4	1	1.9	.974	OF-81, 3B-2
4 yrs.		189	.256	.352	457	117	25	2	5	1.1	45	57	33	77	3	43	9	253	8	6	2	2.0	.978	OF-132, 3B-3
WORLD SERIES																								
1945	CHI N	2	.000	.000	2	0	0	0	0	0.0	0	0	0	2	0	2	0	0	0	0	0	0.0	—	

Hank Sauer

SAUER, HENRY JOHN BR TR 6′ 3″ 198 lbs.
Brother of Ed Sauer.
B. Mar. 17, 1917, Pittsburgh, Pa.

Year	Team	Games	BA	SA	AB	H	2B	3B	HR	HR%	R	RBI	BB	SO	SB	Pinch Hit AB	Pinch Hit H	PO	A	E	DP	TC/G	FA	G by Pos
1941	CIN N	9	.303	.424	33	10	4	0	0	0.0	4	5	1	4	0	1	1	21	1	1	1	2.9	.957	OF-8
1942		7	.250	.550	20	5	0	0	2	10.0	4	4	2	2	0	3	1	37	4	1	8	10.5	.976	1B-4
1945		31	.293	.431	116	34	1	0	5	4.3	18	20	6	16	2	1	0	100	5	3	4	3.5	.972	OF-28, 1B-3
1948		145	.260	.504	530	138	22	1	35	6.6	78	97	60	**85**	2	2	0	359	22	9	10	2.7	.977	OF-132, 1B-12
1949	2 teams	CIN N (42G –.237) CHI N (96G –.291)																						
"	total	138	.275	.507	509	140	23	1	31	6.1	81	99	55	66	0	3	0	302	16	9	2	2.4	.972	OF-135, 1B-1
1950	CHI N	145	.274	.519	540	148	32	2	32	5.9	85	103	60	67	1	3	2	381	29	13	12	3.0	.969	OF-125, 1B-18
1951		141	.263	.486	525	138	19	4	30	5.7	77	89	45	77	2	8	1	286	19	6	2	2.4	.981	OF-132
1952		151	.270	.531	567	153	31	3	**37**	6.5	89	**121**	77	92	1	0	0	327	17	6	3	2.3	.983	OF-151
1953		108	.263	.473	395	104	16	5	19	4.8	61	60	50	56	0	5	1	221	5	7	1	2.2	.970	OF-105
1954		142	.288	.563	520	150	18	1	41	7.9	98	103	70	68	2	1	0	282	8	11	2	2.1	.963	OF-141
1955		79	.211	.387	261	55	8	1	12	4.6	29	28	26	47	0	10	0	122	4	2	1	1.9	.984	OF-68
1956	STL N	75	.298	.424	151	45	4	0	5	3.3	11	24	25	31	0	31	6	55	2	0	1	1.5	1.000	OF-37
1957	NY N	127	.259	.508	378	98	14	1	26	6.9	46	76	49	59	1	24	7	125	4	1	0	1.3	.992	OF-98
1958	SF N	88	.250	.436	236	59	8	0	12	5.1	27	46	35	37	0	19	2	93	3	5	1	1.5	.950	OF-67
1959		13	.067	.267	15	1	0	0	1	6.7	1	1	0	7	0	12	1	0	0	0	0	0.0	.000	OF-1
15 yrs.		1399	.266	.496	4796	1278	200	19	288	6.0	709	876	561	714	11	123	22	2711	139	74	48	2.3	.975	OF-1228, 1B-38

Doug Saunders

SAUNDERS, DOUGLAS LONG BR TR 6′ 172 lbs.
B. Dec. 13, 1969, Yorba Linda, Calif.

Year	Team	Games	BA	SA	AB	H	2B	3B	HR	HR%	R	RBI	BB	SO	SB	Pinch Hit AB	Pinch Hit H	PO	A	E	DP	TC/G	FA	G by Pos
1993	NY N	28	.209	.239	67	14	2	0	0	0.0	8	0	3	4	0	0	0	37	52	4	19	3.4	.957	2B-22, 3B-4, SS-1

Rusty Saunders

SAUNDERS, RUSSELL COLLIER BR TR 6′ 2″ 205 lbs.
B. Mar. 12, 1906, Trenton, N. J. D. Nov. 24, 1967, Trenton, N. J.

Year	Team	Games	BA	SA	AB	H	2B	3B	HR	HR%	R	RBI	BB	SO	SB	Pinch Hit AB	Pinch Hit H	PO	A	E	DP	TC/G	FA	G by Pos
1927	PHI A	5	.133	.200	15	2	1	0	0	0.0	2	2	3	2	0	1	0	8	1	2	0	2.8	.818	OF-4

Al Sauters

SAUTERS, AL
B. Philadelphia, Pa. Deceased.

Year	Team	Games	BA	SA	AB	H	2B	3B	HR	HR%	R	RBI	BB	SO	SB	Pinch Hit AB	Pinch Hit H	PO	A	E	DP	TC/G	FA	G by Pos
1890	PHI AA	14	.098	.098	41	4	0	0	0	0.0			11		0	0	0	17	20	8	0	3.0	.822	3B-11, OF-2, 2B-2

Don Savage

SAVAGE, DONALD ANTHONY BR TR 6′ 180 lbs.
B. Mar. 5, 1919, Bloomfield, N. J. D. Dec. 25, 1961, Montclair, N. J.

Year	Team	Games	BA	SA	AB	H	2B	3B	HR	HR%	R	RBI	BB	SO	SB	Pinch Hit AB	Pinch Hit H	PO	A	E	DP	TC/G	FA	G by Pos
1944	NY A	71	.264	.385	239	63	7	5	4	1.7	31	24	20	41	1	10	1	66	109	10	11	3.1	.946	3B-60
1945		34	.224	.241	58	13	1	0	0	0.0	5	3	3	14	1	9	2	19	25	5	3	3.1	.898	3B-14, OF-2
2 yrs.		105	.256	.357	297	76	8	5	4	1.3	36	27	23	55	2	19	3	85	134	15	14	3.1	.936	3B-74, OF-2

Jim Savage

SAVAGE, JAMES HAROLD BB TR 5′ 5″ 150 lbs.
B. Aug. 29, 1883, Southington, Conn. D. June 26, 1940, New Castle, Pa.

Year	Team	Games	BA	SA	AB	H	2B	3B	HR	HR%	R	RBI	BB	SO	SB	Pinch Hit AB	Pinch Hit H	PO	A	E	DP	TC/G	FA	G by Pos
1912	PHI N	2	.000	.000	3	0	0	0	0	0.0	1	0	1	0	0	0	0	1	2	1	0	4.0	.750	2B-1
1914	PIT F	132	.284	.347	479	136	9	9	1	0.2	81	26	67		17	3	0	193	101	19	10	2.3	.939	OF-93, 3B-29, SS-11, 2B-3
1915		14	.143	.143	21	3	0	0	0	0.0	0	0	1		0	7	2	4	0	1	0	1.3	.800	OF-3, 3B-1
3 yrs.		148	.276	.336	503	139	9	9	1	0.2	82	26	69	0	17	10	2	198	103	21	10	2.3	.935	OF-96, 3B-30, SS-11, 2B-4

Ted Savage

SAVAGE, THEODORE EDMUND BR TR 6′ 1″ 185 lbs.
Born Ephesian Savage.
B. Feb. 21, 1937, Venice, Ill.

Year	Team	Games	BA	SA	AB	H	2B	3B	HR	HR%	R	RBI	BB	SO	SB	Pinch Hit AB	Pinch Hit H	PO	A	E	DP	TC/G	FA	G by Pos
1962	PHI N	127	.266	.373	335	89	11	2	7	2.1	54	39	40	66	16	21	3	185	4	5	1	1.8	.974	OF-109
1963	PIT N	85	.195	.322	149	29	2	1	5	3.4	22	14	14	31	4	33	5	47	3	3	1	1.1	.943	OF-47
1965	STL N	30	.159	.254	63	10	3	0	1	1.6	7	4	6	9	1	7	2	29	1	2	0	1.6	.938	OF-20
1966		16	.172	.310	29	5	2	1	0	0.0	4	3	4	7	4	9	2	9	0	0	0	1.3	1.000	OF-7
1967	2 teams	STL N (9G –.125) CHI N (96G –.218)																						
"	total	105	.215	.330	233	50	10	1	5	2.1	41	33	41	57	7	17	4	133	7	3	2	1.6	.979	OF-86, 3B-1

Ted Savage *continued*

Year	Team	Games	BA	SA	AB	H	2B	3B	HR	HR%	R	RBI	BB	SO	SB	Pinch Hit AB	Pinch Hit H	PO	A	E	DP	TC/G	FA	G by Pos
1968	2 teams	CHI N (3G –.250) LA N (61G –.206)																						
"	total	64	.209	.313	134	28	6	1	2	1.5	7	7	10	21	1	21	3	64	4	1	1	1.7	.986	OF-41
1969	CIN N	68	.227	.345	110	25	7	0	2	1.8	20	11	20	27	3	27	5	57	0	1	0	3.2	.983	OF-17, 2B-1
1970	MIL A	114	.279	.482	276	77	10	5	12	4.3	43	50	57	44	10	31	6	124	3	6	0	1.6	.955	OF-82, 1B-1
1971	2 teams	MIL A (14G –.176) KC A (19G –.172)																						
"	total	33	.174	.174	46	8	0	0	0	0.0	4	2	8	10	3	18	2	8	2	0	0	0.7	1.000	OF-15
9 yrs.		642	.233	.361	1375	321	51	11	34	2.5	202	163	200	272	49	184	32	656	24	21	5	1.6	.970	OF-424, 2B-1, 1B-1, 3B-1

Bob Saverine

SAVERINE, ROBERT PAUL (Rabbit) BB TR 5′10″ 160 lbs.
B. June 2, 1941, Norwalk, Conn.

Year	Team	Games	BA	SA	AB	H	2B	3B	HR	HR%	R	RBI	BB	SO	SB	Pinch Hit AB	Pinch Hit H	PO	A	E	DP	TC/G	FA	G by Pos
1959	BAL A	1	—	—	0	0	0	0	0	—	1	0	0	0	0	0	0	0	0	0	0	0.0	—	
1962		8	.238	.333	21	5	2	0	0	0.0	2	3	1	3	0	1	0	11	19	0	3	4.3	1.000	2B-7
1963		115	.234	.281	167	39	1	2	1	0.6	21	12	25	44	8	16	6	99	89	2	19	2.1	.989	OF-59, 2B-19, SS-13
1964		46	.147	.176	34	5	1	0	0	0.0	14	0	3	6	3	3	0	12	16	0	1	1.6	1.000	SS-15, OF-2
1966	WAS A	120	.251	.333	406	102	10	4	5	1.2	54	24	27	62	4	19	5	186	228	11	44	3.7	.974	2B-70, 3B-26, SS-11, OF-9
1967		89	.236	.292	233	55	13	0	0	0.0	22	8	17	34	8	25	4	90	127	12	24	3.4	.948	2B-48, SS-10, 3B-8, OF-2
6 yrs.		379	.239	.305	861	206	27	6	6	0.7	114	47	73	149	23	64	15	398	479	25	91	3.0	.972	2B-144, OF-72, SS-49, 3B-34

Carl Sawatski

SAWATSKI, CARL ERNEST (Swats) BL TR 5′10″ 210 lbs.
B. Nov. 4, 1927, Shickshinny, Pa. D. Nov. 24, 1991, Little Rock, Ark.

Year	Team	Games	BA	SA	AB	H	2B	3B	HR	HR%	R	RBI	BB	SO	SB	Pinch Hit AB	Pinch Hit H	PO	A	E	DP	TC/G	FA	G by Pos
1948	CHI N	2	.000	.000	2	0	0	0	0	0.0	0	0	0	0	0	2	0	0	0	0	0	0.0	—	
1950		38	.175	.214	103	18	1	0	1	1.0	4	7	11	19	0	7	0	100	19	2	6	3.8	.983	C-32
1953		43	.220	.322	59	13	3	0	1	1.7	5	5	7	7	0	29	6	45	5	3	0	3.5	.943	C-15
1954	CHI A	43	.183	.294	109	20	3	3	1	0.9	6	12	15	20	0	8	1	133	14	2	4	4.5	.987	C-33
1957	MIL N	58	.238	.448	105	25	4	0	6	5.7	13	17	10	15	0	31	6	121	20	2	2	5.1	.986	C-28
1958	2 teams	MIL N (10G –.100) PHI N (60G –.230)																						
"	total	70	.223	.332	193	43	4	1	5	2.6	13	13	18	47	0	13	4	279	20	4	2	5.4	.987	C-56
1959	PHI N	74	.293	.480	198	58	10	0	9	4.5	15	43	32	36	0	7	1	306	23	7	4	4.9	.979	C-69
1960	STL N	78	.229	.352	179	41	4	0	6	3.4	16	27	22	24	0	27	7	279	25	2	5	4.6	.993	C-67
1961		86	.299	.517	174	52	8	0	10	5.7	23	33	25	17	0	39	10	218	19	1	3	3.9	.996	C-60, OF-1
1962		85	.252	.477	222	56	9	1	13	5.9	26	42	36	38	0	15	2	354	24	1	4	5.4	.997	C-70
1963		56	.238	.410	105	25	0	0	6	5.7	12	14	15	28	2	31	4	125	11	2	0	5.1	.986	C-27
11 yrs.		633	.242	.401	1449	351	46	5	58	4.0	133	213	191	251	2	209	41	1960	180	26	30	4.7	.988	C-457, OF-1
WORLD SERIES																								
1957	MIL N	2	.000	.000	2	0	0	0	0	0.0	0	0	0	2	0	2	0	0	0	0	0	0.0	—	

Carl Sawyer

SAWYER, CARL EVERETT (Huck) BR TR 5′11″ 160 lbs.
B. Oct. 19, 1890, Seattle, Wash. D. Jan. 17, 1957, Los Angeles, Calif.

Year	Team	Games	BA	SA	AB	H	2B	3B	HR	HR%	R	RBI	BB	SO	SB	Pinch Hit AB	Pinch Hit H	PO	A	E	DP	TC/G	FA	G by Pos
1915	WAS A	10	.250	.281	32	8	1	0	0	0.0	8	3	4	5	2	0	0	26	22	2	0	5.0	.960	2B-6, SS-4
1916		16	.194	.226	31	6	1	0	0	0.0	3	2	4	4	3	0	0	27	25	4	5	4.7	.929	2B-6, SS-5, 3B-1
2 yrs.		26	.222	.254	63	14	2	0	0	0.0	11	5	8	9	5	0	0	53	47	6	5	4.8	.943	2B-12, SS-9, 3B-1

Dave Sax

SAX, DAVID JOHN BR TR 6′ 185 lbs.
Brother of Steve Sax.
B. Sept. 22, 1958, Sacramento, Calif.

Year	Team	Games	BA	SA	AB	H	2B	3B	HR	HR%	R	RBI	BB	SO	SB	Pinch Hit AB	Pinch Hit H	PO	A	E	DP	TC/G	FA	G by Pos
1982	LA N	2	.000	.000	2	0	0	0	0	0.0	0	0	0	0	0	1	0	1	0	0	0	1.0	1.000	OF-1
1983		7	.000	.000	8	0	0	0	0	0.0	0	1	0	0	0	4	0	11	0	1	0	3.0	.917	C-4
1985	BOS A	22	.306	.389	36	11	3	0	0	0.0	2	6	3	3	0	0	0	66	0	1	0	3.3	.985	C-16, OF-4
1986		4	.455	.818	11	5	1	0	1	9.1	1	1	0	1	0	1	0	14	1	0	0	5.0	1.000	C-2, 1B-1
1987		2	.000	.000	3	0	0	0	0	0.0	0	0	0	1	0	1	0	9	0	0	1	4.5	1.000	C-2
5 yrs.		37	.267	.383	60	16	4	0	1	1.7	3	8	3	5	0	7	0	101	1	2	1	3.5	.981	C-24, OF-5, 1B-1

Ollie Sax

SAX, ERIK OLIVER BR TR 5′ 8″ 164 lbs.
B. Nov. 5, 1904, Branford, Conn. D. Mar. 21, 1982, Newark, N. J.

Year	Team	Games	BA	SA	AB	H	2B	3B	HR	HR%	R	RBI	BB	SO	SB	Pinch Hit AB	Pinch Hit H	PO	A	E	DP	TC/G	FA	G by Pos
1928	STL A	16	.176	.176	17	3	0	0	0	0.0	4	0	5	3	0	1	0	6	15	1	2	2.4	.955	3B-9

Steve Sax

SAX, STEPHEN LOUIS BR TR 5′11″ 185 lbs.
Brother of Dave Sax.
B. Jan. 29, 1960, Sacramento, Calif.

Year	Team	Games	BA	SA	AB	H	2B	3B	HR	HR%	R	RBI	BB	SO	SB	Pinch Hit AB	Pinch Hit H	PO	A	E	DP	TC/G	FA	G by Pos
1981	LA N	31	.277	.345	119	33	2	0	2	1.7	15	9	7	14	5	2	1	64	93	4	22	5.6	.975	2B-29
1982		150	.282	.359	638	180	23	7	4	0.6	88	47	49	53	49	1	1	347	452	19	83	5.5	.977	2B-149
1983		155	.281	.350	623	175	18	5	5	0.8	94	41	58	73	56	4	1	331	399	30	74	5.0	.961	2B-152
1984		145	.243	.304	569	138	24	4	1	0.2	70	35	47	53	34	3	0	318	450	21	99	5.6	.973	2B-141
1985		136	.279	.318	488	136	8	4	1	0.2	62	42	54	43	27	1	0	330	358	22	84	5.2	.969	2B-135, 3B-1
1986		157	.332	.441	633	210	43	4	6	0.9	91	56	59	58	40	3	1	367	432	16	71	5.3	.980	2B-154
1987		157	.280	.369	610	171	22	7	6	1.0	84	46	44	61	37	5	0	343	420	14	92	5.0	.982	2B-152, OF-1, 3B-1
1988		160	.277	.343	**632**	175	19	4	5	0.8	70	57	45	51	42	2	2	276	429	14	69	4.6	.981	2B-158
1989	NY A	158	.315	.387	**651**	205	26	3	5	0.8	88	63	52	44	43	0	0	312	460	10	117	4.9	.987	2B-158
1990		155	.260	.325	615	160	24	2	4	0.7	70	42	49	46	43	0	0	292	457	10	102	4.9	.987	2B-154
1991		158	.304	.414	652	198	38	2	10	1.5	85	56	41	38	31	0	0	277	454	10	107	4.7	.987	2B-149, 3B-5, DH-4
1992	CHI A	143	.236	.317	567	134	26	4	4	0.7	74	47	43	42	30	1	0	305	390	20	75	5.0	.972	2B-141, DH-1
1993		57	.235	.303	119	28	5	0	1	0.8	20	8	8	6	7	8	0	39	3	0	0	0.8	1.000	OF-32, DH-20, 2B-1
1994	OAK A	7	.250	.333	24	6	0	1	0	0.0	2	1	0	2	0	1	1	16	20	0	3	6.0	1.000	2B-6
14 yrs.		1769	.281	.358	6940	1949	278	47	54	0.8	913	550	556	584	444	31	7	3617	4817	190	998	4.9	.978	2B-1679, OF-33, DH-25, 3B-7
DIVISIONAL PLAYOFF SERIES																								
1981	LA N	1	—	—	0	0	0	0	0	—	0	0	0	0	0	0	0	0	0	0	0	0.0	.000	2B-1
LEAGUE CHAMPIONSHIP SERIES																								
1981	LA N	1	—	—	0	0	0	0	0	—	0	0	0	0	0	0	0	0	1	0	0	1.0	1.000	2B-1
1983		4	.250	.250	16	4	0	0	0	0.0	0	0	1	0	1	0	0	11	12	0	3	5.8	1.000	2B-4
1985		6	.300	.450	20	6	3	0	0	0.0	1	1	1	5	0	0	0	12	20	0	0	5.3	1.000	2B-6
1988		7	.267	.267	30	8	0	0	0	0.0	7	3	3	3	5	0	0	12	22	0	6	4.9	1.000	2B-7
4 yrs.		18	.273	.318	66	18	3	0	0	0.0	8	4	5	8	6 **8th**	0	0	35	55	0	9	5.0	1.000	2B-18

Steve Sax *continued*

WORLD SERIES

Year	Team	Games	BA	SA	AB	H	2B	3B	HR	HR%	R	RBI	BB	SO	SB	Pinch Hit AB	Pinch Hit H	PO	A	E	DP	TC/G	FA	G by Pos
1981	LA N	2	.000	.000	1	0	0	0	0	0.0	0	0	0	0	0	1	0	0	0	0	0	0.0	.000	2B-1
1988		5	.300	.300	20	6	0	0	0	0.0	3	0	1	1	1	0	0	11	11	0	2	4.4	1.000	2B-5
2 yrs.		7	.286	.286	21	6	0	0	0	0.0	3	0	1	1	1	1	0	11	11	0	2	3.7	1.000	2B-6

Jimmy Say

SAY, JAMES I.
Brother of Lew Say.
B. 1862, Baltimore, Md. D. June 23, 1894, Baltimore, Md.

Year	Team	Games	BA	SA	AB	H	2B	3B	HR	HR%	R	RBI	BB	SO	SB	Pinch Hit AB	Pinch Hit H	PO	A	E	DP	TC/G	FA	G by Pos
1882	2 teams	LOU AA (1G –.250) PHI AA (22G –.207)																						
"	total	23	.209	.233	86	18	2	0	0	0.0	13		1			0	0	32	76	16	10	5.4	.871	SS-22, 3B-1
1884	2 teams	WIL U (16G –.220) KC U (2G –.250)																						
"	total	18	.224	.299	67	15	1	2	0	0.0	3		1			0	0	12	22	16	2	2.8	.680	3B-18
1887	CLE AA	16	.375	.547	64	24	5	3	0	0.0	9		1		0	0	0	19	26	18	3	3.9	.714	3B-16
3 yrs.		57	.263	.346	217	57	8	5	0	0.0	25		3		0	0	0	63	124	50	15	4.2	.789	3B-35, SS-22

Lew Say

SAY, LOUIS I. BR TR 5′ 7″ 145 lbs.
Brother of Jimmy Say.
B. Feb. 4, 1854, Baltimore, Md. D. June 5, 1930, Fallston, Md.

Year	Team	Games	BA	SA	AB	H	2B	3B	HR	HR%	R	RBI	BB	SO	SB	Pinch Hit AB	Pinch Hit H	PO	A	E	DP	TC/G	FA	G by Pos
1880	CIN N	48	.199	.251	191	38	8	1	0	0.0	14	15	4	31		0	0	54	164	44	11	5.5	.832	SS-48
1882	PHI AA	49	.226	.291	199	45	4	3	1	0.5	35		8			0	0	69	192	40	7	6.1	.867	SS-49
1883	BAL AA	74	.256	.318	324	83	13	2	1	0.3	52		10			0	0	76	241	82	13	5.4	.794	SS-74
1884	2 teams	BAL U (78G –.239) KC U (17G –.200)																						
"	total	95	.232	.303	409	95	16	2	3	0.7	71		13			0	0	131	302	102	19	5.6	.809	SS-94, 2B-1
4 yrs.		266	.232	.297	1123	261	41	8	5	0.4	172	15	35	31		0	0	330	899	268	50	5.6	.821	SS-265, 2B-1

Jerry Scala

SCALA, GERARD DANIEL BL TR 5′11″ 178 lbs.
B. Sept. 27, 1924, Bayonne, N. J. D. Dec. 14, 1993, Fallston, Md.

Year	Team	Games	BA	SA	AB	H	2B	3B	HR	HR%	R	RBI	BB	SO	SB	Pinch Hit AB	Pinch Hit H	PO	A	E	DP	TC/G	FA	G by Pos
1948	CHI A	3	.000	.000	6	0	0	0	0	0.0	1	0	0	3	0	0	0	5	0	0	0	2.5	1.000	OF-2
1949		37	.250	.350	120	30	7	1	1	0.8	17	13	17	19	3	5	1	83	1	1	0	2.3	.988	OF-37
1950		40	.194	.254	67	13	2	1	0	0.0	8	6	10	10	0	5	3	43	1	0	0	1.9	1.000	OF-23
3 yrs.		80	.223	.306	193	43	9	2	1	0.5	26	19	27	32	3	10	4	131	2	1	0	2.2	.993	OF-62

Frank Scalzi

SCALZI, FRANK JOHN (Skeeter) BR TR 5′ 6″ 160 lbs.
B. June 16, 1913, Lafferty, Ohio D. Aug. 25, 1984, Pittsburgh, Pa.

Year	Team	Games	BA	SA	AB	H	2B	3B	HR	HR%	R	RBI	BB	SO	SB	Pinch Hit AB	Pinch Hit H	PO	A	E	DP	TC/G	FA	G by Pos
1939	NY N	11	.333	.333	18	6	0	0	0	0.0	3	0	3	2	1	2	0	10	18	4	3	5.3	.875	SS-5, 3B-1

Johnny Scalzi

SCALZI, JOHN ANTHONY BR TR 5′ 7″ 170 lbs.
B. Mar. 22, 1907, Stamford, Conn. D. Sept. 27, 1962, Port Chester, N. Y.

Year	Team	Games	BA	SA	AB	H	2B	3B	HR	HR%	R	RBI	BB	SO	SB	Pinch Hit AB	Pinch Hit H	PO	A	E	DP	TC/G	FA	G by Pos
1931	BOS N	2	.000	.000	1	0	0	0	0	0.0	0	0	0	1	0	1	0	0	0	0	0	0.0	—	

Mort Scanlan

SCANLAN, MORTIMER J. 6′ 1″ 186 lbs.
B. Mar. 18, 1861, Chicago, Ill. D. Dec. 29, 1928, Chicago, Ill.

Year	Team	Games	BA	SA	AB	H	2B	3B	HR	HR%	R	RBI	BB	SO	SB	Pinch Hit AB	Pinch Hit H	PO	A	E	DP	TC/G	FA	G by Pos
1890	NY N	3	.000	.000	10	0	0	0	0	0.0	0	0	2	5	1	0	0	28	0	0	2	9.3	1.000	1B-3

Pat Scanlon

SCANLON, JAMES PATRICK BL TR 6′ 180 lbs.
B. Sept. 23, 1952, Minneapolis, Minn.

Year	Team	Games	BA	SA	AB	H	2B	3B	HR	HR%	R	RBI	BB	SO	SB	Pinch Hit AB	Pinch Hit H	PO	A	E	DP	TC/G	FA	G by Pos
1974	MON N	2	.250	.250	4	1	0	0	0	0.0	1	0	0	1	0	1	0	0	3	0	0	3.0	1.000	3B-1
1975		60	.183	.284	109	20	3	1	2	1.8	5	15	17	25	0	26	3	12	57	3	4	2.5	.958	3B-28, 1B-1
1976		11	.185	.333	27	5	1	0	1	3.7	2	2	2	5	0	4	1	11	12	3	0	3.3	.885	3B-7, 1B-1
1977	SD N	47	.190	.266	79	15	3	0	1	1.3	9	11	12	20	0	21	2	22	41	3	5	2.4	.955	2B-15, 3B-11, OF-1
4 yrs.		120	.187	.283	219	41	7	1	4	1.8	17	28	31	51	0	52	6	45	113	9	9	2.6	.946	3B-47, 2B-15, 1B-2, OF-1

Pat Scanlon

SCANLON, PATRICK J.
B. Mar. 25, 1861, Nova Scotia, Canada D. July 17, 1913, Springfield, Mass.

Year	Team	Games	BA	SA	AB	H	2B	3B	HR	HR%	R	RBI	BB	SO	SB	Pinch Hit AB	Pinch Hit H	PO	A	E	DP	TC/G	FA	G by Pos
1884	BOS U	6	.292	.333	24	7	1	0	0	0.0	2		0			0	0	6	2	2	0	1.7	.800	OF-6

Russ Scarritt

SCARRITT, STEPHEN RUSSELL MALLORY BL TR 5′10½″ 165 lbs.
B. Jan. 14, 1903, Pensacola, Fla. D. Dec. 4, 1994, Pensacola, Fla.

Year	Team	Games	BA	SA	AB	H	2B	3B	HR	HR%	R	RBI	BB	SO	SB	Pinch Hit AB	Pinch Hit H	PO	A	E	DP	TC/G	FA	G by Pos
1929	BOS A	151	.294	.411	540	159	26	17	1	0.2	69	71	34	38	13	4	1	302	16	19	6	2.3	.944	OF-145
1930		113	.289	.376	447	129	17	8	2	0.4	48	48	12	49	4	3	0	256	5	9	0	2.5	.967	OF-110
1931		10	.154	.179	39	6	1	0	0	0.0	2	1	2	2	0	1	0	20	1	0	0	2.3	1.000	OF-9
1932	PHI N	11	.182	.182	11	2	0	0	0	0.0	0	0	1	2	0	6	1	2	0	0	0	2.0	1.000	OF-1
4 yrs.		285	.285	.385	1037	296	44	25	3	0.3	119	120	49	91	17	14	2	580	22	28	6	2.4	.956	OF-265

Les Scarsella

SCARSELLA, LESLIE GEORGE BL TL 5′11″ 185 lbs.
B. Nov. 23, 1913, Santa Cruz, Calif. D. Dec. 17, 1958, San Francisco, Calif.

Year	Team	Games	BA	SA	AB	H	2B	3B	HR	HR%	R	RBI	BB	SO	SB	Pinch Hit AB	Pinch Hit H	PO	A	E	DP	TC/G	FA	G by Pos
1935	CIN N	6	.200	.300	10	2	1	0	0	0.0	4	0	3	1	0	2	0	17	3	0	2	10.0	1.000	1B-2
1936		115	.313	.412	485	152	21	9	3	0.6	63	65	14	36	6	0	0	1109	84	13	90	10.5	.989	1B-115
1937		110	.246	.331	329	81	11	4	3	0.9	35	34	17	26	5	27	**9**	607	38	11	55	8.3	.983	1B-65, OF-14
1939		16	.143	.143	14	2	0	0	0	0.0	0	2	0	2	0	14	2	0	0	0	0	0.0	—	
1940	BOS N	15	.300	.417	60	18	1	3	0	0.0	7	8	3	5	2	3	1	137	7	2	17	12.2	.986	1B-12
5 yrs.		262	.284	.378	898	255	34	16	6	0.7	109	109	37	70	13	46	12	1870	132	26	164	9.8	.987	1B-194, OF-14

Steve Scarsone

SCARSONE, STEVEN WAYNE BR TR 6′ 2″ 170 lbs.
B. Apr. 11, 1966, Anaheim, Calif.

Year	Team	Games	BA	SA	AB	H	2B	3B	HR	HR%	R	RBI	BB	SO	SB	Pinch Hit AB	Pinch Hit H	PO	A	E	DP	TC/G	FA	G by Pos
1992	2 teams	PHI N (7G –.154) BAL A (11G –.176)																						
"	total	18	.167	.167	30	5	0	0	0	0.0	3	0	2	12	0	5	1	9	11	2	5	2.0	.909	2B-8, 3B-2, SS-1
1993	SF N	44	.252	.398	103	26	9	0	2	1.9	16	15	4	32	0	10	3	53	44	1	11	2.9	.990	2B-20, 3B-8, 1B-6
1994		52	.272	.408	103	28	8	0	2	1.9	21	13	10	20	0	15	4	66	80	2	23	4.0	.986	2B-22, 3B-8, 1B-6, SS-1
1995		80	.266	.476	233	62	10	3	11	4.7	33	29	18	82	3	8	3	135	112	11	31	3.5	.957	3B-50, 2B-13, 1B-11
4 yrs.		194	.258	.424	469	121	27	3	15	3.2	73	57	34	146	3	38	11	263	247	16	70	3.4	.970	3B-68, 2B-63, 1B-23, SS-2

Paul Schaal

SCHAAL, PAUL — B. Mar. 3, 1943, Pittsburgh, Pa. — BR TR 5′11″ 165 lbs.

Year	Team	Games	BA	SA	AB	H	2B	3B	HR	HR%	R	RBI	BB	SO	SB	Pinch Hit AB	Pinch Hit H	PO	A	E	DP	TC/G	FA	G by Pos
1964	LA A	17	.125	.125	32	4	0	0	0	0.0	3	0	2	5	0	0	0	5	22	2	2	1.6	.931	3B-9, 2B-9
1965	CAL A	155	.224	.313	483	108	12	2	9	1.9	48	45	61	88	6	1	1	101	321	13	20	2.8	.970	3B-153, 2B-1
1966		138	.244	.365	386	94	15	7	6	1.6	59	24	68	56	6	4	0	97	249	19	21	2.8	.948	3B-131
1967		99	.188	.294	272	51	9	1	6	2.2	31	20	38	39	2	7	0	79	158	7	11	2.7	.971	3B-88, SS-2, 2B-1
1968		60	.210	.279	219	46	7	1	2	0.9	22	16	29	25	5	2	0	61	142	9	13	3.7	.958	3B-58
1969	KC A	61	.263	.307	205	54	6	0	1	0.5	22	13	25	27	2	3	0	41	103	15	5	2.6	.906	3B-49, SS-6, 2B-6
1970		124	.268	.355	380	102	12	3	5	1.3	50	35	43	39	7	17	3	95	196	19	19	2.7	.939	3B-97, SS-10, 2B-6
1971		161	.274	.412	548	150	31	6	11	2.0	80	63	103	51	7	0	0	107	335	28	31	2.9	.940	3B-161
1972		127	.228	.326	435	99	19	3	6	1.4	47	41	61	59	1	3	1	77	245	18	16	2.7	.947	3B-123, SS-1
1973		121	.288	.399	396	114	14	3	8	2.0	61	42	63	45	5	1	0	77	237	30	14	2.8	.913	3B-121
1974	2 teams	KC A (12G –.176) CAL A (53G –.248)																						
″	total	65	.236	.317	199	47	7	0	3	1.5	13	24	23	32	2	3	0	35	104	13	13	2.4	.914	3B-63
11 yrs.		1128	.244	.344	3555	869	132	26	57	1.6	436	323	516	466	43	41	5	775	2112	173	165	2.8	.943	3B-1053, 2B-23, SS-19

Germany Schaefer

SCHAEFER, HERMAN A. — B. Feb. 4, 1877, Chicago, Ill. D. May 16, 1919, Saranac Lake, N. Y. — BR TR 5′ 9″ 175 lbs.

Year	Team	Games	BA	SA	AB	H	2B	3B	HR	HR%	R	RBI	BB	SO	SB	Pinch Hit AB	Pinch Hit H	PO	A	E	DP	TC/G	FA	G by Pos
1901	CHI N	2	.600	.800	5	3	1	0	0	0.0	0	0	2		0	0	0	6	4	0	1	5.0	1.000	3B-1, 2B-1
1902		81	.196	.223	291	57	2	3	0	0.0	32	14	19		12	0	0	143	156	43	14	4.2	.874	3B-75, 1B-3, OF-2, SS-1
1905	DET A	153	.244	.318	554	135	17	9	2	0.4	64	47	45		19	0	0	410	394	37	35	5.5	.956	2B-151, SS-3
1906		124	.238	.296	446	106	14	3	2	0.4	48	42	32		31	2	1	368	352	43	45	6.3	.944	2B-114, SS-7
1907		109	.258	.315	372	96	12	3	1	0.3	45	32	30		21	2	0	239	286	23	23	5.1	.958	2B-74, SS-18, 3B-14, OF-1
1908		153	.259	.342	584	151	20	10	3	0.5	96	52	37		40	0	0	319	479	57	58	5.5	.933	SS-68, 2B-58, 3B-29
1909	2 teams	DET A (87G –.250) WAS A (37G –.242)																						
″	total	124	.248	.301	408	101	17	1	1	0.2	39	26	20		14	4	0	235	356	26	42	5.1	.958	2B-118, 3B-1, OF-1
1910	WAS A	74	.275	.345	229	63	6	5	0	0.0	27	14	25		17	10	2	90	113	11	16	3.4	.949	2B-35, OF-26, 3B-2
1911		125	.334	.398	440	147	14	7	0	0.0	74	45	57		22	9	3	1048	71	23	57	9.9	.980	1B-108, OF-7
1912		60	.247	.325	166	41	7	3	0	0.0	21	19	23		11	11	2	169	30	8	7	4.1	.961	OF-19, 2B-15, 1B-15, P-1
1913		52	.320	.350	100	32	1	1	0	0.0	17	7	15	12	6	21	11	91	40	7	6	5.3	.949	2B-17, 1B-5, 3B-2, OF-1, P-1
1914		25	.241	.276	29	7	1	0	0	0.0	6	2	3	5	4	14	3	6	4	1	0	1.8	.909	OF-3, 2B-3
1915	NWK F	59	.214	.286	154	33	5	3	0	0.0	26	8	25		3	15	2	146	31	7	12	4.5	.962	OF-17, 1B-13, 3B-9, 2B-2
1916	NY A	1	—	—	0	0	0	0	0	—	0	0	0	0	0	0	0	0	0	0	0	0.0	.000	OF-1
1918	CLE A	1	.000	.000	5	0	0	0	0	0.0	2	0	0	0	1	0	0	3	3	0	0	6.0	1.000	2B-1
15 yrs.		1143	.257	.320	3783	972	117	48	9	0.2	497	308	333	17	201	88	24	3273	2319	286	316	5.6	.951	2B-589, 1B-144, 3B-133, SS-97, OF-78, P-2
WORLD SERIES																								
1907	DET A	5	.143	.143	21	3	0	0	0	0.0	1	0	0	3	1	0	0	12	21	0	2	6.6	1.000	2B-5
1908		5	.125	.125	16	2	0	0	0	0.0	0	0	1	4	0	0	0	10	11	1	3	4.4	.955	2B-3, 3B-2
2 yrs.		10	.135	.135	37	5	0	0	0	0.0	1	0	1	7	1	0	0	22	32	1	5	5.5	.982	2B-8, 3B-2

Jeff Schaefer

SCHAEFER, JEFFREY SCOTT — B. May 31, 1960, Patchogue, N. Y. — BR TR 5′10″ 170 lbs.

Year	Team	Games	BA	SA	AB	H	2B	3B	HR	HR%	R	RBI	BB	SO	SB	Pinch Hit AB	Pinch Hit H	PO	A	E	DP	TC/G	FA	G by Pos
1989	CHI A	15	.100	.100	10	1	0	0	0	0.0	2	0	0	2	1	0	0	5	7	2	4	1.0	.857	SS-5, 3B-4, 2B-4, DH-1
1990	SEA A	55	.206	.234	107	22	3	0	0	0.0	11	6	3	11	4	2	1	52	87	5	20	2.7	.965	3B-26, SS-24, 2B-3
1991		84	.250	.323	164	41	7	1	1	0.6	19	11	5	25	3	3	0	79	120	6	31	2.3	.971	SS-46, 3B-30, 2B-11, DH-1
1992		65	.114	.186	70	8	2	0	1	1.4	5	3	2	10	0	0	0	36	91	9	10	2.2	.934	SS-33, 3B-21, 2B-7, DH-1
1994	OAK A	6	.125	.125	8	1	0	0	0	0.0	0	0	0	1	0	1	0	4	2	1	0	1.2	.857	3B-3, SS-2, 1B-1
5 yrs.		225	.203	.259	359	73	12	1	2	0.6	37	20	10	49	8	6	1	176	307	23	65	2.3	.955	SS-110, 3B-84, 2B-25, DH-3, 1B-1

Harry Schafer

SCHAFER, HARRY C. (Silk Stocking) — B. Aug. 14, 1846, Philadelphia, Pa. D. Feb. 28, 1935, Philadelphia, Pa. — BR TR 5′ 9½″ 143 lbs.

Year	Team	Games	BA	SA	AB	H	2B	3B	HR	HR%	R	RBI	BB	SO	SB	Pinch Hit AB	Pinch Hit H	PO	A	E	DP	TC/G	FA	G by Pos
1876	BOS N	70	.252	.290	286	72	11	0	0	0.0	47	35	4	11		0	0	122	146	63	8	4.7	.810	3B-70
1877		33	.277	.340	141	39	5	2	0	0.0	20	13	0	7		0	0	34	8	17	1	1.8	.712	OF-23, 3B-9, SS-1
1878		2	.125	.125	8	1	0	0	0	0.0	0	0	0	1		0	0	2	0	0	0	1.0	1.000	OF-2
3 yrs.		105	.257	.303	435	112	16	2	0	0.0	67	48	4	19		0	0	158	154	80	9	3.7	.796	3B-79, OF-25, SS-1

Jimmie Schaffer

SCHAFFER, JIMMIE RONALD — B. Apr. 5, 1936, Limeport, Pa. — BR TR 5′ 9″ 170 lbs.

Year	Team	Games	BA	SA	AB	H	2B	3B	HR	HR%	R	RBI	BB	SO	SB	Pinch Hit AB	Pinch Hit H	PO	A	E	DP	TC/G	FA	G by Pos
1961	STL N	68	.255	.320	153	39	7	0	1	0.7	15	16	9	29	0	1	1	244	23	1	6	3.9	.996	C-68
1962		70	.242	.303	66	16	2	1	0	0.0	7	6	6	16	1	1	0	134	10	1	1	2.1	.993	C-69
1963	CHI N	57	.239	.437	142	34	7	0	7	4.9	17	19	11	35	0	1	0	231	23	1	3	4.7	.996	C-54
1964		54	.205	.320	122	25	6	1	2	1.6	9	9	17	17	2	9	3	143	19	5	1	3.9	.970	C-43
1965	2 teams	CHI A (17G –.194) NY N (24G –.135)																						
″	total	41	.162	.265	68	11	5	1	0	0.0	2	1	4	19	0	7	0	110	8	2	2	3.4	.983	C-35
1966	PHI N	18	.133	.400	15	2	1	0	1	6.7	2	4	1	7	0	2	0	17	3	1	1	3.5	.952	C-6
1967		2	.000	.000	2	0	0	0	0	0.0	1	0	1	1	0	0	0	5	0	0	0	5.0	1.000	C-1
1968	CIN N	4	.167	.167	6	1	0	0	0	0.0	0	1	0	3	0	2	0	4	0	0	0	2.0	1.000	C-2
8 yrs.		314	.223	.340	574	128	28	3	11	1.9	53	56	49	127	3	23	4	888	86	11	14	3.5	.989	C-278

Johnny Schaive

SCHAIVE, JOHN EDWARD — B. Feb. 25, 1934, Springfield, Ill. — BR TR 5′ 8″ 175 lbs.

Year	Team	Games	BA	SA	AB	H	2B	3B	HR	HR%	R	RBI	BB	SO	SB	Pinch Hit AB	Pinch Hit H	PO	A	E	DP	TC/G	FA	G by Pos
1958	WAS A	7	.250	.250	24	6	0	0	0	0.0	1	1	1	4	0	1	0	18	13	0	4	5.2	1.000	2B-6
1959		16	.153	.186	59	9	2	0	0	0.0	3	2	0	7	0	0	0	32	52	2	10	5.4	.977	2B-16
1960		6	.250	.333	12	3	1	0	0	0.0	1	0	0	3	0	3	1	5	6	1	2	3.0	.917	2B-4
1962		82	.253	.409	225	57	15	1	6	2.7	20	29	6	25	0	27	5	53	117	5	8	3.2	.971	3B-49, 2B-6
1963		3	.000	.000	3	0	0	0	0	0.0	0	0	0	1	0	3	0	0	0	0	0	0.0	—	
5 yrs.		114	.232	.350	323	75	18	1	6	1.9	25	32	7	40	0	34	6	108	188	8	24	3.8	.974	3B-49, 2B-32

Ray Schalk

SCHALK, RAYMOND WILLIAM (Cracker) BR TR 5′ 9″ 165 lbs.
B. Aug. 12, 1892, Harvel, Ill. D. May 19, 1970, Chicago, Ill.
Manager 1927–28.
Hall of Fame 1955.

Year	Team	Games	BA	SA	AB	H	2B	3B	HR	HR%	R	RBI	BB	SO	SB	Pinch Hit AB	Pinch Hit H	PO	A	E	DP	TC/G	FA	G by Pos
1912	CHI A	23	.286	.317	63	18	2	0	0	0.0	7	8	3		2	0	0	115	40	14	4	7.3	.917	C-23
1913		128	.244	.314	401	98	15	5	1	0.2	38	38	27	36	14	3	0	599	154	15	18	6.1	.980	C-125
1914		135	.270	.314	392	106	13	2	0	0.0	30	36	38	24	24	9	3	613	183	21	20	6.6	.974	C-124
1915		135	.266	.327	413	110	14	4	1	0.2	46	54	62	21	15	1	1	655	159	13	8	6.2	.984	C-134
1916		129	.232	.305	410	95	12	9	0	0.0	36	41	41	31	30	3	0	653	166	10	25	6.7	.988	C-124
1917		140	.226	.295	424	96	12	4	3	0.7	48	51	59	27	19	1	0	624	148	15	13	5.7	.981	C-139
1918		108	.219	.255	333	73	6	3	0	0.0	35	22	36	22	12	2	1	422	114	12	15	5.2	.978	C-106
1919		131	.282	.320	394	111	9	3	0	0.0	57	34	51	25	11	2	0	551	130	13	14	5.4	.981	C-129
1920		151	.270	.348	485	131	25	5	1	0.2	64	61	68	19	10	0	0	581	138	10	19	4.8	.986	C-151
1921		128	.252	.329	416	105	24	4	0	0.0	32	47	40	36	3	2	0	453	129	9	19	4.7	.985	C-126
1922		142	.281	.371	442	124	22	3	4	0.9	57	60	67	36	12	0	0	591	150	8	16	5.3	.989	C-142
1923		123	.228	.277	382	87	12	2	1	0.3	42	44	39	28	6	2	0	481	93	10	20	4.8	.983	C-121
1924		57	.196	.268	153	30	4	2	1	0.7	15	11	21	10	1	1	0	179	55	10	8	4.4	.959	C-56
1925		125	.274	.332	343	94	18	1	0	0.0	44	52	57	27	11	0	0	368	99	8	15	3.8	.983	C-125
1926		82	.265	.314	226	60	9	1	0	0.0	26	32	27	11	5	1	0	251	45	7	6	3.8	.977	C-80
1927		16	.231	.308	26	6	2	0	0	0.0	2	2	2	1	0	1	0	24	8	0	1	2.1	1.000	C-15
1928		2	1.000	1.000	1	1	0	0	0	0.0	0	1	0	0	1	0	0	4	0	0	0	4.0	1.000	C-1
1929	NY N	5	.000	.000	2	0	0	0	0	0.0	0	0	0	1	0	0	0	7	0	0	0	1.4	1.000	C-5
18 yrs.		1760	.253	.316	5306	1345	199	48	12	0.2	579	594	638	355	176	28	5	7171	1811	175	221	5.3	.981	C-1726
WORLD SERIES																								
1917	CHI A	6	.263	.263	19	5	0	0	0	0.0	1	0	2	1	1	0	0	32	6	2	1	6.7	.950	C-6
1919		8	.304	.304	23	7	0	0	0	0.0	1	2	4	2	1	0	0	29	15	1	1	5.6	.978	C-8
2 yrs.		14	.286	.286	42	12	0	0	0	0.0	2	2	6	3	2	0	0	61	21	3	2	6.1	.965	C-14

Roy Schalk

SCHALK, LeROY JOHN BR TR 5′10″ 168 lbs.
B. Nov. 9, 1908, Chicago, Ill. D. Mar. 11, 1990, Gainesville, Tex.

Year	Team	Games	BA	SA	AB	H	2B	3B	HR	HR%	R	RBI	BB	SO	SB	Pinch Hit AB	Pinch Hit H	PO	A	E	DP	TC/G	FA	G by Pos
1932	NY A	3	.250	.333	12	3	1	0	0	0.0	3	0	2	2	0	0	0	4	9	2	1	5.0	.867	2B-3
1944	CHI A	146	.220	.262	587	129	14	4	1	0.2	47	44	45	52	5	0	0	366	413	29	112	5.5	.964	2B-142, SS-5
1945		133	.248	.302	513	127	23	1	1	0.2	50	65	32	41	3	0	0	380	389	18	90	5.9	.977	2B-133
3 yrs.		282	.233	.281	1112	259	38	5	2	0.2	100	109	79	95	8	0	0	750	811	49	203	5.7	.970	2B-278, SS-5

Gene Schall

SCHALL, EUGENE DAVID BR TR 6′ 3″ 190 lbs.
B. June 5, 1970, Abington, Pa.

Year	Team	Games	BA	SA	AB	H	2B	3B	HR	HR%	R	RBI	BB	SO	SB	Pinch Hit AB	Pinch Hit H	PO	A	E	DP	TC/G	FA	G by Pos
1995	PHI N	24	.231	.262	65	15	2	0	0	0.0	2	5	6	16	0	5	2	114	10	2	8	7.0	.984	1B-14, OF-4

Biff Schaller

SCHALLER, WALTER BL TR 5′11″ 168 lbs.
B. Sept. 23, 1889, Chicago, Ill. D. Oct. 9, 1939, Emeryville, Calif.

Year	Team	Games	BA	SA	AB	H	2B	3B	HR	HR%	R	RBI	BB	SO	SB	Pinch Hit AB	Pinch Hit H	PO	A	E	DP	TC/G	FA	G by Pos
1911	DET A	40	.133	.217	60	8	0	1	1	1.7	8	7	4		1	17	6	27	2	0	1	1.7	1.000	OF-16, 1B-1
1913	CHI A	34	.219	.250	96	21	3	0	0	0.0	12	4	20	16	5	2	0	45	0	4	0	1.5	.918	OF-32
2 yrs.		74	.186	.237	156	29	3	1	1	0.6	20	11	24	16	6	19	6	72	2	4	1	1.6	.949	OF-48, 1B-1

Bobby Schang

SCHANG, ROBERT MARTIN BR TR 5′ 7″ 165 lbs.
Brother of Wally Schang.
B. Dec. 7, 1886, Wales Center, N. Y. D. Aug. 29, 1966, Sacramento, Calif.

Year	Team	Games	BA	SA	AB	H	2B	3B	HR	HR%	R	RBI	BB	SO	SB	Pinch Hit AB	Pinch Hit H	PO	A	E	DP	TC/G	FA	G by Pos
1914	PIT N	11	.229	.314	35	8	1	1	0	0.0	0	1	0	10	0	1	0	42	12	2	1	5.6	.964	C-10
1915	2 teams	PIT N (56G –.184) NY N (12G –.143)																						
″	total	68	.178	.260	146	26	6	3	0	0.0	14	5	18	37	3	9	0	167	50	9	4	4.4	.960	C-51
1927	STL N	3	.200	.200	5	1	0	0	0	0.0	0	0	0	0	0	0	0	3	1	0	0	1.3	1.000	C-3
3 yrs.		82	.188	.269	186	35	7	4	0	0.0	14	6	18	47	3	10	0	212	63	11	5	4.5	.962	C-64

Wally Schang

SCHANG, WALTER HENRY BB TR 5′10″ 180 lbs.
Brother of Bobby Schang.
B. Aug. 22, 1889, South Wales, N. Y. D. Mar. 6, 1965, St. Louis, Mo.

Year	Team	Games	BA	SA	AB	H	2B	3B	HR	HR%	R	RBI	BB	SO	SB	Pinch Hit AB	Pinch Hit H	PO	A	E	DP	TC/G	FA	G by Pos
1913	PHI A	77	.266	.415	207	55	16	3	3	1.4	32	30	34	44	4	4	1	317	97	14	9	6.0	.967	C-71
1914		107	.287	.404	307	88	11	8	3	1.0	44	45	32	33	7	5	1	498	154	30	11	6.8	.956	C-100
1915		116	.248	.343	359	89	9	11	1	0.3	64	44	66	47	18	5	1	240	139	40	12	3.8	.905	3B-43, OF-41, C-26
1916		110	.266	.420	338	90	15	8	7	2.1	41	38	38	44	14	11	0	266	77	19	6	3.7	.948	OF-61, C-36
1917		118	.285	.415	316	90	14	9	3	0.9	41	36	29	24	6	18	2	293	127	20	13	4.5	.955	C-79, 3B-12, OF-7
1918	BOS A	88	.244	.284	225	55	7	1	0	0.0	36	20	46	35	4	8	3	207	58	14	5	3.5	.950	C-57, OF-16, 3B-5, SS-1
1919		113	.306	.373	330	101	16	3	0	0.0	43	55	71	42	15	5	0	359	131	14	15	4.9	.972	C-103
1920		122	.305	.450	387	118	30	7	4	1.0	58	51	64	37	7	8	1	377	83	18	8	4.2	.962	C-73, OF-40
1921	NY A	134	.316	.453	424	134	30	5	6	1.4	77	55	78	35	7	2	0	500	101	19	13	4.7	.969	C-132
1922		124	.319	.412	408	130	21	7	1	0.2	46	53	53	36	12	5	1	456	102	14	12	4.6	.976	C-124
1923		84	.276	.342	272	75	8	2	2	0.7	39	29	27	17	5	2	0	292	60	11	6	4.5	.970	C-81
1924		114	.292	.427	356	104	19	7	5	1.4	46	52	48	43	2	4	0	423	89	15	9	4.8	.972	C-109
1925		73	.240	.335	167	40	8	1	2	1.2	17	24	17	9	3	11	2	172	55	6	8	4.0	.974	C-58
1926	STL A	103	.330	.516	285	94	19	5	8	2.8	36	50	32	20	5	17	7	232	75	10	7	3.7	.968	C-82, OF-3
1927		97	.319	.449	263	84	15	2	5	1.9	40	42	41	33	3	18	6	213	73	7	10	3.9	.976	C-75
1928		91	.286	.404	245	70	10	5	3	1.2	41	39	68	26	8	7	3	263	46	5	5	3.8	.984	C-82
1929		94	.237	.378	249	59	10	5	5	2.0	43	36	74	22	1	7	1	268	56	4	6	3.9	.988	C-85
1930	PHI A	45	.174	.272	92	16	4	1	1	1.1	16	9	17	15	0	6	1	126	18	4	2	4.1	.973	C-36
1931	DET A	30	.184	.211	76	14	2	0	0	0.0	9	2	14	11	1	0	0	91	20	4	6	3.8	.965	C-30
19 yrs.		1840	.284	.401	5306	1506	264	90	59	1.1	769	710	849	573	122	143	30	5593	1561	268	163	4.4	.964	C-1439, OF-168, 3B-60, SS-1
WORLD SERIES																								
1913	PHI A	4	.357	.714	14	5	0	1	1	7.1	2	6	2	4	0	0	0	16	4	1	1	5.3	.952	C-4
1914		4	.167	.250	12	2	1	0	0	0.0	1	0	1	4	0	0	0	17	3	1	0	5.3	.952	C-4
1918	BOS A	5	.444	.444	9	4	0	0	0	0.0	1	1	2	3	1	2	1	9	4	0	0	2.6	1.000	C-5

Wally Schang *continued*

Year	Team	Games	BA	SA	AB	H	2B	3B	HR	HR%	R	RBI	BB	SO	SB	Pinch Hit AB	Pinch Hit H	PO	A	E	DP	TC/G	FA	G by Pos
1921	**NY A**	8	.286	.429	21	6	1	1	0	0.0	1	1	5	4	0	0	0	39	11	0	3	6.3	1.000	C-8
1922		5	.188	.250	16	3	1	0	0	0.0	0	0	0	3	0	0	0	19	4	0	0	4.6	1.000	C-5
1923		6	.318	.364	22	7	1	0	0	0.0	3	0	1	2	0	0	0	21	2	1	0	4.0	.958	C-6
6 yrs.		32	.287	.404	94	27	4	2	1	1.1	8	8	11	20	1	2	1	121	28	3	4	4.8	.980	C-32

Art Scharein

SCHAREIN, ARTHUR OTTO (Scoop) BR TR 6′ 175 lbs.
Brother of George Scharein.
B. June 30, 1905, Decatur, Ill. D. July 2, 1969, San Antonio, Tex.

Year	Team	Games	BA	SA	AB	H	2B	3B	HR	HR%	R	RBI	BB	SO	SB	Pinch Hit AB	Pinch Hit H	PO	A	E	DP	TC/G	FA	G by Pos
1932	**STL A**	81	.304	.380	303	92	19	2	0	0.0	43	42	25	10	4	0	0	107	189	12	26	3.8	.961	3B-77, SS-3, 2B-2
1933		123	.204	.244	471	96	13	3	0	0.0	49	26	41	21	7	2	0	158	286	22	43	3.7	.953	3B-95, SS-24, 2B-7
1934		1	.500	.500	2	1	0	0	0	0.0	0	2	0	0	0	2	1	0	0	0	0	0.0	—	
3 yrs.		205	.244	.298	776	189	32	5	0	0.0	92	70	66	31	11	4	1	265	475	34	69	3.7	.956	3B-172, SS-27, 2B-9

George Scharein

SCHAREIN, GEORGE ALBERT (Tom) BR TR 6′ 1″ 174 lbs.
Brother of Art Scharein.
B. Nov. 21, 1914, Decatur, Ill. D. Dec. 23, 1981, Decatur, Ill.

Year	Team	Games	BA	SA	AB	H	2B	3B	HR	HR%	R	RBI	BB	SO	SB	Pinch Hit AB	Pinch Hit H	PO	A	E	DP	TC/G	FA	G by Pos
1937	**PHI N**	146	.241	.284	511	123	20	1	0	0.0	44	57	36	47	13	0	0	335	456	44	98	5.7	.947	SS-146
1938		117	.238	.308	390	93	16	4	1	0.3	47	29	16	33	11	1	0	246	327	37	57	5.2	.939	SS-77, 2B-39, 3B-1
1939		118	.238	.293	399	95	17	1	1	0.3	35	33	13	40	4	0	0	258	331	26	69	5.3	.958	SS-117
1940		7	.294	.294	17	5	0	0	0	0.0	0	0	0	3	0	0	0	13	13	5	2	4.4	.839	SS-7
4 yrs.		388	.240	.294	1317	316	53	6	2	0.2	126	119	65	123	28	1	0	852	1127	112	226	5.4	.946	SS-347, 2B-39, 3B-1

Nick Scharf

SCHARF, EDWARD T. TR
B. July 1858, Baltimore, Md. D. May 12, 1937, Baltimore, Md.

Year	Team	Games	BA	SA	AB	H	2B	3B	HR	HR%	R	RBI	BB	SO	SB	Pinch Hit AB	Pinch Hit H	PO	A	E	DP	TC/G	FA	G by Pos
1882	**BAL AA**	10	.205	.359	39	8	1	1	1	2.6	4		0			0	0	16	1	6	0	2.3	.739	OF-9, 3B-1
1883		3	.154	.231	13	2	1	0	0	0.0	1		1			0	0	3	6	5	1	4.7	.643	SS-3
2 yrs.		13	.192	.327	52	10	2	1	1	1.9	5		1			0	0	19	7	11	1	2.8	.703	OF-9, SS-3, 3B-1

Al Scheer

SCHEER, ALLEN G. BL TR 5′ 9″ 165 lbs.
B. Oct. 21, 1888, Dayton, Ohio D. May 6, 1959, Logansport, Ind.

Year	Team	Games	BA	SA	AB	H	2B	3B	HR	HR%	R	RBI	BB	SO	SB	Pinch Hit AB	Pinch Hit H	PO	A	E	DP	TC/G	FA	G by Pos
1913	**BKN N**	6	.227	.227	22	5	0	0	0	0.0	3	0	2	4	1	0	0	3	1	1	0	0.8	.800	OF-6
1914	**IND F**	120	.306	.427	363	111	23	6	3	0.8	63	45	49		9	13	5	152	21	13	2	1.7	.930	OF-102, 2B-4, SS-1
1915	**NWK F**	155	.267	.375	546	146	25	14	2	0.4	75	60	65		31	0	0	287	16	9	5	2.0	.971	OF-155
3 yrs.		281	.281	.392	931	262	48	20	5	0.5	141	105	116	4	41	13	5	442	38	23	7	1.9	.954	OF-263, 2B-4, SS-1

Heinie Scheer

SCHEER, HENRY WILLIAM BR TR 5′ 8″ 146 lbs.
B. July 31, 1900, New York, N. Y. D. Mar. 21, 1976, New Haven, Conn.

Year	Team	Games	BA	SA	AB	H	2B	3B	HR	HR%	R	RBI	BB	SO	SB	Pinch Hit AB	Pinch Hit H	PO	A	E	DP	TC/G	FA	G by Pos
1922	**PHI A**	51	.170	.281	135	23	3	0	4	3.0	10	12	3	25	1	10	2	71	124	7	9	5.1	.965	2B-31, 3B-9
1923		69	.238	.314	210	50	8	1	2	1.0	26	21	17	41	3	4	0	147	156	9	30	5.1	.971	2B-61
2 yrs.		120	.212	.301	345	73	11	1	6	1.7	36	33	20	66	4	14	2	218	280	16	39	5.1	.969	2B-92, 3B-9

Fritz Scheeren

SCHEEREN, FREDERICK (Dutch) BR TR 6′ 180 lbs.
B. Sept. 8, 1891, Kokomo, Ind. D. June 17, 1973, Oil City, Pa.

Year	Team	Games	BA	SA	AB	H	2B	3B	HR	HR%	R	RBI	BB	SO	SB	Pinch Hit AB	Pinch Hit H	PO	A	E	DP	TC/G	FA	G by Pos
1914	**PIT N**	11	.290	.452	31	9	0	1	1	3.2	4	2	1	6	1	1	0	14	0	3	0	1.7	.824	OF-10
1915		4	.000	.000	3	0	0	0	0	0.0	0	0	0	0	0	3	0	0	0	0	0	0.0	.000	OF-1
2 yrs.		15	.265	.412	34	9	0	1	1	2.9	4	2	1	6	1	4	0	14	0	3	0	1.5	.824	OF-11

Bob Scheffing

SCHEFFING, ROBERT BODEN BR TR 6′ 2″ 180 lbs.
B. Aug. 11, 1913, Overland, Mo. D. Oct. 26, 1985, Phoenix, Ariz.
Manager 1957–59, 1961–63.

Year	Team	Games	BA	SA	AB	H	2B	3B	HR	HR%	R	RBI	BB	SO	SB	Pinch Hit AB	Pinch Hit H	PO	A	E	DP	TC/G	FA	G by Pos
1941	**CHI N**	51	.242	.326	132	32	8	0	1	0.8	9	20	5	19	2	17	3	126	17	5	1	4.4	.966	C-34
1942		44	.196	.284	102	20	3	0	2	2.0	7	12	7	11	2	12	1	122	16	2	6	4.4	.986	C-32
1946		63	.278	.330	115	32	4	1	0	0.0	8	18	12	18	0	19	**7**	97	10	0	3	2.5	1.000	C-43
1947		110	.264	.364	363	96	11	5	5	1.4	33	50	25	25	2	13	5	379	52	7	4	4.5	.984	C-97
1948		102	.300	.427	293	88	18	2	5	1.7	23	45	22	27	0	23	6	332	36	4	5	4.8	.989	C-78
1949		55	.268	.383	149	40	6	1	3	2.0	12	19	9	9	0	14	3	152	18	4	3	4.3	.977	C-40
1950	**2 teams**	**CHI N** (12G –.188)	**CIN N** (21G –.277)																					
″	**total**	33	.254	.365	63	16	1	0	2	3.2	4	7	4	4	0	19	5	54	2	1	2	4.1	.982	C-14
1951	**2 teams**	**CIN N** (47G –.254)	**STL N** (12G –.111)																					
″	**total**	59	.236	.293	140	33	2	0	2	1.4	9	16	19	14	0	7	3	182	15	4	1	3.9	.980	C-52
8 yrs.		517	.263	.360	1357	357	53	9	20	1.5	105	187	103	127	6	124	33	1444	166	27	25	4.2	.984	C-390

Ted Scheffler

SCHEFFLER, THEODORE J. BR TR 5′10″ 160 lbs.
B. Apr. 5, 1864, New York, N. Y. D. Feb. 24, 1949, Jamaica, N. Y.

Year	Team	Games	BA	SA	AB	H	2B	3B	HR	HR%	R	RBI	BB	SO	SB	Pinch Hit AB	Pinch Hit H	PO	A	E	DP	TC/G	FA	G by Pos
1888	**DET N**	27	.202	.255	94	19	3	1	0	0.0	17	4	9	9	4	0	0	49	1	9	1	2.2	.847	OF-27
1890	**ROC AA**	119	.245	.319	445	109	12	6	3	0.7	111		78		77	0	0	197	29	22	6	2.1	.911	OF-119, C-1
2 yrs.		146	.237	.308	539	128	15	7	3	0.6	128	4	87	9	81	0	0	246	30	31	7	2.1	.899	OF-146, C-1

Carl Scheib

SCHEIB, CARL ALVIN BR TR 6′ 1″ 192 lbs.
B. Jan. 1, 1927, Gratz, Pa.

Year	Team	Games	BA	SA	AB	H	2B	3B	HR	HR%	R	RBI	BB	SO	SB	Pinch Hit AB	Pinch Hit H	PO	A	E	DP	TC/G	FA	G by Pos
1943	**PHI A**	6	.000	.000	5	0	0	0	0	0.0	0	0	0	3	0	0	0	1	1	0	0	0.3	1.000	P-6
1944		15	.300	.500	10	3	2	0	0	0.0	1	0	0	2	0	0	0	0	13	0	0	0.9	1.000	P-15
1945		4	.000	.000	2	0	0	0	0	0.0	0	0	0	0	0	0	0	1	2	0	0	0.8	1.000	P-4
1947		22	.133	.133	45	6	0	0	0	0.0	4	3	1	3	0	1	0	3	13	1	2	0.8	.941	P-21
1948		52	.298	.490	104	31	8	3	2	1.9	14	21	8	17	0	16	7	16	36	1	5	1.6	.981	P-32, OF-2
1949		47	.236	.264	72	17	2	0	0	0.0	9	10	8	10	0	9	2	6	24	3	3	0.9	.909	P-38
1950		50	.250	.346	52	13	0	1	1	1.9	6	6	1	9	0	7	1	3	16	0	2	0.4	1.000	P-43
1951		48	.396	.623	53	21	2	2	2	3.8	9	8	1	5	0	2	1	14	43	1	3	1.3	.983	P-46
1952		44	.220	.220	82	18	0	0	0	0.0	4	7	0	9	1	14	2	19	26	2	3	1.6	.957	P-30
1953		35	.195	.195	41	8	0	0	0	0.0	4	4	2	1	0	8	2	4	16	1	1	0.8	.952	P-28
1954	**2 teams**	**PHI A** (1G –.000)	**STL N** (3G –.000)																					
″	**total**	4	.000	.000	2	0	0	0	0	0.0	0	0	0	0	0	0	0	1	1	0	0	0.5	1.000	P-4
11 yrs.		327	.250	.338	468	117	14	6	5	1.1	51	59	21	59	1	57	15	68	191	9	19	1.0	.966	P-267, OF-2

Frank Scheibeck

SCHEIBECK, FRANK S. (Archer) BR TR 5′ 7″ 145 lbs.
B. June 28, 1865, Detroit, Mich. D. Oct. 22, 1956, Detroit, Mich.

Year	Team	Games	BA	SA	AB	H	2B	3B	HR	HR%	R	RBI	BB	SO	SB	Pinch Hit AB	Pinch Hit H	PO	A	E	DP	TC/G	FA	G by Pos
1887	CLE AA	3	.222	.222	9	2	0	0	0	0.0	2		2		0	0	0	1	3	4	0	2.7	.500	3B-1, SS-1, P-1
1888	DET N	1	.000	.000	4	0	0	0	0	0.0	0	0	0	0	0	0	0	2	0	2	0	4.0	.500	SS-1
1890	TOL AA	134	.241	.295	485	117	13	5	1	0.2	72		76		57	0	0	282	412	92	35	5.9	.883	SS-134
1894	2 teams	PIT N (28G –.353) WAS N (52G –.230)																						
″	total	80	.272	.342	298	81	4	7	1	0.3	69	27	56	33	18	4	1	152	242	55	21	5.8	.878	SS-63, OF-9, 3B-3, 2B-2
1895	WAS N	48	.186	.240	167	31	5	2	0	0.0	17	25	17	21	5	0	0	105	149	35	18	6.0	.879	SS-44, 3B-2, 2B-2
1899		27	.287	.351	94	27	4	1	0	0.0	19	9	11		5	0	0	46	75	17	3	5.1	.877	SS-27
1901	CLE A	93	.213	.264	329	70	11	3	0	0.0	33	38	18		3	1	0	176	268	51	26	5.4	.897	SS-92
1906	DET A	3	.100	.100	10	1	0	0	0	0.0	1	0	2		0	0	0	8	8	2	2	6.0	.889	2B-3
8 yrs.		389	.236	.292	1396	329	37	18	2	0.1	213	99	182	54	88	5	1	772	1157	258	105	5.7	.882	SS-362, OF-9, 2B-7, 3B-6, P-1

Richie Scheinblum

SCHEINBLUM, RICHARD ALAN BB TR 6′ 1″ 180 lbs.
B. Nov. 5, 1942, New York, N. Y.

Year	Team	Games	BA	SA	AB	H	2B	3B	HR	HR%	R	RBI	BB	SO	SB	Pinch Hit AB	Pinch Hit H	PO	A	E	DP	TC/G	FA	G by Pos
1965	CLE A	4	.000	.000	1	0	0	0	0	0.0	1	0	0	0	0	1	0	0	0	0	0	0.0	—	
1967		18	.318	.439	66	21	4	2	0	0.0	8	6	5	10	0	0	0	33	0	2	0	1.9	.943	OF-18
1968		19	.218	.309	55	12	5	0	0	0.0	3	5	5	8	0	2	0	34	0	0	0	2.1	1.000	OF-16
1969		102	.186	.236	199	37	5	1	1	0.5	13	13	19	30	0	**54**	14	71	4	2	1	1.5	.974	OF-50
1971	WAS A	27	.143	.204	49	7	3	0	0	0.0	5	4	8	5	0	13	3	23	5	2	1	2.3	.933	OF-13
1972	KC A	134	.300	.418	450	135	21	4	8	1.8	60	66	58	40	0	16	7	215	6	8	2	1.9	.965	OF-119
1973	2 teams	CIN N (29G –.222) CAL A (77G –.328)																						
″	total	106	.307	.406	283	87	12	2	4	1.4	33	29	45	31	0	21	6	114	5	4	1	1.5	.967	OF-73, DH-7
1974	3 teams	CAL A (10G –.154) KC A (36G –.181) STL N (6G –.333)																						
″	total	52	.183	.200	115	21	2	0	0	0.0	8	4	9	11	0	27	5	13	0	1	0	0.5	.929	DH-18, OF-10
8 yrs.		462	.263	.352	1218	320	52	9	13	1.1	131	127	149	135	0	134	35	503	20	19	5	1.7	.965	OF-299, DH-25

Danny Schell

SCHELL, CLYDE DANIEL BR TR 6′ 1″ 195 lbs.
B. Dec. 26, 1927, Fostoria, Mich. D. May 11, 1972, Mayville, Mich.

Year	Team	Games	BA	SA	AB	H	2B	3B	HR	HR%	R	RBI	BB	SO	SB	Pinch Hit AB	Pinch Hit H	PO	A	E	DP	TC/G	FA	G by Pos
1954	PHI N	92	.283	.434	272	77	14	3	7	2.6	25	33	17	31	0	24	5	143	4	4	0	2.2	.974	OF-69
1955		2	.000	.000	2	0	0	0	0	0.0	0	0	0	1	0	2	0	0	0	0	0	0.0	—	
2 yrs.		94	.281	.431	274	77	14	3	7	2.6	25	33	17	32	0	26	5	143	4	4	0	2.2	.974	OF-69

Al Schellhase

SCHELLHASE, ALBERT HERMAN (Schelley) BL TR 5′ 8″ 148 lbs.
B. Sept. 13, 1864, Evansville, Ind. D. Jan. 3, 1919, Evansville, Ind.

Year	Team	Games	BA	SA	AB	H	2B	3B	HR	HR%	R	RBI	BB	SO	SB	Pinch Hit AB	Pinch Hit H	PO	A	E	DP	TC/G	FA	G by Pos
1890	BOS N	9	.138	.138	29	4	0	0	0	0.0	1	1	1	10	0	0	0	18	5	5	0	3.1	.821	OF-5, C-2, SS-1, 3B-1
1891	LOU AA	6	.125	.125	16	2	0	0	0	0.0	3	0	1	1	2	0	0	18	8	2	0	4.7	.929	C-6
2 yrs.		15	.133	.133	45	6	0	0	0	0.0	4	1	2	11	2	0	0	36	13	7	0	3.7	.875	C-8, OF-5, SS-1, 3B-1

Fred Schemanske

SCHEMANSKE, FREDERICK GEORGE (Buck) BR TR 6′ 2″ 190 lbs.
B. Apr. 28, 1903, Detroit, Mich. D. Feb. 18, 1960, Detroit, Mich.

Year	Team	Games	BA	SA	AB	H	2B	3B	HR	HR%	R	RBI	BB	SO	SB	Pinch Hit AB	Pinch Hit H	PO	A	E	DP	TC/G	FA	G by Pos
1923	WAS A	2	1.000	1.000	2	2	0	0	0	0.0	0	2	1	0	0	2	2	0	0	0	0	0.0	.000	P-1

Mike Schemer

SCHEMER, MICHAEL (Lefty) BL TL 6′ 180 lbs.
B. Nov. 20, 1917, Baltimore, Md. D. Apr. 22, 1983, Miami, Fla.

Year	Team	Games	BA	SA	AB	H	2B	3B	HR	HR%	R	RBI	BB	SO	SB	Pinch Hit AB	Pinch Hit H	PO	A	E	DP	TC/G	FA	G by Pos
1945	NY N	31	.333	.407	108	36	3	1	1	0.9	10	10	6	1	2	4	0	268	28	2	21	11.0	.993	1B-27
1946		1	.000	.000	1	0	0	0	0	0.0	0	0	0	0	0	1	0	0	0	0	0	0.0	—	
2 yrs.		32	.330	.404	109	36	3	1	1	0.9	10	10	6	1	2	5	0	268	28	2	21	11.0	.993	1B-27

Bill Schenck

SCHENCK, WILLIAM G. 5′ 7″ 171 lbs.
B. Brooklyn, N. Y. Deceased.

Year	Team	Games	BA	SA	AB	H	2B	3B	HR	HR%	R	RBI	BB	SO	SB	Pinch Hit AB	Pinch Hit H	PO	A	E	DP	TC/G	FA	G by Pos
1882	LOU AA	60	.260	.333	231	60	11	3	0	0.0	37		8			0	0	70	114	45	5	3.7	.803	3B-58, SS-2, P-2
1884	RIC AA	42	.205	.291	151	31	4	0	3	2.0	14		1			0	0	40	122	34	8	4.7	.827	SS-40, 2B-2
1885	BKN AA	1	.000	.000	4	0	0	0	0	0.0	0		0			0	0	2	1	0	0	3.0	1.000	3B-1
3 yrs.		103	.236	.313	386	91	15	3	3	0.8	51		9			0	0	112	237	79	13	4.1	.815	3B-59, SS-42, 2B-2, P-2

Hank Schenz

SCHENZ, HENRY LEONARD BR TR 5′ 9½″ 175 lbs.
B. Apr. 11, 1919, New Richmond, Ohio D. May 12, 1988, Cincinnati, Ohio.

Year	Team	Games	BA	SA	AB	H	2B	3B	HR	HR%	R	RBI	BB	SO	SB	Pinch Hit AB	Pinch Hit H	PO	A	E	DP	TC/G	FA	G by Pos
1946	CHI N	6	.182	.182	11	2	0	0	0	0.0	0	1	0	0	1	0	0	2	4	0	1	1.2	1.000	3B-5
1947		7	.071	.071	14	1	0	0	0	0.0	2	0	2	1	0	0	0	2	9	1	0	2.4	.917	3B-5
1948		96	.261	.326	337	88	17	1	1	0.3	43	14	18	15	3	10	1	187	196	10	45	4.7	.975	2B-78, 3B-5
1949		7	.429	.429	14	6	0	0	0	0.0	2	1	1	0	2	0	0	1	9	0	3	2.0	1.000	3B-5
1950	PIT N	58	.228	.337	101	23	4	2	1	1.0	17	5	6	7	0	14	5	47	59	1	20	2.9	.991	2B-21, 3B-12, SS-4
1951	2 teams	PIT N (25G –.213) NY N (8G –.000)																						
″	total	33	.213	.230	61	13	1	0	0	0.0	6	3	0	2	0	1	0	40	36	3	17	3.8	.962	2B-19, 3B-2
6 yrs.		207	.247	.310	538	133	22	3	2	0.4	70	24	27	25	6	25	6	279	313	15	86	3.9	.975	2B-118, 3B-34, SS-4
WORLD SERIES																								
1951	NY N	1	—	—	0	0	0	0	0	—	0	0	0	0	0	0	0	0	0	0	0	0.0	—	

Joe Schepner

SCHEPNER, JOSEPH MAURICE (Gentleman Joe) BR TR 5′10″ 160 lbs.
B. Aug. 10, 1895, Aliquippa, Pa. D. July 25, 1959, Mobile, Ala.

Year	Team	Games	BA	SA	AB	H	2B	3B	HR	HR%	R	RBI	BB	SO	SB	Pinch Hit AB	Pinch Hit H	PO	A	E	DP	TC/G	FA	G by Pos
1919	STL A	14	.208	.292	48	10	4	0	0	0.0	2	6	1	5	0	1	0	18	18	2	2	2.9	.947	3B-13

Bob Scherbarth

SCHERBARTH, ROBERT ELMER BR TR 6′ 180 lbs.
B. Jan. 18, 1926, Milwaukee, Wis.

Year	Team	Games	BA	SA	AB	H	2B	3B	HR	HR%	R	RBI	BB	SO	SB	Pinch Hit AB	Pinch Hit H	PO	A	E	DP	TC/G	FA	G by Pos
1950	BOS A	1	—	—	0	0	0	0	0	—	0	0	0	0	0	0	0	0	0	0	0	0.0	.000	C-1

Harry Scherer

SCHERER, HARRY
B. Baltimore, Md. Deceased.

Year	Team	Games	BA	SA	AB	H	2B	3B	HR	HR%	R	RBI	BB	SO	SB	Pinch Hit AB	Pinch Hit H	PO	A	E	DP	TC/G	FA	G by Pos
1889	LOU AA	1	.333	.333	3	1	0	0	0	0.0	0	0	0	0	0	0	0	2	0	2	0	4.0	.500	OF-1

Lou Schiappacasse

SCHIAPPACASSE, LOUIS JOSEPH (Skippy) BR TR
B. Mar. 29, 1881, Ann Arbor, Mich. D. Sept. 20, 1910, Ann Arbor, Mich.

Year	Team	Games	BA	SA	AB	H	2B	3B	HR	HR%	R	RBI	BB	SO	SB	Pinch Hit AB	Pinch Hit H	PO	A	E	DP	TC/G	FA	G by Pos
1902	DET A	2	.000	.000	5	0	0	0	0	0.0	0	1	1		0	0	0	0	0	1	0	0.5	.000	OF-2

Morrie Schick

SCHICK, MAURICE FRANCIS BR TR 5′11″ 170 lbs.
B. Apr. 17, 1892, Chicago, Ill. D. Oct. 25, 1979, Hazel Crest, Ill.

Year	Team	Games	BA	SA	AB	H	2B	3B	HR	HR%	R	RBI	BB	SO	SB	Pinch Hit AB	Pinch Hit H	PO	A	E	DP	TC/G	FA	G by Pos
1917	CHI N	14	.147	.147	34	5	0	0	0	0.0	3	3	3	10	0	0	0	21	3	1	0	2.1	.960	OF-12

Chuck Schilling

SCHILLING, CHARLES THOMAS BR TR 5′10″ 160 lbs.
B. Oct. 25, 1937, Brooklyn, N. Y.

Year	Team	Games	BA	SA	AB	H	2B	3B	HR	HR%	R	RBI	BB	SO	SB	Pinch Hit AB	Pinch Hit H	PO	A	E	DP	TC/G	FA	G by Pos
1961	BOS A	158	.259	.327	646	167	25	2	5	0.8	87	62	78	77	7	1	0	397	449	8	121	5.4	.991	2B-158
1962		119	.230	.327	413	95	17	1	7	1.7	48	35	29	48	1	0	0	267	331	9	85	5.1	.985	2B-118
1963		146	.234	.319	576	135	25	0	8	1.4	63	33	41	72	3	4	0	276	369	10	74	4.6	.985	2B-143
1964		47	.196	.233	163	32	6	0	0	0.0	18	7	15	22	0	5	3	89	101	5	20	4.6	.974	2B-42
1965		71	.240	.333	171	41	3	2	3	1.8	14	9	13	17	0	28	6	90	116	5	22	5.1	.976	2B-41
5 yrs.		541	.239	.317	1969	470	76	5	23	1.2	230	146	176	236	11	38	9	1119	1366	37	322	5.0	.985	2B-502

Bill Schindler

SCHINDLER, WILLIAM GIBBONS BR TR 5′11″ 160 lbs.
B. July 10, 1896, Perryville, Mo. D. Feb. 6, 1979, Perryville, Mo.

Year	Team	Games	BA	SA	AB	H	2B	3B	HR	HR%	R	RBI	BB	SO	SB	Pinch Hit AB	Pinch Hit H	PO	A	E	DP	TC/G	FA	G by Pos
1920	STL N	1	.000	.000	2	0	0	0	0	0.0	0	0	0	1	0	0	0	3	0	0	0	3.0	1.000	C-1

Dutch Schirick

SCHIRICK, HARRY ERNEST BR TR 5′ 8″ 160 lbs.
B. June 15, 1890, Ruby, N. Y. D. Nov. 12, 1968, Kingston, N. Y.

Year	Team	Games	BA	SA	AB	H	2B	3B	HR	HR%	R	RBI	BB	SO	SB	Pinch Hit AB	Pinch Hit H	PO	A	E	DP	TC/G	FA	G by Pos
1914	STL A	1	—	—	0	0	0	0	0	—	0	0	1	0	2	0	0	0	0	0	0	0.0	—	

Harry Schlafly

SCHLAFLY, HARRY LINTON BR TR 5′11″ 182 lbs.
B. Sept. 20, 1878, Port Washington, Ohio D. June 27, 1919, Canton, Ohio.
Manager 1914–15.

Year	Team	Games	BA	SA	AB	H	2B	3B	HR	HR%	R	RBI	BB	SO	SB	Pinch Hit AB	Pinch Hit H	PO	A	E	DP	TC/G	FA	G by Pos
1902	CHI N	10	.323	.516	31	10	0	3	0	0.0	5	5	6		2	0	0	14	15	3	1	2.9	.906	OF-5, 2B-4, 3B-2
1906	WAS A	123	.246	.329	426	105	13	8	2	0.5	60	30	50		29	0	0	341	358	28	42	5.9	.961	2B-123
1907		24	.135	.216	74	10	0	0	2	2.7	10	4	22		7	0	0	67	49	9	5	5.2	.928	2B-24
1914	BUF F	51	.260	.378	127	33	7	1	2	1.6	16	19	12		3	14	5	116	73	6	9	5.9	.969	2B-23, 1B-7, 3B-1, OF-1, C-1
4 yrs.		208	.240	.334	658	158	20	12	6	0.9	91	58	90		41	14	5	538	495	46	57	5.6	.957	2B-174, 1B-7, OF-6, 3B-3, C-1

Admiral Schlei

SCHLEI, GEORGE HENRY BR TR 5′ 8½″ 179 lbs.
B. Jan. 12, 1878, Cincinnati, Ohio D. Jan. 24, 1958, Huntington, W. Va.

Year	Team	Games	BA	SA	AB	H	2B	3B	HR	HR%	R	RBI	BB	SO	SB	Pinch Hit AB	Pinch Hit H	PO	A	E	DP	TC/G	FA	G by Pos
1904	CIN N	97	.237	.285	291	69	8	3	0	0.0	25	32	17		7	7	1	384	123	12	5	5.9	.977	C-88
1905		99	.226	.280	314	71	8	3	1	0.3	32	36	22		9	4	2	455	156	23	17	6.7	.964	C-89, 1B-6
1906		116	.245	.351	388	95	13	8	4	1.0	44	54	29		7	4	1	671	156	28	21	7.6	.967	C-91, 1B-21
1907		84	.272	.301	246	67	3	2	0	0.0	28	27	28		5	11	3	287	111	10	6	5.7	.975	C-67, 1B-3, OF-2
1908		92	.220	.277	300	66	6	4	1	0.3	31	22	22		2	4	1	355	96	18	10	5.3	.962	C-88
1909	NY N	92	.244	.287	279	68	12	0	0	0.0	25	30	40		4	3	0	493	127	24	9	7.2	.963	C-89
1910		55	.192	.232	99	19	2	1	0	0.0	10	8	14	10	4	6	1	165	43	3	4	4.3	.986	C-49
1911		1	.000	.000	1	0	0	0	0	0.0	0	0	0	1	0	1	0	0	0	0	0	0.0	—	
8 yrs.		636	.237	.296	1918	455	52	21	6	0.3	195	209	172	11	38	40	9	2810	812	118	72	6.3	.968	C-561, 1B-30, OF-2

Rudy Schlesinger

SCHLESINGER, WILLIAM CORDES BR TR 6′ 2″ 175 lbs.
B. Nov. 5, 1941, Cincinnati, Ohio.

Year	Team	Games	BA	SA	AB	H	2B	3B	HR	HR%	R	RBI	BB	SO	SB	Pinch Hit AB	Pinch Hit H	PO	A	E	DP	TC/G	FA	G by Pos
1965	BOS A	1	.000	.000	1	0	0	0	0	0.0	0	0	0	0	0	1	0	0	0	0	0	0.0	—	

Dutch Schliebner

SCHLIEBNER, FREDERICK PAUL BR TR 5′10″ 180 lbs.
B. May 19, 1891, Charlottenburg, Germany D. Apr. 15, 1975, Toledo, Ohio.

Year	Team	Games	BA	SA	AB	H	2B	3B	HR	HR%	R	RBI	BB	SO	SB	Pinch Hit AB	Pinch Hit H	PO	A	E	DP	TC/G	FA	G by Pos
1923	2 teams	BKN N (19G –.250) STL A (127G –.275)																						
″	total	146	.271	.362	520	141	23	6	4	0.8	61	56	44	67	4	0	0	1331	96	17	121	9.9	.988	1B-146

Jay Schlueter

SCHLUETER, JAY D. BR TR 6′ 182 lbs.
B. July 31, 1949, Phoenix, Ariz.

Year	Team	Games	BA	SA	AB	H	2B	3B	HR	HR%	R	RBI	BB	SO	SB	Pinch Hit AB	Pinch Hit H	PO	A	E	DP	TC/G	FA	G by Pos
1971	HOU N	7	.333	.333	3	1	0	0	0	0.0	1	0	0	1	0	2	1	3	0	0	0	1.5	1.000	OF-2

Norm Schlueter

SCHLUETER, NORMAN JOHN BR TR 5′10″ 175 lbs.
B. Sept. 25, 1916, Belleville, Ill.

Year	Team	Games	BA	SA	AB	H	2B	3B	HR	HR%	R	RBI	BB	SO	SB	Pinch Hit AB	Pinch Hit H	PO	A	E	DP	TC/G	FA	G by Pos
1938	CHI A	35	.229	.288	118	27	5	1	0	0.0	11	7	4	15	1	1	0	107	13	6	3	3.7	.952	C-34
1939		34	.232	.304	56	13	2	1	0	0.0	5	8	1	11	2	2	0	81	2	1	0	2.6	.988	C-32
1944	CLE A	49	.123	.156	122	15	4	0	0	0.0	2	11	12	22	0	6	0	122	9	2	4	3.1	.985	C-43
3 yrs.		118	.186	.236	296	55	11	2	0	0.0	18	26	17	48	3	9	0	310	24	9	7	3.1	.974	C-109

Ray Schmandt

SCHMANDT, RAYMOND HENRY BR TR 6′ 1″ 175 lbs.
B. Jan. 25, 1896, St. Louis, Mo. D. Feb. 2, 1969, St. Louis, Mo.

Year	Team	Games	BA	SA	AB	H	2B	3B	HR	HR%	R	RBI	BB	SO	SB	Pinch Hit AB	Pinch Hit H	PO	A	E	DP	TC/G	FA	G by Pos
1915	STL A	3	.000	.000	4	0	0	0	0	0.0	0	0	0	1	0	2	0	8	0	0	0	8.0	1.000	1B-1
1918	BKN N	34	.307	.421	114	35	5	4	0	0.0	11	18	7	7	1	0	0	79	90	12	8	5.3	.934	2B-34
1919		47	.165	.197	127	21	4	0	0	0.0	8	10	4	13	0	10	2	138	66	11	13	6.0	.949	2B-18, 1B-12, 3B-6
1920		28	.238	.302	63	15	2	1	0	0.0	7	7	3	4	1	6	3	165	17	1	16	9.1	.995	1B-20
1921		95	.306	.366	350	107	8	5	1	0.3	42	43	11	22	3	2	0	941	52	11	74	10.9	.989	1B-92
1922		110	.268	.341	396	106	17	3	2	0.5	54	44	21	28	6	0	0	1017	65	12	83	9.9	.989	1B-110
6 yrs.		317	.269	.337	1054	284	36	13	3	0.3	122	122	46	75	11	20	5	2348	290	47	194	9.2	.982	1B-235, 2B-52, 3B-6
WORLD SERIES																								
1920	BKN N	1	.000	.000	1	0	0	0	0	0.0	0	0	0	0	0	1	0	0	0	0	0	0.0	—	

George Schmees

SCHMEES, GEORGE EDWARD (Rocky) BL TL 6′ 190 lbs.
B. Sept. 6, 1924, Cincinnati, Ohio.

Year	Team	Games	BA	SA	AB	H	2B	3B	HR	HR%	R	RBI	BB	SO	SB	Pinch Hit AB	Pinch Hit H	PO	A	E	DP	TC/G	FA	G by Pos
1952	2 teams	STL A (34G –.131) BOS A (42G –.203)																						
″	total	76	.168	.216	125	21	4	1	0	0.0	17	6	12	29	0	12	0	91	7	4	1	1.9	.961	OF-48, 1B-4, P-2

Bob Schmidt

SCHMIDT, ROBERT BENJAMIN BR TR 6′ 2″ 205 lbs.
B. Apr. 22, 1933, St. Louis, Mo.

Year	Team	Games	BA	SA	AB	H	2B	3B	HR	HR%	R	RBI	BB	SO	SB	Pinch Hit AB	Pinch Hit H	PO	A	E	DP	TC/G	FA	G by Pos
1958	SF N	127	.244	.412	393	96	20	2	14	3.6	46	54	33	59	0	6	2	616	54	12	10	5.5	.982	C-123
1959		71	.243	.376	181	44	7	1	5	2.8	17	20	13	24	0	3	0	307	30	0	1	4.8	1.000	C-70
1960		110	.267	.378	344	92	12	1	8	2.3	31	37	26	51	0	3	0	631	31	13	6	6.3	.981	C-108

Bob Schmidt *continued*

Year	Team	Games	BA	SA	AB	H	2B	3B	HR	HR%	R	RBI	BB	SO	SB	Pinch Hit AB	Pinch Hit H	PO	A	E	DP	TC/G	FA	G by Pos
1961	2 teams	SF N (2G –.167) CIN N (27G –.129)																						
"	total	29	.132	.171	76	10	0	0	1	1.3	4	5	8	15	0	0	0	154	7	1	1	5.6	.994	C-29
1962	WAS A	88	.242	.414	256	62	14	0	10	3.9	28	31	14	37	0	4	1	342	40	1	3	4.4	.997	C-88
1963		9	.200	.267	15	3	1	0	0	0.0	3	0	3	5	0	5	0	18	0	0	0	3.0	1.000	C-6
1965	NY A	20	.250	.350	40	10	1	0	1	2.5	4	3	3	8	0	0	0	93	4	1	0	4.9	.990	C-20
7 yrs.		454	.243	.381	1305	317	55	4	39	3.0	133	150	100	199	0	21	3	2161	166	28	21	5.3	.988	C-444

Boss Schmidt

SCHMIDT, CHARLES BB TR 5′11″ 200 lbs.
Brother of Walter Schmidt.
B. Sept. 12, 1880, Coal Hill, Ark. D. Nov. 14, 1932, Clarksville, Ark.

Year	Team	Games	BA	SA	AB	H	2B	3B	HR	HR%	R	RBI	BB	SO	SB	Pinch Hit AB	Pinch Hit H	PO	A	E	DP	TC/G	FA	G by Pos
1906	DET A	68	.218	.264	216	47	4	3	0	0.0	13	10	6		1	1	0	257	104	16	4	5.6	.958	C-67
1907		104	.244	.295	349	85	6	6	0	0.0	32	23	5		8	1	0	446	132	34	14	5.9	.944	C-104
1908		122	.265	.320	419	111	14	3	1	0.2	45	38	16		5	1	1	541	184	37	12	6.3	.951	C-121
1909		84	.209	.269	253	53	8	2	1	0.4	21	28	7		7	2	1	315	107	20	7	5.4	.955	C-81, OF-1
1910		71	.259	.381	197	51	7	7	1	0.5	22	23	2		2	5	2	239	80	9	1	5.0	.973	C-66
1911		28	.283	.370	46	13	2	1	0	0.0	4	2	0		0	17	6	29	10	0	0	3.9	1.000	C-9, OF-1
6 yrs.		477	.243	.307	1480	360	41	22	3	0.2	137	124	36		23	27	10	1827	617	116	38	5.7	.955	C-448, OF-2
WORLD SERIES																								
1907	DET A	4	.167	.167	12	2	0	0	0	0.0	0	0	2	1	0	1	0	16	9	2	0	9.0	.926	C-3
1908		4	.071	.071	14	1	0	0	0	0.0	0	1	0	2	0	0	0	22	7	0	1	7.3	1.000	C-4
1909		6	.222	.333	18	4	2	0	0	0.0	0	4	2	0	0	0	0	31	11	5	3	7.8	.894	C-6
3 yrs.		14	.159	.205	44	7	2	0	0	0.0	0	5	4	3	0	1	0	69	27	7	4	7.9	.932	C-13

Butch Schmidt

SCHMIDT, CHARLES JOHN BL TL 6′ 1½″ 200 lbs.
B. July 19, 1886, Baltimore, Md. D. Sept. 4, 1952, Baltimore, Md.

Year	Team	Games	BA	SA	AB	H	2B	3B	HR	HR%	R	RBI	BB	SO	SB	Pinch Hit AB	Pinch Hit H	PO	A	E	DP	TC/G	FA	G by Pos
1909	NY A	1	.000	.000	2	0	0	0	0	0.0	0	0	0		0	0	0	0	1	1	0	2.0	.500	P-1
1913	BOS N	22	.308	.423	78	24	2	2	1	1.3	6	14	2	5	1	0	0	166	12	3	5	8.2	.983	1B-22
1914		147	.285	.356	537	153	17	9	1	0.2	67	71	43	55	14	0	0	1485	88	16	109	10.8	.990	1B-147
1915		127	.251	.352	458	115	26	7	2	0.4	46	60	36	59	3	0	0	1221	60	17	80	10.2	.987	1B-127
4 yrs.		297	.272	.358	1075	292	45	18	4	0.4	119	145	81	119	18	0	0	2872	161	37	194	10.3	.988	1B-296, P-1
WORLD SERIES																								
1914	BOS N	4	.294	.294	17	5	0	0	0	0.0	2	2	0	2	1	0	0	52	3	0	3	13.8	1.000	1B-4

Dave Schmidt

SCHMIDT, DAVID FREDERICK BR TR 6′ 1″ 190 lbs.
B. Dec. 22, 1956, Mesa, Ariz.

Year	Team	Games	BA	SA	AB	H	2B	3B	HR	HR%	R	RBI	BB	SO	SB	Pinch Hit AB	Pinch Hit H	PO	A	E	DP	TC/G	FA	G by Pos
1981	BOS A	15	.238	.405	42	10	1	0	2	4.8	6	3	7	17	0	1	1	53	4	0	0	3.8	1.000	C-15

Mike Schmidt

SCHMIDT, MICHAEL JACK BR TR 6′ 2″ 195 lbs.
B. Sept. 27, 1949, Dayton, Ohio.
Hall of Fame 1995.

Year	Team	Games	BA	SA	AB	H	2B	3B	HR	HR%	R	RBI	BB	SO	SB	Pinch Hit AB	Pinch Hit H	PO	A	E	DP	TC/G	FA	G by Pos
1972	PHI N	13	.206	.294	34	7	0	0	1	2.9	2	3	5	15	0	1	0	10	25	2	3	3.1	.946	3B-11, 2B-1
1973		132	.196	.373	367	72	11	0	18	4.9	43	52	62	136	8	9	2	119	256	18	32	3.0	.954	3B-125, 2B-4, 1B-2, SS-2
1974		162	.282	**.546**	568	160	28	7	**36**	**6.3**	108	116	106	**138**	23	0	0	134	404	26	40	3.5	.954	3B-162
1975		158	.249	.523	562	140	34	3	**38**	6.8	93	95	101	**180**	29	1	0	139	390	26	32	3.4	.953	3B-151, SS-10
1976		160	.262	.524	584	153	31	4	**38**	6.5	112	107	100	**149**	14	0	0	139	377	21	29	3.4	.961	3B-160
1977		154	.274	.574	544	149	27	11	38	7.0	114	101	104	122	15	2	0	109	401	20	34	3.5	.962	3B-149, SS-2, 2B-1
1978		145	.251	.435	513	129	27	2	21	4.1	93	78	91	103	19	4	1	98	325	16	34	3.1	.964	3B-139, SS-1
1979		160	.253	.564	541	137	25	4	45	8.3	109	114	**120**	115	9	2	0	115	363	23	38	3.2	.954	3B-157, SS-2
1980		150	.286	**.624**	548	157	25	8	**48**	**8.8**	104	**121**	89	119	12	1	0	98	372	27	31	3.3	.946	3B-149
1981		102	.316	**.644**	354	112	19	2	**31**	**8.8**	**78**	**91**	**73**	71	12	1	1	74	249	15	20	3.3	.956	3B-101
1982		148	.280	**.547**	514	144	26	3	35	6.8	108	87	**107**	131	14	0	0	110	324	23	28	3.1	.950	3B-148
1983		154	.255	.524	534	136	16	4	**40**	**7.5**	104	109	**128**	**148**	7	0	0	108	333	19	29	3.0	.959	3B-153, SS-2
1984		151	.277	.536	528	146	23	3	**36**	**6.8**	93	**106**	92	116	5	4	3	93	330	26	20	3.0	.942	3B-145, 1B-2, SS-1
1985		158	.277	.532	549	152	31	5	33	6.0	89	93	87	117	1	4	1	911	193	18	97	7.0	.984	1B-106, 3B-54, SS-1
1986		160	.290	**.547**	552	160	29	1	**37**	**6.7**	97	**119**	89	84	1	8	2	347	238	8	53	3.7	.987	3B-124, 1B-35
1987		147	.293	.548	522	153	28	0	35	6.7	88	113	83	80	2	6	1	138	319	13	35	3.1	.972	3B-138, 1B-9, SS-3
1988		108	.249	.405	390	97	21	2	12	3.1	52	62	49	42	3	5	0	76	223	19	17	3.0	.940	3B-104, 1B-3
1989		42	.203	.372	148	30	7	0	6	4.1	19	28	21	17	0	0	0	18	71	8	8	2.3	.918	3B-42
18 yrs.		2404	.267	.527	8352	2234	408	59	548 **7th**	6.6 **8th**	1506	1595	1507	1883 **3rd**	174	48	11	2836	5193	328	580	3.5	.961	3B-2212, 1B-157, SS-24, 2B-6
DIVISIONAL PLAYOFF SERIES																								
1981	PHI N	5	.250	.500	16	4	1	0	1	6.3	3	2	4	2	0	0	0	6	10	1	0	3.4	.941	3B-5
LEAGUE CHAMPIONSHIP SERIES																								
1976	PHI N	3	.308	.462	13	4	2	0	0	0.0	1	2	0	1	0	0	0	4	9	1	2	4.7	.929	3B-3
1977		4	.063	.063	16	1	0	0	0	0.0	2	1	2	3	0	0	0	4	15	0	0	4.8	1.000	3B-4
1978		4	.200	.333	15	3	2	0	0	0.0	1	1	2	2	0	0	0	3	18	2	0	5.8	.913	3B-4
1980		5	.208	.250	24	5	1	0	0	0.0	1	1	1	6	1	0	0	3	17	1	2	4.2	.952	3B-5
1983		4	.467	.800	15	7	2	0	1	6.7	5	2	2	3	0	0	0	6	8	1	0	3.8	.933	3B-4
5 yrs.		20	.241	.361	83	20	7 **1st**	0	1	1.2	10	7	7	15	1	0	0	20	67	5	4	4.6	.946	3B-20
WORLD SERIES																								
1980	PHI N	6	.381	.714	21	8	1	0	2	9.5	6	7	4	3	0	0	0	9	8	0	1	2.8	1.000	3B-6
1983		5	.050	.050	20	1	0	0	0	0.0	0	0	0	6	0	0	0	1	10	1	1	2.4	.917	3B-5
2 yrs.		11	.220	.390	41	9	1	0	2	4.9	6	7	4	9	0	0	0	10	18	1	2	2.6	.966	3B-11

Walter Schmidt

SCHMIDT, WALTER JOSEPH BR TR 5′ 9″ 159 lbs.
Brother of Boss Schmidt.
B. Mar. 20, 1887, Coal Hill, Ark. D. July 4, 1973, Modesto, Calif.

Year	Team	Games	BA	SA	AB	H	2B	3B	HR	HR%	R	RBI	BB	SO	SB	Pinch Hit AB	Pinch Hit H	PO	A	E	DP	TC/G	FA	G by Pos
1916	PIT N	64	.190	.250	184	35	1	2	2	1.1	16	15	10	13	3	3	1	232	88	8	6	5.8	.976	C-57
1917		75	.246	.284	183	45	7	0	0	0.0	9	17	11	11	4	7	1	229	84	7	9	5.2	.978	C-61
1918		105	.238	.276	323	77	6	3	0	0.0	31	27	17	19	7	1	1	373	153	10	19	5.2	.981	C-104

Walter Schmidt *continued*

Year	Team	Games	BA	SA	AB	H	2B	3B	HR	HR%	R	RBI	BB	SO	SB	Pinch Hit AB	Pinch Hit H	PO	A	E	DP	TC/G	FA	G by Pos
1919		85	.251	.300	267	67	9	2	0	0.0	23	29	23	9	5	0	0	315	110	8	8	5.1	.982	C-85
1920		94	.277	.329	310	86	8	4	0	0.0	22	20	24	15	9	1	0	323	109	13	10	4.8	.971	C-92
1921		114	.282	.321	393	111	9	3	0	0.0	30	38	12	13	10	3	0	438	120	8	15	5.1	.986	C-111
1922		40	.329	.414	152	50	11	1	0	0.0	21	22	1	5	2	0	0	159	22	1	1	4.6	.995	C-40
1923		97	.248	.281	335	83	7	2	0	0.0	39	37	22	12	10	1	1	279	88	7	10	3.9	.981	C-96
1924		58	.243	.299	177	43	3	2	1	0.6	16	20	13	5	6	0	0	166	51	3	6	3.9	.986	C-57
1925	**STL N**	37	.253	.299	87	22	2	1	0	0.0	9	9	4	3	1	4	1	84	33	4	2	3.9	.967	C-31
10 yrs.		769	.257	.303	2411	619	63	20	3	0.1	216	234	137	105	57	20	5	2598	858	69	86	4.8	.980	C-734

Hank Schmulbach

SCHMULBACH, HENRY ALRIVES BL TR 5′11″ 165 lbs.
B. Jan. 17, 1925, East St. Louis, Ill.

Year	Team	Games	BA	SA	AB	H	2B	3B	HR	HR%	R	RBI	BB	SO	SB	Pinch Hit AB	Pinch Hit H	PO	A	E	DP	TC/G	FA	G by Pos
1943	**STL A**	1	—	—	0	0	0	0	0	—	1	0	0	0	0	0	0	0	0	0	0	0.0	—	

Dave Schneck

SCHNECK, DAVID LEE BL TL 5′10″ 200 lbs.
B. June 18, 1949, Allentown, Pa.

Year	Team	Games	BA	SA	AB	H	2B	3B	HR	HR%	R	RBI	BB	SO	SB	Pinch Hit AB	Pinch Hit H	PO	A	E	DP	TC/G	FA	G by Pos
1972	**NY N**	37	.187	.317	123	23	3	2	3	2.4	7	10	10	26	0	4	0	63	1	1	0	2.0	.985	OF-33
1973		13	.194	.250	36	7	0	1	0	0.0	2	0	1	4	0	1	0	28	0	0	0	2.3	1.000	OF-12
1974		93	.205	.315	254	52	11	1	5	2.0	23	25	16	43	4	6	1	179	7	5	2	2.3	.974	OF-84
3 yrs.		143	.199	.310	413	82	14	4	8	1.9	32	35	27	73	4	11	1	270	8	6	2	2.2	.979	OF-129

Red Schoendienst

SCHOENDIENST, ALBERT FRED BB TR 6′ 170 lbs.
B. Feb. 2, 1923, Germantown, Ill.
Manager 1965–76, 1980, 1990.
Hall of Fame 1989.

Year	Team	Games	BA	SA	AB	H	2B	3B	HR	HR%	R	RBI	BB	SO	SB	Pinch Hit AB	Pinch Hit H	PO	A	E	DP	TC/G	FA	G by Pos
1945	**STL N**	137	.278	.343	565	157	22	6	1	0.2	89	47	21	17	**26**	7	2	302	30	10	11	2.7	.971	OF-118, SS-10, 2B-1
1946		142	.281	.343	606	170	28	5	0	0.0	94	34	37	27	12	1	0	363	379	13	96	5.2	.983	2B-128, 3B-12, SS-4
1947		151	.253	.332	**659**	167	25	9	3	0.5	91	48	48	27	6	3	1	364	417	19	111	5.4	.976	2B-142, 3B-5, OF-1
1948		119	.272	.373	408	111	21	4	4	1.0	64	36	28	16	1	17	4	230	269	10	57	5.3	.980	2B-96
1949		151	.297	.356	640	190	25	2	3	0.5	102	54	51	18	8	1	1	428	471	16	110	5.7	.983	2B-138, SS-14, 3B-6, OF-2
1950		153	.276	.403	**642**	177	**43**	9	7	1.1	81	63	33	32	3	0	0	425	437	14	134	5.7	.984	2B-143, SS-10, 3B-1
1951		135	.289	.405	553	160	32	7	6	1.1	88	54	35	23	0	1	1	354	419	10	120	5.9	.987	2B-124, SS-8
1952		152	.303	.424	620	188	40	7	7	1.1	91	67	42	30	9	0	0	417	460	20	111	5.8	.978	2B-142, 3B-11, SS-3
1953		146	.342	.502	564	193	35	5	15	2.7	107	79	60	23	3	6	4	365	430	14	109	5.8	.983	2B-140
1954		148	.315	.428	610	192	38	8	5	0.8	98	79	54	22	4	4	1	394	477	18	137	6.2	.980	2B-144
1955		145	.268	.376	553	148	21	3	11	2.0	68	51	54	28	7	2	0	296	381	10	96	4.8	.985	2B-142
1956	**2 teams**	**STL N** (40G –.314) **NY N** (92G –.296)																						
″	**total**	132	.302	.370	487	147	21	3	2	0.4	61	29	41	15	1	10	4	298	308	4	74	5.0	.993	2B-121
1957	**2 teams**	**NY N** (57G –.307) **MIL N** (93G –.310)																						
″	**total**	150	.309	.451	648	**200**	31	8	15	2.3	91	65	33	15	4	1	0	379	448	12	113	5.6	.986	2B-149, OF-2
1958	**MIL N**	106	.262	.328	427	112	23	1	1	0.2	47	24	31	21	3	2	0	233	301	7	77	5.2	.987	2B-105
1959		5	.000	.000	3	0	0	0	0	0.0	0	0	0	0	0	1	0	1	1	1	0	0.8	.667	2B-4
1960		68	.257	.319	226	58	9	1	1	0.4	21	19	17	13	1	4	0	120	148	10	34	4.5	.964	2B-62
1961	**STL N**	72	.300	.400	120	36	9	0	1	0.8	9	12	12	6	1	48	16	43	42	4	10	2.8	.955	2B-32
1962		98	.301	.371	143	43	4	0	2	1.4	21	12	9	12	0	**72**	**22**	33	48	1	10	3.3	.988	2B-21, 3B-4
1963		6	.000	.000	5	0	0	0	0	0.0	0	0	0	1	0	5	0	0	0	0	0	0.0	—	
19 yrs.		2216	.289	.387	8479	2449	427	78	84	1.0	1223	773	606	346	89	185	56	5045	5466	193	1410	5.2	.982	2B-1834, OF-123, SS-49, 3B-39
WORLD SERIES																								
1946	**STL N**	7	.233	.267	30	7	1	0	0	0.0	3	1	0	2	1	0	0	17	21	1	5	5.6	.974	2B-7
1957	**MIL N**	5	.278	.333	18	5	1	0	0	0.0	0	2	0	1	0	0	0	5	10	0	4	3.0	1.000	2B-5
1958		7	.300	.467	30	9	3	1	0	0.0	5	0	2	1	0	0	0	18	19	1	3	5.4	.974	2B-7
3 yrs.		19	.269	.359	78	21	5	1	0	0.0	8	3	2	4	1	0	0	40	50	2	12	4.8	.978	2B-19

Jumbo Schoeneck

SCHOENECK, LEWIS W. (Lon) BR TR 6′2″ 223 lbs.
B. Mar. 3, 1862, Chicago, Ill. D. Jan. 20, 1930, Chicago, Ill.

Year	Team	Games	BA	SA	AB	H	2B	3B	HR	HR%	R	RBI	BB	SO	SB	Pinch Hit AB	Pinch Hit H	PO	A	E	DP	TC/G	FA	G by Pos
1884	**3 teams**	**CHI U** (72G –.325) **PIT U** (18G –.286) **BAL U** (16G –.250)																						
″	**total**	106	.308	.387	426	131	24	2	2	0.5	61		8			0	0	1063	31	49	30	10.8	.957	1B-105, SS-1
1888	**IND N**	48	.237	.260	169	40	4	0	0	0.0	15	20	9	24	11	0	0	501	16	14	19	10.6	.974	1B-48, P-2
1889		16	.242	.339	62	15	2	2	0	0.0	3	8	3	3	1	0	0	164	12	4	7	11.3	.978	1B-16
3 yrs.		170	.283	.350	657	186	30	4	2	0.3	79	28	20	27	12	0	0	1728	59	67	56	10.8	.964	1B-169, P-2, SS-1

Dick Schofield

SCHOFIELD, JOHN RICHARD (Ducky) BB TR 5′9″ 163 lbs.
Father of Dick Schofield.
B. Jan. 7, 1935, Springfield, Ill.

Year	Team	Games	BA	SA	AB	H	2B	3B	HR	HR%	R	RBI	BB	SO	SB	Pinch Hit AB	Pinch Hit H	PO	A	E	DP	TC/G	FA	G by Pos
1953	**STL N**	33	.179	.333	39	7	0	0	2	5.1	9	4	2	11	0	1	0	19	36	5	8	4.0	.917	SS-15
1954		43	.143	.429	7	1	0	1	0	0.0	17	1	0	3	1	3	1	4	3	0	1	0.6	1.000	SS-11
1955		12	.000	.000	4	0	0	0	0	0.0	3	0	0	1	0	2	0	1	1	0	0	0.7	1.000	SS-3
1956		16	.100	.167	30	3	2	0	0	0.0	3	1	0	6	0	4	0	11	13	2	4	2.9	.923	SS-9
1957		65	.161	.161	56	9	0	0	0	0.0	10	1	7	13	1	11	1	21	34	3	8	2.5	.948	SS-23
1958	**2 teams**	**STL N** (39G –.213) **PIT N** (26G –.148)																						
″	**total**	65	.200	.267	135	27	4	1	1	0.7	20	10	26	21	0	14	3	54	96	9	18	4.7	.943	SS-32, 3B-2
1959	**PIT N**	81	.234	.338	145	34	10	1	1	0.7	21	9	16	22	1	14	3	90	105	7	25	5.2	.965	2B-28, SS-8, OF-3
1960		65	.333	.392	102	34	4	1	0	0.0	9	10	16	20	0	19	5	58	78	6	18	4.2	.958	SS-23, 2B-10, 3B-1
1961		60	.192	.244	78	15	2	1	0	0.0	16	2	10	19	0	18	3	30	54	4	10	3.1	.955	3B-11, SS-9, 2B-5, OF-3
1962		54	.288	.375	104	30	3	0	2	1.9	19	10	17	22	0	26	8	18	37	3	4	2.5	.948	3B-20, 2B-2, SS-1
1963		138	.246	.303	541	133	18	2	3	0.6	54	32	69	83	2	0	0	279	422	23	107	5.2	.968	SS-117, 2B-20, 3B-1
1964		121	.246	.349	398	98	22	5	3	0.8	50	36	54	60	1	10	0	184	349	28	78	5.1	.950	SS-111
1965	**2 teams**	**PIT N** (31G –.229) **SF N** (101G –.203)																						
″	**total**	132	.209	.256	488	102	15	1	2	0.4	52	25	48	69	3	11	1	194	373	11	78	4.8	.981	SS-121
1966	**3 teams**	**SF N** (11G –.063) **NY A** (25G –.155) **LA N** (20G –.257)																						
″	**total**	56	.194	.208	144	28	2	0	0	0.0	19	6	19	18	1	4	1	47	121	13	14	3.7	.928	SS-30, 3B-19
1967	**LA N**	84	.216	.293	232	50	10	1	2	0.9	23	15	31	40	1	6	0	109	218	8	37	4.5	.976	SS-69, 2B-4, 3B-2

Dick Schofield *continued*

Year	Team	Games	BA	SA	AB	H	2B	3B	HR	HR%	R	RBI	BB	SO	SB	Pinch Hit AB	Pinch Hit H	PO	A	E	DP	TC/G	FA	G by Pos
1968	STL N	69	.220	.315	127	28	7	1	1	0.8	14	8	13	31	1	11	0	109	116	6	22	3.5	.974	SS-43, 2B-23
1969	BOS A	94	.257	.350	226	58	9	3	2	0.9	30	20	29	44	0	33	11	97	150	7	30	4.1	.972	2B-37, SS-11, 3B-9, OF-5
1970		76	.187	.245	139	26	1	2	1	0.7	16	14	21	26	0	43	7	37	64	6	8	3.2	.944	2B-15, 3B-15, SS-3
1971	2 teams	STL N (34G –.217) MIL A (23G –.107)																						
"	total	57	.182	.261	88	16	4	0	1	1.1	9	7	12	17	0	17	5	35	71	3	14	2.1	.972	SS-21, 2B-15, 3B-15
19 yrs.		1321	.227	.297	3083	699	113	20	21	0.7	394	211	390	526	12	247	49	1397	2341	144	484	4.2	.963	SS-660, 2B-159, 3B-95, OF-11
WORLD SERIES																								
1960	PIT N	3	.333	.333	3	1	0	0	0	0.0	0	0	1	0	0	3	1	2	0	0	0	1.0	1.000	SS-2
1968	STL N	2	—	—	0	0	0	0	0	—	0	0	0	0	0	0	0	0	0	0	0	0.0	—	
2 yrs.		5	.333	.333	3	1	0	0	0	0.0	0	0	1	0	0	3	1	2	0	0	0	1.0	1.000	SS-2

Dick Schofield

SCHOFIELD, RICHARD CRAIG BR TR 5′10″ 175 lbs.
Son of Dick Schofield.
B. Nov. 21, 1962, Springfield, Ill.

Year	Team	Games	BA	SA	AB	H	2B	3B	HR	HR%	R	RBI	BB	SO	SB	Pinch Hit AB	Pinch Hit H	PO	A	E	DP	TC/G	FA	G by Pos
1983	CAL A	21	.204	.407	54	11	2	0	3	5.6	4	4	6	8	0	0	0	24	67	7	10	4.7	.929	SS-21
1984		140	.193	.263	400	77	10	3	4	1.0	39	21	33	79	4	0	0	218	420	12	95	4.6	.982	SS-140
1985		147	.219	.331	438	96	19	3	8	1.8	50	41	35	70	11	1	0	261	397	25	108	4.6	.963	SS-147
1986		139	.249	.397	458	114	17	6	13	2.8	67	57	48	55	23	0	0	246	389	18	103	4.8	.972	SS-137
1987		134	.251	.355	479	120	17	3	9	1.9	52	46	37	63	19	0	0	205	351	9	76	4.2	.984	SS-131, 2B-2, DH-1
1988		155	.239	.317	527	126	11	6	6	1.1	61	34	40	57	20	0	0	278	492	13	125	5.1	.983	SS-155
1989		91	.228	.318	302	69	11	2	4	1.3	42	26	28	47	9	1	1	118	276	7	56	4.5	.983	SS-90
1990		99	.255	.297	310	79	8	1	1	0.3	41	18	52	61	3	0	0	170	318	17	77	5.1	.966	SS-99
1991		134	.225	.260	427	96	9	3	0	0.0	44	31	50	69	8	3	0	186	398	15	83	4.5	.975	SS-133
1992	2 teams	CAL A (1G –.333) NY N (142G –.205)																						
"	total	143	.206	.286	423	87	18	2	4	0.9	52	36	61	82	11	0	0	208	392	7	78	4.3	.988	SS-142
1993	TOR A	36	.191	.236	110	21	1	2	0	0.0	11	5	16	25	3	0	0	61	106	4	23	4.8	.977	SS-36
1994		95	.255	.342	325	83	14	1	4	1.2	38	32	34	62	7	0	0	150	235	11	58	4.2	.972	SS-95
1995	2 teams	LA N (9G –.100) CAL A (12G –.250)																						
"	total	21	.200	.200	30	6	0	0	0	0.0	1	2	5	5	0	6	1	11	32	0	5	2.7	1.000	SS-15, 3B-1
13 yrs.		1355	.230	.316	4283	985	137	32	56	1.3	502	353	445	683	118	11	2	2136	3873	145	897	4.6	.976	SS-1341, 2B-2, 3B-1, DH-1
LEAGUE CHAMPIONSHIP SERIES																								
1986	CAL A	7	.300	.433	30	9	1	0	1	3.3	4	2	1	5	1	0	0	12	23	2	3	5.3	.946	SS-7

Otto Schomberg

SCHOMBERG, OTTO H. BL TL
Born Otto H. Shambrick.
B. Nov. 14, 1864, Milwaukee, Wis. D. May 3, 1927, Ottawa, Kans.

Year	Team	Games	BA	SA	AB	H	2B	3B	HR	HR%	R	RBI	BB	SO	SB	Pinch Hit AB	Pinch Hit H	PO	A	E	DP	TC/G	FA	G by Pos
1886	PIT AA	72	.272	.358	246	67	6	6	1	0.4	53		57			0	0	702	6	25	34	10.2	.966	1B-72
1887	IND N	112	.308	.463	419	129	18	16	5	1.2	91	83	56	32	21	0	0	1216	28	55	76	11.5	.958	1B-112, OF-1
1888		30	.214	.304	112	24	5	1	1	0.9	11	10	10	12	6	0	0	151	3	8	8	5.4	.951	OF-15, 1B-15
3 yrs.		214	.283	.407	777	220	29	23	7	0.9	155	93	123	44	27	0	0	2069	37	88	118	10.2	.960	1B-199, OF-16

Jerry Schoonmaker

SCHOONMAKER, JERALD LEE BR TR 5′11″ 190 lbs.
B. Dec. 14, 1933, Seymour, Mo.

Year	Team	Games	BA	SA	AB	H	2B	3B	HR	HR%	R	RBI	BB	SO	SB	Pinch Hit AB	Pinch Hit H	PO	A	E	DP	TC/G	FA	G by Pos
1955	WAS A	20	.152	.261	46	7	0	1	1	2.2	5	4	5	11	1	3	0	22	2	1	0	1.7	.960	OF-15
1957		30	.087	.130	23	2	1	0	0	0.0	5	0	2	11	0	7	0	15	0	0	0	1.2	1.000	OF-13
2 yrs.		50	.130	.217	69	9	1	1	1	1.4	10	4	7	22	1	10	0	37	2	1	0	1.4	.975	OF-28

Paul Schramka

SCHRAMKA, PAUL EDWARD BL TL 6′ 185 lbs.
B. Mar. 22, 1928, Milwaukee, Wis.

Year	Team	Games	BA	SA	AB	H	2B	3B	HR	HR%	R	RBI	BB	SO	SB	Pinch Hit AB	Pinch Hit H	PO	A	E	DP	TC/G	FA	G by Pos
1953	CHI N	2	—	—	0	0	0	0	0	—	0	0	0	0	0	0	0	0	0	0	0	0.0	.000	OF-1

Ossee Schreckengost

SCHRECKENGOST, OSSEE FREEMAN BR TR 5′10″ 180 lbs.
B. Apr. 11, 1875, New Bethlehem, Pa. D. July 9, 1914, Philadelphia, Pa.

Year	Team	Games	BA	SA	AB	H	2B	3B	HR	HR%	R	RBI	BB	SO	SB	Pinch Hit AB	Pinch Hit H	PO	A	E	DP	TC/G	FA	G by Pos
1897	LOU N	1	.000	.000	3	0	0	0	0	0.0	0	0	0		0	0	0	2	1	0	0	3.0	1.000	C-1
1898	CLE N	10	.314	.543	35	11	2	3	0	0.0	5	10	0		1	1	0	33	10	7	1	5.6	.860	C-9
1899	2 teams	STL N (72G –.278) CLE N (43G –.313)																						
"	total	115	.290	.375	427	124	20	5	2	0.5	57	47	21		18	6	0	637	110	40	41	7.1	.949	C-64, 1B-43, OF-2, 2B-1, SS-1
1901	BOS A	86	.304	.386	280	85	13	5	0	0.0	37	38	19		6	9	**3**	301	102	30	9	5.7	.931	C-72, 1B-4
1902	2 teams	CLE A (18G –.338) PHI A (79G –.324)																						
"	total	97	.327	.402	358	117	17	2	2	0.6	50	52	9		5	2	0	619	117	28	11	8.0	.963	C-71, 1B-24, OF-1
1903	PHI A	92	.255	.353	306	78	13	4	3	1.0	26	30	11		0	5	1	597	110	18	8	8.3	.975	C-77, 1B-10
1904		95	.186	.232	311	58	9	1	1	0.3	23	21	5		3	3	1	666	77	14	5	8.1	.982	C-84, 1B-9
1905		121	.272	.346	416	113	19	6	0	0.0	30	45	3		9	7	1	800	114	15	11	8.1	.984	C-112, 1B-2
1906		98	.284	.358	338	96	20	1	1	0.3	29	41	10		5	5	0	568	112	19	8	7.5	.973	C-89, 1B-4
1907		101	.272	.334	356	97	16	3	0	0.0	30	38	17		4	2	0	643	145	12	4	7.9	.985	C-99, 1B-2
1908	2 teams	PHI A (71G –.222) CHI A (6G –.188)																						
"	total	77	.220	.260	223	49	7	1	0	0.0	17	16	7		1	5	3	404	96	11	5	7.0	.978	C-72, 1B-1
11 yrs.		893	.271	.345	3053	828	136	31	9	0.3	304	338	102		52	45	9	5270	994	194	103	7.6	.970	C-750, 1B-99, OF-3, 2B-1, SS-1
WORLD SERIES																								
1905	PHI A	3	.222	.333	9	2	1	0	0	0.0	2	0	0	0	0	0	0	17	4	0	1	7.0	1.000	C-3

Hank Schreiber

SCHREIBER, HENRY WALTER BR TR 5′11″ 165 lbs.
B. July 12, 1891, Cleveland, Ohio D. Feb. 23, 1968, Indianapolis, Ind.

Year	Team	Games	BA	SA	AB	H	2B	3B	HR	HR%	R	RBI	BB	SO	SB	Pinch Hit AB	Pinch Hit H	PO	A	E	DP	TC/G	FA	G by Pos
1914	CHI A	1	.000	.000	2	0	0	0	0	0.0	0	0	0	1	0	0	0	0	0	0	0	0.0	.000	OF-1
1917	BOS N	2	.286	.286	7	2	0	0	0	0.0	1	0	0	1	0	0	0	3	1	0	0	2.0	1.000	SS-1, 3B-1
1919	CIN N	19	.224	.293	58	13	4	0	0	0.0	5	4	0	12	0	0	0	14	50	1	6	3.4	.985	3B-17, SS-2
1921	NY N	4	.333	.333	6	2	0	0	0	0.0	2	2	1	1	0	0	0	5	6	2	0	2.6	.846	2B-2, SS-2, 3B-1
1926	CHI N	10	.056	.111	18	1	1	0	0	0.0	2	0	0	1	0	0	0	7	11	0	0	2.6	1.000	3B-3, SS-3, 2B-1
5 yrs.		36	.198	.253	91	18	5	0	0	0.0	10	6	1	16	0	0	0	29	68	3	6	2.9	.970	3B-22, SS-8, 2B-3, OF-1

Ted Schreiber

SCHREIBER, THEODORE HENRY BR TR 5′11″ 175 lbs.
B. July 11, 1938, Brooklyn, N. Y.

Year	Team	Games	BA	SA	AB	H	2B	3B	HR	HR%	R	RBI	BB	SO	SB	Pinch Hit AB	Pinch Hit H	PO	A	E	DP	TC/G	FA	G by Pos
1963	NY N	39	.160	.160	50	8	0	0	0	0.0	1	2	4	14	0	10	0	15	44	1	3	2.1	.983	3B-17, SS-9, 2B-3

Pop Schriver

SCHRIVER, WILLIAM FREDERICK BR TR 5′10″ 185 lbs.
B. June 11, 1865, Brooklyn, N. Y. D. Dec. 27, 1932, Brooklyn, N. Y.

Year	Team	Games	BA	SA	AB	H	2B	3B	HR	HR%	R	RBI	BB	SO	SB	Pinch Hit AB	Pinch Hit H	PO	A	E	DP	TC/G	FA	G by Pos
1886	BKN AA	8	.048	.048	21	1	0	0	0	0.0	2		2			0	0	12	6	3	0	2.6	.857	OF-5, C-3
1888	PHI N	40	.194	.284	134	26	5	2	1	0.7	15	23	7	21	2	0	0	156	63	36	3	6.4	.859	C-27, SS-6, 3B-6, OF-1
1889		55	.265	.327	211	56	10	0	1	0.5	24	19	16	8	5	0	0	241	99	36	6	6.8	.904	C-48, 2B-6, 3B-1
1890		57	.274	.368	223	61	9	6	0	0.0	37	35	22	15	9	0	0	272	63	33	12	6.5	.910	C-34, 1B-10, 3B-8, 2B-3, OF-2
1891	CHI N	27	.333	.467	90	30	1	4	1	1.1	15	21	10	9	1	0	0	135	27	6	3	5.8	.964	C-27, 1B-2
1892		92	.224	.301	326	73	10	6	1	0.3	40	34	27	25	4	0	0	379	103	37	5	5.6	.929	C-82, OF-10
1893		64	.284	.397	229	65	8	3	4	1.7	49	34	14	9	4	3	0	224	63	23	8	5.1	.926	C-56, OF-5
1894		96	.275	.352	349	96	12	3	3	0.9	55	47	29	21	9	1	0	310	106	36	13	4.7	.920	C-88, SS-3, 3B-3, 1B-2
1895	NY N	24	.315	.391	92	29	2	1	1	1.1	16	16	9	10	3	0	0	127	24	16	6	7.0	.904	C-18, 1B-6
1897	CIN N	61	.303	.433	178	54	12	4	1	0.6	29	30	19		3	5	1	147	42	8	3	3.7	.959	C-53
1898	PIT N	95	.229	.295	315	72	15	3	0	0.0	25	32	23		0	2	0	307	95	18	6	4.5	.957	C-92, 1B-1
1899		91	.282	.389	301	85	19	5	1	0.3	31	49	23		4	5	1	356	95	16	9	5.4	.966	C-78, 1B-8
1900		37	.293	.402	92	27	7	0	1	1.1	11	12	10		0	9	3	95	21	5	1	4.8	.959	C-24, 1B-1
1901	STL N	53	.271	.367	166	45	7	3	1	0.6	17	23	12		2	9	**3**	273	61	10	13	8.0	.971	C-24, 1B-19
14 yrs.		800	.264	.354	2727	720	117	40	16	0.6	366	375	223	118	46	34	8	3034	868	283	88	5.5	.932	C-654, 1B-49, OF-23, 3B-18, 2B-9, SS-9

Bob Schroder

SCHRODER, ROBERT JAMES BL TR 6′ 175 lbs.
B. Dec. 30, 1944, Ridgefield, N. J.

Year	Team	Games	BA	SA	AB	H	2B	3B	HR	HR%	R	RBI	BB	SO	SB	Pinch Hit AB	Pinch Hit H	PO	A	E	DP	TC/G	FA	G by Pos
1965	SF N	31	.222	.222	9	2	0	0	0	0.0	4	1	1	1	0	6	2	4	6	0	1	2.0	1.000	2B-4, 3B-1
1966		10	.242	.242	33	8	0	0	0	0.0	0	2	0	2	0	1	0	9	17	1	2	3.0	.963	SS-9
1967		62	.230	.259	135	31	4	0	0	0.0	20	7	15	15	1	17	3	60	88	1	12	3.0	.993	2B-45, 3B-4
1968		35	.159	.227	44	7	1	1	0	0.0	5	2	7	3	0	11	1	11	20	2	2	1.8	.939	2B-12, SS-4, 3B-2
4 yrs.		138	.217	.249	221	48	5	1	0	0.0	29	12	23	21	1	35	6	84	131	4	17	2.7	.982	2B-61, SS-13, 3B-7

Bill Schroeder

SCHROEDER, ALFRED WILLIAM III BR TR 6′ 2″ 210 lbs.
B. Sept. 7, 1958, Baltimore, Md.

Year	Team	Games	BA	SA	AB	H	2B	3B	HR	HR%	R	RBI	BB	SO	SB	Pinch Hit AB	Pinch Hit H	PO	A	E	DP	TC/G	FA	G by Pos
1983	MIL A	23	.178	.356	73	13	2	1	3	4.1	7	7	3	23	0	0	0	92	5	2	1	4.3	.980	C-23
1984		61	.257	.486	210	54	6	0	14	6.7	29	25	8	54	0	1	0	277	24	4	2	4.9	.987	C-58, DH-3, 1B-1
1985		53	.242	.407	194	47	8	0	8	4.1	18	25	12	61	0	0	0	216	23	3	5	4.6	.988	C-48, DH-4, 1B-1
1986		64	.212	.373	217	46	14	0	7	3.2	32	19	9	59	1	0	0	307	25	1	13	5.2	.997	C-35, 1B-19, DH-10
1987		75	.332	.548	250	83	12	0	14	5.6	35	42	16	56	5	4	0	373	27	2	8	5.5	.995	C-67, 1B-4, DH-2
1988		41	.156	.295	122	19	2	0	5	4.1	9	10	6	36	0	0	0	197	21	0	3	5.3	1.000	C-30, 1B-10, DH-1
1989	CAL A	41	.203	.348	138	28	2	0	6	4.3	16	15	3	44	0	0	0	252	32	3	10	7.0	.990	C-33, 1B-8
1990		18	.224	.483	58	13	3	0	4	6.9	7	9	1	10	0	0	0	100	10	0	2	6.1	1.000	C-15, 1B-3
8 yrs.		376	.240	.426	1262	303	49	1	61	4.8	153	152	58	343	6	5	0	1814	167	15	44	5.3	.992	C-309, 1B-46, DH-20

Rick Schu

SCHU, RICHARD SPENCER BR TR 6′ 170 lbs.
B. Jan. 26, 1962, Philadelphia, Pa.

Year	Team	Games	BA	SA	AB	H	2B	3B	HR	HR%	R	RBI	BB	SO	SB	Pinch Hit AB	Pinch Hit H	PO	A	E	DP	TC/G	FA	G by Pos
1984	PHI N	17	.276	.621	29	8	2	1	2	6.9	12	5	6	6	0	2	0	7	13	1	3	1.4	.952	3B-15
1985		112	.252	.373	416	105	21	4	7	1.7	54	24	38	78	8	1	0	86	191	20	19	2.7	.933	3B-111
1986		92	.274	.447	208	57	10	1	8	3.8	32	25	18	44	2	29	7	42	94	13	6	2.6	.913	3B-58
1987		92	.235	.403	196	46	6	3	7	3.6	24	23	20	36	0	24	2	193	71	10	11	3.8	.964	3B-45, 1B-28
1988	BAL A	89	.256	.363	270	69	9	4	4	1.5	22	20	21	49	6	5	1	94	110	11	8	2.5	.949	3B-72, DH-9, 1B-4
1989	2 teams	BAL A (1G –.000) DET A (98G –.214)																						
″	total	99	.214	.335	266	57	11	0	7	2.6	25	21	24	37	1	10	2	59	126	12	14	1.9	.939	3B-83, DH-9, 2B-6, SS-3, 1B-3
1990	CAL A	61	.268	.433	157	42	8	0	6	3.8	19	14	11	25	0	11	2	104	81	11	16	3.4	.944	3B-38, 1B-15, OF-4, 2B-1
1991	PHI N	17	.091	.091	22	2	0	0	0	0.0	1	2	1	7	0	13	1	15	1	1	0	4.3	.941	3B-3, 1B-1
8 yrs.		579	.247	.385	1564	386	67	13	41	2.6	189	134	139	282	17	95	15	600	687	79	77	2.7	.942	3B-425, 1B-51, DH-18, 2B-7, OF-4, SS-3

Heinie Schuble

SCHUBLE, HENRY GEORGE BR TR 5′ 9″ 152 lbs.
B. Nov. 1, 1906, Houston, Tex. D. Oct. 2, 1990, Baytown, Tex.

Year	Team	Games	BA	SA	AB	H	2B	3B	HR	HR%	R	RBI	BB	SO	SB	Pinch Hit AB	Pinch Hit H	PO	A	E	DP	TC/G	FA	G by Pos
1927	STL N	65	.257	.358	218	56	6	2	4	1.8	29	28	7	27	0	0	0	120	192	29	36	5.2	.915	SS-65
1929	DET A	92	.233	.353	258	60	11	7	2	0.8	35	28	19	23	3	1	0	142	217	47	43	4.6	.884	SS-86, 3B-2
1932		101	.271	.409	340	92	20	6	5	1.5	57	52	24	37	14	2	0	112	204	19	24	3.7	.943	3B-76, SS-15
1933		49	.219	.281	96	21	4	1	0	0.0	12	6	5	17	2	9	4	19	46	4	1	2.7	.942	3B-23, SS-2, 2B-1
1934		11	.267	.400	15	4	2	0	0	0.0	2	2	1	4	0	4	0	4	9	0	1	2.2	1.000	SS-3, 3B-2, 2B-1
1935		11	.250	.250	8	2	0	0	0	0.0	3	0	1	0	0	2	1	1	4	2	2	2.3	.714	3B-2, 2B-1
1936	STL N	2	—	—	0	0	0	0	0	—	0	0	0	0	0	0	0	0	0	0	0	0.0	.000	3B-1
7 yrs.		331	.251	.367	935	235	43	16	11	1.2	138	116	57	108	19	18	5	398	672	101	107	4.2	.914	SS-171, 3B-106, 2B-3

Wes Schulmerich

SCHULMERICH, EDWARD WESLEY BR TR 5′11″ 210 lbs.
B. Aug. 21, 1901, Hillsboro, Ore. D. June 26, 1985, Corvallis, Ore.

Year	Team	Games	BA	SA	AB	H	2B	3B	HR	HR%	R	RBI	BB	SO	SB	Pinch Hit AB	Pinch Hit H	PO	A	E	DP	TC/G	FA	G by Pos
1931	BOS N	95	.309	.422	327	101	17	7	2	0.6	36	43	28	30	0	6	3	190	6	7	0	2.3	.966	OF-87
1932		119	.260	.421	404	105	22	5	11	2.7	47	57	27	61	5	18	4	232	11	8	5	2.5	.968	OF-101
1933	2 teams	BOS N (29G –.247) PHI N (97G –.334)																						
″	total	126	.318	.456	450	143	25	5	9	2.0	63	72	37	55	1	7	2	256	9	6	0	2.3	.978	OF-118
1934	2 teams	PHI N (15G –.250) CIN N (74G –.263)																						
″	total	89	.261	.375	261	68	9	3	5	1.9	23	20	26	51	1	19	8	146	2	4	1	2.2	.974	OF-69
4 yrs.		429	.289	.424	1442	417	73	20	27	1.9	169	192	118	197	7	50	17	824	28	25	6	2.3	.971	OF-375

Art Schult

SCHULT, ARTHUR WILLIAM (Dutch) BR TR 6′ 3″ 210 lbs.
B. June 20, 1928, Brooklyn, N. Y.

Year	Team	Games	BA	SA	AB	H	2B	3B	HR	HR%	R	RBI	BB	SO	SB	Pinch Hit AB	Pinch Hit H	PO	A	E	DP	TC/G	FA	G by Pos
1953	NY A	7	—	—	0	0	0	0	0	—	3	0	0	0	0	0	0	0	0	0	0	0.0	—	
1956	CIN N	5	.429	.429	7	3	0	0	0	0.0	3	2	1	1	0	3	2	0	0	0	0	0.0	.000	OF-1
1957	2 teams	CIN N (21G –.265) WAS A (77G –.263)																						
″	total	98	.263	.363	281	74	16	0	4	1.4	34	39	14	32	0	26	5	379	15	6	35	5.6	.985	OF-36, 1B-35

Art Schult *continued*

Year	Team	Games	BA	SA	AB	H	2B	3B	HR	HR%	R	RBI	BB	SO	SB	Pinch Hit AB	Pinch Hit H	PO	A	E	DP	TC/G	FA	G by Pos
1959	CHI N	42	.271	.381	118	32	7	0	2	1.7	17	14	7	14	0	9	2	152	6	2	15	4.2	.988	1B-23, OF-15
1960		12	.133	.200	15	2	1	0	0	0.0	1	1	1	3	0	7	1	4	0	0	0	0.8	1.000	OF-4, 1B-1
5 yrs.		164	.264	.363	421	111	24	0	6	1.4	58	56	23	50	0	45	10	535	21	8	50	4.9	.986	1B-59, OF-56

Fred Schulte

SCHULTE, FRED WILLIAM (Fritz)
Born Fred William Schult.
B. Jan. 13, 1901, Belvidere, Ill. D. May 20, 1983, Belvidere, Ill.

BR TR 6′ 1″ 183 lbs.

Year	Team	Games	BA	SA	AB	H	2B	3B	HR	HR%	R	RBI	BB	SO	SB	Pinch Hit AB	Pinch Hit H	PO	A	E	DP	TC/G	FA	G by Pos
1927	STL A	60	.317	.503	189	60	16	5	3	1.6	32	34	20	14	5	8	4	117	3	11	0	2.7	.916	OF-49
1928		146	.286	.424	556	159	44	6	7	1.3	90	85	51	60	6	1	1	419	21	12	6	3.2	.973	OF-143
1929		121	.307	.404	446	137	24	5	3	0.7	63	71	59	44	8	5	1	361	12	4	2	3.3	.989	OF-116
1930		113	.278	.401	392	109	23	5	5	1.3	59	62	41	44	12	7	1	297	7	11	6	3.1	.965	OF-98, 1B-5
1931		134	.304	.436	553	168	32	7	9	1.6	100	65	56	49	6	0	0	361	13	11	4	2.9	.971	OF-134
1932		146	.294	.425	565	166	35	6	9	1.6	106	73	71	44	5	8	5	370	12	8	4	2.9	.979	OF-129, 1B-5
1933	WAS A	144	.295	.402	550	162	30	7	5	0.9	98	87	61	27	10	1	0	433	10	9	4	3.2	.980	OF-142
1934		136	.298	.399	524	156	32	6	3	0.6	72	73	53	34	3	2	1	351	5	5	0	2.7	.986	OF-134
1935		75	.268	.357	224	60	6	4	2	0.9	33	23	26	22	0	22	5	96	2	2	0	1.8	.980	OF-55
1936	PIT N	74	.261	.328	238	62	7	3	1	0.4	28	17	20	20	1	17	7	129	1	3	1	2.4	.977	OF-55
1937		29	.100	.100	20	2	0	0	0	0.0	5	3	4	3	0	12	1	4	0	1	0	1.3	.800	OF-4
11 yrs.		1178	.292	.409	4257	1241	249	54	47	1.1	686	593	462	361	56	83	26	2938	86	77	27	2.9	.975	OF-1059, 1B-10
WORLD SERIES																								
1933	WAS A	5	.333	.524	21	7	1	0	1	4.8	1	4	1	1	0	0	0	9	0	0	0	1.8	1.000	OF-5

Ham Schulte

SCHULTE, HERMAN JOSEPH
Born Herman Joseph Schultehenrich.
Brother of Len Schulte.
B. Sept. 1, 1912, St. Louis, Mo. D. Dec. 21, 1993, St. Charles, Mo.

BR TR 5′ 8½″ 158 lbs.

Year	Team	Games	BA	SA	AB	H	2B	3B	HR	HR%	R	RBI	BB	SO	SB	Pinch Hit AB	Pinch Hit H	PO	A	E	DP	TC/G	FA	G by Pos
1940	PHI N	120	.236	.294	436	103	18	2	1	0.2	44	21	32	30	3	1	0	283	320	13	72	5.1	.979	2B-119, SS-1

Jack Schulte

SCHULTE, JOHN HERMAN FRANK
B. Nov. 15, 1881, Cincinnati, Ohio D. Aug. 17, 1975, Roseville, Mich.

BR TR 5′ 9″ 180 lbs.

Year	Team	Games	BA	SA	AB	H	2B	3B	HR	HR%	R	RBI	BB	SO	SB	Pinch Hit AB	Pinch Hit H	PO	A	E	DP	TC/G	FA	G by Pos
1906	BOS N	2	.000	.000	7	0	0	0	0	0.0	0	0	0		0	0	0	3	3	0	0	3.0	1.000	SS-2

Johnny Schulte

SCHULTE, JOHN CLEMENT
B. Sept. 8, 1896, Fredericktown, Mo. D. June 28, 1978, St. Louis, Mo.

BL TR 5′11″ 190 lbs.

Year	Team	Games	BA	SA	AB	H	2B	3B	HR	HR%	R	RBI	BB	SO	SB	Pinch Hit AB	Pinch Hit H	PO	A	E	DP	TC/G	FA	G by Pos
1923	STL A	7	.000	.000	3	0	0	0	0	0.0	1	1	4	0	0	2	0	5	1	0	1	3.0	1.000	1B-1, C-1
1927	STL N	64	.288	.538	156	45	8	2	9	5.8	35	32	47	19	1	3	1	172	45	10	6	3.8	.956	C-59
1928	PHI N	65	.248	.407	113	28	2	2	4	3.5	14	17	15	12	0	26	6	70	23	5	4	2.9	.949	C-34
1929	CHI N	31	.261	.304	69	18	3	0	0	0.0	6	9	7	11	0	1	1	74	16	2	3	3.1	.978	C-30
1932	**2 teams**	**STL A** (15G –.208) **BOS N** (10G –.222)																						
″	**total**	25	.212	.364	33	7	2	0	1	3.0	3	5	3	7	0	8	1	35	2	3	1	2.5	.925	C-16
5 yrs.		192	.262	.436	374	98	15	4	14	3.7	59	64	76	49	1	40	9	356	87	20	15	3.3	.957	C-140, 1B-1

Len Schulte

SCHULTE, LEONARD BERNARD
Born Leonard Bernard Schultehenrich.
Brother of Ham Schulte.
B. Dec. 5, 1916, St. Charles, Mo. D. May 6, 1986, Orlando, Fla.

BR TR 5′10″ 160 lbs.

Year	Team	Games	BA	SA	AB	H	2B	3B	HR	HR%	R	RBI	BB	SO	SB	Pinch Hit AB	Pinch Hit H	PO	A	E	DP	TC/G	FA	G by Pos
1944	STL A	1	—	—	0	0	0	0	0	—	0	0	1	0	0	0	0	0	0	0	0	0.0	—	
1945		119	.247	.288	430	106	16	1	0	0.0	37	36	24	35	0	3	0	167	245	23	24	3.6	.947	3B-71, 2B-37, SS-14
1946		4	.400	.400	5	2	0	0	0	0.0	1	2	0	0	0	3	1	2	3	0	0	2.5	1.000	3B-1, 2B-1
3 yrs.		124	.248	.290	435	108	16	1	0	0.0	38	38	25	35	0	6	1	169	248	23	24	3.5	.948	3B-72, 2B-38, SS-14

Wildfire Schulte

SCHULTE, FRANK M.
B. Sept. 17, 1882, Cohocton, N. Y. D. Oct. 2, 1949, Oakland, Calif.

BL TR 5′11″ 170 lbs.

Year	Team	Games	BA	SA	AB	H	2B	3B	HR	HR%	R	RBI	BB	SO	SB	Pinch Hit AB	Pinch Hit H	PO	A	E	DP	TC/G	FA	G by Pos
1904	CHI N	20	.286	.476	84	24	4	3	2	2.4	16	13	2		1	0	0	34	3	2	0	2.0	.949	OF-20
1905		123	.274	.367	493	135	15	14	1	0.2	67	47	32		16	0	0	189	14	4	0	1.7	.981	OF-123
1906		146	.281	.396	563	158	18	**13**	7	1.2	77	60	31		25	0	0	218	18	6	7	1.7	.975	OF-146
1907		97	.287	.386	342	98	14	7	2	0.6	44	32	22		7	5	1	130	11	4	1	1.6	.972	OF-91
1908		102	.236	.306	386	91	20	2	1	0.3	42	43	29		15	0	0	148	11	1	3	1.6	.994	OF-102
1909		140	.264	.357	538	142	16	11	4	0.7	57	60	24		23	0	0	169	14	6	1	1.4	.968	OF-140
1910		151	.301	.460	559	168	29	15	**10**	1.8	93	68	39	57	22	1	0	221	18	8	5	1.6	.968	OF-150
1911		154	.300	**.534**	577	173	30	21	**21**	**3.6**	105	**121**	76	68	23	0	0	246	19	8	8	1.8	.971	OF-154
1912		139	.264	.423	553	146	27	11	13	2.4	90	70	53	70	17	0	0	219	19	12	6	1.8	.952	OF-139
1913		132	.279	.414	495	138	28	6	9	1.8	85	72	39	68	21	2	1	180	13	9	2	1.6	.955	OF-129
1914		137	.241	.351	465	112	22	7	5	1.1	54	61	39	55	16	3	1	217	9	11	2	1.8	.954	OF-134
1915		151	.249	.373	550	137	20	6	12	2.2	66	69	49	68	19	3	1	280	24	12	3	2.1	.962	OF-147
1916	**2 teams**	**CHI N** (72G –.296) **PIT N** (55G –.254)																						
″	**total**	127	.278	.373	407	113	16	4	5	1.2	43	41	37	54	14	9	1	197	10	9	0	1.9	.958	OF-113
1917	**2 teams**	**PIT N** (30G –.214) **PHI N** (64G –.215)																						
″	**total**	94	.214	.294	252	54	15	1	1	0.4	32	22	26	36	9	21	5	96	4	6	0	1.5	.943	OF-70
1918	WAS A	93	.288	.363	267	77	14	3	0	0.0	35	44	47	36	5	16	5	145	10	5	4	2.1	.969	OF-75
15 yrs.		1806	.270	.395	6531	1766	288	124	93	1.4	906	823	545	512	233	60	15	2689	197	103	42	1.7	.966	OF-1733
WORLD SERIES																								
1906	CHI N	6	.269	.385	26	7	3	0	0	0.0	1	3	1	3	0	0	0	6	1	0	1	1.2	1.000	OF-6
1907		5	.250	.250	20	5	0	0	0	0.0	3	2	1	2	1	0	0	6	2	2	0	2.0	.800	OF-5
1908		5	.389	.500	18	7	0	1	0	0.0	4	2	2	1	2	0	0	3	0	0	0	0.6	1.000	OF-5
1910		5	.353	.529	17	6	3	0	0	0.0	3	2	2	3	0	0	0	4	0	1	0	1.0	.800	OF-5
4 yrs.		21	.309	.407	81	25	6	1	0	0.0	11	9	6	9	3	0	0	19	3	3	1	1.2	.880	OF-21

Howie Schultz

SCHULTZ, HOWARD HENRY (Steeple, Stretch)
B. July 3, 1922, St. Paul, Minn.

BR TR 6′ 6″ 200 lbs.

Year	Team	Games	BA	SA	AB	H	2B	3B	HR	HR%	R	RBI	BB	SO	SB	Pinch Hit AB	Pinch Hit H	PO	A	E	DP	TC/G	FA	G by Pos
1943	BKN N	45	.269	.352	182	49	12	0	1	0.5	20	34	6	24	3	0	0	386	33	6	27	9.4	.986	1B-45
1944		138	.255	.390	526	134	32	3	11	2.1	59	83	24	67	6	6	5	1091	85	14	90	8.8	.988	1B-136

Howie Schultz *continued*

Year	Team	Games	BA	SA	AB	H	2B	3B	HR	HR%	R	RBI	BB	SO	SB	Pinch Hit AB	Pinch Hit H	PO	A	E	DP	TC/G	FA	G by Pos
1945		39	.239	.345	142	34	8	2	1	0.7	18	19	10	14	2	1	0	334	32	6	35	9.8	.984	1B-38
1946		90	.253	.353	249	63	14	1	3	1.2	27	27	16	34	2	3	0	576	58	7	65	7.4	.989	1B-87
1947	**2 teams**	**BKN N** (2G –.000) **PHI N** (114G –.223)																						
"	**total**	116	.223	.319	404	90	19	1	6	1.5	30	35	21	70	0	1	0	987	67	7	92	9.2	.993	1B-115
1948	**2 teams**	**PHI N** (6G –.077) **CIN N** (36G –.167)																						
"	**total**	42	.153	.224	85	13	0	0	2	2.4	9	10	5	9	2	10	2	177	7	3	17	6.4	.984	1B-29
6 yrs.		470	.241	.349	1588	383	85	7	24	1.5	163	208	82	218	15	21	7	3551	282	43	326	8.6	.989	1B-450

Joe Schultz

SCHULTZ, JOSEPH CHARLES, JR. (Dode) BL TR 5′11″ 180 lbs.
Son of Joe Schultz.
B. Aug. 29, 1918, Chicago, Ill. D. Jan. 10, 1996, St. Louis, Mo.
Manager 1969, 1973.

Year	Team	Games	BA	SA	AB	H	2B	3B	HR	HR%	R	RBI	BB	SO	SB	Pinch Hit AB	Pinch Hit H	PO	A	E	DP	TC/G	FA	G by Pos
1939	**PIT N**	4	.286	.429	14	4	2	0	0	0.0	3	2	2	0	0	0	0	24	1	0	0	6.3	1.000	C-4
1940		16	.194	.250	36	7	0	1	0	0.0	2	4	2	1	0	3	2	29	4	3	0	2.8	.917	C-13
1941		2	.500	.500	2	1	0	0	0	0.0	1	0	0	0	0	0	0	0	0	0	0	0.0	—	
1943	**STL A**	46	.239	.293	92	22	5	0	0	0.0	6	8	9	8	0	23	6	83	9	2	1	3.6	.979	C-26
1944		3	.250	.250	8	2	0	0	0	0.0	1	0	0	1	0	1	0	8	1	2	0	3.7	.818	C-3
1945		41	.295	.341	44	13	2	0	0	0.0	1	8	3	1	0	**35**	**11**	15	1	1	0	4.3	.941	C-4
1946		42	.386	.456	57	22	4	0	0	0.0	1	14	11	2	0	23	**10**	42	0	0	2	2.5	1.000	C-17
1947		43	.184	.263	38	7	0	0	1	2.6	3	1	4	5	0	**38**	7	0	0	0	0	0.0	—	
1948		43	.189	.189	37	7	0	0	0	0.0	0	9	6	3	0	**37**	7	0	0	0	0	0.0	—	
9 yrs.		240	.259	.314	328	85	13	1	1	0.3	18	46	37	21	0	160	43	201	16	8	3	3.4	.964	C-67

Joe Schultz

SCHULTZ, JOSEPH CHARLES, SR. (Germany) BR TR 5′11½″ 172 lbs.
Father of Joe Schultz.
B. July 24, 1893, Pittsburgh, Pa. D. Apr. 13, 1941, Columbia, S. C.

Year	Team	Games	BA	SA	AB	H	2B	3B	HR	HR%	R	RBI	BB	SO	SB	Pinch Hit AB	Pinch Hit H	PO	A	E	DP	TC/G	FA	G by Pos
1912	**BOS N**	4	.250	.333	12	3	1	0	0	0.0	1	4	0	2	0	0	0	6	8	3	1	4.3	.824	2B-4
1913		9	.222	.222	18	4	0	0	0	0.0	2	1	2	7	0	1	0	11	1	0	0	2.0	1.000	OF-5, 2B-1
1915	**2 teams**	**BKN N** (56G –.292) **CHI N** (7G –.250)																						
"	**total**	63	.289	.344	128	37	3	2	0	0.0	14	7	10	20	3	29	8	46	46	11	3	1.8	.893	3B-55, 2B-2, SS-1
1916	**PIT N**	77	.260	.319	204	53	8	2	0	0.0	18	22	7	14	6	20	5	75	86	22	3	3.3	.880	2B-24, 3B-24, OF-6, SS-1
1919	**STL N**	88	.253	.328	229	58	9	1	2	0.9	24	21	11	7	4	**31**	**8**	87	15	4	2	2.0	.962	OF-49, 2B-5
1920		99	.263	.309	320	84	5	5	0	0.0	38	32	21	11	5	14	2	147	7	9	3	2.0	.945	OF-80
1921		92	.309	.469	275	85	20	3	6	2.2	37	45	15	11	4	18	6	137	14	6	4	2.2	.962	OF-67, 3B-3, 1B-2
1922		112	.314	.392	344	108	13	4	2	0.6	50	64	19	10	3	22	8	195	7	5	1	2.3	.976	OF-89
1923		2	.286	.286	7	2	0	0	0	0.0	0	1	1	0	0	0	0	5	0	0	0	2.5	1.000	OF-2
1924	**2 teams**	**STL N** (12G –.167) **PHI N** (88G –.282)																						
"	**total**	100	.277	.385	296	82	15	1	5	1.7	35	31	23	18	6	17	6	138	7	6	0	1.9	.960	OF-78
1925	**2 teams**	**PHI N** (24G –.344) **CIN N** (33G –.323)																						
"	**total**	57	.333	.421	126	42	9	1	0	0.0	16	21	7	2	4	18	3	51	4	4	1	1.6	.932	OF-35, 2B-1
11 yrs.		703	.285	.370	1959	558	83	19	15	0.8	235	249	116	102	35	170	46	898	195	70	18	2.2	.940	OF-411, 3B-82, 2B-37, 1B-2, SS-2

John Schultz

SCHULTZ, JOHN
B. St. Louis, Mo. Deceased.

Year	Team	Games	BA	SA	AB	H	2B	3B	HR	HR%	R	RBI	BB	SO	SB	Pinch Hit AB	Pinch Hit H	PO	A	E	DP	TC/G	FA	G by Pos
1891	**STL AA**	1	.000	.000	2	0	0	0	0	0.0	0	0	0	0	0	0	0	1	1	0	0	2.0	1.000	C-1

Jeff Schulz

SCHULZ, JEFFREY ALAN BL TR 6′ 1″ 190 lbs.
B. June 2, 1961, Evansville, Ind.

Year	Team	Games	BA	SA	AB	H	2B	3B	HR	HR%	R	RBI	BB	SO	SB	Pinch Hit AB	Pinch Hit H	PO	A	E	DP	TC/G	FA	G by Pos
1989	**KC A**	7	.222	.222	9	2	0	0	0	0.0	0	1	0	2	0	2	2	6	0	0	0	1.2	1.000	OF-5
1990		30	.258	.364	66	17	5	1	0	0.0	5	6	6	13	0	10	1	33	0	2	0	1.5	.943	OF-22, DH-1
1991	**PIT N**	3	.000	.000	3	0	0	0	0	0.0	0	0	0	2	0	3	0	0	0	0	0	0.0	—	
3 yrs.		40	.244	.333	78	19	5	1	0	0.0	5	7	6	17	0	15	3	39	0	2	0	1.5	.951	OF-27, DH-1

Bill Schuster

SCHUSTER, WILLIAM CHARLES (Broadway) BR TR 5′ 9″ 164 lbs.
B. Aug. 4, 1912, Buffalo, N. Y. D. June 28, 1987, El Monte, Calif.

Year	Team	Games	BA	SA	AB	H	2B	3B	HR	HR%	R	RBI	BB	SO	SB	Pinch Hit AB	Pinch Hit H	PO	A	E	DP	TC/G	FA	G by Pos
1937	**PIT N**	3	.500	.500	6	3	0	0	0	0.0	2	1	1	0	0	0	0	3	6	0	2	4.5	1.000	SS-2
1939	**BOS N**	2	.000	.000	3	0	0	0	0	0.0	0	0	0	1	0	0	0	2	3	1	0	3.0	.833	SS-1, 3B-1
1943	**CHI N**	13	.294	.373	51	15	2	1	0	0.0	3	0	3	2	0	0	0	34	52	2	14	6.8	.977	SS-13
1944		60	.221	.299	154	34	7	1	1	0.6	14	14	12	16	4	11	3	71	109	9	21	4.3	.952	SS-38, 2B-6
1945		45	.191	.277	47	9	2	1	0	0.0	8	2	7	4	2	2	0	38	40	4	8	3.2	.951	SS-22, 2B-3, 3B-1
5 yrs.		123	.234	.310	261	61	11	3	1	0.4	27	17	23	23	6	13	3	148	210	16	45	4.3	.957	SS-76, 2B-9, 3B-2
WORLD SERIES																								
1945	**CHI N**	2	.000	.000	1	0	0	0	0	0.0	1	0	0	0	0	0	0	1	2	0	0	3.0	1.000	SS-1

Bill Schwartz

SCHWARTZ, WILLIAM CHARLES (Blab) BR TR 6′ 2″ 185 lbs.
B. Apr. 22, 1884, Cleveland, Ohio D. Aug. 29, 1961, Nashville, Tenn.

Year	Team	Games	BA	SA	AB	H	2B	3B	HR	HR%	R	RBI	BB	SO	SB	Pinch Hit AB	Pinch Hit H	PO	A	E	DP	TC/G	FA	G by Pos
1904	**CLE A**	24	.151	.174	86	13	2	0	0	0.0	5	0	0		4	1	0	244	6	6	4	11.1	.977	1B-22, 3B-1

Pop Schwartz

SCHWARTZ, WILLIAM AUGUST (Scooper Bill) BR TR 6′ 1″ 195 lbs.
B. Apr. 3, 1864, Jamestown, Ky. D. Dec. 22, 1940, Newport, Ky.

Year	Team	Games	BA	SA	AB	H	2B	3B	HR	HR%	R	RBI	BB	SO	SB	Pinch Hit AB	Pinch Hit H	PO	A	E	DP	TC/G	FA	G by Pos
1883	**COL AA**	2	.250	.250	4	1	0	0	0	0.0	0		0			0	0	6	0	5	0	5.5	.545	1B-1, C-1
1884	**CIN U**	29	.236	.302	106	25	4	0	1	0.9	14		3			0	0	163	35	40	1	8.2	.832	C-25, OF-3, 3B-1
2 yrs.		31	.236	.300	110	26	4	0	1	0.9	14		3			0	0	169	35	45	1	8.0	.819	C-26, OF-3, 3B-1, 1B-1

Randy Schwartz

SCHWARTZ, DOUGLAS RANDALL BL TL 6′ 3″ 230 lbs.
B. Feb. 9, 1944, Los Angeles, Calif.

Year	Team	Games	BA	SA	AB	H	2B	3B	HR	HR%	R	RBI	BB	SO	SB	Pinch Hit AB	Pinch Hit H	PO	A	E	DP	TC/G	FA	G by Pos
1965	**KC A**	6	.286	.286	7	2	0	0	0	0.0	0	1	0	4	0	3	1	9	2	0	0	5.5	1.000	1B-2
1966		10	.091	.091	11	1	0	0	0	0.0	0	1	1	3	0	9	1	8	0	0	1	4.0	1.000	1B-2
2 yrs.		16	.167	.167	18	3	0	0	0	0.0	0	2	1	7	0	12	2	17	2	0	1	4.8	1.000	1B-4

Bill Schwarz

SCHWARZ, WILLIAM DeWITT TR
B. Jan. 30, 1891, Birmingham, Ala. D. June 24, 1949, Jacksonville, Fla.

Year	Team		Games	BA	SA	AB	H	2B	3B	HR	HR%	R	RBI	BB	SO	SB	Pinch Hit AB	Pinch Hit H	PO	A	E	DP	TC/G	FA	G by Pos
1914	NY	A	1	.000	.000	1	0	0	0	0	0.0	0	0	0	1	0	0	0	1	1	0	0	2.0	1.000	C-1

Al Schweitzer

SCHWEITZER, ALBERT CASPER (Cheese) BR TR 5′7½″ 170 lbs.
B. Dec. 23, 1882, Cleveland, Ohio D. Jan. 27, 1969, Newark, Ohio.

Year	Team		Games	BA	SA	AB	H	2B	3B	HR	HR%	R	RBI	BB	SO	SB	Pinch Hit AB	Pinch Hit H	PO	A	E	DP	TC/G	FA	G by Pos
1908	STL	A	64	.291	.352	182	53	4	2	1	0.5	22	14	20		6	9	1	86	14	5	3	1.9	.952	OF-55
1909			27	.224	.250	76	17	2	0	0	0.0	7	2	5		3	5	0	26	2	2	0	1.4	.933	OF-22
1910			113	.230	.285	379	87	11	2	2	0.5	37	37	36		26	3	1	149	15	11	3	1.6	.937	OF-109
1911			76	.215	.295	237	51	11	4	0	0.0	31	34	43		12	8	0	100	13	8	4	1.8	.934	OF-68
4 yrs.			280	.238	.299	874	208	28	8	3	0.3	97	87	104		47	25	2	361	44	26	10	1.7	.940	OF-254

Pius Schwert

SCHWERT, PIUS LOUIS BR TR 5′10½″ 160 lbs.
B. Nov. 22, 1892, Angola, N. Y. D. Mar. 11, 1941, Washington, D. C.

Year	Team		Games	BA	SA	AB	H	2B	3B	HR	HR%	R	RBI	BB	SO	SB	Pinch Hit AB	Pinch Hit H	PO	A	E	DP	TC/G	FA	G by Pos
1914	NY	A	2	.000	.000	5	0	0	0	0	0.0	0	0	2	2	0	0	0	3	7	1	0	5.5	.909	C-2
1915			9	.278	.444	18	5	3	0	0	0.0	6	6	1	6	0	0	0	27	8	1	0	4.0	.972	C-9
2 yrs.			11	.217	.348	23	5	3	0	0	0.0	6	6	3	8	0	0	0	30	15	2	0	4.3	.957	C-11

Art Schwind

SCHWIND, ARTHUR EDWIN BB TR 5′8″ 150 lbs.
B. Nov. 4, 1889, Fort Wayne, Ind. D. Jan. 13, 1968, Sullivan, Ill.

Year	Team		Games	BA	SA	AB	H	2B	3B	HR	HR%	R	RBI	BB	SO	SB	Pinch Hit AB	Pinch Hit H	PO	A	E	DP	TC/G	FA	G by Pos
1912	BOS	N	1	.500	.500	2	1	0	0	0	0.0	0	0	0	0	0	0	0	0	0	0	0	0.0	.000	3B-1

Jerry Schypinski

SCHYPINSKI, GERALD ALBERT BL TR 5′10″ 170 lbs.
B. Sept. 16, 1931, Detroit, Mich.

Year	Team		Games	BA	SA	AB	H	2B	3B	HR	HR%	R	RBI	BB	SO	SB	Pinch Hit AB	Pinch Hit H	PO	A	E	DP	TC/G	FA	G by Pos
1955	KC	A	22	.217	.246	69	15	2	0	0	0.0	7	5	1	6	0	0	0	27	52	5	12	3.7	.940	SS-21, 2B-2

Mike Scioscia

SCIOSCIA, MICHAEL LORRI BL TR 6′2″ 200 lbs.
B. Nov. 27, 1958, Upper Darby, Pa.

Year	Team		Games	BA	SA	AB	H	2B	3B	HR	HR%	R	RBI	BB	SO	SB	Pinch Hit AB	Pinch Hit H	PO	A	E	DP	TC/G	FA	G by Pos
1980	LA	N	54	.254	.328	134	34	5	1	1	0.7	8	8	12	9	1	1	0	226	26	2	5	4.7	.992	C-54
1981			93	.276	.331	290	80	10	0	2	0.7	27	29	36	18	0	2	1	493	48	7	4	6.0	.987	C-91
1982			129	.219	.296	365	80	11	1	5	1.4	31	38	44	31	2	8	0	631	57	10	10	5.7	.986	C-123
1983			12	.314	.486	35	11	3	0	1	2.9	3	7	5	2	0	1	0	55	4	0	0	5.4	1.000	C-11
1984			114	.273	.370	341	93	18	0	5	1.5	29	38	52	26	2	7	0	701	64	12	8	6.9	.985	C-112
1985			141	.296	.420	429	127	26	3	7	1.6	47	53	77	21	3	7	1	818	66	13	8	6.5	.986	C-139
1986			122	.251	.345	374	94	18	1	5	1.3	36	26	62	23	3	10	1	756	64	15	4	7.0	.982	C-119
1987			142	.265	.364	461	122	26	1	6	1.3	44	38	55	23	7	11	4	925	80	11	11	7.4	.989	C-138
1988			130	.257	.324	408	105	18	0	3	0.7	29	35	38	31	0	7	1	748	63	7	10	6.7	.991	C-123
1989			133	.250	.363	408	102	16	0	10	2.5	40	44	52	29	0	6	2	822	82	11	12	7.0	.988	C-130
1990			135	.264	.405	435	115	25	0	12	2.8	46	66	55	31	4	5	0	842	58	10	9	6.9	.989	C-132
1991			119	.264	.391	345	91	16	2	8	2.3	39	40	47	32	4	8	3	677	51	7	8	6.4	.990	C-115
1992			117	.221	.282	348	77	6	3	3	0.9	19	24	32	31	3	13	2	641	74	9	8	6.7	.988	C-108
13 yrs.			1441	.259	.356	4373	1131	198	12	68	1.6	398	446	567	307	29	86	15	8335	737	114	97	6.6	.988	C-1395
DIVISIONAL PLAYOFF SERIES																									
1981	LA	N	4	.154	.154	13	2	0	0	0	0.0	0	1	1	2	0	0	0	21	3	0	0	6.0	1.000	C-4
LEAGUE CHAMPIONSHIP SERIES																									
1981	LA	N	5	.133	.333	15	2	0	0	1	6.7	1	1	2	1	0	0	0	27	1	0	0	5.6	1.000	C-5
1985			6	.250	.250	16	4	0	0	0	0.0	2	1	4	0	0	0	0	31	4	1	0	6.0	.972	C-6
1988			7	.364	.545	22	8	1	0	1	4.5	3	2	1	2	0	0	0	37	4	0	1	5.9	1.000	C-7
3 yrs.			18	.264	.396	53	14	1	0	2	3.8	6	4	7	3	0	0	0	95	9	1	1	5.8	.990	C-18
WORLD SERIES																									
1981	LA	N	3	.250	.250	4	1	0	0	0	0.0	1	0	1	0	0	1	0	7	1	0	0	2.7	1.000	C-3
1988			4	.214	.214	14	3	0	0	0	0.0	0	1	0	2	0	0	0	28	0	1	0	7.3	.966	C-4
2 yrs.			7	.222	.222	18	4	0	0	0	0.0	1	1	1	2	0	1	0	35	1	1	0	5.3	.973	C-7

Lou Scoffic

SCOFFIC, LOUIS (Weaser) BR TR 5′10″ 182 lbs.
B. May 20, 1913, Herrin, Ill.

Year	Team		Games	BA	SA	AB	H	2B	3B	HR	HR%	R	RBI	BB	SO	SB	Pinch Hit AB	Pinch Hit H	PO	A	E	DP	TC/G	FA	G by Pos
1936	STL	N	4	.429	.429	7	3	0	0	0	0.0	2	2	1	2	0	0	0	7	0	1	0	2.7	.875	OF-3

Daryl Sconiers

SCONIERS, DARYL ANTHONY BL TL 6′2″ 185 lbs.
B. Oct. 3, 1958, San Bernardino, Calif.

Year	Team		Games	BA	SA	AB	H	2B	3B	HR	HR%	R	RBI	BB	SO	SB	Pinch Hit AB	Pinch Hit H	PO	A	E	DP	TC/G	FA	G by Pos
1981	CAL	A	15	.269	.385	52	14	1	1	1	1.9	6	7	1	10	0	1	0	95	8	0	11	6.9	1.000	1B-12, DH-3
1982			12	.154	.154	13	2	0	0	0	0.0	0	2	2	1	0	7	1	23	1	0	5	6.0	1.000	1B-3, DH-1
1983			106	.274	.430	314	86	19	3	8	2.5	49	46	17	41	4	28	8	473	23	8	46	5.9	.984	1B-57, DH-27, OF-1
1984			57	.244	.344	160	39	4	0	4	2.5	14	17	13	16	1	10	6	355	26	4	27	9.2	.990	1B-41, DH-1
1985			44	.286	.429	98	28	6	1	2	2.0	14	12	15	18	2	14	3	35	1	1	2	1.4	.973	DH-20, 1B-6
5 yrs.			234	.265	.399	637	169	30	5	15	2.4	83	84	48	86	7	60	18	981	59	13	91	6.1	.988	1B-119, DH-52, OF-1

Scott

SCOTT
Deceased.

Year	Team		Games	BA	SA	AB	H	2B	3B	HR	HR%	R	RBI	BB	SO	SB	Pinch Hit AB	Pinch Hit H	PO	A	E	DP	TC/G	FA	G by Pos
1884	BAL	U	13	.226	.340	53	12	1	1	1	1.9	10		2			0	0	9	2	1	1	0.9	.917	OF-13, 3B-1

Dick Scott

SCOTT, RICHARD EDWARD BR TR 6′1″ 170 lbs.
B. July 19, 1962, Ellsworth, Me.

Year	Team		Games	BA	SA	AB	H	2B	3B	HR	HR%	R	RBI	BB	SO	SB	Pinch Hit AB	Pinch Hit H	PO	A	E	DP	TC/G	FA	G by Pos
1989	OAK	A	3	.000	.000	2	0	0	0	0	0.0	0	1	0	0	0	0	0	0	0	0	0	0.0	.000	SS-3

Donnie Scott

SCOTT, DONALD MALCOLM BB TR 5′11″ 185 lbs.
B. Aug. 16, 1961, Dunedin, Fla.

Year	Team		Games	BA	SA	AB	H	2B	3B	HR	HR%	R	RBI	BB	SO	SB	Pinch Hit AB	Pinch Hit H	PO	A	E	DP	TC/G	FA	G by Pos
1983	TEX	A	2	.000	.000	4	0	0	0	0	0.0	0	0	0	0	0	0	0	8	2	0	0	5.0	1.000	C-2
1984			81	.221	.298	235	52	9	0	3	1.3	16	20	20	44	0	0	0	400	41	12	9	5.7	.974	C-80
1985	SEA	A	80	.222	.357	185	41	13	0	4	2.2	18	23	15	41	1	20	2	277	31	6	1	4.2	.981	C-74
1991	CIN	N	10	.158	.158	19	3	0	0	0	0.0	0	0	0	2	0	2	0	19	0	0	0	2.4	1.000	C-8
4 yrs.			173	.217	.314	443	96	22	0	7	1.6	34	43	35	87	1	22	2	704	74	18	10	4.9	.977	C-164

Everett Scott

SCOTT, LEWIS EVERETT (Deacon) BR TR 5′ 8″ 148 lbs.
B. Nov. 19, 1892, Bluffton, Ind. D. Nov. 2, 1960, Fort Wayne, Ind.

Year	Team	Games	BA	SA	AB	H	2B	3B	HR	HR%	R	RBI	BB	SO	SB	Pinch Hit AB	Pinch Hit H	PO	A	E	DP	TC/G	FA	G by Pos
1914	BOS A	144	.239	.301	539	129	15	6	2	0.4	66	37	32	43	9	1	1	324	408	39	50	5.4	.949	SS-143
1915		100	.201	.231	359	72	11	0	0	0.0	25	28	17	21	4	0	0	198	298	20	31	5.2	.961	SS-100
1916		123	.232	.295	366	85	19	2	0	0.0	37	27	23	24	8	0	0	217	342	19	36	4.7	.967	SS-121, 3B-1, 2B-1
1917		157	.241	.313	528	127	24	7	0	0.0	40	50	20	46	12	0	0	315	483	39	64	5.3	.953	SS-157
1918		126	.221	.269	443	98	11	5	0	0.0	40	43	12	16	11	0	0	270	419	17	38	5.6	.976	SS-126
1919		138	.278	.316	507	141	19	0	0	0.0	41	38	19	26	8	0	0	276	423	17	63	5.2	.976	SS-138
1920		154	.269	.369	569	153	21	12	4	0.7	41	61	21	15	4	0	0	330	496	23	64	5.5	.973	SS-154
1921		154	.262	.335	576	151	21	9	1	0.2	65	60	27	21	5	0	0	380	528	26	94	6.1	.972	SS-154
1922	NY A	154	.269	.345	557	150	23	5	3	0.5	64	45	23	22	2	0	0	302	538	31	74	5.7	.964	SS-154
1923		152	.246	.325	533	131	16	4	6	1.1	48	60	13	19	1	0	0	245	414	27	65	4.5	.961	SS-152
1924		153	.250	.316	548	137	12	6	4	0.7	56	64	21	15	3	0	0	322	455	27	80	5.3	.966	SS-153
1925	2 teams	NY A (22G –.217) WAS A (33G –.272)																						
″	total	55	.252	.301	163	41	6	1	0	0.0	13	22	6	6	1	4	2	96	130	11	35	4.7	.954	SS-48, 3B-2
1926	2 teams	CHI A (40G –.252) CIN N (4G –.667)																						
″	total	44	.268	.349	149	40	10	1	0	0.0	16	14	9	8	1	1	0	78	126	11	20	5.0	.949	SS-43
13 yrs.		1654	.249	.315	5837	1455	208	58	20	0.3	552	549	243	282	69	6	3	3353	5060	307	714	5.3	.965	SS-1643, 3B-3, 2B-1
WORLD SERIES																								
1915	BOS A	5	.056	.056	18	1	0	0	0	0.0	0	0	0	3	0	0	0	8	12	0	1	4.0	1.000	SS-5
1916		5	.125	.250	16	2	0	1	0	0.0	1	1	1	1	0	0	0	9	25	2	3	7.2	.944	SS-5
1918		6	.100	.100	20	2	0	0	0	0.0	0	0	1	1	0	0	0	11	25	0	3	6.0	1.000	SS-6
1922	NY A	5	.143	.143	14	2	0	0	0	0.0	0	1	1	0	0	0	0	14	15	0	6	5.8	1.000	SS-5
1923		6	.318	.318	22	7	0	0	0	0.0	2	3	0	1	0	0	0	8	20	1	4	4.8	.966	SS-6
5 yrs.		27	.156	.178	90	14	0	1	0	0.0	3	5	3	6	0	0	0	50	97	3	17	5.6	.980	SS-27

Gary Scott

SCOTT, GARY THOMAS BR TR 6′ 175 lbs.
B. Aug. 22, 1968, New Rochelle, N. Y.

Year	Team	Games	BA	SA	AB	H	2B	3B	HR	HR%	R	RBI	BB	SO	SB	Pinch Hit AB	Pinch Hit H	PO	A	E	DP	TC/G	FA	G by Pos
1991	CHI N	31	.165	.241	79	13	3	0	1	1.3	8	5	13	14	0	0	0	13	50	2	6	2.1	.969	3B-31
1992		36	.156	.240	96	15	2	0	2	2.1	8	11	5	14	0	4	0	18	43	5	3	2.1	.924	3B-30, SS-2
2 yrs.		67	.160	.240	175	28	5	0	3	1.7	16	16	18	28	0	4	0	31	93	7	9	2.1	.947	3B-61, SS-2

George Scott

SCOTT, GEORGE CHARLES, JR. (Boomer) BR TR 6′ 2″ 200 lbs.
B. Mar. 23, 1944, Greenville, Miss.

Year	Team	Games	BA	SA	AB	H	2B	3B	HR	HR%	R	RBI	BB	SO	SB	Pinch Hit AB	Pinch Hit H	PO	A	E	DP	TC/G	FA	G by Pos
1966	BOS A	162	.245	.433	601	147	18	7	27	4.5	73	90	65	**152**	4	1	1	1362	121	16	131	9.2	.989	1B-158, 3B-5
1967		159	.303	.465	565	171	21	7	19	3.4	74	82	63	119	10	5	3	1321	94	19	115	9.3	.987	1B-152, 3B-2
1968		124	.171	.237	350	60	14	0	3	0.9	23	25	26	88	3	12	1	810	65	11	69	7.5	.988	1B-112, 3B-6
1969		152	.253	.384	549	139	14	5	16	2.9	63	52	61	74	4	0	0	542	226	18	78	4.9	.977	3B-109, 1B-53
1970		127	.296	.467	480	142	24	5	16	3.3	50	63	44	95	4	0	0	551	149	18	55	5.7	.975	3B-68, 1B-59
1971		146	.263	.441	537	141	16	4	24	4.5	72	78	41	102	0	3	1	1256	75	11	122	9.4	.992	1B-143
1972	MIL A	152	.266	.426	578	154	24	4	20	3.5	71	88	43	130	16	3	1	1223	119	15	108	8.4	.989	1B-139, 3B-23
1973		158	.306	.488	604	185	30	4	24	4.0	98	107	61	94	9	1	1	1388	118	9	144	9.6	.994	1B-157, DH-1
1974		158	.281	.432	604	170	36	2	17	2.8	74	82	59	90	9	1	0	1345	114	12	137	9.4	.992	1B-148, DH-9
1975		158	.285	.515	617	176	26	4	**36**	5.8	86	**109**	51	97	6	1	0	1205	116	15	119	8.3	.989	1B-144, DH-12, 3B-5
1976		156	.274	.414	606	166	21	5	18	3.0	73	77	53	118	0	1	0	1393	107	13	133	9.8	.991	1B-155
1977	BOS A	157	.269	.500	584	157	26	5	33	5.7	103	95	57	112	1	0	0	1446	115	24	150	10.1	.985	1B-157
1978		120	.233	.379	412	96	16	4	12	2.9	51	54	44	86	1	2	0	1052	55	10	99	9.3	.991	1B-113, DH-7
1979	3 teams	BOS A (45G –.224) KC A (44G –.267) NY A (16G –.318)																						
″	total	105	.254	.387	346	88	20	4	6	1.7	46	49	31	61	2	10	2	737	46	10	67	7.9	.987	1B-83, DH-17, 3B-1
14 yrs.		2034	.268	.435	7433	1992	306	60	271	3.6	957	1051	699	1418	69	40	10	15631	1520	201	1527	8.5	.988	1B-1773, 3B-219, DH-46
WORLD SERIES																								
1967	BOS A	7	.231	.346	26	6	1	1	0	0.0	3	0	3	6	0	0	0	70	3	0	3	10.4	1.000	1B-7

Jack Scott

SCOTT, JOHN WILLIAM BL TR 6′ 2½″ 199 lbs.
B. Apr. 18, 1892, Ridgeway, N. C. D. Nov. 30, 1959, Durham, N. C.

Year	Team	Games	BA	SA	AB	H	2B	3B	HR	HR%	R	RBI	BB	SO	SB	Pinch Hit AB	Pinch Hit H	PO	A	E	DP	TC/G	FA	G by Pos
1916	PIT N	3	.000	.000	2	0	0	0	0	0.0	0	0	1	1	0	1	0	1	1	0	0	2.0	1.000	P-1
1917	BOS N	7	.125	.125	16	2	0	0	0	0.0	0	0	0	4	0	0	0	1	8	1	0	1.4	.900	P-7
1919		24	.175	.200	40	7	1	0	0	0.0	4	4	1	8	0	3	0	4	16	1	0	1.0	.952	P-19, OF-1
1920		44	.212	.242	99	21	3	0	0	0.0	5	4	5	16	0	0	0	8	65	6	1	1.8	.924	P-44
1921		51	.341	.455	88	30	5	1	1	1.1	14	12	5	7	0	3	0	4	56	3	2	1.3	.952	P-47
1922	2 teams	CIN N (1G –.000) NY N (17G –.267)																						
″	total	18	.258	.258	31	8	0	0	0	0.0	2	4	1	3	0	0	0	0	14	1	0	0.8	.933	P-18
1923	NY N	40	.316	.405	79	25	4	0	1	1.3	12	10	3	5	1	0	0	6	43	2	1	1.3	.961	P-40
1925		41	.241	.345	87	21	4	1	1	1.1	7	6	8	15	0	5	1	11	63	1	3	2.1	.987	P-36
1926		51	.337	.470	83	28	4	2	1	1.2	8	13	3	6	0	1	0	12	49	2	4	1.3	.968	P-50
1927	PHI N	83	.289	.368	114	33	6	0	1	0.9	6	17	9	9	0	28	7	7	51	3	1	1.3	.951	P-48
1928	NY N	16	.267	.333	15	4	1	0	0	0.0	3	2	1	2	0	0	0	3	11	1	2	0.9	.933	P-16
1929		30	.308	.423	26	8	3	0	0	0.0	6	1	2	0	0	0	0	6	22	0	1	0.9	1.000	P-30
12 yrs.		408	.275	.354	680	187	31	4	5	0.7	67	73	39	76	1	41	8	63	399	21	15	1.4	.957	P-356, OF-1
WORLD SERIES																								
1922	NY N	1	.250	.250	4	1	0	0	0	0.0	0	0	0	1	0	0	0	1	1	0	0	2.0	1.000	P-1
1923		2	.000	.000	1	0	0	0	0	0.0	0	0	0	0	0	0	0	0	1	0	0	1.0	1.000	P-1
2 yrs.		3	.200	.200	5	1	0	0	0	0.0	0	0	0	1	0	0	0	1	2	0	0	1.5	1.000	P-2

Jim Scott

SCOTT, JAMES WALTER BR TR 5′ 9½″ 165 lbs.
B. Sept. 22, 1888, Shenandoah, Pa. D. May 12, 1972, So. Pasadena, Fla.

Year	Team	Games	BA	SA	AB	H	2B	3B	HR	HR%	R	RBI	BB	SO	SB	Pinch Hit AB	Pinch Hit H	PO	A	E	DP	TC/G	FA	G by Pos
1914	PIT F	8	.250	.292	24	6	1	0	0	0.0	2	1	5		1	0	0	13	19	8	4	5.0	.800	SS-8

John Scott

SCOTT, JOHN HENRY BR TR 6′ 2″ 165 lbs.
B. Jan. 24, 1952, Jackson, Miss.

Year	Team	Games	BA	SA	AB	H	2B	3B	HR	HR%	R	RBI	BB	SO	SB	Pinch Hit AB	Pinch Hit H	PO	A	E	DP	TC/G	FA	G by Pos
1974	SD N	14	.067	.067	15	1	0	0	0	0.0	3	0	0	4	1	0	0	8	1	0	0	1.1	1.000	OF-8
1975		25	.000	.000	9	0	0	0	0	0.0	6	0	0	2	2	9	0	0	0	0	0	0.0	.000	OF-1
1977	TOR A	79	.240	.305	233	56	9	0	2	0.9	26	15	8	39	10	4	0	127	3	5	2	2.0	.963	OF-67, DH-2
3 yrs.		118	.222	.280	257	57	9	0	2	0.8	35	15	8	45	13	13	0	135	4	5	2	1.8	.965	OF-76, DH-2

LeGrant Scott

SCOTT, LeGRANT EDWARD
B. July 25, 1910, Cleveland, Ohio D. Nov. 12, 1993, Birmingham, Ala.
BL TL 5′ 8½″ 170 lbs.

Year	Team	Games	BA	SA	AB	H	2B	3B	HR	HR%	R	RBI	BB	SO	SB	Pinch Hit AB	Pinch Hit H	PO	A	E	DP	TC/G	FA	G by Pos
1939	PHI N	76	.280	.366	232	65	15	1	1	0.4	31	26	22	14	5	18	5	109	7	5	1	2.2	.959	OF-55

Milt Scott

SCOTT, MILTON PARKER (Mikado Milt)
B. Jan. 17, 1866, Chicago, Ill. D. Nov. 3, 1938, Baltimore, Md.
BR 5′ 9″ 160 lbs.

Year	Team	Games	BA	SA	AB	H	2B	3B	HR	HR%	R	RBI	BB	SO	SB	Pinch Hit AB	Pinch Hit H	PO	A	E	DP	TC/G	FA	G by Pos
1882	CHI N	1	.400	.400	5	2	0	0	0	0.0	1	0	0	0		0	0	3	0	0	0	3.0	1.000	1B-1
1884	DET N	110	.247	.329	438	108	17	5	3	0.7	29		9	62		0	0	1120	26	38	37	10.8	.968	1B-110
1885	2 teams	DET N (38G –.264) PIT AA (55G –.248)																						
″	total	93	.254	.299	358	91	14	1	0	0.0	29	12	9	16		0	0	1017	34	23	45	11.5	.979	1B-93
1886	BAL AA	137	.190	.242	484	92	11	4	2	0.4	48		22			0	0	1347	59	38	38	10.5	.974	1B-137, P-1
4 yrs.		341	.228	.288	1285	293	42	10	5	0.4	107	12	40	78		0	0	3487	119	99	120	10.8	.973	1B-341, P-1

Pete Scott

SCOTT, FLOYD JOHN
B. Dec. 21, 1898, Woodland, Calif. D. May 3, 1953, Daly City, Calif.
BR TR 5′11½″ 175 lbs.

Year	Team	Games	BA	SA	AB	H	2B	3B	HR	HR%	R	RBI	BB	SO	SB	Pinch Hit AB	Pinch Hit H	PO	A	E	DP	TC/G	FA	G by Pos
1926	CHI N	77	.286	.413	189	54	13	1	3	1.6	34	34	22	31	3	4	1	116	9	5	3	2.2	.962	OF-59, 3B-1
1927		71	.314	.442	156	49	18	1	0	0.0	28	21	19	18	1	31	7	70	3	1	1	2.1	.986	OF-36
1928	PIT N	60	.311	.497	177	55	10	4	5	2.8	33	33	18	14	1	6	2	186	8	4	6	4.0	.980	OF-42, 1B-8
3 yrs.		208	.303	.450	522	158	41	6	8	1.5	95	88	59	63	5	41	10	372	20	10	10	2.8	.975	OF-137, 1B-8, 3B-1

Rodney Scott

SCOTT, RODNEY DARRELL
B. Oct. 16, 1953, Indianapolis, Ind.
BB TR 6′ 160 lbs.
BR 1975

Year	Team	Games	BA	SA	AB	H	2B	3B	HR	HR%	R	RBI	BB	SO	SB	Pinch Hit AB	Pinch Hit H	PO	A	E	DP	TC/G	FA	G by Pos
1975	KC A	48	.067	.067	15	1	0	0	0	0.0	13	0	1	3	4	1	0	8	12	2	2	0.6	.909	DH-22, 2B-9, SS-8
1976	MON N	7	.400	.400	10	4	0	0	0	0.0	3	0	1	1	2	0	0	6	8	0	2	1.6	1.000	2B-6, SS-3
1977	OAK A	133	.261	.294	364	95	4	4	0	0.0	56	20	43	50	33	8	3	200	273	21	49	3.3	.957	2B-71, SS-70, 3B-5, OF-1, DH-1
1978	CHI N	78	.282	.313	227	64	5	1	0	0.0	41	15	43	41	27	3	0	77	119	14	17	2.6	.933	3B-60, OF-10, SS-6, 2B-6
1979	MON N	151	.238	.294	562	134	12	5	3	0.5	69	42	66	82	39	1	1	362	421	21	82	5.3	.974	2B-113, SS-39
1980		154	.224	.293	567	127	13	**13**	0	0.0	84	46	70	75	63	3	2	339	432	18	88	5.3	.977	2B-129, SS-21
1981		95	.205	.250	336	69	9	3	0	0.0	43	26	50	35	30	0	0	187	278	8	41	5.1	.983	2B-93
1982	2 teams	MON N (14G –.200) NY A (10G –.192)																						
″	total	24	.196	.196	51	10	0	0	0	0.0	7	1	7	4	7	2	0	31	42	2	8	3.4	.973	2B-16, SS-6
8 yrs.		690	.236	.285	2132	504	43	26	3	0.1	316	150	281	291	205	18	6	1210	1585	86	289	4.1	.970	2B-443, SS-153, 3B-65, DH-23, OF-11
LEAGUE CHAMPIONSHIP SERIES																								
1981	MON N	5	.167	.167	18	3	0	0	0	0.0	0	0	1	3	1	0	0	12	14	1	7	5.4	.963	2B-5

Tony Scott

SCOTT, ANTHONY
B. Sept. 18, 1951, Cincinnati, Ohio.
BB TR 6′ 164 lbs.

Year	Team	Games	BA	SA	AB	H	2B	3B	HR	HR%	R	RBI	BB	SO	SB	Pinch Hit AB	Pinch Hit H	PO	A	E	DP	TC/G	FA	G by Pos
1973	MON N	11	.000	.000	1	0	0	0	0	0.0	2	0	0	1	0	1	0	0	0	1	0	0.3	.000	OF-3
1974		19	.286	.286	7	2	0	0	0	0.0	2	1	1	3	1	1	1	7	0	0	0	0.4	1.000	OF-16
1975		92	.182	.238	143	26	4	2	0	0.0	19	11	12	38	5	8	1	94	6	4	0	1.5	.962	OF-71
1977	STL N	95	.291	.397	292	85	16	3	3	1.0	38	41	33	48	13	10	1	223	5	1	0	2.6	.996	OF-89
1978		96	.228	.283	219	50	5	2	1	0.5	28	14	14	41	5	30	6	100	6	6	0	1.5	.946	OF-77
1979		153	.259	.361	587	152	22	10	6	1.0	69	68	34	92	37	3	1	427	14	7	5	3.0	.984	OF-151
1980		143	.251	.311	415	104	19	3	0	0.0	51	28	35	68	22	8	2	324	5	1	2	2.5	.997	OF-134
1981	2 teams	STL N (45G –.227) HOU N (55G –.293)																						
″	total	100	.264	.359	401	106	18	4	4	1.0	49	39	20	54	18	0	0	247	7	2	0	2.6	.992	OF-99
1982	HOU N	132	.239	.293	460	110	16	3	1	0.2	43	29	15	56	18	10	2	262	7	5	0	2.1	.982	OF-129
1983		80	.226	.301	186	42	6	1	2	1.1	20	17	11	39	5	27	5	89	2	0	1	1.5	1.000	OF-61
1984	2 teams	HOU N (25G –.190) MON N (45G –.254)																						
″	total	70	.239	.293	92	22	5	0	0	0.0	10	5	11	24	1	38	10	30	1	0	0	1.3	1.000	OF-23
11 yrs.		991	.249	.327	2803	699	111	28	17	0.6	331	253	186	464	125	136	29	1803	53	27	8	2.2	.986	OF-853
DIVISIONAL PLAYOFF SERIES																								
1981	HOU N	5	.150	.150	20	3	0	0	0	0.0	0	2	1	6	0	0	0	9	0	0	0	1.8	1.000	OF-5

Jim Scranton

SCRANTON, JAMES DEAN
B. Apr. 5, 1960, Torrence, Calif.
BR TR 6′ 180 lbs.

Year	Team	Games	BA	SA	AB	H	2B	3B	HR	HR%	R	RBI	BB	SO	SB	Pinch Hit AB	Pinch Hit H	PO	A	E	DP	TC/G	FA	G by Pos
1984	KC A	2	.000	.000	2	0	0	0	0	0.0	0	0	0	0	0	1	0	0	1	0	1	0.5	1.000	SS-1, 3B-1
1985		6	.000	.000	4	0	0	0	0	0.0	1	0	0	0	0	0	0	1	8	0	1	1.8	1.000	SS-5
2 yrs.		8	.000	.000	6	0	0	0	0	0.0	1	0	0	0	0	1	0	1	9	0	2	1.4	1.000	SS-6, 3B-1

Chuck Scrivener

SCRIVENER, WAYNE ALLISON
B. Oct. 3, 1947, Alexandria, Va.
BR TR 5′ 9″ 170 lbs.

Year	Team	Games	BA	SA	AB	H	2B	3B	HR	HR%	R	RBI	BB	SO	SB	Pinch Hit AB	Pinch Hit H	PO	A	E	DP	TC/G	FA	G by Pos
1975	DET A	4	.250	.313	16	4	1	0	0	0.0	0	0	0	1	1	0	0	2	8	0	0	2.0	1.000	3B-3, SS-2
1976		80	.221	.288	222	49	7	1	2	0.9	28	16	19	34	1	2	0	137	230	12	47	4.5	.968	2B-43, SS-37, 3B-5
1977		61	.083	.083	72	6	0	0	0	0.0	10	2	5	9	0	0	0	50	89	3	16	2.3	.979	SS-50, 2B-8, 3B-3
3 yrs.		145	.190	.242	310	59	8	1	2	0.6	38	18	24	44	2	2	0	189	327	15	63	3.5	.972	SS-89, 2B-51, 3B-11

Tony Scruggs

SCRUGGS, ANTHONY RAYMOND
B. Mar. 19, 1966, Riverside, Calif.
BR TR 6′ 1″ 210 lbs.

Year	Team	Games	BA	SA	AB	H	2B	3B	HR	HR%	R	RBI	BB	SO	SB	Pinch Hit AB	Pinch Hit H	PO	A	E	DP	TC/G	FA	G by Pos
1991	TEX A	5	.000	.000	6	0	0	0	0	0.0	1	0	0	1	0	1	0	5	0	0	0	1.0	1.000	OF-5

Ken Sears

SEARS, KENNETH EUGENE (Ziggy)
B. July 6, 1917, Streator, Ill. D. July 17, 1968, Bridgeport, Tex.
BL TR 6′ 1″ 200 lbs.

Year	Team	Games	BA	SA	AB	H	2B	3B	HR	HR%	R	RBI	BB	SO	SB	Pinch Hit AB	Pinch Hit H	PO	A	E	DP	TC/G	FA	G by Pos
1943	NY A	60	.278	.348	187	52	7	0	2	1.1	22	22	11	18	1	10	3	233	31	7	5	5.4	.974	C-50
1946	STL A	7	.333	.333	15	5	0	0	0	0.0	1	1	3	0	0	3	1	10	0	0	0	2.5	1.000	C-4
2 yrs.		67	.282	.347	202	57	7	0	2	1.0	23	23	14	18	1	13	4	243	31	7	5	5.2	.975	C-54

Jimmy Sebring

SEBRING, JAMES DENNISON
B. Mar. 22, 1882, Liberty, Pa. D. Dec. 22, 1909, Williamsport, Pa.
BL TR 6′ 180 lbs.

Year	Team	Games	BA	SA	AB	H	2B	3B	HR	HR%	R	RBI	BB	SO	SB	Pinch Hit AB	Pinch Hit H	PO	A	E	DP	TC/G	FA	G by Pos
1902	PIT N	19	.325	.475	80	26	4	4	0	0.0	15	15	5		2	0	0	33	5	1	2	2.1	.974	OF-19
1903		124	.277	.383	506	140	16	13	4	0.8	71	64	32		20	0	0	208	20	18	11	2.0	.927	OF-124
1904	2 teams	PIT N (80G –.269) CIN N (56G –.225)																						
″	total	136	.250	.323	527	132	20	9	0	0.0	50	56	31		16	0	0	234	27	7	8	2.0	.974	OF-136

Jimmy Sebring *continued*

Year	Team	Games	BA	SA	AB	H	2B	3B	HR	HR%	R	RBI	BB	SO	SB	Pinch Hit AB	Pinch Hit H	PO	A	E	DP	TC/G	FA	G by Pos
1905	**CIN N**	58	.286	.406	217	62	10	5	2	0.9	31	28	14		11	2	0	63	6	9	2	1.4	.885	OF-56
1909	**2 teams**	**BKN N** (25G –.099) **WAS A** (1G –.000)																						
"	**total**	26	.099	.136	81	8	1	1	0	0.0	11	5	11		3	0	0	35	4	2	1	1.6	.951	OF-26
5 yrs.		363	.261	.355	1411	368	51	32	6	0.4	178	168	93		52	2	0	573	62	37	24	1.9	.945	OF-361
WORLD SERIES																								
1903	**PIT N**	8	.367	.533	30	11	0	1	1	3.3	3	5	1	4	0	0	0	13	1	0	0	1.8	1.000	OF-8

Frank Secory

SECORY, FRANK EDWARD BR TR 6′ 1″ 200 lbs.
B. Aug. 24, 1912, Mason City, Iowa D. Apr. 7, 1995, Port Huron, Mich.

Year	Team	Games	BA	SA	AB	H	2B	3B	HR	HR%	R	RBI	BB	SO	SB	Pinch Hit AB	Pinch Hit H	PO	A	E	DP	TC/G	FA	G by Pos
1940	**DET A**	1	.000	.000	1	0	0	0	0	0.0	0	0	0	1	0	1	0	0	0	0	0	0.0	—	
1942	**CIN N**	2	.000	.000	5	0	0	0	0	0.0	1	1	3	2	0	0	0	6	0	1	0	3.5	.857	OF-2
1944	**CHI N**	22	.321	.554	56	18	1	0	4	7.1	10	17	6	8	1	4	0	44	0	0	0	2.6	1.000	OF-17
1945		35	.158	.175	57	9	1	0	0	0.0	4	6	2	7	0	21	2	20	0	0	0	1.7	1.000	OF-12
1946		33	.233	.512	43	10	3	0	3	7.0	6	12	6	6	0	22	4	10	0	2	0	1.3	.833	OF-9
5 yrs.		93	.228	.389	162	37	5	0	7	4.3	21	36	17	24	1	48	6	80	0	3	0	2.1	.964	OF-40
WORLD SERIES																								
1945	**CHI N**	5	.400	.400	5	2	0	0	0	0.0	0	0	0	2	0	5	2	0	0	0	0	0.0	—	

Charlie See

SEE, CHARLES HENRY (Chad) BL TR 5′10½″ 175 lbs.
B. Oct. 13, 1896, Pleasantville, N. Y. D. July 19, 1948, Bridgeport, Conn.

Year	Team	Games	BA	SA	AB	H	2B	3B	HR	HR%	R	RBI	BB	SO	SB	Pinch Hit AB	Pinch Hit H	PO	A	E	DP	TC/G	FA	G by Pos
1919	**CIN N**	8	.286	.286	14	4	0	0	0	0.0	1	1	1	0	0	2	0	5	0	1	0	1.5	.833	OF-4
1920		47	.305	.354	82	25	4	0	0	0.0	9	15	1	7	2	24	8	49	5	2	2	3.1	.964	OF-17, P-1
1921		37	.245	.340	106	26	5	1	1	0.9	11	7	7	5	3	7	2	58	4	3	1	2.2	.954	OF-29
3 yrs.		92	.272	.342	202	55	9	1	1	0.5	21	23	9	12	5	33	10	112	9	6	3	2.5	.953	OF-50, P-1

Larry See

SEE, RALPH LAURENCE BR TR 6′ 1″ 195 lbs.
B. June 20, 1960, Norwalk, Calif.

Year	Team	Games	BA	SA	AB	H	2B	3B	HR	HR%	R	RBI	BB	SO	SB	Pinch Hit AB	Pinch Hit H	PO	A	E	DP	TC/G	FA	G by Pos
1986	**LA N**	13	.250	.350	20	5	2	0	0	0.0	1	2	2	7	0	4	1	41	6	1	3	5.3	.979	1B-9
1988	**TEX A**	13	.130	.130	23	3	0	0	0	0.0	0	0	1	8	0	0	0	13	1	1	2	3.0	.933	1B-2, C-2, 3B-1
2 yrs.		26	.186	.233	43	8	2	0	0	0.0	1	2	3	15	0	4	1	54	7	2	5	4.5	.968	1B-11, C-2, 3B-1

Bob Seeds

SEEDS, IRA ROBERT (Suitcase Bob) BR TR 6′ 180 lbs.
B. Feb. 24, 1907, Ringgold, Tex. D. Oct. 28, 1993, Erick, Okla.

Year	Team	Games	BA	SA	AB	H	2B	3B	HR	HR%	R	RBI	BB	SO	SB	Pinch Hit AB	Pinch Hit H	PO	A	E	DP	TC/G	FA	G by Pos
1930	**CLE A**	85	.285	.379	277	79	11	3	3	1.1	37	32	12	22	1	15	4	156	6	8	0	2.4	.953	OF-70
1931		48	.306	.373	134	41	4	1	1	0.7	26	10	11	11	1	9	1	63	4	2	0	2.0	.971	OF-33, 1B-2
1932	**2 teams**	**CLE A** (2G –.000) **CHI A** (116G –.290)																						
"	**total**	118	.288	.370	438	126	18	6	2	0.5	53	45	31	37	5	4	0	234	7	9	1	2.2	.964	OF-113
1933	**BOS A**	82	.243	.335	230	56	13	4	0	0.0	26	23	21	20	1	7	2	422	22	8	33	6.2	.982	1B-41, OF-32
1934	**2 teams**	**BOS A** (8G –.167) **CLE A** (61G –.247)																						
"	**total**	69	.245	.297	192	47	8	1	0	0.0	28	19	21	14	2	15	3	83	2	2	0	1.8	.977	OF-49
1936	**NY A**	13	.262	.571	42	11	1	0	4	9.5	12	10	5	3	3	1	0	24	5	1	1	2.5	.967	OF-9, 3B-3
1938	**NY N**	81	.291	.443	296	86	12	3	9	3.0	35	52	20	33	0	2	0	147	6	2	2	2.0	.987	OF-76
1939		63	.266	.393	173	46	5	1	5	2.9	33	26	22	31	1	12	2	77	2	2	0	1.6	.975	OF-50
1940		56	.290	.426	155	45	5	2	4	2.6	18	16	17	19	0	15	4	64	3	1	0	1.7	.985	OF-40
9 yrs.		615	.277	.382	1937	537	77	21	28	1.4	268	233	160	190	14	80	16	1270	57	35	37	2.6	.974	OF-472, 1B-43, 3B-3
WORLD SERIES																								
1936	**NY A**	1	—	—	0	0	0	0	0	—	0	0	0	0	0	0	0	0	0	0	0	0.0	—	

Pat Seerey

SEEREY, JAMES PATRICK BR TR 5′10″ 200 lbs.
B. Mar. 17, 1923, Wilburton, Okla. D. Apr. 28, 1986, Jennings, Mo.

Year	Team	Games	BA	SA	AB	H	2B	3B	HR	HR%	R	RBI	BB	SO	SB	Pinch Hit AB	Pinch Hit H	PO	A	E	DP	TC/G	FA	G by Pos
1943	**CLE A**	26	.222	.306	72	16	3	0	1	1.4	8	5	4	19	0	9	2	35	3	1	0	2.4	.974	OF-16
1944		101	.234	.412	342	80	16	0	15	**4.4**	39	39	19	**99**	0	18	3	196	8	3	1	2.4	.986	OF-86
1945		126	.237	.401	414	98	22	2	14	3.4	56	56	66	**97**	1	8	0	227	7	6	3	2.1	.975	OF-117
1946		117	.225	.470	404	91	17	2	26	6.4	57	62	65	**101**	2	2	0	248	4	5	1	2.2	.981	OF-115
1947		82	.171	.352	216	37	4	1	11	5.1	24	29	34	66	0	12	1	105	7	5	1	1.7	.957	OF-68
1948	**2 teams**	**CLE A** (10G –.261) **CHI A** (95G –.229)																						
"	**total**	105	.231	.419	363	84	11	0	19	5.2	51	70	90	**102**	0	3	0	204	9	4	5	2.2	.982	OF-100
1949	**CHI A**	4	.000	.000	4	0	0	0	0	0.0	1	0	3	1	0	2	0	1	0	0	0	0.5	1.000	OF-2
7 yrs.		561	.224	.412	1815	406	73	5	86	4.7	236	261	281	485	3	54	6	1016	38	24	11	2.1	.978	OF-504

Emmett Seery

SEERY, JOHN EMMETT BL TR
B. Feb. 13, 1861, Princeville, Ill. D. Aug. 7, 1930, Saranac Lake, N. Y.

Year	Team	Games	BA	SA	AB	H	2B	3B	HR	HR%	R	RBI	BB	SO	SB	Pinch Hit AB	Pinch Hit H	PO	A	E	DP	TC/G	FA	G by Pos
1884	**2 teams**	**BAL U** (105G –.311) **KC U** (1G –.500)																						
"	**total**	106	.313	.411	467	146	26	7	2	0.4	115		21			0	0	166	30	39	4	2.1	.834	OF-105, C-3, 3B-2
1885	**STL N**	59	.162	.208	216	35	7	0	1	0.5	20	14	16	37		0	0	96	18	17	1	2.2	.870	OF-59, 3B-1
1886		126	.238	.327	453	108	22	6	2	0.4	73	48	57	**82**		0	0	176	21	27	2	1.8	.879	OF-126, P-2
1887	**IND N**	122	.224	.353	465	104	18	15	4	0.9	104	28	71	68	48	0	0	220	25	30	2	2.2	.891	OF-122, SS-1
1888		133	.220	.330	500	110	20	10	5	1.0	87	50	64	73	80	0	0	260	21	19	6	2.2	.937	OF-133, SS-1
1889		127	.314	.454	526	165	26	12	8	1.5	123	59	67	59	19	0	0	220	20	24	4	2.1	.909	OF-127
1890	**BKN P**	104	.223	.297	394	88	12	7	1	0.3	78	50	70	36	44	0	0	216	21	28	3	2.5	.894	OF-104
1891	**CIN AA**	97	.285	.411	372	106	15	10	4	1.1	77	36	81	52	19	0	0	160	17	20	3	2.0	.898	OF-97
1892	**LOU N**	42	.201	.253	154	31	6	1	0	0.0	18	15	24	19	6	0	0	65	10	3	1	1.9	.962	OF-42
9 yrs.		916	.252	.356	3547	893	152	68	27	0.8	695	300	471	426	216	0	0	1579	183	207	26	2.1	.895	OF-915, 3B-3, C-3, SS-2, P-2

Kevin Sefcik

SEFCIK, KEVIN JOHN BR TR 5′11″ 175 lbs.
B. Feb. 10, 1971, Tinley Park, Ill.

Year	Team	Games	BA	SA	AB	H	2B	3B	HR	HR%	R	RBI	BB	SO	SB	Pinch Hit AB	Pinch Hit H	PO	A	E	DP	TC/G	FA	G by Pos
1995	**PHI N**	5	.000	.000	4	0	0	0	0	0.0	1	0	0	2	0	2	0	0	1	0	1	0.5	1.000	3B-2

Kal Segrist

SEGRIST, KAL HILL BR TR 6′ 180 lbs.
B. Apr. 14, 1931, Greenville, Tex.

Year	Team	Games	BA	SA	AB	H	2B	3B	HR	HR%	R	RBI	BB	SO	SB	Pinch Hit AB	Pinch Hit H	PO	A	E	DP	TC/G	FA	G by Pos
1952	**NY A**	13	.043	.043	23	1	0	0	0	0.0	3	1	3	1	0	1	0	15	19	1	5	2.9	.971	2B-11, 3B-1
1955	**BAL A**	7	.333	.333	9	3	0	0	0	0.0	1	0	2	0	0	2	1	1	7	0	0	1.6	1.000	3B-3, 2B-1, 1B-1
2 yrs.		20	.125	.125	32	4	0	0	0	0.0	4	1	5	1	0	3	1	16	26	1	5	2.5	.977	2B-12, 3B-4, 1B-1

David Segui

SEGUI, DAVID VINCENT
Son of Diego Segui.
B. June 19, 1966, Kansas City, Kans.

BB TL 6′ 1″ 170 lbs.

Year	Team	Games	BA	SA	AB	H	2B	3B	HR	HR%	R	RBI	BB	SO	SB	Pinch Hit AB	Pinch Hit H	PO	A	E	DP	TC/G	FA	G by Pos
1990	**BAL A**	40	.244	.350	123	30	7	0	2	1.6	14	15	11	15	0	0	0	283	26	3	24	7.8	.990	1B-36, DH-4
1991		86	.278	.340	212	59	7	0	2	0.9	15	22	12	19	1	24	6	264	23	3	22	3.7	.990	1B-42, OF-33, DH-4
1992		115	.233	.296	189	44	9	0	1	0.5	21	17	20	23	1	11	4	406	35	1	42	3.9	.998	1B-95, OF-18
1993		146	.273	.400	450	123	27	0	10	2.2	54	60	58	53	2	2	0	1152	98	5	122	8.7	.996	1B-144, DH-1
1994	**NY N**	92	.241	.387	336	81	17	1	10	3.0	46	43	33	43	0	1	0	696	52	5	65	7.6	.993	1B-78, OF-21
1995	**2 teams**	**NY N** (33G –.329) **MON N** (97G –.305)																						
"	**total**	130	.309	.461	456	141	25	4	12	2.6	68	68	40	47	2	9	4	898	73	3	71	7.9	.997	1B-104, OF-20
6 yrs.		609	.271	.391	1766	478	92	5	37	2.1	218	225	174	200	6	47	14	3699	307	20	346	6.7	.995	1B-499, OF-92, DH-9

Kurt Seibert

SEIBERT, KURT ELLIOTT
B. Oct. 16, 1955, Cheverly, Md.

BB TR 6′ 165 lbs.

Year	Team	Games	BA	SA	AB	H	2B	3B	HR	HR%	R	RBI	BB	SO	SB	Pinch Hit AB	Pinch Hit H	PO	A	E	DP	TC/G	FA	G by Pos
1979	**CHI N**	7	.000	.000	2	0	0	0	0	0.0	2	0	0	1	0	1	0	2	0	0	0	2.0	1.000	3B-1

Rick Seilheimer

SEILHEIMER, RICKY ALLEN
B. Aug. 30, 1960, Brenham, Tex.

BL TR 5′11″ 185 lbs.

Year	Team	Games	BA	SA	AB	H	2B	3B	HR	HR%	R	RBI	BB	SO	SB	Pinch Hit AB	Pinch Hit H	PO	A	E	DP	TC/G	FA	G by Pos
1980	**CHI A**	21	.212	.365	52	11	3	1	1	1.9	4	3	4	15	1	0	0	62	8	4	2	3.5	.946	C-21

Kevin Seitzer

SEITZER, KEVIN LEE
B. Mar. 26, 1962, Springfield, Ill.

BR TR 5′11″ 180 lbs.

Year	Team	Games	BA	SA	AB	H	2B	3B	HR	HR%	R	RBI	BB	SO	SB	Pinch Hit AB	Pinch Hit H	PO	A	E	DP	TC/G	FA	G by Pos
1986	**KC A**	28	.323	.448	96	31	4	1	2	2.1	16	11	19	14	0	1	1	224	19	3	17	8.2	.988	1B-22, OF-5, 3B-3
1987		161	.323	.470	641	**207**	33	8	15	2.3	105	83	80	85	12	0	0	290	315	24	51	3.7	.962	3B-141, 1B-25, OF-3
1988		149	.304	.406	559	170	32	5	5	0.9	90	60	72	64	10	1	0	93	297	26	33	2.8	.938	3B-147, OF-1, DH-1
1989		160	.281	.337	597	168	17	2	4	0.7	78	48	102	76	17	0	0	118	277	20	30	2.4	.952	3B-159, SS-6, OF-3, 1B-2
1990		158	.275	.370	622	171	31	5	6	1.0	91	38	67	66	7	5	3	118	281	19	36	2.6	.955	3B-152, 2B-10
1991		85	.265	.350	234	62	11	3	1	0.4	28	25	29	21	4	20	11	45	127	11	8	2.6	.940	3B-68, DH-3
1992	**MIL A**	148	.270	.367	540	146	35	1	5	0.9	74	71	57	44	13	0	0	102	277	12	18	2.6	.969	3B-146, 2B-2, 1B-1
1993	**2 teams**	**OAK A** (73G –.255) **MIL A** (47G –.290)																						
"	**total**	120	.269	.396	417	112	16	2	11	2.6	45	57	44	48	7	13	2	276	151	12	43	3.5	.973	3B-79, 1B-31, DH-6, OF-4, 2B-3, SS-1, P-1
1994	**MIL A**	80	.314	.453	309	97	24	2	5	1.6	44	49	30	38	2	1	1	329	104	11	51	5.4	.975	3B-43, 1B-35, DH-4
1995		132	.311	.421	492	153	33	3	5	1.0	56	69	64	57	2	2	1	340	179	10	55	3.8	.981	3B-88, 1B-36, DH-14
10 yrs.		1221	.292	.398	4507	1317	236	32	59	1.3	627	511	564	513	74	43	19	1935	2027	148	342	3.3	.964	3B-1026, 1B-152, DH-28, OF-16, 2B-15, SS-7, P-1

Kip Selbach

SELBACH, ALBERT KARL
B. Mar. 24, 1872, Columbus, Ohio D. Feb. 17, 1956, Columbus, Ohio.

BR TR 5′ 7″ 190 lbs.

Year	Team	Games	BA	SA	AB	H	2B	3B	HR	HR%	R	RBI	BB	SO	SB	Pinch Hit AB	Pinch Hit H	PO	A	E	DP	TC/G	FA	G by Pos
1894	**WAS N**	97	.306	.511	372	114	21	17	7	1.9	69	71	51	20	21	0	0	205	62	38	7	3.1	.875	OF-80, SS-19
1895		129	.322	.483	516	166	21	**22**	6	1.2	115	55	69	28	31	0	0	320	64	39	6	3.3	.908	OF-118, SS-6, 2B-5
1896		127	.304	.423	487	148	17	13	5	1.0	100	100	76	28	49	2	2	303	13	18	3	2.7	.946	OF-126
1897		124	.313	.461	486	152	25	16	5	1.0	113	59	80		46	0	0	305	14	15	2	2.7	.955	OF-124
1898		132	.303	.417	515	156	28	11	3	0.6	88	60	64		25	0	0	320	30	19	6	2.8	.949	OF-131, SS-1
1899	**CIN N**	140	.296	.407	521	154	27	11	3	0.6	104	87	70		38	0	0	355	27	19	10	2.9	.953	OF-140
1900	**NY N**	141	.337	.461	523	176	29	12	4	0.8	98	68	72		36	0	0	327	25	18	8	2.6	.951	OF-141
1901		125	.289	.376	502	145	29	6	1	0.2	89	56	45		8	0	0	215	11	14	2	1.9	.942	OF-125
1902	**BAL A**	128	.320	.427	503	161	27	9	3	0.6	86	60	58		22	1	1	286	17	19	3	2.5	.941	OF-127
1903	**WAS A**	141	.250	.354	536	134	23	12	3	0.6	68	49	41		20	0	0	251	11	12	2	1.9	.956	OF-140, 3B-1
1904	**2 teams**	**WAS A** (48G –.275) **BOS A** (98G –.258)																						
"	**total**	146	.264	.356	554	146	27	12	0	0.0	65	44	72		19	0	0	293	13	16	3	2.2	.950	OF-146
1905	**BOS A**	124	.246	.342	418	103	16	6	4	1.0	54	47	67		12	5	1	186	8	15	1	1.8	.928	OF-116
1906		60	.211	.268	228	48	9	2	0	0.0	15	23	18		7	2	0	109	6	4	2	2.1	.966	OF-58
13 yrs.		1614	.293	.411	6161	1803	299	149	44	0.7	1064	779	783	76	334	10	4	3475	301	246	55	2.5	.939	OF-1572, SS-26, 2B-5, 3B-1

George Selkirk

SELKIRK, GEORGE ALEXANDER (Twinkletoes)
B. Jan. 4, 1908, Huntsville, Ont., Canada. D. Jan. 19, 1987, Ft. Lauderdale, Fla.

BL TR 6′ 1″ 182 lbs.

Year	Team	Games	BA	SA	AB	H	2B	3B	HR	HR%	R	RBI	BB	SO	SB	Pinch Hit AB	Pinch Hit H	PO	A	E	DP	TC/G	FA	G by Pos
1934	**NY A**	46	.313	.449	176	55	7	1	5	2.8	23	38	15	17	1	0	0	90	3	1	1	2.0	.989	OF-46
1935		128	.312	.487	491	153	29	12	11	2.2	64	94	44	36	2	2	1	269	9	7	1	2.2	.975	OF-127
1936		137	.308	.511	493	152	28	9	18	3.7	93	107	94	60	13	0	0	290	10	8	3	2.3	.974	OF-135
1937		78	.328	.629	256	84	13	5	18	7.0	49	68	34	24	8	5	1	140	9	2	1	2.2	.987	OF-69
1938		99	.254	.409	335	85	12	5	10	3.0	58	62	68	52	9	2	0	176	7	5	3	2.0	.973	OF-95
1939		128	.306	.517	418	128	17	4	21	5.0	103	101	103	49	12	5	0	254	4	3	1	2.1	.989	OF-124
1940		118	.269	.491	379	102	17	5	19	5.0	68	71	84	43	3	7	2	220	9	9	6	2.1	.962	OF-111
1941		70	.220	.360	164	36	5	0	6	3.7	30	25	28	30	1	19	4	84	4	3	2	1.9	.967	OF-47
1942		42	.192	.231	78	15	3	0	0	0.0	15	10	16	8	0	19	4	36	0	0	0	1.9	1.000	OF-19
9 yrs.		846	.290	.483	2790	810	131	41	108	3.9	503	576	486	319	49	59	12	1559	55	38	18	2.1	.977	OF-773
WORLD SERIES																								
1936	**NY A**	6	.333	.667	24	8	0	1	2	8.3	6	3	4	4	0	0	0	9	0	1	0	1.7	.900	OF-6
1937		5	.263	.316	19	5	1	0	0	0.0	5	6	2	0	0	0	0	7	0	0	0	1.4	1.000	OF-5
1938		3	.200	.200	10	2	0	0	0	0.0	0	1	2	1	0	0	0	3	0	0	0	1.0	1.000	OF-3
1939		4	.167	.250	12	2	1	0	0	0.0	0	0	3	2	0	0	0	9	0	0	0	2.3	1.000	OF-4
1941		2	.500	.500	2	1	0	0	0	0.0	0	0	0	0	0	2	1	0	0	0	0	0.0	—	
1942		1	.000	.000	1	0	0	0	0	0.0	0	0	0	0	0	1	0	0	0	0	0	0.0	—	
6 yrs.		21	.265	.412	68	18	2	1	2	2.9	11	10	11	7	0	3	1	28	0	1	0	1.6	.966	OF-18

Rube Sellers

SELLERS, OLIVER
B. Mar. 7, 1881, Duquesne, Pa. D. Jan. 14, 1952, Pittsburgh, Pa.

BR TR 5′10″ 180 lbs.

Year	Team	Games	BA	SA	AB	H	2B	3B	HR	HR%	R	RBI	BB	SO	SB	Pinch Hit AB	Pinch Hit H	PO	A	E	DP	TC/G	FA	G by Pos
1910	**BOS N**	12	.156	.156	32	5	0	0	0	0.0	3	2	6	5	1	3	0	12	0	0	0	1.3	1.000	OF-9

Carey Selph

SELPH, CAREY ISOM
B. Dec. 5, 1901, Donaldson, Ark. D. Feb. 24, 1976, Houston, Tex.

BR TR 5′ 9½″ 175 lbs.

Year	Team	Games	BA	SA	AB	H	2B	3B	HR	HR%	R	RBI	BB	SO	SB	Pinch Hit AB	Pinch Hit H	PO	A	E	DP	TC/G	FA	G by Pos
1929	**STL N**	25	.235	.294	51	12	1	1	0	0.0	8	7	6	4	1	5	1	23	29	1	3	3.3	.981	2B-16
1932	**CHI A**	116	.283	.371	396	112	19	8	0	0.0	50	51	31	9	7	18	2	128	215	28	28	3.8	.925	3B-71, 2B-26
2 yrs.		141	.277	.362	447	124	20	9	0	0.0	58	58	37	13	8	23	3	151	244	29	31	3.8	.932	3B-71, 2B-42

Mike Sember

SEMBER, MICHAEL DAVID — BR TR 6′ 185 lbs.
B. Feb. 24, 1953, Hammond, Ind.

Year	Team	Games	BA	SA	AB	H	2B	3B	HR	HR%	R	RBI	BB	SO	SB	Pinch Hit AB	Pinch Hit H	PO	A	E	DP	TC/G	FA	G by Pos
1977	CHI N	3	.250	.250	4	1	0	0	0	0.0	0	0	0	2	0	2	0	2	2	0	1	4.0	1.000	2B-1
1978		9	.333	.333	3	1	0	0	0	0.0	2	0	1	1	0	2	1	1	3	1	1	0.6	.800	3B-7, SS-1
2 yrs.		12	.286	.286	7	2	0	0	0	0.0	2	0	1	3	0	4	1	3	5	1	2	1.0	.889	3B-7, SS-1, 2B-1

Andy Seminick

SEMINICK, ANDREW WASIL — BR TR 5′11″ 187 lbs.
B. Sept. 12, 1920, Pierce, W. Va.

Year	Team	Games	BA	SA	AB	H	2B	3B	HR	HR%	R	RBI	BB	SO	SB	Pinch Hit AB	Pinch Hit H	PO	A	E	DP	TC/G	FA	G by Pos
1943	PHI N	22	.181	.292	72	13	2	0	2	2.8	9	5	7	22	0	0	0	83	14	7	2	4.5	.933	C-22, OF-1
1944		22	.222	.286	63	14	2	1	0	0.0	9	4	6	17	2	4	0	58	8	2	1	3.8	.971	C-11, OF-7
1945		80	.239	.394	188	45	7	2	6	3.2	18	26	18	38	3	6	0	202	39	9	3	3.3	.964	C-70, 3B-4, OF-1
1946		124	.264	.414	406	107	15	5	12	3.0	55	52	39	86	2	6	0	461	61	14	12	4.5	.974	C-118
1947		111	.252	.427	337	85	16	2	13	3.9	48	50	58	69	4	3	0	438	53	11	6	4.7	.978	C-107
1948		125	.225	.368	391	88	11	3	13	3.3	49	44	58	68	4	1	0	541	74	22	8	5.1	.965	C-124
1949		109	.243	.503	334	81	11	2	24	7.2	52	68	69	74	0	8	1	411	54	12	6	4.9	.975	C-98
1950		130	.288	.524	393	113	15	3	24	6.1	55	68	68	50	0	7	2	551	54	15	9	5.0	.976	C-124
1951		101	.227	.375	291	66	8	1	11	3.8	42	37	63	67	1	9	0	378	47	9	6	4.8	.979	C-91
1952	CIN N	108	.256	.435	336	86	16	1	14	4.2	38	50	35	65	1	9	1	416	47	13	7	4.8	.973	C-99
1953		119	.235	.413	387	91	12	0	19	4.9	46	64	49	82	2	7	1	436	44	9	2	4.4	.982	C-112
1954		86	.235	.389	247	58	9	4	7	2.8	25	30	48	39	0	5	3	327	44	4	11	4.6	.989	C-82
1955	2 teams CIN N (6G –.133) PHI N (93G –.246)																							
″	total	99	.240	.405	304	73	12	1	12	3.9	33	35	32	62	1	6	0	461	45	3	6	5.5	.994	C-93
1956	PHI N	60	.199	.360	161	32	3	1	7	4.3	16	23	31	38	3	6	0	266	23	7	2	5.5	.976	C-54
1957		8	.091	.091	11	1	0	0	0	0.0	0	0	1	3	0	0	0	22	1	0	0	2.9	1.000	C-8
15 yrs.		1304	.243	.417	3921	953	139	26	164	4.2	495	556	582	780	23	77	8	5051	608	137	81	4.7	.976	C-1213, OF-9, 3B-4
WORLD SERIES																								
1950	PHI N	4	.182	.182	11	2	0	0	0	0.0	0	0	1	3	0	0	0	14	2	1	0	4.3	.941	C-4

Sonny Senerchia

SENERCHIA, EMANUEL ROBERT — BR TR 6′ 1″ 195 lbs.
B. Apr. 6, 1931, Newark, N. J.

Year	Team	Games	BA	SA	AB	H	2B	3B	HR	HR%	R	RBI	BB	SO	SB	Pinch Hit AB	Pinch Hit H	PO	A	E	DP	TC/G	FA	G by Pos
1952	PIT N	29	.220	.360	100	22	5	0	3	3.0	5	11	4	21	0	1	0	30	31	3	3	2.3	.953	3B-28

Paul Sentell

SENTELL, LEOPOLD THEODORE — BR TR 5′ 9″ 176 lbs.
B. Aug. 27, 1879, New Orleans, La. D. Apr. 27, 1923, Cincinnati, Ohio.

Year	Team	Games	BA	SA	AB	H	2B	3B	HR	HR%	R	RBI	BB	SO	SB	Pinch Hit AB	Pinch Hit H	PO	A	E	DP	TC/G	FA	G by Pos
1906	PHI N	63	.229	.281	192	44	5	1	1	0.5	19	14	14		15	8	0	72	105	19	4	3.6	.903	3B-33, 2B-19, OF-2, SS-1
1907		3	.000	.000	3	0	0	0	0	0.0	0	0	1		0	0	0	0	1	0	0	0.3	1.000	SS-2, OF-1
2 yrs.		66	.226	.277	195	44	5	1	1	0.5	19	14	15		15	8	0	72	106	19	4	3.4	.904	3B-33, 2B-19, SS-3, OF-3

Ted Sepkowski

SEPKOWSKI, THEODORE WALTER — BL TR 5′11″ 190 lbs.
Born Theodore Walter Sczepkowski.
B. Nov. 9, 1923, Baltimore, Md.

Year	Team	Games	BA	SA	AB	H	2B	3B	HR	HR%	R	RBI	BB	SO	SB	Pinch Hit AB	Pinch Hit H	PO	A	E	DP	TC/G	FA	G by Pos
1942	CLE A	5	.100	.100	10	1	0	0	0	0.0	0	0	0	3	0	2	0	6	8	3	0	8.5	.824	2B-2
1946		2	.500	.625	8	4	1	0	0	0.0	2	1	0	0	0	0	0	3	2	1	1	3.0	.833	3B-2
1947	2 teams CLE A (10G –.125) NY A (2G –.000)																							
″	total	12	.125	.250	8	1	1	0	0	0.0	1	0	1	1	0	8	1	0	0	0	0	0.0	.000	OF-1
3 yrs.		19	.231	.308	26	6	2	0	0	0.0	3	1	1	4	0	10	1	9	10	4	1	4.6	.826	3B-2, 2B-2, OF-1

Bill Serena

SERENA, WILLIAM ROBERT — BR TR 5′ 9½″ 175 lbs.
B. Oct. 2, 1924, Alameda, Calif.

Year	Team	Games	BA	SA	AB	H	2B	3B	HR	HR%	R	RBI	BB	SO	SB	Pinch Hit AB	Pinch Hit H	PO	A	E	DP	TC/G	FA	G by Pos
1949	CHI N	12	.216	.378	37	8	3	0	1	2.7	3	7	7	9	0	1	0	9	15	2	0	2.4	.923	3B-11
1950		127	.239	.421	435	104	20	4	17	3.9	56	61	65	75	1	2	1	122	274	23	24	3.4	.945	3B-125
1951		13	.333	.538	39	13	3	1	1	2.6	8	4	11	4	0	0	0	15	17	2	1	2.8	.941	3B-12
1952		122	.274	.469	390	107	21	5	15	3.8	49	61	39	83	1	14	4	198	234	8	30	4.1	.982	3B-58, 2B-49
1953		93	.251	.433	275	69	10	5	10	3.6	30	52	41	46	0	13	4	135	160	7	31	3.9	.977	2B-49, 3B-28
1954		41	.159	.381	63	10	0	1	4	6.3	8	13	14	18	0	22	4	5	26	2	0	2.4	.939	3B-12, 2B-2
6 yrs.		408	.251	.439	1239	311	57	16	48	3.9	154	198	177	235	2	52	13	484	726	44	86	3.6	.965	3B-246, 2B-100

Paul Serna

SERNA, PAUL DAVID — BR TR 5′ 8″ 170 lbs.
B. Nov. 16, 1958, El Centro, Calif.

Year	Team	Games	BA	SA	AB	H	2B	3B	HR	HR%	R	RBI	BB	SO	SB	Pinch Hit AB	Pinch Hit H	PO	A	E	DP	TC/G	FA	G by Pos
1981	SEA A	30	.255	.404	94	24	2	0	4	4.3	11	9	3	11	2	0	0	42	92	6	12	4.7	.957	SS-23, 2B-7
1982		65	.225	.296	169	38	3	0	3	1.8	15	8	4	13	0	3	0	63	126	9	23	3.0	.955	SS-31, 2B-18, 3B-15, DH-2
2 yrs.		95	.236	.335	263	62	5	0	7	2.7	26	17	7	24	2	3	0	105	218	15	35	3.5	.956	SS-54, 2B-25, 3B-15, DH-2

Scott Servais

SERVAIS, SCOTT DANIEL — BR TR 6′ 2″ 195 lbs.
B. June 14, 1967, LaCrosse, Wis.

Year	Team	Games	BA	SA	AB	H	2B	3B	HR	HR%	R	RBI	BB	SO	SB	Pinch Hit AB	Pinch Hit H	PO	A	E	DP	TC/G	FA	G by Pos
1991	HOU N	16	.162	.243	37	6	3	0	0	0.0	0	6	4	8	0	2	0	77	4	1	0	5.9	.988	C-14
1992		77	.239	.283	205	49	9	0	0	0.0	12	15	11	25	0	7	1	386	27	2	5	5.7	.995	C-73
1993		85	.244	.415	258	63	11	0	11	4.3	24	32	22	45	0	5	0	493	40	2	9	6.5	.996	C-82
1994		78	.195	.371	251	49	15	1	9	3.6	27	41	10	44	0	0	0	481	29	2	1	6.6	.996	C-78
1995	2 teams HOU N (28G –.225) CHI N (52G –.286)																							
″	total	80	.265	.496	264	70	22	0	13	4.9	38	47	32	52	2	2	0	526	48	12	4	7.3	.980	C-80
5 yrs.		336	.233	.392	1015	237	60	1	33	3.3	101	141	79	174	2	16	1	1963	148	19	19	6.5	.991	C-327

Walter Sessi

SESSI, WALTER ANTHONY (Watsie) — BL TL 6′ 3″ 225 lbs.
B. July 23, 1918, Finleyville, Pa.

Year	Team	Games	BA	SA	AB	H	2B	3B	HR	HR%	R	RBI	BB	SO	SB	Pinch Hit AB	Pinch Hit H	PO	A	E	DP	TC/G	FA	G by Pos
1941	STL N	5	.000	.000	13	0	0	0	0	0.0	2	0	1	2	0	2	0	3	0	1	0	1.3	.750	OF-3
1946		15	.143	.357	14	2	0	0	1	7.1	2	2	1	4	0	14	2	0	0	0	0	0.0	—	
2 yrs.		20	.074	.185	27	2	0	0	1	3.7	4	2	2	6	0	16	2	3	0	1	0	1.3	.750	OF-3

John Sevcik

SEVCIK, JOHN JOSEPH — BR TR 6′ 2″ 205 lbs.
B. July 11, 1942, Oak Park, Ill.

Year	Team	Games	BA	SA	AB	H	2B	3B	HR	HR%	R	RBI	BB	SO	SB	Pinch Hit AB	Pinch Hit H	PO	A	E	DP	TC/G	FA	G by Pos
1965	MIN A	12	.063	.125	16	1	1	0	0	0.0	1	0	1	5	0	2	0	32	5	0	1	3.4	1.000	C-11

Hank Severeid

SEVEREID, HENRY LEVAI BR TR 6′ 175 lbs.
B. June 1, 1891, Story City, Iowa D. Dec. 17, 1968, San Antonio, Tex.

Year	Team	Games	BA	SA	AB	H	2B	3B	HR	HR%	R	RBI	BB	SO	SB	Pinch Hit AB	Pinch Hit H	PO	A	E	DP	TC/G	FA	G by Pos
1911	CIN N	37	.304	.446	56	17	6	1	0	0.0	5	10	3	6	0	17	4	51	12	6	2	3.1	.913	C-22
1912		50	.237	.289	114	27	0	3	0	0.0	10	13	8	11	0	15	3	132	16	8	3	4.7	.949	C-20, 1B-7, OF-6
1913		8	.000	.000	6	0	0	0	0	0.0	0	0	1	1	0	5	0	2	0	0	0	0.7	1.000	C-2, OF-1
1915	STL A	80	.222	.276	203	45	6	1	1	0.5	12	22	16	25	2	15	1	247	66	11	2	5.1	.966	C-64
1916		100	.273	.314	293	80	8	2	0	0.0	23	34	26	17	3	8	1	320	99	10	6	4.7	.977	C-89, 3B-1, 1B-1
1917		143	.265	.333	501	133	23	4	1	0.2	45	57	28	20	6	2	0	532	157	24	10	5.1	.966	C-139, 1B-1
1918		51	.256	.286	133	34	4	0	0	0.0	8	11	18	4	4	7	3	148	44	11	4	4.8	.946	C-42
1919		112	.248	.293	351	87	12	2	0	0.0	16	36	21	13	2	9	1	401	106	9	12	5.0	.983	C-103
1920		123	.277	.348	422	117	14	5	2	0.5	46	49	33	11	5	6	1	480	111	10	11	5.1	.983	C-117
1921		143	.324	.415	472	153	23	7	2	0.4	66	78	42	9	7	14	2	481	117	17	11	4.9	.972	C-126
1922		137	.321	.427	517	166	32	7	3	0.6	49	78	28	12	1	3	0	552	123	11	10	5.1	.984	C-134
1923		122	.308	.419	432	133	27	6	3	0.7	50	51	31	11	3	6	4	513	88	4	9	5.2	.993	C-116
1924		137	.308	.398	432	133	23	2	4	0.9	37	48	36	15	1	6	1	436	104	6	12	4.2	.989	C-129
1925	2 teams	STL A (34G –.367) WAS A (50G –.355)																						
″	total	84	.361	.461	219	79	17	1	1	0.5	26	35	22	8	0	14	3	243	40	3	6	4.3	.990	C-66
1926	2 teams	WAS A (22G –.206) NY A (41G –.268)																						
″	total	63	.255	.323	161	41	9	1	0	0.0	15	17	16	6	1	6	1	171	32	3	4	3.7	.985	C-56
15 yrs.		1390	.289	.367	4312	1245	204	42	17	0.4	408	539	329	169	35	133	25	4709	1115	133	102	4.8	.978	C-1225, 1B-9, OF-7, 3B-1
WORLD SERIES																								
1925	WAS A	1	.333	.333	3	1	0	0	0	0.0	0	0	0	0	0	0	0	6	0	1	0	7.0	.857	C-1
1926	NY A	7	.273	.318	22	6	1	0	0	0.0	1	1	1	2	0	0	0	37	7	0	0	6.3	1.000	C-7
2 yrs.		8	.280	.320	25	7	1	0	0	0.0	1	1	1	2	0	0	0	43	7	1	0	6.4	.980	C-8

Rich Severson

SEVERSON, RICHARD ALLEN BR TR 6′ 174 lbs.
B. Jan. 18, 1945, Artesia, Calif.

Year	Team	Games	BA	SA	AB	H	2B	3B	HR	HR%	R	RBI	BB	SO	SB	Pinch Hit AB	Pinch Hit H	PO	A	E	DP	TC/G	FA	G by Pos
1970	KC A	77	.250	.317	240	60	11	1	1	0.4	22	22	16	33	0	6	1	127	202	12	45	4.5	.965	SS-50, 2B-25
1971		16	.300	.433	30	9	0	2	0	0.0	4	1	3	5	0	3	1	15	35	2	11	4.0	.962	2B-6, SS-6, 3B-1
2 yrs.		93	.256	.330	270	69	11	3	1	0.4	26	23	19	38	0	9	2	142	237	14	56	4.5	.964	SS-56, 2B-31, 3B-1

Ed Seward

SEWARD, EDWARD WILLIAM TR 5′ 7″ 175 lbs.
Born Edward William Sourhardt.
B. June 29, 1867, Cleveland, Ohio D. July 30, 1947, Cleveland, Ohio.

Year	Team	Games	BA	SA	AB	H	2B	3B	HR	HR%	R	RBI	BB	SO	SB	Pinch Hit AB	Pinch Hit H	PO	A	E	DP	TC/G	FA	G by Pos
1885	PRO N	1	.000	.000	3	0	0	0	0	0.0	0	0	0	2		0	0	0	4	0	0	4.0	1.000	P-1
1887	PHI AA	74	.188	.282	266	50	10	0	5	1.9	31		16		14	0	0	63	83	18	2	2.2	.890	P-55, OF-21
1888		64	.142	.209	225	32	3	3	2	0.9	27	14	18		12	0	0	32	127	19	5	2.8	.893	P-57, OF-7
1889		46	.217	.336	143	31	5	3	2	1.4	22	17	22	19	6	0	0	25	67	9	1	2.1	.911	P-39, OF-8, 2B-1
1890		26	.139	.194	72	10	4	0	0	0.0	7		8		3	0	0	19	27	10	2	2.1	.821	P-21, OF-6
1891	CLE N	7	.211	.316	19	4	2	0	0	0.0	2	1	3	4	0	0	0	8	1	1	0	1.4	.900	OF-3, P-3, 1B-1
6 yrs.		218	.174	.261	728	127	24	6	9	1.2	89	32	67	25	35	0	0	147	309	57	10	2.3	.889	P-176, OF-45, 1B-1, 2B-1

George Seward

SEWARD, GEORGE E. 5′ 7½″ 145 lbs.
B. St. Louis, Mo. Deceased.

Year	Team	Games	BA	SA	AB	H	2B	3B	HR	HR%	R	RBI	BB	SO	SB	Pinch Hit AB	Pinch Hit H	PO	A	E	DP	TC/G	FA	G by Pos
1876	NY N	1	.000	.000	3	0	0	0	0	0.0	0	0	0	0		0	0	2	3	0	0	5.0	1.000	2B-1
1882	STL AA	38	.215	.236	144	31	1	1	0	0.0	23		12			0	0	58	17	19	2	2.3	.798	OF-35, C-5
2 yrs.		39	.211	.231	147	31	1	1	0	0.0	23	0	12	0		0	0	60	20	19	2	2.4	.808	OF-35, C-5, 2B-1

Joe Sewell

SEWELL, JOSEPH WHEELER BL TR 5′ 6½″ 155 lbs.
Brother of Tommy Sewell. Brother of Luke Sewell.
B. Oct. 9, 1898, Titus, Ala. D. Mar. 6, 1990, Mobile, Ala.
Hall of Fame 1977.

Year	Team	Games	BA	SA	AB	H	2B	3B	HR	HR%	R	RBI	BB	SO	SB	Pinch Hit AB	Pinch Hit H	PO	A	E	DP	TC/G	FA	G by Pos
1920	CLE A	22	.329	.414	70	23	4	1	0	0.0	14	12	9	4	1	0	0	44	70	15	11	5.9	.884	SS-22
1921		154	.318	.444	572	182	36	12	4	0.7	101	91	80	17	7	0	0	319	480	47	75	5.5	.944	SS-154
1922		153	.299	.385	558	167	28	7	2	0.4	80	83	73	20	10	1	0	322	497	52	79	5.8	.940	SS-139, 2B-12
1923		153	.353	.479	553	195	41	10	3	0.5	98	109	98	12	9	2	0	286	497	59	82	5.6	.930	SS-151
1924		153	.316	.429	594	188	**45**	5	4	0.7	99	104	67	13	3	0	0	349	514	36	76	5.9	.960	SS-153
1925		155	.336	.424	608	204	37	7	1	0.2	78	98	64	4	7	0	0	324	535	29	80	5.7	.967	SS-153, 2B-3
1926		154	.324	.433	578	187	41	5	4	0.7	91	85	65	6	17	0	0	326	463	37	86	5.4	.955	SS-154
1927		153	.316	.424	569	180	48	5	1	0.2	83	92	51	7	3	0	0	361	480	33	80	5.7	.962	SS-153
1928		155	.323	.418	588	190	40	2	4	0.7	79	70	58	9	7	0	0	319	499	33	106	5.5	.961	SS-137, 3B-19
1929		152	.315	.427	578	182	38	3	7	1.2	90	73	48	4	6	0	0	163	336	13	28	3.4	.975	3B-152
1930		109	.289	.371	353	102	17	6	0	0.0	44	48	42	3	1	8	1	83	184	14	16	2.9	.950	3B-97
1931	NY A	130	.302	.388	484	146	22	1	6	1.2	102	64	62	8	1	8	1	132	230	18	15	3.1	.953	3B-121, 2B-1
1932		124	.272	.392	503	137	21	3	11	2.2	95	68	56	3	0	1	0	122	221	9	15	2.9	.974	3B-122
1933		135	.273	.323	524	143	18	1	2	0.4	87	54	71	4	2	5	3	123	224	13	27	2.7	.964	3B-131
14 yrs.		1902	.312	.413	7132	2226	436	68	49	0.7	1141	1051	844	114	74	25	5	3273	5230	408	776	4.8	.954	SS-1216, 3B-642, 2B-16
WORLD SERIES																								
1920	CLE A	7	.174	.174	23	4	0	0	0	0.0	0	0	2	1	0	0	0	11	28	6	3	6.4	.867	SS-7
1932	NY A	4	.333	.400	15	5	1	0	0	0.0	4	3	4	0	0	0	0	4	6	1	1	2.8	.909	3B-4
2 yrs.		11	.237	.263	38	9	1	0	0	0.0	4	3	6	1	0	0	0	15	34	7	4	5.1	.875	SS-7, 3B-4

Luke Sewell

SEWELL, JAMES LUTHER BR TR 5′ 9″ 160 lbs.
Brother of Tommy Sewell. Brother of Joe Sewell.
B. Jan. 5, 1901, Titus, Ala. D. May 14, 1987, Akron, Ohio.
Manager 1941–46, 1949–52.

Year	Team	Games	BA	SA	AB	H	2B	3B	HR	HR%	R	RBI	BB	SO	SB	Pinch Hit AB	Pinch Hit H	PO	A	E	DP	TC/G	FA	G by Pos
1921	CLE A	3	.000	.000	6	0	0	0	0	0.0	0	1	0	3	0	0	0	7	4	0	0	3.7	1.000	C-3
1922		41	.264	.322	87	23	5	0	0	0.0	14	10	5	8	1	1	0	108	21	5	2	3.5	.963	C-38
1923		10	.200	.400	10	2	0	1	0	0.0	2	1	1	0	0	2	0	5	5	2	0	1.7	.833	C-7
1924		63	.291	.358	165	48	9	1	0	0.0	27	17	22	13	1	3	1	171	42	9	5	4.0	.959	C-56
1925		74	.232	.295	220	51	10	2	0	0.0	30	18	33	18	6	4	1	222	54	8	13	4.2	.972	C-66, OF-2
1926		126	.238	.293	433	103	16	4	0	0.0	41	46	36	27	9	1	0	437	91	9	3	4.3	.983	C-125
1927		128	.294	.377	470	138	27	6	0	0.0	52	53	20	23	4	2	0	402	119	20	14	4.3	.963	C-126
1928		122	.270	.375	411	111	16	9	3	0.7	52	52	26	27	3	4	1	430	117	16	13	4.8	.972	C-118

Year	Team	Games	BA	SA	AB	H	2B	3B	HR	HR%	R	RBI	BB	SO	SB	Pinch Hit AB	Pinch Hit H	PO	A	E	DP	TC/G	FA	G by Pos
Luke Sewell *continued*																								
1929		124	.236	.300	406	96	17	3	1	0.2	41	39	29	26	6	0	0	433	81	18	11	4.3	.966	C-124
1930		76	.257	.353	292	75	21	2	1	0.3	40	43	14	9	5	0	0	283	49	9	5	4.5	.974	C-76
1931		108	.275	.384	375	103	30	4	1	0.3	45	53	36	17	1	3	1	384	61	9	5	4.3	.980	C-105
1932		87	.253	.353	300	76	20	2	2	0.7	36	52	38	24	4	2	0	306	50	8	8	4.3	.978	C-84
1933	WAS A	141	.264	.357	474	125	30	4	2	0.4	65	61	48	24	7	0	0	516	61	6	12	4.1	.990	C-141
1934		72	.237	.329	207	49	7	3	2	1.0	21	21	22	10	0	7	2	215	30	2	11	3.8	.992	C-50, OF-7, 1B-6, 3B-1, 2B-1
1935	CHI A	118	.285	.359	421	120	19	3	2	0.5	52	67	32	18	3	5	0	399	83	6	10	4.4	.988	C-112
1936		128	.251	.350	451	113	20	5	5	1.1	59	73	54	16	11	2	0	461	87	9	12	4.4	.984	C-126
1937		122	.269	.357	412	111	21	6	1	0.2	51	61	46	18	4	3	2	502	72	9	11	4.9	.985	C-118
1938		65	.213	.242	211	45	4	1	0	0.0	23	27	20	20	0	0	0	205	55	4	7	4.1	.985	C-65
1939	CLE A	16	.150	.200	20	3	1	0	0	0.0	1	1	3	1	0	0	0	24	4	1	0	1.8	.966	C-15, 1B-1
1942	STL A	6	.083	.083	12	1	0	0	0	0.0	1	0	1	5	0	0	0	12	5	1	1	3.0	.944	C-6
20 yrs.		1630	.259	.341	5383	1393	273	56	20	0.4	653	696	486	307	65	39	8	5522	1091	151	143	4.3	.978	C-1561, OF-9, 1B-7, 3B-1, 2B-1
WORLD SERIES																								
1933	WAS A	5	.176	.176	17	3	0	0	0	0.0	1	1	2	0	1	0	0	23	2	0	0	5.0	1.000	C-5
Tommy Sewell — SEWELL, THOMAS WESLEY. Brother of Joe Sewell. Brother of Luke Sewell. B. Apr. 16, 1906, Titus, Ala. D. July 30, 1956, Montgomery, Ala. BL TR 5′7½″ 155 lbs.																								
1927	CHI N	1	.000	.000	1	0	0	0	0	0.0	0	0	0	0	0	1	0	0	0	0	0	0.0	—	
Jimmy Sexton — SEXTON, JIMMY DALE. B. Dec. 15, 1951, Mobile, Ala. BR TR 5′10″ 175 lbs.																								
1977	SEA A	14	.216	.378	37	8	1	1	1	2.7	5	3	2	6	1	0	0	12	40	4	10	4.7	.929	SS-12
1978	HOU N	88	.206	.298	141	29	3	2	2	1.4	17	6	13	28	16	6	1	62	104	5	19	2.5	.971	SS-58, 3B-8, 2B-3
1979		52	.209	.209	43	9	0	0	0	0.0	8	1	7	7	1	17	3	11	24	2	6	2.2	.946	SS-11, 3B-4, 2B-2
1981	OAK A	7	.000	.000	3	0	0	0	0	0.0	3	0	0	2	2	0	0	0	3	0	0	1.5	1.000	3B-1, DH-1
1982		69	.245	.317	139	34	4	0	2	1.4	19	14	9	24	16	0	0	63	118	9	19	3.2	.953	SS-47, 3B-8, DH-5
1983	STL N	6	.111	.222	9	1	1	0	0	0.0	1	0	1	4	0	1	0	4	8	0	2	2.0	1.000	SS-4, 3B-2
6 yrs.		236	.218	.298	372	81	9	3	5	1.3	53	24	32	71	36	24	4	152	297	20	56	2.8	.957	SS-132, 3B-23, DH-6, 2B-5
Tom Sexton — SEXTON, THOMAS WILLIAM. B. Mar. 14, 1865, Rock Island, Ill. D. Feb. 8, 1934, Rock Island, Ill.																								
1884	MIL U	12	.234	.277	47	11	2	0	0	0.0	9		4			0	0	8	21	5	1	2.8	.853	SS-12
Socks Seybold — SEYBOLD, RALPH ORLANDO. B. Nov. 23, 1870, Washingtonville, Ohio. D. Dec. 22, 1921, Greensburg, Pa. BR TR 5′11″ 175 lbs.																								
1899	CIN N	22	.224	.306	85	19	5	1	0	0.0	13	8	6		2	0	0	40	4	4	0	2.2	.917	OF-22
1901	PHI A	114	.333	.499	457	152	24	14	8	1.8	74	90	40		15	0	0	301	17	10	9	2.9	.970	OF-100, 1B-14
1902		137	.316	.506	522	165	27	12	**16**	**3.1**	91	97	43		6	0	0	246	11	10	3	2.0	.963	OF-136
1903		137	.299	.462	522	156	**45**	8	8	1.5	78	84	38		5	0	0	340	17	13	10	2.7	.965	OF-120, 1B-18
1904		143	.292	.396	510	149	26	9	3	0.6	56	64	42		12	3	0	272	16	9	9	2.1	.970	OF-129, 1B-13
1905		132	.270	.400	488	132	37	4	6	1.2	65	59	42		5	0	0	213	13	4	5	1.7	.983	OF-132
1906		116	.316	.418	411	130	23	2	5	1.2	41	59	30		9	2	0	150	10	13	3	1.5	.925	OF-114
1907		147	.271	.362	564	153	28	4	5	0.9	58	92	40		10	0	0	201	19	6	7	1.5	.973	OF-147
1908		48	.215	.231	130	28	2	0	0	0.0	5	3	12		2	12	2	32	3	3	0	1.1	.921	OF-34
9 yrs.		996	.294	.423	3689	1084	217	54	51	1.4	481	556	293		66	17	2	1795	110	72	46	2.0	.964	OF-934, 1B-45
WORLD SERIES																								
1905	PHI A	5	.125	.125	16	2	0	0	0	0.0	0	0	2	3	0	0	0	5	1	0	1	1.2	1.000	OF-5
Cy Seymour — SEYMOUR, JAMES BENTLEY. B. Dec. 9, 1872, Albany, N. Y. D. Sept. 20, 1919, New York, N. Y. BL TL 6′ 200 lbs.																								
1896	NY N	12	.219	.219	32	7	0	0	0	0.0	2	0	0	7	0	1	0	5	19	4	1	2.3	.857	P-11, OF-1
1897		44	.241	.336	137	33	5	1	2	1.5	13	14	4		3	0	0	24	98	20	5	3.2	.859	P-38, OF-6
1898		80	.276	.347	297	82	5	2	4	1.3	41	23	9		8	0	0	72	120	25	9	2.7	.885	P-45, OF-35, 2B-1
1899		50	.327	.409	159	52	3	2	2	1.3	25	27	4		2	6	1	50	92	30	3	3.9	.826	P-32, OF-8, 1B-3, 3B-1
1900		23	.300	.300	40	12	0	0	0	0.0	9	2	3		0	6	1	9	20	7	0	2.1	.806	P-13, OF-3, 1B-1
1901	BAL A	134	.303	.373	547	166	19	8	1	0.2	84	77	28		38	0	0	278	24	18	5	2.4	.944	OF-133, 1B-1
1902	2 teams	BAL A (72G –.268)	CIN N (62G –.349)																					
″	total	134	.305	.404	515	157	16	10	5	1.0	66	78	30		20	0	0	260	23	19	5	2.2	.937	OF-133, 3B-1, P-1
1903	CIN N	135	.342	.478	558	191	25	15	7	1.3	85	72	33		25	0	0	318	14	36	2	2.7	.902	OF-135
1904		131	.313	.439	531	166	26	13	5	0.9	71	58	29		11	1	1	308	20	17	4	2.7	.951	OF-130
1905		149	**.377**	**.559**	581	**219**	**40**	**21**	8	1.4	95	**121**	51		21	0	0	347	25	21	12	2.6	.947	OF-149
1906	2 teams	CIN N (79G –.257)	NY N (72G –.320)																					
″	total	151	.286	.378	576	165	19	5	8	1.4	70	80	42		29	0	0	331	17	10	6	2.4	.972	OF-151
1907	NY N	131	.294	.400	473	139	25	8	3	0.6	46	75	36		21	5	0	300	8	8	4	2.5	.975	OF-126
1908		156	.267	.339	587	157	23	2	5	0.9	60	92	30		18	1	0	340	29	20	9	2.5	.949	OF-155
1909		80	.311	.400	280	87	12	5	1	0.4	37	30	25		14	6	1	138	11	5	3	2.1	.968	OF-74
1910		79	.265	.334	287	76	9	4	1	0.3	32	40	23	18	10	2	0	137	9	10	1	2.1	.936	OF-76
1913	BOS N	39	.178	.205	73	13	2	0	0	0.0	2	10	7	7	2	15	3	34	4	2	0	2.2	.950	OF-18
16 yrs.		1528	.304	.405	5673	1722	229	96	52	0.9	738	799	354	32	222	43	7	2951	533	252	69	2.5	.933	OF-1333, P-140, 1B-5, 3B-2, 2B-1
Ralph Shafer — SHAFER, RALPH NEWTON. B. Mar. 17, 1894, Cincinnati, Ohio. D. Feb. 5, 1950, Akron, Ohio. 5′11″																								
1914	PIT N	1	—	—	0	0	0	0	0	—	0	0	0	0	0	0	0	0	0	0	0	0.0	—	
Tillie Shafer — SHAFER, ARTHUR JOSEPH. B. Mar. 22, 1889, Los Angeles, Calif. D. Jan. 10, 1962, Los Angeles, Calif. BB TR 5′10″ 165 lbs.																								
1909	NY N	38	.179	.226	84	15	2	1	0	0.0	11	7	14		6	5	0	33	56	15	2	3.4	.856	3B-16, 2B-13, OF-2
1910		29	.190	.238	21	4	1	0	0	0.0	5	1	0	6	0	6	1	5	13	2	2	1.7	.900	3B-8, 2B-2, SS-2

Tillie Shafer *continued*

Year	Team	Games	BA	SA	AB	H	2B	3B	HR	HR%	R	RBI	BB	SO	SB	Pinch Hit AB	Pinch Hit H	PO	A	E	DP	TC/G	FA	G by Pos
1912		78	.288	.325	163	47	4	1	0	0.0	48	23	30	19	22	7	1	80	119	22	10	3.8	.900	SS-31, 2B-20, 3B-7
1913		138	.287	.398	508	146	17	12	5	1.0	74	52	61	55	32	1	0	220	254	43	26	3.8	.917	3B-79, 2B-25, SS-17, OF-15
4 yrs.		283	.273	.360	776	212	24	14	5	0.6	138	83	105	80	60	19	2	338	442	82	40	3.6	.905	3B-110, 2B-60, SS-50, OF-17
WORLD SERIES																								
1912	NY N	3	—	—	0	0	0	0	0	—	0	0	0	0	0	0	0	1	4	0	0	1.7	1.000	SS-3
1913		5	.158	.316	19	3	1	1	0	0.0	2	1	2	3	0	0	0	8	0	0	0	1.3	1.000	OF-5, 3B-1
2 yrs.		8	.158	.316	19	3	1	1	0	0.0	2	1	2	3	0	0	0	9	4	0	0	1.4	1.000	OF-5, SS-3, 3B-1

Frank Shaffer

SHAFFER, FRANK
Deceased.

Year	Team	Games	BA	SA	AB	H	2B	3B	HR	HR%	R	RBI	BB	SO	SB	Pinch Hit AB	Pinch Hit H	PO	A	E	DP	TC/G	FA	G by Pos
1884	3 teams ALT U (19G –.284) KC U (44G –.171) BAL U (3G –.077)																							
″	total	66	.199	.235	251	50	5	2	0	0.0	30		18			0	0	95	22	29	0	2.1	.801	OF-61, C-4, 3B-2, SS-1, 2B-1

Orator Shaffer

SHAFFER, GEORGE BL TR 5′ 9″ 165 lbs.
Brother of Taylor Shaffer.
B. 1852, Philadelphia, Pa. Deceased.

Year	Team	Games	BA	SA	AB	H	2B	3B	HR	HR%	R	RBI	BB	SO	SB	Pinch Hit AB	Pinch Hit H	PO	A	E	DP	TC/G	FA	G by Pos
1877	LOU N	61	.285	.392	260	74	9	5	3	1.2	38	34	9	17		0	0	133	21	28	1	3.0	.846	OF-60, 1B-1
1878	IND N	63	.338	.455	266	90	19	6	0	0.0	48	30	13	20		0	0	105	28	25	2	2.5	.842	OF-63
1879	CHI N	73	.304	.345	316	96	13	0	0	0.0	53	35	6	28		0	0	99	51	38	3	2.6	.798	OF-72, 3B-1
1880	CLE N	83	.266	.361	338	90	14	9	0	0.0	62	21	17	36		0	0	128	35	18	5	2.2	.901	OF-83
1881		85	.257	.338	343	88	13	6	1	0.3	48	34	23	20		0	0	122	24	20	4	2.0	.880	OF-85
1882		84	.214	.300	313	67	14	2	3	1.0	37	28	27	27		0	0	111	17	31	2	1.9	.805	OF-84
1883	BUF N	95	.292	.334	401	117	11	3	0	0.0	67		27	39		0	0	182	41	36	3	2.7	.861	OF-95
1884	STL U	106	.360	.501	467	168	**40**	10	2	0.4	130		30			0	0	132	40	26	4	1.8	.869	OF-100, 2B-7, 1B-1
1885	2 teams STL N (69G –.195) PHI AA (2G –.222)																							
″	total	71	.195	.259	266	52	11	3	0	0.0	31	18	20	31		0	0	107	28	12	0	2.1	.918	OF-71
1886	PHI AA	21	.268	.378	82	22	3	3	0	0.0	15		8			0	0	40	4	10	2	2.6	.815	OF-21
1890		100	.282	.354	390	110	15	5	1	0.3	55		47		29	0	0	169	19	8	7	1.9	.959	OF-98, 1B-3
11 yrs.		842	.283	.369	3442	974	162	52	10	0.3	584	200	227	218	29	0	0	1328	308	252	33	2.2	.867	OF-832, 2B-7, 1B-5, 3B-1

Taylor Shaffer

SHAFFER, TAYLOR
Brother of Orator Shaffer.
B. July 1870, Philadelphia, Pa. Deceased.

Year	Team	Games	BA	SA	AB	H	2B	3B	HR	HR%	R	RBI	BB	SO	SB	Pinch Hit AB	Pinch Hit H	PO	A	E	DP	TC/G	FA	G by Pos
1890	PHI AA	69	.172	.215	261	45	3	4	0	0.0	28		28		19	0	0	214	195	35	39	6.4	.921	2B-69

Art Shamsky

SHAMSKY, ARTHUR LOUIS BL TL 6′ 1″ 168 lbs.
B. Oct. 14, 1941, St. Louis, Mo.

Year	Team	Games	BA	SA	AB	H	2B	3B	HR	HR%	R	RBI	BB	SO	SB	Pinch Hit AB	Pinch Hit H	PO	A	E	DP	TC/G	FA	G by Pos
1965	CIN N	64	.260	.427	96	25	4	3	2	2.1	13	10	10	29	1	45	13	31	2	1	0	1.8	.971	OF-18, 1B-1
1966		96	.231	.521	234	54	5	0	21	9.0	41	47	32	45	0	24	5	104	3	3	1	1.5	.973	OF-74
1967		76	.197	.293	147	29	3	1	3	2.0	6	13	15	34	0	34	10	59	2	1	1	1.5	.984	OF-40
1968	NY N	116	.238	.406	345	82	14	4	12	3.5	30	48	21	58	1	23	1	239	12	3	8	2.6	.988	OF-82, 1B-17
1969		100	.300	.488	303	91	9	3	14	4.6	42	47	36	32	1	13	5	192	2	2	7	2.3	.990	OF-78, 1B-9
1970		122	.293	.432	403	118	19	2	11	2.7	48	49	49	33	1	11	2	482	37	2	30	4.6	.996	OF-58, 1B-56
1971		68	.185	.370	135	25	6	2	5	3.7	13	18	21	18	1	24	3	59	6	1	2	1.7	.985	OF-38, 1B-1
1972	2 teams CHI N (15G –.125) OAK A (8G –.000)																							
″	total	23	.087	.087	23	2	0	0	0	0.0	1	1	4	5	0	15	2	30	1	0	1	7.8	1.000	1B-4
8 yrs.		665	.253	.427	1686	426	60	15	68	4.0	194	233	188	254	5	189	41	1196	65	13	50	2.7	.990	OF-388, 1B-88
LEAGUE CHAMPIONSHIP SERIES																								
1969	NY N	3	.538	.538	13	7	0	0	0	0.0	3	1	0	3	0	0	0	3	0	0	0	1.0	1.000	OF-3
WORLD SERIES																								
1969	NY N	3	.000	.000	6	0	0	0	0	0.0	0	0	0	0	0	2	0	1	0	0	0	1.0	1.000	OF-1

Wally Shaner

SHANER, WALTER DEDAKER (Skinny) BR TR 6′ 2″ 195 lbs.
B. May 24, 1900, Lynchburg, Va. D. Nov. 13, 1992, Las Vegas, Nev.

Year	Team	Games	BA	SA	AB	H	2B	3B	HR	HR%	R	RBI	BB	SO	SB	Pinch Hit AB	Pinch Hit H	PO	A	E	DP	TC/G	FA	G by Pos
1923	CLE A	3	.250	.250	4	1	0	0	0	0.0	1	0	1	1	0	0	0	2	0	0	0	0.7	1.000	OF-2, 3B-1
1926	BOS A	69	.283	.366	191	54	12	2	0	0.0	20	21	17	13	1	18	2	106	3	4	2	2.4	.965	OF-48
1927		122	.273	.406	406	111	33	6	3	0.7	54	49	21	35	11	11	1	231	16	12	3	2.4	.954	OF-108, 1B-1
1929	CIN N	13	.321	.429	28	9	0	0	1	3.6	5	4	4	5	1	2	1	80	1	0	9	8.1	1.000	1B-8, OF-2
4 yrs.		207	.278	.394	629	175	45	8	4	0.6	80	74	43	54	13	31	4	419	20	16	14	2.7	.965	OF-160, 1B-9, 3B-1

Howard Shanks

SHANKS, HOWARD SAMUEL (Hank) BR TR 5′11″ 170 lbs.
B. July 21, 1890, Chicago, Ill. D. July 30, 1941, Monaca, Pa.

Year	Team	Games	BA	SA	AB	H	2B	3B	HR	HR%	R	RBI	BB	SO	SB	Pinch Hit AB	Pinch Hit H	PO	A	E	DP	TC/G	FA	G by Pos
1912	WAS A	115	.231	.308	399	92	14	7	1	0.3	52	47	40		21	2	0	189	14	8	2	1.9	.962	OF-113
1913		109	.254	.315	390	99	11	5	1	0.3	38	37	15	40	24	0	0	207	13	5	3	2.1	.978	OF-109
1914		143	.224	.332	500	112	22	10	4	0.8	44	64	29	51	18	3	0	276	14	14	3	2.2	.954	OF-139
1915		141	.250	.321	492	123	19	8	0	0.0	52	47	30	42	12	2	1	226	128	18	15	2.7	.952	OF-80, 3B-49, 2B-10
1916		140	.253	.321	471	119	15	7	1	0.2	51	48	41	34	23	4	2	313	92	17	15	3.1	.960	OF-88, 3B-31, SS-8, 1B-7
1917		126	.202	.260	430	87	15	5	0	0.0	45	28	33	37	15	6	0	296	267	38	49	5.1	.937	SS-90, OF-26, 1B-2
1918		120	.257	.326	436	112	19	4	1	0.2	42	56	31	21	23	6	2	284	154	22	22	4.0	.952	OF-64, 2B-47, 3B-3
1919		135	.248	.299	491	122	8	7	1	0.2	33	54	25	48	13	1	1	329	359	57	11	5.6	.923	SS-94, 2B-34, OF-6
1920		128	.268	.363	444	119	16	7	4	0.9	56	37	29	43	11	6	0	294	154	17	12	3.9	.963	3B-63, OF-35, 1B-14, 2B-5, SS-1
1921		154	.302	.452	562	170	25	**19**	7	1.2	81	69	57	38	11	0	0	218	330	23	35	3.7	.960	3B-154
1922		84	.283	.397	272	77	10	9	1	0.4	35	32	25	25	6	3	0	125	112	16	16	3.1	.937	3B-54, OF-27
1923	BOS A	131	.254	.336	464	118	19	5	3	0.6	38	57	19	37	6	5	0	188	261	25	34	3.7	.947	3B-85, 2B-36, OF-6, SS-2
1924		72	.259	.373	193	50	16	3	0	0.0	22	25	20	11	1	5	0	118	129	9	23	3.8	.965	SS-37, 3B-22, OF-4, 2B-2, 1B-2
1925	NY A	66	.258	.310	155	40	3	1	1	0.6	15	18	20	15	1	13	4	68	87	6	13	3.2	.963	3B-26, 2B-21, OF-4
14 yrs.		1664	.253	.337	5699	1440	212	97	25	0.4	604	619	414	442	185	56	10	3131	2114	275	253	3.5	.950	OF-701, 3B-487, SS-232, 2B-155, 1B-25

Year	Team	Games	BA	SA	AB	H	2B	3B	HR	HR%	R	RBI	BB	SO	SB	Pinch Hit AB	Pinch Hit H	PO	A	E	DP	TC/G	FA	G by Pos

Doc Shanley

SHANLEY, HARRY ROOT BR TR 5′11″ 174 lbs.
B. Jan. 30, 1889, Grandbury, Tex. D. Dec. 13, 1934, St. Petersburg, Fla.

Year	Team	Games	BA	SA	AB	H	2B	3B	HR	HR%	R	RBI	BB	SO	SB	PH AB	PH H	PO	A	E	DP	TC/G	FA	G by Pos
1912	**STL A**	5	.000	.000	8	0	0	0	0	0.0	1	1	2		0	0	0	7	3	2	1	3.0	.833	SS-4

Jim Shanley

SHANLEY, JAMES H.
B. May 4, 1854, Brooklyn, N. Y. D. Nov. 4, 1904, Brooklyn, N. Y.

Year	Team	Games	BA	SA	AB	H	2B	3B	HR	HR%	R	RBI	BB	SO	SB	PH AB	PH H	PO	A	E	DP	TC/G	FA	G by Pos
1876	**NY N**	2	.125	.125	8	1	0	0	0	0.0	0	0	0	0		0	0	3	0	2	0	2.5	.600	OF-2

Warren Shannabrook

SHANNABROOK, WARREN H. BR TR 6′ 170 lbs.
B. Nov. 30, 1880, Massillon, Ohio D. Mar. 10, 1964, North Canton, Ohio.

Year	Team	Games	BA	SA	AB	H	2B	3B	HR	HR%	R	RBI	BB	SO	SB	PH AB	PH H	PO	A	E	DP	TC/G	FA	G by Pos
1906	**WAS A**	1	.000	.000	2	0	0	0	0	0.0	0	0	0		0	0	0	0	1	0	0	1.0	1.000	3B-1

Dan Shannon

SHANNON, DANIEL WEBSTER 5′ 9″ 175 lbs.
B. Mar. 23, 1865, Bridgeport, Conn. D. Oct. 25, 1913, Bridgeport, Conn.
Manager 1889, 1891.

Year	Team	Games	BA	SA	AB	H	2B	3B	HR	HR%	R	RBI	BB	SO	SB	PH AB	PH H	PO	A	E	DP	TC/G	FA	G by Pos
1889	**LOU AA**	121	.257	.373	498	128	22	12	4	0.8	90	48	42	52	26	0	0	307	391	69	59	6.3	.910	2B-121
1890	**2 teams**	**PHI P** (19G –.240) **NY P** (83G –.216)																						
″	***total***	102	.221	.326	399	88	12	9	4	1.0	74	60	29	46	25	0	0	208	328	54	39	5.8	.908	2B-96, SS-6
1891	**WAS AA**	19	.134	.164	67	9	2	0	0	0.0	7	3	6	9	3	0	0	45	51	11	6	5.6	.897	SS-14, 2B-5
3 yrs.		242	.233	.339	964	225	36	21	8	0.8	171	111	77	107	54	0	0	560	770	134	104	6.0	.908	2B-222, SS-20

Frank Shannon

SHANNON, JOHN FRANCIS (Tod) 5′ 3″ 155 lbs.
B. Dec. 3, 1873, San Francisco, Calif. D. Feb. 27, 1934, Boston, Mass.

Year	Team	Games	BA	SA	AB	H	2B	3B	HR	HR%	R	RBI	BB	SO	SB	PH AB	PH H	PO	A	E	DP	TC/G	FA	G by Pos
1892	**WAS N**	1	.250	.250	4	1	0	0	0	0.0	0	2	0	2	0	0	0	3	2	3	0	8.0	.625	SS-1
1896	**LOU N**	31	.157	.209	115	18	1	1	1	0.9	14	15	13	15	3	0	0	66	78	29	9	5.6	.832	SS-28, 3B-3
2 yrs.		32	.160	.210	119	19	1	1	1	0.8	14	17	13	17	3	0	0	69	80	32	9	5.7	.823	SS-29, 3B-3

Joe Shannon

SHANNON, JOSEPH ALOYSIUS BR TR 5′11″ 170 lbs.
Brother of Red Shannon.
B. Feb. 11, 1897, Jersey City, N. J. D. July 28, 1955, Jersey City, N. J.

Year	Team	Games	BA	SA	AB	H	2B	3B	HR	HR%	R	RBI	BB	SO	SB	PH AB	PH H	PO	A	E	DP	TC/G	FA	G by Pos
1915	**BOS N**	5	.200	.200	10	2	0	0	0	0.0	3	1	0	3	0	2	1	4	3	1	0	2.7	.875	OF-2, 2B-1

Mike Shannon

SHANNON, THOMAS MICHAEL (Moonman) BR TR 6′ 3″ 195 lbs.
B. July 15, 1939, St. Louis, Mo.

Year	Team	Games	BA	SA	AB	H	2B	3B	HR	HR%	R	RBI	BB	SO	SB	PH AB	PH H	PO	A	E	DP	TC/G	FA	G by Pos
1962	**STL N**	10	.133	.133	15	2	0	0	0	0.0	3	0	1	3	0	0	0	7	1	0	0	1.1	1.000	OF-7
1963		32	.308	.423	26	8	0	0	1	3.8	3	2	0	6	0	4	1	15	2	1	0	0.7	.944	OF-26
1964		88	.261	.415	253	66	8	2	9	3.6	30	43	19	54	4	2	0	110	7	2	2	1.4	.983	OF-88
1965		124	.221	.352	244	54	17	3	3	1.2	32	25	28	46	2	19	2	193	6	1	2	1.9	.995	OF-101, C-4
1966		137	.288	.462	459	132	20	6	16	3.5	61	64	37	106	8	9	2	248	10	4	4	2.0	.985	OF-129, C-1
1967		130	.245	.369	482	118	18	3	12	2.5	53	77	37	89	2	2	1	98	241	29	18	2.9	.921	3B-122, OF-6
1968		156	.266	.401	576	153	29	2	15	2.6	62	79	37	114	1	0	0	110	310	21	25	2.8	.952	3B-156
1969		150	.254	.365	551	140	15	5	12	2.2	51	55	49	87	1	2	1	123	258	22	22	2.7	.945	3B-149
1970		52	.213	.287	174	37	9	2	0	0.0	18	22	16	20	1	5	1	32	59	8	4	1.9	.919	3B-51
9 yrs.		879	.255	.387	2780	710	116	23	68	2.4	313	367	224	525	19	43	8	936	894	88	77	2.3	.954	3B-478, OF-357, C-5
WORLD SERIES																								
1964	**STL N**	7	.214	.321	28	6	0	0	1	3.6	6	2	0	9	1	0	0	13	2	0	1	2.1	1.000	OF-7
1967		7	.208	.375	24	5	1	0	1	4.2	3	2	1	4	0	0	0	5	13	2	1	2.9	.900	3B-7
1968		7	.276	.414	29	8	1	0	1	3.4	3	4	1	5	0	0	0	5	10	1	1	2.3	.938	3B-7
3 yrs.		21	.235	.370	81	19	2	0	3	3.7	12	8	2	18	1	0	0	23	25	3	3	2.4	.941	3B-14, OF-7

Owen Shannon

SHANNON, OWEN DENNIS IGNATIUS BR TR
B. Dec. 22, 1879, Omaha, Neb. D. Apr. 10, 1918, Omaha, Neb.

Year	Team	Games	BA	SA	AB	H	2B	3B	HR	HR%	R	RBI	BB	SO	SB	PH AB	PH H	PO	A	E	DP	TC/G	FA	G by Pos
1903	**STL A**	9	.214	.286	28	6	2	0	0	0.0	1	3	1		0	0	0	43	6	2	0	5.7	.961	C-8, 1B-1
1907	**WAS A**	4	.143	.143	7	1	0	0	0	0.0	0	0	0		0	0	0	13	7	0	0	5.0	1.000	C-4
2 yrs.		13	.200	.257	35	7	2	0	0	0.0	1	3	1		0	0	0	56	13	2	0	5.5	.972	C-12, 1B-1

Red Shannon

SHANNON, MAURICE JOSEPH BB TR 5′11″ 170 lbs.
Brother of Joe Shannon.
B. Feb. 11, 1897, Jersey City, N. J. D. Apr. 12, 1970, Jersey City, N. J.

Year	Team	Games	BA	SA	AB	H	2B	3B	HR	HR%	R	RBI	BB	SO	SB	PH AB	PH H	PO	A	E	DP	TC/G	FA	G by Pos
1915	**BOS N**	1	.000	.000	3	0	0	0	0	0.0	0	0	0	0	0	0	0	3	3	1	1	7.0	.857	2B-1
1917	**PHI A**	11	.286	.286	35	10	0	0	0	0.0	8	7	6	9	2	1	0	18	31	7	2	5.6	.875	SS-10
1918		72	.240	.311	225	54	6	5	0	0.0	23	16	42	52	5	0	0	155	223	39	40	5.9	.906	SS-45, 2B-26
1919	**2 teams**	**PHI A** (39G –.271) **BOS A** (80G –.259)																						
″	***total***	119	.263	.344	445	117	18	9	0	0.0	50	31	29	**70**	11	3	1	237	344	21	50	5.2	.965	2B-116
1920	**2 teams**	**WAS A** (62G –.288) **PHI A** (25G –.170)																						
″	***total***	87	.255	.335	310	79	9	8	0	0.0	34	33	26	44	3	1	0	132	225	25	23	4.4	.935	SS-55, 2B-16, 3B-15
1921	**PHI A**	1	.000	.000	1	0	0	0	0	0.0	0	0	0	0	0	1	0	0	0	0	0	0.0	—	
1926	**CHI N**	19	.333	.431	51	17	5	0	0	0.0	9	4	6	3	0	5	2	25	42	3	6	5.4	.957	SS-13
7 yrs.		310	.259	.336	1070	277	38	22	0	0.0	124	91	109	178	21	11	3	570	868	96	122	5.2	.937	2B-159, SS-123, 3B-15

Spike Shannon

SHANNON, WILLIAM PORTER BB TR 5′11″ 180 lbs.
B. Feb. 7, 1878, Pittsburgh, Pa. D. May 16, 1940, Minneapolis, Minn.

Year	Team	Games	BA	SA	AB	H	2B	3B	HR	HR%	R	RBI	BB	SO	SB	PH AB	PH H	PO	A	E	DP	TC/G	FA	G by Pos
1904	**STL N**	134	.280	.318	500	140	10	3	1	0.2	84	26	50		34	1	0	246	18	6	10	2.0	.978	OF-133
1905		140	.268	.309	544	146	16	3	0	0.0	73	41	47		27	0	0	299	7	5	3	2.2	.984	OF-140
1906	**2 teams**	**STL N** (80G –.258) **NY N** (76G –.254)																						
″	***total***	156	.256	.275	589	151	9	1	0	0.0	78	50	70		33	0	0	274	13	10	5	1.9	.966	OF-156
1907	**NY N**	155	.265	.308	**585**	155	12	5	1	0.2	**104**	33	82		33	0	0	282	18	7	3	2.0	.977	OF-155
1908	**2 teams**	**NY N** (77G –.224) **PIT N** (32G –.197)																						
″	***total***	109	.215	.243	395	85	2	3	1	0.3	44	33	37		18	2	0	202	10	8	3	2.1	.964	OF-106
5 yrs.		694	.259	.293	2613	677	49	15	3	0.1	383	183	286		145	3	0	1303	66	36	24	2.0	.974	OF-690

Wally Shannon

SHANNON, WALTER CHARLES BL TR 6′ 178 lbs.
B. Jan. 23, 1933, Cleveland, Ohio D. Feb. 8, 1992, Creve Coeur, Mo.

Year	Team	Lg	Games	BA	SA	AB	H	2B	3B	HR	HR%	R	RBI	BB	SO	SB	Pinch Hit AB	Pinch Hit H	PO	A	E	DP	TC/G	FA	G by Pos
1959	STL	N	47	.284	.337	95	27	5	0	0	0.0	5	5	0	12	0	28	9	40	35	3	9	2.5	.962	SS-21, 2B-10
1960			18	.174	.174	23	4	0	0	0	0.0	2	1	3	6	0	9	1	10	23	0	4	2.1	1.000	2B-15, SS-1
2 yrs.			65	.263	.305	118	31	5	0	0	0.0	7	6	3	18	0	37	10	50	58	3	13	2.4	.973	2B-25, SS-22

Billy Shantz

SHANTZ, WILMER EBERT BR TR 6′ 1″ 160 lbs.
Brother of Bobby Shantz.
B. July 31, 1927, Pottstown, Pa. D. Dec. 13, 1993, Lauderhill, Fla.

Year	Team	Lg	Games	BA	SA	AB	H	2B	3B	HR	HR%	R	RBI	BB	SO	SB	Pinch Hit AB	Pinch Hit H	PO	A	E	DP	TC/G	FA	G by Pos
1954	PHI	A	51	.256	.366	164	42	9	3	1	0.6	13	17	17	23	0	0	0	170	28	5	1	4.0	.975	C-51
1955	KC	A	79	.258	.300	217	56	4	1	1	0.5	18	12	11	14	0	1	0	261	27	3	8	3.7	.990	C-78
1960	NY	A	1	—	—	0	0	0	0	0	—	0	0	0	0	0	0	0	1	0	0	0	1.0	1.000	C-1
3 yrs.			131	.257	.328	381	98	13	4	2	0.5	31	29	28	37	0	1	0	432	55	8	9	3.8	.984	C-130

Ralph Sharman

SHARMAN, RALPH EDWARD (Bally) BR TR 5′11″ 176 lbs.
B. Apr. 11, 1895, Cleveland, Ohio D. May 24, 1918, Camp Sheridan, Ala.

Year	Team	Lg	Games	BA	SA	AB	H	2B	3B	HR	HR%	R	RBI	BB	SO	SB	Pinch Hit AB	Pinch Hit H	PO	A	E	DP	TC/G	FA	G by Pos
1917	PHI	A	13	.297	.405	37	11	2	1	0	0.0	3	2	3	2	1	2	0	16	7	1	0	2.4	.958	OF-10

Dick Sharon

SHARON, RICHARD LOUIS BR TR 6′ 2″ 195 lbs.
B. Apr. 15, 1950, San Mateo, Calif.

Year	Team	Lg	Games	BA	SA	AB	H	2B	3B	HR	HR%	R	RBI	BB	SO	SB	Pinch Hit AB	Pinch Hit H	PO	A	E	DP	TC/G	FA	G by Pos
1973	DET	A	91	.242	.410	178	43	9	0	7	3.9	20	16	10	31	2	3	1	124	5	4	1	1.5	.970	OF-91
1974			60	.217	.295	129	28	4	0	2	1.6	12	10	14	29	4	5	0	84	3	1	1	1.6	.989	OF-56
1975	SD	N	91	.194	.313	160	31	7	0	4	2.5	14	20	26	35	0	33	8	91	1	5	0	1.7	.948	OF-57
3 yrs.			242	.218	.345	467	102	20	0	13	2.8	46	46	50	95	6	41	9	299	9	10	2	1.6	.969	OF-204

Bill Sharp

SHARP, WILLIAM HOWARD BL TL 5′10″ 178 lbs.
B. Jan. 18, 1950, Lima, Ohio.

Year	Team	Lg	Games	BA	SA	AB	H	2B	3B	HR	HR%	R	RBI	BB	SO	SB	Pinch Hit AB	Pinch Hit H	PO	A	E	DP	TC/G	FA	G by Pos
1973	CHI	A	77	.276	.408	196	54	8	3	4	2.0	23	22	19	28	2	5	2	146	10	3	2	2.2	.981	OF-70, DH-1
1974			100	.253	.344	320	81	13	2	4	1.3	45	24	25	37	0	3	1	210	3	3	0	2.2	.986	OF-99
1975	2 teams		CHI A (18G –.200) MIL A (125G –.255)																						
″	total		143	.250	.338	408	102	27	3	1	0.2	38	38	21	29	0	10	1	310	12	3	4	2.4	.991	OF-138
1976	MIL	A	78	.244	.267	180	44	4	0	0	0.0	16	11	10	15	1	17	5	108	7	3	2	1.9	.975	OF-56, DH-7
4 yrs.			398	.255	.341	1104	281	52	8	9	0.8	122	95	75	109	3	35	9	774	32	12	8	2.2	.985	OF-363, DH-8

Bud Sharpe

SHARPE, BAYARD HESTON BL TR
B. Aug. 6, 1881, West Chester, Pa. D. May 31, 1916, Haddock, Ga.

Year	Team	Lg	Games	BA	SA	AB	H	2B	3B	HR	HR%	R	RBI	BB	SO	SB	Pinch Hit AB	Pinch Hit H	PO	A	E	DP	TC/G	FA	G by Pos
1905	BOS	N	46	.182	.224	170	31	3	2	0	0.0	8	11	7		0	1	0	73	20	7	3	2.2	.930	OF-42, C-3, 1B-1
1910	2 teams		BOS N (115G –.239) PIT N (4G –.188)																						
″	total		119	.237	.286	455	108	14	4	0	0.0	32	30	14	33	4	2	1	1159	84	17	72	10.8	.987	1B-117
2 yrs.			165	.222	.269	625	139	17	6	0	0.0	40	41	21	33	4	3	1	1232	104	24	75	8.3	.982	1B-118, OF-42, C-3

Mike Sharperson

SHARPERSON, MICHAEL TYRONE BR TR 6′ 3″ 190 lbs.
B. Oct. 4, 1961, Orangeburg, S. C.

Year	Team	Lg	Games	BA	SA	AB	H	2B	3B	HR	HR%	R	RBI	BB	SO	SB	Pinch Hit AB	Pinch Hit H	PO	A	E	DP	TC/G	FA	G by Pos
1987	2 teams		TOR A (32G –.208) LA N (10G –.273)																						
″	total		42	.225	.287	129	29	6	1	0	0.0	11	10	11	20	2	0	0	68	97	5	18	3.8	.971	2B-38, 3B-7
1988	LA	N	46	.271	.288	59	16	1	0	0	0.0	8	4	1	12	0	22	3	19	31	2	5	1.7	.962	2B-20, 3B-6, SS-4
1989			27	.250	.357	28	7	3	0	0	0.0	2	5	4	7	0	15	3	11	8	0	2	2.1	1.000	2B-4, 1B-2, 3B-2, SS-1
1990			129	.297	.373	357	106	14	2	3	0.8	42	36	46	39	15	19	7	152	193	15	23	2.6	.958	3B-106, SS-15, 2B-9, 1B-6
1991			105	.278	.375	216	60	11	2	2	0.9	24	20	25	24	1	22	6	89	107	4	15	2.0	.980	3B-68, SS-16, 1B-10, 2B-5
1992			128	.300	.394	317	95	21	0	3	0.9	48	36	47	33	2	38	8	120	220	13	31	2.8	.963	2B-63, 3B-60, SS-2
1993			73	.256	.367	90	23	4	0	2	2.2	13	10	5	17	2	47	12	29	38	5	9	2.6	.931	2B-17, 3B-6, SS-3, OF-1, 1B-1
1995	ATL	N	7	.143	.286	7	1	1	0	0	0.0	1	2	0	2	0	6	0	0	0	0	0	0.0	.000	3B-1
8 yrs.			557	.280	.364	1203	337	61	5	10	0.8	149	123	139	154	22	169	39	488	694	44	103	2.6	.964	3B-256, 2B-156, SS-41, 1B-19, OF-1
LEAGUE CHAMPIONSHIP SERIES																									
1988	LA	N	2	.000	.000	1	0	0	0	0	0.0	0	1	1	0	0	1	0	1	0	0	0	0.5	1.000	3B-1, SS-1

John Sharrott

SHARROTT, JOHN HENRY BL TL 5′ 9″ 165 lbs.
B. Aug. 13, 1869, Bangor, Me. D. Dec. 31, 1927, Los Angeles, Calif.

Year	Team	Lg	Games	BA	SA	AB	H	2B	3B	HR	HR%	R	RBI	BB	SO	SB	Pinch Hit AB	Pinch Hit H	PO	A	E	DP	TC/G	FA	G by Pos
1890	NY	N	32	.202	.266	109	22	3	2	0	0.0	16	14	0	14	6	0	0	11	46	15	0	2.1	.792	P-25, OF-9
1891			10	.333	.500	30	10	2	0	1	3.3	5	7	1	2	3	0	0	4	15	1	0	2.0	.950	P-10
1892			4	.125	.125	8	1	0	0	0	0.0	1	0	0	1	0	0	0	1	0	2	0	0.8	.333	OF-3, P-1
1893	PHI	N	50	.250	.336	152	38	4	3	1	0.7	25	22	8	14	6	4	**2**	52	19	14	0	1.9	.835	OF-33, P-12
4 yrs.			96	.237	.321	299	71	9	5	2	0.7	47	43	9	31	15	4	2	68	80	32	0	1.9	.822	P-48, OF-45

Shag Shaughnessy

SHAUGHNESSY, FRANCIS JOSEPH BR TR 6′ 1½″ 185 lbs.
B. Apr. 8, 1883, Amboy, Ill. D. May 15, 1969, Montreal, Que., Canada.

Year	Team	Lg	Games	BA	SA	AB	H	2B	3B	HR	HR%	R	RBI	BB	SO	SB	Pinch Hit AB	Pinch Hit H	PO	A	E	DP	TC/G	FA	G by Pos
1905	WAS	A	1	.000	.000	3	0	0	0	0	0.0	0	0	0		0	0	0	2	0	1	0	3.0	.667	OF-1
1908	PHI	A	8	.310	.310	29	9	0	0	0	0.0	2	1	2		3	0	0	13	0	0	0	1.6	1.000	OF-8
2 yrs.			9	.281	.281	32	9	0	0	0	0.0	2	1	2		3	0	0	15	0	1	0	1.8	.938	OF-9

Jon Shave

SHAVE, JONATHAN TAYLOR BR TR 6′ 185 lbs.
B. Nov. 4, 1967, Waycross, Ga.

Year	Team	Lg	Games	BA	SA	AB	H	2B	3B	HR	HR%	R	RBI	BB	SO	SB	Pinch Hit AB	Pinch Hit H	PO	A	E	DP	TC/G	FA	G by Pos
1993	TEX	A	17	.319	.362	47	15	2	0	0	0.0	3	7	0	8	1	0	0	22	37	3	9	3.6	.952	SS-9, 2B-8

Al Shaw

SHAW, ALBERT SIMPSON BL TR 5′ 8½″ 165 lbs.
B. Mar. 1, 1881, Toledo, Ill. D. Dec. 30, 1974, Danville, Ill.

Year	Team	Lg	Games	BA	SA	AB	H	2B	3B	HR	HR%	R	RBI	BB	SO	SB	Pinch Hit AB	Pinch Hit H	PO	A	E	DP	TC/G	FA	G by Pos
1907	STL	N	8	.304	.304	23	7	0	0	0	0.0	2	1	3		1	0	0	17	1	1	0	2.4	.947	OF-8
1908			107	.264	.330	367	97	13	4	1	0.3	40	19	25		9	10	5	186	28	19	8	2.4	.918	OF-91, SS-4, 3B-1
1909			114	.248	.344	331	82	12	7	2	0.6	45	34	55		15	15	3	189	14	13	1	2.3	.940	OF-92
1914	BKN	F	112	.324	.473	376	122	27	7	5	1.3	81	49	44		24	7	5	198	14	10	4	2.2	.955	OF-102
1915	KC	F	132	.281	.415	448	126	22	10	6	1.3	67	67	46		15	6	1	184	11	12	0	1.7	.942	OF-124
5 yrs.			473	.281	.392	1545	434	74	28	14	0.9	235	170	173		64	38	14	774	68	55	13	2.1	.939	OF-417, SS-4, 3B-1

Year	Team	Games	BA	SA	AB	H	2B	3B	HR	HR%	R	RBI	BB	SO	SB	Pinch Hit AB	Pinch Hit H	PO	A	E	DP	TC/G	FA	G by Pos

Al Shaw

SHAW, ALFRED BR TR 5′ 8″ 170 lbs.
B. Oct. 3, 1874, Burslem, England D. Mar. 25, 1958, Uhrichsville, Ohio.

Year	Team	Games	BA	SA	AB	H	2B	3B	HR	HR%	R	RBI	BB	SO	SB	Pinch Hit AB	Pinch Hit H	PO	A	E	DP	TC/G	FA	G by Pos
1901	DET A	55	.269	.327	171	46	7	0	1	0.6	20	23	10		2	4	0	217	50	17	12	5.3	.940	C-42, 1B-9, 3B-2, SS-1
1907	BOS A	76	.192	.227	198	38	1	3	0	0.0	10	7	18		4	1	0	296	106	13	11	5.6	.969	C-73, 1B-1
1908	CHI A	32	.082	.102	49	4	1	0	0	0.0	0	2	2		0	3	0	87	15	5	1	3.7	.953	C-29
1909	BOS N	17	.098	.098	41	4	0	0	0	0.0	1	0	5		0	2	0	58	21	2	0	5.8	.975	C-14
4 yrs.		180	.200	.240	459	92	9	3	1	0.2	31	32	35		6	10	0	658	192	37	24	5.2	.958	C-158, 1B-10, 3B-2, SS-1

Ben Shaw

SHAW, BENJAMIN NATHANIEL BR TR 5′11½″ 190 lbs.
B. June 18, 1893, La Center, Ky. D. Mar. 16, 1959, Cleveland, Ohio.

Year	Team	Games	BA	SA	AB	H	2B	3B	HR	HR%	R	RBI	BB	SO	SB	Pinch Hit AB	Pinch Hit H	PO	A	E	DP	TC/G	FA	G by Pos
1917	PIT N	2	.000	.000	2	0	0	0	0	0.0	0	0	0	0	0	2	0	0	0	0	0	0.0	—	
1918		21	.194	.222	36	7	1	0	0	0.0	5	2	2	2	0	1	0	67	2	1	3	5.0	.986	1B-9, C-5
2 yrs.		23	.184	.211	38	7	1	0	0	0.0	5	2	2	2	0	3	0	67	2	1	3	5.0	.986	1B-9, C-5

Dupee Shaw

SHAW, FREDERICK LANDER BL TL 5′ 8″ 165 lbs.
B. May 31, 1859, Charlestown, Mass. D. June 11, 1938, Everett, Mass.

Year	Team	Games	BA	SA	AB	H	2B	3B	HR	HR%	R	RBI	BB	SO	SB	Pinch Hit AB	Pinch Hit H	PO	A	E	DP	TC/G	FA	G by Pos
1883	DET N	38	.206	.227	141	29	3	0	0	0.0	13		3	36		0	0	21	50	7	5	1.9	.910	P-26, OF-15
1884	2 teams	DET N (36G –.191) BOS U (44G –.242)																						
″	total	80	.218	.277	289	63	12	1	1	0.3	29		9	21		0	0	39	116	34	3	2.2	.820	P-67, OF-19
1885	PRO N	49	.133	.145	165	22	2	0	0	0.0	17	9	4	38		0	0	11	76	8	2	1.9	.916	P-49, OF-2
1886	WAS N	45	.088	.101	148	13	2	0	0	0.0	13	6	14	44		0	0	13	70	3	1	1.9	.965	P-45, OF-1
1887		21	.186	.214	70	13	2	0	0	0.0	7	3	8	14	1	0	0	4	24	2	0	1.4	.933	P-21
1888		3	.000	.000	10	0	0	0	0	0.0	0	0	0	3	0	0	0	0	2	0	0	0.7	1.000	P-3
6 yrs.		236	.170	.202	823	140	21	1	1	0.1	79	18	38	156	1	0	0	88	338	54	11	1.9	.887	P-211, OF-37

Hunky Shaw

SHAW, ROYAL N. BB TR 5′ 8″ 165 lbs.
B. Sept. 29, 1884, Yakima, Wash. D. July 3, 1969, Yakima, Wash.

Year	Team	Games	BA	SA	AB	H	2B	3B	HR	HR%	R	RBI	BB	SO	SB	Pinch Hit AB	Pinch Hit H	PO	A	E	DP	TC/G	FA	G by Pos
1908	PIT N	1	.000	.000	1	0	0	0	0	0.0	0	0	0		0	1	0	0	0	0	0	0.0	—	

Danny Shay

SHAY, DANIEL C. TR 5′10″
Born Daniel C. Shea.
B. Nov. 8, 1876, Springfield, Ohio D. Dec. 1, 1927, Kansas City, Mo.

Year	Team	Games	BA	SA	AB	H	2B	3B	HR	HR%	R	RBI	BB	SO	SB	Pinch Hit AB	Pinch Hit H	PO	A	E	DP	TC/G	FA	G by Pos
1901	CLE A	19	.227	.307	75	17	2	2	0	0.0	4	10	2		0	0	0	38	53	10	3	5.3	.901	SS-19
1904	STL N	99	.256	.303	340	87	11	1	1	0.3	45	18	39		36	1	0	153	324	46	30	5.3	.912	SS-97, 2B-2
1905		78	.238	.288	281	67	12	1	0	0.0	30	28	35		11	0	0	172	230	35	22	5.6	.920	SS-39, 2B-39
1907	NY N	35	.190	.266	79	15	1	1	1	1.3	10	6	12		5	11	2	40	53	10	3	4.3	.903	2B-13, SS-9, OF-2
4 yrs.		231	.240	.294	775	186	26	5	2	0.3	89	62	88		52	12	2	403	660	101	58	5.3	.913	SS-164, 2B-54, OF-2

Marty Shay

SHAY, ARTHUR JOSEPH BR TR 5′ 7½″ 148 lbs.
B. Apr. 25, 1896, Boston, Mass. D. Feb. 20, 1951, Worcester, Mass.

Year	Team	Games	BA	SA	AB	H	2B	3B	HR	HR%	R	RBI	BB	SO	SB	Pinch Hit AB	Pinch Hit H	PO	A	E	DP	TC/G	FA	G by Pos
1916	CHI N	2	.286	.286	7	2	0	0	0	0.0	0	0	0	1	0	0	0	6	5	1	2	6.0	.917	SS-2
1924	BOS N	19	.235	.309	68	16	3	1	0	0.0	4	2	5	5	2	0	0	38	40	4	10	4.1	.951	2B-19, SS-1
2 yrs.		21	.240	.307	75	18	3	1	0	0.0	4	2	5	6	2	0	0	44	45	5	12	4.3	.947	2B-19, SS-3

Gerry Shea

SHEA, GERALD J. TR 5′ 7″ 160 lbs.
B. July 26, 1881, St. Louis, Mo. D. May 3, 1964, Berkeley, Mo.

Year	Team	Games	BA	SA	AB	H	2B	3B	HR	HR%	R	RBI	BB	SO	SB	Pinch Hit AB	Pinch Hit H	PO	A	E	DP	TC/G	FA	G by Pos
1905	STL N	2	.333	.333	6	2	0	0	0	0.0	0	0	0		0	0	0	7	4	1	1	6.0	.917	C-2

Merv Shea

SHEA, MERVYN DAVID JOHN BR TR 5′11″ 175 lbs.
B. Sept. 5, 1900, San Francisco, Calif. D. Jan. 27, 1953, Sacramento, Calif.

Year	Team	Games	BA	SA	AB	H	2B	3B	HR	HR%	R	RBI	BB	SO	SB	Pinch Hit AB	Pinch Hit H	PO	A	E	DP	TC/G	FA	G by Pos
1927	DET A	34	.176	.318	85	15	6	3	0	0.0	5	9	7	15	0	3	0	94	17	6	1	3.8	.949	C-31
1928		39	.235	.329	85	20	2	3	0	0.0	8	9	9	11	2	7	0	93	24	6	2	4.1	.951	C-30
1929		50	.290	.383	162	47	6	0	3	1.9	23	24	19	18	2	3	0	157	32	7	4	3.9	.964	C-50
1933	2 teams	BOS A (16G –.143) STL A (94G –.262)																						
″	total	110	.242	.299	335	81	14	1	1	0.3	27	35	47	33	2	8	2	376	71	2	17	4.4	.996	C-101
1934	CHI A	62	.159	.176	176	28	3	0	0	0.0	8	5	24	19	0	2	0	240	35	8	4	4.7	.972	C-60
1935		46	.230	.246	122	28	2	0	0	0.0	8	13	30	9	0	2	0	161	30	2	2	4.5	.990	C-43
1936		14	.125	.125	24	3	0	0	0	0.0	3	2	6	5	0	0	0	32	3	0	0	2.5	1.000	C-14
1937		25	.211	.225	71	15	1	0	0	0.0	7	5	15	10	1	0	0	91	21	4	1	4.6	.966	C-25
1938	BKN N	48	.183	.225	120	22	5	0	0	0.0	14	12	28	20	1	0	0	149	19	4	2	3.7	.977	C-47
1939	DET A	4	.000	.000	2	0	0	0	0	0.0	0	0	0	1	0	0	0	1	0	1	0	0.5	.500	C-4
1944	PHI N	7	.267	.467	15	4	0	0	1	6.7	2	1	4	4	0	1	0	18	2	1	0	3.5	.952	C-6
11 yrs.		439	.220	.277	1197	263	39	7	5	0.4	105	115	189	145	8	26	2	1412	254	41	33	4.2	.976	C-411

Nap Shea

SHEA, JOHN EDWARD BR TR 5′ 5″ 155 lbs.
B. May 23, 1874, Ware, Mass. D. July 8, 1968, Bloomfield Hills, Mich.

Year	Team	Games	BA	SA	AB	H	2B	3B	HR	HR%	R	RBI	BB	SO	SB	Pinch Hit AB	Pinch Hit H	PO	A	E	DP	TC/G	FA	G by Pos
1902	PHI N	3	.125	.125	8	1	0	0	0	0.0	1	0	1		0	0	0	13	2	0	0	5.0	1.000	C-3

Danny Sheaffer

SHEAFFER, DANNY TODD BR TR 6′ 185 lbs.
B. Aug. 2, 1961, Jacksonville, Fla.

Year	Team	Games	BA	SA	AB	H	2B	3B	HR	HR%	R	RBI	BB	SO	SB	Pinch Hit AB	Pinch Hit H	PO	A	E	DP	TC/G	FA	G by Pos
1987	BOS A	25	.121	.182	66	8	1	0	1	1.5	5	5	0	14	0	1	1	121	5	3	1	5.2	.977	C-25
1989	CLE A	7	.063	.063	16	1	0	0	0	0.0	1	0	2	2	0	1	0	4	0	0	0	0.7	1.000	DH-3, 3B-2, OF-1
1993	CLR N	82	.278	.384	216	60	9	1	4	1.9	26	32	8	15	2	7	2	337	32	2	6	4.9	.995	C-65, 1B-7, OF-2, 3B-1
1994		44	.218	.282	110	24	4	0	1	0.9	11	12	10	11	0	11	3	181	17	1	3	6.0	.995	C-30, 1B-2, OF-1
1995	STL N	76	.231	.361	208	48	10	1	5	2.4	24	30	23	38	0	6	1	391	44	3	7	6.2	.993	C-67, 1B-3, 3B-1
5 yrs.		234	.229	.328	616	141	24	2	11	1.8	67	79	43	80	2	26	7	1034	98	9	17	5.4	.992	C-187, 1B-12, OF-4, 3B-4, DH-3

Dave Shean

SHEAN, DAVID WILLIAM BR TR 5′11″ 175 lbs.
B. July 9, 1883, Arlington, Mass. D. May 22, 1963, Boston, Mass.

Year	Team	Games	BA	SA	AB	H	2B	3B	HR	HR%	R	RBI	BB	SO	SB	Pinch Hit AB	Pinch Hit H	PO	A	E	DP	TC/G	FA	G by Pos
1906	PHI A	22	.213	.307	75	16	3	2	0	0.0	7	3	5		6	0	0	41	58	2	5	4.6	.980	2B-22
1908	PHI N	14	.146	.188	48	7	2	0	0	0.0	4	2	1		1	0	0	27	34	9	2	5.0	.871	SS-14
1909	2 teams	PHI N (36G –.232) BOS N (75G –.247)																						
″	total	111	.243	.317	379	92	13	6	1	0.3	46	33	31		17	10	3	295	245	19	40	5.5	.966	2B-86, 1B-11, OF-3, SS-1
1910	BOS N	150	.239	.304	543	130	12	7	3	0.6	52	36	42	45	16	2	1	408	493	44	92	6.4	.953	2B-148
1911	CHI N	54	.193	.221	145	28	4	0	0	0.0	17	15	8	15	4	9	1	81	107	12	17	4.7	.940	2B-23, SS-19, 3B-1

Dave Shean *continued*

Year	Team	Lg	Games	BA	SA	AB	H	2B	3B	HR	HR%	R	RBI	BB	SO	SB	Pinch Hit AB	Pinch Hit H	PO	A	E	DP	TC/G	FA	G by Pos
1912	BOS	N	4	.300	.300	10	3	0	0	0	0.0	1	0	1	2	0	1	0	2	9	1	2	3.0	.917	SS-4
1917	CIN	N	131	.210	.267	442	93	9	5	2	0.5	36	35	22	39	10	0	0	332	412	30	69	5.9	.961	2B-131
1918	BOS	A	115	.264	.315	425	112	16	3	0	0.0	58	34	40	25	11	0	0	241	341	20	38	5.2	.967	2B-115
1919			29	.140	.140	100	14	0	0	0	0.0	4	8	5	7	1	0	0	70	85	3	18	5.4	.981	2B-29
9 yrs.			630	.228	.285	2167	495	59	23	6	0.3	225	166	155	133	66	22	5	1497	1784	140	283	5.6	.959	2B-554, SS-38, 1B-11, OF-3, 3B-1
WORLD SERIES																									
1918	BOS	A	6	.211	.263	19	4	1	0	0	0.0	2	0	4	3	1	0	0	15	17	0	3	5.3	1.000	2B-6

Ray Shearer

SHEARER, RAY SOLOMON BR TR 6′ 200 lbs.
B. Sept. 19, 1929, Jacobus, Pa. D. Feb. 21, 1982, York, Pa.

Year	Team	Lg	Games	BA	SA	AB	H	2B	3B	HR	HR%	R	RBI	BB	SO	SB	Pinch Hit AB	Pinch Hit H	PO	A	E	DP	TC/G	FA	G by Pos
1957	MIL	N	2	.500	.500	2	1	0	0	0	0.0	1	0	1	1	0	1	1	0	0	0	0	0.0	.000	OF-1

John Shearon

SHEARON, JOHN M.
B. 1870, Pittsburgh, Pa. D. Feb. 1, 1923, Bradford, Pa.

Year	Team	Lg	Games	BA	SA	AB	H	2B	3B	HR	HR%	R	RBI	BB	SO	SB	Pinch Hit AB	Pinch Hit H	PO	A	E	DP	TC/G	FA	G by Pos
1891	CLE	N	30	.242	.266	124	30	1	1	0	0.0	10	13	1	15	6	0	0	32	13	8	1	1.6	.849	OF-28, P-6
1896			16	.172	.203	64	11	0	1	0	0.0	6	3	4	6	3	0	0	18	0	4	0	1.4	.818	OF-16
2 yrs.			46	.218	.245	188	41	1	2	0	0.0	16	16	5	21	9	0	0	50	13	12	1	1.5	.840	OF-44, P-6

Jimmy Sheckard

SHECKARD, SAMUEL JAMES TILDEN BL TR 5′ 9″ 175 lbs.
B. Nov. 23, 1878, Upper Chanceford, Pa. D. Jan. 15, 1947, Lancaster, Pa.

Year	Team	Lg	Games	BA	SA	AB	H	2B	3B	HR	HR%	R	RBI	BB	SO	SB	Pinch Hit AB	Pinch Hit H	PO	A	E	DP	TC/G	FA	G by Pos
1897	BKN	N	13	.286	.612	49	14	3	2	3	6.1	12	14	6		5	0	0	21	41	20	5	6.3	.756	SS-11, OF-2
1898			105	.277	.392	408	113	17	9	4	1.0	51	64	37		8	0	0	213	13	19	2	2.3	.922	OF-105, 3B-1
1899	BAL	N	147	.295	.382	536	158	18	10	3	0.6	104	75	56		**77**	0	0	306	33	20	14	2.4	.944	OF-146, 1B-1
1900	BKN	N	85	.300	.454	273	82	19	10	1	0.4	74	39	42		30	6	1	171	13	15	3	2.6	.925	OF-78
1901			133	.353	**.536**	558	197	31	**19**	11	2.0	116	104	47		35	0	0	296	37	30	6	2.7	.917	OF-121, 3B-12
1902	2 teams		BAL A (4G –.267)	BKN N (123G –.270)																					
″	total		127	.269	.375	501	135	21	10	4	0.8	89	37	58		25	0	0	289	12	11	6	2.5	.965	OF-127
1903	BKN	N	139	.332	.476	515	171	29	9	**9**	1.7	99	75	75		**67**	0	0	314	36	18	7	2.6	.951	OF-139
1904			143	.239	.314	507	121	23	6	1	0.2	70	46	56		21	0	0	296	16	15	5	2.3	.954	OF-141, 2B-2
1905			130	.292	.398	480	140	20	11	3	0.6	58	41	61		23	0	0	266	24	10	6	2.3	.967	OF-129
1906	CHI	N	149	.262	.353	549	144	27	10	1	0.2	90	45	67		30	0	0	264	13	4	1	1.9	.986	OF-149
1907			142	.267	.324	484	129	23	1	1	0.2	76	36	76		31	1	0	223	13	6	2	1.7	.975	OF-142
1908			115	.231	.305	403	93	18	3	2	0.5	54	22	62		18	0	0	201	13	10	3	1.9	.955	OF-115
1909			148	.255	.335	525	134	29	5	1	0.2	81	43	72		15	0	0	277	18	10	5	2.1	.967	OF-148
1910			144	.256	.363	507	130	27	6	5	1.0	82	51	83	53	22	1	1	308	21	8	3	2.4	.976	OF-143
1911			156	.276	.388	539	149	26	11	4	0.7	**121**	50	**147**	58	32	0	0	332	32	14	12	2.4	.963	OF-156
1912			146	.245	.342	523	128	22	10	3	0.6	85	47	**122**	81	15	0	0	332	26	14	4	2.5	.962	OF-146
1913	2 teams		STL N (52G –.199)	CIN N (47G –.190)																					
″	total		99	.194	.238	252	49	3	4	0	0.0	34	24	68	41	11	12	2	134	10	6	3	1.8	.960	OF-84
17 yrs.			2121	.274	.379	7609	2087	356	136	56	0.7	1296	813	1135	233	465	20	4	4243	371	230	87	2.3	.953	OF-2071, 3B-13, SS-11, 2B-2, 1B-1
WORLD SERIES																									
1906	CHI	N	6	.000	.000	21	0	0	0	0	0.0	0	1	2	4	1	0	0	10	1	0	1	1.8	1.000	OF-6
1907			5	.238	.333	21	5	2	0	0	0.0	0	2	0	1	1	0	0	10	0	0	0	2.0	1.000	OF-5
1908			5	.238	.333	21	5	2	0	0	0.0	2	1	2	3	1	0	0	7	1	0	0	1.6	1.000	OF-5
1910			5	.286	.429	14	4	2	0	0	0.0	5	1	7	2	1	0	0	8	2	1	0	2.2	.909	OF-5
4 yrs.			21	.182	.260	77	14	6	0	0	0.0	7	5	11	10	4	0	0	35	4	1	1	1.9	.975	OF-21

Biff Sheehan

SHEEHAN, TIMOTHY JAMES TR 5′ 9″ 165 lbs.
B. Feb. 13, 1868, Hartford, Conn. D. Oct. 21, 1923, Hartford, Conn.

Year	Team	Lg	Games	BA	SA	AB	H	2B	3B	HR	HR%	R	RBI	BB	SO	SB	Pinch Hit AB	Pinch Hit H	PO	A	E	DP	TC/G	FA	G by Pos
1895	STL	N	52	.317	.417	180	57	3	6	1	0.6	24	18	20	6	7	0	0	151	10	9	7	3.3	.947	OF-41, 1B-11
1896			6	.158	.158	19	3	0	0	0	0.0	0	1	4	0	0	0	0	10	0	0	0	1.7	1.000	OF-6
2 yrs.			58	.302	.392	199	60	3	6	1	0.5	24	19	24	6	7	0	0	161	10	9	7	3.1	.950	OF-47, 1B-11

Daniel Sheehan

SHEEHAN, DANIEL
B. Washington, D. C. Deceased.

Year	Team	Lg	Games	BA	SA	AB	H	2B	3B	HR	HR%	R	RBI	BB	SO	SB	Pinch Hit AB	Pinch Hit H	PO	A	E	DP	TC/G	FA	G by Pos
1884	2 teams		WAS U (7G –.143)	WIL U (2G –.167)																					
″	total		9	.147	.206	34	5	0	1	0	0.0	2		2			0	0	11	1	5	0	1.7	.706	OF-9, 3B-1

Jack Sheehan

SHEEHAN, JOHN THOMAS BB TR 5′ 8½″ 165 lbs.
B. Apr. 15, 1893, Chicago, Ill. D. May 29, 1987, West Palm Beach, Fla.

Year	Team	Lg	Games	BA	SA	AB	H	2B	3B	HR	HR%	R	RBI	BB	SO	SB	Pinch Hit AB	Pinch Hit H	PO	A	E	DP	TC/G	FA	G by Pos
1920	BKN	N	3	.400	.600	5	2	1	0	0	0.0	0	0	1	0	0	0	0	2	6	2	0	3.3	.800	SS-2, 3B-1
1921			5	.000	.000	12	0	0	0	0	0.0	2	0	0	1	0	0	0	6	8	1	1	3.8	.933	2B-2, SS-1, 3B-1
2 yrs.			8	.118	.176	17	2	1	0	0	0.0	2	0	1	1	0	0	0	8	14	3	1	3.6	.880	SS-3, 2B-2, 3B-2
WORLD SERIES																									
1920	BKN	N	3	.182	.182	11	2	0	0	0	0.0	0	0	0	1	0	0	0	3	5	2	0	3.3	.800	3B-3

Jim Sheehan

SHEEHAN, JAMES THOMAS (Big Jim) BR TR 6′ 2″ 196 lbs.
B. July 3, 1913, New Haven, Conn.

Year	Team	Lg	Games	BA	SA	AB	H	2B	3B	HR	HR%	R	RBI	BB	SO	SB	Pinch Hit AB	Pinch Hit H	PO	A	E	DP	TC/G	FA	G by Pos
1936	NY	N	1	.000	.000	4	0	0	0	0	0.0	0	0	0	2	0	0	0	5	0	1	0	6.0	.833	C-1

Tommy Sheehan

SHEEHAN, THOMAS H. BR TR 5′ 8″ 160 lbs.
B. Nov. 6, 1877, Sacramento, Calif. D. May 22, 1959, Panama City, Panama.

Year	Team	Lg	Games	BA	SA	AB	H	2B	3B	HR	HR%	R	RBI	BB	SO	SB	Pinch Hit AB	Pinch Hit H	PO	A	E	DP	TC/G	FA	G by Pos
1900	NY	N	1	.000	.000	2	0	0	0	0	0.0	0	0	0		0	0	0	0	0	0	0	0.0	.000	SS-1
1906	PIT	N	95	.241	.289	315	76	6	3	1	0.3	28	34	18		13	5	1	104	166	15	11	3.2	.947	3B-90
1907			75	.274	.310	226	62	2	3	0	0.0	23	25	23		10	6	2	74	161	19	3	3.8	.925	3B-57, SS-10
1908	BKN	N	146	.214	.261	468	100	18	2	0	0.0	45	29	53		9	1	1	174	280	34	13	3.4	.930	3B-145
4 yrs.			317	.235	.280	1011	238	26	8	1	0.1	96	88	94		32	12	4	352	607	68	27	3.4	.934	3B-292, SS-11

Bud Sheely

SHEELY, HOLLIS KIMBALL BL TR 6′ 1″ 200 lbs.
Son of Earl Sheely.
B. Nov. 26, 1920, Spokane, Wash. D. Oct. 17, 1985, Sacramento, Calif.

Year	Team	Games	BA	SA	AB	H	2B	3B	HR	HR%	R	RBI	BB	SO	SB	Pinch Hit AB	Pinch Hit H	PO	A	E	DP	TC/G	FA	G by Pos
1951	CHI A	34	.180	.202	89	16	2	0	0	0.0	2	7	6	7	0	1	0	127	11	2	3	4.2	.986	C-33
1952		36	.240	.267	75	18	2	0	0	0.0	1	3	12	7	0	6	2	105	12	1	1	3.8	.992	C-31
1953		31	.217	.239	46	10	1	0	0	0.0	4	2	9	8	0	10	4	60	2	0	1	3.6	1.000	C-17
3 yrs.		101	.210	.233	210	44	5	0	0	0.0	7	12	27	22	0	17	6	292	25	3	5	4.0	.991	C-81

Earl Sheely

SHEELY, EARL HOMER (Whitey) BR TR 6′ 3½″ 195 lbs.
Father of Bud Sheely.
B. Feb. 12, 1893, Bushnell, Ill. D. Sept. 16, 1952, Seattle, Wash.

Year	Team	Games	BA	SA	AB	H	2B	3B	HR	HR%	R	RBI	BB	SO	SB	Pinch Hit AB	Pinch Hit H	PO	A	E	DP	TC/G	FA	G by Pos
1921	CHI A	154	.304	.428	563	171	25	6	11	2.0	68	95	57	34	4	0	0	1637	119	22	121	11.5	.988	1B-154
1922		149	.317	.437	526	167	37	4	6	1.1	72	80	60	27	4	0	0	1512	103	12	101	10.9	.993	1B-149
1923		156	.296	.372	570	169	25	3	4	0.7	74	88	79	30	5	0	0	1563	96	14	113	10.7	.992	1B-156
1924		146	.320	.411	535	171	34	3	3	0.6	84	103	95	28	7	0	0	1423	79	14	97	10.4	.991	1B-146
1925		153	.315	.442	600	189	43	3	9	1.5	93	111	68	23	3	0	0	1565	95	20	136	11.0	.988	1B-153
1926		145	.299	.417	525	157	40	2	6	1.1	77	89	75	13	3	0	0	1380	84	8	87	10.2	.995	1B-144
1927		45	.209	.279	129	27	3	0	2	1.6	11	16	20	5	1	8	1	315	15	6	25	9.3	.982	1B-36
1929	PIT N	139	.293	.392	485	142	22	4	6	1.2	63	88	75	24	6	0	0	1292	83	5	102	9.9	.996	1B-139
1931	BOS N	147	.273	.314	538	147	15	2	1	0.2	30	77	34	21	0	3	0	1374	70	12	108	10.2	.992	1B-143
9 yrs.		1234	.300	.399	4471	1340	244	27	48	1.1	572	747	563	205	33	11	1	12061	744	113	890	10.6	.991	1B-1220

Charlie Sheerin

SHEERIN, CHARLES JOSEPH BR TR 5′11½″ 198 lbs.
B. Apr. 17, 1909, Brooklyn, N. Y. D. Sept. 27, 1986, Valley Stream, N. Y.

Year	Team	Games	BA	SA	AB	H	2B	3B	HR	HR%	R	RBI	BB	SO	SB	Pinch Hit AB	Pinch Hit H	PO	A	E	DP	TC/G	FA	G by Pos
1936	PHI N	39	.264	.319	72	19	4	0	0	0.0	4	4	7	18	0	2	1	22	54	5	3	2.3	.938	2B-17, 3B-13, SS-5

Larry Sheets

SHEETS, LARRY KENT BL TR 6′ 4″ 210 lbs.
B. Dec. 6, 1959, Staunton, Va.

Year	Team	Games	BA	SA	AB	H	2B	3B	HR	HR%	R	RBI	BB	SO	SB	Pinch Hit AB	Pinch Hit H	PO	A	E	DP	TC/G	FA	G by Pos
1984	BAL A	8	.438	.688	16	7	1	0	1	6.3	3	2	1	3	0	1	0	12	1	0	0	1.9	1.000	OF-7
1985		113	.262	.442	328	86	8	0	17	5.2	43	50	28	52	0	16	4	12	1	1	1	0.1	.929	DH-93, OF-9, 1B-1
1986		112	.272	.488	338	92	17	1	18	5.3	42	60	21	56	2	13	2	90	8	3	4	1.0	.970	DH-58, OF-32, C-6, 1B-4, 3B-2
1987		135	.316	.563	469	148	23	0	31	6.6	74	94	31	67	1	6	3	243	7	7	3	1.9	.973	OF-124, DH-7, 1B-3
1988		136	.230	.343	452	104	19	1	10	2.2	38	47	42	72	1	12	5	159	12	4	3	1.4	.977	OF-76, DH-50, 1B-3
1989		102	.243	.359	304	74	12	1	7	2.3	33	33	26	58	1	18	6	0	0	0	0	0.0	.000	DH-88
1990	DET A	131	.261	.403	360	94	17	2	10	2.8	40	52	24	42	1	21	4	98	7	2	1	0.9	.981	OF-79, DH-44
1993	SEA A	11	.118	.176	17	2	1	0	0	0.0	0	1	2	1	0	5	1	1	0	0	0	0.2	1.000	DH-5, OF-1
8 yrs.		748	.266	.437	2284	607	98	5	94	4.1	273	339	175	351	6	92	25	615	36	17	12	1.0	.975	DH-345, OF-328, 1B-11, C-6, 3B-2

Gary Sheffield

SHEFFIELD, GARY ANTONIAN BR TR 5′11″ 190 lbs.
B. Nov. 18, 1968, Tampa, Fla.

Year	Team	Games	BA	SA	AB	H	2B	3B	HR	HR%	R	RBI	BB	SO	SB	Pinch Hit AB	Pinch Hit H	PO	A	E	DP	TC/G	FA	G by Pos
1988	MIL A	24	.237	.400	80	19	1	0	4	5.0	12	12	7	7	3	0	0	39	48	3	9	3.8	.967	SS-24
1989		95	.247	.337	368	91	18	0	5	1.4	34	32	27	33	10	0	0	100	238	16	44	3.7	.955	SS-70, 3B-21, DH-4
1990		125	.294	.421	487	143	30	1	10	2.1	67	67	44	41	25	0	0	98	254	25	16	3.0	.934	3B-125
1991		50	.194	.320	175	34	12	2	2	1.1	25	22	19	15	5	0	0	29	65	8	7	2.1	.922	3B-43, DH-5
1992	SD N	146	**.330**	.580	557	184	34	3	33	5.9	87	100	48	40	5	2	1	99	299	16	25	2.9	.961	3B-144
1993	2 teams	SD N (68G –.295) FLA N (72G –.292)																						
″	total	140	.294	.476	494	145	20	5	20	4.0	67	73	47	64	17	4	1	79	225	34	15	2.5	.899	3B-133
1994	FLA N	87	.276	.584	322	89	16	1	27	8.4	61	78	51	50	12	1	1	153	7	5	2	1.9	.970	OF-87
1995		63	.324	.587	213	69	8	0	16	7.5	46	46	55	45	19	0	0	108	5	7	1	2.0	.942	OF-61
8 yrs.		730	.287	.478	2696	774	139	12	117	4.3	399	430	298	295	96	7	3	705	1141	114	119	2.7	.942	3B-466, OF-148, SS-94, DH-9

John Shelby

SHELBY, JOHN T. (T-Bone) BB TR 6′ 1″ 175 lbs.
B. Feb. 23, 1958, Lexington, Ky.

Year	Team	Games	BA	SA	AB	H	2B	3B	HR	HR%	R	RBI	BB	SO	SB	Pinch Hit AB	Pinch Hit H	PO	A	E	DP	TC/G	FA	G by Pos
1981	BAL A	7	.000	.000	2	0	0	0	0	0.0	2	0	0	1	2	0	0	1	0	0	0	0.3	1.000	OF-4
1982		26	.314	.486	35	11	3	0	1	2.9	8	2	0	5	0	3	1	20	1	0	1	0.9	1.000	OF-24
1983		126	.258	.363	325	84	15	2	5	1.5	52	27	18	64	15	27	7	200	9	4	3	1.8	.981	OF-115, DH-1
1984		128	.209	.313	383	80	12	5	6	1.6	44	30	20	71	12	12	4	261	9	2	1	2.2	.993	OF-124
1985		69	.283	.434	205	58	6	2	7	3.4	28	27	7	44	5	12	3	148	4	3	0	2.5	.981	OF-59, DH-3, 2B-1
1986		135	.228	.364	404	92	14	4	11	2.7	54	49	18	75	18	19	6	222	5	5	2	1.9	.978	OF-121, DH-2
1987	2 teams	BAL A (21G –.188) LA N (120G –.277)																						
″	total	141	.272	.453	508	138	26	0	22	4.3	65	72	32	110	16	3	1	294	9	8	3	2.3	.974	OF-136, DH-1
1988	LA N	140	.263	.395	494	130	23	6	10	2.0	65	64	44	128	16	0	0	329	7	6	1	2.4	.982	OF-140
1989		108	.183	.229	345	63	11	1	1	0.3	28	12	25	92	10	11	0	220	3	2	1	2.3	.991	OF-98
1990	2 teams	LA N (25G –.250) DET A (78G – 248)																						
″	total	103	.248	.362	246	61	10	3	4	1.6	24	22	10	58	4	27	7	146	5	4	3	1.8	.974	OF-80, DH-5
1991	DET A	53	.154	.287	143	22	8	1	3	2.1	19	8	8	23	0	6	1	108	4	2	0	2.2	.982	OF-47, DH-4
11 yrs.		1036	.239	.364	3090	739	128	24	70	2.3	389	313	182	671	98	120	30	1949	56	36	15	2.1	.982	OF-948, DH-16, 2B-1
LEAGUE CHAMPIONSHIP SERIES																								
1983	BAL A	3	.222	.222	9	2	0	0	0	0.0	1	0	1	3	1	0	0	3	0	0	0	1.5	1.000	OF-2
1988	LA N	7	.167	.167	24	4	0	0	0	0.0	3	3	5	12	2	0	0	19	0	0	0	2.7	1.000	OF-7
2 yrs.		10	.182	.182	33	6	0	0	0	0.0	4	3	6	15	3	0	0	22	0	0	0	2.4	1.000	OF-9
WORLD SERIES																								
1983	BAL A	5	.444	.444	9	4	0	0	0	0.0	1	1	0	4	0	3	0	10	0	0	0	2.0	1.000	OF-5
1988	LA N	5	.222	.278	18	4	1	0	0	0.0	0	1	2	7	1	0	0	14	0	0	0	2.8	1.000	OF-5
2 yrs.		10	.296	.333	27	8	1	0	0	0.0	1	2	2	11	1	3	0	24	0	0	0	2.4	1.000	OF-10

Bob Sheldon

SHELDON, BOB MITCHELL BL TR 6′ 170 lbs.
B. Nov. 27, 1950, Montebello, Calif.

Year	Team	Games	BA	SA	AB	H	2B	3B	HR	HR%	R	RBI	BB	SO	SB	Pinch Hit AB	Pinch Hit H	PO	A	E	DP	TC/G	FA	G by Pos
1974	MIL A	10	.118	.294	17	2	1	1	0	0.0	4	0	4	2	0	1	0	1	4	0	0	0.7	1.000	DH-4, 2B-3
1975		53	.287	.337	181	52	3	3	0	0.0	17	14	13	14	0	6	3	87	122	5	33	4.3	.977	2B-44, DH-6
1977		31	.203	.297	64	13	4	1	0	0.0	9	3	6	9	0	8	2	7	9	0	2	0.7	1.000	DH-17, 2B-5
3 yrs.		94	.256	.324	262	67	8	5	0	0.0	30	17	23	25	0	15	5	95	135	5	35	3.0	.979	2B-52, DH-27

Year	Team	Games	BA	SA	AB	H	2B	3B	HR	HR%	R	RBI	BB	SO	SB	Pinch Hit AB	Pinch Hit H	PO	A	E	DP	TC/G	FA	G by Pos

Hugh Shelley

SHELLEY, HUBERT LENEIRRE BR TR 6′ 170 lbs.
B. Oct. 26, 1910, Rogers, Tex. D. June 16, 1978, Beaumont, Tex.

Year	Team	Games	BA	SA	AB	H	2B	3B	HR	HR%	R	RBI	BB	SO	SB	Pinch Hit AB	Pinch Hit H	PO	A	E	DP	TC/G	FA	G by Pos
1935	DET A	7	.250	.250	8	2	0	0	0	0.0	1	1	2	1	0	2	1	5	0	0	0	1.0	1.000	OF-5

Ben Shelton

SHELTON, BENJAMIN DAVIS BR TL 6′ 3½″ 215 lbs.
B. Sept. 21, 1969, Chicago, Ill.

Year	Team	Games	BA	SA	AB	H	2B	3B	HR	HR%	R	RBI	BB	SO	SB	Pinch Hit AB	Pinch Hit H	PO	A	E	DP	TC/G	FA	G by Pos
1993	PIT N	15	.250	.542	24	6	1	0	2	8.3	3	7	3	3	0	7	1	17	2	1	1	2.5	.950	OF-6, 1B-2

Skeeter Shelton

SHELTON, ANDREW KEMPER BR TR 5′11″ 175 lbs.
B. June 29, 1888, Huntington, W. Va. D. Jan. 9, 1954, Huntington, W. Va.

Year	Team	Games	BA	SA	AB	H	2B	3B	HR	HR%	R	RBI	BB	SO	SB	Pinch Hit AB	Pinch Hit H	PO	A	E	DP	TC/G	FA	G by Pos
1915	NY A	10	.025	.025	40	1	0	0	0	0.0	1	0	2	10	0	0	0	20	2	0	0	2.2	1.000	OF-10

Steve Shemo

SHEMO, STEPHEN MICHAEL BR TR 5′11″ 175 lbs.
B. Apr. 9, 1915, Swoyersville, Pa. D. Apr. 13, 1992, Eden, N. C.

Year	Team	Games	BA	SA	AB	H	2B	3B	HR	HR%	R	RBI	BB	SO	SB	Pinch Hit AB	Pinch Hit H	PO	A	E	DP	TC/G	FA	G by Pos
1944	BOS N	18	.290	.355	31	9	2	0	0	0.0	3	1	1	3	0	0	0	26	34	2	4	3.4	.968	2B-16, 3B-2
1945		17	.239	.261	46	11	1	0	0	0.0	4	7	1	3	0	0	0	23	21	3	1	2.9	.936	2B-12, 3B-3, SS-1
2 yrs.		35	.260	.299	77	20	3	0	0	0.0	7	8	2	6	0	0	0	49	55	5	5	3.2	.954	2B-28, 3B-5, SS-1

Jack Shepard

SHEPARD, JACK LEROY BR TR 6′ 2″ 195 lbs.
B. May 13, 1931, Clovis, Calif. D. Dec. 31, 1994, Atherton, Calif.

Year	Team	Games	BA	SA	AB	H	2B	3B	HR	HR%	R	RBI	BB	SO	SB	Pinch Hit AB	Pinch Hit H	PO	A	E	DP	TC/G	FA	G by Pos
1953	PIT N	2	.250	.250	4	1	0	0	0	0.0	0	0	0	2	0	0	0	6	0	2	0	4.0	.750	C-2
1954		82	.304	.396	227	69	8	2	3	1.3	24	22	26	33	0	14	4	257	46	7	5	4.6	.977	C-67
1955		94	.239	.314	264	63	10	2	2	0.8	24	23	33	25	1	18	5	288	34	6	6	4.3	.982	C-77
1956		100	.242	.383	256	62	11	2	7	2.7	24	30	25	37	1	15	4	359	36	4	4	4.5	.990	C-86, 1B-2
4 yrs.		278	.260	.362	751	195	29	6	12	1.6	72	75	84	97	2	47	13	910	116	19	15	4.5	.982	C-232, 1B-2

Ray Shepardson

SHEPARDSON, RAYMOND FRANCIS BR TR 5′11½″ 170 lbs.
B. May 3, 1897, Little Falls, N. Y. D. Nov. 8, 1975, Little Falls, N. Y.

Year	Team	Games	BA	SA	AB	H	2B	3B	HR	HR%	R	RBI	BB	SO	SB	Pinch Hit AB	Pinch Hit H	PO	A	E	DP	TC/G	FA	G by Pos
1924	STL N	3	.000	.000	6	0	0	0	0	0.0	1	0	0	3	0	0	0	5	2	0	0	2.3	1.000	C-3

Ron Shepherd

SHEPHERD, RONALD WAYNE BR TR 6′ 4″ 180 lbs.
B. Oct. 27, 1960, Longview, Tex.

Year	Team	Games	BA	SA	AB	H	2B	3B	HR	HR%	R	RBI	BB	SO	SB	Pinch Hit AB	Pinch Hit H	PO	A	E	DP	TC/G	FA	G by Pos
1984	TOR A	12	.000	.000	4	0	0	0	0	0.0	0	0	0	3	0	0	0	2	1	0	0	0.3	1.000	OF-5, DH-4
1985		38	.114	.171	35	4	2	0	0	0.0	7	1	2	12	3	8	0	24	0	0	0	0.8	1.000	OF-16, DH-15
1986		65	.203	.348	69	14	4	0	2	2.9	16	4	3	22	0	8	1	30	0	0	0	0.6	1.000	OF-32, DH-16
3 yrs.		115	.167	.278	108	18	6	0	2	1.9	23	5	5	37	3	16	1	56	1	0	0	0.6	1.000	OF-53, DH-35

Neill Sheridan

SHERIDAN, NEILL RAWLINS (Wild Horse) BR TR 6′ 1½″ 195 lbs.
B. Nov. 20, 1921, Sacramento, Calif.

Year	Team	Games	BA	SA	AB	H	2B	3B	HR	HR%	R	RBI	BB	SO	SB	Pinch Hit AB	Pinch Hit H	PO	A	E	DP	TC/G	FA	G by Pos
1948	BOS A	2	.000	.000	1	0	0	0	0	0.0	0	0	0	1	0	1	0	0	0	0	0	0.0	—	

Pat Sheridan

SHERIDAN, PATRICK ARTHUR BL TR 6′ 3″ 175 lbs.
B. Dec. 4, 1957, Ann Arbor, Mich.

Year	Team	Games	BA	SA	AB	H	2B	3B	HR	HR%	R	RBI	BB	SO	SB	Pinch Hit AB	Pinch Hit H	PO	A	E	DP	TC/G	FA	G by Pos
1981	KC A	3	.000	.000	1	0	0	0	0	0.0	0	0	0	1	0	0	0	2	0	0	0	0.7	1.000	OF-3
1983		109	.270	.381	333	90	12	2	7	2.1	43	36	20	64	12	19	5	237	6	3	2	2.5	.988	OF-100
1984		138	.283	.399	481	136	24	4	8	1.7	64	53	41	91	19	8	4	273	8	4	1	2.1	.986	OF-134
1985		78	.228	.335	206	47	9	2	3	1.5	18	17	23	38	11	10	1	116	3	2	0	1.7	.983	OF-69, DH-1
1986	DET A	98	.237	.360	236	56	9	1	6	2.5	41	19	21	57	9	5	0	172	1	4	0	1.9	.977	OF-90, DH-5
1987		141	.259	.361	421	109	19	3	6	1.4	57	49	44	90	18	16	2	236	6	6	1	1.8	.976	OF-137
1988		127	.254	.403	347	88	9	5	11	3.2	47	47	44	64	8	16	2	203	2	4	0	1.8	.981	OF-111, DH-3
1989	2 teams	DET A (50G –.242) SF N (70G –.205)																						
″	total	120	.221	.335	281	62	6	4	6	2.1	36	29	30	66	8	20	2	163	4	3	1	1.6	.982	OF-101, DH-8
1991	NY A	62	.204	.336	113	23	3	0	4	3.5	13	7	13	30	1	25	5	46	3	0	0	1.4	1.000	OF-34, DH-2
9 yrs.		876	.253	.371	2419	611	91	21	51	2.1	319	257	236	501	86	119	21	1448	33	26	5	1.9	.983	OF-779, DH-19
LEAGUE CHAMPIONSHIP SERIES																								
1984	KC A	3	.000	.000	6	0	0	0	0	0.0	1	0	3	3	0	0	0	9	0	1	0	3.3	.900	OF-3
1985		7	.150	.450	20	3	0	0	2	10.0	4	3	2	3	0	2	1	13	0	0	0	2.2	1.000	OF-6
1987	DET A	5	.300	.700	10	3	1	0	1	10.0	2	2	0	2	1	0	0	7	1	0	0	2.0	1.000	OF-4
1989	SF N	5	.154	.308	13	2	0	1	0	0.0	1	0	0	4	0	0	0	9	1	0	0	2.0	1.000	OF-5
4 yrs.		20	.163	.408	49	8	1	1	3	6.1 **10th**	8	5	5	12	1	2	1	38	2	1	0	2.3	.976	OF-18
WORLD SERIES																								
1985	KC A	5	.222	.333	18	4	2	0	0	0.0	0	1	0	7	0	1	1	6	0	0	0	1.2	1.000	OF-5
1989	SF N	1	.000	.000	2	0	0	0	0	0.0	0	0	0	0	0	0	0	0	0	0	0	0.0	.000	OF-1
2 yrs.		6	.200	.300	20	4	2	0	0	0.0	0	1	0	7	0	1	1	6	0	0	0	1.0	1.000	OF-6

Red Sheridan

SHERIDAN, EUGENE ANTHONY (Gene) BR TR 5′10½″ 160 lbs.
B. Nov. 14, 1896, Brooklyn, N. Y. D. Nov. 25, 1975, Queens Village, N. Y.

Year	Team	Games	BA	SA	AB	H	2B	3B	HR	HR%	R	RBI	BB	SO	SB	Pinch Hit AB	Pinch Hit H	PO	A	E	DP	TC/G	FA	G by Pos
1918	BKN N	2	.250	.250	4	1	0	0	0	0.0	0	0	1	0	1	0	0	3	2	0	0	2.5	1.000	2B-2
1920		3	.000	.000	2	0	0	0	0	0.0	0	0	0	1	0	0	0	3	3	0	2	2.0	1.000	SS-3
2 yrs.		5	.167	.167	6	1	0	0	0	0.0	0	0	1	1	1	0	0	6	5	0	2	2.2	1.000	SS-3, 2B-2

Ed Sherling

SHERLING, EDWARD CREECH (Shine) BR TR 6′ 1″ 185 lbs.
B. July 17, 1897, Coalburg, Ala. D. Nov. 16, 1965, Enterprise, Ala.

Year	Team	Games	BA	SA	AB	H	2B	3B	HR	HR%	R	RBI	BB	SO	SB	Pinch Hit AB	Pinch Hit H	PO	A	E	DP	TC/G	FA	G by Pos
1924	PHI A	4	.500	1.000	2	1	1	0	0	0.0	2	0	0	0	0	2	1	0	0	0	0	0.0	—	

Monk Sherlock

SHERLOCK, JOHN CLINTON BR TR 5′10″ 175 lbs.
Brother of Vince Sherlock.
B. Oct. 26, 1904, Buffalo, N. Y. D. Nov. 26, 1985, Buffalo, N. Y.

Year	Team	Games	BA	SA	AB	H	2B	3B	HR	HR%	R	RBI	BB	SO	SB	Pinch Hit AB	Pinch Hit H	PO	A	E	DP	TC/G	FA	G by Pos
1930	PHI N	92	.324	.398	299	97	18	2	0	0.0	51	38	27	28	0	15	6	639	66	8	59	9.4	.989	1B-70, 2B-5, OF-1

Vince Sherlock

SHERLOCK, VINCENT THOMAS BR TR 6′ 180 lbs.
Brother of Monk Sherlock.
B. Mar. 27, 1909, Buffalo, N. Y.

Year	Team	Games	BA	SA	AB	H	2B	3B	HR	HR%	R	RBI	BB	SO	SB	Pinch Hit AB	Pinch Hit H	PO	A	E	DP	TC/G	FA	G by Pos
1935	BKN N	9	.462	.500	26	12	1	0	0	0.0	4	6	1	2	1	0	0	23	16	4	1	5.4	.907	2B-8

Darrell Sherman

SHERMAN, DARRELL EDWARD
B. Dec. 4, 1967, Los Angeles, Calif.
BL TL 5′ 9″ 160 lbs.

Year	Team	Lg	Games	BA	SA	AB	H	2B	3B	HR	HR%	R	RBI	BB	SO	SB	Pinch Hit AB	Pinch Hit H	PO	A	E	DP	TC/G	FA	G by Pos
1993	SD	N	37	.222	.238	63	14	1	0	0	0.0	8	2	6	8	2	12	5	47	0	0	0	1.8	1.000	OF-26

Dennis Sherrill

SHERRILL, DENNIS LEE
B. May 3, 1956, Miami, Fla.
BR TR 6′ 165 lbs.

Year	Team	Lg	Games	BA	SA	AB	H	2B	3B	HR	HR%	R	RBI	BB	SO	SB	Pinch Hit AB	Pinch Hit H	PO	A	E	DP	TC/G	FA	G by Pos
1978	NY	A	2	.000	.000	1	0	0	0	0	0.0	1	0	0	1	0	0	0	0	0	0	0	0.0		DH-1, 3B-1
1980			3	.250	.250	4	1	0	0	0	0.0	0	0	0	1	0	0	0	5	1	0	0	2.0	1.000	SS-2, 2B-1
2 yrs.			5	.200	.200	5	1	0	0	0	0.0	1	0	0	2	0	0	0	5	1	0	0	1.2	1.000	SS-2, 2B-1, DH-1, 3B-1

Norm Sherry

SHERRY, NORMAN BURT
Brother of Larry Sherry.
B. July 16, 1931, New York, N. Y.
Manager 1976–77.
BR TR 5′11″ 180 lbs.

Year	Team	Lg	Games	BA	SA	AB	H	2B	3B	HR	HR%	R	RBI	BB	SO	SB	Pinch Hit AB	Pinch Hit H	PO	A	E	DP	TC/G	FA	G by Pos
1959	LA	N	2	.333	.333	3	1	0	0	0	0.0	0	2	0	0	0	0	0	4	0	0	0	2.0	1.000	C-2
1960			47	.283	.500	138	39	4	1	8	5.8	22	19	12	29	0	5	1	282	15	2	3	6.8	.993	C-44
1961			47	.256	.397	121	31	2	0	5	4.1	10	21	9	30	0	10	1	253	16	2	3	6.0	.993	C-45
1962			35	.182	.307	88	16	2	0	3	3.4	7	16	6	17	0	1	1	221	13	2	2	6.9	.992	C-34
1963	NY	N	63	.136	.184	147	20	1	0	2	1.4	6	11	10	26	1	2	1	265	26	6	6	4.9	.980	C-61
5 yrs.			194	.215	.346	497	107	9	1	18	3.6	45	69	37	102	1	18	4	1025	70	12	14	6.0	.989	C-186

Barry Shetrone

SHETRONE, BARRY STEVEN
B. July 6, 1938, Baltimore, Md.
BL TR 6′ 2″ 190 lbs.

Year	Team	Lg	Games	BA	SA	AB	H	2B	3B	HR	HR%	R	RBI	BB	SO	SB	Pinch Hit AB	Pinch Hit H	PO	A	E	DP	TC/G	FA	G by Pos
1959	BAL	A	33	.203	.241	79	16	1	1	0	0.0	8	5	5	9	3	6	0	36	0	2	0	1.7	.947	OF-23
1960			1	—	—	0	0	0	0	0	—	1	0	0	0	0	0	0	0	0	0	0	0.0	—	
1961			3	.143	.143	7	1	0	0	0	0.0	0	1	0	2	0	1	0	3	0	0	0	1.5	1.000	OF-2
1962			21	.250	.417	24	6	1	0	1	4.2	3	1	0	5	0	12	4	11	0	0	0	1.8	1.000	OF-6
1963	WAS	A	2	.000	.000	2	0	0	0	0	0.0	0	0	0	0	0	2	0	0	0	0	0	0.0	—	
5 yrs.			60	.205	.268	112	23	2	1	1	0.9	12	7	5	16	3	21	4	50	0	2	0	1.7	.962	OF-31

John Shetzline

SHETZLINE, JOHN HENRY
B. 1850, Philadelphia, Pa. D. Dec. 15, 1892, Philadelphia, Pa.
5′11½″ 190 lbs.

Year	Team	Lg	Games	BA	SA	AB	H	2B	3B	HR	HR%	R	RBI	BB	SO	SB	Pinch Hit AB	Pinch Hit H	PO	A	E	DP	TC/G	FA	G by Pos
1882	BAL	AA	73	.220	.270	282	62	8	3	0	0.0	23		5			0	0	151	189	73	16	5.6	.823	3B-52, 2B-20, SS-1, OF-1

Jimmy Shevlin

SHEVLIN, JAMES CORNELIUS
B. July 9, 1909, Cincinnati, Ohio D. Oct. 30, 1974, Ft. Lauderdale, Fla.
BL TL 5′10½″ 155 lbs.

Year	Team	Lg	Games	BA	SA	AB	H	2B	3B	HR	HR%	R	RBI	BB	SO	SB	Pinch Hit AB	Pinch Hit H	PO	A	E	DP	TC/G	FA	G by Pos
1930	DET	A	28	.143	.143	14	2	0	0	0	0.0	4	2	2	3	0	2	0	55	3	0	0	2.3	1.000	1B-25
1932	CIN	N	7	.208	.292	24	5	2	0	0	0.0	3	4	4	0	4	0	0	63	4	1	3	9.7	.985	1B-7
1934			18	.308	.359	39	12	2	0	0	0.0	6	6	6	5	0	8	3	69	6	0	8	7.5	1.000	1B-10
3 yrs.			53	.247	.299	77	19	4	0	0	0.0	13	12	12	8	4	10	3	187	13	1	11	4.8	.995	1B-42

Pete Shields

SHIELDS, FRANCIS LeROY
B. Sept. 21, 1891, Swiftwater, Miss. D. Feb. 11, 1961, Jackson, Miss.
BR TR 6′ 175 lbs.

Year	Team	Lg	Games	BA	SA	AB	H	2B	3B	HR	HR%	R	RBI	BB	SO	SB	Pinch Hit AB	Pinch Hit H	PO	A	E	DP	TC/G	FA	G by Pos
1915	CLE	A	23	.208	.292	72	15	6	0	0	0.0	4	6	4	14	3	0	0	208	13	6	5	9.9	.974	1B-23

Tommy Shields

SHIELDS, THOMAS CHARLES
B. Aug. 14, 1964, Fairfax, Va.
BL TR 6′ 180 lbs.

Year	Team	Lg	Games	BA	SA	AB	H	2B	3B	HR	HR%	R	RBI	BB	SO	SB	Pinch Hit AB	Pinch Hit H	PO	A	E	DP	TC/G	FA	G by Pos
1992	BAL	A	2	—	—	0	0	0	0	0	—	0	0	0	0	0	0	0	0	0	0	0	0.0	—	
1993	CHI	N	20	.176	.206	34	6	1	0	0	0.0	4	1	2	10	0	7	1	8	22	0	4	1.9	1.000	2B-7, 3B-7, 1B-1, OF-1
2 yrs.			22	.176	.206	34	6	1	0	0	0.0	4	1	2	10	0	7	1	8	22	0	4	1.9	1.000	2B-7, 3B-7, 1B-1, OF-1

Jim Shilling

SHILLING, JAMES ROBERT
B. May 14, 1914, Tulsa, Okla. D. Sept. 12, 1986, Tulsa, Okla.
BR TR 5′11″ 175 lbs.

Year	Team	Lg	Games	BA	SA	AB	H	2B	3B	HR	HR%	R	RBI	BB	SO	SB	Pinch Hit AB	Pinch Hit H	PO	A	E	DP	TC/G	FA	G by Pos
1939	2 teams		CLE A (31G –.276) PHI N (11G –.303)																						
″	total		42	.282	.420	131	37	8	5	0	0.0	11	16	8	13	1	1	0	82	102	14	24	4.7	.929	2B-32, SS-6, 3B-3, OF-1

Ginger Shinault

SHINAULT, ENOCH ERSKINE
B. Sept. 7, 1892, Benton, Ark. D. Dec. 29, 1930, Denver, Colo.
BR TR 5′11″ 170 lbs.

Year	Team	Lg	Games	BA	SA	AB	H	2B	3B	HR	HR%	R	RBI	BB	SO	SB	Pinch Hit AB	Pinch Hit H	PO	A	E	DP	TC/G	FA	G by Pos
1921	CLE	A	22	.379	.414	29	11	1	0	0	0.0	5	3	6	5	1	1	0	27	17	4	1	2.2	.917	C-22
1922			13	.133	.200	15	2	1	0	0	0.0	1	0	0	2	0	2	0	11	1	3	1	1.4	.800	C-11
2 yrs.			35	.295	.341	44	13	2	0	0	0.0	6	3	6	7	1	3	0	38	18	7	2	1.9	.889	C-33

Bill Shindle

SHINDLE, WILLIAM
B. Dec. 5, 1863, Gloucester, N. J. D. June 3, 1936, Lakeland, N. J.
BR TR 5′ 8½″ 155 lbs.

Year	Team	Lg	Games	BA	SA	AB	H	2B	3B	HR	HR%	R	RBI	BB	SO	SB	Pinch Hit AB	Pinch Hit H	PO	A	E	DP	TC/G	FA	G by Pos
1886	DET	N	7	.269	.269	26	7	0	0	0	0.0	4	4	0	5		0	0	3	24	3	1	4.3	.900	SS-7
1887			22	.286	.369	84	24	3	2	0	0.0	17	12	7	10	13	0	0	25	30	13	5	3.1	.809	3B-21, OF-1
1888	BAL	AA	135	.208	.272	514	107	14	8	1	0.2	61	53	20		52	0	0	218	340	47	26	4.5	.922	3B-135
1889			138	.314	.397	567	178	24	7	3	0.5	122	64	42	37	56	0	0	225	323	88	25	4.6	.862	3B-138
1890	PHI	P	132	.322	.481	584	188	21	21	10	1.7	127	90	40	30	51	0	0	268	444	122	67	6.3	.854	SS-130, 3B-2
1891	PHI	N	103	.210	.246	415	87	13	1	0	0.0	68	38	33	39	17	0	0	157	260	58	25	4.6	.878	3B-100, SS-3
1892	BAL	N	143	.252	.357	619	156	20	18	3	0.5	100	50	35	34	24	0	0	225	406	90	28	5.0	.875	3B-134, SS-9
1893			125	.261	.351	521	136	22	11	1	0.2	100	75	66	17	17	0	0	176	308	63	24	4.4	.885	3B-125
1894	BKN	N	116	.296	.405	476	141	22	9	4	0.8	94	96	29	20	19	0	0	192	226	48	12	4.0	.897	3B-116
1895			118	.279	.350	477	133	21	2	3	0.6	91	69	47	28	17	0	0	142	257	46	16	3.8	.897	3B-116
1896			131	.279	.366	516	144	24	9	1	0.2	75	61	24	20	24	0	0	144	251	38	20	3.3	.912	3B-131
1897			134	.284	.382	542	154	32	6	3	0.6	83	105	35		23	0	0	185	241	45	13	3.5	.904	3B-134
1898			120	.225	.266	466	105	10	3	1	0.2	50	41	10		3	0	0	154	278	42	23	4.0	.911	3B-120
13 yrs.			1424	.269	.356	5807	1560	226	97	30	0.5	992	758	388	240	316	0	0	2114	3388	703	285	4.4	.887	3B-1272, SS-149, OF-1

Razor Shines

SHINES, ANTHONY RAYMOND
B. July 18, 1956, Durham, N. C.
BB TR 6′ 1″ 210 lbs.

Year	Team	Lg	Games	BA	SA	AB	H	2B	3B	HR	HR%	R	RBI	BB	SO	SB	Pinch Hit AB	Pinch Hit H	PO	A	E	DP	TC/G	FA	G by Pos
1983	MON	N	3	.500	.500	2	1	0	0	0	0.0	0	0	0	0	0	1	1	0	0	0	0	0.0	.000	OF-1
1984			12	.300	.350	20	6	1	0	0	0.0	0	2	0	3	0	9	2	26	0	0	2	6.5	1.000	1B-3, 3B-1
1985			47	.120	.120	50	6	0	0	0	0.0	0	3	4	9	0	36	5	34	4	2	1	6.7	.950	1B-5, P-1
1987			6	.222	.222	9	2	0	0	0	0.0	0	0	1	0	1	4	0	13	1	0	2	7.0	1.000	1B-2
4 yrs.			68	.185	.198	81	15	1	0	0	0.0	0	5	5	12	1	50	8	73	5	2	5	6.2	.975	1B-10, 3B-1, P-1, OF-1

Ralph Shinners

SHINNERS, RALPH PETER BR TR 6′ 180 lbs.
B. Oct. 4, 1895, Monches, Wis. D. July 23, 1962, Milwaukee, Wis.

Year	Team		Games	BA	SA	AB	H	2B	3B	HR	HR%	R	RBI	BB	SO	SB	Pinch Hit AB	Pinch Hit H	PO	A	E	DP	TC/G	FA	G by Pos
1922	NY	N	56	.252	.311	135	34	4	2	0	0.0	16	15	5	22	3	12	2	84	2	8	2	2.5	.915	OF-37
1923			33	.154	.231	13	2	1	0	0	0.0	5	0	2	1	0	9	1	8	0	0	0	1.3	1.000	OF-6
1925	STL	N	74	.295	.430	251	74	9	2	7	2.8	39	36	12	19	8	7	3	161	2	3	1	2.5	.982	OF-66
3 yrs.			163	.276	.383	399	110	14	4	7	1.8	60	51	19	42	11	28	6	253	4	11	3	2.5	.959	OF-109

Tim Shinnick

SHINNICK, TIMOTHY JAMES (Good Eye) BB TR 5′9″ 150 lbs.
B. Nov. 6, 1867, Exeter, N. H. D. May 18, 1944, Exeter, N. H.

Year	Team		Games	BA	SA	AB	H	2B	3B	HR	HR%	R	RBI	BB	SO	SB	Pinch Hit AB	Pinch Hit H	PO	A	E	DP	TC/G	FA	G by Pos
1890	LOU	AA	133	.256	.339	493	126	16	11	1	0.2	87		62		62	0	0	297	353	53	45	5.3	.925	2B-130, 3B-3
1891			126	.220	.298	436	96	9	11	1	0.2	77	52	54	46	36	0	0	233	338	58	47	5.0	.908	2B-118, 3B-7, SS-1
2 yrs.			259	.239	.320	929	222	25	22	2	0.2	164	52	116	46	98	0	0	530	691	111	92	5.1	.917	2B-248, 3B-10, SS-1

Bill Shipke

SHIPKE, WILLIAM MARTIN (Muskrat Bill) BR TR 5′7″ 145 lbs.
Born William Martin Shipkrethaver.
B. Nov. 18, 1882, St. Louis, Mo. D. Sept. 10, 1940, Omaha, Neb.

Year	Team		Games	BA	SA	AB	H	2B	3B	HR	HR%	R	RBI	BB	SO	SB	Pinch Hit AB	Pinch Hit H	PO	A	E	DP	TC/G	FA	G by Pos
1906	CLE	A	2	.000	.000	6	0	0	0	0	0.0	0	0	0		0	0	0	6	8	1	2	7.5	.933	2B-2
1907	WAS	A	64	.196	.249	189	37	3	2	1	0.5	17	9	15		6	1	0	57	127	11	2	3.1	.944	3B-63
1908			111	.208	.276	341	71	7	8	0	0.0	40	20	38		15	0	0	111	190	23	11	2.9	.929	3B-110, 2B-1
1909			9	.125	.188	16	2	1	0	0	0.0	2	0	2		0	0	0	6	14	2	1	3.7	.909	3B-5, SS-1
4 yrs.			186	.199	.261	552	110	11	10	1	0.2	59	29	55		21	1	0	180	339	37	16	3.1	.933	3B-178, 2B-3, SS-1

Craig Shipley

SHIPLEY, CRAIG BARRY BR TR 6′1″ 175 lbs.
B. Jan. 7, 1963, Parramatta, Australia

Year	Team		Games	BA	SA	AB	H	2B	3B	HR	HR%	R	RBI	BB	SO	SB	Pinch Hit AB	Pinch Hit H	PO	A	E	DP	TC/G	FA	G by Pos
1986	LA	N	12	.111	.148	27	3	1	0	0	0.0	3	4	2	5	0	0	0	16	18	3	4	3.1	.919	SS-10, 3B-1, 2B-1
1987			26	.257	.286	35	9	1	0	0	0.0	3	2	0	6	0	2	0	15	28	3	2	1.9	.935	SS-18, 3B-6
1989	NY	N	4	.143	.143	7	1	0	0	0	0.0	3	0	0	1	0	0	0	0	4	0	0	0.8	1.000	SS-3, 3B-2
1991	SD	N	37	.275	.341	91	25	3	0	1	1.1	6	6	2	14	0	4	0	39	70	7	14	3.5	.940	SS-19, 2B-14
1992			52	.248	.305	105	26	6	0	0	0.0	7	7	2	21	1	14	6	52	74	1	18	3.0	.992	SS-23, 2B-11, 3B-8
1993			105	.235	.326	230	54	9	0	4	1.7	25	22	10	31	12	28	6	84	121	7	15	2.3	.967	SS-38, 3B-37, 2B-12, OF-5
1994			81	.333	.475	240	80	14	4	4	1.7	32	30	9	28	6	13	6	65	108	9	12	2.2	.951	3B-53, SS-14, 2B-13, OF-2, 1B-1
1995	HOU	N	92	.263	.345	232	61	8	1	3	1.3	23	24	8	28	6	25	9	44	114	3	7	2.0	.981	3B-65, SS-11, 2B-5, 1B-1
8 yrs.			409	.268	.359	967	259	42	5	12	1.2	102	95	33	134	25	86	27	315	537	33	72	2.4	.963	3B-172, SS-136, 2B-56, OF-7, 1B-2

Art Shires

SHIRES, CHARLES ARTHUR (Art the Great) BL TR 6′1″ 195 lbs.
B. Aug. 13, 1907, Italy, Tex. D. July 13, 1967, Italy, Tex.

Year	Team		Games	BA	SA	AB	H	2B	3B	HR	HR%	R	RBI	BB	SO	SB	Pinch Hit AB	Pinch Hit H	PO	A	E	DP	TC/G	FA	G by Pos
1928	CHI	A	33	.341	.431	123	42	6	1	1	0.8	20	11	13	10	0	1	1	282	28	3	22	9.8	.990	1B-32
1929			100	.312	.433	353	110	20	7	3	0.8	41	41	32	20	4	9	1	816	58	9	78	9.8	.990	1B-88, 2B-2
1930	2 teams		CHI A (37G –.258) WAS A (38G –.369)																						
″	total		75	.302	.387	212	64	10	1	2	0.9	25	37	11	11	3	19	6	468	26	10	37	9.3	.980	1B-54
1932	BOS	N	82	.238	.339	298	71	9	3	5	1.7	32	30	25	21	1	2	0	715	48	9	61	9.4	.988	1B-82
4 yrs.			290	.291	.395	986	287	45	12	11	1.1	118	119	81	62	8	31	8	2281	160	31	198	9.6	.987	1B-256, 2B-2

Bart Shirley

SHIRLEY, BARTON ARVIN BR TR 5′10″ 183 lbs.
B. Jan. 4, 1940, Corpus Christi, Tex.

Year	Team		Games	BA	SA	AB	H	2B	3B	HR	HR%	R	RBI	BB	SO	SB	Pinch Hit AB	Pinch Hit H	PO	A	E	DP	TC/G	FA	G by Pos
1964	LA	N	18	.274	.323	62	17	1	1	0	0.0	6	7	4	8	0	0	0	19	41	3	5	3.5	.952	3B-10, SS-8
1966			12	.200	.200	5	1	0	0	0	0.0	2	0	0	2	0	4	1	3	2	0	0	1.0	1.000	SS-5
1967	NY	N	6	.000	.000	12	0	0	0	0	0.0	1	0	0	5	0	2	0	2	9	1	1	4.0	.917	2B-3
1968	LA	N	39	.181	.217	83	15	3	0	0	0.0	6	4	10	13	0	1	0	44	80	7	20	3.4	.947	SS-21, 2B-18
4 yrs.			75	.204	.241	162	33	4	1	0	0.0	15	11	14	28	0	7	1	68	132	11	26	3.2	.948	SS-34, 2B-21, 3B-10

Mule Shirley

SHIRLEY, ERNEST RAEFORD BL TL 5′11″ 180 lbs.
B. May 24, 1901, Snow Hill, N. C. D. Aug. 4, 1955, Goldsboro, N. C.

Year	Team		Games	BA	SA	AB	H	2B	3B	HR	HR%	R	RBI	BB	SO	SB	Pinch Hit AB	Pinch Hit H	PO	A	E	DP	TC/G	FA	G by Pos
1924	WAS	A	30	.234	.312	77	18	2	2	0	0.0	12	16	3	7	0	4	2	176	14	3	17	7.4	.984	1B-25, C-1
1925			14	.130	.174	23	3	1	0	0	0.0	2	2	1	7	0	5	1	49	3	0	4	5.8	1.000	1B-9
2 yrs.			44	.210	.280	100	21	3	2	0	0.0	14	18	4	14	0	9	3	225	17	3	21	7.0	.988	1B-34, C-1
WORLD SERIES																									
1924	WAS	A	3	.500	.500	2	1	0	0	0	0.0	1	1	0	0	0	2	1	0	0	0	0	0.0	—	

Ivey Shiver

SHIVER, IVEY MERWIN (Chick) BR TR 6′1½″ 190 lbs.
B. Jan. 22, 1907, Sylvester, Ga. D. Aug. 31, 1972, Savannah, Ga.

Year	Team		Games	BA	SA	AB	H	2B	3B	HR	HR%	R	RBI	BB	SO	SB	Pinch Hit AB	Pinch Hit H	PO	A	E	DP	TC/G	FA	G by Pos
1931	DET	A	2	.111	.111	9	1	0	0	0	0.0	2	0	0	3	0	0	0	3	0	0	0	1.5	1.000	OF-2
1934	CIN	N	19	.203	.322	59	12	1	0	2	3.4	6	6	3	15	1	4	1	26	0	0	0	1.7	1.000	OF-15
2 yrs.			21	.191	.294	68	13	1	0	2	2.9	8	6	3	18	1	4	1	29	0	0	0	1.7	1.000	OF-17

George Shoch

SHOCH, GEORGE QUINTUS BR TR 5′6″ 158 lbs.
B. Jan. 6, 1859, Philadelphia, Pa. D. Sept. 30, 1937, Philadelphia, Pa.

Year	Team		Games	BA	SA	AB	H	2B	3B	HR	HR%	R	RBI	BB	SO	SB	Pinch Hit AB	Pinch Hit H	PO	A	E	DP	TC/G	FA	G by Pos
1886	WAS	N	26	.295	.368	95	28	2	1	1	1.1	11	18	2	13		0	0	29	3	5	0	1.4	.865	OF-25, SS-1
1887			70	.239	.292	264	63	9	1	1	0.4	47	18	21	16	29	0	0	125	43	25	5	2.8	.870	OF-63, SS-6, 2B-1
1888			90	.183	.240	317	58	6	3	2	0.6	46	24	25	22	23	0	0	143	175	38	7	4.0	.893	SS-52, OF-35, P-1, 2B-1
1889			30	.239	.257	109	26	2	0	0	0.0	12	11	20	5	9	0	0	52	9	6	1	2.2	.910	OF-29, SS-1
1891	MIL	AA	34	.315	.409	127	40	7	1	1	0.8	29	16	18	5	12	0	0	64	103	15	4	5.4	.918	SS-25, 3B-9
1892	BAL	N	76	.276	.354	308	85	15	3	1	0.3	42	50	24	19	14	0	0	133	216	51	17	5.3	.873	SS-57, OF-12, 3B-7
1893	BKN	N	94	.263	.339	327	86	17	1	2	0.6	53	54	48	13	9	0	0	159	118	27	9	3.1	.911	OF-46, 3B-37, SS-11, 2B-3
1894			64	.322	.402	239	77	6	5	1	0.4	47	37	26	6	16	0	0	130	77	17	6	3.5	.924	OF-35, 3B-14, 2B-9, SS-6
1895			61	.259	.366	216	56	9	7	0	0.0	49	29	32	6	7	0	0	98	63	14	6	2.9	.920	OF-39, 2B-13, SS-6, 3B-3
1896			76	.292	.364	250	73	7	4	1	0.4	36	28	33	10	11	1	0	124	192	19	17	4.4	.943	2B-62, OF-10, 3B-3, SS-1
1897			85	.278	.324	284	79	9	2	0	0.0	42	38	49		6	0	0	231	281	39	30	6.5	.929	2B-68, SS-13, OF-4
11 yrs.			706	.265	.334	2536	671	89	28	10	0.4	414	323	298	115	136	1	0	1288	1280	256	102	4.0	.909	OF-298, SS-179, 2B-157, 3B-73, P-1

Costen Shockley

SHOCKLEY, JOHN COSTEN
B. Feb. 8, 1942, Georgetown, Del.
BL TL 6′ 2″ 200 lbs.

Year	Team	Games	BA	SA	AB	H	2B	3B	HR	HR%	R	RBI	BB	SO	SB	Pinch Hit AB	Pinch Hit H	PO	A	E	DP	TC/G	FA	G by Pos
1964	PHI N	11	.229	.314	35	8	0	0	1	2.9	4	2	2	8	0	2	0	57	4	2	7	7.0	.968	1B-9
1965	CAL A	40	.187	.262	107	20	2	0	2	1.9	5	17	9	16	0	6	1	245	17	1	25	8.2	.996	1B-31, OF-1
2 yrs.		51	.197	.275	142	28	2	0	3	2.1	9	19	11	24	0	8	1	302	21	3	32	8.0	.991	1B-40, OF-1

Charlie Shoemaker

SHOEMAKER, CHARLES LOUIS
B. Aug. 10, 1939, Los Angeles, Calif. D. May 31, 1990, Mount Penn, Pa.
BL TR 5′10″ 155 lbs.

Year	Team	Games	BA	SA	AB	H	2B	3B	HR	HR%	R	RBI	BB	SO	SB	Pinch Hit AB	Pinch Hit H	PO	A	E	DP	TC/G	FA	G by Pos
1961	KC A	7	.385	.462	26	10	2	0	0	0.0	5	1	2	2	0	1	0	17	18	0	3	5.8	1.000	2B-6
1962		5	.182	.182	11	2	0	0	0	0.0	1	0	0	2	0	1	0	5	9	0	1	3.5	1.000	2B-4
1964		16	.212	.327	52	11	2	2	0	0.0	6	3	0	9	0	1	0	29	25	2	4	4.0	.964	2B-14
3 yrs.		28	.258	.348	89	23	4	2	0	0.0	12	4	2	13	0	3	0	51	52	2	8	4.4	.981	2B-24

Strick Shofner

SHOFNER, FRANK STRICKLAND
B. July 23, 1919, Crawford, Tex.
BL TR 5′10½″ 187 lbs.

Year	Team	Games	BA	SA	AB	H	2B	3B	HR	HR%	R	RBI	BB	SO	SB	Pinch Hit AB	Pinch Hit H	PO	A	E	DP	TC/G	FA	G by Pos
1947	BOS A	5	.154	.308	13	2	0	1	0	0.0	1	0	0	3	0	1	0	3	7	0	1	2.5	1.000	3B-4

Eddie Shokes

SHOKES, EDWARD CHRISTOPHER
B. Jan. 27, 1920, Charleston, S. C.
BL TL 6′ 170 lbs.

Year	Team	Games	BA	SA	AB	H	2B	3B	HR	HR%	R	RBI	BB	SO	SB	Pinch Hit AB	Pinch Hit H	PO	A	E	DP	TC/G	FA	G by Pos
1941	CIN N	1	.000	.000	1	0	0	0	0	0.0	0	0	0	1	0	1	0	0	0	0	0	0.0	—	
1946		31	.120	.133	83	10	1	0	0	0.0	3	5	18	21	1	1	0	262	14	1	26	9.6	.996	1B-29
2 yrs.		32	.119	.131	84	10	1	0	0	0.0	3	5	18	22	1	2	0	262	14	1	26	9.6	.996	1B-29

Ray Shook

SHOOK, RAYMOND CURTIS
B. Nov. 18, 1889, Perry, Ohio D. Sept. 16, 1970, South Bend, Ind.
BR TR 5′ 7½″ 155 lbs.

Year	Team	Games	BA	SA	AB	H	2B	3B	HR	HR%	R	RBI	BB	SO	SB	Pinch Hit AB	Pinch Hit H	PO	A	E	DP	TC/G	FA	G by Pos
1916	CHI A	1	—	—	0	0	0	0	0	—	0	0	0	0	0	0	0	0	0	0	0	0.0	—	

Ron Shoop

SHOOP, RONALD LEE
B. Sept. 19, 1931, Rural Valley, Pa.
BR TR 5′11″ 180 lbs.

Year	Team	Games	BA	SA	AB	H	2B	3B	HR	HR%	R	RBI	BB	SO	SB	Pinch Hit AB	Pinch Hit H	PO	A	E	DP	TC/G	FA	G by Pos
1959	DET A	3	.143	.143	7	1	0	0	0	0.0	1	1	0	1	0	0	0	8	0	0	0	2.7	1.000	C-3

Tom Shopay

SHOPAY, THOMAS MICHAEL
B. Feb. 21, 1945, Bristol, Conn.
BL TR 5′ 9½″ 160 lbs.

Year	Team	Games	BA	SA	AB	H	2B	3B	HR	HR%	R	RBI	BB	SO	SB	Pinch Hit AB	Pinch Hit H	PO	A	E	DP	TC/G	FA	G by Pos
1967	NY A	8	.296	.556	27	8	1	0	2	7.4	2	6	1	5	2	1	0	9	2	1	0	1.7	.917	OF-7
1969		28	.083	.125	48	4	0	1	0	0.0	2	0	2	10	0	13	2	26	0	0	0	2.4	1.000	OF-11
1971	BAL A	47	.257	.284	74	19	2	0	0	0.0	10	5	3	7	2	30	8	18	1	0	0	1.5	1.000	OF-13
1972		49	.225	.225	40	9	0	0	0	0.0	3	2	5	12	0	32	7	4	0	0	0	1.3	1.000	OF-3
1975		40	.161	.194	31	5	1	0	0	0.0	4	2	4	7	3	11	2	17	3	0	0	1.2	1.000	OF-13, DH-3, C-1
1976		14	.200	.200	20	4	0	0	0	0.0	4	1	3	3	1	4	1	14	1	0	0	1.3	1.000	OF-11, C-1
1977		67	.188	.275	69	13	3	0	1	1.4	15	4	8	7	3	10	2	53	2	0	1	1.0	1.000	OF-52, DH-2
7 yrs.		253	.201	.259	309	62	7	1	3	1.0	40	20	26	51	11	101	22	141	9	1	1	1.3	.993	OF-110, DH-5, C-2
WORLD SERIES																								
1971	BAL A	5	.000	.000	4	0	0	0	0	0.0	0	0	0	0	0	4	0	0	0	0	0	0.0	—	

Dave Short

SHORT, DAVID ORVIS
B. May 11, 1917, Magnolia, Ark. D. Nov. 22, 1983, Shreveport, La.
BL TR 5′11½″ 162 lbs.

Year	Team	Games	BA	SA	AB	H	2B	3B	HR	HR%	R	RBI	BB	SO	SB	Pinch Hit AB	Pinch Hit H	PO	A	E	DP	TC/G	FA	G by Pos
1940	CHI A	4	.333	.333	3	1	0	0	0	0.0	1	0	1	2	0	3	1	0	0	0	0	0.0	—	
1941		3	.000	.000	8	0	0	0	0	0.0	0	0	2	1	0	1	0	4	0	1	0	2.5	.800	OF-2
2 yrs.		7	.091	.091	11	1	0	0	0	0.0	1	0	3	3	0	4	1	4	0	1	0	2.5	.800	OF-2

Chick Shorten

SHORTEN, CHARLES HENRY
B. Apr. 19, 1892, Scranton, Pa. D. Oct. 23, 1965, Scranton, Pa.
BL TL 6′ 175 lbs.

Year	Team	Games	BA	SA	AB	H	2B	3B	HR	HR%	R	RBI	BB	SO	SB	Pinch Hit AB	Pinch Hit H	PO	A	E	DP	TC/G	FA	G by Pos
1915	BOS A	6	.214	.286	14	3	1	0	0	0.0	1	0	0	2	0	1	0	6	1	0	0	1.4	1.000	OF-5
1916		53	.295	.330	112	33	2	1	0	0.0	14	11	10	8	1	17	3	46	0	0	0	1.4	1.000	OF-33
1917		69	.179	.226	168	30	4	2	0	0.0	12	16	10	10	2	24	5	82	2	2	0	2.0	.977	OF-43
1919	DET A	95	.315	.370	270	85	9	3	0	0.0	37	22	22	13	5	19	5	143	2	4	2	2.0	.973	OF-75
1920		116	.288	.354	364	105	9	6	1	0.3	35	40	28	14	2	15	5	168	14	2	3	1.9	.989	OF-99
1921		92	.272	.350	217	59	11	3	0	0.0	33	23	20	11	2	**37**	**9**	101	3	2	2	2.0	.981	OF-52, C-1
1922	STL A	55	.275	.489	131	36	12	5	2	1.5	22	16	16	8	0	20	5	58	2	0	1	1.9	1.000	OF-32
1924	CIN N	41	.275	.319	69	19	3	0	0	0.0	7	6	4	2	0	21	6	13	1	0	0	0.9	1.000	OF-15
8 yrs.		527	.275	.349	1345	370	51	20	3	0.2	161	134	110	68	12	154	38	617	25	10	8	1.8	.985	OF-354, C-1
WORLD SERIES																								
1916	BOS A	2	.571	.571	7	4	0	0	0	0.0	0	2	0	1	0	0	0	3	0	0	0	1.5	1.000	OF-2

Burt Shotton

SHOTTON, BURTON EDWIN (Barney)
B. Oct. 18, 1884, Brownhelm, Ohio D. July 29, 1962, Lake Wales, Fla.
Manager 1928–34, 1947–50.
BL TR 5′11″ 175 lbs.

Year	Team	Games	BA	SA	AB	H	2B	3B	HR	HR%	R	RBI	BB	SO	SB	Pinch Hit AB	Pinch Hit H	PO	A	E	DP	TC/G	FA	G by Pos
1909	STL A	17	.262	.295	61	16	0	1	0	0.0	5	0	5		3	0	0	41	2	4	0	2.8	.915	OF-17
1911		139	.255	.302	572	146	11	8	0	0.0	85	36	51		26	0	0	356	21	20	2	2.9	.950	OF-139
1912		154	.290	.353	580	168	15	8	2	0.3	87	40	86		35	0	0	381	20	25	7	2.8	.941	OF-154
1913		147	.297	.373	549	163	23	8	1	0.2	105	28	**99**	63	43	1	0	357	29	20	11	2.8	.951	OF-146
1914		154	.269	.333	579	156	19	9	0	0.0	82	38	64	66	40	2	0	359	15	24	4	2.6	.940	OF-152
1915		156	.283	.360	559	158	18	11	1	0.2	93	30	118	62	43	2	0	295	15	23	4	2.2	.931	OF-154
1916		157	.282	.343	**618**	174	23	6	1	0.2	97	36	**111**	67	41	0	0	357	25	20	6	2.6	.950	OF-157
1917		118	.224	.259	398	89	9	1	1	0.3	47	20	62	47	16	5	0	182	10	16	6	1.9	.923	OF-107
1918	WAS A	126	.261	.321	505	132	16	7	0	0.0	68	21	67	28	25	3	1	277	15	18	6	2.5	.942	OF-122
1919	STL N	85	.285	.381	270	77	13	5	1	0.4	35	20	22	25	17	14	1	104	10	9	2	1.8	.927	OF-67
1920		62	.228	.272	180	41	5	0	1	0.6	28	12	18	14	5	7	1	85	9	4	2	1.9	.959	OF-51
1921		38	.250	.375	48	12	1	1	1	2.1	9	7	7	4	0	22	7	21	2	1	1	2.2	.958	OF-11
1922		34	.200	.233	30	6	1	0	0	0.0	5	2	4	6	0	26	5	1	0	0	0	0.3	1.000	OF-3
1923		1	—	—	0	0	0	0	0	—	1	0	0	0	0	0	0	0	0	0	0	0.0	—	
14 yrs.		1388	.270	.333	4949	1338	154	65	9	0.2	747	290	714	382	294	82	15	2816	173	184	51	2.5	.942	OF-1280

John Shoupe

SHOUPE, JOHN F. BL TL 5′ 7″ 140 lbs.
B. Sept. 30, 1851, Cincinnati, Ohio D. Feb. 13, 1920, Cincinnati, Ohio.

Year	Team	Games	BA	SA	AB	H	2B	3B	HR	HR%	R	RBI	BB	SO	SB	Pinch Hit AB	Pinch Hit H	PO	A	E	DP	TC/G	FA	G by Pos
1879	TRO N	11	.091	.091	44	4	0	0	0	0.0	5	1	0	3		0	0	13	33	12	0	5.3	.793	SS-10, 2B-1
1882	STL AA	2	.000	.000	7	0	0	0	0	0.0	1		0			0	0	5	8	0	0	6.5	1.000	2B-2
1884	WAS U	1	.750	.750	4	3	0	0	0	0.0	1		0			0	0	4	2	1	1	7.0	.857	OF-1
3 yrs.		14	.127	.127	55	7	0	0	0	0.0	7	1	0	3		0	0	22	43	13	1	5.6	.833	SS-10, 2B-3, OF-1

John Shovlin

SHOVLIN, JOHN JOSEPH (Brode) BR TR 5′ 7″ 163 lbs.
B. Jan. 14, 1891, Drifton, Pa. D. Feb. 16, 1976, Bethesda, Md.

Year	Team	Games	BA	SA	AB	H	2B	3B	HR	HR%	R	RBI	BB	SO	SB	Pinch Hit AB	Pinch Hit H	PO	A	E	DP	TC/G	FA	G by Pos
1911	PIT N	2	.000	.000	1	0	0	0	0	0.0	1	0	0	1	0	1	0	0	0	0	0	0.0	—	
1919	STL A	9	.200	.200	35	7	0	0	0	0.0	4	1	5	2	0	0	0	19	25	3	5	5.2	.936	2B-9
1920		7	.286	.286	7	2	0	0	0	0.0	2	2	0	0	0	2	0	3	5	0	0	1.6	1.000	SS-5
3 yrs.		18	.209	.209	43	9	0	0	0	0.0	7	3	5	3	0	3	0	22	30	3	5	3.9	.945	2B-9, SS-5

George Shuba

SHUBA, GEORGE THOMAS (Shotgun) BL TR 5′11″ 180 lbs.
B. Dec. 13, 1924, Youngstown, Ohio.

Year	Team	Games	BA	SA	AB	H	2B	3B	HR	HR%	R	RBI	BB	SO	SB	Pinch Hit AB	Pinch Hit H	PO	A	E	DP	TC/G	FA	G by Pos
1948	BKN N	63	.267	.379	161	43	6	0	4	2.5	21	32	34	31	1	6	2	87	1	6	1	1.7	.936	OF-56
1949		1	.000	.000	1	0	0	0	0	0.0	0	0	0	0	0	1	0	0	0	0	0	0.0	—	
1950		34	.207	.396	111	23	8	2	3	2.7	15	12	13	22	2	5	1	56	4	1	2	2.3	.984	OF-27
1952		94	.305	.465	256	78	12	1	9	3.5	40	40	38	29	1	25	8	116	2	1	0	1.8	.992	OF-67
1953		74	.254	.426	169	43	12	1	5	3.0	19	23	17	20	1	29	7	59	1	1	1	1.4	.984	OF-44
1954		45	.154	.323	65	10	5	0	2	3.1	3	10	7	10	0	30	4	21	0	2	0	1.8	.913	OF-13
1955		44	.275	.373	51	14	2	0	1	2.0	8	8	11	10	0	29	11	10	0	1	0	1.2	.909	OF-9
7 yrs.		355	.259	.413	814	211	45	4	24	2.9	106	125	120	122	5	125	33	349	8	12	4	1.7	.967	OF-216
WORLD SERIES																								
1952	BKN N	4	.300	.400	10	3	1	0	0	0.0	0	0	0	4	0	1	0	7	0	0	0	2.3	1.000	OF-3
1953		2	1.000	4.000	1	1	0	0	1	100.0	1	2	0	0	0	1	1	0	0	0	0	0.0	—	
1955		1	.000	.000	1	0	0	0	0	0.0	0	0	0	0	0	1	0	0	0	0	0	0.0	—	
3 yrs.		7	.333	.667	12	4	1	0	1	8.3	1	2	0	4	0	3	1	7	0	0	0	2.3	1.000	OF-3

Frank Shugart

SHUGART, FRANK HARRY BL TR 5′ 8″ 170 lbs.
Born Frank Harry Shugarts. BB 1897
B. Dec. 10, 1866, Luthersburg, Pa. D. Sept. 9, 1944, Clearfield, Pa.

Year	Team	Games	BA	SA	AB	H	2B	3B	HR	HR%	R	RBI	BB	SO	SB	Pinch Hit AB	Pinch Hit H	PO	A	E	DP	TC/G	FA	G by Pos
1890	CHI P	29	.189	.330	106	20	5	5	0	0.0	8	15	5	13	5	0	0	38	71	14	11	4.1	.886	SS-25, OF-5
1891	PIT N	75	.275	.403	320	88	19	8	2	0.6	57	33	20	26	21	0	0	172	235	44	34	6.0	.902	SS-75
1892		137	.267	.352	554	148	19	14	0	0.0	94	62	47	48	28	0	0	309	475	100	43	6.5	.887	SS-134, C-2, OF-1
1893	2 teams	PIT N (52G –.262) STL N (59G –.280)																						
″	total	111	.272	.346	456	124	17	7	1	0.2	78	60	41	25	25	0	0	207	279	72	26	5.0	.871	SS-74, OF-29, 3B-9
1894	STL N	133	.292	.436	527	154	19	18	7	1.3	103	72	38	37	21	0	0	309	53	42	6	3.0	.896	OF-122, SS-7, 3B-7
1895	LOU N	113	.264	.374	473	125	14	13	4	0.8	61	70	31	25	14	0	0	243	263	71	42	5.0	.877	SS-88, OF-27
1897	PHI N	40	.252	.417	163	41	8	2	5	3.1	20	25	8		5	0	0	104	128	34	15	6.7	.872	SS-40
1901	CHI A	107	.251	.345	415	104	9	12	2	0.5	62	47	28		12	0	0	223	338	73	32	5.9	.885	SS-107
8 yrs.		745	.267	.377	3014	804	110	79	21	0.7	483	384	218	174	131	0	0	1605	1842	450	209	5.2	.885	SS-550, OF-184, 3B-16, C-2

Terry Shumpert

SHUMPERT, TERRANCE DARNELL BR TR 5′11″ 190 lbs.
B. Aug. 16, 1966, Paducah, Ky.

Year	Team	Games	BA	SA	AB	H	2B	3B	HR	HR%	R	RBI	BB	SO	SB	Pinch Hit AB	Pinch Hit H	PO	A	E	DP	TC/G	FA	G by Pos
1990	KC A	32	.275	.363	91	25	6	1	0	0.0	7	8	2	17	3	0	0	56	74	3	15	4.4	.977	2B-27, DH-3
1991		144	.217	.322	369	80	16	4	5	1.4	45	34	30	75	17	0	0	249	368	16	81	4.4	.975	2B-144
1992		36	.149	.255	94	14	5	1	1	1.1	6	11	3	17	2	0	0	50	77	4	17	3.7	.969	2B-33, SS-1, DH-1
1993		8	.100	.100	10	1	0	0	0	0.0	0	0	2	2	1	0	0	11	11	0	3	2.8	1.000	2B-8
1994		64	.240	.426	183	44	6	2	8	4.4	28	24	13	39	18	1	0	69	129	8	16	3.2	.961	2B-38, 3B-24, DH-2, SS-1
1995	BOS A	21	.234	.298	47	11	3	0	0	0.0	6	3	4	13	3	2	0	21	35	2	7	3.4	.966	2B-8, 3B-5, SS-3, DH-1
6 yrs.		305	.220	.339	794	175	36	8	14	1.8	92	80	54	163	44	3	0	456	694	33	139	4.0	.972	2B-258, 3B-29, DH-7, SS-5

Vince Shupe

SHUPE, VINCENT WILLIAM BL TL 5′11″ 180 lbs.
B. Sept. 5, 1921, East Canton, Ohio D. Apr. 5, 1962, Canton, Ohio.

Year	Team	Games	BA	SA	AB	H	2B	3B	HR	HR%	R	RBI	BB	SO	SB	Pinch Hit AB	Pinch Hit H	PO	A	E	DP	TC/G	FA	G by Pos
1945	BOS N	78	.269	.297	283	76	8	0	0	0.0	22	15	17	16	3	1	1	650	53	8	81	9.2	.989	1B-77

Eddie Sicking

SICKING, EDWARD JOSEPH BR TR 5′ 9½″ 165 lbs.
B. Mar. 30, 1897, St. Bernard, Ohio D. Aug. 30, 1978, Madeira, Ohio.

Year	Team	Games	BA	SA	AB	H	2B	3B	HR	HR%	R	RBI	BB	SO	SB	Pinch Hit AB	Pinch Hit H	PO	A	E	DP	TC/G	FA	G by Pos
1916	CHI N	1	.000	.000	1	0	0	0	0	0.0	0	0	0	0	0	1	0	0	0	0	0	0.0	—	
1918	NY N	46	.250	.280	132	33	4	0	0	0.0	9	12	6	11	2	3	0	63	75	9	2	3.3	.939	3B-24, 2B-18, SS-3
1919	2 teams	NY N (6G –.333) PHI N (61G –.216)																						
″	total	67	.225	.245	200	45	2	1	0	0.0	18	18	9	17	4	3	0	127	180	16	40	5.2	.950	SS-41, 2B-21
1920	2 teams	NY N (46G –.172) CIN N (37G –.268)																						
″	total	83	.218	.249	257	56	6	1	0	0.0	23	26	23	15	8	1	0	140	204	23	26	4.5	.937	2B-40, 3B-30, SS-12
1927	PIT N	6	.143	.286	7	1	1	0	0	0.0	1	3	1	0	0	0	0	6	8	0	1	2.8	1.000	2B-5
5 yrs.		203	.226	.255	597	135	13	2	0	0.0	51	59	39	43	14	8	0	336	467	48	69	4.4	.944	2B-84, SS-56, 3B-54

Joe Siddall

SIDDALL, JOSEPH TODD BL TR 6′ 1″ 200 lbs.
B. Oct. 25, 1967, Windsor, Ont., Canada.

Year	Team	Games	BA	SA	AB	H	2B	3B	HR	HR%	R	RBI	BB	SO	SB	Pinch Hit AB	Pinch Hit H	PO	A	E	DP	TC/G	FA	G by Pos
1993	MON N	19	.100	.150	20	2	1	0	0	0.0	0	1	1	5	0	3	0	33	5	0	0	2.2	1.000	C-15, OF-1, 1B-1
1995		7	.300	.300	10	3	0	0	0	0.0	4	1	3	3	0	0	0	14	1	2	0	2.4	.882	C-7
2 yrs.		26	.167	.200	30	5	1	0	0	0.0	4	2	4	8	0	3	0	47	6	2	0	2.3	.964	C-22, OF-1, 1B-1

Norm Siebern

SIEBERN, NORMAN LEROY BL TR 6′ 2″ 200 lbs.
B. July 26, 1933, St. Louis, Mo.

Year	Team	Games	BA	SA	AB	H	2B	3B	HR	HR%	R	RBI	BB	SO	SB	Pinch Hit AB	Pinch Hit H	PO	A	E	DP	TC/G	FA	G by Pos
1956	NY A	54	.204	.333	162	33	1	4	4	2.5	27	21	19	38	1	6	0	100	1	3	0	2.0	.971	OF-51
1958		136	.300	.454	460	138	19	5	14	3.0	79	55	66	87	5	2	1	259	8	5	2	2.0	.982	OF-133
1959		120	.271	.403	380	103	17	0	11	2.9	52	53	41	71	3	20	9	190	3	2	1	2.1	.990	OF-93, 1B-2
1960	KC A	144	.279	.471	520	145	31	6	19	3.7	69	69	72	68	0	4	1	777	43	10	58	5.8	.988	OF-75, 1B-69
1961		153	.296	.475	560	166	36	5	18	3.2	68	98	82	92	2	2	0	990	79	12	89	6.9	.989	1B-109, OF-47
1962		162	.308	.495	600	185	25	6	25	4.2	114	117	110	88	3	0	0	1405	127	10	122	9.5	.994	1B-162
1963		152	.272	.410	556	151	25	2	16	2.9	80	83	79	82	1	5	2	1223	103	12	95	9.1	.991	1B-131, OF-16
1964	BAL A	150	.245	.379	478	117	24	2	12	2.5	92	56	**106**	87	2	6	0	1171	101	6	121	8.6	.995	1B-149

Norm Siebern *continued*

Year	Team	Games	BA	SA	AB	H	2B	3B	HR	HR%	R	RBI	BB	SO	SB	Pinch Hit AB	Pinch Hit H	PO	A	E	DP	TC/G	FA	G by Pos
1965		106	.256	.407	297	76	13	4	8	2.7	44	32	50	49	1	28	2	631	48	6	64	9.0	.991	1B-76
1966	CAL A	125	.247	.339	336	83	14	1	5	1.5	29	41	63	61	0	23	6	1014	65	7	96	11.0	.994	1B-99
1967	2 teams	SF N (46G –.155) BOS A (33G –.205)																						
"	total	79	.176	.245	102	18	1	3	0	0.0	8	11	20	21	0	45	7	138	11	1	9	4.8	.993	1B-28, OF-3
1968	BOS A	27	.067	.067	30	2	0	0	0	0.0	0	0	0	5	0	24	1	8	1	0	1	2.3	1.000	1B-2, OF-2
12 yrs.		1408	.272	.423	4481	1217	206	38	132	2.9	662	636	708	749	18	165	29	7906	590	74	658	6.9	.991	1B-827, OF-420
WORLD SERIES																								
1956	NY A	1	.000	.000	1	0	0	0	0	0.0	0	0	0	0	0	1	0	0	0	0	0	0.0	—	
1958		3	.125	.125	8	1	0	0	0	0.0	1	0	3	2	0	0	0	5	0	0	0	1.7	1.000	OF-3
1967	BOS A	3	.333	.333	3	1	0	0	0	0.0	0	1	0	0	0	2	0	0	0	0	0	0.0	.000	OF-1
3 yrs.		7	.167	.167	12	2	0	0	0	0.0	1	1	3	2	0	3	0	5	0	0	0	1.3	1.000	OF-4

Dick Siebert

SIEBERT, RICHARD WALTHER BL TL 6′ 170 lbs.
Father of Paul Siebert.
B. Feb. 19, 1912, Fall River, Mass. D. Dec. 9, 1978, Minneapolis, Minn.

Year	Team	Games	BA	SA	AB	H	2B	3B	HR	HR%	R	RBI	BB	SO	SB	Pinch Hit AB	Pinch Hit H	PO	A	E	DP	TC/G	FA	G by Pos
1932	BKN N	6	.286	.286	7	2	0	0	0	0.0	1	0	2	2	0	3	1	13	0	0	0	2.2	1.000	1B-6
1936		2	.000	.000	2	0	0	0	0	0.0	0	0	0	0	0	1	0	0	1	0	0	1.0	1.000	OF-1
1937	STL N	22	.184	.237	38	7	2	0	0	0.0	3	2	4	8	1	13	3	44	3	1	2	6.9	.979	1B-7
1938	2 teams	STL N (1G –1.000) PHI A (48G –.284)																						
"	total	49	.287	.359	195	56	8	3	0	0.0	24	28	10	9	2	3	2	403	41	0	35	9.7	1.000	1B-46
1939	PHI A	101	.294	.423	402	118	28	3	6	1.5	58	47	21	22	4	2	0	874	74	9	73	9.7	.991	1B-99
1940		154	.286	.383	595	170	31	6	5	0.8	69	77	33	34	8	0	0	1322	119	22	112	9.5	.985	1B-154
1941		123	.334	.460	467	156	28	8	5	1.1	63	79	37	22	1	0	0	1102	106	12	95	9.9	.990	1B-123
1942		153	.260	.333	612	159	25	7	2	0.3	57	74	24	17	4	0	0	1345	104	16	109	9.6	.989	1B-152
1943		146	.251	.328	558	140	26	7	1	0.2	50	72	33	21	6	1	0	1332	111	15	117	10.1	.990	1B-145
1944		132	.306	.423	468	143	27	5	6	1.3	52	52	62	17	2	0	0	759	53	10	60	6.2	.988	1B-74, OF-58
1945		147	.267	.358	573	153	29	1	7	1.2	62	51	50	33	2	0	0	1427	135	14	129	10.7	.991	1B-147
11 yrs.		1035	.282	.379	3917	1104	204	40	32	0.8	439	482	276	185	30	23	6	8621	747	99	732	9.4	.990	1B-953, OF-59

Fred Siefke

SIEFKE, FREDERICK EDWIN 5′11″ 168 lbs.
B. Mar. 5, 1870, New York, N. Y. D. Apr. 18, 1893, New York, N. Y.

Year	Team	Games	BA	SA	AB	H	2B	3B	HR	HR%	R	RBI	BB	SO	SB	Pinch Hit AB	Pinch Hit H	PO	A	E	DP	TC/G	FA	G by Pos
1890	BKN AA	16	.138	.172	58	8	2	0	0	0.0	1		5		2	0	0	16	44	14	2	4.6	.811	3B-16

John Siegel

SIEGEL, JOHN
B. York, Pa. Deceased.

Year	Team	Games	BA	SA	AB	H	2B	3B	HR	HR%	R	RBI	BB	SO	SB	Pinch Hit AB	Pinch Hit H	PO	A	E	DP	TC/G	FA	G by Pos
1884	PHI U	8	.226	.290	31	7	2	0	0	0.0	4		1			0	0	8	8	14	0	3.8	.533	3B-8

Johnny Siegle

SIEGLE, JOHN HERBERT BR TR 5′10″ 165 lbs.
B. July 8, 1874, Urbana, Ohio D. Feb. 12, 1968, Urbana, Ohio.

Year	Team	Games	BA	SA	AB	H	2B	3B	HR	HR%	R	RBI	BB	SO	SB	Pinch Hit AB	Pinch Hit H	PO	A	E	DP	TC/G	FA	G by Pos
1905	CIN N	17	.304	.446	56	17	1	2	1	1.8	9	8	7		0	1	1	23	1	1	0	1.6	.960	OF-16
1906		22	.118	.206	68	8	2	2	0	0.0	4	7	3		0	1	0	46	1	2	1	2.3	.959	OF-21
2 yrs.		39	.202	.315	124	25	3	4	1	0.8	13	15	10		0	2	1	69	2	3	1	2.0	.959	OF-37

Oscar Siemer

SIEMER, OSCAR SYLVESTER (Cotton) BR TR 5′ 9″ 162 lbs.
B. Aug. 14, 1901, St. Louis, Mo. D. Dec. 5, 1959, St. Louis, Mo.

Year	Team	Games	BA	SA	AB	H	2B	3B	HR	HR%	R	RBI	BB	SO	SB	Pinch Hit AB	Pinch Hit H	PO	A	E	DP	TC/G	FA	G by Pos
1925	BOS N	16	.304	.413	46	14	0	1	1	2.2	5	6	1	0	0	0	0	35	10	5	1	3.1	.900	C-16
1926		31	.205	.219	73	15	1	0	0	0.0	3	5	2	7	0	1	0	81	11	8	2	3.3	.920	C-30
2 yrs.		47	.244	.294	119	29	1	1	1	0.8	8	11	3	7	0	1	0	116	21	13	3	3.3	.913	C-46

Ruben Sierra

SIERRA, RUBEN ANGEL BB TR 6′ 1″ 175 lbs.
Born Ruben Angel Sierra (Garcia).
B. Oct. 6, 1965, Rio Piedras, Puerto Rico.

Year	Team	Games	BA	SA	AB	H	2B	3B	HR	HR%	R	RBI	BB	SO	SB	Pinch Hit AB	Pinch Hit H	PO	A	E	DP	TC/G	FA	G by Pos
1986	TEX A	113	.264	.476	382	101	13	10	16	4.2	50	55	22	65	7	6	1	200	7	6	1	1.9	.972	OF-107, DH-3
1987		158	.263	.470	**643**	169	35	4	30	4.7	97	109	39	114	16	2	0	272	17	11	6	1.9	.963	OF-157
1988		156	.254	.424	615	156	32	2	23	3.7	77	91	44	91	18	3	1	310	11	7	3	2.1	.979	OF-153, DH-1
1989		162	.306	**.543**	634	194	35	**14**	29	4.6	101	**119**	43	82	8	0	0	313	13	9	2	2.1	.973	OF-162
1990		159	.280	.426	608	170	37	2	16	2.6	70	96	49	86	9	2	1	283	7	10	1	1.9	.967	OF-151, DH-7
1991		161	.307	.502	661	203	44	5	25	3.8	110	116	56	91	16	1	1	305	15	7	3	2.0	.979	OF-161
1992	2 teams	TEX A (124G –.278) OAK A (27G –.277)																						
"	total	151	.278	.443	601	167	34	7	17	2.8	83	87	45	68	14	3	1	283	6	7	0	2.0	.976	OF-144, DH-6
1993	OAK A	158	.233	.390	630	147	23	5	22	3.5	77	101	52	97	25	2	0	291	9	7	3	1.9	.977	OF-133, DH-25
1994		110	.268	.484	426	114	21	1	23	5.4	71	92	23	64	8	3	2	155	8	9	2	1.6	.948	OF-98, DH-10
1995	2 teams	OAK A (70G –.265) NY A (56G –.260)																						
"	total	126	.263	.449	479	126	32	0	19	4.0	73	86	46	76	5	5	2	107	2	5	0	0.9	.956	OF-72, DH-53
10 yrs.		1454	.272	.460	5679	1547	306	50	220	3.9	809	952	419	834	126	27	9	2519	95	78	21	1.9	.971	OF-1338, DH-105
DIVISIONAL PLAYOFF SERIES																								
1995	NY A	5	.174	.522	23	4	2	0	2	8.7	2	5	2	7	0	0	0	0	0	0	0	0.0	.000	DH-5
LEAGUE CHAMPIONSHIP SERIES																								
1992	OAK A	6	.333	.625	24	8	2	1	1	4.2	4	7	2	1	1	0	0	12	0	0	0	2.0	1.000	OF-6

Roy Sievers

SIEVERS, ROY EDWARD (Squirrel) BR TR 6′ 1″ 195 lbs.
B. Nov. 18, 1926, St. Louis, Mo.

Year	Team	Games	BA	SA	AB	H	2B	3B	HR	HR%	R	RBI	BB	SO	SB	Pinch Hit AB	Pinch Hit H	PO	A	E	DP	TC/G	FA	G by Pos
1949	STL A	140	.306	.471	471	144	28	1	16	3.4	84	91	70	75	1	7	2	317	25	10	2	2.7	.972	OF-125, 3B-7
1950		113	.238	.395	370	88	20	4	10	2.7	46	57	34	42	1	15	2	248	48	8	6	3.1	.974	OF-78, 3B-21
1951		31	.225	.303	89	20	2	1	1	1.1	10	11	9	21	0	8	1	63	1	1	0	2.6	.985	OF-25
1952		11	.200	.300	30	6	3	0	0	0.0	3	5	1	4	0	5	0	58	3	2	8	9.0	.968	1B-7
1953		92	.270	.407	285	77	15	0	8	2.8	37	35	32	47	0	17	3	604	31	5	64	8.4	.992	1B-76
1954	WAS A	145	.232	.446	514	119	26	6	24	4.7	75	102	80	77	2	5	0	350	15	9	8	2.7	.976	OF-133, 1B-8
1955		144	.271	.489	509	138	20	8	25	4.9	74	106	73	66	1	2	0	363	17	4	16	2.6	.990	OF-129, 1B-17, 3B-2
1956		152	.253	.467	550	139	27	2	29	5.3	92	95	100	88	0	0	0	784	54	9	76	5.5	.989	OF-78, 1B-76
1957		152	.301	.579	572	172	23	5	**42**	7.3	99	**114**	76	55	1	2	2	413	15	6	23	2.9	.986	OF-130, 1B-21
1958		148	.295	.544	550	162	18	1	39	7.1	85	108	53	63	3	4	1	476	26	5	36	3.4	.990	OF-114, 1B-33

Roy Sievers *continued*

Year	Team	Games	BA	SA	AB	H	2B	3B	HR	HR%	R	RBI	BB	SO	SB	Pinch Hit AB	Pinch Hit H	PO	A	E	DP	TC/G	FA	G by Pos
1959		115	.242	.455	385	93	19	0	21	5.5	55	49	53	62	1	7	1	870	72	11	72	9.0	.988	1B-93, OF-13
1960	CHI A	127	.295	.534	444	131	22	0	28	6.3	87	93	74	69	1	9	1	1085	63	8	117	9.6	.993	1B-114, OF-6
1961		141	.295	.537	492	145	26	6	27	5.5	76	92	61	62	1	10	4	1096	94	8	93	9.1	.993	1B-132
1962	PHI N	144	.262	.455	477	125	19	5	21	4.4	61	80	56	80	2	12	1	977	93	10	102	7.9	.991	1B-130, OF-7
1963		138	.240	.418	450	108	19	2	19	4.2	46	82	43	72	0	18	6	981	77	12	93	8.5	.989	1B-126
1964	2 teams	PHI N (49G –.183) WAS A (33G –.172)																						
"	total	82	.180	.348	178	32	4	1	8	4.5	12	27	22	34	0	29	6	328	26	2	37	7.4	.994	1B-48
1965	WAS A	12	.190	.238	21	4	1	0	0	0.0	3	0	4	3	0	4	1	51	1	0	6	7.4	1.000	1B-7
17 yrs.		1887	.267	.475	6387	1703	292	42	318	5.0	945	1147	841	920	14	154	31	9064	661	110	759	5.6	.989	1B-888, OF-838, 3B-30

Frank Siffell

SIFFELL, FRANK
B. 1861, Germany D. Oct. 26, 1909, Philadelphia, Pa.

Year	Team	Games	BA	SA	AB	H	2B	3B	HR	HR%	R	RBI	BB	SO	SB	Pinch Hit AB	Pinch Hit H	PO	A	E	DP	TC/G	FA	G by Pos
1884	PHI AA	7	.176	.235	17	3	1	0	0	0.0	3		0			0	0	22	6	4	0	4.6	.875	C-7
1885		3	.100	.100	10	1	0	0	0	0.0	0		0			0	0	9	0	3	1	4.0	.750	C-2, OF-1
2 yrs.		10	.148	.185	27	4	1	0	0	0.0	3		0			0	0	31	6	7	1	4.4	.841	C-9, OF-1

Frank Sigafoos

SIGAFOOS, FRANCIS LEONARD BR TR 5′9″ 170 lbs.
B. Mar. 21, 1904, Easton, Pa. D. Apr. 12, 1968, Indianapolis, Ind.

Year	Team	Games	BA	SA	AB	H	2B	3B	HR	HR%	R	RBI	BB	SO	SB	Pinch Hit AB	Pinch Hit H	PO	A	E	DP	TC/G	FA	G by Pos
1926	PHI A	13	.256	.256	43	11	0	0	0	0.0	4	2	0	3	0	1	0	12	31	4	5	3.9	.915	SS-12
1929	2 teams	DET A (14G –.174) CHI A (7G –.333)																						
"	total	21	.192	.231	26	5	1	0	0	0.0	4	3	7	5	0	1	0	17	18	3	3	2.2	.921	3B-6, 2B-6, SS-5
1931	CIN N	21	.169	.200	65	11	2	0	0	0.0	6	8	0	6	0	4	1	14	24	5	2	2.5	.884	3B-15, SS-2
3 yrs.		55	.201	.224	134	27	3	0	0	0.0	14	13	7	14	0	6	1	43	73	12	10	2.8	.906	3B-21, SS-19, 2B-6

Paddy Siglin

SIGLIN, WESLEY PETER BR TR 5′10″ 160 lbs.
B. Sept. 24, 1891, Aurelia, Iowa D. Aug. 5, 1956, Oakland, Calif.

Year	Team	Games	BA	SA	AB	H	2B	3B	HR	HR%	R	RBI	BB	SO	SB	Pinch Hit AB	Pinch Hit H	PO	A	E	DP	TC/G	FA	G by Pos
1914	PIT N	14	.154	.154	39	6	0	0	0	0.0	4	2	4	6	1	3	1	24	17	4	1	4.1	.911	2B-11
1915		6	.286	.286	7	2	0	0	0	0.0	1	0	1	2	1	3	0	1	3	1	0	5.0	.800	2B-1
1916		3	.250	.250	4	1	0	0	0	0.0	0	0	0	2	0	0	0	4	2	1	3	2.3	.857	2B-3
3 yrs.		23	.180	.180	50	9	0	0	0	0.0	5	2	5	10	2	6	1	29	22	6	4	3.8	.895	2B-15

Tripp Sigman

SIGMAN, WESLEY TRIPLETT BL TR 6′ 180 lbs.
B. Jan. 17, 1899, Mooresville, N. C. D. Mar. 8, 1971, Augusta, Ga.

Year	Team	Games	BA	SA	AB	H	2B	3B	HR	HR%	R	RBI	BB	SO	SB	Pinch Hit AB	Pinch Hit H	PO	A	E	DP	TC/G	FA	G by Pos
1929	PHI N	10	.517	.759	29	15	1	0	2	6.9	8	9	3	1	0	0	0	17	0	1	0	1.8	.944	OF-10
1930		52	.270	.450	100	27	4	1	4	4.0	15	6	6	9	1	32	8	39	2	3	0	2.3	.932	OF-19
2 yrs.		62	.326	.519	129	42	5	1	6	4.7	23	15	9	10	1	32	8	56	2	4	0	2.1	.935	OF-29

Eddie Silber

SILBER, EDWARD JAMES BR TR 5′11″ 170 lbs.
B. June 6, 1914, Philadelphia, Pa. D. Oct. 26, 1976, Dunedin, Fla.

Year	Team	Games	BA	SA	AB	H	2B	3B	HR	HR%	R	RBI	BB	SO	SB	Pinch Hit AB	Pinch Hit H	PO	A	E	DP	TC/G	FA	G by Pos
1937	STL A	22	.313	.337	83	26	2	0	0	0.0	10	4	5	13	0	1	1	27	0	4	0	1.5	.871	OF-21
1939		1	.000	.000	1	0	0	0	0	0.0	0	0	0	1	0	1	0	0	0	0	0	0.0	—	
2 yrs.		23	.310	.333	84	26	2	0	0	0.0	10	4	5	14	0	2	1	27	0	4	0	1.5	.871	OF-21

Ed Silch

SILCH, EDWARD (Baldy) TR 6′2″ 180 lbs.
B. Feb. 22, 1865, St. Louis, Mo. D. Jan. 15, 1895, St. Louis, Mo.

Year	Team	Games	BA	SA	AB	H	2B	3B	HR	HR%	R	RBI	BB	SO	SB	Pinch Hit AB	Pinch Hit H	PO	A	E	DP	TC/G	FA	G by Pos
1888	BKN AA	14	.271	.354	48	13	4	0	0	0.0	5	3	4		4	0	0	19	1	3	0	1.6	.870	OF-14

Danny Silva

SILVA, DANIEL JAMES BR TR 6′ 170 lbs.
B. Oct. 5, 1896, Everett, Mass. D. Apr. 4, 1974, Hyannis, Mass.

Year	Team	Games	BA	SA	AB	H	2B	3B	HR	HR%	R	RBI	BB	SO	SB	Pinch Hit AB	Pinch Hit H	PO	A	E	DP	TC/G	FA	G by Pos
1919	WAS A	1	.250	.250	4	1	0	0	0	0.0	0	0	0	0	0	0	0	1	4	0	0	5.0	1.000	3B-1

Al Silvera

SILVERA, AARON ALBERT BR TR 6′ 180 lbs.
B. Aug. 26, 1935, San Diego, Calif.

Year	Team	Games	BA	SA	AB	H	2B	3B	HR	HR%	R	RBI	BB	SO	SB	Pinch Hit AB	Pinch Hit H	PO	A	E	DP	TC/G	FA	G by Pos
1955	CIN N	13	.143	.143	7	1	0	0	0	0.0	3	2	0	1	0	6	1	0	0	0	0	0.0	.000	OF-1
1956		1	—	—	0	0	0	0	0	—	0	0	0	0	0	0	0	0	0	0	0	0.0	—	
2 yrs.		14	.143	.143	7	1	0	0	0	0.0	3	2	0	1	0	6	1	0	0	0	0	0.0		OF-1

Charlie Silvera

SILVERA, CHARLES ANTHONY RYAN (Swede) BR TR 5′10″ 175 lbs.
B. Oct. 13, 1924, San Francisco, Calif.

Year	Team	Games	BA	SA	AB	H	2B	3B	HR	HR%	R	RBI	BB	SO	SB	Pinch Hit AB	Pinch Hit H	PO	A	E	DP	TC/G	FA	G by Pos
1948	NY A	4	.571	.714	14	8	0	1	0	0.0	1	1	0	1	0	0	0	17	1	0	0	4.5	1.000	C-4
1949		58	.315	.331	130	41	2	0	0	0.0	8	13	18	5	2	6	3	177	22	3	5	4.0	.985	C-51
1950		18	.160	.160	25	4	0	0	0	0.0	2	1	1	2	0	3	1	46	1	2	1	3.3	.959	C-15
1951		18	.275	.392	51	14	3	0	1	2.0	5	7	5	3	0	0	0	66	6	0	2	4.0	1.000	C-18
1952		20	.327	.382	55	18	3	0	0	0.0	4	11	5	2	0	0	0	54	8	0	1	3.1	1.000	C-20
1953		42	.280	.341	82	23	3	1	0	0.0	11	12	9	5	0	2	1	114	15	1	1	3.3	.992	C-39, 3B-1
1954		20	.270	.297	37	10	1	0	0	0.0	1	4	3	2	0	2	0	72	5	3	1	4.4	.963	C-18
1955		14	.192	.192	26	5	0	0	0	0.0	1	1	6	4	0	2	0	47	4	0	1	4.6	1.000	C-11
1956		7	.222	.222	9	2	0	0	0	0.0	0	0	2	3	0	0	0	9	1	1	0	1.6	.909	C-7
1957	CHI N	26	.208	.264	53	11	3	0	0	0.0	1	2	4	5	0	0	0	97	11	2	2	4.2	.982	C-26
10 yrs.		227	.282	.328	482	136	15	2	1	0.2	34	52	53	32	2	15	5	699	74	12	14	3.7	.985	C-209, 3B-1
WORLD SERIES																								
1949	NY A	1	.000	.000	2	0	0	0	0	0.0	0	0	0	0	0	0	0	6	0	0	0	6.0	1.000	C-1

Luis Silverio

SILVERIO, LUIS PASCUAL BR TR 5′11″ 165 lbs.
Born Luis Pascual Silverio (Delmonte).
B. Oct. 23, 1956, Villa Gonzalez, Dominican Republic.

Year	Team	Games	BA	SA	AB	H	2B	3B	HR	HR%	R	RBI	BB	SO	SB	Pinch Hit AB	Pinch Hit H	PO	A	E	DP	TC/G	FA	G by Pos
1978	KC A	8	.545	.909	11	6	2	1	0	0.0	7	3	2	3	1	0	0	5	0	1	0	0.8	.833	OF-6, DH-2

Tom Silverio

SILVERIO, TOMAS ROBERTO
Born Tomas Roberto Silverio (Veloz).
B. Oct. 14, 1945, Santiago, Dominican Republic.
BL TL 5′10″ 170 lbs.

Year	Team	Games	BA	SA	AB	H	2B	3B	HR	HR%	R	RBI	BB	SO	SB	Pinch Hit AB	Pinch Hit H	PO	A	E	DP	TC/G	FA	G by Pos
1970	CAL A	15	.000	.000	15	0	0	0	0	0.0	1	0	2	4	0	10	0	8	0	0	0	1.3	1.000	OF-5, 1B-1
1971		3	.333	.333	3	1	0	0	0	0.0	0	0	0	0	0	3	1	0	0	0	0	0.0	.000	OF-1
1972		13	.167	.167	12	2	0	0	0	0.0	1	0	0	5	0	7	1	1	0	0	0	0.3	1.000	OF-4
3 yrs.		31	.100	.100	30	3	0	0	0	0.0	2	0	2	9	0	20	2	9	0	0	0	0.8	1.000	OF-10, 1B-1

Dave Silvestri

SILVESTRI, DAVID JOSEPH
B. Sept. 29, 1967, St. Louis, Mo.
BR TR 6′ 180 lbs.

Year	Team	Games	BA	SA	AB	H	2B	3B	HR	HR%	R	RBI	BB	SO	SB	Pinch Hit AB	Pinch Hit H	PO	A	E	DP	TC/G	FA	G by Pos
1992	NY A	7	.308	.615	13	4	0	2	0	0.0	3	1	0	3	0	1	0	4	12	2	3	3.0	.889	SS-6
1993		7	.286	.476	21	6	1	0	1	4.8	4	4	5	3	0	0	0	9	20	3	4	4.6	.906	SS-4, 3B-3
1994		12	.111	.389	18	2	0	1	1	5.6	3	2	4	9	0	1	0	14	16	1	3	2.6	.968	2B-9, 3B-2, SS-1
1995	2 teams	NY A (17G –.095) MON N (39G –.264)																						
″	total	56	.226	.387	93	21	6	0	3	3.2	16	11	13	36	2	15	6	62	48	1	8	2.6	.991	2B-10, SS-10, 1B-8, 3B-8, DH-4, OF-3
4 yrs.		82	.228	.421	145	33	7	3	5	3.4	26	18	22	51	2	17	6	89	96	7	18	2.8	.964	SS-21, 2B-19, 3B-13, 1B-8, DH-4, OF-3

Ken Silvestri

SILVESTRI, KENNETH JOSEPH (Hawk)
B. May 3, 1916, Chicago, Ill. D. Mar. 31, 1992, Tallahassee, Fla.
Manager 1967.
BB TR 6′ 1″ 200 lbs.

Year	Team	Games	BA	SA	AB	H	2B	3B	HR	HR%	R	RBI	BB	SO	SB	Pinch Hit AB	Pinch Hit H	PO	A	E	DP	TC/G	FA	G by Pos
1939	CHI A	22	.173	.293	75	13	3	0	2	2.7	6	5	6	13	0	2	1	74	15	5	3	4.7	.947	C-20
1940		28	.250	.583	24	6	2	0	2	8.3	5	10	4	7	0	24	6	1	0	0	0	1.0	1.000	C-1
1941	NY A	17	.250	.450	40	10	5	0	1	2.5	6	4	7	6	0	3	0	43	6	0	2	3.8	1.000	C-13
1946		13	.286	.333	21	6	1	0	0	0.0	4	1	3	7	0	1	0	40	3	1	1	3.7	.977	C-12
1947		3	.200	.200	10	2	0	0	0	0.0	0	0	2	2	0	0	0	7	1	0	0	2.7	1.000	C-3
1949	PHI N	4	.000	.000	4	0	0	0	0	0.0	1	0	2	1	0	2	0	8	2	0	0	3.3	1.000	C-1, 2B-1, SS-1
1950		11	.250	.350	20	5	0	1	0	0.0	2	4	4	3	0	2	1	25	1	0	0	2.9	1.000	C-9
1951		4	.222	.222	9	2	0	0	0	0.0	2	1	3	2	0	0	0	3	1	0	0	1.3	1.000	C-3
8 yrs.		102	.217	.355	203	44	11	1	5	2.5	26	25	31	41	0	34	8	201	29	6	6	3.7	.975	C-62, 2B-1, SS-1
WORLD SERIES																								
1950	PHI N	1	—	—	0	0	0	0	0	—	0	0	0	0	0	0	0	1	0	0	0	1.0	1.000	C-1

Al Simmons

SIMMONS, ALOYSIUS HARRY (Bucketfoot Al)
Born Aloys Szymanski.
B. May 22, 1902, Milwaukee, Wis. D. May 26, 1956, Milwaukee, Wis.
Hall of Fame 1953.
BR TR 5′11″ 190 lbs.

Year	Team	Games	BA	SA	AB	H	2B	3B	HR	HR%	R	RBI	BB	SO	SB	Pinch Hit AB	Pinch Hit H	PO	A	E	DP	TC/G	FA	G by Pos
1924	PHI A	152	.308	.431	594	183	31	9	8	1.3	69	102	30	60	16	0	0	390	17	10	4	2.7	.976	OF-152
1925		153	.384	.596	**658**	**253**	43	12	24	3.6	122	129	35	41	7	0	0	447	8	16	2	3.1	.966	OF-153
1926		147	.343	.566	581	199	53	10	19	3.3	90	109	48	49	10	0	0	333	11	9	5	2.4	.975	OF-147
1927		106	.392	.645	406	159	36	11	15	3.7	86	108	31	30	10	0	0	247	10	4	2	2.5	.985	OF-105
1928		119	.351	.558	464	163	33	9	15	3.2	78	107	31	30	1	3	2	231	10	3	2	2.1	.988	OF-114
1929		143	.365	.642	581	212	41	9	34	5.9	114	**157**	31	38	4	0	0	349	19	4	2	2.6	.989	OF-142
1930		138	**.381**	.708	554	211	41	16	36	6.5	**152**	165	39	34	9	2	1	275	10	3	1	2.1	.990	OF-136
1931		128	**.390**	.641	513	200	37	13	22	4.3	105	128	47	45	3	0	0	287	10	4	0	2.4	.987	OF-128
1932		154	.322	.548	**670**	**216**	28	9	35	5.2	144	151	47	76	4	0	0	290	9	6	4	2.0	.980	OF-154
1933	CHI A	146	.331	.481	605	200	29	10	14	2.3	85	119	39	49	5	1	0	372	15	4	1	2.7	.990	OF-145
1934		138	.344	.530	558	192	36	7	18	3.2	102	104	53	58	3	0	0	286	14	4	3	2.2	.987	OF-138
1935		128	.267	.427	525	140	22	7	16	3.0	68	79	33	43	4	3	0	349	5	7	1	2.9	.981	OF-126
1936	DET A	143	.327	.484	568	186	38	6	13	2.3	96	112	49	35	6	4	1	364	8	5	2	2.7	.987	OF-138, 1B-1
1937	WAS A	103	.279	.434	419	117	21	10	8	1.9	60	84	27	35	3	1	0	240	7	4	5	2.5	.984	OF-102
1938		125	.302	.511	470	142	23	6	21	4.5	79	95	38	40	2	9	2	232	4	4	1	2.1	.983	OF-117
1939	2 teams	BOS N (93G –.282) CIN N (9G –.143)																						
″	total	102	.274	.410	351	96	17	5	7	2.0	39	44	24	43	0	14	2	172	8	4	2	2.1	.978	OF-87
1940	PHI A	37	.309	.395	81	25	4	0	1	1.2	7	19	4	8	0	16	8	51	1	2	0	3.0	.963	OF-18
1941		9	.125	.167	24	3	1	0	0	0.0	1	1	1	2	0	4	0	16	0	0	0	3.2	1.000	OF-5
1943	BOS A	40	.203	.263	133	27	5	0	1	0.8	9	12	8	21	0	7	0	66	3	1	1	2.1	.986	OF-33
1944	PHI A	4	.500	.500	6	3	0	0	0	0.0	1	2	0	0	0	2	1	3	0	0	0	1.5	1.000	OF-2
20 yrs.		2215	.334	.535	8761	2927	539	149	307	3.5	1507	1827	615	737	87	66	17	5000	169	94	38	2.5	.982	OF-2142, 1B-1
WORLD SERIES																								
1929	PHI A	5	.300	.650	20	6	1	0	2	10.0	6	5	1	4	0	0	0	4	0	0	0	0.8	1.000	OF-5
1930		6	.364	.727	22	8	2	0	2	9.1	4	4	2	2	0	0	0	12	1	0	0	2.2	1.000	OF-6
1931		7	.333	.630	27	9	2	0	2	7.4	4	8	3	3	0	0	0	19	0	0	0	2.7	1.000	OF-7
1939	CIN N	1	.250	.500	4	1	1	0	0	0.0	1	0	0	0	0	0	0	3	0	0	0	3.0	1.000	OF-1
4 yrs.		19	.329	.658	73	24	6	0	6	8.2	15	17	6	9	0	0	0	38	1	0	0	2.1	1.000	OF-19
				5th						8th														

Hack Simmons

SIMMONS, GEORGE WASHINGTON
B. Jan. 29, 1885, Brooklyn, N. Y. D. Apr. 26, 1942, Arverne, N. Y.
BR TR 5′ 8″ 179 lbs.

Year	Team	Games	BA	SA	AB	H	2B	3B	HR	HR%	R	RBI	BB	SO	SB	Pinch Hit AB	Pinch Hit H	PO	A	E	DP	TC/G	FA	G by Pos
1910	DET A	42	.227	.273	110	25	3	1	0	0.0	12	9	10		1	10	3	240	28	6	10	8.8	.978	1B-22, 3B-7, OF-2
1912	NY A	110	.239	.292	401	96	17	2	0	0.0	45	41	33		19	4	0	299	219	24	30	5.2	.956	2B-88, 1B-13, SS-4
1914	BAL F	114	.270	.352	352	95	16	5	1	0.3	50	38	32		7	13	7	154	75	17	9	2.3	.931	OF-73, 2B-26, 1B-4, SS-2, 3B-1
1915		39	.205	.341	88	18	7	1	1	1.1	8	14	10		1	13	5	32	21	3	0	2.2	.946	OF-13, 2B-13
4 yrs.		305	.246	.317	951	234	43	9	2	0.2	115	102	85		28	40	15	725	343	50	49	4.2	.955	2B-127, OF-88, 1B-39, 3B-8, SS-6

John Simmons

SIMMONS, JOHN EARL
B. July 7, 1924, Birmingham, Ala.
BR TR 6′ 1½″ 192 lbs.

Year	Team	Games	BA	SA	AB	H	2B	3B	HR	HR%	R	RBI	BB	SO	SB	Pinch Hit AB	Pinch Hit H	PO	A	E	DP	TC/G	FA	G by Pos
1949	WAS A	62	.215	.215	93	20	0	0	0	0.0	12	5	11	6	0	23	5	34	1	0	0	1.3	1.000	OF-26

Nelson Simmons

SIMMONS, NELSON BERNARD III — BB TR 6′ 1″ 195 lbs.
B. June 27, 1963, Washington, D. C.

Year	Team	Games	BA	SA	AB	H	2B	3B	HR	HR%	R	RBI	BB	SO	SB	Pinch Hit AB	Pinch Hit H	PO	A	E	DP	TC/G	FA	G by Pos
1984	DET A	9	.433	.500	30	13	2	0	0	0.0	4	3	2	5	1	1	0	8	0	0	0	0.9	1.000	OF-5, DH-4
1985		75	.239	.402	251	60	11	0	10	4.0	31	33	26	41	1	8	2	67	2	4	1	1.1	.945	OF-38, DH-31
1987	BAL A	16	.265	.388	49	13	1	1	1	2.0	3	4	3	8	0	3	1	24	2	0	1	1.9	1.000	OF-13, DH-1
3 yrs.		100	.261	.409	330	86	14	1	11	3.3	38	40	31	54	2	12	3	99	4	4	2	1.2	.963	OF-56, DH-36

Ted Simmons

SIMMONS, TED LYLE — BB TR 5′11″ 193 lbs.
B. Aug. 9, 1949, Highland Park, Mich.

Year	Team	Games	BA	SA	AB	H	2B	3B	HR	HR%	R	RBI	BB	SO	SB	Pinch Hit AB	Pinch Hit H	PO	A	E	DP	TC/G	FA	G by Pos
1968	STL N	2	.333	.333	3	1	0	0	0	0.0	0	0	1	1	0	0	0	3	1	0	0	2.0	1.000	C-2
1969		5	.214	.357	14	3	0	1	0	0.0	0	3	1	1	0	1	0	22	0	1	0	5.8	.957	C-4
1970		82	.243	.317	284	69	8	2	3	1.1	29	24	37	37	2	4	1	466	37	5	2	6.4	.990	C-79
1971		133	.304	.424	510	155	32	4	7	1.4	64	77	36	50	1	6	1	747	52	9	11	6.2	.989	C-130
1972		152	.303	.465	594	180	36	6	16	2.7	70	96	29	57	1	2	0	967	93	13	15	7.2	.988	C-135, 1B-15
1973		161	.310	.438	619	192	36	2	13	2.1	62	91	61	47	2	1	0	932	78	14	14	6.4	.986	C-153, 1B-6, OF-2
1974		152	.272	.447	599	163	33	6	20	3.3	66	103	47	35	0	2	1	813	87	15	18	6.0	.984	C-141, 1B-12
1975		157	.332	.491	581	193	32	3	18	3.1	80	100	63	35	1	5	1	818	64	15	5	5.7	.983	C-154, OF-2, 1B-2
1976		150	.291	.394	546	159	35	3	5	0.9	60	75	73	35	0	7	4	726	88	10	25	5.4	.988	C-113, 1B-30, OF-7, 3B-2
1977		150	.318	.500	516	164	25	3	21	4.1	82	95	79	37	2	17	2	683	75	10	5	5.3	.987	C-143, OF-1
1978		152	.287	.512	516	148	40	5	22	4.3	71	80	77	39	1	10	3	703	88	10	6	5.1	.988	C-134, OF-23
1979		123	.283	.507	448	127	22	0	26	5.8	68	87	61	34	0	4	0	606	69	10	10	5.6	.985	C-122
1980		145	.303	.505	495	150	33	2	21	4.2	84	98	59	45	1	15	3	528	71	10	12	4.5	.984	C-129, OF-5
1981	MIL A	100	.216	.376	380	82	13	3	14	3.7	45	61	23	32	0	3	1	333	41	8	7	3.8	.979	C-75, DH-22, 1B-4
1982		137	.269	.451	539	145	29	0	23	4.3	73	97	32	40	0	2	1	570	62	3	8	4.7	.995	C-121, DH-15
1983		153	.308	.448	600	185	39	3	13	2.2	76	108	41	51	4	4	0	395	41	11	4	2.9	.975	C-86, DH-66
1984		132	.221	.300	497	110	23	2	4	0.8	44	52	30	40	3	6	1	352	52	8	37	3.2	.981	DH-77, 1B-37, 3B-14
1985		143	.273	.402	528	144	28	2	12	2.3	60	76	57	32	1	3	1	291	26	3	23	2.2	.991	DH-99, 1B-28, C-15, 3B-2
1986	ATL N	76	.252	.386	127	32	5	0	4	3.1	14	25	12	14	1	47	11	167	18	6	13	5.8	.969	1B-14, C-10, 3B-9
1987		73	.277	.390	177	49	8	0	4	2.3	20	30	21	23	1	29	9	282	35	5	25	7.2	.984	1B-28, C-15, 3B-2
1988		78	.196	.308	107	21	6	0	2	1.9	6	11	15	9	0	47	5	140	14	3	8	5.4	.981	1B-19, C-10
21 yrs.		2456	.285	.437	8680	2472	483	47	248	2.9	1074	1389	855	694	21	215	45	10544	1092	169	248	5.1	.986	C-1771, DH-279, 1B-195, OF-40, 3B-29

DIVISIONAL PLAYOFF SERIES

Year	Team	Games	BA	SA	AB	H	2B	3B	HR	HR%	R	RBI	BB	SO	SB	Pinch Hit AB	Pinch Hit H	PO	A	E	DP	TC/G	FA	G by Pos
1981	MIL A	5	.211	.421	19	4	1	0	1	5.3	1	4	2	2	0	0	0	23	2	1	0	5.2	.962	C-5

LEAGUE CHAMPIONSHIP SERIES

Year	Team	Games	BA	SA	AB	H	2B	3B	HR	HR%	R	RBI	BB	SO	SB	Pinch Hit AB	Pinch Hit H	PO	A	E	DP	TC/G	FA	G by Pos
1982	MIL A	5	.167	.167	18	3	0	0	0	0.0	3	1	1	4	0	0	0	36	3	0	0	7.8	1.000	C-5

WORLD SERIES

Year	Team	Games	BA	SA	AB	H	2B	3B	HR	HR%	R	RBI	BB	SO	SB	Pinch Hit AB	Pinch Hit H	PO	A	E	DP	TC/G	FA	G by Pos
1982	MIL A	7	.174	.435	23	4	0	0	2	8.7	2	3	5	3	0	0	0	28	2	1	0	4.4	.968	C-7

Mike Simms

SIMMS, MICHAEL HOWARD — BR TR 6′ 4″ 185 lbs.
B. Jan. 12, 1967, Orange, Calif.

Year	Team	Games	BA	SA	AB	H	2B	3B	HR	HR%	R	RBI	BB	SO	SB	Pinch Hit AB	Pinch Hit H	PO	A	E	DP	TC/G	FA	G by Pos
1990	HOU N	12	.308	.615	13	4	1	0	1	7.7	3	2	0	4	0	5	0	20	1	0	2	3.5	1.000	1B-6
1991		49	.203	.317	123	25	5	0	3	2.4	18	16	18	38	1	8	1	44	4	6	0	1.3	.889	OF-41
1992		15	.250	.417	24	6	1	0	1	4.2	1	3	2	9	0	6	1	10	2	0	0	1.2	1.000	OF-9, 1B-1
1994		6	.083	.167	12	1	1	0	0	0.0	1	0	0	5	1	2	0	6	0	1	0	2.3	.857	OF-3
1995		50	.256	.512	121	31	4	0	9	7.4	14	24	13	28	1	11	2	221	18	1	19	6.5	.996	1B-25, OF-12
5 yrs.		132	.229	.413	293	67	12	0	14	4.8	37	45	33	84	3	32	4	301	25	8	21	3.4	.976	OF-65, 1B-32

Henry Simon

SIMON, HENRY JOSEPH — BR TR
B. Aug. 25, 1862, Hawkinsville, N. Y. D. Jan. 1, 1925, Albany, N. Y.

Year	Team	Games	BA	SA	AB	H	2B	3B	HR	HR%	R	RBI	BB	SO	SB	Pinch Hit AB	Pinch Hit H	PO	A	E	DP	TC/G	FA	G by Pos
1887	CLE AA	3	.100	.100	10	1	0	0	0	0.0	1		0		0	0	0	3	0	0	0	1.0	1.000	OF-3
1890	2 teams	BKN AA (89G –.257) SYR AA (38G –.301)																						
″	total	127	.270	.376	529	143	22	14	2	0.4	99		51		35	0	0	238	19	14	5	2.1	.948	OF-127
2 yrs.		130	.267	.371	539	144	22	14	2	0.4	100		51		35	0	0	241	19	14	5	2.1	.949	OF-130

Mike Simon

SIMON, MICHAEL EDWARD — BR TR 5′11″ 188 lbs.
B. Apr. 13, 1883, Hayden, Ind. D. June 10, 1963, Los Angeles, Calif.

Year	Team	Games	BA	SA	AB	H	2B	3B	HR	HR%	R	RBI	BB	SO	SB	Pinch Hit AB	Pinch Hit H	PO	A	E	DP	TC/G	FA	G by Pos
1909	PIT N	11	.167	.167	18	3	0	0	0	0.0	2	2	1		0	1	1	28	5	3	1	4.0	.917	C-9
1910		22	.200	.240	50	10	0	1	0	0.0	3	5	1	2	1	7	0	40	12	0	0	3.7	1.000	C-14
1911		71	.228	.274	215	49	4	3	0	0.0	19	22	10	14	1	3	0	320	75	13	6	6.0	.968	C-68
1912		42	.301	.336	113	34	2	1	0	0.0	10	11	5	9	1	2	0	172	43	2	5	5.4	.991	C-40
1913		92	.247	.298	255	63	6	2	1	0.4	23	17	10	15	3	0	0	393	151	14	6	6.1	.975	C-92
1914	STL F	93	.207	.261	276	57	11	2	0	0.0	21	21	18		2	13	2	433	132	9	9	7.4	.984	C-78
1915	BKN F	47	.176	.225	142	25	5	1	0	0.0	7	12	9		1	2	0	175	60	2	4	5.3	.992	C-45
7 yrs.		378	.225	.273	1069	241	28	10	1	0.1	85	90	54	40	9	28	3	1561	478	43	31	6.0	.979	C-346

Syl Simon

SIMON, SYLVESTER ADAM — BR TR 5′10½″ 170 lbs.
B. Dec. 14, 1897, Evansville, Ind. D. Feb. 28, 1973, Chandler, Ind.

Year	Team	Games	BA	SA	AB	H	2B	3B	HR	HR%	R	RBI	BB	SO	SB	Pinch Hit AB	Pinch Hit H	PO	A	E	DP	TC/G	FA	G by Pos
1923	STL A	1	.000	.000	1	0	0	0	0	0.0	0	0	0	0	0	1	0	0	0	0	0	0.0	—	
1924		22	.250	.344	32	8	1	1	0	0.0	5	6	2	5	0	10	2	8	17	4	1	2.6	.862	3B-6, SS-5
2 yrs.		23	.242	.333	33	8	1	1	0	0.0	5	6	2	5	0	11	2	8	17	4	1	2.6	.862	3B-6, SS-5

Mel Simons

SIMONS, MELBERN ELLIS (Butch) — BL TR 5′10″ 175 lbs.
B. July 1, 1900, Carlyle, Ill. D. Nov. 10, 1974, Paducah, Ky.

Year	Team	Games	BA	SA	AB	H	2B	3B	HR	HR%	R	RBI	BB	SO	SB	Pinch Hit AB	Pinch Hit H	PO	A	E	DP	TC/G	FA	G by Pos
1931	CHI A	68	.275	.323	189	52	9	0	0	0.0	24	12	12	17	1	6	1	112	3	6	0	2.1	.950	OF-59
1932		7	.000	.000	5	0	0	0	0	0.0	0	0	0	1	0	1	0	2	0	0	0	0.3	1.000	OF-6
2 yrs.		75	.268	.314	194	52	9	0	0	0.0	24	12	12	18	1	7	1	114	3	6	0	1.9	.951	OF-65

Dick Simpson

SIMPSON, RICHARD CHARLES — BR TR 6′ 4″ 176 lbs.
B. July 28, 1943, Washington, D. C.

Year	Team	Games	BA	SA	AB	H	2B	3B	HR	HR%	R	RBI	BB	SO	SB	Pinch Hit AB	Pinch Hit H	PO	A	E	DP	TC/G	FA	G by Pos
1962	LA A	6	.250	.375	8	2	1	0	0	0.0	1	1	2	3	0	2	0	7	0	0	0	1.8	1.000	OF-4
1964		21	.140	.280	50	7	1	0	2	4.0	11	4	8	15	2	0	0	27	0	0	0	1.7	1.000	OF-16
1965	CAL A	8	.222	.259	27	6	1	0	0	0.0	2	3	2	8	1	0	0	14	0	2	0	2.0	.875	OF-8
1966	CIN N	92	.238	.405	84	20	2	0	4	4.8	26	14	10	32	0	18	2	35	0	3	0	0.6	.921	OF-64
1967		44	.259	.370	54	14	3	0	1	1.9	8	6	7	11	0	9	4	34	2	1	0	1.4	.973	OF-26

Dick Simpson *continued*

Year	Team	Games	BA	SA	AB	H	2B	3B	HR	HR%	R	RBI	BB	SO	SB	Pinch Hit AB	Pinch Hit H	PO	A	E	DP	TC/G	FA	G by Pos
1968	2 teams	STL N (26G –.232) HOU N (59G –.186)																						
"	total	85	.197	.322	233	46	7	2	6	2.6	36	19	28	82	4	3	0	89	3	2	1	1.3	.979	OF-71
1969	2 teams	NY A (6G –.273) SEA A (26G –.176)																						
"	total	32	.194	.355	62	12	4	0	2	3.2	10	9	7	23	3	8	0	26	1	0	0	1.2	1.000	OF-22
7 yrs.		288	.207	.338	518	107	19	2	15	2.9	94	56	64	174	10	40	6	232	6	8	1	1.2	.967	OF-211

Harry Simpson

SIMPSON, HARRY LEON (Suitcase)
B. Dec. 3, 1925, Atlanta, Ga. D. Apr. 3, 1979, Akron, Ohio.
BL TR 6′ 1″ 180 lbs.

Year	Team	Games	BA	SA	AB	H	2B	3B	HR	HR%	R	RBI	BB	SO	SB	Pinch Hit AB	Pinch Hit H	PO	A	E	DP	TC/G	FA	G by Pos
1951	CLE A	122	.229	.313	332	76	7	0	7	2.1	51	24	45	48	6	10	2	458	20	8	29	4.1	.984	OF-68, 1B-50
1952		146	.266	.396	545	145	21	10	10	1.8	66	65	56	82	5	1	1	502	19	5	25	3.4	.990	OF-127, 1B-28
1953		82	.227	.335	242	55	3	1	7	2.9	25	22	18	27	0	10	1	130	4	4	1	1.9	.971	OF-69, 1B-2
1955	2 teams	CLE A (3G –.000) KC A (112G –.301)																						
"	total	115	.300	.413	397	119	16	7	5	1.3	43	52	36	61	3	11	4	272	7	6	4	2.8	.979	OF-100, 1B-3
1956	KC A	141	.293	.490	543	159	22	**11**	21	3.9	76	105	47	82	2	3	0	457	18	11	34	3.4	.977	OF-111, 1B-32
1957	2 teams	KC A (50G –.296) NY A (75G –.250)																						
"	total	125	.270	.452	403	109	16	**9**	13	3.2	51	63	31	64	1	20	4	470	37	5	40	4.6	.990	OF-63, 1B-48
1958	2 teams	NY A (24G –.216) KC A (78G –.264)																						
"	total	102	.255	.384	263	67	9	2	7	2.7	22	33	32	45	0	30	5	429	19	5	44	6.6	.989	1B-43, OF-26
1959	3 teams	KC A (8G –.286) CHI A (38G –.187) PIT N (9G –.267)																						
"	total	55	.212	.385	104	22	7	1	3	2.9	9	17	6	20	0	34	6	62	2	2	2	3.3	.970	OF-15, 1B-5
8 yrs.		888	.266	.408	2829	752	101	41	73	2.6	343	381	271	429	17	119	23	2780	126	46	179	3.7	.984	OF-579, 1B-211
WORLD SERIES																								
1957	NY A	5	.083	.083	12	1	0	0	0	0.0	0	1	0	4	0	1	0	24	1	0	2	6.3	1.000	1B-4

Joe Simpson

SIMPSON, JOE ALLEN
B. Dec. 31, 1951, Purcell, Okla.
BL TL 6′ 3″ 175 lbs.

Year	Team	Games	BA	SA	AB	H	2B	3B	HR	HR%	R	RBI	BB	SO	SB	Pinch Hit AB	Pinch Hit H	PO	A	E	DP	TC/G	FA	G by Pos
1975	LA N	9	.333	.333	6	2	0	0	0	0.0	3	0	0	2	0	1	0	5	0	0	0	0.8	1.000	OF-6
1976		23	.133	.167	30	4	1	0	0	0.0	2	0	1	6	0	0	0	24	0	0	0	1.2	1.000	OF-20
1977		29	.174	.174	23	4	0	0	0	0.0	2	1	2	6	1	0	0	24	2	1	1	0.9	.963	OF-28, 1B-1
1978		10	.400	.400	5	2	0	0	0	0.0	1	1	0	2	0	0	0	8	0	0	0	0.8	1.000	OF-10
1979	SEA A	120	.283	.347	265	75	11	0	2	0.8	29	27	11	21	6	9	2	162	10	6	4	1.6	.966	OF-105, DH-3
1980		129	.249	.332	365	91	15	3	3	0.8	42	34	28	43	17	11	1	220	12	7	3	2.0	.971	OF-119, 1B-3
1981		91	.222	.302	288	64	11	3	2	0.7	32	30	15	41	12	7	1	219	5	5	1	2.6	.978	OF-88
1982		105	.257	.351	296	76	14	4	2	0.7	39	23	22	48	8	7	3	177	7	3	0	1.9	.984	OF-97
1983	KC A	91	.168	.218	119	20	2	2	0	0.0	16	8	11	21	1	2	0	242	18	2	20	2.7	.992	1B-54, OF-38, DH-2, P-2
9 yrs.		607	.242	.317	1397	338	54	12	9	0.6	166	124	90	190	45	37	7	1081	54	24	29	2.0	.979	OF-511, 1B-58, DH-5, P-2

Duke Sims

SIMS, DUANE B.
B. June 5, 1941, Salt Lake City, Utah.
BL TR 6′ 2″ 197 lbs.

Year	Team	Games	BA	SA	AB	H	2B	3B	HR	HR%	R	RBI	BB	SO	SB	Pinch Hit AB	Pinch Hit H	PO	A	E	DP	TC/G	FA	G by Pos
1964	CLE A	2	.000	.000	6	0	0	0	0	0.0	0	0	0	2	0	1	0	13	0	0	0	13.0	1.000	C-1
1965		48	.178	.331	118	21	0	0	6	5.1	9	15	15	33	0	12	2	228	22	5	2	6.4	.980	C-40
1966		52	.263	.444	133	35	2	2	6	4.5	12	19	11	31	0	9	0	260	15	7	2	5.9	.975	C-48
1967		88	.202	.379	272	55	8	2	12	4.4	25	37	30	64	3	5	2	561	56	7	7	7.3	.989	C-85
1968		122	.249	.399	361	90	21	0	11	3.0	48	44	62	68	1	9	2	722	60	16	23	6.7	.980	C-84, 1B-31, OF-4
1969		114	.236	.426	326	77	8	0	18	5.5	40	45	66	80	1	13	1	639	52	6	8	6.6	.991	C-102, OF-3, 1B-1
1970		110	.264	.499	345	91	12	0	23	6.7	46	56	46	59	0	9	1	505	34	8	18	5.3	.985	C-39, OF-36, 1B-29
1971	LA N	90	.274	.400	230	63	7	2	6	2.6	23	25	30	39	0	18	2	345	33	3	5	5.1	.992	C-74
1972	2 teams	LA N (51G –.192) DET A (38G –.316)																						
"	total	89	.241	.357	249	60	11	0	6	2.4	18	30	36	41	0	12	3	395	27	6	5	5.6	.986	C-73, OF-4
1973	2 teams	DET A (80G –.242) NY A (4G –.333)																						
"	total	84	.245	.387	261	64	10	0	9	3.4	34	31	33	37	1	9	1	389	40	9	7	5.7	.979	C-69, OF-6, DH-2
1974	2 teams	NY A (5G –.133) TEX A (39G –.208)																						
"	total	44	.198	.281	121	24	1	0	3	2.5	8	8	9	29	0	7	3	149	21	5	4	4.7	.971	C-31, DH-5, OF-1
11 yrs.		843	.239	.401	2422	580	80	6	100	4.1	263	310	338	483	6	104	17	4206	360	72	81	6.0	.984	C-646, 1B-61, OF-54, DH-7
LEAGUE CHAMPIONSHIP SERIES																								
1972	DET A	4	.214	.500	14	3	2	1	0	0.0	0	0	1	2	0	0	0	3	0	1	0	1.0	.750	OF-2, C-2

Greg Sims

SIMS, GREGORY EMMETT
B. June 28, 1946, San Francisco, Calif.
BB TR 6′ 190 lbs.

Year	Team	Games	BA	SA	AB	H	2B	3B	HR	HR%	R	RBI	BB	SO	SB	Pinch Hit AB	Pinch Hit H	PO	A	E	DP	TC/G	FA	G by Pos
1966	HOU N	7	.167	.167	6	1	0	0	0	0.0	1	0	1	3	0	5	1	1	0	1	0	2.0	.500	OF-1

Matt Sinatro

SINATRO, MATTHEW STEPHEN
B. Mar. 22, 1960, Hartford, Conn.
BR TR 5′ 9″ 174 lbs.

Year	Team	Games	BA	SA	AB	H	2B	3B	HR	HR%	R	RBI	BB	SO	SB	Pinch Hit AB	Pinch Hit H	PO	A	E	DP	TC/G	FA	G by Pos
1981	ATL N	12	.281	.375	32	9	1	1	0	0.0	4	4	5	4	1	0	0	56	10	0	1	5.5	1.000	C-12
1982		37	.136	.198	81	11	2	0	1	1.2	10	4	4	9	0	0	0	112	25	0	1	3.9	1.000	C-35
1983		7	.167	.167	12	2	0	0	0	0.0	0	2	2	1	0	0	0	24	5	1	1	4.3	.967	C-7
1984		2	.000	.000	4	0	0	0	0	0.0	0	0	0	0	0	0	0	4	0	0	0	2.0	1.000	C-2
1987	OAK A	6	.000	.000	3	0	0	0	0	0.0	0	0	0	1	0	2	0	4	0	0	0	0.7	1.000	C-6
1988		10	.333	.556	9	3	2	0	0	0.0	1	5	0	1	0	0	0	21	2	0	1	2.6	1.000	C-9
1989	DET A	13	.120	.120	25	3	0	0	0	0.0	2	1	1	3	0	0	0	42	2	0	0	3.4	1.000	C-13
1990	SEA A	30	.300	.320	50	15	1	0	0	0.0	2	4	4	10	1	2	0	112	16	1	1	4.6	.992	C-28
1991		5	.250	.250	8	2	0	0	0	0.0	1	1	1	1	0	0	0	18	3	0	0	4.2	1.000	C-5
1992		18	.107	.107	28	3	0	0	0	0.0	0	0	0	5	0	0	0	43	4	0	1	2.6	1.000	C-18
10 yrs.		140	.190	.234	252	48	6	1	1	0.4	20	21	17	35	2	4	0	436	67	2	6	3.7	.996	C-135

Hosea Siner

SINER, HOSEA JOHN
B. Mar. 20, 1885, Shelburn, Ind. D. June 10, 1948, Sullivan, Ind.
BR TR 5′10½″ 185 lbs.

Year	Team	Games	BA	SA	AB	H	2B	3B	HR	HR%	R	RBI	BB	SO	SB	Pinch Hit AB	Pinch Hit H	PO	A	E	DP	TC/G	FA	G by Pos
1909	BOS N	10	.130	.130	23	3	0	0	0	0.0	1	1	2		0	2	0	10	10	2	1	3.1	.909	3B-5, SS-1, 2B-1

Duane Singleton

SINGLETON, DUANE EARL BL TR 6′ 1″ 170 lbs.
B. Aug. 6, 1972, Staten Island, N. Y.

Year	Team	Games	BA	SA	AB	H	2B	3B	HR	HR%	R	RBI	BB	SO	SB	Pinch Hit AB	Pinch Hit H	PO	A	E	DP	TC/G	FA	G by Pos
1994	**MIL A**	2	—	—	0	0	0	0	0	—	0	0	0	0	0	0	0	1	0	0	0	0.5	1.000	OF-2
1995		13	.065	.065	31	2	0	0	0	0.0	0	0	1	10	1	0	0	22	1	0	0	2.1	1.000	OF-11
2 yrs.		15	.065	.065	31	2	0	0	0	0.0	0	0	1	10	1	0	0	23	1	0	0	1.8	1.000	OF-13

Ken Singleton

SINGLETON, KENNETH WAYNE BB TR 6′ 4″ 210 lbs.
B. June 10, 1947, New York, N. Y.

Year	Team	Games	BA	SA	AB	H	2B	3B	HR	HR%	R	RBI	BB	SO	SB	Pinch Hit AB	Pinch Hit H	PO	A	E	DP	TC/G	FA	G by Pos
1970	**NY N**	69	.263	.379	198	52	8	0	5	2.5	22	26	30	48	1	18	4	90	1	3	0	1.8	.968	OF-51
1971		115	.245	.393	298	73	5	0	13	4.4	34	46	61	64	0	23	6	143	5	4	0	1.6	.974	OF-96
1972	**MON N**	142	.274	.410	507	139	23	2	14	2.8	77	50	70	99	5	5	1	236	9	7	3	1.8	.972	OF-137
1973		162	.302	.479	560	169	26	2	23	4.1	100	103	123	91	2	3	0	278	20	5	3	1.9	.983	OF-161
1974		148	.276	.376	511	141	20	2	9	1.8	68	74	93	84	5	5	1	224	7	11	0	1.7	.955	OF-143
1975	**BAL A**	155	.300	.454	586	176	37	4	15	2.6	88	55	118	82	3	1	0	283	9	3	2	1.9	.990	OF-155
1976		154	.278	.403	544	151	25	2	13	2.4	62	70	79	76	2	1	0	278	9	5	2	1.9	.983	OF-134, DH-19
1977		152	.328	.507	536	176	24	0	24	4.5	90	99	107	101	0	0	0	278	8	4	2	1.9	.986	OF-150, DH-1
1978		149	.293	.462	502	147	21	2	20	4.0	67	81	98	94	0	3	0	244	1	6	0	1.7	.976	OF-140, DH-5
1979		159	.295	.533	570	168	29	1	35	6.1	93	111	109	118	3	0	0	247	8	5	2	1.6	.981	OF-143, DH-16
1980		156	.304	.485	583	177	28	3	24	4.1	85	104	92	94	0	0	0	248	3	4	1	1.6	.984	OF-151, DH-5
1981		103	.278	.435	363	101	16	1	13	3.6	48	49	61	59	0	1	0	125	2	0	2	1.2	1.000	OF-72, DH-30
1982		156	.251	.381	561	141	27	2	14	2.5	71	77	86	93	0	4	1	10	0	0	0	0.1	1.000	DH-148, OF-5
1983		151	.276	.436	507	140	21	3	18	3.6	52	84	99	83	0	6	4	0	0	0	0	0.0	.000	DH-150
1984		111	.215	.289	363	78	7	1	6	1.7	28	36	37	60	0	17	2	0	0	0	0	0.0	.000	DH-103
15 yrs.		2082	.282	.436	7189	2029	317	25	246	3.4	985	1065	1263	1246	21	87	19	2684	82	57	17	1.4	.980	OF-1538, DH-477
LEAGUE CHAMPIONSHIP SERIES																								
1979	**BAL A**	4	.375	.500	16	6	2	0	0	0.0	4	2	1	2	0	0	0	5	1	0	0	1.5	1.000	OF-4
1983		4	.250	.417	12	3	2	0	0	0.0	0	1	2	2	0	0	0	0	0	0	0	0.0	.000	DH-4
2 yrs.		8	.321	.464	28	9	4	0	0	0.0	4	3	3	4	0	0	0	5	1	0	0	0.8	1.000	DH-4, OF-4
WORLD SERIES																								
1979	**BAL A**	7	.357	.393	28	10	1	0	0	0.0	1	2	2	5	0	0	0	9	0	0	0	1.3	1.000	OF-7
1983		2	.000	.000	1	0	0	0	0	0.0	0	1	1	1	0	1	0	0	0	0	0	0.0	—	
2 yrs.		9	.345	.379	29	10	1	0	0	0.0	1	3	3	6	0	1	0	9	0	0	0	1.3	1.000	OF-7

Fred Sington

SINGTON, FREDERIC WILLIAM BR TR 6′ 2″ 215 lbs.
B. Feb. 24, 1910, Birmingham, Ala.

Year	Team	Games	BA	SA	AB	H	2B	3B	HR	HR%	R	RBI	BB	SO	SB	Pinch Hit AB	Pinch Hit H	PO	A	E	DP	TC/G	FA	G by Pos
1934	**WAS A**	9	.286	.343	35	10	2	0	0	0.0	2	6	4	3	0	0	0	13	1	1	0	1.7	.933	OF-9
1935		20	.182	.182	22	4	0	0	0	0.0	1	3	5	1	0	11	2	7	1	1	0	2.3	.889	OF-4
1936		25	.319	.436	94	30	8	0	1	1.1	13	28	15	9	0	0	0	52	1	3	0	2.2	.946	OF-25
1937		78	.237	.377	228	54	15	4	3	1.3	27	36	37	33	1	14	0	120	4	5	0	2.0	.961	OF-64
1938	**BKN N**	17	.358	.623	53	19	6	1	2	3.8	10	5	13	5	1	0	0	29	0	0	0	1.7	1.000	OF-17
1939		32	.274	.369	84	23	5	0	1	1.2	13	7	15	15	0	6	2	44	1	1	1	2.1	.978	OF-22
6 yrs.		181	.271	.401	516	140	36	5	7	1.4	66	85	89	66	2	31	4	265	8	11	1	2.0	.961	OF-141

Dick Sipek

SIPEK, RICHARD FRANCIS BL TR 5′ 9″ 170 lbs.
B. Jan. 16, 1923, Chicago, Ill.

Year	Team	Games	BA	SA	AB	H	2B	3B	HR	HR%	R	RBI	BB	SO	SB	Pinch Hit AB	Pinch Hit H	PO	A	E	DP	TC/G	FA	G by Pos
1945	**CIN N**	82	.244	.308	156	38	6	2	0	0.0	14	13	9	15	0	45	10	68	2	2	0	2.3	.972	OF-31

John Sipin

SIPIN, JOHN WHITE BR TR 6′ 1½″ 175 lbs.
B. Aug. 29, 1946, Watsonville, Calif.

Year	Team	Games	BA	SA	AB	H	2B	3B	HR	HR%	R	RBI	BB	SO	SB	Pinch Hit AB	Pinch Hit H	PO	A	E	DP	TC/G	FA	G by Pos
1969	**SD N**	68	.223	.319	229	51	12	2	2	0.9	22	9	8	44	2	5	2	106	173	7	41	4.8	.976	2B-60

Dick Sisler

SISLER, RICHARD ALLAN BL TR 6′ 2″ 205 lbs.
Son of George Sisler. Brother of Dave Sisler.
B. Nov. 2, 1920, St. Louis, Mo.
Manager 1964–65.

Year	Team	Games	BA	SA	AB	H	2B	3B	HR	HR%	R	RBI	BB	SO	SB	Pinch Hit AB	Pinch Hit H	PO	A	E	DP	TC/G	FA	G by Pos
1946	**STL N**	83	.260	.362	235	61	11	2	3	1.3	17	42	14	28	0	13	4	334	31	6	31	5.6	.984	1B-37, OF-29
1947		46	.203	.257	74	15	2	1	0	0.0	4	9	3	8	0	30	4	84	6	2	3	6.1	.978	1B-10, OF-5
1948	**PHI N**	121	.274	.408	446	122	21	3	11	2.5	60	56	47	46	1	2	0	986	73	18	88	9.0	.983	1B-120
1949		121	.289	.415	412	119	19	6	7	1.7	42	50	25	38	0	23	6	815	40	11	93	9.0	.987	1B-96
1950		141	.296	.442	523	155	29	4	13	2.5	79	83	64	50	1	2	1	293	9	4	0	2.2	.987	OF-137
1951		125	.287	.414	428	123	20	5	8	1.9	46	52	40	39	1	11	4	233	8	8	3	2.2	.968	OF-111
1952	**2 teams**	**CIN N** (11G –.185) **STL N** (119G –.261)																						
″	**total**	130	.256	.404	445	114	15	6	13	2.9	51	64	32	40	3	6	1	1033	84	17	116	9.4	.985	1B-114, OF-7
1953	**STL N**	32	.256	.326	43	11	1	1	0	0.0	3	4	1	4	0	22	5	42	6	0	5	4.8	1.000	1B-10
8 yrs.		799	.276	.406	2606	720	118	28	55	2.1	302	360	226	253	6	109	25	3820	257	66	339	6.1	.984	1B-387, OF-289
WORLD SERIES																								
1946	**STL N**	2	.000	.000	2	0	0	0	0	0.0	0	0	0	0	0	2	0	0	0	0	0	0.0	—	
1950	**PHI N**	4	.059	.059	17	1	0	0	0	0.0	0	1	0	5	0	0	0	10	1	0	0	2.8	1.000	OF-4
2 yrs.		6	.053	.053	19	1	0	0	0	0.0	0	1	0	5	0	2	0	10	1	0	0	2.8	1.000	OF-4

George Sisler

SISLER, GEORGE HAROLD (Gorgeous George) BL TL 5′11″ 170 lbs.
Father of Dick Sisler. Father of Dave Sisler.
B. Mar. 24, 1893, Manchester, Ohio D. Mar. 26, 1973, Richmond Heights, Mo.
Manager 1924–26.
Hall of Fame 1939.

Year	Team	Games	BA	SA	AB	H	2B	3B	HR	HR%	R	RBI	BB	SO	SB	Pinch Hit AB	Pinch Hit H	PO	A	E	DP	TC/G	FA	G by Pos
1915	**STL A**	81	.285	.369	274	78	10	2	3	1.1	28	29	7	27	10	0	0	413	38	7	21	5.7	.985	1B-37, OF-29, P-15
1916		151	.305	.400	580	177	21	11	4	0.7	83	76	40	37	34	2	0	1523	97	24	87	11.2	.985	1B-139, OF-3, P-3, 3B-2
1917		135	.353	.453	539	190	30	9	2	0.4	60	52	30	19	37	0	0	1386	106	24	97	11.2	.984	1B-133, 2B-2
1918		114	.341	.440	452	154	21	9	2	0.4	69	41	40	17	**45**	0	0	1244	97	13	65	11.7	.990	1B-114, P-2
1919		132	.352	.530	511	180	31	15	10	2.0	96	83	27	20	28	1	1	1249	120	13	62	10.5	.991	1B-131
1920		154	**.407**	.632	**631**	**257**[1]	49	18	19	3.0	137	122	46	19	42	0	0	1477	140	16	87	10.5	.990	1B-154, P-1
1921		138	.371	.560	582	216	38	18	12	2.1	125	104	34	27	**35**	0	0	1267	108	10	86	10.0	.993	1B-138
1922		142	**.420**	.594	586	**246**	42	**18**	8	1.4	**134**	105	49	14	**51**	1	0	1293	125	17	116	10.2	.988	1B-141
1924		151	.305	.421	636	194	27	10	9	1.4	94	74	31	29	19	0	0	1319	111	23	114	9.6	.984	1B-151
1925		150	.345	.479	649	224	21	15	12	1.8	100	105	27	24	11	0	0	1330	133	26	120	9.9	.983	1B-150, P-1

George Sisler *continued*

Year	Team	Games	BA	SA	AB	H	2B	3B	HR	HR%	R	RBI	BB	SO	SB	Pinch Hit AB	Pinch Hit H	PO	A	E	DP	TC/G	FA	G by Pos
1926		150	.290	.398	613	178	21	12	7	1.1	78	71	30	30	12	0	0	1467	88	21	141	10.5	.987	1B-149, P-1
1927		149	.327	.430	614	201	32	8	5	0.8	87	97	24	15	**27**	0	0	1374	131	24	138	10.3	.984	1B-149
1928	**2 teams**	**WAS A** (20G –.245) **BOS N** (118G –.340)																						
″	**total**	138	.331	.419	540	179	27	4	4	0.7	72	70	31	17	11	10	3	1241	86	15	103	10.4	.989	1B-123, OF-5, P-1
1929	**BOS N**	154	.326	.424	629	205	40	8	2	0.3	67	79	33	17	6	0	0	1398	111	28	131	10.0	.982	1B-154
1930		116	.309	.397	431	133	15	7	3	0.7	54	67	23	15	7	8	2	915	81	13	103	9.4	.987	1B-107
15 yrs.		2055	.340	.468	8267	2812	425	164	102	1.2	1284	1175	472	327	375	22	6	18896	1572	274	1471	10.2	.987	1B-1970, OF-37, P-24, 2B-2, 3B-2

Sibby Sisti

SISTI, SEBASTIAN DANIEL BR TR 5′11″ 175 lbs.
B. July 26, 1920, Buffalo, N. Y.

Year	Team	Games	BA	SA	AB	H	2B	3B	HR	HR%	R	RBI	BB	SO	SB	Pinch Hit AB	Pinch Hit H	PO	A	E	DP	TC/G	FA	G by Pos
1939	**BOS N**	63	.228	.284	215	49	7	1	1	0.5	19	11	12	38	4	1	0	136	152	8	8	4.9	.973	2B-34, 3B-17, SS-10
1940		123	.251	.353	459	115	19	5	6	1.3	73	34	36	64	4	2	0	142	225	22	28	3.3	.943	3B-102, 2B-16
1941		140	.259	.320	541	140	24	3	1	0.2	72	45	38	76	7	1	0	169	291	44	29	3.6	.913	3B-137, SS-2, 2B-2
1942		129	.211	.287	407	86	11	4	4	1.0	50	35	45	55	5	2	0	306	351	20	66	5.4	.970	2B-124, OF-1
1946		1	—	—	0	0	0	0	0	—	0	0	0	0	0	0	0	0	0	0	0	0.0	.000	3B-1
1947		56	.281	.373	153	43	8	0	2	1.3	22	15	20	17	2	3	1	93	122	12	24	4.4	.947	SS-51, 2B-1
1948		83	.244	.290	221	54	6	2	0	0.0	30	21	31	34	0	2	1	140	173	14	32	4.7	.957	2B-44, SS-26
1949		101	.257	.358	268	69	12	0	5	1.9	39	22	34	42	1	6	3	156	80	7	11	2.8	.971	OF-48, 2B-21, SS-18, 3B-1
1950		69	.171	.276	105	18	3	1	2	1.9	21	11	16	19	1	7	3	72	69	9	11	2.6	.940	SS-23, 2B-19, 3B-13, OF-1, 1B-1
1951		114	.279	.362	362	101	20	2	2	0.6	46	38	32	50	4	4	2	239	230	18	47	5.7	.963	2B-52, SS-25, 3B-6, 1B-1, OF-1
1952		90	.212	.310	245	52	10	1	4	1.6	19	24	14	43	2	13	1	142	129	16	22	3.5	.944	2B-33, OF-23, SS-18, 3B-9
1953	**MIL N**	38	.217	.261	23	5	1	0	0	0.0	8	4	5	2	0	1	0	13	18	2	3	1.4	.939	2B-13, SS-6, 3B-4
1954		9	—	—	0	0	0	0	0	—	2	0	0	0	0	0	0	0	0	0	0	0.0	—	
13 yrs.		1016	.244	.324	2999	732	121	19	27	0.9	401	260	283	440	30	42	11	1608	1840	172	281	4.0	.952	2B-359, 3B-290, SS-179, OF-74, 1B-2
WORLD SERIES																								
1948	**BOS N**	2	.000	.000	1	0	0	0	0	0.0	0	0	0	0	0	1	0	0	0	0	0	0.0	.000	2B-2

Ed Sixsmith

SIXSMITH, EDWARD BR TR
B. Feb. 26, 1863, Philadelphia, Pa. D. Dec. 12, 1926, Philadelphia, Pa.

Year	Team	Games	BA	SA	AB	H	2B	3B	HR	HR%	R	RBI	BB	SO	SB	Pinch Hit AB	Pinch Hit H	PO	A	E	DP	TC/G	FA	G by Pos
1884	**PHI N**	1	.000	.000	2	0	0	0	0	0.0	0		0	0		0	0	1	0	0	0	1.0	1.000	C-1

Ted Sizemore

SIZEMORE, THEODORE CRAWFORD BR TR 5′10″ 165 lbs.
B. Apr. 15, 1945, Gadsden, Ala.

Year	Team	Games	BA	SA	AB	H	2B	3B	HR	HR%	R	RBI	BB	SO	SB	Pinch Hit AB	Pinch Hit H	PO	A	E	DP	TC/G	FA	G by Pos
1969	**LA N**	159	.271	.342	590	160	20	5	4	0.7	69	46	45	40	5	0	0	347	469	24	93	5.1	.971	2B-118, SS-46, OF-1
1970		96	.306	.350	340	104	10	1	1	0.3	40	34	34	19	5	3	2	209	239	9	50	4.7	.980	2B-86, OF-9, SS-2
1971	**STL N**	135	.264	.333	478	126	14	5	3	0.6	53	42	42	26	4	6	3	277	379	18	79	4.6	.973	2B-93, SS-39, OF-15, 3B-1
1972		120	.264	.335	439	116	17	4	2	0.5	53	38	37	36	8	13	1	222	342	14	68	5.2	.976	2B-111
1973		142	.282	.334	521	147	22	1	1	0.2	69	54	68	34	6	1	0	313	463	15	84	5.6	.981	2B-139, 3B-3
1974		129	.250	.296	504	126	17	0	2	0.4	68	47	70	37	8	2	0	336	412	16	109	5.9	.979	2B-128, SS-1, OF-1
1975		153	.240	.301	562	135	23	1	3	0.5	56	49	45	37	1	1	1	329	405	21	82	4.9	.972	2B-153
1976	**LA N**	84	.241	.278	266	64	8	1	0	0.0	18	18	15	22	2	13	5	178	191	7	51	4.9	.981	2B-71, 3B-3, C-2
1977	**PHI N**	152	.281	.355	519	146	20	3	4	0.8	64	47	52	40	8	1	0	348	427	11	104	5.2	.986	2B-152
1978		108	.219	.254	351	77	12	0	0	0.0	38	25	25	29	8	1	0	232	302	12	61	5.1	.978	2B-107
1979	**2 teams**	**CHI N** (98G –.248) **BOS A** (26G –.261)																						
″	**total**	124	.251	.330	418	105	24	0	3	0.7	48	30	36	30	4	3	0	285	397	16	92	5.6	.977	2B-122, C-2
1980	**BOS A**	9	.217	.261	23	5	1	0	0	0.0	1	0	0	0	0	1	0	16	22	3	7	5.1	.927	2B-8
12 yrs.		1411	.262	.321	5011	1311	188	21	23	0.5	577	430	469	350	59	45	12	3092	4048	166	880	5.2	.977	2B-1288, SS-88, OF-26, 3B-7, C-4
LEAGUE CHAMPIONSHIP SERIES																								
1977	**PHI N**	4	.231	.231	13	3	0	0	0	0.0	1	0	2	0	0	0	0	10	8	2	2	5.0	.900	2B-4
1978		4	.385	.538	13	5	0	1	0	0.0	3	1	1	0	0	0	0	7	8	0	4	3.8	1.000	2B-4
2 yrs.		8	.308	.385	26	8	0	1	0	0.0	4	1	3	0	0	0	0	17	16	2	6	4.4	.943	2B-8

Frank Skaff

SKAFF, FRANCIS MICHAEL BR TR 5′10″ 185 lbs.
B. Sept. 30, 1913, LaCrosse, Wis. D. Apr. 12, 1988, Towson, Md.
Manager 1966.

Year	Team	Games	BA	SA	AB	H	2B	3B	HR	HR%	R	RBI	BB	SO	SB	Pinch Hit AB	Pinch Hit H	PO	A	E	DP	TC/G	FA	G by Pos
1935	**BKN N**	6	.545	.818	11	6	1	1	0	0.0	4	3	0	2	0	3	1	4	2	1	0	2.3	.857	3B-3
1943	**PHI A**	32	.281	.391	64	18	2	1	1	1.6	8	8	6	11	0	7	1	116	20	4	12	6.4	.971	1B-18, 3B-3, SS-1
2 yrs.		38	.320	.453	75	24	3	2	1	1.3	12	11	6	13	0	10	2	120	22	5	12	5.9	.966	1B-18, 3B-6, SS-1

Dave Skaggs

SKAGGS, DAVID LINDSEY BR TR 6′ 2″ 200 lbs.
B. June 12, 1951, Santa Monica, Calif.

Year	Team	Games	BA	SA	AB	H	2B	3B	HR	HR%	R	RBI	BB	SO	SB	Pinch Hit AB	Pinch Hit H	PO	A	E	DP	TC/G	FA	G by Pos
1977	**BAL A**	80	.287	.352	216	62	9	1	1	0.5	22	24	20	34	0	0	0	344	34	2	4	4.8	.995	C-80
1978		36	.151	.186	86	13	1	1	0	0.0	6	2	9	14	0	1	0	149	17	2	2	4.8	.988	C-35
1979		63	.248	.328	137	34	8	0	1	0.7	9	14	13	14	0	0	0	222	24	4	1	4.0	.984	C-63
1980	**2 teams**	**BAL A** (2G –.200) **CAL A** (24G –.197)																						
″	**total**	26	.197	.239	71	14	0	0	1	1.4	7	9	9	14	0	0	0	94	6	3	3	4.0	.971	C-26
4 yrs.		205	.241	.302	510	123	18	2	3	0.6	44	49	51	76	0	1	0	809	81	11	10	4.4	.988	C-204
LEAGUE CHAMPIONSHIP SERIES																								
1979	**BAL A**	1	.000	.000	4	0	0	0	0	0.0	0	0	0	0	0	0	0	3	1	0	0	4.0	1.000	C-1
WORLD SERIES																								
1979	**BAL A**	1	.333	.333	3	1	0	0	0	0.0	1	0	0	0	0	0	0	2	2	0	0	4.0	1.000	C-1

Bud Sketchley

SKETCHLEY, HARRY CLEMENT BL TL 5′10½″ 180 lbs.
B. Mar. 30, 1919, Virden, Man., Canada D. Dec. 19, 1979, Los Angeles, Calif.

Year	Team	Games	BA	SA	AB	H	2B	3B	HR	HR%	R	RBI	BB	SO	SB	Pinch Hit AB	Pinch Hit H	PO	A	E	DP	TC/G	FA	G by Pos
1942	**CHI A**	13	.194	.222	36	7	1	0	0	0.0	1	3	7	4	0	1	0	19	1	1	0	1.8	.952	OF-12

Roe Skidmore

SKIDMORE, ROBERT ROE BR TR 6′ 3″ 188 lbs.
B. Oct. 30, 1945, Decatur, Ill.

Year	Team	Games	BA	SA	AB	H	2B	3B	HR	HR%	R	RBI	BB	SO	SB	Pinch Hit AB	Pinch Hit H	PO	A	E	DP	TC/G	FA	G by Pos
1970	CHI N	1	1.000	1.000	1	1	0	0	0	0.0	0	0	0	0	0	1	1	0	0	0	0	0.0	—	

Bill Skiff

SKIFF, WILLIAM FRANKLIN BR TR 5′10″ 170 lbs.
B. Oct. 16, 1895, New Rochelle, N. Y. D. Dec. 25, 1976, Bronxville, N. Y.

Year	Team	Games	BA	SA	AB	H	2B	3B	HR	HR%	R	RBI	BB	SO	SB	Pinch Hit AB	Pinch Hit H	PO	A	E	DP	TC/G	FA	G by Pos
1921	PIT N	16	.289	.333	45	13	2	0	0	0.0	7	11	0	4	1	2	1	46	8	1	1	4.2	.982	C-13
1926	NY A	6	.091	.091	11	1	0	0	0	0.0	0	0	0	1	0	0	0	8	1	0	1	1.5	1.000	C-6
2 yrs.		22	.250	.286	56	14	2	0	0	0.0	7	11	0	5	1	2	1	54	9	1	2	3.4	.984	C-19

Al Skinner

SKINNER, ALEXANDER
Deceased.

Year	Team	Games	BA	SA	AB	H	2B	3B	HR	HR%	R	RBI	BB	SO	SB	Pinch Hit AB	Pinch Hit H	PO	A	E	DP	TC/G	FA	G by Pos
1884	2 teams	BAL U (1G –.333) CHI U (1G –.333)																						
″	total	2	.333	.333	6	2	0	0	0	0.0	1		0			0	0	2	0	0	0	1.0	1.000	OF-2

Bob Skinner

SKINNER, ROBERT RALPH BL TR 6′ 4″ 190 lbs.
Father of Joel Skinner.
B. Oct. 3, 1931, La Jolla, Calif.
Manager 1968–69, 1977.

Year	Team	Games	BA	SA	AB	H	2B	3B	HR	HR%	R	RBI	BB	SO	SB	Pinch Hit AB	Pinch Hit H	PO	A	E	DP	TC/G	FA	G by Pos
1954	PIT N	132	.249	.370	470	117	15	9	8	1.7	67	46	47	59	4	11	6	1026	84	16	87	9.4	.986	1B-118, OF-2
1956		113	.202	.326	233	47	8	3	5	2.1	29	29	26	50	1	**54**	9	217	8	2	21	3.7	.991	OF-36, 1B-24, 3B-1
1957		126	.305	.468	387	118	12	6	13	3.4	58	45	38	50	10	27	8	232	17	8	9	2.5	.969	OF-93, 1B-9, 3B-1
1958		144	.321	.491	529	170	33	9	13	2.5	93	70	58	55	12	3	1	232	19	6	2	1.8	.977	OF-141
1959		143	.280	.399	547	153	18	4	13	2.4	78	61	67	65	10	1	0	285	9	11	1	2.1	.964	OF-142, 1B-1
1960		145	.273	.431	571	156	33	6	15	2.6	83	86	59	86	11	5	2	250	13	5	2	1.9	.981	OF-141
1961		119	.268	.360	381	102	20	3	3	0.8	61	42	51	49	3	18	4	175	5	5	1	1.9	.973	OF-97
1962		144	.302	.504	510	154	29	7	20	3.9	87	75	76	89	10	4	3	210	6	9	0	1.6	.960	OF-139
1963	2 teams	PIT N (34G –.270) CIN N (72G –.253)																						
″	total	106	.259	.380	316	82	15	7	3	0.9	43	25	34	64	5	22	6	131	4	1	1	1.6	.993	OF-83
1964	2 teams	CIN N (25G –.220) STL N (55G –.271)																						
″	total	80	.254	.367	177	45	8	0	4	2.3	16	21	15	32	0	37	8	62	4	5	0	1.7	.930	OF-43
1965	STL N	80	.309	.493	152	47	5	4	5	3.3	25	26	12	30	1	47	**15**	43	0	3	0	1.4	.935	OF-33
1966		49	.156	.244	45	7	1	0	1	2.2	2	5	2	17	0	45	7	0	0	0	0	0.0	—	
12 yrs.		1381	.277	.421	4318	1198	197	58	103	2.4	642	531	485	646	67	274	69	2863	169	71	124	2.8	.977	OF-950, 1B-152, 3B-2
WORLD SERIES																								
1960	PIT N	2	.200	.200	5	1	0	0	0	0.0	2	1	1	0	1	0	0	4	1	0	1	2.5	1.000	OF-2
1964	STL N	4	.667	1.000	3	2	1	0	0	0.0	0	1	1	0	0	3	2	0	0	0	0	0.0	—	
2 yrs.		6	.375	.500	8	3	1	0	0	0.0	2	2	2	0	1	3	2	4	1	0	1	2.5	1.000	OF-2

Camp Skinner

SKINNER, ELISHA HARRISON BL TR 5′11″ 165 lbs.
B. June 25, 1897, Douglasville, Ga. D. Aug. 4, 1944, Douglasville, Ga.

Year	Team	Games	BA	SA	AB	H	2B	3B	HR	HR%	R	RBI	BB	SO	SB	Pinch Hit AB	Pinch Hit H	PO	A	E	DP	TC/G	FA	G by Pos
1922	NY A	27	.182	.182	33	6	0	0	0	0.0	1	2	0	4	1	24	4	9	0	0	0	2.3	1.000	OF-4
1923	BOS A	7	.231	.385	13	3	2	0	0	0.0	1	1	0	0	0	5	2	0	0	0	0	0.0	.000	OF-2
2 yrs.		34	.196	.239	46	9	2	0	0	0.0	2	3	0	4	1	29	6	9	0	0	0	1.5	1.000	OF-6

Joel Skinner

SKINNER, JOEL PATRICK BR TR 6′ 4″ 195 lbs.
Son of Bob Skinner.
B. Feb. 21, 1961, La Jolla, Calif.

Year	Team	Games	BA	SA	AB	H	2B	3B	HR	HR%	R	RBI	BB	SO	SB	Pinch Hit AB	Pinch Hit H	PO	A	E	DP	TC/G	FA	G by Pos
1983	CHI A	6	.273	.273	11	3	0	0	0	0.0	2	1	0	1	0	0	0	20	4	1	1	4.2	.960	C-6
1984		43	.212	.237	80	17	2	0	0	0.0	4	3	7	19	1	0	0	171	11	2	1	4.3	.989	C-43
1985		22	.341	.545	44	15	4	1	1	2.3	9	5	5	13	0	2	0	94	8	3	0	5.0	.971	C-21
1986	2 teams	CHI A (60G –.201) NY A (54G –.259)																						
″	total	114	.232	.314	315	73	9	1	5	1.6	23	37	16	83	1	0	0	507	37	9	9	4.9	.984	C-114
1987	NY A	64	.137	.230	139	19	4	0	3	2.2	9	14	8	46	0	1	0	232	18	4	2	4.0	.984	C-64
1988		88	.227	.335	251	57	15	0	4	1.6	23	23	14	72	0	0	0	396	16	4	5	4.7	.990	C-85, OF-2, 1B-1
1989	CLE A	79	.230	.303	178	41	10	0	1	0.6	10	13	9	42	1	0	0	280	22	3	1	3.9	.990	C-79
1990		49	.252	.338	139	35	4	1	2	1.4	16	16	7	44	0	0	0	222	16	1	3	4.9	.996	C-49
1991		99	.243	.303	284	69	14	0	1	0.4	23	24	14	67	0	0	0	504	38	5	4	5.5	.991	C-99
9 yrs.		564	.228	.311	1441	329	62	3	17	1.2	119	136	80	387	3	3	0	2426	170	32	26	4.7	.988	C-560, OF-2, 1B-1

Lou Skizas

SKIZAS, LOUIS PETER (The Nervous Greek) BR TR 5′11″ 175 lbs.
B. June 2, 1932, Chicago, Ill.

Year	Team	Games	BA	SA	AB	H	2B	3B	HR	HR%	R	RBI	BB	SO	SB	Pinch Hit AB	Pinch Hit H	PO	A	E	DP	TC/G	FA	G by Pos
1956	2 teams	NY A (6G –.167) KC A (83G –.316)																						
″	total	89	.314	.479	303	95	11	3	11	3.6	39	40	15	19	3	15	3	148	9	4	0	2.2	.975	OF-74
1957	KC A	119	.245	.431	376	92	14	1	18	4.8	34	44	27	15	5	24	2	148	62	8	5	2.0	.963	OF-76, 3B-32
1958	DET A	23	.242	.394	33	8	2	0	1	3.0	4	2	5	1	0	13	2	4	7	3	0	1.6	.786	OF-5, 3B-4
1959	CHI A	8	.077	.077	13	1	0	0	0	0.0	3	0	3	2	0	2	0	6	1	0	0	1.2	1.000	OF-6
4 yrs.		239	.270	.443	725	196	27	4	30	4.1	80	86	50	37	8	54	7	306	79	15	5	2.0	.962	OF-161, 3B-36

Bill Skowron

SKOWRON, WILLIAM JOSEPH (Moose) BR TR 5′11″ 195 lbs.
B. Dec. 18, 1930, Chicago, Ill.

Year	Team	Games	BA	SA	AB	H	2B	3B	HR	HR%	R	RBI	BB	SO	SB	Pinch Hit AB	Pinch Hit H	PO	A	E	DP	TC/G	FA	G by Pos
1954	NY A	87	.340	.577	215	73	12	9	7	3.3	37	41	19	18	2	22	7	399	45	7	48	6.6	.984	1B-61, 3B-5, 2B-2
1955		108	.319	.524	288	92	17	3	12	4.2	46	61	21	32	1	35	6	520	40	7	63	7.4	.988	1B-74, 3B-3
1956		134	.308	.528	464	143	21	6	23	5.0	78	90	50	60	4	12	2	969	86	8	138	8.7	.992	1B-120, 3B-2
1957		122	.304	.470	457	139	15	5	17	3.7	54	88	31	60	3	9	3	1026	86	9	116	9.7	.992	1B-115
1958		126	.273	.424	465	127	22	3	14	3.0	61	73	28	69	1	7	3	1041	72	13	112	9.4	.988	1B-118, 3B-2
1959		74	.298	.539	282	84	13	5	15	5.3	39	59	20	47	1	3	1	626	43	6	68	9.4	.991	1B-72
1960		146	.309	.528	538	166	34	3	26	4.8	63	91	38	95	2	6	1	1202	115	12	130	9.4	.991	1B-142
1961		150	.267	.472	561	150	23	4	28	5.0	76	89	35	108	0	1	0	1228	102	10	146	9.0	.993	1B-149
1962		140	.270	.473	478	129	16	6	23	4.8	63	80	36	99	0	12	4	1054	77	10	101	8.5	.991	1B-135
1963	LA N	89	.203	.287	237	48	8	0	4	1.7	19	19	13	49	0	24	6	518	34	5	44	8.3	.991	1B-66, 3B-1
1964	2 teams	WAS A (73G –.271) CHI A (73G –.293)																						
″	total	146	.282	.428	535	151	21	3	17	3.2	47	79	30	92	0	13	3	1212	80	5	94	9.5	.996	1B-136
1965	CHI A	146	.274	.424	559	153	24	3	18	3.2	63	78	32	77	1	1	1	1297	74	8	116	9.5	.994	1B-145

Bill Skowron *continued*

Year	Team	Games	BA	SA	AB	H	2B	3B	HR	HR%	R	RBI	BB	SO	SB	Pinch Hit AB	Pinch Hit H	PO	A	E	DP	TC/G	FA	G by Pos
1966		120	.249	.359	337	84	15	2	6	1.8	27	29	26	45	1	23	3	722	60	7	75	8.1	.991	1B-98
1967	2 teams	CHI A (8G –.000) CAL A (62G –.220)																						
"	total	70	.206	.260	131	27	2	1	1	0.8	8	11	4	19	0	37	7	338	16	3	15	11.2	.992	1B-32
14 yrs.		1658	.282	.459	5547	1566	243	53	211	3.8	681	888	383	870	16	205	47	12152	930	110	1266	8.9	.992	1B-1463, 3B-13, 2B-2
WORLD SERIES																								
1955	NY A	5	.333	.750	12	4	2	0	1	8.3	2	3	0	1	0	2	0	22	3	1	1	8.7	.962	1B-3
1956		3	.100	.400	10	1	0	0	1	10.0	1	4	0	3	0	1	0	21	4	1	3	13.0	.962	1B-2
1957		2	.000	.000	4	0	0	0	0	0.0	0	0	0	0	0	1	0	5	2	0	1	3.5	1.000	1B-2
1958		7	.259	.481	27	7	0	0	2	7.4	3	7	1	4	0	0	0	55	4	0	4	8.4	1.000	1B-7
1960		7	.375	.625	32	12	2	0	2	6.3	7	6	0	6	0	0	0	70	6	0	9	10.9	1.000	1B-7
1961		5	.353	.529	17	6	0	0	1	5.9	3	5	3	4	0	0	0	46	5	0	1	10.2	1.000	1B-5
1962		6	.222	.333	18	4	0	1	0	0.0	1	1	1	5	0	0	0	52	1	0	3	8.8	1.000	1B-6
1963	LA N	4	.385	.615	13	5	0	0	1	7.7	2	3	1	3	0	0	0	30	4	0	1	8.5	1.000	1B-4
8 yrs.		39	.293	.519	133	39	4	1	8	6.0	19	29	6	26	0	4	0	301	29	2	23	9.2	.994	1B-36
									7th			**6th**		**6th**										

Bob Skube

SKUBE, ROBERT JACOB BL TL 6′ 182 lbs.
B. Oct. 8, 1957, Northridge, Calif.

Year	Team	Games	BA	SA	AB	H	2B	3B	HR	HR%	R	RBI	BB	SO	SB	Pinch Hit AB	Pinch Hit H	PO	A	E	DP	TC/G	FA	G by Pos
1982	MIL A	4	.667	.667	3	2	0	0	0	0.0	0	0	0	0	0	3	2	0	0	0	0	0.0		OF-1, DH-1
1983		12	.200	.320	25	5	1	1	0	0.0	2	9	4	7	0	2	0	22	0	0	0	2.0	1.000	OF-8, DH-2, 1B-1
2 yrs.		16	.250	.357	28	7	1	1	0	0.0	2	9	4	7	0	5	2	22	0	0	0	1.7	1.000	OF-9, DH-3, 1B-1

Gordon Slade

SLADE, GORDON LEIGH (Oskie) BR TR 5′10½″ 160 lbs.
B. Oct. 9, 1904, Salt Lake City, Utah D. Jan. 2, 1974, Long Beach, Calif.

Year	Team	Games	BA	SA	AB	H	2B	3B	HR	HR%	R	RBI	BB	SO	SB	Pinch Hit AB	Pinch Hit H	PO	A	E	DP	TC/G	FA	G by Pos
1930	BKN N	25	.216	.351	37	8	2	0	1	2.7	8	2	3	5	0	0	0	22	53	5	13	3.8	.938	SS-21
1931		85	.239	.313	272	65	13	2	1	0.4	27	29	23	28	2	0	0	174	276	26	54	5.7	.945	SS-82, 3B-2
1932		79	.240	.320	250	60	15	1	1	0.4	23	23	11	26	3	1	1	119	201	17	36	4.3	.950	SS-55, 3B-23
1933	STL N	39	.113	.129	62	7	1	0	0	0.0	6	3	6	7	1	3	0	34	61	6	11	3.2	.941	SS-31, 2B-1
1934	CIN N	138	.285	.369	555	158	19	8	4	0.7	61	52	25	34	6	1	0	302	443	28	83	5.7	.964	SS-97, 2B-39
1935		71	.281	.347	196	55	10	0	1	0.5	22	14	16	16	0	7	2	91	115	11	20	3.4	.949	SS-30, 2B-19, OF-8, 3B-7
6 yrs.		437	.257	.335	1372	353	60	11	8	0.6	147	123	84	116	12	12	3	742	1149	93	217	4.8	.953	SS-316, 2B-59, 3B-32, OF-8

Art Sladen

SLADEN, ARTHUR W.
B. Oct. 28, 1860, Lowell, Mass. D. Feb. 28, 1914, Dracut, Mass.

Year	Team	Games	BA	SA	AB	H	2B	3B	HR	HR%	R	RBI	BB	SO	SB	Pinch Hit AB	Pinch Hit H	PO	A	E	DP	TC/G	FA	G by Pos
1884	BOS U	2	.000	.000	7	0	0	0	0	0.0	0		0			0	0	1	0	0	0	0.5	1.000	OF-2

Jimmy Slagle

SLAGLE, JAMES FRANKLIN (Rabbit, Shorty, The Human Mosquito) BL TR 5′ 7″ 144 lbs.
B. July 11, 1873, Worthville, Pa. D. May 10, 1956, Chicago, Ill.

Year	Team	Games	BA	SA	AB	H	2B	3B	HR	HR%	R	RBI	BB	SO	SB	Pinch Hit AB	Pinch Hit H	PO	A	E	DP	TC/G	FA	G by Pos
1899	WAS N	147	.272	.324	599	163	15	8	0	0.0	92	41	55		22	1	0	407	20	21	8	3.1	.953	OF-146
1900	PHI N	141	.287	.347	574	165	16	9	0	0.0	115	45	60		34	0	0	320	22	29	5	2.6	.922	OF-141
1901	2 teams	PHI N (48G –.202) BOS N (66G –.271)																						
"	total	114	.242	.288	438	106	13	2	1	0.2	55	27	50		19	0	0	197	23	16	6	2.1	.932	OF-114
1902	CHI N	115	.315	.357	454	143	11	4	0	0.0	64	28	53		40	2	1	262	15	10	5	2.5	.965	OF-113
1903		139	.298	.357	543	162	20	6	0	0.0	104	44	81		33	0	0	292	16	21	8	2.4	.936	OF-139
1904		120	.260	.333	481	125	12	10	1	0.2	73	31	41		28	0	0	194	15	18	7	1.9	.921	OF-120
1905		155	.269	.317	568	153	19	4	0	0.0	96	37	97		27	0	0	306	27	13	6	2.2	.962	OF-155
1906		127	.239	.279	498	119	8	6	0	0.0	71	33	63		25	0	0	276	9	7	5	2.3	.976	OF-127
1907		136	.258	.294	489	126	6	6	0	0.0	71	32	76		28	0	0	239	15	10	5	2.0	.962	OF-135
1908		104	.222	.239	352	78	4	1	0	0.0	38	26	43		17	2	0	199	6	5	2	2.1	.976	OF-101
10 yrs.		1298	.268	.317	4996	1340	124	56	2	0.0	779	344	619		273	5	1	2692	168	150	57	2.3	.950	OF-1291
WORLD SERIES																								
1907	CHI N	5	.273	.273	22	6	0	0	0	0.0	3	4	2	5	6	0	0	13	0	1	0	2.8	.929	OF-5

Jack Slattery

SLATTERY, JOHN TERRENCE BR TR 6′ 2″ 191 lbs.
B. Jan. 6, 1878, South Boston, Mass. D. July 17, 1949, Boston, Mass.
Manager 1928.

Year	Team	Games	BA	SA	AB	H	2B	3B	HR	HR%	R	RBI	BB	SO	SB	Pinch Hit AB	Pinch Hit H	PO	A	E	DP	TC/G	FA	G by Pos
1901	BOS A	1	.333	.333	3	1	0	0	0	0.0	1	1	1		0	0	0	3	2	0	0	5.0	1.000	C-1
1903	2 teams	CLE A (4G –.000) CHI A (63G –.218)																						
"	total	67	.207	.239	222	46	3	2	0	0.0	9	20	2		2	4	0	270	52	12	6	5.3	.964	C-56, 1B-7
1906	STL N	3	.286	.286	7	2	0	0	0	0.0	0	0	1		0	1	0	12	1	0	0	6.5	1.000	C-2
1909	WAS A	32	.214	.250	56	12	2	0	0	0.0	4	6	2		1	15	4	93	11	5	3	6.1	.954	1B-11, C-7
4 yrs.		103	.212	.243	288	61	5	2	0	0.0	14	27	6		3	20	4	378	66	17	9	5.5	.963	C-66, 1B-18

Mike Slattery

SLATTERY, MICHAEL J. BL TL 6′ 2″ 210 lbs.
B. Nov. 26, 1866, Boston, Mass. D. Oct. 16, 1904, Boston, Mass.

Year	Team	Games	BA	SA	AB	H	2B	3B	HR	HR%	R	RBI	BB	SO	SB	Pinch Hit AB	Pinch Hit H	PO	A	E	DP	TC/G	FA	G by Pos
1884	BOS U	106	.208	.232	413	86	6	2	0	0.0	60		4			0	0	231	31	47	7	2.9	.848	OF-96, 1B-11
1888	NY N	103	.246	.315	391	96	12	6	1	0.3	50	35	13	28	26	0	0	187	16	18	3	2.1	.919	OF-103
1889		12	.292	.396	48	14	2	0	1	2.1	7	12	4	3	2	0	0	21	2	4	1	2.3	.852	OF-12
1890	NY P	97	.307	.445	411	126	20	11	5	1.2	80	67	27	25	18	0	0	175	5	19	1	2.1	.905	OF-97
1891	2 teams	CIN N (41G –.209) WAS AA (15G –.283)																						
"	total	56	.229	.280	218	50	4	2	1	0.5	32	21	14	15	7	0	0	115	5	10	2	2.3	.923	OF-56
5 yrs.		374	.251	.325	1481	372	44	21	8	0.5	229	135	62	71	53	0	0	729	59	98	14	2.4	.889	OF-364, 1B-11

Don Slaught

SLAUGHT, DONALD MARTIN (Sluggo) BR TR 6′ 1″ 190 lbs.
B. Sept. 11, 1958, Long Beach, Calif.

Year	Team	Games	BA	SA	AB	H	2B	3B	HR	HR%	R	RBI	BB	SO	SB	Pinch Hit AB	Pinch Hit H	PO	A	E	DP	TC/G	FA	G by Pos
1982	KC A	43	.278	.409	115	32	6	0	3	2.6	14	8	9	12	0	0	0	156	7	1	1	3.8	.994	C-43
1983		83	.312	.388	276	86	13	4	0	0.0	21	28	11	27	3	5	2	299	18	12	7	4.1	.964	C-79, DH-1
1984		124	.264	.379	409	108	27	4	4	1.0	48	42	20	55	0	5	2	547	44	11	8	4.9	.982	C-123, DH-1
1985	TEX A	102	.280	.423	343	96	17	4	8	2.3	34	35	20	41	5	1	0	550	33	6	4	5.8	.990	C-102
1986		95	.264	.449	314	83	17	1	13	4.1	39	46	16	59	3	3	3	533	40	4	1	6.2	.993	C-91, DH-2
1987		95	.224	.405	237	53	15	2	8	3.4	25	16	24	51	0	22	5	429	39	7	5	5.3	.985	C-85, DH-5
1988	NY A	97	.283	.450	322	91	25	1	9	2.8	33	43	24	54	1	6	2	496	24	11	4	5.6	.979	C-94, DH-1

Don Slaught *continued*

Year	Team	Lg	Games	BA	SA	AB	H	2B	3B	HR	HR%	R	RBI	BB	SO	SB	Pinch Hit AB	Pinch Hit H	PO	A	E	DP	TC/G	FA	G by Pos
1989			117	.251	.371	350	88	21	3	5	1.4	34	38	30	57	1	12	3	493	44	5	8	5.0	.991	C-105, DH-3
1990	PIT	N	84	.300	.457	230	69	18	3	4	1.7	27	29	27	27	0	16	5	345	36	8	4	5.0	.979	C-78
1991			77	.295	.395	220	65	17	1	1	0.5	19	29	21	32	1	13	2	338	31	5	4	5.3	.987	C-69, 3B-1
1992			87	.345	.482	255	88	17	3	4	1.6	26	37	17	23	2	14	4	365	35	5	4	5.1	.988	C-79
1993			116	.300	.440	377	113	19	2	10	2.7	34	55	29	56	2	13	6	539	51	4	10	5.7	.993	C-105
1994			76	.287	.342	240	69	7	0	2	0.8	21	21	34	31	0	2	0	425	36	3	4	6.3	.994	C-74
1995			35	.304	.357	112	34	6	0	0	0.0	13	13	9	8	0	4	2	220	9	1	2	7.0	.996	C-33
14 yrs.			1231	.283	.413	3800	1075	225	28	71	1.9	388	440	291	533	18	116	36	5735	447	83	66	5.3	.987	C-1160, DH-13, 3B-1
LEAGUE CHAMPIONSHIP SERIES																									
1984	KC	A	3	.364	.364	11	4	0	0	0	0.0	0	0	0	0	0	0	0	17	0	3	0	6.7	.850	C-3
1990	PIT	N	4	.091	.182	11	1	1	0	0	0.0	0	1	2	3	0	0	0	22	1	1	0	6.0	.958	C-4
1991			6	.235	.235	17	4	0	0	0	0.0	0	1	1	4	0	1	1	30	5	0	1	5.8	1.000	C-6
1992			5	.333	.667	12	4	1	0	1	8.3	5	5	6	3	0	1	0	17	1	0	0	3.6	1.000	C-5
4 yrs.			18	.255	.353	51	13	2	0	1	2.0	5	7	9	10	0	2	1	86	7	4	1	5.4	.959	C-18

Enos Slaughter

SLAUGHTER, ENOS BRADSHER (Country) BL TR 5′ 9½″ 180 lbs.
B. Apr. 27, 1916, Roxboro, N. C.
Hall of Fame 1985.

Year	Team	Lg	Games	BA	SA	AB	H	2B	3B	HR	HR%	R	RBI	BB	SO	SB	Pinch Hit AB	Pinch Hit H	PO	A	E	DP	TC/G	FA	G by Pos
1938	STL	N	112	.276	.438	395	109	20	10	8	2.0	59	58	32	38	1	20	2	189	7	6	0	2.2	.970	OF-92
1939			149	.320	.482	604	193	**52**	5	12	2.0	95	86	44	53	2	0	0	348	18	12	5	2.5	.968	OF-149
1940			140	.306	.504	516	158	25	13	17	3.3	96	73	50	35	8	7	2	267	8	3	5	2.1	.989	OF-132
1941			113	.311	.496	425	132	22	9	13	3.1	71	76	53	28	4	2	0	173	5	10	1	1.7	.947	OF-108
1942			152	.318	.494	591	**188**	31	**17**	13	2.2	100	98	88	30	9	1	0	287	15	4	2	2.0	.987	OF-151
1946			156	.300	.465	609	183	30	8	18	3.0	100	**130**	69	41	9	0	0	284	23	6	6	2.0	.981	OF-156
1947			147	.294	.452	551	162	31	13	10	1.8	100	86	59	27	4	4	0	306	15	6	5	2.3	.982	OF-142
1948			146	.321	.470	549	176	27	11	11	2.0	91	90	81	29	4	0	0	330	9	10	1	2.4	.971	OF-146
1949			151	.336	.511	568	191	34	**13**	13	2.3	92	96	79	37	3	1	0	330	10	6	1	2.3	.983	OF-150
1950			148	.290	.415	556	161	26	7	10	1.8	82	101	66	33	3	3	2	260	9	6	1	1.9	.978	OF-145
1951			123	.281	.391	409	115	17	8	4	1.0	48	64	68	25	7	11	2	198	10	1	3	2.0	.995	OF-106
1952			140	.300	.445	510	153	17	12	11	2.2	73	101	70	25	6	3	1	250	11	3	3	1.9	.989	OF-137
1953			143	.291	.433	492	143	34	9	6	1.2	64	89	80	28	4	7	2	235	2	1	0	1.7	.996	OF-137
1954	NY	A	69	.248	.336	125	31	4	2	1	0.8	19	19	28	8	0	31	11	37	0	1	0	1.3	.974	OF-30
1955	2 teams		NY A (10G –.111) KC A (108G –.322)																						
″	total		118	.315	.442	276	87	12	4	5	1.8	50	35	41	18	2	42	**16**	126	5	2	2	1.7	.985	OF-77
1956	2 teams		KC A (91G –.278) NY A (24G –.289)																						
″	total		115	.281	.392	306	86	18	5	2	0.7	52	27	34	26	2	45	11	133	2	2	0	1.8	.985	OF-76
1957	NY	A	96	.254	.368	209	53	7	1	5	2.4	24	34	40	19	0	33	8	97	2	0	0	1.5	1.000	OF-64
1958			77	.304	.435	138	42	4	1	4	2.9	21	19	21	16	2	**48**	13	43	1	2	0	1.3	.957	OF-35
1959	2 teams		NY A (74G –.172) MIL N (11G –.167)																						
″	total		85	.171	.342	117	20	2	0	6	5.1	10	22	16	22	1	48	7	32	0	1	0	1.0	.970	OF-32
19 yrs.			2380	.300	.453	7946	2383	413	148	169	2.1	1247	1304	1019	538	71	306	77	3925	152	82	35	2.0	.980	OF-2065
WORLD SERIES																									
1942	STL	N	5	.263	.474	19	5	1	0	1	5.3	3	2	3	2	0	0	0	9	1	1	0	2.2	.909	OF-5
1946			7	.320	.560	25	8	1	1	1	4.0	5	2	4	3	1	0	0	20	1	0	1	3.0	1.000	OF-7
1956	NY	A	6	.350	.500	20	7	0	0	1	5.0	6	4	4	0	0	0	0	8	1	0	0	1.5	1.000	OF-6
1957			5	.250	.333	12	3	1	0	0	0.0	2	0	3	2	0	0	0	7	0	0	0	1.4	1.000	OF-5
1958			4	.000	.000	3	0	0	0	0	0.0	1	0	1	1	0	3	0	0	0	0	0	0.0	—	
5 yrs.			27	.291	.468	79	23	3	1	3	3.8	17	8	15	8	1	3	0	44	3	1	1	2.1	.979	OF-23

Scottie Slayback

SLAYBACK, ELBERT BR TR 5′ 8″ 165 lbs.
B. Oct. 5, 1901, Paducah, Ky. D. Nov. 30, 1979, Cincinnati, Ohio.

Year	Team	Lg	Games	BA	SA	AB	H	2B	3B	HR	HR%	R	RBI	BB	SO	SB	Pinch Hit AB	Pinch Hit H	PO	A	E	DP	TC/G	FA	G by Pos
1926	NY	N	2	.000	.000	8	0	0	0	0	0.0	0	0	0	0	0	0	0	4	4	1	0	4.5	.889	2B-2

Bruce Sloan

SLOAN, BRUCE ADAMS (Fatso) BL TL 5′ 9″ 195 lbs.
B. Oct. 4, 1914, McAlester, Okla. D. Sept. 24, 1973, Oklahoma City, Okla.

Year	Team	Lg	Games	BA	SA	AB	H	2B	3B	HR	HR%	R	RBI	BB	SO	SB	Pinch Hit AB	Pinch Hit H	PO	A	E	DP	TC/G	FA	G by Pos
1944	NY	N	59	.269	.356	104	28	4	1	1	1.0	7	9	13	8	0	34	8	29	0	2	0	1.5	.935	OF-21

Tod Sloan

SLOAN, YALE YEASTMAN BL TR 6′ 175 lbs.
B. Dec. 24, 1890, Madisonville, Tenn. D. Sept. 12, 1956, Akron, Ohio.

Year	Team	Lg	Games	BA	SA	AB	H	2B	3B	HR	HR%	R	RBI	BB	SO	SB	Pinch Hit AB	Pinch Hit H	PO	A	E	DP	TC/G	FA	G by Pos
1913	STL	A	7	.269	.308	26	7	1	0	0	0.0	2	2	1	9	1	0	0	17	2	1	1	2.9	.950	OF-7
1917			109	.230	.281	313	72	6	2	2	0.6	32	25	28	34	8	27	5	120	10	5	4	1.8	.963	OF-77
1919			27	.238	.349	63	15	1	3	0	0.0	9	6	12	3	0	4	2	23	5	2	1	1.5	.933	OF-20
3 yrs.			143	.234	.294	402	94	8	5	2	0.5	43	33	41	46	9	31	7	160	17	8	6	1.8	.957	OF-104

Ron Slocum

SLOCUM, RONALD REECE BR TR 6′ 2″ 185 lbs.
B. July 2, 1945, Modesto, Calif.

Year	Team	Lg	Games	BA	SA	AB	H	2B	3B	HR	HR%	R	RBI	BB	SO	SB	Pinch Hit AB	Pinch Hit H	PO	A	E	DP	TC/G	FA	G by Pos
1969	SD	N	13	.292	.458	24	7	1	0	1	4.2	6	5	0	5	0	1	0	3	16	1	1	2.2	.950	2B-4, 3B-4, SS-1
1970			60	.141	.268	71	10	2	2	1	1.4	8	11	8	24	0	0	0	72	58	7	9	2.4	.949	C-19, SS-17, 3B-11, 2B-9
1971			7	.000	.000	18	0	0	0	0	0.0	1	0	0	8	0	0	0	7	12	2	0	3.5	.905	3B-6
3 yrs.			80	.150	.265	113	17	3	2	2	1.8	15	16	8	37	0	1	0	82	86	10	10	2.5	.944	3B-21, C-19, SS-18, 2B-13

Craig Smajstrla

SMAJSTRLA, CRAIG LEE (Smash) BB TR 5′ 9″ 165 lbs.
B. June 19, 1962, Houston, Tex.

Year	Team	Lg	Games	BA	SA	AB	H	2B	3B	HR	HR%	R	RBI	BB	SO	SB	Pinch Hit AB	Pinch Hit H	PO	A	E	DP	TC/G	FA	G by Pos
1988	HOU	N	8	.000	.000	3	0	0	0	0	0.0	2	0	0	1	0	2	0	1	0	0	0	0.5	1.000	2B-2

Charlie Small

SMALL, CHARLES ALBERT BL TR 5′11″ 186 lbs.
B. Oct. 24, 1905, Auburn, Me. D. Jan. 14, 1953, Auburn, Me.

Year	Team	Lg	Games	BA	SA	AB	H	2B	3B	HR	HR%	R	RBI	BB	SO	SB	Pinch Hit AB	Pinch Hit H	PO	A	E	DP	TC/G	FA	G by Pos
1930	BOS	A	25	.167	.222	18	3	1	0	0	0.0	1	0	2	5	1	17	3	1	0	0	0	1.0	1.000	OF-1

Hank Small

SMALL, GEORGE HENRY BR TR 6′ 3″ 205 lbs.
B. July 31, 1953, Atlanta, Ga.

Year	Team	Lg	Games	BA	SA	AB	H	2B	3B	HR	HR%	R	RBI	BB	SO	SB	Pinch Hit AB	Pinch Hit H	PO	A	E	DP	TC/G	FA	G by Pos
1978	ATL	N	1	.000	.000	4	0	0	0	0	0.0	0	0	0	0	0	0	0	12	1	0	1	13.0	1.000	1B-1

Jim Small

SMALL, JAMES ARTHUR BL TL 6′ 1½″ 180 lbs.
B. Mar. 8, 1937, Portland, Ore.

Year	Team	Games	BA	SA	AB	H	2B	3B	HR	HR%	R	RBI	BB	SO	SB	Pinch Hit AB	Pinch Hit H	PO	A	E	DP	TC/G	FA	G by Pos
1955	DET A	12	.000	.000	4	0	0	0	0	0.0	2	0	1	1	0	2	0	2	1	0	0	0.8	1.000	OF-4
1956		58	.319	.407	91	29	4	2	0	0.0	13	10	6	10	0	15	7	47	0	3	0	1.9	.940	OF-26
1957		36	.214	.262	42	9	2	0	0	0.0	7	0	2	11	0	13	2	15	0	0	0	1.1	1.000	OF-14
1958	KC A	2	.000	.000	4	0	0	0	0	0.0	0	0	1	0	0	1	0	2	0	0	0	2.0	1.000	OF-1
4 yrs.		108	.270	.340	141	38	6	2	0	0.0	22	10	10	22	0	31	9	66	1	3	0	1.6	.957	OF-45

Roy Smalley

SMALLEY, ROY FREDERICK, JR. BR TR 6′ 3″ 190 lbs.
Father of Roy Smalley.
B. June 9, 1926, Springfield, Mo.

Year	Team	Games	BA	SA	AB	H	2B	3B	HR	HR%	R	RBI	BB	SO	SB	Pinch Hit AB	Pinch Hit H	PO	A	E	DP	TC/G	FA	G by Pos
1948	CHI N	124	.216	.302	361	78	11	4	4	1.1	25	36	23	76	0	0	0	189	351	34	70	4.6	.941	SS-124
1949		135	.245	.382	477	117	21	10	8	1.7	57	35	36	77	2	3	1	265	438	39	91	5.6	.947	SS-132
1950		154	.230	.413	557	128	21	9	21	3.8	58	85	49	**114**	2	0	0	332	541	51	115	6.0	.945	SS-154
1951		79	.231	.395	238	55	7	4	8	3.4	24	31	25	53	0	4	2	117	190	15	42	4.4	.953	SS-74
1952		87	.222	.341	261	58	14	1	5	1.9	36	30	29	58	0	5	1	139	200	17	33	4.3	.952	SS-82
1953		82	.249	.356	253	63	9	0	6	2.4	20	25	28	57	0	5	1	153	191	25	39	4.8	.932	SS-77
1954	MIL N	25	.222	.306	36	8	0	0	1	2.8	5	7	4	9	0	8	2	36	26	1	11	3.5	.984	SS-9, 2B-7, 1B-2
1955	PHI N	92	.196	.327	260	51	11	1	7	2.7	33	39	39	58	0	3	1	138	206	9	32	4.0	.975	SS-87, 3B-1, 2B-1
1956		65	.226	.315	168	38	9	3	0	0.0	14	16	23	29	0	4	0	81	142	12	32	3.9	.949	SS-60
1957		28	.161	.323	31	5	0	1	1	3.2	5	1	1	9	0	6	0	11	21	2	5	1.7	.941	SS-20
1958		1	.000	.000	2	0	0	0	0	0.0	0	0	0	1	0	0	0	3	2	2	1	7.0	.714	SS-1
11 yrs.		872	.227	.360	2644	601	103	33	61	2.3	277	305	257	541	4	38	8	1464	2308	207	471	4.8	.948	SS-820, 2B-8, 1B-2, 3B-1

Roy Smalley

SMALLEY, ROY FREDERICK III BB TR 6′ 1″ 185 lbs.
Son of Roy Smalley.
B. Oct. 25, 1952, Los Angeles, Calif.

Year	Team	Games	BA	SA	AB	H	2B	3B	HR	HR%	R	RBI	BB	SO	SB	Pinch Hit AB	Pinch Hit H	PO	A	E	DP	TC/G	FA	G by Pos
1975	TEX A	78	.228	.296	250	57	8	0	3	1.2	22	33	30	42	4	2	1	108	232	20	44	4.6	.944	SS-59, 2B-19, C-1
1976	2 teams	TEX A (41G –.225) MIN A (103G –.271)																						
″	total	144	.259	.324	513	133	18	3	3	0.6	61	44	76	106	2	0	0	274	447	26	90	5.1	.965	SS-108, 2B-38
1977	MIN A	150	.231	.315	584	135	21	5	6	1.0	93	56	74	89	5	1	0	255	504	33	116	5.3	.958	SS-150
1978		158	.273	.433	586	160	31	3	19	3.2	80	77	85	70	2	1	1	287	527	25	121	5.3	.970	SS-157
1979		162	.271	.441	621	168	28	3	24	3.9	94	95	80	80	2	0	0	305	572	29	146	5.6	.968	SS-161, 1B-1
1980		133	.278	.405	486	135	24	1	12	2.5	64	63	65	63	3	4	1	226	448	17	103	5.3	.975	SS-125, 1B-3, DH-3
1981		56	.263	.443	167	44	7	1	7	4.2	24	22	31	24	0	5	1	62	89	8	14	3.0	.950	SS-37, DH-15, 1B-1
1982	2 teams	MIN A (4G –.154) NY A (142G –.257)																						
″	total	146	.255	.413	499	127	15	2	20	4.0	57	67	71	104	0	7	0	142	367	15	55	3.5	.971	SS-93, 3B-53, DH-4, 2B-1
1983	NY A	130	.275	.452	451	124	24	1	18	4.0	70	62	58	68	3	4	1	289	295	21	58	4.4	.965	SS-91, 3B-26, 1B-22
1984	2 teams	NY A (67G –.239) CHI A (47G –.170)																						
″	total	114	.212	.349	344	73	12	1	11	3.2	32	39	37	65	3	21	6	90	158	16	24	2.6	.939	3B-73, SS-16, DH-7, 1B-6
1985	MIN A	129	.258	.402	388	100	20	0	12	3.1	57	45	60	65	0	26	7	70	133	3	18	1.7	.985	DH-56, SS-49, 3B-14, 1B-1
1986		143	.246	.438	459	113	20	4	20	4.4	59	57	68	80	1	19	6	14	34	1	5	0.3	.980	DH-114, SS-19, 3B-8
1987		110	.275	.411	309	85	16	1	8	2.6	32	34	36	52	2	31	6	9	11	3	0	0.3	.870	DH-73, 3B-14, SS-4
13 yrs.		1653	.257	.395	5657	1454	244	25	163	2.9	745	694	771	908	27	121	30	2131	3817	217	794	3.8	.965	SS-1069, DH-272, 3B-188, 2B-58, 1B-34, C-1
WORLD SERIES																								
1987	MIN A	4	.500	1.000	2	1	1	0	0	0.0	0	0	2	0	0	2	1	0	0	0	0	0.0	—	

Will Smalley

SMALLEY, WILLIAM DARWIN BR TR
B. June 27, 1871, Oakland, Calif. D. Oct. 11, 1891, Bay City, Mich.

Year	Team	Games	BA	SA	AB	H	2B	3B	HR	HR%	R	RBI	BB	SO	SB	Pinch Hit AB	Pinch Hit H	PO	A	E	DP	TC/G	FA	G by Pos
1890	CLE N	136	.213	.239	502	107	11	1	0	0.0	62	42	60	44	10	0	0	221	327	64	27	4.5	.895	3B-136
1891	WAS AA	11	.158	.211	38	6	0	1	0	0.0	5	3	5	2	0	0	0	14	23	11	2	4.4	.771	3B-9, 2B-2
2 yrs.		147	.209	.237	540	113	11	2	0	0.0	67	45	65	46	10	0	0	235	350	75	29	4.5	.886	3B-145, 2B-2

Joe Smaza

SMAZA, JOSEPH PAUL BL TL 5′11″ 175 lbs.
B. July 7, 1923, Detroit, Mich. D. May 30, 1979, Royal Oak, Mich.

Year	Team	Games	BA	SA	AB	H	2B	3B	HR	HR%	R	RBI	BB	SO	SB	Pinch Hit AB	Pinch Hit H	PO	A	E	DP	TC/G	FA	G by Pos
1946	CHI A	2	.200	.200	5	1	0	0	0	0.0	2	0	0	0	0	0	0	0	0	0	0	0.0	.000	OF-1

Bill Smiley

SMILEY, WILLIAM B.
B. 1856, Baltimore, Md. D. July 11, 1884, Baltimore, Md.

Year	Team	Games	BA	SA	AB	H	2B	3B	HR	HR%	R	RBI	BB	SO	SB	Pinch Hit AB	Pinch Hit H	PO	A	E	DP	TC/G	FA	G by Pos
1882	2 teams	STL AA (59G –.212) BAL AA (16G –.148)																						
″	total	75	.199	.226	301	60	4	2	0	0.0	33		6			0	0	193	212	60	28	6.0	.871	2B-73, SS-2, OF-2

Al Smith

SMITH, ALPHONSE EUGENE (Fuzzy) BR TR 6′½″ 189 lbs.
B. Feb. 7, 1928, Kirkwood, Mo.

Year	Team	Games	BA	SA	AB	H	2B	3B	HR	HR%	R	RBI	BB	SO	SB	Pinch Hit AB	Pinch Hit H	PO	A	E	DP	TC/G	FA	G by Pos
1953	CLE A	47	.240	.360	150	36	9	0	3	2.0	28	14	20	25	2	2	1	67	2	6	0	1.8	.920	OF-39, 3B-2
1954		131	.281	.435	481	135	29	6	11	2.3	101	50	88	65	2	2	0	265	34	10	4	2.3	.968	OF-109, 3B-21, SS-4
1955		154	.306	.473	607	186	27	4	22	3.6	**123**	77	93	77	11	0	0	242	67	12	6	1.9	.963	OF-120, 3B-45, SS-5, 2B-1
1956		141	.274	.433	526	144	26	5	16	3.0	87	71	84	72	6	1	0	270	44	10	3	2.1	.969	OF-122, 3B-28, 2B-1
1957		135	.247	.377	507	125	23	5	11	2.2	78	49	79	70	12	1	0	195	159	26	17	2.8	.932	3B-84, OF-50
1958	CHI A	139	.252	.396	480	121	23	5	12	2.5	61	58	48	77	3	3	1	249	9	8	2	1.9	.970	OF-138, 3B-1
1959		129	.237	.396	472	112	16	4	17	3.6	65	55	46	74	7	1	0	303	8	6	2	2.5	.981	OF-128, 3B-1
1960		142	.315	.451	536	169	31	3	12	2.2	80	72	50	65	8	1	0	252	5	9	2	1.9	.966	OF-141
1961		147	.278	.506	532	148	29	4	28	5.3	88	93	56	67	4	5	2	181	164	15	12	2.4	.958	3B-80, OF-71
1962		142	.292	.462	511	149	23	8	16	3.1	62	82	57	60	3	4	2	123	191	20	8	2.3	.940	3B-105, OF-39
1963	BAL A	120	.272	.405	368	100	17	1	10	2.7	45	39	32	74	9	21	5	160	6	5	0	1.8	.971	OF-97
1964	2 teams	CLE A (61G –.162) BOS A (29G –.216)																						
″	total	90	.176	.310	187	33	5	1	6	3.2	25	16	21	42	0	30	4	84	16	3	1	1.5	.971	OF-56, 3B-12
12 yrs.		1517	.272	.429	5357	1458	258	46	164	3.1	843	676	674	768	67	71	15	2391	705	130	57	2.2	.960	OF-1110, 3B-379, SS-9, 2B-2
WORLD SERIES																								
1954	CLE A	4	.214	.429	14	3	0	0	1	7.1	2	2	2	2	0	0	0	4	0	0	0	1.0	1.000	OF-4
1959	CHI A	6	.250	.400	20	5	3	0	0	0.0	1	1	4	4	0	0	0	10	0	0	0	1.7	1.000	OF-6
2 yrs.		10	.235	.412	34	8	3	0	1	2.9	3	3	6	6	0	0	0	14	0	0	0	1.4	1.000	OF-10

Bernie Smith

SMITH, CALVIN BERNARD BR TR 5′ 9″ 164 lbs.
B. Sept. 4, 1941, Ponchatoula, La.

Year	Team	Games	BA	SA	AB	H	2B	3B	HR	HR%	R	RBI	BB	SO	SB	Pinch Hit AB	Pinch Hit H	PO	A	E	DP	TC/G	FA	G by Pos
1970	MIL A	44	.276	.382	76	21	3	1	1	1.3	8	6	11	12	1	17	5	46	0	1	0	1.2	.979	OF-39
1971		15	.139	.250	36	5	1	0	1	2.8	1	3	0	5	0	5	0	11	1	1	0	1.1	.923	OF-12
2 yrs.		59	.232	.339	112	26	4	1	2	1.8	9	9	11	17	1	22	5	57	1	2	0	1.2	.967	OF-51

Bill Smith

SMITH, WILLIAM E. 5′11″ 178 lbs.
B. Toronto, Ont., Canada D. Aug. 9, 1886, Toronto, Ont., Canada.

Year	Team	Games	BA	SA	AB	H	2B	3B	HR	HR%	R	RBI	BB	SO	SB	Pinch Hit AB	Pinch Hit H	PO	A	E	DP	TC/G	FA	G by Pos
1884	CLE N	1	.000	.000	3	0	0	0	0	0.0	0	0	0	2		0	0	0	0	0	0	0.0	.000	OF-1

Billy Smith

SMITH, BILLY EDWARD BB TR 6′ 2½″ 185 lbs.
B. July 14, 1953, Hodge, La.

Year	Team	Games	BA	SA	AB	H	2B	3B	HR	HR%	R	RBI	BB	SO	SB	Pinch Hit AB	Pinch Hit H	PO	A	E	DP	TC/G	FA	G by Pos
1975	CAL A	59	.203	.252	143	29	5	1	0	0.0	10	14	12	27	1	0	0	95	99	14	19	3.4	.933	SS-50, 1B-6, DH-4, 3B-2
1976		13	.375	.375	8	3	0	0	0	0.0	0	0	0	2	0	3	1	0	5	3	1	0.7	.625	SS-10, DH-1
1977	BAL A	109	.215	.300	367	79	12	2	5	1.4	44	29	33	71	3	4	1	268	278	7	80	4.9	.987	2B-104, SS-5, 1B-2, 3B-1
1978		85	.260	.384	250	65	12	2	5	2.0	29	30	27	40	3	3	0	147	210	5	43	4.3	.986	2B-83, SS-2
1979		68	.249	.434	189	47	9	4	6	3.2	18	33	15	33	1	3	0	108	151	7	35	3.9	.974	2B-63, SS-5
1981	SF N	36	.180	.230	61	11	0	0	1	1.6	6	5	9	16	0	12	4	32	50	2	11	2.9	.976	SS-21, 2B-5, 3B-3
6 yrs.		370	.230	.335	1018	234	38	9	17	1.7	107	111	96	189	8	25	6	650	793	38	189	4.0	.974	2B-255, SS-93, 1B-8, 3B-6, DH-5
LEAGUE CHAMPIONSHIP SERIES																								
1979	BAL A	1	.000	.000	4	0	0	0	0	0.0	0	0	0	1	0	0	0	1	2	0	2	3.0	1.000	2B-1
WORLD SERIES																								
1979	BAL A	4	.286	.286	7	2	0	0	0	0.0	1	0	2	0	0	1	1	4	3	0	1	3.5	1.000	2B-2

Bob Smith

SMITH, ROBERT ELDRIDGE BR TR 5′10″ 175 lbs.
B. Apr. 22, 1895, Rogersville, Tenn. D. July 19, 1987, Waycross, Ga.

Year	Team	Games	BA	SA	AB	H	2B	3B	HR	HR%	R	RBI	BB	SO	SB	Pinch Hit AB	Pinch Hit H	PO	A	E	DP	TC/G	FA	G by Pos
1923	BOS N	115	.251	.309	375	94	16	3	0	0.0	30	40	17	35	4	3	1	256	388	35	78	6.2	.948	SS-101, 2B-8
1924		106	.228	.297	347	79	12	3	2	0.6	32	38	15	26	5	2	0	198	313	23	59	5.2	.957	SS-80, 3B-23
1925		58	.282	.379	174	49	9	4	0	0.0	17	23	5	6	2	8	0	78	145	17	20	4.8	.929	SS-21, 2B-15, P-13, OF-1
1926		40	.298	.417	84	25	6	2	0	0.0	10	13	2	4	0	7	4	9	60	2	6	2.2	.972	P-33
1927		54	.248	.321	109	27	3	1	1	0.9	10	10	2	4	0	13	2	22	63	3	3	2.1	.966	P-41
1928		39	.250	.304	92	23	2	0	1	1.1	11	8	1	6	2	1	0	16	66	3	5	2.2	.965	P-38
1929		39	.172	.283	99	17	4	2	1	1.0	12	8	2	8	1	0	0	21	75	2	7	2.5	.980	P-34, SS-5
1930		39	.235	.259	81	19	2	0	0	0.0	7	4	0	5	0	1	0	16	47	1	3	1.7	.984	P-38
1931	CHI N	36	.218	.241	87	19	2	0	0	0.0	7	4	5	2	0	0	0	8	55	0	4	1.8	1.000	P-36
1932		36	.238	.381	42	10	4	1	0	0.0	5	4	0	2	1	0	0	8	36	0	4	1.2	1.000	P-34, 2B-2
1933	2 teams	CIN N (23G –.200) BOS N (14G –.200)																						
″	total	37	.200	.267	45	9	1	1	0	0.0	3	3	1	1	1	1	1	1	34	2	4	1.2	.946	P-30, SS-1
1934	BOS N	42	.250	.278	36	9	1	0	0	0.0	5	3	0	1	0	0	0	7	30	0	2	0.9	1.000	P-39
1935		47	.270	.270	63	17	0	0	0	0.0	3	4	1	5	0	1	1	10	39	1	1	1.1	.980	P-46
1936		35	.222	.267	45	10	2	0	0	0.0	1	4	0	4	0	0	0	8	34	0	2	1.2	1.000	P-35
1937		19	.200	.200	10	2	0	0	0	0.0	1	0	1	1	0	0	0	1	6	0	0	0.4	1.000	P-18
15 yrs.		742	.242	.309	1689	409	64	17	5	0.3	154	166	52	110	16	37	9	659	1391	89	198	3.1	.958	P-435, SS-208, 2B-25, 3B-23, OF-1
WORLD SERIES																								
1932	CHI N	1	—	—	0	0	0	0	0	—	0	0	0	0	0	0	0	0	0	0	0	0.0	.000	P-1

Bobby Gene Smith

SMITH, BOBBY GENE BR TR 5′11″ 180 lbs.
B. May 28, 1934, Hood River, Ore.

Year	Team	Games	BA	SA	AB	H	2B	3B	HR	HR%	R	RBI	BB	SO	SB	Pinch Hit AB	Pinch Hit H	PO	A	E	DP	TC/G	FA	G by Pos
1957	STL N	93	.211	.308	185	39	7	1	3	1.6	24	18	13	35	1	11	1	138	6	4	4	1.9	.973	OF-79
1958		28	.284	.386	88	25	3	0	2	2.3	8	5	2	18	1	1	0	57	2	0	0	2.2	1.000	OF-27
1959		43	.217	.317	60	13	1	1	1	1.7	11	7	1	9	0	7	2	31	3	1	1	1.1	.971	OF-32
1960	PHI N	98	.286	.382	217	62	5	2	4	1.8	24	27	10	28	2	35	11	126	5	0	1	1.8	1.000	OF-70, 3B-1
1961		79	.253	.328	174	44	7	0	2	1.1	16	18	15	32	0	31	6	91	8	3	1	2.2	.971	OF-47
1962	3 teams	NY N (8G –.136) CHI N (13G –.172) STL N (91G –.231)																						
″	total	112	.210	.287	181	38	9	1	1	0.6	17	16	12	22	1	18	2	86	5	0	1	1.0	1.000	OF-93
1965	CAL A	23	.228	.281	57	13	3	0	0	0.0	1	5	2	10	0	7	2	22	1	0	0	1.5	1.000	OF-15
7 yrs.		476	.243	.331	962	234	35	5	13	1.4	101	96	55	154	5	110	24	551	30	8	8	1.6	.986	OF-363, 3B-1

Brick Smith

SMITH, BRICK DUDLEY BR TR 6′ 4″ 225 lbs.
B. May 2, 1959, Charlotte, N. C.

Year	Team	Games	BA	SA	AB	H	2B	3B	HR	HR%	R	RBI	BB	SO	SB	Pinch Hit AB	Pinch Hit H	PO	A	E	DP	TC/G	FA	G by Pos
1987	SEA A	5	.125	.125	8	1	0	0	0	0.0	1	0	2	4	0	1	1	24	2	1	1	6.8	.963	1B-3, DH-1
1988		4	.100	.100	10	1	0	0	0	0.0	1	1	0	1	0	0	0	27	4	0	3	7.8	1.000	1B-4
2 yrs.		9	.111	.111	18	2	0	0	0	0.0	2	1	2	5	0	1	1	51	6	1	4	7.3	.983	1B-7, DH-1

Broadway Aleck Smith

SMITH, ALEXANDER BENJAMIN TR
B. 1871, New York, N. Y. D. July 9, 1919, New York, N. Y.

Year	Team	Games	BA	SA	AB	H	2B	3B	HR	HR%	R	RBI	BB	SO	SB	Pinch Hit AB	Pinch Hit H	PO	A	E	DP	TC/G	FA	G by Pos
1897	BKN N	66	.300	.376	237	71	13	1	1	0.4	36	39	4		12	0	0	188	54	20	10	3.9	.924	C-43, OF-18, 1B-6
1898		52	.261	.342	199	52	6	5	0	0.0	25	23	3		7	2	0	106	33	18	5	3.1	.885	OF-26, C-20, 2B-2, 3B-2, 1B-1
1899	2 teams	BKN N (17G –.180) BAL N (41G –.383)																						
″	total	58	.315	.403	181	57	6	5	0	0.0	23	31	6		7	1	0	166	40	13	4	3.9	.941	C-53, OF-2, 1B-1
1900	BKN N	7	.240	.240	25	6	0	0	0	0.0	2	3	1		2	0	0	9	10	3	0	3.1	.864	3B-6, C-1
1901	NY N	26	.141	.167	78	11	0	1	0	0.0	5	6	0		3	1	0	107	22	7	0	5.4	.949	C-25
1902	BAL A	41	.234	.255	145	34	3	0	0	0.0	10	21	8		5	0	0	135	34	7	5	4.2	.960	C-27, 1B-7, OF-4, 2B-3, 3B-1
1903	BOS A	11	.303	.333	33	10	1	0	0	0.0	4	4	0		0	1	0	44	11	4	1	5.9	.932	C-10
1904	CHI N	10	.207	.241	29	6	1	0	0	0.0	2	1	3		1	2	0	8	3	2	1	1.6	.846	OF-6, 3B-1, C-1
1906	NY N	16	.179	.179	28	5	0	0	0	0.0	0	2	1		1	4	1	41	7	0	4	4.0	1.000	C-8, 1B-3, OF-1
9 yrs.		287	.264	.324	955	252	30	12	1	0.1	107	130	26		38	11	1	804	214	74	30	3.9	.932	C-188, OF-57, 1B-18, 3B-10, 2B-5

Bull Smith

SMITH, LEWIS OSCAR BR TR 6′ 180 lbs.
B. Aug. 20, 1880, Plum, W. Va. D. May 1, 1928, Charleston, W. Va.

Year	Team	Games	BA	SA	AB	H	2B	3B	HR	HR%	R	RBI	BB	SO	SB	Pinch Hit AB	Pinch Hit H	PO	A	E	DP	TC/G	FA	G by Pos
1904	PIT N	13	.143	.190	42	6	0	1	0	0.0	2	0	1		0	0	0	22	2	4	0	2.2	.857	OF-13
1906	CHI N	1	.000	.000	1	0	0	0	0	0.0	0	0	0		0	1	0	0	0	0	0	0.0	—	
1911	WAS A	1	—	—	0	0	0	0	0	—	0	0	0		0	0	0	0	0	0	0	0.0	—	
3 yrs.		15	.140	.186	43	6	0	1	0	0.0	2	0	1		0	1	0	22	2	4	0	2.2	.857	OF-13

Carr Smith

SMITH, EMANUEL CARR BR TR 6′ 1″ 175 lbs.
B. Apr. 8, 1901, Kernersville, N. C. D. Apr. 14, 1989, Miami, Fla.

Year	Team	Games	BA	SA	AB	H	2B	3B	HR	HR%	R	RBI	BB	SO	SB	Pinch Hit AB	Pinch Hit H	PO	A	E	DP	TC/G	FA	G by Pos
1923	WAS A	5	.111	.222	9	1	1	0	0	0.0	0	1	0	0	0	1	0	4	0	0	0	1.0	1.000	OF-4
1924		5	.200	.200	10	2	0	0	0	0.0	1	0	0	3	0	1	0	3	0	0	0	0.8	1.000	OF-4
2 yrs.		10	.158	.211	19	3	1	0	0	0.0	1	1	0	3	0	2	0	7	0	0	0	0.9	1.000	OF-8

Charley Smith

SMITH, CHARLES WILLIAM BR TR 6′ 1″ 170 lbs.
B. Sept. 15, 1937, Charleston, S. C. D. Nov. 29, 1994, Reno, Nev.

Year	Team	Games	BA	SA	AB	H	2B	3B	HR	HR%	R	RBI	BB	SO	SB	Pinch Hit AB	Pinch Hit H	PO	A	E	DP	TC/G	FA	G by Pos
1960	LA N	18	.167	.217	60	10	1	1	0	0.0	2	5	1	15	0	0	0	14	27	2	2	2.4	.953	3B-18
1961	2 teams	LA N (9G –.250) PHI N (112G –.248)																						
″	total	121	.248	.375	435	108	14	4	11	2.5	47	50	24	82	3	5	1	107	233	28	28	3.2	.924	3B-98, SS-17
1962	CHI A	65	.207	.276	145	30	4	0	2	1.4	11	17	9	32	0	13	2	26	76	6	12	2.0	.944	3B-54
1963		4	.286	.571	7	2	0	1	0	0.0	0	1	0	2	0	3	1	3	5	0	4	8.0	1.000	SS-1
1964	2 teams	CHI A (2G –.143) NY N (127G –.239)																						
″	total	129	.238	.402	450	107	12	1	20	4.4	45	58	20	102	2	7	2	159	231	31	28	3.1	.926	3B-87, SS-36, OF-13
1965	NY N	135	.244	.393	499	122	20	3	16	3.2	49	62	17	123	2	3	0	123	288	18	29	3.1	.958	3B-131, SS-6, 2B-1
1966	STL N	116	.266	.396	391	104	13	4	10	2.6	34	43	22	81	0	8	3	89	216	11	27	2.9	.965	3B-107, SS-1
1967	NY A	135	.224	.336	425	95	15	3	9	2.1	38	38	32	110	0	20	6	92	283	21	22	3.4	.947	3B-115
1968		46	.229	.357	70	16	4	1	1	1.4	2	7	5	18	0	31	10	19	30	2	3	3.9	.961	3B-13
1969	CHI N	2	.000	.000	2	0	0	0	0	0.0	0	0	0	0	0	2	0	0	0	0	0	0.0	—	
10 yrs.		771	.239	.370	2484	594	83	18	69	2.8	228	281	130	565	7	92	25	632	1389	119	155	3.1	.944	3B-623, SS-61, OF-13, 2B-1

Chris Smith

SMITH, CHRISTOPHER WILLIAM BB TR 6′ 185 lbs.
B. July 18, 1957, Torrance, Calif.

Year	Team	Games	BA	SA	AB	H	2B	3B	HR	HR%	R	RBI	BB	SO	SB	Pinch Hit AB	Pinch Hit H	PO	A	E	DP	TC/G	FA	G by Pos
1981	MON N	7	.000	.000	7	0	0	0	0	0.0	0	0	0	2	0	7	0	0	1	0	0	1.0	1.000	2B-1
1982		2	.000	.000	2	0	0	0	0	0.0	0	0	0	1	0	2	0	0	0	0	0	0.0	—	
1983	SF N	22	.328	.493	67	22	6	1	1	1.5	13	11	7	12	0	3	3	118	8	3	6	6.4	.977	1B-15, OF-4, 3B-1
3 yrs.		31	.289	.434	76	22	6	1	1	1.3	13	11	7	15	0	12	3	118	9	3	6	6.2	.977	1B-15, OF-4, 3B-1, 2B-1

Dick Smith

SMITH, RICHARD ARTHUR BR TR 6′ 2″ 205 lbs.
B. May 17, 1939, Lebanon, Ore.

Year	Team	Games	BA	SA	AB	H	2B	3B	HR	HR%	R	RBI	BB	SO	SB	Pinch Hit AB	Pinch Hit H	PO	A	E	DP	TC/G	FA	G by Pos
1963	NY N	20	.238	.286	42	10	0	1	0	0.0	4	3	5	10	3	5	1	26	0	0	0	2.2	1.000	OF-10, 1B-2
1964		46	.223	.309	94	21	6	1	0	0.0	14	3	1	29	6	8	1	151	11	2	11	5.3	.988	1B-18, OF-13
1965	LA N	10	.000	.000	6	0	0	0	0	0.0	0	1	0	3	0	0	0	1	0	0	0	0.1	1.000	OF-9
3 yrs.		76	.218	.289	142	31	6	2	0	0.0	18	7	6	42	9	13	2	178	11	2	11	3.7	.990	OF-32, 1B-20

Dick Smith

SMITH, RICHARD HARRISON BR TR 5′ 8″ 160 lbs.
B. July 21, 1927, Blandburg, Pa.

Year	Team	Games	BA	SA	AB	H	2B	3B	HR	HR%	R	RBI	BB	SO	SB	Pinch Hit AB	Pinch Hit H	PO	A	E	DP	TC/G	FA	G by Pos
1951	PIT N	12	.174	.174	46	8	0	0	0	0.0	2	4	8	8	0	0	0	14	30	3	6	3.9	.936	3B-12
1952		29	.106	.121	66	7	1	0	0	0.0	8	5	9	3	0	2	0	24	50	3	8	3.2	.961	3B-16, SS-4, 2B-4
1953		13	.163	.209	43	7	0	1	0	0.0	4	2	6	6	0	0	0	18	56	3	10	5.9	.961	SS-13
1954		12	.097	.194	31	3	1	1	0	0.0	2	0	6	5	0	3	0	7	21	2	3	3.3	.933	3B-9
1955		4	—	—	0	0	0	0	0	—	1	0	1	0	0	0	0	0	0	0	0	0.0	.000	SS-1
5 yrs.		70	.134	.167	186	25	2	2	0	0.0	17	11	30	22	0	5	0	63	157	11	27	3.9	.952	3B-37, SS-18, 2B-4

Dick Smith

SMITH, RICHARD KELLY BR TR 6′ 5″ 200 lbs.
B. Aug. 25, 1944, Lincolnton, N. C.

Year	Team	Games	BA	SA	AB	H	2B	3B	HR	HR%	R	RBI	BB	SO	SB	Pinch Hit AB	Pinch Hit H	PO	A	E	DP	TC/G	FA	G by Pos
1969	WAS A	21	.107	.107	28	3	0	0	0	0.0	2	0	4	7	0	8	0	10	0	1	0	1.2	.909	OF-9

Dwight Smith

SMITH, JOHN DWIGHT BL TR 5′11″ 175 lbs.
B. Nov. 8, 1963, Tallahassee, Fla.

Year	Team	Games	BA	SA	AB	H	2B	3B	HR	HR%	R	RBI	BB	SO	SB	Pinch Hit AB	Pinch Hit H	PO	A	E	DP	TC/G	FA	G by Pos
1989	CHI N	109	.324	.493	343	111	19	6	9	2.6	52	52	31	51	9	15	8	188	7	5	3	2.0	.975	OF-102
1990		117	.262	.376	290	76	15	0	6	2.1	34	27	28	46	11	34	8	139	4	2	2	1.8	.986	OF-81
1991		90	.228	.347	167	38	7	2	3	1.8	16	21	11	32	2	45	11	73	3	3	1	1.9	.962	OF-42
1992		109	.276	.392	217	60	10	3	3	1.4	28	24	13	40	9	49	14	93	2	2	0	1.5	.979	OF-63
1993		111	.300	.494	310	93	17	5	11	3.5	51	35	25	51	8	24	9	163	5	8	2	2.0	.955	OF-89
1994	2 teams	CAL A (45G –.262) BAL A (28G –.311)																						
″	total	73	.281	.459	196	55	7	2	8	4.1	31	30	12	37	2	19	5	81	2	7	1	1.6	.922	OF-53, DH-5
1995	ATL N	103	.252	.412	131	33	8	2	3	2.3	16	21	13	35	0	69	16	24	0	2	0	1.0	.923	OF-25
7 yrs.		712	.282	.434	1654	466	83	20	43	2.6	228	210	133	292	41	255	71	761	23	29	9	1.8	.964	OF-455, DH-5
DIVISIONAL PLAYOFF SERIES																								
1995	ATL N	4	.667	1.000	3	2	1	0	0	0.0	0	1	0	0	0	3	2	0	0	0	0	0.0	—	
LEAGUE CHAMPIONSHIP SERIES																								
1989	CHI N	4	.200	.267	15	3	1	0	0	0.0	2	0	2	2	1	0	0	10	0	0	0	2.5	1.000	OF-4
1995	ATL N	2	.000	.000	2	0	0	0	0	0.0	0	0	0	0	0	2	0	0	0	0	0	0.0	—	
2 yrs.		6	.176	.235	17	3	1	0	0	0.0	2	0	2	2	1	2	0	10	0	0	0	2.5	1.000	OF-4
WORLD SERIES																								
1995	ATL N	3	.500	.500	2	1	0	0	0	0.0	0	0	1	0	0	2	1	0	0	0	0	0.0	—	

Earl Smith

SMITH, EARL CALVIN BR TR 6′ 185 lbs.
B. Mar. 14, 1928, Sunnyside, Wash.

Year	Team	Games	BA	SA	AB	H	2B	3B	HR	HR%	R	RBI	BB	SO	SB	Pinch Hit AB	Pinch Hit H	PO	A	E	DP	TC/G	FA	G by Pos
1955	PIT N	5	.063	.063	16	1	0	0	0	0.0	1	0	4	2	0	0	0	11	0	0	0	2.2	1.000	OF-5

Earl Smith

SMITH, EARL LEONARD BB TR 5′11″ 170 lbs.
B. Jan. 20, 1891, Oak Hill, Ohio D. Mar. 14, 1943, Portsmouth, Ohio.

Year	Team	Games	BA	SA	AB	H	2B	3B	HR	HR%	R	RBI	BB	SO	SB	Pinch Hit AB	Pinch Hit H	PO	A	E	DP	TC/G	FA	G by Pos
1916	CHI N	14	.259	.370	27	7	1	1	0	0.0	2	4	2	5	1	7	1	4	0	1	0	0.7	.800	OF-7
1917	STL A	52	.281	.387	199	56	7	7	0	0.0	31	10	15	21	5	1	1	114	12	3	5	2.5	.977	OF-51
1918		89	.269	.339	286	77	10	5	0	0.0	28	32	13	16	13	8	4	164	14	9	4	2.3	.952	OF-81
1919		88	.250	.349	252	63	12	5	1	0.4	21	36	18	27	1	14	5	155	13	5	4	2.5	.971	OF-68
1920		103	.306	.436	353	108	21	8	3	0.8	45	55	13	18	11	16	2	107	150	23	3	3.3	.918	3B-70, OF-15

Earl Smith *continued*

Year	Team	Games	BA	SA	AB	H	2B	3B	HR	HR%	R	RBI	BB	SO	SB	Pinch Hit AB	Pinch Hit H	PO	A	E	DP	TC/G	FA	G by Pos
1921	2 teams	STL A (25G –.333) WAS A (59G –.217)																						
″	total	84	.252	.364	258	65	9	4	4	1.6	27	26	13	23	1	20	6	113	34	13	2	2.6	.919	OF-47, 3B-14
1922	WAS A	65	.259	.351	205	53	12	2	1	0.5	22	23	8	17	4	10	2	92	16	9	3	2.3	.923	OF-49, 3B-1
7 yrs.		495	.272	.375	1580	429	72	32	9	0.6	176	186	82	127	36	76	21	749	239	63	21	2.6	.940	OF-318, 3B-85

Earl Smith

SMITH, EARL SUTTON (Oil) BL TR 5′10½″ 180 lbs.
B. Feb. 14, 1897, Hot Springs, Ark. D. June 8, 1963, Little Rock, Ark.

Year	Team	Games	BA	SA	AB	H	2B	3B	HR	HR%	R	RBI	BB	SO	SB	Pinch Hit AB	Pinch Hit H	PO	A	E	DP	TC/G	FA	G by Pos
1919	NY N	21	.250	.361	36	9	2	1	0	0.0	5	8	3	3	1	6	0	26	10	1	0	2.5	.973	C-14, 2B-1
1920		91	.294	.340	262	77	7	1	1	0.4	20	30	18	16	5	8	4	252	73	8	12	4.1	.976	C-82
1921		89	.336	.537	229	77	8	4	10	4.4	35	51	27	8	4	8	3	195	56	9	4	3.3	.965	C-78
1922		90	.278	.474	234	65	11	4	9	3.8	29	39	37	12	1	12	3	214	56	6	3	3.7	.978	C-75
1923	2 teams	NY N (24G –.206) BOS N (72G –.288)																						
″	total	96	.276	.418	225	62	16	2	4	1.8	24	23	26	11	0	**35**	6	173	58	6	9	5.2	.975	C-46
1924	2 teams	BOS N (33G –.271) PIT N (39G –.369)																						
″	total	72	.335	.494	170	57	13	1	4	2.4	13	29	19	7	2	21	**10**	167	36	7	4	4.4	.967	C-48
1925	PIT N	109	.313	.471	329	103	22	3	8	2.4	34	64	31	13	4	12	5	317	77	13	15	4.2	.968	C-96
1926		105	.346	.438	292	101	17	2	2	0.7	29	46	28	7	1	7	5	307	63	14	10	3.9	.964	C-98
1927		66	.270	.376	189	51	3	1	5	2.6	16	25	21	11	0	5	3	187	32	3	2	3.6	.986	C-61
1928	2 teams	PIT N (32G –.247) STL N (24G –.224)																						
″	total	56	.238	.336	143	34	8	0	2	1.4	11	18	16	11	0	8	0	130	17	3	4	3.3	.980	C-46
1929	STL N	57	.345	.421	145	50	8	0	1	0.7	9	22	18	6	0	7	2	131	21	6	1	3.2	.962	C-50
1930		8	.000	.000	10	0	0	0	0	0.0	0	0	3	1	0	0	0	18	3	2	0	3.8	.913	C-6
12 yrs.		860	.303	.432	2264	686	115	19	46	2.0	225	355	247	106	18	129	41	2117	502	78	64	3.8	.971	C-700, 2B-1
WORLD SERIES																								
1921	NY N	3	.000	.000	7	0	0	0	0	0.0	0	0	1	0	0	1	0	7	2	1	1	5.0	.900	C-2
1922		4	.143	.143	7	1	0	0	0	0.0	0	0	0	2	0	3	0	2	1	0	0	3.0	1.000	C-1
1925	PIT N	6	.350	.400	20	7	1	0	0	0.0	0	0	1	2	0	0	0	28	7	1	1	6.0	.972	C-6
1927		3	.000	.000	8	0	0	0	0	0.0	0	0	0	0	0	1	0	10	1	1	0	6.0	.917	C-2
1928	STL N	1	.750	.750	4	3	0	0	0	0.0	0	0	0	0	0	0	0	3	1	0	0	4.0	1.000	C-1
5 yrs.		17	.239	.261	46	11	1	0	0	0.0	0	0	2	4	0	5	0	50	12	3	2	5.4	.954	C-12

Edgar Smith

SMITH, ALBERT EDGAR TR 6′ 200 lbs.
B. Oct. 15, 1860, North Haven, Conn. Deceased.

Year	Team	Games	BA	SA	AB	H	2B	3B	HR	HR%	R	RBI	BB	SO	SB	Pinch Hit AB	Pinch Hit H	PO	A	E	DP	TC/G	FA	G by Pos
1883	BOS N	30	.217	.313	115	25	5	3	0	0.0	10	16	5	11		0	0	56	3	6	3	2.1	.908	OF-30, C-1

Edgar Smith

SMITH, EDGAR EUGENE BR TR 5′10″ 160 lbs.
B. June 12, 1862, Providence, R. I. D. Nov. 3, 1892, Providence, R. I.

Year	Team	Games	BA	SA	AB	H	2B	3B	HR	HR%	R	RBI	BB	SO	SB	Pinch Hit AB	Pinch Hit H	PO	A	E	DP	TC/G	FA	G by Pos
1883	2 teams	PRO N (2G –.222) PHI N (1G –.750)																						
″	total	3	.385	.462	13	5	1	0	0	0.0	3		0	2		0	0	3	0	1	0	0.7	.750	OF-3, 1B-2, P-1
1884	WAS AA	14	.088	.123	57	5	0	1	0	0.0	5		1			0	0	19	14	9	4	2.8	.786	OF-12, P-3
1885	PRO N	1	.250	.250	4	1	0	0	0	0.0	0	0	0	0		0	0	0	3	1	0	4.0	.750	P-1
1890	CLE N	8	.292	.375	24	7	0	1	0	0.0	2	4	4	1	0	0	0	3	14	2	1	2.4	.895	P-6, OF-2
4 yrs.		26	.184	.235	98	18	1	2	0	0.0	10	4	5	3	0	0	0	25	31	13	5	2.3	.812	OF-17, P-11, 1B-2

Elmer Smith

SMITH, ELMER ELLSWORTH BL TL 5′11″ 178 lbs.
B. Mar. 23, 1868, Pittsburgh, Pa. D. Nov. 3, 1945, Pittsburgh, Pa.

Year	Team	Games	BA	SA	AB	H	2B	3B	HR	HR%	R	RBI	BB	SO	SB	Pinch Hit AB	Pinch Hit H	PO	A	E	DP	TC/G	FA	G by Pos
1886	CIN AA	9	.286	.393	28	8	1	1	0	0.0	6		9			0	0	1	3	2	0	0.6	.667	P-9, OF-1
1887		52	.253	.371	186	47	10	6	0	0.0	26		11		5	0	0	9	67	13	2	1.6	.854	P-52, OF-2
1888		40	.225	.271	129	29	4	1	0	0.0	15	9	20		2	0	0	4	58	12	0	1.8	.838	P-40, OF-2
1889		29	.277	.410	83	23	3	1	2	2.4	12	17	7	18	1	0	0	2	21	5	0	1.0	.821	P-29
1892	PIT N	138	.274	.384	511	140	16	14	4	0.8	86	63	82	43	22	0	0	232	38	37	0	2.2	.879	OF-124, P-17
1893		128	.346	.525	518	179	26	23	7	1.4	121	103	77	23	26	0	0	271	20	25	7	2.5	.921	OF-128
1894		125	.356	.538	489	174	33	19	6	1.2	128	72	65	12	33	0	0	275	18	21	8	2.5	.933	OF-125, P-1
1895		124	.302	.388	480	145	14	12	1	0.2	88	81	55	25	34	1	0	250	16	31	2	2.4	.896	OF-123
1896		122	.362	.500	484	175	21	14	6	1.2	121	94	74	18	33	0	0	302	14	18	6	2.7	.946	OF-122
1897		123	.310	.463	467	145	19	17	6	1.3	99	54	70		25	0	0	245	19	28	1	2.4	.904	OF-123
1898	CIN N	123	.342	.432	486	166	21	10	1	0.2	79	66	69		20	0	0	280	15	16	5	2.5	.949	OF-123, P-1
1899		87	.298	.381	339	101	13	6	1	0.3	65	24	47		10	0	0	178	12	16	3	2.4	.922	OF-87
1900	2 teams	CIN N (29G –.279) NY N (87G –.260)																						
″	total	116	.265	.369	423	112	13	11	3	0.7	62	52	42		19	4	0	154	13	10	3	1.6	.944	OF-110
1901	2 teams	PIT N (4G –.000) BOS N (18G –.175)																						
″	total	22	.159	.222	63	10	2	1	0	0.0	5	3	8		2	4	0	21	1	4	0	1.6	.846	OF-16
14 yrs.		1238	.310	.434	4686	1454	196	136	37	0.8	913	638	636	139	232	9	0	2224	315	238	37	2.2	.914	OF-1086, P-149

Elmer Smith

SMITH, ELMER JOHN BL TR 5′10″ 165 lbs.
B. Sept. 21, 1892, Sandusky, Ohio D. Aug. 3, 1984, Columbia, Ky.

Year	Team	Games	BA	SA	AB	H	2B	3B	HR	HR%	R	RBI	BB	SO	SB	Pinch Hit AB	Pinch Hit H	PO	A	E	DP	TC/G	FA	G by Pos
1914	CLE A	13	.321	.377	53	17	3	0	0	0.0	5	8	2	11	1	0	0	29	2	0	0	2.4	1.000	OF-13
1915		144	.248	.366	476	118	23	12	3	0.6	37	67	36	75	10	19	6	202	15	18	4	1.9	.923	OF-123
1916	2 teams	CLE A (79G –.277) WAS A (45G –.214)																						
″	total	124	.249	.386	381	95	25	6	5	1.3	37	67	36	63	7	18	7	152	12	4	4	1.6	.976	OF-102
1917	2 teams	WAS A (35G –.222) CLE A (64G –.261)																						
″	total	99	.245	.338	278	68	9	4	3	1.1	29	39	18	32	7	26	4	124	9	8	2	2.0	.943	OF-69
1919	CLE A	114	.278	.438	395	110	24	6	9	2.3	60	54	41	30	15	3	0	167	12	8	8	1.7	.957	OF-111
1920		129	.316	.520	456	144	37	10	12	2.6	82	103	53	35	5	0	0	217	8	7	1	1.8	.970	OF-129
1921		129	.290	.508	431	125	28	9	16	3.7	98	84	56	46	0	2	0	183	16	6	1	1.6	.971	OF-127
1922	2 teams	BOS A (73G –.286) NY A (21G –.185)																						
″	total	94	.275	.453	258	71	13	6	7	2.7	44	37	28	26	0	21	6	130	8	8	4	2.1	.945	OF-69
1923	NY A	70	.306	.475	183	56	6	2	7	3.8	30	35	21	21	3	21	11	86	5	5	2	2.0	.948	OF-47
1925	CIN N	96	.271	.451	284	77	13	7	8	2.8	47	46	28	20	6	13	5	139	8	5	5	1.9	.967	OF-80
10 yrs.		1012	.276	.437	3195	881	181	62	70	2.2	469	540	319	359	54	123	39	1429	95	69	31	1.8	.957	OF-870

Elmer Smith *continued*

Year	Team	Lg	Games	BA	SA	AB	H	2B	3B	HR	HR%	R	RBI	BB	SO	SB	Pinch Hit AB	Pinch Hit H	PO	A	E	DP	TC/G	FA	G by Pos
WORLD SERIES																									
1920	CLE	A	5	.308	.692	13	4	0	1	1	7.7	1	6	1	1	0	1	0	7	1	0	0	1.6	1.000	OF-5
1922	NY	A	2	.000	.000	2	0	0	0	0	0.0	0	0	0	2	0	2	0	0	0	0	0	0.0	—	
2 yrs.			7	.267	.600	15	4	0	1	1	6.7	1	6	1	3	0	3	0	7	1	0	0	1.6	1.000	OF-5

Ernie Smith

SMITH, ERNEST HENRY BR TR 5′8″ 155 lbs.
B. Oct. 11, 1899, Totowa, N. J. D. Apr. 6, 1973, Brooklyn, N. Y.

Year	Team	Lg	Games	BA	SA	AB	H	2B	3B	HR	HR%	R	RBI	BB	SO	SB	Pinch Hit AB	Pinch Hit H	PO	A	E	DP	TC/G	FA	G by Pos
1930	CHI	A	24	.241	.278	79	19	3	0	0	0.0	5	3	5	6	2	3	1	45	58	9	8	5.3	.920	SS-21

Frank Smith

SMITH, FRANK L.
B. Nov. 24, 1857 D. Oct. 11, 1928, Canandaigua, N. Y.

Year	Team	Lg	Games	BA	SA	AB	H	2B	3B	HR	HR%	R	RBI	BB	SO	SB	Pinch Hit AB	Pinch Hit H	PO	A	E	DP	TC/G	FA	G by Pos
1884	PIT	AA	10	.250	.306	36	9	0	1	0	0.0	3		0			0	0	39	7	4	1	5.0	.920	C-7, OF-3

Fred Smith

SMITH, FRED VINCENT BR TR 5′11½″ 185 lbs.
Brother of Charlie Smith.
B. July 29, 1891, Cleveland, Ohio D. May 28, 1961, Cleveland, Ohio.

Year	Team	Lg	Games	BA	SA	AB	H	2B	3B	HR	HR%	R	RBI	BB	SO	SB	Pinch Hit AB	Pinch Hit H	PO	A	E	DP	TC/G	FA	G by Pos
1913	BOS	N	92	.228	.281	285	65	9	3	0	0.0	35	27	29	55	7	2	1	104	150	27	11	3.2	.904	3B-59, 2B-14, SS-11, OF-4
1914	BUF	F	145	.220	.300	473	104	12	10	2	0.4	48	45	49		24	0	0	216	282	36	23	3.6	.933	3B-127, SS-19, 1B-1
1915	2 teams		BUF F (35G –.237) BKN F (110G –.247)																						
″	total		145	.244	.351	499	122	18	10	5	1.0	49	69	38		23	2	0	301	419	62	43	5.5	.921	SS-126, 3B-16
1917	STL	N	56	.182	.224	165	30	0	2	1	0.6	11	17	17	22	4	1	0	63	113	9	6	3.4	.951	3B-51, 2B-2, SS-1
4 yrs.			438	.226	.305	1422	321	39	25	8	0.6	143	158	133	77	58	5	1	684	964	134	83	4.1	.925	3B-253, SS-157, 2B-16, OF-4, 1B-1

George Smith

SMITH, GEORGE CORNELIUS BR TR 5′10″ 170 lbs.
B. July 7, 1937, St. Petersburg, Fla. D. June 15, 1987, St. Petersburg, Fla.

Year	Team	Lg	Games	BA	SA	AB	H	2B	3B	HR	HR%	R	RBI	BB	SO	SB	Pinch Hit AB	Pinch Hit H	PO	A	E	DP	TC/G	FA	G by Pos
1963	DET	A	52	.216	.287	171	37	8	2	0	0.0	16	17	18	34	4	0	0	120	157	5	28	5.4	.982	2B-52
1964			5	.286	.286	7	2	0	0	0	0.0	1	2	1	4	1	1	1	2	5	0	2	2.3	1.000	2B-3
1965			32	.094	.151	53	5	0	0	1	1.9	6	1	3	18	0	5	0	33	33	1	10	2.4	.985	2B-22, SS-3, 3B-3
1966	BOS	A	128	.213	.340	403	86	19	4	8	2.0	41	37	37	86	4	4	0	268	331	24	85	4.9	.961	2B-109, SS-19
4 yrs.			217	.205	.309	634	130	27	6	9	1.4	64	57	59	142	9	10	1	423	526	30	125	4.6	.969	2B-186, SS-22, 3B-3

Germany Smith

SMITH, GEORGE J. BR TR 6′ 175 lbs.
B. Apr. 21, 1863, Pittsburgh, Pa. D. Dec. 1, 1927, Altoona, Pa.

Year	Team	Lg	Games	BA	SA	AB	H	2B	3B	HR	HR%	R	RBI	BB	SO	SB	Pinch Hit AB	Pinch Hit H	PO	A	E	DP	TC/G	FA	G by Pos
1884	2 teams		ALT U (25G –.315) CLE N (72G –.254)																						
″	total		97	.271	.381	399	108	22	5	4	1.0	40	26	3	45		0	0	195	331	69	27	6.1	.884	SS-55, 2B-42, P-1
1885	BKN	AA	108	.258	.379	419	108	17	11	4	1.0	63		10			0	0	161	455	81	23	6.5	.884	SS-108
1886			105	.246	.329	426	105	17	6	2	0.5	66		19			0	0	142	381	85	30	5.7	.860	SS-105, OF-1, C-1
1887			103	.294	.439	435	128	19	16	4	0.9	79		13		26	0	0	161	389	72	23	6.0	.884	SS-101, 3B-2
1888			103	.214	.296	402	86	10	7	3	0.7	47	61	22		27	0	0	155	352	94	29	5.8	.844	SS-103, 2B-1
1889			121	.231	.314	446	103	22	3	3	0.7	89	53	40	42	35	0	0	182	417	67	37	5.5	.899	SS-120, OF-1
1890	BKN	N	129	.191	.231	481	92	6	5	1	0.2	76	47	42	23	24	0	0	232	468	74	49	6.0	.904	SS-129
1891	CIN	N	138	.201	.260	512	103	11	5	3	0.6	50	53	38	32	16	0	0	240	507	75	40	6.0	.909	SS-138
1892			139	.239	.336	506	121	13	6	8	1.6	58	63	42	52	19	0	0	239	561	70	55	6.3	.920	SS-139
1893			130	.236	.314	500	118	18	6	3	0.6	63	56	38	20	14	0	0	250	500	53	67	6.2	.934	SS-130
1894			127	.263	.371	482	127	33	5	3	0.6	73	76	41	28	15	0	0	233	501	72	75	6.3	.911	SS-127
1895			127	.300	.394	503	151	23	6	4	0.8	75	74	34	24	13	0	0	251	457	59	58	6.0	.923	SS-127
1896			120	.287	.388	456	131	22	9	2	0.4	65	71	28	22	22	0	0	207	407	49	47	5.5	.926	SS-120
1897	BKN	N	112	.201	.255	428	86	17	3	0	0.0	47	29	14		1	0	0	201	399	61	36	5.9	.908	SS-112
1898	STL	N	51	.159	.204	157	25	2	1	1	0.6	16	9	24		1	0	0	79	167	26	14	5.3	.904	SS-51
15 yrs.			1710	.243	.331	6552	1592	252	94	45	0.7	907	618	408	288	213	0	0	2928	6292	1007	610	6.0	.902	SS-1665, 2B-43, OF-2, 3B-2, C-1, P-1

Greg Smith

SMITH, GREGORY ALAN BB TR 5′11″ 170 lbs.
B. Apr. 5, 1967, Baltimore, Md.

Year	Team	Lg	Games	BA	SA	AB	H	2B	3B	HR	HR%	R	RBI	BB	SO	SB	Pinch Hit AB	Pinch Hit H	PO	A	E	DP	TC/G	FA	G by Pos
1989	CHI	N	4	.400	.400	5	2	0	0	0	0.0	1	2	0	0	0	1	0	4	3	2	1	4.5	.778	2B-2
1990			18	.205	.295	44	9	2	1	0	0.0	4	5	2	5	1	2	1	20	38	3	8	4.4	.951	SS-7, 2B-7
1991	LA	N	5	.000	.000	3	0	0	0	0	0.0	1	0	0	2	0	3	0	0	0	0	0	0.0	.000	2B-1
3 yrs.			27	.212	.288	52	11	2	1	0	0.0	6	7	2	7	1	6	1	24	41	5	9	4.1	.929	2B-10, SS-7

Hal Smith

SMITH, HAROLD RAYMOND (Cura) BR TR 5′10½″ 186 lbs.
B. June 1, 1931, Barling, Ark.

Year	Team	Lg	Games	BA	SA	AB	H	2B	3B	HR	HR%	R	RBI	BB	SO	SB	Pinch Hit AB	Pinch Hit H	PO	A	E	DP	TC/G	FA	G by Pos
1956	STL	N	75	.282	.401	227	64	12	0	5	2.2	27	23	15	22	1	9	3	300	34	6	3	5.2	.982	C-66
1957			100	.279	.351	333	93	12	3	2	0.6	25	37	18	18	2	4	2	468	42	5	8	5.3	.990	C-97
1958			77	.227	.268	220	50	4	1	1	0.5	13	24	14	14	0	5	0	346	22	4	4	5.2	.989	C-71
1959			142	.270	.403	452	122	15	3	13	2.9	35	50	15	28	2	1	0	758	60	9	13	5.9	.989	C-141
1960			127	.228	.294	337	77	16	0	2	0.6	20	28	29	33	1	5	1	664	61	7	9	5.9	.990	C-124
1961			45	.248	.296	125	31	4	1	0	0.0	6	10	11	12	0	1	0	261	28	2	6	6.5	.993	C-45
1965	PIT	N	4	.000	.000	3	0	0	0	0	0.0	0	0	0	1	0	0	0	13	0	0	0	3.3	1.000	C-4
7 yrs.			570	.258	.345	1697	437	63	8	23	1.4	126	172	102	128	6	25	6	2810	247	33	43	5.6	.989	C-548

Hal Smith

SMITH, HAROLD WAYNE BR TR 6′ 195 lbs.
B. Dec. 7, 1930, West Frankfort, Ill.

Year	Team	Lg	Games	BA	SA	AB	H	2B	3B	HR	HR%	R	RBI	BB	SO	SB	Pinch Hit AB	Pinch Hit H	PO	A	E	DP	TC/G	FA	G by Pos
1955	BAL	A	135	.271	.373	424	115	23	4	4	0.9	41	52	30	21	1	11	4	497	58	8	9	4.5	.986	C-125
1956	2 teams		BAL A (78G –.262) KC A (36G –.275)																						
″	total		114	.267	.380	371	99	23	2	5	1.3	31	42	20	34	2	8	0	496	55	5	14	5.2	.991	C-107
1957	KC	A	107	.303	.483	360	109	26	0	13	3.6	41	41	14	44	2	8	1	463	55	9	8	5.1	.983	C-103
1958			99	.273	.394	315	86	19	2	5	1.6	32	46	25	47	0	10	5	313	112	8	19	4.9	.982	3B-43, C-31, 1B-14
1959			108	.288	.380	292	84	12	0	5	1.7	36	31	34	39	0	12	4	210	129	15	15	3.6	.958	3B-77, C-22
1960	PIT	N	77	.295	.508	258	76	18	2	11	4.3	37	45	22	48	1	6	2	356	30	6	5	5.5	.985	C-71
1961			67	.223	.321	193	43	10	0	3	1.6	12	26	11	38	0	2	1	290	18	3	1	4.8	.990	C-65
1962	HOU	N	109	.235	.380	345	81	14	0	12	3.5	32	35	24	55	0	14	3	580	72	10	10	6.6	.985	C-92, 3B-6, 1B-2

Hal Smith *continued*

Year	Team	Games	BA	SA	AB	H	2B	3B	HR	HR%	R	RBI	BB	SO	SB	Pinch Hit AB	Pinch Hit H	PO	A	E	DP	TC/G	FA	G by Pos
1963		31	.241	.276	58	14	2	0	0	0.0	1	2	4	15	0	19	3	65	2	1	1	6.2	.985	C-11
1964	CIN N	32	.121	.136	66	8	1	0	0	0.0	6	3	12	20	1	12	2	105	8	2	1	5.8	.983	C-20
10 yrs.		879	.267	.394	2682	715	148	10	58	2.2	269	323	196	361	7	102	25	3375	539	67	83	5.0	.983	C-647, 3B-126, 1B-16
WORLD SERIES																								
1960	PIT N	3	.375	.750	8	3	0	0	1	12.5	1	3	0	0	0	0	0	14	1	0	0	5.0	1.000	C-3

Hap Smith

SMITH, HENRY JOSEPH BL TR 6′ 185 lbs.
B. July 14, 1883, Coquille, Ore. D. Feb. 26, 1961, San Jose, Calif.

Year	Team	Games	BA	SA	AB	H	2B	3B	HR	HR%	R	RBI	BB	SO	SB	Pinch Hit AB	Pinch Hit H	PO	A	E	DP	TC/G	FA	G by Pos
1910	BKN N	35	.237	.263	76	18	2	0	0	0.0	6	5	4	14	4	17	3	33	4	1	2	2.4	.974	OF-16

Harry Smith

SMITH, HARRY THOMAS BR TR
B. Oct. 31, 1874, Yorkshire, England D. Feb. 17, 1933, Salem, N. J.
Manager 1909.

Year	Team	Games	BA	SA	AB	H	2B	3B	HR	HR%	R	RBI	BB	SO	SB	Pinch Hit AB	Pinch Hit H	PO	A	E	DP	TC/G	FA	G by Pos
1901	PHI A	11	.324	.353	34	11	1	0	0	0.0	3	3	2		1	1	1	21	10	3	0	3.4	.912	C-9, OF-1
1902	PIT N	50	.189	.222	185	35	4	1	0	0.0	14	12	4		4	0	0	265	49	9	3	6.5	.972	C-50
1903		61	.175	.208	212	37	3	2	0	0.0	15	19	12		2	0	0	259	75	9	2	5.6	.974	C-60, OF-1
1904		47	.248	.284	141	35	3	1	0	0.0	17	18	16		5	0	0	155	61	8	7	4.8	.964	C-44, OF-3
1905		1	.000	.000	3	0	0	0	0	0.0	0	1	0		1	0	0	4	1	0	1	5.0	1.000	C-1
1906		1	.000	.000	1	0	0	0	0	0.0	0	0	0		0	0	0	4	0	1	0	5.0	.800	C-1
1907		18	.263	.289	38	10	1	0	0	0.0	4	1	4		0	0	0	46	16	4	2	3.7	.939	C-18
1908	BOS N	41	.246	.315	130	32	2	2	1	0.8	13	16	7		2	3	0	143	52	5	2	5.3	.975	C-38
1909		43	.168	.221	113	19	4	1	0	0.0	9	4	5		3	12	2	133	39	5	5	5.7	.972	C-31
1910		70	.238	.286	147	35	4	0	1	0.7	8	15	5	14	5	32	6	138	66	11	3	5.7	.949	C-38
10 yrs.		343	.213	.255	1004	214	22	7	2	0.2	83	89	55	14	23	48	9	1168	369	55	25	5.4	.965	C-290, OF-5
WORLD SERIES																								
1903	PIT N	1	.000	.000	3	0	0	0	0	0.0	0	0	0	0	0	0	0	2	1	1	0	4.0	.750	C-1

Harry Smith

SMITH, HARRY W. BR TR 6′ 175 lbs.
B. Feb. 5, 1856, N. Vernon, Ind. D. June 4, 1898, Queensville, Ind.

Year	Team	Games	BA	SA	AB	H	2B	3B	HR	HR%	R	RBI	BB	SO	SB	Pinch Hit AB	Pinch Hit H	PO	A	E	DP	TC/G	FA	G by Pos
1877	2 teams	CHI N (24G –.202) CIN N (10G –.250)																						
″	total	34	.215	.254	130	28	3	1	0	0.0	11	6	5	11		0	0	100	48	29	3	4.7	.836	2B-17, OF-13, C-8
1889	LOU AA	1	.500	.500	2	1	0	0	0	0.0	0	1	0	1	0	0	0	2	0	1	0	1.5	.667	C-1, OF-1
2 yrs.		35	.220	.258	132	29	3	1	0	0.0	11	7	5	12	0	0	0	102	48	30	3	4.5	.833	2B-17, OF-14, C-9

Harry Smith

SMITH, JAMES HARRY BR TR 5′10″ 180 lbs.
B. May 15, 1890, Baltimore, Md. D. Apr. 1, 1922, Charlotte, N. C.

Year	Team	Games	BA	SA	AB	H	2B	3B	HR	HR%	R	RBI	BB	SO	SB	Pinch Hit AB	Pinch Hit H	PO	A	E	DP	TC/G	FA	G by Pos
1914	NY N	5	.429	.429	7	3	0	0	0	0.0	0	2	3	1	1	1	0	18	4	0	0	5.5	1.000	C-4
1915	2 teams	NY N (21G –.125) BKN F (28G –.200)																						
″	total	49	.175	.227	97	17	0	1	1	1.0	6	7	13	12	2	7	2	117	29	5	0	4.0	.967	C-37, OF-1
1917	CIN N	8	.118	.118	17	2	0	0	0	0.0	0	1	2	7	0	1	0	34	11	1	0	6.6	.978	C-7
1918		13	.185	.370	27	5	1	2	0	0.0	4	4	3	6	1	5	1	22	3	0	1	3.6	1.000	C-6, OF-1
4 yrs.		75	.182	.250	148	27	1	3	1	0.7	10	14	21	26	4	14	3	191	47	6	1	4.4	.975	C-54, OF-2

Harvey Smith

SMITH, HARVEY FETTERHOFF BL TR 5′ 8″ 160 lbs.
B. July 24, 1871, Union Deposit, Pa. D. Nov. 12, 1962, Harrisburg, Pa.

Year	Team	Games	BA	SA	AB	H	2B	3B	HR	HR%	R	RBI	BB	SO	SB	Pinch Hit AB	Pinch Hit H	PO	A	E	DP	TC/G	FA	G by Pos
1896	WAS N	36	.275	.359	131	36	7	2	0	0.0	21	17	12	7	9	0	0	31	87	19	5	3.8	.861	3B-36

Heinie Smith

SMITH, GEORGE HENRY BR TR 5′ 9½″ 160 lbs.
B. Oct. 24, 1871, Pittsburgh, Pa. D. June 25, 1939, Buffalo, N. Y.
Manager 1902.

Year	Team	Games	BA	SA	AB	H	2B	3B	HR	HR%	R	RBI	BB	SO	SB	Pinch Hit AB	Pinch Hit H	PO	A	E	DP	TC/G	FA	G by Pos
1897	LOU N	21	.263	.342	76	20	3	0	1	1.3	7	7	3		1	0	0	46	57	8	8	5.3	.928	2B-21
1898		35	.190	.223	121	23	4	0	0	0.0	14	13	6		6	2	1	74	87	16	8	5.4	.910	2B-33
1899	PIT N	15	.283	.377	53	15	3	1	0	0.0	9	12	5		2	0	0	34	46	14	3	5.9	.851	2B-15, SS-1
1901	NY N	9	.207	.448	29	6	2	1	1	3.4	5	4	1		1	0	0	13	20	1	0	3.8	.971	2B-7, P-2
1902		138	.252	.297	511	129	19	2	0	0.0	46	33	17		32	0	0	347	403	37	58	5.7	.953	2B-138
1903	DET A	93	.223	.283	336	75	11	3	1	0.3	36	22	19		12	0	0	200	267	36	30	5.4	.928	2B-93
6 yrs.		311	.238	.296	1126	268	42	7	3	0.3	117	91	51		54	2	1	714	880	112	107	5.5	.934	2B-307, P-2, SS-1

Jack Smith

SMITH, JACK BL TL 5′ 8″ 165 lbs.
B. June 23, 1895, Chicago, Ill. D. May 2, 1972, Westchester, Ill.

Year	Team	Games	BA	SA	AB	H	2B	3B	HR	HR%	R	RBI	BB	SO	SB	Pinch Hit AB	Pinch Hit H	PO	A	E	DP	TC/G	FA	G by Pos
1915	STL N	4	.188	.313	16	3	0	1	0	0.0	2	0	1	5	0	0	0	5	0	0	0	1.3	1.000	OF-4
1916		130	.244	.339	357	87	6	5	6	1.7	43	34	20	50	24	7	1	212	12	12	4	2.0	.949	OF-120
1917		137	.297	.398	462	137	16	11	3	0.6	64	34	38	65	25	8	4	233	12	10	6	2.0	.961	OF-128
1918		42	.211	.235	166	35	2	1	0	0.0	24	4	7	21	5	0	0	87	9	6	6	2.4	.941	OF-42
1919		119	.223	.277	408	91	16	3	0	0.0	47	15	26	29	30	0	0	197	19	9	6	2.0	.960	OF-111
1920		91	.332	.444	313	104	22	5	1	0.3	53	28	25	23	14	4	1	144	12	6	1	2.0	.963	OF-83
1921		116	.328	.477	411	135	22	9	7	1.7	86	33	21	24	11	4	0	179	11	9	3	1.9	.955	OF-103
1922		143	.310	.449	510	158	23	12	8	1.6	117	46	50	30	18	4	1	282	11	15	3	2.3	.951	OF-136
1923		124	.310	.415	407	126	16	6	5	1.2	98	41	27	20	32	3	0	247	11	7	3	2.5	.974	OF-107
1924		124	.283	.362	459	130	18	6	2	0.4	91	33	33	27	24	6	1	251	18	9	8	2.4	.968	OF-114
1925		80	.251	.379	243	61	11	4	4	1.6	53	31	19	13	20	10	4	152	7	7	2	2.6	.958	OF-64
1926	2 teams	STL N (1G –.000) BOS N (96G –.311)																						
″	total	97	.310	.387	323	100	15	2	2	0.6	46	25	28	13	11	9	0	206	8	6	0	2.7	.973	OF-83
1927	BOS N	84	.317	.410	183	58	6	4	1	0.5	27	24	16	12	8	30	8	106	7	6	1	2.5	.950	OF-48
1928		96	.280	.343	254	71	9	2	1	0.4	30	32	21	14	6	25	**9**	165	4	2	0	2.6	.988	OF-65
1929		19	.250	.250	20	5	0	0	0	0.0	2	2	2	2	0	3	0	10	0	2	0	1.3	.833	OF-9
15 yrs.		1406	.287	.385	4532	1301	182	71	40	0.9	783	382	334	348	228	113	29	2476	141	106	43	2.2	.961	OF-1217

Jack Smith

SMITH, JOHN JOSEPH BR TR 5′ 9″
Born John Joseph Coffee.
B. Aug. 8, 1893, Oswayo, Pa. D. Dec. 4, 1962, New York, N. Y.

Year	Team	Games	BA	SA	AB	H	2B	3B	HR	HR%	R	RBI	BB	SO	SB	Pinch Hit AB	Pinch Hit H	PO	A	E	DP	TC/G	FA	G by Pos
1912	DET A	1	—	—	0	0	0	0	0	—	0	0	0	0	0	0	0	2	1	0	1	3.0	1.000	3B-1

Jimmy Smith

SMITH, JAMES LAWRENCE BB TR 5′ 9″ 158 lbs.
Born James Lawrence Greenfield. BR 1914
B. May 15, 1895, Pittsburgh, Pa. D. Jan. 1, 1974, Pittsburgh, Pa.

Year	Team	Games	BA	SA	AB	H	2B	3B	HR	HR%	R	RBI	BB	SO	SB	Pinch Hit AB	Pinch Hit H	PO	A	E	DP	TC/G	FA	G by Pos
1914	CHI F	3	.500	.667	6	3	1	0	0	0.0	1	1	0		0	0	0	3	5	0	2	2.7	1.000	SS-3
1915	2 teams	CHI F (95G –.217) BAL F (33G –.176)																						
″	total	128	.207	.293	426	88	12	5	5	1.2	41	41	25		7	0	0	273	333	70	37	5.4	.896	SS-125, 2B-1
1916	PIT N	36	.188	.219	96	18	1	1	0	0.0	4	5	6	22	0	0	0	58	78	12	6	4.5	.919	SS-27, 3B-6
1917	NY N	36	.229	.302	96	22	5	1	0	0.0	12	2	9	18	6	0	0	53	83	4	5	3.9	.971	2B-29, SS-7
1918	BOS N	34	.225	.363	102	23	3	4	1	1.0	8	14	3	13	1	0	0	65	51	12	7	4.7	.906	SS-9, 2B-7, OF-6, 3B-5
1919	CIN N	28	.275	.525	40	11	1	3	1	2.5	9	10	4	8	1	0	0	18	26	3	5	2.5	.936	3B-6, SS-5, 2B-4, OF-4
1921	PHI N	67	.231	.320	247	57	8	1	4	1.6	31	22	11	28	2	0	0	125	239	11	19	5.7	.971	2B-66
1922		38	.219	.254	114	25	1	0	1	0.9	13	6	5	9	1	2	0	67	94	8	17	4.6	.953	SS-23, 2B-13, 3B-1
8 yrs.		370	.219	.306	1127	247	32	15	12	1.1	119	101	63	98	18	2	0	662	909	120	98	4.9	.929	SS-199, 2B-120, 3B-18, OF-10
WORLD SERIES																								
1919	CIN N	1	—	—	0	0	0	0	0	—	0	0	0	0	0	0	0	0	0	0	0	0.0	—	

Jimmy Smith

SMITH, JAMES LORNE BR TR 6′ 3″ 180 lbs.
B. Sept. 8, 1954, Santa Monica, Calif.

Year	Team	Games	BA	SA	AB	H	2B	3B	HR	HR%	R	RBI	BB	SO	SB	Pinch Hit AB	Pinch Hit H	PO	A	E	DP	TC/G	FA	G by Pos
1982	PIT N	42	.238	.333	42	10	2	1	0	0.0	5	4	5	7	0	1	0	34	50	7	10	2.8	.923	SS-29, 2B-3, 3B-1

Joe Smith

SMITH, JOSEPH BR TR 5′ 8″ 190 lbs.
Born Salvatore Giuseppe Persico.
B. Dec. 29, 1893, New York, N. Y. D. June 12, 1974, Yonkers, N. Y.

Year	Team	Games	BA	SA	AB	H	2B	3B	HR	HR%	R	RBI	BB	SO	SB	Pinch Hit AB	Pinch Hit H	PO	A	E	DP	TC/G	FA	G by Pos
1913	NY A	13	.156	.156	32	5	0	0	0	0.0	1	2	1	14	1	0	0	43	17	3	1	4.8	.952	C-13

John Smith

SMITH, JOHN J. 5′11″ 210 lbs.
B. 1858, New York, N. Y. Deceased.

Year	Team	Games	BA	SA	AB	H	2B	3B	HR	HR%	R	RBI	BB	SO	SB	Pinch Hit AB	Pinch Hit H	PO	A	E	DP	TC/G	FA	G by Pos
1882	2 teams	TRO N (35G –.242) WOR N (19G –.243)																						
″	total	54	.242	.320	219	53	7	5	0	0.0	37	19	8	34		0	0	543	19	29	31	10.9	.951	1B-54

John Smith

SMITH, JOHN MARSHALL (Jack) BB TR 6′ 1″ 165 lbs.
B. Sept. 27, 1906, Washington, D. C. D. May 9, 1982, Silver Spring, Md.

Year	Team	Games	BA	SA	AB	H	2B	3B	HR	HR%	R	RBI	BB	SO	SB	Pinch Hit AB	Pinch Hit H	PO	A	E	DP	TC/G	FA	G by Pos
1931	BOS A	4	.133	.133	15	2	0	0	0	0.0	2	1	2	1	1	0	0	46	0	0	1	11.5	1.000	1B-4

Jud Smith

SMITH, GRANT JUDSON BR TR
B. Jan. 13, 1869, Green Oak, Mich. D. Dec. 7, 1947, Los Angeles, Calif.

Year	Team	Games	BA	SA	AB	H	2B	3B	HR	HR%	R	RBI	BB	SO	SB	Pinch Hit AB	Pinch Hit H	PO	A	E	DP	TC/G	FA	G by Pos
1893	2 teams	CIN N (17G –.233) STL N (4G –.077)																						
″	total	21	.196	.268	56	11	1	0	1	1.8	8	5	10	7	1	0	0	19	23	10	5	2.6	.808	3B-10, OF-9, SS-1
1896	PIT N	10	.343	.457	35	12	2	1	0	0.0	6	4	2	2	3	0	0	19	21	4	3	4.4	.909	3B-10
1898	WAS N	66	.303	.415	234	71	7	5	3	1.3	33	28	22		11	0	0	140	112	28	10	4.3	.900	3B-47, SS-10, 1B-7, 2B-1
1901	PIT N	6	.143	.190	21	3	1	0	0	0.0	1	0	3		0	0	0	7	11	1	0	3.2	.947	3B-6
4 yrs.		103	.280	.382	346	97	11	6	4	1.2	48	37	37	9	15	0	0	185	167	43	18	3.9	.891	3B-73, SS-11, OF-9, 1B-7, 2B-1

Keith Smith

SMITH, KEITH LAVARNE BR TR 5′ 9″ 178 lbs.
B. May 3, 1953, Palmetto, Fla.

Year	Team	Games	BA	SA	AB	H	2B	3B	HR	HR%	R	RBI	BB	SO	SB	Pinch Hit AB	Pinch Hit H	PO	A	E	DP	TC/G	FA	G by Pos
1977	TEX A	23	.239	.388	67	16	4	0	2	3.0	13	6	4	7	2	3	1	38	1	1	0	1.8	.975	OF-22
1979	STL N	6	.231	.231	13	3	0	0	0	0.0	1	0	0	1	0	0	0	14	1	0	0	3.0	1.000	OF-5
1980		24	.129	.161	31	4	1	0	0	0.0	3	2	2	2	0	17	3	10	0	0	0	1.4	1.000	OF-7
3 yrs.		53	.207	.306	111	23	5	0	2	1.8	17	8	6	10	2	20	4	62	2	1	0	1.9	.985	OF-34

Keith Smith

SMITH, PATRICK KEITH BB TR 6′ 1″ 175 lbs.
B. Oct. 20, 1961, Los Angeles, Calif.

Year	Team	Games	BA	SA	AB	H	2B	3B	HR	HR%	R	RBI	BB	SO	SB	Pinch Hit AB	Pinch Hit H	PO	A	E	DP	TC/G	FA	G by Pos
1984	NY A	2	.000	.000	4	0	0	0	0	0.0	0	0	0	2	0	0	0	2	10	1	1	6.5	.923	SS-2
1985		4	—	—	0	0	0	0	0	—	1	0	0	0	0	0	0	0	1	0	0	0.3	1.000	SS-3
2 yrs.		6	.000	.000	4	0	0	0	0	0.0	1	0	0	2	0	0	0	2	11	1	1	2.8	.929	SS-5

Ken Smith

SMITH, KENNETH EARL BL TR 6′ 1″ 195 lbs.
B. Feb. 12, 1958, Youngstown, Ohio.

Year	Team	Games	BA	SA	AB	H	2B	3B	HR	HR%	R	RBI	BB	SO	SB	Pinch Hit AB	Pinch Hit H	PO	A	E	DP	TC/G	FA	G by Pos
1981	ATL N	5	.333	.667	3	1	1	0	0	0.0	0	0	0	1	0	0	0	6	1	0	0	1.8	1.000	1B-4
1982		48	.293	.317	41	12	1	0	0	0.0	6	3	6	13	0	35	8	15	1	0	0	1.8	1.000	1B-6, OF-3
1983		30	.167	.417	12	2	0	0	1	8.3	2	2	1	5	1	8	1	27	6	0	3	2.5	1.000	1B-13
3 yrs.		83	.268	.357	56	15	2	0	1	1.8	8	5	7	19	1	43	9	48	8	0	3	2.2	1.000	1B-23, OF-3

Klondike Smith

SMITH, ARMSTRONG FREDERICK BL TL 5′ 9″ 160 lbs.
B. Jan. 4, 1887, London, England D. Nov. 15, 1959, Springfield, Mass.

Year	Team	Games	BA	SA	AB	H	2B	3B	HR	HR%	R	RBI	BB	SO	SB	Pinch Hit AB	Pinch Hit H	PO	A	E	DP	TC/G	FA	G by Pos
1912	NY A	7	.185	.222	27	5	1	0	0	0.0	0	0	0		1	0	0	10	0	0	0	1.4	1.000	OF-7

L. Smith

SMITH, L.
Deceased.

Year	Team	Games	BA	SA	AB	H	2B	3B	HR	HR%	R	RBI	BB	SO	SB	Pinch Hit AB	Pinch Hit H	PO	A	E	DP	TC/G	FA	G by Pos
1882	BAL AA	1	.000	.000	3	0	0	0	0	0.0	0		0			0	0	1	0	1	0	2.0	.500	OF-1

Leo Smith

SMITH, LIONEL H. 5′ 6″ 142 lbs.
B. May 13, 1859, Brooklyn, N. Y. D. Aug. 30, 1935, Brooklyn, N. Y.

Year	Team	Games	BA	SA	AB	H	2B	3B	HR	HR%	R	RBI	BB	SO	SB	Pinch Hit AB	Pinch Hit H	PO	A	E	DP	TC/G	FA	G by Pos
1890	ROC AA	35	.188	.250	112	21	1	3	0	0.0	11		14		1	0	0	66	115	10	15	5.5	.948	SS-35

Lonnie Smith

SMITH, LONNIE BR TR 5′ 9″ 170 lbs.
B. Dec. 22, 1955, Chicago, Ill.

Year	Team	Games	BA	SA	AB	H	2B	3B	HR	HR%	R	RBI	BB	SO	SB	Pinch Hit AB	Pinch Hit H	PO	A	E	DP	TC/G	FA	G by Pos
1978	PHI N	17	.000	.000	4	0	0	0	0	0.0	6	0	4	3	4	1	0	5	1	0	0	0.5	1.000	OF-11
1979		17	.167	.233	30	5	2	0	0	0.0	4	3	1	7	2	4	0	19	1	0	0	1.8	1.000	OF-11
1980		100	.339	.443	298	101	14	4	3	1.0	69	20	26	48	33	8	2	121	2	4	0	1.5	.969	OF-82
1981		62	.324	.472	176	57	14	3	2	1.1	40	11	18	14	21	5	3	89	10	3	2	2.0	.971	OF-51
1982	STL N	156	.307	.434	592	182	35	8	8	1.4	**120**	69	64	74	68	9	1	303	16	10	3	2.2	.970	OF-149
1983		130	.321	.453	492	158	31	5	8	1.6	83	45	41	55	43	5	1	225	14	15	4	2.0	.941	OF-126
1984		145	.250	.341	504	126	20	4	6	1.2	77	49	70	90	50	3	1	184	18	11	0	1.5	.948	OF-140

Lonnie Smith *continued*

Year	Team	Games	BA	SA	AB	H	2B	3B	HR	HR%	R	RBI	BB	SO	SB	Pinch Hit AB	Pinch Hit H	PO	A	E	DP	TC/G	FA	G by Pos
1985	**2 teams**	**STL N** (28G –.260) **KC A** (120G –.257)																						
"	**total**	148	.257	.358	544	140	25	6	6	1.1	92	48	56	89	52	2	0	238	11	9	4	1.8	.965	OF-147
1986	**KC A**	134	.287	.411	508	146	25	7	8	1.6	80	44	46	78	26	4	2	245	5	9	1	2.0	.965	OF-118, DH-10
1987		48	.251	.359	167	42	7	1	3	1.8	26	8	24	31	9	1	0	52	2	5	0	1.3	.915	OF-32, DH-15
1988	**ATL N**	43	.237	.342	114	27	3	0	3	2.6	14	9	10	25	4	14	3	59	2	2	0	1.8	.968	OF-35
1989		134	.315	.533	482	152	34	4	21	4.4	89	79	76	95	25	3	0	289	3	2	0	2.2	.993	OF-132
1990		135	.305	.459	466	142	27	9	9	1.9	72	42	58	69	10	19	5	254	6	12	2	2.2	.956	OF-122
1991		122	.275	.394	353	97	19	1	7	2.0	58	44	50	64	9	22	4	134	5	5	2	1.5	.965	OF-99
1992		84	.247	.437	158	39	8	2	6	3.8	23	33	17	37	4	43	8	60	2	3	0	1.9	.954	OF-35
1993	**2 teams**	**PIT N** (94G –.286) **BAL A** (9G –.208)																						
"	**total**	103	.278	.448	223	62	6	4	8	3.6	43	27	51	52	9	31	8	109	2	2	0	1.6	.982	OF-64, DH-5
1994	**BAL A**	35	.203	.254	59	12	3	0	0	0.0	13	2	11	18	1	6	1	2	1	0	0	0.1	1.000	DH-30, OF-2
17 yrs.		1613	.288	.420	5170	1488	273	58	98	1.9	909	533	623	849	370	180	39	2388	101	92	18	1.8	.964	OF-1356, DH-60
DIVISIONAL PLAYOFF SERIES																								
1981	**PHI N**	5	.263	.316	19	5	1	0	0	0.0	1	0	0	4	0	0	0	6	1	0	0	1.4	1.000	OF-5
LEAGUE CHAMPIONSHIP SERIES																								
1980	**PHI N**	3	.600	.600	5	3	0	0	0	0.0	2	0	0	0	1	0	0	2	1	0	1	1.5	1.000	OF-2
1982	**STL N**	3	.273	.273	11	3	0	0	0	0.0	1	1	0	1	0	0	0	2	0	0	0	0.7	1.000	OF-3
1985	**KC A**	7	.250	.321	28	7	2	0	0	0.0	2	1	3	6	1	0	0	8	3	1	0	1.7	.917	OF-7
1991	**ATL N**	7	.250	.375	24	6	3	0	0	0.0	3	0	4	5	1	0	0	10	2	0	1	1.7	1.000	OF-7
1992		6	.333	.667	6	2	0	1	0	0.0	1	1	0	0	0	6	2	0	0	0	0	0.0	—	
5 yrs.		26 **9th**	.284	.378	74	21	5	1	0	0.0	9	3	7	12	3	6	2	22	6	1	2	1.5	.966	OF-19
WORLD SERIES																								
1980	**PHI N**	6	.263	.316	19	5	1	0	0	0.0	2	1	1	1	0	0	0	4	1	0	0	1.0	1.000	OF-4, DH-1
1982	**STL N**	7	.321	.536	28	9	4	1	0	0.0	6	1	1	5	2	0	0	11	0	0	0	1.6	1.000	OF-6, DH-1
1985	**KC A**	7	.333	.444	27	9	3	0	0	0.0	4	4	3	8	2	0	0	7	2	0	0	1.3	1.000	OF-7
1991	**ATL N**	7	.231	.577	26	6	0	0	3	11.5	5	3	3	4	1	0	0	2	0	0	0	0.3	1.000	DH-4, OF-3
1992		5	.167	.417	12	2	0	0	1	8.3	1	5	1	4	0	0	0	0	0	0	0	0.0	.000	DH-3
5 yrs.		32	.277	.473	112	31	8 **6th**	1	4	3.6	18	14	9	22	5	0	0	24	3	0	0	0.9	1.000	OF-20, DH-9

Mark Smith

SMITH, MARK EDWARD BR TR 6′ 3″ 205 lbs.
B. May 7, 1970, Pasadena, Calif.

Year	Team	Games	BA	SA	AB	H	2B	3B	HR	HR%	R	RBI	BB	SO	SB	Pinch Hit AB	Pinch Hit H	PO	A	E	DP	TC/G	FA	G by Pos
1994	**BAL A**	3	.143	.143	7	1	0	0	0	0.0	0	2	0	2	0	0	0	8	0	0	0	2.7	1.000	OF-3
1995		37	.231	.365	104	24	5	0	3	2.9	11	15	12	22	3	4	1	60	2	0	0	1.8	1.000	OF-32, DH-3
2 yrs.		40	.225	.351	111	25	5	0	3	2.7	11	17	12	24	3	4	1	68	2	0	0	1.8	1.000	OF-35, DH-3

Mayo Smith

SMITH, EDWARD MAYO BL TR 6′ 183 lbs.
B. Jan. 17, 1915, New London, Mo. D. Nov. 24, 1977, Boynton Beach, Fla.
Manager 1955–59, 1967–70.

Year	Team	Games	BA	SA	AB	H	2B	3B	HR	HR%	R	RBI	BB	SO	SB	Pinch Hit AB	Pinch Hit H	PO	A	E	DP	TC/G	FA	G by Pos
1945	**PHI A**	73	.212	.236	203	43	5	0	0	0.0	18	11	36	13	0	6	4	120	4	3	0	2.0	.976	OF-65

Mike Smith

SMITH, ELWOOD HOPE BL TR 5′11½″ 170 lbs.
B. Nov. 16, 1904, Norfolk, Va. D. May 31, 1981, Chesapeake, Va.

Year	Team	Games	BA	SA	AB	H	2B	3B	HR	HR%	R	RBI	BB	SO	SB	Pinch Hit AB	Pinch Hit H	PO	A	E	DP	TC/G	FA	G by Pos
1926	**NY N**	4	.143	.143	7	1	0	0	0	0.0	0	0	0	2	0	3	0	3	0	0	0	3.0	1.000	OF-1

Milt Smith

SMITH, MILTON BR TR 5′10″ 165 lbs.
B. Mar. 27, 1929, Columbus, Ga.

Year	Team	Games	BA	SA	AB	H	2B	3B	HR	HR%	R	RBI	BB	SO	SB	Pinch Hit AB	Pinch Hit H	PO	A	E	DP	TC/G	FA	G by Pos
1955	**CIN N**	36	.196	.333	102	20	3	1	3	2.9	15	8	13	24	2	2	1	30	61	7	4	3.0	.929	3B-28, 2B-5

Nate Smith

SMITH, NATHANIEL BEVERLY BR TR 5′11″ 170 lbs.
B. Apr. 26, 1935, Chicago, Ill.

Year	Team	Games	BA	SA	AB	H	2B	3B	HR	HR%	R	RBI	BB	SO	SB	Pinch Hit AB	Pinch Hit H	PO	A	E	DP	TC/G	FA	G by Pos
1962	**BAL A**	5	.222	.333	9	2	1	0	0	0.0	3	0	1	4	0	2	1	17	1	0	1	6.0	1.000	C-3

Ollie Smith

SMITH, OLIVER H. BL TL
B. 1868, Mt. Vernon, Ohio Deceased.

Year	Team	Games	BA	SA	AB	H	2B	3B	HR	HR%	R	RBI	BB	SO	SB	Pinch Hit AB	Pinch Hit H	PO	A	E	DP	TC/G	FA	G by Pos
1894	**LOU N**	38	.299	.425	134	40	6	1	3	2.2	26	20	27	15	13	0	0	63	5	9	0	2.0	.883	OF-38

Ozzie Smith

SMITH, OSBORNE EARL (The Wizard) BB TR 5′11″ 150 lbs.
B. Dec. 26, 1954, Mobile, Ala.

Year	Team	Games	BA	SA	AB	H	2B	3B	HR	HR%	R	RBI	BB	SO	SB	Pinch Hit AB	Pinch Hit H	PO	A	E	DP	TC/G	FA	G by Pos
1978	**SD N**	159	.258	.312	590	152	17	6	1	0.2	69	46	47	43	40	1	0	264	548	25	98	5.3	.970	SS-159
1979		156	.211	.262	587	124	18	6	0	0.0	77	27	37	37	28	0	0	256	555	20	86	5.4	.976	SS-155
1980		158	.230	.276	609	140	18	5	0	0.0	67	35	71	49	57	0	0	288	621	24	113	5.9	.974	SS-158
1981		110	.222	.256	**450**	100	11	2	0	0.0	53	21	41	37	22	0	0	220	422	16	72	6.0	.976	SS-110
1982	**STL N**	140	.248	.314	488	121	24	1	2	0.4	58	43	68	32	25	1	0	279	535	13	101	5.9	.984	SS-139
1983		159	.243	.335	552	134	30	6	3	0.5	69	50	64	36	34	2	0	304	519	21	100	5.3	.975	SS-158
1984		124	.257	.337	412	106	20	5	1	0.2	53	44	56	17	35	0	0	233	437	12	94	5.5	.982	SS-124
1985		158	.276	.361	537	148	22	3	6	1.1	70	54	65	27	31	0	0	264	549	14	111	5.2	.983	SS-158
1986		153	.280	.333	514	144	19	4	0	0.0	67	54	79	27	31	8	2	229	453	15	96	4.8	.978	SS-144
1987		158	.303	.383	600	182	40	4	0	0.0	104	75	89	36	43	2	1	245	516	10	111	4.9	.987	SS-158
1988		153	.270	.336	575	155	27	1	3	0.5	80	51	74	43	57	2	0	234	519	22	79	5.2	.972	SS-150
1989		155	.273	.361	593	162	30	8	2	0.3	82	50	55	37	29	2	1	209	483	17	73	4.6	.976	SS-153
1990		143	.254	.305	512	130	21	1	1	0.2	61	50	61	33	32	2	0	212	378	12	66	4.3	.980	SS-140
1991		150	.285	.367	550	157	30	3	3	0.5	96	50	83	36	35	0	0	244	387	8	79	4.3	.987	SS-150
1992		132	.295	.342	518	153	20	2	0	0.0	73	31	59	34	43	0	0	232	420	10	82	5.0	.985	SS-132
1993		141	.288	.356	545	157	22	6	1	0.2	75	53	43	18	21	5	0	251	451	19	98	5.4	.974	SS-134
1994		98	.262	.349	381	100	18	3	3	0.8	51	30	38	26	6	2	0	136	292	8	65	4.5	.982	SS-96
1995		44	.199	.244	156	31	5	1	0	0.0	16	11	17	12	4	3	0	60	128	7	27	4.8	.964	SS-41
18 yrs.		2491	.261	.327	9169	2396	392	67	26	0.3	1221	775	1047	580	573	30	4	4160	8213	273	1551	5.1	.978	SS-2459

Ozzie Smith *continued*

LEAGUE CHAMPIONSHIP SERIES

Year	Team	Games	BA	SA	AB	H	2B	3B	HR	HR%	R	RBI	BB	SO	SB	Pinch Hit AB	Pinch Hit H	PO	A	E	DP	TC/G	FA	G by Pos
1982	STL N	3	.556	.556	9	5	0	0	0	0.0	0	3	3	0	1	0	0	4	11	0	1	5.0	1.000	SS-3
1985		6	.435	.696	23	10	1	1	1	4.3	4	3	3	1	1	0	0	6	16	0	2	3.7	1.000	SS-6
1987		7	.200	.280	25	5	0	1	0	0.0	2	1	3	4	0	0	0	10	19	1	4	4.3	.967	SS-7
3 yrs.		16	.351	.491	57	20	1	2	1	1.8	6	7	9	5	2	0	0	20	46	1	7	4.2	.985	SS-16
			9th					4th																

WORLD SERIES

Year	Team	Games	BA	SA	AB	H	2B	3B	HR	HR%	R	RBI	BB	SO	SB	Pinch Hit AB	Pinch Hit H	PO	A	E	DP	TC/G	FA	G by Pos
1982	STL N	7	.208	.208	24	5	0	0	0	0.0	3	1	3	0	1	0	0	22	17	0	5	5.6	1.000	SS-7
1985		7	.087	.087	23	2	0	0	0	0.0	1	0	4	0	1	0	0	10	16	1	5	3.9	.963	SS-7
1987		7	.214	.214	28	6	0	0	0	0.0	3	2	2	3	2	0	0	7	19	0	1	3.7	1.000	SS-7
3 yrs.		21	.173	.173	75	13	0	0	0	0.0	7	3	9	3	4	0	0	39	52	1	11	4.4	.989	SS-21

Paddy Smith

SMITH, LAWRENCE PATRICK BL TR 6′ 195 lbs.
B. May 16, 1894, Pelham, N. Y. D. Dec. 2, 1990, New Rochelle, N. Y.

Year	Team	Games	BA	SA	AB	H	2B	3B	HR	HR%	R	RBI	BB	SO	SB	Pinch Hit AB	Pinch Hit H	PO	A	E	DP	TC/G	FA	G by Pos
1920	BOS A	2	.000	.000	2	0	0	0	0	0.0	0	0	0	1	0	1	0	0	0	0	0	0.0	.000	C-1

Paul Smith

SMITH, PAUL LESLIE BL TL 5′ 8″ 165 lbs.
B. Mar. 19, 1931, New Castle, Pa.

Year	Team	Games	BA	SA	AB	H	2B	3B	HR	HR%	R	RBI	BB	SO	SB	Pinch Hit AB	Pinch Hit H	PO	A	E	DP	TC/G	FA	G by Pos
1953	PIT N	118	.283	.380	389	110	12	7	4	1.0	41	44	24	23	3	23	8	653	54	11	53	7.7	.985	1B-74, OF-19
1957		81	.253	.340	150	38	4	0	3	2.0	12	11	12	17	0	45	9	53	2	0	0	1.6	1.000	OF-33, 1B-1
1958	2 teams	PIT N (6G –.333) CHI N (18G –.150)																						
″	total	24	.174	.174	23	4	0	0	0	0.0	1	1	6	4	0	13	3	14	2	1	0	4.3	.941	1B-4
3 yrs.		223	.270	.361	562	152	16	7	7	1.2	54	56	42	44	3	81	20	720	58	12	53	6.0	.985	1B-79, OF-52

Paul Smith

SMITH, PAUL STONER BL TR 6′ 1″ 190 lbs.
B. May 7, 1888, Mt. Zion, Ill. D. July 3, 1958, Decatur, Ill.

Year	Team	Games	BA	SA	AB	H	2B	3B	HR	HR%	R	RBI	BB	SO	SB	Pinch Hit AB	Pinch Hit H	PO	A	E	DP	TC/G	FA	G by Pos
1916	CIN N	10	.227	.273	44	10	0	1	0	0.0	5	1	1	8	3	0	0	13	1	0	0	1.4	1.000	OF-10

Pop Smith

SMITH, CHARLES MARVIN BR TR 5′11″ 170 lbs.
B. Oct. 12, 1856, Digby, Nova Scotia, Canada D. Apr. 18, 1927, Boston, Mass.

Year	Team	Games	BA	SA	AB	H	2B	3B	HR	HR%	R	RBI	BB	SO	SB	Pinch Hit AB	Pinch Hit H	PO	A	E	DP	TC/G	FA	G by Pos
1880	CIN N	83	.207	.290	334	69	10	9	0	0.0	35	27	6	36		0	0	282	243	89	32	7.4	.855	2B-83
1881	3 teams	CLE N (10G –.118) WOR N (11G –.073) BUF N (3G –.000)																						
″	total	24	.081	.081	86	7	0	0	0	0.0	5	6	6	18		0	0	55	34	12	5	4.2	.881	3B-10, OF-8, 2B-6
1882	2 teams	PHI AA (20G –.092) LOU AA (3G –.182)																						
″	total	23	.105	.105	76	8	0	0	0	0.0	11		12			0	0	32	67	27	0	5.5	.786	3B-11, SS-7, OF-3, 2B-2
1883	COL AA	97	.262	.410	405	106	14	**17**	4	1.0	82		22			0	0	286	296	74	40	6.6	.887	2B-73, 3B-24, P-3
1884		108	.238	.364	445	106	18	10	6	1.3	78		20			0	0	324	394	75	55	7.3	.905	2B-108
1885	PIT AA	106	.249	.331	453	113	11	13	0	0.0	85		25			0	0	372	384	64	53	7.7	.922	2B-106
1886		126	.217	.308	483	105	20	9	2	0.4	75		42			0	0	221	456	75	36	5.9	.900	SS-98, 2B-28, C-1
1887	PIT N	122	.215	.285	456	98	12	7	2	0.4	69	54	30	48	30	0	0	296	417	65	39	6.4	.916	2B-89, SS-33
1888		131	.206	.270	481	99	15	2	4	0.8	61	52	22	78	37	0	0	222	431	70	42	5.5	.903	SS-75, 2B-56
1889	2 teams	PIT N (72G –.209) BOS N (59G –.260)																						
″	total	131	.232	.339	466	108	23	6	5	1.1	47	59	47	**68**	23	0	0	253	392	72	51	5.4	.900	SS-117, 2B-9, OF-3, 3B-3
1890	BOS N	134	.229	.322	463	106	16	12	1	0.2	82	53	80	**81**	39	0	0	236	403	58	41	5.2	.917	2B-134, SS-1
1891	WAS AA	27	.178	.244	90	16	2	2	0	0.0	13	13	13	16	2	0	0	63	87	18	12	6.0	.893	2B-19, SS-5, 3B-4
12 yrs.		1112	.222	.313	4238	941	141	87	24	0.6	643	264	325	345	131	0	0	2642	3604	699	406	6.2	.899	2B-713, SS-336, 3B-52, OF-14, P-3, C-1

Ray Smith

SMITH, RAYMOND EDWARD BR TR 6′ 1″ 185 lbs.
B. Sept. 18, 1955, Glendale, Calif.

Year	Team	Games	BA	SA	AB	H	2B	3B	HR	HR%	R	RBI	BB	SO	SB	Pinch Hit AB	Pinch Hit H	PO	A	E	DP	TC/G	FA	G by Pos
1981	MIN A	15	.200	.300	40	8	1	0	1	2.5	4	1	0	3	0	0	0	65	3	0	0	4.5	1.000	C-15
1982		9	.217	.304	23	5	0	1	0	0.0	1	1	1	3	0	0	0	44	2	0	0	5.1	1.000	C-9
1983		59	.224	.257	152	34	5	0	0	0.0	11	8	10	12	1	0	0	272	27	5	3	5.2	.984	C-59
3 yrs.		83	.219	.270	215	47	6	1	1	0.5	16	10	11	18	1	0	0	381	32	5	3	5.0	.988	C-83

Red Smith

SMITH, JAMES CARLISLE BR TR 5′11″ 165 lbs.
B. Apr. 6, 1890, Greenville, S. C. D. Oct. 11, 1966, Atlanta, Ga.

Year	Team	Games	BA	SA	AB	H	2B	3B	HR	HR%	R	RBI	BB	SO	SB	Pinch Hit AB	Pinch Hit H	PO	A	E	DP	TC/G	FA	G by Pos
1911	BKN N	28	.261	.333	111	29	6	1	0	0.0	10	19	5	13	5	0	0	30	51	9	7	3.2	.900	3B-28
1912		128	.286	.393	486	139	28	6	4	0.8	75	57	54	51	22	3	1	156	251	27	16	3.5	.938	3B-125
1913		151	.296	.441	540	160	**40**	10	6	1.1	70	76	45	67	22	0	0	175	295	34	13	3.3	.933	3B-151
1914	2 teams	BKN N (90G –.245) BOS N (60G –.314)																						
″	total	150	.272	.395	537	146	27	9	7	1.3	69	85	58	50	15	0	0	220	332	37	28	3.9	.937	3B-150
1915	BOS N	157	.264	.352	549	145	34	4	2	0.4	66	65	67	49	10	0	0	170	292	26	26	3.1	.947	3B-157
1916		150	.259	.348	509	132	16	10	3	0.6	48	60	53	55	13	0	0	166	299	36	15	3.3	.928	3B-150
1917		147	.295	.392	505	149	31	6	2	0.4	60	62	53	61	16	1	0	141	264	33	27	3.0	.925	3B-147
1918		119	.298	.373	429	128	20	3	2	0.5	55	65	45	47	8	0	0	123	291	35	16	3.8	.922	3B-119
1919		87	.245	.282	241	59	6	0	1	0.4	24	25	40	22	6	15	4	128	64	9	5	2.8	.955	OF-48, 3B-23
9 yrs.		1117	.278	.377	3907	1087	208	49	27	0.7	477	514	420	415	117	19	5	1309	2139	246	153	3.4	.933	3B-1050, OF-48

Red Smith

SMITH, MARVIN HAROLD BL TR 5′ 7″ 165 lbs.
B. July 17, 1900, Ashley, Ill. D. Feb. 19, 1961, Los Angeles, Calif.

Year	Team	Games	BA	SA	AB	H	2B	3B	HR	HR%	R	RBI	BB	SO	SB	Pinch Hit AB	Pinch Hit H	PO	A	E	DP	TC/G	FA	G by Pos
1925	PHI A	20	.286	.286	14	4	0	0	0	0.0	1	1	2	5	0	0	0	7	15	4	1	1.4	.846	SS-16, 3B-2

Red Smith

SMITH, RICHARD PAUL BR TR 5′10″ 185 lbs.
B. May 18, 1904, Brokaw, Wis. D. Mar. 8, 1978, Toledo, Ohio.

Year	Team	Games	BA	SA	AB	H	2B	3B	HR	HR%	R	RBI	BB	SO	SB	Pinch Hit AB	Pinch Hit H	PO	A	E	DP	TC/G	FA	G by Pos
1927	NY N	1	—	—	0	0	0	0	0	—	0	0	0	0	0	0	0	1	0	0	0	1.0	1.000	C-1

Red Smith

SMITH, WILLARD JEHU BR TR 5′ 8″ 165 lbs.
B. Apr. 11, 1892, Logansport, Ind. D. July 17, 1972, Noblesville, Ind.

Year	Team	Games	BA	SA	AB	H	2B	3B	HR	HR%	R	RBI	BB	SO	SB	Pinch Hit AB	Pinch Hit H	PO	A	E	DP	TC/G	FA	G by Pos
1917	PIT N	11	.143	.190	21	3	1	0	0	0.0	1	2	3	4	1	4	1	20	11	0	1	5.2	1.000	C-6
1918		15	.167	.208	24	4	1	0	0	0.0	1	3	3	0	0	4	0	27	4	2	2	3.3	.939	C-10
2 yrs.		26	.156	.200	45	7	2	0	0	0.0	2	5	6	4	1	8	1	47	15	2	3	4.0	.969	C-16

Reggie Smith

SMITH, CARL REGINALD — B. Apr. 2, 1945, Shreveport, La. — BB TR 6′ 180 lbs.

Year	Team	Games	BA	SA	AB	H	2B	3B	HR	HR%	R	RBI	BB	SO	SB	Pinch Hit AB	Pinch Hit H	PO	A	E	DP	TC/G	FA	G by Pos
1966	BOS A	6	.154	.192	26	4	1	0	0	0.0	1	0	0	5	0	0	0	17	0	1	0	3.0	.944	OF-6
1967		158	.246	.389	565	139	24	6	15	2.7	78	61	57	95	16	10	1	353	32	7	11	2.6	.982	OF-144, 2B-6
1968		155	.265	.430	558	148	**37**	5	15	2.7	78	69	64	77	22	0	0	390	8	6	1	2.6	.985	OF-155
1969		143	.309	.527	543	168	29	7	25	4.6	87	93	54	67	7	4	1	321	8	14	1	2.5	.959	OF-139
1970		147	.303	.497	580	176	32	7	22	3.8	109	74	51	60	10	2	0	361	15	9	1	2.7	.977	OF-145
1971		159	.283	.489	618	175	**33**	2	30	4.9	85	96	63	82	11	0	0	386	15	14	2	2.6	.966	OF-159
1972		131	.270	.475	467	126	25	4	21	4.5	75	74	68	63	15	2	0	247	8	5	2	2.0	.981	OF-129
1973		115	.303	.515	423	128	23	2	21	5.0	79	69	68	49	3	1	0	282	8	5	2	2.6	.983	OF-104, DH-8, 1B-1
1974	STL N	143	.309	.528	517	160	26	9	23	4.4	79	100	71	70	4	10	4	286	9	7	3	2.3	.977	OF-132, 1B-1
1975		135	.302	.488	477	144	26	3	19	4.0	67	76	63	59	9	7	3	650	39	15	51	5.2	.979	OF-69, 1B-66, 3B-1
1976	2 teams	STL N (47G –.218) LA N (65G –.280)																						
″	total	112	.253	.453	395	100	15	5	18	4.6	55	49	32	70	3	8	4	314	48	4	20	3.5	.989	OF-74, 1B-17, 3B-14
1977	LA N	148	.307	.576	488	150	27	4	32	6.6	104	87	104	76	7	6	1	240	7	5	0	1.8	.980	OF-140
1978		128	.295	.559	447	132	27	2	29	6.5	82	93	70	90	12	2	0	220	8	12	4	1.9	.950	OF-126
1979		68	.274	.466	234	64	13	1	10	4.3	41	32	31	50	6	5	2	159	5	2	0	2.7	.988	OF-62
1980		92	.322	.508	311	100	13	0	15	4.8	47	55	41	63	5	6	3	153	15	1	5	2.0	.994	OF-84
1981		41	.200	.314	35	7	1	0	1	2.9	5	8	7	8	0	31	6	15	1	0	1	8.0	1.000	1B-2
1982	SF N	106	.284	.470	349	99	11	0	18	5.2	51	56	46	46	7	6	1	792	78	16	61	8.9	.982	1B-99
17 yrs.		1987	.287	.489	7033	2020	363	57	314	4.5	1123	1092	890	1030	137	100	26	5186	304	123	165	3.0	.978	OF-1668, 1B-186, 3B-15, DH-8, 2B-6
DIVISIONAL PLAYOFF SERIES																								
1981	LA N	2	.000	.000	1	0	0	0	0	0.0	0	1	0	1	0	1	0	0	0	0	0	0.0	—	
LEAGUE CHAMPIONSHIP SERIES																								
1977	LA N	4	.188	.313	16	3	0	1	0	0.0	2	1	2	5	1	0	0	7	0	1	0	2.0	.875	OF-4
1978		4	.188	.250	16	3	1	0	0	0.0	2	1	0	2	0	0	0	5	0	1	0	1.5	.833	OF-4
1981		1	1.000	1.000	1	1	0	0	0	0.0	0	1	0	0	0	1	1	0	0	0	0	0.0	—	
3 yrs.		9	.212	.303	33	7	1	1	0	0.0	4	3	2	7	1	1	1	12	0	2	0	1.8	.857	OF-8
WORLD SERIES																								
1967	BOS A	7	.250	.542	24	6	1	0	2	8.3	3	3	2	2	0	0	0	14	0	0	0	2.0	1.000	OF-7
1977	LA N	6	.273	.727	22	6	1	0	3	13.6	7	5	4	3	0	0	0	14	1	0	0	2.5	1.000	OF-6
1978		6	.200	.320	25	5	0	0	1	4.0	3	5	2	6	0	0	0	11	1	1	0	2.2	.923	OF-6
1981		2	.500	.500	2	1	0	0	0	0.0	0	0	0	1	0	2	1	0	0	0	0	0.0	—	
4 yrs.		21	.247	.521	73	18	2	0	6	8.2 **8th**	13	13	8	12	0	2	1	39	2	1	0	2.2	.976	OF-19

Skyrocket Smith

SMITH, SAMUEL J. — B. Mar. 19, 1868, Baltimore, Md. D. Apr. 26, 1916, St. Louis, Mo. — BR 6′ 2″ 170 lbs.

Year	Team	Games	BA	SA	AB	H	2B	3B	HR	HR%	R	RBI	BB	SO	SB	Pinch Hit AB	Pinch Hit H	PO	A	E	DP	TC/G	FA	G by Pos
1888	LOU AA	58	.238	.335	206	49	9	4	1	0.5	27	31	24		5	0	0	568	22	18	15	10.5	.970	1B-58

Stub Smith

SMITH, JAMES A. — B. Nov. 26, 1876, Elmwood, Ill. Deceased. — BL TR 5′ 6″ 145 lbs.

Year	Team	Games	BA	SA	AB	H	2B	3B	HR	HR%	R	RBI	BB	SO	SB	Pinch Hit AB	Pinch Hit H	PO	A	E	DP	TC/G	FA	G by Pos
1898	BOS N	3	.100	.100	10	1	0	0	0	0.0	1	0	0		0	0	0	5	9	1	0	5.0	.933	SS-3

Syd Smith

SMITH, SYDNEY E. — B. Aug. 31, 1883, Smithville, S. C. D. June 5, 1961, Orangeburg, S. C. — BR TR 5′10″ 190 lbs.

Year	Team	Games	BA	SA	AB	H	2B	3B	HR	HR%	R	RBI	BB	SO	SB	Pinch Hit AB	Pinch Hit H	PO	A	E	DP	TC/G	FA	G by Pos
1908	2 teams	PHI A (46G –.203) STL A (27G –.184)																						
″	total	73	.196	.309	204	40	12	4	1	0.5	14	15	8		2	10	1	352	75	11	7	6.3	.975	C-61, 1B-6, OF-2
1910	CLE A	9	.333	.370	27	9	1	0	0	0.0	1	3	3		0	0	0	33	13	2	3	5.3	.958	C-9
1911		58	.299	.383	154	46	8	1	1	0.6	8	21	11		0	7	3	270	62	7	10	6.8	.979	C-48, 3B-1, 1B-1
1914	PIT N	5	.273	.273	11	3	0	0	0	0.0	1	1	0	1	0	2	0	12	3	0	0	5.0	1.000	C-3
1915		1	.000	.000	1	0	0	0	0	0.0	0	0	0	0	0	1	0	0	0	0	0	0.0	—	
5 yrs.		146	.247	.340	397	98	21	5	2	0.5	24	40	22	1	2	20	4	667	153	20	20	6.4	.976	C-121, 1B-7, OF-2, 3B-1

Tommy Smith

SMITH, TOMMY ALEXANDER — B. Aug. 1, 1948, Albemarle, N. C. — BL TR 6′ 4″ 210 lbs.

Year	Team	Games	BA	SA	AB	H	2B	3B	HR	HR%	R	RBI	BB	SO	SB	Pinch Hit AB	Pinch Hit H	PO	A	E	DP	TC/G	FA	G by Pos
1973	CLE A	14	.244	.439	41	10	2	0	2	4.9	6	3	1	2	1	0	0	27	0	0	0	2.1	1.000	OF-13
1974		23	.097	.129	31	3	1	0	0	0.0	4	0	2	7	0	2	0	29	1	2	0	1.8	.938	OF-17, DH-1
1975		8	.125	.125	8	1	0	0	0	0.0	0	2	0	1	0	1	0	4	0	0	0	0.7	1.000	OF-3, DH-3
1976		55	.256	.323	164	42	3	1	2	1.2	17	12	8	8	8	2	0	90	4	2	0	1.8	.979	OF-50, DH-2
1977	SEA A	21	.259	.370	27	7	1	1	0	0.0	1	4	0	6	0	8	2	10	3	0	0	0.9	1.000	OF-14
5 yrs.		121	.232	.317	271	63	7	2	4	1.5	28	21	11	24	9	13	2	160	8	4	0	1.7	.977	OF-97, DH-6

Tony Smith

SMITH, ANTHONY — B. May 14, 1884, Chicago, Ill. D. Feb. 27, 1964, Galveston, Tex. — BR TR 5′ 9″ 150 lbs.

Year	Team	Games	BA	SA	AB	H	2B	3B	HR	HR%	R	RBI	BB	SO	SB	Pinch Hit AB	Pinch Hit H	PO	A	E	DP	TC/G	FA	G by Pos
1907	WAS A	51	.187	.209	139	26	1	1	0	0.0	12	8	18		3	0	0	99	141	21	11	5.1	.920	SS-51
1910	BKN N	106	.181	.227	321	58	10	1	1	0.3	31	16	69	53	9	0	0	262	329	37	57	5.9	.941	SS-101, 3B-6
1911		13	.150	.175	40	6	1	0	0	0.0	3	2	8	7	1	0	0	21	38	8	7	5.2	.881	SS-10, 2B-3
3 yrs.		170	.180	.218	500	90	12	2	1	0.2	46	26	95	60	13	0	0	382	508	66	75	5.6	.931	SS-162, 3B-6, 2B-3

Vinnie Smith

SMITH, VINCENT AMBROSE — B. Dec. 7, 1915, Richmond, Va. D. Dec. 14, 1979, Virginia Beach, Va. — BR TR 6′ 1″ 176 lbs.

Year	Team	Games	BA	SA	AB	H	2B	3B	HR	HR%	R	RBI	BB	SO	SB	Pinch Hit AB	Pinch Hit H	PO	A	E	DP	TC/G	FA	G by Pos
1941	PIT N	9	.303	.333	33	10	1	0	0	0.0	3	5	1	5	0	0	0	27	5	2	0	3.8	.941	C-9
1946		7	.190	.190	21	4	0	0	0	0.0	2	0	1	5	0	0	0	25	4	1	0	4.3	.967	C-7
2 yrs.		16	.259	.278	54	14	1	0	0	0.0	5	5	2	10	0	0	0	52	9	3	0	4.0	.953	C-16

Wally Smith

SMITH, WALLACE H. — B. Mar. 13, 1889, Philadelphia, Pa. D. June 10, 1930, Florence, Ariz. — BR TR 5′11½″ 180 lbs.

Year	Team	Games	BA	SA	AB	H	2B	3B	HR	HR%	R	RBI	BB	SO	SB	Pinch Hit AB	Pinch Hit H	PO	A	E	DP	TC/G	FA	G by Pos
1911	STL N	81	.216	.330	194	42	6	5	2	1.0	23	19	21	33	5	16	2	63	139	14	7	3.6	.935	3B-26, SS-25, 2B-8, OF-1
1912		75	.256	.324	219	56	5	5	0	0.0	22	26	29	27	4	12	0	136	130	10	11	4.6	.964	3B-32, SS-22, 1B-6
1914	WAS A	45	.196	.258	97	19	4	1	0	0.0	11	8	3	12	3	11	1	99	35	4	7	4.3	.971	2B-12, SS-7, 1B-7, 3B-5, OF-1
3 yrs.		201	.229	.314	510	117	15	11	2	0.4	56	53	53	72	12	39	3	298	304	28	25	4.1	.956	3B-63, SS-54, 2B-20, 1B-13, OF-2

Wib Smith

SMITH, WILBUR FLOYD BL TR 5'10½" 165 lbs.
B. Aug. 30, 1886, Evart, Mich. D. Nov. 18, 1959, Fargo, N. D.

Year	Team	Games	BA	SA	AB	H	2B	3B	HR	HR%	R	RBI	BB	SO	SB	Pinch Hit AB	Pinch Hit H	PO	A	E	DP	TC/G	FA	G by Pos
1909	STL A	17	.190	.190	42	8	0	0	0	0.0	3	2	0		0	3	1	36	11	9	0	4.0	.839	C-13, 1B-1

Willie Smith

SMITH, WILLIE (Wonderful Willie) BL TL 6' 182 lbs.
B. Feb. 11, 1939, Anniston, Ala.

Year	Team	Games	BA	SA	AB	H	2B	3B	HR	HR%	R	RBI	BB	SO	SB	Pinch Hit AB	Pinch Hit H	PO	A	E	DP	TC/G	FA	G by Pos
1963	DET A	17	.125	.125	8	1	0	0	0	0.0	2	0	0	1	0	2	0	1	4	0	0	0.5	1.000	P-11
1964	LA A	118	.301	.465	359	108	14	6	11	3.1	46	51	8	39	7	23	10	129	8	3	1	1.4	.979	OF-87, P-15
1965	CAL A	136	.261	.423	459	120	14	9	14	3.1	52	57	32	60	9	21	4	196	12	5	2	1.7	.977	OF-123, 1B-2
1966		90	.185	.236	195	36	3	2	1	0.5	18	20	12	37	1	41	5	71	4	2	1	1.5	.974	OF-52
1967	CLE A	21	.219	.281	32	7	2	0	0	0.0	0	2	1	10	0	16	4	12	0	1	0	1.9	.923	OF-4, 1B-3
1968	2 teams	CLE A (33G –.143) CHI N (55G –.275)																						
"	total	88	.245	.402	184	45	10	2	5	2.7	14	28	15	47	0	36	10	113	6	0	6	2.2	1.000	OF-39, 1B-11, P-3
1969	CHI N	103	.246	.441	195	48	9	1	9	4.6	21	25	25	49	1	40	12	185	9	3	14	3.5	.985	OF-33, 1B-24
1970		87	.216	.371	167	36	9	1	5	3.0	15	24	11	32	2	40	9	318	11	2	32	7.5	.994	1B-43, OF-1
1971	CIN N	31	.164	.255	55	9	2	0	1	1.8	3	4	3	9	0	20	0	80	9	0	10	8.9	1.000	1B-10
9 yrs.		691	.248	.395	1654	410	63	21	46	2.8	171	211	107	284	20	239	54	1105	63	16	66	2.6	.986	OF-339, 1B-93, P-29

Homer Smoot

SMOOT, HOMER VERNON BL TR 5'10" 190 lbs.
B. Mar. 23, 1878, Galestown, Md. D. Mar. 25, 1928, Salisbury, Md.

Year	Team	Games	BA	SA	AB	H	2B	3B	HR	HR%	R	RBI	BB	SO	SB	Pinch Hit AB	Pinch Hit H	PO	A	E	DP	TC/G	FA	G by Pos
1902	STL N	129	.311	.380	518	161	19	4	3	0.6	58	48	23		20	0	0	284	14	22	5	2.5	.931	OF-129
1903		129	.296	.396	500	148	22	8	4	0.8	67	49	32		17	0	0	231	14	15	3	2.0	.942	OF-129
1904		137	.281	.365	520	146	23	6	3	0.6	58	66	37		23	0	0	270	17	10	6	2.2	.966	OF-137
1905		139	.311	.433	534	166	21	16	4	0.7	73	58	33		21	1	0	295	18	8	6	2.3	.975	OF-138
1906	2 teams	STL N (86G –.248) CIN N (60G –.259)																						
"	total	146	.252	.327	563	142	17	11	1	0.2	52	48	24		3	1	0	283	18	16	4	2.2	.950	OF-145
5 yrs.		680	.290	.380	2635	763	102	45	15	0.6	308	269	149		84	2	0	1363	81	71	24	2.2	.953	OF-678

Henry Smoyer

SMOYER, HENRY NEITZ (Hennie) BR TR 5' 6"
Born Henry Neitz Smowery.
B. Apr. 24, 1890, Fredericksburg, Pa. D. Feb. 28, 1958, Du Bois, Pa.

Year	Team	Games	BA	SA	AB	H	2B	3B	HR	HR%	R	RBI	BB	SO	SB	Pinch Hit AB	Pinch Hit H	PO	A	E	DP	TC/G	FA	G by Pos
1912	STL A	6	.214	.214	14	3	0	0	0	0.0	1	0	2		0	0	0	5	12	0	1	2.8	1.000	SS-4, 3B-2

Frank Smykal

SMYKAL, FRANK JOHN BR TR 5' 7" 150 lbs.
Born Frank John Smejkal.
B. Oct. 13, 1889, Chicago, Ill. D. Aug. 11, 1950, Chicago, Ill.

Year	Team	Games	BA	SA	AB	H	2B	3B	HR	HR%	R	RBI	BB	SO	SB	Pinch Hit AB	Pinch Hit H	PO	A	E	DP	TC/G	FA	G by Pos
1916	PIT N	6	.300	.300	10	3	0	0	0	0.0	1	2	3	1	1	0	0	3	14	3	1	3.3	.850	SS-5, 3B-1

Clancy Smyres

SMYRES, CLARENCE MELVIN BB TR 5'11½" 175 lbs.
B. May 24, 1922, Culver City, Calif.

Year	Team	Games	BA	SA	AB	H	2B	3B	HR	HR%	R	RBI	BB	SO	SB	Pinch Hit AB	Pinch Hit H	PO	A	E	DP	TC/G	FA	G by Pos
1944	BKN N	5	.000	.000	2	0	0	0	0	0.0	1	0	0	0	0	2	0	0	0	0	0	0.0	—	

Red Smyth

SMYTH, JAMES DANIEL BL TR 5' 9" 152 lbs.
B. Jan. 30, 1893, Holly Springs, Miss. D. Apr. 14, 1958, Inglewood, Calif.

Year	Team	Games	BA	SA	AB	H	2B	3B	HR	HR%	R	RBI	BB	SO	SB	Pinch Hit AB	Pinch Hit H	PO	A	E	DP	TC/G	FA	G by Pos
1915	BKN N	19	.136	.182	22	3	1	0	0	0.0	3	3	4	2	1	4	0	14	1	0	0	1.7	1.000	OF-9
1916		2	.000	.000	5	0	0	0	0	0.0	0	0	0	3	0	1	0	3	2	0	1	2.5	1.000	2B-2
1917	2 teams	BKN N (29G –.125) STL N (28G –.208)																						
"	total	57	.188	.229	96	18	0	2	0	0.0	10	5	8	15	3	24	5	30	3	7	1	1.4	.825	OF-25, 3B-4
1918	STL N	40	.212	.257	113	24	1	2	0	0.0	19	4	16	11	3	1	0	56	31	5	2	2.6	.946	OF-25, 2B-11
4 yrs.		118	.191	.233	236	45	2	4	0	0.0	32	12	28	31	7	30	5	103	37	12	4	2.0	.921	OF-59, 2B-13, 3B-4

Jack Sneed

SNEED, JONATHAN L. 5' 8" 160 lbs.
B. Columbus, Ohio D. Jan. 4, 1899, Memphis, Tenn.

Year	Team	Games	BA	SA	AB	H	2B	3B	HR	HR%	R	RBI	BB	SO	SB	Pinch Hit AB	Pinch Hit H	PO	A	E	DP	TC/G	FA	G by Pos
1884	IND AA	27	.216	.284	102	22	4	0	1	1.0	14		6			0	0	45	4	11	0	2.2	.817	OF-27
1890	2 teams	TOL AA (9G –.200) COL AA (128G –.291)																						
"	total	137	.286	.381	514	147	13	15	2	0.4	117		71		44	0	0	177	27	29	6	1.7	.876	OF-135, SS-2
1891	COL AA	99	.257	.322	366	94	9	6	1	0.3	66	61	55	29	24	0	0	142	10	18	4	1.7	.894	OF-99
3 yrs.		263	.268	.349	982	263	26	21	4	0.4	197	61	132	29	68	0	0	364	41	58	10	1.8	.875	OF-261, SS-2

Charlie Snell

SNELL, CHARLES ANTHONY BR TR 5'11" 160 lbs.
Born Charles Anthony Schnell.
B. Nov. 29, 1893, Hampstead, Md. D. Apr. 4, 1988, Reading, Pa.

Year	Team	Games	BA	SA	AB	H	2B	3B	HR	HR%	R	RBI	BB	SO	SB	Pinch Hit AB	Pinch Hit H	PO	A	E	DP	TC/G	FA	G by Pos
1912	STL A	8	.211	.263	19	4	1	0	0	0.0	0	0	3		0	0	0	35	13	3	1	6.4	.941	C-8

Wally Snell

SNELL, WALTER HENRY (Doc) BR TR 5'10" 170 lbs.
B. Apr. 19, 1889, West Bridgewater, Mass. D. July 23, 1980, Providence, R. I.

Year	Team	Games	BA	SA	AB	H	2B	3B	HR	HR%	R	RBI	BB	SO	SB	Pinch Hit AB	Pinch Hit H	PO	A	E	DP	TC/G	FA	G by Pos
1913	BOS A	5	.375	.375	8	3	0	0	0	0.0	1	0	0	0	1	4	2	6	2	0	1	8.0	1.000	C-1

Duke Snider

SNIDER, EDWIN DONALD (The Silver Fox) BL TR 6'½" 198 lbs.
B. Sept. 19, 1926, Los Angeles, Calif.
Hall of Fame 1980.

Year	Team	Games	BA	SA	AB	H	2B	3B	HR	HR%	R	RBI	BB	SO	SB	Pinch Hit AB	Pinch Hit H	PO	A	E	DP	TC/G	FA	G by Pos
1947	BKN N	40	.241	.301	83	20	3	1	0	0.0	6	5	3	24	2	15	4	48	0	1	0	2.0	.980	OF-25
1948		53	.244	.450	160	39	6	6	5	3.1	22	21	12	27	4	6	2	87	5	1	0	2.0	.989	OF-47
1949		146	.292	.493	552	161	28	7	23	4.2	100	92	56	**92**	12	1	1	355	12	6	2	2.6	.984	OF-145
1950		152	.321	.553	620	**199**	31	10	31	5.0	109	107	58	79	16	1	1	378	15	7	1	2.6	.983	OF-151
1951		150	.277	.483	606	168	26	6	29	4.8	96	101	62	97	14	0	0	382	12	5	1	2.7	.987	OF-150
1952		144	.303	.494	534	162	25	7	21	3.9	80	92	55	77	7	2	1	341	13	3	3	2.5	.992	OF-141
1953		153	.336	**.627**	590	198	38	4	42	7.1	**132**	126	82	90	16	4	3	370	7	5	3	2.5	.987	OF-151
1954		149	.341	.647	584	199	39	10	40	6.8	**120**	130	84	**96**	6	1	1	360	8	7	1	2.5	.981	OF-148
1955		148	.309	.628	538	166	34	6	42	7.8	**126**	**136**	104	87	9	1	0	348	9	4	0	2.5	.989	OF-146
1956		151	.292	**.598**	542	158	33	2	**43**	7.9	112	101	**99**	101	3	1	1	358	11	6	1	2.5	.984	OF-150
1957		139	.274	.587	508	139	25	7	40	**7.9**	91	92	77	**104**	3	3	2	304	6	3	1	2.3	.990	OF-136
1958	LA N	106	.312	.505	327	102	12	3	15	4.6	45	58	32	49	2	15	4	151	4	2	0	1.7	.987	OF-92
1959		126	.308	.535	370	114	11	2	23	6.2	59	88	58	71	1	21	7	157	2	4	1	1.5	.975	OF-107
1960		101	.243	.519	235	57	13	5	14	6.0	38	36	46	54	1	25	6	108	3	4	1	1.5	.965	OF-75
1961		85	.296	.562	233	69	8	3	16	6.9	35	56	29	43	1	18	4	113	6	3	3	1.8	.975	OF-66

Duke Snider *continued*

Year	Team		Games	BA	SA	AB	H	2B	3B	HR	HR%	R	RBI	BB	SO	SB	Pinch Hit AB	Pinch Hit H	PO	A	E	DP	TC/G	FA	G by Pos
1962			80	.278	.481	158	44	11	3	5	3.2	28	30	36	32	2	33	6	56	3	2	0	1.6	.967	OF-39
1963	NY	N	129	.243	.401	354	86	8	3	14	4.0	44	45	56	74	0	29	6	139	5	2	0	1.4	.986	OF-106
1964	SF	N	91	.210	.323	167	35	7	0	4	2.4	16	17	22	40	0	47	10	44	2	1	0	1.1	.979	OF-43
18 yrs.			2143	.295	.540	7161	2116	358	85	407	5.7	1259	1333	971	1237	99	223	59	4099	123	66	18	2.2	.985	OF-1918
WORLD SERIES																									
1949	BKN	N	5	.143	.190	21	3	1	0	0	0.0	2	0	0	8	0	0	0	18	1	0	0	3.8	1.000	OF-5
1952			7	.345	.828	29	10	2	0	4	13.8	5	8	1	5	1	0	0	23	0	0	0	3.3	1.000	OF-7
1953			6	.320	.560	25	8	3	0	1	4.0	3	5	2	6	0	0	0	17	1	0	1	3.0	1.000	OF-6
1955			7	.320	.840	25	8	1	0	4	16.0	5	7	2	6	0	0	0	13	0	0	0	1.9	1.000	OF-7
1956			7	.304	.478	23	7	1	0	1	4.3	5	4	6	8	0	0	0	20	0	0	0	2.9	1.000	OF-7
1959	LA	N	4	.200	.500	10	2	0	0	1	10.0	1	2	2	0	0	1	0	5	0	2	0	2.3	.714	OF-3
6 yrs.			36	.286	.594	133	38	8	0	11	8.3	21	26	13	33	1	1	0	96	2	2	1	2.9	.980	OF-35
								6th		4th	7th	10th	7th		3rd										

Van Snider

SNIDER, VAN VOORHEES BL TR 6′ 3″ 185 lbs.
B. Aug. 11, 1963, Birmingham, Ala.

Year	Team		Games	BA	SA	AB	H	2B	3B	HR	HR%	R	RBI	BB	SO	SB	Pinch Hit AB	Pinch Hit H	PO	A	E	DP	TC/G	FA	G by Pos
1988	CIN	N	11	.214	.357	28	6	1	0	1	3.6	4	6	0	13	0	4	0	15	0	0	0	1.9	1.000	OF-8
1989			8	.143	.143	7	1	0	0	0	0.0	1	0	0	5	0	2	0	6	0	0	0	1.0	1.000	OF-6
2 yrs.			19	.200	.314	35	7	1	0	1	2.9	5	6	0	18	0	6	0	21	0	0	0	1.5	1.000	OF-14

Roxy Snipes

SNIPES, WYATT EURE (Rock) BL TR 6′ 185 lbs.
B. Oct. 28, 1896, Marion, S. C. D. May 1, 1941, Fayetteville, N. C.

Year	Team		Games	BA	SA	AB	H	2B	3B	HR	HR%	R	RBI	BB	SO	SB	Pinch Hit AB	Pinch Hit H	PO	A	E	DP	TC/G	FA	G by Pos
1923	CHI	A	1	.000	.000	1	0	0	0	0	0.0	0	0	0	0	0	1	0	0	0	0	0	0.0	—	

Chappie Snodgrass

SNODGRASS, AMZIE BEAL BR TR 5′10″ 165 lbs.
B. Mar. 18, 1870, Springfield, Ohio D. Sept. 9, 1951, New York, N. Y.

Year	Team		Games	BA	SA	AB	H	2B	3B	HR	HR%	R	RBI	BB	SO	SB	Pinch Hit AB	Pinch Hit H	PO	A	E	DP	TC/G	FA	G by Pos
1901	BAL	A	3	.100	.100	10	1	0	0	0	0.0	0	1	0		0	0	0	3	0	3	0	3.0	.500	OF-2

Fred Snodgrass

SNODGRASS, FREDERICK CHARLES (Snow) BR TR 5′11½″ 175 lbs.
B. Oct. 19, 1887, Ventura, Calif. D. Apr. 5, 1974, Ventura, Calif.

Year	Team		Games	BA	SA	AB	H	2B	3B	HR	HR%	R	RBI	BB	SO	SB	Pinch Hit AB	Pinch Hit H	PO	A	E	DP	TC/G	FA	G by Pos
1908	NY	N	6	.250	.250	4	1	0	0	0	0.0	2	1	0		1	1	0	4	1	0	0	1.7	1.000	C-3
1909			28	.300	.414	70	21	5	0	1	1.4	10	6	7		10	6	1	36	4	3	1	2.0	.930	OF-19, C-2, 1B-1
1910			123	.321	.432	396	127	22	8	2	0.5	69	44	71	52	33	10	3	300	22	10	6	3.0	.970	OF-101, 1B-9, 3B-1, C-1
1911			151	.294	.388	534	157	27	10	1	0.2	83	77	72	59	51	0	0	305	37	9	8	2.3	.974	OF-149, 2B-1, 1B-1
1912			146	.269	.364	535	144	24	9	3	0.6	91	69	70	65	43	2	0	472	36	21	16	3.6	.960	OF-116, 1B-28, 2B-1
1913			141	.291	.383	457	133	21	6	3	0.7	65	49	53	44	27	3	0	317	19	11	1	2.5	.968	OF-133, 1B-3, 2B-1
1914			113	.263	.334	392	103	20	4	0	0.0	54	44	37	43	25	6	1	313	21	7	10	3.0	.979	OF-96, 1B-14, 2B-1, 3B-1
1915	2 teams	NY N (103G –.194) BOS N (23G –.278)																							
″	total		126	.215	.248	331	71	11	0	0	0.0	46	29	42	42	11	4	1	239	14	16	4	2.1	.941	OF-121, 1B-5
1916	BOS	N	112	.249	.317	382	95	13	5	1	0.3	33	32	34	54	14	1	0	274	19	5	5	2.7	.983	OF-110
9 yrs.			946	.275	.359	3101	852	143	42	11	0.4	453	351	386	359	215	33	6	2260	173	82	51	2.7	.967	OF-845, 1B-61, C-6, 2B-4, 3B-2
WORLD SERIES																									
1911	NY	N	6	.105	.105	19	2	0	0	0	0.0	1	1	2	7	0	0	0	9	0	0	0	1.5	1.000	OF-6
1912			8	.212	.273	33	7	2	0	0	0.0	2	2	2	5	1	0	0	17	1	1	0	2.4	.947	OF-8
1913			2	.333	.333	3	1	0	0	0	0.0	0	0	0	0	0	0	0	3	1	0	0	2.0	1.000	OF-1, 1B-1
3 yrs.			16	.182	.218	55	10	2	0	0	0.0	3	3	4	12	1	0	0	29	2	1	0	2.0	.969	OF-15, 1B-1

Chris Snopek

SNOPEK, CHRISTOPHER CHARLES BR TR 6′ 1″ 180 lbs.
B. Sept. 20, 1970, Cynthiana, Ky.

Year	Team		Games	BA	SA	AB	H	2B	3B	HR	HR%	R	RBI	BB	SO	SB	Pinch Hit AB	Pinch Hit H	PO	A	E	DP	TC/G	FA	G by Pos
1995	CHI	A	22	.324	.426	68	22	4	0	1	1.5	12	7	9	12	1	1	1	25	31	2	5	2.5	.966	3B-17, SS-6

J. T. Snow

SNOW, JACK THOMAS BB TL 6′ 2″ 200 lbs.
B. Feb. 26, 1968, Long Beach, Calif.

Year	Team		Games	BA	SA	AB	H	2B	3B	HR	HR%	R	RBI	BB	SO	SB	Pinch Hit AB	Pinch Hit H	PO	A	E	DP	TC/G	FA	G by Pos
1992	NY	A	7	.143	.214	14	2	1	0	0	0.0	1	2	5	5	0	0	0	43	2	0	7	7.5	1.000	1B-6
1993	CAL	A	129	.241	.408	419	101	18	2	16	3.8	60	57	55	88	3	2	0	1010	81	6	103	8.5	.995	1B-129
1994			61	.220	.345	223	49	4	0	8	3.6	22	30	19	48	0	0	0	489	37	2	56	8.7	.996	1B-61
1995			143	.289	.465	544	157	22	1	24	4.4	80	102	52	91	2	0	0	1161	56	4	106	8.5	.997	1B-143
4 yrs.			340	.257	.420	1200	309	45	3	48	4.0	163	191	131	232	5	2	0	2703	176	12	272	8.5	.996	1B-339

Bernie Snyder

SNYDER, BERNARD AUSTIN BR TR 6′ 165 lbs.
B. Aug. 25, 1913, Philadelphia, Pa.

Year	Team		Games	BA	SA	AB	H	2B	3B	HR	HR%	R	RBI	BB	SO	SB	Pinch Hit AB	Pinch Hit H	PO	A	E	DP	TC/G	FA	G by Pos
1935	PHI	A	10	.344	.375	32	11	1	0	0	0.0	5	3	1	2	0	2	0	24	19	5	4	5.3	.896	2B-5, SS-4

Charlie Snyder

SNYDER, CHARLES BR TR
B. Camden, N. J. D. Mar. 10, 1901, Philadelphia, Pa.

Year	Team		Games	BA	SA	AB	H	2B	3B	HR	HR%	R	RBI	BB	SO	SB	Pinch Hit AB	Pinch Hit H	PO	A	E	DP	TC/G	FA	G by Pos
1890	PHI	AA	9	.273	.303	33	9	1	0	0	0.0	5		2		0	0	0	21	5	11	0	3.7	.703	OF-5, C-5

Cooney Snyder

SNYDER, FRANK C. 6′ 3″ 180 lbs.
B. Toronto, Ont., Canada D. Mar. 9, 1917, Toronto, Ont., Canada.

Year	Team		Games	BA	SA	AB	H	2B	3B	HR	HR%	R	RBI	BB	SO	SB	Pinch Hit AB	Pinch Hit H	PO	A	E	DP	TC/G	FA	G by Pos
1898	LOU	N	17	.164	.164	61	10	0	0	0	0.0	4	6	3		0	0	0	43	15	4	1	3.6	.935	C-17

Cory Snyder

SNYDER, JAMES CORY BR TR 6′ 4″ 175 lbs.
B. Nov. 11, 1962, Inglewood, Calif.

Year	Team		Games	BA	SA	AB	H	2B	3B	HR	HR%	R	RBI	BB	SO	SB	Pinch Hit AB	Pinch Hit H	PO	A	E	DP	TC/G	FA	G by Pos
1986	CLE	A	103	.272	.500	416	113	21	1	24	5.8	58	69	16	123	2	0	0	213	84	10	22	2.6	.967	OF-74, SS-34, 3B-11, DH-1
1987			157	.236	.456	577	136	24	2	33	5.7	74	82	31	166	5	7	2	313	53	15	9	2.4	.961	OF-139, SS-18
1988			142	.272	.483	511	139	24	3	26	5.1	71	75	42	101	5	1	0	314	16	5	0	2.4	.985	OF-141
1989			132	.215	.360	489	105	17	0	18	3.7	49	59	23	134	6	8	0	297	32	1	7	2.5	.997	OF-125, SS-7, DH-2
1990			123	.233	.404	438	102	27	3	14	3.2	46	55	21	118	1	4	1	229	18	7	4	2.0	.972	OF-120, SS-5
1991	2 teams	CHI A (50G –.188) TOR A (21G –.143)																							
″	total		71	.175	.265	166	29	4	1	3	1.8	14	17	9	60	0	15	2	195	17	3	10	3.0	.986	OF-43, 1B-22, 3B-3, DH-3
1992	SF	N	124	.269	.444	390	105	22	2	14	3.6	48	57	23	96	4	15	2	301	53	6	18	3.1	.983	OF-70, 1B-27, 3B-14, 2B-4, SS-3

Cory Snyder *continued*

Year	Team	Games	BA	SA	AB	H	2B	3B	HR	HR%	R	RBI	BB	SO	SB	Pinch Hit AB	Pinch Hit H	PO	A	E	DP	TC/G	FA	G by Pos
1993	LA N	143	.266	.397	516	137	33	1	11	2.1	61	56	47	**147**	4	5	1	210	46	9	8	1.7	.966	OF-115, 3B-23, 1B-12, SS-2
1994		73	.235	.392	153	36	6	0	6	3.9	18	18	14	47	1	20	4	92	23	7	9	1.7	.943	OF-50, 1B-9, 3B-6, SS-4, 2B-3
9 yrs.		1068	.247	.425	3656	902	178	13	149	4.1	439	488	226	992	28	75	12	2164	342	63	87	2.4	.975	OF-877, SS-73, 1B-70, 3B-57, 2B-7, DH-6

Frank Snyder

SNYDER, FRANK ELTON (Pancho) BR TR 6′ 2″ 185 lbs.
B. May 27, 1893, San Antonio, Tex. D. Jan. 5, 1962, San Antonio, Tex.

Year	Team	Games	BA	SA	AB	H	2B	3B	HR	HR%	R	RBI	BB	SO	SB	Pinch Hit AB	Pinch Hit H	PO	A	E	DP	TC/G	FA	G by Pos
1912	STL N	11	.111	.111	18	2	0	0	0	0.0	2	0	2	7	1	0	0	25	9	3	0	3.4	.919	C-11
1913		7	.190	.286	21	4	0	1	0	0.0	1	2	0	4	0	0	0	31	12	2	0	6.4	.956	C-7
1914		100	.230	.310	326	75	15	4	1	0.3	19	25	13	28	1	2	0	419	130	12	12	5.7	.979	C-98
1915		144	.298	.387	473	141	22	7	2	0.4	41	55	39	49	3	1	0	592	204	14	9	5.6	.983	C-144
1916		132	.259	.308	406	105	12	4	0	0.0	23	39	18	31	7	13	5	731	138	19	35	7.5	.979	C-72, 1B-46, SS-1
1917		115	.236	.288	313	74	9	2	1	0.3	18	33	27	43	4	18	6	341	134	12	10	5.2	.975	C-94
1918		39	.250	.330	112	28	7	1	0	0.0	5	10	6	13	4	9	2	127	40	6	4	5.8	.965	C-27, 1B-3
1919	2 teams	STL N (50G –.182) NY N (32G –.228)																						
″	total	82	.199	.256	246	49	10	2	0	0.0	14	25	13	22	3	2	1	244	113	6	6	4.5	.983	C-79, 1B-1
1920	NY N	87	.250	.364	264	66	13	4	3	1.1	26	27	17	18	2	3	0	269	92	8	6	4.4	.978	C-84
1921		108	.320	.453	309	99	13	2	8	2.6	36	45	27	24	3	5	2	299	98	6	7	4.0	.985	C-101
1922		104	.343	.487	318	109	21	5	5	1.6	34	51	23	25	1	5	2	272	74	7	10	3.6	.980	C-97
1923		120	.256	.356	402	103	13	6	5	1.2	37	63	24	29	5	8	5	428	90	5	12	4.7	.990	C-112
1924		118	.302	.412	354	107	18	3	5	1.4	37	53	30	43	3	8	3	308	79	5	8	3.6	.987	C-110
1925		107	.240	.375	325	78	9	1	11	3.4	21	51	20	49	0	11	5	336	71	6	7	4.3	.985	C-96
1926		55	.216	.365	148	32	3	2	5	3.4	10	16	13	13	0	0	0	168	38	4	3	3.8	.981	C-55
1927	STL N	63	.258	.299	194	50	5	0	1	0.5	7	30	9	18	0	1	1	174	37	4	5	3.5	.981	C-62
16 yrs.		1392	.265	.360	4229	1122	170	44	47	1.1	331	525	281	416	37	86	32	4764	1359	119	134	4.8	.981	C-1249, 1B-50, SS-1
WORLD SERIES																								
1921	NY N	7	.364	.545	22	8	1	0	1	4.5	4	3	0	2	0	1	0	43	5	0	0	8.0	1.000	C-6
1922		4	.333	.333	15	5	0	0	0	0.0	1	0	0	1	0	0	0	23	5	1	1	7.3	.966	C-4
1923		5	.118	.294	17	2	0	0	1	5.9	1	2	0	2	0	0	0	24	3	0	1	5.4	1.000	C-5
1924		1	.000	.000	1	0	0	0	0	0.0	0	0	0	0	0	1	0	0	0	0	0	0.0	—	
4 yrs.		17	.273	.400	55	15	1	0	2	3.6	6	5	0	5	0	2	0	90	13	1	2	6.9	.990	C-15

Jack Snyder

SNYDER, JOHN WILLIAM BR TR 5′ 9″ 168 lbs.
B. Oct. 6, 1886, Allegheny County, Pa. D. Dec. 13, 1981, Brownsville, Pa.

Year	Team	Games	BA	SA	AB	H	2B	3B	HR	HR%	R	RBI	BB	SO	SB	Pinch Hit AB	Pinch Hit H	PO	A	E	DP	TC/G	FA	G by Pos
1914	BUF F	1	—	—	0	0	0	0	0	—	0	0	1		0	0	0	0	0	0	0	0.0	.000	C-1
1917	BKN N	7	.273	.273	11	3	0	0	0	0.0	1	1	0	2	0	1	0	11	4	0	0	3.0	1.000	C-5
2 yrs.		8	.273	.273	11	3	0	0	0	0.0	1	1	1	2	0	1	0	11	4	0	0	2.5	1.000	C-6

Jerry Snyder

SNYDER, GERALD GEORGE BR TR 6′ 170 lbs.
B. July 21, 1929, Jenks, Okla.

Year	Team	Games	BA	SA	AB	H	2B	3B	HR	HR%	R	RBI	BB	SO	SB	Pinch Hit AB	Pinch Hit H	PO	A	E	DP	TC/G	FA	G by Pos
1952	WAS A	36	.158	.193	57	9	2	0	0	0.0	5	2	5	8	1	7	0	37	55	5	12	4.2	.948	2B-19, SS-4
1953		29	.339	.403	62	21	4	0	0	0.0	10	4	5	8	1	0	0	33	58	3	10	4.5	.968	SS-17, 2B-4
1954		64	.234	.266	154	36	3	1	0	0.0	17	17	15	18	3	1	0	88	148	7	32	4.8	.971	SS-48, 2B-3
1955		46	.224	.271	107	24	5	0	0	0.0	7	5	6	6	1	6	1	78	68	4	24	3.6	.973	2B-22, SS-20
1956		43	.270	.345	148	40	3	1	2	1.4	14	14	10	9	1	1	0	64	124	9	28	4.7	.954	SS-35, 2B-7
1957		42	.151	.194	93	14	1	0	1	1.1	6	4	4	9	0	12	3	43	59	3	16	3.6	.971	SS-15, 2B-13, 3B-1
1958		6	.111	.111	9	1	0	0	0	0.0	1	1	1	1	0	2	0	8	2	0	1	3.3	1.000	2B-2, SS-1
7 yrs.		266	.230	.279	630	145	18	2	3	0.5	60	47	46	59	7	29	4	351	514	31	123	4.2	.965	SS-140, 2B-70, 3B-1

Jimmy Snyder

SNYDER, JAMES ROBERT BR TR 6′ 1″ 185 lbs.
B. Aug. 15, 1932, Dearborn, Mich.
Manager 1988.

Year	Team	Games	BA	SA	AB	H	2B	3B	HR	HR%	R	RBI	BB	SO	SB	Pinch Hit AB	Pinch Hit H	PO	A	E	DP	TC/G	FA	G by Pos
1961	MIN A	3	.000	.000	5	0	0	0	0	0.0	0	0	0	1	0	0	0	4	3	0	1	2.3	1.000	2B-3
1962		12	.100	.100	10	1	0	0	0	0.0	1	1	0	0	0	0	0	8	8	1	3	2.8	.941	2B-5, 1B-1
1964		26	.155	.225	71	11	2	0	1	1.4	3	9	4	11	0	0	0	49	51	1	16	4.0	.990	2B-25
3 yrs.		41	.140	.198	86	12	2	0	1	1.2	4	10	4	12	0	0	0	61	62	2	20	3.7	.984	2B-33, 1B-1

Pop Snyder

SNYDER, CHARLES N. BR TR 5′11½″ 184 lbs.
B. Oct. 6, 1854, Washington, D. C. D. Oct. 29, 1924, Washington, D. C.
Manager 1882–84, 1891.

Year	Team	Games	BA	SA	AB	H	2B	3B	HR	HR%	R	RBI	BB	SO	SB	Pinch Hit AB	Pinch Hit H	PO	A	E	DP	TC/G	FA	G by Pos
1876	LOU N	56	.196	.237	224	44	4	1	1	0.4	21	9	2	7		0	0	252	87	68	3	6.9	.833	C-55, OF-4
1877		61	.258	.327	248	64	7	2	2	0.8	23	28	3	14		0	0	292	103	40	8	6.9	.908	C-61, SS-1, OF-1
1878	BOS N	60	.212	.235	226	48	5	0	0	0.0	21	14	1	19		0	0	344	92	42	2	8.0	.912	C-58, OF-2
1879		81	.237	.322	329	78	16	3	2	0.6	42	35	5	31		0	0	398	142	44	10	7.1	.925	C-80, OF-2
1881		62	.228	.265	219	50	8	0	0	0.0	14	16	3	23		0	0	261	110	44	0	6.6	.894	C-60, SS-1, OF-1, 2B-1
1882	CIN AA	72	.291	.353	309	90	12	2	1	0.3	49		9			0	0	368	95	44	3	6.9	.913	C-70, 1B-2, OF-1
1883		58	.256	.360	250	64	14	6	0	0.0	38		8			0	0	286	78	36	4	6.8	.910	C-57, SS-2
1884		67	.257	.358	268	69	9	9	0	0.0	32		7			0	0	363	137	41	6	8.0	.924	C-65, 1B-2, OF-1
1885		39	.237	.322	152	36	4	3	1	0.7	13		6			0	0	192	64	35	3	7.5	.880	C-38, 1B-1
1886		60	.186	.250	220	41	8	3	0	0.0	33		13			0	0	329	80	44	11	7.4	.903	C-41, 1B-19, OF-1
1887	CLE AA	74	.255	.340	282	72	12	6	0	0.0	33		9		5	0	0	404	148	56	12	8.0	.908	C-63, 1B-13
1888		64	.215	.270	237	51	7	3	0	0.0	22	14	6		9	0	0	335	131	48	12	7.9	.907	C-58, 1B-4, OF-3
1889	CLE N	22	.193	.229	83	16	3	0	0	0.0	5	12	2	12	4	0	0	88	39	13	5	6.4	.907	C-22
1890	CLE P	13	.188	.208	48	9	1	0	0	0.0	5	12	1	9	1	0	0	52	16	3	1	5.5	.958	C-13
1891	WAS AA	8	.185	.259	27	5	0	1	0	0.0	4	2	0	3	0	0	0	51	6	0	0	7.1	1.000	1B-4, C-3, OF-1
15 yrs.		797	.236	.303	3122	737	110	39	7	0.2	355	142	75	118	19	0	0	4015	1328	558	80	7.3	.905	C-744, 1B-45, OF-17, SS-4, 2B-1

Redleg Snyder

SNYDER, EMANUEL SEBASTIAN
Born Emanuel Sebastian Schneider.
B. Dec. 12, 1854, Camden, N. J. D. Nov. 11, 1933, Camden, N. J.
BR TR 5'10" 175 lbs.

Year	Team	Games	BA	SA	AB	H	2B	3B	HR	HR%	R	RBI	BB	SO	SB	Pinch Hit AB	Pinch Hit H	PO	A	E	DP	TC/G	FA	G by Pos
1876	CIN N	55	.151	.176	205	31	3	1	0	0.0	10	12	1	19		0	0	168	6	37	1	3.8	.825	OF-55
1884	WIL U	17	.192	.192	52	10	0	0	0	0.0	4		1			0	0	155	5	4	8	9.6	.976	1B-16, OF-1
2 yrs.		72	.160	.179	257	41	3	1	0	0.0	14	12	2	19		0	0	323	11	41	9	5.2	.891	OF-56, 1B-16

Russ Snyder

SNYDER, RUSSELL HENRY
B. June 22, 1934, Oak, Neb.
BL TR 6' 1" 190 lbs.

Year	Team	Games	BA	SA	AB	H	2B	3B	HR	HR%	R	RBI	BB	SO	SB	Pinch Hit AB	Pinch Hit H	PO	A	E	DP	TC/G	FA	G by Pos
1959	KC A	73	.313	.420	243	76	13	2	3	1.2	41	21	19	29	6	8	2	127	9	2	2	2.2	.986	OF-64
1960		125	.260	.365	304	79	10	5	4	1.3	45	26	20	28	7	32	5	135	4	2	2	1.5	.986	OF-91
1961	BAL A	115	.292	.375	312	91	13	5	1	0.3	46	13	20	32	5	8	0	168	3	6	0	1.6	.966	OF-108
1962		139	.305	.435	416	127	19	4	9	2.2	47	40	17	46	7	21	6	218	8	6	2	1.9	.974	OF-121
1963		148	.256	.364	429	110	21	2	7	1.6	51	36	40	48	18	22	4	238	5	3	1	1.9	.988	OF-130
1964		56	.290	.355	93	27	3	0	1	1.1	11	7	11	22	0	18	3	34	0	1	0	0.9	.971	OF-40
1965		132	.270	.322	345	93	11	2	1	0.3	49	29	27	38	3	23	4	188	4	0	0	1.8	1.000	OF-106
1966		117	.306	.413	373	114	21	5	3	0.8	66	41	38	37	2	15	2	209	6	3	2	2.1	.986	OF-104
1967		108	.236	.324	275	65	8	2	4	1.5	40	23	32	48	5	33	4	127	3	2	0	1.9	.985	OF-69
1968	2 teams	CHI A (38G –.134)	CLE A (68G –.281)																					
"	total	106	.241	.318	299	72	10	2	3	1.0	32	28	29	37	1	29	6	133	4	1	3	1.8	.993	OF-76, 1B-1
1969	CLE A	122	.248	.308	266	66	10	0	2	0.8	26	24	25	33	3	41	7	144	2	6	1	1.8	.961	OF-84
1970	MIL A	124	.232	.315	276	64	11	0	4	1.4	34	31	16	40	1	28	6	140	1	5	0	1.4	.966	OF-106
12 yrs.		1365	.271	.363	3631	984	150	29	42	1.2	488	319	294	438	58	278	49	1861	49	37	13	1.8	.981	OF-1099, 1B-1
WORLD SERIES																								
1966	BAL A	3	.167	.167	6	1	0	0	0	0.0	1	1	2	0	0	0	0	2	0	0	0	0.7	1.000	OF-3

Louis Sockalexis

SOCKALEXIS, LOUIS M. (Chief)
B. Oct. 24, 1871, Old Town, Me. D. Dec. 24, 1913, Burlington, Me.
BL TR 5'11" 185 lbs.

Year	Team	Games	BA	SA	AB	H	2B	3B	HR	HR%	R	RBI	BB	SO	SB	Pinch Hit AB	Pinch Hit H	PO	A	E	DP	TC/G	FA	G by Pos
1897	CLE N	66	.338	.460	278	94	9	8	3	1.1	43	42	18		16	0	0	117	10	16	3	2.2	.888	OF-66
1898		21	.224	.254	67	15	2	0	0	0.0	11	10	1		0	4	1	21	6	1	3	1.8	.964	OF-16
1899		7	.273	.318	22	6	1	0	0	0.0	0	3	1		0	2	0	7	2	2	1	2.2	.818	OF-5
3 yrs.		94	.313	.414	367	115	12	8	3	0.8	54	55	20		16	6	1	145	18	19	7	2.1	.896	OF-87

Bill Sodd

SODD, WILLIAM
B. Sept. 18, 1914, Fort Worth, Tex.
BR TR 6' 2" 210 lbs.

Year	Team	Games	BA	SA	AB	H	2B	3B	HR	HR%	R	RBI	BB	SO	SB	Pinch Hit AB	Pinch Hit H	PO	A	E	DP	TC/G	FA	G by Pos
1937	CLE A	1	.000	.000	1	0	0	0	0	0.0	0	0	0	1	0	1	0	0	0	0	0	0.0	—	

Eric Soderholm

SODERHOLM, ERIC THANE
B. Sept. 24, 1948, Cortland, N. Y.
BR TR 5'11" 187 lbs.

Year	Team	Games	BA	SA	AB	H	2B	3B	HR	HR%	R	RBI	BB	SO	SB	Pinch Hit AB	Pinch Hit H	PO	A	E	DP	TC/G	FA	G by Pos
1971	MIN A	21	.156	.266	64	10	4	0	1	1.6	9	4	10	17	0	0	0	17	48	4	2	3.5	.942	3B-20
1972		93	.188	.359	287	54	10	0	13	4.5	28	39	19	48	3	11	3	66	163	14	17	3.1	.942	3B-79
1973		35	.297	.423	111	33	7	2	1	0.9	22	9	21	16	1	3	1	26	67	8	5	3.0	.921	3B-33, SS-1
1974		141	.276	.392	464	128	18	3	10	2.2	63	51	48	68	7	6	0	101	273	17	19	3.0	.957	3B-130, SS-1
1975		117	.286	.415	419	120	17	2	11	2.6	62	58	53	66	3	1	0	94	277	12	14	3.3	.969	3B-113, DH-3
1977	CHI A	130	.280	.500	460	129	20	3	25	5.4	77	67	47	47	2	0	0	99	249	8	18	2.8	.978	3B-126, DH-3
1978		143	.258	.431	457	118	17	1	20	4.4	57	67	39	44	2	7	4	128	249	14	17	2.8	.964	3B-128, DH-11, 2B-1
1979	2 teams	CHI A (56G –.252)	TEX A (63G –.272)																					
"	total	119	.261	.395	357	93	14	2	10	2.8	46	53	31	28	0	14	3	84	203	8	17	2.7	.973	3B-93, DH-14, 1B-2
1980	NY A	95	.287	.462	275	79	13	1	11	4.0	38	35	27	25	0	11	3	15	65	4	4	1.0	.952	DH-51, 3B-37
9 yrs.		894	.264	.421	2894	764	120	14	102	3.5	402	383	295	359	18	53	14	630	1594	89	113	2.7	.962	3B-759, DH-82, 1B-2, SS-2, 2B-1
LEAGUE CHAMPIONSHIP SERIES																								
1980	NY A	2	.167	.167	6	1	0	0	0	0.0	0	0	0	0	0	0	0	0	0	0	0	0.0	.000	DH-2

Rick Sofield

SOFIELD, RICHARD MICHAEL
B. Dec. 16, 1956, Cheyenne, Wyo.
BL TR 6' 1" 195 lbs.

Year	Team	Games	BA	SA	AB	H	2B	3B	HR	HR%	R	RBI	BB	SO	SB	Pinch Hit AB	Pinch Hit H	PO	A	E	DP	TC/G	FA	G by Pos
1979	MIN A	35	.301	.355	93	28	5	0	0	0.0	8	12	12	27	2	3	1	61	1	3	1	1.9	.954	OF-35
1980		131	.247	.374	417	103	18	4	9	2.2	52	49	24	92	4	13	4	267	7	6	0	2.2	.979	OF-126, DH-2
1981		41	.176	.196	102	18	2	0	0	0.0	9	5	8	22	3	7	1	54	5	1	0	1.8	.983	OF-34
3 yrs.		207	.243	.342	612	149	25	4	9	1.5	69	66	44	141	9	23	6	382	13	10	1	2.1	.975	OF-195, DH-2

Luis Sojo

SOJO, LUIS BELTRAN
Born Luis Beltran Sojo (Sojo).
B. Jan. 3, 1966, Caracas, Venezuela.
BR TR 5'11" 172 lbs.

Year	Team	Games	BA	SA	AB	H	2B	3B	HR	HR%	R	RBI	BB	SO	SB	Pinch Hit AB	Pinch Hit H	PO	A	E	DP	TC/G	FA	G by Pos
1990	TOR A	33	.225	.300	80	18	3	0	1	1.3	14	9	5	5	1	4	0	34	31	5	7	2.2	.929	2B-15, OF-5, SS-5, 3B-4, DH-3
1991	CAL A	113	.258	.327	364	94	14	1	3	0.8	38	20	14	26	4	0	0	233	335	11	78	5.2	.981	2B-107, SS-2, OF-1, 3B-1, DH-1
1992		106	.272	.378	368	100	12	3	7	1.9	37	43	14	24	7	4	1	196	293	9	73	4.5	.982	2B-96, 3B-9, SS-5
1993	TOR A	19	.170	.213	47	8	2	0	0	0.0	5	6	4	2	0	1	0	24	35	2	8	3.2	.967	2B-8, SS-8, 3B-3
1994	SEA A	63	.277	.423	213	59	9	2	6	2.8	32	22	8	25	2	2	1	97	186	7	36	4.3	.976	2B-40, SS-24, DH-2, 3B-1
1995		102	.289	.416	339	98	18	2	7	2.1	50	39	23	19	4	3	1	141	220	9	38	3.5	.976	SS-80, 2B-19, OF-6
6 yrs.		436	.267	.371	1411	377	58	8	24	1.7	176	139	68	101	18	14	3	725	1100	43	240	4.2	.977	2B-285, SS-124, 3B-18, OF-12, DH-6
DIVISIONAL PLAYOFF SERIES																								
1995	SEA A	5	.250	.250	20	5	0	0	0	0.0	0	3	0	3	0	0	0	9	15	1	3	5.0	.960	SS-5
LEAGUE CHAMPIONSHIP SERIES																								
1995	SEA A	6	.250	.350	20	5	2	0	0	0.0	0	1	0	2	0	0	0	9	18	1	7	4.7	.964	SS-6

Tony Solaita

SOLAITA, TOLIA
B. Jan. 15, 1947, Nuuyli, American Samoa D. Feb. 10, 1990, Tafuna, American Somoa.
BL TL 6' 210 lbs.

Year	Team	Games	BA	SA	AB	H	2B	3B	HR	HR%	R	RBI	BB	SO	SB	Pinch Hit AB	Pinch Hit H	PO	A	E	DP	TC/G	FA	G by Pos
1968	NY A	1	.000	.000	1	0	0	0	0	0.0	0	0	0	1	0	0	0	5	0	0	1	5.0	1.000	1B-1
1974	KC A	96	.268	.406	239	64	12	0	7	2.9	31	30	35	70	0	13	4	508	40	5	36	6.9	.991	1B-65, DH-14, OF-1
1975		93	.260	.515	231	60	11	0	16	6.9	35	44	39	79	0	15	3	282	28	2	24	4.3	.994	DH-37, 1B-35
1976	2 teams	KC A (31G –.235)	CAL A (63G –.270)																					
"	total	94	.261	.403	283	74	13	0	9	3.2	29	42	40	61	1	13	4	485	57	2	33	6.8	.996	1B-59, DH-21
1977	CAL A	116	.241	.417	324	78	15	0	14	4.3	40	53	56	77	1	23	8	641	57	7	50	7.3	.990	1B-91, DH-6

Tony Solaita *continued*

Year	Team	Games	BA	SA	AB	H	2B	3B	HR	HR%	R	RBI	BB	SO	SB	Pinch Hit AB	Pinch Hit H	PO	A	E	DP	TC/G	FA	G by Pos
1978		60	.223	.287	94	21	3	0	1	1.1	10	14	16	25	0	34	9	85	7	0	7	3.2	1.000	DH-18, 1B-11
1979	2 teams	MON N (29G –.286) TOR A (36G –.265)																						
"	total	65	.271	.431	144	39	12	1	3	2.1	19	20	28	32	0	14	2	124	10	1	15	3.0	.993	DH-26, 1B-19
7 yrs.		525	.255	.421	1316	336	66	1	50	3.8	164	203	214	345	2	112	30	2130	199	17	166	5.8	.993	1B-281, DH-122, OF-1

Moe Solomon

SOLOMON, MOSE HIRSCH (The Rabbi of Swat) BL TL 5′ 9½″ 180 lbs.
B. Dec. 8, 1900, New York, N. Y. D. June 25, 1966, Miami, Fla.

Year	Team	Games	BA	SA	AB	H	2B	3B	HR	HR%	R	RBI	BB	SO	SB	Pinch Hit AB	Pinch Hit H	PO	A	E	DP	TC/G	FA	G by Pos
1923	NY N	2	.375	.500	8	3	1	0	0	0.0	0	1	0	1	0	0	0	5	0	1	0	3.0	.833	OF-2

Moose Solters

SOLTERS, JULIUS JOSEPH BR TR 6′ 190 lbs.
Born Julius Joseph Soltesz.
B. Mar. 22, 1906, Pittsburgh, Pa. D. Sept. 28, 1975, Pittsburgh, Pa.

Year	Team	Games	BA	SA	AB	H	2B	3B	HR	HR%	R	RBI	BB	SO	SB	Pinch Hit AB	Pinch Hit H	PO	A	E	DP	TC/G	FA	G by Pos
1934	BOS A	101	.299	.447	365	109	25	4	7	1.9	61	58	18	50	9	13	4	197	11	15	1	2.5	.933	OF-89
1935	2 teams	BOS A (24G –.241) STL A (127G –.330)																						
"	total	151	.319	.498	631	201	45	7	18	2.9	94	112	36	42	11	3	1	382	20	6	2	2.8	.985	OF-148
1936	STL A	152	.291	.467	628	183	45	7	17	2.7	100	134	41	76	3	3	0	356	16	17	5	2.6	.956	OF-147
1937	CLE A	152	.323	.533	589	190	42	11	20	3.4	90	109	42	56	6	3	0	283	19	15	3	2.1	.953	OF-149
1938		67	.201	.291	199	40	6	3	2	1.0	30	22	13	28	4	23	4	91	4	3	3	2.1	.969	OF-46
1939	2 teams	CLE A (41G –.275) STL A (40G –.206)																						
"	total	81	.236	.343	233	55	13	3	2	0.9	33	33	19	35	3	27	7	112	3	9	0	2.3	.927	OF-55
1940	CHI A	116	.308	.472	428	132	28	3	12	2.8	65	80	27	54	3	9	1	266	6	8	2	2.6	.971	OF-107
1941		76	.259	.375	251	65	9	4	4	1.6	24	43	18	31	3	12	3	135	7	5	1	2.3	.966	OF-63
1943		42	.155	.186	97	15	0	0	1	1.0	6	8	7	5	0	19	2	30	2	2	0	1.6	.941	OF-21
9 yrs.		938	.289	.449	3421	990	213	42	83	2.4	503	599	221	377	42	112	22	1852	88	80	17	2.4	.960	OF-825

Jock Somerlott

SOMERLOTT, JOHN WESLEY BR TR 6′ 160 lbs.
B. Oct. 26, 1882, Flint, Ind. D. Apr. 21, 1965, Butler, Ind.

Year	Team	Games	BA	SA	AB	H	2B	3B	HR	HR%	R	RBI	BB	SO	SB	Pinch Hit AB	Pinch Hit H	PO	A	E	DP	TC/G	FA	G by Pos
1910	WAS A	16	.222	.222	63	14	0	0	0	0.0	6	2	3		2	0	0	161	8	1	4	10.6	.994	1B-16
1911		13	.175	.175	40	7	0	0	0	0.0	2	2	0		2	1	1	117	10	1	7	10.7	.992	1B-12
2 yrs.		29	.204	.204	103	21	0	0	0	0.0	8	4	3		4	1	1	278	18	2	11	10.6	.993	1B-28

Ed Somerville

SOMERVILLE, EDWARD G. BR TR
B. Mar. 1, 1853, Philadelphia, Pa. D. Oct. 1, 1877, London, Ont., Canada.

Year	Team	Games	BA	SA	AB	H	2B	3B	HR	HR%	R	RBI	BB	SO	SB	Pinch Hit AB	Pinch Hit H	PO	A	E	DP	TC/G	FA	G by Pos
1876	LOU N	64	.188	.215	256	48	5	1	0	0.0	29	14	1	6		0	0	210	251	69	22	8.3	.870	2B-64

Joe Sommer

SOMMER, JOSEPH JOHN BR TR
B. Nov. 20, 1858, Covington, Ky. D. Jan. 16, 1938, Cincinnati, Ohio.

Year	Team	Games	BA	SA	AB	H	2B	3B	HR	HR%	R	RBI	BB	SO	SB	Pinch Hit AB	Pinch Hit H	PO	A	E	DP	TC/G	FA	G by Pos
1880	CIN N	24	.182	.193	88	16	1	0	0	0.0	10	6	0	2		0	0	42	4	5	1	2.0	.902	OF-22, 3B-1, SS-1, C-1
1882	CIN AA	80	.288	.364	**354**	102	12	6	1	0.3	82		24			0	0	188	9	16	2	2.7	.925	OF-80
1883		97	.278	.346	413	115	5	7	3	0.7	79		20			0	0	175	17	33	1	2.3	.853	OF-94, 3B-3, P-1
1884	BAL AA	107	.269	.359	479	129	11	10	4	0.8	96		8			0	0	138	176	58	11	3.5	.844	3B-97, OF-9, 2B-1
1885		110	.251	.331	471	118	23	6	1	0.2	84		24			0	0	245	21	24	2	2.5	.917	OF-107, SS-2, 3B-2, P-2, 1B-1
1886		139	.209	.261	560	117	18	4	1	0.2	79		24			0	0	290	124	45	14	3.2	.902	OF-95, 2B-32, 3B-11, SS-3, P-1
1887		131	.266	.311	463	123	11	5	0	0.0	88		63		29	0	0	237	84	44	10	2.7	.879	OF-110, 2B-13, 3B-10, SS-2, P-1
1888		79	.219	.253	297	65	10	0	0	0.0	31	35	18		13	0	0	115	109	30	13	3.1	.882	OF-44, SS-34, 2B-2, 1B-1
1889		106	.220	.272	386	85	13	2	1	0.3	51	36	42	49	18	0	0	173	26	15	7	2.0	.930	OF-105, SS-1
1890	2 teams	CLE N (9G –.229) BAL AA (38G –.256)																						
"	total	47	.250	.305	164	41	5	2	0	0.0	17	0	15	3	10	0	0	84	5	14	3	2.1	.864	OF-47, P-1
10 yrs.		920	.248	.309	3675	911	109	42	11	0.3	617	77	238	54	70	0	0	1687	575	284	64	2.7	.888	OF-713, 3B-124, 2B-48, SS-43, P-6, 1B-2, C-1

Bill Sommers

SOMMERS, WILLIAM DUNN BR TR 6′ 170 lbs.
B. Feb. 17, 1923, Brooklyn, N. Y.

Year	Team	Games	BA	SA	AB	H	2B	3B	HR	HR%	R	RBI	BB	SO	SB	Pinch Hit AB	Pinch Hit H	PO	A	E	DP	TC/G	FA	G by Pos
1950	STL A	65	.255	.307	137	35	5	1	0	0.0	24	14	25	14	0	11	1	53	83	9	10	2.5	.938	3B-37, 2B-21

Pete Sommers

SOMMERS, JOSEPH ANDREWS BR TR 5′11½″ 181 lbs.
B. Oct. 26, 1866, Cleveland, Ohio D. July 22, 1908, Cleveland, Ohio.

Year	Team	Games	BA	SA	AB	H	2B	3B	HR	HR%	R	RBI	BB	SO	SB	Pinch Hit AB	Pinch Hit H	PO	A	E	DP	TC/G	FA	G by Pos
1887	NY AA	33	.181	.233	116	21	3	0	1	0.9	9		7		6	0	0	124	44	35	5	6.2	.828	C-31, OF-1, 1B-1
1888	BOS N	4	.231	.308	13	3	1	0	0	0.0	1	0	0	3	0	0	0	20	2	3	0	6.3	.880	C-4
1889	2 teams	CHI N (12G –.222) IND N (23G –.250)																						
"	total	35	.240	.372	129	31	7	2	2	1.6	17	22	3	24	2	0	0	150	32	25	3	5.9	.879	C-32, OF-3
1890	2 teams	NY N (17G –.106) CLE N (9G –.206)																						
"	total	26	.148	.222	81	12	2	2	0	0.0	8	2	6	15	0	0	0	127	30	19	3	6.5	.892	C-19, 1B-5, OF-3
4 yrs.		98	.198	.286	339	67	13	4	3	0.9	35	24	16	42	8	0	0	421	108	82	11	6.2	.866	C-86, OF-7, 1B-6

Bill Sorrell

SORRELL, WILLIAM BL TR 6′ 190 lbs.
B. Oct. 14, 1940, Morehead, Ky.

Year	Team	Games	BA	SA	AB	H	2B	3B	HR	HR%	R	RBI	BB	SO	SB	Pinch Hit AB	Pinch Hit H	PO	A	E	DP	TC/G	FA	G by Pos
1965	PHI N	10	.385	.615	13	5	0	0	1	7.7	2	2	2	1	0	7	3	0	0	0	0	0.0	.000	3B-1
1967	SF N	18	.176	.235	17	3	1	0	0	0.0	1	1	3	2	0	10	2	1	0	0	0	0.2	1.000	OF-5
1970	KC A	57	.267	.370	135	36	2	0	4	3.0	12	14	10	13	1	23	6	37	48	9	3	2.6	.904	3B-29, OF-4, 1B-3
3 yrs.		85	.267	.376	165	44	3	0	5	3.0	15	17	15	16	1	40	11	38	48	9	3	2.3	.905	3B-30, OF-9, 1B-3

Chick Sorrells

SORRELLS, RAYMOND EDWIN (Red) BR TR 5′ 9″ 155 lbs.
B. July 31, 1896, Stringtown, Okla. D. July 20, 1983, Terrell, Tex.

Year	Team	Games	BA	SA	AB	H	2B	3B	HR	HR%	R	RBI	BB	SO	SB	Pinch Hit AB	Pinch Hit H	PO	A	E	DP	TC/G	FA	G by Pos
1922	CLE A	2	.000	.000	1	0	0	0	0	0.0	0	0	0	0	0	0	0	0	3	0	0	3.0	1.000	SS-1

Paul Sorrento

SORRENTO, PAUL ANTHONY BL TR 6′ 2″ 195 lbs.
B. Nov. 17, 1965, Somerville, Mass.

Year	Team	Games	BA	SA	AB	H	2B	3B	HR	HR%	R	RBI	BB	SO	SB	Pinch Hit AB	Pinch Hit H	PO	A	E	DP	TC/G	FA	G by Pos
1989	MIN A	14	.238	.238	21	5	0	0	0	0.0	2	1	5	4	0	3	0	13	0	0	1	1.3	1.000	1B-5, DH-5
1990		41	.207	.380	121	25	4	1	5	4.1	11	13	12	31	1	6	2	118	7	1	14	3.3	.992	DH-23, 1B-15
1991		26	.255	.553	47	12	2	0	4	8.5	6	13	4	11	0	12	3	70	7	0	7	5.1	1.000	1B-13, DH-2
1992	CLE A	140	.269	.443	458	123	24	1	18	3.9	52	60	51	89	0	14	2	996	78	8	108	8.2	.993	1B-121, DH-11
1993		148	.257	.434	463	119	26	1	18	3.9	75	65	58	121	3	13	3	1015	86	6	107	7.5	.995	1B-144, OF-3, DH-1

Paul Sorrento *continued*

Year	Team	Games	BA	SA	AB	H	2B	3B	HR	HR%	R	RBI	BB	SO	SB	Pinch Hit AB	Pinch Hit H	PO	A	E	DP	TC/G	FA	G by Pos
1994		95	.280	.453	322	90	14	0	14	4.3	43	62	34	68	0	8	2	798	58	4	79	9.1	.995	1B-86, DH-8
1995		104	.235	.511	323	76	14	0	25	7.7	50	79	51	71	1	9	1	816	57	7	87	8.6	.992	1B-91, DH-11
7 yrs.		568	.256	.451	1755	450	84	3	84	4.8	239	293	215	395	5	65	13	3826	293	26	403	7.7	.994	1B-475, DH-61, OF-3
DIVISIONAL PLAYOFF SERIES																								
1995	CLE A	3	.300	.300	10	3	0	0	0	0.0	2	1	2	3	0	0	0	27	5	2	0	11.3	.941	1B-3
LEAGUE CHAMPIONSHIP SERIES																								
1991	MIN A	1	.000	.000	1	0	0	0	0	0.0	0	0	0	1	0	1	0	0	0	0	0	0.0	—	
1995	CLE A	4	.154	.231	13	2	1	0	0	0.0	2	0	2	3	0	0	0	34	1	2	1	9.3	.946	1B-4
2 yrs.		5	.143	.214	14	2	1	0	0	0.0	2	0	2	4	0	1	0	34	1	2	1	9.3	.946	1B-4
WORLD SERIES																								
1991	MIN A	3	.000	.000	2	0	0	0	0	0.0	0	0	1	2	0	2	0	1	1	0	1	2.0	1.000	1B-1
1995	CLE A	6	.182	.273	11	2	1	0	0	0.0	0	0	0	4	0	3	1	19	2	1	2	7.3	.955	1B-3
2 yrs.		9	.154	.231	13	2	1	0	0	0.0	0	0	1	6	0	5	1	20	3	1	3	6.0	.958	1B-4

Sammy Sosa

SOSA, SAMUEL BR TR 6′ 165 lbs.
Born Samuel Sosa (Peralta).
B. Nov. 12, 1968, San Pedro de Macoris, Dominican Republic.

Year	Team	Games	BA	SA	AB	H	2B	3B	HR	HR%	R	RBI	BB	SO	SB	Pinch Hit AB	Pinch Hit H	PO	A	E	DP	TC/G	FA	G by Pos
1989	2 teams	TEX A (25G –.238) CHI A (33G –.273)																						
″	total	58	.257	.366	183	47	8	0	4	2.2	27	13	11	47	7	4	0	94	2	4	0	1.7	.960	OF-52, DH-6
1990	CHI A	153	.233	.404	532	124	26	10	15	2.8	72	70	33	150	32	0	0	315	14	13	1	2.3	.962	OF-152
1991		116	.203	.335	316	64	10	1	10	3.2	39	33	14	98	13	7	2	214	6	6	0	2.0	.973	OF-111, DH-2
1992	CHI N	67	.260	.393	262	68	7	2	8	3.1	41	25	19	63	15	0	0	145	4	6	1	2.3	.961	OF-67
1993		159	.261	.485	598	156	25	5	33	5.5	92	93	38	135	36	2	1	344	17	9	4	2.3	.976	OF-158
1994		105	.300	.545	426	128	17	6	25	5.9	59	70	25	92	22	0	0	248	5	7	0	2.5	.973	OF-105
1995		144	.268	.500	564	151	17	3	36	6.4	89	119	58	134	34	1	0	320	13	13	2	2.4	.962	OF-143
7 yrs.		802	.256	.449	2881	738	110	27	131	4.5	419	423	198	719	159	14	3	1680	61	58	8	2.3	.968	OF-788, DH-8

Denny Sothern

SOTHERN, DENNIS ELWOOD BR TR 5′11″ 175 lbs.
B. Jan. 20, 1904, Washington, D. C. D. Dec. 7, 1977, Durham, N. C.

Year	Team	Games	BA	SA	AB	H	2B	3B	HR	HR%	R	RBI	BB	SO	SB	Pinch Hit AB	Pinch Hit H	PO	A	E	DP	TC/G	FA	G by Pos
1926	PHI N	14	.245	.434	53	13	1	0	3	5.7	5	10	4	10	0	1	1	38	1	1	0	3.1	.975	OF-13
1928		141	.285	.375	579	165	27	5	5	0.9	82	38	34	53	17	2	2	358	19	14	7	2.9	.964	OF-136
1929		76	.306	.449	294	90	21	3	5	1.7	52	27	16	24	13	1	0	193	9	7	2	2.9	.967	OF-71
1930	2 teams	PHI N (90G –.280) PIT N (17G –.176)																						
″	total	107	.266	.392	398	106	30	1	6	1.5	70	40	25	41	8	8	4	251	15	9	6	2.8	.967	OF-97
1931	BKN N	19	.161	.194	31	5	1	0	0	0.0	10	0	4	8	0	3	1	23	0	1	0	2.4	.958	OF-10
5 yrs.		357	.280	.394	1355	379	80	9	19	1.4	219	115	83	136	38	15	8	863	44	32	15	2.9	.966	OF-327

Steve Souchock

SOUCHOCK, STEPHEN (Bud) BR TR 6′ 2½″ 203 lbs.
B. Mar. 3, 1919, Yatesboro, Pa.

Year	Team	Games	BA	SA	AB	H	2B	3B	HR	HR%	R	RBI	BB	SO	SB	Pinch Hit AB	Pinch Hit H	PO	A	E	DP	TC/G	FA	G by Pos
1946	NY A	47	.302	.477	86	26	3	3	2	2.3	15	10	7	13	0	17	5	180	9	7	19	9.8	.964	1B-20
1948		44	.203	.322	118	24	3	1	3	2.5	11	11	7	13	3	11	2	231	13	3	25	7.7	.988	1B-32
1949	CHI A	84	.234	.409	252	59	13	5	7	2.8	29	37	25	38	5	17	4	346	21	6	30	5.4	.984	OF-39, 1B-30
1951	DET A	91	.245	.505	188	46	10	3	11	5.9	33	28	18	27	0	34	7	94	4	6	1	1.7	.942	OF-59, 2B-1, 1B-1
1952		92	.249	.487	265	66	16	4	13	4.9	40	45	21	28	1	17	4	195	31	8	7	3.0	.966	OF-56, 3B-13, 1B-9
1953		89	.302	.489	278	84	13	3	11	4.0	29	46	8	35	5	10	3	147	7	6	3	2.0	.962	OF-80, 1B-1
1954		25	.179	.462	39	7	0	1	3	7.7	6	8	2	10	1	14	2	15	4	0	0	1.7	1.000	OF-9, 3B-2
1955		1	1.000	1.000	1	1	0	0	0	0.0	0	1	0	0	0	1	1	0	0	0	0	0.0	—	
8 yrs.		473	.255	.457	1227	313	58	20	50	4.1	163	186	88	164	15	121	28	1208	89	36	85	3.8	.973	OF-243, 1B-93, 3B-15, 2B-1

Clyde Southwick

SOUTHWICK, CLYDE AUBRA BL TR 6′ 180 lbs.
B. Nov. 3, 1886, Maxwell, Iowa D. Oct. 14, 1961, Freeport, Ill.

Year	Team	Games	BA	SA	AB	H	2B	3B	HR	HR%	R	RBI	BB	SO	SB	Pinch Hit AB	Pinch Hit H	PO	A	E	DP	TC/G	FA	G by Pos
1911	STL A	4	.250	.250	12	3	0	0	0	0.0	3	0	1		0	0	0	11	4	1	0	4.0	.938	C-4

Bill Southworth

SOUTHWORTH, WILLIAM FREDERICK BR TR 6′ 2″ 205 lbs.
B. Nov. 10, 1945, Madison, Wis.

Year	Team	Games	BA	SA	AB	H	2B	3B	HR	HR%	R	RBI	BB	SO	SB	Pinch Hit AB	Pinch Hit H	PO	A	E	DP	TC/G	FA	G by Pos
1964	MIL N	3	.286	.714	7	2	0	0	1	14.3	2	2	0	3	0	1	0	0	2	0	0	1.0	1.000	3B-2

Billy Southworth

SOUTHWORTH, WILLIAM HARRISON BL TR 5′9″ 170 lbs.
B. Mar. 9, 1893, Harvard, Neb. D. Nov. 15, 1969, Columbus, Ohio.
Manager 1929, 1940–51.

Year	Team	Games	BA	SA	AB	H	2B	3B	HR	HR%	R	RBI	BB	SO	SB	Pinch Hit AB	Pinch Hit H	PO	A	E	DP	TC/G	FA	G by Pos
1913	CLE A	1	—	—	0	0	0	0	0	—	0	0	0	0	0	0	0	0	0	0	0	0.0	.000	OF-1
1915		60	.220	.288	177	39	2	5	0	0.0	25	8	36	12	2	8	0	90	7	6	3	2.3	.942	OF-44
1918	PIT N	64	.341	.443	246	84	5	7	2	0.8	37	43	26	9	19	0	0	137	12	3	4	2.4	.980	OF-64
1919		121	.280	.400	453	127	14	**14**	4	0.9	56	61	32	22	23	0	0	253	17	9	5	2.3	.968	OF-121
1920		146	.284	.374	546	155	17	13	2	0.4	64	53	52	20	23	2	0	337	12	3	3	2.5	.991	OF-142
1921	BOS N	141	.308	.441	569	175	25	15	7	1.2	86	79	36	13	22	0	0	288	25	8	6	2.3	.975	OF-141
1922		43	.323	.475	158	51	4	4	4	2.5	27	18	18	1	4	2	0	100	7	5	0	2.7	.955	OF-41
1923		153	.319	.448	611	195	29	16	6	1.0	95	78	61	23	14	0	0	329	26	22	6	2.5	.942	OF-151, 2B-2
1924	NY N	94	.256	.335	281	72	13	0	3	1.1	40	36	32	16	1	16	2	167	5	12	2	2.5	.935	OF-75
1925		123	.292	.391	473	138	19	5	6	1.3	79	44	51	11	6	1	0	289	7	11	1	2.6	.964	OF-120
1926	2 teams	NY N (36G –.328) STL N (99G –.317)																						
″	total	135	.320	.497	507	162	28	7	16	3.2	99	99	33	10	14	5	4	290	7	9	1	2.4	.971	OF-127
1927	STL N	92	.301	.402	306	92	15	5	2	0.7	52	39	23	7	10	9	2	153	6	5	2	2.0	.970	OF-83
1929		19	.188	.250	32	6	2	0	0	0.0	1	3	2	4	0	13	1	12	0	0	0	2.4	1.000	OF-5
13 yrs.		1192	.297	.415	4359	1296	173	91	52	1.2	661	561	402	148	138	56	9	2445	131	93	33	2.4	.965	OF-1115, 2B-2
WORLD SERIES																								
1924	NY N	5	.000	.000	1	0	0	0	0	0.0	1	0	0	0	0	1	0	1	1	0	0	1.0	1.000	OF-2
1926	STL N	7	.345	.552	29	10	1	1	1	3.4	6	4	0	0	1	0	0	8	3	0	1	1.6	1.000	OF-7
2 yrs.		12	.333	.533	30	10	1	1	1	3.3	7	4	0	0	1	1	0	9	4	0	1	1.4	1.000	OF-9

Len Sowders

SOWDERS, LEONARD 5′11½″ 172 lbs.
Brother of Bill Sowders. Brother of John Sowders.
B. June 29, 1861, Louisville, Ky. D. Nov. 19, 1888, Indianapolis, Ind.

Year	Team	Games	BA	SA	AB	H	2B	3B	HR	HR%	R	RBI	BB	SO	SB	Pinch Hit AB	Pinch Hit H	PO	A	E	DP	TC/G	FA	G by Pos
1886	BAL AA	23	.263	.329	76	20	3	1	0	0.0	10		12			0	0	33	4	4	0	1.7	.902	OF-23, 1B-1

Al Spalding

SPALDING, ALBERT GOODWILL BR TR 6′ 1″ 170 lbs.
B. Sept. 2, 1850, Byron, Ill. D. Sept. 9, 1915, San Diego, Calif.
Manager 1876–77.
Hall of Fame 1939.

Year	Team	Games	BA	SA	AB	H	2B	3B	HR	HR%	R	RBI	BB	SO	SB	Pinch Hit AB	Pinch Hit H	PO	A	E	DP	TC/G	FA	G by Pos
1876	CHI N	66	.312	.373	292	91	14	2	0	0.0	54	44	6	3		0	0	58	94	10	7	2.2	.938	P-61, OF-10, 1B-3
1877		60	.256	.331	254	65	7	6	0	0.0	29	35	3	16		0	0	511	82	33	29	9.8	.947	1B-45, 2B-13, P-4, 3B-2
1878		1	.500	.500	4	2	0	0	0	0.0	0	0	0	0		0	0	3	0	4	0	7.0	.429	2B-1
3 yrs.		127	.287	.355	550	158	21	8	0	0.0	83	79	9	19		0	0	572	176	47	36	5.7	.941	P-65, 1B-48, 2B-14, OF-10, 3B-2

Dick Spalding

SPALDING, CHARLES HARRY BL TL 5′11″ 185 lbs.
B. Oct. 13, 1893, Philadelphia, Pa. D. Feb. 3, 1950, Philadelphia, Pa.

Year	Team	Games	BA	SA	AB	H	2B	3B	HR	HR%	R	RBI	BB	SO	SB	Pinch Hit AB	Pinch Hit H	PO	A	E	DP	TC/G	FA	G by Pos
1927	PHI N	115	.296	.346	442	131	16	3	0	0.0	68	25	38	40	5	1	0	250	7	2	1	2.3	.992	OF-113
1928	WAS A	16	.348	.348	23	8	0	0	0	0.0	1	0	0	4	0	2	0	9	0	0	0	0.8	1.000	OF-11
2 yrs.		131	.299	.346	465	139	16	3	0	0.0	69	25	38	44	5	3	0	259	7	2	1	2.2	.993	OF-124

Al Spangler

SPANGLER, ALBERT DONALD BL TL 6′ 175 lbs.
B. July 8, 1933, Philadelphia, Pa.

Year	Team	Games	BA	SA	AB	H	2B	3B	HR	HR%	R	RBI	BB	SO	SB	Pinch Hit AB	Pinch Hit H	PO	A	E	DP	TC/G	FA	G by Pos
1959	MIL N	6	.417	.583	12	5	0	1	0	0.0	3	0	1	1	1	1	1	6	0	0	0	1.5	1.000	OF-4
1960		101	.267	.352	105	28	5	2	0	0.0	26	6	14	17	6	4	0	88	4	1	1	1.0	.989	OF-92
1961		68	.268	.289	97	26	2	0	0	0.0	23	6	28	9	4	16	3	56	2	0	0	1.3	1.000	OF-44
1962	HOU N	129	.285	.388	418	119	10	9	5	1.2	51	35	70	46	7	8	1	183	7	8	2	1.6	.960	OF-121
1963		120	.281	.386	430	121	25	4	4	0.9	52	27	50	38	5	7	3	215	5	3	1	2.0	.987	OF-113
1964		135	.245	.334	449	110	18	5	4	0.9	51	38	41	43	7	10	2	185	3	7	1	1.5	.964	OF-127
1965	2 teams	HOU N (38G –.214)	CAL A (51G –.260)																					
″	total	89	.236	.269	208	49	2	1	1	0.5	35	8	22	17	5	26	4	76	3	3	0	1.4	.963	OF-57
1966	CAL A	6	.667	.667	9	6	0	0	0	0.0	2	0	2	2	0	3	3	3	0	0	0	1.0	1.000	OF-3
1967	CHI N	62	.254	.308	130	33	7	0	0	0.0	18	13	23	17	2	23	4	71	0	1	0	1.8	.986	OF-41
1968		88	.271	.390	177	48	9	3	2	1.1	21	18	20	24	0	41	10	71	2	2	1	1.6	.973	OF-48
1969		82	.211	.315	213	45	8	1	4	1.9	23	23	21	16	0	26	1	75	1	4	0	1.4	.950	OF-58
1970		21	.143	.429	14	2	1	0	1	7.1	2	1	3	3	0	11	2	5	0	0	0	0.8	1.000	OF-6
1971		5	.400	.400	5	2	0	0	0	0.0	0	0	0	1	0	5	2	0	0	0	0	0.0	—	
13 yrs.		912	.262	.351	2267	594	87	26	21	0.9	307	175	295	234	37	181	36	1034	27	29	6	1.5	.973	OF-714

Bob Speake

SPEAKE, ROBERT CHARLES (Spook) BL TL 6′ 1″ 178 lbs.
B. Aug. 22, 1930, Springfield, Mo.

Year	Team	Games	BA	SA	AB	H	2B	3B	HR	HR%	R	RBI	BB	SO	SB	Pinch Hit AB	Pinch Hit H	PO	A	E	DP	TC/G	FA	G by Pos
1955	CHI N	95	.218	.429	261	57	9	5	12	4.6	36	43	28	71	3	24	5	159	11	6	8	2.8	.966	OF-55, 1B-8
1957		129	.232	.404	418	97	14	5	16	3.8	65	50	38	68	5	23	9	480	41	7	21	5.3	.987	OF-60, 1B-39
1958	SF N	66	.211	.380	71	15	3	0	3	4.2	9	10	13	15	0	41	7	13	2	1	0	1.6	.938	OF-10
1959		15	.091	.091	11	1	0	0	0	0.0	0	1	1	4	0	11	1	0	0	0	0	0.0	—	
4 yrs.		305	.223	.406	761	170	26	10	31	4.1	110	104	80	158	8	99	22	652	54	14	29	4.2	.981	OF-125, 1B-47

Tris Speaker

SPEAKER, TRISTRAM E. (Spoke, The Grey Eagle) BL TL 5′11½″ 193 lbs.
B. Apr. 4, 1888, Hubbard, Tex. D. Dec. 8, 1958, Lake Whitney, Tex.
Manager 1919–26.
Hall of Fame 1937.

Year	Team	Games	BA	SA	AB	H	2B	3B	HR	HR%	R	RBI	BB	SO	SB	Pinch Hit AB	Pinch Hit H	PO	A	E	DP	TC/G	FA	G by Pos
1907	BOS A	7	.158	.158	19	3	0	0	0	0.0	0	1	1		0	3	0	4	2	0	1	1.5	1.000	OF-4
1908		31	.220	.288	118	26	2	3	0	0.0	12	9	4		2	0	0	57	8	0	3	2.1	1.000	OF-31
1909		143	.309	.443	544	168	26	13	7	1.3	73	77	38		35	1	0	319	35	10	12	2.6	.973	OF-142
1910		141	.340	.468	538	183	20	14	7	1.3	92	65	52		35	0	0	337	20	16	7	2.7	.957	OF-140
1911		141	.334	.502	500	167	34	13	8	1.6	88	80	59		25	3	2	297	26	15	5	2.4	.956	OF-138
1912		153	.383	.567	580	222	**53**	12	**10**	1.7	136	98	82		52	0	0	372	35	18	9	2.8	.958	OF-153
1913		141	.363	.533	520	189	35	22	3	0.6	94	81	65	22	46	2	0	374	30	25	7	3.1	.942	OF-139
1914		158	.338	.503	571	**193**	**46**	18	4	0.7	101	90	77	25	42	1	0	425	30	15	14	3.0	.968	OF-156, 1B-1, P-1
1915		150	.322	.411	547	176	25	12	0	0.0	108	69	81	14	29	0	0	378	21	10	8	2.7	.976	OF-150
1916	CLE A	151	**.386**	**.502**	546	**211**	**41**	8	2	0.4	102	83	82	20	35	0	0	359	25	10	10	2.6	.975	OF-151
1917		142	.352	.486	523	184	42	11	2	0.4	90	60	67	14	30	0	0	365	23	8	5	2.8	.980	OF-142
1918		127	.318	.435	471	150	**33**	11	0	0.0	73	61	64	9	27	0	0	352	15	10	6	3.0	.973	OF-127
1919		134	.296	.433	494	146	38	12	2	0.4	83	63	73	12	15	0	0	375	25	7	6	3.0	.983	OF-134
1920		150	.388	.562	552	214	**50**	11	8	1.4	137	107	97	13	10	1	0	363	24	9	8	2.7	.977	OF-149
1921		132	.362	.538	506	183	**52**	14	3	0.6	107	74	68	12	2	4	2	345	15	6	2	2.9	.984	OF-128
1922		131	.378	.606	426	161	**48**	8	11	2.6	85	71	77	11	8	17	**9**	285	13	5	6	2.8	.983	OF-110
1923		150	.380	.610	574	218	**59**	11	17	3.0	133	130	93	15	10	0	0	369	26	13	7	2.7	.968	OF-150
1924		135	.344	.510	486	167	36	9	9	1.9	94	65	72	13	5	7	3	323	20	13	3	2.8	.963	OF-128
1925		117	.389	.578	429	167	35	5	12	2.8	79	87	70	12	5	4	1	311	16	11	9	3.1	.967	OF-109
1926		150	.304	.469	539	164	52	8	7	1.3	96	86	94	15	6	1	0	394	20	8	7	2.8	.981	OF-149
1927	WAS A	141	.327	.444	523	171	43	6	2	0.4	71	73	55	8	9	4	0	423	24	12	23	3.4	.974	OF-120, 1B-17
1928	PHI A	64	.267	.450	191	51	22	2	3	1.6	28	29	10	5	5	12	3	111	8	3	1	2.4	.975	OF-50
22 yrs.		2789	.345	.500	10197	3514	792	223	117	1.1	1882	1559	1381	220	433	60	20	6938	461	224	159	2.8	.971	OF-2700, 1B-18, P-1
			5th			**5th**	**1st**	**6th**			**8th**													
WORLD SERIES																								
1912	BOS A	8	.300	.467	30	9	1	2	0	0.0	4	2	4	2	1	0	0	21	2	2	2	3.1	.920	OF-8
1915		5	.294	.412	17	5	0	1	0	0.0	2	0	4	1	0	0	0	10	0	0	0	2.0	1.000	OF-5
1920	CLE A	7	.320	.480	25	8	2	1	0	0.0	6	1	3	1	0	0	0	18	0	0	0	2.6	1.000	OF-7
3 yrs.		20	.306	.458	72	22	3	4	0	0.0	12	3	11	4	1	0	0	49	2	2	2	2.7	.962	OF-20
								1st																

Horace Speed

SPEED, HORACE ARTHUR B. Oct. 4, 1951, Los Angeles, Calif. BR TR 6′ 1″ 180 lbs.

Year	Team	Games	BA	SA	AB	H	2B	3B	HR	HR%	R	RBI	BB	SO	SB	Pinch Hit AB	Pinch Hit H	PO	A	E	DP	TC/G	FA	G by Pos
1975	SF N	17	.133	.200	15	2	1	0	0	0.0	2	1	1	8	0	1	0	9	0	1	0	1.1	.900	OF-9
1978	CLE A	70	.226	.283	106	24	4	1	0	0.0	13	4	14	31	2	4	0	85	1	2	0	1.4	.977	OF-61, DH-3
1979		26	.143	.143	14	2	0	0	0	0.0	6	1	5	7	2	0	0	14	0	2	0	0.8	.875	OF-16, DH-4
3 yrs.		113	.207	.259	135	28	5	1	0	0.0	21	6	20	46	4	5	0	108	1	5	0	1.2	.956	OF-86, DH-7

Tim Spehr

SPEHR, TIMOTHY JOSEPH B. July 2, 1966, Excelsior Springs, Mo. BR TR 6′ 2″ 205 lbs.

Year	Team	Games	BA	SA	AB	H	2B	3B	HR	HR%	R	RBI	BB	SO	SB	Pinch Hit AB	Pinch Hit H	PO	A	E	DP	TC/G	FA	G by Pos
1991	KC A	37	.189	.378	74	14	5	0	3	4.1	7	14	9	18	1	1	0	190	19	3	3	5.7	.986	C-37
1993	MON N	53	.230	.368	87	20	6	0	2	2.3	14	10	6	20	2	3	0	166	22	9	3	4.0	.954	C-49
1994		52	.250	.389	36	9	3	1	0	0.0	8	5	4	11	2	2	1	104	6	0	1	2.3	1.000	C-46, OF-2
1995		41	.257	.486	35	9	5	0	1	2.9	4	3	6	7	0	2	1	92	12	1	0	2.8	.990	C-38
4 yrs.		183	.224	.392	232	52	19	1	6	2.6	33	32	25	56	5	8	2	552	59	13	7	3.6	.979	C-170, OF-2

Chris Speier

SPEIER, CHRIS EDWARD B. June 28, 1950, Alameda, Calif. BR TR 6′ 1″ 175 lbs.

Year	Team	Games	BA	SA	AB	H	2B	3B	HR	HR%	R	RBI	BB	SO	SB	Pinch Hit AB	Pinch Hit H	PO	A	E	DP	TC/G	FA	G by Pos
1971	SF N	157	.235	.323	601	141	17	6	8	1.3	74	46	56	90	4	2	1	239	517	33	95	5.1	.958	SS-156
1972		150	.269	.400	562	151	25	2	15	2.7	74	71	82	92	9	0	0	243	517	20	69	5.2	.974	SS-150
1973		153	.249	.356	542	135	17	4	11	2.0	58	71	66	69	4	3	2	255	471	33	92	5.0	.957	SS-150, 2B-1
1974		141	.250	.361	501	125	19	5	9	1.8	55	53	62	64	3	4	2	215	453	21	84	5.0	.970	SS-135, 2B-4
1975		141	.271	.415	487	132	30	5	10	2.1	60	69	70	50	4	4	0	247	421	12	81	5.0	.982	SS-136, 3B-1
1976		145	.226	.297	495	112	18	4	3	0.6	51	40	60	52	2	5	1	241	464	19	85	4.9	.974	SS-135, 2B-7, 3B-5, 1B-1
1977	2 teams	SF N (6G –.176) MON N (139G –.235)																						
″	total	145	.234	.339	548	128	31	6	5	0.9	59	38	67	81	1	2	0	239	455	23	77	5.0	.968	SS-143
1978	MON N	150	.251	.329	501	126	18	3	5	1.0	47	51	60	75	1	2	0	245	467	18	93	4.9	.975	SS-148
1979		113	.227	.331	344	78	13	1	7	2.0	31	26	43	45	0	0	0	194	355	17	52	5.1	.970	SS-112
1980		128	.265	.330	388	103	14	4	1	0.3	35	32	52	38	0	0	0	187	397	21	62	4.7	.965	SS-127, 2B-1
1981		96	.225	.290	307	69	10	2	2	0.7	33	25	38	29	1	0	0	175	280	17	57	4.9	.964	SS-96
1982		156	.257	.360	530	136	26	4	7	1.3	41	60	47	67	1	1	0	291	405	13	76	4.6	.982	SS-155
1983		88	.257	.341	261	67	12	2	2	0.8	31	22	29	37	2	5	1	117	203	14	32	3.8	.958	SS-74, 3B-12, 2B-2
1984	3 teams	MON N (25G –.150) STL N (38G –.178) MIN A (12G –.212)																						
″	total	75	.178	.272	191	34	7	1	3	1.6	12	10	13	34	0	16	3	70	180	5	35	3.9	.980	SS-59, 3B-6
1985	CHI N	106	.243	.349	218	53	11	0	4	1.8	16	24	17	34	1	12	5	87	177	11	43	2.7	.960	SS-58, 3B-31, 2B-13
1986		95	.284	.452	155	44	8	0	6	3.9	21	23	15	32	2	17	7	62	106	3	15	2.1	.982	3B-53, SS-23, 2B-7
1987	SF N	111	.249	.394	317	79	13	0	11	3.5	39	39	42	51	4	14	5	118	229	4	41	2.9	.989	2B-55, 3B-44, SS-22
1988		82	.216	.333	171	37	9	1	3	1.8	26	18	23	39	3	10	1	70	142	3	26	2.7	.986	2B-45, 3B-22, SS-12
1989		28	.243	.351	37	9	4	0	0	0.0	7	2	5	9	0	10	3	19	20	1	6	1.7	.975	3B-9, SS-9, 2B-4, 1B-1
19 yrs.		2260	.246	.349	7156	1759	302	50	112	1.6	770	720	847	988	42	107	31	3314	6259	288	1121	4.4	.971	SS-1900, 3B-183, 2B-139, 1B-2
DIVISIONAL PLAYOFF SERIES																								
1981	MON N	5	.400	.533	15	6	2	0	0	0.0	4	3	4	2	0	0	0	16	15	0	0	6.2	1.000	SS-5
LEAGUE CHAMPIONSHIP SERIES																								
1971	SF N	4	.357	.643	14	5	1	0	1	7.1	4	1	1	0	0	0	0	3	14	1	0	4.5	.944	SS-4
1981	MON N	5	.188	.188	16	3	0	0	0	0.0	0	0	2	0	0	0	0	15	16	2	6	6.6	.939	SS-5
1987	SF N	3	.000	.000	5	0	0	0	0	0.0	0	0	0	2	0	2	0	1	3	0	0	4.0	1.000	2B-1
3 yrs.		12	.229	.343	35	8	1	0	1	2.9	4	1	3	2	0	2	0	19	33	3	6	5.5	.945	SS-9, 2B-1

Bob Spence

SPENCE, JOHN ROBERT B. Feb. 10, 1946, San Diego, Calif. BL TR 6′ 4″ 215 lbs.

Year	Team	Games	BA	SA	AB	H	2B	3B	HR	HR%	R	RBI	BB	SO	SB	Pinch Hit AB	Pinch Hit H	PO	A	E	DP	TC/G	FA	G by Pos
1969	CHI A	12	.154	.192	26	4	1	0	0	0.0	0	3	0	9	0	7	0	40	2	0	5	7.0	1.000	1B-6
1970		46	.223	.362	130	29	4	1	4	3.1	11	15	11	32	0	9	1	305	28	2	36	9.1	.994	1B-37
1971		14	.148	.148	27	4	0	0	0	0.0	2	1	5	6	0	5	0	69	2	1	6	10.3	.986	1B-7
3 yrs.		72	.202	.306	183	37	5	1	4	2.2	13	19	16	47	0	21	1	414	32	3	47	9.0	.993	1B-50

Stan Spence

SPENCE, STANLEY ORVILLE B. Mar. 20, 1915, South Portsmouth, Ky. D. Jan. 9, 1983, Kinston, N. C. BL TL 5′10½″ 180 lbs.

Year	Team	Games	BA	SA	AB	H	2B	3B	HR	HR%	R	RBI	BB	SO	SB	Pinch Hit AB	Pinch Hit H	PO	A	E	DP	TC/G	FA	G by Pos
1940	BOS A	51	.279	.426	68	19	2	1	2	2.9	5	13	4	9	0	33	11	15	0	0	0	1.0	1.000	OF-15
1941		86	.232	.340	203	47	10	3	2	1.0	22	28	18	14	1	33	6	99	6	0	2	2.0	1.000	OF-52, 1B-1
1942	WAS A	149	.323	.432	629	203	27	**15**	4	0.6	94	79	62	16	5	0	0	395	7	11	0	2.8	.973	OF-149
1943		149	.267	.405	570	152	23	10	12	2.1	72	88	84	39	8	1	0	396	12	7	1	2.8	.983	OF-148
1944		153	.316	.486	592	187	31	8	18	3.0	83	100	69	28	3	0	0	454	29	6	9	3.2	.988	OF-150, 1B-3
1946		152	.292	.497	578	169	50	10	16	2.8	83	87	62	31	1	1	0	412	15	8	3	2.9	.982	OF-150
1947		147	.279	.441	506	141	22	6	16	3.2	62	73	81	41	2	5	0	408	12	7	3	3.0	.984	OF-142
1948	BOS A	114	.235	.391	391	92	17	4	12	3.1	71	61	82	33	0	9	3	316	10	6	7	3.1	.982	OF-92, 1B-14
1949	2 teams	BOS A (7G –.150) STL A (104G –.245)																						
″	total	111	.240	.416	334	80	14	3	13	3.9	49	46	58	37	1	16	2	219	11	1	2	2.5	.996	OF-90, 1B-1
9 yrs.		1112	.282	.437	3871	1090	196	60	95	2.5	541	575	520	248	21	98	22	2714	102	46	27	2.8	.984	OF-988, 1B-19

Ben Spencer

SPENCER, LLOYD BENJAMIN B. May 15, 1890, Patapsco, Md. D. Sept. 1, 1970, Finksburg, Md. BL TL 5′ 8″ 160 lbs.

Year	Team	Games	BA	SA	AB	H	2B	3B	HR	HR%	R	RBI	BB	SO	SB	Pinch Hit AB	Pinch Hit H	PO	A	E	DP	TC/G	FA	G by Pos
1913	WAS A	8	.286	.429	21	6	1	1	0	0.0	2	2	2	4	0	0	0	10	1	1	0	1.5	.917	OF-8

Chet Spencer

SPENCER, CHESTER ARTHUR B. Mar. 4, 1883, South Webster, Ohio D. Nov. 10, 1938, Portsmouth, Ohio. BL TR 6′ 180 lbs.

Year	Team	Games	BA	SA	AB	H	2B	3B	HR	HR%	R	RBI	BB	SO	SB	Pinch Hit AB	Pinch Hit H	PO	A	E	DP	TC/G	FA	G by Pos
1906	BOS N	8	.148	.185	27	4	1	0	0	0.0	1	0	0		0	0	0	6	1	1	0	1.0	.875	OF-8

Daryl Spencer

SPENCER, DARYL DEAN (Big Dee) B. July 13, 1929, Wichita, Kans. BR TR 6′ 2½″ 185 lbs.

Year	Team	Games	BA	SA	AB	H	2B	3B	HR	HR%	R	RBI	BB	SO	SB	Pinch Hit AB	Pinch Hit H	PO	A	E	DP	TC/G	FA	G by Pos
1952	NY N	7	.294	.412	17	5	0	1	0	0.0	0	3	1	4	0	1	0	7	14	0	2	3.5	1.000	SS-3, 3B-3
1953		118	.208	.424	408	85	18	5	20	4.9	55	56	42	74	0	3	0	179	269	32	52	4.0	.933	SS-53, 3B-36, 2B-32
1956		146	.221	.342	489	108	13	2	14	2.9	46	42	35	65	1	2	0	288	377	18	74	4.6	.974	2B-70, SS-66, 3B-12
1957		148	.249	.376	534	133	31	2	11	2.1	65	50	50	50	3	2	0	301	468	37	118	5.3	.954	SS-110, 2B-36, 3B-6
1958	SF N	148	.256	.406	539	138	20	5	17	3.2	71	74	73	60	1	0	0	262	472	34	102	5.1	.956	SS-134, 2B-17

Daryl Spencer *continued*

Year	Team	Games	BA	SA	AB	H	2B	3B	HR	HR%	R	RBI	BB	SO	SB	Pinch Hit AB	Pinch Hit H	PO	A	E	DP	TC/G	FA	G by Pos
1959		152	.265	.369	555	147	20	1	12	2.2	59	62	58	67	5	1	0	350	417	24	84	5.1	.970	2B-151, SS-4
1960	STL N	148	.258	.404	507	131	20	3	16	3.2	70	58	81	74	1	2	1	242	359	32	74	4.1	.949	SS-138, 2B-16
1961	2 teams	STL N (37G –.254) LA N (60G –.243)																						
"	total	97	.248	.395	319	79	11	0	12	3.8	46	48	43	52	1	1	0	114	208	13	42	3.5	.961	3B-57, SS-40
1962	LA N	77	.236	.318	157	37	5	1	2	1.3	24	12	32	31	0	13	1	38	101	10	7	2.2	.933	3B-57, SS-10
1963	2 teams	LA N (7G –.111) CIN N (50G –.239)																						
"	total	57	.232	.293	164	38	7	0	1	0.6	21	23	34	39	1	7	0	47	95	3	9	2.8	.979	3B-51
10 yrs.		1098	.244	.380	3689	901	145	20	105	2.8	457	428	449	516	13	32	2	1828	2780	203	564	4.4	.958	SS-558, 2B-322, 3B-222

Jim Spencer

SPENCER, JAMES LLOYD BL TL 6′ 2″ 195 lbs.
B. July 30, 1946, Hanover, Pa.

Year	Team	Games	BA	SA	AB	H	2B	3B	HR	HR%	R	RBI	BB	SO	SB	Pinch Hit AB	Pinch Hit H	PO	A	E	DP	TC/G	FA	G by Pos
1968	CAL A	19	.191	.206	68	13	1	0	0	0.0	2	5	3	10	0	0	0	152	18	1	15	9.0	.994	1B-19
1969		113	.254	.383	386	98	14	3	10	2.6	39	31	26	53	1	8	2	926	66	9	81	9.4	.991	1B-107
1970		146	.274	.399	511	140	20	4	12	2.3	61	68	28	61	0	6	2	1212	85	7	131	9.2	.995	1B-142
1971		148	.237	.392	510	121	21	2	18	3.5	50	59	48	63	0	7	1	1296	93	5	117	9.6	.996	1B-145
1972		82	.222	.259	212	47	5	0	1	0.5	13	14	12	25	0	22	4	289	23	3	25	5.3	.990	1B-35, OF-24
1973	2 teams	CAL A (29G –.241) TEX A (102G –.267)																						
"	total	131	.262	.362	439	115	16	5	6	1.4	45	54	43	50	0	8	0	994	74	1	134	8.4	.999	1B-125, DH-3
1974	TEX A	118	.278	.392	352	98	11	4	7	2.0	36	44	22	27	1	8	3	389	27	1	36	3.7	.998	1B-60, DH-54
1975		132	.266	.397	403	107	18	1	11	2.7	50	47	35	43	0	8	3	844	70	5	92	7.4	.995	1B-99, DH-25
1976	CHI A	150	.253	.367	518	131	13	2	14	2.7	53	70	49	52	6	4	0	1206	112	2	116	9.1	.998	1B-143, DH-2
1977		128	.247	.400	470	116	16	1	18	3.8	56	69	36	50	1	2	1	977	90	10	76	8.6	.991	1B-125
1978	NY A	71	.227	.440	150	34	9	1	7	4.7	12	24	15	32	0	24	7	90	7	0	4	1.9	1.000	DH-35, 1B-15
1979		106	.288	.593	295	85	15	3	23	7.8	60	53	38	25	0	16	3	232	17	2	35	2.6	.992	DH-71, 1B-26
1980		97	.236	.421	259	61	9	0	13	5.0	38	43	30	44	1	22	8	567	41	6	51	6.8	.990	1B-75, DH-15
1981	2 teams	NY A (25G –.143) OAK A (54G –.205)																						
"	total	79	.188	.274	234	44	8	0	4	1.7	20	13	19	27	1	13	4	516	53	1	47	7.8	.998	1B-73
1982	OAK A	33	.168	.277	101	17	3	1	2	2.0	6	5	3	20	0	3	2	230	22	2	30	7.9	.992	1B-32
15 yrs.		1553	.250	.387	4908	1227	179	27	146	3.0	541	599	407	582	11	151	40	9920	798	55	990	7.4	.995	1B-1221, DH-205, OF-24
DIVISIONAL PLAYOFF SERIES																								
1981	OAK A	1	.250	.500	4	1	1	0	0	0.0	0	0	0	0	0	0	0	6	2	0	0	8.0	1.000	1B-1
LEAGUE CHAMPIONSHIP SERIES																								
1980	NY A	1	.000	.000	1	0	0	0	0	0.0	0	0	0	0	0	1	0	0	0	0	0	0.0	—	
1981	OAK A	2	.000	.000	2	0	0	0	0	0.0	0	0	0	0	0	2	0	4	2	0	1	3.0	1.000	1B-2
2 yrs.		3	.000	.000	3	0	0	0	0	0.0	0	0	0	0	0	3	0	4	2	0	1	3.0	1.000	1B-2
WORLD SERIES																								
1978	NY A	4	.167	.167	12	2	0	0	0	0.0	3	0	2	4	0	1	0	23	2	0	4	8.3	1.000	1B-3

Roy Spencer

SPENCER, ROY HAMPTON BR TR 5′10″ 168 lbs.
B. Feb. 22, 1900, Scranton, N. C. D. Feb. 8, 1973, Port Charlotte, Fla.

Year	Team	Games	BA	SA	AB	H	2B	3B	HR	HR%	R	RBI	BB	SO	SB	Pinch Hit AB	Pinch Hit H	PO	A	E	DP	TC/G	FA	G by Pos
1925	PIT N	14	.214	.250	28	6	1	0	0	0.0	1	2	1	3	1	3	0	18	1	2	2	1.9	.905	C-11
1926		28	.395	.465	43	17	3	0	0	0.0	5	4	1	0	0	10	6	29	3	1	0	2.1	.970	C-16
1927		38	.283	.337	92	26	3	1	0	0.0	9	13	3	3	0	4	2	98	15	3	2	3.4	.974	C-34
1929	WAS A	50	.155	.216	116	18	4	0	1	0.9	18	9	8	15	0	5	1	128	20	5	2	3.7	.967	C-41
1930		93	.255	.315	321	82	11	4	0	0.0	32	36	18	27	3	0	0	395	44	5	3	4.8	.989	C-93
1931		145	.275	.327	483	133	16	3	1	0.2	48	60	35	21	0	0	0	642	69	11	9	5.0	.985	C-145
1932		102	.246	.284	317	78	9	0	1	0.3	28	41	24	17	0	3	1	313	44	8	9	3.7	.978	C-98
1933	CLE A	75	.203	.242	227	46	5	2	0	0.0	26	23	23	17	0	3	1	258	42	3	4	4.2	.990	C-72
1934		5	.143	.286	7	1	1	0	0	0.0	0	2	0	1	0	1	1	7	2	0	0	2.3	1.000	C-4
1936	NY N	19	.278	.333	18	5	1	0	0	0.0	3	3	2	3	0	2	1	18	3	0	0	1.5	1.000	C-14
1937	BKN N	51	.205	.256	117	24	2	2	0	0.0	5	4	8	17	0	5	0	177	27	0	2	4.5	1.000	C-45
1938		16	.267	.333	45	12	1	1	0	0.0	2	6	5	6	0	0	0	55	5	2	0	3.9	.968	C-16
12 yrs.		636	.247	.298	1814	448	57	13	3	0.2	177	203	128	130	4	36	13	2138	275	40	33	4.2	.984	C-589
WORLD SERIES																								
1927	PIT N	1	.000	.000	1	0	0	0	0	0.0	0	0	0	0	0	0	0	0	0	0	0	0.0	.000	C-1

Tom Spencer

SPENCER, HUBERT THOMAS BR TR 6′ 170 lbs.
B. Feb. 28, 1951, Gallipolis, Ohio.

Year	Team	Games	BA	SA	AB	H	2B	3B	HR	HR%	R	RBI	BB	SO	SB	Pinch Hit AB	Pinch Hit H	PO	A	E	DP	TC/G	FA	G by Pos
1978	CHI A	29	.185	.200	65	12	1	0	0	0.0	3	4	2	9	0	7	0	52	2	0	0	1.9	1.000	OF-27, DH-2

Tubby Spencer

SPENCER, EDWARD RUSSELL BR TR 5′10″ 215 lbs.
B. Jan. 26, 1884, Oil City, Pa. D. Feb. 1, 1945, San Francisco, Calif.

Year	Team	Games	BA	SA	AB	H	2B	3B	HR	HR%	R	RBI	BB	SO	SB	Pinch Hit AB	Pinch Hit H	PO	A	E	DP	TC/G	FA	G by Pos
1905	STL A	35	.235	.278	115	27	1	2	0	0.0	6	11	7		2	1	1	134	41	7	1	5.4	.962	C-34
1906		58	.176	.218	188	33	6	1	0	0.0	15	17	7		4	3	0	226	60	20	3	5.7	.935	C-54
1907		71	.265	.322	230	61	11	1	0	0.0	27	24	7		1	8	2	250	80	15	6	5.5	.957	C-63
1908		91	.210	.238	286	60	6	1	0	0.0	19	28	17		1	2	1	398	109	9	9	5.8	.983	C-89
1909	BOS A	28	.162	.176	74	12	1	0	0	0.0	6	9	6		2	2	0	94	24	1	0	4.6	.992	C-26
1911	PHI N	11	.156	.281	32	5	1	0	1	3.1	2	3	3	7	0	0	0	47	15	5	2	6.1	.925	C-11
1916	DET A	19	.370	.481	54	20	1	1	1	1.9	7	10	6	6	2	0	0	58	21	1	1	4.2	.988	C-19
1917		70	.240	.313	192	46	8	3	0	0.0	13	22	15	15	0	8	0	250	57	7	10	5.1	.978	C-62
1918		66	.219	.284	155	34	8	1	0	0.0	11	8	19	18	1	17	3	153	46	7	3	4.2	.966	C-48, 1B-1
9 yrs.		449	.225	.277	1326	298	43	10	2	0.2	106	132	87	46	13	41	7	1610	453	72	35	5.2	.966	C-406, 1B-1

Vern Spencer

SPENCER, VERNON MURRAY BL TR 5′ 7″ 165 lbs.
B. Feb. 4, 1894, Wixom, Mich. D. June 3, 1971, Wixom, Mich.

Year	Team	Games	BA	SA	AB	H	2B	3B	HR	HR%	R	RBI	BB	SO	SB	Pinch Hit AB	Pinch Hit H	PO	A	E	DP	TC/G	FA	G by Pos
1920	NY N	45	.200	.257	140	28	2	3	0	0.0	15	19	11	17	4	3	0	76	6	6	1	2.2	.932	OF-40

Paul Speraw

SPERAW, PAUL BACHMAN (Birdie, Polly) BR TR 5′ 8½″ 145 lbs.
B. Oct. 5, 1893, Annville, Pa. D. Feb. 22, 1962, Cedar Rapids, Iowa.

Year	Team	Games	BA	SA	AB	H	2B	3B	HR	HR%	R	RBI	BB	SO	SB	Pinch Hit AB	Pinch Hit H	PO	A	E	DP	TC/G	FA	G by Pos
1920	STL A	1	.000	.000	2	0	0	0	0	0.0	0	0	0	0	0	0	0	1	1	0	0	2.0	1.000	3B-1

Ed Sperber

SPERBER, EDWIN GEORGE
B. Jan. 21, 1895, Cincinnati, Ohio D. Jan. 5, 1976, Cincinnati, Ohio.
BL TL 5′11″ 175 lbs.

Year	Team	Games	BA	SA	AB	H	2B	3B	HR	HR%	R	RBI	BB	SO	SB	Pinch Hit AB	Pinch Hit H	PO	A	E	DP	TC/G	FA	G by Pos
1924	BOS N	24	.288	.373	59	17	2	0	1	1.7	8	12	10	9	3	2	0	25	1	3	0	1.7	.897	OF-17
1925		2	.000	.000	2	0	0	0	0	0.0	0	0	0	0	0	2	0	0	0	0	0	0.0	—	
2 yrs.		26	.279	.361	61	17	2	0	1	1.6	8	12	10	9	3	4	0	25	1	3	0	1.7	.897	OF-17

Rob Sperring

SPERRING, ROBERT WALTER
B. Oct. 10, 1949, San Francisco, Calif.
BR TR 6′1″ 185 lbs.

Year	Team	Games	BA	SA	AB	H	2B	3B	HR	HR%	R	RBI	BB	SO	SB	Pinch Hit AB	Pinch Hit H	PO	A	E	DP	TC/G	FA	G by Pos
1974	CHI N	42	.206	.262	107	22	3	0	1	0.9	9	5	9	28	1	1	0	64	101	10	16	4.1	.943	2B-35, SS-8
1975		65	.208	.271	144	30	4	1	1	0.7	25	9	16	31	0	1	0	70	115	12	18	3.1	.939	3B-22, 2B-17, SS-16, OF-8
1976		43	.258	.290	93	24	3	0	0	0.0	8	7	9	25	0	1	0	36	40	1	5	1.8	.987	3B-20, SS-15, 2B-4, OF-3
1977	HOU N	58	.186	.233	129	24	3	0	1	0.8	6	9	12	23	0	10	3	57	98	6	15	3.0	.963	SS-22, 2B-20, 3B-11
4 yrs.		208	.211	.262	473	100	13	1	3	0.6	48	30	46	107	1	13	3	227	354	29	54	3.0	.952	2B-76, SS-61, 3B-53, OF-11

Stan Sperry

SPERRY, STANLEY KENNETH
B. Feb. 19, 1914, Evansville, Wis. D. Sept. 27, 1962, Evansville, Wis.
BL TR 5′10½″ 164 lbs.

Year	Team	Games	BA	SA	AB	H	2B	3B	HR	HR%	R	RBI	BB	SO	SB	Pinch Hit AB	Pinch Hit H	PO	A	E	DP	TC/G	FA	G by Pos
1936	PHI N	20	.135	.216	37	5	3	0	0	0.0	2	4	3	5	0	3	1	23	22	5	4	3.3	.900	2B-15
1938	PHI A	60	.273	.320	253	69	6	3	0	0.0	28	27	15	9	1	0	0	121	185	13	26	5.3	.959	2B-60
2 yrs.		80	.255	.307	290	74	9	3	0	0.0	30	31	18	14	1	3	1	144	207	18	30	4.9	.951	2B-75

Bill Spiers

SPIERS, WILLIAM JAMES
B. June 5, 1966, Orangeburg, S. C.
BL TR 6′2″ 190 lbs.

Year	Team	Games	BA	SA	AB	H	2B	3B	HR	HR%	R	RBI	BB	SO	SB	Pinch Hit AB	Pinch Hit H	PO	A	E	DP	TC/G	FA	G by Pos
1989	MIL A	114	.255	.333	345	88	9	3	4	1.2	44	33	21	63	10	4	3	164	295	21	62	4.3	.956	SS-89, 3B-12, DH-4, 2B-4, 1B-2
1990		112	.242	.317	363	88	15	3	2	0.6	44	36	16	45	11	2	1	159	326	12	72	4.5	.976	SS-111
1991		133	.283	.401	414	117	13	6	8	1.9	71	54	34	55	14	1	0	201	345	17	93	4.3	.970	SS-128, DH-2, OF-1
1992		12	.313	.438	16	5	2	0	0	0.0	2	2	1	4	1	1	0	6	6	0	0	1.1	1.000	SS-5, 2B-4, DH-1, 3B-1
1993		113	.238	.303	340	81	8	4	2	0.6	43	36	29	51	9	3	1	213	231	13	55	3.9	.972	2B-104, OF-7, SS-4, DH-1
1994		73	.252	.308	214	54	10	1	0	0.0	27	17	19	42	7	10	0	70	128	8	26	2.7	.961	3B-35, SS-35, DH-3, OF-2, 1B-1
1995	NY N	63	.208	.264	72	15	2	1	0	0.0	5	11	12	15	0	40	9	13	30	7	3	2.9	.860	3B-11, 2B-6
7 yrs.		620	.254	.335	1764	448	59	18	16	0.9	236	189	132	275	52	61	14	826	1361	78	311	4.0	.966	SS-372, 2B-118, 3B-59, DH-11, OF-10, 1B-3

Harry Spies

SPIES, HENRY
B. June 12, 1866, New Orleans, La. D. July 8, 1942, Los Angeles, Calif.
BR TR 5′11½″ 170 lbs.

Year	Team	Games	BA	SA	AB	H	2B	3B	HR	HR%	R	RBI	BB	SO	SB	Pinch Hit AB	Pinch Hit H	PO	A	E	DP	TC/G	FA	G by Pos
1895	2 teams	CIN N (14G –.220)	LOU N (72G –.268)																					
″	total	86	.261	.371	326	85	14	8	2	0.6	44	40	14	21	4	0	0	573	71	33	38	7.7	.951	1B-49, C-38, SS-1

Ed Spiezio

SPIEZIO, EDWARD WAYNE
B. Oct. 31, 1941, Joliet, Ill.
BR TR 5′11″ 180 lbs.

Year	Team	Games	BA	SA	AB	H	2B	3B	HR	HR%	R	RBI	BB	SO	SB	Pinch Hit AB	Pinch Hit H	PO	A	E	DP	TC/G	FA	G by Pos
1964	STL N	12	.333	.333	12	4	0	0	0	0.0	0	0	0	1	0	12	4	0	0	0	0	0.0	—	
1965		10	.167	.167	18	3	0	0	0	0.0	0	5	1	4	0	7	2	1	7	0	0	2.7	1.000	3B-3
1966		26	.219	.397	73	16	5	1	2	2.7	4	10	5	11	1	6	0	14	32	6	3	2.7	.885	3B-19
1967		55	.210	.314	105	22	2	0	3	2.9	9	10	7	18	2	27	8	24	35	2	4	2.3	.967	3B-19, OF-7
1968		29	.157	.157	51	8	0	0	0	0.0	1	2	5	6	1	14	4	20	5	0	1	1.9	1.000	OF-11, 3B-2
1969	SD N	121	.234	.369	355	83	9	0	13	3.7	29	43	38	64	1	23	5	93	198	19	10	3.1	.939	3B-98, OF-1
1970		110	.285	.462	316	90	18	1	12	3.8	45	42	43	42	4	21	7	66	178	12	10	2.8	.953	3B-93
1971		97	.231	.338	308	71	10	1	7	2.3	16	36	22	50	6	7	2	57	168	9	12	2.5	.962	3B-91, OF-1
1972	2 teams	SD N (20G –.138)	CHI A (74G –.238)																					
″	total	94	.229	.294	306	70	12	1	2	0.7	22	26	14	49	1	17	1	69	176	12	12	3.3	.953	3B-79
9 yrs.		554	.238	.355	1544	367	56	4	39	2.5	126	174	135	245	16	134	33	344	799	60	52	2.8	.950	3B-404, OF-20
WORLD SERIES																								
1967	STL N	1	.000	.000	1	0	0	0	0	0.0	0	0	0	0	0	1	0	0	0	0	0	0.0	—	
1968		1	1.000	1.000	1	1	0	0	0	0.0	0	0	0	0	0	1	1	0	0	0	0	0.0	—	
2 yrs.		2	.500	.500	2	1	0	0	0	0.0	0	0	0	0	0	2	1							

Charlie Spikes

SPIKES, LESLIE CHARLES
B. Jan. 23, 1951, Bogalusa, La.
BR TR 6′3″ 215 lbs.

Year	Team	Games	BA	SA	AB	H	2B	3B	HR	HR%	R	RBI	BB	SO	SB	Pinch Hit AB	Pinch Hit H	PO	A	E	DP	TC/G	FA	G by Pos
1972	NY A	14	.147	.176	34	5	1	0	0	0.0	2	3	1	13	0	5	0	14	1	0	1	1.7	1.000	OF-9
1973	CLE A	140	.237	.409	506	120	12	3	23	4.5	68	73	45	103	5	2	1	202	13	8	0	1.6	.964	OF-111, DH-26
1974		155	.271	.431	568	154	23	1	22	3.9	63	80	34	100	10	1	0	284	16	10	3	2.0	.968	OF-154
1975		111	.229	.380	345	79	13	3	11	3.2	41	33	30	51	7	17	7	176	13	5	5	1.8	.974	OF-103, DH-2
1976		101	.237	.326	334	79	11	5	3	0.9	34	31	23	50	5	8	0	185	7	3	0	2.0	.985	OF-98, DH-2
1977		32	.232	.347	95	22	2	0	3	3.2	13	11	11	17	0	7	1	34	1	1	1	1.2	.972	OF-27, DH-2
1978	DET A	10	.250	.286	28	7	1	0	0	0.0	1	2	2	6	0	0	0	9	1	1	1	1.2	.909	OF-9
1979	ATL N	66	.280	.462	93	26	8	0	3	3.2	12	21	5	30	0	47	16	16	0	3	0	1.3	.842	OF-15
1980		41	.278	.306	36	10	1	0	0	0.0	6	2	3	18	0	31	10	4	0	0	0	0.6	1.000	OF-7
9 yrs.		670	.246	.389	2039	502	72	12	65	3.2	240	256	154	388	27	118	35	924	52	31	11	1.8	.969	OF-533, DH-32

Harry Spilman

SPILMAN, WILLIAM HARRY
B. July 18, 1954, Albany, Ga.
BL TR 6′1″ 180 lbs.

Year	Team	Games	BA	SA	AB	H	2B	3B	HR	HR%	R	RBI	BB	SO	SB	Pinch Hit AB	Pinch Hit H	PO	A	E	DP	TC/G	FA	G by Pos
1978	CIN N	4	.250	.250	4	1	0	0	0	0.0	1	0	0	1	0	4	1	0	0	0	0	0.0	—	
1979		43	.214	.268	56	12	3	0	0	0.0	7	5	7	5	0	22	5	64	11	0	3	4.7	1.000	1B-12, 3B-4
1980		65	.267	.426	101	27	4	0	4	4.0	14	19	9	19	0	41	12	132	15	2	11	6.8	.987	1B-18, OF-2, C-1, 3B-1
1981	2 teams	CIN N (23G –.167)	HOU N (28G –.294)																					
″	total	51	.241	.259	58	14	1	0	0	0.0	9	4	5	10	0	29	9	62	5	1	3	3.8	.985	1B-15, 3B-3
1982	HOU N	38	.279	.459	61	17	2	0	3	4.9	7	11	5	10	0	26	6	86	5	1	5	8.4	.989	1B-11
1983		42	.167	.244	78	13	3	0	1	1.3	7	9	5	12	0	20	1	138	8	0	5	5.8	1.000	1B-19, C-6
1984		32	.264	.375	72	19	2	0	2	2.8	14	15	12	10	0	10	1	143	9	3	14	6.0	.981	1B-18, C-8
1985		44	.136	.197	66	9	1	0	1	1.5	3	4	3	7	0	20	4	134	4	0	15	6.6	1.000	1B-19, C-2
1986	2 teams	DET A (24G –.245)	SF N (58G –.287)																					
″	total	82	.273	.441	143	39	9	0	5	3.5	18	30	15	21	0	42	16	147	18	2	8	4.0	.988	1B-20, DH-11, 3B-7, C-2, OF-1, 2B-1
1987	SF N	83	.267	.356	90	24	5	0	1	1.1	5	14	9	20	1	61	13	40	7	2	5	2.5	.959	3B-10, 1B-9, C-1

Harry Spilman *continued*

Year	Team	Games	BA	SA	AB	H	2B	3B	HR	HR%	R	RBI	BB	SO	SB	Pinch Hit AB	Pinch Hit H	PO	A	E	DP	TC/G	FA	G by Pos
1988	2 teams	SF N (40G –.175) HOU N (7G –.000)																						
"	total	47	.156	.289	45	7	1	1	1	2.2	4	3	4	9	0	34	4	24	3	1	3	2.8	.964	1B-7, C-2, OF-1
1989	HOU N	32	.278	.361	36	10	3	0	0	0.0	7	3	7	2	0	19	4	47	4	0	2	5.1	1.000	1B-9, C-1
12 yrs.		563	.237	.348	810	192	34	1	18	2.2	96	117	81	126	1	328	76	1017	89	12	74	5.1	.989	1B-157, 3B-25, C-23, DH-11, OF-4, 2B-1
DIVISIONAL PLAYOFF SERIES																								
1981	HOU N	1	.000	.000	1	0	0	0	0	0.0	0	0	0	0	0	1	0	0	0	0	0	0.0	—	
LEAGUE CHAMPIONSHIP SERIES																								
1979	CIN N	2	.000	.000	2	0	0	0	0	0.0	0	0	0	0	0	2	0	0	0	0	0	0.0	—	
1987	SF N	3	.500	2.000	2	1	0	0	1	50.0	1	1	0	0	0	2	1	0	0	0	0	0.0	—	
2 yrs.		5	.250	1.000	4	1	0	0	1	25.0	1	1	0	0	0	4	1							

Hal Spindel

SPINDEL, HAROLD STEWART
B. May 27, 1913, Chandler, Okla.
BR TR 6′ 185 lbs.

Year	Team	Games	BA	SA	AB	H	2B	3B	HR	HR%	R	RBI	BB	SO	SB	Pinch Hit AB	Pinch Hit H	PO	A	E	DP	TC/G	FA	G by Pos
1939	STL A	48	.269	.311	119	32	3	1	0	0.0	13	11	8	7	0	15	6	126	14	1	4	4.4	.993	C-32
1945	PHI N	36	.230	.264	87	20	3	0	0	0.0	7	8	6	7	0	4	0	93	14	4	6	3.6	.964	C-31
1946		1	.333	.333	3	1	0	0	0	0.0	0	1	0	0	0	0	0	3	0	0	0	3.0	1.000	C-1
3 yrs.		85	.254	.292	209	53	6	1	0	0.0	20	20	14	14	0	19	6	222	28	5	10	4.0	.980	C-64

Andy Spognardi

SPOGNARDI, ANDREA ETTORE
B. Oct. 18, 1908, Boston, Mass.
BL TR 5′ 9½″ 160 lbs.

Year	Team	Games	BA	SA	AB	H	2B	3B	HR	HR%	R	RBI	BB	SO	SB	Pinch Hit AB	Pinch Hit H	PO	A	E	DP	TC/G	FA	G by Pos
1932	BOS A	17	.294	.324	34	10	1	0	0	0.0	9	1	6	6	0	1	1	14	38	1	6	3.8	.981	2B-9, SS-3, 3B-2

Al Spohrer

SPOHRER, ALFRED RAY
B. Dec. 3, 1902, Philadelphia, Pa. D. July 17, 1972, Plymouth, N. H.
BR TR 5′10½″ 175 lbs.

Year	Team	Games	BA	SA	AB	H	2B	3B	HR	HR%	R	RBI	BB	SO	SB	Pinch Hit AB	Pinch Hit H	PO	A	E	DP	TC/G	FA	G by Pos
1928	2 teams	NY N (3G –.000) BOS N (48G –.218)																						
"	total	51	.214	.238	126	27	3	0	0	0.0	15	9	5	11	1	3	1	104	22	3	1	2.5	.977	C-51
1929	BOS N	114	.272	.398	342	93	21	8	2	0.6	42	48	26	35	1	4	1	314	57	18	5	3.6	.954	C-109
1930		112	.317	.441	356	113	22	8	2	0.6	44	37	22	24	3	3	1	322	36	16	4	3.5	.957	C-108
1931		114	.240	.317	350	84	17	5	0	0.0	23	27	22	27	2	3	0	392	54	8	5	4.1	.982	C-111
1932		104	.269	.316	335	90	12	2	0	0.0	31	33	15	26	2	3	0	374	62	4	2	4.4	.991	C-100
1933		67	.250	.310	184	46	6	1	1	0.5	11	12	11	13	3	2	0	150	26	5	4	2.8	.972	C-65
1934		100	.223	.279	265	59	15	0	0	0.0	25	17	14	18	1	0	0	296	45	8	5	3.6	.977	C-98
1935		92	.242	.288	260	63	7	1	1	0.4	22	16	9	12	0	2	0	230	45	12	4	3.2	.958	C-90
8 yrs.		754	.259	.336	2218	575	103	25	6	0.3	213	199	124	166	13	20	3	2182	347	74	30	3.6	.972	C-732

Jim Spotts

SPOTTS, JAMES RUSSELL
B. Apr. 10, 1909, Honeybrook, Pa. D. June 15, 1964, Medford, N. J.
BR TR 5′10½″ 175 lbs.

Year	Team	Games	BA	SA	AB	H	2B	3B	HR	HR%	R	RBI	BB	SO	SB	Pinch Hit AB	Pinch Hit H	PO	A	E	DP	TC/G	FA	G by Pos
1930	PHI N	3	.000	.000	2	0	0	0	0	0.0	1	0	0	1	0	1	0	2	0	0	0	1.0	1.000	C-2

Charlie Sprague

SPRAGUE, CHARLES WELLINGTON
B. Oct. 10, 1864, Cleveland, Ohio D. Dec. 31, 1912, Des Moines, Iowa.
BL TL 5′11″ 150 lbs.

Year	Team	Games	BA	SA	AB	H	2B	3B	HR	HR%	R	RBI	BB	SO	SB	Pinch Hit AB	Pinch Hit H	PO	A	E	DP	TC/G	FA	G by Pos
1887	CHI N	3	.154	.154	13	2	0	0	0	0.0	0	0	0	2	0	0	0	0	2	1	0	0.8	.667	P-3, OF-1
1889	CLE N	2	.143	.143	7	1	0	0	0	0.0	2	1	1	0	1	0	0	0	6	1	1	3.5	.857	P-2
1890	TOL AA	55	.236	.337	199	47	5	6	1	0.5	25		16		10	0	0	60	18	8	1	1.5	.907	OF-40, P-19
3 yrs.		60	.228	.320	219	50	5	6	1	0.5	27	1	17	2	11	0	0	60	26	10	2	1.5	.896	OF-41, P-24

Ed Sprague

SPRAGUE, EDWARD NELSON, JR.
Son of Ed Sprague.
B. July 25, 1967, Castro Valley, Calif.
BR TR 6′ 2″ 215 lbs.

Year	Team	Games	BA	SA	AB	H	2B	3B	HR	HR%	R	RBI	BB	SO	SB	Pinch Hit AB	Pinch Hit H	PO	A	E	DP	TC/G	FA	G by Pos
1991	TOR A	61	.275	.394	160	44	7	0	4	2.5	17	20	19	43	0	1	1	167	72	14	14	4.1	.945	3B-35, 1B-22, C-2, DH-2
1992		22	.234	.340	47	11	2	0	1	2.1	6	7	3	7	0	3	2	82	5	1	1	4.0	.989	C-15, 1B-4, DH-2, 3B-1
1993		150	.260	.386	546	142	31	1	12	2.2	50	73	32	85	1	0	0	127	232	17	21	2.5	.955	3B-150
1994		109	.240	.373	405	97	19	1	11	2.7	38	44	23	95	1	0	0	118	147	14	20	2.5	.950	3B-107, 1B-3
1995		144	.244	.407	521	127	27	2	18	3.5	77	74	58	96	0	0	0	167	234	17	23	2.8	.959	3B-139, 1B-7, DH-2
5 yrs.		486	.251	.389	1679	421	86	4	46	2.7	188	218	135	326	2	4	3	661	690	63	79	2.9	.955	3B-432, 1B-36, C-17, DH-6
LEAGUE CHAMPIONSHIP SERIES																								
1992	TOR A	2	.500	.500	2	1	0	0	0	0.0	0	0	0	1	0	2	1	0	0	0	0	0.0	—	
1993		6	.286	.381	21	6	0	1	0	0.0	0	4	2	4	0	0	0	5	9	0	1	2.3	1.000	3B-6
2 yrs.		8	.304	.391	23	7	0	1	0	0.0	0	4	2	5	0	2	1	5	9	0	1	2.3	1.000	3B-6
WORLD SERIES																								
1992	TOR A	3	.500	2.000	2	1	0	0	1	50.0	1	2	1	0	0	2	1	0	0	0	0	0.0	.000	1B-1
1993		5	.067	.067	15	1	0	0	0	0.0	0	2	1	6	0	1	0	4	9	2	1	3.0	.867	3B-4, 1B-1
2 yrs.		8	.118	.294	17	2	0	0	1	5.9	1	4	2	6	0	3	1	4	9	2	1	2.5	.867	3B-4, 1B-2

Harry Spratt

SPRATT, HENRY LEE
B. July 10, 1888, Broadford, Va. D. July 3, 1969, Washington, Pa.
BL TR 5′ 8½″ 175 lbs.

Year	Team	Games	BA	SA	AB	H	2B	3B	HR	HR%	R	RBI	BB	SO	SB	Pinch Hit AB	Pinch Hit H	PO	A	E	DP	TC/G	FA	G by Pos
1911	BOS N	62	.240	.357	154	37	4	4	2	1.3	22	13	13	25	1	19	5	82	75	19	9	4.5	.892	SS-26, 2B-5, OF-4, 3B-4
1912		27	.258	.438	89	23	3	2	3	3.4	6	15	7	11	2	4	0	22	58	15	6	4.1	.842	SS-23
2 yrs.		89	.247	.387	243	60	7	6	5	2.1	28	28	20	36	3	23	5	104	133	34	15	4.4	.875	SS-49, 2B-5, OF-4, 3B-4

George Spriggs

SPRIGGS, GEORGE HERMAN
B. May 22, 1941, Jewell, Md.
BL TR 5′11″ 175 lbs.

Year	Team	Games	BA	SA	AB	H	2B	3B	HR	HR%	R	RBI	BB	SO	SB	Pinch Hit AB	Pinch Hit H	PO	A	E	DP	TC/G	FA	G by Pos
1965	PIT N	9	.500	.500	2	1	0	0	0	0.0	5	0	0	0	2	1	0	0	0	0	0	0.0	.000	OF-1
1966		9	.143	.143	7	1	0	0	0	0.0	0	0	0	3	0	7	1	0	0	0	0	0.0	—	
1967		38	.175	.228	57	10	1	1	0	0.0	14	5	6	20	3	21	3	15	0	0	0	1.2	1.000	OF-13
1969	KC A	23	.138	.276	29	4	2	1	0	0.0	4	0	3	8	0	14	1	7	0	0	0	1.2	1.000	OF-6
1970		51	.208	.292	130	27	2	3	1	0.8	12	7	14	32	4	10	2	57	4	3	0	1.8	.953	OF-36
5 yrs.		130	.191	.271	225	43	5	5	1	0.4	35	12	23	63	9	53	7	79	4	3	0	1.5	.965	OF-56

Year	Team	Games	BA	SA	AB	H	2B	3B	HR	HR%	R	RBI	BB	SO	SB	Pinch Hit AB	Pinch Hit H	PO	A	E	DP	TC/G	FA	G by Pos

Steve Springer

SPRINGER, STEVEN MICHAEL BR TR 6′ 190 lbs.
B. Feb. 11, 1961, Long Beach, Calif.

Year	Team	Games	BA	SA	AB	H	2B	3B	HR	HR%	R	RBI	BB	SO	SB	Pinch Hit AB	Pinch Hit H	PO	A	E	DP	TC/G	FA	G by Pos
1990	CLE A	4	.167	.167	12	2	0	0	0	0.0	1	1	0	6	0	1	0	2	3	0	0	1.3	1.000	3B-3, DH-1
1992	NY N	4	.400	.600	5	2	1	0	0	0.0	0	0	0	1	0	2	0	0	0	0	0	0.0	—	
2 yrs.		8	.235	.294	17	4	1	0	0	0.0	1	1	0	7	0	3	0	2	3	0	0	1.3	1.000	3B-3, DH-1

Joe Sprinz

SPRINZ, JOSEPH CONRAD (Mule) BR TR 5′11″ 185 lbs.
B. Aug. 3, 1902, St. Louis, Mo. D. Jan. 11, 1994, Fremont, Calif.

Year	Team	Games	BA	SA	AB	H	2B	3B	HR	HR%	R	RBI	BB	SO	SB	Pinch Hit AB	Pinch Hit H	PO	A	E	DP	TC/G	FA	G by Pos
1930	CLE A	17	.178	.200	45	8	1	0	0	0.0	5	2	4	4	0	0	0	64	13	0	2	4.5	1.000	C-17
1931		1	.000	.000	3	0	0	0	0	0.0	0	0	0	0	0	0	0	2	1	0	0	3.0	1.000	C-1
1933	STL N	3	.200	.200	5	1	0	0	0	0.0	1	0	1	1	0	0	0	18	1	0	0	6.3	1.000	C-3
3 yrs.		21	.170	.189	53	9	1	0	0	0.0	6	2	5	5	0	0	0	84	15	0	2	4.7	1.000	C-21

Freddy Spurgeon

SPURGEON, FRED BR TR 5′11½″ 160 lbs.
B. Oct. 9, 1900, Wabash, Ind. D. Nov. 5, 1970, Kalamazoo, Mich.

Year	Team	Games	BA	SA	AB	H	2B	3B	HR	HR%	R	RBI	BB	SO	SB	Pinch Hit AB	Pinch Hit H	PO	A	E	DP	TC/G	FA	G by Pos
1924	CLE A	3	.125	.250	8	1	1	0	0	0.0	0	0	0	0	0	0	0	5	10	2	1	5.7	.882	2B-3
1925		107	.287	.327	376	108	9	3	0	0.0	50	32	15	21	8	2	0	158	259	25	31	4.2	.943	3B-56, 2B-46, SS-3
1926		149	.295	.355	614	181	31	3	0	0.0	101	49	27	36	7	0	0	341	479	32	93	5.7	.962	2B-149
1927		57	.251	.313	179	45	6	1	1	0.6	30	19	18	14	8	1	1	124	150	18	28	5.6	.938	2B-52
4 yrs.		316	.285	.339	1177	335	47	7	1	0.1	181	100	60	71	23	3	1	628	898	77	153	5.2	.952	2B-250, 3B-56, SS-3

Ed Spurney

SPURNEY, EDWARD FREDERICK
B. Jan. 19, 1872, Cleveland, Ohio D. Oct. 12, 1932, Cleveland, Ohio.

Year	Team	Games	BA	SA	AB	H	2B	3B	HR	HR%	R	RBI	BB	SO	SB	Pinch Hit AB	Pinch Hit H	PO	A	E	DP	TC/G	FA	G by Pos
1891	PIT N	3	.286	.429	7	2	1	0	0	0.0	2	0	2	1	0	0	0	1	7	1	0	3.0	.889	SS-3

Mike Squires

SQUIRES, MICHAEL LYNN BL TL 5′11″ 185 lbs.
B. Mar. 5, 1952, Kalamazoo, Mich.

Year	Team	Games	BA	SA	AB	H	2B	3B	HR	HR%	R	RBI	BB	SO	SB	Pinch Hit AB	Pinch Hit H	PO	A	E	DP	TC/G	FA	G by Pos
1975	CHI A	20	.231	.231	65	15	0	0	0	0.0	5	4	8	5	3	0	0	155	12	2	14	8.4	.988	1B-20
1977		3	.000	.000	3	0	0	0	0	0.0	0	0	0	1	0	2	0	8	1	0	0	9.0	1.000	1B-1
1978		46	.280	.367	150	42	9	2	0	0.0	25	19	16	21	4	1	1	361	20	1	29	8.5	.997	1B-45
1979		122	.264	.325	295	78	10	1	2	0.7	44	22	22	9	15	6	1	744	60	4	62	7.3	.995	1B-110, OF-1
1980		131	.283	.350	343	97	11	3	2	0.6	38	33	33	24	8	14	4	905	68	5	79	8.4	.995	1B-114, C-2
1981		92	.265	.296	294	78	9	0	0	0.0	35	25	22	17	7	6	2	729	58	6	68	8.9	.992	1B-88, OF-1
1982		116	.267	.359	195	52	9	3	1	0.5	33	21	14	13	3	14	3	512	48	3	59	5.2	.995	1B-109
1983		143	.222	.281	153	34	4	1	1	0.7	21	11	22	11	3	23	4	515	40	2	55	4.3	.996	1B-124, DH-5, 3B-1
1984		104	.183	.195	82	15	1	0	0	0.0	9	6	6	7	2	22	3	234	25	0	29	2.8	1.000	1B-77, 3B-13, OF-3, P-1
1985		2	—	—	0	0	0	0	0	—	1	0	0	0	0	0	0	0	0	0	0	0.0	—	
10 yrs.		779	.260	.318	1580	411	53	10	6	0.4	211	141	143	108	45	88	18	4163	332	23	395	6.3	.995	1B-688, 3B-14, DH-5, OF-5, C-2, P-1

LEAGUE CHAMPIONSHIP SERIES

Year	Team	Games	BA	SA	AB	H	2B	3B	HR	HR%	R	RBI	BB	SO	SB	Pinch Hit AB	Pinch Hit H	PO	A	E	DP	TC/G	FA	G by Pos
1983	CHI A	4	.000	.000	4	0	0	0	0	0.0	0	0	0	0	0	2	0	5	0	0	0	1.7	1.000	1B-3

Marv Staehle

STAEHLE, MARVIN GUSTAVE BL TR 5′10″ 165 lbs.
B. Mar. 13, 1942, Oak Park, Ill.

Year	Team	Games	BA	SA	AB	H	2B	3B	HR	HR%	R	RBI	BB	SO	SB	Pinch Hit AB	Pinch Hit H	PO	A	E	DP	TC/G	FA	G by Pos
1964	CHI A	6	.400	.400	5	2	0	0	0	0.0	0	2	0	0	1	5	2	0	0	0	0	0.0	—	
1965		7	.429	.429	7	3	0	0	0	0.0	0	2	0	0	0	7	3	0	0	0	0	0.0	—	
1966		8	.133	.133	15	2	0	0	0	0.0	2	0	4	2	1	2	0	9	14	0	5	3.8	1.000	2B-6
1967		32	.111	.130	54	6	1	0	0	0.0	1	1	4	8	1	8	0	29	35	0	4	2.9	1.000	2B-17, SS-5
1969	MON N	6	.412	.706	17	7	2	0	1	5.9	4	1	2	0	0	2	1	6	11	1	2	4.5	.944	2B-4
1970		104	.218	.252	321	70	9	1	0	0.0	41	26	39	21	1	13	2	153	210	14	53	4.1	.963	2B-91, SS-1
1971	ATL N	22	.111	.111	36	4	0	0	0	0.0	5	1	5	4	0	11	0	21	28	0	5	6.1	1.000	2B-7, 3B-1
7 yrs.		185	.207	.244	455	94	12	1	1	0.2	53	33	54	35	4	48	8	218	298	15	69	4.0	.972	2B-125, SS-6, 3B-1

Bob Stafford

STAFFORD, ROBERT M.
B. June 26, 1872, Oak Ridge, N. C. D. Aug. 20, 1916, Moores Springs, N. C.

Year	Team	Games	BA	SA	AB	H	2B	3B	HR	HR%	R	RBI	BB	SO	SB	Pinch Hit AB	Pinch Hit H	PO	A	E	DP	TC/G	FA	G by Pos
1890	PHI AA	1	.000	.000	2	0	0	0	0	0.0	0		0		0	0	0	0	0	0	0	0.0	.000	OF-1

General Stafford

STAFFORD, JAMES JOSEPH BR TR 5′8″ 165 lbs.
Brother of John Stafford.
B. July 9, 1868, Webster, Mass. D. Sept. 18, 1923, Worcester, Mass.

Year	Team	Games	BA	SA	AB	H	2B	3B	HR	HR%	R	RBI	BB	SO	SB	Pinch Hit AB	Pinch Hit H	PO	A	E	DP	TC/G	FA	G by Pos
1890	BUF P	15	.143	.163	49	7	1	0	0	0.0	11	3	7	8	2	0	0	9	21	5	2	2.2	.857	P-12, OF-4
1893	NY N	67	.281	.388	281	79	7	4	5	1.8	58	27	25	31	19	0	0	129	8	15	4	2.3	.901	OF-67
1894		14	.217	.283	46	10	1	1	0	0.0	10	4	10	7	2	1	0	29	11	9	3	3.8	.816	3B-6, OF-5, 1B-1, 2B-1
1895		124	.279	.346	463	129	12	5	3	0.6	79	73	40	32	42	0	0	265	336	61	44	5.3	.908	2B-110, OF-12, 3B-2
1896		59	.287	.335	230	66	9	1	0	0.0	28	40	13	18	15	0	0	93	26	12	5	2.2	.908	OF-53, SS-6
1897	2 teams	NY N (7G –.087) LOU N (111G –.278)																						
″	total	118	.268	.371	455	122	16	5	7	1.5	68	56	34		14	1	0	222	360	75	34	5.6	.886	SS-105, OF-12, 3B-1
1898	2 teams	LOU N (49G –.298) BOS N (37G –.260)																						
″	total	86	.283	.319	304	86	5	0	2	0.7	47	33	23		10	1	0	162	88	23	9	3.1	.916	OF-57, 2B-28, 1B-1, 3B-1
1899	2 teams	BOS N (55G –.302) WAS N (31G –.246)																						
″	total	86	.280	.370	300	84	9	3	4	1.3	40	54	12		13	5	1	168	98	30	13	3.6	.899	OF-41, 2B-22, SS-18, 3B-2
8 yrs.		569	.274	.350	2128	583	60	19	21	1.0	341	290	164	96	117	8	1	1077	948	230	114	4.0	.898	OF-251, 2B-161, SS-129, 3B-12, P-12, 1B-2

Heinie Stafford

STAFFORD, HENRY ALEXANDER BR TR 5′7″ 160 lbs.
B. Nov. 1, 1891, Orleans, Vt. D. Jan. 29, 1972, Lake Worth, Fla.

Year	Team	Games	BA	SA	AB	H	2B	3B	HR	HR%	R	RBI	BB	SO	SB	Pinch Hit AB	Pinch Hit H	PO	A	E	DP	TC/G	FA	G by Pos
1916	NY N	1	.000	.000	1	0	0	0	0	0.0	0	0	0	0	0	1	0	0	0	0	0	0.0	—	

Steve Staggs

STAGGS, STEPHEN ROBERT BR TR 5′9″ 150 lbs.
B. May 6, 1951, Anchorage, Alaska.

Year	Team	Games	BA	SA	AB	H	2B	3B	HR	HR%	R	RBI	BB	SO	SB	Pinch Hit AB	Pinch Hit H	PO	A	E	DP	TC/G	FA	G by Pos
1977	TOR A	72	.258	.357	291	75	11	6	2	0.7	37	28	36	38	5	1	0	169	194	13	35	5.2	.965	2B-72
1978	OAK A	47	.244	.321	78	19	2	2	0	0.0	10	0	19	17	2	4	2	59	68	3	10	2.8	.977	2B-40, SS-2, DH-2, 3B-2
2 yrs.		119	.255	.350	369	94	13	8	2	0.5	47	28	55	55	7	5	2	228	262	16	45	4.3	.968	2B-112, SS-2, DH-2, 3B-2

Chick Stahl

STAHL, CHARLES SYLVESTER BL TL 5′10″ 160 lbs.
B. Jan. 10, 1873, Avila, Ind. D. Mar. 28, 1907, West Baden, Ind.
Manager 1906.

Year	Team	Games	BA	SA	AB	H	2B	3B	HR	HR%	R	RBI	BB	SO	SB	Pinch Hit AB	Pinch Hit H	PO	A	E	DP	TC/G	FA	G by Pos
1897	BOS N	114	.354	.499	469	166	30	13	4	0.9	111	97	38		18	1	0	164	17	14	4	1.8	.928	OF-111
1898		125	.308	.407	467	144	21	8	3	0.6	72	52	46		6	0	0	199	14	7	4	1.8	.968	OF-125
1899		148	.351	.495	576	202	23	18	8	1.4	122	53	72		33	0	0	253	27	10	6	1.9	.966	OF-148, P-1
1900		136	.295	.421	553	163	23	16	5	0.9	88	82	34		27	1	1	277	22	10	4	2.3	.968	OF-135
1901	BOS A	131	.309	.445	515	159	20	16	6	1.2	106	72	54		29	0	0	277	12	13	3	2.3	.957	OF-131
1902		127	.323	.421	508	164	22	11	2	0.4	92	58	37		24	2	2	244	15	12	2	2.2	.956	OF-125
1903		77	.274	.375	299	82	12	6	2	0.7	60	44	28		10	3	0	135	11	6	2	2.1	.961	OF-74
1904		157	.295	.421	587	173	27	**19**	3	0.5	84	67	64		11	0	0	293	6	12	0	2.0	.961	OF-157
1905		134	.258	.308	500	129	17	4	0	0.0	61	47	50		18	0	0	249	11	6	4	2.0	.977	OF-134
1906		155	.286	.366	595	170	24	6	4	0.7	62	51	47		13	0	0	344	24	15	9	2.5	.961	OF-155
10 yrs.		1304	.306	.417	5069	1552	219	117	37	0.7	858	623	470		189	7	3	2435	159	105	38	2.1	.961	OF-1295, P-1
WORLD SERIES																								
1903	BOS A	8	.303	.515	33	10	1	3 4th	0	0.0	6	3	1	2	2	0	0	14	1	0	0	1.9	1.000	OF-8

Jake Stahl

STAHL, GARLAND BR TR 6′ 2″ 195 lbs.
B. Apr. 13, 1879, Elkhart, Ill. D. Sept. 18, 1922, Monrovia, Calif.
Manager 1905–06, 1912–13.

Year	Team	Games	BA	SA	AB	H	2B	3B	HR	HR%	R	RBI	BB	SO	SB	Pinch Hit AB	Pinch Hit H	PO	A	E	DP	TC/G	FA	G by Pos
1903	BOS A	40	.239	.446	92	22	3	5	2	2.2	14	8	4		1	**11**	**5**	105	27	6	0	4.8	.957	C-28, OF-1
1904	WAS A	142	.262	.381	520	136	29	12	3	0.6	54	50	21		25	0	0	1259	89	33	53	9.7	.976	1B-119, OF-23
1905		141	.244	.365	501	122	22	12	5	1.0	66	66	28		41	1	0	1593	94	21	51	12.2	.988	1B-140
1906		137	.222	.274	482	107	9	8	0	0.0	38	51	21		30	1	0	1322	78	24	51	10.5	.983	1B-136
1908	2 teams	NY A (74G –.255) BOS A (79G –.248)																						
″	total	153	.252	.374	532	134	27	16	2	0.4	63	65	31		30	1	0	1008	62	22	37	7.2	.980	1B-85, OF-67
1909	BOS A	127	.294	.434	435	128	19	12	6	1.4	62	60	43		16	1	0	1353	50	20	57	11.3	.986	1B-126
1910		144	.271	.424	531	144	19	16	**10**	**1.9**	68	77	42		22	2	0	1488	60	23	46	11.1	.985	1B-142
1912		95	.301	.429	326	98	21	6	3	0.9	40	60	31		13	3	1	853	49	18	37	10.0	.980	1B-92
1913		2	.000	.000	2	0	0	0	0	0.0	0	0	0	1	0	2	0	0	0	0	0	0.0	—	
9 yrs.		981	.260	.382	3421	891	149	87	31	0.9	405	437	221	1	178	22	6	8981	509	167	332	10.1	.983	1B-840, OF-91, C-28
WORLD SERIES																								
1912	BOS A	8	.281	.344	32	9	2	0	0	0.0	3	2	0	6	2	0	0	77	3	1	4	10.1	.988	1B-8

Larry Stahl

STAHL, LARRY FLOYD BL TL 6′ 175 lbs.
B. June 29, 1941, Belleville, Ill.

Year	Team	Games	BA	SA	AB	H	2B	3B	HR	HR%	R	RBI	BB	SO	SB	Pinch Hit AB	Pinch Hit H	PO	A	E	DP	TC/G	FA	G by Pos
1964	KC A	15	.261	.478	46	12	1	0	3	6.5	7	6	1	10	0	5	1	20	1	1	1	2.2	.955	OF-10
1965		28	.198	.395	81	16	2	1	4	4.9	9	14	5	16	1	7	1	47	1	0	0	2.3	1.000	OF-21
1966		119	.250	.365	312	78	11	5	5	1.6	37	34	17	63	5	31	7	142	6	3	1	1.6	.980	OF-94
1967	NY N	71	.239	.290	155	37	5	0	1	0.6	9	18	8	25	2	30	5	90	4	3	0	2.3	.969	OF-43
1968		53	.235	.344	183	43	7	2	3	1.6	15	10	21	38	3	3	1	155	8	2	4	2.9	.988	OF-47, 1B-9
1969	SD N	95	.198	.315	162	32	6	2	3	1.9	10	10	17	31	3	44	6	136	16	2	8	3.1	.987	OF-37, 1B-13
1970		52	.182	.212	66	12	2	0	0	0.0	5	3	2	14	2	33	7	16	1	0	0	0.9	1.000	OF-20
1971		114	.253	.399	308	78	13	4	8	2.6	27	36	26	59	4	26	8	201	12	2	7	2.6	.991	OF-75, 1B-7
1972		107	.226	.347	297	67	9	3	7	2.4	31	20	31	67	1	28	5	141	4	2	1	1.9	.986	OF-76, 1B-1
1973	CIN N	76	.225	.333	111	25	2	2	2	1.8	17	12	14	34	1	45	11	44	3	0	3	1.5	1.000	OF-29, 1B-2
10 yrs.		730	.232	.351	1721	400	58	19	36	2.1	167	163	142	357	22	252	52	992	56	15	25	2.2	.986	OF-452, 1B-32
LEAGUE CHAMPIONSHIP SERIES																								
1973	CIN N	4	.500	.500	4	2	0	0	0	0.0	1	0	0	1	0	4	2	0	0	0	0	0.0	—	

Scott Stahoviak

STAHOVIAK, SCOTT EDMUND BL TR 6′ 5″ 210 lbs.
B. Mar. 6, 1970, Waukegan, Ill.

Year	Team	Games	BA	SA	AB	H	2B	3B	HR	HR%	R	RBI	BB	SO	SB	Pinch Hit AB	Pinch Hit H	PO	A	E	DP	TC/G	FA	G by Pos
1993	MIN A	20	.193	.263	57	11	4	0	0	0.0	1	1	3	22	0	5	0	9	38	4	1	2.7	.922	3B-19
1995		94	.266	.373	263	70	19	0	3	1.1	28	23	30	61	5	10	2	503	91	5	49	6.5	.992	1B-69, 3B-22, DH-1
2 yrs.		114	.253	.353	320	81	23	0	3	0.9	29	24	33	83	5	15	2	512	129	9	50	5.9	.986	1B-69, 3B-41, DH-1

Roy Staiger

STAIGER, ROY JOSEPH (Linus) BR TR 6′ 200 lbs.
B. Jan. 6, 1950, Tulsa, Okla.

Year	Team	Games	BA	SA	AB	H	2B	3B	HR	HR%	R	RBI	BB	SO	SB	Pinch Hit AB	Pinch Hit H	PO	A	E	DP	TC/G	FA	G by Pos
1975	NY N	13	.158	.211	19	3	1	0	0	0.0	2	0	0	4	0	0	0	5	11	0	0	1.2	1.000	3B-13
1976		95	.220	.273	304	67	8	1	2	0.7	23	26	25	35	3	1	0	55	209	9	18	2.9	.967	3B-93, SS-1
1977		40	.252	.374	123	31	9	0	2	1.6	16	11	4	20	1	0	0	23	76	7	4	2.9	.934	3B-36, SS-1
1979	NY A	4	.273	.364	11	3	1	0	0	0.0	1	1	1	0	0	0	0	2	7	0	1	2.3	1.000	3B-4
4 yrs.		152	.228	.300	457	104	19	1	4	0.9	42	38	30	59	4	1	0	85	303	16	23	2.7	.960	3B-146, SS-2

Tuck Stainback

STAINBACK, GEORGE TUCKER BR TR 5′11½″ 175 lbs.
B. Aug. 4, 1911, Los Angeles, Calif. D. Nov. 29, 1992, Camarillo, Calif.

Year	Team	Games	BA	SA	AB	H	2B	3B	HR	HR%	R	RBI	BB	SO	SB	Pinch Hit AB	Pinch Hit H	PO	A	E	DP	TC/G	FA	G by Pos
1934	CHI N	104	.306	.379	359	110	14	3	2	0.6	47	46	8	42	7	8	3	186	5	9	1	2.1	.955	OF-96, 3B-1
1935		47	.255	.394	94	24	4	0	3	3.2	16	11	0	13	1	10	3	40	1	3	0	1.6	.932	OF-28
1936		44	.173	.253	75	13	3	0	1	1.3	13	5	6	14	1	9	1	38	1	0	0	1.5	1.000	OF-26
1937		72	.231	.287	160	37	7	1	0	0.0	18	14	7	16	3	10	2	99	4	2	1	2.1	.981	OF-49
1938	3 teams	STL N (6G –.000) PHI N (30G –.259) BKN N (35G –.327)																						
″	total	71	.282	.374	195	55	9	3	1	0.5	26	31	5	10	2	17	4	107	2	2	0	2.2	.982	OF-50
1939	BKN N	68	.269	.348	201	54	7	0	3	1.5	22	19	4	23	0	10	2	121	0	8	0	2.3	.938	OF-55
1940	DET A	15	.225	.275	40	9	2	0	0	0.0	4	1	1	9	0	5	1	26	4	1	0	3.4	.968	OF-9
1941		94	.245	.325	200	49	8	1	2	1.0	19	10	3	21	6	8	1	107	3	6	0	1.5	.948	OF-80
1942	NY A	15	.200	.200	10	2	0	0	0	0.0	0	0	0	2	0	1	0	6	0	0	0	2.0	1.000	OF-3
1943		71	.260	.325	231	60	11	2	0	0.0	31	10	7	16	3	5	3	141	3	1	2	2.4	.993	OF-61
1944		30	.218	.256	78	17	3	0	0	0.0	13	5	3	7	1	5	1	44	1	2	0	2.0	.957	OF-24
1945		95	.257	.352	327	84	12	2	5	1.5	40	32	13	20	0	9	2	233	10	8	6	3.0	.968	OF-83
1946	PHI A	91	.244	.292	291	71	10	2	0	0.0	35	20	7	20	3	23	5	153	5	6	1	2.5	.963	OF-66
13 yrs.		817	.259	.333	2261	585	90	14	17	0.8	284	204	64	213	27	120	28	1301	39	48	11	2.2	.965	OF-630, 3B-1

Tuck Stainback *continued*

Year	Team	Games	BA	SA	AB	H	2B	3B	HR	HR%	R	RBI	BB	SO	SB	Pinch Hit AB	Pinch Hit H	PO	A	E	DP	TC/G	FA	G by Pos
WORLD SERIES																								
1942	NY A	2	—	—	0	0	0	0	0	—	0	0	0	0	0	0	0	0	0	0	0	0.0	—	
1943		5	.176	.176	17	3	0	0	0	0.0	0	0	0	2	0	0	0	7	1	0	0	1.6	1.000	OF-5
2 yrs.		7	.176	.176	17	3	0	0	0	0.0	0	0	0	2	0	0	0	7	1	0	0	1.6	1.000	OF-5

Matt Stairs

STAIRS, MATTHEW WADE BL TR 5′ 9″ 175 lbs.
B. Feb. 27, 1968, Fredericton, N. B., Canada.

Year	Team	Games	BA	SA	AB	H	2B	3B	HR	HR%	R	RBI	BB	SO	SB	Pinch Hit AB	Pinch Hit H	PO	A	E	DP	TC/G	FA	G by Pos
1992	MON N	13	.167	.233	30	5	2	0	0	0.0	2	5	7	7	0	3	1	14	0	1	0	1.5	.933	OF-10
1993		6	.375	.500	8	3	1	0	0	0.0	1	2	0	1	0	5	2	1	0	0	0	1.0	1.000	OF-1
1995	BOS A	39	.261	.398	88	23	7	1	1	1.1	8	17	4	14	0	16	4	19	2	2	0	0.9	.913	OF-23, DH-2
3 yrs.		58	.246	.365	126	31	10	1	1	0.8	11	24	11	22	0	24	7	34	2	3	0	1.1	.923	OF-34, DH-2
DIVISIONAL PLAYOFF SERIES																								
1995	BOS A	1	.000	.000	1	0	0	0	0	0.0	0	0	0	1	0	1	0	0	0	0	0	0.0	—	

Gale Staley

STALEY, GEORGE GAYLORD BL TR 5′ 8½″ 167 lbs.
B. May 2, 1899, De Pere, Wis. D. Apr. 19, 1989, Walnut Creek, Calif.

Year	Team	Games	BA	SA	AB	H	2B	3B	HR	HR%	R	RBI	BB	SO	SB	Pinch Hit AB	Pinch Hit H	PO	A	E	DP	TC/G	FA	G by Pos
1925	CHI N	7	.423	.500	26	11	2	0	0	0.0	2	3	2	1	0	0	0	19	28	1	7	6.9	.979	2B-7

Virgil Stallcup

STALLCUP, THOMAS VIRGIL (Red) BR TR 6′ 3″ 185 lbs.
B. Jan. 3, 1922, Ravensford, N. C. D. May 2, 1989, Greenville, S. C.

Year	Team	Games	BA	SA	AB	H	2B	3B	HR	HR%	R	RBI	BB	SO	SB	Pinch Hit AB	Pinch Hit H	PO	A	E	DP	TC/G	FA	G by Pos
1947	CIN N	8	.000	.000	1	0	0	0	0	0.0	1	0	0	1	0	0	0	0	0	0	0	0.0	.000	SS-1
1948		149	.228	.315	539	123	30	4	3	0.6	40	65	18	52	2	1	1	264	433	32	84	4.9	.956	SS-148
1949		141	.254	.336	575	146	28	5	3	0.5	49	45	9	44	1	0	0	256	437	27	87	5.1	.963	SS-141
1950		136	.251	.356	483	121	23	2	8	1.7	44	54	17	39	4	0	0	253	389	18	79	4.9	.973	SS-136
1951		121	.241	.346	428	103	17	2	8	1.9	33	49	6	40	2	4	0	190	333	17	61	4.6	.969	SS-117
1952	2 teams CIN N (2G –.000) STL N (29G –.129)																							
″	total	31	.125	.156	32	4	1	0	0	0.0	4	1	1	5	0	14	3	5	16	0	4	1.6	1.000	SS-13
1953	STL N	1	.000	.000	1	0	0	0	0	0.0	0	0	0	0	0	1	0	0	0	0	0	0.0	—	
7 yrs.		587	.241	.334	2059	497	99	13	22	1.1	171	214	51	181	9	20	4	968	1608	94	315	4.8	.965	SS-556

George Staller

STALLER, GEORGE WALBORN (Stopper) BL TL 5′11″ 190 lbs.
B. Apr. 1, 1916, Rutherford Heights, Pa. D. July 3, 1992, Harrisburgh, Pa.

Year	Team	Games	BA	SA	AB	H	2B	3B	HR	HR%	R	RBI	BB	SO	SB	Pinch Hit AB	Pinch Hit H	PO	A	E	DP	TC/G	FA	G by Pos
1943	PHI A	21	.271	.459	85	23	1	3	3	3.5	14	12	5	6	1	0	0	42	1	1	0	2.2	.977	OF-20

George Stallings

STALLINGS, GEORGE TWEEDY (The Miracle Man) BR TR 6′ 1″ 187 lbs.
B. Nov. 17, 1867, Augusta, Ga. D. May 13, 1929, Haddock, Ga.
Manager 1897–98, 1901, 1909–10, 1913–20.

Year	Team	Games	BA	SA	AB	H	2B	3B	HR	HR%	R	RBI	BB	SO	SB	Pinch Hit AB	Pinch Hit H	PO	A	E	DP	TC/G	FA	G by Pos
1890	BKN N	4	.000	.000	11	0	0	0	0	0.0	1	0	1	3	0	0	0	13	1	1	0	3.8	.933	C-4
1897	PHI N	2	.222	.333	9	2	1	0	0	0.0	1	0	0		0	0	0	18	1	1	1	10.0	.950	OF-1, 1B-1
1898		1	—	—	0	0	0	0	0	—	1	0	0		0	0	0	0	0	0	0	0.0	—	
3 yrs.		7	.100	.150	20	2	1	0	0	0.0	3	0	1	3	0	0	0	31	2	2	1	5.8	.943	C-4, OF-1, 1B-1

Oscar Stanage

STANAGE, OSCAR HARLAND BR TR 5′11″ 190 lbs.
B. Mar. 17, 1883, Tulare, Calif. D. Nov. 11, 1964, Detroit, Mich.

Year	Team	Games	BA	SA	AB	H	2B	3B	HR	HR%	R	RBI	BB	SO	SB	Pinch Hit AB	Pinch Hit H	PO	A	E	DP	TC/G	FA	G by Pos
1906	CIN N	1	.000	.000	1	0	0	0	0	0.0	0	0	0		0	0	0	1	0	0	0	1.0	1.000	C-1
1909	DET A	77	.262	.341	252	66	8	6	0	0.0	17	21	11		2	0	0	324	80	15	12	5.4	.964	C-77
1910		88	.207	.284	275	57	7	4	2	0.7	24	25	20		1	4	0	344	148	25	6	6.2	.952	C-84
1911		141	.264	.336	503	133	13	7	3	0.6	45	51	20		3	0	0	599	212	41	13	6.0	.952	C-141
1912		119	.261	.305	394	103	9	4	0	0.0	35	41	34		3	0	0	440	168	32	14	5.4	.950	C-119
1913		80	.224	.295	241	54	13	2	0	0.0	19	21	21	35	5	2	2	277	106	16	6	5.2	.960	C-77
1914		122	.193	.233	400	77	8	4	0	0.0	16	25	24	58	2	0	0	532	190	30	11	6.2	.960	C-122
1915		100	.223	.277	300	67	9	2	1	0.3	27	31	20	41	5	0	0	395	111	19	0	5.3	.964	C-100
1916		94	.237	.316	291	69	17	3	0	0.0	16	30	17	48	3	0	0	387	108	15	11	5.4	.971	C-94
1917		99	.205	.259	297	61	14	1	0	0.0	19	30	20	35	3	4	1	385	88	11	13	5.1	.977	C-95
1918		54	.253	.290	186	47	4	0	1	0.5	9	14	11	18	2	2	0	234	56	8	10	5.7	.973	C-47, 1B-5
1919		38	.242	.317	120	29	4	1	1	0.8	9	15	7	12	1	1	0	150	39	5	8	5.2	.974	C-36, 1B-1
1920		78	.231	.303	238	55	17	0	0	0.0	12	17	14	21	0	1	0	248	75	14	4	4.3	.958	C-78
1925		3	.200	.200	5	1	0	0	0	0.0	0	0	0	0	0	0	0	2	0	0	0	0.7	1.000	C-3
14 yrs.		1094	.234	.295	3503	819	123	34	8	0.2	248	321	219	268	30	14	3	4318	1381	231	108	5.5	.961	C-1074, 1B-6
WORLD SERIES																								
1909	DET A	2	.200	.200	5	1	0	0	0	0.0	0	2	0	2	0	0	0	12	2	0	0	7.0	1.000	C-2

Jerry Standaert

STANDAERT, JEROME JOHN BR TR 5′10″ 168 lbs.
B. Nov. 2, 1901, Chicago, Ill. D. Aug. 4, 1964, Chicago, Ill.

Year	Team	Games	BA	SA	AB	H	2B	3B	HR	HR%	R	RBI	BB	SO	SB	Pinch Hit AB	Pinch Hit H	PO	A	E	DP	TC/G	FA	G by Pos
1925	BKN N	1	.000	.000	1	0	0	0	0	0.0	0	0	0	1	0	1	0	0	0	0	0	0.0	—	
1926		66	.345	.451	113	39	8	2	0	0.0	13	14	5	7	0	22	6	40	46	8	5	2.3	.915	2B-21, 3B-14, SS-6
1929	BOS A	19	.167	.278	18	3	2	0	0	0.0	1	4	3	2	0	8	1	21	2	1	2	2.4	.958	1B-10
3 yrs.		86	.318	.424	132	42	10	2	0	0.0	14	18	8	10	0	31	7	61	48	9	7	2.3	.924	2B-21, 3B-14, 1B-10, SS-6

Pete Stanicek

STANICEK, PETER LOUIS BB TR 5′11″ 175 lbs.
Brother of Steve Stanicek.
B. Apr. 16, 1963, Harvey, Ill.

Year	Team	Games	BA	SA	AB	H	2B	3B	HR	HR%	R	RBI	BB	SO	SB	Pinch Hit AB	Pinch Hit H	PO	A	E	DP	TC/G	FA	G by Pos
1987	BAL A	30	.274	.301	113	31	3	0	0	0.0	9	9	8	19	8	0	0	37	46	4	15	2.8	.954	2B-19, DH-10, 3B-2
1988		83	.230	.310	261	60	7	1	4	1.5	29	17	28	45	12	10	2	149	24	4	7	2.2	.977	OF-65, 2B-16, DH-1
2 yrs.		113	.243	.307	374	91	10	1	4	1.1	38	26	36	64	20	10	2	186	70	8	22	2.3	.970	OF-65, 2B-35, DH-11, 3B-2

Steve Stanicek

STANICEK, STEPHEN BLAIR BR TR 6′ 190 lbs.
Brother of Pete Stanicek.
B. June 19, 1961, Lake Forest, Ill.

Year	Team	Games	BA	SA	AB	H	2B	3B	HR	HR%	R	RBI	BB	SO	SB	Pinch Hit AB	Pinch Hit H	PO	A	E	DP	TC/G	FA	G by Pos
1987	MIL A	4	.286	.286	7	2	0	0	0	0.0	2	0	0	2	0	3	1	0	0	0	0	0.0	.000	DH-1
1989	PHI N	9	.111	.111	9	1	0	0	0	0.0	0	1	0	3	0	9	1	0	0	0	0	0.0	—	
2 yrs.		13	.188	.188	16	3	0	0	0	0.0	2	1	0	5	0	12	2	0	0	0	0	0.0		DH-1

Tom Stankard

STANKARD, THOMAS FRANCIS BR TR 6′ 190 lbs.
B. Mar. 20, 1882, Waltham, Mass. D. June 13, 1958, Waltham, Mass.

Year	Team	Games	BA	SA	AB	H	2B	3B	HR	HR%	R	RBI	BB	SO	SB	Pinch Hit AB	Pinch Hit H	PO	A	E	DP	TC/G	FA	G by Pos
1904	PIT N	2	.000	.000	2	0	0	0	0	0.0	0	0	0		0	0	0	1	1	0	0	1.0	1.000	SS-1, 3B-1

Andy Stankiewicz

STANKIEWICZ, ANDREW NEAL BR TR 5′ 9″ 165 lbs.
B. Aug. 10, 1964, Inglewood, Calif.

Year	Team	Games	BA	SA	AB	H	2B	3B	HR	HR%	R	RBI	BB	SO	SB	Pinch Hit AB	Pinch Hit H	PO	A	E	DP	TC/G	FA	G by Pos
1992	NY A	116	.268	.347	400	107	22	2	2	0.5	52	25	38	42	9	3	0	185	346	12	74	4.7	.978	SS-81, 2B-34, DH-1
1993		16	.000	.000	9	0	0	0	0	0.0	5	0	1	1	0	0	0	7	15	0	4	1.8	1.000	2B-6, 3B-4, SS-1, DH-1
1994	HOU N	37	.259	.370	54	14	3	0	1	1.9	10	5	12	12	1	8	3	12	45	0	7	2.4	1.000	SS-17, 2B-6, 3B-1
1995		43	.115	.135	52	6	1	0	0	0.0	6	7	12	19	4	12	3	20	59	1	6	3.5	.988	SS-14, 2B-6, 3B-3
4 yrs.		212	.247	.322	515	127	26	2	3	0.6	73	37	63	74	14	23	6	224	465	13	91	4.0	.981	SS-113, 2B-52, 3B-8, DH-2

Eddie Stanky

STANKY, EDWARD RAYMOND (Muggsy, The Brat) BR TR 5′ 8″ 170 lbs.
B. Sept. 3, 1916, Philadelphia, Pa.
Manager 1952–55, 1966–68, 1977.

Year	Team	Games	BA	SA	AB	H	2B	3B	HR	HR%	R	RBI	BB	SO	SB	Pinch Hit AB	Pinch Hit H	PO	A	E	DP	TC/G	FA	G by Pos
1943	CHI N	142	.245	.278	510	125	15	1	0	0.0	92	47	92	42	4	0	0	379	441	31	85	5.9	.964	2B-131, SS-12, 3B-2
1944	2 teams	CHI N (13G –.240) BKN N (89G –.276)																						
″	total	102	.273	.325	286	78	9	3	0	0.0	36	16	46	15	4	5	0	207	224	21	37	4.4	.954	2B-61, SS-38, 3B-4
1945	BKN N	153	.258	.333	555	143	29	5	1	0.2	**128**	39	**148**	42	6	0	0	429	441	34	101	5.9	.962	2B-153, SS-1
1946		144	.273	.352	483	132	24	7	0	0.0	98	36	**137**	56	8	2	0	356	359	17	88	5.2	.977	2B-141
1947		146	.252	.329	559	141	24	5	3	0.5	97	53	103	39	3	0	0	402	406	12	123	5.6	.985	2B-146
1948	BOS N	67	.320	.417	247	79	14	2	2	0.8	49	29	61	13	3	1	1	168	202	7	45	5.7	.981	2B-66
1949		138	.285	.358	506	144	24	5	1	0.2	90	42	113	41	3	3	0	357	354	15	92	5.4	.979	2B-135
1950	NY N	152	.300	.412	527	158	25	5	8	1.5	115	52	**144**	50	9	0	0	407	418	20	128	5.6	.976	2B-151
1951		145	.247	.369	515	127	17	2	14	2.7	88	43	127	63	8	4	0	356	412	18	117	5.6	.977	2B-140
1952	STL N	53	.229	.277	83	19	4	0	0	0.0	13	7	19	9	0	26	9	41	44	0	9	4.3	1.000	2B-20
1953		17	.267	.267	30	8	0	0	0	0.0	5	1	6	4	0	5	0	16	22	0	4	4.8	1.000	2B-8
11 yrs.		1259	.268	.348	4301	1154	185	35	29	0.7	811	365	996	374	48	46	10	3118	3323	175	829	5.5	.974	2B-1152, SS-51, 3B-6
WORLD SERIES																								
1947	BKN N	7	.240	.280	25	6	1	0	0	0.0	4	2	3	2	0	0	0	18	19	1	5	5.4	.974	2B-7
1948	BOS N	6	.286	.357	14	4	1	0	0	0.0	0	1	7	1	0	0	0	8	12	0	2	3.3	1.000	2B-6
1951	NY N	6	.136	.136	22	3	0	0	0	0.0	3	1	3	2	0	0	0	14	16	1	3	5.2	.968	2B-6
3 yrs.		19	.213	.246	61	13	2	0	0	0.0	7	4	13	5	0	0	0	40	47	2	10	4.7	.978	2B-19

Fred Stanley

STANLEY, FREDERICK BLAIR (Chicken) BR TR 5′10″ 165 lbs.
B. Aug. 13, 1947, Farnhamville, Iowa. BB 1969–1971

Year	Team	Games	BA	SA	AB	H	2B	3B	HR	HR%	R	RBI	BB	SO	SB	Pinch Hit AB	Pinch Hit H	PO	A	E	DP	TC/G	FA	G by Pos
1969	SEA A	17	.279	.372	43	12	2	1	0	0.0	2	4	3	8	1	1	0	22	29	2	8	3.3	.962	SS-15, 2B-1
1970	MIL A	6	—	—	0	0	0	0	0	—	1	0	0	0	0	0	0	1	1	0	0	1.0	1.000	2B-2
1971	CLE A	60	.225	.302	129	29	4	0	2	1.6	14	12	27	25	1	0	0	61	145	6	29	3.7	.972	SS-55, 2B-3
1972	2 teams	CLE A (6G –.167) SD N (39G –.200)																						
″	total	45	.196	.227	97	19	3	0	0	0.0	16	2	14	22	1	4	1	68	75	3	16	3.0	.979	SS-22, 2B-22, 3B-4
1973	NY A	26	.212	.288	66	14	0	1	1	1.5	6	5	7	16	0	0	0	42	72	2	11	4.8	.983	SS-21, 2B-3
1974		33	.184	.184	38	7	0	0	0	0.0	2	3	3	2	1	1	0	32	59	1	14	2.7	.989	SS-19, 2B-15
1975		117	.222	.250	252	56	5	1	0	0.0	34	15	21	27	3	0	0	161	249	9	53	3.6	.979	SS-83, 2B-33, 3B-1
1976		110	.238	.273	260	62	2	2	1	0.4	32	20	34	29	1	1	0	148	252	8	36	3.6	.980	SS-110, 2B-3
1977		48	.261	.326	46	12	0	0	1	2.2	6	7	8	6	1	0	0	36	48	3	7	1.9	.966	SS-42, 3B-3, 2B-2
1978		81	.219	.281	160	35	7	0	1	0.6	14	9	25	31	0	0	0	88	152	9	26	2.9	.964	SS-71, 2B-11, 3B-4
1979		57	.200	.270	100	20	1	0	2	2.0	9	14	5	17	0	0	0	42	113	8	23	2.9	.951	SS-31, 3B-16, 2B-8, 1B-1
1980		49	.209	.244	86	18	3	0	0	0.0	13	5	5	5	0	0	0	39	86	7	18	2.8	.947	SS-19, 2B-17, 3B-12
1981	OAK A	66	.193	.221	145	28	4	0	0	0.0	15	7	15	23	2	0	0	96	120	3	25	3.2	.986	SS-62, 2B-6
1982		101	.193	.250	228	44	7	0	2	0.9	33	17	29	32	0	0	0	116	226	13	43	3.5	.963	SS-98, 2B-2
14 yrs.		816	.216	.263	1650	356	38	5	10	0.6	197	120	196	243	11	7	1	952	1627	74	309	3.2	.972	SS-648, 2B-128, 3B-40, 1B-1
DIVISIONAL PLAYOFF SERIES																								
1981	OAK A	3	.000	.000	6	0	0	0	0	0.0	0	0	1	1	0	0	0	7	8	0	0	5.0	1.000	SS-3
LEAGUE CHAMPIONSHIP SERIES																								
1976	NY A	5	.333	.467	15	5	2	0	0	0.0	1	0	2	0	0	0	0	7	15	1	2	4.6	.957	SS-5
1977		2	—	—	0	0	0	0	0	—	0	0	0	0	0	0	0	1	0	0	0	0.5	1.000	SS-2
1978		2	.200	.200	5	1	0	0	0	0.0	0	0	0	2	0	0	0	3	3	0	0	3.0	1.000	2B-2
1981	OAK A	2	.333	.333	3	1	0	0	0	0.0	0	1	0	1	0	0	0	4	2	0	0	3.0	1.000	SS-2
4 yrs.		11	.304	.391	23	7	2	0	0	0.0	1	1	2	3	0	0	0	15	20	1	2	3.3	.972	SS-9, 2B-2
WORLD SERIES																								
1976	NY A	4	.167	.333	6	1	1	0	0	0.0	1	1	3	1	0	0	0	4	7	1	3	3.0	.917	SS-4
1977		1	—	—	0	0	0	0	0	—	0	0	0	0	0	0	0	1	0	0	0	1.0	1.000	SS-1
1978		3	.200	.400	5	1	1	0	0	0.0	0	0	1	0	0	0	0	5	2	0	1	2.3	1.000	2B-3
3 yrs.		8	.182	.364	11	2	2	0	0	0.0	1	1	4	1	0	0	0	10	9	1	4	2.5	.950	SS-5, 2B-3

Jimmy Stanley

STANLEY, JAMES FRANCIS BB TR 5′ 6″ 148 lbs.
B. 1889, Chicago, Ill.

Year	Team	Games	BA	SA	AB	H	2B	3B	HR	HR%	R	RBI	BB	SO	SB	Pinch Hit AB	Pinch Hit H	PO	A	E	DP	TC/G	FA	G by Pos
1914	CHI F	54	.194	.224	98	19	3	0	0	0.0	13	4	19		2	6	0	51	64	16	8	2.9	.878	SS-40, 3B-3, 2B-1, OF-1

Joe Stanley

STANLEY, JOSEPH
B. N. J. Deceased.

Year	Team	Games	BA	SA	AB	H	2B	3B	HR	HR%	R	RBI	BB	SO	SB	Pinch Hit AB	Pinch Hit H	PO	A	E	DP	TC/G	FA	G by Pos
1884	BAL U	6	.238	.286	21	5	1	0	0	0.0	3		0			0	0	3	1	5	0	1.5	.444	OF-6

Joe Stanley

STANLEY, JOSEPH BERNARD BB TR 5′ 9½″ 150 lbs.
Brother of Buck Stanley.
B. Apr. 2, 1881, Washington, D. C. D. Sept. 13, 1967, Detroit, Mich.

Year	Team	Games	BA	SA	AB	H	2B	3B	HR	HR%	R	RBI	BB	SO	SB	Pinch Hit AB	Pinch Hit H	PO	A	E	DP	TC/G	FA	G by Pos
1897	WAS N	1	.000	.000	1	0	0	0	0	0.0	0	0	0		0	0	0	0	0	0	0	0.0	.000	P-1
1902	WAS A	3	.333	.333	12	4	0	0	0	0.0	2	1	0		0	0	0	5	0	1	0	2.0	.833	OF-3
1903	BOS N	86	.250	.331	308	77	12	5	1	0.3	40	47	18		10	5	0	119	23	19	2	2.0	.882	OF-77, SS-1, P-1
1904		3	.000	.000	8	0	0	0	0	0.0	0	0	0		0	0	0	2	2	1	0	1.7	.800	OF-3
1905	WAS A	28	.261	.337	92	24	2	1	1	1.1	13	17	7		4	1	0	47	4	3	0	2.0	.944	OF-27

Joe Stanley *continued*

Year	Team	Lg	Games	BA	SA	AB	H	2B	3B	HR	HR%	R	RBI	BB	SO	SB	Pinch Hit AB	Pinch Hit H	PO	A	E	DP	TC/G	FA	G by Pos
1906			73	.163	.199	221	36	0	4	0	0.0	18	9	20		6	10	1	78	7	6	0	1.4	.934	OF-64, P-1
1909	CHI	N	22	.135	.154	52	7	1	0	0	0.0	4	2	6		0	6	0	17	1	1	0	1.2	.947	OF-16
7 yrs.			216	.213	.272	694	148	15	10	2	0.3	77	76	51		20	22	1	268	37	31	2	1.7	.908	OF-190, P-3, SS-1

Mickey Stanley

STANLEY, MITCHELL JACK
B. July 20, 1942, Grand Rapids, Mich.
BR TR 6′ 1″ 185 lbs.

Year	Team	Lg	Games	BA	SA	AB	H	2B	3B	HR	HR%	R	RBI	BB	SO	SB	Pinch Hit AB	Pinch Hit H	PO	A	E	DP	TC/G	FA	G by Pos
1964	DET	A	4	.273	.273	11	3	0	0	0	0.0	3	1	0	1	0	0	0	5	0	0	0	1.3	1.000	OF-4
1965			30	.239	.368	117	28	6	0	3	2.6	14	13	3	12	1	0	0	69	1	1	0	2.4	.986	OF-29
1966			92	.289	.426	235	68	15	4	3	1.3	28	19	17	20	2	9	3	163	6	0	1	2.1	1.000	OF-82
1967			145	.210	.312	333	70	7	3	7	2.1	38	24	29	46	9	13	1	264	7	4	5	2.0	.985	OF-128, 1B-8
1968			153	.259	.364	583	151	16	6	11	1.9	88	60	42	57	4	6	0	405	40	4	13	2.9	.991	OF-130, 1B-15, SS-9, 2B-1
1969			149	.235	.367	592	139	28	1	16	2.7	73	70	52	56	8	7	2	342	138	10	24	3.0	.980	OF-101, SS-59, 1B-4
1970			142	.252	.396	568	143	21	11	13	2.3	83	47	45	56	10	5	2	384	9	1	10	2.8	.997	OF-132, 1B-9
1971			139	.292	.404	401	117	14	5	7	1.7	43	41	24	44	1	6	3	315	10	4	3	2.4	.988	OF-139
1972			142	.234	.395	435	102	16	6	14	3.2	45	55	29	49	1	5	3	309	9	2	1	2.3	.994	OF-139
1973			157	.244	.384	602	147	23	5	17	2.8	81	57	48	65	0	0	0	420	10	3	3	2.8	.993	OF-157
1974			99	.221	.325	394	87	13	2	8	2.0	40	34	26	63	5	1	0	341	14	4	11	3.5	.989	OF-91, 1B-12, 2B-1
1975			52	.256	.390	164	42	7	3	3	1.8	26	19	15	27	1	3	2	183	22	2	9	4.1	.990	OF-28, 1B-14, 3B-7, DH-1
1976			84	.257	.402	214	55	17	1	4	1.9	34	29	14	19	2	19	6	187	47	5	14	3.4	.979	OF-38, 1B-17, 3B-11, SS-3, 2B-2
1977			75	.230	.387	222	51	9	1	8	3.6	30	23	18	30	0	13	3	128	5	4	3	2.1	.971	OF-57, SS-3, 1B-3, DH-2
1978			53	.265	.384	151	40	9	0	3	2.0	15	8	9	19	0	12	2	173	9	2	16	4.0	.989	OF-34, 1B-12
15 yrs.			1516	.248	.377	5022	1243	201	48	117	2.3	641	500	371	564	44	99	27	3688	327	46	113	2.7	.989	OF-1289, 1B-94, SS-74, 3B-18, 2B-4, DH-3
LEAGUE CHAMPIONSHIP SERIES																									
1972	DET	A	4	.333	.333	6	2	0	0	0	0.0	0	0	0	0	0	1	0	7	0	0	0	2.3	1.000	OF-3
WORLD SERIES																									
1968	DET	A	7	.214	.286	28	6	0	1	0	0.0	4	0	2	4	0	0	0	15	16	2	3	3.0	.939	SS-7, OF-4

Mike Stanley

STANLEY, ROBERT MICHAEL
B. June 25, 1963, Fort Lauderdale, Fla.
BR TR 6′ 1″ 185 lbs.

Year	Team	Lg	Games	BA	SA	AB	H	2B	3B	HR	HR%	R	RBI	BB	SO	SB	Pinch Hit AB	Pinch Hit H	PO	A	E	DP	TC/G	FA	G by Pos
1986	TEX	A	15	.333	.533	30	10	3	0	1	3.3	4	1	3	7	1	5	2	14	8	1	2	1.5	.957	3B-7, C-4, DH-3, OF-1
1987			78	.273	.403	216	59	8	1	6	2.8	34	37	31	48	3	6	4	389	26	7	7	5.7	.983	C-61, 1B-12, OF-1
1988			94	.229	.297	249	57	8	0	3	1.2	21	27	37	62	0	15	3	342	17	4	4	5.0	.989	C-64, 1B-7, 3B-2
1989			67	.246	.311	122	30	3	1	1	0.8	9	11	12	29	1	23	6	117	8	3	3	2.3	.977	C-25, DH-21, 1B-7, 3B-3
1990			103	.249	.333	189	47	8	1	2	1.1	21	19	30	25	1	27	7	261	25	4	2	3.2	.986	C-63, DH-14, 3B-8, 1B-6
1991			95	.249	.381	181	45	13	1	3	1.7	25	25	34	44	0	27	6	288	20	6	2	3.8	.981	C-58, 1B-12, 3B-6, DH-6, OF-1
1992	NY	A	68	.249	.428	173	43	7	0	8	4.6	24	27	33	45	0	5	1	287	30	6	5	5.0	.981	C-55, DH-6, 1B-4
1993			130	.305	.534	423	129	17	1	26	6.1	70	84	57	85	1	11	3	652	46	3	5	5.7	.996	C-122, DH-2
1994			82	.300	.545	290	87	20	0	17	5.9	54	57	39	56	0	1	0	444	33	5	3	5.8	.990	C-72, 1B-7, DH-4
1995			118	.268	.481	399	107	29	1	18	4.5	63	83	57	106	1	2	0	651	35	5	3	5.9	.993	C-107, DH-10
10 yrs.			850	.270	.439	2272	614	116	6	85	3.7	325	371	333	507	8	122	32	3445	248	44	36	4.8	.988	C-631, DH-66, 1B-55, 3B-26, OF-3
DIVISIONAL PLAYOFF SERIES																									
1995	NY	A	4	.313	.500	16	5	0	0	1	6.3	2	3	2	1	0	0	0	30	0	1	0	7.8	.968	C-4

John Stansbury

STANSBURY, JOHN JAMES
B. Dec. 6, 1885, Phillipsburg, N. J. D. Dec. 26, 1970, Easton, Pa.
BR TR 5′ 9″ 165 lbs.

Year	Team	Lg	Games	BA	SA	AB	H	2B	3B	HR	HR%	R	RBI	BB	SO	SB	Pinch Hit AB	Pinch Hit H	PO	A	E	DP	TC/G	FA	G by Pos
1918	BOS	A	20	.128	.149	47	6	1	0	0	0.0	3	2	6	3	0	0	0	16	37	1	5	2.7	.981	3B-18, OF-2

Buck Stanton

STANTON, GEORGE WASHINGTON
B. June 19, 1906, Stantonsburg, N. C. D. Jan. 1, 1992, San Antonio, Tex.
BL TL 5′10″ 150 lbs.

Year	Team	Lg	Games	BA	SA	AB	H	2B	3B	HR	HR%	R	RBI	BB	SO	SB	Pinch Hit AB	Pinch Hit H	PO	A	E	DP	TC/G	FA	G by Pos
1931	STL	A	13	.200	.333	15	3	2	0	0	0.0	3	0	0	6	0	10	1	3	0	1	0	4.0	.750	OF-1

Harry Stanton

STANTON, HARRY ANDREW
B. St. Louis, Mo. Deceased.
TR

Year	Team	Lg	Games	BA	SA	AB	H	2B	3B	HR	HR%	R	RBI	BB	SO	SB	Pinch Hit AB	Pinch Hit H	PO	A	E	DP	TC/G	FA	G by Pos
1900	STL	N	1	—	—	0	0	0	0	0	—	0	0	0		0	0	0	0	0	0	0	0.0	.000	C-1

Leroy Stanton

STANTON, LEROY BOBBY (Lee)
B. Apr. 10, 1946, Latta, S. C.
BR TR 6′ 1″ 195 lbs.

Year	Team	Lg	Games	BA	SA	AB	H	2B	3B	HR	HR%	R	RBI	BB	SO	SB	Pinch Hit AB	Pinch Hit H	PO	A	E	DP	TC/G	FA	G by Pos
1970	NY	N	4	.250	.750	4	1	0	1	0	0.0	0	0	0	0	0	3	0	1	0	0	0	1.0	1.000	OF-1
1971			5	.190	.238	21	4	1	0	0	0.0	2	2	2	4	0	0	0	9	0	0	0	1.8	1.000	OF-5
1972	CAL	A	127	.251	.393	402	101	15	3	12	3.0	44	39	22	100	2	7	1	225	6	4	2	1.9	.983	OF-124
1973			119	.235	.356	306	72	9	2	8	2.6	41	34	27	88	3	11	5	160	5	6	2	1.6	.965	OF-107
1974			118	.267	.407	415	111	21	2	11	2.7	48	62	33	107	10	7	1	226	11	6	0	2.1	.975	OF-114
1975			137	.261	.416	440	115	20	3	14	3.2	67	82	52	85	18	10	0	230	16	10	2	1.9	.961	OF-131, DH-1
1976			93	.190	.281	231	44	13	1	2	0.9	12	25	24	57	2	15	3	128	1	2	0	1.6	.985	OF-79, DH-4
1977	SEA	A	133	.275	.511	454	125	24	1	27	5.9	56	90	42	115	0	11	4	175	9	9	2	1.6	.953	OF-91, DH-33
1978			93	.182	.248	302	55	11	0	3	1.0	24	24	34	80	1	5	0	59	1	0	0	0.7	1.000	DH-59, OF-30
9 yrs.			829	.244	.388	2575	628	114	13	77	3.0	294	358	236	636	36	69	14	1213	49	37	8	1.7	.972	OF-682, DH-97

Tom Stanton

STANTON, THOMAS PATRICK
B. Oct. 25, 1874, St. Louis, Mo. D. Jan. 17, 1957, St. Louis, Mo.
BB TR 5′10″ 175 lbs.

Year	Team	Lg	Games	BA	SA	AB	H	2B	3B	HR	HR%	R	RBI	BB	SO	SB	Pinch Hit AB	Pinch Hit H	PO	A	E	DP	TC/G	FA	G by Pos
1904	CHI	N	1	.000	.000	3	0	0	0	0	0.0	0	0	0		0	0	0	4	1	0	0	5.0	1.000	C-1

Joe Staples

STAPLES, JOSEPH F.
B. Buffalo, N. Y. Deceased.

Year	Team	Lg	Games	BA	SA	AB	H	2B	3B	HR	HR%	R	RBI	BB	SO	SB	Pinch Hit AB	Pinch Hit H	PO	A	E	DP	TC/G	FA	G by Pos
1885	BUF	N	7	.045	.045	22	1	0	0	0	0.0	0	0	0	9		0	0	7	4	7	1	2.6	.611	OF-6, 2B-1

Dave Stapleton

STAPLETON, DAVID LESLIE BR TR 6′ 1″ 178 lbs.
B. Jan 16, 1954, Fairhope, Ala.

Year	Team	Games	BA	SA	AB	H	2B	3B	HR	HR%	R	RBI	BB	SO	SB	Pinch Hit AB	Pinch Hit H	PO	A	E	DP	TC/G	FA	G by Pos
1980	**BOS A**	106	.321	.463	449	144	33	5	7	1.6	61	45	13	32	3	4	1	269	338	12	101	5.5	.981	2B-94, 1B-8, OF-6, DH-3, 3B-2
1981		93	.285	.423	355	101	17	1	10	2.8	45	42	21	22	0	4	0	260	204	17	50	5.0	.965	SS-33, 3B-25, 2B-23, 1B-12, DH-3
1982		150	.264	.398	538	142	28	1	14	2.6	66	65	31	40	2	5	0	1032	179	13	116	8.1	.989	1B-106, SS-27, 2B-9, 3B-5, DH-4, OF-1
1983		151	.247	.363	542	134	31	1	10	1.8	54	66	40	44	1	1	0	1249	105	10	132	9.1	.993	1B-145, 2B-5
1984		13	.231	.282	39	9	2	0	0	0.0	4	1	3	3	0	2	1	86	8	0	5	8.5	1.000	1B-10, DH-1
1985		30	.227	.318	66	15	6	0	0	0.0	4	2	4	11	0	6	1	41	36	1	11	2.9	.987	2B-14, 1B-8, DH-5
1986		39	.128	.154	39	5	1	0	0	0.0	4	3	2	10	0	2	2	85	16	0	13	2.7	1.000	1B-29, 2B-6, 3B-2
7 yrs.		582	.271	.398	2028	550	118	8	41	2.0	238	224	114	162	6	24	5	3022	886	53	428	6.8	.987	1B-318, 2B-151, SS-60, 3B-34, DH-16, OF-7
LEAGUE CHAMPIONSHIP SERIES																								
1986	**BOS A**	4	.667	.667	3	2	0	0	0	0.0	2	0	1	0	0	0	0	10	0	0	1	2.5	1.000	1B-4
WORLD SERIES																								
1986	**BOS A**	3	.000	.000	1	0	0	0	0	0.0	0	0	0	0	0	0	0	3	2	0	0	1.7	1.000	1B-3

Willie Stargell

STARGELL, WILVER DORNEL (Pops) BL TL 6′ 2″ 188 lbs.
B. Mar. 6, 1940, Earlsboro, Okla.
Hall of Fame 1988.

Year	Team	Games	BA	SA	AB	H	2B	3B	HR	HR%	R	RBI	BB	SO	SB	Pinch Hit AB	Pinch Hit H	PO	A	E	DP	TC/G	FA	G by Pos
1962	**PIT N**	10	.290	.452	31	9	3	1	0	0.0	1	4	3	10	0	2	0	12	1	1	0	1.6	.929	OF-9
1963		108	.243	.428	304	74	11	6	11	3.6	34	47	19	85	0	25	2	226	12	9	18	3.0	.964	OF-65, 1B-16
1964		117	.273	.501	421	115	19	7	21	5.0	53	78	17	92	1	12	2	565	24	10	50	5.5	.983	OF-59, 1B-50
1965		144	.272	.501	533	145	25	8	27	5.1	68	107	39	127	1	5	1	268	14	8	8	2.0	.972	OF-137, 1B-7
1966		140	.315	.581	485	153	30	0	33	6.8	84	102	48	109	2	9	3	300	13	11	17	2.3	.966	OF-127, 1B-15
1967		134	.271	.465	462	125	18	6	20	4.3	54	73	67	103	1	6	1	447	27	11	26	3.6	.977	OF-98, 1B-37
1968		128	.237	.441	435	103	15	1	24	5.5	57	67	47	105	5	5	0	254	19	9	12	2.2	.968	OF-113, 1B-13
1969		145	.307	.556	522	160	31	6	29	5.6	89	92	61	120	1	8	1	333	14	7	21	2.5	.980	OF-116, 1B-23
1970		136	.264	.511	474	125	18	3	31	6.5	70	85	44	119	0	9	4	184	17	5	1	1.6	.976	OF-125, 1B-1
1971		141	.295	.628	511	151	26	0	**48**	9.4	104	125	83	**154**	0	3	1	237	8	4	4	1.8	.984	OF-135
1972		138	.293	.558	495	145	28	2	33	6.7	75	112	65	129	1	5	0	931	41	17	96	7.4	.983	1B-101, OF-32
1973		148	.299	**.646**	522	156	**43**	3	**44**	8.4	106	**119**	80	129	0	7	2	261	14	7	1	2.0	.975	OF-142
1974		140	.301	.537	508	153	37	4	25	4.9	90	96	87	106	0	3	0	256	8	9	1	2.0	.967	OF-135, 1B-1
1975		124	.295	.516	461	136	32	2	22	4.8	71	90	58	109	0	2	1	1121	54	10	112	9.7	.992	1B-122
1976		117	.257	.458	428	110	20	3	20	4.7	54	65	50	101	2	7	0	1037	53	13	76	9.9	.988	1B-111
1977		63	.274	.548	186	51	12	0	13	7.0	29	35	31	55	0	10	2	449	27	7	26	8.8	.986	1B-55
1978		122	.295	.567	390	115	18	2	28	7.2	60	97	50	93	3	10	3	875	57	6	76	8.4	.994	1B-112
1979		126	.281	.552	424	119	19	0	32	7.5	60	82	47	105	0	15	7	949	47	3	102	8.8	.997	1B-113
1980		67	.262	.485	202	53	10	1	11	5.4	28	38	26	52	0	11	3	460	33	4	54	9.2	.992	1B-54
1981		38	.283	.350	60	17	4	0	0	0.0	2	9	5	9	0	26	8	70	0	0	10	7.8	1.000	1B-9
1982		74	.233	.411	73	17	4	0	3	4.1	6	17	10	24	0	56	14	43	3	0	2	5.8	1.000	1B-8
21 yrs.		2360	.282	.529	7927	2232	423	55	475	6.0	1195	1540	937	1936 **2nd**	17	236	55	9278	486	151	713	4.6	.985	OF-1293, 1B-848
LEAGUE CHAMPIONSHIP SERIES																								
1970	**PIT N**	3	.500	.583	12	6	1	0	0	0.0	0	1	1	1	0	0	0	4	0	0	0	1.3	1.000	OF-3
1971		4	.000	.000	14	0	0	0	0	0.0	1	0	2	6	0	0	0	6	0	0	0	1.5	1.000	OF-4
1972		5	.063	.125	16	1	1	0	0	0.0	1	1	2	5	0	0	0	32	3	0	1	5.8	1.000	1B-5, OF-1
1974		4	.400	.800	15	6	0	0	2	13.3	3	4	1	2	0	0	0	13	0	0	0	3.3	1.000	OF-4
1975		3	.182	.273	11	2	1	0	0	0.0	1	0	1	3	0	0	0	15	0	0	2	5.0	1.000	1B-3
1979		3	.455	1.182	11	5	2	0	2	18.2	2	6	3	2	0	0	0	32	2	0	2	11.3	1.000	1B-3
6 yrs.		22	.253	.468	79	20	5	0	4	5.1	8	12	10	19 **6th**	0	0	0	102	5	0	5	4.7	1.000	OF-12, 1B-11
WORLD SERIES																								
1971	**PIT N**	7	.208	.250	24	5	1	0	0	0.0	3	1	7	9	0	0	0	11	1	0	1	1.7	1.000	OF-7
1979		7	.400	.833	30	12	4	0	3	10.0	7	7	0	6	0	0	0	59	2	2	9	9.0	.968	1B-7
2 yrs.		14	.315	.574	54	17	5	0	3	5.6	10	8	7	15	0	0	0	70	3	2	10	5.4	.973	1B-7, OF-7

Dolly Stark

STARK, MONROE RANDOLPH BR TR 5′ 9″ 160 lbs.
B. Jan. 19, 1885, Ripley, Miss. D. Dec. 1, 1924, Memphis, Tenn.

Year	Team	Games	BA	SA	AB	H	2B	3B	HR	HR%	R	RBI	BB	SO	SB	Pinch Hit AB	Pinch Hit H	PO	A	E	DP	TC/G	FA	G by Pos
1909	**CLE A**	19	.200	.200	60	12	0	0	0	0.0	4	1	6		4	0	0	36	41	11	3	4.6	.875	SS-19
1910	**BKN N**	30	.165	.194	103	17	3	0	0	0.0	7	8	7	19	2	0	0	68	90	19	13	5.9	.893	SS-30
1911		70	.295	.326	193	57	4	1	0	0.0	25	19	20	24	6	11	3	115	138	19	20	4.9	.930	SS-34, 2B-18, 3B-3
1912		8	.182	.182	22	4	0	0	0	0.0	2	2	1	3	2	1	0	13	20	4	3	5.3	.892	SS-7
4 yrs.		127	.238	.262	378	90	7	1	0	0.0	38	30	34	46	14	12	3	232	289	53	39	5.2	.908	SS-90, 2B-18, 3B-3

Matt Stark

STARK, MATTHEW SCOTT BR TR 6′ 4″ 225 lbs.
B. Jan. 21, 1965, Whittier, Calif.

Year	Team	Games	BA	SA	AB	H	2B	3B	HR	HR%	R	RBI	BB	SO	SB	Pinch Hit AB	Pinch Hit H	PO	A	E	DP	TC/G	FA	G by Pos
1987	**TOR A**	5	.083	.083	12	1	0	0	0	0.0	0	0	0	0	0	2	0	25	1	0	0	5.2	1.000	C-5
1990	**CHI A**	8	.250	.313	16	4	1	0	0	0.0	0	3	1	6	0	2	0	0	0	0	0	0.0	.000	DH-6
2 yrs.		13	.179	.214	28	5	1	0	0	0.0	0	3	1	6	0	4	0	25	1	0	0	2.4	1.000	DH-6, C-5

George Starnagle

STARNAGLE, GEORGE HENRY BR TR 5′11″ 175 lbs.
Born George Henry Steuernagel.
B. Oct. 6, 1873, Belleville, Ill. D. Feb. 15, 1946, Belleville, Ill.

Year	Team	Games	BA	SA	AB	H	2B	3B	HR	HR%	R	RBI	BB	SO	SB	Pinch Hit AB	Pinch Hit H	PO	A	E	DP	TC/G	FA	G by Pos
1902	**CLE A**	1	.000	.000	3	0	0	0	0	0.0	0	0	0		0	0	0	2	0	1	0	3.0	.667	C-1

Charlie Starr

STARR, CHARLES WATKIN TR
B. Aug. 30, 1878, Pike County, Ohio D. Oct. 18, 1937, Pasadena, Calif.

Year	Team	Games	BA	SA	AB	H	2B	3B	HR	HR%	R	RBI	BB	SO	SB	Pinch Hit AB	Pinch Hit H	PO	A	E	DP	TC/G	FA	G by Pos
1905	**STL A**	24	.206	.206	97	20	0	0	0	0.0	10	6	7		0	2	0	26	56	5	3	3.6	.943	2B-18, 3B-6
1908	**PIT N**	20	.186	.220	59	11	2	0	0	0.0	8	8	13		6	1	0	22	51	7	3	4.2	.913	2B-12, SS-5, 3B-2
1909	**2 teams**	**BOS N** (61G –.222) **PHI N** (3G –.000)																						
″	**total**	64	.219	.256	219	48	2	3	0	0.0	16	6	31		7	3	0	116	161	21	20	4.7	.930	2B-54, SS-6, 3B-3
3 yrs.		108	.211	.237	375	79	4	3	0	0.0	34	20	51		13	6	0	164	268	33	26	4.4	.929	2B-84, SS-11, 3B-11

Chick Starr

STARR, WILLIAM
B. Feb. 26, 1911, Brooklyn, N. Y. D. Aug. 12, 1991, La Jolla, Calif.
BR TR 6′ 1″ 175 lbs.

Year	Team	Games	BA	SA	AB	H	2B	3B	HR	HR%	R	RBI	BB	SO	SB	Pinch Hit AB	Pinch Hit H	PO	A	E	DP	TC/G	FA	G by Pos
1935	WAS A	12	.208	.208	24	5	0	0	0	0.0	1	1	0	1	0	0	0	28	6	1	2	2.9	.971	C-12
1936		1	—	—	0	0	0	0	0	—	0	0	0	0	0	0	0	0	0	0	0	0.0	.000	C-1
2 yrs.		13	.208	.208	24	5	0	0	0	0.0	1	1	0	1	0	0	0	28	6	1	2	2.7	.971	C-13

Joe Start

START, JOSEPH (Old Reliable)
B. Oct. 14, 1842, New York, N. Y. D. Mar. 27, 1927, Providence, R. I.
BL TL 5′ 9″ 165 lbs.

Year	Team	Games	BA	SA	AB	H	2B	3B	HR	HR%	R	RBI	BB	SO	SB	Pinch Hit AB	Pinch Hit H	PO	A	E	DP	TC/G	FA	G by Pos
1876	NY N	56	.277	.299	264	73	6	0	0	0.0	40	21	1	2		0	0	547	10	21	11	10.3	.964	1B-56
1877	HAR N	60	.332	.399	271	90	3	6	1	0.4	55	21	6	2		0	0	704	10	27	25	12.4	.964	1B-60
1878	CHI N	61	.351	.439	**285**	**100**	12	5	1	0.4	58	27	2	3		0	0	719	13	33	28	12.5	.957	1B-61
1879	PRO N	66	.319	.404	317	101	11	5	2	0.6	70	37	7	4		0	0	779	11	22	24	12.3	.973	1B-65, OF-1
1880		82	.278	.354	345	96	14	6	0	0.0	53	27	13	20		0	0	954	10	29	30	12.1	.971	1B-82
1881		79	.328	.397	348	114	12	6	0	0.0	56	29	9	7		0	0	837	17	33	50	11.2	.963	1B-79
1882		82	.329	.407	356	117	8	10	0	0.0	58		11	7		0	0	905	21	25	54	11.6	.974	1B-82
1883		87	.284	.373	370	105	16	7	1	0.3	63		22	16		0	0	923	29	43	48	11.4	.957	1B-87
1884		93	.276	.344	381	105	10	5	2	0.5	80		35	25		0	0	939	21	20	31	10.5	.980	1B-93
1885		101	.275	.326	374	103	11	4	0	0.0	47	41	39	10		0	0	1036	35	31	42	10.9	.972	1B-101
1886	WAS N	31	.221	.270	122	27	4	1	0	0.0	10	17	5	13		0	0	348	7	10	16	11.8	.973	1B-31
11 yrs.		798	.300	.370	3433	1031	107	55	7	0.2	590	220	150	109		0	0	8691	184	294	359	11.5	.968	1B-797, OF-1

Dave Staton

STATON, DAVID ALAN
B. Apr. 12, 1968, Seattle, Wash.
BR TR 6′ 5″ 215 lbs.

Year	Team	Games	BA	SA	AB	H	2B	3B	HR	HR%	R	RBI	BB	SO	SB	Pinch Hit AB	Pinch Hit H	PO	A	E	DP	TC/G	FA	G by Pos
1993	SD N	17	.262	.690	42	11	3	0	5	11.9	7	9	3	12	0	6	3	66	14	0	10	6.7	1.000	1B-12
1994		29	.182	.394	66	12	2	0	4	6.1	6	6	10	18	0	7	0	152	20	0	9	8.6	1.000	1B-20
2 yrs.		46	.213	.509	108	23	5	0	9	8.3	13	15	13	30	0	13	3	218	34	0	19	7.9	1.000	1B-32

Joe Staton

STATON, JOSEPH (Slim)
B. Mar. 8, 1948, Seattle, Wash.
BL TL 6′ 3″ 175 lbs.

Year	Team	Games	BA	SA	AB	H	2B	3B	HR	HR%	R	RBI	BB	SO	SB	Pinch Hit AB	Pinch Hit H	PO	A	E	DP	TC/G	FA	G by Pos
1972	DET A	6	.000	.000	2	0	0	0	0	0.0	1	0	0	1	0	0	0	5	0	0	0	2.5	1.000	1B-2
1973		9	.235	.235	17	4	0	0	0	0.0	2	3	0	3	1	2	0	25	6	1	1	6.4	.969	1B-5
2 yrs.		15	.211	.211	19	4	0	0	0	0.0	3	3	0	4	1	2	0	30	6	1	1	5.3	.973	1B-7

Rusty Staub

STAUB, DANIEL JOSEPH (Le Grand Orange)
B. Apr. 1, 1944, New Orleans, La.
BL TR 6′ 2″ 190 lbs.

Year	Team	Games	BA	SA	AB	H	2B	3B	HR	HR%	R	RBI	BB	SO	SB	Pinch Hit AB	Pinch Hit H	PO	A	E	DP	TC/G	FA	G by Pos
1963	HOU N	150	.224	.308	513	115	17	4	6	1.2	43	45	59	58	0	5	0	963	63	11	52	6.6	.989	1B-109, OF-49
1964		89	.216	.346	292	63	10	2	8	2.7	26	35	21	31	1	8	3	512	30	9	34	6.3	.984	1B-49, OF-38
1965		131	.256	.412	410	105	20	1	14	3.4	43	63	52	57	3	16	5	203	12	11	1	2.0	.951	OF-112, 1B-1
1966		153	.280	.412	554	155	28	3	13	2.3	60	81	58	61	2	6	3	291	15	12	3	2.1	.962	OF-148, 1B-1
1967		149	.333	.473	546	182	**44**	1	10	1.8	71	74	60	47	0	5	1	269	10	11	2	2.0	.962	OF-144
1968		161	.291	.387	591	172	37	1	6	1.0	54	72	73	57	2	0	0	1336	94	13	100	8.9	.991	1B-147, OF-15
1969	MON N	158	.302	.526	549	166	26	5	29	5.3	89	79	110	61	3	2	1	265	16	10	2	1.9	.966	OF-156
1970		160	.274	.497	569	156	23	7	30	5.3	98	94	112	93	12	3	2	308	14	5	4	2.0	.985	OF-160
1971		162	.311	.482	599	186	34	6	19	3.2	94	97	74	42	9	5	1	290	20	18	5	2.0	.945	OF-162
1972	NY N	66	.293	.452	239	70	11	0	9	3.8	32	38	31	13	0	1	0	108	4	2	2	1.8	.982	OF-65
1973		152	.279	.421	585	163	36	1	15	2.6	77	76	74	52	1	0	0	297	17	7	5	2.1	.978	OF-152
1974		151	.258	.406	561	145	22	2	19	3.4	65	78	77	39	2	4	2	262	19	5	5	1.9	.983	OF-147
1975		155	.282	.448	574	162	30	4	19	3.3	93	105	77	55	2	2	1	267	15	4	3	1.9	.986	OF-153
1976	DET A	161	.299	.433	589	176	28	3	15	2.5	73	96	83	49	3	0	0	218	8	7	3	1.4	.970	OF-126, DH-36
1977		158	.278	.448	623	173	34	3	22	3.5	84	101	59	47	1	2	0	0	0	0	0	0.0	.000	DH-156
1978		162	.273	.435	642	175	30	1	24	3.7	75	121	76	35	3	0	0	0	0	0	0	0.0	.000	DH-162
1979	2 teams	DET A (68G –.236)	MON N (38G –.267)																					
″	total	106	.244	.404	332	81	15	1	12	3.6	41	54	46	28	1	14	2	156	7	1	11	1.8	.994	DH-66, 1B-22, OF-1
1980	TEX A	109	.300	.459	340	102	23	2	9	2.6	42	55	39	18	1	15	5	262	14	6	28	2.8	.979	DH-57, 1B-30, OF-14
1981	NY N	70	.317	.466	161	51	9	0	5	3.1	9	21	22	12	1	24	9	339	20	4	26	8.9	.989	1B-41
1982		112	.242	.324	219	53	9	0	3	1.4	11	27	24	10	0	57	12	172	19	2	12	4.3	.990	OF-27, 1B-18
1983		104	.296	.426	115	34	6	0	3	2.6	5	28	14	10	0	**81**	**24**	40	5	2	6	4.7	.957	OF-5, 1B-5
1984		78	.264	.361	72	19	4	0	1	1.4	2	18	4	9	0	**66**	**18**	13	0	0	2	4.3	1.000	1B-3
1985		54	.267	.400	45	12	3	0	1	2.2	2	8	10	4	0	42	11	1	0	0	0	1.0	1.000	OF-1
23 yrs.		2951 **8th**	.279	.431	9720	2716	499	47	292	3.0	1189	1466	1255	888	47	358	100	6572	402	140	306	2.8	.980	OF-1675, DH-477, 1B-426
LEAGUE CHAMPIONSHIP SERIES																								
1973	NY N	4	.200	.800	15	3	0	0	3	20.0	4	5	3	2	0	0	0	10	0	0	0	2.5	1.000	OF-4
WORLD SERIES																								
1973	NY N	7	.423	.615	26	11	2	0	1	3.8	1	6	2	2	0	0	0	5	0	0	0	0.8	1.000	OF-6

Ebba St. Claire

ST. CLAIRE, EDWARD JOSEPH
Father of Randy St. Claire.
B. Aug. 5, 1921, Whitehall, N. Y. D. Aug. 22, 1982, Whitehall, N. Y.
BB TR 6′ 1″ 219 lbs.

Year	Team	Games	BA	SA	AB	H	2B	3B	HR	HR%	R	RBI	BB	SO	SB	Pinch Hit AB	Pinch Hit H	PO	A	E	DP	TC/G	FA	G by Pos
1951	BOS N	72	.282	.391	220	62	17	2	1	0.5	22	25	12	24	0	10	3	267	29	7	5	4.9	.977	C-62
1952		39	.213	.287	108	23	2	0	2	1.9	5	4	8	12	0	5	1	151	21	5	4	5.2	.972	C-34
1953	MIL N	33	.200	.313	80	16	3	0	2	2.5	7	5	3	9	0	7	1	106	11	1	3	4.4	.992	C-27
1954	NY N	20	.262	.429	42	11	1	0	2	4.8	5	6	12	7	0	4	1	72	7	2	3	5.1	.975	C-16
4 yrs.		164	.249	.356	450	112	23	2	7	1.6	39	40	35	52	0	26	6	596	68	15	15	4.9	.978	C-139

Jigger Statz

STATZ, ARNOLD JOHN
B. Oct. 20, 1897, Waukegan, Ill. D. Mar. 16, 1988, Corona Del Mar, Calif.
BR TR 5′ 7½″ 150 lbs.
BB 1922

Year	Team	Games	BA	SA	AB	H	2B	3B	HR	HR%	R	RBI	BB	SO	SB	Pinch Hit AB	Pinch Hit H	PO	A	E	DP	TC/G	FA	G by Pos
1919	NY N	21	.300	.367	60	18	2	1	0	0.0	7	6	3	8	2	0	0	45	0	1	0	2.0	.978	OF-18, 2B-5
1920	2 teams	NY N (16G –.133)	BOS A (2G –.000)																					
″	total	18	.121	.182	33	4	0	1	0	0.0	0	5	2	9	0	3	0	17	1	1	1	1.4	.947	OF-14
1922	CHI N	110	.297	.366	462	137	19	5	1	0.2	77	34	41	31	16	0	0	309	16	14	4	3.1	.959	OF-110
1923		154	.319	.440	**655**	209	33	8	10	1.5	110	70	56	42	29	0	0	438	26	12	7	3.1	.975	OF-154
1924		135	.277	.352	549	152	22	5	3	0.5	69	49	37	50	13	2	1	377	26	19	5	3.2	.955	OF-131, 2B-1

Jigger Statz *continued*

Year	Team	Games	BA	SA	AB	H	2B	3B	HR	HR%	R	RBI	BB	SO	SB	Pinch Hit AB	Pinch Hit H	PO	A	E	DP	TC/G	FA	G by Pos
1925		38	.257	.378	148	38	6	3	2	1.4	21	14	11	16	4	1	0	112	3	7	0	3.3	.943	OF-37
1927	BKN N	130	.274	.355	507	139	24	7	1	0.2	64	21	26	43	10	4	0	371	15	4	5	3.2	.990	OF-122, 2B-1
1928		77	.234	.292	171	40	8	1	0	0.0	28	16	18	12	3	5	2	108	3	4	2	1.5	.965	OF-77, 2B-1
8 yrs.		683	.285	.373	2585	737	114	31	17	0.7	376	215	194	211	77	15	3	1777	90	62	24	2.9	.968	OF-663, 2B-8

Dan Stearns

STEARNS, DANIEL ECKFORD BL TR 6′ 1″ 185 lbs.
B. Oct. 17, 1861, Buffalo, N. Y. D. June 28, 1944, Glendale, Calif.

Year	Team	Games	BA	SA	AB	H	2B	3B	HR	HR%	R	RBI	BB	SO	SB	Pinch Hit AB	Pinch Hit H	PO	A	E	DP	TC/G	FA	G by Pos
1880	BUF N	28	.183	.260	104	19	6	1	0	0.0	8	13	3	23		0	0	39	24	20	3	2.4	.759	OF-20, C-8, 3B-5, SS-1
1881	DET N	3	.091	.182	11	1	1	0	0	0.0	1	0	0	2		0	0	1	9	4	1	4.7	.714	SS-3
1882	CIN AA	49	.257	.322	214	55	10	2	0	0.0	28		6			0	0	337	16	30	16	7.7	.922	1B-35, OF-12, 2B-2, SS-1
1883	BAL AA	93	.246	.327	382	94	10	9	1	0.3	54		**34**			0	0	985	38	58	38	11.6	.946	1B-92, OF-1
1884		100	.237	.306	396	94	12	3	3	0.8	61		28			0	0	959	48	54	36	10.5	.949	1B-100, 2B-1
1885	2 teams	BAL AA (67G –.186)	BUF N (30G –.200)																					
″	total	97	.190	.274	358	68	9	9	1	0.3	47	9	46	23		0	0	746	73	42	42	8.5	.951	1B-75, SS-19, C-4, OF-3
1889	KC AA	139	.286	.386	560	160	24	13	2	0.4	96	87	56	69	67	0	0	1400	60	52	75	10.9	.966	1B-135, 3B-4
7 yrs.		509	.242	.325	2025	491	72	37	7	0.3	295	109	173	117	67	0	0	4467	268	260	211	9.6	.948	1B-437, OF-36, SS-24, C-12, 3B-9, 2B-3

John Stearns

STEARNS, JOHN HARDIN (Dude) BR TR 6′ 185 lbs.
B. Aug. 21, 1951, Denver, Colo.

Year	Team	Games	BA	SA	AB	H	2B	3B	HR	HR%	R	RBI	BB	SO	SB	Pinch Hit AB	Pinch Hit H	PO	A	E	DP	TC/G	FA	G by Pos
1974	PHI N	1	.500	.500	2	1	0	0	0	0.0	0	0	0	0	0	1	1	1	0	0	0	1.0	1.000	C-1
1975	NY N	59	.189	.284	169	32	5	1	3	1.8	25	10	17	15	4	8	1	297	40	2	9	6.3	.994	C-54
1976		32	.262	.379	103	27	6	0	2	1.9	13	10	16	11	1	3	0	200	20	3	2	7.4	.987	C-30
1977		139	.251	.397	431	108	25	1	12	2.8	52	55	77	76	9	9	1	772	79	17	15	6.5	.980	C-127, 1B-6
1978		143	.264	.413	477	126	24	1	15	3.1	65	73	70	57	25	4	2	711	84	12	7	5.7	.985	C-141, 3B-1
1979		155	.243	.355	538	131	29	2	9	1.7	58	66	52	57	15	12	1	754	107	16	29	5.7	.982	C-121, 1B-16, 3B-11, OF-6
1980		91	.285	.370	319	91	25	1	0	0.0	42	45	33	24	7	5	2	552	62	8	17	6.8	.987	C-74, 1B-16, 3B-1
1981		80	.271	.333	273	74	12	1	1	0.4	25	24	24	17	12	6	1	360	52	7	11	5.3	.983	C-66, 1B-9, 3B-4
1982		98	.293	.415	352	103	25	3	4	1.1	46	28	30	35	17	6	2	384	74	10	9	5.0	.979	C-81, 3B-12
1983		4	—	—	0	0	0	0	0	—	2	0	0	0	1	0	0	0	0	0	0	0.0	—	
1984		8	.176	.235	17	3	1	0	0	0.0	6	1	4	2	1	2	1	28	2	0	4	5.0	1.000	C-4, 1B-2
11 yrs.		810	.260	.375	2681	696	152	10	46	1.7	334	312	323	294	91	56	12	4059	520	75	103	5.9	.984	C-699, 1B-49, 3B-29, OF-6

John Stedronsky

STEDRONSKY, JOHN
B. Cleveland, Ohio Deceased.

Year	Team	Games	BA	SA	AB	H	2B	3B	HR	HR%	R	RBI	BB	SO	SB	Pinch Hit AB	Pinch Hit H	PO	A	E	DP	TC/G	FA	G by Pos
1879	CHI N	4	.083	.083	12	1	0	0	0	0.0	0	0	0	3		0	0	4	11	4	1	4.8	.789	3B-4

Farmer Steelman

STEELMAN, MORRIS JAMES TR
B. June 29, 1875, Millville, N. J. D. Sept. 16, 1944, Merchantville, N. J.

Year	Team	Games	BA	SA	AB	H	2B	3B	HR	HR%	R	RBI	BB	SO	SB	Pinch Hit AB	Pinch Hit H	PO	A	E	DP	TC/G	FA	G by Pos
1899	LOU N	4	.067	.200	15	1	0	1	0	0.0	2	2	2		0	0	0	11	2	1	0	3.5	.929	C-4
1900	BKN N	1	.000	.000	4	0	0	0	0	0.0	0	0	0		0	0	0	4	2	0	0	6.0	1.000	C-1
1901	2 teams	BKN N (1G –.333)	PHI A (27G –.261)																					
″	total	28	.264	.286	91	24	2	0	0	0.0	5	7	10		4	0	0	66	29	1	2	3.6	.990	C-15, OF-12
1902	PHI A	10	.188	.219	32	6	1	0	0	0.0	1	6	2		2	0	0	28	6	1	2	3.5	.971	OF-5, C-5
4 yrs.		43	.218	.254	142	31	3	1	0	0.0	8	15	14		6	0	0	109	39	3	4	3.6	.980	C-25, OF-17

James Steels

STEELS, JAMES EARL BL TL 5′10″ 185 lbs.
B. May 30, 1961, Jackson, Miss.

Year	Team	Games	BA	SA	AB	H	2B	3B	HR	HR%	R	RBI	BB	SO	SB	Pinch Hit AB	Pinch Hit H	PO	A	E	DP	TC/G	FA	G by Pos
1987	SD N	62	.191	.235	68	13	1	1	0	0.0	9	6	11	14	3	31	8	23	1	1	0	0.9	.960	OF-28
1988	TEX A	36	.189	.208	53	10	1	0	0	0.0	4	5	0	15	2	9	2	41	2	1	2	1.5	.977	OF-17, DH-7, 1B-6
1989	SF N	13	.083	.083	12	1	0	0	0	0.0	0	0	2	4	0	7	0	15	2	0	0	4.3	1.000	1B-3, OF-1
3 yrs.		111	.180	.211	133	24	2	1	0	0.0	13	11	13	33	5	47	10	79	5	2	2	1.4	.977	OF-46, 1B-9, DH-7

Fred Steere

STEERE, FREDERICK EUGENE
B. Aug. 16, 1872, S. Scituate, R. I. D. Mar. 13, 1942, San Mateo, Calif.

Year	Team	Games	BA	SA	AB	H	2B	3B	HR	HR%	R	RBI	BB	SO	SB	Pinch Hit AB	Pinch Hit H	PO	A	E	DP	TC/G	FA	G by Pos
1894	PIT N	10	.205	.205	39	8	0	0	0	0.0	3	4	2	1	2	0	0	15	28	5	4	4.8	.896	SS-10

John Stefero

STEFERO, JOHN ROBERT BL TR 5′ 8″ 185 lbs.
B. Sept. 22, 1959, Sumter, S. C.

Year	Team	Games	BA	SA	AB	H	2B	3B	HR	HR%	R	RBI	BB	SO	SB	Pinch Hit AB	Pinch Hit H	PO	A	E	DP	TC/G	FA	G by Pos
1983	BAL A	9	.455	.545	11	5	1	0	0	0.0	2	4	3	2	0	2	0	20	3	2	0	2.8	.920	C-9
1986		52	.233	.300	120	28	2	0	2	1.7	14	13	16	25	0	6	2	221	20	4	2	4.8	.984	C-50, 2B-1
1987	MON N	18	.196	.250	56	11	0	0	1	1.8	4	3	3	17	0	2	0	90	12	2	0	6.1	.981	C-17
3 yrs.		79	.235	.299	187	44	3	0	3	1.6	20	20	22	44	0	10	2	331	35	8	2	4.9	.979	C-76, 2B-1

Dave Stegman

STEGMAN, DAVID WILLIAM BR TR 5′11″ 190 lbs.
B. Jan. 30, 1954, Inglewood, Calif.

Year	Team	Games	BA	SA	AB	H	2B	3B	HR	HR%	R	RBI	BB	SO	SB	Pinch Hit AB	Pinch Hit H	PO	A	E	DP	TC/G	FA	G by Pos
1978	DET A	8	.286	.643	14	4	2	0	1	7.1	3	3	1	2	0	0	0	11	0	0	0	1.6	1.000	OF-7
1979		12	.194	.484	31	6	0	0	3	9.7	6	5	2	3	1	1	0	35	0	0	0	2.9	1.000	OF-12
1980		65	.177	.262	130	23	5	0	2	1.5	12	9	14	23	1	6	1	82	1	1	0	1.4	.988	OF-57, DH-2
1982	NY A	2	—	—	0	0	0	0	0	—	0	0	0	0	0	0	0	0	0	0	0	0.0	—	
1983	CHI A	30	.170	.208	53	9	2	0	0	0.0	5	4	10	9	0	3	0	31	1	0	0	1.1	1.000	OF-29
1984		55	.261	.380	92	24	1	2	2	2.2	13	11	4	18	3	5	2	65	1	1	0	1.4	.985	OF-46, DH-3
6 yrs.		172	.206	.325	320	66	10	2	8	2.5	39	32	31	55	5	15	3	224	3	2	0	1.5	.991	OF-151, DH-5

Bill Stein

STEIN, WILLIAM ALLEN BR TR 5′10″ 170 lbs.
B. Jan. 21, 1947, Battle Creek, Mich.

Year	Team	Games	BA	SA	AB	H	2B	3B	HR	HR%	R	RBI	BB	SO	SB	Pinch Hit AB	Pinch Hit H	PO	A	E	DP	TC/G	FA	G by Pos
1972	STL N	14	.314	.543	35	11	0	1	2	5.7	2	3	0	7	1	6	3	5	4	0	0	1.1	1.000	OF-4, 3B-4
1973		32	.218	.255	55	12	2	0	0	0.0	4	2	7	18	0	18	3	37	1	0	1	2.9	1.000	OF-10, 1B-2, 3B-1
1974	CHI A	13	.279	.302	43	12	1	0	0	0.0	5	5	7	8	0	6	0	7	20	4	0	2.4	.871	3B-11, DH-2
1975		76	.270	.350	226	61	7	1	3	1.3	23	21	18	32	2	6	0	87	118	9	21	3.0	.958	2B-28, 3B-24, DH-18, OF-1
1976		117	.268	.347	392	105	15	2	4	1.0	32	36	22	67	4	8	2	161	243	19	39	3.5	.955	2B-58, 3B-58, DH-1, 1B-1, OF-1, SS-1

Bill Stein *continued*

Year	Team	Games	BA	SA	AB	H	2B	3B	HR	HR%	R	RBI	BB	SO	SB	Pinch Hit AB	Pinch Hit H	PO	A	E	DP	TC/G	FA	G by Pos
1977	**SEA A**	151	.259	.394	556	144	26	5	13	2.3	53	67	29	79	3	1	0	146	255	15	20	2.7	.964	3B-147, DH-3, SS-2
1978		114	.261	.370	403	105	24	4	4	1.0	41	37	37	56	1	2	0	72	244	24	21	3.0	.929	3B-111, DH-1
1979		88	.248	.384	250	62	9	2	7	2.8	28	27	17	28	1	8	0	64	162	7	20	2.7	.970	3B-67, 2B-17, SS-3
1980		67	.268	.379	198	53	5	1	5	2.5	16	27	16	25	1	11	1	119	115	4	21	3.9	.983	3B-34, 2B-14, 1B-8, DH-5
1981	**TEX A**	53	.330	.435	115	38	6	0	2	1.7	21	22	7	15	1	20	**9**	166	26	2	10	5.0	.990	1B-20, OF-8, 3B-7, 2B-3, SS-1
1982		85	.239	.299	184	44	8	0	1	0.5	14	16	12	23	0	34	**12**	72	122	6	28	2.7	.970	2B-34, 3B-28, SS-6, DH-3, 1B-2, OF-1
1983		78	.310	.409	232	72	15	1	2	0.9	21	33	8	31	2	18	6	222	103	5	40	4.6	.985	2B-32, 1B-23, 3B-10, DH-6
1984		27	.279	.302	43	12	1	0	0	0.0	3	3	5	9	0	13	2	16	17	1	4	1.6	.971	2B-11, DH-4, 1B-3, 3B-3
1985		44	.253	.354	79	20	3	1	1	1.3	5	12	1	15	0	24	10	52	20	2	4	2.4	.973	3B-11, 1B-8, DH-6, OF-3, 2B-3
14 yrs.		959	.267	.370	2811	751	122	18	44	1.6	268	311	186	413	16	175	48	1226	1450	98	229	3.2	.965	3B-516, 2B-200, 1B-67, DH-49, OF-28, SS-13

Justin Stein

STEIN, JUSTIN MARION (Ott)
B. Aug. 9, 1911, St. Louis, Mo. D. May 1, 1992, Creve Coeur, Mo.
BR TR 5′11″ 180 lbs.

Year	Team	Games	BA	SA	AB	H	2B	3B	HR	HR%	R	RBI	BB	SO	SB	Pinch Hit AB	Pinch Hit H	PO	A	E	DP	TC/G	FA	G by Pos
1938	**2 teams**	**PHI N** (11G –.256) **CIN N** (11G –.333)																						
″	**total**	22	.281	.333	57	16	1	1	0	0.0	9	3	2	5	0	2	1	19	36	7	5	3.3	.887	3B-7, SS-7, 2B-5

Terry Steinbach

STEINBACH, TERRY LEE
B. Mar. 2, 1962, New Ulm, Minn.
BR TR 6′ 1″ 195 lbs.

Year	Team	Games	BA	SA	AB	H	2B	3B	HR	HR%	R	RBI	BB	SO	SB	Pinch Hit AB	Pinch Hit H	PO	A	E	DP	TC/G	FA	G by Pos
1986	**OAK A**	6	.333	.733	15	5	0	0	2	13.3	3	4	1	0	0	2	1	21	4	1	1	5.2	.962	C-5
1987		122	.284	.463	391	111	16	3	16	4.1	66	56	32	66	1	7	4	642	44	10	6	5.9	.986	C-107, 3B-10, 1B-1
1988		104	.265	.402	351	93	19	1	9	2.6	42	51	33	47	3	4	2	536	58	9	10	5.5	.985	C-84, 3B-9, 1B-8, DH-7, OF-1
1989		130	.273	.352	454	124	13	1	7	1.5	37	42	30	66	1	8	2	612	47	11	14	5.0	.984	C-103, OF-14, 1B-10, DH-4, 3B-3
1990		114	.251	.372	379	95	15	2	9	2.4	32	57	19	66	0	14	4	401	31	5	1	3.9	.989	C-83, DH-25, 1B-3
1991		129	.274	.386	456	125	31	1	6	1.3	50	67	22	70	2	7	4	639	53	15	11	5.5	.979	C-117, 1B-9, DH-2
1992		128	.279	.411	438	122	20	1	12	2.7	48	53	45	58	2	5	0	598	72	10	10	5.2	.985	C-124, 1B-5, DH-2
1993		104	.285	.416	389	111	19	1	10	2.6	47	43	25	65	3	4	1	524	47	7	18	5.4	.988	C-86, 1B-15, DH-6
1994		103	.285	.442	369	105	21	2	11	3.0	51	57	26	62	2	0	0	592	60	1	7	6.3	.998	C-93, DH-6, 1B-5
1995		114	.278	.458	406	113	26	1	15	3.7	43	65	25	74	1	3	1	686	57	6	6	6.6	.992	C-111, 1B-2
10 yrs.		1054	.275	.411	3648	1004	180	13	97	2.7	419	495	258	574	15	54	19	5251	473	75	84	5.5	.987	C-913, 1B-58, DH-52, 3B-22, OF-15
LEAGUE CHAMPIONSHIP SERIES																								
1988	**OAK A**	2	.250	.250	4	1	0	0	0	0.0	0	0	2	0	0	0	0	12	0	0	0	6.0	1.000	C-2
1989		4	.200	.200	15	3	0	0	0	0.0	0	1	1	5	0	0	0	17	0	0	0	4.3	1.000	C-3, DH-1
1990		3	.455	.455	11	5	0	0	0	0.0	2	1	1	2	0	0	0	11	0	0	0	3.7	1.000	C-3
1992		6	.292	.417	24	7	0	0	1	4.2	1	5	2	7	0	0	0	30	7	0	0	6.2	1.000	C-6
4 yrs.		15	.296	.352	54	16	0	0	1	1.9	3	7	6	14	0	0	0	70	7	0	0	5.1	1.000	C-14, DH-1
WORLD SERIES																								
1988	**OAK A**	3	.364	.455	11	4	1	0	0	0.0	0	0	0	2	0	0	0	11	3	0	0	4.7	1.000	C-2, DH-1
1989		4	.250	.563	16	4	0	1	1	6.3	3	7	2	1	0	0	0	27	2	0	0	7.3	1.000	C-4
1990		3	.125	.125	8	1	0	0	0	0.0	0	0	0	1	0	0	0	8	1	0	0	3.0	1.000	C-3
3 yrs.		10	.257	.429	35	9	1	1	1	2.9	3	7	2	4	0	0	0	46	6	0	0	5.2	1.000	C-9, DH-1

Hank Steinbacher

STEINBACHER, HENRY JOHN
B. Mar. 22, 1913, Sacramento, Calif. D. Apr. 3, 1977, Sacramento, Calif.
BL TR 5′11″ 180 lbs.

Year	Team	Games	BA	SA	AB	H	2B	3B	HR	HR%	R	RBI	BB	SO	SB	Pinch Hit AB	Pinch Hit H	PO	A	E	DP	TC/G	FA	G by Pos
1937	**CHI A**	26	.260	.384	73	19	4	1	1	1.4	13	9	4	7	2	11	1	24	0	1	0	1.7	.960	OF-15
1938		106	.331	.459	399	132	23	8	4	1.0	59	61	41	19	1	4	1	202	7	8	2	2.1	.963	OF-101
1939		71	.171	.234	111	19	2	1	1	0.9	16	15	21	8	0	39	8	38	1	0	0	1.8	1.000	OF-22
3 yrs.		203	.292	.407	583	170	29	10	6	1.0	88	85	66	34	3	54	10	264	8	9	2	2.0	.968	OF-138

Gene Steinbrenner

STEINBRENNER, EUGENE GASS
B. Nov. 17, 1892, Pittsburgh, Pa. D. Apr. 25, 1970, Pittsburgh, Pa.
BR TR 5′ 8½″ 155 lbs.

Year	Team	Games	BA	SA	AB	H	2B	3B	HR	HR%	R	RBI	BB	SO	SB	Pinch Hit AB	Pinch Hit H	PO	A	E	DP	TC/G	FA	G by Pos
1912	**PHI N**	3	.222	.333	9	2	1	0	0	0.0	0	1	0	3	0	0	0	4	5	1	1	3.3	.900	2B-3

Bill Steinecke

STEINECKE, WILLIAM ROBERT
B. Feb. 7, 1907, Cincinnati, Ohio D. July 20, 1986, St. Augustine, Fla.
BR TR 5′ 8½″ 175 lbs.

Year	Team	Games	BA	SA	AB	H	2B	3B	HR	HR%	R	RBI	BB	SO	SB	Pinch Hit AB	Pinch Hit H	PO	A	E	DP	TC/G	FA	G by Pos
1931	**PIT N**	4	.000	.000	4	0	0	0	0	0.0	0	0	0	1	0	3	0	0	0	0	0	0.0	.000	C-1

Ben Steiner

STEINER, BENJAMIN SAUNDERS
B. July 28, 1921, Alexandria, Va. D. Oct. 27, 1988, Venice, Calif.
BL TR 5′11″ 165 lbs.

Year	Team	Games	BA	SA	AB	H	2B	3B	HR	HR%	R	RBI	BB	SO	SB	Pinch Hit AB	Pinch Hit H	PO	A	E	DP	TC/G	FA	G by Pos
1945	**BOS A**	78	.257	.332	304	78	8	3	3	1.0	39	20	31	29	10	1	0	202	213	14	63	5.6	.967	2B-77
1946		3	.250	.250	4	1	0	0	0	0.0	1	0	0	0	0	0	0	2	1	1	0	4.0	.750	3B-1
1947	**DET A**	1	—	—	0	0	0	0	0	—	1	0	0	0	0	0	0	0	0	0	0	0.0	—	
3 yrs.		82	.256	.331	308	79	8	3	3	1.0	41	20	31	29	10	1	0	204	214	15	63	5.6	.965	2B-77, 3B-1

Red Steiner

STEINER, JAMES HARRY
B. Jan. 7, 1915, Los Angeles, Calif.
BL TR 5′11″ 175 lbs.

Year	Team	Games	BA	SA	AB	H	2B	3B	HR	HR%	R	RBI	BB	SO	SB	Pinch Hit AB	Pinch Hit H	PO	A	E	DP	TC/G	FA	G by Pos
1945	**2 teams**	**CLE A** (12G –.150) **BOS A** (26G –.203)																						
″	**total**	38	.190	.203	79	15	1	0	0	0.0	6	6	15	6	0	1	1	76	14	1	5	2.6	.989	C-35

Harry Steinfeldt

STEINFELDT, HARRY M.
B. Sept. 29, 1877, St. Louis, Mo. D. Aug. 17, 1914, Bellevue, Ky.
BR TR 5′ 9½″ 180 lbs.

Year	Team	Games	BA	SA	AB	H	2B	3B	HR	HR%	R	RBI	BB	SO	SB	Pinch Hit AB	Pinch Hit H	PO	A	E	DP	TC/G	FA	G by Pos
1898	**CIN N**	88	.295	.393	308	91	18	6	0	0.0	47	43	27		9	0	0	202	158	41	17	4.4	.898	2B-31, OF-29, 3B-22, SS-5, 1B-4
1899		107	.244	.326	386	94	16	8	0	0.0	62	43	40		19	0	0	189	262	45	19	4.6	.909	3B-59, 2B-40, SS-8, OF-2
1900		136	.248	.343	513	127	29	7	2	0.4	58	66	27		14	0	0	309	403	48	52	5.6	.937	3B-67, 2B-64, OF-2, SS-2
1901		105	.249	.380	382	95	18	7	6	1.6	40	47	28		10	0	0	198	269	42	28	4.8	.917	3B-55, 2B-50
1902		129	.278	.355	479	133	20	7	1	0.2	53	49	24		12	0	0	191	316	50	30	4.3	.910	3B-129, OF-1
1903		118	.312	.481	439	137	**32**	12	6	1.4	71	83	47		13	0	0	201	261	35	12	4.2	.930	3B-104, SS-14
1904		99	.244	.318	349	85	11	6	1	0.3	35	52	29		16	1	0	153	168	41	13	3.7	.887	3B-98
1905		114	.271	.367	384	104	16	9	1	0.3	49	39	30		15	8	1	154	223	33	16	3.9	.920	3B-103, 2B-1, OF-1, 1B-1

Harry Steinfeldt *continued*

Year	Team	Lg	Games	BA	SA	AB	H	2B	3B	HR	HR%	R	RBI	BB	SO	SB	Pinch Hit AB	Pinch Hit H	PO	A	E	DP	TC/G	FA	G by Pos
1906	CHI	N	151	.327	.430	539	**176**	27	10	3	0.6	81	**83**	47		29	0	0	160	254	20	13	2.9	.954	3B-150, 2B-1
1907			152	.266	.336	542	144	25	5	1	0.2	52	70	37		19	1	0	161	307	16	18	3.2	.967	3B-151
1908			150	.241	.306	539	130	20	6	1	0.2	63	62	36		12	1	0	166	275	28	15	3.1	.940	3B-150
1909			151	.252	.337	528	133	27	6	2	0.4	73	59	57		22	0	0	183	299	31	16	3.4	.940	3B-151
1910			129	.252	.317	448	113	21	1	2	0.4	70	58	36	29	10	1	0	137	246	22	16	3.2	.946	3B-128
1911	BOS	N	19	.254	.365	63	16	4	0	1	1.6	5	8	6	3	1	0	0	23	24	11	2	3.1	.810	3B-19
14 yrs.			1648	.268	.360	5899	1578	284	90	27	0.5	759	762	471	32	201	12	1	2427	3465	463	267	3.9	.927	3B-1386, 2B-187, OF-35, SS-29, 1B-5
WORLD SERIES																									
1906	CHI	N	6	.250	.300	20	5	1	0	0	0.0	2	2	1	0	1	0	0	3	9	1	0	2.2	.923	3B-6
1907			5	.471	.647	17	8	1	1	0	0.0	2	2	1	2	1	0	0	10	7	0	1	3.4	1.000	3B-5
1908			5	.250	.250	16	4	0	0	0	0.0	3	3	2	5	1	0	0	4	11	1	0	3.2	.938	3B-5
1910			5	.100	.150	20	2	1	0	0	0.0	0	1	0	4	0	0	0	2	12	4	0	3.6	.778	3B-5
4 yrs.			21	.260	.329	73	19	3	1	0	0.0	7	8	4	11	2	0	0	19	39	6	1	3.0	.906	3B-21

Bill Stellbauer

STELLBAUER, WILLIAMS JENNINGS BR TR 5′10″ 175 lbs.
B. Mar. 20, 1894, Bremond, Tex. D. Feb. 16, 1974, New Braunfels, Tex.

Year	Team	Lg	Games	BA	SA	AB	H	2B	3B	HR	HR%	R	RBI	BB	SO	SB	Pinch Hit AB	Pinch Hit H	PO	A	E	DP	TC/G	FA	G by Pos
1916	PHI	A	25	.271	.354	48	13	2	1	0	0.0	2	5	6	7	2	9	2	18	0	3	0	1.5	.857	OF-14

Rick Stelmaszek

STELMASZEK, RICHARD FRANCIS BL TR 6′1″ 195 lbs.
B. Oct. 8, 1948, Chicago, Ill.

Year	Team	Lg	Games	BA	SA	AB	H	2B	3B	HR	HR%	R	RBI	BB	SO	SB	Pinch Hit AB	Pinch Hit H	PO	A	E	DP	TC/G	FA	G by Pos
1971	WAS	A	6	.000	.000	9	0	0	0	0	0.0	0	0	0	3	0	3	0	4	1	0	0	1.7	1.000	C-3
1973	2 teams		TEX A (7G –.111) CAL A (22G –.154)																						
″	total		29	.143	.171	35	5	1	0	0	0.0	2	3	7	9	0	0	0	71	5	0	1	2.6	1.000	C-29
1974	CHI	N	25	.227	.341	44	10	2	0	1	2.3	2	7	10	6	0	10	2	55	2	1	1	3.6	.983	C-16
3 yrs.			60	.170	.239	88	15	3	0	1	1.1	4	10	17	18	0	13	2	130	8	1	2	2.9	.993	C-48

Fred Stem

STEM, FREDERICK BOOTHE BL TR 6′2″ 160 lbs.
B. Sept. 22, 1885, Oxford, N. C. D. Sept. 5, 1964, Darlington, S. C.

Year	Team	Lg	Games	BA	SA	AB	H	2B	3B	HR	HR%	R	RBI	BB	SO	SB	Pinch Hit AB	Pinch Hit H	PO	A	E	DP	TC/G	FA	G by Pos
1908	BOS	N	19	.278	.306	72	20	0	1	0	0.0	9	3	2		1	1	0	192	9	1	9	11.2	.995	1B-18
1909			73	.208	.241	245	51	2	3	0	0.0	13	11	12		5	5	0	656	62	8	31	10.7	.989	1B-68
2 yrs.			92	.224	.256	317	71	2	4	0	0.0	22	14	14		6	6	0	848	71	9	40	10.8	.990	1B-86

Casey Stengel

STENGEL, CHARLES DILLON (The Old Professor) BL TL 5′11″ 175 lbs.
B. July 30, 1890, Kansas City, Mo. D. Sept. 29, 1975, Glendale, Calif.
Manager 1934–36, 1938–43, 1949–60, 1962–65.
Hall of Fame 1966.

Year	Team	Lg	Games	BA	SA	AB	H	2B	3B	HR	HR%	R	RBI	BB	SO	SB	Pinch Hit AB	Pinch Hit H	PO	A	E	DP	TC/G	FA	G by Pos
1912	BKN	N	17	.316	.386	57	18	1	0	1	1.8	9	13	15	9	5	0	0	36	1	4	0	2.4	.902	OF-17
1913			124	.272	.393	438	119	16	8	7	1.6	60	43	56	58	19	5	1	270	16	12	1	2.5	.960	OF-119
1914			126	.316	.425	412	130	13	10	4	1.0	55	60	56	55	19	4	0	173	15	7	3	1.6	.964	OF-121
1915			132	.237	.353	459	109	20	12	3	0.7	52	50	34	46	5	1	0	220	13	10	2	1.9	.959	OF-129
1916			127	.279	.424	462	129	27	8	8	1.7	66	53	33	51	11	6	2	206	14	8	4	1.9	.965	OF-121
1917			150	.257	.375	549	141	23	12	6	1.1	69	73	60	62	18	0	0	256	30	9	9	2.0	.969	OF-150
1918	PIT	N	39	.246	.320	122	30	4	1	1	0.8	18	12	16	14	11	3	0	64	7	2	3	2.7	.973	OF-27
1919			89	.293	.424	321	94	10	10	4	1.2	38	43	35	35	12	2	0	195	7	9	3	2.4	.957	OF-87
1920	PHI	N	129	.292	.436	445	130	25	6	9	2.0	53	50	38	35	7	10	3	212	16	11	1	2.0	.954	OF-118
1921	2 teams		PHI N (24G –.305) NY N (18G –.227)																						
″	total		42	.284	.358	81	23	4	1	0	0.0	11	6	7	12	1	13	3	33	5	2	2	1.0	.950	OF-42
1922	NY	N	84	.368	.564	250	92	8	10	7	2.8	48	48	21	17	4	1	0	179	7	6	2	2.5	.969	OF-77
1923			75	.339	.505	218	74	11	5	5	2.3	39	43	20	18	6	15	3	115	4	2	1	2.1	.983	OF-57
1924	BOS	N	131	.280	.382	461	129	20	6	5	1.1	57	39	45	39	13	4	0	211	12	5	4	1.8	.978	OF-126
1925			12	.077	.077	13	1	0	0	0	0.0	0	2	1	2	0	9	0	1	0	0	0	1.0	1.000	OF-1
14 yrs.			1277	.284	.410	4288	1219	182	89	60	1.4	575	535	437	453	131	73	12	2171	147	87	35	2.0	.964	OF-1192
WORLD SERIES																									
1916	BKN	N	4	.364	.364	11	4	0	0	0	0.0	2	0	0	1	0	0	0	3	1	1	0	1.7	.800	OF-3
1922	NY	N	2	.400	.400	5	2	0	0	0	0.0	0	0	0	1	0	0	0	4	0	0	0	2.0	1.000	OF-2
1923			6	.417	.917	12	5	0	0	2	16.7	3	4	4	0	0	1	0	11	0	0	0	1.8	1.000	OF-6
3 yrs.			12	.393	.607	28	11	0	0	2	7.1	5	4	4	2	0	1	0	18	1	1	0	1.8	.950	OF-11

Mike Stenhouse

STENHOUSE, MICHAEL STEVEN BL TR 6′1″ 195 lbs.
Son of Dave Stenhouse.
B. May 29, 1958, Pueblo, Colo.

Year	Team	Lg	Games	BA	SA	AB	H	2B	3B	HR	HR%	R	RBI	BB	SO	SB	Pinch Hit AB	Pinch Hit H	PO	A	E	DP	TC/G	FA	G by Pos
1982	MON	N	1	.000	.000	1	0	0	0	0	0.0	0	0	0	1	0	1	0	0	0	0	0	0.0	—	
1983			24	.125	.150	40	5	1	0	0	0.0	2	2	4	10	0	9	0	37	2	0	3	2.8	1.000	OF-9, 1B-5
1984			80	.183	.297	175	32	8	0	4	2.3	14	16	26	32	0	26	5	118	5	2	8	2.0	.984	OF-48, 1B-14
1985	MIN	A	81	.223	.335	179	40	5	0	5	2.8	23	21	29	18	1	23	5	83	10	3	4	1.9	.969	DH-27, OF-16, 1B-8
1986	BOS	A	21	.095	.143	21	2	1	0	0	0.0	1	1	12	5	0	8	1	23	3	0	3	3.7	1.000	OF-4, 1B-3
5 yrs.			207	.190	.291	416	79	15	0	9	2.2	40	40	71	66	1	67	11	261	20	5	18	2.1	.983	OF-77, 1B-30, DH-27

Rennie Stennett

STENNETT, RENALDO ANTONIO BR TR 5′11″ 160 lbs.
Born Renaldo Antonio Stennett (Porte).
B. Apr. 5, 1951, Colon, Panama.

Year	Team	Lg	Games	BA	SA	AB	H	2B	3B	HR	HR%	R	RBI	BB	SO	SB	Pinch Hit AB	Pinch Hit H	PO	A	E	DP	TC/G	FA	G by Pos
1971	PIT	N	50	.353	.458	153	54	5	4	1	0.7	24	15	7	9	1	15	3	82	106	9	22	5.5	.954	2B-36
1972			109	.286	.376	370	106	14	5	3	0.8	43	30	9	43	4	21	5	197	173	10	45	4.0	.974	2B-49, OF-41, SS-6
1973			128	.242	.358	466	113	18	3	10	2.1	45	55	16	63	2	17	4	281	348	14	84	4.9	.978	2B-84, SS-43, OF-5
1974			157	.291	.374	673	196	29	3	7	1.0	84	56	32	51	8	1	0	444	475	19	115	6.0	.980	2B-154, OF-2
1975			148	.286	.383	616	176	25	7	7	1.1	89	62	33	42	5	4	0	379	463	18	98	6.0	.979	2B-144
1976			157	.257	.341	654	168	31	9	2	0.3	59	60	19	32	18	1	1	432	506	19	111	5.9	.980	2B-157, SS-4
1977			116	.336	.430	453	152	20	4	5	1.1	53	51	29	24	28	3	2	269	315	11	70	5.3	.982	2B-113
1978			106	.243	.309	333	81	9	2	3	0.9	30	35	13	22	2	17	3	167	215	13	40	4.6	.967	2B-80, 3B-6

Rennie Stennett *continued*

Year	Team	Games	BA	SA	AB	H	2B	3B	HR	HR%	R	RBI	BB	SO	SB	Pinch Hit AB	Pinch Hit H	PO	A	E	DP	TC/G	FA	G by Pos
1979		108	.238	.292	319	76	13	2	0	0.0	31	24	24	25	1	6	2	172	282	12	63	4.6	.974	2B-102
1980	**SF N**	120	.244	.302	397	97	13	2	2	0.5	34	37	22	31	4	13	1	244	293	15	53	5.0	.973	2B-111
1981		38	.230	.264	87	20	0	0	1	1.1	8	7	3	6	2	20	5	48	46	0	9	4.9	1.000	2B-19
11 yrs.		1237	.274	.359	4521	1239	177	41	41	0.9	500	432	207	348	75	118	26	2715	3222	140	710	5.3	.977	2B-1049, SS-53, OF-48, 3B-6
LEAGUE CHAMPIONSHIP SERIES																								
1972	**PIT N**	5	.286	.286	21	6	0	0	0	0.0	2	1	1	0	0	0	0	0	0	0	0	0.0		OF-5, 2B-1
1974		4	.063	.063	16	1	0	0	0	0.0	1	0	1	1	0	0	0	10	10	1	1	5.3	.952	2B-4
1975		3	.214	.214	14	3	0	0	0	0.0	0	0	0	1	0	0	0	3	8	0	2	2.8	1.000	2B-3, SS-1
1979		1	—	—	0	0	0	0	0	—	0	0	0	0	0	0	0	0	1	0	0	1.0	1.000	2B-1
4 yrs.		13	.196	.196	51	10	0	0	0	0.0	3	1	2	2	0	0	0	13	19	1	3	2.2	.970	2B-9, OF-5, SS-1
WORLD SERIES																								
1979	**PIT N**	1	1.000	1.000	1	1	0	0	0	0.0	0	0	0	0	0	1	1	0	0	0	0	0.0	—	

Jake Stenzel

STENZEL, JACOB CHARLES BR TR 5′10″ 168 lbs.
Born Jacob Charles Stelzle.
B. June 24, 1867, Cincinnati, Ohio D. Jan. 6, 1919, Cincinnati, Ohio.

Year	Team	Games	BA	SA	AB	H	2B	3B	HR	HR%	R	RBI	BB	SO	SB	Pinch Hit AB	Pinch Hit H	PO	A	E	DP	TC/G	FA	G by Pos
1890	**CHI N**	11	.268	.293	41	11	1	0	0	0.0	3	3	1	0	0	0	0	31	6	2	0	3.3	.949	OF-6, C-6
1892	**PIT N**	3	.000	.000	9	0	0	0	0	0.0	0	0	1	3	1	0	0	3	2	0	0	1.7	1.000	OF-2, C-1
1893		60	.362	.509	224	81	13	4	4	1.8	57	37	24	17	16	**6**	1	109	18	20	3	2.5	.864	OF-45, C-12, 2B-1, SS-1
1894		131	.354	.580	522	185	39	20	13	2.5	148	121	75	13	61	0	0	311	23	27	6	2.8	.925	OF-131
1895		129	.374	.539	514	192	38	13	7	1.4	114	97	57	25	53	0	0	257	23	27	6	2.4	.912	OF-129
1896		114	.361	.486	479	173	26	14	2	0.4	104	82	32	13	57	0	0	250	13	23	5	2.5	.920	OF-114, 1B-1
1897	**BAL N**	131	.353	.487	536	189	**43**	7	5	0.9	113	116	36		69	0	0	264	12	20	2	2.3	.932	OF-131
1898	**2 teams**	**BAL N** (35G –.254) **STL N** (108G –.282)																						
″	**total**	143	.275	.365	542	149	20	13	1	0.2	97	55	53		25	0	0	314	14	21	3	2.4	.940	OF-143
1899	**2 teams**	**STL N** (35G –.273) **CIN N** (9G –.310)																						
″	**total**	44	.280	.363	157	44	10	0	1	0.6	26	22	20		10	3	0	85	3	4	1	2.3	.957	OF-40
9 yrs.		766	.339	.481	3024	1024	190	71	33	1.1	662	533	299	71	292	9	1	1624	114	144	26	2.5	.923	OF-741, C-19, 2B-1, 1B-1, SS-1

Gene Stephens

STEPHENS, GLEN EUGENE BL TR 6′ 3½″ 175 lbs.
B. Jan. 20, 1933, Gravette, Ark.

Year	Team	Games	BA	SA	AB	H	2B	3B	HR	HR%	R	RBI	BB	SO	SB	Pinch Hit AB	Pinch Hit H	PO	A	E	DP	TC/G	FA	G by Pos
1952	**BOS A**	21	.226	.321	53	12	5	0	0	0.0	10	5	3	8	4	4	1	24	1	1	0	2.0	.962	OF-13
1953		78	.204	.290	221	45	6	2	3	1.4	30	18	29	56	3	1	0	113	2	4	0	1.7	.966	OF-72
1955		109	.293	.459	157	46	9	4	3	1.9	25	18	20	34	0	23	4	82	7	5	1	1.3	.947	OF-75
1956		104	.270	.349	63	17	2	0	1	1.6	22	7	12	12	0	24	7	57	2	1	0	0.8	.983	OF-71
1957		120	.266	.399	173	46	6	4	3	1.7	25	26	26	20	0	29	5	70	4	1	2	0.8	.987	OF-90
1958		134	.219	.363	270	59	10	1	9	3.3	38	25	22	46	1	22	3	149	5	4	2	1.4	.975	OF-110
1959		92	.278	.367	270	75	13	1	3	1.1	34	39	29	33	5	7	3	141	11	3	0	1.8	.981	OF-85
1960	**2 teams**	**BOS A** (35G –.229) **BAL A** (84G –.238)																						
″	**total**	119	.235	.354	302	71	15	0	7	2.3	47	22	39	47	9	11	2	180	7	4	0	1.8	.979	OF-108
1961	**2 teams**	**BAL A** (32G –.190) **KC A** (62G –.208)																						
″	**total**	94	.203	.295	241	49	8	1	4	1.7	26	28	30	34	4	11	2	148	8	4	5	1.9	.975	OF-84
1962	**KC A**	5	.000	.000	4	0	0	0	0	0.0	0	0	1	1	0	4	0	0	0	0	0	0.0	—	
1963	**CHI A**	6	.389	.556	18	7	0	0	1	5.6	5	2	1	3	0	0	0	8	2	1	0	2.2	.909	OF-5
1964		82	.234	.355	141	33	4	2	3	2.1	21	17	21	28	1	19	7	91	2	3	1	1.6	.969	OF-59
12 yrs.		964	.240	.355	1913	460	78	15	37	1.9	283	207	233	322	27	155	34	1063	51	31	11	1.5	.973	OF-772

Jim Stephens

STEPHENS, JAMES WALTER (Little Nemo) BR TR 5′ 6½″ 157 lbs.
B. Dec. 10, 1883, Salineville, Ohio D. Jan. 2, 1965, Oxford, Ala.

Year	Team	Games	BA	SA	AB	H	2B	3B	HR	HR%	R	RBI	BB	SO	SB	Pinch Hit AB	Pinch Hit H	PO	A	E	DP	TC/G	FA	G by Pos
1907	**STL A**	58	.202	.272	173	35	6	3	0	0.0	15	11	15		3	2	0	200	63	9	4	4.9	.967	C-56
1908		47	.200	.240	150	30	4	1	0	0.0	14	6	9		0	2	0	193	68	11	4	6.0	.960	C-45
1909		79	.220	.283	223	49	5	0	3	1.3	18	18	13		5	7	0	335	103	9	9	6.2	.980	C-72
1910		99	.241	.298	299	72	3	7	0	0.0	24	23	16		2	3	1	418	156	17	18	6.2	.971	C-96
1911		70	.231	.302	212	49	5	5	0	0.0	11	17	17		1	2	0	223	94	17	7	5.1	.949	C-66
1912		74	.249	.332	205	51	7	5	0	0.0	13	22	7		3	8	0	262	110	18	10	5.9	.954	C-66
6 yrs.		427	.227	.291	1262	286	30	21	3	0.2	95	97	77		14	24	1	1631	594	81	52	5.8	.965	C-401

Ray Stephens

STEPHENS, CARL RAY BR TR 6′ 190 lbs.
B. Sept. 22, 1962, Houston, Tex.

Year	Team	Games	BA	SA	AB	H	2B	3B	HR	HR%	R	RBI	BB	SO	SB	Pinch Hit AB	Pinch Hit H	PO	A	E	DP	TC/G	FA	G by Pos
1990	**STL N**	5	.133	.400	15	2	1	0	1	6.7	2	1	0	3	0	0	0	31	2	0	0	6.6	1.000	C-5
1991		6	.286	.286	7	2	0	0	0	0.0	0	0	1	3	0	0	0	16	2	0	0	3.0	1.000	C-6
1992	**TEX A**	8	.154	.154	13	2	0	0	0	0.0	0	0	0	5	0	3	0	12	2	0	0	2.0	1.000	C-6, DH-1
3 yrs.		19	.171	.286	35	6	1	0	1	2.9	2	1	1	11	0	3	0	59	6	0	0	3.6	1.000	C-17, DH-1

Vern Stephens

STEPHENS, VERNON DECATUR (Buster, Junior) BR TR 5′10″ 185 lbs.
B. Oct. 23, 1920, McAlister, N. M. D. Nov. 3, 1968, Long Beach, Calif.

Year	Team	Games	BA	SA	AB	H	2B	3B	HR	HR%	R	RBI	BB	SO	SB	Pinch Hit AB	Pinch Hit H	PO	A	E	DP	TC/G	FA	G by Pos
1941	**STL A**	3	.500	.500	2	1	0	0	0	0.0	0	0	0	0	0	1	0	0	1	1	0	2.0	.500	SS-1
1942		145	.294	.433	575	169	26	6	14	2.4	84	92	41	53	1	1	1	290	415	42	82	5.2	.944	SS-144
1943		137	.289	.482	512	148	27	3	22	4.3	75	91	54	73	3	3	1	240	342	34	51	4.6	.945	SS-123, OF-11
1944		145	.293	.462	559	164	32	1	20	3.6	91	**109**	62	54	2	1	0	239	480	35	71	5.3	.954	SS-143
1945		149	.289	.473	571	165	27	3	**24**	**4.2**	90	89	55	70	2	1	1	258	450	30	71	5.0	.959	SS-144, 3B-4
1946		115	.307	.460	450	138	19	4	14	3.1	67	64	35	49	0	3	0	224	343	30	71	5.3	.950	SS-112
1947		150	.279	.406	562	157	18	4	15	2.7	74	83	70	61	8	0	0	283	494	24	113	5.4	.970	SS-149
1948	**BOS A**	155	.269	.471	635	171	25	8	29	4.6	114	137	77	56	1	0	0	269	540	24	113	5.4	.971	SS-155
1949		155	.290	.539	610	177	31	2	39	6.4	113	**159**	101	73	2	0	0	257	508	27	128	5.1	.966	SS-155
1950		149	.295	.511	628	185	34	6	30	4.8	125	**144**	65	43	1	3	0	258	431	13	115	4.8	.981	SS-146
1951		109	.300	.501	377	113	21	2	17	4.5	62	78	38	33	1	17	4	105	209	7	19	3.5	.978	3B-89, SS-2
1952		92	.254	.383	295	75	13	2	7	2.4	35	44	39	31	2	9	2	110	227	16	48	4.3	.955	SS-53, 3B-29
1953	**2 teams**	**CHI A** (44G –.186) **STL A** (46G –.321)																						
″	**total**	90	.262	.361	294	77	14	0	5	1.7	30	31	31	42	2	4	0	84	162	8	16	2.9	.969	3B-84, SS-3

Vern Stephens *continued*

Year	Team	Lg	Games	BA	SA	AB	H	2B	3B	HR	HR%	R	RBI	BB	SO	SB	Pinch Hit AB	Pinch Hit H	PO	A	E	DP	TC/G	FA	G by Pos
1954	BAL	A	101	.285	.403	365	104	17	1	8	2.2	31	46	17	36	0	5	0	102	186	10	19	3.1	.966	3B-96
1955	2 teams		BAL A (3G –.167) CHI A (22G –.250)																						
"	total		25	.242	.435	62	15	3	0	3	4.8	10	7	7	11	0	6	1	13	39	0	4	2.6	1.000	3B-20
15 yrs.			1720	.286	.460	6497	1859	307	42	247	3.8	1001	1174	692	685	25	54	10	2732	4827	301	921	4.7	.962	SS-1330, 3B-322, OF-11
WORLD SERIES																									
1944	STL	A	6	.227	.273	22	5	1	0	0	0.0	2	0	3	3	0	0	0	9	19	3	4	5.2	.903	SS-6

Bobby Stephenson

STEPHENSON, ROBERT LLOYD BR TR 6′ 165 lbs.
B. Aug. 11, 1928, Blair, Okla.

Year	Team	Lg	Games	BA	SA	AB	H	2B	3B	HR	HR%	R	RBI	BB	SO	SB	Pinch Hit AB	Pinch Hit H	PO	A	E	DP	TC/G	FA	G by Pos
1955	STL	N	67	.243	.270	111	27	3	0	0	0.0	19	6	5	18	2	6	0	65	80	8	21	2.7	.948	SS-48, 2B-7, 3B-1

Dummy Stephenson

STEPHENSON, REUBEN CRANDOL BR TR 5′11½″ 180 lbs.
B. Sept. 22, 1869, Petersburg, N. J. D. Dec. 1, 1924, Trenton, N. J.

Year	Team	Lg	Games	BA	SA	AB	H	2B	3B	HR	HR%	R	RBI	BB	SO	SB	Pinch Hit AB	Pinch Hit H	PO	A	E	DP	TC/G	FA	G by Pos
1892	PHI	N	8	.270	.351	37	10	3	0	0	0.0	4	5	0	2	0	0	0	11	1	3	0	1.9	.800	OF-8

Joe Stephenson

STEPHENSON, JOSEPH CHESTER BR TR 6′ 2″ 185 lbs.
Father of Jerry Stephenson.
B. June 30, 1921, Detroit, Mich.

Year	Team	Lg	Games	BA	SA	AB	H	2B	3B	HR	HR%	R	RBI	BB	SO	SB	Pinch Hit AB	Pinch Hit H	PO	A	E	DP	TC/G	FA	G by Pos
1943	NY	N	9	.250	.292	24	6	1	0	0	0.0	4	1	0	5	0	1	0	30	6	1	1	6.2	.973	C-6
1944	CHI	N	4	.125	.125	8	1	0	0	0	0.0	1	0	1	3	1	1	0	13	2	0	0	5.0	1.000	C-3
1947	CHI	A	16	.143	.143	35	5	0	0	0	0.0	3	3	1	7	0	1	0	42	5	2	0	3.8	.959	C-13
3 yrs.			29	.179	.194	67	12	1	0	0	0.0	8	4	2	15	1	3	0	85	13	3	1	4.6	.970	C-22

Johnny Stephenson

STEPHENSON, JOHN HERMAN BL TR 5′11″ 180 lbs.
B. Apr. 13, 1941, South Portsmouth, Ky.

Year	Team	Lg	Games	BA	SA	AB	H	2B	3B	HR	HR%	R	RBI	BB	SO	SB	Pinch Hit AB	Pinch Hit H	PO	A	E	DP	TC/G	FA	G by Pos
1964	NY	N	37	.158	.211	57	9	0	0	1	1.8	2	2	4	18	0	21	2	10	18	6	1	1.5	.824	3B-14, OF-8
1965			62	.215	.355	121	26	5	0	4	3.3	9	15	8	19	0	29	6	147	13	3	1	3.3	.982	C-47, OF-2
1966			63	.196	.238	143	28	1	1	1	0.7	17	11	8	28	0	25	4	187	30	6	4	4.2	.973	C-52, OF-1
1967	CHI	N	18	.224	.327	49	11	3	1	0	0.0	3	5	1	6	0	3	1	67	8	0	2	5.8	1.000	C-13
1968			2	.000	.000	2	0	0	0	0	0.0	0	0	0	0	0	2	0	0	0	0	0	0.0	—	
1969	SF	N	22	.222	.296	27	6	2	0	0	0.0	2	3	0	4	0	15	4	15	1	3	0	1.9	.842	C-9, 3B-1
1970			23	.070	.093	43	3	1	0	0	0.0	3	6	2	7	0	14	3	52	8	0	1	6.0	1.000	C-9, OF-1
1971	CAL	A	98	.219	.312	279	61	17	0	3	1.1	24	25	22	21	0	16	1	434	33	4	3	5.4	.992	C-88
1972			66	.274	.349	146	40	3	1	2	1.4	14	17	11	8	0	21	8	273	12	2	2	5.1	.993	C-56
1973			60	.246	.311	122	30	5	0	1	0.8	9	9	7	7	0	10	4	233	11	5	1	4.4	.980	C-56
10 yrs.			451	.216	.296	989	214	37	3	12	1.2	83	93	63	118	0	156	33	1418	134	29	15	4.4	.982	C-330, 3B-15, OF-12

Phil Stephenson

STEPHENSON, PHILLIP RAYMOND BL TL 6′ 1″ 195 lbs.
B. Sept. 19, 1960, Guthrie, Okla.

Year	Team	Lg	Games	BA	SA	AB	H	2B	3B	HR	HR%	R	RBI	BB	SO	SB	Pinch Hit AB	Pinch Hit H	PO	A	E	DP	TC/G	FA	G by Pos
1989	2 teams		CHI N (17G –.143) SD N (10G –.353)																						
"	total		27	.237	.395	38	9	0	0	2	5.3	4	2	5	5	1	14	2	42	4	1	3	4.3	.979	1B-8, OF-3
1990	SD	N	103	.209	.335	182	38	9	1	4	2.2	26	19	30	43	2	35	7	345	36	1	33	6.4	.997	1B-60
1991			11	.286	.286	7	2	0	0	0	0.0	0	0	2	3	0	7	2	0	0	0	0	0.0	—	
1992			53	.155	.211	71	11	2	1	0	0.0	5	8	10	11	0	29	5	48	3	1	2	2.4	.981	OF-15, 1B-7
4 yrs.			194	.201	.312	298	60	11	2	6	2.0	35	29	47	62	3	85	16	435	43	3	38	5.2	.994	1B-75, OF-18

Riggs Stephenson

STEPHENSON, JACKSON RIGGS (Old Hoss) BR TR 5′10″ 185 lbs.
B. Jan. 5, 1898, Akron, Ala. D. Nov. 15, 1985, Tuscaloosa, Ala.

Year	Team	Lg	Games	BA	SA	AB	H	2B	3B	HR	HR%	R	RBI	BB	SO	SB	Pinch Hit AB	Pinch Hit H	PO	A	E	DP	TC/G	FA	G by Pos
1921	CLE	A	65	.330	.461	206	68	17	2	2	1.0	45	34	23	15	4	6	0	122	155	17	32	5.3	.942	2B-54, 3B-2
1922			86	.339	.511	233	79	24	5	2	0.9	47	32	27	18	3	24	6	76	135	12	11	3.6	.946	3B-34, 2B-25, OF-3
1923			91	.319	.475	301	96	20	6	5	1.7	48	65	15	25	6	21	4	205	214	13	49	6.2	.970	2B-66, OF-3, 3B-1
1924			71	.371	.504	240	89	20	0	4	1.7	33	44	27	10	1	6	1	126	180	12	20	4.9	.962	2B-58, OF-7
1925			19	.296	.444	54	16	3	1	1	1.9	8	9	7	3	1	3	2	33	2	2	1	2.3	.946	OF-16
1926	CHI	N	82	.338	.456	281	95	18	3	3	1.1	40	44	31	16	2	6	2	126	7	7	0	1.9	.950	OF-74
1927			152	.344	.491	579	199	**46**	9	7	1.2	101	82	65	28	8	0	0	309	25	10	7	2.3	.971	OF-146, 3B-6
1928			137	.324	.477	512	166	36	9	8	1.6	75	90	68	29	8	2	1	268	10	5	1	2.1	.982	OF-135
1929			136	.362	.562	495	179	36	6	17	3.4	91	110	67	21	10	5	3	245	9	4	4	2.0	.984	OF-130
1930			109	.367	.478	341	125	21	1	5	1.5	56	68	32	20	2	27	11	132	5	6	1	1.8	.958	OF-80
1931			80	.319	.414	263	84	14	4	1	0.4	34	52	37	14	1	14	2	134	1	2	1	1.7	.985	OF-80
1932			147	.324	.443	583	189	49	4	4	0.7	86	85	54	27	3	0	0	298	7	5	2	2.1	.984	OF-147
1933			97	.329	.436	346	114	17	4	4	1.2	45	51	34	16	5	3	0	187	5	3	2	2.1	.985	OF-91
1934			38	.216	.216	74	16	0	0	0	0.0	5	7	7	5	0	22	5	26	3	0	1	1.9	1.000	OF-15
14 yrs.			1310	.336	.473	4508	1515	321	54	63	1.4	714	773	494	247	54	139	37	2287	758	98	132	2.7	.969	OF-927, 2B-203, 3B-43
WORLD SERIES																									
1929	CHI	N	5	.316	.368	19	6	1	0	0	0.0	3	3	2	2	0	0	0	13	1	0	0	2.8	1.000	OF-5
1932			4	.444	.500	18	8	1	0	0	0.0	2	4	0	0	0	0	0	4	0	0	0	1.0	1.000	OF-4
2 yrs.			9	.378	.432	37	14	2	0	0	0.0	5	7	2	2	0	0	0	17	1	0	0	2.0	1.000	OF-9

Walter Stephenson

STEPHENSON, WALTER McQUEEN (Tarzan) BR TR 6′ 180 lbs.
B. Mar. 27, 1911, Saluda, N. C. D. July 4, 1993, Shreveport, La.

Year	Team	Lg	Games	BA	SA	AB	H	2B	3B	HR	HR%	R	RBI	BB	SO	SB	Pinch Hit AB	Pinch Hit H	PO	A	E	DP	TC/G	FA	G by Pos
1935	CHI	N	16	.385	.500	26	10	1	1	0	0.0	2	2	1	5	0	9	2	17	6	0	1	3.8	1.000	C-6
1936			6	.083	.083	12	1	0	0	0	0.0	0	1	0	5	0	2	0	10	1	0	0	2.8	1.000	C-4
1937	PHI	N	10	.261	.261	23	6	0	0	0	0.0	1	2	2	3	0	2	0	24	5	1	1	4.3	.967	C-7
3 yrs.			32	.279	.328	61	17	1	1	0	0.0	3	5	3	13	0	13	2	51	12	1	2	3.8	.984	C-17
WORLD SERIES																									
1935	CHI	N	1	.000	.000	1	0	0	0	0	0.0	0	0	0	1	0	1	0	0	0	0	0	0.0	—	

Dutch Sterrett

STERRETT, CHARLES HURLBUT BR TR 5′11½″ 165 lbs.
B. Oct. 1, 1889, Milroy, Pa. D. Dec. 9, 1965, Baltimore, Md.

Year	Team	Lg	Games	BA	SA	AB	H	2B	3B	HR	HR%	R	RBI	BB	SO	SB	Pinch Hit AB	Pinch Hit H	PO	A	E	DP	TC/G	FA	G by Pos
1912	NY	A	66	.265	.357	230	61	4	7	1	0.4	30	32	11		8	1	0	259	22	5	4	4.3	.983	OF-38, 1B-17, C-10, 2B-1
1913			21	.171	.171	35	6	0	0	0	0.0	0	3	1	5	1	13	0	48	3	1	1	6.5	.981	1B-6, OF-1, C-1
2 yrs.			87	.253	.332	265	67	4	7	1	0.4	30	35	12	5	9	14	0	307	25	6	5	4.6	.982	OF-39, 1B-23, C-11, 2B-1

Bobby Stevens

STEVENS, ROBERT JORDAN — BL TR 5′ 8″ 149 lbs.
B. Apr. 17, 1907, Chevy Chase, Md.

Year	Team	Games	BA	SA	AB	H	2B	3B	HR	HR%	R	RBI	BB	SO	SB	Pinch Hit AB	Pinch Hit H	PO	A	E	DP	TC/G	FA	G by Pos
1931	PHI N	12	.343	.343	35	12	0	0	0	0.0	3	4	2	2	0	2	0	19	21	6	5	4.6	.870	SS-10

Chuck Stevens

STEVENS, CHARLES AUGUSTUS — BB TL 6′ 1″ 180 lbs.
B. July 10, 1918, Van Houten, N. M.

Year	Team	Games	BA	SA	AB	H	2B	3B	HR	HR%	R	RBI	BB	SO	SB	Pinch Hit AB	Pinch Hit H	PO	A	E	DP	TC/G	FA	G by Pos
1941	STL A	4	.154	.154	13	2	0	0	0	0.0	2	2	0	1	0	0	0	28	0	1	3	7.3	.966	1B-4
1946		122	.248	.326	432	107	17	4	3	0.7	53	27	47	62	4	2	0	1020	86	6	98	9.3	.995	1B-120
1948		85	.261	.341	287	75	12	4	1	0.3	34	26	41	26	2	0	0	737	56	7	89	9.4	.991	1B-85
3 yrs.		211	.251	.329	732	184	29	8	4	0.5	89	55	88	89	6	2	0	1785	142	14	190	9.3	.993	1B-209

Ed Stevens

STEVENS, EDWARD LEE (Big Ed) — BL TL 6′ 1″ 190 lbs.
B. Jan. 12, 1925, Galveston, Tex.

Year	Team	Games	BA	SA	AB	H	2B	3B	HR	HR%	R	RBI	BB	SO	SB	Pinch Hit AB	Pinch Hit H	PO	A	E	DP	TC/G	FA	G by Pos
1945	BKN N	55	.274	.433	201	55	14	3	4	2.0	29	29	32	20	0	0	0	478	38	7	40	9.5	.987	1B-55
1946		103	.242	.426	310	75	13	7	10	3.2	34	60	27	44	2	4	1	716	48	11	59	7.8	.986	1B-99
1947		5	.154	.231	13	2	1	0	0	0.0	0	0	1	5	0	1	0	29	4	1	2	6.8	.971	1B-5
1948	PIT N	128	.254	.396	429	109	19	6	10	2.3	47	69	35	53	4	10	3	1021	83	4	94	9.5	.996	1B-117
1949		67	.262	.371	221	58	10	1	4	1.8	22	32	22	24	1	9	0	533	58	3	65	10.2	.995	1B-58
1950		17	.196	.239	46	9	2	0	0	0.0	2	3	4	5	0	4	2	92	8	0	11	8.3	1.000	1B-12
6 yrs.		375	.252	.398	1220	308	59	17	28	2.3	134	193	121	151	7	28	6	2869	239	26	271	9.1	.992	1B-346

Lee Stevens

STEVENS, DeWAIN LEE — BL TL 6′ 4″ 205 lbs.
B. July 10, 1967, Kansas City, Mo.

Year	Team	Games	BA	SA	AB	H	2B	3B	HR	HR%	R	RBI	BB	SO	SB	Pinch Hit AB	Pinch Hit H	PO	A	E	DP	TC/G	FA	G by Pos
1990	CAL A	67	.214	.339	248	53	10	0	7	2.8	28	32	22	75	1	3	0	597	36	4	62	9.5	.994	1B-67
1991		18	.293	.414	58	17	7	0	0	0.0	8	9	6	12	1	0	0	100	6	1	5	5.3	.991	1B-11, OF-9
1992		106	.221	.349	312	69	19	0	7	2.2	25	37	29	64	1	12	3	764	49	4	88	8.8	.995	1B-91, DH-2
3 yrs.		191	.225	.351	618	139	36	0	14	2.3	61	78	57	151	3	15	3	1461	91	9	155	8.7	.994	1B-169, OF-9, DH-2

R C Stevens

STEVENS, R C — BR TL 6′ 5″ 219 lbs.
B. July 22, 1934, Moultrie, Ga.

Year	Team	Games	BA	SA	AB	H	2B	3B	HR	HR%	R	RBI	BB	SO	SB	Pinch Hit AB	Pinch Hit H	PO	A	E	DP	TC/G	FA	G by Pos
1958	PIT N	59	.267	.556	90	24	3	1	7	7.8	16	18	5	25	0	6	1	212	21	2	28	4.5	.991	1B-52
1959		3	.286	.714	7	2	0	0	1	14.3	2	1	0	0	0	2	0	11	1	0	1	12.0	1.000	1B-1
1960		9	.000	.000	3	0	0	0	0	0.0	1	0	0	1	0	2	0	10	2	0	2	1.7	1.000	1B-7
1961	WAS A	33	.129	.145	62	8	1	0	0	0.0	2	2	7	15	1	6	1	147	20	0	18	6.7	1.000	1B-25
4 yrs.		104	.210	.395	162	34	4	1	8	4.9	21	21	12	41	1	16	2	380	44	2	49	5.0	.995	1B-85

Todd Steverson

STEVERSON, TODD ANTHONY — BR TR 6′ 2″ 194 lbs.
B. Nov. 15, 1971, Los Angeles, Calif.

Year	Team	Games	BA	SA	AB	H	2B	3B	HR	HR%	R	RBI	BB	SO	SB	Pinch Hit AB	Pinch Hit H	PO	A	E	DP	TC/G	FA	G by Pos
1995	DET A	30	.262	.405	42	11	0	0	2	4.8	11	6	6	10	2	3	1	22	1	0	0	0.8	1.000	OF-27, DH-1

Ace Stewart

STEWART, ASA — BR TR 5′10″ 176 lbs.
B. Feb. 14, 1869, Terre Haute, Ind. D. Apr. 17, 1912, Terre Haute, Ind.

Year	Team	Games	BA	SA	AB	H	2B	3B	HR	HR%	R	RBI	BB	SO	SB	Pinch Hit AB	Pinch Hit H	PO	A	E	DP	TC/G	FA	G by Pos
1895	CHI N	97	.241	.384	365	88	8	10	8	2.2	52	76	39	40	14	0	0	252	281	52	53	6.0	.911	2B-97

Bill Stewart

STEWART, WILLIAM WAYNE — BR TR 5′11″ 200 lbs.
B. Apr. 12, 1928, Bay City, Mich.

Year	Team	Games	BA	SA	AB	H	2B	3B	HR	HR%	R	RBI	BB	SO	SB	Pinch Hit AB	Pinch Hit H	PO	A	E	DP	TC/G	FA	G by Pos
1955	KC A	11	.111	.167	18	2	1	0	0	0.0	2	0	1	6	0	4	0	7	1	0	1	1.3	1.000	OF-6

Bud Stewart

STEWART, EDWARD PERRY — BL TR 5′11″ 160 lbs.
B. June 15, 1916, Sacramento, Calif.

Year	Team	Games	BA	SA	AB	H	2B	3B	HR	HR%	R	RBI	BB	SO	SB	Pinch Hit AB	Pinch Hit H	PO	A	E	DP	TC/G	FA	G by Pos
1941	PIT N	73	.267	.308	172	46	7	0	0	0.0	27	10	12	17	3	25	**10**	71	5	3	2	1.9	.962	OF-41
1942		82	.219	.306	183	40	8	4	0	0.0	21	20	22	16	2	28	6	87	23	3	0	2.3	.973	OF-34, 3B-10, 2B-6
1948	2 teams	NY A (6G –.200) WAS A (118G –.279)																						
"	total	124	.278	.438	406	113	18	13	7	1.7	57	69	49	27	8	9	1	265	5	7	1	2.4	.975	OF-114
1949	WAS A	118	.284	.425	388	110	23	4	8	2.1	58	43	49	33	6	11	4	207	8	4	3	2.1	.982	OF-105
1950		118	.267	.370	378	101	15	6	4	1.1	46	35	46	33	5	18	2	202	10	2	3	2.1	.991	OF-100
1951	CHI A	95	.276	.465	217	60	13	5	6	2.8	40	40	29	9	1	31	**9**	111	4	2	0	1.9	.983	OF-63
1952		92	.267	.378	225	60	10	0	5	2.2	23	30	28	17	3	34	6	108	1	2	0	1.9	.982	OF-60
1953		53	.271	.407	59	16	2	0	2	3.4	16	13	14	3	1	34	10	12	0	0	0	0.8	1.000	OF-16
1954		18	.077	.077	13	1	0	0	0	0.0	0	0	3	2	0	12	1	3	0	0	0	1.5	1.000	OF-2
9 yrs.		773	.268	.393	2041	547	96	32	32	1.6	288	260	252	157	29	202	49	1066	56	23	9	2.1	.980	OF-535, 3B-10, 2B-6

Glen Stewart

STEWART, GLEN WELDON (Gabby) — BR TR 6′ 175 lbs.
B. Sept. 29, 1912, Tullahoma, Tenn.

Year	Team	Games	BA	SA	AB	H	2B	3B	HR	HR%	R	RBI	BB	SO	SB	Pinch Hit AB	Pinch Hit H	PO	A	E	DP	TC/G	FA	G by Pos
1940	NY N	15	.138	.172	29	4	1	0	0	0.0	1	0	1	2	0	4	1	7	21	3	3	2.8	.903	3B-6, SS-5
1943	PHI N	110	.211	.265	336	71	10	1	2	0.6	23	24	32	41	1	8	1	222	286	23	51	5.1	.957	SS-77, 2B-18, 1B-8, C-1
1944		118	.220	.276	377	83	11	5	0	0.0	32	29	28	40	0	4	1	126	263	13	23	3.5	.968	3B-83, SS-32, 2B-1
3 yrs.		243	.213	.267	742	158	22	6	2	0.3	56	53	61	83	1	16	3	355	570	39	77	4.2	.960	SS-114, 3B-89, 2B-19, 1B-8, C-1

Jimmy Stewart

STEWART, JAMES FRANKLIN — BB TR 6′ 165 lbs.
B. June 11, 1939, Opelika, Ala.

Year	Team	Games	BA	SA	AB	H	2B	3B	HR	HR%	R	RBI	BB	SO	SB	Pinch Hit AB	Pinch Hit H	PO	A	E	DP	TC/G	FA	G by Pos
1963	CHI N	13	.297	.351	37	11	2	0	0	0.0	1	1	1	7	1	5	1	13	29	1	8	4.3	.977	SS-9, 2B-1
1964		132	.253	.316	415	105	17	0	3	0.7	59	33	49	61	10	31	9	217	308	13	64	4.8	.976	2B-61, SS-45, OF-4, 3B-1
1965		116	.223	.284	282	63	9	4	0	0.0	26	19	30	53	13	41	6	117	58	8	11	1.8	.956	OF-55, SS-48
1966		57	.178	.244	90	16	4	1	0	0.0	4	4	7	12	1	31	6	36	3	0	0	1.7	1.000	OF-15, 2B-4, SS-2, 3B-2
1967	2 teams	CHI N (6G –.167) CHI A (24G –.167)																						
"	total	30	.167	.167	24	4	0	0	0	0.0	6	2	1	6	1	13	1	9	8	3	4	1.5	.850	OF-6, 2B-5, SS-2
1969	CIN N	119	.253	.357	221	56	3	4	4	1.8	26	24	19	33	4	38	9	89	42	4	9	1.5	.970	OF-66, 2B-18, 3B-6, SS-1
1970		101	.267	.343	105	28	3	1	1	1.0	15	8	8	13	5	39	13	46	36	3	8	1.1	.965	OF-48, 2B-18, 3B-9, 1B-1, C-1
1971		80	.232	.305	82	19	2	2	0	0.0	7	9	9	12	3	**48**	11	13	22	2	3	1.1	.946	OF-19, 3B-9, 2B-6
1972	HOU N	68	.219	.313	96	21	5	2	0	0.0	14	9	6	9	0	40	7	83	18	0	5	3.4	1.000	OF-11, 1B-9, 2B-8, 3B-2
1973		61	.191	.191	68	13	0	0	0	0.0	6	3	9	12	0	44	8	5	17	0	2	1.8	1.000	3B-8, OF-3, 2B-1
10 yrs.		777	.237	.305	1420	336	45	14	8	0.6	164	112	139	218	38	330	71	628	541	34	114	2.4	.972	OF-227, 2B-122, SS-107, 3B-37, 1B-10, C-1

Jimmy Stewart *continued*

Year	Team		Games	BA	SA	AB	H	2B	3B	HR	HR%	R	RBI	BB	SO	SB	Pinch Hit AB	Pinch Hit H	PO	A	E	DP	TC/G	FA	G by Pos
LEAGUE CHAMPIONSHIP SERIES																									
1970	CIN	N	1	.000	.000	2	0	0	0	0	0.0	0	0	0	0	0	0	0	0	0	0	0	0.0	.000	OF-1
WORLD SERIES																									
1970	CIN	N	2	.000	.000	2	0	0	0	0	0.0	0	0	0	1	0	2	0	0	0	0	0	0.0	—	

Mark Stewart

STEWART, MARK (Big Slick)
B. Oct. 11, 1889, Whitlock, Tenn. D. Jan. 17, 1932, Memphis, Tenn.
BL TR 6′1″ 180 lbs.

Year	Team		Games	BA	SA	AB	H	2B	3B	HR	HR%	R	RBI	BB	SO	SB	Pinch Hit AB	Pinch Hit H	PO	A	E	DP	TC/G	FA	G by Pos
1913	CIN	N	1	.000	.000	1	0	0	0	0	0.0	0	0	0	0	0	0	0	0	0	0	0	0.0	.000	C-1

Neb Stewart

STEWART, WALTER NESBITT
B. May 21, 1918, South Charleston, Ohio D. June 8, 1990, London, Ont., Canada.
BR TR 6′1″ 195 lbs.

Year	Team		Games	BA	SA	AB	H	2B	3B	HR	HR%	R	RBI	BB	SO	SB	Pinch Hit AB	Pinch Hit H	PO	A	E	DP	TC/G	FA	G by Pos
1940	PHI	N	10	.129	.129	31	4	0	0	0	0.0	3	0	1	5	0	0	0	15	2	1	1	2.0	.944	OF-9

Shannon Stewart

STEWART, SHANNON HAROLD
B. Feb. 25, 1974, Cincinnati, Ohio.
BR TR 6′ 175 lbs.

Year	Team		Games	BA	SA	AB	H	2B	3B	HR	HR%	R	RBI	BB	SO	SB	Pinch Hit AB	Pinch Hit H	PO	A	E	DP	TC/G	FA	G by Pos
1995	TOR	A	12	.211	.211	38	8	0	0	0	0.0	2	1	5	5	2	0	0	20	1	1	0	1.8	.955	OF-12

Stuffy Stewart

STEWART, JOHN FRANKLIN
B. Jan. 31, 1894, Jasper, Fla. D. Dec. 30, 1980, Lake City, Fla.
BR TR 5′9½″ 160 lbs.

Year	Team		Games	BA	SA	AB	H	2B	3B	HR	HR%	R	RBI	BB	SO	SB	Pinch Hit AB	Pinch Hit H	PO	A	E	DP	TC/G	FA	G by Pos
1916	STL	N	9	.176	.176	17	3	0	0	0	0.0	0	1	0	3	0	0	0	11	9	4	2	3.0	.833	2B-8
1917			13	.000	.000	9	0	0	0	0	0.0	4	0	0	4	0	1	0	3	1	0	0	0.4	1.000	OF-7, 2B-2
1922	PIT	N	3	.154	.154	13	2	0	0	0	0.0	3	0	0	1	0	0	0	5	9	2	2	5.3	.875	2B-3
1923	BKN	N	4	.364	.727	11	4	1	0	1	9.1	3	1	1	1	0	0	0	4	7	3	1	4.7	.786	2B-3
1925	WAS	A	7	.353	.412	17	6	1	0	0	0.0	3	3	1	2	1	0	0	4	10	1	1	2.5	.933	3B-5, 2B-1
1926			62	.270	.397	63	17	6	1	0	0.0	27	9	6	6	8	3	1	33	48	2	8	3.2	.976	2B-25, 3B-1
1927			56	.240	.318	129	31	6	2	0	0.0	24	4	8	15	12	3	0	61	95	10	15	4.3	.940	2B-37, 3B-2
1929			22	.000	.000	6	0	0	0	0	0.0	10	0	1	0	0	2	0	3	4	0	0	2.3	1.000	2B-3
8 yrs.			176	.238	.325	265	63	14	3	1	0.4	74	18	17	32	21	9	1	124	183	22	29	3.4	.933	2B-82, 3B-8, OF-7

Tuffy Stewart

STEWART, CHARLES EUGENE
B. July 31, 1883, Chicago, Ill. D. Nov. 18, 1934, Chicago, Ill.
BL TL 5′10″ 167 lbs.

Year	Team		Games	BA	SA	AB	H	2B	3B	HR	HR%	R	RBI	BB	SO	SB	Pinch Hit AB	Pinch Hit H	PO	A	E	DP	TC/G	FA	G by Pos
1913	CHI	N	9	.125	.250	8	1	1	0	0	0.0	1	2	2	5	1	5	0	2	0	0	0	2.0	1.000	OF-1
1914			2	.000	.000	1	0	0	0	0	0.0	0	0	0	0	0	1	0	0	0	0	0	0.0	—	
2 yrs.			11	.111	.222	9	1	1	0	0	0.0	1	2	2	5	1	6	0	2	0	0	0	2.0	1.000	OF-1

Royle Stillman

STILLMAN, ROYLE ELDON
B. Jan. 2, 1951, Santa Monica, Calif.
BL TL 5′11″ 180 lbs.

Year	Team		Games	BA	SA	AB	H	2B	3B	HR	HR%	R	RBI	BB	SO	SB	Pinch Hit AB	Pinch Hit H	PO	A	E	DP	TC/G	FA	G by Pos
1975	BAL	A	13	.429	.429	14	6	0	0	0	0.0	1	1	1	3	0	4	1	3	0	0	0	1.5	1.000	OF-2
1976			20	.091	.091	22	2	0	0	0	0.0	0	1	3	4	0	15	1	2	0	0	0	0.3	1.000	DH-5, 1B-2
1977	CHI	A	56	.210	.361	119	25	7	1	3	2.5	18	13	17	21	2	17	3	47	0	1	0	1.2	.979	OF-26, DH-13, 1B-1
3 yrs.			89	.213	.329	155	33	7	1	3	1.9	19	15	21	28	2	36	5	52	0	1	0	1.1	.981	OF-28, DH-18, 1B-3

Kurt Stillwell

STILLWELL, KURT ANDREW
Son of Ron Stillwell.
B. June 4, 1965, Glendale, Calif.
BB TR 5′11″ 165 lbs.

Year	Team		Games	BA	SA	AB	H	2B	3B	HR	HR%	R	RBI	BB	SO	SB	Pinch Hit AB	Pinch Hit H	PO	A	E	DP	TC/G	FA	G by Pos
1986	CIN	N	104	.229	.258	279	64	6	1	0	0.0	31	26	30	47	6	20	6	107	205	16	40	4.1	.951	SS-80
1987			131	.258	.375	395	102	20	7	4	1.0	54	33	32	50	4	29	8	144	247	23	38	3.8	.944	SS-51, 2B-37, 3B-20
1988	KC	A	128	.251	.399	459	115	28	5	10	2.2	63	53	47	76	6	4	0	170	349	13	60	4.3	.976	SS-124
1989			130	.261	.380	463	121	20	7	7	1.5	52	54	42	64	9	4	1	179	334	16	65	4.1	.970	SS-130
1990			144	.249	.352	506	126	35	4	3	0.6	60	51	39	60	0	9	2	181	350	24	79	3.9	.957	SS-141
1991			122	.265	.361	385	102	17	1	6	1.6	44	51	33	56	3	18	2	163	263	18	66	3.8	.959	SS-118
1992	SD	N	114	.227	.298	379	86	15	3	2	0.5	35	24	26	58	4	5	1	250	266	16	66	4.8	.970	2B-111
1993	2 teams		SD N (57G –.215) CAL A (22G –.262)																						
"	total		79	.231	.302	182	42	6	2	1	0.5	11	14	15	33	6	28	7	93	114	14	21	3.8	.937	SS-37, 2B-18, 3B-3
8 yrs.			952	.249	.349	3048	758	147	30	33	1.1	350	306	264	444	38	117	27	1287	2128	140	435	4.1	.961	SS-681, 2B-166, 3B-23

Ron Stillwell

STILLWELL, RONALD ROY
Father of Kurt Stillwell.
B. Dec. 3, 1939, Los Angeles, Calif.
BR TR 5′11″ 165 lbs.

Year	Team		Games	BA	SA	AB	H	2B	3B	HR	HR%	R	RBI	BB	SO	SB	Pinch Hit AB	Pinch Hit H	PO	A	E	DP	TC/G	FA	G by Pos
1961	WAS	A	8	.125	.188	16	2	1	0	0	0.0	3	1	1	4	0	1	1	4	9	1	4	2.8	.929	SS-5
1962			6	.273	.273	22	6	0	0	0	0.0	5	2	2	2	0	0	0	16	12	0	3	4.0	1.000	2B-6, SS-1
2 yrs.			14	.211	.237	38	8	1	0	0	0.0	8	3	3	6	0	1	1	20	21	1	7	3.5	.976	2B-6, SS-6

Craig Stimac

STIMAC, CRAIG STEVEN
B. Nov. 18, 1954, Oak Park, Ill.
BR TR 6′2″ 185 lbs.

Year	Team		Games	BA	SA	AB	H	2B	3B	HR	HR%	R	RBI	BB	SO	SB	Pinch Hit AB	Pinch Hit H	PO	A	E	DP	TC/G	FA	G by Pos
1980	SD	N	20	.220	.260	50	11	2	0	0	0.0	5	7	1	6	0	8	2	51	16	2	2	5.3	.971	C-11, 3B-2
1981			9	.111	.111	9	1	0	0	0	0.0	0	0	0	3	0	9	1	0	0	0	0	0.0	—	
2 yrs.			29	.203	.237	59	12	2	0	0	0.0	5	7	1	9	0	17	3	51	16	2	2	5.3	.971	C-11, 3B-2

Kelly Stinnett

STINNETT, KELLY LEE
B. Feb. 14, 1970, Lawton, Okla.
BR TR 5′11″ 195 lbs.

Year	Team		Games	BA	SA	AB	H	2B	3B	HR	HR%	R	RBI	BB	SO	SB	Pinch Hit AB	Pinch Hit H	PO	A	E	DP	TC/G	FA	G by Pos
1994	NY	N	47	.253	.360	150	38	6	2	2	1.3	20	14	11	28	2	4	0	211	20	5	2	5.4	.979	C-44
1995			77	.219	.332	196	43	8	1	4	2.0	23	18	29	65	2	9	1	380	22	7	1	6.1	.983	C-67
2 yrs.			124	.234	.344	346	81	14	3	6	1.7	43	32	40	93	4	13	1	591	42	12	3	5.8	.981	C-111

Bob Stinson

STINSON, GORRELL ROBERT
B. Oct. 11, 1945, Elkin, N. C.
BB TR 5′11″ 180 lbs.
BR 1969

Year	Team		Games	BA	SA	AB	H	2B	3B	HR	HR%	R	RBI	BB	SO	SB	Pinch Hit AB	Pinch Hit H	PO	A	E	DP	TC/G	FA	G by Pos
1969	LA	N	4	.375	.375	8	3	0	0	0	0.0	1	2	0	2	0	0	0	20	0	1	0	5.3	.952	C-4
1970			4	.000	.000	3	0	0	0	0	0.0	1	0	0	1	0	0	0	3	0	0	0	1.0	1.000	C-3
1971	STL	N	17	.211	.263	19	4	1	0	0	0.0	3	1	1	7	0	2	1	36	0	1	0	4.1	.973	C-6, OF-3
1972	HOU	N	27	.171	.200	35	6	1	0	0	0.0	3	2	1	6	0	15	1	26	2	1	0	1.9	.966	C-12, OF-3
1973	MON	N	48	.261	.414	111	29	6	1	3	2.7	12	12	17	15	0	10	3	174	9	4	2	5.2	.979	C-35, 3B-1

Bob Stinson *continued*

Year	Team		Games	BA	SA	AB	H	2B	3B	HR	HR%	R	RBI	BB	SO	SB	Pinch Hit AB	Pinch Hit H	PO	A	E	DP	TC/G	FA	G by Pos
1974			38	.172	.230	87	15	2	0	1	1.1	4	6	15	16	1	12	3	122	14	0	4	4.7	1.000	C-29
1975	KC	A	63	.265	.361	147	39	9	1	1	0.7	18	9	18	29	1	4	0	257	33	2	4	4.6	.993	C-59, 2B-1, DH-1, OF-1, 1B-1
1976			79	.263	.335	209	55	7	1	2	1.0	26	25	25	29	3	2	0	304	30	7	4	4.3	.979	C-79
1977	SEA	A	105	.269	.394	297	80	11	1	8	2.7	27	32	37	50	0	11	2	494	43	9	11	5.5	.984	C-99, DH-1
1978			124	.258	.404	364	94	14	3	11	3.0	46	55	45	42	2	7	1	472	60	7	7	4.3	.987	C-123, DH-1
1979			95	.243	.348	247	60	8	0	6	2.4	19	28	33	38	1	7	1	376	29	9	2	4.5	.978	C-91
1980			48	.215	.262	107	23	2	0	1	0.9	6	8	9	19	0	12	1	135	8	3	2	3.2	.979	C-45
12 yrs.			652	.250	.356	1634	408	61	7	33	2.0	166	180	201	254	8	82	13	2419	228	44	36	4.5	.984	C-585, OF-7, DH-3, 2B-1, 1B-1, 3B-1
LEAGUE CHAMPIONSHIP SERIES																									
1976	KC	A	2	.000	.000	1	0	0	0	0	0.0	0	0	0	0	0	1	0	0	0	0	0	0.0	.000	C-1

Snuffy Stirnweiss

STIRNWEISS, GEORGE HENRY BR TR 5′ 8½″ 175 lbs.
B. Oct. 26, 1918, New York, N. Y. D. Sept. 15, 1958, Newark, N. J.

Year	Team		Games	BA	SA	AB	H	2B	3B	HR	HR%	R	RBI	BB	SO	SB	Pinch Hit AB	Pinch Hit H	PO	A	E	DP	TC/G	FA	G by Pos
1943	NY	A	83	.219	.288	274	60	8	4	1	0.4	34	25	47	37	11	3	0	124	200	20	55	4.8	.942	SS-68, 2B-4
1944			154	.319	.460	643	**205**	35	**16**	8	1.2	**125**	43	73	87	**55**	0	0	433	481	17	113	6.0	.982	2B-154
1945			152	**.309**	**.476**	**632**	**195**	32	**22**	10	1.6	**107**	64	78	62	**33**	0	0	432	492	29	119	6.3	.970	2B-152
1946			129	.251	.318	487	122	19	7	0	0.0	75	37	66	58	18	3	0	159	299	8	49	3.6	.983	3B-79, 2B-46, SS-4
1947			148	.256	.342	571	146	18	8	5	0.9	102	41	89	47	5	0	0	337	402	13	107	5.1	.983	2B-148
1948			141	.252	.336	515	130	20	7	3	0.6	90	32	86	62	5	0	0	346	364	5	103	5.1	.993	2B-141
1949			70	.261	.338	157	41	8	2	0	0.0	29	11	29	20	3	5	1	124	109	6	34	4.3	.975	2B-51, 3B-4
1950	2 teams		NY A (7G –.000) STL A (93G –.218)																						
″	total		100	.216	.287	328	71	16	2	1	0.3	32	24	51	49	3	2	1	200	215	13	51	4.2	.970	2B-66, 3B-32, SS-5
1951	CLE	A	50	.216	.261	88	19	1	0	1	1.1	10	4	22	25	1	9	1	49	77	1	18	4.7	.992	2B-25, 3B-2
1952			1	—	—	0	0	0	0	0	—	0	0	0	0	0	0	0	0	0	0	0	0.0	.000	3B-1
10 yrs.			1028	.268	.371	3695	989	157	68	29	0.8	604	281	541	447	134	22	3	2204	2639	112	649	5.0	.977	2B-787, 3B-118, SS-77
WORLD SERIES																									
1943	NY	A	1	.000	.000	1	0	0	0	0	0.0	1	0	0	0	0	1	0	0	0	0	0	0.0	—	
1947			7	.259	.333	27	7	0	1	0	0.0	3	3	8	8	0	0	0	17	21	0	2	5.4	1.000	2B-7
1949			1	—	—	0	0	0	0	0	—	0	0	0	0	0	0	0	0	0	0	0	0.0	—	
3 yrs.			9	.250	.321	28	7	0	1	0	0.0	4	3	8	8	0	1	0	17	21	0	2	5.4	1.000	2B-7

Jack Stivetts

STIVETTS, JOHN ELMER (Happy Jack) BR TR 6′ 2″ 185 lbs.
B. Mar. 31, 1868, Ashland, Pa. D. Apr. 18, 1930, Ashland, Pa.

Year	Team		Games	BA	SA	AB	H	2B	3B	HR	HR%	R	RBI	BB	SO	SB	Pinch Hit AB	Pinch Hit H	PO	A	E	DP	TC/G	FA	G by Pos
1889	STL	AA	27	.228	.304	79	18	2	2	0	0.0	12	7	3	13	0	0	0	12	43	6	0	2.3	.902	P-26, OF-1
1890			67	.288	.500	226	65	15	6	7	3.1	36		16		2	0	0	65	89	17	6	2.6	.901	P-54, OF-10, 1B-3
1891			85	.305	.421	302	92	10	2	7	2.3	45	54	10	32	4	**2**	0	51	113	17	4	2.1	.906	P-64, OF-24
1892	BOS	N	70	.296	.408	240	71	14	2	3	1.3	40	36	27	28	8	0	0	53	97	16	8	2.3	.904	P-53, OF-18, 1B-1
1893			49	.297	.448	172	51	5	6	3	1.7	32	25	12	14	6	1	0	31	55	7	3	1.9	.925	P-37, OF-8, 3B-3
1894			68	.328	.533	244	80	12	7	8	3.3	55	64	16	21	3	**5**	**2**	79	53	13	5	2.2	.910	P-45, OF-16, 1B-4
1895			46	.190	.278	158	30	6	4	0	0.0	20	24	6	18	1	2	1	76	53	4	5	3.0	.970	P-38, 1B-5, OF-2
1896			67	.344	.480	221	76	9	6	3	1.4	42	49	12	10	4	5	4	90	62	15	4	2.8	.910	P-42, OF-12, 1B-5, 3B-1
1897			61	.367	.533	199	73	9	9	2	1.0	41	37	15		2	10	3	68	45	8	3	2.4	.934	OF-29, P-18, 2B-2, 1B-2
1898			41	.252	.333	111	28	1	1	2	1.8	16	16	10		1	10	2	97	22	10	4	4.0	.922	OF-14, 1B-10, SS-4, 2B-2, P-2
1899	CLE	N	18	.205	.282	39	8	1	1	0	0.0	8	2	6		0	3	0	14	20	1	0	2.2	.971	OF-7, P-7, 3B-1, SS-1
11 yrs.			599	.297	.438	1991	592	84	46	35	1.8	347	314	133	136	31	38	12	636	652	114	42	2.5	.919	P-386, OF-141, 1B-30, SS-5, 3B-5, 2B-4

Milt Stock

STOCK, MILTON JOSEPH BR TR 5′ 8″ 154 lbs.
B. July 11, 1893, Chicago, Ill. D. July 16, 1977, Fairhope, Ala.

Year	Team		Games	BA	SA	AB	H	2B	3B	HR	HR%	R	RBI	BB	SO	SB	Pinch Hit AB	Pinch Hit H	PO	A	E	DP	TC/G	FA	G by Pos
1913	NY	N	7	.176	.235	17	3	1	0	0	0.0	2	1	2	1	2	0	0	12	19	6	4	37.0	.838	SS-1
1914			115	.263	.340	365	96	17	1	3	0.8	52	41	34	21	11	0	0	97	266	23	17	3.4	.940	3B-113, SS-1
1915	PHI	N	69	.260	.330	227	59	7	3	1	0.4	37	15	22	26	6	10	1	64	108	5	7	3.0	.972	3B-55, SS-4
1916			132	.281	.360	509	143	25	6	1	0.2	61	43	27	33	21	3	1	150	259	23	29	3.3	.947	3B-117, SS-15
1917			150	.264	.349	564	149	27	6	3	0.5	76	53	51	34	25	0	0	176	315	33	20	3.4	.937	3B-133, SS-19
1918			123	.274	.314	481	132	14	1	1	0.2	62	42	35	22	20	1	0	132	273	23	16	3.5	.946	3B-123
1919	STL	N	135	.307	.356	492	151	16	4	0	0.0	56	52	49	21	17	0	0	219	393	29	47	4.7	.955	2B-77, 3B-58
1920			155	.319	.382	**639**	204	28	6	0	0.0	85	76	40	27	15	0	0	158	300	30	23	3.1	.939	3B-155
1921			149	.307	.388	587	180	27	6	3	0.5	96	84	48	26	11	0	0	148	243	25	21	2.8	.940	3B-149
1922			151	.305	.418	581	177	33	9	5	0.9	85	79	42	29	7	1	0	175	247	22	22	3.0	.950	3B-149, SS-1
1923			151	.289	.363	603	174	33	3	2	0.3	63	96	40	21	9	1	0	166	261	20	24	3.0	.955	3B-150, 2B-1
1924	BKN	N	142	.242	.292	561	136	14	4	2	0.4	66	52	26	32	3	0	0	139	200	25	14	2.6	.931	3B-142
1925			146	.328	.408	615	202	28	9	1	0.2	98	62	38	28	8	0	0	315	489	19	75	5.6	.977	2B-141, 3B-5
1926			3	.000	.000	8	0	0	0	0	0.0	0	0	1	0	0	0	0	4	8	1	1	4.3	.923	2B-3
14 yrs.			1628	.289	.361	6249	1806	270	58	22	0.4	839	696	455	321	155	16	2	1955	3381	284	320	3.5	.949	3B-1349, 2B-222, SS-41
WORLD SERIES																									
1915	PHI	N	5	.118	.176	17	2	1	0	0	0.0	1	0	1	0	0	0	0	1	8	0	0	1.8	1.000	3B-5

Kevin Stocker

STOCKER, KEVIN DOUGLAS BB TR 6′ 1″ 175 lbs.
B. Feb. 13, 1970, Spokane, Wash.

Year	Team		Games	BA	SA	AB	H	2B	3B	HR	HR%	R	RBI	BB	SO	SB	Pinch Hit AB	Pinch Hit H	PO	A	E	DP	TC/G	FA	G by Pos
1993	PHI	N	70	.324	.417	259	84	12	3	2	0.8	46	31	30	43	5	0	0	118	202	14	44	4.8	.958	SS-70
1994			82	.273	.351	271	74	11	2	2	0.7	38	28	44	41	2	0	0	118	253	16	46	4.7	.959	SS-82
1995			125	.218	.274	412	90	14	3	1	0.2	42	32	43	75	6	0	0	148	383	17	71	4.4	.969	SS-125
3 yrs.			277	.263	.335	942	248	37	8	5	0.5	126	91	117	159	13	0	0	384	838	47	161	4.6	.963	SS-277
LEAGUE CHAMPIONSHIP SERIES																									
1993	PHI	N	6	.182	.227	22	4	1	0	0	0.0	0	1	2	5	0	0	0	9	14	1	1	4.0	.958	SS-6
WORLD SERIES																									
1993	PHI	N	6	.211	.263	19	4	1	0	0	0.0	1	1	5	5	0	0	0	8	13	0	4	3.5	1.000	SS-6

Len Stockwell

STOCKWELL, LEONARD CLARK BR TR 5′11″ 165 lbs.
B. Aug. 25, 1859, Cordova, Ill. D. Jan. 28, 1905, Niles, Calif.

Year	Team		Games	BA	SA	AB	H	2B	3B	HR	HR%	R	RBI	BB	SO	SB	Pinch Hit AB	Pinch Hit H	PO	A	E	DP	TC/G	FA	G by Pos
1879	**CLE**	**N**	2	.000	.000	6	0	0	0	0	0.0	0	0	0	2		0	0	2	2	0	1	2.0	1.000	OF-2
1884	**LOU**	**AA**	2	.111	.111	9	1	0	0	0	0.0	0		0			0	0	4	2	2	0	2.7	.750	OF-2, C-1
1890	**CLE**	**N**	2	.286	.429	7	2	1	0	0	0.0	2	0	0	3	0	0	0	10	1	3	0	7.0	.786	OF-1, 1B-1
3 yrs.			6	.136	.182	22	3	1	0	0	0.0	2	0	0	5	0	0	0	16	5	5	1	3.7	.808	OF-5, 1B-1, C-1

Al Stokes

STOKES, ALBERT JOHN BR TR 5′ 9″ 175 lbs.
Born Albert John Stocek.
B. Jan. 1, 1900, Chicago, Ill. D. Dec. 19, 1986, Grantham, N. H.

Year	Team		Games	BA	SA	AB	H	2B	3B	HR	HR%	R	RBI	BB	SO	SB	Pinch Hit AB	Pinch Hit H	PO	A	E	DP	TC/G	FA	G by Pos
1925	**BOS**	**A**	17	.212	.250	52	11	0	1	0	0.0	7	1	4	8	0	0	0	40	23	2	3	3.8	.969	C-17
1926			30	.163	.267	86	14	3	3	0	0.0	7	6	8	28	0	1	0	70	24	7	3	3.5	.931	C-29
2 yrs.			47	.181	.261	138	25	3	4	0	0.0	14	7	12	36	0	1	0	110	47	9	6	3.6	.946	C-46

Gene Stone

STONE, EUGENE DANIEL BL TL 5′11″ 190 lbs.
B. Jan. 16, 1944, Burbank, Calif.

Year	Team		Games	BA	SA	AB	H	2B	3B	HR	HR%	R	RBI	BB	SO	SB	Pinch Hit AB	Pinch Hit H	PO	A	E	DP	TC/G	FA	G by Pos
1969	**PHI**	**N**	18	.214	.286	28	6	0	1	0	0.0	4	0	4	9	0	10	2	43	1	0	3	8.8	1.000	1B-5

George Stone

STONE, GEORGE ROBERT BL TL 5′ 9″ 175 lbs.
B. Sept. 3, 1877, Lost Nation, Iowa D. Jan. 3, 1945, Clinton, Iowa.

Year	Team		Games	BA	SA	AB	H	2B	3B	HR	HR%	R	RBI	BB	SO	SB	Pinch Hit AB	Pinch Hit H	PO	A	E	DP	TC/G	FA	G by Pos
1903	**BOS**	**A**	2	.000	.000	2	0	0	0	0	0.0	0	0	0		0	2	0	0	0	0	0	0.0	—	
1905	**STL**	**A**	154	.296	.410	**632**	**187**	25	13	7	1.1	76	52	44		26	0	0	278	15	14	5	2.0	.954	OF-154
1906			154	**.358**	**.501**	581	208	25	20	6	1.0	91	71	52		35	0	0	295	10	10	3	2.0	.968	OF-154
1907			155	.320	.399	596	191	13	11	4	0.7	77	59	59		23	0	0	276	12	9	5	1.9	.970	OF-155
1908			148	.281	.369	588	165	21	8	5	0.9	89	31	55		20	0	0	274	11	16	3	2.0	.947	OF-148
1909			83	.287	.339	310	89	5	4	1	0.3	33	15	24		8	2	0	147	8	12	4	2.1	.928	OF-81
1910			152	.256	.329	562	144	17	12	0	0.0	60	40	48		20	5	1	220	20	7	2	1.7	.972	OF-147
7 yrs.			848	.301	.396	3271	984	106	68	23	0.7	426	268	282		132	9	1	1490	76	68	22	1.9	.958	OF-839

Jeff Stone

STONE, JEFFREY GLEN BL TR 6′ 175 lbs.
B. Dec. 26, 1960, Kennett, Mo.

Year	Team		Games	BA	SA	AB	H	2B	3B	HR	HR%	R	RBI	BB	SO	SB	Pinch Hit AB	Pinch Hit H	PO	A	E	DP	TC/G	FA	G by Pos
1983	**PHI**	**N**	9	.750	1.750	4	3	0	2	0	0.0	2	3	0	1	4	1	1	0	0	0	0	0.0	.000	OF-1
1984			51	.362	.465	185	67	4	6	1	0.5	27	15	9	26	27	5	0	75	1	7	0	1.8	.916	OF-46
1985			88	.265	.337	264	70	4	3	3	1.1	36	11	15	50	15	18	5	82	4	3	0	1.3	.966	OF-69
1986			82	.277	.406	249	69	6	4	6	2.4	32	19	20	52	19	21	7	103	8	2	1	1.9	.982	OF-58
1987			66	.256	.352	125	32	7	1	1	0.8	19	16	8	38	3	37	9	32	3	0	1	1.4	1.000	OF-25
1988	**BAL**	**A**	26	.164	.180	61	10	1	0	0	0.0	4	1	4	11	4	7	2	23	3	1	1	1.2	.963	OF-21, DH-1
1989	**2 teams**		**TEX A** (22G –.167)	**BOS A** (18G –.200)																					
″	**total**		40	.176	.275	51	9	1	2	0	0.0	8	6	4	7	3	12	1	8	0	0	0	0.3	1.000	DH-18, OF-14
1990	**BOS**	**A**	10	.500	.500	2	1	0	0	0	0.0	1	1	0	1	0	1	0	0	0	0	0	0.0	.000	DH-2
8 yrs.			372	.277	.375	941	261	23	18	11	1.2	129	72	60	186	75	102	25	323	19	13	3	1.4	.963	OF-234, DH-21

John Stone

STONE, JOHN THOMAS (Rocky) BL TR 6′ 1″ 178 lbs.
B. Oct. 10, 1905, Lynchburg, Tenn. D. Nov. 30, 1955, Shelbyville, Tenn.

Year	Team		Games	BA	SA	AB	H	2B	3B	HR	HR%	R	RBI	BB	SO	SB	Pinch Hit AB	Pinch Hit H	PO	A	E	DP	TC/G	FA	G by Pos
1928	**DET**	**A**	26	.354	.549	113	40	10	3	2	1.8	20	21	5	8	1	0	0	49	2	2	0	2.0	.962	OF-26
1929			51	.260	.400	150	39	11	2	2	1.3	23	15	11	13	1	15	4	68	4	1	0	2.0	.986	OF-36
1930			126	.313	.455	422	132	29	11	3	0.7	60	56	32	49	6	18	4	222	5	8	1	2.2	.966	OF-108
1931			147	.327	.464	584	191	28	11	10	1.7	86	76	56	48	13	0	0	319	11	14	6	2.3	.959	OF-147
1932			144	.297	.486	582	173	35	12	17	2.9	106	108	58	64	2	3	0	334	11	14	2	2.5	.961	OF-141
1933			148	.280	.434	574	161	33	11	11	1.9	86	80	54	37	1	5	3	280	11	9	1	2.1	.970	OF-141
1934	**WAS**	**A**	113	.315	.465	419	132	28	7	7	1.7	77	67	52	26	1	4	2	245	13	9	3	2.4	.966	OF-112
1935			125	.315	.460	454	143	27	18	1	0.2	78	78	39	29	4	14	2	224	12	11	4	2.2	.955	OF-114
1936			123	.341	.545	437	149	22	11	15	3.4	95	90	60	26	8	6	2	249	12	9	5	2.4	.967	OF-114
1937			139	.330	.480	542	179	33	15	6	1.1	84	88	66	36	6	1	0	300	15	5	3	2.3	.984	OF-137
1938			56	.244	.380	213	52	12	4	3	1.4	24	28	30	16	2	1	0	107	5	3	0	2.2	.974	OF-53
11 yrs.			1198	.310	.468	4490	1391	268	105	77	1.7	739	707	463	352	45	67	17	2397	101	85	25	2.3	.967	OF-1129

Ron Stone

STONE, HARRY RONALD BL TL 6′ 2″ 185 lbs.
B. Sept. 9, 1942, Corning, Calif.

Year	Team		Games	BA	SA	AB	H	2B	3B	HR	HR%	R	RBI	BB	SO	SB	Pinch Hit AB	Pinch Hit H	PO	A	E	DP	TC/G	FA	G by Pos
1966	**KC**	**A**	26	.273	.318	22	6	1	0	0	0.0	2	0	0	2	1	15	4	14	2	2	3	2.6	.889	OF-4, 1B-3
1969	**PHI**	**N**	103	.239	.293	222	53	7	1	1	0.5	22	24	29	28	3	28	2	85	6	2	0	1.3	.978	OF-69
1970			123	.262	.358	321	84	12	5	3	0.9	30	39	38	45	5	23	4	164	5	6	1	1.7	.966	OF-99, 1B-6
1971			95	.227	.314	185	42	8	1	2	1.1	16	23	25	36	2	43	7	93	6	4	2	1.9	.961	OF-51, 1B-3
1972			41	.167	.204	54	9	0	1	0	0.0	3	3	9	11	0	22	3	24	3	0	0	1.8	1.000	OF-15
5 yrs.			388	.241	.318	804	194	28	8	6	0.7	73	89	101	122	11	131	20	380	22	14	6	1.7	.966	OF-238, 1B-12

Tige Stone

STONE, WILLIAM ARTHUR BR TR 5′ 8″ 145 lbs.
B. Sept. 18, 1901, Macon, Ga. D. Jan. 1, 1960, Jacksonville, Fla.

Year	Team		Games	BA	SA	AB	H	2B	3B	HR	HR%	R	RBI	BB	SO	SB	Pinch Hit AB	Pinch Hit H	PO	A	E	DP	TC/G	FA	G by Pos
1923	**STL**	**N**	5	1.000	1.000	1	1	0	0	0	0.0	0	0	2	0	0	0	0	0	2	0	0	0.4	1.000	OF-4, P-1

John Stoneham

STONEHAM, JOHN ANDREW BL TR 5′ 9½″ 168 lbs.
B. Nov. 8, 1908, Wood River, Ill.

Year	Team		Games	BA	SA	AB	H	2B	3B	HR	HR%	R	RBI	BB	SO	SB	Pinch Hit AB	Pinch Hit H	PO	A	E	DP	TC/G	FA	G by Pos
1933	**CHI**	**A**	10	.120	.240	25	3	0	0	1	4.0	4	3	2	2	0	0	0	13	0	0	0	1.4	1.000	OF-9

Howie Storie

STORIE, HOWARD EDWARD BR TR 5′10″ 175 lbs.
B. May 15, 1911, Pittsfield, Mass. D. July 27, 1968, Pittsfield, Mass.

Year	Team		Games	BA	SA	AB	H	2B	3B	HR	HR%	R	RBI	BB	SO	SB	Pinch Hit AB	Pinch Hit H	PO	A	E	DP	TC/G	FA	G by Pos
1931	**BOS**	**A**	6	.118	.118	17	2	0	0	0	0.0	2	0	3	2	0	0	0	20	3	0	0	3.8	1.000	C-6
1932			6	.375	.375	8	3	0	0	0	0.0	0	0	0	0	0	1	0	11	0	0	0	2.2	1.000	C-5
2 yrs.			12	.200	.200	25	5	0	0	0	0.0	2	0	3	2	0	1	0	31	3	0	0	3.1	1.000	C-11

Alan Storke

STORKE, ALAN MARSHALL BR TR 6′ 1″
B. Sept. 27, 1884, Auburn, N. Y. D. Mar. 18, 1910, Newton, Mass.

Year	Team		Games	BA	SA	AB	H	2B	3B	HR	HR%	R	RBI	BB	SO	SB	Pinch Hit AB	Pinch Hit H	PO	A	E	DP	TC/G	FA	G by Pos
1906	**PIT**	**N**	5	.250	.333	12	3	1	0	0	0.0	1	1	1		1	2	1	2	9	1	1	4.0	.917	3B-2, SS-1
1907			112	.258	.317	357	92	6	6	1	0.3	24	39	16		6	10	3	275	160	28	19	4.5	.940	3B-67, 1B-23, 2B-7, SS-5

Alan Storke *continued*

Year	Team	Games	BA	SA	AB	H	2B	3B	HR	HR%	R	RBI	BB	SO	SB	Pinch Hit AB	Pinch Hit H	PO	A	E	DP	TC/G	FA	G by Pos
1908		64	.252	.322	202	51	5	3	1	0.5	20	12	9		4	8	0	487	28	8	19	9.3	.985	1B-49, 3B-6, 2B-1
1909	2 teams	PIT N (37G –.254) STL N (48G –.282)																						
″	total	85	.271	.318	292	79	10	2	0	0.0	23	22	19		6	4	1	280	189	15	26	6.0	.969	SS-44, 1B-19, 3B-14, 2B-4
4 yrs.		266	.261	.319	863	225	22	11	2	0.2	68	74	45		17	24	5	1044	386	52	65	6.1	.965	1B-91, 3B-89, SS-50, 2B-12

Lin Storti

STORTI, LINDO IVAN BB TR 5′11″ 165 lbs.
B. Dec. 5, 1906, Santa Monica, Calif. D. July 24, 1982, Ontario, Calif.

Year	Team	Games	BA	SA	AB	H	2B	3B	HR	HR%	R	RBI	BB	SO	SB	Pinch Hit AB	Pinch Hit H	PO	A	E	DP	TC/G	FA	G by Pos
1930	STL A	7	.321	.429	28	9	1	1	0	0.0	6	2	2	6	0	1	0	19	20	1	8	6.7	.975	2B-6
1931		86	.220	.337	273	60	15	4	3	1.1	32	26	15	50	0	9	2	91	149	18	24	3.5	.930	3B-67, 2B-7
1932		53	.259	.383	193	50	11	2	3	1.6	19	26	5	20	1	2	0	50	81	6	8	2.7	.956	3B-51
1933		70	.195	.310	210	41	7	4	3	1.4	26	21	25	31	2	13	3	105	113	8	26	4.0	.965	3B-32, 2B-24
4 yrs.		216	.227	.345	704	160	34	11	9	1.3	83	75	47	107	3	25	5	265	363	33	66	3.5	.950	3B-150, 2B-37

Tom Stouch

STOUCH, THOMAS CARL BR TR 6′ 2″ 165 lbs.
B. Dec. 2, 1870, Perrysville, Ohio D. Oct. 7, 1956, Lancaster, Pa.

Year	Team	Games	BA	SA	AB	H	2B	3B	HR	HR%	R	RBI	BB	SO	SB	Pinch Hit AB	Pinch Hit H	PO	A	E	DP	TC/G	FA	G by Pos
1898	LOU N	4	.313	.375	16	5	1	0	0	0.0	4	6	1		0	0	0	8	9	3	1	5.0	.850	2B-4

George Stovall

STOVALL, GEORGE THOMAS (Firebrand) BR TR 6′ 2″ 180 lbs.
Brother of Jesse Stovall.
B. Nov. 23, 1878, Independence, Mo. D. Nov. 5, 1951, Burlington, Iowa.
Manager 1911–15.

Year	Team	Games	BA	SA	AB	H	2B	3B	HR	HR%	R	RBI	BB	SO	SB	Pinch Hit AB	Pinch Hit H	PO	A	E	DP	TC/G	FA	G by Pos
1904	CLE A	52	.297	.379	182	54	10	1	1	0.5	18	31	2		4	1	0	391	44	12	20	8.8	.973	1B-38, 2B-9, OF-3, 3B-1
1905		111	.272	.368	419	114	31	3	1	0.2	41	47	13		13	3	0	751	161	30	35	8.6	.968	1B-59, 2B-46, OF-4
1906		116	.273	.339	443	121	19	5	0	0.0	54	37	8		15	9	3	666	153	21	53	8.1	.975	1B-55, 3B-30, 2B-19
1907		124	.236	.305	466	110	17	6	1	0.2	38	36	18		13	0	0	1382	71	25	90	11.9	.983	1B-122, 3B-2
1908		138	.292	.380	534	156	29	6	2	0.4	71	45	17		14	0	0	1524	89	16	79	11.8	.990	1B-132, OF-5, SS-1
1909		145	.246	.322	565	139	17	10	2	0.4	60	49	6		25	0	0	1478	109	19	80	11.1	.988	1B-145
1910		142	.261	.313	521	136	19	4	0	0.0	47	52	14		16	7	2	1404	91	18	60	11.3	.988	1B-132, 2B-2
1911		126	.271	.338	458	124	17	7	0	0.0	48	79	21		11	5	1	1076	92	19	56	9.9	.984	1B-118, 2B-2
1912	STL A	115	.254	.322	398	101	17	5	0	0.0	35	45	14		11	21	4	845	68	16	64	9.9	.983	1B-94
1913		89	.287	.363	303	87	14	3	1	0.3	34	24	7	23	7	13	2	751	65	10	38	10.9	.988	1B-76
1914	KC F	124	.284	.398	450	128	20	5	7	1.6	51	75	23		6	8	2	1201	70	14	82	11.0	.989	1B-116, 3B-1
1915		130	.231	.287	480	111	21	3	0	0.0	48	44	31		8	1	0	1417	87	20	61	11.8	.987	1B-129
12 yrs.		1412	.265	.340	5219	1381	231	58	15	0.3	545	564	174	23	143	68	14	12886	1100	220	718	10.6	.985	1B-1216, 2B-78, 3B-34, OF-12, SS-1

Harry Stovey

STOVEY, HARRY DUFFIELD BR TR 5′11½″ 180 lbs.
Born Harry Duffield Stowe.
B. Dec. 20, 1856, Philadelphia, Pa. D. Sept. 20, 1937, New Bedford, Mass.
Manager 1881, 1885.

Year	Team	Games	BA	SA	AB	H	2B	3B	HR	HR%	R	RBI	BB	SO	SB	Pinch Hit AB	Pinch Hit H	PO	A	E	DP	TC/G	FA	G by Pos
1880	WOR N	83	.265	.454	355	94	21	**14**	**6**	1.7	76	28	12	46		0	0	514	18	35	21	6.7	.938	OF-46, 1B-37, P-2
1881		75	.270	.402	341	92	25	7	2	0.6	57	30	12	23		0	0	592	17	32	26	8.5	.950	1B-57, OF-18
1882		84	.289	.422	360	104	13	10	5	1.4	90	26	22	34		0	0	557	25	45	27	7.5	.928	1B-43, OF-41
1883	PHI AA	94	.302	**.504**	421	127	**31**	6	**14**	**3.3**	**110**		26			0	0	985	23	39	31	10.8	.963	1B-93, OF-3, P-1
1884		104	.326	.545	448	146	22	**23**	10	2.2	**124**		26			0	0	1061	32	45	46	10.9	.960	1B-104
1885		112	.315	.488	486	153	27	9	**13**	**2.7**	**130**		39			0	0	927	36	44	49	9.0	.956	1B-82, OF-30
1886		123	.294	.440	489	144	28	11	**7**	**1.4**	115		64			0	0	798	25	56	30	7.0	.936	OF-63, 1B-62, P-1
1887		124	.286	.421	497	142	31	12	4	0.8	125		56		74	0	0	613	35	36	22	5.4	.947	OF-80, 1B-46
1888		130	.287	.460	530	152	25	**20**	9	1.7	127	65	62		87	0	0	329	16	14	10	2.7	.961	OF-118, 1B-13
1889		137	.308	**.525**	556	171	38	13	**19**	**3.4**	**152**	**119**	77	68	63	0	0	287	38	37	9	2.6	.898	OF-137, 1B-1
1890	BOS P	118	.297	.470	481	143	25	11	12	2.5	142	83	81	38	**97**	0	0	189	24	19	4	1.7	.918	OF-134, 1B-1
1891	BOS N	134	.279	**.498**	544	152	31	**20**	**16**	2.9	118	95	78	**69**	57	0	0	233	22	25	4	2.1	.911	OF-135, 1B-1
1892	2 teams	BOS N (38G –.164) BAL N (74G –.272)																						
″	total	112	.235	.371	429	101	22	12	4	0.9	79	67	54	51	40	0	0	285	14	27	7	2.9	.917	OF-102, 1B-10
1893	2 teams	BAL N (8G –.154) BKN N (48G –.251)																						
″	total	56	.239	.353	201	48	8	6	1	0.5	47	34	52	14	23	1	0	133	4	16	0	2.8	.895	OF-55
14 yrs.		1486	.288	.461	6138	1769	347	174	122	2.0	1492	547	661	343	441	1	0	7503	329	470	286	5.5	.943	OF-962, 1B-550, P-4

Ray Stoviak

STOVIAK, RAYMOND THOMAS BL TL 6′ 1″ 195 lbs.
B. June 6, 1915, Scottdale, Pa.

Year	Team	Games	BA	SA	AB	H	2B	3B	HR	HR%	R	RBI	BB	SO	SB	Pinch Hit AB	Pinch Hit H	PO	A	E	DP	TC/G	FA	G by Pos
1938	PHI N	10	.000	.000	10	0	0	0	0	0.0	1	0	0	3	0	3	0	1	1	0	0	0.5	1.000	OF-4

Joe Strain

STRAIN, JOSEPH ALLAN, JR. BR TR 5′10″ 169 lbs.
B. Apr. 30, 1954, Denver, Colo.

Year	Team	Games	BA	SA	AB	H	2B	3B	HR	HR%	R	RBI	BB	SO	SB	Pinch Hit AB	Pinch Hit H	PO	A	E	DP	TC/G	FA	G by Pos
1979	SF N	67	.241	.292	257	62	8	1	1	0.4	27	12	13	21	8	0	0	147	189	6	32	5.0	.982	2B-67, 3B-1
1980		77	.286	.317	189	54	6	0	0	0.0	26	16	10	10	1	30	8	88	113	4	16	4.2	.980	2B-42, 3B-6, SS-1
1981	CHI N	25	.189	.203	74	14	1	0	0	0.0	7	1	5	7	0	3	2	38	81	3	10	6.1	.975	2B-20
3 yrs.		169	.250	.288	520	130	15	1	1	0.2	60	29	28	38	9	33	10	273	383	13	58	4.9	.981	2B-129, 3B-7, SS-1

Paul Strand

STRAND, PAUL EDWARD BL TL 6′½″ 190 lbs.
B. Dec. 19, 1893, Carbonado, Wash. D. July 2, 1974, Salt Lake City, Utah.

Year	Team	Games	BA	SA	AB	H	2B	3B	HR	HR%	R	RBI	BB	SO	SB	Pinch Hit AB	Pinch Hit H	PO	A	E	DP	TC/G	FA	G by Pos
1913	BOS N	7	.167	.167	6	1	0	0	0	0.0	0	0	0	0	0	0	0	1	6	1	0	1.1	.875	P-7
1914		16	.105	.211	19	2	2	0	0	0.0	2	3	1	5	0	1	0	0	13	3	1	1.0	.813	P-16
1915		45	.091	.091	22	2	0	0	0	0.0	3	2	0	4	0	9	2	4	3	1	0	0.7	.875	P-6, OF-5
1924	PHI A	47	.228	.329	167	38	9	4	0	0.0	15	13	8	9	3	3	0	80	3	1	0	1.9	.988	OF-44
4 yrs.		115	.201	.290	214	43	11	4	0	0.0	20	18	9	18	3	13	2	85	25	6	1	1.5	.948	OF-49, P-29

Johnny Strands

STRANDS, JOHN LAWRENCE BR TR 5′10½″ 165 lbs.
B. Dec. 5, 1885, Chicago, Ill. D. Jan. 19, 1957, Forest Park, Ill.

Year	Team	Games	BA	SA	AB	H	2B	3B	HR	HR%	R	RBI	BB	SO	SB	Pinch Hit AB	Pinch Hit H	PO	A	E	DP	TC/G	FA	G by Pos
1915	NWK F	35	.187	.293	75	14	3	1	1	1.3	7	11	6		1	12	2	26	29	4	3	2.6	.932	3B-12, 2B-9, OF-2

Sammy Strang

STRANG, SAMUEL NICKLIN (The Dixie Thrush) BB TR 5′ 8″ 160 lbs.
Born Samuel Strang Nicklin.
B. Dec. 16, 1876, Chattanooga, Tenn. D. Mar. 13, 1932, Chattanooga, Tenn.

Year	Team	Games	BA	SA	AB	H	2B	3B	HR	HR%	R	RBI	BB	SO	SB	Pinch Hit AB	Pinch Hit H	PO	A	E	DP	TC/G	FA	G by Pos
1896	LOU N	14	.261	.261	46	12	0	0	0	0.0	6	7	6	6	4	0	0	19	30	12	5	4.4	.803	SS-14
1900	CHI N	27	.284	.314	102	29	3	0	0	0.0	15	9	8		1	0	0	30	62	16	5	4.0	.852	3B-16, SS-9, 2B-2
1901	NY N	135	.282	.341	493	139	14	6	1	0.2	55	34	59		40	0	0	189	304	60	27	4.0	.892	3B-91, 2B-37, OF-5, SS-4
1902	2 teams	CHI A (137G –.295) CHI N (3G –.364)																						
″	total	140	.296	.364	547	162	18	5	3	0.5	109	46	76		39	0	0	175	338	63	23	4.1	.891	3B-139, 2B-2
1903	BKN N	135	.272	.333	508	138	21	5	0	0.0	101	38	75		46	0	0	166	251	38	13	3.4	.916	3B-124, OF-8, 2B-3
1904		77	.192	.244	271	52	11	0	1	0.4	28	9	45		16	0	0	114	185	39	15	4.4	.885	2B-63, 3B-12, SS-1
1905	NY N	111	.259	.347	294	76	9	4	3	1.0	51	29	58		23	14	**8**	123	144	25	11	3.0	.914	2B-47, OF-38, SS-9, 1B-1, 3B-1
1906		113	.319	.435	313	100	16	4	4	1.3	50	49	54		21	9	1	188	194	25	14	3.9	.939	2B-57, OF-39, SS-4, 3B-3, 1B-1
1907		123	.252	.382	306	77	20	4	4	1.3	56	30	60		21	**19**	4	174	61	12	8	2.6	.951	OF-70, 2B-13, 3B-7, 1B-5, SS-1
1908		28	.094	.094	53	5	0	0	0	0.0	8	2	23		5	4	2	29	47	12	5	4.0	.864	2B-14, OF-5, SS-3
10 yrs.		903	.269	.343	2933	790	112	28	16	0.5	479	253	464	6	216	46	15	1207	1616	302	126	3.7	.903	3B-393, 2B-238, OF-165, SS-45, 1B-7
WORLD SERIES																								
1905	NY N	1	.000	.000	1	0	0	0	0	0.0	0	0	0	1	0	1	0	0	0	0	0	0.0	—	

Alan Strange

STRANGE, ALAN COCHRANE (Inky) BR TR 5′ 9″ 162 lbs.
B. Nov. 7, 1906, Philadelphia, Pa. D. June 27, 1994, Seattle, Wash.

Year	Team	Games	BA	SA	AB	H	2B	3B	HR	HR%	R	RBI	BB	SO	SB	Pinch Hit AB	Pinch Hit H	PO	A	E	DP	TC/G	FA	G by Pos
1934	STL A	127	.233	.288	430	100	17	2	1	0.2	39	45	48	28	3	2	0	260	392	31	84	5.5	.955	SS-125
1935	2 teams	STL A (49G –.231) WAS A (20G –.185)																						
″	total	69	.219	.279	201	44	8	2	0	0.0	11	22	21	8	0	2	0	131	184	12	39	5.0	.963	SS-65
1940	STL A	54	.186	.269	167	31	8	3	0	0.0	26	6	22	12	2	13	3	73	128	7	28	5.3	.966	SS-35, 2B-4
1941		45	.232	.268	112	26	4	0	0	0.0	14	11	15	5	1	7	1	74	80	4	17	4.5	.975	SS-32, 1B-2, 3B-1
1942		19	.270	.324	37	10	2	0	0	0.0	3	5	3	0	0	3	0	16	28	3	3	3.4	.936	3B-10, SS-3, 2B-1
5 yrs.		314	.223	.282	947	211	39	7	1	0.1	93	89	109	53	6	27	4	554	812	57	171	5.1	.960	SS-260, 3B-11, 2B-5, 1B-2

Doug Strange

STRANGE, JOSEPH DOUGLAS BB TR 6′ 2″ 170 lbs.
B. Apr. 13, 1964, Greenville, S. C.

Year	Team	Games	BA	SA	AB	H	2B	3B	HR	HR%	R	RBI	BB	SO	SB	Pinch Hit AB	Pinch Hit H	PO	A	E	DP	TC/G	FA	G by Pos
1989	DET A	64	.214	.260	196	42	4	1	1	0.5	16	14	17	36	3	3	0	53	118	19	17	2.6	.900	3B-54, SS-9, 2B-9, DH-1
1991	CHI N	3	.444	.556	9	4	1	0	0	0.0	0	1	0	1	1	0	0	1	3	1	0	1.7	.800	3B-3
1992		52	.160	.202	94	15	1	0	1	1.1	7	5	10	15	1	10	1	24	51	6	4	1.8	.926	3B-33, 2B-12
1993	TEX A	145	.256	.360	484	124	29	0	7	1.4	58	60	43	69	6	12	4	276	374	13	83	4.6	.980	2B-135, 3B-9, SS-1
1994		73	.212	.341	226	48	12	1	5	2.2	26	26	15	38	1	6	1	88	174	11	39	4.0	.960	2B-53, 3B-13, OF-3
1995	SEA A	74	.271	.394	155	42	9	2	2	1.3	19	21	10	25	0	32	10	39	70	5	2	2.2	.956	3B-41, 2B-5, OF-4, DH-1
6 yrs.		411	.236	.332	1164	275	56	4	16	1.4	126	127	95	184	12	63	16	481	790	55	145	3.4	.959	2B-214, 3B-153, SS-10, OF-7, DH-2
DIVISIONAL PLAYOFF SERIES																								
1995	SEA A	2	.000	.000	4	0	0	0	0	0.0	0	1	1	1	0	1	0	0	0	0	0	0.0	.000	3B-2
LEAGUE CHAMPIONSHIP SERIES																								
1995	SEA A	4	.000	.000	4	0	0	0	0	0.0	0	0	0	2	0	2	0	2	3	0	0	2.5	1.000	3B-2

Asa Stratton

STRATTON, ASA EVANS
B. Feb. 10, 1853, Grafton, Mass. D. Aug. 14, 1925, Fitchburg, Mass.

Year	Team	Games	BA	SA	AB	H	2B	3B	HR	HR%	R	RBI	BB	SO	SB	Pinch Hit AB	Pinch Hit H	PO	A	E	DP	TC/G	FA	G by Pos
1881	WOR N	1	.250	.250	4	1	0	0	0	0.0	0	0	0	2		0	0	0	1	2	0	3.0	.333	SS-1

Scott Stratton

STRATTON, C. SCOTT BL TR 6′ 180 lbs.
B. Oct. 2, 1869, Campbellsburg, Ky. D. Mar. 8, 1939, Louisville, Ky.

Year	Team	Games	BA	SA	AB	H	2B	3B	HR	HR%	R	RBI	BB	SO	SB	Pinch Hit AB	Pinch Hit H	PO	A	E	DP	TC/G	FA	G by Pos
1888	LOU AA	67	.257	.309	249	64	8	1	1	0.4	35	29	12		10	0	0	66	70	17	1	2.2	.889	OF-38, P-33
1889		62	.288	.415	229	66	7	5	4	1.7	30	34	13	36	10	0	0	198	57	21	15	4.2	.924	OF-29, P-19, 1B-17
1890		55	.323	.392	189	61	3	5	0	0.0	29		16		8	0	0	29	111	4	2	2.6	.972	P-50, OF-5
1891	2 teams	PIT N (2G –.125) LOU AA (34G –.235)																						
″	total	36	.228	.244	123	28	2	0	0	0.0	10	8	11	16	8	0	0	88	70	11	11	4.7	.935	P-22, 1B-8, OF-6
1892	LOU N	63	.256	.347	219	56	2	9	0	0.0	22	23	17	21	9	0	0	83	94	17	8	3.0	.912	P-42, OF-17, 1B-6
1893		61	.226	.308	221	50	8	5	0	0.0	34	16	25	15	6	0	0	66	96	8	4	2.7	.953	P-38, OF-23, 1B-1
1894	2 teams	LOU N (13G –.324) CHI N (23G –.375)																						
″	total	36	.361	.564	133	48	6	6	3	2.3	38	27	10	3	4	2	0	44	33	4	5	2.4	.951	P-22, OF-10, 1B-2
1895	CHI N	10	.292	.417	24	7	1	1	0	0.0	3	2	4	2	1	1	0	10	10	5	0	2.8	.800	P-5, OF-4
8 yrs.		390	.274	.364	1387	380	37	32	8	0.6	201	139	108	93	56	3	0	584	541	87	46	3.1	.928	P-231, OF-132, 1B-34

Joe Straub

STRAUB, JOSEPH J. BR TR 5′10″ 160 lbs.
B. Jan. 19, 1858, Milwaukee, Wis. D. Feb. 13, 1929, Pueblo, Colo.

Year	Team	Games	BA	SA	AB	H	2B	3B	HR	HR%	R	RBI	BB	SO	SB	Pinch Hit AB	Pinch Hit H	PO	A	E	DP	TC/G	FA	G by Pos
1880	TRO N	3	.250	.250	12	3	0	0	0	0.0	1	3	1	3		0	0	13	9	5	0	9.0	.815	C-3
1882	PHI AA	8	.188	.250	32	6	2	0	0	0.0	2		1			0	0	34	11	10	0	6.9	.818	C-7, OF-1
1883	COL AA	27	.130	.130	100	13	0	0	0	0.0	4		4			0	0	182	22	22	8	8.4	.903	C-14, 1B-12, OF-1
3 yrs.		38	.153	.167	144	22	2	0	0	0.0	7	3	6	3		0	0	229	42	37	8	8.1	.880	C-24, 1B-12, OF-2

Joe Strauss

STRAUSS, JOSEPH (The Socker) BR TR
Born Joseph Strasser.
B. Nov. 16, 1858, Cincinnati, Ohio D. June 24, 1906, Cincinnati, Ohio.

Year	Team	Games	BA	SA	AB	H	2B	3B	HR	HR%	R	RBI	BB	SO	SB	Pinch Hit AB	Pinch Hit H	PO	A	E	DP	TC/G	FA	G by Pos
1884	KC U	16	.200	.250	60	12	3	0	0	0.0	4		1			0	0	31	17	14	1	3.9	.774	OF-10, C-3, 2B-2, 3B-1
1885	LOU AA	2	.167	.167	6	1	0	0	0	0.0	0		0			0	0	6	0	2	0	4.0	.750	C-1, OF-1
1886	2 teams	LOU AA (74G –.215) BKN AA (9G –.250)																						
″	total	83	.219	.288	333	73	6	7	1	0.3	42		9			0	0	123	34	25	0	2.1	.863	OF-80, C-3, P-2
3 yrs.		101	.216	.281	399	86	9	7	1	0.3	46		10			0	0	160	51	41	1	2.4	.837	OF-91, C-7, 2B-2, P-2, 3B-1

Darryl Strawberry

STRAWBERRY, DARRYL EUGENE (The Straw Man) BL TL 6′ 6″ 190 lbs.
B. Mar. 12, 1962, Los Angeles, Calif.

Year	Team	Games	BA	SA	AB	H	2B	3B	HR	HR%	R	RBI	BB	SO	SB	Pinch Hit AB	Pinch Hit H	PO	A	E	DP	TC/G	FA	G by Pos
1983	NY N	122	.257	.512	420	108	15	7	26	6.2	63	74	47	128	19	4	0	232	8	4	0	2.1	.984	OF-117
1984		147	.251	.467	522	131	27	4	26	5.0	75	97	75	131	27	4	2	276	11	6	3	2.0	.980	OF-146
1985		111	.277	.557	393	109	15	4	29	7.4	78	79	73	96	26	2	0	211	5	2	2	2.0	.991	OF-110
1986		136	.259	.507	475	123	27	5	27	5.7	76	93	72	141	28	8	0	226	10	6	3	1.8	.975	OF-131
1987		154	.284	.583	532	151	32	5	39	7.3	108	104	97	122	36	3	1	272	6	8	3	1.9	.972	OF-151

Darryl Strawberry *continued*

Year	Team	Games	BA	SA	AB	H	2B	3B	HR	HR%	R	RBI	BB	SO	SB	Pinch Hit AB	Pinch Hit H	PO	A	E	DP	TC/G	FA	G by Pos
1988		153	.269	**.545**	543	146	27	3	**39**	**7.2**	101	101	85	127	29	2	0	297	4	9	3	2.1	.971	OF-150
1989		134	.225	.466	476	107	26	1	29	6.1	69	77	61	105	11	6	1	272	4	8	2	2.2	.972	OF-131
1990		152	.277	.518	542	150	18	1	37	**6.8**	92	108	70	110	15	5	0	268	10	3	4	1.9	.989	OF-149
1991	LA N	139	.265	.491	505	134	22	4	28	5.5	86	99	75	125	10	3	1	209	11	5	2	1.7	.978	OF-136
1992		43	.237	.385	156	37	8	0	5	3.2	20	25	19	34	3	2	1	67	2	1	0	1.7	.986	OF-42
1993		32	.140	.310	100	14	2	0	5	5.0	12	12	16	19	1	3	1	37	1	4	0	1.4	.905	OF-29
1994	SF N	29	.239	.424	92	22	3	1	4	4.3	13	17	19	22	0	0	0	61	1	2	1	2.4	.969	OF-27
1995	NY A	32	.276	.448	87	24	4	1	3	3.4	15	13	10	22	0	5	1	18	2	2	1	0.8	.909	DH-15, OF-11
13 yrs.		1384	.259	.505	4843	1256	226	36	297	6.1	808	899	719	1182	205	47	8	2446	75	60	24	1.9	.977	OF-1330, DH-15
DIVISIONAL PLAYOFF SERIES																								
1995	NY A	2	.000	.000	2	0	0	0	0	0.0	0	0	0	1	0	2	0	0	0	0	0	0.0	—	
LEAGUE CHAMPIONSHIP SERIES																								
1986	NY N	6	.227	.545	22	5	1	0	2	9.1	4	5	3	12	1	0	0	9	0	0	0	1.5	1.000	OF-6
1988		7	.300	.467	30	9	2	0	1	3.3	5	6	2	5	0	0	0	11	0	0	0	1.6	1.000	OF-7
2 yrs.		13	.269	.500	52	14	3	0	3	5.8	9	11	5	17 10th	1	0	0	20	0	0	0	1.5	1.000	OF-13
WORLD SERIES																								
1986	NY N	7	.208	.375	24	5	1	0	1	4.2	4	1	4	6	3	0	0	19	0	0	0	2.7	1.000	OF-7

Gabby Street

STREET, CHARLES EVARD (Old Sarge) BR TR 5′11″ 180 lbs.
B. Sept. 30, 1882, Huntsville, Ala. D. Feb. 6, 1951, Joplin, Mo.
Manager 1929–33, 1938.

Year	Team	Games	BA	SA	AB	H	2B	3B	HR	HR%	R	RBI	BB	SO	SB	Pinch Hit AB	Pinch Hit H	PO	A	E	DP	TC/G	FA	G by Pos
1904	CIN N	11	.121	.152	33	4	1	0	0	0.0	1	0	1		2	0	0	55	17	2	0	6.7	.973	C-11
1905	3 teams	CIN N (2G –.000) BOS N (3G –.167) CIN N (29G –.253)																						
″	total	34	.238	.305	105	25	5	1	0	0.0	8	8	8		2	3	0	123	54	8	1	6.2	.957	C-30
1908	WAS A	131	.206	.279	394	81	12	7	1	0.3	31	32	40		5	3	2	578	167	21	14	6.0	.973	C-128
1909		137	.211	.246	407	86	12	1	0	0.0	25	29	26		2	0	0	714	210	18	18	6.9	.981	C-137
1910		89	.202	.237	257	52	6	0	1	0.4	13	16	23		1	3	1	417	151	13	8	6.8	.978	C-86
1911		72	.222	.264	216	48	7	1	0	0.0	16	14	14		4	1	0	362	102	13	10	6.7	.973	C-71
1912	NY A	28	.182	.216	88	16	1	1	0	0.0	4	6	7		1	0	0	141	43	8	4	6.9	.958	C-28
1931	STL N	1	.000	.000	1	0	0	0	0	0.0	0	0	0	0	0	0	0	1	1	0	0	2.0	1.000	C-1
8 yrs.		503	.208	.256	1501	312	44	11	2	0.1	98	105	119	0	17	10	3	2391	745	83	55	6.5	.974	C-492

Walt Streuli

STREULI, WALTER HERBERT BR TR 6′2″ 195 lbs.
B. Sept. 26, 1935, Memphis, Tenn.

Year	Team	Games	BA	SA	AB	H	2B	3B	HR	HR%	R	RBI	BB	SO	SB	Pinch Hit AB	Pinch Hit H	PO	A	E	DP	TC/G	FA	G by Pos
1954	DET A	1	—	—	0	0	0	0	0	—	0	0	1	0	0	0	0	1	0	0	0	1.0	1.000	C-1
1955		2	.250	.500	4	1	1	0	0	0.0	1	1	0	0	0	0	0	7	0	0	0	3.5	1.000	C-2
1956		3	.250	.375	8	2	1	0	0	0.0	0	1	1	2	0	0	0	13	1	1	1	5.0	.933	C-3
3 yrs.		6	.250	.417	12	3	2	0	0	0.0	1	2	2	2	0	0	0	21	1	1	1	3.8	.957	C-6

John Strick

STRICK, JOHN QUINCY ADAMS
B. Louisville, Ky. Deceased.

Year	Team	Games	BA	SA	AB	H	2B	3B	HR	HR%	R	RBI	BB	SO	SB	Pinch Hit AB	Pinch Hit H	PO	A	E	DP	TC/G	FA	G by Pos
1882	LOU AA	32	.164	.236	110	18	6	1	0	0.0	17		9			0	0	110	45	22	6	5.1	.876	C-21, OF-6, 2B-6, SS-1, 1B-1

Cub Stricker

STRICKER, JOHN A. BR TR 5′3″ 133 lbs.
Born John A. Streaker.
B. June 8, 1859, Philadelphia, Pa. D. Nov. 19, 1937, Philadelphia, Pa.
Manager 1892.

Year	Team	Games	BA	SA	AB	H	2B	3B	HR	HR%	R	RBI	BB	SO	SB	Pinch Hit AB	Pinch Hit H	PO	A	E	DP	TC/G	FA	G by Pos
1882	PHI AA	72	.217	.246	272	59	6	1	0	0.0	34		15			0	0	240	252	52	29	7.3	.904	2B-72, P-2, OF-1
1883		89	.273	.306	330	90	8	0	1	0.3	67		19			0	0	260	226	95	23	6.5	.836	2B-88, C-2
1884		107	.231	.333	399	92	16	11	1	0.3	59		19			0	0	281	257	81	40	5.6	.869	2B-107, P-1, OF-1, C-1
1885		106	.234	.279	398	93	9	3	1	0.3	71		21			0	0	284	304	81	41	6.3	.879	2B-106
1887	CLE AA	131	.264	.326	534	141	19	4	2	0.4	122		53		86	0	0	469	387	92	63	7.0	.903	2B-126, SS-6, P-3
1888		127	.233	.290	493	115	13	6	1	0.2	80	33	50		60	0	0	397	366	58	58	6.3	.929	2B-122, OF-6, P-2
1889	CLE N	136	.251	.288	566	142	10	4	1	0.2	83	47	58	18	32	0	0	437	437	64	65	6.9	.932	2B-135, SS-1
1890	CLE P	127	.244	.320	544	133	19	8	2	0.4	93	65	54	16	24	0	0	325	438	90	61	6.6	.894	2B-109, SS-20
1891	BOS AA	139	.216	.261	514	111	15	4	0	0.0	96	46	63	34	54	0	0	405	418	51	78	6.3	.942	2B-139
1892	2 teams	STL N (28G –.204) BAL N (75G –.264)																						
″	total	103	.248	.316	367	91	6	5	3	0.8	57	48	42	25	18	0	0	279	298	48	39	6.1	.923	2B-102, SS-1
1893	WAS N	59	.183	.225	218	40	7	1	0	0.0	28	20	20	12	4	0	0	168	146	36	23	5.9	.897	2B-39, OF-12, SS-4, 3B-4
11 yrs.		1196	.239	.294	4635	1107	128	47	12	0.3	790	259	414	105	278	0	0	3545	3529	748	520	6.5	.904	2B-1145, SS-32, OF-20, P-8, 3B-4, C-3

George Strickland

STRICKLAND, GEORGE BEVAN (Bo) BR TR 6′1″ 175 lbs.
B. Jan. 10, 1926, New Orleans, La.
Manager 1964, 1966.

Year	Team	Games	BA	SA	AB	H	2B	3B	HR	HR%	R	RBI	BB	SO	SB	Pinch Hit AB	Pinch Hit H	PO	A	E	DP	TC/G	FA	G by Pos
1950	PIT N	23	.111	.111	27	3	0	0	0	0.0	0	2	3	8	0	1	1	22	24	1	7	2.3	.979	SS-19, 3B-1
1951		138	.216	.333	454	98	12	7	9	2.0	59	47	65	83	4	0	0	255	426	37	97	5.2	.948	SS-125, 2B-13
1952	2 teams	PIT N (76G –.177) CLE A (31G –.216)																						
″	total	107	.188	.287	320	60	10	2	6	1.9	25	30	35	60	4	1	0	212	313	25	74	5.2	.955	SS-58, 2B-46, 3B-1, 1B-1
1953	CLE A	123	.284	.379	419	119	17	4	5	1.2	43	47	51	52	0	0	0	238	400	17	103	5.3	.974	SS-122, 1B-1
1954		112	.213	.313	361	77	12	3	6	1.7	42	37	55	62	2	0	0	193	321	21	61	4.8	.961	SS-112
1955		130	.209	.273	388	81	9	5	2	0.5	34	34	49	60	1	1	0	221	360	14	84	4.6	.976	SS-128
1956		85	.211	.292	171	36	1	2	3	1.8	22	17	22	27	0	2	0	118	145	5	34	3.3	.981	2B-28, SS-28, 3B-26
1957		89	.234	.308	201	47	8	2	1	0.5	21	19	26	29	0	2	0	146	164	6	38	3.5	.981	2B-48, SS-23, 3B-19
1959		132	.238	.302	441	105	15	2	3	0.7	55	48	52	64	1	1	0	153	281	18	54	3.4	.960	3B-80, SS-50, 2B-4
1960		32	.167	.238	42	7	0	0	1	2.4	4	3	4	8	0	3	0	11	31	1	6	1.5	.977	SS-14, 3B-12, 2B-2
10 yrs.		971	.224	.311	2824	633	84	27	36	1.3	305	284	362	453	12	11	1	1569	2465	145	558	4.3	.965	SS-679, 2B-141, 3B-139, 1B-2
WORLD SERIES																								
1954	CLE A	3	.000	.000	9	0	0	0	0	0.0	0	0	0	2	0	0	0	6	8	1	1	5.0	.933	SS-3

George Strief

STRIEF, GEORGE ANDREW
B. Oct. 16, 1856, Cincinnati, Ohio D. Apr. 1, 1946, Cleveland, Ohio.
BR TR 5′ 7″ 172 lbs.

Year	Team	Games	BA	SA	AB	H	2B	3B	HR	HR%	R	RBI	BB	SO	SB	Pinch Hit AB	Pinch Hit H	PO	A	E	DP	TC/G	FA	G by Pos
1879	**CLE N**	71	.174	.208	264	46	7	1	0	0.0	24	15	10	23		0	0	141	51	26	4	3.1	.881	OF-55, 2B-16
1882	**PIT AA**	79	.195	.286	297	58	9	6	2	0.7	45		13			0	0	241	208	41	29	6.2	.916	2B-78, SS-1
1883	**STL AA**	82	.225	.265	302	68	9	0	1	0.3	22		12			0	0	220	217	47	28	5.9	.903	2B-67, OF-15
1884	**4 teams**	**STL AA** (48G –.201) **KC U** (15G –.107) **PIT U** (15G –.208) **CLE N** (8G –.241)																						
″	**total**	86	.189	.273	322	61	17	2	2	0.6	35	0	20	5		0	0	174	104	36	14	3.7	.885	OF-49, 2B-34, 3B-2, 1B-1
1885	**PHI AA**	44	.274	.377	175	48	8	5	0	0.0	19		9			0	0	62	82	19	10	3.7	.883	3B-19, SS-10, OF-8, 2B-7
5 yrs.		362	.207	.275	1360	281	50	14	5	0.4	145	15	64	28		0	0	838	662	169	85	4.6	.899	2B-202, OF-127, 3B-21, SS-11, 1B-1

Lou Stringer

STRINGER, LOUIS BERNARD
B. May 13, 1917, Grand Rapids, Mich.
BR TR 5′11″ 173 lbs.

Year	Team	Games	BA	SA	AB	H	2B	3B	HR	HR%	R	RBI	BB	SO	SB	Pinch Hit AB	Pinch Hit H	PO	A	E	DP	TC/G	FA	G by Pos
1941	**CHI N**	145	.246	.352	512	126	31	4	5	1.0	59	53	59	86	3	0	0	359	462	38	85	6.0	.956	2B-137, SS-7
1942		121	.236	.352	406	96	10	5	9	2.2	45	41	31	55	3	7	3	268	343	29	59	5.6	.955	2B-113, 3B-1
1946		80	.244	.311	209	51	3	1	3	1.4	26	19	26	34	0	5	0	135	152	13	17	4.7	.957	2B-62, SS-1, 3B-1
1948	**BOS A**	4	.091	.364	11	1	0	0	1	9.1	1	1	0	3	0	2	0	5	13	1	5	9.5	.947	2B-2
1949		35	.268	.439	41	11	4	0	1	2.4	10	6	5	10	0	9	1	25	20	1	12	5.1	.978	2B-9
1950		24	.294	.353	17	5	1	0	0	0.0	7	2	0	4	1	9	2	4	7	2	2	2.6	.846	3B-3, SS-1, 2B-1
6 yrs.		409	.242	.348	1196	290	49	10	19	1.6	148	122	121	192	7	32	6	796	997	84	180	5.6	.955	2B-324, SS-9, 3B-5

Joe Stripp

STRIPP, JOSEPH VALENTINE (Jersey Joe)
B. Feb. 3, 1903, Harrison, N. J. D. June 10, 1989, Orlando, Fla.
BR TR 5′11½″ 175 lbs.

Year	Team	Games	BA	SA	AB	H	2B	3B	HR	HR%	R	RBI	BB	SO	SB	Pinch Hit AB	Pinch Hit H	PO	A	E	DP	TC/G	FA	G by Pos
1928	**CIN N**	42	.288	.403	139	40	7	3	1	0.7	18	17	8	8	0	2	1	42	34	7	2	2.1	.916	OF-21, 3B-17, SS-1
1929		64	.214	.299	187	40	3	2	3	1.6	24	20	24	15	2	7	2	49	120	7	4	3.1	.960	3B-55, 2B-2
1930		130	.306	.431	464	142	37	6	3	0.6	74	64	51	37	15	6	0	774	133	7	83	7.4	.992	1B-75, 3B-48
1931		105	.324	.415	426	138	26	2	3	0.7	71	42	21	31	5	1	1	183	197	14	37	3.8	.964	3B-96, 1B-9
1932	**BKN N**	138	.303	.438	534	162	36	9	6	1.1	94	64	36	30	14	0	0	485	237	19	61	5.4	.974	3B-93, 1B-43
1933		141	.277	.346	537	149	20	7	1	0.2	69	51	26	23	5	1	1	170	264	15	17	3.2	.967	3B-140
1934		104	.315	.404	384	121	19	6	1	0.3	50	40	22	20	2	1	0	157	152	16	25	3.1	.951	3B-96, 1B-7, SS-1
1935		109	.306	.391	373	114	13	5	3	0.8	44	43	22	15	2	4	2	180	169	10	24	3.5	.972	3B-88, 1B-15, OF-1
1936		110	.317	.399	439	139	31	1	1	0.2	51	60	22	12	2	3	1	132	174	10	13	3.0	.968	3B-106
1937		90	.243	.300	300	73	10	2	1	0.3	37	26	20	18	1	9	3	208	102	9	13	3.8	.972	3B-66, 1B-14, SS-3
1938	**2 teams**	**STL N** (54G –.286) **BOS N** (59G –.275)																						
″	**total**	113	.280	.327	428	120	17	0	1	0.2	43	37	28	17	2	4	2	114	187	9	21	2.8	.971	3B-109
11 yrs.		1146	.294	.384	4211	1238	219	43	24	0.6	575	464	280	226	50	38	13	2494	1769	123	300	4.0	.972	3B-914, 1B-163, OF-22, SS-5, 2B-2

Allie Strobel

STROBEL, ALBERT IRVING
B. June 11, 1884, Boston, Mass. D. Feb. 10, 1955, Hollywood, Calif.
BR TR 6′ 160 lbs.

Year	Team	Games	BA	SA	AB	H	2B	3B	HR	HR%	R	RBI	BB	SO	SB	Pinch Hit AB	Pinch Hit H	PO	A	E	DP	TC/G	FA	G by Pos
1905	**BOS N**	5	.105	.105	19	2	0	0	0	0.0	1	2	0		0	0	0	5	7	0	1	2.4	1.000	3B-4, OF-1
1906		100	.202	.262	317	64	10	3	1	0.3	28	24	29		2	1	0	193	283	30	33	5.1	.941	2B-93, SS-6, OF-1
2 yrs.		105	.196	.253	336	66	10	3	1	0.3	29	26	29		2	1	0	198	290	30	34	4.9	.942	2B-93, SS-6, 3B-4, OF-2

Jim Stroner

STRONER, JAMES MELVIN
B. May 29, 1901, Chicago, Ill. D. Dec. 6, 1975, Tarboro, N. C.
BR TR 5′10″ 175 lbs.

Year	Team	Games	BA	SA	AB	H	2B	3B	HR	HR%	R	RBI	BB	SO	SB	Pinch Hit AB	Pinch Hit H	PO	A	E	DP	TC/G	FA	G by Pos
1929	**PIT N**	6	.375	.500	8	3	1	0	0	0.0	0	0	1	0	0	3	2	1	3	3	0	3.5	.571	3B-2

Ed Stroud

STROUD, EDWIN MARVIN (The Creeper)
B. Oct. 31, 1939, Lapine, Ala.
BL TR 5′11″ 180 lbs.

Year	Team	Games	BA	SA	AB	H	2B	3B	HR	HR%	R	RBI	BB	SO	SB	Pinch Hit AB	Pinch Hit H	PO	A	E	DP	TC/G	FA	G by Pos
1966	**CHI A**	12	.167	.222	36	6	2	0	0	0.0	3	1	2	8	3	0	0	20	0	0	0	1.8	1.000	OF-11
1967	**2 teams**	**CHI A** (20G –.296) **WAS A** (87G –.201)																						
″	**total**	107	.212	.281	231	49	5	4	1	0.4	42	13	26	34	15	6	0	131	3	2	1	1.5	.985	OF-91
1968	**WAS A**	105	.239	.376	306	73	10	10	4	1.3	41	23	20	50	9	22	2	139	2	3	1	1.7	.979	OF-84
1969		123	.252	.393	206	52	5	6	4	1.9	35	29	30	33	12	44	14	109	1	2	0	1.3	.982	OF-85
1970		129	.266	.349	433	115	11	5	5	1.2	69	32	40	79	29	19	6	271	8	2	3	2.4	.993	OF-118
1971	**CHI A**	53	.177	.248	141	25	4	3	0	0.0	19	2	11	20	4	14	2	51	0	0	0	1.2	1.000	OF-44
6 yrs.		529	.237	.336	1353	320	37	28	14	1.0	209	100	129	224	72	105	24	721	14	9	5	1.7	.988	OF-433

Steve Stroughter

STROUGHTER, STEPHEN LEWIS
B. Mar. 15, 1952, Visalia, Calif.
BL TR 6′ 2″ 190 lbs.

Year	Team	Games	BA	SA	AB	H	2B	3B	HR	HR%	R	RBI	BB	SO	SB	Pinch Hit AB	Pinch Hit H	PO	A	E	DP	TC/G	FA	G by Pos
1982	**SEA A**	26	.170	.255	47	8	1	0	1	2.1	4	3	3	9	0	10	1	7	1	0	0	0.7	1.000	DH-9, OF-3

Amos Strunk

STRUNK, AMOS AARON
B. Nov. 22, 1889, Philadelphia, Pa. D. July 22, 1979, Llanerch, Pa.
BL TL 5′11½″ 175 lbs.

Year	Team	Games	BA	SA	AB	H	2B	3B	HR	HR%	R	RBI	BB	SO	SB	Pinch Hit AB	Pinch Hit H	PO	A	E	DP	TC/G	FA	G by Pos
1908	**PHI A**	12	.235	.265	34	8	1	0	0	0.0	4	0	4		0	1	1	27	1	3	1	2.8	.903	OF-11
1909		11	.114	.114	35	4	0	0	0	0.0	1	2	1		2	2	0	10	2	0	0	1.3	1.000	OF-9
1910		16	.333	.375	48	16	0	1	0	0.0	9	2	3		4	0	0	33	1	0	0	2.4	1.000	OF-14
1911		74	.256	.321	215	55	7	2	1	0.5	42	21	35		13	7	2	145	11	6	5	2.5	.963	OF-62, 1B-2
1912		120	.289	.400	412	119	13	12	3	0.7	58	63	47		29	3	2	278	16	3	3	2.5	.990	OF-118
1913		93	.305	.425	292	89	11	12	0	0.0	30	46	29	23	14	11	4	168	9	7	3	2.3	.962	OF-80
1914		122	.275	.342	404	111	15	3	2	0.5	58	45	57	38	25	2	0	280	14	4	3	2.5	.987	OF-120
1915		132	.297	.427	485	144	28	16	1	0.2	76	45	56	45	17	2	0	413	32	9	21	3.5	.980	OF-111, 1B-19
1916		150	.316	.421	544	172	30	9	3	0.6	71	49	66	59	21	0	0	368	24	8	14	2.7	.980	OF-143, 1B-7
1917		148	.281	.361	540	152	26	7	1	0.2	83	45	68	37	16	0	0	346	13	5	5	2.5	.986	OF-146
1918	**BOS A**	114	.257	.344	413	106	18	9	0	0.0	50	35	36	13	20	1	0	230	13	3	4	2.2	.988	OF-113
1919	**2 teams**	**BOS A** (48G –.272) **PHI A** (60G –.211)																						
″	**total**	108	.241	.323	378	91	17	7	0	0.0	42	30	36	28	6	5	2	216	11	6	0	2.3	.974	OF-100
1920	**2 teams**	**PHI A** (58G –.297) **CHI A** (51G –.230)																						
″	**total**	109	.265	.335	385	102	16	4	1	0.3	55	34	49	24	1	7	1	195	5	3	0	2.0	.985	OF-103
1921	**CHI A**	121	.332	.451	401	133	19	10	3	0.7	68	69	38	27	7	8	3	214	10	7	2	2.1	.970	OF-111
1922		92	.289	.350	311	90	11	4	0	0.0	36	33	33	28	9	10	3	246	13	3	6	3.1	.989	OF-75, 1B-9

Amos Strunk *continued*

Year	Team	Games	BA	SA	AB	H	2B	3B	HR	HR%	R	RBI	BB	SO	SB	Pinch Hit AB	Pinch Hit H	PO	A	E	DP	TC/G	FA	G by Pos
1923		54	.315	.315	54	17	0	0	0	0.0	7	8	8	5	1	**39**	**12**	18	0	1	0	2.7	.947	OF-4, 1B-3
1924	**2 teams**	**CHI A** (1G –.000) **PHI A** (30G –.143)																						
"	**total**	31	.140	.140	43	6	0	0	0	0.0	5	1	7	4	0	20	3	7	0	0	0	0.9	1.000	OF-8
17 yrs.		1507	.283	.373	4994	1415	212	96	15	0.3	695	528	573	331	185	118	33	3194	175	68	67	2.5	.980	OF-1328, 1B-40
WORLD SERIES																								
1910	**PHI A**	4	.278	.444	18	5	1	1	0	0.0	2	2	2	5	0	0	0	10	1	1	0	3.0	.917	OF-4
1911		1	—	—	0	0	0	0	0	—	0	0	0	0	0	0	0	0	0	0	0	0.0	—	
1913		5	.118	.118	17	2	0	0	0	0.0	3	0	2	2	0	0	0	13	0	0	0	2.6	1.000	OF-5
1914		2	.286	.286	7	2	0	0	0	0.0	0	0	0	2	0	0	0	4	0	0	0	2.0	1.000	OF-2
1918	**BOS A**	6	.174	.304	23	4	1	1	0	0.0	1	0	0	5	0	0	0	8	2	0	0	1.7	1.000	OF-6
5 yrs.		18	.200	.292	65	13	2	2	0	0.0	6	2	4	14	0	0	0	35	3	1	0	2.3	.974	OF-17

Al Struve

STRUVE, ALBERT
B. St. Louis, Mo. Deceased.

Year	Team	Games	BA	SA	AB	H	2B	3B	HR	HR%	R	RBI	BB	SO	SB	Pinch Hit AB	Pinch Hit H	PO	A	E	DP	TC/G	FA	G by Pos
1884	**STL AA**	2	.286	.286	7	2	0	0	0	0.0	2		0			0	0	6	6	0	0	6.0	1.000	C-1, OF-1

Bill Stuart

STUART, WILLIAM ALEXANDER (Chauncey) 5′11″ 170 lbs.
B. Aug. 28, 1873, Boalsburg, Pa. D. Oct. 14, 1928, Fort Worth, Tex.

Year	Team	Games	BA	SA	AB	H	2B	3B	HR	HR%	R	RBI	BB	SO	SB	Pinch Hit AB	Pinch Hit H	PO	A	E	DP	TC/G	FA	G by Pos
1895	**PIT N**	19	.247	.286	77	19	3	0	0	0.0	5	10	2	6	2	0	0	39	61	10	5	5.8	.909	SS-17, 2B-2
1899	**NY N**	1	.000	.000	3	0	0	0	0	0.0	0	0	0		0	0	0	2	2	0	0	4.0	1.000	2B-1
2 yrs.		20	.237	.275	80	19	3	0	0	0.0	5	10	2	6	2	0	0	41	63	10	5	5.7	.912	SS-17, 2B-3

Dick Stuart

STUART, RICHARD LEE (Dr. Strangeglove) BR TR 6′ 4″ 212 lbs.
B. Nov. 7, 1932, San Francisco, Calif.

Year	Team	Games	BA	SA	AB	H	2B	3B	HR	HR%	R	RBI	BB	SO	SB	Pinch Hit AB	Pinch Hit H	PO	A	E	DP	TC/G	FA	G by Pos
1958	**PIT N**	67	.268	.543	254	68	12	5	16	6.3	38	48	11	75	0	3	0	529	49	16	69	9.3	.973	1B-64
1959		118	.297	.549	397	118	15	2	27	6.8	64	78	42	86	1	16	5	831	81	22	87	8.8	.976	1B-105, OF-1
1960		122	.260	.479	438	114	17	5	23	5.3	48	83	39	107	0	13	4	920	77	14	90	9.4	.986	1B-108
1961		138	.301	.581	532	160	28	8	35	6.6	83	117	34	**121**	0	3	1	1152	99	21	141	9.6	.983	1B-132, OF-1
1962		114	.228	.398	394	90	11	4	16	4.1	52	64	32	94	0	13	3	868	78	17	98	9.5	.982	1B-101
1963	**BOS A**	157	.261	.521	612	160	25	4	42	6.9	81	**118**	44	144	0	2	1	1207	134	29	100	8.8	.979	1B-155
1964		156	.279	.491	603	168	27	1	33	5.5	73	114	37	130	0	1	0	1159	104	24	105	8.3	.981	1B-155
1965	**PHI N**	149	.234	.429	538	126	19	1	28	5.2	53	95	39	136	1	8	1	1119	98	17	100	8.6	.986	1B-143, 3B-1
1966	**2 teams**	**NY N** (31G –.218) **LA N** (38G –.264)																						
"	**total**	69	.242	.365	178	43	1	0	7	3.9	11	22	20	43	0	16	3	407	34	8	36	9.4	.982	1B-48
1969	**CAL A**	22	.157	.255	51	8	2	0	1	2.0	3	4	3	21	0	9	1	102	4	1	11	8.2	.991	1B-13
10 yrs.		1112	.264	.489	3997	1055	157	30	228	5.7	506	743	301	957	2	84	19	8294	758	169	837	9.0	.982	1B-1024, OF-2, 3B-1
WORLD SERIES																								
1960	**PIT N**	6	.150	.150	20	3	0	0	0	0.0	0	0	0	3	0	0	0	45	0	0	6	7.5	1.000	1B-6
1966	**LA N**	2	.000	.000	2	0	0	0	0	0.0	0	0	0	1	0	2	0	0	0	0	0	0.0	—	
2 yrs.		8	.136	.136	22	3	0	0	0	0.0	0	0	0	4	0	2	0	45	0	0	6	7.5	1.000	1B-6

Luke Stuart

STUART, LUTHER LANE BR TR 5′ 8″ 165 lbs.
B. May 23, 1892, Alamance County, N. C. D. June 15, 1947, Winston-Salem, N. C.

Year	Team	Games	BA	SA	AB	H	2B	3B	HR	HR%	R	RBI	BB	SO	SB	Pinch Hit AB	Pinch Hit H	PO	A	E	DP	TC/G	FA	G by Pos
1921	**STL A**	3	.333	1.333	3	1	0	0	1	33.3	2	2	0	1	0	0	0	1	1	0	0	0.7	1.000	2B-3

Franklin Stubbs

STUBBS, FRANKLIN LEE BL TL 6′ 2″ 205 lbs.
B. Oct. 21, 1960, Richland, N. C.

Year	Team	Games	BA	SA	AB	H	2B	3B	HR	HR%	R	RBI	BB	SO	SB	Pinch Hit AB	Pinch Hit H	PO	A	E	DP	TC/G	FA	G by Pos
1984	**LA N**	87	.194	.341	217	42	2	3	8	3.7	22	17	24	63	2	22	4	417	37	4	31	6.5	.991	1B-51, OF-20
1985		10	.222	.222	9	2	0	0	0	0.0	0	2	0	3	0	7	2	11	0	0	1	2.8	1.000	1B-4
1986		132	.226	.421	420	95	11	1	23	5.5	55	58	37	107	7	12	0	244	14	7	3	1.9	.974	OF-124, 1B-13
1987		129	.233	.415	386	90	16	3	16	4.1	48	52	31	85	8	11	3	830	79	5	65	7.1	.995	1B-111, OF-18
1988		115	.223	.376	242	54	13	0	8	3.3	30	34	23	61	11	26	8	530	57	13	41	6.2	.978	1B-84, OF-13
1989		69	.291	.466	103	30	6	0	4	3.9	11	15	16	27	3	26	6	70	5	3	5	2.2	.962	OF-28, 1B-7
1990	**HOU N**	146	.261	.475	448	117	23	2	23	5.1	59	71	48	114	19	11	3	609	43	6	42	4.6	.991	1B-72, OF-71
1991	**MIL A**	103	.213	.359	362	77	16	2	11	3.0	48	38	35	71	13	4	0	828	82	9	78	9.2	.990	1B-92, OF-4, DH-4
1992		92	.229	.368	288	66	11	1	9	3.1	37	42	27	68	11	10	3	525	63	8	44	7.0	.987	1B-68, DH-16, OF-1
1995	**DET A**	62	.250	.397	116	29	11	0	2	1.7	13	19	19	27	0	25	5	155	5	5	13	3.8	.970	1B-20, OF-20, DH-3
10 yrs.		945	.232	.404	2591	602	109	12	104	4.0	323	348	260	626	74	154	34	4219	385	60	323	5.5	.987	1B-522, OF-299, DH-23
LEAGUE CHAMPIONSHIP SERIES																								
1988	**LA N**	4	.250	.250	8	2	0	0	0	0.0	0	0	0	4	0	2	0	16	2	0	2	6.0	1.000	1B-3
WORLD SERIES																								
1988	**LA N**	5	.294	.412	17	5	2	0	0	0.0	3	2	1	3	0	0	0	34	0	0	3	6.8	1.000	1B-5

Larry Stubing

STUBING, LAWRENCE GEORGE (Moose) BL TL 6′ 3″ 220 lbs.
B. Mar. 31, 1938, Bronx, N. Y.
Manager 1988.

Year	Team	Games	BA	SA	AB	H	2B	3B	HR	HR%	R	RBI	BB	SO	SB	Pinch Hit AB	Pinch Hit H	PO	A	E	DP	TC/G	FA	G by Pos
1967	**CAL A**	5	.000	.000	5	0	0	0	0	0.0	0	0	0	4	0	5	0	0	0	0	0	0.0	—	

Bill Stumpf

STUMPF, WILLIAM FREDERICK BR TR 6′½″ 175 lbs.
B. Mar. 21, 1892, Baltimore, Md. D. Feb. 14, 1966, Crownsville, Md.

Year	Team	Games	BA	SA	AB	H	2B	3B	HR	HR%	R	RBI	BB	SO	SB	Pinch Hit AB	Pinch Hit H	PO	A	E	DP	TC/G	FA	G by Pos
1912	**NY A**	40	.240	.240	129	31	0	0	0	0.0	8	10	6		5	0	0	74	93	21	10	4.7	.888	SS-27, 2B-8, 3B-4, 1B-1
1913		12	.207	.241	29	6	1	0	0	0.0	5	1	3	3	0	1	0	14	23	8	2	3.8	.822	SS-6, 2B-5, OF-1
2 yrs.		52	.234	.241	158	37	1	0	0	0.0	13	11	9	3	5	1	0	88	116	29	12	4.5	.876	SS-33, 2B-13, 3B-4, OF-1, 1B-1

George Stumpf

STUMPF, GEORGE FREDERICK BL TL 5′ 8″ 155 lbs.
B. Dec. 15, 1910, New Orleans, La. D. Mar. 6, 1993, Metairie, La.

Year	Team	Games	BA	SA	AB	H	2B	3B	HR	HR%	R	RBI	BB	SO	SB	Pinch Hit AB	Pinch Hit H	PO	A	E	DP	TC/G	FA	G by Pos
1931	**BOS A**	7	.250	.357	28	7	1	1	0	0.0	2	4	1	2	0	0	0	14	0	0	0	2.0	1.000	OF-7
1932		79	.201	.254	169	34	2	2	1	0.6	18	18	18	21	1	25	4	78	2	4	0	1.6	.952	OF-51
1933		22	.341	.415	41	14	3	0	0	0.0	8	5	4	2	4	5	1	22	0	0	0	1.5	1.000	OF-15
1936	**CHI A**	10	.273	.318	22	6	1	0	0	0.0	3	5	2	1	0	5	3	9	1	0	0	2.5	1.000	OF-4
4 yrs.		118	.235	.296	260	61	7	3	1	0.4	31	32	25	26	5	35	8	123	3	4	0	1.7	.969	OF-77

Guy Sturdy

STURDY, GUY R.
B. Aug. 7, 1899, Sherman, Tex. D. May 4, 1965, Marshall, Tex.
BL TL 6′½″ 180 lbs.

Year	Team	Lg	Games	BA	SA	AB	H	2B	3B	HR	HR%	R	RBI	BB	SO	SB	Pinch Hit AB	Pinch Hit H	PO	A	E	DP	TC/G	FA	G by Pos
1927	STL	A	5	.429	.476	21	9	1	0	0	0.0	5	5	1	0	1	0	0	35	2	1	2	7.6	.974	1B-5
1928			54	.222	.311	45	10	1	0	1	2.2	3	8	8	4	1	**44**	**10**	2	0	0	0	2.0	1.000	1B-1
2 yrs.			59	.288	.364	66	19	2	0	1	1.5	8	13	9	4	2	44	10	37	2	1	2	6.7	.975	1B-6

Bobby Sturgeon

STURGEON, ROBERT HOWARD
B. Aug. 6, 1919, Clinton, Ind.
BR TR 6′ 175 lbs.

Year	Team	Lg	Games	BA	SA	AB	H	2B	3B	HR	HR%	R	RBI	BB	SO	SB	Pinch Hit AB	Pinch Hit H	PO	A	E	DP	TC/G	FA	G by Pos
1940	CHI	N	7	.190	.238	21	4	1	0	0	0.0	1	2	0	1	0	0	0	19	20	7	5	6.6	.848	SS-7
1941			129	.245	.293	433	106	15	3	0	0.0	45	25	9	30	5	0	0	215	366	27	68	4.8	.956	SS-126, 3B-1, 2B-1
1942			63	.247	.302	162	40	7	1	0	0.0	8	7	4	13	2	2	0	113	163	4	33	4.4	.986	2B-32, SS-29, 3B-2
1946			100	.296	.361	294	87	12	2	1	0.3	26	21	10	18	0	7	3	160	209	22	44	4.2	.944	SS-72, 2B-21
1947			87	.254	.341	232	59	10	5	0	0.0	16	21	7	12	0	10	3	137	202	6	43	4.3	.983	SS-45, 2B-30, 3B-5
1948	BOS	N	34	.218	.282	78	17	3	1	0	0.0	10	4	4	5	0	4	2	43	46	7	9	3.7	.927	2B-18, SS-4, 3B-4
6 yrs.			420	.257	.318	1220	313	48	12	1	0.1	106	80	34	79	7	23	8	687	1006	73	202	4.4	.959	SS-283, 2B-102, 3B-12

Dean Sturgis

STURGIS, DEAN DONNELL
B. Dec. 1, 1892, Beloit, Wis. D. June 4, 1950, Uniontown, Pa.
BR TR 6′ 1″ 180 lbs.

Year	Team	Lg	Games	BA	SA	AB	H	2B	3B	HR	HR%	R	RBI	BB	SO	SB	Pinch Hit AB	Pinch Hit H	PO	A	E	DP	TC/G	FA	G by Pos
1914	PHI	A	4	.250	.250	4	1	0	0	0	0.0	1	0	1	2	0	2	0	4	1	0	0	5.0	1.000	C-1

Johnny Sturm

STURM, JOHN PETER JOSEPH
B. Jan. 23, 1916, St. Louis, Mo.
BL TL 6′ 1″ 185 lbs.

Year	Team	Lg	Games	BA	SA	AB	H	2B	3B	HR	HR%	R	RBI	BB	SO	SB	Pinch Hit AB	Pinch Hit H	PO	A	E	DP	TC/G	FA	G by Pos
1941	NY	A	124	.239	.300	524	125	17	3	3	0.6	58	36	37	50	3	0	0	1099	85	12	117	9.6	.990	1B-124
WORLD SERIES																									
1941	NY	A	5	.286	.286	21	6	0	0	0	0.0	0	2	0	2	1	0	0	48	1	0	5	9.8	1.000	1B-5

George Stutz

STUTZ, GEORGE (Kid)
B. Feb. 12, 1893, Philadelphia, Pa. D. Dec. 29, 1930, Philadelphia, Pa.
BR TR 5′ 5″ 150 lbs.

Year	Team	Lg	Games	BA	SA	AB	H	2B	3B	HR	HR%	R	RBI	BB	SO	SB	Pinch Hit AB	Pinch Hit H	PO	A	E	DP	TC/G	FA	G by Pos
1926	PHI	N	6	.000	.000	9	0	0	0	0	0.0	0	0	0	2	0	1	0	8	7	1	2	3.2	.938	SS-5

Lena Styles

STYLES, WILLIAM GRAVES
B. Nov. 27, 1899, Gurley, Ala. D. Mar. 14, 1956, Huntsville, Ala.
BR TR 6′ 1″ 185 lbs.

Year	Team	Lg	Games	BA	SA	AB	H	2B	3B	HR	HR%	R	RBI	BB	SO	SB	Pinch Hit AB	Pinch Hit H	PO	A	E	DP	TC/G	FA	G by Pos
1919	PHI	A	8	.273	.318	22	6	1	0	0	0.0	0	5	1	6	0	0	0	31	7	1	1	4.9	.974	C-8
1920			24	.260	.360	50	13	3	1	0	0.0	5	5	6	7	1	7	1	94	15	3	5	7.0	.973	C-9, 1B-7
1921			4	.200	.200	5	1	0	0	0	0.0	0	0	0	2	0	2	1	1	1	4	0	3.0	.333	C-2
1930	CIN	N	7	.250	.417	12	3	0	1	0	0.0	2	1	1	2	0	1	0	13	3	2	0	3.0	.889	C-5, 1B-1
1931			34	.241	.276	87	21	3	0	0	0.0	7	5	8	7	0	3	0	68	7	4	0	2.5	.949	C-31
5 yrs.			77	.250	.313	176	44	7	2	0	0.0	14	16	16	24	1	13	2	207	33	14	6	4.0	.945	C-55, 1B-8

Chris Stynes

STYNES, CHRISTOPHER DESMOND
B. Jan. 19, 1973, Queens, N. Y.
BR TR 5′ 9″ 175 lbs.

Year	Team	Lg	Games	BA	SA	AB	H	2B	3B	HR	HR%	R	RBI	BB	SO	SB	Pinch Hit AB	Pinch Hit H	PO	A	E	DP	TC/G	FA	G by Pos
1995	KC	A	22	.171	.200	35	6	1	0	0	0.0	7	2	4	3	0	3	1	22	35	1	12	3.2	.983	2B-17, DH-1

Neil Stynes

STYNES, CORNELIUS WILLIAM
B. Dec. 10, 1868, Arlington, Mass. D. Mar. 26, 1944, Somerville, Mass.
BR TR 6′ 165 lbs.

Year	Team	Lg	Games	BA	SA	AB	H	2B	3B	HR	HR%	R	RBI	BB	SO	SB	Pinch Hit AB	Pinch Hit H	PO	A	E	DP	TC/G	FA	G by Pos
1890	CLE	P	2	.000	.000	8	0	0	0	0	0.0	0	0	0	0	0	0	0	11	0	3	0	7.0	.786	C-2

Ken Suarez

SUAREZ, KENNETH RAYMOND
B. Apr. 12, 1943, Tampa, Fla.
BR TR 5′ 9″ 175 lbs.

Year	Team	Lg	Games	BA	SA	AB	H	2B	3B	HR	HR%	R	RBI	BB	SO	SB	Pinch Hit AB	Pinch Hit H	PO	A	E	DP	TC/G	FA	G by Pos
1966	KC	A	35	.145	.174	69	10	0	1	0	0.0	5	2	15	26	2	1	0	145	20	8	7	5.1	.954	C-34
1967			39	.238	.413	63	15	5	0	2	3.2	7	9	16	21	1	2	0	170	20	4	2	5.4	.979	C-36
1968	CLE	A	17	.100	.100	10	1	0	0	0	0.0	1	0	1	3	0	3	0	22	2	0	0	1.6	1.000	C-12, 2B-1, OF-1, 3B-1
1969			36	.294	.388	85	25	5	0	1	1.2	7	9	15	12	1	0	0	191	20	2	3	5.9	.991	C-36
1971			50	.203	.285	123	25	7	0	1	0.8	10	9	18	15	0	2	0	268	14	2	3	5.9	.993	C-48
1972	TEX	A	25	.152	.182	33	5	1	0	0	0.0	2	4	1	4	0	11	1	53	2	2	0	3.4	.965	C-17
1973			93	.248	.299	278	69	11	0	1	0.4	25	27	33	16	1	4	1	501	44	6	4	6.1	.989	C-90
7 yrs.			295	.227	.297	661	150	29	1	5	0.8	57	60	99	97	5	23	2	1350	122	24	19	5.4	.984	C-273, 2B-1, OF-1, 3B-1

Luis Suarez

SUAREZ, LUIS ABELARDO
B. Aug. 24, 1916, Alto Songo, Cuba D. June 5, 1991, Havana, Cuba.
BR TR 5′11″ 170 lbs.

Year	Team	Lg	Games	BA	SA	AB	H	2B	3B	HR	HR%	R	RBI	BB	SO	SB	Pinch Hit AB	Pinch Hit H	PO	A	E	DP	TC/G	FA	G by Pos
1944	WAS	A	1	.000	.000	2	0	0	0	0	0.0	0	0	0	0	0	0	0	0	2	0	0	2.0	1.000	3B-1

Tony Suck

SUCK, CHARLES ANTHONY
Born Charles Anthony Zuck.
B. June 11, 1858, Chicago, Ill. D. Jan. 29, 1895, Chicago, Ill.
5′ 9″ 164 lbs.

Year	Team	Lg	Games	BA	SA	AB	H	2B	3B	HR	HR%	R	RBI	BB	SO	SB	Pinch Hit AB	Pinch Hit H	PO	A	E	DP	TC/G	FA	G by Pos
1883	BUF	N	2	.000	.000	7	0	0	0	0	0.0	1		1	4		0	0	4	0	3	0	3.5	.571	C-1, OF-1
1884	3 teams		CHI U (43G –.144) PIT U (10G –.171) BAL U (3G –.300)																						
″	total		56	.157	.167	198	31	2	0	0	0.0	20		13			0	0	242	90	50	4	6.5	.869	C-31, SS-15, OF-12, 3B-1
2 yrs.			58	.151	.161	205	31	2	0	0	0.0	21		14	4		0	0	246	90	53	4	6.4	.864	C-32, SS-15, OF-13, 3B-1

Bill Sudakis

SUDAKIS, WILLIAM PAUL (Suds)
B. Mar. 27, 1946, Joliet, Ill.
BB TR 6′ 1″ 190 lbs.

Year	Team	Lg	Games	BA	SA	AB	H	2B	3B	HR	HR%	R	RBI	BB	SO	SB	Pinch Hit AB	Pinch Hit H	PO	A	E	DP	TC/G	FA	G by Pos
1968	LA	N	24	.276	.471	87	24	4	2	3	3.4	11	12	15	14	1	0	0	25	57	4	3	3.6	.953	3B-24
1969			132	.234	.383	462	108	17	5	14	3.0	50	53	40	94	3	12	1	98	272	21	26	3.2	.946	3B-121
1970			94	.264	.461	269	71	11	0	14	5.2	37	44	35	46	4	21	5	194	100	14	9	3.9	.955	C-38, 3B-37, OF-3, 1B-1
1971			41	.193	.337	83	16	3	0	3	3.6	10	7	12	22	0	21	4	90	16	0	1	4.4	1.000	C-19, 3B-3, 1B-1, OF-1
1972	NY	N	18	.143	.204	49	7	0	0	1	2.0	3	7	6	14	0	6	1	88	8	2	3	8.2	.980	1B-7, C-5
1973	TEX	A	82	.255	.494	235	60	11	0	15	6.4	32	43	23	53	0	14	5	216	62	5	21	3.9	.982	3B-29, 1B-24, C-9, DH-8, OF-2
1974	NY	A	89	.232	.344	259	60	8	0	7	2.7	26	39	25	48	0	15	2	280	26	4	31	4.1	.987	DH-39, 1B-33, 3B-3, C-1
1975	2 teams		CAL A (30G –.121) CLE A (20G –.196)																						
″	total		50	.154	.231	104	16	2	0	2	1.9	8	9	16	22	1	19	1	121	7	1	10	3.4	.992	1B-14, DH-13, C-11
8 yrs.			530	.234	.393	1548	362	56	7	59	3.8	177	214	172	313	9	108	19	1112	548	51	104	3.8	.970	3B-217, C-83, 1B-80, DH-60, OF-6

Pete Suder

SUDER, PETER (Pecky) BR TR 6′ 175 lbs.
B. Apr. 16, 1916, Aliquippa, Pa.

Year	Team		Games	BA	SA	AB	H	2B	3B	HR	HR%	R	RBI	BB	SO	SB	Pinch Hit AB	Pinch Hit H	PO	A	E	DP	TC/G	FA	G by Pos
1941	PHI	A	139	.245	.339	531	130	20	9	4	0.8	45	52	19	47	1	0	0	180	279	21	28	3.5	.956	3B-136, SS-3
1942			128	.256	.340	476	122	20	4	4	0.8	46	54	24	39	4	2	0	242	344	22	59	4.5	.964	SS-69, 3B-34, 2B-31
1943			131	.221	.291	475	105	14	5	3	0.6	30	41	14	40	1	1	0	272	323	17	68	4.6	.972	2B-95, 3B-32, SS-5
1946			128	.281	.352	455	128	20	3	2	0.4	38	50	18	37	1	11	2	247	284	22	56	4.7	.960	SS-67, 3B-33, 2B-12, 1B-3, OF-2
1947			145	.241	.337	528	127	28	4	5	0.9	45	60	35	44	0	1	0	310	418	12	96	5.1	.984	2B-140, SS-3, 3B-2
1948			148	.241	.345	519	125	23	5	7	1.3	64	60	60	60	1	0	0	342	461	10	114	5.5	.988	2B-148
1949			118	.267	.416	445	119	24	6	10	2.2	44	75	23	35	0	0	0	240	331	17	94	4.6	.971	2B-89, 3B-36, SS-2
1950			77	.246	.383	248	61	10	0	8	3.2	34	35	23	31	2	4	1	167	181	9	55	5.0	.975	2B-47, 3B-11, SS-10, 1B-4
1951			123	.245	.298	440	108	18	1	1	0.2	46	42	30	42	5	0	0	321	355	11	107	5.5	.984	2B-103, SS-18, 3B-3
1952			74	.241	.303	228	55	7	2	1	0.4	22	20	16	17	1	0	0	136	179	8	40	4.3	.975	2B-43, SS-17, 3B-16
1953			115	.286	.350	454	130	11	3	4	0.9	44	35	17	35	3	0	0	189	290	11	44	4.2	.978	3B-72, 2B-38, SS-7
1954			69	.200	.263	205	41	11	1	0	0.0	8	16	7	16	0	13	3	100	134	9	25	4.3	.963	2B-35, 3B-20, SS-2
1955	KC	A	26	.210	.284	81	17	4	1	0	0.0	3	1	2	13	0	2	0	51	44	1	17	4.0	.990	2B-24
13 yrs.			1421	.249	.337	5085	1268	210	44	49	1.0	469	541	288	456	19	34	6	2797	3623	170	803	4.7	.974	2B-805, 3B-395, SS-203, 1B-7, OF-2

Willie Sudhoff

SUDHOFF, JOHN WILLIAM (Wee Willie) BR TR 5′ 7″ 165 lbs.
B. Sept. 17, 1874, St. Louis, Mo. D. May 25, 1917, St. Louis, Mo.

Year	Team		Games	BA	SA	AB	H	2B	3B	HR	HR%	R	RBI	BB	SO	SB	Pinch Hit AB	Pinch Hit H	PO	A	E	DP	TC/G	FA	G by Pos
1897	STL	N	11	.238	.262	42	10	1	0	0	0.0	7	3	1		0	0	0	8	29	3	2	3.6	.925	P-11
1898			41	.158	.192	120	19	2	1	0	0.0	5	4	5		0	0	0	15	114	12	5	3.4	.915	P-41
1899	2 teams	CLE N (11G –.065) STL N (26G –.206)																							
″	total		37	.162	.212	99	16	1	2	0	0.0	11	8	12		0	0	0	11	99	11	3	3.3	.909	P-37
1900	STL	N	35	.189	.217	106	20	1	1	0	0.0	15	6	11		8	1	0	26	57	12	1	2.7	.874	P-16, OF-12, 3B-7
1901			38	.176	.278	108	19	2	3	1	0.9	11	17	10		0	0	0	14	84	5	4	2.7	.951	P-38
1902	STL	A	31	.169	.195	77	13	2	0	0	0.0	6	5	4		3	0	0	8	84	10	4	3.3	.902	P-30, OF-1
1903			41	.182	.227	110	20	1	2	0	0.0	11	6	3		1	2	0	15	104	5	0	3.3	.960	P-38
1904			30	.165	.200	85	14	3	0	0	0.0	5	7	6		0	0	0	13	104	3	4	4.0	.975	P-27, OF-3
1905			32	.186	.244	86	16	3	1	0	0.0	6	3	7		1	0	0	20	96	4	0	3.8	.967	P-32
1906	WAS	A	9	.429	.429	7	3	0	0	0	0.0	0	0	0		0	0	0	1	11	1	0	1.4	.923	P-9
10 yrs.			305	.179	.225	840	150	16	10	1	0.1	77	59	59		13	3	0	131	782	66	23	3.2	.933	P-279, OF-16, 3B-7

William Suero

SUERO, WILLIAMS BR TR 5′ 9″ 175 lbs.
Born Williams Suero (Urban).
B. Nov. 7, 1966, Santo Domingo, Dominican Republic
D. Nov. 30, 1995, Santo Domingo, Dominican Republic.

Year	Team		Games	BA	SA	AB	H	2B	3B	HR	HR%	R	RBI	BB	SO	SB	Pinch Hit AB	Pinch Hit H	PO	A	E	DP	TC/G	FA	G by Pos
1992	MIL	A	18	.188	.250	16	3	1	0	0	0.0	4	0	2	1	1	0	0	11	22	1	5	1.9	.971	2B-15, DH-2, SS-1
1993			15	.286	.286	14	4	0	0	0	0.0	0	0	1	3	0	6	3	6	13	1	2	2.2	.950	2B-8, 3B-1
2 yrs.			33	.233	.267	30	7	1	0	0	0.0	4	0	3	4	1	6	3	17	35	2	7	2.0	.963	2B-23, DH-2, 3B-1, SS-1

Joe Sugden

SUGDEN, JOSEPH BB TR 5′10″ 180 lbs.
B. July 31, 1870, Philadelphia, Pa. D. June 28, 1959, Philadelphia, Pa.

Year	Team		Games	BA	SA	AB	H	2B	3B	HR	HR%	R	RBI	BB	SO	SB	Pinch Hit AB	Pinch Hit H	PO	A	E	DP	TC/G	FA	G by Pos
1893	PIT	N	27	.261	.370	92	24	4	3	0	0.0	20	12	10	11	1	0	0	81	27	5	3	4.2	.956	C-27
1894			39	.331	.496	139	46	13	2	2	1.4	23	23	14	2	3	0	0	120	43	21	5	4.7	.886	C-31, 3B-4, SS-3, OF-1
1895			49	.310	.368	155	48	4	1	1	0.6	28	17	16	12	4	0	0	176	57	25	4	5.3	.903	C-49
1896			80	.296	.359	301	89	5	7	0	0.0	42	36	19	9	5	0	0	337	73	21	16	5.3	.951	C-70, 1B-7, OF-4
1897			84	.222	.271	288	64	6	4	0	0.0	31	38	18		9	0	0	342	83	27	8	5.4	.940	C-81, 1B-3
1898	STL	N	89	.253	.284	289	73	7	1	0	0.0	29	34	23		5	7	2	272	91	21	13	4.6	.945	C-60, OF-15, 1B-8
1899	CLE	N	76	.276	.304	250	69	5	1	0	0.0	19	14	11		2	2	1	213	111	23	14	4.7	.934	C-66, OF-4, 1B-3, 3B-1
1901	CHI	A	48	.275	.333	153	42	7	1	0	0.0	21	19	13		4	2	0	200	49	7	4	5.4	.973	C-42, 1B-5
1902	STL	A	69	.246	.300	203	50	7	2	0	0.0	25	15	20		2	3	1	210	69	13	9	4.4	.955	C-61, 1B-4, P-1
1903			79	.216	.232	241	52	4	0	0	0.0	18	22	25		4	5	0	391	84	8	10	6.5	.983	C-66, 1B-8
1904			105	.262	.297	347	91	6	3	0	0.0	25	30	28		6	1	0	645	102	9	22	7.1	.988	C-79, 1B-28
1905			85	.173	.188	266	46	4	0	0	0.0	21	23	23		3	4	0	496	114	10	7	7.8	.984	C-71, 1B-9
1912	DET	A	1	.250	.250	4	1	0	0	0	0.0	1	0	0		0	0	0	13	3	1	0	17.0	.941	1B-1
13 yrs.			831	.255	.303	2728	695	72	25	3	0.1	303	283	220	34	48	24	4	3496	906	191	115	5.7	.958	C-703, 1B-76, OF-24, 3B-5, SS-3, P-1

Gus Suhr

SUHR, AUGUST RICHARD BL TR 6′ 180 lbs.
B. Jan. 3, 1906, San Francisco, Calif.

Year	Team		Games	BA	SA	AB	H	2B	3B	HR	HR%	R	RBI	BB	SO	SB	Pinch Hit AB	Pinch Hit H	PO	A	E	DP	TC/G	FA	G by Pos
1930	PIT	N	151	.286	.480	542	155	26	14	17	3.1	93	107	80	56	11	0	0	1445	79	13	142	10.2	.992	1B-151
1931			87	.211	.333	270	57	13	4	4	1.5	26	32	38	25	4	8	4	684	39	5	72	9.6	.993	1B-76
1932			154	.263	.398	581	153	31	16	5	0.9	78	81	63	39	7	0	0	1388	84	18	111	9.7	.988	1B-154
1933			154	.267	.413	566	151	31	11	10	1.8	72	75	72	52	2	0	0	1451	90	14	151	10.1	.991	1B-154
1934			151	.283	.459	573	162	36	13	13	2.3	67	103	66	52	4	0	0	1326	75	9	108	9.3	.994	1B-151
1935			153	.272	.437	529	144	33	12	10	1.9	68	81	70	54	6	2	1	1316	73	15	83	9.3	.989	1B-149, OF-2
1936			156	.312	.467	583	182	33	12	11	1.9	111	118	95	34	8	0	0	1432	93	10	100	9.8	.993	1B-156
1937			151	.278	.402	575	160	28	14	5	0.9	69	97	83	42	2	0	0	1452	91	11	108	10.3	.993	1B-151
1938			145	.294	.430	530	156	35	14	3	0.6	82	64	87	37	4	0	0	1512	81	12	150	11.1	.993	1B-145
1939	2 teams	PIT N (63G –.289) PHI N (60G –.318)																							
″	total		123	.303	.408	402	122	22	4	4	1.0	44	55	59	37	5	8	1	1041	60	7	92	9.9	.994	1B-112
1940	PHI	N	10	.160	.400	25	4	0	0	2	8.0	4	5	5	5	0	3	1	57	1	2	5	8.6	.967	1B-7
11 yrs.			1435	.279	.428	5176	1446	288	114	84	1.6	714	818	718	433	53	21	7	13104	766	116	1122	9.9	.992	1B-1406, OF-2

Clyde Sukeforth

SUKEFORTH, CLYDE LeROY (Sukey) BL TR 5′10″ 155 lbs.
B. Nov. 30, 1901, Washington, Me.
Manager 1947.

Year	Team		Games	BA	SA	AB	H	2B	3B	HR	HR%	R	RBI	BB	SO	SB	Pinch Hit AB	Pinch Hit H	PO	A	E	DP	TC/G	FA	G by Pos
1926	CIN	N	1	.000	.000	1	0	0	0	0	0.0	0	0	0	1	0	1	0	0	0	0	0	0.0	—	
1927			38	.190	.224	58	11	2	0	0	0.0	12	2	7	2	2	3	1	52	12	2	1	2.8	.970	C-24
1928			33	.132	.208	53	7	2	1	0	0.0	5	3	3	5	0	4	0	48	8	2	1	2.2	.966	C-26
1929			84	.354	.451	237	84	16	2	1	0.4	31	33	17	6	8	3	2	171	40	4	4	2.8	.981	C-76
1930			94	.284	.345	296	84	9	3	1	0.3	30	19	17	12	1	7	1	234	46	7	8	3.5	.976	C-82

Clyde Sukeforth *continued*

Year	Team	Games	BA	SA	AB	H	2B	3B	HR	HR%	R	RBI	BB	SO	SB	Pinch Hit AB	Pinch Hit H	PO	A	E	DP	TC/G	FA	G by Pos
1931		112	.256	.322	351	90	15	4	0	0.0	22	25	38	13	0	4	1	300	59	13	9	3.5	.965	C-106
1932	BKN N	59	.234	.342	111	26	4	4	0	0.0	14	12	6	10	1	22	3	95	13	1	2	3.0	.991	C-36
1933		20	.056	.056	36	2	0	0	0	0.0	1	0	2	1	0	0	0	50	7	1	2	3.2	.983	C-18
1934		27	.163	.186	43	7	1	0	0	0.0	5	1	1	6	0	5	0	38	4	0	2	2.3	1.000	C-18
1945		18	.294	.314	51	15	1	0	0	0.0	2	1	4	1	0	5	0	53	1	3	0	4.4	.947	C-13
10 yrs.		486	.264	.331	1237	326	50	14	2	0.2	122	96	95	57	12	54	8	1041	190	33	29	3.2	.974	C-399

Guy Sularz

SULARZ, GUY PATRICK
B. Nov. 7, 1955, Minneapolis, Minn.
BR TR 5′11″ 165 lbs.

Year	Team	Games	BA	SA	AB	H	2B	3B	HR	HR%	R	RBI	BB	SO	SB	Pinch Hit AB	Pinch Hit H	PO	A	E	DP	TC/G	FA	G by Pos
1980	SF N	25	.246	.292	65	16	1	1	0	0.0	3	3	9	6	1	0	0	50	79	3	14	5.1	.977	2B-21, 3B-5
1981		10	.200	.200	20	4	0	0	0	0.0	0	2	2	4	0	3	1	9	24	0	3	4.7	1.000	2B-6, 3B-1
1982		63	.228	.287	101	23	3	0	1	1.0	15	7	9	11	3	6	0	57	100	7	23	2.7	.957	SS-37, 3B-14, 2B-9
1983		10	.100	.100	20	2	0	0	0	0.0	3	0	3	2	0	1	0	10	20	2	3	3.2	.938	SS-6, 3B-4
4 yrs.		108	.218	.262	206	45	4	1	1	0.5	21	12	23	23	4	10	1	126	223	12	43	3.5	.967	SS-43, 2B-36, 3B-24

Ernie Sulik

SULIK, ERNEST RICHARD
B. July 7, 1910, San Francisco, Calif. D. May 31, 1963, Oakland, Calif.
BL TL 5′10″ 178 lbs.

Year	Team	Games	BA	SA	AB	H	2B	3B	HR	HR%	R	RBI	BB	SO	SB	Pinch Hit AB	Pinch Hit H	PO	A	E	DP	TC/G	FA	G by Pos
1936	PHI N	122	.287	.386	404	116	14	4	6	1.5	69	36	40	22	4	14	2	227	6	7	1	2.3	.971	OF-105

Andy Sullivan

SULLIVAN, ANDREW B.
B. Aug. 30, 1884, Southborough, Mass. D. Feb. 14, 1920, Framingham, Mass.
TR

Year	Team	Games	BA	SA	AB	H	2B	3B	HR	HR%	R	RBI	BB	SO	SB	Pinch Hit AB	Pinch Hit H	PO	A	E	DP	TC/G	FA	G by Pos
1904	BOS N	1	.000	.000	1	0	0	0	0	0.0	0	0	1		0	0	0	2	0	0	0	2.0	1.000	SS-1

Bill Sullivan

SULLIVAN, WILLIAM F.
B. July 4, 1853, Holyoke, Mass. D. Nov. 13, 1884, Holyoke, Mass.

Year	Team	Games	BA	SA	AB	H	2B	3B	HR	HR%	R	RBI	BB	SO	SB	Pinch Hit AB	Pinch Hit H	PO	A	E	DP	TC/G	FA	G by Pos
1878	CHI N	2	.167	.167	6	1	0	0	0	0.0	1	0	0	0		0	0	1	0	0	0	0.5	1.000	OF-2

Billy Sullivan

SULLIVAN, WILLIAM JOSEPH, JR.
Son of Billy Sullivan.
B. Oct. 23, 1910, Chicago, Ill. D. Jan. 4, 1994, Sarasota, Fla.
BL TR 6′ 170 lbs.

Year	Team	Games	BA	SA	AB	H	2B	3B	HR	HR%	R	RBI	BB	SO	SB	Pinch Hit AB	Pinch Hit H	PO	A	E	DP	TC/G	FA	G by Pos
1931	CHI A	92	.275	.364	363	100	16	5	2	0.6	48	33	20	14	4	7	4	104	152	24	9	3.3	.914	3B-83, OF-2, 1B-1
1932		93	.316	.384	307	97	16	1	1	0.3	31	45	20	9	1	19	3	511	66	13	46	8.0	.978	1B-52, 3B-17, C-5
1933		54	.192	.208	125	24	0	1	0	0.0	9	13	10	5	0	22	5	232	15	8	22	8.5	.969	1B-22, C-8
1935	CIN N	85	.266	.361	241	64	9	4	2	0.8	29	36	19	16	4	21	7	383	78	8	41	7.7	.983	1B-40, 3B-15, 2B-6
1936	CLE A	93	.351	.508	319	112	32	6	2	0.6	39	48	16	9	5	11	5	355	52	12	13	5.2	.971	C-72, 3B-5, 1B-3, OF-1
1937		72	.286	.446	168	48	12	3	3	1.8	26	22	17	7	1	24	5	199	23	9	4	5.3	.961	C-38, 1B-5, 3B-1
1938	STL A	111	.277	.381	375	104	16	1	7	1.9	35	49	20	10	8	8	1	484	69	5	17	5.3	.991	C-99, 1B-6
1939		118	.289	.416	332	96	17	5	5	1.5	53	50	34	18	3	33	9	251	17	12	7	3.4	.957	OF-59, C-19, 1B-4
1940	DET A	78	.309	.450	220	68	14	4	3	1.4	36	41	31	11	2	15	5	296	43	10	5	5.5	.971	C-57, 3B-6
1941		85	.282	.393	234	66	15	1	3	1.3	29	29	35	11	0	21	6	339	33	9	7	6.0	.976	C-63
1942	BKN N	43	.267	.337	101	27	2	1	1	1.0	11	14	12	6	1	1	0	140	13	6	2	3.9	.962	C-41
1947	PIT N	38	.255	.309	55	14	3	0	0	0.0	1	8	6	3	1	25	5	42	4	0	1	3.8	1.000	C-12
12 yrs.		962	.289	.395	2840	820	152	32	29	1.0	347	388	240	119	30	207	55	3336	565	116	174	5.4	.971	C-414, 1B-133, 3B-127, OF-62, 2B-6
WORLD SERIES																								
1940	DET A	5	.154	.154	13	2	0	0	0	0.0	3	0	5	2	0	1	0	24	2	0	0	6.5	1.000	C-4

Billy Sullivan

SULLIVAN, WILLIAM JOSEPH, SR.
Father of Billy Sullivan.
B. Feb. 1, 1875, Oakland, Wis. D. Jan. 28, 1965, Newberg, Ore.
Manager 1909.
BR TR 5′ 9″ 155 lbs.

Year	Team	Games	BA	SA	AB	H	2B	3B	HR	HR%	R	RBI	BB	SO	SB	Pinch Hit AB	Pinch Hit H	PO	A	E	DP	TC/G	FA	G by Pos
1899	BOS N	22	.270	.378	74	20	2	0	2	2.7	10	12	1		2	0	0	94	26	6	3	5.7	.952	C-22
1900		72	.273	.399	238	65	6	0	8	3.4	36	41	9		4	3	2	232	77	9	11	4.7	.972	C-66, SS-1, 2B-1
1901	CHI A	98	.245	.351	367	90	15	6	4	1.1	54	56	10		12	0	0	396	104	19	13	5.3	.963	C-97, 3B-1
1902		76	.243	.323	263	64	12	3	1	0.4	36	26	6		11	2	0	254	81	11	10	4.7	.968	C-70, OF-2, 1B-2
1903		32	.189	.252	111	21	4	0	1	0.9	10	7	5		3	1	0	123	35	2	1	5.2	.988	C-31
1904		108	.229	.307	371	85	18	4	1	0.3	29	44	12		11	1	0	463	130	22	10	5.7	.964	C-107
1905		99	.201	.269	323	65	10	3	2	0.6	25	26	13		14	3	0	404	104	13	10	5.4	.975	C-93, 1B-2, 3B-1
1906		118	.214	.297	387	83	18	4	2	0.5	37	33	22		10	0	0	475	134	16	7	5.3	.974	C-118
1907		112	.174	.221	339	59	8	4	0	0.0	30	36	21		6	3	0	479	119	10	13	5.6	.984	C-108, 2B-1
1908		137	.191	.228	430	82	8	4	0	0.0	40	29	22		15	1	0	553	156	11	11	5.3	.985	C-137
1909		97	.162	.174	265	43	3	0	0	0.0	11	16	17		9	0	0	452	119	10	6	6.0	.983	C-97
1910		45	.183	.225	142	26	4	1	0	0.0	10	6	7		0	0	0	290	71	9	5	8.2	.976	C-45
1911		89	.215	.273	256	55	9	3	0	0.0	26	31	16		1	0	0	447	114	8	13	6.4	.986	C-89
1912		39	.209	.253	91	19	2	1	0	0.0	9	15	9		0	0	0	147	52	5	4	5.2	.975	C-39
1914		1	—	—	0	0	0	0	0	—	0	0	0	0	0	0	0	1	0	0	0	1.0	1.000	C-1
1916	DET A	1	—	—	0	0	0	0	0	—	0	0	0	0	0	0	0	0	0	0	0	0.0	.000	C-1
16 yrs.		1146	.212	.280	3657	777	119	33	21	0.6	363	378	170	0	98	14	2	4810	1322	151	117	5.6	.976	C-1121, 1B-4, 3B-2, OF-2, 2B-2, SS-1
WORLD SERIES																								
1906	CHI A	6	.000	.000	21	0	0	0	0	0.0	0	0	0	9	0	0	0	35	10	1	1	7.7	.978	C-6

Chub Sullivan

SULLIVAN, JOHN FRANK
B. Jan. 12, 1856, Boston, Mass. D. Sept. 12, 1881, Boston, Mass.
BR TR 6′ 164 lbs.

Year	Team	Games	BA	SA	AB	H	2B	3B	HR	HR%	R	RBI	BB	SO	SB	Pinch Hit AB	Pinch Hit H	PO	A	E	DP	TC/G	FA	G by Pos
1877	CIN N	8	.250	.250	32	8	0	0	0	0.0	4	4	1	0		0	0	66	1	4	1	8.9	.944	1B-8
1878		61	.258	.291	244	63	4	2	0	0.0	29	20	2	9		0	0	680	23	18	33	11.8	.975	1B-61
1880	WOR N	43	.259	.331	166	43	6	3	0	0.0	22	0	4	6		0	0	447	12	8	19	10.9	.983	1B-43
3 yrs.		112	.258	.303	442	114	10	5	0	0.0	55	24	7	15		0	0	1193	36	30	53	11.2	.976	1B-112

Dan Sullivan

SULLIVAN, DANIEL C. (Link)
B. May 9, 1857, Providence, R. I. D. Oct. 26, 1893, Providence, R. I.
TR 5′11″ 194 lbs.

Year	Team	Games	BA	SA	AB	H	2B	3B	HR	HR%	R	RBI	BB	SO	SB	Pinch Hit AB	Pinch Hit H	PO	A	E	DP	TC/G	FA	G by Pos
1882	LOU AA	67	.273	.315	286	78	8	2	0	0.0	44		9			0	0	311	115	64	4	7.1	.869	C-54, 3B-10, OF-4, SS-1
1883		37	.211	.272	147	31	5	2	0	0.0	8		3			0	0	157	35	27	2	5.9	.877	C-32, OF-2, 3B-2, SS-1
1884		63	.239	.320	247	59	8	6	0	0.0	27		9			0	0	341	61	30	2	6.8	.931	C-63, OF-1
1885	2 teams	LOU AA (13G –.182) STL AA (17G –.117)																						
″	total	30	.144	.173	104	15	3	0	0	0.0	7		8			0	0	157	38	11	3	6.9	.947	C-26, 1B-4
1886	PIT AA	1	.000	.000	4	0	0	0	0	0.0	0		0			0	0	2	1	2	0	5.0	.600	C-1
5 yrs.		198	.232	.288	788	183	24	10	0	0.0	86		29			0	0	968	250	134	11	6.7	.901	C-176, 3B-12, OF-7, 1B-4, SS-2

Denny Sullivan

SULLIVAN, DENNIS J.
B. June 26, 1858, Boston, Mass. D. Dec. 31, 1925, Boston, Mass.
TR 5′ 9″ 170 lbs.

Year	Team	Games	BA	SA	AB	H	2B	3B	HR	HR%	R	RBI	BB	SO	SB	Pinch Hit AB	Pinch Hit H	PO	A	E	DP	TC/G	FA	G by Pos
1879	PRO N	5	.263	.368	19	5	2	0	0	0.0	5	2	1	1		0	0	1	5	8	0	2.8	.429	3B-4, OF-1
1880	BOS N	1	.250	.250	4	1	0	0	0	0.0	1	1	0	1		0	0	6	0	1	0	7.0	.857	C-1
2 yrs.		6	.261	.348	23	6	2	0	0	0.0	6	3	1	2		0	0	7	5	9	0	3.5	.571	3B-4, C-1, OF-1

Denny Sullivan

SULLIVAN, DENNIS WILLIAM
B. Sept. 28, 1882, Hillsboro, Wis. D. June 2, 1956, Los Angeles, Calif.
BL TR 5′10″

Year	Team	Games	BA	SA	AB	H	2B	3B	HR	HR%	R	RBI	BB	SO	SB	Pinch Hit AB	Pinch Hit H	PO	A	E	DP	TC/G	FA	G by Pos
1905	WAS A	3	.000	.000	11	0	0	0	0	0.0	0	0	1		0	0	0	3	0	0	0	1.0	1.000	OF-3
1907	BOS A	144	.245	.283	551	135	18	0	1	0.2	73	26	44		16	0	0	296	16	8	3	2.2	.975	OF-144
1908	2 teams	BOS A (101G –.241) CLE A (3G –.000)																						
″	total	104	.237	.295	359	85	7	7	0	0.0	33	25	14		15	4	0	195	18	4	4	2.1	.982	OF-101
1909	CLE A	3	.500	.500	2	1	0	0	0	0.0	0	0	0		0	1	1	0	0	0	0	0.0	.000	OF-2
4 yrs.		254	.239	.285	923	221	25	7	1	0.1	106	51	59		31	5	1	494	34	12	7	2.2	.978	OF-250

Eddie Sullivan

Playing record listed under Eddie Collins.

Haywood Sullivan

SULLIVAN, HAYWOOD COOPER
Father of Marc Sullivan.
B. Dec. 15, 1930, Donalsonville, Ga.
Manager 1965.
BR TR 6′ 4″ 210 lbs.

Year	Team	Games	BA	SA	AB	H	2B	3B	HR	HR%	R	RBI	BB	SO	SB	Pinch Hit AB	Pinch Hit H	PO	A	E	DP	TC/G	FA	G by Pos
1955	BOS A	2	.000	.000	6	0	0	0	0	0.0	1	0	0	1	0	0	0	11	1	0	0	6.0	1.000	C-2
1957		2	.000	.000	1	0	0	0	0	0.0	0	0	0	0	0	1	0	2	0	0	0	2.0	1.000	C-1
1959		4	.000	.000	2	0	0	0	0	0.0	0	0	1	1	0	1	0	4	0	0	0	2.0	1.000	C-2
1960		52	.161	.242	124	20	1	0	3	2.4	9	10	16	24	0	2	0	237	13	2	5	5.0	.992	C-50
1961	KC A	117	.242	.356	331	80	16	2	6	1.8	42	40	46	45	1	12	4	494	44	10	19	5.0	.982	C-88, 1B-16, OF-5
1962		95	.248	.332	274	68	7	2	4	1.5	33	29	31	54	1	2	1	449	31	10	2	5.2	.980	C-94, 1B-1
1963		40	.212	.283	113	24	6	1	0	0.0	9	8	15	15	0	5	0	226	15	2	3	6.6	.992	C-37
7 yrs.		312	.226	.318	851	192	30	5	13	1.5	94	87	109	140	2	23	5	1423	104	24	29	5.2	.985	C-274, 1B-17, OF-5

Jack Sullivan

SULLIVAN, CARL MANCEL
B. Feb. 22, 1918, Princeton, Tex. D. Oct. 15, 1992, Dallas, Tex.
BR TR 5′11″ 185 lbs.

Year	Team	Games	BA	SA	AB	H	2B	3B	HR	HR%	R	RBI	BB	SO	SB	Pinch Hit AB	Pinch Hit H	PO	A	E	DP	TC/G	FA	G by Pos
1944	DET A	1	.000	.000	1	0	0	0	0	0.0	0	0	0	0	0	0	0	1	0	0	0	1.0	1.000	2B-1

Joe Sullivan

SULLIVAN, JOSEPH DANIEL
B. Jan. 6, 1870, Charlestown, Mass. D. Nov. 2, 1897, Charlestown, Mass.
5′10″ 178 lbs.

Year	Team	Games	BA	SA	AB	H	2B	3B	HR	HR%	R	RBI	BB	SO	SB	Pinch Hit AB	Pinch Hit H	PO	A	E	DP	TC/G	FA	G by Pos
1893	WAS N	128	.266	.360	508	135	16	13	2	0.4	72	64	36	24	7	0	0	233	396	102	34	5.7	.860	SS-128
1894	2 teams	WAS N (17G –.250) PHI N (75G –.352)																						
″	total	92	.335	.440	364	122	13	8	3	0.8	70	68	29	12	13	1	0	207	264	60	34	5.8	.887	SS-81, 2B-8, OF-1, 3B-1
1895	PHI N	94	.338	.389	373	126	7	3	2	0.5	75	50	24	20	15	0	0	195	270	63	32	5.6	.881	SS-89, OF-6
1896	2 teams	PHI N (48G –.251) STL N (51G –.292)																						
″	total	99	.273	.350	403	110	9	5	4	1.0	70	45	27	24	14	0	0	196	28	12	2	2.3	.949	OF-90, 2B-7, SS-2, 3B-2
4 yrs.		413	.299	.382	1648	493	45	29	11	0.7	287	227	116	80	49	1	0	831	958	237	102	4.9	.883	SS-300, OF-97, 2B-15, 3B-3

John Sullivan

SULLIVAN, JOHN EUGENE
B. Feb. 16, 1873, Chicago, Ill. D. June 5, 1924, St. Paul, Minn.
TR

Year	Team	Games	BA	SA	AB	H	2B	3B	HR	HR%	R	RBI	BB	SO	SB	Pinch Hit AB	Pinch Hit H	PO	A	E	DP	TC/G	FA	G by Pos
1905	DET A	12	.161	.161	31	5	0	0	0	0.0	4	4	4		0	0	0	56	21	2	0	6.6	.975	C-12
1908	PIT N	1	.000	.000	1	0	0	0	0	0.0	0	0	0		0	0	0	1	1	0	0	2.0	1.000	C-1
2 yrs.		13	.156	.156	32	5	0	0	0	0.0	4	4	4		0	0	0	57	22	2	0	6.2	.975	C-13

John Sullivan

SULLIVAN, JOHN LAWRENCE
B. Mar. 21, 1890, Williamsport, Pa. D. Apr. 1, 1966, Milton, Pa.
BR TR 5′11″ 180 lbs.

Year	Team	Games	BA	SA	AB	H	2B	3B	HR	HR%	R	RBI	BB	SO	SB	Pinch Hit AB	Pinch Hit H	PO	A	E	DP	TC/G	FA	G by Pos
1920	BOS N	82	.296	.396	250	74	14	4	1	0.4	36	28	29	29	3	6	3	164	11	4	6	2.5	.978	OF-66, 1B-6
1921	2 teams	BOS N (5G –.000) CHI N (76G –.329)																						
″	total	81	.322	.461	245	79	14	4	4	1.6	28	41	19	26	3	14	3	122	3	5	0	2.0	.962	OF-65
2 yrs.		163	.309	.428	495	153	28	8	5	1.0	64	69	48	55	6	20	6	286	14	9	6	2.3	.971	OF-131, 1B-6

John Sullivan

SULLIVAN, JOHN PAUL
B. Nov. 2, 1920, Chicago, Ill.
BR TR 5′10″ 170 lbs.

Year	Team	Games	BA	SA	AB	H	2B	3B	HR	HR%	R	RBI	BB	SO	SB	Pinch Hit AB	Pinch Hit H	PO	A	E	DP	TC/G	FA	G by Pos
1942	WAS A	94	.235	.286	357	84	16	1	0	0.0	38	42	25	30	2	1	0	217	235	31	51	5.3	.936	SS-92
1943		134	.208	.250	456	95	12	2	1	0.2	49	55	57	59	6	0	0	276	445	41	89	5.7	.946	SS-133
1944		138	.251	.280	471	118	12	1	0	0.0	49	30	52	43	3	0	0	276	426	50	89	5.4	.934	SS-138
1947		49	.256	.271	133	34	0	1	0	0.0	13	5	22	14	0	1	0	85	131	8	29	5.5	.964	SS-40, 2B-1
1948		85	.208	.243	173	36	4	1	0	0.0	25	12	22	25	2	9	0	100	155	14	34	4.4	.948	SS-57, 2B-4
1949	STL A	105	.226	.284	243	55	8	3	0	0.0	29	18	38	35	5	3	0	151	187	20	42	3.6	.944	SS-71, 3B-23, 2B-6
6 yrs.		605	.230	.270	1833	422	52	9	1	0.1	203	162	216	206	18	14	0	1105	1579	164	334	5.0	.942	SS-531, 3B-23, 2B-11

John Sullivan

SULLIVAN, JOHN PETER
B. Jan. 3, 1941, Somerville, N. J.
BL TR 6′ 195 lbs.

Year	Team	Games	BA	SA	AB	H	2B	3B	HR	HR%	R	RBI	BB	SO	SB	Pinch Hit AB	Pinch Hit H	PO	A	E	DP	TC/G	FA	G by Pos
1963	DET A	3	.000	.000	5	0	0	0	0	0.0	0	0	2	1	0	0	0	9	1	0	0	5.0	1.000	C-2
1964		2	.000	.000	3	0	0	0	0	0.0	0	0	0	1	0	0	0	2	2	0	0	2.0	1.000	C-2
1965		34	.267	.337	86	23	0	0	2	2.3	5	11	9	13	0	4	1	163	14	1	1	6.1	.994	C-29

John Sullivan *continued*

Year	Team		Games	BA	SA	AB	H	2B	3B	HR	HR%	R	RBI	BB	SO	SB	Pinch Hit AB	Pinch Hit H	PO	A	E	DP	TC/G	FA	G by Pos
1967	NY	N	65	.218	.252	147	32	5	0	0	0.0	4	6	6	26	0	26	4	201	17	2	2	3.9	.991	C-57
1968	PHI	N	12	.222	.222	18	4	0	0	0	0.0	0	1	2	4	0	7	1	26	3	1	1	3.8	.967	C-8
5 yrs.			116	.228	.270	259	59	5	0	2	0.8	9	18	19	45	0	37	6	401	37	4	4	4.5	.991	C-98

Marc Sullivan

SULLIVAN, MARC COOPER BR TR 6′ 4″ 198 lbs.
Son of Haywood Sullivan.
B. July 25, 1958, Quincy, Mass.

Year	Team		Games	BA	SA	AB	H	2B	3B	HR	HR%	R	RBI	BB	SO	SB	Pinch Hit AB	Pinch Hit H	PO	A	E	DP	TC/G	FA	G by Pos
1982	BOS	A	2	.333	.333	6	2	0	0	0	0.0	0	0	0	2	0	0	0	9	2	0	1	5.5	1.000	C-2
1984			2	.500	.500	6	3	0	0	0	0.0	1	1	1	0	0	0	0	19	0	1	0	10.0	.950	C-2
1985			32	.174	.290	69	12	2	0	2	2.9	10	3	6	15	0	0	0	129	8	1	1	4.3	.993	C-32
1986			41	.193	.252	119	23	4	0	1	0.8	15	14	7	32	0	0	0	203	13	3	1	5.3	.986	C-41
1987			60	.169	.237	160	27	5	0	2	1.3	11	10	4	43	0	0	0	303	29	2	6	5.6	.994	C-60
5 yrs.			137	.186	.258	360	67	11	0	5	1.4	37	28	18	92	0	0	0	663	52	7	9	5.3	.990	C-137

Marty Sullivan

SULLIVAN, MARTIN C. BR TR
B. Oct. 20, 1862, Lowell, Mass. D. Jan. 6, 1894, Lowell, Mass.

Year	Team		Games	BA	SA	AB	H	2B	3B	HR	HR%	R	RBI	BB	SO	SB	Pinch Hit AB	Pinch Hit H	PO	A	E	DP	TC/G	FA	G by Pos
1887	CHI	N	115	.284	.424	472	134	13	16	7	1.5	98	77	36	53	35	0	0	189	10	36	0	2.0	.847	OF-115, P-1
1888			75	.236	.379	314	74	12	6	7	2.2	40	39	15	32	9	0	0	114	13	10	7	1.8	.927	OF-75
1889	IND	N	69	.285	.398	256	73	11	3	4	1.6	45	35	50	31	15	0	0	191	9	15	8	3.1	.930	OF-64, 1B-5
1890	BOS	N	121	.285	.386	505	144	19	7	6	1.2	82	61	56	48	33	0	0	242	16	13	1	2.2	.952	OF-120, 3B-1
1891	2 teams	BOS N (17G –.224) CLE N (1G –.250)																							
″	total		18	.225	.324	71	16	1	0	2	2.8	15	8	5	4	7	0	0	24	1	2	0	1.5	.926	OF-18
5 yrs.			398	.273	.395	1618	441	56	32	26	1.6	280	220	162	168	99	0	0	760	49	76	16	2.2	.914	OF-392, 1B-5, 3B-1, P-1

Mike Sullivan

SULLIVAN, MICHAEL JOSEPH BR TR 5′ 8½″ 165 lbs.
B. June 10, 1860, Webster, Mass. D. June 16, 1929, Webster, Mass.

Year	Team		Games	BA	SA	AB	H	2B	3B	HR	HR%	R	RBI	BB	SO	SB	Pinch Hit AB	Pinch Hit H	PO	A	E	DP	TC/G	FA	G by Pos
1888	PHI	AA	28	.277	.455	112	31	5	6	1	0.9	20	19	3		10	0	0	34	19	20	0	2.6	.726	OF-18, 3B-10

Pat Sullivan

SULLIVAN, PATRICK J. TR 5′11″ 165 lbs.
B. Dec. 22, 1862, Milwaukee, Wis. Deceased.

Year	Team		Games	BA	SA	AB	H	2B	3B	HR	HR%	R	RBI	BB	SO	SB	Pinch Hit AB	Pinch Hit H	PO	A	E	DP	TC/G	FA	G by Pos
1884	KC	U	31	.193	.254	114	22	2	1	1	0.9	15		4			0	0	47	40	25	5	3.5	.777	3B-21, OF-9, P-1, C-1

Russ Sullivan

SULLIVAN, RUSSELL GUY BL TR 6′ 196 lbs.
B. Feb. 19, 1923, Fredericksburg, Va.

Year	Team		Games	BA	SA	AB	H	2B	3B	HR	HR%	R	RBI	BB	SO	SB	Pinch Hit AB	Pinch Hit H	PO	A	E	DP	TC/G	FA	G by Pos
1951	DET	A	7	.192	.346	26	5	1	0	1	3.8	2	1	2	1	0	0	0	14	1	1	0	2.3	.938	OF-7
1952			15	.327	.577	52	17	2	1	3	5.8	7	5	3	5	1	1	1	17	2	4	0	1.6	.826	OF-14
1953			23	.250	.389	72	18	5	1	1	1.4	7	6	13	5	0	3	0	42	4	2	1	2.4	.958	OF-20
3 yrs.			45	.267	.447	150	40	8	2	5	3.3	16	12	18	11	1	4	1	73	7	7	1	2.1	.920	OF-41

Sleeper Sullivan

SULLIVAN, THOMAS JEFFERSON BR TR 175 lbs.
B. St. Louis, Mo. D. Sept. 25, 1899, Camden, N. J.

Year	Team		Games	BA	SA	AB	H	2B	3B	HR	HR%	R	RBI	BB	SO	SB	Pinch Hit AB	Pinch Hit H	PO	A	E	DP	TC/G	FA	G by Pos
1881	BUF	N	35	.190	.223	121	23	4	0	0	0.0	13	15	1	21		0	0	111	33	27	1	4.8	.842	C-31, OF-5
1882	STL	AA	51	.181	.229	188	34	3	3	0	0.0	24		3			0	0	232	46	53	4	6.5	.840	C-50, P-1
1883			8	.222	.296	27	6	0	1	0	0.0	2		0			0	0	38	12	4	1	6.8	.926	C-6, OF-2
1884	STL	U	2	.111	.111	9	1	0	0	0	0.0	0		0			0	0	6	1	2	0	3.0	.778	C-1, P-1, OF-1
4 yrs.			96	.186	.229	345	64	7	4	0	0.0	39	15	4	21		0	0	387	92	86	6	5.8	.848	C-88, OF-8, P-2

Suter Sullivan

SULLIVAN, SUTER G. 6′ 170 lbs.
B. Oct. 14, 1872, Baltimore, Md. D. Apr. 19, 1925, Baltimore, Md.

Year	Team		Games	BA	SA	AB	H	2B	3B	HR	HR%	R	RBI	BB	SO	SB	Pinch Hit AB	Pinch Hit H	PO	A	E	DP	TC/G	FA	G by Pos
1898	STL	N	42	.222	.243	144	32	3	0	0	0.0	10	12	13		1	2	0	75	78	19	7	4.2	.890	SS-23, OF-10, 2B-6, P-1, 1B-1
1899	CLE	N	127	.245	.292	473	116	16	3	0	0.0	37	55	25		16	0	0	161	248	29	22	3.4	.934	3B-101, OF-20, SS-3, 1B-3, 2B-2
2 yrs.			169	.240	.280	617	148	19	3	0	0.0	47	67	38		17	2	0	236	326	48	29	3.6	.921	3B-101, OF-30, SS-26, 2B-8, 1B-4, P-1

Ted Sullivan

SULLIVAN, THEODORE PAUL
B. 1851, County Clare, Ireland D. July 5, 1929, Washington, D. C.
Manager 1883–84, 1888.

Year	Team		Games	BA	SA	AB	H	2B	3B	HR	HR%	R	RBI	BB	SO	SB	Pinch Hit AB	Pinch Hit H	PO	A	E	DP	TC/G	FA	G by Pos
1884	KC	U	3	.333	.333	9	3	0	0	0	0.0	0		1			0	0	1	3	4	0	2.7	.500	OF-2, SS-1

Tom Sullivan

SULLIVAN, THOMAS BRANDON BR TR 6′ 190 lbs.
B. Dec. 19, 1906, Nome, Alaska D. Aug. 16, 1944, Seattle, Wash.

Year	Team		Games	BA	SA	AB	H	2B	3B	HR	HR%	R	RBI	BB	SO	SB	Pinch Hit AB	Pinch Hit H	PO	A	E	DP	TC/G	FA	G by Pos
1925	CIN	N	1	.000	.000	1	0	0	0	0	0.0	0	0	0	0	0	0	0	1	0	0	0	1.0	1.000	C-1

Homer Summa

SUMMA, HOMER WAYNE BL TR 5′10½″ 170 lbs.
B. Nov. 3, 1898, Gentry, Mo. D. Jan. 29, 1966, Los Angeles, Calif.

Year	Team		Games	BA	SA	AB	H	2B	3B	HR	HR%	R	RBI	BB	SO	SB	Pinch Hit AB	Pinch Hit H	PO	A	E	DP	TC/G	FA	G by Pos
1920	PIT	N	10	.318	.455	22	7	1	1	0	0.0	1	1	3	1	1	4	1	18	1	1	0	3.3	.950	OF-6
1922	CLE	A	12	.348	.609	46	16	3	3	1	2.2	9	6	1	1	1	0	0	14	3	0	0	1.4	1.000	OF-12
1923			137	.328	.419	525	172	27	6	3	0.6	92	69	33	20	9	1	1	216	15	11	5	1.8	.955	OF-136
1924			111	.290	.390	390	113	21	6	2	0.5	55	38	11	16	4	14	2	167	10	11	2	2.0	.941	OF-95
1925			75	.330	.384	224	74	10	1	0	0.0	28	25	13	6	3	17	2	86	4	5	0	1.7	.947	OF-54, 3B-2
1926			154	.308	.403	581	179	31	6	4	0.7	74	76	47	9	15	0	0	328	18	9	5	2.3	.975	OF-154
1927			145	.286	.402	574	164	41	7	4	0.7	72	74	32	18	6	0	0	242	12	12	3	1.8	.955	OF-145
1928			134	.284	.365	504	143	26	3	3	0.6	60	57	20	15	4	2	0	223	12	7	5	1.8	.971	OF-132
1929	PHI	A	37	.272	.321	81	22	4	0	0	0.0	12	10	2	1	1	12	2	48	1	1	0	2.1	.980	OF-24
1930			25	.278	.407	54	15	2	1	1	1.9	10	5	4	1	0	7	2	29	1	2	0	2.1	.938	OF-15
10 yrs.			840	.302	.398	3001	905	166	34	18	0.6	413	361	166	88	44	57	10	1371	77	59	20	1.9	.961	OF-773, 3B-2
WORLD SERIES																									
1929	PHI	A	1	.000	.000	1	0	0	0	0	0.0	0	0	0	1	0	1	0	0	0	0	0	0.0	—	

Champ Summers

SUMMERS, JOHN JUNIOR II BL TR 6′ 2″ 205 lbs.
B. June 15, 1946, Bremerton, Wash.

Year	Team		Games	BA	SA	AB	H	2B	3B	HR	HR%	R	RBI	BB	SO	SB	Pinch Hit AB	Pinch Hit H	PO	A	E	DP	TC/G	FA	G by Pos
1974	OAK	A	20	.125	.167	24	3	1	0	0	0.0	2	3	1	5	0	7	1	6	0	0	0	0.4	1.000	OF-12, DH-2
1975	CHI	N	76	.231	.341	91	21	5	1	1	1.1	14	16	10	13	0	46	14	16	0	2	0	1.0	.889	OF-18

Champp Summers *continued*

Year	Team	Games	BA	SA	AB	H	2B	3B	HR	HR%	R	RBI	BB	SO	SB	Pinch Hit AB	Pinch Hit H	PO	A	E	DP	TC/G	FA	G by Pos
1976		83	.206	.294	126	26	2	0	3	2.4	11	13	13	31	1	47	12	95	5	1	10	2.7	.990	OF-26, 1B-10, C-1
1977	CIN N	59	.171	.342	76	13	4	0	3	3.9	11	6	6	16	0	38	6	24	2	0	0	1.5	1.000	OF-16, 3B-1
1978		13	.257	.400	35	9	2	0	1	2.9	4	3	7	4	2	0	0	14	0	1	0	1.3	.933	OF-12
1979	2 teams	CIN N (27G –.200) DET A (90G –.313)																						
"	total	117	.291	.556	306	89	14	2	21	6.9	57	62	53	48	7	23	5	166	10	3	5	1.8	.983	OF-82, DH-10, 1B-10
1980	DET A	120	.297	.504	347	103	19	1	17	4.9	61	60	52	52	4	26	7	60	1	3	0	0.6	.953	DH-64, OF-47, 1B-1
1981		64	.255	.358	165	42	8	0	3	1.8	16	21	19	35	1	14	3	26	1	1	0	0.5	.964	DH-37, OF-18
1982	SF N	70	.248	.384	125	31	5	0	4	3.2	15	19	16	17	0	31	10	46	3	4	0	1.6	.925	OF-31, 1B-3
1983		29	.136	.136	22	3	0	0	0	0.0	3	3	7	8	0	20	3	2	0	0	0	2.0	1.000	OF-1
1984	SD N	47	.185	.296	54	10	3	0	1	1.9	5	12	4	15	0	36	7	53	1	0	8	6.8	1.000	1B-8
11 yrs.		698	.255	.425	1371	350	63	4	54	3.9	199	218	188	244	15	288	68	508	23	15	23	1.3	.973	OF-263, DH-113, 1B-32, 3B-1, C-1
LEAGUE CHAMPIONSHIP SERIES																								
1984	SD N	2	.000	.000	2	0	0	0	0	0.0	0	0	0	1	0	0	0	0	0	0	0	0.0	—	
WORLD SERIES																								
1984	SD N	1	.000	.000	1	0	0	0	0	0.0	0	0	0	1	0	1	0	0	0	0	0	0.0	—	

Kid Summers

SUMMERS, WILLIAM TR
B. Toronto, Ont., Canada D. Oct. 16, 1895, Toronto, Ont., Canada.

Year	Team	Games	BA	SA	AB	H	2B	3B	HR	HR%	R	RBI	BB	SO	SB	Pinch Hit AB	Pinch Hit H	PO	A	E	DP	TC/G	FA	G by Pos
1893	STL N	2	.000	.000	1	0	0	0	0	0.0	1	0	0	0	0	0	0	1	1	2	0	2.0	.500	OF-1, C-1

Carl Sumner

SUMNER, CARL RINGDAHL (Lefty) BL TL 5′ 8″ 160 lbs.
B. Sept. 28, 1908, Cambridge, Mass.

Year	Team	Games	BA	SA	AB	H	2B	3B	HR	HR%	R	RBI	BB	SO	SB	Pinch Hit AB	Pinch Hit H	PO	A	E	DP	TC/G	FA	G by Pos
1928	BOS A	16	.276	.379	29	8	1	1	0	0.0	6	3	5	6	0	3	1	12	0	1	0	1.3	.923	OF-10

Art Sunday

SUNDAY, ARTHUR BL TL 5′ 9″ 193 lbs.
Born August Wacher.
B. Jan. 21, 1862, Springfield, Ohio Deceased.

Year	Team	Games	BA	SA	AB	H	2B	3B	HR	HR%	R	RBI	BB	SO	SB	Pinch Hit AB	Pinch Hit H	PO	A	E	DP	TC/G	FA	G by Pos
1890	BKN P	24	.265	.349	83	22	5	1	0	0.0	26	13	15	9	0	0	0	28	2	3	0	1.4	.909	OF-24

Billy Sunday

SUNDAY, WILLIAM ASHLEY (The Evangelist) BL TR 5′10″ 160 lbs.
B. Nov. 19, 1862, Ames, Iowa D. Nov. 6, 1935, Chicago, Ill.

Year	Team	Games	BA	SA	AB	H	2B	3B	HR	HR%	R	RBI	BB	SO	SB	Pinch Hit AB	Pinch Hit H	PO	A	E	DP	TC/G	FA	G by Pos
1883	CHI N	14	.241	.315	54	13	4	0	0	0.0	6		1	18		0	0	10	1	6	0	1.2	.647	OF-14
1884		43	.222	.324	176	39	4	1	4	2.3	25		4	36		0	0	45	8	27	1	1.9	.662	OF-43
1885		46	.256	.343	172	44	3	3	2	1.2	36	20	12	33		0	0	46	6	11	2	1.4	.825	OF-46
1886		28	.243	.301	103	25	2	2	0	0.0	16	6	7	26		0	0	50	3	5	0	2.1	.914	OF-28
1887		50	.291	.427	199	58	6	6	3	1.5	41	32	21	20	34	0	0	78	4	25	2	2.1	.766	OF-50
1888	PIT N	120	.236	.275	505	119	14	3	0	0.0	69	15	12	36	71	0	0	297	27	21	5	2.9	.939	OF-120
1889		81	.240	.327	321	77	10	6	2	0.6	62	25	27	33	47	0	0	157	17	10	2	2.3	.946	OF-81
1890	2 teams	PIT N (86G –.257) PHI N (31G –.261)																						
"	total	117	.258	.302	477	123	12	3	1	0.2	82	39	50	27	86	0	0	250	30	31	11	2.6	.900	OF-117, P-1
8 yrs.		499	.248	.317	2007	498	55	24	12	0.6	337	137	134	229	238	0	0	933	96	136	23	2.3	.883	OF-499, P-1

Jim Sundberg

SUNDBERG, JAMES HOWARD BR TR 6′ 190 lbs.
B. May 18, 1951, Galesburg, Ill.

Year	Team	Games	BA	SA	AB	H	2B	3B	HR	HR%	R	RBI	BB	SO	SB	Pinch Hit AB	Pinch Hit H	PO	A	E	DP	TC/G	FA	G by Pos
1974	TEX A	132	.247	.323	368	91	13	3	3	0.8	45	36	62	61	2	1	0	722	69	8	15	6.1	.990	C-132
1975		155	.199	.256	472	94	9	0	6	1.3	45	36	51	77	3	0	0	791	101	17	11	5.9	.981	C-155
1976		140	.228	.310	448	102	24	2	3	0.7	33	34	37	61	0	1	1	719	96	7	11	5.9	.991	C-140
1977		149	.291	.389	453	132	20	3	6	1.3	61	65	53	77	2	1	1	801	103	5	12	6.1	.994	C-149
1978		149	.278	.380	518	144	23	6	6	1.2	54	58	64	70	2	1	0	769	91	3	14	5.8	.997	C-148, DH-1
1979		150	.275	.368	495	136	23	4	5	1.0	50	64	51	51	3	1	0	754	75	4	13	5.6	.995	C-150
1980		151	.273	.384	505	138	24	1	10	2.0	59	63	64	67	2	3	2	853	76	7	7	6.2	.993	C-151
1981		102	.277	.366	339	94	17	2	3	0.9	42	28	50	48	2	2	1	465	52	2	9	5.2	.996	C-98, OF-2
1982		139	.251	.383	470	118	22	5	10	2.1	37	47	49	57	2	7	1	612	69	6	15	5.2	.991	C-132, OF-1
1983		131	.201	.254	378	76	14	0	2	0.5	30	28	35	64	0	1	0	618	56	5	2	5.2	.993	C-131
1984	MIL A	110	.261	.399	348	91	19	4	7	2.0	43	43	38	63	1	3	0	556	55	3	6	5.6	.995	C-109
1985	KC A	115	.245	.381	367	90	12	4	10	2.7	38	35	33	67	0	5	3	572	41	5	10	5.5	.992	C-112
1986		140	.212	.322	429	91	9	1	12	2.8	41	42	57	91	1	8	2	686	46	4	11	5.5	.995	C-134
1987	CHI N	61	.201	.302	139	28	2	0	4	2.9	9	15	19	40	0	8	3	273	34	2	2	5.4	.994	C-57
1988	2 teams	CHI N (24G –.241) TEX A (38G –.286)																						
"	total	62	.269	.428	145	39	5	0	6	4.1	21	22	13	32	0	9	1	229	16	0	3	4.4	1.000	C-56
1989	TEX A	76	.197	.299	147	29	7	1	2	1.4	13	8	23	37	0	5	1	353	27	3	3	5.2	.992	C-73, DH-1
16 yrs.		1962	.248	.348	6021	1493	243	36	95	1.6	621	624	699	963	20	56	16	9773	1007	81	144	5.6	.993	C-1927, OF-3, DH-2
LEAGUE CHAMPIONSHIP SERIES																								
1985	KC A	7	.167	.417	24	4	1	1	1	4.2	3	6	1	7	0	0	0	42	2	1	1	6.4	.978	C-7
WORLD SERIES																								
1985	KC A	7	.250	.333	24	6	2	0	0	0.0	6	1	6	4	0	0	0	47	3	0	1	7.1	1.000	C-7

B. J. Surhoff

SURHOFF, WILLIAM JAMES BL TR 6′ 1″ 185 lbs.
Brother of Rich Surhoff.
B. Aug. 4, 1964, Bronx, N. Y.

Year	Team	Games	BA	SA	AB	H	2B	3B	HR	HR%	R	RBI	BB	SO	SB	Pinch Hit AB	Pinch Hit H	PO	A	E	DP	TC/G	FA	G by Pos
1987	MIL A	115	.299	.423	395	118	22	3	7	1.8	50	68	36	30	11	10	3	648	56	11	12	6.6	.985	C-98, 3B-10, 1B-1
1988		139	.245	.318	493	121	21	0	5	1.0	47	38	31	49	21	9	2	550	94	8	3	4.6	.988	C-106, 3B-31, 1B-2, SS-1, OF-1
1989		126	.248	.339	436	108	17	4	5	1.1	42	55	25	29	14	5	0	530	58	10	7	4.8	.983	C-106, DH-12, 3B-6
1990		135	.276	.376	474	131	21	4	6	1.3	55	59	41	37	18	8	2	619	62	12	11	5.1	.983	C-125, 3B-11
1991		143	.289	.372	505	146	19	4	5	1.0	57	68	26	33	5	10	2	665	71	4	11	5.2	.995	C-127, DH-6, 3B-5, OF-2, 2B-1
1992		139	.252	.321	480	121	19	1	4	0.8	63	62	46	41	14	4	1	699	74	6	25	5.4	.992	C-109, 1B-17, DH-9, OF-7, 3B-3
1993		148	.274	.391	552	151	38	3	7	1.3	66	79	36	47	12	5	2	175	220	18	21	2.6	.956	3B-121, OF-24, 1B-8, C-3, DH-1

B. J. Surhoff *continued*

Year	Team	Games	BA	SA	AB	H	2B	3B	HR	HR%	R	RBI	BB	SO	SB	Pinch Hit AB	Pinch Hit H	PO	A	E	DP	TC/G	FA	G by Pos
1994		40	.261	.485	134	35	11	2	5	3.7	20	22	16	14	0	1	0	121	29	4	12	3.7	.974	3B-18, C-12, 1B-8, OF-3, DH-1
1995		117	.320	.492	415	133	26	3	13	3.1	72	73	37	43	7	3	0	529	44	5	45	4.3	.991	OF-60, 1B-55, C-18, DH-3
9 yrs.		1102	.274	.380	3884	1064	194	24	57	1.5	472	524	294	323	102	55	12	4536	708	78	147	4.7	.985	C-704, 3B-205, OF-97, 1B-91, DH-32, 2B-1, SS-1

George Susce

SUSCE, GEORGE CYRIL METHODIUS (Good Kid) BR TR 5′11½″ 200 lbs.
Father of George Susce.
B. Aug. 13, 1908, Pittsburgh, Pa. D. Feb. 25, 1986, Sarasota, Fla.

Year	Team	Games	BA	SA	AB	H	2B	3B	HR	HR%	R	RBI	BB	SO	SB	Pinch Hit AB	Pinch Hit H	PO	A	E	DP	TC/G	FA	G by Pos
1929	PHI N	17	.294	.647	17	5	3	0	1	5.9	5	1	1	2	0	5	0	9	0	1	0	0.9	.900	C-11
1932	DET A	2	—	—	0	0	0	0	0	—	0	0	0	0	0	0	0	1	0	0	0	0.5	1.000	C-2
1939	PIT N	31	.227	.333	75	17	3	1	1	1.3	8	4	12	5	0	0	0	111	14	2	2	4.1	.984	1B-31
1940	STL A	61	.212	.248	113	24	4	0	0	0.0	6	13	9	9	1	0	0	168	21	3	3	3.1	.984	C-61
1941	CLE A	1	—	—	0	0	0	0	0	—	0	0	0	0	0	0	0	1	0	0	0	1.0	1.000	C-1
1942		2	1.000	1.000	1	1	0	0	0	0.0	1	0	1	0	0	0	0	2	0	0	0	1.0	1.000	C-2
1943		3	.000	.000	1	0	0	0	0	0.0	0	0	0	0	0	0	0	0	2	0	0	0.7	1.000	C-3
1944		29	.230	.246	61	14	1	0	0	0.0	3	4	2	5	0	0	0	78	13	5	3	3.3	.948	C-29
8 yrs.		146	.228	.299	268	61	11	1	2	0.7	23	22	25	21	1	5	0	370	50	11	8	3.1	.974	C-109, 1B-31

Pete Susko

SUSKO, PETER JONATHAN BL TL 5′11″ 172 lbs.
B. July 2, 1904, Laura, Ohio D. May 22, 1978, Jacksonville, Fla.

Year	Team	Games	BA	SA	AB	H	2B	3B	HR	HR%	R	RBI	BB	SO	SB	Pinch Hit AB	Pinch Hit H	PO	A	E	DP	TC/G	FA	G by Pos
1934	WAS A	58	.286	.362	224	64	5	3	2	0.9	25	25	18	10	3	0	0	608	40	8	58	11.3	.988	1B-58

Butch Sutcliffe

SUTCLIFFE, CHARLES INIGO BR TR 5′8½″ 165 lbs.
B. July 22, 1915, Fall River, Mass. D. Mar. 2, 1994, Fall River, Mass.

Year	Team	Games	BA	SA	AB	H	2B	3B	HR	HR%	R	RBI	BB	SO	SB	Pinch Hit AB	Pinch Hit H	PO	A	E	DP	TC/G	FA	G by Pos
1938	BOS N	4	.250	.250	4	1	0	0	0	0.0	1	2	2	1	0	0	0	8	0	2	0	3.3	.800	C-3

Sy Sutcliffe

SUTCLIFFE, EDWARD ELMER BL 6′2″ 170 lbs.
B. Apr. 15, 1862, Wheaton, Ill. D. Feb. 13, 1893, Wheaton, Ill.

Year	Team	Games	BA	SA	AB	H	2B	3B	HR	HR%	R	RBI	BB	SO	SB	Pinch Hit AB	Pinch Hit H	PO	A	E	DP	TC/G	FA	G by Pos
1884	CHI N	4	.200	.267	15	3	1	0	0	0.0	4		2	4		0	0	34	6	1	1	10.3	.976	C-4
1885	2 teams	CHI N (11G –.186) STL N (16G –.122)																						
″	total	27	.152	.196	92	14	2	1	0	0.0	7	8	7	15		0	0	108	28	24	0	5.7	.850	C-25, OF-3
1888	DET N	49	.257	.314	191	49	5	3	0	0.0	17	23	5	14	6	0	0	172	127	39	13	6.9	.885	SS-24, C-14, 1B-5, OF-4, 2B-2
1889	CLE N	46	.248	.311	161	40	3	2	1	0.6	17	21	14	6	5	0	0	253	74	31	10	7.8	.913	C-37, 1B-8, OF-1
1890	CLE P	99	.329	.422	386	127	14	8	2	0.5	62	60	33	16	10	0	0	286	126	58	11	4.5	.877	C-84, OF-15, SS-4, 3B-2
1891	WAS AA	53	.353	.453	201	71	8	3	2	1.0	29	33	17	17	8	0	0	118	41	21	4	3.0	.883	OF-35, C-22, SS-3, 3B-1
1892	BAL N	66	.279	.377	276	77	10	7	1	0.4	41	27	14	15	12	0	0	678	24	31	39	11.1	.958	1B-66
7 yrs.		344	.288	.371	1322	381	43	24	6	0.5	177	172	92	87	41	0	0	1649	426	205	78	6.4	.910	C-186, 1B-79, OF-58, SS-31, 3B-3, 2B-2

Gary Sutherland

SUTHERLAND, GARY LYNN BR TR 6′ 185 lbs.
Brother of Darrell Sutherland.
B. Sept. 27, 1944, Glendale, Calif.

Year	Team	Games	BA	SA	AB	H	2B	3B	HR	HR%	R	RBI	BB	SO	SB	Pinch Hit AB	Pinch Hit H	PO	A	E	DP	TC/G	FA	G by Pos
1966	PHI N	3	.000	.000	3	0	0	0	0	0.0	0	0	0	0	0	2	0	1	2	0	1	3.0	1.000	SS-1
1967		103	.247	.320	231	57	12	1	1	0.4	23	19	17	22	0	22	4	110	115	15	33	2.6	.938	SS-66, OF-25
1968		67	.275	.326	138	38	7	0	0	0.0	16	15	8	15	0	31	9	48	73	3	10	2.8	.976	2B-17, SS-10, 3B-10, OF-7
1969	MON N	141	.239	.307	544	130	26	1	3	0.6	63	35	37	31	5	1	0	328	389	21	112	4.8	.972	2B-139, SS-15, OF-1
1970		116	.206	.259	359	74	10	0	3	0.8	37	26	31	22	2	23	4	182	264	12	73	4.1	.974	2B-97, SS-15, 3B-1
1971		111	.257	.332	304	78	7	2	4	1.3	25	26	18	12	3	19	3	157	253	21	60	4.0	.951	2B-56, SS-46, OF-4, 3B-2
1972	HOU N	5	.125	.125	8	1	0	0	0	0.0	0	1	0	0	0	4	0	1	2	0	0	1.5	1.000	3B-1, 2B-1
1973		16	.259	.352	54	14	5	0	0	0.0	8	3	3	5	0	2	1	37	31	2	11	4.7	.971	2B-14, SS-1
1974	DET A	149	.254	.313	619	157	20	1	5	0.8	60	49	26	37	1	2	1	340	380	18	103	4.6	.976	2B-147, SS-10, 3B-4
1975		129	.258	.330	503	130	12	3	6	1.2	51	39	45	41	0	1	0	278	365	21	83	5.2	.968	2B-128
1976	2 teams	DET A (42G –.205) MIL A (59G –.217)																						
″	total	101	.211	.272	232	49	7	2	1	0.4	19	15	15	19	0	12	2	161	204	11	52	3.9	.971	2B-87, DH-8, 1B-2
1977	SD N	80	.243	.301	103	25	3	0	1	1.0	5	11	7	15	0	38	12	39	53	5	12	1.8	.948	2B-30, 3B-21, 1B-4
1978	STL N	10	.167	.167	6	1	0	0	0	0.0	1	0	0	0	0	6	1	0	3	0	0	3.0	1.000	2B-1
13 yrs.		1031	.243	.308	3104	754	109	10	24	0.8	308	239	207	219	11	163	37	1682	2134	129	550	4.1	.967	2B-717, SS-164, 3B-39, OF-37, DH-8, 1B-6

Leo Sutherland

SUTHERLAND, LEONARDO BL TL 5′10″ 165 lbs.
Born Leonardo Sutherland (Cantin).
B. Apr. 6, 1958, Santiago, Cuba.

Year	Team	Games	BA	SA	AB	H	2B	3B	HR	HR%	R	RBI	BB	SO	SB	Pinch Hit AB	Pinch Hit H	PO	A	E	DP	TC/G	FA	G by Pos
1980	CHI A	34	.258	.292	89	23	3	0	0	0.0	9	5	1	11	4	10	4	50	0	3	0	2.3	.943	OF-23
1981		11	.167	.167	12	2	0	0	0	0.0	6	0	3	1	2	1	0	6	0	0	0	0.9	1.000	OF-7
2 yrs.		45	.248	.277	101	25	3	0	0	0.0	15	5	4	12	6	11	4	56	0	3	0	2.0	.949	OF-30

Glenn Sutko

SUTKO, GLENN EDWARD BR TR 6′3″ 225 lbs.
B. May 9, 1968, Atlanta, Ga.

Year	Team	Games	BA	SA	AB	H	2B	3B	HR	HR%	R	RBI	BB	SO	SB	Pinch Hit AB	Pinch Hit H	PO	A	E	DP	TC/G	FA	G by Pos
1990	CIN N	1	.000	.000	1	0	0	0	0	0.0	0	0	0	1	0	0	0	3	0	0	0	3.0	1.000	C-1
1991		10	.100	.100	10	1	0	0	0	0.0	0	1	2	6	0	1	0	16	5	3	0	2.7	.875	C-9
2 yrs.		11	.091	.091	11	1	0	0	0	0.0	0	1	2	7	0	1	0	19	5	3	0	2.7	.889	C-10

Ezra Sutton

SUTTON, EZRA BALLOU BR TR 5′8½″ 153 lbs.
B. Sept. 17, 1850, Palmyra, N. Y. D. June 20, 1907, Braintree, Mass.

Year	Team	Games	BA	SA	AB	H	2B	3B	HR	HR%	R	RBI	BB	SO	SB	Pinch Hit AB	Pinch Hit H	PO	A	E	DP	TC/G	FA	G by Pos
1876	PHI N	54	.297	.419	236	70	12	7	1	0.4	45	31	3	2		0	0	390	52	58	13	8.9	.884	1B-29, 2B-15, 3B-8, OF-4
1877	BOS N	58	.292	.379	253	74	10	6	0	0.0	43	39	4	10		0	0	104	122	36	10	4.5	.863	SS-36, 3B-22
1878		60	.226	.301	239	54	9	3	1	0.4	31	29	2	14		0	0	82	121	25	9	3.8	.890	3B-59, SS-1
1879		84	.248	.310	339	84	13	4	0	0.0	54	34	2	18		0	0	89	210	47	18	4.1	.864	SS-51, 3B-33
1880		76	.250	.295	288	72	9	2	0	0.0	41	25	7	7		0	0	114	188	35	19	4.4	.896	SS-39, 3B-37
1881		83	.291	.351	333	97	12	4	0	0.0	43	31	13	9		0	0	114	161	39	10	3.8	.876	3B-81, SS-2
1882		81	.251	.301	319	80	8	1	2	0.6	44	38	24	25		0	0	104	151	42	6	3.7	.859	3B-77, SS-4
1883		94	.324	.486	414	134	28	15	3	0.7	101	73	17	12		0	0	123	157	42	14	3.4	.870	3B-93, SS-1, OF-1
1884		110	.346	.455	468	**162**	28	7	3	0.6	102		29	22		0	0	119	186	31	7	3.1	.908	3B-110
1885		110	.313	.425	457	143	23	8	4	0.9	78	47	17	25		0	0	157	222	53	26	3.9	.877	3B-91, SS-16, 2B-2, 1B-1

Ezra Sutton *continued*

Year	Team	Lg	Games	BA	SA	AB	H	2B	3B	HR	HR%	R	RBI	BB	SO	SB	Pinch Hit AB	Pinch Hit H	PO	A	E	DP	TC/G	FA	G by Pos
1886			116	.277	.361	499	138	21	6	3	0.6	83	48	26	21		0	0	181	204	56	19	3.8	.873	OF-43, SS-28, 3B-28, 2B-18
1887			77	.304	.429	326	99	14	9	3	0.9	58	46	13	6	17	0	0	178	234	58	12	5.9	.877	SS-37, OF-18, 2B-13, 3B-11
1888			28	.218	.291	110	24	3	1	1	0.9	16	16	7	3	10	0	0	33	49	15	4	3.5	.845	3B-27, SS-1
13 yrs.			1031	.288	.381	4281	1231	190	73	21	0.5	739	457	164	174	27	0	0	1788	2057	537	167	4.2	.877	3B-677, SS-216, OF-66, 2B-48, 1B-30

Dale Sveum

SVEUM, DALE CURTIS BB TR 6′ 2″ 185 lbs.
B. Nov. 23, 1963, Richmond, Calif.

Year	Team	Lg	Games	BA	SA	AB	H	2B	3B	HR	HR%	R	RBI	BB	SO	SB	Pinch Hit AB	Pinch Hit H	PO	A	E	DP	TC/G	FA	G by Pos
1986	**MIL**	**A**	91	.246	.366	317	78	13	2	7	2.2	35	35	32	63	4	2	0	92	179	30	19	3.3	.900	3B-65, SS-13, 2B-13
1987			153	.252	.454	535	135	27	3	25	4.7	86	95	40	133	2	1	1	242	396	23	89	4.3	.965	SS-142, 2B-13
1988			129	.242	.347	467	113	14	4	9	1.9	41	51	21	122	1	0	0	209	375	27	94	4.7	.956	SS-127, 2B-1, DH-1
1990			48	.197	.282	117	23	7	0	1	0.9	15	12	12	30	0	6	0	59	63	6	10	2.7	.953	3B-22, 2B-16, SS-5, 1B-5
1991			90	.241	.365	266	64	19	1	4	1.5	33	43	32	78	2	6	0	85	189	10	33	3.0	.965	SS-51, 3B-38, DH-3, 2B-2
1992	**2 teams**		**PHI N** (54G –.178)	**CHI A** (40G –.219)																					
″	**total**		94	.197	.297	249	49	13	0	4	1.6	28	28	28	68	1	19	1	121	198	16	38	4.0	.952	SS-71, 3B-7, 1B-6
1993	**OAK**	**A**	30	.177	.304	79	14	2	1	2	2.5	12	6	16	21	0	7	3	128	17	3	13	5.1	.980	1B-14, 3B-7, 2B-4, DH-2, SS-1, OF-1
1994	**SEA**	**A**	10	.185	.296	27	5	0	0	1	3.7	3	2	2	10	0	4	0	2	8	1	0	1.6	.909	DH-4, 3B-3
8 yrs.			645	.234	.368	2057	481	95	11	53	2.6	253	272	183	525	10	45	5	938	1425	116	296	3.9	.953	SS-410, 3B-142, 2B-49, 1B-25, DH-10, OF-1

Harry Swacina

SWACINA, HARRY JOSEPH (Swats) BR TR 6′ 2″ 190 lbs.
B. Aug. 22, 1881, St. Louis, Mo. D. June 21, 1944, Birmingham, Ala.

Year	Team	Lg	Games	BA	SA	AB	H	2B	3B	HR	HR%	R	RBI	BB	SO	SB	Pinch Hit AB	Pinch Hit H	PO	A	E	DP	TC/G	FA	G by Pos
1907	**PIT**	**N**	26	.200	.232	95	19	1	1	0	0.0	9	10	4		1	0	0	246	12	1	9	10.0	.996	1B-26
1908			53	.216	.261	176	38	6	1	0	0.0	7	13	5		4	2	1	501	19	9	19	10.6	.983	1B-50
1914	**BAL**	**F**	158	.280	.348	**617**	173	26	8	0	0.0	70	90	14		15	0	0	1616	104	26	74	11.1	.985	1B-158
1915			85	.246	.306	301	74	13	1	1	0.3	24	38	9		9	8	1	735	58	11	50	10.6	.986	1B-75, 2B-1
4 yrs.			322	.256	.315	1189	304	46	11	1	0.1	110	151	32		29	10	2	3098	193	47	152	10.8	.986	1B-309, 2B-1

Andy Swan

SWAN, ANDREW J.
B. May 11, 1845, Tewksbury, Mass. D. Aug. 27, 1885, Lawrence, Mass.

Year	Team	Lg	Games	BA	SA	AB	H	2B	3B	HR	HR%	R	RBI	BB	SO	SB	Pinch Hit AB	Pinch Hit H	PO	A	E	DP	TC/G	FA	G by Pos
1884	**2 teams**		**WAS AA** (5G –.143)	**RIC AA** (3G –.500)																					
″	**total**		8	.258	.290	31	8	1	0	0	0.0	5		0			0	0	58	1	7	0	8.3	.894	1B-6, 3B-2

Pinky Swander

SWANDER, EDWARD O. BL TR 5′ 9″ 180 lbs.
B. July 4, 1880, Portsmouth, Ohio D. Oct. 24, 1944, Springfield, Mass.

Year	Team	Lg	Games	BA	SA	AB	H	2B	3B	HR	HR%	R	RBI	BB	SO	SB	Pinch Hit AB	Pinch Hit H	PO	A	E	DP	TC/G	FA	G by Pos
1903	**STL**	**A**	14	.275	.392	51	14	2	2	0	0.0	9	6	10		0	0	0	13	2	3	0	1.3	.833	OF-14
1904			1	.000	.000	1	0	0	0	0	0.0	0	0	0		0	1	0	0	0	0	0	0.0	—	
2 yrs.			15	.269	.385	52	14	2	2	0	0.0	9	6	10		0	1	0	13	2	3	0	1.3	.833	OF-14

Bill Swanson

SWANSON, WILLIAM ANDREW BB TR 5′ 6″ 156 lbs.
B. Oct. 12, 1888, New York, N. Y. D. Oct. 14, 1954, New York, N. Y.

Year	Team	Lg	Games	BA	SA	AB	H	2B	3B	HR	HR%	R	RBI	BB	SO	SB	Pinch Hit AB	Pinch Hit H	PO	A	E	DP	TC/G	FA	G by Pos
1914	**BOS**	**A**	11	.200	.300	20	4	2	0	0	0.0	0	1	3	4	0	1	0	10	12	3	0	2.5	.880	2B-6, 3B-3, SS-1

Evar Swanson

SWANSON, ERNEST EVAR BR TR 5′ 9″ 170 lbs.
B. Oct. 15, 1902, DeKalb, Ill. D. July 17, 1973, Galesburg, Ill.

Year	Team	Lg	Games	BA	SA	AB	H	2B	3B	HR	HR%	R	RBI	BB	SO	SB	Pinch Hit AB	Pinch Hit H	PO	A	E	DP	TC/G	FA	G by Pos
1929	**CIN**	**N**	145	.300	.423	574	172	35	12	4	0.7	100	43	41	47	33	2	1	317	9	10	2	2.4	.970	OF-142
1930			95	.309	.399	301	93	15	3	2	0.7	43	22	11	17	4	15	1	178	5	7	1	2.7	.963	OF-71
1932	**CHI**	**A**	14	.308	.404	52	16	3	1	0	0.0	9	8	8	3	3	0	0	24	0	1	0	1.8	.960	OF-14
1933			144	.306	.384	539	165	25	7	1	0.2	102	63	93	35	19	6	2	281	7	8	0	2.1	.973	OF-139
1934			117	.298	.343	426	127	9	5	0	0.0	71	34	59	31	10	9	2	193	4	4	1	1.9	.980	OF-105
5 yrs.			515	.303	.390	1892	573	87	28	7	0.4	325	170	212	133	69	32	6	993	25	30	4	2.2	.971	OF-471

Karl Swanson

SWANSON, KARL EDWARD BL TR 5′10″ 155 lbs.
B. Dec. 17, 1903, North Henderson, Ill.

Year	Team	Lg	Games	BA	SA	AB	H	2B	3B	HR	HR%	R	RBI	BB	SO	SB	Pinch Hit AB	Pinch Hit H	PO	A	E	DP	TC/G	FA	G by Pos
1928	**CHI**	**A**	22	.141	.156	64	9	1	0	0	0.0	2	6	4	7	3	0	0	33	66	6	9	5.0	.943	2B-21
1929			2	.000	.000	1	0	0	0	0	0.0	0	0	0	0	0	1	0	0	0	0	0	0.0	—	
2 yrs.			24	.138	.154	65	9	1	0	0	0.0	2	6	4	7	3	1	0	33	66	6	9	5.0	.943	2B-21

Stan Swanson

SWANSON, STANLEY LAWRENCE BR TR 5′11″ 168 lbs.
B. May 19, 1944, Yuba City, Calif.

Year	Team	Lg	Games	BA	SA	AB	H	2B	3B	HR	HR%	R	RBI	BB	SO	SB	Pinch Hit AB	Pinch Hit H	PO	A	E	DP	TC/G	FA	G by Pos
1971	**MON**	**N**	49	.245	.330	106	26	3	0	2	1.9	14	11	10	13	1	10	3	54	0	0	0	1.4	1.000	OF-38

Ed Swartwood

SWARTWOOD, CYRUS EDWARD BL TR 198 lbs.
B. Jan. 12, 1859, Rockford, Ill. D. May 15, 1924, Pittsburgh, Pa.

Year	Team	Lg	Games	BA	SA	AB	H	2B	3B	HR	HR%	R	RBI	BB	SO	SB	Pinch Hit AB	Pinch Hit H	PO	A	E	DP	TC/G	FA	G by Pos
1881	**BUF**	**N**	1	.333	.333	3	1	0	0	0	0.0	0	0	1	0		0	0	1	0	1	0	2.0	.500	OF-1
1882	**PIT**	**AA**	76	.329	.498	325	107	**18**	11	5	1.5	**86**		21			0	0	133	10	32	3	2.3	.817	OF-73, 1B-4
1883			94	**.356**	.475	413	**147**	24	8	3	0.7	86		24			0	0	703	32	63	28	8.0	.921	1B-60, OF-37, C-3
1884			102	.288	.366	399	115	19	6	0	0.0	74		33			0	0	349	46	54	20	4.4	.880	OF-79, 1B-22, 3B-1, P-1
1885	**BKN**	**AA**	99	.266	.331	399	106	8	9	0	0.0	80		36			0	0	179	9	26	1	2.1	.879	OF-95, 1B-4, SS-1, C-1
1886			122	.280	.369	471	132	13	10	3	0.6	95		**70**			0	0	190	33	29	4	2.0	.885	OF-122, C-1
1887			91	.253	.344	363	92	14	8	1	0.3	72		46		29	0	0	129	23	30	5	2.0	.835	OF-91
1890	**TOL**	**AA**	126	.327	.444	462	151	23	11	3	0.6	106		80		53	0	0	224	23	20	2	2.1	.925	OF-126, P-1
1892	**PIT**	**N**	13	.238	.262	42	10	1	0	0	0.0	8	4	13	11	1	0	0	22	6	2	2	2.3	.933	OF-13
9 yrs.			724	.299	.400	2877	861	120	63	15	0.5	607	4	324	11	83	0	0	1930	182	257	65	3.2	.892	OF-637, 1B-90, C-5, P-2, SS-1, 3B-1

Charlie Sweasy

SWEASY, CHARLES JAMES BR TR 5′ 9″ 172 lbs.
Born Charles James Swasey.
B. Nov. 2, 1847, Newark, N. J. D. Mar. 30, 1908, Newark, N. J.

Year	Team	Lg	Games	BA	SA	AB	H	2B	3B	HR	HR%	R	RBI	BB	SO	SB	Pinch Hit AB	Pinch Hit H	PO	A	E	DP	TC/G	FA	G by Pos
1876	**CIN**	**N**	56	.204	.244	225	46	5	2	0	0.0	18	10	2	5		0	0	169	158	54	30	6.8	.858	2B-55, OF-1
1878	**PRO**	**N**	55	.175	.189	212	37	3	0	0	0.0	23	8	7	23		0	0	141	183	59	20	7.0	.846	2B-55
2 yrs.			111	.190	.217	437	83	8	2	0	0.0	41	18	9	28		0	0	310	341	113	50	6.9	.852	2B-110, OF-1

Bill Sweeney

SWEENEY, WILLIAM JOHN BR TR 5′11″ 175 lbs.
B. Mar. 6, 1886, Covington, Ky. D. May 26, 1948, Cambridge, Mass.

Year	Team	Games	BA	SA	AB	H	2B	3B	HR	HR%	R	RBI	BB	SO	SB	Pinch Hit AB	Pinch Hit H	PO	A	E	DP	TC/G	FA	G by Pos
1907	2 teams	CHI N (3G –.100) BOS N (58G –.262)																						
″	total	61	.254	.264	201	51	2	0	0	0.0	25	19	16		9	2	0	88	112	30	9	4.0	.870	3B-23, SS-18, OF-11, 2B-5, 1B-1
1908	BOS N	127	.244	.294	418	102	15	3	0	0.0	44	40	45		17	3	2	175	282	35	14	3.9	.929	3B-123, SS-2, 2B-1
1909		138	.243	.300	493	120	19	3	1	0.2	45	36	37		25	0	0	222	326	52	26	4.3	.913	3B-112, SS-26
1910		150	.267	.357	499	133	22	4	5	1.0	43	46	61	28	25	4	3	439	369	66	73	5.9	.924	SS-110, 3B-21, 1B-17
1911		137	.314	.417	523	164	33	6	3	0.6	92	63	77	26	33	1	1	372	410	46	61	6.1	.944	2B-136
1912		153	.344	.445	593	204	31	13	1	0.2	84	100	68	34	27	0	0	459	475	40	76	6.4	.959	2B-153
1913		139	.257	.315	502	129	17	6	0	0.0	65	47	66	50	18	2	1	301	391	45	42	5.4	.939	2B-137
1914	CHI N	134	.218	.276	463	101	14	5	1	0.2	45	38	53	15	18	0	0	301	426	35	40	5.7	.954	2B-134
8 yrs.		1039	.272	.344	3692	1004	153	40	11	0.3	443	389	423	153	172	12	7	2357	2791	349	341	5.3	.937	2B-566, 3B-279, SS-156, 1B-18, OF-11

Bill Sweeney

SWEENEY, WILLIAM JOSEPH BR TR 5′11″ 180 lbs.
B. Dec. 29, 1904, Cleveland, Ohio D. Apr. 18, 1957, San Diego, Calif.

Year	Team	Games	BA	SA	AB	H	2B	3B	HR	HR%	R	RBI	BB	SO	SB	Pinch Hit AB	Pinch Hit H	PO	A	E	DP	TC/G	FA	G by Pos
1928	DET A	89	.252	.333	309	78	15	5	0	0.0	47	19	15	28	12	8	1	677	55	5	51	9.4	.993	1B-75, OF-3
1930	BOS A	88	.309	.412	243	75	13	0	4	1.6	32	30	9	15	5	25	4	541	30	2	49	10.1	.997	1B-56, 3B-1
1931		131	.295	.373	498	147	30	3	1	0.2	48	58	20	30	5	6	4	1283	92	9	89	11.2	.993	1B-124
3 yrs.		308	.286	.370	1050	300	58	8	5	0.5	127	107	44	73	22	39	9	2501	177	16	189	10.4	.994	1B-255, OF-3, 3B-1

Charlie Sweeney

SWEENEY, CHARLES FRANCIS (Buck)
B. Apr. 15, 1890, Pittsburgh, Pa. D. Mar. 15, 1955, Pittsburgh, Pa.

Year	Team	Games	BA	SA	AB	H	2B	3B	HR	HR%	R	RBI	BB	SO	SB	Pinch Hit AB	Pinch Hit H	PO	A	E	DP	TC/G	FA	G by Pos
1914	PHI A	1	.000	.000	1	0	0	0	0	0.0	0	0	0	1	0	0	0	1	0	0	0	1.0	1.000	OF-1

Charlie Sweeney

SWEENEY, CHARLES J. BR TR 5′10½″ 160 lbs.
B. Apr. 13, 1863, San Francisco, Calif. D. Apr. 4, 1902, San Francisco, Calif.

Year	Team	Games	BA	SA	AB	H	2B	3B	HR	HR%	R	RBI	BB	SO	SB	Pinch Hit AB	Pinch Hit H	PO	A	E	DP	TC/G	FA	G by Pos
1882	PRO N	1	.000	.000	4	0	0	0	0	0.0	0		0	1		0	0	0	1	1	0	2.0	.500	OF-1
1883		22	.218	.253	87	19	3	0	0	0.0	9		2	10		0	0	29	38	10	1	2.9	.870	P-20, OF-7
1884	2 teams	PRO N (41G –.298) STL U (45G –.316)																						
″	total	86	.307	.404	339	104	23	2	2	0.6	55		21	17		0	0	92	127	15	5	2.5	.936	P-60, OF-30, 1B-2
1885	STL N	71	.206	.240	267	55	7	1	0	0.0	27	24	12	33		0	0	81	67	27	3	2.4	.846	OF-39, P-35
1886		17	.250	.281	64	16	2	0	0	0.0	4	7	3	10		0	0	9	26	5	1	2.4	.875	P-11, OF-4, SS-2
1887	CLE AA	36	.226	.316	133	30	4	4	0	0.0	22		21		11	0	0	173	17	20	4	5.7	.905	1B-20, OF-10, P-3, SS-2, 3B-2
6 yrs.		233	.251	.317	894	224	39	7	2	0.2	117	31	59	71	11	0	0	384	276	78	14	3.0	.894	P-129, OF-91, 1B-22, SS-4, 3B-2

Dan Sweeney

SWEENEY, DANIEL J. 5′ 5″ 160 lbs.
B. Jan. 28, 1868, Philadelphia, Pa. D. July 13, 1913, Louisville, Ky.

Year	Team	Games	BA	SA	AB	H	2B	3B	HR	HR%	R	RBI	BB	SO	SB	Pinch Hit AB	Pinch Hit H	PO	A	E	DP	TC/G	FA	G by Pos
1895	LOU N	22	.267	.356	90	24	5	0	1	1.1	18	16	17	2	2	0	0	26	2	7	0	1.6	.800	OF-22

Hank Sweeney

SWEENEY, HENRY LEON BL TL 6′ 185 lbs.
B. Dec. 28, 1915, Franklin, Tenn. D. May 6, 1980, Columbia, Tenn.

Year	Team	Games	BA	SA	AB	H	2B	3B	HR	HR%	R	RBI	BB	SO	SB	Pinch Hit AB	Pinch Hit H	PO	A	E	DP	TC/G	FA	G by Pos
1944	PIT N	1	.000	.000	2	0	0	0	0	0.0	0	0	0	1	0	0	0	9	1	0	0	10.0	1.000	1B-1

Jeff Sweeney

SWEENEY, EDWARD FRANCIS BR TR 6′ 1″ 200 lbs.
B. July 19, 1888, Chicago, Ill. D. July 4, 1947, Chicago, Ill.

Year	Team	Games	BA	SA	AB	H	2B	3B	HR	HR%	R	RBI	BB	SO	SB	Pinch Hit AB	Pinch Hit H	PO	A	E	DP	TC/G	FA	G by Pos
1908	NY A	32	.146	.171	82	12	2	0	0	0.0	4	2	5		0	5	0	134	26	9	3	6.3	.947	C-25, OF-1, 1B-1
1909		67	.267	.284	176	47	3	0	0	0.0	19	21	16		3	2	0	293	84	21	8	6.1	.947	C-62, 1B-3
1910		78	.200	.256	215	43	4	4	0	0.0	25	13	17		12	1	0	388	106	13	2	6.5	.974	C-78
1911		83	.231	.301	229	53	6	5	0	0.0	17	18	14		8	0	0	394	94	18	8	6.1	.964	C-83
1912		110	.268	.308	351	94	12	1	0	0.0	37	30	27		6	2	1	548	167	34	9	6.9	.955	C-108
1913		117	.265	.322	351	93	10	2	2	0.6	35	40	37	41	11	3	1	512	180	26	9	6.4	.964	C-112, 1B-1
1914		87	.213	.264	258	55	8	1	1	0.4	25	22	35	30	19	8	2	369	120	10	7	6.4	.980	C-78
1915		53	.190	.204	137	26	2	0	0	0.0	12	5	25	12	3	0	0	213	59	7	4	5.3	.975	C-53
1919	PIT N	17	.095	.119	42	4	1	0	0	0.0	0	0	5	6	1	2	1	34	17	3	2	3.6	.944	C-15
9 yrs.		644	.232	.277	1841	427	48	13	3	0.2	174	151	181	89	63	23	5	2885	853	141	52	6.3	.964	C-614, 1B-5, OF-1

Jerry Sweeney

SWEENEY, JEREMIAH H. 5′ 9½″ 157 lbs.
B. 1860, Boston, Mass. D. Aug. 25, 1891, Boston, Mass.

Year	Team	Games	BA	SA	AB	H	2B	3B	HR	HR%	R	RBI	BB	SO	SB	Pinch Hit AB	Pinch Hit H	PO	A	E	DP	TC/G	FA	G by Pos
1884	KC U	31	.264	.287	129	34	3	0	0	0.0	16		4			0	0	304	14	14	15	10.7	.958	1B-31

Mark Sweeney

SWEENEY, MARK PATRICK BL TL 6′ 1″ 195 lbs.
B. Oct. 26, 1969, Framingham, Mass.

Year	Team	Games	BA	SA	AB	H	2B	3B	HR	HR%	R	RBI	BB	SO	SB	Pinch Hit AB	Pinch Hit H	PO	A	E	DP	TC/G	FA	G by Pos
1995	STL N	37	.273	.377	77	21	2	0	2	2.6	5	13	10	15	1	15	8	153	11	2	20	8.3	.988	1B-19, OF-1

Mike Sweeney

SWEENEY, MICHAEL JOHN BR TR 6′ 1″ 195 lbs.
B. July 22, 1973, Orange, Calif.

Year	Team	Games	BA	SA	AB	H	2B	3B	HR	HR%	R	RBI	BB	SO	SB	Pinch Hit AB	Pinch Hit H	PO	A	E	DP	TC/G	FA	G by Pos
1995	KC A	4	.250	.250	4	1	0	0	0	0.0	1	0	0	0	0	3	1	7	0	1	0	2.0	.875	C-4

Pete Sweeney

SWEENEY, PETER JAY BR TR
B. Dec. 31, 1863, Calif. D. Aug. 22, 1901, San Francisco, Calif.

Year	Team	Games	BA	SA	AB	H	2B	3B	HR	HR%	R	RBI	BB	SO	SB	Pinch Hit AB	Pinch Hit H	PO	A	E	DP	TC/G	FA	G by Pos
1888	WAS N	11	.182	.227	44	8	0	1	0	0.0	3	5	0	4	0	0	0	22	13	9	1	4.0	.795	3B-8, OF-3
1889	2 teams	WAS N (49G –.228) STL AA (9G –.368)																						
″	total	58	.251	.329	231	58	9	3	1	0.4	21	31	12	31	10	0	0	86	99	50	7	4.1	.787	3B-55, OF-2, 2B-1
1890	3 teams	STL AA (49G –.179) LOU AA (2G –.143) PHI AA (14G –.163)																						
″	total	65	.175	.220	246	43	5	3	0	0.0	29		25		9	0	0	176	117	45	14	5.1	.867	2B-32, 3B-23, OF-6, 1B-3, SS-2
3 yrs.		134	.209	.269	521	109	14	7	1	0.2	53	36	37	35	19	0	0	284	229	104	22	4.6	.831	3B-86, 2B-33, OF-11, 1B-3, SS-2

Rooney Sweeney

SWEENEY, JOHN J. 5′ 8″ 155 lbs.
B. 1860, New York, N. Y. Deceased.

Year	Team	Games	BA	SA	AB	H	2B	3B	HR	HR%	R	RBI	BB	SO	SB	Pinch Hit AB	Pinch Hit H	PO	A	E	DP	TC/G	FA	G by Pos
1883	BAL AA	25	.208	.297	101	21	5	2	0	0.0	13		4			0	0	101	42	19	3	6.2	.883	C-23, OF-3
1884	BAL U	48	.226	.274	186	42	7	1	0	0.0	37		15			0	0	218	61	35	1	6.3	.889	C-33, OF-16, 3B-1
1885	STL N	3	.091	.091	11	1	0	0	0	0.0	1	0	0	4		0	0	8	2	1	0	3.7	.909	OF-2, C-1
3 yrs.		76	.215	.275	298	64	12	3	0	0.0	51	0	19	4		0	0	327	105	55	4	6.2	.887	C-57, OF-21, 3B-1

Rick Sweet

SWEET, RICKY JOE BB TR 6′ 1″ 200 lbs.
B. Sept. 7, 1952, Longview, Wash. BL 1978

Year	Team	Games	BA	SA	AB	H	2B	3B	HR	HR%	R	RBI	BB	SO	SB	Pinch Hit AB	Pinch Hit H	PO	A	E	DP	TC/G	FA	G by Pos
1978	SD N	88	.221	.270	226	50	8	0	1	0.4	15	11	27	22	1	12	0	337	33	6	3	4.9	.984	C-76
1982	2 teams	NY N (3G –.333) SEA A (88G –.256)																						
″	total	91	.257	.333	261	67	6	1	4	1.5	29	24	20	25	3	21	2	431	26	3	6	5.5	.993	C-83
1983	SEA A	93	.221	.269	249	55	9	0	1	0.4	18	22	13	26	2	20	8	413	34	6	6	5.3	.987	C-85
3 yrs.		272	.234	.292	736	172	23	1	6	0.8	62	57	60	73	6	53	10	1181	93	15	15	5.3	.988	C-244

Ham Sweigert

SWEIGERT, HAMPTON
Deceased.

Year	Team	Games	BA	SA	AB	H	2B	3B	HR	HR%	R	RBI	BB	SO	SB	Pinch Hit AB	Pinch Hit H	PO	A	E	DP	TC/G	FA	G by Pos
1890	PHI AA	1	.000	.000	1	0	0	0	0	0.0	0		1		1	0	0	1	1	0	0	2.0	1.000	OF-1

Augie Swentor

SWENTOR, AUGUST WILLIAM BR TR 6′ 185 lbs.
B. Nov. 21, 1899, Seymour, Conn. D. Nov. 10, 1969, Waterbury, Conn.

Year	Team	Games	BA	SA	AB	H	2B	3B	HR	HR%	R	RBI	BB	SO	SB	Pinch Hit AB	Pinch Hit H	PO	A	E	DP	TC/G	FA	G by Pos
1922	CHI A	1	.000	.000	1	0	0	0	0	0.0	0	0	0	1	0	0	0	0	0	0	0	0.0	.000	C-1

Pop Swett

SWETT, WILLIAM E.
B. Apr. 16, 1870, San Francisco, Calif. D. Nov. 22, 1934, San Francisco, Calif.

Year	Team	Games	BA	SA	AB	H	2B	3B	HR	HR%	R	RBI	BB	SO	SB	Pinch Hit AB	Pinch Hit H	PO	A	E	DP	TC/G	FA	G by Pos
1890	BOS P	37	.191	.330	94	18	4	3	1	1.1	16	12	16	26	4	0	0	83	12	21	1	3.1	.819	C-34, OF-3

Bob Swift

SWIFT, ROBERT VIRGIL BR TR 5′11½″ 180 lbs.
B. Mar. 6, 1915, Salina, Kans. D. Oct. 17, 1966, Detroit, Mich.
Manager 1965–66.

Year	Team	Games	BA	SA	AB	H	2B	3B	HR	HR%	R	RBI	BB	SO	SB	Pinch Hit AB	Pinch Hit H	PO	A	E	DP	TC/G	FA	G by Pos
1940	STL A	130	.244	.299	398	97	20	1	0	0.0	37	39	28	39	1	2	0	389	55	9	8	3.5	.980	C-128
1941		63	.259	.300	170	44	7	0	0	0.0	13	21	22	11	2	5	1	180	22	3	3	3.5	.985	C-58
1942	2 teams	STL A (29G –.197) PHI A (60G –.229)																						
″	total	89	.220	.257	268	59	7	0	1	0.4	12	23	16	22	1	1	0	334	50	9	5	4.5	.977	C-88
1943	PHI A	77	.192	.237	224	43	5	1	1	0.4	16	11	35	16	0	0	0	278	53	8	9	4.4	.976	C-77
1944	DET A	80	.255	.320	247	63	11	1	1	0.4	15	19	27	27	2	4	1	288	48	6	4	4.5	.982	C-76
1945		95	.233	.251	279	65	5	0	0	0.0	19	24	25	22	1	1	0	358	60	5	12	4.5	.988	C-94
1946		42	.234	.308	107	25	2	0	2	1.9	13	10	14	7	0	0	0	187	14	4	2	4.9	.980	C-42
1947		97	.251	.301	279	70	11	0	1	0.4	23	21	33	16	2	1	0	401	45	5	6	4.6	.989	C-97
1948		113	.223	.284	292	65	6	0	4	1.4	23	33	51	29	1	1	0	476	55	5	13	4.8	.991	C-112
1949		74	.238	.302	189	45	6	0	2	1.1	16	18	26	20	0	6	1	232	26	3	6	3.8	.989	C-69
1950		67	.227	.303	132	30	4	0	2	1.5	14	9	25	6	0	1	0	201	20	1	3	3.4	.995	C-66
1951		44	.192	.192	104	20	0	0	0	0.0	8	5	12	10	0	1	0	146	17	3	3	3.9	.982	C-43
1952		28	.138	.155	58	8	1	0	0	0.0	3	4	7	7	0	0	0	118	12	3	1	4.8	.977	C-28
1953		2	.333	.667	3	1	1	0	0	0.0	0	1	2	1	0	0	0	13	0	0	0	6.5	1.000	C-2
14 yrs.		1001	.231	.280	2750	635	86	3	14	0.5	212	238	323	233	10	23	3	3601	477	64	75	4.2	.985	C-980
WORLD SERIES																								
1945	DET A	3	.250	.250	4	1	0	0	0	0.0	1	0	2	0	0	0	0	9	1	0	0	3.3	1.000	C-3

Charlie Swindells

SWINDELLS, CHARLES JAY BR TR 5′11½″ 180 lbs.
B. Oct. 26, 1878, Rockford, Ill. D. July 22, 1940, Portland, Ore.

Year	Team	Games	BA	SA	AB	H	2B	3B	HR	HR%	R	RBI	BB	SO	SB	Pinch Hit AB	Pinch Hit H	PO	A	E	DP	TC/G	FA	G by Pos
1904	STL N	3	.125	.125	8	1	0	0	0	0.0	0	0	0		0	0	0	14	1	0	0	5.0	1.000	C-3

Steve Swisher

SWISHER, STEVEN EUGENE BR TR 6′ 2″ 205 lbs.
B. Aug. 9, 1951, Parkersburg, W. Va.

Year	Team	Games	BA	SA	AB	H	2B	3B	HR	HR%	R	RBI	BB	SO	SB	Pinch Hit AB	Pinch Hit H	PO	A	E	DP	TC/G	FA	G by Pos
1974	CHI N	90	.214	.286	280	60	5	0	5	1.8	21	27	37	63	0	0	0	493	50	7	8	6.1	.987	C-90
1975		93	.213	.303	254	54	16	2	1	0.4	20	22	30	57	1	0	0	426	36	10	5	5.1	.979	C-93
1976		109	.236	.326	377	89	13	3	5	1.3	25	42	20	82	2	4	1	574	49	11	6	5.9	.983	C-107
1977		74	.190	.298	205	39	7	0	5	2.4	21	15	9	47	0	4	1	327	38	9	3	5.2	.976	C-72
1978	STL N	45	.278	.365	115	32	5	1	1	0.9	11	10	8	14	1	3	1	202	13	2	0	5.2	.991	C-42
1979		38	.151	.233	73	11	1	1	1	1.4	4	3	6	17	0	5	0	105	6	3	2	3.5	.974	C-33
1980		18	.250	.292	24	6	1	0	0	0.0	2	2	1	7	0	9	2	21	1	1	0	2.9	.957	C-8
1981	SD N	16	.143	.143	28	4	0	0	0	0.0	2	0	2	11	0	7	1	33	1	1	0	3.5	.971	C-10
1982		26	.172	.293	58	10	1	0	2	3.4	2	3	5	24	0	0	0	93	9	2	0	4.0	.981	C-26
9 yrs.		509	.216	.303	1414	305	49	7	20	1.4	108	124	118	322	4	32	6	2274	203	46	24	5.2	.982	C-481

Ron Swoboda

SWOBODA, RONALD ALAN (Rocky) BR TR 6′ 2″ 195 lbs.
B. June 30, 1944, Baltimore, Md.

Year	Team	Games	BA	SA	AB	H	2B	3B	HR	HR%	R	RBI	BB	SO	SB	Pinch Hit AB	Pinch Hit H	PO	A	E	DP	TC/G	FA	G by Pos
1965	NY N	135	.228	.424	399	91	15	3	19	4.8	52	50	33	102	2	26	7	188	9	11	2	1.9	.947	OF-112
1966		112	.222	.342	342	76	9	4	8	2.3	34	50	31	76	4	19	8	145	7	2	0	1.6	.987	OF-97
1967		134	.281	.419	449	126	17	3	13	2.9	47	53	41	96	3	9	2	333	25	13	7	2.9	.965	OF-108, 1B-20
1968		132	.242	.373	450	109	14	6	11	2.4	46	59	52	113	8	9	4	217	14	6	4	1.9	.975	OF-125
1969		109	.235	.361	327	77	10	2	9	2.8	38	52	43	90	1	9	2	163	5	2	0	1.8	.988	OF-97
1970		115	.233	.392	245	57	8	2	9	3.7	29	40	40	72	2	20	5	117	3	2	1	1.2	.984	OF-100
1971	2 teams	MON N (39G –.253) NY A (54G –.261)																						
″	total	93	.258	.352	213	55	6	4	2	0.9	24	26	38	51	0	29	4	119	5	4	0	1.8	.969	OF-73
1972	NY A	63	.248	.345	113	28	8	0	1	0.9	9	12	17	29	0	26	4	61	2	1	2	1.7	.984	OF-35, 1B-2
1973		35	.116	.186	43	5	0	0	1	2.3	6	2	4	18	0	1	1	23	0	0	0	1.0	1.000	OF-20, DH-4
9 yrs.		928	.242	.379	2581	624	87	24	73	2.8	285	344	299	647	20	148	37	1366	70	41	16	1.9	.972	OF-767, 1B-22, DH-4
WORLD SERIES																								
1969	NY N	4	.400	.467	15	6	1	0	0	0.0	1	1	1	3	0	0	0	14	0	0	0	3.5	1.000	OF-4

Lou Sylvester

SYLVESTER, LOUIS J.
B. Feb. 14, 1855, Springfield, Ill. Deceased.
BR TR 5′ 3″ 165 lbs.

Year	Team	Games	BA	SA	AB	H	2B	3B	HR	HR%	R	RBI	BB	SO	SB	Pinch Hit AB	Pinch Hit H	PO	A	E	DP	TC/G	FA	G by Pos
1884	CIN U	82	.267	.372	333	89	13	8	2	0.6	67		18			0	0	111	28	39	2	2.0	.781	OF-81, P-6, SS-2
1886	2 teams	LOU AA (45G –.227) CIN AA (17G –.182)																						
"	total	62	.215	.311	209	45	5	3	3	1.4	51		36			0	0	80	13	9	5	1.6	.912	OF-62
1887	STL AA	29	.223	.339	112	25	4	3	1	0.9	20		13		13	0	0	55	8	6	4	2.3	.913	OF-29, 2B-1
3 yrs.		173	.243	.347	654	159	22	14	6	0.9	138		67		13	0	0	246	49	54	11	1.9	.845	OF-172, P-6, SS-2, 2B-1

Joe Szekely

SZEKELY, JOSEPH
B. Feb. 2, 1925, Cleveland, Ohio.
BR TR 5′11″ 180 lbs.

Year	Team	Games	BA	SA	AB	H	2B	3B	HR	HR%	R	RBI	BB	SO	SB	Pinch Hit AB	Pinch Hit H	PO	A	E	DP	TC/G	FA	G by Pos
1953	CIN N	5	.077	.077	13	1	0	0	0	0.0	0	0	0	3	0	2	0	4	2	0	1	2.0	1.000	OF-3

Ken Szotkiewicz

SZOTKIEWICZ, KENNETH JOHN
B. Feb. 25, 1947, Wilmington, Del.
BL TR 6′ 165 lbs.

Year	Team	Games	BA	SA	AB	H	2B	3B	HR	HR%	R	RBI	BB	SO	SB	Pinch Hit AB	Pinch Hit H	PO	A	E	DP	TC/G	FA	G by Pos
1970	DET A	47	.107	.226	84	9	1	0	3	3.6	9	9	12	29	0	3	0	32	101	4	20	3.1	.971	SS-44

Jerry Tabb

TABB, JERRY LYNN
B. Mar. 17, 1952, Altus, Okla.
BL TR 6′ 2″ 195 lbs.

Year	Team	Games	BA	SA	AB	H	2B	3B	HR	HR%	R	RBI	BB	SO	SB	Pinch Hit AB	Pinch Hit H	PO	A	E	DP	TC/G	FA	G by Pos
1976	CHI N	11	.292	.292	24	7	0	0	0	0.0	2	0	3	2	0	6	1	52	2	0	4	9.0	1.000	1B-6
1977	OAK A	51	.222	.368	144	32	3	0	6	4.2	8	19	10	26	0	10	2	288	16	2	26	7.5	.993	1B-36, DH-5
1978		12	.111	.111	9	1	0	0	0	0.0	0	1	2	5	0	9	1	3	0	0	0	0.8	1.000	1B-2, DH-2
3 yrs.		74	.226	.345	177	40	3	0	6	3.4	10	20	15	33	0	25	4	343	18	2	30	7.1	.994	1B-44, DH-7

Pat Tabler

TABLER, PATRICK SEAN
B. Feb. 2, 1958, Hamilton, Ohio.
BR TR 6′ 3″ 175 lbs.

Year	Team	Games	BA	SA	AB	H	2B	3B	HR	HR%	R	RBI	BB	SO	SB	Pinch Hit AB	Pinch Hit H	PO	A	E	DP	TC/G	FA	G by Pos
1981	CHI N	35	.188	.267	101	19	3	1	1	1.0	11	5	13	26	0	0	0	70	93	3	17	4.7	.982	2B-35
1982		25	.235	.365	85	20	4	2	1	1.2	9	7	6	20	0	0	0	23	33	3	3	2.4	.949	3B-25
1983	CLE A	124	.291	.409	430	125	23	5	6	1.4	56	65	56	63	2	5	2	197	55	11	6	2.3	.958	OF-80, 3B-25, DH-6, 2B-2
1984		144	.290	.410	473	137	21	3	10	2.1	66	68	47	62	3	6	1	532	89	7	54	4.2	.989	1B-67, OF-43, 3B-36, DH-1, 2B-1
1985		117	.275	.371	404	111	18	3	5	1.2	47	59	27	55	0	8	4	744	77	14	78	7.3	.983	1B-92, DH-18, 3B-4, 2B-1
1986		130	.326	.433	473	154	29	2	6	1.3	61	48	29	75	3	9	1	846	84	9	87	7.5	.990	1B-107, DH-18
1987		151	.307	.439	553	170	34	3	11	2.0	66	86	51	84	5	7	2	650	75	12	49	5.0	.984	1B-82, DH-66
1988	2 teams	CLE A (41G –.224) KC A (89G –.309)																						
"	total	130	.282	.358	444	125	22	3	2	0.5	53	66	46	68	3	8	2	182	10	5	11	1.6	.975	DH-69, OF-37, 1B-17, 3B-1
1989	KC A	123	.259	.308	390	101	11	1	2	0.5	36	42	37	42	0	13	2	217	25	4	11	2.1	.984	OF-55, DH-39, 1B-20, 2B-3, 3B-1
1990	2 teams	KC A (75G –.272) NY N (17G –.279)																						
"	total	92	.273	.370	238	65	15	1	2	0.8	18	29	23	29	0	18	4	121	11	2	8	1.7	.985	OF-52, DH-15, 3B-6, 1B-5
1991	TOR A	82	.216	.270	185	40	5	1	1	0.5	20	21	29	21	0	21	9	183	14	3	11	2.6	.985	DH-57, 1B-20, OF-1
1992		49	.252	.289	135	34	5	0	0	0.0	11	16	11	14	0	7	0	288	22	0	20	6.9	1.000	1B-34, OF-8, DH-2, 3B-1
12 yrs.		1202	.282	.379	3911	1101	190	25	47	1.2	454	512	375	559	16	102	27	4053	588	73	355	4.1	.985	1B-444, DH-291, OF-276, 3B-99, 2B-42
LEAGUE CHAMPIONSHIP SERIES																								
1991	TOR A	2	.000	.000	1	0	0	0	0	0.0	0	0	1	0	0	1	0	0	0	0	0	0.0	.000	DH-2
WORLD SERIES																								
1992	TOR A	2	.000	.000	2	0	0	0	0	0.0	0	0	0	0	0	2	0	0	0	0	0	0.0	—	

Greg Tabor

TABOR, GREGORY STEVEN
B. May 21, 1961, Castro Valley, Calif.
BR TR 6′ 165 lbs.

Year	Team	Games	BA	SA	AB	H	2B	3B	HR	HR%	R	RBI	BB	SO	SB	Pinch Hit AB	Pinch Hit H	PO	A	E	DP	TC/G	FA	G by Pos
1987	TEX A	9	.111	.222	9	1	1	0	0	0.0	4	1	0	4	0	0	0	4	11	1	2	3.2	.938	2B-4, DH-1

Jim Tabor

TABOR, JAMES REUBIN (Rawhide)
B. Nov. 5, 1916, New Hope, Ala. D. Aug. 22, 1953, Sacramento, Calif.
BR TR 6′ 2″ 175 lbs.

Year	Team	Games	BA	SA	AB	H	2B	3B	HR	HR%	R	RBI	BB	SO	SB	Pinch Hit AB	Pinch Hit H	PO	A	E	DP	TC/G	FA	G by Pos
1938	BOS A	19	.316	.491	57	18	3	2	1	1.8	8	8	1	6	0	5	2	18	30	8	4	4.3	.857	3B-11, SS-2
1939		149	.289	.447	577	167	33	8	14	2.4	76	95	40	54	16	1	1	144	338	40	32	3.5	.923	3B-148
1940		120	.285	.510	459	131	28	6	21	4.6	73	81	42	58	14	0	0	143	267	33	25	3.7	.926	3B-120
1941		126	.279	.446	498	139	29	3	16	3.2	65	101	36	48	17	2	1	123	277	30	24	3.4	.930	3B-125
1942		139	.252	.366	508	128	18	2	12	2.4	56	75	37	47	6	0	0	168	236	33	24	3.2	.924	3B-138
1943		137	.242	.374	537	130	26	3	13	2.4	57	85	43	54	7	3	1	137	261	26	32	3.1	.939	3B-133, OF-2
1944		116	.285	.445	438	125	25	3	13	3.0	58	72	31	38	4	2	0	125	258	20	14	3.5	.950	3B-114
1946	PHI N	124	.268	.374	463	124	15	2	10	2.2	53	50	36	51	3	0	0	156	221	18	17	3.2	.954	3B-124
1947		75	.235	.339	251	59	14	0	4	1.6	27	31	20	21	2	7	1	68	96	15	8	2.7	.916	3B-67
9 yrs.		1005	.270	.418	3788	1021	191	29	104	2.7	473	598	286	377	69	20	6	1082	1984	223	180	3.3	.932	3B-980, OF-2, SS-2

Jeff Tackett

TACKETT, JEFFREY WILSON
B. Dec. 1, 1965, Fresno, Calif.
BR TR 6′ 2″ 200 lbs.

Year	Team	Games	BA	SA	AB	H	2B	3B	HR	HR%	R	RBI	BB	SO	SB	Pinch Hit AB	Pinch Hit H	PO	A	E	DP	TC/G	FA	G by Pos
1991	BAL A	6	.125	.125	8	1	0	0	0	0.0	1	0	2	2	0	0	0	22	0	0	0	3.7	1.000	C-6
1992		65	.240	.380	179	43	8	1	5	2.8	21	24	17	28	0	1	0	311	32	1	5	5.3	.997	C-64, 3B-1
1993		38	.172	.207	87	15	3	0	0	0.0	8	9	13	28	0	0	0	167	16	2	1	4.7	.989	C-38, P-1
1994		26	.226	.434	53	12	3	1	2	3.8	5	9	5	13	0	0	0	86	11	2	0	3.8	.980	C-26
4 yrs.		135	.217	.336	327	71	14	2	7	2.1	35	42	37	71	0	1	0	586	59	5	6	4.8	.992	C-134, P-1, 3B-1

Doug Taitt

TAITT, DOUGLAS JOHN (Poco)
B. Aug. 3, 1902, Bay City, Mich. D. Dec. 12, 1970, Portland, Ore.
BL TR 6′ 176 lbs.

Year	Team	Games	BA	SA	AB	H	2B	3B	HR	HR%	R	RBI	BB	SO	SB	Pinch Hit AB	Pinch Hit H	PO	A	E	DP	TC/G	FA	G by Pos
1928	BOS A	143	.299	.434	482	144	28	14	3	0.6	51	61	36	32	13	3	0	252	19	7	8	2.0	.975	OF-139, P-1
1929	2 teams	BOS A (26G –.277) CHI A (47G –.169)																						
"	total	73	.206	.265	189	39	11	0	0	0.0	17	18	16	18	0	21	6	90	7	4	3	2.0	.960	OF-51
1931	PHI N	38	.225	.298	151	34	4	2	1	0.7	13	15	4	14	0	0	0	95	4	1	0	2.6	.990	OF-38
1932		4	.000	.000	2	0	0	0	0	0.0	0	1	2	0	0	2	0	0	0	0	0	0.0	—	
4 yrs.		258	.263	.369	824	217	43	16	4	0.5	81	95	58	64	13	26	6	437	30	12	11	2.1	.975	OF-228, P-1

Dale Talbot

TALBOT, ROBERT DALE BR TR 6′ 170 lbs.
B. June 6, 1927, Visalia, Calif.

Year	Team	Games	BA	SA	AB	H	2B	3B	HR	HR%	R	RBI	BB	SO	SB	Pinch Hit AB	Pinch Hit H	PO	A	E	DP	TC/G	FA	G by Pos
1953	CHI N	8	.333	.400	30	10	0	1	0	0.0	5	0	0	4	1	0	0	20	3	0	1	3.3	1.000	OF-7
1954		114	.241	.305	403	97	15	4	1	0.2	45	19	16	25	3	1	0	245	10	4	1	2.4	.985	OF-110
2 yrs.		122	.247	.312	433	107	15	5	1	0.2	50	19	16	29	4	1	0	265	13	4	2	2.4	.986	OF-117

Tim Talton

TALTON, MARION LEE BL TR 6′ 3″ 200 lbs.
B. Jan. 14, 1939, Pikeville, N. C.

Year	Team	Games	BA	SA	AB	H	2B	3B	HR	HR%	R	RBI	BB	SO	SB	Pinch Hit AB	Pinch Hit H	PO	A	E	DP	TC/G	FA	G by Pos
1966	KC A	37	.340	.547	53	18	3	1	2	3.8	8	6	1	5	0	25	10	73	5	0	7	3.4	1.000	C-14, 1B-9
1967		46	.254	.339	59	15	3	1	0	0.0	7	5	7	13	0	32	9	67	5	2	0	3.2	.973	C-22, 1B-1
2 yrs.		83	.295	.438	112	33	6	2	2	1.8	15	11	8	18	0	57	19	140	10	2	7	3.3	.987	C-36, 1B-10

John Tamargo

TAMARGO, JOHN FELIX BB TR 5′10″ 170 lbs.
B. Nov. 7, 1951, Tampa, Fla.

Year	Team	Games	BA	SA	AB	H	2B	3B	HR	HR%	R	RBI	BB	SO	SB	Pinch Hit AB	Pinch Hit H	PO	A	E	DP	TC/G	FA	G by Pos
1976	STL N	10	.300	.300	10	3	0	0	0	0.0	2	1	3	0	0	7	2	4	0	0	0	4.0	1.000	C-1
1977		4	.000	.000	4	0	0	0	0	0.0	0	0	0	2	0	3	0	1	0	0	0	1.0	1.000	C-1
1978	2 teams	STL N (6G –.000) SF N (36G –.239)																						
″	total	42	.224	.316	98	22	4	1	1	1.0	6	8	18	9	1	11	1	157	9	6	4	5.4	.965	C-32
1979	2 teams	SF N (30G –.200) MON N (12G –.381)																						
″	total	42	.247	.383	81	20	5	0	2	2.5	7	11	7	11	0	21	6	80	6	1	4	4.1	.989	C-21
1980	MON N	37	.275	.392	51	14	3	0	1	2.0	4	13	6	5	0	23	7	36	3	1	2	3.3	.975	C-12
5 yrs.		135	.242	.348	244	59	12	1	4	1.6	19	33	34	27	1	65	16	278	18	8	10	4.5	.974	C-67

Leo Tankersley

TANKERSLEY, LAWRENCE WILLIAM BR TR 6′ 176 lbs.
B. June 8, 1901, Terrell, Tex. D. Sept. 18, 1980, Dallas, Tex.

Year	Team	Games	BA	SA	AB	H	2B	3B	HR	HR%	R	RBI	BB	SO	SB	Pinch Hit AB	Pinch Hit H	PO	A	E	DP	TC/G	FA	G by Pos
1925	CHI A	1	.000	.000	3	0	0	0	0	0.0	0	0	0	0	0	0	0	1	0	0	0	1.0	1.000	C-1

Jesse Tannehill

TANNEHILL, JESSE NILES (Tanny) BB TL 5′ 8″ 150 lbs.
BL 1903
Brother of Lee Tannehill.
B. July 14, 1874, Dayton, Ky. D. Sept. 22, 1956, Dayton, Ky.

Year	Team	Games	BA	SA	AB	H	2B	3B	HR	HR%	R	RBI	BB	SO	SB	Pinch Hit AB	Pinch Hit H	PO	A	E	DP	TC/G	FA	G by Pos
1894	CIN N	5	.000	.000	11	0	0	0	0	0.0	0	1	1	2	0	0	0	1	2	2	0	1.0	.600	P-5
1897	PIT N	56	.266	.332	184	49	8	2	0	0.0	22	22	18		4	2	0	89	53	13	1	2.9	.916	OF-33, P-21
1898		60	.289	.408	152	44	9	3	1	0.7	25	17	7		4	8	3	28	95	5	2	2.6	.961	P-43, OF-7
1899		47	.258	.341	132	34	5	3	0	0.0	17	10	8		2	6	1	9	95	5	7	2.6	.954	P-41, OF-1
1900		34	.336	.400	110	37	7	0	0	0.0	19	17	5		2	1	1	14	65	6	1	2.6	.929	P-29, OF-4
1901		42	.244	.333	135	33	3	3	1	0.7	19	12	6		0	0	0	23	53	7	1	2.0	.916	P-32, OF-10
1902		44	.291	.365	148	43	6	1	1	0.7	27	17	12		3	2	0	25	57	4	3	2.0	.953	P-26, OF-16
1903	NY A	40	.234	.351	111	26	6	2	1	0.9	18	13	8		1	3	0	14	83	3	2	2.7	.970	P-32, OF-5
1904	BOS A	45	.197	.311	122	24	2	6	0	0.0	14	6	9		1	10	**2**	12	107	1	4	3.4	.992	P-33, OF-2
1905		37	.226	.280	93	21	2	0	1	1.1	11	12	16		1	0	0	9	97	6	3	3.0	.946	P-37
1906		31	.278	.354	79	22	2	2	0	0.0	12	4	6		1	4	1	15	58	4	1	2.9	.948	P-27
1907		21	.196	.294	51	10	3	1	0	0.0	2	6	2		0	2	0	9	42	1	3	2.9	.981	P-18
1908	2 teams	BOS A (1G –.500) WAS A (26G –.256)																						
″	total	27	.267	.289	45	12	1	0	0	0.0	1	3	2		0	15	3	5	34	4	2	3.9	.907	P-11
1909	WAS A	16	.167	.194	36	6	1	0	0	0.0	2	1	5		0	4	0	14	9	0	1	1.9	1.000	OF-9, P-3
1911	CIN N	1	.000	.000	1	0	0	0	0	0.0	0	0	0	1	0	0	0	0	1	0	0	1.0	1.000	P-1
15 yrs.		506	.256	.338	1410	361	55	23	5	0.4	189	141	105	3	19	57	11	267	851	61	31	2.6	.948	P-359, OF-87

Lee Tannehill

TANNEHILL, LEE FORD BR TR 5′11″ 170 lbs.
Brother of Jesse Tannehill.
B. Oct. 26, 1880, Dayton, Ky. D. Feb. 16, 1938, Live Oak, Fla.

Year	Team	Games	BA	SA	AB	H	2B	3B	HR	HR%	R	RBI	BB	SO	SB	Pinch Hit AB	Pinch Hit H	PO	A	E	DP	TC/G	FA	G by Pos
1903	CHI A	138	.225	.276	503	113	14	3	2	0.4	48	50	25		10	0	0	291	457	76	58	6.0	.908	SS-138
1904		153	.229	.303	547	125	31	5	0	0.0	50	61	20		14	0	0	180	369	31	22	3.8	.947	3B-153
1905		142	.200	.244	480	96	17	2	0	0.0	38	39	45		8	0	0	168	358	39	17	4.0	.931	3B-142
1906		116	.183	.220	378	69	8	3	0	0.0	26	33	31		7	0	0	173	332	27	13	4.6	.949	3B-99, SS-17
1907		33	.241	.259	108	26	2	0	0	0.0	9	11	8		3	0	0	25	91	11	4	3.8	.913	3B-31, SS-2
1908		141	.216	.259	482	104	15	3	0	0.0	44	35	25		6	0	0	142	354	35	21	3.8	.934	3B-136, SS-5
1909		155	.222	.281	531	118	21	5	0	0.0	39	47	31		12	0	0	229	419	41	32	4.4	.940	3B-91, SS-64
1910		67	.222	.278	230	51	10	0	1	0.4	17	21	11		3	0	0	267	156	13	21	6.5	.970	SS-38, 1B-23, 3B-6
1911		141	.254	.310	516	131	17	6	0	0.0	60	49	32		0	0	0	385	493	38	53	6.5	.959	SS-102, 2B-27, 3B-8, 1B-5
1912		3	.000	.000	3	0	0	0	0	0.0	0	0	1		0	0	0	2	2	2	1	2.0	.667	3B-3
10 yrs.		1089	.220	.273	3778	833	135	27	3	0.1	331	346	229		63	0	0	1862	3031	313	242	4.8	.940	3B-669, SS-366, 1B-28, 2B-27
WORLD SERIES																								
1906	CHI A	3	.111	.111	9	1	0	0	0	0.0	1	0	0	2	0	0	0	1	12	0	0	4.3	1.000	SS-3

Chuck Tanner

TANNER, CHARLES WILLIAM BL TL 6′ 185 lbs.
Father of Bruce Tanner.
B. July 4, 1929, New Castle, Pa.
Manager 1970–88.

Year	Team	Games	BA	SA	AB	H	2B	3B	HR	HR%	R	RBI	BB	SO	SB	Pinch Hit AB	Pinch Hit H	PO	A	E	DP	TC/G	FA	G by Pos
1955	MIL N	97	.247	.383	243	60	9	3	6	2.5	27	27	27	32	0	32	7	101	4	2	0	1.7	.981	OF-62
1956		60	.238	.317	63	15	2	0	1	1.6	6	4	10	10	0	44	10	4	0	1	0	0.6	.800	OF-8
1957	2 teams	MIL N (22G –.246) CHI N (95G –.286)																						
″	total	117	.279	.408	387	108	19	2	9	2.3	47	48	28	24	0	16	4	191	5	2	2	2.0	.990	OF-100
1958	CHI N	73	.262	.437	103	27	6	0	4	3.9	10	17	9	10	1	**53**	12	21	0	1	0	1.5	.955	OF-15
1959	CLE A	14	.250	.354	48	12	2	0	1	2.1	6	5	2	9	0	4	0	18	0	0	0	1.8	1.000	OF-10
1960		21	.280	.320	25	7	1	0	0	0.0	2	4	4	6	1	15	3	5	0	0	0	1.3	1.000	OF-4
1961	LA A	7	.125	.125	8	1	0	0	0	0.0	0	0	2	2	0	4	1	0	0	0	0	0.0	.000	OF-1
1962		7	.125	.125	8	1	0	0	0	0.0	0	0	0	0	0	6	1	0	0	0	0	0.0	.000	OF-2
8 yrs.		396	.261	.388	885	231	39	5	21	2.4	98	105	82	93	2	174	38	340	9	6	2	1.8	.983	OF-202

Walter Tappan

TAPPAN, WALTER VAN DORN (Tap) BR TR 5′ 9″ 150 lbs.
B. Oct. 8, 1890, Carlinville, Ill. D. Dec. 19, 1967, Lynwood, Calif.

Year	Team	Games	BA	SA	AB	H	2B	3B	HR	HR%	R	RBI	BB	SO	SB	Pinch Hit AB	Pinch Hit H	PO	A	E	DP	TC/G	FA	G by Pos
1914	KC F	18	.205	.308	39	8	1	0	1	2.6	1	3	1		1	0	0	7	28	5	2	2.7	.875	SS-8, 3B-6, 2B-1

El Tappe

TAPPE, ELVIN WALTER
B. May 21, 1927, Quincy, Ill.
Manager 1961–62.

BR TR 5′11″ 180 lbs.

Year	Team	Games	BA	SA	AB	H	2B	3B	HR	HR%	R	RBI	BB	SO	SB	Pinch Hit AB	Pinch Hit H	PO	A	E	DP	TC/G	FA	G by Pos
1954	CHI N	46	.185	.210	119	22	3	0	0	0.0	5	4	10	9	0	0	0	185	22	3	2	4.6	.986	C-46
1955		2	—	—	0	0	0	0	0	—	0	0	0	0	0	0	0	3	1	0	0	2.0	1.000	C-2
1956		3	.000	.000	1	0	0	0	0	0.0	0	0	1	0	0	0	0	4	0	0	0	1.3	1.000	C-3
1958		17	.214	.214	28	6	0	0	0	0.0	2	4	3	1	0	1	0	46	4	2	0	3.3	.962	C-16
1960		51	.233	.301	103	24	7	0	0	0.0	11	3	11	12	0	2	0	215	27	2	4	5.0	.992	C-49
1962		26	.208	.208	53	11	0	0	0	0.0	3	6	4	3	0	0	0	101	13	0	4	4.4	1.000	C-26
6 yrs.		145	.207	.240	304	63	10	0	0	0.0	21	17	29	25	0	3	0	554	67	7	10	4.4	.989	C-142

Ted Tappe

TAPPE, THEODORE NASH
B. Feb. 2, 1931, Seattle, Wash.

BL TR 6′3″ 185 lbs.

Year	Team	Games	BA	SA	AB	H	2B	3B	HR	HR%	R	RBI	BB	SO	SB	Pinch Hit AB	Pinch Hit H	PO	A	E	DP	TC/G	FA	G by Pos
1950	CIN N	7	.200	.800	5	1	0	0	1	20.0	1	1	1	1	0	5	1	0	0	0	0	0.0	—	
1951		4	.333	.333	3	1	0	0	0	0.0	0	0	0	0	0	3	1	0	0	0	0	0.0	—	
1955	CHI N	23	.260	.540	50	13	2	0	4	8.0	12	10	11	11	0	8	2	18	1	0	0	1.3	1.000	OF-15
3 yrs.		34	.259	.552	58	15	2	0	5	8.6	13	11	12	12	0	16	4	18	1	0	0	1.3	1.000	OF-15

Tony Tarasco

TARASCO, ANTONIO GIACINTO
B. Dec. 9, 1970, New York, N. Y.

BL TR 6′ 185 lbs.

Year	Team	Games	BA	SA	AB	H	2B	3B	HR	HR%	R	RBI	BB	SO	SB	Pinch Hit AB	Pinch Hit H	PO	A	E	DP	TC/G	FA	G by Pos
1993	ATL N	24	.229	.286	35	8	2	0	0	0.0	6	2	0	5	0	13	4	11	0	0	0	0.9	1.000	OF-12
1994		87	.273	.432	132	36	6	0	5	3.8	16	19	9	17	5	46	10	42	1	0	0	0.9	1.000	OF-46
1995	MON N	126	.249	.404	438	109	18	4	14	3.2	64	40	51	78	24	8	2	229	7	5	2	2.1	.979	OF-117
3 yrs.		237	.253	.403	605	153	26	4	19	3.1	86	61	60	100	29	67	16	282	8	5	2	1.7	.983	OF-175
LEAGUE CHAMPIONSHIP SERIES																								
1993	ATL N	2	.000	.000	1	0	0	0	0	0.0	0	0	0	1	0	0	0	0	0	0	0	0.0	.000	OF-2

Arlie Tarbert

TARBERT, WILBUR ARLINGTON
B. Sept. 10, 1904, Cleveland, Ohio D. Nov. 27, 1946, Cleveland, Ohio.

BR TR 6′ 160 lbs.

Year	Team	Games	BA	SA	AB	H	2B	3B	HR	HR%	R	RBI	BB	SO	SB	Pinch Hit AB	Pinch Hit H	PO	A	E	DP	TC/G	FA	G by Pos
1927	BOS A	33	.188	.203	69	13	1	0	0	0.0	5	5	3	12	0	2	0	30	4	2	0	1.3	.944	OF-27
1928		6	.176	.235	17	3	1	0	0	0.0	1	2	1	1	1	0	0	8	0	2	0	1.7	.800	OF-6
2 yrs.		39	.186	.209	86	16	2	0	0	0.0	6	7	4	13	1	2	0	38	4	4	0	1.4	.913	OF-33

Danny Tartabull

TARTABULL, DANILO
Born Danilo Tartabull (Mora).
Son of Jose Tartabull.
B. Oct. 30, 1962, San Juan, Puerto Rico.

BR TR 6′1″ 185 lbs.

Year	Team	Games	BA	SA	AB	H	2B	3B	HR	HR%	R	RBI	BB	SO	SB	Pinch Hit AB	Pinch Hit H	PO	A	E	DP	TC/G	FA	G by Pos
1984	SEA A	10	.300	.650	20	6	1	0	2	10.0	3	7	2	3	0	1	0	8	21	2	5	3.4	.935	SS-8, 2B-1
1985		19	.328	.525	61	20	7	1	1	1.6	8	7	8	14	1	3	1	28	43	4	11	3.8	.947	SS-16, 3B-4
1986		137	.270	.489	511	138	25	6	25	4.9	76	96	61	157	4	2	1	233	111	18	28	2.7	.950	OF-101, 2B-31, DH-3, 3B-1
1987	KC A	158	.309	.541	582	180	27	3	34	5.8	95	101	79	136	9	3	0	228	11	6	1	1.6	.976	OF-149, DH-6
1988		146	.274	.515	507	139	38	3	26	5.1	80	102	76	119	8	4	1	227	8	9	1	1.7	.963	OF-130, DH-13
1989		133	.268	.440	441	118	22	0	18	4.1	54	62	69	123	4	4	1	108	3	2	0	0.9	.982	OF-71, DH-55
1990		88	.268	.473	313	84	19	0	15	4.8	41	60	36	93	1	4	1	81	1	3	0	1.0	.965	OF-52, DH-32
1991		132	.316	**.593**	484	153	35	3	31	6.4	78	100	65	121	6	1	0	190	4	7	0	1.5	.965	OF-124, DH-6
1992	NY A	123	.266	.489	421	112	19	0	25	5.9	72	85	103	115	2	3	0	142	3	3	1	1.2	.980	OF-69, DH-53
1993		138	.250	.503	513	128	33	2	31	6.0	87	102	92	156	0	0	0	88	3	2	2	0.7	.978	DH-88, OF-50
1994		104	.256	.464	399	102	24	1	19	4.8	68	67	66	111	1	3	1	43	1	0	0	0.4	1.000	DH-78, OF-26
1995	2 teams	NY A (59G –.224)	OAK A (24G –.261)																					
″	total	83	.236	.379	280	66	16	0	8	2.9	34	35	43	82	0	6	3	28	1	0	1	0.4	1.000	DH-61, OF-19
12 yrs.		1271	.275	.498	4532	1246	266	19	235	5.2	696	824	700	1230	36	34	9	1404	210	56	50	1.3	.966	OF-791, DH-395, 2B-32, SS-24, 3B-5

Jose Tartabull

TARTABULL, JOSE MILAGES
Born Jose Milages Tartabull (Guzman).
Father of Danny Tartabull.
B. Nov. 27, 1938, Cienfuegos, Cuba.

BL TL 5′11″ 165 lbs.

Year	Team	Games	BA	SA	AB	H	2B	3B	HR	HR%	R	RBI	BB	SO	SB	Pinch Hit AB	Pinch Hit H	PO	A	E	DP	TC/G	FA	G by Pos
1962	KC A	107	.277	.329	310	86	6	5	0	0.0	49	22	20	19	19	19	5	185	6	5	0	2.3	.974	OF-85
1963		79	.240	.326	242	58	8	5	1	0.4	27	19	17	17	16	6	1	135	3	2	1	2.0	.986	OF-71
1964		104	.200	.220	100	20	2	0	0	0.0	9	3	5	12	4	41	5	42	3	1	1	0.8	.978	OF-59
1965		68	.312	.413	218	68	11	4	1	0.5	28	19	18	20	11	13	7	133	5	2	0	2.6	.986	OF-54
1966	2 teams	KC A (37G –.236)	BOS A (68G –.277)																					
″	total	105	.261	.332	322	84	9	7	0	0.0	41	15	17	24	19	24	3	160	2	1	0	2.1	.994	OF-79
1967	BOS A	115	.223	.243	247	55	1	2	0	0.0	36	10	23	26	6	32	9	90	3	1	1	1.1	.989	OF-83
1968		72	.281	.324	139	39	6	0	0	0.0	24	6	6	5	2	30	8	59	1	1	0	1.4	.984	OF-43
1969	OAK A	75	.267	.316	266	71	11	1	0	0.0	28	11	9	11	3	11	2	134	2	1	0	2.2	.993	OF-63
1970		24	.231	.385	13	3	2	0	0	0.0	5	2	0	2	1	7	0	3	0	0	0	0.5	1.000	OF-6
9 yrs.		749	.261	.320	1857	484	56	24	2	0.1	247	107	115	136	81	183	40	941	25	14	3	1.8	.986	OF-543
WORLD SERIES																								
1967	BOS A	7	.154	.154	13	2	0	0	0	0.0	1	0	1	2	0	1	0	7	0	0	0	1.2	1.000	OF-6

LaSchelle Tarver

TARVER, LaSCHELLE
B. Jan. 30, 1959, Modesto, Calif.

BL TL 5′11″ 165 lbs.

Year	Team	Games	BA	SA	AB	H	2B	3B	HR	HR%	R	RBI	BB	SO	SB	Pinch Hit AB	Pinch Hit H	PO	A	E	DP	TC/G	FA	G by Pos
1986	BOS A	13	.120	.120	25	3	0	0	0	0.0	3	1	1	4	0	1	0	16	0	0	0	1.8	1.000	OF-9

Willie Tasby

TASBY, WILLIE
B. Jan. 8, 1933, Shreveport, La.

BR TR 5′11″ 170 lbs.

Year	Team	Games	BA	SA	AB	H	2B	3B	HR	HR%	R	RBI	BB	SO	SB	Pinch Hit AB	Pinch Hit H	PO	A	E	DP	TC/G	FA	G by Pos
1958	BAL A	18	.200	.320	50	10	3	0	1	2.0	6	1	7	15	1	1	0	30	0	0	0	1.9	1.000	OF-16
1959		142	.250	.378	505	126	16	5	13	2.6	69	48	34	80	3	4	1	320	13	11	4	2.5	.968	OF-137
1960	2 teams	BAL A (39G –.212)	BOS A (105G –.281)																					
″	total	144	.268	.362	470	126	19	2	7	1.5	77	40	60	66	4	7	3	279	7	6	1	2.1	.979	OF-138

Year	Team	Games	BA	SA	AB	H	2B	3B	HR	HR%	R	RBI	BB	SO	SB	Pinch Hit AB	Pinch Hit H	PO	A	E	DP	TC/G	FA	G by Pos

Willie Tasby *continued*

Year	Team	Games	BA	SA	AB	H	2B	3B	HR	HR%	R	RBI	BB	SO	SB	Pinch Hit AB	Pinch Hit H	PO	A	E	DP	TC/G	FA	G by Pos
1961	WAS A	141	.251	.389	494	124	13	2	17	3.4	54	63	58	94	4	0	0	332	5	5	0	2.5	.985	OF-139
1962	2 teams	WAS A (11G –.206) CLE A (75G –.241)																						
"	total	86	.236	.318	233	55	7	0	4	1.7	29	17	27	47	0	16	1	119	2	1	0	1.6	.992	OF-76, 3B-1
1963	CLE A	52	.224	.371	116	26	3	1	4	3.4	11	5	15	25	0	14	0	54	0	1	0	1.4	.982	OF-37, 2B-1
6 yrs.		583	.250	.367	1868	467	61	10	46	2.5	246	174	201	327	12	42	5	1134	27	24	5	2.2	.980	OF-543, 2B-1, 3B-1

Bennie Tate

TATE, HENRY BENNETT BL TR 5′ 8″ 165 lbs.
B. Dec. 3, 1901, Whitwell, Tenn. D. Oct. 27, 1973, W. Frankfort, Ill.

Year	Team	Games	BA	SA	AB	H	2B	3B	HR	HR%	R	RBI	BB	SO	SB	Pinch Hit AB	Pinch Hit H	PO	A	E	DP	TC/G	FA	G by Pos
1924	WAS A	21	.302	.349	43	13	2	0	0	0.0	2	7	1	2	0	6	3	33	4	7	0	3.1	.841	C-14
1925		16	.481	.593	27	13	3	0	0	0.0	0	7	2	2	0	2	1	36	6	2	2	3.1	.955	C-14
1926		59	.268	.352	142	38	5	2	1	0.7	17	13	15	1	0	9	2	109	35	6	3	3.3	.960	C-45
1927		61	.313	.389	131	41	5	1	1	0.8	12	24	8	4	0	16	5	148	24	4	4	4.5	.977	C-39
1928		57	.246	.295	122	30	6	0	0	0.0	10	15	10	4	0	25	9	111	21	2	1	4.5	.985	C-30
1929		81	.294	.362	265	78	12	3	0	0.0	26	30	16	8	2	6	3	291	49	10	10	4.7	.971	C-74
1930	2 teams	WAS A (14G –.250) CHI A (72G –.317)																						
"	total	86	.312	.372	250	78	11	2	0	0.0	27	29	18	11	2	5	2	231	42	6	5	3.5	.978	C-79
1931	CHI A	89	.267	.333	273	73	12	3	0	0.0	27	22	26	10	1	4	1	310	69	5	11	4.5	.987	C-85
1932	2 teams	CHI A (4G –.100) BOS A (81G –.245)																						
"	total	85	.240	.339	283	68	12	5	2	0.7	22	26	21	6	0	5	3	253	53	8	7	3.9	.975	C-80
1934	CHI N	11	.125	.125	24	3	0	0	0	0.0	1	0	1	3	0	3	0	12	3	0	0	1.9	1.000	C-8
10 yrs.		566	.279	.351	1560	435	68	16	4	0.3	144	173	118	51	5	81	29	1534	306	50	43	4.0	.974	C-468
WORLD SERIES																								
1924	WAS A	3	—	—	0	0	0	0	0	—	0	1	3	0	0	0	0	0	0	0	0	0.0	—	

Hugh Tate

TATE, HUGH HENRY BR TR 5′11″ 190 lbs.
B. May 19, 1880, Everett, Pa. D. Aug. 7, 1956, Greenville, Pa.

Year	Team	Games	BA	SA	AB	H	2B	3B	HR	HR%	R	RBI	BB	SO	SB	Pinch Hit AB	Pinch Hit H	PO	A	E	DP	TC/G	FA	G by Pos
1905	WAS A	4	.300	.500	10	3	0	1	0	0.0	2	2	0		1	1	0	4	0	0	0	1.3	1.000	OF-3

Lee Tate

TATE, LEE WILLIE (Skeeter) BR TR 5′10″ 165 lbs.
B. Mar. 18, 1932, Black Rock, Ark.

Year	Team	Games	BA	SA	AB	H	2B	3B	HR	HR%	R	RBI	BB	SO	SB	Pinch Hit AB	Pinch Hit H	PO	A	E	DP	TC/G	FA	G by Pos
1958	STL N	10	.200	.257	35	7	2	0	0	0.0	4	1	4	3	0	1	0	16	22	2	5	4.4	.950	SS-9
1959		41	.140	.260	50	7	1	1	1	2.0	5	4	5	7	0	0	0	33	49	6	10	2.0	.932	SS-39, 3B-2, 2B-2
2 yrs.		51	.165	.259	85	14	3	1	1	1.2	9	5	9	10	0	1	0	49	71	8	15	2.5	.938	SS-48, 3B-2, 2B-2

Pop Tate

TATE, EDWARD CHRISTOPHER (Dimples) BR TL 5′10″ 178 lbs.
B. Dec. 22, 1860, Richmond, Va. D. June 25, 1932, Richmond, Va.

Year	Team	Games	BA	SA	AB	H	2B	3B	HR	HR%	R	RBI	BB	SO	SB	Pinch Hit AB	Pinch Hit H	PO	A	E	DP	TC/G	FA	G by Pos
1885	BOS N	4	.154	.154	13	2	0	0	0	0.0	1	2	1	3		0	0	19	13	5	0	9.3	.865	C-4
1886		31	.226	.274	106	24	3	1	0	0.0	13	3	7	17		0	0	163	44	27	2	7.5	.885	C-31
1887		60	.260	.307	231	60	5	3	0	0.0	34	27	8	9	7	0	0	217	111	27	6	5.8	.924	C-53, OF-8
1888		41	.230	.311	148	34	7	1	1	0.7	18	6	8	7	3	0	0	188	64	43	6	7.0	.854	C-41, OF-1
1889	BAL AA	72	.182	.241	253	46	6	3	1	0.4	28	27	13	37	4	0	0	371	77	30	4	6.6	.937	C-62, 1B-10
1890		19	.183	.225	71	13	1	1	0	0.0	7		4		3	0	0	112	18	7	3	7.2	.949	C-11, 1B-8
6 yrs.		227	.218	.274	822	179	22	9	2	0.2	101	65	41	73	17	0	0	1070	327	139	21	6.7	.910	C-202, 1B-18, OF-9

Jarvis Tatum

TATUM, JARVIS BR TR 6′ 185 lbs.
B. Oct. 11, 1946, Fresno, Calif.

Year	Team	Games	BA	SA	AB	H	2B	3B	HR	HR%	R	RBI	BB	SO	SB	Pinch Hit AB	Pinch Hit H	PO	A	E	DP	TC/G	FA	G by Pos
1968	CAL A	17	.176	.196	51	9	1	0	0	0.0	7	2	0	9	0	3	0	25	0	0	0	2.3	1.000	OF-11
1969		10	.318	.318	22	7	0	0	0	0.0	2	0	0	6	0	4	0	6	0	1	0	1.4	.857	OF-5
1970		75	.238	.276	181	43	7	0	0	0.0	28	6	17	35	1	13	1	108	2	2	0	1.9	.982	OF-58
3 yrs.		102	.232	.264	254	59	8	0	0	0.0	37	8	17	50	1	20	1	139	2	3	0	1.9	.979	OF-74

Jim Tatum

TATUM, JAMES RAY BR TR 6′ 2″ 200 lbs.
B. Oct. 9, 1967, San Diego, Calif.

Year	Team	Games	BA	SA	AB	H	2B	3B	HR	HR%	R	RBI	BB	SO	SB	Pinch Hit AB	Pinch Hit H	PO	A	E	DP	TC/G	FA	G by Pos
1992	MIL A	5	.125	.125	8	1	0	0	0	0.0	0	0	1	2	0	0	0	6	2	0	0	1.6	1.000	3B-5
1993	CLR N	92	.204	.286	98	20	5	0	1	1.0	7	12	5	27	0	67	17	45	5	2	7	2.5	.962	1B-12, 3B-6, OF-3
1995		34	.235	.324	34	8	1	1	0	0.0	4	4	1	7	0	30	7	4	0	0	0	1.3	1.000	OF-2, C-1
3 yrs.		131	.207	.286	140	29	6	1	1	0.7	11	16	7	36	0	97	24	55	7	2	7	2.2	.969	1B-12, 3B-11, OF-5, C-1

Tommy Tatum

TATUM, V. T. BR TR 6′ 185 lbs.
B. July 16, 1919, Decatur, Tex. D. Nov. 7, 1989, Oklahoma City, Okla.

Year	Team	Games	BA	SA	AB	H	2B	3B	HR	HR%	R	RBI	BB	SO	SB	Pinch Hit AB	Pinch Hit H	PO	A	E	DP	TC/G	FA	G by Pos
1941	BKN N	8	.167	.250	12	2	1	0	0	0.0	1	1	1	3	0	4	0	4	0	0	0	1.0	1.000	OF-4
1947	2 teams	BKN N (4G –.000) CIN N (69G –.273)																						
"	total	73	.264	.330	182	48	5	2	1	0.5	19	16	16	17	7	7	0	120	6	0	3	2.4	1.000	OF-52, 2B-1
2 yrs.		81	.258	.325	194	50	6	2	1	0.5	20	17	17	20	7	11	0	124	6	0	3	2.3	1.000	OF-56, 2B-1

Eddie Taubensee

TAUBENSEE, EDWARD KENNETH BL TR 6′ 4″ 205 lbs.
B. Oct. 31, 1968, Beeville, Tex.

Year	Team	Games	BA	SA	AB	H	2B	3B	HR	HR%	R	RBI	BB	SO	SB	Pinch Hit AB	Pinch Hit H	PO	A	E	DP	TC/G	FA	G by Pos
1991	CLE A	26	.242	.303	66	16	2	1	0	0.0	5	8	5	16	0	2	0	89	6	2	1	3.9	.979	C-25
1992	HOU N	104	.222	.323	297	66	15	0	5	1.7	23	28	31	78	2	4	0	557	66	5	6	6.1	.992	C-103
1993		94	.250	.389	288	72	11	1	9	3.1	26	42	21	44	1	7	2	551	41	5	5	6.6	.992	C-90
1994	2 teams	HOU N (5G –.100) CIN N (61G –.294)																						
"	total	66	.283	.476	187	53	8	2	8	4.3	29	21	15	31	2	4	0	380	19	4	1	6.1	.990	C-66
1995	CIN N	80	.284	.491	218	62	14	2	9	4.1	32	44	22	52	2	14	6	338	22	6	2	5.4	.984	C-65, 1B-3
5 yrs.		370	.255	.402	1056	269	50	6	31	2.9	115	143	94	221	7	31	8	1915	154	22	15	5.9	.989	C-349, 1B-3
LEAGUE CHAMPIONSHIP SERIES																								
1995	CIN N	2	.500	.500	2	1	0	0	0	0.0	0	0	0	0	0	1	0	0	0	0	0	0.0	.000	C-1

Fred Tauby

TAUBY, FRED JOSEPH BR TR 5′ 9½″ 168 lbs.
Born Fred Joseph Taubensee.
B. Mar. 27, 1906, Canton, Ohio D. Nov. 23, 1955, Concordia, Calif.

Year	Team		Games	BA	SA	AB	H	2B	3B	HR	HR%	R	RBI	BB	SO	SB	Pinch Hit AB	Pinch Hit H	PO	A	E	DP	TC/G	FA	G by Pos
1935	CHI	A	13	.125	.156	32	4	1	0	0	0.0	5	2	2	3	0	4	0	15	2	0	1	2.4	1.000	OF-7
1937	PHI	N	11	.000	.000	20	0	0	0	0	0.0	2	3	0	5	1	3	0	8	0	0	0	1.1	1.000	OF-7
2 yrs.			24	.077	.096	52	4	1	0	0	0.0	7	5	2	8	1	7	0	23	2	0	1	1.8	1.000	OF-14

Don Taussig

TAUSSIG, DONALD FRANKLIN BR TR 6′ 180 lbs.
B. Feb. 19, 1932, New York, N. Y.

Year	Team		Games	BA	SA	AB	H	2B	3B	HR	HR%	R	RBI	BB	SO	SB	Pinch Hit AB	Pinch Hit H	PO	A	E	DP	TC/G	FA	G by Pos
1958	SF	N	39	.200	.260	50	10	0	0	1	2.0	10	4	3	8	0	3	1	28	0	0	0	0.8	1.000	OF-36
1961	STL	N	98	.287	.447	188	54	14	5	2	1.1	27	25	16	34	2	8	2	123	6	1	2	1.5	.992	OF-87
1962	HOU	N	16	.200	.320	25	5	0	0	1	4.0	1	1	2	11	0	11	3	10	0	0	0	2.5	1.000	OF-4
3 yrs.			153	.262	.399	263	69	14	5	4	1.5	38	30	21	53	2	22	6	161	6	1	2	1.3	.994	OF-127

Jesus Tavarez

TAVAREZ, JESUS RAFAEL BB TR 6′ 170 lbs.
Born Jesus Rafael Tavarez (Alcantras).
B. Mar. 26, 1971, Santo Domingo, Dominican Republic.

Year	Team		Games	BA	SA	AB	H	2B	3B	HR	HR%	R	RBI	BB	SO	SB	Pinch Hit AB	Pinch Hit H	PO	A	E	DP	TC/G	FA	G by Pos
1994	FLA	N	17	.179	.179	39	7	0	0	0	0.0	4	4	1	5	1	6	2	28	1	0	0	2.6	1.000	OF-11
1995			63	.289	.374	190	55	6	2	2	1.1	31	13	16	27	7	2	0	119	1	0	1	2.0	1.000	OF-61
2 yrs.			80	.271	.341	229	62	6	2	2	0.9	35	17	17	32	8	8	2	147	2	0	1	2.1	1.000	OF-72

Jackie Tavener

TAVENER, JOHN ADAM BL TR 5′ 5″ 138 lbs.
B. Dec. 27, 1897, Celina, Ohio D. Sept. 14, 1969, Fort Worth, Tex.

Year	Team		Games	BA	SA	AB	H	2B	3B	HR	HR%	R	RBI	BB	SO	SB	Pinch Hit AB	Pinch Hit H	PO	A	E	DP	TC/G	FA	G by Pos
1921	DET	A	2	.000	.000	4	0	0	0	0	0.0	0	0	0	1	0	0	0	3	4	0	0	3.5	1.000	SS-2
1925			134	.245	.318	453	111	11	11	0	0.0	45	47	39	60	5	0	0	229	398	24	73	4.9	.963	SS-134
1926			156	.265	.365	532	141	22	14	1	0.2	65	58	52	53	8	0	0	300	470	39	92	5.2	.952	SS-156
1927			116	.274	.406	419	115	22	9	5	1.2	60	59	36	38	20	1	0	246	356	33	79	5.6	.948	SS-114
1928			132	.260	.406	473	123	24	15	5	1.1	59	52	33	51	13	0	0	302	405	42	81	5.7	.944	SS-131
1929	CLE	A	92	.212	.304	250	53	9	4	2	0.8	25	27	26	28	1	0	0	158	275	25	59	5.1	.945	SS-89
6 yrs.			632	.255	.364	2131	543	88	53	13	0.6	254	243	186	231	47	1	0	1238	1908	163	384	5.3	.951	SS-626

Alex Taveras

TAVERAS, ALEJANDRO ANTONIO BR TR 5′10″ 155 lbs.
Born Alejandro Antonio Taveras (Betances).
B. Oct. 9, 1955, Santiago, Dominican Republic.

Year	Team		Games	BA	SA	AB	H	2B	3B	HR	HR%	R	RBI	BB	SO	SB	Pinch Hit AB	Pinch Hit H	PO	A	E	DP	TC/G	FA	G by Pos
1976	HOU	N	14	.217	.217	46	10	0	0	0	0.0	3	2	2	1	1	0	0	26	44	3	4	5.2	.959	SS-7, 2B-7
1982	LA	N	11	.333	.667	3	1	1	0	0	0.0	1	2	0	1	0	0	0	3	10	0	0	1.3	1.000	2B-4, 3B-4, SS-2
1983			10	.000	.000	4	0	0	0	0	0.0	0	0	0	1	0	0	0	3	5	0	1	1.3	1.000	SS-3, 2B-2, 3B-1
3 yrs.			35	.208	.226	53	11	1	0	0	0.0	4	4	2	3	1	0	0	32	59	3	5	3.1	.968	2B-13, SS-12, 3B-5

Frank Taveras

TAVERAS, FRANKLIN CRISOSTOMO BR TR 6′ 155 lbs.
Born Franklin Crisostomo Taveras (Fabian).
B. Dec. 24, 1949, Las Matas de Santa Cruz, Dominican Republic.

Year	Team		Games	BA	SA	AB	H	2B	3B	HR	HR%	R	RBI	BB	SO	SB	Pinch Hit AB	Pinch Hit H	PO	A	E	DP	TC/G	FA	G by Pos
1971	PIT	N	1	—	—	0	0	0	0	0	—	0	0	0	0	0	0	0	0	0	0	0	0.0	—	
1972			4	.000	.000	3	0	0	0	0	0.0	0	0	1	1	0	0	0	2	2	0	1	1.0	1.000	SS-4
1974			126	.246	.270	333	82	4	2	0	0.0	33	26	25	41	13	0	0	170	321	31	60	4.2	.941	SS-124
1975			134	.212	.257	378	80	9	4	0	0.0	44	23	37	42	17	0	0	200	369	28	74	4.5	.953	SS-132
1976			144	.258	.297	519	134	8	6	0	0.0	76	24	44	79	58	1	0	210	481	35	74	5.1	.952	SS-141
1977			147	.252	.331	544	137	20	10	1	0.2	72	29	38	71	**70**	0	0	178	449	25	62	4.5	.962	SS-146
1978			157	.278	.353	654	182	31	9	0	0.0	81	38	29	60	46	0	0	216	448	38	80	4.5	.946	SS-157
1979	2 teams		PIT N (11G –.244) NY N (153G –.263)																						
″	total		164	.262	.335	680	178	29	9	1	0.1	93	34	33	74	44	1	1	287	464	28	92	4.8	.964	SS-164
1980	NY	N	141	.279	.327	562	157	27	0	0	0.0	65	25	23	64	32	5	0	237	347	25	63	4.3	.959	SS-140
1981			84	.230	.290	283	65	11	3	0	0.0	30	11	12	36	16	4	1	120	202	24	44	4.4	.931	SS-79
1982	MON	N	48	.161	.241	87	14	5	1	0	0.0	9	4	7	6	4	2	1	58	70	6	18	3.0	.955	SS-26, 2B-19
11 yrs.			1150	.255	.313	4043	1029	144	44	2	0.0	503	214	249	474	300	13	3	1678	3153	240	568	4.5	.953	SS-1113, 2B-19
LEAGUE CHAMPIONSHIP SERIES																									
1974	PIT	N	2	.000	.000	2	0	0	0	0	0.0	0	0	0	0	1	0	0	2	1	0	0	1.5	1.000	SS-2
1975			3	.143	.143	7	1	0	0	0	0.0	0	1	1	2	0	0	0	4	6	0	2	3.3	1.000	SS-3
2 yrs.			5	.111	.111	9	1	0	0	0	0.0	0	1	1	2	1	0	0	6	7	0	2	2.6	1.000	SS-5

Bennie Taylor

TAYLOR, BENJAMIN EUGENE BL TL 6′ 195 lbs.
B. Sept. 30, 1927, Metropolis, Ill.

Year	Team		Games	BA	SA	AB	H	2B	3B	HR	HR%	R	RBI	BB	SO	SB	Pinch Hit AB	Pinch Hit H	PO	A	E	DP	TC/G	FA	G by Pos
1951	STL	A	33	.258	.398	93	24	2	1	3	3.2	14	6	9	22	1	7	2	195	14	6	21	8.6	.972	1B-25
1952	DET	A	7	.167	.167	18	3	0	0	0	0.0	0	0	0	5	0	3	0	36	2	0	4	9.5	1.000	1B-4
1955	MIL	N	12	.100	.100	10	1	0	0	0	0.0	2	0	2	4	0	9	1	1	0	0	0	1.0	1.000	1B-1
3 yrs.			52	.231	.339	121	28	2	1	3	2.5	16	6	11	31	1	19	3	232	16	6	25	8.5	.976	1B-30

Bill Taylor

TAYLOR, WILLIAM MICHAEL (Moose) BL TL 6′ 3″ 212 lbs.
B. Dec. 30, 1929, Alhambra, Calif.

Year	Team		Games	BA	SA	AB	H	2B	3B	HR	HR%	R	RBI	BB	SO	SB	Pinch Hit AB	Pinch Hit H	PO	A	E	DP	TC/G	FA	G by Pos
1954	NY	N	55	.185	.292	65	12	1	0	2	3.1	4	10	3	15	0	42	9	6	0	0	0	0.7	1.000	OF-9
1955			65	.266	.516	64	17	4	0	4	6.3	9	12	1	16	0	**60**	**15**	0	0	0	0	0.0	.000	OF-2
1956			1	.250	.500	4	1	1	0	0	0.0	0	0	0	1	0	0	0	0	0	0	0	0.0	.000	OF-1
1957	2 teams		NY N (11G –.000) DET A (9G –.348)																						
″	total		20	.250	.406	32	8	2	0	1	3.1	4	3	1	5	0	13	2	5	0	0	0	1.0	1.000	OF-5
1958	DET	A	8	.375	.375	8	3	0	0	0	0.0	0	1	0	2	0	6	3	1	0	0	0	1.0	1.000	OF-1
5 yrs.			149	.237	.405	173	41	8	0	7	4.0	17	26	5	39	0	121	29	12	0	0	0	0.7	1.000	OF-18

Billy Taylor

TAYLOR, WILLIAM HENRY (Bollicky) BR TR 5′11½″ 204 lbs.
B. 1855, Washington, D. C. D. May 14, 1900, Jacksonville, Fla.

Year	Team		Games	BA	SA	AB	H	2B	3B	HR	HR%	R	RBI	BB	SO	SB	Pinch Hit AB	Pinch Hit H	PO	A	E	DP	TC/G	FA	G by Pos
1881	3 teams		WOR N (6G –.107) DET N (1G –.500) CLE N (24G –.243)																						
″	total		31	.222	.252	135	30	4	0	0	0.0	9	15	0	10		0	0	67	9	15	1	2.8	.835	OF-28, 3B-2, P-2
1882	PIT	AA	70	.281	.455	299	84	16	12	4	1.3	40		7			0	0	377	73	60	7	7.0	.882	C-27, 1B-23, 3B-14, OF-8, P-1
1883			83	.260	.350	369	96	13	7	2	0.5	43		9			0	0	263	66	58	4	3.9	.850	OF-37, C-33, P-19, 1B-9
1884	2 teams		STL U (43G –.366) PHI AA (30G –.252)																						
″	total		73	.323	.471	297	96	29	3	3	1.0	52		9			0	0	122	118	37	5	3.6	.866	P-63, 1B-10, OF-4
1885	PHI	AA	6	.190	.190	21	4	0	0	0	0.0	0		0			0	0	0	5	4	0	1.5	.556	P-6

Billy Taylor *continued*

Year	Team	Games	BA	SA	AB	H	2B	3B	HR	HR%	R	RBI	BB	SO	SB	Pinch Hit AB	Pinch Hit H	PO	A	E	DP	TC/G	FA	G by Pos
1886	BAL AA	10	.308	.359	39	12	0	1	0	0.0	4		1			0	0	18	14	3	0	3.5	.914	P-8, 1B-1, C-1
1887	PHI AA	1	.250	.250	4	1	0	0	0	0.0	0		0		0	0	0	0	1	0	0	1.0	1.000	P-1
7 yrs.		274	.277	.393	1164	323	62	23	9	0.8	148	15	26	10	0	0	0	847	286	177	17	4.4	.865	P-100, OF-77, C-61, 1B-43, 3B-16

Bob Taylor

TAYLOR, ROBERT LEE BL TR 5′ 9″ 170 lbs.
B. Mar. 20, 1944, Leland, Miss.

Year	Team	Games	BA	SA	AB	H	2B	3B	HR	HR%	R	RBI	BB	SO	SB	Pinch Hit AB	Pinch Hit H	PO	A	E	DP	TC/G	FA	G by Pos
1970	SF N	63	.190	.262	84	16	0	0	2	2.4	12	10	12	13	0	28	6	27	1	0	1	1.0	1.000	OF-26, C-1

Carl Taylor

TAYLOR, CARL MEANS BR TR 6′ 2″ 200 lbs.
B. Jan. 20, 1944, Sarasota, Fla.

Year	Team	Games	BA	SA	AB	H	2B	3B	HR	HR%	R	RBI	BB	SO	SB	Pinch Hit AB	Pinch Hit H	PO	A	E	DP	TC/G	FA	G by Pos
1968	PIT N	44	.211	.225	71	15	1	0	0	0.0	5	7	10	10	1	10	1	83	10	2	1	3.1	.979	C-29, OF-2
1969		104	.348	.457	221	77	10	1	4	1.8	30	33	31	36	0	41	17	267	16	8	26	4.8	.973	OF-36, 1B-24
1970	STL N	104	.249	.388	245	61	12	2	6	2.4	39	45	41	30	5	42	11	176	11	3	11	3.1	.984	OF-46, 1B-15, 3B-1
1971	2 teams	KC A (20G –.179) PIT N (7G –.167)																						
″	total	27	.176	.216	51	9	0	1	0	0.0	4	3	5	18	0	13	2	31	0	1	0	1.8	.969	OF-18
1972	KC A	63	.265	.301	113	30	2	1	0	0.0	17	11	17	16	4	26	8	161	9	7	7	4.5	.960	C-21, OF-7, 1B-6, 3B-5
1973		69	.228	.283	145	33	6	1	0	0.0	18	16	32	20	2	1	0	270	20	6	2	4.5	.980	C-63, 1B-2, DH-1
6 yrs.		411	.266	.352	846	225	31	6	10	1.2	113	115	136	130	12	133	39	988	66	27	47	3.9	.975	C-113, OF-109, 1B-47, 3B-6, DH-1

Chink Taylor

TAYLOR, C. L. BR TR 5′ 9″ 160 lbs.
B. Feb. 9, 1898, Burnet, Tex. D. July 7, 1980, Temple, Tex.

Year	Team	Games	BA	SA	AB	H	2B	3B	HR	HR%	R	RBI	BB	SO	SB	Pinch Hit AB	Pinch Hit H	PO	A	E	DP	TC/G	FA	G by Pos
1925	CHI N	8	.000	.000	6	0	0	0	0	0.0	2	0	0	0	0	2	0	2	0	0	0	1.0	1.000	OF-2

Danny Taylor

TAYLOR, DANIEL TURNEY BR TR 5′10″ 190 lbs.
B. Dec. 23, 1900, Lash, Pa. D. Oct. 11, 1972, Latrobe, Pa.

Year	Team	Games	BA	SA	AB	H	2B	3B	HR	HR%	R	RBI	BB	SO	SB	Pinch Hit AB	Pinch Hit H	PO	A	E	DP	TC/G	FA	G by Pos
1926	WAS A	21	.300	.400	50	15	0	1	1	2.0	10	5	5	7	1	5	2	17	1	0	0	1.5	1.000	OF-12
1929	CHI N	2	.000	.000	3	0	0	0	0	0.0	0	0	1	1	0	1	0	1	0	0	0	1.0	1.000	OF-1
1930		74	.283	.402	219	62	14	3	2	0.9	43	37	27	34	6	14	7	97	3	3	0	2.0	.971	OF-52
1931		88	.300	.448	270	81	13	6	5	1.9	48	41	31	46	4	18	6	170	3	2	0	2.6	.989	OF-67
1932	2 teams	CHI N (6G –.227) BKN N (105G –.324)																						
″	total	111	.319	.489	417	133	24	7	11	2.6	87	51	36	42	14	3	0	289	8	5	1	3.0	.983	OF-102
1933	BKN N	103	.285	.469	358	102	21	9	9	2.5	75	40	47	45	11	11	3	247	4	6	1	2.8	.977	OF-91
1934		120	.299	.440	405	121	24	6	7	1.7	62	57	63	47	12	10	2	188	8	5	1	1.9	.975	OF-108
1935		112	.290	.432	352	102	19	5	7	2.0	51	59	46	32	6	9	4	193	4	6	0	2.1	.970	OF-99
1936		43	.293	.397	116	34	6	0	2	1.7	12	15	11	14	2	8	1	49	2	1	1	1.7	.981	OF-31
9 yrs.		674	.297	.446	2190	650	121	37	44	2.0	388	305	267	268	56	79	25	1251	33	28	4	2.3	.979	OF-563

Dwight Taylor

TAYLOR, DWIGHT BERNARD BL TL 5′ 9″ 172 lbs.
B. Mar. 24, 1960, Los Angeles, Calif.

Year	Team	Games	BA	SA	AB	H	2B	3B	HR	HR%	R	RBI	BB	SO	SB	Pinch Hit AB	Pinch Hit H	PO	A	E	DP	TC/G	FA	G by Pos
1986	KC A	4	.000	.000	2	0	0	0	0	0.0	1	0	0	0	0	1	0	0	0	0	0	0.0		DH-2, OF-1

Eddie Taylor

TAYLOR, EDWARD JAMES BR TR 5′ 6½″ 160 lbs.
B. Nov. 17, 1901, Chicago, Ill. D. Jan. 30, 1992, Chula Vista, Calif.

Year	Team	Games	BA	SA	AB	H	2B	3B	HR	HR%	R	RBI	BB	SO	SB	Pinch Hit AB	Pinch Hit H	PO	A	E	DP	TC/G	FA	G by Pos
1926	BOS N	92	.268	.313	272	73	8	2	0	0.0	37	33	38	26	4	0	0	117	174	13	28	3.2	.957	3B-62, SS-33

Fred Taylor

TAYLOR, FREDERICK RANKIN BL TR 6′ 3″ 201 lbs.
B. Dec. 3, 1924, Zanesville, Ohio.

Year	Team	Games	BA	SA	AB	H	2B	3B	HR	HR%	R	RBI	BB	SO	SB	Pinch Hit AB	Pinch Hit H	PO	A	E	DP	TC/G	FA	G by Pos
1950	WAS A	6	.125	.125	16	2	0	0	0	0.0	1	0	1	2	0	3	0	27	3	1	5	10.3	.968	1B-3
1951		6	.167	.250	12	2	1	0	0	0.0	1	0	0	4	0	4	0	24	1	1	4	13.0	.962	1B-2
1952		10	.263	.316	19	5	1	0	0	0.0	3	4	3	2	0	5	2	34	6	0	4	8.0	1.000	1B-5
3 yrs.		22	.191	.234	47	9	2	0	0	0.0	5	4	4	8	0	12	2	85	10	2	13	9.7	.979	1B-10

Harry Taylor

TAYLOR, HARRY LEONARD BL 6′ 2″ 160 lbs.
B. Apr. 4, 1866, Halsey Valley, N. Y. D. July 12, 1955, Buffalo, N. Y.

Year	Team	Games	BA	SA	AB	H	2B	3B	HR	HR%	R	RBI	BB	SO	SB	Pinch Hit AB	Pinch Hit H	PO	A	E	DP	TC/G	FA	G by Pos
1890	LOU AA	134	.306	.344	553	169	7	7	0	0.0	115		68		45	0	0	1330	112	36	59	10.9	.976	1B-118, SS-12, 2B-4, C-1
1891		91	.296	.351	348	103	7	3	2	0.6	80	35	55	31	15	0	0	911	47	21	56	10.5	.979	1B-90, 2B-1, 3B-1, C-1
1892	LOU N	125	.260	.278	493	128	7	1	0	0.0	66	34	58	23	24	0	0	498	74	29	29	4.7	.952	OF-73, 1B-34, 2B-14, 3B-5, SS-2
1893	BAL N	88	.283	.322	360	102	9	1	1	0.3	50	54	32	11	24	0	0	882	43	23	58	10.8	.976	1B-88
4 yrs.		438	.286	.322	1754	502	30	12	3	0.2	311	123	213	65	108	0	0	3621	276	109	202	9.0	.973	1B-330, OF-73, 2B-19, SS-14, 3B-6, C-2

Harry Taylor

TAYLOR, HARRY WARREN (Handsome Harry) BL TL 6′ 1½″ 185 lbs.
B. Dec. 26, 1907, McKeesport, Pa. D. Apr. 27, 1969, Toledo, Ohio.

Year	Team	Games	BA	SA	AB	H	2B	3B	HR	HR%	R	RBI	BB	SO	SB	Pinch Hit AB	Pinch Hit H	PO	A	E	DP	TC/G	FA	G by Pos
1932	CHI N	10	.125	.125	8	1	0	0	0	0.0	1	0	1	1	0	7	1	5	0	0	0	5.0	1.000	1B-1

Hawk Taylor

TAYLOR, ROBERT DALE BR TR 6′ 1″ 187 lbs.
B. Apr. 3, 1939, Metropolis, Ill.

Year	Team	Games	BA	SA	AB	H	2B	3B	HR	HR%	R	RBI	BB	SO	SB	Pinch Hit AB	Pinch Hit H	PO	A	E	DP	TC/G	FA	G by Pos
1957	MIL N	7	.000	.000	1	0	0	0	0	0.0	2	0	0	0	0	1	0	0	0	0	0	0.0	.000	C-1
1958		4	.125	.250	8	1	1	0	0	0.0	1	0	0	3	0	0	0	5	0	0	0	1.3	1.000	OF-4
1961		20	.192	.308	26	5	0	0	1	3.8	1	1	3	11	0	12	2	8	1	0	0	1.5	1.000	OF-5, C-1
1962		20	.255	.255	47	12	0	0	0	0.0	3	2	2	10	0	8	2	23	1	1	0	2.3	.960	OF-11
1963		16	.069	.069	29	2	0	0	0	0.0	1	0	1	12	0	9	0	14	0	0	0	1.8	1.000	OF-8
1964	NY N	92	.240	.329	225	54	8	0	4	1.8	20	23	8	33	0	34	8	210	28	5	5	4.0	.979	C-45, OF-16
1965		25	.152	.413	46	7	0	0	4	8.7	5	10	1	8	0	13	0	51	6	3	0	3.8	.950	C-15, 1B-1
1966		53	.174	.275	109	19	2	0	3	2.8	5	12	3	19	0	28	4	140	18	3	10	3.8	.981	C-29, 1B-13

Hawk Taylor *continued*

Year	Team	Games	BA	SA	AB	H	2B	3B	HR	HR%	R	RBI	BB	SO	SB	Pinch Hit AB	Pinch Hit H	PO	A	E	DP	TC/G	FA	G by Pos
1967	2 teams NY N (13G –.243) CAL A (23G –.308)																							
″	total	36	.281	.382	89	25	6	0	1	1.1	8	7	6	16	0	5	1	140	18	3	3	5.2	.981	C-31
1969	KC A	64	.270	.427	89	24	5	0	3	3.4	7	21	6	18	0	49	13	38	2	2	1	1.8	.952	OF-18, C-6
1970		57	.164	.218	55	9	3	0	0	0.0	3	6	6	16	0	46	9	12	2	1	1	3.8	.933	C-3, 1B-1
11 yrs.		394	.218	.319	724	158	25	0	16	2.2	56	82	36	146	0	205	39	641	76	18	20	3.5	.976	C-131, OF-62, 1B-15

Jack Taylor

TAYLOR, JOHN W. (Brakeman)
B. Jan. 14, 1874, New Straightsville, Ohio D. Mar. 4, 1938, Columbus, Ohio.
BR TR 5′10″ 170 lbs.

Year	Team	Games	BA	SA	AB	H	2B	3B	HR	HR%	R	RBI	BB	SO	SB	Pinch Hit AB	Pinch Hit H	PO	A	E	DP	TC/G	FA	G by Pos
1898	CHI N	5	.200	.333	15	3	2	0	0	0.0	4	2	3		0	0	0	0	9	0	1	1.8	1.000	P-5
1899		42	.266	.360	139	37	9	2	0	0.0	25	17	16		0	1	1	24	88	8	8	2.9	.933	P-41
1900		28	.235	.333	81	19	3	1	1	1.2	7	6	3		1	0	0	10	42	7	2	2.1	.881	P-28
1901		35	.217	.274	106	23	6	0	0	0.0	12	2	4		0	2	0	24	78	6	3	3.3	.944	P-33
1902		55	.237	.280	186	44	6	1	0	0.0	18	17	8		6	1	0	42	133	9	5	3.4	.951	P-36, 3B-12, OF-3, 1B-2, 2B-1
1903		40	.222	.310	126	28	3	4	0	0.0	13	17	6		3	0	0	16	91	7	2	2.9	.939	P-37, 3B-1, 2B-1
1904	STL N	42	.211	.301	133	28	3	3	1	0.8	9	8	4		3	0	0	14	109	6	1	3.1	.953	P-41
1905		39	.190	.264	121	23	5	2	0	0.0	11	12	8		4	0	0	12	82	3	1	2.5	.969	P-37, 3B-2
1906	2 teams STL N (17G –.208) CHI N (17G –.208)																							
″	total	34	.208	.236	106	22	3	0	0	0.0	9	5	14		1	0	0	12	95	2	2	3.2	.982	P-34
1907	CHI N	18	.191	.234	47	9	2	0	0	0.0	2	1	0		0	0	0	6	40	0	1	2.6	1.000	P-18
10 yrs.		338	.223	.292	1060	236	42	13	2	0.2	110	87	66		18	4	1	160	767	48	26	2.9	.951	P-310, 3B-15, OF-3, 1B-2, 2B-2

Joe Taylor

TAYLOR, JOE CEPHUS (Cash)
B. Mar. 2, 1926, Chapman, Ala.
BR TR 6′1″ 185 lbs.

Year	Team	Games	BA	SA	AB	H	2B	3B	HR	HR%	R	RBI	BB	SO	SB	Pinch Hit AB	Pinch Hit H	PO	A	E	DP	TC/G	FA	G by Pos
1954	PHI A	18	.224	.328	58	13	1	1	1	1.7	5	8	2	9	0	3	2	32	1	2	0	2.2	.943	OF-16
1957	CIN N	33	.262	.439	107	28	7	0	4	3.7	14	9	6	24	0	6	2	63	3	2	1	2.5	.971	OF-27
1958	2 teams STL N (18G –.304) BAL A (36G –.273)																							
″	total	54	.280	.440	100	28	7	0	3	3.0	13	12	9	23	0	25	7	44	1	1	1	1.8	.978	OF-26
1959	BAL A	14	.156	.281	32	5	1	0	1	3.1	2	2	11	15	0	1	0	10	0	0	0	0.8	1.000	OF-12
4 yrs.		119	.249	.401	297	74	16	1	9	3.0	34	31	28	71	0	35	11	149	5	5	2	2.0	.969	OF-81

Leo Taylor

TAYLOR, LEO THOMAS (Chink)
B. May 13, 1901, Walla Walla, Wash. D. May 20, 1982, Seattle, Wash.
BR TR 5′10½″ 150 lbs.

Year	Team	Games	BA	SA	AB	H	2B	3B	HR	HR%	R	RBI	BB	SO	SB	Pinch Hit AB	Pinch Hit H	PO	A	E	DP	TC/G	FA	G by Pos
1923	CHI A	2	—	—	0	0	0	0	0	—	0	0	0	0	0	0	0	0	0	0	0	0.0	—	

Oak Taylor

TAYLOR, EDWARD S.
B. Feb. 3, 1855, Belfast, Me. D. Feb. 19, 1888, San Francisco, Calif.

Year	Team	Games	BA	SA	AB	H	2B	3B	HR	HR%	R	RBI	BB	SO	SB	Pinch Hit AB	Pinch Hit H	PO	A	E	DP	TC/G	FA	G by Pos
1877	HAR N	2	.375	.375	8	3	0	0	0	0.0	0	0	0	2		0	0	2	0	0	0	1.0	1.000	OF-2
1884	PIT AA	41	.211	.250	152	32	4	1	0	0.0	22		6			0	0	68	7	19	0	2.3	.798	OF-41
2 yrs.		43	.219	.256	160	35	4	1	0	0.0	22	0	6	2		0	0	70	7	19	0	2.2	.802	OF-43

Sammy Taylor

TAYLOR, SAMUEL DOUGLAS
B. Feb. 27, 1933, Woodruff, S. C.
BL TR 6′2″ 185 lbs.

Year	Team	Games	BA	SA	AB	H	2B	3B	HR	HR%	R	RBI	BB	SO	SB	Pinch Hit AB	Pinch Hit H	PO	A	E	DP	TC/G	FA	G by Pos
1958	CHI N	96	.259	.372	301	78	12	2	6	2.0	30	36	27	46	2	12	4	460	23	6	4	5.6	.988	C-87
1959		110	.269	.428	353	95	13	2	13	3.7	41	43	35	47	1	9	1	497	37	10	1	5.0	.982	C-109
1960		74	.207	.327	150	31	9	0	3	2.0	14	17	6	18	0	36	6	152	24	4	2	4.2	.978	C-43
1961		89	.238	.391	235	56	8	2	8	3.4	26	23	23	39	0	14	0	319	25	4	5	4.6	.989	C-75
1962	2 teams CHI N (7G –.133) NY N (68G –.222)																							
″	total	75	.214	.318	173	37	5	2	3	1.7	12	21	26	20	0	16	3	225	26	2	3	4.5	.992	C-56
1963	3 teams NY N (22G –.257) CIN N (3G –.000) CLE A (4G –.300)																							
″	total	29	.235	.275	51	12	0	1	0	0.0	4	7	5	11	0	14	5	68	5	1	2	4.4	.986	C-17
6 yrs.		473	.245	.375	1263	309	47	9	33	2.6	127	147	122	181	3	101	19	1721	140	27	17	4.9	.986	C-387

Sandy Taylor

TAYLOR, JAMES B.
Deceased.
5′10½″ 175 lbs.

Year	Team	Games	BA	SA	AB	H	2B	3B	HR	HR%	R	RBI	BB	SO	SB	Pinch Hit AB	Pinch Hit H	PO	A	E	DP	TC/G	FA	G by Pos
1879	TRO N	24	.216	.258	97	21	4	0	0	0.0	10	8	1	8		0	0	37	2	12	0	2.1	.765	OF-24

Tommy Taylor

TAYLOR, THOMAS LIVINGSTONE CARLTON
B. Sept. 17, 1892, Mexia, Tex. D. Apr. 5, 1956, Greenville, Miss.
BR TR 5′8½″ 160 lbs.

Year	Team	Games	BA	SA	AB	H	2B	3B	HR	HR%	R	RBI	BB	SO	SB	Pinch Hit AB	Pinch Hit H	PO	A	E	DP	TC/G	FA	G by Pos
1924	WAS A	26	.260	.329	73	19	3	1	0	0.0	11	10	2	8	2	6	1	23	17	4	4	2.3	.909	3B-16, 2B-2, OF-1
WORLD SERIES																								
1924	WAS A	3	.000	.000	2	0	0	0	0	0.0	0	0	0	2	0	0	0	0	3	1	0	2.0	.750	3B-2

Tony Taylor

TAYLOR, ANTONIO NEMESIO
Born Antonio Nemesio Taylor (Sanchez).
B. Dec. 19, 1935, Central Alara, Cuba.
BR TR 5′9″ 170 lbs.

Year	Team	Games	BA	SA	AB	H	2B	3B	HR	HR%	R	RBI	BB	SO	SB	Pinch Hit AB	Pinch Hit H	PO	A	E	DP	TC/G	FA	G by Pos
1958	CHI N	140	.235	.314	497	117	15	3	6	1.2	63	27	40	93	21	0	0	311	374	23	103	5.1	.968	2B-137, 3B-1
1959		150	.280	.393	624	175	30	8	8	1.3	96	38	45	86	23	0	0	355	456	25	105	5.5	.970	2B-149, SS-2
1960	2 teams CHI N (19G –.263) PHI N (127G –.287)																							
″	total	146	.284	.377	581	165	25	7	5	0.9	80	44	41	98	26	2	0	321	411	23	87	5.2	.970	2B-142, 3B-4
1961	PHI N	106	.250	.323	400	100	17	3	2	0.5	47	26	29	59	11	14	3	233	279	10	74	5.6	.981	2B-91, 3B-3
1962		152	.259	.342	625	162	21	5	7	1.1	87	43	68	82	20	2	1	372	385	22	101	5.1	.972	2B-150, SS-2
1963		157	.281	.367	640	180	20	10	5	0.8	102	49	42	99	23	4	0	325	412	10	88	4.6	.987	2B-149, 3B-13
1964		154	.251	.316	570	143	13	6	4	0.7	62	46	46	74	13	3	1	325	358	16	94	4.7	.977	2B-150
1965		106	.229	.319	323	74	14	3	3	0.9	41	27	22	58	5	14	1	169	222	17	52	4.5	.958	2B-86, 3B-5
1966		125	.242	.346	434	105	14	8	5	1.2	47	40	31	56	8	8	1	187	281	9	45	4.0	.981	2B-68, 3B-52
1967		132	.238	.312	462	110	16	6	2	0.4	55	34	42	74	10	8	3	524	182	9	73	4.9	.987	1B-58, 3B-44, 2B-42, SS-3
1968		145	.250	.311	547	137	20	2	3	0.5	59	38	39	60	22	3	0	115	324	16	26	3.2	.965	3B-138, 2B-5, 1B-1
1969		138	.262	.339	557	146	24	5	3	0.5	68	30	42	62	19	5	2	262	294	15	66	4.1	.974	3B-71, 2B-57, 1B-10
1970		124	.301	.462	439	132	26	9	9	2.1	74	55	50	67	9	14	6	220	215	5	48	3.8	.989	2B-59, 3B-38, OF-18, SS-1
1971	2 teams PHI N (36G –.234) DET A (55G –.287)																							
″	total	91	.267	.372	288	77	12	3	4	1.4	36	24	21	21	7	18	5	173	173	2	43	4.3	.994	2B-65, 3B-14, 1B-2
1972	DET A	78	.303	.404	228	69	12	4	1	0.4	33	20	14	34	5	20	6	130	122	8	26	3.4	.969	2B-67, 3B-8, 1B-1

Tony Taylor *continued*

Year	Team	Games	BA	SA	AB	H	2B	3B	HR	HR%	R	RBI	BB	SO	SB	Pinch Hit AB	Pinch Hit H	PO	A	E	DP	TC/G	FA	G by Pos
1973		84	.229	.338	275	63	9	3	5	1.8	35	24	17	29	9	9	0	151	168	4	37	3.9	.988	2B-72, 1B-6, 3B-4, DH-1
1974	**PHI N**	62	.328	.484	64	21	4	0	2	3.1	5	13	6	6	0	46	**17**	34	4	0	1	2.4	1.000	1B-7, 3B-5, 2B-4
1975		79	.243	.340	103	25	5	1	1	1.0	13	17	17	18	3	**54**	12	34	35	5	2	3.2	.932	3B-16, 1B-4, 2B-3
1976		26	.261	.304	23	6	1	0	0	0.0	2	3	1	7	0	21	5	0	1	0	1	0.3	1.000	2B-2, 3B-1
19 yrs.		2195	.261	.352	7680	2007	298	86	75	1.0	1005	598	613	1083	234	245	63	4241	4696	219	1072	4.5	.976	2B-1498, 3B-417, 1B-89, OF-18, SS-8, DH-1
LEAGUE CHAMPIONSHIP SERIES																								
1972	**DET A**	4	.133	.267	15	2	2	0	0	0.0	0	0	0	2	0	0	0	5	9	0	2	3.5	1.000	2B-4

Wally Taylor

TAYLOR, WILLIAM H. 5′10″ 160 lbs.
B. Dec. 1870, Pittsburgh, Pa. D. Sept. 12, 1905, Cincinnati, Ohio.

Year	Team	Games	BA	SA	AB	H	2B	3B	HR	HR%	R	RBI	BB	SO	SB	Pinch Hit AB	Pinch Hit H	PO	A	E	DP	TC/G	FA	G by Pos
1898	**LOU N**	9	.250	.292	24	6	1	0	0	0.0	2	2	1		1	1	0	10	14	5	0	3.6	.828	3B-7, 2B-1

Zack Taylor

TAYLOR, JAMES WREN BR TR 5′11½″ 180 lbs.
B. July 27, 1898, Yulee, Fla. D. Sept. 19, 1974, Orlando, Fla.
Manager 1946, 1948–51.

Year	Team	Games	BA	SA	AB	H	2B	3B	HR	HR%	R	RBI	BB	SO	SB	Pinch Hit AB	Pinch Hit H	PO	A	E	DP	TC/G	FA	G by Pos
1920	**BKN N**	9	.385	.538	13	5	2	0	0	0.0	3	5	0	2	0	0	0	11	4	2	0	1.9	.882	C-9
1921		30	.196	.235	102	20	0	2	0	0.0	6	8	1	8	2	0	0	106	33	5	5	4.8	.965	C-30
1922		7	.214	.214	14	3	0	0	0	0.0	0	2	1	1	0	1	0	16	3	1	0	2.9	.950	C-7
1923		96	.288	.356	337	97	11	6	0	0.0	29	46	9	13	2	11	4	354	118	16	6	5.8	.967	C-84
1924		99	.290	.348	345	100	9	4	1	0.3	36	39	14	14	0	6	2	388	96	6	13	5.3	.988	C-93
1925		109	.310	.403	352	109	16	4	3	0.9	33	44	17	19	0	12	2	294	102	17	12	4.3	.959	C-96
1926	**BOS N**	125	.255	.319	432	110	22	3	0	0.0	36	42	28	27	1	1	0	394	123	8	17	4.3	.985	C-123
1927	**2 teams**	**BOS N** (30G –.240) **NY N** (83G –.233)																						
″	**total**	113	.234	.291	354	83	9	4	1	0.3	26	35	25	25	2	5	1	404	79	11	11	4.6	.978	C-108
1928	**BOS N**	125	.251	.308	399	100	15	1	2	0.5	36	30	33	29	2	1	0	367	83	7	8	3.7	.985	C-124
1929	**2 teams**	**BOS N** (34G –.248) **CHI N** (64G –.274)																						
″	**total**	98	.266	.367	316	84	23	3	1	0.3	37	41	26	27	0	3	0	348	71	11	7	4.5	.974	C-95
1930	**CHI N**	32	.232	.305	95	22	2	1	1	1.1	12	11	2	12	0	2	0	92	18	0	1	3.9	1.000	C-28
1931		8	.250	.250	4	1	0	0	0	0.0	0	0	2	1	0	1	0	5	2	0	0	1.4	1.000	C-5
1932		21	.200	.233	30	6	1	0	0	0.0	2	3	1	4	0	7	1	39	4	0	0	3.1	1.000	C-14
1933		16	.000	.000	11	0	0	0	0	0.0	0	0	0	1	0	4	0	8	0	0	0	0.7	1.000	C-12
1934	**NY A**	4	.143	.143	7	1	0	0	0	0.0	0	0	0	1	0	1	0	3	2	0	0	1.7	1.000	C-3
1935	**BKN N**	26	.130	.185	54	7	3	0	0	0.0	2	5	2	8	0	0	0	51	14	2	2	2.6	.970	C-26
16 yrs.		918	.261	.329	2865	748	113	28	9	0.3	258	311	161	192	9	55	10	2880	752	86	82	4.3	.977	C-857
WORLD SERIES																								
1929	**CHI N**	5	.176	.176	17	3	0	0	0	0.0	0	3	0	3	0	0	0	31	4	0	0	7.0	1.000	C-5

Birdie Tebbetts

TEBBETTS, GEORGE ROBERT BR TR 5′11½″ 170 lbs.
B. Nov. 10, 1912, Burlington, Vt.
Manager 1954–58, 1961–66.

Year	Team	Games	BA	SA	AB	H	2B	3B	HR	HR%	R	RBI	BB	SO	SB	Pinch Hit AB	Pinch Hit H	PO	A	E	DP	TC/G	FA	G by Pos
1936	**DET A**	10	.303	.545	33	10	1	2	1	3.0	7	4	5	3	0	0	0	51	5	1	0	5.7	.982	C-10
1937		50	.191	.290	162	31	4	3	2	1.2	15	16	10	13	0	2	0	155	25	7	1	3.9	.963	C-48
1938		53	.294	.385	143	42	6	2	1	0.7	16	25	12	13	1	9	3	108	20	2	4	2.5	.985	C-53
1939		106	.261	.372	341	89	22	2	4	1.2	37	53	25	20	2	6	1	449	64	16	10	5.3	.970	C-100
1940		111	.296	.412	379	112	24	4	4	1.1	46	46	35	14	4	2	0	572	89	17	10	6.3	.975	C-107
1941		110	.284	.376	359	102	19	4	2	0.6	28	47	38	29	1	12	3	461	83	13	11	5.7	.977	C-98
1942		99	.247	.292	308	76	11	0	1	0.3	24	27	39	17	4	2	2	446	69	12	10	5.4	.977	C-97
1946		87	.243	.307	280	68	11	2	1	0.4	20	34	28	23	1	0	0	486	53	10	4	6.3	.982	C-87
1947	**2 teams**	**DET A** (20G –.094) **BOS A** (90G –.299)																						
″	**total**	110	.267	.308	344	92	11	0	1	0.3	23	30	24	33	2	1	0	427	65	10	10	4.6	.980	C-109
1948	**BOS A**	128	.280	.381	446	125	26	2	5	1.1	54	68	62	32	5	1	0	470	56	10	8	4.3	.981	C-126
1949		122	.270	.342	404	109	14	0	5	1.2	42	48	62	22	8	4	1	481	51	11	13	4.6	.980	C-118
1950		79	.310	.444	268	83	10	1	8	3.0	33	45	29	26	1	3	1	285	44	4	5	4.5	.988	C-74
1951	**CLE A**	55	.263	.350	137	36	6	0	2	1.5	8	18	8	7	0	11	5	145	27	4	1	4.0	.977	C-44
1952		42	.248	.317	101	25	4	0	1	1.0	4	8	12	9	0	5	2	131	15	2	0	4.0	.986	C-37
14 yrs.		1162	.270	.358	3705	1000	169	22	38	1.0	357	469	389	261	29	58	18	4667	666	119	87	4.9	.978	C-1108
WORLD SERIES																								
1940	**DET A**	4	.000	.000	11	0	0	0	0	0.0	0	0	0	0	0	1	0	13	3	1	1	5.7	.941	C-3

Patsy Tebeau

TEBEAU, OLIVER WENDELL BR TR 5′8″ 163 lbs.
Brother of White Wings Tebeau.
B. Dec. 5, 1864, St. Louis, Mo. D. May 15, 1918, St. Louis, Mo.
Manager 1890–00.

Year	Team	Games	BA	SA	AB	H	2B	3B	HR	HR%	R	RBI	BB	SO	SB	Pinch Hit AB	Pinch Hit H	PO	A	E	DP	TC/G	FA	G by Pos
1887	**CHI N**	20	.162	.206	68	11	3	0	0	0.0	8	10	4	4	8	0	0	19	34	9	4	3.1	.855	3B-20
1889	**CLE N**	136	.282	.390	521	147	20	6	8	1.5	72	76	37	41	26	0	0	185	287	54	26	3.9	.897	3B-136
1890	**CLE P**	110	.300	.418	450	135	26	6	5	1.1	86	74	34	20	14	0	0	204	246	66	25	4.7	.872	3B-110
1891	**CLE N**	61	.261	.329	249	65	8	3	1	0.4	38	41	16	13	12	0	0	102	150	33	13	4.6	.884	3B-61, OF-1
1892		86	.244	.318	340	83	13	3	2	0.6	47	49	23	34	6	0	0	154	172	31	22	4.2	.913	3B-74, 2B-5, 1B-4, SS-3
1893		116	.329	.440	486	160	32	8	2	0.4	90	102	32	11	19	0	0	659	186	44	36	7.7	.951	1B-57, 3B-56, 2B-3
1894		125	.302	.390	523	158	23	7	3	0.6	82	89	35	35	30	0	0	1110	84	32	73	9.6	.974	1B-115, 2B-10, 3B-2, SS-1
1895		63	.318	.405	264	84	13	2	2	0.8	50	52	16	18	8	0	0	519	68	8	32	9.3	.987	1B-49, 2B-9, 3B-6
1896		132	.269	.343	543	146	22	6	2	0.4	56	94	21	22	20	0	0	1372	102	27	91	11.0	.982	1B-122, 3B-7, 2B-5, SS-1, P-1
1897		109	.267	.347	412	110	15	9	0	0.0	62	59	30		11	0	0	957	99	12	51	9.5	.989	1B-92, 2B-18, 3B-2, SS-1
1898		131	.258	.304	477	123	11	4	1	0.2	53	63	53		5	0	0	1057	162	30	55	9.3	.976	1B-91, 2B-34, SS-7, 3B-3
1899	**STL N**	77	.246	.313	281	69	10	3	1	0.4	27	26	18		5	0	0	676	68	22	34	9.8	.971	1B-65, SS-11, 2B-1, 3B-1
1900		1	.000	.000	4	0	0	0	0	0.0	0	0	0		0	0	0	4	3	3	0	10.0	.700	SS-1
13 yrs.		1167	.280	.364	4618	1291	196	57	27	0.6	671	735	319	198	164	0	0	7018	1661	371	462	7.6	.959	1B-595, 3B-478, 2B-85, SS-25, P-1, OF-1

Pussy Tebeau

TEBEAU, CHARLES ALSTON
B. Feb. 22, 1870, Worcester, Mass. D. Mar. 25, 1950, Pittsfield, Mass.
5′10″ 175 lbs.

Year	Team		Games	BA	SA	AB	H	2B	3B	HR	HR%	R	RBI	BB	SO	SB	Pinch Hit AB	Pinch Hit H	PO	A	E	DP	TC/G	FA	G by Pos
1895	CLE	N	2	.500	.500	6	3	0	0	0	0.0	3	1	2	1	1	0	0	3	1	0	0	2.0	1.000	OF-2

White Wings Tebeau

TEBEAU, GEORGE E. (Hard Call)
Brother of Patsy Tebeau.
B. Dec. 26, 1861, St. Louis, Mo. D. Feb. 4, 1923, Denver, Colo.
BR TR 5′9″ 175 lbs.

Year	Team		Games	BA	SA	AB	H	2B	3B	HR	HR%	R	RBI	BB	SO	SB	Pinch Hit AB	Pinch Hit H	PO	A	E	DP	TC/G	FA	G by Pos
1887	CIN	AA	85	.296	.403	318	94	12	5	4	1.3	57		31		37	0	0	176	17	24	2	2.6	.889	OF-84, P-1
1888			121	.229	.338	411	94	12	12	3	0.7	72	51	61		37	0	0	195	20	21	3	2.0	.911	OF-121
1889			135	.252	.381	496	125	21	11	7	1.4	110	70	69	62	61	0	0	249	18	34	4	2.2	.887	OF-134, 1B-1
1890	TOL	AA	94	.268	.370	381	102	16	10	1	0.3	71		51		55	0	0	182	14	10	1	2.2	.951	OF-94, P-1
1894	2 teams	WAS N (61G –.225) CLE N (40G –.313)																							
″	total		101	.261	.366	372	97	19	10	0	0.0	73	53	62	38	26	0	0	292	13	35	14	3.4	.897	OF-88, 1B-12, 3B-1
1895	CLE	N	91	.326	.409	337	110	16	6	0	0.0	57	68	50	28	12	0	0	480	25	17	12	5.7	.967	OF-49, 1B-42
6 yrs.			627	.269	.376	2315	622	96	54	15	0.6	440	242	324	128	228	0	0	1574	107	141	36	2.9	.923	OF-570, 1B-55, P-2, 3B-1

Dick Teed

TEED, RICHARD LEROY
B. Mar. 8, 1926, Springfield, Mass.
BB TR 5′11″ 180 lbs.

Year	Team		Games	BA	SA	AB	H	2B	3B	HR	HR%	R	RBI	BB	SO	SB	Pinch Hit AB	Pinch Hit H	PO	A	E	DP	TC/G	FA	G by Pos
1953	BKN	N	1	.000	.000	1	0	0	0	0	0.0	0	0	0	1	0	1	0	0	0	0	0	0.0	—	

Wil Tejada

TEJADA, WILFREDO ARISTIDES
Born Wilfredo Aristides Tejada (Andujar).
B. Nov. 12, 1962, Santo Domingo, Dominican Republic.
BR TR 6′ 175 lbs.

Year	Team		Games	BA	SA	AB	H	2B	3B	HR	HR%	R	RBI	BB	SO	SB	Pinch Hit AB	Pinch Hit H	PO	A	E	DP	TC/G	FA	G by Pos
1986	MON	N	10	.240	.280	25	6	1	0	0	0.0	1	2	2	8	0	0	0	40	8	0	1	4.8	1.000	C-10
1988			8	.267	.400	15	4	2	0	0	0.0	1	2	0	4	0	1	0	37	1	0	0	5.4	1.000	C-7
2 yrs.			18	.250	.325	40	10	3	0	0	0.0	2	4	2	12	0	1	0	77	9	0	1	5.1	1.000	C-17

Johnny Temple

TEMPLE, JOHN ELLIS
B. Aug. 8, 1927, Lexington, N. C. D. Jan. 9, 1994, Anderson, S. C.
BR TR 5′11″ 175 lbs.

Year	Team		Games	BA	SA	AB	H	2B	3B	HR	HR%	R	RBI	BB	SO	SB	Pinch Hit AB	Pinch Hit H	PO	A	E	DP	TC/G	FA	G by Pos
1952	CIN	N	30	.196	.258	97	19	3	0	1	1.0	8	5	5	1	2	6	2	63	57	2	18	5.5	.984	2B-22
1953			63	.264	.327	110	29	4	0	1	0.9	14	9	7	12	1	8	5	71	90	6	20	3.8	.964	2B-44
1954			146	.307	.366	505	155	14	8	0	0.0	60	44	62	24	21	0	0	428	374	22	117	5.7	.973	2B-144
1955			150	.281	.325	588	165	20	3	0	0.0	94	50	80	32	19	1	1	408	410	24	119	5.6	.971	2B-149, SS-1
1956			154	.285	.332	**632**	180	18	3	2	0.3	88	41	58	40	14	0	0	389	432	16	89	5.4	.981	2B-154, OF-1
1957			145	.284	.341	557	158	24	4	0	0.0	85	37	**94**	34	19	1	0	391	372	20	81	5.4	.974	2B-145
1958			141	.306	.402	542	166	31	6	3	0.6	82	47	91	41	15	0	0	396	354	16	91	5.4	.979	2B-141, 1B-1
1959			149	.311	.430	598	186	35	6	8	1.3	102	67	72	40	14	0	0	322	390	19	96	4.9	.974	2B-149
1960	CLE	A	98	.268	.323	381	102	13	1	2	0.5	50	19	32	20	11	4	3	182	191	10	58	4.1	.974	2B-77, 3B-17
1961			129	.276	.347	518	143	22	3	3	0.6	73	30	61	36	9	0	0	239	317	18	79	4.4	.969	2B-129
1962	2 teams	BAL A (78G –.263) HOU N (31G –.263)																							
″	total		109	.263	.310	365	96	12	1	1	0.3	42	29	43	33	8	12	1	178	228	12	50	4.3	.971	2B-97, 3B-1
1963	HOU	N	100	.264	.317	322	85	12	1	1	0.3	22	17	41	24	7	9	2	146	188	16	19	3.9	.954	2B-61, 3B-29
1964	CIN	N	6	.000	.000	3	0	0	0	0	0.0	0	0	2	1	0	3	0	0	0	0	0	0.0	—	
13 yrs.			1420	.284	.351	5218	1484	208	36	22	0.4	720	395	648	338	140	44	14	3213	3403	181	837	5.0	.973	2B-1312, 3B-47, 1B-1, OF-1, SS-1

Garry Templeton

TEMPLETON, GARRY LEWIS (Jump Steady)
B. Mar. 24, 1956, Lockney, Tex.
BB TR 5′11″ 175 lbs.

Year	Team		Games	BA	SA	AB	H	2B	3B	HR	HR%	R	RBI	BB	SO	SB	Pinch Hit AB	Pinch Hit H	PO	A	E	DP	TC/G	FA	G by Pos
1976	STL	N	53	.291	.362	213	62	8	2	1	0.5	32	17	7	33	11	1	0	111	172	24	41	5.8	.922	SS-53
1977			153	.322	.449	621	200	19	**18**	8	1.3	94	79	15	70	28	2	0	285	453	32	98	5.1	.958	SS-151
1978			155	.280	.377	647	181	31	**13**	2	0.3	82	47	22	87	34	2	0	285	523	40	108	5.5	.953	SS-155
1979			154	.314	.458	672	**211**	32	**19**	9	1.3	105	62	18	91	26	1	0	292	525	34	102	5.7	.960	SS-150
1980			118	.319	.417	504	161	19	9	4	0.8	83	43	18	43	31	2	0	223	451	29	85	6.1	.959	SS-115
1981			80	.288	.393	333	96	16	8	1	0.3	47	33	14	55	8	4	0	160	272	18	54	5.9	.960	SS-76
1982	SD	N	141	.247	.352	563	139	25	8	6	1.1	76	64	26	82	27	6	1	220	422	26	70	4.9	.961	SS-136
1983			126	.263	.335	460	121	20	2	3	0.7	39	40	21	57	16	3	0	219	355	24	66	4.9	.960	SS-123
1984			148	.258	.320	493	127	19	3	2	0.4	40	35	39	81	8	2	0	225	407	26	79	4.5	.960	SS-146
1985			148	.282	.377	546	154	30	2	6	1.1	63	55	41	88	16	0	0	245	460	23	96	4.9	.968	SS-148
1986			147	.247	.308	510	126	21	2	2	0.4	42	44	35	86	10	9	4	207	358	20	60	4.1	.966	SS-144
1987			148	.222	.296	510	113	13	5	5	1.0	42	48	42	92	14	1	0	253	447	20	77	4.9	.972	SS-146
1988			110	.249	.354	362	90	15	7	3	0.8	35	36	20	50	8	5	0	170	316	16	62	4.7	.968	SS-105, 3B-2
1989			142	.255	.354	506	129	26	3	6	1.2	43	40	23	80	1	3	0	232	409	20	74	4.7	.970	SS-140
1990			144	.248	.362	505	125	25	3	9	1.8	45	59	24	59	1	9	2	214	367	26	74	4.5	.957	SS-135
1991	2 teams	SD N (32G –.193) NY N (80G –.228)																							
″	total		112	.221	.304	276	61	10	2	3	1.1	25	26	10	38	3	36	4	210	141	8	30	4.2	.978	SS-41, 1B-25, 3B-17, OF-2
16 yrs.			2079	.271	.369	7721	2096	329	106	70	0.9	893	728	375	1092	242	86	11	3551	6078	386	1176	5.0	.961	SS-1964, 1B-25, 3B-19, OF-2
LEAGUE CHAMPIONSHIP SERIES																									
1984	SD	N	5	.333	.400	15	5	1	0	0	0.0	2	2	2	0	1	0	0	19	11	1	3	6.2	.968	SS-5
WORLD SERIES																									
1984	SD	N	5	.316	.368	19	6	1	0	0	0.0	1	0	0	3	0	0	0	8	11	0	1	3.8	1.000	SS-5

Gene Tenace

TENACE, FURY GENE
Born Fiore Gino Tennaci.
B. Oct. 10, 1946, Russellton, Pa.
Manager 1991.
BR TR 6′ 190 lbs.

Year	Team		Games	BA	SA	AB	H	2B	3B	HR	HR%	R	RBI	BB	SO	SB	Pinch Hit AB	Pinch Hit H	PO	A	E	DP	TC/G	FA	G by Pos
1969	OAK	A	16	.158	.237	38	6	0	0	1	2.6	1	2	1	15	0	5	0	61	6	0	0	5.2	1.000	C-13
1970			38	.305	.562	105	32	6	0	7	6.7	19	20	23	30	0	7	2	180	18	2	7	6.7	.990	C-30
1971			65	.274	.430	179	49	7	0	7	3.9	26	25	29	34	2	13	4	300	20	2	3	6.1	.994	C-52, OF-1
1972			82	.225	.339	227	51	5	3	5	2.2	22	32	24	42	0	17	7	329	23	7	5	5.2	.981	C-49, OF-9, 1B-7, 3B-2, 2B-2
1973			160	.259	.443	510	132	18	2	24	4.7	83	84	101	94	2	2	0	1218	71	14	108	7.6	.989	1B-134, C-33, DH-3, 2B-1
1974			158	.211	.411	484	102	17	1	26	5.4	71	73	**110**	105	2	0	0	1110	83	10	83	6.4	.992	1B-106, C-79, 2B-3
1975			158	.255	.464	498	127	17	0	29	5.8	83	87	106	127	7	0	0	942	84	11	37	5.3	.989	C-125, 1B-68, DH-1
1976			128	.249	.458	417	104	19	1	22	5.3	64	66	81	91	5	3	0	840	56	8	50	6.6	.991	1B-70, C-65, DH-2
1977	SD	N	147	.233	.410	437	102	24	4	15	3.4	66	61	**125**	119	5	5	0	820	112	16	33	6.4	.983	C-99, 1B-36, 3B-14
1978			142	.224	.409	401	90	18	4	16	4.0	60	61	101	98	6	7	1	944	79	8	68	6.8	.992	1B-80, C-71, 3B-1

Gene Tenace *continued*

Year	Team	Games	BA	SA	AB	H	2B	3B	HR	HR%	R	RBI	BB	SO	SB	Pinch Hit AB	Pinch Hit H	PO	A	E	DP	TC/G	FA	G by Pos
1979		151	.263	.445	463	122	16	4	20	4.3	61	67	105	106	2	7	2	995	83	8	65	6.5	.993	C-94, 1B-72
1980		133	.222	.424	316	70	11	1	17	5.4	46	50	92	63	4	16	2	540	56	11	16	4.9	.982	C-104, 1B-19
1981	**STL N**	58	.233	.403	129	30	7	0	5	3.9	26	22	38	26	0	12	3	165	22	3	4	4.2	.984	C-38, 1B-7
1982		66	.258	.500	124	32	9	0	7	5.6	18	18	36	31	1	12	3	188	24	1	4	4.8	.995	C-37, 1B-7
1983	**PIT N**	53	.177	.258	62	11	5	0	0	0.0	7	6	12	17	0	29	3	99	6	2	6	4.7	.981	1B-19, C-3, OF-1
15 yrs.		1555	.241	.429	4390	1060	179	20	201	4.6	653	674	984	998	36	135	27	8731	743	103	489	6.2	.989	C-892, 1B-625, 3B-17, OF-11, DH-6, 2B-6
LEAGUE CHAMPIONSHIP SERIES																								
1971	**OAK A**	1	.000	.000	3	0	0	0	0	0.0	0	0	1	1	0	0	0	8	0	0	0	8.0	1.000	C-1
1972		5	.059	.059	17	1	0	0	0	0.0	1	1	3	5	0	0	0	21	5	1	0	3.9	.963	C-5, 2B-2
1973		5	.235	.294	17	4	1	0	0	0.0	3	0	2	4	1	0	0	43	3	0	2	5.8	1.000	1B-5, C-3
1974		4	.000	.000	11	0	0	0	0	0.0	1	1	4	4	1	0	0	35	2	0	3	9.3	1.000	1B-4
1975		3	.000	.000	9	0	0	0	0	0.0	0	0	3	2	0	0	0	19	1	0	3	5.0	1.000	C-3, 1B-1
5 yrs.		18	.088	.105	57	5	1	0	0	0.0	5	2	13 **7th**	16	2	0	0	126	11	1	8	5.8	.993	C-12, 1B-10, 2B-2
WORLD SERIES																								
1972	**OAK A**	7	.348	.913	23	8	1	0	4	17.4	5	9	2	4	0	0	0	51	6	1	1	8.3	.983	C-6, 1B-1
1973		7	.158	.211	19	3	1	0	0	0.0	0	3	11	7	0	0	0	57	2	2	6	6.1	.967	1B-7, C-3
1974		5	.222	.222	9	2	0	0	0	0.0	0	0	3	4	0	0	0	20	1	0	3	4.2	1.000	1B-5
1982	**STL N**	5	.000	.000	6	0	0	0	0	0.0	0	0	1	2	0	4	0	0	0	0	0	0.0	.000	DH-1
4 yrs.		24	.228	.474	57	13	2	0	4	7.0	5	12	17	17	0	4	0	128	9	3	10	6.1	.979	1B-13, C-9, DH-1

Tom Tennant

TENNANT, THOMAS FRANCIS BL TL 5′11″ 165 lbs.
B. July 3, 1882, Monroe, Wis. D. Feb. 15, 1955, San Carlos, Calif.

Year	Team	Games	BA	SA	AB	H	2B	3B	HR	HR%	R	RBI	BB	SO	SB	Pinch Hit AB	Pinch Hit H	PO	A	E	DP	TC/G	FA	G by Pos
1912	**STL A**	2	.000	.000	2	0	0	0	0	0.0	1	0	0		0	2	0	0	0	0	0	0.0	—	

Fred Tenney

TENNEY, FRED CLAY
B. July 9, 1859, Marlborough, N. H. D. June 15, 1919, Fall River, Mass.

Year	Team	Games	BA	SA	AB	H	2B	3B	HR	HR%	R	RBI	BB	SO	SB	Pinch Hit AB	Pinch Hit H	PO	A	E	DP	TC/G	FA	G by Pos
1884	**3 teams**	**WAS U** (32G –.235) **BOS U** (4G –.118) **WIL U** (1G –.000)																						
″	**total**	37	.216	.252	139	30	3	1	0	0.0	18	0	6	0	0	0	0	80	11	16	3	2.8	.850	OF-27, 1B-6, P-5

Fred Tenney

TENNEY, FREDERICK BL TL 5′ 9″ 155 lbs.
B. Nov. 26, 1871, Georgetown, Mass. D. July 3, 1952, Boston, Mass.
Manager 1905–07, 1911.

Year	Team	Games	BA	SA	AB	H	2B	3B	HR	HR%	R	RBI	BB	SO	SB	Pinch Hit AB	Pinch Hit H	PO	A	E	DP	TC/G	FA	G by Pos
1894	**BOS N**	27	.395	.570	86	34	7	1	2	2.3	23	21	12	9	6	0	0	64	22	11	3	3.6	.887	C-20, OF-6, 1B-1
1895		49	.272	.353	173	47	9	1	1	0.6	35	21	24	5	6	0	0	109	24	7	2	2.9	.950	OF-28, C-21
1896		88	.336	.411	348	117	14	3	2	0.6	64	49	36	12	18	1	0	183	40	14	4	2.7	.941	OF-60, C-27
1897		132	.318	.376	**566**	180	24	3	1	0.2	125	85	49		34	0	0	1250	82	16	69	10.2	.988	1B-128, OF-4
1898		117	.328	.400	488	160	25	5	0	0.0	106	62	33		23	0	0	1090	66	23	71	10.0	.980	1B-117, C-1
1899		150	.347	.439	603	209	19	17	1	0.2	115	67	63		28	0	0	1474	99	35	107	10.7	.978	1B-150
1900		112	.279	.339	437	122	13	5	1	0.2	77	56	39		17	1	0	1021	82	21	50	10.1	.981	1B-111
1901		115	.278	.317	457	127	13	1	1	0.2	63	22	37		15	0	0	1069	88	29	58	10.3	.976	1B-113, C-2
1902		134	.315	.376	489	154	18	3	2	0.4	88	30	73		21	0	0	1251	105	21	75	10.3	.985	1B-134
1903		122	.313	.396	447	140	22	3	3	0.7	79	41	70		21	0	0	1145	93	33	60	10.4	.974	1B-122
1904		147	.270	.341	533	144	17	9	1	0.2	76	37	57		17	0	0	1457	115	24	66	10.8	.985	1B-144, OF-4
1905		149	.288	.332	549	158	18	3	0	0.0	84	28	67		17	1	0	1557	152	32	68	11.7	.982	1B-148, P-1
1906		143	.283	.340	544	154	12	8	1	0.2	61	28	58		17	0	0	1456	118	28	78	11.2	.983	1B-143
1907		150	.273	.334	554	151	18	8	0	0.0	83	26	82		15	1	0	1587	113	19	86	11.5	.989	1B-149
1908	**NY N**	156	.256	.304	583	149	20	1	2	0.3	**101**	49	72		17	0	0	1634	117	18	68	11.3	.990	1B-156
1909		101	.235	.291	375	88	8	2	3	0.8	43	30	52		8	1	0	1046	72	16	53	11.6	.986	1B-98
1911	**BOS N**	102	.263	.328	369	97	13	4	1	0.3	52	36	50	17	5	4	1	901	64	15	47	10.3	.985	1B-93, OF-2
17 yrs.		1994	.294	.358	7601	2231	270	77	22	0.3	1275	688	874	43	285	9	1	18294	1452	362	965	10.1	.982	1B-1807, OF-104, C-71, P-1

Frank Tepedino

TEPEDINO, FRANK RONALD BL TL 5′11″ 185 lbs.
B. Nov. 23, 1947, Brooklyn, N. Y.

Year	Team	Games	BA	SA	AB	H	2B	3B	HR	HR%	R	RBI	BB	SO	SB	Pinch Hit AB	Pinch Hit H	PO	A	E	DP	TC/G	FA	G by Pos
1967	**NY A**	9	.400	.400	5	2	0	0	0	0.0	0	0	1	1	0	5	2	2	0	0	0	2.0	1.000	1B-1
1969		13	.231	.231	39	9	0	0	0	0.0	6	4	4	4	1	1	0	19	0	1	0	1.5	.950	OF-13
1970		16	.316	.421	19	6	2	0	0	0.0	2	2	1	2	0	11	4	10	0	0	0	5.0	1.000	1B-1, OF-1
1971	**2 teams**	**NY A** (6G –.000) **MIL A** (53G –.198)																						
″	**total**	59	.188	.250	112	21	1	0	2	1.8	11	7	4	17	2	28	3	190	22	3	18	7.4	.986	1B-28, OF-1
1972	**NY A**	8	.000	.000	8	0	0	0	0	0.0	0	0	0	1	0	8	0	0	0	0	0	0.0	—	
1973	**ATL N**	74	.304	.419	148	45	5	0	4	2.7	20	29	13	21	0	24	9	331	28	3	30	6.2	.992	1B-58
1974		78	.231	.272	169	39	5	1	0	0.0	11	16	9	13	1	33	8	307	26	4	35	7.3	.988	1B-46
1975		8	.000	.000	7	0	0	0	0	0.0	0	0	1	2	0	7	0	0	0	0	0	0.0	—	
8 yrs.		265	.241	.306	507	122	13	1	6	1.2	50	58	33	61	4	117	26	859	76	11	83	6.3	.988	1B-134, OF-15

Joe Tepsic

TEPSIC, JOSEPH JOHN BR TR 5′ 9″ 170 lbs.
B. Sept. 18, 1923, Slovan, Pa.

Year	Team	Games	BA	SA	AB	H	2B	3B	HR	HR%	R	RBI	BB	SO	SB	Pinch Hit AB	Pinch Hit H	PO	A	E	DP	TC/G	FA	G by Pos
1946	**BKN N**	15	.000	.000	5	0	0	0	0	0.0	2	0	1	1	0	3	0	1	0	0	0	1.0	1.000	OF-1

Jerry Terrell

TERRELL, JERRY WAYNE BR TR 5′11″ 165 lbs.
B. July 13, 1946, Waseca, Minn. BB 1974

Year	Team	Games	BA	SA	AB	H	2B	3B	HR	HR%	R	RBI	BB	SO	SB	Pinch Hit AB	Pinch Hit H	PO	A	E	DP	TC/G	FA	G by Pos
1973	**MIN A**	124	.265	.315	438	116	15	2	1	0.2	43	32	21	56	13	3	1	170	298	18	55	3.1	.963	SS-81, 3B-30, DH-30, 2B-14, OF-1
1974		116	.245	.314	229	56	4	6	0	0.0	43	19	11	27	3	7	1	114	179	9	35	3.1	.970	SS-34, 2B-26, 3B-21, DH-12, OF-3, 1B-2
1975		108	.286	.345	385	110	16	2	1	0.3	48	36	19	27	4	4	1	267	232	14	60	4.5	.973	SS-41, 2B-39, 1B-15, 3B-12, OF-6, DH-2
1976		89	.246	.275	171	42	3	1	0	0.0	29	8	9	15	11	5	1	82	122	8	27	2.3	.962	2B-31, 3B-26, SS-16, DH-12, OF-6
1977		93	.224	.266	214	48	6	0	1	0.5	32	20	11	21	10	13	3	58	129	6	20	2.1	.969	3B-59, 2B-14, DH-9, SS-7, 1B-1, OF-1

Jerry Terrell *continued*

Year	Team		Games	BA	SA	AB	H	2B	3B	HR	HR%	R	RBI	BB	SO	SB	Pinch Hit AB	Pinch Hit H	PO	A	E	DP	TC/G	FA	G by Pos
1978	KC	A	73	.203	.211	133	27	1	0	0	0.0	14	8	4	13	8	3	2	88	103	4	15	2.7	.979	3B-31, 3B-25, SS-11, 1B-5
1979			31	.300	.450	40	12	3	0	1	2.5	5	2	1	1	1	5	0	10	28	1	4	1.3	.974	3B-19, 2B-7, DH-2, P-1, SS-1
1980			23	.063	.063	16	1	0	0	0	0.0	4	0	0	0	0	1	1	29	7	0	2	2.4	1.000	OF-7, 2B-3, 1B-3, P-1, DH-1
8 yrs.			657	.253	.304	1626	412	48	11	4	0.2	218	125	76	160	50	41	10	818	1098	60	218	3.0	.970	3B-192, SS-191, 2B-165, DH-68, 1B-26, OF-24, P-2

Tom Terrell

TERRELL, JOHN THOMAS
B. June 29, 1867, Louisville, Ky. D. July 9, 1893, Louisville, Ky.

Year	Team		Games	BA	SA	AB	H	2B	3B	HR	HR%	R	RBI	BB	SO	SB	Pinch Hit AB	Pinch Hit H	PO	A	E	DP	TC/G	FA	G by Pos
1886	LOU	AA	1	.250	.250	4	1	0	0	0	0.0	0		0			0	0	4	0	0	0	2.0	1.000	C-1, OF-1

Adonis Terry

TERRY, WILLIAM H. BR TR 5′11½″ 168 lbs.
B. Aug. 7, 1864, Westfield, Mass. D. Feb. 24, 1915, Milwaukee, Wis.

Year	Team		Games	BA	SA	AB	H	2B	3B	HR	HR%	R	RBI	BB	SO	SB	Pinch Hit AB	Pinch Hit H	PO	A	E	DP	TC/G	FA	G by Pos
1884	BKN	AA	68	.233	.300	240	56	10	3	0	0.0	16		8			0	0	56	85	37	2	2.5	.792	P-57, OF-13
1885			71	.170	.208	264	45	1	3	1	0.4	23		10			0	0	90	46	15	2	2.1	.901	OF-47, P-25, 3B-1
1886			75	.237	.344	299	71	8	9	2	0.7	34		10			0	0	99	117	35	3	3.2	.861	P-34, OF-32, SS-13
1887			86	.293	.392	352	103	6	10	3	0.9	56		16		27	0	0	128	90	26	2	2.7	.893	OF-49, P-40, SS-2
1888			30	.252	.304	115	29	6	0	0	0.0	13	8	5		7	0	0	34	44	6	3	2.6	.929	P-23, OF-7, 1B-2
1889			49	.300	.450	160	48	6	6	2	1.3	29	26	14	14	8	0	0	88	88	10	4	3.6	.946	P-41, 1B-10
1890	BKN	N	99	.278	.408	363	101	17	9	4	1.1	63	59	40	34	32	0	0	127	79	19	6	2.2	.916	OF-54, P-46, 1B-1
1891			30	.209	.308	91	19	7	1	0	0.0	10	6	9	26	4	0	0	12	35	4	1	1.7	.922	P-25, OF-5
1892	2 teams		BAL N (1G –.000) PIT N (31G –.160)																						
″	total		32	.154	.288	104	16	0	4	2	1.9	10	11	10	12	2	0	0	27	51	7	0	2.7	.918	P-31, OF-1
1893	PIT	N	26	.254	.394	71	18	4	3	0	0.0	9	11	3	11	1	0	0	9	37	4	2	1.9	.920	P-26
1894	2 teams		PIT N (1G –.000) CHI N (30G –.347)																						
″	total		31	.347	.432	95	33	4	2	0	0.0	19	17	11	12	3	0	0	21	27	6	1	1.6	.889	P-24, OF-7, 1B-2
1895	CHI	N	40	.219	.292	137	30	3	2	1	0.7	18	10	2	17	1	0	0	17	83	13	3	2.8	.885	P-38, SS-1, OF-1
1896			30	.263	.343	99	26	4	2	0	0.0	14	15	8	12	4	0	0	18	43	2	0	2.1	.968	P-30
1897			1	.000	.000	3	0	0	0	0	0.0	1	0	0		0	0	0	0	3	1	0	4.0	.750	P-1
14 yrs.			668	.249	.344	2393	595	76	54	15	0.6	315	163	146	138	89	0	0	726	828	185	29	2.5	.894	P-441, OF-216, SS-16, 1B-15, 3B-1

Bill Terry

TERRY, WILLIAM HAROLD (Memphis Bill) BL TL 6′ 1″ 200 lbs.
B. Oct. 30, 1896, Atlanta, Ga. D. Jan. 9, 1989, Jacksonville, Fla.
Manager 1932–41.
Hall of Fame 1954.

Year	Team		Games	BA	SA	AB	H	2B	3B	HR	HR%	R	RBI	BB	SO	SB	Pinch Hit AB	Pinch Hit H	PO	A	E	DP	TC/G	FA	G by Pos
1923	NY	N	3	.143	.143	7	1	0	0	0	0.0	1	0	2	2	0	1	0	22	1	0	1	11.5	1.000	1B-2
1924			77	.239	.399	163	39	7	2	5	3.1	26	24	17	18	1	**38**	9	325	14	4	30	8.2	.988	1B-42
1925			133	.319	.474	489	156	31	6	11	2.2	75	70	42	52	4	6	2	1270	77	14	83	10.8	.990	1B-126
1926			98	.289	.453	225	65	12	5	5	2.2	26	43	22	17	3	38	12	418	34	9	36	8.9	.980	1B-38, OF-14
1927			150	.326	.529	580	189	32	13	20	3.4	101	121	46	53	1	0	0	1621	105	12	135	11.6	.993	1B-150
1928			149	.326	.518	568	185	36	11	17	3.0	100	101	64	36	7	0	0	1584	78	12	148	11.2	.993	1B-149
1929			150	.372	.522	607	226	39	5	14	2.3	103	117	48	35	10	0	0	1575	111	12	146	11.3	.993	1B-149, OF-1
1930			154	**.401**	.619	633	**254**	39	15	23	3.6	139	129	57	33	8	0	0	1538	128	17	128	10.9	.990	1B-154
1931			153	.349	.529	611	213	43	**20**	9	1.5	**121**	112	47	36	8	0	0	1411	105	16	108	10.0	.990	1B-153
1932			154	.350	.580	643	225	42	11	28	4.4	124	117	32	23	4	0	0	1493	137	14	125	10.7	.991	1B-154
1933			123	.322	.423	475	153	20	5	6	1.3	68	58	40	23	3	6	4	1246	76	11	103	11.4	.992	1B-117
1934			153	.354	.463	602	213	30	6	8	1.3	109	83	60	47	0	0	0	1592	105	10	131	11.2	.994	1B-153
1935			145	.341	.451	596	203	32	8	6	1.0	91	64	41	55	7	2	1	1379	99	6	105	10.4	.996	1B-143
1936			79	.310	.424	229	71	10	5	2	0.9	36	39	19	19	0	22	6	525	41	2	55	10.1	.996	1B-56
14 yrs.			1721	.341	.506	6428	2193	373	112	154	2.4	1120	1078	537	449	56	113	34	15999	1111	139	1334	10.8	.992	1B-1586, OF-15
WORLD SERIES																									
1924	NY	N	5	.429	.786	14	6	0	1	1	7.1	3	1	3	1	0	1	0	43	2	0	2	11.3	1.000	1B-4
1933			5	.273	.455	22	6	1	0	1	4.5	3	1	0	0	0	0	0	50	1	0	3	10.2	1.000	1B-5
1936			6	.240	.240	25	6	0	0	0	0.0	1	5	1	4	0	0	0	45	8	0	5	8.8	1.000	1B-6
3 yrs.			16	.295	.443	61	18	1	1	2	3.3	7	7	4	5	0	1	0	138	11	0	10	9.9	1.000	1B-15

Zeb Terry

TERRY, ZEBULON ALEXANDER BR TR 5′ 8″ 129 lbs.
B. June 17, 1891, Denison, Tex. D. Mar. 14, 1988, Los Angeles, Calif.

Year	Team		Games	BA	SA	AB	H	2B	3B	HR	HR%	R	RBI	BB	SO	SB	Pinch Hit AB	Pinch Hit H	PO	A	E	DP	TC/G	FA	G by Pos
1916	CHI	A	94	.190	.249	269	51	8	4	0	0.0	20	17	33	36	4	1	1	148	243	27	36	4.5	.935	SS-93
1917			2	.000	.000	1	0	0	0	0	0.0	0	0	2	0	0	0	0	0	1	0	0	1.0	1.000	SS-1
1918	BOS	N	28	.305	.362	105	32	2	2	0	0.0	17	8	8	14	1	0	0	57	114	4	14	6.5	.977	SS-27
1919	PIT	N	129	.227	.278	472	107	12	6	0	0.0	46	27	31	26	12	2	1	207	395	25	41	4.9	.960	SS-127
1920	CHI	N	133	.280	.369	496	139	26	9	0	0.0	56	52	44	22	12	0	0	291	471	25	62	5.9	.968	SS-70, 2B-63
1921			123	.275	.328	488	134	18	1	2	0.4	59	45	27	19	1	1	0	272	413	20	57	5.7	.972	2B-123
1922			131	.286	.343	496	142	24	2	0	0.0	56	67	34	16	2	0	0	310	461	29	77	6.1	.964	2B-125, SS-4, 3B-3
7 yrs.			640	.260	.322	2327	605	90	24	2	0.1	254	216	179	133	32	4	2	1285	2098	130	287	5.5	.963	SS-322, 2B-311, 3B-3

Wayne Terwilliger

TERWILLIGER, WILLARD WAYNE (Twig) BR TR 5′11″ 165 lbs.
B. June 27, 1925, Clare, Mich.

Year	Team		Games	BA	SA	AB	H	2B	3B	HR	HR%	R	RBI	BB	SO	SB	Pinch Hit AB	Pinch Hit H	PO	A	E	DP	TC/G	FA	G by Pos
1949	CHI	N	36	.223	.313	112	25	2	1	2	1.8	11	10	16	22	0	1	0	77	103	4	11	5.4	.978	2B-34
1950			133	.242	.362	480	116	22	3	10	2.1	63	32	43	63	13	4	1	314	380	24	80	5.6	.967	2B-126, 3B-1, OF-1, 1B-1
1951	2 teams		CHI N (50G –.214) BKN N (37G –.280)																						
″	total		87	.227	.256	242	55	7	0	0	0.0	37	14	37	28	4	7	3	167	187	13	47	5.0	.965	2B-73, 3B-1
1953	WAS	A	134	.252	.347	464	117	24	4	4	0.9	62	46	64	65	7	1	1	333	395	13	108	5.6	.982	2B-133
1954			106	.208	.270	337	70	10	1	3	0.9	42	24	32	40	3	1	0	227	274	16	77	5.0	.969	2B-90, 3B-10, SS-3
1955	NY	N	80	.257	.339	257	66	16	1	1	0.4	29	18	36	42	2	0	0	212	240	7	70	5.7	.985	2B-78, SS-1, 3B-1
1956			14	.222	.278	18	4	1	0	0	0.0	0	0	0	5	0	4	0	14	9	1	3	4.0	.958	2B-6
1959	KC	A	74	.267	.361	180	48	11	0	2	1.1	27	18	19	31	2	6	0	144	167	9	42	4.8	.972	2B-63, SS-2, 3B-1
1960			2	.000	.000	1	0	0	0	0	0.0	0	0	0	0	0	0	0	1	1	0	1	1.0	1.000	2B-2
9 yrs.			666	.240	.325	2091	501	93	10	22	1.1	271	162	247	296	31	24	5	1489	1756	87	439	5.3	.974	2B-605, 3B-14, SS-6, OF-1, 1B-1

Al Tesch

TESCH, ALBERT JOHN, JR. (Tiny) — BB TR 5′10″ 155 lbs.
B. Jan. 27, 1891, Jersey City, N. J. D. Aug. 3, 1947, Jersey City, N. J.

Year	Team	Games	BA	SA	AB	H	2B	3B	HR	HR%	R	RBI	BB	SO	SB	Pinch Hit AB	Pinch Hit H	PO	A	E	DP	TC/G	FA	G by Pos
1915	BKN F	8	.286	.429	7	2	1	0	0	0.0	2	2	0		0	1	0	5	8	2	1	5.0	.867	2B-3

Nick Testa

TESTA, NICHOLAS — BR TR 5′ 8″ 180 lbs.
B. June 29, 1928, New York, N. Y.

Year	Team	Games	BA	SA	AB	H	2B	3B	HR	HR%	R	RBI	BB	SO	SB	Pinch Hit AB	Pinch Hit H	PO	A	E	DP	TC/G	FA	G by Pos
1958	SF N	1	—	—	0	0	0	0	0	—	0	0	0	0	0	0	0	0	0	1	0	1.0	.000	C-1

Dick Tettelbach

TETTELBACH, RICHARD MORLEY (Tut) — BR TR 6′ 195 lbs.
B. June 26, 1929, New Haven, Conn. D. Jan. 26, 1995, East Harwich, Mass.

Year	Team	Games	BA	SA	AB	H	2B	3B	HR	HR%	R	RBI	BB	SO	SB	Pinch Hit AB	Pinch Hit H	PO	A	E	DP	TC/G	FA	G by Pos
1955	NY A	2	.000	.000	5	0	0	0	0	0.0	0	0	0	0	0	0	0	0	1	0	0	0.5	1.000	OF-2
1956	WAS A	18	.156	.281	64	10	1	2	1	1.6	10	9	14	15	0	0	0	37	2	0	0	2.2	1.000	OF-18
1957		9	.182	.182	11	2	0	0	0	0.0	2	1	4	2	0	3	1	9	0	1	0	3.3	.900	OF-3
3 yrs.		29	.150	.250	80	12	1	2	1	1.3	12	10	18	17	0	3	1	46	3	1	0	2.2	.980	OF-23

Mickey Tettleton

TETTLETON, MICKEY LEE — BB TR 6′ 2″ 190 lbs.
B. Sept. 16, 1960, Oklahoma City, Okla.

Year	Team	Games	BA	SA	AB	H	2B	3B	HR	HR%	R	RBI	BB	SO	SB	Pinch Hit AB	Pinch Hit H	PO	A	E	DP	TC/G	FA	G by Pos
1984	OAK A	33	.263	.355	76	20	2	1	1	1.3	10	5	11	21	0	3	0	112	10	1	1	3.8	.992	C-32
1985		78	.251	.351	211	53	12	0	3	1.4	23	15	28	59	2	3	1	344	24	4	9	4.8	.989	C-76, DH-1
1986		90	.204	.389	211	43	9	0	10	4.7	26	35	39	51	7	2	0	463	32	8	6	5.7	.984	C-89
1987		82	.194	.322	211	41	3	0	8	3.8	19	26	30	65	1	2	0	435	29	6	1	5.7	.987	C-80, 1B-1, DH-1
1988	BAL A	86	.261	.424	283	74	11	1	11	3.9	31	37	28	70	0	9	0	361	31	3	1	4.9	.992	C-80
1989		117	.258	.509	411	106	21	2	26	6.3	72	65	73	117	3	3	1	297	42	2	1	2.9	.994	C-75, DH-43
1990		135	.223	.381	444	99	21	2	15	3.4	68	51	106	160	2	2	1	458	39	5	4	3.7	.990	C-90, DH-40, 1B-5, OF-1
1991	DET A	154	.263	.491	501	132	17	2	31	6.2	85	89	101	131	3	13	4	562	55	6	2	4.1	.990	C-125, DH-24, OF-3, 1B-1
1992		157	.238	.469	525	125	25	0	32	6.1	82	83	**122**	137	0	4	1	481	47	2	11	3.4	.996	C-113, DH-40, 1B-3, OF-2
1993		152	.245	.492	522	128	25	4	32	6.1	79	110	109	139	3	4	1	724	47	6	43	4.5	.992	1B-59, C-56, OF-55, DH-4
1994		107	.248	.463	339	84	18	2	17	5.0	57	51	97	98	0	2	1	367	30	5	7	3.4	.988	C-53, 1B-24, DH-22, OF-18
1995	TEX A	134	.238	.510	429	102	19	1	32	7.5	76	78	107	110	0	2	0	185	10	3	8	1.5	.985	OF-63, DH-58, 1B-9, C-3
12 yrs.		1325	.242	.450	4163	1007	183	15	218	5.2	628	645	851	1158	21	49	10	4789	396	51	94	3.9	.990	C-872, DH-233, OF-142, 1B-102

Tim Teufel

TEUFEL, TIMOTHY SHAWN — BR TR 6′ 175 lbs.
B. July 7, 1958, Greenwich, Conn.

Year	Team	Games	BA	SA	AB	H	2B	3B	HR	HR%	R	RBI	BB	SO	SB	Pinch Hit AB	Pinch Hit H	PO	A	E	DP	TC/G	FA	G by Pos
1983	MIN A	21	.308	.538	78	24	7	1	3	3.8	11	6	2	8	0	2	0	47	58	1	14	5.3	.991	2B-18, SS-1, DH-1
1984		157	.262	.400	568	149	30	3	14	2.5	76	61	76	73	1	0	0	315	485	13	81	5.2	.984	2B-157
1985		138	.260	.399	434	113	24	3	10	2.3	58	50	48	70	4	6	1	237	352	12	67	4.4	.980	2B-137, DH-1
1986	NY N	93	.247	.369	279	69	20	1	4	1.4	35	31	32	42	1	16	3	143	174	9	28	3.7	.972	2B-84, 1B-3, 3B-1
1987		97	.308	.545	299	92	29	0	14	4.7	55	61	44	53	3	18	8	139	214	11	44	3.9	.970	2B-92, 1B-1
1988		90	.234	.352	273	64	20	0	4	1.5	35	31	29	41	0	14	4	175	213	7	49	4.5	.982	2B-84, 1B-3
1989		83	.256	.333	219	56	7	2	2	0.9	27	15	32	50	1	12	3	261	112	10	30	5.2	.974	2B-40, 1B-33
1990		80	.246	.480	175	43	11	0	10	5.7	28	24	15	33	0	29	8	141	58	4	16	3.5	.980	1B-24, 2B-24, 3B-10
1991	2 teams	NY N (20G –.118) SD N (97G –.228)																						
″	total	117	.217	.370	341	74	16	0	12	3.5	41	44	51	77	9	12	1	178	205	9	27	3.1	.977	2B-66, 3B-53, 1B-6
1992	SD N	101	.224	.337	246	55	10	0	6	2.4	23	25	31	45	2	19	2	137	163	7	23	3.7	.977	2B-52, 3B-26, 1B-5
1993		96	.250	.430	200	50	11	2	7	3.5	26	31	27	39	2	32	3	109	124	3	22	3.4	.987	2B-52, 3B-9, 1B-8
11 yrs.		1073	.254	.404	3112	789	185	12	86	2.8	415	379	387	531	23	160	33	1882	2158	86	401	4.2	.979	2B-806, 3B-99, 1B-83, DH-2, SS-1
LEAGUE CHAMPIONSHIP SERIES																								
1986	NY N	2	.167	.167	6	1	0	0	0	0.0	0	0	0	0	0	0	0	2	8	0	1	5.0	1.000	2B-2
1988		1	.000	.000	3	0	0	0	0	0.0	0	0	0	1	0	0	0	1	3	0	0	4.0	1.000	2B-1
2 yrs.		3	.111	.111	9	1	0	0	0	0.0	0	0	0	1	0	0	0	3	11	0	1	4.7	1.000	2B-3
WORLD SERIES																								
1986	NY N	3	.444	.889	9	4	1	0	1	11.1	1	1	0	2	0	0	0	3	3	1	1	2.3	.857	2B-3

George Textor

TEXTOR, GEORGE BERNHARDT (Tex) — BB TR 5′10½″ 174 lbs.
B. Dec. 27, 1888, Newport, Ky. D. Mar. 10, 1954, Massillon, Ohio.

Year	Team	Games	BA	SA	AB	H	2B	3B	HR	HR%	R	RBI	BB	SO	SB	Pinch Hit AB	Pinch Hit H	PO	A	E	DP	TC/G	FA	G by Pos
1914	IND F	22	.175	.175	57	10	0	0	0	0.0	2	4	2		0	1	0	72	34	5	7	5.3	.955	C-21
1915	NWK F	3	.333	.333	6	2	0	0	0	0.0	1	0	0		0	0	0	5	1	0	0	2.0	1.000	C-3
2 yrs.		25	.190	.190	63	12	0	0	0	0.0	3	4	2		0	1	0	77	35	5	7	4.9	.957	C-24

Moe Thacker

THACKER, MORRIS BENTON — BR TR 6′ 3″ 205 lbs.
B. May 21, 1934, Louisville, Ky.

Year	Team	Games	BA	SA	AB	H	2B	3B	HR	HR%	R	RBI	BB	SO	SB	Pinch Hit AB	Pinch Hit H	PO	A	E	DP	TC/G	FA	G by Pos
1958	CHI N	11	.250	.542	24	6	1	0	2	8.3	4	3	1	7	0	2	1	34	6	2	1	4.7	.952	C-9
1960		54	.156	.167	90	14	1	0	0	0.0	5	6	14	20	1	4	1	170	23	4	2	3.9	.980	C-50
1961		25	.171	.171	35	6	0	0	0	0.0	3	2	11	11	0	0	0	67	5	2	0	3.0	.973	C-25
1962		65	.187	.234	107	20	5	0	0	0.0	8	9	14	40	0	1	0	219	34	1	8	3.9	.996	C-65
1963	STL N	3	.000	.000	4	0	0	0	0	0.0	0	0	0	3	0	0	0	9	1	0	0	3.3	1.000	C-3
5 yrs.		158	.177	.227	260	46	7	0	2	0.8	20	20	40	81	1	7	2	499	69	9	11	3.8	.984	C-152

Ron Theobald

THEOBALD, RONALD MERRILL — BR TR 5′ 8″ 165 lbs.
B. July 28, 1943, Oakland, Calif.

Year	Team	Games	BA	SA	AB	H	2B	3B	HR	HR%	R	RBI	BB	SO	SB	Pinch Hit AB	Pinch Hit H	PO	A	E	DP	TC/G	FA	G by Pos
1971	MIL A	126	.276	.325	388	107	12	2	1	0.3	50	23	38	39	11	12	5	233	312	15	81	5.0	.973	2B-111, 3B-1, SS-1
1972		125	.220	.256	391	86	11	0	1	0.3	45	19	68	38	0	14	4	193	299	6	68	4.4	.988	2B-113
2 yrs.		251	.248	.290	779	193	23	2	2	0.3	95	42	106	77	11	26	9	426	611	21	149	4.7	.980	2B-224, 3B-1, SS-1

George Theodore

THEODORE, GEORGE BASIL (The Stork) — BR TR 6′ 4″ 190 lbs.
B. Nov. 13, 1947, Salt Lake City, Utah.

Year	Team	Games	BA	SA	AB	H	2B	3B	HR	HR%	R	RBI	BB	SO	SB	Pinch Hit AB	Pinch Hit H	PO	A	E	DP	TC/G	FA	G by Pos
1973	NY N	45	.259	.319	116	30	4	0	1	0.9	14	15	10	13	1	11	2	80	5	1	4	2.3	.988	OF-33, 1B-4
1974		60	.158	.211	76	12	1	0	1	1.3	7	1	8	14	0	30	5	97	3	3	7	4.0	.971	1B-14, OF-12
2 yrs.		105	.219	.276	192	42	5	0	2	1.0	21	16	18	27	1	41	7	177	8	4	11	3.0	.979	OF-45, 1B-18
WORLD SERIES																								
1973	NY N	2	.000	.000	2	0	0	0	0	0.0	0	0	0	0	0	1	0	1	0	0	0	1.0	1.000	OF-1

Tommy Thevenow

THEVENOW, THOMAS JOSEPH
B. Sept. 6, 1903, Madison, Ind. D. July 29, 1957, Madison, Ind.
BR TR 5'10" 155 lbs.

Year	Team	Games	BA	SA	AB	H	2B	3B	HR	HR%	R	RBI	BB	SO	SB	Pinch Hit AB	Pinch Hit H	PO	A	E	DP	TC/G	FA	G by Pos
1924	STL N	23	.202	.270	89	18	4	1	0	0.0	4	7	1	6	1	0	0	61	95	8	15	7.1	.951	SS-23
1925		50	.269	.331	175	47	7	2	0	0.0	17	17	7	12	3	0	0	98	169	14	18	5.6	.950	SS-50
1926		156	.256	.311	563	144	15	5	2	0.4	64	63	27	26	8	0	0	371	597	45	98	6.5	.956	SS-156
1927		59	.194	.236	191	37	6	1	0	0.0	23	4	14	8	2	0	0	111	199	18	38	5.6	.945	SS-59
1928		69	.205	.287	171	35	8	3	0	0.0	11	13	20	12	0	0	0	104	166	19	29	4.3	.934	SS-64, 3B-3, 1B-1
1929	PHI N	90	.227	.262	317	72	11	0	0	0.0	30	35	25	25	3	0	0	188	296	24	56	5.6	.953	SS-90
1930		156	.286	.326	573	164	21	1	0	0.0	57	78	23	26	1	0	0	344	554	56	113	6.1	.941	SS-156
1931	PIT N	120	.213	.248	404	86	12	1	0	0.0	35	38	28	22	0	0	0	245	432	25	92	5.8	.964	SS-120
1932		59	.237	.284	194	46	3	3	0	0.0	12	26	7	12	0	6	0	82	126	14	24	4.4	.937	SS-29, 3B-22
1933		73	.312	.340	253	79	5	1	0	0.0	20	34	3	5	2	9	1	143	180	9	33	5.1	.973	2B-61, SS-3, 3B-1
1934		122	.271	.316	446	121	16	2	0	0.0	37	54	20	20	0	6	2	214	280	19	37	4.3	.963	2B-75, 3B-44, SS-1
1935		110	.238	.304	408	97	9	9	0	0.0	38	47	12	23	1	7	1	142	216	17	18	3.6	.955	3B-82, SS-13, 2B-8
1936	CIN N	106	.234	.268	321	75	7	2	0	0.0	25	36	15	23	2	1	0	178	248	23	49	4.0	.949	SS-68, 2B-33, 3B-12
1937	BOS N	21	.118	.176	34	4	0	1	0	0.0	5	2	4	2	0	1	0	14	32	3	3	2.5	.939	SS-12, 3B-6, 2B-2
1938	PIT N	15	.200	.200	25	5	0	0	0	0.0	2	2	4	0	0	1	0	13	31	2	7	3.3	.957	2B-9, SS-4, 3B-1
15 yrs.		1229	.247	.294	4164	1030	124	32	2	0.0	380	456	210	222	23	31	4	2308	3621	296	630	5.2	.952	SS-848, 2B-188, 3B-171, 1B-1
WORLD SERIES																								
1926	STL N	7	.417	.583	24	10	1	0	1	4.2	5	4	0	1	0	0	0	10	26	2	5	5.4	.947	SS-7
1928		1	—	—	0	0	0	0	0	—	0	0	0	0	0	0	0	1	0	0	0	1.0	1.000	SS-1
2 yrs.		8	.417	.583	24	10	1	0	1	4.2	5	4	0	1	0	0	0	11	26	2	5	4.9	.949	SS-8

Andres Thomas

THOMAS, ANDRES
Born Andres Perez (Thomas).
B. Nov. 10, 1963, Boca Chica, Dominican Republic.
BR TR 6'1" 170 lbs.

Year	Team	Games	BA	SA	AB	H	2B	3B	HR	HR%	R	RBI	BB	SO	SB	Pinch Hit AB	Pinch Hit H	PO	A	E	DP	TC/G	FA	G by Pos
1985	ATL N	15	.278	.278	18	5	0	0	0	0.0	6	2	0	2	0	1	1	6	17	2	2	2.5	.920	SS-10
1986		102	.251	.372	323	81	17	2	6	1.9	26	32	8	49	4	6	3	143	290	19	62	4.7	.958	SS-97
1987		82	.231	.312	324	75	11	0	5	1.5	29	39	14	50	6	1	0	128	276	20	56	5.2	.953	SS-81
1988		153	.252	.360	606	153	22	2	13	2.1	54	68	14	95	7	3	1	230	456	29	90	4.8	.959	SS-150
1989		141	.213	.316	554	118	18	0	13	2.3	41	57	12	62	3	2	0	231	400	29	81	4.8	.956	SS-138
1990		84	.219	.302	278	61	8	0	5	1.8	26	30	11	43	2	10	4	104	200	10	43	4.1	.968	SS-72, 3B-5
6 yrs.		577	.234	.334	2103	493	76	4	42	2.0	182	228	59	301	22	23	9	842	1639	109	334	4.7	.958	SS-548, 3B-5

Bill Thomas

THOMAS, WILLIAM MISKEY
Brother of Roy Thomas.
B. Dec. 8, 1877, Norristown, Pa. D. Jan. 14, 1950, Evansburg, Pa.
BR TR 5'10" 190 lbs.

Year	Team	Games	BA	SA	AB	H	2B	3B	HR	HR%	R	RBI	BB	SO	SB	Pinch Hit AB	Pinch Hit H	PO	A	E	DP	TC/G	FA	G by Pos
1902	PHI N	6	.118	.118	17	2	0	0	0	0.0	1	0	1		0	1	0	9	3	2	1	2.8	.857	OF-3, 2B-1, 1B-1

Bud Thomas

THOMAS, JOHN TILLMAN
B. Mar. 10, 1929, Sedalia, Mo.
BR TR 6' 160 lbs.

Year	Team	Games	BA	SA	AB	H	2B	3B	HR	HR%	R	RBI	BB	SO	SB	Pinch Hit AB	Pinch Hit H	PO	A	E	DP	TC/G	FA	G by Pos
1951	STL A	14	.350	.500	20	7	0	0	1	5.0	3	1	0	3	2	0	0	12	18	0	4	2.1	1.000	SS-14

Danny Thomas

THOMAS, DANNY LEE
B. May 9, 1951, Birmingham, Ala. D. July 3, 1980, Mobile, Ala.
BR TR 6'2" 190 lbs.

Year	Team	Games	BA	SA	AB	H	2B	3B	HR	HR%	R	RBI	BB	SO	SB	Pinch Hit AB	Pinch Hit H	PO	A	E	DP	TC/G	FA	G by Pos
1976	MIL A	32	.276	.457	105	29	5	1	4	3.8	13	15	14	28	1	0	0	60	3	3	1	2.1	.955	OF-32
1977		22	.271	.457	70	19	3	2	2	2.9	11	11	8	11	0	3	1	22	0	0	0	1.2	1.000	OF-9, DH-9
2 yrs.		54	.274	.457	175	48	8	3	6	3.4	24	26	22	39	1	3	1	82	3	3	1	1.8	.966	OF-41, DH-9

Derrel Thomas

THOMAS, DERREL OSBORN
B. Jan. 14, 1951, Los Angeles, Calif.
BB TR 6' 160 lbs.

Year	Team	Games	BA	SA	AB	H	2B	3B	HR	HR%	R	RBI	BB	SO	SB	Pinch Hit AB	Pinch Hit H	PO	A	E	DP	TC/G	FA	G by Pos
1971	HOU N	5	.000	.000	5	0	0	0	0	0.0	0	0	0	2	0	0	0	3	2	0	1	5.0	1.000	2B-1
1972	SD N	130	.230	.310	500	115	15	5	5	1.0	48	36	41	73	9	2	0	290	357	26	77	5.0	.961	2B-83, SS-49, OF-3
1973		113	.238	.260	404	96	7	1	0	0.0	41	22	34	52	15	6	2	211	324	37	66	4.7	.935	SS-74, 2B-47
1974		141	.247	.333	523	129	24	6	3	0.6	48	41	51	58	7	5	3	310	336	18	53	4.4	.973	2B-104, 3B-22, OF-20, SS-5
1975	SF N	144	.276	.381	540	149	21	9	6	1.1	99	48	57	56	28	2	1	349	372	19	100	5.2	.974	2B-141, OF-1
1976		81	.232	.301	272	63	5	4	2	0.7	38	19	29	26	10	11	2	163	215	15	52	5.4	.962	2B-69, OF-2, SS-1, 3B-1
1977		148	.267	.379	506	135	13	10	8	1.6	75	44	46	70	15	19	5	307	158	14	24	3.4	.971	OF-78, 2B-27, SS-26, 3B-6, 1B-3
1978	SD N	128	.227	.293	352	80	10	2	3	0.9	36	26	35	37	11	7	1	328	168	12	39	3.2	.976	OF-77, 2B-40, 3B-26, 1B-14
1979	LA N	141	.256	.350	406	104	15	4	5	1.2	47	44	41	49	18	11	1	298	38	5	8	2.3	.985	OF-119, 3B-18, 2B-5, SS-3, 1B-1
1980		117	.266	.357	297	79	18	3	1	0.3	32	22	26	48	7	8	3	203	175	14	39	3.1	.964	OF-52, SS-49, 2B-18, C-5, 3B-4
1981		80	.248	.321	218	54	4	0	4	1.8	25	24	25	23	7	3	0	133	144	14	30	3.5	.952	2B-30, SS-26, OF-18, 3B-10
1982		66	.265	.306	98	26	2	1	0	0.0	13	2	10	12	2	5	0	58	58	4	14	1.8	.967	OF-28, 2B-18, 3B-14, SS-6
1983		118	.250	.375	192	48	6	6	2	1.0	38	8	27	36	9	16	3	134	51	5	11	1.7	.974	OF-82, SS-13, 2B-9, 3B-7
1984	2 teams	MON N (108G –.255)	CAL A (14G –.138)																					
"	total	122	.243	.309	272	66	12	3	0	0.0	29	22	23	37	0	14	0	130	136	11	34	1.9	.960	SS-66, OF-55, 2B-15, 3B-7, 1B-1
1985	PHI N	63	.207	.359	92	19	2	0	4	4.3	16	12	11	14	2	35	7	31	38	7	4	2.5	.908	SS-21, OF-7, C-1, 2B-1, 3B-1
15 yrs.		1597	.249	.332	4677	1163	154	54	43	0.9	585	370	456	593	140	144	28	2948	2572	201	552	3.5	.965	2B-608, OF-542, SS-339, 3B-116, 1B-19, C-6

Year	Team	Games	BA	SA	AB	H	2B	3B	HR	HR%	R	RBI	BB	SO	SB	Pinch Hit AB	Pinch Hit H	PO	A	E	DP	TC/G	FA	G by Pos
DIVISIONAL PLAYOFF SERIES																								
1981	LA N	4	.000	.000	2	0	0	0	0	0.0	1	0	0	1	0	1	0	0	0	0	0	0.0	.000	OF-4
LEAGUE CHAMPIONSHIP SERIES																								
1981	LA N	2	1.000	1.000	1	1	0	0	0	0.0	2	0	0	0	0	1	1	1	0	0	0	0.5	1.000	OF-1, 3B-1
1983		4	.444	.556	9	4	1	0	0	0.0	0	0	0	3	1	1	0	7	0	0	0	1.8	1.000	OF-4
2 yrs.		6	.500	.600	10	5	1	0	0	0.0	2	0	0	3	1	2	1	8	0	0	0	1.3	1.000	OF-5, 3B-1
WORLD SERIES																								
1981	LA N	5	.000	.000	7	0	0	0	0	0.0	2	1	1	2	0	2	0	4	2	0	2	1.2	1.000	OF-3, SS-1, 3B-1

Frank Thomas

THOMAS, FRANK EDWARD (The Big Hurt) BR TR 6′ 5″ 240 lbs.
B. May 27, 1968, Columbus, Ga.

Year	Team	Games	BA	SA	AB	H	2B	3B	HR	HR%	R	RBI	BB	SO	SB	Pinch Hit AB	Pinch Hit H	PO	A	E	DP	TC/G	FA	G by Pos
1990	CHI A	60	.330	.529	191	63	11	3	7	3.7	39	31	44	54	0	1	1	428	26	5	53	7.8	.989	1B-51, DH-8
1991		158	.318	.553	559	178	31	2	32	5.7	104	109	**138**	112	1	1	1	459	27	2	43	3.1	.996	DH-101, 1B-56
1992		160	.323	.536	573	185	**46**	2	24	4.2	108	115	**122**	88	6	1	0	1428	92	13	112	9.6	.992	1B-158, DH-2
1993		153	.317	.607	549	174	36	0	41	7.5	106	128	112	54	4	0	0	1222	83	15	128	8.6	.989	1B-150, DH-4
1994		113	.353	**.729**	399	141	34	1	38	**9.5**	**106**	101	**109**	61	2	1	0	735	45	7	74	7.0	.991	1B-99, DH-13
1995		145	.308	.606	493	152	27	0	40	8.1	102	111	**136**	74	3	3	0	743	35	7	66	5.5	.991	1B-91, DH-53
6 yrs.		789	.323	.593	2764	893	185	8	182	6.6	565	595	661	443	16	7	2	5015	308	49	476	6.8	.991	1B-605, DH-181
LEAGUE CHAMPIONSHIP SERIES																								
1993	CHI A	6	.353	.529	17	6	0	0	1	5.9	2	3	10	5	0	0	0	24	3	0	3	4.5	1.000	1B-4, DH-2

Frank Thomas

THOMAS, FRANK JOSEPH BR TR 6′ 3″ 200 lbs.
B. June 11, 1929, Pittsburgh, Pa.

Year	Team	Games	BA	SA	AB	H	2B	3B	HR	HR%	R	RBI	BB	SO	SB	Pinch Hit AB	Pinch Hit H	PO	A	E	DP	TC/G	FA	G by Pos
1951	PIT N	39	.264	.392	148	39	9	2	2	1.4	21	16	9	15	0	3	1	87	5	0	2	2.5	1.000	OF-37
1952		6	.095	.095	21	2	0	0	0	0.0	1	0	1	1	0	0	0	8	1	0	0	1.8	1.000	OF-5
1953		128	.255	.505	455	116	22	1	30	6.6	68	102	50	93	1	9	1	306	17	8	1	2.8	.976	OF-118
1954		153	.298	.497	577	172	32	7	23	4.0	81	94	51	74	3	1	1	418	14	5	2	2.9	.989	OF-153
1955		142	.245	.431	510	125	16	2	25	4.9	72	72	60	76	2	3	1	307	8	5	3	2.3	.984	OF-139
1956		157	.282	.461	588	166	24	3	25	4.3	69	80	36	61	0	2	0	216	179	18	22	2.4	.956	3B-111, OF-56, 2B-4
1957		151	.290	.460	594	172	30	1	23	3.9	72	89	44	66	3	0	0	729	119	25	60	5.4	.971	1B-71, OF-59, 3B-31
1958		149	.281	.528	562	158	26	4	35	6.2	89	109	42	79	0	1	0	160	243	30	22	2.9	.931	3B-139, OF-8, 1B-2
1959	CIN N	108	.225	.380	374	84	18	2	12	3.2	41	47	27	56	0	8	1	206	126	19	19	3.2	.946	3B-64, OF-33, 1B-14
1960	CHI N	135	.238	.399	479	114	12	1	21	4.4	54	64	28	74	1	11	4	528	92	17	40	4.8	.973	1B-50, OF-49, 3B-33
1961	2 teams	CHI N (15G –.260) MIL N (124G –.284)																						
″	total	139	.281	.497	473	133	15	3	27	5.7	65	73	31	78	2	11	1	300	12	10	8	2.4	.969	OF-119, 1B-17
1962	NY N	156	.266	.496	571	152	23	3	34	6.0	69	94	48	95	2	11	4	311	36	14	8	2.5	.961	OF-126, 1B-11, 3B-10
1963		126	.260	.393	420	109	9	1	15	3.6	34	60	33	48	0	15	4	304	17	4	10	2.9	.988	OF-96, 1B-15, 3B-1
1964	2 teams	NY N (60G –.254) PHI N (39G –.294)																						
″	total	99	.271	.415	340	92	17	1	10	2.9	39	45	15	41	1	14	4	498	46	9	49	6.1	.984	1B-58, OF-31, 3B-2
1965	3 teams	PHI N (35G –.260) HOU N (23G –.172) MIL N (15G –.212)																						
″	total	73	.220	.345	168	37	9	0	4	2.4	17	17	9	36	0	29	3	262	15	5	24	5.4	.982	1B-33, OF-16, 3B-3
1966	CHI N	5	.000	.000	5	0	0	0	0	0.0	0	0	0	1	0	5	0	0	0	0	0	0.0	—	
16 yrs.		1766	.266	.454	6285	1671	262	31	286	4.6	792	962	484	894	15	123	25	4640	930	169	270	3.3	.971	OF-1045, 3B-394, 1B-271, 2B-4

Fred Thomas

THOMAS, FREDERICK HARVEY BR TR 5′10″ 160 lbs.
B. Dec. 19, 1892, Milwaukee, Wis. D. Jan. 15, 1986, Rice Lake, Wis.

Year	Team	Games	BA	SA	AB	H	2B	3B	HR	HR%	R	RBI	BB	SO	SB	Pinch Hit AB	Pinch Hit H	PO	A	E	DP	TC/G	FA	G by Pos
1918	BOS A	44	.257	.306	144	37	2	1	1	0.7	19	11	15	20	4	1	0	54	97	5	4	3.7	.968	3B-41, SS-1
1919	PHI A	124	.212	.294	453	96	11	10	2	0.4	42	23	43	52	12	0	0	168	242	24	14	3.5	.945	3B-124
1920	2 teams	PHI A (76G –.231) WAS A (3G –.143)																						
″	total	79	.229	.286	262	60	6	3	1	0.4	27	11	26	18	8	1	0	106	181	12	13	4.0	.960	3B-63, SS-12
3 yrs.		247	.225	.293	859	193	19	14	4	0.5	88	45	84	90	24	2	0	328	520	41	31	3.7	.954	3B-228, SS-13
WORLD SERIES																								
1918	BOS A	6	.118	.118	17	2	0	0	0	0.0	0	1	1	2	0	0	0	6	10	0	0	2.7	1.000	3B-6

George Thomas

THOMAS, GEORGE EDWARD BR TR 6′ 3½″ 190 lbs.
B. Nov. 29, 1937, Minneapolis, Minn.

Year	Team	Games	BA	SA	AB	H	2B	3B	HR	HR%	R	RBI	BB	SO	SB	Pinch Hit AB	Pinch Hit H	PO	A	E	DP	TC/G	FA	G by Pos
1957	DET A	1	.000	.000	1	0	0	0	0	0.0	0	0	0	1	0	1	0	0	0	1	0	1.0	.000	3B-1
1958		1	—	—	0	0	0	0	0	—	0	0	0	0	0	0	0	0	0	0	0	0.0	.000	OF-1
1961	2 teams	DET A (17G –.000) LA A (79G –.280)																						
″	total	96	.274	.458	288	79	12	1	13	4.5	41	59	21	70	3	5	0	99	64	13	6	2.0	.926	OF-47, 3B-38, SS-1
1962	LA A	56	.238	.381	181	43	10	2	4	2.2	13	12	21	37	0	5	1	107	4	5	1	2.3	.957	OF-51
1963	2 teams	LA A (53G –.210) DET A (44G –.239)																						
″	total	97	.221	.330	276	61	11	2	5	1.8	27	26	20	54	2	11	0	178	24	7	4	2.2	.967	OF-79, 3B-10, 1B-4, 2B-1
1964	DET A	105	.286	.464	308	88	15	2	12	3.9	39	44	18	53	4	18	6	165	5	2	1	1.9	.988	OF-90, 3B-1
1965		79	.213	.308	169	36	5	1	3	1.8	19	10	12	39	2	17	2	88	4	5	0	1.6	.948	OF-59, 2B-1
1966	BOS A	69	.237	.347	173	41	4	0	5	2.9	25	20	23	33	1	13	3	99	12	0	1	1.9	1.000	OF-48, 3B-6, C-2, 1B-2
1967		65	.213	.270	89	19	2	0	1	1.1	10	6	3	23	0	18	2	57	4	2	0	1.3	.968	OF-43, 1B-3, C-1
1968		12	.200	.500	10	2	0	0	1	10.0	3	1	1	3	1	1	0	9	0	0	0	1.0	1.000	OF-9
1969		29	.353	.451	51	18	3	1	0	0.0	9	8	3	11	0	6	1	85	6	2	9	3.9	.978	OF-12, 1B-10, C-1, 3B-1
1970		38	.343	.485	99	34	8	0	2	2.0	13	13	11	12	0	6	3	40	4	4	1	1.5	.917	OF-26, 3B-6
1971	2 teams	BOS A (9G –.077) MIN A (23G –.267)																						
″	total	32	.209	.233	43	9	1	0	0	0.0	4	3	5	7	0	18	5	7	1	1	0	0.5	.889	OF-16, 3B-1, 1B-1
13 yrs.		680	.255	.389	1688	430	71	9	46	2.7	203	202	138	343	13	119	23	934	128	42	23	1.9	.962	OF-481, 3B-64, 1B-20, C-4, 2B-2, SS-1
WORLD SERIES																								
1967	BOS A	2	.000	.000	2	0	0	0	0	0.0	0	0	0	1	0	1	0	1	0	0	0	1.0	1.000	OF-1

Gorman Thomas

THOMAS, JAMES GORMAN BR TR 6′ 2″ 210 lbs.
B. Dec. 12, 1950, Charleston, S. C.

Year	Team	Games	BA	SA	AB	H	2B	3B	HR	HR%	R	RBI	BB	SO	SB	Pinch Hit AB	Pinch Hit H	PO	A	E	DP	TC/G	FA	G by Pos
1973	MIL A	59	.187	.284	155	29	7	1	2	1.3	16	11	14	61	5	4	1	87	1	4	1	1.7	.957	OF-50, DH-3, 3B-1
1974		17	.261	.478	46	12	4	0	2	4.3	10	11	8	15	4	3	1	26	0	0	0	1.7	1.000	OF-13, DH-2
1975		121	.179	.371	240	43	12	2	10	4.2	34	28	31	84	4	2	1	215	5	9	1	1.9	.961	OF-113, DH-6
1976		99	.198	.361	227	45	9	2	8	3.5	27	36	31	67	2	12	1	211	4	4	0	2.3	.982	OF-94, 3B-1, DH-1
1978		137	.246	.515	452	111	24	1	32	7.1	70	86	73	133	3	0	0	345	5	6	0	2.6	.983	OF-137
1979		156	.244	.539	557	136	29	0	**45**	**8.1**	97	123	98	**175**	1	0	0	435	4	4	0	2.8	.991	OF-152, DH-4
1980		162	.239	.471	628	150	26	3	38	6.1	78	105	58	**170**	8	0	0	455	6	7	1	2.9	.985	OF-160, DH-2
1981		103	.259	.493	363	94	22	0	21	5.8	54	65	50	85	4	0	0	221	8	5	3	2.3	.979	OF-97, DH-6
1982		158	.245	.506	567	139	29	1	**39**	6.9	96	112	84	143	3	1	0	427	11	4	4	2.8	.991	OF-157
1983	2 teams	MIL A (46G –.183) CLE A (106G –.221)																						
″	total	152	.209	.379	535	112	23	1	22	4.1	72	69	80	148	10	0	0	439	7	7	2	3.0	.985	OF-152

Gorman Thomas *continued*

Year	Team	Games	BA	SA	AB	H	2B	3B	HR	HR%	R	RBI	BB	SO	SB	Pinch Hit AB	Pinch Hit H	PO	A	E	DP	TC/G	FA	G by Pos
1984	SEA A	35	.157	.213	108	17	3	0	1	0.9	6	13	28	27	0	0	0	45	2	0	0	1.3	1.000	OF-34, DH-1
1985		135	.215	.450	484	104	16	1	32	6.6	76	87	84	126	3	2	0	0	0	0	0	0.0	.000	DH-133
1986	2 teams	SEA A (57G –.194)	MIL A (44G –.179)																					
″	total	101	.187	.371	315	59	8	1	16	5.1	45	36	58	105	3	12	0	47	3	1	3	0.5	.980	DH-88, 1B-6
13 yrs.		1435	.225	.448	4677	1051	212	13	268	5.7	681	782	697	1339	50	36	4	2953	56	51	15	2.2	.983	OF-1159, DH-246, 1B-6, 3B-2
DIVISIONAL PLAYOFF SERIES																								
1981	MIL A	5	.118	.294	17	2	0	0	1	5.9	2	1	1	9	0	0	0	12	0	0	0	2.4	1.000	OF-3, DH-2
LEAGUE CHAMPIONSHIP SERIES																								
1982	MIL A	5	.067	.267	15	1	0	0	1	6.7	1	3	2	7	0	0	0	13	0	0	0	2.6	1.000	OF-5
WORLD SERIES																								
1982	MIL A	7	.115	.115	26	3	0	0	0	0.0	0	3	2	7	0	0	0	15	0	0	0	2.1	1.000	OF-7

Herb Thomas

THOMAS, HERBERT MARK BR TR 5′ 4½″ 157 lbs.
B. May 26, 1902, Sampson City, Fla. D. Dec. 4, 1991, Starke, Fla.

Year	Team	Games	BA	SA	AB	H	2B	3B	HR	HR%	R	RBI	BB	SO	SB	Pinch Hit AB	Pinch Hit H	PO	A	E	DP	TC/G	FA	G by Pos
1924	BOS N	32	.220	.291	127	28	4	1	1	0.8	12	8	9	8	5	0	0	109	6	2	1	3.7	.983	OF-32
1925		5	.235	.353	17	4	0	1	0	0.0	2	0	2	0	0	0	0	10	16	1	1	5.4	.963	2B-5
1927	2 teams	BOS N (24G –.230)	NY N (13G –.176)																					
″	total	37	.220	.341	91	20	7	2	0	0.0	13	7	4	10	2	8	0	36	44	3	7	3.6	.964	2B-17, OF-3, SS-3
3 yrs.		74	.221	.315	235	52	11	4	1	0.4	27	15	15	18	7	8	0	155	66	6	9	3.8	.974	OF-35, 2B-22, SS-3

Ira Thomas

THOMAS, IRA FELIX BR TR 6′ 2″ 200 lbs.
B. Jan. 22, 1881, Ballston Spa, N. Y. D. Oct. 11, 1958, Philadelphia, Pa.

Year	Team	Games	BA	SA	AB	H	2B	3B	HR	HR%	R	RBI	BB	SO	SB	Pinch Hit AB	Pinch Hit H	PO	A	E	DP	TC/G	FA	G by Pos
1906	NY A	44	.200	.243	115	23	1	2	0	0.0	12	15	8		2	2	0	145	38	12	1	4.6	.938	C-42
1907		80	.192	.269	208	40	5	4	1	0.5	20	24	10		5	16	2	264	92	17	8	5.5	.954	C-66, 1B-2
1908	DET A	40	.307	.317	101	31	1	0	0	0.0	6	8	5		0	11	4	124	15	4	3	4.9	.972	C-29
1909	PHI A	84	.223	.281	256	57	9	3	0	0.0	22	31	18		4	0	0	479	112	9	5	7.1	.985	C-84
1910		60	.278	.361	180	50	8	2	1	0.6	14	19	6		2	0	0	324	86	14	8	7.1	.967	C-60
1911		103	.273	.340	297	81	14	3	0	0.0	33	39	23		4	0	0	499	150	17	12	6.5	.974	C-103
1912		46	.216	.295	139	30	4	2	1	0.7	14	13	8		3	0	0	207	58	8	5	5.9	.971	C-46
1913		21	.283	.396	53	15	4	1	0	0.0	3	6	4	8	0	0	0	88	25	2	1	5.5	.983	C-21
1914		2	.000	.000	3	0	0	0	0	0.0	0	0	0	0	0	1	0	6	1	0	0	7.0	1.000	C-1
1915		1	—	—	0	0	0	0	0	—	0	0	0	0	0	0	0	0	1	0	0	1.0	1.000	C-1
10 yrs.		481	.242	.308	1352	327	46	17	3	0.2	124	155	82	8	20	30	6	2136	578	83	43	6.1	.970	C-453, 1B-2
WORLD SERIES																								
1908	DET A	2	.500	.750	4	2	1	0	0	0.0	0	1	1	0	0	1	1	9	2	0	0	11.0	1.000	C-1
1910	PHI A	4	.250	.250	12	3	0	0	0	0.0	2	1	4	1	0	0	0	27	8	1	1	9.0	.972	C-4
1911		4	.083	.083	12	1	0	0	0	0.0	1	1	1	2	0	0	0	31	5	0	0	9.0	1.000	C-4
3 yrs.		10	.214	.250	28	6	1	0	0	0.0	3	3	6	3	0	1	1	67	15	1	1	9.2	.988	C-9

Kite Thomas

THOMAS, KEITH MARSHALL BR TR 6′ 1½″ 195 lbs.
B. Apr. 27, 1923, Kansas City, Kans. D. Jan. 7, 1995, Rocky Mount, N. C.

Year	Team	Games	BA	SA	AB	H	2B	3B	HR	HR%	R	RBI	BB	SO	SB	Pinch Hit AB	Pinch Hit H	PO	A	E	DP	TC/G	FA	G by Pos
1952	PHI A	75	.250	.474	116	29	6	1	6	5.2	24	18	20	27	0	35	8	44	1	2	0	1.6	.957	OF-29
1953	2 teams	PHI A (24G –.122)	WAS A (38G –.293)																					
″	total	62	.215	.308	107	23	3	2	1	0.9	11	14	14	13	0	30	7	45	1	2	0	2.0	.958	OF-23, C-1
2 yrs.		137	.233	.395	223	52	9	3	7	3.1	35	32	34	40	0	65	15	89	2	4	0	1.8	.958	OF-52, C-1

Lee Thomas

THOMAS, JAMES LEROY BL TL 6′ 2″ 195 lbs.
B. Feb. 5, 1936, Peoria, Ill.

Year	Team	Games	BA	SA	AB	H	2B	3B	HR	HR%	R	RBI	BB	SO	SB	Pinch Hit AB	Pinch Hit H	PO	A	E	DP	TC/G	FA	G by Pos
1961	2 teams	NY A (2G –.500)	LA A (130G –.284)																					
″	total	132	.285	.491	452	129	11	5	24	5.3	77	70	47	74	0	18	5	426	19	11	27	3.8	.976	OF-86, 1B-34
1962	LA A	160	.290	.467	583	169	21	2	26	4.5	88	104	55	74	6	3	0	868	47	18	67	5.7	.981	1B-90, OF-74
1963		149	.220	.316	528	116	12	6	9	1.7	52	55	53	82	6	6	2	1032	85	5	89	7.6	.996	1B-104, OF-43
1964	2 teams	LA A (47G –.273)	BOS A (107G –.257)																					
″	total	154	.262	.398	573	150	27	3	15	2.6	58	66	52	51	3	1	0	252	10	5	2	1.7	.981	OF-154, 1B-2
1965	BOS A	151	.271	.464	521	141	27	4	22	4.2	74	75	72	42	6	9	1	1064	98	19	86	8.0	.984	1B-127, OF-20
1966	2 teams	ATL N (39G –.198)	CHI N (75G –.242)																					
″	total	114	.222	.324	275	61	5	1	7	2.5	26	24	24	30	1	33	9	425	35	5	35	6.4	.989	1B-56, OF-17
1967	CHI N	77	.220	.283	191	42	4	1	2	1.0	16	23	15	22	1	22	4	131	7	2	9	2.6	.986	OF-43, 1B-10
1968	HOU N	90	.194	.229	201	39	4	0	1	0.5	14	11	14	22	2	39	7	80	8	2	3	1.8	.978	OF-48, 1B-2
8 yrs.		1027	.255	.397	3324	847	111	22	106	3.2	405	428	332	397	25	131	28	4278	309	67	318	5.1	.986	OF-485, 1B-425

Leo Thomas

THOMAS, LEO RAYMOND (Tommy) BR TR 5′11½″ 178 lbs.
B. July 26, 1923, Turlock, Calif.

Year	Team	Games	BA	SA	AB	H	2B	3B	HR	HR%	R	RBI	BB	SO	SB	Pinch Hit AB	Pinch Hit H	PO	A	E	DP	TC/G	FA	G by Pos
1950	STL A	35	.198	.273	121	24	6	0	1	0.8	19	9	20	14	0	0	0	35	72	4	7	3.2	.964	3B-35
1952	2 teams	STL A (41G –.234)	CHI A (19G –.167)																					
″	total	60	.223	.270	148	33	5	1	0	0.0	13	18	23	11	2	6	1	53	99	10	11	3.2	.938	3B-46, SS-3, 2B-1
2 yrs.		95	.212	.271	269	57	11	1	1	0.4	32	27	43	25	2	6	1	88	171	14	18	3.2	.949	3B-81, SS-3, 2B-1

Pinch Thomas

THOMAS, CHESTER DAVID BL TR 5′ 9½″ 173 lbs.
B. Jan. 24, 1888, Camp Point, Ill. D. Dec. 24, 1953, Modesto, Calif.

Year	Team	Games	BA	SA	AB	H	2B	3B	HR	HR%	R	RBI	BB	SO	SB	Pinch Hit AB	Pinch Hit H	PO	A	E	DP	TC/G	FA	G by Pos
1912	BOS A	12	.200	.200	30	6	0	0	0	0.0	0	5	2		1	0	0	42	14	2	1	4.8	.966	C-12
1913		37	.286	.374	91	26	1	2	1	1.1	6	15	2	11	1	7	2	135	41	3	2	6.0	.983	C-30
1914		63	.192	.200	130	25	1	0	0	0.0	9	5	18	17	1	1	0	236	47	10	6	4.7	.966	C-61, 1B-1
1915		86	.236	.296	203	48	4	4	0	0.0	21	21	13	20	3	3	2	325	81	13	7	5.1	.969	C-82
1916		99	.264	.333	216	57	10	1	1	0.5	21	21	33	13	4	6	2	321	86	8	7	4.6	.981	C-90
1917		83	.238	.272	202	48	7	0	0	0.0	24	24	27	9	2	6	3	296	69	5	8	4.8	.986	C-77
1918	CLE A	32	.247	.274	73	18	0	1	0	0.0	2	5	6	6	0	8	4	85	24	6	1	4.8	.948	C-24
1919		34	.109	.109	46	5	0	0	0	0.0	2	2	4	3	0	13	0	39	9	1	0	2.3	.980	C-21
1920		9	.333	.444	9	3	1	0	0	0.0	2	0	3	1	0	1	0	14	3	0	0	2.4	1.000	C-7
1921		21	.257	.343	35	9	3	0	0	0.0	1	4	10	2	0	2	0	27	3	4	0	1.8	.882	C-19
10 yrs.		476	.237	.284	1035	245	27	8	2	0.2	88	102	118	82	12	47	13	1520	377	52	32	4.6	.973	C-423, 1B-1

Pinch Thomas *continued*

Year	Team	Games	BA	SA	AB	H	2B	3B	HR	HR%	R	RBI	BB	SO	SB	Pinch Hit AB	Pinch Hit H	PO	A	E	DP	TC/G	FA	G by Pos
WORLD SERIES																								
1915	BOS A	2	.200	.200	5	1	0	0	0	0.0	0	0	0	0	0	0	0	10	3	0	1	6.5	1.000	C-2
1916		3	.143	.429	7	1	0	1	0	0.0	0	0	0	1	0	0	0	10	4	0	0	4.7	1.000	C-3
1920	CLE A	1	—	—	0	0	0	0	0	—	0	0	0	0	0	0	0	1	0	0	0	1.0	1.000	C-1
3 yrs.		6	.167	.333	12	2	0	1	0	0.0	0	0	0	1	0	0	0	21	7	0	1	4.7	1.000	C-6

Ray Thomas

THOMAS, RAYMOND JOSEPH BR TR 5′11″ 175 lbs.
B. July 9, 1910, Dover, N. H. D. Dec. 6, 1993, Wilson, N. C.

Year	Team	Games	BA	SA	AB	H	2B	3B	HR	HR%	R	RBI	BB	SO	SB	Pinch Hit AB	Pinch Hit H	PO	A	E	DP	TC/G	FA	G by Pos
1938	BKN N	1	.333	.333	3	1	0	0	0	0.0	1	0	0	0	0	0	0	5	0	0	0	5.0	1.000	C-1

Red Thomas

THOMAS, ROBERT WILLIAM BR TR 5′11″ 165 lbs.
B. Apr. 25, 1898, Hargrove, Ala. D. Mar. 29, 1962, Fremont, Ohio.

Year	Team	Games	BA	SA	AB	H	2B	3B	HR	HR%	R	RBI	BB	SO	SB	Pinch Hit AB	Pinch Hit H	PO	A	E	DP	TC/G	FA	G by Pos
1921	CHI N	8	.267	.467	30	8	3	0	1	3.3	5	5	4	5	0	0	0	24	1	1	0	3.3	.962	OF-8

Roy Thomas

THOMAS, ROY ALLEN BL TL 5′11″ 150 lbs.
Brother of Bill Thomas.
B. Mar. 24, 1874, Norristown, Pa. D. Nov. 20, 1959, Norristown, Pa.

Year	Team	Games	BA	SA	AB	H	2B	3B	HR	HR%	R	RBI	BB	SO	SB	Pinch Hit AB	Pinch Hit H	PO	A	E	DP	TC/G	FA	G by Pos
1899	PHI N	150	.325	.362	547	178	12	4	0	0.0	137	47	115		42	1	0	454	23	20	14	3.3	.960	OF-135, 1B-14
1900		140	.316	.335	531	168	4	3	0	0.0	**131**	33	**115**		37	1	0	303	19	14	6	2.4	.958	OF-139, P-1
1901		129	.309	.334	479	148	5	2	1	0.2	102	28	**100**		27	0	0	283	9	10	2	2.3	.967	OF-129
1902		138	.286	.322	500	143	4	7	0	0.0	89	24	**107**		17	0	0	277	23	8	3	2.2	.974	OF-138
1903		130	.327	.365	477	156	11	2	1	0.2	88	27	**107**		17	0	0	318	19	13	3	2.7	.963	OF-130
1904		139	.290	.345	496	144	6	6	3	0.6	92	29	**102**		28	0	0	321	21	9	4	2.5	.974	OF-139
1905		147	.317	.358	562	178	11	6	0	0.0	118	31	93		23	0	0	373	27	7	6	2.8	.983	OF-147
1906		142	.254	.302	493	125	10	7	0	0.0	81	16	**107**		22	0	0	340	12	5	5	2.5	.986	OF-142
1907		121	.243	.301	419	102	15	3	1	0.2	70	23	**83**		11	0	0	274	15	6	4	2.4	.980	OF-121
1908	2 teams PHI N (6G –.167) PIT N (102G –.256)																							
"	total	108	.251	.334	410	103	11	10	1	0.2	54	24	51		11	0	0	282	7	7	4	2.8	.976	OF-107
1909	BOS N	83	.263	.302	281	74	9	1	0	0.0	36	11	47		5	5	2	155	9	4	1	2.4	.976	OF-71
1910	PHI N	23	.183	.239	71	13	0	2	0	0.0	7	4	7	5	4	3	0	38	2	2	0	2.1	.952	OF-20
1911		21	.167	.233	30	5	2	0	0	0.0	5	2	8	6	0	7	1	14	3	0	0	1.5	1.000	OF-11
13 yrs.		1471	.290	.333	5296	1537	100	53	7	0.1	1010	299	1042	11	244	17	3	3432	189	105	52	2.6	.972	OF-1429, 1B-14, P-1

Valmy Thomas

THOMAS, VALMY BR TR 5′9″ 165 lbs.
B. Oct. 21, 1928, Santurce, Puerto Rico.

Year	Team	Games	BA	SA	AB	H	2B	3B	HR	HR%	R	RBI	BB	SO	SB	Pinch Hit AB	Pinch Hit H	PO	A	E	DP	TC/G	FA	G by Pos
1957	NY N	88	.249	.390	241	60	10	3	6	2.5	30	31	16	29	0	1	0	396	31	4	8	4.9	.991	C-88
1958	SF N	63	.259	.357	143	37	5	0	3	2.1	14	16	13	24	1	2	0	244	17	2	4	4.3	.992	C-61
1959	PHI N	66	.200	.236	140	28	2	0	1	0.7	5	7	9	19	1	0	0	310	25	7	3	5.2	.980	C-65, 3B-1
1960	BAL A	8	.063	.063	16	1	0	0	0	0.0	0	0	1	0	0	0	0	27	2	0	1	3.6	1.000	C-8
1961	CLE A	27	.209	.314	86	18	3	0	2	2.3	7	6	6	7	0	0	0	151	17	2	6	6.3	.988	C-27
5 yrs.		252	.230	.329	626	144	20	3	12	1.9	56	60	45	79	2	3	0	1128	92	15	22	4.9	.988	C-249, 3B-1

Walt Thomas

THOMAS, WILLIAM WALTER BR TR 5′8″
B. Apr. 28, 1884, Altoona, Pa. D. June 6, 1950, Altoona, Pa.

Year	Team	Games	BA	SA	AB	H	2B	3B	HR	HR%	R	RBI	BB	SO	SB	Pinch Hit AB	Pinch Hit H	PO	A	E	DP	TC/G	FA	G by Pos
1908	BOS N	5	.154	.154	13	2	0	0	0	0.0	2	1	3		2	0	0	7	12	3	1	4.4	.864	SS-5

Art Thomason

THOMASON, ARTHUR WILSON (Sillie) BL TL 5′8″ 150 lbs.
B. Feb. 12, 1889, Liberty, Mo. D. May 2, 1944, Kansas City, Mo.

Year	Team	Games	BA	SA	AB	H	2B	3B	HR	HR%	R	RBI	BB	SO	SB	Pinch Hit AB	Pinch Hit H	PO	A	E	DP	TC/G	FA	G by Pos
1910	CLE A	17	.158	.193	57	9	0	1	0	0.0	3	2	5		3	0	0	26	5	2	1	1.9	.939	OF-17

Gary Thomasson

THOMASSON, GARY LEAH BL TL 6′1″ 180 lbs.
B. July 29, 1951, San Diego, Calif.

Year	Team	Games	BA	SA	AB	H	2B	3B	HR	HR%	R	RBI	BB	SO	SB	Pinch Hit AB	Pinch Hit H	PO	A	E	DP	TC/G	FA	G by Pos
1972	SF N	10	.333	.444	27	9	1	1	0	0.0	5	1	1	7	0	2	1	60	1	0	7	6.8	1.000	1B-7, OF-2
1973		112	.285	.413	235	67	10	4	4	1.7	35	30	22	43	2	18	4	312	15	6	15	3.7	.982	1B-47, OF-43
1974		120	.244	.327	315	77	14	3	2	0.6	41	29	38	56	7	30	6	235	17	7	9	2.8	.973	OF-76, 1B-15
1975		114	.227	.347	326	74	12	3	7	2.1	44	32	37	48	9	17	4	293	18	7	14	3.5	.978	OF-74, 1B-17
1976		103	.259	.424	328	85	20	5	8	2.4	45	38	30	45	8	16	4	436	20	12	28	5.0	.974	OF-54, 1B-39
1977		145	.256	.451	446	114	24	6	17	3.8	63	71	75	102	16	16	5	404	11	14	15	3.0	.967	OF-113, 1B-31
1978	2 teams OAK A (47G –.201) NY A (55G –.276)																							
"	total	102	.233	.367	270	63	8	2	8	3.0	37	36	28	66	4	7	2	212	11	7	1	2.3	.970	OF-94, 1B-5, DH-1
1979	LA N	115	.248	.422	315	78	11	1	14	4.4	39	45	43	70	4	18	2	196	4	4	1	2.0	.980	OF-100, 1B-1
1980		80	.216	.270	111	24	3	0	1	0.9	6	12	17	26	0	45	11	38	1	1	0	1.3	.975	OF-31, 1B-1
9 yrs.		901	.249	.391	2373	591	103	25	61	2.6	315	294	291	463	50	169	39	2186	98	58	90	3.1	.975	OF-587, 1B-163, DH-1
LEAGUE CHAMPIONSHIP SERIES																								
1978	NY A	3	.000	.000	1	0	0	0	0	0.0	0	0	0	0	0	1	0	2	0	0	0	0.7	1.000	OF-3
WORLD SERIES																								
1978	NY A	3	.250	.250	4	1	0	0	0	0.0	0	0	0	1	0	0	0	3	0	0	0	1.0	1.000	OF-3

Jim Thome

THOME, JAMES HOWARD BL TR 6′3″ 190 lbs.
B. Aug. 27, 1970, Peoria, Ill.

Year	Team	Games	BA	SA	AB	H	2B	3B	HR	HR%	R	RBI	BB	SO	SB	Pinch Hit AB	Pinch Hit H	PO	A	E	DP	TC/G	FA	G by Pos
1991	CLE A	27	.255	.367	98	25	4	2	1	1.0	7	9	5	16	1	0	0	12	60	8	6	3.0	.900	3B-27
1992		40	.205	.299	117	24	3	1	2	1.7	8	12	10	34	2	1	0	21	61	11	3	2.3	.882	3B-40
1993		47	.266	.474	154	41	11	0	7	4.5	28	22	29	36	2	2	0	29	86	6	10	2.6	.950	3B-47
1994		98	.268	.523	321	86	20	1	20	6.2	58	52	46	84	3	7	2	62	173	15	12	2.7	.940	3B-94
1995		137	.314	.558	452	142	29	3	25	5.5	92	73	97	113	4	5	0	75	214	16	19	2.3	.948	3B-134, DH-1
5 yrs.		349	.278	.494	1142	318	67	7	55	4.8	193	168	187	283	12	15	2	199	594	56	50	2.5	.934	3B-342, DH-1
DIVISIONAL PLAYOFF SERIES																								
1995	CLE A	3	.154	.385	13	2	0	0	1	7.7	1	3	1	6	0	0	0	6	6	0	1	4.0	1.000	3B-3
LEAGUE CHAMPIONSHIP SERIES																								
1995	CLE A	5	.267	.667	15	4	0	0	2	13.3	2	5	2	3	0	0	0	1	5	1	0	1.4	.857	3B-5
WORLD SERIES																								
1995	CLE A	6	.211	.421	19	4	1	0	1	5.3	1	2	2	5	0	1	1	3	5	1	0	1.5	.889	3B-6

Bobby Thompson

THOMPSON, BOBBY LaRUE
B. Nov. 3, 1953, Charlotte, N. C.

BB TR 5′11″ 175 lbs.

Year	Team	Games	BA	SA	AB	H	2B	3B	HR	HR%	R	RBI	BB	SO	SB	Pinch Hit AB	Pinch Hit H	PO	A	E	DP	TC/G	FA	G by Pos
1978	TEX A	64	.225	.350	120	27	3	3	2	1.7	23	12	9	26	7	0	0	109	1	2	0	2.0	.982	OF-52, DH-3

Danny Thompson

THOMPSON, DANNY LEON
B. Feb. 1, 1947, Wichita, Kans. D. Dec. 10, 1976, Rochester, Minn.

BR TR 6′ 183 lbs.

Year	Team	Games	BA	SA	AB	H	2B	3B	HR	HR%	R	RBI	BB	SO	SB	Pinch Hit AB	Pinch Hit H	PO	A	E	DP	TC/G	FA	G by Pos
1970	MIN A	96	.219	.248	302	66	9	0	0	0.0	25	22	7	39	0	3	1	156	229	6	39	3.2	.985	2B-81, 3B-37, SS-6
1971		48	.263	.298	57	15	2	0	0	0.0	10	7	7	12	0	20	5	13	24	4	2	2.0	.902	3B-17, 2B-3, SS-1
1972		144	.276	.356	573	158	22	6	4	0.7	54	48	34	57	3	0	0	247	468	32	76	5.2	.957	SS-144
1973		99	.225	.282	347	78	13	2	1	0.3	29	36	16	41	1	2	0	131	326	24	50	5.0	.950	SS-95, 3B-1
1974		97	.250	.326	264	66	6	1	4	1.5	25	25	22	29	1	6	0	131	192	13	41	3.6	.961	SS-88, 3B-5, DH-1
1975		112	.270	.355	355	96	11	2	5	1.4	25	37	18	30	0	6	2	147	261	26	41	3.9	.940	SS-100, 3B-7, DH-3, 2B-1
1976	2 teams	MIN A (34G –.234) TEX A (64G –.214)																						
″	total	98	.222	.253	320	71	7	0	1	0.3	21	19	16	27	3	8	2	118	220	6	35	3.5	.983	SS-44, 3B-39, 2B-14, DH-1
7 yrs.		694	.248	.310	2218	550	70	11	15	0.7	189	194	120	235	8	45	10	943	1720	111	284	4.0	.960	SS-478, 3B-106, 2B-99, DH-5
LEAGUE CHAMPIONSHIP SERIES																								
1970	MIN A	3	.125	.250	8	1	1	0	0	0.0	0	0	1	0	0	0	0	2	3	1	1	2.0	.833	2B-3

Don Thompson

THOMPSON, DONALD NEWLIN
B. Dec. 28, 1923, Swepsonville, N. C.

BL TL 6′ 185 lbs.

Year	Team	Games	BA	SA	AB	H	2B	3B	HR	HR%	R	RBI	BB	SO	SB	Pinch Hit AB	Pinch Hit H	PO	A	E	DP	TC/G	FA	G by Pos
1949	BOS N	7	.182	.182	11	2	0	0	0	0.0	0	0	0	2	0	5	0	4	0	1	0	2.5	.800	OF-2
1951	BKN N	80	.229	.254	118	27	3	0	0	0.0	25	6	12	12	2	11	3	75	3	1	1	1.3	.987	OF-61
1953		96	.242	.294	153	37	5	0	1	0.7	25	12	14	13	2	13	0	84	5	1	1	1.1	.989	OF-81
1954		34	.040	.040	25	1	0	0	0	0.0	2	1	5	5	0	5	0	14	1	0	0	0.5	1.000	OF-29
4 yrs.		217	.218	.254	307	67	8	0	1	0.3	52	19	31	32	4	34	3	177	9	3	2	1.1	.984	OF-173
WORLD SERIES																								
1953	BKN N	2	—	—	0	0	0	0	0	—	0	0	0	0	0	0	0	0	1	0	0	0.5	1.000	OF-2

Frank Thompson

THOMPSON, FRANK E.
B. July 2, 1895, Springfield, Mo. D. June 27, 1940, Jasper County, Mo.

BR TR 5′ 8″ 155 lbs.

Year	Team	Games	BA	SA	AB	H	2B	3B	HR	HR%	R	RBI	BB	SO	SB	Pinch Hit AB	Pinch Hit H	PO	A	E	DP	TC/G	FA	G by Pos
1920	STL A	22	.170	.170	53	9	0	0	0	0.0	7	5	13	10	1	2	0	17	27	8	2	3.3	.846	3B-14, 2B-2

Fresco Thompson

THOMPSON, LAFAYETTE FRESCO (Tommy)
B. June 6, 1902, Centreville, Ala. D. Nov. 20, 1968, Fullerton, Calif.

BR TR 5′ 8″ 150 lbs.

Year	Team	Games	BA	SA	AB	H	2B	3B	HR	HR%	R	RBI	BB	SO	SB	Pinch Hit AB	Pinch Hit H	PO	A	E	DP	TC/G	FA	G by Pos
1925	PIT N	14	.243	.351	37	9	2	1	0	0.0	4	8	4	1	2	2	0	19	24	1	6	3.7	.977	2B-12
1926	NY N	2	.625	.625	8	5	0	0	0	0.0	1	1	2	0	1	0	0	2	8	0	0	5.0	1.000	2B-2
1927	PHI N	153	.303	.409	597	181	32	14	1	0.2	78	70	34	36	19	0	0	424	485	35	97	6.2	.963	2B-153
1928		152	.287	.390	634	182	34	11	3	0.5	99	50	42	27	19	0	0	409	509	32	109	6.3	.966	2B-152
1929		148	.324	.419	623	202	41	3	4	0.6	115	53	75	34	16	0	0	395	512	33	103	6.4	.965	2B-148
1930		122	.282	.395	478	135	34	4	4	0.8	77	46	35	29	7	8	3	287	386	32	95	6.3	.955	2B-112
1931	BKN N	74	.265	.326	181	48	6	1	1	0.6	26	21	23	16	5	4	1	102	135	13	40	3.2	.948	2B-63, SS-10, 3B-5
1932		3	.000	.000	1	0	0	0	0	0.0	0	0	0	0	0	1	0	0	0	0	0	0.0	—	
1934	NY N	1	.000	.000	1	0	0	0	0	0.0	0	0	0	0	0	1	0	0	0	0	0	0.0	—	
9 yrs.		669	.298	.398	2560	762	149	34	13	0.5	400	249	215	143	69	16	4	1638	2059	146	450	5.8	.962	2B-642, SS-10, 3B-5

Hank Thompson

THOMPSON, HENRY CURTIS
B. Dec. 8, 1925, Oklahoma City, Okla. D. Sept. 30, 1969, Fresno, Calif.

BL TR 5′ 9″ 174 lbs.

Year	Team	Games	BA	SA	AB	H	2B	3B	HR	HR%	R	RBI	BB	SO	SB	Pinch Hit AB	Pinch Hit H	PO	A	E	DP	TC/G	FA	G by Pos
1947	STL A	27	.256	.295	78	20	1	1	0	0.0	10	5	10	7	2	8	3	55	55	5	15	6.1	.957	2B-19
1949	NY N	75	.280	.444	275	77	10	4	9	3.3	51	34	42	30	5	4	1	198	180	15	44	5.6	.962	2B-69, 3B-1
1950		148	.289	.463	512	148	17	6	20	3.9	82	91	83	60	8	1	0	154	305	26	44	3.3	.946	3B-138, OF-10
1951		87	.235	.386	264	62	8	4	8	3.0	37	33	43	23	1	14	1	64	120	15	16	2.8	.925	3B-71
1952		128	.260	.454	423	110	13	9	17	4.0	67	67	50	38	4	9	3	236	108	16	11	3.0	.956	OF-72, 3B-46, 2B-4
1953		114	.302	.567	388	117	15	8	24	6.2	80	74	60	39	6	4	1	99	195	13	18	2.8	.958	3B-101, OF-9, 2B-1
1954		136	.263	.482	448	118	18	1	26	5.8	76	86	90	58	3	5	0	126	269	23	27	3.1	.945	3B-130, 2B-2, OF-1
1955		135	.245	.398	432	106	13	1	17	3.9	65	63	84	56	2	9	1	115	276	23	25	3.1	.944	3B-124, 2B-7, SS-1
1956		83	.235	.415	183	43	9	0	8	4.4	24	29	31	26	2	24	8	36	95	14	7	2.6	.903	3B-44, OF-10, SS-1
9 yrs.		933	.267	.453	3003	801	104	34	129	4.3	492	482	493	337	33	78	18	1083	1603	150	207	3.3	.947	3B-655, OF-102, 2B-102, SS-2
WORLD SERIES																								
1951	NY N	5	.143	.143	14	2	0	0	0	0.0	2	0	5	2	0	0	0	5	0	2	0	1.4	.714	OF-5
1954		4	.364	.455	11	4	1	0	0	0.0	6	2	7	1	0	0	0	5	11	0	1	4.0	1.000	3B-4
2 yrs.		9	.240	.280	25	6	1	0	0	0.0	8	2	12	3	0	0	0	10	11	2	1	2.6	.913	OF-5, 3B-4

Homer Thompson

THOMPSON, HOMER THOMAS
Brother of Tommy Thompson.
B. June 1, 1891, Spring City, Tenn. D. Sept. 12, 1957, Atlanta, Ga.

BR TR 5′ 9″ 160 lbs.

Year	Team	Games	BA	SA	AB	H	2B	3B	HR	HR%	R	RBI	BB	SO	SB	Pinch Hit AB	Pinch Hit H	PO	A	E	DP	TC/G	FA	G by Pos
1912	NY A	1	—	—	0	0	0	0	0	—	0	0	0		0	0	0	1	0	1	0	2.0	.500	C-1

Jason Thompson

THOMPSON, JASON DOLPH
B. July 6, 1954, Hollywood, Calif.

BL TL 6′ 4″ 200 lbs.

Year	Team	Games	BA	SA	AB	H	2B	3B	HR	HR%	R	RBI	BB	SO	SB	Pinch Hit AB	Pinch Hit H	PO	A	E	DP	TC/G	FA	G by Pos
1976	DET A	123	.218	.376	412	90	12	1	17	4.1	45	54	68	72	2	3	0	1157	88	8	104	10.7	.994	1B-117
1977		158	.270	.487	585	158	24	5	31	5.3	87	105	73	91	0	0	0	1599	97	16	135	10.8	.991	1B-158
1978		153	.287	.472	589	169	25	3	26	4.4	79	96	74	96	0	1	0	1503	92	11	153	10.6	.993	1B-151
1979		145	.246	.404	492	121	16	1	20	4.1	58	79	70	90	2	8	2	1176	91	8	135	9.0	.994	1B-140, DH-2
1980	2 teams	DET A (36G –.214) CAL A (102G –.317)																						
″	total	138	.288	.475	438	126	19	0	21	4.8	69	90	83	86	2	14	4	679	51	0	66	5.7	1.000	1B-83, DH-45
1981	PIT N	86	.242	.502	223	54	13	0	15	6.7	36	42	59	49	0	13	4	590	46	7	65	8.2	.989	1B-78
1982		156	.284	.511	550	156	32	0	31	5.6	87	101	101	107	1	0	0	1395	105	10	114	9.7	.993	1B-155
1983		152	.259	.406	517	134	20	1	18	3.5	70	76	99	128	1	2	0	1266	89	9	131	9.0	.993	1B-151
1984		154	.254	.389	543	138	22	0	17	3.1	61	74	87	73	0	3	1	1337	74	14	111	9.4	.990	1B-152
1985		123	.241	.378	402	97	17	1	12	3.0	42	61	84	58	0	6	1	995	82	9	69	9.5	.992	1B-114
1986	MON N	30	.196	.275	51	10	4	0	0	0.0	6	4	18	12	0	12	1	121	4	5	7	8.7	.962	1B-15
11 yrs.		1418	.261	.438	4802	1253	204	12	208	4.3	640	782	816	862	8	62	13	11818	819	97	1090	9.4	.992	1B-1314, DH-47

Milt Thompson

THOMPSON, MILTON BERNARD
B. Jan. 5, 1959, Washington, D. C.
BL TR 5′11″ 170 lbs.

Year	Team	Games	BA	SA	AB	H	2B	3B	HR	HR%	R	RBI	BB	SO	SB	Pinch Hit AB	Pinch Hit H	PO	A	E	DP	TC/G	FA	G by Pos
1984	ATL N	25	.303	.374	99	30	1	0	2	2.0	16	4	11	11	14	2	2	37	6	2	1	1.8	.956	OF-25
1985		73	.302	.363	182	55	7	2	0	0.0	17	6	7	36	9	30	13	78	2	3	0	1.7	.964	OF-49
1986	PHI N	96	.251	.341	299	75	7	1	6	2.0	38	23	26	62	19	10	1	212	1	2	1	2.4	.991	OF-89
1987		150	.302	.425	527	159	26	9	7	1.3	86	43	42	87	46	15	5	354	4	4	1	2.5	.989	OF-146
1988		122	.288	.357	378	109	16	2	2	0.5	53	33	39	59	17	16	4	278	5	5	1	2.6	.983	OF-112
1989	STL N	155	.290	.393	545	158	28	8	4	0.7	60	68	39	91	27	10	1	348	5	8	1	2.5	.978	OF-147
1990		135	.218	.328	418	91	14	7	6	1.4	42	30	39	60	25	21	4	232	4	7	0	2.1	.971	OF-116
1991		115	.307	.442	326	100	16	5	6	1.8	55	34	32	53	16	28	10	207	8	2	1	2.4	.991	OF-91
1992		109	.293	.404	208	61	9	1	4	1.9	31	17	16	39	18	58	16	74	1	2	1	1.7	.974	OF-45
1993	PHI N	129	.262	.350	340	89	14	2	4	1.2	42	44	40	57	9	25	8	162	6	1	1	1.6	.994	OF-106
1994	2 teams	PHI N (87G –.273)			HOU N (9G –.286)													126	2	0	1	1.5	1.000	OF-85
"	total	96	.274	.353	241	66	7	0	4	1.7	34	33	24	30	9	13	2	45	2	1	1	1.4	.979	OF-34
1995	HOU N	92	.220	.333	132	29	9	0	2	1.5	14	19	14	37	4	54	13							
12 yrs.		1297	.277	.376	3695	1022	154	37	47	1.3	488	354	329	622	213	282	79	2153	46	37	10	2.1	.983	OF-1045
LEAGUE CHAMPIONSHIP SERIES																								
1993	PHI N	6	.231	.308	13	3	1	0	0	0.0	2	0	1	2	0	1	0	8	0	1	0	1.8	.889	OF-5
WORLD SERIES																								
1993	PHI N	6	.313	.688	16	5	1	1	1	6.3	3	6	1	2	0	0	0	10	0	1	0	1.8	.909	OF-6

Robby Thompson

THOMPSON, ROBERT RANDALL
B. May 10, 1962, West Palm Beach, Fla.
BR TR 5′11″ 165 lbs.

Year	Team	Games	BA	SA	AB	H	2B	3B	HR	HR%	R	RBI	BB	SO	SB	Pinch Hit AB	Pinch Hit H	PO	A	E	DP	TC/G	FA	G by Pos
1986	SF N	149	.271	.370	549	149	27	3	7	1.3	73	47	42	112	12	1	0	255	451	17	97	4.8	.976	2B-149, SS-1
1987		132	.262	.419	420	110	26	5	10	2.4	62	44	40	91	16	4	2	246	341	17	99	4.8	.972	2B-126
1988		138	.264	.384	477	126	24	6	7	1.5	66	48	40	111	14	5	1	255	365	14	88	4.7	.978	2B-134
1989		148	.241	.400	547	132	26	**11**	13	2.4	91	50	51	133	12	0	0	307	425	8	88	5.0	.989	2B-148
1990		144	.245	.392	498	122	22	3	15	3.0	67	56	34	96	14	3	1	287	441	8	94	5.2	.989	2B-142
1991		144	.262	.447	492	129	24	5	19	3.9	74	48	63	95	14	0	0	320	402	11	98	5.1	.985	2B-144
1992		128	.260	.415	443	115	25	1	14	3.2	54	49	43	75	5	8	1	296	382	15	101	5.8	.978	2B-120
1993		128	.312	.496	494	154	30	2	19	3.8	85	65	45	97	10	2	1	273	384	8	95	5.2	.988	2B-128
1994		35	.209	.349	129	27	8	2	2	1.6	13	7	15	32	3	0	0	67	121	2	24	5.4	.989	2B-35
1995		95	.223	.339	336	75	15	0	8	2.4	51	23	42	76	1	4	1	181	238	3	49	4.6	.993	2B-91
10 yrs.		1241	.260	.407	4385	1139	227	38	114	2.6	636	437	415	918	101	27	7	2487	3550	103	833	5.0	.983	2B-1217, SS-1
LEAGUE CHAMPIONSHIP SERIES																								
1987	SF N	7	.100	.350	20	2	0	1	1	5.0	4	2	5	7	2	1	0	11	19	1	6	5.2	.968	2B-6
1989		5	.278	.611	18	5	0	0	2	11.1	5	3	3	2	0	0	0	10	13	0	4	4.6	1.000	2B-5
2 yrs.		12	.184	.474	38	7	0	1	3	7.9	9	5	8	9	2	1	0	21	32	1	10	4.9	.981	2B-11
WORLD SERIES																								
1989	SF N	4	.091	.091	11	1	0	0	0	0.0	0	2	0	4	0	1	1	4	10	0	2	3.5	1.000	2B-4

Ryan Thompson

THOMPSON, RYAN ORLANDO
B. Nov. 4, 1967, Chestertown, Md.
BR TR 6′ 3″ 200 lbs.

Year	Team	Games	BA	SA	AB	H	2B	3B	HR	HR%	R	RBI	BB	SO	SB	Pinch Hit AB	Pinch Hit H	PO	A	E	DP	TC/G	FA	G by Pos
1992	NY N	30	.222	.389	108	24	7	1	3	2.8	15	10	8	24	2	1	0	77	2	1	0	2.8	.988	OF-29
1993		80	.250	.444	288	72	19	2	11	3.8	34	26	19	81	2	1	1	228	4	3	0	3.1	.987	OF-76
1994		98	.225	.434	334	75	14	1	18	5.4	39	59	28	94	1	0	0	274	5	3	1	2.9	.989	OF-98
1995		75	.251	.378	267	67	13	0	7	2.6	39	31	19	77	3	1	1	193	4	3	3	2.7	.985	OF-74
4 yrs.		283	.239	.417	997	238	53	4	39	3.9	127	126	74	276	8	3	2	772	15	10	4	2.9	.987	OF-277

Sam Thompson

THOMPSON, SAMUEL LUTHER (Big Sam)
B. Mar. 5, 1860, Danville, Ind. D. Nov. 7, 1922, Detroit, Mich.
Hall of Fame 1974.
BL TL 6′ 2″ 207 lbs.

Year	Team	Games	BA	SA	AB	H	2B	3B	HR	HR%	R	RBI	BB	SO	SB	Pinch Hit AB	Pinch Hit H	PO	A	E	DP	TC/G	FA	G by Pos
1885	DET N	63	.303	.500	254	77	11	9	7	2.8	58	44	16	22		0	0	86	24	14	0	2.0	.887	OF-62, 3B-1
1886		122	.310	.445	503	156	18	13	8	1.6	101	89	35	31		0	0	194	29	13	11	1.9	.945	OF-122
1887		127	**.372**	**.571**	**545**	**203**	29	**23**	11	2.0	118	**166**	32	19	22	0	0	217	24	24	7	2.1	.909	OF-127
1888		56	.282	.466	238	67	10	8	6	2.5	51	40	23	10	5	0	0	86	4	12	0	1.8	.882	OF-56
1889	PHI N	128	.296	.492	533	158	36	4	**20**	**3.8**	103	111	36	22	24	0	0	173	19	21	7	1.7	.901	OF-128
1890		132	.313	.443	549	**172**	**41**	9	4	0.7	116	102	42	29	25	0	0	170	29	13	5	1.6	.939	OF-132
1891		133	.294	.415	554	163	23	10	8	1.4	108	90	52	20	29	0	0	234	32	18	6	2.1	.937	OF-133
1892		153	.305	.432	609	186	28	11	9	1.5	109	104	59	19	28	0	0	223	28	17	7	1.8	.937	OF-153
1893		131	.370	.530	**600**	**222**	**37**	13	11	1.8	130	126	50	17	18	0	0	178	17	15	3	1.6	.929	OF-131, 1B-1
1894		102	.407	.686	437	178	29	27	13	3.0	108	141	40	13	24	0	0	159	12	4	2	1.7	.977	OF-102
1895		119	.392	**.654**	538	211	45	21	**18**	3.3	131	**165**	31	11	27	1	1	186	31	13	2	1.9	.943	OF-118
1896		119	.298	.449	517	154	28	7	12	2.3	103	100	28	13	12	0	0	231	28	7	11	2.2	.974	OF-119
1897		3	.231	.385	13	3	0	1	0	0.0	2	3	1		0	0	0	4	1	1	0	2.0	.833	OF-3
1898		14	.349	.571	63	22	5	3	1	1.6	14	15	4		2	0	0	19	5	0	0	1.7	1.000	OF-14
1906	DET A	8	.226	.290	31	7	0	1	0	0.0	4	3	1		0	0	0	14	0	0	0	1.8	1.000	OF-8
15 yrs.		1410	.331	.505	5984	1979	340	160	128	2.1	1256	1299	450	226	216	1	1	2174	283	172	61	1.9	.935	OF-1408, 1B-1, 3B-1

Scot Thompson

THOMPSON, VERNON SCOT
B. Dec. 7, 1955, Grove City, Pa.
BL TL 6′ 3″ 195 lbs.

Year	Team	Games	BA	SA	AB	H	2B	3B	HR	HR%	R	RBI	BB	SO	SB	Pinch Hit AB	Pinch Hit H	PO	A	E	DP	TC/G	FA	G by Pos
1978	CHI N	19	.417	.500	36	15	3	0	0	0.0	7	2	2	4	0	12	6	14	1	0	1	2.1	1.000	OF-5, 1B-2
1979		128	.289	.373	346	100	13	5	2	0.6	36	29	17	37	4	33	12	161	7	5	3	1.7	.971	OF-100
1980		102	.212	.292	226	48	10	1	2	0.9	26	13	28	31	6	21	6	149	6	4	8	2.0	.975	OF-66, 1B-12
1981		57	.165	.209	115	19	5	0	0	0.0	8	8	7	8	2	22	2	56	1	2	0	1.8	.966	OF-30, 1B-3
1982		49	.365	.459	74	27	5	1	0	0.0	11	7	5	4	0	27	7	39	3	0	1	1.6	1.000	OF-23, 1B-4
1983		53	.193	.250	88	17	3	1	0	0.0	4	10	3	14	0	28	6	29	0	0	0	1.0	1.000	OF-29, 1B-1
1984	SF N	120	.306	.355	245	75	7	1	1	0.4	30	31	30	26	5	31	5	562	36	2	48	6.5	.997	1B-87, OF-6
1985	2 teams	SF N (64G –.207)			MON N (34G –.281)													180	18	1	14	6.6	.995	1B-27, OF-3
"	total	98	.224	.266	143	32	6	0	0	0.0	10	10	5	17	0	**62**	9							
8 yrs.		626	.262	.328	1273	333	52	9	5	0.4	132	110	97	141	17	236	53	1190	72	14	75	3.2	.989	OF-262, 1B-136

Shag Thompson

THOMPSON, JAMES ALFRED BL TR 5′ 8½″ 165 lbs.
B. Apr. 29, 1893, Haw River, N. C. D. Jan. 7, 1990, Black Mountain, N. C.

Year	Team	Games	BA	SA	AB	H	2B	3B	HR	HR%	R	RBI	BB	SO	SB	Pinch Hit AB	Pinch Hit H	PO	A	E	DP	TC/G	FA	G by Pos
1914	PHI A	16	.172	.241	29	5	0	1	0	0.0	3	2	7	8	1	5	1	13	3	1	1	2.1	.941	OF-8
1915		17	.333	.394	33	11	2	0	0	0.0	5	2	4	6	0	7	2	11	2	0	1	1.9	1.000	OF-7
1916		15	.000	.000	17	0	0	0	0	0.0	4	0	7	6	1	3	0	16	0	0	0	2.3	1.000	OF-7
3 yrs.		48	.203	.253	79	16	2	1	0	0.0	12	4	18	20	2	15	3	40	5	1	2	2.1	.978	OF-22

Tim Thompson

THOMPSON, CHARLES LEMOINE BL TR 5′11″ 190 lbs.
B. Mar. 1, 1924, Coalport, Pa.

Year	Team	Games	BA	SA	AB	H	2B	3B	HR	HR%	R	RBI	BB	SO	SB	Pinch Hit AB	Pinch Hit H	PO	A	E	DP	TC/G	FA	G by Pos
1954	BKN N	10	.154	.231	13	2	1	0	0	0.0	2	1	1	1	0	5	1	10	0	1	0	3.7	.909	C-2, OF-1
1956	KC A	92	.272	.347	268	73	13	2	1	0.4	21	27	17	23	2	23	4	328	38	7	7	5.5	.981	C-68
1957		81	.204	.339	230	47	10	0	7	3.0	25	19	18	26	0	19	1	272	29	2	7	4.9	.993	C-62
1958	DET A	4	.167	.167	6	1	0	0	0	0.0	1	0	3	2	0	1	0	8	1	0	0	2.3	1.000	C-4
4 yrs.		187	.238	.338	517	123	24	2	8	1.5	49	47	39	52	2	48	6	618	68	10	14	5.1	.986	C-136, OF-1

Tommy Thompson

THOMPSON, RUPERT LOCKHART BL TR 5′ 9½″ 155 lbs.
B. May 19, 1910, Elkhart, Ill. D. May 24, 1971, Auburn, Calif.

Year	Team	Games	BA	SA	AB	H	2B	3B	HR	HR%	R	RBI	BB	SO	SB	Pinch Hit AB	Pinch Hit H	PO	A	E	DP	TC/G	FA	G by Pos
1933	BOS N	24	.186	.196	97	18	1	0	0	0.0	6	6	4	6	0	0	0	64	3	0	0	2.8	1.000	OF-24
1934		105	.265	.318	343	91	12	3	0	0.0	40	37	13	19	2	23	8	205	12	8	3	2.7	.964	OF-82
1935		112	.273	.343	297	81	7	1	4	1.3	34	30	36	17	2	24	3	184	9	7	3	2.4	.965	OF-85
1936		106	.286	.365	266	76	9	0	4	1.5	37	36	31	12	3	37	10	359	20	5	19	6.0	.987	OF-39, 1B-25
1938	CHI A	19	.111	.111	18	2	0	0	0	0.0	2	2	1	2	0	17	2	2	0	0	1	2.0	1.000	1B-1
1939	2 teams	CHI A (1G –.000) STL A (30G –.302)																						
″	total	31	.302	.395	86	26	5	0	1	1.2	23	8	23	7	0	5	1	40	3	1	0	1.9	.977	OF-23
6 yrs.		397	.266	.328	1107	294	34	4	9	0.8	142	119	108	63	7	106	24	854	47	21	26	3.3	.977	OF-253, 1B-26

Tug Thompson

THOMPSON, JOHN P. TR 5′ 8″ 160 lbs.
B. 1865, London, Ont., Canada.

Year	Team	Games	BA	SA	AB	H	2B	3B	HR	HR%	R	RBI	BB	SO	SB	Pinch Hit AB	Pinch Hit H	PO	A	E	DP	TC/G	FA	G by Pos
1882	CIN AA	1	.200	.200	5	1	0	0	0	0.0	0		0			0	0	0	0	1	0	1.0	.000	OF-1
1884	IND AA	24	.206	.237	97	20	3	0	0	0.0	10		2			0	0	65	16	24	0	4.4	.771	OF-12, C-12
2 yrs.		25	.206	.235	102	21	3	0	0	0.0	10		2			0	0	65	16	25	0	4.2	.764	OF-13, C-12

Bobby Thomson

THOMSON, ROBERT BROWN (The Staten Island Scot) BR TR 6′ 2″ 180 lbs.
B. Oct. 25, 1923, Glasgow, Scotland.

Year	Team	Games	BA	SA	AB	H	2B	3B	HR	HR%	R	RBI	BB	SO	SB	Pinch Hit AB	Pinch Hit H	PO	A	E	DP	TC/G	FA	G by Pos
1946	NY N	18	.315	.537	54	17	4	1	2	3.7	8	9	4	5	0	2	0	18	25	3	0	2.9	.935	3B-16
1947		138	.283	.508	545	154	26	5	29	5.3	105	85	40	78	1	3	0	357	32	12	6	2.9	.970	OF-127, 2B-9
1948		138	.248	.401	471	117	20	2	16	3.4	75	63	30	77	2	9	3	313	10	10	2	2.7	.970	OF-125
1949		156	.309	.518	641	198	35	9	27	4.2	99	109	44	45	10	0	0	488	10	9	4	3.3	.982	OF-156
1950		149	.252	.449	563	142	22	7	25	4.4	79	85	55	45	3	0	0	394	15	9	5	2.8	.978	OF-149
1951		148	.293	.562	518	152	27	8	32	6.2	89	101	73	57	5	2	0	258	139	20	14	2.9	.952	OF-77, 3B-69
1952		153	.270	.482	608	164	29	**14**	24	3.9	89	108	52	74	5	0	0	234	187	18	13	2.9	.959	3B-91, OF-63
1953		154	.288	.472	608	175	22	6	26	4.3	80	106	43	57	4	0	0	391	16	7	0	2.7	.983	OF-154
1954	MIL N	43	.232	.323	99	23	3	0	2	2.0	7	15	12	29	0	14	5	45	3	1	2	1.9	.980	OF-26
1955		101	.257	.414	343	88	12	3	12	3.5	40	56	34	52	2	13	2	182	5	6	0	2.1	.969	OF-91
1956		142	.235	.408	451	106	10	4	20	4.4	59	74	43	75	2	5	0	262	17	10	0	2.1	.965	OF-136, 3B-3
1957	2 teams	MIL N (41G –.236) NY N (81G –.242)																						
″	total	122	.240	.410	363	87	12	7	12	3.3	39	61	27	66	3	13	2	202	7	2	0	1.9	.991	OF-109, 3B-1
1958	CHI N	152	.283	.466	547	155	27	5	21	3.8	67	82	56	76	0	1	1	358	16	5	4	2.5	.987	OF-148, 3B-4
1959		122	.259	.398	374	97	15	2	11	2.9	55	52	35	50	1	9	4	223	9	3	4	2.0	.987	OF-116
1960	2 teams	BOS A (40G –.263) BAL A (3G –.000)																						
″	total	43	.250	.417	120	30	3	1	5	4.2	12	20	11	18	0	13	3	75	1	4	3	2.7	.950	OF-29, 1B-1
15 yrs.		1779	.270	.462	6305	1705	267	74	264	4.2	903	1026	559	804	38	84	20	3800	492	119	57	2.6	.973	OF-1506, 3B-184, 2B-9, 1B-1
WORLD SERIES																								
1951	NY N	6	.238	.286	21	5	1	0	0	0.0	1	2	5	0	0	0	0	12	15	2	0	4.8	.931	3B-6

Dickie Thon

THON, RICHARD WILLIAM BR TR 5′11″ 160 lbs.
B. June 20, 1958, South Bend, Ind.

Year	Team	Games	BA	SA	AB	H	2B	3B	HR	HR%	R	RBI	BB	SO	SB	Pinch Hit AB	Pinch Hit H	PO	A	E	DP	TC/G	FA	G by Pos
1979	CAL A	35	.339	.393	56	19	3	0	0	0.0	6	8	5	10	0	0	0	38	46	8	13	2.7	.913	2B-24, SS-8, DH-1, 3B-1
1980		80	.255	.315	267	68	12	2	0	0.0	32	15	10	28	7	13	2	70	128	10	28	3.0	.952	SS-22, 2B-21, DH-15, 3B-10, 1B-1
1981	HOU N	49	.274	.337	95	26	6	0	0	0.0	13	3	9	13	6	2	0	53	63	6	13	2.7	.951	2B-28, SS-13, 3B-5
1982		136	.276	.397	496	137	31	**10**	3	0.6	73	36	37	48	37	9	4	183	412	17	82	4.8	.972	SS-119, 3B-8, 2B-1
1983		154	.286	.457	619	177	28	9	20	3.2	81	79	54	73	34	0	0	258	533	28	114	5.3	.966	SS-154
1984		5	.353	.471	17	6	0	1	0	0.0	3	1	0	4	0	0	0	8	13	0	1	4.2	1.000	SS-5
1985		84	.251	.355	251	63	6	1	6	2.4	26	29	18	50	8	6	1	106	218	11	48	4.2	.967	SS-79
1986		106	.248	.335	278	69	13	1	3	1.1	24	21	29	49	6	20	5	142	210	10	39	3.5	.972	SS-104
1987		32	.212	.273	66	14	1	0	1	1.5	6	3	16	13	3	9	3	21	53	6	7	2.6	.925	SS-31
1988	SD N	95	.264	.337	258	68	12	2	1	0.4	36	18	33	49	19	19	3	84	171	12	29	3.7	.955	SS-70, 2B-2, 3B-1
1989	PHI N	136	.271	.434	435	118	18	4	15	3.4	45	60	33	81	6	7	3	174	380	16	65	4.4	.972	SS-129
1990		149	.255	.350	552	141	20	4	8	1.4	54	48	37	77	12	6	1	222	439	25	86	4.6	.964	SS-148
1991		146	.252	.351	539	136	18	4	9	1.7	44	44	25	84	11	1	0	234	412	21	65	4.6	.969	SS-146
1992	TEX A	95	.247	.367	275	68	15	3	4	1.5	30	37	20	40	12	8	3	117	225	15	38	4.1	.958	SS-87
1993	MIL A	85	.269	.331	245	66	10	1	1	0.4	23	33	22	39	6	16	4	80	119	7	19	2.3	.966	SS-28, 3B-25, 2B-22, DH-14
15 yrs.		1387	.264	.374	4449	1176	193	42	71	1.6	496	435	348	658	167	116	29	1790	3422	192	647	4.1	.964	SS-1143, 2B-98, 3B-50, DH-30, 1B-1
DIVISIONAL PLAYOFF SERIES																								
1981	HOU N	4	.182	.182	11	2	0	0	0	0.0	0	0	1	0	0	1	0	5	10	1	0	4.0	.938	SS-4
LEAGUE CHAMPIONSHIP SERIES																								
1979	CAL A	1	—	—	0	0	0	0	0	—	1	0	0	0	0	0	0	0	0	0	0	0.0	.000	SS-1
1986	HOU N	6	.250	.500	12	3	0	0	1	8.3	1	1	0	1	0	1	0	6	9	0	2	2.5	1.000	SS-6
2 yrs.		7	.250	.500	12	3	0	0	1	8.3	2	1	0	1	0	1	0	6	9	0	2	2.1	1.000	SS-7

Jack Thoney

THONEY, JOHN (Bullet Jack)
Born John Thoeny.
B. Dec. 8, 1879, Ft. Thomas, Ky. D. Oct. 24, 1948, Covington, Ky.
BR TR 5′10″ 175 lbs.

Year	Team	Games	BA	SA	AB	H	2B	3B	HR	HR%	R	RBI	BB	SO	SB	Pinch Hit AB	Pinch Hit H	PO	A	E	DP	TC/G	FA	G by Pos
1902	2 teams	CLE A (28G –.286) BAL A (3G –.000)																						
″	total	31	.259	.336	116	30	7	1	0	0.0	15	11	10		5	1	0	51	57	20	4	4.3	.844	2B-14, SS-11, 3B-3, OF-2
1903	CLE A	32	.205	.254	122	25	3	0	1	0.8	10	9	2		7	2	0	65	13	11	3	2.9	.876	OF-24, 2B-5, 3B-2
1904	2 teams	WAS A (17G –.300) NY A (36G –.188)																						
″	total	53	.227	.283	198	45	7	2	0	0.0	23	18	9		11	1	0	87	46	23	4	2.9	.853	OF-27, 3B-26
1908	BOS A	109	.255	.325	416	106	5	9	2	0.5	58	30	13		16	8	3	208	12	12	2	2.3	.948	OF-101
1909		13	.125	.150	40	5	1	0	0	0.0	1	3	2		2	3	0	23	1	1	1	2.5	.960	OF-10
1911		26	.250	.250	20	5	0	0	0	0.0	5	2	0		1	20	5	0	0	0	0	0.0	—	
6 yrs.		264	.237	.298	912	216	23	12	3	0.3	112	73	36		42	35	8	434	129	67	14	2.8	.894	OF-164, 3B-31, 2B-19, SS-11

Andre Thornton

THORNTON, ANDRE
B. Aug. 13, 1949, Tuskegee, Ala.
BR TR 6′ 3″ 200 lbs.

Year	Team	Games	BA	SA	AB	H	2B	3B	HR	HR%	R	RBI	BB	SO	SB	Pinch Hit AB	Pinch Hit H	PO	A	E	DP	TC/G	FA	G by Pos
1973	CHI N	17	.200	.286	35	7	3	0	0	0.0	3	2	7	9	0	9	3	81	10	1	3	10.2	.989	1B-9
1974		107	.261	.439	303	79	16	4	10	3.3	41	46	48	50	2	19	6	760	70	7	61	9.2	.992	1B-90, 3B-1
1975		120	.293	.516	372	109	21	4	18	4.8	70	60	88	63	3	9	1	984	77	13	88	9.3	.988	1B-113, 3B-2
1976	2 teams	CHI N (27G –.200) MON N (69G –.191)																						
″	total	96	.194	.373	268	52	11	2	11	4.1	28	38	48	46	4	21	4	542	46	6	60	7.5	.990	1B-68, OF-11
1977	CLE A	131	.263	.527	433	114	20	5	28	6.5	77	70	70	82	3	7	1	1026	71	6	97	8.8	.995	1B-117, DH-9
1978		145	.262	.516	508	133	22	4	33	6.5	97	105	93	72	4	1	1	1327	106	7	106	9.9	.995	1B-145
1979		143	.233	.449	515	120	31	1	26	5.0	89	93	90	93	5	0	0	1089	82	7	100	8.2	.994	1B-130, DH-13
1981		69	.239	.372	226	54	12	0	6	2.7	22	30	23	37	3	6	3	67	5	1	7	1.1	.986	DH-53, 1B-11
1982		161	.273	.484	589	161	26	1	32	5.4	90	116	109	81	6	0	0	76	5	0	5	0.5	1.000	DH-152, 1B-8
1983		141	.281	.439	508	143	27	1	17	3.3	78	77	87	72	4	2	1	201	21	2	20	1.6	.991	DH-114, 1B-27
1984		155	.271	.484	587	159	26	0	33	5.6	91	99	91	79	6	0	0	86	9	2	11	0.6	.979	DH-144, 1B-11
1985		124	.236	.408	461	109	13	0	22	4.8	49	88	47	75	3	2	1	0	0	0	0	0.0	.000	DH-122
1986		120	.229	.392	401	92	14	0	17	4.2	49	66	65	67	4	12	5	0	0	0	0	0.0	.000	DH-110
1987		36	.118	.141	85	10	2	0	0	0.0	8	5	10	25	1	15	2	0	0	0	0	0.0	.000	DH-21
14 yrs.		1565	.254	.452	5291	1342	244	22	253	4.8	792	895	876	851	48	103	28	6239	502	52	558	4.6	.992	DH-738, 1B-729, OF-11, 3B-3

Lou Thornton

THORNTON, LOUIS, JR.
B. Apr. 26, 1963, Montgomery, Ala.
BL TR 6′ 170 lbs.

Year	Team	Games	BA	SA	AB	H	2B	3B	HR	HR%	R	RBI	BB	SO	SB	Pinch Hit AB	Pinch Hit H	PO	A	E	DP	TC/G	FA	G by Pos
1985	TOR A	56	.236	.319	72	17	1	1	1	1.4	18	8	2	24	1	3	1	44	0	2	0	0.9	.957	OF-35, DH-16
1987		12	.500	.500	2	1	0	0	0	0.0	5	0	1	0	0	0	0	0	0	0	0	0.0	.000	OF-4
1988		11	.000	.000	2	0	0	0	0	0.0	1	0	0	0	0	0	0	1	0	0	0	0.1	1.000	OF-10
1989	NY N	13	.308	.385	13	4	1	0	0	0.0	5	1	0	1	2	1	0	9	0	0	0	1.5	1.000	OF-6
1990		3	—	—	0	0	0	0	0	—	0	0	0	0	0	0	0	1	0	0	0	0.5	1.000	OF-2
5 yrs.		95	.247	.326	89	22	2	1	1	1.1	29	9	3	25	3	4	1	55	0	2	0	0.8	.965	OF-57, DH-16
LEAGUE CHAMPIONSHIP SERIES																								
1985	TOR A	2	—	—	0	0	0	0	0	—	1	0	0	0	0	0	0	0	0	0	0	0.0	—	

Otis Thornton

THORNTON, OTIS BENJAMIN
B. June 30, 1945, Docena, Ala.
BR TR 6′ 1″ 186 lbs.

Year	Team	Games	BA	SA	AB	H	2B	3B	HR	HR%	R	RBI	BB	SO	SB	Pinch Hit AB	Pinch Hit H	PO	A	E	DP	TC/G	FA	G by Pos
1973	HOU N	2	.000	.000	3	0	0	0	0	0.0	0	1	0	2	0	1	0	4	0	0	1	2.0	1.000	C-2

Walter Thornton

THORNTON, WALTER MILLER
B. Feb. 18, 1875, Lewiston, Me. D. July 14, 1960, Los Angeles, Calif.
BL TL 6′ 1″ 180 lbs.

Year	Team	Games	BA	SA	AB	H	2B	3B	HR	HR%	R	RBI	BB	SO	SB	Pinch Hit AB	Pinch Hit H	PO	A	E	DP	TC/G	FA	G by Pos
1895	CHI N	8	.318	.500	22	7	1	0	1	4.5	4	7	3	1	0	0	0	7	5	1	0	1.6	.923	P-7, 1B-1
1896		9	.364	.455	22	8	0	1	0	0.0	6	1	5	2	2	1	0	8	3	3	0	1.8	.786	P-5, OF-3
1897		75	.321	.400	265	85	9	6	0	0.0	39	55	30		13	1	0	85	33	24	1	1.9	.831	OF-59, P-16
1898		62	.295	.338	210	62	5	2	0	0.0	34	14	22		8	2	0	74	53	17	5	2.3	.882	OF-34, P-28
4 yrs.		154	.312	.382	519	162	15	9	1	0.2	83	77	60	3	23	4	0	174	94	45	6	2.0	.856	OF-96, P-56, 1B-1

Bob Thorpe

THORPE, BENJAMIN ROBERT
B. Nov. 19, 1926, Caryville, Fla.
BR TR 6′ 1½″ 190 lbs.

Year	Team	Games	BA	SA	AB	H	2B	3B	HR	HR%	R	RBI	BB	SO	SB	Pinch Hit AB	Pinch Hit H	PO	A	E	DP	TC/G	FA	G by Pos
1951	BOS N	2	.500	1.500	2	1	0	1	0	0.0	1	1	0	0	0	2	1	0	0	0	0	0.0	—	
1952		81	.260	.332	292	76	8	2	3	1.0	20	26	5	42	3	9	4	132	9	4	3	2.0	.972	OF-72
1953	MIL N	27	.162	.189	37	6	1	0	0	0.0	1	5	1	6	0	9	1	12	0	0	0	0.7	1.000	OF-18
3 yrs.		110	.251	.323	331	83	9	3	3	0.9	22	32	6	48	3	20	6	144	9	4	3	1.7	.975	OF-90

Jim Thorpe

THORPE, JAMES FRANCIS
B. May 28, 1887, Prague, Okla. D. Mar. 28, 1953, Long Beach, Calif.
BR TR 6′ 1″ 185 lbs.
BB 1915

Year	Team	Games	BA	SA	AB	H	2B	3B	HR	HR%	R	RBI	BB	SO	SB	Pinch Hit AB	Pinch Hit H	PO	A	E	DP	TC/G	FA	G by Pos
1913	NY N	19	.143	.229	35	5	0	0	1	2.9	6	2	1	9	2	6	2	15	2	1	1	2.0	.944	OF-9
1914		30	.194	.226	31	6	1	0	0	0.0	5	2	0	4	1	22	5	3	0	1	0	1.0	.750	OF-4
1915		17	.231	.327	52	12	3	1	0	0.0	8	1	2	16	4	1	0	28	0	2	0	2.0	.933	OF-15
1917	2 teams	CIN N (77G –.247) NY N (26G –.193)																						
″	total	103	.237	.357	308	73	5	10	4	1.3	41	40	14	45	12	14	3	174	7	8	2	2.2	.958	OF-87
1918	NY N	58	.248	.381	113	28	4	4	1	0.9	15	11	4	18	3	11	3	57	2	1	1	1.4	.983	OF-44
1919	2 teams	NY N (2G –.333) BOS N (60G –.327)																						
″	total	62	.327	.428	159	52	7	3	1	0.6	16	26	6	30	7	11	1	88	2	8	2	2.3	.918	OF-40, 1B-2
6 yrs.		289	.252	.362	698	176	20	18	7	1.0	91	82	27	122	29	65	14	365	13	21	6	2.0	.947	OF-199, 1B-2
WORLD SERIES																								
1917	NY N	1	—	—	0	0	0	0	0	—	0	0	0	0	0	0	0	0	0	0	0	0.0	.000	OF-1

Buck Thrasher

THRASHER, FRANK EDWARD
B. Aug. 6, 1889, Watkinsville, Ga. D. June 12, 1938, Cleveland, Tenn.
BL TR 5′11″ 182 lbs.

Year	Team	Games	BA	SA	AB	H	2B	3B	HR	HR%	R	RBI	BB	SO	SB	Pinch Hit AB	Pinch Hit H	PO	A	E	DP	TC/G	FA	G by Pos
1916	PHI A	7	.310	.448	29	9	2	1	0	0.0	4	4	2	1	0	0	0	9	0	0	0	1.3	1.000	OF-7
1917		23	.234	.286	77	18	2	1	0	0.0	5	2	3	12	0	1	0	29	1	2	0	1.5	.938	OF-22
2 yrs.		30	.255	.330	106	27	4	2	0	0.0	9	6	5	13	0	1	0	38	1	2	0	1.4	.951	OF-29

Faye Throneberry

THRONEBERRY, MAYNARD FAYE BL TR 5'11" 185 lbs.
Brother of Marv Throneberry.
B. June 22, 1931, Memphis, Tenn.

Year	Team	Games	BA	SA	AB	H	2B	3B	HR	HR%	R	RBI	BB	SO	SB	Pinch Hit AB	Pinch Hit H	PO	A	E	DP	TC/G	FA	G by Pos
1952	BOS A	98	.258	.361	310	80	11	3	5	1.6	38	23	33	67	16	12	1	141	9	7	5	1.8	.955	OF-86
1955		60	.257	.472	144	37	7	3	6	4.2	20	27	14	31	0	24	5	69	3	3	0	2.2	.960	OF-34
1956		24	.220	.320	50	11	2	0	1	2.0	6	3	3	16	0	11	2	20	0	2	0	1.7	.909	OF-13
1957	2 teams	BOS A (1G –.000) WAS A (68G –.185)																						
"	total	69	.184	.276	196	36	8	2	2	1.0	21	12	17	38	0	7	0	116	2	2	0	2.1	.983	OF-58
1958	WAS A	44	.184	.356	87	16	1	1	4	4.6	12	7	4	28	0	17	5	35	1	0	0	1.4	1.000	OF-26
1959		117	.251	.388	327	82	11	2	10	3.1	36	42	33	61	6	28	3	136	7	7	2	1.7	.953	OF-86
1960		85	.248	.325	157	39	7	1	1	0.6	18	23	18	33	1	40	12	52	2	3	0	1.7	.947	OF-34
1961	LA A	24	.194	.226	31	6	1	0	0	0.0	1	0	5	10	0	16	3	8	1	0	0	1.8	1.000	OF-5
8 yrs.		521	.236	.358	1302	307	48	12	29	2.2	152	137	127	284	23	155	31	577	25	24	7	1.8	.962	OF-342

Marv Throneberry

THRONEBERRY, MARVIN EUGENE (Marvelous Marv) BL TL 6' 1" 190 lbs.
Brother of Faye Throneberry.
B. Sept. 2, 1933, Collierville, Tenn. D. June 23, 1994, Fisherville, Tenn.

Year	Team	Games	BA	SA	AB	H	2B	3B	HR	HR%	R	RBI	BB	SO	SB	Pinch Hit AB	Pinch Hit H	PO	A	E	DP	TC/G	FA	G by Pos
1955	NY A	1	1.000	1.500	2	2	1	0	0	0.0	1	3	0	0	1	0	0	3	1	0	0	4.0	1.000	1B-1
1958		60	.227	.427	150	34	5	2	7	4.7	30	19	19	40	1	12	0	322	21	4	42	7.7	.988	1B-40, OF-5
1959		80	.240	.391	192	46	5	0	8	4.2	27	22	18	51	0	15	1	346	29	4	40	5.7	.989	1B-54, OF-13
1960	KC A	104	.250	.445	236	59	9	2	11	4.7	29	41	23	60	0	33	8	508	40	5	56	7.8	.991	1B-71
1961	2 teams	KC A (40G –.238) BAL A (56G –.208)																						
"	total	96	.226	.403	226	51	5	1	11	4.9	26	35	31	50	0	26	7	330	35	4	37	5.6	.989	1B-41, OF-25
1962	2 teams	BAL A (9G –.000) NY N (116G –.244)																						
"	total	125	.238	.415	366	87	11	3	16	4.4	30	49	38	89	1	26	5	788	77	17	87	8.9	.981	1B-97, OF-2
1963	NY N	14	.143	.214	14	2	1	0	0	0.0	0	1	1	5	0	10	2	9	0	0	1	3.0	1.000	1B-3
7 yrs.		480	.237	.416	1186	281	37	8	53	4.5	143	170	130	295	3	122	23	2306	203	34	263	7.2	.987	1B-307, OF-45
WORLD SERIES																								
1958	NY A	1	.000	.000	1	0	0	0	0	0.0	0	0	0	1	0	1	0	0	0	0	0	0.0	—	

Bob Thurman

THURMAN, ROBERT BURNS BL TL 6' 1" 205 lbs.
B. May 14, 1917, Wichita, Kans.

Year	Team	Games	BA	SA	AB	H	2B	3B	HR	HR%	R	RBI	BB	SO	SB	Pinch Hit AB	Pinch Hit H	PO	A	E	DP	TC/G	FA	G by Pos
1955	CIN N	82	.217	.408	152	33	2	3	7	4.6	19	22	17	26	0	44	9	54	2	3	0	1.6	.949	OF-36
1956		80	.295	.532	139	41	5	2	8	5.8	25	22	10	14	0	48	9	39	2	2	1	1.5	.953	OF-29
1957		74	.247	.542	190	47	4	2	16	8.4	38	40	15	33	0	34	9	75	3	1	1	1.8	.987	OF-44
1958		94	.230	.382	178	41	7	4	4	2.2	23	20	20	38	1	48	11	80	2	2	1	2.0	.976	OF-41
1959		4	.250	.250	4	1	0	0	0	0.0	1	2	0	1	0	4	1	0	0	0	0	0.0	—	
5 yrs.		334	.246	.465	663	163	18	11	35	5.3	106	106	62	112	1	178	39	248	9	8	3	1.8	.970	OF-150

Gary Thurman

THURMAN, GARY MONTEZ BR TR 5'10" 170 lbs.
B. Nov. 12, 1964, Indianapolis, Ind.

Year	Team	Games	BA	SA	AB	H	2B	3B	HR	HR%	R	RBI	BB	SO	SB	Pinch Hit AB	Pinch Hit H	PO	A	E	DP	TC/G	FA	G by Pos
1987	KC A	27	.296	.321	81	24	2	0	0	0.0	12	5	8	20	7	0	0	61	5	2	1	2.5	.971	OF-27
1988		35	.167	.182	66	11	1	0	0	0.0	6	2	4	20	5	1	0	36	1	2	0	1.2	.949	OF-32, DH-1
1989		72	.195	.241	87	17	2	1	0	0.0	24	5	15	26	16	1	0	54	2	3	0	0.9	.949	OF-60, DH-4
1990		23	.233	.283	60	14	3	0	0	0.0	5	3	2	12	1	0	0	32	0	0	0	1.5	1.000	OF-21
1991		80	.277	.359	184	51	9	0	2	1.1	24	13	11	42	15	5	2	129	2	4	0	1.9	.970	OF-72
1992		88	.245	.305	200	49	6	3	0	0.0	25	20	9	34	9	8	1	138	5	2	0	1.9	.986	OF-67, DH-8
1993	DET A	75	.213	.281	89	19	2	2	0	0.0	22	13	11	30	7	1	1	54	3	3	1	1.0	.950	OF-53, DH-6
1995	SEA A	13	.320	.400	25	8	2	0	0	0.0	3	3	1	3	5	1	0	15	0	0	0	1.7	1.000	OF-9
8 yrs.		413	.244	.301	792	193	27	6	2	0.3	121	64	61	187	65	17	4	519	18	16	2	1.5	.971	OF-341, DH-19

Sloppy Thurston

THURSTON, HOLLIS JOHN BR TR 5'11" 165 lbs.
B. June 2, 1899, Fremont, Neb. D. Sept. 14, 1973, Los Angeles, Calif.

Year	Team	Games	BA	SA	AB	H	2B	3B	HR	HR%	R	RBI	BB	SO	SB	Pinch Hit AB	Pinch Hit H	PO	A	E	DP	TC/G	FA	G by Pos
1923	2 teams	STL A (2G –.000) CHI A (45G –.316)																						
"	total	47	.316	.405	79	25	5	1	0	0.0	10	4	2	6	0	1	0	6	50	2	2	1.3	.966	P-46
1924	CHI A	51	.254	.377	122	31	6	3	1	0.8	15	9	5	14	0	10	3	15	75	3	1	2.4	.968	P-38, OF-1
1925		44	.286	.417	84	24	7	2	0	0.0	2	13	5	13	0	6	2	15	55	2	4	2.0	.972	P-36
1926		38	.311	.377	61	19	4	0	0	0.0	5	5	3	6	0	5	0	4	30	1	1	1.1	.971	P-31
1927	WAS A	42	.315	.467	92	29	4	2	2	2.2	11	17	5	10	1	9	1	12	46	4	4	2.1	.935	P-29
1930	BKN N	36	.200	.320	50	10	3	0	1	2.0	3	11	0	16	0	10	2	3	30	0	0	1.4	1.000	P-24
1931		24	.217	.333	60	13	2	1	1	1.7	8	8	2	10	0	0	0	3	30	2	3	1.5	.943	P-24
1932		29	.304	.429	56	17	5	1	0	0.0	7	5	2	9	0	1	0	10	34	0	2	1.6	1.000	P-28
1933		32	.159	.205	44	7	2	0	0	0.0	4	7	0	7	0	0	0	3	40	1	0	1.4	.977	P-32
9 yrs.		343	.270	.383	648	175	38	10	5	0.8	65	79	24	91	1	42	8	71	390	15	17	1.6	.968	P-288, OF-1

Eddie Tiemeyer

TIEMEYER, EDWARD CARL BR TR 5'11½" 185 lbs.
B. May 9, 1885, Cincinnati, Ohio D. Sept. 27, 1946, Cincinnati, Ohio.

Year	Team	Games	BA	SA	AB	H	2B	3B	HR	HR%	R	RBI	BB	SO	SB	Pinch Hit AB	Pinch Hit H	PO	A	E	DP	TC/G	FA	G by Pos
1906	CIN N	5	.182	.182	11	2	0	0	0	0.0	3	0	1		0	1	0	1	6	0	1	1.8	1.000	3B-3, P-1
1907		1	—	—	0	0	0	0	0	—	1	0	1		0	0	0	0	0	0	0	0.0	—	
1909	NY A	3	.375	.500	8	3	1	0	0	0.0	1	0	1		0	0	0	25	0	1	0	8.7	.962	1B-3
3 yrs.		9	.263	.316	19	5	1	0	0	0.0	5	0	3		0	1	0	26	6	1	1	4.7	.970	3B-3, 1B-3, P-1

Mike Tiernan

TIERNAN, MICHAEL JOSEPH (Silent Mike) BL TL 5'11" 165 lbs.
B. Jan. 21, 1867, Trenton, N. J. D. Nov. 9, 1918, New York, N. Y.

Year	Team	Games	BA	SA	AB	H	2B	3B	HR	HR%	R	RBI	BB	SO	SB	Pinch Hit AB	Pinch Hit H	PO	A	E	DP	TC/G	FA	G by Pos
1887	NY N	103	.287	.452	407	117	13	12	10	2.5	82	62	32	31	28	0	0	150	13	25	3	1.7	.867	OF-103, P-5
1888		113	.293	.427	443	130	16	8	9	2.0	75	52	42	42	52	0	0	174	16	8	2	1.8	.960	OF-113
1889		122	.335	.501	499	167	22	14	11	2.2	**147**	73	**96**	32	33	0	0	179	19	23	2	1.8	.896	OF-122
1890		133	.304	**.495**	553	168	25	21	13	2.4	132	59	68	53	56	0	0	210	13	26	5	1.9	.896	OF-133
1891		134	.306	.494	542	166	30	12	**16**	**3.0**	111	73	69	32	53	0	0	138	16	17	4	1.3	.901	OF-134
1892		116	.287	.400	450	129	16	10	5	1.1	79	66	57	46	20	0	0	155	15	19	2	1.6	.899	OF-116
1893		125	.309	.481	511	158	19	12	15	2.9	114	102	72	24	26	0	0	178	12	15	2	1.6	.927	OF-125
1894		112	.276	.417	424	117	19	13	5	1.2	84	77	54	21	28	1	0	169	9	15	1	1.7	.922	OF-111
1895		120	.347	.527	476	165	23	21	7	1.5	127	70	66	19	36	0	0	184	8	11	2	1.7	.946	OF-119
1896		133	.369	.516	521	192	24	16	7	1.3	132	89	77	18	35	0	0	213	15	7	4	1.8	.970	OF-133

Mike Tiernan *continued*

Year	Team	Games	BA	SA	AB	H	2B	3B	HR	HR%	R	RBI	BB	SO	SB	Pinch Hit AB	Pinch Hit H	PO	A	E	DP	TC/G	FA	G by Pos
1897		127	.330	.451	528	174	29	10	5	0.9	123	72	61		40	0	0	178	11	14	2	1.6	.931	OF-127
1898		103	.280	.398	415	116	15	11	4	1.0	90	49	43		19	0	0	130	12	4	2	1.4	.973	OF-103
1899		35	.255	.314	137	35	4	2	0	0.0	17	7	10		2	0	0	42	3	3	1	1.4	.938	OF-35
13 yrs.		1476	.311	.463	5906	1834	255	162	107	1.8	1313	851	747	318	428	1	0	2100	162	187	32	1.7	.924	OF-1474, P-5

Bill Tierney

TIERNEY, WILLIAM J.
B. May 14, 1858, Boston, Mass. D. Sept. 21, 1898, Boston, Mass.

Year	Team	Games	BA	SA	AB	H	2B	3B	HR	HR%	R	RBI	BB	SO	SB	Pinch Hit AB	Pinch Hit H	PO	A	E	DP	TC/G	FA	G by Pos
1882	CIN AA	1	.000	.000	5	0	0	0	0	0.0	1		0			0	0	10	1	1	0	12.0	.917	1B-1
1884	BAL U	1	.333	.333	3	1	0	0	0	0.0	0		1			0	0	1	0	0	0	1.0	1.000	OF-1
2 yrs.		2	.125	.125	8	1	0	0	0	0.0	1		1			0	0	11	1	1	0	6.5	.923	OF-1, 1B-1

Cotton Tierney

TIERNEY, JAMES ARTHUR BR TR 5′ 8″ 175 lbs.
B. Feb. 10, 1894, Kansas City, Kans. D. Apr. 18, 1953, Kansas City, Mo.

Year	Team	Games	BA	SA	AB	H	2B	3B	HR	HR%	R	RBI	BB	SO	SB	Pinch Hit AB	Pinch Hit H	PO	A	E	DP	TC/G	FA	G by Pos
1920	PIT N	12	.239	.348	46	11	5	0	0	0.0	4	8	3	4	1	0	0	20	40	2	4	5.2	.968	2B-10, SS-2
1921		117	.299	.405	442	132	22	8	3	0.7	49	52	24	31	4	3	0	200	243	18	37	4.0	.961	2B-72, 3B-37, OF-4, SS-3
1922		122	.345	.515	441	152	26	14	7	1.6	58	86	22	40	7	13	3	184	305	20	53	4.7	.961	2B-105, OF-2, SS-1, 3B-1
1923	2 teams	PIT N (29G –.292) PHI N (121G –.317)																						
″	total	150	.312	.447	600	187	36	3	13	2.2	90	88	26	52	5	0	0	323	515	27	105	5.8	.969	2B-143, OF-5, 3B-2
1924	BOS N	136	.259	.331	505	131	16	1	6	1.2	38	58	22	37	11	2	1	266	434	26	88	5.3	.964	2B-115, 3B-22
1925	BKN N	93	.257	.362	265	68	14	4	2	0.8	27	39	12	23	0	**28**	7	60	105	6	8	2.7	.965	3B-61, 2B-1, 1B-1
6 yrs.		630	.296	.415	2299	681	119	30	31	1.3	266	331	109	187	28	46	11	1053	1642	99	295	4.8	.965	2B-446, 3B-123, OF-11, SS-6, 1B-1

John Tilley

TILLEY, JOHN C. BR 5′ 7″ 154 lbs.
B. New York, N. Y. Deceased.

Year	Team	Games	BA	SA	AB	H	2B	3B	HR	HR%	R	RBI	BB	SO	SB	Pinch Hit AB	Pinch Hit H	PO	A	E	DP	TC/G	FA	G by Pos
1882	CLE N	15	.089	.143	56	5	1	1	0	0.0	2	4	2	11		0	0	32	4	6	1	2.8	.857	OF-15
1884	2 teams	TOL AA (17G –.179) STP U (9G –.154)																						
″	total	26	.171	.207	82	14	3	0	0	0.0	7		7			0	0	26	1	8	0	1.3	.771	OF-26
2 yrs.		41	.138	.181	138	19	4	1	0	0.0	9	4	9	11		0	0	58	5	14	1	1.9	.818	OF-41

Bob Tillman

TILLMAN, JOHN ROBERT BR TR 6′ 4″ 205 lbs.
B. Mar. 24, 1937, Nashville, Tenn.

Year	Team	Games	BA	SA	AB	H	2B	3B	HR	HR%	R	RBI	BB	SO	SB	Pinch Hit AB	Pinch Hit H	PO	A	E	DP	TC/G	FA	G by Pos
1962	BOS A	81	.229	.454	249	57	6	4	14	5.6	28	38	19	65	0	16	3	389	19	7	1	6.3	.983	C-66
1963		96	.225	.349	307	69	10	2	8	2.6	24	32	34	64	0	2	1	621	26	5	5	6.9	.992	C-95
1964		131	.278	.445	425	118	18	1	17	4.0	43	61	49	74	0	0	0	897	49	11	5	7.3	.989	C-131
1965		111	.215	.307	368	79	10	3	6	1.6	20	35	40	69	0	6	1	676	45	9	6	6.9	.988	C-106
1966		78	.230	.314	204	47	8	0	3	1.5	12	24	22	35	0	9	3	372	24	4	5	5.6	.990	C-72
1967	2 teams	BOS A (30G –.188) NY A (22G –.254)																						
″	total	52	.220	.307	127	28	2	0	3	2.4	9	13	10	35	0	10	2	203	24	6	6	5.7	.974	C-41
1968	ATL N	86	.220	.301	236	52	4	0	5	2.1	16	20	16	55	1	10	2	359	29	4	7	5.2	.990	C-75
1969		69	.195	.411	190	37	5	0	12	6.3	18	29	18	47	0	1	0	309	15	4	5	4.8	.988	C-69
1970		71	.238	.408	223	53	5	0	11	4.9	19	30	20	66	0	1	0	404	22	5	0	6.2	.988	C-70
9 yrs.		775	.232	.371	2329	540	68	10	79	3.4	189	282	228	510	1	55	12	4230	253	55	40	6.3	.988	C-725
LEAGUE CHAMPIONSHIP SERIES																								
1969	ATL N	1	—	—	0	0	0	0	0	—	0	0	0	0	0	0	0	2	0	0	0	2.0	1.000	C-1

Rusty Tillman

TILLMAN, KERRY JEROME BR TR 6′ 175 lbs.
B. Aug. 29, 1960, Jacksonville, Fla.

Year	Team	Games	BA	SA	AB	H	2B	3B	HR	HR%	R	RBI	BB	SO	SB	Pinch Hit AB	Pinch Hit H	PO	A	E	DP	TC/G	FA	G by Pos
1982	NY N	12	.154	.231	13	2	1	0	0	0.0	4	0	0	4	1	5	2	2	0	0	0	0.7	1.000	OF-3
1986	OAK A	22	.256	.359	39	10	1	0	1	2.6	6	6	3	11	2	5	0	20	0	1	0	1.2	.952	OF-17
1988	SF N	4	.250	1.000	4	1	0	0	1	25.0	1	3	2	1	0	3	0	1	0	0	0	1.0	1.000	OF-1
3 yrs.		38	.232	.375	56	13	2	0	2	3.6	11	9	5	16	3	13	2	23	0	1	0	1.1	.958	OF-21

Ozzie Timmons

TIMMONS, OSBORNE LLEWELLYN BR TR 6′ 2″ 205 lbs.
B. Sept. 18, 1970, Tampa, Fla.

Year	Team	Games	BA	SA	AB	H	2B	3B	HR	HR%	R	RBI	BB	SO	SB	Pinch Hit AB	Pinch Hit H	PO	A	E	DP	TC/G	FA	G by Pos
1995	CHI N	77	.263	.474	171	45	10	1	8	4.7	30	28	13	32	3	26	5	63	1	2	1	1.2	.970	OF-55

Ron Tingley

TINGLEY, RONALD IRVIN BR TR 6′ 2″ 160 lbs.
B. May 27, 1959, Presque Isle, Me.

Year	Team	Games	BA	SA	AB	H	2B	3B	HR	HR%	R	RBI	BB	SO	SB	Pinch Hit AB	Pinch Hit H	PO	A	E	DP	TC/G	FA	G by Pos
1982	SD N	8	.100	.100	20	2	0	0	0	0.0	0	0	0	7	0	0	0	40	4	2	1	5.8	.957	C-8
1988	CLE A	9	.167	.292	24	4	0	0	1	4.2	1	2	2	8	0	1	1	48	6	0	1	6.0	1.000	C-9
1989	CAL A	4	.333	.333	3	1	0	0	0	0.0	0	0	1	0	0	0	0	7	1	1	0	2.3	.889	C-4
1990		5	.000	.000	3	0	0	0	0	0.0	0	0	1	1	0	0	0	12	0	0	0	2.4	1.000	C-5
1991		45	.200	.287	115	23	7	0	1	0.9	11	13	8	34	1	0	0	222	32	3	2	5.7	.988	C-45
1992		71	.197	.299	127	25	2	1	3	2.4	15	8	13	35	0	3	0	270	35	4	2	4.5	.987	C-69
1993		58	.200	.278	90	18	7	0	0	0.0	7	12	9	22	1	0	0	200	20	1	3	3.8	.995	C-58
1994	2 teams	FLA N (19G –.173) CHI A (5G –.000)																						
″	total	24	.158	.298	57	9	3	1	1	1.8	4	2	5	20	0	2	1	107	10	1	1	5.1	.992	C-23
1995	DET A	54	.226	.403	124	28	8	1	4	3.2	14	18	15	38	0	0	0	199	19	2	0	4.1	.991	C-53, 1B-1
9 yrs.		278	.195	.307	563	110	27	3	10	1.8	52	55	54	165	2	6	2	1105	127	14	10	4.5	.989	C-274, 1B-1

Joe Tinker

TINKER, JOSEPH BERT BR TR 5′ 9″ 175 lbs.
B. July 27, 1880, Muscotah, Kans. D. July 27, 1948, Orlando, Fla.
Manager 1913–16.
Hall of Fame 1946.

Year	Team	Games	BA	SA	AB	H	2B	3B	HR	HR%	R	RBI	BB	SO	SB	Pinch Hit AB	Pinch Hit H	PO	A	E	DP	TC/G	FA	G by Pos
1902	CHI N	133	.273	.343	501	137	19	5	2	0.4	54	54	26		27	0	0	253	468	74	48	6.0	.907	SS-124, 3B-8
1903		124	.291	.380	460	134	21	7	2	0.4	67	70	37		27	0	0	246	400	67	37	5.8	.906	SS-107, 3B-17
1904		141	.221	.318	488	108	12	13	3	0.6	55	41	29		41	0	0	331	465	64	54	6.1	.926	SS-140, OF-1
1905		149	.247	.320	547	135	18	8	2	0.4	70	66	34		31	0	0	345	527	56	67	6.2	.940	SS-149
1906		148	.233	.289	523	122	18	4	1	0.2	75	64	43		30	0	0	289	474	46	55	5.5	.943	SS-147, 3B-1
1907		117	.221	.271	402	89	11	3	1	0.2	36	36	25		20	3	0	215	390	39	45	5.7	.939	SS-113
1908		157	.266	.392	548	146	23	14	6	1.1	67	68	32		30	0	0	314	570	39	48	5.9	.958	SS-157
1909		143	.256	.372	516	132	26	11	4	0.8	56	57	17		23	0	0	320	470	50	49	5.9	.940	SS-143

Joe Tinker *continued*

Year	Team	Games	BA	SA	AB	H	2B	3B	HR	HR%	R	RBI	BB	SO	SB	Pinch Hit AB	Pinch Hit H	PO	A	E	DP	TC/G	FA	G by Pos
1910		133	.288	.397	473	136	25	9	3	0.6	48	69	24	35	20	2	0	277	411	42	54	5.6	.942	SS-131
1911		144	.278	.390	536	149	24	12	4	0.7	61	69	39	31	30	0	0	333	486	55	56	6.1	.937	SS-143
1912		142	.282	.351	550	155	24	7	0	0.0	80	75	38	21	25	0	0	354	470	50	73	6.2	.943	SS-142
1913	CIN N	110	.317	.445	382	121	20	13	1	0.3	47	57	20	26	10	1	0	237	337	19	34	5.4	.968	SS-101, 3B-9
1914	CHI F	126	.256	.349	438	112	21	7	2	0.5	50	46	38		19	1	0	271	408	38	48	5.7	.947	SS-125
1915		31	.269	.328	67	18	2	1	0	0.0	7	9	13		3	4	1	27	58	8	4	3.7	.914	SS-16, 2B-5, 3B-4
1916	CHI N	7	.100	.100	10	1	0	0	0	0.0	0	1	1	1	0	1	0	4	9	1	0	2.3	.929	SS-4, 3B-2
15 yrs.		1805	.263	.354	6441	1695	264	114	31	0.5	773	782	416	114	336	12	1	3816	5943	648	672	5.8	.938	SS-1742, 3B-41, 2B-5, OF-1
WORLD SERIES																								
1906	CHI N	6	.167	.167	18	3	0	0	0	0.0	4	1	2	2	2	0	0	10	20	2	0	5.3	.938	SS-6
1907		5	.154	.154	13	2	0	0	0	0.0	4	1	3	3	2	0	0	15	23	3	5	8.2	.927	SS-5
1908		5	.263	.421	19	5	0	0	1	5.3	2	5	0	2	1	0	0	8	19	0	2	5.4	1.000	SS-5
1910		5	.333	.444	18	6	2	0	0	0.0	2	0	2	2	1	0	0	11	14	2	2	5.4	.926	SS-5
4 yrs.		21	.235	.309	68	16	2	0	1	1.5	12	7	7	9	6	0	0	44	76	7	9	6.0	.945	SS-21

Lee Tinsley

TINSLEY, LEE OWEN BB TR 5′11″ 190 lbs.
B. Mar. 4, 1969, Shelbyville, Ky.

Year	Team	Games	BA	SA	AB	H	2B	3B	HR	HR%	R	RBI	BB	SO	SB	Pinch Hit AB	Pinch Hit H	PO	A	E	DP	TC/G	FA	G by Pos
1993	SEA A	11	.158	.368	19	3	1	0	1	5.3	2	2	2	9	0	5	1	9	0	1	0	1.3	.900	OF-6, DH-2
1994	BOS A	78	.222	.292	144	32	4	0	2	1.4	27	14	19	36	13	4	0	114	1	1	1	1.7	.991	OF-60, DH-9
1995		100	.284	.402	341	97	17	1	7	2.1	61	41	39	74	18	4	2	227	4	5	1	2.4	.979	OF-97
3 yrs.		189	.262	.369	504	132	22	1	10	2.0	90	57	60	119	31	13	3	350	5	7	2	2.1	.981	OF-163, DH-11
DIVISIONAL PLAYOFF SERIES																								
1995	BOS A	1	.000	.000	5	0	0	0	0	0.0	0	0	1	2	0	0	0	1	0	0	0	1.0	1.000	OF-1

Eric Tipton

TIPTON, ERIC GORDON (Blue Devil, Dukie) BR TR 5′11″ 190 lbs.
B. Apr. 20, 1915, Petersburg, Va.

Year	Team	Games	BA	SA	AB	H	2B	3B	HR	HR%	R	RBI	BB	SO	SB	Pinch Hit AB	Pinch Hit H	PO	A	E	DP	TC/G	FA	G by Pos
1939	PHI A	47	.231	.337	104	24	4	2	1	1.0	12	14	13	7	2	11	2	65	0	4	0	2.0	.942	OF-34
1940		2	.125	.375	8	1	0	1	0	0.0	2	0	1	1	0	0	0	3	0	0	0	1.5	1.000	OF-2
1941		1	.500	.500	4	2	0	0	0	0.0	0	0	0	0	0	0	0	2	0	0	0	2.0	1.000	OF-1
1942	CIN N	63	.222	.353	207	46	5	5	4	1.9	22	18	25	14	1	5	2	126	3	3	0	2.3	.977	OF-58
1943		140	.288	.424	493	142	26	7	9	1.8	82	49	85	36	1	0	0	298	8	5	2	2.2	.984	OF-139
1944		140	.301	.390	479	144	28	3	3	0.6	62	36	59	32	5	1	0	329	8	6	1	2.5	.983	OF-139
1945		108	.242	.344	331	80	17	1	5	1.5	32	34	40	37	11	22	4	192	2	6	1	2.4	.970	OF-83
7 yrs.		501	.270	.383	1626	439	80	19	22	1.4	212	151	223	127	20	39	8	1015	21	24	4	2.3	.977	OF-456

Joe Tipton

TIPTON, JOE HICKS BR TR 5′11″ 185 lbs.
B. Feb. 18, 1922, McCaysville, Ga. D. Mar. 1, 1994, Birmingham, Ala.

Year	Team	Games	BA	SA	AB	H	2B	3B	HR	HR%	R	RBI	BB	SO	SB	Pinch Hit AB	Pinch Hit H	PO	A	E	DP	TC/G	FA	G by Pos
1948	CLE A	47	.289	.356	90	26	3	0	1	1.1	11	13	4	10	0	6	0	84	18	3	4	2.6	.971	C-40
1949	CHI A	67	.204	.309	191	39	5	3	3	1.6	20	19	27	17	1	14	1	203	32	2	4	4.5	.992	C-53
1950	PHI A	64	.266	.402	184	49	5	1	6	3.3	15	20	19	16	0	5	1	201	24	3	3	3.9	.987	C-59
1951		72	.239	.324	213	51	9	0	3	1.4	23	20	51	25	1	0	0	230	52	9	12	4.0	.969	C-72
1952	2 teams	PHI A (23G –.191) CLE A (43G –.248)																						
″	total	66	.225	.416	173	39	6	0	9	5.2	21	30	36	31	1	5	2	198	36	5	2	4.1	.979	C-58
1953	CLE A	47	.229	.413	109	25	2	0	6	5.5	17	13	19	13	0	5	0	114	18	0	1	2.9	1.000	C-46
1954	WAS A	54	.223	.293	157	35	6	1	1	0.6	9	10	30	30	0	2	0	220	30	2	6	4.8	.992	C-52
7 yrs.		417	.236	.355	1117	264	36	5	29	2.6	116	125	186	142	3	37	4	1250	210	24	32	3.9	.984	C-380
WORLD SERIES																								
1948	CLE A	1	.000	.000	1	0	0	0	0	0.0	0	0	0	1	0	1	0	0	0	0	0	0.0	—	

Tom Tischinski

TISCHINSKI, THOMAS ARTHUR BR TR 5′10″ 190 lbs.
B. July 12, 1944, Kansas City, Mo.

Year	Team	Games	BA	SA	AB	H	2B	3B	HR	HR%	R	RBI	BB	SO	SB	Pinch Hit AB	Pinch Hit H	PO	A	E	DP	TC/G	FA	G by Pos
1969	MIN A	37	.191	.191	47	9	0	0	0	0.0	2	2	8	8	0	5	1	77	5	0	2	2.6	1.000	C-32
1970		24	.196	.261	46	9	0	0	1	2.2	6	2	9	6	0	2	0	90	7	1	0	4.5	.990	C-22
1971		21	.130	.217	23	3	2	0	0	0.0	0	2	1	4	0	0	0	49	6	1	3	2.7	.982	C-21
3 yrs.		82	.181	.224	116	21	2	0	1	0.9	8	6	18	18	0	7	1	216	18	2	5	3.1	.992	C-75

John Titus

TITUS, JOHN FRANKLIN (Silent John) BL TL 5′9″ 156 lbs.
B. Feb. 21, 1876, St. Clair, Pa. D. Jan. 8, 1943, St. Clair, Pa.

Year	Team	Games	BA	SA	AB	H	2B	3B	HR	HR%	R	RBI	BB	SO	SB	Pinch Hit AB	Pinch Hit H	PO	A	E	DP	TC/G	FA	G by Pos
1903	PHI N	72	.286	.404	280	80	15	6	2	0.7	38	34	19		5	0	0	126	13	7	2	2.0	.952	OF-72
1904		146	.294	.387	504	148	25	5	4	0.8	60	55	46		15	5	1	258	21	14	7	2.1	.952	OF-140
1905		147	.308	.436	548	169	36	14	2	0.4	99	89	69		11	0	0	255	24	11	4	2.0	.962	OF-147
1906		145	.267	.339	484	129	22	5	1	0.2	67	57	78		12	3	1	236	23	7	7	1.9	.974	OF-142
1907		145	.275	.382	523	144	23	12	3	0.6	72	63	47		9	3	1	198	21	17	3	1.7	.928	OF-142
1908		149	.286	.360	539	154	24	5	2	0.4	75	48	53		27	0	0	215	22	9	3	1.7	.963	OF-149
1909		151	.270	.350	540	146	22	6	3	0.6	69	46	66		23	2	0	241	23	8	6	1.8	.971	OF-148
1910		143	.241	.325	535	129	26	5	3	0.6	91	35	93	44	20	1	0	226	22	6	4	1.8	.976	OF-142
1911		76	.284	.453	236	67	14	1	8	3.4	35	26	32	16	3	15	4	85	10	2	3	1.6	.979	OF-60
1912	2 teams	PHI N (45G –.274) BOS N (96G –.325)																						
″	total	141	.309	.446	502	155	32	11	5	1.0	99	70	82	34	11	3	0	205	14	11	2	1.7	.952	OF-138
1913	BOS N	87	.297	.420	269	80	14	2	5	1.9	33	38	35	22	4	11	2	94	8	9	1	1.5	.919	OF-75
11 yrs.		1402	.282	.385	4960	1401	253	72	38	0.8	738	561	620	116	140	43	9	2139	201	101	42	1.8	.959	OF-1355

Bill Tobin

TOBIN, WILLIAM F. BL
B. Oct. 10, 1854, Hartford, Conn. D. Oct. 10, 1912, Hartford, Conn.

Year	Team	Games	BA	SA	AB	H	2B	3B	HR	HR%	R	RBI	BB	SO	SB	Pinch Hit AB	Pinch Hit H	PO	A	E	DP	TC/G	FA	G by Pos
1880	2 teams	WOR N (5G –.125) TRO N (33G –.162)																						
″	total	38	.158	.178	152	24	1	1	0	0.0	15	11	4	25		0	0	357	8	16	27	10.0	.958	1B-38

Jack Tobin

TOBIN, JOHN THOMAS BL TL 5′8″ 142 lbs.
B. May 4, 1892, St. Louis, Mo. D. Dec. 10, 1969, St. Louis, Mo.

Year	Team	Games	BA	SA	AB	H	2B	3B	HR	HR%	R	RBI	BB	SO	SB	Pinch Hit AB	Pinch Hit H	PO	A	E	DP	TC/G	FA	G by Pos
1914	STL F	139	.270	.393	529	143	24	10	7	1.3	81	35	51		20	2	0	185	31	11	3	1.7	.952	OF-132
1915		158	.294	.406	**625**	**184**	26	13	6	1.0	92	51	68		31	0	0	279	21	11	3	2.0	.965	OF-158

Jack Tobin *continued*

Year	Team	Games	BA	SA	AB	H	2B	3B	HR	HR%	R	RBI	BB	SO	SB	Pinch Hit AB	Pinch Hit H	PO	A	E	DP	TC/G	FA	G by Pos
1916	STL A	77	.213	.253	150	32	4	1	0	0.0	16	10	12	13	7	26	5	46	2	9	0	1.4	.842	OF-41
1918		122	.277	.338	480	133	19	5	0	0.0	59	36	48	26	13	0	0	244	20	8	8	2.2	.971	OF-122
1919		127	.327	.438	486	159	22	7	6	1.2	54	57	36	24	8	3	0	247	16	13	5	2.2	.953	OF-123
1920		147	.341	.452	593	202	34	10	4	0.7	94	62	39	23	21	0	0	293	18	13	1	2.2	.960	OF-147
1921		150	.352	.487	**671**	236	31	18	8	1.2	132	59	35	22	7	0	0	277	28	14	5	2.1	.956	OF-150
1922		146	.331	.474	625	207	34	8	13	2.1	122	66	56	22	7	0	0	221	15	15	5	1.7	.940	OF-145
1923		151	.317	.476	637	202	32	15	13	2.0	91	73	42	13	8	0	0	269	14	9	3	1.9	.969	OF-151
1924		136	.299	.390	569	170	30	8	2	0.4	87	48	50	12	6	4	0	248	19	12	5	2.1	.957	OF-131
1925		77	.301	.389	193	58	11	0	2	1.0	25	27	9	5	8	29	6	79	1	1	2	1.9	.988	OF-39, 1B-3
1926	2 teams	WAS A (27G –.212) BOS A (51G –.273)																						
"	total	78	.264	.322	242	64	9	1	1	0.4	31	17	16	3	6	14	1	89	7	3	1	1.7	.970	OF-58
1927	BOS A	111	.310	.390	374	116	18	3	2	0.5	52	40	36	9	5	13	3	152	10	9	4	1.8	.947	OF-93
13 yrs.		1619	.309	.420	6174	1906	294	99	64	1.0	936	581	498	172	147	91	15	2629	202	128	45	2.0	.957	OF-1490, 1B-3

Jim Tobin

TOBIN, JAMES ANTHONY (Abba Dabba) BR TR 6′ 185 lbs.
Brother of Johnny Tobin.
B. Dec. 27, 1912, Oakland, Calif. D. May 19, 1969, Oakland, Calif.

Year	Team	Games	BA	SA	AB	H	2B	3B	HR	HR%	R	RBI	BB	SO	SB	Pinch Hit AB	Pinch Hit H	PO	A	E	DP	TC/G	FA	G by Pos
1937	PIT N	21	.441	.559	34	15	4	0	0	0.0	7	6	4	3	0	1	0	5	10	1	0	0.8	.938	P-20
1938		56	.243	.320	103	25	6	1	0	0.0	8	11	9	12	0	14	2	11	41	0	1	1.3	1.000	P-40
1939		43	.243	.392	74	18	3	1	2	2.7	9	11	2	12	0	17	1	2	26	0	2	1.1	1.000	P-25
1940	BOS N	20	.279	.349	43	12	3	0	0	0.0	5	3	1	10	0	5	0	6	16	1	1	1.5	.957	P-15
1941		43	.184	.233	103	19	5	0	0	0.0	6	9	10	31	1	10	0	15	71	3	4	2.7	.966	P-33
1942		47	.246	.421	114	28	2	0	6	5.3	14	15	16	23	0	7	1	14	93	6	6	3.1	.947	P-37
1943		46	.280	.374	107	30	4	0	2	1.9	8	12	6	16	0	11	4	17	67	6	7	2.6	.933	P-33, 1B-1
1944		62	.190	.302	116	22	5	1	2	1.7	13	18	16	28	0	14	2	13	93	3	4	2.5	.972	P-43
1945	2 teams	BOS N (41G –.143) DET A (17G –.120)																						
"	total	58	.137	.314	102	14	3	0	5	4.9	11	17	20	27	0	10	0	20	63	1	6	2.0	.988	P-41
9 yrs.		396	.230	.345	796	183	35	3	17	2.1	81	102	84	162	1	89	10	103	480	21	31	2.1	.965	P-287, 1B-1
WORLD SERIES																								
1945	DET A	1	.000	.000	1	0	0	0	0	0.0	0	0	0	0	0	0	0	0	1	0	0	1.0	1.000	P-1

Johnny Tobin

TOBIN, JOHN MARTIN (Tip) BR TR 6′ 3″ 187 lbs.
B. Sept. 15, 1906, Jamaica Plain, Mass. D. Aug. 6, 1983, Rhinebeck, N. Y.

Year	Team	Games	BA	SA	AB	H	2B	3B	HR	HR%	R	RBI	BB	SO	SB	Pinch Hit AB	Pinch Hit H	PO	A	E	DP	TC/G	FA	G by Pos
1932	NY N	1	.000	.000	1	0	0	0	0	0.0	0	0	0	0	0	1	0	0	0	0	0	0.0	—	

Johnny Tobin

TOBIN, JOHN PATRICK (Jackie) BL TR 6′ 165 lbs.
Brother of Jim Tobin.
B. Jan. 8, 1921, Oakland, Calif. D. Jan. 18, 1982, Oakland, Calif.

Year	Team	Games	BA	SA	AB	H	2B	3B	HR	HR%	R	RBI	BB	SO	SB	Pinch Hit AB	Pinch Hit H	PO	A	E	DP	TC/G	FA	G by Pos
1945	BOS A	84	.252	.288	278	70	6	2	0	0.0	25	21	26	24	2	6	3	101	161	13	20	3.5	.953	3B-72, 2B-5, OF-1

Al Todd

TODD, ALFRED CHESTER BR TR 6′ 1″ 198 lbs.
B. Jan. 7, 1902, Troy, N. Y. D. Mar. 8, 1985, Elmira, N. Y.

Year	Team	Games	BA	SA	AB	H	2B	3B	HR	HR%	R	RBI	BB	SO	SB	Pinch Hit AB	Pinch Hit H	PO	A	E	DP	TC/G	FA	G by Pos
1932	PHI N	33	.229	.300	70	16	5	0	0	0.0	8	9	1	9	1	7	1	58	4	7	2	2.8	.899	C-25
1933		73	.206	.235	136	28	4	0	0	0.0	13	10	4	18	1	34	7	97	21	2	3	3.3	.983	C-34, OF-2
1934		91	.318	.444	302	96	22	2	4	1.3	33	41	10	39	3	8	4	291	32	8	7	4.0	.976	C-82
1935		107	.290	.390	328	95	18	3	3	0.9	40	42	19	35	3	20	5	292	37	11	5	3.9	.968	C-87
1936	PIT N	76	.273	.371	267	73	10	5	2	0.7	28	28	11	24	4	6	2	332	39	9	2	5.4	.976	C-70
1937		133	.307	.428	514	158	18	10	8	1.6	51	86	16	36	2	5	2	603	89	20	15	5.6	.972	C-128
1938		133	.265	.375	491	130	19	7	7	1.4	52	75	18	31	2	1	0	574	89	10	7	5.1	.985	C-132
1939	BKN N	86	.278	.380	245	68	10	0	5	2.0	28	32	13	16	1	13	5	284	35	5	5	4.4	.985	C-73
1940	CHI N	104	.255	.346	381	97	13	2	6	1.6	31	42	11	29	1	0	0	418	59	8	11	4.7	.984	C-104
1941		6	.167	.167	6	1	0	0	0	0.0	1	0	0	1	0	6	1	0	0	0	0	0.0	—	
1943		21	.133	.133	45	6	0	0	0	0.0	1	1	1	5	0	4	1	62	7	1	2	4.1	.986	C-17
11 yrs.		863	.276	.377	2785	768	119	29	35	1.3	286	366	104	243	18	104	28	3011	412	81	59	4.6	.977	C-752, OF-2

Phil Todt

TODT, PHILIP JULIUS BL TL 6′ 175 lbs.
B. Aug. 9, 1901, St. Louis, Mo. D. Nov. 15, 1973, St. Louis, Mo.

Year	Team	Games	BA	SA	AB	H	2B	3B	HR	HR%	R	RBI	BB	SO	SB	Pinch Hit AB	Pinch Hit H	PO	A	E	DP	TC/G	FA	G by Pos
1924	BOS A	52	.262	.408	103	27	8	2	1	1.0	17	14	6	9	0	**30**	4	160	11	3	8	7.9	.983	1B-18, OF-4
1925		141	.278	.439	544	151	29	13	11	2.0	62	75	44	29	3	1	0	1408	100	13	126	10.9	.991	1B-140
1926		154	.255	.362	599	153	19	12	7	1.2	56	69	40	38	3	0	0	1755	126	22	114	12.4	.988	1B-154
1927		140	.236	.337	516	122	22	6	6	1.2	55	52	28	23	6	1	0	1401	112	13	121	11.0	.991	1B-139
1928		144	.252	.406	539	136	31	8	12	2.2	61	73	26	47	6	1	0	1486	94	5	96	11.0	.997	1B-144
1929		153	.262	.391	534	140	37	10	4	0.7	49	64	31	28	6	0	0	1467	102	14	128	10.3	.991	1B-153
1930		111	.269	.439	383	103	22	5	11	2.9	49	62	24	33	4	6	1	1001	65	8	84	10.3	.993	1B-104
1931	PHI A	62	.244	.411	197	48	14	2	5	2.5	23	44	8	22	1	8	2	403	13	2	36	8.0	.995	1B-52
8 yrs.		957	.258	.395	3415	880	182	58	57	1.7	372	453	207	229	29	47	7	9081	623	80	713	10.8	.992	1B-904, OF-4
WORLD SERIES																								
1931	PHI A	1	—	—	0	0	0	0	0	—	0	0	1	0	0	0	0	0	0	0	0	0.0	—	

Bobby Tolan

TOLAN, ROBERT BL TL 5′11″ 170 lbs.
B. Nov. 19, 1945, Los Angeles, Calif.

Year	Team	Games	BA	SA	AB	H	2B	3B	HR	HR%	R	RBI	BB	SO	SB	Pinch Hit AB	Pinch Hit H	PO	A	E	DP	TC/G	FA	G by Pos
1965	STL N	17	.188	.217	69	13	2	0	0	0.0	8	6	0	4	2	0	0	32	0	1	0	1.9	.970	OF-17
1966		43	.172	.280	93	16	5	1	1	1.1	10	6	6	15	1	12	3	41	1	2	0	1.6	.955	OF-26, 1B-1
1967		110	.253	.370	265	67	7	3	6	2.3	35	32	19	43	12	33	10	225	9	1	8	2.5	.996	OF-80, 1B-13
1968		92	.230	.335	278	64	12	1	5	1.8	28	17	13	42	9	23	2	199	12	4	8	2.8	.981	OF-67, 1B-9
1969	CIN N	152	.305	.474	637	194	25	10	21	3.3	104	93	27	92	26	2	0	362	6	10	3	2.5	.974	OF-150
1970		152	.316	.475	589	186	34	6	16	2.7	112	80	62	94	**57**	5	1	349	7	8	0	2.4	.978	OF-150
1972		149	.283	.386	604	171	28	5	8	1.3	88	82	44	88	42	1	0	401	9	4	3	2.8	.990	OF-149
1973		129	.206	.304	457	94	14	2	9	2.0	42	51	27	68	15	12	3	279	9	10	1	2.5	.966	OF-120
1974	SD N	95	.266	.384	357	95	16	1	8	2.2	45	40	20	41	7	4	0	161	5	5	0	1.9	.971	OF-88
1975		147	.255	.338	506	129	19	4	5	1.0	58	43	28	45	11	14	2	336	20	7	8	2.5	.981	OF-120, 1B-27

Bobby Tolan *continued*

Year	Team	Games	BA	SA	AB	H	2B	3B	HR	HR%	R	RBI	BB	SO	SB	Pinch Hit AB	Pinch Hit H	PO	A	E	DP	TC/G	FA	G by Pos
1976	PHI N	110	.261	.342	272	71	7	0	5	1.8	32	35	7	39	10	33	4	395	14	5	36	4.9	.988	1B-50, OF-35
1977	2 teams PHI N (15G –.125) PIT N (49G –.203)																							
"	total	64	.189	.300	90	17	4	0	2	2.2	8	10	5	14	1	40	8	125	7	1	10	4.9	.992	1B-25, OF-2
1979	SD N	22	.190	.286	21	4	0	1	0	0.0	2	2	0	2	0	13	3	10	2	0	2	2.0	1.000	1B-5, OF-1
13 yrs.		1282	.265	.382	4238	1121	173	34	86	2.0	572	497	258	587	193	192	36	2915	101	58	79	2.7	.981	OF-1005, 1B-130
LEAGUE CHAMPIONSHIP SERIES																								
1970	CIN N	3	.417	.667	12	5	0	0	1	8.3	3	2	1	1	1	0	0	5	0	0	0	1.7	1.000	OF-3
1972		5	.238	.381	21	5	1	1	0	0.0	3	4	0	4	0	0	0	13	0	0	0	2.6	1.000	OF-5
1976	PHI N	3	.000	.000	2	0	0	0	0	0.0	0	0	1	0	0	2	0	1	0	0	0	0.5	1.000	OF-1, 1B-1
3 yrs.		11	.286	.457	35	10	1	1	1	2.9	6	6	2	5	1	2	0	19	0	0	0	1.9	1.000	OF-9, 1B-1
WORLD SERIES																								
1967	STL N	3	.000	.000	2	0	0	0	0	0.0	1	0	1	1	0	2	0	0	0	0	0	0.0	—	
1968		1	.000	.000	1	0	0	0	0	0.0	0	0	0	1	0	1	0	0	0	0	0	0.0	—	
1970	CIN N	5	.211	.421	19	4	1	0	1	5.3	5	1	3	2	1	0	0	4	0	1	0	1.0	.800	OF-5
1972		7	.269	.308	26	7	1	0	0	0.0	2	6	1	4	5	0	0	11	0	1	0	1.7	.917	OF-7
4 yrs.		16	.229	.333	48	11	2	0	1	2.1	8	7	5	8	6	3	0	15	0	2	0	1.4	.882	OF-12

Jose Tolentino

TOLENTINO, JOSE FRANCO
Born Jose Tolentino (Franco).
B. June 3, 1961, Mexico City, Mexico.

BL TL 6′ 1″ 195 lbs.

Year	Team	Games	BA	SA	AB	H	2B	3B	HR	HR%	R	RBI	BB	SO	SB	Pinch Hit AB	Pinch Hit H	PO	A	E	DP	TC/G	FA	G by Pos
1991	HOU N	44	.259	.389	54	14	4	0	1	1.9	6	6	4	9	0	30	6	53	5	1	3	5.4	.983	1B-10, OF-1

Wayne Tolleson

TOLLESON, JIMMY WAYNE
B. Nov. 22, 1955, Spartanburg, S. C.

BB TR 5′ 9″ 160 lbs.

Year	Team	Games	BA	SA	AB	H	2B	3B	HR	HR%	R	RBI	BB	SO	SB	Pinch Hit AB	Pinch Hit H	PO	A	E	DP	TC/G	FA	G by Pos
1981	TEX A	14	.167	.167	24	4	0	0	0	0.0	6	1	1	5	2	1	0	5	8	0	0	1.6	1.000	3B-6, SS-2
1982		38	.114	.129	70	8	1	0	0	0.0	6	2	5	14	1	0	0	47	70	5	20	3.9	.959	SS-26, 3B-4, 2B-1
1983		134	.260	.315	470	122	13	2	3	0.6	64	20	40	68	33	0	0	268	372	17	81	4.7	.974	2B-112, SS-26, DH-1
1984		118	.213	.251	338	72	9	2	0	0.0	35	9	27	47	22	0	0	195	287	10	62	4.0	.980	2B-109, SS-7, 3B-5, DH-1, OF-1
1985		123	.313	.381	323	101	9	5	1	0.3	45	18	21	46	21	5	1	149	255	14	48	3.3	.967	SS-81, 2B-29, 3B-12, DH-6
1986	2 teams CHI A (81G –.250) NY A (60G –.284)																							
"	total	141	.265	.339	475	126	16	5	3	0.6	61	43	52	76	17	3	0	147	327	14	50	3.2	.971	SS-74, 3B-72, 2B-3, DH-2, OF-2
1987	NY A	121	.221	.241	349	77	4	0	1	0.3	48	22	43	72	5	0	0	162	326	15	66	4.1	.970	SS-119, 3B-3
1988		21	.254	.288	59	15	2	0	0	0.0	8	5	8	12	1	1	0	28	54	3	9	3.7	.965	2B-12, 3B-10, SS-1
1989		80	.164	.250	140	23	5	2	1	0.7	16	9	16	23	5	10	0	45	107	7	20	2.0	.956	3B-28, SS-28, 2B-12, DH-10
1990		73	.149	.189	74	11	1	1	0	0.0	12	4	6	21	1	5	1	57	86	2	26	2.2	.986	SS-45, 2B-13, DH-5, 3B-3
10 yrs.		863	.241	.293	2322	559	60	17	9	0.4	301	133	219	384	108	25	2	1103	1892	87	382	3.5	.972	SS-409, 2B-291, 3B-143, DH-25, OF-3

Tim Tolman

TOLMAN, TIMOTHY LEE
B. Apr. 20, 1956, Santa Monica, Calif.

BR TR 6′ 190 lbs.

Year	Team	Games	BA	SA	AB	H	2B	3B	HR	HR%	R	RBI	BB	SO	SB	Pinch Hit AB	Pinch Hit H	PO	A	E	DP	TC/G	FA	G by Pos
1981	HOU N	4	.125	.125	8	1	0	0	0	0.0	0	0	0	0	0	2	0	2	0	0	0	0.7	1.000	OF-3
1982		15	.192	.385	26	5	2	0	1	3.8	4	3	4	3	0	7	1	17	1	0	2	3.0	1.000	OF-5, 1B-1
1983		43	.196	.375	56	11	4	0	2	3.6	4	10	6	9	0	30	4	55	2	0	6	5.7	1.000	1B-7, OF-3
1984		14	.176	.235	17	3	1	0	0	0.0	2	0	0	3	0	10	1	6	0	0	0	1.5	1.000	OF-3, 1B-1
1985		31	.140	.302	43	6	1	0	2	4.7	4	8	1	10	0	17	3	24	2	0	1	1.7	1.000	OF-9, 1B-6
1986	DET A	16	.176	.206	34	6	1	0	0	0.0	4	2	6	4	1	1	0	23	0	0	2	1.4	1.000	DH-9, OF-4, 1B-3
1987		9	.083	.167	12	1	1	0	0	0.0	3	1	7	2	0	1	0	8	0	0	0	0.9	1.000	OF-7, DH-2
7 yrs.		132	.168	.296	196	33	10	0	5	2.6	21	24	24	31	1	68	9	135	5	0	11	2.2	1.000	OF-34, 1B-18, DH-11

Chick Tolson

TOLSON, CHARLES JULIUS (Slug)
B. May 3, 1895, Washington, D. C. D. Apr. 16, 1965, Washington, D. C.

BR TR 6′ 185 lbs.

Year	Team	Games	BA	SA	AB	H	2B	3B	HR	HR%	R	RBI	BB	SO	SB	Pinch Hit AB	Pinch Hit H	PO	A	E	DP	TC/G	FA	G by Pos
1925	CLE A	3	.250	.250	12	3	0	0	0	0.0	0	0	2	1	0	0	0	32	2	0	1	11.3	1.000	1B-3
1926	CHI N	57	.313	.450	80	25	6	1	1	1.3	4	8	5	8	0	**40**	**14**	104	7	1	11	8.6	.991	1B-13
1927		39	.296	.481	54	16	4	0	2	3.7	6	17	4	9	0	27	7	74	5	0	3	9.9	1.000	1B-8
1929		32	.257	.330	109	28	5	0	1	0.9	13	19	9	16	0	0	0	289	16	7	21	9.8	.978	1B-32
1930		13	.300	.350	20	6	1	0	0	0.0	0	1	6	5	1	7	2	43	4	1	6	9.6	.979	1B-5
5 yrs.		144	.284	.393	275	78	16	1	4	1.5	23	45	26	39	1	74	23	542	34	9	42	9.6	.985	1B-61
WORLD SERIES																								
1929	CHI N	1	.000	.000	1	0	0	0	0	0.0	0	0	0	1	0	1	0	0	0	0	0	0.0	—	

Andy Tomberlin

TOMBERLIN, ANDY LEE
B. Nov. 7, 1966, Monroe, N. C.

BL TL 5′11″ 160 lbs.

Year	Team	Games	BA	SA	AB	H	2B	3B	HR	HR%	R	RBI	BB	SO	SB	Pinch Hit AB	Pinch Hit H	PO	A	E	DP	TC/G	FA	G by Pos
1993	PIT N	27	.286	.405	42	12	0	1	1	2.4	4	5	2	14	0	18	4	9	1	0	0	1.4	1.000	OF-7
1994	BOS A	17	.194	.333	36	7	0	1	1	2.8	1	1	6	12	1	4	1	12	2	0	1	0.8	1.000	OF-11, DH-5, P-1
1995	OAK A	46	.212	.353	85	18	0	0	4	4.7	15	10	5	22	4	6	2	45	1	1	0	1.1	.979	OF-42, DH-1
3 yrs.		90	.227	.362	163	37	0	2	6	3.7	20	16	13	48	5	28	7	66	4	1	1	1.1	.986	OF-60, DH-6, P-1

George Tomer

TOMER, GEORGE CLARENCE
B. Nov. 26, 1895, Perry, Iowa D. Dec. 15, 1984, Perry, Iowa.

BL TR 6′ 180 lbs.

Year	Team	Games	BA	SA	AB	H	2B	3B	HR	HR%	R	RBI	BB	SO	SB	Pinch Hit AB	Pinch Hit H	PO	A	E	DP	TC/G	FA	G by Pos
1913	STL A	1	.000	.000	1	0	0	0	0	0.0	0	0	0	1	0	1	0	0	0	0	0	0.0	—	

Phil Tomney

TOMNEY, PHILIP H.
B. July 17, 1863, Reading, Pa. D. Mar. 18, 1892, Reading, Pa.

BR TR 5′ 7″ 155 lbs.

Year	Team	Games	BA	SA	AB	H	2B	3B	HR	HR%	R	RBI	BB	SO	SB	Pinch Hit AB	Pinch Hit H	PO	A	E	DP	TC/G	FA	G by Pos
1888	LOU AA	34	.150	.175	120	18	3	0	0	0.0	15	4	7		11	0	0	40	117	21	7	5.2	.882	SS-34
1889		112	.213	.293	376	80	8	5	4	1.1	61	38	46	47	26	0	0	229	454	114	57	7.1	.857	SS-112
1890		108	.277	.376	386	107	21	7	1	0.3	72		43		27	0	0	180	406	64	31	6.0	.902	SS-108
3 yrs.		254	.232	.313	882	205	32	12	5	0.6	148	42	96	47	64	0	0	449	977	199	95	6.4	.878	SS-254

Tony Tonneman

TONNEMAN, CHARLES RICHARD
B. Sept. 10, 1881, Chicago, Ill. D. Aug. 7, 1951, Prescott, Ariz.

BR TR 5′10½″ 175 lbs.

Year	Team	Games	BA	SA	AB	H	2B	3B	HR	HR%	R	RBI	BB	SO	SB	Pinch Hit AB	Pinch Hit H	PO	A	E	DP	TC/G	FA	G by Pos
1911	BOS A	2	.200	.400	5	1	1	0	0	0.0	0	3	1		0	0	0	16	2	2	0	10.0	.900	C-2

Bert Tooley

TOOLEY, ALBERT R.
B. Aug. 30, 1886, Howell, Mich. D. Aug. 17, 1976, Marshall, Mich.
BR TR 5′10″ 155 lbs.

Year	Team	Games	BA	SA	AB	H	2B	3B	HR	HR%	R	RBI	BB	SO	SB	Pinch Hit AB	Pinch Hit H	PO	A	E	DP	TC/G	FA	G by Pos
1911	BKN N	119	.206	.252	433	89	11	3	1	0.2	55	29	53	63	18	3	1	226	340	46	42	5.4	.925	SS-114
1912		77	.234	.317	265	62	6	5	2	0.8	34	37	19	21	12	0	0	147	214	47	23	5.4	.885	SS-76
2 yrs.		196	.216	.277	698	151	17	8	3	0.4	89	66	72	84	30	3	1	373	554	93	65	5.4	.909	SS-190

Specs Toporcer

TOPORCER, GEORGE
B. Feb. 9, 1899, New York, N. Y. D. May 17, 1989, Huntington Station, N. Y.
BL TR 5′10½″ 165 lbs.

Year	Team	Games	BA	SA	AB	H	2B	3B	HR	HR%	R	RBI	BB	SO	SB	Pinch Hit AB	Pinch Hit H	PO	A	E	DP	TC/G	FA	G by Pos
1921	STL N	22	.264	.283	53	14	1	0	0	0.0	4	2	3	4	1	6	1	25	42	4	6	5.1	.944	2B-12, SS-2
1922		116	.324	.455	352	114	25	6	3	0.9	56	36	24	18	2	15	6	173	255	30	35	4.6	.934	SS-91, 3B-6, OF-1, 2B-1
1923		97	.254	.340	303	77	11	3	3	1.0	45	35	41	14	4	8	3	193	240	24	57	5.3	.947	2B-52, SS-33, 3B-1, 1B-1
1924		70	.313	.409	198	62	10	3	1	0.5	30	24	11	14	2	10	1	56	105	8	8	2.8	.953	3B-33, SS-25, 2B-3
1925		83	.284	.384	268	76	13	4	2	0.7	38	26	36	15	7	8	2	149	231	16	41	5.4	.960	SS-66, 2B-7
1926		64	.250	.330	88	22	3	2	0	0.0	13	9	8	9	1	23	9	24	40	1	3	2.0	.985	2B-27, SS-5, 3B-1
1927		86	.248	.321	290	72	13	4	0	0.0	37	19	27	16	5	8	3	98	160	13	23	3.2	.952	3B-54, SS-27, 2B-2, 1B-1
1928		8	.000	.000	14	0	0	0	0	0.0	0	0	0	3	0	6	0	12	3	0	1	7.5	1.000	2B-1, 1B-1
8 yrs.		546	.279	.373	1566	437	76	22	9	0.6	223	151	150	93	22	84	25	730	1076	96	174	4.2	.950	SS-249, 2B-105, 3B-95, 1B-3, OF-1
WORLD SERIES																								
1926	STL N	1	—	—	0	0	0	0	0	—	0	1	0	0	0	0	0	0	0	0	0	0.0	—	

Jeff Torborg

TORBORG, JEFFREY ALLEN
B. Nov. 26, 1941, Plainfield, N. J.
Manager 1977–79, 1989–93.
BR TR 6′½″ 195 lbs.

Year	Team	Games	BA	SA	AB	H	2B	3B	HR	HR%	R	RBI	BB	SO	SB	Pinch Hit AB	Pinch Hit H	PO	A	E	DP	TC/G	FA	G by Pos
1964	LA N	28	.233	.302	43	10	1	1	0	0.0	4	4	3	8	0	1	0	80	4	2	1	3.2	.977	C-27
1965		56	.240	.347	150	36	5	1	3	2.0	8	13	10	26	0	6	1	300	19	3	1	6.1	.991	C-53
1966		46	.225	.275	120	27	3	0	1	0.8	4	13	10	23	0	2	0	269	17	4	2	6.4	.986	C-45
1967		76	.214	.276	196	42	4	1	2	1.0	11	12	13	31	1	1	1	413	30	5	3	6.0	.989	C-75
1968		37	.161	.183	93	15	2	0	0	0.0	2	4	6	10	0	0	0	206	20	2	10	6.2	.991	C-37
1969		51	.185	.218	124	23	4	0	0	0.0	7	7	9	17	1	1	0	251	26	1	5	5.6	.996	C-50
1970		64	.231	.313	134	31	8	0	1	0.7	11	17	14	15	1	2	1	275	16	5	2	4.7	.983	C-63
1971	CAL A	55	.203	.244	123	25	5	0	0	0.0	6	5	3	6	0	6	0	208	17	3	9	4.7	.987	C-49
1972		59	.209	.229	153	32	3	0	0	0.0	5	8	14	21	0	1	0	383	28	1	5	7.1	.998	C-58
1973		102	.220	.259	255	56	7	0	1	0.4	20	18	21	32	0	0	0	611	37	6	2	6.4	.991	C-102
10 yrs.		574	.214	.265	1391	297	42	3	8	0.6	78	101	103	189	3	20	3	2996	214	32	40	5.8	.990	C-559

Earl Torgeson

TORGESON, CLIFFORD EARL (The Earl of Snohomish)
B. Jan. 1, 1924, Snohomish, Wash. D. Nov. 8, 1990, Everett, Wash.
BL TL 6′3″ 180 lbs.

Year	Team	Games	BA	SA	AB	H	2B	3B	HR	HR%	R	RBI	BB	SO	SB	Pinch Hit AB	Pinch Hit H	PO	A	E	DP	TC/G	FA	G by Pos
1947	BOS N	128	.281	.481	399	112	20	6	16	4.0	73	78	82	59	11	11	1	1033	76	18	83	9.6	.984	1B-117
1948		134	.253	.397	438	111	23	5	10	2.3	70	67	81	54	19	4	2	1069	81	8	85	9.0	.993	1B-129
1949		25	.260	.450	100	26	5	1	4	4.0	17	19	13	4	4	0	0	242	8	3	21	10.1	.988	1B-25
1950		156	.290	.472	576	167	30	3	23	4.0	**120**	87	119	69	15	0	0	1365	110	21	126	9.6	.986	1B-156
1951		155	.263	.437	581	153	21	4	24	4.1	99	92	102	70	20	0	0	1330	107	17	137	9.4	.988	1B-155
1952		122	.230	.314	382	88	17	0	5	1.3	49	34	81	38	11	12	2	935	74	12	86	9.3	.988	1B-105, OF-5
1953	PHI N	111	.274	.470	379	104	25	8	11	2.9	58	64	53	57	7	6	1	916	65	13	83	9.5	.987	1B-105
1954		135	.271	.371	490	133	22	6	5	1.0	63	54	75	52	7	1	0	1146	74	12	103	9.3	.990	1B-133
1955	2 teams	PHI N (47G –.267) DET A (89G –.283)																						
″	total	136	.278	.396	450	125	15	4	10	2.2	87	67	93	49	11	9	3	1044	79	8	106	9.0	.993	1B-126
1956	DET A	117	.264	.425	318	84	9	3	12	3.8	61	42	78	47	6	27	10	623	32	5	62	8.0	.992	1B-83
1957	2 teams	DET A (30G –.240) CHI A (86G –.295)																						
″	total	116	.286	.429	301	86	13	3	8	2.7	58	51	61	54	7	28	8	710	36	1	83	8.5	.999	1B-87, OF-1
1958	CHI A	96	.266	.468	188	50	8	0	10	5.3	37	30	48	29	7	24	9	470	30	11	54	7.0	.978	1B-73
1959		127	.220	.357	277	61	5	3	9	3.2	40	45	62	55	7	24	5	717	37	13	58	7.4	.983	1B-103
1960		68	.263	.404	57	15	2	0	2	3.5	12	9	21	8	1	41	12	54	4	1	3	5.9	.983	1B-10
1961	2 teams	CHI A (20G –.067) NY A (22G –.111)																						
″	total	42	.091	.091	33	3	0	0	0	0.0	4	1	11	8	0	23	2	30	2	1	7	3.7	.970	1B-9
15 yrs.		1668	.265	.417	4969	1318	215	46	149	3.0	848	740	980	653	133	210	55	11684	815	144	1097	8.9	.989	1B-1416, OF-6
WORLD SERIES																								
1948	BOS N	5	.389	.556	18	7	3	0	0	0.0	2	1	2	1	1	0	0	44	5	0	2	9.8	1.000	1B-5
1959	CHI A	3	.000	.000	1	0	0	0	0	0.0	1	0	1	0	0	1	0	0	0	0	0	0.0	.000	1B-1
2 yrs.		8	.368	.526	19	7	3	0	0	0.0	3	1	3	1	1	1	0	44	5	0	2	8.2	1.000	1B-6

Red Torphy

TORPHY, WALTER ANTHONY
B. Nov. 6, 1891, Fall River, Mass. D. Feb. 11, 1980, Fall River, Mass.
BR TR 5′11″ 169 lbs.

Year	Team	Games	BA	SA	AB	H	2B	3B	HR	HR%	R	RBI	BB	SO	SB	Pinch Hit AB	Pinch Hit H	PO	A	E	DP	TC/G	FA	G by Pos
1920	BOS N	3	.200	.333	15	3	2	0	0	0.0	1	2	0	1	0	0	0	31	0	1	2	10.7	.969	1B-3

Frank Torre

TORRE, FRANK JOSEPH
Brother of Joe Torre.
B. Dec. 30, 1931, Brooklyn, N. Y.
BL TL 6′4″ 200 lbs.

Year	Team	Games	BA	SA	AB	H	2B	3B	HR	HR%	R	RBI	BB	SO	SB	Pinch Hit AB	Pinch Hit H	PO	A	E	DP	TC/G	FA	G by Pos
1956	MIL N	111	.258	.296	159	41	6	0	0	0.0	17	16	11	4	1	23	5	390	42	3	34	4.9	.993	1B-89
1957		129	.272	.393	364	99	19	5	5	1.4	46	40	29	19	0	15	5	859	71	4	89	8.0	.996	1B-117
1958		138	.309	.444	372	115	22	5	6	1.6	41	55	42	14	2	17	6	960	80	6	85	8.6	.994	1B-122
1959		115	.228	.304	263	60	15	1	1	0.4	23	33	35	12	0	28	7	622	46	4	43	7.7	.994	1B-87
1960		21	.205	.227	44	9	1	0	0	0.0	2	5	3	2	0	3	1	105	4	0	12	6.4	1.000	1B-17
1962	PHI N	108	.310	.381	168	52	8	2	0	0.0	13	20	24	6	1	33	4	347	37	8	40	5.2	.980	1B-76
1963		92	.250	.375	112	28	7	2	1	0.9	8	10	11	7	0	32	8	253	28	3	26	5.1	.989	1B-56
7 yrs.		714	.273	.372	1482	404	78	15	13	0.9	150	179	155	64	4	151	36	3536	308	28	329	6.9	.993	1B-564
WORLD SERIES																								
1957	MIL N	7	.300	.900	10	3	0	0	2	20.0	2	3	2	0	0	1	0	37	2	0	4	5.6	1.000	1B-7
1958		7	.176	.176	17	3	0	0	0	0.0	0	1	2	0	0	3	0	40	2	2	4	6.3	.955	1B-7
2 yrs.		14	.222	.444	27	6	0	0	2	7.4	2	4	4	0	0	4	0	77	4	2	8	5.9	.976	1B-14

Joe Torre

TORRE, JOSEPH PAUL
Brother of Frank Torre.
B. July 18, 1940, Brooklyn, N. Y.
Manager 1977–84, 1990–95.

BR TR 6′ 2″ 212 lbs.

Year	Team	Games	BA	SA	AB	H	2B	3B	HR	HR%	R	RBI	BB	SO	SB	Pinch Hit AB	Pinch Hit H	PO	A	E	DP	TC/G	FA	G by Pos
1960	MIL N	2	.500	.500	2	1	0	0	0	0.0	0	0	0	1	0	2	1	0	0	0	0	0.0	—	
1961		113	.278	.424	406	113	21	4	10	2.5	40	42	28	60	3	3	2	494	50	10	4	4.9	.982	C-112
1962		80	.282	.395	220	62	8	1	5	2.3	23	26	24	24	1	16	6	325	39	5	4	5.9	.986	C-63
1963		142	.293	.431	501	147	19	4	14	2.8	57	71	42	79	1	7	1	919	76	6	45	7.0	.994	C-105, 1B-37, OF-2
1964		154	.321	.498	601	193	36	5	20	3.3	87	109	36	67	2	2	1	1081	94	7	53	7.1	.994	C-96, 1B-70
1965		148	.291	.489	523	152	21	1	27	5.2	68	80	61	79	0	5	2	1022	73	8	43	7.4	.993	C-100, 1B-49
1966	ATL N	148	.315	.560	546	172	20	3	36	6.6	83	101	60	61	0	3	1	874	87	12	33	6.5	.988	C-114, 1B-36
1967		135	.277	.444	477	132	18	1	20	4.2	67	68	49	75	2	6	1	785	81	8	33	6.4	.991	C-114, 1B-23
1968		115	.271	.377	424	115	11	2	10	2.4	45	55	34	72	1	1	0	733	48	2	26	6.5	.997	C-92, 1B-29
1969	STL N	159	.289	.447	602	174	29	6	18	3.0	72	101	66	85	0	1	0	1360	91	7	117	9.1	.995	1B-144, C-17
1970		161	.325	.498	624	203	27	9	21	3.4	89	100	70	91	2	0	0	651	162	19	16	5.1	.977	C-90, 3B-73, 1B-1
1971		161	**.363**	.555	634	**230**	34	8	24	3.8	97	**137**	63	70	4	0	0	136	271	21	22	2.7	.951	3B-161
1972		149	.289	.419	544	157	26	6	11	2.0	71	81	54	64	3	6	4	336	198	15	34	3.8	.973	3B-117, 1B-27
1973		141	.287	.403	519	149	17	2	13	2.5	67	69	65	78	2	0	0	881	128	12	83	5.9	.988	1B-114, 3B-58
1974		147	.282	.401	529	149	28	1	11	2.1	59	70	69	88	1	4	2	1173	121	14	145	8.3	.989	1B-139, 3B-18
1975	NY N	114	.247	.357	361	89	16	3	6	1.7	33	35	35	55	0	22	5	172	157	15	26	3.2	.956	3B-83, 1B-24
1976		114	.306	.406	310	95	10	3	5	1.6	36	31	21	35	1	35	8	593	52	7	42	8.0	.989	1B-78, 3B-4
1977		26	.176	.294	51	9	3	0	1	2.0	2	9	2	10	0	11	2	83	3	1	9	5.1	.989	1B-16, 3B-1
18 yrs.		2209	.297	.452	7874	2342	344	59	252	3.2	996	1185	779	1094	23	124	36	11618	1731	169	735	6.1	.987	C-903, 1B-787, 3B-515, OF-2

Felix Torres

TORRES, FELIX
Born Felix Torres (Sanchez).
B. May 1, 1932, Ponce, Puerto Rico.

BR TR 5′11″ 165 lbs.

Year	Team	Games	BA	SA	AB	H	2B	3B	HR	HR%	R	RBI	BB	SO	SB	Pinch Hit AB	Pinch Hit H	PO	A	E	DP	TC/G	FA	G by Pos
1962	LA A	127	.259	.392	451	117	19	4	11	2.4	44	74	28	73	0	6	1	110	250	24	20	3.1	.938	3B-123
1963		138	.261	.361	463	121	32	1	4	0.9	40	51	30	73	1	12	3	110	237	23	30	3.0	.938	3B-122, 1B-2
1964		100	.231	.397	277	64	10	0	12	4.3	25	28	13	56	1	23	3	89	123	7	12	2.9	.968	3B-72, 1B-3
3 yrs.		365	.254	.381	1191	302	61	5	27	2.3	109	153	71	202	2	41	7	309	610	54	62	3.0	.945	3B-317, 1B-5

Gil Torres

TORRES, DON GILBERTO
Born Don Gilberto Torres (Nunez).
Son of Ricardo Torres.
B. Aug. 23, 1915, Regla, Cuba D. Jan. 11, 1983, Regla, Cuba.

BR TR 6′ 155 lbs.

Year	Team	Games	BA	SA	AB	H	2B	3B	HR	HR%	R	RBI	BB	SO	SB	Pinch Hit AB	Pinch Hit H	PO	A	E	DP	TC/G	FA	G by Pos
1940	WAS A	2	—	—	0	0	0	0	0	—	0	0	0	0	0	0	0	0	1	0	0	0.5	1.000	P-2
1944		134	.267	.328	524	140	20	6	0	0.0	42	58	21	24	10	0	0	167	322	24	35	3.7	.953	3B-123, 2B-10, 1B-4
1945		147	.237	.276	562	133	12	5	0	0.0	39	48	21	29	7	0	0	274	440	35	65	5.1	.953	SS-145, 3B-2
1946		63	.254	.297	185	47	8	0	0	0.0	18	13	11	12	3	5	0	82	137	11	20	3.9	.952	SS-31, 3B-18, 2B-7, P-3
4 yrs.		346	.252	.301	1271	320	40	11	0	0.0	99	119	53	65	20	5	0	523	900	70	120	4.3	.953	SS-176, 3B-143, 2B-17, P-5, 1B-4

Hector Torres

TORRES, HECTOR EPITACIO
Born Hector Epitacio Torres (Marroquin).
B. Sept. 16, 1945, Monterrey, Mexico.

BR TR 6′ 175 lbs.

Year	Team	Games	BA	SA	AB	H	2B	3B	HR	HR%	R	RBI	BB	SO	SB	Pinch Hit AB	Pinch Hit H	PO	A	E	DP	TC/G	FA	G by Pos
1968	HOU N	128	.223	.258	466	104	11	1	1	0.2	44	24	18	64	2	1	0	159	393	24	55	4.5	.958	SS-127, 2B-1
1969		34	.159	.217	69	11	1	0	1	1.4	5	8	2	12	0	14	3	30	38	4	7	3.3	.944	SS-22
1970		31	.246	.323	65	16	1	2	0	0.0	6	5	6	8	0	4	1	34	51	4	9	3.2	.955	SS-22, 2B-6
1971	CHI N	31	.224	.276	58	13	3	0	0	0.0	4	2	4	10	0	4	1	12	45	3	7	2.7	.950	SS-18, 2B-4
1972	MON N	83	.155	.221	181	28	4	1	2	1.1	14	7	13	26	0	7	1	112	167	9	34	3.6	.969	2B-60, SS-16, OF-2, 3B-1, P-1
1973	HOU N	38	.091	.106	66	6	1	0	0	0.0	3	2	7	13	0	3	0	32	75	5	10	3.2	.955	SS-22, 2B-13
1975	SD N	112	.259	.335	352	91	12	0	5	1.4	31	26	22	32	2	0	0	128	338	13	55	3.6	.973	SS-75, 3B-42, 2B-16
1976		74	.195	.279	215	42	6	0	4	1.9	8	15	16	31	2	8	0	72	168	12	30	3.6	.952	SS-63, 3B-4, 2B-3
1977	TOR A	91	.241	.346	266	64	7	3	5	1.9	33	26	16	33	1	2	1	144	240	10	38	4.2	.975	SS-68, 2B-23, 3B-2
9 yrs.		622	.216	.281	1738	375	46	7	18	1.0	148	115	104	229	7	43	7	723	1515	84	245	3.8	.964	SS-433, 2B-126, 3B-49, OF-2, P-1

Ricardo Torres

TORRES, RICARDO J.
Born Ricardo J. Torres (Martinez).
Father of Gil Torres.
B. Apr. 16, 1891, Regla, Cuba D. Apr. 17, 1960, Regla, Cuba.

BR TR 5′11″ 160 lbs.

Year	Team	Games	BA	SA	AB	H	2B	3B	HR	HR%	R	RBI	BB	SO	SB	Pinch Hit AB	Pinch Hit H	PO	A	E	DP	TC/G	FA	G by Pos
1920	WAS A	16	.333	.367	30	10	1	0	0	0.0	8	3	1	4	0	2	1	49	2	0	1	4.3	1.000	1B-7, C-5
1921		2	.333	.333	3	1	0	0	0	0.0	1	0	1	1	0	0	0	3	0	1	0	2.0	.750	C-2
1922		4	.000	.000	4	0	0	0	0	0.0	0	0	0	1	0	1	0	2	3	0	0	1.7	1.000	C-3
3 yrs.		22	.297	.324	37	11	1	0	0	0.0	9	3	2	6	0	3	1	54	5	1	1	3.5	.983	C-10, 1B-7

Rusty Torres

TORRES, ROSENDO
Born Rosendo Torres (Hernandez).
B. Sept. 30, 1948, Aguadilla, Puerto Rico.

BB TR 5′10″ 175 lbs.

Year	Team	Games	BA	SA	AB	H	2B	3B	HR	HR%	R	RBI	BB	SO	SB	Pinch Hit AB	Pinch Hit H	PO	A	E	DP	TC/G	FA	G by Pos
1971	NY A	9	.385	.731	26	10	3	0	2	7.7	5	3	0	8	0	4	0	13	0	0	0	2.6	1.000	OF-5
1972		80	.211	.291	199	42	7	0	3	1.5	15	13	18	44	0	22	7	86	4	2	0	1.5	.978	OF-62
1973	CLE A	122	.205	.304	312	64	8	1	7	2.2	31	28	50	62	6	7	3	191	9	5	1	1.8	.976	OF-114
1974		108	.187	.260	150	28	2	0	3	2.0	19	12	13	24	2	12	1	110	8	5	0	1.3	.959	OF-94, DH-1
1976	CAL A	120	.205	.356	264	54	16	3	6	2.3	37	27	36	39	4	3	0	195	5	2	0	1.8	.990	OF-105, DH-6, 3B-1
1977		58	.156	.312	77	12	1	1	3	3.9	9	10	10	18	0	2	1	60	1	1	0	1.1	.984	OF-54
1978	CHI A	16	.318	.591	44	14	3	0	3	6.8	7	6	6	7	0	1	0	27	0	1	0	2.0	.964	OF-14
1979		90	.253	.424	170	43	5	0	8	4.7	26	24	23	37	0	12	1	117	4	3	0	1.5	.976	OF-85
1980	KC A	51	.167	.167	72	12	0	0	0	0.0	10	3	8	7	1	1	1	67	4	2	1	1.8	.973	OF-40, DH-1
9 yrs.		654	.212	.334	1314	279	45	5	35	2.7	159	126	164	246	13	64	14	866	35	21	2	1.6	.977	OF-573, DH-8, 3B-1

Kelvin Torve

TORVE, KELVIN CURTIS BL TR 6′ 3″ 205 lbs.
B. Jan. 10, 1960, Rapid City, S. D.

Year	Team	Games	BA	SA	AB	H	2B	3B	HR	HR%	R	RBI	BB	SO	SB	Pinch Hit AB	Pinch Hit H	PO	A	E	DP	TC/G	FA	G by Pos
1988	MIN A	12	.188	.375	16	3	0	0	1	6.3	1	2	1	2	0	6	1	14	1	0	1	3.8	1.000	1B-4
1990	NY N	20	.289	.395	38	11	4	0	0	0.0	0	2	4	9	0	9	3	65	0	0	6	6.5	1.000	1B-9, OF-1
1991		10	.000	.000	8	0	0	0	0	0.0	0	0	0	1	0	8	0	0	2	0	0	2.0	1.000	1B-1
3 yrs.		42	.226	.339	62	14	4	0	1	1.6	1	4	5	12	0	23	4	79	3	0	7	5.5	1.000	1B-14, OF-1

Cesar Tovar

TOVAR, CESAR LEONARDO (Pepito) BR TR 5′ 9″ 155 lbs.
Born Cesar Leonardo Perez (Tovar).
B. July 3, 1940, Caracas, Venezuela D. July 14, 1994, Caracas, Venezuela.

Year	Team	Games	BA	SA	AB	H	2B	3B	HR	HR%	R	RBI	BB	SO	SB	Pinch Hit AB	Pinch Hit H	PO	A	E	DP	TC/G	FA	G by Pos
1965	MIN A	18	.200	.240	25	5	1	0	0	0.0	3	2	2	3	2	4	0	5	14	3	2	2.4	.864	2B-4, 3B-2, OF-2, SS-1
1966		134	.260	.335	465	121	19	5	2	0.4	57	41	44	50	16	2	0	254	274	14	44	4.1	.974	2B-76, SS-31, OF-24
1967		164	.267	.365	**649**	173	32	7	6	0.9	98	47	46	51	19	0	0	307	184	17	23	2.7	.967	OF-74, 3B-70, 2B-36, SS-9
1968		157	.272	.372	613	167	31	6	6	1.0	89	47	34	41	35	3	0	247	235	26	24	2.4	.949	OF-78, 3B-75, SS-35, 2B-18, C-1, P-1, 1B-1
1969		158	.288	.415	535	154	25	5	11	2.1	99	52	37	37	45	12	3	315	134	13	30	2.7	.972	OF-113, 2B-41, 3B-20
1970		161	.300	.442	650	195	**36**	**13**	10	1.5	120	54	52	47	30	3	0	389	25	14	6	2.6	.967	OF-151, 2B-8, 3B-4
1971		157	.311	.368	657	**204**	29	3	1	0.2	94	45	45	39	18	1	0	352	27	7	5	2.4	.982	OF-154, 3B-7, 2B-2
1972		141	.265	.334	548	145	20	6	2	0.4	86	31	39	39	21	3	0	287	10	5	2	2.2	.983	OF-139
1973	PHI N	97	.268	.357	328	88	18	4	1	0.3	49	21	29	35	6	14	4	113	113	12	32	2.6	.950	3B-46, OF-24, 2B-22
1974	TEX A	138	.292	.377	562	164	24	6	4	0.7	78	58	47	33	13	1	0	331	13	7	3	2.5	.980	OF-135, DH-3
1975	2 teams	TEX A (102G –.258)	OAK A (19G –.231)																					
″	total	121	.256	.313	453	116	17	0	3	0.7	58	31	30	28	20	12	1	59	6	5	1	0.6	.929	DH-73, OF-31, 2B-5, 3B-3, SS-1
1976	2 teams	OAK A (29G –.178)	NY A (13G –.154)																					
″	total	42	.167	.179	84	14	1	0	0	0.0	3	6	8	7	1	12	2	27	8	1	3	1.0	.972	OF-20, DH-14, 2B-3
12 yrs.		1488	.278	.368	5569	1546	253	55	46	0.8	834	435	413	410	226	67	10	2686	1043	124	175	2.5	.968	OF-945, 3B-227, 2B-215, DH-90, SS-77, P-1, C-1, 1B-1
LEAGUE CHAMPIONSHIP SERIES																								
1969	MIN A	3	.077	.077	13	1	0	0	0	0.0	0	0	1	2	0	0	0	10	0	0	0	3.3	1.000	OF-3
1970		3	.385	.538	13	5	0	1	0	0.0	2	1	0	0	0	0	0	0	0	0	0	0.0		OF-3, 2B-1
1975	OAK A	2	.500	.500	2	1	0	0	0	0.0	2	0	1	0	0	1	0	2	2	1	0	5.0	.800	2B-1
3 yrs.		8	.250	.321	28	7	0	1	0	0.0	4	1	2	2	0	1	0	12	2	1	0	1.9	.933	OF-6, 2B-2

Babe Towne

TOWNE, JAY KING BR TR 5′10″ 180 lbs.
B. Mar. 12, 1880, Coon Rapids, Iowa D. Oct. 29, 1938, Des Moines, Iowa.

Year	Team	Games	BA	SA	AB	H	2B	3B	HR	HR%	R	RBI	BB	SO	SB	Pinch Hit AB	Pinch Hit H	PO	A	E	DP	TC/G	FA	G by Pos
1906	CHI A	13	.278	.278	36	10	0	0	0	0.0	3	6	7		0	1	0	39	9	4	0	4.3	.923	C-12
WORLD SERIES																								
1906	CHI A	1	.000	.000	1	0	0	0	0	0.0	0	0	0	0	0	1	0	0	0	0	0	0.0	—	

George Townsend

TOWNSEND, GEORGE HODGSON BR TR 5′ 7½″ 180 lbs.
B. June 4, 1867, Hartsdale, N. Y. D. Mar. 15, 1930, New Haven, Conn.

Year	Team	Games	BA	SA	AB	H	2B	3B	HR	HR%	R	RBI	BB	SO	SB	Pinch Hit AB	Pinch Hit H	PO	A	E	DP	TC/G	FA	G by Pos
1887	PHI AA	31	.193	.220	109	21	3	0	0	0.0	12		3		8	0	0	102	39	22	1	5.3	.865	C-28, OF-3
1888		42	.155	.193	161	25	6	0	0	0.0	13	12	4		2	0	0	225	76	31	2	7.9	.907	C-42
1890	BAL AA	18	.239	.328	67	16	4	1	0	0.0	6		4		3	0	0	72	34	8	2	6.3	.930	C-18
1891		61	.191	.255	204	39	5	4	0	0.0	29	18	20	21	3	0	0	192	68	26	5	4.7	.909	C-58, OF-3
4 yrs.		152	.187	.238	541	101	18	5	0	0.0	60	30	31	21	16	0	0	591	217	87	10	5.9	.903	C-146, OF-6

Jim Toy

TOY, JAMES MADISON BR TR 5′ 6″ 160 lbs.
B. Feb. 20, 1858, Beaver Falls, Pa. D. Mar. 13, 1919, Beaver Falls, Pa.

Year	Team	Games	BA	SA	AB	H	2B	3B	HR	HR%	R	RBI	BB	SO	SB	Pinch Hit AB	Pinch Hit H	PO	A	E	DP	TC/G	FA	G by Pos
1887	CLE AA	109	.222	.300	423	94	20	5	1	0.2	56		17		8	0	0	764	65	34	55	7.6	.961	1B-82, OF-11, C-10, 3B-8, SS-3
1890	BKN AA	44	.181	.200	160	29	3	0	0	0.0	11		11		2	0	0	148	86	36	4	6.1	.867	C-44
2 yrs.		153	.211	.273	583	123	23	5	1	0.2	67		28		10	0	0	912	151	70	59	7.2	.938	1B-82, C-54, OF-11, 3B-8, SS-3

Jim Traber

TRABER, JAMES JOSEPH BL TL 6′ 194 lbs.
B. Dec. 26, 1961, Columbus, Ohio.

Year	Team	Games	BA	SA	AB	H	2B	3B	HR	HR%	R	RBI	BB	SO	SB	Pinch Hit AB	Pinch Hit H	PO	A	E	DP	TC/G	FA	G by Pos
1984	BAL A	10	.238	.238	21	5	0	0	0	0.0	3	2	2	4	0	3	1	0	0	0	0	0.0	.000	DH-9
1986		65	.255	.472	212	54	7	0	13	6.1	28	44	18	31	0	7	2	243	23	5	28	4.7	.982	1B-29, DH-21, OF-8
1988		103	.222	.324	352	78	6	0	10	2.8	25	45	19	42	1	9	2	481	59	6	51	5.6	.989	1B-57, DH-30, OF-11
1989		86	.209	.295	234	49	8	0	4	1.7	14	26	19	41	4	16	3	514	54	1	59	7.7	.998	1B-69, DH-5
4 yrs.		264	.227	.352	819	186	21	0	27	3.3	70	117	58	118	5	35	8	1238	136	12	138	5.8	.991	1B-155, DH-65, OF-19

Dick Tracewski

TRACEWSKI, RICHARD JOSEPH BR TR 5′11″ 160 lbs.
B. Feb. 3, 1935, Eynon, Pa.
Manager 1979.

Year	Team	Games	BA	SA	AB	H	2B	3B	HR	HR%	R	RBI	BB	SO	SB	Pinch Hit AB	Pinch Hit H	PO	A	E	DP	TC/G	FA	G by Pos
1962	LA N	15	.000	.000	2	0	0	0	0	0.0	3	0	2	0	0	1	0	1	4	0	0	1.3	1.000	SS-4
1963		104	.226	.258	217	49	2	1	1	0.5	23	10	19	39	2	0	0	105	216	14	34	3.2	.958	SS-81, 2B-23
1964		106	.247	.326	304	75	13	4	1	0.3	31	26	31	61	3	4	2	152	218	15	35	3.7	.961	2B-56, 3B-30, SS-19
1965		78	.215	.263	186	40	6	0	1	0.5	17	20	25	30	2	8	1	51	132	12	7	2.6	.938	3B-53, 2B-14, SS-7
1966	DET A	81	.194	.218	124	24	1	1	0	0.0	15	7	10	32	1	7	0	71	100	10	27	2.5	.945	2B-70, SS-3
1967		74	.280	.383	107	30	4	2	1	0.9	19	9	8	20	1	9	3	54	90	3	17	2.2	.980	SS-44, 2B-12, 3B-10
1968		90	.156	.236	212	33	3	1	4	1.9	30	15	24	51	3	9	1	82	157	5	27	3.0	.980	SS-51, 3B-16, 2B-14
1969		66	.139	.165	79	11	2	0	0	0.0	10	4	15	20	3	3	1	59	87	5	20	2.5	.967	SS-41, 2B-13, 3B-6
8 yrs.		614	.213	.272	1231	262	31	9	8	0.6	148	91	134	253	15	41	8	575	1004	64	167	2.9	.961	SS-250, 2B-202, 3B-115
WORLD SERIES																								
1963	LA N	4	.154	.154	13	2	0	0	0	0.0	1	0	1	2	0	0	0	7	7	1	1	3.8	.933	2B-4
1965		6	.118	.118	17	2	0	0	0	0.0	0	0	1	5	0	1	0	11	11	1	4	3.8	.957	2B-6
1968	DET A	2	—	—	0	0	0	0	0	—	1	0	0	0	0	0	0	0	0	0	0	0.0	.000	3B-1
3 yrs.		12	.133	.133	30	4	0	0	0	0.0	2	0	2	7	0	1	0	18	18	2	5	3.5	.947	2B-10, 3B-1

Jim Tracy

TRACY, JAMES EDWIN BL TR 6′ 185 lbs.
B. Dec. 31, 1955, Hamilton, Ohio.

Year	Team	Games	BA	SA	AB	H	2B	3B	HR	HR%	R	RBI	BB	SO	SB	Pinch Hit AB	Pinch Hit H	PO	A	E	DP	TC/G	FA	G by Pos
1980	CHI N	42	.254	.402	122	31	3	3	3	2.5	12	9	13	37	2	12	2	44	0	2	1	1.4	.957	OF-31, 1B-1
1981		45	.238	.302	63	15	2	1	0	0.0	6	5	12	14	1	29	5	16	0	0	0	1.5	1.000	OF-11
2 yrs.		87	.249	.368	185	46	5	4	3	1.6	18	14	25	51	3	41	7	60	0	2	1	1.4	.968	OF-42, 1B-1

Bill Traffley

TRAFFLEY, WILLIAM FRANKLIN
Brother of John Traffley.
B. Dec. 21, 1859, Staten Island, N. Y. D. June 23, 1908, Des Moines, Iowa.
BR TR 5′11½″ 185 lbs.

Year	Team	Games	BA	SA	AB	H	2B	3B	HR	HR%	R	RBI	BB	SO	SB	Pinch Hit AB	Pinch Hit H	PO	A	E	DP	TC/G	FA	G by Pos
1878	CHI N	2	.111	.111	9	1	0	0	0	0.0	1	1	0	1		0	0	7	3	0	0	5.0	1.000	C-2
1883	CIN AA	30	.200	.248	105	21	5	0	0	0.0	17		4			0	0	121	34	28	2	5.9	.847	C-29, SS-2
1884	BAL AA	53	.176	.252	210	37	4	6	0	0.0	25		3			0	0	336	57	30	6	7.8	.929	C-47, OF-6, 1B-1
1885		69	.154	.220	254	39	4	5	1	0.4	27		17			0	0	365	112	32	7	6.9	.937	C-61, OF-10, 2B-3
1886		25	.212	.235	85	18	0	1	0	0.0	15		10			0	0	163	35	10	4	8.3	.952	C-25
5 yrs.		179	.175	.235	663	116	13	12	1	0.2	85	1	34	1		0	0	992	241	100	19	7.2	.925	C-164, OF-16, 2B-3, SS-2, 1B-1

John Traffley

TRAFFLEY, JOHN M.
Brother of Bill Traffley.
B. 1862, Chicago, Ill. D. May 15, 1900, Baltimore, Md.
5′ 9″ 180 lbs.

Year	Team	Games	BA	SA	AB	H	2B	3B	HR	HR%	R	RBI	BB	SO	SB	Pinch Hit AB	Pinch Hit H	PO	A	E	DP	TC/G	FA	G by Pos
1889	LOU AA	1	.500	.500	2	1	0	0	0	0.0	0	0	0	0	0	0	0	0	0	1	0	1.0	.000	OF-1

Walt Tragesser

TRAGESSER, WALTER JOSEPH
B. June 14, 1887, Lafayette, Ind. D. Dec. 14, 1970, Lafayette, Ind.
BR TR 6′ 175 lbs.

Year	Team	Games	BA	SA	AB	H	2B	3B	HR	HR%	R	RBI	BB	SO	SB	Pinch Hit AB	Pinch Hit H	PO	A	E	DP	TC/G	FA	G by Pos
1913	BOS N	2	—	—	0	0	0	0	0	—	0	0	0	0	0	0	0	1	0	0	0	0.5	1.000	C-2
1915		7	.000	.000	7	0	0	0	0	0.0	1	0	0	2	0	0	0	15	2	1	1	2.6	.944	C-7
1916		41	.204	.222	54	11	1	0	0	0.0	3	4	5	10	0	11	1	73	27	3	2	3.6	.971	C-29
1917		98	.222	.269	297	66	10	2	0	0.0	23	25	15	36	5	4	2	433	105	16	11	5.7	.971	C-98
1918		7	.000	.000	1	0	0	0	0	0.0	0	0	0	0	0	0	0	4	1	1	0	0.9	.833	C-7
1919	2 teams BOS N (20G –.175) PHI N (35G –.237)																							
″	total	55	.221	.279	154	34	9	0	0	0.0	10	11	11	41	5	6	2	182	69	12	7	5.5	.954	C-48
1920	PHI N	62	.210	.386	176	37	11	1	6	3.4	17	26	4	36	4	8	2	157	46	12	4	4.1	.944	C-52
7 yrs.		272	.215	.295	689	148	31	3	6	0.9	54	66	35	125	14	29	7	865	250	45	25	4.8	.961	C-243

Red Tramback

TRAMBACK, STEPHEN JOSEPH
B. Oct. 1, 1915, Iselin, Pa. D. Dec. 28, 1979, Buffalo, N. Y.
BL TL 6′ 175 lbs.

Year	Team	Games	BA	SA	AB	H	2B	3B	HR	HR%	R	RBI	BB	SO	SB	Pinch Hit AB	Pinch Hit H	PO	A	E	DP	TC/G	FA	G by Pos
1940	NY N	2	.250	.250	4	1	0	0	0	0.0	0	0	1	1	1	1	0	2	0	1	0	3.0	.667	OF-1

Alan Trammell

TRAMMELL, ALAN STUART
B. Feb. 21, 1958, Garden Grove, Calif.
BR TR 6′ 165 lbs.

Year	Team	Games	BA	SA	AB	H	2B	3B	HR	HR%	R	RBI	BB	SO	SB	Pinch Hit AB	Pinch Hit H	PO	A	E	DP	TC/G	FA	G by Pos
1977	DET A	19	.186	.186	43	8	0	0	0	0.0	6	0	4	12	0	0	0	15	34	2	5	2.7	.961	SS-19
1978		139	.268	.339	448	120	14	6	2	0.4	49	34	45	56	3	0	0	239	421	14	95	4.8	.979	SS-139
1979		142	.276	.357	460	127	11	4	6	1.3	68	50	43	55	17	0	0	245	388	26	99	4.6	.961	SS-142
1980		146	.300	.404	560	168	21	5	9	1.6	107	65	69	63	12	2	0	225	412	13	89	4.5	.980	SS-144
1981		105	.258	.327	392	101	15	3	2	0.5	52	31	49	31	10	1	1	181	347	9	65	5.1	.983	SS-105
1982		157	.258	.395	489	126	34	3	9	1.8	66	57	52	47	19	0	0	259	459	16	97	4.7	.978	SS-157
1983		142	.319	.471	505	161	31	2	14	2.8	83	66	57	64	30	0	0	236	367	13	71	4.4	.979	SS-140
1984		139	.314	.468	555	174	34	5	14	2.5	85	69	60	63	19	3	1	180	314	10	71	3.7	.980	SS-114, DH-22
1985		149	.258	.380	605	156	21	7	13	2.1	79	57	50	71	14	0	0	225	400	15	89	4.3	.977	SS-149
1986		151	.277	.469	574	159	33	7	21	3.7	107	75	59	57	25	1	0	238	445	22	99	4.7	.969	SS-149, DH-2
1987		151	.343	.551	597	205	34	3	28	4.7	109	105	60	47	21	3	0	222	421	19	94	4.4	.971	SS-149
1988		128	.311	.464	466	145	24	1	15	3.2	73	69	46	46	7	2	2	195	355	11	67	4.5	.980	SS-125
1989		121	.243	.334	449	109	20	3	5	1.1	54	43	45	45	10	2	1	188	396	9	71	5.0	.985	SS-117, DH-2
1990		146	.304	.449	559	170	37	1	14	2.5	71	89	68	55	12	2	0	232	409	14	102	4.5	.979	SS-142, DH-3
1991		101	.248	.373	375	93	20	0	9	2.4	57	55	37	39	11	4	1	131	296	9	60	4.4	.979	SS-92, DH-6
1992		29	.275	.392	102	28	7	1	1	1.0	11	11	15	4	2	0	0	46	80	3	16	4.8	.977	SS-27
1993		112	.329	.496	401	132	25	3	12	3.0	72	60	38	38	12	11	2	113	238	9	31	3.2	.975	SS-63, 3B-35, OF-8, DH-6
1994		76	.267	.414	292	78	17	1	8	2.7	38	28	16	35	3	6	1	117	180	10	43	4.1	.967	SS-63, DH-11
1995		74	.269	.350	223	60	12	0	2	0.9	28	23	27	19	3	11	4	86	158	5	34	3.8	.980	SS-60, DH-6
19 yrs.		2227	.287	.419	8095	2320	410	55	184	2.3	1215	987	840	847	230	48	13	3373	6120	229	1298	4.4	.976	SS-2096, DH-58, 3B-35, OF-8
LEAGUE CHAMPIONSHIP SERIES																								
1984	DET A	3	.364	.818	11	4	0	1	1	9.1	2	3	3	1	0	0	0	1	8	0	0	3.0	1.000	SS-3
1987		5	.200	.250	20	4	1	0	0	0.0	3	2	1	2	0	0	0	6	9	1	1	3.2	.938	SS-5
2 yrs.		8	.258	.452	31	8	1	1	1	3.2	5	5	4	3	0	0	0	7	17	1	1	3.1	.960	SS-8
WORLD SERIES																								
1984	DET A	5	.450	.800	20	9	1	0	2	10.0	5	6	2	2	1	0	0	8	9	1	0	3.6	.944	SS-5

Cecil Travis

TRAVIS, CECIL HOWELL
B. Aug. 8, 1913, Riverdale, Ga.
BL TR 6′ 1½″ 185 lbs.

Year	Team	Games	BA	SA	AB	H	2B	3B	HR	HR%	R	RBI	BB	SO	SB	Pinch Hit AB	Pinch Hit H	PO	A	E	DP	TC/G	FA	G by Pos
1933	WAS A	18	.302	.326	43	13	1	0	0	0.0	7	2	2	5	0	3	0	8	30	1	1	2.6	.974	3B-15
1934		109	.319	.403	392	125	22	4	1	0.3	48	53	24	37	1	10	1	88	210	20	23	3.2	.937	3B-99
1935		138	.318	.397	534	170	28	7	0	0.0	85	61	41	28	4	7	2	164	258	16	30	3.4	.963	3B-114, OF-16
1936		138	.317	.433	517	164	34	10	2	0.4	77	92	39	21	4	10	4	244	231	31	58	3.9	.939	SS-71, OF-53, 2B-4, 3B-2
1937		135	.344	.439	526	181	27	7	3	0.6	72	66	39	34	3	5	3	229	396	23	99	5.0	.965	SS-129
1938		146	.335	.432	567	190	30	5	5	0.9	96	67	58	22	6	2	0	304	457	40	113	5.6	.950	SS-143
1939		130	.292	.403	476	139	20	9	5	1.1	55	63	34	25	0	10	3	194	359	24	74	4.9	.958	SS-118
1940		136	.322	.445	528	170	37	11	2	0.4	60	76	48	23	0	0	0	164	340	38	50	4.0	.930	3B-113, SS-23
1941		152	.359	.520	608	**218**	39	19	7	1.2	106	101	52	25	2	0	0	293	427	27	103	4.9	.964	SS-136, 3B-16
1945		15	.241	.315	54	13	2	1	0	0.0	4	10	4	5	0	1	0	18	28	4	4	3.6	.920	3B-14
1946		137	.252	.318	465	117	22	3	1	0.2	45	56	45	47	2	6	1	187	290	31	60	3.9	.939	SS-75, 3B-56
1947		74	.216	.260	204	44	4	1	1	0.5	10	10	16	19	1	24	3	53	112	9	15	3.2	.948	3B-39, SS-15
12 yrs.		1328	.314	.416	4914	1544	266	77	27	0.5	665	657	402	291	23	78	17	1946	3138	264	630	4.3	.951	SS-710, 3B-468, OF-69, 2B-4

Brian Traxler

TRAXLER, BRIAN LEE
B. Sept. 26, 1967, Waukegan, Ill.
BL TL 5′10″ 200 lbs.

Year	Team	Games	BA	SA	AB	H	2B	3B	HR	HR%	R	RBI	BB	SO	SB	Pinch Hit AB	Pinch Hit H	PO	A	E	DP	TC/G	FA	G by Pos
1990	LA N	9	.091	.182	11	1	1	0	0	0.0	0	0	0	4	0	8	1	6	2	0	0	2.7	1.000	1B-3

Jim Tray

TRAY, JAMES
B. Feb. 14, 1860, Jackson, Mich. D. July 28, 1905, Jackson, Mich.
5′11″ 180 lbs.

Year	Team	Games	BA	SA	AB	H	2B	3B	HR	HR%	R	RBI	BB	SO	SB	Pinch Hit AB	Pinch Hit H	PO	A	E	DP	TC/G	FA	G by Pos
1884	IND AA	6	.286	.286	21	6	0	0	0	0.0	2		2			0	0	45	5	5	0	9.2	.909	C-4, 1B-2

Pie Traynor

TRAYNOR, HAROLD JOSEPH BR TR 6′ 170 lbs.
B. Nov. 11, 1899, Framingham, Mass. D. Mar. 16, 1972, Pittsburgh, Pa.
Manager 1934–39.
Hall of Fame 1948.

Year	Team	Games	BA	SA	AB	H	2B	3B	HR	HR%	R	RBI	BB	SO	SB	Pinch Hit AB	Pinch Hit H	PO	A	E	DP	TC/G	FA	G by Pos
1920	PIT N	17	.212	.308	52	11	3	1	0	0.0	6	2	3	6	1	0	0	35	39	12	4	5.1	.860	SS-17
1921		7	.263	.263	19	5	0	0	0	0.0	0	2	1	2	0	2	1	4	9	1	0	3.5	.929	3B-3, SS-1
1922		142	.282	.375	571	161	17	12	4	0.7	89	81	27	28	17	1	0	186	278	31	26	3.5	.937	3B-124, SS-18
1923		153	.338	.489	616	208	19	**19**	12	1.9	108	101	34	19	28	0	0	191	310	26	30	3.4	.951	3B-153
1924		142	.294	.417	545	160	26	13	5	0.9	86	82	37	26	24	1	0	179	268	15	31	3.3	.968	3B-141
1925		150	.320	.464	591	189	39	14	6	1.0	114	106	52	19	15	0	0	228	305	24	42	3.7	.957	3B-150, SS-1
1926		152	.317	.436	574	182	25	17	3	0.5	83	92	38	14	8	1	0	191	294	24	40	3.4	.953	3B-148, SS-3
1927		149	.342	.455	573	196	32	9	5	0.9	93	106	22	11	11	0	0	225	293	20	25	3.5	.963	3B-143, SS-9
1928		144	.337	.462	569	192	38	12	3	0.5	91	124	28	10	12	0	0	175	296	27	15	3.5	.946	3B-144
1929		130	.356	.472	540	192	27	12	4	0.7	94	108	30	7	13	0	0	148	238	20	23	3.1	.951	3B-130
1930		130	.366	.509	497	182	22	11	9	1.8	90	119	48	19	7	0	0	130	268	25	18	3.3	.941	3B-130
1931		155	.298	.416	615	183	37	15	2	0.3	81	103	54	28	6	0	0	172	284	37	21	3.2	.925	3B-155
1932		135	.329	.433	513	169	27	10	2	0.4	74	68	32	20	6	7	2	173	222	27	14	3.3	.936	3B-127
1933		154	.304	.372	624	190	27	6	1	0.2	85	82	35	24	5	0	0	176	300	27	16	3.3	.946	3B-154
1934		119	.309	.410	444	137	22	10	1	0.2	62	61	21	27	3	7	4	116	176	14	16	2.8	.954	3B-110
1935		57	.279	.373	204	57	10	3	1	0.5	24	36	10	17	2	5	0	59	84	18	2	3.2	.888	3B-49, 1B-1
1937		5	.167	.167	12	2	0	0	0	0.0	3	0	0	1	0	0	0	2	8	0	0	3.3	1.000	3B-3
17 yrs.		1941	.320	.435	7559	2416	371	164	58	0.8	1183	1273	472	278	158	24	7	2390	3672	348	323	3.3	.946	3B-1864, SS-49, 1B-1
WORLD SERIES																								
1925	PIT N	7	.346	.615	26	9	0	2	1	3.8	2	4	3	1	1	0	0	6	18	0	2	3.4	1.000	3B-7
1927		4	.200	.267	15	3	1	0	0	0.0	1	0	0	1	0	0	0	5	9	1	1	3.8	.933	3B-4
2 yrs.		11	.293	.488	41	12	1	2	1	2.4	3	4	3	2	1	0	0	11	27	1	3	3.5	.974	3B-11

Fred Treacey

TREACEY, FREDERICK S. TR 5′ 9½″ 145 lbs.
Brother of Pete Treacey.
B. 1847, Brooklyn, N. Y. Deceased.

Year	Team	Games	BA	SA	AB	H	2B	3B	HR	HR%	R	RBI	BB	SO	SB	Pinch Hit AB	Pinch Hit H	PO	A	E	DP	TC/G	FA	G by Pos
1876	NY N	57	.211	.238	256	54	5	1	0	0.0	47	18	1	5		0	0	202	9	39	1	4.4	.844	OF-57

Pete Treacey

TREACEY, PETER
Brother of Fred Treacey.
B. 1852, Brooklyn, N. Y. Deceased.

Year	Team	Games	BA	SA	AB	H	2B	3B	HR	HR%	R	RBI	BB	SO	SB	Pinch Hit AB	Pinch Hit H	PO	A	E	DP	TC/G	FA	G by Pos
1876	NY N	2	.000	.000	5	0	0	0	0	0.0	1	0	1	0		0	0	0	3	1	0	2.0	.750	SS-2

Ray Treadaway

TREADAWAY, EDGAR RAYMOND BL TR 5′ 6″ 165 lbs.
B. Oct. 31, 1907, Ragland, Ala. D. Oct. 12, 1935, Chattanooga, Tenn.

Year	Team	Games	BA	SA	AB	H	2B	3B	HR	HR%	R	RBI	BB	SO	SB	Pinch Hit AB	Pinch Hit H	PO	A	E	DP	TC/G	FA	G by Pos
1930	WAS A	6	.211	.316	19	4	2	0	0	0.0	1	1	0	3	0	2	1	5	5	2	1	3.0	.833	3B-4

George Treadway

TREADWAY, GEORGE B. BL 6′ 175 lbs.
B. Nov. 11, 1866, Greenup County, Ky. Deceased.

Year	Team	Games	BA	SA	AB	H	2B	3B	HR	HR%	R	RBI	BB	SO	SB	Pinch Hit AB	Pinch Hit H	PO	A	E	DP	TC/G	FA	G by Pos
1893	BAL N	115	.260	.376	458	119	16	17	1	0.2	78	67	57	50	24	0	0	192	27	24	4	2.1	.901	OF-115
1894	BKN N	123	.328	.518	479	157	27	26	4	0.8	124	102	72	43	27	1	0	274	16	35	2	2.6	.892	OF-122, 1B-1
1895		86	.257	.378	339	87	14	3	7	2.1	54	54	33	22	9	0	0	117	7	16	4	1.6	.886	OF-86
1896	LOU N	2	.143	.143	7	1	0	0	0	0.0	0	1	1	0	0	0	0	16	1	6	0	11.5	.739	OF-1, 1B-1
4 yrs.		326	.284	.428	1283	364	57	46	12	0.9	256	224	163	115	60	1	0	599	51	81	10	2.2	.889	OF-324, 1B-2

Jeff Treadway

TREADWAY, HUGH JEFFERY BL TR 5′10″ 170 lbs.
B. Jan. 22, 1963, Columbus, Ga.

Year	Team	Games	BA	SA	AB	H	2B	3B	HR	HR%	R	RBI	BB	SO	SB	Pinch Hit AB	Pinch Hit H	PO	A	E	DP	TC/G	FA	G by Pos
1987	CIN N	23	.333	.452	84	28	4	0	2	2.4	9	4	2	6	1	2	1	44	48	4	14	4.6	.958	2B-21
1988		103	.252	.362	301	76	19	4	2	0.7	30	23	27	30	2	7	4	189	253	8	50	4.5	.982	2B-97, 3B-2
1989	ATL N	134	.277	.378	473	131	18	3	8	1.7	58	40	30	38	3	11	3	273	341	12	80	4.9	.981	2B-123, 3B-6
1990		128	.283	.403	474	134	20	2	11	2.3	56	59	25	42	3	6	2	241	360	15	72	5.0	.976	2B-122
1991		106	.320	.418	306	98	17	2	3	1.0	41	32	23	19	2	14	4	155	206	15	33	4.0	.960	2B-93
1992		61	.222	.286	126	28	6	1	0	0.0	5	5	9	16	1	17	3	53	85	1	25	3.0	.993	2B-45, 3B-1
1993	CLE A	97	.303	.403	221	67	14	1	2	0.9	25	27	14	21	1	36	9	46	111	10	13	2.6	.940	3B-42, 2B-19, DH-4
1994	LA N	52	.299	.343	67	20	3	0	0	0.0	14	5	5	8	1	27	13	21	37	3	7	2.3	.951	2B-24, 3B-3
1995	2 teams	LA N (17G –.118) MON N (41G –.240)																						
″	total	58	.209	.269	67	14	2	1	0	0.0	6	13	5	4	0	40	6	13	16	0	3	1.9	1.000	2B-12, 3B-3
9 yrs.		762	.281	.383	2119	596	103	14	28	1.3	244	208	140	184	14	160	45	1035	1457	68	297	4.1	.973	2B-556, 3B-57, DH-4
LEAGUE CHAMPIONSHIP SERIES																								
1991	ATL N	1	.333	.333	3	1	0	0	0	0.0	0	0	0	0	0	0	0	2	2	0	1	4.0	1.000	2B-1
1992		3	.667	.667	3	2	0	0	0	0.0	1	0	0	1	0	2	1	0	1	0	0	1.0	1.000	2B-1
2 yrs.		4	.500	.500	6	3	0	0	0	0.0	1	0	0	1	0	2	1	2	3	0	1	2.5	1.000	2B-2
WORLD SERIES																								
1991	ATL N	3	.250	.250	4	1	0	0	0	0.0	1	0	1	2	0	1	0	1	3	1	1	5.0	.800	2B-1
1992		1	.000	.000	1	0	0	0	0	0.0	0	0	0	0	0	1	0	0	0	0	0	0.0	—	
2 yrs.		4	.200	.200	5	1	0	0	0	0.0	1	0	1	2	0	2	0	1	3	1	1	5.0	.800	2B-1

Red Treadway

TREADWAY, THADFORD LEON BL TR 5′10″ 175 lbs.
B. Apr. 28, 1920, Athalone, N. C. D. May 26, 1994, Atlanta, Ga.

Year	Team	Games	BA	SA	AB	H	2B	3B	HR	HR%	R	RBI	BB	SO	SB	Pinch Hit AB	Pinch Hit H	PO	A	E	DP	TC/G	FA	G by Pos
1944	NY N	50	.300	.353	170	51	5	2	0	0.0	23	5	13	11	2	10	4	87	3	4	0	2.5	.957	OF-38
1945		88	.241	.330	224	54	4	2	4	1.8	31	23	20	13	3	25	5	107	3	7	0	2.0	.940	OF-60
2 yrs.		138	.266	.340	394	105	9	4	4	1.0	54	28	33	24	5	35	9	194	6	11	0	2.2	.948	OF-98

Frank Trechock

TRECHOCK, FRANK ADAM BR TR 5′10″ 175 lbs.
B. Dec. 24, 1915, Windber, Pa. D. Jan. 16, 1989, Minneapolis, Minn.

Year	Team	Games	BA	SA	AB	H	2B	3B	HR	HR%	R	RBI	BB	SO	SB	Pinch Hit AB	Pinch Hit H	PO	A	E	DP	TC/G	FA	G by Pos
1937	WAS A	1	.500	.500	4	2	0	0	0	0.0	0	0	0	1	0	0	0	2	4	2	2	8.0	.750	SS-1

Nick Tremark

TREMARK, NICHOLAS JOSEPH
B. Oct. 15, 1912, Yonkers, N. Y.

BL TL 5′ 5″ 150 lbs.

Year	Team	Games	BA	SA	AB	H	2B	3B	HR	HR%	R	RBI	BB	SO	SB	Pinch Hit AB	Pinch Hit H	PO	A	E	DP	TC/G	FA	G by Pos
1934	BKN N	17	.250	.286	28	7	1	0	0	0.0	3	6	2	2	0	7	1	16	0	0	0	1.8	1.000	OF-9
1935		10	.231	.308	13	3	1	0	0	0.0	1	3	1	1	0	5	2	6	0	0	0	1.5	1.000	OF-4
1936		8	.250	.313	32	8	2	0	0	0.0	6	1	3	2	0	0	0	16	2	0	0	2.3	1.000	OF-8
3 yrs.		35	.247	.301	73	18	4	0	0	0.0	10	10	6	5	0	12	3	38	2	0	0	1.9	1.000	OF-21

Chris Tremie

TREMIE, CHRISTOPHER JAMES
B. Oct. 17, 1969, Houston, Tex.

BR TR 6′ 200 lbs.

Year	Team	Games	BA	SA	AB	H	2B	3B	HR	HR%	R	RBI	BB	SO	SB	Pinch Hit AB	Pinch Hit H	PO	A	E	DP	TC/G	FA	G by Pos
1995	CHI A	10	.167	.167	24	4	0	0	0	0.0	0	0	1	2	0	1	0	39	2	1	0	4.2	.976	C-9, DH-1

Overton Tremper

TREMPER, CARLTON OVERTON
B. Mar. 22, 1906, Brooklyn, N. Y.

BR TR 5′10″ 163 lbs.

Year	Team	Games	BA	SA	AB	H	2B	3B	HR	HR%	R	RBI	BB	SO	SB	Pinch Hit AB	Pinch Hit H	PO	A	E	DP	TC/G	FA	G by Pos
1927	BKN N	36	.233	.233	60	14	0	0	0	0.0	4	4	0	2	0	8	1	13	2	0	0	0.8	1.000	OF-18
1928		10	.194	.323	31	6	2	1	0	0.0	1	1	0	1	0	1	1	11	2	0	0	1.3	1.000	OF-10
2 yrs.		46	.220	.264	91	20	2	1	0	0.0	5	5	0	3	0	9	2	24	4	0	0	1.0	1.000	OF-28

Mike Tresh

TRESH, MICHAEL
Father of Tom Tresh.
B. Feb. 23, 1914, Hazleton, Pa. D. Oct. 4, 1966, Detroit, Mich.

BR TR 5′11″ 170 lbs.

Year	Team	Games	BA	SA	AB	H	2B	3B	HR	HR%	R	RBI	BB	SO	SB	Pinch Hit AB	Pinch Hit H	PO	A	E	DP	TC/G	FA	G by Pos
1938	CHI A	10	.241	.310	29	7	2	0	0	0.0	3	2	8	4	0	0	0	37	8	1	1	4.6	.978	C-10
1939		119	.259	.284	352	91	5	2	0	0.0	49	38	64	30	3	0	0	480	59	8	7	4.6	.985	C-119
1940		135	.281	.340	480	135	15	5	1	0.2	62	64	49	40	3	0	0	619	69	12	7	5.2	.983	C-135
1941		115	.251	.282	390	98	10	1	0	0.0	38	33	38	27	1	0	0	488	81	11	12	5.0	.981	C-115
1942		72	.232	.275	233	54	8	1	0	0.0	21	15	28	24	2	0	0	258	37	7	2	4.2	.977	C-72
1943		86	.215	.226	279	60	3	0	0	0.0	20	20	37	20	2	0	0	321	62	7	4	4.6	.982	C-85
1944		93	.260	.292	312	81	8	1	0	0.0	22	25	37	15	0	0	0	370	47	8	5	4.6	.981	C-93
1945		150	.249	.273	458	114	11	0	0	0.0	50	47	65	37	6	0	0	575	102	11	7	4.6	.984	C-150
1946		80	.217	.258	217	47	5	2	0	0.0	28	21	36	24	0	1	0	330	48	2	13	4.8	.995	C-79
1947		90	.241	.277	274	66	6	2	0	0.0	19	20	26	26	2	1	0	313	38	9	10	4.0	.975	C-89
1948		39	.250	.287	108	27	1	0	1	0.9	10	11	9	9	0	5	2	99	16	2	1	3.4	.983	C-34
1949	CLE A	38	.216	.216	37	8	0	0	0	0.0	4	1	5	7	0	0	0	71	8	0	3	2.1	1.000	C-38
12 yrs.		1027	.249	.283	3169	788	74	14	2	0.1	326	297	402	263	19	7	2	3961	575	78	72	4.5	.983	C-1019

Tom Tresh

TRESH, THOMAS MICHAEL
Son of Mike Tresh.
B. Sept. 20, 1937, Detroit, Mich.

BB TR 6′ 1″ 180 lbs.

Year	Team	Games	BA	SA	AB	H	2B	3B	HR	HR%	R	RBI	BB	SO	SB	Pinch Hit AB	Pinch Hit H	PO	A	E	DP	TC/G	FA	G by Pos
1961	NY A	9	.250	.250	8	2	0	0	0	0.0	1	0	0	1	0	3	1	3	7	0	1	3.3	1.000	SS-3
1962		157	.286	.441	622	178	26	5	20	3.2	94	93	67	74	4	2	0	290	315	20	51	4.1	.968	SS-111, OF-43
1963		145	.269	.487	520	140	28	5	25	4.8	91	71	83	79	3	1	0	305	6	6	1	2.2	.981	OF-144
1964		153	.246	.402	533	131	25	5	16	3.0	75	73	73	110	13	7	1	259	7	1	0	1.8	.996	OF-146
1965		156	.279	.477	602	168	29	6	26	4.3	94	74	59	92	5	2	0	283	11	9	1	2.0	.970	OF-154
1966		151	.233	.421	537	125	12	4	27	5.0	76	68	86	89	5	3	1	224	191	12	18	2.9	.972	OF-84, 3B-64
1967		130	.219	.377	448	98	23	3	14	3.1	45	53	50	86	1	10	1	198	9	6	1	1.8	.972	OF-118
1968		152	.195	.308	507	99	18	3	11	2.2	60	52	76	97	10	6	1	244	410	32	70	4.7	.953	SS-119, OF-27
1969	2 teams	NY A (45G –.182) DET A (94G –.224)																						
″	total	139	.211	.350	474	100	18	3	14	3.0	59	46	56	70	4	10	1	215	313	17	58	4.2	.969	SS-118, OF-11, 3B-1
9 yrs.		1192	.245	.411	4251	1041	179	34	153	3.6	595	530	550	698	45	44	6	2021	1269	103	201	3.0	.970	OF-727, SS-351, 3B-65
WORLD SERIES																								
1962	NY A	7	.321	.464	28	9	1	0	1	3.6	5	4	1	4	2	0	0	14	0	0	0	2.0	1.000	OF-7
1963		4	.200	.400	15	3	0	0	1	6.7	1	2	1	6	0	0	0	3	0	0	0	0.8	1.000	OF-4
1964		7	.273	.636	22	6	2	0	2	9.1	4	7	6	7	0	0	0	11	0	0	0	1.6	1.000	OF-7
3 yrs.		18	.277	.508	65	18	3	0	4	6.2	10	13	8	17	2	0	0	28	0	0	0	1.6	1.000	OF-18

Alex Trevino

TREVINO, ALEJANDRO
Born Alejandro Trevino (Castro).
Brother of Bobby Trevino.
B. Aug. 26, 1957, Monterrey, Mexico.

BR TR 5′10″ 165 lbs.

Year	Team	Games	BA	SA	AB	H	2B	3B	HR	HR%	R	RBI	BB	SO	SB	Pinch Hit AB	Pinch Hit H	PO	A	E	DP	TC/G	FA	G by Pos
1978	NY N	6	.250	.250	12	3	0	0	0	0.0	3	0	1	2	0	1	0	12	4	0	0	2.7	1.000	C-5, 3B-1
1979		79	.271	.333	207	56	11	1	0	0.0	24	20	20	27	2	16	5	229	71	9	14	4.4	.971	C-36, 3B-27, 2B-8
1980		106	.256	.299	355	91	11	2	0	0.0	26	37	13	41	0	12	3	450	76	16	7	5.4	.970	C-86, 3B-14, 2B-1
1981		56	.262	.275	149	39	2	0	0	0.0	17	10	13	19	3	10	3	215	25	9	1	4.8	.964	C-45, 2B-4, OF-2, 3B-1
1982	CIN N	120	.251	.304	355	89	10	3	1	0.3	24	33	34	34	3	7	1	725	61	17	7	6.8	.979	C-116, 3B-2
1983		74	.216	.293	167	36	8	1	1	0.6	14	13	17	20	0	7	2	359	32	5	2	5.8	.987	C-63, 3B-4, 2B-1
1984	2 teams	CIN N (6G –.167) ATL N (79G –.244)																						
″	total	85	.243	.335	272	66	16	0	3	1.1	36	28	16	29	5	7	1	403	61	5	5	5.7	.989	C-83
1985	SF N	57	.217	.408	157	34	10	1	6	3.8	17	19	20	24	0	2	0	299	19	7	1	5.8	.978	C-55, 3B-1
1986	LA N	89	.262	.386	202	53	13	0	4	2.0	31	26	27	35	0	31	7	304	46	11	4	5.6	.970	C-63, 1B-1
1987		72	.222	.347	144	32	7	1	3	2.1	16	16	6	28	1	33	7	206	22	3	3	4.8	.987	C-45, OF-2, 3B-1
1988	HOU N	78	.249	.368	193	48	17	0	2	1.0	19	13	24	29	5	5	1	360	24	9	5	5.2	.977	C-74, OF-1
1989		59	.290	.405	131	38	7	1	2	1.5	15	16	7	18	0	21	1	173	13	2	2	5.2	.989	C-32, 3B-2, 1B-2
1990	3 teams	HOU N (42G –.188) NY N (9G –.300) CIN N (7G –.429)																						
″	total	58	.221	.314	86	19	5	0	1	1.2	3	13	7	11	0	22	7	172	9	4	0	4.6	.978	C-39, 1B-1
13 yrs.		939	.249	.333	2430	604	117	10	23	0.9	245	244	205	317	19	174	38	3907	463	97	51	5.5	.978	C-742, 3B-53, 2B-14, OF-5, 1B-4

Bobby Trevino

TREVINO, CARLOS
Born Carlos (Castro).
Brother of Alex Trevino.
B. Aug. 15, 1943, Monterrey, Mexico.

BR TR 6′ 2″ 185 lbs.

Year	Team	Games	BA	SA	AB	H	2B	3B	HR	HR%	R	RBI	BB	SO	SB	Pinch Hit AB	Pinch Hit H	PO	A	E	DP	TC/G	FA	G by Pos
1968	CAL A	17	.225	.250	40	9	1	0	0	0.0	1	1	2	9	0	6	0	24	1	1	0	2.4	.962	OF-11

Gus Triandos

TRIANDOS, GUS CONSTANTINE
B. July 30, 1930, San Francisco, Calif.
BR TR 6′ 3″ 205 lbs.

Year	Team	Games	BA	SA	AB	H	2B	3B	HR	HR%	R	RBI	BB	SO	SB	Pinch Hit AB	Pinch Hit H	PO	A	E	DP	TC/G	FA	G by Pos
1953	NY A	18	.157	.255	51	8	2	0	1	2.0	5	6	3	9	0	3	1	117	7	2	8	7.4	.984	1B-12, C-5
1954		2	.000	.000	1	0	0	0	0	0.0	0	0	0	1	0	1	0	0	0	0	0	0.0	.000	C-1
1955	BAL A	140	.277	.399	481	133	17	3	12	2.5	47	65	40	55	0	14	2	966	84	13	95	7.6	.988	1B-103, C-36, 3B-1
1956		131	.279	.462	452	126	18	1	21	4.6	47	88	48	73	0	5	1	790	89	12	39	6.3	.987	C-89, 1B-52
1957		129	.254	.445	418	106	21	1	19	4.5	44	72	38	73	0	17	1	580	64	5	13	5.4	.992	C-120
1958		137	.245	.456	474	116	10	0	30	6.3	59	79	60	65	1	8	2	698	61	10	11	5.8	.987	C-132
1959		126	.216	.430	393	85	7	1	25	6.4	43	73	65	56	0	3	0	597	63	13	5	5.4	.981	C-125
1960		109	.269	.418	364	98	18	0	12	3.3	36	54	41	62	0	4	0	516	45	6	5	5.4	.989	C-105
1961		115	.244	.426	397	97	21	0	17	4.3	35	63	44	60	0	4	0	642	55	8	9	6.2	.989	C-114
1962		66	.159	.280	207	33	7	0	6	2.9	20	23	29	43	0	4	1	355	28	6	2	6.2	.985	C-63
1963	DET A	106	.239	.407	327	78	13	0	14	4.3	28	41	32	67	0	13	3	535	29	1	4	6.3	.998	C-90
1964	PHI N	73	.250	.426	188	47	9	0	8	4.3	17	33	26	41	0	16	4	379	25	6	4	6.3	.985	C-64, 1B-1
1965	2 teams	PHI N (30G –.171)	HOU N (24G –.181)																					
″	total	54	.175	.240	154	27	4	0	2	1.3	8	11	14	31	0	8	3	268	15	8	2	6.1	.973	C-48
13 yrs.		1206	.244	.413	3907	954	147	6	167	4.3	389	608	440	636	1	100	18	6443	565	90	197	6.1	.987	C-992, 1B-168, 3B-1

Manny Trillo

TRILLO, JESUS MANUEL (Indio)
Born Jesus Manuel Marcano (Trillo).
B. Dec. 25, 1950, Carapito, Venezuela.
BR TR 6′ 1″ 150 lbs.

Year	Team	Games	BA	SA	AB	H	2B	3B	HR	HR%	R	RBI	BB	SO	SB	Pinch Hit AB	Pinch Hit H	PO	A	E	DP	TC/G	FA	G by Pos
1973	OAK A	17	.250	.417	12	3	2	0	0	0.0	0	3	0	4	0	0	0	15	17	2	5	2.1	.941	2B-16
1974		21	.152	.152	33	5	0	0	0	0.0	3	2	2	8	0	0	0	31	43	4	10	3.7	.949	2B-21
1975	CHI N	154	.248	.316	545	135	12	2	7	1.3	55	70	45	78	1	1	0	350	509	29	103	5.8	.967	2B-153, SS-1
1976		158	.239	.311	582	139	24	3	4	0.7	42	59	53	70	17	1	0	350	527	17	103	5.7	.981	2B-156, SS-1
1977		152	.280	.377	504	141	18	5	7	1.4	51	57	44	58	3	5	0	330	467	25	81	5.5	.970	2B-149
1978		152	.261	.332	552	144	17	5	4	0.7	53	55	50	67	0	2	2	354	505	19	99	5.9	.978	2B-149
1979	PHI N	118	.260	.357	431	112	22	1	6	1.4	40	42	20	59	4	0	0	270	368	10	84	5.5	.985	2B-118
1980		141	.292	.412	531	155	25	9	7	1.3	68	43	32	46	8	0	0	360	467	11	91	6.0	.987	2B-140
1981		94	.287	.395	349	100	14	3	6	1.7	37	36	26	37	10	0	0	245	286	7	61	5.7	.987	2B-94
1982		149	.271	.319	549	149	24	1	0	0.0	52	39	33	53	8	0	0	343	441	5	101	5.3	.994	2B-149
1983	2 teams	CLE A (88G –.272)	MON N (31G –.264)																					
″	total	119	.270	.342	441	119	21	1	3	0.7	49	45	31	64	1	0	0	229	355	8	81	5.0	.986	2B-118
1984	SF N	98	.254	.342	401	102	21	1	4	1.0	45	36	25	55	0	1	0	218	294	6	67	5.2	.988	2B-96, 3B-4
1985		125	.224	.288	451	101	16	2	3	0.7	36	25	40	44	2	5	0	263	361	13	73	5.3	.980	2B-120, 3B-1
1986	CHI N	81	.296	.382	152	45	10	0	1	0.7	22	19	16	21	0	14	3	114	63	5	14	2.6	.973	3B-53, 1B-11, 2B-6
1987		108	.294	.444	214	63	8	0	8	3.7	27	26	25	37	0	23	7	301	53	4	35	3.7	.989	1B-47, 3B-35, 2B-10, SS-6
1988		76	.250	.299	164	41	5	0	1	0.6	15	14	8	32	2	20	2	177	81	3	19	4.3	.989	1B-24, 3B-17, 2B-13, SS-7
1989	CIN N	17	.205	.205	39	8	0	0	0	0.0	3	0	2	9	0	4	1	27	18	1	2	3.3	.978	2B-10, 1B-3, SS-1
17 yrs.		1780	.263	.345	5950	1562	239	33	61	1.0	598	571	452	742	56	76	15	3977	4855	169	1029	5.2	.981	2B-1518, 3B-110, 1B-85, SS-16
DIVISIONAL PLAYOFF SERIES																								
1981	PHI N	5	.188	.188	16	3	0	0	0	0.0	1	1	4	0	0	0	0	15	10	0	0	5.0	1.000	2B-5
LEAGUE CHAMPIONSHIP SERIES																								
1974	OAK A	1	—	—	0	0	0	0	0	—	1	0	0	0	0	0	0	0	0	0	0	0.0	—	
1980	PHI N	5	.381	.571	21	8	2	1	0	0.0	1	4	0	2	0	0	0	18	25	1	4	8.8	.977	2B-5
2 yrs.		6	.381	.571	21	8	2	1	0	0.0	2	4	0	2	0	0	0	18	25	1	4	8.8	.977	2B-5
WORLD SERIES																								
1980	PHI N	6	.217	.304	23	5	2	0	0	0.0	4	2	0	0	0	0	0	14	25	1	6	6.7	.975	2B-6

Coaker Triplett

TRIPLETT, HERMAN COAKER
B. Dec. 18, 1911, Boone, N. C. D. Jan. 30, 1992, Boone, N. C.
BR TR 5′11″ 185 lbs.

Year	Team	Games	BA	SA	AB	H	2B	3B	HR	HR%	R	RBI	BB	SO	SB	Pinch Hit AB	Pinch Hit H	PO	A	E	DP	TC/G	FA	G by Pos
1938	CHI N	12	.250	.361	36	9	2	1	0	0.0	4	2	0	1	0	3	0	15	1	0	0	1.8	1.000	OF-9
1941	STL N	76	.286	.400	185	53	6	3	3	1.6	29	21	18	27	0	25	5	78	4	3	0	1.8	.965	OF-46
1942		64	.273	.390	154	42	7	4	1	0.6	18	23	17	15	1	16	2	82	2	3	0	1.9	.966	OF-46
1943	2 teams	STL N (9G –.080)	PHI N (105G –.272)																					
″	total	114	.260	.439	385	100	16	4	15	3.9	46	56	29	34	2	16	4	197	11	6	0	2.2	.972	OF-96
1944	PHI N	84	.234	.288	184	43	5	1	1	0.5	15	25	19	10	1	36	8	90	3	1	1	2.1	.989	OF-44
1945		120	.240	.333	363	87	11	1	7	1.9	36	46	40	27	6	28	5	202	3	12	1	2.4	.945	OF-92
6 yrs.		470	.256	.375	1307	334	47	14	27	2.1	148	173	123	114	10	124	24	664	24	25	2	2.1	.965	OF-333

Hal Trosky

TROSKY, HAROLD ARTHUR, SR.
Born Harold Arthur Troyavesky.
Father of Hal Trosky.
B. Nov. 11, 1912, Norway, Iowa D. June 18, 1979, Cedar Rapids, Iowa.
BL TR 6′ 2″ 207 lbs.
BB 1935

Year	Team	Games	BA	SA	AB	H	2B	3B	HR	HR%	R	RBI	BB	SO	SB	Pinch Hit AB	Pinch Hit H	PO	A	E	DP	TC/G	FA	G by Pos
1933	CLE A	11	.295	.477	44	13	1	2	1	2.3	6	8	2	12	0	0	0	91	4	1	6	8.7	.990	1B-11
1934		154	.330	.598	625	206	45	9	35	5.6	117	142	58	49	2	0	0	1487	86	22	145	10.4	.986	1B-154
1935		154	.271	.468	632	171	33	7	26	4.1	84	113	46	60	1	1	1	1567	88	11	129	10.9	.993	1B-153
1936		151	.343	.644	629	216	45	9	42	6.7	124	**162**	36	58	6	0	0	1368	86	22	126	9.7	.985	1B-151, 2B-1
1937		153	.298	.547	601	179	36	9	32	5.3	104	128	65	60	3	1	0	1403	76	10	131	9.8	.993	1B-152
1938		150	.334	.542	554	185	40	9	19	3.4	106	110	67	40	5	1	1	1232	102	10	124	9.1	.993	1B-148
1939		122	.335	.589	448	150	31	4	25	5.6	89	104	52	28	2	4	0	1004	97	9	97	9.4	.992	1B-118
1940		140	.295	.529	522	154	39	4	25	4.8	85	93	79	45	1	0	0	1207	70	11	129	9.3	.991	1B-139
1941		89	.294	.455	310	91	17	0	11	3.5	43	51	44	21	1	4	2	727	54	9	77	9.3	.989	1B-85
1944	CHI A	135	.241	.374	497	120	32	2	10	2.0	55	70	62	30	3	4	1	1310	57	9	122	10.6	.993	1B-130
1946		88	.254	.334	299	76	12	3	2	0.7	22	31	34	37	4	6	1	729	33	7	63	9.6	.991	1B-80
11 yrs.		1347	.302	.522	5161	1561	331	58	228	4.4	835	1012	545	440	28	21	6	12125	753	121	1149	9.8	.991	1B-1321, 2B-1

Mike Trost

TROST, MICHAEL J.
B. 1866, Philadelphia, Pa. D. Mar. 24, 1901, Philadelphia, Pa.
TR 6′½″ 180 lbs.

Year	Team	Games	BA	SA	AB	H	2B	3B	HR	HR%	R	RBI	BB	SO	SB	Pinch Hit AB	Pinch Hit H	PO	A	E	DP	TC/G	FA	G by Pos
1890	STL AA	17	.255	.353	51	13	2	0	1	2.0	10		6		4	0	0	70	13	9	0	5.4	.902	C-13, OF-4
1895	LOU N	3	.083	.083	12	1	0	0	0	0.0	1	1	0	1	1	0	0	17	0	0	1	5.7	1.000	1B-3
2 yrs.		20	.222	.302	63	14	2	0	1	1.6	11	1	6	1	5	0	0	87	13	9	1	5.4	.917	C-13, OF-4, 1B-3

Sam Trott

TROTT, SAMUEL W.
B. Mar. 1859, Washington, D. C. D. June 5, 1925, Catonsville, Md.
Manager 1891.
BL TL 5′ 9″ 190 lbs.

Year	Team	Games	BA	SA	AB	H	2B	3B	HR	HR%	R	RBI	BB	SO	SB	Pinch Hit AB	Pinch Hit H	PO	A	E	DP	TC/G	FA	G by Pos
1880	BOS N	39	.208	.256	125	26	4	1	0	0.0	14	9	3	5		0	0	177	56	28	0	6.5	.893	C-36, OF-4
1881	DET N	6	.200	.360	25	5	2	1	0	0.0	3	2	1	3		0	0	27	6	5	0	6.3	.868	C-6
1882		32	.240	.310	129	31	7	1	0	0.0	11	12	0	13		0	0	207	53	33	6	8.4	.887	C-23, SS-3, 2B-3, 1B-3, OF-2, 3B-1
1883		75	.244	.298	295	72	14	1	0	0.0	27		10	23		0	0	273	135	58	20	5.6	.876	2B-42, C-34, OF-6, 1B-1
1884	BAL AA	71	.257	.401	284	73	17	9	2	0.7	36		4			0	0	513	105	46	15	9.4	.931	C-60, 2B-6, OF-5
1885		21	.273	.341	88	24	2	2	0	0.0	12		5			0	0	91	32	21	6	6.0	.854	C-17, OF-4, 2B-2, SS-1
1887		85	.257	.330	300	77	16	3	0	0.0	44		27		8	0	0	428	136	53	11	7.2	.914	C-69, 2B-11, OF-3, 1B-2, SS-1
1888		31	.278	.454	108	30	11	4	0	0.0	19	22	4		1	0	0	164	36	22	4	6.9	.901	C-27, OF-3, 2B-1, 1B-1
8 yrs.		360	.250	.340	1354	338	73	22	2	0.1	166	45	54	44	9	0	0	1880	559	266	62	7.2	.902	C-272, 2B-65, OF-27, 1B-7, SS-5, 3B-1

Quincy Troupe

TROUPPE, QUINCY THOMAS
B. Dec. 25, 1912, Dublin, Ga. D. Aug. 12, 1993, Creve Coeur, Mo.
BB TR 6′ 2½″ 225 lbs.

Year	Team	Games	BA	SA	AB	H	2B	3B	HR	HR%	R	RBI	BB	SO	SB	Pinch Hit AB	Pinch Hit H	PO	A	E	DP	TC/G	FA	G by Pos
1952	CLE A	6	.100	.100	10	1	0	0	0	0.0	1	0	1	3	0	0	0	22	3	0	0	4.2	1.000	C-6

Dasher Troy

TROY, JOHN JOSEPH
B. May 8, 1856, New York, N. Y. D. Mar. 30, 1938, Ozone Park, N. Y.
BR TR 5′ 5″ 154 lbs.

Year	Team	Games	BA	SA	AB	H	2B	3B	HR	HR%	R	RBI	BB	SO	SB	Pinch Hit AB	Pinch Hit H	PO	A	E	DP	TC/G	FA	G by Pos
1881	DET N	11	.341	.409	44	15	3	0	0	0.0	2	4	3	8		0	0	13	23	7	4	3.9	.837	3B-7, 2B-4
1882	2 teams	DET N (40G –.243) PRO N (4G –.235)																						
″	total	44	.243	.308	169	41	7	2	0	0.0	23	14	5	11		0	0	79	111	46	10	5.1	.805	2B-31, SS-15
1883	NY N	85	.215	.269	316	68	7	5	0	0.0	37		9	33		0	0	202	262	70	26	6.3	.869	2B-73, SS-12
1884	NY AA	107	.264	.378	421	111	22	10	2	0.5	80		19			0	0	224	314	74	25	5.7	.879	2B-107
1885		45	.220	.305	177	39	3	3	2	1.1	24		5			0	0	128	103	38	17	6.0	.859	2B-42, OF-2, SS-1
5 yrs.		292	.243	.327	1127	274	42	20	4	0.4	166	18	41	52		0	0	646	813	235	82	5.8	.861	2B-257, SS-28, 3B-7, OF-2

Fred Truax

TRUAX, FREDERICK W.
B. 1868 D. Dec. 18, 1899, Omaha, Neb.

Year	Team	Games	BA	SA	AB	H	2B	3B	HR	HR%	R	RBI	BB	SO	SB	Pinch Hit AB	Pinch Hit H	PO	A	E	DP	TC/G	FA	G by Pos
1890	PIT N	1	.333	.333	3	1	0	0	0	0.0	0	1	1	1	0	0	0	1	0	0	1	1.0	1.000	OF-1

Harry Truby

TRUBY, HARRY GARVIN (Bird Eye)
B. May 12, 1870, Ironton, Ohio D. Mar. 21, 1953, Ironton, Ohio.
TR 5′11″ 185 lbs.

Year	Team	Games	BA	SA	AB	H	2B	3B	HR	HR%	R	RBI	BB	SO	SB	Pinch Hit AB	Pinch Hit H	PO	A	E	DP	TC/G	FA	G by Pos
1895	CHI N	33	.336	.361	119	40	3	0	0	0.0	17	16	10	7	7	0	0	98	93	10	21	6.1	.950	2B-33
1896	2 teams	CHI N (29G –.257) PIT N (8G –.156)																						
″	total	37	.234	.319	141	33	2	2	2	1.4	14	34	8	9	5	0	0	96	99	13	24	5.8	.938	2B-36
2 yrs.		70	.281	.338	260	73	5	2	2	0.8	31	50	18	16	12	0	0	194	192	23	45	5.9	.944	2B-69

Frank Truesdale

TRUESDALE, FRANK DAY
B. Mar. 31, 1884, St. Louis, Mo. D. Aug. 27, 1943, Albuquerque, N. M.
BB TR 5′ 8″ 145 lbs.

Year	Team	Games	BA	SA	AB	H	2B	3B	HR	HR%	R	RBI	BB	SO	SB	Pinch Hit AB	Pinch Hit H	PO	A	E	DP	TC/G	FA	G by Pos
1910	STL A	123	.219	.253	415	91	7	2	1	0.2	39	25	48		29	1	0	279	313	56	41	5.3	.914	2B-123
1911		1	—	—	0	0	0	0	0	—	1	0	0		0	0	0	0	0	0	0	0.0	—	
1914	NY A	77	.212	.230	217	46	4	0	0	0.0	23	13	39	35	11	3	1	123	189	18	20	4.6	.945	2B-67, 3B-4
1918	BOS A	15	.278	.306	36	10	1	0	0	0.0	6	2	4	5	1	4	1	14	28	4	2	4.6	.913	2B-10
4 yrs.		216	.220	.249	668	147	12	2	1	0.1	69	40	91	40	41	8	2	416	530	78	63	5.0	.924	2B-200, 3B-4

Ed Trumbull

TRUMBULL, EDWARD J.
Born Edward J. Trembly.
B. Nov. 3, 1860, Chicopee, Mass. D. Jan. 14, 1937, Kingston, Pa.

Year	Team	Games	BA	SA	AB	H	2B	3B	HR	HR%	R	RBI	BB	SO	SB	Pinch Hit AB	Pinch Hit H	PO	A	E	DP	TC/G	FA	G by Pos
1884	WAS AA	25	.116	.140	86	10	2	0	0	0.0	5		2			0	0	24	24	14	1	2.5	.774	OF-15, P-10

Greg Tubbs

TUBBS, GREGORY ALAN
B. Aug. 31, 1962, Smithville, Tenn.
BR TR 5′ 9″ 195 lbs.

Year	Team	Games	BA	SA	AB	H	2B	3B	HR	HR%	R	RBI	BB	SO	SB	Pinch Hit AB	Pinch Hit H	PO	A	E	DP	TC/G	FA	G by Pos
1993	CIN N	35	.186	.237	59	11	0	0	1	1.7	10	2	14	10	3	9	0	38	1	1	0	1.9	.975	OF-21

Michael Tucker

TUCKER, MICHAEL ANTHONY
B. June 25, 1971, South Boston, Va.
BL TR 6′ 2″ 185 lbs.

Year	Team	Games	BA	SA	AB	H	2B	3B	HR	HR%	R	RBI	BB	SO	SB	Pinch Hit AB	Pinch Hit H	PO	A	E	DP	TC/G	FA	G by Pos
1995	KC A	62	.260	.384	177	46	10	0	4	2.3	23	17	18	51	2	6	0	67	3	1	0	1.2	.986	OF-36, DH-22

Ollie Tucker

TUCKER, OLIVER DINWIDDIE
B. Jan. 27, 1902, Radiant, Va. D. July 13, 1940, Radiant, Va.
BL TR 5′11″ 190 lbs.

Year	Team	Games	BA	SA	AB	H	2B	3B	HR	HR%	R	RBI	BB	SO	SB	Pinch Hit AB	Pinch Hit H	PO	A	E	DP	TC/G	FA	G by Pos
1927	WAS A	20	.208	.292	24	5	2	0	0	0.0	1	8	4	2	0	10	1	9	0	0	0	1.8	1.000	OF-5
1928	CLE A	14	.128	.191	47	6	0	0	1	2.1	5	2	7	3	0	0	0	18	3	0	0	1.5	1.000	OF-14
2 yrs.		34	.155	.225	71	11	2	0	1	1.4	6	10	11	5	0	10	1	27	3	0	0	1.6	1.000	OF-19

Scooter Tucker

TUCKER, EDDIE JACK
B. Nov. 18, 1966, Greenville, Miss.
BR TR 6′ 2″ 205 lbs.

Year	Team	Games	BA	SA	AB	H	2B	3B	HR	HR%	R	RBI	BB	SO	SB	Pinch Hit AB	Pinch Hit H	PO	A	E	DP	TC/G	FA	G by Pos
1992	HOU N	20	.120	.140	50	6	1	0	0	0.0	5	3	3	13	1	1	0	75	6	2	0	4.4	.976	C-19
1993		9	.192	.231	26	5	1	0	0	0.0	1	3	2	3	0	1	0	56	3	0	0	7.4	1.000	C-8
1995	2 teams	HOU N (5G –.286) CLE A (17G –.000)																						
″	total	22	.074	.185	27	2	0	0	1	3.7	3	1	5	4	0	3	0	60	4	1	0	3.3	.985	C-20
3 yrs.		51	.126	.175	103	13	2	0	1	1.0	9	7	10	20	1	5	0	191	13	3	0	4.4	.986	C-47

Thurman Tucker

TUCKER, THURMAN LOWELL (Joe E.)
B. Sept. 26, 1917, Gordon, Tex. D. May 7, 1993, Oklahoma City, Okla.
BL TR 5′10½″ 165 lbs.

Year	Team	Games	BA	SA	AB	H	2B	3B	HR	HR%	R	RBI	BB	SO	SB	Pinch Hit AB	Pinch Hit H	PO	A	E	DP	TC/G	FA	G by Pos
1942	CHI A	7	.125	.208	24	3	0	1	0	0.0	2	1	0	4	0	2	0	8	1	1	0	2.0	.900	OF-5
1943		139	.235	.303	528	124	15	6	3	0.6	81	39	79	72	29	6	1	399	14	5	1	3.2	.988	OF-132
1944		124	.287	.361	446	128	15	6	2	0.4	59	46	57	40	13	1	0	414	12	4	2	3.6	.991	OF-120
1946		121	.288	.354	438	126	20	3	1	0.2	62	36	54	45	9	8	3	276	11	3	1	2.6	.990	OF-110
1947		89	.236	.315	254	60	9	4	1	0.4	28	17	38	25	10	19	4	171	5	4	2	2.8	.978	OF-65
1948	CLE A	83	.260	.343	242	63	13	2	1	0.4	52	19	31	17	11	10	3	172	5	0	2	2.7	1.000	OF-66
1949		80	.244	.289	197	48	5	2	0	0.0	28	14	18	19	4	22	2	119	2	2	0	2.4	.984	OF-52

Thurman Tucker *continued*

Year	Team	Games	BA	SA	AB	H	2B	3B	HR	HR%	R	RBI	BB	SO	SB	Pinch Hit AB	Pinch Hit H	PO	A	E	DP	TC/G	FA	G by Pos
1950		57	.178	.228	101	18	2	0	1	1.0	13	7	14	14	1	18	3	58	2	2	1	1.8	.968	OF-34
1951		1	.000	.000	1	0	0	0	0	0.0	0	0	0	1	0	1	0	0	0	0	0	0.0	—	
9 yrs.		701	.255	.325	2231	570	79	24	9	0.4	325	179	291	237	77	87	16	1617	52	21	9	2.9	.988	OF-584
WORLD SERIES																								
1948	CLE A	1	.333	.333	3	1	0	0	0	0.0	1	0	1	0	0	0	0	3	1	0	1	4.0	1.000	OF-1

Tommy Tucker

TUCKER, THOMAS JOSEPH BB TR 5′11″ 165 lbs.
B. Oct. 28, 1863, Holyoke, Mass. D. Oct. 22, 1935, Montague, Mass.

Year	Team	Games	BA	SA	AB	H	2B	3B	HR	HR%	R	RBI	BB	SO	SB	Pinch Hit AB	Pinch Hit H	PO	A	E	DP	TC/G	FA	G by Pos
1887	BAL AA	136	.275	.372	524	144	15	9	6	1.1	114		29		85	0	0	1346	50	35	49	10.5	.976	1B-136
1888		136	.287	.400	520	149	17	12	6	1.2	74	61	16		43	0	0	1365	59	38	64	10.7	.974	1B-129, OF-7, P-1
1889		134	**.372**	.484	527	**196**	22	11	5	0.9	103	99	42	26	63	0	0	1165	48	48	63	9.3	.962	1B-123, OF-12
1890	BOS N	132	.295	.362	539	159	17	8	1	0.2	104	62	56	22	43	0	0	1341	39	29	53	10.7	.979	1B-132
1891		140	.270	.328	548	148	16	5	2	0.4	103	69	37	30	26	0	0	1313	55	34	66	9.9	.976	1B-140, P-1
1892		149	.282	.341	542	153	15	7	1	0.2	85	62	45	35	22	0	0	1484	51	45	96	10.6	.972	1B-149
1893		121	.284	.362	486	138	13	2	7	1.4	83	91	27	31	8	0	0	1252	39	27	89	10.9	.980	1B-121
1894		123	.330	.420	500	165	24	6	3	0.6	112	100	53	21	18	0	0	1108	68	18	82	9.6	.985	1B-123, OF-1
1895		125	.249	.335	462	115	19	6	3	0.6	87	73	61	29	15	0	0	1159	82	28	78	10.2	.978	1B-125
1896		122	.304	.395	474	144	27	5	2	0.4	74	72	30	29	6	0	0	1214	72	20	72	10.7	.985	1B-122
1897	2 teams	BOS N (4G –.214) WAS N (93G –.338)																						
″	total	97	.333	.456	366	122	20	5	5	1.4	52	65	29		18	0	0	897	46	17	58	9.9	.982	1B-97
1898	2 teams	BKN N (73G –.279) STL N (72G –.238)																						
″	total	145	.260	.318	535	139	16	6	1	0.2	53	54	30		2	0	0	1552	85	30	84	11.5	.982	1B-145
1899	CLE N	127	.241	.296	456	110	19	3	0	0.0	40	40	24		3	0	0	1229	58	30	71	10.4	.977	1B-127
13 yrs.		1687	.290	.373	6479	1882	240	85	42	0.6	1084	848	479	223	352	0	0	16425	752	399	925	10.4	.977	1B-1669, OF-20, P-2

Brian Turang

TURANG, BRIAN CRAIG BR TR 5′10″ 170 lbs.
B. June 14, 1967, Long Beach, Calif.

Year	Team	Games	BA	SA	AB	H	2B	3B	HR	HR%	R	RBI	BB	SO	SB	Pinch Hit AB	Pinch Hit H	PO	A	E	DP	TC/G	FA	G by Pos
1993	SEA A	40	.250	.343	140	35	11	1	0	0.0	22	7	17	20	6	2	1	72	2	1	0	1.8	.987	OF-38, 3B-2, 2B-1, DH-1
1994		38	.188	.277	112	21	5	1	1	0.9	9	8	7	25	3	1	0	52	10	2	3	1.6	.969	OF-30, 2B-5, DH-4
2 yrs.		78	.222	.313	252	56	16	2	1	0.4	31	15	24	45	9	3	1	124	12	3	3	1.7	.978	OF-68, 2B-6, DH-5, 3B-2

Jerry Turbidy

TURBIDY, JEREMIAH BR TR 5′ 8″ 165 lbs.
B. July 4, 1852, Dudley, Mass. D. Sept. 5, 1920, Webster, Mass.

Year	Team	Games	BA	SA	AB	H	2B	3B	HR	HR%	R	RBI	BB	SO	SB	Pinch Hit AB	Pinch Hit H	PO	A	E	DP	TC/G	FA	G by Pos
1884	KC U	13	.224	.306	49	11	4	0	0	0.0	5		3			0	0	24	54	16	4	7.2	.830	SS-13

Eddie Turchin

TURCHIN, EDWARD LAWRENCE (Smiley) BR TR 5′10″ 165 lbs.
B. Feb. 10, 1917, New York, N. Y. D. Feb. 8, 1982, Brookhaven, N. Y.

Year	Team	Games	BA	SA	AB	H	2B	3B	HR	HR%	R	RBI	BB	SO	SB	Pinch Hit AB	Pinch Hit H	PO	A	E	DP	TC/G	FA	G by Pos
1943	CLE A	11	.231	.231	13	3	0	0	0	0.0	4	1	3	1	0	0	0	5	9	1	1	2.5	.933	3B-4, SS-2

Pete Turgeon

TURGEON, EUGENE JOSEPH BR TR 5′ 6″ 145 lbs.
B. Jan. 3, 1897, Minneapolis, Minn. D. Jan. 24, 1977, Wichita Falls, Tex.

Year	Team	Games	BA	SA	AB	H	2B	3B	HR	HR%	R	RBI	BB	SO	SB	Pinch Hit AB	Pinch Hit H	PO	A	E	DP	TC/G	FA	G by Pos
1923	CHI N	3	.167	.167	6	1	0	0	0	0.0	1	0	0	0	0	0	0	4	3	1	2	4.0	.875	SS-2

Chris Turner

TURNER, CHRISTOPHER WAN BR TR 6′ 2″ 190 lbs.
B. Mar. 23, 1969, Bowling Green, Ky.

Year	Team	Games	BA	SA	AB	H	2B	3B	HR	HR%	R	RBI	BB	SO	SB	Pinch Hit AB	Pinch Hit H	PO	A	E	DP	TC/G	FA	G by Pos
1993	CAL A	25	.280	.387	75	21	5	0	1	1.3	9	13	9	16	1	0	0	116	14	1	0	5.2	.992	C-25
1994		58	.242	.322	149	36	7	1	1	0.7	23	12	10	29	3	2	0	268	29	1	0	5.2	.997	C-57
1995		5	.100	.100	10	1	0	0	0	0.0	0	1	0	3	0	1	0	17	2	0	0	4.8	1.000	C-4
3 yrs.		88	.248	.333	234	58	12	1	2	0.9	32	26	19	48	4	3	0	401	45	2	0	5.2	.996	C-86

Earl Turner

TURNER, EARL EDWIN BR TR 5′ 9″ 170 lbs.
B. May 6, 1923, Pittsfield, Mass.

Year	Team	Games	BA	SA	AB	H	2B	3B	HR	HR%	R	RBI	BB	SO	SB	Pinch Hit AB	Pinch Hit H	PO	A	E	DP	TC/G	FA	G by Pos
1948	PIT N	2	.000	.000	1	0	0	0	0	0.0	0	0	0	0	0	1	0	0	0	0	0	0.0	.000	C-1
1950		40	.243	.365	74	18	0	0	3	4.1	10	5	4	13	1	6	1	101	11	3	3	3.4	.974	C-34
2 yrs.		42	.240	.360	75	18	0	0	3	4.0	10	5	4	13	1	7	1	101	11	3	3	3.3	.974	C-35

Jerry Turner

TURNER, JOHN WEBBER BL TL 5′ 9″ 180 lbs.
B. Jan. 17, 1954, Texarkana, Ark.

Year	Team	Games	BA	SA	AB	H	2B	3B	HR	HR%	R	RBI	BB	SO	SB	Pinch Hit AB	Pinch Hit H	PO	A	E	DP	TC/G	FA	G by Pos
1974	SD N	17	.292	.313	48	14	1	0	0	0.0	4	2	3	5	2	6	3	14	1	0	0	1.2	1.000	OF-13
1975		11	.273	.273	22	6	0	0	0	0.0	1	0	2	1	0	6	3	10	0	1	0	2.8	.909	OF-4
1976		105	.267	.413	281	75	16	5	5	1.8	41	37	32	38	12	25	5	115	6	5	0	1.7	.960	OF-74
1977		118	.246	.412	289	71	16	1	10	3.5	43	48	31	43	12	45	12	114	10	7	2	1.9	.947	OF-69
1978		106	.280	.436	225	63	9	1	8	3.6	28	37	21	32	6	49	**20**	91	5	3	0	1.7	.970	OF-58
1979		138	.248	.368	448	111	23	2	9	2.0	55	61	34	58	4	28	5	197	7	9	2	1.9	.958	OF-115
1980		85	.288	.379	153	44	5	0	3	2.0	22	18	10	18	8	47	13	44	2	0	1	1.4	1.000	OF-34
1981	2 teams	SD N (33G –.226) CHI A (10G –.167)																						
″	total	43	.209	.349	43	9	0	0	2	4.7	6	8	5	5	0	29	5	7	0	1	0	1.6	.875	OF-5
1982	DET A	85	.248	.376	210	52	3	0	8	3.8	21	27	20	37	1	24	4	10	0	1	0	0.2	.909	DH-50, OF-13
1983	SD N	25	.130	.130	23	3	0	0	0	0.0	1	0	1	8	0	23	3	0	0	0	0	0.0	.000	OF-1
10 yrs.		733	.257	.387	1742	448	73	9	45	2.6	222	238	159	245	45	282	73	602	31	27	5	1.5	.959	OF-386, DH-50

Shane Turner

TURNER, SHANE LEE BL TR 5′10″ 180 lbs.
B. Jan. 8, 1963, Los Angeles, Calif.

Year	Team	Games	BA	SA	AB	H	2B	3B	HR	HR%	R	RBI	BB	SO	SB	Pinch Hit AB	Pinch Hit H	PO	A	E	DP	TC/G	FA	G by Pos
1988	PHI N	18	.171	.171	35	6	0	0	0	0.0	1	1	5	9	0	5	1	8	14	1	2	1.8	.957	3B-8, SS-5
1991	BAL A	4	.000	.000	1	0	0	0	0	0.0	0	0	0	0	0	1	0	0	1	0	0	0.5	1.000	2B-1, DH-1
1992	SEA A	34	.270	.338	74	20	5	0	0	0.0	8	5	9	15	2	5	1	21	29	5	5	1.7	.909	3B-18, OF-15
3 yrs.		56	.236	.282	110	26	5	0	0	0.0	9	6	14	24	2	11	2	29	44	6	7	1.6	.924	3B-26, OF-15, SS-5, 2B-1, DH-1

Terry Turner

TURNER, TERRENCE LAMONT (Cotton) BR TR 5′ 8″ 149 lbs.
B. Feb. 28, 1881, Sandy Lake, Pa. D. July 18, 1960, Cleveland, Ohio.

Year	Team	Games	BA	SA	AB	H	2B	3B	HR	HR%	R	RBI	BB	SO	SB	Pinch Hit AB	Pinch Hit H	PO	A	E	DP	TC/G	FA	G by Pos
1901	PIT N	2	.429	.429	7	3	0	0	0	0.0	0	1	0		0	0	0	3	7	2	0	6.0	.833	3B-2
1904	CLE A	111	.235	.295	404	95	9	6	1	0.2	41	45	11		5	0	0	191	376	36	28	5.4	.940	SS-111
1905		154	.263	.359	582	153	16	14	4	0.7	48	72	14		17	0	0	285	430	41	49	4.9	.946	SS-154

Terry Turner *continued*

Year	Team	Games	BA	SA	AB	H	2B	3B	HR	HR%	R	RBI	BB	SO	SB	Pinch Hit AB	Pinch Hit H	PO	A	E	DP	TC/G	FA	G by Pos
1906		147	.291	.372	584	170	27	7	2	0.3	85	62	35		27	0	0	287	570	36	61	6.1	.960	SS-147
1907		148	.242	.307	524	127	20	7	0	0.0	57	46	19		27	1	0	258	477	39	67	5.3	.950	SS-145
1908		60	.239	.303	201	48	11	1	0	0.0	21	19	15		18	7	1	65	68	6	4	2.6	.957	OF-36, SS-17
1909		53	.250	.322	208	52	7	4	0	0.0	25	16	14		14	1	0	112	176	11	21	5.8	.963	SS-26, 2B-26
1910		150	.230	.275	574	132	14	6	0	0.0	71	33	53		31	1	0	249	449	25	50	4.9	.965	SS-94, 3B-46, 2B-9
1911		117	.252	.333	417	105	16	9	0	0.0	59	28	34		29	0	0	174	245	19	16	3.7	.957	3B-94, 2B-14, SS-10
1912		103	.308	.368	370	114	14	4	0	0.0	54	33	31		19	0	0	129	199	17	21	3.3	.951	3B-103
1913		120	.247	.302	388	96	13	4	0	0.0	61	44	55	35	13	3	1	188	279	18	35	4.1	.963	3B-71, 2B-25, SS-21
1914		120	.245	.327	428	105	14	9	1	0.2	43	33	44	36	17	0	0	168	290	15	23	3.9	.968	3B-103, 2B-17
1915		95	.252	.313	262	66	14	1	0	0.0	35	14	29	13	12	3	0	92	190	10	14	4.1	.966	2B-51, 3B-20
1916		124	.262	.311	428	112	15	3	0	0.0	52	38	40	29	15	5	1	164	308	14	28	4.1	.971	3B-77, 2B-42
1917		69	.206	.244	180	37	7	0	0	0.0	16	15	14	19	4	5	0	86	119	4	7	3.3	.981	3B-40, 2B-23, SS-1
1918		74	.249	.296	233	58	7	2	0	0.0	24	23	22	15	6	1	1	77	170	5	6	3.5	.980	3B-46, 2B-26, SS-1
1919	**PHI A**	38	.189	.213	127	24	3	0	0	0.0	7	6	5	9	2	1	0	61	114	8	16	4.9	.956	SS-19, 2B-17, 3B-1
17 yrs.		1685	.253	.318	5917	1497	207	77	8	0.1	699	528	435	156	256	28	4	2589	4467	306	446	4.5	.958	SS-746, 3B-603, 2B-250, OF-36

Tom Turner

TURNER, THOMAS RICHARD BR TR 6′½″ 215 lbs.
B. Sept. 8, 1916, Custer, Okla. D. May 14, 1986, Kennewick, Wash.

Year	Team	Games	BA	SA	AB	H	2B	3B	HR	HR%	R	RBI	BB	SO	SB	Pinch Hit AB	Pinch Hit H	PO	A	E	DP	TC/G	FA	G by Pos
1940	**CHI A**	37	.208	.260	96	20	1	2	0	0.0	11	6	3	12	1	7	1	110	13	4	0	4.4	.969	C-29
1941		38	.238	.278	126	30	5	0	0	0.0	7	8	9	15	2	3	1	166	21	4	3	5.5	.979	C-35
1942		56	.242	.352	182	44	9	1	3	1.6	18	21	19	15	0	2	1	199	35	7	5	4.5	.971	C-54
1943		51	.240	.338	154	37	7	1	2	1.3	16	11	13	21	1	2	0	186	34	5	5	4.6	.978	C-49
1944	**2 teams**	**CHI A** (36G –.230) **STL A** (15G –.320)																						
″	**total**	51	.246	.341	138	34	7	0	2	1.4	11	17	7	21	0	4	0	149	18	7	3	3.7	.960	C-47
5 yrs.		233	.237	.320	696	165	29	4	7	1.0	63	63	51	84	4	18	3	810	121	27	16	4.5	.972	C-214
WORLD SERIES																								
1944	**STL A**	1	.000	.000	1	0	0	0	0	0.0	0	0	0	0	0	1	0	0	0	0	0	0.0	—	

Tuck Turner

TURNER, GEORGE A. BB TL 5′6½″ 155 lbs.
B. Feb. 13, 1873, West Brighton, N. Y. D. July 16, 1945, Staten Island, N. Y.

Year	Team	Games	BA	SA	AB	H	2B	3B	HR	HR%	R	RBI	BB	SO	SB	Pinch Hit AB	Pinch Hit H	PO	A	E	DP	TC/G	FA	G by Pos
1893	**PHI N**	36	.323	.406	155	50	4	3	1	0.6	32	13	9	19	7	0	0	79	5	6	2	2.5	.933	OF-36
1894		80	.416	.540	339	141	21	9	1	0.3	91	82	23	13	11	1	0	134	7	13	1	1.9	.916	OF-78, P-1
1895		59	.386	.510	210	81	8	6	2	1.0	51	43	25	11	14	4	**2**	89	5	17	0	2.0	.847	OF-55
1896	**2 teams**	**PHI N** (13G –.219) **STL N** (51G –.246)																						
″	**total**	64	.243	.362	235	57	9	8	1	0.4	42	27	22	26	12	4	0	84	8	5	1	1.6	.948	OF-59
1897	**STL N**	103	.291	.404	416	121	17	12	2	0.5	58	41	35		8	1	0	146	10	9	3	1.6	.945	OF-102
1898		35	.199	.255	141	28	8	0	0	0.0	20	7	14		1	1	0	50	2	4	1	1.6	.929	OF-34
6 yrs.		377	.320	.429	1496	478	67	38	7	0.5	294	213	128	69	53	11	2	582	37	54	8	1.8	.920	OF-364, P-1

Bill Tuttle

TUTTLE, WILLIAM ROBERT BR TR 6′ 190 lbs.
B. July 4, 1929, Elwood, Ill.

Year	Team	Games	BA	SA	AB	H	2B	3B	HR	HR%	R	RBI	BB	SO	SB	Pinch Hit AB	Pinch Hit H	PO	A	E	DP	TC/G	FA	G by Pos
1952	**DET A**	7	.240	.240	25	6	0	0	0	0.0	2	2	0	1	0	1	0	19	0	0	0	3.2	1.000	OF-6
1954		147	.266	.385	530	141	20	11	7	1.3	64	58	62	60	5	3	1	364	18	6	3	2.7	.985	OF-145
1955		154	.279	.400	603	168	23	4	14	2.3	102	78	76	54	6	1	0	442	12	7	2	3.0	.985	OF-154
1956		140	.253	.357	546	138	22	4	9	1.6	61	65	38	48	5	4	2	348	13	9	2	2.7	.976	OF-137
1957		133	.251	.328	451	113	12	4	5	1.1	49	47	44	41	2	3	1	331	5	6	1	2.7	.982	OF-128
1958	**KC A**	148	.231	.358	511	118	14	9	11	2.2	77	51	74	58	7	10	1	311	12	4	2	2.3	.988	OF-145
1959		126	.300	.413	463	139	19	6	7	1.5	74	43	48	38	10	4	2	294	17	5	3	2.6	.984	OF-121
1960		151	.256	.347	559	143	21	3	8	1.4	75	40	66	52	1	5	2	381	16	5	3	2.7	.988	OF-148
1961	**2 teams**	**KC A** (25G –.262) **MIN A** (113G –.246)																						
″	**total**	138	.249	.335	454	113	14	5	5	1.1	53	46	52	50	1	3	0	199	167	18	16	2.2	.953	OF-89, 3B-85, 2B-2
1962	**MIN A**	110	.211	.285	123	26	4	1	1	0.8	21	13	19	14	1	6	1	71	2	2	0	0.7	.973	OF-104
1963		16	.000	.000	3	0	0	0	0	0.0	0	0	1	0	0	2	0	7	1	0	0	0.6	1.000	OF-14
11 yrs.		1270	.259	.363	4268	1105	149	47	67	1.6	578	443	480	416	38	42	10	2767	263	62	32	2.4	.980	OF-1191, 3B-85, 2B-2

Guy Tutwiler

TUTWILER, GUY ISBELL (King Tut) BL TR 6′ 175 lbs.
B. July 17, 1889, Coalburg, Ala. D. Aug. 15, 1930, Birmingham, Ala.

Year	Team	Games	BA	SA	AB	H	2B	3B	HR	HR%	R	RBI	BB	SO	SB	Pinch Hit AB	Pinch Hit H	PO	A	E	DP	TC/G	FA	G by Pos
1911	**DET A**	13	.188	.250	32	6	2	0	0	0.0	3	3	2		0	3	0	14	11	6	0	3.4	.806	2B-6, OF-3
1913		14	.213	.255	47	10	0	1	0	0.0	4	7	4	12	2	0	0	140	10	2	10	10.9	.987	1B-14
2 yrs.		27	.203	.253	79	16	2	1	0	0.0	7	10	6	12	2	3	0	154	21	8	10	8.0	.956	1B-14, 2B-6, OF-3

Old Hoss Twineham

TWINEHAM, ARTHUR W. BL TL 6′1½″ 190 lbs.
B. Nov. 26, 1866, Galesburg, Ill. Deceased.

Year	Team	Games	BA	SA	AB	H	2B	3B	HR	HR%	R	RBI	BB	SO	SB	Pinch Hit AB	Pinch Hit H	PO	A	E	DP	TC/G	FA	G by Pos
1893	**STL N**	14	.313	.354	48	15	2	0	0	0.0	8	11	1	2	0	0	0	48	16	5	1	4.9	.928	C-14
1894		38	.315	.386	127	40	4	1	1	0.8	22	16	9	11	2	0	0	147	38	12	1	5.2	.939	C-38
2 yrs.		52	.314	.377	175	55	6	1	1	0.6	30	27	10	13	2	0	0	195	54	17	2	5.1	.936	C-52

Larry Twitchell

TWITCHELL, LAWRENCE GRANT BR TR 6′ 185 lbs.
B. Feb. 18, 1864, Cleveland, Ohio D. Aug. 23, 1930, Cleveland, Ohio.

Year	Team	Games	BA	SA	AB	H	2B	3B	HR	HR%	R	RBI	BB	SO	SB	Pinch Hit AB	Pinch Hit H	PO	A	E	DP	TC/G	FA	G by Pos
1886	**DET N**	4	.063	.063	16	1	0	0	0	0.0	0	0	0	2		0	0	2	8	0	1	1.7	1.000	P-4, OF-2
1887		65	.333	.432	264	88	14	6	0	0.0	44	51	8	19	12	0	0	89	16	13	2	1.7	.890	OF-53, P-15
1888		131	.244	.324	524	128	19	4	5	1.0	71	67	28	45	14	0	0	195	15	28	4	1.8	.882	OF-131, P-2
1889	**CLE N**	134	.275	.366	549	151	16	11	4	0.7	73	95	29	37	17	0	0	220	10	21	0	1.9	.916	OF-134, P-1
1890	**2 teams**	**CLE P** (56G –.223) **BUF P** (44G –.221)																						
″	**total**	100	.222	.294	405	90	9	4	4	1.0	57	53	40	29	8	0	0	125	47	22	2	1.9	.887	OF-88, P-12, 1B-3
1891	**COL AA**	57	.277	.379	224	62	9	4	2	0.9	32	35	20	28	10	0	0	70	10	9	0	1.4	.899	OF-56, P-6
1892	**WAS N**	51	.219	.318	192	42	9	5	0	0.0	20	20	11	31	8	0	0	80	11	13	1	2.0	.875	OF-48, SS-3, 3B-1
1893	**LOU N**	45	.310	.422	187	58	12	3	1	0.5	37	31	17	20	7	0	0	91	6	14	0	2.5	.874	OF-45
1894		52	.267	.400	210	56	16	3	2	1.0	28	32	15	20	8	0	0	103	17	12	4	2.5	.909	OF-51, P-1
9 yrs.		639	.263	.356	2571	676	104	40	18	0.7	362	384	168	231	84	0	0	975	140	132	14	1.9	.894	OF-608, P-41, SS-3, 1B-3, 3B-1

Babe Twombly

TWOMBLY, CLARENCE EDWARD BL TR 5′10″ 165 lbs.
Brother of George Twombly.
B. Jan. 18, 1896, Jamaica Plain, Mass. D. Nov. 23, 1974, San Clemente, Calif.

Year	Team	Lg	Games	BA	SA	AB	H	2B	3B	HR	HR%	R	RBI	BB	SO	SB	Pinch Hit AB	Pinch Hit H	PO	A	E	DP	TC/G	FA	G by Pos
1920	CHI	N	78	.235	.284	183	43	1	1	2	1.1	25	14	17	20	5	22	4	91	7	3	0	2.1	.970	OF-45, 2B-2
1921			87	.377	.451	175	66	8	1	1	0.6	22	18	11	10	4	**38**	**15**	81	11	3	0	2.1	.968	OF-45
2 yrs.			165	.304	.366	358	109	9	2	3	0.8	47	32	28	30	9	60	19	172	18	6	0	2.1	.969	OF-90, 2B-2

George Twombly

TWOMBLY, GEORGE FREDERICK (Silent George) BR TR 5′ 9″ 165 lbs.
Brother of Babe Twombly.
B. June 4, 1892, Boston, Mass. D. Feb. 17, 1975, Lexington, Mass.

Year	Team	Lg	Games	BA	SA	AB	H	2B	3B	HR	HR%	R	RBI	BB	SO	SB	Pinch Hit AB	Pinch Hit H	PO	A	E	DP	TC/G	FA	G by Pos
1914	CIN	N	68	.233	.275	240	56	0	5	0	0.0	22	19	14	27	12	0	0	111	11	4	2	1.9	.968	OF-68
1915			46	.197	.227	66	13	0	1	0	0.0	5	5	8	8	5	14	4	30	2	0	0	0.7	1.000	OF-46
1916			3	.000	.000	5	0	0	0	0	0.0	0	0	1	1	0	2	0	2	0	0	0	2.0	1.000	OF-1
1917	BOS	N	32	.186	.216	102	19	1	1	0	0.0	8	9	18	5	4	1	0	61	1	4	1	2.2	.939	OF-29, 1B-1
1919	WAS	A	1	.000	.000	4	0	0	0	0	0.0	0	0	0	0	0	0	0	0	0	0	0	0.0	.000	OF-1
5 yrs.			150	.211	.247	417	88	1	7	0	0.0	35	33	41	41	21	17	4	204	14	8	3	1.5	.965	OF-145, 1B-1

Jim Tyack

TYACK, JAMES FREDERICK BL TR 6′ 2″ 195 lbs.
B. Jan. 9, 1911, Florence, Mont. D. Jan. 3, 1995, Bakersfield, Calif.

Year	Team	Lg	Games	BA	SA	AB	H	2B	3B	HR	HR%	R	RBI	BB	SO	SB	Pinch Hit AB	Pinch Hit H	PO	A	E	DP	TC/G	FA	G by Pos
1943	PHI	A	54	.258	.323	155	40	8	1	0	0.0	11	23	14	9	1	12	2	82	4	2	0	2.3	.977	OF-38

Fred Tyler

TYLER, FREDERICK FRANKLIN BR TR 5′10½″ 180 lbs.
Brother of Lefty Tyler.
B. Dec. 16, 1891, Derry, N. H. D. Oct. 14, 1945, East Derry, N. H.

Year	Team	Lg	Games	BA	SA	AB	H	2B	3B	HR	HR%	R	RBI	BB	SO	SB	Pinch Hit AB	Pinch Hit H	PO	A	E	DP	TC/G	FA	G by Pos
1914	BOS	N	18	.333	.333	24	8	0	0	0	0.0	2	2	0	2	0	0	0	21	8	0	1	4.8	1.000	C-6

Johnnie Tyler

TYLER, JOHN ANTHONY (Ty Ty) BB TR 6′ 175 lbs.
Born John Tylka. BL 1934
B. July 30, 1906, Mount Pleasant, Pa. D. July 11, 1972, Mount Pleasant, Pa.

Year	Team	Lg	Games	BA	SA	AB	H	2B	3B	HR	HR%	R	RBI	BB	SO	SB	Pinch Hit AB	Pinch Hit H	PO	A	E	DP	TC/G	FA	G by Pos
1934	BOS	N	3	.167	.167	6	1	0	0	0	0.0	0	1	0	3	0	2	0	3	1	0	0	4.0	1.000	OF-1
1935			13	.340	.553	47	16	2	1	2	4.3	7	11	4	3	0	1	0	24	1	3	0	2.5	.893	OF-11
2 yrs.			16	.321	.509	53	17	2	1	2	3.8	7	12	4	6	0	3	0	27	2	3	0	2.7	.906	OF-12

Lefty Tyler

TYLER, GEORGE ALBERT BL TL 6′ 175 lbs.
Brother of Fred Tyler.
B. Dec. 14, 1889, Derry, N. H. D. Sept. 29, 1953, Lowell, Mass.

Year	Team	Lg	Games	BA	SA	AB	H	2B	3B	HR	HR%	R	RBI	BB	SO	SB	Pinch Hit AB	Pinch Hit H	PO	A	E	DP	TC/G	FA	G by Pos
1910	BOS	N	2	.500	.500	4	2	0	0	0	0.0	0	0	1	0	0	0	0	0	2	0	0	1.0	1.000	P-2
1911			28	.164	.197	61	10	2	0	0	0.0	10	2	8	9	0	0	0	8	58	8	2	2.6	.892	P-28
1912			42	.198	.229	96	19	3	0	0	0.0	8	5	4	16	0	0	0	15	75	5	3	2.3	.947	P-42
1913			43	.206	.275	102	21	7	0	0	0.0	13	10	11	16	0	3	1	13	107	9	1	3.3	.930	P-39
1914			38	.202	.213	94	19	1	0	0	0.0	6	4	4	20	0	0	0	16	57	5	3	2.1	.936	P-38
1915			45	.261	.375	88	23	7	0	1	1.1	11	6	4	19	0	10	1	6	50	1	1	1.8	.982	P-32
1916			39	.204	.355	93	19	3	1	3	3.2	10	20	9	15	0	3	0	9	72	3	3	2.5	.964	P-34
1917			55	.231	.261	134	31	4	0	0	0.0	8	11	17	19	0	12	3	105	80	2	10	4.3	.989	P-32, 1B-11
1918	CHI	N	38	.210	.220	100	21	1	0	0	0.0	9	8	9	15	0	2	0	17	88	3	3	3.3	.972	P-33
1919			6	.143	.143	7	1	0	0	0	0.0	0	1	3	2	0	0	0	1	13	0	1	2.3	1.000	P-6
1920			29	.262	.338	65	17	3	1	0	0.0	6	6	9	7	0	2	2	15	64	2	3	3.0	.975	P-27
1921			19	.231	.308	26	6	2	0	0	0.0	4	2	1	5	0	7	2	3	10	0	1	1.3	1.000	P-10
12 yrs.			384	.217	.274	870	189	33	2	4	0.5	85	75	80	143	0	39	9	208	676	38	31	2.8	.959	P-323, 1B-11
WORLD SERIES																									
1914	BOS	N	1	.000	.000	3	0	0	0	0	0.0	0	0	0	1	0	0	0	1	5	0	0	6.0	1.000	P-1
1918	CHI	N	3	.200	.200	5	1	0	0	0	0.0	0	2	2	0	0	0	0	2	9	1	0	4.0	.917	P-3
2 yrs.			4	.125	.125	8	1	0	0	0	0.0	0	2	2	1	0	0	0	3	14	1	0	4.5	.944	P-4

Earl Tyree

TYREE, EARL CARLTON BR TR 5′ 8″ 160 lbs.
B. Mar. 4, 1890, Huntsville, Ill. D. May 17, 1954, Rushville, Ill.

Year	Team	Lg	Games	BA	SA	AB	H	2B	3B	HR	HR%	R	RBI	BB	SO	SB	Pinch Hit AB	Pinch Hit H	PO	A	E	DP	TC/G	FA	G by Pos
1914	CHI	N	1	.000	.000	4	0	0	0	0	0.0	1	0	0	0	0	0	0	2	1	0	0	3.0	1.000	C-1

Jim Tyrone

TYRONE, JAMES VERNON BR TR 6′ 1″ 185 lbs.
Brother of Wayne Tyrone.
B. Jan. 29, 1949, Alice, Tex.

Year	Team	Lg	Games	BA	SA	AB	H	2B	3B	HR	HR%	R	RBI	BB	SO	SB	Pinch Hit AB	Pinch Hit H	PO	A	E	DP	TC/G	FA	G by Pos
1972	CHI	N	13	.000	.000	8	0	0	0	0	0.0	1	0	0	3	1	3	0	6	1	0	0	1.8	1.000	OF-4
1974			57	.185	.321	81	15	0	1	3	3.7	19	3	6	8	1	28	7	26	2	1	0	0.9	.966	OF-32, 3B-1
1975			11	.227	.318	22	5	0	1	0	0.0	0	3	1	4	1	5	1	7	1	0	0	1.0	1.000	OF-8
1977	OAK	A	96	.245	.340	294	72	11	1	5	1.7	32	26	25	62	3	11	5	168	5	9	0	2.1	.951	OF-81, DH-4, 1B-1, SS-1
4 yrs.			177	.227	.328	405	92	11	3	8	2.0	52	32	32	77	6	47	13	207	9	10	0	1.7	.956	OF-125, DH-4, 1B-1, SS-1, 3B-1

Wayne Tyrone

TYRONE, OSCAR WAYNE BR TR 6′ 1″ 185 lbs.
Brother of Jim Tyrone.
B. Aug. 1, 1950, Alice, Tex.

Year	Team	Lg	Games	BA	SA	AB	H	2B	3B	HR	HR%	R	RBI	BB	SO	SB	Pinch Hit AB	Pinch Hit H	PO	A	E	DP	TC/G	FA	G by Pos
1976	CHI	N	30	.228	.298	57	13	1	0	1	1.8	3	8	3	21	0	14	4	39	10	0	6	2.9	1.000	OF-7, 3B-5, 1B-5

Mike Tyson

TYSON, MICHAEL RAY BR TR 5′ 9″ 170 lbs.
B. Jan. 13, 1950, Rocky Mount, N. C.

Year	Team	Lg	Games	BA	SA	AB	H	2B	3B	HR	HR%	R	RBI	BB	SO	SB	Pinch Hit AB	Pinch Hit H	PO	A	E	DP	TC/G	FA	G by Pos
1972	STL	N	13	.189	.216	37	7	1	0	0	0.0	1	0	1	9	0	0	0	26	36	3	4	5.0	.954	2B-11, SS-2
1973			144	.243	.299	469	114	15	4	1	0.2	48	33	23	66	2	0	0	239	401	33	80	4.7	.951	SS-128, 2B-16
1974			151	.223	.287	422	94	14	5	1	0.2	35	37	22	70	4	0	0	247	434	31	115	4.6	.956	SS-143, 2B-12
1975			122	.266	.342	368	98	16	3	2	0.5	45	37	24	39	5	2	0	184	308	15	52	4.1	.970	SS-95, 2B-24, 3B-5
1976			76	.286	.445	245	70	12	9	3	1.2	26	28	16	34	3	1	0	158	237	12	54	5.5	.971	2B-74
1977			138	.246	.342	418	103	15	2	7	1.7	42	57	30	48	3	2	0	267	423	15	99	5.2	.979	2B-135
1978			125	.233	.300	377	88	16	0	3	0.8	26	26	24	41	2	4	1	246	306	13	78	4.6	.977	2B-124
1979			75	.221	.363	190	42	8	2	5	2.6	18	20	13	28	2	9	2	125	184	8	42	4.5	.975	2B-71
1980	CHI	N	123	.238	.337	341	81	19	3	3	0.9	34	23	15	61	1	6	2	222	329	18	69	4.9	.968	2B-117
1981			50	.185	.272	92	17	2	0	2	2.2	6	8	7	15	1	13	4	50	76	8	14	3.6	.940	2B-36, SS-1
10 yrs.			1017	.241	.327	2959	714	118	28	27	0.9	281	269	175	411	23	37	9	1764	2734	156	607	4.7	.966	2B-620, SS-369, 3B-5

Turkey Tyson

TYSON, CECIL WASHINGTON
B. Dec. 6, 1914, Elm City, N. C.
BL TR 6′ 5½″ 225 lbs.

Year	Team	Games	BA	SA	AB	H	2B	3B	HR	HR%	R	RBI	BB	SO	SB	Pinch Hit AB	Pinch Hit H	PO	A	E	DP	TC/G	FA	G by Pos
1944	PHI N	1	.000	.000	1	0	0	0	0	0.0	0	0	0	0	0	1	0	0	0	0	0	0.0	—	

Ty Tyson

TYSON, ALBERT THOMAS
B. June 1, 1892, Wilkes-Barre, Pa. D. Aug. 16, 1953, Buffalo, N. Y.
BR TR 5′11″ 169 lbs.

Year	Team	Games	BA	SA	AB	H	2B	3B	HR	HR%	R	RBI	BB	SO	SB	Pinch Hit AB	Pinch Hit H	PO	A	E	DP	TC/G	FA	G by Pos
1926	NY N	97	.293	.373	335	98	16	1	3	0.9	40	35	15	28	6	4	1	232	9	5	5	2.7	.980	OF-92
1927		43	.264	.352	159	42	7	2	1	0.6	24	17	10	19	5	1	1	73	5	6	1	2.0	.929	OF-41
1928	BKN N	59	.271	.348	210	57	11	1	1	0.5	25	21	10	14	3	1	0	130	6	5	3	2.6	.965	OF-55
3 yrs.		199	.280	.361	704	197	34	4	5	0.7	89	73	35	61	14	6	2	435	20	16	9	2.5	.966	OF-188

Bob Uecker

UECKER, ROBERT GEORGE
B. Jan. 26, 1935, Milwaukee, Wis.
BR TR 6′ 1″ 190 lbs.

Year	Team	Games	BA	SA	AB	H	2B	3B	HR	HR%	R	RBI	BB	SO	SB	Pinch Hit AB	Pinch Hit H	PO	A	E	DP	TC/G	FA	G by Pos
1962	MIL N	33	.250	.328	64	16	2	0	1	1.6	5	8	7	15	0	7	2	101	10	2	4	4.7	.982	C-24
1963		13	.250	.375	16	4	2	0	0	0.0	3	0	2	5	0	7	2	21	2	1	1	4.0	.958	C-6
1964	STL N	40	.198	.236	106	21	1	0	1	0.9	8	6	17	24	0	0	0	201	20	3	2	5.6	.987	C-40
1965		53	.228	.317	145	33	7	0	2	1.4	17	10	24	27	0	5	0	240	29	4	1	5.6	.985	C-49
1966	PHI N	78	.208	.338	207	43	6	0	7	3.4	15	30	22	36	0	4	0	368	33	6	7	5.4	.985	C-76
1967	2 teams	PHI N (18G –.171) ATL N (62G –.146)																						
″	total	80	.150	.218	193	29	4	0	3	1.6	17	20	24	60	0	6	1	348	36	11	3	5.2	.972	C-76
6 yrs.		297	.200	.287	731	146	22	0	14	1.9	65	74	96	167	0	29	5	1279	130	27	18	5.3	.981	C-271

Frenchy Uhalt

UHALT, BERNARD BARTHOLOMEW
B. Apr. 27, 1910, Bakersfield, Calif.
BL TR 5′10″ 180 lbs.

Year	Team	Games	BA	SA	AB	H	2B	3B	HR	HR%	R	RBI	BB	SO	SB	Pinch Hit AB	Pinch Hit H	PO	A	E	DP	TC/G	FA	G by Pos
1934	CHI A	57	.242	.285	165	40	5	1	0	0.0	28	16	29	12	6	13	4	85	2	6	1	2.3	.935	OF-40

Ted Uhlaender

UHLAENDER, THEODORE OTTO
B. Oct. 21, 1940, Chicago Heights, Ill.
BL TR 6′ 2″ 190 lbs.

Year	Team	Games	BA	SA	AB	H	2B	3B	HR	HR%	R	RBI	BB	SO	SB	Pinch Hit AB	Pinch Hit H	PO	A	E	DP	TC/G	FA	G by Pos
1965	MIN A	13	.182	.182	22	4	0	0	0	0.0	1	1	0	2	1	8	2	7	1	0	0	2.0	1.000	OF-4
1966		105	.226	.286	367	83	12	2	2	0.5	39	22	27	33	10	3	0	258	4	4	2	2.7	.985	OF-100
1967		133	.258	.381	415	107	19	7	6	1.4	41	49	13	45	4	11	2	255	6	1	3	2.2	.996	OF-118
1968		140	.283	.389	488	138	21	5	7	1.4	52	52	28	46	16	2	0	283	3	4	1	2.2	.986	OF-129
1969		152	.273	.356	554	151	18	2	8	1.4	93	62	44	52	15	5	3	278	8	1	1	1.9	.997	OF-150
1970	CLE A	141	.268	.391	473	127	21	2	11	2.3	56	46	39	44	3	11	5	225	5	2	1	1.7	.991	OF-134
1971		141	.288	.352	500	144	20	3	2	0.4	52	47	38	44	3	11	2	245	6	2	0	1.9	.992	OF-131
1972	CIN N	73	.159	.186	113	18	3	0	0	0.0	9	6	13	11	0	41	3	37	3	1	0	1.5	.976	OF-27
8 yrs.		898	.263	.353	2932	772	114	21	36	1.2	343	285	202	277	52	92	17	1588	36	15	8	2.1	.991	OF-793
LEAGUE CHAMPIONSHIP SERIES																								
1969	MIN A	2	.167	.167	6	1	0	0	0	0.0	0	0	0	0	0	0	0	4	0	1	0	2.5	.800	OF-2
1972	CIN N	2	.500	.500	2	1	0	0	0	0.0	0	0	0	0	0	2	1	0	0	0	0	0.0	—	
2 yrs.		4	.250	.250	8	2	0	0	0	0.0	0	0	0	0	0	2	1	4	0	1	0	2.5	.800	OF-2
WORLD SERIES																								
1972	CIN N	4	.250	.500	4	1	1	0	0	0.0	0	0	0	1	0	4	1	0	0	0	0	0.0	—	

George Uhle

UHLE, GEORGE ERNEST (The Bull)
B. Sept. 18, 1898, Cleveland, Ohio D. Feb. 26, 1985, Lakewood, Ohio.
BR TR 6′ 190 lbs.

Year	Team	Games	BA	SA	AB	H	2B	3B	HR	HR%	R	RBI	BB	SO	SB	Pinch Hit AB	Pinch Hit H	PO	A	E	DP	TC/G	FA	G by Pos
1919	CLE A	26	.302	.395	43	13	2	1	0	0.0	7	6	1	5	0	0	0	10	33	4	1	1.8	.915	P-26
1920		27	.344	.344	32	11	0	0	0	0.0	4	2	2	2	1	0	0	6	21	0	0	1.0	1.000	P-27
1921		48	.245	.362	94	23	2	3	1	1.1	21	18	6	9	0	0	0	15	46	4	2	1.5	.938	P-41, C-1
1922		56	.266	.376	109	29	8	2	0	0.0	21	14	13	6	1	2	2	16	53	5	5	1.5	.932	P-50
1923		58	.361	.472	144	52	10	3	0	0.0	23	22	7	10	2	3	0	18	89	2	9	2.0	.982	P-54
1924		59	.308	.411	107	33	6	1	1	0.9	10	19	4	8	0	26	**11**	19	42	0	5	2.2	1.000	P-28
1925		56	.279	.365	104	29	3	3	0	0.0	10	13	7	7	0	22	5	12	39	3	2	1.9	.944	P-29
1926		50	.227	.273	132	30	3	0	1	0.8	16	11	10	12	2	8	1	30	67	7	3	2.7	.933	P-39
1927		43	.266	.380	79	21	7	1	0	0.0	4	14	5	12	0	18	5	6	31	1	3	1.5	.974	P-25
1928		55	.286	.388	98	28	3	2	1	1.0	9	17	8	4	0	20	4	10	59	2	4	2.3	.972	P-31
1929	DET A	40	.343	.370	108	37	1	1	0	0.0	18	13	6	6	0	7	1	13	39	4	2	1.8	.929	P-32
1930		59	.308	.427	117	36	4	2	2	1.7	15	21	8	13	0	21	5	10	29	1	2	1.2	.975	P-33
1931		53	.244	.378	90	22	6	0	2	2.2	8	7	8	8	0	21	3	3	38	0	1	1.4	1.000	P-29
1932		38	.182	.273	55	10	3	1	0	0.0	2	4	6	5	0	5	1	5	25	0	2	0.9	1.000	P-33
1933	3 teams	DET A (1G –.000) NY N (8G –.000) NY A (12G –.400)																						
″	total	21	.320	.360	25	8	1	0	0	0.0	2	1	5	5	0	2	0	1	13	0	1	0.7	1.000	P-19
1934	NY A	10	.600	1.000	5	3	0	1	0	0.0	1	1	0	0	0	0	0	1	1	0	0	0.2	1.000	P-10
1936	CLE A	24	.381	.571	21	8	1	0	1	4.8	1	4	2	0	0	14	6	0	0	0	0	0.0	.000	P-7
17 yrs.		723	.288	.383	1363	393	60	21	9	0.7	172	187	98	112	6	169	44	175	625	33	42	1.6	.960	P-513, C-1
WORLD SERIES																								
1920	CLE A	2	—	—	0	0	0	0	0	—	0	0	0	0	0	0	0	0	1	0	0	1.0	1.000	P-1

Maury Uhler

UHLER, MAURICE WILLIAM
B. Dec. 14, 1886, Pikesville, Md. D. May 4, 1918, Baltimore, Md.
BR TR 5′11″ 165 lbs.

Year	Team	Games	BA	SA	AB	H	2B	3B	HR	HR%	R	RBI	BB	SO	SB	Pinch Hit AB	Pinch Hit H	PO	A	E	DP	TC/G	FA	G by Pos
1914	CIN N	46	.214	.250	56	12	2	0	0	0.0	12	3	5	11	4	3	0	40	1	3	0	1.2	.932	OF-36

Charlie Uhlir

UHLIR, CHARLES KAREL
B. July 30, 1912, Chicago, Ill. D. July 8, 1984, Spirit Lake, Iowa.
BL TL 5′ 7½″ 150 lbs.

Year	Team	Games	BA	SA	AB	H	2B	3B	HR	HR%	R	RBI	BB	SO	SB	Pinch Hit AB	Pinch Hit H	PO	A	E	DP	TC/G	FA	G by Pos
1934	CHI A	14	.148	.148	27	4	0	0	0	0.0	3	3	2	6	0	5	1	9	0	0	0	1.5	1.000	OF-6

Mike Ulisney

ULISNEY, MICHAEL EDWARD (Slugs)
B. Sept. 28, 1917, Greenwald, Pa.
BR TR 5′ 9″ 165 lbs.

Year	Team	Games	BA	SA	AB	H	2B	3B	HR	HR%	R	RBI	BB	SO	SB	Pinch Hit AB	Pinch Hit H	PO	A	E	DP	TC/G	FA	G by Pos
1945	BOS N	11	.389	.611	18	7	1	0	1	5.6	4	4	1	0	0	5	2	4	1	2	0	1.8	.714	C-4

Scott Ullger

ULLGER, SCOTT MATTHEW
B. June 10, 1956, New York, N. Y.
BR TR 6′ 3″ 196 lbs.

Year	Team	Games	BA	SA	AB	H	2B	3B	HR	HR%	R	RBI	BB	SO	SB	Pinch Hit AB	Pinch Hit H	PO	A	E	DP	TC/G	FA	G by Pos
1983	MIN A	35	.190	.241	79	15	4	0	0	0.0	8	5	5	21	0	3	0	186	11	2	14	5.9	.990	1B-30, 3B-3, DH-1

George Ulrich

ULRICH, GEORGE T.
B. June 5, 1869, Philadelphia, Pa. Deceased.

Year	Team	Games	BA	SA	AB	H	2B	3B	HR	HR%	R	RBI	BB	SO	SB	Pinch Hit AB	Pinch Hit H	PO	A	E	DP	TC/G	FA	G by Pos
1892	WAS N	6	.292	.333	24	7	1	0	0	0.0	1	0	0	4	2	0	0	9	14	2	1	3.6	.920	3B-3, SS-2, C-2
1893	CIN N	1	.000	.000	3	0	0	0	0	0.0	0	0	0	0	1	0	0	1	0	0	0	1.0	1.000	OF-1
1896	NY N	14	.178	.200	45	8	1	0	0	0.0	4	1	1	1	0	0	0	20	6	5	1	2.2	.839	OF-11, 3B-3
3 yrs.		21	.208	.236	72	15	2	0	0	0.0	5	1	1	5	3	0	0	30	20	7	2	2.6	.877	OF-12, 3B-6, SS-2, C-2

Tommy Umphlett

UMPHLETT, THOMAS MULLEN BR TR 6′ 2″ 180 lbs.
B. May 12, 1930, Scotland Neck, N. C.

Year	Team	Games	BA	SA	AB	H	2B	3B	HR	HR%	R	RBI	BB	SO	SB	Pinch Hit AB	Pinch Hit H	PO	A	E	DP	TC/G	FA	G by Pos
1953	BOS A	137	.283	.376	495	140	27	5	3	0.6	53	59	34	30	4	1	0	382	12	7	1	2.9	.983	OF-136
1954	WAS A	114	.219	.269	342	75	8	3	1	0.3	21	33	17	42	1	15	0	169	13	2	4	1.8	.989	OF-101
1955		110	.217	.266	323	70	10	0	2	0.6	34	19	24	35	2	8	1	237	8	3	1	2.4	.988	OF-103
3 yrs.		361	.246	.314	1160	285	45	8	6	0.5	108	111	75	107	7	24	1	788	33	12	6	2.5	.986	OF-340

Bob Unglaub

UNGLAUB, ROBERT ALEXANDER BR TR 5′11″ 178 lbs.
B. July 31, 1881, Baltimore, Md. D. Nov. 29, 1916, Baltimore, Md.
Manager 1907.

Year	Team	Games	BA	SA	AB	H	2B	3B	HR	HR%	R	RBI	BB	SO	SB	Pinch Hit AB	Pinch Hit H	PO	A	E	DP	TC/G	FA	G by Pos
1904	2 teams	NY A (6G –.211) BOS A (9G –.154)																						
″	total	15	.188	.219	32	6	1	0	0	0.0	3	4	1		0	4	0	12	10	6	1	2.5	.786	3B-6, 2B-3, SS-2
1905	BOS A	43	.223	.281	121	27	5	1	0	0.0	18	11	6		2	12	2	87	55	10	3	4.9	.934	3B-21, 2B-8, 1B-2
1907		139	.254	.338	544	138	17	13	1	0.2	49	62	23		14	0	0	1504	84	22	71	11.6	.986	1B-139
1908	2 teams	BOS A (72G –.263) WAS A (72G –.308)																						
″	total	144	.286	.360	542	155	21	8	1	0.2	46	54	15		14	1	0	894	232	31	38	8.1	.973	1B-76, 3B-39, 2B-27
1909	WAS A	130	.265	.350	480	127	14	9	3	0.6	43	41	22		15	1	0	669	121	13	39	6.2	.984	1B-57, OF-43, 2B-25, 3B-4
1910		124	.234	.274	431	101	9	4	0	0.0	29	44	21		21	1	0	1230	79	20	51	10.7	.985	1B-124
6 yrs.		595	.258	.328	2150	554	67	35	5	0.2	188	216	88		66	19	2	4396	581	102	203	8.8	.980	1B-398, 3B-70, 2B-63, OF-43, SS-2

Tim Unroe

UNROE, TIMOTHY BRIAN BR TR 6′ 3″ 200 lbs.
B. Oct. 7, 1970, Round Lake Beach, Ill.

Year	Team	Games	BA	SA	AB	H	2B	3B	HR	HR%	R	RBI	BB	SO	SB	Pinch Hit AB	Pinch Hit H	PO	A	E	DP	TC/G	FA	G by Pos
1995	MIL A	2	.250	.250	4	1	0	0	0	0.0	0	0	0	0	0	0	0	11	0	0	3	5.5	1.000	1B-2

Al Unser

UNSER, ALBERT BERNARD BR TR 6′ 1″ 175 lbs.
Father of Del Unser.
B. Oct. 12, 1912, Morrisonville, Ill. D. July 7, 1995, Decatur, Ill.

Year	Team	Games	BA	SA	AB	H	2B	3B	HR	HR%	R	RBI	BB	SO	SB	Pinch Hit AB	Pinch Hit H	PO	A	E	DP	TC/G	FA	G by Pos
1942	DET A	4	.375	.375	8	3	0	0	0	0.0	2	0	0	2	0	0	0	11	3	0	0	3.5	1.000	C-4
1943		38	.248	.297	101	25	5	0	0	0.0	14	4	15	15	0	0	0	143	20	3	4	4.5	.982	C-37
1944		11	.120	.320	25	3	0	1	1	4.0	2	5	3	2	0	5	2	12	7	3	2	3.7	.864	2B-5, C-1
1945	CIN N	67	.265	.387	204	54	10	3	3	1.5	23	21	14	24	0	5	2	207	30	11	5	4.1	.956	C-61
4 yrs.		120	.251	.355	338	85	15	4	4	1.2	41	30	32	43	0	10	4	373	60	17	11	4.2	.962	C-103, 2B-5

Del Unser

UNSER, DELBERT BERNARD BL TL 6′ 1″ 180 lbs.
Son of Al Unser.
B. Dec. 9, 1944, Decatur, Ill.

Year	Team	Games	BA	SA	AB	H	2B	3B	HR	HR%	R	RBI	BB	SO	SB	Pinch Hit AB	Pinch Hit H	PO	A	E	DP	TC/G	FA	G by Pos
1968	WAS A	156	.230	.277	635	146	13	7	1	0.2	66	30	46	66	11	1	1	392	22	5	10	2.7	.988	OF-156, 1B-1
1969		153	.286	.382	581	166	19	**8**	7	1.2	69	57	58	54	8	11	3	339	8	10	3	2.4	.972	OF-149
1970		119	.258	.326	322	83	5	1	5	1.6	37	30	30	29	1	21	2	173	8	3	2	1.8	.984	OF-103
1971		153	.255	.355	581	148	19	6	9	1.5	63	41	59	68	11	2	0	394	10	8	2	2.7	.981	OF-151
1972	CLE A	132	.238	.277	383	91	12	0	1	0.3	29	17	28	46	5	15	4	248	10	3	1	2.2	.989	OF-119
1973	PHI N	136	.289	.427	440	127	20	4	11	2.5	64	52	47	55	5	12	2	329	14	4	4	2.6	.988	OF-132
1974		142	.264	.399	454	120	18	5	11	2.4	72	61	50	62	6	13	2	300	13	6	0	2.4	.981	OF-135
1975	NY N	147	.294	.392	531	156	18	2	10	1.9	65	53	37	76	4	3	1	362	13	5	2	2.6	.987	OF-144
1976	2 teams	NY N (77G –.228) MON N (69G –.227)																						
″	total	146	.228	.355	496	113	19	4	12	2.4	57	40	29	84	7	7	1	288	10	3	2	2.1	.990	OF-142
1977	MON N	113	.273	.453	289	79	14	1	12	4.2	33	40	33	41	2	21	4	280	13	3	15	3.0	.990	OF-72, 1B-27
1978		130	.196	.257	179	35	5	0	2	1.1	16	15	24	29	2	37	3	232	12	2	16	2.5	.992	1B-64, OF-33
1979	PHI N	95	.298	.482	141	42	8	0	6	4.3	26	29	14	33	2	46	14	118	5	3	6	2.4	.976	OF-30, 1B-22
1980		96	.264	.391	110	29	6	4	0	0.0	15	10	10	21	0	38	12	116	13	0	7	2.4	1.000	1B-31, OF-23
1981		62	.153	.203	59	9	3	0	0	0.0	5	6	13	9	0	26	5	63	5	0	4	2.0	1.000	1B-18, OF-16
1982		19	.000	.000	14	0	0	0	0	0.0	0	0	3	2	0	11	0	9	1	0	1	1.4	1.000	1B-5, OF-2
15 yrs.		1799	.258	.358	5215	1344	179	42	87	1.7	617	481	481	675	64	264	54	3643	157	55	75	2.4	.986	OF-1407, 1B-168
LEAGUE CHAMPIONSHIP SERIES																								
1980	PHI N	5	.400	.600	5	2	1	0	0	0.0	2	1	0	2	0	3	1	2	0	0	0	1.0	1.000	OF-2
WORLD SERIES																								
1980	PHI N	3	.500	.833	6	3	2	0	0	0.0	2	2	0	1	0	2	2	1	0	0	0	0.3	1.000	OF-3

John Upham

UPHAM, JOHN LESLIE BL TL 6′ 180 lbs.
B. Dec. 29, 1941, Windsor, Ont., Canada.

Year	Team	Games	BA	SA	AB	H	2B	3B	HR	HR%	R	RBI	BB	SO	SB	Pinch Hit AB	Pinch Hit H	PO	A	E	DP	TC/G	FA	G by Pos
1967	CHI N	8	.667	.667	3	2	0	0	0	0.0	1	0	0	0	0	3	2	0	0	0	0	0.0	.000	P-5
1968		13	.200	.200	10	2	0	0	0	0.0	0	0	0	3	0	6	1	0	3	0	0	0.8	1.000	P-2, OF-2
2 yrs.		21	.308	.308	13	4	0	0	0	0.0	1	0	0	3	0	9	3	0	3	0	0	0.3	1.000	P-7, OF-2

Dixie Upright

UPRIGHT, ROY T. BL TL 6′ 175 lbs.
Born R T Upright.
B. May 30, 1926, Kannapolis, N. C. D. Nov. 13, 1986, Concord, N. C.

Year	Team	Games	BA	SA	AB	H	2B	3B	HR	HR%	R	RBI	BB	SO	SB	Pinch Hit AB	Pinch Hit H	PO	A	E	DP	TC/G	FA	G by Pos
1953	STL A	9	.250	.625	8	2	0	0	1	12.5	3	1	1	3	0	8	2	0	0	0	0	0.0	—	

Willie Upshaw

UPSHAW, WILLIE CLAY BL TL 6′ 185 lbs.
B. Apr. 27, 1957, Blanco, Tex.

Year	Team	Games	BA	SA	AB	H	2B	3B	HR	HR%	R	RBI	BB	SO	SB	Pinch Hit AB	Pinch Hit H	PO	A	E	DP	TC/G	FA	G by Pos
1978	TOR A	95	.237	.304	224	53	8	2	1	0.4	26	17	21	35	4	12	1	131	4	7	5	1.8	.951	OF-52, DH-18, 1B-10
1980		34	.213	.344	61	13	3	1	1	1.6	10	5	6	14	1	9	2	51	7	1	11	2.2	.983	1B-14, DH-12, OF-1
1981		61	.171	.324	111	19	3	1	4	3.6	15	10	11	16	2	17	4	72	6	0	8	1.8	1.000	DH-15, OF-14, 1B-14
1982		160	.267	.443	580	155	25	7	21	3.6	77	75	52	91	8	2	0	1438	101	17	123	9.7	.989	1B-155, DH-5
1983		160	.306	.515	579	177	26	7	27	4.7	99	104	61	98	10	4	1	1294	117	21	131	8.9	.985	1B-159, DH-1

Willie Upshaw *continued*

Year	Team	Games	BA	SA	AB	H	2B	3B	HR	HR%	R	RBI	BB	SO	SB	Pinch Hit AB	Pinch Hit H	PO	A	E	DP	TC/G	FA	G by Pos
1984		152	.278	.464	569	158	31	9	19	3.3	79	84	55	86	10	0	0	1246	103	14	133	9.0	.990	1B-151, DH-1
1985		148	.275	.447	501	138	31	5	15	3.0	79	65	48	71	8	2	0	1157	104	10	111	8.6	.992	1B-147, DH-1
1986		155	.251	.368	573	144	28	6	9	1.6	85	60	78	87	23	2	0	1314	131	12	118	9.4	.992	1B-154, DH-1
1987		150	.244	.391	512	125	22	4	15	2.9	68	58	58	78	10	7	2	1169	127	9	114	8.9	.993	1B-146
1988	CLE A	149	.245	.369	493	121	22	3	11	2.2	58	50	62	66	12	7	2	1162	102	12	93	8.9	.991	1B-144
10 yrs.		1264	.262	.419	4203	1103	199	45	123	2.9	596	528	452	642	88	62	12	9034	802	103	847	8.2	.990	1B-1094, OF-67, DH-54
LEAGUE CHAMPIONSHIP SERIES																								
1985	TOR A	7	.231	.308	26	6	2	0	0	0.0	2	1	1	4	0	0	0	53	7	1	3	8.7	.984	1B-7

Tom Upton

UPTON, THOMAS HERBERT (Muscles)
Brother of Bill Upton.
B. Dec. 29, 1926, Esther, Mo.
BR TR 6′ 160 lbs.

Year	Team	Games	BA	SA	AB	H	2B	3B	HR	HR%	R	RBI	BB	SO	SB	Pinch Hit AB	Pinch Hit H	PO	A	E	DP	TC/G	FA	G by Pos
1950	STL A	124	.237	.296	389	92	5	6	2	0.5	50	30	52	45	7	5	0	199	333	30	65	4.8	.947	SS-115, 2B-2, 3B-1
1951		52	.198	.275	131	26	4	3	0	0.0	9	12	12	22	1	0	0	80	105	10	33	4.1	.949	SS-47
1952	WAS A	5	.000	.000	5	0	0	0	0	0.0	1	0	1	0	0	0	0	3	8	0	1	3.7	1.000	SS-3
3 yrs.		181	.225	.288	525	118	9	9	2	0.4	60	42	65	67	8	5	0	282	446	40	99	4.6	.948	SS-165, 2B-2, 3B-1

Luke Urban

URBAN, LOUIS JOHN
B. Mar. 22, 1898, Fall River, Mass. D. Dec. 7, 1980, Somerset, Mass.
BR TR 5′ 8″ 168 lbs.

Year	Team	Games	BA	SA	AB	H	2B	3B	HR	HR%	R	RBI	BB	SO	SB	Pinch Hit AB	Pinch Hit H	PO	A	E	DP	TC/G	FA	G by Pos
1927	BOS N	35	.288	.333	111	32	5	0	0	0.0	11	10	3	6	1	1	1	59	30	5	1	2.8	.947	C-34
1928		15	.176	.176	17	3	0	0	0	0.0	0	2	0	1	0	5	1	12	5	0	0	3.4	1.000	C-5
2 yrs.		50	.273	.313	128	35	5	0	0	0.0	11	12	3	7	1	6	2	71	35	5	1	2.8	.955	C-39

Billy Urbanski

URBANSKI, WILLIAM MICHAEL
B. June 5, 1903, Linoleumville, N. Y. D. July 12, 1973, Perth Amboy, N. J.
BR TR 5′ 8″ 165 lbs.

Year	Team	Games	BA	SA	AB	H	2B	3B	HR	HR%	R	RBI	BB	SO	SB	Pinch Hit AB	Pinch Hit H	PO	A	E	DP	TC/G	FA	G by Pos
1931	BOS N	82	.238	.307	303	72	13	4	0	0.0	22	17	10	32	3	0	0	103	188	11	23	3.5	.964	3B-68, SS-19
1932		136	.272	.387	563	153	25	8	8	1.4	80	46	28	60	8	0	0	316	461	44	91	6.0	.946	SS-136
1933		144	.251	.302	566	142	21	4	0	0.0	65	35	33	48	4	1	0	299	473	38	91	5.7	.953	SS-143
1934		146	.293	.397	605	177	30	6	7	1.2	104	53	56	37	4	1	0	298	457	31	84	5.4	.961	SS-145
1935		132	.230	.286	514	118	17	0	4	0.8	53	30	40	32	3	0	0	258	356	40	52	5.1	.939	SS-129
1936		122	.261	.316	494	129	17	5	0	0.0	55	26	31	42	2	3	1	224	280	31	63	4.5	.942	SS-80, 3B-38
1937		1	.000	.000	1	0	0	0	0	0.0	0	0	0	1	0	1	0	0	0	0	0	0.0	—	
7 yrs.		763	.260	.337	3046	791	123	27	19	0.6	379	207	198	252	24	6	1	1498	2215	195	404	5.2	.950	SS-652, 3B-106

Jose Uribe

URIBE, JOSE ALTAGRACIA
Played as Jose Gonzalez in 1984.
Born Jose Altagracia Gonzalez (Uribe).
B. Jan. 21, 1959, San Cristobal, Dominican Republic.
BB TR 5′10″ 156 lbs.
BR 1984

Year	Team	Games	BA	SA	AB	H	2B	3B	HR	HR%	R	RBI	BB	SO	SB	Pinch Hit AB	Pinch Hit H	PO	A	E	DP	TC/G	FA	G by Pos
1984	STL N	8	.211	.211	19	4	0	0	0	0.0	4	3	0	2	1	0	0	7	15	1	4	3.8	.957	SS-5, 2B-1
1985	SF N	147	.237	.315	476	113	20	4	3	0.6	46	26	30	57	8	2	0	209	438	26	77	4.6	.961	SS-145, 2B-1
1986		157	.223	.280	453	101	15	1	3	0.7	46	43	61	76	22	2	1	249	444	16	95	4.5	.977	SS-156
1987		95	.291	.424	309	90	16	5	5	1.6	44	30	24	35	12	3	1	145	286	13	62	4.7	.971	SS-95
1988		141	.252	.318	493	124	10	7	3	0.6	47	35	36	69	14	0	0	212	404	19	77	4.5	.970	SS-140
1989		151	.221	.280	453	100	12	6	1	0.2	34	30	34	74	6	0	0	225	436	18	85	4.5	.973	SS-150
1990		138	.248	.304	415	103	8	6	1	0.2	35	24	29	49	5	4	1	182	373	20	73	4.3	.965	SS-134
1991		90	.221	.303	231	51	8	4	1	0.4	23	12	20	33	3	1	0	98	218	11	35	3.8	.966	SS-87
1992		66	.241	.346	162	39	9	1	2	1.2	24	13	14	25	2	1	0	75	157	7	37	3.9	.971	SS-62
1993	HOU N	45	.245	.264	53	13	1	0	0	0.0	4	3	8	5	1	1	1	34	51	5	20	2.2	.944	SS-41
10 yrs.		1038	.241	.314	3064	738	99	34	19	0.6	307	219	256	425	74	14	4	1436	2822	136	565	4.3	.969	SS-1015, 2B-2
LEAGUE CHAMPIONSHIP SERIES																								
1987	SF N	7	.269	.308	26	7	1	0	0	0.0	1	2	0	4	1	0	0	11	21	1	7	4.7	.970	SS-7
1989		5	.235	.294	17	4	1	0	0	0.0	2	1	1	5	1	0	0	6	9	2	2	3.4	.882	SS-5
2 yrs.		12	.256	.302	43	11	2	0	0	0.0	3	3	1	9	2	0	0	17	30	3	9	4.2	.940	SS-12
WORLD SERIES																								
1989	SF N	3	.200	.200	5	1	0	0	0	0.0	1	0	0	0	0	0	0	1	3	0	0	1.3	1.000	SS-3

Lou Ury

URY, LOUIS NEWTON
B. Apr. 1877, Fort Scott, Kans. D. Mar. 4, 1918, Kansas City, Mo.
TR 6′

Year	Team	Games	BA	SA	AB	H	2B	3B	HR	HR%	R	RBI	BB	SO	SB	Pinch Hit AB	Pinch Hit H	PO	A	E	DP	TC/G	FA	G by Pos
1903	STL N	2	.143	.143	7	1	0	0	0	0.0	0	0	0		0	0	0	23	1	0	1	12.0	1.000	1B-2

Bob Usher

USHER, ROBERT ROYCE
B. Mar. 1, 1925, San Diego, Calif.
BR TR 6′ 1½″ 180 lbs.

Year	Team	Games	BA	SA	AB	H	2B	3B	HR	HR%	R	RBI	BB	SO	SB	Pinch Hit AB	Pinch Hit H	PO	A	E	DP	TC/G	FA	G by Pos
1946	CIN N	92	.204	.270	152	31	5	1	1	0.7	16	14	13	27	2	1	0	104	9	2	3	1.4	.983	OF-80, 3B-1
1947		9	.182	.318	22	4	0	0	1	4.5	2	1	2	2	0	0	0	16	1	0	0	2.1	1.000	OF-8
1950		106	.259	.368	321	83	17	0	6	1.9	51	35	27	38	3	10	2	190	7	3	1	2.1	.985	OF-95
1951		114	.208	.310	303	63	12	2	5	1.7	27	25	19	36	4	13	2	218	9	6	4	2.4	.974	OF-98
1952	CHI N	1	—	—	0	0	0	0	0	—	0	0	1	0	0	0	0	0	0	0	0	0.0	—	
1957	2 teams	CLE A (10G –.125) WAS A (96G –.261)																						
″	total	106	.257	.337	303	78	7	1	5	1.7	37	27	28	33	0	4	0	231	7	5	2	2.4	.979	OF-99, 3B-1
6 yrs.		428	.235	.329	1101	259	41	4	18	1.6	133	102	90	136	9	28	4	759	33	16	10	2.1	.980	OF-380, 3B-2

Dutch Ussat

USSAT, WILLIAM AUGUST
B. Apr. 11, 1904, Dayton, Ohio D. May 29, 1959, Dayton, Ohio.
BR TR 6′ 1″ 170 lbs.

Year	Team	Games	BA	SA	AB	H	2B	3B	HR	HR%	R	RBI	BB	SO	SB	Pinch Hit AB	Pinch Hit H	PO	A	E	DP	TC/G	FA	G by Pos
1925	CLE A	1	.000	.000	1	0	0	0	0	0.0	0	0	0	0	0	0	0	0	1	0	0	1.0	1.000	2B-1
1927		4	.188	.313	16	3	0	1	0	0.0	4	2	2	1	0	0	0	5	6	0	1	2.8	1.000	3B-4
2 yrs.		5	.176	.294	17	3	0	1	0	0.0	4	2	2	1	0	0	0	5	7	0	1	2.4	1.000	3B-4, 2B-1

Tex Vache

VACHE, ERNEST LEWIS
B. Nov. 17, 1894, Santa Monica, Calif. D. June 11, 1953, Los Angeles, Calif.
BR TR 6′ 1″ 200 lbs.

Year	Team	Games	BA	SA	AB	H	2B	3B	HR	HR%	R	RBI	BB	SO	SB	Pinch Hit AB	Pinch Hit H	PO	A	E	DP	TC/G	FA	G by Pos
1925	BOS A	110	.313	.464	252	79	15	7	3	1.2	41	48	21	33	2	**49**	10	87	2	9	0	1.8	.908	OF-53

Gene Vadeboncoeur

VADEBONCOEUR, EUGENE ONESIME BR TR 5′ 6″ 150 lbs.
B. July 15, 1858, Louiseville, Que., Canada. D. Oct. 16, 1935, Haverhill, Mass.

Year	Team	Games	BA	SA	AB	H	2B	3B	HR	HR%	R	RBI	BB	SO	SB	Pinch Hit AB	Pinch Hit H	PO	A	E	DP	TC/G	FA	G by Pos
1884	PHI N	4	.214	.214	14	3	0	0	0	0.0	1		1	2		0	0	13	9	4	0	6.5	.846	C-4

Harry Vahrenhorst

VAHRENHORST, HARRY HENRY BR TR 6′ 1″ 175 lbs.
B. Feb. 13, 1885, St. Louis, Mo. D. Oct. 10, 1943, St. Louis, Mo.

Year	Team	Games	BA	SA	AB	H	2B	3B	HR	HR%	R	RBI	BB	SO	SB	Pinch Hit AB	Pinch Hit H	PO	A	E	DP	TC/G	FA	G by Pos
1904	STL A	1	.000	.000	1	0	0	0	0	0.0	0	0	0		0	1	0	0	0	0	0	0.0	—	

Mike Vail

VAIL, MICHAEL LEWIS BR TR 6′ 1″ 180 lbs.
B. Nov. 10, 1951, San Francisco, Calif.

Year	Team	Games	BA	SA	AB	H	2B	3B	HR	HR%	R	RBI	BB	SO	SB	Pinch Hit AB	Pinch Hit H	PO	A	E	DP	TC/G	FA	G by Pos
1975	NY N	38	.302	.420	162	49	8	1	3	1.9	17	17	9	37	0	1	1	92	9	3	1	2.9	.971	OF-36
1976		53	.217	.266	143	31	5	1	0	0.0	8	9	6	19	0	17	4	63	1	4	0	1.9	.941	OF-35
1977		108	.262	.398	279	73	12	1	8	2.9	29	35	19	58	0	30	4	159	5	6	2	2.0	.965	OF-85
1978	2 teams	CLE A (14G –.235) CHI N (74G –.333)																						
″	total	88	.318	.439	214	68	8	3	4	1.9	17	35	4	33	1	35	13	68	1	1	0	1.3	.986	OF-54, 3B-1, DH-1
1979	CHI N	87	.335	.520	179	60	8	2	7	3.9	28	35	14	27	0	44	12	51	4	2	0	1.4	.965	OF-39, 3B-2
1980		114	.298	.423	312	93	17	2	6	1.9	30	47	14	77	2	45	8	126	5	5	1	1.8	.963	OF-77
1981	CIN N	31	.161	.161	31	5	0	0	0	0.0	1	3	0	9	0	28	5	3	0	0	0	1.0	1.000	OF-3
1982		78	.254	.381	189	48	10	1	4	2.1	9	29	6	33	0	29	8	72	7	1	0	1.5	.988	OF-52
1983	2 teams	SF N (18G –.154) MON N (34G –.283)																						
″	total	52	.241	.354	79	19	3	0	2	2.5	6	7	8	17	0	25	5	50	5	1	1	2.4	.982	OF-17, 1B-5, 3B-1
1984	LA N	16	.063	.063	16	1	0	0	0	0.0	1	2	1	7	0	13	1	0	0	0	0	0.0	.000	OF-1
10 yrs.		665	.279	.400	1604	447	71	11	34	2.1	146	219	81	317	3	267	61	684	37	23	5	1.8	.969	OF-399, 1B-5, 3B-4, DH-1

Roy Valdes

VALDES, ROGELIO LAZARO BR TR 5′11″ 185 lbs.
Born Rogelio Lazaro Valdes (Rojas).
B. Feb. 20, 1920, Havana, Cuba

Year	Team	Games	BA	SA	AB	H	2B	3B	HR	HR%	R	RBI	BB	SO	SB	Pinch Hit AB	Pinch Hit H	PO	A	E	DP	TC/G	FA	G by Pos
1944	WAS A	1	.000	.000	1	0	0	0	0	0.0	0	0	0	0	0	1	0	0	0	0	0	0.0	—	

Sandy Valdespino

VALDESPINO, HILARIO BL TL 5′ 8″ 170 lbs.
Born Hilario Valdespino (Borroto).
B. Jan. 24, 1939, San Jose de las Lajas, Cuba.

Year	Team	Games	BA	SA	AB	H	2B	3B	HR	HR%	R	RBI	BB	SO	SB	Pinch Hit AB	Pinch Hit H	PO	A	E	DP	TC/G	FA	G by Pos
1965	MIN A	108	.261	.322	245	64	8	2	1	0.4	38	22	20	28	7	47	10	94	4	1	1	1.7	.990	OF-57
1966		52	.176	.259	108	19	1	1	2	1.9	11	9	4	24	2	27	2	36	0	0	0	1.6	1.000	OF-23
1967		99	.165	.216	97	16	2	0	1	1.0	9	3	5	22	3	33	7	40	3	1	0	0.7	.977	OF-65
1968	ATL N	36	.233	.279	86	20	1	0	1	1.2	8	4	10	20	0	15	1	40	0	1	0	2.0	.976	OF-20
1969	2 teams	HOU N (41G –.244) SEA A (20G –.211)																						
″	total	61	.236	.268	157	37	5	0	0	0.0	20	14	16	26	2	22	3	60	4	4	0	1.9	.941	OF-36
1970	MIL A	8	.000	.000	9	0	0	0	0	0.0	0	0	0	4	0	7	0	0	0	0	0	0.0	.000	OF-1
1971	KC A	18	.317	.508	63	20	6	0	2	3.2	10	15	2	5	0	4	2	18	1	1	0	1.3	.950	OF-15
7 yrs.		382	.230	.295	765	176	23	3	7	0.9	96	67	57	129	14	155	25	288	12	8	1	1.4	.974	OF-217
WORLD SERIES																								
1965	MIN A	5	.273	.364	11	3	1	0	0	0.0	1	0	0	1	0	3	1	6	0	0	0	3.0	1.000	OF-2

Julio Valdez

VALDEZ, JULIO JULIAN BB TR 6′ 2″ 160 lbs.
BR 1980
Born Julio Julian Castillo (Valdez).
B. June 3, 1956, San Cristobal, Dominican Republic.

Year	Team	Games	BA	SA	AB	H	2B	3B	HR	HR%	R	RBI	BB	SO	SB	Pinch Hit AB	Pinch Hit H	PO	A	E	DP	TC/G	FA	G by Pos
1980	BOS A	8	.263	.474	19	5	1	0	1	5.3	4	4	0	5	2	0	0	17	26	3	10	5.8	.935	SS-8
1981		17	.217	.217	23	5	0	0	0	0.0	1	3	0	2	0	0	0	12	30	2	3	2.6	.955	SS-17
1982		28	.250	.300	20	5	1	0	0	0.0	3	1	0	7	1	2	1	16	24	1	5	1.6	.976	SS-22, DH-3
1983		12	.120	.120	25	3	0	0	0	0.0	3	0	1	4	0	0	0	16	16	2	3	2.8	.941	2B-9, SS-2, DH-1
4 yrs.		65	.207	.264	87	18	2	0	1	1.1	11	8	1	18	3	2	1	61	96	8	21	2.7	.952	SS-49, 2B-9, DH-4

Jose Valdivielso

VALDIVIELSO, JOSE BR TR 6′ 1″ 175 lbs.
Born Jose Martinez Valdivielso (Lopez).
B. May 22, 1934, Matanzas, Cuba.

Year	Team	Games	BA	SA	AB	H	2B	3B	HR	HR%	R	RBI	BB	SO	SB	Pinch Hit AB	Pinch Hit H	PO	A	E	DP	TC/G	FA	G by Pos
1955	WAS A	94	.221	.316	294	65	12	5	2	0.7	32	28	21	38	1	0	0	160	317	22	69	5.3	.956	SS-94
1956		90	.236	.333	246	58	8	2	4	1.6	18	29	29	36	3	1	0	144	266	23	58	4.8	.947	SS-90
1959		24	.286	.286	14	4	0	0	0	0.0	1	0	1	3	0	1	1	13	18	0	6	1.5	1.000	SS-21
1960		117	.213	.246	268	57	1	1	2	0.7	23	19	20	36	1	0	0	179	294	23	68	4.3	.954	SS-115, 3B-1
1961	MIN A	76	.195	.248	149	29	5	0	1	0.7	15	9	8	19	1	0	0	67	107	6	20	2.5	.967	SS-43, 2B-15, 3B-14
5 yrs.		401	.219	.290	971	213	26	8	9	0.9	89	85	79	132	6	2	1	563	1002	74	221	4.2	.955	SS-363, 2B-15, 3B-15

John Valentin

VALENTIN, JOHN WILLIAM BR TR 6′ 170 lbs.
B. Feb. 18, 1967, Mineola, N. Y.

Year	Team	Games	BA	SA	AB	H	2B	3B	HR	HR%	R	RBI	BB	SO	SB	Pinch Hit AB	Pinch Hit H	PO	A	E	DP	TC/G	FA	G by Pos
1992	BOS A	58	.276	.427	185	51	13	0	5	2.7	21	25	20	17	1	0	0	79	182	10	45	4.7	.963	SS-58
1993		144	.278	.447	468	130	40	3	11	2.4	50	66	49	77	3	1	0	238	432	20	96	4.8	.971	SS-144
1994		84	.316	.505	301	95	26	2	9	3.0	53	49	42	38	3	1	0	134	239	8	54	4.5	.979	SS-83, DH-1
1995		135	.298	.533	520	155	37	2	27	5.2	108	102	81	67	20	0	0	225	413	18	94	4.9	.973	SS-135
4 yrs.		421	.292	.486	1474	431	116	7	52	3.5	232	242	192	199	27	2	0	676	1266	56	289	4.7	.972	SS-420, DH-1
DIVISIONAL PLAYOFF SERIES																								
1995	BOS A	3	.250	.583	12	3	1	0	1	8.3	1	2	3	1	0	0	0	5	5	1	0	3.7	.909	SS-3

Jose Valentin

VALENTIN, JOSE ANTONIO BB TR 5′10″ 175 lbs.
Born Jose Antonio Valentin (Rosario).
B. Oct. 12, 1969, Manati, Puerto Rico.

Year	Team	Games	BA	SA	AB	H	2B	3B	HR	HR%	R	RBI	BB	SO	SB	Pinch Hit AB	Pinch Hit H	PO	A	E	DP	TC/G	FA	G by Pos
1992	MIL A	4	.000	.000	3	0	0	0	0	0.0	1	1	0	0	0	0	0	1	1	1	0	1.5	.667	2B-1, SS-1
1993		19	.245	.396	53	13	1	2	1	1.9	10	7	7	16	1	0	0	20	51	6	9	4.1	.922	SS-19
1994		97	.239	.421	285	68	19	0	11	3.9	47	46	38	75	12	0	0	150	336	20	71	4.9	.960	SS-83, 2B-18, 3B-1, DH-1
1995		112	.219	.402	338	74	23	3	11	3.3	62	49	37	83	16	0	0	163	335	15	82	4.8	.971	SS-104, DH-3, 3B-1
4 yrs.		232	.228	.408	679	155	43	5	23	3.4	120	103	82	174	29	0	0	334	723	42	162	4.7	.962	SS-207, 2B-19, DH-4, 3B-2

Bob Valentine

VALENTINE, ROBERT
Deceased.

Year	Team	Games	BA	SA	AB	H	2B	3B	HR	HR%	R	RBI	BB	SO	SB	Pinch Hit AB	Pinch Hit H	PO	A	E	DP	TC/G	FA	G by Pos
1876	NY N	1	.000	.000	3	0	0	0	0	0.0	0	0	0	0		0	0	2	0	4	0	6.0	.333	C-1

Bobby Valentine

VALENTINE, ROBERT JOHN BR TR 5′10″ 189 lbs.
B. May 13, 1950, Stamford, Conn.
Manager 1985–92.

Year	Team	Games	BA	SA	AB	H	2B	3B	HR	HR%	R	RBI	BB	SO	SB	Pinch Hit AB	Pinch Hit H	PO	A	E	DP	TC/G	FA	G by Pos
1969	LA N	5	—	—	0	0	0	0	0	—	3	0	0	0	0	0	0	0	0	0	0	0.0	—	
1971		101	.249	.310	281	70	10	2	1	0.4	32	25	15	20	5	14	5	123	176	16	31	3.4	.949	SS-37, 3B-23, 2B-21, OF-11
1972		119	.274	.335	391	107	11	2	3	0.8	42	32	27	33	5	10	1	178	245	23	38	3.9	.948	2B-49, 3B-39, OF-16, SS-10
1973	CAL A	32	.302	.397	126	38	5	2	1	0.8	12	13	5	9	6	0	0	63	75	6	11	4.4	.958	SS-25, OF-8
1974		117	.261	.329	371	97	10	3	3	0.8	39	39	25	25	8	9	3	160	116	17	10	2.5	.942	OF-62, SS-36, 3B-15, DH-4, 2B-1
1975	2 teams	CAL A (26G –.281) SD N (7G –.133)																						
″	total	33	.250	.319	72	18	2	0	1	1.4	6	6	8	3	1	10	2	31	1	2	2	3.1	.941	OF-6, 1B-3, 3B-2
1976	SD N	15	.367	.449	49	18	4	0	0	0.0	3	4	6	2	0	1	0	55	6	0	2	4.4	1.000	OF-10, 1B-4
1977	2 teams	SD N (44G –.179) NY N (42G –.133)																						
″	total	86	.153	.220	150	23	4	0	2	1.3	13	13	13	19	0	44	9	119	64	3	16	3.4	.984	SS-24, 1B-16, 3B-14
1978	NY N	69	.269	.331	160	43	7	0	1	0.6	17	18	19	18	1	15	4	78	109	6	13	3.6	.969	2B-45, 3B-9
1979	SEA A	62	.276	.337	98	27	6	0	0	0.0	9	7	22	5	1	20	7	32	38	2	5	1.3	.972	SS-29, OF-15, 3B-4, 2B-4, C-2, DH-1
10 yrs.		639	.260	.326	1698	441	59	9	12	0.7	176	157	140	134	27	123	31	839	830	75	128	3.2	.957	SS-161, OF-128, 2B-120, 3B-106, 1B-23, DH-5, C-2

Ellis Valentine

VALENTINE, ELLIS CLARENCE BR TR 6′ 4″ 205 lbs.
B. July 30, 1954, Helena, Ark.

Year	Team	Games	BA	SA	AB	H	2B	3B	HR	HR%	R	RBI	BB	SO	SB	Pinch Hit AB	Pinch Hit H	PO	A	E	DP	TC/G	FA	G by Pos
1975	MON N	12	.364	.576	33	12	4	0	1	3.0	2	3	2	4	0	2	0	12	1	2	1	1.4	.867	OF-11
1976		94	.279	.410	305	85	15	2	7	2.3	36	39	30	51	14	4	0	162	12	5	4	2.0	.972	OF-88
1977		127	.293	.504	508	149	28	2	25	4.9	63	76	30	58	13	1	0	232	9	7	1	2.0	.972	OF-126
1978		151	.289	.489	570	165	35	2	25	4.4	75	76	35	88	13	4	3	296	24	10	3	2.3	.970	OF-146
1979		146	.276	.454	548	151	29	3	21	3.8	73	82	22	74	11	2	1	281	10	5	2	2.1	.983	OF-144
1980		86	.315	.524	311	98	22	2	13	4.2	40	67	25	44	5	2	1	154	6	5	1	2.0	.970	OF-83
1981	2 teams	MON N (22G –.211) NY N (48G –.207)																						
″	total	70	.208	.359	245	51	11	1	8	3.3	23	36	11	49	0	4	2	115	8	4	0	1.9	.969	OF-68
1982	NY N	111	.288	.407	337	97	14	1	8	2.4	33	48	5	38	1	16	3	159	10	3	4	1.8	.983	OF-98
1983	CAL A	86	.240	.435	271	65	10	2	13	4.8	30	43	18	48	2	3	2	152	5	6	1	1.9	.963	OF-85
1985	TEX A	11	.211	.395	38	8	1	0	2	5.3	5	4	2	8	0	2	1	7	0	0	0	0.6	1.000	OF-7, DH-4
10 yrs.		894	.278	.458	3166	881	169	15	123	3.9	380	474	180	462	59	40	13	1570	85	47	17	2.0	.972	OF-856, DH-4

Fred Valentine

VALENTINE, FRED LEE (Squeaky) BB TR 6′ 1″ 190 lbs.
B. Jan. 19, 1935, Clarksdale, Miss.

Year	Team	Games	BA	SA	AB	H	2B	3B	HR	HR%	R	RBI	BB	SO	SB	Pinch Hit AB	Pinch Hit H	PO	A	E	DP	TC/G	FA	G by Pos
1959	BAL A	12	.316	.316	19	6	0	0	0	0.0	0	1	3	4	0	0	0	7	1	1	0	1.1	.889	OF-8
1963		26	.268	.293	41	11	1	0	0	0.0	5	1	8	5	0	12	4	15	0	0	0	1.5	1.000	OF-10
1964	WAS A	102	.226	.307	212	48	5	0	4	1.9	20	20	21	44	4	37	5	86	2	2	1	1.6	.978	OF-57
1965		12	.241	.241	29	7	0	0	0	0.0	6	1	4	5	3	2	1	23	0	0	0	2.1	1.000	OF-11
1966		146	.276	.455	508	140	29	7	16	3.1	77	59	51	63	22	7	3	304	7	7	3	2.3	.978	OF-138, 1B-2
1967		151	.234	.346	457	107	16	1	11	2.4	52	44	56	76	17	22	6	258	7	3	0	2.0	.989	OF-136
1968	2 teams	WAS A (37G –.238) BAL A (47G –.187)																						
″	total	84	.214	.339	192	41	5	2	5	2.6	20	12	13	31	1	33	1	67	4	1	2	1.4	.986	OF-53
7 yrs.		533	.247	.373	1458	360	56	10	36	2.5	180	138	156	228	47	113	20	760	21	14	6	1.9	.982	OF-413, 1B-2

Benny Valenzuela

VALENZUELA, BENJAMIN BELTRAN (Papelero) BR TR 5′10″ 175 lbs.
B. June 2, 1933, Los Mochis, Mexico

Year	Team	Games	BA	SA	AB	H	2B	3B	HR	HR%	R	RBI	BB	SO	SB	Pinch Hit AB	Pinch Hit H	PO	A	E	DP	TC/G	FA	G by Pos
1958	STL N	10	.214	.286	14	3	1	0	0	0.0	0	0	1	0	0	5	2	3	4	1	0	2.7	.875	3B-3

Dave Valle

VALLE, DAVID BR TR 6′ 2″ 200 lbs.
B. Oct. 30, 1960, Bayside, N. Y.

Year	Team	Games	BA	SA	AB	H	2B	3B	HR	HR%	R	RBI	BB	SO	SB	Pinch Hit AB	Pinch Hit H	PO	A	E	DP	TC/G	FA	G by Pos
1984	SEA A	13	.296	.444	27	8	1	0	1	3.7	4	4	1	5	0	0	0	56	5	0	0	4.7	1.000	C-13
1985		31	.157	.171	70	11	1	0	0	0.0	2	4	1	17	0	0	0	117	7	3	0	4.1	.976	C-31
1986		22	.340	.679	53	18	3	0	5	9.4	10	15	7	7	0	8	2	90	3	2	3	5.9	.979	C-12, 1B-4
1987		95	.256	.435	324	83	16	3	12	3.7	40	53	15	46	2	10	1	422	34	5	2	5.9	.989	C-75, 1B-2, OF-1
1988		93	.231	.400	290	67	15	2	10	3.4	29	50	18	38	0	10	5	490	47	6	8	6.2	.989	C-84, DH-3, 1B-1
1989		94	.237	.354	316	75	10	3	7	2.2	32	34	29	32	0	3	2	496	52	4	3	5.9	.993	C-93
1990		107	.214	.331	308	66	15	0	7	2.3	37	33	45	48	1	3	0	633	44	2	9	6.5	.997	C-104, 1B-1
1991		132	.194	.299	324	63	8	1	8	2.5	38	32	34	49	0	3	0	676	52	6	9	5.6	.992	C-129, 1B-2
1992		124	.240	.362	367	88	16	1	9	2.5	39	30	27	58	0	3	2	606	62	7	10	5.5	.990	C-122
1993		135	.258	.395	423	109	19	0	13	3.1	48	63	48	56	1	0	0	881	71	5	13	7.1	.995	C-135
1994	2 teams	BOS A (30G –.158) MIL A (16G –.389)																						
″	total	46	.232	.375	112	26	8	1	2	1.8	14	10	18	22	0	2	0	204	7	3	1	4.9	.986	C-40, DH-2, 1B-2
1995	TEX A	36	.240	.280	75	18	3	0	0	0.0	7	5	6	18	1	2	0	157	13	1	2	4.8	.994	C-29, 1B-7
12 yrs.		928	.235	.369	2689	632	115	11	74	2.8	300	333	249	396	5	44	12	4828	397	44	60	5.9	.992	C-867, 1B-19, DH-5, OF-1

Hector Valle

VALLE, HECTOR JOSE BR TR 5′ 9″ 180 lbs.
B. Oct. 27, 1940, Vega Baja, Puerto Rico.

Year	Team	Games	BA	SA	AB	H	2B	3B	HR	HR%	R	RBI	BB	SO	SB	Pinch Hit AB	Pinch Hit H	PO	A	E	DP	TC/G	FA	G by Pos
1965	LA N	9	.308	.308	13	4	0	0	0	0.0	1	2	2	3	0	2	1	20	1	0	0	3.5	1.000	C-6

Elmer Valo

VALO, ELMER WILLIAM BL TR 5′11″ 190 lbs.
B. Mar. 5, 1921, Ribnik, Czechoslovakia.

Year	Team	Games	BA	SA	AB	H	2B	3B	HR	HR%	R	RBI	BB	SO	SB	Pinch Hit AB	Pinch Hit H	PO	A	E	DP	TC/G	FA	G by Pos
1940	PHI A	6	.348	.348	23	8	0	0	0	0.0	6	0	3	0	2	0	0	18	0	0	0	3.0	1.000	OF-6
1941		15	.420	.580	50	21	0	1	2	4.0	13	6	4	2	0	4	1	22	0	0	0	2.2	1.000	OF-10
1942		133	.251	.336	459	115	13	10	2	0.4	64	40	70	21	13	9	2	264	5	10	0	2.3	.964	OF-122
1943		77	.221	.297	249	55	6	2	3	1.2	31	18	35	13	2	13	1	134	4	2	0	2.2	.986	OF-63
1946		108	.307	.411	348	107	21	6	1	0.3	59	31	60	18	9	15	5	182	7	5	0	2.2	.974	OF-90
1947		112	.300	.405	370	111	12	6	5	1.4	60	36	64	21	11	5	1	205	9	6	0	2.1	.973	OF-104
1948		113	.305	.394	383	117	17	4	3	0.8	72	46	81	13	10	3	1	231	4	4	1	2.2	.983	OF-109
1949		150	.283	.404	547	155	27	12	5	0.9	86	85	119	32	14	0	0	395	8	8	0	2.7	.981	OF-150
1950		129	.280	.406	446	125	16	5	10	2.2	62	46	83	22	12	6	1	264	9	5	3	2.4	.982	OF-117
1951		123	.302	.446	444	134	27	8	7	1.6	75	55	75	20	11	8	2	247	5	5	0	2.2	.981	OF-116

Elmer Valo *continued*

Year	Team	Games	BA	SA	AB	H	2B	3B	HR	HR%	R	RBI	BB	SO	SB	Pinch Hit AB	Pinch Hit H	PO	A	E	DP	TC/G	FA	G by Pos
1952		129	.281	.407	388	109	26	4	5	1.3	69	47	101	16	12	10	1	223	7	9	1	2.0	.962	OF-121
1953		50	.224	.259	85	19	3	0	0	0.0	15	9	22	7	0	19	4	46	1	0	1	1.9	1.000	OF-25
1954		95	.214	.330	224	48	11	6	1	0.4	28	33	51	18	2	22	1	135	3	5	1	2.3	.965	OF-62
1955	**KC A**	112	.364	.484	283	103	17	4	3	1.1	50	37	52	18	5	31	14	147	5	2	2	2.1	.987	OF-72
1956	**2 teams**	**KC A** (9G –.222) **PHI N** (98G –.289)																						
″	**total**	107	.287	.400	300	86	13	3	5	1.7	41	39	49	22	7	16	5	167	4	6	0	2.0	.966	OF-88
1957	**BKN N**	81	.273	.422	161	44	10	1	4	2.5	14	26	25	16	0	34	8	57	0	0	0	1.6	1.000	OF-36
1958	**LA N**	65	.248	.317	101	25	2	1	1	1.0	9	14	12	11	0	36	9	24	0	0	0	0.9	1.000	OF-26
1959	**CLE A**	34	.292	.292	24	7	0	0	0	0.0	3	5	7	0	0	24	7	1	0	0	0	0.5	1.000	OF-2
1960	**2 teams**	**NY A** (8G –.000) **WAS A** (76G –.281)																						
″	**total**	84	.261	.304	69	18	3	0	0	0.0	7	16	19	5	0	59	14	5	1	0	0	0.8	1.000	OF-8
1961	**2 teams**	**MIN A** (33G –.156) **PHI N** (50G –.186)																						
″	**total**	83	.173	.267	75	13	4	0	1	1.3	4	12	11	9	0	72	13	2	0	0	0	1.0	1.000	OF-2
20 yrs.		1806	.282	.391	5029	1420	228	73	58	1.2	768	601	943	284	110	386	90	2769	72	67	9	2.2	.977	OF-1329

Deacon Van Buren

VAN BUREN, EDWARD EUGENE BL TR 5′10″ 175 lbs.
B. Dec. 14, 1870, LaSalle County, Ill. D. June 29, 1957, Portland, Ore.

Year	Team	Games	BA	SA	AB	H	2B	3B	HR	HR%	R	RBI	BB	SO	SB	Pinch Hit AB	Pinch Hit H	PO	A	E	DP	TC/G	FA	G by Pos
1904	**2 teams**	**BKN N** (1G –1.000) **PHI N** (12G –.233)																						
″	**total**	13	.250	.295	44	11	2	0	0	0.0	2	3	3		2	1	1	23	2	1	1	2.2	.962	OF-12

Ty Van Burkleo

VAN BURKLEO, TYLER LEE BL TL 6′ 5″ 230 lbs.
B. Oct. 7, 1963, Oakland, Calif.

Year	Team	Games	BA	SA	AB	H	2B	3B	HR	HR%	R	RBI	BB	SO	SB	Pinch Hit AB	Pinch Hit H	PO	A	E	DP	TC/G	FA	G by Pos
1993	**CAL A**	12	.152	.333	33	5	3	0	1	3.0	2	1	6	9	1	1	0	99	3	0	8	8.5	1.000	1B-12
1994	**CLR N**	2	.000	.000	5	0	0	0	0	0.0	0	0	0	1	0	1	0	15	1	0	1	8.0	1.000	1B-2
2 yrs.		14	.132	.289	38	5	3	0	1	2.6	2	1	6	10	1	2	0	114	4	0	9	8.4	1.000	1B-14

Al Van Camp

VAN CAMP, ALBERT JOSEPH BR TR 5′11½″ 175 lbs.
B. Sept. 7, 1903, Moline, Ill. D. Feb. 2, 1981, Bensenville, Ill.

Year	Team	Games	BA	SA	AB	H	2B	3B	HR	HR%	R	RBI	BB	SO	SB	Pinch Hit AB	Pinch Hit H	PO	A	E	DP	TC/G	FA	G by Pos
1928	**CLE A**	5	.235	.294	17	4	1	0	0	0.0	0	2	0	1	1	0	0	47	1	1	1	9.8	.980	1B-5
1931	**BOS A**	102	.275	.346	324	89	15	4	0	0.0	34	33	20	24	3	16	6	324	18	3	17	4.1	.991	OF-59, 1B-25
1932		34	.223	.301	103	23	4	2	0	0.0	10	6	4	17	0	7	0	249	18	4	20	10.8	.985	1B-25
3 yrs.		141	.261	.333	444	116	20	6	0	0.0	44	41	24	42	4	23	6	620	37	8	38	5.8	.988	OF-59, 1B-55

Carl Vandagrift

VANDAGRIFT, CARL WILLIAM BR TR 5′ 8″ 155 lbs.
B. Apr. 22, 1883, Cantrall, Ill. D. Oct. 9, 1920, Fort Wayne, Ind.

Year	Team	Games	BA	SA	AB	H	2B	3B	HR	HR%	R	RBI	BB	SO	SB	Pinch Hit AB	Pinch Hit H	PO	A	E	DP	TC/G	FA	G by Pos
1914	**IND F**	43	.250	.279	136	34	4	0	0	0.0	25	9	9		7	0	0	78	89	14	9	4.0	.923	2B-28, 3B-12, SS-5

John Vander Wal

VANDER WAL, JOHN HENRY BL TL 6′ 1″ 180 lbs.
B. Apr. 29, 1966, Grand Rapids, Mich.

Year	Team	Games	BA	SA	AB	H	2B	3B	HR	HR%	R	RBI	BB	SO	SB	Pinch Hit AB	Pinch Hit H	PO	A	E	DP	TC/G	FA	G by Pos
1991	**MON N**	21	.213	.361	61	13	4	1	1	1.6	4	8	1	18	0	4	1	29	0	0	0	1.7	1.000	OF-17
1992		105	.239	.352	213	51	8	2	4	1.9	21	20	24	36	3	35	6	122	6	2	3	2.0	.985	OF-57, 1B-7
1993		106	.233	.372	215	50	7	4	5	2.3	34	30	27	30	6	30	7	271	14	4	17	3.6	.986	1B-42, OF-38
1994	**CLR N**	91	.245	.427	110	27	3	1	5	4.5	12	15	16	31	2	**58**	**14**	106	3	0	11	5.2	1.000	1B-14, OF-7
1995		105	.347	.594	101	35	8	1	5	5.0	15	21	16	23	1	**72**	**28**[1]	51	4	2	3	2.8	.965	OF-10, 1B-10
5 yrs.		428	.251	.406	700	176	30	9	20	2.9	86	94	84	138	12	199	56	579	27	8	34	3.0	.987	OF-129, 1B-73
DIVISIONAL PLAYOFF SERIES																								
1995	**CLR N**	4	.000	.000	4	0	0	0	0	0.0	0	0	0	2	0	4	0	0	0	0	0	0.0	—	

Fred Van Dusen

VAN DUSEN, FREDERICK WILLIAM BL TL 6′ 3″ 180 lbs.
B. July 31, 1937, Jackson Heights, N. Y.

Year	Team	Games	BA	SA	AB	H	2B	3B	HR	HR%	R	RBI	BB	SO	SB	Pinch Hit AB	Pinch Hit H	PO	A	E	DP	TC/G	FA	G by Pos
1955	**PHI N**	1	—	—	0	0	0	0	0	—	0	0	0	0	0	0	0	0	0	0	0	0.0	—	

Bill Van Dyke

VAN DYKE, WILLIAM JENNINGS BR TR 5′ 8″ 170 lbs.
B. Dec. 15, 1863, Paris, Ill. D. May 5, 1933, El Paso, Tex.

Year	Team	Games	BA	SA	AB	H	2B	3B	HR	HR%	R	RBI	BB	SO	SB	Pinch Hit AB	Pinch Hit H	PO	A	E	DP	TC/G	FA	G by Pos
1890	**TOL AA**	129	.257	.341	502	129	14	11	2	0.4	74		25		73	0	0	211	52	30	3	2.2	.898	OF-110, 3B-18, 2B-2, C-1
1892	**STL N**	4	.125	.125	16	2	0	0	0	0.0	2	1	0	1	0	0	0	7	0	1	0	2.0	.875	OF-4
1893	**BOS N**	3	.250	.333	12	3	1	0	0	0.0	2	1	0	1	1	0	0	4	0	0	0	1.3	1.000	OF-3
3 yrs.		136	.253	.334	530	134	15	11	2	0.4	78	2	25	2	74	0	0	222	52	31	3	2.2	.898	OF-117, 3B-18, 2B-2, C-1

Dave Van Gorder

VAN GORDER, DAVID THOMAS BR TR 6′ 2″ 205 lbs.
B. Mar. 27, 1957, Los Angeles, Calif.

Year	Team	Games	BA	SA	AB	H	2B	3B	HR	HR%	R	RBI	BB	SO	SB	Pinch Hit AB	Pinch Hit H	PO	A	E	DP	TC/G	FA	G by Pos
1982	**CIN N**	51	.182	.219	137	25	3	1	0	0.0	4	7	14	19	1	1	0	273	18	4	3	5.8	.986	C-51
1984		38	.228	.248	101	23	2	0	0	0.0	10	6	12	17	0	2	0	194	11	0	1	5.5	1.000	C-36, 1B-1
1985		73	.238	.325	151	36	7	0	2	1.3	12	24	9	19	0	4	1	255	11	3	2	3.8	.989	C-70
1986		9	.000	.000	10	0	0	0	0	0.0	0	0	1	2	0	1	0	20	0	0	0	2.9	1.000	C-7
1987	**BAL A**	12	.238	.381	21	5	0	0	1	4.8	4	1	3	6	0	1	0	44	1	1	0	3.8	.978	C-12
5 yrs.		183	.212	.267	420	89	12	1	3	0.7	30	38	39	63	1	9	1	786	41	8	6	4.7	.990	C-176, 1B-1

George Van Haltren

VAN HALTREN, GEORGE EDWARD MARTIN BL TL 5′11″ 170 lbs.
B. Mar. 30, 1866, St. Louis, Mo. D. Sept. 29, 1945, Oakland, Calif.
Manager 1892.

Year	Team	Games	BA	SA	AB	H	2B	3B	HR	HR%	R	RBI	BB	SO	SB	Pinch Hit AB	Pinch Hit H	PO	A	E	DP	TC/G	FA	G by Pos
1887	**CHI N**	45	.203	.279	172	35	4	0	3	1.7	30	17	15	15	12	0	0	47	26	8	2	1.7	.901	OF-27, P-20
1888		81	.283	.437	318	90	9	14	4	1.3	46	34	22	34	21	0	0	98	62	17	0	2.0	.904	OF-57, P-30
1889		134	.309	.433	543	168	20	10	9	1.7	126	81	82	41	28	0	0	230	35	32	5	2.2	.892	OF-130, SS-3, 2B-1
1890	**BKN P**	92	.335	.444	376	126	8	9	5	1.3	84	54	41	23	35	0	0	143	90	22	7	2.6	.914	OF-67, P-28, SS-3
1891	**BAL AA**	139	.318	.443	566	180	14	15	9	1.6	136	83	71	46	75	0	0	275	190	82	22	3.7	.850	OF-81, SS-59, P-6, 2B-2
1892	**2 teams**	**BAL N** (135G –.302) **PIT N** (13G –.200)																						
″	**total**	148	.293	.409	611	179	22	14	7	1.1	115	62	76	34	55	0	0	270	47	52	9	2.4	.859	OF-142, P-4, 3B-3, SS-2, 1B-2
1893	**PIT N**	124	.338	.423	529	179	14	11	3	0.6	129	79	75	25	37	1	0	245	69	49	6	2.9	.865	OF-111, SS-12, 2B-2
1894	**NY N**	137	.331	.430	519	172	22	4	7	1.3	109	104	55	22	43	0	0	299	29	31	5	2.6	.914	OF-137
1895		131	.340	.503	521	177	23	19	8	1.5	113	103	57	29	32	0	0	252	27	27	3	2.3	.912	OF-131, P-1
1896		133	.351	.484	562	197	18	**21**	5	0.9	136	74	55	36	39	0	0	273	26	15	4	2.3	.952	OF-133, P-2

George Van Haltren *continued*

Year	Team	Games	BA	SA	AB	H	2B	3B	HR	HR%	R	RBI	BB	SO	SB	Pinch Hit AB	Pinch Hit H	PO	A	E	DP	TC/G	FA	G by Pos
1897		129	.330	.417	564	186	22	9	3	0.5	117	64	40		50	0	0	267	31	20	4	2.5	.937	OF-129
1898		156	.312	.413	**654**	204	28	16	2	0.3	129	68	59		36	0	0	299	22	29	5	2.2	.917	OF-156
1899		151	.301	.356	604	182	21	3	2	0.3	117	58	74		31	0	0	284	31	23	8	2.2	.932	OF-151
1900		141	.315	.398	571	180	30	7	1	0.2	114	51	50		**45**	0	0	325	28	23	7	2.6	.939	OF-141, P-1
1901		135	.342	.414	544	186	22	7	1	0.2	82	47	51		24	0	0	263	27	18	5	2.3	.942	OF-135, P-1
1902		24	.261	.318	88	23	1	2	0	0.0	14	7	17		6	0	0	43	6	4	1	2.2	.925	OF-24
1903		84	.257	.286	280	72	6	1	0	0.0	42	28	28		14	8	1	136	3	6	1	1.9	.959	OF-75
17 yrs.		1984	.316	.418	8022	2536	284	162	69	0.9	1639	1014	868	305	583	9	1	3749	749	458	94	2.5	.908	OF-1827, P-93, SS-79, 2B-5, 3B-3, 1B-2

John Vann

VANN, JOHN SILAS
B. June 7, 1893, Fairland, Okla. D. June 10, 1958, Shreveport, La.
BR TR

Year	Team	Games	BA	SA	AB	H	2B	3B	HR	HR%	R	RBI	BB	SO	SB	Pinch Hit AB	Pinch Hit H	PO	A	E	DP	TC/G	FA	G by Pos
1913	**STL N**	1	.000	.000	1	0	0	0	0	0.0	0	0	0	1	0	1	0	0	0	0	0	0.0	—	

Jay Van Noy

VAN NOY, JAY LOWELL
B. Nov. 4, 1928, Garland, Utah.
BL TR 6′ 1″ 200 lbs.

Year	Team	Games	BA	SA	AB	H	2B	3B	HR	HR%	R	RBI	BB	SO	SB	Pinch Hit AB	Pinch Hit H	PO	A	E	DP	TC/G	FA	G by Pos
1951	**STL N**	6	.000	.000	7	0	0	0	0	0.0	1	0	1	6	0	4	0	2	0	0	0	2.0	1.000	OF-1

Maurice Van Robays

VAN ROBAYS, MAURICE RENE (Bomber)
B. Nov. 15, 1914, Detroit, Mich. D. Mar. 1, 1965, Detroit, Mich.
BR TR 6′½″ 190 lbs.

Year	Team	Games	BA	SA	AB	H	2B	3B	HR	HR%	R	RBI	BB	SO	SB	Pinch Hit AB	Pinch Hit H	PO	A	E	DP	TC/G	FA	G by Pos
1939	**PIT N**	27	.314	.457	105	33	9	0	2	1.9	13	16	6	10	0	1	0	36	3	3	1	1.6	.929	OF-25, 2B-1
1940		145	.273	.402	572	156	27	7	11	1.9	82	116	33	58	2	2	1	276	10	11	3	2.1	.963	OF-143, 1B-1
1941		129	.282	.381	457	129	23	5	4	0.9	62	78	41	29	0	6	3	292	9	8	3	2.6	.974	OF-121
1942		100	.232	.311	328	76	13	5	1	0.3	29	46	30	24	0	14	3	199	6	3	3	2.5	.986	OF-84
1943		69	.288	.432	236	68	17	7	1	0.4	32	35	18	19	0	9	4	120	5	8	1	2.2	.940	OF-60
1946		59	.212	.308	146	31	5	3	1	0.7	14	12	11	15	0	20	3	70	2	3	0	1.9	.960	OF-37, 1B-2
6 yrs.		529	.267	.380	1844	493	94	27	20	1.1	232	303	139	155	2	52	14	993	35	36	11	2.2	.966	OF-470, 1B-3, 2B-1

Andy Van Slyke

VAN SLYKE, ANDREW JAMES (Slick)
B. Dec. 21, 1960, Utica, N. Y.
BL TR 6′ 1″ 190 lbs.

Year	Team	Games	BA	SA	AB	H	2B	3B	HR	HR%	R	RBI	BB	SO	SB	Pinch Hit AB	Pinch Hit H	PO	A	E	DP	TC/G	FA	G by Pos
1983	**STL N**	101	.262	.421	309	81	15	5	8	2.6	51	38	46	64	21	5	1	203	59	6	16	2.5	.978	OF-69, 3B-30, 1B-9
1984		137	.244	.368	361	88	16	4	7	1.9	45	50	63	71	28	11	4	357	82	8	40	3.1	.982	OF-81, 3B-32, 1B-30
1985		146	.259	.439	424	110	25	6	13	3.1	61	55	47	54	34	19	4	237	13	1	6	1.7	.996	OF-142, 1B-2
1986		137	.270	.452	418	113	23	7	13	3.1	48	61	47	85	21	10	2	415	34	8	25	3.1	.982	OF-110, 1B-38
1987	**PIT N**	157	.293	.507	564	165	36	11	21	3.7	93	82	56	122	34	7	1	338	10	4	9	2.3	.989	OF-150, 1B-1
1988		154	.288	.506	587	169	23	**15**	25	4.3	101	100	57	126	30	5	0	406	12	4	2	2.8	.991	OF-152
1989		130	.237	.370	476	113	18	9	9	1.9	64	53	47	100	16	10	1	344	9	4	6	2.9	.989	OF-123, 1B-2
1990		136	.284	.465	493	140	26	6	17	3.4	67	77	66	89	14	4	0	326	6	8	0	2.6	.976	OF-133
1991		138	.265	.446	491	130	24	7	17	3.5	87	83	71	85	10	4	0	273	8	1	1	2.1	.996	OF-135
1992		154	.324	.505	614	**199**	**45**	12	14	2.3	103	89	58	99	12	0	0	421	11	5	3	2.8	.989	OF-154
1993		83	.310	.449	323	100	13	4	8	2.5	42	50	24	40	11	6	0	205	2	1	1	2.7	.995	OF-78
1994		105	.246	.358	374	92	18	3	6	1.6	41	30	52	72	7	7	1	238	9	2	1	2.5	.992	OF-99
1995	**2 teams**	**BAL A** (17G –.159)	**PHI N** (63G –.243)																					
″	**total**	80	.224	.343	277	62	11	2	6	2.2	32	24	33	56	7	8	0	159	7	3	2	2.3	.982	OF-73
13 yrs.		1658	.274	.443	5711	1562	293	91	164	2.9	835	792	667	1063	245	96	14	3922	262	55	112	2.6	.987	OF-1499, 1B-82, 3B-62
LEAGUE CHAMPIONSHIP SERIES																								
1985	**STL N**	5	.091	.091	11	1	0	0	0	0.0	1	1	2	1	0	0	0	7	0	0	0	1.4	1.000	OF-5
1990	**PIT N**	6	.208	.333	24	5	1	1	0	0.0	3	3	1	7	1	0	0	13	1	0	0	2.3	1.000	OF-6
1991		7	.160	.360	25	4	2	0	1	4.0	3	2	5	5	1	0	0	18	1	0	0	2.7	1.000	OF-7
1992		7	.276	.448	29	8	3	1	0	0.0	1	4	1	5	0	0	0	20	0	0	0	2.9	1.000	OF-7
4 yrs.		25	.202	.348	89 **10th**	18	6 **7th**	2 **4th**	1	1.1	8	10	9	18 **7th**	2	0	0	58	2	0	0	2.4	1.000	OF-25
WORLD SERIES																								
1985	**STL N**	6	.091	.091	11	1	0	0	0	0.0	0	0	0	5	0	0	0	8	0	0	0	1.3	1.000	OF-6

Ike Van Zandt

VAN ZANDT, CHARLES ISAAC
B. 1877, Brooklyn, N. Y. D. Sept. 14, 1908, Nashua, N. H.
BL

Year	Team	Games	BA	SA	AB	H	2B	3B	HR	HR%	R	RBI	BB	SO	SB	Pinch Hit AB	Pinch Hit H	PO	A	E	DP	TC/G	FA	G by Pos
1901	**NY N**	3	.167	.167	6	1	0	0	0	0.0	1	0	0		0	0	0	1	0	3	0	1.3	.250	P-2, OF-1
1904	**CHI N**	3	.000	.000	11	0	0	0	0	0.0	0	0	0		0	0	0	3	0	0	0	1.0	1.000	OF-3
1905	**STL A**	94	.233	.295	322	75	15	1	1	0.3	31	20	7		7	**18**	**4**	76	9	11	0	1.3	.885	OF-74, 1B-1, P-1
3 yrs.		100	.224	.283	339	76	15	1	1	0.3	32	20	7		7	18	4	80	9	14	0	1.3	.864	OF-78, P-3, 1B-1

Dick Van Zant

VAN ZANT, RICHARD (Foghorn Dick)
B. Nov. 1864, Richmond, Ind. D. Aug. 6, 1912, Richmond, Ind.

Year	Team	Games	BA	SA	AB	H	2B	3B	HR	HR%	R	RBI	BB	SO	SB	Pinch Hit AB	Pinch Hit H	PO	A	E	DP	TC/G	FA	G by Pos
1888	**CLE AA**	10	.258	.290	31	8	1	0	0	0.0	1	1	1		1	0	0	7	22	8	2	3.7	.784	3B-10

Hedi Vargas

VARGAS, HEDIBERTO
Born Hediberto Vargas (Rodriguez).
B. Feb. 23, 1959, Guanica, Puerto Rico.
BR TR 6′ 4″ 205 lbs.

Year	Team	Games	BA	SA	AB	H	2B	3B	HR	HR%	R	RBI	BB	SO	SB	Pinch Hit AB	Pinch Hit H	PO	A	E	DP	TC/G	FA	G by Pos
1982	**PIT N**	8	.375	.500	8	3	1	0	0	0.0	1	3	0	2	0	3	2	16	1	0	1	3.4	1.000	1B-5
1984		18	.226	.290	31	7	2	0	0	0.0	3	2	3	5	0	6	4	51	4	1	6	4.3	.982	1B-13
2 yrs.		26	.256	.333	39	10	3	0	0	0.0	4	5	3	7	0	9	6	67	5	1	7	4.1	.986	1B-18

Buck Varner

VARNER, GLEN GANN
B. Aug. 17, 1930, Hixson, Tenn.
BL TR 5′10″ 170 lbs.

Year	Team	Games	BA	SA	AB	H	2B	3B	HR	HR%	R	RBI	BB	SO	SB	Pinch Hit AB	Pinch Hit H	PO	A	E	DP	TC/G	FA	G by Pos
1952	**WAS A**	2	.000	.000	4	0	0	0	0	0.0	0	0	1	1	0	1	0	1	0	0	0	1.0	1.000	OF-1

Pete Varney

VARNEY, RICHARD FRED
B. Apr. 10, 1949, Roxbury, Mass.
BR TR 6′ 3″ 235 lbs.

Year	Team	Games	BA	SA	AB	H	2B	3B	HR	HR%	R	RBI	BB	SO	SB	Pinch Hit AB	Pinch Hit H	PO	A	E	DP	TC/G	FA	G by Pos
1973	**CHI A**	5	.000	.000	4	0	0	0	0	0.0	0	0	1	0	0	0	0	10	0	0	0	2.0	1.000	C-5
1974		9	.250	.250	28	7	0	0	0	0.0	1	2	1	8	0	0	0	47	5	1	0	5.9	.981	C-9

Pete Varney *continued*

Year	Team	Games	BA	SA	AB	H	2B	3B	HR	HR%	R	RBI	BB	SO	SB	Pinch Hit AB	Pinch Hit H	PO	A	E	DP	TC/G	FA	G by Pos
1975		36	.271	.393	107	29	5	1	2	1.9	12	8	6	28	2	3	0	151	14	2	1	4.6	.988	C-34, DH-2
1976	2 teams	CHI A (14G –.244) ATL N (5G –.100)																						
"	total	19	.216	.431	51	11	2	0	3	5.9	5	5	2	11	0	0	0	85	7	1	1	4.9	.989	C-19
4 yrs.		69	.247	.374	190	47	7	1	5	2.6	18	15	10	47	2	3	0	293	26	4	2	4.7	.988	C-67, DH-2

Gary Varsho

VARSHO, GARY ANDREW
B. June 20, 1961, Marshfield, Wis.
BL TR 5′11″ 190 lbs.

Year	Team	Games	BA	SA	AB	H	2B	3B	HR	HR%	R	RBI	BB	SO	SB	Pinch Hit AB	Pinch Hit H	PO	A	E	DP	TC/G	FA	G by Pos
1988	CHI N	46	.274	.315	73	20	3	0	0	0.0	6	5	1	6	5	28	11	29	0	3	0	1.8	.906	OF-18
1989		61	.184	.276	87	16	4	2	0	0.0	10	6	4	13	3	36	5	25	1	2	0	1.3	.929	OF-21
1990		46	.250	.333	48	12	4	0	0	0.0	10	1	1	6	2	43	11	2	0	0	0	0.7	1.000	OF-3
1991	PIT N	99	.273	.417	187	51	11	2	4	2.1	23	23	19	34	9	41	9	95	2	1	1	1.7	.990	OF-54, 1B-3
1992		103	.222	.370	162	36	6	3	4	2.5	22	22	10	32	5	55	13	62	1	1	0	1.5	.984	OF-44
1993	CIN N	77	.232	.358	95	22	6	0	2	2.1	8	11	9	19	1	44	9	27	1	0	1	1.3	1.000	OF-22
1994	PIT N	67	.256	.402	82	21	6	3	0	0.0	15	5	4	19	0	28	8	25	0	2	0	0.7	.926	OF-36, 1B-1
1995	PHI N	72	.252	.282	103	26	1	1	0	0.0	7	11	7	17	2	46	12	31	0	2	0	1.3	.939	OF-25
8 yrs.		571	.244	.355	837	204	41	11	10	1.2	101	84	55	146	27	321	78	296	5	11	2	1.4	.965	OF-223, 1B-4
LEAGUE CHAMPIONSHIP SERIES																								
1991	PIT N	2	.500	.500	2	1	0	0	0	0.0	0	0	0	1	0	2	1	0	0	0	0	0.0	—	
1992		2	.500	.500	2	1	0	0	0	0.0	0	0	0	0	0	2	1	0	0	0	0	0.0	.000	OF-1
2 yrs.		4	.500	.500	4	2	0	0	0	0.0	0	0	0	1	0	4	2	0	0	0	0	0.0		OF-1

Jim Vatcher

VATCHER, JAMES ERNEST
B. May 27, 1966, Santa Monica, Calif.
BR TR 5′ 9″ 165 lbs.

Year	Team	Games	BA	SA	AB	H	2B	3B	HR	HR%	R	RBI	BB	SO	SB	Pinch Hit AB	Pinch Hit H	PO	A	E	DP	TC/G	FA	G by Pos
1990	2 teams	PHI N (36G –.261) ATL N (21G –.259)																						
"	total	57	.260	.356	73	19	2	1	1	1.4	7	7	5	15	0	32	10	27	0	0	0	0.9	1.000	OF-30
1991	SD N	17	.200	.200	20	4	0	0	0	0.0	3	2	4	6	1	8	2	8	1	1	0	0.9	.900	OF-11
1992		13	.250	.313	16	4	1	0	0	0.0	1	2	3	6	0	0	0	13	1	0	0	1.1	1.000	OF-13
3 yrs.		87	.248	.321	109	27	3	1	1	0.9	11	11	12	27	1	40	12	48	2	1	0	0.9	.980	OF-54

Arky Vaughan

VAUGHAN, JOSEPH FLOYD
B. Mar. 9, 1912, Clifty, Ark. D. Aug. 30, 1952, Eagleville, Calif.
Hall of Fame 1985.
BL TR 5′10½″ 175 lbs.

Year	Team	Games	BA	SA	AB	H	2B	3B	HR	HR%	R	RBI	BB	SO	SB	Pinch Hit AB	Pinch Hit H	PO	A	E	DP	TC/G	FA	G by Pos
1932	PIT N	129	.318	.412	497	158	15	10	4	0.8	71	61	39	26	10	1	0	247	403	46	74	5.4	.934	SS-128
1933		152	.314	.478	573	180	29	**19**	9	1.6	85	97	64	23	3	0	0	310	487	46	95	5.5	.945	SS-152
1934		149	.333	.511	558	186	41	11	12	2.2	115	94	**94**	38	10	0	0	329	480	41	77	5.7	.952	SS-149
1935		137	**.385**	**.607**	499	192	34	10	19	3.8	108	99	**97**	18	4	0	0	249	422	35	55	5.2	.950	SS-137
1936		156	.335	.474	568	190	30	11	9	1.6	**122**	78	**118**	21	6	0	0	327	477	47	86	5.5	.945	SS-156
1937		126	.322	.463	469	151	17	**17**	5	1.1	71	72	54	22	7	6	2	257	335	27	58	5.2	.956	SS-108, OF-12
1938		148	.322	.444	541	174	35	5	7	1.3	88	68	104	21	14	1	0	306	507	33	107	5.8	.961	SS-147
1939		152	.306	.424	595	182	30	11	6	1.0	94	62	70	20	12	0	0	330	531	34	103	5.9	.962	SS-152
1940		156	.300	.453	594	178	40	**15**	7	1.2	**113**	95	88	25	12	0	0	309	546	52	94	5.8	.943	SS-155, 3B-2
1941		106	.316	.455	374	118	20	7	6	1.6	69	38	50	13	8	4	0	174	298	21	43	4.9	.957	SS-97, 3B-3
1942	BKN N	128	.277	.341	495	137	18	4	2	0.4	82	49	51	17	8	3	1	130	225	14	22	3.0	.962	3B-119, SS-5, 2B-1
1943		149	.305	.413	610	186	39	6	5	0.8	**112**	66	60	13	**20**	1	0	237	375	21	57	4.1	.967	SS-99, 3B-55
1947		64	.325	.444	126	41	5	2	2	1.6	24	25	27	11	4	26	10	56	20	0	3	2.4	1.000	OF-22, 3B-10
1948		65	.244	.341	123	30	3	0	3	2.4	19	22	21	8	0	29	8	47	14	0	1	1.8	1.000	OF-26, 3B-8
14 yrs.		1817	.318	.453	6622	2103	356	128	96	1.4	1173	926	937	276	118	71	21	3308	5120	417	875	5.1	.953	SS-1485, 3B-197, OF-60, 2B-1
WORLD SERIES																								
1947	BKN N	3	.500	1.000	2	1	1	0	0	0.0	0	0	1	0	0	2	1	0	0	0	0	0.0	—	

Glenn Vaughan

VAUGHAN, GLENN EDWARD (Sparky)
B. Feb. 15, 1944, Compton, Calif.
BB TR 5′11″ 170 lbs.

Year	Team	Games	BA	SA	AB	H	2B	3B	HR	HR%	R	RBI	BB	SO	SB	Pinch Hit AB	Pinch Hit H	PO	A	E	DP	TC/G	FA	G by Pos
1963	HOU N	9	.167	.167	30	5	0	0	0	0.0	1	0	2	5	1	0	0	13	20	3	1	3.6	.917	SS-9, 3B-1

Bobby Vaughn

VAUGHN, ROBERT
B. June 4, 1885, Stamford, N. Y. D. Apr. 11, 1965, Seattle, Wash.
BR TR 5′ 9″ 150 lbs.

Year	Team	Games	BA	SA	AB	H	2B	3B	HR	HR%	R	RBI	BB	SO	SB	Pinch Hit AB	Pinch Hit H	PO	A	E	DP	TC/G	FA	G by Pos
1909	NY A	5	.143	.143	14	2	0	0	0	0.0	1	0	1		1	0	0	10	5	2	0	3.4	.882	2B-4, SS-1
1915	STL F	144	.280	.351	521	146	19	9	0	0.0	69	32	58		24	1	0	274	382	36	48	4.7	.948	2B-127, SS-12, 3B-8
2 yrs.		149	.277	.346	535	148	19	9	0	0.0	70	32	59		25	1	0	284	387	38	48	4.7	.946	2B-131, SS-13, 3B-8

Farmer Vaughn

VAUGHN, HENRY FRANCIS
B. Mar. 1, 1864, Ruraldale, Ohio D. Feb. 21, 1914, Cincinnati, Ohio.
BR TR 6′ 3″ 177 lbs.

Year	Team	Games	BA	SA	AB	H	2B	3B	HR	HR%	R	RBI	BB	SO	SB	Pinch Hit AB	Pinch Hit H	PO	A	E	DP	TC/G	FA	G by Pos
1886	CIN AA	1	.000	.000	3	0	0	0	0	0.0	0		0			0	0	8	3	1	0	12.0	.917	C-1
1888	LOU AA	51	.196	.254	189	37	4	2	1	0.5	15	21	4		4	0	0	164	49	28	6	4.5	.884	OF-28, C-25
1889		90	.239	.322	360	86	11	5	3	0.8	39	45	7	41	13	0	0	441	121	51	18	6.5	.917	C-54, OF-20, 1B-18, 3B-3
1890	NY P	44	.265	.325	166	44	7	0	1	0.6	27	22	10	9	6	0	0	113	22	19	3	3.5	.877	C-30, OF-12, 3B-1, 2B-1
1891	2 teams	CIN AA (51G –.257) MIL AA (25G –.333)																						
"	total	76	.285	.354	274	78	14	1	1	0.4	34	23	18	20	8	0	0	324	82	32	12	5.5	.927	C-64, OF-7, 1B-6, 3B-2, P-1
1892	CIN N	91	.254	.329	346	88	10	5	2	0.6	45	50	16	13	10	0	0	394	80	33	22	5.2	.935	C-67, 1B-14, OF-11, 3B-6
1893		121	.280	.371	483	135	17	12	1	0.2	68	108	35	17	16	0	0	533	95	26	27	5.3	.960	C-80, OF-23, 1B-21
1894		72	.310	.479	284	88	15	6	7	2.5	50	64	12	11	5	1	0	362	64	26	19	5.6	.942	C-43, 1B-27, OF-8, SS-3
1895		92	.305	.404	334	102	23	5	0	0.0	60	48	17	10	15	0	0	379	96	30	13	5.4	.941	C-77, 1B-15, 2B-1, 3B-1
1896		114	.293	.395	433	127	20	9	2	0.5	71	66	16	7	7	2	2	740	82	21	41	7.4	.975	1B-57, C-57
1897		54	.291	.407	199	58	13	5	0	0.0	21	30	2		2	4	0	393	31	10	20	8.7	.977	1B-35, C-15
1898		78	.305	.389	275	84	12	4	1	0.4	35	46	11		4	6	4	462	50	17	28	7.3	.968	1B-39, C-33
1899		31	.176	.185	108	19	1	0	0	0.0	9	2	3		2	2	1	239	24	8	12	9.3	.970	1B-21, C-7, OF-1
13 yrs.		915	.274	.364	3454	946	147	54	19	0.6	474	525	151	128	92	15	7	4552	799	302	221	6.0	.947	C-553, 1B-253, OF-110, 3B-13, SS-3, 2B-2, P-1

Year	Team	Games	BA	SA	AB	H	2B	3B	HR	HR%	R	RBI	BB	SO	SB	Pinch Hit AB	Pinch Hit H	PO	A	E	DP	TC/G	FA	G by Pos

Fred Vaughn

VAUGHN, FREDERICK THOMAS (Muscles)
B. Oct. 18, 1918, Coalinga, Calif. D. Mar. 2, 1964, Lake Wales, Fla.
BR TR 5′10″ 185 lbs.

Year	Team	Games	BA	SA	AB	H	2B	3B	HR	HR%	R	RBI	BB	SO	SB	PH AB	PH H	PO	A	E	DP	TC/G	FA	G by Pos
1944	WAS A	30	.257	.321	109	28	2	1	1	0.9	10	21	9	24	2	1	1	62	78	10	16	5.2	.933	2B-26, 3B-3
1945		80	.235	.302	268	63	7	4	1	0.4	28	25	23	48	0	4	1	177	189	21	35	5.0	.946	2B-76, SS-1
2 yrs.		110	.241	.308	377	91	9	5	2	0.5	38	46	32	72	2	5	2	239	267	31	51	5.1	.942	2B-102, 3B-3, SS-1

Greg Vaughn

VAUGHN, GREGORY LAMONT
B. July 3, 1965, Sacramento, Calif.
BR TR 6′ 195 lbs.

Year	Team	Games	BA	SA	AB	H	2B	3B	HR	HR%	R	RBI	BB	SO	SB	PH AB	PH H	PO	A	E	DP	TC/G	FA	G by Pos
1989	MIL A	38	.265	.425	113	30	3	0	5	4.4	18	23	13	23	4	1	0	32	1	2	0	0.9	.943	OF-24, DH-13
1990		120	.220	.432	382	84	26	2	17	4.5	51	61	33	91	7	5	0	195	8	7	1	1.8	.967	OF-106, DH-8
1991		145	.244	.456	542	132	24	5	27	5.0	81	98	62	125	2	2	0	315	5	2	1	2.2	.994	OF-135, DH-10
1992		141	.228	.409	501	114	18	2	23	4.6	77	78	60	123	15	4	0	288	6	3	0	2.2	.990	OF-131, DH-7
1993		154	.267	.482	569	152	28	2	30	5.3	97	97	89	118	10	2	0	214	1	3	1	1.4	.986	OF-94, DH-58
1994		95	.254	.478	370	94	24	1	19	5.1	59	55	51	93	9	0	0	162	5	3	0	1.8	.982	OF-81, DH-14
1995		108	.224	.408	392	88	19	1	17	4.3	67	59	55	89	10	4	1	0	0	0	0	0.0	.000	DH-104
7 yrs.		801	.242	.445	2869	694	142	13	138	4.8	450	471	363	662	57	18	1	1206	26	20	3	1.6	.984	OF-571, DH-214

Mo Vaughn

VAUGHN, MAURICE SAMUEL
B. Dec. 15, 1967, Norwalk, Conn.
BL TR 6′ 1″ 225 lbs.

Year	Team	Games	BA	SA	AB	H	2B	3B	HR	HR%	R	RBI	BB	SO	SB	PH AB	PH H	PO	A	E	DP	TC/G	FA	G by Pos
1991	BOS A	74	.260	.370	219	57	12	0	4	1.8	21	32	26	43	2	9	3	378	26	6	43	6.3	.985	1B-49, DH-16
1992		113	.234	.400	355	83	16	2	13	3.7	42	57	47	67	3	13	4	741	57	15	76	7.7	.982	1B-85, DH-20
1993		152	.297	.525	539	160	34	1	29	5.4	86	101	79	130	4	2	0	1110	70	16	104	8.0	.987	1B-131, DH-19
1994		111	.310	.576	394	122	25	1	26	6.6	65	82	57	112	4	3	0	879	57	10	103	8.8	.989	1B-107, DH-1
1995		140	.300	.575	550	165	28	3	39	7.1	98	**126**	68	**150**	11	0	0	1262	94	11	126	9.8	.992	1B-138, DH-2
5 yrs.		590	.285	.510	2057	587	115	7	111	5.4	312	398	277	502	24	27	7	4370	304	58	452	8.3	.988	1B-510, DH-58
DIVISIONAL PLAYOFF SERIES																								
1995	BOS A	3	.000	.000	14	0	0	0	0	0.0	0	0	1	7	0	0	0	27	2	0	0	9.7	1.000	1B-3

Bobby Veach

VEACH, ROBERT HAYES
B. June 29, 1888, Island, Ky. D. Aug. 7, 1945, Detroit, Mich.
BL TR 5′11″ 160 lbs.

Year	Team	Games	BA	SA	AB	H	2B	3B	HR	HR%	R	RBI	BB	SO	SB	PH AB	PH H	PO	A	E	DP	TC/G	FA	G by Pos
1912	DET A	23	.342	.430	79	27	5	1	0	0.0	8	15	5		2	1	0	46	5	4	0	2.5	.927	OF-22
1913		138	.269	.354	494	133	22	10	0	0.0	54	64	53	31	22	1	0	250	16	24	3	2.1	.917	OF-137
1914		149	.275	.369	531	146	19	14	1	0.2	56	72	50	29	20	3	3	282	22	11	6	2.2	.965	OF-145
1915		152	.313	.434	569	178	**40**	10	3	0.5	81	**112**	68	43	16	0	0	297	19	8	4	2.1	.975	OF-152
1916		150	.306	.433	566	173	33	15	3	0.5	92	91	52	41	24	0	0	342	14	12	4	2.5	.967	OF-150
1917		154	.319	.457	571	182	31	12	8	1.4	79	**103**	61	44	21	0	0	356	17	17	5	2.5	.956	OF-154
1918		127	.279	.391	499	139	21	13	3	0.6	59	**78**	35	23	21	0	0	277	14	7	3	2.3	.977	OF-127, P-1
1919		139	.355	.519	538	**191**	**45**	**17**	3	0.6	87	101	33	33	19	1	1	338	14	12	3	2.6	.967	OF-138
1920		154	.307	.474	612	188	39	15	11	1.8	92	113	36	22	11	0	0	357	26	13	4	2.6	.967	OF-154
1921		150	.338	.529	612	207	43	13	16	2.6	110	128	48	31	14	1	0	384	21	11	4	2.8	.974	OF-149
1922		155	.327	.468	618	202	34	13	9	1.5	96	126	42	27	9	0	0	375	16	7	3	2.6	.982	OF-154
1923		114	.321	.406	293	94	13	3	2	0.7	45	39	29	21	10	22	8	127	6	8	0	1.6	.943	OF-85, C-1
1924	BOS A	142	.295	.426	519	153	35	9	5	1.0	77	99	47	18	5	12	3	268	15	13	2	2.3	.956	OF-130
1925	3 teams	BOS A (1G –.200)	NY A (56G –.353)	WAS A (18G –.243)																				
″	total	75	.323	.430	158	51	13	2	0	0.0	17	25	12	4	1	26	6	53	6	3	1	1.4	.952	OF-45
14 yrs.		1822	.310	.442	6659	2064	393	147	64	1.0	953	1166	571	367	195	67	21	3752	211	150	42	2.4	.964	OF-1742, C-1, P-1
WORLD SERIES																								
1925	WAS A	2	.000	.000	1	0	0	0	0	0.0	0	1	0	0	0	1	0	0	0	0	0	0.0	—	

Peek-A-Boo Veach

VEACH, WILLIAM WALTER
B. June 15, 1862, Indianapolis, Ind. D. Nov. 12, 1937, Indianapolis, Ind.

Year	Team	Games	BA	SA	AB	H	2B	3B	HR	HR%	R	RBI	BB	SO	SB	PH AB	PH H	PO	A	E	DP	TC/G	FA	G by Pos
1884	KC U	27	.134	.183	82	11	1	0	1	1.2	9		9			0	0	33	28	6	4	2.4	.910	OF-14, P-12, 1B-1, 2B-1
1887	LOU AA	1	.000	.000	3	0	0	0	0	0.0	0		1		0	0	0	2	1	1	0	4.0	.750	P-1
1890	2 teams	CLE N (64G –.235)	PIT N (8G –.300)																					
″	total	72	.243	.351	268	65	11	6	2	0.7	30	37	41	31	9	0	0	721	44	23	38	10.9	.971	1B-72
3 yrs.		100	.215	.309	353	76	12	6	3	0.8	39	37	51	31	9	0	0	756	73	30	42	8.5	.965	1B-73, OF-14, P-13, 2B-1

Coot Veal

VEAL, ORVILLE INMAN
B. July 9, 1932, Sandersville, Ga.
BR TR 6′ 1″ 165 lbs.

Year	Team	Games	BA	SA	AB	H	2B	3B	HR	HR%	R	RBI	BB	SO	SB	PH AB	PH H	PO	A	E	DP	TC/G	FA	G by Pos
1958	DET A	58	.256	.324	207	53	10	2	0	0.0	29	16	14	21	1	0	0	95	160	5	30	4.5	.981	SS-58
1959		77	.202	.247	89	18	1	0	1	1.1	12	15	8	7	0	0	0	57	96	6	16	2.2	.962	SS-72
1960		27	.297	.406	64	19	5	1	0	0.0	8	8	11	7	0	2	1	30	55	1	10	3.3	.988	SS-22, 3B-3, 2B-1
1961	WAS A	69	.202	.248	218	44	10	0	0	0.0	21	8	19	29	1	4	0	130	172	8	43	4.9	.974	SS-63
1962	PIT N	1	.000	.000	1	0	0	0	0	0.0	0	0	0	1	0	1	0	0	0	0	0	0.0	—	
1963	DET A	15	.219	.219	32	7	0	0	0	0.0	5	4	4	4	0	4	2	14	35	1	1	4.2	.980	SS-12
6 yrs.		247	.231	.288	611	141	26	3	1	0.2	75	51	56	69	2	11	3	326	518	21	100	3.7	.976	SS-227, 3B-3, 2B-1

Jesus Vega

VEGA, JESUS ANTONIO
Born Jesus Antonio Vega (Morales).
B. Oct. 14, 1955, Bayamon, Puerto Rico.
BR TR 6′ 1″ 176 lbs.

Year	Team	Games	BA	SA	AB	H	2B	3B	HR	HR%	R	RBI	BB	SO	SB	PH AB	PH H	PO	A	E	DP	TC/G	FA	G by Pos
1979	MIN A	4	.000	.000	7	0	0	0	0	0.0	0	0	0	2	0	3	0	0	0	0	0	0.0	.000	DH-3
1980		12	.167	.167	30	5	0	0	0	0.0	3	4	3	7	1	3	0	1	1	0	0	0.2	1.000	DH-9, 1B-2
1982		71	.266	.372	199	53	6	0	5	2.5	23	29	8	19	6	20	5	106	8	3	9	2.0	.974	DH-39, 1B-18, OF-1
3 yrs.		87	.246	.335	236	58	6	0	5	2.1	26	33	11	28	7	26	5	107	9	3	9	1.7	.975	DH-51, 1B-20, OF-1

Randy Velarde

VELARDE, RANDY LEE
B. Nov. 24, 1962, Midland, Tex.
BR TR 6′ 185 lbs.

Year	Team	Games	BA	SA	AB	H	2B	3B	HR	HR%	R	RBI	BB	SO	SB	PH AB	PH H	PO	A	E	DP	TC/G	FA	G by Pos
1987	NY A	8	.182	.182	22	4	0	0	0	0.0	1	1	0	6	0	0	0	8	20	2	3	3.8	.933	SS-8
1988		48	.174	.357	115	20	6	0	5	4.3	18	12	8	24	1	0	0	72	98	8	26	3.6	.955	2B-24, SS-14, 3B-11
1989		33	.340	.480	100	34	4	2	2	2.0	12	11	7	14	0	2	1	26	61	4	16	2.5	.956	3B-27, SS-9
1990		95	.210	.319	229	48	6	2	5	2.2	21	19	20	53	0	7	1	70	159	12	18	2.4	.950	3B-74, SS-15, OF-5, 2B-3, DH-3
1991		80	.245	.332	184	45	11	1	1	0.5	19	15	18	43	3	7	4	64	148	15	24	2.7	.934	3B-50, SS-31, OF-2
1992		121	.272	.386	412	112	24	1	7	1.7	57	46	38	78	7	3	2	179	257	15	50	3.6	.967	SS-75, 3B-26, OF-23, 2B-3
1993		85	.301	.469	226	68	13	2	7	3.1	28	24	18	39	2	13	4	102	92	9	20	2.2	.956	OF-50, SS-26, 3B-16, DH-1

Randy Velarde *continued*

Year	Team		Games	BA	SA	AB	H	2B	3B	HR	HR%	R	RBI	BB	SO	SB	Pinch Hit AB	Pinch Hit H	PO	A	E	DP	TC/G	FA	G by Pos
1994			77	.279	.439	280	78	16	1	9	3.2	47	34	22	61	4	0	0	94	188	19	37	3.4	.937	SS-49, 3B-27, OF-7, 2B-5
1995			111	.278	.392	367	102	19	1	7	1.9	60	46	55	64	5	2	0	170	258	10	48	3.4	.977	2B-62, SS-28, OF-20, 3B-19
9 yrs.			658	.264	.392	1935	511	99	10	43	2.2	263	208	186	382	22	34	12	785	1281	94	242	3.0	.956	SS-255, 3B-250, OF-107, 2B-97, DH-4
DIVISIONAL PLAYOFF SERIES																									
1995	NY	A	5	.176	.176	17	3	0	0	0	0.0	3	1	6	4	0	0	0	15	11	1	1	3.4	.963	2B-4, OF-2, 3B-2

Guillermo Velasquez

VELASQUEZ, GUILLERMO BL TR 6′ 3″ 220 lbs.
Born Guillermo Velasquez (Burgara).
B. Apr. 23, 1968, Mexicali, Mexico.

Year	Team		Games	BA	SA	AB	H	2B	3B	HR	HR%	R	RBI	BB	SO	SB	Pinch Hit AB	Pinch Hit H	PO	A	E	DP	TC/G	FA	G by Pos
1992	SD	N	15	.304	.435	23	7	0	0	1	4.3	1	5	1	7	0	11	2	15	1	1	1	3.4	.941	1B-3, OF-2
1993			79	.210	.287	143	30	2	0	3	2.1	7	20	13	35	0	32	8	225	21	4	20	5.7	.984	1B-38, OF-6
2 yrs.			94	.223	.307	166	37	2	0	4	2.4	8	25	14	42	0	43	10	240	22	5	21	5.4	.981	1B-41, OF-8

Freddie Velazquez

VELAZQUEZ, FEDERICO ANTONIO BR TR 6′ 1″ 185 lbs.
Born Federico Antonio Velazquez (Velasquez).
B. Dec. 6, 1937, Santo Domingo, Dominican Republic.

Year	Team		Games	BA	SA	AB	H	2B	3B	HR	HR%	R	RBI	BB	SO	SB	Pinch Hit AB	Pinch Hit H	PO	A	E	DP	TC/G	FA	G by Pos
1969	SEA	A	6	.125	.250	16	2	2	0	0	0.0	1	2	1	3	0	1	0	27	0	0	0	5.4	1.000	C-5
1973	ATL	N	15	.348	.391	23	8	1	0	0	0.0	2	3	1	3	0	6	1	36	3	1	0	3.6	.975	C-11
2 yrs.			21	.256	.333	39	10	3	0	0	0.0	3	5	2	6	0	7	1	63	3	1	0	4.2	.985	C-16

Otto Velez

VELEZ, OTONIEL BR TR 6′ 185 lbs.
Born Otoniel Velez (Franceschi).
B. Nov. 29, 1950, Ponce, Puerto Rico.

Year	Team		Games	BA	SA	AB	H	2B	3B	HR	HR%	R	RBI	BB	SO	SB	Pinch Hit AB	Pinch Hit H	PO	A	E	DP	TC/G	FA	G by Pos
1973	NY	A	23	.195	.325	77	15	4	0	2	2.6	9	7	15	24	0	0	0	45	2	2	0	2.1	.959	OF-23
1974			27	.209	.343	67	14	1	1	2	3.0	9	10	15	24	0	2	0	140	8	3	8	5.8	.980	1B-21, OF-3, 3B-2
1975			6	.250	.250	8	2	0	0	0	0.0	0	1	2	0	0	3	1	11	0	0	1	5.5	1.000	1B-1, DH-1
1976			49	.266	.394	94	25	6	0	2	2.1	11	10	23	26	0	14	3	89	2	2	5	2.4	.978	OF-24, 1B-8, DH-5, 3B-1
1977	TOR	A	120	.256	.458	360	92	19	3	16	4.4	50	62	65	87	4	17	2	140	5	4	1	1.4	.973	OF-79, DH-28
1978			91	.266	.448	248	66	14	2	9	3.6	29	38	45	41	1	20	8	161	12	3	4	2.1	.983	OF-74, DH-9, 1B-1
1979			99	.288	.529	274	79	21	0	15	5.5	45	48	46	45	0	19	5	159	5	4	3	1.9	.976	OF-73, DH-9, 1B-6
1980			104	.269	.487	357	96	12	3	20	5.6	54	62	54	86	0	3	1	36	3	1	2	0.4	.975	DH-97, 1B-3
1981			80	.212	.404	240	51	9	2	11	4.6	32	28	55	60	0	5	1	9	0	0	0	0.1	1.000	DH-74, 1B-1
1982			28	.192	.269	52	10	1	0	1	1.9	4	5	13	15	1	7	1	0	0	0	0	0.0	.000	DH-24
1983	CLE	A	10	.080	.080	25	2	0	0	0	0.0	1	1	3	6	0	2	0	0	0	0	0	0.0	.000	DH-8
11 yrs.			637	.251	.441	1802	452	87	11	78	4.3	244	272	336	414	6	92	22	790	37	19	24	1.5	.978	OF-276, DH-255, 1B-41, 3B-3
LEAGUE CHAMPIONSHIP SERIES																									
1976	NY	A	1	.000	.000	1	0	0	0	0	0.0	0	0	0	0	0	1	0	0	0	0	0	0.0	—	
WORLD SERIES																									
1976	NY	A	3	.000	.000	3	0	0	0	0	0.0	0	0	0	3	0	3	0	0	0	0	0	0.0	—	

Art Veltman

VELTMAN, ARTHUR PATRICK BR TR 6′ 175 lbs.
B. Mar. 24, 1906, Mobile, Ala. D. Oct. 1, 1980, San Antonio, Tex.

Year	Team		Games	BA	SA	AB	H	2B	3B	HR	HR%	R	RBI	BB	SO	SB	Pinch Hit AB	Pinch Hit H	PO	A	E	DP	TC/G	FA	G by Pos
1926	CHI	A	5	.250	.250	4	1	0	0	0	0.0	1	0	1	1	0	3	1	0	1	0	0	1.0	1.000	SS-1
1928	NY	N	1	.333	1.000	3	1	0	1	0	0.0	1	0	1	0	0	0	0	3	0	0	0	3.0	1.000	OF-1
1929			2	.000	.000	1	0	0	0	0	0.0	1	0	2	0	0	0	0	1	0	0	0	1.0	1.000	C-1
1931	BOS	N	1	.000	.000	1	0	0	0	0	0.0	0	0	0	0	0	1	0	0	0	0	0	0.0	—	
1932	NY	N	2	.000	.000	1	0	0	0	0	0.0	0	0	0	1	0	1	0	0	0	0	0	0.0	—	
1934	PIT	N	12	.107	.107	28	3	0	0	0	0.0	1	2	0	1	0	1	0	26	2	0	0	2.5	1.000	C-11
6 yrs.			23	.132	.184	38	5	0	1	0	0.0	4	2	4	3	0	6	1	30	3	0	0	2.4	1.000	C-12, OF-1, SS-1

Max Venable

VENABLE, WILLIAM McKINLEY, JR. BL TR 5′10″ 185 lbs.
B. June 6, 1957, Phoenix, Ariz.

Year	Team		Games	BA	SA	AB	H	2B	3B	HR	HR%	R	RBI	BB	SO	SB	Pinch Hit AB	Pinch Hit H	PO	A	E	DP	TC/G	FA	G by Pos
1979	SF	N	55	.165	.200	85	14	1	1	0	0.0	12	3	10	18	3	17	5	30	2	3	0	1.4	.914	OF-25
1980			64	.268	.304	138	37	5	0	0	0.0	13	10	15	22	8	26	9	61	0	0	0	1.5	1.000	OF-40
1981			18	.188	.313	32	6	0	2	0	0.0	2	1	4	3	3	12	1	12	0	0	0	2.4	1.000	OF-5
1982			71	.224	.280	125	28	2	1	1	0.8	17	7	7	16	9	17	3	66	6	1	2	1.4	.986	OF-53
1983			94	.219	.364	228	50	7	4	6	2.6	28	27	22	34	15	22	6	141	5	1	0	2.2	.993	OF-66
1984	MON	N	38	.239	.352	71	17	2	0	2	2.8	7	7	3	7	1	13	4	33	0	0	0	1.2	1.000	OF-27
1985	CIN	N	77	.289	.422	135	39	12	3	0	0.0	21	10	6	17	11	35	13	60	3	0	0	1.6	1.000	OF-39
1986			108	.211	.313	147	31	7	1	2	1.4	17	15	17	24	7	51	8	63	0	2	0	1.1	.969	OF-57
1987			7	.143	.143	7	1	0	0	0	0.0	2	2	0	0	0	2	1	3	0	0	0	0.8	1.000	OF-4
1989	CAL	A	20	.358	.434	53	19	4	0	0	0.0	7	4	1	16	0	6	1	21	0	0	0	1.6	1.000	OF-13
1990			93	.259	.402	189	49	9	3	4	2.1	26	21	24	31	5	16	3	112	3	3	1	1.5	.975	OF-77, DH-1
1991			82	.246	.358	187	46	8	2	3	1.6	24	21	11	30	2	16	3	86	3	3	0	1.4	.967	OF-65, DH-3
12 yrs.			727	.241	.345	1397	337	57	17	18	1.3	176	128	120	218	64	233	57	688	22	13	3	1.5	.982	OF-471, DH-4

Robin Ventura

VENTURA, ROBIN MARK BL TR 6′ 1″ 185 lbs.
B. July 14, 1967, Santa Maria, Calif.

Year	Team		Games	BA	SA	AB	H	2B	3B	HR	HR%	R	RBI	BB	SO	SB	Pinch Hit AB	Pinch Hit H	PO	A	E	DP	TC/G	FA	G by Pos
1989	CHI	A	16	.178	.244	45	8	3	0	0	0.0	5	7	8	6	0	1	0	17	33	2	2	3.3	.962	3B-16
1990			150	.249	.318	493	123	17	1	5	1.0	48	54	55	53	1	7	2	116	268	25	32	2.8	.939	3B-147, 1B-1
1991			157	.284	.442	606	172	25	1	23	3.8	92	100	80	67	2	3	0	225	291	18	37	2.9	.966	3B-151, 1B-31
1992			157	.282	.431	592	167	38	1	16	2.7	85	93	93	71	2	0	0	141	375	23	29	3.4	.957	3B-157, 1B-2
1993			157	.262	.433	554	145	27	1	22	4.0	85	94	105	82	1	2	0	119	278	14	27	2.6	.966	3B-155, 1B-4
1994			109	.282	.459	401	113	15	1	18	4.5	57	78	61	69	3	1	0	88	180	20	22	2.6	.931	3B-108, 1B-3, SS-1
1995			135	.295	.498	492	145	22	0	26	5.3	79	93	75	98	4	4	2	202	216	19	25	3.1	.957	3B-122, 1B-18, DH-1
7 yrs.			881	.274	.427	3183	873	147	5	110	3.5	451	519	477	446	13	18	4	908	1641	121	174	2.9	.955	3B-856, 1B-59, DH-1, SS-1
LEAGUE CHAMPIONSHIP SERIES																									
1993	CHI	A	6	.200	.350	20	4	0	0	1	5.0	2	5	6	6	0	0	0	9	6	1	0	2.3	.938	3B-6, 1B-1

Vince Ventura

VENTURA, VINCENT
B. Apr. 18, 1917, New York, N. Y.
BR TR 6′ 1½″ 190 lbs.

Year	Team	Games	BA	SA	AB	H	2B	3B	HR	HR%	R	RBI	BB	SO	SB	Pinch Hit AB	Pinch Hit H	PO	A	E	DP	TC/G	FA	G by Pos
1945	WAS A	18	.207	.207	58	12	0	0	0	0.0	4	2	4	4	0	3	1	30	1	4	0	2.3	.886	OF-15

Quilvio Veras

VERAS, QUILVIO ALBERTO
Born Quilvio Alberto Veras (Perez).
B. Apr. 3, 1971, Santo Domingo, Dominican Republic
BB TR 5′ 9″ 166 lbs.

Year	Team	Games	BA	SA	AB	H	2B	3B	HR	HR%	R	RBI	BB	SO	SB	Pinch Hit AB	Pinch Hit H	PO	A	E	DP	TC/G	FA	G by Pos
1995	FLA N	124	.261	.373	440	115	20	7	5	1.1	86	32	80	68	**56**	2	0	300	315	9	85	5.0	.986	2B-122, OF-2

Emil Verban

VERBAN, EMIL MATTHEW (Dutch, The Antelope)
B. Aug. 27, 1915, Lincoln, Ill. D. June 8, 1989, Quincy, Ill.
BR TR 5′11″ 165 lbs.

Year	Team	Games	BA	SA	AB	H	2B	3B	HR	HR%	R	RBI	BB	SO	SB	Pinch Hit AB	Pinch Hit H	PO	A	E	DP	TC/G	FA	G by Pos
1944	STL N	146	.257	.293	498	128	14	2	0	0.0	51	43	19	14	0	0	0	319	380	23	105	4.9	.968	2B-146
1945		155	.278	.342	597	166	22	8	0	0.0	59	72	19	15	4	0	0	398	406	18	95	5.3	.978	2B-155
1946	2 teams	STL N (1G –.000) PHI N (138G –.275)																						
″	total	139	.274	.331	474	130	17	5	0	0.0	44	34	21	18	5	1	0	353	381	28	83	5.5	.963	2B-138
1947	PHI N	155	.285	.341	540	154	14	8	0	0.0	50	42	23	8	5	0	0	450	453	17	111	5.9	.982	2B-155
1948	2 teams	PHI N (55G –.231) CHI N (56G –.294)																						
″	total	111	.269	.333	417	112	20	2	1	0.2	51	27	15	12	4	1	0	238	290	17	72	5.0	.969	2B-110
1949	CHI N	98	.289	.327	343	99	11	1	0	0.0	38	22	8	2	3	7	1	218	249	17	60	5.5	.965	2B-88
1950	2 teams	CHI N (45G –.108) BOS N (4G –.000)																						
″	total	49	.095	.119	42	4	1	0	0	0.0	8	1	3	5	0	13	1	20	21	4	8	3.0	.911	2B-10, SS-3, 3B-1, OF-1
7 yrs.		853	.272	.325	2911	793	99	26	1	0.0	301	241	108	74	21	22	2	1996	2180	124	534	5.3	.971	2B-802, SS-3, 3B-1, OF-1
WORLD SERIES																								
1944	STL N	6	.412	.412	17	7	0	0	0	0.0	1	2	2	0	0	0	0	15	7	0	2	3.7	1.000	2B-6

Gene Verble

VERBLE, GENE KERMIT (Satchel)
B. June 29, 1928, Concord, N. C.
BR TR 5′10″ 163 lbs.

Year	Team	Games	BA	SA	AB	H	2B	3B	HR	HR%	R	RBI	BB	SO	SB	Pinch Hit AB	Pinch Hit H	PO	A	E	DP	TC/G	FA	G by Pos
1951	WAS A	68	.203	.243	177	36	3	2	0	0.0	16	15	18	10	1	16	2	101	124	5	28	4.8	.978	SS-28, 2B-19, 3B-1
1953		13	.190	.190	21	4	0	0	0	0.0	4	2	2	1	0	1	0	10	18	0	4	3.5	1.000	SS-8
2 yrs.		81	.202	.237	198	40	3	2	0	0.0	20	17	20	11	1	17	2	111	142	5	32	4.6	.981	SS-36, 2B-19, 3B-1

Frank Verdi

VERDI, FRANK MICHAEL
B. June 2, 1926, Brooklyn, N. Y.
BR TR 5′10½″ 170 lbs.

Year	Team	Games	BA	SA	AB	H	2B	3B	HR	HR%	R	RBI	BB	SO	SB	Pinch Hit AB	Pinch Hit H	PO	A	E	DP	TC/G	FA	G by Pos
1953	NY A	1	—	—	0	0	0	0	0	—	0	0	0	0	0	0	0	0	0	0	0	0.0	.000	SS-1

Johnny Vergez

VERGEZ, JOHN LOUIS
B. July 9, 1906, Oakland, Calif. D. July 15, 1991, Davis, Calif.
BR TR 5′ 8″ 165 lbs.

Year	Team	Games	BA	SA	AB	H	2B	3B	HR	HR%	R	RBI	BB	SO	SB	Pinch Hit AB	Pinch Hit H	PO	A	E	DP	TC/G	FA	G by Pos
1931	NY N	152	.278	.396	565	157	24	2	13	2.3	67	81	29	65	11	0	0	146	268	30	23	2.9	.932	3B-152
1932		118	.261	.380	376	98	21	3	6	1.6	42	43	25	36	1	3	1	94	212	23	22	2.9	.930	3B-111, SS-1
1933		123	.271	.448	458	124	21	6	16	3.5	57	72	39	66	1	0	0	101	222	25	17	2.8	.928	3B-123
1934		108	.200	.328	320	64	18	1	7	2.2	31	27	28	55	1	3	0	86	195	17	11	2.9	.943	3B-104
1935	PHI N	148	.249	.363	546	136	27	4	9	1.6	56	63	46	67	8	0	0	188	222	20	25	2.9	.953	3B-148, SS-2
1936	2 teams	PHI N (15G –.275) STL N (8G –.167)																						
″	total	23	.241	.345	58	14	3	0	1	1.7	5	6	4	14	0	2	0	19	21	2	3	2.1	.952	3B-20
6 yrs.		672	.255	.385	2323	593	114	16	52	2.2	258	292	171	303	22	8	1	634	1140	117	101	2.9	.938	3B-658, SS-3

Mickey Vernon

VERNON, JAMES BARTON
B. Apr. 22, 1918, Marcus Hook, Pa.
Manager 1961–63.
BL TL 6′ 2″ 170 lbs.

Year	Team	Games	BA	SA	AB	H	2B	3B	HR	HR%	R	RBI	BB	SO	SB	Pinch Hit AB	Pinch Hit H	PO	A	E	DP	TC/G	FA	G by Pos
1939	WAS A	76	.257	.351	276	71	15	4	1	0.4	23	30	24	28	1	0	0	690	40	11	75	9.9	.985	1B-75
1940		5	.158	.158	19	3	0	0	0	0.0	0	0	0	3	0	1	0	41	2	0	5	10.8	1.000	1B-4
1941		138	.299	.443	531	159	27	11	9	1.7	73	93	43	51	9	6	2	1186	80	10	122	9.7	.992	1B-132
1942		151	.271	.388	621	168	34	6	9	1.4	76	86	39	63	25	0	0	1360	95	26	109	9.8	.982	1B-151
1943		145	.268	.387	553	148	29	8	7	1.3	89	70	66	55	24	1	1	1351	75	14	125	10.1	.990	1B-143
1946		148	**.353**	.508	587	207	**51**	8	8	1.4	88	85	49	64	14	1	1	1320	101	15	133	9.8	.990	1B-147
1947		154	.265	.388	600	159	29	12	7	1.2	77	85	49	42	12	0	0	1299	105	19	123	9.2	.987	1B-154
1948		150	.242	.332	558	135	27	7	3	0.5	78	48	54	43	15	1	0	1297	113	15	123	9.5	.989	1B-150
1949	CLE A	153	.291	.443	584	170	27	4	18	3.1	72	83	58	51	9	0	0	1438	155	14	168	10.5	.991	1B-153
1950	2 teams	CLE A (28G –.189) WAS A (90G –.306)																						
″	total	118	.281	.400	417	117	17	3	9	2.2	55	75	62	39	8	8	1	959	78	9	121	9.5	.991	1B-110
1951	WAS A	141	.293	.423	546	160	30	7	9	1.6	69	87	53	45	7	3	3	1157	87	8	121	9.1	.994	1B-137
1952		154	.251	.394	569	143	33	9	10	1.8	71	80	89	66	7	0	0	1291	115	10	139	9.3	.993	1B-153
1953		152	**.337**	.518	608	205	**43**	11	15	2.5	101	115	63	57	4	0	0	1376	94	12	158	9.8	.992	1B-152
1954		151	.290	.492	597	173	**33**	14	20	3.4	90	97	61	61	1	3	2	1365	76	11	144	9.8	.992	1B-148
1955		150	.301	.452	538	162	23	8	14	2.6	74	85	74	50	0	7	2	1258	69	8	137	9.3	.994	1B-144
1956	BOS A	119	.310	.511	403	125	28	4	15	3.7	67	84	57	40	1	10	4	930	58	11	96	9.3	.989	1B-108
1957		102	.241	.393	270	65	18	1	7	2.6	36	38	41	35	0	22	6	662	51	6	47	10.3	.992	1B-70
1958	CLE A	119	.293	.439	355	104	22	3	8	2.3	49	55	44	56	0	24	7	774	50	11	90	8.7	.987	1B-96
1959	MIL N	74	.220	.363	91	20	4	0	3	3.3	8	14	7	20	0	59	13	65	4	2	3	5.1	.972	1B-10, OF-4
1960	PIT N	9	.125	.125	8	1	0	0	0	0.0	0	1	1	0	0	8	1	0	0	0	0	0.0	—	
20 yrs.		2409	.286	.428	8731	2495	490	120	172	2.0	1196	1311	934	869	137	154	43	19819	1448	212	2044	9.6	.990	1B-2237, OF-4

Zoilo Versalles

VERSALLES, ZOILO CASANOVA (Zorro)
Born Zoilo Casanova Versalles (Rodriguez).
B. Dec. 18, 1939, Havana, Cuba D. June 9, 1995, Bloomington, Minn.
BR TR 5′10″ 146 lbs.

Year	Team	Games	BA	SA	AB	H	2B	3B	HR	HR%	R	RBI	BB	SO	SB	Pinch Hit AB	Pinch Hit H	PO	A	E	DP	TC/G	FA	G by Pos
1959	WAS A	29	.153	.203	59	9	0	0	1	1.7	4	1	4	15	1	0	0	41	59	6	13	3.7	.943	SS-29
1960		15	.133	.267	45	6	2	2	0	0.0	2	4	2	5	0	0	0	30	42	5	6	5.1	.935	SS-15
1961	MIN A	129	.280	.390	510	143	25	5	7	1.4	65	53	25	61	16	0	0	229	371	30	74	4.9	.952	SS-129
1962		160	.241	.373	568	137	18	3	17	3.0	69	67	37	71	5	0	0	335	501	26	127	5.4	.970	SS-160
1963		159	.261	.401	621	162	31	**13**	10	1.6	74	54	33	66	7	0	0	301	448	30	87	4.9	.961	SS-159
1964		160	.259	.431	659	171	33	**10**	20	3.0	94	64	42	88	14	1	1	271	427	31	89	4.6	.957	SS-160
1965		160	.273	.462	**666**	182	**45**	**12**	19	2.9	**126**	77	41	**122**	27	0	0	248	487	39	105	4.8	.950	SS-160
1966		137	.249	.346	543	135	20	6	7	1.3	73	36	40	85	10	2	0	195	377	35	69	4.5	.942	SS-135
1967		160	.200	.282	581	116	16	7	6	1.0	63	50	33	113	5	0	0	229	454	30	81	4.5	.958	SS-159
1968	LA N	122	.196	.266	403	79	16	3	2	0.5	29	24	26	84	6	2	1	204	380	28	62	5.1	.954	SS-119

Zoilo Versalles *continued*

Year	Team	Games	BA	SA	AB	H	2B	3B	HR	HR%	R	RBI	BB	SO	SB	Pinch Hit AB	Pinch Hit H	PO	A	E	DP	TC/G	FA	G by Pos
1969	**2 teams** **CLE A** (72G –.226) **WAS A** (31G –.267)																							
"	**total**	103	.236	.305	292	69	13	2	1	0.3	30	19	24	60	4	13	4	121	185	11	29	3.1	.965	2B-52, 3B-35, SS-16
1971	**ATL N**	66	.191	.325	194	37	11	0	5	2.6	21	22	11	40	2	9	1	63	107	13	13	3.3	.929	3B-30, SS-24, 2B-1
12 yrs.		1400	.242	.367	5141	1246	230	63	95	1.8	650	471	318	810	97	27	7	2267	3838	284	755	4.6	.956	SS-1265, 3B-65, 2B-53
WORLD SERIES																								
1965	**MIN A**	7	.286	.500	28	8	1	1	1	3.6	3	4	2	7	1	0	0	13	12	0	3	3.6	1.000	SS-7

Tom Veryzer

VERYZER, THOMAS MARTIN BR TR 6′ 1½″ 175 lbs.
B. Feb. 11, 1953, Port Jefferson, N. Y.

Year	Team	Games	BA	SA	AB	H	2B	3B	HR	HR%	R	RBI	BB	SO	SB	Pinch Hit AB	Pinch Hit H	PO	A	E	DP	TC/G	FA	G by Pos
1973	**DET A**	18	.300	.400	20	6	0	1	0	0.0	1	2	2	4	0	0	0	6	12	3	1	1.2	.857	SS-18
1974		22	.236	.382	55	13	2	0	2	3.6	4	9	5	8	1	1	0	18	33	4	4	2.8	.927	SS-20
1975		128	.252	.327	404	102	13	1	5	1.2	37	48	23	76	2	0	0	215	358	24	62	4.7	.960	SS-128
1976		97	.234	.277	354	83	8	2	1	0.3	31	25	21	44	1	0	0	164	313	17	53	5.1	.966	SS-97
1977		125	.197	.254	350	69	12	1	2	0.6	31	28	16	44	0	0	0	185	377	18	62	4.7	.969	SS-124
1978	**CLE A**	130	.271	.340	421	114	18	4	1	0.2	48	32	13	36	1	0	0	177	375	21	58	4.4	.963	SS-129
1979		149	.220	.254	449	99	9	3	0	0.0	41	34	34	54	2	0	0	238	446	18	90	4.7	.974	SS-148
1980		109	.271	.321	358	97	12	0	2	0.6	28	28	10	25	0	0	0	169	331	15	59	4.8	.971	SS-108
1981		75	.244	.262	221	54	4	0	0	0.0	13	14	10	10	1	0	0	121	207	10	48	4.5	.970	SS-75
1982	**NY N**	40	.333	.370	54	18	2	0	0	0.0	6	4	3	4	1	0	0	40	44	7	4	2.2	.923	2B-26, SS-16
1983	**CHI N**	59	.205	.273	88	18	3	0	1	1.1	5	3	3	13	0	11	3	27	73	2	17	2.3	.980	SS-28, 3B-17
1984		44	.189	.203	74	14	1	0	0	0.0	5	4	3	11	0	0	0	44	63	5	13	2.5	.955	SS-36, 3B-5, 2B-4
12 yrs.		996	.241	.294	2848	687	84	12	14	0.5	250	231	143	329	9	12	3	1404	2632	144	471	4.3	.966	SS-927, 2B-30, 3B-22
LEAGUE CHAMPIONSHIP SERIES																								
1984	**CHI N**	3	.000	.000	1	0	0	0	0	0.0	0	0	0	0	0	0	0	0	0	0	0	0.0		SS-1, 3B-1

Ernie Vick

VICK, HENRY ARTHUR BR TR 5′ 9½″ 185 lbs.
B. July 2, 1900, Toledo, Ohio D. July 16, 1980, Ann Arbor, Mich.

Year	Team	Games	BA	SA	AB	H	2B	3B	HR	HR%	R	RBI	BB	SO	SB	Pinch Hit AB	Pinch Hit H	PO	A	E	DP	TC/G	FA	G by Pos
1922	**STL N**	3	.333	.667	6	2	2	0	0	0.0	1	0	0	0	0	0	0	7	0	1	1	2.7	.875	C-3
1924		16	.348	.391	23	8	1	0	0	0.0	2	0	3	3	0	0	0	26	11	1	4	2.4	.974	C-16
1925		14	.188	.313	32	6	2	1	0	0.0	3	3	3	1	0	5	0	34	5	3	0	4.7	.929	C-9
1926		24	.196	.235	51	10	2	0	0	0.0	6	4	3	4	0	1	0	40	11	3	1	2.3	.944	C-23
4 yrs.		57	.232	.313	112	26	7	1	0	0.0	12	7	9	8	0	6	0	107	27	8	6	2.8	.944	C-51

Sammy Vick

VICK, SAMUEL BRUCE BR TR 5′10½″ 163 lbs.
B. Apr. 12, 1895, Batesville, Miss. D. Aug. 17, 1986, Memphis, Tenn.

Year	Team	Games	BA	SA	AB	H	2B	3B	HR	HR%	R	RBI	BB	SO	SB	Pinch Hit AB	Pinch Hit H	PO	A	E	DP	TC/G	FA	G by Pos
1917	**NY A**	10	.278	.361	36	10	3	0	0	0.0	4	2	1	6	2	0	0	14	1	2	0	1.7	.882	OF-10
1918		2	.667	.667	3	2	0	0	0	0.0	1	1	0	0	0	1	0	0	0	0	0	0.0	.000	OF-1
1919		106	.248	.344	407	101	15	9	2	0.5	59	27	35	55	9	5	1	166	11	9	2	1.9	.952	OF-100
1920		51	.220	.297	118	26	7	1	0	0.0	21	11	14	20	1	17	6	56	0	3	0	1.8	.949	OF-33
1921	**BOS A**	44	.260	.325	77	20	3	1	0	0.0	5	9	1	10	0	28	8	21	1	0	0	1.5	1.000	OF-14, C-1
5 yrs.		213	.248	.335	641	159	28	11	2	0.3	90	50	51	91	12	51	15	257	13	14	2	1.8	.951	OF-158, C-1

George Vico

VICO, GEORGE STEVE (Sam) BL TR 6′ 4″ 200 lbs.
B. Aug. 9, 1923, San Fernando, Calif. D. Jan. 13, 1994, Redondo Beach, Calif.

Year	Team	Games	BA	SA	AB	H	2B	3B	HR	HR%	R	RBI	BB	SO	SB	Pinch Hit AB	Pinch Hit H	PO	A	E	DP	TC/G	FA	G by Pos
1948	**DET A**	144	.267	.392	521	139	23	9	8	1.5	50	58	39	39	2	2	0	1169	85	15	112	8.9	.988	1B-142
1949		67	.190	.338	142	27	5	2	4	2.8	15	18	21	17	0	13	2	372	32	6	36	7.7	.985	1B-53
2 yrs.		211	.250	.380	663	166	28	11	12	1.8	65	76	60	56	2	15	2	1541	117	21	148	8.6	.987	1B-195

Jose Vidal

VIDAL, JOSE (Papito) BR TR 6′ 190 lbs.
Born Jose Vidal (Nicolas).
B. Apr. 3, 1940, Batey Lechugas, Dominican Republic.

Year	Team	Games	BA	SA	AB	H	2B	3B	HR	HR%	R	RBI	BB	SO	SB	Pinch Hit AB	Pinch Hit H	PO	A	E	DP	TC/G	FA	G by Pos
1966	**CLE A**	17	.188	.281	32	6	1	1	0	0.0	4	3	5	11	0	4	0	16	0	0	0	1.5	1.000	OF-11
1967		16	.118	.118	34	4	0	0	0	0.0	4	0	7	12	0	4	1	20	1	0	0	2.1	1.000	OF-10
1968		37	.167	.278	54	9	0	0	2	3.7	5	5	2	15	3	11	1	22	2	0	0	0.9	1.000	OF-26, 1B-1
1969	**SEA A**	18	.192	.385	26	5	0	1	1	3.8	7	2	4	8	1	5	0	11	0	1	0	2.0	.917	OF-6
4 yrs.		88	.164	.260	146	24	1	2	3	2.1	20	10	18	46	4	24	2	69	3	1	0	1.4	.986	OF-53, 1B-1

Hector Villanueva

VILLANUEVA, HECTOR BR TR 6′ 1″ 220 lbs.
Born Hector Villanueva (Balasquide).
B. Oct. 2, 1964, San Juan, Puerto Rico.

Year	Team	Games	BA	SA	AB	H	2B	3B	HR	HR%	R	RBI	BB	SO	SB	Pinch Hit AB	Pinch Hit H	PO	A	E	DP	TC/G	FA	G by Pos
1990	**CHI N**	52	.272	.509	114	31	4	1	7	6.1	14	18	4	27	1	18	3	170	10	2	6	4.9	.989	C-23, 1B-14
1991		71	.276	.542	192	53	10	1	13	6.8	23	32	21	30	0	13	3	276	27	6	4	5.1	.981	C-55, 1B-6
1992		51	.152	.259	112	17	6	0	2	1.8	9	13	11	24	0	16	4	181	24	4	4	6.1	.981	C-28, 1B-6
1993	**STL N**	17	.145	.327	55	8	1	0	3	5.5	7	9	4	17	0	0	0	86	3	0	0	5.2	1.000	C-17
4 yrs.		191	.230	.442	473	109	21	2	25	5.3	53	72	40	98	1	47	10	713	64	12	14	5.3	.985	C-123, 1B-26

Fernando Vina

VINA, FERNANDO BL TR 5′ 9″ 170 lbs.
B. Apr. 16, 1969, Sacramento, Calif.

Year	Team	Games	BA	SA	AB	H	2B	3B	HR	HR%	R	RBI	BB	SO	SB	Pinch Hit AB	Pinch Hit H	PO	A	E	DP	TC/G	FA	G by Pos
1993	**SEA A**	24	.222	.267	45	10	2	0	0	0.0	5	2	4	3	6	1	0	28	40	0	12	3.1	1.000	2B-16, SS-4, DH-2
1994	**NY N**	79	.250	.298	124	31	6	0	0	0.0	20	6	12	11	3	34	6	46	59	4	5	2.7	.963	2B-13, 3B-12, SS-9, OF-6
1995	**MIL A**	113	.257	.361	288	74	7	7	3	1.0	46	29	22	28	6	6	1	194	247	8	73	4.2	.982	2B-99, SS-6, 3B-2
3 yrs.		216	.252	.335	457	115	15	7	3	0.7	71	37	38	42	15	41	7	268	346	12	90	3.7	.981	2B-128, SS-19, 3B-14, OF-6, DH-2

Charlie Vinson

VINSON, CHARLES ANTHONY BL TL 6′ 3″ 207 lbs.
B. Jan. 5, 1944, Washington, D. C.

Year	Team	Games	BA	SA	AB	H	2B	3B	HR	HR%	R	RBI	BB	SO	SB	Pinch Hit AB	Pinch Hit H	PO	A	E	DP	TC/G	FA	G by Pos
1966	**CAL A**	13	.182	.409	22	4	2	0	1	4.5	3	6	5	9	0	0	0	72	2	0	8	6.7	1.000	1B-11

Rube Vinson

VINSON, ERNEST AUGUSTUS
B. Mar. 20, 1879, Dover, Del. D. Oct. 12, 1951, Chester, Pa.
5′ 9″ 168 lbs.

Year	Team	Games	BA	SA	AB	H	2B	3B	HR	HR%	R	RBI	BB	SO	SB	Pinch Hit AB	Pinch Hit H	PO	A	E	DP	TC/G	FA	G by Pos
1904	CLE A	15	.306	.327	49	15	1	0	0	0.0	12	2	10		2	0	0	24	6	0	0	2.0	1.000	OF-15
1905		38	.195	.233	133	26	3	1	0	0.0	12	9	7		4	2	0	65	1	5	0	2.0	.930	OF-36
1906	CHI A	7	.250	.250	24	6	0	0	0	0.0	2	3	2		1	1	1	6	0	4	0	2.5	.600	OF-4
3 yrs.		60	.228	.257	206	47	4	1	0	0.0	26	14	19		7	3	1	95	7	9	0	2.0	.919	OF-55

Jim Viox

VIOX, JAMES HENRY
B. Dec. 30, 1890, Lockland, Ohio D. Jan. 6, 1969, Erlanger, Ky.
BR TR 5′ 7″ 150 lbs.

Year	Team	Games	BA	SA	AB	H	2B	3B	HR	HR%	R	RBI	BB	SO	SB	Pinch Hit AB	Pinch Hit H	PO	A	E	DP	TC/G	FA	G by Pos
1912	PIT N	33	.186	.343	70	13	2	3	1	1.4	8	7	3	5	2	8	0	21	30	4	2	2.5	.927	3B-10, SS-8, OF-3, 2B-1
1913		137	.317	.427	492	156	32	8	2	0.4	86	65	64	28	14	2	1	241	334	30	30	4.5	.950	2B-124, SS-10
1914		143	.265	.326	506	134	18	5	1	0.2	52	57	63	33	9	1	0	256	402	45	43	5.0	.936	2B-138, SS-2, OF-2
1915		150	.256	.334	503	129	17	8	2	0.4	56	45	75	31	12	2	1	252	387	31	35	4.5	.954	2B-135, 3B-13, OF-2
1916		43	.250	.326	132	33	7	0	1	0.8	12	17	17	11	2	6	1	41	75	9	6	3.5	.928	2B-25, 3B-11
5 yrs.		506	.273	.358	1703	465	76	24	7	0.4	214	191	222	108	39	19	3	811	1228	119	116	4.5	.945	2B-423, 3B-34, SS-20, OF-7

Bill Virdon

VIRDON, WILLIAM CHARLES
B. June 9, 1931, Hazel Park, Mich.
Manager 1972–84.
BL TR 6′ 175 lbs.

Year	Team	Games	BA	SA	AB	H	2B	3B	HR	HR%	R	RBI	BB	SO	SB	Pinch Hit AB	Pinch Hit H	PO	A	E	DP	TC/G	FA	G by Pos
1955	STL N	144	.281	.433	534	150	18	6	17	3.2	58	68	36	64	2	9	1	339	7	12	1	2.5	.966	OF-142
1956	2 teams	STL N (24G –.211)	PIT N (133G –.334)																					
″	total	157	.319	.445	580	185	23	10	10	1.7	77	46	38	71	6	6	0	387	12	5	2	2.6	.988	OF-154
1957	PIT N	144	.251	.383	561	141	28	11	8	1.4	59	50	33	69	3	5	1	403	13	6	2	3.0	.986	OF-141
1958		144	.267	.387	604	161	24	11	9	1.5	75	46	52	70	5	1	0	401	11	3	0	2.9	.993	OF-143
1959		144	.254	.355	519	132	24	2	8	1.5	67	41	55	65	7	0	0	404	16	9	5	3.0	.979	OF-144
1960		120	.264	.406	409	108	16	9	8	2.0	60	40	40	44	8	9	3	272	10	5	0	2.6	.983	OF-109
1961		146	.260	.369	599	156	22	8	9	1.5	81	58	49	45	5	1	0	384	6	6	4	2.7	.985	OF-145
1962		156	.247	.345	663	164	27	**10**	6	0.9	82	47	36	65	5	0	0	360	11	9	0	2.4	.976	OF-156
1963		142	.269	.374	554	149	22	6	8	1.4	58	53	43	55	1	0	0	323	6	4	2	2.3	.988	OF-142
1964		145	.243	.298	473	115	11	3	3	0.6	59	27	30	48	1	10	2	243	5	6	1	1.9	.976	OF-134
1965		135	.279	.370	481	134	22	5	4	0.8	58	24	30	49	4	11	1	260	3	8	1	2.1	.970	OF-128
1968		6	.333	1.333	3	1	0	0	1	33.3	1	2	0	2	0	2	1	1	0	0	0	0.3	1.000	OF-4
12 yrs.		1583	.267	.379	5980	1596	237	81	91	1.5	735	502	442	647	47	54	9	3777	100	73	18	2.6	.982	OF-1542
WORLD SERIES																								
1960	PIT N	7	.241	.345	29	7	3	0	0	0.0	2	5	1	3	1	0	0	18	0	1	0	2.7	.947	OF-7

Ozzie Virgil

VIRGIL, OSVALDO JOSE, JR.
Born Osvaldo Jose Virgil (Lopez).
Son of Ozzie Virgil.
B. Dec. 7, 1956, Mayaguez, Puerto Rico.
BR TR 6′ 1″ 205 lbs.

Year	Team	Games	BA	SA	AB	H	2B	3B	HR	HR%	R	RBI	BB	SO	SB	Pinch Hit AB	Pinch Hit H	PO	A	E	DP	TC/G	FA	G by Pos
1980	PHI N	1	.200	.400	5	1	1	0	0	0.0	1	0	0	1	0	0	0	4	0	0	0	4.0	1.000	C-1
1981		6	.000	.000	6	0	0	0	0	0.0	0	0	0	2	0	5	0	2	0	0	0	2.0	1.000	C-1
1982		49	.238	.386	101	24	6	0	3	3.0	11	8	10	26	0	14	3	173	14	7	3	5.5	.964	C-35
1983		55	.214	.393	140	30	7	0	6	4.3	11	23	8	34	0	8	2	228	24	9	2	5.1	.966	C-51
1984		141	.261	.434	456	119	21	2	18	3.9	61	68	45	91	1	8	2	722	58	6	6	5.7	.992	C-137
1985		131	.246	.432	426	105	16	3	19	4.5	47	55	49	85	0	12	4	667	52	4	11	6.0	.994	C-120
1986	ATL N	114	.223	.373	359	80	9	0	15	4.2	45	48	63	73	1	5	0	682	93	13	9	7.1	.984	C-111
1987		123	.247	.471	429	106	13	1	27	6.3	57	72	47	81	0	3	0	654	74	8	12	6.0	.989	C-122
1988		107	.256	.372	320	82	10	0	9	2.8	23	31	22	54	2	15	7	448	45	5	3	5.2	.990	C-96
1989	TOR A	9	.182	.545	11	2	1	0	1	9.1	2	2	4	3	0	2	1	1	0	0	0	0.1	1.000	DH-6, C-1
1990		3	.000	.000	5	0	0	0	0	0.0	0	0	0	3	0	0	0	1	0	0	0	0.3	1.000	C-2, DH-1
11 yrs.		739	.243	.416	2258	549	84	6	98	4.3	258	307	248	453	4	72	19	3582	360	52	46	5.8	.987	C-677, DH-7
LEAGUE CHAMPIONSHIP SERIES																								
1983	PHI N	1	.000	.000	1	0	0	0	0	0.0	0	0	0	1	0	1	0	0	0	0	0	0.0	—	
WORLD SERIES																								
1983	PHI N	3	.500	.500	2	1	0	0	0	0.0	0	1	0	0	0	2	1	1	0	0	0	1.0	1.000	C-1

Ozzie Virgil

VIRGIL, OSVALDO JOSE, SR.
Born Osvaldo Jose Virgil (Pichardo).
Father of Ozzie Virgil.
B. May 17, 1933, Monte Cristi, Dominican Republic.
BR TR 6′ 1″ 174 lbs.

Year	Team	Games	BA	SA	AB	H	2B	3B	HR	HR%	R	RBI	BB	SO	SB	Pinch Hit AB	Pinch Hit H	PO	A	E	DP	TC/G	FA	G by Pos
1956	NY N	3	.417	.667	12	5	1	1	0	0.0	2	2	0	0	1	0	0	3	1	1	1	1.7	.800	3B-3
1957		96	.235	.305	226	53	0	2	4	1.8	26	24	14	27	2	8	2	64	111	12	10	2.1	.936	3B-62, OF-24, SS-1
1958	DET A	49	.244	.363	193	47	10	2	3	1.6	19	19	8	20	1	1	0	55	101	3	7	3.2	.981	3B-49
1960		62	.227	.356	132	30	4	2	3	2.3	16	13	4	14	1	8	2	52	85	4	13	2.5	.972	3B-42, 2B-8, SS-5, C-1
1961	2 teams	DET A (20G –.133)	KC A (11G –.143)																					
″	total	31	.137	.196	51	7	0	0	1	2.0	2	1	1	8	0	12	3	23	17	3	3	2.0	.930	3B-13, C-6, SS-1, 2B-1
1962	BAL A	1	—	—	0	0	0	0	0	—	0	0	1	0	0	0	0	0	0	0	0	0.0	—	
1965	PIT N	39	.265	.367	49	13	2	0	1	2.0	3	5	2	10	0	18	6	36	17	1	4	2.0	.981	C-15, 3B-7, 2B-5
1966	SF N	42	.213	.303	89	19	2	0	2	2.2	7	9	4	12	1	12	1	110	26	3	5	4.0	.978	3B-13, C-13, 1B-5, OF-2, 2B-2
1969		1	.000	.000	1	0	0	0	0	0.0	0	0	0	0	0	1	0	0	0	0	0	0.0	—	
9 yrs.		324	.231	.331	753	174	19	7	14	1.9	75	73	34	91	6	60	14	343	358	27	43	2.6	.963	3B-189, C-35, OF-26, 2B-16, SS-7, 1B-5

Jake Virtue

VIRTUE, JACOB KITCHLINE
B. Mar. 2, 1865, Philadelphia, Pa. D. Feb. 3, 1943, Camden, N. J.
BB TL 5′ 9½″ 165 lbs.

Year	Team	Games	BA	SA	AB	H	2B	3B	HR	HR%	R	RBI	BB	SO	SB	Pinch Hit AB	Pinch Hit H	PO	A	E	DP	TC/G	FA	G by Pos
1890	CLE N	62	.305	.404	223	68	6	5	2	0.9	39	25	49	15	9	0	0	633	21	12	33	10.7	.982	1B-62
1891		139	.261	.364	517	135	19	14	2	0.4	82	72	75	40	15	0	0	1465	44	44	70	11.2	.972	1B-139
1892		147	.282	.391	557	157	15	20	2	0.4	98	89	84	68	14	0	0	1500	61	26	61	10.8	.984	1B-147
1893		97	.265	.368	378	100	16	10	1	0.3	87	60	54	14	11	0	0	820	76	28	50	9.5	.970	1B-73, OF-13, SS-5, 3B-5, P-1
1894		29	.258	.326	89	23	4	1	0	0.0	15	10	13	3	1	4	0	65	8	7	0	3.0	.913	OF-21, 2B-3, 1B-2, P-1
5 yrs.		474	.274	.376	1764	483	60	50	7	0.4	321	256	275	140	50	4	0	4483	210	117	214	10.2	.976	1B-423, OF-34, SS-5, 3B-5, 2B-3, P-2

Joe Visner

VISNER, JOSEPH PAUL BL TR 5′11″ 180 lbs.
Born Joseph Paul Vezina.
B. Sept. 27, 1859, Minneapolis, Minn. D. June 17, 1945, Fosston, Minn.

Year	Team		Games	BA	SA	AB	H	2B	3B	HR	HR%	R	RBI	BB	SO	SB	Pinch Hit AB	Pinch Hit H	PO	A	E	DP	TC/G	FA	G by Pos
1885	**BAL**	**AA**	4	.231	.231	13	3	0	0	0	0.0	2		2			0	0	6	0	2	0	2.0	.750	OF-4
1889	**BKN**	**AA**	80	.258	.447	295	76	12	10	8	2.7	56	68	36	36	13	0	0	237	74	42	8	4.3	.881	C-53, OF-29
1890	**PIT**	**P**	127	.265	.395	521	138	15	**22**	3	0.6	110	71	76	44	18	0	0	198	18	26	4	1.9	.893	OF-127
1891	**2 teams**	**WAS AA** (18G –.279) **STL AA** (6G –.148)																							
″	**total**		24	.242	.379	95	23	2	4	1	1.1	15	8	8	10	2	0	0	33	4	8	0	1.8	.822	OF-23, 3B-1, C-1
4 yrs.			235	.260	.408	924	240	29	36	12	1.3	183	147	122	90	33	0	0	474	96	78	12	2.7	.880	OF-183, C-54, 3B-1

Joe Vitiello

VITIELLO, JOSEPH DAVID BR TR 6′ 2″ 215 lbs.
B. Apr. 11, 1970, Cambridge, Mass.

Year	Team		Games	BA	SA	AB	H	2B	3B	HR	HR%	R	RBI	BB	SO	SB	Pinch Hit AB	Pinch Hit H	PO	A	E	DP	TC/G	FA	G by Pos
1995	**KC**	**A**	53	.254	.446	130	33	4	0	7	5.4	13	21	8	25	0	11	2	51	3	1	3	1.2	.982	DH-38, 1B-8

Ossie Vitt

VITT, OSCAR JOSEPH BR TR 5′10″ 150 lbs.
B. Jan. 4, 1890, San Francisco, Calif. D. Jan. 31, 1963, Oakland, Calif.
Manager 1938–40.

Year	Team		Games	BA	SA	AB	H	2B	3B	HR	HR%	R	RBI	BB	SO	SB	Pinch Hit AB	Pinch Hit H	PO	A	E	DP	TC/G	FA	G by Pos
1912	**DET**	**A**	73	.245	.289	273	67	4	4	0	0.0	39	19	18		17	7	1	109	99	11	8	3.3	.950	OF-27, 3B-24, 2B-15
1913			99	.240	.304	359	86	11	3	2	0.6	45	33	31	18	5	2	0	174	283	23	25	4.9	.952	2B-78, 3B-17, OF-2
1914			66	.251	.287	195	49	7	0	0	0.0	35	8	31	8	10	8	0	68	155	9	13	4.2	.961	2B-36, 3B-16, OF-2, SS-1
1915			152	.250	.334	560	140	18	13	1	0.2	116	48	80	22	26	0	0	191	325	19	19	3.5	.964	3B-151, 2B-2
1916			153	.226	.295	597	135	17	12	0	0.0	88	42	75	28	18	0	0	210	389	22	32	4.1	.965	3B-151, SS-2
1917			140	.254	.303	512	130	13	6	0	0.0	65	47	56	15	18	0	0	164	260	27	18	3.2	.940	3B-140
1918			81	.240	.273	267	64	5	2	0	0.0	29	17	32	6	5	3	0	128	159	14	17	3.9	.953	3B-66, 2B-9, OF-3
1919	**BOS**	**A**	133	.243	.277	469	114	10	3	0	0.0	64	40	44	11	9	0	0	129	254	13	24	3.0	.967	3B-133
1920			87	.220	.291	296	65	10	4	1	0.3	50	28	43	10	5	1	0	99	208	8	17	3.7	.975	3B-64, 2B-21
1921			78	.190	.246	232	44	11	1	0	0.0	29	12	45	13	1	2	1	75	138	9	16	2.9	.959	3B-71, OF-3, 1B-2
10 yrs.			1062	.238	.295	3760	894	106	48	4	0.1	560	294	455	131	114	23	2	1347	2270	155	189	3.6	.959	3B-833, 2B-161, OF-37, SS-3, 1B-2

Jose Vizcaino

VIZCAINO, JOSE LUIS BB TR 6′ 1″ 150 lbs.
Born Jose Luis Vizcaino (Pimental).
B. Mar. 26, 1968, San Cristobal, Dominican Republic.

Year	Team		Games	BA	SA	AB	H	2B	3B	HR	HR%	R	RBI	BB	SO	SB	Pinch Hit AB	Pinch Hit H	PO	A	E	DP	TC/G	FA	G by Pos
1989	**LA**	**N**	7	.200	.200	10	2	0	0	0	0.0	2	0	0	1	0	1	1	6	9	2	2	3.4	.882	SS-5
1990			37	.275	.333	51	14	1	1	0	0.0	3	2	4	8	1	15	2	23	27	2	6	3.1	.962	SS-11, 2B-6
1991	**CHI**	**N**	93	.262	.297	145	38	5	0	0	0.0	7	10	5	18	2	6	1	49	118	7	19	1.8	.960	3B-57, SS-33, 2B-9
1992			86	.225	.298	285	64	10	4	1	0.4	25	17	14	35	3	6	1	93	195	9	34	3.5	.970	SS-50, 3B-29, 2B-5
1993			151	.287	.358	551	158	19	4	4	0.7	74	54	46	71	12	8	2	217	410	17	72	4.1	.974	SS-81, 3B-44, 2B-34
1994	**NY**	**N**	103	.256	.324	410	105	13	3	3	0.7	47	33	33	62	1	2	1	137	291	13	55	4.3	.971	SS-102
1995			135	.287	.365	509	146	21	5	3	0.6	66	56	35	76	8	1	0	189	412	10	78	4.5	.984	SS-134, 2B-1
7 yrs.			612	.269	.338	1961	527	69	17	11	0.6	224	172	137	271	27	39	8	714	1462	60	266	3.7	.973	SS-416, 3B-130, 2B-55

Omar Vizquel

VIZQUEL, OMAR ENRIQUE BB TR 5′ 9″ 155 lbs.
Born Omar Enrique Vizquel (Gonzalez).
B. May 15, 1967, Caracas, Venezuela.

Year	Team		Games	BA	SA	AB	H	2B	3B	HR	HR%	R	RBI	BB	SO	SB	Pinch Hit AB	Pinch Hit H	PO	A	E	DP	TC/G	FA	G by Pos
1989	**SEA**	**A**	143	.220	.261	387	85	7	3	1	0.3	45	20	28	40	1	2	0	208	388	18	102	4.3	.971	SS-143
1990			81	.247	.298	255	63	3	2	2	0.8	19	18	18	22	4	0	0	103	239	7	48	4.3	.980	SS-81
1991			142	.230	.293	426	98	16	4	1	0.2	42	41	45	37	7	8	0	224	422	13	105	4.7	.980	SS-138, 2B-1
1992			136	.294	.352	483	142	20	4	0	0.0	49	21	32	38	15	5	0	223	403	7	92	4.7	.989	SS-136
1993			158	.255	.298	560	143	14	2	2	0.4	68	31	50	71	12	1	1	245	475	15	108	4.7	.980	SS-155, DH-2
1994	**CLE**	**A**	69	.273	.325	286	78	10	1	1	0.3	39	33	23	23	13	1	1	114	204	6	53	4.7	.981	SS-69
1995			136	.266	.351	542	144	28	0	6	1.1	87	56	59	59	29	1	0	211	407	9	85	4.6	.986	SS-136
7 yrs.			865	.256	.314	2939	753	98	16	13	0.4	349	220	255	290	81	18	2	1328	2538	75	593	4.6	.981	SS-858, DH-2, 2B-1
DIVISIONAL PLAYOFF SERIES																									
1995	**CLE**	**A**	3	.167	.250	12	2	1	0	0	0.0	2	4	2	2	1	0	0	4	11	0	0	5.0	1.000	SS-3
LEAGUE CHAMPIONSHIP SERIES																									
1995	**CLE**	**A**	6	.087	.130	23	2	1	0	0	0.0	2	2	5	2	3	0	0	9	21	0	3	5.0	1.000	SS-6
WORLD SERIES																									
1995	**CLE**	**A**	6	.174	.261	23	4	0	1	0	0.0	3	1	3	5	1	0	0	12	22	0	7	5.7	1.000	SS-6

Otto Vogel

VOGEL, OTTO HENRY BR TR 6′ 195 lbs.
B. Oct. 26, 1899, Mendota, Ill. D. July 19, 1969, Iowa City, Iowa.

Year	Team		Games	BA	SA	AB	H	2B	3B	HR	HR%	R	RBI	BB	SO	SB	Pinch Hit AB	Pinch Hit H	PO	A	E	DP	TC/G	FA	G by Pos
1923	**CHI**	**N**	41	.210	.272	81	17	0	1	1	1.2	10	6	7	11	2	6	1	37	4	3	1	1.8	.932	OF-24, 3B-1
1924			70	.267	.372	172	46	11	2	1	0.6	28	24	10	26	4	9	2	101	10	5	2	2.1	.957	OF-53, 3B-2
2 yrs.			111	.249	.340	253	63	11	3	2	0.8	38	30	17	37	6	15	3	138	14	8	3	2.0	.950	OF-77, 3B-3

Jack Voigt

VOIGT, JOHN DAVID BR TR 6′ 1″ 170 lbs.
B. May 17, 1966, Sarasota, Fla.

Year	Team		Games	BA	SA	AB	H	2B	3B	HR	HR%	R	RBI	BB	SO	SB	Pinch Hit AB	Pinch Hit H	PO	A	E	DP	TC/G	FA	G by Pos
1992	**BAL**	**A**	1	—	—	0	0	0	0	0	—	0	0	0	0	0	0	0	0	0	0	0	0.0	—	
1993			64	.296	.500	152	45	11	1	6	3.9	32	23	25	33	1	10	2	101	6	1	3	1.8	.991	OF-43, DH-8, 1B-5, 3B-3
1994			59	.241	.340	141	34	5	0	3	2.1	15	20	18	25	0	3	1	114	5	2	2	2.0	.983	OF-54, 1B-6, DH-2
1995	**2 teams**	**BAL A** (3G –1.000) **TEX A** (33G –.161)																							
″	**total**		36	.175	.317	63	11	3	0	2	3.2	9	8	10	14	0	3	1	56	3	1	3	1.8	.983	OF-25, 1B-6, DH-2
4 yrs.			160	.253	.404	356	90	19	1	11	3.1	56	51	53	72	1	16	4	271	14	4	8	1.9	.986	OF-122, 1B-17, DH-12, 3B-3

Clyde Vollmer

VOLLMER, CLYDE FREDERICK BR TR 6′ 1″ 185 lbs.
B. Sept. 24, 1921, Cincinnati, Ohio.

Year	Team		Games	BA	SA	AB	H	2B	3B	HR	HR%	R	RBI	BB	SO	SB	Pinch Hit AB	Pinch Hit H	PO	A	E	DP	TC/G	FA	G by Pos
1942	**CIN**	**N**	12	.093	.163	43	4	0	0	1	2.3	2	4	1	5	0	1	0	32	0	0	0	2.9	1.000	OF-11
1946			9	.182	.182	22	4	0	0	0	0.0	1	1	1	3	2	1	0	9	0	0	0	1.3	1.000	OF-7
1947			78	.219	.303	155	34	10	0	1	0.6	19	13	9	18	0	11	3	125	2	2	0	2.0	.984	OF-66
1948	**2 teams**	**CIN N** (7G –.111) **WAS A** (1G –.400)																							
″	**total**		8	.214	.214	14	3	0	0	0	0.0	1	0	1	2	0	5	1	3	0	0	0	1.0	1.000	OF-3
1949	**WAS**	**A**	129	.253	.391	443	112	17	1	14	3.2	58	59	53	62	1	13	5	324	3	6	1	2.9	.982	OF-114

Clyde Vollmer *continued*

Year	Team	Games	BA	SA	AB	H	2B	3B	HR	HR%	R	RBI	BB	SO	SB	Pinch Hit AB	Pinch Hit H	PO	A	E	DP	TC/G	FA	G by Pos
1950	2 teams	WAS A (6G –.286) BOS A (57G –.284)																						
"	total	63	.284	.454	183	52	10	0	7	3.8	39	38	23	40	2	19	4	85	4	4	0	2.2	.957	OF-42
1951	BOS A	115	.251	.456	386	97	9	2	22	5.7	66	85	55	66	0	6	1	206	5	3	0	2.0	.986	OF-106
1952		90	.264	.476	250	66	12	4	11	4.4	35	50	39	47	2	20	5	143	3	0	1	2.1	1.000	OF-70
1953	2 teams	BOS A (1G –.000) WAS A (118G –.260)																						
"	total	119	.260	.392	408	106	15	3	11	2.7	54	74	49	59	0	12	4	227	8	5	1	2.3	.979	OF-106
1954	WAS A	62	.256	.342	117	30	4	0	2	1.7	8	15	12	28	0	31	6	33	2	0	1	1.3	1.000	OF-26
10 yrs.		685	.251	.402	2021	508	77	10	69	3.4	283	339	243	330	7	119	29	1187	27	20	4	2.2	.984	OF-551

Fritz Von Kolnitz

VON KOLNITZ, ALFRED HOLMES
B. May 20, 1893, Charleston, S. C. D. Mar. 18, 1948, Mount Pleasant, S. C.
BR TR 5′10½″ 175 lbs.

Year	Team	Games	BA	SA	AB	H	2B	3B	HR	HR%	R	RBI	BB	SO	SB	Pinch Hit AB	Pinch Hit H	PO	A	E	DP	TC/G	FA	G by Pos
1914	CIN N	41	.221	.240	104	23	2	0	0	0.0	8	6	6	16	4	7	0	31	44	9	2	2.5	.893	3B-20, OF-11, C-2, 1B-1
1915		50	.192	.269	78	15	4	1	0	0.0	6	6	7	11	1	20	6	15	22	3	4	1.3	.925	3B-18, SS-6, 1B-3, C-2, OF-1
1916	CHI A	24	.227	.295	44	10	3	0	0	0.0	1	7	2	6	0	10	3	9	11	2	1	1.7	.909	3B-13
3 yrs.		115	.212	.261	226	48	9	1	0	0.0	15	19	15	33	5	37	9	55	77	14	7	1.9	.904	3B-51, OF-12, SS-6, C-4, 1B-4

Joe Vosmik

VOSMIK, JOSEPH FRANKLIN
B. Apr. 4, 1910, Cleveland, Ohio D. Jan. 27, 1962, Cleveland, Ohio.
BR TR 6′ 185 lbs.

Year	Team	Games	BA	SA	AB	H	2B	3B	HR	HR%	R	RBI	BB	SO	SB	Pinch Hit AB	Pinch Hit H	PO	A	E	DP	TC/G	FA	G by Pos
1930	CLE A	9	.231	.308	26	6	2	0	0	0.0	1	4	1	1	0	2	0	13	1	1	1	3.0	.933	OF-5
1931		149	.320	.464	591	189	36	14	7	1.2	80	117	38	30	7	2	1	315	12	10	2	2.3	.970	OF-147
1932		153	.312	.462	621	194	39	12	10	1.6	106	97	58	42	2	0	0	432	12	5	4	2.9	.989	OF-153
1933		119	.263	.381	438	115	20	10	4	0.9	53	56	42	13	0	5	1	242	15	4	3	2.3	.985	OF-113
1934		104	.341	.477	405	138	33	2	6	1.5	71	78	35	10	1	1	1	199	7	5	2	2.0	.976	OF-104
1935		152	.348	.537	620	**216**	**47**	**20**	10	1.6	93	110	59	30	2	2	1	347	5	5	3	2.4	.986	OF-150
1936		138	.287	.413	506	145	29	7	7	1.4	76	94	79	21	5	2	2	258	11	6	1	2.0	.978	OF-136
1937	STL A	144	.325	.455	594	193	47	9	4	0.7	81	93	49	38	2	1	1	333	12	10	4	2.5	.972	OF-143
1938	BOS A	146	.324	.446	621	**201**	37	6	9	1.4	121	86	59	26	0	0	0	302	14	7	4	2.2	.978	OF-146
1939		145	.276	.388	554	153	29	6	7	1.3	89	84	66	33	4	0	0	296	9	8	0	2.2	.974	OF-144
1940	BKN N	116	.282	.354	404	114	14	6	1	0.2	45	42	22	21	0	17	5	193	9	5	1	2.1	.976	OF-99
1941		25	.196	.196	56	11	0	0	0	0.0	0	4	4	4	0	7	1	12	0	0	0	0.7	1.000	OF-18
1944	WAS A	14	.194	.250	36	7	2	0	0	0.0	2	9	2	3	0	2	2	16	0	0	0	1.3	1.000	OF-12
13 yrs.		1414	.307	.438	5472	1682	335	92	65	1.2	818	874	514	272	23	41	15	2958	107	66	25	2.3	.979	OF-1370

Alex Voss

VOSS, ALEXANDER
B. May 16, 1858, Roswell, Ga. D. Aug. 31, 1906, Cincinnati, Ohio.
BR TR 6′ 1″ 180 lbs.

Year	Team	Games	BA	SA	AB	H	2B	3B	HR	HR%	R	RBI	BB	SO	SB	Pinch Hit AB	Pinch Hit H	PO	A	E	DP	TC/G	FA	G by Pos
1884	2 teams	WAS U (63G –.192) KC U (14G –.089)																						
"	total	77	.176	.207	290	51	9	0	0	0.0	34		5			0	0	180	113	36	11	3.8	.891	P-34, OF-21, 3B-16, 1B-15, SS-1

Bill Voss

VOSS, WILLIAM EDWARD
B. Oct. 31, 1943, Glendale, Calif.
BL TL 6′ 2″ 160 lbs.

Year	Team	Games	BA	SA	AB	H	2B	3B	HR	HR%	R	RBI	BB	SO	SB	Pinch Hit AB	Pinch Hit H	PO	A	E	DP	TC/G	FA	G by Pos
1965	CHI A	11	.182	.333	33	6	0	1	1	3.0	4	3	3	5	0	0	0	12	0	0	0	1.2	1.000	OF-10
1966		2	.000	.000	2	0	0	0	0	0.0	0	0	0	2	0	1	0	1	0	0	0	1.0	1.000	OF-1
1967		13	.091	.091	22	2	0	0	0	0.0	4	0	0	1	1	0	0	14	0	0	0	1.3	1.000	OF-11
1968		61	.156	.216	167	26	2	1	2	1.2	14	15	16	34	5	7	2	73	5	3	3	1.5	.963	OF-55
1969	CAL A	133	.261	.332	349	91	11	4	2	0.6	33	40	35	40	5	16	6	187	11	1	4	1.8	.995	OF-111, 1B-2
1970		80	.243	.348	181	44	4	3	3	1.7	21	30	23	18	2	26	6	86	7	2	1	1.7	.979	OF-55
1971	MIL A	97	.251	.375	275	69	4	0	10	3.6	31	30	24	45	2	20	5	151	1	2	1	1.9	.987	OF-79
1972	3 teams	MIL A (27G –.083) OAK A (40G –.227) STL N (11G –.267)																						
"	total	78	.196	.284	148	29	8	1	1	0.7	12	9	16	22	0	30	5	78	3	1	0	1.7	.988	OF-47
8 yrs.		475	.227	.317	1177	267	29	10	19	1.6	119	127	117	167	15	100	24	602	27	9	9	1.7	.986	OF-369, 1B-2

Phil Voyles

VOYLES, PHILIP VANCE
B. May 12, 1900, Murphy, N. C. D. Nov. 3, 1972, Marlboro, Mass.
BL TR 5′11½″ 175 lbs.

Year	Team	Games	BA	SA	AB	H	2B	3B	HR	HR%	R	RBI	BB	SO	SB	Pinch Hit AB	Pinch Hit H	PO	A	E	DP	TC/G	FA	G by Pos
1929	BOS N	20	.235	.294	68	16	0	2	0	0.0	9	14	6	8	0	0	0	45	2	4	0	2.5	.922	OF-20

George Vukovich

VUKOVICH, GEORGE STEPHEN
B. June 24, 1956, Chicago, Ill.
BL TR 6′ 198 lbs.

Year	Team	Games	BA	SA	AB	H	2B	3B	HR	HR%	R	RBI	BB	SO	SB	Pinch Hit AB	Pinch Hit H	PO	A	E	DP	TC/G	FA	G by Pos
1980	PHI N	78	.224	.276	58	13	1	1	0	0.0	6	8	6	9	0	45	11	14	0	1	0	0.5	.933	OF-28
1981		20	.385	.500	26	10	0	0	1	3.8	5	4	1	0	1	11	5	10	0	0	0	1.1	1.000	OF-9
1982		123	.272	.391	335	91	18	2	6	1.8	41	42	32	47	2	23	5	168	4	4	3	1.7	.977	OF-102
1983	CLE A	124	.247	.330	312	77	13	2	3	1.0	31	44	24	37	3	10	3	203	3	3	0	1.7	.986	OF-122
1984		134	.304	.439	437	133	22	5	9	2.1	38	60	34	61	1	13	2	316	13	2	5	2.5	.994	OF-130
1985		149	.244	.350	434	106	22	0	8	1.8	43	45	30	75	2	20	5	250	4	3	0	1.9	.988	OF-137
6 yrs.		628	.268	.379	1602	430	76	10	27	1.7	164	203	127	229	9	122	31	961	24	13	8	1.9	.987	OF-528
DIVISIONAL PLAYOFF SERIES																								
1981	PHI N	5	.444	.778	9	4	0	0	1	11.1	1	2	0	3	0	4	3	6	0	0	0	2.0	1.000	OF-3
LEAGUE CHAMPIONSHIP SERIES																								
1980	PHI N	4	.000	.000	3	0	0	0	0	0.0	0	0	0	0	0	3	0	0	0	0	0	0.0	.000	OF-1

John Vukovich

VUKOVICH, JOHN CHRISTOPHER
B. July 31, 1947, Sacramento, Calif.
Manager 1986, 1988.
BR TR 6′ 1″ 187 lbs.

Year	Team	Games	BA	SA	AB	H	2B	3B	HR	HR%	R	RBI	BB	SO	SB	Pinch Hit AB	Pinch Hit H	PO	A	E	DP	TC/G	FA	G by Pos
1970	PHI N	3	.125	.125	8	1	0	0	0	0.0	1	0	1	0	0	0	0	4	8	2	1	4.7	.857	SS-2, 3B-1
1971		74	.166	.189	217	36	5	0	0	0.0	11	14	12	34	2	0	0	58	137	9	8	2.8	.956	3B-74
1973	MIL A	55	.125	.195	128	16	3	0	2	1.6	10	9	9	40	0	1	0	86	67	5	7	2.9	.968	3B-40, 1B-13, SS-1
1974		38	.188	.313	80	15	1	0	3	3.8	5	11	1	16	2	1	0	46	68	5	10	3.1	.958	3B-12, SS-12, 2B-11, 1B-4
1975	CIN N	31	.211	.289	38	8	3	0	0	0.0	4	2	4	5	0	0	0	12	37	4	4	1.7	.925	3B-31
1976	PHI N	4	.125	.500	8	1	0	0	1	12.5	2	2	0	2	0	0	0	6	2	0	0	1.6	1.000	3B-4, 1B-1
1977		2	.000	.000	2	0	0	0	0	0.0	0	0	0	1	0	2	0	0	0	0	0	0.0	—	
1979		10	.200	.267	15	3	1	0	0	0.0	0	1	0	3	0	0	0	2	13	0	1	1.5	1.000	3B-7, 2B-3

John Vukovich *continued*

Year	Team	Games	BA	SA	AB	H	2B	3B	HR	HR%	R	RBI	BB	SO	SB	Pinch Hit AB	Pinch Hit H	PO	A	E	DP	TC/G	FA	G by Pos
1980		49	.161	.210	62	10	1	1	0	0.0	4	5	2	7	0	4	1	18	35	2	0	1.1	.964	3B-34, 2B-9, SS-5, 1B-1
1981		11	.000	.000	1	0	0	0	0	0.0	0	0	0	1	0	0	0	4	4	1	0	0.8	.889	3B-9, 2B-1, 1B-1
10 yrs.		277	.161	.222	559	90	14	1	6	1.1	37	44	29	109	4	8	1	236	371	28	31	2.3	.956	3B-212, 2B-24, 1B-20, SS-20

Frank Waddey

WADDEY, FRANK ORUM BL TL 5′10½″ 185 lbs.
B. Aug. 21, 1905, Memphis, Tenn. D. Oct. 21, 1990, Knoxville, Tenn.

Year	Team	Games	BA	SA	AB	H	2B	3B	HR	HR%	R	RBI	BB	SO	SB	Pinch Hit AB	Pinch Hit H	PO	A	E	DP	TC/G	FA	G by Pos
1931	STL A	14	.273	.318	22	6	1	0	0	0.0	3	2	2	3	0	7	2	6	0	0	0	0.9	1.000	OF-7

Gale Wade

WADE, GALEARD LEE BL TR 6′ 1½″ 185 lbs.
B. Jan. 20, 1929, Hollister, Mo.

Year	Team	Games	BA	SA	AB	H	2B	3B	HR	HR%	R	RBI	BB	SO	SB	Pinch Hit AB	Pinch Hit H	PO	A	E	DP	TC/G	FA	G by Pos
1955	CHI N	9	.182	.303	33	6	1	0	1	3.0	5	1	4	3	0	0	0	12	1	2	0	1.7	.867	OF-9
1956		10	.000	.000	12	0	0	0	0	0.0	0	0	1	0	0	3	0	7	0	1	0	2.7	.875	OF-3
2 yrs.		19	.133	.222	45	6	1	0	1	2.2	5	1	5	3	0	3	0	19	1	3	0	1.9	.870	OF-12

Ham Wade

WADE, ABRAHAM LINCOLN BR TR 5′ 8″ 155 lbs.
B. Dec. 20, 1880, Spring City, Pa. D. July 21, 1968, Riverside, N. J.

Year	Team	Games	BA	SA	AB	H	2B	3B	HR	HR%	R	RBI	BB	SO	SB	Pinch Hit AB	Pinch Hit H	PO	A	E	DP	TC/G	FA	G by Pos
1907	NY N	1	—	—	0	0	0	0	0	—	0	0	0		0	0	0	2	0	0	0	2.0	1.000	OF-1

Rip Wade

WADE, RICHARD FRANK BL TR 5′11″ 174 lbs.
B. Jan. 12, 1898, Duluth, Minn. D. June 16, 1957, Sandstone, Minn.

Year	Team	Games	BA	SA	AB	H	2B	3B	HR	HR%	R	RBI	BB	SO	SB	Pinch Hit AB	Pinch Hit H	PO	A	E	DP	TC/G	FA	G by Pos
1923	WAS A	33	.232	.406	69	16	2	2	2	2.9	8	14	5	10	0	8	1	26	3	1	1	1.6	.967	OF-19

Woodie Wagenhorst

WAGENHORST, ELLWOOD OTTO 5′11″ 165 lbs.
B. June 3, 1863, Kutztown, Pa. D. Feb. 12, 1946, Washington, D. C.

Year	Team	Games	BA	SA	AB	H	2B	3B	HR	HR%	R	RBI	BB	SO	SB	Pinch Hit AB	Pinch Hit H	PO	A	E	DP	TC/G	FA	G by Pos
1888	PHI N	2	.125	.125	8	1	0	0	0	0.0	2	0	0	1	0	0	0	2	2	1	1	2.5	.800	3B-2

Bill Wagner

WAGNER, WILLIAM JOSEPH BR TR 6′ 187 lbs.
B. Jan. 2, 1894, Jessup, Iowa D. Jan. 11, 1951, Waterloo, Iowa.

Year	Team	Games	BA	SA	AB	H	2B	3B	HR	HR%	R	RBI	BB	SO	SB	Pinch Hit AB	Pinch Hit H	PO	A	E	DP	TC/G	FA	G by Pos
1914	PIT N	3	.000	.000	1	0	0	0	0	0.0	0	0	0	0	0	0	0	1	1	0	0	0.7	1.000	C-3
1915		5	.000	.000	5	0	0	0	0	0.0	0	0	1	2	0	1	0	6	5	0	0	3.7	1.000	C-3
1916		19	.237	.342	38	9	0	2	0	0.0	2	2	5	8	0	4	1	54	19	5	3	5.2	.936	C-15
1917		53	.205	.278	151	31	7	2	0	0.0	15	9	11	22	1	6	2	239	49	14	7	6.2	.954	C-37, 1B-12
1918	BOS N	13	.213	.277	47	10	0	0	1	2.1	2	7	4	5	0	0	0	43	12	5	0	4.6	.917	C-13
5 yrs.		93	.207	.281	242	50	7	4	1	0.4	19	18	21	37	1	11	3	343	86	24	10	5.5	.947	C-71, 1B-12

Butts Wagner

WAGNER, ALBERT BR TR 5′10″ 170 lbs.
Brother of Honus Wagner.
B. Sept. 17, 1871, Chartiers, Pa. D. Nov. 26, 1928, Pittsburgh, Pa.

Year	Team	Games	BA	SA	AB	H	2B	3B	HR	HR%	R	RBI	BB	SO	SB	Pinch Hit AB	Pinch Hit H	PO	A	E	DP	TC/G	FA	G by Pos
1898	2 teams	WAS N (63G –.224) BKN N (11G –.237)																						
″	total	74	.226	.307	261	59	12	3	1	0.4	22	34	16		4	1	0	97	126	46	9	3.7	.829	3B-50, OF-10, SS-8, 2B-5

Hal Wagner

WAGNER, HAROLD EDWARD BL TR 6′ 165 lbs.
B. July 2, 1915, East Riverton, N. J. D. Aug. 4, 1979, Riverside, N. J.

Year	Team	Games	BA	SA	AB	H	2B	3B	HR	HR%	R	RBI	BB	SO	SB	Pinch Hit AB	Pinch Hit H	PO	A	E	DP	TC/G	FA	G by Pos
1937	PHI A	1	—	—	0	0	0	0	0	—	0	0	0	0	0	0	0	1	0	0	1	1.0	1.000	C-1
1938		33	.227	.273	88	20	2	1	0	0.0	10	8	8	9	0	3	1	87	16	3	2	3.5	.972	C-30
1939		5	.125	.125	8	1	0	0	0	0.0	0	0	0	3	0	0	0	11	3	0	0	2.8	1.000	C-5
1940		34	.253	.347	75	19	5	1	0	0.0	9	10	11	6	0	5	2	91	16	4	4	4.0	.964	C-28
1941		46	.221	.336	131	29	8	2	1	0.8	18	15	19	9	1	4	0	144	19	4	4	4.0	.976	C-42
1942		104	.236	.313	288	68	17	1	1	0.3	26	30	24	29	1	12	2	371	47	6	7	4.5	.986	C-94
1943		111	.239	.315	289	69	17	1	1	0.3	22	26	36	17	3	14	3	340	56	8	3	4.1	.980	C-99
1944	2 teams	PHI A (5G –.250) BOS A (66G –.332)																						
″	total	71	.330	.436	227	75	13	4	1	0.4	21	38	29	14	1	7	2	300	30	10	4	5.2	.971	C-65
1946	BOS A	117	.230	.322	370	85	12	2	6	1.6	39	52	69	32	3	0	0	553	39	10	3	5.2	.983	C-116
1947	2 teams	BOS A (21G –.231) DET A (71G –.288)																						
″	total	92	.273	.383	256	70	13	0	5	2.0	24	39	37	21	0	1	1	357	34	5	4	4.3	.987	C-92
1948	2 teams	DET A (54G –.202) PHI N (3G –.000)																						
″	total	57	.195	.221	113	22	3	0	0	0.0	10	10	20	11	1	2	0	165	14	2	4	3.4	.989	C-53
1949	PHI N	1	.000	.000	4	0	0	0	0	0.0	0	0	0	1	0	0	0	3	0	1	0	4.0	.750	C-1
12 yrs.		672	.248	.334	1849	458	90	12	15	0.8	179	228	253	152	10	48	11	2423	274	53	36	4.4	.981	C-626
WORLD SERIES																								
1946	BOS A	5	.000	.000	13	0	0	0	0	0.0	0	0	0	1	0	0	0	20	2	0	0	4.4	1.000	C-5

Heinie Wagner

WAGNER, CHARLES F. BR TR 5′ 9″ 183 lbs.
B. Sept. 23, 1880, New York, N. Y. D. Mar. 20, 1943, New Rochelle, N. Y.
Manager 1930.

Year	Team	Games	BA	SA	AB	H	2B	3B	HR	HR%	R	RBI	BB	SO	SB	Pinch Hit AB	Pinch Hit H	PO	A	E	DP	TC/G	FA	G by Pos
1902	NY N	17	.214	.232	56	12	1	0	0	0.0	4	2	0		3	0	0	31	44	12	5	5.1	.862	SS-17
1906	BOS A	9	.281	.281	32	9	0	0	0	0.0	1	4	1		2	0	0	16	34	3	2	5.9	.943	2B-9
1907		111	.213	.275	385	82	10	4	2	0.5	29	21	31		20	0	0	284	393	51	31	6.6	.930	SS-109, 3B-1, 2B-1
1908		153	.247	.293	526	130	11	5	1	0.2	62	46	27		20	0	0	373	569	61	51	6.6	.939	SS-153
1909		124	.256	.333	430	110	16	7	1	0.2	51	49	35		18	0	0	283	415	50	40	6.0	.933	SS-123, 2B-1
1910		142	.273	.360	491	134	26	7	1	0.2	61	52	44		26	2	0	303	424	57	40	5.6	.927	SS-140
1911		80	.257	.379	261	67	13	8	1	0.4	34	38	29		15	8	2	181	198	38	25	5.8	.909	2B-40, SS-32
1912		144	.274	.359	504	138	25	6	2	0.4	75	68	62		21	0	0	332	391	61	43	5.4	.922	SS-144
1913		110	.227	.326	365	83	14	8	2	0.5	43	34	40	29	9	1	0	281	318	40	37	5.9	.937	SS-105, 2B-4
1915		84	.240	.296	267	64	11	2	0	0.0	38	29	37	34	8	3	0	164	197	28	18	4.8	.928	2B-79, 3B-1, OF-1
1916		6	.500	.625	8	4	1	0	0	0.0	2	0	3	0	2	0	0	5	12	0	0	2.8	1.000	3B-4, SS-1, 2B-1
1918		3	.125	.125	8	1	0	0	0	0.0	0	0	1	0	0	0	0	2	7	1	2	3.3	.900	2B-2, 3B-1
12 yrs.		983	.250	.326	3333	834	128	47	10	0.3	400	343	310	63	144	14	2	2255	3002	402	294	5.8	.929	SS-824, 2B-137, 3B-7, OF-1
WORLD SERIES																								
1912	BOS A	8	.167	.200	30	5	1	0	0	0.0	1	0	3	6	1	0	0	24	24	3	0	6.4	.941	SS-8

Year	Team	Games	BA	SA	AB	H	2B	3B	HR	HR%	R	RBI	BB	SO	SB	Pinch Hit AB	Pinch Hit H	PO	A	E	DP	TC/G	FA	G by Pos

Honus Wagner

WAGNER, JOHN PETER (The Flying Dutchman)
Brother of Butts Wagner.
B. Feb. 24, 1874, Chartiers, Pa. D. Dec. 6, 1955, Carnegie, Pa.
Manager 1917.
Hall of Fame 1936.
BR TR 5′11″ 200 lbs.

Year	Team	Games	BA	SA	AB	H	2B	3B	HR	HR%	R	RBI	BB	SO	SB	Pinch Hit AB	Pinch Hit H	PO	A	E	DP	TC/G	FA	G by Pos
1897	LOU N	61	.338	.468	237	80	17	4	2	0.8	37	39	15		19	0	0	124	37	16	7	2.9	.910	OF-52, 2B-9
1898		151	.299	.410	588	176	29	3	10	1.7	80	105	31		27	2	1	847	192	43	57	7.2	.960	1B-75, 3B-65, 2B-10
1899		147	.336	.494	571	192	43	13	7	1.2	98	113	40		37	1	0	260	201	28	20	3.3	.943	3B-75, OF-61, 2B-7, 1B-4
1900	PIT N	135	**.381**	**.573**	527	201	**45**	**22**	4	0.8	107	100	41		38	1	0	216	45	13	9	2.0	.953	OF-118, 3B-9, 2B-7, 1B-3, P-1
1901		141	.353	.491	556	196	37	11	6	1.1	100	**126**	53		**49**	0	0	297	280	48	35	4.4	.923	SS-62, OF-54, 3B-24, 2B-1
1902		137	.329	**.467**	538	177	**33**	16	3	0.6	**105**	**91**	43		**42**	0	0	532	176	32	33	5.3	.957	OF-61, SS-44, 1B-32, 2B-1, P-1
1903		129	**.355**	.518	512	182	30	**19**	5	1.0	97	101	44		46	0	0	386	401	52	53	6.5	.938	SS-111, OF-12, 1B-6
1904		132	**.349**	**.520**	490	171	**44**	14	4	0.8	97	75	59		**53**	1	0	319	376	51	46	5.6	.932	SS-121, OF-8, 1B-3, 2B-2
1905		147	.363	.505	548	199	32	14	6	1.1	114	101	54		57	0	0	363	517	60	64	6.4	.936	SS-145, OF-2
1906		142	**.339**	.459	516	175	**38**	9	2	0.4	**103**	71	58		53	1	0	338	474	52	57	6.2	.940	SS-137, OF-2, 3B-1
1907		142	**.350**	**.513**	515	180	**38**	14	6	1.2	98	82	46		**61**	0	0	358	429	49	33	5.9	.941	SS-138, 1B-4
1908		151	**.354**	**.542**	568	**201**	**39**	**19**	10	1.8	100	**109**	54		**53**	0	0	354	469	50	47	5.8	.943	SS-151
1909		137	**.339**	**.489**	495	168	**39**	10	5	1.0	92	**100**	66		35	0	0	344	430	49	58	6.0	.940	SS-136, OF-1
1910		150	.320	.432	556	**178**	34	8	4	0.7	90	81	59	47	24	0	0	442	427	52	67	6.1	.944	SS-138, 1B-11, 2B-2
1911		130	**.334**	.507	473	158	23	16	9	1.9	87	89	67	34	20	0	0	472	321	47	76	6.5	.944	SS-101, 1B-28, OF-1
1912		145	.324	.496	558	181	35	20	7	1.3	91	102	59	38	26	0	0	341	462	32	74	5.8	.962	SS-143
1913		114	.300	.385	413	124	18	4	3	0.7	51	56	26	40	21	7	1	289	323	24	47	6.1	.962	SS-105
1914		150	.252	.317	552	139	15	9	1	0.2	60	50	51	51	23	1	0	344	460	43	46	5.6	.949	SS-132, 3B-17, 1B-1
1915		151	.274	.422	566	155	32	17	6	1.1	68	78	39	64	22	4	1	421	428	38	62	5.8	.957	SS-131, 2B-12, 1B-10
1916		123	.287	.370	432	124	15	9	1	0.2	45	39	34	36	11	6	1	417	282	35	46	6.1	.952	SS-92, 1B-24, 2B-4
1917		74	.265	.304	230	61	7	1	0	0.0	15	24	24	17	5	7	1	466	51	10	27	7.8	.981	1B-47, 3B-18, 2B-2, SS-1
21 yrs.		2789	.327	.466	10441	3418	643	252	101	1.0	1735	1732	963	327	722	31	5	7930	6781	824	964	5.6	.947	SS-1888, OF-372, 1B-248, 3B-209, 2B-57, P-2
						7th	**8th**	**3rd**							**8th**									
WORLD SERIES																								
1903	PIT N	8	.222	.259	27	6	1	0	0	0.0	2	3	3	4	3	0	0	13	27	6	4	5.8	.870	SS-8
1909		7	.333	.500	24	8	2	1	0	0.0	4	6	4	2	6	0	0	13	23	2	1	5.4	.947	SS-7
2 yrs.		15	.275	.373	51	14	3	1	0	0.0	6	9	7	6	9	0	0	26	50	8	5	5.6	.905	SS-15
															6th									

Joe Wagner

WAGNER, JOSEPH BERNARD
B. Apr. 24, 1889, New York, N. Y. D. Nov. 15, 1948, Bronx, N. Y.
BR TR 5′11″ 165 lbs.

Year	Team	Games	BA	SA	AB	H	2B	3B	HR	HR%	R	RBI	BB	SO	SB	Pinch Hit AB	Pinch Hit H	PO	A	E	DP	TC/G	FA	G by Pos
1915	CIN N	75	.178	.223	197	35	5	2	0	0.0	17	13	8	35	4	7	2	114	149	10	28	4.4	.963	2B-46, SS-14, 3B-2

Leon Wagner

WAGNER, LEON LAMAR (Daddy Wags)
B. May 13, 1934, Chattanooga, Tenn.
BL TR 6′ 1″ 195 lbs.

Year	Team	Games	BA	SA	AB	H	2B	3B	HR	HR%	R	RBI	BB	SO	SB	Pinch Hit AB	Pinch Hit H	PO	A	E	DP	TC/G	FA	G by Pos
1958	SF N	74	.317	.534	221	70	9	0	13	5.9	31	35	18	34	1	18	4	89	5	5	0	1.7	.949	OF-57
1959		87	.225	.419	129	29	4	3	5	3.9	20	22	25	24	0	52	10	48	0	3	0	1.8	.941	OF-28
1960	STL N	39	.214	.357	98	21	2	0	4	4.1	12	11	17	17	0	7	1	48	4	2	0	1.7	.963	OF-32
1961	LA A	133	.280	.517	453	127	19	2	28	6.2	74	79	48	65	5	16	3	187	12	6	2	1.8	.971	OF-116
1962		160	.268	.500	612	164	21	5	37	6.0	96	107	50	87	7	3	1	269	7	8	1	1.8	.972	OF-156
1963		149	.291	.456	550	160	11	1	26	4.7	73	90	49	73	5	9	2	254	7	11	1	1.9	.960	OF-141
1964	CLE A	163	.253	.434	641	162	19	2	31	4.8	94	100	56	121	14	2	1	254	5	11	0	1.7	.959	OF-163
1965		144	.294	.495	517	152	18	1	28	5.4	91	79	60	52	12	11	3	175	3	8	0	1.4	.957	OF-134
1966		150	.279	.441	549	153	20	0	23	4.2	70	66	46	69	5	10	3	185	4	2	0	1.4	.990	OF-139
1967		135	.242	.386	433	105	15	1	15	3.5	56	54	37	76	3	15	4	142	4	3	1	1.3	.980	OF-117
1968	2 teams	CLE A (38G –.184)	CHI A (69G –.284)																					
″	total	107	.261	.332	211	55	12	0	1	0.5	19	24	27	37	2	**46**	11	51	0	6	0	1.0	.895	OF-56
1969	SF N	11	.333	.333	12	4	0	0	0	0.0	0	2	2	1	0	7	3	3	0	0	0	3.0	1.000	OF-1
12 yrs.		1352	.272	.455	4426	1202	150	15	211	4.8	636	669	435	656	54	196	46	1705	51	65	5	1.6	.964	OF-1140

Mark Wagner

WAGNER, MARK DUANE
B. Mar. 4, 1954, Conneaut, Ohio
BR TR 6′ 165 lbs.

Year	Team	Games	BA	SA	AB	H	2B	3B	HR	HR%	R	RBI	BB	SO	SB	Pinch Hit AB	Pinch Hit H	PO	A	E	DP	TC/G	FA	G by Pos
1976	DET A	39	.261	.330	115	30	2	3	0	0.0	9	12	6	18	0	0	0	60	135	11	25	5.3	.947	SS-39
1977		22	.146	.250	48	7	0	1	1	2.1	4	3	4	12	0	0	0	15	58	6	10	3.6	.924	SS-21, 2B-1
1978		39	.239	.284	109	26	1	2	0	0.0	10	6	3	11	1	1	1	57	81	5	18	3.7	.965	SS-35, 2B-4
1979		75	.274	.315	146	40	3	0	1	0.7	16	13	16	25	3	1	1	88	146	8	28	3.3	.967	SS-41, 2B-29, 3B-2, DH-1
1980		45	.236	.250	72	17	1	0	0	0.0	5	3	7	11	0	2	0	43	61	7	8	2.6	.937	SS-28, 3B-9, 2B-6
1981	TEX A	50	.259	.365	85	22	4	1	1	1.2	15	14	8	13	1	2	0	54	87	5	18	3.0	.966	SS-43, 2B-4, 3B-2
1982		60	.240	.274	179	43	4	1	0	0.0	14	8	10	28	1	0	0	77	197	13	32	4.8	.955	SS-60
1983		2	.000	.000	2	0	0	0	0	0.0	0	0	0	1	0	0	0	2	4	0	0	3.0	1.000	SS-2
1984	OAK A	82	.230	.310	87	20	5	1	0	0.0	8	12	7	11	2	1	0	73	83	6	15	1.9	.963	SS-58, 3B-15, 2B-8, DH-3, P-1
9 yrs.		414	.243	.299	843	205	20	9	3	0.4	81	71	61	130	8	7	2	469	852	61	154	3.4	.956	SS-327, 2B-52, 3B-28, DH-4, P-1

Kermit Wahl

WAHL, KERMIT EMERSON
B. Nov. 18, 1922, Columbia, S. D. D. Sept. 16, 1987, Tucson, Ariz.
BR TR 5′11″ 170 lbs.

Year	Team	Games	BA	SA	AB	H	2B	3B	HR	HR%	R	RBI	BB	SO	SB	Pinch Hit AB	Pinch Hit H	PO	A	E	DP	TC/G	FA	G by Pos
1944	CIN N	4	.000	.000	1	0	0	0	0	0.0	0	0	0	0	0	0	0	0	0	0	0	0.0	.000	3B-1
1945		71	.201	.263	194	39	8	2	0	0.0	18	10	23	22	2	0	0	139	180	17	22	4.8	.949	2B-32, SS-31, 3B-7
1947		39	.173	.210	81	14	0	0	1	1.2	8	4	6	12	0	5	1	39	50	2	5	2.9	.978	3B-20, SS-9, 2B-2
1950	PHI A	89	.257	.343	280	72	12	3	2	0.7	26	27	30	30	1	7	2	111	197	17	29	4.0	.948	3B-61, SS-18, 2B-2
1951	2 teams	PHI A (20G –.186)	STL A (8G –.333)																					
″	total	28	.233	.291	86	20	3	1	0	0.0	6	9	9	8	0	4	0	28	49	3	7	3.3	.962	3B-24
5 yrs.		231	.226	.294	642	145	23	6	3	0.5	58	50	68	72	3	16	3	317	476	39	63	4.0	.953	3B-113, SS-58, 2B-36

Eddie Waitkus

WAITKUS, EDWARD STEPHEN
B. Sept. 4, 1919, Cambridge, Mass. D. Sept. 15, 1972, Jamaica Plain, Mass.
BL TL 6′ 170 lbs.

Year	Team	Games	BA	SA	AB	H	2B	3B	HR	HR%	R	RBI	BB	SO	SB	Pinch Hit AB	Pinch Hit H	PO	A	E	DP	TC/G	FA	G by Pos
1941	CHI N	12	.179	.179	28	5	0	0	0	0.0	1	0	0	3	0	3	1	71	3	4	8	8.7	.949	1B-9
1946		113	.304	.408	441	134	24	5	4	0.9	50	55	23	14	3	5	2	992	81	4	76	10.2	.996	1B-106
1947		130	.292	.381	514	150	28	6	2	0.4	60	35	32	17	3	2	0	1161	101	8	109	10.1	.994	1B-126

Eddie Waitkus *continued*

Year	Team	Games	BA	SA	AB	H	2B	3B	HR	HR%	R	RBI	BB	SO	SB	Pinch Hit AB	Pinch Hit H	PO	A	E	DP	TC/G	FA	G by Pos
1948		139	.295	.416	562	166	27	10	7	1.2	87	44	43	19	11	2	0	1107	92	10	77	8.9	.992	1B-116, OF-20
1949	PHI N	54	.306	.426	209	64	16	3	1	0.5	41	28	33	12	3	0	0	452	36	3	51	9.1	.994	1B-54
1950		154	.284	.359	641	182	32	5	2	0.3	102	44	55	29	3	1	1	1387	99	10	142	9.7	.993	1B-154
1951		145	.257	.320	610	157	27	4	1	0.2	65	46	53	22	0	2	0	1214	94	10	121	9.2	.992	1B-144
1952		146	.289	.375	499	144	29	4	2	0.4	51	49	64	23	2	3	0	1281	95	12	119	9.7	.991	1B-143
1953		81	.291	.356	247	72	9	2	1	0.4	24	16	13	23	1	20	7	480	37	6	65	8.9	.989	1B-59
1954	BAL A	95	.283	.383	311	88	17	4	2	0.6	35	33	28	25	0	15	4	618	48	0	72	8.5	1.000	1B-78
1955	2 teams	BAL A (38G –.259) PHI N (33G –.280)																						
"	total	71	.271	.344	192	52	6	1	2	1.0	12	23	28	17	2	11	4	430	30	6	46	8.2	.987	1B-57
11 yrs.		1140	.285	.374	4254	1214	215	44	24	0.6	528	373	372	204	28	64	19	9193	716	73	886	9.4	.993	1B-1046, OF-20
WORLD SERIES																								
1950	PHI N	4	.267	.333	15	4	1	0	0	0.0	0	0	2	0	0	0	0	34	3	0	1	9.3	1.000	1B-4

Charlie Waitt

WAITT, CHARLES C. 5′11″ 165 lbs.
B. Oct. 14, 1853, Hallowell, Me. D. Oct. 21, 1912, San Francisco, Calif.

Year	Team	Games	BA	SA	AB	H	2B	3B	HR	HR%	R	RBI	BB	SO	SB	Pinch Hit AB	Pinch Hit H	PO	A	E	DP	TC/G	FA	G by Pos
1877	CHI N	10	.098	.098	41	4	0	0	0	0.0	2	2	0	3		0	0	20	3	6	1	2.9	.793	OF-10
1882	BAL AA	72	.156	.172	250	39	4	0	0	0.0	19		13			0	0	142	11	22	2	2.4	.874	OF-72
1883	PHI N	1	.333	.333	3	1	0	0	0	0.0	0		0	1		0	0	1	0	2	0	3.0	.333	OF-1
3 yrs.		83	.150	.163	294	44	4	0	0	0.0	21	2	13	4		0	0	163	14	30	3	2.5	.855	OF-83

Don Wakamatsu

WAKAMATSU, WILBUR DONALD BR TR 6′ 2″ 200 lbs.
B. Feb. 22, 1963, Hood River, Ore.

Year	Team	Games	BA	SA	AB	H	2B	3B	HR	HR%	R	RBI	BB	SO	SB	Pinch Hit AB	Pinch Hit H	PO	A	E	DP	TC/G	FA	G by Pos
1991	CHI A	18	.226	.226	31	7	0	0	0	0.0	2	0	1	6	0	1	1	47	2	0	2	2.7	1.000	C-18

Dick Wakefield

WAKEFIELD, RICHARD CUMMINGS BL TR 6′ 4″ 210 lbs.
Son of Howard Wakefield.
B. May 6, 1921, Chicago, Ill. D. Aug. 26, 1985, Redford, Mich.

Year	Team	Games	BA	SA	AB	H	2B	3B	HR	HR%	R	RBI	BB	SO	SB	Pinch Hit AB	Pinch Hit H	PO	A	E	DP	TC/G	FA	G by Pos
1941	DET A	7	.143	.143	7	1	0	0	0	0.0	0	0	0	1	0	6	1	1	0	0	0	1.0	1.000	OF-1
1943		155	.316	.434	**633**	**200**	**38**	8	7	1.1	91	79	62	60	4	0	0	314	11	14	1	2.2	.959	OF-155
1944		78	.355	.576	276	98	15	5	12	4.3	53	53	55	29	2	0	0	155	3	6	1	2.1	.963	OF-78
1946		111	.268	.412	396	106	11	5	12	3.0	64	59	59	55	3	4	0	210	6	8	1	2.2	.964	OF-104
1947		112	.283	.416	368	104	15	5	8	2.2	59	51	80	44	1	10	4	197	10	11	2	2.2	.950	OF-101
1948		110	.276	.472	322	89	20	5	11	3.4	50	53	70	55	0	22	7	198	3	11	1	2.5	.948	OF-86
1949		59	.206	.389	126	26	3	1	6	4.8	17	19	32	24	0	18	3	71	3	0	1	2.3	1.000	OF-32
1950	NY A	3	.500	.500	2	1	0	0	0	0.0	0	1	1	1	0	2	1	0	0	0	0	0.0	—	
1952	NY N	3	.000	.000	2	0	0	0	0	0.0	0	0	1	0	0	2	0	0	0	0	0	0.0	—	
9 yrs.		638	.293	.447	2132	625	102	29	56	2.6	334	315	360	269	10	64	16	1146	36	50	7	2.2	.959	OF-557

Howard Wakefield

WAKEFIELD, HOWARD JOHN BR TR 6′ 1″ 205 lbs.
Father of Dick Wakefield.
B. Apr. 2, 1884, Bucyrus, Ohio D. Apr. 16, 1941, Chicago, Ill.

Year	Team	Games	BA	SA	AB	H	2B	3B	HR	HR%	R	RBI	BB	SO	SB	Pinch Hit AB	Pinch Hit H	PO	A	E	DP	TC/G	FA	G by Pos
1905	CLE A	9	.160	.160	25	4	0	0	0	0.0	3	1	0		0	1	0	18	7	2	0	3.4	.926	C-8
1906	WAS A	77	.280	.355	211	59	9	2	1	0.5	17	21	7		6	16	**9**	237	59	17	5	5.2	.946	C-60
1907	CLE A	26	.135	.189	37	5	2	0	0	0.0	4	3	3		0	15	2	37	3	3	2	3.9	.930	C-11
3 yrs.		112	.249	.315	273	68	11	2	1	0.4	24	25	10		6	32	11	292	69	22	7	4.8	.943	C-79

Matt Walbeck

WALBECK, MATTHEW LOVICK BB TR 5′11″ 195 lbs.
B. Oct. 2, 1969, Sacramento, Calif.

Year	Team	Games	BA	SA	AB	H	2B	3B	HR	HR%	R	RBI	BB	SO	SB	Pinch Hit AB	Pinch Hit H	PO	A	E	DP	TC/G	FA	G by Pos
1993	CHI N	11	.200	.367	30	6	2	0	1	3.3	2	6	1	6	0	3	1	49	2	0	0	4.6	1.000	C-11
1994	MIN A	97	.204	.284	338	69	12	0	5	1.5	31	35	17	37	1	3	0	496	45	4	0	5.7	.993	C-95, DH-1
1995		115	.257	.316	393	101	18	1	1	0.3	40	44	25	71	3	3	0	604	35	6	3	5.7	.991	C-113
3 yrs.		223	.231	.304	761	176	32	1	7	0.9	73	85	43	114	4	9	1	1149	82	10	3	5.6	.992	C-219, DH-1

Ed Walczak

WALCZAK, EDWIN JOSEPH (Husky) BR TR 5′11″ 180 lbs.
B. Sept. 21, 1918, Arctic, R. I.

Year	Team	Games	BA	SA	AB	H	2B	3B	HR	HR%	R	RBI	BB	SO	SB	Pinch Hit AB	Pinch Hit H	PO	A	E	DP	TC/G	FA	G by Pos
1945	PHI N	20	.211	.263	57	12	3	0	0	0.0	6	2	6	9	0	0	0	49	44	4	14	5.1	.959	2B-17, SS-2

Fred Walden

WALDEN, THOMAS FRED BR TR
B. June 25, 1890, Fayette, Mo. D. Sept. 27, 1955, Jefferson Barracks, Mo.

Year	Team	Games	BA	SA	AB	H	2B	3B	HR	HR%	R	RBI	BB	SO	SB	Pinch Hit AB	Pinch Hit H	PO	A	E	DP	TC/G	FA	G by Pos
1912	STL A	1	—	—	0	0	0	0	0	—	0	0	0		0	0	0	0	0	1	0	1.0	.000	C-1

Irv Waldron

WALDRON, IRVING J. (Wally) BR TR
B. Jan. 21, 1876, Hillside, N. Y. D. July 22, 1944, Worcester, Mass.

Year	Team	Games	BA	SA	AB	H	2B	3B	HR	HR%	R	RBI	BB	SO	SB	Pinch Hit AB	Pinch Hit H	PO	A	E	DP	TC/G	FA	G by Pos
1901	2 teams	MIL A (62G –.297) WAS A (79G –.322)																						
"	total	141	.311	.378	**598**	186	22	9	0	0.0	102	51	38		20	1	1	237	16	21	0	2.0	.923	OF-140

Jim Walewander

WALEWANDER, JAMES BB TR 5′10″ 160 lbs.
B. May 2, 1961, Chicago, Ill.

Year	Team	Games	BA	SA	AB	H	2B	3B	HR	HR%	R	RBI	BB	SO	SB	Pinch Hit AB	Pinch Hit H	PO	A	E	DP	TC/G	FA	G by Pos
1987	DET A	53	.241	.389	54	13	3	1	1	1.9	24	4	7	6	2	2	0	26	58	1	12	1.9	.988	2B-24, 3B-17, SS-3
1988		88	.211	.240	175	37	5	0	0	0.0	23	6	12	26	11	2	0	125	154	6	38	4.0	.979	2B-61, SS-8, 3B-3
1990	NY A	9	.200	.400	5	1	1	0	0	0.0	1	1	0	0	1	1	0	4	5	0	0	1.3	1.000	3B-2, 2B-2, DH-2, SS-1
1993	CAL A	12	.125	.125	8	1	0	0	0	0.0	2	3	5	1	1	0	0	9	13	0	4	2.2	1.000	SS-6, 2B-2, DH-2
4 yrs.		162	.215	.273	242	52	9	1	1	0.4	50	14	24	33	15	5	0	164	230	7	54	3.0	.983	2B-89, 3B-22, SS-18, DH-4

Chico Walker

WALKER, CLEOTHA BB TR 5′ 9″ 170 lbs.
B. Nov. 25, 1957, Jackson, Miss.

Year	Team	Games	BA	SA	AB	H	2B	3B	HR	HR%	R	RBI	BB	SO	SB	Pinch Hit AB	Pinch Hit H	PO	A	E	DP	TC/G	FA	G by Pos
1980	BOS A	19	.211	.263	57	12	0	0	1	1.8	3	5	6	10	3	1	1	15	31	2	7	2.7	.958	2B-11, DH-7
1981		6	.353	.353	17	6	0	0	0	0.0	3	2	1	2	0	1	0	4	10	0	1	2.8	1.000	2B-5
1983		4	.400	1.200	5	2	0	2	0	0.0	2	1	0	0	0	1	0	4	1	0	0	1.7	1.000	OF-3
1984		3	.000	.000	2	0	0	0	0	0.0	0	1	0	1	0	2	0	0	1	0	0	1.0	1.000	2B-1
1985	CHI N	21	.083	.083	12	1	0	0	0	0.0	3	0	0	5	1	8	1	4	0	0	0	0.5	1.000	OF-6, 2B-2
1986		28	.277	.376	101	28	3	2	1	1.0	21	7	10	20	15	2	0	42	1	2	0	1.7	.956	OF-26
1987		47	.200	.238	105	21	4	0	0	0.0	15	7	12	23	11	6	0	37	0	1	0	1.1	.974	OF-33, 3B-2

Chico Walker *continued*

Year	Team	Games	BA	SA	AB	H	2B	3B	HR	HR%	R	RBI	BB	SO	SB	Pinch Hit AB	Pinch Hit H	PO	A	E	DP	TC/G	FA	G by Pos
1988	CAL A	33	.154	.167	78	12	1	0	0	0.0	8	2	6	15	2	10	0	33	20	2	1	2.1	.964	OF-17, 2B-7, 3B-2
1991	CHI N	124	.257	.337	374	96	10	1	6	1.6	51	34	33	57	13	32	13	106	89	8	9	1.8	.961	3B-57, OF-53, 2B-6
1992	2 teams	CHI N (19G –.115) NY N (107G –.308)																						
"	total	126	.289	.391	253	73	12	1	4	1.6	26	38	27	50	15	57	10	54	85	8	6	1.9	.946	3B-38, OF-21, 2B-18
1993	NY N	115	.225	.338	213	48	7	1	5	2.3	18	19	14	29	7	65	15	68	82	8	11	2.5	.949	2B-24, 3B-23, OF-15
11 yrs.		526	.246	.329	1217	299	37	7	17	1.4	150	116	109	212	67	185	40	367	320	31	35	1.9	.957	OF-174, 3B-122, 2B-74, DH-7

Curt Walker

WALKER, WILLIAM CURTIS BL TR 5′ 9½″ 170 lbs.
B. July 3, 1896, Beeville, Tex. D. Dec. 9, 1955, Beeville, Tex.

Year	Team	Games	BA	SA	AB	H	2B	3B	HR	HR%	R	RBI	BB	SO	SB	Pinch Hit AB	Pinch Hit H	PO	A	E	DP	TC/G	FA	G by Pos
1919	NY A	1	.000	.000	1	0	0	0	0	0.0	0	0	0	0	0	1	0	0	0	0	0	0.0	—	
1920	NY N	8	.071	.071	14	1	0	0	0	0.0	0	0	1	3	0	4	0	5	0	0	0	1.3	1.000	OF-4
1921	2 teams	NY N (64G –.286) PHI N (21G –.338)																						
"	total	85	.301	.435	269	81	15	6	3	1.1	41	43	20	13	4	1	1	277	18	7	5	3.8	.977	OF-79
1922	PHI N	148	.337	.499	581	196	36	11	12	2.1	102	89	56	46	11	1	0	295	24	15	8	2.3	.955	OF-147
1923		140	.281	.378	527	148	26	5	5	0.9	66	66	45	31	12	2	1	284	19	17	5	2.3	.947	OF-140, 1B-1
1924	2 teams	PHI N (24G –.296) CIN N (109G –.300)																						
"	total	133	.299	.436	468	140	27	11	5	1.1	66	54	51	19	7	4	1	239	15	8	5	2.0	.969	OF-129
1925	CIN N	145	.318	.460	509	162	22	16	6	1.2	86	71	57	31	14	3	0	332	12	6	4	2.5	.983	OF-141
1926		155	.306	.450	571	175	24	20	6	1.1	83	78	60	31	3	3	0	325	21	14	8	2.4	.961	OF-152
1927		146	.292	.395	527	154	16	10	6	1.1	60	80	47	19	5	4	0	316	15	15	8	2.5	.957	OF-141
1928		123	.279	.412	427	119	15	12	6	1.4	64	73	49	14	19	1	1	289	9	14	3	2.6	.955	OF-122
1929		141	.313	.474	492	154	28	15	7	1.4	76	83	85	17	17	2	1	298	11	10	2	2.3	.969	OF-138
1930		134	.307	.460	472	145	26	11	8	1.7	74	51	64	30	4	11	6	241	5	9	2	2.1	.965	OF-120
12 yrs.		1359	.304	.440	4858	1475	235	117	64	1.3	718	688	535	254	96	37	11	2901	149	115	50	2.4	.964	OF-1313, 1B-1

Dixie Walker

WALKER, FRED (The People's Cherce) BL TR 6′ 1″ 175 lbs.
Brother of Harry Walker. Son of Dixie Walker.
B. Sept. 24, 1910, Villa Rica, Ga. D. May 17, 1982, Birmingham, Ala.

Year	Team	Games	BA	SA	AB	H	2B	3B	HR	HR%	R	RBI	BB	SO	SB	Pinch Hit AB	Pinch Hit H	PO	A	E	DP	TC/G	FA	G by Pos
1931	NY A	2	.300	.500	10	3	2	0	0	0.0	1	1	0	4	0	0	0	3	0	0	0	1.5	1.000	OF-2
1933		98	.274	.500	328	90	15	7	15	4.6	68	51	26	28	2	18	4	194	7	8	1	2.7	.962	OF-77
1934		17	.118	.118	17	2	0	0	0	0.0	2	0	1	3	0	12	2	1	0	0	0	1.0	1.000	OF-1
1935		8	.154	.231	13	2	1	0	0	0.0	1	1	0	1	0	5	1	3	0	1	0	2.0	.750	OF-2
1936	2 teams	NY A (6G –.350) CHI A (26G –.271)																						
"	total	32	.289	.389	90	26	2	2	1	1.1	15	16	15	9	2	10	2	55	2	0	0	2.6	1.000	OF-22
1937	CHI A	154	.302	.449	593	179	28	**16**	9	1.5	105	95	78	26	1	0	0	270	10	14	1	1.9	.952	OF-154
1938	DET A	127	.308	.434	454	140	27	6	6	1.3	84	43	65	32	5	10	3	224	8	5	1	2.1	.979	OF-114
1939	2 teams	DET A (43G –.305) BKN N (61G –.280)																						
"	total	104	.290	.412	379	110	10	9	6	1.6	57	57	35	18	5	6	2	237	9	8	4	2.6	.969	OF-96
1940	BKN N	143	.308	.435	556	171	37	8	6	1.1	75	66	42	21	3	6	4	360	6	10	3	2.8	.973	OF-136
1941		148	.311	.452	531	165	32	8	9	1.7	88	71	70	18	4	2	0	309	19	8	8	2.3	.976	OF-146
1942		118	.290	.412	393	114	28	1	6	1.5	57	54	47	15	1	6	2	207	8	3	2	2.0	.986	OF-110
1943		138	.302	.411	540	163	32	6	5	0.9	83	71	49	24	3	2	1	262	20	9	2	2.1	.969	OF-136
1944		147	**.357**	.529	535	191	37	8	13	2.4	77	91	72	27	6	7	2	260	17	11	4	2.1	.962	OF-140
1945		154	.300	.438	607	182	42	9	8	1.3	102	**124**	75	16	6	1	0	346	18	3	4	2.4	.992	OF-153
1946		150	.319	.448	576	184	29	9	9	1.6	80	116	67	28	14	1	0	237	15	8	3	1.7	.969	OF-149
1947		148	.306	.427	529	162	31	3	9	1.7	77	94	97	26	6	1	0	261	9	10	0	1.9	.964	OF-147
1948	PIT N	129	.316	.392	408	129	19	3	2	0.5	39	54	52	18	1	16	3	168	4	4	0	1.6	.977	OF-112
1949		88	.282	.331	181	51	4	1	1	0.6	26	18	26	11	0	40	**13**	82	5	4	2	2.2	.956	OF-39, 1B-3
18 yrs.		1905	.306	.437	6740	2064	376	96	105	1.6	1037	1023	817	325	59	143	39	3479	157	106	35	2.2	.972	OF-1736, 1B-3
WORLD SERIES																								
1941	BKN N	5	.222	.333	18	4	2	0	0	0.0	3	0	2	1	0	0	0	14	0	0	0	2.8	1.000	OF-5
1947		7	.222	.370	27	6	1	0	1	3.7	1	4	3	1	1	0	0	9	1	0	0	1.4	1.000	OF-7
2 yrs.		12	.222	.356	45	10	3	0	1	2.2	4	4	5	2	1	0	0	23	1	0	0	2.0	1.000	OF-12

Duane Walker

WALKER, DUANE ALLEN BL TL 6′ 180 lbs.
B. Mar. 13, 1957, Pasadena, Tex.

Year	Team	Games	BA	SA	AB	H	2B	3B	HR	HR%	R	RBI	BB	SO	SB	Pinch Hit AB	Pinch Hit H	PO	A	E	DP	TC/G	FA	G by Pos
1982	CIN N	86	.218	.322	239	52	10	0	5	2.1	26	22	27	58	9	14	2	110	7	1	1	1.7	.992	OF-69
1983		109	.236	.324	225	53	12	1	2	0.9	14	29	20	43	6	48	16	104	4	5	0	1.9	.956	OF-60
1984		83	.292	.528	195	57	10	3	10	5.1	35	28	33	35	7	14	4	110	3	6	0	1.8	.950	OF-68
1985	2 teams	CIN N (37G –.167) TEX A (53G –.174)																						
"	total	90	.172	.322	180	31	4	1	7	3.9	19	17	21	47	3	40	7	66	6	2	1	1.4	.973	OF-42, DH-10
1988	STL N	24	.182	.227	22	4	1	0	0	0.0	1	3	2	7	0	19	4	2	0	0	0	0.4	1.000	OF-4, 1B-1
5 yrs.		392	.229	.367	861	197	37	5	24	2.8	95	99	103	190	25	135	33	392	20	14	2	1.7	.967	OF-243, DH-10, 1B-1

Ernie Walker

WALKER, ERNEST ROBERT BL TR 6′ 165 lbs.
Brother of Dixie Walker.
B. Sept. 17, 1890, Blossburg, Ala. D. Apr. 1, 1965, Pell City, Ala.

Year	Team	Games	BA	SA	AB	H	2B	3B	HR	HR%	R	RBI	BB	SO	SB	Pinch Hit AB	Pinch Hit H	PO	A	E	DP	TC/G	FA	G by Pos
1913	STL A	7	.214	.214	14	3	0	0	0	0.0	0	2	0	5	0	5	2	5	0	0	0	2.5	1.000	OF-2
1914		71	.298	.405	131	39	5	3	1	0.8	19	14	13	26	6	29	**10**	45	3	2	0	1.4	.960	OF-36
1915		50	.211	.284	109	23	4	2	0	0.0	15	9	23	32	5	14	3	36	1	5	3	1.3	.881	OF-33
3 yrs.		128	.256	.343	254	65	9	5	1	0.4	34	25	36	63	11	48	15	86	4	7	3	1.4	.928	OF-71

Fleet Walker

WALKER, MOSES FLEETWOOD BR TR 159 lbs.
Brother of Welday Walker.
B. Oct. 7, 1856, Mt. Pleasant, Ohio D. May 11, 1924, Cleveland, Ohio.

Year	Team	Games	BA	SA	AB	H	2B	3B	HR	HR%	R	RBI	BB	SO	SB	Pinch Hit AB	Pinch Hit H	PO	A	E	DP	TC/G	FA	G by Pos
1884	TOL AA	42	.263	.316	152	40	2	3	0	0.0	23		8			0	0	221	70	37	4	7.8	.887	C-41, OF-1

Frank Walker

WALKER, CHARLES FRANKLIN BR TR 5′11″ 165 lbs.
B. Sept. 22, 1894, Enoree, S. C. D. Sept. 16, 1974, Bristol, Tenn.

Year	Team	Games	BA	SA	AB	H	2B	3B	HR	HR%	R	RBI	BB	SO	SB	Pinch Hit AB	Pinch Hit H	PO	A	E	DP	TC/G	FA	G by Pos
1917	DET A	2	.000	.000	2	0	0	0	0	0.0	0	0	0	1	0	0	0	0	0	0	0	0.0	—	
1918		55	.198	.311	167	33	10	3	1	0.6	10	20	7	29	3	7	1	102	5	9	1	2.6	.922	OF-45
1920	PHI A	24	.231	.297	91	21	2	2	0	0.0	10	10	5	14	0	0	0	57	1	1	0	2.5	.983	OF-24

Frank Walker *continued*

Year	Team	Games	BA	SA	AB	H	2B	3B	HR	HR%	R	RBI	BB	SO	SB	Pinch Hit AB	Pinch Hit H	PO	A	E	DP	TC/G	FA	G by Pos
1921		19	.227	.318	66	15	3	0	1	1.5	6	6	8	11	1	0	0	46	3	2	0	2.7	.961	OF-19
1925	NY N	39	.222	.272	81	18	1	0	1	1.2	12	5	9	11	1	7	1	45	3	2	1	2.4	.960	OF-21
5 yrs.		139	.214	.300	407	87	16	5	3	0.7	38	41	29	66	5	14	2	250	12	14	2	2.5	.949	OF-109

Gee Walker

WALKER, GERALD HOLMES BR TR 5′11″ 188 lbs.
Brother of Hub Walker.
B. Mar. 19, 1908, Gulfport, Miss. D. Mar. 20, 1981, Jackson, Miss.

Year	Team	Games	BA	SA	AB	H	2B	3B	HR	HR%	R	RBI	BB	SO	SB	Pinch Hit AB	Pinch Hit H	PO	A	E	DP	TC/G	FA	G by Pos
1931	DET A	59	.296	.423	189	56	17	2	1	0.5	20	28	14	21	10	9	4	99	2	5	1	2.4	.953	OF-44
1932		126	.323	.465	480	155	32	6	8	1.7	71	78	13	38	30	8	1	309	9	17	1	2.9	.949	OF-116
1933		127	.280	.424	483	135	29	7	9	1.9	68	64	15	49	26	12	2	234	10	15	3	2.3	.942	OF-113
1934		98	.300	.418	347	104	19	2	6	1.7	54	39	19	20	20	17	5	191	5	11	2	2.6	.947	OF-80
1935		98	.301	.453	362	109	22	6	7	1.9	52	53	15	21	6	14	7	204	2	10	1	2.5	.954	OF-85
1936		134	.353	.536	550	194	55	5	12	2.2	105	93	23	30	17	9	1	280	14	16	5	2.5	.948	OF-125
1937		151	.335	.499	635	213	42	4	18	2.8	105	113	41	74	23	0	0	316	9	15	2	2.3	.956	OF-151
1938	CHI A	120	.305	.493	442	135	23	6	16	3.6	69	87	38	32	9	12	4	197	9	9	2	2.0	.958	OF-107
1939		149	.291	.443	598	174	30	11	13	2.2	95	111	28	43	17	2	0	365	11	13	3	2.6	.967	OF-147
1940	WAS A	140	.294	.432	595	175	29	7	13	2.2	87	96	24	58	21	0	0	285	10	10	2	2.2	.967	OF-140
1941	CLE A	121	.283	.431	445	126	26	11	6	1.3	56	48	18	46	12	13	5	257	9	5	0	2.6	.982	OF-105
1942	CIN N	119	.230	.322	422	97	20	2	5	1.2	40	50	31	44	11	8	1	277	7	8	2	2.7	.973	OF-110
1943		114	.245	.329	429	105	23	2	3	0.7	48	54	12	38	6	6	1	231	8	5	3	2.3	.980	OF-106
1944		121	.278	.366	478	133	21	3	5	1.0	56	62	23	48	7	3	1	293	3	10	0	2.6	.967	OF-117
1945		106	.253	.320	316	80	11	2	2	0.6	28	21	16	38	8	35	9	127	7	7	1	2.0	.950	OF-67, 3B-3
15 yrs.		1783	.294	.430	6771	1991	399	76	124	1.8	954	997	330	600	223	148	41	3665	115	156	28	2.4	.960	OF-1613, 3B-3
WORLD SERIES																								
1934	DET A	3	.333	.333	3	1	0	0	0	0.0	0	1	0	1	0	3	1	0	0	0	0	0.0	—	
1935		3	.250	.250	4	1	0	0	0	0.0	1	0	1	0	0	2	0	0	0	0	0	0.0	.000	OF-1
2 yrs.		6	.286	.286	7	2	0	0	0	0.0	1	1	1	1	0	5	1	0	0	0	0	0.0		OF-1

Greg Walker

WALKER, GREGORY LEE BL TR 6′ 3″ 205 lbs.
B. Oct. 6, 1959, Douglas, Ga.

Year	Team	Games	BA	SA	AB	H	2B	3B	HR	HR%	R	RBI	BB	SO	SB	Pinch Hit AB	Pinch Hit H	PO	A	E	DP	TC/G	FA	G by Pos
1982	CHI A	11	.412	1.000	17	7	2	1	2	11.8	3	7	2	3	0	4	2	0	0	0	0	0.0	.000	DH-4
1983		118	.270	.440	307	83	16	3	10	3.3	32	55	28	57	2	35	13	426	19	7	40	5.7	.985	1B-59, DH-21
1984		136	.294	.532	442	130	29	2	24	5.4	62	75	35	66	8	16	3	791	51	4	66	6.9	.995	1B-101, DH-21
1985		163	.258	.454	601	155	38	4	24	4.0	77	92	44	100	5	9	3	1217	97	8	116	8.4	.994	1B-151, DH-7
1986		78	.277	.493	282	78	10	6	13	4.6	37	51	29	44	1	3	1	670	57	5	57	9.4	.993	1B-77, DH-1
1987		157	.256	.465	566	145	33	2	27	4.8	85	94	75	112	2	4	0	1402	80	9	135	9.5	.994	1B-154, DH-3
1988		99	.247	.374	377	93	22	1	8	2.1	45	42	29	77	0	1	0	935	41	7	93	10.0	.993	1B-98
1989		77	.210	.335	233	49	14	0	5	2.1	25	26	23	50	0	9	0	373	17	5	38	5.6	.987	1B-48, DH-23
1990	2 teams	CHI A (2G –.200) BAL A (14G –.147)																						
″	total	16	.154	.154	39	6	0	0	0	0.0	2	2	3	11	1	3	0	14	1	0	2	1.2	1.000	DH-12, 1B-1
9 yrs.		855	.260	.449	2864	746	164	19	113	3.9	368	444	268	520	19	84	22	5828	363	45	547	8.0	.993	1B-689, DH-92
LEAGUE CHAMPIONSHIP SERIES																								
1983	CHI A	2	.333	.333	3	1	0	0	0	0.0	0	0	1	2	0	1	0	8	0	0	2	8.0	1.000	1B-1

Harry Walker

WALKER, HARRY WILLIAM (The Hat) BL TR 6′ 2″ 175 lbs.
Brother of Dixie Walker. Son of Dixie Walker.
B. Oct. 22, 1916, Pascagoula, Miss.
Manager 1955, 1965–72.

Year	Team	Games	BA	SA	AB	H	2B	3B	HR	HR%	R	RBI	BB	SO	SB	Pinch Hit AB	Pinch Hit H	PO	A	E	DP	TC/G	FA	G by Pos
1940	STL N	7	.185	.259	27	5	2	0	0	0.0	2	6	0	2	0	0	0	21	2	0	0	3.3	1.000	OF-7
1941		7	.267	.333	15	4	1	0	0	0.0	3	1	2	1	0	0	0	7	0	1	0	1.6	.875	OF-5
1942		74	.314	.398	191	60	12	2	0	0.0	38	16	11	14	2	16	0	116	6	4	0	2.2	.968	OF-56, 2B-2
1943		148	.294	.376	564	166	28	6	2	0.4	76	53	40	24	5	4	1	322	14	13	4	2.4	.963	OF-144, 2B-1
1946		112	.237	.338	346	82	14	6	3	0.9	53	27	30	29	12	11	3	273	15	7	5	3.0	.976	OF-92, 1B-8
1947	2 teams	STL N (10G –.200) PHI N (130G –.371)																						
″	total	140	**.363**	.487	513	186	29	**16**	1	0.2	81	41	63	39	13	2	0	383	15	14	4	2.9	.966	OF-136, 1B-4
1948	PHI N	112	.292	.355	332	97	11	2	2	0.6	34	23	33	30	4	26	7	220	8	4	2	2.7	.983	OF-81, 1B-4, 3B-1
1949	2 teams	CHI N (42G –.264) CIN N (86G –.318)																						
″	total	128	.300	.378	473	142	21	5	2	0.4	73	37	45	23	6	11	2	246	10	11	1	2.3	.959	OF-116, 1B-1
1950	STL N	60	.207	.240	150	31	5	0	0	0.0	17	7	18	12	0	6	0	102	3	3	1	2.3	.972	OF-46, 1B-2
1951		8	.308	.346	26	8	1	0	0	0.0	6	2	2	1	0	0	0	20	1	0	2	3.0	1.000	OF-6, 1B-1
1955		11	.357	.500	14	5	2	0	0	0.0	2	1	1	0	0	9	4	2	1	0	1	3.0	1.000	OF-1
11 yrs.		807	.296	.383	2651	786	126	37	10	0.4	385	214	245	175	42	85	17	1712	75	57	20	2.6	.969	OF-690, 1B-20, 2B-3, 3B-1
WORLD SERIES																								
1942	STL N	1	.000	.000	1	0	0	0	0	0.0	0	0	0	1	0	1	0	0	0	0	0	0.0	—	
1943		5	.167	.222	18	3	1	0	0	0.0	0	0	0	2	0	1	1	10	0	2	0	2.4	.833	OF-5
1946		7	.412	.529	17	7	2	0	0	0.0	3	6	4	2	0	1	0	14	0	0	0	2.0	1.000	OF-7
3 yrs.		13	.278	.361	36	10	3	0	0	0.0	3	6	4	5	0	3	1	24	0	2	0	2.2	.923	OF-12

Hub Walker

WALKER, HARVEY WILLOS BL TR 5′10½″ 175 lbs.
Brother of Gee Walker.
B. Aug. 17, 1906, Gulfport, Miss. D. Nov. 26, 1982, San Jose, Calif.

Year	Team	Games	BA	SA	AB	H	2B	3B	HR	HR%	R	RBI	BB	SO	SB	Pinch Hit AB	Pinch Hit H	PO	A	E	DP	TC/G	FA	G by Pos
1931	DET A	90	.286	.345	252	72	13	1	0	0.0	27	16	23	25	10	12	2	170	4	7	1	2.7	.961	OF-66
1935		9	.160	.280	25	4	3	0	0	0.0	4	1	3	4	0	2	1	19	0	0	0	2.7	1.000	OF-7
1936	CIN N	92	.275	.399	258	71	18	1	4	1.6	49	23	35	32	8	13	1	162	4	5	2	2.3	.971	OF-73, 1B-1, C-1
1937		78	.249	.339	221	55	9	4	1	0.5	33	19	34	24	7	12	3	137	5	1	3	2.3	.993	OF-58, 2B-3
1945	DET A	28	.130	.130	23	3	0	0	0	0.0	4	1	9	4	1	15	1	5	0	0	0	0.7	1.000	OF-7
5 yrs.		297	.263	.353	779	205	43	6	5	0.6	117	60	104	89	26	54	8	493	13	13	6	2.4	.975	OF-211, 2B-3, 1B-1, C-1
WORLD SERIES																								
1945	DET A	2	.500	1.000	2	1	1	0	0	0.0	1	0	0	0	0	2	1	0	0	0	0	0.0	—	

Joe Walker

WALKER, JOSEPH RICHARD (Speed)
B. Jan. 23, 1898, Munhall, Pa. D. June 20, 1959, West Mifflin, Pa.
BR TR 6′ 170 lbs.

Year	Team	Games	BA	SA	AB	H	2B	3B	HR	HR%	R	RBI	BB	SO	SB	Pinch Hit AB	Pinch Hit H	PO	A	E	DP	TC/G	FA	G by Pos
1923	STL N	2	.286	.286	7	2	0	0	0	0.0	1	0	0	1	0	0	0	19	0	0	1	9.5	1.000	1B-2

Johnny Walker

WALKER, JOHN MILES
B. Dec. 11, 1896, Toulon, Ill. D. Aug. 19, 1976, Hollywood, Fla.
BR TR 6′ 175 lbs.

Year	Team	Games	BA	SA	AB	H	2B	3B	HR	HR%	R	RBI	BB	SO	SB	Pinch Hit AB	Pinch Hit H	PO	A	E	DP	TC/G	FA	G by Pos
1919	PHI A	3	.000	.000	9	0	0	0	0	0.0	0	0	0	2	0	0	0	15	1	1	0	5.7	.941	C-3
1920		9	.227	.273	22	5	1	0	0	0.0	0	5	0	1	0	3	1	20	4	1	0	4.2	.960	C-6
1921		113	.258	.329	423	109	14	5	2	0.5	41	45	9	29	5	7	2	1022	56	12	71	10.3	.989	1B-99, C-7
3 yrs.		125	.251	.319	454	114	15	5	2	0.4	41	50	9	32	5	10	3	1057	61	14	71	9.8	.988	1B-99, C-16

Larry Walker

WALKER, LARRY KENNETH ROBERT
B. Dec. 1, 1966, Maple Ridge, B. C., Canada.
BL TR 6′ 2″ 185 lbs.

Year	Team	Games	BA	SA	AB	H	2B	3B	HR	HR%	R	RBI	BB	SO	SB	Pinch Hit AB	Pinch Hit H	PO	A	E	DP	TC/G	FA	G by Pos
1989	MON N	20	.170	.170	47	8	0	0	0	0.0	4	4	5	13	1	7	0	19	2	0	1	1.4	1.000	OF-15
1990		133	.241	.434	419	101	18	3	19	4.5	59	51	49	112	21	11	1	249	12	4	5	2.1	.985	OF-124
1991		137	.290	.458	487	141	30	2	16	3.3	59	64	42	102	14	2	1	536	36	6	30	4.1	.990	OF-102, 1B-39
1992		143	.301	.506	528	159	31	4	23	4.4	85	93	41	97	18	3	1	269	16	2	2	2.1	.993	OF-139
1993		138	.265	.469	490	130	24	5	22	4.5	85	86	80	76	29	2	0	316	16	6	4	2.5	.982	OF-132, 1B-4
1994		103	.322	.587	395	127	**44**	2	19	4.8	76	86	47	74	15	1	0	423	29	9	21	4.5	.980	OF-68, 1B-35
1995	CLR N	131	.306	.607	494	151	31	5	36	7.3	96	101	49	72	16	1	1	225	13	3	0	1.9	.988	OF-129
7 yrs.		805	.286	.504	2860	817	178	21	135	4.7	464	485	313	546	114	27	4	2037	124	30	63	2.8	.986	OF-709, 1B-78
DIVISIONAL PLAYOFF SERIES																								
1995	CLR N	4	.214	.429	14	3	0	0	1	7.1	3	3	3	4	1	0	0	3	0	0	0	0.8	1.000	OF-4

Oscar Walker

WALKER, OSCAR
B. Mar. 18, 1854, Brooklyn, N. Y. D. May 20, 1889, Brooklyn, N. Y.
BL TL 5′10″ 166 lbs.

Year	Team	Games	BA	SA	AB	H	2B	3B	HR	HR%	R	RBI	BB	SO	SB	Pinch Hit AB	Pinch Hit H	PO	A	E	DP	TC/G	FA	G by Pos
1879	BUF N	72	.275	.380	287	79	15	6	1	0.3	35	35	8	38		0	0	828	30	49	52	12.6	.946	1B-72
1880		34	.230	.317	126	29	4	2	1	0.8	12	15	6	18		0	0	267	10	27	17	8.7	.911	1B-24, OF-11
1882	STL AA	76	.239	.396	318	76	15	7	**7**	**2.2**	48		10			0	0	172	18	32	5	2.9	.856	OF-75, 2B-1, 1B-1
1884	BKN AA	95	.270	.359	382	103	12	8	2	0.5	59		9			0	0	476	20	31	12	5.5	.941	OF-59, 1B-36
1885	BAL AA	4	.000	.000	13	0	0	0	0	0.0	1		0			0	0	4	0	2	0	1.5	.667	OF-4
5 yrs.		281	.255	.366	1126	287	46	23	11	1.0	155	50	33	56		0	0	1747	78	141	86	6.9	.928	OF-149, 1B-133, 2B-1

Rube Walker

WALKER, ALBERT BLUFORD
B. May 16, 1926, Lenoir, N. C. D. Dec. 12, 1992, Morganton, N. C.
BL TR 6′ 175 lbs.

Year	Team	Games	BA	SA	AB	H	2B	3B	HR	HR%	R	RBI	BB	SO	SB	Pinch Hit AB	Pinch Hit H	PO	A	E	DP	TC/G	FA	G by Pos
1948	CHI N	79	.275	.409	171	47	8	0	5	2.9	17	26	24	17	0	32	7	178	22	4	3	4.6	.980	C-44
1949		56	.244	.331	172	42	4	1	3	1.7	11	22	9	18	0	12	3	166	23	7	2	4.6	.964	C-43
1950		74	.230	.357	213	49	7	1	6	2.8	19	16	18	34	0	14	1	240	34	7	6	4.5	.975	C-62
1951	2 teams	CHI N (37G –.234) BKN N (36G –.243)																						
″	total	73	.238	.348	181	43	8	0	4	2.2	15	14	18	27	0	17	3	173	23	6	4	3.7	.970	C-54
1952	BKN N	46	.259	.338	139	36	8	0	1	0.7	9	19	8	17	0	6	1	217	16	3	2	5.9	.987	C-40
1953		43	.242	.400	95	23	6	0	3	3.2	5	9	7	11	0	14	5	120	12	3	2	4.8	.978	C-28
1954		50	.181	.323	155	28	7	0	5	3.2	12	23	24	17	0	3	0	259	19	1	4	5.9	.996	C-47
1955		48	.252	.359	103	26	5	0	2	1.9	6	13	15	11	1	10	2	147	10	2	3	4.5	.987	C-35
1956		54	.212	.329	146	31	6	1	3	2.1	5	20	7	18	0	9	2	184	20	3	4	4.8	.986	C-43
1957		60	.181	.265	166	30	8	0	2	1.2	12	23	15	33	2	10	3	230	20	2	3	5.0	.992	C-50
1958	LA N	25	.114	.227	44	5	2	0	1	2.3	3	7	5	10	0	5	1	62	5	1	1	3.4	.985	C-20
11 yrs.		608	.227	.341	1585	360	69	3	35	2.2	114	192	150	213	3	132	28	1976	204	39	34	4.8	.982	C-466
WORLD SERIES																								
1956	BKN N	2	.000	.000	2	0	0	0	0	0.0	0	0	0	0	0	2	0	0	0	0	0	0.0	—	

Tilly Walker

WALKER, CLARENCE WILLIAM
B. Sept. 4, 1887, Telford, Tenn. D. Sept. 21, 1959, Unicoi, Tenn.
BR TR 5′11″ 165 lbs.

Year	Team	Games	BA	SA	AB	H	2B	3B	HR	HR%	R	RBI	BB	SO	SB	Pinch Hit AB	Pinch Hit H	PO	A	E	DP	TC/G	FA	G by Pos
1911	WAS A	95	.278	.334	356	99	6	4	2	0.6	44	39	15		12	0	0	163	14	16	1	2.1	.917	OF-94
1912		36	.273	.309	110	30	2	1	0	0.0	22	9	8		11	4	0	37	6	8	3	1.6	.843	OF-31, 2B-1
1913	STL A	23	.294	.365	85	25	4	1	0	0.0	7	11	2	9	5	0	0	36	5	4	0	2.0	.911	OF-23
1914		151	.298	.441	517	154	24	16	6	1.2	67	78	51	72	29	5	2	311	30	10	5	2.4	.972	OF-145
1915		144	.269	.365	510	137	20	7	5	1.0	53	49	36	77	20	4	2	333	27	23	5	2.8	.940	OF-139
1916	BOS A	128	.266	.394	467	124	29	11	3	0.6	68	46	23	45	14	0	0	290	12	13	4	2.5	.959	OF-128
1917		106	.246	.359	337	83	18	7	2	0.6	41	37	25	38	6	9	3	225	20	7	7	2.6	.972	OF-96
1918	PHI A	114	.295	.423	414	122	20	0	**11**	2.7	56	48	41	44	8	5	2	242	25	13	4	2.6	.954	OF-109
1919		125	.292	.450	456	133	30	6	10	2.2	47	64	26	41	8	7	2	253	13	19	4	2.5	.933	OF-115
1920		149	.268	.419	585	157	23	7	17	2.9	79	82	40	59	9	0	0	318	26	22	5	2.5	.940	OF-149
1921		142	.304	.504	556	169	32	5	23	4.1	89	101	73	41	3	0	0	337	24	17	3	2.7	.955	OF-142
1922		153	.283	.549	565	160	31	4	37	6.5	111	99	61	64	4	3	0	309	19	15	4	2.3	.956	OF-148
1923		52	.275	.413	109	30	5	2	2	1.8	12	16	14	11	1	22	6	52	1	0	1	2.0	1.000	OF-26
13 yrs.		1418	.281	.427	5067	1423	244	71	118	2.3	696	679	415	501	130	59	17	2906	222	167	46	2.4	.949	OF-1345, 2B-1
WORLD SERIES																								
1916	BOS A	3	.273	.455	11	3	0	1	0	0.0	1	1	1	2	0	0	0	4	1	0	0	1.7	1.000	OF-3

Tony Walker

WALKER, ANTHONY BRUCE
B. July 1, 1959, San Diego, Calif.
BR TR 6′ 2″ 205 lbs.

Year	Team	Games	BA	SA	AB	H	2B	3B	HR	HR%	R	RBI	BB	SO	SB	Pinch Hit AB	Pinch Hit H	PO	A	E	DP	TC/G	FA	G by Pos
1986	HOU N	84	.222	.367	90	20	7	0	2	2.2	19	10	11	15	11	7	1	73	0	1	0	1.1	.986	OF-68

Wallie Walker

WALKER, WALTER S.
B. May 12, 1860, Berlin, Mich. D. Feb. 28, 1922, Pontiac, Mich.
TR 5′10½″ 162 lbs.

Year	Team	Games	BA	SA	AB	H	2B	3B	HR	HR%	R	RBI	BB	SO	SB	Pinch Hit AB	Pinch Hit H	PO	A	E	DP	TC/G	FA	G by Pos
1884	DET N	1	.250	.250	4	1	0	0	0	0.0	1		0			0	0	5	1	2	0	8.0	.750	C-1

Welday Walker

WALKER, WELDAY WILBERFORCE
Brother of Fleet Walker.
B. July 27, 1860, Steubenville, Ohio D. Nov. 23, 1937, Steubenville, Ohio.

Year	Team	Games	BA	SA	AB	H	2B	3B	HR	HR%	R	RBI	BB	SO	SB	Pinch Hit AB	Pinch Hit H	PO	A	E	DP	TC/G	FA	G by Pos
1884	TOL AA	5	.222	.278	18	4	1	0	0	0.0	1		0			0	0	4	0	2	0	1.2	.667	OF-5

Joe Wall

WALL, JOSEPH FRANCIS (Gummy)
B. July 24, 1873, Brooklyn, N. Y. D. July 17, 1936, Brooklyn, N. Y.
BL TL

Year	Team	Games	BA	SA	AB	H	2B	3B	HR	HR%	R	RBI	BB	SO	SB	Pinch Hit AB	Pinch Hit H	PO	A	E	DP	TC/G	FA	G by Pos
1901	NY N	4	.500	.500	8	4	0	0	0	0.0	0	1	0		0	1	1	3	0	0	0	1.0	1.000	C-2, OF-1
1902	2 teams	NY N (6G –.357) BKN N (5G –.167)																						
"	total	11	.250	.313	32	8	2	0	0	0.0	2	0	5		0	3	1	23	4	3	0	3.8	.900	C-5, OF-3
2 yrs.		15	.300	.350	40	12	2	0	0	0.0	2	1	5		0	4	2	26	4	3	0	3.0	.909	C-7, OF-4

Bobby Wallace

WALLACE, RHODERICK JOHN (Rhody)
B. Nov. 4, 1873, Pittsburgh, Pa. D. Nov. 3, 1960, Torrance, Calif.
Manager 1911–12, 1937.
Hall of Fame 1953.
BR TR 5′ 8″ 170 lbs.

Year	Team	Games	BA	SA	AB	H	2B	3B	HR	HR%	R	RBI	BB	SO	SB	Pinch Hit AB	Pinch Hit H	PO	A	E	DP	TC/G	FA	G by Pos
1894	CLE N	4	.154	.231	13	2	1	0	0	0.0	0	1	0	1	0	0	0	3	9	0	0	3.0	1.000	P-4
1895		30	.214	.296	98	21	2	3	0	0.0	16	10	6	17	0	0	0	15	66	8	2	3.0	.910	P-30
1896		45	.235	.336	149	35	6	3	1	0.7	19	17	11	21	2	0	0	44	35	5	4	1.8	.940	OF-23, P-22, 1B-1
1897		131	.335	.504	516	173	33	21	4	0.8	99	112	48		14	0	0	191	250	35	10	3.6	.926	3B-130, OF-1
1898		154	.270	.371	593	160	25	13	3	0.5	81	99	63		7	0	0	248	365	39	23	4.2	.940	3B-141, 2B-13
1899	STL N	151	.295	.454	577	170	28	14	12	2.1	91	108	54		17	0	0	322	536	73	53	6.1	.922	SS-100, 3B-52
1900		126	.268	.381	485	130	25	9	4	0.8	72	70	40		7	0	0	329	449	55	31	6.6	.934	SS-126, 3B-1
1901		135	.322	.448	556	179	34	15	2	0.4	69	91	20		15	0	0	326	542	66	67	7.0	.929	SS-134
1902	STL A	133	.287	.394	495	142	32	9	1	0.2	71	63	45		18	1	0	301	475	42	64	6.2	.949	SS-131, OF-1, P-1
1903		136	.245	.356	519	127	21	17	1	0.2	63	54	28		10	0	0	282	468	62	53	6.0	.924	SS-135
1904		139	.273	.351	550	150	29	4	2	0.4	57	69	42		20	0	0	303	482	44	37	6.0	.947	SS-139
1905		156	.271	.349	587	159	25	9	1	0.2	67	59	45		13	0	0	385	506	62	40	6.1	.935	SS-156
1906		139	.258	.345	476	123	21	7	2	0.4	64	67	58		24	1	1	309	461	41	47	5.9	.949	SS-138
1907		147	.257	.320	538	138	20	7	0	0.0	56	70	54		16	0	0	338	517	54	54	6.2	.941	SS-147
1908		137	.253	.324	487	123	24	4	1	0.2	59	60	52		5	0	0	286	510	41	45	6.1	.951	SS-137
1909		116	.238	.285	403	96	12	2	1	0.2	36	35	38		7	0	0	242	336	32	39	5.3	.948	SS-87, 3B-29
1910		138	.258	.323	508	131	19	7	0	0.0	47	37	49		12	0	0	316	444	43	43	5.8	.946	SS-98, 3B-40
1911		125	.232	.271	410	95	12	2	0	0.0	35	31	46		8	0	0	282	417	42	49	5.9	.943	SS-124, 2B-1
1912		99	.241	.316	323	78	14	5	0	0.0	39	31	43		3	1	0	210	296	31	35	5.5	.942	SS-86, 3B-10, 2B-2
1913		53	.211	.245	147	31	5	0	0	0.0	11	21	14	16	1	7	0	75	119	12	8	4.6	.942	SS-38, 3B-7
1914		26	.219	.274	73	16	2	1	0	0.0	3	5	5	13	1	5	1	27	49	9	2	4.0	.894	SS-19, 3B-2
1915		9	.231	.385	13	3	0	1	0	0.0	1	4	5	0	0	0	0	11	17	5	4	3.7	.848	SS-9
1916		14	.278	.278	18	5	0	0	0	0.0	0	1	2	1	0	0	0	8	27	2	1	2.6	.946	3B-9, SS-5
1917	STL N	8	.100	.100	10	1	0	0	0	0.0	0	2	0	1	0	3	1	5	6	1	0	1.7	.917	3B-5, SS-2
1918		32	.153	.163	98	15	1	0	0	0.0	3	4	6	9	1	3	2	61	83	10	13	5.1	.935	2B-17, SS-12, 3B-1
25 yrs.		2383	.266	.359	8642	2303	391	153	35	0.4	1059	1121	774	79	201	21	5	4919	7465	814	724	5.6	.938	SS-1823, 3B-427, P-57, 2B-33, OF-25, 1B-1

Doc Wallace

WALLACE, FREDERICK RENSHAW
B. Sept. 30, 1893, Church Hill, Md. D. Dec. 31, 1964, Haverford, Pa.
BR TR 5′ 6½″ 135 lbs.

Year	Team	Games	BA	SA	AB	H	2B	3B	HR	HR%	R	RBI	BB	SO	SB	Pinch Hit AB	Pinch Hit H	PO	A	E	DP	TC/G	FA	G by Pos
1919	PHI N	2	.250	.250	4	1	0	0	0	0.0	0	0	0	1	0	0	0	3	4	1	0	4.0	.875	SS-2

Don Wallace

WALLACE, DONALD ALLEN
B. Aug. 25, 1940, Sapulpa, Okla.
BL TR 5′ 8″ 165 lbs.

Year	Team	Games	BA	SA	AB	H	2B	3B	HR	HR%	R	RBI	BB	SO	SB	Pinch Hit AB	Pinch Hit H	PO	A	E	DP	TC/G	FA	G by Pos
1967	CAL A	23	.000	.000	6	0	0	0	0	0.0	2	0	3	2	0	3	0	4	3	0	1	1.2	1.000	2B-4, 3B-1, 1B-1

Jack Wallace

WALLACE, CLARENCE EUGENE
B. Aug. 6, 1890, Winnfield, La. D. Oct. 15, 1960, Winnfield, La.
BR TR 5′10½″ 175 lbs.

Year	Team	Games	BA	SA	AB	H	2B	3B	HR	HR%	R	RBI	BB	SO	SB	Pinch Hit AB	Pinch Hit H	PO	A	E	DP	TC/G	FA	G by Pos
1915	CHI N	2	.286	.286	7	2	0	0	0	0.0	1	1	0	2	0	0	0	13	6	0	0	9.5	1.000	C-2

Jim Wallace

WALLACE, JAMES L.
B. Nov. 14, 1881, Boston, Mass. D. May 16, 1953, Revere, Mass.
BL TL 5′ 9″ 150 lbs.

Year	Team	Games	BA	SA	AB	H	2B	3B	HR	HR%	R	RBI	BB	SO	SB	Pinch Hit AB	Pinch Hit H	PO	A	E	DP	TC/G	FA	G by Pos
1905	PIT N	7	.207	.241	29	6	1	0	0	0.0	3	3	3		2	0	0	10	3	1	0	2.0	.929	OF-7

Tim Wallach

WALLACH, TIMOTHY CHARLES
B. Sept. 14, 1957, Huntington Park, Calif.
BR TR 6′ 3″ 220 lbs.

Year	Team	Games	BA	SA	AB	H	2B	3B	HR	HR%	R	RBI	BB	SO	SB	Pinch Hit AB	Pinch Hit H	PO	A	E	DP	TC/G	FA	G by Pos
1980	MON N	5	.182	.455	11	2	0	0	1	9.1	1	2	1	5	0	2	0	12	0	0	0	3.0	1.000	OF-3, 1B-1
1981		71	.236	.344	212	50	9	1	4	1.9	19	13	15	37	0	6	1	207	31	1	9	3.6	.996	OF-35, 1B-16, 3B-15
1982		158	.268	.471	596	160	31	3	28	4.7	89	97	36	81	6	3	1	132	287	23	23	2.8	.948	3B-156, OF-2, 1B-1
1983		156	.269	.434	581	156	33	3	19	3.3	54	70	55	97	0	0	0	151	265	19	25	2.8	.956	3B-156
1984		160	.246	.395	582	143	25	4	18	3.1	55	72	50	101	3	0	0	162	332	21	29	3.2	.959	3B-160, SS-1
1985		155	.260	.450	569	148	36	3	22	3.9	70	81	38	79	9	2	0	148	383	18	34	3.6	.967	3B-154
1986		134	.233	.396	480	112	22	1	18	3.8	50	71	44	72	8	1	0	94	270	16	26	2.9	.958	3B-132
1987		153	.298	.514	593	177	**42**	4	26	4.4	89	123	37	98	9	3	0	128	292	21	21	2.9	.952	3B-150, P-1
1988		159	.257	.389	592	152	32	5	12	2.0	52	69	38	88	2	8	2	124	329	18	32	3.1	.962	3B-153, 2B-1
1989		154	.277	.419	573	159	**42**	0	13	2.3	76	77	58	81	3	1	1	113	302	18	20	2.8	.958	3B-153, P-1
1990		161	.296	.471	626	185	37	5	21	3.4	69	98	42	80	6	0	0	128	309	21	23	2.8	.954	3B-161
1991		151	.225	.334	577	130	22	1	13	2.3	60	73	50	100	2	0	0	107	310	14	27	2.9	.968	3B-149
1992		150	.223	.331	537	120	29	1	9	1.7	53	59	50	90	2	3	0	689	244	15	59	6.1	.984	3B-85, 1B-71
1993	LA N	133	.222	.342	477	106	19	1	12	2.5	42	62	32	70	0	5	0	121	229	15	15	2.8	.959	3B-130, 1B-1
1994		113	.280	.502	414	116	21	1	23	5.6	68	78	46	80	0	1	0	81	174	11	9	2.4	.959	3B-113
1995		97	.266	.428	327	87	22	2	9	2.8	24	38	27	69	0	1	0	61	156	5	9	2.3	.977	3B-96, 1B-1
16 yrs.		2110	.259	.418	7747	2003	422	35	248	3.2	871	1083	619	1228	50	36	5	2458	3913	236	361	3.1	.964	3B-1963, 1B-91, OF-40, P-2, 2B-1, SS-1
DIVISIONAL PLAYOFF SERIES																								
1981	MON N	4	.250	.500	4	1	1	0	0	0.0	1	0	4	0	0	0	0	4	0	0	0	1.3	1.000	OF-3
1995	LA N	3	.083	.083	12	1	0	0	0	0.0	0	0	1	3	0	0	0	1	2	0	0	1.0	1.000	3B-3
2 yrs.		7	.125	.188	16	2	1	0	0	0.0	1	0	5	3	0	0	0	5	2	0	0	1.2	1.000	3B-3, OF-3
LEAGUE CHAMPIONSHIP SERIES																								
1981	MON N	1	.000	.000	1	0	0	0	0	0.0	0	0	0	0	0	1	0	0	0	0	0	0.0	—	

Jack Wallaesa

WALLAESA, JOHN
B. Aug. 31, 1919, Easton, Pa. D. Dec. 27, 1986, Easton, Pa.
BB TR 6′ 3″ 191 lbs.
BR 1940

Year	Team	Games	BA	SA	AB	H	2B	3B	HR	HR%	R	RBI	BB	SO	SB	Pinch Hit AB	Pinch Hit H	PO	A	E	DP	TC/G	FA	G by Pos
1940	PHI A	6	.150	.150	20	3	0	0	0	0.0	0	2	0	2	0	0	0	9	19	3	3	5.2	.903	SS-6
1942		36	.256	.359	117	30	4	1	2	1.7	13	13	1	26	0	0	0	62	76	12	16	4.2	.920	SS-36
1946		63	.196	.314	194	38	4	2	5	2.6	16	11	14	47	1	3	1	111	130	22	31	4.5	.916	SS-59
1947	CHI A	81	.195	.351	205	40	9	1	7	3.4	25	32	23	51	2	27	4	130	96	5	22	4.6	.978	SS-27, OF-22, 3B-1
1948		33	.188	.250	48	9	0	0	1	2.1	2	3	1	12	0	27	6	11	17	0	5	4.7	1.000	SS-5, OF-1
5 yrs.		219	.205	.325	584	120	17	4	15	2.6	56	61	39	138	3	57	11	323	338	42	77	4.5	.940	SS-133, OF-23, 3B-1

Norm Wallen

WALLEN, NORMAN EDWARD
Born Norman Edward Walentoski.
B. Feb. 13, 1917, Milwaukee, Wis.
BR TR 5′11½″ 175 lbs.

Year	Team	Games	BA	SA	AB	H	2B	3B	HR	HR%	R	RBI	BB	SO	SB	Pinch Hit AB	Pinch Hit H	PO	A	E	DP	TC/G	FA	G by Pos
1945	BOS N	4	.133	.267	15	2	0	1	0	0.0	1	1	1	1	0	0	0	3	5	2	0	2.5	.800	3B-4

Tye Waller

WALLER, ELLIOTT TYRONE
B. Mar. 14, 1957, Fresno, Calif.
BR TR 6′ 180 lbs.

Year	Team	Games	BA	SA	AB	H	2B	3B	HR	HR%	R	RBI	BB	SO	SB	Pinch Hit AB	Pinch Hit H	PO	A	E	DP	TC/G	FA	G by Pos
1980	STL N	5	.083	.083	12	1	0	0	0	0.0	3	0	1	5	0	0	0	1	2	0	0	0.6	1.000	3B-5
1981	CHI N	30	.268	.451	71	19	2	1	3	4.2	10	13	4	18	2	1	1	18	35	1	2	1.9	.981	3B-22, OF-3, 2B-3
1982		17	.238	.238	21	5	0	0	0	0.0	4	1	2	5	0	6	2	10	1	1	0	1.5	.917	OF-7, 3B-1
1987	HOU N	11	.167	.333	6	1	1	0	0	0.0	1	0	0	3	0	4	1	2	0	0	0	0.7	1.000	OF-3
4 yrs.		63	.236	.364	110	26	3	1	3	2.7	18	14	7	31	2	11	4	31	38	2	2	1.6	.972	3B-28, OF-13, 2B-3

Denny Walling

WALLING, DENNIS MARTIN
B. Apr. 17, 1954, Neptune, N. J.
BL TR 6′ 180 lbs.

Year	Team	Games	BA	SA	AB	H	2B	3B	HR	HR%	R	RBI	BB	SO	SB	Pinch Hit AB	Pinch Hit H	PO	A	E	DP	TC/G	FA	G by Pos
1975	OAK A	6	.125	.250	8	1	1	0	0	0.0	0	2	0	4	0	4	1	3	0	0	0	1.0	1.000	OF-3
1976		3	.273	.273	11	3	0	0	0	0.0	1	0	0	3	0	0	0	8	0	1	0	3.0	.889	OF-3
1977	HOU N	6	.286	.381	21	6	0	1	0	0.0	1	6	2	4	0	1	1	14	0	0	0	2.8	1.000	OF-5
1978		120	.251	.356	247	62	11	3	3	1.2	30	36	30	24	9	39	10	140	4	3	2	1.9	.980	OF-78
1979		82	.327	.497	147	48	8	4	3	2.0	21	31	17	21	3	37	14	65	2	1	0	1.6	.985	OF-42
1980		100	.299	.387	284	85	6	5	3	1.1	30	29	35	26	4	21	4	525	31	6	46	6.9	.989	1B-63, OF-19
1981		65	.234	.367	158	37	6	0	5	3.2	23	23	28	17	2	18	6	226	9	2	18	4.4	.992	OF-27, 1B-27
1982		85	.205	.267	146	30	4	1	1	0.7	22	14	23	19	4	30	6	167	11	1	8	3.4	.994	OF-32, 1B-20
1983		100	.296	.444	135	40	5	3	3	2.2	24	19	15	16	2	37	8	134	29	6	13	2.5	.964	1B-42, OF-13, 3B-13
1984		87	.281	.402	249	70	11	5	3	1.2	37	31	16	28	7	26	7	116	102	7	21	3.0	.969	3B-52, 1B-16, OF-6
1985		119	.270	.394	345	93	20	1	7	2.0	44	45	25	26	5	23	2	326	124	12	31	4.2	.974	3B-51, 1B-46, OF-13
1986		130	.312	.479	382	119	23	1	13	3.4	54	58	36	31	1	31	12	108	161	9	8	2.4	.968	3B-102, OF-11, 1B-4
1987		110	.283	.418	325	92	21	4	5	1.5	45	33	39	37	5	15	8	175	119	10	21	3.0	.967	3B-79, 1B-16, OF-7
1988	2 teams	HOU N (65G –.244) STL N (19G –.224)																						
″	total	84	.239	.325	234	56	13	2	1	0.4	22	21	17	25	2	20	3	73	112	9	17	2.7	.954	3B-56, OF-12, 1B-4
1989	STL N	69	.304	.430	79	24	7	0	1	1.3	9	11	14	12	0	32	11	67	9	4	4	2.3	.950	1B-20, 3B-9, OF-6
1990		78	.220	.283	127	28	5	0	1	0.8	7	19	8	15	0	46	11	103	26	0	5	3.8	1.000	1B-15, 3B-11, OF-8
1991	TEX A	24	.091	.114	44	4	1	0	0	0.0	1	2	3	8	0	10	3	10	13	1	0	1.3	.958	3B-14, OF-5
1992	HOU N	3	.333	.333	3	1	0	0	0	0.0	1	0	0	0	0	3	1	0	0	0	0	0.0	—	
18 yrs.		1271	.271	.390	2945	799	142	30	49	1.7	372	380	308	316	44	393	108 **8th**	2260	752	72	194	3.2	.977	3B-387, OF-290, 1B-273
DIVISIONAL PLAYOFF SERIES																								
1981	HOU N	3	.333	.333	6	2	0	0	0	0.0	0	1	0	1	0	1	1	6	1	1	0	4.0	.875	OF-1, 1B-1
LEAGUE CHAMPIONSHIP SERIES																								
1980	HOU N	3	.111	.111	9	1	0	0	0	0.0	2	2	1	0	0	1	0	6	0	0	0	2.0	1.000	OF-2, 1B-1
1986		5	.158	.211	19	3	1	0	0	0.0	1	2	0	4	0	2	1	3	6	0	0	1.8	1.000	3B-5
2 yrs.		8	.143	.179	28	4	1	0	0	0.0	3	4	1	4	0	3	1	9	6	0	0	1.9	1.000	3B-5, OF-2, 1B-1

Joe Wallis

WALLIS, HAROLD JOSEPH (Tarzan)
B. Jan. 9, 1952, East St. Louis, Ill.
BB TR 5′10″ 185 lbs.

Year	Team	Games	BA	SA	AB	H	2B	3B	HR	HR%	R	RBI	BB	SO	SB	Pinch Hit AB	Pinch Hit H	PO	A	E	DP	TC/G	FA	G by Pos
1975	CHI N	16	.286	.446	56	16	2	2	1	1.8	9	4	5	14	2	3	1	31	1	0	0	2.1	1.000	OF-15
1976		121	.254	.361	338	86	11	5	5	1.5	51	21	33	62	3	26	4	193	11	5	3	2.3	.976	OF-90
1977		56	.250	.362	80	20	3	0	2	2.5	14	8	16	25	0	16	2	36	2	1	0	1.1	.974	OF-35
1978	2 teams	CHI N (28G –.309) OAK A (85G –.237)																						
″	total	113	.249	.377	334	83	18	2	7	2.1	35	32	31	55	1	10	2	223	8	4	5	2.2	.983	OF-105, DH-1
1979	OAK A	23	.141	.205	78	11	2	0	1	1.3	6	3	10	18	1	0	0	41	1	0	0	1.8	1.000	OF-23
5 yrs.		329	.244	.359	886	216	36	9	16	1.8	115	68	95	174	7	55	9	524	23	10	8	2.1	.982	OF-268, DH-1

Lee Walls

WALLS, RAY LEE
B. Jan. 6, 1933, San Diego, Calif. D. Oct. 11, 1993, Los Angeles, Calif.
BR TR 6′ 3″ 205 lbs.

Year	Team	Games	BA	SA	AB	H	2B	3B	HR	HR%	R	RBI	BB	SO	SB	Pinch Hit AB	Pinch Hit H	PO	A	E	DP	TC/G	FA	G by Pos
1952	PIT N	32	.188	.287	80	15	0	1	2	2.5	6	5	8	22	0	10	1	44	2	0	1	2.4	1.000	OF-19
1956		143	.274	.432	474	130	20	11	11	2.3	72	54	50	83	3	10	1	284	11	11	1	2.3	.964	OF-133, 3B-1
1957	2 teams	PIT N (8G –.182) CHI N (117G –.240)																						
″	total	125	.237	.338	388	92	11	5	6	1.5	45	33	29	72	6	22	8	188	7	3	0	1.9	.985	OF-101, 3B-1
1958	CHI N	136	.304	.493	513	156	19	3	24	4.7	80	72	47	62	4	4	2	241	10	2	1	1.9	.992	OF-132
1959		120	.257	.393	354	91	18	3	8	2.3	43	33	42	73	0	4	0	203	1	7	0	1.8	.967	OF-119
1960	2 teams	CIN N (29G –.274) PHI N (65G –.199)																						
″	total	94	.223	.325	265	59	9	3	4	1.5	31	26	31	52	5	20	5	130	51	8	10	2.4	.958	OF-37, 3B-34, 1B-9
1961	PHI N	91	.280	.425	261	73	6	4	8	3.1	32	30	19	48	2	19	4	247	59	8	33	4.4	.975	1B-28, 3B-26, OF-18
1962	LA N	60	.266	.312	109	29	3	1	0	0.0	9	17	10	21	1	27	13	98	12	2	4	3.5	.982	OF-17, 1B-11, 3B-4
1963		64	.233	.349	86	20	1	0	3	3.5	12	11	7	25	0	39	7	55	12	1	3	2.7	.985	OF-18, 1B-5, 3B-2
1964		37	.179	.214	28	5	1	0	0	0.0	1	3	2	12	0	28	5	1	0	0	0	0.1	1.000	OF-6, C-1
10 yrs.		902	.262	.398	2558	670	88	31	66	2.6	331	284	245	470	21	183	46	1491	165	42	53	2.4	.975	OF-600, 3B-68, 1B-53, C-1

Austin Walsh

WALSH, AUSTIN EDWARD
B. Sept. 1, 1891, Cambridge, Mass. D. Jan. 26, 1955, Glendale, Calif.
BL TL 5′11″ 175 lbs.

Year	Team	Games	BA	SA	AB	H	2B	3B	HR	HR%	R	RBI	BB	SO	SB	Pinch Hit AB	Pinch Hit H	PO	A	E	DP	TC/G	FA	G by Pos
1914	CHI F	57	.240	.331	121	29	6	1	1	0.8	14	10	4		0	22	3	0	0	0	0	0.0	.000	OF-30

Dee Walsh

WALSH, LEO THOMAS BB TR 5′ 9½″ 165 lbs.
B. Mar. 28, 1890, St. Louis, Mo. D. July 14, 1971, St. Louis, Mo.

Year	Team		Games	BA	SA	AB	H	2B	3B	HR	HR%	R	RBI	BB	SO	SB	Pinch Hit AB	Pinch Hit H	PO	A	E	DP	TC/G	FA	G by Pos
1913	STL	A	23	.170	.208	53	9	0	1	0	0.0	8	5	6	11	3	0	0	36	63	7	6	4.6	.934	SS-22, 3B-1
1914			7	.087	.087	23	2	0	0	0	0.0	1	1	2	4	1	0	0	14	20	3	5	5.3	.919	SS-7
1915			59	.220	.253	150	33	5	0	0	0.0	13	6	14	25	6	4	1	71	21	6	0	2.0	.939	OF-45, 3B-2, P-1, SS-1, 2B-1
3 yrs.			89	.195	.226	226	44	5	1	0	0.0	22	12	22	40	10	4	1	121	104	16	11	3.0	.934	OF-45, SS-30, 3B-3, P-1, 2B-1

Ed Walsh

WALSH, EDWARD AUGUSTINE (Big Ed) BR TR 6′ 1″ 193 lbs.
Father of Ed Walsh.
B. May 14, 1881, Plains, Pa. D. May 26, 1959, Pompano Beach, Fla.
Manager 1924.
Hall of Fame 1946.

Year	Team		Games	BA	SA	AB	H	2B	3B	HR	HR%	R	RBI	BB	SO	SB	Pinch Hit AB	Pinch Hit H	PO	A	E	DP	TC/G	FA	G by Pos
1904	CHI	A	18	.220	.366	41	9	1	1	1	2.4	5	4	3		1	0	0	8	35	1	2	2.4	.977	P-18
1905			29	.155	.190	58	9	2	0	0	0.0	5	2	4		0	2	0	13	42	2	1	2.1	.965	P-22, OF-5
1906			42	.141	.212	99	14	3	2	0	0.0	12	4	3		0	1	0	30	108	6	2	3.5	.958	P-41
1907			57	.162	.247	154	25	6	2	1	0.6	7	10	0		2	1	0	35	227	4	2	4.8	.985	P-56
1908			66	.172	.248	157	27	7	1	1	0.6	10	10	7		2	0	0	41	190	6	9	3.6	.975	P-66
1909			32	.214	.274	84	18	5	0	0	0.0	5	11	6		4	0	0	23	93	1	2	3.7	.991	P-31, OF-1
1910			52	.217	.283	138	30	3	3	0	0.0	12	4	5		5	7	1	21	154	9	5	4.1	.951	P-45
1911			62	.206	.226	155	32	3	0	0	0.0	22	9	1		0	7	2	27	159	8	5	3.5	.959	P-56
1912			64	.243	.287	136	33	4	1	0	0.0	12	12	14		0	2	1	22	143	15	3	2.9	.917	P-62
1913			17	.156	.188	32	5	1	0	0	0.0	1	2	1	7	0	1	0	6	32	3	1	2.6	.927	P-16
1914			10	.063	.125	16	1	1	0	0	0.0	0	0	1	4	0	2	0	7	15	1	0	2.9	.957	P-8
1915			5	.364	.364	11	4	0	0	0	0.0	0	1	0	1	0	2	1	3	4	0	0	2.3	1.000	P-3
1916			2	—	—	0	0	0	0	0	—	0	0	0	0	0	0	0	0	2	0	0	1.0	1.000	P-2
1917	BOS	N	4	.250	.250	4	1	0	0	0	0.0	1	0	1	2	0	0	0	1	7	1	0	2.3	.889	P-4
14 yrs.			460	.192	.252	1085	208	36	10	3	0.3	92	69	46	14	14	25	5	237	1211	57	32	3.5	.962	P-430, OF-6
WORLD SERIES																									
1906	CHI	A	2	.000	.000	4	0	0	0	0	0.0	1	0	3	3	0	0	0	0	5	1	0	3.0	.833	P-2

Jimmy Walsh

WALSH, JAMES CHARLES BL TR 5′10½″ 170 lbs.
B. Sept. 22, 1885, Killala, Ireland D. July 3, 1962, Syracuse, N. Y.

Year	Team		Games	BA	SA	AB	H	2B	3B	HR	HR%	R	RBI	BB	SO	SB	Pinch Hit AB	Pinch Hit H	PO	A	E	DP	TC/G	FA	G by Pos
1912	PHI	A	31	.252	.364	107	27	8	2	0	0.0	11	15	12		7	1	0	70	1	4	1	2.5	.947	OF-30
1913			94	.254	.340	303	77	16	5	0	0.0	56	27	38	40	15	4	1	184	11	8	4	2.3	.961	OF-88
1914	2 teams		NY A (43G –.191) PHI A (67G –.236)																						
″	total		110	.219	.338	352	77	12	9	4	1.1	48	47	59	48	12	6	1	221	20	9	6	2.4	.964	OF-97, 1B-3, 3B-3, SS-1
1915	PHI	A	117	.206	.278	417	86	15	6	1	0.2	48	20	57	64	22	3	0	240	16	6	1	2.3	.977	OF-109, 3B-2, 1B-1
1916	2 teams		PHI A (114G –.233) BOS A (13G –.125)																						
″	total		127	.229	.298	406	93	13	6	1	0.2	47	29	58	38	30	4	0	185	16	12	4	1.7	.944	OF-119, 3B-2, 1B-1
1917	BOS	A	57	.265	.330	185	49	6	3	0	0.0	25	12	25	14	6	7	2	103	8	2	0	2.4	.982	OF-47
6 yrs.			536	.231	.316	1770	409	70	31	6	0.3	235	150	249	204	92	25	4	1003	72	41	16	2.2	.963	OF-490, 3B-7, 1B-5, SS-1
WORLD SERIES																									
1914	PHI	A	3	.333	.500	6	2	1	0	0	0.0	0	1	3	1	0	0	0	2	0	0	0	1.0	1.000	OF-2
1916	BOS	A	1	.000	.000	3	0	0	0	0	0.0	0	0	0	0	0	0	0	1	0	0	0	1.0	1.000	OF-1
2 yrs.			4	.222	.333	9	2	1	0	0	0.0	0	1	3	1	0	0	0	3	0	0	0	1.0	1.000	OF-3

Jimmy Walsh

WALSH, MICHAEL TIMOTHY (Runt) BR TR 5′ 9″ 174 lbs.
B. Mar. 25, 1886, Lima, Ohio D. Jan. 21, 1947, Baltimore, Md.

Year	Team		Games	BA	SA	AB	H	2B	3B	HR	HR%	R	RBI	BB	SO	SB	Pinch Hit AB	Pinch Hit H	PO	A	E	DP	TC/G	FA	G by Pos
1910	PHI	N	88	.248	.343	242	60	8	3	3	1.2	28	31	25	38	5	20	3	122	101	23	11	3.7	.907	OF-27, 2B-26, SS-9, 3B-5
1911			94	.270	.370	289	78	20	3	1	0.3	29	31	21	30	5	10	2	148	79	12	14	2.8	.950	OF-48, 2B-14, SS-9, 3B-7, C-4, P-1, 1B-1
1912			51	.267	.387	150	40	6	3	2	1.3	16	19	8	20	3	10	1	69	112	10	12	4.0	.948	2B-31, 3B-12, C-5
1913			26	.333	.467	30	10	4	0	0	0.0	3	5	1	5	1	12	3	9	10	1	3	1.8	.950	2B-6, SS-3, 3B-1, OF-1
1914	BAL	F	120	.308	.456	428	132	25	4	10	2.3	54	65	22		18	3	1	126	220	26	18	3.2	.930	3B-113, SS-1, 2B-1, OF-1
1915	2 teams		BAL F (106G –.302) STL F (17G –.194)																						
″	total		123	.294	.410	432	127	21	1	9	2.1	48	61	24		13	7	1	138	204	24	15	3.2	.934	3B-115
6 yrs.			502	.285	.404	1571	447	84	14	25	1.6	178	212	101	93	45	62	11	612	726	96	73	3.3	.933	3B-253, 2B-78, OF-77, SS-22, C-9, P-1, 1B-1

Joe Walsh

WALSH, JOSEPH FRANCIS BR TR 6′ 2″ 170 lbs.
B. Oct. 14, 1886, Minersville, Pa. D. Jan. 6, 1967, Buffalo, N. Y.

Year	Team		Games	BA	SA	AB	H	2B	3B	HR	HR%	R	RBI	BB	SO	SB	Pinch Hit AB	Pinch Hit H	PO	A	E	DP	TC/G	FA	G by Pos
1910	NY	A	1	.000	.000	3	0	0	0	0	0.0	0	2	0		0	0	0	1	2	0	0	3.0	1.000	C-1
1911			4	.222	.333	9	2	1	0	0	0.0	2	0	0		0	1	0	4	1	0	0	1.7	1.000	C-3
2 yrs.			5	.167	.250	12	2	1	0	0	0.0	2	2	0		0	1	0	5	3	0	0	2.0	1.000	C-4

Joe Walsh

WALSH, JOSEPH PATRICK (Tweet) BR TR 5′10″ 155 lbs.
B. Mar. 13, 1917, Roxbury, Mass.

Year	Team		Games	BA	SA	AB	H	2B	3B	HR	HR%	R	RBI	BB	SO	SB	Pinch Hit AB	Pinch Hit H	PO	A	E	DP	TC/G	FA	G by Pos
1938	BOS	N	4	.000	.000	8	0	0	0	0	0.0	0	0	0	2	0	0	0	6	3	1	1	2.5	.900	SS-4

Joe Walsh

WALSH, JOSEPH R.
B. Nov. 5, 1864, Chicago, Ill. D. Aug. 8, 1911, Omaha, Neb.

Year	Team		Games	BA	SA	AB	H	2B	3B	HR	HR%	R	RBI	BB	SO	SB	Pinch Hit AB	Pinch Hit H	PO	A	E	DP	TC/G	FA	G by Pos
1891	BAL	AA	26	.210	.260	100	21	0	1	1	1.0	14	10	6	18	4	0	0	65	84	19	16	6.5	.887	SS-13, 2B-13

John Walsh

WALSH, JOHN GABRIEL BR TR 5′ 8½″ 162 lbs.
B. Mar. 25, 1879, Wilkes-Barre, Pa. D. Apr. 25, 1947, Jamaica, N. Y.

Year	Team		Games	BA	SA	AB	H	2B	3B	HR	HR%	R	RBI	BB	SO	SB	Pinch Hit AB	Pinch Hit H	PO	A	E	DP	TC/G	FA	G by Pos
1903	PHI	N	1	.000	.000	3	0	0	0	0	0.0	0	0	0		0	0	0	0	2	0	0	2.0	1.000	3B-1

Tom Walsh

WALSH, THOMAS JOSEPH BR TR 5′11″ 170 lbs.
B. Feb. 28, 1885, Davenport, Iowa D. Mar. 16, 1963, Naples, Fla.

Year	Team		Games	BA	SA	AB	H	2B	3B	HR	HR%	R	RBI	BB	SO	SB	Pinch Hit AB	Pinch Hit H	PO	A	E	DP	TC/G	FA	G by Pos
1906	CHI	N	2	.000	.000	1	0	0	0	0	0.0	0	0	0		0	0	0	1	1	0	0	1.0	1.000	C-2

Walt Walsh

WALSH, WALTER WILLIAM BR TR 5′11″ 170 lbs.
B. Apr. 30, 1897, Newark, N. J. D. Jan. 15, 1966, Avon-by-the-Sea, N. J.

Year	Team		Games	BA	SA	AB	H	2B	3B	HR	HR%	R	RBI	BB	SO	SB	Pinch Hit AB	Pinch Hit H	PO	A	E	DP	TC/G	FA	G by Pos
1920	PHI	N	2	—	—	0	0	0	0	0	—	0	0	0	0	0	0	0	0	0	0	0	0.0	—	

Bucky Walters

WALTERS, WILLIAM HENRY — BR TR 6′ 1″ 180 lbs.
B. Apr. 19, 1909, Philadelphia, Pa. D. Apr. 20, 1991, Abington, Pa.
Manager 1948–49.

Year	Team	Games	BA	SA	AB	H	2B	3B	HR	HR%	R	RBI	BB	SO	SB	Pinch Hit AB	Pinch Hit H	PO	A	E	DP	TC/G	FA	G by Pos
1931	BOS N	9	.211	.263	38	8	2	0	0	0.0	2	0	0	3	0	0	0	7	22	1	0	3.3	.967	3B-6, 2B-3
1932		22	.187	.253	75	14	3	1	0	0.0	8	4	2	18	0	0	0	17	44	6	8	3.0	.910	3B-22
1933	BOS A	52	.256	.390	195	50	8	3	4	2.1	27	28	19	24	1	2	1	58	107	10	14	3.5	.943	3B-43, 2B-7
1934	2 teams	BOS A (23G –.216)	PHI N (83G –.260)																					
″	total	106	.250	.410	388	97	24	7	8	2.1	46	56	22	66	1	0	0	116	200	21	19	3.1	.938	3B-103, 2B-3, P-2
1935	PHI N	49	.250	.292	96	24	2	1	0	0.0	14	6	9	12	0	14	4	15	48	1	4	2.0	.984	P-24, OF-5, 2B-2, 3B-1
1936		64	.240	.364	121	29	10	1	1	0.8	12	16	7	15	0	17	4	15	98	3	6	2.8	.974	P-40, 3B-1, 2B-1
1937		56	.277	.343	137	38	6	0	1	0.7	15	16	5	16	1	10	4	12	85	1	8	2.2	.990	P-37, 3B-8
1938	2 teams	PHI N (15G –.286)	CIN N (36G –.141)																					
″	total	51	.192	.253	99	19	3	0	1	1.0	16	8	8	23	1	5	0	6	66	2	5	1.9	.973	P-39
1939	CIN N	40	.325	.433	120	39	8	1	1	0.8	16	16	5	12	1	1	0	16	77	2	10	2.4	.979	P-39
1940		37	.205	.256	117	24	3	0	1	0.9	11	18	4	14	2	1	0	13	56	4	7	2.0	.945	P-36
1941		39	.189	.245	106	20	6	0	0	0.0	6	9	7	13	0	2	0	18	68	2	6	2.4	.977	P-37
1942		40	.242	.384	99	24	6	1	2	2.0	13	13	3	13	0	3	0	13	60	3	6	2.2	.961	P-34, OF-1
1943		37	.267	.400	90	24	7	1	1	1.1	11	12	6	15	1	3	0	19	49	2	7	2.1	.971	P-34
1944		37	.280	.318	107	30	4	0	0	0.0	9	13	8	18	0	3	1	15	55	0	7	2.1	1.000	P-34
1945		24	.230	.426	61	14	3	0	3	4.9	11	8	3	14	2	2	0	6	33	1	3	1.8	.975	P-22
1946		24	.127	.164	55	7	2	0	0	0.0	6	5	4	12	2	1	0	10	37	3	7	2.3	.940	P-22
1947		20	.267	.311	45	12	2	0	0	0.0	3	4	2	13	0	0	0	6	19	1	0	1.3	.962	P-20
1948		7	.267	.267	15	4	0	0	0	0.0	1	2	0	2	0	0	0	1	11	0	0	1.7	1.000	P-7
1950	BOS N	1	.000	.000	2	0	0	0	0	0.0	0	0	0	0	0	0	0	1	0	0	0	1.0	1.000	P-1
19 yrs.		715	.243	.344	1966	477	99	16	23	1.2	227	234	114	303	12	64	14	364	1135	63	117	2.5	.960	P-428, 3B-184, 2B-16, OF-6
WORLD SERIES																								
1939	CIN N	2	.000	.000	3	0	0	0	0	0.0	0	0	0	0	0	0	0	0	3	0	1	1.5	1.000	P-2
1940		2	.286	.857	7	2	1	0	1	14.3	2	2	0	1	0	0	0	0	4	0	0	2.0	1.000	P-2
2 yrs.		4	.200	.600	10	2	1	0	1	10.0	2	2	0	1	0	0	0	0	7	0	1	1.8	1.000	P-4

Dan Walters

WALTERS, DANIEL GENE — BR TR 6′ 4″ 225 lbs.
B. Aug. 15, 1966, Brunswick, Me.

Year	Team	Games	BA	SA	AB	H	2B	3B	HR	HR%	R	RBI	BB	SO	SB	Pinch Hit AB	Pinch Hit H	PO	A	E	DP	TC/G	FA	G by Pos
1992	SD N	57	.251	.391	179	45	11	1	4	2.2	14	22	10	28	1	3	0	329	25	3	5	6.5	.992	C-55
1993		27	.202	.266	94	19	3	0	1	1.1	6	10	7	13	0	1	0	138	21	5	1	6.3	.970	C-26
2 yrs.		84	.234	.348	273	64	14	1	5	1.8	20	32	17	41	1	4	0	467	46	8	6	6.4	.985	C-81

Fred Walters

WALTERS, FRED JAMES (Whale) — BR TR 6′ 1″ 210 lbs.
B. Sept. 4, 1912, Laurel, Miss. D. Feb. 1, 1980, Laurel, Miss.

Year	Team	Games	BA	SA	AB	H	2B	3B	HR	HR%	R	RBI	BB	SO	SB	Pinch Hit AB	Pinch Hit H	PO	A	E	DP	TC/G	FA	G by Pos
1945	BOS A	40	.172	.194	93	16	2	0	0	0.0	2	5	10	9	1	2	1	108	35	1	2	3.8	.993	C-38

Ken Walters

WALTERS, KENNETH ROGERS — BR TR 6′ 1″ 180 lbs.
B. Nov. 11, 1933, Fresno, Calif.

Year	Team	Games	BA	SA	AB	H	2B	3B	HR	HR%	R	RBI	BB	SO	SB	Pinch Hit AB	Pinch Hit H	PO	A	E	DP	TC/G	FA	G by Pos
1960	PHI N	124	.239	.319	426	102	10	0	8	1.9	42	37	16	50	4	13	1	220	17	3	4	2.0	.988	OF-119
1961		86	.228	.328	180	41	8	2	2	1.1	23	14	5	25	2	19	5	96	7	2	3	1.7	.981	OF-56, 1B-5, 3B-1
1963	CIN N	49	.187	.253	75	14	2	0	1	1.3	6	7	4	14	0	29	5	24	0	2	0	1.2	.923	OF-21, 1B-1
3 yrs.		259	.231	.314	681	157	20	2	11	1.6	71	58	25	89	6	61	11	340	24	7	7	1.8	.981	OF-196, 1B-6, 3B-1

Roxy Walters

WALTERS, ALFRED JOHN — BR TR 5′ 8½″ 160 lbs.
B. Nov. 5, 1892, San Francisco, Calif. D. June 3, 1956, Alameda, Calif.

Year	Team	Games	BA	SA	AB	H	2B	3B	HR	HR%	R	RBI	BB	SO	SB	Pinch Hit AB	Pinch Hit H	PO	A	E	DP	TC/G	FA	G by Pos
1915	NY A	2	.333	.333	3	1	0	0	0	0.0	0	0	0	0	0	0	0	8	3	0	1	5.5	1.000	C-2
1916		66	.266	.340	203	54	9	3	0	0.0	13	23	14	42	2	1	0	346	102	12	13	7.1	.974	C-65
1917		61	.263	.275	171	45	2	0	0	0.0	16	14	9	22	2	4	1	263	73	11	6	6.1	.968	C-57
1918		64	.199	.236	191	38	5	1	0	0.0	18	12	9	18	3	4	1	211	49	13	7	4.6	.952	C-50, OF-9
1919	BOS A	48	.193	.207	135	26	2	0	0	0.0	7	9	7	15	1	1	1	162	54	4	3	4.7	.982	C-47
1920		88	.198	.248	258	51	11	1	0	0.0	25	28	30	21	2	0	0	354	94	9	15	5.3	.980	C-85, 1B-2
1921		54	.201	.237	169	34	4	1	0	0.0	17	13	10	11	3	0	0	232	53	3	11	5.3	.990	C-54
1922		38	.194	.214	98	19	2	0	0	0.0	4	6	6	8	0	1	1	117	30	5	5	4.2	.967	C-36
1923		40	.250	.288	104	26	4	0	0	0.0	9	5	2	6	0	1	1	111	36	4	2	4.1	.974	C-36, 2B-1
1924	CLE A	32	.257	.284	74	19	2	0	0	0.0	10	5	10	6	0	0	0	75	34	2	4	3.5	.982	C-25, 2B-7
1925		5	.200	.200	20	4	0	0	0	0.0	0	0	0	2	0	0	0	8	7	0	1	3.0	1.000	C-5
11 yrs.		498	.222	.259	1426	317	41	6	0	0.0	119	115	97	151	13	12	5	1887	535	63	68	5.2	.975	C-462, OF-9, 2B-8, 1B-2

Danny Walton

WALTON, DANIEL JAMES (Mickey) — BR TR 6′ 195 lbs.
B. July 14, 1947, Los Angeles, Calif. — BB 1975–1977, 1980

Year	Team	Games	BA	SA	AB	H	2B	3B	HR	HR%	R	RBI	BB	SO	SB	Pinch Hit AB	Pinch Hit H	PO	A	E	DP	TC/G	FA	G by Pos
1968	HOU N	2	.000	.000	2	0	0	0	0	0.0	0	0	0	1	0	2	0	0	0	0	0	0.0	—	
1969	SEA A	23	.217	.370	92	20	1	2	3	3.3	12	10	5	26	2	0	0	40	2	1	1	1.9	.977	OF-23
1970	MIL A	117	.257	.441	397	102	20	1	17	4.3	32	66	51	126	2	6	2	162	4	6	0	1.5	.965	OF-114, 3B-1
1971	2 teams	MIL A (30G –.203)	NY A (5G –.143)																					
″	total	35	.193	.337	83	16	3	0	3	3.6	6	11	7	29	0	10	2	28	0	2	0	1.3	.933	OF-23, 3B-1
1973	MIN A	37	.177	.333	96	17	1	1	4	4.2	13	8	17	28	0	5	0	18	3	0	0	0.7	1.000	OF-18, DH-11, 3B-1
1975		42	.175	.254	63	11	2	0	1	1.6	4	8	4	18	0	32	7	27	1	1	4	1.9	.966	1B-7, DH-6, C-2
1976	LA N	18	.133	.133	15	2	0	0	0	0.0	0	2	1	2	0	15	2	0	0	0	0	0.0	—	
1977	HOU N	13	.190	.190	21	4	0	0	0	0.0	0	1	0	5	0	8	2	41	2	2	1	9.0	.956	1B-5
1980	TEX A	10	.200	.200	10	2	0	0	0	0.0	2	1	3	5	0	7	2	0	0	0	0	0.0	.000	DH-1
9 yrs.		297	.223	.376	779	174	27	4	28	3.6	69	107	88	240	4	85	17	316	12	12	6	1.6	.965	OF-178, DH-18, 1B-12, 3B-3, C-2

Jerome Walton

WALTON, JEROME O'TERRELL — BR TR 6′ 1″ 175 lbs.
B. July 8, 1965, Newnan, Ga.

Year	Team	Games	BA	SA	AB	H	2B	3B	HR	HR%	R	RBI	BB	SO	SB	Pinch Hit AB	Pinch Hit H	PO	A	E	DP	TC/G	FA	G by Pos
1989	CHI N	116	.293	.385	475	139	23	3	5	1.1	64	46	27	77	24	0	0	289	2	3	1	2.6	.990	OF-115
1990		101	.263	.329	392	103	16	2	2	0.5	63	21	50	70	14	0	0	247	3	6	0	2.6	.977	OF-98
1991		123	.219	.330	270	59	13	1	5	1.9	42	17	19	55	7	25	5	170	2	3	1	1.7	.983	OF-101
1992		30	.127	.164	55	7	0	1	0	0.0	7	1	9	13	1	5	0	34	0	2	0	1.5	.944	OF-24
1993	CAL A	5	.000	.000	2	0	0	0	0	0.0	2	0	1	2	1	0	0	2	0	0	0	0.5	1.000	DH-3, OF-1

Jerome Walton *continued*

Year	Team	Lg	Games	BA	SA	AB	H	2B	3B	HR	HR%	R	RBI	BB	SO	SB	Pinch Hit AB	Pinch Hit H	PO	A	E	DP	TC/G	FA	G by Pos
1994	CIN	N	46	.309	.412	68	21	4	0	1	1.5	10	9	4	12	1	15	2	58	1	1	2	1.8	.983	OF-26, 1B-7
1995			102	.290	.525	162	47	12	1	8	4.9	32	22	17	25	10	17	3	110	2	2	0	1.2	.982	OF-89, 1B-3
7 yrs.			523	.264	.367	1424	376	68	8	21	1.5	220	116	127	254	58	62	10	910	10	17	4	2.0	.982	OF-454, 1B-10, DH-3
DIVISIONAL PLAYOFF SERIES																									
1995	CIN	N	3	.000	.000	3	0	0	0	0	0.0	0	0	1	1	0	1	0	3	0	0	0	1.0	1.000	OF-3
LEAGUE CHAMPIONSHIP SERIES																									
1989	CHI	N	5	.364	.364	22	8	0	0	0	0.0	4	2	2	2	0	0	0	11	0	0	0	2.2	1.000	OF-5
1995	CIN	N	2	.000	.000	7	0	0	0	0	0.0	0	0	0	2	0	0	0	6	0	0	0	3.0	1.000	OF-2
2 yrs.			7	.276	.276	29	8	0	0	0	0.0	4	2	2	4	0	0	0	17	0	0	0	2.4	1.000	OF-7

Reggie Walton

WALTON, REGINALD SHERARD BR TR 6′ 3″ 205 lbs.
B. Oct. 24, 1952, Kansas City, Mo.

Year	Team	Lg	Games	BA	SA	AB	H	2B	3B	HR	HR%	R	RBI	BB	SO	SB	Pinch Hit AB	Pinch Hit H	PO	A	E	DP	TC/G	FA	G by Pos
1980	SEA	A	31	.277	.422	83	23	6	0	2	2.4	8	9	3	10	2	5	2	26	0	2	0	1.0	.929	OF-17, DH-11
1981			12	.000	.000	6	0	0	0	0	0.0	1	0	1	2	0	4	0	0	0	0	0	0.0		OF-4, DH-1
1982	PIT	N	13	.200	.267	15	3	1	0	0	0.0	1	0	1	1	0	10	0	0	0	0	0	0.0	.000	OF-2
3 yrs.			56	.250	.375	104	26	7	0	2	1.9	10	9	5	13	2	19	2	26	0	2	0	0.8	.929	OF-23, DH-12

Bill Wambsganss

WAMBSGANSS, WILLIAM ADOLPH BR TR 5′11″ 175 lbs.
B. Mar. 19, 1894, Cleveland, Ohio D. Dec. 8, 1985, Lakewood, Ohio.

Year	Team	Lg	Games	BA	SA	AB	H	2B	3B	HR	HR%	R	RBI	BB	SO	SB	Pinch Hit AB	Pinch Hit H	PO	A	E	DP	TC/G	FA	G by Pos
1914	CLE	A	43	.217	.287	143	31	6	2	0	0.0	12	12	8	24	2	0	0	72	117	18	16	5.2	.913	SS-36, 2B-4
1915			121	.195	.227	375	73	4	4	0	0.0	30	21	36	50	8	6	0	169	306	35	28	4.5	.931	2B-78, 3B-35
1916			136	.246	.293	475	117	14	4	0	0.0	57	45	41	40	13	1	0	252	410	52	53	5.3	.927	SS-106, 2B-24, 3B-5
1917			141	.255	.313	499	127	17	6	0	0.0	52	43	37	42	16	1	0	332	443	38	70	5.8	.953	2B-138, 1B-2
1918			87	.295	.356	315	93	15	2	0	0.0	34	40	21	21	16	0	0	204	251	23	35	5.5	.952	2B-87
1919			139	.278	.344	526	146	17	6	2	0.4	60	60	32	24	18	0	0	342	436	30	60	5.8	.963	2B-139
1920			153	.244	.317	565	138	16	11	1	0.2	83	55	54	26	9	0	0	414	489	38	75	6.2	.960	2B-153
1921			107	.285	.393	410	117	28	5	2	0.5	80	46	44	27	13	0	0	271	263	20	51	5.3	.964	2B-103, 3B-2
1922			143	.262	.325	538	141	22	6	0	0.0	89	47	60	26	17	1	0	326	418	34	79	5.5	.956	2B-125, SS-16, C-1
1923			101	.290	.380	345	100	20	4	1	0.3	59	59	43	15	12	3	0	255	278	20	47	5.9	.964	2B-88, 3B-4, SS-2
1924	BOS	A	156	.274	.354	636	174	41	5	0	0.0	93	49	54	32	14	0	0	459	490	37	98	6.4	.962	2B-155
1925			111	.231	.294	360	83	12	4	1	0.3	50	41	52	21	3	1	0	301	330	27	65	6.0	.959	2B-103, 1B-6
1926	PHI	A	54	.352	.407	54	19	3	0	0	0.0	11	1	8	8	1	20	4	14	31	3	5	2.1	.938	SS-15, 2B-8
13 yrs.			1492	.259	.327	5241	1359	215	59	7	0.1	710	519	490	356	142	33	4	3411	4262	375	682	5.6	.953	2B-1205, SS-175, 3B-46, 1B-8, C-1
WORLD SERIES																									
1920	CLE	A	7	.154	.154	26	4	0	0	0	0.0	3	1	2	1	0	0	0	22	17	0	4	5.6	1.000	2B-7

Lloyd Waner

WANER, LLOYD JAMES (Little Poison) BL TR 5′ 9″ 150 lbs.
Brother of Paul Waner.
B. Mar. 16, 1906, Harrah, Okla. D. July 22, 1982, Oklahoma City, Okla.
Hall of Fame 1967.

Year	Team	Lg	Games	BA	SA	AB	H	2B	3B	HR	HR%	R	RBI	BB	SO	SB	Pinch Hit AB	Pinch Hit H	PO	A	E	DP	TC/G	FA	G by Pos
1927	PIT	N	150	.355	.410	629	223	17	6	2	0.3	**133**	27	37	23	14	0	0	397	9	10	0	2.8	.976	OF-150, 2B-1
1928			152	.335	.434	**659**	221	22	14	5	0.8	121	61	40	13	8	0	0	418	15	9	4	2.9	.980	OF-152
1929			151	.353	.479	**662**	234	28	**20**	5	0.8	134	74	37	20	6	0	0	450	22	6	6	3.2	.987	OF-151
1930			68	.362	.427	260	94	8	3	1	0.4	32	36	5	5	3	2	1	165	6	3	1	2.7	.983	OF-65
1931			154	.314	.407	**681**	**214**	25	13	4	0.6	90	57	39	16	7	0	0	485	22	11	5	3.4	.979	OF-153, 2B-1
1932			134	.333	.435	565	188	27	11	3	0.5	90	38	31	11	6	2	1	426	9	6	0	3.4	.986	OF-131
1933			121	.276	.324	500	138	14	5	0	0.0	59	26	22	8	3	6	4	267	9	5	2	2.5	.982	OF-114
1934			140	.283	.352	611	173	27	6	1	0.2	95	48	38	12	6	1	0	405	8	9	1	3.0	.979	OF-139
1935			122	.309	.402	537	166	22	14	0	0.0	83	46	22	10	1	1	1	350	5	4	1	3.0	.989	OF-121
1936			106	.321	.399	414	133	13	8	1	0.2	67	31	31	5	1	11	1	245	2	4	2	2.7	.984	OF-92
1937			129	.330	.393	537	177	23	4	1	0.2	80	45	34	12	3	5	2	312	8	4	0	2.6	.988	OF-123
1938			147	.313	.401	619	194	25	7	5	0.8	79	57	28	11	5	3	0	341	15	5	5	2.5	.986	OF-144
1939			112	.285	.340	379	108	15	3	0	0.0	49	24	17	13	0	17	3	227	13	2	2	2.6	.992	OF-92, 3B-1
1940			72	.259	.277	166	43	3	0	0	0.0	30	3	5	5	2	18	6	90	3	1	1	2.2	.989	OF-42
1941	3 teams	PIT N (3G –.250) BOS N (19G –.412) CIN N (55G –.256)																							
″	total		77	.292	.324	219	64	5	1	0	0.0	26	11	12	0	1	11	4	102	4	2	1	1.8	.981	OF-60
1942	PHI	N	100	.261	.307	287	75	7	3	0	0.0	23	10	16	6	1	22	4	170	6	6	0	2.4	.967	OF-75
1944	2 teams	BKN N (15G –.286) PIT N (19G –.357)																							
″	total		34	.321	.321	28	9	0	0	0	0.0	5	3	5	0	0	18	7	12	0	0	0	1.1	1.000	OF-11
1945	PIT	N	23	.263	.263	19	5	0	0	0	0.0	5	1	1	3	0	17	5	2	1	0	0	1.0	1.000	OF-3
18 yrs.			1992	.316	.394	7772	2459	281	118	28	0.4	1201	598	420	173	67	134	39	4864	157	87	31	2.8	.983	OF-1818, 2B-2, 3B-1
WORLD SERIES																									
1927	PIT	N	4	.400	.600	15	6	1	1	0	0.0	5	0	1	0	0	0	0	9	1	2	0	3.0	.833	OF-4

Paul Waner

WANER, PAUL GLEE (Big Poison) BL TL 5′ 8½″ 153 lbs.
Brother of Lloyd Waner.
B. Apr. 16, 1903, Harrah, Okla. D. Aug. 29, 1965, Sarasota, Fla.
Hall of Fame 1952.

Year	Team	Lg	Games	BA	SA	AB	H	2B	3B	HR	HR%	R	RBI	BB	SO	SB	Pinch Hit AB	Pinch Hit H	PO	A	E	DP	TC/G	FA	G by Pos
1926	PIT	N	144	.336	.528	536	180	35	**22**	8	1.5	101	79	66	19	11	3	0	307	21	8	3	2.4	.976	OF-139
1927			155	**.380**	.543	623	**237**	40	**17**	9	1.4	113	**131**	60	14	5	0	0	430	25	10	12	3.0	.978	OF-143, 1B-14
1928			152	.370	.547	602	223	**50**	19	6	1.0	**142**	86	77	16	6	0	0	533	22	12	17	3.7	.979	OF-131, 1B-24
1929			151	.336	.534	596	200	43	15	15	2.5	131	100	89	24	15	1	0	398	18	5	7	2.8	.988	OF-143, 1B-7
1930			145	.368	.525	589	217	32	18	8	1.4	117	77	57	18	18	2	0	344	9	15	4	2.6	.959	OF-143
1931			150	.322	.453	559	180	35	10	6	1.1	88	70	73	21	6	2	0	441	31	9	18	3.3	.981	OF-138, 1B-10
1932			154	.341	.505	630	215	**62**	10	7	1.1	107	82	56	24	13	0	0	367	13	10	3	2.5	.974	OF-154
1933			154	.309	.456	618	191	38	16	7	1.1	101	70	60	20	3	0	0	346	16	7	2	2.4	.981	OF-154
1934			146	**.362**	.539	599	**217**	32	16	14	2.3	**122**	90	68	24	8	1	1	323	15	5	1	2.4	.985	OF-145
1935			139	.321	.477	549	176	29	12	11	2.0	98	78	61	22	2	3	1	283	13	5	2	2.2	.983	OF-136

Paul Waner *continued*

Year	Team	Games	BA	SA	AB	H	2B	3B	HR	HR%	R	RBI	BB	SO	SB	Pinch Hit AB	Pinch Hit H	PO	A	E	DP	TC/G	FA	G by Pos
1936		148	**.373**	.520	585	218	53	9	5	0.9	107	94	74	29	7	3	1	323	15	14	7	2.4	.960	OF-145
1937		154	.354	.441	619	219	30	9	2	0.3	94	74	63	34	4	2	0	298	19	11	6	2.1	.966	OF-150, 1B-3
1938		148	.280	.378	625	175	31	6	6	1.0	77	69	47	28	2	11	0	284	11	7	0	2.1	.977	OF-147
1939		125	.328	.438	461	151	30	6	3	0.7	62	45	35	18	0	11	3	206	12	5	4	2.1	.978	OF-106
1940		89	.290	.378	238	69	16	1	1	0.4	32	32	23	14	0	34	6	150	9	2	12	3.0	.988	OF-45, 1B-8
1941	**2 teams**	**BKN N** (11G –.171) **BOS N** (95G –.279)																						
″	**total**	106	.267	.328	329	88	10	2	2	0.6	45	50	55	14	1	18	3	160	8	8	3	2.0	.955	OF-86, 1B-1
1942	**BOS N**	114	.258	.324	333	86	17	1	1	0.3	43	39	62	20	2	17	2	150	6	5	3	1.7	.969	OF-94
1943	**BKN N**	82	.311	.396	225	70	16	0	1	0.4	29	26	35	9	0	21	10	116	4	5	1	2.2	.960	OF-57
1944	**2 teams**	**BKN N** (83G –.287) **NY A** (9G –.143)																						
″	**total**	92	.280	.322	143	40	4	1	0	0.0	17	17	29	8	1	45	**13**	54	3	1	0	1.8	.983	OF-32
1945	**NY A**	1	—	—	0	0	0	0	0	—	0	0	1	0	0	0	0	0	0	0	0	0.0	—	
20 yrs.		2549	.333	.473	9459	3152	603 **10th**	190 **10th**	112	1.2	1626	1309	1091	376	104	164	40	5513	270	144	105	2.5	.976	OF-2288, 1B-67
WORLD SERIES																								
1927	**PIT N**	4	.333	.400	15	5	1	0	0	0.0	0	3	0	1	0	0	0	8	0	0	0	2.0	1.000	OF-4

Jack Wanner

WANNER, CLARENCE CURTIS BR TR 5′11½″ 190 lbs.
B. Nov. 29, 1885, Geneseo, Ill. D. May 28, 1919, Geneseo, Ill.

Year	Team	Games	BA	SA	AB	H	2B	3B	HR	HR%	R	RBI	BB	SO	SB	Pinch Hit AB	Pinch Hit H	PO	A	E	DP	TC/G	FA	G by Pos
1909	**NY A**	3	.125	.125	8	1	0	0	0	0.0	0	0	2		1	1	0	1	5	4	1	5.0	.600	SS-2

Pee Wee Wanninger

WANNINGER, PAUL LOUIS BL TR 5′ 7″ 150 lbs.
B. Dec. 12, 1902, Birmingham, Ala. D. Mar. 7, 1981, North Augusta, S. C.

Year	Team	Games	BA	SA	AB	H	2B	3B	HR	HR%	R	RBI	BB	SO	SB	Pinch Hit AB	Pinch Hit H	PO	A	E	DP	TC/G	FA	G by Pos
1925	**NY A**	117	.236	.305	403	95	13	6	1	0.2	35	22	11	34	3	1	1	219	306	31	61	4.8	.944	SS-111, 3B-3, 2B-1
1927	**2 teams**	**BOS A** (18G –.200) **CIN N** (28G –.247)																						
″	**total**	46	.229	.268	153	35	2	2	0	0.0	18	9	12	9	2	2	0	88	146	17	32	5.8	.932	SS-43
2 yrs.		163	.234	.295	556	130	15	8	1	0.2	53	31	23	43	5	3	1	307	452	48	93	5.1	.941	SS-154, 3B-3, 2B-1

Aaron Ward

WARD, AARON LEE BR TR 5′10½″ 160 lbs.
B. Aug. 28, 1896, Booneville, Ark. D. Jan. 30, 1961, New Orleans, La.

Year	Team	Games	BA	SA	AB	H	2B	3B	HR	HR%	R	RBI	BB	SO	SB	Pinch Hit AB	Pinch Hit H	PO	A	E	DP	TC/G	FA	G by Pos
1917	**NY A**	8	.115	.115	26	3	0	0	0	0.0	0	1	1	5	0	1	0	12	13	2	3	3.9	.926	SS-7
1918		20	.125	.156	32	4	1	0	0	0.0	2	1	2	7	1	1	0	23	25	2	5	2.6	.960	SS-11, OF-4, 2B-4
1919		27	.206	.265	34	7	2	0	0	0.0	5	2	5	6	0	14	4	43	14	1	5	5.3	.983	1B-5, 3B-3, SS-2, 2B-1
1920		127	.256	.387	496	127	18	7	11	2.2	62	54	33	**84**	7	1	0	169	344	18	36	4.2	.966	3B-114, SS-12
1921		153	.306	.423	556	170	30	10	5	0.9	77	75	42	68	6	0	0	306	487	28	68	5.3	.966	2B-123, 3B-33
1922		154	.267	.357	558	149	19	5	7	1.3	69	68	45	64	7	0	0	358	490	23	74	5.7	.974	2B-152, 3B-2
1923		152	.284	.422	567	161	26	11	10	1.8	79	82	56	65	8	0	0	387	493	18	86	5.9	.980	2B-152
1924		120	.253	.395	400	101	13	10	8	2.0	42	66	40	45	1	0	0	303	385	19	60	5.8	.973	2B-120, SS-1
1925		125	.246	.337	439	108	22	3	4	0.9	41	38	49	49	1	2	0	264	336	20	59	5.0	.968	2B-113, 3B-10
1926		22	.323	.387	31	10	2	0	0	0.0	5	3	2	6	0	15	5	13	7	0	0	4.0	1.000	2B-4, 3B-1
1927	**CHI A**	145	.270	.391	463	125	25	8	5	1.1	75	56	63	56	6	1	0	283	450	27	66	5.3	.964	2B-138, 3B-6
1928	**CLE A**	6	.111	.111	9	1	0	0	0	0.0	0	0	1	2	0	0	0	4	13	4	5	3.5	.810	3B-3, SS-2, 2B-1
12 yrs.		1059	.268	.383	3611	966	158	54	50	1.4	457	446	339	457	37	35	9	2165	3057	162	467	5.3	.970	2B-808, 3B-172, SS-35, 1B-5, OF-4
WORLD SERIES																								
1921	**NY A**	8	.231	.231	26	6	0	0	0	0.0	1	4	2	6	0	0	0	18	34	2	4	6.8	.963	2B-8
1922		5	.154	.615	13	2	0	0	2	15.4	3	3	3	3	0	0	0	13	16	1	4	6.0	.967	2B-5
1923		6	.417	.542	24	10	0	0	1	4.2	4	2	1	3	1	0	0	11	27	0	3	6.3	1.000	2B-6
3 yrs.		19	.286	.429	63	18	0	0	3	4.8	8	9	6	12	1	0	0	42	77	3	11	6.4	.975	2B-19

Chris Ward

WARD, CHRIS GILBERT BL TL 6′ 180 lbs.
B. May 18, 1949, Oakland, Calif.

Year	Team	Games	BA	SA	AB	H	2B	3B	HR	HR%	R	RBI	BB	SO	SB	Pinch Hit AB	Pinch Hit H	PO	A	E	DP	TC/G	FA	G by Pos
1972	**CHI N**	1	.000	.000	1	0	0	0	0	0.0	0	0	0	0	0	1	0	0	0	0	0	0.0	—	
1974		92	.204	.255	137	28	4	0	1	0.7	8	15	18	13	0	49	9	94	6	1	4	3.6	.990	OF-22, 1B-6
2 yrs.		93	.203	.254	138	28	4	0	1	0.7	8	15	18	13	0	50	9	94	6	1	4	3.6	.990	OF-22, 1B-6

Chuck Ward

WARD, CHARLES WILLIAM BR TR 5′11½″ 170 lbs.
B. July 30, 1894, St. Louis, Mo. D. Apr. 4, 1969, Indian Rocks, Fla.

Year	Team	Games	BA	SA	AB	H	2B	3B	HR	HR%	R	RBI	BB	SO	SB	Pinch Hit AB	Pinch Hit H	PO	A	E	DP	TC/G	FA	G by Pos
1917	**PIT N**	125	.236	.279	423	100	12	3	0	0.0	25	43	32	43	5	1	0	226	347	52	53	5.0	.917	SS-112, 2B-8, 3B-5
1918	**BKN N**	2	.333	.333	6	2	0	0	0	0.0	0	3	0	0	0	0	0	0	3	0	0	1.5	1.000	3B-2
1919		45	.233	.267	150	35	1	2	0	0.0	7	8	7	11	0	0	0	47	79	11	0	3.0	.920	3B-45
1920		19	.155	.169	71	11	1	0	0	0.0	7	4	3	3	1	0	0	46	44	7	5	5.1	.928	SS-19
1921		12	.071	.107	28	2	1	0	0	0.0	1	0	4	2	0	0	0	25	34	4	7	5.3	.937	SS-12
1922		33	.275	.352	91	25	5	1	0	0.0	12	14	5	8	1	0	0	54	89	10	13	4.6	.935	SS-31, 3B-2
6 yrs.		236	.228	.269	769	175	20	6	0	0.0	52	72	51	67	7	1	0	398	596	84	78	4.6	.922	SS-174, 3B-54, 2B-8

Gary Ward

WARD, GARY LAMELL BR TR 6′ 2″ 195 lbs.
B. Dec. 6, 1953, Los Angeles, Calif.

Year	Team	Games	BA	SA	AB	H	2B	3B	HR	HR%	R	RBI	BB	SO	SB	Pinch Hit AB	Pinch Hit H	PO	A	E	DP	TC/G	FA	G by Pos
1979	**MIN A**	10	.286	.286	14	4	0	0	0	0.0	2	1	3	3	0	1	0	8	0	0	0	1.0	1.000	OF-5, DH-3
1980		13	.463	.780	41	19	6	2	1	2.4	11	10	3	6	0	2	0	14	0	0	0	1.2	1.000	OF-12
1981		85	.264	.359	295	78	7	6	3	1.0	42	29	28	48	5	5	1	185	8	5	4	2.4	.975	OF-80, DH-2
1982		152	.289	.519	570	165	33	7	28	4.9	85	91	37	105	13	5	2	343	13	4	3	2.4	.989	OF-150, DH-2
1983		157	.278	.440	623	173	34	5	19	3.0	76	88	44	98	8	4	0	374	24	9	6	2.6	.978	OF-152, DH-2
1984	**TEX A**	153	.284	.447	602	171	21	7	21	3.5	97	79	55	95	7	4	0	376	11	5	1	2.6	.987	OF-148, DH-5
1985		154	.287	.433	593	170	28	7	15	2.5	77	70	39	97	26	1	1	304	11	10	2	2.1	.969	OF-153, DH-1
1986		105	.316	.405	380	120	15	2	5	1.3	54	51	31	72	12	0	0	237	8	1	3	2.3	.996	OF-104, DH-1
1987	**NY A**	146	.248	.384	529	131	22	1	16	3.0	65	78	33	101	9	12	8	318	10	3	11	2.3	.991	OF-94, DH-36, 1B-15
1988		91	.225	.312	231	52	8	0	4	1.7	26	24	24	41	0	17	5	220	5	2	9	3.4	.991	OF-54, 1B-11, 3B-2
1989	**2 teams**	**NY A** (8G –.294) **DET A** (105G –.251)																						
″	**total**	113	.253	.397	292	74	11	2	9	3.1	27	30	24	59	1	32	6	234	16	3	15	2.3	.988	OF-57, DH-27, 1B-26
1990	**DET A**	106	.256	.392	309	79	11	2	9	2.9	32	46	30	50	2	14	5	164	2	2	1	1.7	.988	OF-85, DH-13, 1B-2
12 yrs.		1285	.276	.425	4479	1236	196	41	130	2.9	594	597	351	775	83	97	28	2777	108	44	55	2.4	.985	OF-1094, DH-92, 1B-54, 3B-2

Year	Team	Games	BA	SA	AB	H	2B	3B	HR	HR%	R	RBI	BB	SO	SB	Pinch Hit AB	Pinch Hit H	PO	A	E	DP	TC/G	FA	G by Pos

Hap Ward

WARD, JOSEPH NICHOLS BR
B. Nov. 15, 1885, Leesburg, N. J. D. Sept. 13, 1979, Elmer, N. J.

Year	Team	Games	BA	SA	AB	H	2B	3B	HR	HR%	R	RBI	BB	SO	SB	Pinch Hit AB	Pinch Hit H	PO	A	E	DP	TC/G	FA	G by Pos
1912	DET A	1	.000	.000	2	0	0	0	0	0.0	0	0	0		0	0	0	2	0	0	0	2.0	1.000	OF-1

Jay Ward

WARD, JOHN FRANCIS BR TR 6′ 1″ 185 lbs.
B. Sept. 9, 1938, Brookfield, Mo.

Year	Team	Games	BA	SA	AB	H	2B	3B	HR	HR%	R	RBI	BB	SO	SB	Pinch Hit AB	Pinch Hit H	PO	A	E	DP	TC/G	FA	G by Pos
1963	MIN A	9	.067	.133	15	1	1	0	0	0.0	0	2	1	5	0	2	0	3	5	0	0	1.6	1.000	3B-4, OF-1
1964		12	.226	.290	31	7	2	0	0	0.0	4	2	6	13	0	1	0	25	21	1	4	3.9	.979	2B-9, OF-3
1970	CIN N	6	.000	.000	3	0	0	0	0	0.0	0	0	2	1	0	2	0	4	1	0	1	1.3	1.000	3B-2, 1B-1, 2B-1
3 yrs.		27	.163	.224	49	8	3	0	0	0.0	4	4	9	19	0	5	0	32	27	1	5	2.9	.983	2B-10, 3B-6, OF-4, 1B-1

Jim Ward

WARD, JAMES H. H.
B. Mar. 2, 1855, Boston, Mass. D. June 4, 1886, Boston, Mass.

Year	Team	Games	BA	SA	AB	H	2B	3B	HR	HR%	R	RBI	BB	SO	SB	Pinch Hit AB	Pinch Hit H	PO	A	E	DP	TC/G	FA	G by Pos
1876	PHI N	1	.500	.500	4	2	0	0	0	0.0	1	1	0	1		0	0	5	1	2	0	8.0	.750	C-1

Joe Ward

WARD, JOSEPH A. TR
B. Sept. 2, 1884, Philadelphia, Pa. D. Aug. 11, 1934, Philadelphia, Pa.

Year	Team	Games	BA	SA	AB	H	2B	3B	HR	HR%	R	RBI	BB	SO	SB	Pinch Hit AB	Pinch Hit H	PO	A	E	DP	TC/G	FA	G by Pos
1906	PHI N	35	.295	.450	129	38	8	6	0	0.0	12	11	5		2	5	1	41	50	7	2	3.2	.929	3B-27, 2B-3, SS-1
1909	2 teams	NY A (9G –.179) PHI N (74G –.266)																						
″	total	83	.255	.311	212	54	8	2	0	0.0	24	23	10		9	27	5	139	112	22	17	3.8	.919	2B-55, SS-8, 1B-6, OF-2
1910	PHI N	48	.145	.177	124	18	2	1	0	0.0	11	13	3	11	1	14	2	296	25	8	11	9.7	.976	1B-32, SS-1, 3B-1
3 yrs.		166	.237	.314	465	110	18	9	0	0.0	47	47	18	11	12	46	8	476	187	37	30	5.1	.947	2B-58, 1B-38, 3B-28, SS-10, OF-2

John Ward

WARD, JOHN E.
B. Washington, D. C. Deceased.

Year	Team	Games	BA	SA	AB	H	2B	3B	HR	HR%	R	RBI	BB	SO	SB	Pinch Hit AB	Pinch Hit H	PO	A	E	DP	TC/G	FA	G by Pos
1884	WAS U	1	.250	.250	4	1	0	0	0	0.0	0		0			0	0	0	0	1	0	1.0	.000	OF-1

Kevin Ward

WARD, KEVIN MICHAEL BR TR 6′ 1″ 195 lbs.
B. Sept. 28, 1961, Lansdale, Pa.

Year	Team	Games	BA	SA	AB	H	2B	3B	HR	HR%	R	RBI	BB	SO	SB	Pinch Hit AB	Pinch Hit H	PO	A	E	DP	TC/G	FA	G by Pos
1991	SD N	44	.243	.402	107	26	7	2	2	1.9	13	8	9	27	1	10	3	54	0	1	0	1.7	.982	OF-33
1992		81	.197	.293	147	29	5	0	3	2.0	12	12	14	38	2	36	6	68	2	4	0	1.5	.946	OF-51
2 yrs.		125	.217	.339	254	55	12	2	5	2.0	25	20	23	65	3	46	9	122	2	5	0	1.5	.961	OF-84

Monte Ward

WARD, JOHN MONTGOMERY BL TR 5′ 9″ 165 lbs.
B. Mar. 3, 1860, Bellefonte, Pa. D. Mar. 4, 1925, Augusta, Ga. BB 1888
Manager 1880, 1884, 1890–94.
Hall of Fame 1964.

Year	Team	Games	BA	SA	AB	H	2B	3B	HR	HR%	R	RBI	BB	SO	SB	Pinch Hit AB	Pinch Hit H	PO	A	E	DP	TC/G	FA	G by Pos
1878	PRO N	37	.196	.312	138	27	5	4	1	0.7	14	15	2	13		0	0	23	74	15	4	3.0	.866	P-37
1879		83	.286	.349	364	104	9	4	2	0.5	71	41	7	14		0	0	55	167	23	4	2.6	.906	P-70, 3B-16, OF-8
1880		86	.228	.272	356	81	12	2	0	0.0	53	27	6	16		0	0	74	203	17	5	3.0	.942	P-70, 3B-25, OF-2
1881		85	.244	.328	357	87	18	6	0	0.0	56	53	5	10		0	0	110	130	29	11	2.9	.892	OF-40, P-39, SS-13
1882		83	.245	.296	355	87	10	4	0	0.0	58		13	22		0	0	105	105	31	8	2.8	.871	OF-50, P-33, SS-4
1883	NY N	88	.255	.395	380	97	18	7	7	1.8	76		8	25		0	0	154	116	42	4	3.2	.865	OF-56, P-33, 3B-5, SS-2, 2B-1
1884		113	.253	.322	482	122	11	8	2	0.4	98		28	47		0	0	201	206	58	19	4.0	.875	OF-59, 2B-47, P-9
1885		111	.226	.285	446	101	8	9	0	0.0	72		17	39		0	0	167	350	55	36	5.2	.904	SS-111
1886		122	.273	.340	491	134	17	5	2	0.4	82	81	19	46		0	0	91	369	69	36	4.3	.870	SS-122
1887		129	.338	.391	**545**	184	16	5	1	0.2	114	53	29	12	**111**	0	0	226	469	61	53	5.9	.919	SS-129
1888		122	.251	.310	510	128	14	5	2	0.4	70	49	9	13	38	0	0	185	331	86	39	4.9	.857	SS-122
1889		114	.299	.349	479	143	13	4	1	0.2	87	67	27	7	62	0	0	245	339	76	38	5.7	.885	SS-108, 2B-7
1890	BKN P	128	.337	.428	561	189	15	12	4	0.7	134	60	51	22	63	0	0	303	450	105	59	6.7	.878	SS-128
1891	BKN N	105	.277	.329	441	122	13	5	0	0.0	85	39	36	10	57	0	0	235	352	72	36	6.3	.891	SS-87, 2B-18
1892		148	.265	.301	614	163	13	3	1	0.2	109	47	82	19	**88**	0	0	377	472	74	48	6.2	.920	2B-148
1893	NY N	135	.328	.415	588	193	27	9	2	0.3	129	77	47	5	46	1	0	348	464	73	41	6.6	.918	2B-134
1894		136	.265	.306	540	143	12	5	0	0.0	100	77	34	6	39	0	0	331	446	64	52	6.2	.924	2B-136
17 yrs.		1825	.275	.341	7647	2105	231	97	25	0.3	1408	686	420	326	504	1	0	3230	5043	950	493	4.9	.897	SS-826, 2B-491, P-291, OF-215, 3B-46

Pete Ward

WARD, PETER THOMAS BL TR 6′ 1″ 185 lbs.
B. July 26, 1939, Montreal, Que., Canada.

Year	Team	Games	BA	SA	AB	H	2B	3B	HR	HR%	R	RBI	BB	SO	SB	Pinch Hit AB	Pinch Hit H	PO	A	E	DP	TC/G	FA	G by Pos
1962	BAL A	8	.143	.238	21	3	2	0	0	0.0	1	2	4	5	0	1	1	10	0	0	0	1.7	1.000	OF-6
1963	CHI A	157	.295	.482	600	177	34	6	22	3.7	80	84	52	77	7	3	1	158	303	38	28	3.2	.924	3B-154, SS-1, 2B-1
1964		144	.282	.473	539	152	28	3	23	4.3	61	94	56	76	1	5	1	126	309	19	24	3.3	.958	3B-138
1965		138	.247	.367	507	125	25	3	10	2.0	62	57	56	83	2	5	1	97	320	21	22	3.2	.952	3B-134, 2B-1
1966		84	.219	.291	251	55	7	1	3	1.2	22	28	24	49	3	9	0	112	42	3	6	2.0	.981	OF-59, 3B-16, 1B-5
1967		146	.233	.392	467	109	16	2	18	3.9	49	62	61	109	3	6	3	409	55	7	26	3.1	.985	OF-89, 1B-39, 3B-22
1968		125	.216	.366	399	86	15	0	15	3.8	43	50	76	85	4	6	1	325	170	12	25	3.9	.976	3B-77, 1B-31, OF-22
1969		105	.246	.372	199	49	7	0	6	3.0	22	32	33	38	0	46	**17**	193	48	3	13	4.4	.988	1B-25, 3B-21, OF-9
1970	NY A	66	.260	.377	77	20	2	2	1	1.3	5	18	9	17	0	44	10	83	3	0	7	6.6	1.000	1B-13
9 yrs.		973	.254	.405	3060	776	136	17	98	3.2	345	427	371	539	20	125	35	1513	1250	103	151	3.3	.964	3B-562, OF-185, 1B-113, 2B-2, SS-1

Piggy Ward

WARD, FRANK GRAY BB TR 5′ 9½″ 196 lbs.
B. Apr. 16, 1867, Chambersburg, Pa. D. Oct. 24, 1912, Altoona, Pa.

Year	Team	Games	BA	SA	AB	H	2B	3B	HR	HR%	R	RBI	BB	SO	SB	Pinch Hit AB	Pinch Hit H	PO	A	E	DP	TC/G	FA	G by Pos
1883	PHI N	1	.000	.000	5	0	0	0	0	0.0	0		0	2		0	0	0	2	0	0	2.0	1.000	3B-1
1889		7	.160	.200	25	4	1	0	0	0.0	0	4	0	7	1	0	0	13	16	7	0	5.1	.806	2B-6, OF-1
1891	PIT N	6	.333	.333	18	6	0	0	0	0.0	3	2	3	3	3	**1**	0	5	0	1	0	1.2	.833	OF-5
1892	BAL N	56	.290	.392	186	54	6	5	1	0.5	28	33	31	18	10	0	0	84	44	16	7	2.6	.889	OF-43, 2B-7, SS-5, C-1
1893	2 teams	BAL N (11G –.245) CIN N (42G –.280)																						
″	total	53	.271	.337	199	54	5	4	0	0.0	55	15	42	12	31	1	0	100	9	19	4	2.5	.852	OF-49, 1B-3
1894	WAS N	98	.303	.375	347	105	11	7	0	0.0	86	36	80	31	41	2	1	195	246	52	22	5.2	.895	2B-79, OF-12, SS-3, 3B-1
6 yrs.		221	.286	.360	780	223	23	16	1	0.1	172	90	156	73	86	4	1	397	317	95	33	3.7	.883	OF-110, 2B-92, SS-8, 1B-3, 3B-2, C-1

Preston Ward

WARD, PRESTON MEYER
B. July 24, 1927, Columbia, Mo.
BL TR 6′ 4″ 190 lbs.

Year	Team	Games	BA	SA	AB	H	2B	3B	HR	HR%	R	RBI	BB	SO	SB	Pinch Hit AB	Pinch Hit H	PO	A	E	DP	TC/G	FA	G by Pos
1948	BKN N	42	.260	.370	146	38	9	2	1	0.7	9	21	15	23	0	3	0	268	20	3	21	7.7	.990	1B-38
1950	CHI N	80	.253	.368	285	72	11	2	6	2.1	31	33	27	42	3	14	1	734	73	4	78	10.7	.995	1B-76
1953	2 teams	CHI N (33G –.230) PIT N (88G –.210)																						
″	total	121	.215	.346	381	82	12	1	12	3.1	45	39	62	60	4	9	2	791	65	9	74	7.7	.990	1B-85, OF-27
1954	PIT N	117	.269	.383	360	97	16	2	7	1.9	37	48	39	61	0	18	4	419	69	15	34	5.0	.970	1B-48, OF-42, 3B-11
1955		84	.212	.380	179	38	7	4	5	2.8	16	25	22	28	0	30	6	384	35	1	41	8.6	.998	1B-48, OF-1
1956	2 teams	PIT N (16G –.333) CLE A (87G –.253)																						
″	total	103	.267	.450	180	48	10	1	7	3.9	21	32	22	24	0	26	8	260	25	3	20	3.3	.990	1B-60, OF-22, 3B-5
1957	CLE A	10	.182	.273	11	2	1	0	0	0.0	2	0	0	2	0	9	1	3	0	0	0	3.0	1.000	1B-1
1958	2 teams	CLE A (48G –.338) KC A (81G –.254)																						
″	total	129	.284	.397	416	118	13	2	10	2.4	50	45	37	63	0	18	4	523	116	14	46	5.4	.979	1B-60, 3B-58, OF-2
1959	KC A	58	.248	.358	109	27	4	1	2	1.8	8	19	7	12	0	32	8	161	7	4	14	7.5	.977	1B-22, OF-1
9 yrs.		744	.253	.380	2067	522	83	15	50	2.4	219	262	231	315	7	159	34	3543	410	53	328	6.6	.987	1B-438, OF-95, 3B-74

Rube Ward

WARD, JOHN ANDREW
B. Feb. 6, 1879, New Lexington, Ohio D. Jan. 17, 1945, Akron, Ohio.

Year	Team	Games	BA	SA	AB	H	2B	3B	HR	HR%	R	RBI	BB	SO	SB	Pinch Hit AB	Pinch Hit H	PO	A	E	DP	TC/G	FA	G by Pos
1902	BKN N	13	.290	.323	31	9	1	0	0	0.0	4	2	2		0	2	0	16	1	3	0	1.8	.850	OF-11

Turner Ward

WARD, TURNER MAX
B. Apr. 11, 1965, Orlando, Fla.
BB TR 6′ 2″ 200 lbs.

Year	Team	Games	BA	SA	AB	H	2B	3B	HR	HR%	R	RBI	BB	SO	SB	Pinch Hit AB	Pinch Hit H	PO	A	E	DP	TC/G	FA	G by Pos
1990	CLE A	14	.348	.500	46	16	2	1	1	2.2	10	10	3	8	3	0	0	20	2	1	0	1.6	.957	OF-13, DH-1
1991	2 teams	CLE A (40G –.230) TOR A (8G –.308)																						
″	total	48	.239	.301	113	27	7	0	0	0.0	12	7	11	18	0	3	1	70	1	0	0	1.6	1.000	OF-44
1992	TOR A	18	.345	.552	29	10	3	0	1	3.4	7	3	4	4	0	4	0	18	1	0	0	1.6	1.000	OF-12
1993		72	.192	.311	167	32	4	2	4	2.4	20	28	23	26	3	7	2	97	2	1	0	1.5	.990	OF-65, 1B-1
1994	MIL A	102	.232	.357	367	85	15	2	9	2.5	55	45	52	68	6	1	0	260	9	4	1	2.7	.985	OF-99, 3B-1
1995		44	.264	.395	129	34	3	1	4	3.1	19	16	14	21	6	4	1	81	5	1	1	2.1	.989	OF-40, DH-1
6 yrs.		298	.240	.361	851	204	34	6	19	2.2	123	109	107	145	18	19	4	546	20	7	2	2.1	.988	OF-273, DH-2, 3B-1, 1B-1

Buzzy Wares

WARES, CLYDE ELLSWORTH
B. Mar. 23, 1886, Vandalia, Mich. D. May 26, 1964, South Bend, Ind.
BR TR 5′10″ 150 lbs.

Year	Team	Games	BA	SA	AB	H	2B	3B	HR	HR%	R	RBI	BB	SO	SB	Pinch Hit AB	Pinch Hit H	PO	A	E	DP	TC/G	FA	G by Pos
1913	STL A	10	.286	.343	35	10	2	0	0	0.0	5	1	1	3	2	1	0	20	16	1	4	4.1	.973	2B-9
1914		81	.209	.265	215	45	10	1	0	0.0	20	23	28	35	10	1	0	146	214	36	26	5.2	.909	SS-68, 2B-8
2 yrs.		91	.220	.276	250	55	12	1	0	0.0	25	24	29	38	12	2	0	166	230	37	30	5.1	.915	SS-68, 2B-17

Fred Warner

WARNER, FREDERICK JOHN RODNEY
B. 1855, Philadelphia, Pa. D. Feb. 13, 1886, Philadelphia, Pa.
5′ 7″ 155 lbs.

Year	Team	Games	BA	SA	AB	H	2B	3B	HR	HR%	R	RBI	BB	SO	SB	Pinch Hit AB	Pinch Hit H	PO	A	E	DP	TC/G	FA	G by Pos
1876	PHI N	1	.000	.000	3	0	0	0	0	0.0	0	0	0	0		0	0	3	0	2	0	5.0	.600	OF-1
1878	IND N	43	.248	.273	165	41	4	0	0	0.0	19	10	2	15		0	0	44	124	18	9	4.3	.903	SS-41, OF-2
1879	CLE N	76	.244	.304	316	77	11	4	0	0.0	32	22	2	20		0	0	127	113	48	5	3.8	.833	3B-54, OF-21, 1B-1
1883	PHI N	39	.227	.284	141	32	6	1	0	0.0	13		5	21		0	0	49	55	29	4	3.4	.782	3B-38, OF-1
1884	BKN AA	84	.222	.241	352	78	4	0	1	0.3	40		17			0	0	94	149	52	13	3.5	.824	3B-83, OF-1
5 yrs.		243	.233	.272	977	228	25	5	1	0.1	104	32	26	56		0	0	317	441	149	31	3.7	.836	3B-175, SS-41, OF-26, 1B-1

Hooks Warner

WARNER, HOKE HAYDEN
B. May 22, 1894, Del Rio, Tex. D. Feb. 19, 1947, San Francisco, Calif.
BL TR 5′10½″ 170 lbs.

Year	Team	Games	BA	SA	AB	H	2B	3B	HR	HR%	R	RBI	BB	SO	SB	Pinch Hit AB	Pinch Hit H	PO	A	E	DP	TC/G	FA	G by Pos
1916	PIT N	44	.238	.292	168	40	1	1	2	1.2	12	14	6	19	6	0	0	62	59	13	5	3.1	.903	3B-42, 2B-1
1917		3	.200	.200	5	1	0	0	0	0.0	0	0	0	1	0	1	1	5	2	0	0	7.0	1.000	3B-1
1919		6	.125	.125	8	1	0	0	0	0.0	0	2	3	1	0	1	1	3	6	2	0	3.7	.818	3B-3
1921	CHI N	14	.211	.237	38	8	1	0	0	0.0	4	3	2	1	1	3	0	4	18	1	1	2.3	.957	3B-10
4 yrs.		67	.228	.274	219	50	2	1	2	0.9	16	19	11	22	7	5	2	74	85	16	6	3.1	.909	3B-56, 2B-1

Jack Warner

WARNER, JOHN JOSEPH
B. Aug. 15, 1872, New York, N. Y. D. Dec. 21, 1943, Queens, N. Y.
BL TR 5′11″ 165 lbs.

Year	Team	Games	BA	SA	AB	H	2B	3B	HR	HR%	R	RBI	BB	SO	SB	Pinch Hit AB	Pinch Hit H	PO	A	E	DP	TC/G	FA	G by Pos
1895	2 teams	BOS N (3G –.143) LOU N (67G –.267)																						
″	total	70	.264	.310	239	63	4	2	1	0.4	22	21	12	16	10	0	0	219	54	21	5	4.1	.929	C-67, 1B-3, 2B-1
1896	2 teams	LOU N (33G –.227) NY N (19G –.259)																						
″	total	52	.238	.262	164	39	2	1	0	0.0	18	13	13	17	4	0	0	207	54	18	4	5.4	.935	C-51, 1B-1
1897	NY N	110	.275	.320	397	109	6	3	2	0.5	50	51	26		8	0	0	513	127	32	17	6.1	.952	C-110
1898		110	.257	.322	373	96	14	5	0	0.0	40	42	22		9	0	0	538	139	22	10	6.4	.969	C-109, OF-1
1899		88	.266	.300	293	78	8	1	0	0.0	38	19	15		15	3	0	329	125	22	9	5.6	.954	C-82, 1B-3
1900		34	.250	.287	108	27	4	0	0	0.0	15	13	8		1	3	1	98	49	8	5	5.0	.948	C-31
1901		87	.241	.268	291	70	6	1	0	0.0	19	20	3		3	3	0	361	107	16	11	5.8	.967	C-84
1902	BOS A	65	.234	.320	222	52	5	7	0	0.0	19	12	13		0	0	0	252	81	7	8	5.3	.979	C-64
1903	NY N	89	.284	.347	285	81	8	5	0	0.0	38	34	7		5	3	1	450	123	8	9	6.8	.986	C-85
1904		86	.199	.233	287	57	5	1	1	0.3	29	15	14		7	0	0	427	115	10	7	6.4	.982	C-86
1905	2 teams	STL N (41G –.255) DET A (36G –.202)																						
″	total	77	.230	.297	256	59	4	5	1	0.4	21	19	14		4	0	0	350	103	16	6	6.1	.966	C-77
1906	2 teams	DET A (50G –.242) WAS A (32G –.204)																						
″	total	82	.227	.293	256	58	8	3	1	0.4	20	19	14		7	1	0	348	136	13	5	6.1	.974	C-81
1907	WAS A	72	.256	.280	207	53	5	0	0	0.0	11	17	12		3	8	1	271	64	10	4	5.4	.971	C-64
1908		51	.241	.276	116	28	2	1	0	0.0	8	8	8		7	8	1	181	38	4	2	5.3	.982	C-41, 1B-1
14 yrs.		1073	.249	.297	3494	870	81	35	6	0.2	348	303	181	33	83	29	4	4544	1315	207	102	5.8	.966	C-1032, 1B-8, OF-1, 2B-1

Jack Warner

WARNER, JOHN RALPH
B. Aug. 29, 1903, Evansville, Ind. D. Mar. 13, 1986, Mt. Vernon, Ill.
BR TR 5′ 9½″ 165 lbs.

Year	Team	Games	BA	SA	AB	H	2B	3B	HR	HR%	R	RBI	BB	SO	SB	Pinch Hit AB	Pinch Hit H	PO	A	E	DP	TC/G	FA	G by Pos
1925	DET A	10	.333	.333	39	13	0	0	0	0.0	7	2	3	6	0	0	0	3	15	0	3	1.8	1.000	3B-10
1926		100	.251	.315	311	78	8	6	0	0.0	41	34	38	24	8	2	0	108	177	13	10	3.0	.956	3B-95, SS-3
1927		139	.267	.343	559	149	22	9	1	0.2	78	45	47	45	15	1	0	156	277	24	34	3.3	.947	3B-138
1928		75	.214	.272	206	44	4	4	0	0.0	33	13	16	15	4	1	0	71	120	12	10	3.4	.941	3B-52, SS-7
1929	BKN N	17	.274	.306	62	17	2	0	0	0.0	3	4	7	6	3	0	0	34	52	5	8	5.4	.945	SS-17

Jack Warner *continued*

Year	Team	Games	BA	SA	AB	H	2B	3B	HR	HR%	R	RBI	BB	SO	SB	Pinch Hit AB	Pinch Hit H	PO	A	E	DP	TC/G	FA	G by Pos
1930		21	.320	.360	25	8	1	0	0	0.0	4	0	2	7	1	3	1	5	12	0	0	0.8	1.000	3B-21
1931		9	.500	.500	4	2	0	0	0	0.0	2	0	1	1	0	0	0	2	5	0	0	2.3	1.000	SS-2, 3B-1
1933	PHI N	107	.224	.274	340	76	15	1	0	0.0	31	22	28	33	1	5	1	203	291	17	53	5.0	.967	2B-71, 3B-30, SS-1
8 yrs.		478	.250	.312	1546	387	52	20	1	0.1	199	120	142	137	32	12	2	582	949	71	118	3.6	.956	3B-347, 2B-71, SS-30

Jackie Warner

WARNER, JOHN JOSEPH BR TR 6′ 180 lbs.
B. Aug. 1, 1943, Monrovia, Calif.

Year	Team	Games	BA	SA	AB	H	2B	3B	HR	HR%	R	RBI	BB	SO	SB	Pinch Hit AB	Pinch Hit H	PO	A	E	DP	TC/G	FA	G by Pos
1966	CAL A	45	.211	.431	123	26	4	1	7	5.7	22	16	9	55	0	4	0	59	1	1	0	1.6	.984	OF-37

Hal Warnock

WARNOCK, HAROLD CHARLES BL TR 6′ 2″ 180 lbs.
B. Jan. 6, 1912, New York, N. Y.

Year	Team	Games	BA	SA	AB	H	2B	3B	HR	HR%	R	RBI	BB	SO	SB	Pinch Hit AB	Pinch Hit H	PO	A	E	DP	TC/G	FA	G by Pos
1935	STL A	6	.286	.571	7	2	2	0	0	0.0	1	0	0	3	0	6	1	1	0	0	0	0.5	1.000	OF-2

Bennie Warren

WARREN, BENNIE LOUIS BR TR 6′ 1″ 184 lbs.
B. Mar. 2, 1912, Elk City, Okla. D. May 11, 1994, Oklahoma City, Okla.

Year	Team	Games	BA	SA	AB	H	2B	3B	HR	HR%	R	RBI	BB	SO	SB	Pinch Hit AB	Pinch Hit H	PO	A	E	DP	TC/G	FA	G by Pos
1939	PHI N	18	.232	.286	56	13	0	0	1	1.8	4	7	7	7	0	1	1	60	8	3	2	4.2	.958	C-17
1940		106	.246	.398	289	71	6	1	12	4.2	33	34	40	46	1	7	4	326	63	11	9	4.1	.973	C-97, 1B-1
1941		121	.214	.342	345	74	13	2	9	2.6	34	35	44	66	0	11	4	412	84	14	16	4.6	.973	C-110
1942		90	.209	.356	225	47	6	3	7	3.1	19	20	24	36	0	9	0	267	51	10	4	4.2	.970	C-78, 1B-1
1946	NY N	39	.159	.377	69	11	1	1	4	5.8	7	8	14	21	0	7	0	103	8	4	0	3.8	.965	C-30
1947		3	.200	.200	5	1	0	0	0	0.0	0	0	0	1	0	0	0	2	0	0	0	0.7	1.000	C-3
6 yrs.		377	.219	.360	989	217	26	7	33	3.3	97	104	129	177	1	35	9	1170	214	42	31	4.2	.971	C-335, 1B-2

Bill Warren

WARREN, WILLIAM HACKNEY (Hack) BL TR 5′ 8″ 165 lbs.
B. Feb. 11, 1887, Cairo, Ill. D. Jan. 28, 1960, Whiteville, Tenn.

Year	Team	Games	BA	SA	AB	H	2B	3B	HR	HR%	R	RBI	BB	SO	SB	Pinch Hit AB	Pinch Hit H	PO	A	E	DP	TC/G	FA	G by Pos
1914	IND F	26	.240	.280	50	12	2	0	0	0.0	5	5	5		2	3	0	64	17	6	1	3.8	.931	C-23
1915	NWK F	5	.333	.333	3	1	0	0	0	0.0	0	1	0		0	3	1	2	0	0	0	1.0	1.000	1B-1, C-1
2 yrs.		31	.245	.283	53	13	2	0	0	0.0	5	6	5		2	6	1	66	17	6	1	3.6	.933	C-24, 1B-1

Rabbit Warstler

WARSTLER, HAROLD BURTON BR TR 5′ 7½″ 150 lbs.
B. Sept. 13, 1903, North Canton, Ohio D. May 31, 1964, North Canton, Ohio.

Year	Team	Games	BA	SA	AB	H	2B	3B	HR	HR%	R	RBI	BB	SO	SB	Pinch Hit AB	Pinch Hit H	PO	A	E	DP	TC/G	FA	G by Pos
1930	BOS A	55	.185	.253	162	30	2	3	1	0.6	16	13	20	21	0	0	0	100	149	14	30	4.9	.947	SS-54
1931		66	.243	.304	181	44	5	3	0	0.0	20	10	15	27	2	5	0	102	167	19	26	4.7	.934	2B-42, SS-19
1932		115	.211	.276	388	82	15	5	0	0.0	26	34	22	43	9	3	0	254	373	41	84	6.2	.939	SS-107
1933		92	.217	.273	322	70	13	1	1	0.3	44	17	42	36	2	1	0	150	275	22	40	5.1	.951	SS-87
1934	PHI A	117	.236	.303	419	99	19	3	1	0.2	56	36	51	30	9	4	0	232	396	22	88	6.0	.966	2B-107, SS-2
1935		138	.250	.337	496	124	20	7	3	0.6	62	59	56	53	8	0	0	309	486	34	94	6.0	.959	2B-136, 3B-2
1936	2 teams PHI A (66G –.250) BOS N (74G –.211)																							
″	total	140	.228	.281	540	123	14	6	1	0.2	54	41	58	49	2	0	0	296	543	35	104	6.2	.960	SS-74, 2B-66
1937	BOS N	149	.223	.276	555	124	20	0	3	0.5	57	36	51	62	4	0	0	298	493	49	85	5.6	.942	SS-149
1938		142	.231	.270	467	108	10	4	0	0.0	37	40	48	38	3	0	0	295	445	49	76	5.6	.938	SS-135, 2B-7
1939		114	.243	.292	342	83	11	3	0	0.0	34	24	24	31	2	1	0	194	301	20	75	4.6	.961	SS-49, 2B-43, 3B-21
1940	2 teams BOS N (33G –.211) CHI N (45G –.226)																							
″	total	78	.222	.264	216	48	4	1	1	0.5	25	22	18	24	1	6	0	122	184	16	35	4.5	.950	2B-41, SS-29, 3B-2
11 yrs.		1206	.229	.287	4088	935	133	36	11	0.3	431	332	405	414	42	20	0	2352	3812	321	737	5.5	.951	SS-705, 2B-442, 3B-25

Bill Warwick

WARWICK, FIRMAN NEWTON BR TR 6′½″ 180 lbs.
B. Nov. 26, 1897, Philadelphia, Pa. D. Dec. 19, 1984, San Antonio, Tex.

Year	Team	Games	BA	SA	AB	H	2B	3B	HR	HR%	R	RBI	BB	SO	SB	Pinch Hit AB	Pinch Hit H	PO	A	E	DP	TC/G	FA	G by Pos
1921	PIT N	1	.000	.000	1	0	0	0	0	0.0	0	0	0	0	0	0	0	0	1	1	0	2.0	.500	C-1
1925	STL N	13	.293	.488	41	12	1	2	1	2.4	8	6	5	5	0	0	0	33	4	0	0	2.8	1.000	C-13
1926		9	.357	.357	14	5	0	0	0	0.0	0	2	0	2	0	0	0	19	5	2	0	2.9	.923	C-9
3 yrs.		23	.304	.446	56	17	1	2	1	1.8	8	8	5	7	0	0	0	52	10	3	0	2.8	.954	C-23

Carl Warwick

WARWICK, CARL WAYNE BR TL 5′10″ 170 lbs.
B. Feb. 27, 1937, Dallas, Tex.

Year	Team	Games	BA	SA	AB	H	2B	3B	HR	HR%	R	RBI	BB	SO	SB	Pinch Hit AB	Pinch Hit H	PO	A	E	DP	TC/G	FA	G by Pos
1961	2 teams LA N (19G –.091) STL N (55G –.250)																							
″	total	74	.239	.374	163	39	6	2	4	2.5	29	17	20	36	3	13	4	96	2	3	1	1.7	.970	OF-60
1962	2 teams STL N (13G –.348) HOU N (130G –.260)																							
″	total	143	.264	.404	500	132	17	1	17	3.4	67	64	40	79	4	13	4	271	13	4	1	2.1	.986	OF-138
1963	HOU N	150	.254	.348	528	134	19	5	7	1.3	49	47	49	70	3	10	2	260	8	3	2	1.9	.989	OF-141, 1B-2
1964	STL N	88	.259	.373	158	41	7	1	3	1.9	14	15	11	30	2	43	11	53	3	4	2	1.2	.933	OF-49
1965	2 teams STL N (50G –.156) BAL A (9G –.000)																							
″	total	59	.132	.176	91	12	2	1	0	0.0	6	6	7	20	1	36	4	49	1	1	4	1.8	.980	OF-24, 1B-4
1966	CHI N	16	.227	.227	22	5	0	0	0	0.0	3	0	0	6	0	7	2	8	1	0	0	0.9	1.000	OF-10
6 yrs.		530	.248	.360	1462	363	51	10	31	2.1	168	149	127	241	13	122	27	737	28	15	10	1.8	.981	OF-422, 1B-6
WORLD SERIES																								
1964	STL N	5	.750	.750	4	3	0	0	0	0.0	2	1	1	0	0	4	3	0	0	0	0	0.0	—	

Jimmy Wasdell

WASDELL, JAMES CHARLES BL TL 5′11″ 185 lbs.
B. May 15, 1914, Cleveland, Ohio D. Aug. 6, 1983, New Port Richey, Fla.

Year	Team	Games	BA	SA	AB	H	2B	3B	HR	HR%	R	RBI	BB	SO	SB	Pinch Hit AB	Pinch Hit H	PO	A	E	DP	TC/G	FA	G by Pos
1937	WAS A	32	.255	.418	110	28	4	4	2	1.8	13	12	7	13	0	4	1	196	11	1	19	7.4	.995	1B-21, OF-7
1938		53	.236	.307	140	33	2	1	2	1.4	19	16	12	12	5	18	4	234	12	1	26	7.7	.996	1B-26, OF-6
1939		29	.303	.367	109	33	5	1	0	0.0	12	13	9	16	3	1	0	255	15	10	24	10.0	.964	1B-28
1940	2 teams WAS A (10G –.086) BKN N (77G –.278)																							
″	total	87	.253	.374	265	67	15	4	3	1.1	38	37	20	31	4	14	5	268	8	7	12	4.2	.975	OF-42, 1B-25
1941	BKN N	94	.298	.419	265	79	14	3	4	1.5	39	48	16	15	2	23	4	185	7	4	5	2.8	.980	OF-54, 1B-15
1942	PIT N	122	.259	.318	409	106	11	2	3	0.7	44	38	47	22	1	16	1	246	12	11	5	2.6	.959	OF-97, 1B-7
1943	2 teams PIT N (4G –.500) PHI N (141G –.261)																							
″	total	145	.261	.344	524	137	19	6	4	0.8	54	68	48	22	6	5	4	857	61	13	62	6.7	.986	1B-82, OF-56
1944	PHI N	133	.277	.355	451	125	20	3	3	0.7	47	40	45	17	0	9	2	286	6	5	6	2.4	.983	OF-121, 1B-4

Jimmy Wasdell *continued*

Year	Team	Games	BA	SA	AB	H	2B	3B	HR	HR%	R	RBI	BB	SO	SB	Pinch Hit AB	Pinch Hit H	PO	A	E	DP	TC/G	FA	G by Pos
1945		134	.300	.412	500	150	19	8	7	1.4	65	60	32	11	7	8	5	739	47	12	52	6.2	.985	OF-65, 1B-63
1946	2 teams	PHI N (26G –.255) CLE A (32G –.268)																						
"	total	58	.261	.337	92	24	0	2	1	1.1	8	9	7	6	1	36	10	43	4	4	9	2.5	.922	OF-14, 1B-6
1947	CLE A	1	.000	.000	1	0	0	0	0	0.0	0	0	0	0	0	1	0	0	0	0	0	0.0	—	
11 yrs.		888	.273	.365	2866	782	109	34	29	1.0	339	341	243	165	29	135	36	3309	183	68	220	4.8	.981	OF-462, 1B-277
WORLD SERIES																								
1941	BKN N	3	.200	.400	5	1	1	0	0	0.0	0	2	0	0	0	3	1	2	0	0	0	2.0	1.000	OF-1

Link Wasem

WASEM, LINCOLN WILLIAM BR TR 5′ 9½″ 180 lbs.
B. Jan. 30, 1911, Birmingham, Ohio D. Mar. 6, 1979, South Laguna, Calif.

Year	Team	Games	BA	SA	AB	H	2B	3B	HR	HR%	R	RBI	BB	SO	SB	Pinch Hit AB	Pinch Hit H	PO	A	E	DP	TC/G	FA	G by Pos
1937	BOS N	2	.000	.000	1	0	0	0	0	0.0	0	0	0	0	0	0	0	2	12	0	0	7.0	1.000	C-2

Libe Washburn

WASHBURN, LIBEUS BB TL 5′10″ 180 lbs.
B. June 16, 1874, Lynn, N. H. D. Mar. 22, 1940, Malone, N. Y.

Year	Team	Games	BA	SA	AB	H	2B	3B	HR	HR%	R	RBI	BB	SO	SB	Pinch Hit AB	Pinch Hit H	PO	A	E	DP	TC/G	FA	G by Pos
1902	NY N	6	.444	.444	9	4	0	0	0	0.0	1	0	2		1	3	1	4	0	0	0	1.3	1.000	OF-3
1903	PHI N	8	.167	.167	18	3	0	0	0	0.0	1	1	1		0	2	0	3	7	0	0	1.7	1.000	P-4, OF-2
2 yrs.		14	.259	.259	27	7	0	0	0	0.0	2	1	3		1	5	1	7	7	0	0	1.6	1.000	OF-5, P-4

Claudell Washington

WASHINGTON, CLAUDELL BL TL 6′ 190 lbs.
B. Aug. 31, 1954, Los Angeles, Calif.

Year	Team	Games	BA	SA	AB	H	2B	3B	HR	HR%	R	RBI	BB	SO	SB	Pinch Hit AB	Pinch Hit H	PO	A	E	DP	TC/G	FA	G by Pos
1974	OAK A	73	.285	.376	221	63	10	5	0	0.0	16	19	13	44	6	8	3	63	2	1	0	0.9	.985	DH-38, OF-32
1975		148	.308	.424	590	182	24	7	10	1.7	86	77	32	80	40	2	1	305	8	7	1	2.2	.978	OF-148
1976		134	.257	.353	490	126	20	6	5	1.0	65	53	30	90	37	3	2	276	10	11	2	2.3	.963	OF-126, DH-6
1977	TEX A	129	.284	.420	521	148	31	2	12	2.3	63	68	25	112	21	2	0	255	11	6	3	2.1	.978	OF-127, DH-1
1978	2 teams	TEX A (12G –.167) CHI A (86G –.264)																						
"	total	98	.253	.376	356	90	16	5	6	1.7	34	33	13	69	5	6	2	170	6	8	0	2.0	.957	OF-89, DH-5
1979	CHI A	131	.280	.454	471	132	33	5	13	2.8	79	66	28	93	19	13	4	256	7	7	3	2.2	.974	OF-122, DH-3
1980	2 teams	CHI A (32G –.289) NY N (79G –.275)																						
"	total	111	.278	.452	374	104	20	6	11	2.9	53	54	25	82	21	17	1	164	13	6	2	1.9	.967	OF-93, DH-2
1981	ATL N	85	.291	.425	320	93	22	3	5	1.6	37	37	15	47	12	5	3	145	5	1	0	1.9	.993	OF-79
1982		150	.266	.416	563	150	24	6	16	2.8	94	80	50	107	33	7	0	221	9	12	3	1.7	.950	OF-139
1983		134	.278	.413	496	138	24	8	9	1.8	75	44	35	103	31	7	2	218	8	6	3	1.8	.974	OF-128
1984		120	.286	.469	416	119	21	2	17	4.1	62	61	59	77	21	12	2	170	4	6	0	1.7	.967	OF-107
1985		122	.276	.455	398	110	14	6	15	3.8	62	43	40	66	14	26	6	122	3	5	1	1.3	.962	OF-99
1986	2 teams	ATL N (40G –.270) NY A (54G –.237)																						
"	total	94	.254	.434	272	69	16	0	11	4.0	36	30	21	59	10	28	5	110	1	3	0	1.5	.974	OF-76
1987	NY A	102	.279	.420	312	87	17	0	9	2.9	42	44	27	54	10	21	4	166	3	2	1	2.0	.988	OF-72, DH-13
1988		126	.308	.442	455	140	22	3	11	2.4	62	64	24	74	15	19	4	309	5	5	1	2.7	.984	OF-117
1989	CAL A	110	.273	.428	418	114	18	4	13	3.1	53	42	27	84	13	6	2	187	6	5	2	1.9	.975	OF-100, DH-7
1990	2 teams	CAL A (12G –.176) NY A (33G –.163)																						
"	total	45	.167	.228	114	19	2	1	1	0.9	7	9	4	25	4	11	3	61	3	0	0	2.0	1.000	OF-30, DH-2
17 yrs.		1912	.278	.420	6787	1884	334	69	164	2.4	926	824	468	1266	312	193	44	3198	104	91	22	1.9	.973	OF-1684, DH-77
LEAGUE CHAMPIONSHIP SERIES																								
1974	OAK A	4	.273	.364	11	3	1	0	0	0.0	1	0	0	0	0	1	1	11	0	0	0	3.7	1.000	OF-3
1975		3	.250	.333	12	3	1	0	0	0.0	1	1	0	2	0	0	0	1	0	2	0	1.0	.333	OF-2, DH-1
1982	ATL N	3	.333	.333	9	3	0	0	0	0.0	0	0	2	2	0	0	0	5	1	0	0	2.0	1.000	OF-3
3 yrs.		10	.281	.344	32	9	2	0	0	0.0	2	1	2	4	0	1	1	17	1	2	0	2.2	.900	OF-8, DH-1
WORLD SERIES																								
1974	OAK A	5	.571	.571	7	4	0	0	0	0.0	1	0	1	1	0	1	1	3	0	0	0	0.6	1.000	OF-5

George Washington

WASHINGTON, SLOAN VERNON BL TR 5′11½″ 190 lbs.
B. June 4, 1907, Linden, Tex. D. Feb. 17, 1985, Linden, Tex.

Year	Team	Games	BA	SA	AB	H	2B	3B	HR	HR%	R	RBI	BB	SO	SB	Pinch Hit AB	Pinch Hit H	PO	A	E	DP	TC/G	FA	G by Pos
1935	CHI A	108	.283	.437	339	96	22	3	8	2.4	40	47	10	18	1	29	9	137	10	4	2	1.9	.974	OF-79
1936		20	.163	.265	49	8	2	0	1	2.0	6	5	1	4	0	6	1	13	2	1	0	1.3	.938	OF-12
2 yrs.		128	.268	.415	388	104	24	3	9	2.3	46	52	11	22	1	35	10	150	12	5	2	1.8	.970	OF-91

Herb Washington

WASHINGTON, HERBERT LEE BR TR 6′ 170 lbs.
B. Nov. 16, 1951, Belzoni, Miss.

Year	Team	Games	BA	SA	AB	H	2B	3B	HR	HR%	R	RBI	BB	SO	SB	Pinch Hit AB	Pinch Hit H	PO	A	E	DP	TC/G	FA	G by Pos
1974	OAK A	92	—	—	0	0	0	0	0	—	29	0	0	0	29	0	0	0	0	0	0	0.0	—	
1975		13	—	—	0	0	0	0	0	—	4	0	0	0	2	0	0	0	0	0	0	0.0	—	
2 yrs.		105			0	0	0	0	0		33	0	0	0	31	0	0							
LEAGUE CHAMPIONSHIP SERIES																								
1974	OAK A	2	—	—	0	0	0	0	0	—	0	0	0	0	0	0	0	0	0	0	0	0.0	—	
WORLD SERIES																								
1974	OAK A	3	—	—	0	0	0	0	0	—	0	0	0	0	0	0	0	0	0	0	0	0.0	—	

LaRue Washington

WASHINGTON, LaRUE BR TR 6′ 170 lbs.
B. Sept. 7, 1953, Long Beach, Calif.

Year	Team	Games	BA	SA	AB	H	2B	3B	HR	HR%	R	RBI	BB	SO	SB	Pinch Hit AB	Pinch Hit H	PO	A	E	DP	TC/G	FA	G by Pos
1978	TEX A	3	.000	.000	3	0	0	0	0	0.0	0	0	0	1	0	0	0	0	5	0	2	1.7	1.000	2B-2, DH-1
1979		25	.278	.278	18	5	0	0	0	0.0	5	2	4	0	2	0	0	16	1	0	0	1.1	1.000	OF-13, 3B-1, DH-1
2 yrs.		28	.238	.238	21	5	0	0	0	0.0	5	2	4	1	2	0	0	16	6	0	2	1.2	1.000	OF-13, 2B-2, DH-2, 3B-1

Ron Washington

WASHINGTON, RONALD BR TR 5′11″ 156 lbs.
B. Apr. 29, 1952, New Orleans, La.

Year	Team	Games	BA	SA	AB	H	2B	3B	HR	HR%	R	RBI	BB	SO	SB	Pinch Hit AB	Pinch Hit H	PO	A	E	DP	TC/G	FA	G by Pos
1977	LA N	10	.368	.368	19	7	0	0	0	0.0	4	1	0	2	1	0	0	4	14	3	2	2.1	.857	SS-10
1981	MIN A	28	.226	.286	84	19	3	1	0	0.0	8	5	4	14	4	0	0	64	80	8	19	5.4	.947	SS-26, OF-2
1982		119	.271	.368	451	122	17	6	5	1.1	48	39	14	79	3	2	0	201	269	13	58	3.7	.973	SS-91, 2B-37, 3B-1
1983		99	.246	.325	317	78	7	3	4	1.3	28	26	22	50	10	4	1	140	246	16	54	4.1	.960	SS-81, 2B-14, DH-1, 3B-1
1984		88	.294	.447	197	58	11	5	3	1.5	25	23	4	31	1	12	2	77	134	4	24	2.5	.981	SS-71, 2B-9, DH-4, 3B-2

Ron Washington *continued*

Year	Team	Games	BA	SA	AB	H	2B	3B	HR	HR%	R	RBI	BB	SO	SB	Pinch Hit AB	Pinch Hit H	PO	A	E	DP	TC/G	FA	G by Pos
1985		69	.274	.400	135	37	6	4	1	0.7	24	14	8	15	5	12	2	55	100	7	14	2.3	.957	SS-31, 2B-24, DH-7, 3B-7, 1B-1
1986		48	.257	.459	74	19	3	0	4	5.4	15	11	3	21	1	10	2	12	20	2	6	0.8	.941	2B-16, DH-15, SS-7, 3B-3
1987	BAL A	26	.203	.304	79	16	3	1	1	1.3	7	6	1	15	0	0	0	19	42	0	3	2.2	1.000	3B-20, 2B-3, DH-2, OF-2, SS-1
1988	CLE A	69	.256	.363	223	57	14	2	2	0.9	30	21	9	35	3	4	3	95	162	17	29	4.0	.938	SS-54, 3B-8, 2B-7
1989	HOU N	7	.143	.286	7	1	1	0	0	0.0	1	0	0	4	0	5	0	0	1	0	0	0.5	1.000	3B-1, 2B-1
10 yrs.		563	.261	.368	1586	414	65	22	20	1.3	190	146	65	266	28	49	10	667	1068	70	209	3.2	.961	SS-372, 2B-111, 3B-43, DH-29, OF-4, 1B-1

U. L. Washington

WASHINGTON, U. L.
B. Oct. 27, 1953, Stringtown, Okla.
BB TR 5′11″ 175 lbs.

Year	Team	Games	BA	SA	AB	H	2B	3B	HR	HR%	R	RBI	BB	SO	SB	Pinch Hit AB	Pinch Hit H	PO	A	E	DP	TC/G	FA	G by Pos
1977	KC A	10	.200	.350	20	4	1	1	0	0.0	0	1	5	4	1	0	0	13	21	5	4	3.9	.872	SS-9, DH-1
1978		69	.264	.295	129	34	2	1	0	0.0	10	9	10	20	12	1	1	79	92	9	18	2.6	.950	SS-49, 2B-19, DH-1
1979		101	.254	.358	268	68	12	5	2	0.7	32	25	20	44	10	3	0	174	243	18	68	4.3	.959	SS-50, 2B-46, DH-3, 3B-1
1980		153	.273	.375	549	150	16	11	6	1.1	79	53	53	78	20	2	1	237	467	32	86	4.8	.957	SS-152
1981		98	.227	.307	339	77	19	1	2	0.6	40	29	41	43	10	0	0	135	297	12	58	4.5	.973	SS-98
1982		119	.286	.412	437	125	19	3	10	2.3	64	60	38	48	23	2	0	173	371	22	63	4.8	.961	SS-117, DH-1
1983		144	.236	.320	547	129	19	6	5	0.9	76	41	48	78	40	3	0	201	448	36	91	4.9	.947	SS-140, DH-1
1984		63	.224	.276	170	38	6	0	1	0.6	18	10	14	31	4	0	0	81	166	10	40	4.2	.961	SS-61
1985	MON N	68	.249	.352	193	48	9	4	1	0.5	24	17	15	33	6	20	3	76	130	7	29	3.9	.967	2B-43, SS-9, 3B-3
1986	PIT N	72	.200	.259	135	27	0	4	0	0.0	14	10	15	27	6	29	5	50	97	8	25	2.9	.948	SS-51, 2B-3
1987		10	.300	.300	10	3	0	0	0	0.0	1	0	2	3	0	6	2	1	4	1	0	3.0	.833	SS-1, 3B-1
11 yrs.		907	.251	.343	2797	703	103	36	27	1.0	358	255	261	409	132	66	12	1220	2336	160	482	4.3	.957	SS-737, 2B-111, DH-7, 3B-5
DIVISIONAL PLAYOFF SERIES																								
1981	KC A	3	.222	.222	9	2	0	0	0	0.0	0	0	0	1	0	0	0	7	11	1	0	6.3	.947	SS-3
LEAGUE CHAMPIONSHIP SERIES																								
1980	KC A	3	.364	.455	11	4	1	0	0	0.0	1	1	2	3	0	0	0	5	7	0	2	4.0	1.000	SS-3
1984		2	.000	.000	1	0	0	0	0	0.0	0	0	0	1	0	1	0	0	0	0	0	0.0	—	
2 yrs.		5	.333	.417	12	4	1	0	0	0.0	1	1	2	4	0	1	0	5	7	0	2	4.0	1.000	SS-3
WORLD SERIES																								
1980	KC A	6	.273	.273	22	6	0	0	0	0.0	1	2	0	6	0	0	0	8	20	1	4	4.8	.966	SS-6

Mark Wasinger

WASINGER, MARK THOMAS
B. Aug. 4, 1961, Monterey, Calif.
BR TR 6′ 165 lbs.

Year	Team	Games	BA	SA	AB	H	2B	3B	HR	HR%	R	RBI	BB	SO	SB	Pinch Hit AB	Pinch Hit H	PO	A	E	DP	TC/G	FA	G by Pos
1986	SD N	3	.000	.000	8	0	0	0	0	0.0	0	1	0	2	0	0	0	2	2	3	1	1.8	.571	3B-3, 2B-1
1987	SF N	44	.275	.350	80	22	3	0	1	1.3	16	3	8	14	2	11	1	21	50	1	9	2.2	.986	3B-21, 2B-10, SS-2
1988		3	.000	.000	2	0	0	0	0	0.0	1	0	0	0	0	1	0	0	0	0	0	0.0	.000	3B-1
3 yrs.		50	.244	.311	90	22	3	0	1	1.1	17	4	8	16	2	12	1	23	52	4	10	2.1	.949	3B-25, 2B-11, SS-2

John Wathan

WATHAN, JOHN DAVID (Duke)
B. Oct. 4, 1949, Cedar Rapids, Iowa.
Manager 1987–92.
BR TR 6′ 2″ 205 lbs.

Year	Team	Games	BA	SA	AB	H	2B	3B	HR	HR%	R	RBI	BB	SO	SB	Pinch Hit AB	Pinch Hit H	PO	A	E	DP	TC/G	FA	G by Pos
1976	KC A	27	.286	.310	42	12	1	0	0	0.0	5	5	2	5	0	2	1	63	4	1	1	2.6	.985	C-23, 1B-3
1977		55	.328	.471	119	39	5	3	2	1.7	18	21	5	8	2	18	6	156	9	2	2	4.0	.988	C-35, 1B-5, DH-2
1978		67	.300	.395	190	57	10	1	2	1.1	19	28	3	12	2	13	6	385	28	2	20	6.1	.995	1B-47, C-21
1979		90	.206	.302	199	41	7	3	2	1.0	26	28	7	24	2	31	5	336	24	3	30	4.2	.992	1B-49, C-23, DH-11, OF-3
1980		126	.305	.406	453	138	14	7	6	1.3	57	58	50	42	17	10	3	472	33	8	19	4.1	.984	C-77, OF-35, 1B-12
1981		89	.252	.312	301	76	9	3	1	0.3	24	19	19	23	11	4	0	316	28	7	1	3.9	.980	C-73, OF-16, 1B-1
1982		121	.270	.328	448	121	11	3	3	0.7	79	51	48	46	36	2	0	482	40	10	5	4.3	.981	C-120, 1B-3
1983		128	.245	.314	437	107	18	3	2	0.5	49	32	27	56	28	5	2	615	58	9	29	4.9	.987	C-92, 1B-37, OF-9
1984		97	.181	.269	171	31	7	1	2	1.2	17	10	21	34	6	4	1	304	31	6	10	3.5	.982	C-59, 1B-33, DH-4, OF-1
1985		60	.234	.324	145	34	8	1	1	0.7	11	9	17	15	1	2	0	259	29	4	6	5.1	.986	C-49, 1B-6, DH-2
10 yrs.		860	.262	.343	2505	656	90	25	21	0.8	305	261	199	265	105	91	24	3388	284	52	123	4.4	.986	C-572, 1B-196, OF-64, DH-19
DIVISIONAL PLAYOFF SERIES																								
1981	KC A	3	.300	.300	10	3	0	0	0	0.0	1	0	1	1	0	0	0	11	4	1	0	5.3	.938	C-3
LEAGUE CHAMPIONSHIP SERIES																								
1976	KC A	1	—	—	0	0	0	0	0	—	0	0	0	0	0	0	0	0	0	0	0	0.0	.000	C-1
1977		4	.000	.000	6	0	0	0	0	0.0	0	0	0	3	0	2	0	19	0	0	0	4.8	1.000	1B-2, C-1, DH-1
1978		1	.000	.000	3	0	0	0	0	0.0	0	0	0	0	0	0	0	7	0	0	0	7.0	1.000	1B-1
1980		3	.000	.000	6	0	0	0	0	0.0	1	0	3	1	0	1	0	7	0	0	0	2.3	1.000	OF-3
1984		1	.000	.000	1	0	0	0	0	0.0	0	0	0	0	0	1	0	0	0	0	0	0.0	—	
5 yrs.		10	.000	.000	16	0	0	0	0	0.0	1	0	3	4	0	4	0	33	0	0	0	3.7	1.000	OF-3, 1B-3, C-2, DH-1
WORLD SERIES																								
1980	KC A	3	.286	.286	7	2	0	0	0	0.0	1	1	2	1	0	1	0	7	1	0	0	2.7	1.000	C-2, OF-1
1985		2	.000	.000	1	0	0	0	0	0.0	0	0	0	1	0	1	0	0	0	0	0	0.0	—	
2 yrs.		5	.250	.250	8	2	0	0	0	0.0	1	1	2	2	0	2	0	7	1	0	0	2.7	1.000	C-2, OF-1

Bill Watkins

WATKINS, WILLIAM HENRY
B. May 5, 1858, Brantford, Ont., Canada D. June 9, 1937, Port Huron, Mich.
Manager 1884–89, 1893, 1898–99.
5′10″ 156 lbs.

Year	Team	Games	BA	SA	AB	H	2B	3B	HR	HR%	R	RBI	BB	SO	SB	Pinch Hit AB	Pinch Hit H	PO	A	E	DP	TC/G	FA	G by Pos
1884	IND AA	34	.205	.236	127	26	4	0	0	0.0	16		5			0	0	45	63	15	4	3.6	.878	3B-23, 2B-9, SS-2

Dave Watkins

WATKINS, DAVID ROGER
B. Mar. 15, 1944, Owensboro, Ky.
BR TR 5′10″ 185 lbs.

Year	Team	Games	BA	SA	AB	H	2B	3B	HR	HR%	R	RBI	BB	SO	SB	Pinch Hit AB	Pinch Hit H	PO	A	E	DP	TC/G	FA	G by Pos
1969	PHI N	69	.176	.284	148	26	2	1	4	2.7	17	12	22	53	2	11	1	247	20	5	2	4.5	.982	C-54, OF-5, 3B-1

Ed Watkins

WATKINS, JAMES EDWARD
B. June 21, 1877, Philadelphia, Pa. D. Mar. 29, 1933, Kelvin, Ariz.

Year	Team	Games	BA	SA	AB	H	2B	3B	HR	HR%	R	RBI	BB	SO	SB	Pinch Hit AB	Pinch Hit H	PO	A	E	DP	TC/G	FA	G by Pos
1902	PHI N	1	.000	.000	3	0	0	0	0	0.0	0	0	1		0	0	0	1	0	0	0	1.0	1.000	OF-1

George Watkins

WATKINS, GEORGE ARCHIBALD BL TR 6′ 175 lbs.
B. June 4, 1900, Freestone County, Tex. D. June 1, 1970, Houston, Tex.

Year	Team	Games	BA	SA	AB	H	2B	3B	HR	HR%	R	RBI	BB	SO	SB	Pinch Hit AB	Pinch Hit H	PO	A	E	DP	TC/G	FA	G by Pos
1930	STL N	119	.373	.621	391	146	32	7	17	4.3	85	87	24	49	5	15	5	279	18	11	16	3.0	.964	OF-89, 1B-13, 2B-1
1931		131	.288	.477	503	145	30	13	13	2.6	93	51	31	66	15	2	0	263	12	12	4	2.2	.958	OF-129
1932		137	.312	.461	458	143	35	3	9	2.0	67	63	45	46	18	6	2	267	11	15	1	2.4	.949	OF-120
1933		138	.278	.371	525	146	24	5	5	1.0	66	62	39	62	11	3	0	295	9	15	3	2.4	.953	OF-135
1934	NY N	105	.247	.389	296	73	18	3	6	2.0	38	33	24	34	2	16	3	165	3	10	1	2.2	.944	OF-81
1935	PHI N	150	.270	.413	600	162	25	5	17	2.8	80	76	40	78	3	2	1	325	18	15	4	2.4	.958	OF-148
1936	2 teams	PHI N (19G –.243) BKN N (105G –.255)																						
″	total	124	.253	.387	434	110	28	6	6	1.4	61	48	43	47	7	8	2	206	6	9	2	1.9	.959	OF-115
7 yrs.		904	.288	.443	3207	925	192	42	73	2.3	490	420	246	382	61	52	13	1800	77	87	31	2.4	.956	OF-817, 1B-13, 2B-1
WORLD SERIES																								
1930	STL N	4	.167	.417	12	2	0	0	1	8.3	2	1	1	3	0	0	0	5	0	1	0	1.5	.833	OF-4
1931		5	.286	.571	14	4	1	0	1	7.1	4	2	2	1	1	0	0	8	0	0	0	1.6	1.000	OF-5
2 yrs.		9	.231	.500	26	6	1	0	2	7.7	6	3	3	4	1	0	0	13	0	1	0	1.6	.929	OF-9

Neal Watlington

WATLINGTON, JULIUS NEAL BL TR 6′ 195 lbs.
B. Dec. 25, 1922, Yanceyville, N. C.

Year	Team	Games	BA	SA	AB	H	2B	3B	HR	HR%	R	RBI	BB	SO	SB	Pinch Hit AB	Pinch Hit H	PO	A	E	DP	TC/G	FA	G by Pos
1953	PHI A	21	.159	.182	44	7	1	0	0	0.0	4	3	3	8	0	12	2	37	7	1	2	5.0	.978	C-9

Art Watson

WATSON, ARTHUR STANHOPE (Watty) BL TR 5′11″ 170 lbs.
B. Jan. 11, 1884, Jeffersonville, Ind. D. May 9, 1950, Buffalo, N. Y.

Year	Team	Games	BA	SA	AB	H	2B	3B	HR	HR%	R	RBI	BB	SO	SB	Pinch Hit AB	Pinch Hit H	PO	A	E	DP	TC/G	FA	G by Pos
1914	BKN F	22	.283	.478	46	13	4	1	1	2.2	7	3	1		0	2	1	66	20	2	1	4.9	.977	C-18
1915	2 teams	BKN F (9G –.263) BUF F (22G –.467)																						
″	total	31	.388	.592	49	19	1	3	1	2.0	10	14	3		0	16	6	27	9	5	2	2.9	.878	C-13, OF-1
2 yrs.		53	.337	.537	95	32	5	4	2	2.1	17	17	4		0	18	7	93	29	7	3	4.0	.946	C-31, OF-1

Bob Watson

WATSON, ROBERT JOSE (Bull) BR TR 6′ 1½″ 201 lbs.
B. Apr. 10, 1946, Los Angeles, Calif.

Year	Team	Games	BA	SA	AB	H	2B	3B	HR	HR%	R	RBI	BB	SO	SB	Pinch Hit AB	Pinch Hit H	PO	A	E	DP	TC/G	FA	G by Pos
1966	HOU N	1	.000	.000	1	0	0	0	0	0.0	0	0	0	0	0	1	0	0	0	0	0	0.0	—	
1967		6	.214	.429	14	3	0	0	1	7.1	1	2	0	3	0	3	0	21	2	1	0	8.0	.958	1B-3
1968		45	.229	.321	140	32	7	0	2	1.4	13	8	13	32	1	5	0	46	0	6	0	1.3	.885	OF-40
1969		20	.275	.350	40	11	3	0	0	0.0	3	3	6	5	0	5	3	46	3	0	4	4.1	1.000	OF-6, 1B-5, C-1
1970		97	.272	.443	327	89	19	2	11	3.4	48	61	24	59	1	13	5	707	40	6	54	8.4	.992	1B-83, C-6, OF-1
1971		129	.288	.395	468	135	17	3	9	1.9	49	67	41	56	0	3	1	470	18	7	28	3.8	.986	OF-87, 1B-45
1972		147	.312	.464	548	171	27	4	16	2.9	74	86	53	83	1	2	0	231	7	5	3	1.7	.979	OF-143, 1B-2
1973		158	.312	.449	573	179	24	3	16	2.8	97	94	85	73	1	2	0	433	11	12	7	2.7	.974	OF-142, 1B-26, C-3
1974		150	.298	.412	524	156	19	4	11	2.1	69	67	60	61	3	8	2	298	12	4	9	1.8	.987	OF-140, 1B-35
1975		132	.324	.495	485	157	27	1	18	3.7	67	85	40	50	3	8	2	1089	70	8	106	9.2	.993	1B-118, OF-9
1976		157	.313	.458	585	183	31	3	16	2.7	76	102	62	64	3	3	0	1395	96	15	126	9.7	.990	1B-155
1977		151	.289	.498	554	160	38	6	22	4.0	77	110	57	69	5	5	3	1331	118	9	100	10.0	.994	1B-146
1978		139	.289	.451	461	133	25	4	14	3.0	51	79	51	57	3	9	0	974	95	9	63	8.4	.992	1B-128
1979	2 teams	HOU N (49G –.239) BOS A (84G –.337)																						
″	total	133	.303	.469	475	144	23	4	16	3.4	63	71	45	56	3	6	0	896	80	10	81	7.7	.990	1B-102, DH-26
1980	NY A	130	.307	.456	469	144	25	3	13	2.8	62	68	48	56	2	11	3	851	63	9	87	7.4	.990	1B-104, DH-21
1981		59	.212	.385	156	33	3	3	6	3.8	15	12	24	17	0	13	3	367	25	1	42	7.0	.997	1B-50, DH-6
1982	2 teams	NY A (7G –.235) ATL N (57G –.246)																						
″	total	64	.244	.420	131	32	6	1	5	3.8	19	25	17	20	1	25	6	248	8	0	23	7.1	1.000	1B-33, OF-2, DH-1
1983	ATL N	65	.309	.490	149	46	9	0	6	4.0	14	37	18	23	0	27	11	280	19	5	23	8.9	.984	1B-34
1984		49	.212	.329	85	18	4	0	2	2.4	4	12	9	12	0	29	6	165	12	3	17	9.5	.983	1B-19
19 yrs.		1832	.295	.447	6185	1826	307	41	184	3.0	802	989	653	796	27	178	45	9848	679	110	773	6.2	.990	1B-1088, OF-570, DH-54, C-10
DIVISIONAL PLAYOFF SERIES																								
1981	NY A	5	.438	.438	16	7	0	0	0	0.0	2	1	1	1	0	0	0	36	3	1	0	8.0	.975	1B-5
LEAGUE CHAMPIONSHIP SERIES																								
1980	NY A	3	.500	.917	12	6	3	1	0	0.0	0	0	0	0	0	0	0	28	5	1	2	11.3	.971	1B-3
1981		3	.250	.250	12	3	0	0	0	0.0	0	1	0	1	0	0	0	17	0	0	5	5.7	1.000	1B-3
2 yrs.		6	.375	.583	24	9	3	1	0	0.0	0	1	0	1	0	0	0	45	5	1	7	8.5	.980	1B-6
WORLD SERIES																								
1981	NY A	6	.318	.636	22	7	1	0	2	9.1	2	7	3	0	0	0	0	51	0	0	2	8.5	1.000	1B-6

Johnny Watson

WATSON, JOHN THOMAS BL TR 6′ 175 lbs.
B. Jan. 16, 1908, Tazewell, Va. D. Apr. 29, 1965, Huntington, W. Va.

Year	Team	Games	BA	SA	AB	H	2B	3B	HR	HR%	R	RBI	BB	SO	SB	Pinch Hit AB	Pinch Hit H	PO	A	E	DP	TC/G	FA	G by Pos
1930	DET A	4	.250	.417	12	3	2	0	0	0.0	1	3	1	2	0	0	0	6	10	3	2	4.8	.842	SS-4

Allie Watt

WATT, ALBERT BAILEY BR TR 5′ 8″ 154 lbs.
Brother of Frank Watt.
B. Dec. 12, 1899, Philadelphia, Pa. D. Mar. 15, 1968, Norfolk, Va.

Year	Team	Games	BA	SA	AB	H	2B	3B	HR	HR%	R	RBI	BB	SO	SB	Pinch Hit AB	Pinch Hit H	PO	A	E	DP	TC/G	FA	G by Pos
1920	WAS A	1	1.000	2.000	1	1	1	0	0	0.0	0	1	0	0	0	0	0	0	1	0	0	1.0	1.000	2B-1

Cliff Watwood

WATWOOD, JOHN CLIFFORD (Lefty) BL TL 6′ 1″ 186 lbs.
B. Aug. 17, 1905, Alexander City, Ala. D. Mar. 1, 1980, Goodwater, Ala.

Year	Team	Games	BA	SA	AB	H	2B	3B	HR	HR%	R	RBI	BB	SO	SB	Pinch Hit AB	Pinch Hit H	PO	A	E	DP	TC/G	FA	G by Pos
1929	CHI A	85	.302	.410	278	84	12	6	2	0.7	33	18	22	21	6	7	2	188	7	12	2	2.7	.942	OF-77
1930		133	.302	.393	427	129	25	4	2	0.5	75	51	52	35	5	19	4	707	46	11	59	7.3	.986	1B-62, OF-43
1931		128	.283	.368	367	104	16	6	1	0.3	51	47	56	30	9	17	5	277	14	16	3	2.9	.948	OF-102, 1B-4
1932	2 teams	CHI A (13G –.306) BOS A (95G –.248)																						
″	total	108	.257	.298	315	81	13	0	0	0.0	31	30	21	14	7	27	9	273	20	14	17	4.0	.954	OF-59, 1B-18
1933	BOS A	13	.133	.133	30	4	0	0	0	0.0	2	2	3	3	0	3	0	19	0	1	0	2.2	.950	OF-9
1939	PHI N	2	.167	.167	6	1	0	0	0	0.0	0	0	0	0	0	0	0	14	0	1	0	7.5	.933	1B-2
6 yrs.		469	.283	.363	1423	403	66	16	5	0.4	192	148	154	103	27	73	20	1478	87	55	81	4.3	.966	OF-290, 1B-86

Bob Way

WAY, ROBERT CLINTON BR TR 5′10½″ 168 lbs.
B. Apr. 2, 1906, Emlenton, Pa. D. June 20, 1974, Pittsburgh, Pa.

Year	Team	Games	BA	SA	AB	H	2B	3B	HR	HR%	R	RBI	BB	SO	SB	Pinch Hit AB	Pinch Hit H	PO	A	E	DP	TC/G	FA	G by Pos
1927	CHI A	5	.333	.333	3	1	0	0	0	0.0	3	1	0	1	0	3	1	1	0	0	0	1.0	1.000	2B-1

Roy Weatherly

WEATHERLY, CYRIL ROY (Stormy) BL TR 5′ 6½″ 170 lbs.
B. Feb. 25, 1915, Warren, Tex. D. Jan. 19, 1991, Woodville, Tex.

Year	Team	Games	BA	SA	AB	H	2B	3B	HR	HR%	R	RBI	BB	SO	SB	Pinch Hit AB	Pinch Hit H	PO	A	E	DP	TC/G	FA	G by Pos
1936	CLE A	84	.335	.519	349	117	28	6	8	2.3	64	53	16	29	3	0	0	164	15	5	2	2.2	.973	OF-84
1937		53	.201	.343	134	27	4	0	5	3.7	19	13	6	14	1	13	1	48	6	2	1	1.4	.964	OF-38, 3B-1
1938		83	.262	.386	210	55	14	3	2	1.0	32	18	14	14	8	25	5	110	7	3	3	2.2	.975	OF-55
1939		95	.310	.406	323	100	16	6	1	0.3	43	32	19	23	7	17	4	146	3	6	1	2.0	.961	OF-76
1940		135	.303	.464	578	175	35	11	12	2.1	90	59	27	26	9	0	0	370	10	12	3	2.9	.969	OF-135
1941		102	.289	.399	363	105	21	5	3	0.8	59	37	32	20	2	14	5	208	1	7	1	2.5	.968	OF-88
1942		128	.258	.368	473	122	23	7	5	1.1	61	39	35	25	8	13	5	324	7	3	4	2.9	.991	OF-117
1943	NY A	77	.264	.389	280	74	8	3	7	2.5	37	28	18	9	4	8	2	174	2	3	0	2.6	.983	OF-68
1946		2	.500	.500	2	1	0	0	0	0.0	0	0	0	0	0	2	1	0	0	0	0	0.0	—	
1950	NY N	52	.261	.391	69	18	3	3	0	0.0	10	11	13	10	0	32	9	21	2	0	0	1.5	1.000	OF-15
10 yrs.		811	.286	.418	2781	794	152	44	43	1.5	415	290	180	170	42	124	32	1565	53	41	15	2.5	.975	OF-676, 3B-1
WORLD SERIES																								
1943	NY A	1	.000	.000	1	0	0	0	0	0.0	0	0	0	0	0	1	0	0	0	0	0	0.0	—	

Art Weaver

WEAVER, ARTHUR COGGSHALL TR 6′ 1″ 160 lbs.
B. Apr. 7, 1879, Wichita, Kans. D. Mar. 23, 1917, Denver, Colo.

Year	Team	Games	BA	SA	AB	H	2B	3B	HR	HR%	R	RBI	BB	SO	SB	Pinch Hit AB	Pinch Hit H	PO	A	E	DP	TC/G	FA	G by Pos
1902	STL N	11	.182	.242	33	6	2	0	0	0.0	2	3	1		0	0	0	40	17	1	1	5.3	.983	C-11
1903	2 teams STL N (16G –.245) PIT N (16G –.229)																							
″	total	32	.237	.258	97	23	0	1	0	0.0	12	8	6		1	0	0	149	44	6	3	6.2	.970	C-27, 1B-5
1905	STL A	28	.120	.163	92	11	2	1	0	0.0	5	3	1		0	0	0	139	38	7	4	6.6	.962	C-28
1908	CHI A	15	.200	.229	35	7	1	0	0	0.0	1	1	1		0	0	0	32	9	2	2	2.9	.953	C-15
4 yrs.		86	.183	.218	257	47	5	2	0	0.0	20	15	9		1	0	0	360	108	16	10	5.6	.967	C-81, 1B-5

Buck Weaver

WEAVER, GEORGE DANIEL BR TR 5′11″ 170 lbs.
B. Aug. 18, 1890, Pottstown, Pa. D. Jan. 31, 1956, Chicago, Ill. BB 1917–1920

Year	Team	Games	BA	SA	AB	H	2B	3B	HR	HR%	R	RBI	BB	SO	SB	Pinch Hit AB	Pinch Hit H	PO	A	E	DP	TC/G	FA	G by Pos
1912	CHI A	147	.224	.300	523	117	21	8	1	0.2	55	43	9		12	0	0	342	425	71	53	5.7	.915	SS-147
1913		151	.272	.356	533	145	17	8	4	0.8	51	52	15	60	20	0	0	392	520	70	73	6.5	.929	SS-151
1914		136	.246	.327	541	133	20	9	2	0.4	64	28	20	40	14	2	0	367	389	59	50	6.1	.928	SS-134
1915		148	.268	.355	563	151	18	11	3	0.5	83	49	32	58	24	0	0	281	470	49	54	5.4	.939	SS-148
1916		151	.227	.309	582	132	27	6	3	0.5	78	38	30	48	22	0	0	266	385	36	49	4.5	.948	3B-85, SS-66
1917		118	.284	.362	447	127	16	5	3	0.7	64	32	27	29	19	1	0	174	257	21	27	3.9	.954	3B-107, SS-10
1918		112	.300	.352	420	126	12	5	0	0.0	37	29	11	24	20	2	1	201	339	33	51	5.2	.942	SS-98, 3B-11, 2B-1
1919		140	.296	.401	**571**	169	33	9	3	0.5	89	75	11	21	22	0	0	200	341	20	28	4.0	.964	3B-97, SS-43
1920		151	.331	.420	629	208	34	8	2	0.3	102	74	28	23	19	0	0	209	351	36	33	3.9	.940	3B-126, SS-25
9 yrs.		1254	.272	.355	4809	1308	198	69	21	0.4	623	420	183	303	172	5	1	2432	3477	395	418	5.0	.937	SS-822, 3B-426, 2B-1
WORLD SERIES																								
1917	CHI A	6	.333	.381	21	7	1	0	0	0.0	3	1	0	2	0	0	0	13	14	4	4	5.2	.871	SS-6
1919		8	.324	.500	34	11	4	1	0	0.0	4	0	0	2	0	0	0	9	18	0	0	3.4	1.000	3B-8
2 yrs.		14	.327	.455	55	18	5	1	0	0.0	7	1	0	4	0	0	0	22	32	4	4	4.1	.931	3B-8, SS-6

Farmer Weaver

WEAVER, WILLIAM B. BL
B. Mar. 23, 1865, Parkersburg, W. Va. D. Jan. 23, 1943, Akron, Ohio.

Year	Team	Games	BA	SA	AB	H	2B	3B	HR	HR%	R	RBI	BB	SO	SB	Pinch Hit AB	Pinch Hit H	PO	A	E	DP	TC/G	FA	G by Pos
1888	LOU AA	26	.250	.277	112	28	1	1	0	0.0	12	8	3		12	0	0	37	6	6	0	1.9	.878	OF-26
1889		124	.291	.349	499	145	17	6	0	0.0	62	60	40	22	21	0	0	257	36	28	4	2.5	.913	OF-123, C-2, 3B-1, 2B-1
1890		130	.289	.386	557	161	27	9	3	0.5	101		29		45	0	0	233	25	22	5	2.2	.921	OF-127, SS-2, 3B-1
1891		133	.282	.356	556	157	24	7	1	0.2	74	53	33	23	30	0	0	306	34	15	7	2.6	.958	OF-130, C-4
1892	LOU N	138	.254	.296	551	140	15	4	0	0.0	58	57	40	17	30	0	0	245	36	36	5	2.2	.886	OF-122, C-15, 1B-10
1893		106	.292	.376	439	128	17	7	2	0.5	79	49	27	12	17	0	0	208	37	19	5	2.5	.928	OF-85, C-21
1894	2 teams LOU N (64G –.221) PIT N (30G –.348)																							
″	total	94	.262	.343	359	94	12	4	3	0.8	35	48	13	12	7	1	0	264	75	26	15	3.8	.929	OF-36, C-31, SS-12, 1B-10, 3B-5, 2B-1
7 yrs.		751	.278	.348	3073	853	113	38	9	0.3	421	275	185	86	162	1	0	1550	249	152	41	2.6	.922	OF-649, C-73, 1B-20, SS-14, 3B-7, 2B-2

Jim Weaver

WEAVER, JAMES FRANCIS BL TL 6′ 4″ 190 lbs.
B. Oct. 10, 1959, Kingston, N. Y.

Year	Team	Games	BA	SA	AB	H	2B	3B	HR	HR%	R	RBI	BB	SO	SB	Pinch Hit AB	Pinch Hit H	PO	A	E	DP	TC/G	FA	G by Pos
1985	DET A	12	.143	.286	7	1	1	0	0	0.0	2	0	1	4	0	2	0	1	0	0	0	0.1	1.000	OF-4, DH-4
1987	SEA A	7	.000	.000	4	0	0	0	0	0.0	2	0	2	3	1	1	0	4	1	0	0	1.3	1.000	OF-4
1989	SF N	12	.200	.350	20	4	3	0	0	0.0	2	2	0	7	1	2	0	7	0	0	0	0.9	1.000	OF-8
3 yrs.		31	.161	.290	31	5	4	0	0	0.0	6	2	3	14	2	5	0	12	1	0	0	0.6	1.000	OF-16, DH-4

Sam Weaver

WEAVER, SAMUEL H. BR TR 5′10″ 185 lbs.
B. July 10, 1855, Philadelphia, Pa. D. Feb. 1, 1914, Philadelphia, Pa.

Year	Team	Games	BA	SA	AB	H	2B	3B	HR	HR%	R	RBI	BB	SO	SB	Pinch Hit AB	Pinch Hit H	PO	A	E	DP	TC/G	FA	G by Pos
1878	MIL N	48	.200	.235	170	34	4	1	0	0.0	15	3	11	14		0	0	37	80	18	1	2.5	.867	P-45, OF-9
1882	PHI AA	43	.232	.252	155	36	3	0	0	0.0	19		12			0	0	18	127	9	1	3.5	.942	P-42, OF-2
1883	LOU AA	55	.192	.232	203	39	6	1	0	0.0	22		13			0	0	41	82	10	4	2.4	.925	P-48, OF-6, 1B-1
1884	PHI U	20	.214	.238	84	18	2	0	0	0.0	11		2			0	0	20	29	11	0	2.6	.817	P-17, OF-6
1886	PHI AA	2	.143	.143	7	1	0	0	0	0.0	0		0			0	0	5	1	0	1	2.0	1.000	P-2, 1B-1
5 yrs.		168	.207	.237	619	128	15	2	0	0.0	67	3	38	14		0	0	121	319	48	7	2.7	.902	P-154, OF-23, 1B-2

Billy Webb

WEBB, WILLIAM JOSEPH BR TR 5′10″ 161 lbs.
B. June 25, 1895, Chicago, Ill. D. Jan. 12, 1943, Chicago, Ill.

Year	Team	Games	BA	SA	AB	H	2B	3B	HR	HR%	R	RBI	BB	SO	SB	Pinch Hit AB	Pinch Hit H	PO	A	E	DP	TC/G	FA	G by Pos
1917	PIT N	5	.200	.200	15	3	0	0	0	0.0	1	0	2	3	0	1	0	9	13	1	1	5.8	.957	2B-3, SS-1

Earl Webb

WEBB, WILLIAM EARL BL TR 6′ 1″ 185 lbs.
B. Sept. 17, 1897, Bon Air, Tenn. D. May 23, 1965, Jamestown, Tenn.

Year	Team	Games	BA	SA	AB	H	2B	3B	HR	HR%	R	RBI	BB	SO	SB	Pinch Hit AB	Pinch Hit H	PO	A	E	DP	TC/G	FA	G by Pos
1925	NY N	4	.000	.000	3	0	0	0	0	0.0	0	0	1	1	0	3	0	0	0	0	0	0.0	—	
1927	CHI N	102	.301	.506	332	100	18	4	14	4.2	58	52	48	31	3	15	3	171	14	8	5	2.2	.959	OF-86
1928		62	.250	.407	140	35	7	3	3	2.1	22	23	14	17	0	24	8	65	4	1	0	2.3	.986	OF-31
1930	BOS A	127	.323	.523	449	145	30	6	16	3.6	61	66	44	56	2	8	2	200	8	9	4	1.9	.959	OF-116
1931		151	.333	.528	589	196	**67**[1]	3	14	2.4	96	103	70	51	2	0	0	270	21	16	5	2.0	.948	OF-151

Earl Webb *continued*

Year	Team	Games	BA	SA	AB	H	2B	3B	HR	HR%	R	RBI	BB	SO	SB	Pinch Hit AB	Pinch Hit H	PO	A	E	DP	TC/G	FA	G by Pos
1932	**2 teams**	**BOS A** (52G –.281) **DET A** (87G –.287)																						
"	**total**	139	.285	.417	530	151	28	9	8	1.5	72	78	64	33	1	1	0	251	16	12	4	2.1	.957	OF-134, 1B-2
1933	**2 teams**	**DET A** (6G –.273) **CHI A** (58G –.290)																						
"	**total**	64	.288	.356	118	34	5	0	1	0.8	17	11	19	13	0	**30**	8	129	5	7	8	5.0	.950	OF-18, 1B-10
7 yrs.		649	.306	.478	2161	661	155	25	56	2.6	326	333	260	202	8	81	21	1086	68	53	26	2.2	.956	OF-536, 1B-12

Skeeter Webb

WEBB, JAMES LAVERNE BR TR 5′ 9½″ 150 lbs.
B. Nov. 4, 1909, Meridian, Miss. D. July 8, 1986, Meridian, Miss.

Year	Team	Games	BA	SA	AB	H	2B	3B	HR	HR%	R	RBI	BB	SO	SB	Pinch Hit AB	Pinch Hit H	PO	A	E	DP	TC/G	FA	G by Pos
1932	**STL N**	1	—	—	0	0	0	0	0	—	0	0	0	0	0	0	0	0	0	0	0	0.0	.000	SS-1
1938	**CLE A**	20	.276	.310	58	16	2	0	0	0.0	11	2	8	7	1	0	0	29	32	4	7	3.6	.938	SS-13, 3B-3, 2B-2
1939		81	.264	.346	269	71	14	1	2	0.7	28	26	15	24	1	0	0	165	203	27	40	4.9	.932	SS-81
1940	**CHI A**	84	.237	.290	334	79	11	2	1	0.3	33	29	30	33	3	2	0	152	247	13	46	5.0	.968	2B-74, SS-7, 3B-1
1941		29	.190	.214	84	16	2	0	0	0.0	7	6	3	9	1	3	1	55	64	10	13	5.0	.922	2B-18, SS-5, 3B-3
1942		32	.170	.213	94	16	2	1	0	0.0	5	4	4	13	1	0	0	62	87	6	14	5.3	.961	2B-29
1943		58	.235	.277	213	50	5	2	0	0.0	15	22	6	19	5	3	0	118	169	14	35	5.6	.953	2B-54
1944		139	.211	.271	513	108	19	6	0	0.0	44	30	20	39	7	0	0	221	480	39	88	5.3	.947	SS-135, 2B-5
1945	**DET A**	118	.199	.238	407	81	12	2	0	0.0	43	21	30	35	8	0	0	245	368	25	79	5.5	.961	SS-104, 2B-11
1946		64	.219	.237	169	37	1	1	0	0.0	12	17	9	18	3	1	0	105	155	7	30	4.6	.974	2B-50, SS-8
1947		50	.203	.241	79	16	3	0	0	0.0	13	6	7	9	3	2	0	52	78	2	10	3.7	.985	2B-30, SS-6
1948	**PHI A**	23	.148	.185	54	8	2	0	0	0.0	5	3	0	9	0	0	0	24	42	2	12	4.0	.971	2B-9, SS-8
12 yrs.		699	.219	.268	2274	498	73	15	3	0.1	216	166	132	215	33	11	1	1228	1925	149	374	5.0	.955	SS-368, 2B-282, 3B-7
WORLD SERIES																								
1945	**DET A**	7	.185	.185	27	5	0	0	0	0.0	4	1	3	1	0	0	0	9	24	1	3	4.9	.971	SS-7

Harry Weber

WEBER, HARRY
B. Indianapolis, Ind. Deceased.

Year	Team	Games	BA	SA	AB	H	2B	3B	HR	HR%	R	RBI	BB	SO	SB	Pinch Hit AB	Pinch Hit H	PO	A	E	DP	TC/G	FA	G by Pos
1884	**IND AA**	3	.000	.000	8	0	0	0	0	0.0	0		0			0	0	17	10	7	0	11.3	.794	C-3

Joe Weber

WEBER, JOSEPH EDWARD
B. Feb. 15, 1862, Hamilton, Ont., Canada D. Dec. 15, 1921, Hamilton, Ont., Canada.

Year	Team	Games	BA	SA	AB	H	2B	3B	HR	HR%	R	RBI	BB	SO	SB	Pinch Hit AB	Pinch Hit H	PO	A	E	DP	TC/G	FA	G by Pos
1884	**DET N**	2	.000	.000	8	0	0	0	0	0.0	0		0	2		0	0	2	1	1	0	2.0	.750	OF-2

Lenny Webster

WEBSTER, LEONARD IRELL BR TR 5′ 9″ 185 lbs.
B. Feb. 10, 1965, New Orleans, La.

Year	Team	Games	BA	SA	AB	H	2B	3B	HR	HR%	R	RBI	BB	SO	SB	Pinch Hit AB	Pinch Hit H	PO	A	E	DP	TC/G	FA	G by Pos
1989	**MIN A**	14	.300	.400	20	6	2	0	0	0.0	3	1	3	2	0	1	1	32	0	0	0	2.3	1.000	C-14
1990		2	.333	.500	6	2	1	0	0	0.0	1	0	1	1	0	0	0	9	0	0	0	4.5	1.000	C-2
1991		18	.294	.588	34	10	1	0	3	8.8	7	8	6	10	0	2	0	61	10	1	1	4.2	.986	C-17
1992		53	.280	.407	118	33	10	1	1	0.8	10	13	9	11	0	6	5	190	11	1	3	4.0	.995	C-49, DH-1
1993		49	.198	.245	106	21	2	0	1	0.9	14	8	11	8	1	3	0	177	13	0	1	4.1	1.000	C-45, DH-1
1994	**MON N**	57	.273	.448	143	39	10	0	5	3.5	13	23	16	24	0	13	1	237	19	1	0	5.6	.996	C-46
1995	**PHI N**	49	.267	.407	150	40	9	0	4	2.7	18	14	16	27	0	6	0	275	17	3	1	6.9	.990	C-43
7 yrs.		242	.262	.399	577	151	35	1	14	2.4	66	67	62	83	1	31	7	981	70	6	6	4.8	.994	C-216, DH-2

Mitch Webster

WEBSTER, MITCHELL DEAN BB TL 6′½″ 170 lbs.
B. May 16, 1959, Larned, Kans.

Year	Team	Games	BA	SA	AB	H	2B	3B	HR	HR%	R	RBI	BB	SO	SB	Pinch Hit AB	Pinch Hit H	PO	A	E	DP	TC/G	FA	G by Pos
1983	**TOR A**	11	.182	.182	11	2	0	0	0	0.0	2	0	1	1	0	1	0	5	0	0	0	0.6	1.000	OF-7, DH-2
1984		26	.227	.409	22	5	2	1	0	0.0	9	4	1	7	0	7	1	16	0	2	1	0.9	.889	OF-10, DH-9, 1B-1
1985	**2 teams**	**TOR A** (4G –.000) **MON N** (74G –.274)																						
"	**total**	78	.272	.484	213	58	8	2	11	5.2	32	30	20	33	15	9	1	133	3	1	0	2.0	.993	OF-66, DH-2
1986	**MON N**	151	.290	.431	576	167	31	**13**	8	1.4	89	49	57	78	36	4	1	325	12	8	3	2.4	.977	OF-146
1987		156	.281	.435	588	165	30	8	15	2.6	101	63	70	95	33	7	4	266	8	5	0	1.8	.982	OF-153
1988	**2 teams**	**MON N** (81G –.255) **CHI N** (70G –.265)																						
"	**total**	151	.260	.356	523	136	16	8	6	1.1	69	39	55	87	22	17	3	322	3	6	0	2.4	.982	OF-136
1989	**CHI N**	98	.257	.364	272	70	12	4	3	1.1	40	19	30	55	14	30	4	161	3	6	0	2.3	.965	OF-74
1990	**CLE A**	128	.252	.407	437	110	20	6	12	2.7	58	55	20	61	22	12	4	345	3	5	2	2.8	.986	OF-118, 1B-3, DH-3
1991	**3 teams**	**CLE A** (13G –.125) **PIT N** (36G –.175) **LA N** (58G –.284)																						
"	**total**	107	.207	.325	203	42	8	5	2	1.0	23	19	21	61	2	35	7	111	2	2	1	1.5	.983	OF-75, 1B-1
1992	**LA N**	135	.267	.420	262	70	12	5	6	2.3	33	35	27	49	11	47	**17**	130	0	3	0	1.5	.977	OF-90
1993		88	.244	.337	172	42	6	2	2	1.2	26	14	11	24	4	35	6	75	1	4	0	1.4	.950	OF-56
1994		82	.274	.464	84	23	4	0	4	4.8	16	12	8	13	1	31	9	29	0	0	0	0.6	1.000	OF-48
1995		54	.179	.286	56	10	1	1	1	1.8	6	3	4	14	0	35	6	12	0	0	0	0.5	1.000	OF-25
13 yrs.		1265	.263	.401	3419	900	150	55	70	2.0	504	342	325	578	160	270	63	1930	35	42	7	2.0	.979	OF-1004, DH-16, 1B-5
DIVISIONAL PLAYOFF SERIES																								
1995	**LA N**	2	.000	.000	2	0	0	0	0	0.0	0	0	0	0	0	2	0	0	0	0	0	0.0	—	
LEAGUE CHAMPIONSHIP SERIES																								
1989	**CHI N**	3	.333	.333	3	1	0	0	0	0.0	0	0	0	0	0	1	0	0	0	0	0	0.0	.000	OF-2

Ramon Webster

WEBSTER, RAMON ALBERTO BL TL 6′ 185 lbs.
B. Aug. 31, 1942, Colon, Panama.

Year	Team	Games	BA	SA	AB	H	2B	3B	HR	HR%	R	RBI	BB	SO	SB	Pinch Hit AB	Pinch Hit H	PO	A	E	DP	TC/G	FA	G by Pos
1967	**KC A**	122	.256	.411	360	92	15	4	11	3.1	41	51	32	44	5	26	5	639	43	8	43	7.0	.988	1B-83, OF-15
1968	**OAK A**	66	.214	.327	196	42	11	1	3	1.5	17	23	12	24	3	11	6	454	27	6	33	8.9	.988	1B-55
1969		64	.260	.325	77	20	0	1	1	1.3	5	13	12	8	0	39	10	89	8	0	6	7.5	1.000	1B-13
1970	**SD N**	95	.259	.336	116	30	3	0	2	1.7	12	11	11	12	1	70	17	99	7	2	14	6.8	.981	1B-15, OF-1
1971	**3 teams**	**SD N** (10G –.125) **CHI N** (16G –.313) **OAK A** (7G –.000)																						
"	**total**	33	.207	.276	29	6	2	0	0	0.0	1	0	3	6	0	27	4	3	1	0	1	2.0	1.000	1B-2
5 yrs.		380	.244	.365	778	190	31	6	17	2.2	76	98	70	94	9	173	42	1284	86	16	97	7.5	.988	1B-168, OF-16

Ray Webster

WEBSTER, RAYMOND GEORGE BR TR 6′ 175 lbs.
B. Nov. 15, 1937, Grass Valley, Calif.

Year	Team	Games	BA	SA	AB	H	2B	3B	HR	HR%	R	RBI	BB	SO	SB	Pinch Hit AB	Pinch Hit H	PO	A	E	DP	TC/G	FA	G by Pos
1959	**CLE A**	40	.203	.338	74	15	2	1	2	2.7	10	10	5	7	1	8	1	34	45	8	13	3.1	.908	2B-24, 3B-4
1960	**BOS A**	7	.000	.000	3	0	0	0	0	0.0	1	1	1	0	0	3	0	1	1	0	1	2.0	1.000	2B-1
2 yrs.		47	.195	.325	77	15	2	1	2	2.6	11	11	6	7	1	11	1	35	46	8	14	3.1	.910	2B-25, 3B-4

Pete Weckbecker

WECKBECKER, PETER 5′ 7″ 150 lbs.
B. Aug. 30, 1864, Butler, Pa. D. May 16, 1935, Hampton, Va.

Year	Team	Games	BA	SA	AB	H	2B	3B	HR	HR%	R	RBI	BB	SO	SB	Pinch Hit AB	Pinch Hit H	PO	A	E	DP	TC/G	FA	G by Pos
1889	IND N	1	.000	.000	1	0	0	0	0	0.0	0	2	0	0	0	0	0	2	0	0	0	2.0	1.000	C-1
1890	LOU AA	32	.238	.248	101	24	1	0	0	0.0	17		8		7	0	0	158	33	12	2	6.3	.941	C-32
2 yrs.		33	.235	.245	102	24	1	0	0	0.0	17	2	8	0	7	0	0	160	33	12	2	6.2	.941	C-33

Eric Wedge

WEDGE, ERIC MICHAEL BR TR 6′ 3″ 215 lbs.
B. Jan. 27, 1968, Fort Wayne, Ind.

Year	Team	Games	BA	SA	AB	H	2B	3B	HR	HR%	R	RBI	BB	SO	SB	Pinch Hit AB	Pinch Hit H	PO	A	E	DP	TC/G	FA	G by Pos
1991	BOS A	1	1.000	1.000	1	1	0	0	0	0.0	0	0	0	0	0	1	1	0	0	0	0	0.0	.000	DH-1
1992		27	.250	.500	68	17	2	0	5	7.4	11	11	13	18	0	5	2	19	2	0	1	0.8	1.000	DH-20, C-5
1993	CLR N	9	.182	.182	11	2	0	0	0	0.0	2	1	0	4	0	8	2	6	1	0	0	7.0	1.000	C-1
1994	BOS A	2	.000	.000	6	0	0	0	0	0.0	0	0	1	3	0	0	0	0	0	0	0	0.0	.000	DH-2
4 yrs.		39	.233	.430	86	20	2	0	5	5.8	13	12	14	25	0	14	5	25	3	0	1	1.0	1.000	DH-23, C-6

Charlie Weeden

WEEDEN, CHARLES ALBERT BL TL 6′ 200 lbs.
B. Dec. 21, 1882, Northwood, N. H. D. Jan. 7, 1939, Northwood, N. H.

Year	Team	Games	BA	SA	AB	H	2B	3B	HR	HR%	R	RBI	BB	SO	SB	Pinch Hit AB	Pinch Hit H	PO	A	E	DP	TC/G	FA	G by Pos
1911	BOS N	1	.000	.000	1	0	0	0	0	0.0	0	0	0	0	0	1	0	0	0	0	0	0.0	—	

Johnny Weekly

WEEKLY, JOHNNY BR TR 6′ 200 lbs.
B. June 14, 1937, Waterproof, La. D. Nov. 24, 1974, Walnut Creek, Calif.

Year	Team	Games	BA	SA	AB	H	2B	3B	HR	HR%	R	RBI	BB	SO	SB	Pinch Hit AB	Pinch Hit H	PO	A	E	DP	TC/G	FA	G by Pos
1962	HOU N	13	.192	.462	26	5	1	0	2	7.7	3	2	7	4	0	6	1	8	0	0	0	1.1	1.000	OF-7
1963		34	.225	.375	80	18	3	0	3	3.8	4	14	7	14	0	12	3	36	2	0	0	1.7	1.000	OF-23
1964		6	.133	.133	15	2	0	0	0	0.0	0	3	1	3	0	1	0	9	1	0	0	2.0	1.000	OF-5
3 yrs.		53	.207	.364	121	25	4	0	5	4.1	7	19	15	21	0	19	4	53	3	0	0	1.6	1.000	OF-35

John Wehner

WEHNER, JOHN PAUL BR TR 6′ 3″ 205 lbs.
B. June 29, 1967, Pittsburgh, Pa.

Year	Team	Games	BA	SA	AB	H	2B	3B	HR	HR%	R	RBI	BB	SO	SB	Pinch Hit AB	Pinch Hit H	PO	A	E	DP	TC/G	FA	G by Pos
1991	PIT N	37	.340	.406	106	36	7	0	0	0.0	15	7	7	17	3	3	2	23	65	6	9	2.6	.936	3B-36
1992		55	.179	.228	123	22	6	0	0	0.0	11	4	12	22	3	12	5	96	64	4	17	3.2	.976	3B-34, 1B-13, 2B-5
1993		29	.143	.143	35	5	0	0	0	0.0	3	0	6	10	0	9	0	17	8	0	3	1.3	1.000	OF-13, 3B-3, 2B-3
1994		2	.250	.500	4	1	1	0	0	0.0	1	3	0	1	0	1	1	0	2	0	0	2.0	1.000	3B-1
1995		52	.308	.364	107	33	0	3	0	0.0	13	5	10	17	3	14	2	35	29	0	2	1.5	1.000	OF-23, 3B-19, SS-1, C-1
5 yrs.		175	.259	.312	375	97	14	3	0	0.0	43	19	35	67	9	39	10	171	168	10	31	2.3	.971	3B-93, OF-36, 1B-13, 2B-8, SS-1, C-1
LEAGUE CHAMPIONSHIP SERIES																								
1992	PIT N	2	.000	.000	2	0	0	0	0	0.0	0	0	0	2	0	2	0	0	0	0	0	0.0	—	

Ralph Weigel

WEIGEL, RALPH RICHARD (Wig) BR TR 6′ 1″ 180 lbs.
B. Oct. 2, 1921, Coldwater, Ohio D. Apr. 15, 1992, Memphis, Tenn.

Year	Team	Games	BA	SA	AB	H	2B	3B	HR	HR%	R	RBI	BB	SO	SB	Pinch Hit AB	Pinch Hit H	PO	A	E	DP	TC/G	FA	G by Pos
1946	CLE A	6	.167	.167	12	2	0	0	0	0.0	0	0	0	2	1	0	0	16	0	0	0	2.7	1.000	C-6
1948	CHI A	66	.233	.313	163	38	7	3	0	0.0	8	26	13	18	1	24	6	109	19	4	4	3.2	.970	C-39, OF-2
1949	WAS A	34	.233	.267	60	14	2	0	0	0.0	4	4	8	6	0	12	2	55	9	1	4	3.1	.985	C-21
3 yrs.		106	.230	.294	235	54	9	3	0	0.0	12	30	21	26	2	36	8	180	28	5	8	3.1	.977	C-66, OF-2

Podgie Weihe

WEIHE, JOHN GARIBALDI BR TR 5′11″ 175 lbs.
B. Nov. 13, 1862, Cincinnati, Ohio D. Apr. 15, 1914, Cincinnati, Ohio.

Year	Team	Games	BA	SA	AB	H	2B	3B	HR	HR%	R	RBI	BB	SO	SB	Pinch Hit AB	Pinch Hit H	PO	A	E	DP	TC/G	FA	G by Pos
1883	CIN AA	1	.250	.250	4	1	0	0	0	0.0	1		0			0	0	4	0	0	0	4.0	1.000	OF-1
1884	IND AA	63	.254	.367	256	65	13	2	4	1.6	29		9			0	0	110	26	24	4	2.5	.850	OF-58, 2B-4, 1B-3
2 yrs.		64	.254	.365	260	66	13	2	4	1.5	30		9			0	0	114	26	24	4	2.5	.854	OF-59, 2B-4, 1B-3

Elmer Weingartner

WEINGARTNER, ELMER WILLIAM (Dutch) BR TR 5′11″ 178 lbs.
B. Aug. 13, 1918, Cleveland, Ohio.

Year	Team	Games	BA	SA	AB	H	2B	3B	HR	HR%	R	RBI	BB	SO	SB	Pinch Hit AB	Pinch Hit H	PO	A	E	DP	TC/G	FA	G by Pos
1945	CLE A	20	.231	.256	39	9	1	0	0	0.0	5	1	4	11	0	0	0	29	32	9	7	3.5	.871	SS-20

Phil Weintraub

WEINTRAUB, PHILIP BL TL 6′ 1″ 195 lbs.
B. Oct. 12, 1907, Chicago, Ill. D. June 21, 1987, Palm Springs, Calif.

Year	Team	Games	BA	SA	AB	H	2B	3B	HR	HR%	R	RBI	BB	SO	SB	Pinch Hit AB	Pinch Hit H	PO	A	E	DP	TC/G	FA	G by Pos
1933	NY N	8	.200	.400	15	3	0	0	1	6.7	3	1	3	2	0	1	1	4	0	2	0	1.0	.667	OF-6
1934		31	.351	.378	74	26	2	0	0	0.0	13	15	15	10	0	10	1	34	0	2	0	1.8	.944	OF-20
1935		64	.241	.348	112	27	3	3	1	0.9	18	6	17	13	0	29	5	152	11	4	9	6.4	.976	1B-19, OF-7
1937	2 teams	CIN N (49G –.271) NY N (66 –.333)																						
″	total	55	.274	.430	186	51	12	4	3	1.6	30	21	20	26	1	6	1	79	3	2	1	1.8	.976	OF-48
1938	PHI N	100	.311	.422	351	109	23	2	4	1.1	51	45	64	43	1	2	0	913	75	12	70	10.2	.988	1B-98
1944	NY N	104	.316	.524	361	114	18	9	13	3.6	55	77	59	59	0	5	2	928	72	8	72	10.2	.992	1B-99
1945		82	.272	.417	283	77	9	1	10	3.5	45	42	54	29	2	4	1	774	60	6	49	10.9	.993	1B-77
7 yrs.		444	.295	.440	1382	407	67	19	32	2.3	215	207	232	182	4	57	11	2884	221	36	201	8.4	.989	1B-293, OF-81

Al Weis

WEIS, ALBERT JOHN BB TR 6′ 160 lbs.
BR 1969–1971
B. Apr. 2, 1938, Franklin Square, N. Y.

Year	Team	Games	BA	SA	AB	H	2B	3B	HR	HR%	R	RBI	BB	SO	SB	Pinch Hit AB	Pinch Hit H	PO	A	E	DP	TC/G	FA	G by Pos
1962	CHI A	7	.083	.083	12	1	0	0	0	0.0	2	0	2	3	1	0	0	3	13	3	0	3.2	.842	SS-4, 2B-1, 3B-1
1963		99	.271	.314	210	57	9	0	0	0.0	41	18	18	37	15	9	2	123	168	10	41	4.0	.967	2B-48, SS-27, 3B-1
1964		133	.247	.302	328	81	4	4	2	0.6	36	23	22	41	22	6	1	205	267	21	65	3.9	.957	2B-116, SS-9, OF-2
1965		103	.296	.393	135	40	4	3	1	0.7	29	12	12	22	4	6	2	117	130	6	31	3.0	.976	2B-74, SS-7, OF-2, 3B-2
1966		129	.155	.187	187	29	4	1	0	0.0	20	9	17	50	3	0	0	151	218	10	52	3.3	.974	2B-96, SS-18
1967		50	.245	.283	53	13	2	0	0	0.0	9	4	1	7	3	0	0	30	62	1	5	2.1	.989	2B-32, SS-13
1968	NY N	90	.172	.204	274	47	6	0	1	0.4	15	14	21	63	3	3	0	138	244	14	43	4.4	.965	SS-59, 2B-29, 3B-2
1969		103	.215	.291	247	53	9	2	2	0.8	20	23	15	51	3	3	0	138	218	13	50	3.8	.965	SS-52, 2B-43, 3B-1
1970		75	.207	.306	121	25	7	1	1	0.8	20	11	7	21	1	2	0	75	81	8	13	2.8	.951	2B-44, SS-15
1971		11	.000	.000	11	0	0	0	0	0.0	3	1	2	4	0	4	0	5	6	0	2	1.6	1.000	2B-5, 3B-2
10 yrs.		800	.219	.275	1578	346	45	11	7	0.4	195	115	117	299	55	33	5	985	1407	86	302	3.5	.965	2B-488, SS-204, 3B-9, OF-4
LEAGUE CHAMPIONSHIP SERIES																								
1969	NY N	3	.000	.000	1	0	0	0	0	0.0	0	0	0	0	0	0	0	1	3	0	1	1.3	1.000	2B-3
WORLD SERIES																								
1969	NY N	5	.455	.727	11	5	0	0	1	9.1	1	3	4	2	0	0	0	8	5	1	0	2.8	.929	2B-5

Butch Weis

WEIS, ARTHUR JOHN
B. Mar. 2, 1901, St. Louis, Mo.
BL TL 5′11″ 180 lbs.

Year	Team	Games	BA	SA	AB	H	2B	3B	HR	HR%	R	RBI	BB	SO	SB	Pinch Hit AB	Pinch Hit H	PO	A	E	DP	TC/G	FA	G by Pos
1922	CHI N	2	.500	.500	2	1	0	0	0	0.0	2	0	0	0	0	2	1	0	0	0	0	0.0	—	
1923		22	.231	.269	26	6	1	0	0	0.0	2	2	5	8	0	13	3	9	0	0	0	1.5	1.000	OF-6
1924		39	.278	.353	133	37	8	1	0	0.0	19	23	15	14	4	1	1	81	8	2	2	2.5	.978	OF-36
1925		67	.267	.361	180	48	5	3	2	1.1	16	25	23	22	2	20	3	78	3	3	0	1.8	.964	OF-46
4 yrs.		130	.270	.352	341	92	14	4	2	0.6	39	50	43	44	6	36	8	168	11	5	2	2.1	.973	OF-88

Bud Weiser

WEISER, HARRY BUDSON
B. Jan. 8, 1891, Shamokin, Pa. D. July 31, 1961, Shamokin, Pa.
BR TR 5′11″ 165 lbs.

Year	Team	Games	BA	SA	AB	H	2B	3B	HR	HR%	R	RBI	BB	SO	SB	Pinch Hit AB	Pinch Hit H	PO	A	E	DP	TC/G	FA	G by Pos
1915	PHI N	37	.141	.172	64	9	2	0	0	0.0	6	8	7	12	2	8	3	26	0	3	0	1.5	.897	OF-20
1916		4	.300	.400	10	3	1	0	0	0.0	1	1	0	3	0	0	0	5	0	0	0	1.3	1.000	OF-4
2 yrs.		41	.162	.203	74	12	3	0	0	0.0	7	9	7	15	2	8	3	31	0	3	0	1.4	.912	OF-24

Gary Weiss

WEISS, GARY LEE
B. Dec. 27, 1955, Brenham, Tex.
BB TR 5′10″ 170 lbs.

Year	Team	Games	BA	SA	AB	H	2B	3B	HR	HR%	R	RBI	BB	SO	SB	Pinch Hit AB	Pinch Hit H	PO	A	E	DP	TC/G	FA	G by Pos
1980	LA N	8	—	—	0	0	0	0	0	—	2	0	0	0	0	0	0	0	0	0	0	0.0	—	
1981		14	.105	.105	19	2	0	0	0	0.0	2	1	1	4	0	1	0	12	11	2	8	1.9	.920	SS-13
2 yrs.		22	.105	.105	19	2	0	0	0	0.0	4	1	1	4	0	1	0	12	11	2	8	1.9	.920	SS-13

Joe Weiss

WEISS, JOSEPH HAROLD
B. Jan. 27, 1894, Chicago, Ill. D. July 7, 1967, Cedar Rapids, Iowa.
BR TR 6′ 175 lbs.

Year	Team	Games	BA	SA	AB	H	2B	3B	HR	HR%	R	RBI	BB	SO	SB	Pinch Hit AB	Pinch Hit H	PO	A	E	DP	TC/G	FA	G by Pos
1915	CHI F	29	.224	.282	85	19	1	2	0	0.0	6	11	3		0	0	0	239	10	2	7	8.7	.992	1B-29

Walt Weiss

WEISS, WALTER WILLIAM
B. Nov. 28, 1963, Tuxedo, N. Y.
BB TR 6′ 175 lbs.

Year	Team	Games	BA	SA	AB	H	2B	3B	HR	HR%	R	RBI	BB	SO	SB	Pinch Hit AB	Pinch Hit H	PO	A	E	DP	TC/G	FA	G by Pos
1987	OAK A	16	.462	.615	26	12	4	0	0	0.0	3	1	2	2	1	1	0	8	30	1	4	3.5	.974	SS-11
1988		147	.250	.321	452	113	17	3	3	0.7	44	39	35	56	4	1	0	254	431	15	83	4.8	.979	SS-147
1989		84	.233	.318	236	55	11	0	3	1.3	30	21	21	39	6	0	0	106	195	15	44	3.8	.953	SS-84
1990		138	.265	.321	445	118	17	1	2	0.4	50	35	46	53	9	3	1	194	373	12	77	4.2	.979	SS-137
1991		40	.226	.286	133	30	6	1	0	0.0	15	13	12	14	6	1	1	64	99	5	21	4.2	.970	SS-40
1992		103	.212	.241	316	67	5	2	0	0.0	36	21	43	39	6	1	0	144	270	19	57	4.2	.956	SS-103
1993	FLA N	158	.266	.308	500	133	14	2	1	0.2	50	39	79	73	7	6	0	229	406	15	80	4.2	.977	SS-153
1994	CLR N	110	.251	.303	423	106	11	4	1	0.2	58	32	56	58	12	2	0	157	318	13	68	4.4	.973	SS-110
1995		137	.260	.321	427	111	17	3	1	0.2	65	25	98	57	15	1	0	202	407	16	98	4.6	.974	SS-136
9 yrs.		933	.252	.308	2958	745	102	16	11	0.4	351	226	392	391	66	16	2	1358	2529	111	532	4.3	.972	SS-921
DIVISIONAL PLAYOFF SERIES																								
1995	CLR N	4	.167	.167	12	2	0	0	0	0.0	1	0	3	3	1	0	0	6	12	0	4	4.5	1.000	SS-4
LEAGUE CHAMPIONSHIP SERIES																								
1988	OAK A	4	.333	.467	15	5	2	0	0	0.0	2	2	0	4	0	0	0	7	10	0	3	4.3	1.000	SS-4
1989		4	.111	.222	9	1	1	0	0	0.0	2	0	1	1	1	0	0	5	9	0	2	3.5	1.000	SS-4
1990		2	.000	.000	7	0	0	0	0	0.0	2	0	2	2	0	0	0	2	7	1	1	5.0	.900	SS-2
1992		3	.167	.167	6	1	0	0	0	0.0	1	0	2	1	2	0	0	5	6	0	1	3.7	1.000	SS-3
4 yrs.		13	.189	.270	37	7	3	0	0	0.0	7	2	5	8	3	0	0	19	32	1	7	4.0	.981	SS-13
WORLD SERIES																								
1988	OAK A	5	.063	.063	16	1	0	0	0	0.0	1	0	0	2	1	0	0	5	11	1	1	3.4	.941	SS-5
1989		4	.133	.333	15	2	0	0	1	6.7	3	1	2	2	0	0	0	7	8	0	1	3.8	1.000	SS-4
2 yrs.		9	.097	.194	31	3	0	0	1	3.2	4	1	2	4	1	0	0	12	19	1	2	3.6	.969	SS-9

Johnny Welaj

WELAJ, JOHN LUDWIG
B. May 27, 1914, Moss Creek, Pa.
BR TR 6′ 164 lbs.

Year	Team	Games	BA	SA	AB	H	2B	3B	HR	HR%	R	RBI	BB	SO	SB	Pinch Hit AB	Pinch Hit H	PO	A	E	DP	TC/G	FA	G by Pos
1939	WAS A	63	.274	.363	201	55	11	2	1	0.5	23	33	13	20	13	7	2	113	2	3	1	2.1	.975	OF-55
1940		88	.256	.340	215	55	9	0	3	1.4	31	21	19	20	8	20	7	132	1	3	0	2.6	.978	OF-53
1941		49	.208	.250	96	20	4	0	0	0.0	16	5	6	16	3	22	7	47	0	1	0	2.5	.979	OF-19
1943	PHI A	93	.242	.306	281	68	16	1	0	0.0	45	15	15	17	12	10	1	187	3	8	0	2.8	.960	OF-72
4 yrs.		293	.250	.323	793	198	40	3	4	0.5	115	74	53	73	36	59	17	479	6	15	1	2.5	.970	OF-199

Curt Welch

WELCH, CURTIS BENTON
B. Feb. 11, 1862, East Liverpool, Ohio D. Aug. 29, 1896, East Liverpool, Ohio.
BR TR 5′10″ 175 lbs.

Year	Team	Games	BA	SA	AB	H	2B	3B	HR	HR%	R	RBI	BB	SO	SB	Pinch Hit AB	Pinch Hit H	PO	A	E	DP	TC/G	FA	G by Pos
1884	TOL AA	109	.224	.304	425	95	24	5	0	0.0	61		10			0	0	212	29	31	4	2.4	.886	OF-106, C-2, 2B-2, 1B-1, P-1
1885	STL AA	112	.271	.363	432	117	18	8	2	0.5	84		23			0	0	236	25	15	5	2.5	.946	OF-112
1886		138	.281	.393	563	158	31	13	2	0.4	114		29			0	0	300	19	18	5	2.4	.947	OF-138, 2B-2
1887		131	.278	.379	544	151	32	7	3	0.6	98		25		89	0	0	370	47	35	10	3.4	.923	OF-123, 2B-8, 1B-1
1888	PHI AA	136	.282	.357	549	155	22	8	1	0.2	125	61	33		95	0	0	277	25	19	6	2.3	.941	OF-135, 2B-3
1889		125	.271	.370	516	140	**39**	6	0	0.0	134	39	67	30	66	0	0	282	29	26	10	2.7	.923	OF-125
1890	2 teams	PHI AA (103G –.268) BAL AA (19G –.132)																						
″	total	122	.248	.332	464	115	25	4	2	0.4	116		58		72	0	0	269	28	23	9	2.6	.928	OF-120, 1B-2, P-1
1891	BAL AA	132	.268	.368	514	138	22	10	3	0.6	122	55	77	42	50	0	0	306	103	24	18	3.2	.945	OF-113, 2B-21, SS-2
1892	2 teams	BAL N (63G –.236) CIN N (25G –.202)																						
″	total	88	.227	.278	331	75	1	5	2	0.6	56	29	43	17	21	0	0	189	6	19	2	2.4	.911	OF-88
1893	LOU N	14	.170	.191	47	8	1	0	0	0.0	5	2	16	4	1	0	0	29	2	3	0	2.4	.912	OF-14
10 yrs.		1107	.263	.352	4385	1152	215	66	15	0.3	915	186	381	93	394	0	0	2470	313	213	69	2.7	.929	OF-1074, 2B-36, 1B-4, C-2, SS-2, P-2

Frank Welch

WELCH, FRANK TIGUER (Bugger)
B. Aug. 10, 1897, Birmingham, Ala. D. July 25, 1957, Birmingham, Ala.
BR TR 5′ 9″ 175 lbs.

Year	Team	Games	BA	SA	AB	H	2B	3B	HR	HR%	R	RBI	BB	SO	SB	Pinch Hit AB	Pinch Hit H	PO	A	E	DP	TC/G	FA	G by Pos
1919	PHI A	15	.167	.333	54	9	1	1	2	3.7	5	7	7	10	0	0	0	38	2	4	0	2.9	.909	OF-15
1920		100	.258	.367	360	93	17	5	4	1.1	43	40	26	41	2	3	0	194	14	14	4	2.3	.937	OF-97
1921		115	.285	.412	403	115	18	6	7	1.7	48	45	34	43	6	10	4	251	16	16	1	2.7	.943	OF-104
1922		114	.259	.408	375	97	17	3	11	2.9	43	49	40	40	3	9	4	191	12	11	2	2.1	.949	OF-104
1923		125	.297	.413	421	125	19	9	4	1.0	56	55	48	40	1	7	0	253	13	9	4	2.4	.967	OF-117
1924		94	.290	.399	293	85	13	2	5	1.7	47	31	35	27	2	20	7	120	15	2	2	1.9	.985	OF-74
1925		85	.277	.401	202	56	5	4	4	2.0	40	41	29	14	2	24	4	85	6	3	3	1.6	.968	OF-57

Frank Welch *continued*

Year	Team	Games	BA	SA	AB	H	2B	3B	HR	HR%	R	RBI	BB	SO	SB	Pinch Hit AB	Pinch Hit H	PO	A	E	DP	TC/G	FA	G by Pos
1926		75	.282	.408	174	49	8	1	4	2.3	26	23	26	9	2	19	3	75	4	2	1	1.7	.975	OF-49
1927	BOS A	15	.179	.250	28	5	2	0	0	0.0	2	4	5	1	0	8	2	9	3	0	1	2.0	1.000	OF-6
9 yrs.		738	.274	.398	2310	634	100	31	41	1.8	310	295	250	225	18	100	24	1216	85	61	18	2.2	.955	OF-623

Herb Welch

WELCH, HERBERT M. (Dutch) BL TR 5′ 6″ 154 lbs.
B. Oct. 19, 1898, Roellen, Tenn. D. Apr. 13, 1967, Memphis, Tenn.

Year	Team	Games	BA	SA	AB	H	2B	3B	HR	HR%	R	RBI	BB	SO	SB	Pinch Hit AB	Pinch Hit H	PO	A	E	DP	TC/G	FA	G by Pos
1925	BOS A	13	.289	.342	38	11	0	1	0	0.0	2	2	0	6	0	0	0	25	42	8	9	5.8	.893	SS-13

Mickey Welch

WELCH, MICHAEL FRANCIS (Smiling Mickey) BR TR 5′ 8″ 160 lbs.
B. July 4, 1859, Brooklyn, N. Y. D. July 30, 1941, Concord, N. H.
Hall of Fame 1973.

Year	Team	Games	BA	SA	AB	H	2B	3B	HR	HR%	R	RBI	BB	SO	SB	Pinch Hit AB	Pinch Hit H	PO	A	E	DP	TC/G	FA	G by Pos
1880	TRO N	66	.287	.390	251	72	20	3	0	0.0	25	27	5	24		0	0	36	86	23	4	2.2	.841	P-65, OF-2
1881		40	.203	.270	148	30	10	0	0	0.0	12	11	1	16		0	0	20	39	7	3	1.6	.894	P-40
1882		38	.245	.305	151	37	6	0	1	0.7	26	17	5	16		0	0	15	46	11	4	1.8	.847	P-33, OF-8
1883	NY N	84	.234	.331	320	75	12	5	3	0.9	42		10	38		0	0	71	63	38	4	1.9	.779	P-54, OF-38
1884		71	.241	.357	249	60	14	3	3	1.2	47		16	49		0	0	25	78	14	6	1.6	.880	P-65, OF-7
1885		56	.206	.276	199	41	8	0	2	1.0	28		14	39		0	0	16	70	14	0	1.8	.860	P-56
1886		59	.216	.254	213	46	4	2	0	0.0	17	18	7	47		0	0	19	82	5	0	1.7	.953	P-59, OF-3
1887		40	.243	.338	148	36	4	2	2	1.4	16	15	6	1	2	0	0	17	51	12	0	2.0	.850	P-40, OF-1
1888		47	.189	.254	169	32	5	0	2	1.2	16	10	1	33	4	0	0	16	75	17	1	2.3	.843	P-47
1889		45	.192	.237	156	30	5	1	0	0.0	20	12	5	27	0	0	0	13	59	4	2	1.7	.947	P-45
1890		37	.179	.211	123	22	4	0	0	0.0	15	10	9	25	1	0	0	10	43	4	1	1.5	.930	P-37
1891		22	.141	.141	71	10	0	0	0	0.0	4	4	3	13	0	0	0	7	21	4	0	1.5	.875	P-22
1892		1	.333	.333	3	1	0	0	0	0.0	0	0	0	1	0	0	0	0	1	0	0	1.0	1.000	P-1
13 yrs.		606	.224	.298	2201	492	92	16	13	0.6	268	124	82	329	7	0	0	265	714	153	25	1.8	.865	P-564, OF-59

Milt Welch

WELCH, MILTON EDWARD BR TR 5′10″ 175 lbs.
B. July 26, 1924, Farmersville, Ill.

Year	Team	Games	BA	SA	AB	H	2B	3B	HR	HR%	R	RBI	BB	SO	SB	Pinch Hit AB	Pinch Hit H	PO	A	E	DP	TC/G	FA	G by Pos
1945	DET A	1	.000	.000	2	0	0	0	0	0.0	0	0	0	1	0	0	0	3	1	0	1	4.0	1.000	C-1

Tub Welch

WELCH, JAMES T. TR 5′11″ 230 lbs.
B. July 3, 1866, St. Louis, Mo. Deceased.

Year	Team	Games	BA	SA	AB	H	2B	3B	HR	HR%	R	RBI	BB	SO	SB	Pinch Hit AB	Pinch Hit H	PO	A	E	DP	TC/G	FA	G by Pos
1890	TOL AA	35	.287	.361	108	31	3	1	1	0.9	15		8		7	0	0	188	44	23	4	7.3	.910	C-25, 1B-10
1895	LOU N	47	.242	.301	153	37	4	1	1	0.7	18	8	13	7	2	0	0	254	41	21	17	6.6	.934	C-28, 1B-20
2 yrs.		82	.261	.326	261	68	7	2	2	0.8	33	8	21	7	9	0	0	442	85	44	21	6.9	.923	C-53, 1B-30

Harry Welchonce

WELCHONCE, HARRY MONROE BL TR 6′ 170 lbs.
B. Nov. 20, 1883, North Point, Pa. D. Feb. 26, 1977, Arcadia, Calif.

Year	Team	Games	BA	SA	AB	H	2B	3B	HR	HR%	R	RBI	BB	SO	SB	Pinch Hit AB	Pinch Hit H	PO	A	E	DP	TC/G	FA	G by Pos
1911	PHI N	26	.212	.273	66	14	4	0	0	0.0	9	6	7	8	0	9	3	25	1	2	0	1.6	.929	OF-17

Mike Welday

WELDAY, LYNDON EARL BL TL
B. Dec. 19, 1879, Conway, Iowa D. May 28, 1942, Leavenworth, Kans.

Year	Team	Games	BA	SA	AB	H	2B	3B	HR	HR%	R	RBI	BB	SO	SB	Pinch Hit AB	Pinch Hit H	PO	A	E	DP	TC/G	FA	G by Pos
1907	CHI A	24	.229	.314	35	8	1	1	0	0.0	2	0	6		0	6	1	13	2	1	0	1.1	.938	OF-15
1909		29	.189	.189	74	14	0	0	0	0.0	3	5	4		2	8	2	35	4	5	1	2.2	.886	OF-20
2 yrs.		53	.202	.229	109	22	1	1	0	0.0	5	5	10		2	14	3	48	6	6	1	1.7	.900	OF-35

Ollie Welf

WELF, OLIVER HENRY BR TL 5′ 9″ 160 lbs.
B. Jan. 17, 1889, Cleveland, Ohio D. June 15, 1967, Cleveland, Ohio.

Year	Team	Games	BA	SA	AB	H	2B	3B	HR	HR%	R	RBI	BB	SO	SB	Pinch Hit AB	Pinch Hit H	PO	A	E	DP	TC/G	FA	G by Pos
1916	CLE A	1	—	—	0	0	0	0	0	—	0	0	0	0	0	0	0	0	0	0	0	0.0	—	

Bob Wellman

WELLMAN, ROBERT JOSEPH BR TR 6′ 4″ 210 lbs.
B. July 15, 1925, Norwood, Ohio D. Dec. 20, 1994, Covington, Ky.

Year	Team	Games	BA	SA	AB	H	2B	3B	HR	HR%	R	RBI	BB	SO	SB	Pinch Hit AB	Pinch Hit H	PO	A	E	DP	TC/G	FA	G by Pos
1948	PHI A	4	.200	.400	10	2	0	1	0	0.0	1	0	3	2	0	1	0	26	1	1	2	9.3	.964	1B-2, OF-1
1950		11	.333	.533	15	5	0	0	1	6.7	1	1	0	3	0	8	2	4	0	0	0	2.0	1.000	OF-2
2 yrs.		15	.280	.480	25	7	0	1	1	4.0	2	1	3	5	0	9	2	30	1	1	2	6.4	.969	OF-3, 1B-2

Brad Wellman

WELLMAN, BRAD EUGENE BR TR 6′ 165 lbs.
B. Aug. 17, 1959, Lodi, Calif.

Year	Team	Games	BA	SA	AB	H	2B	3B	HR	HR%	R	RBI	BB	SO	SB	Pinch Hit AB	Pinch Hit H	PO	A	E	DP	TC/G	FA	G by Pos
1982	SF N	6	.250	.250	4	1	0	0	0	0.0	1	0	0	1	0	2	0	0	1	0	0	0.5	1.000	2B-2
1983		82	.214	.247	182	39	3	0	1	0.5	15	16	22	39	5	4	0	94	167	9	27	3.6	.967	2B-74, SS-2
1984		93	.226	.291	265	60	9	1	2	0.8	23	25	19	41	10	6	3	151	258	11	37	4.3	.974	2B-54, SS-33, 3B-10
1985		71	.236	.310	174	41	11	1	0	0.0	16	16	4	33	5	6	1	66	107	9	15	2.8	.951	2B-36, 3B-25, SS-3
1986		12	.154	.154	13	2	0	0	0	0.0	0	1	1	2	0	2	1	3	10	0	1	1.3	1.000	SS-8, 3B-1, 2B-1
1987	LA N	3	.250	.250	4	1	0	0	0	0.0	1	1	0	1	0	0	0	3	3	0	1	2.0	1.000	3B-1, SS-1, 2B-1
1988	KC A	71	.271	.327	107	29	3	0	1	0.9	11	6	6	23	1	2	1	67	101	6	27	2.7	.966	2B-46, SS-15, 3B-4
1989		103	.230	.287	178	41	4	0	2	1.1	30	12	7	36	5	1	0	104	184	2	42	2.8	.993	2B-64, SS-34, 3B-3, DH-1
8 yrs.		441	.231	.287	927	214	30	2	6	0.6	97	77	59	176	26	23	6	488	831	37	150	3.2	.973	2B-278, SS-96, 3B-44, DH-1

Boomer Wells

WELLS, GREGORY DeWAYNE BR TR 6′ 5″ 218 lbs.
B. Apr. 25, 1954, McIntosh, Ala.

Year	Team	Games	BA	SA	AB	H	2B	3B	HR	HR%	R	RBI	BB	SO	SB	Pinch Hit AB	Pinch Hit H	PO	A	E	DP	TC/G	FA	G by Pos
1981	TOR A	32	.247	.315	73	18	5	0	0	0.0	7	5	5	12	0	8	3	146	10	1	10	6.3	.994	1B-22, DH-3
1982	MIN A	15	.204	.296	54	11	1	2	0	0.0	5	3	1	8	0	1	1	74	2	3	6	5.3	.962	1B-10, DH-5
2 yrs.		47	.228	.307	127	29	6	2	0	0.0	12	8	6	20	0	9	4	220	12	4	16	5.9	.983	1B-32, DH-8

Jake Wells

WELLS, JACOB BR TR 5′11″ 167 lbs.
B. Aug. 9, 1863, Memphis, Tenn. D. Mar. 16, 1927, Hendersonville, N. C.

Year	Team	Games	BA	SA	AB	H	2B	3B	HR	HR%	R	RBI	BB	SO	SB	Pinch Hit AB	Pinch Hit H	PO	A	E	DP	TC/G	FA	G by Pos
1888	DET N	16	.158	.175	57	9	1	0	0	0.0	5	2	0	5	0	0	0	96	25	11	2	8.3	.917	C-16
1890	STL AA	30	.238	.267	105	25	3	0	0	0.0	17		10		1	0	0	166	43	13	3	7.2	.941	C-28, OF-3
2 yrs.		46	.210	.235	162	34	4	0	0	0.0	22	2	10	5	1	0	0	262	68	24	5	7.5	.932	C-44, OF-3

Leo Wells

WELLS, LEO DONALD
B. July 18, 1917, Kansas City, Kans.
BR TR 5'10" 180 lbs.

Year	Team	Games	BA	SA	AB	H	2B	3B	HR	HR%	R	RBI	BB	SO	SB	Pinch Hit AB	Pinch Hit H	PO	A	E	DP	TC/G	FA	G by Pos
1942	CHI A	35	.194	.274	62	12	2	0	1	1.6	8	4	4	5	1	13	5	23	53	2	10	4.3	.974	SS-12, 3B-6
1946		45	.189	.260	127	24	4	1	1	0.8	11	11	12	34	3	2	0	39	92	8	7	3.5	.942	3B-38, SS-2
2 yrs.		80	.190	.265	189	36	6	1	2	1.1	19	15	16	39	4	15	5	62	145	10	17	3.7	.954	3B-44, SS-14

Jimmy Welsh

WELSH, JAMES DANIEL
B. Oct. 9, 1902, Denver, Colo. D. Oct. 30, 1970, Oakland, Calif.
BL TR 6'1" 174 lbs.

Year	Team	Games	BA	SA	AB	H	2B	3B	HR	HR%	R	RBI	BB	SO	SB	Pinch Hit AB	Pinch Hit H	PO	A	E	DP	TC/G	FA	G by Pos
1925	BOS N	122	.312	.440	484	151	25	8	7	1.4	69	63	20	24	7	3	0	241	36	11	7	2.4	.962	OF-116, 2B-3
1926		134	.278	.378	490	136	18	11	3	0.6	69	57	33	28	6	4	0	283	23	11	8	2.5	.965	OF-129
1927		131	.288	.423	497	143	26	7	9	1.8	72	54	23	27	11	1	0	381	24	13	6	3.2	.969	OF-129, 1B-1
1928	NY N	124	.307	.431	476	146	22	5	9	1.9	77	54	29	30	4	3	1	310	8	6	3	2.8	.981	OF-117
1929	2 teams	NY N (38G –.248) BOS N (53G –.290)																						
"	total	91	.273	.403	315	86	15	7	4	1.3	49	24	22	12	4	3	0	220	10	7	2	2.8	.970	OF-86
1930	BOS N	113	.275	.389	422	116	21	9	3	0.7	51	36	29	23	5	2	1	329	8	7	2	3.1	.980	OF-110
6 yrs.		715	.290	.411	2684	778	127	47	35	1.3	387	288	156	144	37	16	2	1764	109	55	28	2.8	.971	OF-687, 2B-3, 1B-1

Lew Wendell

WENDELL, LEWIS CHARLES
B. Mar. 22, 1892, New York, N. Y. D. July 11, 1953, Brooklyn, N. Y.
BR TR 5'11" 178 lbs.

Year	Team	Games	BA	SA	AB	H	2B	3B	HR	HR%	R	RBI	BB	SO	SB	Pinch Hit AB	Pinch Hit H	PO	A	E	DP	TC/G	FA	G by Pos
1915	NY N	20	.222	.306	36	8	1	1	0	0.0	0	5	2	7	0	3	0	33	13	4	1	2.5	.920	C-20
1916		2	.000	.000	2	0	0	0	0	0.0	0	0	0	2	0	2	0	0	0	0	0	0.0	—	
1924	PHI N	21	.250	.281	32	8	1	0	0	0.0	3	2	3	5	0	3	1	25	6	0	0	1.8	1.000	C-17
1925		18	.077	.077	26	2	0	0	0	0.0	0	3	1	3	0	8	0	16	4	2	0	2.4	.909	C-9
1926		1	.000	.000	4	0	0	0	0	0.0	0	0	0	0	0	0	0	0	1	2	0	3.0	.333	C-1
5 yrs.		62	.180	.220	100	18	2	1	0	0.0	3	10	6	17	0	16	1	74	24	8	1	2.3	.925	C-47

Jack Wentz

WENTZ, JOHN GEORGE
Born John George Wernz.
B. Mar. 4, 1863, Louisville, Ky. D. Sept. 14, 1907, Louisville, Ky.
BR TR 5'10½" 175 lbs.

Year	Team	Games	BA	SA	AB	H	2B	3B	HR	HR%	R	RBI	BB	SO	SB	Pinch Hit AB	Pinch Hit H	PO	A	E	DP	TC/G	FA	G by Pos
1891	LOU AA	1	.250	.250	4	1	0	0	0	0.0	0	0	0	0	0	0	0	2	2	2	0	6.0	.667	2B-1

Stan Wentzel

WENTZEL, STANLEY AARON
B. Jan. 13, 1917, Lorane, Pa. D. Nov. 18, 1991, St. Lawrence, Pa.
BR TR 6'1" 200 lbs.

Year	Team	Games	BA	SA	AB	H	2B	3B	HR	HR%	R	RBI	BB	SO	SB	Pinch Hit AB	Pinch Hit H	PO	A	E	DP	TC/G	FA	G by Pos
1945	BOS N	4	.211	.316	19	4	0	1	0	0.0	3	6	0	3	1	0	0	8	0	0	0	2.0	1.000	OF-4

Julie Wera

WERA, JULIAN VALENTINE
B. Feb. 9, 1902, Winona, Minn. D. Dec. 12, 1975, Rochester, Minn.
BR TR 5'8" 164 lbs.

Year	Team	Games	BA	SA	AB	H	2B	3B	HR	HR%	R	RBI	BB	SO	SB	Pinch Hit AB	Pinch Hit H	PO	A	E	DP	TC/G	FA	G by Pos
1927	NY A	38	.238	.381	42	10	3	0	1	2.4	7	8	1	5	0	4	0	17	15	0	0	1.7	1.000	3B-19
1929		5	.417	.417	12	5	0	0	0	0.0	1	2	1	1	0	1	0	0	5	0	0	1.3	1.000	3B-4
2 yrs.		43	.278	.389	54	15	3	0	1	1.9	8	10	2	6	0	5	0	17	20	0	0	1.6	1.000	3B-23

Bill Werber

WERBER, WILLIAM MURRAY
B. June 20, 1908, Berwyn, Md.
BR TR 5'10" 170 lbs.

Year	Team	Games	BA	SA	AB	H	2B	3B	HR	HR%	R	RBI	BB	SO	SB	Pinch Hit AB	Pinch Hit H	PO	A	E	DP	TC/G	FA	G by Pos
1930	NY A	4	.286	.286	14	4	0	0	0	0.0	5	2	3	1	0	0	0	12	9	1	3	5.5	.955	SS-3, 3B-1
1933	2 teams	NY A (3G –.000) BOS A (108G –.259)																						
"	total	111	.258	.377	427	110	30	6	3	0.7	64	39	33	39	15	4	1	169	259	39	43	4.2	.916	SS-71, 3B-39, 2B-2
1934	BOS A	152	.321	.472	623	200	41	10	11	1.8	129	67	77	37	**40**	0	0	179	392	43	39	4.0	.930	3B-130, SS-22
1935		124	.255	.424	462	118	30	3	14	3.0	84	61	69	41	**29**	1	0	174	264	27	20	3.8	.942	3B-123
1936		145	.275	.407	535	147	29	6	10	1.9	89	67	89	37	23	0	0	202	167	21	16	2.7	.946	3B-101, OF-45, 2B-1
1937	PHI A	128	.292	.414	493	144	31	4	7	1.4	85	70	74	39	**35**	2	0	141	260	17	25	3.3	.959	3B-125, OF-3
1938		134	.259	.397	499	129	22	7	11	2.2	92	69	93	37	19	0	0	168	266	30	21	3.5	.935	3B-134
1939	CIN N	147	.289	.389	599	173	35	5	5	0.8	**115**	57	91	46	15	0	0	165	308	34	32	3.4	.933	3B-147
1940		143	.277	.416	584	162	35	5	12	2.1	105	48	68	40	16	0	0	139	287	17	24	3.1	.962	3B-143
1941		109	.239	.299	418	100	9	2	4	1.0	56	46	53	24	14	1	0	120	256	16	30	3.7	.959	3B-107
1942	NY N	98	.205	.249	370	76	9	2	1	0.3	51	13	51	22	9	3	1	79	227	24	14	3.5	.927	3B-93
11 yrs.		1295	.271	.392	5024	1363	271	50	78	1.6	875	539	701	363	215	11	2	1548	2695	269	267	3.5	.940	3B-1143, SS-96, OF-48, 2B-3
WORLD SERIES																								
1939	CIN N	4	.250	.250	16	4	0	0	0	0.0	1	2	2	0	0	0	0	3	5	0	0	2.0	1.000	3B-4
1940		7	.370	.519	27	10	4	0	0	0.0	5	2	4	2	0	0	0	9	16	2	3	3.9	.926	3B-7
2 yrs.		11	.326	.419	43	14	4	0	0	0.0	6	4	6	2	0	0	0	12	21	2	3	3.2	.943	3B-11

Perry Werden

WERDEN, PERCIVAL WHERITT (Moose)
B. July 21, 1865, St. Louis, Mo. D. Jan. 9, 1934, Minneapolis, Minn.
BR TR 6'2" 220 lbs.

Year	Team	Games	BA	SA	AB	H	2B	3B	HR	HR%	R	RBI	BB	SO	SB	Pinch Hit AB	Pinch Hit H	PO	A	E	DP	TC/G	FA	G by Pos
1884	STL U	18	.237	.263	76	18	2	0	0	0.0	7		2			0	0	17	36	6	1	2.7	.898	P-16, OF-6
1888	WAS N	3	.300	.300	10	3	0	0	0	0.0	0	2	1	4	0	0	0	6	0	1	0	2.3	.857	OF-3
1890	TOL AA	128	.295	.456	498	147	22	**20**	6	1.2	113		78		59	0	0	1190	61	35	57	10.0	.973	1B-124, OF-5
1891	BAL AA	139	.290	.424	552	160	20	18	6	1.1	102	104	52	59	46	0	0	1422	58	30	79	10.9	.980	1B-139
1892	STL N	149	.258	.355	598	154	22	6	8	1.3	73	84	59	52	20	0	0	1467	102	28	81	10.7	.982	1B-149
1893		125	.276	.442	500	138	22	**29**	1	0.2	73	94	49	25	11	0	0	1194	82	43	75	10.6	.967	1B-124, OF-1
1897	LOU N	131	.302	.429	506	153	21	14	5	1.0	76	83	40		14	0	0	1318	116	23	70	11.1	.984	1B-131
7 yrs.		693	.282	.414	2740	773	109	87	26	0.9	444	367	281	140	150	0	0	6614	455	166	363	10.4	.977	1B-667, P-16, OF-15

Johnny Werhas

WERHAS, JOHN CHARLES (Peaches)
B. Feb. 7, 1938, Highland Park, Mich.
BR TR 6'2" 200 lbs.

Year	Team	Games	BA	SA	AB	H	2B	3B	HR	HR%	R	RBI	BB	SO	SB	Pinch Hit AB	Pinch Hit H	PO	A	E	DP	TC/G	FA	G by Pos
1964	LA N	29	.193	.241	83	16	2	1	0	0.0	6	8	13	12	0	1	0	30	49	4	4	3.0	.952	3B-28
1965		4	.000	.000	3	0	0	0	0	0.0	1	0	1	2	0	2	0	3	0	0	0	3.0	1.000	1B-1
1967	2 teams	LA N (7G –.143) CAL A (49G –.160)																						
"	total	56	.159	.268	82	13	1	1	2	2.4	8	6	10	25	0	23	3	30	37	2	2	2.0	.971	3B-30, 1B-4, OF-1
3 yrs.		89	.173	.250	168	29	3	2	2	1.2	15	14	24	39	0	26	3	63	86	6	6	2.4	.961	3B-58, 1B-5, OF-1

Don Werner

WERNER, DONALD PAUL
B. Mar. 8, 1953, Appleton, Wis.
BR TR 6'1" 175 lbs.

Year	Team	Games	BA	SA	AB	H	2B	3B	HR	HR%	R	RBI	BB	SO	SB	Pinch Hit AB	Pinch Hit H	PO	A	E	DP	TC/G	FA	G by Pos
1975	CIN N	7	.125	.125	8	1	0	0	0	0.0	0	0	0	0	0	0	0	10	2	1	0	1.9	.923	C-7
1976		3	.500	.750	4	2	1	0	0	0.0	0	1	1	1	0	0	0	7	2	0	0	3.0	1.000	C-3

Don Werner *continued*

Year	Team	Games	BA	SA	AB	H	2B	3B	HR	HR%	R	RBI	BB	SO	SB	Pinch Hit AB	Pinch Hit H	PO	A	E	DP	TC/G	FA	G by Pos
1977		10	.174	.435	23	4	0	0	2	8.7	3	4	2	3	0	0	0	40	4	0	2	4.4	1.000	C-10
1978		50	.150	.186	113	17	2	1	0	0.0	7	11	14	30	1	1	1	214	21	3	4	4.9	.987	C-49
1980		24	.172	.203	64	11	2	0	0	0.0	2	5	7	10	1	1	1	119	6	5	1	5.4	.962	C-24
1981	TEX A	2	.250	.250	8	2	0	0	0	0.0	1	0	0	2	0	0	0	0	0	0	0	0.0	.000	DH-2
1982		22	.203	.237	59	12	2	0	0	0.0	4	3	3	7	0	0	0	91	5	2	2	4.5	.980	C-22
7 yrs.		118	.176	.229	279	49	7	1	2	0.7	17	24	27	53	2	2	2	481	40	11	9	4.5	.979	C-115, DH-2

Joe Werrick

WERRICK, JOSEPH ABRAHAM BR TR 5′ 9″ 151 lbs.
B. Oct. 25, 1861, St. Paul, Minn. D. May 10, 1943, St. Peter, Minn.

Year	Team	Games	BA	SA	AB	H	2B	3B	HR	HR%	R	RBI	BB	SO	SB	Pinch Hit AB	Pinch Hit H	PO	A	E	DP	TC/G	FA	G by Pos
1884	STP U	9	.074	.074	27	2	0	0	0	0.0	3		1			0	0	8	26	11	0	5.0	.756	SS-9
1886	LOU AA	136	.250	.351	561	140	20	14	3	0.5	75		33			0	0	162	257	72	9	3.6	.853	3B-136
1887		136	.285	.413	533	152	21	13	7	1.3	90		38		49	0	0	153	286	89	12	3.9	.831	3B-136
1888		111	.215	.278	413	89	12	7	0	0.0	49	51	30		15	0	0	135	226	79	11	4.0	.820	3B-89, SS-11, 2B-8, OF-3
4 yrs.		392	.250	.348	1534	383	53	34	10	0.7	217	51	102		64	0	0	458	795	251	32	3.8	.833	3B-361, SS-20, 2B-8, OF-3

Don Wert

WERT, DONALD RALPH BR TR 5′10″ 162 lbs.
B. July 29, 1938, Strasburg, Pa.

Year	Team	Games	BA	SA	AB	H	2B	3B	HR	HR%	R	RBI	BB	SO	SB	Pinch Hit AB	Pinch Hit H	PO	A	E	DP	TC/G	FA	G by Pos
1963	DET A	78	.259	.382	251	65	6	2	7	2.8	31	25	24	51	3	4	0	85	173	10	20	3.5	.963	3B-47, 2B-21, SS-8
1964		148	.257	.362	525	135	18	5	9	1.7	63	55	50	74	3	3	0	134	293	16	33	3.0	.964	3B-142, SS-4
1965		162	.261	.363	609	159	22	2	12	2.0	81	54	73	71	5	0	0	164	337	12	34	3.1	.977	3B-161, SS-3, 2B-1
1966		150	.268	.370	559	150	20	2	11	2.0	56	70	64	69	6	0	0	128	253	11	20	2.6	.972	3B-150
1967		142	.257	.341	534	137	23	2	6	1.1	60	40	44	59	1	2	0	113	282	9	22	2.9	.978	3B-140, SS-1
1968		150	.200	.299	536	107	15	1	12	2.2	44	37	37	79	0	1	1	144	284	15	22	2.9	.966	3B-150, SS-2
1969		132	.225	.355	423	95	11	1	14	3.3	46	50	49	60	3	2	0	114	259	13	20	3.0	.966	3B-129
1970		128	.218	.303	363	79	13	0	6	1.7	34	33	44	56	1	15	2	95	193	14	20	2.5	.954	3B-117, 2B-2
1971	WAS A	20	.050	.075	40	2	1	0	0	0.0	2	2	4	10	0	7	0	9	23	2	2	2.3	.941	3B-7, SS-7, 2B-1
9 yrs.		1110	.242	.343	3840	929	129	15	77	2.0	417	366	389	529	22	34	3	986	2097	102	193	2.9	.968	3B-1043, 2B-25, SS-25
WORLD SERIES																								
1968	DET A	6	.118	.118	17	2	0	0	0	0.0	1	2	6	5	0	0	0	5	14	0	1	3.2	1.000	3B-6

Dennis Werth

WERTH, DENNIS DEAN BR TR 6′ 1″ 200 lbs.
B. Dec. 29, 1952, Lincoln, Ill.

Year	Team	Games	BA	SA	AB	H	2B	3B	HR	HR%	R	RBI	BB	SO	SB	Pinch Hit AB	Pinch Hit H	PO	A	E	DP	TC/G	FA	G by Pos
1979	NY A	3	.250	.250	4	1	0	0	0	0.0	1	0	0	0	0	2	0	5	1	0	0	6.0	1.000	1B-1
1980		39	.308	.492	65	20	3	0	3	4.6	15	12	12	19	0	9	1	82	3	2	9	2.9	.977	1B-12, OF-8, DH-8, 3B-1, C-1
1981		34	.109	.127	55	6	1	0	0	0.0	7	1	12	12	1	5	0	104	11	0	7	3.4	1.000	1B-19, OF-8, DH-4, C-3
1982	KC A	41	.133	.133	15	2	0	0	0	0.0	5	2	4	2	0	1	0	94	9	1	10	2.8	.990	1B-35, C-2
4 yrs.		117	.209	.302	139	29	4	0	3	2.2	28	15	28	33	1	17	1	285	24	3	26	3.1	.990	1B-67, OF-16, DH-12, C-6, 3B-1

Del Wertz

WERTZ, DWIGHT LYMAN MOODY BR TR 5′10″ 160 lbs.
B. Oct. 11, 1888, Canton, Ohio D. May 26, 1958, Sarasota, Fla.

Year	Team	Games	BA	SA	AB	H	2B	3B	HR	HR%	R	RBI	BB	SO	SB	Pinch Hit AB	Pinch Hit H	PO	A	E	DP	TC/G	FA	G by Pos
1914	BUF F	3	—	—	0	0	0	0	0	—	1	0	0		0	0	0	1	0	0	0	1.0	1.000	SS-1

Vic Wertz

WERTZ, VICTOR WOODROW BL TR 6′ 186 lbs.
B. Feb. 9, 1925, York, Pa. D. July 7, 1983, Detroit, Mich.

Year	Team	Games	BA	SA	AB	H	2B	3B	HR	HR%	R	RBI	BB	SO	SB	Pinch Hit AB	Pinch Hit H	PO	A	E	DP	TC/G	FA	G by Pos
1947	DET A	102	.288	.432	333	96	22	4	6	1.8	60	44	47	66	2	18	5	160	6	6	0	2.1	.965	OF-82
1948		119	.248	.396	391	97	19	9	7	1.8	49	67	48	70	0	19	4	196	11	10	3	2.2	.954	OF-98
1949		155	.304	.465	608	185	26	6	20	3.3	96	133	80	61	2	0	0	302	14	6	4	2.1	.981	OF-155
1950		149	.308	.533	559	172	37	4	27	4.8	99	123	91	55	0	4	2	286	5	10	3	2.1	.967	OF-145
1951		138	.285	.511	501	143	24	4	27	5.4	86	94	78	61	0	6	0	254	7	3	1	2.0	.989	OF-131
1952	2 teams	DET A (85G –.246) STL A (37G –.346)																						
"	total	122	.277	.506	415	115	20	3	23	5.5	68	70	69	64	1	8	2	198	8	5	3	1.8	.976	OF-115
1953	STL A	128	.268	.466	440	118	18	6	19	4.3	61	70	72	44	1	8	2	243	15	7	4	2.2	.974	OF-121
1954	2 teams	BAL A (29G –.202) CLE A (94G –.275)																						
"	total	123	.257	.422	389	100	15	2	15	3.9	38	61	45	57	0	7	1	614	57	9	58	5.9	.987	1B-83, OF-32
1955	CLE A	74	.253	.475	257	65	11	2	14	5.4	30	55	32	33	1	5	2	462	34	8	50	7.0	.984	1B-63, OF-9
1956		136	.264	.509	481	127	22	0	32	6.7	65	106	75	87	0	1	0	971	77	9	99	7.9	.991	1B-133
1957		144	.282	.485	515	145	21	0	28	5.4	84	105	78	87	2	4	0	1025	83	14	122	8.1	.988	1B-139
1958		25	.279	.512	43	12	1	0	3	7.0	5	12	5	7	0	16	3	44	5	1	5	6.3	.980	1B-8
1959	BOS A	94	.275	.413	247	68	13	0	7	2.8	38	49	22	32	0	33	7	440	38	4	44	7.5	.992	1B-64
1960		131	.282	.460	443	125	22	0	19	4.3	45	103	37	54	0	18	10	841	78	12	89	8.0	.987	1B-117
1961	2 teams	BOS A (99G –.262) DET A (8G –.167)																						
"	total	107	.260	.424	323	84	16	2	11	3.4	33	61	38	44	0	18	3	664	67	7	65	8.6	.991	1B-86
1962	DET A	74	.324	.486	105	34	2	0	5	4.8	7	18	5	13	0	53	**17**	75	9	1	5	5.3	.988	1B-16
1963	2 teams	DET A (6G –.000) MIN A (35G –.136)																						
"	total	41	.122	.306	49	6	0	0	3	6.1	3	7	6	6	0	30	4	32	5	0	2	6.2	1.000	1B-6
17 yrs.		1862	.277	.469	6099	1692	289	42	266	4.4	867	1178	828	841	9	248	62	6807	519	112	557	4.6	.985	OF-888, 1B-715
WORLD SERIES																								
1954	CLE A	4	.500	.938	16	8	2	1	1	6.3	2	3	2	2	0	0	0	33	6	1	2	10.0	.975	1B-4

Jim Wessinger

WESSINGER, JAMES MICHAEL BR TR 5′10″ 165 lbs.
B. Sept. 25, 1955, Utica, N. Y.

Year	Team	Games	BA	SA	AB	H	2B	3B	HR	HR%	R	RBI	BB	SO	SB	Pinch Hit AB	Pinch Hit H	PO	A	E	DP	TC/G	FA	G by Pos
1979	ATL N	10	.000	.000	7	0	0	0	0	0.0	2	0	1	4	0	2	0	2	3	1	0	3.0	.833	2B-2

Billy West

WEST, WILLIAM NELSON
B. Aug. 21, 1840, Philadelphia, Pa. D. Aug. 18, 1891, Radnor, Pa.

Year	Team	Games	BA	SA	AB	H	2B	3B	HR	HR%	R	RBI	BB	SO	SB	Pinch Hit AB	Pinch Hit H	PO	A	E	DP	TC/G	FA	G by Pos
1876	NY N	1	.000	.000	4	0	0	0	0	0.0	0	0	0	0		0	0	1	3	0	1	4.0	1.000	2B-1

Buck West

WEST, MILTON DOUGLAS BL TR 5′10″ 200 lbs.
B. Aug. 29, 1860, Spring Hill, Ohio D. Jan. 13, 1929, Mansfield, Ohio.

Year	Team	Games	BA	SA	AB	H	2B	3B	HR	HR%	R	RBI	BB	SO	SB	Pinch Hit AB	Pinch Hit H	PO	A	E	DP	TC/G	FA	G by Pos
1884	CIN AA	33	.244	.397	131	32	2	9	0	0.0	20		2			0	0	46	1	10	0	1.7	.825	OF-33
1890	CLE N	37	.245	.338	151	37	6	1	2	1.3	20	29	7	11	4	0	0	50	9	12	1	1.9	.831	OF-37
2 yrs.		70	.245	.365	282	69	8	10	2	0.7	40	29	9	11	4	0	0	96	10	22	1	1.8	.828	OF-70

Dick West

WEST, RICHARD THOMAS BR TR 6′ 2″ 180 lbs.
B. Nov. 24, 1915, Louisville, Ky.

Year	Team	Games	BA	SA	AB	H	2B	3B	HR	HR%	R	RBI	BB	SO	SB	Pinch Hit AB	Pinch Hit H	PO	A	E	DP	TC/G	FA	G by Pos
1938	CIN N	1	.000	.000	1	0	0	0	0	0.0	0	0	0	0	0	1	0	0	0	0	0	0.0	—	
1939		6	.211	.211	19	4	0	0	0	0.0	1	4	1	4	0	1	1	11	0	0	0	1.8	1.000	OF-5, C-1
1940		7	.393	.571	28	11	2	0	1	3.6	4	6	0	2	1	0	0	19	2	0	0	3.0	1.000	C-7
1941		67	.215	.285	172	37	5	2	1	0.6	15	17	6	23	4	1	0	209	21	7	3	3.7	.970	C-64
1942		33	.177	.253	79	14	3	0	1	1.3	9	8	5	13	1	6	0	86	13	1	1	4.3	.990	C-17, OF-6
1943		3	—	—	0	0	0	0	0	—	1	0	0	0	0	0	0	0	0	0	0	0.0	—	
6 yrs.		117	.221	.298	299	66	10	2	3	1.0	30	35	12	42	6	9	1	325	36	8	4	3.7	.978	C-89, OF-11

Max West

WEST, MAX EDWARD BL TR 6′ 1½″ 182 lbs.
B. Nov. 28, 1916, Dexter, Mo.

Year	Team	Games	BA	SA	AB	H	2B	3B	HR	HR%	R	RBI	BB	SO	SB	Pinch Hit AB	Pinch Hit H	PO	A	E	DP	TC/G	FA	G by Pos
1938	BOS N	123	.234	.368	418	98	16	5	10	2.4	47	63	38	38	5	3	0	268	8	4	4	2.4	.986	OF-109, 1B-7
1939		130	.285	.497	449	128	26	6	19	4.2	67	82	51	55	1	5	3	287	8	8	2	2.4	.974	OF-124
1940		141	.261	.372	524	137	27	5	7	1.3	72	72	65	54	2	3	1	558	40	11	34	4.4	.982	OF-102, 1B-36
1941		138	.277	.426	484	134	28	4	12	2.5	63	68	72	68	5	6	3	302	13	6	5	2.4	.981	OF-132
1942		134	.254	.409	452	115	22	0	16	3.5	54	56	68	59	4	3	2	913	51	12	67	7.2	.988	1B-85, OF-50
1946	2 teams	BOS N (1G –.000) CIN N (72G –.213)																						
″	total	73	.212	.350	203	43	13	0	5	2.5	16	18	32	37	1	12	1	115	6	6	3	2.2	.953	OF-58, 1B-1
1948	PIT N	87	.178	.370	146	26	4	0	8	5.5	19	21	27	29	1	32	5	209	20	2	14	4.8	.991	1B-32, OF-16
7 yrs.		826	.254	.407	2676	681	136	20	77	2.9	338	380	353	340	19	64	15	2652	146	49	129	3.8	.983	OF-591, 1B-161

Max West

WEST, WALTER MAXWELL BR TR 5′11″ 165 lbs.
B. July 14, 1904, Sunset, Tex. D. Apr. 25, 1971, Houston, Tex.

Year	Team	Games	BA	SA	AB	H	2B	3B	HR	HR%	R	RBI	BB	SO	SB	Pinch Hit AB	Pinch Hit H	PO	A	E	DP	TC/G	FA	G by Pos
1928	BKN N	7	.286	.429	21	6	1	1	0	0.0	4	1	4	1	0	1	0	12	3	2	1	2.4	.882	OF-7
1929		5	.250	.375	8	2	1	0	0	0.0	1	1	1	0	0	2	1	2	0	0	0	1.0	1.000	OF-2
2 yrs.		12	.276	.414	29	8	2	1	0	0.0	5	2	5	1	0	3	1	14	3	2	1	2.1	.895	OF-9

Sammy West

WEST, SAMUEL FILMORE BL TL 5′11″ 165 lbs.
B. Oct. 5, 1904, Longview, Tex. D. Nov. 23, 1985, Lubbock, Tex.

Year	Team	Games	BA	SA	AB	H	2B	3B	HR	HR%	R	RBI	BB	SO	SB	Pinch Hit AB	Pinch Hit H	PO	A	E	DP	TC/G	FA	G by Pos
1927	WAS A	38	.239	.328	67	16	4	1	0	0.0	9	6	8	8	1	19	4	28	3	2	0	1.8	.939	OF-18
1928		125	.302	.442	378	114	30	7	3	0.8	59	40	20	23	5	7	0	210	13	1	0	1.9	.996	OF-116
1929		142	.267	.347	510	136	16	8	3	0.6	60	75	45	41	9	3	1	376	25	9	8	2.9	.978	OF-139
1930		120	.328	.474	411	135	22	10	6	1.5	75	67	37	34	5	0	0	310	8	9	1	2.8	.972	OF-118
1931		132	.333	.481	526	175	43	13	3	0.6	77	91	30	37	6	0	0	402	13	4	3	3.3	.990	OF-127
1932		146	.287	.412	554	159	27	12	6	1.1	88	83	48	57	4	3	0	450	15	10	7	3.3	.979	OF-143
1933	STL A	133	.300	.458	517	155	25	12	11	2.1	93	48	59	49	10	6	1	329	14	4	3	2.7	.988	OF-127
1934		122	.326	.469	482	157	22	10	9	1.9	90	55	62	55	3	2	0	303	14	9	3	2.7	.972	OF-120
1935		138	.300	.442	527	158	37	4	10	1.9	93	70	75	46	1	3	3	449	7	5	2	3.4	.989	OF-135
1936		152	.278	.381	533	148	26	4	7	1.3	78	70	94	70	2	3	0	442	10	8	2	3.1	.983	OF-148
1937		122	.328	.473	457	150	37	4	7	1.5	68	58	46	28	1	14	3	298	17	4	6	3.0	.987	OF-105
1938	2 teams	STL A (44G –.309) WAS A (92G –.302)																						
″	total	136	.305	.420	509	155	27	7	6	1.2	68	74	47	30	2	9	2	322	4	7	3	2.6	.979	OF-126
1939	WAS A	115	.282	.397	390	110	20	8	3	0.8	52	52	67	29	1	6	0	365	13	6	12	3.6	.984	OF-89, 1B-17
1940		57	.253	.364	99	25	6	1	1	1.0	7	18	16	13	0	26	8	113	7	1	13	5.8	.992	1B-12, OF-9
1941		26	.270	.270	37	10	0	0	0	0.0	3	6	11	2	1	12	4	19	0	0	0	2.4	1.000	OF-8
1942	CHI A	49	.232	.265	151	35	5	0	0	0.0	14	25	31	18	2	2	0	112	1	2	1	2.6	.983	OF-45
16 yrs.		1753	.299	.425	6148	1838	347	101	75	1.2	934	838	696	540	53	115	26	4528	164	81	64	3.0	.983	OF-1573, 1B-29

Oscar Westerberg

WESTERBERG, OSCAR WILLIAM BB TR
B. July 8, 1882, Alameda, Calif. D. Apr. 17, 1909, Alameda, Calif.

Year	Team	Games	BA	SA	AB	H	2B	3B	HR	HR%	R	RBI	BB	SO	SB	Pinch Hit AB	Pinch Hit H	PO	A	E	DP	TC/G	FA	G by Pos
1907	BOS N	2	.333	.333	6	2	0	0	0	0.0	0	1	1		0	0	0	3	3	0	1	3.0	1.000	SS-2

Jim Westlake

WESTLAKE, JAMES PATRICK BL TL 6′ 1″ 190 lbs.
Brother of Wally Westlake.
B. July 3, 1930, Sacramento, Calif.

Year	Team	Games	BA	SA	AB	H	2B	3B	HR	HR%	R	RBI	BB	SO	SB	Pinch Hit AB	Pinch Hit H	PO	A	E	DP	TC/G	FA	G by Pos
1955	PHI N	1	.000	.000	1	0	0	0	0	0.0	0	0	0	1	0	1	0	0	0	0	0	0.0	—	

Wally Westlake

WESTLAKE, WALDON THOMAS BR TR 6′ 186 lbs.
Brother of Jim Westlake.
B. Nov. 8, 1920, Gridley, Calif.

Year	Team	Games	BA	SA	AB	H	2B	3B	HR	HR%	R	RBI	BB	SO	SB	Pinch Hit AB	Pinch Hit H	PO	A	E	DP	TC/G	FA	G by Pos
1947	PIT N	112	.273	.459	407	111	17	4	17	4.2	59	69	27	63	5	2	0	239	8	3	0	2.3	.988	OF-109
1948		132	.285	.456	428	122	10	6	17	4.0	78	65	46	40	2	8	2	274	8	7	2	2.3	.976	OF-125
1949		147	.282	.490	525	148	24	8	23	4.4	77	104	45	69	6	4	0	319	12	6	4	2.4	.982	OF-143
1950		139	.285	.493	477	136	15	6	24	5.0	69	95	48	78	1	15	3	329	4	3	3	2.7	.991	OF-123
1951	2 teams	PIT N (50G –.282) STL N (73G –.255)																						
″	total	123	.266	.462	448	119	12	5	22	4.9	64	84	33	68	1	9	1	203	96	15	14	2.8	.952	OF-79, 3B-34
1952	3 teams	STL N (21G –.216) CIN N (59G –.202) CLE A (29G –.232)																						
″	total	109	.212	.288	326	69	11	1	4	1.2	47	33	47	56	2	6	0	231	12	1	2	2.3	.996	OF-104
1953	CLE A	82	.330	.495	218	72	7	1	9	4.1	42	46	35	29	2	7	0	128	3	5	2	1.9	.963	OF-72
1954		85	.263	.454	240	63	9	2	11	4.6	36	42	26	37	0	11	2	131	1	5	0	2.0	.964	OF-70
1955	2 teams	CLE A (16G –.250) BAL A (8G –.125)																						
″	total	24	.182	.227	44	8	2	0	0	0.0	2	1	9	10	0	5	1	18	1	0	0	1.4	1.000	OF-14
1956	PHI N	5	.000	.000	4	0	0	0	0	0.0	0	0	1	3	0	4	0	0	0	0	0	0.0	—	
10 yrs.		958	.272	.450	3117	848	107	33	127	4.1	474	539	317	453	19	71	9	1872	145	45	27	2.4	.978	OF-839, 3B-34
WORLD SERIES																								
1954	CLE A	2	.143	.143	7	1	0	0	0	0.0	0	0	1	3	0	0	0	6	0	1	0	3.5	.857	OF-2

Al Weston

WESTON, ALFRED JOHN BR TR 6′ 195 lbs.
B. Dec. 11, 1905, Lynn, Mass.

Year	Team	Games	BA	SA	AB	H	2B	3B	HR	HR%	R	RBI	BB	SO	SB	Pinch Hit AB	Pinch Hit H	PO	A	E	DP	TC/G	FA	G by Pos
1929	BOS N	3	.000	.000	3	0	0	0	0	0.0	0	0	0	2	0	3	0	0	0	0	0	0.0	—	

Wes Westrum

WESTRUM, WESLEY NOREEN BR TR 5′11″ 185 lbs.
B. Nov. 28, 1922, Clearbrook, Minn.
Manager 1965–67, 1974–75.

Year	Team	Games	BA	SA	AB	H	2B	3B	HR	HR%	R	RBI	BB	SO	SB	Pinch Hit AB	Pinch Hit H	PO	A	E	DP	TC/G	FA	G by Pos
1947	NY N	6	.417	.500	12	5	1	0	0	0.0	1	2	0	2	0	4	1	8	2	0	0	5.0	1.000	C-2
1948		66	.160	.296	125	20	3	1	4	3.2	14	16	20	36	3	2	0	179	25	4	4	3.3	.981	C-63
1949		64	.243	.402	169	41	4	1	7	4.1	23	28	37	39	1	2	0	224	18	5	4	4.0	.980	C-62
1950		140	.236	.437	437	103	13	3	23	5.3	68	71	92	73	2	0	0	608	71	1	21	4.9	.999	C-139
1951		124	.219	.418	361	79	12	0	20	5.5	59	70	104	93	1	2	0	554	62	8	9	5.1	.987	C-122
1952		114	.220	.385	322	71	11	0	14	4.3	47	43	76	68	1	2	0	481	64	12	11	5.0	.978	C-112
1953		107	.224	.366	290	65	5	0	12	4.1	40	30	56	73	2	1	0	441	56	9	9	4.7	.982	C-106, 3B-1
1954		98	.187	.305	246	46	3	1	8	3.3	25	27	45	60	0	0	0	419	45	7	8	4.8	.985	C-98
1955		69	.212	.307	137	29	1	0	4	2.9	11	18	24	18	0	1	0	280	27	4	5	4.6	.987	C-68
1956		68	.220	.356	132	29	5	2	3	2.3	10	8	25	28	0	1	1	297	27	6	7	4.9	.982	C-67
1957		63	.165	.209	91	15	1	0	1	1.1	4	2	10	24	0	0	0	148	21	6	4	2.8	.966	C-63
11 yrs.		919	.217	.373	2322	503	59	8	96	4.1	302	315	489	514	10	15	2	3639	418	62	82	4.6	.985	C-902, 3B-1
WORLD SERIES																								
1951	NY N	6	.235	.294	17	4	1	0	0	0.0	1	0	5	3	0	0	0	29	2	1	0	5.3	.969	C-6
1954		4	.273	.273	11	3	0	0	0	0.0	0	3	1	3	0	0	0	23	0	0	0	5.8	1.000	C-4
2 yrs.		10	.250	.286	28	7	1	0	0	0.0	1	3	6	6	0	0	0	52	2	1	0	5.5	.982	C-10

Jeff Wetherby

WETHERBY, JEFFREY BARRET BL TL 6′ 2″ 195 lbs.
B. Oct. 18, 1963, Granada Hills, Calif.

Year	Team	Games	BA	SA	AB	H	2B	3B	HR	HR%	R	RBI	BB	SO	SB	Pinch Hit AB	Pinch Hit H	PO	A	E	DP	TC/G	FA	G by Pos
1989	ATL N	52	.208	.354	48	10	2	1	1	2.1	5	7	4	6	1	36	8	8	0	0	0	0.9	1.000	OF-9

Buzz Wetzel

WETZEL, FRANKLIN BURTON BR TR 5′ 9½″ 177 lbs.
B. July 7, 1893, Columbus, Ind. D. Mar. 5, 1942, Hollywood, Calif.

Year	Team	Games	BA	SA	AB	H	2B	3B	HR	HR%	R	RBI	BB	SO	SB	Pinch Hit AB	Pinch Hit H	PO	A	E	DP	TC/G	FA	G by Pos
1920	STL A	6	.474	.632	19	9	1	1	0	0.0	5	5	4	1	0	1	1	12	1	2	0	3.0	.867	OF-5
1921		61	.210	.277	119	25	2	0	2	1.7	16	10	9	20	0	32	5	52	1	1	0	2.0	.981	OF-27
2 yrs.		67	.246	.326	138	34	3	1	2	1.4	21	15	13	21	0	33	6	64	2	3	0	2.2	.957	OF-32

Bill Whaley

WHALEY, WILLIAM CARL BR TR 5′11″ 178 lbs.
B. Feb. 10, 1899, Indianapolis, Ind. D. Mar. 3, 1943, Indianapolis, Ind.

Year	Team	Games	BA	SA	AB	H	2B	3B	HR	HR%	R	RBI	BB	SO	SB	Pinch Hit AB	Pinch Hit H	PO	A	E	DP	TC/G	FA	G by Pos
1923	STL A	23	.240	.320	50	12	2	1	0	0.0	5	1	4	2	0	8	1	25	2	0	0	2.1	1.000	OF-13

Bert Whaling

WHALING, ALBERT JAMES BR TR 6′ 185 lbs.
B. June 22, 1888, Los Angeles, Calif. D. Jan. 21, 1965, Sawtelle, Calif.

Year	Team	Games	BA	SA	AB	H	2B	3B	HR	HR%	R	RBI	BB	SO	SB	Pinch Hit AB	Pinch Hit H	PO	A	E	DP	TC/G	FA	G by Pos
1913	BOS N	79	.242	.299	211	51	8	2	0	0.0	22	25	10	32	3	2	1	328	84	4	4	5.4	.990	C-77
1914		60	.209	.250	172	36	7	0	0	0.0	18	12	21	28	2	0	0	272	91	7	7	6.3	.981	C-59
1915		72	.221	.274	190	42	6	2	0	0.0	10	13	8	38	0	2	0	292	68	5	2	5.1	.986	C-72
3 yrs.		211	.225	.276	573	129	21	4	0	0.0	50	50	39	98	5	4	1	892	243	16	13	5.5	.986	C-208

Mack Wheat

WHEAT, McKINLEY DAVIS BR TR 5′11½″ 167 lbs.
Brother of Zack Wheat.
B. June 9, 1893, Polo, Mo. D. Aug. 14, 1979, Los Banos, Calif.

Year	Team	Games	BA	SA	AB	H	2B	3B	HR	HR%	R	RBI	BB	SO	SB	Pinch Hit AB	Pinch Hit H	PO	A	E	DP	TC/G	FA	G by Pos
1915	BKN N	8	.071	.071	14	1	0	0	0	0.0	0	0	0	5	0	0	0	19	3	1	1	2.9	.957	C-8
1916		2	.000	.000	2	0	0	0	0	0.0	0	0	0	1	0	0	0	5	0	0	0	2.5	1.000	C-2
1917		29	.133	.150	60	8	1	0	0	0.0	2	0	1	12	1	0	0	77	23	3	0	3.8	.971	C-18, OF-9
1918		57	.217	.293	157	34	7	1	1	0.6	11	3	8	24	2	8	2	162	50	8	1	4.9	.964	C-38, OF-7
1919		47	.205	.232	112	23	3	0	0	0.0	5	8	2	22	1	1	0	131	39	10	3	4.7	.944	C-38
1920	PHI N	78	.226	.335	230	52	10	3	3	1.3	15	20	8	35	3	2	0	262	105	15	8	5.2	.961	C-74
1921		10	.185	.333	27	5	2	1	0	0.0	1	4	0	3	0	1	1	39	11	1	1	5.7	.980	C-9
7 yrs.		231	.204	.279	602	123	23	5	4	0.7	34	35	19	102	7	12	3	695	231	38	14	4.7	.961	C-187, OF-16

Zack Wheat

WHEAT, ZACHARY DAVIS (Buck) BL TR 5′10″ 170 lbs.
Brother of Mack Wheat.
B. May 23, 1888, Hamilton, Mo. D. Mar. 11, 1972, Sedalia, Mo.
Hall of Fame 1959.

Year	Team	Games	BA	SA	AB	H	2B	3B	HR	HR%	R	RBI	BB	SO	SB	Pinch Hit AB	Pinch Hit H	PO	A	E	DP	TC/G	FA	G by Pos
1909	BKN N	26	.304	.431	102	31	7	3	0	0.0	15	4	6		1	0	0	54	5	3	1	2.4	.952	OF-26
1910		156	.284	.403	606	172	36	15	2	0.3	78	55	47	80	16	0	0	354	21	15	6	2.5	.962	OF-156
1911		140	.287	.412	534	153	26	13	5	0.9	55	76	29	58	21	4	2	287	12	14	0	2.3	.955	OF-136
1912		123	.305	.450	453	138	28	7	8	1.8	70	65	39	40	16	3	0	285	13	10	2	2.5	.968	OF-122
1913		138	.301	.430	535	161	28	10	7	1.3	64	71	25	45	19	2	0	338	13	8	7	2.7	.978	OF-135
1914		145	.319	.452	533	170	26	9	9	1.7	66	89	47	50	20	1	0	331	21	14	5	2.5	.962	OF-144
1915		146	.258	.360	528	136	15	12	5	0.9	64	66	52	42	21	2	1	345	18	18	4	2.6	.953	OF-144
1916		149	.312	**.461**	568	177	32	13	9	1.6	76	73	43	49	19	0	0	333	14	9	0	2.4	.975	OF-149
1917		109	.312	.423	362	113	15	11	1	0.3	38	41	20	18	5	10	2	216	12	5	5	2.1	.979	OF-109
1918		105	**.335**	.386	409	137	15	3	0	0.0	39	51	16	17	9	0	0	219	11	5	2	2.2	.979	OF-105
1919		137	.297	.409	536	159	23	11	5	0.9	70	62	33	27	15	0	0	297	9	9	2	2.3	.971	OF-137
1920		148	.328	.463	583	191	26	13	9	1.5	89	73	48	21	8	0	0	287	10	9	5	2.1	.971	OF-148
1921		148	.320	.484	568	182	31	10	14	2.5	91	85	44	19	11	0	0	283	18	11	3	2.1	.965	OF-148
1922		152	.335	.503	600	201	29	12	16	2.7	92	112	45	22	9	0	0	317	14	3	1	2.2	.991	OF-152
1923		98	.375	.510	349	131	13	5	8	2.3	63	65	23	12	3	11	4	135	4	14	1	1.8	.908	OF-87
1924		141	.375	.549	566	212	41	8	14	2.5	92	97	49	18	3	1	0	288	13	11	4	2.2	.965	OF-139
1925		150	.359	.541	616	221	42	14	14	2.3	125	103	45	22	3	1	0	320	7	13	2	2.3	.962	OF-149
1926		111	.290	.411	411	119	31	2	5	1.2	68	35	21	14	4	9	2	202	9	10	3	2.2	.955	OF-102
1927	PHI A	88	.324	.393	247	80	12	1	1	0.4	34	38	18	5	2	24	6	105	8	2	1	1.9	.983	OF-62
19 yrs.		2410	.317	.450	9106	2884	476	172	132	1.4	1289	1261	650	559	205	68	17	4996	232	183	54	2.3	.966	OF-2350
WORLD SERIES																								
1916	BKN N	5	.211	.316	19	4	0	1	0	0.0	2	1	2	2	1	0	0	14	0	1	0	3.0	.933	OF-5
1920		7	.333	.407	27	9	2	0	0	0.0	2	2	1	2	0	0	0	16	0	2	0	2.6	.889	OF-7
2 yrs.		12	.283	.370	46	13	2	1	0	0.0	4	3	3	4	1	0	0	30	0	3	0	2.8	.909	OF-12

Woody Wheaton

WHEATON, ELWOOD PIERCE BL TL 5′ 8½″ 160 lbs.
B. Oct. 3, 1914, Philadelphia, Pa.

Year	Team	Games	BA	SA	AB	H	2B	3B	HR	HR%	R	RBI	BB	SO	SB	Pinch Hit AB	Pinch Hit H	PO	A	E	DP	TC/G	FA	G by Pos
1943	PHI A	7	.200	.267	30	6	2	0	0	0.0	2	2	3	2	0	0	0	20	1	0	0	3.0	1.000	OF-7
1944		30	.186	.220	59	11	2	0	0	0.0	1	5	5	3	1	11	2	29	6	1	1	1.9	.972	P-11, OF-8
2 yrs.		37	.191	.236	89	17	4	0	0	0.0	3	7	8	5	1	11	2	49	7	1	1	2.2	.982	OF-15, P-11

Dick Wheeler

WHEELER, RICHARD BR TR 5′11″ 185 lbs.
Born Richard Wheeler Maynard.
B. Jan. 14, 1898, Keene, N. H. D. Feb. 12, 1962, Lexington, Mass.

Year	Team	Games	BA	SA	AB	H	2B	3B	HR	HR%	R	RBI	BB	SO	SB	Pinch Hit AB	Pinch Hit H	PO	A	E	DP	TC/G	FA	G by Pos
1918	STL N	3	.000	.000	6	0	0	0	0	0.0	0	0	0	3	0	1	0	0	0	0	0	0.0	.000	OF-2

Don Wheeler

WHEELER, DONALD WESLEY (Scotty) BR TR 5′10″ 175 lbs.
B. Sept. 29, 1922, Minneapolis, Minn.

Year	Team	Games	BA	SA	AB	H	2B	3B	HR	HR%	R	RBI	BB	SO	SB	Pinch Hit AB	Pinch Hit H	PO	A	E	DP	TC/G	FA	G by Pos
1949	CHI A	67	.240	.323	192	46	9	2	1	0.5	17	22	27	19	2	8	1	210	36	6	4	4.3	.976	C-58

Ed Wheeler

WHEELER, EDWARD BB TR 5′10″ 160 lbs.
B. June 15, 1878, Sherman, Mich. D. Aug. 15, 1960, Ft. Worth, Tex.

Year	Team	Games	BA	SA	AB	H	2B	3B	HR	HR%	R	RBI	BB	SO	SB	Pinch Hit AB	Pinch Hit H	PO	A	E	DP	TC/G	FA	G by Pos
1902	BKN N	30	.125	.125	96	12	0	0	0	0.0	4	5	3		1	3	0	55	54	19	4	4.9	.852	3B-11, 2B-10, SS-5

Ed Wheeler

WHEELER, EDWARD RAYMOND BR TR 5′ 9″ 160 lbs.
B. May 24, 1917, Los Angeles, Calif. D. Aug. 4, 1983, Centralia, Wash.

Year	Team	Games	BA	SA	AB	H	2B	3B	HR	HR%	R	RBI	BB	SO	SB	Pinch Hit AB	Pinch Hit H	PO	A	E	DP	TC/G	FA	G by Pos
1945	CLE A	46	.194	.222	72	14	2	0	0	0.0	12	2	8	13	1	7	3	29	23	5	1	2.0	.912	3B-14, SS-11, 2B-3

George Wheeler

WHEELER, GEORGE HARRISON (Heavy) BL TR 5′ 9½″ 180 lbs.
B. Nov. 10, 1881, Shelburn, Ind. D. June 14, 1918, Clinton, Ind.

Year	Team	Games	BA	SA	AB	H	2B	3B	HR	HR%	R	RBI	BB	SO	SB	Pinch Hit AB	Pinch Hit H	PO	A	E	DP	TC/G	FA	G by Pos
1910	CIN N	3	.000	.000	3	0	0	0	0	0.0	0	0	0	2	0	3	0	0	0	0	0	0.0	—	

Harry Wheeler

WHEELER, HARRY EUGENE BR TR 5′11″ 165 lbs.
B. Mar. 3, 1858, Versailles, Ind. D. Oct. 9, 1900, Cincinnati, Ohio.
Manager 1884.

Year	Team	Games	BA	SA	AB	H	2B	3B	HR	HR%	R	RBI	BB	SO	SB	Pinch Hit AB	Pinch Hit H	PO	A	E	DP	TC/G	FA	G by Pos
1878	PRO N	7	.148	.148	27	4	0	0	0	0.0	7	1	2	15		0	0	2	5	1	0	1.1	.875	P-7
1879	CIN N	1	.000	.000	3	0	0	0	0	0.0	0	0	0	2		0	0	2	0	0	0	1.0	1.000	OF-1, P-1
1880	2 teams	CLE N (1G –.250) CIN N (17G –.092)																						
″	total	18	.101	.130	69	7	2	0	0	0.0	1	2	0	15		0	0	39	5	14	1	3.2	.759	OF-18
1882	CIN AA	76	.250	.355	344	86	11	11	1	0.3	59		7			0	0	175	19	35	11	2.9	.847	OF-64, 1B-12, P-4
1883	COL AA	82	.226	.283	371	84	6	6	1	0.3	42		6			0	0	131	17	38	2	2.2	.796	OF-82, P-1, 2B-1
1884	5 teams	STL AA (5G –.263) KC U (14G –.258) CHI U (20G –.224) PIT U (17G –.233) BAL U (17G –.261)																						
″	total	73	.244	.305	308	75	10	3	1	0.3	43		22			0	0	99	10	32	0	1.9	.773	OF-72, P-1
6 yrs.		257	.228	.298	1122	256	29	20	3	0.3	152	3	37	32		0	0	448	56	120	14	2.4	.808	OF-237, P-14, 1B-12, 2B-1

Bobby Wheelock

WHEELOCK, WARREN H. BR TR 5′ 8″ 150 lbs.
B. Aug. 6, 1864, Charlestown, Mass. D. Mar. 13, 1928, Boston, Mass.

Year	Team	Games	BA	SA	AB	H	2B	3B	HR	HR%	R	RBI	BB	SO	SB	Pinch Hit AB	Pinch Hit H	PO	A	E	DP	TC/G	FA	G by Pos
1887	BOS N	48	.253	.337	166	42	4	2	2	1.2	32	15	15	15	20	0	0	73	72	22	5	3.2	.868	OF-28, SS-20, 2B-4
1890	COL AA	52	.237	.295	190	45	6	1	1	0.5	24		25		34	0	0	92	162	33	12	5.5	.885	SS-52
1891		136	.229	.263	498	114	15	1	0	0.0	82	39	78	55	52	0	0	248	474	81	65	5.9	.899	SS-136
3 yrs.		236	.235	.285	854	201	25	4	3	0.4	138	54	118	70	106	0	0	413	708	136	82	5.2	.892	SS-208, OF-28, 2B-4

Jim Whelan

WHELAN, JAMES FRANCIS BR TR 5′ 8½″ 165 lbs.
B. May 11, 1890, Kansas City, Mo. D. Nov. 29, 1929, Dayton, Ohio.

Year	Team	Games	BA	SA	AB	H	2B	3B	HR	HR%	R	RBI	BB	SO	SB	Pinch Hit AB	Pinch Hit H	PO	A	E	DP	TC/G	FA	G by Pos
1913	STL N	1	.000	.000	1	0	0	0	0	0.0	0	0	0	0	0	1	0	0	0	0	0	0.0	—	

Tom Whelan

WHELAN, THOMAS JOSEPH BR TR 5′11″ 175 lbs.
B. Jan. 3, 1894, Lynn, Mass. D. June 26, 1957, Boston, Mass.

Year	Team	Games	BA	SA	AB	H	2B	3B	HR	HR%	R	RBI	BB	SO	SB	Pinch Hit AB	Pinch Hit H	PO	A	E	DP	TC/G	FA	G by Pos
1920	BOS N	1	.000	.000	1	0	0	0	0	0.0	0	0	1	1	0	0	0	4	0	0	0	4.0	1.000	1B-1

Pete Whisenant

WHISENANT, PETER BR TR 6′ 2″ 190 lbs.
B. Dec. 14, 1929, Asheville, N. C.

Year	Team	Games	BA	SA	AB	H	2B	3B	HR	HR%	R	RBI	BB	SO	SB	Pinch Hit AB	Pinch Hit H	PO	A	E	DP	TC/G	FA	G by Pos
1952	BOS N	24	.192	.231	52	10	2	0	0	0.0	3	7	4	13	1	9	1	34	2	1	2	2.6	.973	OF-14
1955	STL N	58	.191	.304	115	22	5	1	2	1.7	10	9	5	29	2	20	5	76	4	3	1	2.1	.964	OF-40
1956	CHI N	103	.239	.414	314	75	16	3	11	3.5	37	46	24	53	8	8	2	242	6	2	0	2.7	.992	OF-93
1957	CIN N	67	.211	.456	90	19	3	2	5	5.6	18	11	5	24	0	20	8	54	0	1	0	1.3	.982	OF-43
1958		85	.236	.463	203	48	9	2	11	5.4	33	40	18	37	3	25	6	122	3	0	1	1.9	1.000	OF-66, 2B-1
1959		36	.239	.479	71	17	2	0	5	7.0	13	11	8	18	0	14	1	27	1	1	1	1.4	.966	OF-21
1960	3 teams	CIN N (1G –.000) CLE A (7G –.167) WAS A (58G –.226)																						
″	total	66	.221	.369	122	27	9	0	3	2.5	19	9	19	16	2	15	2	69	2	0	0	1.4	1.000	OF-49
1961	2 teams	MIN A (10G –.000) CIN N (26G –.200)																						
″	total	36	.143	.143	21	3	0	0	0	0.0	7	1	3	6	1	13	1	6	2	1	0	0.5	.889	OF-17, 3B-1, C-1
8 yrs.		475	.224	.399	988	221	46	8	37	3.7	140	134	86	196	17	124	26	630	20	9	5	1.9	.986	OF-343, C-1, 3B-1, 2B-1

Larry Whisenton

WHISENTON, LARRY BL TL 6′ 1″ 190 lbs.
B. July 3, 1956, St. Louis, Mo.

Year	Team	Games	BA	SA	AB	H	2B	3B	HR	HR%	R	RBI	BB	SO	SB	Pinch Hit AB	Pinch Hit H	PO	A	E	DP	TC/G	FA	G by Pos
1977	ATL N	4	.250	.250	4	1	0	0	0	0.0	1	1	0	3	0	4	1	0	0	0	0	0.0	—	
1978		6	.188	.250	16	3	1	0	0	0.0	1	2	1	2	0	1	0	5	0	0	0	1.3	1.000	OF-4
1979		13	.243	.351	37	9	2	1	0	0.0	3	1	3	3	1	0	0	28	3	0	0	2.4	1.000	OF-13
1981		9	.200	.200	5	1	0	0	0	0.0	1	0	2	1	0	5	1	0	0	1	0	0.5	.000	OF-2
1982		84	.238	.399	143	34	7	2	4	2.8	21	17	23	33	2	45	8	53	1	2	0	1.6	.964	OF-34
5 yrs.		116	.234	.371	205	48	10	3	4	2.0	27	21	29	42	3	55	10	86	4	3	0	1.8	.968	OF-53
LEAGUE CHAMPIONSHIP SERIES																								
1982	ATL N	2	.000	.000	2	0	0	0	0	0.0	0	0	0	1	0	2	0	0	0	0	0	0.0	—	

Lew Whistler

WHISTLER, LEWIS W. TR 5′10½″ 178 lbs.
Born Lewis W. Wissler.
B. Mar. 10, 1868, St. Louis, Mo. D. Dec. 30, 1959, St. Louis, Mo.

Year	Team	Games	BA	SA	AB	H	2B	3B	HR	HR%	R	RBI	BB	SO	SB	Pinch Hit AB	Pinch Hit H	PO	A	E	DP	TC/G	FA	G by Pos
1890	NY N	45	.288	.459	170	49	9	7	2	1.2	27	29	20	37	8	0	0	490	10	9	28	11.3	.982	1B-45
1891		72	.245	.374	265	65	8	7	4	1.5	39	38	24	45	4	0	0	143	128	49	11	4.4	.847	SS-33, OF-22, 1B-7, 2B-6, 3B-5

Lew Whistler *continued*

Year	Team	Games	BA	SA	AB	H	2B	3B	HR	HR%	R	RBI	BB	SO	SB	Pinch Hit AB	Pinch Hit H	PO	A	E	DP	TC/G	FA	G by Pos
1892	2 teams	BAL N (52G –.225)	LOU N (80G –.235)																					
"	total	132	.231	.346	494	114	10	13	7	1.4	74	55	48	67	26	0	0	1329	88	36	75	10.8	.975	1B-123, 2B-10, OF-1
1893	2 teams	LOU N (13G –.213)	STL N (10G –.237)																					
"	total	23	.224	.271	85	19	2	1	0	0.0	10	11	8	7	1	0	0	153	9	9	9	7.4	.947	1B-14, OF-9
4 yrs.		272	.244	.366	1014	247	29	28	13	1.3	150	133	100	156	39	0	0	2115	235	103	123	8.9	.958	1B-189, SS-33, OF-32, 2B-16, 3B-5

Lou Whitaker

WHITAKER, LOUIS RODMAN (Sweet Lou)
B. May 12, 1957, Brooklyn, N. Y.
BL TR 5′11″ 160 lbs.

Year	Team	Games	BA	SA	AB	H	2B	3B	HR	HR%	R	RBI	BB	SO	SB	Pinch Hit AB	Pinch Hit H	PO	A	E	DP	TC/G	FA	G by Pos
1977	DET A	11	.250	.281	32	8	1	0	0	0.0	5	2	4	6	2	0	0	17	18	0	2	3.9	1.000	2B-9
1978		139	.285	.357	484	138	12	7	3	0.6	71	58	61	65	7	6	3	301	458	17	95	5.6	.978	2B-136, DH-2
1979		127	.286	.378	423	121	14	8	3	0.7	75	42	78	66	20	5	0	280	369	9	103	5.2	.986	2B-126
1980		145	.233	.283	477	111	19	1	1	0.2	68	45	73	79	8	8	2	340	428	12	93	5.5	.985	2B-143
1981		109	.263	.373	335	88	14	4	5	1.5	48	36	40	42	5	2	1	227	354	9	77	5.5	.985	2B-108
1982		152	.286	.434	560	160	22	8	15	2.7	76	65	48	58	11	4	1	331	470	10	120	5.4	.988	2B-149, DH-1
1983		161	.320	.457	643	206	40	6	12	1.9	94	72	67	70	17	7	3	299	447	13	92	4.7	.983	2B-160
1984		143	.289	.407	558	161	25	1	13	2.3	90	56	62	63	6	6	1	290	405	15	83	5.0	.979	2B-142
1985		152	.280	.457	608	170	29	8	21	3.5	102	73	80	56	6	4	0	314	414	11	101	4.9	.985	2B-150
1986		144	.269	.437	584	157	26	6	20	3.4	95	73	63	70	13	6	4	276	421	11	98	5.0	.984	2B-141
1987		149	.265	.427	604	160	38	6	16	2.6	110	59	71	108	13	3	1	275	416	17	99	4.8	.976	2B-148
1988		115	.275	.419	403	111	18	2	12	3.0	54	55	66	61	2	9	3	218	284	8	53	4.6	.984	2B-110
1989		148	.251	.462	509	128	21	1	28	5.5	77	85	89	59	6	6	0	327	393	11	99	4.9	.985	2B-146, DH-2
1990		132	.237	.407	472	112	22	2	18	3.8	75	60	74	71	8	11	1	286	372	6	98	5.1	.991	2B-130, DH-1
1991		138	.279	.489	470	131	26	2	23	4.9	94	78	90	45	4	13	4	255	361	4	91	4.5	.994	2B-135, DH-3
1992		130	.278	.461	453	126	26	0	19	4.2	77	71	81	46	6	8	0	256	312	9	73	4.5	.984	2B-119, DH-10
1993		119	.290	.449	383	111	32	1	9	2.3	72	67	78	46	3	16	5	236	322	11	75	5.2	.981	2B-110
1994		92	.301	.491	322	97	21	2	12	3.7	67	43	41	47	2	12	2	135	246	12	43	4.5	.969	2B-83, DH-5
1995		84	.293	.518	249	73	14	0	14	5.6	36	44	31	41	4	21	5	107	162	4	32	3.8	.985	2B-63, DH-8
19 yrs.		2390	.276	.426	8569	2369	420	65	244	2.8	1386	1084	1197	1099	143	147	36	4770	6652	189	1527	5.0	.984	2B-2308, DH-32
LEAGUE CHAMPIONSHIP SERIES																								
1984	DET A	3	.143	.143	14	2	0	0	0	0.0	3	0	0	3	0	0	0	5	6	0	0	3.7	1.000	2B-3
1987		5	.176	.353	17	3	0	0	1	5.9	4	1	7	3	1	0	0	11	14	0	1	5.0	1.000	2B-5
2 yrs.		8	.161	.258	31	5	0	0	1	3.2	7	1	7	6	1	0	0	16	20	0	1	4.5	1.000	2B-8
WORLD SERIES																								
1984	DET A	5	.278	.389	18	5	2	0	0	0.0	6	0	4	4	0	0	0	15	18	0	2	6.6	1.000	2B-5

Steve Whitaker

WHITAKER, STEPHEN EDWARD
B. May 7, 1943, Tacoma, Wash.
BL TR 6′ 180 lbs.

Year	Team	Games	BA	SA	AB	H	2B	3B	HR	HR%	R	RBI	BB	SO	SB	Pinch Hit AB	Pinch Hit H	PO	A	E	DP	TC/G	FA	G by Pos
1966	NY A	31	.246	.491	114	28	3	2	7	6.1	15	15	9	24	0	0	0	61	3	3	0	2.2	.955	OF-31
1967		122	.243	.358	441	107	12	3	11	2.5	37	50	23	89	2	10	4	202	12	4	6	1.9	.982	OF-114
1968		28	.117	.150	60	7	2	0	0	0.0	3	3	8	18	0	13	2	20	2	2	0	1.7	.917	OF-14
1969	SEA A	69	.250	.440	116	29	2	1	6	5.2	15	13	12	29	2	25	5	45	5	2	0	1.3	.962	OF-39
1970	SF N	16	.111	.148	27	3	1	0	0	0.0	3	4	2	14	0	6	2	6	0	1	0	0.8	.857	OF-9
5 yrs.		266	.230	.367	758	174	20	6	24	3.2	73	85	54	174	4	54	13	334	22	12	6	1.8	.967	OF-207

Bill White

WHITE, WILLIAM BARNEY
B. June 25, 1923, Paris, Tex.
BR TR 5′11″ 186 lbs.

Year	Team	Games	BA	SA	AB	H	2B	3B	HR	HR%	R	RBI	BB	SO	SB	Pinch Hit AB	Pinch Hit H	PO	A	E	DP	TC/G	FA	G by Pos
1945	BKN N	4	.000	.000	1	0	0	0	0	0.0	2	0	1	1	0	0	0	1	1	0	0	2.0	1.000	SS-1

Bill White

WHITE, WILLIAM DeKOVA
B. Jan. 28, 1934, Lakewood, Fla.
BL TL 6′ 185 lbs.

Year	Team	Games	BA	SA	AB	H	2B	3B	HR	HR%	R	RBI	BB	SO	SB	Pinch Hit AB	Pinch Hit H	PO	A	E	DP	TC/G	FA	G by Pos
1956	NY N	138	.256	.459	508	130	23	7	22	4.3	63	59	47	72	15	0	0	1256	111	15	106	9.9	.989	1B-138, OF-2
1958	SF N	26	.241	.379	29	7	1	0	1	3.4	5	4	7	5	1	16	4	19	1	0	2	4.0	1.000	1B-3, OF-2
1959	STL N	138	.302	.470	517	156	33	9	12	2.3	77	72	34	61	15	5	1	579	27	9	33	3.8	.985	OF-92, 1B-71
1960		144	.283	.455	554	157	27	10	16	2.9	81	79	42	83	12	3	0	1058	66	13	109	7.5	.989	1B-123, OF-29
1961		153	.286	.472	591	169	28	11	20	3.4	89	90	64	84	8	3	0	1373	104	17	125	9.9	.989	1B-151
1962		159	.324	.482	614	199	31	3	20	3.3	93	102	58	69	9	1	0	1260	97	10	116	7.9	.993	1B-146, OF-27
1963		162	.304	.491	658	200	26	8	27	4.1	106	109	59	100	10	0	0	1389	105	13	126	9.3	.991	1B-162
1964		160	.303	.474	631	191	37	4	21	3.3	92	102	52	103	7	0	0	1513	101	6	125	10.1	.996	1B-160
1965		148	.289	.481	543	157	26	3	24	4.4	82	73	63	86	3	4	1	1308	109	11	114	9.9	.992	1B-144
1966	PHI N	159	.276	.451	577	159	23	6	22	3.8	85	103	68	109	16	4	0	1422	109	9	118	9.7	.994	1B-158
1967		110	.250	.360	308	77	6	2	8	2.6	29	33	52	61	6	14	0	775	52	6	85	8.8	.993	1B-95
1968		127	.239	.361	385	92	16	2	9	2.3	34	40	39	79	0	20	5	982	77	6	94	9.6	.994	1B-111
1969	STL N	49	.211	.228	57	12	1	0	0	0.0	7	4	11	15	1	31	5	81	7	0	7	5.9	1.000	1B-15
13 yrs.		1673	.286	.455	5972	1706	278	65	202	3.4	843	870	596	927	103	101	16	13015	966	115	1160	8.7	.992	1B-1477, OF-152
WORLD SERIES																								
1964	STL N	7	.111	.148	27	3	1	0	0	0.0	2	2	2	6	1	0	0	62	3	0	4	9.3	1.000	1B-7

Bill White

WHITE, WILLIAM DIGHTON
B. May 1, 1860, Bridgeport, Ohio D. Dec. 31, 1924, Bellaire, Ohio.

Year	Team	Games	BA	SA	AB	H	2B	3B	HR	HR%	R	RBI	BB	SO	SB	Pinch Hit AB	Pinch Hit H	PO	A	E	DP	TC/G	FA	G by Pos
1884	PIT AA	74	.227	.320	291	66	7	10	0	0.0	25		13			0	0	75	206	69	14	4.7	.803	SS-60, 3B-10, OF-4
1886	LOU AA	135	.257	.329	557	143	17	10	1	0.2	96		37			0	0	212	431	96	48	5.4	.870	SS-135, P-1
1887		132	.252	.313	512	129	7	9	2	0.4	85		47		41	0	0	204	431	96	45	5.5	.869	SS-132
1888	2 teams	LOU AA (49G –.278)	STL AA (76G –.175)																					
"	total	125	.218	.288	473	103	8	8	3	0.6	66	60	28		21	0	0	199	368	86	16	5.2	.868	SS-112, 3B-11, 2B-2
4 yrs.		466	.241	.312	1833	441	39	37	6	0.3	272	60	125		62	0	0	690	1436	347	123	5.3	.860	SS-439, 3B-21, OF-4, 2B-2, P-1

Bill White

WHITE, WILLIAM EDWARD
B. Milner, Ga. Deceased.

Year	Team	Games	BA	SA	AB	H	2B	3B	HR	HR%	R	RBI	BB	SO	SB	Pinch Hit AB	Pinch Hit H	PO	A	E	DP	TC/G	FA	G by Pos
1879	PRO N	1	.250	.250	4	1	0	0	0	0.0	1	0	0	1		0	0	12	0	0	1	12.0	1.000	1B-1

C. B. White

WHITE, C. B.
B. Wakeman, Ohio Deceased.

Year	Team	Lg	Games	BA	SA	AB	H	2B	3B	HR	HR%	R	RBI	BB	SO	SB	Pinch Hit AB	Pinch Hit H	PO	A	E	DP	TC/G	FA	G by Pos
1883	**PHI**	**N**	1	.000	.000	1	0	0	0	0	0.0	0		0	0		0	0	3	1	1	0	2.5	.800	SS-1, 3B-1

Charlie White

WHITE, CHARLES BL TR 5′11″ 192 lbs.
B. Aug. 12, 1928, Kinston, N. C.

Year	Team	Lg	Games	BA	SA	AB	H	2B	3B	HR	HR%	R	RBI	BB	SO	SB	Pinch Hit AB	Pinch Hit H	PO	A	E	DP	TC/G	FA	G by Pos
1954	**MIL**	**N**	50	.237	.312	93	22	4	0	1	1.1	14	8	9	8	0	24	4	101	4	2	0	3.8	.981	C-28
1955			12	.233	.267	30	7	1	0	0	0.0	3	4	5	7	0	1	0	39	2	0	0	4.1	1.000	C-10
2 yrs.			62	.236	.301	123	29	5	0	1	0.8	17	12	14	15	0	25	4	140	6	2	0	3.9	.986	C-38

Deacon White

WHITE, JAMES LAURIE BL TR 5′11″ 175 lbs.
Brother of Will White.
B. Dec. 7, 1847, Caton, N. Y. D. July 7, 1939, Aurora, Ill.
Manager 1879.

Year	Team	Lg	Games	BA	SA	AB	H	2B	3B	HR	HR%	R	RBI	BB	SO	SB	Pinch Hit AB	Pinch Hit H	PO	A	E	DP	TC/G	FA	G by Pos
1876	**CHI**	**N**	66	.343	.419	303	104	18	1	1	0.3	66	**60**	7	3		0	0	318	51	69	3	6.2	.842	C-63, OF-3, 1B-3, P-1, 3B-1
1877	**BOS**	**N**	59	**.387**	**.545**	266	**103**	14	**11**	2	0.8	51	**49**	8	3		0	0	384	22	24	16	7.0	.944	1B-35, OF-19, C-7
1878	**CIN**	**N**	61	.314	.337	258	81	4	1	0	0.0	41	29	10	5		0	0	277	71	39	4	6.0	.899	C-48, OF-16, 3B-1
1879			78	.330	.423	333	110	16	6	1	0.3	55	52	6	9		0	0	349	96	55	3	6.1	.890	C-59, OF-21, 1B-2
1880			35	.298	.355	141	42	4	2	0	0.0	21	7	9	7		0	0	59	9	17	3	2.3	.800	OF-33, 1B-3, 2B-1
1881	**BUF**	**N**	78	.310	.411	319	99	24	4	0	0.0	58	53	9	8		0	0	371	119	70	24	7.1	.875	1B-26, 2B-25, OF-17, 3B-7, C-4
1882			83	.282	.341	337	95	17	0	1	0.3	51		15	16		0	0	173	150	55	8	4.6	.854	3B-63, C-20
1883			94	.292	.353	391	114	14	5	0	0.0	62		23	18		0	0	183	165	67	11	4.2	.839	3B-77, C-22
1884			110	.325	.442	452	147	16	11	5	1.1	82		32	13		0	0	130	203	66	13	3.6	.835	3B-108, C-3
1885			98	.292	.337	404	118	6	6	0	0.0	54	57	12	11		0	0	118	198	40	12	3.6	.888	3B-98
1886	**DET**	**N**	124	.289	.354	491	142	19	5	1	0.2	65	76	31	35		0	0	131	245	68	18	3.6	.847	3B-124
1887			111	.303	.416	449	136	20	11	3	0.7	71	75	26	15	20	0	0	152	227	65	19	4.0	.854	3B-106, OF-3, 1B-2
1888			125	.298	.381	527	157	22	5	4	0.8	75	71	21	24	12	0	0	146	244	65	19	3.6	.857	3B-125
1889	**PIT**	**N**	55	.253	.307	225	57	10	1	0	0.0	35	26	16	18	2	0	0	98	97	26	10	4.0	.882	3B-52, 1B-3
1890	**BUF**	**P**	122	.260	.308	439	114	13	4	0	0.0	62	47	67	30	3	0	0	670	202	47	52	7.5	.949	3B-64, 1B-57, P-1, SS-1
15 yrs.			1299	.303	.382	5335	1619	217	73	18	0.3	849	602	292	215	37	0	0	3559	2099	773	215	4.9	.880	3B-826, C-226, 1B-131, OF-112, 2B-26, P-2, SS-1

Derrick White

WHITE, DERRICK RAMON BR TR 6′ 1″ 220 lbs.
B. Oct. 12, 1969, San Rafael, Calif.

Year	Team	Lg	Games	BA	SA	AB	H	2B	3B	HR	HR%	R	RBI	BB	SO	SB	Pinch Hit AB	Pinch Hit H	PO	A	E	DP	TC/G	FA	G by Pos
1993	**MON**	**N**	17	.224	.408	49	11	3	0	2	4.1	6	4	2	12	2	0	0	129	8	1	16	8.1	.993	1B-17
1995	**DET**	**A**	39	.188	.229	48	9	2	0	0	0.0	3	2	0	7	1	6	1	55	5	2	4	1.9	.968	1B-16, OF-9, DH-8
2 yrs.			56	.206	.320	97	20	5	0	2	2.1	9	6	2	19	3	6	1	184	13	3	20	4.0	.985	1B-33, OF-9, DH-8

Devon White

WHITE, DEVON MARKES BB TR 6′ 1″ 170 lbs.
B. Dec. 29, 1962, Kingston, Jamaica.

Year	Team	Lg	Games	BA	SA	AB	H	2B	3B	HR	HR%	R	RBI	BB	SO	SB	Pinch Hit AB	Pinch Hit H	PO	A	E	DP	TC/G	FA	G by Pos
1985	**CAL**	**A**	21	.143	.143	7	1	0	0	0	0.0	7	0	1	3	3	0	0	10	1	0	0	0.7	1.000	OF-16
1986			28	.235	.353	51	12	1	1	1	2.0	8	3	6	8	6	0	0	49	0	2	0	1.8	.961	OF-28
1987			159	.263	.443	639	168	33	5	24	3.8	103	87	39	135	32	0	0	424	16	9	3	2.8	.980	OF-159
1988			122	.259	.389	455	118	22	2	11	2.4	76	51	23	84	17	5	2	364	7	9	2	3.3	.976	OF-116
1989			156	.245	.371	636	156	18	13	12	1.9	86	56	31	129	44	1	0	430	10	5	3	2.9	.989	OF-154, DH-1
1990			125	.217	.343	443	96	17	3	11	2.5	57	44	44	116	21	3	0	302	11	9	4	2.6	.972	OF-122
1991	**TOR**	**A**	156	.282	.455	642	181	40	10	17	2.6	110	60	55	135	33	0	0	439	8	1	2	2.9	.998	OF-156
1992			153	.248	.390	641	159	26	7	17	2.7	98	60	47	133	37	0	0	443	8	7	2	3.0	.985	OF-152, DH-1
1993			146	.273	.438	598	163	42	6	15	2.5	116	52	57	127	34	0	0	399	6	3	2	2.8	.993	OF-145
1994			100	.270	.457	403	109	24	6	13	3.2	67	49	21	80	11	1	1	267	3	6	1	2.8	.978	OF-98
1995			101	.283	.431	427	121	23	5	10	2.3	61	53	29	97	11	1	0	260	7	3	0	2.7	.989	OF-100
11 yrs.			1267	.260	.413	4942	1284	246	58	131	2.7	789	515	353	1047	249	11	3	3387	77	54	19	2.8	.985	OF-1246, DH-2
LEAGUE CHAMPIONSHIP SERIES																									
1986	**CAL**	**A**	3	.500	.500	2	1	0	0	0	0.0	2	0	0	1	0	0	0	2	0	0	0	0.7	1.000	OF-3
1991	**TOR**	**A**	5	.364	.409	22	8	1	0	0	0.0	5	0	2	3	3	0	0	16	0	0	0	3.2	1.000	OF-5
1992			6	.348	.435	23	8	2	0	0	0.0	2	2	5	6	0	0	0	16	0	1	0	2.8	.941	OF-6
1993			6	.444	.667	27	12	1	1	1	3.7	3	2	1	5	0	0	0	15	0	0	0	2.5	1.000	OF-6
4 yrs.			20	.392	.514	74	29	4	1	1	1.4	12	4	8	15	3	0	0	49	0	1	0	2.5	.980	OF-20
				2nd			**6th**																		
WORLD SERIES																									
1992	**TOR**	**A**	6	.231	.269	26	6	1	0	0	0.0	2	2	0	6	1	0	0	22	1	0	1	3.8	1.000	OF-6
1993			6	.292	.708	24	7	3	2	1	4.2	8	7	4	7	1	0	0	16	0	0	0	2.7	1.000	OF-6
2 yrs.			12	.260	.480	50	13	4	2	1	2.0	10	9	4	13	2	0	0	38	1	0	1	3.3	1.000	OF-12

Doc White

WHITE, GUY HARRIS BL TL 6′ 1″ 165 lbs.
B. Apr. 9, 1879, Washington, D. C. D. Feb. 19, 1969, Silver Spring, Md.

Year	Team	Lg	Games	BA	SA	AB	H	2B	3B	HR	HR%	R	RBI	BB	SO	SB	Pinch Hit AB	Pinch Hit H	PO	A	E	DP	TC/G	FA	G by Pos
1901	**PHI**	**N**	31	.274	.358	95	26	3	1	1	1.1	15	10	2		1	0	0	7	72	4	0	2.6	.952	P-31, OF-1
1902			61	.263	.307	179	47	3	1	1	0.6	17	15	11		5	5	1	35	84	12	0	2.4	.908	P-36, OF-19
1903	**CHI**	**A**	38	.202	.232	99	20	3	0	0	0.0	10	5	19		1	0	0	27	98	4	5	3.4	.969	P-37, OF-1
1904			33	.158	.184	76	12	2	0	0	0.0	7	2	10		3	0	0	33	68	5	2	3.3	.953	P-30, OF-2
1905			37	.163	.233	86	14	4	1	0	0.0	7	7	4		3	0	0	20	77	4	2	2.7	.960	P-36, OF-1
1906			28	.185	.231	65	12	1	1	0	0.0	11	3	13		3	0	0	17	77	8	1	3.5	.922	P-28, OF-1
1907			48	.222	.233	90	20	1	0	0	0.0	12	2	12		2	0	0	33	103	2	1	2.9	.986	P-46, OF-2
1908			51	.229	.239	109	25	1	0	0	0.0	12	10	12		4	6	1	30	116	2	7	3.4	.986	P-41, OF-3
1909			72	.234	.292	192	45	1	5	0	0.0	24	7	33		7	8	1	71	54	8	1	2.1	.940	OF-40, P-24
1910			56	.198	.238	126	25	1	2	0	0.0	14	8	14		2	8	0	44	79	3	4	2.7	.976	P-33, OF-14
1911			39	.256	.295	78	20	1	1	0	0.0	12	6	7		1	0	0	20	57	6	2	2.2	.928	P-34, 1B-2, OF-1
1912			33	.125	.179	56	7	1	1	0	0.0	5	0	7		0	1	0	5	46	0	1	1.6	1.000	P-32
1913			20	.120	.120	25	3	0	0	0	0.0	1	0	3	1	0	0	0	4	44	2	0	2.5	.960	P-19, 1B-1
13 yrs.			547	.216	.259	1276	276	22	13	2	0.2	147	75	147	1	32	28	3	346	975	60	26	2.7	.957	P-427, OF-85, 1B-3
WORLD SERIES																									
1906	**CHI**	**A**	3	.000	.000	3	0	0	0	0	0.0	0	0	1	0	0	0	0	1	3	0	0	1.3	1.000	P-3

Don White

WHITE, DONALD WILLIAM BR TR 6′ 1″ 195 lbs.
B. Jan. 8, 1919, Everett, Wash. D. June 15, 1987, Carlsbad, Calif.

Year	Team	Games	BA	SA	AB	H	2B	3B	HR	HR%	R	RBI	BB	SO	SB	Pinch Hit AB	Pinch Hit H	PO	A	E	DP	TC/G	FA	G by Pos
1948	PHI A	86	.245	.328	253	62	14	2	1	0.4	29	28	19	16	0	13	2	122	37	9	6	2.4	.946	OF-54, 3B-17
1949		57	.213	.249	169	36	6	0	0	0.0	12	10	14	12	2	8	3	91	9	2	2	2.0	.980	OF-47, 3B-4
2 yrs.		143	.232	.296	422	98	20	2	1	0.2	41	38	33	28	2	21	5	213	46	11	8	2.2	.959	OF-101, 3B-21

Ed White

WHITE, EDWARD PERRY BR TR 6′ 2″ 200 lbs.
B. Apr. 6, 1926, Anniston, Ala. D. Sept. 28, 1982, Lakeland, Fla.

Year	Team	Games	BA	SA	AB	H	2B	3B	HR	HR%	R	RBI	BB	SO	SB	Pinch Hit AB	Pinch Hit H	PO	A	E	DP	TC/G	FA	G by Pos
1955	CHI A	3	.500	.500	4	2	0	0	0	0.0	0	0	1	1	0	1	0	2	0	0	0	1.0	1.000	OF-2

Elder White

WHITE, ELDER LAFAYETTE BR TR 5′11″ 165 lbs.
B. Dec. 23, 1934, Colerain, N. C.

Year	Team	Games	BA	SA	AB	H	2B	3B	HR	HR%	R	RBI	BB	SO	SB	Pinch Hit AB	Pinch Hit H	PO	A	E	DP	TC/G	FA	G by Pos
1962	CHI N	23	.151	.189	53	8	2	0	0	0.0	4	1	8	11	3	6	1	25	47	1	6	4.6	.986	SS-15, 2B-1

Frank White

WHITE, FRANK, JR. BR TR 5′11″ 165 lbs.
B. Sept. 4, 1950, Greenville, Miss.

Year	Team	Games	BA	SA	AB	H	2B	3B	HR	HR%	R	RBI	BB	SO	SB	Pinch Hit AB	Pinch Hit H	PO	A	E	DP	TC/G	FA	G by Pos
1973	KC A	51	.223	.281	139	31	6	1	0	0.0	20	5	8	23	3	1	0	71	121	12	36	4.3	.941	SS-37, 2B-11
1974		99	.221	.294	204	45	6	3	1	0.5	19	18	5	33	3	3	0	119	189	12	40	3.3	.962	2B-50, SS-29, 3B-16, DH-3
1975		111	.250	.365	304	76	10	2	7	2.3	43	36	20	39	11	0	0	180	272	11	56	4.0	.976	2B-67, SS-42, 3B-4, DH-2
1976		152	.229	.307	446	102	17	6	2	0.4	39	46	19	42	20	0	0	296	479	23	89	4.8	.971	2B-130, SS-37
1977		152	.245	.342	474	116	21	5	5	1.1	59	50	25	67	23	0	0	310	437	8	86	4.8	.989	2B-152, SS-4
1978		143	.275	.399	461	127	24	6	7	1.5	66	50	26	59	13	3	0	325	385	16	96	5.2	.978	2B-140
1979		127	.266	.403	467	124	26	4	10	2.1	73	48	25	54	28	1	0	317	332	12	78	5.3	.982	2B-125
1980		154	.264	.357	560	148	23	4	7	1.3	70	60	19	69	19	3	0	395	448	10	103	5.6	.988	2B-153
1981		94	.250	.376	364	91	17	1	9	2.5	35	38	19	50	4	1	1	226	263	6	70	5.3	.988	2B-93
1982		145	.298	.469	524	156	45	6	11	2.1	71	56	16	65	10	1	0	361	389	17	99	5.3	.978	2B-144
1983		146	.260	.406	549	143	35	6	11	2.0	52	77	20	51	13	3	2	390	442	8	123	5.8	.990	2B-145
1984		129	.271	.445	479	130	22	5	17	3.5	58	56	27	72	5	1	0	299	425	11	97	5.7	.985	2B-129
1985		149	.249	.414	563	140	25	1	22	3.9	62	69	28	86	10	0	0	342	490	17	101	5.7	.980	2B-149
1986		151	.272	.465	566	154	37	3	22	3.9	76	84	43	88	4	6	1	317	441	10	92	5.0	.987	2B-151, SS-1, 3B-1
1987		154	.245	.400	563	138	32	2	17	3.0	67	78	51	86	1	1	0	320	458	10	89	5.2	.987	2B-152, DH-1
1988		150	.235	.330	537	126	25	1	8	1.5	48	58	21	67	7	6	2	293	426	4	88	4.8	.994	2B-148, DH-3
1989		135	.256	.328	418	107	22	1	2	0.5	34	36	30	52	3	4	0	238	407	10	64	4.9	.985	2B-132, OF-1
1990		82	.216	.307	241	52	14	1	2	0.8	20	21	10	32	1	2	0	142	218	8	51	4.6	.978	2B-79, OF-1
18 yrs.		2324	.255	.383	7859	2006	407	58	160	2.0	912	886	412	1035	178	36	6	4941	6622	205	1458	5.0	.983	2B-2150, SS-150, 3B-21, DH-9, OF-2
DIVISIONAL PLAYOFF SERIES																								
1981	KC A	3	.182	.182	11	2	0	0	0	0.0	1	0	1	1	0	0	0	5	6	1	0	4.0	.917	2B-3
LEAGUE CHAMPIONSHIP SERIES																								
1976	KC A	4	.125	.125	8	1	0	0	0	0.0	2	0	0	1	0	0	0	6	11	0	3	4.3	1.000	2B-4
1977		5	.278	.333	18	5	1	0	0	0.0	1	2	0	4	1	0	0	13	16	0	1	5.8	1.000	2B-5
1978		4	.231	.231	13	3	0	0	0	0.0	1	2	0	0	0	0	0	9	12	0	3	5.3	1.000	2B-4
1980		3	.545	.909	11	6	1	0	1	9.1	3	3	0	0	1	0	0	9	10	1	3	6.7	.950	2B-3
1984		3	.083	.083	12	1	0	0	0	0.0	1	0	0	3	0	0	0	7	3	0	2	3.3	1.000	2B-3
1985		7	.200	.200	25	5	0	0	0	0.0	1	3	1	2	0	0	0	9	28	0	4	5.3	1.000	2B-7
6 yrs.		26 **9th**	.241	.299	87	21	2	0	1	1.1	9	10	1	10	2	0	0	53	80	1	16	5.2	.993	2B-26
WORLD SERIES																								
1980	KC A	6	.080	.080	25	2	0	0	0	0.0	0	0	1	5	1	0	0	13	21	2	6	6.0	.944	2B-6
1985		7	.250	.464	28	7	3	0	1	3.6	4	6	3	4	1	0	0	10	20	0	2	4.3	1.000	2B-7
2 yrs.		13	.170	.283	53	9	3	0	1	1.9	4	6	4	9	2	0	0	23	41	2	8	5.1	.970	2B-13

Fuzz White

WHITE, ALBERT EUGENE BL TR 6′ 175 lbs.
B. June 27, 1918, Springfield, Mo.

Year	Team	Games	BA	SA	AB	H	2B	3B	HR	HR%	R	RBI	BB	SO	SB	Pinch Hit AB	Pinch Hit H	PO	A	E	DP	TC/G	FA	G by Pos
1940	STL A	2	.000	.000	2	0	0	0	0	0.0	0	0	0	0	0	2	0	0	0	0	0	0.0	—	
1947	NY N	7	.231	.231	13	3	0	0	0	0.0	3	0	0	0	0	1	0	11	0	0	0	2.2	1.000	OF-5
2 yrs.		9	.200	.200	15	3	0	0	0	0.0	3	0	0	0	0	3	0	11	0	0	0	2.2	1.000	OF-5

Jack White

WHITE, JOHN PETER BB TR 5′ 7½″ 150 lbs.
B. Aug. 31, 1905, New York, N. Y. D. June 19, 1971, Flushing, N. Y.

Year	Team	Games	BA	SA	AB	H	2B	3B	HR	HR%	R	RBI	BB	SO	SB	Pinch Hit AB	Pinch Hit H	PO	A	E	DP	TC/G	FA	G by Pos
1927	CIN N	5	.000	.000	4	0	0	0	0	0.0	1	0	0	0	0	0	0	3	5	0	1	1.6	1.000	2B-3, SS-2
1928		1	.000	.000	3	0	0	0	0	0.0	0	0	0	1	0	0	0	5	0	1	0	6.0	.833	2B-1
2 yrs.		6	.000	.000	7	0	0	0	0	0.0	1	0	0	1	0	0	0	8	5	1	1	2.3	.929	2B-4, SS-2

Jack White

WHITE, JOHN WALLACE BR TR 5′ 6″
B. Jan. 19, 1878, Traders Point, Ind. D. Sept. 30, 1963, Indianapolis, Ind.

Year	Team	Games	BA	SA	AB	H	2B	3B	HR	HR%	R	RBI	BB	SO	SB	Pinch Hit AB	Pinch Hit H	PO	A	E	DP	TC/G	FA	G by Pos
1904	BOS N	1	.000	.000	5	0	0	0	0	0.0	1	0	0		0	0	0	2	1	0	0	3.0	1.000	OF-1

Jerry White

WHITE, JEROME CARDELL BB TR 5′10″ 164 lbs.
B. Aug. 23, 1952, Shirley, Mass.

Year	Team	Games	BA	SA	AB	H	2B	3B	HR	HR%	R	RBI	BB	SO	SB	Pinch Hit AB	Pinch Hit H	PO	A	E	DP	TC/G	FA	G by Pos
1974	MON N	9	.400	.700	10	4	1	1	0	0.0	0	2	0	0	3	0	0	6	0	0	0	0.9	1.000	OF-7
1975		39	.299	.423	97	29	4	1	2	2.1	14	7	10	7	5	3	0	81	1	2	1	2.8	.976	OF-30
1976		114	.245	.313	278	68	11	1	2	0.7	32	21	27	31	15	17	2	157	4	3	0	1.8	.982	OF-92
1977		16	.190	.190	21	4	0	0	0	0.0	4	1	1	3	1	10	2	5	0	0	0	0.6	1.000	OF-8
1978	2 teams	MON N (18G –.200) CHI N (59G –.272)																						
″	total	77	.267	.329	146	39	6	0	1	0.7	24	10	24	19	5	12	3	102	4	2	1	1.9	.981	OF-57
1979	MON N	88	.297	.428	138	41	7	1	3	2.2	30	18	21	23	8	38	12	55	2	1	1	1.3	.983	OF-43
1980		110	.262	.430	214	56	9	3	7	3.3	22	23	30	37	8	29	6	101	5	6	1	1.3	.946	OF-84
1981		59	.218	.353	119	26	5	1	3	2.5	11	11	13	17	5	18	5	58	2	3	1	1.6	.952	OF-39
1982		69	.243	.365	115	28	6	1	2	1.7	13	13	8	26	3	39	10	40	1	0	0	1.4	1.000	OF-30
1983		40	.147	.176	34	5	1	0	0	0.0	4	0	12	8	4	23	2	13	0	0	0	1.0	1.000	OF-13
1986	STL N	25	.125	.250	24	3	0	0	1	4.2	1	3	2	3	0	19	2	5	0	0	0	0.8	1.000	OF-6
11 yrs.		646	.253	.363	1196	303	50	9	21	1.8	155	109	148	174	57	208	44	623	19	17	5	1.6	.974	OF-409

Jerry White *continued*

Year	Team	Games	BA	SA	AB	H	2B	3B	HR	HR%	R	RBI	BB	SO	SB	Pinch Hit AB	Pinch Hit H	PO	A	E	DP	TC/G	FA	G by Pos
DIVISIONAL PLAYOFF SERIES																								
1981	**MON N**	5	.167	.222	18	3	1	0	0	0.0	3	1	2	2	3	0	0	11	0	0	0	2.2	1.000	OF-5
LEAGUE CHAMPIONSHIP SERIES																								
1981	**MON N**	5	.313	.563	16	5	1	0	1	6.3	2	3	3	1	1	0	0	6	0	0	0	1.2	1.000	OF-5

Jo-Jo White

WHITE, JOYNER CLIFFORD BL TR 5′11″ 165 lbs.
Father of Mike White.
B. June 1, 1909, Red Oak, Ga. D. Oct. 9, 1986, Tacoma, Wash.
Manager 1960.

Year	Team	Games	BA	SA	AB	H	2B	3B	HR	HR%	R	RBI	BB	SO	SB	Pinch Hit AB	Pinch Hit H	PO	A	E	DP	TC/G	FA	G by Pos
1932	**DET A**	79	.260	.346	208	54	6	3	2	1.0	25	21	22	19	6	25	9	96	6	4	2	2.3	.962	OF-47
1933		91	.252	.359	234	59	9	5	2	0.9	43	34	27	26	5	26	**10**	122	4	3	1	2.4	.977	OF-54
1934		115	.313	.385	384	120	18	5	0	0.0	97	44	69	39	28	12	2	225	9	10	2	2.4	.959	OF-100
1935		114	.240	.345	412	99	13	12	2	0.5	82	32	68	42	19	13	4	247	7	10	1	2.7	.962	OF-98
1936		58	.275	.333	51	14	3	0	0	0.0	11	6	9	10	2	30	10	14	1	1	0	0.9	.938	OF-18
1937		94	.246	.308	305	75	5	7	0	0.0	50	21	50	40	12	5	2	216	4	6	0	2.8	.973	OF-82
1938		78	.262	.301	206	54	6	1	0	0.0	40	15	28	15	3	18	3	141	4	5	0	2.7	.967	OF-55
1943	**PHI A**	139	.248	.316	500	124	17	7	1	0.2	69	30	61	51	12	5	1	335	8	12	2	2.7	.966	OF-133
1944	**2 teams**	**PHI A** (85G –.221) **CIN N** (24G –.235)																						
″	**total**	109	.224	.261	352	79	6	2	1	0.3	39	26	50	34	5	7	1	217	9	9	2	2.4	.962	OF-97, SS-1
9 yrs.		877	.256	.328	2652	678	83	42	8	0.3	456	229	384	276	92	141	42	1613	52	60	10	2.5	.965	OF-684, SS-1
WORLD SERIES																								
1934	**DET A**	7	.130	.130	23	3	0	0	0	0.0	6	0	8	4	1	0	0	22	0	1	0	3.3	.957	OF-7
1935		5	.263	.263	19	5	0	0	0	0.0	3	1	5	7	0	0	0	14	0	0	0	2.8	1.000	OF-5
2 yrs.		12	.190	.190	42	8	0	0	0	0.0	9	1	13	11	1	0	0	36	0	1	0	3.1	.973	OF-12

Mike White

WHITE, JOYNER MICHAEL BR TR 5′ 8″ 160 lbs.
Son of Jo-Jo White.
B. Dec. 18, 1938, Detroit, Mich.

Year	Team	Games	BA	SA	AB	H	2B	3B	HR	HR%	R	RBI	BB	SO	SB	Pinch Hit AB	Pinch Hit H	PO	A	E	DP	TC/G	FA	G by Pos
1963	**HOU N**	3	.286	.286	7	2	0	0	0	0.0	0	0	0	0	0	1	0	10	3	0	0	6.5	1.000	2B-2
1964		89	.271	.332	280	76	11	3	0	0.0	30	27	20	47	1	13	2	151	41	5	12	2.3	.975	OF-72, 2B-10, 3B-3
1965		8	.000	.000	9	0	0	0	0	0.0	0	0	1	2	0	7	0	0	1	0	0	1.0	1.000	3B-1
3 yrs.		100	.264	.321	296	78	11	3	0	0.0	30	27	21	49	1	21	2	161	45	5	12	2.4	.976	OF-72, 2B-12, 3B-4

Myron White

WHITE, MYRON ALAN BL TL 5′11″ 180 lbs.
B. Aug. 1, 1957, Long Beach, Calif.

Year	Team	Games	BA	SA	AB	H	2B	3B	HR	HR%	R	RBI	BB	SO	SB	Pinch Hit AB	Pinch Hit H	PO	A	E	DP	TC/G	FA	G by Pos
1978	**LA N**	7	.500	.500	4	2	0	0	0	0.0	1	1	0	1	0	0	0	2	0	0	0	0.5	1.000	OF-4

Rondell White

WHITE, RONDELL BERNARD BR TR 6′ 1″ 193 lbs.
B. Feb. 23, 1972, Milledgeville, Ga.

Year	Team	Games	BA	SA	AB	H	2B	3B	HR	HR%	R	RBI	BB	SO	SB	Pinch Hit AB	Pinch Hit H	PO	A	E	DP	TC/G	FA	G by Pos
1993	**MON N**	23	.260	.411	73	19	3	1	2	2.7	9	15	7	16	1	1	0	33	0	0	0	1.6	1.000	OF-21
1994		40	.278	.464	97	27	10	1	2	2.1	16	13	9	18	1	10	0	34	1	2	0	1.3	.946	OF-29
1995		130	.295	.464	474	140	33	4	13	2.7	87	57	41	87	25	9	2	268	5	4	2	2.3	.986	OF-119
3 yrs.		193	.289	.458	644	186	46	6	17	2.6	112	85	57	121	27	20	2	335	6	6	2	2.1	.983	OF-169

Roy White

WHITE, ROY HILTON BB TR 5′10″ 160 lbs.
B. Dec. 27, 1943, Los Angeles, Calif.

Year	Team	Games	BA	SA	AB	H	2B	3B	HR	HR%	R	RBI	BB	SO	SB	Pinch Hit AB	Pinch Hit H	PO	A	E	DP	TC/G	FA	G by Pos
1965	**NY A**	14	.333	.381	42	14	2	0	0	0.0	7	3	4	7	2	2	2	16	4	0	0	1.8	1.000	OF-10, 2B-1
1966		115	.225	.345	316	71	13	2	7	2.2	39	20	37	43	14	22	7	159	6	7	2	2.0	.959	OF-82, 2B-2
1967		70	.224	.290	214	48	8	0	2	0.9	22	18	19	25	10	16	1	79	29	10	1	2.2	.915	OF-36, 3B-17
1968		159	.267	.414	577	154	20	7	17	2.9	89	62	73	50	20	4	1	283	14	1	4	1.9	.997	OF-154
1969		130	.290	.426	448	130	30	5	7	1.6	55	74	81	51	18	5	0	267	9	3	1	2.2	.989	OF-126
1970		162	.296	.473	609	180	30	6	22	3.6	109	94	95	66	24	1	0	315	6	2	0	2.0	.994	OF-161
1971		147	.292	.469	524	153	22	7	19	3.6	86	84	86	66	14	2	0	306	8	0	1	2.2	1.000	OF-145
1972		155	.270	.376	556	150	29	0	10	1.8	76	54	**99**	59	23	0	0	323	8	2	1	2.1	.994	OF-155
1973		162	.246	.374	**639**	157	22	3	18	2.8	88	60	78	81	16	0	0	339	4	8	0	2.2	.977	OF-162
1974		136	.275	.393	473	130	19	8	7	1.5	68	43	67	44	15	18	3	141	2	1	1	1.2	.993	OF-67, DH-53
1975		148	.290	.430	556	161	32	5	12	2.2	81	59	72	50	16	4	1	361	12	6	3	2.6	.984	OF-135, 1B-7, DH-2
1976		156	.286	.409	626	179	29	3	14	2.2	**104**	65	83	52	31	0	0	380	9	5	1	2.5	.987	OF-156
1977		143	.268	.405	519	139	25	2	14	2.7	72	52	75	58	18	4	0	301	7	6	4	2.3	.981	OF-135, DH-4
1978		103	.269	.393	346	93	13	3	8	2.3	44	43	42	35	10	9	0	128	1	1	0	1.3	.992	OF-74, DH-23
1979		81	.215	.288	205	44	6	0	3	1.5	24	27	23	21	2	19	5	45	3	0	0	0.9	1.000	DH-29, OF-27
15 yrs.		1881	.271	.404	6650	1803	300	51	160	2.4	964	758	934	708	233	106	20	3443	122	52	19	2.1	.986	OF-1625, DH-111, 3B-17, 1B-7, 2B-3
LEAGUE CHAMPIONSHIP SERIES																								
1976	**NY A**	5	.294	.471	17	5	3	0	0	0.0	4	3	5	1	1	0	0	17	0	0	0	3.4	1.000	OF-5
1977		5	.400	.800	5	2	2	0	0	0.0	2	0	1	0	0	1	0	2	0	1	0	1.5	.667	OF-1, DH-1
1978		4	.313	.563	16	5	1	0	1	6.3	5	1	1	2	0	0	0	3	0	0	0	0.8	1.000	OF-3, DH-1
3 yrs.		14	.316	.553	38	12	6	0	1	2.6	11	4	7	3	1	1	0	22	0	1	0	2.1	.957	OF-9, DH-2
							7th																	
WORLD SERIES																								
1976	**NY A**	4	.133	.133	15	2	0	0	0	0.0	0	0	3	0	0	0	0	13	0	0	0	3.3	1.000	OF-4
1977		2	.000	.000	2	0	0	0	0	0.0	0	0	0	0	0	2	0	0	0	0	0	0.0	.000	
1978		6	.333	.458	24	8	0	0	1	4.2	9	4	4	5	2	0	0	15	0	0	0	2.5	1.000	OF-6
3 yrs.		12	.244	.317	41	10	0	0	1	2.4	9	4	7	5	2	2	0	28	0	0	0	2.3	1.000	OF-10

Sam White

WHITE, SAMUEL LAMBETH BL TR 6′ 185 lbs.
B. Aug. 23, 1892, Preston, England D. Nov. 11, 1929, Philadelphia, Pa.

Year	Team	Games	BA	SA	AB	H	2B	3B	HR	HR%	R	RBI	BB	SO	SB	Pinch Hit AB	Pinch Hit H	PO	A	E	DP	TC/G	FA	G by Pos
1919	**BOS N**	1	.000	.000	1	0	0	0	0	0.0	0	0	0	0	0	0	0	0	5	0	0	5.0	1.000	C-1

Sammy White

WHITE, SAMUEL CHARLES BR TR 6' 3" 195 lbs.
B. July 7, 1928, Wenatchee, Wash. D. Aug. 5, 1991, Princeville, Hawaii.

Year	Team	Games	BA	SA	AB	H	2B	3B	HR	HR%	R	RBI	BB	SO	SB	Pinch Hit AB	Pinch Hit H	PO	A	E	DP	TC/G	FA	G by Pos
1951	BOS A	4	.182	.182	11	2	0	0	0	0.0	0	0	0	3	0	0	0	15	1	0	2	4.0	1.000	C-4
1952		115	.281	.423	381	107	20	2	10	2.6	35	49	16	43	2	5	0	464	59	9	7	4.8	.983	C-110
1953		136	.273	.435	476	130	34	2	13	2.7	59	64	29	48	3	7	2	588	68	9	9	5.1	.986	C-131
1954		137	.282	.426	493	139	25	2	14	2.8	46	75	21	50	1	4	0	677	80	16	11	5.8	.979	C-133
1955		143	.261	.392	544	142	30	4	11	2.0	65	64	44	58	1	0	0	671	71	12	8	5.3	.984	C-143
1956		114	.245	.332	392	96	15	2	5	1.3	28	44	35	40	2	0	0	547	60	10	13	5.4	.984	C-114
1957		111	.215	.276	340	73	10	1	3	0.9	24	31	25	38	0	0	0	489	49	8	13	4.9	.985	C-111
1958		102	.259	.378	328	85	15	3	6	1.8	25	35	21	37	1	0	0	450	38	6	8	4.8	.988	C-102
1959		119	.284	.347	377	107	13	4	1	0.3	34	42	23	39	4	1	0	557	56	6	8	5.2	.990	C-119
1961	MIL N	21	.222	.286	63	14	1	0	1	1.6	1	5	2	9	0	0	0	107	5	3	0	5.8	.974	C-20
1962	PHI N	41	.216	.320	97	21	4	0	2	2.1	7	12	2	16	0	2	0	173	19	5	4	4.9	.975	C-40
11 yrs.		1043	.262	.377	3502	916	167	20	66	1.9	324	421	218	381	14	19	2	4738	506	84	83	5.2	.984	C-1027

Warren White

WHITE, WILLIAM WARREN
Deceased.

Year	Team	Games	BA	SA	AB	H	2B	3B	HR	HR%	R	RBI	BB	SO	SB	Pinch Hit AB	Pinch Hit H	PO	A	E	DP	TC/G	FA	G by Pos
1884	WAS U	4	.056	.056	18	1	0	0	0	0.0	2		0			0	0	9	7	7	0	5.8	.696	3B-2, SS-1, 2B-1

Ed Whited

WHITED, EDWARD MORRIS BR TR 6' 3" 195 lbs.
B. Feb. 9, 1964, Bristol, Pa.

Year	Team	Games	BA	SA	AB	H	2B	3B	HR	HR%	R	RBI	BB	SO	SB	Pinch Hit AB	Pinch Hit H	PO	A	E	DP	TC/G	FA	G by Pos
1989	ATL N	36	.162	.243	74	12	3	0	1	1.4	5	4	6	15	1	4	0	23	33	5	3	1.9	.918	3B-29, 1B-3

Burgess Whitehead

WHITEHEAD, BURGESS URQUHART (Whitey) BR TR 5'10½" 160 lbs.
B. June 29, 1910, Tarboro, N. C. D. Nov. 25, 1993, Windsor, N. C.

Year	Team	Games	BA	SA	AB	H	2B	3B	HR	HR%	R	RBI	BB	SO	SB	Pinch Hit AB	Pinch Hit H	PO	A	E	DP	TC/G	FA	G by Pos
1933	STL N	12	.286	.286	7	2	0	0	0	0.0	2	1	0	1	0	0	0	4	7	0	1	0.9	1.000	SS-9, 2B-3
1934		100	.277	.355	332	92	13	5	1	0.3	55	24	12	19	5	1	0	158	220	16	38	3.8	.959	2B-48, SS-29, 3B-28
1935		107	.263	.305	338	89	10	2	0	0.0	45	33	11	14	5	12	2	188	240	10	47	4.7	.977	2B-80, 3B-8, SS-6
1936	NY N	154	.278	.356	632	176	31	3	4	0.6	99	47	29	32	14	0	0	442	552	32	107	6.7	.969	2B-153
1937		152	.286	.359	574	164	15	6	5	0.9	64	52	28	20	7	0	0	394	514	24	106	6.1	.974	2B-152
1939		95	.239	.293	335	80	6	3	2	0.6	31	24	24	19	1	0	0	240	336	17	63	6.2	.971	2B-91, SS-4, 3B-1
1940		133	.282	.340	568	160	9	6	4	0.7	68	36	26	17	9	0	0	238	336	16	50	4.4	.973	3B-74, 2B-57, SS-4
1941		116	.228	.293	403	92	15	4	1	0.2	41	23	14	10	7	0	0	288	285	18	60	5.6	.970	2B-104, 3B-1
1946	PIT N	55	.220	.260	127	28	1	2	0	0.0	10	5	6	6	3	12	2	66	66	5	14	3.9	.964	2B-30, 3B-4, SS-1
9 yrs.		924	.266	.331	3316	883	100	31	17	0.5	415	245	150	138	51	25	4	2018	2556	138	486	5.3	.971	2B-718, 3B-116, SS-53
WORLD SERIES																								
1934	STL N	1	—	—	0	0	0	0	0	—	0	0	0	0	0	0	0	1	0	0	0	1.0	1.000	SS-1
1936	NY N	6	.048	.048	21	1	0	0	0	0.0	1	2	1	3	0	0	0	14	20	0	5	5.7	1.000	2B-6
1937		5	.250	.375	16	4	2	0	0	0.0	1	0	2	0	1	0	0	8	17	1	5	5.2	.962	2B-5
3 yrs.		12	.135	.189	37	5	2	0	0	0.0	2	2	3	3	1	0	0	23	37	1	10	5.1	.984	2B-11, SS-1

Milt Whitehead

WHITEHEAD, MILTON P. BB
B. 1862 D. Aug. 15, 1901, Highland, Calif.

Year	Team	Games	BA	SA	AB	H	2B	3B	HR	HR%	R	RBI	BB	SO	SB	Pinch Hit AB	Pinch Hit H	PO	A	E	DP	TC/G	FA	G by Pos
1884	2 teams	STL U (99G –.211) KC U (5G –.136)																						
"	total	104	.207	.255	415	86	15	1	1	0.2	63		8			0	0	101	291	93	19	4.6	.808	SS-95, 2B-4, OF-2, 3B-2, P-1, C-1

Gil Whitehouse

WHITEHOUSE, GILBERT ARTHUR BB TR 5'10½" 170 lbs.
B. Oct. 15, 1893, Somerville, Mass. D. Feb. 14, 1926, Brewer, Me.

Year	Team	Games	BA	SA	AB	H	2B	3B	HR	HR%	R	RBI	BB	SO	SB	Pinch Hit AB	Pinch Hit H	PO	A	E	DP	TC/G	FA	G by Pos
1912	BOS N	2	.000	.000	6	0	0	0	0	0.0	0	0	0	3	0	0	0	4	0	2	0	3.0	.667	C-2
1915	NWK F	35	.225	.308	120	27	6	2	0	0.0	16	9	6		3	6	1	36	8	2	1	1.5	.957	OF-28, C-1, P-1
2 yrs.		37	.214	.294	126	27	6	2	0	0.0	16	9	6	3	3	6	1	40	8	4	1	1.6	.923	OF-28, C-3, P-1

Gurdon Whiteley

WHITELEY, GURDON W. 5'11" 190 lbs.
B. Oct. 5, 1859, Ashaway, R. I. D. Nov. 24, 1924, Cranston, R. I.

Year	Team	Games	BA	SA	AB	H	2B	3B	HR	HR%	R	RBI	BB	SO	SB	Pinch Hit AB	Pinch Hit H	PO	A	E	DP	TC/G	FA	G by Pos
1884	CLE N	8	.147	.147	34	5	0	0	0	0.0	4	0	1	8		0	0	9	3	3	2	1.9	.800	OF-8
1885	BOS N	33	.185	.252	135	25	2	2	1	0.7	14	7	1	25		0	0	48	9	17	2	2.2	.770	OF-32, C-1
2 yrs.		41	.178	.231	169	30	2	2	1	0.6	18	7	2	33		0	0	57	12	20	4	2.2	.775	OF-40, C-1

George Whiteman

WHITEMAN, GEORGE BR TR 5' 7" 160 lbs.
B. Dec. 23, 1882, Peoria, Ill. D. Feb. 10, 1947, Houston, Tex.

Year	Team	Games	BA	SA	AB	H	2B	3B	HR	HR%	R	RBI	BB	SO	SB	Pinch Hit AB	Pinch Hit H	PO	A	E	DP	TC/G	FA	G by Pos
1907	BOS A	3	.182	.182	11	2	0	0	0	0.0	0	1	0		0	1	0	2	0	0	0	1.0	1.000	OF-2
1913	NY A	11	.344	.500	32	11	3	1	0	0.0	8	2	7	2	2	0	0	29	1	2	1	2.9	.938	OF-11
1918	BOS A	71	.266	.346	214	57	14	0	1	0.5	24	28	20	9	9	2	0	95	5	7	1	1.6	.935	OF-69
3 yrs.		85	.272	.358	257	70	17	1	1	0.4	32	31	27	11	11	3	0	126	6	9	2	1.7	.936	OF-82
WORLD SERIES																								
1918	BOS A	6	.250	.350	20	5	0	1	0	0.0	2	1	2	1	1	0	0	15	2	1	1	3.0	.944	OF-6

Mark Whiten

WHITEN, MARK ANTHONY BB TR 6' 3" 210 lbs.
B. Nov. 25, 1966, Pensacola, Fla.

Year	Team	Games	BA	SA	AB	H	2B	3B	HR	HR%	R	RBI	BB	SO	SB	Pinch Hit AB	Pinch Hit H	PO	A	E	DP	TC/G	FA	G by Pos
1990	TOR A	33	.273	.375	88	24	1	1	2	2.3	12	7	7	14	2	3	0	60	3	0	0	2.0	1.000	OF-30, DH-2
1991	2 teams	TOR A (46G –.221) CLE A (70G –.256)																						
"	total	116	.243	.388	407	99	18	7	9	2.2	46	45	30	85	4	5	0	256	13	7	2	2.5	.975	OF-109, DH-3
1992	CLE A	148	.254	.360	508	129	19	4	9	1.8	73	43	72	102	16	1	1	321	14	7	1	2.3	.980	OF-144, DH-2
1993	STL N	152	.253	.423	562	142	13	4	25	4.4	81	99	58	110	15	6	2	329	9	10	1	2.4	.971	OF-148
1994		92	.293	.485	334	98	18	2	14	4.2	57	53	37	75	10	2	1	234	9	9	0	2.8	.964	OF-90
1995	2 teams	BOS A (32G –.185) PHI N (60G –.269)																						
"	total	92	.241	.400	320	77	13	1	12	3.8	51	47	39	86	8	7	2	157	8	4	1	1.9	.976	OF-86, DH-1
6 yrs.		633	.256	.406	2219	569	82	19	71	3.2	320	294	243	472	55	24	6	1357	56	37	5	2.4	.974	OF-607, DH-8

Fred Whitfield

WHITFIELD, FRED DWIGHT BL TL 6' 1" 190 lbs.
B. Jan. 7, 1938, Vandiver, Ala.

Year	Team	Games	BA	SA	AB	H	2B	3B	HR	HR%	R	RBI	BB	SO	SB	Pinch Hit AB	Pinch Hit H	PO	A	E	DP	TC/G	FA	G by Pos
1962	STL N	73	.266	.475	158	42	7	1	8	5.1	20	34	7	30	1	33	11	282	25	4	32	8.2	.987	1B-38
1963	CLE A	109	.251	.500	346	87	17	3	21	6.1	44	54	24	61	0	17	4	690	51	10	64	8.2	.987	1B-92
1964		101	.270	.423	293	79	13	1	10	3.4	29	29	12	58	0	24	4	596	36	5	63	8.1	.992	1B-79

Fred Whitfield *continued*

Year	Team	Lg	Games	BA	SA	AB	H	2B	3B	HR	HR%	R	RBI	BB	SO	SB	Pinch Hit AB	Pinch Hit H	PO	A	E	DP	TC/G	FA	G by Pos
1965			132	.293	.513	468	137	23	1	26	5.6	49	90	16	42	2	18	9	932	80	7	79	8.4	.993	1B-122
1966			137	.241	.440	502	121	15	2	27	5.4	59	78	27	76	1	4	0	1104	76	11	96	9.0	.991	1B-132
1967			100	.218	.362	257	56	10	0	9	3.5	24	31	25	45	3	32	9	494	40	4	51	8.2	.993	1B-66
1968	CIN	N	87	.257	.409	171	44	8	0	6	3.5	15	32	9	29	0	46	**11**	285	21	6	28	7.6	.981	1B-41
1969			74	.149	.189	74	11	0	0	1	1.4	2	8	18	27	0	**51**	8	57	8	1	5	4.7	.985	1B-14
1970	MON	N	4	.067	.067	15	1	0	0	0	0.0	0	0	1	3	0	0	0	34	7	1	3	10.5	.976	1B-4
9 yrs.			817	.253	.443	2284	578	93	8	108	4.7	242	356	139	371	7	225	56	4474	344	49	421	8.3	.990	1B-588

Terry Whitfield

WHITFIELD, TERRY BERTLAND
B. Jan. 12, 1953, Blythe, Calif.
BL TR 6′ 1½″ 197 lbs.

Year	Team	Lg	Games	BA	SA	AB	H	2B	3B	HR	HR%	R	RBI	BB	SO	SB	Pinch Hit AB	Pinch Hit H	PO	A	E	DP	TC/G	FA	G by Pos
1974	NY	A	2	.200	.200	5	1	0	0	0	0.0	0	0	0	1	0	1	0	0	0	0	0	0.0	.000	OF-1
1975			28	.272	.309	81	22	1	1	0	0.0	9	7	1	17	1	2	2	42	3	1	0	1.8	.978	OF-25, DH-1
1976			1	—	—	0	0	0	0	0	—	0	0	0	0	0	0	0	0	0	0	0	0.0	.000	OF-1
1977	SF	N	114	.285	.433	326	93	21	3	7	2.1	41	36	20	46	2	32	11	167	4	5	0	2.1	.972	OF-84
1978			149	.289	.400	488	141	20	2	10	2.0	70	32	33	69	5	10	3	249	7	3	2	1.8	.988	OF-141
1979			133	.287	.396	394	113	20	4	5	1.3	52	44	36	47	5	31	7	167	10	8	3	1.7	.957	OF-106
1980			118	.296	.396	321	95	16	2	4	1.2	38	26	20	44	4	25	5	140	11	2	1	1.6	.987	OF-95
1984	LA	N	87	.244	.356	180	44	8	0	4	2.2	15	18	17	35	1	29	8	76	4	1	0	1.4	.988	OF-58
1985			79	.260	.413	104	27	7	0	3	2.9	8	16	6	27	0	50	14	23	2	2	0	1.0	.926	OF-28
1986			19	.071	.071	14	1	0	0	0	0.0	0	0	5	2	0	12	1	1	0	0	0	1.0	1.000	OF-1
10 yrs.			730	.281	.394	1913	537	93	12	33	1.7	233	179	138	288	18	192	51	865	41	22	6	1.7	.976	OF-540, DH-1
LEAGUE CHAMPIONSHIP SERIES																									
1985	LA	N	1	—	—	0	0	0	0	0	—	0	0	0	0	0	0	0	0	0	0	0	0.0	—	

Ed Whiting

WHITING, EDWARD C.
Played as Ed Zieber in 1886.
B. 1860, Philadelphia, Pa. Deceased.
BL TR 188 lbs.

Year	Team	Lg	Games	BA	SA	AB	H	2B	3B	HR	HR%	R	RBI	BB	SO	SB	Pinch Hit AB	Pinch Hit H	PO	A	E	DP	TC/G	FA	G by Pos
1882	BAL	AA	74	.260	.338	308	80	14	5	0	0.0	43		7			0	0	320	109	85	9	6.7	.835	C-72, 1B-3, OF-2
1883	LOU	AA	58	.292	.417	240	70	16	4	2	0.8	35		9			0	0	269	68	46	6	6.4	.880	C-50, OF-6, 2B-2, 1B-1, 3B-1
1884			42	.223	.306	157	35	7	3	0	0.0	16		9			0	0	225	56	34	10	7.2	.892	C-40, OF-2, 1B-2
1886	WAS	N	6	.000	.000	21	0	0	0	0	0.0	0	0	1	12		0	0	22	12	3	0	6.2	.919	C-6
4 yrs.			180	.255	.347	726	185	37	12	2	0.3	94	0	26	12		0	0	836	245	168	25	6.7	.865	C-168, OF-10, 1B-6, 2B-2, 3B-1

Dick Whitman

WHITMAN, DICK CORWIN
B. Nov. 9, 1920, Woodburn, Ore.
BL TR 5′11″ 170 lbs.

Year	Team	Lg	Games	BA	SA	AB	H	2B	3B	HR	HR%	R	RBI	BB	SO	SB	Pinch Hit AB	Pinch Hit H	PO	A	E	DP	TC/G	FA	G by Pos
1946	BKN	N	104	.260	.362	265	69	15	3	2	0.8	39	31	22	19	5	14	4	178	5	0	0	2.2	1.000	OF-85
1947			4	.400	.400	10	4	0	0	0	0.0	1	2	1	0	0	1	1	7	0	0	0	2.3	1.000	OF-3
1948			60	.291	.370	165	48	13	0	0	0.0	24	20	14	12	4	12	5	93	3	1	0	2.0	.990	OF-48
1949			23	.184	.224	49	9	2	0	0	0.0	8	2	4	4	0	12	2	20	0	1	0	1.9	.952	OF-11
1950	PHI	N	75	.250	.303	132	33	7	0	0	0.0	21	12	10	10	1	39	**12**	56	2	1	0	1.8	.983	OF-32
1951			19	.118	.118	17	2	0	0	0	0.0	0	0	0	1	0	13	2	0	0	0	0	0.0	.000	OF-6
6 yrs.			285	.259	.335	638	165	37	3	2	0.3	93	67	51	46	10	91	26	354	10	3	0	2.0	.992	OF-185
WORLD SERIES																									
1949	BKN	N	1	.000	.000	1	0	0	0	0	0.0	0	0	0	1	0	1	0	0	0	0	0	0.0	—	
1950	PHI	N	3	.000	.000	2	0	0	0	0	0.0	0	0	1	0	0	2	0	0	0	0	0	0.0	—	
2 yrs.			4	.000	.000	3	0	0	0	0	0.0	0	0	1	1	0	3	0							

Frank Whitman

WHITMAN, WALTER FRANKLIN (Hooker)
B. Aug. 15, 1924, Marengo, Ind.
BR TR 6′ 2″ 175 lbs.

Year	Team	Lg	Games	BA	SA	AB	H	2B	3B	HR	HR%	R	RBI	BB	SO	SB	Pinch Hit AB	Pinch Hit H	PO	A	E	DP	TC/G	FA	G by Pos
1946	CHI	A	17	.063	.063	16	1	0	0	0	0.0	7	1	2	6	0	0	0	20	14	2	2	4.5	.944	SS-6, 2B-1, 1B-1
1948			3	.000	.000	6	0	0	0	0	0.0	0	0	0	3	0	2	0	1	2	3	1	6.0	.500	SS-1
2 yrs.			20	.045	.045	22	1	0	0	0	0.0	7	1	2	9	0	2	0	21	16	5	3	4.7	.881	SS-7, 2B-1, 1B-1

Dan Whitmer

WHITMER, DANIEL CHARLES
B. Nov. 23, 1955, Redlands, Calif.
BR TR 6′ 3″ 195 lbs.

Year	Team	Lg	Games	BA	SA	AB	H	2B	3B	HR	HR%	R	RBI	BB	SO	SB	Pinch Hit AB	Pinch Hit H	PO	A	E	DP	TC/G	FA	G by Pos
1980	CAL	A	48	.241	.276	87	21	3	0	0	0.0	8	7	4	21	1	0	0	190	12	0	2	4.2	1.000	C-48
1981	TOR	A	7	.111	.222	9	1	1	0	0	0.0	0	0	1	2	0	0	0	12	3	0	2	2.1	1.000	C-7
2 yrs.			55	.229	.271	96	22	4	0	0	0.0	8	7	5	23	1	0	0	202	15	0	4	3.9	1.000	C-55

Darrell Whitmore

WHITMORE, DARRELL LAMONT
B. Nov. 18, 1968, Front Royal, Va.
BL TR 6′ 1″ 210 lbs.

Year	Team	Lg	Games	BA	SA	AB	H	2B	3B	HR	HR%	R	RBI	BB	SO	SB	Pinch Hit AB	Pinch Hit H	PO	A	E	DP	TC/G	FA	G by Pos
1993	FLA	N	76	.204	.300	250	51	8	2	4	1.6	24	19	10	72	4	6	0	140	3	3	1	2.1	.979	OF-69
1994			9	.227	.273	22	5	1	0	0	0.0	1	0	3	5	0	2	0	14	0	0	0	2.3	1.000	OF-6
1995			27	.190	.276	58	11	2	0	1	1.7	6	2	5	15	0	13	2	24	0	1	0	1.6	.960	OF-16
3 yrs.			112	.203	.294	330	67	11	2	5	1.5	31	21	18	92	4	21	2	178	3	4	1	2.0	.978	OF-91

Art Whitney

WHITNEY, ARTHUR WILSON
Brother of Frank Whitney.
B. Jan. 16, 1858, Brockton, Mass. D. Aug. 15, 1943, Lowell, Mass.
BR TR 5′ 8″ 155 lbs.

Year	Team	Lg	Games	BA	SA	AB	H	2B	3B	HR	HR%	R	RBI	BB	SO	SB	Pinch Hit AB	Pinch Hit H	PO	A	E	DP	TC/G	FA	G by Pos
1880	WOR	N	76	.222	.308	302	67	13	5	1	0.3	38	36	9	15		0	0	83	162	40	6	3.8	.860	3B-76
1881	DET	N	58	.182	.262	214	39	7	5	0	0.0	23	9	7	15		0	0	73	141	38	10	4.3	.849	3B-58
1882	2 teams		PRO N (11G –.075) DET N (31G –.183)																						
″	total		42	.155	.155	155	24	0	0	0	0.0	12	4	3	23		0	0	65	100	32	9	4.5	.838	3B-22, SS-19, P-3
1884	PIT	AA	23	.298	.340	94	28	4	0	0	0.0	10		1			0	0	33	49	8	1	3.9	.911	3B-21, SS-1, OF-1
1885			90	.233	.282	373	87	10	4	0	0.0	53		16			0	0	116	244	33	23	4.4	.916	SS-75, 3B-8, 2B-4, OF-3
1886			136	.239	.280	511	122	13	4	0	0.0	70		51			0	0	168	345	61	30	4.2	.894	3B-95, SS-42, P-1
1887	PIT	N	119	.260	.304	431	112	11	4	0	0.0	57	51	55	18	10	0	0	166	237	33	13	3.7	.924	3B-119
1888	NY	N	90	.220	.256	328	72	1	4	1	0.3	28	28	8	22	7	0	0	90	184	35	11	3.4	.887	3B-90

Art Whitney *continued*

Year	Team	Games	BA	SA	AB	H	2B	3B	HR	HR%	R	RBI	BB	SO	SB	Pinch Hit AB	Pinch Hit H	PO	A	E	DP	TC/G	FA	G by Pos
1889		129	.218	.258	473	103	12	2	1	0.2	71	59	56	39	19	0	0	160	265	57	27	3.7	.882	3B-129, P-1
1890	NY P	119	.219	.260	442	97	12	3	0	0.0	71	45	64	19	8	0	0	176	257	74	23	4.3	.854	3B-88, SS-31
1891	2 teams	CIN AA (93G –.199) STL AA (3G –.000)																						
″	total	96	.193	.240	358	69	6	1	3	0.8	42	33	32	22	8	0	0	129	211	37	12	3.9	.902	3B-96
11 yrs.		978	.223	.269	3681	820	89	32	6	0.2	475	265	302	173	52	0	0	1259	2195	448	165	4.0	.885	3B-802, SS-168, P-5, 2B-4, OF-4

Frank Whitney

WHITNEY, FRANK THOMAS (Jumbo) BR TR 5′ 7½″ 152 lbs.
Brother of Art Whitney.
B. Feb. 18, 1856, Brockton, Mass. D. Oct. 30, 1943, Baltimore, Md.

Year	Team	Games	BA	SA	AB	H	2B	3B	HR	HR%	R	RBI	BB	SO	SB	Pinch Hit AB	Pinch Hit H	PO	A	E	DP	TC/G	FA	G by Pos
1876	BOS N	34	.237	.302	139	33	7	1	0	0.0	27	15	1	3		0	0	75	8	20	4	2.9	.806	OF-34, 2B-1

Jim Whitney

WHITNEY, JAMES EVANS (Grasshopper Jim) BL TR 6′ 2″ 172 lbs.
B. Nov. 10, 1857, Conklin, N. Y. D. May 21, 1891, Binghamton, N. Y.

Year	Team	Games	BA	SA	AB	H	2B	3B	HR	HR%	R	RBI	BB	SO	SB	Pinch Hit AB	Pinch Hit H	PO	A	E	DP	TC/G	FA	G by Pos
1881	BOS N	75	.255	.337	282	72	17	3	0	0.0	37	32	19	18		0	0	40	100	32	3	2.1	.814	P-66, OF-15, 1B-2
1882		61	.323	.510	251	81	18	7	5	**2.0**	49	48	24	13		0	0	57	88	19	3	2.6	.884	P-49, OF-9, 1B-6
1883		96	.281	.433	409	115	27	10	5	1.2	78	57	25	29		0	0	89	100	27	4	2.1	.875	P-62, OF-40, 1B-2
1884		66	.259	.393	270	70	17	5	3	1.1	41		16	38		0	0	135	80	10	3	3.1	.956	P-41, OF-15, 1B-15, 3B-1
1885		72	.234	.290	290	68	8	4	0	0.0	35	36	17	24		0	0	86	133	26	4	3.4	.894	P-51, OF-17, 1B-5
1886	KC N	67	.239	.340	247	59	13	3	2	0.8	25	23	29	39		0	0	39	119	18	6	2.6	.898	P-46, OF-22, 3B-1
1887	WAS N	54	.264	.398	201	53	9	6	2	1.0	29	22	18	24	10	0	0	16	93	13	5	2.3	.893	P-47, OF-7
1888		42	.170	.191	141	24	0	0	1	0.7	13	17	7	20	3	0	0	24	67	12	2	2.4	.883	P-39, OF-3, 1B-1
1889	IND N	10	.375	.563	32	12	4	1	0	0.0	6	4	5	6	2	0	0	5	9	0	0	1.4	1.000	P-9, OF-1
1890	PHI AA	7	.238	.238	21	5	0	0	0	0.0	3		1		0	0	0	1	8	1	1	1.4	.900	P-6, OF-1
10 yrs.		550	.261	.375	2144	559	113	39	18	0.8	316	239	161	211	15	0	0	492	797	158	31	2.5	.891	P-416, OF-130, 1B-31, 3B-2

Pinky Whitney

WHITNEY, ARTHUR CARTER BR TR 5′10″ 165 lbs.
B. Jan. 2, 1905, San Antonio, Tex. D. Sept. 1, 1987, Center, Tex.

Year	Team	Games	BA	SA	AB	H	2B	3B	HR	HR%	R	RBI	BB	SO	SB	Pinch Hit AB	Pinch Hit H	PO	A	E	DP	TC/G	FA	G by Pos
1928	PHI N	151	.301	.426	585	176	35	4	10	1.7	73	103	36	30	3	2	0	171	293	22	27	3.3	.955	3B-149
1929		154	.327	.482	612	200	43	14	8	1.3	89	115	61	35	7	0	0	168	333	17	29	3.4	.967	3B-154
1930		149	.342	.465	606	207	41	5	8	1.3	87	117	40	41	3	1	0	186	313	18	29	3.5	.965	3B-148
1931		130	.287	.433	501	144	36	5	9	1.8	64	74	30	38	6	2	0	131	217	19	1	2.9	.948	3B-128
1932		154	.298	.449	624	186	33	11	13	2.1	93	124	35	66	6	0	0	194	293	21	36	3.3	.959	3B-151, 2B-5
1933	2 teams	PHI N (31G –.264) BOS N (100G –.246)																						
″	total	131	.250	.366	503	126	21	2	11	2.2	54	68	33	31	3	1	0	146	288	11	29	3.3	.975	3B-115, 2B-18
1934	BOS N	146	.259	.377	563	146	26	2	12	2.1	58	79	25	54	7	0	0	172	345	17	31	3.6	.968	3B-111, 2B-36, SS-2
1935		126	.273	.367	458	125	23	4	4	0.9	41	60	24	36	2	1	0	196	305	17	25	4.2	.967	3B-74, 2B-49
1936	2 teams	BOS N (10G –.175) PHI N (114G –.294)																						
″	total	124	.284	.375	451	128	17	3	6	1.3	45	64	39	37	2	2	1	121	230	16	17	3.0	.956	3B-121, 2B-1
1937	PHI N	138	.341	.446	487	166	19	4	8	1.6	56	79	43	44	6	8	1	136	238	7	17	2.9	.982	3B-130
1938		102	.277	.343	300	83	9	1	3	1.0	27	38	27	22	0	20	4	101	134	14	14	3.1	.944	3B-75, 1B-4, 2B-2
1939		34	.187	.253	75	14	0	1	1	1.3	9	6	7	4	0	13	2	106	30	1	13	6.2	.993	1B-12, 2B-8, 3B-2
12 yrs.		1539	.295	.415	5765	1701	303	56	93	1.6	696	927	400	438	45	50	8	1828	3019	180	268	3.4	.964	3B-1358, 2B-119, 1B-16, SS-2

Ernie Whitt

WHITT, LEO ERNEST BL TR 6′ 2″ 200 lbs.
B. June 13, 1952, Detroit, Mich.

Year	Team	Games	BA	SA	AB	H	2B	3B	HR	HR%	R	RBI	BB	SO	SB	Pinch Hit AB	Pinch Hit H	PO	A	E	DP	TC/G	FA	G by Pos
1976	BOS A	8	.222	.500	18	4	2	0	1	5.6	4	3	2	2	0	1	0	24	0	0	0	3.0	1.000	C-8
1977	TOR A	23	.171	.244	41	7	3	0	0	0.0	4	6	2	12	0	9	1	62	4	0	0	4.7	1.000	C-14
1978		2	.000	.000	4	0	0	0	0	0.0	0	0	1	1	0	1	0	7	1	0	0	8.0	1.000	C-1
1980		106	.237	.353	295	70	12	2	6	2.0	23	34	22	30	1	1	0	436	56	7	11	4.8	.986	C-105
1981		74	.236	.297	195	46	9	0	1	0.5	16	16	20	30	5	4	0	297	46	3	5	4.8	.991	C-72
1982		105	.261	.440	284	74	14	2	11	3.9	28	42	26	34	3	21	7	406	30	8	0	4.5	.982	C-98, DH-1
1983		123	.256	.459	344	88	15	2	17	4.9	53	56	50	55	1	17	5	554	50	5	4	5.1	.992	C-119
1984		124	.238	.425	315	75	12	1	15	4.8	35	46	43	49	0	16	5	583	40	4	8	5.3	.994	C-118
1985		139	.245	.444	412	101	21	2	19	4.6	55	64	47	59	3	16	2	649	38	8	6	5.2	.988	C-134
1986		131	.268	.448	395	106	19	2	16	4.1	48	56	35	39	0	11	3	709	41	7	7	5.9	.991	C-129
1987		135	.269	.455	446	120	24	1	19	4.3	57	75	44	50	0	12	1	803	55	5	10	6.6	.994	C-131
1988		127	.251	.410	398	100	11	2	16	4.0	63	70	61	38	4	11	0	643	43	4	10	5.6	.994	C-123
1989		129	.262	.416	385	101	24	1	11	2.9	42	53	52	53	5	16	3	550	43	5	5	4.9	.992	C-115, DH-8
1990	ATL N	67	.172	.250	180	31	8	0	2	1.1	14	10	23	27	0	9	3	296	42	3	1	5.8	.991	C-59
1991	BAL A	35	.242	.274	62	15	2	0	0	0.0	5	3	8	12	0	16	4	72	8	0	0	3.6	1.000	C-20, DH-2
15 yrs.		1328	.249	.410	3774	938	176	15	134	3.6	447	534	436	491	22	161	34	6091	497	59	67	5.3	.991	C-1246, DH-11
LEAGUE CHAMPIONSHIP SERIES																								
1985	TOR A	7	.190	.238	21	4	1	0	0	0.0	1	2	2	4	0	0	0	50	3	0	1	7.6	1.000	C-7
1989		5	.125	.313	16	2	0	0	1	6.3	1	3	2	3	0	0	0	32	2	0	0	6.8	1.000	C-5
2 yrs.		12	.162	.270	37	6	1	0	1	2.7	2	5	4	7	0	0	0	82	5	0	1	7.3	1.000	C-12

Possum Whitted

WHITTED, GEORGE BOSTIC BR TR 5′ 8½″ 168 lbs.
B. Feb. 4, 1890, Durham, N. C. D. Oct. 16, 1962, Wilmington, N. C.

Year	Team	Games	BA	SA	AB	H	2B	3B	HR	HR%	R	RBI	BB	SO	SB	Pinch Hit AB	Pinch Hit H	PO	A	E	DP	TC/G	FA	G by Pos
1912	STL N	12	.261	.326	46	12	3	0	0	0.0	7	7	3	5	1	0	0	19	17	6	1	3.5	.857	3B-12
1913		122	.221	.271	402	89	10	5	0	0.0	44	38	31	44	9	15	3	225	207	27	27	4.3	.941	OF-40, SS-37, 3B-21, 2B-7, 1B-2
1914	2 teams	STL N (20G –.129) BOS N (66G –.261)																						
″	total	86	.245	.349	249	61	12	4	2	0.8	39	32	18	21	11	6	1	167	71	15	10	3.2	.941	OF-41, 3B-16, 2B-16, 1B-4, SS-3
1915	PHI N	125	.281	.339	448	126	17	3	1	0.2	46	43	29	47	24	1	0	339	21	10	5	3.2	.973	OF-109, 1B-7
1916		147	.281	.399	526	148	20	12	6	1.1	68	68	19	46	29	1	0	383	16	14	8	2.7	.966	OF-136, 1B-16
1917		149	.280	.373	553	155	24	9	3	0.5	69	70	30	56	10	0	0	306	35	9	2	2.2	.974	OF-141, 1B-10, 3B-6, 2B-1
1918		24	.244	.291	86	21	4	0	0	0.0	7	3	4	10	4	2	1	52	3	1	1	2.4	.982	OF-22, 1B-1
1919	2 teams	PHI N (78G –.249) PIT N (35G –.389)																						
″	total	113	.293	.402	420	123	21	8	3	0.7	47	53	20	24	12	2	1	491	102	13	29	5.8	.979	OF-48, 1B-35, 2B-20, 3B-2

Possum Whitted *continued*

Year	Team	Games	BA	SA	AB	H	2B	3B	HR	HR%	R	RBI	BB	SO	SB	Pinch Hit AB	Pinch Hit H	PO	A	E	DP	TC/G	FA	G by Pos
1920	PIT N	134	.261	.338	494	129	11	12	1	0.2	53	74	35	36	11	0	0	263	234	16	24	3.8	.969	3B-125, 1B-10, OF-1
1921		108	.283	.427	403	114	23	7	7	1.7	60	63	26	21	5	1	0	276	13	3	10	2.7	.990	OF-102, 1B-7
1922	BKN N	1	.000	.000	1	0	0	0	0	0.0	0	0	0	0	0	1	0	0	0	0	0	0.0	—	
11 yrs.		1021	.270	.362	3628	978	145	60	23	0.6	440	451	215	310	116	29	6	2521	719	114	117	3.4	.966	OF-640, 3B-182, 1B-92, 2B-44, SS-40
WORLD SERIES																								
1914	BOS N	4	.214	.357	14	3	0	1	0	0.0	2	2	3	1	1	0	0	5	0	0	0	1.3	1.000	OF-4
1915	PHI N	5	.067	.067	15	1	0	0	0	0.0	0	1	1	0	1	0	0	12	0	0	0	2.0	1.000	OF-5, 1B-1
2 yrs.		9	.138	.207	29	4	0	1	0	0.0	2	3	4	1	2	0	0	17	0	0	0	1.7	1.000	OF-9, 1B-1

Bob Wicker

WICKER, ROBERT KITRIDGE
B. May 24, 1878, Bedford, Ind. D. Jan. 22, 1955, Evanston, Ill.
BR TR 6′ 2″ 180 lbs.

Year	Team	Games	BA	SA	AB	H	2B	3B	HR	HR%	R	RBI	BB	SO	SB	Pinch Hit AB	Pinch Hit H	PO	A	E	DP	TC/G	FA	G by Pos
1901	STL N	3	.333	.333	3	1	0	0	0	0.0	1	0	0		0	1	0	0	0	0	0	0.0	.000	P-1
1902		31	.234	.260	77	18	2	0	0	0.0	6	3	3		2	6	1	22	47	10	3	3.2	.873	P-22, OF-3
1903	2 teams	STL N (1G –.000) CHI N (32G –.245)																						
″	total	33	.240	.330	100	24	5	2	0	0.0	19	8	4		1	0	0	13	45	9	2	2.0	.866	P-33
1904	CHI N	50	.219	.226	155	34	1	0	0	0.0	17	9	4		4	0	0	48	34	7	1	1.8	.921	P-30, OF-20
1905		25	.139	.139	72	10	0	0	0	0.0	5	3	4		1	0	0	8	36	2	3	1.8	.957	P-22, OF-3
1906	2 teams	CHI N (10G –.100) CIN N (20G –.180)																						
″	total	30	.157	.229	70	11	1	2	0	0.0	6	4	7		2	0	0	13	38	6	2	1.9	.895	P-30
6 yrs.		172	.205	.241	477	98	9	4	0	0.0	54	27	22		10	7	1	104	200	34	11	2.1	.899	P-138, OF-26

Floyd Wicker

WICKER, FLOYD EULISS
B. Sept. 12, 1943, Burlington, N. C.
BL TR 6′ 2″ 175 lbs.

Year	Team	Games	BA	SA	AB	H	2B	3B	HR	HR%	R	RBI	BB	SO	SB	Pinch Hit AB	Pinch Hit H	PO	A	E	DP	TC/G	FA	G by Pos
1968	STL N	5	.500	.500	4	2	0	0	0	0.0	2	0	0	0	0	4	2	0	0	0	0	0.0	—	
1969	MON N	41	.103	.103	39	4	0	0	0	0.0	2	2	2	20	0	29	3	11	0	0	0	1.0	1.000	OF-11
1970	MIL A	15	.195	.293	41	8	1	0	1	2.4	3	3	1	8	0	6	1	16	0	0	0	1.3	1.000	OF-12
1971	2 teams	MIL A (11G –.125) SF N (9G –.143)																						
″	total	20	.138	.138	29	4	0	0	0	0.0	3	1	4	5	0	10	1	12	1	0	0	1.9	1.000	OF-7
4 yrs.		81	.159	.195	113	18	1	0	1	0.9	10	6	7	33	0	49	7	39	1	0	0	1.3	1.000	OF-30

Al Wickland

WICKLAND, ALBERT
B. Jan. 27, 1888, Chicago, Ill. D. Mar. 14, 1980, Port Washington, Wis.
BL TL 5′ 7″ 155 lbs.

Year	Team	Games	BA	SA	AB	H	2B	3B	HR	HR%	R	RBI	BB	SO	SB	Pinch Hit AB	Pinch Hit H	PO	A	E	DP	TC/G	FA	G by Pos
1913	CIN N	26	.215	.405	79	17	5	5	0	0.0	7	8	6	19	3	2	0	57	2	1	1	2.5	.983	OF-24
1914	CHI F	157	.276	.405	536	148	31	10	6	1.1	74	68	**81**		17	0	0	252	23	11	3	1.8	.962	OF-157
1915	2 teams	CHI F (30G –.244) PIT F (110G –.301)																						
″	total	140	.291	.375	475	138	14	10	2	0.4	74	35	65		26	7	1	266	14	10	2	2.2	.966	OF-133
1918	BOS N	95	.262	.398	332	87	7	13	4	1.2	55	32	53	39	12	0	0	183	11	5	2	2.1	.975	OF-95
1919	NY A	26	.152	.174	46	7	1	0	0	0.0	2	1	2	10	0	10	1	14	0	0	0	0.9	1.000	OF-15
5 yrs.		444	.270	.386	1468	397	58	38	12	0.8	212	144	207	68	58	19	2	772	50	27	8	2.0	.968	OF-424

Chris Widger

WIDGER, CHRISTOPHER JON
B. May 21, 1971, Wilmington, Del.
BR TR 6′ 3″ 195 lbs.

Year	Team	Games	BA	SA	AB	H	2B	3B	HR	HR%	R	RBI	BB	SO	SB	Pinch Hit AB	Pinch Hit H	PO	A	E	DP	TC/G	FA	G by Pos
1995	SEA A	23	.200	.267	45	9	0	0	1	2.2	2	2	3	11	0	3	0	64	1	0	0	2.8	1.000	C-19, OF-3, DH-1
DIVISIONAL PLAYOFF SERIES																								
1995	SEA A	2	.000	.000	3	0	0	0	0	0.0	0	0	0	3	0	0	0	14	0	0	0	7.0	1.000	C-2
LEAGUE CHAMPIONSHIP SERIES																								
1995	SEA A	3	.000	.000	1	0	0	0	0	0.0	0	0	0	1	0	0	0	7	0	0	0	2.3	1.000	C-3

Tom Wiedenbauer

WIEDENBAUER, THOMAS JOHN
B. Nov. 5, 1958, Menomonie, Wis.
BR TR 6′ 1″ 180 lbs.

Year	Team	Games	BA	SA	AB	H	2B	3B	HR	HR%	R	RBI	BB	SO	SB	Pinch Hit AB	Pinch Hit H	PO	A	E	DP	TC/G	FA	G by Pos
1979	HOU N	4	.667	.833	6	4	1	0	0	0.0	0	2	0	2	0	0	0	3	0	0	0	1.0	1.000	OF-3

Stump Wiedman

WIEDMAN, GEORGE EDWARD
B. Feb. 17, 1861, Rochester, N. Y. D. Mar. 3, 1905, New York, N. Y.
BR TR 5′ 7½″ 165 lbs.

Year	Team	Games	BA	SA	AB	H	2B	3B	HR	HR%	R	RBI	BB	SO	SB	Pinch Hit AB	Pinch Hit H	PO	A	E	DP	TC/G	FA	G by Pos
1880	BUF N	23	.103	.115	78	8	1	0	0	0.0	8	3	2	11		0	0	21	20	5	0	1.5	.891	P-17, OF-13
1881	DET N	13	.255	.277	47	12	1	0	0	0.0	8	5	2	2		0	0	3	15	0	0	1.4	1.000	P-13
1882		50	.218	.264	193	42	7	1	0	0.0	20	20	2	19		0	0	39	76	12	2	2.4	.906	P-46, OF-6, SS-1
1883		79	.185	.220	313	58	6	1	1	0.3	34		4	38		0	0	81	94	26	4	2.2	.871	P-52, OF-35, 2B-4
1884		81	.163	.183	300	49	6	0	0	0.0	24		13	41		0	0	89	62	37	3	2.3	.803	OF-53, P-26, 2B-1, SS-1
1885		44	.157	.203	153	24	2	1	1	0.7	7	14	8	32		0	0	19	60	18	1	1.3	.814	OF-38, P-38, 2B-1
1886	KC N	51	.168	.179	179	30	2	0	0	0.0	13	7	5	46		0	0	26	106	9	5	2.6	.936	P-51, OF-3
1887	3 teams	DET N (21G –.207) NY AA (14G –.152) NY N (1G –.333)																						
″	total	36	.191	.229	131	25	3	1	0	0.0	17	11	7	3	8	0	0	20	59	13	0	2.4	.859	P-34, OF-5
1888	NY N	2	.000	.000	7	0	0	0	0	0.0	1	1	2	1	0	0	0	3	2	2	0	3.5	.714	P-2
9 yrs.		379	.177	.207	1401	248	28	4	2	0.1	132	61	45	193	8	0	0	301	494	122	15	2.1	.867	P-279, OF-153, 2B-6, SS-2

Tom Wieghaus

WIEGHAUS, THOMAS ROBERT
B. Feb. 1, 1957, Chicago Heights, Ill.
BR TR 6′ 195 lbs.

Year	Team	Games	BA	SA	AB	H	2B	3B	HR	HR%	R	RBI	BB	SO	SB	Pinch Hit AB	Pinch Hit H	PO	A	E	DP	TC/G	FA	G by Pos
1981	MON N	1	.000	.000	1	0	0	0	0	0.0	0	0	0	0	0	0	0	5	0	0	0	5.0	1.000	C-1
1983		1	—	—	0	0	0	0	0	—	0	0	0	0	0	0	0	1	0	0	0	1.0	1.000	C-1
1984	HOU N	6	.000	.000	10	0	0	0	0	0.0	0	1	1	3	0	0	0	30	3	0	0	5.5	1.000	C-6
3 yrs.		8	.000	.000	11	0	0	0	0	0.0	0	1	1	3	0	0	0	36	3	0	0	4.9	1.000	C-8

Whitey Wietelmann

WIETELMANN, WILLIAM FREDERICK
B. Mar. 15, 1919, Zanesville, Ohio.
BB TR 6′ 170 lbs.
BR 1939–1941

Year	Team	Games	BA	SA	AB	H	2B	3B	HR	HR%	R	RBI	BB	SO	SB	Pinch Hit AB	Pinch Hit H	PO	A	E	DP	TC/G	FA	G by Pos
1939	BOS N	23	.203	.217	69	14	1	0	0	0.0	2	5	2	9	1	0	0	38	69	5	12	4.9	.955	SS-22, 2B-1
1940		35	.195	.220	41	8	1	0	0	0.0	3	1	5	5	0	4	0	20	27	2	9	1.8	.959	2B-15, 3B-9, SS-3
1941		16	.091	.091	33	3	0	0	0	0.0	1	0	1	2	0	1	0	26	29	0	3	3.2	1.000	2B-10, SS-5, 3B-2
1942		13	.206	.265	34	7	2	0	0	0.0	4	0	4	5	0	0	0	19	29	3	6	4.3	.941	SS-11, 2B-1
1943		153	.215	.245	534	115	14	1	0	0.0	33	39	46	40	9	0	0	307	581	40	91	6.1	.957	SS-153

Whitey Wietelmann *continued*

Year	Team	Games	BA	SA	AB	H	2B	3B	HR	HR%	R	RBI	BB	SO	SB	Pinch Hit AB	Pinch Hit H	PO	A	E	DP	TC/G	FA	G by Pos
1944		125	.240	.302	417	100	18	1	2	0.5	46	32	33	25	0	0	0	269	351	30	75	5.1	.954	SS-103, 2B-23, 3B-1
1945		123	.271	.348	428	116	15	3	4	0.9	53	33	39	27	4	0	0	303	338	21	76	5.1	.968	2B-87, SS-39, 3B-2, P-1
1946		44	.205	.205	78	16	0	0	0	0.0	7	5	14	8	0	12	2	40	39	7	6	2.8	.919	SS-16, 3B-8, 2B-4, P-3
1947	PIT N	48	.234	.305	128	30	4	1	1	0.8	21	7	12	10	0	7	0	69	68	13	14	3.5	.913	SS-22, 2B-14, 3B-6, 1B-1
9 yrs.		580	.232	.282	1762	409	55	6	7	0.4	170	122	156	131	14	24	2	1091	1531	121	292	4.9	.956	SS-374, 2B-155, 3B-28, P-4, 1B-1

Alan Wiggins

WIGGINS, ALAN ANTHONY BB TR 6′ 2″ 160 lbs.
B. Feb. 17, 1958, Los Angeles, Calif. D. Jan. 6, 1991, Los Angeles, Calif.

Year	Team	Games	BA	SA	AB	H	2B	3B	HR	HR%	R	RBI	BB	SO	SB	Pinch Hit AB	Pinch Hit H	PO	A	E	DP	TC/G	FA	G by Pos
1981	SD N	15	.357	.357	14	5	0	0	0	0.0	4	0	1	0	2	4	2	6	0	2	0	2.0	.750	OF-4
1982		72	.256	.303	254	65	3	3	1	0.4	40	15	13	19	33	3	0	140	8	5	2	2.2	.967	OF-68, 2B-1
1983		144	.276	.324	503	139	20	2	0	0.0	83	22	65	43	66	2	0	572	35	8	31	4.1	.987	OF-105, 1B-45
1984		158	.258	.329	596	154	19	7	3	0.5	106	34	75	57	70	0	0	391	410	32	95	5.3	.962	2B-157
1985	2 teams	SD N (10G –.054) BAL A (76G –.285)																						
″	total	86	.260	.319	335	87	12	4	0	0.0	46	21	31	20	30	0	0	170	207	14	62	4.6	.964	2B-85
1986	BAL A	71	.251	.272	239	60	3	1	0	0.0	30	11	22	20	21	1	0	121	151	6	40	4.1	.978	2B-66, DH-1
1987		85	.232	.268	306	71	4	2	1	0.3	37	15	28	34	20	10	3	86	98	4	21	2.3	.979	DH-44, 2B-33, OF-5
7 yrs.		631	.259	.309	2247	581	61	19	5	0.2	346	118	235	193	242	20	5	1486	909	71	251	4.0	.971	2B-342, OF-182, DH-45, 1B-45
LEAGUE CHAMPIONSHIP SERIES																								
1984	SD N	5	.316	.316	19	6	0	0	0	0.0	4	1	2	2	0	0	0	11	11	0	1	4.4	1.000	2B-5
WORLD SERIES																								
1984	SD N	5	.364	.409	22	8	1	0	0	0.0	2	1	0	2	1	0	0	13	6	2	1	4.2	.905	2B-5

Del Wilber

WILBER, DELBERT QUENTIN (Babe) BR TR 6′ 3″ 200 lbs.
B. Feb. 24, 1919, Lincoln Park, Mich.
Manager 1973.

Year	Team	Games	BA	SA	AB	H	2B	3B	HR	HR%	R	RBI	BB	SO	SB	Pinch Hit AB	Pinch Hit H	PO	A	E	DP	TC/G	FA	G by Pos
1946	STL N	4	.000	.000	4	0	0	0	0	0.0	0	0	1	0	0	0	0	0	0	0	0	0.0	.000	C-4
1947		51	.232	.333	99	23	8	1	0	0.0	7	12	5	13	0	15	5	108	10	2	2	3.5	.983	C-34
1948		27	.190	.224	58	11	2	0	0	0.0	5	10	4	9	0	1	0	67	7	4	1	3.0	.949	C-26
1949		2	.250	.250	4	1	0	0	0	0.0	0	0	0	0	0	0	0	5	1	0	0	3.0	1.000	C-2
1951	PHI N	84	.278	.429	245	68	7	3	8	3.3	30	34	17	26	0	10	1	326	26	8	5	4.9	.978	C-73
1952	2 teams	PHI N (2G –.000) BOS A (47G –.267)																						
″	total	49	.263	.416	137	36	10	1	3	2.2	7	23	7	21	1	10	4	160	22	1	5	4.7	.995	C-39
1953	BOS A	58	.241	.500	112	27	6	1	7	6.3	16	29	6	21	0	28	4	108	7	2	2	3.9	.983	C-28, 1B-2
1954		24	.131	.246	61	8	2	1	1	1.6	2	7	4	6	0	6	1	49	8	3	2	3.3	.950	C-18
8 yrs.		299	.242	.389	720	174	35	7	19	2.6	67	115	44	96	1	70	15	823	81	20	17	4.1	.978	C-224, 1B-2

Claude Wilborn

WILBORN, CLAUDE EDWARD BL TR 6′ 1″ 180 lbs.
B. Sept. 1, 1912, Woodsdale, N. C. D. Nov. 13, 1992, Roxboro, N. C.

Year	Team	Games	BA	SA	AB	H	2B	3B	HR	HR%	R	RBI	BB	SO	SB	Pinch Hit AB	Pinch Hit H	PO	A	E	DP	TC/G	FA	G by Pos
1940	BOS N	5	.000	.000	7	0	0	0	0	0.0	0	0	0	1	0	2	0	1	0	1	0	0.7	.500	OF-3

Ted Wilborn

WILBORN, THADDEAUS INGLEHART BB TR 6′ 165 lbs.
B. Dec. 16, 1958, Waco, Tex.

Year	Team	Games	BA	SA	AB	H	2B	3B	HR	HR%	R	RBI	BB	SO	SB	Pinch Hit AB	Pinch Hit H	PO	A	E	DP	TC/G	FA	G by Pos
1979	TOR A	22	.000	.000	12	0	0	0	0	0.0	3	0	1	7	0	0	0	7	0	1	0	0.7	.875	OF-7, DH-4
1980	NY A	8	.250	.250	8	2	0	0	0	0.0	2	1	0	1	0	1	0	6	1	0	1	2.3	1.000	OF-3
2 yrs.		30	.100	.100	20	2	0	0	0	0.0	5	1	1	8	0	1	0	13	1	1	1	1.1	.933	OF-10, DH-4

Wiley

WILEY
Deceased.

Year	Team	Games	BA	SA	AB	H	2B	3B	HR	HR%	R	RBI	BB	SO	SB	Pinch Hit AB	Pinch Hit H	PO	A	E	DP	TC/G	FA	G by Pos
1884	WAS U	1	.000	.000	4	0	0	0	0	0.0	0		0			0	0	0	1	2	0	3.0	.333	3B-1

Rob Wilfong

WILFONG, ROBERT DANIEL BL TR 6′ 1″ 180 lbs.
B. Sept. 1, 1953, Pasadena, Calif.

Year	Team	Games	BA	SA	AB	H	2B	3B	HR	HR%	R	RBI	BB	SO	SB	Pinch Hit AB	Pinch Hit H	PO	A	E	DP	TC/G	FA	G by Pos
1977	MIN A	73	.246	.281	171	42	1	1	1	0.6	22	13	17	26	10	2	0	114	164	12	40	4.3	.959	2B-66, DH-1
1978		92	.266	.322	199	53	8	0	1	0.5	23	11	19	27	8	1	0	152	196	5	37	4.2	.986	2B-80, DH-5
1979		140	.313	.458	419	131	22	6	9	2.1	71	59	29	54	11	16	5	287	379	14	92	5.0	.979	2B-133, OF-3
1980		131	.248	.368	416	103	16	5	8	1.9	55	45	34	61	10	14	5	245	338	4	85	4.7	.993	2B-120, OF-6
1981		93	.246	.331	305	75	11	3	3	1.0	32	19	29	43	2	8	0	183	268	9	52	4.9	.980	2B-93
1982	2 teams	MIN A (25G –.160) CAL A (55G –.245)																						
″	total	80	.208	.273	183	38	5	2	1	0.5	24	16	14	30	4	19	2	69	155	5	32	3.8	.978	2B-50, 3B-5, OF-3, SS-2, DH-1
1983	CAL A	65	.254	.339	177	45	7	1	2	1.1	17	17	10	25	0	8	3	107	144	2	33	4.3	.992	2B-39, 3B-13, SS-6, DH-1
1984		108	.248	.362	307	76	13	2	6	2.0	31	33	20	53	3	18	5	162	268	12	48	4.3	.973	2B-97, SS-4, DH-1
1985		83	.189	.258	217	41	3	0	4	1.8	16	13	16	32	4	11	2	124	216	5	45	4.9	.986	2B-69, DH-2
1986		92	.219	.309	288	63	11	3	3	1.0	25	33	16	34	1	8	2	135	257	7	48	4.4	.982	2B-90
1987	SF N	2	.125	.500	8	1	0	0	1	12.5	2	2	1	2	1	0	0	2	3	1	2	3.0	.833	2B-2
11 yrs.		959	.248	.345	2690	668	97	23	39	1.4	318	261	205	387	54	105	24	1580	2388	76	514	4.5	.981	2B-839, 3B-18, SS-12, OF-12, DH-11
LEAGUE CHAMPIONSHIP SERIES																								
1982	CAL A	2	.000	.000	1	0	0	0	0	0.0	0	0	0	1	0	1	0	0	0	0	0	0.0	—	
1986		4	.308	.385	13	4	1	0	0	0.0	1	2	0	2	0	1	1	9	10	0	4	4.8	1.000	2B-4
2 yrs.		6	.286	.357	14	4	1	0	0	0.0	1	2	0	3	0	2	1	9	10	0	4	4.8	1.000	2B-4

Jim Wilhelm

WILHELM, JAMES WEBSTER BR TR 6′ 3″ 190 lbs.
B. Sept. 20, 1952, San Rafael, Calif.

Year	Team	Games	BA	SA	AB	H	2B	3B	HR	HR%	R	RBI	BB	SO	SB	Pinch Hit AB	Pinch Hit H	PO	A	E	DP	TC/G	FA	G by Pos
1978	SD N	10	.368	.474	19	7	2	0	0	0.0	2	4	0	2	1	0	0	9	0	0	0	0.9	1.000	OF-10
1979		39	.243	.340	103	25	4	3	0	0.0	8	8	2	12	1	10	2	61	4	1	0	2.2	.985	OF-30
2 yrs.		49	.262	.361	122	32	6	3	0	0.0	10	12	2	14	2	10	2	70	4	1	0	1.9	.987	OF-40

Spider Wilhelm

WILHELM, CHARLES ERNEST BR TR 5′ 9″ 170 lbs.
B. May 23, 1929, Baltimore, Md. D. Oct. 20, 1992, Venice, Fla.

Year	Team	Games	BA	SA	AB	H	2B	3B	HR	HR%	R	RBI	BB	SO	SB	Pinch Hit AB	Pinch Hit H	PO	A	E	DP	TC/G	FA	G by Pos
1953	PHI A	7	.286	.429	7	2	1	0	0	0.0	1	0	0	3	0	1	1	2	5	1	0	1.3	.875	SS-6

Year	Team	Games	BA	SA	AB	H	2B	3B	HR	HR%	R	RBI	BB	SO	SB	Pinch Hit AB	Pinch Hit H	PO	A	E	DP	TC/G	FA	G by Pos

Joe Wilhoit

WILHOIT, JOSEPH WILLIAM
B. Dec. 20, 1885, Hiawatha, Kans. D. Sept. 25, 1930, Santa Barbara, Calif.
BL TR 6′ 2″ 175 lbs.

Year	Team	Games	BA	SA	AB	H	2B	3B	HR	HR%	R	RBI	BB	SO	SB	Pinch Hit AB	Pinch Hit H	PO	A	E	DP	TC/G	FA	G by Pos
1916	BOS N	116	.230	.300	383	88	13	4	2	0.5	44	38	27	45	18	6	1	177	12	4	3	1.8	.979	OF-108
1917	3 teams	BOS N (54G –.274) PIT N (9G –.200) NY N (34G –.340)																						
″	total	97	.285	.341	246	70	7	2	1	0.4	29	18	26	21	5	25	5	88	9	6	1	1.5	.942	OF-66, 1B-1
1918	NY N	64	.274	.341	135	37	3	3	0	0.0	13	15	17	14	4	6	1	71	7	2	2	1.5	.975	OF-55
1919	BOS A	6	.333	.333	18	6	0	0	0	0.0	7	2	5	2	1	1	0	8	0	0	0	1.6	1.000	OF-5
4 yrs.		283	.257	.321	782	201	23	9	3	0.4	93	73	75	82	28	38	7	344	28	12	6	1.6	.969	OF-234, 1B-1
WORLD SERIES																								
1917	NY N	2	.000	.000	1	0	0	0	0	0.0	0	0	1	0	0	1	0	0	0	0	0	0.0	—	

Denney Wilie

WILIE, DENNIS ERNEST
B. Sept. 22, 1890, Mt. Calm, Tex. D. June 20, 1966, Hayward, Calif.
BL TL 5′ 8″ 155 lbs.

Year	Team	Games	BA	SA	AB	H	2B	3B	HR	HR%	R	RBI	BB	SO	SB	Pinch Hit AB	Pinch Hit H	PO	A	E	DP	TC/G	FA	G by Pos
1911	STL N	28	.235	.333	51	12	3	1	0	0.0	10	3	8	11	3	10	1	18	2	0	0	1.3	1.000	OF-15
1912		30	.229	.271	48	11	0	1	0	0.0	2	6	7	9	0	8	2	21	1	2	0	1.5	.917	OF-16
1915	CLE A	45	.252	.344	131	33	4	1	2	1.5	14	10	26	18	2	8	0	80	1	8	0	2.5	.910	OF-35
3 yrs.		103	.243	.326	230	56	7	3	2	0.9	26	19	41	38	5	26	3	119	4	10	0	2.0	.925	OF-66

Harry Wilke

WILKE, HENRY JOSEPH
B. Dec. 14, 1900, Cincinnati, Ohio D. June 21, 1991, Hamilton, Ohio.
BR TR 5′10½″ 171 lbs.

Year	Team	Games	BA	SA	AB	H	2B	3B	HR	HR%	R	RBI	BB	SO	SB	Pinch Hit AB	Pinch Hit H	PO	A	E	DP	TC/G	FA	G by Pos
1927	CHI N	3	.000	.000	9	0	0	0	0	0.0	0	0	0	1	0	0	0	2	5	0	0	2.3	1.000	3B-3

Curtis Wilkerson

WILKERSON, CURTIS VERNON
B. Apr. 26, 1961, Petersburg, Va.
BB TR 5′ 9″ 158 lbs.

Year	Team	Games	BA	SA	AB	H	2B	3B	HR	HR%	R	RBI	BB	SO	SB	Pinch Hit AB	Pinch Hit H	PO	A	E	DP	TC/G	FA	G by Pos
1983	TEX A	16	.171	.229	35	6	0	1	0	0.0	7	1	2	5	3	1	0	18	31	1	5	3.8	.980	SS-9, 3B-2, 2B-2
1984		153	.248	.279	484	120	12	0	1	0.2	47	26	22	72	12	0	0	227	391	30	73	4.0	.954	SS-116, 2B-47
1985		129	.244	.308	360	88	11	6	0	0.0	35	22	22	63	14	2	1	165	328	21	65	3.9	.959	SS-110, 2B-19, DH-2
1986		110	.237	.305	236	56	10	3	0	0.0	27	15	11	42	9	3	0	125	199	13	56	2.9	.961	2B-60, SS-56, DH-2
1987		85	.268	.391	138	37	5	3	2	1.4	28	14	6	16	6	3	1	79	98	6	18	2.3	.967	SS-33, 2B-28, 3B-18
1988		117	.293	.358	338	99	12	5	0	0.0	41	28	26	43	9	6	0	186	299	15	58	4.1	.970	2B-87, SS-24, 3B-11
1989	CHI N	77	.244	.313	160	39	4	2	1	0.6	18	10	8	33	4	28	11	42	91	8	10	2.9	.943	3B-26, 2B-15, SS-7, OF-1
1990		77	.220	.258	186	41	5	1	0	0.0	21	16	7	36	2	13	5	49	93	14	7	2.3	.910	3B-52, 2B-14, SS-1, OF-1
1991	PIT N	85	.188	.277	191	36	9	1	2	1.0	20	18	15	40	2	33	7	73	124	2	24	3.4	.990	2B-30, SS-15, 3B-14
1992	KC A	111	.250	.311	296	74	10	1	2	0.7	27	29	18	47	18	4	1	148	257	10	56	3.6	.976	SS-69, 2B-39, 3B-5, DH-1
1993		12	.143	.143	28	4	0	0	0	0.0	1	0	1	6	2	0	0	8	25	0	3	2.4	1.000	2B-10, SS-4
11 yrs.		972	.245	.305	2452	600	78	23	8	0.3	272	179	138	403	81	93	26	1120	1936	120	375	3.4	.962	SS-444, 2B-351, 3B-128, DH-5, OF-2
LEAGUE CHAMPIONSHIP SERIES																								
1989	CHI N	3	.500	.500	2	1	0	0	0	0.0	1	0	0	0	0	2	1	0	0	0	0	0.0	.000	3B-1
1991	PIT N	4	.000	.000	4	0	0	0	0	0.0	0	0	0	3	0	4	0	0	0	0	0	0.0	—	
2 yrs.		7	.167	.167	6	1	0	0	0	0.0	1	0	0	3	0	6	1	0	0	0	0	0.0		3B-1

Bobby Wilkins

WILKINS, ROBERT LINWOOD
B. Aug. 11, 1922, Denton, N. C.
BR TR 5′ 9″ 165 lbs.

Year	Team	Games	BA	SA	AB	H	2B	3B	HR	HR%	R	RBI	BB	SO	SB	Pinch Hit AB	Pinch Hit H	PO	A	E	DP	TC/G	FA	G by Pos
1944	PHI A	24	.240	.240	25	6	0	0	0	0.0	7	3	1	4	0	2	0	12	21	2	3	3.9	.943	SS-9
1945		62	.260	.299	154	40	6	0	0	0.0	22	4	10	17	2	1	0	79	118	16	23	4.8	.925	SS-40, OF-4
2 yrs.		86	.257	.291	179	46	6	0	0	0.0	29	7	11	21	2	3	0	91	139	18	26	4.7	.927	SS-49, OF-4

Rick Wilkins

WILKINS, RICHARD DAVID
B. June 4, 1967, Jacksonville, Fla.
BL TR 6′ 2″ 210 lbs.

Year	Team	Games	BA	SA	AB	H	2B	3B	HR	HR%	R	RBI	BB	SO	SB	Pinch Hit AB	Pinch Hit H	PO	A	E	DP	TC/G	FA	G by Pos
1991	CHI N	86	.222	.355	203	45	9	0	6	3.0	21	22	19	56	3	5	2	373	42	3	6	5.1	.993	C-82
1992		83	.270	.414	244	66	9	1	8	3.3	20	22	28	53	0	15	5	408	47	3	5	6.3	.993	C-73
1993		136	.303	.561	446	135	23	1	30	6.7	78	73	50	99	2	9	4	717	89	3	9	6.1	.996	C-133
1994		100	.227	.387	313	71	25	2	7	2.2	44	39	40	86	4	9	0	550	51	4	1	6.2	.993	C-95, 1B-2
1995	2 teams	CHI N (50G –.191) HOU N (15G –.250)																						
″	total	65	.203	.322	202	41	3	0	7	3.5	30	19	46	61	0	3	0	381	34	4	2	6.5	.990	C-62, 1B-2
5 yrs.		470	.254	.433	1408	358	69	4	58	4.1	193	175	183	355	9	41	11	2429	263	17	23	6.0	.994	C-445, 1B-4

Ed Wilkinson

WILKINSON, EDWARD HENRY
B. June 20, 1890, Jacksonville, Ore. D. Apr. 9, 1918, Tucson, Ariz.
BR TR 6′ 170 lbs.

Year	Team	Games	BA	SA	AB	H	2B	3B	HR	HR%	R	RBI	BB	SO	SB	Pinch Hit AB	Pinch Hit H	PO	A	E	DP	TC/G	FA	G by Pos
1911	NY A	10	.231	.231	13	3	0	0	0	0.0	2	1	0		0	2	0	4	1	1	0	1.5	.833	OF-3, 2B-1

Bob Will

WILL, ROBERT LEE (Butch)
B. July 15, 1931, Berwyn, Ill.
BL TL 5′10½″ 175 lbs.

Year	Team	Games	BA	SA	AB	H	2B	3B	HR	HR%	R	RBI	BB	SO	SB	Pinch Hit AB	Pinch Hit H	PO	A	E	DP	TC/G	FA	G by Pos
1957	CHI N	70	.223	.277	112	25	3	0	1	0.9	13	10	5	21	1	36	8	51	1	2	0	1.8	.963	OF-30
1958		6	.250	.250	4	1	0	0	0	0.0	1	0	2	0	0	4	1	0	0	0	0	0.0	.000	OF-1
1960		138	.255	.373	475	121	20	9	6	1.3	58	53	47	54	1	20	5	224	10	2	2	2.0	.992	OF-121
1961		86	.257	.336	113	29	9	0	0	0.0	9	8	15	19	0	**52**	11	36	0	1	1	1.2	.973	OF-30, 1B-1
1962		87	.239	.337	92	22	3	0	2	2.2	6	15	13	22	0	67	17	14	0	0	0	1.6	1.000	OF-9
1963		23	.174	.174	23	4	0	0	0	0.0	0	1	1	3	0	20	4	10	0	0	1	10.0	1.000	1B-1
6 yrs.		410	.247	.344	819	202	35	9	9	1.1	87	87	83	119	2	199	46	335	11	5	4	1.8	.986	OF-191, 1B-2

Jerry Willard

WILLARD, GERALD DUANE, JR.
B. Mar. 14, 1960, Oxnard, Calif.
BL TR 6′ 2″ 200 lbs.

Year	Team	Games	BA	SA	AB	H	2B	3B	HR	HR%	R	RBI	BB	SO	SB	Pinch Hit AB	Pinch Hit H	PO	A	E	DP	TC/G	FA	G by Pos
1984	CLE A	87	.224	.386	246	55	8	1	10	4.1	21	37	26	55	1	12	1	335	35	7	7	4.9	.981	C-76, DH-1
1985		104	.270	.383	300	81	13	0	7	2.3	39	36	28	59	0	10	2	427	52	5	11	5.0	.990	C-96, DH-1
1986	OAK A	75	.267	.385	161	43	7	0	4	2.5	17	26	22	28	0	7	4	300	12	2	1	4.0	.994	C-71, DH-7
1987		7	.167	.167	6	1	0	0	0	0.0	1	0	2	1	0	1	0	1	0	0	1	0.2	1.000	DH-3, 1B-1, 3B-1
1990	CHI A	3	.000	.000	3	0	0	0	0	0.0	0	0	0	2	0	2	0	0	0	0	0	0.0	.000	C-1
1991	ATL N	17	.214	.429	14	3	0	0	1	7.1	1	4	2	5	0	12	2	3	0	0	0	3.0	1.000	C-1
1992	2 teams	ATL N (26G –.348) MON N (21G –.120)																						
″	total	47	.229	.375	48	11	1	0	2	4.2	2	8	2	10	0	39	9	19	3	1	0	3.8	.957	1B-5, C-1
1994	SEA A	6	.200	.800	5	1	0	0	1	20.0	1	3	1	1	0	4	1	0	0	0	0	0.0		DH-1, C-1
8 yrs.		346	.249	.384	783	195	29	1	25	3.2	82	114	83	161	1	87	19	1085	102	15	20	4.5	.988	C-247, DH-13, 1B-6, 3B-1

Jerry Willard *continued*

Year	Team		Games	BA	SA	AB	H	2B	3B	HR	HR%	R	RBI	BB	SO	SB	Pinch Hit AB	Pinch Hit H	PO	A	E	DP	TC/G	FA	G by Pos
LEAGUE CHAMPIONSHIP SERIES																									
1991	ATL	N	2	.000	.000	2	0	0	0	0	0.0	0	0	0	1	0	2	0	0	0	0	0	0.0	—	
WORLD SERIES																									
1991	ATL	N	1	—	—	0	0	0	0	0	—	0	1	0	0	0	0	0	0	0	0	0	0.0	—	

Art Williams

WILLIAMS, ARTHUR FRANKLIN TR
B. Aug. 26, 1877, Somerville, Mass. D. May 16, 1941, Arlington, Va.

Year	Team		Games	BA	SA	AB	H	2B	3B	HR	HR%	R	RBI	BB	SO	SB	Pinch Hit AB	Pinch Hit H	PO	A	E	DP	TC/G	FA	G by Pos
1902	CHI	N	47	.231	.250	160	37	3	0	0	0.0	17	14	15		9	4	0	226	15	11	10	5.9	.956	OF-24, 1B-19

Bernie Williams

WILLIAMS, BERNABE BB TR 6′ 2″ 180 lbs.
Born Bernabe Williams (Figueroa).
B. Sept. 13, 1968, San Juan, Puerto Rico.

Year	Team		Games	BA	SA	AB	H	2B	3B	HR	HR%	R	RBI	BB	SO	SB	Pinch Hit AB	Pinch Hit H	PO	A	E	DP	TC/G	FA	G by Pos
1991	NY	A	85	.238	.350	320	76	19	4	3	0.9	43	34	48	57	10	0	0	230	3	5	0	2.8	.979	OF-85
1992			62	.280	.406	261	73	14	2	5	1.9	39	26	29	36	7	0	0	187	5	1	2	3.1	.995	OF-62
1993			139	.268	.400	567	152	31	4	12	2.1	67	68	53	106	9	0	0	366	5	4	0	2.7	.989	OF-139
1994			108	.289	.453	408	118	29	1	12	2.9	80	57	61	54	16	3	1	277	7	3	1	2.7	.990	OF-107
1995			144	.307	.487	563	173	29	9	18	3.2	93	82	75	98	8	0	0	431	1	8	0	3.1	.982	OF-144
5 yrs.			538	.279	.427	2119	592	122	20	50	2.4	322	267	266	351	50	3	1	1491	21	21	3	2.9	.986	OF-537
DIVISIONAL PLAYOFF SERIES																									
1995	NY	A	5	.429	.810	21	9	2	0	2	9.5	8	5	7	3	1	0	0	13	0	0	0	2.6	1.000	OF-5

Bernie Williams

WILLIAMS, BERNARD BR TR 6′ 1″ 175 lbs.
B. Oct. 8, 1948, Alameda, Calif.

Year	Team		Games	BA	SA	AB	H	2B	3B	HR	HR%	R	RBI	BB	SO	SB	Pinch Hit AB	Pinch Hit H	PO	A	E	DP	TC/G	FA	G by Pos
1970	SF	N	7	.313	.438	16	5	2	0	0	0.0	2	1	2	1	1	1	0	9	1	0	1	1.7	1.000	OF-6
1971			35	.178	.233	73	13	1	0	1	1.4	8	5	12	24	1	9	1	28	0	2	0	1.1	.933	OF-27
1972			46	.191	.397	68	13	3	1	3	4.4	12	9	7	22	0	17	4	34	1	0	0	2.3	1.000	OF-15
1974	SD	N	14	.133	.133	15	2	0	0	0	0.0	1	0	0	6	0	9	1	2	0	0	0	0.7	1.000	OF-3
4 yrs.			102	.192	.308	172	33	6	1	4	2.3	23	15	21	53	2	36	6	73	2	2	1	1.5	.974	OF-51

Billy Williams

WILLIAMS, BILLY LEO BL TR 6′ 1″ 175 lbs.
B. June 15, 1938, Whistler, Ala.
Hall of Fame 1987.

Year	Team		Games	BA	SA	AB	H	2B	3B	HR	HR%	R	RBI	BB	SO	SB	Pinch Hit AB	Pinch Hit H	PO	A	E	DP	TC/G	FA	G by Pos
1959	CHI	N	18	.152	.212	33	5	0	1	0	0.0	0	2	1	7	0	6	0	18	0	0	0	1.8	1.000	OF-10
1960			12	.277	.489	47	13	0	2	2	4.3	4	7	5	12	0	0	0	25	0	1	0	2.2	.962	OF-12
1961			146	.278	.484	529	147	20	7	25	4.7	75	86	45	70	6	13	6	220	9	11	3	1.8	.954	OF-135
1962			159	.298	.466	618	184	22	8	22	3.6	94	91	70	72	9	0	0	273	18	10	4	1.9	.967	OF-159
1963			161	.286	.497	612	175	36	9	25	4.1	87	95	68	78	7	1	0	298	13	4	2	2.0	.987	OF-160
1964			162	.312	.532	645	201	39	2	33	5.1	100	98	59	84	10	1	0	233	14	13	0	1.6	.950	OF-162
1965			164	.315	.552	645	203	39	6	34	5.3	115	108	65	76	10	0	0	296	10	10	2	1.9	.968	OF-164
1966			162	.276	.461	648	179	23	5	29	4.5	100	91	69	61	6	0	0	319	9	8	3	2.1	.976	OF-162
1967			162	.278	.481	634	176	21	12	28	4.4	92	84	68	67	6	0	0	271	3	3	1	1.7	.989	OF-162
1968			163	.288	.500	642	185	30	8	30	4.7	91	98	48	53	4	0	0	261	4	9	0	1.7	.967	OF-163
1969			163	.293	.474	642	188	33	10	21	3.3	103	95	59	70	3	2	0	250	15	12	2	1.7	.957	OF-159
1970			161	.322	.586	636	**205**	34	4	42	6.6	**137**	129	72	65	7	0	0	259	13	3	1	1.7	.989	OF-160
1971			157	.301	.505	594	179	27	5	28	4.7	86	93	77	44	7	5	1	284	8	7	3	1.9	.977	OF-154
1972			150	**.333**	**.606**	574	191	34	6	37	6.4	95	122	62	59	3	2	1	275	13	4	5	2.0	.986	OF-144, 1B-5
1973			156	.288	.438	576	166	22	2	20	3.5	72	86	76	72	4	3	1	420	34	6	15	2.9	.987	OF-138, 1B-19
1974			117	.280	.453	404	113	22	0	16	4.0	55	68	67	44	4	10	2	635	53	11	50	6.5	.984	1B-65, OF-43
1975	OAK	A	155	.244	.419	520	127	20	1	23	4.4	68	81	76	68	0	3	1	30	3	1	5	0.2	.971	DH-145, 1B-7
1976			120	.211	.339	351	74	12	0	11	3.1	36	41	58	44	4	13	3	0	0	0	0	0.0		DH-106, OF-1
18 yrs.			2488	.290	.492	9350	2711	434	88	426	4.6	1410	1475	1045	1046	90	59	15	4367	219	113	96	1.9	.976	OF-2088, DH-251, 1B-96
LEAGUE CHAMPIONSHIP SERIES																									
1975	OAK	A	3	.000	.000	8	0	0	0	0	0.0	0	0	1	1	0	1	0	0	0	0	0	0.0	.000	DH-2

Billy Williams

WILLIAMS, WILLIAM BL TR 6′ 3″ 195 lbs.
B. June 13, 1933, Newberry, S. C.

Year	Team		Games	BA	SA	AB	H	2B	3B	HR	HR%	R	RBI	BB	SO	SB	Pinch Hit AB	Pinch Hit H	PO	A	E	DP	TC/G	FA	G by Pos
1969	SEA	A	4	.000	.000	10	0	0	0	0	0.0	1	0	0	3	0	0	0	1	2	0	0	1.0	1.000	OF-3

Bob Williams

WILLIAMS, ROBERT ELIAS BR TR 6′ 190 lbs.
B. Apr. 27, 1884, Monday, Ohio D. Aug. 6, 1962, Nelsonville, Ohio.

Year	Team		Games	BA	SA	AB	H	2B	3B	HR	HR%	R	RBI	BB	SO	SB	Pinch Hit AB	Pinch Hit H	PO	A	E	DP	TC/G	FA	G by Pos
1911	NY	A	20	.191	.234	47	9	2	0	0	0.0	3	8	5		1	0	0	73	24	6	1	5.2	.942	C-20
1912			20	.136	.159	44	6	1	0	0	0.0	7	3	9		0	0	0	91	16	8	0	5.8	.930	C-20
1913			6	.158	.158	19	3	0	0	0	0.0	0	0	1	3	0	0	0	25	9	1	0	5.8	.971	C-6
3 yrs.			46	.164	.191	110	18	3	0	0	0.0	10	11	15	3	1	0	0	189	49	15	1	5.5	.941	C-46

Buff Williams

WILLIAMS, ALVA MITCHEL BR TR 5′11½″ 187 lbs.
B. Jan. 31, 1882, Carthage, Ill. D. July 23, 1933, Keokuk, Iowa.

Year	Team		Games	BA	SA	AB	H	2B	3B	HR	HR%	R	RBI	BB	SO	SB	Pinch Hit AB	Pinch Hit H	PO	A	E	DP	TC/G	FA	G by Pos
1911	BOS	A	95	.239	.303	284	68	8	5	0	0.0	36	31	24		9	0	0	727	73	20	28	8.6	.976	1B-57, C-38
1912	WAS	A	57	.318	.439	157	50	11	4	0	0.0	14	22	7		2	10	2	234	74	7	6	7.0	.978	C-45
1913			65	.283	.406	106	30	6	2	1	0.9	9	12	9	16	3	29	6	117	21	2	6	4.5	.986	C-18, 1B-8, OF-5
1914			81	.278	.379	169	47	6	4	1	0.6	17	22	13	19	2	25	6	252	58	6	0	6.0	.981	C-44, 1B-8, OF-1
1915			91	.244	.325	197	48	8	4	0	0.0	14	31	18	20	4	30	3	363	67	10	10	7.9	.977	C-40, 1B-15, 3B-1
1916			76	.267	.337	202	54	10	2	0	0.0	16	20	15	19	5	14	2	390	30	6	21	7.3	.986	1B-34, C-23, 3B-1
1918	CLE	A	28	.239	.324	71	17	2	2	0	0.0	5	7	9	6	2	6	1	190	10	4	11	9.3	.980	1B-21, C-1
7 yrs.			493	.265	.352	1186	314	51	23	2	0.2	111	145	95	80	27	114	20	2273	333	55	82	7.4	.979	C-209, 1B-143, OF-6, 3B-2

Cy Williams

WILLIAMS, FRED BL TL 6′ 2″ 180 lbs.
B. Dec. 21, 1887, Wadena, Ind. D. Apr. 23, 1974, Eagle River, Wis.

Year	Team		Games	BA	SA	AB	H	2B	3B	HR	HR%	R	RBI	BB	SO	SB	Pinch Hit AB	Pinch Hit H	PO	A	E	DP	TC/G	FA	G by Pos
1912	CHI	N	28	.242	.290	62	15	1	1	0	0.0	3	1	6	14	2	5	0	36	3	0	0	1.8	1.000	OF-22
1913			49	.224	.359	156	35	3	3	4	2.6	17	32	5	26	5	5	2	77	4	2	0	1.9	.976	OF-44
1914			55	.202	.266	94	19	2	2	0	0.0	12	5	13	13	2	22	4	46	2	3	0	1.9	.941	OF-27
1915			151	.257	.398	518	133	22	6	13	2.5	59	64	26	49	15	1	1	347	14	12	2	2.5	.968	OF-151
1916			118	.279	.459	405	113	19	9	**12**	**3.0**	55	66	51	64	6	2	0	260	7	3	0	2.3	.989	OF-116

Cy Williams *continued*

Year	Team	Games	BA	SA	AB	H	2B	3B	HR	HR%	R	RBI	BB	SO	SB	Pinch Hit AB	Pinch Hit H	PO	A	E	DP	TC/G	FA	G by Pos
1917		138	.241	.338	468	113	22	4	5	1.1	53	42	38	**78**	8	1	1	340	23	15	4	2.8	.960	OF-136
1918	PHI N	94	.276	.373	351	97	14	1	6	1.7	49	39	27	30	10	1	0	229	10	8	4	2.7	.968	OF-91
1919		109	.278	.393	435	121	21	1	9	**2.1**	54	39	30	43	9	1	0	278	13	9	2	2.8	.970	OF-108
1920		148	.325	.497	590	192	36	10	**15**	2.5	88	72	32	45	18	1	0	388	22	12	4	2.9	.972	OF-147
1921		146	.320	.488	562	180	28	6	18	3.2	67	75	30	32	5	0	0	382	29	9	5	2.9	.979	OF-146
1922		151	.308	.514	584	180	30	6	26	4.5	98	92	74	49	11	1	0	376	19	11	2	2.7	.973	OF-150
1923		136	.293	.576	535	157	22	3	**41**	**7.7**	98	114	59	57	11	1	0	350	9	7	3	2.7	.981	OF-135
1924		148	.328	.552	558	183	31	11	24	4.3	101	93	67	49	7	3	0	368	13	15	0	2.7	.962	OF-145
1925		107	.331	.522	314	104	11	5	13	4.1	78	60	53	34	4	10	5	173	12	2	3	1.9	.989	OF-96
1926		107	.345	**.568**	336	116	13	4	18	**5.4**	63	53	38	35	2	13	4	143	14	6	3	1.8	.963	OF-93
1927		131	.274	.502	492	135	18	2	**30**	**6.1**	86	98	61	57	0	1	0	241	22	8	8	2.1	.970	OF-130
1928		99	.256	.445	238	61	9	0	12	5.0	31	37	54	34	0	20	7	118	9	0	0	1.8	1.000	OF-69
1929		66	.292	.554	65	19	2	0	5	7.7	11	21	22	9	0	38	9	27	1	1	0	2.6	.966	OF-11
1930		21	.471	.588	17	8	2	0	0	0.0	1	2	4	3	0	16	8	1	0	0	0	0.3	1.000	OF-3
19 yrs.		2002	.292	.470	6780	1981	306	74	251	3.7	1024	1005	690	721	115	142	41	4180	226	123	40	2.5	.973	OF-1820

Dallas Williams

WILLIAMS, DALLAS McKINLEY, JR.
B. Feb. 28, 1958, Brooklyn, N. Y.
BL TL 5′11″ 165 lbs.

Year	Team	Games	BA	SA	AB	H	2B	3B	HR	HR%	R	RBI	BB	SO	SB	Pinch Hit AB	Pinch Hit H	PO	A	E	DP	TC/G	FA	G by Pos
1981	BAL A	2	.500	.500	2	1	0	0	0	0.0	0	0	0	0	0	2	1	1	0	0	0	1.0	1.000	OF-1
1983	CIN N	18	.056	.056	36	2	0	0	0	0.0	2	1	3	6	0	8	0	18	0	0	0	1.5	1.000	OF-12
2 yrs.		20	.079	.079	38	3	0	0	0	0.0	2	1	3	6	0	10	1	19	0	0	0	1.5	1.000	OF-13

Dana Williams

WILLIAMS, DANA LAMOUNT
B. Mar. 20, 1963, Weirton, W. Va.
BR TR 5′10″ 170 lbs.

Year	Team	Games	BA	SA	AB	H	2B	3B	HR	HR%	R	RBI	BB	SO	SB	Pinch Hit AB	Pinch Hit H	PO	A	E	DP	TC/G	FA	G by Pos
1989	BOS A	8	.200	.400	5	1	1	0	0	0.0	1	0	0	1	0	1	0	0	1	0	0	0.3	1.000	DH-2, OF-1

Davey Williams

WILLIAMS, DAVID CARLOUS
B. Nov. 2, 1927, Dallas, Tex.
BR TR 5′10″ 160 lbs.

Year	Team	Games	BA	SA	AB	H	2B	3B	HR	HR%	R	RBI	BB	SO	SB	Pinch Hit AB	Pinch Hit H	PO	A	E	DP	TC/G	FA	G by Pos
1949	NY N	13	.240	.360	50	12	1	1	1	2.0	7	5	7	4	0	0	0	19	22	2	5	3.3	.953	2B-13
1951		30	.266	.375	64	17	1	0	2	3.1	17	8	5	8	1	2	0	38	43	0	7	3.7	1.000	2B-22
1952		138	.254	.385	540	137	26	3	13	2.4	70	55	48	63	2	0	0	279	375	18	102	4.9	.973	2B-138
1953		112	.297	.368	340	101	11	2	3	0.9	51	34	44	19	2	10	3	191	254	8	54	4.8	.982	2B-95
1954		142	.222	.316	544	121	18	3	9	1.7	65	46	43	33	1	1	0	353	396	14	112	5.4	.982	2B-142
1955		82	.251	.324	247	62	4	1	4	1.6	25	15	17	17	0	12	4	139	162	10	39	4.4	.968	2B-71
6 yrs.		517	.252	.351	1785	450	61	10	32	1.8	235	163	164	144	6	25	7	1019	1252	52	319	4.8	.978	2B-481
WORLD SERIES																								
1951	NY N	2	.000	.000	1	0	0	0	0	0.0	0	0	0	0	0	1	0	0	0	0	0	0.0	—	
1954		4	.000	.000	11	0	0	0	0	0.0	0	1	2	2	0	0	0	10	9	1	2	5.0	.950	2B-4
2 yrs.		6	.000	.000	12	0	0	0	0	0.0	0	1	2	2	0	1	0	10	9	1	2	5.0	.950	2B-4

Denny Williams

WILLIAMS, EVON DANIEL
B. Dec. 13, 1899, Portland, Ore. D. Mar. 23, 1929, San Clemente, Calif.
BL TR 5′ 8½″ 150 lbs.

Year	Team	Games	BA	SA	AB	H	2B	3B	HR	HR%	R	RBI	BB	SO	SB	Pinch Hit AB	Pinch Hit H	PO	A	E	DP	TC/G	FA	G by Pos
1921	CIN N	10	.000	.000	7	0	0	0	0	0.0	0	0	0	2	0	6	0	1	0	0	0	1.0	1.000	OF-1
1924	BOS A	25	.365	.400	85	31	3	0	0	0.0	17	4	10	5	3	5	0	34	1	1	0	1.9	.972	OF-19
1925		68	.229	.261	218	50	1	3	0	0.0	28	13	17	11	2	13	3	117	4	6	1	2.4	.953	OF-52
1928		16	.222	.222	18	4	0	0	0	0.0	1	1	1	1	0	9	1	5	0	0	0	0.8	1.000	OF-6
4 yrs.		119	.259	.290	328	85	4	3	0	0.0	46	18	28	19	5	33	4	157	5	7	1	2.2	.959	OF-78

Dewey Williams

WILLIAMS, DEWEY EDGAR (Dee)
B. Feb. 5, 1916, Durham, N. C.
BR TR 6′ 160 lbs.

Year	Team	Games	BA	SA	AB	H	2B	3B	HR	HR%	R	RBI	BB	SO	SB	Pinch Hit AB	Pinch Hit H	PO	A	E	DP	TC/G	FA	G by Pos
1944	CHI N	79	.240	.282	262	63	7	2	0	0.0	23	27	23	18	2	1	0	317	50	7	7	4.9	.981	C-77
1945		59	.280	.400	100	28	2	2	2	2.0	16	5	13	13	0	4	1	114	20	3	1	2.5	.978	C-54
1946		4	.200	.200	5	1	0	0	0	0.0	0	0	0	2	0	2	1	3	1	0	0	2.0	1.000	C-2
1947		3	.000	.000	2	0	0	0	0	0.0	0	0	0	1	0	2	0	0	0	0	0	0.0	.000	C-1
1948	CIN N	48	.168	.221	95	16	2	0	1	1.1	9	5	10	18	0	1	0	137	11	6	1	3.3	.961	C-47
5 yrs.		193	.233	.293	464	108	11	4	3	0.6	48	37	46	52	2	10	2	571	82	16	9	3.7	.976	C-181
WORLD SERIES																								
1945	CHI N	2	.000	.000	2	0	0	0	0	0.0	0	0	0	1	0	1	0	1	1	0	0	2.0	1.000	C-1

Dib Williams

WILLIAMS, EDWIN DIBRELL
B. Jan. 19, 1910, Greenbrier, Ark. D. Apr. 2, 1992, Searcy, Ark.
BR TR 5′11½″ 175 lbs.

Year	Team	Games	BA	SA	AB	H	2B	3B	HR	HR%	R	RBI	BB	SO	SB	Pinch Hit AB	Pinch Hit H	PO	A	E	DP	TC/G	FA	G by Pos
1930	PHI A	67	.262	.393	191	50	10	3	3	1.6	24	22	15	19	2	5	0	109	151	12	23	4.6	.956	2B-39, SS-19, 3B-1
1931		86	.269	.384	294	79	12	2	6	2.0	41	40	19	21	2	3	1	168	237	27	63	5.2	.938	SS-72, 2B-10, OF-1
1932		62	.251	.363	215	54	10	1	4	1.9	30	24	22	23	0	6	0	124	181	17	32	5.8	.947	2B-53, SS-3
1933		115	.289	.444	408	118	20	5	11	2.7	52	73	32	35	1	0	0	265	320	47	51	5.5	.926	SS-84, 2B-29, 1B-2
1934		66	.273	.361	205	56	10	1	2	1.0	25	17	21	18	0	12	3	111	174	13	31	5.4	.956	2B-53, SS-2
1935	**2 teams**	**PHI A** (4G –.100)	**BOS A** (75G –.251)																					
″	**total**	79	.245	.326	261	64	12	0	3	1.1	26	25	24	24	2	3	0	127	159	12	21	3.9	.960	2B-31, 3B-30, SS-15, 1B-1
6 yrs.		475	.267	.385	1574	421	74	12	29	1.8	198	201	133	140	7	29	4	904	1222	128	221	5.1	.943	2B-215, SS-195, 3B-31, 1B-3, OF-1
WORLD SERIES																								
1931	PHI A	7	.320	.360	25	8	1	0	0	0.0	2	1	2	9	0	0	0	7	24	0	2	4.4	1.000	SS-7

Dick Williams

WILLIAMS, RICHARD HIRSCHFELD
B. May 7, 1929, St. Louis, Mo.
Manager 1967–69, 1971–88.
BR TR 6′ 190 lbs.

Year	Team	Games	BA	SA	AB	H	2B	3B	HR	HR%	R	RBI	BB	SO	SB	Pinch Hit AB	Pinch Hit H	PO	A	E	DP	TC/G	FA	G by Pos
1951	BKN N	23	.200	.333	60	12	3	1	1	1.7	5	5	4	10	0	8	2	21	1	0	0	1.5	1.000	OF-15
1952		36	.309	.397	68	21	4	1	0	0.0	13	11	2	10	0	6	1	51	3	0	2	2.0	1.000	OF-25, 3B-1, 1B-1
1953		30	.218	.364	55	12	2	0	2	3.6	4	5	3	10	0	5	0	24	0	2	0	1.1	.923	OF-24
1954		16	.147	.235	34	5	0	0	1	2.9	5	2	2	7	0	3	0	12	0	0	0	0.9	1.000	OF-14
1956	**2 teams**	**BKN N** (7G –.286)	**BAL A** (87G –.286)																					
″	**total**	94	.286	.450	360	103	18	4	11	3.1	45	37	30	41	5	8	2	249	17	4	4	2.6	.985	OF-81, 2B-10, 1B-10, 3B-4

Dick Williams *continued*

Year	Team	Games	BA	SA	AB	H	2B	3B	HR	HR%	R	RBI	BB	SO	SB	Pinch Hit AB	Pinch Hit H	PO	A	E	DP	TC/G	FA	G by Pos
1957	**2 teams**	**BAL A** (47G –.234)	**CLE A** (67G –.283)																					
″	**total**	114	.261	.374	372	97	17	2	7	1.9	49	34	26	40	3	11	2	244	72	8	20	3.0	.975	OF-63, 3B-34, 1B-12
1958	**BAL A**	128	.276	.347	409	113	17	0	4	1.0	36	32	37	47	0	13	0	359	61	8	27	2.9	.981	OF-70, 3B-45, 1B-26, 2B-7
1959	**KC A**	130	.266	.436	488	130	33	1	16	3.3	72	75	28	60	4	8	1	349	181	13	42	3.9	.976	3B-80, 1B-32, OF-23, 2B-3
1960		127	.288	.448	420	121	31	0	12	2.9	47	65	39	68	0	15	5	376	131	11	28	4.5	.979	3B-57, 1B-34, OF-25
1961	**BAL A**	103	.206	.345	310	64	15	2	8	2.6	37	24	20	38	0	16	6	209	16	3	11	2.4	.987	OF-75, 1B-20, 3B-2
1962		82	.247	.315	178	44	7	1	1	0.6	20	18	14	26	0	31	13	180	13	0	13	3.6	1.000	OF-29, 1B-21, 3B-4
1963	**BOS A**	79	.257	.360	136	35	8	0	2	1.5	15	12	15	25	0	48	**16**	64	28	1	4	2.7	.989	3B-17, 1B-11, OF-7
1964		61	.159	.406	69	11	2	0	5	7.2	10	11	7	10	0	25	3	50	21	1	6	1.8	.986	1B-21, 3B-13, OF-5
13 yrs.		1023	.260	.392	2959	768	157	12	70	2.4	358	331	227	392	12	197	51	2188	544	51	157	3.0	.982	OF-456, 3B-257, 1B-188, 2B-20
WORLD SERIES																								
1953	**BKN N**	3	.500	.500	2	1	0	0	0	0.0	0	0	1	1	0	2	1	0	0	0	0	0.0	—	

Earl Williams

WILLIAMS, EARL BAXTER BR TR 6′½″ 185 lbs.
B. Jan. 27, 1903, Cumberland Gap, Tenn. D. Mar. 10, 1958, Knoxville, Tenn.

Year	Team	Games	BA	SA	AB	H	2B	3B	HR	HR%	R	RBI	BB	SO	SB	Pinch Hit AB	Pinch Hit H	PO	A	E	DP	TC/G	FA	G by Pos
1928	**BOS N**	3	.000	.000	2	0	0	0	0	0.0	0	0	0	1	0	2	0	1	0	0	0	1.0	1.000	C-1

Earl Williams

WILLIAMS, EARL CRAIG, JR. BR TR 6′3″ 215 lbs.
B. July 14, 1948, Newark, N. J.

Year	Team	Games	BA	SA	AB	H	2B	3B	HR	HR%	R	RBI	BB	SO	SB	Pinch Hit AB	Pinch Hit H	PO	A	E	DP	TC/G	FA	G by Pos
1970	**ATL N**	10	.368	.579	19	7	4	0	0	0.0	4	5	3	4	0	4	2	23	8	0	4	4.4	1.000	1B-4, 3B-3
1971		145	.260	.491	497	129	14	1	33	6.6	64	87	42	80	0	12	3	596	117	18	38	5.0	.975	C-72, 3B-42, 1B-31
1972		151	.258	.457	565	146	24	2	28	5.0	72	87	62	118	0	1	0	740	87	23	18	5.4	.973	C-116, 3B-21, 1B-20
1973	**BAL A**	132	.237	.425	459	109	18	1	22	4.8	58	83	66	107	0	4	0	733	52	8	41	5.8	.990	C-95, 1B-42
1974		118	.254	.395	413	105	16	0	14	3.4	47	52	40	79	0	4	0	707	50	8	44	6.2	.990	C-75, 1B-47, DH-1
1975	**ATL N**	111	.240	.360	383	92	13	0	11	2.9	42	50	34	63	0	12	1	896	56	12	80	9.5	.988	1B-90, C-11
1976	**2 teams**	**ATL N** (61G –.212)	**MON N** (61G –.237)																					
″	**total**	122	.225	.406	374	84	13	2	17	4.5	35	55	33	65	0	17	5	715	64	9	50	6.9	.989	1B-64, C-51
1977	**OAK A**	100	.241	.391	348	84	13	0	13	3.7	39	38	18	58	2	5	1	305	26	3	14	3.0	.991	DH-45, C-36, 1B-29
8 yrs.		889	.247	.424	3058	756	115	6	138	4.5	361	457	298	574	2	59	12	4715	460	81	289	5.9	.985	C-456, 1B-327, 3B-66, DH-46
LEAGUE CHAMPIONSHIP SERIES																								
1973	**BAL A**	5	.278	.556	18	5	2	0	1	5.6	2	4	2	2	0	0	0	43	2	0	2	9.0	1.000	1B-4, C-1
1974		2	.000	.000	6	0	0	0	0	0.0	0	0	0	2	0	0	0	16	1	1	3	9.0	.944	1B-2
2 yrs.		7	.208	.417	24	5	2	0	1	4.2	2	4	2	4	0	0	0	59	3	1	5	9.0	.984	1B-6, C-1

Eddie Williams

WILLIAMS, EDWARD LAQUAN BR TR 6′ 175 lbs.
B. Nov. 1, 1964, Shreveport, La.

Year	Team	Games	BA	SA	AB	H	2B	3B	HR	HR%	R	RBI	BB	SO	SB	Pinch Hit AB	Pinch Hit H	PO	A	E	DP	TC/G	FA	G by Pos
1986	**CLE A**	5	.143	.143	7	1	0	0	0	0.0	2	1	0	3	0	2	0	0	0	0	0	0.0	.000	OF-4
1987		22	.172	.281	64	11	4	0	1	1.6	9	4	9	19	0	0	0	17	37	1	6	2.5	.982	3B-22
1988		10	.190	.190	21	4	0	0	0	0.0	3	1	0	3	0	0	0	3	18	0	0	2.1	1.000	3B-10
1989	**CHI A**	66	.274	.358	201	55	8	0	3	1.5	25	10	18	31	1	1	0	37	123	16	21	2.7	.909	3B-65
1990	**SD N**	14	.286	.571	42	12	3	0	3	7.1	5	4	5	6	0	2	0	5	21	3	2	2.2	.897	3B-13
1994		49	.331	.594	175	58	11	1	11	6.3	32	42	15	26	0	2	0	382	29	5	28	8.9	.988	1B-46, 3B-1
1995		97	.260	.426	296	77	11	1	12	4.1	35	47	23	47	0	16	2	571	48	7	53	7.7	.989	1B-81
7 yrs.		263	.270	.433	806	218	37	2	30	3.7	111	109	70	135	1	23	2	1015	276	32	110	5.5	.976	1B-127, 3B-111, OF-4

George Williams

WILLIAMS, GEORGE BR TR 5′11″ 165 lbs.
B. Oct. 23, 1939, Detroit, Mich.

Year	Team	Games	BA	SA	AB	H	2B	3B	HR	HR%	R	RBI	BB	SO	SB	Pinch Hit AB	Pinch Hit H	PO	A	E	DP	TC/G	FA	G by Pos
1961	**PHI N**	17	.250	.250	36	9	0	0	0	0.0	4	1	4	4	0	1	0	23	36	2	9	4.1	.967	2B-15
1962	**HOU N**	5	.375	.500	8	3	1	0	0	0.0	1	2	0	1	0	2	0	1	5	0	1	2.0	1.000	2B-3
1964	**KC A**	37	.209	.275	91	19	6	0	0	0.0	10	2	6	12	0	6	0	41	58	4	18	4.0	.961	2B-20, SS-2, OF-2, 3B-2
3 yrs.		59	.230	.281	135	31	7	0	0	0.0	15	5	10	17	0	9	0	65	99	6	28	3.9	.965	2B-38, SS-2, OF-2, 3B-2

George Williams

WILLIAMS, GEORGE ERIK BB TR 5′10″ 190 lbs.
B. Apr. 22, 1969, La Crosse, Wis.

Year	Team	Games	BA	SA	AB	H	2B	3B	HR	HR%	R	RBI	BB	SO	SB	Pinch Hit AB	Pinch Hit H	PO	A	E	DP	TC/G	FA	G by Pos
1995	**OAK A**	29	.291	.494	79	23	5	1	3	3.8	13	14	11	21	0	7	3	58	7	3	0	3.0	.956	C-13, DH-10

Gerald Williams

WILLIAMS, GERALD FLOYD BR TR 6′2″ 190 lbs.
B. Aug. 10, 1966, New Orleans, La.

Year	Team	Games	BA	SA	AB	H	2B	3B	HR	HR%	R	RBI	BB	SO	SB	Pinch Hit AB	Pinch Hit H	PO	A	E	DP	TC/G	FA	G by Pos
1992	**NY A**	15	.296	.704	27	8	2	0	3	11.1	7	6	0	3	2	0	0	20	1	2	0	1.9	.913	OF-12
1993		42	.149	.269	67	10	2	3	0	0.0	11	6	1	14	2	4	1	41	2	2	0	1.2	.956	OF-37
1994		57	.291	.523	86	25	8	0	4	4.7	19	13	4	17	1	6	1	43	2	2	0	1.0	.957	OF-43, DH-2
1995		100	.247	.467	182	45	18	2	6	3.3	33	28	22	34	4	13	2	138	6	1	0	1.6	.993	OF-92, DH-1
4 yrs.		214	.243	.461	362	88	30	5	13	3.6	70	53	27	68	9	23	4	242	11	7	0	1.4	.973	OF-184, DH-3
DIVISIONAL PLAYOFF SERIES																								
1995	**NY A**	5	.000	.000	5	0	0	0	0	0.0	1	0	2	3	0	0	0	7	1	0	0	1.6	1.000	OF-5

Gus Williams

WILLIAMS, AUGUST JOSEPH (Gloomy Gus) BL TL 6′ 185 lbs.
Brother of Harry Williams.
B. May 7, 1888, Omaha, Neb. D. Apr. 16, 1964, Sterling, Ill.

Year	Team	Games	BA	SA	AB	H	2B	3B	HR	HR%	R	RBI	BB	SO	SB	Pinch Hit AB	Pinch Hit H	PO	A	E	DP	TC/G	FA	G by Pos
1911	**STL A**	9	.269	.385	26	7	3	0	0	0.0	1	0	0		0	2	1	13	0	2	0	2.1	.867	OF-7
1912		64	.292	.444	216	63	13	7	2	0.9	32	32	27		18	2	0	94	12	8	3	1.8	.930	OF-62
1913		147	.273	.400	538	147	21	16	5	0.9	72	53	57	87	31	3	0	225	26	13	7	1.8	.951	OF-143
1914		143	.253	.339	499	126	19	6	4	0.8	51	47	36	**120**	35	1	0	200	24	16	2	1.7	.933	OF-141
1915		45	.202	.277	119	24	2	2	1	0.8	15	11	6	16	11	6	0	35	2	2	1	1.1	.949	OF-35
5 yrs.		408	.263	.374	1398	367	58	31	12	0.9	171	143	126	223	95	14	1	567	64	41	13	1.7	.939	OF-388

Harry Williams

WILLIAMS, HARRY PETER BR TR 6′1½″ 200 lbs.
Brother of Gus Williams.
B. June 23, 1890, Omaha, Neb. D. Dec. 21, 1963, Huntington Park, Calif.

Year	Team	Games	BA	SA	AB	H	2B	3B	HR	HR%	R	RBI	BB	SO	SB	Pinch Hit AB	Pinch Hit H	PO	A	E	DP	TC/G	FA	G by Pos
1913	**NY A**	27	.256	.354	82	21	3	1	1	1.2	18	12	15	10	6	0	0	244	12	5	7	9.7	.981	1B-27
1914		59	.163	.230	178	29	5	2	1	0.6	9	17	26	26	3	1	0	577	25	15	19	10.6	.976	1B-58
2 yrs.		86	.192	.269	260	50	8	3	2	0.8	27	29	41	36	9	1	0	821	37	20	26	10.3	.977	1B-85

Jim Williams

WILLIAMS, JAMES ALFRED
B. Apr. 29, 1947, Zachary, La.
BR TR 6′ 2″ 190 lbs.

Year	Team	Lg	Games	BA	SA	AB	H	2B	3B	HR	HR%	R	RBI	BB	SO	SB	Pinch Hit AB	Pinch Hit H	PO	A	E	DP	TC/G	FA	G by Pos
1969	SD	N	13	.280	.320	25	7	1	0	0	0.0	4	2	3	11	0	6	3	9	0	1	0	1.7	.900	OF-6
1970			11	.286	.286	14	4	0	0	0	0.0	4	0	1	3	1	4	1	6	0	0	0	1.0	1.000	OF-6
2 yrs.			24	.282	.308	39	11	1	0	0	0.0	8	2	4	14	1	10	4	15	0	1	0	1.3	.938	OF-12

Jimmy Williams

WILLIAMS, JAMES THOMAS (Buttons)
B. Dec. 20, 1876, St. Louis, Mo. D. Jan. 16, 1965, St. Petersburg, Fla.
BR TR 5′ 9″ 175 lbs.

Year	Team	Lg	Games	BA	SA	AB	H	2B	3B	HR	HR%	R	RBI	BB	SO	SB	Pinch Hit AB	Pinch Hit H	PO	A	E	DP	TC/G	FA	G by Pos
1899	PIT	N	152	.355	.532	617	219	28	**27**	9	1.5	126	116	60		26	0	0	251	354	66	14	4.4	.902	3B-152
1900			106	.264	.389	416	110	15	11	5	1.2	72	68	32		18	0	0	156	265	54	22	4.4	.886	3B-103, SS-4
1901	BAL	A	130	.317	.495	501	159	26	**21**	7	1.4	113	96	56		21	0	0	339	412	52	47	6.2	.935	2B-130
1902			125	.313	.500	498	156	27	**21**	8	1.6	83	83	36		14	2	0	275	369	48	47	5.6	.931	2B-104, 3B-19, 1B-1
1903	NY	A	132	.267	.392	502	134	30	12	3	0.6	60	82	39		9	0	0	266	438	32	59	5.6	.957	2B-132
1904			146	.263	.354	559	147	31	7	2	0.4	62	74	38		14	0	0	315	465	40	52	5.6	.951	2B-146
1905			129	.228	.343	470	107	20	8	6	1.3	54	60	50		14	0	0	335	332	25	51	5.4	.964	2B-129
1906			139	.277	.373	501	139	25	7	3	0.6	62	77	44		8	0	0	336	412	32	34	5.6	.959	2B-139
1907			139	.270	.359	504	136	17	11	2	0.4	53	63	35		14	0	0	357	393	26	45	5.6	.966	2B-139
1908	STL	A	148	.236	.321	539	127	20	7	4	0.7	63	53	55		7	0	0	352	445	31	50	5.6	.963	2B-148
1909			110	.195	.235	374	73	3	6	0	0.0	32	22	29		6	1	0	221	280	20	42	4.8	.962	2B-109
11 yrs.			1456	.275	.396	5481	1507	242	138	49	0.9	780	794	474		151	3	0	3203	4165	426	463	5.4	.945	2B-1176, 3B-274, SS-4, 1B-1

Jimy Williams

WILLIAMS, JAMES FRANCIS
B. Oct. 4, 1943, Santa Maria, Calif.
Manager 1986–89.
BR TR 5′10″ 170 lbs.

Year	Team	Lg	Games	BA	SA	AB	H	2B	3B	HR	HR%	R	RBI	BB	SO	SB	Pinch Hit AB	Pinch Hit H	PO	A	E	DP	TC/G	FA	G by Pos
1966	STL	N	13	.273	.273	11	3	0	0	0	0.0	1	1	1	5	0	1	0	2	5	0	1	0.7	1.000	SS-7, 2B-3
1967			1	.000	.000	2	0	0	0	0	0.0	0	0	0	1	0	0	0	6	1	0	0	7.0	1.000	SS-1
2 yrs.			14	.231	.231	13	3	0	0	0	0.0	1	1	1	6	0	1	0	8	6	0	1	1.3	1.000	SS-8, 2B-3

Ken Williams

WILLIAMS, KENNETH ROY
B. June 28, 1890, Grant's Pass, Ore. D. Jan. 22, 1959, Grant's Pass, Ore.
BL TR 6′ 170 lbs.

Year	Team	Lg	Games	BA	SA	AB	H	2B	3B	HR	HR%	R	RBI	BB	SO	SB	Pinch Hit AB	Pinch Hit H	PO	A	E	DP	TC/G	FA	G by Pos
1915	CIN	N	71	.242	.324	219	53	10	4	0	0.0	22	16	15	20	4	9	3	117	11	7	4	2.2	.948	OF-62
1916			10	.111	.111	27	3	0	0	0	0.0	1	1	2	5	1	1	0	19	2	1	1	2.2	.955	OF-10
1918	STL	A	2	.000	.000	1	0	0	0	0	0.0	0	1	1	0	0	0	0	0	0	0	0	0.0	—	
1919			65	.300	.467	227	68	10	5	6	2.6	32	35	26	25	7	2	0	168	10	12	3	3.0	.937	OF-63
1920			141	.307	.480	521	160	34	13	10	1.9	90	72	41	26	18	1	1	331	17	14	6	2.6	.961	OF-138
1921			146	.347	.561	547	190	31	7	24	4.4	115	117	74	42	20	0	0	331	24	26	3	2.6	.932	OF-145
1922			153	.332	.627	585	194	34	11	**39**	6.7	128	**155**	74	31	37	0	0	372	16	12	4	2.6	.970	OF-153
1923			147	.357	.623	555	198	37	12	29	5.2	106	91	79	32	18	1	0	333	23	12	5	2.5	.967	OF-145
1924			114	.324	.533	398	129	21	4	18	4.5	78	84	69	17	20	5	1	257	13	9	2	2.6	.968	OF-109
1925			102	.331	**.613**	411	136	31	5	25	**6.1**	83	105	37	14	10	0	0	242	11	12	4	2.6	.955	OF-102
1926			108	.280	.510	347	97	15	7	17	4.9	55	74	39	23	5	12	3	189	12	11	2	2.3	.948	OF-91, 2B-1
1927			131	.323	.527	421	136	23	6	17	4.0	70	74	57	30	9	14	3	260	15	10	4	2.5	.965	OF-113
1928	BOS	A	133	.303	.413	462	140	25	1	8	1.7	59	67	37	15	4	6	1	253	10	8	0	2.1	.970	OF-127
1929			74	.345	.540	139	48	14	2	3	2.2	21	21	15	7	1	30	10	83	3	3	3	2.3	.966	OF-36, 1B-2
14 yrs.			1397	.319	.531	4860	1552	285	77	196	4.0	860	913	566	287	154	81	22	2955	167	137	41	2.5	.958	OF-1294, 1B-2, 2B-1

Kenny Williams

WILLIAMS, KENNETH ROYAL
B. Apr. 6, 1964, Berkeley, Calif.
BR TR 6′ 2″ 187 lbs.

Year	Team	Lg	Games	BA	SA	AB	H	2B	3B	HR	HR%	R	RBI	BB	SO	SB	Pinch Hit AB	Pinch Hit H	PO	A	E	DP	TC/G	FA	G by Pos
1986	CHI	A	15	.129	.226	31	4	0	0	1	3.2	2	1	1	11	1	0	0	18	1	0	1	1.7	1.000	OF-10, DH-1
1987			116	.281	.422	391	110	18	2	11	2.8	48	50	10	83	21	1	0	303	5	6	2	2.7	.981	OF-115
1988			73	.159	.305	220	35	4	2	8	3.6	18	28	10	64	6	2	1	87	69	17	4	2.4	.902	OF-38, 3B-32, DH-3
1989	DET	A	94	.205	.302	258	53	5	1	6	2.3	29	23	18	63	9	10	1	180	11	4	3	2.2	.979	OF-87, DH-1, 1B-1
1990	2 teams		DET A (57G –.133)	TOR A (49G –.194)																					
″	total		106	.161	.226	155	25	8	1	0	0.0	23	13	10	42	9	18	2	103	5	0	2	1.2	1.000	OF-77, DH-15
1991	2 teams		TOR A (13G –.207)	MON N (34G –.271)																					
″	total		47	.253	.394	99	25	7	2	1	1.0	16	4	7	27	3	10	2	58	4	2	0	1.8	.969	OF-33, DH-2
6 yrs.			451	.218	.339	1154	252	42	8	27	2.3	136	119	56	290	49	41	6	749	95	29	12	2.1	.967	OF-360, 3B-32, DH-22, 1B-1

Mark Williams

WILLIAMS, MARK WESTLEY
B. July 28, 1953, Elmira, N. Y.
BL TL 6′ 180 lbs.

Year	Team	Lg	Games	BA	SA	AB	H	2B	3B	HR	HR%	R	RBI	BB	SO	SB	Pinch Hit AB	Pinch Hit H	PO	A	E	DP	TC/G	FA	G by Pos
1977	OAK	A	3	.000	.000	2	0	0	0	0	0.0	0	1	1	1	0	2	0	1	0	0	0	1.0	1.000	OF-1

Matt Williams

WILLIAMS, MATTHEW DERRICK
B. Nov. 28, 1965, Bishop, Calif.
BR TR 6′ 2″ 205 lbs.

Year	Team	Lg	Games	BA	SA	AB	H	2B	3B	HR	HR%	R	RBI	BB	SO	SB	Pinch Hit AB	Pinch Hit H	PO	A	E	DP	TC/G	FA	G by Pos
1987	SF	N	84	.188	.339	245	46	9	2	8	3.3	28	21	16	68	4	3	2	110	234	9	52	4.1	.975	SS-70, 3B-17
1988			52	.205	.410	156	32	6	1	8	5.1	17	19	8	41	0	2	0	48	108	7	9	2.9	.957	3B-43, SS-14
1989			84	.202	.455	292	59	18	1	18	6.2	31	50	14	72	1	3	0	90	168	10	15	2.6	.963	3B-73, SS-30
1990			159	.277	.488	617	171	27	2	33	5.3	87	**122**	33	138	7	1	1	140	306	19	33	2.9	.959	3B-159
1991			157	.268	.499	589	158	24	5	34	5.8	72	98	33	128	5	3	0	134	295	16	32	2.8	.964	3B-155, SS-4
1992			146	.227	.384	529	120	13	5	20	3.8	58	66	39	109	7	5	1	105	289	23	33	2.9	.945	3B-144
1993			145	.294	.561	579	170	33	4	38	6.6	105	110	27	80	1	1	0	117	266	12	34	2.7	.970	3B-144
1994			112	.267	.607	445	119	16	3	**43**	9.7	74	96	33	87	1	2	0	79	234	12	21	3.0	.963	3B-110
1995			76	.336	.647	283	95	17	1	23	8.1	53	65	30	58	2	2	0	49	178	10	10	3.2	.958	3B-74
9 yrs.			1015	.260	.497	3735	970	163	24	225	6.0	525	647	233	781	28	22	4	872	2078	118	239	3.0	.962	3B-919, SS-118
LEAGUE CHAMPIONSHIP SERIES																									
1989	SF	N	5	.300	.650	20	6	1	0	2	10.0	2	9	0	2	0	0	0	5	12	0	2	2.8	1.000	3B-5, SS-1
WORLD SERIES																									
1989	SF	N	4	.125	.313	16	2	0	0	1	6.3	1	1	0	6	0	0	0	4	12	0	2	2.3	1.000	SS-4, 3B-3

Otto Williams

WILLIAMS, OTTO GEORGE
B. Nov. 2, 1877, Newark, N. J. D. Mar. 19, 1937, Omaha, Neb.
BR TR 5′ 8″ 165 lbs.

Year	Team	Lg	Games	BA	SA	AB	H	2B	3B	HR	HR%	R	RBI	BB	SO	SB	Pinch Hit AB	Pinch Hit H	PO	A	E	DP	TC/G	FA	G by Pos
1902	STL	N	2	.400	.400	5	2	0	0	0	0.0	0	2	1		1	0	0	5	8	3	0	8.0	.813	SS-2
1903	2 teams		STL N (53G –.203)	CHI N (38G –.223)																					
″	total		91	.211	.252	317	67	9	2	0	0.0	24	22	13		14	0	0	189	275	48	26	5.7	.906	SS-78, 2B-8, 1B-3, 3B-1

Otto Williams *continued*

Year	Team	Lg	Games	BA	SA	AB	H	2B	3B	HR	HR%	R	RBI	BB	SO	SB	Pinch Hit AB	Pinch Hit H	PO	A	E	DP	TC/G	FA	G by Pos
1904	**CHI**	**N**	57	.200	.232	185	37	4	1	0	0.0	21	8	13		9	2	1	161	67	9	3	4.4	.962	OF-21, 1B-11, SS-10, 2B-6, 3B-6
1906	**WAS**	**A**	20	.137	.137	51	7	0	0	0	0.0	3	2	2		0	3	0	36	41	6	4	4.9	.928	SS-8, 2B-6, 1B-2, 3B-1
4 yrs.			170	.203	.237	558	113	13	3	0	0.0	48	34	29		24	5	1	391	391	66	33	5.2	.922	SS-98, OF-21, 2B-20, 1B-16, 3B-8

Pap Williams

WILLIAMS, FRED BR TR 6′ 1″ 200 lbs.
B. July 17, 1913, Meridian, Miss. D. Nov. 2, 1993, Meridian, Miss.

Year	Team	Lg	Games	BA	SA	AB	H	2B	3B	HR	HR%	R	RBI	BB	SO	SB	Pinch Hit AB	Pinch Hit H	PO	A	E	DP	TC/G	FA	G by Pos
1945	**CLE**	**A**	16	.211	.211	19	4	0	0	0	0.0	0	0	1	2	0	12	2	13	2	0	2	5.0	1.000	1B-3

Reggie Williams

WILLIAMS, REGINALD BERNARD BB TR 6′ 1″ 180 lbs.
B. May 5, 1966, Laurens, S. C.

Year	Team	Lg	Games	BA	SA	AB	H	2B	3B	HR	HR%	R	RBI	BB	SO	SB	Pinch Hit AB	Pinch Hit H	PO	A	E	DP	TC/G	FA	G by Pos
1992	**CAL**	**A**	14	.231	.346	26	6	1	1	0	0.0	5	2	1	10	0	0	0	26	0	0	0	2.0	1.000	OF-12, DH-1
1995	**LA**	**N**	15	.091	.091	11	1	0	0	0	0.0	2	1	2	3	0	1	0	6	0	0	0	0.4	1.000	OF-14
2 yrs.			29	.189	.270	37	7	1	1	0	0.0	7	3	3	13	0	1	0	32	0	0	0	1.2	1.000	OF-26, DH-1

Reggie Williams

WILLIAMS, REGINALD DEWAYNE BR TR 5′11″ 185 lbs.
B. Aug. 29, 1960, Memphis, Tenn.

Year	Team	Lg	Games	BA	SA	AB	H	2B	3B	HR	HR%	R	RBI	BB	SO	SB	Pinch Hit AB	Pinch Hit H	PO	A	E	DP	TC/G	FA	G by Pos
1985	**LA**	**N**	22	.333	.333	9	3	0	0	0	0.0	4	0	0	4	1	3	1	8	1	1	0	0.7	.900	OF-15
1986			128	.277	.376	303	84	14	2	4	1.3	35	32	23	57	9	11	1	179	5	3	2	1.5	.984	OF-124
1987			39	.111	.111	36	4	0	0	0	0.0	6	4	5	9	1	9	0	21	0	2	0	0.8	.913	OF-30
1988	**CLE**	**A**	11	.226	.387	31	7	2	0	1	3.2	7	3	0	6	0	1	1	13	1	0	0	1.3	1.000	OF-11
4 yrs.			200	.259	.351	379	98	16	2	5	1.3	52	39	28	76	11	24	3	221	7	6	2	1.3	.974	OF-180

Rinaldo Williams

WILLIAMS, RINALDO LEWIS BL TR
B. Dec. 18, 1893, Santa Cruz, Calif. D. Apr. 24, 1966, Cottonwood, Ariz.

Year	Team	Lg	Games	BA	SA	AB	H	2B	3B	HR	HR%	R	RBI	BB	SO	SB	Pinch Hit AB	Pinch Hit H	PO	A	E	DP	TC/G	FA	G by Pos
1914	**BKN**	**F**	4	.267	.400	15	4	2	0	0	0.0	1	0	0		0	0	0	4	8	1	0	3.3	.923	3B-4

Ted Williams

WILLIAMS, THEODORE SAMUEL (The Splendid Splinter, The Thumper) BL TR 6′ 3″ 205 lbs.
B. Aug. 30, 1918, San Diego, Calif.
Manager 1969–72.
Hall of Fame 1966.

Year	Team	Lg	Games	BA	SA	AB	H	2B	3B	HR	HR%	R	RBI	BB	SO	SB	Pinch Hit AB	Pinch Hit H	PO	A	E	DP	TC/G	FA	G by Pos
1939	**BOS**	**A**	149	.327	.609	565	185	44	11	31	5.5	131	**145**	107	64	2	0	0	318	11	19	3	2.3	.945	OF-149
1940			144	.344	.594	561	193	43	14	23	4.1	**134**	113	96	54	4	0	0	302	15	13	2	2.3	.961	OF-143, P-1
1941			143	**.406**	**.735**	456	185	33	3	**37**	**8.1**	**135**	120	**145**	27	2	9	3	262	11	11	2	2.1	.961	OF-133
1942			150	**.356**	**.648**	522	186	34	5	**36**	**6.9**	**141**	**137**	**145**	51	3	0	0	313	15	4	4	2.2	.988	OF-150
1946			150	.342	**.667**	514	176	37	8	38	7.4	**142**	123	**156**	44	0	0	0	325	7	10	2	2.3	.971	OF-150
1947			156	**.343**	**.634**	528	181	40	9	**32**	**6.1**	**125**	**114**	**162**	47	0	0	0	347	10	9	2	2.3	.975	OF-156
1948			137	**.369**	**.615**	509	188	**44**	3	25	4.9	124	127	**126**	41	4	2	0	289	9	5	2	2.3	.983	OF-134
1949			155	.343	**.650**	566	194	**39**	3	**43**	**7.6**	**150**	**159**	**162**	48	1	0	0	337	12	6	3	2.3	.983	OF-155
1950			89	.317	.647	334	106	24	1	28	8.4	82	97	82	21	3	1	1	165	7	8	0	2.1	.956	OF-86
1951			148	.318	**.556**	531	169	28	4	30	5.6	109	126	**144**	45	1	0	0	315	12	4	6	2.3	.988	OF-147
1952			6	.400	.900	10	4	0	1	1	10.0	2	3	2	2	0	4	1	4	0	0	0	2.0	1.000	OF-2
1953			37	.407	.901	91	37	6	0	13	14.3	17	34	19	10	0	10	2	31	1	1	1	1.3	.970	OF-26
1954			117	.345	**.635**	386	133	23	1	29	**7.5**	93	89	**136**	32	0	4	2	213	5	4	0	1.9	.982	OF-115
1955			98	.356	.703	320	114	21	3	28	8.8	77	83	91	24	2	2	1	170	5	2	0	1.9	.989	OF-93
1956			136	.345	.605	400	138	28	2	24	6.0	71	82	102	39	0	20	5	174	7	5	2	1.7	.973	OF-110
1957			132	**.388**	**.731**	420	163	28	1	38	**9.0**	96	87	119	43	0	5	3	215	2	1	0	1.7	.995	OF-125
1958			129	**.328**	.584	411	135	23	2	26	6.3	81	85	98	49	1	11	3	154	3	7	0	1.4	.957	OF-114
1959			103	.254	.419	272	69	15	0	10	3.7	32	43	52	27	0	24	11	94	4	3	0	1.3	.970	OF-76
1960			113	.316	.645	310	98	15	0	29	9.4	56	72	75	41	1	19	1	131	6	1	1	1.6	.993	OF-87
19 yrs.			2292	.344	.634	7706	2654	525	71	521	6.8	1798	1839	2019	709	24	111	33	4159	142	113	30	2.1	.974	OF-2151, P-1
				7th	**2nd**					**10th**	**4th**		**10th**	**2nd**											
WORLD SERIES																									
1946	**BOS**	**A**	7	.200	.200	25	5	0	0	0	0.0	2	1	5	5	0	0	0	16	2	0	2	2.6	1.000	OF-7

Walt Williams

WILLIAMS, WALTER ALLEN (No-Neck) BR TR 5′ 6″ 165 lbs.
B. Dec. 19, 1943, Brownwood, Tex.

Year	Team	Lg	Games	BA	SA	AB	H	2B	3B	HR	HR%	R	RBI	BB	SO	SB	Pinch Hit AB	Pinch Hit H	PO	A	E	DP	TC/G	FA	G by Pos
1964	**HOU**	**N**	10	.000	.000	9	0	0	0	0	0.0	1	0	0	2	1	2	0	4	0	0	0	0.8	1.000	OF-5
1967	**CHI**	**A**	104	.240	.353	275	66	16	3	3	1.1	35	15	17	20	3	30	4	112	6	2	2	1.6	.983	OF-73
1968			63	.241	.308	133	32	6	0	1	0.8	6	8	4	17	0	28	5	47	2	0	1	1.4	1.000	OF-34
1969			135	.304	.374	471	143	22	1	3	0.6	59	32	26	33	6	24	7	183	13	3	4	1.8	.985	OF-111
1970			110	.251	.343	315	79	18	1	3	1.0	43	15	19	30	3	29	8	119	12	7	1	1.7	.949	OF-79
1971			114	.294	.424	361	106	17	3	8	2.2	43	35	24	27	5	27	9	157	5	0	2	1.8	1.000	OF-90, 3B-1
1972			77	.249	.317	221	55	7	1	2	0.9	22	11	13	20	6	23	4	93	6	1	2	1.7	.990	OF-57, 3B-1
1973	**CLE**	**A**	104	.289	.406	350	101	15	1	8	2.3	43	38	14	29	9	17	4	123	7	4	0	1.5	.970	OF-61, DH-26
1974	**NY**	**A**	43	.113	.113	53	6	0	0	0	0.0	5	3	1	10	1	15	1	20	1	1	0	0.8	.955	OF-24, DH-3
1975			82	.281	.400	185	52	5	1	5	2.7	27	16	8	23	0	31	**10**	57	4	1	0	1.1	.984	OF-31, DH-17, 2B-6
10 yrs.			842	.270	.365	2373	640	106	11	33	1.4	284	173	126	211	34	226	52	915	56	19	12	1.6	.981	OF-565, DH-46, 2B-6, 3B-2

Wash Williams

WILLIAMS, WASHINGTON J. 5′11″ 180 lbs.
B. Philadelphia, Pa. D. Aug. 9, 1892, Philadelphia, Pa.

Year	Team	Lg	Games	BA	SA	AB	H	2B	3B	HR	HR%	R	RBI	BB	SO	SB	Pinch Hit AB	Pinch Hit H	PO	A	E	DP	TC/G	FA	G by Pos
1884	**RIC**	**AA**	2	.250	.250	8	2	0	0	0	0.0	0		0			0	0	1	0	1	0	1.0	.500	OF-2
1885	**CHI**	**N**	1	.250	.250	4	1	0	0	0	0.0	0	0	0	0		0	0	1	1	1	0	1.5	.667	OF-1, P-1
2 yrs.			3	.250	.250	12	3	0	0	0	0.0	0	0	0	0		0	0	2	1	2	0	1.3	.600	OF-3, P-1

Woody Williams

WILLIAMS, WOODROW WILSON BR TR 5′11″ 175 lbs.
B. Aug. 21, 1912, Pamplin, Va. D. Feb. 24, 1995, Appomattox, Va.

Year	Team	Lg	Games	BA	SA	AB	H	2B	3B	HR	HR%	R	RBI	BB	SO	SB	Pinch Hit AB	Pinch Hit H	PO	A	E	DP	TC/G	FA	G by Pos
1938	**BKN**	**N**	20	.333	.392	51	17	1	1	0	0.0	6	6	4	1	1	0	0	28	28	4	4	3.2	.933	SS-18, 3B-1
1943	**CIN**	**N**	30	.377	.435	69	26	2	1	0	0.0	8	11	1	3	0	5	1	37	47	6	7	3.8	.933	2B-12, 3B-7, SS-5
1944			155	.240	.289	**653**	157	23	3	1	0.2	73	35	44	24	7	0	0	377	542	27	97	6.1	.971	2B-155
1945			133	.237	.266	482	114	14	0	0	0.0	46	27	39	24	6	0	0	295	393	22	61	5.3	.969	2B-133
4 yrs.			338	.250	.292	1255	314	40	5	1	0.1	133	79	88	52	14	5	1	737	1010	59	169	5.5	.967	2B-300, SS-23, 3B-8

Howie Williamson

WILLIAMSON, NATHANIEL HOWARD (Cow) BL TL 6′ 1″ 170 lbs.
B. Dec. 23, 1904, Little Rock, Ark. D. Aug. 15, 1969, Texarkana, Ark.

Year	Team	Games	BA	SA	AB	H	2B	3B	HR	HR%	R	RBI	BB	SO	SB	Pinch Hit AB	Pinch Hit H	PO	A	E	DP	TC/G	FA	G by Pos
1928	STL N	10	.222	.222	9	2	0	0	0	0.0	0	0	1	4	0	9	2	0	0	0	0	0.0	—	

Ned Williamson

WILLIAMSON, EDWARD NAGLE BR TR 5′11″ 210 lbs.
B. Oct. 24, 1857, Philadelphia, Pa. D. Mar. 3, 1894, Willow Springs, Ark.

Year	Team	Games	BA	SA	AB	H	2B	3B	HR	HR%	R	RBI	BB	SO	SB	Pinch Hit AB	Pinch Hit H	PO	A	E	DP	TC/G	FA	G by Pos
1878	IND N	63	.232	.300	250	58	10	2	1	0.4	31	19	5	15		0	0	88	128	33	6	4.0	.867	3B-63
1879	CHI N	80	.294	.447	320	94	20	13	1	0.3	66	36	24	31		0	0	183	199	49	15	5.4	.886	3B-70, 1B-6, C-4
1880		75	.251	.328	311	78	20	2	0	0.0	65	31	15	26		0	0	147	176	34	9	4.6	.905	3B-63, C-11, 2B-3
1881		82	.268	.347	343	92	12	6	1	0.3	56	48	19	19		0	0	135	220	36	13	4.5	.908	3B-76, 2B-4, P-3, SS-2, C-1
1882		83	.282	.408	348	98	27	4	3	0.9	66	60	27	21		0	0	108	211	43	16	4.3	.881	3B-83, P-1
1883		98	.276	.438	402	111	**49**	5	2	0.5	83		22	48		0	0	115	257	88	20	4.6	.809	3B-97, C-3, P-1
1884		107	.278	.554	417	116	18	8	**27**	**6.5**	84		42	56		0	0	155	271	67	26	4.4	.864	3B-99, C-10, P-2
1885		113	.238	.324	407	97	16	5	3	0.7	87	64	**75**	60		0	0	120	261	45	18	3.7	.894	3B-113, P-2, C-1
1886		121	.216	.335	430	93	17	8	6	1.4	69	58	80	71		0	0	162	356	79	36	4.7	.868	SS-121, C-4, P-2
1887		127	.267	.437	439	117	20	14	9	2.1	77	78	73	57	45	0	0	133	362	61	31	4.3	.890	SS-127, P-1
1888		132	.250	.385	452	113	9	14	8	1.8	75	73	65	71	25	0	0	120	375	65	48	4.2	.884	SS-132
1889		47	.237	.283	173	41	3	1	1	0.6	16	30	23	22	2	0	0	48	130	33	7	4.5	.844	SS-47
1890	CHI P	73	.195	.264	261	51	7	4	1	0.4	34	26	36	35	3	0	0	75	149	51	12	3.8	.815	3B-52, SS-21
13 yrs.		1201	.255	.384	4553	1159	228	86	63	1.4	809	523	506	532	75	0	0	1589	3095	684	257	4.4	.873	3B-716, SS-450, C-34, P-12, 2B-7, 1B-6

Julius Willigrod

WILLIGROD, JULIUS BL
B. Calif. D. Sept. 27, 1906, San Francisco, Calif.

Year	Team	Games	BA	SA	AB	H	2B	3B	HR	HR%	R	RBI	BB	SO	SB	Pinch Hit AB	Pinch Hit H	PO	A	E	DP	TC/G	FA	G by Pos
1882	2 teams	DET N (1G –.333) CLE N (9G –.139)																						
″	total	10	.154	.231	39	6	1	1	0	0.0	5	2	3	8		0	0	13	2	3	0	1.8	.833	OF-9, SS-1

Hugh Willingham

WILLINGHAM, THOMAS HUGH BR TR 6′ 180 lbs.
B. May 30, 1906, Dalhart, Tex. D. June 15, 1988, El Reno, Okla.

Year	Team	Games	BA	SA	AB	H	2B	3B	HR	HR%	R	RBI	BB	SO	SB	Pinch Hit AB	Pinch Hit H	PO	A	E	DP	TC/G	FA	G by Pos
1930	CHI A	3	.250	.250	4	1	0	0	0	0.0	2	0	2	1	0	2	1	1	3	0	0	4.0	1.000	2B-1
1931	PHI N	23	.257	.457	35	9	2	1	1	2.9	5	3	2	9	0	5	1	24	18	6	5	4.4	.875	SS-8, 3B-2, OF-1
1932		4	.000	.000	2	0	0	0	0	0.0	0	0	0	0	0	2	0	0	0	0	0	0.0	—	
1933		1	.000	.000	1	0	0	0	0	0.0	0	0	0	0	0	1	0	0	0	0	0	0.0	—	
4 yrs.		31	.238	.405	42	10	2	1	1	2.4	7	3	4	10	0	10	2	25	21	6	5	4.3	.885	SS-8, 3B-2, OF-1, 2B-1

Wills

WILLS
Deceased.

Year	Team	Games	BA	SA	AB	H	2B	3B	HR	HR%	R	RBI	BB	SO	SB	Pinch Hit AB	Pinch Hit H	PO	A	E	DP	TC/G	FA	G by Pos
1884	2 teams	WAS AA (4G –.133) KC U (5G –.143)																						
″	total	9	.139	.222	36	5	3	0	0	0.0	3		0			0	0	10	5	1	0	1.8	.938	OF-9

Bump Wills

WILLS, ELLIOTT TAYLOR BB TR 5′ 9″ 172 lbs.
Son of Maury Wills.
B. July 27, 1952, Washington, D. C.

Year	Team	Games	BA	SA	AB	H	2B	3B	HR	HR%	R	RBI	BB	SO	SB	Pinch Hit AB	Pinch Hit H	PO	A	E	DP	TC/G	FA	G by Pos
1977	TEX A	152	.287	.410	541	155	28	6	9	1.7	87	62	65	96	28	3	0	321	492	15	89	5.4	.982	2B-150, SS-2, DH-1, 1B-1
1978		157	.250	.347	539	135	17	4	9	1.7	78	57	63	91	52	3	0	350	526	17	84	5.7	.981	2B-156
1979		146	.273	.350	543	148	21	3	5	0.9	90	46	53	58	35	2	1	337	468	20	95	5.7	.976	2B-146
1980		146	.263	.360	578	152	31	5	5	0.9	102	58	51	71	34	0	0	340	473	13	112	5.7	.984	2B-144
1981		102	.251	.307	410	103	13	2	2	0.5	51	41	32	49	12	0	0	268	326	10	70	5.9	.983	2B-101, DH-1
1982	CHI N	128	.272	.377	419	114	18	4	6	1.4	64	38	46	76	35	21	6	199	297	19	45	5.0	.963	2B-103
6 yrs.		831	.266	.360	3030	807	128	24	36	1.2	472	302	310	441	196	27	7	1815	2582	94	495	5.6	.979	2B-800, SS-2, DH-2, 1B-1

Dave Wills

WILLS, DAVIS BOWLES BL TL
B. Jan. 26, 1877, Charlottesville, Va. D. Oct. 12, 1959, Washington, D. C.

Year	Team	Games	BA	SA	AB	H	2B	3B	HR	HR%	R	RBI	BB	SO	SB	Pinch Hit AB	Pinch Hit H	PO	A	E	DP	TC/G	FA	G by Pos
1899	LOU N	24	.223	.277	94	21	3	1	0	0.0	15	12	2		1	0	0	259	8	12	9	11.6	.957	1B-24

Maury Wills

WILLS, MAURICE MORNING BB TR 5′11″ 170 lbs.
Father of Bump Wills.
B. Oct. 2, 1932, Washington, D. C.
Manager 1980–81.

Year	Team	Games	BA	SA	AB	H	2B	3B	HR	HR%	R	RBI	BB	SO	SB	Pinch Hit AB	Pinch Hit H	PO	A	E	DP	TC/G	FA	G by Pos
1959	LA N	83	.260	.298	242	63	5	2	0	0.0	27	7	13	27	7	0	0	121	220	12	39	4.3	.966	SS-82
1960		148	.295	.331	516	152	15	2	0	0.0	75	27	35	47	**50**	0	0	260	431	40	78	5.0	.945	SS-145
1961		148	.282	.339	**613**	173	12	10	1	0.2	105	31	59	50	**35**	1	0	253	428	29	104	4.8	.959	SS-148
1962		165	.299	.373	**695**	208	13	**10**	6	0.9	130	48	51	57	**104**	0	0	295	493	36	86	5.0	.956	SS-165
1963		134	.302	.349	527	159	19	3	0	0.0	83	34	44	48	**40**	0	0	197	381	26	54	4.3	.957	SS-109, 3B-33
1964		158	.275	.324	630	173	15	5	2	0.3	81	34	41	73	**53**	4	0	275	428	27	77	4.7	.963	SS-149, 3B-6
1965		158	.286	.329	650	186	14	7	0	0.0	92	33	40	64	**94**	2	0	267	535	25	89	5.3	.970	SS-155
1966		143	.273	.308	594	162	14	2	1	0.2	60	39	34	60	38	1	0	231	460	23	80	5.0	.968	SS-139, 3B-4
1967	PIT N	149	.302	.365	616	186	12	9	3	0.5	92	45	31	44	29	3	1	102	346	24	32	3.2	.949	3B-144, SS-2
1968		153	.278	.316	627	174	12	6	0	0.0	76	31	45	57	52	3	0	115	308	18	32	2.9	.959	3B-141, SS-10
1969	2 teams	MON N (47G –.222) LA N (104G –.297)																						
″	total	151	.274	.335	623	171	10	8	4	0.6	80	47	59	61	40	1	1	240	496	28	92	5.1	.963	SS-150, 2B-1
1970	LA N	132	.270	.318	522	141	19	3	0	0.0	77	34	50	34	28	5	1	171	397	24	58	4.6	.959	SS-126, 3B-4
1971		149	.281	.329	601	169	14	3	3	0.5	73	44	40	44	15	6	1	220	486	17	87	4.9	.976	SS-144, 3B-4
1972		71	.129	.167	132	17	3	1	0	0.0	16	4	10	18	1	5	1	39	103	2	20	2.5	.986	SS-31, 3B-26
14 yrs.		1942	.281	.331	7588	2134	177	71	20	0.3	1067	458	552	684	586	31	5	2786	5512	331	928	4.5	.962	SS-1555, 3B-362, 2B-1
WORLD SERIES																								
1959	LA N	6	.250	.250	20	5	0	0	0	0.0	2	1	0	3	1	0	0	10	21	1	3	5.3	.969	SS-6
1963		4	.133	.133	15	2	0	0	0	0.0	1	0	1	3	1	0	0	5	10	1	0	4.0	.938	SS-4
1965		7	.367	.467	30	11	3	0	0	0.0	3	3	1	3	3	0	0	14	26	0	6	5.7	1.000	SS-7
1966		4	.077	.077	13	1	0	0	0	0.0	0	0	3	3	1	0	0	12	15	0	3	6.8	1.000	SS-4
4 yrs.		21	.244	.282	78	19	3	0	0	0.0	6	4	5	12	6	0	0	41	72	2	12	5.5	.983	SS-21

Kid Willson

WILLSON, FRANK HOXIE BL TL 6′ 1″ 190 lbs.
B. Nov. 3, 1895, Bloomington, Neb. D. Apr. 17, 1964, Union Gap, Wash.

Year	Team	Games	BA	SA	AB	H	2B	3B	HR	HR%	R	RBI	BB	SO	SB	Pinch Hit AB	Pinch Hit H	PO	A	E	DP	TC/G	FA	G by Pos
1918	CHI A	4	.000	.000	1	0	0	0	0	0.0	2	0	1	1	0	1	0	0	0	0	0	0.0	—	
1927		7	.100	.100	10	1	0	0	0	0.0	1	1	0	2	0	4	0	6	0	0	0	3.0	1.000	OF-2
2 yrs.		11	.091	.091	11	1	0	0	0	0.0	3	1	1	3	0	5	0	6	0	0	0	3.0	1.000	OF-2

Walt Wilmot

WILMOT, WALTER ROBERT BB TR
B. Oct. 18, 1863, Plover, Wis. D. Feb. 1, 1929, Chicago, Ill.

Year	Team	Games	BA	SA	AB	H	2B	3B	HR	HR%	R	RBI	BB	SO	SB	Pinch Hit AB	Pinch Hit H	PO	A	E	DP	TC/G	FA	G by Pos
1888	WAS N	119	.224	.321	473	106	16	9	4	0.8	61	43	23	55	46	0	0	260	19	41	4	2.7	.872	OF-119
1889		108	.289	.484	432	125	19	**19**	9	2.1	88	57	51	32	40	0	0	232	22	20	4	2.5	.927	OF-108
1890	CHI N	139	.278	.420	571	159	15	12	**14**	2.5	114	99	64	44	76	0	0	320	26	23	4	2.7	.938	OF-139
1891		121	.279	.414	498	139	14	10	11	2.2	102	71	55	21	42	0	0	223	15	20	0	2.1	.922	OF-121
1892		92	.216	.287	380	82	7	7	2	0.5	47	35	40	20	31	0	0	197	8	22	0	2.5	.903	OF-92
1893		94	.301	.431	392	118	14	14	3	0.8	69	61	40	8	39	1	0	198	16	31	1	2.6	.873	OF-93
1894		133	.330	.471	597	197	45	12	5	0.8	134	130	35	23	74	0	0	264	16	41	5	2.4	.872	OF-133
1895		108	.283	.395	466	132	16	6	8	1.7	86	72	30	19	28	0	0	226	19	23	5	2.5	.914	OF-108
1897	NY N	11	.265	.412	34	9	2	0	1	2.9	8	4	2		1	1	0	13	2	1	0	1.8	.938	OF-9
1898		35	.239	.341	138	33	4	2	2	1.4	16	22	9		4	1	0	35	4	5	0	1.3	.886	OF-34
10 yrs.		960	.276	.405	3981	1100	152	91	59	1.5	725	594	349	222	381	3	0	1968	147	227	23	2.4	.903	OF-956

Archie Wilson

WILSON, ARCHIE CLIFTON BR TR 5′11″ 175 lbs.
B. Nov. 25, 1923, Los Angeles, Calif.

Year	Team	Games	BA	SA	AB	H	2B	3B	HR	HR%	R	RBI	BB	SO	SB	Pinch Hit AB	Pinch Hit H	PO	A	E	DP	TC/G	FA	G by Pos
1951	NY A	4	.000	.000	4	0	0	0	0	0.0	0	0	0	0	0	2	0	3	0	0	0	1.5	1.000	OF-2
1952	3 teams	NY A (3G –.500) WAS A (26G –.208) BOS A (18G –.263)																						
″	total	47	.228	.309	136	31	5	3	0	0.0	9	17	7	14	0	9	3	84	1	3	1	2.4	.966	OF-37
2 yrs.		51	.221	.300	140	31	5	3	0	0.0	9	17	7	14	0	11	3	87	1	3	1	2.3	.967	OF-39

Art Wilson

WILSON, ARTHUR EARL (Dutch) BR TR 5′ 8″ 170 lbs.
B. Dec. 11, 1885, Macon, Ill. D. June 12, 1960, Chicago, Ill.

Year	Team	Games	BA	SA	AB	H	2B	3B	HR	HR%	R	RBI	BB	SO	SB	Pinch Hit AB	Pinch Hit H	PO	A	E	DP	TC/G	FA	G by Pos
1908	NY N	1	—	—	0	0	0	0	0	—	0	0	0		0	0	0	0	0	0	0	0.0	—	
1909		19	.238	.333	42	10	2	1	0	0.0	4	5	4		0	1	0	50	11	1	1	3.4	.984	C-18
1910		26	.269	.385	52	14	4	1	0	0.0	10	5	9	6	2	0	0	95	22	3	4	4.6	.975	C-25, 1B-1
1911		66	.303	.431	109	33	9	1	1	0.9	17	17	19	12	6	2	0	200	34	9	2	3.8	.963	C-64
1912		65	.289	.413	121	35	6	0	3	2.5	17	19	13	14	2	3	1	213	30	10	5	4.1	.960	C-61
1913		54	.190	.215	79	15	0	1	0	0.0	5	8	11	11	1	2	1	144	38	6	5	3.7	.968	C-49, 1B-2
1914	CHI F	137	.291	.466	440	128	31	8	10	2.3	78	64	70		13	4	2	674	212	24	19	6.9	.974	C-132
1915		96	.305	.439	269	82	11	2	7	2.6	44	31	65		8	7	2	391	96	10	6	5.7	.980	C-87
1916	2 teams	PIT N (53G –.258) CHI N (36G –.193)																						
″	total	89	.227	.298	242	55	8	3	1	0.4	16	17	19	41	5	14	2	307	80	13	6	5.5	.967	C-73
1917	CHI N	81	.213	.303	211	45	9	2	2	0.9	17	25	32	36	6	4	2	361	92	15	5	6.2	.968	C-75
1918	BOS N	89	.246	.289	280	69	8	2	0	0.0	15	19	24	31	5	2	0	292	96	9	7	4.7	.977	C-85
1919		71	.257	.309	191	49	8	1	0	0.0	14	16	25	19	2	5	1	214	82	7	4	4.7	.977	C-64, 1B-1
1920		16	.053	.053	19	1	0	0	0	0.0	0	0	1	1	0	7	0	4	5	1	0	1.3	.900	3B-6, C-2
1921	CLE A	2	.000	.000	1	0	0	0	0	0.0	0	0	0	0	0	0	0	1	1	0	0	1.0	1.000	C-2
14 yrs.		812	.261	.364	2056	536	96	22	24	1.2	237	226	292	171	50	51	11	2946	799	108	64	5.2	.972	C-737, 3B-6, 1B-4
WORLD SERIES																								
1911	NY N	1	.000	.000	1	0	0	0	0	0.0	0	0	0	0	0	0	0	1	0	0	0	1.0	1.000	C-1
1912		2	1.000	1.000	1	1	0	0	0	0.0	0	0	0	0	0	0	0	2	1	1	0	2.0	.750	C-2
1913		3	.000	.000	3	0	0	0	0	0.0	0	0	0	2	0	0	0	4	1	0	0	1.7	1.000	C-3
3 yrs.		6	.200	.200	5	1	0	0	0	0.0	0	0	0	2	0	0	0	7	2	1	0	1.7	.900	C-6

Artie Wilson

WILSON, ARTHUR LEE BL TR 5′11″ 162 lbs.
B. Oct. 28, 1920, Springfield, Ala.

Year	Team	Games	BA	SA	AB	H	2B	3B	HR	HR%	R	RBI	BB	SO	SB	Pinch Hit AB	Pinch Hit H	PO	A	E	DP	TC/G	FA	G by Pos
1951	NY N	19	.182	.182	22	4	0	0	0	0.0	2	1	2	1	2	11	2	14	11	1	5	3.3	.962	2B-3, SS-3, 1B-2

Bill Wilson

WILSON, WILLIAM DONALD BR TR 6′ 2″ 200 lbs.
B. Nov. 6, 1928, Central City, Neb.

Year	Team	Games	BA	SA	AB	H	2B	3B	HR	HR%	R	RBI	BB	SO	SB	Pinch Hit AB	Pinch Hit H	PO	A	E	DP	TC/G	FA	G by Pos
1950	CHI A	3	.000	.000	6	0	0	0	0	0.0	0	0	2	2	0	0	0	3	0	0	0	1.5	1.000	OF-2
1953		9	.059	.059	17	1	0	0	0	0.0	1	1	0	7	0	4	0	9	0	0	0	3.0	1.000	OF-3
1954	2 teams	CHI A (20G –.171) PHI A (94G –.238)																						
″	total	114	.232	.411	358	83	11	1	17	4.7	47	38	46	64	1	5	0	303	7	5	4	2.9	.984	OF-110
1955	KC A	98	.223	.432	273	61	12	0	15	5.5	39	38	24	63	1	14	3	186	4	6	0	2.4	.969	OF-82, P-1
4 yrs.		224	.222	.407	654	145	23	1	32	4.9	87	77	72	136	2	23	3	501	11	11	4	2.6	.979	OF-197, P-1

Bill Wilson

WILSON, WILLIAM G. TR
B. Oct. 28, 1867, Hannibal, Mo. D. May 9, 1924, St. Paul, Minn.

Year	Team	Games	BA	SA	AB	H	2B	3B	HR	HR%	R	RBI	BB	SO	SB	Pinch Hit AB	Pinch Hit H	PO	A	E	DP	TC/G	FA	G by Pos
1890	PIT N	83	.214	.270	304	65	11	3	0	0.0	30	21	22	50	5	0	0	409	90	60	22	6.8	.893	C-38, OF-25, 1B-18, SS-1
1897	LOU N	105	.213	.273	381	81	12	4	1	0.3	43	41	18		9	1	0	339	114	30	7	4.6	.938	C-103, 3B-1
1898		29	.167	.245	102	17	1	2	1	1.0	5	13	5		3	0	0	97	34	16	2	5.1	.891	C-28, 1B-1
3 yrs.		217	.207	.268	787	163	24	9	2	0.3	78	75	45	50	17	1	0	845	238	106	31	5.5	.911	C-169, OF-25, 1B-19, 3B-1, SS-1

Bob Wilson

WILSON, ROBERT BR TR 5′11″ 197 lbs.
B. Nov. 22, 1925, Dallas, Tex. D. Apr. 23, 1985, Dallas, Tex.

Year	Team	Games	BA	SA	AB	H	2B	3B	HR	HR%	R	RBI	BB	SO	SB	Pinch Hit AB	Pinch Hit H	PO	A	E	DP	TC/G	FA	G by Pos
1958	LA N	3	.200	.200	5	1	0	0	0	0.0	0	0	0	1	0	2	1	1	0	0	0	1.0	1.000	OF-1

Charlie Wilson

WILSON, CHARLES WOODROW (Swamp Baby) BB TR 5′10½″ 178 lbs.
B. Jan. 13, 1905, Clinton, S. C. D. Dec. 19, 1970, Rochester, N. Y.

Year	Team	Games	BA	SA	AB	H	2B	3B	HR	HR%	R	RBI	BB	SO	SB	Pinch Hit AB	Pinch Hit H	PO	A	E	DP	TC/G	FA	G by Pos
1931	BOS N	16	.190	.310	58	11	4	0	1	1.7	7	11	3	5	0	0	0	9	24	3	0	2.6	.917	3B-14
1932	STL N	24	.198	.323	96	19	3	3	1	1.0	7	2	3	8	0	0	0	28	73	7	14	4.5	.935	SS-24
1933		1	.000	.000	1	0	0	0	0	0.0	0	0	0	1	0	0	0	0	0	0	0	0.0	.000	SS-1
1935		16	.323	.323	31	10	0	0	0	0.0	1	1	2	2	0	7	4	6	8	1	1	1.9	.933	3B-8
4 yrs.		57	.215	.317	186	40	7	3	2	1.1	15	14	8	16	0	7	4	43	105	11	15	3.4	.931	SS-25, 3B-22

Craig Wilson

WILSON, CRAIG BR TR 5′11″ 175 lbs.
B. Nov. 28, 1964, Annapolis, Md.

Year	Team	Games	BA	SA	AB	H	2B	3B	HR	HR%	R	RBI	BB	SO	SB	Pinch Hit AB	Pinch Hit H	PO	A	E	DP	TC/G	FA	G by Pos
1989	STL N	6	.250	.250	4	1	0	0	0	0.0	1	1	1	2	0	4	1	1	0	1	0	1.0	.500	3B-2
1990		55	.248	.264	121	30	2	0	0	0.0	13	7	8	14	0	23	9	45	30	1	5	2.1	.987	3B-13, OF-13, 2B-9, 1B-1
1991		60	.171	.195	82	14	2	0	0	0.0	5	13	6	10	0	37	11	30	14	2	6	1.9	.957	3B-12, OF-5, 1B-4, 2B-3
1992		61	.311	.368	106	33	6	0	0	0.0	6	13	10	18	1	25	6	24	47	3	8	2.3	.959	3B-18, 2B-11, OF-3
1993	KC A	21	.265	.347	49	13	1	0	1	2.0	6	3	7	6	1	6	1	8	22	1	4	1.8	.968	3B-15, 2B-1, OF-1
5 yrs.		203	.251	.290	362	91	11	0	1	0.3	31	37	32	50	2	95	28	108	113	8	23	2.1	.965	3B-60, 2B-24, OF-22, 1B-5

Dan Wilson

WILSON, DANIEL ALLEN BR TR 6′ 3″ 190 lbs.
B. Mar. 25, 1969, Arlington Heights, Ill.

Year	Team	Games	BA	SA	AB	H	2B	3B	HR	HR%	R	RBI	BB	SO	SB	Pinch Hit AB	Pinch Hit H	PO	A	E	DP	TC/G	FA	G by Pos
1992	CIN N	12	.360	.400	25	9	1	0	0	0.0	2	3	3	8	0	4	2	42	4	0	0	5.1	1.000	C-9
1993		36	.224	.263	76	17	3	0	0	0.0	6	8	9	16	0	3	1	146	9	1	2	4.5	.994	C-35
1994	SEA A	91	.216	.312	282	61	14	2	3	1.1	24	27	10	57	1	0	0	602	41	9	2	7.2	.986	C-91
1995		119	.278	.416	399	111	22	3	9	2.3	40	51	33	63	2	1	1	897	51	5	2	8.0	.995	C-119
4 yrs.		258	.253	.363	782	198	40	5	12	1.5	72	89	55	144	3	8	4	1687	105	15	6	7.1	.992	C-254
DIVISIONAL PLAYOFF SERIES																								
1995	SEA A	5	.118	.118	17	2	0	0	0	0.0	0	1	2	6	0	0	0	34	1	0	1	7.0	1.000	C-5
LEAGUE CHAMPIONSHIP SERIES																								
1995	SEA A	6	.000	.000	16	0	0	0	0	0.0	0	0	0	4	0	0	0	35	3	1	0	6.5	.974	C-6

Earl Wilson

WILSON, EARL LAWRENCE BR TR 6′ 3″ 216 lbs.
B. Oct. 2, 1934, Ponchatoula, La.

Year	Team	Games	BA	SA	AB	H	2B	3B	HR	HR%	R	RBI	BB	SO	SB	Pinch Hit AB	Pinch Hit H	PO	A	E	DP	TC/G	FA	G by Pos
1959	BOS A	9	.500	.750	8	4	2	0	0	0.0	0	4	0	1	0	0	0	2	5	1	0	0.9	.875	P-9
1960		15	.174	.217	23	4	1	0	0	0.0	3	2	1	7	0	0	0	6	10	1	1	1.3	.941	P-13
1962		35	.174	.333	69	12	2	0	3	4.3	8	8	5	19	0	0	0	19	22	3	2	1.4	.932	P-31
1963		38	.208	.333	72	15	0	3	1	1.4	5	7	7	18	0	0	0	17	36	3	1	1.5	.946	P-37
1964		54	.205	.466	73	15	4	0	5	6.8	19	13	9	22	0	1	0	14	29	2	0	1.4	.956	P-33
1965		47	.177	.405	79	14	0	0	6	7.6	13	12	13	29	0	0	0	24	26	3	2	1.5	.943	P-36
1966	2 teams	BOS A (18G –.250) DET A (27G –.234)																						
″	total	45	.240	.500	96	23	0	2	7	7.3	20	22	8	36	0	4	1	36	39	5	4	2.1	.938	P-38
1967	DET A	52	.185	.315	108	20	2	0	4	3.7	8	15	8	39	0	12	2	26	42	0	2	1.7	1.000	P-39
1968		40	.227	.489	88	20	0	1	7	8.0	9	17	2	35	0	6	0	26	30	4	3	1.8	.933	P-34
1969		37	.132	.132	76	10	0	0	0	0.0	6	6	10	37	0	2	0	8	38	4	3	1.4	.920	P-35
1970	2 teams	DET A (18G –.194) SD N (15G –.059)																						
″	total	33	.146	.292	48	7	1	0	2	4.2	4	5	4	28	0	0	0	7	18	2	1	0.8	.926	P-33
11 yrs.		405	.195	.369	740	144	12	6	35	4.7	95	111	67	271	0	25	3	185	295	28	19	1.5	.945	P-338
WORLD SERIES																								
1968	DET A	1	.000	.000	1	0	0	0	0	0.0	0	0	0	1	0	0	0	0	2	0	0	2.0	1.000	P-1

Eddie Wilson

WILSON, EDWARD FRANCIS BL TL 5′11″ 165 lbs.
B. Sept. 7, 1909, Hamden, Conn. D. Apr. 11, 1979, Hamden, Conn.

Year	Team	Games	BA	SA	AB	H	2B	3B	HR	HR%	R	RBI	BB	SO	SB	Pinch Hit AB	Pinch Hit H	PO	A	E	DP	TC/G	FA	G by Pos
1936	BKN N	52	.347	.457	173	60	8	1	3	1.7	28	25	14	25	3	5	0	72	3	6	0	1.7	.926	OF-47
1937		36	.222	.389	54	12	4	1	1	1.9	11	8	17	14	1	9	1	27	1	1	0	1.4	.966	OF-21
2 yrs.		88	.317	.441	227	72	12	2	4	1.8	39	33	31	39	4	14	1	99	4	7	0	1.6	.936	OF-68

Frank Wilson

WILSON, FRANCIS EDWARD (Squash) BL TR 6′ 185 lbs.
B. Apr. 20, 1901, Malden, Mass. D. Nov. 25, 1974, Leicester, Mass.

Year	Team	Games	BA	SA	AB	H	2B	3B	HR	HR%	R	RBI	BB	SO	SB	Pinch Hit AB	Pinch Hit H	PO	A	E	DP	TC/G	FA	G by Pos
1924	BOS N	61	.237	.284	215	51	7	0	1	0.5	20	15	23	22	3	5	2	140	5	4	1	2.7	.973	OF-55
1925		12	.419	.516	31	13	1	1	0	0.0	3	0	4	1	2	1	0	23	1	0	0	2.4	1.000	OF-10
1926		87	.237	.309	236	56	11	3	0	0.0	22	23	20	21	3	28	7	121	6	9	1	2.4	.934	OF-56
1928	2 teams	CLE A (2G –.000) STL A (6G –.000)																						
″	total	8	.000	.000	6	0	0	0	0	0.0	1	0	1	0	0	5	0	0	0	0	0	0.0	.000	OF-1
4 yrs.		168	.246	.307	488	120	19	4	1	0.2	46	38	48	44	8	39	9	284	12	13	2	2.5	.958	OF-122

Gary Wilson

WILSON, JAMES GARRETT BR TR 5′ 7″ 168 lbs.
B. Jan. 12, 1877, Baltimore, Md. D. May 1, 1969, Randallstown, Md.

Year	Team	Games	BA	SA	AB	H	2B	3B	HR	HR%	R	RBI	BB	SO	SB	Pinch Hit AB	Pinch Hit H	PO	A	E	DP	TC/G	FA	G by Pos
1902	BOS A	2	.125	.125	8	1	0	0	0	0.0	0	1	0		0	0	0	6	6	3	2	7.5	.800	2B-2

Glenn Wilson

WILSON, GLENN DWIGHT BR TR 6′ 1″ 190 lbs.
B. Dec. 22, 1958, Baytown, Tex.

Year	Team	Games	BA	SA	AB	H	2B	3B	HR	HR%	R	RBI	BB	SO	SB	Pinch Hit AB	Pinch Hit H	PO	A	E	DP	TC/G	FA	G by Pos
1982	DET A	84	.292	.457	322	94	15	1	12	3.7	39	34	15	51	2	2	0	215	8	3	1	2.7	.987	OF-80, DH-4
1983		144	.268	.408	503	135	25	6	11	2.2	55	65	25	79	1	7	3	225	12	3	2	1.7	.988	OF-143
1984	PHI N	132	.240	.372	341	82	21	3	6	1.8	28	31	17	56	7	19	2	153	7	7	0	1.5	.958	OF-109, 3B-4
1985		161	.275	.424	608	167	39	5	14	2.3	73	102	35	117	7	5	2	343	18	12	4	2.4	.968	OF-158
1986		155	.271	.413	584	158	30	4	15	2.6	70	84	42	91	5	3	0	331	20	4	5	2.3	.989	OF-154
1987		154	.264	.381	569	150	21	2	14	2.5	55	54	38	82	3	2	1	315	19	11	2	2.2	.968	OF-154, P-1
1988	2 teams	SEA A (78G –.250) PIT N (37G –.270)																						
″	total	115	.256	.341	410	105	18	1	5	1.2	39	32	18	70	1	3	1	206	5	4	2	1.9	.981	OF-110, DH-2
1989	2 teams	PIT N (100G –.282) HOU N (28G –.216)																						
″	total	128	.266	.421	432	115	26	4	11	2.5	50	64	37	53	1	15	4	249	13	6	2	2.2	.978	OF-110, 1B-10
1990	HOU N	118	.245	.364	368	90	14	0	10	2.7	42	55	26	64	0	15	3	227	12	6	6	2.2	.976	OF-108, 1B-1
1993	PIT N	10	.143	.143	14	2	0	0	0	0.0	0	0	0	9	0	4	0	5	2	1	0	1.6	.875	OF-5
10 yrs.		1201	.265	.398	4151	1098	209	26	98	2.4	451	521	253	672	27	75	16	2269	116	57	24	2.1	.977	OF-1131, 1B-11, DH-6, 3B-4, P-1

Grady Wilson

WILSON, GRADY HERBERT BR TR 6′½″ 170 lbs.
B. Nov. 23, 1922, Columbus, Ga.

Year	Team	Games	BA	SA	AB	H	2B	3B	HR	HR%	R	RBI	BB	SO	SB	Pinch Hit AB	Pinch Hit H	PO	A	E	DP	TC/G	FA	G by Pos
1948	PIT N	12	.100	.200	10	1	1	0	0	0.0	1	1	0	3	0	0	0	7	4	2	2	1.9	.846	SS-7

Hack Wilson

WILSON, LEWIS ROBERT BR TR 5′ 6″ 190 lbs.
B. Apr. 26, 1900, Ellwood City, Pa. D. Nov. 23, 1948, Baltimore, Md.
Hall of Fame 1979.

Year	Team	Games	BA	SA	AB	H	2B	3B	HR	HR%	R	RBI	BB	SO	SB	Pinch Hit AB	Pinch Hit H	PO	A	E	DP	TC/G	FA	G by Pos
1923	NY N	3	.200	.200	10	2	0	0	0	0.0	0	0	0	1	0	0	0	6	0	1	0	2.3	.857	OF-3
1924		107	.295	.486	383	113	19	12	10	2.6	62	57	44	46	4	4	0	230	8	8	2	2.4	.967	OF-103

Year	Team	Games	BA	SA	AB	H	2B	3B	HR	HR%	R	RBI	BB	SO	SB	Pinch Hit AB	Pinch Hit H	PO	A	E	DP	TC/G	FA	G by Pos

Hack Wilson *continued*

Year	Team	Games	BA	SA	AB	H	2B	3B	HR	HR%	R	RBI	BB	SO	SB	Pinch Hit AB	Pinch Hit H	PO	A	E	DP	TC/G	FA	G by Pos
1925		62	.239	.422	180	43	7	4	6	3.3	28	30	21	33	5	5	2	75	3	2	2	1.6	.975	OF-50
1926	CHI N	142	.321	.539	529	170	36	8	**21**	4.0	97	109	**69**	61	10	2	1	348	11	10	5	2.6	.973	OF-140
1927		146	.318	.579	551	175	30	12	**30**	5.4	119	129	71	**70**	13	0	0	400	13	14	3	2.9	.967	OF-146
1928		145	.313	.588	520	163	32	9	**31**	**6.0**	89	120	77	**94**	4	2	0	321	11	14	2	2.4	.960	OF-143
1929		150	.345	.618	574	198	30	5	39	6.8	135	**159**	78	**83**	3	0	0	380	14	12	4	2.7	.970	OF-150
1930		155	.356	**.723**	585	208	35	6	**56**	**9.6**	146	**190**[1]	**105**	**84**	3	0	0	357	9	19	2	2.5	.951	OF-155
1931		112	.261	.435	395	103	22	4	13	3.3	66	61	63	69	1	8	2	210	9	5	1	2.2	.978	OF-103
1932	BKN N	135	.297	.538	481	143	37	5	23	4.8	77	123	51	**85**	2	7	1	220	14	11	4	2.0	.955	OF-125
1933		117	.267	.389	360	96	13	2	9	2.5	41	54	52	50	7	16	5	192	21	10	3	2.3	.955	OF-90, 2B-5
1934	2 teams	BKN N (67G –.262)		PHI N (7G –.100)																				
"	total	74	.245	.365	192	47	5	0	6	3.1	24	30	43	37	0	20	5	82	3	2	6	1.8	.977	OF-49
12 yrs.		1348	.307	.545	4760	1461	266	67	244	5.1	884	1062	674	713	52	64	16	2821	116	108	34	2.4	.965	OF-1257, 2B-5
WORLD SERIES																								
1924	NY N	7	.233	.267	30	7	1	0	0	0.0	1	3	1	9	0	0	0	19	1	0	0	2.9	1.000	OF-7
1929	CHI N	5	.471	.588	17	8	0	1	0	0.0	2	0	4	3	0	0	0	14	0	1	0	3.0	.933	OF-5
2 yrs.		12	.319	.383	47	15	1	1	0	0.0	3	3	5	12	0	0	0	33	1	1	0	2.9	.971	OF-12

Henry Wilson

WILSON, HENRY C.
B. Apr. 8, 1877, Baltimore, Md. Deceased.

Year	Team	Games	BA	SA	AB	H	2B	3B	HR	HR%	R	RBI	BB	SO	SB	Pinch Hit AB	Pinch Hit H	PO	A	E	DP	TC/G	FA	G by Pos
1898	BAL N	1	.000	.000	2	0	0	0	0	0.0	0	0	1		0	0	0	3	2	0	0	5.0	1.000	C-1

Hickie Wilson

WILSON, GEORGE ARCHER
B. Brooklyn, N. Y. D. Nov. 28, 1914, Brooklyn, N. Y.
5′ 8″ 175 lbs.

Year	Team	Games	BA	SA	AB	H	2B	3B	HR	HR%	R	RBI	BB	SO	SB	Pinch Hit AB	Pinch Hit H	PO	A	E	DP	TC/G	FA	G by Pos
1884	BKN AA	24	.232	.280	82	19	4	0	0	0.0	13		5			0	0	80	16	12	5	4.2	.889	OF-12, C-10, 1B-3, 2B-1

Icehouse Wilson

WILSON, GEORGE PEACOCK
B. Sept. 14, 1912, Maricopa, Calif. D. Oct. 13, 1973, Moraga, Calif.
BR TR 6′ 186 lbs.

Year	Team	Games	BA	SA	AB	H	2B	3B	HR	HR%	R	RBI	BB	SO	SB	Pinch Hit AB	Pinch Hit H	PO	A	E	DP	TC/G	FA	G by Pos
1934	DET A	1	.000	.000	1	0	0	0	0	0.0	0	0	0	0	0	1	0	0	0	0	0	0.0	—	

Jim Wilson

WILSON, JAMES GEORGE
B. Dec. 29, 1960, Corvallis, Ore.
BR TR 6′ 3″ 230 lbs.

Year	Team	Games	BA	SA	AB	H	2B	3B	HR	HR%	R	RBI	BB	SO	SB	Pinch Hit AB	Pinch Hit H	PO	A	E	DP	TC/G	FA	G by Pos
1985	CLE A	4	.357	.357	14	5	0	0	0	0.0	2	4	1	3	0	0	0	23	0	0	1	5.8	1.000	1B-2, DH-2
1989	SEA A	5	.000	.000	8	0	0	0	0	0.0	0	0	0	3	0	4	0	0	0	0	0	0.0	.000	DH-5
2 yrs.		9	.227	.227	22	5	0	0	0	0.0	2	4	1	6	0	4	0	23	0	0	1	2.6	1.000	DH-7, 1B-2

Jimmie Wilson

WILSON, JAMES (Ace)
B. July 23, 1900, Philadelphia, Pa. D. May 31, 1947, Bradenton, Fla.
Manager 1934–38, 1941–44.
BR TR 6′ 1½″ 200 lbs.

Year	Team	Games	BA	SA	AB	H	2B	3B	HR	HR%	R	RBI	BB	SO	SB	Pinch Hit AB	Pinch Hit H	PO	A	E	DP	TC/G	FA	G by Pos
1923	PHI N	85	.262	.310	252	66	9	0	1	0.4	27	25	4	17	4	10	3	238	50	15	10	4.3	.950	C-69, OF-2
1924		95	.279	.421	280	78	16	3	6	2.1	32	39	17	12	5	11	2	249	93	12	16	4.2	.966	C-82, 1B-2, OF-1
1925		108	.328	.430	335	110	19	3	3	0.9	42	54	32	25	5	16	4	275	50	6	9	3.7	.982	C-89, OF-1
1926		90	.305	.398	279	85	10	2	4	1.4	40	32	25	20	3	11	3	228	78	16	5	4.1	.950	C-79
1927		128	.275	.332	443	122	15	2	2	0.5	50	45	34	15	13	4	1	377	82	12	12	3.8	.975	C-124
1928	2 teams	PHI N (21G –.300)		STL N (120G –.258)																				
"	total	141	.264	.351	481	127	30	3	2	0.4	56	63	54	32	12	0	0	469	103	9	17	4.2	.985	C-140
1929	STL N	120	.325	.464	394	128	27	8	4	1.0	59	71	43	19	4	1	1	410	80	14	16	4.2	.972	C-119
1930		107	.318	.434	362	115	25	7	1	0.3	54	58	28	17	8	8	3	456	67	7	11	5.0	.987	C-107
1931		115	.274	.337	383	105	20	2	0	0.0	45	51	28	15	5	5	0	498	75	9	15	5.3	.985	C-110
1932		92	.248	.343	274	68	16	2	2	0.7	36	28	15	18	9	10	3	344	58	8	11	5.2	.980	C-75, 1B-3, 2B-1
1933		113	.255	.309	369	94	17	0	1	0.3	34	45	23	33	6	5	1	498	58	10	13	5.3	.982	C-107
1934	PHI N	91	.292	.365	277	81	11	0	3	1.1	25	35	14	10	1	13	4	265	42	4	7	3.9	.987	C-77, 2B-1, 1B-1
1935		93	.279	.359	290	81	20	0	1	0.3	38	37	19	19	4	14	4	329	44	7	9	4.8	.982	C-78, 2B-1
1936		85	.278	.343	230	64	12	0	1	0.4	25	27	12	21	5	20	8	196	31	9	5	3.7	.962	C-63, 1B-1
1937		39	.276	.345	87	24	3	0	1	1.1	15	8	6	4	1	16	0	93	13	3	2	4.5	.972	C-22, 1B-2
1938		3	.000	.000	2	0	0	0	0	0.0	0	0	0	1	0	2	0	1	1	0	0	2.0	1.000	C-1
1939	CIN N	4	.333	.333	3	1	0	0	0	0.0	0	0	0	1	0	2	1	0	0	0	0	0.0	.000	C-1
1940		16	.243	.297	37	9	2	0	0	0.0	2	3	2	1	1	0	0	46	10	1	0	3.6	.982	C-16
18 yrs.		1525	.284	.370	4778	1358	252	32	32	0.7	580	621	356	280	86	148	38	4972	935	142	158	4.4	.977	C-1359, 1B-9, OF-4, 2B-3
WORLD SERIES																								
1928	STL N	3	.091	.182	11	1	1	0	0	0.0	1	1	0	3	0	0	0	14	2	2	0	6.0	.889	C-3
1930		4	.267	.333	15	4	1	0	0	0.0	0	2	0	1	0	0	0	23	0	0	0	5.8	1.000	C-4
1931		7	.217	.217	23	5	0	0	0	0.0	0	2	1	1	0	0	0	50	3	1	1	7.7	.981	C-7
1940	CIN N	6	.353	.353	17	6	0	0	0	0.0	2	0	1	2	1	0	0	26	2	0	1	4.7	1.000	C-6
4 yrs.		20	.242	.273	66	16	2	0	0	0.0	3	5	2	7	1	0	0	113	7	3	2	6.2	.976	C-20

Les Wilson

WILSON, LESTER WILBUR (Tug)
B. July 17, 1885, St. Louis, Mich. D. Apr. 4, 1969, Edmonds, Wash.
BL TR 5′11″ 170 lbs.

Year	Team	Games	BA	SA	AB	H	2B	3B	HR	HR%	R	RBI	BB	SO	SB	Pinch Hit AB	Pinch Hit H	PO	A	E	DP	TC/G	FA	G by Pos
1911	BOS A	5	.000	.000	7	0	0	0	0	0.0	0	0	2		0	1	0	4	0	0	0	1.3	1.000	OF-3

Mike Wilson

WILSON, SAMUEL MARSHALL
B. Dec. 2, 1896, Edge Hill, Pa. D. May 16, 1978, Boynton Beach, Fla.
BR TR 5′10½″ 160 lbs.

Year	Team	Games	BA	SA	AB	H	2B	3B	HR	HR%	R	RBI	BB	SO	SB	Pinch Hit AB	Pinch Hit H	PO	A	E	DP	TC/G	FA	G by Pos
1921	PIT N	5	.000	.000	4	0	0	0	0	0.0	0	0	0	0	0	0	0	3	2	1	0	1.2	.833	C-5

Mookie Wilson

WILSON, WILLIAM HAYWARD
B. Feb. 9, 1956, Bamberg, S. C.
BB TR 5′10″ 170 lbs.

Year	Team	Games	BA	SA	AB	H	2B	3B	HR	HR%	R	RBI	BB	SO	SB	Pinch Hit AB	Pinch Hit H	PO	A	E	DP	TC/G	FA	G by Pos
1980	NY N	27	.248	.352	105	26	5	3	0	0.0	16	4	12	19	7	0	0	72	1	2	0	2.9	.973	OF-26
1981		92	.271	.372	328	89	8	8	3	0.9	49	14	20	59	24	10	1	226	3	4	2	2.9	.983	OF-80
1982		159	.279	.369	639	178	25	9	5	0.8	90	55	32	102	58	7	2	415	12	5	4	2.8	.988	OF-156
1983		152	.276	.367	**638**	176	25	6	7	1.1	91	51	18	103	54	7	0	422	5	7	1	2.9	.984	OF-148
1984		154	.276	.409	587	162	28	10	10	1.7	88	54	26	90	46	8	5	396	8	4	6	2.8	.990	OF-146
1985		93	.276	.424	337	93	16	8	6	1.8	56	26	28	52	24	8	1	216	0	8	0	2.7	.964	OF-83
1986		123	.289	.430	381	110	17	5	9	2.4	61	45	32	72	25	20	7	228	7	5	2	2.1	.979	OF-114

Mookie Wilson *continued*

Year	Team	Games	BA	SA	AB	H	2B	3B	HR	HR%	R	RBI	BB	SO	SB	Pinch Hit AB	Pinch Hit H	PO	A	E	DP	TC/G	FA	G by Pos
1987		124	.299	.455	385	115	19	7	9	2.3	58	34	35	85	21	32	10	205	3	8	2	2.0	.963	OF-109
1988		112	.296	.431	378	112	17	5	8	2.1	61	41	27	63	15	22	7	200	4	5	1	2.0	.976	OF-104
1989	2 teams	NY N (80G –.205)	TOR A (54G –.298)																					
"	total	134	.251	.329	487	122	19	2	5	1.0	54	35	13	84	19	22	4	263	4	5	1	2.2	.982	OF-125
1990	TOR A	147	.265	.355	588	156	36	4	3	0.5	81	51	31	102	23	0	0	370	5	3	2	2.6	.992	OF-141, DH-6
1991		86	.241	.349	241	58	12	4	2	0.8	26	28	8	35	11	9	1	71	2	2	0	1.0	.973	OF-41, DH-34
12 yrs.		1403	.274	.386	5094	1397	227	71	67	1.3	731	438	282	866	327	145	38	3084	54	58	21	2.4	.982	OF-1273, DH-40
LEAGUE CHAMPIONSHIP SERIES																								
1986	NY N	6	.115	.115	26	3	0	0	0	0.0	2	1	1	7	1	0	0	16	1	0	1	2.8	1.000	OF-6
1988		4	.154	.154	13	2	0	0	0	0.0	2	1	2	2	0	1	0	6	0	0	0	2.0	1.000	OF-3
1989	TOR A	5	.263	.263	19	5	0	0	0	0.0	2	2	2	2	1	0	0	10	0	0	0	2.0	1.000	OF-5
1991		3	.250	.250	8	2	0	0	0	0.0	1	0	1	3	1	0	0	4	0	0	0	2.0	1.000	OF-2
4 yrs.		18	.182	.182	66	12	0	0	0	0.0	7	4	6	14	3	1	0	36	1	0	1	2.3	1.000	OF-16
WORLD SERIES																								
1986	NY N	7	.269	.308	26	7	1	0	0	0.0	3	0	1	6	3	0	0	15	2	0	0	2.4	1.000	OF-7

Neil Wilson

WILSON, SAMUEL O'NEILL
B. June 14, 1935, Lexington, Tenn.
BL TR 6′ 1″ 175 lbs.

Year	Team	Games	BA	SA	AB	H	2B	3B	HR	HR%	R	RBI	BB	SO	SB	Pinch Hit AB	Pinch Hit H	PO	A	E	DP	TC/G	FA	G by Pos
1960	SF N	6	.000	.000	10	0	0	0	0	0.0	0	0	1	2	0	0	0	23	0	1	0	4.0	.958	C-6

Nigel Wilson

WILSON, NIGEL EDWARD
B. Jan. 12, 1970, Oshawa, Ont., Canada.
BL TL 6′ 1″ 185 lbs.

Year	Team	Games	BA	SA	AB	H	2B	3B	HR	HR%	R	RBI	BB	SO	SB	Pinch Hit AB	Pinch Hit H	PO	A	E	DP	TC/G	FA	G by Pos
1993	FLA N	7	.000	.000	16	0	0	0	0	0.0	0	0	0	11	0	4	0	4	0	0	0	1.3	1.000	OF-3
1995	CIN N	5	.000	.000	7	0	0	0	0	0.0	0	0	0	4	0	3	0	2	0	0	0	1.0	1.000	OF-2
2 yrs.		12	.000	.000	23	0	0	0	0	0.0	0	0	0	15	0	7	0	6	0	0	0	1.2	1.000	OF-5

Owen Wilson

WILSON, JOHN OWEN (Chief)
B. Aug. 21, 1883, Austin, Tex. D. Feb. 22, 1954, Bertram, Tex.
BL TR 6′ 2″ 185 lbs.

Year	Team	Games	BA	SA	AB	H	2B	3B	HR	HR%	R	RBI	BB	SO	SB	Pinch Hit AB	Pinch Hit H	PO	A	E	DP	TC/G	FA	G by Pos
1908	PIT N	144	.227	.285	529	120	8	7	3	0.6	47	43	22		12	0	0	258	20	13	3	2.0	.955	OF-144
1909		154	.272	.374	569	155	22	12	4	0.7	64	59	19		17	0	0	292	19	14	7	2.1	.957	OF-154
1910		146	.276	.373	536	148	14	13	4	0.7	59	50	21	68	8	0	0	255	23	8	5	2.0	.972	OF-146
1911		148	.300	.472	544	163	34	12	12	2.2	72	107	41	55	10	1	1	273	20	7	10	2.1	.977	OF-146
1912		152	.300	.513	583	175	19	**36**[1]	11	1.9	80	95	35	67	16	0	0	324	20	14	5	2.4	.961	OF-152
1913		155	.266	.386	580	154	12	14	10	1.7	71	73	32	62	9	0	0	301	14	10	3	2.1	.969	OF-155
1914	STL N	154	.259	.393	580	150	27	12	9	1.6	64	73	32	66	14	0	0	312	34	6	11	2.3	.983	OF-154
1915		107	.276	.374	348	96	13	6	3	0.9	33	39	19	43	8	2	0	234	20	4	3	2.4	.984	OF-107
1916		120	.239	.299	355	85	8	2	3	0.8	30	32	20	46	4	6	0	181	11	9	3	1.8	.955	OF-113
9 yrs.		1280	.269	.391	4624	1246	157	114	59	1.3	520	571	241	407	98	9	1	2430	181	85	50	2.1	.968	OF-1271
WORLD SERIES																								
1909	PIT N	7	.154	.192	26	4	1	0	0	0.0	2	1	0	2	1	0	0	1	1	1	0	0.4	.667	OF-7

Parke Wilson

WILSON, PARKE ASEL
B. Oct. 26, 1867, Keithsburg, Ill. D. Dec. 20, 1934, Hermosa Beach, Calif.
BR TR 5′11″ 166 lbs.

Year	Team	Games	BA	SA	AB	H	2B	3B	HR	HR%	R	RBI	BB	SO	SB	Pinch Hit AB	Pinch Hit H	PO	A	E	DP	TC/G	FA	G by Pos
1893	NY N	31	.246	.351	114	28	4	1	2	1.8	16	21	7	9	5	0	0	106	20	4	1	4.2	.969	C-31
1894		49	.331	.434	175	58	5	5	1	0.6	35	32	14	5	8	0	0	246	28	31	9	6.2	.898	C-34, 1B-15
1895		67	.235	.273	238	56	9	0	0	0.0	32	30	14	16	11	0	0	313	68	29	20	6.1	.929	C-53, 1B-11, 3B-3
1896		75	.237	.245	253	60	2	0	0	0.0	33	23	13	14	9	2	0	278	64	23	4	5.0	.937	C-71, 1B-2
1897		46	.299	.396	154	46	9	3	0	0.0	29	22	15		5	1	0	222	26	13	9	5.8	.950	C-30, 1B-10, OF-4, 2B-1
1898		1	.000	.000	4	0	0	0	0	0.0	0	0	0		0	0	0	0	0	0	0	0.0	.000	OF-1
1899		97	.268	.329	328	88	8	6	0	0.0	49	42	43		16	2	0	416	140	49	34	6.1	.919	C-31, 1B-29, SS-19, 3B-15, OF-6
7 yrs.		366	.265	.325	1266	336	37	15	3	0.2	194	170	106	44	54	5	0	1581	346	149	77	5.7	.928	C-250, 1B-67, SS-19, 3B-18, OF-11, 2B-1

Red Wilson

WILSON, ROBERT JAMES
B. Mar. 7, 1929, Milwaukee, Wis.
BR TR 5′10″ 160 lbs.

Year	Team	Games	BA	SA	AB	H	2B	3B	HR	HR%	R	RBI	BB	SO	SB	Pinch Hit AB	Pinch Hit H	PO	A	E	DP	TC/G	FA	G by Pos
1951	CHI A	4	.273	.364	11	3	1	0	0	0.0	1	0	1	2	0	0	0	9	2	0	0	2.8	1.000	C-4
1952		2	.000	.000	3	0	0	0	0	0.0	0	0	0	1	0	0	0	8	1	0	0	4.5	1.000	C-2
1953		71	.250	.299	164	41	6	1	0	0.0	21	10	26	12	2	7	1	282	24	6	1	5.0	.981	C-63
1954	2 teams	CHI A (8G –.200)	DET A (54G –.282)																					
"	total	62	.274	.389	190	52	11	1	3	1.6	24	23	28	14	3	1	0	289	28	1	8	5.2	.997	C-61
1955	DET A	78	.220	.282	241	53	9	0	2	0.8	26	17	26	23	1	8	1	292	25	5	5	4.5	.984	C-72
1956		78	.289	.452	228	66	12	2	7	3.1	32	38	42	18	2	1	0	393	34	4	7	5.5	.991	C-78
1957		59	.242	.348	178	43	8	1	3	1.7	21	13	24	19	2	0	0	277	29	0	5	5.2	1.000	C-59
1958		103	.299	.379	298	89	13	1	3	1.0	31	29	35	30	10	3	0	565	34	5	6	6.0	.992	C-101
1959		67	.263	.408	228	60	17	2	4	1.8	28	35	10	23	2	3	0	374	25	5	8	6.3	.988	C-64
1960	2 teams	DET A (45G –.216)	CLE A (32G –.216)																					
"	total	77	.216	.275	222	48	7	0	2	0.9	22	24	22	21	3	2	1	392	34	7	1	5.8	.984	C-75
10 yrs.		601	.258	.356	1763	455	84	8	24	1.4	206	189	214	163	25	25	3	2881	236	33	41	5.4	.990	C-579

Squanto Wilson

WILSON, GEORGE FRANCIS
B. Mar. 29, 1889, Old Town, Me. D. Mar. 26, 1967, Winthrop, Me.
BB TR 5′ 9½″ 170 lbs.

Year	Team	Games	BA	SA	AB	H	2B	3B	HR	HR%	R	RBI	BB	SO	SB	Pinch Hit AB	Pinch Hit H	PO	A	E	DP	TC/G	FA	G by Pos
1911	DET A	5	.188	.188	16	3	0	0	0	0.0	2	0	2		0	0	0	20	7	3	0	6.0	.900	C-5
1914	BOS A	1	—	—	0	0	0	0	0	—	0	0	0	0	0	0	0	0	0	0	0	0.0	.000	1B-1
2 yrs.		6	.188	.188	16	3	0	0	0	0.0	2	0	2	0	0	0	0	20	7	3	0	5.0	.900	C-5, 1B-1

Tack Wilson

WILSON, MICHAEL
B. May 16, 1956, Shreveport, La.
BR TR 5′10″ 186 lbs.

Year	Team	Games	BA	SA	AB	H	2B	3B	HR	HR%	R	RBI	BB	SO	SB	Pinch Hit AB	Pinch Hit H	PO	A	E	DP	TC/G	FA	G by Pos
1983	MIN A	5	.250	.500	4	1	1	0	0	0.0	4	1	0	0	0	0	0	1	0	0	0	0.3	1.000	DH-2, OF-1
1987	CAL A	7	.500	.500	2	1	0	0	0	0.0	5	0	1	0	0	0	0	1	0	0	0	0.2	1.000	OF-4, DH-2
2 yrs.		12	.333	.500	6	2	1	0	0	0.0	9	1	1	0	0	0	0	2	0	0	0	0.2	1.000	OF-5, DH-4

Ted Wilson

WILSON, GEORGE WASHINGTON (Teddy) BL TR 6′ 1½″ 185 lbs.
B. Aug. 30, 1925, Cherryville, N. C. D. Oct. 29, 1974, Gastonia, N. C.

Year	Team	Games	BA	SA	AB	H	2B	3B	HR	HR%	R	RBI	BB	SO	SB	Pinch Hit AB	Pinch Hit H	PO	A	E	DP	TC/G	FA	G by Pos
1952	2 teams	CHI A (8G –.111) NY N (62G –.241)																						
″	total	70	.231	.339	121	28	7	0	2	1.7	9	17	4	16	0	**48**	12	62	0	3	2	2.7	.954	OF-22, 1B-2
1953	NY N	11	.125	.125	8	1	0	0	0	0.0	0	0	2	2	0	8	1	0	0	0	0	0.0	—	
1956	2 teams	NY N (53G –.132) NY A (11G –.167)																						
″	total	64	.138	.188	80	11	1	0	1	1.3	6	2	8	14	0	48	8	16	1	1	0	1.3	.944	OF-14
3 yrs.		145	.191	.273	209	40	8	0	3	1.4	15	19	14	32	0	104	21	78	1	4	2	2.2	.952	OF-36, 1B-2
WORLD SERIES																								
1956	NY A	1	.000	.000	1	0	0	0	0	0.0	0	0	0	1	0	1	0	0	0	0	0	0.0	—	

Tom Wilson

WILSON, THOMAS G. (Slats) BB TR 6′ 1½″ 160 lbs.
B. June 3, 1890, Fleming, Kans. D. Mar. 7, 1953, San Pedro, Calif.

Year	Team	Games	BA	SA	AB	H	2B	3B	HR	HR%	R	RBI	BB	SO	SB	Pinch Hit AB	Pinch Hit H	PO	A	E	DP	TC/G	FA	G by Pos
1914	WAS A	1	.000	.000	1	0	0	0	0	0.0	0	0	0	0	0	0	0	0	0	0	0	0.0	.000	C-1

Willie Wilson

WILSON, WILLIE JAMES BB TR 6′ 3″ 190 lbs.
B. July 9, 1955, Montgomery, Ala.

Year	Team	Games	BA	SA	AB	H	2B	3B	HR	HR%	R	RBI	BB	SO	SB	Pinch Hit AB	Pinch Hit H	PO	A	E	DP	TC/G	FA	G by Pos
1976	KC A	12	.167	.167	6	1	0	0	0	0.0	0	0	0	2	2	0	0	6	1	1	0	1.3	.875	OF-6
1977		13	.324	.382	34	11	2	0	0	0.0	10	1	1	8	6	0	0	24	0	1	0	2.3	.960	OF-9, DH-2
1978		127	.217	.278	198	43	8	2	0	0.0	43	16	16	33	46	0	0	171	6	4	2	1.5	.978	OF-112, DH-6
1979		154	.315	.420	588	185	18	13	6	1.0	113	49	28	92	**83**	0	0	384	13	6	0	2.6	.985	OF-152, DH-2
1980		161	.326	.421	**705**[1]	**230**	28	**15**	3	0.4	**133**	49	28	81	79	3	0	482	9	6	1	3.1	.988	OF-159
1981		102	.303	.364	439	133	10	7	1	0.2	54	32	18	42	34	0	0	299	14	4	3	3.1	.987	OF-101
1982		136	**.332**	.431	585	194	19	**15**	3	0.5	87	46	26	81	37	1	0	376	4	5	0	2.9	.987	OF-135
1983		137	.276	.352	576	159	22	8	2	0.3	90	33	33	75	59	3	1	354	3	9	0	2.7	.975	OF-136
1984		128	.301	.390	541	163	24	9	2	0.4	81	44	39	56	47	0	0	383	6	4	2	3.1	.990	OF-128
1985		141	.278	.408	605	168	25	**21**	4	0.7	87	43	29	94	43	0	0	378	4	2	1	2.7	.995	OF-140
1986		156	.269	.366	631	170	20	7	9	1.4	77	44	31	97	34	6	0	408	4	3	2	2.7	.993	OF-155
1987		146	.279	.377	610	170	18	**15**	4	0.7	97	30	32	88	59	1	0	342	3	1	1	2.4	.997	OF-143, DH-2
1988		147	.262	.333	591	155	17	**11**	1	0.2	81	37	22	106	35	4	1	365	1	4	0	2.6	.989	OF-142
1989		112	.253	.358	383	97	17	7	3	0.8	58	43	27	78	24	2	2	252	2	6	0	2.4	.977	OF-108, DH-1
1990		115	.290	.371	307	89	13	3	2	0.7	49	42	30	57	24	9	0	187	2	0	1	1.8	1.000	OF-106, DH-1
1991	OAK A	113	.238	.313	294	70	14	4	0	0.0	38	28	18	43	20	21	6	176	2	3	0	1.9	.983	OF-87, DH-9
1992		132	.270	.333	396	107	15	5	0	0.0	38	37	35	65	28	10	3	355	2	7	2	2.9	.981	OF-120, DH-5
1993	CHI N	105	.258	.348	221	57	11	3	1	0.5	29	11	11	40	7	37	9	109	1	1	0	1.4	.991	OF-82
1994		17	.238	.429	21	5	0	2	0	0.0	4	0	1	6	1	6	2	9	0	0	0	0.9	1.000	OF-10
19 yrs.		2154	.285	.376	7731	2207	281	147	41	0.5	1169	585	425	1144	668 **10th**	103	24	5060	77	67	15	2.5	.987	OF-2031, DH-28
DIVISIONAL PLAYOFF SERIES																								
1981	KC A	3	.308	.308	13	4	0	0	0	0.0	0	1	0	0	0	0	0	6	0	0	0	2.0	1.000	OF-3
LEAGUE CHAMPIONSHIP SERIES																								
1978	KC A	3	.250	.250	4	1	0	0	0	0.0	0	0	0	2	0	0	0	2	0	0	0	0.7	1.000	OF-3
1980		3	.308	.615	13	4	2	1	0	0.0	2	4	1	2	0	0	0	6	1	0	0	2.3	1.000	OF-3
1984		3	.154	.154	13	2	0	0	0	0.0	0	0	1	2	0	0	0	10	0	0	0	3.3	1.000	OF-3
1985		7	.310	.414	29	9	0	0	1	3.4	5	2	1	5	1	0	0	12	0	0	0	1.7	1.000	OF-7
1992	OAK A	6	.227	.273	22	5	1	0	0	0.0	0	0	1	5	7	0	0	16	0	0	0	2.3	1.000	OF-6, DH-1
5 yrs.		22	.259	.358	81	21	3	1	1	1.2	7	6	4	16	8 **4th**	0	0	46	1	0	0	2.0	1.000	OF-22, DH-1
WORLD SERIES																								
1980	KC A	6	.154	.192	26	4	1	0	0	0.0	3	0	4	12	2	0	0	15	1	0	0	2.7	1.000	OF-6
1985		7	.367	.433	30	11	0	1	0	0.0	2	3	1	4	3	0	0	19	1	0	0	2.9	1.000	OF-7
2 yrs.		13	.268	.321	56	15	1	1	0	0.0	5	3	5	16	5	0	0	34	2	0	0	2.8	1.000	OF-13

Ed Winceniak

WINCENIAK, EDWARD JOSEPH BR TR 5′ 9″ 165 lbs.
B. Apr. 16, 1929, Chicago, Ill.

Year	Team	Games	BA	SA	AB	H	2B	3B	HR	HR%	R	RBI	BB	SO	SB	Pinch Hit AB	Pinch Hit H	PO	A	E	DP	TC/G	FA	G by Pos
1956	CHI N	15	.118	.118	17	2	0	0	0	0.0	1	0	1	3	0	7	0	6	3	1	0	2.0	.900	3B-4, 2B-1
1957		17	.240	.360	50	12	3	0	1	2.0	5	8	2	9	0	5	1	20	20	2	5	3.5	.952	SS-5, 3B-4, 2B-3
2 yrs.		32	.209	.299	67	14	3	0	1	1.5	6	8	3	12	0	12	1	26	23	3	5	3.1	.942	3B-8, SS-5, 2B-4

Gordie Windhorn

WINDHORN, GORDON RAY BR TR 6′ 1″ 185 lbs.
B. Dec. 19, 1933, Watseka, Ill.

Year	Team	Games	BA	SA	AB	H	2B	3B	HR	HR%	R	RBI	BB	SO	SB	Pinch Hit AB	Pinch Hit H	PO	A	E	DP	TC/G	FA	G by Pos
1959	NY A	7	.000	.000	11	0	0	0	0	0.0	0	0	0	3	0	3	0	4	0	0	0	1.0	1.000	OF-4
1961	LA N	34	.242	.545	33	8	2	1	2	6.1	10	6	4	3	0	8	1	16	1	1	0	1.1	.944	OF-17
1962	2 teams	KC A (14G –.158) LA A (40G –.178)																						
″	total	54	.172	.281	64	11	7	0	0	0.0	10	2	7	13	1	12	0	30	0	0	0	0.7	1.000	OF-41
3 yrs.		95	.176	.333	108	19	9	1	2	1.9	20	8	11	19	1	23	1	50	1	1	0	0.8	.981	OF-62

Bill Windle

WINDLE, WILLIS BREWER BL TL 5′11½″ 170 lbs.
B. Dec. 13, 1904, Galena, Kans. D. Dec. 8, 1981, Corpus Christi, Tex.

Year	Team	Games	BA	SA	AB	H	2B	3B	HR	HR%	R	RBI	BB	SO	SB	Pinch Hit AB	Pinch Hit H	PO	A	E	DP	TC/G	FA	G by Pos
1928	PIT N	1	1.000	2.000	1	1	1	0	0	0.0	1	0	0	0	0	0	0	1	0	0	0	1.0	1.000	1B-1
1929		2	.000	.000	1	0	0	0	0	0.0	0	0	0	1	0	0	0	3	0	0	0	1.5	1.000	1B-2
2 yrs.		3	.500	1.000	2	1	1	0	0	0.0	1	0	0	1	0	0	0	4	0	0	0	1.3	1.000	1B-3

Bobby Wine

WINE, ROBERT PAUL, SR. BR TR 6′ 1″ 187 lbs.
Father of Robbie Wine.
B. Sept. 17, 1938, New York, N. Y.
Manager 1985.

Year	Team	Games	BA	SA	AB	H	2B	3B	HR	HR%	R	RBI	BB	SO	SB	Pinch Hit AB	Pinch Hit H	PO	A	E	DP	TC/G	FA	G by Pos
1960	PHI N	4	.143	.143	14	2	0	0	0	0.0	1	0	0	2	0	0	0	9	10	0	4	4.8	1.000	SS-4
1962		112	.244	.331	311	76	15	0	4	1.3	30	25	11	49	2	2	0	149	263	8	54	3.9	.981	SS-89, 3B-20
1963		142	.215	.306	418	90	14	3	6	1.4	29	44	14	83	1	2	0	224	369	17	73	4.4	.972	SS-132, 3B-8
1964		126	.212	.304	283	60	8	3	4	1.4	28	34	25	37	1	6	3	159	266	15	57	3.5	.966	SS-108, 3B-16
1965		139	.228	.292	394	90	8	1	5	1.3	31	33	31	69	0	1	0	223	387	21	85	4.5	.967	SS-135, 1B-4
1966		46	.236	.292	89	21	5	0	0	0.0	8	5	6	13	0	3	0	57	91	4	19	3.6	.974	SS-40, OF-2
1967		135	.190	.267	363	69	12	5	2	0.6	27	28	29	77	3	0	0	206	392	12	91	4.5	.980	SS-134, 1B-2

Bobby Wine *continued*

Year	Team	Games	BA	SA	AB	H	2B	3B	HR	HR%	R	RBI	BB	SO	SB	Pinch Hit AB	Pinch Hit H	PO	A	E	DP	TC/G	FA	G by Pos
1968		27	.169	.296	71	12	3	0	2	2.8	5	7	6	17	0	1	0	37	68	3	12	4.2	.972	SS-25, 3B-1
1969	**MON N**	121	.200	.251	370	74	8	1	3	0.8	23	25	28	49	0	2	0	214	367	31	98	5.1	.949	SS-118, 1B-1, 3B-1
1970		159	.232	.303	501	116	21	3	3	0.6	40	51	39	94	0	1	1	284	481	19	137	4.9	.976	SS-159
1971		119	.200	.235	340	68	9	0	1	0.3	25	16	25	46	0	0	0	221	321	10	76	4.6	.982	SS-119
1972		34	.222	.278	18	4	1	0	0	0.0	2	0	0	2	0	8	1	12	15	1	2	1.1	.964	3B-21, SS-4, 2B-1
12 yrs.		1164	.215	.286	3172	682	104	16	30	0.9	249	268	214	538	7	26	5	1795	3030	141	708	4.3	.972	SS-1067, 3B-67, 1B-7, OF-2, 2B-1

Robbie Wine

WINE, ROBERT PAUL, JR. BR TR 6′ 2″ 190 lbs.
Son of Bobby Wine.
B. July 13, 1962, Norristown, Pa.

Year	Team	Games	BA	SA	AB	H	2B	3B	HR	HR%	R	RBI	BB	SO	SB	Pinch Hit AB	Pinch Hit H	PO	A	E	DP	TC/G	FA	G by Pos
1986	**HOU N**	9	.250	.333	12	3	1	0	0	0.0	2	0	1	4	0	1	0	28	5	0	0	4.1	1.000	C-8
1987		14	.103	.138	29	3	1	0	0	0.0	1	0	1	10	0	3	0	40	7	1	2	4.0	.979	C-12
2 yrs.		23	.146	.195	41	6	2	0	0	0.0	3	0	2	14	0	4	0	68	12	1	2	4.1	.988	C-20

Ralph Winegarner

WINEGARNER, RALPH LEE BR TR 6′ 182 lbs.
B. Oct. 29, 1909, Benton, Kans. D. Apr. 14, 1988, Wichita, Kans.

Year	Team	Games	BA	SA	AB	H	2B	3B	HR	HR%	R	RBI	BB	SO	SB	Pinch Hit AB	Pinch Hit H	PO	A	E	DP	TC/G	FA	G by Pos
1930	**CLE A**	5	.455	.500	22	10	1	0	0	0.0	5	2	1	7	0	0	0	5	13	3	2	4.2	.857	3B-5
1932		7	.143	.143	7	1	0	0	0	0.0	1	0	0	5	0	2	0	0	3	1	1	0.8	.750	P-5
1934		32	.196	.294	51	10	2	0	1	2.0	9	5	3	11	0	10	1	2	17	0	0	0.8	1.000	P-22, OF-1
1935		65	.310	.488	84	26	4	1	3	3.6	11	17	9	12	1	29	11	21	21	3	3	1.4	.933	P-25, OF-4, 3B-3, 1B-1
1936		18	.125	.125	16	2	0	0	0	0.0	0	2	1	6	0	10	2	0	1	0	0	0.1	1.000	P-9
1949	**STL A**	9	.400	1.000	5	2	0	0	1	20.0	2	2	1	2	0	0	0	1	1	0	0	0.2	1.000	P-9
6 yrs.		136	.276	.405	185	51	7	1	5	2.7	28	28	15	43	1	51	14	29	56	7	6	1.1	.924	P-70, 3B-8, OF-5, 1B-1

Dave Winfield

WINFIELD, DAVID MARK BR TR 6′ 6″ 220 lbs.
B. Oct. 3, 1951, St. Paul, Minn.

Year	Team	Games	BA	SA	AB	H	2B	3B	HR	HR%	R	RBI	BB	SO	SB	Pinch Hit AB	Pinch Hit H	PO	A	E	DP	TC/G	FA	G by Pos
1973	**SD N**	56	.277	.383	141	39	4	1	3	2.1	9	12	12	19	0	17	8	65	1	3	0	1.9	.957	OF-36, 1B-1
1974		145	.265	.438	498	132	18	4	20	4.0	57	75	40	96	9	15	4	276	11	12	2	2.3	.960	OF-131
1975		143	.267	.403	509	136	20	2	15	2.9	74	76	69	82	23	2	0	302	9	9	1	2.3	.972	OF-138
1976		137	.283	.431	492	139	26	4	13	2.6	81	69	65	78	26	2	1	304	15	6	4	2.4	.982	OF-134
1977		157	.275	.467	615	169	29	7	25	4.1	104	92	58	75	16	2	1	368	15	11	3	2.5	.972	OF-156
1978		158	.308	.499	587	181	30	5	24	4.1	88	97	55	81	21	5	1	328	8	7	1	2.2	.980	OF-154, 1B-2
1979		159	.308	.558	597	184	27	10	34	5.7	97	**118**	85	71	15	2	0	344	14	5	3	2.3	.986	OF-157
1980		162	.276	.450	558	154	25	6	20	3.6	89	87	79	83	23	9	3	273	20	4	4	1.9	.987	OF-159
1981	**NY A**	105	.294	.464	388	114	25	1	13	3.4	52	68	43	41	11	4	3	196	1	3	0	1.9	.985	OF-102, DH-1
1982		140	.280	.560	539	151	24	8	37	6.9	84	106	45	64	5	1	0	279	17	8	2	2.2	.974	OF-135, DH-4
1983		152	.283	.513	598	169	26	8	32	5.4	99	116	58	77	15	3	2	313	5	7	2	2.2	.978	OF-151
1984		141	.340	.515	567	193	34	4	19	3.4	106	100	53	71	6	0	0	306	3	2	1	2.2	.994	OF-140
1985		155	.275	.471	633	174	34	6	26	4.1	105	114	52	96	19	1	1	316	13	3	3	2.2	.991	OF-152, DH-2
1986		154	.262	.462	565	148	31	5	24	4.2	90	104	77	106	6	7	1	292	9	5	5	2.0	.984	OF-145, DH-6, 3B-2
1987		156	.275	.457	575	158	22	1	27	4.7	83	97	76	96	5	4	2	253	6	3	1	1.7	.989	OF-145, DH-8
1988		149	.322	.530	559	180	37	2	25	4.5	96	107	69	88	9	4	0	276	3	3	1	1.9	.989	OF-141, DH-4
1990	**2 teams**	**NY A** (20G –.213) **CAL A** (112G –.275)																						
″	**total**	132	.267	.453	475	127	21	2	21	4.4	70	78	52	81	0	7	1	177	7	2	1	1.4	.989	OF-120, DH-10
1991	**CAL A**	150	.262	.472	568	149	27	4	28	4.9	75	86	56	109	7	1	0	198	7	2	1	1.4	.990	OF-115, DH-34
1992	**TOR A**	156	.290	.491	583	169	33	3	26	4.5	92	108	82	89	2	0	0	52	1	0	0	0.3	1.000	DH-130, OF-26
1993	**MIN A**	143	.271	.442	547	148	27	2	21	3.8	72	76	45	106	2	5	2	91	3	0	3	0.7	1.000	DH-105, OF-31, 1B-5
1994		77	.252	.425	294	74	15	3	10	3.4	35	43	31	51	2	0	0	3	0	0	0	0.0	1.000	DH-76, OF-1
1995	**CLE A**	46	.191	.287	115	22	5	0	2	1.7	11	4	14	26	1	10	2	0	0	0	0	0.0	.000	DH-39
22 yrs.		2973	.283	.475	11003	3110	540	88	465	4.2	1669	1833	1216	1686	223	101	32	5012	168	95	38	1.8	.982	OF-2469, DH-419, 1B-8, 3B-2
		7th			**6th**																			
DIVISIONAL PLAYOFF SERIES																								
1981	**NY A**	5	.350	.500	20	7	3	0	0	0.0	2	0	1	5	0	0	0	10	1	0	0	2.2	1.000	OF-5
LEAGUE CHAMPIONSHIP SERIES																								
1981	**NY A**	3	.154	.231	13	2	1	0	0	0.0	2	2	2	2	1	0	0	6	0	0	0	2.0	1.000	OF-3
1992	**TOR A**	6	.250	.542	24	6	1	0	2	8.3	7	3	4	2	0	0	0	0	0	0	0	0.0	.000	DH-6
2 yrs.		9	.216	.432	37	8	2	0	2	5.4	9	5	6	4	1	0	0	6	0	0	0	0.7	1.000	DH-6, OF-3
WORLD SERIES																								
1981	**NY A**	6	.045	.045	22	1	0	0	0	0.0	0	1	5	4	1	0	0	13	1	0	0	2.3	1.000	OF-6
1992	**TOR A**	6	.227	.273	22	5	1	0	0	0.0	0	3	2	3	0	0	0	7	0	0	0	1.2	1.000	OF-3, DH-3
2 yrs.		12	.136	.159	44	6	1	0	0	0.0	0	4	7	7	1	0	0	20	1	0	0	1.8	1.000	OF-9, DH-3

Al Wingo

WINGO, ABSALOM HOLBROOK (Red) BL TR 5′11″ 180 lbs.
Brother of Ivy Wingo.
B. May 6, 1898, Norcross, Ga. D. Oct. 9, 1964, Detroit, Mich.

Year	Team	Games	BA	SA	AB	H	2B	3B	HR	HR%	R	RBI	BB	SO	SB	Pinch Hit AB	Pinch Hit H	PO	A	E	DP	TC/G	FA	G by Pos
1919	**PHI A**	15	.305	.424	59	18	1	3	0	0.0	9	2	4	12	0	0	0	21	1	5	0	1.8	.815	OF-15
1924	**DET A**	78	.287	.413	150	43	12	2	1	0.7	21	26	21	13	2	29	10	59	3	5	2	1.6	.925	OF-43
1925		130	.370	.527	440	163	34	10	5	1.1	104	68	69	31	14	7	1	282	16	9	6	2.5	.971	OF-122
1926		108	.282	.356	298	84	19	0	1	0.3	45	45	52	32	4	24	6	155	13	14	2	2.4	.923	OF-74, 3B-2
1927		75	.234	.321	137	32	8	2	0	0.0	15	20	25	14	1	33	6	43	6	6	2	1.6	.891	OF-34
1928		87	.285	.380	242	69	13	2	2	0.8	30	30	40	17	2	12	0	144	5	5	1	2.2	.968	OF-71
6 yrs.		493	.308	.423	1326	409	87	19	9	0.7	224	191	211	119	23	105	23	704	44	44	13	2.2	.944	OF-359, 3B-2

Ed Wingo

WINGO, EDMUND ARMAND BR TR 5′ 5″ 145 lbs.
Born Edmund Armand LaRiviere.
B. Oct. 8, 1895, Ste. Anne de Bellevue, Canada D. Dec. 5, 1964, Lachine, Que., Canada.

Year	Team	Games	BA	SA	AB	H	2B	3B	HR	HR%	R	RBI	BB	SO	SB	Pinch Hit AB	Pinch Hit H	PO	A	E	DP	TC/G	FA	G by Pos
1920	**PHI A**	1	.250	.250	4	1	0	0	0	0.0	0	1	0	0	0	0	0	8	1	0	0	9.0	1.000	C-1

Ivy Wingo

WINGO, IVEY BROWN BL TR 5′10″ 160 lbs.
Brother of Al Wingo.
B. July 8, 1890, Gainesville, Ga. D. Mar. 1, 1941, Norcross, Ga.
Manager 1916.

Year	Team	Games	BA	SA	AB	H	2B	3B	HR	HR%	R	RBI	BB	SO	SB	Pinch Hit AB	Pinch Hit H	PO	A	E	DP	TC/G	FA	G by Pos
1911	STL N	25	.211	.246	57	12	2	0	0	0.0	4	3	3	7	0	6	0	65	22	8	3	5.3	.916	C-18
1912		100	.265	.394	310	82	18	8	2	0.6	38	44	23	45	8	9	1	360	148	23	11	5.8	.957	C-92
1913		111	.256	.344	305	78	5	8	2	0.7	25	35	17	41	18	10	4	393	139	31	14	5.5	.945	C-97, 1B-5, OF-1
1914		80	.300	.426	237	71	8	5	4	1.7	24	26	18	17	15	4	2	276	93	16	7	5.5	.958	C-70
1915	CIN N	119	.221	.316	339	75	11	6	3	0.9	26	29	13	33	10	17	2	415	124	20	15	5.7	.964	C-97, OF-1
1916		119	.245	.349	347	85	8	11	2	0.6	30	40	25	27	4	10	5	463	170	28	15	6.2	.958	C-107
1917		121	.266	.376	399	106	16	11	2	0.5	37	39	25	13	9	1	0	459	151	21	12	5.3	.967	C-120
1918		100	.254	.337	323	82	15	6	0	0.0	36	31	19	18	6	2	1	321	111	13	13	4.5	.971	C-93, OF-5
1919		76	.273	.371	245	67	12	6	0	0.0	30	27	23	19	4	1	0	266	106	12	6	5.1	.969	C-75
1920		108	.264	.338	364	96	11	5	2	0.5	32	38	19	13	6	0	0	370	117	21	14	4.7	.959	C-107, 2B-2
1921		97	.268	.363	295	79	7	6	3	1.0	20	38	21	14	3	4	1	318	101	19	11	4.7	.957	C-92, OF-1
1922		80	.285	.392	260	74	13	3	3	1.2	24	45	23	11	1	2	0	211	81	11	6	3.9	.964	C-78
1923		61	.263	.357	171	45	9	2	1	0.6	10	24	9	11	1	4	1	172	44	7	2	3.9	.969	C-57
1924		66	.286	.370	192	55	5	4	1	0.5	21	23	14	8	1	1	0	220	50	3	7	4.1	.989	C-65, 1B-1
1925		55	.205	.253	146	30	7	0	0	0.0	6	12	11	8	1	0	0	154	38	7	7	3.6	.965	C-55
1926		7	.200	.200	10	2	0	0	0	0.0	0	1	1	0	0	0	0	12	1	0	0	1.9	1.000	C-7
1929		1	.000	.000	1	0	0	0	0	0.0	0	0	0	0	0	0	0	0	0	0	0	0.0	.000	C-1
17 yrs.		1326	.260	.356	4001	1039	147	81	25	0.6	363	455	264	285	87	71	17	4475	1496	240	143	5.0	.961	C-1231, OF-8, 1B-6, 2B-2
WORLD SERIES																								
1919	CIN N	3	.571	.571	7	4	0	0	0	0.0	1	1	3	1	0	0	0	8	3	0	0	3.7	1.000	C-3

George Winkelman

WINKELMAN, GEORGE EDWARD BL TL
B. June 14, 1861, Philadelphia, Pa. D. May 19, 1960, Washington, D. C.

Year	Team	Games	BA	SA	AB	H	2B	3B	HR	HR%	R	RBI	BB	SO	SB	Pinch Hit AB	Pinch Hit H	PO	A	E	DP	TC/G	FA	G by Pos
1883	LOU AA	4	.000	.000	13	0	0	0	0	0.0	2		1			0	0	8	2	6	0	4.0	.625	OF-4
1886	WAS N	1	.200	.200	5	1	0	0	0	0.0	0	0	0	1	0	0	0	0	0	0	0	0.0		OF-1, P-1
2 yrs.		5	.056	.056	18	1	0	0	0	0.0	2	0	1	1	0	0	0	8	2	6	0	2.7	.625	OF-5, P-1

Herm Winningham

WINNINGHAM, HERMAN SON BL TR 5′11″ 185 lbs.
B. Dec. 1, 1961, Orangeburg, S. C.

Year	Team	Games	BA	SA	AB	H	2B	3B	HR	HR%	R	RBI	BB	SO	SB	Pinch Hit AB	Pinch Hit H	PO	A	E	DP	TC/G	FA	G by Pos
1984	NY N	14	.407	.519	27	11	1	1	0	0.0	5	5	1	7	2	4	1	7	0	0	0	0.7	1.000	OF-10
1985	MON N	125	.237	.317	312	74	6	5	3	1.0	30	21	28	72	20	13	6	229	6	4	2	2.1	.983	OF-116
1986		90	.216	.346	185	40	6	3	4	2.2	23	11	18	51	12	23	3	97	2	2	1	1.5	.980	OF-66, SS-1
1987		137	.239	.349	347	83	20	3	4	1.2	34	41	34	68	29	20	5	225	5	6	1	1.8	.975	OF-131
1988	2 teams	MON N (47G –.233) CIN N (53G –.230)																						
″	total	100	.232	.286	203	47	3	4	0	0.0	16	21	17	45	12	21	4	128	1	1	0	1.8	.992	OF-72
1989	CIN N	115	.251	.355	251	63	11	3	3	1.2	40	13	24	50	14	29	7	146	3	3	0	1.8	.980	OF-85
1990		84	.256	.425	160	41	8	5	3	1.9	20	17	14	31	6	20	5	89	3	0	0	1.4	1.000	OF-64
1991		98	.225	.290	169	38	6	1	1	0.6	17	4	11	40	4	33	13	99	2	5	0	1.6	.953	OF-66
1992	BOS A	105	.235	.291	234	55	8	1	1	0.4	27	14	10	53	6	38	**12**	112	7	3	1	1.7	.975	OF-67, DH-6
9 yrs.		868	.239	.334	1888	452	69	26	19	1.0	212	147	157	417	105	201	56	1132	29	24	5	1.7	.980	OF-677, DH-6, SS-1
LEAGUE CHAMPIONSHIP SERIES																								
1990	CIN N	3	.286	.429	7	2	1	0	0	0.0	1	1	1	1	1	1	0	7	0	0	0	3.5	1.000	OF-2
WORLD SERIES																								
1990	CIN N	2	.500	.500	4	2	0	0	0	0.0	1	0	0	0	0	1	0	3	0	0	0	3.0	1.000	OF-1

Tom Winsett

WINSETT, JOHN THOMAS (Long Tom) BL TR 6′ 2″ 190 lbs.
B. Nov. 24, 1909, McKenzie, Tenn. D. July 20, 1987, Memphis, Tenn.

Year	Team	Games	BA	SA	AB	H	2B	3B	HR	HR%	R	RBI	BB	SO	SB	Pinch Hit AB	Pinch Hit H	PO	A	E	DP	TC/G	FA	G by Pos
1930	BOS A	1	.000	.000	1	0	0	0	0	0.0	0	0	0	1	0	0	0	0	0	0	0	0.0	—	
1931		64	.197	.250	76	15	1	0	1	1.3	6	7	4	21	0	**52**	11	13	1	0	0	1.8	1.000	OF-8
1933		6	.083	.083	12	1	0	0	0	0.0	1	0	1	6	0	2	0	1	0	0	0	0.3	1.000	OF-4
1935	STL N	7	.500	.583	12	6	1	0	0	0.0	2	2	2	3	0	5	2	0	0	0	0	0.0	.000	OF-2
1936	BKN N	22	.235	.353	85	20	7	0	1	1.2	13	18	11	14	0	1	1	42	3	0	0	2.1	1.000	OF-21
1937		118	.237	.351	350	83	15	5	5	1.4	32	42	45	64	3	15	5	209	6	9	1	2.2	.960	OF-101, P-1
1938		12	.300	.433	30	9	1	0	1	3.3	6	7	6	4	0	2	0	15	0	2	0	1.9	.882	OF-9
7 yrs.		230	.237	.341	566	134	25	5	8	1.4	60	76	69	113	3	77	19	280	10	11	1	2.1	.963	OF-145, P-1

Matt Winters

WINTERS, MATTHEW LITTLETON BL TR 6′ 3″ 215 lbs.
B. Mar. 18, 1960, Buffalo, N. Y.

Year	Team	Games	BA	SA	AB	H	2B	3B	HR	HR%	R	RBI	BB	SO	SB	Pinch Hit AB	Pinch Hit H	PO	A	E	DP	TC/G	FA	G by Pos
1989	KC A	42	.234	.346	107	25	6	0	2	1.9	14	9	14	23	0	7	1	45	1	3	0	1.4	.939	OF-31, DH-3

Kettle Wirts

WIRTS, ELWOOD VERNON BR TR 5′11″ 170 lbs.
B. Oct. 31, 1897, Consumnes, Calif. D. July 12, 1968, Sacramento, Calif.

Year	Team	Games	BA	SA	AB	H	2B	3B	HR	HR%	R	RBI	BB	SO	SB	Pinch Hit AB	Pinch Hit H	PO	A	E	DP	TC/G	FA	G by Pos
1921	CHI N	7	.182	.182	11	2	0	0	0	0.0	0	1	0	3	0	2	2	13	3	0	1	3.2	1.000	C-5
1922		31	.172	.259	58	10	2	0	1	1.7	7	6	12	15	0	3	0	55	6	2	1	2.3	.968	C-27
1923		5	.200	.200	5	1	0	0	0	0.0	2	1	2	0	0	0	0	10	0	0	0	3.3	1.000	C-3
1924	CHI A	6	.083	.083	12	1	0	0	0	0.0	0	0	2	2	1	0	0	9	7	0	0	3.2	1.000	C-5
4 yrs.		49	.163	.221	86	14	2	0	1	1.2	9	8	16	20	1	5	2	87	16	2	2	2.6	.981	C-40

Bill Wise

WISE, WILLIAM E.
B. Mar. 15, 1861, Washington, D. C. D. May 5, 1940, Washington, D. C.

Year	Team	Games	BA	SA	AB	H	2B	3B	HR	HR%	R	RBI	BB	SO	SB	Pinch Hit AB	Pinch Hit H	PO	A	E	DP	TC/G	FA	G by Pos
1882	BAL AA	5	.100	.150	20	2	1	0	0	0.0	2		0			0	0	4	7	2	1	2.6	.846	P-3, OF-2
1884	WAS U	85	.233	.307	339	79	17	1	2	0.6	51		12			0	0	80	137	49	7	2.6	.816	P-50, OF-43, 3B-8, SS-2, 1B-1
1886	WAS N	1	.000	.000	3	0	0	0	0	0.0	0	0	0	1		0	0	0	0	0	0	0.0	.000	P-1
3 yrs.		91	.224	.296	362	81	18	1	2	0.6	53	0	12	1		0	0	84	144	51	8	2.5	.817	P-54, OF-45, 3B-8, SS-2, 1B-1

Casey Wise

WISE, KENDALL COLE BB TR 6′ 170 lbs.
Son of Hughie Wise.
B. Sept. 8, 1932, Lafayette, Ind.

Year	Team	Games	BA	SA	AB	H	2B	3B	HR	HR%	R	RBI	BB	SO	SB	Pinch Hit AB	Pinch Hit H	PO	A	E	DP	TC/G	FA	G by Pos
1957	CHI N	43	.179	.226	106	19	3	1	0	0.0	12	7	11	14	0	4	0	69	84	10	21	4.5	.939	2B-31, SS-5
1958	MIL N	31	.197	.211	71	14	1	0	0	0.0	8	0	4	8	1	8	0	27	50	1	7	4.3	.987	2B-10, SS-7, 3B-1

Casey Wise *continued*

Year	Team	Games	BA	SA	AB	H	2B	3B	HR	HR%	R	RBI	BB	SO	SB	Pinch Hit AB	Pinch Hit H	PO	A	E	DP	TC/G	FA	G by Pos
1959		22	.171	.237	76	13	2	0	1	1.3	11	5	10	5	0	1	0	48	44	3	15	3.8	.968	2B-20, SS-5
1960	DET A	30	.147	.294	68	10	0	2	2	2.9	6	5	4	9	1	3	0	33	59	1	12	3.3	.989	2B-17, SS-10, 3B-1
4 yrs.		126	.174	.240	321	56	6	3	3	0.9	37	17	29	36	2	16	0	177	237	15	55	4.0	.965	2B-78, SS-27, 3B-2
WORLD SERIES																								
1958	MIL N	2	.000	.000	1	0	0	0	0	0.0	0	0	0	1	0	1	0	0	0	0	0	0.0	—	

Hughie Wise

WISE, HUGH EDWARD
Father of Casey Wise.
B. Mar. 9, 1906, Campbellsville, Ky. D. July 21, 1987, Plantation, Fla.
BB TR 6′ 178 lbs.

Year	Team	Games	BA	SA	AB	H	2B	3B	HR	HR%	R	RBI	BB	SO	SB	Pinch Hit AB	Pinch Hit H	PO	A	E	DP	TC/G	FA	G by Pos
1930	DET A	2	.333	.333	6	2	0	0	0	0.0	0	0	0	0	0	0	0	9	2	0	0	5.5	1.000	C-2

Nick Wise

WISE, NICHOLAS JOSEPH
B. June 15, 1866, Boston, Mass. D. Jan. 15, 1923, Boston, Mass.
BR TR 5′11″ 194 lbs.

Year	Team	Games	BA	SA	AB	H	2B	3B	HR	HR%	R	RBI	BB	SO	SB	Pinch Hit AB	Pinch Hit H	PO	A	E	DP	TC/G	FA	G by Pos
1888	BOS N	1	.000	.000	3	0	0	0	0	0.0	0	0	0	0	0	0	0	0	0	0	0	0.0		OF-1, C-1

Sam Wise

WISE, SAMUEL WASHINGTON
B. Aug. 18, 1857, Akron, Ohio D. Jan. 22, 1910, Akron, Ohio.
BL TR 5′10½″ 170 lbs.

Year	Team	Games	BA	SA	AB	H	2B	3B	HR	HR%	R	RBI	BB	SO	SB	Pinch Hit AB	Pinch Hit H	PO	A	E	DP	TC/G	FA	G by Pos
1881	DET N	1	.500	.500	4	2	0	0	0	0.0	0	0	0	2		0	0	1	3	3	0	7.0	.571	3B-1
1882	BOS N	78	.221	.326	298	66	11	4	4	1.3	44	34	5	45		0	0	90	199	54	13	4.4	.843	SS-72, 3B-6
1883		96	.271	.397	406	110	25	7	4	1.0	73	58	13	74		0	0	134	274	88	21	5.2	.823	SS-96
1884		114	.214	.319	426	91	15	9	4	0.9	60		25	**104**		0	0	175	330	70	21	5.0	.878	SS-107, 2B-7
1885		107	.283	.406	424	120	20	10	4	0.9	71	46	25	61		0	0	196	338	86	35	5.8	.861	SS-79, 2B-22, OF-6
1886		96	.289	.432	387	112	19	12	4	1.0	71	72	33	61		0	0	592	100	55	27	7.9	.926	1B-57, 2B-20, SS-18
1887		113	.334	.522	467	156	27	17	9	1.9	103	92	36	44	43	0	0	231	289	81	29	5.2	.865	SS-72, OF-27, 2B-16
1888		105	.240	.372	417	100	19	12	4	1.0	66	40	34	66	33	0	0	242	281	62	37	5.5	.894	SS-89, 3B-6, 1B-5, OF-4, 2B-2
1889	WAS N	121	.250	.341	472	118	15	8	4	0.8	79	62	61	62	24	0	0	245	323	76	36	5.3	.882	2B-72, SS-26, 3B-13, OF-10
1890	BUF P	119	.293	.430	505	148	29	11	6	1.2	95	102	46	45	19	0	0	328	375	73	58	6.5	.906	2B-119
1891	BAL AA	103	.247	.317	388	96	14	5	1	0.3	70	48	62	52	33	0	0	229	308	68	32	5.9	.888	2B-99, SS-4
1893	WAS N	122	.311	.457	521	162	27	17	5	1.0	102	77	49	27	20	0	0	345	380	79	53	6.6	.902	2B-91, 3B-31
12 yrs.		1175	.272	.397	4715	1281	221	112	49	1.0	834	631	389	643	172	0	0	2808	3200	795	362	5.8	.883	SS-563, 2B-448, 1B-62, 3B-57, OF-47

Phil Wisner

WISNER, PHILIP N.
B. July 1869, Washington, D. C. D. July 5, 1936, Washington, D. C.
TR

Year	Team	Games	BA	SA	AB	H	2B	3B	HR	HR%	R	RBI	BB	SO	SB	Pinch Hit AB	Pinch Hit H	PO	A	E	DP	TC/G	FA	G by Pos
1895	WAS N	1	—	—	0	0	0	0	0	—	0	0	0	0	0	0	0	0	1	3	0	4.0	.250	SS-1

Dave Wissman

WISSMAN, DAVID ALVIN
B. Feb. 17, 1941, Greenfield, Mass.
BL TR 6′ 2″ 178 lbs.

Year	Team	Games	BA	SA	AB	H	2B	3B	HR	HR%	R	RBI	BB	SO	SB	Pinch Hit AB	Pinch Hit H	PO	A	E	DP	TC/G	FA	G by Pos
1964	PIT N	16	.148	.148	27	4	0	0	0	0.0	2	0	1	9	0	6	2	11	0	0	0	1.1	1.000	OF-10

Tex Wisterzil

WISTERZIL, GEORGE JOHN
B. Mar. 7, 1891, Detroit, Mich. D. June 27, 1964, San Antonio, Tex.
BR TR 5′ 9½″ 150 lbs.

Year	Team	Games	BA	SA	AB	H	2B	3B	HR	HR%	R	RBI	BB	SO	SB	Pinch Hit AB	Pinch Hit H	PO	A	E	DP	TC/G	FA	G by Pos
1914	BKN F	149	.257	.328	534	137	18	10	0	0.0	54	66	34		17	0	0	207	294	23	24	3.5	.956	3B-149, 2B-1
1915	3 teams BKN F (36G –.311) CHI F (49G –.244) STL F (8G –.208)																							
″	total	93	.265	.320	294	78	8	4	0	0.0	29	39	31		12	5	0	123	194	14	13	3.8	.958	3B-87
2 yrs.		242	.260	.325	828	215	26	14	0	0.0	83	105	65		29	5	0	330	488	37	37	3.6	.957	3B-236, 2B-1

Mickey Witek

WITEK, NICHOLAS JOSEPH
B. Dec. 19, 1915, Luzerne, Pa. D. Sept. 24, 1990, Kingston, Pa.
BR TR 5′10″ 170 lbs.

Year	Team	Games	BA	SA	AB	H	2B	3B	HR	HR%	R	RBI	BB	SO	SB	Pinch Hit AB	Pinch Hit H	PO	A	E	DP	TC/G	FA	G by Pos
1940	NY N	119	.256	.293	433	111	7	0	3	0.7	34	31	24	17	2	1	1	257	412	29	62	5.8	.958	SS-89, 2B-32
1941		26	.362	.447	94	34	5	0	1	1.1	11	16	4	2	0	0	0	70	70	10	17	6.5	.933	2B-23
1942		148	.260	.344	553	144	19	6	5	0.9	72	48	36	20	2	1	0	371	441	18	72	5.6	.978	2B-147
1943		153	.314	.370	622	195	17	0	6	1.0	68	55	41	23	1	0	0	401	505	31	90	6.1	.967	2B-153
1946		82	.264	.366	284	75	13	2	4	1.4	32	29	28	10	1	7	2	138	150	20	23	4.0	.935	2B-42, 3B-35
1947		51	.219	.313	160	35	4	1	3	1.9	22	17	15	12	1	8	0	105	128	6	28	5.6	.975	2B-40, 3B-3
1949	NY A	1	1.000	1.000	1	1	0	0	0	0.0	0	0	0	0	0	1	1	0	0	0	0	0.0	—	
7 yrs.		580	.277	.347	2147	595	65	9	22	1.0	239	196	148	84	7	18	4	1342	1706	114	292	5.6	.964	2B-437, SS-89, 3B-38

Corky Withrow

WITHROW, RAYMOND WALLACE
B. Nov. 28, 1937, High Coal, W. Va.
BR TR 6′ 3½″ 197 lbs.

Year	Team	Games	BA	SA	AB	H	2B	3B	HR	HR%	R	RBI	BB	SO	SB	Pinch Hit AB	Pinch Hit H	PO	A	E	DP	TC/G	FA	G by Pos
1963	STL N	6	.000	.000	9	0	0	0	0	0.0	0	1	0	2	0	4	0	3	0	0	0	1.5	1.000	OF-2

Frank Withrow

WITHROW, FRANK BLAINE (Kid)
B. June 14, 1891, Greenwood, Mo. D. Sept. 5, 1966, Omaha, Neb.
BR TR 5′11½″ 187 lbs.

Year	Team	Games	BA	SA	AB	H	2B	3B	HR	HR%	R	RBI	BB	SO	SB	Pinch Hit AB	Pinch Hit H	PO	A	E	DP	TC/G	FA	G by Pos
1920	PHI N	48	.182	.227	132	24	4	1	0	0.0	8	12	8	26	0	0	0	164	51	6	10	4.6	.973	C-48
1922		10	.333	.429	21	7	2	0	0	0.0	3	3	3	5	0	2	0	24	6	3	1	4.1	.909	C-8
2 yrs.		58	.203	.255	153	31	6	1	0	0.0	11	15	11	31	0	2	0	188	57	9	11	4.5	.965	C-56

Ron Witmeyer

WITMEYER, RONALD HERMAN
B. June 28, 1967, West Islip, N. Y.
BL TL 6′ 3″ 215 lbs.

Year	Team	Games	BA	SA	AB	H	2B	3B	HR	HR%	R	RBI	BB	SO	SB	Pinch Hit AB	Pinch Hit H	PO	A	E	DP	TC/G	FA	G by Pos
1991	OAK A	11	.053	.053	19	1	0	0	0	0.0	0	0	0	5	0	4	0	32	3	0	2	4.4	1.000	1B-8

Whitey Witt

WITT, LAWTON WALTER
Born Ladislaw Waldemar Wittkowski.
B. Sept. 28, 1895, Orange, Mass. D. July 14, 1988, Salem County, N. J.
BL TR 5′ 7″ 150 lbs.

Year	Team	Games	BA	SA	AB	H	2B	3B	HR	HR%	R	RBI	BB	SO	SB	Pinch Hit AB	Pinch Hit H	PO	A	E	DP	TC/G	FA	G by Pos
1916	PHI A	143	.245	.337	563	138	16	15	2	0.4	64	36	55	71	19	1	0	299	423	78	59	5.6	.902	SS-142
1917		128	.252	.299	452	114	13	4	0	0.0	62	28	65	45	12	4	0	209	370	40	41	5.0	.935	SS-111, OF-7, 3B-6
1919		122	.267	.326	460	123	15	6	0	0.0	56	33	46	26	11	4	1	267	166	19	25	3.9	.958	OF-59, 2B-56, 3B-2
1920		65	.321	.413	218	70	11	3	1	0.5	29	25	27	16	2	2	0	99	30	5	5	2.2	.963	OF-49, 2B-11, SS-2
1921		154	.315	.418	629	198	31	11	4	0.6	100	45	77	52	16	0	0	288	15	13	3	2.1	.959	OF-154
1922	NY A	140	.297	.364	528	157	11	6	4	0.8	98	40	**89**	29	5	1	1	312	9	8	1	2.4	.976	OF-139
1923		146	.314	.408	596	187	18	10	6	1.0	113	56	67	42	2	2	0	357	14	8	4	2.6	.979	OF-144

Whitey Witt *continued*

Year	Team	Games	BA	SA	AB	H	2B	3B	HR	HR%	R	RBI	BB	SO	SB	Pinch Hit AB	Pinch Hit H	PO	A	E	DP	TC/G	FA	G by Pos
1924		147	.297	.362	600	178	26	5	1	0.2	88	36	45	20	9	3	0	362	11	9	1	2.7	.976	OF-143
1925		31	.200	.300	40	8	2	1	0	0.0	9	0	6	2	1	9	3	19	1	0	0	2.0	1.000	OF-10
1926	BKN N	63	.259	.294	85	22	1	1	0	0.0	13	3	12	6	1	28	6	44	2	4	1	2.3	.920	OF-22
10 yrs.		1139	.287	.364	4171	1195	144	62	18	0.4	632	302	489	309	78	54	11	2256	1041	184	140	3.3	.947	OF-727, SS-255, 2B-67, 3B-8
WORLD SERIES																								
1922	NY A	5	.222	.389	18	4	1	1	0	0.0	1	0	1	2	0	0	0	7	1	0	0	1.6	1.000	OF-5
1923		6	.240	.320	25	6	2	0	0	0.0	1	4	1	1	0	0	0	18	1	0	0	3.2	1.000	OF-6
2 yrs.		11	.233	.349	43	10	3	1	0	0.0	2	4	2	3	0	0	0	25	2	0	0	2.5	1.000	OF-11

Jerry Witte

WITTE, JEROME CHARLES BR TR 6′ 1″ 190 lbs.
B. July 30, 1915, St. Louis, Mo.

Year	Team	Games	BA	SA	AB	H	2B	3B	HR	HR%	R	RBI	BB	SO	SB	Pinch Hit AB	Pinch Hit H	PO	A	E	DP	TC/G	FA	G by Pos
1946	STL A	18	.192	.301	73	14	2	0	2	2.7	7	4	0	18	0	0	0	140	8	5	15	8.5	.967	1B-18
1947		34	.141	.242	99	14	2	1	2	2.0	4	12	11	22	0	8	0	218	16	4	21	8.8	.983	1B-27
2 yrs.		52	.163	.267	172	28	4	1	4	2.3	11	16	11	40	0	8	0	358	24	9	36	8.7	.977	1B-45

John Wockenfuss

WOCKENFUSS, JOHNNY BILTON BR TR 6′ 190 lbs.
B. Feb. 27, 1949, Welch, W. Va.

Year	Team	Games	BA	SA	AB	H	2B	3B	HR	HR%	R	RBI	BB	SO	SB	Pinch Hit AB	Pinch Hit H	PO	A	E	DP	TC/G	FA	G by Pos
1974	DET A	13	.138	.172	29	4	1	0	0	0.0	1	2	3	2	0	0	0	45	10	4	2	4.5	.932	C-13
1975		35	.229	.432	118	27	6	3	4	3.4	15	13	10	15	0	1	0	195	23	4	4	6.5	.982	C-34
1976		60	.222	.361	144	32	7	2	3	2.1	18	10	17	14	0	1	0	221	19	15	5	4.3	.941	C-59
1977		53	.274	.500	164	45	8	1	9	5.5	26	25	14	18	0	9	2	181	20	3	2	4.2	.985	C-37, OF-9, DH-3
1978		71	.283	.422	187	53	5	0	7	3.7	23	22	21	14	0	17	6	89	2	2	0	1.5	.978	OF-60, DH-2
1979		87	.264	.506	231	61	9	1	15	6.5	27	46	18	40	2	20	5	318	26	3	22	4.6	.991	1B-31, C-20, DH-18, OF-6
1980		126	.274	.449	372	102	13	2	16	4.3	56	65	68	64	1	17	4	575	47	11	44	4.9	.983	1B-52, DH-28, C-25, OF-23
1981		70	.215	.395	172	37	4	0	9	5.2	20	25	28	22	0	13	1	197	6	3	27	2.9	.985	DH-39, 1B-25, C-5, OF-1
1982		70	.301	.472	193	58	9	0	8	4.1	28	32	29	21	0	11	4	228	14	2	9	3.5	.992	C-24, 1B-17, DH-17, OF-10, 3B-1
1983		92	.269	.420	245	66	8	1	9	3.7	32	44	31	37	1	24	7	225	21	2	10	3.0	.992	DH-39, C-29, 1B-13, 3B-1, OF-1
1984	PHI N	86	.289	.417	180	52	3	1	6	3.3	20	24	30	24	1	27	6	323	20	7	21	5.6	.980	1B-39, C-21, 3B-2
1985		32	.162	.162	37	6	0	0	0	0.0	1	2	8	7	0	24	5	44	1	0	5	5.0	1.000	1B-7, C-2
12 yrs.		795	.262	.432	2072	543	73	11	86	4.2	267	310	277	278	5	164	40	2641	209	56	151	4.1	.981	C-269, 1B-184, DH-146, OF-110, 3B-4

Andy Woehr

WOEHR, ANDREW EMIL BR TR 5′11″ 165 lbs.
B. Feb. 4, 1896, Fort Wayne, Ind. D. July 24, 1990, Fort Wayne, Ind.

Year	Team	Games	BA	SA	AB	H	2B	3B	HR	HR%	R	RBI	BB	SO	SB	Pinch Hit AB	Pinch Hit H	PO	A	E	DP	TC/G	FA	G by Pos
1923	PHI N	13	.341	.390	41	14	2	0	0	0.0	3	3	1	1	0	0	0	15	24	1	4	3.1	.975	3B-13
1924		50	.217	.309	152	33	4	5	0	0.0	11	17	5	8	2	3	0	46	58	9	8	2.5	.920	3B-44, 2B-1
2 yrs.		63	.244	.326	193	47	6	5	0	0.0	14	20	6	9	2	3	0	61	82	10	12	2.6	.935	3B-57, 2B-1

Joe Woerlin

WOERLIN, JOSEPH
B. Oct. 9, 1864, France D. June 22, 1919, St. Louis, Mo.

Year	Team	Games	BA	SA	AB	H	2B	3B	HR	HR%	R	RBI	BB	SO	SB	Pinch Hit AB	Pinch Hit H	PO	A	E	DP	TC/G	FA	G by Pos
1895	WAS N	1	.333	.333	3	1	0	0	0	0.0	1	0	0	0	0	0	0	0	3	0	0	3.0	1.000	SS-1

Jim Wohlford

WOHLFORD, JAMES EUGENE (Wolfie) BR TR 5′11″ 175 lbs.
B. Feb. 28, 1951, Visalia, Calif.

Year	Team	Games	BA	SA	AB	H	2B	3B	HR	HR%	R	RBI	BB	SO	SB	Pinch Hit AB	Pinch Hit H	PO	A	E	DP	TC/G	FA	G by Pos
1972	KC A	15	.240	.280	25	6	1	0	0	0.0	3	0	2	6	0	4	0	7	12	1	1	2.5	.950	2B-8
1973		45	.266	.385	109	29	1	3	2	1.8	21	10	11	12	1	5	1	31	2	0	1	1.0	1.000	DH-19, OF-13
1974		143	.271	.343	501	136	16	7	2	0.4	55	44	39	74	16	9	2	273	7	5	4	2.1	.982	OF-138, DH-1
1975		116	.255	.312	353	90	10	5	0	0.0	45	30	34	37	12	14	2	175	9	9	1	1.8	.953	OF-102, DH-4
1976		107	.249	.307	293	73	10	2	1	0.3	47	24	29	24	22	16	2	190	8	5	1	2.1	.975	OF-93, DH-3, 2B-1
1977	MIL A	129	.248	.320	391	97	16	3	2	0.5	41	36	21	49	17	4	1	246	7	5	1	2.0	.981	OF-125, 2B-1, DH-1
1978		46	.297	.415	118	35	7	2	1	0.8	16	19	6	10	3	8	2	52	2	1	0	1.4	.982	OF-35, DH-4
1979		63	.263	.366	175	46	13	1	1	0.6	19	17	8	28	6	2	1	126	0	4	0	2.2	.969	OF-55, DH-5
1980	SF N	91	.280	.368	193	54	6	4	1	0.5	17	24	13	23	1	48	12	89	3	2	0	1.9	.979	OF-49, 3B-1
1981		50	.162	.250	68	11	3	0	1	1.5	4	7	4	9	0	40	5	3	1	0	0	0.4	1.000	OF-10
1982		97	.256	.336	250	64	12	1	2	0.8	37	25	30	36	8	27	5	122	4	1	0	1.8	.992	OF-72
1983	MON N	83	.277	.355	141	39	8	0	1	0.7	7	14	5	14	0	31	11	80	2	1	0	1.4	.988	OF-61
1984		95	.300	.451	213	64	13	2	5	2.3	20	29	14	19	3	39	8	85	4	1	2	1.5	.989	OF-59, 3B-2
1985		70	.192	.272	125	24	5	1	1	0.8	7	15	16	18	0	21	5	58	1	0	0	1.4	1.000	OF-43
1986		70	.266	.383	94	25	4	2	1	1.1	10	11	9	17	0	41	8	22	6	0	0	1.0	1.000	OF-22, 3B-6
15 yrs.		1220	.260	.343	3049	793	125	33	21	0.7	349	305	241	376	89	309	65	1559	68	35	11	1.8	.979	OF-877, DH-37, 2B-10, 3B-9
LEAGUE CHAMPIONSHIP SERIES																								
1976	KC A	5	.182	.182	11	2	0	0	0	0.0	3	0	3	1	2	1	1	7	0	0	0	1.4	1.000	OF-5

John Wojcik

WOJCIK, JOHN JOSEPH BL TR 6′ 175 lbs.
B. Apr. 6, 1942, Olean, N. Y.

Year	Team	Games	BA	SA	AB	H	2B	3B	HR	HR%	R	RBI	BB	SO	SB	Pinch Hit AB	Pinch Hit H	PO	A	E	DP	TC/G	FA	G by Pos
1962	KC A	16	.302	.395	43	13	4	0	0	0.0	8	9	13	4	3	4	2	21	1	0	0	1.8	1.000	OF-12
1963		19	.186	.186	59	11	0	0	0	0.0	7	2	8	8	2	2	0	34	1	0	0	2.1	1.000	OF-17
1964		6	.136	.136	22	3	0	0	0	0.0	1	0	2	8	0	0	0	10	0	0	0	1.7	1.000	OF-6
3 yrs.		41	.218	.250	124	27	4	0	0	0.0	16	11	23	20	5	6	2	65	2	0	0	1.9	1.000	OF-35

Chicken Wolf

WOLF, WILLIAM VAN WINKLE BR TR 5′ 9″ 190 lbs.
B. May 12, 1862, Louisville, Ky. D. May 16, 1903, Louisville, Ky.
Manager 1889.

Year	Team	Games	BA	SA	AB	H	2B	3B	HR	HR%	R	RBI	BB	SO	SB	Pinch Hit AB	Pinch Hit H	PO	A	E	DP	TC/G	FA	G by Pos
1882	LOU AA	78	.299	.384	318	95	11	8	0	0.0	46		9			0	0	98	45	21	3	2.0	.872	OF-70, SS-9, 1B-1, P-1
1883		98	.262	.360	389	102	17	9	1	0.3	59		5			0	0	244	66	42	9	3.4	.881	OF-78, C-20, SS-5, 2B-1
1884		110	.300	.414	**486**	146	24	11	3	0.6	79		4			0	0	227	43	35	4	2.7	.885	OF-101, C-11, 1B-1, 3B-1, SS-1
1885		112	.292	.416	483	141	23	17	1	0.2	79		11			0	0	184	23	20	5	2.0	.912	OF-111, C-2, 3B-1, P-1
1886		130	.272	.363	545	148	17	12	3	0.6	93		27			0	0	267	40	27	13	2.5	.919	OF-122, 1B-8, C-3, 2B-1, P-1
1887		137	.281	.381	569	160	28	13	1	0.2	103		34		45	0	0	302	31	24	11	2.6	.933	OF-128, 1B-11
1888		128	.286	.379	538	154	28	11	0	0.0	80	67	25		41	0	0	189	168	63	13	3.2	.850	OF-85, SS-39, 3B-4, C-3, 1B-1

Chicken Wolf *continued*

Year	Team	Games	BA	SA	AB	H	2B	3B	HR	HR%	R	RBI	BB	SO	SB	Pinch Hit AB	Pinch Hit H	PO	A	E	DP	TC/G	FA	G by Pos
1889		130	.291	.377	546	159	20	9	3	0.5	72	57	29	34	18	0	0	362	96	35	23	3.7	.929	OF-88, 1B-16, 2B-13, SS-10, 3B-7
1890		134	**.363**	.479	543	**197**	29	11	4	0.7	100		43		46	0	0	210	38	18	6	2.0	.932	OF-123, 3B-12
1891		136	.256	.324	528	135	17	8	1	0.2	67	81	42	36	13	0	0	222	30	19	10	2.0	.930	OF-131, 1B-5, 3B-1
1892	STL N	3	.143	.143	14	2	0	0	0	0.0	1	1	0	1	0	0	0	1	0	0	0	0.3	1.000	OF-3
11 yrs.		1196	.290	.388	4959	1439	214	109	17	0.3	779	206	229	71	163	0	0	2306	580	304	97	2.6	.905	OF-1040, SS-64, 1B-43, C-39, 3B-26, 2B-15, P-3

Ray Wolf

WOLF, RAYMOND BERNARD BR TR 5′11″ 175 lbs.
B. July 15, 1904, Chicago, Ill. D. Oct. 6, 1979, Fort Worth, Tex.

Year	Team	Games	BA	SA	AB	H	2B	3B	HR	HR%	R	RBI	BB	SO	SB	Pinch Hit AB	Pinch Hit H	PO	A	E	DP	TC/G	FA	G by Pos
1927	CIN N	1	.000	.000	1	0	0	0	0	0.0	0	0	0	0	0	0	0	3	0	0	0	3.0	1.000	1B-1

Harry Wolfe

WOLFE, HAROLD (Whitey) BR TR 5′ 8″ 160 lbs.
B. Nov. 24, 1890, Worcester, Mass. D. July 28, 1971, Ft. Wayne, Ind.

Year	Team	Games	BA	SA	AB	H	2B	3B	HR	HR%	R	RBI	BB	SO	SB	Pinch Hit AB	Pinch Hit H	PO	A	E	DP	TC/G	FA	G by Pos
1917	2 teams	CHI N (9G –.400) PIT N (3G –.000)																						
″	total	12	.200	.200	10	2	0	0	0	0.0	1	1	2	5	0	3	0	7	6	1	2	2.8	.929	OF-2, SS-2, 2B-1

Larry Wolfe

WOLFE, LAURENCE MARCY BR TR 5′11″ 170 lbs.
B. Mar. 2, 1953, Melbourne, Fla.

Year	Team	Games	BA	SA	AB	H	2B	3B	HR	HR%	R	RBI	BB	SO	SB	Pinch Hit AB	Pinch Hit H	PO	A	E	DP	TC/G	FA	G by Pos
1977	MIN A	8	.240	.280	25	6	1	0	0	0.0	3	6	1	0	0	3	2	9	13	0	1	2.8	1.000	3B-8
1978		88	.234	.323	235	55	10	1	3	1.3	25	25	36	27	0	7	2	66	163	12	11	2.7	.950	3B-81, SS-7
1979	BOS A	47	.244	.410	78	19	4	0	3	3.8	12	15	17	21	0	8	4	48	70	5	15	3.0	.959	2B-27, 3B-9, SS-2, C-1, 1B-1, DH-1
1980		18	.130	.304	23	3	1	0	1	4.3	3	4	0	5	0	3	1	3	8	0	2	0.6	1.000	3B-14, DH-4
4 yrs.		161	.230	.338	361	83	16	1	7	1.9	43	50	54	53	0	21	9	126	254	17	29	2.6	.957	3B-112, 2B-27, SS-9, DH-5, 1B-1, C-1

Polly Wolfe

WOLFE, ROY CHAMBERLAIN BL TR 5′10″ 170 lbs.
B. Sept. 1, 1888, Knoxville, Ill. D. Nov. 21, 1938, Morris, Ill.

Year	Team	Games	BA	SA	AB	H	2B	3B	HR	HR%	R	RBI	BB	SO	SB	Pinch Hit AB	Pinch Hit H	PO	A	E	DP	TC/G	FA	G by Pos
1912	CHI A	1	.000	.000	1	0	0	0	0	0.0	0	0	0		0	1	0	0	0	0	0	0.0	—	
1914		9	.214	.214	28	6	0	0	0	0.0	0	0	3	6	1	1	0	7	0	1	0	1.0	.875	OF-8
2 yrs.		10	.207	.207	29	6	0	0	0	0.0	0	0	3	6	1	2	0	7	0	1	0	1.0	.875	OF-8

Abe Wolstenholme

WOLSTENHOLME, ABRAHAM LINCOLN
B. Mar. 4, 1861, Philadelphia, Pa. D. Mar. 4, 1916, Philadelphia, Pa.

Year	Team	Games	BA	SA	AB	H	2B	3B	HR	HR%	R	RBI	BB	SO	SB	Pinch Hit AB	Pinch Hit H	PO	A	E	DP	TC/G	FA	G by Pos
1883	PHI N	3	.091	.182	11	1	1	0	0	0.0	0		0	0		0	0	4	4	3	0	3.7	.727	C-2, OF-1

Harry Wolter

WOLTER, HARRY MEIGS BL TL 5′10″ 175 lbs.
B. July 11, 1884, Monterey, Calif. D. July 7, 1970, Palo Alto, Calif.

Year	Team	Games	BA	SA	AB	H	2B	3B	HR	HR%	R	RBI	BB	SO	SB	Pinch Hit AB	Pinch Hit H	PO	A	E	DP	TC/G	FA	G by Pos
1907	3 teams	CIN N (4G –.133) PIT N (1G –.000) STL N (16G –.340)																						
″	total	21	.286	.286	63	18	0	0	0	0.0	5	7	3		1	4	0	20	5	1	1	1.5	.962	OF-13, P-4
1909	BOS A	54	.244	.378	119	29	2	4	2	1.7	14	10	9		2	13	1	189	26	9	6	6.2	.960	1B-17, P-10, OF-9
1910	NY A	135	.267	.361	479	128	15	9	4	0.8	84	42	66		39	2	0	192	11	13	3	1.7	.940	OF-130
1911		122	.304	.440	434	132	17	15	4	0.9	78	36	62		28	3	2	192	20	12	9	1.9	.946	OF-113, 1B-2
1912		12	.344	.469	32	11	2	1	0	0.0	8	1	10		5	3	0	11	1	1	0	1.4	.923	OF-9
1913		126	.254	.339	425	108	18	6	2	0.5	53	43	80	50	13	3	1	228	15	14	1	2.1	.946	OF-121
1917	CHI N	117	.249	.331	353	88	15	7	0	0.0	44	28	38	40	7	16	7	134	14	9	5	1.6	.943	OF-97, 1B-1
7 yrs.		587	.270	.369	1905	514	69	42	12	0.6	286	167	268	90	95	44	11	966	92	59	25	2.1	.947	OF-492, 1B-20, P-14

Harry Wolverton

WOLVERTON, HARRY STERLING BL TR 5′11″ 205 lbs.
B. Dec. 6, 1873, Mt. Vernon, Ohio D. Feb. 4, 1937, Oakland, Calif.
Manager 1912.

Year	Team	Games	BA	SA	AB	H	2B	3B	HR	HR%	R	RBI	BB	SO	SB	Pinch Hit AB	Pinch Hit H	PO	A	E	DP	TC/G	FA	G by Pos
1898	CHI N	13	.327	.347	49	16	1	0	0	0.0	4	2	1		1	0	0	21	35	10	1	5.1	.848	3B-13
1899		99	.285	.386	389	111	14	11	1	0.3	50	49	30		14	0	0	124	228	58	12	4.1	.859	3B-98, SS-1
1900	2 teams	CHI N (3G –.182) PHI N (101G –.282)																						
″	total	104	.279	.368	394	110	10	8	3	0.8	44	58	22		5	0	0	124	239	49	16	4.0	.881	3B-104
1901	PHI N	93	.309	.369	379	117	15	4	0	0.0	42	43	22		13	0	0	114	190	26	9	3.5	.921	3B-93
1902	2 teams	WAS A (59G –.249) PHI N (34G –.294)																						
″	total	93	.265	.327	385	102	11	5	1	0.3	47	39	22		11	0	0	130	230	34	19	4.2	.914	3B-93
1903	PHI N	123	.308	.383	494	152	13	12	0	0.0	72	53	18		10	0	0	182	247	27	8	3.7	.941	3B-123
1904		102	.266	.329	398	106	15	5	0	0.0	43	49	26		18	0	0	143	191	27	15	3.5	.925	3B-102
1905	BOS N	122	.225	.300	463	104	15	7	2	0.4	38	55	23		10	0	0	139	256	28	12	3.5	.934	3B-122
1912	NY A	33	.300	.360	50	15	1	1	0	0.0	6	4	2		1	26	10	13	10	5	1	4.0	.821	3B-7
9 yrs.		782	.278	.352	3001	833	95	53	7	0.2	346	352	166		83	26	10	990	1626	264	93	3.8	.908	3B-755, SS-1

Sid Womack

WOMACK, SIDNEY KIRK (Tex) BR TR 5′10½″ 185 lbs.
B. Oct. 2, 1896, Greensburg, La. D. Aug. 28, 1958, Jackson, Miss.

Year	Team	Games	BA	SA	AB	H	2B	3B	HR	HR%	R	RBI	BB	SO	SB	Pinch Hit AB	Pinch Hit H	PO	A	E	DP	TC/G	FA	G by Pos
1926	BOS N	1	.000	.000	3	0	0	0	0	0.0	0	1	0	0	0	0	0	3	1	0	0	4.0	1.000	C-1

Tony Womack

WOMACK, ANTHONY DARRELL BL TR 5′ 9″ 160 lbs.
B. Sept. 25, 1969, Danville, Va.

Year	Team	Games	BA	SA	AB	H	2B	3B	HR	HR%	R	RBI	BB	SO	SB	Pinch Hit AB	Pinch Hit H	PO	A	E	DP	TC/G	FA	G by Pos
1993	PIT N	15	.083	.083	24	2	0	0	0	0.0	5	0	3	3	2	3	0	11	22	1	6	5.7	.971	SS-6
1994		5	.333	.333	12	4	0	0	0	0.0	4	1	2	3	0	0	0	3	6	2	2	2.2	.818	2B-3, SS-2
2 yrs.		20	.167	.167	36	6	0	0	0	0.0	9	1	5	6	2	3	0	14	28	3	8	4.1	.933	SS-8, 2B-3

Bob Wood

WOOD, ROBERT LYNN BR TR 5′ 8½″ 153 lbs.
B. July 28, 1865, Thorn Hill, Ohio D. May 22, 1943, Churchill, Ohio.

Year	Team	Games	BA	SA	AB	H	2B	3B	HR	HR%	R	RBI	BB	SO	SB	Pinch Hit AB	Pinch Hit H	PO	A	E	DP	TC/G	FA	G by Pos
1898	CIN N	39	.275	.330	109	30	6	0	0	0.0	14	16	9		1	8	3	109	29	8	1	4.7	.945	C-29, OF-1, 1B-1
1899		62	.314	.443	194	61	11	7	0	0.0	34	24	25		3	2	1	174	52	14	5	4.1	.942	C-53, OF-2, 3B-2, 1B-1
1900		45	.266	.338	139	37	8	1	0	0.0	17	22	10		3	11	1	69	56	12	5	4.0	.912	C-18, 3B-15, OF-1
1901	CLE A	98	.292	.384	346	101	23	3	1	0.3	45	49	12		6	4	1	328	121	25	12	5.0	.947	C-84, 3B-4, OF-3, SS-1, 2B-1, 1B-1
1902		81	.295	.380	258	76	18	2	0	0.0	23	40	27		1	9	2	347	70	19	11	6.1	.956	C-52, 1B-16, OF-2, 2B-1, 3B-1

Bob Wood *continued*

Year	Team	Games	BA	SA	AB	H	2B	3B	HR	HR%	R	RBI	BB	SO	SB	Pinch Hit AB	Pinch Hit H	PO	A	E	DP	TC/G	FA	G by Pos
1904	DET A	49	.246	.320	175	43	6	2	1	0.6	15	17	5		1	2	0	232	69	8	5	6.6	.974	C-47
1905		8	.083	.125	24	2	1	0	0	0.0	1	0	1		0	1	0	26	13	5	0	6.3	.886	C-7
7 yrs.		382	.281	.369	1245	350	73	15	2	0.2	149	168	89		15	37	8	1285	410	91	39	5.2	.949	C-290, 3B-22, 1B-19, OF-9, 2B-2, SS-1

Doc Wood

WOOD, CHARLES SPENCER BR TR 5′10″ 150 lbs.
B. Feb. 28, 1900, Batesville, Miss. D. Nov. 3, 1974, New Orleans, La.

Year	Team	Games	BA	SA	AB	H	2B	3B	HR	HR%	R	RBI	BB	SO	SB	Pinch Hit AB	Pinch Hit H	PO	A	E	DP	TC/G	FA	G by Pos
1923	PHI A	3	.333	.333	3	1	0	0	0	0.0	0	0	0	0	0	0	0	0	5	1	1	2.0	.833	SS-3

Fred Wood

WOOD, FRED S. 5′ 5″ 150 lbs.
Brother of Pete Wood.
B. 1863, Hamilton, Ont., Canada D. Aug. 23, 1933, New York, N. Y.

Year	Team	Games	BA	SA	AB	H	2B	3B	HR	HR%	R	RBI	BB	SO	SB	Pinch Hit AB	Pinch Hit H	PO	A	E	DP	TC/G	FA	G by Pos
1884	DET N	12	.048	.048	42	2	0	0	0	0.0	4		3	18		0	0	41	14	13	1	4.9	.809	C-7, OF-6, SS-1
1885	BUF N	1	.250	.250	4	1	0	0	0	0.0	0	0	0	0		0	0	4	1	1	1	6.0	.833	C-1
2 yrs.		13	.065	.065	46	3	0	0	0	0.0	4	0	3	18		0	0	45	15	14	2	4.9	.811	C-8, OF-6, SS-1

George Wood

WOOD, GEORGE A. (Dandy) BL TR 5′10½″ 175 lbs.
B. Nov. 9, 1858, Boston, Mass. D. Apr. 4, 1924, Harrisburg, Pa.
Manager 1891.

Year	Team	Games	BA	SA	AB	H	2B	3B	HR	HR%	R	RBI	BB	SO	SB	Pinch Hit AB	Pinch Hit H	PO	A	E	DP	TC/G	FA	G by Pos
1880	WOR N	81	.245	.324	327	80	16	5	0	0.0	37	28	10	37		0	0	128	11	17	1	1.9	.891	OF-80, 3B-2, 1B-1
1881	DET N	80	.297	.421	337	100	18	9	2	0.6	54	32	19	32		0	0	132	18	24	4	2.2	.862	OF-80
1882		84	.269	.421	375	101	12	12	**7**	1.9	69	29	14	30		0	0	161	14	23	8	2.4	.884	OF-84
1883		99	.302	.444	441	133	26	11	5	1.1	81		25	37		0	0	226	18	34	3	2.8	.878	OF-99, P-1
1884		114	.252	.378	473	119	16	10	8	1.7	79		39	75		0	0	190	18	24	1	2.0	.897	OF-114, 3B-1
1885		82	.290	.428	362	105	19	8	5	1.4	62	28	13	19		0	0	125	40	21	3	2.2	.887	OF-70, 3B-12, P-1, SS-1
1886	PHI N	106	.273	.407	450	123	18	15	4	0.9	81	50	23	75		0	0	156	33	22	3	2.0	.896	OF-97, SS-6, 3B-3
1887		113	.289	.497	491	142	22	19	14	2.9	118	66	40	51	19	0	0	164	34	28	4	2.0	.876	OF-104, SS-3, 3B-3, 2B-3
1888		106	.229	.342	433	99	19	6	6	1.4	67	15	39	44	20	0	0	176	19	22	3	2.0	.899	OF-104, 3B-2, P-2
1889	2 teams	PHI N (97G –.251) BAL AA (3G –.200)																						
″	total	100	.250	.352	432	108	21	4	5	1.2	78	54	53	35	18	0	0	175	27	19	1	2.2	.914	OF-95, SS-6, P-1
1890	PHI P	132	.289	.429	539	156	20	14	9	1.7	115	102	51	35	20	0	0	255	35	34	10	2.4	.895	OF-132, 3B-1
1891	PHI AA	132	.309	.413	528	163	18	14	3	0.6	105	61	72	52	22	0	0	236	43	26	13	2.3	.915	OF-122, 3B-6, SS-5
1892	2 teams	BAL N (21G –.224) CIN N (30G –.196)																						
″	total	51	.208	.279	183	38	3	5	0	0.0	19	24	20	25	5	0	0	74	11	11	2	1.9	.885	OF-51
13 yrs.		1280	.273	.403	5371	1467	228	132	68	1.3	965	489	418	547	104	0	0	2198	321	305	56	2.2	.892	OF-1232, 3B-30, SS-21, P-5, 2B-3, 1B-1

Harry Wood

WOOD, HAROLD AUSTIN BL TR 5′10″ 155 lbs.
B. Feb. 10, 1885, Waterville, Me. D. May 18, 1955, Bethesda, Md.

Year	Team	Games	BA	SA	AB	H	2B	3B	HR	HR%	R	RBI	BB	SO	SB	Pinch Hit AB	Pinch Hit H	PO	A	E	DP	TC/G	FA	G by Pos
1903	CIN N	2	.000	.000	3	0	0	0	0	0.0	0	0	1		0	1	0	0	0	0	0	0.0	.000	OF-2

Jake Wood

WOOD, JACOB BR TR 6′ 1″ 163 lbs.
B. June 22, 1937, Elizabeth, N. J.

Year	Team	Games	BA	SA	AB	H	2B	3B	HR	HR%	R	RBI	BB	SO	SB	Pinch Hit AB	Pinch Hit H	PO	A	E	DP	TC/G	FA	G by Pos
1961	DET A	162	.258	.376	663	171	17	**14**	11	1.7	96	69	58	**141**	30	1	0	380	396	25	83	4.9	.969	2B-162
1962		111	.226	.346	367	83	10	5	8	2.2	68	30	33	59	24	11	2	185	197	20	33	4.5	.950	2B-90
1963		85	.271	.407	351	95	11	2	11	3.1	50	27	24	61	18	1	0	190	202	17	47	5.0	.958	2B-81, 3B-1
1964		64	.232	.304	125	29	2	2	1	0.8	11	7	4	24	0	29	7	105	30	5	13	5.0	.964	1B-11, 2B-10, 3B-6, OF-1
1965		58	.288	.375	104	30	3	0	2	1.9	12	7	10	19	3	25	9	57	38	2	12	4.2	.979	2B-20, 1B-1, SS-1, 3B-1
1966		98	.252	.343	230	58	9	3	2	0.9	39	27	28	48	4	40	6	124	100	9	26	4.0	.961	2B-52, 3B-4, 1B-2
1967	2 teams	DET A (14G –.050) CIN N (16G –.118)																						
″	total	30	.081	.108	37	3	1	0	0	0.0	3	1	2	10	0	19	2	15	5	1	3	3.5	.952	2B-2, OF-2, 1B-2
7 yrs.		608	.250	.362	1877	469	53	26	35	1.9	279	168	159	362	79	126	26	1056	968	79	217	4.7	.962	2B-417, 1B-16, 3B-12, OF-3, SS-1

Joe Wood

WOOD, JOSEPH PERRY (Little General) BR TR 5′ 9½″ 160 lbs.
B. Oct. 3, 1919, Houston, Tex. D. Mar. 25, 1985, Houston, Tex.

Year	Team	Games	BA	SA	AB	H	2B	3B	HR	HR%	R	RBI	BB	SO	SB	Pinch Hit AB	Pinch Hit H	PO	A	E	DP	TC/G	FA	G by Pos
1943	DET A	60	.323	.415	164	53	4	4	1	0.6	22	17	6	13	2	10	3	70	64	12	6	3.7	.918	2B-22, 3B-18

Ken Wood

WOOD, KENNETH LANIER BR TR 6′ 200 lbs.
B. July 1, 1924, Lincolnton, N. C.

Year	Team	Games	BA	SA	AB	H	2B	3B	HR	HR%	R	RBI	BB	SO	SB	Pinch Hit AB	Pinch Hit H	PO	A	E	DP	TC/G	FA	G by Pos
1948	STL A	10	.083	.167	24	2	0	1	0	0.0	2	2	1	4	0	5	0	10	1	0	0	2.2	1.000	OF-5
1949		7	.000	.000	6	0	0	0	0	0.0	0	0	1	2	0	3	0	0	0	0	0	0.0	.000	OF-3
1950		128	.225	.396	369	83	24	0	13	3.5	42	62	38	58	0	32	4	162	16	9	2	2.0	.952	OF-94
1951		109	.237	.429	333	79	19	0	15	4.5	40	44	27	49	1	10	1	179	7	8	0	1.9	.959	OF-100
1952	2 teams	BOS A (15G –.100) WAS A (61G –.238)																						
″	total	76	.226	.391	230	52	8	6	6	2.6	26	32	33	25	0	8	0	169	6	9	1	2.7	.951	OF-69
1953	WAS A	12	.212	.242	33	7	1	0	0	0.0	0	3	2	3	0	5	1	13	1	0	1	2.0	1.000	OF-7
6 yrs.		342	.224	.393	995	223	52	7	34	3.4	110	143	102	141	1	63	6	533	31	26	4	2.1	.956	OF-278

Roy Wood

WOOD, ROY WINTON (Woody) BR TR 6′ 175 lbs.
B. Aug. 29, 1892, Monticello, Ark. D. Apr. 6, 1974, Fayetteville, Ark.

Year	Team	Games	BA	SA	AB	H	2B	3B	HR	HR%	R	RBI	BB	SO	SB	Pinch Hit AB	Pinch Hit H	PO	A	E	DP	TC/G	FA	G by Pos
1913	PIT N	14	.286	.400	35	10	4	0	0	0.0	4	2	1	8	0	3	0	18	4	2	1	2.7	.917	OF-8, 1B-1
1914	CLE A	72	.236	.305	220	52	6	3	1	0.5	24	15	13	26	6	10	2	209	16	7	13	3.8	.970	OF-41, 1B-20
1915		33	.192	.244	78	15	2	1	0	0.0	5	3	2	13	1	8	1	183	8	2	7	8.4	.990	1B-21, OF-2
3 yrs.		119	.231	.300	333	77	12	4	1	0.3	33	20	16	47	7	21	3	410	28	11	21	4.8	.976	OF-51, 1B-42

Smoky Joe Wood

WOOD, JOE BR TR 5′11″ 180 lbs.
Born Howard Ellsworth Wood.
Father of Joe Wood.
B. Oct. 25, 1889, Kansas City, Mo. D. July 27, 1985, West Haven, Conn.

Year	Team	Games	BA	SA	AB	H	2B	3B	HR	HR%	R	RBI	BB	SO	SB	Pinch Hit AB	Pinch Hit H	PO	A	E	DP	TC/G	FA	G by Pos
1908	BOS A	6	.000	.000	7	0	0	0	0	0.0	1	0	0		0	0	0	3	5	1	1	1.5	.889	P-6
1909		24	.164	.200	55	9	0	1	0	0.0	4	3	2		0	0	0	7	27	1	0	1.5	.971	P-24

Smoky Joe Wood *continued*

Year	Team	Games	BA	SA	AB	H	2B	3B	HR	HR%	R	RBI	BB	SO	SB	Pinch Hit AB	Pinch Hit H	PO	A	E	DP	TC/G	FA	G by Pos
1910		35	.261	.362	69	18	2	1	1	1.4	9	5	5		0	0	0	17	62	2	3	2.3	.975	P-35
1911		44	.261	.420	88	23	4	2	2	2.3	15	11	10		1	0	0	23	67	5	3	2.2	.947	P-44
1912		43	.290	.435	124	36	13	1	1	0.8	17	13	11		0	0	0	41	110	4	2	3.6	.974	P-43
1913		24	.268	.357	56	15	5	0	0	0.0	10	10	4	7	1	1	0	9	55	3	1	2.9	.955	P-23
1914		20	.140	.163	43	6	1	0	0	0.0	2	1	3	14	1	2	0	13	28	0	0	2.3	1.000	P-18
1915		29	.259	.370	54	14	1	1	1	1.9	6	7	5	10	1	0	0	8	48	1	6	2.3	.982	P-25
1917	CLE A	10	.000	.000	6	0	0	0	0	0.0	1	0	0	3	0	2	0	2	5	0	0	1.4	1.000	P-5
1918		119	.296	.403	422	125	22	4	5	1.2	41	66	36	38	8	1	0	273	77	17	7	3.1	.954	OF-95, 2B-19, 1B-4
1919		72	.255	.375	192	49	10	5	1	0.5	30	27	32	21	3	6	0	90	7	7	1	1.6	.933	OF-64, P-1
1920		61	.270	.401	137	37	11	2	1	0.7	25	30	25	16	1	0	0	71	6	1	0	1.4	.987	OF-54, P-1
1921		66	.366	.562	194	71	16	5	4	2.1	32	60	25	17	2	0	0	105	3	3	1	1.7	.973	OF-64
1922		142	.297	.442	505	150	33	8	8	1.6	74	92	50	63	5	1	0	249	18	11	5	2.0	.960	OF-140, 1B-1
14 yrs.		695	.283	.411	1952	553	118	30	24	1.2	267	325	208	189	23	13	0	911	518	56	30	2.2	.962	OF-417, P-225, 2B-19, 1B-5
WORLD SERIES																								
1912	BOS A	4	.286	.286	7	2	0	0	0	0.0	1	1	1	0	0	0	0	1	6	0	1	1.8	1.000	P-4
1920	CLE A	4	.200	.300	10	2	1	0	0	0.0	2	0	1	2	0	1	0	7	0	0	0	1.8	1.000	OF-4
2 yrs.		8	.235	.294	17	4	1	0	0	0.0	3	1	2	2	0	1	0	8	6	0	1	1.8	1.000	OF-4, P-4

Ted Wood

WOOD, EDWARD ROBERT
B. Jan. 4, 1967, Mansfield, Ohio.
BL TL 6′ 2″ 170 lbs.

Year	Team	Games	BA	SA	AB	H	2B	3B	HR	HR%	R	RBI	BB	SO	SB	Pinch Hit AB	Pinch Hit H	PO	A	E	DP	TC/G	FA	G by Pos
1991	SF N	10	.120	.120	25	3	0	0	0	0.0	0	1	2	11	0	3	1	10	0	1	0	1.4	.909	OF-8
1992		24	.207	.293	58	12	2	0	1	1.7	5	3	6	15	0	7	2	35	0	1	0	2.3	.972	OF-16
1993	MON N	13	.192	.231	26	5	1	0	0	0.0	4	3	3	3	0	5	0	16	0	0	0	2.0	1.000	OF-8
3 yrs.		47	.183	.239	109	20	3	0	1	0.9	9	7	11	29	0	15	3	61	0	2	0	2.0	.968	OF-32

Larry Woodall

WOODALL, CHARLES LAWRENCE
B. July 26, 1894, Staunton, Va. D. May 16, 1963, Cambridge, Mass.
BR TR 5′ 9″ 165 lbs.

Year	Team	Games	BA	SA	AB	H	2B	3B	HR	HR%	R	RBI	BB	SO	SB	Pinch Hit AB	Pinch Hit H	PO	A	E	DP	TC/G	FA	G by Pos
1920	DET A	18	.245	.265	49	12	1	0	0	0.0	4	5	2	6	0	2	0	59	20	1	0	5.3	.988	C-15
1921		46	.362	.438	80	29	4	1	0	0.0	10	14	6	7	1	18	5	48	8	2	1	2.4	.966	C-24
1922		50	.344	.392	125	43	2	2	0	0.0	19	18	8	11	0	11	4	117	11	3	1	3.4	.977	C-39
1923		71	.277	.405	148	41	12	2	1	0.7	20	19	22	9	2	9	4	140	32	3	2	2.9	.983	C-60
1924		67	.309	.388	165	51	9	2	0	0.0	23	24	21	5	0	4	0	174	41	3	5	3.5	.986	C-62
1925		75	.205	.240	171	35	4	1	0	0.0	20	13	24	8	1	0	0	165	38	7	4	2.8	.967	C-75
1926		67	.233	.267	146	34	5	0	0	0.0	18	15	15	2	0	5	1	149	37	4	3	3.2	.979	C-59
1927		88	.280	.362	246	69	8	6	0	0.0	28	39	37	9	9	2	0	265	72	1	6	3.9	.997	C-86
1928		65	.210	.247	186	39	5	1	0	0.0	19	13	24	10	3	3	0	218	44	2	3	4.3	.992	C-62
1929		1	.000	.000	1	0	0	0	0	0.0	0	0	0	0	0	1	0	0	0	0	0	0.0	—	
10 yrs.		548	.268	.331	1317	353	50	15	1	0.1	161	160	159	67	16	55	14	1335	303	26	25	3.5	.984	C-482

Darrell Woodard

WOODARD, DARRELL LEE
B. Dec. 10, 1956, Wilmar, Ark.
BR TR 5′11″ 160 lbs.

Year	Team	Games	BA	SA	AB	H	2B	3B	HR	HR%	R	RBI	BB	SO	SB	Pinch Hit AB	Pinch Hit H	PO	A	E	DP	TC/G	FA	G by Pos
1978	OAK A	33	.000	.000	9	0	0	0	0	0.0	10	0	1	1	3	0	0	14	14	1	3	1.8	.966	2B-14, 3B-1, DH-1

Mike Woodard

WOODARD, MICHAEL CARY
B. Mar. 2, 1960, Melrose Park, Ill.
BL TR 5′ 9″ 155 lbs.

Year	Team	Games	BA	SA	AB	H	2B	3B	HR	HR%	R	RBI	BB	SO	SB	Pinch Hit AB	Pinch Hit H	PO	A	E	DP	TC/G	FA	G by Pos
1985	SF N	24	.244	.256	82	20	1	0	0	0.0	12	9	5	3	6	1	1	49	46	1	14	4.2	.990	2B-23
1986		48	.253	.342	79	20	2	1	1	1.3	14	5	10	9	7	21	4	28	43	2	13	2.7	.973	2B-23, SS-2, 3B-2
1987		10	.211	.263	19	4	1	0	0	0.0	0	1	0	1	0	2	0	13	15	0	4	3.5	1.000	2B-8
1988	CHI A	18	.133	.178	45	6	0	1	0	0.0	3	4	1	5	1	1	0	41	37	2	8	5.7	.975	2B-14
4 yrs.		100	.222	.271	225	50	4	2	1	0.4	29	19	16	18	14	25	5	131	141	5	39	3.8	.982	2B-68, SS-2, 3B-2

Red Woodhead

WOODHEAD, JAMES
B. July 9, 1851, Chelsea, Mass. D. Sept. 7, 1881, Boston, Mass.
5′ 6″ 160 lbs.

Year	Team	Games	BA	SA	AB	H	2B	3B	HR	HR%	R	RBI	BB	SO	SB	Pinch Hit AB	Pinch Hit H	PO	A	E	DP	TC/G	FA	G by Pos
1879	SYR N	34	.160	.168	131	21	1	0	0	0.0	4	2	0	23		0	0	52	51	27	4	3.8	.792	3B-34

Gene Woodling

WOODLING, EUGENE RICHARD
B. Aug. 16, 1922, Akron, Ohio.
BL TR 5′ 9½″ 195 lbs.

Year	Team	Games	BA	SA	AB	H	2B	3B	HR	HR%	R	RBI	BB	SO	SB	Pinch Hit AB	Pinch Hit H	PO	A	E	DP	TC/G	FA	G by Pos
1943	CLE A	8	.320	.600	25	8	2	1	1	4.0	5	5	1	3	0	2	1	8	1	0	0	1.5	1.000	OF-6
1946		61	.188	.256	133	25	1	4	0	0.0	8	9	16	13	1	21	3	81	0	0	0	2.2	1.000	OF-37
1947	PIT N	22	.266	.342	79	21	2	2	0	0.0	7	10	7	5	0	1	0	59	1	2	0	3.0	.968	OF-21
1949	NY A	112	.270	.412	296	80	13	7	5	1.7	60	44	52	21	2	13	2	163	5	3	1	1.7	.982	OF-98
1950		122	.283	.412	449	127	20	10	6	1.3	81	60	70	31	5	4	0	263	16	2	3	2.4	.993	OF-118
1951		120	.281	.462	420	118	15	8	15	3.6	65	71	62	37	0	5	1	265	5	2	0	2.3	.993	OF-116
1952		122	.309	.473	408	126	19	6	12	2.9	58	63	59	31	1	5	2	241	12	1	4	2.2	.996	OF-118
1953		125	.306	.468	395	121	26	4	10	2.5	64	58	82	29	2	11	5	240	6	1	2	2.1	.996	OF-119
1954		97	.250	.352	304	76	12	5	3	1.0	33	40	53	35	3	10	3	164	5	3	1	1.9	.983	OF-89
1955	2 teams	BAL A (47G –.221)	CLE A (79G –.278)																					
″	total	126	.257	.384	404	104	21	3	8	2.0	55	53	60	33	3	13	2	205	5	1	1	1.8	.995	OF-117
1956	CLE A	100	.262	.391	317	83	17	0	8	2.5	56	38	69	29	2	13	3	154	3	3	0	1.9	.981	OF-85
1957		133	.321	.521	430	138	25	2	19	4.4	74	78	64	35	0	22	5	225	10	2	0	2.1	.992	OF-113
1958	BAL A	133	.276	.429	413	114	16	1	15	3.6	57	65	66	49	4	19	5	181	7	5	1	1.7	.974	OF-116
1959		140	.300	.455	440	132	22	2	14	3.2	63	77	78	35	1	18	10	210	2	4	0	1.7	.981	OF-124
1960		140	.283	.414	435	123	18	3	11	2.5	68	62	84	40	3	18	8	202	7	1	0	1.7	.995	OF-124
1961	WAS A	110	.313	.471	342	107	16	4	10	2.9	39	57	50	24	1	20	7	154	8	2	0	1.8	.988	OF-90
1962	2 teams	WAS A (44G –.280)	NY N (81G –.274)																					
″	total	125	.276	.424	297	82	12	1	10	3.4	37	40	48	27	1	39	8	109	0	3	0	1.4	.973	OF-78
17 yrs.		1796	.284	.431	5587	1585	257	63	147	2.6	830	830	921	477	29	234	65	2924	93	35	13	1.9	.989	OF-1569
WORLD SERIES																								
1949	NY A	3	.400	.700	10	4	3	0	0	0.0	4	0	3	0	0	0	0	7	0	0	0	2.3	1.000	OF-3
1950		4	.429	.429	14	6	0	0	0	0.0	2	1	2	0	0	1	0	7	0	1	0	2.0	.875	OF-4
1951		6	.167	.500	18	3	1	1	1	5.6	6	1	5	3	0	1	0	18	0	1	0	3.8	.947	OF-5

Gene Woodling *continued*

Year	Team	Games	BA	SA	AB	H	2B	3B	HR	HR%	R	RBI	BB	SO	SB	Pinch Hit AB	Pinch Hit H	PO	A	E	DP	TC/G	FA	G by Pos
1952		7	.348	.609	23	8	1	1	1	4.3	4	1	3	3	0	1	1	18	0	1	0	3.2	.947	OF-6
1953		6	.300	.450	20	6	0	0	1	5.0	5	3	6	2	0	0	0	9	1	0	1	1.7	1.000	OF-6
5 yrs.		26	.318	.529	85	27	5	2	3	3.5	21 **10th**	6	19 **10th**	8	0	3	1	59	1	3	1	2.6	.952	OF-24

Orville Woodruff

WOODRUFF, ORVILLE FRANCIS (Sam)
B. Dec. 27, 1876, Chilo, Ohio D. July 22, 1937, Cincinnati, Ohio.
BR TR 5′ 9″ 160 lbs.

Year	Team	Games	BA	SA	AB	H	2B	3B	HR	HR%	R	RBI	BB	SO	SB	Pinch Hit AB	Pinch Hit H	PO	A	E	DP	TC/G	FA	G by Pos
1904	CIN N	87	.190	.255	306	58	14	3	0	0.0	20	20	19		9	0	0	126	190	30	16	4.0	.913	3B-61, 2B-17, SS-8, OF-1
1910		21	.148	.164	61	9	1	0	0	0.0	6	2	7	8	2	0	0	32	32	7	3	3.4	.901	3B-17, 2B-4
2 yrs.		108	.183	.240	367	67	15	3	0	0.0	26	22	26	8	11	0	0	158	222	37	19	3.9	.911	3B-78, 2B-21, SS-8, OF-1

Pete Woodruff

WOODRUFF, PETER FRANK
B. June 1873, New York, N. Y. Deceased.
BR TR

Year	Team	Games	BA	SA	AB	H	2B	3B	HR	HR%	R	RBI	BB	SO	SB	Pinch Hit AB	Pinch Hit H	PO	A	E	DP	TC/G	FA	G by Pos
1899	NY N	20	.246	.393	61	15	1	1	2	3.3	11	7	9		3	0	0	34	3	1	1	1.9	.974	OF-19, 1B-1

Al Woods

WOODS, ALVIS
B. Aug. 8, 1953, Oakland, Calif.
BL TL 6′ 3″ 190 lbs.

Year	Team	Games	BA	SA	AB	H	2B	3B	HR	HR%	R	RBI	BB	SO	SB	Pinch Hit AB	Pinch Hit H	PO	A	E	DP	TC/G	FA	G by Pos
1977	TOR A	122	.284	.382	440	125	17	4	6	1.4	58	35	36	38	8	4	2	215	6	7	1	1.9	.969	OF-115, DH-4
1978		62	.241	.364	220	53	12	3	3	1.4	19	25	11	23	1	3	1	131	2	3	0	2.3	.978	OF-60
1979		132	.278	.385	436	121	24	4	5	1.1	57	36	40	28	6	2	0	251	10	9	2	2.1	.967	OF-127, DH-2
1980		100	.300	.480	373	112	18	2	15	4.0	54	47	37	35	4	10	2	205	5	2	1	2.1	.991	OF-88, DH-13
1981		85	.247	.309	288	71	15	0	1	0.3	20	21	19	31	3	8	2	179	4	5	0	2.4	.973	OF-77, DH-2
1982		85	.234	.343	201	47	11	1	3	1.5	20	24	21	20	1	20	3	96	2	3	1	1.4	.970	OF-64, DH-10
1986	MIN A	23	.321	.571	28	9	1	0	2	7.1	5	8	3	5	0	16	8	0	0	0	0	0.0	.000	DH-7
7 yrs.		609	.271	.387	1986	538	98	14	35	1.8	233	196	167	180	23	63	18	1077	29	29	5	2.0	.974	OF-531, DH-38

Gary Woods

WOODS, GARY LEE
B. July 20, 1954, Santa Barbara, Calif.
BR TR 6′ 2″ 185 lbs.

Year	Team	Games	BA	SA	AB	H	2B	3B	HR	HR%	R	RBI	BB	SO	SB	Pinch Hit AB	Pinch Hit H	PO	A	E	DP	TC/G	FA	G by Pos
1976	OAK A	6	.125	.125	8	1	0	0	0	0.0	0	0	0	3	0	2	0	7	0	0	0	1.4	1.000	OF-4, DH-1
1977	TOR A	60	.216	.264	227	49	9	1	0	0.0	21	17	7	38	5	1	1	154	4	1	0	2.7	.994	OF-60
1978		8	.158	.211	19	3	1	0	0	0.0	1	0	1	1	1	1	0	12	0	0	0	2.0	1.000	OF-6
1980	HOU N	19	.377	.585	53	20	5	0	2	3.8	8	15	2	9	1	5	3	19	1	0	0	1.4	1.000	OF-14
1981		54	.209	.264	110	23	4	1	0	0.0	10	12	11	22	2	15	3	61	1	1	0	1.6	.984	OF-40
1982	CHI N	117	.269	.388	245	66	15	1	4	1.6	28	30	21	48	3	22	4	161	6	0	1	1.6	1.000	OF-103
1983		93	.242	.353	190	46	9	0	4	2.1	25	22	15	27	5	31	6	97	4	3	0	1.4	.971	OF-73, 2B-1
1984		87	.235	.388	98	23	4	1	3	3.1	13	10	15	21	2	31	7	54	3	0	1	0.9	1.000	OF-62, 2B-3
1985		81	.244	.280	82	20	3	0	0	0.0	11	4	14	18	0	27	7	42	1	0	0	0.8	1.000	OF-56
9 yrs.		525	.243	.337	1032	251	50	4	13	1.3	117	110	86	187	19	135	31	607	20	5	2	1.5	.992	OF-418, 2B-4, DH-1
DIVISIONAL PLAYOFF SERIES																								
1981	HOU N	2	.000	.000	2	0	0	0	0	0.0	0	0	0	1	0	2	0	0	0	0	0	0.0	—	
LEAGUE CHAMPIONSHIP SERIES																								
1980	HOU N	4	.250	.250	8	2	0	0	0	0.0	0	1	1	3	1	2	0	1	0	0	0	0.3	1.000	OF-3
1984	CHI N	1	.000	.000	1	0	0	0	0	0.0	0	0	0	1	0	1	0	1	0	0	0	1.0	1.000	OF-1
2 yrs.		5	.222	.222	9	2	0	0	0	0.0	0	1	1	4	1	3	0	2	0	0	0	0.5	1.000	OF-4

Jim Woods

WOODS, JAMES JEROME (Woody)
B. Sept. 17, 1939, Chicago, Ill.
BR TR 6′ 175 lbs.

Year	Team	Games	BA	SA	AB	H	2B	3B	HR	HR%	R	RBI	BB	SO	SB	Pinch Hit AB	Pinch Hit H	PO	A	E	DP	TC/G	FA	G by Pos
1957	CHI N	2	—	—	0	0	0	0	0	—	1	0	0	0	0	0	0	0	0	0	0	0.0	—	
1960	PHI N	11	.176	.265	34	6	0	0	1	2.9	4	3	3	13	0	0	0	9	22	2	1	3.0	.939	3B-11
1961		23	.229	.417	48	11	3	0	2	4.2	6	9	4	15	0	10	3	12	18	1	3	2.1	.968	3B-15
3 yrs.		36	.207	.354	82	17	3	0	3	3.7	11	12	7	28	0	10	3	21	40	3	4	2.5	.953	3B-26

Ron Woods

WOODS, RONALD LAWRENCE
B. Feb. 1, 1943, Hamilton, Ohio.
BR TR 5′10″ 168 lbs.

Year	Team	Games	BA	SA	AB	H	2B	3B	HR	HR%	R	RBI	BB	SO	SB	Pinch Hit AB	Pinch Hit H	PO	A	E	DP	TC/G	FA	G by Pos
1969	2 teams	DET A (17G –.267) NY A (72G –.175)																						
″	total	89	.183	.263	186	34	5	2	2	1.1	21	10	24	32	2	11	0	135	2	0	0	1.9	1.000	OF-74
1970	NY A	95	.227	.382	225	51	5	3	8	3.6	30	27	33	35	4	19	3	108	6	3	1	1.5	.974	OF-78
1971	2 teams	NY A (25G –.250) MON N (51G –.297)																						
″	total	76	.288	.406	170	49	8	3	2	1.2	30	19	23	20	0	28	5	100	5	2	1	2.0	.981	OF-54
1972	MON N	97	.258	.425	221	57	5	1	10	4.5	21	31	22	33	3	36	7	110	2	1	0	1.5	.991	OF-73
1973		135	.230	.311	318	73	11	3	3	0.9	45	31	56	34	12	28	6	208	7	5	1	1.9	.977	OF-114
1974		90	.205	.228	127	26	0	0	1	0.8	15	12	17	17	6	31	4	75	0	1	0	1.2	.987	OF-61
6 yrs.		582	.233	.342	1247	290	34	12	26	2.1	162	130	175	171	27	153	25	736	22	12	3	1.7	.984	OF-454

Walt Woods

WOODS, WALTER SYDNEY
B. Apr. 28, 1875, Rye, N. H. D. Oct. 30, 1951, Portsmouth, N. H.
BR TR 5′ 9½″ 165 lbs.

Year	Team	Games	BA	SA	AB	H	2B	3B	HR	HR%	R	RBI	BB	SO	SB	Pinch Hit AB	Pinch Hit H	PO	A	E	DP	TC/G	FA	G by Pos
1898	CHI N	48	.175	.182	154	27	1	0	0	0.0	16	8	4		3	0	0	42	87	15	3	2.9	.896	P-27, OF-11, 2B-6, SS-3, 3B-3
1899	LOU N	42	.151	.198	126	19	1	1	1	0.8	15	14	10		5	0	0	38	108	12	2	3.8	.924	P-26, 2B-11, SS-3, OF-2
1900	PIT N	1	.000	.000	1	0	0	0	0	0.0	0	0	0		0	0	0	0	0	0	0	0.0	.000	P-1
3 yrs.		91	.164	.189	281	46	2	1	1	0.4	31	22	14		8	0	0	80	195	27	5	3.2	.911	P-54, 2B-17, OF-13, SS-6, 3B-3

Tracy Woodson

WOODSON, TRACY MICHAEL
B. Oct. 5, 1962, Richmond, Va.
BR TR 6′ 3″ 215 lbs.

Year	Team	Games	BA	SA	AB	H	2B	3B	HR	HR%	R	RBI	BB	SO	SB	Pinch Hit AB	Pinch Hit H	PO	A	E	DP	TC/G	FA	G by Pos
1987	LA N	53	.228	.324	136	31	8	1	1	0.7	14	11	9	21	1	4	1	58	58	4	7	2.3	.967	3B-45, 1B-7
1988		65	.249	.335	173	43	4	1	3	1.7	15	15	7	32	1	9	3	160	60	6	13	3.4	.973	3B-41, 1B-25
1989		4	.000	.000	6	0	0	0	0	0.0	0	0	0	1	0	3	0	1	1	0	0	2.0	1.000	3B-1
1992	STL N	31	.307	.404	114	35	8	0	1	0.9	9	22	3	10	0	2	1	43	38	3	4	2.9	.964	3B-26, 1B-3
1993		62	.208	.234	77	16	2	0	0	0.0	4	2	1	14	0	24	7	56	25	4	10	2.2	.953	3B-28, 1B-11
5 yrs.		215	.247	.328	506	125	22	2	5	1.0	42	50	20	78	2	42	12	318	182	17	34	2.8	.967	3B-141, 1B-46
LEAGUE CHAMPIONSHIP SERIES																								
1988	LA N	3	.250	.250	4	1	0	0	0	0.0	0	0	0	1	0	2	1	3	0	0	0	1.0	1.000	1B-3

Tracy Woodson *continued*

Year	Team	Games	BA	SA	AB	H	2B	3B	HR	HR%	R	RBI	BB	SO	SB	Pinch Hit AB	Pinch Hit H	PO	A	E	DP	TC/G	FA	G by Pos
WORLD SERIES																								
1988	LA N	4	.000	.000	4	0	0	0	0	0.0	0	1	0	0	0	4	0	6	1	0	0	2.3	1.000	1B-3

Woody Woodward

WOODWARD, WILLIAM FREDERICK
B. Sept. 23, 1942, Miami, Fla.
BR TR 6′ 2″ 180 lbs.

Year	Team	Games	BA	SA	AB	H	2B	3B	HR	HR%	R	RBI	BB	SO	SB	Pinch Hit AB	Pinch Hit H	PO	A	E	DP	TC/G	FA	G by Pos
1963	MIL N	10	.000	.000	2	0	0	0	0	0.0	1	0	0	0	0	1	0	1	6	0	0	1.4	1.000	SS-5
1964		77	.209	.243	115	24	2	1	0	0.0	18	11	6	28	0	2	0	75	102	5	27	2.8	.973	2B-40, SS-18, 3B-7, 1B-1
1965		112	.208	.264	265	55	7	4	0	0.0	17	11	10	50	2	2	0	150	252	9	62	3.6	.978	SS-107, 2B-8
1966	ATL N	144	.264	.327	455	120	23	3	0	0.0	46	43	37	54	2	1	0	262	399	23	78	4.5	.966	2B-79, SS-73
1967		136	.226	.270	429	97	15	2	0	0.0	30	25	37	51	0	1	0	300	385	11	86	5.1	.984	2B-120, SS-16
1968	2 teams ATL N (12G –.167) CIN N (56G –.244)																							
″	total	68	.231	.252	143	33	3	0	0	0.0	15	11	8	29	2	5	0	71	123	6	20	3.3	.970	SS-47, 2B-10, 3B-2, 1B-1
1969	CIN N	97	.261	.311	241	63	12	0	0	0.0	36	15	24	40	3	0	0	148	249	14	36	4.3	.966	SS-93, 2B-2
1970		100	.223	.288	264	59	8	3	1	0.4	23	14	20	21	1	2	1	131	250	9	55	3.6	.977	SS-77, 3B-20, 2B-10, 1B-2
1971		136	.242	.282	273	66	9	1	0	0.0	22	18	27	28	4	3	1	129	253	7	49	2.5	.982	SS-85, 3B-63, 2B-9
9 yrs.		880	.236	.287	2187	517	79	14	1	0.0	208	148	169	301	14	17	2	1267	2019	84	413	3.8	.975	SS-521, 2B-278, 3B-92, 1B-4
LEAGUE CHAMPIONSHIP SERIES																								
1970	CIN N	3	.100	.100	10	1	0	0	0	0.0	0	0	1	0	0	0	0	0	0	0	0	0.0		SS-3, 3B-3
WORLD SERIES																								
1970	CIN N	4	.200	.200	5	1	0	0	0	0.0	0	0	0	0	0	1	1	4	5	0	2	3.0	1.000	SS-3

Earl Wooten

WOOTEN, EARL HAZWELL (Junior)
B. Jan. 16, 1924, Pelzer, S. C.
BR TL 5′11″ 160 lbs.

Year	Team	Games	BA	SA	AB	H	2B	3B	HR	HR%	R	RBI	BB	SO	SB	Pinch Hit AB	Pinch Hit H	PO	A	E	DP	TC/G	FA	G by Pos
1947	WAS A	6	.083	.083	24	2	0	0	0	0.0	0	1	0	4	1	0	0	19	0	2	0	3.5	.905	OF-6
1948		88	.256	.322	258	66	8	3	1	0.4	34	23	24	21	2	8	2	230	18	4	6	3.2	.984	OF-73, 1B-6, P-1
2 yrs.		94	.241	.301	282	68	8	3	1	0.4	34	24	24	25	3	8	2	249	18	6	6	3.2	.978	OF-79, 1B-6, P-1

Chuck Workman

WORKMAN, CHARLES THOMAS
B. Jan. 6, 1915, Leeton, Mo. D. Jan. 3, 1953, Kansas City, Mo.
BL TR 6′ 175 lbs.

Year	Team	Games	BA	SA	AB	H	2B	3B	HR	HR%	R	RBI	BB	SO	SB	Pinch Hit AB	Pinch Hit H	PO	A	E	DP	TC/G	FA	G by Pos
1938	CLE A	2	.400	.400	5	2	0	0	0	0.0	1	0	0	0	0	1	0	1	0	1	0	2.0	.500	OF-1
1941		9	.000	.000	4	0	0	0	0	0.0	2	0	1	1	0	4	0	0	0	0	0	0.0	—	
1943	BOS N	153	.249	.328	615	153	17	1	10	1.6	71	67	53	72	12	0	0	343	28	6	9	2.5	.984	OF-149, 1B-3, 3B-1
1944		140	.208	.344	418	87	18	3	11	2.6	46	53	42	41	1	16	4	186	60	6	7	2.1	.976	OF-103, 3B-19
1945		139	.274	.459	514	141	16	2	25	**4.9**	77	87	51	58	9	6	0	150	205	31	18	2.9	.920	3B-107, OF-24
1946	2 teams BOS N (25G –.167) PIT N (58G –.221)																							
″	total	83	.207	.311	193	40	6	1	4	2.1	16	23	14	30	2	24	**7**	132	5	3	1	2.6	.979	OF-52, 3B-1
6 yrs.		526	.242	.368	1749	423	57	7	50	2.9	213	230	161	202	24	51	11	812	298	47	35	2.5	.959	OF-329, 3B-128, 1B-3

Hank Workman

WORKMAN, HENRY KILGARIFF
B. Feb. 5, 1926, Los Angeles, Calif.
BL TR 6′ 1″ 185 lbs.

Year	Team	Games	BA	SA	AB	H	2B	3B	HR	HR%	R	RBI	BB	SO	SB	Pinch Hit AB	Pinch Hit H	PO	A	E	DP	TC/G	FA	G by Pos
1950	NY A	2	.200	.200	5	1	0	0	0	0.0	1	0	0	1	0	1	0	6	0	0	1	6.0	1.000	1B-1

Craig Worthington

WORTHINGTON, CRAIG RICHARD
B. Apr. 17, 1965, Los Angeles, Calif.
BR TR 6′ 160 lbs.

Year	Team	Games	BA	SA	AB	H	2B	3B	HR	HR%	R	RBI	BB	SO	SB	Pinch Hit AB	Pinch Hit H	PO	A	E	DP	TC/G	FA	G by Pos
1988	BAL A	26	.185	.284	81	15	2	0	2	2.5	5	4	9	24	1	0	0	20	53	3	4	2.9	.961	3B-26
1989		145	.247	.384	497	123	23	0	15	3.0	57	70	61	114	1	0	0	113	277	20	22	2.8	.951	3B-145
1990		133	.226	.322	425	96	17	0	8	1.9	46	44	63	96	1	0	0	90	218	18	28	2.5	.945	3B-131, DH-2
1991		31	.225	.373	102	23	3	0	4	3.9	11	12	12	14	0	1	0	26	51	2	3	2.6	.975	3B-30
1992	CLE A	9	.167	.167	24	4	0	0	0	0.0	0	2	2	4	0	0	0	6	18	4	2	3.1	.857	3B-9
1995	2 teams CIN N (10G –.278) TEX A (26G –.221)																							
″	total	36	.233	.395	86	20	5	0	3	3.5	5	8	9	9	0	4	2	39	39	1	6	2.5	.987	3B-28, 1B-4
6 yrs.		380	.231	.351	1215	281	50	0	32	2.6	124	140	156	261	3	5	2	294	656	48	65	2.7	.952	3B-369, 1B-4, DH-2

Red Worthington

WORTHINGTON, ROBERT LEE (Bob)
B. Apr. 24, 1906, Alhambra, Calif. D. Dec. 8, 1963, Sepulveda, Calif.
BR TR 5′11″ 170 lbs.

Year	Team	Games	BA	SA	AB	H	2B	3B	HR	HR%	R	RBI	BB	SO	SB	Pinch Hit AB	Pinch Hit H	PO	A	E	DP	TC/G	FA	G by Pos
1931	BOS N	128	.291	.407	491	143	25	10	4	0.8	47	44	26	38	1	4	0	242	8	3	1	2.0	.988	OF-124
1932		105	.303	.476	435	132	35	8	8	1.8	62	61	15	24	1	1	0	216	8	3	2	2.2	.987	OF-104
1933		17	.156	.244	45	7	4	0	0	0.0	3	0	1	3	0	7	0	17	1	2	0	2.0	.900	OF-10
1934	2 teams BOS N (41G –.246) STL N (1G –.000)																							
″	total	42	.242	.318	66	16	5	0	0	0.0	6	6	6	6	0	27	8	23	0	2	0	2.3	.920	OF-11
4 yrs.		292	.287	.423	1037	298	69	18	12	1.2	118	111	48	71	2	39	8	498	17	10	3	2.1	.981	OF-249

Chuck Wortman

WORTMAN, WILLIAM LEWIS
B. Jan. 5, 1892, Baltimore, Md. D. Aug. 19, 1977, Las Vegas, Nev.
BR TR 5′ 7″ 150 lbs.

Year	Team	Games	BA	SA	AB	H	2B	3B	HR	HR%	R	RBI	BB	SO	SB	Pinch Hit AB	Pinch Hit H	PO	A	E	DP	TC/G	FA	G by Pos
1916	CHI N	69	.201	.261	234	47	4	2	2	0.9	17	16	18	22	4	0	0	124	191	32	24	5.0	.908	SS-69
1917		75	.174	.205	190	33	4	1	0	0.0	24	9	18	23	6	0	0	85	164	22	26	4.0	.919	SS-65, 2B-1, 3B-1
1918		17	.118	.294	17	2	0	0	1	5.9	4	3	1	2	3	0	0	13	13	3	1	2.4	.897	2B-8, SS-4
3 yrs.		161	.186	.238	441	82	8	3	3	0.7	45	28	37	47	13	0	0	222	368	57	51	4.4	.912	SS-138, 2B-9, 3B-1
WORLD SERIES																								
1918	CHI N	1	.000	.000	1	0	0	0	0	0.0	0	0	0	0	0	0	0	1	0	0	0	1.0	1.000	2B-1

Ron Wotus

WOTUS, RONALD ALLAN
B. Mar. 3, 1961, Hartford, Conn.
BR TR 6′ 1″ 165 lbs.

Year	Team	Games	BA	SA	AB	H	2B	3B	HR	HR%	R	RBI	BB	SO	SB	Pinch Hit AB	Pinch Hit H	PO	A	E	DP	TC/G	FA	G by Pos
1983	PIT N	5	.000	.000	3	0	0	0	0	0.0	0	0	0	1	0	2	0	2	2	0	1	1.3	1.000	SS-2, 2B-1
1984		27	.218	.327	55	12	6	0	0	0.0	4	2	6	8	0	2	1	28	72	2	12	4.3	.980	SS-17, 2B-7
2 yrs.		32	.207	.310	58	12	6	0	0	0.0	4	2	6	9	0	4	1	30	74	2	13	3.9	.981	SS-19, 2B-8

Jimmy Woulfe

WOULFE, JAMES JOSEPH
B. Nov. 25, 1859, New Orleans, La. D. Dec. 20, 1924, New Orleans, La.
TR 5′11″

Year	Team	Games	BA	SA	AB	H	2B	3B	HR	HR%	R	RBI	BB	SO	SB	Pinch Hit AB	Pinch Hit H	PO	A	E	DP	TC/G	FA	G by Pos
1884	2 teams CIN AA (8G –.147) PIT AA (15G –.113)																							
″	total	23	.126	.161	87	11	1	1	0	0.0	10		1			0	0	32	4	10	2	2.0	.783	OF-22, 3B-1

Year	Team	Games	BA	SA	AB	H	2B	3B	HR	HR%	R	RBI	BB	SO	SB	Pinch Hit AB	Pinch Hit H	PO	A	E	DP	TC/G	FA	G by Pos

Ab Wright

WRIGHT, ALBERT OWEN BR TR 6′ 1½″ 190 lbs.
B. Nov. 16, 1905, Terlton, Okla.

Year	Team	Games	BA	SA	AB	H	2B	3B	HR	HR%	R	RBI	BB	SO	SB	Pinch Hit AB	Pinch Hit H	PO	A	E	DP	TC/G	FA	G by Pos
1935	CLE A	67	.237	.356	160	38	11	1	2	1.3	17	18	10	17	2	20	3	56	4	1	0	1.3	.984	OF-47
1944	BOS N	71	.256	.410	195	50	9	0	7	3.6	20	35	18	31	0	23	5	88	2	3	1	2.0	.968	OF-47
2 yrs.		138	.248	.386	355	88	20	1	9	2.5	37	53	28	48	2	43	8	144	6	4	1	1.6	.974	OF-94

Al Wright

WRIGHT, ALBERT EDGAR BR TR 6′ 2″ 168 lbs.
B. Nov. 11, 1912, San Francisco, Calif.

Year	Team	Games	BA	SA	AB	H	2B	3B	HR	HR%	R	RBI	BB	SO	SB	Pinch Hit AB	Pinch Hit H	PO	A	E	DP	TC/G	FA	G by Pos
1933	BOS N	4	1.000	1.000	1	1	0	0	0	0.0	0	0	0	0	0	0	0	1	0	1	0	0.7	.500	2B-3

Bill Wright

WRIGHT, WILLIAM HIRAM
Deceased.

Year	Team	Games	BA	SA	AB	H	2B	3B	HR	HR%	R	RBI	BB	SO	SB	Pinch Hit AB	Pinch Hit H	PO	A	E	DP	TC/G	FA	G by Pos
1887	WAS N	1	.667	.667	3	2	0	0	0	0.0	0	0	0	0	0	0	0	7	0	2	0	9.0	.778	C-1

Ceylon Wright

WRIGHT, CEYLON BL TR 5′ 9″ 150 lbs.
B. Aug. 16, 1893, Minneapolis, Minn. D. Nov. 7, 1947, Hines, Ill.

Year	Team	Games	BA	SA	AB	H	2B	3B	HR	HR%	R	RBI	BB	SO	SB	Pinch Hit AB	Pinch Hit H	PO	A	E	DP	TC/G	FA	G by Pos
1916	CHI A	8	.000	.000	18	0	0	0	0	0.0	0	0	1	7	0	0	0	8	19	5	2	4.0	.844	SS-8

Dick Wright

WRIGHT, WILLARD JAMES BR TR 5′10″ 170 lbs.
B. May 5, 1890, Worcester, N. Y. D. Jan. 24, 1952, Bethlehem, Pa.

Year	Team	Games	BA	SA	AB	H	2B	3B	HR	HR%	R	RBI	BB	SO	SB	Pinch Hit AB	Pinch Hit H	PO	A	E	DP	TC/G	FA	G by Pos
1915	BKN F	4	.000	.000	5	0	0	0	0	0.0	0	0	0		0	1	0	5	0	1	0	2.0	.833	C-3

George Wright

WRIGHT, GEORGE BR TR 5′ 9½″ 150 lbs.
Brother of Harry Wright. Brother of Sam Wright.
B. Jan. 28, 1847, Yonkers, N. Y. D. Aug. 21, 1937, Boston, Mass.
Manager 1879.
Hall of Fame 1937.

Year	Team	Games	BA	SA	AB	H	2B	3B	HR	HR%	R	RBI	BB	SO	SB	Pinch Hit AB	Pinch Hit H	PO	A	E	DP	TC/G	FA	G by Pos
1876	BOS N	70	.299	.397	**335**	100	18	6	1	0.3	72	34	8	9		0	0	96	253	44	16	5.5	.888	SS-68, 2B-2, P-1
1877		61	.276	.334	**290**	80	15	1	0	0.0	58	35	9	15		0	0	175	217	55	29	7.3	.877	2B-58, SS-3
1878		59	.225	.251	267	60	5	1	0	0.0	35	12	6	22		0	0	72	197	15	24	4.8	.947	SS-59
1879	PRO N	85	.276	.374	388	107	15	10	1	0.3	79	42	13	20		0	0	96	319	34	17	5.3	.924	SS-85
1880	BOS N	1	.250	.250	4	1	0	0	0	0.0	2	0	0	0		0	0	0	3	0	0	3.0	1.000	SS-1
1881		7	.200	.200	25	5	0	0	0	0.0	4	0	3	1		0	0	7	19	1	3	3.9	.963	SS-7
1882	PRO N	46	.162	.189	185	30	1	2	0	0.0	14		4	36		0	0	46	133	26	16	4.5	.873	SS-46
7 yrs.		329	.256	.323	1494	383	54	20	2	0.1	264	123	43	103		0	0	492	1141	175	105	5.5	.903	SS-269, 2B-60, P-1

George Wright

WRIGHT, GEORGE DEWITT BB TR 5′11″ 180 lbs.
B. Dec. 22, 1958, Oklahoma City, Okla.

Year	Team	Games	BA	SA	AB	H	2B	3B	HR	HR%	R	RBI	BB	SO	SB	Pinch Hit AB	Pinch Hit H	PO	A	E	DP	TC/G	FA	G by Pos
1982	TEX A	150	.264	.377	557	147	20	5	11	2.0	69	50	30	78	3	0	0	398	14	8	3	2.8	.981	OF-149
1983		162	.276	.424	634	175	28	6	18	2.8	79	80	41	82	8	2	0	460	6	7	1	2.9	.985	OF-161
1984		101	.243	.384	383	93	19	4	9	2.3	40	48	15	54	0	2	0	175	3	3	0	1.8	.983	OF-80, DH-18
1985		109	.190	.242	363	69	13	0	2	0.6	21	18	25	49	4	4	0	213	8	2	2	2.1	.991	OF-102, DH-4
1986	2 teams	TEX A (49G –.217) MON N (56G –.188)																						
″	total	105	.202	.291	223	45	8	3	2	0.9	22	12	15	51	4	35	2	109	4	2	0	1.5	.983	OF-74, DH-1
5 yrs.		627	.245	.361	2160	529	88	18	42	1.9	231	208	126	314	19	43	2	1355	35	22	6	2.4	.984	OF-566, DH-23

Glenn Wright

WRIGHT, FORREST GLENN (Buckshot) BR TR 5′11″ 170 lbs.
B. Feb. 6, 1901, Archie, Mo. D. Apr. 6, 1984, Olathe, Kans.

Year	Team	Games	BA	SA	AB	H	2B	3B	HR	HR%	R	RBI	BB	SO	SB	Pinch Hit AB	Pinch Hit H	PO	A	E	DP	TC/G	FA	G by Pos
1924	PIT N	153	.287	.425	**616**	177	28	18	7	1.1	80	111	27	52	14	0	0	310	601	52	102	6.3	.946	SS-153
1925		153	.308	.480	614	189	32	10	18	2.9	97	121	31	32	3	0	0	338	530	56	109	6.0	.939	SS-153, 3B-1
1926		119	.308	.459	458	141	15	15	8	1.7	73	77	19	26	6	3	0	242	382	49	82	5.8	.927	SS-116
1927		143	.281	.388	570	160	26	4	9	1.6	78	105	39	46	4	0	0	296	430	45	82	5.4	.942	SS-143
1928		108	.310	.457	407	126	20	8	8	2.0	63	66	21	53	3	6	1	195	301	39	59	5.2	.927	SS-101, 1B-1, OF-1
1929	BKN N	24	.200	.320	25	5	0	0	1	4.0	4	6	3	6	0	17	2	2	2	2	0	2.0	.667	SS-3
1930		135	.321	.543	532	171	28	12	22	4.1	83	126	32	70	2	1	0	297	462	28	97	5.9	.964	SS-134
1931		77	.284	.448	268	76	9	4	9	3.4	36	32	14	35	1	2	0	151	255	25	52	5.7	.942	SS-75
1932		127	.274	.433	446	122	31	5	10	2.2	50	60	12	57	4	4	0	235	387	40	84	5.3	.940	SS-122, 1B-2
1933		71	.255	.339	192	49	13	0	1	0.5	19	18	11	24	1	9	2	161	134	19	35	5.1	.939	SS-51, 1B-9, 3B-2
1935	CHI A	9	.120	.160	25	3	1	0	0	0.0	1	1	0	6	0	2	0	13	20	2	3	5.0	.943	2B-7
11 yrs.		1119	.294	.446	4153	1219	203	76	93	2.2	584	723	209	407	38	44	5	2240	3504	357	705	5.7	.941	SS-1051, 1B-12, 2B-7, 3B-3, OF-1
WORLD SERIES																								
1925	PIT N	7	.185	.333	27	5	1	0	1	3.7	3	3	1	4	0	0	0	11	24	2	0	5.3	.946	SS-7
1927		4	.154	.154	13	2	0	0	0	0.0	1	2	0	0	0	0	0	5	13	1	2	4.8	.947	SS-4
2 yrs.		11	.175	.275	40	7	1	0	1	2.5	4	5	1	4	0	0	0	16	37	3	2	5.1	.946	SS-11

Harry Wright

WRIGHT, WILLIAM HENRY BR TR 5′ 9½″ 157 lbs.
Brother of Sam Wright. Brother of George Wright.
B. Jan. 10, 1835, Sheffield, England D. Oct. 3, 1895, Atlantic City, N. J.
Manager 1876–93.
Hall of Fame 1953.

Year	Team	Games	BA	SA	AB	H	2B	3B	HR	HR%	R	RBI	BB	SO	SB	Pinch Hit AB	Pinch Hit H	PO	A	E	DP	TC/G	FA	G by Pos
1876	BOS N	1	.000	.000	3	0	0	0	0	0.0	0	0	0	1		0	0	0	0	0	0	0.0	.000	OF-1
1877		1	.000	.000	4	0	0	0	0	0.0	0	0	0	1		0	0	1	1	1	1	3.0	.667	OF-1
2 yrs.		2	.000	.000	7	0	0	0	0	0.0	0	0	0	2		0	0	1	1	1	1	1.5	.667	OF-2

Joe Wright

WRIGHT, JOSEPH S. BL TL 5′ 8″ 175 lbs.
B. 1873, Pittsburgh, Pa. Deceased.

Year	Team	Games	BA	SA	AB	H	2B	3B	HR	HR%	R	RBI	BB	SO	SB	Pinch Hit AB	Pinch Hit H	PO	A	E	DP	TC/G	FA	G by Pos
1895	LOU N	60	.276	.368	228	63	10	4	1	0.4	30	30	12	28	7	0	0	127	4	5	1	2.3	.963	OF-59, C-1
1896	2 teams	LOU N (2G –.286) PIT N (15G –.308)																						
″	total	17	.305	.373	59	18	2	1	0	0.0	5	6	1	3	1	2	1	26	0	1	0	1.8	.963	OF-14, 3B-1
2 yrs.		77	.282	.369	287	81	12	5	1	0.3	35	36	13	31	8	2	1	153	4	6	1	2.2	.963	OF-73, 3B-1, C-1

Pat Wright

WRIGHT, PATRICK W. BB TR 6′ 2″ 190 lbs.
B. July 5, 1868, Pottsville, Pa. D. May 29, 1943, Springfield, Ill.

Year	Team	Games	BA	SA	AB	H	2B	3B	HR	HR%	R	RBI	BB	SO	SB	Pinch Hit AB	Pinch Hit H	PO	A	E	DP	TC/G	FA	G by Pos
1890	CHI N	1	.000	.000	2	0	0	0	0	0.0	0	0	1	0	0	0	0	1	3	0	0	4.0	1.000	2B-1

Rasty Wright

WRIGHT, WILLIAM SMITH
B. Jan. 31, 1863, Birmingham, Mich. D. Oct. 14, 1922, Duluth, Minn.
BL 6′ 1″ 185 lbs.

Year	Team	Games	BA	SA	AB	H	2B	3B	HR	HR%	R	RBI	BB	SO	SB	Pinch Hit AB	Pinch Hit H	PO	A	E	DP	TC/G	FA	G by Pos
1890	2 teams	SYR AA (88G –.305) CLE N (13G –.111)																						
″	total	101	.282	.341	393	111	11	6	0	0.0	89	2	81	4	33	0	0	191	16	21	7	2.3	.908	OF-101

Sam Wright

WRIGHT, SAMUEL
Brother of Harry Wright. Brother of George Wright.
B. Nov. 25, 1848, New York, N. Y. D. May 6, 1928, Boston, Mass.
BR TR 5′ 7½″ 146 lbs.

Year	Team	Games	BA	SA	AB	H	2B	3B	HR	HR%	R	RBI	BB	SO	SB	Pinch Hit AB	Pinch Hit H	PO	A	E	DP	TC/G	FA	G by Pos
1876	BOS N	2	.125	.125	8	1	0	0	0	0.0	0	0	0	0		0	0	1	6	2	0	4.5	.778	SS-2
1880	CIN N	9	.088	.088	34	3	0	0	0	0.0	0	0	0	5		0	0	5	27	4	0	4.0	.889	SS-9
1881	BOS N	1	.250	.250	4	1	0	0	0	0.0	0	0	0	0		0	0	1	3	2	0	6.0	.667	SS-1
3 yrs.		12	.109	.109	46	5	0	0	0	0.0	0	0	0	5		0	0	7	36	8	0	4.3	.843	SS-12

Taffy Wright

WRIGHT, TAFT SHEDRON
B. Aug. 10, 1911, Tabor City, N. C. D. Oct. 22, 1981, Orlando, Fla.
BL TR 5′10″ 180 lbs.

Year	Team	Games	BA	SA	AB	H	2B	3B	HR	HR%	R	RBI	BB	SO	SB	Pinch Hit AB	Pinch Hit H	PO	A	E	DP	TC/G	FA	G by Pos
1938	WAS A	100	.350	.517	263	92	18	10	2	0.8	37	36	13	17	1	**39**	**13**	107	3	2	3	1.9	.982	OF-60
1939		129	.309	.435	499	154	29	11	4	0.8	77	93	38	19	1	6	3	236	10	13	4	2.1	.950	OF-123
1940	CHI A	147	.337	.448	581	196	31	9	5	0.9	79	88	43	25	4	2	1	278	11	11	2	2.1	.963	OF-144
1941		136	.322	.468	513	165	35	5	10	1.9	71	97	60	27	5	1	0	279	8	8	3	2.2	.973	OF-134
1942		85	.333	.410	300	100	13	5	0	0.0	43	47	48	9	1	4	1	176	6	6	1	2.3	.968	OF-81
1946		115	.275	.389	422	116	19	4	7	1.7	46	52	42	17	10	7	2	217	5	2	0	2.1	.991	OF-107
1947		124	.324	.387	401	130	13	0	4	1.0	48	54	48	17	8	18	3	198	6	6	1	2.1	.971	OF-100
1948		134	.279	.365	455	127	15	6	4	0.9	50	61	39	18	2	19	6	227	9	3	3	2.1	.987	OF-114
1949	PHI A	59	.235	.356	149	35	2	5	2	1.3	14	25	16	6	0	19	3	60	5	2	0	1.9	.970	OF-35
9 yrs.		1029	.311	.423	3583	1115	175	55	38	1.1	465	553	347	155	32	115	32	1778	63	53	17	2.1	.972	OF-898

Tom Wright

WRIGHT, THOMAS EVERETTE
B. Sept. 22, 1923, Shelby, N. C.
BL TR 5′11½″ 180 lbs.

Year	Team	Games	BA	SA	AB	H	2B	3B	HR	HR%	R	RBI	BB	SO	SB	Pinch Hit AB	Pinch Hit H	PO	A	E	DP	TC/G	FA	G by Pos
1948	BOS A	3	.500	1.500	2	1	0	1	0	0.0	1	0	0	0	0	2	1	0	0	0	0	0.0	—	
1949		5	.250	.500	4	1	1	0	0	0.0	1	1	1	1	0	4	1	0	0	0	0	0.0	—	
1950		54	.318	.383	107	34	7	0	0	0.0	17	20	6	18	0	28	7	40	1	2	1	1.8	.953	OF-24
1951		28	.222	.317	63	14	1	1	1	1.6	8	9	11	8	0	10	1	19	0	1	0	1.1	.950	OF-18
1952	2 teams	STL A (29G –.242) CHI A (60G –.258)																						
″	total	89	.253	.354	198	50	10	2	2	1.0	21	27	28	36	2	34	**10**	98	4	3	0	2.0	.971	OF-52
1953	CHI A	77	.250	.379	132	33	5	3	2	1.5	14	25	12	21	0	42	13	44	1	1	0	1.4	.978	OF-33
1954	WAS A	76	.246	.333	171	42	4	4	1	0.6	13	17	18	38	0	32	8	84	0	0	0	2.0	1.000	OF-43
1955		7	.000	.000	7	0	0	0	0	0.0	0	0	0	1	0	7	0	0	0	0	0	0.0	—	
1956		2	.000	.000	1	0	0	0	0	0.0	0	0	0	0	0	1	0	0	0	0	0	0.0	—	
9 yrs.		341	.255	.355	685	175	28	11	6	0.9	75	99	76	123	2	160	41	285	6	7	1	1.8	.977	OF-170

Russ Wrightstone

WRIGHTSTONE, RUSSELL GUY
B. Mar. 18, 1893, Bowmansdale, Pa. D. Feb. 25, 1969, Harrisburg, Pa.
BL TR 5′10½″ 176 lbs.

Year	Team	Games	BA	SA	AB	H	2B	3B	HR	HR%	R	RBI	BB	SO	SB	Pinch Hit AB	Pinch Hit H	PO	A	E	DP	TC/G	FA	G by Pos
1920	PHI N	76	.262	.345	206	54	6	1	3	1.5	23	17	10	25	3	16	4	76	109	13	7	3.4	.934	3B-56, SS-2, 2B-1
1921		109	.296	.425	372	110	13	4	9	2.4	59	51	18	20	4	12	2	135	134	19	6	3.0	.934	3B-54, OF-37, 2B-4
1922		99	.305	.441	331	101	18	6	5	1.5	56	33	28	17	4	20	3	118	227	11	29	4.6	.969	3B-40, SS-35, 1B-2
1923		119	.273	.416	392	107	21	7	7	1.8	59	57	21	19	5	16	5	132	216	15	30	3.6	.959	3B-72, SS-21, 2B-9
1924		118	.307	.443	388	119	24	4	7	1.8	55	58	27	15	5	9	2	139	197	21	23	3.2	.941	3B-97, 2B-9, SS-5, OF-1
1925		72	.346	.591	286	99	18	5	14	4.9	48	61	19	18	0	7	6	152	62	16	11	2.7	.930	OF-45, SS-12, 3B-11, 2B-10, 1B-6
1926		112	.307	.432	368	113	23	1	7	1.9	55	57	27	11	5	4	2	549	125	19	64	6.4	.973	1B-53, 3B-37, 2B-13, OF-5
1927		141	.306	.403	533	163	24	5	6	1.1	62	75	48	20	9	3	0	1268	90	15	114	9.9	.989	1B-136, 3B-1, 2B-1
1928	2 teams	PHI N (33G –.209) NY N (30G –.160)																						
″	total	63	.198	.310	116	23	5	1	2	1.7	10	16	17	7	0	28	4	53	3	5	1	1.9	.918	OF-26, 1B-6
9 yrs.		909	.297	.431	2992	889	152	34	60	2.0	427	425	215	152	35	115	28	2622	1163	134	285	4.9	.966	3B-368, 1B-203, OF-114, SS-75, 2B-47

Zeke Wrigley

WRIGLEY, GEORGE WATSON
B. Jan. 18, 1874, Philadelphia, Pa. D. Sept. 28, 1952, Philadelphia, Pa.
5′ 8½″ 150 lbs.

Year	Team	Games	BA	SA	AB	H	2B	3B	HR	HR%	R	RBI	BB	SO	SB	Pinch Hit AB	Pinch Hit H	PO	A	E	DP	TC/G	FA	G by Pos
1896	WAS N	5	.111	.111	9	1	0	0	0	0.0	1	2	1	1	0	1	0	4	15	1	0	5.0	.950	2B-3, SS-1
1897		104	.284	.384	388	110	14	8	3	0.8	65	64	21		5	0	0	175	209	50	18	4.0	.885	OF-36, SS-33, 3B-30, 2B-9
1898		111	.245	.333	400	98	9	10	2	0.5	50	39	20		10	0	0	284	358	72	45	6.4	.899	SS-97, 2B-11, OF-3, 3B-1
1899	2 teams	NY N (4G –.200) BKN N (15G –.204)																						
″	total	19	.203	.297	64	13	2	2	0	0.0	5	12	4		3	0	0	35	42	12	4	4.7	.865	SS-14, 3B-5
4 yrs.		239	.258	.351	861	222	25	20	5	0.6	121	117	46	1	18	1	0	498	624	135	67	5.2	.893	SS-145, OF-39, 3B-36, 2B-23

Rick Wrona

WRONA, RICHARD JAMES
B. Dec. 10, 1963, Tulsa, Okla.
BR TR 6′ 1″ 185 lbs.

Year	Team	Games	BA	SA	AB	H	2B	3B	HR	HR%	R	RBI	BB	SO	SB	Pinch Hit AB	Pinch Hit H	PO	A	E	DP	TC/G	FA	G by Pos
1988	CHI N	4	.000	.000	6	0	0	0	0	0.0	0	0	0	1	0	1	0	11	1	0	0	6.0	1.000	C-2
1989		38	.283	.391	92	26	2	1	2	2.2	11	14	2	21	0	3	2	158	15	3	1	4.8	.983	C-37
1990		16	.172	.172	29	5	0	0	0	0.0	3	0	2	11	1	0	0	55	9	2	2	4.1	.970	C-16
1992	CIN N	11	.174	.174	23	4	0	0	0	0.0	0	0	0	3	0	0	0	52	5	2	0	5.4	.966	C-10, 1B-1
1993	CHI A	4	.125	.125	8	1	0	0	0	0.0	0	1	0	4	0	0	0	12	0	0	0	3.0	1.000	C-4
1994	MIL A	6	.500	1.200	10	5	4	0	1	10.0	2	3	1	1	0	2	1	10	2	1	0	2.2	.923	C-5, 1B-1
6 yrs.		79	.244	.345	168	41	6	1	3	1.8	16	18	5	41	1	6	3	298	32	8	3	4.4	.976	C-74, 1B-2
LEAGUE CHAMPIONSHIP SERIES																								
1989	CHI N	2	.000	.000	5	0	0	0	0	0.0	0	0	0	3	0	0	0	9	1	0	0	5.0	1.000	C-2

Yats Wuestling

WUESTLING, GEORGE
B. Oct. 18, 1903, St. Louis, Mo. D. Apr. 26, 1970, St. Louis, Mo.
BR TR 5′11″ 167 lbs.

Year	Team	Games	BA	SA	AB	H	2B	3B	HR	HR%	R	RBI	BB	SO	SB	Pinch Hit AB	Pinch Hit H	PO	A	E	DP	TC/G	FA	G by Pos
1929	DET A	54	.200	.240	150	30	4	1	0	0.0	13	16	9	24	0	0	0	78	140	13	19	4.3	.944	SS-52, 3B-1, 2B-1
1930	2 teams	DET A (4G –.000) NY A (25G –.190)																						
″	total	29	.164	.194	67	11	0	1	0	0.0	5	3	6	17	0	1	0	41	54	8	12	3.7	.922	SS-25, 3B-3
2 yrs.		83	.189	.226	217	41	4	2	0	0.0	18	19	15	41	0	1	0	119	194	21	31	4.1	.937	SS-77, 3B-4, 2B-1

Joe Wyatt

WYATT, LORAL JOHN
B. Apr. 6, 1900, Petersburg, Ind. D. Dec. 5, 1970, Oblong, Ill.
BR TR 6′ 1″ 175 lbs.

Year	Team	Games	BA	SA	AB	H	2B	3B	HR	HR%	R	RBI	BB	SO	SB	Pinch Hit AB	Pinch Hit H	PO	A	E	DP	TC/G	FA	G by Pos
1924	CLE A	4	.182	.182	11	2	0	0	0	0.0	1	1	2	1	0	0	0	5	0	1	0	1.5	.833	OF-4

Ren Wylie

WYLIE, JAMES RENWICK
B. Dec. 14, 1861, Elizabeth, Pa. D. Aug. 17, 1951, Wilkinsburg, Pa.
BR TR 5′11″ 155 lbs.

Year	Team	Games	BA	SA	AB	H	2B	3B	HR	HR%	R	RBI	BB	SO	SB	Pinch Hit AB	Pinch Hit H	PO	A	E	DP	TC/G	FA	G by Pos
1882	PIT AA	1	.000	.000	3	0	0	0	0	0.0	0		0			0	0	0	1	0	0	1.0	1.000	OF-1

Frank Wyman

WYMAN, FRANK C.
B. May 10, 1862, Haverhill, Mass. D. Feb. 4, 1916, Everett, Mass.

Year	Team	Games	BA	SA	AB	H	2B	3B	HR	HR%	R	RBI	BB	SO	SB	Pinch Hit AB	Pinch Hit H	PO	A	E	DP	TC/G	FA	G by Pos
1884	2 teams	KC U (30G –.218) CHI U (2G –.375)																						
″	total	32	.227	.258	132	30	4	0	0	0.0	17		3			0	0	90	19	26	4	3.8	.807	OF-25, 1B-5, 3B-3, P-3

Butch Wynegar

WYNEGAR, HAROLD DELANO
B. Mar. 14, 1956, York, Pa.
BB TR 6′ 1″ 190 lbs.

Year	Team	Games	BA	SA	AB	H	2B	3B	HR	HR%	R	RBI	BB	SO	SB	Pinch Hit AB	Pinch Hit H	PO	A	E	DP	TC/G	FA	G by Pos
1976	MIN A	149	.260	.363	534	139	21	2	10	1.9	58	69	79	63	0	3	1	650	78	16	6	4.9	.978	C-137, DH-15
1977		144	.261	.370	532	139	22	3	10	1.9	76	79	68	61	2	5	2	676	84	5	8	5.3	.993	C-142, 3B-1
1978		135	.229	.308	454	104	22	1	4	0.9	36	45	47	42	1	8	1	582	70	8	12	5.0	.988	C-131, 3B-1
1979		149	.270	.351	504	136	20	0	7	1.4	74	57	74	36	2	2	0	653	65	6	10	4.9	.992	C-146, DH-2
1980		146	.255	.335	486	124	18	3	5	1.0	61	57	63	36	3	8	2	670	72	9	13	5.3	.988	C-142, DH-1
1981		47	.247	.280	150	37	5	0	0	0.0	11	10	17	9	0	2	0	162	24	1	4	4.1	.995	C-37, DH-9
1982	2 teams	MIN A (24G –.209) NY A (63G –.293)																						
″	total	87	.267	.361	277	74	12	1	4	1.4	36	28	50	33	0	2	0	523	26	5	10	6.4	.991	C-86
1983	NY A	94	.296	.429	301	89	18	2	6	2.0	40	42	52	29	1	4	0	480	29	8	4	5.6	.985	C-93
1984		129	.267	.342	442	118	13	1	6	1.4	48	45	64	36	1	7	1	757	59	6	9	6.5	.993	C-126
1985		102	.223	.320	309	69	15	0	5	1.6	27	32	64	43	0	8	3	547	34	6	7	6.1	.990	C-96
1986		61	.206	.345	194	40	4	1	7	3.6	19	29	30	21	0	8	3	325	22	2	1	6.1	.994	C-57
1987	CAL A	31	.207	.228	92	19	2	0	0	0.0	4	5	9	13	0	3	0	162	12	1	3	6.0	.994	C-28, DH-1
1988		27	.255	.418	55	14	4	1	1	1.8	8	8	8	7	0	4	1	94	8	2	1	4.0	.981	C-26
13 yrs.		1301	.255	.347	4330	1102	176	15	65	1.5	498	506	625	429	10	64	14	6281	583	75	88	5.4	.989	C-1247, DH-28, 3B-2

Early Wynn

WYNN, EARLY (Gus)
B. Jan. 6, 1920, Hartford, Ala.
Hall of Fame 1972.
BB TR 6′ 190 lbs.
BR 1941–1944

Year	Team	Games	BA	SA	AB	H	2B	3B	HR	HR%	R	RBI	BB	SO	SB	Pinch Hit AB	Pinch Hit H	PO	A	E	DP	TC/G	FA	G by Pos
1939	WAS A	3	.167	.167	6	1	0	0	0	0.0	0	1	1	1	0	0	0	1	0	0	0	0.3	1.000	P-3
1941		5	.133	.200	15	2	1	0	0	0.0	1	0	0	5	0	0	0	2	9	1	1	2.4	.917	P-5
1942		30	.217	.246	69	15	2	0	0	0.0	4	7	3	13	0	0	0	5	36	2	3	1.4	.953	P-30
1943		38	.296	.378	98	29	3	1	1	1.0	6	11	1	11	0	1	0	5	49	3	3	1.5	.947	P-37
1944		43	.207	.261	92	19	2	0	1	1.1	4	6	3	21	0	11	1	4	31	1	4	1.1	.972	P-33
1946		25	.319	.426	47	15	2	0	1	2.1	4	9	5	7	0	6	3	7	18	1	2	1.5	.962	P-17
1947		54	.275	.375	120	33	6	0	2	1.7	6	13	1	19	0	20	6	15	33	1	3	1.5	.980	P-33
1948		73	.217	.264	106	23	3	1	0	0.0	9	16	14	22	0	32	3	6	32	2	1	1.2	.950	P-33
1949	CLE A	35	.143	.200	70	10	1	0	1	1.4	3	7	4	10	0	7	0	16	31	0	3	1.8	1.000	P-26
1950		39	.234	.403	77	18	5	1	2	2.6	12	10	10	12	0	5	1	5	36	3	5	1.4	.932	P-32
1951		41	.185	.306	108	20	8	1	1	0.9	8	13	7	9	0	3	0	13	42	1	2	1.5	.982	P-37
1952		44	.222	.242	99	22	2	0	0	0.0	5	10	9	15	0	2	1	20	46	4	2	1.7	.943	P-42
1953		37	.275	.396	91	25	2	0	3	3.3	11	10	7	17	0	1	0	11	36	0	2	1.3	1.000	P-36
1954		40	.183	.215	93	17	3	0	0	0.0	10	4	7	13	0	0	0	17	27	2	1	1.1	.957	P-40
1955		34	.179	.250	84	15	3	0	1	1.2	8	7	6	17	0	2	0	7	27	2	0	1.1	.944	P-32
1956		38	.228	.307	101	23	5	0	1	1.0	5	15	7	22	1	0	0	15	48	3	3	1.7	.955	P-38
1957		40	.116	.116	86	10	0	0	0	0.0	4	4	11	23	0	0	0	10	38	0	5	1.2	1.000	P-40
1958	CHI A	40	.200	.213	75	15	1	0	0	0.0	7	11	10	25	0	0	0	12	25	0	2	0.9	1.000	P-40
1959		37	.244	.389	90	22	7	0	2	2.2	11	8	9	18	0	0	0	6	39	2	2	1.3	.957	P-37
1960		36	.200	.293	75	15	2	1	1	1.3	8	7	14	17	0	0	0	7	28	1	1	1.0	.972	P-36
1961		17	.162	.162	37	6	0	0	0	0.0	4	2	3	11	0	0	0	4	11	0	0	0.9	1.000	P-17
1962		27	.130	.148	54	7	1	0	0	0.0	5	2	7	17	0	0	0	3	20	0	2	0.9	1.000	P-27
1963	CLE A	20	.273	.273	11	3	0	0	0	0.0	1	0	2	5	0	0	0	2	8	0	0	0.5	1.000	P-20
23 yrs.		796	.214	.285	1704	365	59	5	17	1.0	136	173	141	330	1	90	15	193	670	29	47	1.3	.967	P-691
WORLD SERIES																								
1954	CLE A	1	.500	1.000	2	1	1	0	0	0.0	0	0	0	1	0	0	0	1	1	0	0	2.0	1.000	P-1
1959	CHI A	3	.200	.400	5	1	1	0	0	0.0	0	1	0	2	0	0	0	1	3	0	0	1.3	1.000	P-3
2 yrs.		4	.286	.571	7	2	2	0	0	0.0	0	1	0	3	0	0	0	2	4	0	0	1.5	1.000	P-4

Jimmy Wynn

WYNN, JAMES SHERMAN (The Toy Cannon)
B. Mar. 12, 1942, Hamilton, Ohio
BR TR 5′10″ 160 lbs.

Year	Team	Games	BA	SA	AB	H	2B	3B	HR	HR%	R	RBI	BB	SO	SB	Pinch Hit AB	Pinch Hit H	PO	A	E	DP	TC/G	FA	G by Pos
1963	HOU N	70	.244	.372	250	61	10	5	4	1.6	31	27	30	53	4	1	0	124	33	8	3	2.2	.952	OF-53, SS-21, 3B-2
1964		67	.224	.324	219	49	7	0	5	2.3	19	18	24	58	5	3	0	129	8	6	3	2.2	.958	OF-64
1965		157	.275	.470	564	155	30	7	22	3.9	90	73	84	126	43	3	0	382	13	9	1	2.6	.978	OF-155
1966		105	.256	.440	418	107	21	1	18	4.3	62	62	41	81	13	0	0	259	6	6	4	2.6	.978	OF-104
1967		158	.249	.495	594	148	29	3	37	6.2	102	107	74	**137**	16	1	0	364	4	12	1	2.4	.968	OF-157
1968		156	.269	.474	542	146	23	5	26	4.8	85	67	90	131	11	3	0	298	20	4	8	2.1	.988	OF-153
1969		149	.269	.507	495	133	17	1	33	6.7	113	87	**148**	142	23	0	0	318	9	5	3	2.2	.985	OF-149
1970		157	.282	.493	554	156	32	2	27	4.9	82	88	106	96	24	2	1	293	14	4	4	2.1	.987	OF-151
1971		123	.203	.295	404	82	16	0	7	1.7	38	45	56	63	10	9	1	232	9	3	5	2.1	.988	OF-116
1972		145	.273	.470	542	148	29	3	24	4.4	117	90	103	99	17	1	0	284	8	5	2	2.1	.983	OF-144
1973		139	.220	.395	481	106	14	5	20	4.2	90	55	91	102	14	4	0	270	9	4	1	2.1	.986	OF-133
1974	LA N	150	.271	.497	535	145	17	4	32	6.0	104	108	108	104	18	3	0	365	10	3	3	2.6	.992	OF-148
1975		130	.248	.417	412	102	16	0	18	4.4	80	58	110	77	7	10	0	282	6	5	2	2.4	.983	OF-120
1976	ATL N	148	.207	.367	449	93	19	1	17	3.8	75	66	**127**	111	16	8	2	287	17	9	2	2.3	.971	OF-138
1977	2 teams	NY A (30G –.143) MIL A (36G –.197)																						
″	total	66	.175	.237	194	34	5	2	1	0.5	17	13	32	47	4	13	1	50	1	1	0	1.2	.981	OF-25, DH-18
15 yrs.		1920	.250	.436	6653	1665	285	39	291	4.4	1105	964	1224	1427	225	61	5	3937	167	84	42	2.3	.980	OF-1810, SS-21, DH-18, 3B-2

Jimmy Wynn *continued*

Year	Team	Games	BA	SA	AB	H	2B	3B	HR	HR%	R	RBI	BB	SO	SB	Pinch Hit AB	Pinch Hit H	PO	A	E	DP	TC/G	FA	G by Pos
LEAGUE CHAMPIONSHIP SERIES																								
1974	**LA N**	4	.200	.400	10	2	2	0	0	0.0	4	2	9	1	1	0	0	11	0	0	0	2.8	1.000	OF-4
WORLD SERIES																								
1974	**LA N**	5	.188	.438	16	3	1	0	1	6.3	1	2	4	4	0	0	0	5	0	0	0	1.0	1.000	OF-5

Marvell Wynne

WYNNE, MARVELL BL TL 5′11″ 176 lbs.
B. Dec. 17, 1959, Chicago, Ill.

Year	Team	Games	BA	SA	AB	H	2B	3B	HR	HR%	R	RBI	BB	SO	SB	Pinch Hit AB	Pinch Hit H	PO	A	E	DP	TC/G	FA	G by Pos
1983	**PIT N**	103	.243	.355	366	89	16	2	7	1.9	66	26	38	52	12	1	0	223	3	4	2	2.3	.983	OF-102
1984		154	.266	.337	653	174	24	11	0	0.0	77	39	42	81	24	0	0	373	8	4	1	2.5	.990	OF-154
1985		103	.205	.258	337	69	6	3	2	0.6	21	18	18	48	10	3	0	229	7	3	1	2.4	.987	OF-99
1986	**SD N**	137	.264	.417	288	76	19	2	7	2.4	34	37	15	45	11	12	3	203	3	3	2	1.7	.986	OF-125
1987		98	.250	.346	188	47	8	2	2	1.1	17	24	20	37	11	30	6	100	2	2	0	1.5	.981	OF-71
1988		128	.264	.426	333	88	13	4	11	3.3	37	42	31	62	3	23	2	216	5	3	2	2.0	.987	OF-113
1989	**2 teams**	**SD N** (105G –.252) **CHI N** (20G –.188)																						
″	**total**	125	.243	.354	342	83	13	2	7	2.0	27	39	13	48	6	17	2	177	7	6	2	1.7	.968	OF-109
1990	**CHI N**	92	.204	.333	186	38	8	2	4	2.2	21	19	14	25	3	26	4	108	3	1	2	1.7	.991	OF-66
8 yrs.		940	.247	.352	2693	664	107	28	40	1.5	300	244	191	398	80	112	17	1629	38	26	12	2.0	.985	OF-839
LEAGUE CHAMPIONSHIP SERIES																								
1989	**CHI N**	4	.167	.167	6	1	0	0	0	0.0	0	0	0	0	0	2	0	3	0	0	0	1.5	1.000	OF-2

Johnny Wyrostek

WYROSTEK, JOHN BARNEY BL TR 6′ 2″ 180 lbs.
B. July 12, 1919, Fairmont City, Ill. D. Dec. 12, 1986, St. Louis, Mo.

Year	Team	Games	BA	SA	AB	H	2B	3B	HR	HR%	R	RBI	BB	SO	SB	Pinch Hit AB	Pinch Hit H	PO	A	E	DP	TC/G	FA	G by Pos
1942	**PIT N**	9	.114	.171	35	4	0	1	0	0.0	0	3	3	2	0	1	0	18	1	0	1	2.4	1.000	OF-8
1943		51	.152	.190	79	12	3	0	0	0.0	7	1	3	15	0	24	4	34	1	5	0	1.7	.875	OF-20, 3B-2, 2B-1, 1B-1
1946	**PHI N**	145	.281	.383	545	153	30	4	6	1.1	73	45	70	42	7	3	0	388	18	8	4	2.9	.981	OF-142
1947		128	.273	.390	454	124	24	7	5	1.1	68	51	61	45	7	1	0	261	11	8	2	2.2	.971	OF-126
1948	**CIN N**	136	.273	.455	512	140	24	9	17	3.3	74	76	52	63	7	5	0	331	8	8	1	2.7	.977	OF-130
1949		134	.249	.365	474	118	20	4	9	1.9	54	46	58	63	7	5	0	293	10	9	1	2.4	.971	OF-129
1950		131	.285	.418	509	145	34	5	8	1.6	70	76	52	38	1	1	1	258	10	5	4	2.1	.982	OF-129, 1B-4
1951		142	.311	.391	537	167	31	3	2	0.4	52	61	54	54	2	3	2	255	8	8	2	1.9	.970	OF-139
1952	**2 teams**	**CIN N** (30G –.236) **PHI N** (98G –.274)																						
″	**total**	128	.265	.347	427	113	17	6	2	0.5	57	47	62	33	2	11	2	280	16	6	2	2.6	.980	OF-117, 1B-1
1953	**PHI N**	125	.271	.359	409	111	14	2	6	1.5	42	47	38	43	0	15	2	192	11	8	2	1.9	.962	OF-110
1954		92	.239	.351	259	62	12	4	3	1.2	28	28	29	39	0	17	5	277	14	4	21	3.8	.986	OF-55, 1B-22
11 yrs.		1221	.271	.383	4240	1149	209	45	58	1.4	525	481	482	437	33	86	16	2587	108	69	40	2.4	.975	OF-1105, 1B-28, 3B-2, 2B-1

Henry Yaik

YAIK, HENRY 5′11″ 185 lbs.
B. Mar. 1, 1864, Detroit, Mich. D. Sept. 21, 1935, Detroit, Mich.

Year	Team	Games	BA	SA	AB	H	2B	3B	HR	HR%	R	RBI	BB	SO	SB	Pinch Hit AB	Pinch Hit H	PO	A	E	DP	TC/G	FA	G by Pos
1888	**PIT N**	2	.333	.333	6	2	0	0	0	0.0	0	1	1	0	0	0	0	9	3	6	1	9.0	.667	OF-1, C-1

Ad Yale

YALE, WILLIAM M.
B. Apr. 17, 1870, Bristol, Conn. D. Apr. 27, 1948, Bridgeport, Conn.

Year	Team	Games	BA	SA	AB	H	2B	3B	HR	HR%	R	RBI	BB	SO	SB	Pinch Hit AB	Pinch Hit H	PO	A	E	DP	TC/G	FA	G by Pos
1905	**BKN N**	4	.077	.077	13	1	0	0	0	0.0	1	1	1		0	0	0	38	1	0	4	9.8	1.000	1B-4

Hugh Yancy

YANCY, HUGH BR TR 5′11″ 170 lbs.
B. Oct. 16, 1950, Sarasota, Fla.

Year	Team	Games	BA	SA	AB	H	2B	3B	HR	HR%	R	RBI	BB	SO	SB	Pinch Hit AB	Pinch Hit H	PO	A	E	DP	TC/G	FA	G by Pos
1972	**CHI A**	3	.111	.111	9	1	0	0	0	0.0	0	0	0	0	0	0	0	2	6	0	0	2.7	1.000	3B-3
1974		1	—	—	0	0	0	0	0	—	0	0	0	0	0	0	0	0	0	0	0	0.0	.000	DH-1
1976		3	.100	.200	10	1	1	0	0	0.0	0	0	0	3	0	0	0	8	4	0	3	4.0	1.000	2B-3
3 yrs.		7	.105	.158	19	2	1	0	0	0.0	0	0	0	3	0	0	0	10	10	0	3	2.9	1.000	2B-3, 3B-3, DH-1

George Yankowski

YANKOWSKI, GEORGE EDWARD BR TR 6′ 180 lbs.
B. Nov. 19, 1922, Cambridge, Mass.

Year	Team	Games	BA	SA	AB	H	2B	3B	HR	HR%	R	RBI	BB	SO	SB	Pinch Hit AB	Pinch Hit H	PO	A	E	DP	TC/G	FA	G by Pos
1942	**PHI A**	6	.154	.231	13	2	1	0	0	0.0	0	2	0	2	0	0	0	14	3	0	0	2.8	1.000	C-6
1949	**CHI A**	12	.167	.222	18	3	1	0	0	0.0	0	2	0	2	0	6	0	15	3	0	0	3.0	1.000	C-6
2 yrs.		18	.161	.226	31	5	2	0	0	0.0	0	4	0	4	0	6	0	29	6	0	0	2.9	1.000	C-12

George Yantz

YANTZ, GEORGE WEBB BR TR 5′ 6½″ 168 lbs.
B. July 27, 1886, Louisville, Ky. D. Feb. 26, 1967, Louisville, Ky.

Year	Team	Games	BA	SA	AB	H	2B	3B	HR	HR%	R	RBI	BB	SO	SB	Pinch Hit AB	Pinch Hit H	PO	A	E	DP	TC/G	FA	G by Pos
1912	**CHI N**	1	1.000	1.000	1	1	0	0	0	0.0	0	0	0	0	0	0	0	0	0	0	0	0.0	.000	C-1

Yam Yaryan

YARYAN, CLARENCE EVERETT BR TR 5′10½″ 180 lbs.
B. Nov. 5, 1892, Knowlton, Iowa D. Nov. 16, 1964, Birmingham, Ala.

Year	Team	Games	BA	SA	AB	H	2B	3B	HR	HR%	R	RBI	BB	SO	SB	Pinch Hit AB	Pinch Hit H	PO	A	E	DP	TC/G	FA	G by Pos
1921	**CHI A**	45	.304	.422	102	31	8	2	0	0.0	11	15	9	16	0	10	1	72	26	7	1	3.1	.933	C-34
1922		36	.197	.310	71	14	2	0	2	2.8	9	9	6	10	1	8	0	71	14	3	1	3.5	.966	C-25
2 yrs.		81	.260	.376	173	45	10	2	2	1.2	20	24	15	26	1	18	1	143	40	10	2	3.3	.948	C-59

Carl Yastrzemski

YASTRZEMSKI, CARL MICHAEL (Yaz) BL TR 5′11″ 175 lbs.
B. Aug. 22, 1939, Southampton, N. Y.
Hall of Fame 1989.

Year	Team	Games	BA	SA	AB	H	2B	3B	HR	HR%	R	RBI	BB	SO	SB	Pinch Hit AB	Pinch Hit H	PO	A	E	DP	TC/G	FA	G by Pos
1961	**BOS A**	148	.266	.396	583	155	31	6	11	1.9	71	80	50	96	6	1	0	248	12	10	1	1.8	.963	OF-147
1962		160	.296	.469	646	191	43	6	19	2.9	99	94	66	82	7	0	0	329	15	11	3	2.2	.969	OF-160
1963		151	**.321**	.475	570	**183**	**40**	3	14	2.5	91	68	**95**	72	8	0	0	283	18	6	3	2.0	.980	OF-151
1964		151	.289	.451	567	164	29	9	15	2.6	77	67	75	90	6	0	0	372	24	11	4	2.7	.973	OF-148, 3B-2
1965		133	.312	**.536**	494	154	**45**	3	20	4.0	78	72	70	58	7	3	0	222	11	3	2	1.8	.987	OF-130
1966		160	.278	.431	594	165	**39**	2	16	2.7	81	80	84	60	8	3	1	310	15	5	2	2.1	.985	OF-158
1967		161	**.326**	**.622**	579	**189**	31	4	**44**	7.6	**112**	**121**	91	69	10	0	0	297	13	7	1	2.0	.978	OF-161
1968		157	**.301**	.495	539	162	32	2	23	4.3	90	74	**119**	90	13	0	0	315	13	3	4	2.1	.991	OF-155, 1B-3
1969		162	.255	.507	603	154	28	2	40	6.6	96	111	101	91	15	0	0	427	38	6	31	2.9	.987	OF-143, 1B-22
1970		161	.329	**.592**	566	186	29	0	40	7.1	**125**	102	128	66	23	1	0	816	64	14	62	5.5	.984	1B-94, OF-69

Carl Yastrzemski *continued*

Year	Team	Games	BA	SA	AB	H	2B	3B	HR	HR%	R	RBI	BB	SO	SB	Pinch Hit AB	Pinch Hit H	PO	A	E	DP	TC/G	FA	G by Pos
1971		148	.254	.392	508	129	21	2	15	3.0	75	70	106	60	8	2	2	281	16	2	4	2.0	.993	OF-146
1972		125	.264	.391	455	120	18	2	12	2.6	70	68	67	44	5	1	0	498	43	8	35	4.4	.985	OF-83, 1B-42
1973		152	.296	.463	540	160	25	4	19	3.5	82	95	105	58	9	1	0	979	119	18	87	7.3	.984	1B-107, 3B-31, OF-14
1974		148	.301	.445	515	155	25	2	15	2.9	**93**	79	104	48	12	0	0	806	46	6	68	5.7	.993	1B-84, OF-63, DH-4
1975		149	.269	.405	543	146	30	1	14	2.6	91	60	87	67	8	1	0	1217	88	5	103	8.7	.996	1B-140, OF-8, DH-2
1976		155	.267	.432	546	146	23	2	21	3.8	71	102	80	67	5	1	0	922	55	4	78	6.3	.996	1B-94, OF-51, DH-10
1977		150	.296	.505	558	165	27	3	28	5.0	99	102	73	40	11	0	0	344	22	0	5	2.4	1.000	OF-140, 1B-7, DH-6
1978		144	.277	.423	523	145	21	2	17	3.3	70	81	76	44	4	1	0	523	49	5	49	3.9	.991	OF-71, 1B-50, DH-27
1979		147	.270	.450	518	140	28	1	21	4.1	69	87	62	46	3	3	2	529	56	4	42	4.1	.993	DH-56, 1B-51, OF-36
1980		105	.275	.462	364	100	21	1	15	4.1	49	50	44	38	0	6	0	225	13	4	20	2.3	.983	DH-49, OF-39, 1B-16
1981		91	.246	.355	338	83	14	1	7	2.1	36	53	49	28	0	3	0	353	34	3	26	4.5	.992	DH-48, 1B-39
1982		131	.275	.431	459	126	22	1	16	3.5	53	72	59	50	0	15	1	119	10	0	12	1.1	1.000	DH-102, 1B-14, OF-2
1983		119	.266	.408	380	101	24	0	10	2.6	38	56	54	29	0	10	2	22	1	0	1	0.2	1.000	DH-107, 1B-2, OF-1
23 yrs.		3308 **2nd**	.285	.462	11988 **3rd**	3419 **6th**	646 **7th**	59	452	3.8	1816	1844 **9th**	1845 **4th**	1393	168	52	8	10437	775	135	643	3.5	.988	OF-2076, 1B-765, DH-411, 3B-33
LEAGUE CHAMPIONSHIP SERIES																								
1975	**BOS A**	3	.455	.818	11	5	1	0	1	9.1	4	2	1	1	0	0	0	7	2	0	0	3.0	1.000	OF-3
WORLD SERIES																								
1967	**BOS A**	7	.400	.840	25	10	2	0	3	12.0	4	5	4	1	0	0	0	16	2	0	0	2.6	1.000	OF-7
1975		7	.310	.310	29	9	0	0	0	0.0	7	4	4	1	0	0	0	36	1	0	4	4.6	1.000	OF-4, 1B-4
2 yrs.		14	.352	.556	54	19	2	0	3	5.6	11	9	8	2	0	0	0	52	3	0	4	3.7	1.000	OF-11, 1B-4

Al Yates

YATES, ALBERT ARTHUR (Bunny)
B. May 26, 1945, Jersey City, N. J.
BR TR 6′ 2″ 210 lbs.

Year	Team	Games	BA	SA	AB	H	2B	3B	HR	HR%	R	RBI	BB	SO	SB	Pinch Hit AB	Pinch Hit H	PO	A	E	DP	TC/G	FA	G by Pos
1971	**MIL A**	24	.277	.383	47	13	2	0	1	2.1	5	4	3	7	1	11	3	19	2	0	0	1.8	1.000	OF-12

Emil Yde

YDE, EMIL OGDEN
B. Jan. 28, 1900, Great Lakes, Ill. D. Dec. 4, 1968, Leesburg, Fla.
BB TL 5′11″ 165 lbs.
BL 1925

Year	Team	Games	BA	SA	AB	H	2B	3B	HR	HR%	R	RBI	BB	SO	SB	Pinch Hit AB	Pinch Hit H	PO	A	E	DP	TC/G	FA	G by Pos
1924	**PIT N**	50	.239	.352	88	21	1	3	1	1.1	8	9	0	13	0	13	3	5	57	6	4	2.1	.912	P-33
1925		47	.191	.258	89	17	4	1	0	0.0	11	11	2	13	1	4	0	8	46	4	8	1.8	.931	P-33
1926		43	.230	.351	74	17	5	2	0	0.0	11	4	5	7	0	0	0	10	47	4	3	1.6	.934	P-37
1927		23	.167	.278	18	3	0	1	0	0.0	8	1	0	1	0	4	1	2	11	1	0	1.6	.929	P-9
1929	**DET A**	46	.333	.396	48	16	1	1	0	0.0	8	3	3	6	0	13	5	5	16	2	0	0.8	.913	P-29
5 yrs.		209	.233	.328	317	74	11	8	1	0.3	46	28	10	40	1	34	9	30	177	17	15	1.6	.924	P-141
WORLD SERIES																								
1925	**PIT N**	2	.000	.000	1	0	0	0	0	0.0	1	0	0	0	0	0	0	0	0	0	0	0.0	.000	P-1
1927		1	—	—	0	0	0	0	0	—	1	0	0	0	0	0	0	0	0	0	0	0.0	—	
2 yrs.		3	.000	.000	1	0	0	0	0	0.0	2	0	0	0	0	0	0	0	0	0	0	0.0		P-1

Bert Yeabsley

YEABSLEY, ROBERT WATKINS
B. Dec. 17, 1893, Philadelphia, Pa. D. Feb. 8, 1961, Philadelphia, Pa.
BR TR 5′9½″ 175 lbs.

Year	Team	Games	BA	SA	AB	H	2B	3B	HR	HR%	R	RBI	BB	SO	SB	Pinch Hit AB	Pinch Hit H	PO	A	E	DP	TC/G	FA	G by Pos
1919	**PHI N**	3	—	—	0	0	0	0	0	—	0	0	1	0	0	0	0	0	0	0	0	0.0	—	

George Yeager

YEAGER, GEORGE J. (Doc)
B. June 4, 1873, Cincinnati, Ohio D. June 5, 1940, Cincinnati, Ohio.
BR TR 5′10″ 190 lbs.

Year	Team	Games	BA	SA	AB	H	2B	3B	HR	HR%	R	RBI	BB	SO	SB	Pinch Hit AB	Pinch Hit H	PO	A	E	DP	TC/G	FA	G by Pos
1896	**BOS N**	2	.200	.200	5	1	0	0	0	0.0	1	0	0	1	0	0	0	13	0	0	3	6.5	1.000	1B-2
1897		30	.242	.389	95	23	2	3	2	2.1	20	15	7		2	2	0	77	31	11	1	4.3	.908	C-13, OF-10, 2B-4, 3B-1
1898		68	.267	.376	221	59	13	1	3	1.4	37	24	16		1	3	2	303	40	19	6	5.6	.948	C-37, 1B-17, OF-9, SS-2
1899		3	.125	.125	8	1	0	0	0	0.0	1	0	1		0	0	0	11	1	2	0	4.7	.857	OF-2, C-1
1901	**2 teams**	**CLE A** (39G –.223) **PIT N** (26G –.264)																						
″	**total**	65	.239	.278	230	55	7	1	0	0.0	22	24	8		3	5	0	243	81	20	7	5.7	.942	C-45, 1B-6, 3B-4, OF-3, 2B-2
1902	**2 teams**	**NY N** (38G –.204) **BAL A** (11G –.184)																						
″	**total**	49	.199	.233	146	29	3	1	0	0.0	9	10	13		1	7	1	190	52	14	6	6.1	.945	C-38, 1B-3, OF-1
6 yrs.		217	.238	.312	705	168	25	6	5	0.7	90	73	45	1	7	17	3	837	205	66	23	5.5	.940	C-134, 1B-28, OF-25, 2B-6, 3B-5, SS-2

Joe Yeager

YEAGER, JOSEPH F. (Little Joe)
B. Aug. 28, 1875, Philadelphia, Pa. D. July 2, 1937, Detroit, Mich.
BR TR 5′10″ 160 lbs.

Year	Team	Games	BA	SA	AB	H	2B	3B	HR	HR%	R	RBI	BB	SO	SB	Pinch Hit AB	Pinch Hit H	PO	A	E	DP	TC/G	FA	G by Pos
1898	**BKN N**	43	.172	.224	134	23	5	1	0	0.0	12	15	7		1	0	0	21	107	11	3	3.2	.921	P-36, OF-4, SS-2, 2B-1
1899		23	.191	.234	47	9	0	1	0	0.0	12	4	6		0	0	0	21	50	5	10	3.3	.934	SS-11, P-10, 3B-1, OF-1
1900		3	.333	.333	9	3	0	0	0	0.0	0	0	0		0	0	0	0	3	0	0	1.0	1.000	P-2, 3B-1
1901	**DET A**	41	.296	.416	125	37	7	1	2	1.6	18	17	4		3	2	0	33	104	13	12	3.8	.913	P-26, SS-12, 2B-1
1902		50	.242	.360	161	39	6	5	1	0.6	17	23	5		0	1	0	59	94	9	3	3.4	.944	P-19, OF-13, 2B-12, SS-3, 3B-1
1903		109	.256	.323	402	103	15	6	0	0.0	36	43	18		9	0	0	130	186	27	10	3.1	.921	3B-107, SS-1, P-1
1905	**NY A**	115	.267	.342	401	107	16	7	0	0.0	53	42	25		8	3	2	148	242	31	14	3.8	.926	3B-90, SS-21
1906		57	.301	.366	123	37	6	1	0	0.0	20	12	13		3	**18**	3	69	86	10	9	4.3	.939	SS-22, 2B-13, 3B-3
1907	**STL A**	123	.239	.326	436	104	21	7	1	0.2	32	44	31		11	4	1	172	287	31	23	4.1	.937	3B-92, 2B-17, SS-10
1908		10	.333	.400	15	5	1	0	0	0.0	3	1	1		2	5	1	4	12	0	0	3.2	1.000	2B-4, SS-1
10 yrs.		574	.252	.331	1853	467	77	29	4	0.2	203	201	110		37	33	7	657	1171	137	84	3.7	.930	3B-295, P-94, SS-83, 2B-48, OF-18

Steve Yeager

YEAGER, STEPHEN WAYNE
B. Nov. 24, 1948, Huntington, W. Va.
BR TR 6′ 190 lbs.

Year	Team	Games	BA	SA	AB	H	2B	3B	HR	HR%	R	RBI	BB	SO	SB	Pinch Hit AB	Pinch Hit H	PO	A	E	DP	TC/G	FA	G by Pos
1972	**LA N**	35	.274	.406	106	29	0	1	4	3.8	18	15	16	26	0	0	0	220	19	4	2	6.9	.984	C-35
1973		54	.254	.336	134	34	5	0	2	1.5	18	10	15	33	1	4	1	230	24	5	2	5.2	.981	C-50
1974		94	.266	.437	316	84	16	1	12	3.8	41	41	32	77	2	0	0	552	58	5	4	6.6	.992	C-93
1975		135	.228	.347	452	103	16	1	12	2.7	34	54	40	75	2	0	0	806	62	7	4	6.5	.992	C-135
1976		117	.214	.354	359	77	11	3	11	3.1	42	35	30	84	3	1	1	522	77	9	9	5.3	.985	C-115
1977		125	.256	.444	387	99	21	2	16	4.1	53	55	43	84	1	3	0	690	89	18	12	6.5	.977	C-123
1978		94	.193	.276	228	44	7	0	4	1.8	19	23	36	41	0	4	1	373	55	5	3	4.8	.988	C-91
1979		105	.216	.384	310	67	9	2	13	4.2	33	41	29	68	1	2	2	513	56	9	7	5.6	.984	C-103
1980		96	.211	.273	227	48	8	0	2	0.9	20	20	20	54	2	4	1	382	36	7	5	4.5	.984	C-95
1981		42	.209	.337	86	18	2	0	3	3.5	5	7	6	14	0	5	2	142	13	1	1	3.9	.994	C-40

Steve Yeager *continued*

Year	Team	Games	BA	SA	AB	H	2B	3B	HR	HR%	R	RBI	BB	SO	SB	Pinch Hit AB	Pinch Hit H	PO	A	E	DP	TC/G	FA	G by Pos
1982		82	.245	.321	196	48	5	2	2	1.0	13	18	13	28	0	9	2	338	42	4	8	5.1	.990	C-76
1983		113	.203	.379	335	68	8	3	15	4.5	31	41	23	57	1	2	0	579	63	10	10	5.8	.985	C-112
1984		74	.228	.310	197	45	4	0	4	2.0	16	29	20	38	1	17	4	317	30	2	1	5.4	.994	C-65
1985		53	.207	.256	121	25	4	1	0	0.0	4	9	7	24	0	7	1	212	28	2	2	5.0	.992	C-48
1986	SEA A	50	.208	.269	130	27	2	0	2	1.5	10	12	12	23	0	1	0	234	22	0	5	5.2	1.000	C-49
15 yrs.		1269	.228	.355	3584	816	118	16	102	2.8	357	410	342	726	14	59	15	6110	674	88	75	5.6	.987	C-1230
DIVISIONAL PLAYOFF SERIES																								
1981	LA N	2	.400	.600	5	2	1	0	0	0.0	1	0	0	1	0	1	1	6	0	0	0	3.0	1.000	C-2
LEAGUE CHAMPIONSHIP SERIES																								
1974	LA N	3	.000	.000	9	0	0	0	0	0.0	1	0	3	3	1	0	0	14	1	0	0	5.0	1.000	C-3
1977		4	.231	.231	13	3	0	0	0	0.0	1	2	1	3	0	0	0	22	1	0	0	5.8	1.000	C-4
1978		4	.231	.462	13	3	0	0	1	7.7	2	2	2	2	1	0	0	21	2	0	0	5.8	1.000	C-4
1981		1	.500	.500	2	1	0	0	0	0.0	1	0	0	0	0	1	1	2	0	0	0	2.0	1.000	C-1
1983		2	.167	.333	6	1	1	0	0	0.0	0	0	0	0	0	0	0	7	1	0	0	4.0	1.000	C-2
1985		1	.000	.000	2	0	0	0	0	0.0	0	0	1	1	0	0	0	4	0	0	0	4.0	1.000	C-1
6 yrs.		15	.178	.267	45	8	1	0	1	2.2	5	4	7	9	2	1	1	70	5	0	0	5.0	1.000	C-15
WORLD SERIES																								
1974	LA N	4	.364	.455	11	4	1	0	0	0.0	0	1	1	4	0	0	0	32	4	1	1	9.3	.973	C-4
1977		6	.316	.684	19	6	1	0	2	10.5	2	5	1	1	0	0	0	32	6	0	0	6.3	1.000	C-6
1978		5	.231	.308	13	3	1	0	0	0.0	2	0	1	2	0	0	0	23	2	0	0	5.0	1.000	C-5
1981		6	.286	.786	14	4	1	0	2	14.3	2	4	0	2	0	0	0	20	0	0	0	3.3	1.000	C-6
4 yrs.		21	.298	.579	57	17	4	0	4	7.0	6	10	3	9	0	0	0	107	12	1	1	5.7	.992	C-21

Eric Yelding

YELDING, ERIC GIRARD
B. Feb. 22, 1965, Montrose, Ala.
BR TR 5′11″ 170 lbs.

1989	HOU N	70	.233	.256	90	21	2	0	0	0.0	19	9	7	19	11	16	4	37	57	3	9	2.7	.969	SS-15, 2B-13, OF-8
1990		142	.254	.297	511	130	9	5	1	0.2	69	28	39	87	64	2	0	315	124	17	21	3.1	.963	OF-94, SS-40, 2B-10, 3B-3
1991		78	.243	.301	276	67	11	1	1	0.4	19	20	13	46	11	7	3	114	166	20	31	3.9	.933	SS-72, OF-4
1992		9	.250	.250	8	2	0	0	0	0.0	1	0	0	3	0	5	0	1	0	0	0	0.3	1.000	OF-2, SS-2
1993	CHI N	69	.204	.296	108	22	5	1	1	0.9	14	10	11	22	3	22	4	52	86	4	15	3.5	.972	2B-32, 3B-7, SS-1, OF-1
5 yrs.		368	.244	.294	993	242	27	7	3	0.3	122	67	70	177	89	52	11	519	433	44	76	3.3	.956	SS-130, OF-109, 2B-55, 3B-10

Archie Yelle

YELLE, ARCHIE JOSEPH
B. June 11, 1892, Saginaw, Mich. D. May 2, 1983, Woodland, Calif.
BR TR 5′10½″ 170 lbs.

1917	DET A	25	.137	.157	51	7	1	0	0	0.0	4	0	5	4	2	1	0	62	16	2	1	3.3	.975	C-24
1918		56	.174	.194	144	25	3	0	0	0.0	7	7	9	15	0	4	1	172	81	14	5	5.1	.948	C-52
1919		5	.000	.000	4	0	0	0	0	0.0	1	0	1	0	0	0	0	3	1	1	0	1.0	.800	C-5
3 yrs.		86	.161	.181	199	32	4	0	0	0.0	12	7	15	19	2	5	1	237	98	17	6	4.3	.952	C-81

Steve Yerkes

YERKES, STEPHEN DOUGLAS
B. May 15, 1888, Hatboro, Pa. D. Jan. 31, 1971, Lansdale, Pa.
BR TR 5′ 9″ 165 lbs.

1909	BOS A	5	.500	.500	2	1	0	0	0	0.0	0	0	0		0	2	1	0	0	0	0	0.0	.000	SS-3
1911		142	.279	.345	502	140	24	3	1	0.2	70	57	52		14	0	0	288	388	54	39	5.2	.926	SS-116, 2B-14, 3B-11
1912		131	.252	.317	523	132	22	6	0	0.0	73	42	41		4	0	0	244	323	34	39	4.6	.943	2B-131
1913		137	.267	.359	487	130	30	6	1	0.2	67	48	50	32	11	7	1	220	341	25	31	4.5	.957	2B-129
1914	2 teams	BOS A (92G –.218) PIT F (39G –.338)																						
″	total	131	.257	.363	435	112	26	7	2	0.5	41	48	25	23	7	0	0	266	380	18	51	5.1	.973	2B-91, SS-39
1915	PIT F	121	.288	.371	434	125	17	8	1	0.2	44	49	30		17	0	0	255	336	24	42	5.0	.961	2B-114, SS-8
1916	CHI N	44	.263	.358	137	36	6	2	1	0.7	12	10	9	7	1	3	1	79	114	17	14	5.1	.919	2B-41
7 yrs.		711	.268	.350	2520	676	125	32	6	0.2	307	254	207	62	54	12	3	1352	1882	172	216	4.9	.950	2B-520, SS-166, 3B-11
WORLD SERIES																								
1912	BOS A	8	.250	.375	32	8	0	2	0	0.0	3	4	2	3	0	0	0	15	22	1	1	4.8	.974	2B-8

Tom Yewcic

YEWCIC, THOMAS J. (Kibby)
B. May 9, 1932, Conemaugh, Pa.
BR TR 5′11″ 180 lbs.

1957	DET A	1	.000	.000	1	0	0	0	0	0.0	0	0	0	0	0	0	0	4	1	1	0	6.0	.833	C-1

Ed Yewell

YEWELL, EDWIN LEONARD
B. Aug. 22, 1862, Washington, D. C. D. Sept. 15, 1940, Washington, D. C.

1884	2 teams	WAS AA (27G –.247) WAS U (1G –.000)																						
″	total	28	.237	.289	97	23	3	1	0	0.0	14		1			0	0	42	57	20	7	4.1	.832	2B-11, OF-8, 3B-8, SS-2

Earl Yingling

YINGLING, EARL HERSHEY (Chink)
B. Oct. 29, 1888, Chillicothe, Ohio D. Oct. 2, 1962, Columbus, Ohio.
BL TL 5′11½″ 180 lbs.

1911	CLE A	5	.273	.273	11	3	0	0	0	0.0	1	2	1		0	0	0	2	6	0	1	2.0	1.000	P-4
1912	BKN N	25	.250	.313	64	16	2	1	0	0.0	9	3	4	6	0	0	0	7	36	5	0	1.9	.896	P-25
1913		40	.383	.400	60	23	1	0	0	0.0	11	5	9	8	0	11	4	8	34	4	2	1.8	.913	P-26
1914	CIN N	61	.192	.233	120	23	2	0	1	0.8	9	11	9	15	3	13	2	22	45	8	2	1.6	.893	P-34, OF-13
1918	WAS A	8	.467	.467	15	7	0	0	0	0.0	1	2	2	1	0	3	1	4	12	0	3	3.2	1.000	P-5
5 yrs.		139	.267	.304	270	72	5	1	1	0.4	31	23	25	30	3	27	7	43	133	17	8	1.8	.912	P-94, OF-13

Joe Yingling

YINGLING, JOSEPH GRANVILLE
B. July 23, 1866, Baltimore, Md. D. Oct. 24, 1946, Baltimore, Md.
BR TL 5′ 7½″ 145 lbs.

1886	WAS N	1	.000	.000	2	0	0	0	0	0.0	0	0	0	1		0	0	0	1	1	1	2.0	.500	P-1
1894	PHI N	1	.250	.250	4	1	0	0	0	0.0	0	0	0	1	0	0	0	1	2	0	0	3.0	1.000	SS-1
2 yrs.		2	.167	.167	6	1	0	0	0	0.0	0	0	0	2	0	0	0	1	3	1	1	2.5	.800	SS-1, P-1

Bill Yohe

YOHE, WILLIAM CLYDE
B. Sept. 2, 1878, Mt. Elere, Ill. D. Dec. 24, 1938, Bremerton, Wash.
TR 5′ 8″ 180 lbs.

1909	WAS A	21	.208	.236	72	15	2	0	0	0.0	6	4	3		2	2	1	23	47	6	1	4.0	.921	3B-19

Rudy York

YORK, RUDOLPH PRESTON BR TR 6′ 1″ 209 lbs.
B. Aug. 17, 1913, Ragland, Ala. D. Feb. 5, 1970, Rome, Ga.
Manager 1959.

Year	Team	Games	BA	SA	AB	H	2B	3B	HR	HR%	R	RBI	BB	SO	SB	Pinch Hit AB	Pinch Hit H	PO	A	E	DP	TC/G	FA	G by Pos
1934	DET A	3	.167	.167	6	1	0	0	0	0.0	0	0	1	3	0	2	1	4	2	0	0	3.0	1.000	C-2
1937		104	.307	.651	375	115	18	3	35	**9.3**	72	103	41	52	3	7	1	235	93	18	11	3.6	.948	C-54, 3B-41
1938		135	.298	.579	463	138	27	2	33	7.1	85	127	92	74	1	3	0	431	71	10	11	3.9	.980	C-116, OF-14, 1B-1
1939		102	.307	.544	329	101	16	1	20	6.1	66	68	41	50	5	16	2	434	39	5	22	5.6	.990	C-67, 1B-19
1940		155	.316	.583	588	186	46	6	33	5.6	105	134	89	88	3	0	0	1390	107	15	101	9.8	.990	1B-155
1941		155	.259	.456	590	153	29	3	27	4.6	91	111	92	88	3	0	0	1393	110	21	111	9.8	.986	1B-155
1942		153	.260	.428	577	150	26	4	21	3.6	81	90	73	71	3	1	1	1413	146	19	117	10.4	.988	1B-152
1943		155	.271	**.527**	571	155	22	11	**34**	6.0	90	**118**	84	88	5	0	0	1349	149	15	105	9.8	.990	1B-155
1944		151	.276	.439	583	161	27	7	18	3.1	77	98	68	73	5	0	0	1453	107	17	163	10.4	.989	1B-151
1945		155	.264	.413	595	157	25	5	18	3.0	71	87	59	85	6	0	0	1464	113	19	142	10.3	.988	1B-155
1946	BOS A	154	.276	.437	579	160	30	6	17	2.9	78	119	86	93	3	0	0	1327	116	8	154	9.4	.994	1B-154
1947	2 teams	BOS A (48G –.212)			CHI A (102G –.242)																			
"	total	150	.233	.397	584	136	25	4	21	3.6	56	91	58	87	1	0	0	1327	107	7	149	9.6	.995	1B-150
1948	PHI A	31	.157	.157	51	8	0	0	0	0.0	4	6	7	15	0	18	2	77	5	1	10	5.9	.988	1B-14
13 yrs.		1603	.275	.483	5891	1621	291	52	277	4.7	876	1152	791	867	38	47	7	12297	1165	155	1096	8.8	.989	1B-1261, C-239, 3B-41, OF-14
WORLD SERIES																								
1940	DET A	7	.231	.423	26	6	0	1	1	3.8	3	2	4	7	0	0	0	59	2	0	4	8.7	1.000	1B-7
1945		7	.179	.214	28	5	1	0	0	0.0	1	3	3	4	0	0	0	67	8	1	3	10.9	.987	1B-7
1946	BOS A	7	.261	.652	23	6	1	1	2	8.7	6	5	6	4	0	0	0	59	4	1	0	9.1	.984	1B-7
3 yrs.		21	.221	.416	77	17	2	2	3	3.9	10	10	13	15	0	0	0	185	14	2	7	9.6	.990	1B-21

Tom York

YORK, THOMAS JEFFERSON BL 5′ 9″ 165 lbs.
B. July 13, 1851, Brooklyn, N. Y. D. Feb. 17, 1936, New York, N. Y.
Manager 1878, 1881.

Year	Team	Games	BA	SA	AB	H	2B	3B	HR	HR%	R	RBI	BB	SO	SB	Pinch Hit AB	Pinch Hit H	PO	A	E	DP	TC/G	FA	G by Pos
1876	HAR N	67	.259	.369	263	68	12	7	1	0.4	47	39	10	4		0	0	153	8	18	1	2.7	.899	OF-67
1877		56	.283	.422	237	67	16	7	1	0.4	43	37	3	11		0	0	130	5	21	1	2.8	.865	OF-56
1878	PRO N	62	.309	.465	269	83	19	**10**	1	0.4	56	26	8	19		0	0	89	14	15	3	1.9	.873	OF-62
1879		81	.310	.421	342	106	25	5	1	0.3	69	50	19	28		0	0	114	9	14	2	1.7	.898	OF-81
1880		53	.212	.276	203	43	9	2	0	0.0	21	18	8	29		0	0	94	5	7	1	2.0	.934	OF-53
1881		85	.304	.427	316	96	23	5	2	0.6	57	47	29	26		0	0	159	17	29	1	2.4	.859	OF-85
1882		81	.268	.393	321	86	23	7	1	0.3	48		19	14		0	0	159	11	24	3	2.4	.876	OF-81
1883	CLE N	100	.260	.378	381	99	29	5	2	0.5	56		**37**	55		0	0	176	15	30	3	2.2	.864	OF-100
1884	BAL AA	83	.223	.322	314	70	14	7	1	0.3	64		34			0	0	100	7	20	1	1.5	.843	OF-83
1885		22	.264	.356	87	23	4	2	0	0.0	6		8			0	0	41	4	3	1	2.2	.938	OF-22
10 yrs.		690	.271	.387	2733	741	174	57	10	0.4	467	217	175	186		0	0	1215	95	181	17	2.2	.879	OF-690

Tony York

YORK, ANTHONY BATTON BR TR 5′10″ 165 lbs.
B. Nov. 27, 1912, Irene, Tex. D. Apr. 18, 1970, Hillsboro, Tex.

Year	Team	Games	BA	SA	AB	H	2B	3B	HR	HR%	R	RBI	BB	SO	SB	Pinch Hit AB	Pinch Hit H	PO	A	E	DP	TC/G	FA	G by Pos
1944	CHI N	28	.235	.247	85	20	1	0	0	0.0	4	7	4	11	0	0	0	39	81	5	7	4.6	.960	SS-15, 3B-12

Eddie Yost

YOST, EDWARD FREDERICK (The Walking Man) BR TR 5′10″ 170 lbs.
B. Oct. 13, 1926, Brooklyn, N. Y.
Manager 1963.

Year	Team	Games	BA	SA	AB	H	2B	3B	HR	HR%	R	RBI	BB	SO	SB	Pinch Hit AB	Pinch Hit H	PO	A	E	DP	TC/G	FA	G by Pos
1944	WAS A	7	.143	.143	14	2	0	0	0	0.0	3	0	1	2	0	0	0	9	6	2	0	3.4	.882	3B-3, SS-2
1946		8	.080	.120	25	2	1	0	0	0.0	2	1	5	5	2	1	0	7	17	0	1	3.4	1.000	3B-7
1947		115	.238	.292	428	102	17	3	0	0.0	52	14	45	57	3	0	0	125	198	14	11	3.0	.958	3B-114
1948		145	.249	.357	555	138	32	11	2	0.4	74	50	82	51	4	0	0	189	240	15	21	3.1	.966	3B-145
1949		124	.253	.391	435	110	19	7	9	2.1	57	45	91	41	3	1	0	158	232	19	23	3.4	.954	3B-122
1950		155	.295	.405	573	169	26	2	11	1.9	114	58	**141**	63	6	0	0	205	307	30	45	3.5	.945	3B-155
1951		154	.283	.424	568	161	**36**	4	12	2.1	109	65	126	55	6	0	0	209	234	21	22	3.0	.955	3B-152, OF-3
1952		157	.233	.359	587	137	32	3	12	2.0	92	49	**129**	73	4	0	0	212	249	18	26	3.1	.962	3B-157
1953		152	.272	.395	577	157	30	7	9	1.6	107	45	**123**	59	7	0	0	190	300	18	31	3.3	.965	3B-152
1954		155	.256	.380	539	138	26	4	11	2.0	101	47	131	71	7	0	0	170	347	17	29	3.4	.968	3B-155
1955		122	.243	.371	375	91	17	5	7	1.9	64	48	95	54	4	14	3	100	217	19	22	3.1	.943	3B-107
1956		152	.231	.336	515	119	17	2	11	2.1	94	53	**151**	82	8	9	0	182	303	18	31	3.5	.964	3B-135, OF-8
1957		110	.251	.372	414	104	13	5	9	2.2	47	38	73	49	1	4	0	109	207	16	18	3.1	.952	3B-107
1958		134	.224	.323	406	91	16	0	8	2.0	55	37	81	43	3	15	3	122	187	11	21	2.7	.966	3B-114, OF-4, 1B-2
1959	DET A	148	.278	.436	521	145	19	0	21	4.0	**115**	61	**135**	77	9	3	0	168	260	17	21	3.0	.962	3B-146, 2B-1
1960		143	.260	.398	497	129	23	2	14	2.8	78	47	**125**	69	5	5	1	155	208	26	18	2.7	.933	3B-142
1961	LA A	76	.202	.263	213	43	4	0	3	1.4	29	15	50	48	0	8	1	57	103	6	4	2.5	.964	3B-67
1962		52	.240	.346	104	25	9	1	0	0.0	22	10	30	21	0	16	1	69	48	4	5	3.5	.967	3B-28, 1B-7
18 yrs.		2109	.254	.371	7346	1863	337	56	139	1.9	1215	683	1614 **7th**	920	72	76	9	2436	3663	271	349	3.1	.957	3B-2008, OF-15, 1B-9, SS-2, 2B-1

Ned Yost

YOST, EDGAR FREDERICK BR TR 6′ 1″ 190 lbs.
B. Aug. 19, 1955, Eureka, Calif.

Year	Team	Games	BA	SA	AB	H	2B	3B	HR	HR%	R	RBI	BB	SO	SB	Pinch Hit AB	Pinch Hit H	PO	A	E	DP	TC/G	FA	G by Pos
1980	MIL A	15	.161	.161	31	5	0	0	0	0.0	0	0	0	6	0	0	0	41	5	0	0	3.1	1.000	C-15
1981		18	.222	.556	27	6	0	0	3	11.1	4	3	3	6	0	0	0	37	6	2	2	2.8	.956	C-16
1982		40	.276	.429	98	27	6	3	1	1.0	13	8	7	20	3	1	0	121	6	3	2	3.3	.977	C-39, DH-1
1983		61	.224	.352	196	44	5	1	6	3.1	21	28	5	36	1	1	1	252	16	8	2	4.5	.971	C-61
1984	TEX A	80	.182	.273	242	44	4	0	6	2.5	15	25	6	47	1	3	0	368	20	2	1	5.0	.995	C-78
1985	MON N	5	.182	.182	11	2	0	0	0	0.0	1	0	0	2	0	0	0	24	1	1	0	5.2	.962	C-5
6 yrs.		219	.212	.329	605	128	15	4	16	2.6	54	64	21	117	5	5	1	843	54	16	7	4.2	.982	C-214, DH-1
WORLD SERIES																								
1982	MIL A	1	—	—	0	0	0	0	0	—	0	0	1	0	0	0	0	1	0	0	0	1.0	1.000	C-1

Elmer Yoter

YOTER, ELMER ELLSWORTH BR TR 5′ 7″ 155 lbs.
B. June 26, 1900, Plainfield, Pa. D. July 26, 1966, Camp Hill, Pa.

Year	Team	Games	BA	SA	AB	H	2B	3B	HR	HR%	R	RBI	BB	SO	SB	Pinch Hit AB	Pinch Hit H	PO	A	E	DP	TC/G	FA	G by Pos
1921	PHI A	3	.000	.000	3	0	0	0	0	0.0	0	0	0	1	0	3	0	0	0	0	0	0.0	—	
1924	CLE A	19	.273	.318	66	18	1	1	0	0.0	3	7	5	8	0	0	0	18	39	6	1	3.3	.905	3B-19

Elmer Yoter *continued*

Year	Team	Games	BA	SA	AB	H	2B	3B	HR	HR%	R	RBI	BB	SO	SB	Pinch Hit AB	Pinch Hit H	PO	A	E	DP	TC/G	FA	G by Pos
1927	CHI N	13	.222	.333	27	6	1	1	0	0.0	2	5	4	4	0	1	0	4	14	1	0	1.7	.947	3B-11
1928		1	—	—	0	0	0	0	0	—	0	0	0	0	0	0	0	0	0	0	0	0.0	.000	3B-1
4 yrs.		36	.250	.313	96	24	2	2	0	0.0	5	12	9	13	0	4	0	22	53	7	1	2.6	.915	3B-31

Babe Young

YOUNG, NORMAN ROBERT
B. July 1, 1915, Astoria, N. Y. D. Dec. 25, 1983, Everett, Mass.
BL TL 6′ 2½″ 185 lbs.

Year	Team	Games	BA	SA	AB	H	2B	3B	HR	HR%	R	RBI	BB	SO	SB	Pinch Hit AB	Pinch Hit H	PO	A	E	DP	TC/G	FA	G by Pos
1936	NY N	1	.000	.000	1	0	0	0	0	0.0	0	0	0	0	0	1	0	0	0	0	0	0.0	—	
1939		22	.307	.480	75	23	4	0	3	4.0	8	14	5	6	0	0	0	214	9	4	18	10.3	.982	1B-22
1940		149	.286	.441	556	159	27	4	17	3.1	75	101	69	28	4	2	0	1505	86	13	112	10.9	.992	1B-147
1941		152	.265	.462	574	152	28	5	25	4.4	90	104	66	39	1	1	1	1395	87	21	124	10.0	.986	1B-150
1942		101	.279	.460	287	80	17	1	11	3.8	37	59	34	22	1	27	6	260	16	6	13	3.9	.979	OF-54, 1B-18
1946		104	.278	.388	291	81	11	0	7	2.4	30	33	30	21	3	**32**	5	492	24	7	25	7.2	.987	1B-49, OF-24
1947	2 teams	NY N (14G –.071) CIN N (95G –.283)																						
″	total	109	.275	.460	378	104	22	3	14	3.7	55	79	35	27	0	16	2	730	56	8	66	8.5	.990	1B-93
1948	2 teams	CIN N (49G –.231) STL N (41G –.243)																						
″	total	90	.237	.344	241	57	12	4	2	0.8	25	25	35	18	0	18	3	529	29	3	54	8.4	.995	1B-66, OF-1
8 yrs.		728	.273	.436	2403	656	121	17	79	3.3	320	415	274	161	9	97	17	5125	307	62	412	8.8	.989	1B-545, OF-79

Bobby Young

YOUNG, ROBERT GEORGE
B. Jan. 22, 1925, Granite, Md. D. Jan. 28, 1985, Baltimore, Md.
BL TR 6′ 1″ 175 lbs.

Year	Team	Games	BA	SA	AB	H	2B	3B	HR	HR%	R	RBI	BB	SO	SB	Pinch Hit AB	Pinch Hit H	PO	A	E	DP	TC/G	FA	G by Pos
1948	STL N	3	.000	.000	1	0	0	0	0	0.0	0	0	0	1	0	1	0	2	0	0	0	2.0	1.000	3B-1
1951	STL A	147	.260	.316	611	159	13	9	1	0.2	75	31	44	51	8	0	0	361	462	17	118	5.7	.980	2B-147
1952		149	.247	.325	575	142	15	9	4	0.7	59	39	56	48	3	1	1	380	407	13	127	5.4	.984	2B-149
1953		148	.255	.326	537	137	22	2	4	0.7	48	25	41	40	2	0	0	397	363	18	120	5.3	.977	2B-148
1954	BAL A	130	.245	.331	432	106	13	6	4	0.9	43	24	54	42	4	8	1	299	310	15	76	4.9	.976	2B-127
1955	2 teams	BAL A (59G –.199) CLE A (18G –.311)																						
″	total	77	.221	.260	231	51	4	1	1	0.4	12	14	12	25	1	7	2	145	180	5	56	4.7	.985	2B-69, 3B-1
1956	CLE A	1	—	—	0	0	0	0	0	—	0	0	0	0	0	0	0	0	0	0	0	0.0	—	
1958	PHI N	32	.233	.333	60	14	1	1	1	1.7	7	4	1	5	0	9	2	28	33	2	6	3.0	.968	2B-21
8 yrs.		687	.249	.318	2447	609	68	28	15	0.6	244	137	208	212	18	26	6	1612	1755	70	503	5.2	.980	2B-661, 3B-2

Del Young

YOUNG, DELMER EDWARD
Son of Del Young.
B. May 11, 1912, Cleveland, Ohio D. Dec. 8, 1979, San Francisco, Calif.
BB TR 5′11″ 168 lbs.

Year	Team	Games	BA	SA	AB	H	2B	3B	HR	HR%	R	RBI	BB	SO	SB	Pinch Hit AB	Pinch Hit H	PO	A	E	DP	TC/G	FA	G by Pos
1937	PHI N	109	.194	.231	360	70	9	2	0	0.0	36	24	18	55	6	0	0	200	333	28	63	5.2	.950	2B-108
1938		108	.229	.279	340	78	13	2	0	0.0	27	31	20	35	0	2	0	196	307	33	52	5.2	.938	SS-87, 2B-17
1939		77	.263	.364	217	57	9	2	3	1.4	22	20	8	24	1	7	1	109	154	16	28	3.9	.943	SS-55, 2B-17
1940		15	.242	.303	33	8	0	1	0	0.0	2	1	2	1	0	0	0	23	23	2	4	4.4	.958	SS-6, 2B-5
4 yrs.		309	.224	.281	950	213	31	7	3	0.3	87	76	48	115	7	9	1	528	817	79	147	4.8	.945	SS-148, 2B-147

Del Young

YOUNG, DELMER JOHN
Father of Del Young.
B. Oct. 24, 1885, Macon, Mo. D. Dec. 17, 1959, Cleveland, Ohio.
BL TR 5′11″ 195 lbs.

Year	Team	Games	BA	SA	AB	H	2B	3B	HR	HR%	R	RBI	BB	SO	SB	Pinch Hit AB	Pinch Hit H	PO	A	E	DP	TC/G	FA	G by Pos
1909	CIN N	2	.286	.286	7	2	0	0	0	0.0	0	1	1		0	0	0	2	1	0	0	1.5	1.000	OF-2
1914	BUF F	80	.276	.431	174	48	5	5	4	2.3	17	22	3		0	**37**	7	49	2	3	2	1.3	.944	OF-41
1915		12	.133	.133	15	2	0	0	0	0.0	0	0	1		1	9	1	2	0	1	0	1.0	.667	OF-3
3 yrs.		94	.265	.403	196	52	5	5	4	2.0	17	23	5		1	46	8	53	3	4	2	1.3	.933	OF-46

Dick Young

YOUNG, RICHARD ENNIS
B. June 3, 1928, Seattle, Wash.
BL TR 5′11″ 175 lbs.
BB 1952

Year	Team	Games	BA	SA	AB	H	2B	3B	HR	HR%	R	RBI	BB	SO	SB	Pinch Hit AB	Pinch Hit H	PO	A	E	DP	TC/G	FA	G by Pos
1951	PHI N	15	.235	.309	68	16	5	0	0	0.0	7	2	3	6	0	0	0	26	33	5	8	4.3	.922	2B-15
1952		5	.222	.333	9	2	1	0	0	0.0	3	0	1	3	1	2	0	5	4	1	1	5.0	.900	2B-2
2 yrs.		20	.234	.312	77	18	6	0	0	0.0	10	2	4	9	1	2	0	31	37	6	9	4.4	.919	2B-17

Don Young

YOUNG, DONALD WAYNE
B. Oct. 18, 1945, Houston, Tex.
BR TR 6′ 2″ 185 lbs.

Year	Team	Games	BA	SA	AB	H	2B	3B	HR	HR%	R	RBI	BB	SO	SB	Pinch Hit AB	Pinch Hit H	PO	A	E	DP	TC/G	FA	G by Pos
1965	CHI N	11	.057	.143	35	2	0	0	1	2.9	1	2	0	11	0	3	1	14	0	1	0	1.4	.933	OF-11
1969		101	.239	.371	272	65	12	3	6	2.2	36	27	38	74	1	0	0	191	4	5	0	2.0	.975	OF-100
2 yrs.		112	.218	.345	307	67	12	3	7	2.3	37	29	38	85	1	3	1	205	4	6	0	1.9	.972	OF-111

Eric Young

YOUNG, ERIC ORLANDO
B. Nov. 26, 1966, Jacksonville, Fla.
BR TR 5′ 9″ 180 lbs.

Year	Team	Games	BA	SA	AB	H	2B	3B	HR	HR%	R	RBI	BB	SO	SB	Pinch Hit AB	Pinch Hit H	PO	A	E	DP	TC/G	FA	G by Pos
1992	LA N	49	.258	.288	132	34	1	0	1	0.8	9	11	8	9	6	0	0	85	114	9	19	4.8	.957	2B-43
1993	CLR N	144	.269	.353	490	132	16	8	3	0.6	82	42	63	41	42	14	5	254	230	18	44	3.8	.964	2B-79, OF-52
1994		90	.272	.430	228	62	13	1	7	3.1	37	30	38	17	18	21	3	97	4	2	0	1.7	.981	OF-60, 2B-1
1995		120	.317	.473	366	116	21	**9**	6	1.6	68	36	49	29	35	19	4	179	230	11	54	4.4	.974	2B-77, OF-19
4 yrs.		403	.283	.396	1216	344	51	18	17	1.4	196	119	158	96	101	54	12	615	578	40	117	3.7	.968	2B-200, OF-131
DIVISIONAL PLAYOFF SERIES																								
1995	CLR N	4	.438	.688	16	7	1	0	1	6.3	3	2	2	2	1	0	0	8	13	3	3	6.0	.875	2B-4

Ernie Young

YOUNG, ERNEST WESLEY
B. July 8, 1969, Chicago, Ill.
BR TR 6′ 1″ 190 lbs.

Year	Team	Games	BA	SA	AB	H	2B	3B	HR	HR%	R	RBI	BB	SO	SB	Pinch Hit AB	Pinch Hit H	PO	A	E	DP	TC/G	FA	G by Pos
1994	OAK A	11	.067	.100	30	2	1	0	0	0.0	2	3	1	8	0	2	0	22	1	1	0	2.2	.958	OF-10, DH-1
1995		26	.200	.380	50	10	3	0	2	4.0	9	5	8	12	0	2	0	35	0	2	0	1.5	.946	OF-24
2 yrs.		37	.150	.275	80	12	4	0	2	2.5	11	8	9	20	0	4	0	57	1	3	0	1.7	.951	OF-34, DH-1

George Young

YOUNG, GEORGE JOSEPH
B. Apr. 1, 1890, Brooklyn, N. Y. D. Mar. 13, 1950, Brightwaters, N. Y.
BL TR 6′ 185 lbs.

Year	Team	Games	BA	SA	AB	H	2B	3B	HR	HR%	R	RBI	BB	SO	SB	Pinch Hit AB	Pinch Hit H	PO	A	E	DP	TC/G	FA	G by Pos
1913	CLE A	2	.000	.000	2	0	0	0	0	0.0	0	0	0	0	0	2	0	0	0	0	0	0.0	—	

Gerald Young

YOUNG, GERALD ANTHONY
B. Oct. 22, 1964, Tele, Honduras.
BB TR 6′ 2″ 185 lbs.

Year	Team	Games	BA	SA	AB	H	2B	3B	HR	HR%	R	RBI	BB	SO	SB	Pinch Hit AB	Pinch Hit H	PO	A	E	DP	TC/G	FA	G by Pos
1987	HOU N	71	.321	.380	274	88	9	2	1	0.4	44	15	26	27	26	2	1	143	5	3	1	2.3	.980	OF-67
1988		149	.257	.325	576	148	21	9	0	0.0	79	37	66	66	65	5	2	357	10	3	1	2.6	.992	OF-145

Gerald Young *continued*

Year	Team	Games	BA	SA	AB	H	2B	3B	HR	HR%	R	RBI	BB	SO	SB	Pinch Hit AB	Pinch Hit H	PO	A	E	DP	TC/G	FA	G by Pos
1989		146	.233	.276	533	124	17	3	0	0.0	71	38	74	60	34	2	1	412	15	1	5	3.0	.998	OF-143
1990		57	.175	.234	154	27	4	1	1	0.6	15	4	20	23	6	5	0	99	4	1	1	2.1	.990	OF-50
1991		108	.218	.275	142	31	3	1	1	0.7	26	11	24	17	16	23	3	96	4	0	1	1.2	1.000	OF-84
1992		74	.184	.224	76	14	1	1	0	0.0	14	4	10	11	6	20	1	53	0	2	0	1.0	.964	OF-57
1993	CLR N	19	.053	.053	19	1	0	0	0	0.0	5	1	4	1	0	5	0	15	0	2	0	1.5	.882	OF-11
1994	STL N	16	.317	.488	41	13	3	2	0	0.0	5	3	3	8	2	4	1	19	0	0	0	1.7	1.000	OF-11
8 yrs.		640	.246	.304	1815	446	58	19	3	0.2	259	113	227	213	155	66	9	1194	38	12	9	2.2	.990	OF-568

Herman Young

YOUNG, HERMAN JOHN BR TR 5′ 8″ 155 lbs.
B. Apr. 14, 1886, Boston, Mass. D. Dec. 12, 1966, Ipswich, Mass.

Year	Team	Games	BA	SA	AB	H	2B	3B	HR	HR%	R	RBI	BB	SO	SB	Pinch Hit AB	Pinch Hit H	PO	A	E	DP	TC/G	FA	G by Pos
1911	BOS N	9	.240	.240	25	6	0	0	0	0.0	2	0	0	3	0	1	0	10	23	3	3	4.5	.917	3B-5, SS-3

John Young

YOUNG, JOHN THOMAS BL TL 6′ 3″ 210 lbs.
B. Feb. 9, 1949, Los Angeles, Calif.

Year	Team	Games	BA	SA	AB	H	2B	3B	HR	HR%	R	RBI	BB	SO	SB	Pinch Hit AB	Pinch Hit H	PO	A	E	DP	TC/G	FA	G by Pos
1971	DET A	2	.500	.750	4	2	1	0	0	0.0	1	1	0	0	0	1	0	7	0	0	0	7.0	1.000	1B-1

Kevin Young

YOUNG, KEVIN STACEY BR TR 6′ 3″ 210 lbs.
B. June 16, 1969, Alpena, Mich.

Year	Team	Games	BA	SA	AB	H	2B	3B	HR	HR%	R	RBI	BB	SO	SB	Pinch Hit AB	Pinch Hit H	PO	A	E	DP	TC/G	FA	G by Pos
1992	PIT N	10	.571	.571	7	4	0	0	0	0.0	2	4	2	0	1	1	0	3	1	1	0	0.6	.800	3B-7, 1B-1
1993		141	.236	.343	449	106	24	3	6	1.3	38	47	36	82	2	6	2	1122	112	3	108	8.8	.998	1B-135, 3B-6
1994		59	.205	.320	122	25	7	2	1	0.8	15	11	8	34	0	10	0	178	45	3	21	4.1	.987	1B-37, 3B-17, OF-1
1995		56	.232	.381	181	42	9	0	6	3.3	13	22	8	53	1	3	0	58	110	12	9	3.3	.933	3B-48, 1B-6
4 yrs.		266	.233	.350	759	177	40	5	13	1.7	68	84	54	169	4	20	2	1361	268	19	138	6.4	.988	1B-179, 3B-78, OF-1

Mike Young

YOUNG, MICHAEL DARREN BB TR 6′ 2″ 195 lbs.
B. Mar. 20, 1960, Oakland, Calif.

Year	Team	Games	BA	SA	AB	H	2B	3B	HR	HR%	R	RBI	BB	SO	SB	Pinch Hit AB	Pinch Hit H	PO	A	E	DP	TC/G	FA	G by Pos
1982	BAL A	6	.000	.000	2	0	0	0	0	0.0	2	0	0	1	0	2	0	1	0	0	0	0.3	1.000	DH-2, OF-1
1983		25	.167	.278	36	6	2	1	0	0.0	5	2	2	8	1	5	0	25	1	2	0	1.1	.929	OF-22, DH-3
1984		123	.252	.431	401	101	17	2	17	4.2	59	52	58	110	6	7	2	216	4	4	0	1.9	.982	OF-115, DH-1
1985		139	.273	.513	450	123	22	1	28	6.2	72	81	48	104	1	18	6	190	6	5	0	1.6	.975	OF-90, DH-37
1986		117	.252	.371	369	93	15	1	9	2.4	43	42	49	90	3	12	3	149	1	6	0	1.5	.962	OF-69, DH-38
1987		110	.240	.405	363	87	10	1	16	4.4	46	39	46	91	10	10	4	117	0	3	0	1.1	.975	OF-60, DH-47
1988	2 teams	PHI N (75G –.226) MIL A (8G –.000)																						
″	total	83	.206	.313	160	33	14	0	1	0.6	15	14	28	48	0	40	7	76	0	5	0	1.7	.938	OF-44, DH-5
1989	CLE A	32	.186	.237	59	11	0	0	1	1.7	2	5	6	13	1	21	5	1	0	0	0	0.1	1.000	DH-15, OF-1
8 yrs.		635	.247	.414	1840	454	80	6	72	3.9	244	235	237	465	22	115	27	775	12	25	0	1.5	.969	OF-402, DH-148

Pep Young

YOUNG, LEMUEL FLOYD BR TR 5′ 9″ 162 lbs.
B. Aug. 29, 1907, Jamestown, N. C. D. Jan. 14, 1962, Jamestown, N. C.

Year	Team	Games	BA	SA	AB	H	2B	3B	HR	HR%	R	RBI	BB	SO	SB	Pinch Hit AB	Pinch Hit H	PO	A	E	DP	TC/G	FA	G by Pos
1933	PIT N	25	.300	.450	20	6	1	1	0	0.0	3	0	0	5	0	20	5	2	1	0	0	1.5	1.000	2B-1, SS-1
1934		19	.235	.235	17	4	0	0	0	0.0	3	2	0	6	0	4	0	4	9	0	2	3.3	1.000	SS-2, 2B-2
1935		128	.265	.399	494	131	25	10	7	1.4	60	82	21	59	2	0	0	315	326	32	47	5.5	.952	2B-107, 3B-6, OF-6, SS-4
1936		125	.248	.377	475	118	23	10	6	1.3	47	77	29	52	3	1	0	318	361	24	39	5.7	.966	2B-123
1937		113	.260	.390	408	106	20	3	9	2.2	43	54	26	63	4	2	1	195	328	24	52	4.8	.956	SS-45, 3B-39, 2B-30
1938		149	.278	.381	562	156	36	5	4	0.7	58	79	40	64	7	0	0	370	554	26	120	6.4	.973	2B-149
1939		84	.276	.375	293	81	14	3	3	1.0	34	29	23	29	1	0	0	202	270	16	61	5.8	.967	2B-84
1940		54	.250	.382	136	34	8	2	2	1.5	19	20	12	23	1	7	1	61	98	15	16	3.9	.914	2B-33, SS-7, 3B-5
1941	2 teams	CIN N (4G –.167) STL N (2G –.000)																						
″	total	6	.143	.143	14	2	0	0	0	0.0	2	0	0	3	0	3	0	5	7	1	1	4.3	.923	3B-3
1945	STL N	27	.149	.234	47	7	1	0	1	2.1	5	4	1	8	0	5	0	31	30	2	4	2.7	.968	SS-11, 3B-9, 2B-3
10 yrs.		730	.262	.380	2466	645	128	34	32	1.3	274	347	152	312	18	42	7	1503	1984	140	342	5.4	.961	2B-532, SS-70, 3B-62, OF-6

Ralph Young

YOUNG, RALPH STUART BB TR 5′ 5″ 165 lbs.
B. Sept. 19, 1889, Philadelphia, Pa. D. Jan. 24, 1965, Philadelphia, Pa.

Year	Team	Games	BA	SA	AB	H	2B	3B	HR	HR%	R	RBI	BB	SO	SB	Pinch Hit AB	Pinch Hit H	PO	A	E	DP	TC/G	FA	G by Pos
1913	NY A	7	.067	.067	15	1	0	0	0	0.0	2	0	3	3	2	0	0	11	19	5	3	5.0	.857	SS-7
1915	DET A	123	.243	.286	378	92	6	5	0	0.0	44	31	53	31	12	0	0	233	371	32	44	5.3	.950	2B-119
1916		153	.263	.322	528	139	16	6	1	0.2	60	45	62	43	20	0	0	380	436	29	56	5.5	.966	2B-146, SS-6, 3B-1
1917		141	.231	.280	503	116	18	2	1	0.2	64	35	61	35	8	0	0	300	449	33	46	5.5	.958	2B-141
1918		91	.188	.218	298	56	7	1	0	0.0	31	21	54	17	15	0	0	190	271	30	28	5.4	.939	2B-91
1919		125	.211	.268	456	96	13	5	1	0.2	63	25	53	32	8	0	0	312	405	23	39	5.9	.969	2B-121, SS-4
1920		150	.291	.347	594	173	21	6	0	0.0	84	33	85	30	8	0	0	405	436	27	46	5.8	.969	2B-150
1921		107	.299	.334	401	120	8	3	0	0.0	70	29	69	23	11	1	0	285	270	31	44	5.5	.947	2B-106
1922	PHI A	125	.223	.279	470	105	19	2	1	0.2	62	35	55	21	8	5	2	302	350	27	53	5.7	.960	2B-120
9 yrs.		1022	.247	.296	3643	898	108	30	4	0.1	480	254	495	235	92	6	2	2418	3007	237	359	5.6	.958	2B-994, SS-17, 3B-1

Russ Young

YOUNG, RUSSELL CHARLES BB TR 6′ 175 lbs.
B. Sept. 15, 1902, Bryan, Ohio D. May 13, 1984, Roseville, Calif.

Year	Team	Games	BA	SA	AB	H	2B	3B	HR	HR%	R	RBI	BB	SO	SB	Pinch Hit AB	Pinch Hit H	PO	A	E	DP	TC/G	FA	G by Pos
1931	STL A	16	.118	.206	34	4	0	0	1	2.9	2	2	2	4	0	0	0	44	7	0	0	3.2	1.000	C-16

Joel Youngblood

YOUNGBLOOD, JOEL RANDOLPH BR TR 6′ 180 lbs.
B. Aug. 28, 1951, Houston, Tex.

Year	Team	Games	BA	SA	AB	H	2B	3B	HR	HR%	R	RBI	BB	SO	SB	Pinch Hit AB	Pinch Hit H	PO	A	E	DP	TC/G	FA	G by Pos
1976	CIN N	55	.193	.246	57	11	1	1	0	0.0	8	1	2	8	1	33	5	15	3	2	2	1.2	.900	OF-9, 3B-6, 2B-1, C-1
1977	2 teams	STL N (25G –.185) NY N (70G –.253)																						
″	total	95	.244	.316	209	51	13	1	0	0.0	17	12	16	45	1	22	5	107	94	8	21	2.5	.962	OF-33, 2B-33, 3B-16
1978	NY N	113	.252	.436	266	67	12	8	7	2.6	40	30	16	39	4	23	7	160	96	6	21	2.6	.977	OF-50, 2B-39, 3B-9, SS-1
1979		158	.275	.436	590	162	37	5	16	2.7	90	60	60	84	18	4	1	337	57	9	10	2.3	.978	OF-147, 2B-13, 3B-12
1980		146	.276	.381	514	142	26	2	8	1.6	58	69	52	69	14	13	7	318	65	13	11	2.7	.967	OF-121, 3B-21, 2B-6
1981		43	.350	.531	143	50	10	2	4	2.8	16	25	12	19	2	3	0	70	6	3	0	1.9	.962	OF-41
1982	2 teams	NY N (80G –.257) MON N (40G –.200)																						
″	total	120	.240	.318	292	70	14	0	3	1.0	37	29	17	58	2	15	2	149	23	7	3	1.7	.961	OF-98, 2B-8, SS-1, 3B-1
1983	SF N	124	.292	.499	373	109	20	3	17	4.6	59	53	33	59	7	20	4	147	182	19	28	3.1	.945	2B-64, 3B-28, OF-22
1984		134	.254	.358	469	119	17	1	10	2.1	50	51	48	86	5	6	1	102	206	37	12	2.6	.893	3B-117, OF-11, 2B-5
1985		95	.270	.348	230	62	6	0	4	1.7	24	24	30	37	3	32	9	103	6	6	0	2.0	.948	OF-56, 3B-1

Joel Youngblood *continued*

Year	Team		Games	BA	SA	AB	H	2B	3B	HR	HR%	R	RBI	BB	SO	SB	Pinch Hit AB	Pinch Hit H	PO	A	E	DP	TC/G	FA	G by Pos
1986			97	.255	.402	184	47	12	0	5	2.7	20	28	18	34	1	58	16	68	14	3	4	1.4	.965	OF-45, 1B-7, 3B-5, 2B-4, SS-1
1987			69	.253	.385	91	23	3	0	3	3.3	9	11	5	13	1	44	13	24	3	0	0	1.1	1.000	OF-22, 3B-2
1988			83	.252	.285	123	31	4	0	0	0.0	12	16	10	17	1	49	15	48	0	1	0	1.1	.980	OF-45
1989	CIN	N	76	.212	.331	118	25	5	0	3	2.5	13	13	13	21	0	38	8	31	1	1	1	0.7	.970	OF-45
14 yrs.			1408	.265	.392	3659	969	180	23	80	2.2	453	422	332	589	60	360	93	1679	756	115	113	2.2	.955	OF-745, 3B-218, 2B-173, 1B-7, SS-3, C-1

Henry Youngman

YOUNGMAN, HENRY
B. 1865, Indiana, Pa. D. Jan. 24, 1936, Pittsburgh, Pa.
TR

Year	Team		Games	BA	SA	AB	H	2B	3B	HR	HR%	R	RBI	BB	SO	SB	Pinch Hit AB	Pinch Hit H	PO	A	E	DP	TC/G	FA	G by Pos
1890	PIT	N	13	.128	.191	47	6	1	1	0	0.0	6	4	6	9	1	0	0	29	28	16	4	5.6	.781	3B-7, 2B-6

Ross Youngs

YOUNGS, ROYCE MIDDLEBROOK (Pep)
B. Apr. 10, 1897, Shiner, Tex. D. Oct. 22, 1927, San Antonio, Tex.
Hall of Fame 1972.
BL TR 5′ 8″ 162 lbs.

Year	Team		Games	BA	SA	AB	H	2B	3B	HR	HR%	R	RBI	BB	SO	SB	Pinch Hit AB	Pinch Hit H	PO	A	E	DP	TC/G	FA	G by Pos
1917	NY	N	7	.346	.654	26	9	2	3	0	0.0	5	1	1	5	1	0	0	16	2	0	1	2.6	1.000	OF-7
1918			121	.302	.376	474	143	16	8	1	0.2	70	25	44	**49**	10	1	0	197	22	12	3	1.9	.948	OF-120
1919			130	.311	.415	489	152	**31**	7	2	0.4	73	43	51	47	24	0	0	235	23	16	7	2.1	.942	OF-130
1920			153	.351	.477	581	204	27	14	6	1.0	92	78	75	55	18	0	0	288	26	22	7	2.2	.935	OF-153
1921			141	.327	.456	504	165	24	16	3	0.6	90	102	71	47	21	4	2	122	11	3	3	1.0	.978	OF-137
1922			149	.331	.465	559	185	34	10	7	1.3	105	86	55	50	17	1	0	280	28	19	6	2.2	.942	OF-147
1923			152	.336	.446	596	200	33	12	3	0.5	**121**	87	73	36	13	0	0	282	22	13	7	2.1	.959	OF-152
1924			133	.356	.521	526	187	33	12	10	1.9	112	74	77	31	11	1	0	237	19	12	3	2.0	.955	OF-132, 2B-2
1925			130	.264	.372	500	132	24	6	6	1.2	82	53	66	51	17	1	0	219	32	15	3	2.0	.944	OF-127, 2B-3
1926			95	.306	.398	372	114	12	5	4	1.1	62	43	37	19	21	1	1	170	18	5	5	2.1	.974	OF-94
10 yrs.			1211	.322	.441	4627	1491	236	93	42	0.9	812	592	550	390	153	9	3	2046	203	117	45	2.0	.951	OF-1199, 2B-5
WORLD SERIES																									
1921	NY	N	8	.280	.400	25	7	1	1	0	0.0	3	3	7	2	2	0	0	7	1	0	0	1.0	1.000	OF-8
1922			5	.375	.375	16	6	0	0	0	0.0	2	2	3	1	0	0	0	9	2	2	1	2.6	.846	OF-5
1923			6	.348	.478	23	8	0	0	1	4.3	2	3	2	0	0	0	0	5	1	2	0	1.3	.750	OF-6
1924			7	.185	.222	27	5	1	0	0	0.0	3	1	5	6	1	0	0	8	1	0	0	1.3	1.000	OF-7
4 yrs.			26	.286	.363	91	26	2	1	1	1.1	10	9	17	9	3	0	0	29	5	4	1	1.5	.895	OF-26

Eddie Yount

YOUNT, FLOYD EDWIN
B. Dec. 19, 1916, Newton, N. C. D. Oct. 26, 1973, Newton, N. C.
BR TR 6′ 1″ 185 lbs.

Year	Team		Games	BA	SA	AB	H	2B	3B	HR	HR%	R	RBI	BB	SO	SB	Pinch Hit AB	Pinch Hit H	PO	A	E	DP	TC/G	FA	G by Pos
1937	PHI	A	4	.286	.286	7	2	0	0	0	0.0	1	1	0	1	0	2	0	3	0	0	0	1.5	1.000	OF-2
1939	PIT	N	2	.000	.000	2	0	0	0	0	0.0	0	0	0	2	0	2	0	0	0	0	0	0.0	—	
2 yrs.			6	.222	.222	9	2	0	0	0	0.0	1	1	0	3	0	4	0	3	0	0	0	1.5	1.000	OF-2

Robin Yount

YOUNT, ROBIN R.
Brother of Larry Yount.
B. Sept. 16, 1955, Danville, Ill.
BR TR 6′ 165 lbs.

Year	Team		Games	BA	SA	AB	H	2B	3B	HR	HR%	R	RBI	BB	SO	SB	Pinch Hit AB	Pinch Hit H	PO	A	E	DP	TC/G	FA	G by Pos
1974	MIL	A	107	.250	.346	344	86	14	5	3	0.9	48	26	12	46	7	0	0	148	327	19	55	4.6	.962	SS-107
1975			147	.267	.367	558	149	28	2	8	1.4	67	52	33	69	12	2	0	273	402	44	80	5.0	.939	SS-145
1976			161	.252	.301	638	161	19	3	2	0.3	59	54	38	69	16	0	0	290	510	31	104	5.1	.963	SS-161, OF-1
1977			154	.288	.377	605	174	34	4	4	0.7	66	49	41	80	16	3	1	256	449	26	94	4.8	.964	SS-153
1978			127	.293	.428	502	147	23	9	9	1.8	66	71	24	43	16	2	1	246	453	30	78	5.8	.959	SS-125
1979			149	.267	.371	577	154	26	5	8	1.4	72	51	35	52	11	0	0	267	517	25	97	5.4	.969	SS-149
1980			143	.293	.519	611	179	**49**	10	23	3.8	121	87	26	67	20	2	0	239	455	28	89	5.1	.961	SS-133, DH-9
1981			96	.273	.419	377	103	15	5	10	2.7	50	49	22	37	4	1	1	161	370	8	83	5.6	.985	SS-93, DH-3
1982			156	.331	**.578**	635	**210**	**46**	12	29	4.6	129	114	54	63	14	2	1	253	489	24	95	4.9	.969	SS-154, DH-1
1983			149	.308	.503	578	178	42	**10**	17	2.9	102	80	72	58	12	2	2	256	420	19	86	4.7	.973	SS-139, DH-8
1984			160	.298	.441	624	186	27	7	16	2.6	105	80	67	67	14	0	0	199	402	18	80	3.9	.971	SS-120, DH-39
1985			122	.277	.442	466	129	26	3	15	3.2	76	68	49	56	10	0	0	267	5	8	2	2.3	.971	OF-108, DH-12, 1B-3
1986			140	.312	.450	522	163	31	7	9	1.7	82	46	62	73	14	1	0	365	9	2	5	2.7	.995	OF-131, DH-6, 1B-3
1987			158	.312	.479	635	198	25	9	21	3.3	99	103	76	94	19	0	0	380	5	5	2	2.5	.987	OF-150, DH-8
1988			162	.306	.465	621	190	38	**11**	13	2.1	92	91	63	63	22	0	0	444	12	2	2	2.8	.996	OF-158, DH-4
1989			160	.318	.511	614	195	38	9	21	3.4	101	103	63	71	19	0	0	361	8	7	2	2.3	.981	OF-143, DH-17
1990			158	.247	.380	587	145	17	5	17	2.9	98	77	78	89	15	0	0	422	3	4	0	2.7	.991	OF-157, DH-1
1991			130	.260	.376	503	131	20	4	10	2.0	66	77	54	79	6	1	0	315	1	2	1	2.4	.994	OF-117, DH-13
1992			150	.264	.390	557	147	40	3	8	1.4	71	77	53	81	15	1	0	371	6	2	0	2.5	.995	OF-139, DH-11
1993			127	.258	.379	454	117	25	3	8	1.8	62	51	44	93	9	5	1	342	7	1	8	2.8	.997	OF-114, 1B-7, DH-6
20 yrs.			2856 **10th**	.285	.430	11008 **5th**	3142	583	126	251	2.3	1632	1406	966	1350	271	22	7	5855	4850	305	963	3.9	.972	SS-1479, OF-1218, DH-138, 1B-13
DIVISIONAL PLAYOFF SERIES																									
1981	MIL	A	5	.316	.421	19	6	0	1	0	0.0	4	1	2	2	1	0	0	6	16	1	0	4.6	.957	SS-5
LEAGUE CHAMPIONSHIP SERIES																									
1982	MIL	A	5	.250	.250	16	4	0	0	0	0.0	1	0	5	0	0	0	0	11	12	1	4	4.8	.958	SS-5
WORLD SERIES																									
1982	MIL	A	7	.414	.621	29	12	3	0	1	3.4	6	6	2	2	0	0	0	20	19	3	1	6.0	.929	SS-7

Jeff Yurak

YURAK, JEFFREY LYNN
B. Feb. 26, 1954, Pasadena, Calif.
BB TR 6′ 3″ 195 lbs.

Year	Team		Games	BA	SA	AB	H	2B	3B	HR	HR%	R	RBI	BB	SO	SB	Pinch Hit AB	Pinch Hit H	PO	A	E	DP	TC/G	FA	G by Pos
1978	MIL	A	5	.000	.000	5	0	0	0	0	0.0	0	0	1	0	0	3	0	4	0	0	0	4.0	1.000	OF-1

Sal Yvars

YVARS, SALVADOR ANTHONY
B. Feb. 20, 1924, New York, N. Y.
BR TR 5′10″ 187 lbs.

Year	Team		Games	BA	SA	AB	H	2B	3B	HR	HR%	R	RBI	BB	SO	SB	Pinch Hit AB	Pinch Hit H	PO	A	E	DP	TC/G	FA	G by Pos
1947	NY	N	1	.200	.200	5	1	0	0	0	0.0	0	0	0	2	0	0	0	3	1	0	0	4.0	1.000	C-1
1948			15	.211	.316	38	8	1	0	1	2.6	4	6	3	1	0	0	0	50	8	0	2	3.9	1.000	C-15
1949			3	.000	.000	8	0	0	0	0	0.0	0	0	1	1	0	1	0	11	1	0	0	6.0	1.000	C-2
1950			9	.143	.143	14	2	0	0	0	0.0	0	0	1	2	0	0	0	22	4	1	0	3.0	.963	C-9
1951			25	.317	.512	41	13	2	0	2	4.9	9	3	5	7	0	2	0	46	3	3	1	2.3	.942	C-23

Sal Yvars *continued*

Year	Team	Games	BA	SA	AB	H	2B	3B	HR	HR%	R	RBI	BB	SO	SB	Pinch Hit AB	Pinch Hit H	PO	A	E	DP	TC/G	FA	G by Pos
1952		66	.245	.344	151	37	3	0	4	2.6	15	18	10	16	0	7	1	202	40	3	3	4.2	.988	C-59
1953	**2 teams**	**NY N** (23G –.277) **STL N** (30G –.246)																						
"	**total**	53	.260	.308	104	27	2	0	1	1.0	5	7	11	7	0	9	1	146	20	1	4	3.6	.994	C-46
1954	**STL N**	38	.246	.421	57	14	4	0	2	3.5	8	8	6	5	1	18	4	46	9	0	1	2.6	1.000	C-21
8 yrs.		210	.244	.344	418	102	12	0	10	2.4	41	42	37	41	1	37	6	526	86	8	11	3.5	.987	C-176
WORLD SERIES																								
1951	**NY N**	1	.000	.000	1	0	0	0	0	0.0	0	0	0	0	0	1	0	0	0	0	0	0.0	—	

Elmer Zacher

ZACHER, ELMER HENRY (Silver) BR TR 5′ 9″ 190 lbs.
B. Sept. 17, 1883, Buffalo, N. Y. D. Dec. 20, 1944, Buffalo, N. Y.

Year	Team	Games	BA	SA	AB	H	2B	3B	HR	HR%	R	RBI	BB	SO	SB	Pinch Hit AB	Pinch Hit H	PO	A	E	DP	TC/G	FA	G by Pos
1910	**2 teams**	**NY N** (1G –.000) **STL N** (47G –.212)																						
"	**total**	48	.212	.265	132	28	5	1	0	0.0	7	10	10	19	3	9	2	78	7	3	1	2.3	.966	OF-37, 2B-1

Fred Zahner

ZAHNER, FREDERICK JOSEPH
B. June 5, 1870, Louisville, Ky. D. July 24, 1900, Louisville, Ky.

Year	Team	Games	BA	SA	AB	H	2B	3B	HR	HR%	R	RBI	BB	SO	SB	Pinch Hit AB	Pinch Hit H	PO	A	E	DP	TC/G	FA	G by Pos
1894	**LOU N**	13	.200	.244	45	9	0	1	0	0.0	7	3	3	5	2	0	0	31	6	8	2	3.5	.822	C-10, OF-2, 1B-1
1895		21	.224	.286	49	11	1	1	0	0.0	7	6	6	4	0	0	0	28	14	9	0	2.4	.824	C-21
2 yrs.		34	.213	.266	94	20	1	2	0	0.0	14	9	9	9	2	0	0	59	20	17	2	2.8	.823	C-31, OF-2, 1B-1

Frankie Zak

ZAK, FRANK THOMAS BR TR 5′10″ 150 lbs.
B. Feb. 22, 1922, Passaic, N. J. D. Feb. 6, 1972, Passaic, N. J.

Year	Team	Games	BA	SA	AB	H	2B	3B	HR	HR%	R	RBI	BB	SO	SB	Pinch Hit AB	Pinch Hit H	PO	A	E	DP	TC/G	FA	G by Pos
1944	**PIT N**	87	.300	.331	160	48	3	1	0	0.0	33	11	22	18	6	0	0	93	162	14	24	4.0	.948	SS-67
1945		15	.143	.214	28	4	2	0	0	0.0	2	3	3	5	0	0	0	9	26	1	3	3.3	.972	SS-10, 2B-1
1946		21	.200	.200	20	4	0	0	0	0.0	8	0	1	0	0	0	0	13	26	3	5	4.2	.929	SS-10
3 yrs.		123	.269	.303	208	56	5	1	0	0.0	43	14	26	23	6	0	0	115	214	18	32	3.9	.948	SS-87, 2B-1

Jack Zalusky

ZALUSKY, JOHN FRANCIS BR TR 5′11½″ 172 lbs.
B. June 22, 1879, Minneapolis, Minn. D. Aug. 11, 1935, Minneapolis, Minn.

Year	Team	Games	BA	SA	AB	H	2B	3B	HR	HR%	R	RBI	BB	SO	SB	Pinch Hit AB	Pinch Hit H	PO	A	E	DP	TC/G	FA	G by Pos
1903	**NY A**	7	.313	.313	16	5	0	0	0	0.0	2	1	1		0	0	0	18	3	0	0	3.0	1.000	C-6, 1B-1

Eddie Zambrano

ZAMBRANO, EDUARDO JOSE BR TR 6′ 2″ 175 lbs.
Born Eduardo Jose Zambrano (Guerra).
B. Feb. 1, 1966, Maracaibo, Venezuela.

Year	Team	Games	BA	SA	AB	H	2B	3B	HR	HR%	R	RBI	BB	SO	SB	Pinch Hit AB	Pinch Hit H	PO	A	E	DP	TC/G	FA	G by Pos
1993	**CHI N**	8	.294	.294	17	5	0	0	0	0.0	1	2	1	3	0	3	2	14	0	1	1	2.5	.933	OF-4, 1B-2
1994		67	.259	.474	116	30	7	0	6	5.2	17	18	16	29	2	26	7	84	5	2	6	2.3	.978	OF-27, 1B-9, 3B-4
2 yrs.		75	.263	.451	133	35	7	0	6	4.5	18	20	17	32	2	29	9	98	5	3	7	2.3	.972	OF-31, 1B-11, 3B-4

Joe Zapustas

ZAPUSTAS, JOSEPH JOHN BR TR 6′ 1″ 185 lbs.
B. July 25, 1907, Boston, Mass.

Year	Team	Games	BA	SA	AB	H	2B	3B	HR	HR%	R	RBI	BB	SO	SB	Pinch Hit AB	Pinch Hit H	PO	A	E	DP	TC/G	FA	G by Pos
1933	**PHI A**	2	.200	.200	5	1	0	0	0	0.0	0	0	0	0	0	0	0	2	0	0	0	1.0	1.000	OF-2

Jose Zardon

ZARDON, JOSE ANTONIO BR TR 5′11½″ 160 lbs.
Born Jose Antonio Zardon (Sanchez).
B. May 20, 1923, Havana, Cuba.

Year	Team	Games	BA	SA	AB	H	2B	3B	HR	HR%	R	RBI	BB	SO	SB	Pinch Hit AB	Pinch Hit H	PO	A	E	DP	TC/G	FA	G by Pos
1945	**WAS A**	54	.290	.374	131	38	5	3	0	0.0	13	13	7	11	3	2	0	104	2	3	0	2.5	.972	OF-43

Al Zarilla

ZARILLA, ALLEN LEE (Zeke) BL TR 5′11″ 180 lbs.
B. May 1, 1919, Los Angeles, Calif.

Year	Team	Games	BA	SA	AB	H	2B	3B	HR	HR%	R	RBI	BB	SO	SB	Pinch Hit AB	Pinch Hit H	PO	A	E	DP	TC/G	FA	G by Pos
1943	**STL A**	70	.254	.320	228	58	7	1	2	0.9	27	17	17	20	1	11	4	123	5	5	2	2.2	.962	OF-60
1944		100	.299	.448	288	86	13	6	6	2.1	43	45	29	33	1	15	2	167	4	4	1	2.2	.977	OF-79
1946		125	.259	.377	371	96	14	9	4	1.1	46	43	27	37	3	15	1	236	13	7	6	2.4	.973	OF-107
1947		127	.224	.318	380	85	15	6	3	0.8	34	38	40	45	3	16	0	209	6	3	0	2.0	.986	OF-110
1948		144	.329	.482	529	174	39	3	12	2.3	77	74	48	48	11	9	3	322	5	13	0	2.5	.962	OF-136
1949	**2 teams**	**STL A** (15G –.250) **BOS A** (124G –.281)																						
"	**total**	139	.277	.411	530	147	33	4	10	1.9	78	77	56	53	5	2	0	260	6	4	4	2.0	.985	OF-137
1950	**BOS A**	130	.325	.493	471	153	32	10	9	1.9	92	74	76	47	2	1	0	230	12	6	1	1.9	.976	OF-128
1951	**CHI A**	120	.257	.401	382	98	21	2	10	2.6	56	60	60	57	2	3	0	164	7	3	2	1.5	.983	OF-117
1952	**3 teams**	**CHI A** (39G –.232) **STL A** (48G –.238) **BOS A** (21G –.183)																						
"	**total**	108	.225	.325	289	65	10	2	5	1.7	43	24	48	29	5	18	1	141	10	5	0	1.8	.968	OF-86
1953	**BOS A**	57	.194	.224	67	13	2	0	0	0.0	11	4	14	13	0	30	4	17	1	1	0	1.1	.947	OF-18
10 yrs.		1120	.276	.405	3535	975	186	43	61	1.7	507	456	415	382	33	120	15	1869	69	51	16	2.0	.974	OF-978
WORLD SERIES																								
1944	**STL A**	4	.100	.100	10	1	0	0	0	0.0	1	1	0	4	0	2	0	2	0	0	0	0.7	1.000	OF-3

Norm Zauchin

ZAUCHIN, NORBERT HENRY BR TR 6′ 4½″ 220 lbs.
B. Nov. 17, 1929, Royal Oak, Mich.

Year	Team	Games	BA	SA	AB	H	2B	3B	HR	HR%	R	RBI	BB	SO	SB	Pinch Hit AB	Pinch Hit H	PO	A	E	DP	TC/G	FA	G by Pos
1951	**BOS A**	5	.167	.250	12	2	1	0	0	0.0	0	0	0	4	0	1	0	20	2	1	8	5.8	.957	1B-4
1955		130	.239	.430	477	114	10	0	27	5.7	65	93	69	**105**	3	4	2	1137	84	6	106	9.7	.995	1B-126
1956		44	.214	.310	84	18	2	0	2	2.4	12	11	14	22	0	12	1	189	10	2	18	6.5	.990	1B-31
1957		52	.264	.396	91	24	3	0	3	3.3	11	14	9	13	0	21	4	194	15	6	28	6.0	.972	1B-36
1958	**WAS A**	96	.228	.416	303	69	8	2	15	5.0	35	37	38	68	0	5	1	749	56	4	74	8.9	.995	1B-91
1959		19	.211	.394	71	15	4	0	3	4.2	11	4	7	14	2	0	0	203	6	1	17	11.1	.995	1B-19
6 yrs.		346	.233	.408	1038	242	28	2	50	4.8	134	159	137	226	5	43	8	2492	173	20	251	8.7	.993	1B-307

Greg Zaun

ZAUN, GREGORY OWEN BB TR 5′10″ 170 lbs.
B. Apr. 4, 1971, Glendale, Calif.

Year	Team	Games	BA	SA	AB	H	2B	3B	HR	HR%	R	RBI	BB	SO	SB	Pinch Hit AB	Pinch Hit H	PO	A	E	DP	TC/G	FA	G by Pos
1995	**BAL A**	40	.260	.394	104	27	5	0	3	2.9	18	14	16	14	1	2	1	216	13	3	2	5.9	.987	C-39

Zay

ZAY
B. Pittsburgh, Pa. Deceased.

Year	Team	Games	BA	SA	AB	H	2B	3B	HR	HR%	R	RBI	BB	SO	SB	Pinch Hit AB	Pinch Hit H	PO	A	E	DP	TC/G	FA	G by Pos
1886	**BAL AA**	1	.000	.000	1	0	0	0	0	0.0	0		0			0	0	1	0	1	0	1.0	.500	P-1, OF-1

Joe Zdeb

ZDEB, JOSEPH EDMUND BR TR 5′11″ 185 lbs.
B. June 27, 1953, Compton, Ill.

Year	Team	Games	BA	SA	AB	H	2B	3B	HR	HR%	R	RBI	BB	SO	SB	Pinch Hit AB	Pinch Hit H	PO	A	E	DP	TC/G	FA	G by Pos
1977	KC A	105	.297	.374	195	58	5	2	2	1.0	26	23	16	23	6	22	7	93	4	3	0	1.0	.970	OF-93, DH-4, 3B-1
1978		60	.252	.315	127	32	2	3	0	0.0	18	11	7	18	3	17	3	66	2	3	0	1.3	.958	OF-52, 2B-1, DH-1, 3B-1
1979		15	.174	.304	23	4	1	1	0	0.0	3	0	2	4	1	8	1	13	0	0	0	1.4	1.000	OF-9
3 yrs.		180	.272	.348	345	94	8	6	2	0.6	47	34	25	45	10	47	11	172	6	6	0	1.1	.967	OF-154, DH-5, 3B-2, 2B-1
LEAGUE CHAMPIONSHIP SERIES																								
1977	KC A	4	.000	.000	9	0	0	0	0	0.0	0	0	0	2	1	1	0	4	0	0	0	1.0	1.000	OF-4

Dave Zearfoss

ZEARFOSS, DAVID WILLIAM TILDEN TR 5′9″
B. Jan. 1, 1868, Schenectady, N. Y. D. Sept. 12, 1945, Wilmington, Del.

Year	Team	Games	BA	SA	AB	H	2B	3B	HR	HR%	R	RBI	BB	SO	SB	Pinch Hit AB	Pinch Hit H	PO	A	E	DP	TC/G	FA	G by Pos
1896	NY N	19	.217	.267	60	13	1	1	0	0.0	5	6	5	5	2	0	0	53	14	8	1	3.9	.893	C-19
1897		5	.300	.500	10	3	0	1	0	0.0	1	0	0		0	0	0	15	7	3	1	5.0	.880	C-5
1898		1	1.000	1.000	1	1	0	0	0	0.0	0	0	0		0	0	0	2	1	0	0	3.0	1.000	C-1
1904	STL N	27	.212	.237	80	17	2	0	0	0.0	7	9	10		0	1	0	107	33	5	1	5.8	.966	C-25
1905		20	.157	.196	51	8	0	1	0	0.0	2	2	4		0	1	0	62	22	3	0	4.6	.966	C-19
5 yrs.		72	.208	.252	202	42	3	3	0	0.0	15	17	19	5	2	2	0	239	77	19	3	4.9	.943	C-69

George Zeber

ZEBER, GEORGE WILLIAM BB TR 5′11″ 170 lbs.
B. Aug. 29, 1950, Ellwood City, Pa.

Year	Team	Games	BA	SA	AB	H	2B	3B	HR	HR%	R	RBI	BB	SO	SB	Pinch Hit AB	Pinch Hit H	PO	A	E	DP	TC/G	FA	G by Pos
1977	NY A	25	.323	.508	65	21	3	0	3	4.6	8	10	9	11	0	1	0	42	56	4	11	3.8	.961	2B-21, SS-2, DH-2, 3B-2
1978		3	.000	.000	6	0	0	0	0	0.0	0	0	0	0	0	1	0	1	2	1	0	4.0	.750	2B-1
2 yrs.		28	.296	.465	71	21	3	0	3	4.2	8	10	9	11	0	2	0	43	58	5	11	3.8	.953	2B-22, SS-2, DH-2, 3B-2
WORLD SERIES																								
1977	NY A	2	.000	.000	2	0	0	0	0	0.0	0	0	0	2	0	2	0	0	0	0	0	0.0	.000	

Rollie Zeider

ZEIDER, ROLLIE HUBERT (Bunions) BR TR 5′10″ 162 lbs.
B. Nov. 16, 1883, Auburn, Ind. D. Sept. 12, 1967, Garrett, Ind.

Year	Team	Games	BA	SA	AB	H	2B	3B	HR	HR%	R	RBI	BB	SO	SB	Pinch Hit AB	Pinch Hit H	PO	A	E	DP	TC/G	FA	G by Pos
1910	CHI A	136	.217	.243	498	108	9	2	0	0.0	57	31	62		49	0	0	312	372	60	47	5.5	.919	2B-87, SS-45, 3B-4
1911		73	.253	.295	217	55	3	0	2	0.9	39	21	29		28	8	4	358	92	15	16	7.2	.968	1B-29, SS-17, 3B-10, 2B-9
1912		129	.245	.329	420	103	12	10	1	0.2	57	42	50		47	3	1	742	163	27	39	7.6	.971	1B-66, 3B-56, SS-1
1913	2 teams	CHI A (13G –.350) NY A (49G –.233)																						
″	total	62	.246	.257	179	44	2	0	0	0.0	19	14	29	10	6	2	0	153	114	17	13	4.9	.940	SS-23, 2B-20, 3B-8, 1B-7
1914	CHI F	119	.274	.319	452	124	13	2	1	0.2	60	36	44		35	1	0	151	219	26	27	3.4	.934	3B-117, SS-1
1915		129	.227	.279	494	112	22	2	0	0.0	65	34	43		16	0	0	281	350	37	47	5.0	.945	2B-83, 3B-30, SS-21
1916	CHI N	98	.235	.287	345	81	11	2	1	0.3	29	22	26	26	9	1	0	140	199	21	19	3.5	.942	3B-55, 2B-33, OF-7, SS-5, 1B-2
1917		108	.243	.294	354	86	14	2	0	0.0	36	27	28	30	17	15	2	151	226	28	35	4.1	.931	SS-48, 3B-26, 2B-24, OF-1, 1B-1
1918		82	.223	.251	251	56	3	2	0	0.0	31	26	23	20	16	7	1	147	209	16	22	4.6	.957	2B-79, 3B-1, 1B-1
9 yrs.		936	.240	.286	3210	769	89	22	5	0.2	393	253	334	86	223	37	8	2435	1944	247	265	5.0	.947	2B-335, 3B-307, SS-161, 1B-106, OF-8
WORLD SERIES																								
1918	CHI N	2	—	—	0	0	0	0	0	—	0	0	2	0	0	0	0	1	2	0	0	1.5	1.000	3B-2

Todd Zeile

ZEILE, TODD EDWARD BR TR 6′1″ 190 lbs.
B. Sept. 9, 1965, Van Nuys, Calif.

Year	Team	Games	BA	SA	AB	H	2B	3B	HR	HR%	R	RBI	BB	SO	SB	Pinch Hit AB	Pinch Hit H	PO	A	E	DP	TC/G	FA	G by Pos
1989	STL N	28	.256	.354	82	21	3	1	1	1.2	7	8	9	14	0	5	0	125	10	4	1	6.0	.971	C-23
1990		144	.244	.398	495	121	25	3	15	3.0	62	57	67	77	2	3	0	648	106	15	12	5.5	.980	C-105, 3B-24, 1B-11, OF-1
1991		155	.280	.412	565	158	36	3	11	1.9	76	81	62	94	17	0	0	124	290	25	18	2.9	.943	3B-154
1992		126	.257	.364	439	113	18	4	7	1.6	51	48	68	70	7	3	0	80	235	13	19	2.6	.960	3B-124
1993		157	.277	.433	571	158	36	1	17	3.0	82	103	70	76	5	3	1	83	310	33	26	2.8	.923	3B-153
1994		113	.267	.470	415	111	25	1	19	4.6	62	75	52	56	1	2	0	66	224	12	24	2.7	.960	3B-112
1995	2 teams	STL N (34G –.291) CHI N (79G –.227)																						
″	total	113	.246	.397	426	105	22	0	14	3.3	50	52	34	76	1	2	0	361	163	19	44	4.8	.965	3B-75, 1B-35, OF-2
7 yrs.		836	.263	.411	2993	787	165	13	84	2.8	390	424	362	463	33	18	1	1487	1338	121	144	3.6	.959	3B-642, C-128, 1B-46, OF-3

Bart Zeller

ZELLER, BARTON WALLACE BR TR 6′1″ 185 lbs.
B. July 22, 1941, Chicago Heights, Ill.

Year	Team	Games	BA	SA	AB	H	2B	3B	HR	HR%	R	RBI	BB	SO	SB	Pinch Hit AB	Pinch Hit H	PO	A	E	DP	TC/G	FA	G by Pos
1970	STL N	1	—	—	0	0	0	0	0	—	0	0	0	0	0	0	0	1	0	0	0	1.0	1.000	C-1

Gus Zernial

ZERNIAL, GUS EDWARD (Ozark Ike) BR TR 6′2½″ 210 lbs.
B. June 27, 1923, Beaumont, Tex.

Year	Team	Games	BA	SA	AB	H	2B	3B	HR	HR%	R	RBI	BB	SO	SB	Pinch Hit AB	Pinch Hit H	PO	A	E	DP	TC/G	FA	G by Pos
1949	CHI A	73	.318	.500	198	63	17	2	5	2.5	29	38	15	26	0	25	8	73	4	0	0	1.7	1.000	OF-46
1950		143	.280	.484	543	152	16	4	29	5.3	75	93	38	**110**	0	5	1	306	9	10	2	2.4	.969	OF-137
1951	2 teams	CHI A (4G –.105) PHI A (139G –.274)																						
″	total	143	.268	.511	571	153	30	5	**33**	**5.8**	92	**129**	63	**101**	2	1	1	334	18	10	3	2.5	.972	OF-142
1952	PHI A	145	.262	.452	549	144	15	1	29	5.3	76	100	70	87	5	3	1	302	6	9	0	2.2	.972	OF-141
1953		147	.284	.559	556	158	21	3	42	**7.6**	85	108	57	79	4	4	3	300	17	9	2	2.3	.972	OF-141
1954		97	.250	.411	336	84	8	2	14	4.2	42	62	30	60	0	6	2	185	4	9	1	2.2	.955	OF-90, 1B-2
1955	KC A	120	.254	.508	413	105	9	3	30	**7.3**	62	84	30	90	1	17	2	231	9	9	4	2.4	.964	OF-103
1956		109	.224	.445	272	61	12	0	16	5.9	36	44	33	66	2	35	4	111	9	2	1	1.8	.984	OF-69
1957		131	.236	.471	437	103	20	1	27	6.2	56	69	34	84	1	17	4	217	5	12	1	2.1	.949	OF-113, 1B-1
1958	DET A	66	.323	.516	124	40	7	1	5	4.0	8	23	6	25	0	38	**15**	30	1	2	0	1.4	.939	OF-24
1959		60	.227	.417	132	30	4	0	7	5.3	11	26	7	27	0	27	6	198	10	6	20	6.5	.972	1B-32, OF-1
11 yrs.		1234	.265	.486	4131	1093	159	22	237	5.7	572	776	383	755	15	178	47	2287	92	78	34	2.4	.968	OF-1007, 1B-35

Ed Zieber

Playing record listed under Ed Whiting.

Charlie Ziegler

ZIEGLER, CHARLES WALLACE
B. Jan. 13, 1875, Canton, Ohio D. Apr. 18, 1904, Canton, Ohio.

Year	Team	Lg	Games	BA	SA	AB	H	2B	3B	HR	HR%	R	RBI	BB	SO	SB	Pinch Hit AB	Pinch Hit H	PO	A	E	DP	TC/G	FA	G by Pos
1899	CLE	N	2	.250	.250	8	2	0	0	0	0.0	2	0	0		0	0	0	2	5	1	0	4.0	.875	SS-1, 2B-1
1900	PHI	N	3	.273	.273	11	3	0	0	0	0.0	0	1	0		0	0	0	4	4	1	0	3.0	.889	3B-3
2 yrs.			5	.263	.263	19	5	0	0	0	0.0	2	1	0		0	0	0	6	9	2	0	3.4	.882	3B-3, SS-1, 2B-1

Benny Zientara

ZIENTARA, BENEDICT JOSEPH BR TR 5′9″ 165 lbs.
B. Feb. 14, 1920, Chicago, Ill. D. Apr. 16, 1985, Lake Elsinore, Calif.

Year	Team	Lg	Games	BA	SA	AB	H	2B	3B	HR	HR%	R	RBI	BB	SO	SB	Pinch Hit AB	Pinch Hit H	PO	A	E	DP	TC/G	FA	G by Pos
1941	CIN	N	9	.286	.286	21	6	0	0	0	0.0	3	2	1	3	0	0	0	14	18	3	3	5.8	.914	2B-6
1946			78	.289	.339	280	81	10	2	0	0.0	26	16	14	11	3	0	0	114	219	11	38	4.6	.968	2B-39, 3B-36
1947			117	.258	.321	418	108	18	1	2	0.5	60	24	23	23	2	9	5	248	258	12	53	4.6	.977	2B-100, 3B-13
1948			74	.187	.214	187	35	1	2	0	0.0	17	7	12	11	0	7	1	146	144	3	32	4.5	.990	2B-60, 3B-3, SS-2
4 yrs.			278	.254	.304	906	230	29	5	2	0.2	106	49	50	48	5	16	6	522	639	29	126	4.6	.976	2B-205, 3B-52, SS-2

Bill Zies

ZIES, WILLIAM BL
Deceased.

Year	Team	Lg	Games	BA	SA	AB	H	2B	3B	HR	HR%	R	RBI	BB	SO	SB	Pinch Hit AB	Pinch Hit H	PO	A	E	DP	TC/G	FA	G by Pos
1891	STL	AA	2	.333	.333	3	1	0	0	0	0.0	0	0	0	0	0	0	0	5	1	0	0	3.0	1.000	C-2

Chief Zimmer

ZIMMER, CHARLES LOUIS BR TR 6′ 190 lbs.
B. Nov. 23, 1860, Marietta, Ohio D. Aug. 22, 1949, Cleveland, Ohio.
Manager 1903.

Year	Team	Lg	Games	BA	SA	AB	H	2B	3B	HR	HR%	R	RBI	BB	SO	SB	Pinch Hit AB	Pinch Hit H	PO	A	E	DP	TC/G	FA	G by Pos
1884	DET	N	8	.069	.103	29	2	1	0	0	0.0	0		1	14		0	0	31	11	8	3	6.3	.840	C-6, OF-2
1886	NY	AA	6	.158	.158	19	3	0	0	0	0.0	1		1			0	0	33	17	6	0	9.3	.893	C-6
1887	CLE	AA	14	.231	.327	52	12	5	0	0	0.0	9		4		1	0	0	64	13	8	2	6.1	.906	C-12, 1B-2
1888			65	.241	.330	212	51	11	4	0	0.0	27	22	18		15	0	0	345	115	42	7	7.6	.916	C-59, OF-3, 1B-3, SS-1
1889	CLE	N	84	.259	.375	259	67	9	9	1	0.4	47	21	44	35	14	0	0	336	131	35	11	6.0	.930	C-81, 1B-3
1890			125	.214	.291	444	95	16	6	2	0.5	54	57	46	54	15	0	0	480	188	45	14	5.7	.937	C-125
1891			116	.255	.341	440	112	21	4	3	0.7	55	69	33	49	15	0	0	477	184	45	7	6.0	.936	C-116, 3B-1
1892			111	.262	.402	413	108	29	13	1	0.2	63	64	32	47	18	0	0	514	122	42	11	6.1	.938	C-111
1893			57	.308	.454	227	70	13	7	2	0.9	27	41	16	15	4	1	0	169	73	8	10	4.4	.968	C-56, 3B-1
1894			90	.284	.408	341	97	20	5	4	1.2	55	65	17	31	14	1	0	289	100	15	16	4.5	.963	C-89
1895			88	.340	.467	315	107	21	2	5	1.6	60	56	33	30	14	1	0	339	79	11	5	4.9	.974	C-84, 1B-3
1896			91	.277	.375	336	93	18	3	3	0.9	46	46	31	48	4	0	0	338	81	12	9	4.7	.972	C-91, 3B-1
1897			80	.316	.412	294	93	22	3	0	0.0	50	40	25		8	0	0	278	81	9	10	4.6	.976	C-80
1898			20	.238	.270	63	15	2	0	0	0.0	5	4	5		2	1	0	78	20	3	2	5.3	.970	C-19
1899	2 teams		CLE N (20G –.342)	LOU N (75G –.298)																					
″	total		95	.307	.406	335	103	13	4	4	1.2	52	43	27		10	2	1	358	111	13	13	5.2	.973	C-82, 1B-11
1900	PIT	N	82	.295	.395	271	80	7	10	0	0.0	27	35	17		4	2	0	343	101	17	9	5.8	.963	C-78, 1B-2
1901			69	.220	.275	236	52	7	3	0	0.0	17	21	20		6	1	1	285	69	9	4	5.3	.975	C-68
1902			42	.268	.324	142	38	4	2	0	0.0	13	17	11		4	0	0	202	48	8	8	6.1	.969	C-41, 1B-1
1903	PHI	N	37	.220	.288	118	26	3	1	1	0.8	9	19	9		3	2	1	162	50	7	4	6.3	.968	C-35
19 yrs.			1280	.269	.369	4546	1224	222	76	26	0.6	617	620	390	323	151	11	3	5121	1594	343	145	5.5	.951	C-1239, 1B-25, OF-5, 3B-3, SS-1

Don Zimmer

ZIMMER, DONALD WILLIAM (Popeye) BR TR 5′9″ 165 lbs.
B. Jan. 17, 1931, Cincinnati, Ohio
Manager 1972–73, 1976–82, 1988–91.

Year	Team	Lg	Games	BA	SA	AB	H	2B	3B	HR	HR%	R	RBI	BB	SO	SB	Pinch Hit AB	Pinch Hit H	PO	A	E	DP	TC/G	FA	G by Pos
1954	BKN	N	24	.182	.242	33	6	0	1	0	0.0	3	0	3	8	2	2	0	14	32	3	6	3.8	.939	SS-13
1955			88	.239	.443	280	67	10	1	15	5.4	38	50	19	66	5	3	0	184	207	12	63	4.4	.970	2B-62, SS-21, 3B-8
1956			17	.300	.350	20	6	1	0	0	0.0	4	2	0	7	0	0	0	10	11	1	4	1.8	.955	SS-8, 3B-3, 2B-1
1957			84	.219	.327	269	59	9	1	6	2.2	23	19	16	63	1	1	0	114	186	15	24	3.9	.952	3B-39, SS-37, 2B-5
1958	LA	N	127	.262	.415	455	119	15	2	17	3.7	52	60	28	92	14	1	0	281	395	26	102	5.5	.963	SS-114, 3B-12, 2B-1, OF-1
1959			97	.165	.249	249	41	7	1	4	1.6	21	28	37	56	3	4	1	120	240	10	43	3.9	.973	SS-88, 3B-5, 2B-1
1960	CHI	N	132	.258	.389	368	95	16	7	6	1.6	37	35	27	56	8	13	3	211	274	16	31	3.9	.968	2B-75, 3B-45, SS-5, OF-2
1961			128	.252	.403	477	120	25	4	13	2.7	57	40	25	70	5	8	1	284	332	20	100	5.2	.969	2B-116, 3B-5, OF-1
1962	2 teams		NY N (14G –.077)	CIN N (63G –.250)																					
″	total		77	.213	.303	244	52	12	2	2	0.8	19	17	17	40	1	9	4	77	129	11	14	2.9	.949	3B-57, 2B-17, SS-1
1963	2 teams		LA N (22G –.217)	WAS A (83G –.248)																					
″	total		105	.246	.424	321	79	13	1	14	4.4	41	46	21	67	3	14	5	93	191	20	18	3.3	.934	3B-88, 2B-3, SS-1
1964	WAS	A	121	.246	.411	341	84	16	2	12	3.5	38	38	27	94	1	38	10	72	144	10	6	2.4	.956	3B-87, OF-4, C-2, 2B-1
1965			95	.199	.252	226	45	6	0	2	0.9	20	17	26	59	2	27	5	181	81	12	7	3.4	.956	3B-36, C-33, 2B-12
12 yrs.			1095	.235	.372	3283	773	130	22	91	2.8	353	352	246	678	45	120	29	1641	2222	156	418	4.0	.961	3B-385, 2B-294, SS-288, C-35, OF-8
WORLD SERIES																									
1955	BKN	N	4	.222	.222	9	2	0	0	0	0.0	0	2	2	5	0	1	0	4	8	2	3	3.5	.857	2B-4
1959	LA	N	1	.000	.000	1	0	0	0	0	0.0	0	0	0	0	0	0	0	0	1	0	0	1.0	1.000	SS-1
2 yrs.			5	.200	.200	10	2	0	0	0	0.0	0	2	2	5	0	1	0	4	9	2	3	3.0	.867	2B-4, SS-1

Bill Zimmerman

ZIMMERMAN, WILLIAM H. BR TR 5′8½″ 172 lbs.
B. Jan. 20, 1889, Kengen, Germany D. Oct. 4, 1952, Newark, N. J.

Year	Team	Lg	Games	BA	SA	AB	H	2B	3B	HR	HR%	R	RBI	BB	SO	SB	Pinch Hit AB	Pinch Hit H	PO	A	E	DP	TC/G	FA	G by Pos
1915	BKN	N	22	.281	.316	57	16	2	0	0	0.0	3	7	4	8	1	3	0	19	0	3	0	1.2	.864	OF-18

Eddie Zimmerman

ZIMMERMAN, EDWARD DESMOND (Zimmie) BR TR 5′9″ 160 lbs.
B. Jan. 4, 1883, Oceanic, N. J. D. May 6, 1945, Emmaus, Pa.

Year	Team	Lg	Games	BA	SA	AB	H	2B	3B	HR	HR%	R	RBI	BB	SO	SB	Pinch Hit AB	Pinch Hit H	PO	A	E	DP	TC/G	FA	G by Pos
1906	STL	N	5	.214	.214	14	3	0	0	0	0.0	0	1	0		0	0	0	7	6	1	0	2.8	.929	3B-5
1911	BKN	N	122	.185	.264	417	77	10	7	3	0.7	31	36	34	37	9	0	0	167	229	16	24	3.4	.961	3B-122
2 yrs.			127	.186	.262	431	80	10	7	3	0.7	31	37	34	37	9	0	0	174	235	17	24	3.4	.960	3B-127

Heinie Zimmerman

ZIMMERMAN, HENRY BR TR 5′11½″ 176 lbs.
B. Feb. 9, 1887, New York, N. Y. D. Mar. 14, 1969, New York, N. Y.

Year	Team	Lg	Games	BA	SA	AB	H	2B	3B	HR	HR%	R	RBI	BB	SO	SB	Pinch Hit AB	Pinch Hit H	PO	A	E	DP	TC/G	FA	G by Pos
1907	CHI	N	5	.222	.333	9	2	1	0	0	0.0	0	1	0		0	0	0	10	8	4	2	3.7	.818	2B-4, SS-1, OF-1
1908			46	.292	.345	113	33	4	1	0	0.0	17	9	1		2	15	2	48	48	9	2	3.5	.914	2B-20, OF-8, SS-1, 3B-1
1909			65	.273	.344	183	50	9	2	0	0.0	23	21	3		7	18	6	100	93	19	12	3.9	.910	2B-27, 3B-16, SS-12

Heinie Zimmerman *continued*

Year	Team		Games	BA	SA	AB	H	2B	3B	HR	HR%	R	RBI	BB	SO	SB	Pinch Hit AB	Pinch Hit H	PO	A	E	DP	TC/G	FA	G by Pos
1910			99	.284	.394	335	95	16	6	3	0.9	35	38	20	36	7	12	3	164	181	33	28	4.4	.913	2B-33, SS-26, 3B-22, OF-4, 1B-1
1911			143	.307	.462	535	164	22	17	9	1.7	80	85	25	50	23	4	1	388	348	42	52	5.6	.946	2B-108, 3B-20, 1B-11
1912			145	**.372**	**.571**	557	**207**	**41**	14	**14**	2.5	95	**103**	38	60	23	2	0	354	253	39	31	4.5	.940	3B-121, 1B-22
1913			127	.313	.490	447	140	28	12	9	2.0	69	95	41	40	18	1	0	139	232	36	18	3.3	.912	3B-125
1914			146	.296	.424	564	167	36	12	4	0.7	75	87	20	46	17	1	1	196	270	54	19	3.6	.896	3B-119, SS-15, 2B-12
1915			139	.265	.379	520	138	28	11	3	0.6	65	62	21	33	19	1	1	252	344	40	35	4.5	.937	2B-100, 3B-36, SS-4
1916	**2 teams**		**CHI N** (107G –.291) **NY N** (40G –.272)																						
"	**total**		147	.286	.390	549	157	29	5	6	1.1	76	**83**	23	43	24	4	1	155	329	34	23	3.9	.934	3B-115, 2B-14, SS-4
1917	**NY**	**N**	150	.297	.391	585	174	22	9	5	0.9	61	**102**	16	43	13	0	0	154	352	29	24	3.5	.946	3B-149, 2B-5
1918			121	.272	.363	463	126	19	10	1	0.2	43	56	13	23	14	1	1	312	219	17	15	4.6	.969	3B-100, 1B-19
1919			123	.255	.354	444	113	20	6	4	0.9	56	58	21	30	8	0	0	122	268	25	15	3.4	.940	3B-123
13 yrs.			1456	.295	.419	5304	1566	275	105	58	1.1	695	800	242	404	175	59	16	2394	2945	381	276	4.1	.933	3B-947, 2B-323, SS-63, 1B-53, OF-13
WORLD SERIES																									
1907	**CHI**	**N**	1	.000	.000	1	0	0	0	0	0.0	0	0	0	1	0	0	0	0	1	0	0	1.0	1.000	2B-1
1910			5	.235	.294	17	4	1	0	0	0.0	0	2	1	3	1	0	0	10	18	1	1	5.8	.966	2B-5
1917	**NY**	**N**	6	.120	.200	25	3	0	1	0	0.0	1	0	0	0	0	0	0	9	14	2	0	4.2	.920	3B-6
3 yrs.			12	.163	.233	43	7	1	1	0	0.0	1	2	1	4	1	0	0	19	33	3	1	4.6	.945	3B-6, 2B-6

Jerry Zimmerman

ZIMMERMAN, GERALD ROBERT
B. Sept. 21, 1934, Omaha, Neb.

BR TR 6′ 2″ 185 lbs.

Year	Team		Games	BA	SA	AB	H	2B	3B	HR	HR%	R	RBI	BB	SO	SB	Pinch Hit AB	Pinch Hit H	PO	A	E	DP	TC/G	FA	G by Pos
1961	**CIN**	**N**	76	.206	.230	204	42	5	0	0	0.0	8	10	11	21	1	0	0	374	22	10	8	5.3	.975	C-76
1962	**MIN**	**A**	34	.274	.339	62	17	4	0	0	0.0	8	7	3	5	0	0	0	111	9	1	0	3.6	.992	C-34
1963			39	.232	.250	56	13	1	0	0	0.0	3	3	2	8	0	1	0	116	8	0	0	3.2	1.000	C-39
1964			63	.200	.225	120	24	3	0	0	0.0	6	12	10	15	0	3	0	264	22	2	1	4.6	.993	C-63
1965			83	.214	.253	154	33	1	1	1	0.6	8	11	12	23	0	0	0	321	22	1	5	4.2	.997	C-82
1966			60	.252	.328	119	30	4	1	1	0.8	11	15	15	23	0	2	0	264	16	1	5	4.8	.996	C-59
1967			104	.167	.192	234	39	3	0	1	0.4	13	12	22	49	0	0	0	572	44	5	7	6.0	.992	C-104
1968			24	.111	.133	45	5	1	0	0	0.0	3	2	3	10	0	0	0	109	7	1	0	4.9	.991	C-24
8 yrs.			483	.204	.239	994	203	22	2	3	0.3	60	72	78	154	1	6	0	2131	150	21	26	4.8	.991	C-481
WORLD SERIES																									
1961	**CIN**	**N**	2	—	—	0	0	0	0	0	—	0	0	0	0	0	0	0	4	0	0	0	2.0	1.000	C-2
1965	**MIN**	**A**	2	.000	.000	1	0	0	0	0	0.0	0	0	0	0	0	0	0	2	1	0	1	1.5	1.000	C-2
2 yrs.			4	.000	.000	1	0	0	0	0	0.0	0	0	0	0	0	0	0	6	1	0	1	1.8	1.000	C-4

Roy Zimmerman

ZIMMERMAN, ROY FRANKLIN
B. Sept. 13, 1916, Pine Grove, Pa.

BL TL 6′ 2″ 187 lbs.

Year	Team		Games	BA	SA	AB	H	2B	3B	HR	HR%	R	RBI	BB	SO	SB	Pinch Hit AB	Pinch Hit H	PO	A	E	DP	TC/G	FA	G by Pos
1945	**NY**	**N**	27	.276	.439	98	27	1	0	5	5.1	14	15	5	16	1	1	0	226	13	3	13	9.3	.988	1B-25, OF-1

Frank Zinn

ZINN, FRANK PATRICK
B. Dec. 21, 1865, Phoenixville, Pa. D. May 12, 1936, Manayunk, Pa.

5′ 8″ 150 lbs.

Year	Team		Games	BA	SA	AB	H	2B	3B	HR	HR%	R	RBI	BB	SO	SB	Pinch Hit AB	Pinch Hit H	PO	A	E	DP	TC/G	FA	G by Pos
1888	**PHI**	**AA**	2	.000	.000	7	0	0	0	0	0.0	0	0	1		0	0	0	13	2	1	0	8.0	.938	C-2

Guy Zinn

ZINN, GUY
B. Feb. 13, 1887, Hallbrook, W. Va. D. Oct. 6, 1949, Clarksburg, W. Va.

BL TR 5′10½″ 170 lbs.

Year	Team		Games	BA	SA	AB	H	2B	3B	HR	HR%	R	RBI	BB	SO	SB	Pinch Hit AB	Pinch Hit H	PO	A	E	DP	TC/G	FA	G by Pos
1911	**NY**	**A**	9	.148	.296	27	4	0	2	0	0.0	5	1	4		0	1	0	10	2	1	0	1.6	.923	OF-8
1912			106	.262	.394	401	105	15	10	6	1.5	56	55	50		17	0	0	158	9	20	1	1.8	.893	OF-106
1913	**BOS**	**N**	36	.297	.406	138	41	8	2	1	0.7	15	15	4	23	3	1	0	83	8	5	1	2.7	.948	OF-35
1914	**BAL**	**F**	61	.280	.418	225	63	10	6	3	1.3	30	25	16		6	3	1	82	5	6	1	1.6	.935	OF-57
1915			102	.269	.394	312	84	18	3	5	1.6	30	43	35		2	9	1	139	11	8	4	1.8	.949	OF-88
5 yrs.			314	.269	.398	1103	297	51	23	15	1.4	136	139	109	23	28	14	2	472	35	40	7	1.9	.927	OF-294

Bud Zipfel

ZIPFEL, MARION SYLVESTER
B. Nov. 18, 1938, Belleville, Ill.

BL TR 6′ 3″ 200 lbs.

Year	Team		Games	BA	SA	AB	H	2B	3B	HR	HR%	R	RBI	BB	SO	SB	Pinch Hit AB	Pinch Hit H	PO	A	E	DP	TC/G	FA	G by Pos
1961	**WAS**	**A**	50	.200	.371	170	34	7	5	4	2.4	17	18	15	49	1	5	0	429	25	8	40	10.5	.983	1B-44
1962			68	.239	.370	184	44	4	1	6	3.3	21	21	17	43	1	18	2	228	17	8	13	5.2	.968	1B-26, OF-23
2 yrs.			118	.220	.370	354	78	11	6	10	2.8	38	39	32	92	2	23	2	657	42	16	53	7.7	.978	1B-70, OF-23

Richie Zisk

ZISK, RICHARD WALTER
B. Feb. 6, 1949, Brooklyn, N. Y.

BR TR 6′ 1″ 200 lbs.

Year	Team		Games	BA	SA	AB	H	2B	3B	HR	HR%	R	RBI	BB	SO	SB	Pinch Hit AB	Pinch Hit H	PO	A	E	DP	TC/G	FA	G by Pos
1971	**PIT**	**N**	7	.200	.467	15	3	1	0	1	6.7	2	2	4	7	0	1	0	7	0	0	0	1.2	1.000	OF-6
1972			17	.189	.270	37	7	3	0	0	0.0	4	4	7	10	0	5	1	14	1	1	0	1.3	.938	OF-12
1973			103	.324	.526	333	108	23	7	10	3.0	44	54	21	63	0	19	4	139	12	2	4	1.8	.987	OF-84
1974			149	.313	.476	536	168	30	3	17	3.2	75	100	65	91	1	9	4	312	9	5	3	2.3	.985	OF-141
1975			147	.290	.474	504	146	27	3	20	4.0	69	75	68	109	0	6	0	264	7	7	1	2.0	.975	OF-140
1976			155	.289	.465	581	168	35	2	21	3.6	91	89	52	96	1	3	2	300	11	4	2	2.1	.987	OF-152
1977	**CHI**	**A**	141	.290	.514	531	154	17	6	30	5.6	78	101	55	98	0	3	0	210	9	4	3	1.6	.982	OF-109, DH-28
1978	**TEX**	**A**	140	.262	.432	511	134	19	1	22	4.3	68	85	58	76	3	1	0	155	6	2	0	1.2	.988	OF-90, DH-49
1979			144	.262	.416	503	132	21	1	18	3.6	69	64	57	75	1	7	2	234	10	7	6	1.8	.972	OF-134, DH-3
1980			135	.290	.460	448	130	17	1	19	4.2	48	77	39	72	0	19	3	45	3	1	1	0.4	.980	DH-86, OF-37
1981	**SEA**	**A**	94	.311	.485	357	111	12	1	16	4.5	42	43	28	63	0	1	0	0	0	0	0	0.0	.000	DH-93
1982			131	.292	.477	503	147	28	1	21	4.2	61	62	49	89	2	0	0	0	0	0	0	0.0	.000	DH-130
1983			90	.242	.411	285	69	12	0	12	4.2	30	36	30	61	0	10	2	0	0	0	0	0.0	.000	DH-84
13 yrs.			1453	.287	.466	5144	1477	245	26	207	4.0	681	792	533	910	8	84	18	1680	68	33	20	1.3	.981	OF-905, DH-473
LEAGUE CHAMPIONSHIP SERIES																									
1974	**PIT**	**N**	3	.300	.300	10	3	0	0	0	0.0	1	0	0	3	0	1	1	2	0	0	0	1.0	1.000	OF-2
1975			3	.500	.600	10	5	1	0	0	0.0	0	0	2	2	0	0	0	8	0	0	0	2.7	1.000	OF-3
2 yrs.			6	.400	.450	20	8	1	0	0	0.0	1	0	2	5	0	1	1	10	0	0	0	2.0	1.000	OF-5

Billy Zitzmann

ZITZMANN, WILLIAM ARTHUR
B. Nov. 19, 1895, Long Island City, N. Y. D. May 29, 1985, Passaic, N. J.
BR TR 5′10½″ 175 lbs.

Year	Team	Games	BA	SA	AB	H	2B	3B	HR	HR%	R	RBI	BB	SO	SB	Pinch Hit AB	Pinch Hit H	PO	A	E	DP	TC/G	FA	G by Pos
1919	2 teams	PIT N (11G –.192)	CIN N (2G –.000)																					
″	total	13	.185	.222	27	5	1	0	0	0.0	5	2	0	6	2	3	0	11	0	1	0	1.3	.917	OF-9
1925	CIN N	104	.252	.316	301	76	13	3	0	0.0	53	21	35	22	11	6	1	136	6	6	0	1.6	.959	OF-89, SS-1
1926		53	.245	.287	94	23	2	1	0	0.0	21	3	6	7	3	3	0	55	0	2	0	1.8	.965	OF-31
1927		88	.284	.362	232	66	10	4	0	0.0	47	24	20	18	9	0	0	149	24	11	0	2.6	.940	OF-60, SS-8, 3B-3
1928		101	.297	.387	266	79	9	3	3	1.1	53	33	13	22	13	3	0	155	5	7	2	2.1	.958	OF-78, 3B-1
1929		47	.226	.262	84	19	3	0	0	0.0	18	6	9	10	4	1	1	77	0	5	1	3.0	.939	OF-22, 1B-5
6 yrs.		406	.267	.336	1004	268	38	11	3	0.3	197	89	83	85	42	16	2	583	35	32	3	2.1	.951	OF-289, SS-9, 1B-5, 3B-4

Eddie Zosky

ZOSKY, EDWARD JAMES
B. Feb. 10, 1968, Whittier, Calif.
BR TR 6′ 175 lbs.

Year	Team	Games	BA	SA	AB	H	2B	3B	HR	HR%	R	RBI	BB	SO	SB	Pinch Hit AB	Pinch Hit H	PO	A	E	DP	TC/G	FA	G by Pos
1991	TOR A	18	.148	.259	27	4	1	1	0	0.0	2	2	0	8	0	1	0	12	26	0	5	2.1	1.000	SS-18
1992		8	.286	.571	7	2	0	1	0	0.0	1	1	0	2	0	1	1	2	10	1	2	1.6	.923	SS-8
1995	FLA N	6	.200	.200	5	1	0	0	0	0.0	0	0	0	0	0	0	0	1	2	1	1	0.8	.750	SS-4, 2B-1
3 yrs.		32	.179	.308	39	7	1	2	0	0.0	3	3	0	10	0	2	1	15	38	2	8	1.8	.964	SS-30, 2B-1

Bob Zupcic

ZUPCIC, ROBERT
B. Aug. 18, 1966, Pittsburgh, Pa.
BR TR 6′ 4″ 220 lbs.

Year	Team	Games	BA	SA	AB	H	2B	3B	HR	HR%	R	RBI	BB	SO	SB	Pinch Hit AB	Pinch Hit H	PO	A	E	DP	TC/G	FA	G by Pos
1991	BOS A	18	.160	.280	25	4	0	0	1	4.0	3	3	1	6	0	1	0	14	0	2	0	1.0	.875	OF-16
1992		124	.276	.352	392	108	19	1	3	0.8	46	43	25	60	2	10	2	241	11	6	3	2.2	.977	OF-114, DH-5
1993		141	.241	.360	286	69	24	2	2	0.7	40	26	27	54	5	9	2	179	7	4	2	1.5	.979	OF-122, DH-5
1994	2 teams	BOS A (4G –.000)	CHI A (32G –.205)																					
″	total	36	.196	.293	92	18	4	1	1	1.1	10	8	4	17	0	3	2	49	4	0	0	1.6	1.000	OF-30, 3B-2, 1B-1, DH-1
4 yrs.		319	.250	.346	795	199	47	4	7	0.9	99	80	57	137	7	23	6	483	22	12	5	1.7	.977	OF-282, DH-11, 3B-2, 1B-1

Frank Zupo

ZUPO, FRANK JOSEPH (Noodles)
B. Aug. 29, 1939, San Francisco, Calif.
BL TR 5′11″ 182 lbs.

Year	Team	Games	BA	SA	AB	H	2B	3B	HR	HR%	R	RBI	BB	SO	SB	Pinch Hit AB	Pinch Hit H	PO	A	E	DP	TC/G	FA	G by Pos
1957	BAL A	10	.083	.083	12	1	0	0	0	0.0	2	0	1	4	0	4	0	20	1	2	0	2.9	.913	C-8
1958		1	.000	.000	2	0	0	0	0	0.0	0	0	0	1	0	0	0	4	0	0	0	4.0	1.000	C-1
1961		5	.500	.750	4	2	1	0	0	0.0	1	0	1	1	0	0	0	7	0	0	0	1.8	1.000	C-4
3 yrs.		16	.167	.222	18	3	1	0	0	0.0	3	0	2	6	0	4	0	31	1	2	0	2.6	.941	C-13

Paul Zuvella

ZUVELLA, PAUL
B. Oct. 31, 1958, San Mateo, Calif.
BR TR 6′ 173 lbs.

Year	Team	Games	BA	SA	AB	H	2B	3B	HR	HR%	R	RBI	BB	SO	SB	Pinch Hit AB	Pinch Hit H	PO	A	E	DP	TC/G	FA	G by Pos
1982	ATL N	2	.000	.000	1	0	0	0	0	0.0	0	0	0	0	0	0	0	0	4	1	0	5.0	.800	SS-1
1983		3	.000	.000	5	0	0	0	0	0.0	0	0	2	1	0	1	0	1	2	1	0	2.0	.750	SS-2
1984		11	.200	.240	25	5	1	0	0	0.0	2	1	2	3	0	0	0	13	21	0	6	2.8	1.000	SS-6, 2B-6
1985		81	.253	.305	190	48	8	1	0	0.0	16	4	16	14	2	5	1	112	173	8	39	3.7	.973	2B-42, SS-33, 3B-5
1986	NY A	21	.083	.104	48	4	1	0	0	0.0	2	2	5	4	0	0	0	30	54	3	12	4.1	.966	SS-21
1987		14	.176	.176	34	6	0	0	0	0.0	2	0	0	4	0	3	0	20	25	0	5	3.2	1.000	2B-7, SS-6, 3B-1
1988	CLE A	51	.231	.285	130	30	5	1	0	0.0	9	7	8	13	0	1	0	77	112	8	21	4.0	.959	SS-49
1989		24	.276	.414	58	16	2	0	2	3.4	10	6	1	11	0	3	1	14	24	2	1	1.7	.950	SS-15, 3B-5, DH-3
1991	KC A	2	—	—	0	0	0	0	0	—	0	0	0	0	0	0	0	0	0	0	0	0.0	.000	3B-2
9 yrs.		209	.222	.277	491	109	17	2	2	0.4	41	20	34	50	2	13	2	267	415	23	84	3.5	.967	SS-133, 2B-55, 3B-13, DH-3

Dutch Zwilling

ZWILLING, EDWARD HARRISON
B. Nov. 2, 1888, St. Louis, Mo. D. Mar. 27, 1978, La Crescenta, Calif.
BL TL 5′ 6½″ 160 lbs.

Year	Team	Games	BA	SA	AB	H	2B	3B	HR	HR%	R	RBI	BB	SO	SB	Pinch Hit AB	Pinch Hit H	PO	A	E	DP	TC/G	FA	G by Pos
1910	CHI A	27	.184	.241	87	16	5	0	0	0.0	7	5	11		1	0	0	45	2	3	1	1.9	.940	OF-27
1914	CHI F	154	.313	.480	592	185	38	8	**15**	2.5	91	95	46		21	0	0	340	15	14	3	2.4	.962	OF-154
1915		150	.286	.442	548	157	32	7	13	2.4	65	**94**	67		24	1	0	359	20	8	6	2.6	.979	OF-148, 1B-3
1916	CHI N	35	.113	.189	53	6	1	0	1	1.9	4	8	4	6	0	23	4	11	0	0	0	1.1	1.000	OF-10
4 yrs.		366	.284	.435	1280	364	76	15	29	2.3	167	202	128	6	46	24	4	755	37	25	10	2.4	.969	OF-339, 1B-3

PART NINE

Pitcher Register

Alphabetical List of Every Man Who Ever
Pitched in the Major Leagues
And His Pitching, Fielding, and Significant
Batting Records

Pitcher Register

The Pitcher Register is an alphabetical list of every man who pitched in the major leagues from 1876 through today. Included are lifetime totals of Divisional Playoff Series, League Championship Series, and World Series.

Much of this information has never been compiled, especially for the period 1876 through 1919. All information and abbreviations that may appear unfamiliar are explained in the sample format presented below. John Doe, the player used in the sample, is fictitious and serves only to illustrate the information.

John Doe

DOE, JOHN LEE (Slim) TR 6'2"165 lbs.
Played as John Cherry part of 1900.
Born John Lee Doughnut. Brother of Bill Doe.
B. Jan. 1, 1850, New York, N.Y. D. July 1, 1955, New York, N.Y.
Manager 1908–15.
Hall of Fame 1946.

														Relief Pitching			Batting									
Year	Team	W	L	PCT	ERA	G	GS	CG	IP	H	BB	SO	ShO	W	L	SV	AB	H	HR	BA	PO	A	E	DP	TC/G	FA
1884	**STL U**	4	2	.667	3.40	26	0	0	54.2	41	38	40	0	1	1	0	28	12	0	.226	15	20	3	2	1.5	.921
1885	**LOU AA**	14	20	.583	4.12	40	19	10	207.2	193	76	70	0	0	1	0	43	33	0	.289	13	33	2	3	0.9	.958
1886	**CLE N**	10	5	.667	4.08	40	8	4	117	110	55	77	0	0	1	1	40	16	1	.165	7	26	3	1	0.9	.917
1887	**BOS N**	9	3	.750	3.38	27	5	2	88	90	36	34	0	2	3	2	40	12	0	.141	12	27	1	5	1.5	.975
1888	**NY N**	13	4	.765	4.17	39	4	0	110	121	50	236	0	0	1	0	16	6	0	.273	5	10	0	2	0.4	1.000
1889	**3 teams**	**DET N** (10G 4–2)			**PIT N** (32G 0–0)		**PHI N** (31G 4–0)																			
"	**total**	8	2	.800	4.25	22	2	2	91.1	90	41	43	0	0	0	0	3	3	0	.333	6	14	2	2	1.0	.909
1890	**NY P**	13	6	.684	4.43	38	0	0	61.1	57	28	30	0	1	0	1	34	17	0	.185	9	9	3	1	0.6	.857
1900	**CHI N**	18	4	.818	3.71	35	1	0	63.1	58	15	23	0	0	0	2	35	13	1	.146	3	6	1	0	0.3	.900
1901	**NY N**	18	4	.818	**1.98**[1]	35	0	0	77.1	68	40	29	0	3	0	0	25	16	0	.254	7	16	5	1	0.8	.821
1906	**BOS N**	14	10	.583	3.41	31	0	0	58	66	23	24	0	1	3	0	37	16	1	.286	5	8	0	1	0.4	1.000
1907		13	4	.765	2.51	37	0		68	44	30	31	0	1	1	0	9	2	0	.182	10	25	2	0	1.0	.946
1908		0	0	—	3.38	1	1	0	8	8	1	1	0	3	1	3	33	7	0	.226	0	0	0	0	—	—
1914	**CHI F**	3	1	.750	2.78	6	0	0	54.2	41	28	9	0	2	3	3	19	2	0	.222	0	2	0	0	0.3	1.000
13 yrs.		137	55	.714	3.50	377	40	18 **8th**	1059.1	987	461	647	0	21	17	15	492	216	3	.212	92	286	13	7	1.0	.967
DIVISIONAL PLAYOFF SERIES																										
1908	**BOS N**	1	0	1.000	2.81	2	2	0	16	13	3	9	0	0	0	0	0	0	0	—	0	1	0	0	0.5	1.000
LEAGUE CHAMPIONSHIP SERIES																										
1906	**BOS N**	1	0	1.000	0.00	1	1	0	8	5	1	7	0	0	0	0	2	0	0	.000	0	1	0	0	1.0	1.000
1908		0	0	—	3.00	2	0	0	6	4	0	7	0	0	0	0	1	0	0	.000	1	0	1	0	2.0	.500
					1.29	3	1	0	14	9	0	14 9th	0	0	0	0	3	0	0	.000	1	1	1	0	1.5	.667
WORLD SERIES																										
1906	**BOS N**	0	0	—	0.00	2	0	0	1.2	0	1	2	0	0	0	0	0	0	0	—	1	1	0	0	1.0	1.000

Player Information

John Doe

This shortened version of the player's full name is the name most familiar to the fans. All players in this section are alphabetically arranged by the last name part of this name.

Doe, John Lee

Player's full name. The arrangement is last name first, then first and middle name(s).

(Slim)

Player's nickname. Any name appearing in parentheses is a nickname.

TR

The player's throwing style. Doe, for instance, threw right-handed.

6'2"

Player's height.

165 lbs

Player's average playing weight.

Played as John Cherry part of 1900

The player at one time in his major league career played under another name and can be found in box scores or newspaper stories only under that name.

Born John Lee Doughnut

The name the player was given at birth. (For the most part, the player never used this name while playing in the major leagues, but, if he did, it would be listed as "played as," which is explained above under the heading "Played as John Cherry part of 1900.")

Brother of Bill Doe

The player's brother. (Relatives indicated here are fathers, sons, and brothers who played or managed in the major leagues and the National Association.)

B. Jan. 1, 1850, New York, N.Y.

Date and place of birth.

D. July 1, 1955, New York, N.Y.

Date and place of death. (Some players are listed simply as "deceased." Although no certification of death or other information is now available, it is reasonably certain they are dead.)

Manager 1908–15

Doe also served as a major league manager. All men who were managers can also be found in the Manager Register where their complete managerial record is shown.

Hall of Fame 1946

Doe was elected to the Baseball Hall of Fame in 1946.

Column Headings Information

														Relief Pitching			Batting									
Year	Team	W	L	PCT	ERA	G	GS	CG	IP	H	BB	SO	ShO	W	L	SV	AB	H	HR	BA	PO	A	E	DP	TC/G	FA

Total Pitching (including all starting and relief appearances)

W	Wins
L	Losses
PCT	Winning Percentage
ERA	Earned Run Average
G	Games Pitched In
GS	Games Started
CG	Complete Games
IP	Innings Pitched
H	Hits Allowed
BB	Bases on Balls Allowed
SO	Strikeouts
ShO	Shutouts

Relief Pitching

W	Wins
L	Losses
SV	Saves

Batting

AB	At Bats
H	Hits
HR	Home Runs
BA	Batting Average

Fielding

PO	Putouts
A	Assists
E	Errors
DP	Double Plays
TC/G	Total Chances Per Game
FA	Fielding Average

Team and League Information

Year	Team		W	L	PCT	ERA	G	GS	CG	IP	H	BB	SO	ShO	W	L	SV	AB	H	HR	BA	PO	A	E	DP	TC/G	FA
1884	STL	U																									
1885	LOU	AA																									
1886	CLE	N																									
1887	BOS	N																									
1888	NY	N																									
1889	3 teams		DET N (10G 4–2) PIT N (32G 0–0) PHI N (31G 4–0)																								
"	total		8	2	.800	4.25	22	2	2	91.1	90	41	43	0	0	0	0	3	3	0	.333	6	14	2	2	1.0	.909
1890	NY	P																									
1900	CHI	N																									
1901	NY	N																									
1906	BOS	N																									
1907																											
1908																											
1914	CHI	F																									
1915	NY	A																									
13 yrs.			1592																								

Doe's record has been exaggerated so that his playing career spans all the years of the six different major leagues. Directly alongside the year and team information is the symbol for the league:

N National League (1876 to date)
A American League (1901 to date)
F Federal League (1914–15)
AA American Association (1882–91)
P Players' League (1890)
U Union Association (1884)
STL The abbreviation of the city in which the team played. Doe, for example, played for St. Louis in 1884. All teams in this section are listed by an abbreviation of the city or area in which the team played. The abbreviations follow:

ALT	Altoona	IND	Indianapolis
ATL	Atlanta	KC	Kansas City
BAL	Baltimore	LA	Los Angeles
BOS	Boston	LOU	Louisville
BKN	Brooklyn	MIL	Milwaukee
BUF	Buffalo	MIN	Minnesota
CAL	California	MON	Montreal
CHI	Chicago	NWK	Newark
CIN	Cincinnati	NY	New York
CLE	Cleveland	OAK	Oakland
CLR	Colorado	PHI	Philadelphia
COL	Columbus	PIT	Pittsburgh
DET	Detroit	PRO	Providence
FLA	Florida	RIC	Richmond
HAR	Hartford	ROC	Rochester

HOU	Houston	SD	San Diego
SEA	Seattle	TOL	Toledo
SF	San Francisco	TOR	Toronto
STL	St. Louis	TRO	Troy
STP	St. Paul	WAS	Washington
SYR	Syracuse	WIL	Wilmington
TEX	Texas	WOR	Worcester

Blank space appearing beneath a team and league indicates that the team and league are the same. Doe, for example, played for Boston in the National League from 1906 through 1908.

3 Teams Total. Indicates a player played for more than one team in the same year. Doe played for three teams in 1889. The number of games he played and his wins and losses for each team are also shown. Directly beneath this line, following the word "total," is Doe's combined record for all three teams for 1889.

Total Playing Years. This information, which appears as the first item on the pitcher's lifetime total line, indicates the total number of years in which he pitched at least one game. Doe, for example, pitched in at least one game for 13 years.

Statistical Information

John Doe

DOE, JOHN LEE (Slim) TR 6′2″165 lbs.
Played as John Cherry part of 1900.
Born John Lee Doughnut. Brother of Bill Doe.
B. Jan. 1, 1850, New York, N.Y. D. July 1, 1955, New York, N.Y.
Manager 1908–15.
Hall of Fame 1946.

Year	Team		W	L	PCT	ERA	G	GS	CG	IP	H	BB	SO	ShO	Relief Pitching W	Relief Pitching L	Relief Pitching SV	Batting AB	Batting H	Batting HR	BA	PO	A	E	DP	TC/G	FA
1884	**STL**	**U**	4	2	.667	3.40	26	0	0	54.2	41	38	40	0	1	1	0	28	12	0	.226	15	20	3	2	1.5	.921
1885	**LOU**	**AA**	14	20	.583	4.12	40	19	10	207.2	193	76	70	0	0	1	0	43	33	0	.289	13	33	2	3	0.9	.958
1886	**CLE**	**N**	10	5	.667	4.08	40	8	4	117	110	55	77	0	0	1	1	40	16	1	.165	7	26	3	1	0.9	.917
1887	**BOS**	**N**	9	3	.750	3.38	27	5	2	88	90	36	34	0	2	3	2	40	12	0	.141	12	27	1	5	1.5	.975
1888	**NY**	**N**	13	4	.765	4.17	39	4	0	110	121	50	236	0	0	1	0	16	6	0	.273	5	10	0	2	0.4	1.000
1889	**3 teams**		**DET N** (10G 4–2)			**PIT N** (32G 0–0)			**PHI N** (31G 4–0)																		
″	**total**		8	2	.800	4.25	22	2	2	91.1	90	41	43	0	0	0	0	3	3	0	.333	6	14	2	2	1.0	.909
1890	**NY**	**P**	13	6	.684	4.43	38	0	0	61.1	57	28	30	0	1	0	1	34	17	0	.185	9	9	3	1	0.6	.857
1900	**CHI**	**N**	18	4	.818	3.71	35	1	0	63.1	58	15	23	0	0	0	2	35	13	1	.146	3	6	1	0	0.3	.900
1901	**NY**	**N**	18	4	.818	**1.98**[1]	35	0	0	77.1	68	40	29	0	3	0	0	25	16	0	.254	7	16	5	1	0.8	.821
1906	**BOS**	**N**	14	10	.583	3.41	31	0	0	58	66	23	24	0	1	3	0	37	16	1	.286	5	8	0	1	0.4	1.000
1907			13	4	.765	2.51	37	0		68	44	30	31	0	1	1	0	9	2	0	.182	10	25	2	0	1.0	.946
1908			0	0	—	3.38	1	1	0	8	8	1	1	0	3	1	3	33	7	0	.226	0	0	0	0	—	—
1914	**CHI**	**F**	3	1	.750	2.78	6	0	0	54.2	41	28	9	0	2	3	3	19	2	0	.222	0	2	0	0	0.3	1.000
13yrs.			137	55	.714	3.50	377	40	18 8th	1059.1	987	461	647	0	21	17	15	492	216	3	.212	92	286	13	7	1.0	.967

Partial Innings Pitched. These are shown in the Innings Pitched column, and are indicated by a ".1" or ".2" after the total. Doe, for example, pitched 54⅔ innings in 1884.

League Leaders. Statistics that appear in boldfaced print indicate the pitcher led his league that year in a particular statistical category. Doe, for example, led the National League in earned run average in 1901. When there is a tie for league lead, the figures for all the men who tied are shown in boldface.

All-Time Single Season Leaders. (Starts with 1893, the first year that the pitcher's box was moved to its present distance of 60 feet 6 inches.) Indicated by the small number that appears next to the statistic. Doe, for example, is shown by a small number "1" next to his earned run average in 1901. This means he is first on the all-time major league list for having the lowest earned run average in a single season. All pitchers who tied for first are shown by the same number.

Lifetime Leaders. Indicated by the figure that appears beneath the line showing the pitcher's lifetime totals. Doe has an "8th" shown below his lifetime complete games total. This means that, lifetime, Doe ranks eighth among major league pitchers in complete games. Once again, only the top ten are indicated, and players who are tied receive the same number.

Meaningless Averages. Indicated by the use of a dash (—). In the case of Doe, a dash is shown for his 1908 winning percentage. This means that although he pitched in one game he never had a decision. A percentage of .000 would mean that he had at least one loss.

Estimated Earned Run Averages. Any time an earned run average appears in italics, it indicates that not all the earned runs allowed by the pitcher are known, and the information had to be estimated. Doe's 1885 earned run average, for example, appears in italics. It is known that Doe's team, Louisville, allowed 560 runs in 112 games. Of these games, it is known that in 90 of them Louisville allowed 420 runs of which 315 or 75% were earned. Doe pitched 207⅔ innings in 40 games and allowed 134 runs. In 35 of these games, it is known that he allowed 118 runs of which 83 were earned. By multiplying the team's known ratio of earned runs to total runs (75%), by Doe's 16 (134 minus 118) remaining runs allowed, a figure of 12 additional estimated earned runs is calculated. This means that Doe allowed an estimated total of 95 earned runs in 207⅔ innings, for an estimated earned run average of 4.12. In all cases at least 50% of the runs allowed by the team were "known" as a basis for estimating earned run averages. (Any time the symbol "infinity" [∞] is shown for a pitcher's earned run average, it means that the pitcher allowed one or more earned runs during a season without retiring a batter.)

League Leader Qualifications. Throughout baseball there have been different rules used to determine the minimum appearances necessary to qualify for league leader in categories concerning averages (Batting Average, Earned Run Average, etc.). For the rules and the years they were in effect, see Appendix C.

Batting Statistics. Because a pitcher's batting statistics are of relatively minor importance—and the Designated Hitter rule may eliminate pitchers' batting entirely—only the most significant statistics are given: number of hits, home runs, and batting average.

An Asterisk **(*)** shown in the lifetime batting totals means that the pitcher's complete year-by-year and lifetime batting record is listed in the Player Register.

Don Aase

AASE, DONALD WILLIAM
B. Sept. 8, 1954, Orange, Calif.
BR TR 6′ 3″ 190 lbs.

Year	Team	W	L	PCT	ERA	G	GS	CG	IP	H	BB	SO	ShO	Relief Pitching W	Relief Pitching L	Relief Pitching SV	Batting AB	Batting H	Batting HR	BA	PO	A	E	DP	TC/G	FA
1977	BOS A	6	2	.750	3.12	13	13	4	92.1	85	19	49	2	0	0	0	0	0	0	—	5	13	1	0	1.5	.947
1978	CAL A	11	8	.579	4.03	29	29	6	178.2	185	80	93	1	0	0	0	0	0	0	—	16	26	3	2	1.6	.933
1979		9	10	.474	4.82	37	28	7	185	200	77	96	1	1	1	2	0	0	0	—	8	17	2	3	0.7	.926
1980		8	13	.381	4.06	40	21	5	175	193	66	74	1	3	0	2	0	0	0	—	10	22	4	2	0.9	.889
1981		4	4	.500	2.35	39	0	0	65	56	24	38	0	4	4	11	0	0	0	—	2	10	1	1	0.3	.923
1982		3	3	.500	3.46	24	0	0	52	45	23	40	0	3	3	4	0	0	0	—	3	5	0	0	0.3	1.000
1984		4	1	.800	1.62	23	0	0	39	30	19	28	0	4	1	8	0	0	0	—	1	5	1	0	0.3	.857
1985	BAL A	10	6	.625	3.78	54	0	0	88	83	35	67	0	10	6	14	0	0	0	—	8	10	0	0	0.3	1.000
1986		6	7	.462	2.98	66	0	0	81.2	71	28	67	0	6	7	34	0	0	0	—	5	12	1	1	0.3	.944
1987		1	0	1.000	2.25	7	0	0	8	8	4	3	0	1	0	2	0	0	0	—	0	1	0	0	0.1	1.000
1988		0	0	—	4.05	35	0	0	46.2	40	37	28	0	0	0	0	0	0	0	—	2	3	0	1	0.1	1.000
1989	NY N	1	5	.167	3.94	49	0	0	59.1	56	26	34	0	1	5	2	5	0	0	.000	6	8	0	0	0.3	1.000
1990	LA N	3	1	.750	4.97	32	0	0	38	33	19	24	0	3	1	3	0	0	0	—	1	3	0	0	0.1	1.000
13 yrs.		66	60	.524	3.80	448	91	22	1108.2	1085	457	641	5	36	28	82	5	0	0	.000	67	135	13	10	0.5	.940
LEAGUE CHAMPIONSHIP SERIES																										
1979	CAL A	1	0	1.000	1.80	2	0	0	5	4	2	6	0	1	0	0	0	0	0	—	0	1	0	0	0.5	1.000

Bert Abbey

ABBEY, BERT WOOD
B. Nov. 11, 1869, Essex, Vt. D. June 11, 1962, Essex Junction, Vt.
BR TR 5′11″ 175 lbs.

Year	Team	W	L	PCT	ERA	G	GS	CG	IP	H	BB	SO	ShO	Relief Pitching W	Relief Pitching L	Relief Pitching SV	Batting AB	Batting H	Batting HR	BA	PO	A	E	DP	TC/G	FA
1892	WAS N	5	18	.217	3.45	27	22	19	195.2	207	76	77	0	0	2	1	75	9	0	.120	6	55	11	2	2.7	.847
1893	CHI N	2	4	.333	5.46	7	7	5	56	74	20	6	0	0	0	0	26	6	0	.231	3	14	4	1	3.0	.810
1894		2	7	.222	5.18	11	11	10	92	119	37	24	0	0	0	0	39	5	0	.128	2	13	3	0	1.6	.833
1895	2 teams CHI N (1G 0–1) BKN N (8G 5–2)																									
″	total	5	3	.625	4.35	9	7	6	60	76	11	17	0	1	0	0	22	6	0	.273	1	18	0	1	2.1	1.000
1896	BKN N	8	8	.500	5.15	25	18	12	164.1	210	48	37	0	1	1	0	63	12	0	.190	5	34	4	0	1.7	.907
5 yrs.		22	40	.355	4.52	79	65	52	568	686	192	161	0	2	3	1	225	38	0	.169	17	134	22	4	2.2	.873

Charlie Abbey

ABBEY, CHARLES S.
B. Oct. 14, 1866, Falls City, Neb. D. Apr. 27, 1926, San Francisco, Calif.
BL 5′ 8½″ 169 lbs.

Year	Team	W	L	PCT	ERA	G	GS	CG	IP	H	BB	SO	ShO	Relief Pitching W	Relief Pitching L	Relief Pitching SV	Batting AB	Batting H	Batting HR	BA	PO	A	E	DP	TC/G	FA
1896	WAS N	0	0	—	4.50	1	0	0	2	6	0	0	0	0	0	0	*				68	6	5	1	2.5	.937

Dan Abbott

ABBOTT, LEANDER FRANKLIN (Big Dan)
B. Mar. 16, 1862, Portage, Ohio D. Feb. 13, 1930, Ottawa Lake, Mich.
BR TR 5′11″ 190 lbs.

Year	Team	W	L	PCT	ERA	G	GS	CG	IP	H	BB	SO	ShO	Relief Pitching W	Relief Pitching L	Relief Pitching SV	Batting AB	Batting H	Batting HR	BA	PO	A	E	DP	TC/G	FA
1890	TOL AA	0	2	.000	*6.23*	3	1	1	13	19	8	1	0	0	1	1	7	1	0	.143	3	4	0	0	2.3	1.000

Glenn Abbott

ABBOTT, WILLIAM GLENN
B. Feb. 16, 1951, Little Rock, Ark.
BR TR 6′ 6″ 200 lbs.

Year	Team	W	L	PCT	ERA	G	GS	CG	IP	H	BB	SO	ShO	Relief Pitching W	Relief Pitching L	Relief Pitching SV	Batting AB	Batting H	Batting HR	BA	PO	A	E	DP	TC/G	FA
1973	OAK A	1	0	1.000	3.86	5	3	1	18.2	16	7	6	0	0	0	0	0	0	0	—	1	2	0	0	0.6	1.000
1974		5	7	.417	3.00	19	17	3	96	89	34	38	0	0	0	0	0	0	0	—	6	13	3	2	1.2	.864
1975		5	5	.500	4.25	30	15	3	114.1	109	50	51	1	2	0	0	0	0	0	—	9	15	2	0	0.9	.923
1976		2	4	.333	5.52	19	10	0	62	87	16	27	0	1	1	0	0	0	0	—	3	12	0	0	0.8	1.000
1977	SEA A	12	13	.480	4.46	36	34	7	204	212	56	100	0	0	0	0	0	0	0	—	16	28	2	2	1.3	.957
1978		7	15	.318	5.27	29	28	8	155.1	191	44	67	1	0	0	0	0	0	0	—	15	22	3	1	1.4	.925
1979		4	10	.286	5.15	23	19	3	117	138	38	25	0	0	0	0	0	0	0	—	6	18	0	2	1.0	1.000
1980		12	12	.500	4.10	31	31	7	215	228	49	78	2	0	0	0	0	0	0	—	25	39	1	1	2.1	.985
1981		4	9	.308	3.95	22	20	1	130	127	28	35	0	0	0	0	0	0	0	—	11	21	1	1	1.5	.970
1983	2 teams SEA A (14G 5–3) DET A (7G 2–1)																									
″	total	7	4	.636	3.63	21	21	3	129	146	22	49	1	0	0	0	0	0	0		17	9	3	2	1.4	.897
1984	DET A	3	4	.429	5.93	13	8	1	44	62	8	8	0	1	1	0	0	0	0	—	4	8	2	1	1.1	.857
11 yrs.		62	83	.428	4.39	248	206	37	1285.1	1405	352	484	5	4	2	0	0	0	0		113	187	17	12	1.3	.946
LEAGUE CHAMPIONSHIP SERIES																										
1975	OAK A	0	0	—	0.00	1	0	0	1	0	0	0	0	0	0	0	0	0	0	—	0	0	0	0	0.0	.000

Jim Abbott

ABBOTT, JAMES ANTHONY
B. Sept. 19, 1967, Flint, Mich.
BL TL 6′ 3″ 200 lbs.

Year	Team	W	L	PCT	ERA	G	GS	CG	IP	H	BB	SO	ShO	Relief Pitching W	Relief Pitching L	Relief Pitching SV	Batting AB	Batting H	Batting HR	BA	PO	A	E	DP	TC/G	FA
1989	CAL A	12	12	.500	3.92	29	29	4	181.1	190	74	115	2	0	0	0	0	0	0	—	6	26	3	1	1.2	.914
1990		10	14	.417	4.51	33	33	4	211.2	**246**	72	105	1	0	0	0	0	0	0	—	8	36	1	4	1.4	.978
1991		18	11	.621	2.89	34	34	5	243	222	73	158	1	0	0	0	0	0	0	—	19	46	2	3	2.0	.970
1992		7	15	.318	2.77	29	29	7	211	208	68	130	0	0	0	0	0	0	0	—	11	35	0	1	1.6	1.000
1993	NY A	11	14	.440	4.37	32	32	4	214	221	73	95	1	0	0	0	0	0	0	—	4	42	1	3	1.5	.979
1994		9	8	.529	4.55	24	24	2	160.1	167	64	90	0	0	0	0	0	0	0	—	8	23	1	1	1.3	.969
1995	2 teams CHI A (17G 6–4) CAL A (13G 5–4)																									
″	total	11	8	.579	3.70	30	30	4	197	209	64	86	1	0	0	0	0	0	0	—	8	30	0	0	1.3	1.000
7 yrs.		78	82	.488	3.77	211	211	30	1418.1	1463	488	779	6	0	0	0	0	0	0		64	238	8	13	1.5	.974

Kyle Abbott

ABBOTT, LAWRENCE KYLE
B. Feb. 18, 1968, Newburyport, Mass.
BL TL 6′ 4″ 200 lbs.

Year	Team	W	L	PCT	ERA	G	GS	CG	IP	H	BB	SO	ShO	Relief Pitching W	Relief Pitching L	Relief Pitching SV	Batting AB	Batting H	Batting HR	BA	PO	A	E	DP	TC/G	FA
1991	CAL A	1	2	.333	4.58	5	3	0	19.2	22	13	12	0	0	0	0	0	0	0	—	0	5	0	0	1.0	1.000
1992	PHI N	1	14	.067	5.13	31	19	0	133.1	147	45	88	0	0	0	0	29	2	0	.069	3	15	0	0	0.6	1.000
1995		2	0	1.000	3.81	18	0	0	28.1	28	16	21	0	2	0	0	2	1	0	.500	3	4	1	0	0.4	.875
3 yrs.		4	16	.200	4.86	54	22	0	181.1	197	74	121	0	2	0	0	31	3	0	.097	6	24	1	0	0.6	.968

Paul Abbott

ABBOTT, PAUL DAVID
B. Sept. 15, 1967, Van Nuys, Calif.
BR TR 6′ 3″ 185 lbs.

Year	Team	W	L	PCT	ERA	G	GS	CG	IP	H	BB	SO	ShO	Relief Pitching W	Relief Pitching L	Relief Pitching SV	Batting AB	Batting H	Batting HR	BA	PO	A	E	DP	TC/G	FA
1990	MIN A	0	5	.000	5.97	7	7	0	34.2	37	28	25	0	0	0	0	0	0	0	—	2	2	1	1	0.7	.800
1991		3	1	.750	4.75	15	3	0	47.1	38	36	43	0	3	0	0	0	0	0	—	3	4	0	0	0.5	1.000
1992		0	0	—	3.27	6	0	0	11	12	5	13	0	0	0	0	0	0	0	—	2	3	0	1	0.8	1.000
1993	CLE A	0	1	.000	6.38	5	5	0	18.1	19	11	7	0	0	0	0	0	0	0	—	2	3	1	0	1.2	.833
4 yrs.		3	7	.300	5.25	33	15	0	111.1	106	80	88	0	3	0	0	0	0	0		9	12	2	2	0.7	.913

Al Aber

ABER, ALBERT JULIUS (Lefty) BL TL 6′ 2″ 195 lbs.
B. July 31, 1927, Cleveland, Ohio D. May 20, 1993, Garfield Heights, Ohio.

Year	Team	W	L	PCT	ERA	G	GS	CG	IP	H	BB	SO	ShO	Relief W	Relief L	Relief SV	AB	H	HR	BA	PO	A	E	DP	TC/G	FA
1950	CLE A	1	0	1.000	2.00	1	1	1	9	5	4	4	0	0	0	0	2	0	0	.000	1	1	0	0	2.0	1.000
1953	2 teams CLE A (6G 1–1) DET A (17G 4–3)																									
″	total	5	4	.556	4.71	23	10	2	72.2	69	50	38	0	3	1	0	23	3	0	.130	0	17	0	0	0.7	1.000
1954	DET A	5	11	.313	3.97	32	18	4	124.2	121	40	54	0	0	1	3	39	5	0	.128	13	21	2	2	1.1	.944
1955		6	3	.667	3.38	39	1	0	80	86	28	37	0	6	3	3	17	1	0	.059	4	17	3	2	0.6	.875
1956		4	4	.500	3.43	42	0	0	63	65	25	21	0	4	4	7	10	3	0	.300	1	12	1	1	0.3	.929
1957	2 teams DET A (28G 3–3) KC A (3G 0–0)																									
″	total	3	3	.500	7.20	31	0	0	40	52	13	15	0	3	3	1	9	2	0	.222	4	11	0	0	0.5	1.000
6 yrs.		24	25	.490	4.18	168	30	7	389.1	398	160	169	0	16	12	14	100	14	0	.140	23	79	6	5	0.6	.944

Bill Abernathie

ABERNATHIE, WILLIAM EDWARD BR TR 5′10″ 190 lbs.
B. Jan. 30, 1929, Torrance, Calif.

Year	Team	W	L	PCT	ERA	G	GS	CG	IP	H	BB	SO	ShO	Relief W	Relief L	Relief SV	AB	H	HR	BA	PO	A	E	DP	TC/G	FA
1952	CLE A	0	0	—	13.50	1	0	0	2	4	1	0	0	0	0	1	1	0	0	.000	0	0	0	0	0.0	.000

Tal Abernathy

ABERNATHY, TALMADGE LAFAYETTE BR TL 6′ 2″ 210 lbs.
B. Oct. 30, 1921, Bynum, N. C.

Year	Team	W	L	PCT	ERA	G	GS	CG	IP	H	BB	SO	ShO	Relief W	Relief L	Relief SV	AB	H	HR	BA	PO	A	E	DP	TC/G	FA
1942	PHI A	0	0	—	10.13	1	0	0	2.2	2	3	1	0	0	0	0	0	0	0	—	1	1	0	0	2.0	1.000
1943		0	3	.000	12.89	5	2	1	14.2	24	13	10	0	0	1	0	4	1	0	.250	2	3	1	0	1.2	.833
1944		0	0	—	3.00	1	0	0	3	5	1	2	0	0	0	0	1	0	0	.000	0	0	0	0	0.0	.000
3 yrs.		0	3	.000	11.07	7	2	1	20.1	31	17	13	0	0	1	0	5	1	0	.200	3	4	1	0	1.1	.875

Ted Abernathy

ABERNATHY, THEODORE WADE BR TR 6′ 4″ 215 lbs.
B. Mar. 6, 1933, Stanley, N. C.

Year	Team	W	L	PCT	ERA	G	GS	CG	IP	H	BB	SO	ShO	Relief W	Relief L	Relief SV	AB	H	HR	BA	PO	A	E	DP	TC/G	FA
1955	WAS A	5	9	.357	5.96	40	14	3	119.1	136	67	79	2	1	1	0	26	4	0	.154	8	22	1	2	0.8	.968
1956		1	3	.250	4.15	5	4	2	30.1	35	10	18	0	0	0	0	11	2	0	.182	2	13	0	1	3.0	1.000
1957		2	10	.167	6.78	26	16	2	85	100	65	50	0	1	0	0	24	4	0	.167	4	19	0	3	0.9	1.000
1960		0	0	—	12.00	2	0	0	3	4	4	1	0	0	0	0	1	1	0	1.000	0	2	0	0	1.0	1.000
1963	CLE A	7	2	.778	2.88	43	0	0	59.1	54	29	47	0	7	2	12	5	2	0	.400	4	18	2	2	0.6	.917
1964		2	6	.250	4.33	53	0	0	72.2	66	46	57	0	2	6	11	6	0	0	.000	3	24	1	2	0.5	.964
1965	CHI N	4	6	.400	2.57	**84**	0	0	136.1	113	56	104	0	4	6	**31**	18	3	0	.167	11	41	0	3	0.6	1.000
1966	2 teams CHI N (20G 1–3) ATL N (38G 4–4)																									
″	total	5	7	.417	4.55	58	0	0	93	84	53	60	0	5	7	8	12	2	0	.167	11	25	2	0	0.7	.947
1967	CIN N	6	3	.667	1.27	**70**	0	0	106.1	63	41	88	0	6	3	**28**	17	1	0	.059	8	25	4	0	0.5	.892
1968		10	7	.588	2.46	**78**	0	0	135.1	111	55	64	0	10	7	13	17	0	0	.000	14	39	3	0	0.7	.946
1969	CHI N	4	3	.571	3.18	56	0	0	85	75	42	55	0	4	3	3	8	2	0	.250	9	23	2	0	0.6	.941
1970	3 teams CHI N (11G 0–0) STL N (11G 1–0) KC A (36G 9–3)																									
″	total	10	3	.769	2.59	58	0	0	83.1	65	55	59	0	10	3	14	17	3	0	.176	4	21	1	1	0.4	.962
1971	KC A	4	6	.400	2.56	63	0	0	81	60	50	55	0	4	6	23	13	1	0	.077	8	20	2	0	0.5	.933
1972		3	4	.429	1.71	45	0	0	58	44	19	28	0	3	4	5	6	0	0	.000	6	12	3	2	0.5	.857
14 yrs.		63	69	.477	3.46	681	34	7	1148	1010	592	765	2	57	48	148	181	25	0	.138	92	304	21	16	0.6	.950

Woody Abernathy

ABERNATHY, VIRGIL WOODROW BL TL 6′ 170 lbs.
B. Feb. 1, 1915, Forest City, N. C. D. Dec. 5, 1994, Louisville, Ky.

Year	Team	W	L	PCT	ERA	G	GS	CG	IP	H	BB	SO	ShO	Relief W	Relief L	Relief SV	AB	H	HR	BA	PO	A	E	DP	TC/G	FA
1946	NY N	1	1	.500	3.38	15	1	0	40	32	10	6	0	1	0	1	8	0	0	.000	1	6	0	0	0.5	1.000
1947		0	0	—	9.00	1	0	0	2	4	1	0	0	0	0	0	0	0	0	—	0	0	0	0	0.0	.000
2 yrs.		1	1	.500	3.64	16	1	0	42	36	11	6	0	1	0	1	8	0	0	.000	1	6	0	0	0.4	1.000

Harry Ables

ABLES, HARRY TERRELL (Hal, Hans) BR TL 6′ 2½″ 200 lbs.
B. Oct. 4, 1884, Terrell, Tex. D. Feb. 8, 1951, San Antonio, Tex.

Year	Team	W	L	PCT	ERA	G	GS	CG	IP	H	BB	SO	ShO	Relief W	Relief L	Relief SV	AB	H	HR	BA	PO	A	E	DP	TC/G	FA
1905	STL A	0	3	.000	3.82	6	3	1	30.2	37	13	11	0	0	0	0	10	0	0	.000	1	6	0	0	1.2	1.000
1909	CLE A	1	1	.500	2.12	5	3	3	29.2	26	10	24	0	0	0	0	12	0	0	.000	0	5	2	0	1.4	.714
1911	NY A	0	1	.000	9.82	3	2	0	11	16	7	6	0	0	0	0	4	0	0	.000	0	1	0	0	0.3	1.000
3 yrs.		1	5	.167	4.04	14	8	4	71.1	79	30	41	0	0	0	0	26	0	0	.000	1	12	2	0	1.1	.867

George Abrams

ABRAMS, GEORGE ALLEN BR TR 5′ 9″ 170 lbs.
B. Nov. 9, 1899, Seattle, Wash. D. Dec. 5, 1986, Clearwater, Fla.

Year	Team	W	L	PCT	ERA	G	GS	CG	IP	H	BB	SO	ShO	Relief W	Relief L	Relief SV	AB	H	HR	BA	PO	A	E	DP	TC/G	FA
1923	CIN N	0	0	—	9.64	3	0	0	4.2	10	3	1	0	0	0	0	1	1	0	1.000	0	1	0	0	0.3	1.000

Johnny Abrego

ABREGO, JOHNNY RAY BR TR 6′ 185 lbs.
B. July 4, 1962, Corpus Christi, Tex.

Year	Team	W	L	PCT	ERA	G	GS	CG	IP	H	BB	SO	ShO	Relief W	Relief L	Relief SV	AB	H	HR	BA	PO	A	E	DP	TC/G	FA
1985	CHI N	1	1	.500	6.38	6	5	0	24	32	12	13	0	0	0	0	9	0	0	.000	1	6	1	0	1.3	.875

Juan Acevedo

ACEVEDO, JUAN CARLOS BR TR 6′ 2″ 195 lbs.
B. May 5, 1970, Juarez, Mexico.

Year	Team	W	L	PCT	ERA	G	GS	CG	IP	H	BB	SO	ShO	Relief W	Relief L	Relief SV	AB	H	HR	BA	PO	A	E	DP	TC/G	FA
1995	CLR N	4	6	.400	6.44	17	11	0	65.2	82	20	40	0	0	0	0	18	1	0	.056	6	7	1	0	0.8	.929

Jim Acker

ACKER, JAMES JUSTIN BR TR 6′ 2″ 210 lbs.
B. Sept. 24, 1958, Freer, Tex.

Year	Team	W	L	PCT	ERA	G	GS	CG	IP	H	BB	SO	ShO	Relief W	Relief L	Relief SV	AB	H	HR	BA	PO	A	E	DP	TC/G	FA
1983	TOR A	5	1	.833	4.33	38	5	0	97.2	103	38	44	0	2	1	1	0	0	0	—	12	15	0	4	0.7	1.000
1984		3	5	.375	4.38	32	3	0	72	79	25	33	0	3	4	1	0	0	0	—	7	8	1	0	0.5	.938
1985		7	2	.778	3.23	61	0	0	86.1	86	43	42	0	7	2	10	0	0	0	—	10	16	0	1	0.4	1.000
1986	2 teams TOR A (23G 2–4) ATL N (21G 3–8)																									
″	total	5	12	.294	4.01	44	19	0	155	163	48	69	0	2	2	0	28	3	0	.107	16	28	0	4	1.0	1.000
1987	ATL N	4	9	.308	4.16	68	0	0	114.2	109	51	68	0	4	9	14	14	3	0	.214	6	23	0	2	0.4	1.000
1988		0	4	.000	4.71	21	1	0	42	45	14	25	0	0	3	0	5	2	0	.400	3	7	0	0	0.5	1.000
1989	2 teams ATL N (59G 0–6) TOR A (14G 2–1)																									
″	total	2	7	.222	2.43	73	0	0	126	108	32	92	0	2	7	2	7	1	0	.143	13	24	1	0	0.5	.974
1990	TOR A	4	4	.500	3.83	59	0	0	91.2	103	30	54	0	4	4	1	0	0	0	—	5	19	0	0	0.4	1.000
1991		3	5	.375	5.20	54	4	0	88.1	77	36	44	0	2	3	1	0	0	0	—	1	16	0	0	0.3	1.000
1992	SEA A	0	0	—	5.28	17	0	0	30.2	45	12	11	0	0	0	0	0	0	0	—	0	5	0	0	0.3	1.000
10 yrs.		33	49	.402	3.97	467	32	0	904.1	918	329	482	0	26	35	30	54	9	0	.167	73	161	2	11	0.5	.992

Jim Acker *continued*

LEAGUE CHAMPIONSHIP SERIES

Year	Team		W	L	PCT	ERA	G	GS	CG	IP	H	BB	SO	ShO	Relief Pitching W	Relief Pitching L	Relief Pitching SV	Batting AB	Batting H	Batting HR	BA	PO	A	E	DP	TC/G	FA
1985	TOR	A	0	0	—	0.00	2	0	0	6	2	0	5	0	0	0	0	0	0	0	—	0	1	0	0	0.5	1.000
1989			0	0	—	1.42	5	0	0	6.1	4	1	4	0	0	0	0	0	0	0	—	1	1	0	0	0.4	1.000
1991			0	0	—	0.00	1	0	0	0.2	1	0	1	0	0	0	0	0	0	0	—	0	0	0	0	0.0	.000
3 yrs.			0	0		0.69	8	0	0	13	7	1	10	0	0	0	0	0	0	0		1	2	0	0	0.4	1.000

Tom Acker

ACKER, THOMAS JAMES (Shoulders)
B. Mar. 7, 1930, Paterson, N. J.

BR TR 6′ 4″ 215 lbs.

Year	Team		W	L	PCT	ERA	G	GS	CG	IP	H	BB	SO	ShO	Relief Pitching W	Relief Pitching L	Relief Pitching SV	Batting AB	Batting H	Batting HR	BA	PO	A	E	DP	TC/G	FA
1956	CIN	N	4	3	.571	2.37	29	7	1	83.2	60	29	54	1	1	2	1	19	1	0	.053	9	15	0	0	0.8	1.000
1957			10	5	.667	4.97	49	6	1	108.2	122	41	67	0	7	4	4	19	1	0	.053	7	16	0	1	0.5	1.000
1958			4	3	.571	4.55	38	10	3	124.2	126	43	90	0	0	1	1	30	2	0	.067	2	13	1	0	0.4	.938
1959			1	2	.333	4.12	37	0	0	63.1	57	37	45	0	1	2	2	9	1	0	.111	1	5	0	0	0.2	1.000
4 yrs.			19	13	.594	4.12	153	23	5	380.1	365	150	256	1	9	9	8	77	5	0	.065	19	49	1	1	0.5	.986

Fritz Ackley

ACKLEY, FLORIAN FREDERICK
B. Apr. 10, 1937, Hayward, Wis.

BL TR 6′ 1½″ 202 lbs.

Year	Team		W	L	PCT	ERA	G	GS	CG	IP	H	BB	SO	ShO	Relief Pitching W	Relief Pitching L	Relief Pitching SV	Batting AB	Batting H	Batting HR	BA	PO	A	E	DP	TC/G	FA
1963	CHI	A	1	0	1.000	2.08	2	2	0	13	7	7	11	0	0	0	0	5	1	0	.200	0	4	0	0	2.0	1.000
1964			0	0	—	8.53	3	2	0	6.1	10	4	6	0	0	0	0	1	1	0	1.000	0	2	0	0	0.7	1.000
2 yrs.			1	0	1.000	4.19	5	4	0	19.1	17	11	17	0	0	0	0	6	2	0	.333	0	6	0	0	1.2	1.000

Cy Acosta

ACOSTA, CECILIO
Born Cecilio Acosta (Miranda).
B. Nov. 22, 1946, Sabino, Mexico.

BR TR 5′10″ 165 lbs.

Year	Team		W	L	PCT	ERA	G	GS	CG	IP	H	BB	SO	ShO	Relief Pitching W	Relief Pitching L	Relief Pitching SV	Batting AB	Batting H	Batting HR	BA	PO	A	E	DP	TC/G	FA
1972	CHI	A	3	0	1.000	1.56	26	0	0	34.2	25	17	28	0	3	0	5	4	0	0	.000	2	3	1	0	0.2	.833
1973			10	6	.625	2.23	48	0	0	97	66	39	60	0	10	6	18	1	0	0	.000	2	10	2	2	0.3	.857
1974			0	3	.000	3.72	27	0	0	46	43	18	19	0	0	3	3	2	0	0	.000	2	8	1	1	0.4	.909
1975	PHI	N	0	0	—	6.00	6	0	0	9	9	3	2	0	0	0	1	0	0	0	—	0	0	0	0	0.0	.000
4 yrs.			13	9	.591	2.65	107	0	0	186.2	143	77	109	0	13	9	27	7	0	0	.000	6	21	4	3	0.3	.871

Ed Acosta

ACOSTA, EDUARDO ELIXBET
Born Eduardo Elixbet (Lopez).
B. Mar. 9, 1944, Boquete, Panama.

BB TR 6′ 5″ 215 lbs.

Year	Team		W	L	PCT	ERA	G	GS	CG	IP	H	BB	SO	ShO	Relief Pitching W	Relief Pitching L	Relief Pitching SV	Batting AB	Batting H	Batting HR	BA	PO	A	E	DP	TC/G	FA
1970	PIT	N	0	0	—	12.00	3	0	0	3	5	2	1	0	0	0	1	0	0	0	—	0	0	0	0	0.0	.000
1971	SD	N	3	3	.500	2.74	8	6	3	46	43	7	16	1	0	1	0	17	0	0	.000	7	3	0	0	1.3	1.000
1972			3	6	.333	4.45	46	2	0	89	105	30	53	0	2	5	0	12	1	0	.083	3	10	1	1	0.3	.929
3 yrs.			6	9	.400	4.04	57	8	3	138	153	39	70	1	2	6	1	29	1	0	.034	10	13	1	1	0.4	.958

Jose Acosta

ACOSTA, JOSE
Born Jose Acosta (Fernandez).
Brother of Merito Acosta.
B. Mar. 4, 1891, Havana, Cuba D. Nov. 16, 1977, Havana, Cuba.

BR TR 5′ 6″ 134 lbs.

Year	Team		W	L	PCT	ERA	G	GS	CG	IP	H	BB	SO	ShO	Relief Pitching W	Relief Pitching L	Relief Pitching SV	Batting AB	Batting H	Batting HR	BA	PO	A	E	DP	TC/G	FA
1920	WAS	A	5	4	.556	4.03	17	5	4	82.2	92	26	9	1	2	2	1	25	6	0	.240	2	10	1	0	0.8	.923
1921			5	4	.556	4.36	33	7	2	115.2	148	36	30	0	3	1	3	30	2	0	.067	3	26	0	0	0.9	1.000
1922	CHI	A	0	2	.000	8.40	5	1	0	15	25	6	6	0	0	1	0	5	1	0	.200	0	1	0	0	0.2	1.000
3 yrs.			10	10	.500	4.51	55	13	6	213.1	265	68	45	1	5	4	4	60	9	0	.150	5	37	1	0	0.8	.977

Mark Acre

ACRE, MARK ROBERT
B. Sept. 16, 1968, Concord, Calif.

BR TR 6′ 8″ 235 lbs.

Year	Team		W	L	PCT	ERA	G	GS	CG	IP	H	BB	SO	ShO	Relief Pitching W	Relief Pitching L	Relief Pitching SV	Batting AB	Batting H	Batting HR	BA	PO	A	E	DP	TC/G	FA
1994	OAK	A	5	1	.833	3.41	34	0	0	34.1	24	23	21	0	5	1	0	0	0	0	—	0	3	1	0	0.1	.750
1995			1	2	.333	5.71	43	0	0	52	52	28	47	0	1	2	0	0	0	0	—	3	3	0	0	0.1	1.000
2 yrs.			6	3	.667	4.80	77	0	0	86.1	76	51	68	0	6	3	0	0	0	0		3	6	1	0	0.1	.900

Ace Adams

ADAMS, ACE TOWNSEND
B. Mar. 2, 1912, Willows, Calif.

BR TR 5′10½″ 182 lbs.

Year	Team		W	L	PCT	ERA	G	GS	CG	IP	H	BB	SO	ShO	Relief Pitching W	Relief Pitching L	Relief Pitching SV	Batting AB	Batting H	Batting HR	BA	PO	A	E	DP	TC/G	FA
1941	NY	N	4	1	.800	4.82	38	0	0	71	84	35	18	0	4	1	1	12	1	0	.083	0	11	0	0	0.3	1.000
1942			7	4	.636	1.84	**61**	0	0	88	69	31	33	0	7	4	11	10	1	0	.100	1	21	1	3	0.4	.957
1943			11	7	.611	2.82	**70**	3	1	140.1	121	55	46	0	9	**7**	9	32	4	0	.125	3	28	1	1	0.5	.969
1944			8	11	.421	4.25	**65**	4	1	137.2	149	58	32	0	6	**9**	**13**	29	3	0	.103	3	20	0	1	0.4	1.000
1945			11	9	.550	3.42	65	0	0	113	109	44	39	0	**11**	**9**	**15**	16	3	0	.188	7	27	3	2	0.6	.919
1946			0	1	.000	16.88	3	0	0	2.2	9	1	3	0	0	1	0	0	0	0	—	0	1	0	0	0.3	1.000
6 yrs.			41	33	.554	3.47	302	7	2	552.2	541	224	171	0	37	31	49	99	12	0	.121	14	108	5	7	0.4	.961

Babe Adams

ADAMS, CHARLES BENJAMIN
B. May 18, 1882, Tipton, Ind. D. July 27, 1968, Silver Spring, Md.

BL TR 5′11½″ 185 lbs.

Year	Team		W	L	PCT	ERA	G	GS	CG	IP	H	BB	SO	ShO	Relief Pitching W	Relief Pitching L	Relief Pitching SV	Batting AB	Batting H	Batting HR	BA	PO	A	E	DP	TC/G	FA
1906	STL	N	0	1	.000	13.50	1	1	0	4	9	2	0	0	0	0	0	1	0	0	.000	0	3	1	0	4.0	.750
1907	PIT	N	0	2	.000	6.95	4	3	1	22	40	3	11	0	0	0	0	7	2	0	.286	3	7	1	0	2.8	.909
1909			12	3	.800	1.11	25	12	7	130	88	23	65	3	6	0	2	39	2	0	.051	1	33	3	0	1.5	.919
1910			18	9	.667	2.24	34	30	16	245	217	60	101	3	0	1	0	83	16	0	.193	7	44	5	1	1.6	.911
1911			22	12	.647	2.33	40	37	24	293.1	253	42	133	**7**	0	0	0	103	26	0	.252	3	42	1	2	1.1	.978
1912			11	8	.579	2.91	28	21	11	170.1	169	35	63	2	1	1	0	53	12	0	.226	2	36	0	0	1.4	1.000
1913			21	10	.677	2.15	43	37	24	313.2	271	49	144	4	0	1	0	114	33	0	.289	10	74	1	1	2.0	.988
1914			13	16	.448	2.51	40	35	19	283	253	39	91	3	0	1	1	97	16	1	.165	13	62	0	2	1.9	1.000
1915			14	14	.500	2.87	40	30	17	245	229	34	62	2	2	3	2	85	12	0	.141	3	67	0	5	1.8	1.000
1916			2	9	.182	5.72	16	10	4	72.1	91	12	22	1	0	1	0	22	6	0	.273	2	20	0	0	1.4	1.000
1918			1	1	.500	1.19	3	3	2	22.2	15	4	6	1	0	0	0	9	3	0	.333	0	4	0	0	1.3	1.000
1919			17	10	.630	1.98	34	29	23	263.1	213	23	92	7	1	0	1	92	17	0	.185	4	55	0	1	1.7	1.000
1920			17	13	.567	2.16	35	33	19	263	240	18	84	**8**	0	0	2	89	13	1	.146	3	66	2	1	2.0	.972
1921			14	5	.737	2.64	25	20	11	160	155	18	55	2	3	0	0	63	16	0	.254	1	34	0	1	1.4	1.000
1922			8	11	.421	3.57	27	19	12	171.1	191	15	39	4	1	3	0	56	16	1	.286	5	43	1	2	1.8	.980
1923			13	7	.650	4.42	26	22	11	158.2	196	25	38	0	1	1	1	55	15	0	.273	0	29	1	0	1.2	.967
1924			3	1	.750	1.13	9	3	2	39.2	31	3	5	0	1	1	0	11	2	0	.182	1	5	0	0	0.7	1.000

Babe Adams *continued*

Year	Team	Lg	W	L	PCT	ERA	G	GS	CG	IP	H	BB	SO	ShO	Relief Pitching W	Relief Pitching L	Relief Pitching SV	Batting AB	Batting H	Batting HR	BA	PO	A	E	DP	TC/G	FA
1925			6	5	.545	5.42	33	10	3	101.1	129	17	18	0	3	1	3	31	7	0	.226	0	17	0	1	0.5	1.000
1926			2	3	.400	6.14	19	0	0	36.2	51	8	7	0	2	3	3	9	2	0	.222	0	7	1	0	0.4	.875
19 yrs.			194	140	.581	2.76	482	355	206	2995.1	2841	430	1036	47	21	17	15	1019	216	3	.212	58	648	17	17	1.5	.976
WORLD SERIES																											
1909	PIT	N	3	0	1.000	1.33	3	3	3	27	18	6	11	1	0	0	0	9	0	0	.000	0	7	0	0	2.3	1.000
1925			0	0	—	0.00	1	0	0	1	2	0	0	0	0	0	0	0	0	0	—	0	0	0	0	0.0	.000
2 yrs.			3	0	1.000	1.29	4	3	3	28	20	6	11	1	0	0	0	9	0	0	.000	0	7	0	0	1.8	1.000
					1st	9th																					

Bob Adams

ADAMS, ROBERT ANDREW BR TR 6'½" 165 lbs.
B. Jan. 20, 1907, Birmingham, Ala. D. Mar. 6, 1970, Jacksonville, Fla.

Year	Team	Lg	W	L	PCT	ERA	G	GS	CG	IP	H	BB	SO	ShO	Relief Pitching W	Relief Pitching L	Relief Pitching SV	Batting AB	Batting H	Batting HR	BA	PO	A	E	DP	TC/G	FA
1931	PHI	N	0	1	.000	9.00	1	1	0	6	14	1	3	0	0	0	0	3	0	0	.000	1	0	0	0	1.0	1.000
1932			0	0	—	1.50	4	0	0	6	7	2	2	0	0	0	0	0	0	0	—	1	2	0	0	0.8	1.000
2 yrs.			0	1	.000	5.25	5	1	0	12	21	3	5	0	0	0	0	3	0	0	.000	2	2	0	0	0.8	1.000

Bob Adams

ADAMS, ROBERT BURDETTE BR TR 5'11" 168 lbs.
B. July 24, 1901, Holyoke, Mass.

Year	Team	Lg	W	L	PCT	ERA	G	GS	CG	IP	H	BB	SO	ShO	Relief Pitching W	Relief Pitching L	Relief Pitching SV	Batting AB	Batting H	Batting HR	BA	PO	A	E	DP	TC/G	FA
1925	BOS	A	0	0	—	7.94	2	0	0	5.2	10	3	1	0	0	0	0	3	1	0	.333	0	5	0	0	2.5	1.000

Dan Adams

ADAMS, DANIEL LESLIE (Rube) BR TR 5'11½" 165 lbs.
B. June 19, 1889, St. Louis, Mo. D. Oct. 6, 1964, St. Louis, Mo.

Year	Team	Lg	W	L	PCT	ERA	G	GS	CG	IP	H	BB	SO	ShO	Relief Pitching W	Relief Pitching L	Relief Pitching SV	Batting AB	Batting H	Batting HR	BA	PO	A	E	DP	TC/G	FA
1914	KC	F	3	9	.250	3.51	36	14	6	136	141	52	38	0	1	1	3	46	7	1	.152	8	38	3	1	1.4	.939
1915			0	2	.000	4.63	11	2	0	35	41	13	16	0	0	0	0	9	1	0	.111	6	9	0	0	1.4	1.000
2 yrs.			3	11	.214	3.74	47	16	6	171	182	65	54	0	1	1	3	55	8	1	.145	14	47	3	1	1.4	.953

Joe Adams

ADAMS, JOSEPH EDWARD (Wagon Tongue) BR TL 6' 190 lbs.
B. Oct. 28, 1877, Cowden, Ill. D. Oct. 8, 1952, Montgomery City, Mo.

Year	Team	Lg	W	L	PCT	ERA	G	GS	CG	IP	H	BB	SO	ShO	Relief Pitching W	Relief Pitching L	Relief Pitching SV	Batting AB	Batting H	Batting HR	BA	PO	A	E	DP	TC/G	FA
1902	STL	N	0	0	—	9.00	1	0	0	4	9	2	0	0	0	0	0	2	0	0	.000	1	3	0	2	4.0	1.000

Karl Adams

ADAMS, KARL TUTWILER (Rebel) BR TR 6'2" 170 lbs.
B. Aug. 11, 1891, Columbus, Ga. D. Sept. 17, 1967, Everett, Wash.

Year	Team	Lg	W	L	PCT	ERA	G	GS	CG	IP	H	BB	SO	ShO	Relief Pitching W	Relief Pitching L	Relief Pitching SV	Batting AB	Batting H	Batting HR	BA	PO	A	E	DP	TC/G	FA
1914	CIN	N	0	0	—	9.00	4	0	0	8	14	5	5	0	0	0	0	2	1	0	.500	0	4	1	0	1.3	.800
1915	CHI	N	1	9	.100	4.71	26	12	3	107	105	43	57	0	0	1	0	30	0	0	.000	2	29	2	0	1.3	.939
2 yrs.			1	9	.100	5.01	30	12	3	115	119	48	62	0	0	1	0	32	1	0	.031	2	33	3	0	1.3	.921

Red Adams

ADAMS, CHARLES DWIGHT BR TR 6' 185 lbs.
B. Oct. 7, 1921, Parlier, Calif.

Year	Team	Lg	W	L	PCT	ERA	G	GS	CG	IP	H	BB	SO	ShO	Relief Pitching W	Relief Pitching L	Relief Pitching SV	Batting AB	Batting H	Batting HR	BA	PO	A	E	DP	TC/G	FA
1946	CHI	N	0	1	.000	8.25	8	0	0	12	18	7	8	0	0	1	0	1	0	0	.000	0	5	1	1	0.8	.833

Rick Adams

ADAMS, REUBEN ALEXANDER BL TL 6' 165 lbs.
B. Dec. 24, 1878, Paris, Tex. D. Mar. 10, 1955, Paris, Tex.

Year	Team	Lg	W	L	PCT	ERA	G	GS	CG	IP	H	BB	SO	ShO	Relief Pitching W	Relief Pitching L	Relief Pitching SV	Batting AB	Batting H	Batting HR	BA	PO	A	E	DP	TC/G	FA
1905	WAS	A	2	5	.286	3.59	11	6	3	62.2	63	24	25	1	1	0	0	23	4	0	.174	4	20	2	0	2.4	.923

Terry Adams

ADAMS, TERRY WAYNE BR TR 6'3" 180 lbs.
B. Mar. 6, 1973, Mobile, Ala.

Year	Team	Lg	W	L	PCT	ERA	G	GS	CG	IP	H	BB	SO	ShO	Relief Pitching W	Relief Pitching L	Relief Pitching SV	Batting AB	Batting H	Batting HR	BA	PO	A	E	DP	TC/G	FA
1995	CHI	N	1	1	.500	6.50	18	0	0	18	22	10	15	0	1	1	1	0	0	0	—	2	1	0	0	0.2	1.000

Willie Adams

ADAMS, JAMES IRVIN BR TR 6'4" 180 lbs.
B. Sept. 27, 1890, Clearfield, Pa. D. June 18, 1937, Albany, N. Y.

Year	Team	Lg	W	L	PCT	ERA	G	GS	CG	IP	H	BB	SO	ShO	Relief Pitching W	Relief Pitching L	Relief Pitching SV	Batting AB	Batting H	Batting HR	BA	PO	A	E	DP	TC/G	FA
1912	STL	A	2	3	.400	3.88	13	5	0	46.1	50	19	16	0	1	0	0	13	0	0	.000	0	8	1	0	0.7	.889
1913			0	0	—	10.00	4	0	0	9	12	4	5	0	0	0	0	1	0	0	.000	0	1	0	0	0.3	1.000
1914	PIT	F	3	1	.750	3.74	15	2	1	55.1	70	22	14	0	2	0	0	15	1	0	.067	4	11	1	0	1.1	.938
1918	PHI	A	5	12	.294	4.42	32	14	7	169	164	97	39	0	3	0	0	57	8	0	.140	5	50	1	2	1.8	.982
1919			0	0	—	3.86	1	0	0	4.2	7	2	0	0	0	0	0	2	0	0	.000	0	1	0	0	1.0	1.000
5 yrs.			10	16	.385	4.37	65	21	8	284.1	303	144	74	0	6	0	0	88	9	0	.102	9	71	3	2	1.3	.964

Mike Adamson

ADAMSON, JOHN MICHAEL BR TR 6'2" 185 lbs.
B. Sept. 13, 1947, San Diego, Calif.

Year	Team	Lg	W	L	PCT	ERA	G	GS	CG	IP	H	BB	SO	ShO	Relief Pitching W	Relief Pitching L	Relief Pitching SV	Batting AB	Batting H	Batting HR	BA	PO	A	E	DP	TC/G	FA
1967	BAL	A	0	1	.000	8.38	3	2	0	9.2	9	12	8	0	0	0	0	2	1	0	.500	0	0	0	0	0.0	.000
1968			0	2	.000	9.39	2	2	0	7.2	9	4	4	0	0	0	0	3	1	0	.333	0	0	0	0	0.0	.000
1969			0	1	.000	4.50	6	0	0	8	10	6	2	0	0	1	0	1	0	0	.000	2	3	0	0	0.8	1.000
3 yrs.			0	4	.000	7.46	11	4	0	25.1	28	22	14	0	0	1	0	6	2	0	.333	2	3	0	0	0.5	1.000

Dewey Adkins

ADKINS, JOHN DEWEY BR TR 6'2" 195 lbs.
B. May 11, 1918, Norcatur, Kans.

Year	Team	Lg	W	L	PCT	ERA	G	GS	CG	IP	H	BB	SO	ShO	Relief Pitching W	Relief Pitching L	Relief Pitching SV	Batting AB	Batting H	Batting HR	BA	PO	A	E	DP	TC/G	FA
1942	WAS	A	0	0	—	9.95	1	1	0	6.1	7	6	3	0	0	0	0	2	1	0	.500	0	0	0	0	0.0	.000
1943			0	0	—	2.61	7	0	0	10.1	9	5	1	0	0	0	0	0	0	0	—	0	0	0	0	0.0	.000
1949	CHI	N	2	4	.333	5.68	30	5	1	82.1	98	39	43	0	1	1	0	20	4	1	.200	9	18	2	1	1.0	.931
3 yrs.			2	4	.333	5.64	38	6	1	99	114	50	47	0	1	1	0	22	5	1	.227	9	18	2	1	0.8	.931

Doc Adkins

ADKINS, MERLE THERON (Babe) BR TR 5'10½" 220 lbs.
B. Aug. 5, 1872, Troy, Wis. D. Feb. 21, 1934, Durham, N. C.

Year	Team	Lg	W	L	PCT	ERA	G	GS	CG	IP	H	BB	SO	ShO	Relief Pitching W	Relief Pitching L	Relief Pitching SV	Batting AB	Batting H	Batting HR	BA	PO	A	E	DP	TC/G	FA
1902	BOS	A	1	1	.500	4.05	4	2	1	20	30	7	3	0	0	0	0	9	2	0	.222	0	7	0	0	1.8	1.000
1903	NY	A	0	0	—	7.71	2	1	0	7	10	5	0	0	0	0	1	3	0	0	.000	0	0	0	0	0.0	.000
2 yrs.			1	1	.500	5.00	6	3	1	27	40	12	3	0	0	0	1	12	2	0	.167	0	7	0	0	1.2	1.000

Grady Adkins

ADKINS, GRADY EMMETT (Butcher Boy) BR TR 5'11" 175 lbs.
B. June 29, 1897, Jacksonville, Ark. D. Mar. 31, 1966, Little Rock, Ark.

Year	Team	Lg	W	L	PCT	ERA	G	GS	CG	IP	H	BB	SO	ShO	Relief Pitching W	Relief Pitching L	Relief Pitching SV	Batting AB	Batting H	Batting HR	BA	PO	A	E	DP	TC/G	FA
1928	CHI	A	10	16	.385	3.73	36	27	14	224.2	233	89	54	0	3	1	1	70	10	0	.143	8	51	4	2	1.8	.937
1929			2	11	.154	5.33	31	15	5	138.1	168	67	24	0	0	1	0	46	11	0	.239	11	37	1	0	1.6	.980
2 yrs.			12	27	.308	4.34	67	42	19	363	401	156	78	0	3	2	1	116	21	0	.181	19	88	5	2	1.7	.955

Year	Team	W	L	PCT	ERA	G	GS	CG	IP	H	BB	SO	ShO	Relief Pitching W	L	SV	Batting AB	H	HR	BA	PO	A	E	DP	TC/G	FA

Steve Adkins

ADKINS, STEVEN THOMAS
B. Oct. 26, 1964, Chicago, Ill.
BR TL 6′ 6″ 210 lbs.

Year	Team	W	L	PCT	ERA	G	GS	CG	IP	H	BB	SO	ShO	Relief W	Relief L	SV	AB	H	HR	BA	PO	A	E	DP	TC/G	FA
1990	NY A	1	2	.333	6.38	5	5	0	24	19	29	14	0	0	0	0	0	0	0	—	0	3	0	0	0.6	1.000

Juan Agosto

AGOSTO, JUAN ROBERTO
Born Juan Roberto Agosto (Gonzalez).
B. Feb. 23, 1958, Rio Piedras, Puerto Rico.
BL TL 6′ 2″ 190 lbs.

Year	Team	W	L	PCT	ERA	G	GS	CG	IP	H	BB	SO	ShO	Relief W	Relief L	SV	AB	H	HR	BA	PO	A	E	DP	TC/G	FA
1981	CHI A	0	0	—	4.50	2	0	0	6	5	0	3	0	0	0	0	0	0	0	—	0	1	0	0	0.5	1.000
1982		0	0	—	18.00	1	0	0	2	7	0	1	0	0	0	0	0	0	0	—	0	1	0	0	1.0	1.000
1983		2	2	.500	4.10	39	0	0	41.2	41	11	29	0	2	2	7	0	0	0	—	2	8	2	1	0.3	.833
1984		2	1	.667	3.09	49	0	0	55.1	54	34	26	0	2	1	7	0	0	0	—	7	16	1	5	0.5	.958
1985		4	3	.571	3.58	54	0	0	60.1	45	23	39	0	4	3	1	0	0	0	—	10	15	1	0	0.5	.962
1986	2 teams CHI A (9G 0–2) MIN A (17G 1–2)																									
″	total	1	4	.200	8.64	26	1	0	25	49	18	12	0	1	3	1	0	0	0		3	4	2	0	0.3	.778
1987	HOU N	1	1	.500	2.63	27	0	0	27.1	26	10	6	0	1	1	2	1	0	0	.000	3	10	1	1	0.5	.929
1988		10	2	.833	2.26	75	0	0	91.2	74	30	33	0	10	2	4	5	0	0	.000	12	34	2	0	0.6	.958
1989		4	5	.444	2.93	71	0	0	83	81	32	46	0	4	5	1	5	1	0	.200	4	19	3	2	0.4	.885
1990		9	8	.529	4.29	**82**	0	0	92.1	91	39	50	0	9	8	4	2	0	0	.000	11	18	0	1	0.4	1.000
1991	STL N	5	3	.625	4.81	72	0	0	86	92	39	34	0	5	3	2	3	1	0	.333	5	17	2	2	0.3	.917
1992	2 teams STL N (22G 2–4) SEA A (17G 0–0)																									
″	total	2	4	.333	6.12	39	1	0	50	66	12	25	0	2	4	0	4	0	0	.000	1	15	0	1	0.4	1.000
1993	HOU N	0	0	—	6.00	6	0	0	6	8	0	3	0	0	0	0	0	0	0	—	0	0	0	0	0.0	.000
13 yrs.		40	33	.548	4.01	543	2	0	626.2	639	248	307	0	40	32	29	20	2	0	.100	58	158	14	13	0.4	.939
LEAGUE CHAMPIONSHIP SERIES																										
1983	CHI A	0	0	—	0.00	1	0	0	0.1	0	0	0	0	0	0	0	0	0	0	—	0	0	0	0	0.0	.000

Rick Aguilera

AGUILERA, RICHARD WARREN (Aggie)
B. Dec. 31, 1961, San Gabriel, Calif.
BR TR 6′ 4″ 195 lbs.

Year	Team	W	L	PCT	ERA	G	GS	CG	IP	H	BB	SO	ShO	Relief W	Relief L	SV	AB	H	HR	BA	PO	A	E	DP	TC/G	FA
1985	NY N	10	7	.588	3.24	21	19	2	122.1	118	37	74	0	1	0	0	36	10	0	.278	8	16	0	1	1.1	1.000
1986		10	7	.588	3.88	28	20	2	141.2	145	36	104	0	1	1	0	51	8	2	.157	13	26	0	1	1.4	1.000
1987		11	3	.786	3.60	18	17	1	115	124	33	77	0	0	0	0	40	9	1	.225	7	29	2	1	2.1	.947
1988		0	4	.000	6.93	11	3	0	24.2	29	10	16	0	0	2	0	4	1	0	.250	3	5	0	0	0.7	1.000
1989	2 teams NY N (36G 6–6) MIN A (11G 3–5)																									
″	total	9	11	.450	2.79	47	11	3	145	130	38	137	0	6	6	7	7	0	0	.000	6	21	1	2	0.6	.964
1990	MIN A	5	3	.625	2.76	56	0	0	65.1	55	19	61	0	5	3	32	0	0	0	—	2	4	0	0	0.1	1.000
1991		4	5	.444	2.35	63	0	0	69	44	30	61	0	4	5	42	0	0	0	—	7	5	0	0	0.2	1.000
1992		2	6	.250	2.84	64	0	0	66.2	60	17	52	0	2	6	41	0	0	0	—	2	5	0	0	0.1	1.000
1993		4	3	.571	3.11	65	0	0	72.1	60	14	59	0	4	3	34	0	0	0	—	12	8	0	0	0.3	1.000
1994		1	4	.200	3.63	44	0	0	44.2	57	10	46	0	1	4	23	0	0	0	—	4	9	0	0	0.3	1.000
1995	2 teams MIN A (22G 1–1) BOS A (30G 2–2)																									
″	total	3	3	.500	2.60	52	0	0	55.1	46	13	52	0	3	3	32	0	0	0	—	2	8	0	0	0.2	1.000
11 yrs.		59	56	.513	3.25	469	70	8	922	868	257	739	0	27	33	211	138	28	3	.203	66	136	3	5	0.4	.985
DIVISIONAL PLAYOFF SERIES																										
1995	BOS A	0	0	—	13.50	1	0	0	0.2	3	0	1	0	0	0	0	0	0	0	—	0	0	0	0	0.0	.000
LEAGUE CHAMPIONSHIP SERIES																										
1986	NY N	0	0	—	0.00	2	0	0	5	2	2	2	0	0	0	0	0	0	0	—	1	1	0	0	1.0	1.000
1988		0	0	—	1.29	3	0	0	7	3	2	4	0	0	0	0	1	0	0	.000	0	1	0	0	0.3	1.000
1991	MIN A	0	0	—	0.00	3	0	0	3.1	1	0	3	0	0	0	3	0	0	0	—	0	0	0	0	0.0	.000
3 yrs.		0	0		0.59	8	0	0	15.1	6	4	9	0	0	0	3 6th	1	0	0	.000	1	2	0	0	0.4	1.000
WORLD SERIES																										
1986	NY N	1	0	1.000	12.00	2	0	0	3	8	1	4	0	1	0	0	0	0	0	—	0	0	0	0	0.0	.000
1991	MIN A	1	1	.500	1.80	4	0	0	5	6	1	3	0	1	1	2	1	0	0	.000	0	0	0	0	0.0	.000
2 yrs.		2	1	.667	5.63	6	0	0	8	14	2	7	0	2	1	2	1	0	0	.000	0	0	0	0	0.0	

Hank Aguirre

AGUIRRE, HENRY JOHN
B. Jan. 31, 1931, Azusa, Calif. D. Sept. 5, 1994, Bloomfield Hills, Mich.
BR TL 6′ 4″ 205 lbs.
BB 1965–1970

Year	Team	W	L	PCT	ERA	G	GS	CG	IP	H	BB	SO	ShO	Relief W	Relief L	SV	AB	H	HR	BA	PO	A	E	DP	TC/G	FA
1955	CLE A	2	0	1.000	1.42	4	1	1	12.2	6	12	6	1	1	0	0	4	0	0	.000	1	0	0	0	0.3	1.000
1956		3	5	.375	3.72	16	9	2	65.1	63	27	31	1	1	0	1	18	2	0	.111	3	8	2	0	0.8	.846
1957		1	1	.500	5.75	10	1	0	20.1	26	13	9	0	0	1	0	4	0	0	.000	2	2	1	1	0.5	.800
1958	DET A	3	4	.429	3.75	44	3	0	69.2	67	27	38	0	2	2	5	14	3	0	.214	3	14	0	1	0.4	1.000
1959		0	0	—	3.38	3	0	0	2.2	4	3	3	0	0	0	0	0	0	0	—	0	1	0	1	0.3	1.000
1960		5	3	.625	2.85	37	6	1	94.2	75	30	80	0	2	1	10	28	1	0	.036	2	7	1	0	0.3	.900
1961		4	4	.500	3.25	45	0	0	55.1	44	38	32	0	4	4	8	9	0	0	.000	1	7	2	0	0.2	.800
1962		16	8	.667	**2.21**	42	22	11	216	162	65	156	2	4	2	3	75	2	0	.027	7	22	3	0	0.8	.906
1963		14	15	.483	3.67	38	33	14	225.2	222	68	134	3	0	2	0	76	10	0	.132	7	23	1	1	0.8	.968
1964		5	10	.333	3.79	32	27	3	161.2	134	59	88	0	0	0	1	53	3	0	.057	8	12	4	2	0.8	.833
1965		14	10	.583	3.59	32	32	10	208.1	185	60	141	2	0	0	0	70	6	0	.086	8	32	4	0	1.4	.909
1966		3	9	.250	3.82	30	14	2	103.2	104	26	50	0	0	3	0	25	3	0	.120	2	13	4	0	0.6	.789
1967		0	1	.000	2.40	31	1	0	41.1	34	17	33	0	0	1	0	2	1	0	.500	3	7	1	0	0.4	.909
1968	LA N	1	2	.333	0.69	25	0	0	39	32	13	25	0	1	2	3	3	0	0	.000	0	4	2	0	0.2	.667
1969	CHI N	1	0	1.000	2.60	41	0	0	45	45	12	19	0	1	0	1	5	2	0	.400	1	13	0	0	0.3	1.000
1970		3	0	1.000	4.50	17	0	0	14	13	9	11	0	3	0	1	2	0	0	.000	0	2	3	0	0.3	.400
16 yrs.		75	72	.510	3.25	447	149	44	1375.1	1216	479	856	9	19	18	33	388	33	0	.085	48	167	28	6	0.5	.885

Pat Ahearne

AHEARNE, PATRICK HOWARD
B. Dec. 10, 1969, San Francisco, Calif.
BR TR 6′ 3″ 195 lbs.

Year	Team	W	L	PCT	ERA	G	GS	CG	IP	H	BB	SO	ShO	Relief W	Relief L	SV	AB	H	HR	BA	PO	A	E	DP	TC/G	FA
1995	DET A	0	2	.000	11.70	4	3	0	10	20	5	4	0	0	0	0	0	0	0	—	3	1	0	0	1.0	1.000

Eddie Ainsmith

AINSMITH, EDWARD WILBUR
B. Feb. 4, 1892, Cambridge, Mass. D. Sept. 6, 1981, Fort Lauderdale, Fla.
BR TR 5′11″ 180 lbs.

Year	Team	W	L	PCT	ERA	G	GS	CG	IP	H	BB	SO	ShO	Relief W	Relief L	SV	AB	H	HR	BA	PO	A	E	DP	TC/G	FA
1913	WAS A	0	0	—	54.00	1	0	0	0.1	2	0	0	0	0	0	0	*				131	52	7	4	6.3	.963

Raleigh Aitchison

AITCHISON, RALEIGH LEONIDAS (Redskin) BR TL 5′11½″ 175 lbs.
B. Dec. 5, 1887, Tyndall, S. D. D. Sept. 26, 1958, Columbus, Kans.

Year	Team	W	L	PCT	ERA	G	GS	CG	IP	H	BB	SO	ShO	Relief Pitching W	Relief Pitching L	Relief Pitching SV	Batting AB	Batting H	Batting HR	BA	PO	A	E	DP	TC/G	FA
1911	BKN N	0	1	.000	0.00	1	0	0	1.1	1	1	0	0	0	1	0	0	0	0	—	0	0	0	0	0.0	.000
1914		12	7	.632	2.66	26	17	8	172.1	156	60	87	3	1	2	0	51	10	0	.196	8	30	4	0	1.6	.905
1915		0	4	.000	4.96	7	5	2	32.2	36	6	14	0	0	0	0	8	0	0	.000	1	12	3	0	2.3	.813
3 yrs.		12	12	.500	3.01	34	22	10	206.1	193	67	101	3	1	3	0	59	10	0	.169	9	42	7	0	1.7	.879

Jack Aker

AKER, JACK DELANE (Chief) BR TR 6′ 2″ 190 lbs.
B. July 13, 1940, Tulare, Calif.

Year	Team	W	L	PCT	ERA	G	GS	CG	IP	H	BB	SO	ShO	Relief Pitching W	Relief Pitching L	Relief Pitching SV	Batting AB	Batting H	Batting HR	BA	PO	A	E	DP	TC/G	FA
1964	KC A	0	1	.000	8.82	9	0	0	16.1	17	10	7	0	0	1	0	3	0	0	.000	2	5	0	1	0.8	1.000
1965		4	3	.571	3.16	34	0	0	51.1	45	18	26	0	4	3	3	8	0	0	.000	4	11	0	2	0.4	1.000
1966		8	4	.667	1.99	66	0	0	113	81	28	68	0	8	4	**32**	21	2	0	.095	9	32	0	1	0.6	1.000
1967		3	8	.273	4.30	57	0	0	88	87	32	65	0	3	8	12	8	1	0	.125	7	19	0	3	0.5	1.000
1968	OAK A	4	4	.500	4.10	54	0	0	74.2	72	33	44	0	4	4	11	7	1	0	.143	2	14	1	1	0.3	.941
1969	2 teams SEA A (15G 0–2) NY A (38G 8–4)																									
″	total	8	6	.571	3.17	53	0	0	82.1	76	35	47	0	8	6	14	10	1	0	.100	14	18	0	4	0.6	1.000
1970	NY A	4	2	.667	2.06	41	0	0	70	57	20	36	0	4	2	16	16	1	0	.063	4	11	1	0	0.4	.938
1971		4	4	.500	2.57	41	0	0	56	48	26	24	0	4	4	4	3	0	0	.000	10	12	3	0	0.6	.880
1972	2 teams NY A (4G 0–0) CHI N (48G 6–6)																									
″	total	6	6	.500	2.96	52	0	0	73	70	26	37	0	6	6	17	6	0	0	.000	5	20	1	3	0.5	.962
1973	CHI N	4	5	.444	4.08	47	0	0	64	76	23	25	0	4	5	12	7	0	0	.000	6	17	1	3	0.5	.958
1974	2 teams ATL N (17G 0–1) NY N (24G 2–1)																									
″	total	2	2	.500	3.57	41	0	0	58	50	23	25	0	2	2	2	3	1	0	.333	2	8	1	1	0.3	.909
11 yrs.		47	45	.511	3.28	495	0	0	746.2	679	274	404	0	47	45	123	92	7	0	.076	65	167	8	19	0.5	.967

Darrel Akerfelds

AKERFELDS, DARREL WAYNE BR TR 6′ 2″ 210 lbs.
B. June 12, 1962, Denver, Colo.

Year	Team	W	L	PCT	ERA	G	GS	CG	IP	H	BB	SO	ShO	Relief Pitching W	Relief Pitching L	Relief Pitching SV	Batting AB	Batting H	Batting HR	BA	PO	A	E	DP	TC/G	FA
1986	OAK A	0	0	—	6.75	2	0	0	5.1	7	3	5	0	0	0	0	0	0	0	—	1	1	0	0	1.0	1.000
1987	CLE A	2	6	.250	6.75	16	13	1	74.2	84	38	42	0	0	0	0	0	0	0	—	0	11	1	1	0.8	.917
1989	TEX A	0	1	.000	3.27	6	0	0	11	11	5	9	0	0	1	0	0	0	0	—	0	2	0	0	0.3	1.000
1990	PHI N	5	2	.714	3.77	71	0	0	93	65	54	42	0	5	2	3	6	1	0	.167	2	14	1	0	0.2	.941
1991		2	1	.667	5.26	30	0	0	49.2	49	27	31	0	2	1	0	3	0	0	.000	2	12	1	0	0.5	.933
5 yrs.		9	10	.474	5.08	125	13	1	233.2	216	127	129	0	7	4	3	9	1	0	.111	5	40	3	1	0.4	.938

Jerry Akers

AKERS, ALBERT EARL BR TR 5′11″ 175 lbs.
B. Nov. 1, 1887, Shelbyville, Ind. D. May 15, 1979, Bay Pines, Fla.

Year	Team	W	L	PCT	ERA	G	GS	CG	IP	H	BB	SO	ShO	Relief Pitching W	Relief Pitching L	Relief Pitching SV	Batting AB	Batting H	Batting HR	BA	PO	A	E	DP	TC/G	FA
1912	WAS A	1	1	.500	4.87	5	1	0	20.1	24	15	11	0	1	0	0	6	2	0	.333	1	1	1	0	0.6	.667

Gibson Alba

ALBA, GIBSON ALBERTO BL TL 6′ 2″ 160 lbs.
Born Gibson Alberto Alba (Rosado).
B. Jan. 18, 1960, Santiago, Dominican Republic.

Year	Team	W	L	PCT	ERA	G	GS	CG	IP	H	BB	SO	ShO	Relief Pitching W	Relief Pitching L	Relief Pitching SV	Batting AB	Batting H	Batting HR	BA	PO	A	E	DP	TC/G	FA
1988	STL N	0	0	—	2.70	3	0	0	3.1	1	2	3	0	0	0	0	0	0	0	—	0	0	0	0	0.0	.000

Joe Albanese

ALBANESE, JOSEPH PETER BR TR 6′ 3″ 215 lbs.
B. June 26, 1933, New York, N. Y.

Year	Team	W	L	PCT	ERA	G	GS	CG	IP	H	BB	SO	ShO	Relief Pitching W	Relief Pitching L	Relief Pitching SV	Batting AB	Batting H	Batting HR	BA	PO	A	E	DP	TC/G	FA
1958	WAS A	0	0	—	4.50	6	0	0	6	8	2	3	0	0	0	0	0	0	0	—	0	2	0	0	0.3	1.000

Jose Alberro

ALBERRO, JOSE EDGARDO BR TR 6′ 2″ 190 lbs.
B. June 29, 1969, San Juan, Puerto Rico.

Year	Team	W	L	PCT	ERA	G	GS	CG	IP	H	BB	SO	ShO	Relief Pitching W	Relief Pitching L	Relief Pitching SV	Batting AB	Batting H	Batting HR	BA	PO	A	E	DP	TC/G	FA
1995	TEX A	0	0	—	7.40	12	0	0	20.2	26	12	10	0	0	0	0	0	0	0	—	2	4	0	0	0.5	1.000

Cy Alberts

ALBERTS, FREDERICK JOSEPH BR TR 6′ 230 lbs.
B. Jan. 14, 1882, Grand Rapids, Mich. D. Aug. 27, 1917, Fort Wayne, Ind.

Year	Team	W	L	PCT	ERA	G	GS	CG	IP	H	BB	SO	ShO	Relief Pitching W	Relief Pitching L	Relief Pitching SV	Batting AB	Batting H	Batting HR	BA	PO	A	E	DP	TC/G	FA
1910	STL N	1	2	.333	6.18	4	3	2	27.2	35	20	10	0	0	0	0	7	0	0	.000	1	3	0	0	1.0	1.000

Ed Albosta

ALBOSTA, EDWARD JOHN (Rube) BR TR 6′ 1″ 175 lbs.
B. Oct. 27, 1918, Saginaw, Mich.

Year	Team	W	L	PCT	ERA	G	GS	CG	IP	H	BB	SO	ShO	Relief Pitching W	Relief Pitching L	Relief Pitching SV	Batting AB	Batting H	Batting HR	BA	PO	A	E	DP	TC/G	FA
1941	BKN N	0	2	.000	6.23	2	2	0	13	11	8	5	0	0	0	0	4	0	0	.000	0	4	0	0	2.0	1.000
1946	PIT N	0	6	.000	6.13	17	6	0	39.2	41	35	19	0	0	1	0	8	1	0	.125	2	7	0	1	0.5	1.000
2 yrs.		0	8	.000	6.15	19	8	0	52.2	52	43	24	0	0	1	0	12	1	0	.083	2	11	0	1	0.7	1.000

Ed Albrecht

ALBRECHT, EDWARD ARTHUR BR TR 5′10½″ 165 lbs.
B. Feb. 28, 1929, St. Louis, Mo. D. Dec. 29, 1979, Centerville, Iowa.

Year	Team	W	L	PCT	ERA	G	GS	CG	IP	H	BB	SO	ShO	Relief Pitching W	Relief Pitching L	Relief Pitching SV	Batting AB	Batting H	Batting HR	BA	PO	A	E	DP	TC/G	FA
1949	STL A	1	0	1.000	5.40	1	1	1	5	1	4	1	0	0	0	0	2	0	0	.000	0	1	0	0	1.0	1.000
1950		0	1	.000	5.40	2	1	0	6.2	6	7	1	0	0	1	0	1	0	0	.000	0	1	0	0	0.5	1.000
2 yrs.		1	1	.500	5.40	3	2	1	11.2	7	11	2	0	0	1	0	3	0	0	.000	0	2	0	0	0.7	1.000

Vic Albury

ALBURY, VICTOR BL TL 6′ 190 lbs.
B. May 12, 1947, Key West, Fla.

Year	Team	W	L	PCT	ERA	G	GS	CG	IP	H	BB	SO	ShO	Relief Pitching W	Relief Pitching L	Relief Pitching SV	Batting AB	Batting H	Batting HR	BA	PO	A	E	DP	TC/G	FA
1973	MIN A	1	0	1.000	2.70	14	0	0	23.1	13	19	13	0	1	0	0	0	0	0	—	0	0	0	0	0.0	.000
1974		8	9	.471	4.12	32	22	4	164	159	80	85	1	1	0	0	0	0	0	—	5	20	0	4	0.8	1.000
1975		6	7	.462	4.53	32	15	2	135	115	97	72	0	3	0	1	1	0	0	.000	4	24	2	3	0.9	.933
1976		3	1	.750	3.58	23	0	0	50.1	51	24	23	0	3	1	0	0	0	0	—	1	8	0	0	0.4	1.000
4 yrs.		18	17	.514	4.11	101	37	6	372.2	338	220	193	1	8	1	1	1	0	0	.000	10	52	2	7	0.6	.969

Santo Alcala

ALCALA, SANTO BR TR 6′ 5″ 195 lbs.
Born Santo Anibal (Alcala).
B. Dec. 23, 1952, San Pedro de Macoris, Dominican Republic.

Year	Team	W	L	PCT	ERA	G	GS	CG	IP	H	BB	SO	ShO	Relief Pitching W	Relief Pitching L	Relief Pitching SV	Batting AB	Batting H	Batting HR	BA	PO	A	E	DP	TC/G	FA
1976	CIN N	11	4	.733	4.70	30	21	3	132	131	67	67	1	1	1	0	43	6	0	.140	8	17	1	0	0.9	.962
1977	2 teams CIN N (7G 1–1) MON N (31G 2–6)																									
″	total	3	7	.300	4.83	38	12	0	117.1	126	54	73	0	1	0	2	28	2	1	.071	8	11	0	0	0.5	1.000
2 yrs.		14	11	.560	4.76	68	33	3	249.1	257	121	140	1	2	1	2	71	8	1	.113	16	28	1	0	0.7	.978

Dale Alderson

ALDERSON, DALE LEONARD
B. Mar. 8, 1918, Belden, Neb. D. Feb. 12, 1982, Garden Grove, Calif.
BR TR 5'10" 190 lbs.

Year	Team	Lg	W	L	PCT	ERA	G	GS	CG	IP	H	BB	SO	ShO	Relief Pitching W	Relief Pitching L	Relief Pitching SV	Batting AB	Batting H	Batting HR	BA	PO	A	E	DP	TC/G	FA
1943	CHI	N	0	1	.000	6.43	4	2	0	14	21	3	4	0	0	0	0	3	0	0	.000	0	4	0	0	1.0	1.000
1944			0	0	—	6.65	12	1	0	21.2	31	9	7	0	0	0	0	4	0	0	.000	2	7	0	1	0.8	1.000
2 yrs.			0	1	.000	6.56	16	3	0	35.2	52	12	11	0	0	0	0	7	0	0	.000	2	11	0	1	0.8	1.000

Scott Aldred

ALDRED, SCOTT PHILLIP
B. June 12, 1968, Flint, Mich.
BL TL 6'4" 195 lbs.

Year	Team	Lg	W	L	PCT	ERA	G	GS	CG	IP	H	BB	SO	ShO	Relief Pitching W	Relief Pitching L	Relief Pitching SV	Batting AB	Batting H	Batting HR	BA	PO	A	E	DP	TC/G	FA
1990	DET	A	1	2	.333	3.77	4	3	0	14.1	13	10	7	0	0	0	0	0	0	0	—	0	2	0	0	0.5	1.000
1991			2	4	.333	5.18	11	11	1	57.1	58	30	35	0	0	0	0	0	0	0	—	3	8	0	0	1.0	1.000
1992			3	8	.273	6.78	16	13	0	65	80	33	34	0	1	1	0	0	0	0	—	5	10	0	1	0.9	1.000
1993	2 teams CLR N (5G 0–0) MON N (3G 1–0)																										
"	total		1	0	1.000	9.00	8	0	0	12	19	10	9	0	1	0	0	0	0	0		0	2	0	0	0.3	1.000
4 yrs.			7	14	.333	6.05	39	27	1	148.2	170	83	85	0	2	1	0	0	0	0		8	22	0	1	0.8	1.000

Jay Aldrich

ALDRICH, JAY ROBERT
B. Apr. 14, 1961, Alexandria, La.
BR TR 6'3" 210 lbs.

Year	Team	Lg	W	L	PCT	ERA	G	GS	CG	IP	H	BB	SO	ShO	Relief Pitching W	Relief Pitching L	Relief Pitching SV	Batting AB	Batting H	Batting HR	BA	PO	A	E	DP	TC/G	FA
1987	MIL	A	3	1	.750	4.94	31	0	0	58.1	71	13	22	0	0	0	0	0	0	0	—	6	5	1	0	0.4	.917
1989	2 teams MIL A (16G 1–0) ATL N (8G 1–2)																										
"	total		2	2	.500	3.29	24	0	0	38.1	31	19	19	0	2	2	1	1	0	0	.000	4	5	1	1	0.4	.900
1990	BAL	A	1	2	.333	8.25	7	0	0	12	17	7	5	0	1	2	1	0	0	0	—	2	1	0	0	0.4	1.000
3 yrs.			6	5	.545	4.72	62	0	0	108.2	119	39	46	0	3	4	2	1	0	0	.000	12	11	2	1	0.4	.920

Vic Aldridge

ALDRIDGE, VICTOR EDDINGTON
B. Oct. 25, 1893, Indian Springs, Ind. D. Apr. 17, 1973, Terre Haute, Ind.
BR TR 5'9½" 175 lbs.

Year	Team	Lg	W	L	PCT	ERA	G	GS	CG	IP	H	BB	SO	ShO	Relief Pitching W	Relief Pitching L	Relief Pitching SV	Batting AB	Batting H	Batting HR	BA	PO	A	E	DP	TC/G	FA
1917	CHI	N	6	6	.500	3.12	30	7	1	106.2	100	37	44	1	4	1	2	29	4	0	.138	2	44	3	2	1.6	.939
1918			0	1	.000	1.46	3	0	0	12.1	11	6	10	0	0	1	0	3	1	0	.333	0	2	0	0	0.7	1.000
1922			16	15	.516	3.52	36	34	20	258.1	287	56	66	2	1	0	0	100	26	0	.260	3	68	4	2	2.1	.947
1923			16	9	.640	3.48	30	30	15	217	209	67	64	2	0	0	0	71	19	0	.268	6	46	0	3	1.7	1.000
1924			15	12	.556	3.50	32	32	20	244.1	261	80	74	0	0	0	0	85	15	0	.176	4	59	1	3	2.0	.984
1925	PIT	N	15	7	.682	3.63	30	26	14	213.1	218	74	88	1	2	0	0	86	20	1	.233	2	34	1	2	1.2	.973
1926			10	13	.435	4.07	30	26	12	190	204	73	61	1	0	1	1	71	16	0	.225	0	42	3	3	1.5	.933
1927			15	10	.600	4.25	35	34	17	239.1	248	74	86	1	0	0	1	96	21	0	.219	5	35	0	2	1.1	1.000
1928	NY	N	4	7	.364	4.83	22	17	3	119.1	133	45	33	0	0	0	2	40	11	1	.275	4	24	0	2	1.3	1.000
9 yrs.			97	80	.548	3.76	248	206	102	1600.2	1671	512	526	8	7	3	6	581	133	2	.229	26	354	12	19	1.6	.969
WORLD SERIES																											
1925	PIT	N	2	0	1.000	3.93	3	3	2	18.1	18	9	9	0	0	0	0	7	0	0	.000	0	4	0	0	1.3	1.000
1927			0	1	.000	7.36	1	1	0	7.1	10	4	4	0	0	0	0	2	0	0	.000	0	2	0	0	2.0	1.000
2 yrs.			2	1	.667	4.91	4	4	2	25.2	28	13	13	0	0	0	0	9	0	0	.000	0	6	0	0	1.5	1.000

Bob Alexander

ALEXANDER, ROBERT SOMERVILLE
B. Aug. 7, 1922, Vancouver, B. C., Canada. D. Apr. 7, 1993, Oceanside, Calif.
BR TR 6'2½" 205 lbs.

Year	Team	Lg	W	L	PCT	ERA	G	GS	CG	IP	H	BB	SO	ShO	Relief Pitching W	Relief Pitching L	Relief Pitching SV	Batting AB	Batting H	Batting HR	BA	PO	A	E	DP	TC/G	FA
1955	BAL	A	1	0	1.000	13.50	4	0	0	4	8	2	1	0	1	0	0	0	0	0	—	0	0	0	0	0.0	.000
1957	CLE	A	0	1	.000	9.00	5	0	0	7	10	5	1	0	0	1	0	1	0	0	.000	0	0	0	0	0.0	.000
2 yrs.			1	1	.500	10.64	9	0	0	11	18	7	2	0	1	1	0	1	0	0	.000	0	0	0	0	0.0	

Doyle Alexander

ALEXANDER, DOYLE LAFAYETTE
B. Sept. 4, 1950, Cordova, Ala.
BR TR 6'3" 190 lbs.

Year	Team	Lg	W	L	PCT	ERA	G	GS	CG	IP	H	BB	SO	ShO	Relief Pitching W	Relief Pitching L	Relief Pitching SV	Batting AB	Batting H	Batting HR	BA	PO	A	E	DP	TC/G	FA
1971	LA	N	6	6	.500	3.82	17	12	4	92	105	18	30	0	1	0	0	33	9	0	.273	5	12	1	0	1.1	.944
1972	BAL	A	6	8	.429	2.45	35	9	2	106.1	78	30	49	2	4	5	2	25	2	0	.080	14	23	2	1	1.1	.949
1973			12	8	.600	3.86	29	26	10	175	169	52	63	0	1	0	0	0	0	0	—	15	30	2	1	1.6	.957
1974			6	9	.400	4.03	30	12	2	114	127	43	40	0	3	2	0	0	0	0	—	13	30	2	5	1.5	.956
1975			8	8	.500	3.04	32	11	3	133.1	127	47	46	1	3	4	1	0	0	0	—	14	29	2	1	1.4	.956
1976	2 teams BAL A (11G 3–4) NY A (19G 10–5)																										
"	total		13	9	.591	3.36	30	25	7	201	172	63	58	3	2	0	0	0	0	0		11	30	0	2	1.4	1.000
1977	TEX	A	17	11	.607	3.65	34	34	12	237	221	82	82	1	0	0	0	0	0	0	—	17	46	4	4	2.0	.940
1978			9	10	.474	3.86	31	28	7	191	198	71	81	1	0	0	0	0	0	0	—	17	36	4	1	1.8	.930
1979			5	7	.417	4.46	23	18	0	113	114	69	50	0	0	0	0	0	0	0	—	12	23	0	1	1.5	1.000
1980	ATL	N	14	11	.560	4.19	35	35	7	232	227	74	114	1	0	0	0	83	15	0	.181	16	49	4	4	2.0	.942
1981	SF	N	11	7	.611	2.90	24	24	1	152	156	44	77	1	0	0	0	51	9	0	.176	9	16	0	1	1.0	1.000
1982	NY	A	1	7	.125	6.08	16	11	0	66.2	81	14	26	0	0	0	0	0	0	0	—	3	9	1	1	0.8	.923
1983	2 teams NY A (8G 0–2) TOR A (17G 7–6)																										
"	total		7	8	.467	4.41	25	20	5	145	157	33	63	0	1	0	0	0	0	0		13	19	1	1	1.3	.970
1984	TOR	A	17	6	**.739**	3.13	36	35	11	261.2	238	59	139	2	0	0	0	0	0	0	—	18	33	2	4	1.5	.962
1985			17	10	.630	3.45	36	36	6	260.2	268	67	142	1	0	0	0	0	0	0	—	28	32	1	4	1.7	.984
1986	2 teams TOR A (17G 5–4) ATL N (17G 6–6)																										
"	total		11	10	.524	4.14	34	34	5	228.1	255	37	139	0	0	0	0	38	8	0	.211	14	25	3	2	1.2	.929
1987	2 teams ATL N (16G 5–10) DET A (11G 9–0)																										
"	total		14	10	.583	3.01	27	27	6	206	178	53	108	3	0	0	0	35	1	0	.029	10	24	0	2	1.3	1.000
1988	DET	A	14	11	.560	4.32	34	34	5	229	260	46	126	1	0	0	0	0	0	0	—	12	19	2	1	1.0	.939
1989			6	**18**	.250	4.44	33	33	5	223	245	76	95	1	0	0	0	0	0	0	—	23	32	1	1	1.7	.982
19 yrs.			194	174	.527	3.76	561	464	98	3367	3376	978	1528	18	15	11	3	265	44	0	.166	264	517	32	37	1.4	.961
LEAGUE CHAMPIONSHIP SERIES																											
1973	BAL	A	0	1	.000	4.91	1	1	0	3.2	5	0	1	0	0	0	0	0	0	0	—	0	2	0	1	2.0	1.000
1985	TOR	A	0	1	.000	8.71	2	2	0	10.1	14	3	9	0	0	0	0	0	0	0	—	1	0	0	0	0.5	1.000
1987	DET	A	0	2	.000	10.00	2	2	0	9	14	1	5	0	0	0	0	0	0	0	—	2	1	0	0	1.5	1.000
3 yrs.			0	4 **3rd**	.000	8.61	5	5	0	23	33	4	15	0	0	0	0	0	0	0		3	3	0	1	1.2	1.000
WORLD SERIES																											
1976	NY	A	0	1	.000	7.50	1	1	0	6	9	2	1	0	0	0	0	0	0	0	—	0	1	0	1	1.0	1.000

Year	Team		W	L	PCT	ERA	G	GS	CG	IP	H	BB	SO	ShO	Relief Pitching W	L	SV	Batting AB	H	HR	BA	PO	A	E	DP	TC/G	FA
Gerald Alexander																											
ALEXANDER, GERALD PAUL — B. Mar. 26, 1968, Baton Rouge, La. — BR TR 5′11″ 190 lbs.																											
1990	TEX	A	0	0	—	7.71	3	2	0	7	14	5	8	0	0	0	0	0	0	0	—	1	0	0	1	0.3	1.000
1991			5	3	.625	5.24	30	9	0	89.1	93	48	50	0	3	2	0	0	0	0	—	5	14	0	2	0.6	1.000
1992			1	0	1.000	27.00	3	0	0	1.2	5	1	1	0	1	0	0	0	0	0	—	1	0	0	0	0.3	1.000
3 yrs.			6	3	.667	5.79	36	11	0	98	112	54	59	0	4	2	0	0	0	0		7	14	0	3	0.6	1.000
Grover Alexander																											
ALEXANDER, GROVER CLEVELAND (Pete) — B. Feb. 26, 1887, Elba, Neb. D. Nov. 4, 1950, St. Paul, Neb. Hall of Fame 1938. — BR TR 6′ 1″ 185 lbs.																											
1911	PHI	N	**28**	13	.683	2.57	48	37	**31**	**367**	285	129	227	**7**	4	2	3	138	24	0	.174	11	95	4	3	2.3	.964
1912			19	17	.528	2.81	46	34	25	**310.1**	289	105	**195**	3	3	2	2	102	19	2	.186	10	75	3	1	1.9	.966
1913			22	8	.733	2.79	47	35	23	306.1	288	75	159	**9**	4	2	2	103	13	0	.126	10	82	0	3	2.0	1.000
1914			**27**	15	.643	2.38	46	39	**32**	**355**	**327**	76	**214**	6	4	1	1	137	32	0	.234	18	102	3	1	2.6	.976
1915			**31**	10	**.756**	**1.22**	49	42	**36**	**376.1**	253	64	**241**	**12**	1	1	3	130	22	1	.169	22	120	3	4	3.0	.979
1916			**33**	12	.733	**1.55**	48	**45**	**38**	**389**	**323**	50	**167**	**16**[1]	0	0	3	138	33	0	.239	17	102	1	3	2.5	.992
1917			**30**	13	.698	**1.86**	45	**44**	**35**	**387.2**	**336**	58	**201**	**8**	0	0	0	139	30	1	.216	24	108	1	3	3.0	.992
1918	CHI	N	2	1	.667	1.73	3	3	3	26	19	3	15	0	0	0	0	10	1	0	.100	0	8	0	0	2.7	1.000
1919			16	11	.593	**1.72**	30	27	20	235	180	38	121	**9**	0	1	1	70	12	0	.171	6	85	0	2	3.0	1.000
1920			**27**	14	.659	**1.91**	46	**40**	**33**	**363.1**	**335**	69	**173**	7	1	0	5	118	27	1	.229	8	105	2	2	2.5	.983
1921			15	13	.536	3.39	31	30	21	252	286	33	77	**3**	0	0	1	95	29	1	.305	11	60	2	4	2.4	.973
1922			16	13	.552	3.63	33	31	20	245.2	283	34	48	1	1	0	1	85	15	0	.176	9	69	0	5	2.4	1.000
1923			22	12	.647	3.19	39	36	26	305	308	30	72	3	0	1	2	111	24	1	.216	11	90	1	6	2.6	.990
1924			12	5	.706	3.03	21	20	12	169.1	183	25	33	0	0	1	0	65	15	1	.231	4	53	2	2	2.8	.966
1925			15	11	.577	3.39	32	30	20	236	270	29	63	1	0	1	0	79	19	2	.241	7	45	0	4	1.6	1.000
1926	2 teams	CHI N (7G 3–3)	STL N (23G 9–7)																								
″	total		12	10	.545	3.05	30	23	15	200.1	191	31	47	2	2	1	2	65	13	0	.200	3	58	2	1	2.1	.968
1927	STL	N	21	10	.677	2.52	37	30	22	268	261	38	48	2	2	1	3	94	23	0	.245	8	66	0	1	2.0	1.000
1928			16	9	.640	3.36	34	31	18	243.2	262	37	59	1	0	0	2	86	25	1	.291	4	57	0	3	1.8	1.000
1929			9	8	.529	3.89	22	19	8	132	149	23	33	0	1	1	0	41	2	0	.049	5	38	1	2	2.0	.977
1930	PHI	N	0	3	.000	9.14	9	3	0	21.2	40	6	6	0	0	2	0	4	0	0	.000	1	1	0	0	0.2	1.000
20 yrs.			373 **3rd**	208	.642	2.56	696	599	438	5189.2 **10th**	4868	953	2199	90 **2nd**	23	17	31	1810	378	11	.209	189	1419	25	50	2.3	.985
WORLD SERIES																											
1915	PHI	N	1	1	.500	1.53	2	2	2	17.2	14	4	10	0	0	0	0	5	1	0	.200	2	5	0	0	3.5	1.000
1926	STL	N	2	0	1.000	0.89	3	2	2	20.1	12	4	17	0	0	0	1	7	0	0	.000	0	6	1	1	2.3	.857
1928			0	1	.000	19.80	2	1	0	5	10	4	2	0	0	0	0	1	0	0	.000	0	4	0	0	2.0	1.000
3 yrs.			3	2	.600	3.35	7	5	4	43	36	12	29	0	0	0	1	13	1	0	.077	2	15	1	1	2.6	.944
Brian Allard																											
ALLARD, BRIAN MARSHALL — B. Jan. 3, 1958, Spring Valley, Ill. — BR TR 6′ 1″ 175 lbs.																											
1979	TEX	A	1	3	.250	4.36	7	4	2	33	36	13	14	0	0	0	0	0	0	0	—	3	5	0	0	1.1	1.000
1980			0	1	.000	5.79	5	2	0	14	13	10	10	0	0	0	0	0	0	0	—	0	1	1	0	0.4	.500
1981	SEA	A	3	2	.600	3.75	7	7	1	48	48	8	20	0	0	0	0	0	0	0	—	4	6	1	1	1.6	.909
3 yrs.			4	6	.400	4.26	19	13	3	95	97	31	44	0	0	0	0	0	0	0		7	12	2	1	1.1	.905
Bob Allen																											
ALLEN, ROBERT EARL — B. July 2, 1914, Smithville, Tenn. — BR TR 6′ 1″ 165 lbs.																											
1937	PHI	N	0	1	.000	6.75	3	1	0	12	18	8	8	0	0	0	0	3	1	0	.333	0	0	2	0	0.7	.000
Bob Allen																											
ALLEN, ROBERT GRAY — B. Oct. 23, 1937, Tatum, Tex. — BL TL 6′ 2″ 175 lbs.																											
1961	CLE	A	3	2	.600	3.75	48	0	0	81.2	96	40	42	0	3	2	3	12	2	0	.167	4	14	0	0	0.4	1.000
1962			1	1	.500	5.87	30	0	0	30.2	29	25	23	0	1	1	4	5	0	0	.000	4	6	2	1	0.4	.833
1963			1	2	.333	4.66	43	0	0	56	58	29	51	0	1	2	2	5	1	0	.200	2	9	1	2	0.3	.917
1966			2	2	.500	4.21	36	0	0	51.1	56	13	33	0	2	2	5	9	1	0	.111	2	12	1	1	0.4	.933
1967			0	5	.000	2.98	47	0	0	54.1	49	25	50	0	0	5	5	0	0	0	—	4	10	0	0	0.3	1.000
5 yrs.			7	12	.368	4.11	204	0	0	274	288	132	199	0	7	12	19	31	4	0	.129	16	51	4	4	0.3	.944
Frank Allen																											
ALLEN, FRANK LEON (Thin Man) — B. Aug. 26, 1889, Newbern, Ala. D. July 30, 1933, Gainesville, Ala. — BR TL 5′ 9″ 175 lbs.																											
1912	BKN	N	3	9	.250	3.63	20	15	5	109	119	57	58	1	0	0	0	36	6	1	.167	2	28	2	0	1.6	.938
1913			4	18	.182	2.83	34	25	11	174.2	144	81	82	0	0	3	2	51	7	1	.137	6	30	4	0	1.2	.900
1914	2 teams	BKN N (36G 8–14)	PIT F (1G 1–0)																								
″	total		9	14	.391	3.18	37	22	11	178.1	174	57	71	1	1	2	0	49	7	0	.143	4	41	3	2	1.3	.938
1915	PIT	F	23	12	.657	2.51	41	37	24	283.1	230	100	127	6	1	1	0	89	7	0	.079	16	80	6	1	2.5	.941
1916	BOS	N	8	2	.800	2.07	19	14	7	113	102	31	63	2	1	0	1	34	7	0	.206	2	24	2	0	1.5	.929
1917			3	11	.214	3.94	29	14	2	112	124	47	56	0	0	**4**	0	29	5	0	.172	1	23	1	0	0.9	.960
6 yrs.			50	66	.431	2.93	180	127	60	970.1	893	373	457	10	3	10	3	288	39	2	.135	31	226	18	3	1.5	.935
John Allen																											
ALLEN, JOHN MARSHALL — B. Oct. 27, 1890, Berkeley Springs, W. Va. D. Sept. 24, 1967, Hagerstown, Md. — BR TR 6′ 1″ 170 lbs.																											
1914	BAL	F	0	0	—	18.00	1	0	0	2	2	2	2	0	0	0	0	0	0	0	—	0	1	0	0	1.0	1.000
Johnny Allen																											
ALLEN, JOHN THOMAS — B. Sept. 30, 1905, Lenoir, N. C. D. Mar. 29, 1959, St. Petersburg, Fla. — BR TR 6′ 180 lbs.																											
1932	NY	A	17	4	**.810**	3.70	33	21	13	192	162	76	109	3	4	0	4	73	9	1	.123	8	31	3	2	1.3	.929
1933			15	7	.682	4.39	25	24	10	184.2	171	87	119	1	0	0	1	72	13	0	.181	10	29	1	0	1.6	.975
1934			5	2	.714	2.89	13	10	4	71.2	62	32	54	0	0	0	0	26	5	0	.192	1	12	0	2	1.0	1.000
1935			13	6	.684	3.61	23	23	12	167	149	58	113	2	0	0	0	67	15	1	.224	9	33	1	1	1.9	.977
1936	CLE	A	20	10	.667	3.44	36	31	19	243	234	97	165	4	2	1	1	87	14	0	.161	9	50	2	1	1.7	.967
1937			15	1	**.938**	2.55	24	20	14	173	157	60	87	0	0	0	0	67	6	0	.090	7	37	1	1	1.9	.978
1938			14	8	.636	4.18	30	27	13	200	189	81	112	0	1	1	0	79	20	1	.253	14	43	2	3	2.0	.966
1939			9	7	.563	4.58	28	26	9	175	199	56	79	2	0	0	0	71	16	0	.225	17	36	5	7	2.1	.914
1940			9	8	.529	3.44	32	17	5	138.2	126	48	62	3	3	1	5	48	10	0	.208	8	21	0	2	0.9	1.000
1941	2 teams	STL A (20G 2–5)	BKN N (11G 3–0)																								
″	total		5	5	.500	4.71	31	13	3	124.1	127	41	48	0	1	3	1	42	4	1	.095	5	23	2	2	1.0	.933

Johnny Allen *continued*

Year	Team	W	L	PCT	ERA	G	GS	CG	IP	H	BB	SO	ShO	Relief Pitching W	Relief Pitching L	Relief Pitching SV	Batting AB	Batting H	Batting HR	BA	PO	A	E	DP	TC/G	FA
1942	BKN N	10	6	.625	3.20	27	15	5	118	106	39	50	1	1	3	3	39	7	0	.179	3	25	0	3	1.0	1.000
1943	2 teams BKN N (17G 5–1) NY N (15G 1–3)																									
"	total	6	4	.600	3.65	32	1	0	79	79	39	39	0	6	4	3	21	3	0	.143	7	18	2	0	0.8	.926
1944	NY N	4	7	.364	4.07	18	13	2	84	88	24	33	1	0	0	0	24	2	0	.083	6	8	0	0	0.8	1.000
13 yrs.		142	75	.654	3.75	352	241	109	1950.1	1849	738	1070	17	18	13	18	716	124	4	.173	104	366	19	24	1.4	.961
WORLD SERIES																										
1932	NY A	0	0	—	40.50	1	1	0	0.2	5	0	0	0	0	0	0	0	0	0	—	0	0	0	0	0.0	.000
1941	BKN N	0	0	—	0.00	3	0	0	3.2	1	3	0	0	0	0	0	0	0	0	—	0	0	0	0	0.0	.000
2 yrs.		0	0		6.23	4	1	0	4.1	6	3	0	0	0	0	0	0	0	0		0	0	0	0	0.0	

Lloyd Allen

ALLEN, LLOYD CECIL BR TR 6′ 1″ 185 lbs.
B. May 8, 1950, Merced, Calif.

Year	Team	W	L	PCT	ERA	G	GS	CG	IP	H	BB	SO	ShO	Relief Pitching W	Relief Pitching L	Relief Pitching SV	Batting AB	Batting H	Batting HR	BA	PO	A	E	DP	TC/G	FA
1969	CAL A	0	1	.000	5.40	4	1	0	10	5	10	5	0	0	0	0	2	1	0	.500	1	4	0	0	1.3	1.000
1970		1	1	.500	2.63	8	2	0	24	23	11	12	0	0	0	0	4	0	0	.000	2	2	0	1	0.5	1.000
1971		4	6	.400	2.49	54	1	0	94	75	40	72	0	4	6	15	17	5	1	.294	5	17	1	0	0.4	.957
1972		3	7	.300	3.49	42	6	0	85	76	55	53	0	3	3	5	17	2	0	.118	3	10	0	2	0.3	1.000
1973	2 teams CAL A (5G 0–0) TEX A (23G 0–6)																									
"	total	0	6	.000	9.42	28	5	0	49.2	73	44	29	0	0	2	2	0	0	0		3	11	2	1	0.6	.875
1974	2 teams TEX A (14G 0–1) CHI A (6G 0–1)																									
"	total	0	2	.000	7.45	20	2	0	29	31	30	21	0	0	1	0	0	0	0		1	1	0	0	0.1	1.000
1975	CHI A	0	2	.000	11.81	3	2	0	5.1	8	6	2	0	0	0	0	0	0	0	—	0	1	0	1	0.3	1.000
7 yrs.		8	25	.242	4.70	159	19	0	297	291	196	194	0	7	12	22	40	8	1	.200	15	46	3	5	0.4	.953

Myron Allen

ALLEN, MYRON SMITH BR TR 5′ 8″ 150 lbs.
B. Mar. 22, 1854, Kingston, N. Y. D. Mar. 8, 1924, Kingston, N. Y.

Year	Team	W	L	PCT	ERA	G	GS	CG	IP	H	BB	SO	ShO	Relief Pitching W	Relief Pitching L	Relief Pitching SV	Batting AB	Batting H	Batting HR	BA	PO	A	E	DP	TC/G	FA
1883	NY N	0	1	.000	1.13	1	1	1	8	8	3	0	0	0	0	0	4	0	0	.000	1	1	0	0	2.0	1.000
1887	CLE AA	1	0	1.000	1.86	2	0	0	9.2	9	3	1	0	1	0	0	463	128	4	.276	2	2	0	0	4.0	1.000
1888	KC AA	0	2	.000	2.50	2	2	2	18	17	1	2	0	0	0	0	136	29	0	.213	73	17	7	1	2.6	.928
3 yrs.		1	3	.250	2.02	5	3	3	35.2	34	7	3	0	1	0	0	*				306	52	38	8	2.5	.904

Neil Allen

ALLEN, NEIL PATRICK BR TR 6′ 3″ 185 lbs.
B. Jan. 24, 1958, Kansas City, Kans.

Year	Team	W	L	PCT	ERA	G	GS	CG	IP	H	BB	SO	ShO	Relief Pitching W	Relief Pitching L	Relief Pitching SV	Batting AB	Batting H	Batting HR	BA	PO	A	E	DP	TC/G	FA
1979	NY N	6	10	.375	3.55	50	5	0	99	100	47	65	0	6	6	8	14	0	0	.000	9	14	1	1	0.5	.958
1980		7	10	.412	3.71	59	0	0	97	87	40	79	0	7	10	22	14	2	0	.143	4	10	1	0	0.3	.933
1981		7	6	.538	2.96	43	0	0	67	64	26	50	0	7	6	18	5	1	0	.200	4	13	0	1	0.4	1.000
1982		3	7	.300	3.06	50	0	0	64.2	65	30	59	0	3	7	19	6	1	0	.167	1	8	1	1	0.2	.900
1983	2 teams NY N (21G 2–7) STL N (25G 10–6)																									
"	total	12	13	.480	3.94	46	22	5	175.2	179	84	106	3	3	5	2	49	5	0	.102	17	20	0	0	0.8	1.000
1984	STL N	9	6	.600	3.55	57	1	0	119	105	49	66	0	9	5	3	25	6	0	.240	5	22	0	0	0.5	1.000
1985	2 teams STL N (23G 1–4) NY A (17G 1–0)																									
"	total	2	4	.333	4.17	40	1	0	58.1	58	30	26	0	2	3	3	2	0	0	.000	5	8	0	0	0.3	1.000
1986	CHI A	7	2	.778	3.82	22	17	2	113	101	38	57	2	0	0	0	0	0	0	—	15	10	0	0	1.1	1.000
1987	2 teams CHI A (15G 0–7) NY A (8G 0–1)																									
"	total	0	8	.000	5.93	23	11	0	74.1	97	36	42	0	0	0	0	0	0	0		7	7	1	1	0.7	.933
1988	NY A	5	3	.625	3.84	41	2	0	117.1	121	37	61	1	5	1	0	0	0	0	—	6	8	0	0	0.3	1.000
1989	CLE A	0	1	.000	15.00	3	0	0	3	8	0	0	0	0	1	0	0	0	0	—	2	0	0	0	0.7	1.000
11 yrs.		58	70	.453	3.88	434	59	7	988.1	985	417	611	6	42	44	75	115	15	0	.130	75	120	4	4	0.5	.980

Dana Allison

ALLISON, DANA ERIC BR TL 6′ 3″ 215 lbs.
B. Aug. 14, 1966, Front Royal, Va.

Year	Team	W	L	PCT	ERA	G	GS	CG	IP	H	BB	SO	ShO	Relief Pitching W	Relief Pitching L	Relief Pitching SV	Batting AB	Batting H	Batting HR	BA	PO	A	E	DP	TC/G	FA
1991	OAK A	1	1	.500	7.36	11	0	0	11	16	5	4	0	1	1	0	0	0	0	—	0	0	0	0	0.0	.000

Doug Allison

ALLISON, DOUGLAS L. BR TR 5′10½″ 160 lbs.
Brother of Art Allison.
B. July 1845, Philadelphia, Pa. D. Dec. 19, 1916, Washington, D. C.

Year	Team	W	L	PCT	ERA	G	GS	CG	IP	H	BB	SO	ShO	Relief Pitching W	Relief Pitching L	Relief Pitching SV	Batting AB	Batting H	Batting HR	BA	PO	A	E	DP	TC/G	FA
1878	PRO N	0	0	—	1.80	1	0	0	5	11	1	0	0	0	0	0	*				206	43	34	2	6.2	.880

Mack Allison

ALLISON, MACK PENDLETON BR TR 6′ 1″ 185 lbs.
B. Jan. 23, 1887, Owensboro, Ky. D. Mar. 13, 1964, Mount Vernon, Mo.

Year	Team	W	L	PCT	ERA	G	GS	CG	IP	H	BB	SO	ShO	Relief Pitching W	Relief Pitching L	Relief Pitching SV	Batting AB	Batting H	Batting HR	BA	PO	A	E	DP	TC/G	FA
1911	STL A	2	1	.667	2.05	3	3	3	26.1	24	5	2	0	0	0	0	10	2	0	.200	2	5	1	0	2.7	.875
1912		6	17	.261	3.62	31	20	11	169	171	49	43	1	0	3	1	52	7	0	.135	4	46	6	2	1.8	.893
1913		1	3	.250	2.28	11	4	3	51.1	52	13	12	0	0	0	0	14	0	0	.000	0	9	0	0	0.8	1.000
3 yrs.		9	21	.300	3.17	45	27	17	246.2	247	67	57	1	0	3	1	76	9	0	.118	6	60	7	2	1.6	.904

Luis Aloma

ALOMA, LUIS (Witto) BR TR 6′ 2″ 195 lbs.
Born Luis Aloma (Barba).
B. July 23, 1923, Havana, Cuba.

Year	Team	W	L	PCT	ERA	G	GS	CG	IP	H	BB	SO	ShO	Relief Pitching W	Relief Pitching L	Relief Pitching SV	Batting AB	Batting H	Batting HR	BA	PO	A	E	DP	TC/G	FA
1950	CHI A	7	2	.778	3.80	42	0	0	87.2	77	53	49	0	7	2	4	15	1	0	.067	3	13	0	0	0.4	1.000
1951		6	0	1.000	1.82	25	1	1	69.1	52	24	25	1	5	0	3	20	7	0	.350	6	4	0	0	0.4	1.000
1952		3	1	.750	4.28	25	0	0	40	42	11	18	0	3	1	6	7	0	0	.000	3	6	0	0	0.4	1.000
1953		2	0	1.000	4.70	24	0	0	38.1	41	23	23	0	2	0	2	6	0	0	.000	3	5	0	1	0.3	1.000
4 yrs.		18	3	.857	3.44	116	1	1	235.1	212	111	115	1	17	3	15	48	8	0	.167	15	28	0	1	0.4	1.000

Matty Alou

ALOU, MATEO BL TL 5′ 9″ 160 lbs.
Born Mateo Rojas (Alou).
Brother of Jesus Alou. Brother of Felipe Alou.
B. Dec. 22, 1938, Haina, Dominican Republic.

Year	Team	W	L	PCT	ERA	G	GS	CG	IP	H	BB	SO	ShO	Relief Pitching W	Relief Pitching L	Relief Pitching SV	Batting AB	Batting H	Batting HR	BA	PO	A	E	DP	TC/G	FA
1965	SF N	0	0	—	0.00	1	0	0	2	3	1	3	0	0	0	0	*				1	0	0	0	1.0	1.000

Porfi Altamirano

ALTAMIRANO, PORFIRIO BR TR 6′ 175 lbs.
Born Porfirio Altamirano (Ramirez).
B. May 17, 1952, Darillo, Nicaragua.

Year	Team		W	L	PCT	ERA	G	GS	CG	IP	H	BB	SO	ShO	Relief Pitching W	Relief Pitching L	Relief Pitching SV	Batting AB	Batting H	Batting HR	BA	PO	A	E	DP	TC/G	FA
1982	PHI	N	5	1	.833	4.15	29	0	0	39	41	14	26	0	5	1	2	4	1	0	.250	2	8	1	0	0.4	.909
1983			2	3	.400	3.70	31	0	0	41.1	38	15	24	0	2	3	0	2	0	0	.000	2	8	0	0	0.3	1.000
1984	CHI	N	0	0	—	4.76	5	0	0	11.1	8	1	7	0	0	0	0	2	0	0	.000	0	4	0	0	0.8	1.000
3 yrs.			7	4	.636	4.03	65	0	0	91.2	87	30	57	0	7	4	2	8	1	0	.125	4	20	1	0	0.4	.960

Ernie Alten

ALTEN, ERNEST MATTHIAS (Lefty) BR TL 6′ 175 lbs.
B. Dec. 1, 1894, Avon, Ohio D. Sept. 9, 1981, Napa, Calif.

Year	Team		W	L	PCT	ERA	G	GS	CG	IP	H	BB	SO	ShO	Relief Pitching W	Relief Pitching L	Relief Pitching SV	Batting AB	Batting H	Batting HR	BA	PO	A	E	DP	TC/G	FA
1920	DET	A	0	1	.000	9.00	14	1	0	23	40	9	4	0	0	0	0	3	0	0	.000	3	6	0	0	0.6	1.000

Nick Altrock

ALTROCK, NICHOLAS BB TL 5′10″ 197 lbs.
B. Sept. 15, 1876, Cincinnati, Ohio D. Jan. 20, 1965, Washington, D. C.

Year	Team		W	L	PCT	ERA	G	GS	CG	IP	H	BB	SO	ShO	Relief Pitching W	Relief Pitching L	Relief Pitching SV	Batting AB	Batting H	Batting HR	BA	PO	A	E	DP	TC/G	FA
1898	LOU	N	3	3	.500	4.50	11	7	6	70	89	21	13	0	0	0	0	29	7	0	.241	3	26	0	2	2.6	1.000
1902	BOS	A	0	2	.000	2.00	3	2	1	18	19	7	5	0	0	0	1	8	0	0	.000	1	8	2	1	3.7	.818
1903	2 teams	BOS A	(1G 0–1)		CHI A	(12G 4–3)																					
″	total		4	4	.500	2.85	13	9	7	79	72	23	22	1	0	0	0	33	11	0	.333	7	44	3	1	4.2	.944
1904	CHI	A	19	14	.576	2.96	38	36	31	307	274	48	87	6	0	0	1	111	22	1	.198	43	114	5	3	4.3	.969
1905			23	12	.657	1.88	38	34	31	315.2	274	63	97	3	2	1	0	114	14	0	.123	36	132	2	10	4.4	.988
1906			20	13	.606	2.06	38	30	25	287.2	269	42	99	4	**5**	1	0	100	16	0	.160	29	102	4	5	3.5	.970
1907			7	13	.350	2.57	30	21	15	213.2	210	31	61	1	2	1	2	72	13	0	.181	26	89	5	0	4.0	.958
1908			5	7	.417	2.71	23	13	8	136	127	18	21	1	1	0	2	49	10	0	.204	20	67	3	0	3.9	.967
1909	2 teams	CHI A	(1G 0–1)		WAS A	(9G 1–3)																					
″	total		1	4	.200	5.36	10	6	3	47	71	6	11	0	0	0	0	22	1	0	.045	11	16	3	0	2.5	.900
1912	WAS	A	0	1	.000	13.50	1	0	0	1.1	1	2	0	0	0	1	0	1	0	0	.000	3	0	1	0	2.0	.750
1913			0	0	—	4.82	4	0	0	9.1	7	4	2	0	0	0	0	1	0	0	.000	1	4	1	0	1.5	.833
1914			0	0	—	0.00	1	0	0	1	3	0	0	0	0	0	0	0	0	0	—	0	0	0	0	0.0	.000
1915			0	0	—	9.00	1	0	0	3	7	1	2	0	0	0	1	1	0	0	.000	0	0	0	0	0.0	.000
1918			1	2	.333	2.96	5	3	1	24.1	24	6	5	0	0	0	0	8	1	1	.125	3	8	1	1	2.4	.917
1919			0	0	—	∞	1	0	0		4	0	0	0	0	0	0	0	0	0	—	0	0	0	0	0.0	.000
1924			0	0	—	0.00	1	0	0	2	4	0	0	0	0	0	0	1	1	0	1.000	0	2	1	0	3.0	.667
16 yrs.			83	75	.525	2.67	218	161	128	1515	1455	272	425	16	10	4	7	552	97	2	.176	183	612	31	23	3.7	.962
WORLD SERIES																											
1906	CHI	A	1	1	.500	1.00	2	2	2	18	11	2	5	0	0	0	0	4	1	0	.250	6	11	0	2	8.5	1.000

Jose Alvarez

ALVAREZ, JOSE LINO BR TR 5′10″ 170 lbs.
B. Apr. 12, 1956, Tampa, Fla.

Year	Team		W	L	PCT	ERA	G	GS	CG	IP	H	BB	SO	ShO	Relief Pitching W	Relief Pitching L	Relief Pitching SV	Batting AB	Batting H	Batting HR	BA	PO	A	E	DP	TC/G	FA
1981	ATL	N	0	0	—	0.00	1	0	0	2	0	0	2	0	0	0	0	0	0	0	—	0	0	0	0	0.0	.000
1982			0	0	—	4.70	7	0	0	7.2	8	2	6	0	0	0	0	0	0	0	—	0	2	0	0	0.3	1.000
1988			5	6	.455	2.99	60	0	0	102.1	88	53	81	0	5	6	3	8	3	0	.375	11	17	0	4	0.5	1.000
1989			3	3	.500	2.86	30	0	0	50.1	44	24	45	0	3	3	2	3	0	0	.000	5	8	0	1	0.4	1.000
4 yrs.			8	9	.471	2.99	98	0	0	162.1	140	79	134	0	8	9	5	11	3	0	.273	16	27	0	5	0.4	1.000

Tavo Alvarez

ALVAREZ, CESAR OCTAVIO BR TR 6′ 3″ 245 lbs.
B. Nov. 25, 1971, Ciudad Obregon, Mexico.

Year	Team		W	L	PCT	ERA	G	GS	CG	IP	H	BB	SO	ShO	Relief Pitching W	Relief Pitching L	Relief Pitching SV	Batting AB	Batting H	Batting HR	BA	PO	A	E	DP	TC/G	FA
1995	MON	N	1	5	.167	6.75	8	8	0	37.1	46	14	17	0	0	0	0	12	0	0	.000	3	4	1	1	1.0	.875

Wilson Alvarez

ALVAREZ, WILSON EDUARDO BL TL 6′ 1″ 175 lbs.
Born Wilson Eduardo Alvarez (Funemayor).
B. Mar. 24, 1970, Maracaibo, Venezuela.

Year	Team		W	L	PCT	ERA	G	GS	CG	IP	H	BB	SO	ShO	Relief Pitching W	Relief Pitching L	Relief Pitching SV	Batting AB	Batting H	Batting HR	BA	PO	A	E	DP	TC/G	FA
1989	TEX	A	0	1	.000	∞	1	1	0		3	2	0	0	0	0	0	0	0	0	—	0	0	0	0	0.0	.000
1991	CHI	A	3	2	.600	3.51	10	9	2	56.1	47	29	32	1	0	0	0	0	0	0	—	1	7	0	1	0.8	1.000
1992			5	3	.625	5.20	34	9	0	100.1	103	65	66	0	2	2	1	0	0	0	—	4	14	2	1	0.6	.900
1993			15	8	.652	2.95	31	31	1	207.2	168	**122**	155	1	0	0	0	0	0	0	—	5	28	1	2	1.1	.971
1994			12	8	.600	3.45	24	24	2	161.2	147	62	108	1	0	0	0	0	0	0	—	6	13	0	1	0.8	1.000
1995			8	11	.421	4.32	29	29	3	175	171	93	118	0	0	0	0	0	0	0	—	7	31	0	1	1.3	1.000
6 yrs.			43	33	.566	3.81	129	103	8	701	639	373	479	3	2	2	1	0	0	0		23	93	3	6	0.9	.975
LEAGUE CHAMPIONSHIP SERIES																											
1993	CHI	A	1	0	1.000	1.00	1	1	1	9	7	2	6	0	0	0	0	0	0	0	—	0	2	0	1	2.0	1.000

Red Ames

AMES, LEON KESSLING BB TR 5′10½″ 185 lbs.
B. Aug. 2, 1882, Warren, Ohio D. Oct. 8, 1936, Warren, Ohio.

Year	Team		W	L	PCT	ERA	G	GS	CG	IP	H	BB	SO	ShO	Relief Pitching W	Relief Pitching L	Relief Pitching SV	Batting AB	Batting H	Batting HR	BA	PO	A	E	DP	TC/G	FA
1903	NY	N	2	0	1.000	1.29	2	2	2	14	5	8	14	1	0	0	0	6	0	0	.000	0	0	0	0	0.0	.000
1904			4	6	.400	2.27	16	13	11	115	94	38	93	1	0	0	3	40	5	0	.125	5	26	4	1	2.2	.886
1905			22	8	.733	2.74	34	31	21	263	220	105	198	2	1	0	0	97	14	0	.144	12	69	5	1	2.5	.942
1906			12	10	.545	2.66	31	25	15	203.1	166	93	156	1	1	0	1	61	4	0	.066	10	66	5	0	2.6	.938
1907			10	12	.455	2.16	39	26	17	233.1	184	108	146	2	0	3	1	69	12	1	.174	11	76	8	0	2.4	.916
1908			7	4	.636	1.81	18	15	5	114.1	96	27	81	0	1	0	0	36	7	0	.194	5	32	3	4	2.2	.925
1909			15	10	.600	2.70	34	26	20	240	214	81	156	2	1	0	1	81	6	0	.074	11	99	9	1	3.5	.924
1910			12	11	.522	2.22	33	23	13	190.1	161	63	94	3	0	3	0	62	11	1	.177	11	68	8	4	2.6	.908
1911			11	10	.524	2.68	34	23	13	205	170	54	118	1	2	1	1	64	6	0	.094	7	69	7	0	2.4	.916
1912			11	5	.688	2.46	33	22	9	179	194	35	83	2	2	0	1	58	13	0	.224	6	53	1	3	1.8	.983
1913	2 teams	NY N	(8G 2–1)		CIN N	(31G 11–13)																					
″	total		13	14	.481	2.78	39	29	14	227	220	78	110	1	2	1	3	72	8	0	.111	2	67	1	2	1.8	.986
1914	CIN	N	15	**23**	.395	2.64	47	36	18	297	274	94	128	4	1	4	**6**	94	12	1	.128	8	99	9	3	2.5	.922
1915	2 teams	CIN N	(17G 2–4)		STL N	(15G 9–3)																					
″	total		11	7	.611	3.23	32	21	12	181.1	175	56	74	3	0	0	2	55	5	0	.091	5	61	2	1	2.1	.971
1916	STL	N	11	16	.407	2.64	45	25	10	228	225	57	98	2	4	**5**	**7**	68	12	0	.176	3	56	6	0	1.4	.908
1917			15	10	.600	2.71	43	19	10	209	189	57	62	2	**8**	2	3	64	12	0	.188	4	83	2	4	2.1	.978

Red Ames *continued*

Year	Team	W	L	PCT	ERA	G	GS	CG	IP	H	BB	SO	ShO	Relief Pitching W	Relief Pitching L	Relief Pitching SV	Batting AB	Batting H	Batting HR	BA	PO	A	E	DP	TC/G	FA
1918		9	14	.391	2.31	27	25	17	206.2	192	52	68	0	0	0	1	64	10	0	.156	6	57	3	1	2.4	.955
1919	2 teams STL N (23G 3–5) PHI N (3G 0–2)																									
"	total	3	7	.300	5.13	26	8	2	86	114	28	23	0	2	0	2	23	6	0	.261	1	19	1	0	0.8	.952
17 yrs.		183	167	.523	2.63	533	369	209	3192.1	2893	1034	1702	27	25	19	32	1014	143	3	.141	107	1000	74	25	2.2	.937
WORLD SERIES																										
1905	NY N	0	0	—	0.00	1	0	0	1	1	1	1	0	0	0	0	0	0	0	—	0	1	0	0	1.0	1.000
1911		0	1	.000	2.25	2	1	0	8	6	1	6	0	0	0	0	2	1	0	.500	0	2	1	0	1.5	.667
1912		0	0	—	4.50	1	0	0	2	3	1	0	0	0	0	0	0	0	0	—	0	1	0	0	1.0	1.000
3 yrs.		0	1	.000	2.45	4	1	0	11	10	3	7	0	0	0	0	2	1	0	.500	0	4	1	0	1.3	.800

Doc Amole

AMOLE, MORRIS GEORGE BR TL 5′ 9″ 165 lbs.
B. July 5, 1878, Coatesville, Pa. D. Mar. 7, 1912, Wilmington, Del.

Year	Team	W	L	PCT	ERA	G	GS	CG	IP	H	BB	SO	ShO	Relief Pitching W	Relief Pitching L	Relief Pitching SV	Batting AB	Batting H	Batting HR	BA	PO	A	E	DP	TC/G	FA
1897	BAL N	4	4	.500	2.57	11	7	6	70	67	17	19	0	1	0	0	28	3	0	.107	2	19	3	0	2.2	.875
1898	WAS N	0	6	.000	7.84	7	5	4	49.1	83	22	11	0	0	1	0	20	2	0	.100	4	16	3	0	3.3	.870
2 yrs.		4	10	.286	4.75	18	12	10	119.1	150	39	30	0	1	1	0	48	5	0	.104	6	35	6	0	2.6	.872

Vincente Amor

AMOR, VINCENTE BR TR 6′ 3″ 182 lbs.
Born Vincente (Alvarez).
B. Aug. 8, 1932, Havana, Cuba.

Year	Team	W	L	PCT	ERA	G	GS	CG	IP	H	BB	SO	ShO	Relief Pitching W	Relief Pitching L	Relief Pitching SV	Batting AB	Batting H	Batting HR	BA	PO	A	E	DP	TC/G	FA
1955	CHI N	0	1	.000	4.50	4	0	0	6	11	3	3	0	0	1	0	0	0	0	—	0	4	0	0	1.0	1.000
1957	CIN N	1	2	.333	5.93	9	4	1	27.1	39	10	9	0	0	1	0	6	1	0	.167	2	3	0	0	0.6	1.000
2 yrs.		1	3	.250	5.67	13	4	1	33.1	50	13	12	0	0	2	0	6	1	0	.167	2	7	0	0	0.7	1.000

Walter Ancker

ANCKER, WALTER (Gee, Liver) BR TR 6′ 1″ 190 lbs.
B. Apr. 10, 1894, New York, N. Y. D. Feb. 13, 1954, Englewood, N. J.

Year	Team	W	L	PCT	ERA	G	GS	CG	IP	H	BB	SO	ShO	Relief Pitching W	Relief Pitching L	Relief Pitching SV	Batting AB	Batting H	Batting HR	BA	PO	A	E	DP	TC/G	FA
1915	PHI A	0	0	—	3.57	4	1	0	17.2	19	17	4	0	0	0	0	6	0	0	.000	1	5	0	1	1.5	1.000

Larry Andersen

ANDERSEN, LARRY EUGENE BR TR 6′ 3″ 200 lbs.
B. May 6, 1953, Portland, Ore.

Year	Team	W	L	PCT	ERA	G	GS	CG	IP	H	BB	SO	ShO	Relief Pitching W	Relief Pitching L	Relief Pitching SV	Batting AB	Batting H	Batting HR	BA	PO	A	E	DP	TC/G	FA
1975	CLE A	0	0	—	4.76	3	0	0	5.2	4	2	4	0	0	0	0	0	0	0	—	1	1	0	0	0.7	1.000
1977		0	1	.000	3.21	11	0	0	14	10	9	8	0	0	1	0	0	0	0	—	3	6	2	4	1.0	.818
1979		0	0	—	7.41	8	0	0	17	25	4	7	0	0	0	0	0	0	0	—	0	4	0	1	0.5	1.000
1981	SEA A	3	3	.500	2.65	41	0	0	68	57	18	40	0	3	3	5	0	0	0	—	5	9	0	1	0.3	1.000
1982		0	0	—	5.99	40	1	0	79.2	100	23	32	0	0	0	1	0	0	0	—	8	14	0	2	0.6	1.000
1983	PHI N	1	0	1.000	2.39	17	0	0	26.1	19	9	14	0	1	0	0	2	0	0	.000	2	6	0	0	0.5	1.000
1984		3	7	.300	2.38	64	0	0	90.2	85	25	54	0	3	7	4	4	0	0	.000	5	16	4	1	0.4	.840
1985		3	3	.500	4.32	57	0	0	73	78	26	50	0	3	3	3	4	0	0	.000	5	21	2	2	0.5	.929
1986	2 teams PHI N (10G 0–0) HOU N (38G 2–1)																									
"	total	2	1	.667	3.03	48	0	0	77.1	83	26	42	0	2	1	1	6	0	0	.000	10	11	2	3	0.5	.913
1987	HOU N	9	5	.643	3.45	67	0	0	101.2	95	41	94	0	9	5	5	6	1	0	.167	12	10	3	0	0.4	.880
1988		2	4	.333	2.94	53	0	0	82.2	82	20	66	0	2	4	5	6	2	0	.333	9	9	2	1	0.4	.900
1989		4	4	.500	1.54	60	0	0	87.2	63	24	85	0	4	4	3	3	1	0	.333	10	13	4	0	0.4	.852
1990	2 teams HOU N (50G 5–2) BOS A (15G 0–0)																									
"	total	5	2	.714	1.79	65	0	0	95.2	79	27	93	0	5	2	7	3	0	0	.000	13	12	2	1	0.4	.926
1991	SD N	3	4	.429	2.30	38	0	0	47	39	13	40	0	3	4	13	2	0	0	.000	5	7	1	0	0.3	.923
1992		1	1	.500	3.34	34	0	0	35	26	8	35	0	1	1	2	1	0	0	.000	4	5	1	0	0.3	.900
1993	PHI N	3	2	.600	2.92	64	0	0	61.2	54	21	67	0	3	2	0	1	1	0	1.000	3	4	1	1	0.1	.875
1994		1	2	.333	4.41	29	0	0	32.2	33	15	27	0	1	2	0	0	0	0	—	2	3	1	0	0.2	.833
17 yrs.		40	39	.506	3.15	699	1	0	995.2	932	311	758	0	40	39	49	38	5	0	.132	97	151	25	17	0.4	.908
LEAGUE CHAMPIONSHIP SERIES																										
1986	HOU N	0	0	—	0.00	2	0	0	5	1	2	3	0	0	0	0	0	0	0	—	0	0	0	0	0.0	.000
1990	BOS A	0	1	.000	6.00	3	0	0	3	3	3	3	0	0	1	0	0	0	0	—	1	0	0	0	0.3	1.000
1993	PHI N	0	0	—	15.43	3	0	0	2.1	4	1	3	0	0	0	1	0	0	0	—	0	1	0	0	0.3	1.000
3 yrs.		0	1	.000	5.23	8	0	0	10.1	8	6	9	0	0	1	1	0	0	0	—	1	1	0	0	0.3	1.000
WORLD SERIES																										
1983	PHI N	0	0	—	2.25	2	0	0	4	4	0	1	0	0	0	0	0	0	0	—	1	1	0	1	1.0	1.000
1993		0	0	—	12.27	4	0	0	3.2	5	3	3	0	0	0	0	0	0	0	—	0	0	0	0	0.0	.000
2 yrs.		0	0	—	7.04	6	0	0	7.2	9	3	4	0	0	0	0	0	0	0	—	1	1	0	1	0.3	1.000

Allan Anderson

ANDERSON, ALLAN LEE BL TL 5′11½″ 178 lbs.
B. Jan. 7, 1964, Lancaster, Ohio.

Year	Team	W	L	PCT	ERA	G	GS	CG	IP	H	BB	SO	ShO	Relief Pitching W	Relief Pitching L	Relief Pitching SV	Batting AB	Batting H	Batting HR	BA	PO	A	E	DP	TC/G	FA
1986	MIN A	3	6	.333	5.55	21	10	1	84.1	106	30	51	0	1	1	1	0	0	0	—	4	14	1	1	0.9	.947
1987		1	0	1.000	10.95	4	2	0	12.1	20	10	3	0	0	0	0	0	0	0	—	1	0	0	0	0.3	1.000
1988		16	9	.640	**2.45**	30	30	3	202.1	199	37	83	1	0	0	0	0	0	0	—	9	34	2	3	1.5	.956
1989		17	10	.630	3.80	33	33	4	196.2	214	53	69	1	0	0	0	1	0	0	.000	12	27	1	5	1.2	.975
1990		7	18	.280	4.53	31	31	5	188.2	214	39	82	1	0	0	0	0	0	0	—	7	37	0	2	1.4	1.000
1991		5	11	.313	4.96	29	22	2	134.1	148	42	51	0	0	2	0	0	0	0	—	8	19	0	1	0.9	1.000
6 yrs.		49	54	.476	4.11	148	128	15	818.2	901	211	339	3	1	3	1	1	0	0	.000	41	131	4	12	1.2	.977

Bill Anderson

ANDERSON, WILLIAM EDWARD (Lefty) BR TL 6′ 1″ 165 lbs.
B. Nov. 28, 1895, Boston, Mass. D. Mar. 13, 1983, Medford, Mass.

Year	Team	W	L	PCT	ERA	G	GS	CG	IP	H	BB	SO	ShO	Relief Pitching W	Relief Pitching L	Relief Pitching SV	Batting AB	Batting H	Batting HR	BA	PO	A	E	DP	TC/G	FA
1925	BOS N	0	0	—	10.13	2	0	0	2.2	5	2	1	0	0	0	0	1	0	0	.000	0	0	0	0	0.0	.000

Bob Anderson

ANDERSON, ROBERT CARL BR TR 6′ 4½″ 210 lbs.
B. Sept. 29, 1935, East Chicago, Ind.

Year	Team	W	L	PCT	ERA	G	GS	CG	IP	H	BB	SO	ShO	Relief Pitching W	Relief Pitching L	Relief Pitching SV	Batting AB	Batting H	Batting HR	BA	PO	A	E	DP	TC/G	FA
1957	CHI N	0	1	.000	7.71	8	0	0	16.1	20	8	7	0	0	1	0	4	0	0	.000	0	5	2	0	0.9	.714
1958		3	3	.500	3.97	17	8	2	65.2	61	29	51	0	0	0	0	17	2	0	.118	3	11	0	0	0.8	1.000
1959		12	13	.480	4.13	37	36	7	235.1	245	77	113	1	0	0	0	80	6	0	.075	13	43	4	4	1.6	.933
1960		9	11	.450	4.11	38	30	5	203.2	201	68	115	0	0	1	1	71	12	0	.169	10	43	4	2	1.5	.930
1961		7	10	.412	4.26	57	12	1	152	162	56	96	0	4	3	8	42	6	2	.143	14	38	0	7	0.9	1.000

Bob Anderson *continued*

Year	Team	Lg	W	L	PCT	ERA	G	GS	CG	IP	H	BB	SO	ShO	Relief W	Relief L	Relief SV	AB	H	HR	BA	PO	A	E	DP	TC/G	FA
1962			2	7	.222	5.02	57	4	0	107.2	111	60	82	0	1	6	4	23	3	0	.130	4	16	1	1	0.4	.952
1963	DET	A	3	1	.750	3.30	32	3	0	60	58	21	38	0	2	0	0	9	4	0	.444	2	9	2	0	0.4	.846
7 yrs.			36	46	.439	4.26	246	93	15	840.2	858	319	502	1	7	11	13	246	33	2	.134	46	165	13	14	0.9	.942

Brian Anderson

ANDERSON, BRIAN JAMES BL TL 6′ 1″ 190 lbs.
B. Apr. 26, 1972, Portsmouth, Va.

Year	Team	Lg	W	L	PCT	ERA	G	GS	CG	IP	H	BB	SO	ShO	Relief W	Relief L	Relief SV	AB	H	HR	BA	PO	A	E	DP	TC/G	FA
1993	CAL	A	0	0	—	3.97	4	1	0	11.1	11	2	4	0	0	0	0	0	0	0	—	0	1	0	0	0.3	1.000
1994			7	5	.583	5.22	18	18	0	101.2	120	27	47	0	0	0	0	0	0	0	—	6	10	1	0	0.9	.941
1995			6	8	.429	5.87	18	17	1	99.2	110	30	45	0	0	0	0	0	0	0	—	4	16	2	1	1.2	.909
3 yrs.			13	13	.500	5.46	40	36	1	212.2	241	59	96	0	0	0	0	0	0	0		10	27	3	1	1.0	.925

Bud Anderson

ANDERSON, KARL ADAM BR TR 6′ 3″ 210 lbs.
B. May 27, 1956, Westbury, N. Y.

Year	Team	Lg	W	L	PCT	ERA	G	GS	CG	IP	H	BB	SO	ShO	Relief W	Relief L	Relief SV	AB	H	HR	BA	PO	A	E	DP	TC/G	FA
1982	CLE	A	3	4	.429	3.35	25	5	1	80.2	84	30	44	0	2	1	0	0	0	0	—	10	8	1	0	0.8	.947
1983			1	6	.143	4.08	39	1	0	68.1	64	32	32	0	1	5	7	0	0	0	—	3	6	2	0	0.3	.818
2 yrs.			4	10	.286	3.68	64	6	1	149	148	62	76	0	3	6	7	0	0	0		13	14	3	0	0.5	.900

Craig Anderson

ANDERSON, NORMAN CRAIG BR TR 6′ 2″ 205 lbs.
B. July 1, 1938, Washington, D. C.

Year	Team	Lg	W	L	PCT	ERA	G	GS	CG	IP	H	BB	SO	ShO	Relief W	Relief L	Relief SV	AB	H	HR	BA	PO	A	E	DP	TC/G	FA
1961	STL	N	4	3	.571	3.26	25	0	0	38.2	38	12	21	0	4	3	1	9	3	0	.333	3	7	0	0	0.4	1.000
1962	NY	N	3	17	.150	5.35	50	14	2	131.1	150	63	62	0	3	6	4	32	3	0	.094	8	36	2	3	0.9	.957
1963			0	2	.000	8.68	3	2	0	9.1	17	3	6	0	0	0	0	3	1	0	.333	1	2	1	0	1.3	.750
1964			0	1	.000	5.54	4	1	0	13	21	3	5	0	0	0	0	3	0	0	.000	0	3	0	1	0.8	1.000
4 yrs.			7	23	.233	5.10	82	17	2	192.1	226	81	94	0	7	9	5	47	7	0	.149	12	48	3	4	0.8	.952

Dave Anderson

ANDERSON, DAVID S. TL
B. Oct. 10, 1868, Chester, Pa. D. Mar. 22, 1897, Chester, Pa.

Year	Team	Lg	W	L	PCT	ERA	G	GS	CG	IP	H	BB	SO	ShO	Relief W	Relief L	Relief SV	AB	H	HR	BA	PO	A	E	DP	TC/G	FA
1889	PHI	N	0	1	.000	7.43	5	2	1	23	30	14	8	0	0	0	0	11	2	0	.182	0	7	0	0	1.4	1.000
1890	2 teams	PHI N (3G 1–1)	PIT N (13G 2–11)																								
″	total		3	12	.200	5.09	16	15	14	127.1	147	60	48	0	0	0	0	51	4	0	.078	4	42	1	0	2.9	.979
2 yrs.			3	13	.188	5.45	21	17	15	150.1	177	74	56	0	0	0	0	62	6	0	.097	4	49	1	0	2.6	.981

Fred Anderson

ANDERSON, JOHN FREDERICK (Spitball) BR TR 6′ 2″ 180 lbs.
B. Dec. 11, 1885, Calahan, N. C. D. Nov. 8, 1957, Winston-Salem, N. C.

Year	Team	Lg	W	L	PCT	ERA	G	GS	CG	IP	H	BB	SO	ShO	Relief W	Relief L	Relief SV	AB	H	HR	BA	PO	A	E	DP	TC/G	FA
1909	BOS	A	0	0	—	1.13	1	1	0	8	3	1	5	0	0	0	0	3	0	0	.000	0	2	0	1	2.0	1.000
1913			0	6	.000	5.97	10	8	4	57.1	84	21	32	0	0	0	0	20	1	0	.050	5	13	1	0	1.9	.947
1914	BUF	F	13	16	.448	3.08	37	28	21	260.1	243	64	144	2	1	2	0	90	17	0	.189	7	69	3	2	2.1	.962
1915			19	13	.594	2.51	36	28	14	240	192	72	142	5	4	0	0	80	12	0	.150	5	65	4	2	2.1	.946
1916	NY	N	9	13	.409	3.40	38	27	13	188	206	38	98	2	0	1	2	58	8	0	.138	2	38	0	0	1.1	1.000
1917			8	8	.500	1.44	38	18	8	162	122	34	69	1	2	1	3	42	3	0	.071	0	46	1	0	1.2	.979
1918			4	2	.667	2.67	18	4	2	70.2	62	17	24	1	2	1	**3**	19	0	0	.000	4	34	0	0	2.1	1.000
7 yrs.			53	58	.477	2.86	178	114	62	986.1	912	247	514	11	9	5	8	312	41	0	.131	23	267	9	5	1.7	.970
WORLD SERIES																											
1917	NY	N	0	1	.000	18.00	1	0	0	2	5	0	3	0	0	1	0	0	0	0	—	0	1	0	0	1.0	1.000

John Anderson

ANDERSON, JOHN CHARLES BR TR 6′ 1″ 190 lbs.
B. Nov. 23, 1932, St. Paul, Minn.

Year	Team	Lg	W	L	PCT	ERA	G	GS	CG	IP	H	BB	SO	ShO	Relief W	Relief L	Relief SV	AB	H	HR	BA	PO	A	E	DP	TC/G	FA
1958	PHI	N	0	0	—	7.88	5	1	0	16	26	4	9	0	0	0	0	3	0	0	.000	0	2	0	0	0.4	1.000
1960	BAL	A	0	0	—	13.50	4	0	0	4.2	8	4	1	0	0	0	0	0	0	0	—	2	2	0	0	1.0	1.000
1962	2 teams	STL N (5G 0–0)	HOU N (10G 0–0)																								
″	total		0	0		4.13	15	0	0	24	30	6	9	0	0	0	1	2	0	0	.000	1	6	0	0	0.5	1.000
3 yrs.			0	0		6.45	24	1	0	44.2	64	14	19	0	0	0	1	5	0	0	.000	3	10	0	0	0.5	1.000

Larry Anderson

ANDERSON, LAWRENCE DENNIS BR TR 6′ 3″ 190 lbs.
B. Dec. 3, 1952, Maywood, Calif.

Year	Team	Lg	W	L	PCT	ERA	G	GS	CG	IP	H	BB	SO	ShO	Relief W	Relief L	Relief SV	AB	H	HR	BA	PO	A	E	DP	TC/G	FA
1974	MIL	A	0	0	—	0.00	2	0	0	2	2	1	3	0	0	0	0	0	0	0	—	1	0	0	0	0.5	1.000
1975			1	0	1.000	5.04	8	1	1	30.1	36	6	13	1	0	0	0	0	0	0	—	2	5	0	0	0.9	1.000
1977	CHI	A	1	3	.250	9.00	6	0	0	9	10	15	7	0	1	3	0	0	0	0	—	1	0	0	0	0.2	1.000
3 yrs.			2	3	.400	5.66	16	1	1	41.1	48	22	23	1	1	3	0	0	0	0		4	5	0	0	0.6	1.000

Mike Anderson

ANDERSON, MICHAEL ALLEN BR TR 6′ 2″ 200 lbs.
Brother of Kent Anderson.
B. June 22, 1951, Florence, S. C.

Year	Team	Lg	W	L	PCT	ERA	G	GS	CG	IP	H	BB	SO	ShO	Relief W	Relief L	Relief SV	AB	H	HR	BA	PO	A	E	DP	TC/G	FA
1979	PHI	N	0	0	—	0.00	1	0	0	1	2	0	2	0	0	0	0	*				67	1	1	0	2.7	.986

Mike Anderson

ANDERSON, MICHAEL JAMES BR TR 6′ 3″ 200 lbs.
B. July 30, 1966, Austin, Tex.

Year	Team	Lg	W	L	PCT	ERA	G	GS	CG	IP	H	BB	SO	ShO	Relief W	Relief L	Relief SV	AB	H	HR	BA	PO	A	E	DP	TC/G	FA
1993	CIN	N	0	0	—	18.56	3	0	0	5.1	12	3	4	0	0	0	0	1	0	0	.000	0	1	0	0	0.3	1.000

Red Anderson

ANDERSON, ARNOLD REVOLA BR TR 6′ 3″ 210 lbs.
B. June 19, 1912, Lawton, Iowa D. Aug. 7, 1972, Sioux City, Iowa.

Year	Team	Lg	W	L	PCT	ERA	G	GS	CG	IP	H	BB	SO	ShO	Relief W	Relief L	Relief SV	AB	H	HR	BA	PO	A	E	DP	TC/G	FA
1937	WAS	A	0	1	.000	6.75	2	1	0	10.2	11	11	3	0	0	0	0	3	0	0	.000	0	3	1	0	2.0	.750
1940			1	1	.500	3.86	2	2	2	14	12	5	3	0	0	0	0	5	3	0	.600	0	3	0	1	1.5	1.000
1941			4	6	.400	4.18	32	6	1	112	127	53	34	0	2	3	0	31	8	0	.258	3	18	0	1	0.7	1.000
3 yrs.			5	8	.385	4.35	36	9	3	136.2	150	69	40	0	2	3	0	39	11	0	.282	3	24	1	2	0.8	.964

Rick Anderson

ANDERSON, RICHARD ARLEN BR TR 6′ 175 lbs.
B. Nov. 29, 1956, Everett, Wash.

Year	Team	Lg	W	L	PCT	ERA	G	GS	CG	IP	H	BB	SO	ShO	Relief W	Relief L	Relief SV	AB	H	HR	BA	PO	A	E	DP	TC/G	FA
1986	NY	N	2	1	.667	2.72	15	5	0	49.2	45	11	21	0	0	0	1	11	1	0	.091	8	4	0	0	0.8	1.000
1987	KC	A	0	2	.000	13.85	6	2	0	13	26	9	12	0	0	0	0	0	0	0	—	1	3	0	0	0.7	1.000
1988			2	1	.667	4.24	7	3	0	34	41	9	9	0	2	0	0	0	0	0	—	1	3	0	0	0.6	1.000
3 yrs.			4	4	.500	4.75	28	10	0	96.2	112	29	42	0	2	0	1	11	1	0	.091	10	10	0	0	0.7	1.000

Rick Anderson

ANDERSON, RICHARD LEE BR TR 6′ 2″ 210 lbs.
B. Dec. 25, 1953, Inglewood, Calif. D. June 23, 1989, Wilmington, Calif.

Year	Team	W	L	PCT	ERA	G	GS	CG	IP	H	BB	SO	ShO	Relief Pitching W	L	SV	Batting AB	H	HR	BA	PO	A	E	DP	TC/G	FA
1979	NY A	0	0	—	4.50	1	0	0	2	1	4	0	0	0	0	0	0	0	0	—	0	3	0	0	3.0	1.000
1980	SEA A	0	0	—	3.60	5	2	0	10	8	10	7	0	0	0	0	0	0	0	—	0	0	1	0	0.2	.000
2 yrs.		0	0		3.75	6	2	0	12	9	14	7	0	0	0	0	0	0	0		0	3	1	0	0.7	.750

Scott Anderson

ANDERSON, SCOTT RICHARD BR TR 6′ 6″ 190 lbs.
B. Aug. 1, 1962, Corvallis, Ore.

Year	Team	W	L	PCT	ERA	G	GS	CG	IP	H	BB	SO	ShO	Relief Pitching W	L	SV	Batting AB	H	HR	BA	PO	A	E	DP	TC/G	FA
1987	TEX A	0	1	.000	9.53	8	0	0	11.1	17	8	6	0	0	1	0	0	0	0	—	2	3	0	1	0.6	1.000
1990	MON N	0	1	.000	3.00	4	3	0	18	12	5	16	0	0	0	0	4	0	0	.000	0	2	0	0	0.5	1.000
1995	KC A	1	0	1.000	5.33	6	4	0	25.1	29	8	6	0	0	0	0	0	0	0	—	2	3	0	0	0.8	1.000
3 yrs.		1	2	.333	5.43	18	7	0	54.2	58	21	28	0	0	1	0	4	0	0	.000	4	8	0	1	0.7	1.000

Varney Anderson

ANDERSON, VARNEY SAMUEL BR TR 5′10″ 165 lbs.
B. June 18, 1866, Geneva, Ill. D. Nov. 5, 1941, Rockford, Ill.

Year	Team	W	L	PCT	ERA	G	GS	CG	IP	H	BB	SO	ShO	Relief Pitching W	L	SV	Batting AB	H	HR	BA	PO	A	E	DP	TC/G	FA
1889	IND N	0	1	.000	4.50	2	1	1	12	13	9	3	0	0	0	0	5	0	0	.000	0	3	1	0	2.0	.750
1894	WAS N	0	2	.000	7.07	2	2	2	14	15	6	3	0	0	0	0	7	3	0	.429	1	2	1	0	2.0	.750
1895		9	16	.360	5.89	29	25	18	204.2	288	97	35	0	0	0	0	97	28	0	.289	10	49	8	4	2.2	.881
1896		0	1	.000	13.00	2	2	1	9	23	3	0	0	0	0	0	5	3	0	.600	0	0	1	0	0.5	.000
4 yrs.		9	20	.310	6.16	35	30	22	239.2	339	115	41	0	0	0	0	114	34	0	.298	11	54	11	4	2.1	.855

Walter Anderson

ANDERSON, WALTER CARL (Lefty) BL TL 6′ 2″ 160 lbs.
B. Sept. 25, 1897, Grand Rapids, Mich. D. Jan. 6, 1990, Battle Creek, Mich.

Year	Team	W	L	PCT	ERA	G	GS	CG	IP	H	BB	SO	ShO	Relief Pitching W	L	SV	Batting AB	H	HR	BA	PO	A	E	DP	TC/G	FA
1917	PHI A	0	0	—	3.03	14	2	0	38.2	32	21	10	0	0	0	0	7	3	0	.429	4	9	1	0	1.0	.929
1919		1	0	1.000	3.86	3	0	0	14	13	8	10	0	1	0	0	4	0	0	.000	0	4	0	0	1.3	1.000
2 yrs.		1	0	1.000	3.25	17	2	0	52.2	45	29	20	0	1	0	0	11	3	0	.273	4	13	1	0	1.1	.944

Wingo Anderson

ANDERSON, WINGO CHARLIE BR TL 5′10½″ 150 lbs.
B. Aug. 13, 1886, Alvarado, Tex. D. Dec. 19, 1950, Fort Worth, Tex.

Year	Team	W	L	PCT	ERA	G	GS	CG	IP	H	BB	SO	ShO	Relief Pitching W	L	SV	Batting AB	H	HR	BA	PO	A	E	DP	TC/G	FA
1910	CIN N	0	0	—	4.67	7	2	0	17.1	16	17	11	0	0	0	0	5	1	0	.200	2	0	0	0	0.3	1.000

John Andre

ANDRE, JOHN EDWARD (Long John) BL TR 6′ 4″ 200 lbs.
B. Jan. 3, 1923, Brockton, Mass. D. Nov. 25, 1976, Centerville, Mass.

Year	Team	W	L	PCT	ERA	G	GS	CG	IP	H	BB	SO	ShO	Relief Pitching W	L	SV	Batting AB	H	HR	BA	PO	A	E	DP	TC/G	FA
1955	CHI N	0	1	.000	5.80	22	3	0	45	45	28	19	0	0	1	1	9	1	0	.111	2	6	0	0	0.4	1.000

Elbert Andrews

ANDREWS, ELBERT DeVORE BL TR 6′ 175 lbs.
B. Dec. 11, 1901, Greenwood, S. C. D. Nov. 25, 1979, Greenwood, S. C.

Year	Team	W	L	PCT	ERA	G	GS	CG	IP	H	BB	SO	ShO	Relief Pitching W	L	SV	Batting AB	H	HR	BA	PO	A	E	DP	TC/G	FA
1925	PHI A	0	0	—	10.13	6	0	0	8	12	11	0	0	0	0	0	0	0	0	—	0	2	0	0	0.3	1.000

Hub Andrews

ANDREWS, HERBERT CARL (Tuny) BR TR 6′ 170 lbs.
B. Aug. 31, 1922, Burbank, Calif.

Year	Team	W	L	PCT	ERA	G	GS	CG	IP	H	BB	SO	ShO	Relief Pitching W	L	SV	Batting AB	H	HR	BA	PO	A	E	DP	TC/G	FA
1947	NY N	0	0	—	6.23	7	0	0	8.2	14	4	2	0	0	0	0	0	0	0	—	0	2	0	0	0.3	1.000
1948		0	0	—	0.00	1	0	0	3	3	0	0	0	0	0	0	0	0	0	—	0	2	0	0	2.0	1.000
2 yrs.		0	0		4.63	8	0	0	11.2	17	4	2	0	0	0	0	0	0	0		0	4	0	0	0.5	1.000

Ivy Andrews

ANDREWS, IVY PAUL (Poison) BR TR 6′ 1″ 200 lbs.
B. May 6, 1907, Dora, Ala. D. Nov. 24, 1970, Birmingham, Ala.

Year	Team	W	L	PCT	ERA	G	GS	CG	IP	H	BB	SO	ShO	Relief Pitching W	L	SV	Batting AB	H	HR	BA	PO	A	E	DP	TC/G	FA
1931	NY A	2	0	1.000	4.19	7	3	1	34.1	36	8	10	0	1	0	0	11	2	0	.182	1	6	0	2	1.0	1.000
1932	2 teams NY A (4G 2–1) BOS A (25G 8–6)																									
″	total	10	7	.588	3.52	29	20	9	166.1	164	62	37	0	2	1	0	60	9	0	.150	4	34	1	4	1.3	.974
1933	BOS A	7	13	.350	4.95	34	17	5	140	157	61	37	0	3	2	1	42	9	0	.214	5	28	3	0	1.1	.917
1934	STL A	4	11	.267	4.66	43	13	2	139	166	65	51	0	2	4	3	40	14	0	.350	4	17	1	1	0.5	.955
1935		13	7	.650	3.54	50	20	10	213.1	231	53	43	0	3	2	1	68	9	0	.132	7	32	2	4	0.8	.951
1936		7	12	.368	4.84	36	25	11	191.1	221	50	33	0	0	0	1	59	10	0	.169	2	28	1	1	0.9	.968
1937	2 teams CLE A (20G 3–4) NY A (11G 3–2)																									
″	total	6	6	.500	3.81	31	9	4	108.2	125	26	33	2	3	2	1	27	4	0	.148	4	19	1	1	0.8	.958
1938	NY A	1	3	.250	3.00	19	1	1	48	51	17	13	0	1	2	1	12	2	0	.167	3	10	0	0	0.7	1.000
8 yrs.		50	59	.459	4.14	249	108	43	1041	1151	342	257	2	15	13	8	319	59	0	.185	30	174	9	13	0.9	.958
WORLD SERIES																										
1937	NY A	0	0	—	3.18	1	0	0	5.2	6	4	1	0	0	0	0	2	0	0	.000	0	1	0	0	1.0	1.000

John Andrews

ANDREWS, JOHN RICHARD BL TL 5′10″ 175 lbs.
B. Feb. 9, 1949, Monterey Park, Calif.

Year	Team	W	L	PCT	ERA	G	GS	CG	IP	H	BB	SO	ShO	Relief Pitching W	L	SV	Batting AB	H	HR	BA	PO	A	E	DP	TC/G	FA
1973	STL N	1	1	.500	4.42	16	0	0	18.1	16	11	5	0	1	1	0	2	1	0	.500	1	1	0	0	0.1	1.000

Nate Andrews

ANDREWS, NATHAN HARDY BR TR 6′ 195 lbs.
B. Sept. 30, 1913, Pembroke, N. C. D. Apr. 26, 1991, Winston-Salem, N. C.

Year	Team	W	L	PCT	ERA	G	GS	CG	IP	H	BB	SO	ShO	Relief Pitching W	L	SV	Batting AB	H	HR	BA	PO	A	E	DP	TC/G	FA
1937	STL N	0	0	—	4.00	4	1	0	9	12	3	6	0	0	0	0	0	0	0	—	0	4	0	0	1.0	1.000
1939		1	2	.333	6.75	11	1	0	16	24	12	6	0	1	1	0	2	0	0	.000	1	5	0	0	0.5	1.000
1940	CLE A	0	1	.000	6.00	6	0	0	12	16	6	3	0	0	1	0	0	0	0	—	0	5	0	2	0.8	1.000
1941		0	0	—	11.57	2	0	0	2.1	3	2	1	0	0	0	0	1	0	0	.000	0	0	0	0	0.0	.000
1943	BOS N	14	**20**	.412	2.57	36	34	23	283.2	253	75	80	3	0	2	0	90	14	0	.156	11	71	2	2	2.3	.976
1944		16	15	.516	3.22	37	34	16	257.1	263	74	76	3	1	0	2	88	10	0	.114	14	56	2	2	1.9	.972
1945		7	12	.368	4.58	21	19	8	137.2	160	52	26	0	0	1	0	43	9	0	.209	7	28	1	1	1.7	.972
1946	2 teams CIN N (7G 2–4) NY N (3G 1–0)																									
″	total	3	4	.429	4.39	10	9	4	55.1	67	12	18	0	0	0	0	16	2	0	.125	1	10	0	0	1.1	1.000
8 yrs.		41	54	.432	3.46	127	98	51	773.1	798	236	216	6	2	5	2	240	35	0	.146	34	179	5	7	1.7	.977

Fred Andrus

ANDRUS, FREDERICK HOTHAM BR TR 6′ 2″ 185 lbs.
B. Aug. 23, 1850, Washington, Mich. D. Nov. 10, 1937, Detroit, Mich.

Year	Team	W	L	PCT	ERA	G	GS	CG	IP	H	BB	SO	ShO	Relief Pitching W	L	SV	Batting AB	H	HR	BA	PO	A	E	DP	TC/G	FA
1884	CHI N	1	0	1.000	*2.00*	1	1	1	9	11	2	2	0	0	0	0	*				5	0	2	0	0.9	.714

Joaquin Andujar

ANDUJAR, JOAQUIN BB TR 6′ 170 lbs.
B. Dec. 21, 1952, San Pedro de Macoris, Dominican Republic.

Year	Team	Lg	W	L	PCT	ERA	G	GS	CG	IP	H	BB	SO	ShO	Relief W	Relief L	Relief SV	AB	H	HR	BA	PO	A	E	DP	TC/G	FA
1976	**HOU**	**N**	9	10	.474	3.61	28	25	9	172	163	75	59	4	0	0	0	57	8	0	.140	12	24	3	1	1.4	.923
1977			11	8	.579	3.68	26	25	4	159	149	64	69	1	0	0	0	53	10	0	.189	14	38	8	1	2.3	.867
1978			5	7	.417	3.41	35	13	2	111	88	58	55	0	2	3	1	23	3	0	.130	11	27	4	1	1.2	.905
1979			12	12	.500	3.43	46	23	8	194	168	88	77	0	3	2	4	57	5	2	.088	16	50	5	2	1.5	.930
1980			3	8	.273	3.91	35	14	0	122	132	43	75	0	0	2	2	29	5	1	.172	7	27	5	2	1.1	.872
1981	**2 teams**	**HOU N**	(9G 2–3)		**STL N**	(11G 6–1)																					
″	**total**		8	4	.667	4.10	20	11	1	79	85	23	37	0	1	1	0	23	0	0	.000	5	12	2	0	0.9	.895
1982	**STL**	**N**	15	10	.600	2.47	38	37	9	265.2	237	50	137	5	0	0	0	95	15	0	.158	17	51	5	3	1.9	.932
1983			6	16	.273	4.16	39	34	5	225	215	75	125	2	0	0	1	73	6	0	.082	15	62	6	3	2.1	.928
1984			**20**	14	.588	3.34	36	36	12	**261.1**	218	70	147	**4**	0	0	0	84	11	2	.131	15	54	3	2	2.0	.958
1985			21	12	.636	3.40	38	38	10	269.2	265	82	112	2	0	0	0	94	10	0	.106	8	45	6	8	1.6	.898
1986	**OAK**	**A**	12	7	.632	3.82	28	26	7	155.1	139	56	72	1	0	0	1	0	0	0	—	16	21	3	4	1.4	.925
1987			3	5	.375	6.08	13	13	1	60.2	63	26	32	0	0	0	0	0	0	0	—	1	11	2	1	1.1	.857
1988	**HOU**	**N**	2	5	.286	4.00	23	10	0	78.2	94	21	35	0	0	2	0	19	4	0	.211	5	15	2	0	1.0	.909
13 yrs.			127	118	.518	3.58	405	305	68	2153.1	2016	731	1032	19	6	10	9	607	77	5	.127	142	437	54	28	1.6	.915
LEAGUE CHAMPIONSHIP SERIES																											
1980	**HOU**	**N**	0	0	—	0.00	1	0	0	1	0	1	0	0	0	0	1	0	0	0	—	0	0	0	0	0.0	.000
1982	**STL**	**N**	1	0	1.000	2.70	1	1	0	6.2	6	2	4	0	0	0	0	1	0	0	.000	0	1	0	0	1.0	1.000
1985			0	1	.000	6.97	2	2	0	10.1	14	4	9	0	0	0	0	4	1	0	.250	0	0	2	0	1.0	.000
3 yrs.			1	1	.500	5.00	4	3	0	18	20	7	13	0	0	0	1	5	1	0	.200	0	1	2	0	0.8	.333
WORLD SERIES																											
1982	**STL**	**N**	2	0	1.000	1.35	2	2	0	13.1	10	1	4	0	0	0	0	0	0	0	—	1	2	1	0	2.0	.750
1985			0	1	.000	9.00	2	1	0	4	10	4	3	0	0	0	0	1	0	0	.000	0	1	0	0	0.5	1.000
2 yrs.			2	1	.667	3.12	4	3	0	17.1	20	5	7	0	0	0	0	1	0	0	.000	1	3	1	0	1.3	.800

Luis Andujar

ANDUJAR, LUIS BR TR 6′ 2″ 175 lbs.
Born Luis Andujar (Sanchez).
B. Nov. 22, 1972, Bani, Dominican Republic.

Year	Team	Lg	W	L	PCT	ERA	G	GS	CG	IP	H	BB	SO	ShO	Relief W	Relief L	Relief SV	AB	H	HR	BA	PO	A	E	DP	TC/G	FA
1995	**CHI**	**A**	2	1	.667	3.26	5	5	0	30.1	26	14	9	0	0	0	0	0	0	0	—	1	1	0	0	0.4	1.000

Norm Angelini

ANGELINI, NORMAN STANLEY BL TL 5′11″ 175 lbs.
B. Sept. 24, 1947, San Francisco, Calif.

Year	Team	Lg	W	L	PCT	ERA	G	GS	CG	IP	H	BB	SO	ShO	Relief W	Relief L	Relief SV	AB	H	HR	BA	PO	A	E	DP	TC/G	FA
1972	**KC**	**A**	2	1	.667	2.25	21	0	0	16	13	12	16	0	2	1	2	2	0	0	.000	2	1	0	0	0.1	1.000
1973			0	0	—	4.50	7	0	0	4	2	7	3	0	0	0	1	0	0	0	—	0	0	0	0	0.0	.000
2 yrs.			2	1	.667	2.70	28	0	0	20	15	19	19	0	2	1	3	2	0	0	.000	2	1	0	0	0.1	1.000

Cap Anson

ANSON, ADRIAN CONSTANTINE (Pops, Old Anse) BR TR 6′ 227 lbs.
B. Apr. 11, 1852, Marshalltown, Iowa D. Apr. 14, 1922, Chicago, Ill.
Manager 1879–98.
Hall of Fame 1939.

Year	Team	Lg	W	L	PCT	ERA	G	GS	CG	IP	H	BB	SO	ShO	Relief W	Relief L	Relief SV	AB	H	HR	BA	PO	A	E	DP	TC/G	FA
1883	**CHI**	**N**	0	0	—	0.00	2	0	0	3	1	1	0	0	0	0	1	413	127	0	.308	137	147	50	8	4.9	.850
1884			0	1	.000	*18.00*	1	0	0	1	3	1	1	0	0	**1**	0	475	159	21	.335	1216	48	62	86	11.3	.953
2 yrs.			0	1	.000	4.50	3	0	0	4	4	2	1	0	0	1	1	*				21312	1334	725	1222	10.0	.969

Johnny Antonelli

ANTONELLI, JOHN AUGUST BL TL 6′ 1½″ 185 lbs.
B. Apr. 12, 1930, Rochester, N. Y.

Year	Team	Lg	W	L	PCT	ERA	G	GS	CG	IP	H	BB	SO	ShO	Relief W	Relief L	Relief SV	AB	H	HR	BA	PO	A	E	DP	TC/G	FA
1948	**BOS**	**N**	0	0	—	2.25	4	0	0	4	2	3	0	0	0	0	1	0	0	0	—	0	3	0	0	0.8	1.000
1949			3	7	.300	3.56	22	10	3	96	99	42	48	1	0	1	0	25	3	0	.120	5	14	4	0	1.0	.826
1950			2	3	.400	5.93	20	6	2	57.2	81	22	33	1	0	0	0	16	2	0	.125	2	13	1	0	0.8	.938
1953	**MIL**	**N**	12	12	.500	3.18	31	26	11	175.1	167	71	131	2	2	1	1	62	11	0	.177	6	34	1	3	1.3	.976
1954	**NY**	**N**	21	7	**.750**	**2.30**	39	37	18	258.2	209	94	152	**6**	0	0	2	98	16	2	.163	10	54	2	3	1.7	.970
1955			14	16	.467	3.33	38	34	14	235.1	206	82	143	2	0	0	1	82	17	4	.207	7	46	2	2	1.4	.964
1956			20	13	.606	2.86	41	36	15	258.1	225	75	145	**6**	3	0	1	89	14	3	.157	11	49	1	5	1.5	.984
1957			12	18	.400	3.77	40	30	8	212.1	228	67	114	3	3	1	0	72	11	3	.153	9	27	3	3	1.0	.923
1958	**SF**	**N**	16	13	.552	3.28	41	34	13	241.2	216	87	143	0	1	1	3	84	19	1	.226	10	27	4	3	1.0	.902
1959			19	10	.655	3.10	40	38	17	282	247	76	165	**4**	0	0	1	101	16	2	.158	8	44	2	3	1.4	.963
1960			6	7	.462	3.77	41	10	1	112.1	106	47	57	1	4	2	11	34	8	0	.235	2	19	0	0	0.5	1.000
1961	**2 teams**	**CLE A**	(11G 0–4)		**MIL N**	(9G 1–0)																					
″	**total**		1	4	.200	6.75	20	7	0	58.2	84	21	31	0	1	0	0	16	4	0	.250	2	12	1	2	0.8	.933
12 yrs.			126	110	.534	3.34	377	268	102	1992.1	1870	687	1162	26	14	6	21	679	121	15	.178	72	342	21	24	1.2	.952
WORLD SERIES																											
1954	**NY**	**N**	1	0	1.000	0.84	2	1	1	10.2	8	7	12	0	0	0	1	3	0	0	.000	0	1	0	0	0.5	1.000

Bob Apodaca

APODACA, ROBERT JOHN BR TR 5′11″ 170 lbs.
B. Jan. 31, 1950, Los Angeles, Calif.

Year	Team	Lg	W	L	PCT	ERA	G	GS	CG	IP	H	BB	SO	ShO	Relief W	Relief L	Relief SV	AB	H	HR	BA	PO	A	E	DP	TC/G	FA
1973	**NY**	**N**	0	0	—	∞	1	0	0		0	2	0	0	0	0	0	0	0	0	—	0	0	0	0	0.0	.000
1974			6	6	.500	3.50	35	8	1	103	92	42	54	0	1	5	3	25	3	0	.120	7	13	2	2	0.6	.909
1975			3	4	.429	1.48	46	0	0	85	66	28	45	0	3	4	13	11	4	0	.364	8	22	1	1	0.7	.968
1976			3	7	.300	2.80	43	3	0	90	71	29	45	0	3	5	5	16	2	0	.125	8	17	0	1	0.6	1.000
1977			4	8	.333	3.43	59	0	0	84	83	30	53	0	4	8	5	6	1	0	.167	5	17	1	1	0.4	.957
5 yrs.			16	25	.390	2.86	184	11	1	362	312	131	197	0	11	22	26	58	10	0	.172	28	69	4	5	0.5	.960

Luis Aponte

APONTE, LUIS EDUARDO BR TR 6′ 180 lbs.
Born Luis Eduardo Aponte (Yuripe).
B. June 14, 1953, El Tigre, Venezuela.

Year	Team	Lg	W	L	PCT	ERA	G	GS	CG	IP	H	BB	SO	ShO	Relief W	Relief L	Relief SV	AB	H	HR	BA	PO	A	E	DP	TC/G	FA
1980	**BOS**	**A**	0	0	—	1.29	4	0	0	7	6	2	1	0	0	0	0	0	0	0	—	0	2	0	0	0.5	1.000
1981			1	0	1.000	0.56	7	0	0	16	11	3	11	0	1	0	1	0	0	0	—	1	6	0	0	1.0	1.000
1982			2	2	.500	3.18	40	0	0	85	78	25	44	0	2	2	3	0	0	0	—	11	16	0	3	0.7	1.000
1983			5	4	.556	3.63	34	0	0	62	74	23	32	0	5	4	3	0	0	0	—	10	8	0	1	0.5	1.000
1984	**CLE**	**A**	1	0	1.000	4.11	25	0	0	50.1	53	15	25	0	1	0	0	0	0	0	—	1	5	0	0	0.2	1.000
5 yrs.			9	6	.600	3.27	110	0	0	220.1	222	68	113	0	9	6	7	0	0	0		23	37	0	4	0.5	1.000

Kevin Appier

APPIER, ROBERT KEVIN
B. Dec. 6, 1967, Lancaster, Calif.
BR TR 6′ 2″ 180 lbs.

Year	Team	Lg	W	L	PCT	ERA	G	GS	CG	IP	H	BB	SO	ShO	Relief W	Relief L	Relief SV	Batting AB	Batting H	Batting HR	BA	PO	A	E	DP	TC/G	FA
1989	KC	A	1	4	.200	9.14	6	5	0	21.2	34	12	10	0	0	0	0	0	0	0	—	1	0	0	0	0.2	1.000
1990			12	8	.600	2.76	32	24	3	185.2	179	54	127	3	0	0	0	0	0	0	—	15	21	3	3	1.2	.923
1991			13	10	.565	3.42	34	31	6	207.2	205	61	158	3	0	1	0	0	0	0	—	20	26	2	0	1.4	.958
1992			15	8	.652	2.46	30	30	3	208.1	167	68	150	0	0	0	0	0	0	0	—	19	21	1	4	1.4	.976
1993			18	8	.692	**2.56**	34	34	5	238.2	183	81	186	1	0	0	0	0	0	0	—	26	14	1	4	1.2	.976
1994			7	6	.538	3.83	23	23	1	155	137	63	145	0	0	0	0	0	0	0	—	7	13	0	1	0.9	1.000
1995			15	10	.600	3.89	31	31	4	201.1	163	80	185	1	0	0	0	0	0	0	—	16	20	0	3	1.2	1.000
7 yrs.			81	54	.600	3.22	190	178	22	1218.1	1068	419	961	8	0	1	0	0	0	0		104	115	7	15	1.2	.969

Fred Applegate

APPLEGATE, FREDERICK ROMAINE (Snitz)
B. May 9, 1879, Williamsport, Pa. D. Apr. 21, 1968, Williamsport, Pa.
BR TR 6′ 2″ 180 lbs.

Year	Team	Lg	W	L	PCT	ERA	G	GS	CG	IP	H	BB	SO	ShO	Relief W	Relief L	Relief SV	Batting AB	Batting H	Batting HR	BA	PO	A	E	DP	TC/G	FA
1904	PHI	A	1	2	.333	6.43	3	3	3	21	29	8	12	0	0	0	0	7	2	0	.286	0	8	0	0	2.7	1.000

Ed Appleton

APPLETON, EDWARD SAMUEL (Whitey)
B. Feb. 29, 1892, Arlington, Tex. D. Jan. 27, 1932, Arlington, Tex.
BR TR 6′½″ 173 lbs.

Year	Team	Lg	W	L	PCT	ERA	G	GS	CG	IP	H	BB	SO	ShO	Relief W	Relief L	Relief SV	Batting AB	Batting H	Batting HR	BA	PO	A	E	DP	TC/G	FA
1915	BKN	N	4	10	.286	3.32	34	10	5	138.1	133	66	50	0	1	4	0	44	7	0	.159	5	36	4	1	1.3	.911
1916			1	2	.333	3.06	14	3	1	47	49	18	14	0	1	0	1	12	2	0	.167	4	8	1	0	0.9	.923
2 yrs.			5	12	.294	3.25	48	13	6	185.1	182	84	64	0	2	4	1	56	9	0	.161	9	44	5	1	1.2	.914

Pete Appleton

APPLETON, PETER WILLIAM
Played as Pete Jablonowski 1927-33.
Born Peter William Jablonowski.
B. May 20, 1904, Terryville, Conn. D. Jan. 18, 1974, Trenton, N. J.
BR TR 5′11″ 180 lbs.

Year	Team	Lg	W	L	PCT	ERA	G	GS	CG	IP	H	BB	SO	ShO	Relief W	Relief L	Relief SV	Batting AB	Batting H	Batting HR	BA	PO	A	E	DP	TC/G	FA
1927	CIN	N	2	1	.667	1.82	6	2	2	29.2	29	17	3	1	1	0	0	11	6	0	.545	4	8	0	2	2.0	1.000
1928			3	4	.429	4.68	31	1	0	82.2	101	22	20	0	3	4	0	31	10	0	.323	3	28	0	3	1.0	1.000
1930	CLE	A	8	7	.533	4.02	39	7	2	118.2	122	53	45	0	6	5	1	40	8	0	.200	6	30	2	4	1.0	.947
1931			4	4	.500	4.63	29	4	3	79.2	100	29	25	0	1	3	0	24	5	0	.208	4	16	2	1	0.8	.909
1932	2 teams		CLE A (4G 0–0)			BOS A (11G 0–3)																					
″	total		0	3	.000	5.29	15	3	0	51	60	29	16	0	0	0	0	17	3	0	.176	5	20	0	0	1.7	1.000
1933	NY	A	0	0	—	0.00	1	0	0	2	3	1	0	0	0	0	0	0	0	0	—	0	1	0	1	1.0	1.000
1936	WAS	A	14	9	.609	3.53	38	20	12	201.2	199	77	77	1	4	1	3	76	19	0	.250	9	42	1	1	1.4	.981
1937			8	15	.348	4.39	35	18	7	168	167	72	62	4	3	4	2	59	11	0	.186	8	42	1	4	1.5	.980
1938			7	9	.438	4.60	43	10	5	164.1	175	61	62	0	3	4	5	59	15	0	.254	9	29	4	4	1.0	.905
1939			5	10	.333	4.56	40	4	2	102.2	104	48	50	0	4	7	6	25	4	0	.160	4	17	1	2	0.6	.955
1940	CHI	A	4	0	1.000	5.62	25	0	0	57.2	54	28	21	0	4	0	5	17	3	0	.176	4	8	1	1	0.5	.923
1941			0	3	.000	5.27	13	0	0	27.1	27	17	12	0	0	3	1	4	1	0	.250	1	6	0	0	0.5	1.000
1942	2 teams		CHI A (4G 0–0)			STL A (14G 1–1)																					
″	total		1	1	.500	3.09	18	0	0	32	27	14	14	0	1	1	2	6	1	0	.167	1	13	0	1	0.8	1.000
1945	2 teams		STL A (2G 0–0)			WAS A (6G 1–0)																					
″	total		1	0	1.000	4.56	8	2	1	23.2	19	18	13	0	0	0	1	5	1	0	.200	0	5	0	1	0.6	1.000
14 yrs.			57	66	.463	4.30	341	71	34	1141	1187	486	420	6	30	32	26	374	87	0	.233	58	265	12	25	1.0	.964

Luis Aquino

AQUINO, LUIS ANTONIO
Born Luis Antonio Aquino (Colon).
B. May 19, 1964, Santurce, Puerto Rico.
BR TR 6′ 155 lbs.

Year	Team	Lg	W	L	PCT	ERA	G	GS	CG	IP	H	BB	SO	ShO	Relief W	Relief L	Relief SV	Batting AB	Batting H	Batting HR	BA	PO	A	E	DP	TC/G	FA
1986	TOR	A	1	1	.500	6.35	7	0	0	11.1	14	3	5	0	1	1	0	0	0	0	—	1	1	0	0	0.3	1.000
1988	KC	A	1	0	1.000	2.79	7	5	1	29	33	17	11	1	0	0	0	0	0	0	—	2	2	1	1	0.7	.800
1989			6	8	.429	3.50	34	16	2	141.1	148	35	68	1	2	0	0	0	0	0	—	11	23	0	3	1.0	1.000
1990			4	1	.800	3.16	20	3	1	68.1	59	27	28	0	2	0	0	0	0	0	—	4	10	0	2	0.7	1.000
1991			8	4	.667	3.44	38	18	1	157	152	47	80	1	2	0	3	0	0	0	—	14	21	3	3	1.0	.921
1992			3	6	.333	4.52	15	13	0	67.2	81	20	11	0	0	1	0	0	0	0	—	4	16	0	1	1.3	1.000
1993	FLA	N	6	8	.429	3.42	38	13	0	110.2	115	40	67	0	2	2	0	25	2	0	.080	10	30	1	5	1.1	.976
1994			2	1	.667	3.73	29	1	0	50.2	39	22	22	0	2	1	0	6	1	0	.167	5	10	0	2	0.5	1.000
1995	2 teams		MON N (29G 0–2)			SF N (5G 0–1)																					
″	total		0	3	.000	5.10	34	0	0	42.1	57	13	26	0	0	3	2	4	1	0	.250	3	4	0	2	0.2	1.000
9 yrs.			31	32	.492	3.68	222	69	5	678.1	698	224	318	3	11	8	5	35	4	0	.114	54	117	5	19	0.8	.972

Fred Archer

ARCHER, FREDERICK MARVIN (Lefty)
B. Mar. 7, 1910, Johnson City, Tenn. D. Oct. 31, 1981, Charlotte, N. C.
BL TL 6′ 193 lbs.

Year	Team	Lg	W	L	PCT	ERA	G	GS	CG	IP	H	BB	SO	ShO	Relief W	Relief L	Relief SV	Batting AB	Batting H	Batting HR	BA	PO	A	E	DP	TC/G	FA
1936	PHI	A	2	3	.400	6.38	6	5	2	36.2	41	15	9	0	0	0	0	15	4	0	.267	1	6	0	1	1.2	1.000
1937			0	0	—	6.00	1	0	0	3	4	0	2	0	0	0	0	0	0	0	—	0	1	0	0	1.0	1.000
2 yrs.			2	3	.400	6.35	7	5	2	39.2	45	15	11	0	0	0	0	15	4	0	.267	1	7	0	1	1.1	1.000

Jim Archer

ARCHER, JAMES WILLIAM
B. May 25, 1932, Max Meadows, Va.
BR TL 6′ 190 lbs.

Year	Team	Lg	W	L	PCT	ERA	G	GS	CG	IP	H	BB	SO	ShO	Relief W	Relief L	Relief SV	Batting AB	Batting H	Batting HR	BA	PO	A	E	DP	TC/G	FA
1961	KC	A	9	15	.375	3.20	39	27	9	205.1	204	60	110	2	1	1	5	63	4	0	.063	6	36	2	2	1.1	.955
1962			0	1	.000	9.43	18	1	0	27.2	40	10	12	0	0	0	0	1	1	0	1.000	2	3	1	0	0.3	.833
2 yrs.			9	16	.360	3.94	57	28	9	233	244	70	122	2	1	1	5	64	5	0	.078	8	39	3	2	0.9	.940

Rugger Ardizoia

ARDIZOIA, RINALDO JOSEPH
B. Nov. 20, 1919, Oleggio, Italy.
BR TR 5′11″ 180 lbs.

Year	Team	Lg	W	L	PCT	ERA	G	GS	CG	IP	H	BB	SO	ShO	Relief W	Relief L	Relief SV	Batting AB	Batting H	Batting HR	BA	PO	A	E	DP	TC/G	FA
1947	NY	A	0	0	—	9.00	1	0	0	2	4	1	0	0	0	0	0	0	0	0	—	0	1	0	0	1.0	1.000

Frank Arellanes

ARELLANES, FRANK JULIAN
B. Jan. 28, 1882, Santa Cruz, Calif. D. Dec. 13, 1918, San Jose, Calif.
BR TR 6′ 180 lbs.

Year	Team	Lg	W	L	PCT	ERA	G	GS	CG	IP	H	BB	SO	ShO	Relief W	Relief L	Relief SV	Batting AB	Batting H	Batting HR	BA	PO	A	E	DP	TC/G	FA
1908	BOS	A	4	3	.571	1.82	11	8	6	79.1	60	18	33	1	0	0	0	30	5	0	.167	2	19	3	1	2.2	.875
1909			16	12	.571	2.18	45	28	17	230.2	192	43	82	1	3	2	**8**	78	13	0	.167	13	74	7	2	2.1	.926
1910			4	7	.364	2.88	18	13	2	100	106	24	33	0	1	1	0	34	6	1	.176	2	35	2	2	2.2	.949
3 yrs.			24	22	.522	2.28	74	49	25	410	358	85	148	2	4	3	8	142	24	1	.169	17	128	12	5	2.1	.924

Rudy Arias

ARIAS, RODOLFO BL TL 5'10" 165 lbs.
Born Rodolfo Arias (Martinez).
B. June 6, 1931, Las Villas, Cuba.

Year	Team	Lg	W	L	PCT	ERA	G	GS	CG	IP	H	BB	SO	ShO	Relief W	Relief L	Relief SV	Bat AB	Bat H	HR	BA	PO	A	E	DP	TC/G	FA
1959	CHI	A	2	0	1.000	4.09	34	0	0	44	49	20	28	0	2	0	2	4	0	0	.000	3	10	0	0	0.4	1.000

Don Arlich

ARLICH, DONALD LOUIS BL TL 6' 2" 185 lbs.
B. Feb. 15, 1943, Wayne, Mich.

Year	Team	Lg	W	L	PCT	ERA	G	GS	CG	IP	H	BB	SO	ShO	Relief W	Relief L	Relief SV	Bat AB	Bat H	HR	BA	PO	A	E	DP	TC/G	FA
1965	HOU	N	0	0	—	3.00	1	1	0	6	5	1	0	0	0	0	0	2	0	0	.000	0	1	0	0	1.0	1.000
1966			0	1	.000	15.75	7	0	0	4	11	4	1	0	0	1	0	1	0	0	.000	0	0	0	0	0.0	.000
2 yrs.			0	1	.000	8.10	8	1	0	10	16	5	1	0	0	1	0	3	0	0	.000	0	1	0	0	0.1	1.000

Steve Arlin

ARLIN, STEPHEN RALPH BR TR 6' 3½" 195 lbs.
B. Sept. 25, 1945, Seattle, Wash.

Year	Team	Lg	W	L	PCT	ERA	G	GS	CG	IP	H	BB	SO	ShO	Relief W	Relief L	Relief SV	Bat AB	Bat H	HR	BA	PO	A	E	DP	TC/G	FA
1969	SD	N	0	1	.000	9.00	4	1	0	11	13	9	9	0	0	0	0	2	0	0	.000	0	1	0	0	0.3	1.000
1970			1	0	1.000	2.77	2	2	1	13	11	8	3	1	0	0	0	5	0	0	.000	0	4	0	0	2.0	1.000
1971			9	**19**	.321	3.47	36	34	10	228	211	103	156	4	0	0	0	73	9	0	.123	18	23	1	3	1.2	.976
1972			10	**21**	.323	3.60	38	37	12	250	217	**122**	159	3	1	0	0	72	11	0	.153	17	34	3	1	1.4	.944
1973			11	14	.440	5.10	34	27	7	180	196	72	98	3	2	0	0	60	10	0	.167	11	21	0	4	0.9	1.000
1974	2 teams	SD N (16G 1–7) CLE A (11G 2–5)																									
"	total		3	12	.200	6.17	27	22	2	108	144	59	38	0	0	0	1	18	2	0	.111	9	13	5	0	1.0	.815
6 yrs.			34	67	.337	4.32	141	123	32	790	792	373	463	11	3	0	1	230	32	0	.139	55	96	9	8	1.1	.944

Orville Armbrust

ARMBRUST, ORVILLE MARTIN BR TR 5'10" 195 lbs.
B. Mar. 2, 1910, Beirne, Ark. D. Oct. 2, 1967, Mobile, Ala.

Year	Team	Lg	W	L	PCT	ERA	G	GS	CG	IP	H	BB	SO	ShO	Relief W	Relief L	Relief SV	Bat AB	Bat H	HR	BA	PO	A	E	DP	TC/G	FA
1934	WAS	A	1	0	1.000	2.13	3	2	0	12.2	10	3	3	0	0	0	0	4	0	0	.000	1	6	0	0	2.3	1.000

Howard Armstrong

ARMSTRONG, HOWARD ELMER BR TR 5' 9" 165 lbs.
B. Dec. 2, 1889, East Claridon, Ohio D. Mar. 8, 1926, Canisteo, N. Y.

Year	Team	Lg	W	L	PCT	ERA	G	GS	CG	IP	H	BB	SO	ShO	Relief W	Relief L	Relief SV	Bat AB	Bat H	HR	BA	PO	A	E	DP	TC/G	FA
1911	PHI	A	0	1	.000	0.00	1	0	0	3	3	1	0	0	0	1	0	1	0	0	.000	0	2	0	0	2.0	1.000

Jack Armstrong

ARMSTRONG, JACK WILLIAM BR TR 6' 5" 220 lbs.
B. Mar. 7, 1965, Englewood, N. J.

Year	Team	Lg	W	L	PCT	ERA	G	GS	CG	IP	H	BB	SO	ShO	Relief W	Relief L	Relief SV	Bat AB	Bat H	HR	BA	PO	A	E	DP	TC/G	FA
1988	CIN	N	4	7	.364	5.79	14	13	0	65.1	63	38	45	0	0	0	0	21	2	0	.095	3	13	0	0	1.1	1.000
1989			2	3	.400	4.64	9	8	0	42.2	40	21	23	0	0	0	0	8	0	0	.000	1	9	0	0	1.1	1.000
1990			12	9	.571	3.42	29	27	2	166	151	59	110	1	0	0	0	47	5	0	.106	15	20	0	2	1.2	1.000
1991			7	13	.350	5.48	27	24	1	139.2	158	54	93	0	0	0	0	43	4	0	.093	16	16	2	0	1.3	.941
1992	CLE	A	6	15	.286	4.64	35	23	1	166.2	176	67	114	0	3	0	0	0	0	0	—	13	25	4	2	1.2	.905
1993	FLA	N	9	17	.346	4.49	36	33	0	196.1	210	78	118	0	1	0	0	66	10	0	.152	13	28	2	1	1.2	.953
1994	TEX	A	0	1	.000	3.60	2	2	0	10	9	2	7	0	0	0	0	0	0	0	—	1	0	0	0	0.5	1.000
7 yrs.			40	65	.381	4.58	152	130	4	786.2	807	319	510	1	4	0	0	185	21	0	.114	62	111	8	5	1.2	.956
WORLD SERIES																											
1990	CIN	N	0	0	—	0.00	1	0	0	3	1	0	3	0	0	0	0	0	0	0	—	0	0	0	0	0.0	.000

Mike Armstrong

ARMSTRONG, MICHAEL DENNIS BR TR 6' 3" 193 lbs.
B. Mar. 7, 1954, Glen Cove, N. Y.

Year	Team	Lg	W	L	PCT	ERA	G	GS	CG	IP	H	BB	SO	ShO	Relief W	Relief L	Relief SV	Bat AB	Bat H	HR	BA	PO	A	E	DP	TC/G	FA
1980	SD	N	0	0	—	5.79	11	0	0	14	16	13	14	0	0	0	0	3	0	0	.000	1	0	1	0	0.2	.500
1981			0	2	.000	6.00	10	0	0	12	14	11	9	0	0	2	0	0	0	0	—	0	0	0	0	0.0	.000
1982	KC	A	5	5	.500	3.20	52	0	0	112.2	88	43	75	0	5	5	6	0	0	0	—	9	8	0	1	0.3	1.000
1983			10	7	.588	3.86	58	0	0	102.2	86	45	52	0	10	7	3	0	0	0	—	8	12	0	1	0.3	1.000
1984	NY	A	3	2	.600	3.48	36	0	0	54.1	47	26	43	0	3	2	1	0	0	0	—	7	4	1	0	0.3	.917
1985			0	0	—	3.07	9	0	0	14.2	9	2	11	0	0	0	0	0	0	0	—	1	1	0	0	0.2	1.000
1986			0	1	.000	9.35	7	1	0	8.2	13	5	8	0	0	0	0	0	0	0	—	1	1	1	0	0.4	.667
1987	CLE	A	1	0	1.000	8.68	14	0	0	18.2	27	10	9	0	1	0	1	0	0	0	—	1	2	1	0	0.3	.750
8 yrs.			19	17	.528	4.10	197	1	0	337.2	300	155	221	0	19	16	11	3	0	0	.000	28	28	4	2	0.3	.933

Scott Arnold

ARNOLD, SCOTT GENTRY BR TR 6' 2" 210 lbs.
B. Aug. 18, 1962, Lexington, Ky.

Year	Team	Lg	W	L	PCT	ERA	G	GS	CG	IP	H	BB	SO	ShO	Relief W	Relief L	Relief SV	Bat AB	Bat H	HR	BA	PO	A	E	DP	TC/G	FA
1988	STL	N	0	0	—	5.40	6	0	0	6.2	9	4	8	0	0	0	0	0	0	0	—	0	1	0	0	0.2	1.000

Tony Arnold

ARNOLD, TONY DALE BR TR 5'11" 170 lbs.
B. May 3, 1959, El Paso, Tex.

Year	Team	Lg	W	L	PCT	ERA	G	GS	CG	IP	H	BB	SO	ShO	Relief W	Relief L	Relief SV	Bat AB	Bat H	HR	BA	PO	A	E	DP	TC/G	FA
1986	BAL	A	0	2	.000	3.55	11	0	0	25.1	25	11	7	0	0	2	0	0	0	0	—	4	9	0	0	1.2	1.000
1987			0	0	—	5.77	27	0	0	53	71	17	18	0	0	0	0	0	0	0	—	5	17	0	2	0.8	1.000
2 yrs.			0	2	.000	5.06	38	0	0	78.1	96	28	25	0	0	2	0	0	0	0		9	26	0	2	0.9	1.000

Brad Arnsberg

ARNSBERG, BRADLEY JAMES BR TR 6' 4" 205 lbs.
B. Aug. 20, 1963, Seattle, Wash.

Year	Team	Lg	W	L	PCT	ERA	G	GS	CG	IP	H	BB	SO	ShO	Relief W	Relief L	Relief SV	Bat AB	Bat H	HR	BA	PO	A	E	DP	TC/G	FA
1986	NY	A	0	0	—	3.38	2	1	0	8	13	1	3	0	0	0	0	0	0	0	—	0	0	0	0	0.0	.000
1987			1	3	.250	5.59	6	2	0	19.1	22	13	14	0	0	2	0	0	0	0	—	1	5	0	0	1.0	1.000
1989	TEX	A	2	1	.667	4.13	16	1	0	48	45	22	26	0	2	0	1	0	0	0	—	5	10	0	2	0.9	1.000
1990			6	1	.857	2.15	53	0	0	62.2	56	33	44	0	6	1	5	0	0	0	—	5	11	0	2	0.3	1.000
1991			0	1	.000	8.38	9	0	0	9.2	10	5	8	0	0	1	0	0	0	0	—	0	1	1	0	0.2	.500
1992	CLE	A	0	0	—	11.81	8	0	0	10.2	13	11	5	0	0	0	0	0	0	0	—	2	0	0	0	0.3	1.000
6 yrs.			9	6	.600	4.26	94	4	0	158.1	159	85	100	0	8	4	6	0	0	0		13	27	1	4	0.4	.976

Orie Arntzen

ARNTZEN, ORIE EDGAR (Old Folks) BR TR 6' 1" 200 lbs.
B. Oct. 18, 1909, Beverly, Ill. D. Jan. 28, 1970, Cedar Rapids, Iowa.

Year	Team	Lg	W	L	PCT	ERA	G	GS	CG	IP	H	BB	SO	ShO	Relief W	Relief L	Relief SV	Bat AB	Bat H	HR	BA	PO	A	E	DP	TC/G	FA
1943	PHI	A	4	13	.235	4.22	32	20	9	164.1	172	69	66	0	0	0	0	50	8	0	.160	7	19	3	4	0.9	.897

Rene Arocha

AROCHA, RENE
Born Rene Arocha (Magaly).
B. Feb. 24, 1966, Havana, Cuba.
BR TR 6′ 180 lbs.

Year	Team	W	L	PCT	ERA	G	GS	CG	IP	H	BB	SO	ShO	Relief Pitching W	Relief Pitching L	Relief Pitching SV	Batting AB	Batting H	Batting HR	BA	PO	A	E	DP	TC/G	FA
1993	STL N	11	8	.579	3.78	32	29	1	188	197	31	96	0	0	1	0	58	6	0	.103	9	28	4	3	1.3	.902
1994		4	4	.500	4.01	45	7	1	83	94	21	62	1	3	1	11	9	1	0	.111	3	11	0	0	0.3	1.000
1995		3	5	.375	3.99	41	0	0	49.2	55	18	25	0	3	5	0	1	0	0	.000	2	9	0	1	0.3	1.000
3 yrs.		18	17	.514	3.87	118	36	2	320.2	346	70	183	1	6	7	11	68	7	0	.103	14	48	4	4	0.6	.939

Jerry Arrigo

ARRIGO, GERALD WILLIAM
B. June 12, 1941, Chicago, Ill.
BL TL 6′ 1″ 185 lbs.

Year	Team	W	L	PCT	ERA	G	GS	CG	IP	H	BB	SO	ShO	Relief Pitching W	Relief Pitching L	Relief Pitching SV	Batting AB	Batting H	Batting HR	BA	PO	A	E	DP	TC/G	FA
1961	MIN A	0	1	.000	10.24	7	2	0	9.2	9	10	6	0	0	0	0	2	1	0	.500	0	2	0	0	0.3	1.000
1962		0	0	—	18.00	1	0	0	1	3	1	1	0	0	0	0	0	0	0	—	0	0	0	0	0.0	.000
1963		1	2	.333	2.87	5	1	0	15.2	12	4	13	0	1	1	0	4	0	0	.000	2	3	0	0	1.0	1.000
1964		7	4	.636	3.84	41	12	2	105.1	97	45	96	1	3	2	1	29	5	0	.172	3	18	1	0	0.5	.955
1965	CIN N	2	4	.333	6.17	27	5	0	54	75	30	43	0	1	2	2	12	2	1	.167	1	3	0	0	0.1	1.000
1966	2 teams CIN N (3G 0–0) NY N (17G 3–3)																									
″	total	3	3	.500	3.91	20	5	0	50.2	54	19	31	0	2	0	0	11	5	0	.455	4	8	1	2	0.6	.923
1967	CIN N	6	6	.500	3.16	32	5	1	74	61	35	56	1	4	3	1	19	4	0	.211	1	4	0	0	0.2	1.000
1968		12	10	.545	3.33	36	31	5	205.1	181	77	140	1	1	0	0	67	5	0	.075	3	45	1	1	1.4	.980
1969		4	7	.364	4.14	20	16	1	91.1	89	61	35	0	0	0	0	31	5	0	.161	1	8	1	0	0.5	.900
1970	CHI A	0	3	.000	13.15	5	3	0	13	24	9	12	0	0	0	0	4	0	0	.000	0	1	0	0	0.2	1.000
10 yrs.		35	40	.467	4.14	194	80	9	620	605	291	433	3	12	8	4	179	27	1	.151	15	92	4	3	0.6	.964

Fernando Arroyo

ARROYO, FERNANDO
B. Mar. 21, 1952, Sacramento, Calif.
BR TR 6′ 2″ 180 lbs.

Year	Team	W	L	PCT	ERA	G	GS	CG	IP	H	BB	SO	ShO	Relief Pitching W	Relief Pitching L	Relief Pitching SV	Batting AB	Batting H	Batting HR	BA	PO	A	E	DP	TC/G	FA
1975	DET A	2	1	.667	4.56	14	2	1	53.1	56	22	25	0	1	0	0	0	0	0	—	6	11	0	2	1.2	1.000
1977		8	18	.308	4.18	38	28	8	209	227	52	60	1	1	2	0	0	0	0	—	15	63	1	4	2.1	.987
1978		0	0	—	8.31	2	0	0	4.1	8	0	1	0	0	0	0	0	0	0	—	0	1	0	0	0.5	1.000
1979		1	1	.500	8.25	6	0	0	12	17	4	7	0	1	1	0	0	0	0	—	1	2	0	0	0.5	1.000
1980	MIN A	6	6	.500	4.70	21	11	1	92	97	32	27	1	2	0	0	0	0	0	—	9	8	1	0	0.9	.944
1981		7	10	.412	3.94	23	19	2	128	144	34	39	0	0	0	0	0	0	0	—	7	23	0	1	1.3	1.000
1982	2 teams MIN A (6G 0–1) OAK A (10G 0–0)																									
″	total	0	1	.000	5.25	16	0	0	36	40	13	13	0	0	1	0	0	0	0		3	10	1	1	0.8	.929
1986	OAK A	0	0	—	0.00	1	0	0		0	3	0	0	0	0	0	0	0	0	—	0	0	0	0	0.0	.000
8 yrs.		24	37	.393	4.44	121	60	12	534.2	589	160	172	2	5	4	0	0	0	0		41	118	3	8	1.3	.981

Luis Arroyo

ARROYO, LUIS ENRIQUE (Yo-Yo)
B. Feb. 18, 1927, Penuelas, Puerto Rico.
BL TL 5′ 8½″ 178 lbs.

Year	Team	W	L	PCT	ERA	G	GS	CG	IP	H	BB	SO	ShO	Relief Pitching W	Relief Pitching L	Relief Pitching SV	Batting AB	Batting H	Batting HR	BA	PO	A	E	DP	TC/G	FA
1955	STL N	11	8	.579	4.19	35	24	9	159	162	63	68	1	1	0	0	56	13	1	.232	5	20	2	0	0.8	.926
1956	PIT N	3	3	.500	4.71	18	2	1	28.2	36	12	17	0	2	2	0	4	2	0	.500	1	5	0	0	0.3	1.000
1957		3	11	.214	4.68	54	10	0	130.2	151	31	101	0	3	5	1	32	5	0	.156	4	12	1	0	0.3	.941
1959	CIN N	1	0	1.000	3.95	10	0	0	13.2	17	11	8	0	1	0	0	2	0	0	.000	0	5	1	0	0.6	.833
1960	NY A	5	1	.833	2.88	29	0	0	40.2	30	22	29	0	5	1	7	5	0	0	.000	2	7	0	0	0.3	1.000
1961		15	5	.750	2.19	**65**	0	0	119	83	49	87	0	**15**	5	**29**	25	7	0	.280	2	15	1	0	0.3	.944
1962		1	3	.250	4.81	27	0	0	33.2	33	17	21	0	1	3	7	4	2	0	.500	0	5	2	0	0.3	.714
1963		1	1	.500	13.50	6	0	0	6	12	3	5	0	1	1	0	0	0	0	—	0	0	0	0	0.0	.000
8 yrs.		40	32	.556	3.93	244	36	10	531.1	524	208	336	1	29	17	44	128	29	1	.227	14	69	7	0	0.4	.922
WORLD SERIES																										
1960	NY A	0	0	—	13.50	1	0	0	0.2	2	0	1	0	0	0	0	1	0	0	.000	0	0	0	0	0.0	.000
1961		1	0	1.000	2.25	2	0	0	4	4	2	3	0	1	0	0	0	0	0	—	1	1	1	0	1.5	.667
2 yrs.		1	0	1.000	3.86	3	0	0	4.2	6	2	4	0	1	0	0	1	0	0	.000	1	1	1	0	1.0	.667

Rudy Arroyo

ARROYO, RUDOLPH, JR.
B. June 19, 1950, New York, N. Y.
BR TL 6′ 2″ 195 lbs.

Year	Team	W	L	PCT	ERA	G	GS	CG	IP	H	BB	SO	ShO	Relief Pitching W	Relief Pitching L	Relief Pitching SV	Batting AB	Batting H	Batting HR	BA	PO	A	E	DP	TC/G	FA
1971	STL N	0	1	.000	5.25	9	0	0	12	18	5	5	0	0	1	0	1	0	0	.000	0	1	0	0	0.1	1.000

Harry Arundel

ARUNDEL, HARRY
B. Feb. 1855, Philadelphia, Pa. D. Mar. 25, 1904, Cleveland, Ohio.
TR 5′ 6″ 145 lbs.

Year	Team	W	L	PCT	ERA	G	GS	CG	IP	H	BB	SO	ShO	Relief Pitching W	Relief Pitching L	Relief Pitching SV	Batting AB	Batting H	Batting HR	BA	PO	A	E	DP	TC/G	FA
1882	PIT AA	4	10	.286	*4.65*	14	14	13	120	155	23	47	0	0	0	0	53	10	0	.189	5	64	5	0	4.9	.932
1884	PRO N	1	0	1.000	1.00	1	1	1	9	8	4	4	0	0	0	0	3	1	0	.333	0	1	0	0	1.0	1.000
2 yrs.		5	10	.333	4.40	15	15	14	129	163	27	51	0	0	0	0	56	11	0	.196	5	65	5	0	4.7	.933

Ken Ash

ASH, KENNETH LOWTHER
B. Sept. 16, 1901, Anmoore, W. Va. D. Nov. 15, 1979, Clarksburg, W. Va.
BR TR 5′11″ 165 lbs.

Year	Team	W	L	PCT	ERA	G	GS	CG	IP	H	BB	SO	ShO	Relief Pitching W	Relief Pitching L	Relief Pitching SV	Batting AB	Batting H	Batting HR	BA	PO	A	E	DP	TC/G	FA
1925	CHI A	0	0	—	9.00	2	0	0	4	7	0	0	0	0	0	0	0	0	0	—	0	0	0	0	0.0	.000
1928	CIN N	3	3	.500	6.50	8	5	2	36	43	13	6	0	1	0	0	14	1	0	.071	0	10	0	0	1.3	1.000
1929		1	5	.167	4.83	29	7	2	82	91	30	26	0	1	1	2	21	3	0	.143	6	17	1	2	0.8	.958
1930		2	0	1.000	3.43	16	1	1	39.1	37	16	15	0	1	0	0	11	2	0	.182	0	15	0	1	0.9	1.000
4 yrs.		6	8	.429	4.96	55	13	5	161.1	178	59	47	0	3	1	2	46	6	0	.130	6	42	1	3	0.9	.980

Andy Ashby

ASHBY, ANDREW JASON
B. July 11, 1967, Kansas City, Mo.
BR TR 6′ 5″ 180 lbs.

Year	Team	W	L	PCT	ERA	G	GS	CG	IP	H	BB	SO	ShO	Relief Pitching W	Relief Pitching L	Relief Pitching SV	Batting AB	Batting H	Batting HR	BA	PO	A	E	DP	TC/G	FA
1991	PHI N	1	5	.167	6.00	8	8	0	42	41	19	26	0	0	0	0	12	1	0	.083	7	4	0	1	1.4	1.000
1992		1	3	.250	7.54	10	8	0	37	42	21	24	0	0	0	0	11	1	0	.091	1	6	0	0	0.7	1.000
1993	2 teams CLR N (20G 0–4) SD N (12G 3–6)																									
″	total	3	10	.231	6.80	32	21	0	123	168	56	77	0	0	0	1	36	5	0	.139	15	19	0	1	1.1	1.000
1994	SD N	6	11	.353	3.40	24	24	4	164.1	145	43	121	0	0	0	0	49	8	0	.163	14	22	0	0	1.5	1.000
1995		12	10	.545	2.94	31	**31**	2	192.2	180	62	150	2	0	0	0	49	8	0	.163	6	21	1	0	0.9	.964
5 yrs.		23	39	.371	4.46	105	92	6	559	576	201	398	2	0	0	1	157	23	0	.146	43	72	1	2	1.1	.991

Paul Assenmacher

ASSENMACHER, PAUL ANDRE
B. Dec. 10, 1960, Detroit, Mich.
BL TL 6′ 3″ 195 lbs.

Year	Team	W	L	PCT	ERA	G	GS	CG	IP	H	BB	SO	ShO	Relief Pitching W	Relief Pitching L	Relief Pitching SV	Batting AB	Batting H	Batting HR	BA	PO	A	E	DP	TC/G	FA
1986	ATL N	7	3	.700	2.50	61	0	0	68.1	61	26	56	0	7	3	7	6	0	0	.000	5	15	0	1	0.3	1.000
1987		1	1	.500	5.10	52	0	0	54.2	58	24	39	0	1	1	2	4	0	0	.000	2	3	0	0	0.1	1.000
1988		8	7	.533	3.06	64	0	0	79.1	72	32	71	0	8	7	5	3	1	0	.333	6	11	0	2	0.3	1.000

Paul Assenmacher *continued*

Year	Team	W	L	PCT	ERA	G	GS	CG	IP	H	BB	SO	ShO	Relief Pitching W	Relief Pitching L	Relief Pitching SV	Batting AB	Batting H	Batting HR	BA	PO	A	E	DP	TC/G	FA
1989	2 teams ATL N (49G 1–3) CHI N (14G 2–1)																									
"	total	3	4	.429	3.99	63	0	0	76.2	74	28	79	0	3	4	0	5	0	0	.000	3	13	0	0	0.3	1.000
1990	CHI N	7	2	.778	2.80	74	1	0	103	90	36	95	0	7	2	10	8	0	0	.000	1	18	0	0	0.3	1.000
1991		7	8	.467	3.24	75	0	0	102.2	85	31	117	0	7	8	15	4	1	0	.250	4	10	1	0	0.2	.933
1992		4	4	.500	4.10	70	0	0	68	72	26	67	0	4	4	8	4	0	0	.000	3	6	0	1	0.1	1.000
1993	2 teams CHI N (46G 2–1) NY A (26G 2–2)																									
"	total	4	3	.571	3.38	72	0	0	56	54	22	45	0	4	3	0	2	1	0	.500	1	4	1	2	0.1	.833
1994	CHI A	1	2	.333	3.55	44	0	0	33	26	13	29	0	1	2	1	0	0	0	—	2	5	0	2	0.2	1.000
1995	CLE A	6	2	.750	2.82	47	0	0	38.1	32	12	40	0	6	2	0	0	0	0	—	0	5	0	1	0.1	1.000
10 yrs.		48	36	.571	3.40	622	1	0	680	624	250	638	0	48	36	48	36	3	0	.083	27	90	2	9	0.2	.983
DIVISIONAL PLAYOFF SERIES																										
1995	CLE A	0	0	—	0.00	3	0	0	1.2	0	0	3	0	0	0	0	0	0	0	—	0	0	0	0	0.0	.000
LEAGUE CHAMPIONSHIP SERIES																										
1989	CHI N	0	0	—	13.50	2	0	0	0.2	3	0	0	0	0	0	0	0	0	0	—	0	0	0	0	0.0	.000
1995	CLE A	0	0	—	0.00	3	0	0	1.1	0	1	2	0	0	0	0	0	0	0	—	0	0	0	0	0.0	.000
2 yrs.		0	0		4.50	5	0	0	2	3	1	2	0	0	0	0	0	0	0		0	0	0	0	0.0	
WORLD SERIES																										
1995	CLE A	0	0	—	6.75	4	0	0	1.1	1	3	3	0	0	0	0	0	0	0	—	0	0	0	0	0.0	.000

Pedro Astacio

ASTACIO, PEDRO JULIO BR TR 6′ 2″ 174 lbs.
Born Pedro Julio Astacio (Pura).
B. Nov. 28, 1969, Hato Mayor, Dominican Republic.

Year	Team	W	L	PCT	ERA	G	GS	CG	IP	H	BB	SO	ShO	Relief Pitching W	Relief Pitching L	Relief Pitching SV	Batting AB	Batting H	Batting HR	BA	PO	A	E	DP	TC/G	FA
1992	LA N	5	5	.500	1.98	11	11	4	82	80	20	43	4	0	0	0	24	3	0	.125	4	13	2	1	1.7	.895
1993		14	9	.609	3.57	31	31	3	186.1	165	68	122	2	0	0	0	62	10	0	.161	23	17	2	1	1.4	.952
1994		6	8	.429	4.29	23	23	3	149	142	47	108	1	0	0	0	47	3	0	.064	19	13	0	0	1.4	1.000
1995		7	8	.467	4.24	48	11	1	104	103	29	80	1	6	2	0	24	3	0	.125	11	11	0	0	0.5	1.000
4 yrs.		32	30	.516	3.66	113	76	11	521.1	490	164	353	8	6	2	0	157	19	0	.121	57	54	4	2	1.0	.965
DIVISIONAL PLAYOFF SERIES																										
1995	LA N	0	0	—	0.00	3	0	0	3.1	1	0	5	0	0	0	0	0	0	0	—	0	2	0	0	0.7	1.000

Keith Atherton

ATHERTON, KEITH ROWE BR TR 6′ 5″ 190 lbs.
B. Feb. 19, 1959, Newport News, Va.

Year	Team	W	L	PCT	ERA	G	GS	CG	IP	H	BB	SO	ShO	Relief Pitching W	Relief Pitching L	Relief Pitching SV	Batting AB	Batting H	Batting HR	BA	PO	A	E	DP	TC/G	FA
1983	OAK A	2	5	.286	2.77	29	0	0	68.1	53	23	40	0	2	5	4	1	0	0	.000	1	7	0	0	0.3	1.000
1984		7	6	.538	4.33	57	1	0	104	110	39	58	0	7	6	2	0	0	0	—	5	5	1	0	0.2	.909
1985		4	7	.364	4.30	56	0	0	104.2	89	42	77	0	4	7	3	0	0	0	—	4	6	1	0	0.2	.909
1986	2 teams OAK A (13G 1–2) MIN A (47G 5–8)																									
"	total	6	10	.375	4.08	60	0	0	97	100	46	67	0	6	**10**	10	0	0	0		6	11	1	1	0.3	.944
1987	MIN A	7	5	.583	4.54	59	0	0	79.1	81	30	51	0	7	5	2	0	0	0	—	3	12	1	0	0.3	.938
1988		7	5	.583	3.41	49	0	0	74	65	22	43	0	7	5	3	0	0	0	—	3	9	1	0	0.3	.923
1989	CLE A	0	3	.000	4.15	32	0	0	39	48	13	13	0	0	3	2	0	0	0	—	4	1	0	0	0.2	1.000
7 yrs.		33	41	.446	3.99	342	1	0	566.1	546	215	349	0	33	41	26	1	0	0	.000	26	51	5	1	0.2	.939
LEAGUE CHAMPIONSHIP SERIES																										
1987	MIN A	0	0	—	0.00	1	0	0	0.1	1	0	0	0	0	0	0	0	0	0	—	0	0	0	0	0.0	.000
WORLD SERIES																										
1987	MIN A	0	0	—	6.75	2	0	0	1.1	0	1	0	0	0	0	0	0	0	0	—	0	0	0	0	0.0	.000

Jim Atkins

ATKINS, JAMES CURTIS (Buddy) BL TR 6′ 3″ 205 lbs.
B. Mar. 10, 1921, Birmingham, Ala.

Year	Team	W	L	PCT	ERA	G	GS	CG	IP	H	BB	SO	ShO	Relief Pitching W	Relief Pitching L	Relief Pitching SV	Batting AB	Batting H	Batting HR	BA	PO	A	E	DP	TC/G	FA
1950	BOS A	0	0	—	3.86	1	0	0	4.2	4	4	0	0	0	0	0	2	0	0	.000	1	0	0	0	1.0	1.000
1952		0	1	.000	3.48	3	1	0	10.1	11	7	2	0	0	0	0	3	2	0	.667	1	2	0	0	1.0	1.000
2 yrs.		0	1	.000	3.60	4	1	0	15	15	11	2	0	0	0	0	5	2	0	.400	2	2	0	0	1.0	1.000

Tommy Atkins

ATKINS, FRANCIS MONTGOMERY BL TL 5′10½″ 165 lbs.
B. Dec. 9, 1887, Ponca, Neb. D. May 7, 1956, Cleveland, Ohio.

Year	Team	W	L	PCT	ERA	G	GS	CG	IP	H	BB	SO	ShO	Relief Pitching W	Relief Pitching L	Relief Pitching SV	Batting AB	Batting H	Batting HR	BA	PO	A	E	DP	TC/G	FA
1909	PHI A	0	0	—	4.50	1	1	0	6	6	5	4	0	0	0	0	2	0	0	.000	1	3	0	0	4.0	1.000
1910		3	2	.600	2.68	15	3	2	57	53	23	29	0	1	1	2	17	2	0	.118	2	18	0	0	1.3	1.000
2 yrs.		3	2	.600	2.86	16	4	2	63	59	28	33	0	1	1	2	19	2	0	.105	3	21	0	0	1.5	1.000

Al Atkinson

ATKINSON, ALBERT WRIGHT BR TR 5′11½″ 165 lbs.
B. Mar. 9, 1861, Clinton, Ill. D. June 17, 1952, McNatt, Mo.

Year	Team	W	L	PCT	ERA	G	GS	CG	IP	H	BB	SO	ShO	Relief Pitching W	Relief Pitching L	Relief Pitching SV	Batting AB	Batting H	Batting HR	BA	PO	A	E	DP	TC/G	FA
1884	4 teams PHI AA (22G 11–11) CHI U (8G 4–4) PIT U (8G 2–6) BAL U (8G 3–5)																									
"	total	20	26	.435	3.34	46	46	44	393.1	373	54	247	2	0	0	0	180	34	0	.189	20	93	32	2	2.8	.779
1886	PHI AA	25	17	.595	*3.95*	45	45	44	396.2	414	101	154	1	0	0	0	148	18	0	.122	21	59	7	1	1.9	.920
1887		6	8	.429	*5.92*	15	15	11	124.2	156	54	34	0	0	0	0	59	12	1	.203	14	26	4	0	2.3	.909
3 yrs.		51	51	.500	3.96	106	106	99	914.2	943	209	435	3	0	0	0	387	64	1	.165	55	178	43	3	2.4	.844

Bill Atkinson

ATKINSON, WILLIAM CECIL GLENN BL TR 5′ 7″ 165 lbs.
B. Oct. 4, 1954, Chatham, Ont., Canada.

Year	Team	W	L	PCT	ERA	G	GS	CG	IP	H	BB	SO	ShO	Relief Pitching W	Relief Pitching L	Relief Pitching SV	Batting AB	Batting H	Batting HR	BA	PO	A	E	DP	TC/G	FA
1976	MON N	0	0	—	0.00	4	0	0	5	3	1	4	0	0	0	0	0	0	0	—	0	1	0	0	0.3	1.000
1977		7	2	.778	3.36	55	0	0	83	72	29	56	0	7	2	7	5	1	0	.200	6	18	1	0	0.5	.960
1978		2	2	.500	4.40	29	0	0	45	45	28	32	0	2	2	3	4	2	0	.500	2	9	2	1	0.4	.846
1979		2	0	1.000	1.93	10	0	0	14	9	4	7	0	2	0	1	1	0	0	.000	1	0	0	0	0.1	1.000
4 yrs.		11	4	.733	3.43	98	0	0	147	129	62	99	0	11	4	11	10	3	0	.300	9	28	3	1	0.4	.925

Don August

AUGUST, DONALD GLENN (Augie) BR TR 6′ 3″ 190 lbs.
B. July 3, 1963, Inglewood, Calif.

Year	Team	W	L	PCT	ERA	G	GS	CG	IP	H	BB	SO	ShO	Relief Pitching W	Relief Pitching L	Relief Pitching SV	Batting AB	Batting H	Batting HR	BA	PO	A	E	DP	TC/G	FA
1988	MIL A	13	7	.650	3.09	24	22	6	148.1	137	48	66	1	1	0	0	0	0	0	—	22	24	0	2	1.9	1.000
1989		12	12	.500	5.31	31	25	2	142.1	175	58	51	1	2	0	0	0	0	0	—	13	25	2	5	1.3	.950
1990		0	3	.000	6.55	5	0	0	11	13	5	2	0	0	3	0	0	0	0	—	1	2	1	0	0.8	.750
1991		9	8	.529	5.47	28	23	1	138.1	166	47	62	1	1	1	0	0	0	0	—	11	21	0	1	1.1	1.000
4 yrs.		34	30	.531	4.64	88	70	9	440	491	158	181	3	4	4	0	0	0	0		47	72	3	8	1.4	.975

Jerry Augustine

AUGUSTINE, GERALD LEE
B. July 24, 1952, Kewaunee, Wis.
BL TL 6′ 185 lbs.

Year	Team	Lg	W	L	PCT	ERA	G	GS	CG	IP	H	BB	SO	ShO	Relief Pitching W	Relief Pitching L	Relief Pitching SV	Batting AB	Batting H	Batting HR	BA	PO	A	E	DP	TC/G	FA
1975	MIL	A	2	0	1.000	3.04	5	3	1	26.2	26	12	8	0	0	0	0	0	0	0	—	1	3	1	0	1.0	.800
1976			9	12	.429	3.30	39	24	5	171.2	167	56	59	3	1	1	0	0	0	0	—	9	18	1	1	0.7	.964
1977			12	18	.400	4.48	33	33	10	209	222	72	68	1	0	0	0	0	0	0	—	3	42	4	2	1.5	.918
1978			13	12	.520	4.54	35	30	9	188.1	204	61	59	2	1	0	0	0	0	0	—	10	41	0	1	1.5	1.000
1979			9	6	.600	3.45	43	2	0	86	95	30	41	0	9	5	5	0	0	0	—	3	6	0	1	0.2	1.000
1980			4	3	.571	4.50	39	1	0	70	83	36	22	0	4	2	2	0	0	0	—	1	13	0	2	0.4	1.000
1981			2	2	.500	4.28	27	2	0	61	75	18	26	0	1	1	2	0	0	0	—	1	11	1	2	0.5	.923
1982			1	3	.250	5.08	20	2	1	62	63	26	22	0	1	1	0	0	0	0	—	0	4	0	1	0.2	1.000
1983			3	3	.500	5.74	34	7	1	64.1	89	25	40	0	1	1	2	0	0	0	—	4	7	0	0	0.3	1.000
1984			0	0	—	0.00	4	0	0	5.1	4	4	3	0	0	0	0	0	0	0	—	1	1	0	0	0.5	1.000
10 yrs.			55	59	.482	4.23	279	104	27	944.1	1028	340	348	6	18	11	11	0	0	0		33	146	7	10	0.7	.962

Eldon Auker

AUKER, ELDON LeROY (Big Six)
B. Sept. 21, 1910, Norcatur, Kans.
BR TR 6′ 2″ 194 lbs.

Year	Team	Lg	W	L	PCT	ERA	G	GS	CG	IP	H	BB	SO	ShO	Relief Pitching W	Relief Pitching L	Relief Pitching SV	Batting AB	Batting H	Batting HR	BA	PO	A	E	DP	TC/G	FA
1933	DET	A	3	3	.500	5.24	15	6	2	55	63	25	17	1	0	1	0	17	2	0	.118	1	9	0	0	0.7	1.000
1934			15	7	.682	3.42	43	18	10	205	234	56	86	2	6	4	1	74	11	0	.149	9	53	2	3	1.5	.969
1935			18	7	**.720**	3.83	36	25	13	195	213	61	63	2	3	0	0	74	16	0	.216	5	44	0	4	1.4	1.000
1936			13	16	.448	4.89	35	31	14	215.1	263	83	66	2	0	0	0	78	24	0	.308	10	60	4	7	2.1	.946
1937			17	9	.654	3.88	39	32	19	252.2	250	97	73	1	0	1	1	91	18	3	.198	15	72	3	4	2.3	.967
1938			11	10	.524	5.27	27	24	12	160.2	184	56	46	1	0	1	0	57	5	0	.088	12	41	1	1	2.0	.981
1939	BOS	A	9	10	.474	5.36	31	25	6	151	183	61	43	1	1	0	0	53	12	2	.226	9	35	4	2	1.5	.917
1940	STL	A	16	11	.593	3.96	38	35	20	263.2	299	96	78	2	0	0	0	89	19	1	.213	27	51	4	4	2.2	.951
1941			14	15	.483	5.50	34	31	13	216	268	85	60	0	1	2	0	80	10	0	.125	14	43	0	6	1.7	1.000
1942			14	13	.519	4.08	35	34	17	249	**273**	86	62	2	0	0	0	87	14	0	.161	18	52	2	7	2.1	.972
10 yrs.			130	101	.563	4.42	333	261	126	1963.1	2230	706	594	14	11	9	2	700	131	6	.187	120	460	20	38	1.8	.967
WORLD SERIES																											
1934	DET	A	1	1	.500	5.56	2	2	1	11.1	16	5	2	0	0	0	0	4	0	0	.000	0	2	0	1	1.0	1.000
1935			0	0	—	3.00	1	1	0	6	6	2	1	0	0	0	0	2	0	0	.000	0	2	0	0	2.0	1.000
2 yrs.			1	1	.500	4.67	3	3	1	17.1	22	7	3	0	0	0	0	6	0	0	.000	0	4	0	1	1.3	1.000

Joe Ausanio

AUSANIO, JOSEPH JOHN, JR.
B. Dec. 9, 1965, Kingston, N. Y.
BR TR 6′ 1″ 205 lbs.

Year	Team	Lg	W	L	PCT	ERA	G	GS	CG	IP	H	BB	SO	ShO	Relief Pitching W	Relief Pitching L	Relief Pitching SV	Batting AB	Batting H	Batting HR	BA	PO	A	E	DP	TC/G	FA
1994	NY	A	2	1	.667	5.17	13	0	0	15.2	16	6	15	0	2	1	0	0	0	0	—	1	2	0	0	0.2	1.000
1995			2	0	1.000	5.73	28	0	0	37.2	42	23	36	0	2	0	1	0	0	0	—	4	2	0	0	0.2	1.000
2 yrs.			4	1	.800	5.57	41	0	0	53.1	58	29	51	0	4	1	1	0	0	0		5	4	0	0	0.2	1.000

Dennis Aust

AUST, DENNIS KAY
B. Nov. 25, 1940, Tecumseh, Neb.
BR TR 5′11″ 180 lbs.

Year	Team	Lg	W	L	PCT	ERA	G	GS	CG	IP	H	BB	SO	ShO	Relief Pitching W	Relief Pitching L	Relief Pitching SV	Batting AB	Batting H	Batting HR	BA	PO	A	E	DP	TC/G	FA
1965	STL	N	0	0	—	4.91	6	0	0	7.1	6	2	7	0	0	0	1	1	0	0	.000	0	3	0	0	0.5	1.000
1966			0	1	.000	6.52	9	0	0	9.2	12	6	7	0	0	1	1	1	0	0	.000	1	1	0	0	0.2	1.000
2 yrs.			0	1	.000	5.82	15	0	0	17	18	8	14	0	0	1	2	2	0	0	.000	1	4	0	0	0.3	1.000

Jim Austin

AUSTIN, JAMES PARKER
B. Dec. 7, 1963, Farmville, Va.
BR TR 6′ 2″ 200 lbs.

Year	Team	Lg	W	L	PCT	ERA	G	GS	CG	IP	H	BB	SO	ShO	Relief Pitching W	Relief Pitching L	Relief Pitching SV	Batting AB	Batting H	Batting HR	BA	PO	A	E	DP	TC/G	FA
1991	MIL	A	0	0	—	8.31	5	0	0	8.2	8	11	3	0	0	0	0	0	0	0	—	1	2	0	0	0.6	1.000
1992			5	2	.714	1.85	47	0	0	58.1	38	32	30	0	5	2	0	0	0	0	—	2	2	0	0	0.1	1.000
1993			1	2	.333	3.82	31	0	0	33	28	13	15	0	1	2	0	0	0	0	—	1	4	0	0	0.2	1.000
3 yrs.			6	4	.600	3.06	83	0	0	100	74	56	48	0	6	4	0	0	0	0		4	8	0	0	0.1	1.000

Rick Austin

AUSTIN, RICK GERALD
B. Oct. 27, 1946, Seattle, Wash.
BR TL 6′ 4″ 190 lbs.

Year	Team	Lg	W	L	PCT	ERA	G	GS	CG	IP	H	BB	SO	ShO	Relief Pitching W	Relief Pitching L	Relief Pitching SV	Batting AB	Batting H	Batting HR	BA	PO	A	E	DP	TC/G	FA
1970	CLE	A	2	5	.286	4.76	31	8	1	68	74	26	53	1	1	1	3	18	2	0	.111	4	13	0	1	0.5	1.000
1971			0	0	—	5.09	23	0	0	23	25	20	20	0	0	0	1	1	0	0	.000	1	5	0	1	0.3	1.000
1975	MIL	A	2	3	.400	4.05	32	0	0	40	32	32	30	0	2	3	2	0	0	0	—	1	3	0	0	0.1	1.000
1976			0	0	—	5.06	3	0	0	5.1	10	0	3	0	0	0	0	0	0	0	—	0	2	0	1	0.7	1.000
4 yrs.			4	8	.333	4.62	89	8	1	136.1	141	78	106	1	3	4	6	19	2	0	.105	6	23	0	3	0.3	1.000

Al Autry

AUTRY, ALBERT, JR.
B. Feb. 29, 1952, Modesto, Calif.
BR TR 6′ 5″ 225 lbs.

Year	Team	Lg	W	L	PCT	ERA	G	GS	CG	IP	H	BB	SO	ShO	Relief Pitching W	Relief Pitching L	Relief Pitching SV	Batting AB	Batting H	Batting HR	BA	PO	A	E	DP	TC/G	FA
1976	ATL	N	1	0	1.000	5.40	1	1	0	5	4	3	3	0	0	0	0	2	0	0	.000	0	0	0	0	0.0	.000

Steve Avery

AVERY, STEVEN THOMAS
B. Apr. 14, 1970, Trenton, Mich.
BL TL 6′ 4″ 180 lbs.

Year	Team	Lg	W	L	PCT	ERA	G	GS	CG	IP	H	BB	SO	ShO	Relief Pitching W	Relief Pitching L	Relief Pitching SV	Batting AB	Batting H	Batting HR	BA	PO	A	E	DP	TC/G	FA
1990	ATL	N	3	11	.214	5.64	21	20	1	99	121	45	75	1	0	1	0	30	4	0	.133	4	22	2	0	1.3	.929
1991			18	8	.692	3.38	35	35	3	210.1	189	65	137	1	0	0	0	79	17	0	.215	9	31	1	2	1.2	.976
1992			11	11	.500	3.20	35	**35**	2	233.2	216	71	129	2	0	0	0	76	13	0	.171	16	36	3	1	1.6	.945
1993			18	6	.750	2.94	35	35	3	223.1	216	43	125	1	0	0	0	75	12	0	.160	4	47	0	2	1.5	1.000
1994			8	3	.727	4.04	24	24	1	151.2	127	55	122	0	0	0	0	49	5	0	.102	4	26	1	0	1.3	.968
1995			7	13	.350	4.67	29	29	3	173.1	165	52	141	1	0	0	0	53	11	2	.208	3	37	2	2	1.4	.952
6 yrs.			65	52	.556	3.75	179	178	13	1091.1	1034	331	729	6	0	1	0	362	62	2	.171	40	199	9	7	1.4	.964
DIVISIONAL PLAYOFF SERIES																											
1995	ATL	N	0	0	—	13.50	1	0	0	0.2	1	0	1	0	0	0	0	0	0	0	—	0	0	0	0	0.0	.000
LEAGUE CHAMPIONSHIP SERIES																											
1991	ATL	N	2	0	1.000	0.00	2	2	0	16.1	9	4	17	0	0	0	0	7	1	0	.143	1	2	0	0	1.5	1.000
1992			1	1	.500	9.00	3	2	0	8	13	2	3	0	0	0	0	2	0	0	.000	0	0	0	0	0.0	.000
1993			0	0	—	2.77	2	2	0	13	9	6	10	0	0	0	0	4	2	0	.500	0	2	0	0	1.0	1.000
1995			1	0	1.000	0.00	2	1	0	6	2	4	6	0	0	0	0	2	1	0	.500	0	2	0	0	1.0	1.000
4 yrs.			4	1	.800	2.49	9	7	0	43.1	33	16	36	0	0	0	0	15	4	0	.267	1	6	0	0	0.8	1.000
			3rd		**7th**							**10th**	**7th**														
WORLD SERIES																											
1991	ATL	N	0	0	—	3.46	2	2	0	13	10	1	8	0	0	0	0	3	0	0	.000	1	0	0	0	0.5	1.000
1992			0	1	.000	3.75	2	2	0	12	11	3	11	0	0	0	0	1	0	0	.000	0	2	0	0	1.0	1.000
1995			1	0	1.000	1.50	1	1	0	6	3	5	3	0	0	0	0	0	0	0	—	0	0	0	0	0.0	.000
3 yrs.			1	1	.500	3.19	5	5	0	31	24	9	22	0	0	0	0	4	0	0	.000	1	2	0	0	0.6	1.000

Jim Avrea

AVREA, JAMES EPHERIUM (Jay) BR TR 6′ 1½″ 175 lbs.
B. July 6, 1920, Cleburne, Tex. D. June 27, 1987, Dallas, Tex.

Year	Team	W	L	PCT	ERA	G	GS	CG	IP	H	BB	SO	ShO	Relief Pitching W	Relief Pitching L	Relief Pitching SV	Batting AB	Batting H	Batting HR	BA	PO	A	E	DP	TC/G	FA
1950	CIN N	0	0	—	3.38	2	0	0	5.1	6	3	2	0	0	0	0	2	0	0	.000	1	0	0	0	0.5	1.000

Bobby Ayala

AYALA, ROBERT JOSEPH BR TR 6′ 2″ 190 lbs.
B. July 8, 1969, Ventura, Calif.

Year	Team	W	L	PCT	ERA	G	GS	CG	IP	H	BB	SO	ShO	Relief Pitching W	Relief Pitching L	Relief Pitching SV	Batting AB	Batting H	Batting HR	BA	PO	A	E	DP	TC/G	FA
1992	CIN N	2	1	.667	4.34	5	5	0	29	33	13	23	0	0	0	0	9	0	0	.000	3	8	0	1	2.2	1.000
1993		7	10	.412	5.60	43	9	0	98	106	45	65	0	5	4	3	21	2	0	.095	12	10	6	1	0.7	.786
1994	SEA A	4	3	.571	2.86	46	0	0	56.2	42	26	76	0	4	3	18	0	0	0	—	2	5	2	0	0.2	.778
1995		6	5	.545	4.44	63	0	0	71	73	30	77	0	6	5	19	0	0	0	—	7	6	1	0	0.2	.929
4 yrs.		19	19	.500	4.52	157	14	0	254.2	254	114	241	0	15	12	40	30	2	0	.067	24	29	9	2	0.4	.855
DIVISIONAL PLAYOFF SERIES																										
1995	SEA A	0	0	—	54.00	2	0	0	0.2	6	1	0	0	0	0	0	0	0	0	—	0	0	0	0	0.0	.000
LEAGUE CHAMPIONSHIP SERIES																										
1995	SEA A	0	0	—	2.45	2	0	0	3.2	3	3	3	0	0	0	0	0	0	0	—	0	1	0	1	0.5	1.000

Jake Aydelott

AYDELOTT, JACOB STUART 6′ 180 lbs.
B. July 6, 1861, Marion, Ind. D. Oct. 22, 1926, Detroit, Mich.

Year	Team	W	L	PCT	ERA	G	GS	CG	IP	H	BB	SO	ShO	Relief Pitching W	Relief Pitching L	Relief Pitching SV	Batting AB	Batting H	Batting HR	BA	PO	A	E	DP	TC/G	FA
1884	IND AA	5	7	.417	*4.92*	12	12	11	106	129	29	30	0	0	0	0	44	5	0	.114	2	16	6	0	1.8	.750
1886	PHI AA	0	2	.000	4.00	2	2	2	18	21	12	5	0	0	0	0	6	0	0	.000	0	3	0	0	1.5	1.000
2 yrs.		5	9	.357	4.79	14	14	13	124	150	41	35	0	0	0	0	50	5	0	.100	2	19	6	0	1.8	.778

Bill Ayers

AYERS, WILLIAM OSCAR BR TR 6′ 3″ 185 lbs.
B. Sept. 27, 1919, Newnan, Ga. D. Sept. 24, 1980, Newnan, Ga.

Year	Team	W	L	PCT	ERA	G	GS	CG	IP	H	BB	SO	ShO	Relief Pitching W	Relief Pitching L	Relief Pitching SV	Batting AB	Batting H	Batting HR	BA	PO	A	E	DP	TC/G	FA
1947	NY N	0	3	.000	8.15	13	4	0	35.1	46	14	22	0	0	0	1	8	2	0	.250	1	9	1	0	0.8	.909

Doc Ayers

AYERS, YANCY WYATT BR TR 6′ 1″ 185 lbs.
B. May 20, 1890, Fancy Gap, Va. D. May 26, 1968, Pulaski, Va.

Year	Team	W	L	PCT	ERA	G	GS	CG	IP	H	BB	SO	ShO	Relief Pitching W	Relief Pitching L	Relief Pitching SV	Batting AB	Batting H	Batting HR	BA	PO	A	E	DP	TC/G	FA
1913	WAS A	1	1	.500	1.53	4	2	1	17.2	12	4	17	1	0	0	1	7	0	0	.000	0	8	1	0	2.3	.889
1914		12	15	.444	2.54	49	31	8	265.1	221	54	148	3	3	2	3	83	14	0	.169	17	65	10	0	1.9	.891
1915		14	9	.609	2.21	40	16	8	211.1	178	38	96	2	**5**	**4**	3	63	12	0	.190	12	42	6	3	1.5	.900
1916		5	9	.357	3.78	43	17	7	157	173	52	69	0	0	2	2	43	6	0	.140	5	27	5	1	0.9	.865
1917		11	10	.524	2.17	40	15	12	207.2	192	59	78	3	5	4	1	63	13	0	.206	13	55	2	3	1.8	.971
1918		10	12	.455	2.83	40	24	11	219.2	215	63	67	4	3	2	3	66	10	0	.152	8	65	5	1	2.0	.936
1919	2 teams WAS A (11G 0–6) DET A (24G 5–3)																									
″	total	5	9	.357	2.75	35	10	3	137.1	140	45	44	1	4	3	0	36	8	0	.222	5	41	6	4	1.5	.885
1920	DET A	7	14	.333	3.88	46	22	9	208.2	217	62	103	3	0	2	1	59	9	0	.153	4	52	4	1	1.3	.933
1921		0	0	—	9.00	2	1	0	4	9	2	0	0	0	0	0	0	0	0	—	0	0	0	0	0.0	.000
9 yrs.		65	79	.451	2.84	299	138	59	1428.2	1357	379	622	17	20	19	14	420	72	0	.171	64	355	39	13	1.5	.915

Bob Ayrault

AYRAULT, ROBERT JOSEPH BR TR 6′ 4″ 230 lbs.
B. Apr. 27, 1966, South Lake Tahoe, Calif.

Year	Team	W	L	PCT	ERA	G	GS	CG	IP	H	BB	SO	ShO	Relief Pitching W	Relief Pitching L	Relief Pitching SV	Batting AB	Batting H	Batting HR	BA	PO	A	E	DP	TC/G	FA
1992	PHI N	2	2	.500	3.12	30	0	0	43.1	32	17	27	0	2	2	0	0	0	0	—	1	8	0	0	0.3	1.000
1993	2 teams PHI N (10G 2–0) SEA A (14G 1–1)																									
″	total	3	1	.750	5.40	24	0	0	30	36	16	15	0	3	1	0	2	0	0	.000	0	3	0	0	0.1	1.000
2 yrs.		5	3	.625	4.05	54	0	0	73.1	68	33	42	0	5	3	0	2	0	0	.000	1	11	0	0	0.2	1.000

Bob Babcock

BABCOCK, ROBERT ERNEST BR TR 6′ 5″ 210 lbs.
B. Aug. 25, 1949, New Castle, Pa.

Year	Team	W	L	PCT	ERA	G	GS	CG	IP	H	BB	SO	ShO	Relief Pitching W	Relief Pitching L	Relief Pitching SV	Batting AB	Batting H	Batting HR	BA	PO	A	E	DP	TC/G	FA
1979	TEX A	0	0	—	10.80	4	0	0	5	7	7	6	0	0	0	0	0	0	0	—	0	1	0	0	0.3	1.000
1980		1	2	.333	4.70	19	0	0	23	20	8	15	0	1	2	0	0	0	0	—	0	3	0	0	0.2	1.000
1981		1	1	.500	2.17	16	0	0	29	21	16	18	0	1	1	0	0	0	0	—	2	4	0	0	0.4	1.000
3 yrs.		2	3	.400	3.95	39	0	0	57	48	31	39	0	2	3	0	0	0	0	—	2	8	0	0	0.3	1.000

Johnny Babich

BABICH, JOHN CHARLES BR TR 6′ 1½″ 185 lbs.
B. May 14, 1913, Albion, Calif.

Year	Team	W	L	PCT	ERA	G	GS	CG	IP	H	BB	SO	ShO	Relief Pitching W	Relief Pitching L	Relief Pitching SV	Batting AB	Batting H	Batting HR	BA	PO	A	E	DP	TC/G	FA
1934	BKN N	7	11	.389	4.20	25	19	7	135	148	51	62	0	0	2	1	50	7	0	.140	6	36	4	1	1.8	.913
1935		7	14	.333	6.66	37	24	7	143.1	191	52	55	2	0	3	0	49	9	0	.184	6	31	4	1	1.1	.902
1936	BOS N	0	0	—	10.50	3	0	0	6	11	6	1	0	0	0	0	1	0	0	.000	0	2	1	0	1.0	.667
1940	PHI A	14	13	.519	3.73	31	30	16	229.1	222	80	94	1	0	0	0	86	10	0	.116	14	42	2	0	1.9	.966
1941		2	7	.222	6.09	16	14	4	78.1	85	31	19	0	0	1	0	25	10	0	.400	9	19	0	0	1.8	1.000
5 yrs.		30	45	.400	4.93	112	87	34	592	657	220	231	3	0	6	1	211	36	0	.171	35	130	11	2	1.6	.938

Les Backman

BACKMAN, LESTER JOHN BR TR 6′½″ 195 lbs.
B. Mar. 20, 1888, Cleves, Ohio D. Nov. 8, 1975, Cincinnati, Ohio.

Year	Team	W	L	PCT	ERA	G	GS	CG	IP	H	BB	SO	ShO	Relief Pitching W	Relief Pitching L	Relief Pitching SV	Batting AB	Batting H	Batting HR	BA	PO	A	E	DP	TC/G	FA
1909	STL N	3	11	.214	4.14	21	15	8	128.1	146	39	35	0	0	0	0	39	4	0	.103	2	36	1	0	1.9	.974
1910		6	7	.462	3.03	26	11	6	116	117	53	41	0	4	2	1	35	4	0	.114	5	30	3	1	1.5	.921
2 yrs.		9	18	.333	3.61	47	26	14	244.1	263	92	76	0	4	2	1	74	8	0	.108	7	66	4	1	1.6	.948

Eddie Bacon

BACON, EDGAR SUTER
B. Apr. 8, 1895, Franklin County, Ky. D. Oct. 2, 1963, Louisville, Ky.

Year	Team	W	L	PCT	ERA	G	GS	CG	IP	H	BB	SO	ShO	Relief Pitching W	Relief Pitching L	Relief Pitching SV	Batting AB	Batting H	Batting HR	BA	PO	A	E	DP	TC/G	FA
1917	PHI A	0	0	—	6.00	1	0	0	6	5	7	0	0	0	0	0	*				1	7	0	0	8.0	1.000

Mike Bacsik

BACSIK, MICHAEL JAMES BR TR 6′ 2″ 180 lbs.
B. Apr. 1, 1952, Dallas, Tex.

Year	Team	W	L	PCT	ERA	G	GS	CG	IP	H	BB	SO	ShO	Relief Pitching W	Relief Pitching L	Relief Pitching SV	Batting AB	Batting H	Batting HR	BA	PO	A	E	DP	TC/G	FA
1975	TEX A	1	2	.333	3.71	7	3	0	26.2	28	9	13	0	0	0	0	0	0	0	—	2	3	0	0	0.7	1.000
1976		3	2	.600	4.25	23	0	0	55	66	26	21	0	3	2	0	0	0	0	—	3	6	1	0	0.4	.900
1977		0	0	—	22.50	2	0	0	2	9	0	1	0	0	0	0	0	0	0	—	0	1	0	0	0.5	1.000
1979	MIN A	4	2	.667	4.36	31	0	0	66	61	29	33	0	4	2	0	0	0	0	—	4	9	0	0	0.4	1.000
1980		0	0	—	4.30	10	0	0	23	26	11	9	0	0	0	0	0	0	0	—	3	3	0	1	0.6	1.000
5 yrs.		8	6	.571	4.43	73	3	0	172.2	190	75	77	0	7	4	0	0	0	0		12	22	1	1	0.5	.971

Fred Baczewski

BACZEWSKI, FREDERIC JOHN (Lefty)
B. May 15, 1926, St. Paul, Minn. D. Nov. 14, 1976, Culver City, Calif.
BL TL 6′ 2½″ 185 lbs.

Year	Team	Lg	W	L	PCT	ERA	G	GS	CG	IP	H	BB	SO	ShO	Relief Pitching W	Relief Pitching L	Relief Pitching SV	Batting AB	Batting H	Batting HR	BA	PO	A	E	DP	TC/G	FA
1953	**2 teams**		**CHI N** (9G 0–0)	**CIN N** (24G 11–4)																							
″	**total**		11	4	.733	3.64	33	18	10	148.1	145	58	61	1	1	0	1	47	9	1	.191	5	13	4	2	0.7	.818
1954	**CIN**	**N**	6	6	.500	5.26	29	22	4	130	159	53	43	1	0	0	0	42	3	0	.071	12	16	1	1	1.0	.966
1955			0	0	—	18.00	1	0	0	1	2	0	0	0	0	0	0	0	0	0	—	0	0	0	0	0.0	.000
3 yrs.			17	10	.630	4.45	63	40	14	279.1	306	111	104	2	1	0	1	89	12	1	.135	17	29	5	3	0.8	.902

Lore Bader

BADER, LORE VERNE (King)
B. Apr. 27, 1888, Bader, Ill. D. June 2, 1973, Le Roy, Kans.
BL TR 6′ 175 lbs.

Year	Team	Lg	W	L	PCT	ERA	G	GS	CG	IP	H	BB	SO	ShO	Relief Pitching W	Relief Pitching L	Relief Pitching SV	Batting AB	Batting H	Batting HR	BA	PO	A	E	DP	TC/G	FA
1912	**NY**	**N**	2	0	1.000	0.90	2	1	1	10	9	6	3	0	1	0	0	3	0	0	.000	1	3	0	0	2.0	1.000
1917	**BOS**	**A**	2	0	1.000	2.35	15	1	0	38.1	48	18	14	0	1	0	1	10	3	0	.300	1	15	1	1	1.1	.941
1918			1	3	.250	3.33	5	4	2	27	26	12	10	1	0	0	0	9	1	0	.111	1	2	1	0	0.8	.750
3 yrs.			5	3	.625	2.51	22	6	3	75.1	83	36	27	1	2	0	1	22	4	0	.182	3	20	2	1	1.1	.920

Ed Baecht

BAECHT, EDWARD JOSEPH
B. May 15, 1907, Baden, Okla. D. Aug. 15, 1957, Grafton, Ill.
BR TR 6′ 3″ 195 lbs.

Year	Team	Lg	W	L	PCT	ERA	G	GS	CG	IP	H	BB	SO	ShO	Relief Pitching W	Relief Pitching L	Relief Pitching SV	Batting AB	Batting H	Batting HR	BA	PO	A	E	DP	TC/G	FA
1926	**PHI**	**N**	2	0	1.000	6.11	28	1	1	56	73	28	14	0	1	0	0	14	2	0	.143	2	23	2	1	1.0	.926
1927			0	1	.000	12.00	1	1	0	6	12	2	0	0	0	0	0	2	0	0	.000	0	2	0	0	2.0	1.000
1928			1	1	.500	6.00	9	1	0	24	37	9	10	0	1	0	0	7	1	0	.143	0	8	0	0	0.9	1.000
1931	**CHI**	**N**	2	4	.333	3.76	22	6	2	67	64	32	34	0	1	1	0	18	5	0	.278	3	18	0	1	1.0	1.000
1932			0	0	—	0.00	1	0	0	1	1	1	0	0	0	0	0	0	0	0	—	0	0	0	0	0.0	.000
1937	**STL**	**A**	0	0	—	12.79	3	0	0	6.1	13	6	3	0	0	0	0	1	0	0	.000	0	1	0	0	0.3	1.000
6 yrs.			5	6	.455	5.56	64	9	3	160.1	200	78	61	0	3	1	0	42	8	0	.190	5	52	2	2	0.9	.966

Jim Bagby

BAGBY, JAMES CHARLES JACOB, JR.
Son of Jim Bagby.
B. Sept. 8, 1916, Cleveland, Ohio D. Sept. 2, 1988, Marietta, Ga.
BR TR 6′ 2″ 170 lbs.

Year	Team	Lg	W	L	PCT	ERA	G	GS	CG	IP	H	BB	SO	ShO	Relief Pitching W	Relief Pitching L	Relief Pitching SV	Batting AB	Batting H	Batting HR	BA	PO	A	E	DP	TC/G	FA
1938	**BOS**	**A**	15	11	.577	4.21	43	25	10	198.2	218	90	73	1	4	1	2	67	13	0	.194	16	43	3	3	1.4	.952
1939			5	5	.500	7.09	21	11	3	80	119	36	35	0	2	1	0	34	10	1	.294	3	11	1	2	0.7	.933
1940			10	16	.385	4.73	36	21	6	182.2	217	83	57	1	5	5	2	74	15	0	.203	17	38	1	6	1.5	.982
1941	**CLE**	**A**	9	15	.375	4.04	33	27	12	200.2	214	76	53	0	0	0	2	74	18	0	.243	16	42	1	5	1.8	.983
1942			17	9	.654	2.96	38	**35**	16	270.2	267	64	54	4	0	0	1	95	18	1	.189	17	58	4	7	2.1	.949
1943			17	14	.548	3.10	36	**33**	16	**273**	**248**	80	70	3	1	0	1	112	30	0	.268	21	68	2	5	2.5	.978
1944			4	5	.444	4.33	13	10	2	79	101	34	12	0	2	0	0	31	7	1	.226	5	16	2	4	1.8	.913
1945			8	11	.421	3.73	25	19	11	159.1	171	59	38	3	0	1	1	58	17	0	.293	13	47	4	3	2.6	.938
1946	**BOS**	**A**	7	6	.538	3.71	21	11	6	106.2	117	49	16	1	1	1	0	42	5	0	.119	7	19	2	1	1.3	.929
1947	**PIT**	**N**	5	4	.556	4.67	37	6	2	115.2	143	37	23	0	2	2	0	32	7	0	.219	7	28	2	2	1.0	.946
10 yrs.			97	96	.503	3.96	303	198	84	1666.1	1815	608	431	13	17	11	9	619	140	3	.226	122	370	22	38	1.7	.957
WORLD SERIES																											
1946	**BOS**	**A**	0	0	—	3.00	1	0	0	3	6	1	1	0	0	0	0	1	0	0	.000	0	1	0	0	1.0	1.000

Jim Bagby

BAGBY, JAMES CHARLES JACOB, SR. (Sarge)
Father of Jim Bagby.
B. Oct. 5, 1889, Barnett, Ga. D. July 28, 1954, Marietta, Ga.
BB TR 6′ 170 lbs.

Year	Team	Lg	W	L	PCT	ERA	G	GS	CG	IP	H	BB	SO	ShO	Relief Pitching W	Relief Pitching L	Relief Pitching SV	Batting AB	Batting H	Batting HR	BA	PO	A	E	DP	TC/G	FA
1912	**CIN**	**N**	2	0	1.000	3.12	5	1	0	17.1	17	9	10	0	2	0	0	5	0	0	.000	1	4	0	0	1.0	1.000
1916	**CLE**	**A**	16	16	.500	2.55	48	27	14	278.2	253	67	88	3	5	**6**	5	90	15	0	.167	24	62	5	3	1.9	.945
1917			23	13	.639	1.96	49	37	26	320.2	**277**	73	83	8	1	1	7	108	25	0	.231	26	77	3	5	2.2	.972
1918			17	16	.515	2.69	**45**	31	23	271.1	274	78	57	2	2	2	6	99	21	0	.212	15	67	4	1	1.9	.953
1919			17	11	.607	2.80	35	32	21	241.1	258	44	61	0	0	0	3	89	23	1	.258	14	64	4	3	2.3	.951
1920			**31**	12	**.721**	2.89	**48**	**39**	**30**	**339.2**	**338**	79	73	3	**6**	1	0	131	33	1	.252	16	57	2	1	1.6	.973
1921			14	12	.538	4.70	40	26	12	191.2	238	44	37	0	3	2	4	76	15	0	.197	12	42	3	1	1.4	.947
1922			4	5	.444	6.32	25	10	4	98.1	134	39	25	0	1	0	1	42	11	0	.262	6	28	0	0	1.4	1.000
1923	**PIT**	**N**	3	2	.600	5.24	21	6	2	68.2	95	25	16	0	1	1	3	20	1	0	.050	1	10	0	4	0.5	1.000
9 yrs.			127	87	.593	3.10	316	209	132	1827.2	1884	458	450	16	21	13	29	660	144	2	.218	115	411	21	18	1.7	.962
WORLD SERIES																											
1920	**CLE**	**A**	1	1	.500	1.80	2	2	1	15	20	1	3	0	0	0	0	6	2	1	.333	2	3	1	0	3.0	.833

Stan Bahnsen

BAHNSEN, STANLEY RAYMOND
B. Dec. 15, 1944, Council Bluffs, Iowa.
BR TR 6′ 2″ 185 lbs.

Year	Team	Lg	W	L	PCT	ERA	G	GS	CG	IP	H	BB	SO	ShO	Relief Pitching W	Relief Pitching L	Relief Pitching SV	Batting AB	Batting H	Batting HR	BA	PO	A	E	DP	TC/G	FA
1966	**NY**	**A**	1	1	.500	3.52	4	3	1	23	15	7	16	0	0	0	1	7	1	0	.143	1	3	0	0	1.0	1.000
1968			17	12	.586	2.05	37	34	10	267.1	216	68	162	1	0	1	0	81	4	0	.049	15	32	3	1	1.4	.940
1969			9	16	.360	3.83	40	33	5	220.2	222	90	130	2	1	2	1	60	5	0	.083	13	36	3	4	1.3	.942
1970			14	11	.560	3.32	36	35	6	233	227	75	116	2	0	0	0	74	11	0	.149	17	40	4	3	1.7	.934
1971			14	12	.538	3.35	36	34	14	242	221	72	110	3	0	0	0	79	12	0	.152	18	55	4	5	2.1	.948
1972	**CHI**	**A**	21	16	.568	3.60	43	41	5	252.1	263	73	157	1	0	0	0	92	14	0	.152	11	50	2	6	1.5	.968
1973			18	**21**	.462	3.57	42	42	14	282.1	290	117	120	4	0	0	0	0	0	0	—	20	53	4	4	1.8	.948
1974			12	15	.444	4.71	38	35	10	216	230	110	102	1	1	1	0	0	0	0	—	5	39	2	1	1.2	.957
1975	**2 teams**		**CHI A** (12G 4–6)	**OAK A** (21G 6–7)																							
″	**total**		10	13	.435	4.36	33	28	4	167.1	166	77	80	0	0	0	0	1	0	0	.000	10	27	2	1	1.2	.949
1976	**OAK**	**A**	8	7	.533	3.34	35	14	1	143	124	43	82	1	5	1	0	0	0	0	—	13	23	1	0	1.1	.973
1977	**2 teams**		**OAK A** (11G 1–2)	**MON N** (23G 8–9)																							
″	**total**		9	11	.450	5.01	34	24	3	149	166	51	79	1	0	1	1	42	5	0	.119	12	19	4	0	1.0	.886
1978	**MON**	**N**	1	5	.167	3.84	44	1	0	75	74	31	44	0	1	5	7	11	1	0	.091	6	10	2	0	0.4	.889
1979			3	1	.750	3.16	55	0	0	94	80	42	71	0	3	1	5	14	1	1	.071	4	13	2	0	0.3	.895
1980			7	6	.538	3.07	57	0	0	91	80	33	48	0	7	6	4	9	1	0	.111	6	12	0	1	0.3	1.000
1981			2	1	.667	4.96	25	3	0	49	45	24	28	0	2	0	1	9	1	0	.111	2	2	1	0	0.2	.800
1982	**2 teams**		**CAL A** (7G 0–1)	**PHI N** (8G 0–0)																							
″	**total**		0	1	.000	2.74	15	0	0	23	21	11	14	0	0	1	0	0	0	0		1	1	1	0	0.2	.667
16 yrs.			146	149	.495	3.61	574	327	73	2528	2440	924	1359	16	20	19	20	479	56	1	.117	154	415	35	26	1.1	.942
DIVISIONAL PLAYOFF SERIES																											
1981	**MON**	**N**	0	0	—	0.00	1	0	0	1.1	1	1	1	0	0	0	0	0	0	0	—	0	0	0	0	0.0	.000

Ed Bahr

BAHR, EDSON GARFIELD — BR TR 6′ 1½″ 172 lbs.
B. Oct. 16, 1919, Rouleau, Sask., Canada.

Year	Team	W	L	PCT	ERA	G	GS	CG	IP	H	BB	SO	ShO	Relief Pitching W	Relief L	Relief SV	Batting AB	Batting H	HR	BA	PO	A	E	DP	TC/G	FA
1946	PIT N	8	6	.571	2.63	27	14	7	136.2	128	52	44	0	0	0	0	45	8	0	.178	8	28	5	2	1.5	.878
1947		3	5	.375	4.59	19	11	1	82.1	82	43	25	0	1	1	0	23	2	0	.087	2	12	1	1	0.8	.933
2 yrs.		11	11	.500	3.37	46	25	8	219	210	95	69	0	1	1	0	68	10	0	.147	10	40	6	3	1.2	.893

Grover Baichley

BAICHLEY, GROVER CLEVELAND — BR TR 5′ 9½″ 165 lbs.
B. Jan. 7, 1890, Toledo, Ill. D. June 30, 1956, San Jose, Calif.

Year	Team	W	L	PCT	ERA	G	GS	CG	IP	H	BB	SO	ShO	Relief Pitching W	Relief L	Relief SV	Batting AB	Batting H	HR	BA	PO	A	E	DP	TC/G	FA
1914	STL A	0	0	—	5.14	4	0	0	7	9	3	3	0	0	0	0	1	0	0	.000	0	4	0	0	1.0	1.000

Scott Bailes

BAILES, SCOTT ALAN — BL TL 6′ 2″ 170 lbs.
B. Dec. 18, 1961, Chillicothe, Ohio.

Year	Team	W	L	PCT	ERA	G	GS	CG	IP	H	BB	SO	ShO	Relief Pitching W	Relief L	Relief SV	Batting AB	Batting H	HR	BA	PO	A	E	DP	TC/G	FA
1986	CLE A	10	10	.500	4.95	62	10	0	112.2	123	43	60	0	8	7	7	0	0	0	—	4	13	1	0	0.3	.944
1987		7	8	.467	4.64	39	17	0	120.1	145	47	65	0	2	1	6	0	0	0	—	6	19	2	0	0.7	.926
1988		9	14	.391	4.90	37	21	5	145	149	46	53	2	2	3	0	0	0	0	—	14	19	1	0	0.9	.971
1989		5	9	.357	4.28	34	11	0	113.2	116	29	47	0	2	3	0	0	0	0	—	4	20	2	2	0.8	.923
1990	CAL A	2	0	1.000	6.37	27	0	0	35.1	46	20	16	0	2	0	0	0	0	0	—	2	10	1	0	0.5	.923
1991		1	2	.333	4.18	42	0	0	51.2	41	22	41	0	1	2	0	0	0	0	—	3	8	0	0	0.3	1.000
1992		3	1	.750	7.45	32	0	0	38.2	59	28	25	0	3	1	0	0	0	0	—	1	4	0	1	0.2	1.000
7 yrs.		37	44	.457	4.93	273	59	5	617.1	679	235	307	2	20	17	13	0	0	0		34	93	7	3	0.5	.948

Bill Bailey

BAILEY, WILLIAM F. — BL TL 5′11″ 165 lbs.
B. Apr. 12, 1889, Fort Smith, Ark. D. Nov. 2, 1926, Houston, Tex.

Year	Team	W	L	PCT	ERA	G	GS	CG	IP	H	BB	SO	ShO	Relief Pitching W	Relief L	Relief SV	Batting AB	Batting H	HR	BA	PO	A	E	DP	TC/G	FA
1907	STL A	4	1	.800	2.42	6	5	3	48.1	39	15	17	0	0	0	0	20	3	0	.150	2	11	1	0	2.3	.929
1908		3	5	.375	3.04	22	12	7	106.2	85	50	42	0	0	0	0	34	3	0	.088	0	26	3	0	1.3	.897
1909		9	10	.474	2.44	32	20	17	199	174	75	114	1	1	0	0	77	22	0	.286	5	52	2	1	1.7	.966
1910		3	18	.143	3.32	34	20	13	192.1	186	97	90	0	3	1	0	63	13	0	.206	7	57	6	0	2.1	.914
1911		0	3	.000	4.55	7	2	2	31.2	42	16	8	0	0	1	0	11	0	0	.000	2	11	1	1	2.0	.929
1912		0	1	.000	9.28	3	2	0	10.2	15	10	2	0	0	0	0	2	1	0	.500	0	1	0	0	0.3	1.000
1914	BAL F	7	9	.438	3.08	19	18	10	128.2	106	68	131	1	1	0	0	43	7	0	.163	5	45	2	0	2.7	.962
1915	2 teams BAL F (36G 5–19) CHI F (5G 3–1)																									
″	total	8	20	.286	4.27	41	28	14	223.2	202	125	122	5	1	**4**	0	74	17	0	.230	9	61	7	2	1.9	.909
1918	DET A	1	2	.333	5.97	8	4	1	37.2	53	26	13	0	0	0	0	13	1	0	.077	1	14	0	0	1.9	1.000
1921	STL N	2	5	.286	4.26	19	6	3	74	95	22	20	1	1	2	0	22	2	0	.091	2	26	3	1	1.6	.903
1922		0	2	.000	5.40	12	0	0	31.2	38	23	11	0	0	2	0	7	2	0	.286	2	11	1	0	1.2	.929
11 yrs.		37	76	.327	3.57	203	117	70	1084.1	1035	527	570	8	7	10	0	366	71	0	.194	35	315	26	5	1.8	.931

Cory Bailey

BAILEY, PHILLIP CORY — BR TR 6′ 195 lbs.
B. Jan. 24, 1971, Herrin, Ill.

Year	Team	W	L	PCT	ERA	G	GS	CG	IP	H	BB	SO	ShO	Relief Pitching W	Relief L	Relief SV	Batting AB	Batting H	HR	BA	PO	A	E	DP	TC/G	FA
1993	BOS A	0	1	.000	3.45	11	0	0	15.2	12	12	11	0	0	1	0	0	0	0	—	0	5	0	0	0.5	1.000
1994		0	1	.000	12.46	5	0	0	4.1	10	3	4	0	0	1	0	0	0	0	—	0	0	0	0	0.0	.000
1995	STL N	0	0	—	7.36	3	0	0	3.2	2	2	5	0	0	0	0	0	0	0	—	0	1	0	0	0.3	1.000
3 yrs.		0	2	.000	5.70	19	0	0	23.2	24	17	20	0	0	2	0	0	0	0		0	6	0	0	0.3	1.000

Harvey Bailey

BAILEY, HARVEY FRANCIS — TL 6′ 160 lbs.
B. Nov. 24, 1876, Adrian, Mich. D. July 10, 1922, Toledo, Ohio.

Year	Team	W	L	PCT	ERA	G	GS	CG	IP	H	BB	SO	ShO	Relief Pitching W	Relief L	Relief SV	Batting AB	Batting H	HR	BA	PO	A	E	DP	TC/G	FA
1899	BOS N	6	4	.600	3.95	12	11	8	86.2	83	35	26	0	1	0	0	34	8	0	.235	2	17	2	0	1.8	.905
1900		0	0	—	4.95	4	1	0	20	24	11	9	0	0	0	0	9	2	0	.222	1	8	0	0	2.3	1.000
2 yrs.		6	4	.600	4.13	16	12	8	106.2	107	46	35	0	1	0	0	43	10	0	.233	3	25	2	0	1.9	.933

Howard Bailey

BAILEY, HOWARD LEE — BR TL 6′ 195 lbs.
B. July 31, 1957, Grand Haven, Mich.

Year	Team	W	L	PCT	ERA	G	GS	CG	IP	H	BB	SO	ShO	Relief Pitching W	Relief L	Relief SV	Batting AB	Batting H	HR	BA	PO	A	E	DP	TC/G	FA
1981	DET A	1	4	.200	7.30	9	5	0	37	45	13	17	0	0	0	0	0	0	0	—	2	11	0	0	1.4	1.000
1982		0	0	—	0.00	8	0	0	10	6	2	3	0	0	0	1	0	0	0	—	1	2	0	0	0.4	1.000
1983		5	5	.500	4.88	33	3	0	72	69	25	21	0	4	3	0	0	0	0	—	9	10	3	1	0.7	.864
3 yrs.		6	9	.400	5.22	50	8	0	119	120	40	41	0	4	3	1	0	0	0		12	23	3	1	0.8	.921

Jim Bailey

BAILEY, JAMES HOPKINS — BB TL 6′ 2½″ 210 lbs.
Brother of Ed Bailey.
B. Dec. 16, 1934, Strawberry Plains, Tenn.

Year	Team	W	L	PCT	ERA	G	GS	CG	IP	H	BB	SO	ShO	Relief Pitching W	Relief L	Relief SV	Batting AB	Batting H	HR	BA	PO	A	E	DP	TC/G	FA
1959	CIN N	0	1	.000	6.17	3	1	0	11.2	17	6	7	0	0	0	0	3	0	0	.000	0	0	0	0	0.0	.000

King Bailey

BAILEY, LEONARD C. — BL TL 6′ 185 lbs.
B. Nov. 1870, Va. Deceased.

Year	Team	W	L	PCT	ERA	G	GS	CG	IP	H	BB	SO	ShO	Relief Pitching W	Relief L	Relief SV	Batting AB	Batting H	HR	BA	PO	A	E	DP	TC/G	FA
1895	CIN N	1	0	1.000	5.63	1	1	1	8	13	0	0	0	0	0	0	4	2	0	.500	1	2	1	0	4.0	.750

Roger Bailey

BAILEY, CHARLES ROGER — BR TR 6′ 1″ 180 lbs.
B. Oct. 3, 1970, Chattahoochee, Fla.

Year	Team	W	L	PCT	ERA	G	GS	CG	IP	H	BB	SO	ShO	Relief Pitching W	Relief L	Relief SV	Batting AB	Batting H	HR	BA	PO	A	E	DP	TC/G	FA
1995	CLR N	7	6	.538	4.98	39	6	0	81.1	88	39	33	0	3	5	0	16	2	0	.125	3	14	2	2	0.5	.895

Steve Bailey

BAILEY, STEVEN JOHN — BR TR 6′ 1″ 194 lbs.
B. Feb. 12, 1942, Bronx, N. Y.

Year	Team	W	L	PCT	ERA	G	GS	CG	IP	H	BB	SO	ShO	Relief Pitching W	Relief L	Relief SV	Batting AB	Batting H	HR	BA	PO	A	E	DP	TC/G	FA
1967	CLE A	2	5	.286	3.90	32	1	0	64.2	62	42	46	0	2	4	2	10	0	0	.000	10	7	0	1	0.5	1.000
1968		0	1	.000	3.60	2	1	0	5	4	2	1	0	0	0	0	0	0	0	—	0	0	0	0	0.0	.000
2 yrs.		2	6	.250	3.88	34	2	0	69.2	66	44	47	0	2	4	2	10	0	0	.000	10	7	0	1	0.5	1.000

Sweetbreads Bailey

BAILEY, ABRAHAM LINCOLN — BR TR 6′ 205 lbs.
B. Feb. 12, 1895, Joliet, Ill. D. Sept. 27, 1939, Joliet, Ill.

Year	Team	W	L	PCT	ERA	G	GS	CG	IP	H	BB	SO	ShO	Relief Pitching W	Relief L	Relief SV	Batting AB	Batting H	HR	BA	PO	A	E	DP	TC/G	FA
1919	CHI N	3	5	.375	3.15	21	5	0	71.1	75	20	19	0	3	2	0	18	7	0	.389	0	29	0	2	1.4	1.000
1920		1	2	.333	7.12	21	1	0	36.2	38	11	8	0	1	1	0	7	1	0	.143	0	14	0	0	0.7	1.000
1921	2 teams CHI N (3G 0–0) BKN N (7G 0–0)																									
″	total	0	0		4.91	10	0	0	29.1	41	9	8	0	0	0	0	5	0	0	.000	1	8	1	0	1.0	.900
3 yrs.		4	7	.364	4.59	52	6	0	137.1	154	40	35	0	4	3	0	30	8	0	.267	1	51	1	2	1.0	.981

Bob Bailor

BAILOR, ROBERT MICHAEL BR TR 5′11″ 170 lbs.
B. July 10, 1951, Connellsville, Pa.

Year	Team	Lg	W	L	PCT	ERA	G	GS	CG	IP	H	BB	SO	ShO	Relief Pitching W	Relief Pitching L	Relief Pitching SV	Batting AB	Batting H	Batting HR	BA	PO	A	E	DP	TC/G	FA
1980	**TOR**	**A**	0	0	—	9.00	3	0	0	2	4	1	0	0	0	0	0	*				5	9	0	1	4.7	1.000

Loren Bain

BAIN, HERBERT LOREN BR TR 6′ 190 lbs.
B. July 4, 1922, Staples, Minn.

Year	Team	Lg	W	L	PCT	ERA	G	GS	CG	IP	H	BB	SO	ShO	Relief Pitching W	Relief Pitching L	Relief Pitching SV	Batting AB	Batting H	Batting HR	BA	PO	A	E	DP	TC/G	FA
1945	**NY**	**N**	0	0	—	7.88	3	0	0	8	10	4	1	0	0	0	0	3	1	0	.333	0	1	0	0	0.3	1.000

Doug Bair

BAIR, CHARLES DOUGLAS BR TR 6′ 180 lbs.
B. Aug. 22, 1949, Defiance, Ohio.

Year	Team	Lg	W	L	PCT	ERA	G	GS	CG	IP	H	BB	SO	ShO	Relief Pitching W	Relief Pitching L	Relief Pitching SV	Batting AB	Batting H	Batting HR	BA	PO	A	E	DP	TC/G	FA
1976	**PIT**	**N**	0	0	—	5.68	4	0	0	6.1	4	5	4	0	0	0	0	0	0	0	—	1	0	0	0	0.3	1.000
1977	**OAK**	**A**	4	6	.400	3.47	45	0	0	83	78	57	68	0	4	6	8	0	0	0	—	7	14	1	1	0.5	.955
1978	**CIN**	**N**	7	6	.538	1.98	70	0	0	100	87	38	91	0	7	6	28	14	2	0	.143	11	7	1	1	0.3	.947
1979			11	7	.611	4.31	65	0	0	94	93	51	86	0	11	7	16	8	0	0	.000	5	9	1	1	0.2	.933
1980			3	6	.333	4.24	61	0	0	85	91	39	62	0	3	6	6	2	0	0	.000	3	21	0	1	0.4	1.000
1981	**2 teams**	**CIN N** (24G 2–2) **STL N** (11G 2–0)																									
″	**total**		4	2	.667	5.10	35	0	0	54.2	55	19	30	0	4	2	1	6	1	1	.167	2	6	1	0	0.3	.889
1982	**STL**	**N**	5	3	.625	2.55	63	0	0	91.2	69	36	68	0	5	3	8	13	1	0	.077	9	13	1	1	0.4	.957
1983	**2 teams**	**STL N** (26G 1–1) **DET A** (27G 7–3)																									
″	**total**		8	4	.667	3.59	53	1	0	85.1	75	32	60	0	7	4	5	2	0	0	.000	3	10	1	0	0.3	.929
1984	**DET**	**A**	5	3	.625	3.75	47	1	0	93.2	82	36	57	0	5	2	4	0	0	0	—	12	11	0	2	0.5	1.000
1985	**2 teams**	**DET A** (21G 2–0) **STL N** (2G 0–0)																									
″	**total**		2	0	1.000	5.96	23	3	0	51.1	55	27	30	0	1	0	0	0	0	0		4	9	0	0	0.6	1.000
1986	**OAK**	**A**	2	3	.400	3.00	31	0	0	45	37	18	40	0	2	3	4	0	0	0	—	2	7	0	1	0.3	1.000
1987	**PHI**	**N**	2	0	1.000	5.93	11	0	0	13.2	17	5	10	0	2	0	0	1	0	0	.000	1	2	1	0	0.4	.750
1988	**TOR**	**A**	0	0	—	4.05	10	0	0	13.1	14	3	8	0	0	0	0	0	0	0	—	2	1	0	0	0.3	1.000
1989	**PIT**	**N**	2	3	.400	2.27	44	0	0	67.1	52	28	56	0	2	3	1	5	1	0	.200	8	10	1	0	0.4	.947
1990			0	0	—	4.81	22	0	0	24.1	30	11	19	0	0	0	0	1	0	0	.000	2	4	1	1	0.3	.857
15 yrs.			55	43	.561	3.63	584	5	0	908.2	839	405	689	0	53	42	81	52	5	1	.096	72	124	9	9	0.4	.956
LEAGUE CHAMPIONSHIP SERIES																											
1979	**CIN**	**N**	0	1	.000	9.00	1	0	0	1	2	1	0	0	0	1	0	0	0	0	—	0	1	0	0	1.0	1.000
1982	**STL**	**N**	0	0	—	0.00	1	0	0	1	2	3	0	0	0	0	0	0	0	0	—	0	1	0	0	1.0	1.000
2 yrs.			0	1	.000	4.50	2	0	0	2	4	4	0	0	0	1	0	0	0	0		0	2	0	0	1.0	1.000
WORLD SERIES																											
1982	**STL**	**N**	0	1	.000	9.00	3	0	0	2	2	2	3	0	0	1	0	0	0	0	—	0	0	0	0	0.0	.000
1984	**DET**	**A**	0	0	—	0.00	1	0	0	0.2	0	0	1	0	0	0	0	0	0	0	—	0	0	0	0	0.0	.000
2 yrs.			0	1	.000	6.75	4	0	0	2.2	2	2	4	0	0	1	0	0	0	0		0	0	0	0	0.0	

Bob Baird

BAIRD, ROBERT ALLEN BL TL 6′ 4″ 195 lbs.
B. Jan. 16, 1940, Knoxville, Tenn. D. Apr. 11, 1974, Chattanooga, Tenn.

Year	Team	Lg	W	L	PCT	ERA	G	GS	CG	IP	H	BB	SO	ShO	Relief Pitching W	Relief Pitching L	Relief Pitching SV	Batting AB	Batting H	Batting HR	BA	PO	A	E	DP	TC/G	FA
1962	**WAS**	**A**	0	1	.000	6.75	3	3	0	10.2	13	8	3	0	0	0	0	3	0	0	.000	0	2	0	0	0.7	1.000
1963			0	3	.000	7.71	5	3	0	11.2	12	7	7	0	0	0	0	3	1	0	.333	0	1	1	0	0.4	.500
2 yrs.			0	4	.000	7.25	8	6	0	22.1	25	15	10	0	0	0	0	6	1	0	.167	0	3	1	0	0.5	.750

Jersey Bakely

BAKELY, EDWARD ENOCH BR TR
Born Edward Enoch Bakeley.
B. Apr. 17, 1864, Blackwood, N. J. D. Feb. 17, 1915, Philadelphia, Pa.

Year	Team	Lg	W	L	PCT	ERA	G	GS	CG	IP	H	BB	SO	ShO	Relief Pitching W	Relief Pitching L	Relief Pitching SV	Batting AB	Batting H	Batting HR	BA	PO	A	E	DP	TC/G	FA
1883	**PHI**	**AA**	5	3	.625	*3.23*	8	8	7	61.1	65	12	14	0	0	0	0	26	5	0	.192	2	12	1	0	1.7	.933
1884	**3 teams**	**PHI U** (39G 14–25) **WIL U** (2G 0–2) **KC U** (5G 2–3)																									
″	**total**		16	**30**	.348	4.29	46	45	43	394.2	443	**81**	226	1	0	1	0	192	25	0	.130	44	79	30	6	2.7	.804
1888	**CLE**	**AA**	25	33	.431	2.97	61	61	60	532.2	518	128	212	4	0	0	0	194	26	1	.134	22	119	18	3	2.6	.887
1889	**CLE**	**N**	12	22	.353	2.96	36	34	33	304.1	296	106	105	2	0	1	0	111	15	1	.135	19	64	5	5	2.4	.943
1890	**CLE**	**P**	12	25	.324	4.47	43	38	32	326.1	412	147	67	0	0	0	0	138	28	0	.203	11	72	7	1	2.0	.922
1891	**2 teams**	**WAS AA** (13G 2–10) **BAL AA** (8G 4–2)																									
″	**total**		6	12	.333	4.24	21	18	16	163.1	175	90	45	0	1	0	0	66	12	0	.182	6	31	13	1	2.4	.740
6 yrs.			76	125	.378	3.66	215	204	191	1782.2	1909	564	669	7	1	2	0	727	111	2	.153	104	377	74	16	2.4	.867

Dave Bakenhaster

BAKENHASTER, DAVID LEE BR TR 5′10″ 168 lbs.
B. Mar. 5, 1945, Columbus, Ohio.

Year	Team	Lg	W	L	PCT	ERA	G	GS	CG	IP	H	BB	SO	ShO	Relief Pitching W	Relief Pitching L	Relief Pitching SV	Batting AB	Batting H	Batting HR	BA	PO	A	E	DP	TC/G	FA
1964	**STL**	**N**	0	0	—	6.00	2	0	0	3	9	1	0	0	0	0	0	0	0	0	—	0	1	0	0	0.5	1.000

Al Baker

BAKER, ALBERT JONES BR TR 5′11″ 170 lbs.
B. Feb. 28, 1906, Batesville, Miss. D. Nov. 6, 1982, Kenedy, Tex.

Year	Team	Lg	W	L	PCT	ERA	G	GS	CG	IP	H	BB	SO	ShO	Relief Pitching W	Relief Pitching L	Relief Pitching SV	Batting AB	Batting H	Batting HR	BA	PO	A	E	DP	TC/G	FA
1938	**BOS**	**A**	0	0	—	9.39	3	0	0	7.2	13	2	2	0	0	0	0	4	0	0	.000	1	1	0	0	0.7	1.000

Bock Baker

BAKER, CHARLES TL 5′ 9″ 181 lbs.
B. July 17, 1878, Troy, N. Y. D. Aug. 17, 1940, New York, N. Y.

Year	Team	Lg	W	L	PCT	ERA	G	GS	CG	IP	H	BB	SO	ShO	Relief Pitching W	Relief Pitching L	Relief Pitching SV	Batting AB	Batting H	Batting HR	BA	PO	A	E	DP	TC/G	FA
1901	**2 teams**	**CLE A** (1G 0–1) **PHI A** (1G 0–1)																									
″	**total**		0	2	.000	7.71	2	2	1	14	29	12	1	0	0	0	0	7	1	0	.143	0	2	0	1	1.0	1.000

Ernie Baker

BAKER, EARNEST GOULD BR TR 5′10″ 160 lbs.
B. Aug. 8, 1875, Concord, Mich. D. Oct. 25, 1945, Homer, Mich.

Year	Team	Lg	W	L	PCT	ERA	G	GS	CG	IP	H	BB	SO	ShO	Relief Pitching W	Relief Pitching L	Relief Pitching SV	Batting AB	Batting H	Batting HR	BA	PO	A	E	DP	TC/G	FA
1905	**CIN**	**N**	0	0	—	4.50	1	0	0	4	7	0	1	0	0	0	0	2	0	0	.000	0	0	0	0	0.0	.000

Jesse Baker

BAKER, JESSE ORMOND BL TL 5′11″ 188 lbs.
B. June 3, 1888, Anderson Island, Wash. D. Sept. 26, 1972, Tacoma, Wash.

Year	Team	Lg	W	L	PCT	ERA	G	GS	CG	IP	H	BB	SO	ShO	Relief Pitching W	Relief Pitching L	Relief Pitching SV	Batting AB	Batting H	Batting HR	BA	PO	A	E	DP	TC/G	FA
1911	**CHI**	**A**	2	7	.222	3.93	22	8	3	94	101	30	51	0	1	0	1	29	3	0	.103	2	33	1	0	1.6	.972

Kirtley Baker

BAKER, KIRTLEY (Whitey) BR TR 5′ 9″ 160 lbs.
B. June 24, 1869, Aurora, Ind. D. Apr. 15, 1927, Covington, Ky.

Year	Team	Lg	W	L	PCT	ERA	G	GS	CG	IP	H	BB	SO	ShO	Relief Pitching W	Relief Pitching L	Relief Pitching SV	Batting AB	Batting H	Batting HR	BA	PO	A	E	DP	TC/G	FA
1890	**PIT**	**N**	3	19	.136	5.60	25	21	19	178.1	209	86	76	2	1	0	0	68	10	0	.147	11	32	6	2	2.0	.878
1893	**BAL**	**N**	3	8	.273	8.44	15	12	8	91.2	138	58	26	0	0	0	0	57	17	0	.298	16	35	4	1	3.1	.927
1894			0	1	.000	∞	1	0	0		1	2	0	0	0	1	0	4	0	0	.000	3	1	1	0	2.5	.800

Kirtley Baker *continued*

Year	Team	Lg	W	L	PCT	ERA	G	GS	CG	IP	H	BB	SO	ShO	Relief Pitching W	Relief Pitching L	Relief Pitching SV	Batting AB	Batting H	HR	BA	PO	A	E	DP	TC/G	FA
1898	WAS	N	2	3	.400	3.06	6	5	4	47	56	18	7	0	0	0	0	18	5	0	.278	3	8	0	0	1.8	1.000
1899			1	7	.125	6.83	11	6	3	54	79	22	6	0	1	1	0	19	3	0	.158	1	24	4	0	2.6	.862
5 yrs.			9	38	.191	6.28	58	44	34	371	483	186	115	2	2	2	0	166	35	0	.211	34	100	15	3	2.4	.899

Neal Baker

BAKER, NEAL VERNON BR TR 6′ 1″ 175 lbs.
B. Apr. 30, 1904, LaPorte, Tex. D. Jan. 5, 1982, Houston, Tex.

Year	Team	Lg	W	L	PCT	ERA	G	GS	CG	IP	H	BB	SO	ShO	Relief Pitching W	Relief Pitching L	Relief Pitching SV	Batting AB	Batting H	HR	BA	PO	A	E	DP	TC/G	FA
1927	PHI	A	0	0	—	5.71	5	2	0	17.1	27	7	3	0	0	0	0	6	1	0	.167	0	5	0	2	1.0	1.000

Norm Baker

BAKER, NORMAN LESLIE (Bones)
B. Oct. 14, 1862, Philadelphia, Pa. D. Feb. 20, 1949, Hurffville, N. J.

Year	Team	Lg	W	L	PCT	ERA	G	GS	CG	IP	H	BB	SO	ShO	Relief Pitching W	Relief Pitching L	Relief Pitching SV	Batting AB	Batting H	HR	BA	PO	A	E	DP	TC/G	FA
1883	PIT	AA	0	2	.000	*3.32*	3	3	2	19	24	11	5	0	0	0	0	12	0	0	.000	3	1	2	0	1.2	.667
1885	LOU	AA	13	12	.520	*3.40*	25	24	24	217	210	69	79	1	**1**	0	0	87	18	0	.207	5	33	12	1	2.0	.760
1890	BAL	AA	1	1	.500	3.71	2	2	2	17	16	6	10	0	0	0	0	7	0	0	.000	0	5	0	0	2.5	1.000
3 yrs.			14	15	.483	3.42	30	29	28	253	250	86	94	1	1	0	0	106	18	0	.170	8	39	14	1	1.9	.770

Scott Baker

BAKER, SCOTT BL TL 6′ 2″ 175 lbs.
B. May 18, 1970, San Jose, Calif.

Year	Team	Lg	W	L	PCT	ERA	G	GS	CG	IP	H	BB	SO	ShO	Relief Pitching W	Relief Pitching L	Relief Pitching SV	Batting AB	Batting H	HR	BA	PO	A	E	DP	TC/G	FA
1995	OAK	A	0	0	—	9.82	1	0	0	3.2	5	5	3	0	0	0	0	0	0	0	—	0	0	0	0	0.0	.000

Steve Baker

BAKER, STEVEN BYRNE BR TR 6′ 185 lbs.
B. Aug. 30, 1956, Eugene, Ore.

Year	Team	Lg	W	L	PCT	ERA	G	GS	CG	IP	H	BB	SO	ShO	Relief Pitching W	Relief Pitching L	Relief Pitching SV	Batting AB	Batting H	HR	BA	PO	A	E	DP	TC/G	FA
1978	DET	A	2	4	.333	4.55	15	10	0	63.1	66	42	39	0	1	1	0	0	0	0	—	3	5	1	0	0.6	.889
1979			1	7	.125	6.64	21	12	0	84	97	51	54	0	0	1	1	0	0	0	—	3	8	0	1	0.5	1.000
1982	OAK	A	1	1	.500	4.56	5	3	0	25.2	30	4	14	0	0	0	0	0	0	0	—	0	3	1	0	0.8	.750
1983	2 teams	OAK A (35G 3–3) STL N (8G 0–1)																									
″	total		3	4	.429	3.94	43	1	0	64	69	30	24	0	3	3	5	0	0	0		4	7	0	0	0.3	1.000
4 yrs.			7	16	.304	5.13	84	26	0	237	262	127	131	0	4	5	6	0	0	0		10	23	2	1	0.4	.943

Tom Baker

BAKER, THOMAS CALVIN (Rattlesnake) BR TR 6′ 1½″ 180 lbs.
B. June 11, 1913, Nursery, Tex. D. Jan. 3, 1991, Fort Worth, Tex.

Year	Team	Lg	W	L	PCT	ERA	G	GS	CG	IP	H	BB	SO	ShO	Relief Pitching W	Relief Pitching L	Relief Pitching SV	Batting AB	Batting H	HR	BA	PO	A	E	DP	TC/G	FA
1935	BKN	N	1	0	1.000	4.29	11	1	1	42	48	20	10	0	1	0	0	19	9	0	.474	0	5	0	0	0.5	1.000
1936			1	8	.111	4.72	35	8	2	87.2	98	48	35	0	1	2	2	30	7	0	.233	2	21	2	2	0.7	.920
1937	2 teams	BKN N (7G 0–1) NY N (13G 1–0)																									
″	total		1	1	.500	5.03	20	0	0	39.1	44	21	13	0	1	1	0	9	2	0	.222	2	7	1	0	0.5	.900
1938	NY	N	0	0	—	6.75	2	0	0	4	5	3	0	0	0	0	0	0	0	0	—	1	1	0	0	1.0	1.000
4 yrs.			3	9	.250	4.73	68	9	3	173	195	92	58	0	3	3	2	58	18	0	.310	5	34	3	2	0.6	.929

Tom Baker

BAKER, THOMAS HENRY BL TL 6′ 195 lbs.
B. May 6, 1934, Port Townsend, Wash. D. Mar. 9, 1980, Port Townsend, Wash.

Year	Team	Lg	W	L	PCT	ERA	G	GS	CG	IP	H	BB	SO	ShO	Relief Pitching W	Relief Pitching L	Relief Pitching SV	Batting AB	Batting H	HR	BA	PO	A	E	DP	TC/G	FA
1963	CHI	N	0	1	.000	3.00	10	1	0	18	20	7	14	0	0	0	0	3	0	0	.000	1	3	0	0	0.4	1.000

Mike Balas

BALAS, MICHAEL FRANCIS BR TR 6′ 195 lbs.
Born Michael Francis Balaski.
B. May 17, 1910, Lowell, Mass.

Year	Team	Lg	W	L	PCT	ERA	G	GS	CG	IP	H	BB	SO	ShO	Relief Pitching W	Relief Pitching L	Relief Pitching SV	Batting AB	Batting H	HR	BA	PO	A	E	DP	TC/G	FA
1938	BOS	N	0	0	—	6.75	1	0	0	1.1	3	0	0	0	0	0	0	0	0	0	—	0	0	0	0	0.0	.000

Jack Baldschun

BALDSCHUN, JACK EDWARD BR TR 6′1″ 175 lbs.
B. Oct. 16, 1936, Greenville, Ohio.

Year	Team	Lg	W	L	PCT	ERA	G	GS	CG	IP	H	BB	SO	ShO	Relief Pitching W	Relief Pitching L	Relief Pitching SV	Batting AB	Batting H	HR	BA	PO	A	E	DP	TC/G	FA
1961	PHI	N	5	3	.625	3.88	**65**	0	0	99.2	90	49	59	0	5	3	3	11	0	0	.000	9	18	0	0	0.4	1.000
1962			12	7	.623	2.96	67	0	0	112.2	95	48	95	0	**12**	7	13	16	1	0	.063	6	19	1	2	0.4	.962
1963			11	7	.611	2.30	65	0	0	113.2	99	42	89	0	11	7	16	20	0	0	.000	8	27	5	0	0.6	.875
1964			6	9	.400	3.12	71	0	0	118.1	111	40	96	0	6	**9**	21	16	4	0	.250	5	27	4	2	0.5	.889
1965			5	8	.385	3.82	65	0	0	99	102	42	81	0	5	**8**	6	7	0	0	.000	2	22	2	0	0.4	.923
1966	CIN	N	1	5	.167	5.49	42	0	0	57.1	71	25	44	0	1	5	0	3	1	0	.333	1	11	1	2	0.3	.923
1967			0	0	—	4.15	9	0	0	13	15	9	12	0	0	0	0	1	0	0	.000	2	1	0	0	0.3	1.000
1969	SD	N	7	2	.778	4.79	61	0	0	77	80	29	67	0	7	2	1	4	1	0	.250	6	10	1	0	0.3	.941
1970			1	0	1.000	10.38	12	0	0	13	24	4	12	0	1	0	0	0	0	0	—	0	1	0	0	0.1	1.000
9 yrs.			48	41	.539	3.70	457	0	0	703.2	687	298	555	0	48	41	60	78	7	0	.090	39	136	14	6	0.4	.926

Dave Baldwin

BALDWIN, DAVID GEORGE BR TR 6′ 2″ 200 lbs.
B. Mar. 30, 1938, Tucson, Ariz.

Year	Team	Lg	W	L	PCT	ERA	G	GS	CG	IP	H	BB	SO	ShO	Relief Pitching W	Relief Pitching L	Relief Pitching SV	Batting AB	Batting H	HR	BA	PO	A	E	DP	TC/G	FA
1966	WAS	A	0	0	—	3.86	4	0	0	7	8	1	4	0	0	0	0	0	0	0	—	0	0	0	0	0.0	.000
1967			2	4	.333	1.70	58	0	0	68.2	53	20	52	0	2	4	12	4	0	0	.000	2	18	0	0	0.3	1.000
1968			0	2	.000	4.07	40	0	0	42	40	12	30	0	0	2	5	2	0	0	.000	2	9	0	0	0.3	1.000
1969			2	4	.333	4.05	43	0	0	66.2	57	34	51	0	2	4	4	7	0	0	.000	4	7	0	0	0.3	1.000
1970	MIL	A	2	1	.667	2.57	28	0	0	35	25	18	26	0	2	1	1	2	1	0	.500	6	14	0	1	0.7	1.000
1973	CHI	A	0	0	—	3.60	3	0	0	5	7	4	1	0	0	0	0	0	0	0	—	1	1	0	0	0.7	1.000
6 yrs.			6	11	.353	3.09	176	0	0	224.1	190	89	164	0	6	11	22	15	1	0	.067	15	49	0	1	0.4	1.000

Harry Baldwin

BALDWIN, HOWARD EDWARD BR TR 5′11″ 160 lbs.
B. June 30, 1900, Baltimore, Md. D. Jan. 23, 1958, Baltimore, Md.

Year	Team	Lg	W	L	PCT	ERA	G	GS	CG	IP	H	BB	SO	ShO	Relief Pitching W	Relief Pitching L	Relief Pitching SV	Batting AB	Batting H	HR	BA	PO	A	E	DP	TC/G	FA
1924	NY	N	3	1	.750	4.28	10	2	1	33.2	42	11	5	0	2	0	0	11	4	0	.364	1	8	0	0	0.9	1.000
1925			0	0	—	9.00	1	0	0	1	3	1	0	0	0	0	0	0	0	0	—	0	0	0	0	0.0	.000
2 yrs.			3	1	.750	4.41	11	2	1	34.2	45	12	5	0	2	0	0	11	4	0	.364	1	8	0	0	0.8	1.000
WORLD SERIES																											
1924	NY	N	0	0	—	0.00	1	0	0	2	1	0	1	0	0	0	0	0	0	0	—	0	0	0	0	0.0	.000

James Baldwin

BALDWIN, JAMES J. BR TR 6′ 3″ 210 lbs.
B. July 15, 1971, Southern Pines, N. C.

Year	Team	Lg	W	L	PCT	ERA	G	GS	CG	IP	H	BB	SO	ShO	Relief Pitching W	Relief Pitching L	Relief Pitching SV	Batting AB	Batting H	HR	BA	PO	A	E	DP	TC/G	FA
1995	CHI	A	0	1	.000	12.89	6	4	0	14.2	32	9	10	0	0	0	0	0	0	0	—	0	3	1	0	0.7	.750

Kid Baldwin

BALDWIN, CLARENCE GEOGHAN
B. Nov. 1, 1864, Newport, Ky. D. July 10, 1897, Cincinnati, Ohio.
BR TR 5′ 6″ 147 lbs.

Year	Team	Lg	W	L	PCT	ERA	G	GS	CG	IP	H	BB	SO	ShO	Relief W	Relief L	Relief SV	Batting AB	Batting H	HR	BA	PO	A	E	DP	TC/G	FA
1885	CIN	AA	0	0	—	*9.00*	2	1	0	4	5	6	1	0	0	0	0	*				220	92	41	4	6.2	.884

Lady Baldwin

BALDWIN, CHARLES BUSTED
B. Apr. 8, 1859, Oramel, N. Y. D. Mar. 7, 1937, Hastings, Mich.
BL TL 5′11″ 170 lbs.

Year	Team	Lg	W	L	PCT	ERA	G	GS	CG	IP	H	BB	SO	ShO	Relief W	Relief L	Relief SV	Batting AB	Batting H	HR	BA	PO	A	E	DP	TC/G	FA
1884	MIL	U	1	1	.500	*2.65*	2	2	2	17	7	1	21	0	0	0	0	27	6	0	.222	6	3	2	1	1.6	.818
1885	DET	N	11	9	.550	*1.86*	21	20	19	179.1	137	28	135	1	0	0	1	124	30	0	.242	29	44	10	1	2.5	.880
1886			**42**	13	.764	*2.24*	56	56	55	487	371	100	**323**	**7**	0	0	0	204	41	0	.201	21	105	4	7	2.2	.969
1887			13	10	.565	3.84	24	24	24	211	225	61	60	1	0	0	0	85	23	0	.271	7	43	4	1	2.3	.926
1888			3	3	.500	5.43	6	6	5	53	76	15	26	0	0	0	0	23	6	0	.261	0	10	0	0	1.4	1.000
1890	2 teams	BKN N (2G 1–0) BUF P (7G 2–5)																									
″	total		3	5	.375	4.78	9	8	7	69.2	105	28	17	0	0	0	0	31	8	0	.258	1	20	0	0	2.3	1.000
6 yrs.			73	41	.640	2.85	118	116	112	1017	921	233	582	9	0	0	1	494	114	0	.231	64	225	20	10	2.2	.935

Mark Baldwin

BALDWIN, MARCUS ELMORE (Fido)
B. Oct. 29, 1863, Pittsburgh, Pa. D. Nov. 10, 1929, Pittsburgh, Pa.
BR TR 6′ 190 lbs.

Year	Team	Lg	W	L	PCT	ERA	G	GS	CG	IP	H	BB	SO	ShO	Relief W	Relief L	Relief SV	Batting AB	Batting H	HR	BA	PO	A	E	DP	TC/G	FA
1887	CHI	N	18	17	.514	3.40	40	39	35	334	329	122	164	1	0	0	**1**	139	26	4	.187	13	45	8	1	1.4	.879
1888			13	15	.464	2.76	30	30	27	251	241	99	157	2	0	0	0	106	16	1	.151	13	60	6	0	2.4	.924
1889	COL	AA	27	**34**	.443	3.61	**63**	**59**	54	**513.2**	458	**274**	**368**	6	1	**2**	1	208	39	2	.188	33	91	13	1	2.1	.905
1890	CHI	P	**34**	24	.586	3.31	**59**	**57**	**54**	**501**	**498**	**249**	**211**	1	2	0	0	215	45	1	.209	26	146	15	2	3.2	.920
1891	PIT	N	22	28	.440	2.76	53	51	48	437.2	385	227	197	2	1	0	0	177	27	1	.153	37	80	13	4	2.5	.900
1892			26	27	.491	3.47	56	53	45	440.1	447	194	157	0	2	0	0	178	18	1	.101	37	86	18	2	2.5	.872
1893	2 teams	PIT N (1G 0–0) NY N (45G 16–20)																									
″	total		16	20	.444	4.15	46	40	33	333.2	341	142	100	2	2	1	**2**	135	17	0	.126	24	53	7	1	1.8	.917
7 yrs.			156	165	.486	3.36	347	329	296	2811.1	2699	1307	1354	14	8	3	4	1158	188	10	.162	183	561	80	11	2.3	.903

Ollie Baldwin

BALDWIN, ORSON F.
B. Nov. 3, 1881, Carson City, Mich. D. Feb. 16, 1942, Los Angeles, Calif.
TR 185 lbs.

Year	Team	Lg	W	L	PCT	ERA	G	GS	CG	IP	H	BB	SO	ShO	Relief W	Relief L	Relief SV	Batting AB	Batting H	HR	BA	PO	A	E	DP	TC/G	FA
1908	STL	N	1	3	.250	6.14	4	4	0	14.2	16	11	5	0	0	0	0	6	0	0	.000	0	4	0	0	1.0	1.000

Rick Baldwin

BALDWIN, RICKEY ALAN
B. June 1, 1953, Fresno, Calif.
BL TR 6′ 3″ 180 lbs.

Year	Team	Lg	W	L	PCT	ERA	G	GS	CG	IP	H	BB	SO	ShO	Relief W	Relief L	Relief SV	Batting AB	Batting H	HR	BA	PO	A	E	DP	TC/G	FA
1975	NY	N	3	5	.375	3.34	54	0	0	97	97	34	54	0	3	5	6	15	3	0	.200	3	18	2	2	0.4	.913
1976			0	0	—	2.35	11	0	0	23	14	10	9	0	0	0	0	3	1	0	.333	1	4	0	0	0.5	1.000
1977			1	2	.333	4.43	40	0	0	63	62	31	23	0	1	2	1	4	2	0	.500	6	12	0	3	0.4	1.000
3 yrs.			4	7	.364	3.59	105	0	0	183	173	75	86	0	4	7	7	22	6	0	.273	10	34	2	5	0.4	.957

Jeff Ballard

BALLARD, JEFFREY SCOTT
B. Aug. 13, 1963, Billings, Mont.
BL TL 6′ 3″ 210 lbs.

Year	Team	Lg	W	L	PCT	ERA	G	GS	CG	IP	H	BB	SO	ShO	Relief W	Relief L	Relief SV	Batting AB	Batting H	HR	BA	PO	A	E	DP	TC/G	FA
1987	BAL	A	2	8	.200	6.59	14	14	0	69.2	100	35	27	0	0	0	0	0	0	0	—	5	10	0	1	1.1	1.000
1988			8	12	.400	4.40	25	25	6	153.1	167	42	41	1	0	0	0	0	0	0	—	9	13	0	3	0.9	1.000
1989			18	8	.692	3.43	35	35	4	215.1	240	57	62	1	0	0	0	0	0	0	—	13	55	2	6	2.0	.971
1990			2	11	.154	4.93	44	17	0	133.1	152	42	50	0	1	1	0	0	0	0	—	11	20	1	0	0.7	.969
1991			6	12	.333	5.60	26	22	0	123.2	153	28	37	0	0	0	0	0	0	0	—	4	15	1	3	0.8	.950
1993	PIT	N	4	1	.800	4.86	25	5	0	53.2	70	15	16	0	3	0	0	11	4	0	.364	4	12	1	3	0.7	.941
1994			1	1	.500	6.66	28	0	0	24.1	32	10	11	0	1	1	2	2	1	0	.500	1	3	0	0	0.1	1.000
7 yrs.			41	53	.436	4.71	197	118	10	773.1	914	229	244	2	5	2	2	13	5	0	.385	47	128	5	16	0.9	.972

Jay Baller

BALLER, JAY SCOTT
B. Oct. 6, 1960, Stayton, Ore.
BR TR 6′ 6″ 215 lbs.

Year	Team	Lg	W	L	PCT	ERA	G	GS	CG	IP	H	BB	SO	ShO	Relief W	Relief L	Relief SV	Batting AB	Batting H	HR	BA	PO	A	E	DP	TC/G	FA
1982	PHI	N	0	0	—	3.38	4	1	0	8	7	2	7	0	0	0	0	0	0	0	—	0	1	0	0	0.3	1.000
1985	CHI	N	2	3	.400	3.46	20	4	0	52	52	17	31	0	2	0	1	8	0	0	.000	4	6	0	0	0.5	1.000
1986			2	4	.333	5.37	36	0	0	53.2	58	28	42	0	2	4	5	5	0	0	.000	2	4	0	0	0.2	1.000
1987			0	1	.000	6.75	23	0	0	29.1	38	20	27	0	0	1	0	1	1	0	1.000	0	3	1	0	0.2	.750
1990	KC	A	0	1	.000	15.43	3	0	0	2.1	4	2	1	0	0	1	0	0	0	0	—	0	0	0	0	0.0	.000
1992	PHI	N	0	0	—	8.18	8	0	0	11	10	10	9	0	0	0	0	0	0	0	—	1	1	0	0	0.3	1.000
6 yrs.			4	9	.308	5.24	94	5	0	156.1	169	79	117	0	4	6	6	14	1	0	.071	7	15	1	0	0.2	.957

Mark Ballinger

BALLINGER, MARK ALAN
B. Jan. 31, 1949, Glendale, Calif.
BR TR 6′ 6″ 205 lbs.

Year	Team	Lg	W	L	PCT	ERA	G	GS	CG	IP	H	BB	SO	ShO	Relief W	Relief L	Relief SV	Batting AB	Batting H	HR	BA	PO	A	E	DP	TC/G	FA
1971	CLE	A	1	2	.333	4.63	18	0	0	35	30	13	25	0	1	2	0	5	1	0	.200	1	5	0	0	0.3	1.000

Win Ballou

BALLOU, NOBLE WINFIELD (Old Pard)
B. Nov. 30, 1897, Mount Morgan, Ky. D. Jan. 30, 1963, San Francisco, Calif.
BR TL 5′10½″ 170 lbs.

Year	Team	Lg	W	L	PCT	ERA	G	GS	CG	IP	H	BB	SO	ShO	Relief W	Relief L	Relief SV	Batting AB	Batting H	HR	BA	PO	A	E	DP	TC/G	FA
1925	WAS	A	1	1	.500	4.55	10	1	1	27.2	38	13	13	0	1	0	0	7	1	0	.143	0	8	2	1	1.0	.800
1926	STL	A	11	10	.524	4.79	43	13	5	154	186	71	59	0	6	3	2	42	2	1	.048	8	50	4	4	1.4	.935
1927			5	6	.455	4.78	21	11	4	90.1	105	46	17	0	2	1	0	28	1	0	.036	7	20	2	1	1.4	.931
1929	BKN	N	2	3	.400	6.71	25	1	0	57.2	69	38	20	0	2	2	0	16	1	0	.063	5	21	1	1	1.1	.963
4 yrs.			19	20	.487	5.11	99	26	10	329.2	398	168	109	0	11	6	2	93	5	1	.054	20	99	9	7	1.3	.930
WORLD SERIES																											
1925	WAS	A	0	0	—	0.00	2	0	0	1.2	0	1	1	0	0	0	0	0	0	0	—	0	0	0	0	0.0	.000

Tony Balsamo

BALSAMO, ANTHONY FRED
B. Nov. 21, 1937, Brooklyn, N. Y.
BR TR 6′ 2″ 185 lbs.

Year	Team	Lg	W	L	PCT	ERA	G	GS	CG	IP	H	BB	SO	ShO	Relief W	Relief L	Relief SV	Batting AB	Batting H	HR	BA	PO	A	E	DP	TC/G	FA
1962	CHI	N	0	1	.000	6.44	18	0	0	29.1	34	20	27	0	0	1	0	5	1	0	.200	3	6	1	2	0.6	.900

George Bamberger

BAMBERGER, GEORGE IRVIN
B. Aug. 1, 1925, Staten Island, N. Y.
Manager 1978–80, 1982–83, 1985–86.
BR TR 6′ 175 lbs.

Year	Team	Lg	W	L	PCT	ERA	G	GS	CG	IP	H	BB	SO	ShO	Relief W	Relief L	Relief SV	Batting AB	Batting H	HR	BA	PO	A	E	DP	TC/G	FA
1951	NY	N	0	0	—	18.00	2	0	0	2	4	2	1	0	0	0	0	0	0	0	—	0	0	0	0	0.0	.000
1952			0	0	—	9.00	5	0	0	4	6	6	0	0	0	0	0	0	0	0	—	0	1	0	0	0.2	1.000
1959	BAL	A	0	0	—	7.56	3	1	0	8.1	15	2	2	0	0	0	1	2	0	0	.000	0	3	0	0	1.0	1.000
3 yrs.			0	0		9.42	10	1	0	14.1	25	10	3	0	0	0	1	2	0	0	.000	0	4	0	0	0.4	1.000

Sal Bando

BANDO, SALVATORE LEONARD — BR TR 6′ 195 lbs.
Brother of Chris Bando.
B. Feb. 13, 1944, Cleveland, Ohio.

Year	Team	W	L	PCT	ERA	G	GS	CG	IP	H	BB	SO	ShO	Relief W	Relief L	Relief SV	Batting AB	Batting H	Batting HR	BA	PO	A	E	DP	TC/G	FA
1979	MIL A	0	0	—	6.00	1	0	0	3	3	0	0	0	0	0	0	*				5	23	2	1	4.3	.933

Eddie Bane

BANE, EDWARD NORMAN — BR TL 5′ 9″ 160 lbs.
B. Mar. 22, 1952, Chicago, Ill.

Year	Team	W	L	PCT	ERA	G	GS	CG	IP	H	BB	SO	ShO	Relief W	Relief L	Relief SV	Batting AB	Batting H	Batting HR	BA	PO	A	E	DP	TC/G	FA
1973	MIN A	0	5	.000	4.92	23	6	0	60.1	62	30	42	0	0	2	2	0	0	0	—	7	14	3	1	1.0	.875
1975		3	1	.750	2.86	4	4	0	28.1	28	15	14	0	0	0	0	0	0	0	—	1	2	2	0	1.3	.600
1976		4	7	.364	5.11	17	15	1	79.1	92	39	24	0	0	0	0	0	0	0	—	5	4	1	0	0.6	.900
3 yrs.		7	13	.350	4.66	44	25	1	168	182	84	80	0	0	2	2	0	0	0		13	20	6	1	0.9	.846

Dick Baney

BANEY, RICHARD LEE — BR TR 6′ 185 lbs.
B. Nov. 1, 1946, Fullerton, Calif.

Year	Team	W	L	PCT	ERA	G	GS	CG	IP	H	BB	SO	ShO	Relief W	Relief L	Relief SV	Batting AB	Batting H	Batting HR	BA	PO	A	E	DP	TC/G	FA
1969	SEA A	1	0	1.000	3.86	9	1	0	18.2	21	7	9	0	0	0	0	2	0	0	.000	1	1	1	1	0.3	.667
1973	CIN N	2	1	.667	2.93	11	1	0	30.2	26	6	17	0	1	1	2	9	2	0	.222	2	0	0	0	0.2	1.000
1974		1	0	1.000	5.49	22	1	0	41	51	17	12	0	1	0	1	5	0	0	.000	0	2	0	0	0.1	1.000
3 yrs.		4	1	.800	4.28	42	3	0	90.1	98	30	38	0	2	1	3	16	2	0	.125	3	3	1	1	0.2	.857

Dan Bankhead

BANKHEAD, DANIEL ROBERT — BR TR 6′ 1″ 184 lbs.
B. May 3, 1920, Empire, Ala. D. May 2, 1976, Houston, Tex.

Year	Team	W	L	PCT	ERA	G	GS	CG	IP	H	BB	SO	ShO	Relief W	Relief L	Relief SV	Batting AB	Batting H	Batting HR	BA	PO	A	E	DP	TC/G	FA
1947	BKN N	0	0	—	7.20	4	0	0	10	15	8	6	0	0	0	1	4	1	1	.250	1	0	0	0	0.3	1.000
1950		9	4	.692	5.50	41	12	2	129.1	119	88	96	1	5	1	3	39	9	0	.231	6	19	4	3	0.7	.862
1951		0	1	.000	15.43	7	1	0	14	27	14	9	0	0	0	0	2	0	0	.000	1	3	0	0	0.6	1.000
3 yrs.		9	5	.643	6.52	52	13	2	153.1	161	110	111	1	5	1	4	45	10	1	.222	8	22	4	3	0.7	.882

Scott Bankhead

BANKHEAD, MICHAEL SCOTT — BR TR 5′10″ 175 lbs.
B. July 31, 1963, Raleigh, N. C.

Year	Team	W	L	PCT	ERA	G	GS	CG	IP	H	BB	SO	ShO	Relief W	Relief L	Relief SV	Batting AB	Batting H	Batting HR	BA	PO	A	E	DP	TC/G	FA
1986	KC A	8	9	.471	4.61	24	17	0	121	121	37	94	0	2	1	0	0	0	0	—	11	12	1	0	1.0	.958
1987	SEA A	9	8	.529	5.42	27	25	2	149.1	168	37	95	0	0	0	0	0	0	0	—	9	9	0	1	0.7	1.000
1988		7	9	.438	3.07	21	21	2	135	115	38	102	1	0	0	0	0	0	0	—	7	11	0	0	0.9	1.000
1989		14	6	.700	3.34	33	33	3	210.1	187	63	140	2	0	0	0	0	0	0	—	14	19	0	2	1.0	1.000
1990		0	2	.000	11.08	4	4	0	13	18	7	10	0	0	0	0	0	0	0	—	0	0	0	0	0.0	.000
1991		3	6	.333	4.90	17	9	0	60.2	73	21	28	0	1	1	0	0	0	0	—	5	7	0	1	0.7	1.000
1992	CIN N	10	4	.714	2.93	54	0	0	70.2	57	29	53	0	10	4	1	9	2	0	.222	5	2	2	0	0.2	.778
1993	BOS A	2	1	.667	3.50	40	0	0	64.1	59	29	47	0	2	1	0	0	0	0	—	1	4	1	0	0.2	.833
1994		3	2	.600	4.54	27	0	0	37.2	34	12	25	0	3	2	0	0	0	0	—	1	0	0	0	0.0	1.000
1995	NY A	1	1	.500	6.00	20	1	0	39	44	16	20	0	1	1	0	0	0	0	—	2	2	0	0	0.2	1.000
10 yrs.		57	48	.543	4.18	267	110	7	901	876	289	614	3	19	10	1	9	2	0	.222	55	66	4	4	0.5	.968

Bill Banks

BANKS, WILLIAM JOHN — BR TR 5′11″ 150 lbs.
Born William John Yerrick.
B. Feb. 26, 1874, Danville, Pa. D. Sept. 8, 1936, Danville, Pa.

Year	Team	W	L	PCT	ERA	G	GS	CG	IP	H	BB	SO	ShO	Relief W	Relief L	Relief SV	Batting AB	Batting H	Batting HR	BA	PO	A	E	DP	TC/G	FA
1895	BOS N	1	0	1.000	0.00	1	1	0	7	7	4	4	0	0	0	0	3	0	0	.000	0	2	0	0	2.0	1.000
1896		0	3	.000	10.57	4	3	2	23	42	13	6	0	0	0	0	11	3	0	.273	0	3	0	0	0.8	1.000
2 yrs.		1	3	.250	8.10	5	4	2	30	49	17	10	0	0	0	0	14	3	0	.214	0	5	0	0	1.0	1.000

Willie Banks

BANKS, WILLIE ANTHONY — BR TR 6′ 1″ 190 lbs.
B. Feb. 27, 1969, Jersey City, N. J.

Year	Team	W	L	PCT	ERA	G	GS	CG	IP	H	BB	SO	ShO	Relief W	Relief L	Relief SV	Batting AB	Batting H	Batting HR	BA	PO	A	E	DP	TC/G	FA
1991	MIN A	1	1	.500	5.71	5	3	0	17.1	21	12	16	0	0	0	0	0	0	0	—	0	0	0	0	0.0	.000
1992		4	4	.500	5.70	16	12	0	71	80	37	37	0	0	0	0	0	0	0	—	9	5	0	0	0.9	1.000
1993		11	12	.478	4.04	31	30	0	171.1	186	78	138	0	0	0	0	0	0	0	—	13	15	6	1	1.1	.824
1994	CHI N	8	12	.400	5.40	23	23	1	138.1	139	56	91	1	0	0	0	41	5	0	.122	9	13	1	0	1.0	.957
1995	3 teams CHI N (10G 0–1) LA N (6G 0–2) FLA N (9G 2–3)																									
″	total	2	6	.250	5.66	25	15	0	90.2	106	58	62	0	0	1	0	26	7	0	.269	13	10	1	0	1.0	.958
5 yrs.		26	35	.426	5.03	100	83	1	488.2	532	241	344	1	0	1	0	67	12	0	.179	44	43	8	1	0.9	.916

Floyd Bannister

BANNISTER, FLOYD FRANKLIN — BL TL 6′ 1″ 190 lbs.
B. June 10, 1955, Pierre, S. D.

Year	Team	W	L	PCT	ERA	G	GS	CG	IP	H	BB	SO	ShO	Relief W	Relief L	Relief SV	Batting AB	Batting H	Batting HR	BA	PO	A	E	DP	TC/G	FA
1977	HOU N	8	9	.471	4.03	24	23	4	143	138	68	112	1	0	1	0	48	9	0	.188	6	14	0	1	0.8	1.000
1978		3	9	.250	4.83	28	16	2	110	120	63	94	2	0	0	0	31	5	0	.161	1	6	0	2	0.3	1.000
1979	SEA A	10	15	.400	4.05	30	30	6	182	185	68	115	2	0	0	0	0	0	0	—	10	15	0	0	0.8	1.000
1980		9	13	.409	3.47	32	32	8	218	200	66	155	0	0	0	0	0	0	0	—	12	26	1	2	1.2	.974
1981		9	9	.500	4.46	21	20	5	121	128	39	85	2	0	0	0	0	0	0	—	6	15	0	1	1.0	1.000
1982		12	13	.480	3.43	35	35	5	247	225	77	**209**	3	0	0	0	0	0	0	—	8	30	2	1	1.1	.950
1983	CHI A	16	10	.615	3.35	34	34	5	217.1	191	71	193	2	0	0	0	0	0	0	—	8	23	2	0	1.0	.939
1984		14	11	.560	4.83	34	33	4	218	211	80	152	0	0	0	0	1	0	0	.000	3	23	1	0	0.8	.963
1985		10	14	.417	4.87	34	34	4	210.2	211	100	198	1	0	0	0	0	0	0	—	4	22	1	0	0.8	.963
1986		10	14	.417	3.54	28	27	6	165.1	162	48	92	1	1	0	0	0	0	0	—	3	22	1	1	0.9	.962
1987		16	11	.593	3.58	34	34	11	228.2	216	49	124	2	0	0	0	0	0	0	—	10	22	1	0	1.0	.970
1988	KC A	12	13	.480	4.33	31	31	2	189.1	182	68	113	0	0	0	0	0	0	0	—	8	25	1	1	1.1	.971
1989		4	1	.800	4.66	14	14	0	75.1	87	18	35	0	0	0	0	0	0	0	—	3	15	0	3	1.3	1.000
1991	CAL A	0	0	—	3.96	16	0	0	25	25	10	16	0	0	0	0	0	0	0	—	0	1	0	0	0.1	1.000
1992	TEX A	1	1	.500	6.32	36	0	0	37	39	21	30	0	1	1	0	0	0	0	—	4	5	0	0	0.3	1.000
15 yrs.		134	143	.484	4.06	431	363	62	2387.2	2320	846	1723	16	2	2	0	80	14	0	.175	86	264	10	12	0.8	.972
LEAGUE CHAMPIONSHIP SERIES																										
1983	CHI A	0	1	.000	4.50	1	1	0	6	5	1	5	0	0	0	0	0	0	0	—	0	0	0	0	0.0	.000

Jimmy Bannon

BANNON, JAMES HENRY (Foxy Grandpa) — BR TR 5′ 5″ 160 lbs.
Brother of Tom Bannon.
B. May 5, 1871, Amesbury, Mass. D. Mar. 24, 1948, Glen Rock, N. J.

Year	Team	W	L	PCT	ERA	G	GS	CG	IP	H	BB	SO	ShO	Relief W	Relief L	Relief SV	Batting AB	Batting H	Batting HR	BA	PO	A	E	DP	TC/G	FA
1893	STL N	0	1	.000	22.50	1	1	0	4	10	5	1	0	0	0	0	107	36	0	.336	31	10	15	2	2.1	.732
1894	BOS N	0	0	—	0.00	1	0	0	2	4	1	0	0	0	0	0	494	166	13	.336	241	43	41	12	2.5	.874
1895		0	0	—	6.00	1	0	0	3	4	2	1	0	0	0	0	489	171	6	.350	209	31	33	3	2.2	.879
3 yrs.		0	1	.000	12.00	3	1	0	9	18	8	2	0	0	0	0	*				645	141	118	24	2.4	.869

Jack Banta

BANTA, JACKIE KAY
B. June 24, 1925, Hutchinson, Kans.
BL TR 6′ 2½″ 175 lbs.

Year	Team	Lg	W	L	PCT	ERA	G	GS	CG	IP	H	BB	SO	ShO	Relief W	Relief L	Relief SV	Batting AB	Batting H	Batting HR	BA	PO	A	E	DP	TC/G	FA
1947	BKN	N	0	1	.000	7.04	3	1	0	7.2	7	4	3	0	0	1	0	2	0	0	.000	0	5	0	0	1.7	1.000
1948			0	1	.000	8.10	2	1	0	3.1	5	5	1	0	0	0	0	1	0	0	.000	0	0	0	0	0.0	.000
1949			10	6	.625	3.37	48	12	2	152.1	125	68	97	1	6	2	3	46	5	0	.109	8	27	3	3	0.8	.921
1950			4	4	.500	4.35	16	5	1	41.1	39	36	15	0	2	3	2	12	2	0	.167	0	4	0	2	0.3	1.000
4 yrs.			14	12	.538	3.78	69	19	3	204.2	176	113	116	1	8	6	5	61	7	0	.115	8	36	3	5	0.7	.936
WORLD SERIES																											
1949	BKN	N	0	0	—	3.18	3	0	0	5.2	5	1	4	0	0	0	0	1	0	0	.000	0	1	0	0	0.3	1.000

Brian Barber

BARBER, BRIAN SCOTT
B. Mar. 4, 1973, Hamilton, Ohio
BR TR 6′ 1″ 175 lbs.

Year	Team	Lg	W	L	PCT	ERA	G	GS	CG	IP	H	BB	SO	ShO	Relief W	Relief L	Relief SV	Batting AB	Batting H	Batting HR	BA	PO	A	E	DP	TC/G	FA
1995	STL	N	2	1	.667	5.22	9	4	0	29.1	31	16	27	0	0	0	0	8	1	0	.125	1	1	0	0	0.2	1.000

Steve Barber

BARBER, STEPHEN DAVID
B. Feb. 22, 1939, Takoma Park, Md.
BL TL 6′ 195 lbs.

Year	Team	Lg	W	L	PCT	ERA	G	GS	CG	IP	H	BB	SO	ShO	Relief W	Relief L	Relief SV	Batting AB	Batting H	Batting HR	BA	PO	A	E	DP	TC/G	FA
1960	BAL	A	10	7	.588	3.22	36	27	6	181.2	148	**113**	112	1	0	1	2	54	3	0	.056	4	30	2	5	1.0	.944
1961			18	12	.600	3.33	37	34	14	248.1	194	130	150	**8**	0	0	1	80	13	2	.163	13	60	4	8	2.1	.948
1962			9	6	.600	3.46	28	19	5	140.1	145	61	89	2	0	0	0	42	3	0	.071	16	26	2	1	1.6	.955
1963			20	13	.606	2.75	39	36	11	258.2	253	92	180	2	0	1	0	87	12	1	.138	19	43	4	8	1.7	.939
1964			9	13	.409	3.84	36	26	4	157	144	81	118	0	1	1	1	47	7	1	.149	11	37	2	3	1.4	.960
1965			15	10	.600	2.69	37	32	7	220.2	177	81	130	2	1	1	0	65	5	1	.077	12	47	6	1	1.8	.908
1966			10	5	.667	2.29	25	22	5	133.1	104	49	91	3	0	0	0	44	3	0	.068	5	30	2	1	1.5	.946
1967	2 teams	BAL A (15G 4–9) NY A (17G 6–9)																									
″	total		10	18	.357	4.07	32	32	4	172.1	150	115	118	2	0	0	0	51	7	0	.137	11	25	6	2	1.3	.857
1968	NY	A	6	5	.545	3.23	20	19	3	128.1	127	64	87	1	0	0	0	39	2	0	.051	2	24	4	1	1.5	.867
1969	SEA	A	4	7	.364	4.80	25	16	0	86.1	99	48	69	0	0	0	0	25	5	0	.200	3	13	2	2	0.7	.889
1970	2 teams	CHI N (5G 0–1) ATL N (5G 0–1)																									
″	total		0	2	.000	6.20	10	2	0	20.1	27	11	14	0	0	1	0	4	1	0	.250	0	2	0	0	0.2	1.000
1971	ATL	N	3	1	.750	4.80	39	3	0	75	92	25	40	0	3	0	2	13	2	0	.154	4	13	1	0	0.5	.944
1972	2 teams	ATL N (5G 0–0) CAL A (34G 4–4)																									
″	total		4	4	.500	2.80	39	3	0	74	55	36	40	0	3	4	2	12	2	0	.167	3	12	2	0	0.4	.882
1973	CAL	A	3	2	.600	3.53	50	1	0	89.1	90	32	58	0	2	2	4	0	0	0	—	3	10	0	0	0.3	1.000
1974	SF	N	0	1	.000	5.14	13	0	0	14	13	12	13	0	0	1	1	0	0	0	—	0	0	1	0	0.1	.000
15 yrs.			121	106	.533	3.36	466	272	59	1999.2	1818	950	1309	21	10	12	13	563	65	5	.115	106	372	38	32	1.1	.926

Steve Barber

BARBER, STEVEN LEE
B. Mar. 13, 1948, Grand Rapids, Mich.
BR TR 6′ 1″ 190 lbs.

Year	Team	Lg	W	L	PCT	ERA	G	GS	CG	IP	H	BB	SO	ShO	Relief W	Relief L	Relief SV	Batting AB	Batting H	Batting HR	BA	PO	A	E	DP	TC/G	FA
1970	MIN	A	0	0	—	4.67	18	0	0	27	26	18	14	0	0	0	2	2	0	0	.000	1	3	0	0	0.2	1.000
1971			1	0	1.000	6.00	4	2	0	12	8	13	4	0	1	0	0	5	0	0	.000	1	1	0	0	0.5	1.000
2 yrs.			1	0	1.000	5.08	22	2	0	39	34	31	18	0	1	0	2	7	0	0	.000	2	4	0	0	0.3	1.000

Frank Barberich

BARBERICH, FRANK FREDERICK
B. Feb. 3, 1882, New Town, N. Y. D. May 1, 1965, Ocala, Fla.
BB TR 5′10½″ 175 lbs.

Year	Team	Lg	W	L	PCT	ERA	G	GS	CG	IP	H	BB	SO	ShO	Relief W	Relief L	Relief SV	Batting AB	Batting H	Batting HR	BA	PO	A	E	DP	TC/G	FA
1907	BOS	N	1	1	.500	5.84	2	2	1	12.1	19	5	1	0	0	0	0	4	0	0	.000	2	3	0	0	2.5	1.000
1910	BOS	A	0	0	—	7.20	2	0	0	5	7	2	0	0	0	0	0	1	0	0	.000	1	2	0	0	1.5	1.000
2 yrs.			1	1	.500	6.23	4	2	1	17.1	26	7	1	0	0	0	0	5	0	0	.000	3	5	0	0	2.0	1.000

Curt Barclay

BARCLAY, CURTIS CORDELL
B. Aug. 22, 1931, Chicago, Ill. D. Mar. 25, 1985, Missoula, Mont.
BR TR 6′ 3″ 210 lbs.

Year	Team	Lg	W	L	PCT	ERA	G	GS	CG	IP	H	BB	SO	ShO	Relief W	Relief L	Relief SV	Batting AB	Batting H	Batting HR	BA	PO	A	E	DP	TC/G	FA
1957	NY	N	9	9	.500	3.44	37	28	5	183	196	48	67	2	2	0	0	58	11	0	.190	6	48	2	4	1.5	.964
1958	SF	N	1	0	1.000	2.81	6	1	0	16	16	5	6	0	1	0	0	6	4	0	.667	3	2	0	0	0.8	1.000
1959			0	0	—	54.00	1	0	0	0.1	2	2	0	0	0	0	0	0	0	0	—	0	0	1	0	1.0	.000
3 yrs.			10	9	.526	3.48	44	29	5	199.1	214	55	73	2	3	0	0	64	15	0	.234	9	50	3	4	1.4	.952

Ray Bare

BARE, RAYMOND DOUGLAS
B. Apr. 15, 1949, Miami, Fla. D. Mar. 29, 1994, Miami, Fla.
BR TR 6′ 2″ 185 lbs.

Year	Team	Lg	W	L	PCT	ERA	G	GS	CG	IP	H	BB	SO	ShO	Relief W	Relief L	Relief SV	Batting AB	Batting H	Batting HR	BA	PO	A	E	DP	TC/G	FA
1972	STL	N	0	1	.000	0.54	14	0	0	16.2	18	6	5	0	0	1	1	0	0	0	—	0	2	1	0	0.2	.667
1974			1	2	.333	6.00	10	3	0	24	25	9	6	0	1	0	0	5	1	0	.200	4	6	0	1	1.0	1.000
1975	DET	A	8	13	.381	4.48	29	21	6	150.2	174	47	71	1	1	1	0	0	0	0	—	6	31	2	3	1.3	.949
1976			7	8	.467	4.63	30	21	3	134	157	51	59	2	0	0	0	0	0	0	—	6	25	0	2	1.0	1.000
1977			0	2	.000	12.86	5	4	0	14	24	7	4	0	0	0	0	0	0	0	—	2	7	0	2	1.8	1.000
5 yrs.			16	26	.381	4.80	88	49	9	339.1	398	120	145	3	2	2	1	5	1	0	.200	18	71	3	8	1.0	.967

John Barfield

BARFIELD, JOHN DAVID
B. Oct. 15, 1964, Pine Bluff, Ark.
BL TL 6′ 1″ 185 lbs.

Year	Team	Lg	W	L	PCT	ERA	G	GS	CG	IP	H	BB	SO	ShO	Relief W	Relief L	Relief SV	Batting AB	Batting H	Batting HR	BA	PO	A	E	DP	TC/G	FA
1989	TEX	A	0	1	.000	6.17	4	2	0	11.2	15	4	9	0	0	0	0	0	0	0	—	1	1	0	0	0.5	1.000
1990			4	3	.571	4.67	33	0	0	44.1	42	13	17	0	4	3	1	0	0	0	—	4	7	0	0	0.3	1.000
1991			4	4	.500	4.54	28	9	0	83.1	96	22	27	0	2	1	1	0	0	0	—	6	12	3	1	0.8	.857
3 yrs.			8	8	.500	4.72	65	11	0	139.1	153	39	53	0	6	4	2	0	0	0		11	20	3	1	0.5	.912

Clyde Barfoot

BARFOOT, CLYDE RAYMOND
B. July 8, 1891, Richmond, Va. D. Mar. 11, 1971, Highland Park, Calif.
BR TR 6′ 170 lbs.

Year	Team	Lg	W	L	PCT	ERA	G	GS	CG	IP	H	BB	SO	ShO	Relief W	Relief L	Relief SV	Batting AB	Batting H	Batting HR	BA	PO	A	E	DP	TC/G	FA
1922	STL	N	4	5	.444	4.21	42	2	1	117.2	139	30	19	0	3	4	2	34	12	0	.353	2	33	1	1	0.9	.972
1923			3	3	.500	3.73	33	2	1	101.1	112	27	23	1	2	3	1	37	7	0	.189	2	26	2	1	0.9	.933
1926	DET	A	1	2	.333	4.88	11	1	0	31.1	42	9	7	0	1	1	2	5	1	0	.200	2	10	0	2	1.1	1.000
3 yrs.			8	10	.444	4.10	86	5	2	250.1	293	66	49	1	6	8	5	76	20	0	.263	6	69	3	4	0.9	.962

Greg Bargar

BARGAR, GREG ROBERT
B. Jan. 27, 1959, Inglewood, Calif.
BR TR 6′ 2″ 185 lbs.

Year	Team	Lg	W	L	PCT	ERA	G	GS	CG	IP	H	BB	SO	ShO	Relief W	Relief L	Relief SV	Batting AB	Batting H	Batting HR	BA	PO	A	E	DP	TC/G	FA
1983	MON	N	2	0	1.000	6.75	8	3	0	20	23	8	9	0	0	0	0	6	1	0	.167	1	1	0	0	0.3	1.000
1984			0	1	.000	7.88	3	1	0	8	8	7	2	0	0	0	0	1	0	0	.000	1	2	1	0	1.3	.750
1986	STL	N	0	2	.000	5.60	22	0	0	27.1	36	10	12	0	0	2	0	2	0	0	.000	3	7	0	0	0.5	1.000
3 yrs.			2	3	.400	6.34	33	4	0	55.1	67	25	23	0	0	2	0	9	1	0	.111	5	10	1	0	0.5	.938

Cy Barger

BARGER, EROS BOLIVAR BL TR 6′ 160 lbs.
B. May 18, 1885, Jamestown, Ky. D. Sept. 23, 1964, Columbia, Ky.

Year	Team	W	L	PCT	ERA	G	GS	CG	IP	H	BB	SO	ShO	Relief Pitching W	L	SV	Batting AB	H	HR	BA	PO	A	E	DP	TC/G	FA
1906	NY A	0	0	—	10.13	2	1	0	5.1	7	3	3	0	0	0	1	3	1	0	.333	0	1	0	0	0.5	1.000
1907		0	0	—	3.00	1	0	0	6	10	1	0	0	0	0	0	2	0	0	.000	0	0	1	0	1.0	.000
1910	BKN N	15	15	.500	2.88	35	30	25	271.2	267	107	87	2	1	0	1	104	24	0	.231	9	87	1	2	2.8	.990
1911		11	15	.423	3.52	30	30	21	217.1	224	71	60	1	0	0	0	145	33	0	.228	34	68	5	2	2.5	.953
1912		1	9	.100	5.46	16	11	6	94	120	42	30	0	0	0	0	37	7	0	.189	2	29	2	0	2.1	.939
1914	PIT F	10	16	.385	4.34	33	26	18	228.1	252	63	70	1	1	1	1	83	17	0	.205	9	61	2	0	2.1	.972
1915		10	7	.588	2.29	34	13	8	153	130	47	47	1	4	1	5	54	15	0	.278	4	42	0	1	1.4	1.000
7 yrs.		47	62	.431	3.56	151	111	78	975.2	1010	334	297	5	6	2	8	*				58	288	11	5	2.2	.969

Brian Bark

BARK, BRIAN STUART BL TL 5′ 9″ 170 lbs.
B. Aug. 26, 1968, Baltimore, Md.

Year	Team	W	L	PCT	ERA	G	GS	CG	IP	H	BB	SO	ShO	Relief Pitching W	L	SV	Batting AB	H	HR	BA	PO	A	E	DP	TC/G	FA
1995	BOS A	0	0	—	0.00	3	0	0	2.1	2	1	0	0	0	0	0	0	0	0	—	0	0	0	0	0.0	.000

Len Barker

BARKER, LEONARD HAROLD BR TR 6′ 5″ 225 lbs.
B. July 27, 1955, Ft. Knox, Ky.

Year	Team	W	L	PCT	ERA	G	GS	CG	IP	H	BB	SO	ShO	Relief Pitching W	L	SV	Batting AB	H	HR	BA	PO	A	E	DP	TC/G	FA
1976	TEX A	1	0	1.000	2.40	2	2	1	15	7	6	7	0	0	0	0	0	0	0	—	0	2	0	0	1.0	1.000
1977		4	1	.800	2.68	15	3	0	47	36	24	51	0	3	0	1	0	0	0	—	4	8	0	1	0.8	1.000
1978		1	5	.167	4.82	29	0	0	52.1	63	29	33	0	1	5	4	0	0	0	—	2	9	1	1	0.4	.917
1979	CLE A	6	6	.500	4.93	29	19	2	137	146	70	93	0	0	0	0	0	0	0	—	8	13	2	1	0.8	.913
1980		19	12	.613	4.17	36	36	8	246	237	92	**187**	1	0	0	0	0	0	0	—	11	24	0	2	1.0	1.000
1981		8	7	.533	3.92	22	22	9	154	150	46	**127**	3	0	0	0	0	0	0	—	9	21	2	1	1.5	.938
1982		15	11	.577	3.90	33	33	10	244.2	211	88	187	1	0	0	0	0	0	0	—	23	27	2	1	1.6	.962
1983	2 teams CLE A (24G 8–13) ATL N (6G 1–3)																									
″	total	9	16	.360	4.88	30	30	4	182.2	181	66	126	1	0	0	0	8	1	0	.125	9	24	3	3	1.2	.917
1984	ATL N	7	8	.467	3.85	21	20	1	126.1	120	38	95	0	0	0	0	38	2	0	.053	5	34	2	2	2.0	.951
1985		2	9	.182	6.35	20	18	0	73.2	84	37	47	0	0	0	0	17	0	0	.000	2	9	1	0	0.6	.917
1987	MIL A	2	1	.667	5.36	11	11	0	43.2	54	17	22	0	0	0	0	0	0	0	—	3	6	0	0	0.8	1.000
11 yrs.		74	76	.493	4.35	248	194	35	1322.1	1289	513	975	6	4	5	5	63	3	0	.048	76	177	13	12	1.1	.951

Jeff Barkley

BARKLEY, JEFFREY CARVER BB TR 6′ 3″ 178 lbs.
B. Nov. 21, 1959, Hickory, N. C.

Year	Team	W	L	PCT	ERA	G	GS	CG	IP	H	BB	SO	ShO	Relief Pitching W	L	SV	Batting AB	H	HR	BA	PO	A	E	DP	TC/G	FA
1984	CLE A	0	0	—	6.75	3	0	0	4	6	1	4	0	0	0	0	0	0	0	—	0	1	0	0	0.3	1.000
1985		0	3	.000	5.27	21	0	0	41	37	15	30	0	0	3	1	0	0	0	—	4	5	1	0	0.5	.900
2 yrs.		0	3	.000	5.40	24	0	0	45	43	16	34	0	0	3	1	0	0	0		4	6	1	0	0.5	.909

Mike Barlow

BARLOW, MICHAEL ROSWELL BL TR 6′ 6″ 210 lbs.
B. Apr. 30, 1948, Stamford, N. Y.

Year	Team	W	L	PCT	ERA	G	GS	CG	IP	H	BB	SO	ShO	Relief Pitching W	L	SV	Batting AB	H	HR	BA	PO	A	E	DP	TC/G	FA
1975	STL N	0	0	—	4.50	9	0	0	8	11	3	2	0	0	0	0	0	0	0	—	0	1	1	0	0.2	.500
1976	HOU N	2	2	.500	4.50	16	0	0	22	27	17	11	0	2	2	0	3	0	0	.000	0	7	0	0	0.4	1.000
1977	CAL A	4	2	.667	4.58	20	1	0	59	53	27	25	0	3	2	1	0	0	0	—	5	10	2	0	0.9	.882
1978		0	0	—	4.50	1	0	0	2	3	0	1	0	0	0	0	0	0	0	—	0	0	0	0	0.0	.000
1979		1	1	.500	5.13	35	0	0	86	106	30	33	0	1	1	0	0	0	0	—	4	11	0	2	0.4	1.000
1980	TOR A	3	1	.750	4.09	40	1	0	55	57	21	19	0	2	1	5	0	0	0	—	2	9	1	0	0.3	.917
1981		0	0	—	4.20	12	0	0	15	22	6	5	0	0	0	0	0	0	0	—	0	5	0	0	0.4	1.000
7 yrs.		10	6	.625	4.63	133	2	0	247	279	104	96	0	8	6	6	3	0	0	.000	11	43	4	2	0.4	.931
LEAGUE CHAMPIONSHIP SERIES																										
1979	CAL A	0	0	—	0.00	1	0	0	1	0	0	0	0	0	0	0	0	0	0	—	0	0	0	0	0.0	.000

Charlie Barnabe

BARNABE, CHARLES EDWARD BL TL 5′11½″ 164 lbs.
B. June 12, 1900, Russell Gulch, Colo. D. Aug. 16, 1977, Waco, Tex.

Year	Team	W	L	PCT	ERA	G	GS	CG	IP	H	BB	SO	ShO	Relief Pitching W	L	SV	Batting AB	H	HR	BA	PO	A	E	DP	TC/G	FA
1927	CHI A	0	5	.000	5.31	17	5	1	61	86	20	5	0	0	2	0	19	3	0	.158	2	20	0	0	1.3	1.000
1928		0	2	.000	6.52	7	2	0	9.2	17	0	3	0	0	0	0	8	4	1	.500	2	5	0	0	1.0	1.000
2 yrs.		0	7	.000	5.48	24	7	1	70.2	103	20	8	0	0	2	0	27	7	1	.259	4	25	0	0	1.2	1.000

Bob Barnes

BARNES, ROBERT AVERY (Lefty) BL TL 5′11½″ 150 lbs.
B. Jan. 6, 1902, Washburn, Ill. D. Dec. 8, 1993, Peoria, Ill.

Year	Team	W	L	PCT	ERA	G	GS	CG	IP	H	BB	SO	ShO	Relief Pitching W	L	SV	Batting AB	H	HR	BA	PO	A	E	DP	TC/G	FA
1924	CHI A	0	0	—	19.29	2	0	0	4.2	14	0	1	0	0	0	0	2	0	0	.000	0	2	0	0	1.0	1.000

Brian Barnes

BARNES, BRIAN KEITH BL TL 5′ 9″ 170 lbs.
B. Mar. 25, 1967, Roanoke Rapids, N. C.

Year	Team	W	L	PCT	ERA	G	GS	CG	IP	H	BB	SO	ShO	Relief Pitching W	L	SV	Batting AB	H	HR	BA	PO	A	E	DP	TC/G	FA
1990	MON N	1	1	.500	2.89	4	4	1	28	25	7	23	0	0	0	0	9	0	0	.000	4	3	1	0	2.0	.875
1991		5	8	.385	4.22	28	27	1	160	135	84	117	0	0	0	0	49	4	0	.082	7	31	2	1	1.4	.950
1992		6	6	.500	2.97	21	17	0	100	77	46	65	0	0	0	0	29	8	0	.276	5	18	0	0	1.1	1.000
1993		2	6	.250	4.41	52	8	0	100	105	48	60	0	1	3	3	20	3	0	.150	3	15	0	1	0.3	1.000
1994	2 teams CLE A (6G 0–1) LA N (5G 0–0)																									
″	total	0	1	.000	5.89	11	0	0	18.1	22	19	10	0	0	1	0	0	0	0		1	2	1	0	0.4	.750
5 yrs.		14	22	.389	3.94	116	56	2	406.1	364	204	275	0	1	4	3	107	15	0	.140	20	69	4	2	0.8	.957

Frank Barnes

BARNES, FRANK BR TR 6′ 170 lbs.
B. Aug. 26, 1926, Longwood, Miss.

Year	Team	W	L	PCT	ERA	G	GS	CG	IP	H	BB	SO	ShO	Relief Pitching W	L	SV	Batting AB	H	HR	BA	PO	A	E	DP	TC/G	FA
1957	STL N	0	1	.000	4.50	3	1	0	10	13	9	5	0	0	0	0	2	0	0	.000	0	0	0	0	0.0	.000
1958		1	1	.500	7.58	8	1	0	19	19	16	17	0	1	1	0	6	1	0	.167	0	3	1	0	0.5	.750
1960		0	1	.000	3.52	4	1	0	7.2	8	9	8	0	0	0	1	2	0	0	.000	0	0	0	0	0.0	.000
3 yrs.		1	3	.250	5.89	15	3	0	36.2	40	34	30	0	1	1	1	10	1	0	.100	0	3	1	0	0.3	.750

Frank Barnes

BARNES, FRANK SAMUEL (Lefty) BL TL 6′ 2½″ 195 lbs.
B. Jan. 9, 1900, Dallas, Tex. D. Sept. 27, 1967, Houston, Tex.

Year	Team	W	L	PCT	ERA	G	GS	CG	IP	H	BB	SO	ShO	Relief Pitching W	L	SV	Batting AB	H	HR	BA	PO	A	E	DP	TC/G	FA
1929	DET A	0	1	.000	7.20	4	1	0	5	10	3	0	0	0	0	0	1	0	0	.000	0	3	1	0	1.0	.750
1930	NY A	0	1	.000	8.03	2	2	0	12.1	13	13	2	0	0	0	0	6	2	0	.333	0	10	0	0	5.0	1.000
2 yrs.		0	2	.000	7.79	6	3	0	17.1	23	16	2	0	0	0	0	7	2	0	.286	0	13	1	0	2.3	.929

Jesse Barnes

BARNES, JESSE LAWRENCE
Brother of Virgil Barnes.
B. Aug. 26, 1892, Perkins, Okla. D. Sept. 9, 1961, Santa Rosa, N. M.
BL TR 6′ 170 lbs.

Year	Team	W	L	PCT	ERA	G	GS	CG	IP	H	BB	SO	ShO	Relief W	Relief L	Relief SV	Batting AB	Batting H	HR	BA	PO	A	E	DP	TC/G	FA
1915	BOS N	4	0	1.000	1.39	9	3	2	45.1	41	10	16	0	1	0	0	17	3	0	.176	0	10	0	0	1.1	1.000
1916		6	15	.286	2.37	33	18	9	163	154	37	55	3	1	4	1	48	9	0	.188	11	60	2	2	2.2	.973
1917		13	**21**	.382	2.68	50	33	27	295	261	50	107	2	0	3	1	101	24	0	.238	18	96	1	1	2.3	.991
1918	NY N	6	1	.857	1.81	9	9	4	54.2	53	13	12	2	0	0	0	18	4	0	.222	5	25	1	0	3.4	.968
1919		**25**	9	.735	2.40	38	34	23	295.2	263	35	92	4	2	1	1	120	32	0	.267	11	97	3	5	2.9	.973
1920		20	15	.571	2.64	43	34	23	292.2	271	56	63	2	3	2	0	108	22	0	.204	16	93	4	9	2.6	.965
1921		15	9	.625	3.10	42	31	15	258.2	298	44	56	1	1	1	6	92	19	0	.207	24	67	0	4	2.2	1.000
1922		13	8	.619	3.51	37	29	14	212.2	236	38	52	2	0	1	0	77	14	0	.182	10	63	4	5	2.1	.948
1923	2 teams NY N (12G 3–1) BOS N (31G 10–14)																									
"	total	13	15	.464	3.31	43	27	13	231.1	252	56	53	5	2	**4**	3	79	13	0	.165	9	75	2	6	2.0	.977
1924	BOS N	15	**20**	.429	3.23	37	32	21	267.2	292	53	49	**4**	1	2	0	90	20	0	.222	15	68	0	3	2.2	1.000
1925		11	16	.407	4.53	32	28	17	216.1	255	63	55	0	0	1	0	81	16	1	.198	11	39	2	1	1.6	.962
1926	BKN N	10	11	.476	5.24	31	24	10	158	204	35	29	1	0	0	1	59	14	0	.237	7	37	3	1	1.5	.936
1927		2	10	.167	5.72	18	10	2	78.2	106	25	14	0	1	2	0	23	5	0	.217	1	18	0	0	1.1	1.000
13 yrs.		153	150	.505	3.22	422	312	180	2569.2	2686	515	653	26	12	21	13	913	195	1	.214	138	748	22	37	2.2	.976
WORLD SERIES																										
1921	NY N	2	0	1.000	1.65	3	0	0	16.1	6	6	18	0	2	0	0	9	4	0	.444	1	1	0	0	0.7	1.000
1922		0	0	—	1.80	1	1	1	10	8	2	6	0	0	0	0	4	0	0	.000	0	4	0	0	4.0	1.000
2 yrs.		2	0	1.000 1st	1.71	4	1	1	26.1	14	8	24	0	2	0	0	13	4	0	.308	1	5	0	0	1.5	1.000

Junie Barnes

BARNES, JUNE SHOAF (Lefty)
B. Dec. 1, 1911, Linwood, N. C. D. Dec. 31, 1963, Jacksonville, N. C.
BL TL 5′11½″ 170 lbs.

Year	Team	W	L	PCT	ERA	G	GS	CG	IP	H	BB	SO	ShO	Relief W	Relief L	Relief SV	Batting AB	Batting H	HR	BA	PO	A	E	DP	TC/G	FA
1934	CIN N	0	0	—	0.00	2	0	0	0.1	0	1	0	0	0	0	0	0	0	0	—	0	0	0	0	0.0	.000

Rich Barnes

BARNES, RICHARD MONROE
B. July 21, 1959, Palm Beach, Fla.
BR TL 6′ 4″ 180 lbs.

Year	Team	W	L	PCT	ERA	G	GS	CG	IP	H	BB	SO	ShO	Relief W	Relief L	Relief SV	Batting AB	Batting H	HR	BA	PO	A	E	DP	TC/G	FA
1982	CHI A	0	2	.000	4.76	6	2	0	17	21	4	6	0	0	0	1	0	0	0	—	0	4	0	0	0.7	1.000
1983	CLE A	1	1	.500	6.94	4	2	0	11.2	18	10	2	0	1	0	0	0	0	0	—	1	1	0	1	0.5	1.000
2 yrs.		1	3	.250	5.65	10	4	0	28.2	39	14	8	0	1	0	1	0	0	0		1	5	0	1	0.6	1.000

Ross Barnes

BARNES, ROSCOE CHARLES
B. May 8, 1850, Mount Morris, Ill. D. Feb. 5, 1915, Chicago, Ill.
BR TR 5′ 8½″ 145 lbs.

Year	Team	W	L	PCT	ERA	G	GS	CG	IP	H	BB	SO	ShO	Relief W	Relief L	Relief SV	Batting AB	Batting H	HR	BA	PO	A	E	DP	TC/G	FA
1876	CHI N	0	0	—	20.25	1	0	0	1.1	7	0	0	0	0	0	0	*				167	199	36	22	6.0	.910

Virgil Barnes

BARNES, VIRGIL JENNINGS (Zeke)
Brother of Jesse Barnes.
B. Mar. 5, 1897, Ontario, Kans. D. July 24, 1958, Wichita, Kans.
BR TR 6′ 165 lbs.

Year	Team	W	L	PCT	ERA	G	GS	CG	IP	H	BB	SO	ShO	Relief W	Relief L	Relief SV	Batting AB	Batting H	HR	BA	PO	A	E	DP	TC/G	FA
1919	NY N	0	0	—	18.00	1	0	0	2	6	1	1	0	0	0	0	0	0	0	—	0	0	0	0	0.0	.000
1920		0	1	.000	3.86	1	1	0	7	9	1	2	0	0	0	0	1	0	0	.000	0	4	0	0	4.0	1.000
1922		1	0	1.000	3.48	22	2	1	51.2	46	11	16	0	0	0	2	12	2	0	.167	3	13	0	1	0.7	1.000
1923		2	3	.400	3.91	22	2	0	53	59	19	6	0	0	3	1	14	0	0	.000	0	16	0	0	0.7	1.000
1924		16	10	.615	3.06	35	29	15	229.1	239	57	59	1	1	2	3	77	14	0	.182	10	66	1	3	2.2	.987
1925		15	11	.577	3.53	32	27	17	221.2	242	53	53	1	1	1	2	89	9	0	.101	8	54	2	3	2.0	.969
1926		8	13	.381	2.87	31	25	9	185	183	56	54	2	0	0	1	56	3	0	.054	10	42	2	1	1.7	.963
1927		14	11	.560	3.98	35	29	12	228.2	251	51	66	2	2	2	2	83	9	0	.108	6	49	4	1	1.7	.932
1928	2 teams NY N (10G 3–3) BOS N (16G 2–7)																									
"	total	5	10	.333	5.45	26	19	4	115.2	157	44	18	1	0	1	0	39	3	0	.077	2	24	3	1	1.1	.897
9 yrs.		61	59	.508	3.66	205	134	58	1094	1192	293	275	7	4	9	11	371	40	0	.108	39	268	12	10	1.6	.962
WORLD SERIES																										
1923	NY N	0	0	—	0.00	2	0	0	4.2	4	0	4	0	0	0	0	1	0	0	.000	1	2	0	0	1.5	1.000
1924		0	1	.000	5.68	2	2	0	12.2	15	1	9	0	0	0	0	4	0	0	.000	2	3	0	0	2.5	1.000
2 yrs.		0	1	.000	4.15	4	2	0	17.1	19	1	13	0	0	0	0	5	0	0	.000	3	5	0	0	2.0	1.000

Rex Barney

BARNEY, REX EDWARD
B. Dec. 19, 1924, Omaha, Neb.
BR TR 6′ 3″ 185 lbs.

Year	Team	W	L	PCT	ERA	G	GS	CG	IP	H	BB	SO	ShO	Relief W	Relief L	Relief SV	Batting AB	Batting H	HR	BA	PO	A	E	DP	TC/G	FA
1943	BKN N	2	2	.500	6.35	9	8	1	45.1	36	41	23	0	0	1	0	18	1	0	.056	1	7	0	1	0.9	1.000
1946		2	5	.286	5.87	16	9	1	53.2	46	51	36	0	0	0	0	17	4	0	.235	7	6	1	1	0.9	.929
1947		5	2	.714	4.98	28	9	0	77.2	66	59	36	0	2	0	0	27	3	0	.111	1	11	0	4	0.4	1.000
1948		15	13	.536	3.10	44	34	12	246.2	193	122	138	4	1	3	0	84	14	0	.167	5	28	4	1	0.8	.892
1949		9	8	.529	4.41	38	20	6	140.2	108	89	80	2	2	3	1	47	10	0	.213	4	10	2	1	0.4	.875
1950		2	1	.667	6.42	20	1	0	33.2	25	48	23	0	2	1	0	8	1	0	.125	2	3	1	0	0.3	.833
6 yrs.		35	31	.530	4.34	155	81	20	597.2	474	410	336	6	7	8	1	201	33	0	.164	20	65	8	8	0.6	.914
WORLD SERIES																										
1947	BKN N	0	1	.000	2.70	3	1	0	6.2	4	10	3	0	0	0	0	1	0	0	.000	0	1	0	0	0.3	1.000
1949		0	1	.000	16.88	1	1	0	2.2	3	6	2	0	0	0	0	0	0	0	—	1	1	1	0	3.0	.667
2 yrs.		0	2	.000	6.75	4	2	0	9.1	7	16	5	0	0	0	0	1	0	0	.000	1	2	1	0	1.0	.750

Ed Barnhart

BARNHART, EDGAR VERNON
B. Sept. 16, 1904, Providence, Mo. D. Sept. 14, 1984, Columbia, Mo.
BL TR 5′10″ 160 lbs.

Year	Team	W	L	PCT	ERA	G	GS	CG	IP	H	BB	SO	ShO	Relief W	Relief L	Relief SV	Batting AB	Batting H	HR	BA	PO	A	E	DP	TC/G	FA
1924	STL A	0	0	—	0.00	1	0	0	1	0	2	0	0	0	0	0	0	0	0	—	0	1	0	0	1.0	1.000

Les Barnhart

BARNHART, LESLIE EARL
B. Feb. 23, 1905, Hoxie, Kans. D. Oct. 7, 1971, Scottsdale, Ariz.
BR TR 6′ 180 lbs.

Year	Team	W	L	PCT	ERA	G	GS	CG	IP	H	BB	SO	ShO	Relief W	Relief L	Relief SV	Batting AB	Batting H	HR	BA	PO	A	E	DP	TC/G	FA
1928	CLE A	0	1	.000	7.00	2	1	0	9	13	4	1	0	0	0	0	2	1	0	.500	0	0	0	0	0.0	.000
1930		1	0	1.000	6.48	1	1	0	8.1	12	4	1	0	0	0	0	3	0	0	.000	0	3	0	0	3.0	1.000
2 yrs.		1	1	.500	6.75	3	2	0	17.1	25	8	2	0	0	0	0	5	1	0	.200	0	3	0	0	1.0	1.000

George Barnicle

BARNICLE, GEORGE BERNARD BR TR 6′ 2″ 175 lbs.
B. Aug. 26, 1917, Fitchburg, Mass. D. Oct. 10, 1990, Largo, Fla.

Year	Team	W	L	PCT	ERA	G	GS	CG	IP	H	BB	SO	ShO	Relief W	Relief L	Relief SV	Batting AB	Batting H	HR	BA	PO	A	E	DP	TC/G	FA
1939	BOS N	2	2	.500	4.91	6	1	0	18.1	16	8	15	0	2	1	0	5	0	0	.000	1	4	0	0	0.8	1.000
1940		1	0	1.000	7.44	13	2	1	32.2	28	31	11	0	0	0	0	11	0	0	.000	1	9	0	1	0.8	1.000
1941		0	1	.000	6.75	1	1	0	6.2	5	4	2	0	0	0	0	2	0	0	.000	0	2	0	0	2.0	1.000
3 yrs.		3	3	.500	6.55	20	4	1	57.2	49	43	28	0	2	1	0	18	0	0	.000	2	15	0	1	0.9	1.000

Ed Barnowski

BARNOWSKI, EDWARD ANTHONY BR TR 6′ 2″ 195 lbs.
B. Aug. 23, 1943, Scranton, Pa.

Year	Team	W	L	PCT	ERA	G	GS	CG	IP	H	BB	SO	ShO	Relief W	Relief L	Relief SV	Batting AB	Batting H	HR	BA	PO	A	E	DP	TC/G	FA
1965	BAL A	0	0	—	2.08	4	0	0	4.1	3	7	6	0	0	0	0	0	0	0	—	0	0	0	0	0.0	.000
1966		0	0	—	3.00	2	0	0	3	4	1	2	0	0	0	0	0	0	0	—	0	1	0	0	0.5	1.000
2 yrs.		0	0		2.45	6	0	0	7.1	7	8	8	0	0	0	0	0	0	0		0	1	0	0	0.2	1.000

Salome Barojas

BAROJAS, SALOME BR TR 5′ 9″ 160 lbs.
Born Salome Barojas (Romero).
B. June 16, 1957, Cordoba, Mexico.

Year	Team	W	L	PCT	ERA	G	GS	CG	IP	H	BB	SO	ShO	Relief W	Relief L	Relief SV	Batting AB	Batting H	HR	BA	PO	A	E	DP	TC/G	FA
1982	CHI A	6	6	.500	3.54	61	0	0	106.2	96	46	56	0	6	6	21	0	0	0	—	10	28	0	2	0.6	1.000
1983		3	3	.500	2.47	52	0	0	87.1	70	32	38	0	3	3	12	0	0	0	—	2	14	0	1	0.3	1.000
1984	2 teams	CHI A (24G 3–2) SEA A (19G 6–5)																								
″	total	9	7	.563	4.15	43	14	0	134.1	136	60	55	0	3	3	2	0	0	0		8	27	0	1	0.8	1.000
1985	SEA A	0	5	.000	5.98	17	4	0	52.2	65	33	27	0	0	1	0	0	0	0	—	5	7	1	0	0.8	.923
1988	PHI N	0	0	—	8.31	6	0	0	8.2	7	8	1	0	0	0	0	0	0	0	—	0	2	1	0	0.5	.667
5 yrs.		18	21	.462	3.95	179	18	0	389.2	374	179	177	0	12	13	35	0	0	0		25	78	2	4	0.6	.981
LEAGUE CHAMPIONSHIP SERIES																										
1983	CHI A	0	0	—	18.00	2	0	0	1	4	0	0	0	0	0	0	0	0	0	—	0	2	0	0	1.0	1.000

Bob Barr

BARR, ROBERT ALEXANDER BR TR 6′ 175 lbs.
B. Mar. 12, 1908, Newton, Mass.

Year	Team	W	L	PCT	ERA	G	GS	CG	IP	H	BB	SO	ShO	Relief W	Relief L	Relief SV	Batting AB	Batting H	HR	BA	PO	A	E	DP	TC/G	FA
1935	BKN N	0	0	—	3.86	2	0	0	2.1	5	2	0	0	0	0	0	0	0	0	—	0	0	0	0	0.0	.000

Bob Barr

BARR, ROBERT McCLELLAND BR TR 6′ 1″ 192 lbs.
B. Dec. 1856, Washington, D. C. D. Mar. 11, 1930, Washington, D. C.

Year	Team	W	L	PCT	ERA	G	GS	CG	IP	H	BB	SO	ShO	Relief W	Relief L	Relief SV	Batting AB	Batting H	HR	BA	PO	A	E	DP	TC/G	FA
1883	PIT AA	6	18	.250	*4.38*	26	23	19	203.1	263	28	81	0	0	**1**	**1**	142	35	0	.246	62	43	17	2	2.7	.861
1884	2 teams	WAS AA (32G 9–23) IND AA (16G 3–11)																								
″	total	12	34	.261	3.94	48	48	47	413	471	50	207	2	0	0	0	200	32	2	.160	33	80	36	3	2.6	.758
1886	WAS N	3	18	.143	*4.30*	23	23	21	190.2	216	54	80	1	0	0	0	79	13	0	.165	6	36	9	1	2.3	.824
1890	ROC AA	28	**24**	.538	*3.25*	57	54	52	493.1	458	**219**	209	3	1	0	0	201	36	2	.179	20	111	10	2	2.5	.929
1891	NY N	0	4	.000	5.33	5	4	2	27	47	12	11	0	0	0	0	11	1	0	.091	1	6	1	1	1.6	.875
5 yrs.		49	98	.333	3.83	159	152	141	1327.1	1455	363	588	6	1	1	1	*				122	276	73	9	2.5	.845

Jim Barr

BARR, JAMES LELAND BR TR 6′ 3″ 205 lbs.
B. Feb. 10, 1948, Lynwood, Calif.

Year	Team	W	L	PCT	ERA	G	GS	CG	IP	H	BB	SO	ShO	Relief W	Relief L	Relief SV	Batting AB	Batting H	HR	BA	PO	A	E	DP	TC/G	FA
1971	SF N	1	1	.500	3.60	17	0	0	35	33	5	16	0	1	1	0	4	0	0	.000	3	9	1	0	0.8	.923
1972		8	10	.444	2.87	44	18	8	179	166	41	86	2	0	3	2	49	9	0	.184	8	32	2	2	1.0	.952
1973		11	17	.393	3.82	41	33	8	231	240	49	88	3	1	1	2	66	10	0	.152	19	31	0	4	1.2	1.000
1974		13	9	.591	2.74	44	27	11	240	223	47	84	5	1	1	2	71	18	1	.254	16	41	3	4	1.4	.950
1975		13	14	.481	3.06	35	33	12	244	244	58	77	2	2	0	0	76	9	0	.118	28	48	3	2	2.3	.962
1976		15	12	.556	2.89	37	37	8	252.1	260	60	75	3	0	0	0	74	12	0	.162	22	56	4	0	2.2	.951
1977		12	16	.429	4.77	38	38	6	234	286	56	97	2	0	0	0	76	10	0	.132	13	53	5	2	1.9	.930
1978		8	11	.421	3.53	32	25	5	163	180	35	44	2	0	0	1	50	5	0	.100	7	35	4	1	1.4	.913
1979	CAL A	10	12	.455	4.20	36	25	5	197	217	55	69	0	2	1	0	0	0	0	—	6	41	0	5	1.3	1.000
1980		1	4	.200	5.56	24	7	0	68	90	23	22	0	0	0	1	0	0	0	—	1	10	2	0	0.5	.846
1982	SF N	4	3	.571	3.29	53	9	1	128.2	125	20	36	1	1	2	2	32	8	0	.250	15	19	1	2	0.7	.971
1983		5	3	.625	3.98	53	0	0	92.2	106	20	47	0	5	3	2	15	2	0	.133	10	13	1	0	0.5	.958
12 yrs.		101	112	.474	3.56	454	252	64	2064.2	2170	469	741	20	13	12	12	513	83	1	.162	148	388	26	22	1.2	.954
LEAGUE CHAMPIONSHIP SERIES																										
1971	SF N	0	0	—	9.00	1	0	0	1	3	0	2	0	0	0	0	1	0	0	.000	0	0	0	0	0.0	.000

Steve Barr

BARR, STEVEN CHARLES BL TL 6′ 4″ 200 lbs.
B. Sept. 8, 1951, St. Louis, Mo.

Year	Team	W	L	PCT	ERA	G	GS	CG	IP	H	BB	SO	ShO	Relief W	Relief L	Relief SV	Batting AB	Batting H	HR	BA	PO	A	E	DP	TC/G	FA
1974	BOS A	1	0	1.000	4.00	1	1	1	9	7	6	3	0	0	0	0	0	0	0	—	1	2	0	0	3.0	1.000
1975		0	1	.000	2.57	3	2	0	7	11	7	2	0	0	0	0	0	0	0	—	0	1	1	1	0.7	.500
1976	TEX A	2	6	.250	5.56	20	10	3	68	70	44	27	0	0	1	0	0	0	0	—	1	14	3	1	0.9	.833
3 yrs.		3	7	.300	5.14	24	13	4	84	88	57	32	0	0	1	0	0	0	0		2	17	4	2	1.0	.826

Bill Barrett

BARRETT, WILLIAM JOSEPH (Whispering Bill) BR TR 6′ 175 lbs.
B. May 28, 1900, Cambridge, Mass. D. Jan. 26, 1951, Cambridge, Mass.

Year	Team	W	L	PCT	ERA	G	GS	CG	IP	H	BB	SO	ShO	Relief W	Relief L	Relief SV	Batting AB	Batting H	HR	BA	PO	A	E	DP	TC/G	FA
1921	PHI A	1	0	1.000	7.20	4	0	0	5	2	9	2	0	1	0	0	*				13	32	3	1	3.4	.938

Dick Barrett

BARRETT, TRACEY SOUTER (Kewpie) BR TR 5′ 9″ 175 lbs.
Played as Dick Oliver in 1934.
B. Sept. 28, 1906, Montoursville, Pa. D. Oct. 30, 1966, Seattle, Wash.

Year	Team	W	L	PCT	ERA	G	GS	CG	IP	H	BB	SO	ShO	Relief W	Relief L	Relief SV	Batting AB	Batting H	HR	BA	PO	A	E	DP	TC/G	FA
1933	PHI A	4	4	.500	5.76	15	7	3	70.1	74	49	26	0	0	1	0	21	6	0	.286	4	16	1	0	1.4	.952
1934	BOS N	1	3	.250	6.68	15	3	0	32.1	50	12	14	0	1	1	0	7	1	0	.143	1	12	1	0	0.9	.929
1943	2 teams	CHI N (15G 0–4) PHI N (23G 10–9)																								
″	total	10	13	.435	2.90	38	24	10	214.1	189	79	85	2	0	0	1	58	8	0	.138	16	40	1	3	1.5	.982
1944	PHI N	12	18	.400	3.86	37	28	11	221.1	223	88	74	1	3	2	0	74	16	0	.216	9	54	0	2	1.7	1.000
1945		7	**20**	.259	5.43	36	30	8	190.2	216	92	72	0	1	2	1	62	9	0	.145	9	38	2	3	1.4	.959
5 yrs.		34	58	.370	4.30	141	92	32	729	752	320	271	3	5	6	2	222	40	0	.180	39	160	5	8	1.4	.975

Frank Barrett

BARRETT, FRANCIS JOSEPH (Red) BR TR 6′ 2″ 173 lbs.
B. July 1, 1913, Fort Lauderdale, Fla.

Year	Team	W	L	PCT	ERA	G	GS	CG	IP	H	BB	SO	ShO	Relief W	Relief L	Relief SV	Batting AB	Batting H	HR	BA	PO	A	E	DP	TC/G	FA
1939	STL N	0	1	.000	5.40	1	0	0	1.2	1	1	3	0	0	1	0	0	0	0	—	1	0	0	0	1.0	1.000
1944	BOS A	8	7	.533	3.69	38	2	0	90.1	93	42	40	0	7	6	8	28	4	0	.143	5	16	2	1	0.6	.913

Frank Barrett *continued*

Year	Team	Lg	W	L	PCT	ERA	G	GS	CG	IP	H	BB	SO	ShO	Relief Pitching W	Relief Pitching L	Relief Pitching SV	Batting AB	Batting H	Batting HR	BA	PO	A	E	DP	TC/G	FA
1945			4	3	.571	2.62	37	0	0	86	77	29	35	0	4	3	3	20	5	0	.250	4	14	1	1	0.5	.947
1946	BOS	N	2	4	.333	5.09	23	0	0	35.1	35	17	12	0	2	4	1	6	0	0	.000	4	12	1	0	0.7	.941
1950	PIT	N	1	2	.333	4.15	5	0	0	4.1	5	1	0	0	1	2	0	0	0	0	—	1	2	0	1	0.6	1.000
5 yrs.			15	17	.469	3.51	104	2	0	217.2	211	90	90	0	14	16	12	54	9	0	.167	15	44	4	3	0.6	.937

Red Barrett

BARRETT, CHARLES HENRY BR TR 5′11″ 183 lbs.
B. Feb. 14, 1915, Santa Barbara, Calif. D. July 28, 1990, Wilson, N. C.

Year	Team	Lg	W	L	PCT	ERA	G	GS	CG	IP	H	BB	SO	ShO	Relief Pitching W	Relief Pitching L	Relief Pitching SV	Batting AB	Batting H	Batting HR	BA	PO	A	E	DP	TC/G	FA
1937	CIN	N	0	0	—	1.42	1	0	0	6.1	5	2	1	0	0	0	0	3	0	0	.000	0	0	0	0	0.0	.000
1938			2	0	1.000	3.14	6	2	2	28.2	28	15	5	0	0	0	0	7	1	0	.143	5	3	0	0	1.3	1.000
1939			0	0	—	1.69	2	0	0	5.1	5	1	1	0	0	0	0	1	0	0	.000	0	1	0	0	0.5	1.000
1940			1	0	1.000	6.75	3	0	0	2.2	5	1	0	0	1	0	0	0	0	0	—	0	2	0	1	0.7	1.000
1943	BOS	N	12	18	.400	3.18	38	31	14	255	240	63	64	3	0	2	0	81	11	0	.136	17	55	2	9	1.9	.973
1944			9	16	.360	4.06	42	30	11	230.1	257	63	54	1	0	3	2	75	13	0	.173	15	51	3	7	1.6	.957
1945	2 teams	BOS N (9G 2–3)	STL N (36G 21–9)																								
″	total		**23**	12	.657	3.00	45	34	**24**	**284.2**	**287**	54	76	3	1	3	2	98	12	0	.122	24	54	1	1	1.8	.987
1946	STL	N	3	2	.600	4.03	23	9	1	67	75	24	22	1	1	0	2	17	1	0	.059	4	17	0	1	0.9	1.000
1947	BOS	N	11	12	.478	3.55	36	30	12	210.2	200	53	53	3	0	1	1	72	8	0	.111	17	38	3	2	1.6	.948
1948			7	8	.467	3.65	34	13	3	128.1	132	26	40	0	2	3	0	39	7	0	.179	13	26	1	1	1.2	.975
1949			1	1	.500	5.68	23	0	0	44.1	58	10	17	0	1	1	0	5	1	0	.200	3	14	1	0	0.8	.944
11 yrs.			69	69	.500	3.53	253	149	67	1263.1	1292	312	333	11	6	13	7	398	54	0	.136	98	261	11	22	1.5	.970
WORLD SERIES																											
1948	BOS	N	0	0	—	0.00	2	0	0	3.2	1	0	1	0	0	0	0	0	0	0	—	0	0	0	0	0.0	.000

Tim Barrett

BARRETT, TIMOTHY WAYNE BL TR 6′1″ 185 lbs.
B. Jan. 24, 1961, Huntingburg, Ind.

Year	Team	Lg	W	L	PCT	ERA	G	GS	CG	IP	H	BB	SO	ShO	Relief Pitching W	Relief Pitching L	Relief Pitching SV	Batting AB	Batting H	Batting HR	BA	PO	A	E	DP	TC/G	FA
1988	MON	N	0	0	—	5.79	4	0	0	9.1	10	2	5	0	0	0	1	2	0	0	.000	3	1	1	1	1.3	.800

Francisco Barrios

BARRIOS, FRANCISCO JAVIER BR TR 5′11″ 155 lbs.
Born Francisco Javier Barrios (Jimenez).
B. June 10, 1953, Hermosillo, Mexico D. Apr. 9, 1982, Hermosillo, Mexico.

Year	Team	Lg	W	L	PCT	ERA	G	GS	CG	IP	H	BB	SO	ShO	Relief Pitching W	Relief Pitching L	Relief Pitching SV	Batting AB	Batting H	Batting HR	BA	PO	A	E	DP	TC/G	FA
1974	CHI	A	0	0	—	27.00	2	0	0	2	7	2	2	0	0	0	0	0	0	0	—	0	0	0	0	0.0	.000
1976			5	9	.357	4.31	35	14	6	142	136	46	81	0	0	4	3	0	0	0	—	10	14	1	3	0.7	.960
1977			14	7	.667	4.13	33	31	9	231	241	58	119	0	1	0	0	0	0	0	—	20	27	2	2	1.5	.959
1978			9	15	.375	4.05	33	32	9	195.2	180	85	79	2	0	0	0	0	0	0	—	19	38	0	0	1.7	1.000
1979			8	3	.727	3.60	15	15	2	95	88	33	28	0	0	0	0	0	0	0	—	10	8	3	2	1.4	.857
1980			1	1	.500	5.06	3	3	0	16	21	8	2	0	0	0	0	0	0	0	—	0	3	2	0	1.7	.600
1981			1	3	.250	4.00	8	7	1	36	45	14	12	0	0	0	0	0	0	0	—	1	6	1	0	1.0	.875
7 yrs.			38	38	.500	4.15	129	102	27	717.2	718	246	323	2	1	4	3	0	0	0		60	96	9	7	1.3	.945

Frank Barron

BARRON, FRANK JOHN BL TL 6′1″ 175 lbs.
B. Aug. 6, 1890, St. Marys, W. Va. D. Sept. 18, 1964, St. Marys, W. Va.

Year	Team	Lg	W	L	PCT	ERA	G	GS	CG	IP	H	BB	SO	ShO	Relief Pitching W	Relief Pitching L	Relief Pitching SV	Batting AB	Batting H	Batting HR	BA	PO	A	E	DP	TC/G	FA
1914	WAS	A	0	0	—	0.00	1	0	0	1	1	0	1	0	0	0	0	0	0	0	—	1	0	0	0	1.0	1.000

Ed Barry

BARRY, EDWARD (Jumbo) TL 6′3″ 185 lbs.
B. Oct. 2, 1882, Madison, Wis. D. June 19, 1920, Montague, Mass.

Year	Team	Lg	W	L	PCT	ERA	G	GS	CG	IP	H	BB	SO	ShO	Relief Pitching W	Relief Pitching L	Relief Pitching SV	Batting AB	Batting H	Batting HR	BA	PO	A	E	DP	TC/G	FA
1905	BOS	A	1	2	.333	2.88	7	5	2	40.2	38	15	18	0	0	0	0	11	1	0	.091	2	3	0	0	0.7	1.000
1906			0	3	.000	6.00	3	3	3	21	23	5	10	0	0	0	0	9	1	0	.111	1	8	1	0	3.3	.900
1907			0	1	.000	2.08	2	2	1	17.1	13	5	6	0	0	0	0	3	0	0	.000	1	5	1	0	3.5	.857
3 yrs.			1	6	.143	3.53	12	10	6	79	74	25	34	0	0	0	0	23	2	0	.087	4	16	2	0	1.8	.909

Hardin Barry

BARRY, HARDIN (Finn) BR TR 6′ 185 lbs.
B. Mar. 26, 1891, Susanville, Calif. D. Nov. 5, 1969, Carson City, Nev.

Year	Team	Lg	W	L	PCT	ERA	G	GS	CG	IP	H	BB	SO	ShO	Relief Pitching W	Relief Pitching L	Relief Pitching SV	Batting AB	Batting H	Batting HR	BA	PO	A	E	DP	TC/G	FA
1912	PHI	A	0	0	—	7.62	3	0	0	13	18	4	3	0	0	0	0	4	0	0	.000	2	2	0	0	1.3	1.000

Tom Barry

BARRY, THOMAS ARTHUR TR 5′9″ 155 lbs.
B. Apr. 10, 1879, St. Louis, Mo. D. June 4, 1946, St. Louis, Mo.

Year	Team	Lg	W	L	PCT	ERA	G	GS	CG	IP	H	BB	SO	ShO	Relief Pitching W	Relief Pitching L	Relief Pitching SV	Batting AB	Batting H	Batting HR	BA	PO	A	E	DP	TC/G	FA
1904	PHI	N	0	1	.000	40.50	1	1	0	0.2	6	1	1	0	0	0	0	0	0	0	—	0	0	0	0	0.0	.000

Bob Barthelson

BARTHELSON, ROBERT EDWARD BR TR 6′ 185 lbs.
B. July 15, 1924, New Haven, Conn.

Year	Team	Lg	W	L	PCT	ERA	G	GS	CG	IP	H	BB	SO	ShO	Relief Pitching W	Relief Pitching L	Relief Pitching SV	Batting AB	Batting H	Batting HR	BA	PO	A	E	DP	TC/G	FA
1944	NY	N	1	1	.500	4.66	7	1	0	9.2	13	5	4	0	1	1	0	0	0	0	—	0	1	0	0	0.1	1.000

John Barthold

BARTHOLD, JOHN FRANCIS (Hans) BB TR 5′11″ 180 lbs.
B. Apr. 14, 1882, Philadelphia, Pa. D. Nov. 4, 1946, Fairview Village, Pa.

Year	Team	Lg	W	L	PCT	ERA	G	GS	CG	IP	H	BB	SO	ShO	Relief Pitching W	Relief Pitching L	Relief Pitching SV	Batting AB	Batting H	Batting HR	BA	PO	A	E	DP	TC/G	FA
1904	PHI	A	0	0	—	5.06	4	0	0	10.2	12	8	5	0	0	0	0	3	1	0	.333	0	5	0	1	1.3	1.000

Les Bartholomew

BARTHOLOMEW, LESTER JUSTIN BR TL 5′11½″ 195 lbs.
B. Apr. 4, 1903, Madison, Wis. D. Sept. 19, 1972, Barrington, Ill.

Year	Team	Lg	W	L	PCT	ERA	G	GS	CG	IP	H	BB	SO	ShO	Relief Pitching W	Relief Pitching L	Relief Pitching SV	Batting AB	Batting H	Batting HR	BA	PO	A	E	DP	TC/G	FA
1928	PIT	N	0	0	—	7.15	6	0	0	22.2	31	9	6	0	0	0	0	7	1	0	.143	0	5	1	1	1.0	.833
1932	CHI	A	0	0	—	5.06	3	0	0	5.1	5	6	1	0	0	0	0	1	0	0	.000	0	1	0	0	0.3	1.000
2 yrs.			0	0	—	6.75	9	0	0	28	36	15	7	0	0	0	0	8	1	0	.125	0	6	1	1	0.8	.857

Bill Bartley

BARTLEY, WILLIAM JACKSON BR TR 5′11½″ 190 lbs.
B. Jan. 8, 1885, Cincinnati, Ohio D. May 17, 1965, Cincinnati, Ohio.

Year	Team	Lg	W	L	PCT	ERA	G	GS	CG	IP	H	BB	SO	ShO	Relief Pitching W	Relief Pitching L	Relief Pitching SV	Batting AB	Batting H	Batting HR	BA	PO	A	E	DP	TC/G	FA
1903	NY	N	0	0	—	0.00	1	0	0	3	3	4	2	0	0	0	0	1	0	0	.000	0	1	0	0	1.0	1.000
1906	PHI	A	0	0	—	9.35	3	0	0	8.2	10	6	6	0	0	0	1	3	1	0	.333	2	4	0	0	2.0	1.000
1907			0	1	.000	2.24	15	3	2	56.1	44	19	16	0	0	1	0	21	2	0	.095	9	14	2	2	1.7	.920
3 yrs.			0	1	.000	3.04	19	3	2	68	57	29	24	0	0	1	1	25	3	0	.120	11	19	2	2	1.7	.938

Shawn Barton

BARTON, SHAWN EDWARD — BR TL 6′ 3″ 195 lbs.
B. May 14, 1963, Los Angeles, Calif.

Year	Team	Lg	W	L	PCT	ERA	G	GS	CG	IP	H	BB	SO	ShO	Relief W	Relief L	Relief SV	AB	H	HR	BA	PO	A	E	DP	TC/G	FA
1992	SEA	A	0	1	.000	2.92	14	0	0	12.1	10	7	4	0	0	1	0	0	0	0	—	2	3	1	0	0.4	.833
1995	SF	N	4	1	.800	4.26	52	0	0	44.1	37	19	22	0	4	1	1	0	0	0	—	4	8	0	2	0.2	1.000
2 yrs.			4	2	.667	3.97	66	0	0	56.2	47	26	26	0	4	2	1	0	0	0		6	11	1	2	0.3	.944

Charlie Bartson

BARTSON, CHARLES FRANKLIN — 6′ 170 lbs.
B. Mar. 13, 1865, Peoria, Ill. D. June 9, 1936, Peoria, Ill.

Year	Team	Lg	W	L	PCT	ERA	G	GS	CG	IP	H	BB	SO	ShO	Relief W	Relief L	Relief SV	AB	H	HR	BA	PO	A	E	DP	TC/G	FA
1890	CHI	P	8	10	.444	4.26	25	19	16	188	222	66	47	0	1	0	1	75	13	0	.173	10	70	7	1	3.5	.920

Jim Baskette

BASKETTE, JAMES BLAINE (Big Jim) — BR TR 6′ 2″ 185 lbs.
B. Dec. 10, 1887, Athens, Tenn. D. July 30, 1942, Athens, Tenn.

Year	Team	Lg	W	L	PCT	ERA	G	GS	CG	IP	H	BB	SO	ShO	Relief W	Relief L	Relief SV	AB	H	HR	BA	PO	A	E	DP	TC/G	FA
1911	CLE	A	1	2	.333	3.38	4	2	2	21.1	21	9	8	0	0	1	0	6	2	0	.333	4	2	0	0	1.5	1.000
1912			8	4	.667	3.18	29	11	7	116	109	46	51	1	2	1	1	40	5	0	.125	4	19	1	0	0.8	.958
1913			0	0	—	5.79	2	1	0	4.2	8	2	0	0	0	0	0	1	1	0	1.000	0	4	0	0	2.0	1.000
3 yrs.			9	6	.600	3.30	35	14	9	142	138	57	59	1	2	2	1	47	8	0	.170	8	25	1	0	1.0	.971

Dick Bass

BASS, RICHARD WILLIAM — BR TR 6′ 2″ 175 lbs.
B. July 7, 1906, Rogersville, Tenn. D. Feb. 3, 1989, Graceville, Fla.

Year	Team	Lg	W	L	PCT	ERA	G	GS	CG	IP	H	BB	SO	ShO	Relief W	Relief L	Relief SV	AB	H	HR	BA	PO	A	E	DP	TC/G	FA
1939	WAS	A	0	1	.000	6.75	1	1	0	8	7	6	1	0	0	0	0	2	0	0	.000	0	1	0	0	1.0	1.000

Norm Bass

BASS, NORMAN DELANEY — BR TR 6′ 3″ 205 lbs.
B. Jan. 21, 1939, Laurel, Miss.

Year	Team	Lg	W	L	PCT	ERA	G	GS	CG	IP	H	BB	SO	ShO	Relief W	Relief L	Relief SV	AB	H	HR	BA	PO	A	E	DP	TC/G	FA
1961	KC	A	11	11	.500	4.69	40	23	6	170.2	164	82	74	2	0	1	0	59	7	1	.119	5	17	2	2	0.6	.917
1962			2	6	.250	6.09	22	10	0	75.1	96	46	33	0	1	1	0	22	1	0	.045	6	19	0	0	1.1	1.000
1963			0	0	—	11.74	3	1	0	7.2	11	9	4	0	0	0	0	1	0	0	.000	0	1	2	0	1.0	.333
3 yrs.			13	17	.433	5.32	65	34	6	253.2	271	137	111	2	1	2	0	82	8	1	.098	11	37	4	2	0.8	.923

Charlie Bastian

BASTIAN, CHARLES J. — BR TR 5′ 6½″ 145 lbs.
B. July 4, 1860, Philadelphia, Pa. D. Jan. 18, 1932, Pennsauken, N. J.

Year	Team	Lg	W	L	PCT	ERA	G	GS	CG	IP	H	BB	SO	ShO	Relief W	Relief L	Relief SV	AB	H	HR	BA	PO	A	E	DP	TC/G	FA
1884	WIL	U	0	0	—	*3.00*	1	0	0	6	6	0	2	0	0	0	0	*				67	95	14	9	6.1	.920

Joe Batchelder

BATCHELDER, JOSEPH EDWARD (Win) — BR TL 5′ 7″ 165 lbs.
B. July 11, 1898, Wenham, Mass. D. May 5, 1989, Beverly, Mass.

Year	Team	Lg	W	L	PCT	ERA	G	GS	CG	IP	H	BB	SO	ShO	Relief W	Relief L	Relief SV	AB	H	HR	BA	PO	A	E	DP	TC/G	FA
1923	BOS	N	1	0	1.000	7.00	4	1	1	9	12	1	2	0	0	0	0	1	0	0	.000	1	1	0	0	0.5	1.000
1924			0	0	—	3.86	3	0	0	4.2	4	2	2	0	0	0	0	1	0	0	.000	0	2	0	0	0.7	1.000
1925			0	0	—	5.14	4	0	0	7	10	1	2	0	0	0	0	1	0	0	.000	0	4	1	0	1.3	.800
3 yrs.			1	0	1.000	5.66	11	1	1	20.2	26	4	6	0	0	0	0	3	0	0	.000	1	7	1	0	0.8	.889

Richard Batchelor

BATCHELOR, RICHARD ANTHONY — BR TR 6′ 1″ 195 lbs.
B. Apr. 8, 1967, Florence, S. C.

Year	Team	Lg	W	L	PCT	ERA	G	GS	CG	IP	H	BB	SO	ShO	Relief W	Relief L	Relief SV	AB	H	HR	BA	PO	A	E	DP	TC/G	FA
1993	STL	N	0	0	—	8.10	9	0	0	10	14	3	4	0	0	0	0	1	0	0	.000	1	1	0	0	0.2	1.000

Dick Bates

BATES, CHARLES RICHARD — BL TR 6′ 190 lbs.
B. Oct. 7, 1945, McArthur, Ohio.

Year	Team	Lg	W	L	PCT	ERA	G	GS	CG	IP	H	BB	SO	ShO	Relief W	Relief L	Relief SV	AB	H	HR	BA	PO	A	E	DP	TC/G	FA
1969	SEA	A	0	0	—	27.00	1	0	0	1.2	3	3	3	0	0	0	0	0	0	0	—	1	0	0	0	1.0	1.000

Frank Bates

BATES, CREED FRANK — TR
B. Chattanooga, Tenn. Deceased.

Year	Team	Lg	W	L	PCT	ERA	G	GS	CG	IP	H	BB	SO	ShO	Relief W	Relief L	Relief SV	AB	H	HR	BA	PO	A	E	DP	TC/G	FA
1898	CLE	N	2	1	.667	3.10	4	4	4	29	30	11	5	0	0	0	0	9	1	0	.111	2	6	1	1	2.3	.889
1899	2 teams	STL N (2G 0–0) CLE N (20G 1–18)																									
"	total		1	18	.053	6.90	22	19	17	161.2	246	110	13	0	0	0	0	68	15	0	.221	10	41	10	2	2.5	.836
2 yrs.			3	19	.136	6.33	26	23	21	190.2	276	121	18	0	0	0	0	77	16	0	.208	12	47	11	3	2.5	.843

John Bates

BATES, JOHN WILLIAM
B. May 28, 1868, Ohio D. Mar. 24, 1919, Oakland, Calif.

Year	Team	Lg	W	L	PCT	ERA	G	GS	CG	IP	H	BB	SO	ShO	Relief W	Relief L	Relief SV	AB	H	HR	BA	PO	A	E	DP	TC/G	FA
1889	KC	AA	0	1	.000	13.50	1	1	1	8	15	5	3	0	0	0	0	4	0	0	.000	0	0	0	0	0.0	.000

Miguel Batista

BATISTA, MIGUEL JEREZ — BR TR 6′ 160 lbs.
Born Miguel Jerez Batista (Decartes).
B. Feb. 19, 1971, Santo Domingo, Dominican Republic.

Year	Team	Lg	W	L	PCT	ERA	G	GS	CG	IP	H	BB	SO	ShO	Relief W	Relief L	Relief SV	AB	H	HR	BA	PO	A	E	DP	TC/G	FA
1992	PIT	N	0	0	—	9.00	1	0	0	2	4	3	1	0	0	0	0	0	0	0	—	0	0	0	0	0.0	.000

Joe Battin

BATTIN, JOSEPH V. — BR TR
B. Nov. 11, 1851, Philadelphia, Pa. D. Dec. 10, 1937, Akron, Ohio.
Manager 1883–84.

Year	Team	Lg	W	L	PCT	ERA	G	GS	CG	IP	H	BB	SO	ShO	Relief W	Relief L	Relief SV	AB	H	HR	BA	PO	A	E	DP	TC/G	FA
1877	STL	N	0	0	—	4.91	1	0	0	3.2	3	1	1	0	0	0	0	226	45	1	.199	118	146	40	8	4.8	.868
1883	PIT	AA	0	0	—	2.25	2	0	0	4	9	1	0	0	0	0	0	388	83	1	.214	117	136	55	10	5.2	.821
2 yrs.			0	0		3.52	3	0	0	7.2	12	2	1	0	0	0	0	*				593	886	229	45	4.7	.866

Chris Batton

BATTON, CHRISTOPHER SEAN — BR TR 6′ 4″ 195 lbs.
B. Aug. 24, 1954, Los Angeles, Calif.

Year	Team	Lg	W	L	PCT	ERA	G	GS	CG	IP	H	BB	SO	ShO	Relief W	Relief L	Relief SV	AB	H	HR	BA	PO	A	E	DP	TC/G	FA
1976	OAK	A	0	0	—	9.00	2	1	0	4	5	3	4	0	0	0	0	0	0	0	—	0	0	0	0	0.0	.000

Lou Bauer

BAUER, LOUIS WALTER (Kid) — BR TR 6′ 175 lbs.
B. Nov. 30, 1898, Egg Harbor City, N. J. D. Feb. 4, 1979, Pomona, N. J.

Year	Team	Lg	W	L	PCT	ERA	G	GS	CG	IP	H	BB	SO	ShO	Relief W	Relief L	Relief SV	AB	H	HR	BA	PO	A	E	DP	TC/G	FA
1918	PHI	A	0	0	—	∞	1	0	0		0	2	0	0	0	0	0	0	0	0	—	0	0	0	0	0.0	.000

Al Bauers

BAUERS, ALBERT J. — TL
B. 1850, Columbus, Ohio D. Sept. 6, 1913, Wilkes-Barre, Pa.

Year	Team	Lg	W	L	PCT	ERA	G	GS	CG	IP	H	BB	SO	ShO	Relief W	Relief L	Relief SV	AB	H	HR	BA	PO	A	E	DP	TC/G	FA
1884	COL	AA	1	2	.333	*4.68*	3	3	3	25	22	14	13	0	0	0	0	11	3	0	.273	1	5	1	0	2.3	.857
1886	STL	N	0	4	.000	5.97	4	4	3	28.2	31	27	13	0	0	0	0	12	2	0	.167	0	3	1	0	1.0	.750
2 yrs.			1	6	.143	5.37	7	7	6	53.2	53	41	26	0	0	0	0	23	5	0	.217	1	8	2	0	1.6	.818

Russ Bauers

BAUERS, RUSSELL LEE BL TR 6′ 3″ 195 lbs.
B. May 10, 1914, Townsend, Wis. D. Jan. 21, 1995, Hines, Ill.

Year	Team	Lg	W	L	PCT	ERA	G	GS	CG	IP	H	BB	SO	ShO	Relief W	Relief L	Relief SV	AB	H	HR	BA	PO	A	E	DP	TC/G	FA
1936	PIT	N	0	0	—	33.75	1	1	0	1.1	2	4	0	0	0	0	0	0	0	0	—	0	0	0	0	0.0	.000
1937			13	6	.684	2.88	34	19	11	187.2	174	80	118	2	3	1	1	69	15	0	.217	1	58	2	0	1.8	.967
1938			13	14	.481	3.07	40	34	12	243	207	99	117	3	1	2	3	88	21	0	.239	3	38	6	1	1.2	.872
1939			2	4	.333	3.35	15	8	1	53.2	46	25	12	0	1	1	1	19	4	0	.211	0	7	0	3	0.5	1.000
1940			0	2	.000	7.63	15	2	0	30.2	42	18	11	0	0	0	0	7	2	0	.286	1	7	0	1	0.5	1.000
1941			1	3	.250	5.54	8	5	1	37.1	40	25	20	0	0	0	0	14	5	0	.357	0	4	3	1	0.9	.571
1946	CHI	N	2	1	.667	3.53	15	2	2	43.1	45	19	22	0	1	0	1	10	3	0	.300	5	6	1	0	0.8	.917
1950	STL	A	0	0	—	4.50	1	0	0	2	6	1	0	0	0	0	0	0	0	0	—	0	1	0	0	1.0	1.000
8 yrs.			31	30	.508	3.53	129	71	27	599	562	271	300	5	6	4	6	207	50	0	.242	10	121	12	6	1.1	.916

Frank Baumann

BAUMANN, FRANK MATT (The Beau) BL TL 6′ 205 lbs.
B. July 1, 1933, St. Louis, Mo.

Year	Team	Lg	W	L	PCT	ERA	G	GS	CG	IP	H	BB	SO	ShO	Relief W	Relief L	Relief SV	AB	H	HR	BA	PO	A	E	DP	TC/G	FA
1955	BOS	A	2	1	.667	5.82	7	5	0	34	38	17	27	0	1	0	0	13	3	0	.231	0	6	0	0	0.9	1.000
1956			2	1	.667	3.28	7	1	0	24.2	22	14	18	0	1	1	0	9	3	0	.333	1	1	1	0	0.4	.667
1957			1	0	1.000	3.75	4	1	0	12	13	3	7	0	0	0	0	2	1	0	.500	0	1	0	0	0.3	1.000
1958			2	2	.500	4.47	10	7	2	52.1	56	27	31	0	0	0	0	14	3	0	.214	1	6	0	0	0.7	1.000
1959			6	4	.600	4.05	26	10	2	95.2	96	55	48	0	2	0	1	29	6	0	.207	5	20	3	1	1.1	.893
1960	CHI	A	13	6	.684	**2.67**	44	20	7	185.1	169	53	71	2	6	2	3	52	8	0	.154	4	25	1	1	0.7	.967
1961			10	13	.435	5.61	53	23	5	187.2	249	59	75	1	4	4	3	61	16	2	.262	14	37	1	1	1.0	.981
1962			7	6	.538	3.38	40	10	3	119.2	117	36	55	1	4	2	4	30	8	0	.267	5	23	1	3	0.7	.966
1963			2	1	.667	3.04	24	1	0	50.1	52	17	31	0	2	0	1	11	1	0	.091	2	9	0	1	0.5	1.000
1964			0	3	.000	6.19	22	0	0	32	40	16	19	0	0	3	1	4	0	0	.000	1	4	0	0	0.2	1.000
1965	CHI	N	0	1	.000	7.36	4	0	0	3.2	4	3	2	0	0	1	0	0	0	0	—	0	1	0	0	0.3	1.000
11 yrs.			45	38	.542	4.11	241	78	19	797.1	856	300	384	4	20	13	13	225	49	2	.218	33	133	7	7	0.7	.960

George Baumgardner

BAUMGARDNER, GEORGE WASHINGTON BL TR 5′11″ 178 lbs.
B. July 22, 1891, Barboursville, W. Va. D. Dec. 13, 1970, Barboursville, W. Va.

Year	Team	Lg	W	L	PCT	ERA	G	GS	CG	IP	H	BB	SO	ShO	Relief W	Relief L	Relief SV	AB	H	HR	BA	PO	A	E	DP	TC/G	FA
1912	STL	A	11	13	.458	3.38	30	26	18	218.1	222	79	102	2	0	0	0	76	11	0	.145	4	61	1	2	2.2	.985
1913			10	19	.345	3.13	38	31	23	253.1	**267**	84	78	2	0	0	1	78	13	0	.167	8	72	6	1	2.3	.930
1914			14	13	.519	2.79	45	18	9	183.2	152	84	93	3	**6**	**5**	3	53	7	0	.132	4	49	2	0	1.2	.964
1915			0	2	.000	4.43	7	1	1	22.1	29	11	6	0	0	1	0	6	0	0	.000	0	10	1	0	1.6	.909
1916			1	0	1.000	7.88	4	2	0	8	12	5	4	0	0	0	0	2	0	0	.000	0	0	0	0	0.0	.000
5 yrs.			36	47	.434	3.22	124	78	51	685.2	682	263	283	7	6	6	4	215	31	0	.144	16	192	10	3	1.8	.954

Ross Baumgarten

BAUMGARTEN, ROSS BL TL 6′ 1″ 180 lbs.
B. May 27, 1955, Highland Park, Ill.

Year	Team	Lg	W	L	PCT	ERA	G	GS	CG	IP	H	BB	SO	ShO	Relief W	Relief L	Relief SV	AB	H	HR	BA	PO	A	E	DP	TC/G	FA
1978	CHI	A	2	2	.500	5.87	7	4	1	23	29	9	15	1	0	0	0	0	0	0	—	0	2	0	0	0.3	1.000
1979			13	8	.619	3.53	28	28	4	191	175	83	72	3	0	0	0	0	0	0	—	14	28	1	1	1.5	.977
1980			2	12	.143	3.44	24	23	3	136	127	52	66	1	0	0	0	0	0	0	—	5	31	1	3	1.5	.973
1981			5	9	.357	4.06	19	19	2	102	101	40	52	1	0	0	0	0	0	0	—	7	16	0	1	1.2	1.000
1982	PIT	N	0	5	.000	6.55	12	10	0	44	60	27	17	0	0	0	0	12	1	0	.083	2	8	0	1	0.8	1.000
5 yrs.			22	36	.379	3.99	90	84	10	496	492	211	222	6	0	0	0	12	1	0	.083	28	85	2	6	1.3	.983

Harry Baumgartner

BAUMGARTNER, HARRY E. BR TR 5′11″ 175 lbs.
B. Oct. 6, 1892, S. Pittsburg, Tenn. D. Dec. 3, 1930, Augusta, Ga.

Year	Team	Lg	W	L	PCT	ERA	G	GS	CG	IP	H	BB	SO	ShO	Relief W	Relief L	Relief SV	AB	H	HR	BA	PO	A	E	DP	TC/G	FA
1920	DET	A	0	1	.000	4.00	9	0	0	18	18	6	7	0	0	1	0	4	1	0	.250	1	5	0	0	0.7	1.000

Stan Baumgartner

BAUMGARTNER, STANWOOD FULTON BL TL 6′ 175 lbs.
B. Dec. 14, 1894, Houston, Tex. D. Oct. 4, 1955, Philadelphia, Pa.

Year	Team	Lg	W	L	PCT	ERA	G	GS	CG	IP	H	BB	SO	ShO	Relief W	Relief L	Relief SV	AB	H	HR	BA	PO	A	E	DP	TC/G	FA
1914	PHI	N	3	2	.600	3.28	15	3	2	60.1	60	16	24	1	3	0	0	19	1	0	.053	3	11	0	0	0.9	1.000
1915			0	2	.000	2.42	16	1	0	48.1	38	23	27	0	0	1	0	12	1	0	.083	3	17	1	1	1.3	.952
1916			0	0	—	2.25	1	0	0	4	5	1	0	0	0	0	0	1	0	0	.000	0	0	0	0	0.0	.000
1921			3	6	.333	7.02	22	7	2	66.2	103	22	13	0	2	0	0	30	6	0	.200	1	15	1	0	0.7	.941
1922			1	1	.500	6.52	6	1	0	9.2	18	5	2	0	1	0	0	3	1	0	.333	1	3	0	0	0.7	1.000
1924	PHI	A	13	6	.684	2.88	36	16	12	181	181	73	45	1	4	1	4	60	13	0	.217	10	33	3	1	1.3	.935
1925			6	3	.667	3.57	37	12	2	113.1	120	35	18	1	2	1	3	30	7	0	.233	10	25	3	1	1.0	.921
1926			1	1	.500	4.03	10	1	0	22.1	28	10	0	0	1	1	0	3	1	0	.333	2	8	0	0	1.0	1.000
8 yrs.			27	21	.563	3.70	143	41	18	505.2	553	185	129	3	13	4	7	158	30	0	.190	30	112	8	3	1.0	.947

George Bausewine

BAUSEWINE, GEORGE W. 6′ 2″ 207 lbs.
B. Mar. 22, 1869, Philadelphia, Pa. D. July 29, 1947, Norristown, Pa.

Year	Team	Lg	W	L	PCT	ERA	G	GS	CG	IP	H	BB	SO	ShO	Relief W	Relief L	Relief SV	AB	H	HR	BA	PO	A	E	DP	TC/G	FA
1889	PHI	AA	1	4	.200	3.90	7	6	6	55.1	64	33	18	0	0	0	0	21	1	0	.048	0	12	0	0	1.7	1.000

Ed Bauta

BAUTA, EDUARDO BR TR 6′ 3″ 200 lbs.
Born Eduardo Bauta (Galvez).
B. Jan. 6, 1935, Florida Camaguey, Cuba.

Year	Team	Lg	W	L	PCT	ERA	G	GS	CG	IP	H	BB	SO	ShO	Relief W	Relief L	Relief SV	AB	H	HR	BA	PO	A	E	DP	TC/G	FA
1960	STL	N	0	0	—	6.32	9	0	0	15.2	14	11	6	0	0	0	1	1	0	0	.000	0	2	0	0	0.2	1.000
1961			2	0	1.000	1.40	13	0	0	19.1	12	5	12	0	2	0	5	4	2	0	.500	0	3	0	0	0.2	1.000
1962			1	0	1.000	5.01	20	0	0	32.1	28	21	25	0	1	0	1	4	1	0	.250	1	6	0	0	0.3	1.000
1963	**2 teams**	**STL N** (38G 3–4) **NY N** (9G 0–0)																									
″	**total**		3	4	.429	4.27	47	0	0	71.2	77	30	43	0	3	4	3	8	0	0	.000	0	9	0	0	0.2	1.000
1964	NY	N	0	2	.000	5.40	8	0	0	10	17	3	3	0	0	2	1	0	0	0	—	0	5	1	0	0.8	.833
5 yrs.			6	6	.500	4.35	97	0	0	149	148	70	89	0	6	6	11	17	3	0	.176	1	25	1	0	0.3	.963

Jose Bautista

BAUTISTA, JOSE JOAQUIN BR TR 6′ 1″ 177 lbs.
Born Jose Joaquin Bautista (Arias).
B. July 25, 1964, Bani, Dominican Republic.

Year	Team	Lg	W	L	PCT	ERA	G	GS	CG	IP	H	BB	SO	ShO	Relief W	Relief L	Relief SV	AB	H	HR	BA	PO	A	E	DP	TC/G	FA
1988	BAL	A	6	15	.286	4.30	33	25	3	171.2	171	45	76	0	0	1	0	0	0	0	—	27	11	1	3	1.2	.974
1989			3	4	.429	5.31	15	10	0	78	84	15	30	0	0	0	0	0	0	0	—	3	10	1	0	0.9	.929
1990			1	0	1.000	4.05	22	0	0	26.2	28	7	15	0	1	0	0	0	0	0	—	1	2	0	0	0.1	1.000
1991			0	1	.000	16.88	5	0	0	5.1	13	5	3	0	0	1	0	0	0	0	—	0	1	0	0	0.2	1.000
1993	CHI	N	10	3	.769	2.82	58	7	1	111.2	105	27	63	0	6	1	2	21	4	0	.190	14	18	2	2	0.6	.941

Jose Bautista *continued*

Year	Team	Lg	W	L	PCT	ERA	G	GS	CG	IP	H	BB	SO	ShO	Relief Pitching W	Relief Pitching L	Relief Pitching SV	Batting AB	Batting H	Batting HR	BA	PO	A	E	DP	TC/G	FA
1994			4	5	.444	3.89	58	0	0	69.1	75	17	45	0	4	5	1	2	0	0	.000	5	9	0	0	0.2	1.000
1995	SF	N	3	8	.273	6.44	52	6	0	100.2	120	26	45	0	2	5	0	18	0	0	.000	5	11	1	0	0.3	.941
7 yrs.			27	36	.429	4.59	243	48	4	563.1	596	142	277	0	13	13	3	41	4	0	.098	55	62	5	5	0.5	.959

Bill Bayne

BAYNE, WILLIAM LEAR (Beverly) BL TL 5′9″ 160 lbs.
B. Apr. 18, 1899, Pittsburgh, Pa. D. May 22, 1981, St. Louis, Mo.

Year	Team	Lg	W	L	PCT	ERA	G	GS	CG	IP	H	BB	SO	ShO	Relief Pitching W	Relief Pitching L	Relief Pitching SV	Batting AB	Batting H	Batting HR	BA	PO	A	E	DP	TC/G	FA
1919	STL	A	1	1	.500	5.25	2	2	1	12	16	6	0	0	0	0	0	5	2	0	.400	1	4	0	0	2.5	1.000
1920			5	6	.455	3.70	18	13	6	99.2	102	41	38	1	0	0	0	35	6	0	.171	3	16	1	1	1.1	.950
1921			11	5	.688	4.72	47	14	7	164	167	80	82	1	**5**	1	3	60	18	1	.300	9	36	6	0	1.1	.882
1922			4	5	.444	4.56	26	9	3	92.2	86	37	38	0	1	2	2	30	7	0	.233	6	12	0	0	0.7	1.000
1923			2	2	.500	4.50	19	2	0	46	49	31	15	0	2	1	0	13	3	0	.231	3	8	1	1	0.6	.917
1924			1	3	.250	4.17	21	3	0	49.2	46	28	20	0	1	2	0	14	6	0	.429	2	8	2	0	0.6	.833
1928	CLE	A	2	5	.286	5.13	37	6	3	108.2	128	43	39	0	0	3	3	30	11	0	.367	5	32	3	3	1.1	.925
1929	BOS	A	5	5	.500	6.72	27	6	2	84.1	111	29	26	0	4	0	0	25	8	0	.320	4	22	0	3	1.0	1.000
1930			0	0	—	4.50	1	0	0	4	5	1	1	0	0	0	0	2	1	0	.500	0	1	0	0	1.0	1.000
9 yrs.			31	32	.492	4.82	198	55	22	661	710	296	259	2	13	9	8	214	62	1	.290	33	139	13	8	0.9	.930

Walter Beall

BEALL, WALTER ESAU BR TR 5′10″ 178 lbs.
B. July 29, 1899, Washington, D. C. D. Jan. 28, 1959, Suitland, Md.

Year	Team	Lg	W	L	PCT	ERA	G	GS	CG	IP	H	BB	SO	ShO	Relief Pitching W	Relief Pitching L	Relief Pitching SV	Batting AB	Batting H	Batting HR	BA	PO	A	E	DP	TC/G	FA
1924	NY	A	2	0	1.000	3.52	4	2	0	23	19	17	18	0	1	0	0	7	1	0	.143	0	4	0	0	1.0	1.000
1925			0	1	.000	12.71	8	1	0	11.1	11	19	8	0	0	0	0	3	0	0	.000	0	4	0	0	0.5	1.000
1926			2	4	.333	3.53	20	9	1	81.2	71	68	56	0	0	0	1	22	3	0	.136	0	24	6	1	1.5	.800
1927			0	0	—	9.00	1	0	0	1	1	0	0	0	0	0	0	0	0	0	—	0	0	0	0	0.0	.000
1929	WAS	A	1	0	1.000	3.86	3	0	0	7	8	7	3	0	1	0	0	3	0	0	.000	0	3	0	0	1.0	1.000
5 yrs.			5	5	.500	4.43	36	12	1	124	110	111	85	0	2	0	1	35	4	0	.114	0	35	6	1	1.1	.854

Alex Beam

BEAM, ALEXANDER ROGER
B. Nov. 21, 1870, Johnstown, Pa. D. Apr. 17, 1938, Nogales, Ariz.

Year	Team	Lg	W	L	PCT	ERA	G	GS	CG	IP	H	BB	SO	ShO	Relief Pitching W	Relief Pitching L	Relief Pitching SV	Batting AB	Batting H	Batting HR	BA	PO	A	E	DP	TC/G	FA
1889	PIT	N	1	1	.500	6.50	2	2	2	18	11	15	1	0	0	0	0	6	1	0	.167	0	4	3	0	3.5	.571

Ernie Beam

BEAM, ERNEST JOSEPH TR 6′½″ 185 lbs.
B. Mar. 17, 1867, Mansfield, Ohio D. Sept. 13, 1918, Mansfield, Ohio.

Year	Team	Lg	W	L	PCT	ERA	G	GS	CG	IP	H	BB	SO	ShO	Relief Pitching W	Relief Pitching L	Relief Pitching SV	Batting AB	Batting H	Batting HR	BA	PO	A	E	DP	TC/G	FA
1895	PHI	N	0	2	.000	11.31	9	1	1	24.2	33	25	3	0	0	1	**3**	11	2	0	.182	1	4	1	0	0.6	.833

Charlie Beamon

BEAMON, CHARLES ALFONZO, SR. BR TR 5′11″ 195 lbs.
Father of Charlie Beamon.
B. Dec. 25, 1934, Oakland, Calif.

Year	Team	Lg	W	L	PCT	ERA	G	GS	CG	IP	H	BB	SO	ShO	Relief Pitching W	Relief Pitching L	Relief Pitching SV	Batting AB	Batting H	Batting HR	BA	PO	A	E	DP	TC/G	FA
1956	BAL	A	2	0	1.000	1.38	2	1	1	13	9	8	14	1	1	0	0	5	0	0	.000	0	3	0	0	1.5	1.000
1957			0	0	—	5.19	4	1	0	8.2	8	7	5	0	0	0	0	2	0	0	.000	0	2	1	0	0.8	.667
1958			1	3	.250	4.35	21	3	0	49.2	47	21	26	0	1	1	0	10	0	0	.000	6	15	0	4	1.0	1.000
3 yrs.			3	3	.500	3.91	27	5	1	71.1	64	36	45	1	2	1	0	17	0	0	.000	6	20	1	4	1.0	.963

Belve Bean

BEAN, BEVERIC BENTON (Bill) BR TR 6′1½″ 197 lbs.
B. Apr. 23, 1905, Mullin, Tex. D. June 1, 1988, Comanche, Tex.

Year	Team	Lg	W	L	PCT	ERA	G	GS	CG	IP	H	BB	SO	ShO	Relief Pitching W	Relief Pitching L	Relief Pitching SV	Batting AB	Batting H	Batting HR	BA	PO	A	E	DP	TC/G	FA
1930	CLE	A	3	3	.500	5.45	23	3	2	74.1	99	32	19	0	3	1	2	26	9	0	.346	3	17	1	0	0.9	.952
1931			0	1	.000	6.43	4	0	0	7	11	4	3	0	0	1	0	1	0	0	.000	0	3	0	0	0.8	1.000
1933			1	2	.333	5.25	27	2	0	70.1	80	20	41	0	1	1	0	22	4	0	.182	4	16	0	0	0.7	1.000
1934			5	1	.833	3.86	21	1	0	51.1	53	21	20	0	5	0	0	15	3	0	.200	0	14	1	0	0.7	.933
1935	2 teams	CLE A	(16G 0–0)	WAS A	(10G 2–0)																						
″	total		2	0	1.000	7.31	11	2	0	32	45	19	6	0	2	0	0	8	3	1	.375	0	4	0	0	0.4	1.000
5 yrs.			11	7	.611	5.32	86	8	2	235	288	96	89	0	11	3	2	72	19	1	.264	7	54	2	0	0.7	.968

Dave Beard

BEARD, CHARLES DAVID BL TR 6′5″ 190 lbs.
B. Oct. 2, 1959, Atlanta, Ga.

Year	Team	Lg	W	L	PCT	ERA	G	GS	CG	IP	H	BB	SO	ShO	Relief Pitching W	Relief Pitching L	Relief Pitching SV	Batting AB	Batting H	Batting HR	BA	PO	A	E	DP	TC/G	FA
1980	OAK	A	0	1	.000	3.38	13	0	0	16	12	7	12	0	0	1	1	0	0	0	—	0	2	0	0	0.2	1.000
1981			1	1	.500	2.77	8	0	0	13	9	4	15	0	1	1	3	0	0	0	—	2	1	0	0	0.4	1.000
1982			10	9	.526	3.44	54	2	0	91.2	85	35	73	0	10	7	11	0	0	0	—	3	11	2	1	0.3	.875
1983			5	5	.500	5.61	43	0	0	61	55	36	40	0	5	5	10	0	0	0	—	1	3	0	0	0.1	1.000
1984	SEA	A	3	2	.600	5.80	43	0	0	76	88	33	40	0	3	2	5	0	0	0	—	2	12	1	0	0.3	.933
1985	CHI	N	0	0	—	6.39	9	0	0	12.2	16	7	4	0	0	0	0	0	0	0	—	0	2	0	0	0.2	1.000
1989	DET	A	0	2	.000	5.06	2	1	0	5.1	9	2	1	0	0	1	0	0	0	0	—	1	0	0	0	1.0	1.000
7 yrs.			19	20	.487	4.70	172	3	0	275.2	274	124	185	0	19	17	30	0	0	0		9	32	3	1	0.3	.932
DIVISIONAL PLAYOFF SERIES																											
1981	OAK	A	0	0	—	0.00	1	0	0	1.1	0	0	2	0	0	0	1	0	0	0	—	0	0	0	0	0.0	.000
LEAGUE CHAMPIONSHIP SERIES																											
1981	OAK	A	0	0	—	40.50	1	0	0	0.2	5	0	0	0	0	0	0	0	0	0	—	0	1	0	0	1.0	1.000

Mike Beard

BEARD, MICHAEL RICHARD BL TL 6′1″ 185 lbs.
B. June 21, 1950, Little Rock, Ark.

Year	Team	Lg	W	L	PCT	ERA	G	GS	CG	IP	H	BB	SO	ShO	Relief Pitching W	Relief Pitching L	Relief Pitching SV	Batting AB	Batting H	Batting HR	BA	PO	A	E	DP	TC/G	FA
1974	ATL	N	0	0	—	3.00	6	0	0	9	5	1	7	0	0	0	0	0	0	0	—	1	2	0	0	0.5	1.000
1975			4	0	1.000	3.21	34	2	0	70	71	28	27	0	4	0	0	9	1	0	.111	2	13	1	1	0.5	.938
1976			0	2	.000	4.24	30	0	0	34	38	14	8	0	0	2	1	1	0	0	.000	3	9	0	1	0.4	1.000
1977			0	0	—	9.00	4	0	0	5	14	2	1	0	0	0	0	0	0	0	—	0	1	0	0	0.3	1.000
4 yrs.			4	2	.667	3.74	74	2	0	118	128	45	43	0	4	2	1	10	1	0	.100	6	25	1	2	0.4	.969

Ralph Beard

BEARD, RALPH WILLIAM BR TR 6′5″ 200 lbs.
B. Feb. 11, 1929, Cincinnati, Ohio.

Year	Team	Lg	W	L	PCT	ERA	G	GS	CG	IP	H	BB	SO	ShO	Relief Pitching W	Relief Pitching L	Relief Pitching SV	Batting AB	Batting H	Batting HR	BA	PO	A	E	DP	TC/G	FA
1954	STL	N	0	4	.000	3.72	13	10	0	58	62	28	17	0	0	0	0	17	1	0	.059	0	8	1	1	0.7	.889

Gene Bearden

BEARDEN, HENRY EUGENE
B. Sept. 5, 1920, Lexa, Ark.

BL TL 6′ 4″ 198 lbs.

Year	Team		W	L	PCT	ERA	G	GS	CG	IP	H	BB	SO	ShO	Relief Pitching W	Relief Pitching L	Relief Pitching SV	Batting AB	Batting H	Batting HR	BA	PO	A	E	DP	TC/G	FA
1947	CLE	A	0	0	—	81.00	1	0	0	0.1	2	1	0	0	0	0	0	0	0	0	—	0	0	0	0	0.0	.000
1948			20	7	.741	**2.43**	37	29	15	229.2	187	106	80	6	0	2	1	90	23	2	.256	15	52	1	11	1.8	.985
1949			8	8	.500	5.10	32	19	5	127	140	92	41	0	1	1	0	45	5	0	.111	9	42	1	2	1.6	.981
1950	2 teams	CLE A	(14G 1–3)		WAS A	(12G 3–5)																					
″	total		4	8	.333	4.99	26	12	4	113.2	138	65	30	0	1	2	0	35	7	0	.200	8	22	7	1	1.4	.811
1951	2 teams	WAS A	(1G 0–0)		DET A	(37G 3–4)																					
″	total		3	4	.429	4.64	38	5	2	108.2	118	60	39	1	1	2	0	32	6	2	.188	3	21	1	0	0.7	.960
1952	STL	A	7	8	.467	4.30	34	16	3	150.2	158	78	45	0	1	2	0	65	23	0	.354	12	32	2	0	1.4	.957
1953	CHI	A	3	3	.500	2.93	25	3	0	58.1	48	33	24	0	3	1	0	21	4	0	.190	2	11	3	0	0.6	.813
7 yrs.			45	38	.542	3.96	193	84	29	788.1	791	435	259	7	7	10	1	288	68	4	.236	49	180	15	14	1.3	.939
WORLD SERIES																											
1948	CLE	A	1	0	1.000	0.00	2	1	1	10.2	6	1	4	1	0	0	1	4	2	0	.500	0	7	0	1	3.5	1.000

Gary Beare

BEARE, GARY RAY
B. Aug. 22, 1952, San Diego, Calif.

BR TR 6′ 4″ 205 lbs.

Year	Team		W	L	PCT	ERA	G	GS	CG	IP	H	BB	SO	ShO	Relief Pitching W	Relief Pitching L	Relief Pitching SV	Batting AB	Batting H	Batting HR	BA	PO	A	E	DP	TC/G	FA
1976	MIL	A	2	3	.400	3.29	6	5	2	41	43	15	32	0	0	0	0	0	0	0	—	2	4	1	1	1.2	.857
1977			3	3	.500	6.41	17	6	0	59	63	38	32	0	2	0	0	0	0	0	—	5	16	0	0	1.2	1.000
2 yrs.			5	6	.455	5.13	23	11	2	100	106	53	64	0	2	0	0	0	0	0		7	20	1	1	1.2	.964

Larry Bearnarth

BEARNARTH, LAWRENCE DONALD
B. Sept. 11, 1941, New York, N. Y.

BR TR 6′ 2″ 203 lbs.

Year	Team		W	L	PCT	ERA	G	GS	CG	IP	H	BB	SO	ShO	Relief Pitching W	Relief Pitching L	Relief Pitching SV	Batting AB	Batting H	Batting HR	BA	PO	A	E	DP	TC/G	FA
1963	NY	N	3	8	.273	3.42	58	2	0	126.1	127	47	48	0	3	7	4	30	6	0	.200	11	35	3	1	0.8	.939
1964			5	5	.500	4.15	44	1	0	78	79	38	31	0	5	4	3	14	2	0	.143	9	27	0	0	0.8	1.000
1965			3	5	.375	4.60	40	3	0	60.2	75	28	16	0	3	3	1	9	1	0	.111	2	15	2	2	0.5	.895
1966			2	3	.400	4.45	29	1	0	54.2	59	20	27	0	2	2	0	9	1	0	.111	4	14	0	0	0.6	1.000
1971	MIL	A	0	0	—	18.00	2	0	0	3	10	2	2	0	0	0	0	0	0	0	—	1	1	0	0	1.0	1.000
5 yrs.			13	21	.382	4.13	173	7	0	322.2	350	135	124	0	13	16	8	62	10	0	.161	27	92	5	3	0.7	.960

Kevin Bearse

BEARSE, KEVIN GERARD
B. Nov. 7, 1965, Jersey City, N. J.

BL TL 6′ 2″ 195 lbs.

Year	Team		W	L	PCT	ERA	G	GS	CG	IP	H	BB	SO	ShO	Relief Pitching W	Relief Pitching L	Relief Pitching SV	Batting AB	Batting H	Batting HR	BA	PO	A	E	DP	TC/G	FA
1990	CLE	A	0	2	.000	12.91	3	3	0	7.2	16	5	2	0	0	0	0	0	0	0	—	0	1	0	0	0.3	1.000

Chris Beasley

BEASLEY, CHRISTOPHER CHARLES
B. June 23, 1962, Jackson, Tenn.

BR TR 6′ 2″ 190 lbs.

Year	Team		W	L	PCT	ERA	G	GS	CG	IP	H	BB	SO	ShO	Relief Pitching W	Relief Pitching L	Relief Pitching SV	Batting AB	Batting H	Batting HR	BA	PO	A	E	DP	TC/G	FA
1991	CAL	A	0	1	.000	3.38	22	0	0	26.2	26	10	14	0	0	1	0	0	0	0	—	4	4	0	1	0.4	1.000

Eb Beatin

BEATIN, EBENEZER AMBROSE
B. Aug. 10, 1866, Baltimore, Md. D. May 9, 1925, Baltimore, Md.

BR TR 5′ 9″ 162 lbs.

Year	Team		W	L	PCT	ERA	G	GS	CG	IP	H	BB	SO	ShO	Relief Pitching W	Relief Pitching L	Relief Pitching SV	Batting AB	Batting H	Batting HR	BA	PO	A	E	DP	TC/G	FA
1887	DET	N	1	1	.500	4.00	2	2	2	18	13	8	6	0	0	0	0	7	0	0	.000	0	2	0	0	1.0	1.000
1888			5	7	.417	2.86	12	12	12	107	111	16	44	1	0	0	0	56	14	2	.250	8	25	7	0	2.5	.825
1889	CLE	N	20	15	.571	3.57	36	36	35	317.2	316	141	126	3	0	0	0	121	14	1	.116	15	52	6	1	2.0	.918
1890			22	30	.423	3.83	54	54	53	474.1	**518**	186	155	1	0	0	0	191	27	1	.141	30	101	8	7	2.6	.942
1891			0	3	.000	5.28	5	4	2	29	39	21	4	0	0	0	0	13	1	0	.077	0	6	0	0	1.2	1.000
5 yrs.			48	56	.462	3.68	109	108	104	946	997	372	335	5	0	0	0	388	56	4	.144	53	186	21	6	2.3	.919

Jim Beattie

BEATTIE, JAMES LOUIS
B. July 4, 1954, Hampton, Va.

BR TR 6′ 5″ 210 lbs.

Year	Team		W	L	PCT	ERA	G	GS	CG	IP	H	BB	SO	ShO	Relief Pitching W	Relief Pitching L	Relief Pitching SV	Batting AB	Batting H	Batting HR	BA	PO	A	E	DP	TC/G	FA
1978	NY	A	6	9	.400	3.73	25	22	0	128	123	51	65	0	0	0	0	0	0	0	—	14	21	3	2	1.5	.921
1979			3	6	.333	5.21	15	13	1	76	85	41	32	1	0	0	0	0	0	0	—	9	16	1	1	1.7	.962
1980	SEA	A	5	15	.250	4.86	33	29	3	187	205	98	67	0	0	1	0	0	0	0	—	10	30	0	1	1.2	1.000
1981			3	2	.600	2.96	13	9	0	67	59	18	36	0	0	0	1	0	0	0	—	8	11	1	0	1.5	.950
1982			8	12	.400	3.34	28	26	6	172.1	149	65	140	1	0	0	0	0	0	0	—	16	21	1	2	1.4	.974
1983			10	15	.400	3.84	30	29	8	196.2	197	66	132	2	0	0	0	0	0	0	—	18	37	2	5	1.9	.965
1984			12	16	.429	3.41	32	32	12	211	206	75	119	2	0	0	0	0	0	0	—	13	33	0	2	1.4	1.000
1985			5	6	.455	7.29	18	15	1	70.1	93	33	45	1	0	0	0	0	0	0	—	4	6	1	0	0.6	.909
1986			0	6	.000	6.02	9	7	0	40.1	57	14	24	0	0	0	0	0	0	0	—	4	6	0	2	1.1	1.000
9 yrs.			52	87	.374	4.17	203	182	31	1148.2	1174	461	660	7	0	1	1	0	0	0		96	181	9	15	1.4	.969
LEAGUE CHAMPIONSHIP SERIES																											
1978	NY	A	1	0	1.000	1.69	1	1	0	5.1	2	5	3	0	0	0	0	0	0	0	—	2	0	0	0	2.0	1.000
WORLD SERIES																											
1978	NY	A	1	0	1.000	2.00	1	1	1	9	9	4	8	0	0	0	0	0	0	0	—	0	1	0	0	1.0	1.000

Blaine Beatty

BEATTY, GORDON BLAINE
B. Apr. 25, 1964, Victoria, Tex.

BL TL 6′ 2″ 185 lbs.

Year	Team		W	L	PCT	ERA	G	GS	CG	IP	H	BB	SO	ShO	Relief Pitching W	Relief Pitching L	Relief Pitching SV	Batting AB	Batting H	Batting HR	BA	PO	A	E	DP	TC/G	FA
1989	NY	N	0	0	—	1.50	2	1	0	6	5	2	3	0	0	0	0	2	1	0	.500	2	0	0	0	1.0	1.000
1991			0	0	—	2.79	5	0	0	9.2	9	4	7	0	0	0	0	0	0	0	—	1	1	0	0	0.4	1.000
2 yrs.			0	0		2.30	7	1	0	15.2	14	6	10	0	0	0	0	2	1	0	.500	3	1	0	0	0.6	1.000

Johnny Beazley

BEAZLEY, JOHN ANDREW
B. May 25, 1918, Nashville, Tenn. D. Apr. 21, 1990, Nashville, Tenn.

BR TR 6′ 1½″ 190 lbs.

Year	Team		W	L	PCT	ERA	G	GS	CG	IP	H	BB	SO	ShO	Relief Pitching W	Relief Pitching L	Relief Pitching SV	Batting AB	Batting H	Batting HR	BA	PO	A	E	DP	TC/G	FA
1941	STL	N	1	0	1.000	1.00	1	1	1	9	10	3	4	0	0	0	0	3	0	0	.000	0	1	0	0	1.0	1.000
1942			21	6	.778	2.13	43	23	13	215.1	181	73	91	3	6	3	3	73	10	0	.137	10	48	1	1	1.4	.983
1946			7	5	.583	4.46	19	18	5	103	109	55	36	0	0	0	0	33	8	0	.242	10	16	1	1	1.4	.963
1947	BOS	N	2	0	1.000	4.40	9	2	2	28.2	30	19	12	0	0	0	0	7	0	0	.000	3	4	0	0	0.8	1.000
1948			0	1	.000	4.50	3	2	0	16	19	7	4	0	0	0	0	4	0	0	.000	1	2	0	0	1.0	1.000
1949			0	0	—	0.00	1	0	0	2	0	0	0	0	0	0	0	0	0	0	—	0	0	0	0	0.0	.000
6 yrs.			31	12	.721	3.01	76	46	21	374	349	157	147	3	6	3	3	120	18	0	.150	24	71	2	2	1.3	.979

Johnny Beazley *continued*

Year	Team	Lg	W	L	PCT	ERA	G	GS	CG	IP	H	BB	SO	ShO	Relief Pitching W	Relief Pitching L	Relief Pitching SV	Batting AB	Batting H	Batting HR	BA	PO	A	E	DP	TC/G	FA
WORLD SERIES																											
1942	STL	N	2	0	1.000	2.50	2	2	2	18	17	3	6	0	0	0	0	7	1	0	.143	2	0	1	0	1.5	.667
1946			0	0	—	0.00	1	0	0	1	1	0	1	0	0	0	0	0	0	0	—	0	1	0	0	1.0	1.000
2 yrs.			2	0	1.000	2.37	3	2	2	19	18	3	7	0	0	0	0	7	1	0	.143	2	1	1	0	1.3	.750

Buck Becannon

BECANNON, JAMES MELVIN 5′10″ 165 lbs.
B. Aug. 22, 1859, New York, N. Y. D. Nov. 5, 1923, New York, N. Y.

Year	Team	Lg	W	L	PCT	ERA	G	GS	CG	IP	H	BB	SO	ShO	Relief Pitching W	Relief Pitching L	Relief Pitching SV	Batting AB	Batting H	Batting HR	BA	PO	A	E	DP	TC/G	FA
1884	NY	AA	1	0	1.000	*1.50*	1	1	1	6	2	2	2	0	0	0	0	3	0	0	.000	0	2	0	0	2.0	1.000
1885			2	8	.200	*6.25*	10	10	10	85	108	24	13	0	0	0	0	33	10	0	.303	1	17	0	0	1.8	1.000
2 yrs.			3	8	.273	5.93	11	11	11	91	110	26	15	0	0	0	0	41	10	0	.244	3	21	2	0	2.2	.923

Boom-Boom Beck

BECK, WALTER WILLIAM BR TR 6′ 2″ 200 lbs.
B. Oct. 16, 1904, Decatur, Ill. D. May 7, 1987, Champaign, Ill.

Year	Team	Lg	W	L	PCT	ERA	G	GS	CG	IP	H	BB	SO	ShO	Relief Pitching W	Relief Pitching L	Relief Pitching SV	Batting AB	Batting H	Batting HR	BA	PO	A	E	DP	TC/G	FA
1924	STL	A	0	0	—	0.00	1	0	0	1	2	1	0	0	0	0	0	0	0	0	—	0	1	0	0	1.0	1.000
1927			1	0	1.000	5.56	3	1	1	11.1	15	5	6	0	0	0	0	4	1	0	.250	1	1	0	0	0.7	1.000
1928			2	3	.400	4.41	16	4	2	49	52	20	17	0	1	0	0	14	6	0	.429	0	11	1	2	0.8	.917
1933	BKN	N	12	20	.375	3.54	43	**35**	15	257	270	69	89	3	1	1	1	95	18	0	.189	12	52	3	4	1.6	.955
1934			2	6	.250	7.42	22	9	2	57	72	32	24	0	1	1	0	17	4	0	.235	2	17	0	2	0.9	1.000
1939	PHI	N	7	14	.333	4.73	34	16	12	182.2	203	64	77	0	3	4	3	68	9	0	.132	8	37	6	1	1.5	.882
1940			4	9	.308	4.31	29	15	4	129.1	147	41	38	0	2	0	0	36	2	0	.056	10	32	3	0	1.6	.933
1941			1	9	.100	4.63	34	7	2	95.1	104	35	34	0	0	3	0	25	3	0	.120	3	6	1	0	0.3	.900
1942			0	1	.000	4.75	26	1	0	53	69	17	10	0	0	0	0	12	4	0	.333	3	9	1	2	0.5	.923
1943			0	0	—	9.88	4	0	0	13.2	24	5	3	0	0	0	0	4	2	0	.500	4	0	0	0	1.0	1.000
1944	DET	A	1	2	.333	3.89	28	2	0	74	67	27	25	0	1	1	1	22	7	0	.318	0	6	1	1	0.3	.857
1945	2 teams	CIN N	(11G 2–4)	PIT N	(14G 6–1)																						
″	total		8	5	.615	2.68	25	11	6	110.2	96	26	29	0	2	1	1	30	5	0	.167	4	21	0	0	1.0	1.000
12 yrs.			38	69	.355	4.30	265	101	44	1034	1121	342	352	3	11	11	6	327	61	0	.187	47	193	16	12	1.0	.938

Frank Beck

BECK, FRANK J. TR 5′ 9″ 141 lbs.
Born Frank J. Hengstebeck.
B. Sept. 29, 1860, Poughkeepsie, N. Y. D. Feb. 8, 1941, Detroit, Mich.

Year	Team	Lg	W	L	PCT	ERA	G	GS	CG	IP	H	BB	SO	ShO	Relief Pitching W	Relief Pitching L	Relief Pitching SV	Batting AB	Batting H	Batting HR	BA	PO	A	E	DP	TC/G	FA
1884	2 teams	PIT AA	(3G 0–3)	BAL U	(2G 0–2)																						
″	total		0	5	.000	6.62	5	5	4	34	50	10	18	0	0	0	0	32	6	0	.188	3	7	1	0	1.2	.909

George Beck

BECK, ERNEST GEORGE (Eaglebeak) BR TR 5′11″ 165 lbs.
B. Feb. 21, 1890, South Bend, Ind. D. Oct. 29, 1973, South Bend, Ind.

Year	Team	Lg	W	L	PCT	ERA	G	GS	CG	IP	H	BB	SO	ShO	Relief Pitching W	Relief Pitching L	Relief Pitching SV	Batting AB	Batting H	Batting HR	BA	PO	A	E	DP	TC/G	FA
1914	CLE	A	0	0	—	0.00	1	0	0	1	1	0	0	0	0	0	0	0	0	0	—	0	0	0	0	0.0	.000

Rich Beck

BECK, RICHARD HENRY BB TR 6′ 3″ 190 lbs.
B. Jan. 21, 1941, Pasco, Wash.

Year	Team	Lg	W	L	PCT	ERA	G	GS	CG	IP	H	BB	SO	ShO	Relief Pitching W	Relief Pitching L	Relief Pitching SV	Batting AB	Batting H	Batting HR	BA	PO	A	E	DP	TC/G	FA
1965	NY	A	2	1	.667	2.14	3	3	1	21	22	7	10	1	0	0	0	7	0	0	.000	3	4	0	2	2.3	1.000

Rod Beck

BECK, RODNEY ROY BR TR 6′ 1″ 215 lbs.
B. Aug. 3, 1968, Burbank, Calif.

Year	Team	Lg	W	L	PCT	ERA	G	GS	CG	IP	H	BB	SO	ShO	Relief Pitching W	Relief Pitching L	Relief Pitching SV	Batting AB	Batting H	Batting HR	BA	PO	A	E	DP	TC/G	FA
1991	SF	N	1	1	.500	3.78	31	0	0	52.1	53	13	38	0	1	1	1	2	1	0	.500	1	10	0	0	0.4	1.000
1992			3	3	.500	1.76	65	0	0	92	62	15	87	0	3	3	17	2	1	0	.500	2	13	1	0	0.2	.938
1993			3	1	.750	2.16	76	0	0	79.1	57	13	86	0	3	1	48	4	0	0	.000	0	8	1	1	0.1	.889
1994			2	4	.333	2.77	48	0	0	48.2	49	13	39	0	2	4	28	3	0	0	.000	4	4	0	0	0.2	1.000
1995			5	6	.455	4.45	60	0	0	58.2	60	21	42	0	5	6	33	3	1	0	.333	6	7	0	0	0.2	1.000
5 yrs.			14	15	.483	2.80	280	0	0	331	281	75	292	0	14	15	127	14	3	0	.214	13	42	2	1	0.2	.965

Bob Becker

BECKER, ROBERT CHARLES TL
B. Aug. 15, 1875, Syracuse, N. Y. D. Oct. 11, 1951, Syracuse, N. Y.

Year	Team	Lg	W	L	PCT	ERA	G	GS	CG	IP	H	BB	SO	ShO	Relief Pitching W	Relief Pitching L	Relief Pitching SV	Batting AB	Batting H	Batting HR	BA	PO	A	E	DP	TC/G	FA
1897	PHI	N	0	2	.000	5.63	5	2	2	24	32	7	10	0	0	0	0	9	1	0	.111	2	3	1	0	1.2	.833
1898			0	0	—	10.80	1	0	0	5	6	5	0	0	0	0	0	1	0	0	.000	0	2	0	0	2.0	1.000
2 yrs.			0	2	.000	6.52	6	2	2	29	38	12	10	0	0	0	0	10	1	0	.100	2	5	1	0	1.3	.875

Charlie Becker

BECKER, CHARLES S. (Buck) BL TL 6′ 2″ 180 lbs.
B. Oct. 14, 1888, Washington, D. C. D. July 30, 1928, Washington, D. C.

Year	Team	Lg	W	L	PCT	ERA	G	GS	CG	IP	H	BB	SO	ShO	Relief Pitching W	Relief Pitching L	Relief Pitching SV	Batting AB	Batting H	Batting HR	BA	PO	A	E	DP	TC/G	FA
1911	WAS	A	3	5	.375	4.04	11	5	5	71.1	80	23	31	1	0	3	0	22	5	0	.227	1	18	0	0	1.7	1.000
1912			0	0	—	3.00	4	0	0	9	8	6	5	0	0	0	0	2	1	0	.500	0	1	0	0	0.3	1.000
2 yrs.			3	5	.375	3.92	15	5	5	80.1	88	29	36	1	0	3	0	24	6	0	.250	1	19	0	0	1.3	1.000

Jake Beckley

BECKLEY, JACOB PETER (St. Jacob) BL TL 5′10″ 200 lbs.
B. Aug. 4, 1867, Hannibal, Mo. D. June 25, 1918, Kansas City, Mo.
Hall of Fame 1971.

Year	Team	Lg	W	L	PCT	ERA	G	GS	CG	IP	H	BB	SO	ShO	Relief Pitching W	Relief Pitching L	Relief Pitching SV	Batting AB	Batting H	Batting HR	BA	PO	A	E	DP	TC/G	FA
1902	CIN	N	0	1	.000	6.75	1	1	0	4	9	1	2	0	0	0	0	*				744	19	16	38	11.0	.979

Jim Beckman

BECKMAN, JAMES JOSEPH BR TR 5′10″ 172 lbs.
Born Reinhardt Boeckman.
B. Mar. 1, 1905, Cincinnati, Ohio D. Dec. 5, 1974, Montgomery, Ohio.

Year	Team	Lg	W	L	PCT	ERA	G	GS	CG	IP	H	BB	SO	ShO	Relief Pitching W	Relief Pitching L	Relief Pitching SV	Batting AB	Batting H	Batting HR	BA	PO	A	E	DP	TC/G	FA
1927	CIN	N	0	1	.000	5.84	4	1	0	12.1	18	6	0	0	0	0	0	1	0	0	.000	0	0	1	0	0.3	.000
1928			0	1	.000	5.87	6	0	0	15.1	19	9	4	0	0	1	0	3	0	0	.000	0	2	0	1	0.3	1.000
2 yrs.			0	2	.000	5.86	10	1	0	27.2	37	15	4	0	0	1	0	4	0	0	.000	0	2	1	1	0.3	.667

Bill Beckmann

BECKMANN, WILLIAM ALOYSIUS BR TR 6′ 175 lbs.
B. Dec. 8, 1907, Clayton, Mo. D. Jan. 1, 1990, Florissant, Mo.

Year	Team	Lg	W	L	PCT	ERA	G	GS	CG	IP	H	BB	SO	ShO	Relief Pitching W	Relief Pitching L	Relief Pitching SV	Batting AB	Batting H	Batting HR	BA	PO	A	E	DP	TC/G	FA
1939	PHI	A	7	11	.389	5.39	27	19	7	155.1	198	41	20	2	2	0	0	52	13	0	.250	10	19	0	0	1.1	1.000
1940			8	4	.667	4.17	34	9	6	127.1	132	35	47	2	3	2	1	39	8	0	.205	11	13	3	0	0.8	.889

Bill Beckmann *continued*

Year	Team	Lg	W	L	PCT	ERA	G	GS	CG	IP	H	BB	SO	ShO	Relief W	Relief L	Relief SV	Batting AB	Batting H	Batting HR	BA	PO	A	E	DP	TC/G	FA
1941			5	9	.357	4.57	22	15	4	130	141	33	28	0	3	0	1	47	9	0	.191	5	12	2	0	0.9	.895
1942	2 teams	PHI A (5G 0–1) STL N (2G 1–0)																									
"	total		1	1	.500	5.27	7	1	0	27.1	28	10	13	0	1	0	0	5	2	0	.400	0	5	0	0	0.7	1.000
4 yrs.			21	25	.457	4.79	90	44	17	440	499	119	108	4	9	2	2	143	32	0	.224	26	49	5	0	0.9	.938

Joe Beckwith

BECKWITH, THOMAS JOSEPH
B. Jan. 28, 1955, Auburn, Ala.
BL TR 6′ 3″ 180 lbs.

Year	Team	Lg	W	L	PCT	ERA	G	GS	CG	IP	H	BB	SO	ShO	Relief W	Relief L	Relief SV	Batting AB	Batting H	Batting HR	BA	PO	A	E	DP	TC/G	FA
1979	LA	N	1	2	.333	4.38	17	0	0	37	42	15	28	0	1	2	2	5	0	0	.000	5	5	2	0	0.7	.833
1980			3	3	.500	1.95	38	0	0	60	60	23	40	0	3	3	0	2	0	0	.000	1	7	2	0	0.3	.800
1982			2	1	.667	2.70	19	1	0	40	38	14	33	0	2	1	1	7	0	0	.000	2	2	0	0	0.2	1.000
1983			3	4	.429	3.55	42	3	0	71	73	35	50	0	3	2	1	5	1	0	.200	8	13	0	1	0.5	1.000
1984	KC	A	8	4	.667	3.40	49	1	0	100.2	92	25	75	0	8	3	2	0	0	0	—	10	12	0	1	0.4	1.000
1985			1	5	.167	4.07	49	0	0	95	99	32	80	0	1	5	1	0	0	0	—	7	12	2	1	0.4	.905
1986	LA	N	0	0	—	6.87	15	0	0	18.1	28	6	13	0	0	0	0	0	0	0	—	1	0	0	0	0.1	1.000
7 yrs.			18	19	.486	3.54	229	5	0	422	432	150	319	0	18	16	7	19	1	0	.053	34	51	6	3	0.4	.934
LEAGUE CHAMPIONSHIP SERIES																											
1983	LA	N	0	0	—	0.00	2	0	0	2.1	1	2	3	0	0	0	0	0	0	0	—	0	0	0	0	0.0	.000
WORLD SERIES																											
1985	KC	A	0	0	—	0.00	1	0	0	2	1	0	3	0	0	0	0	0	0	0	—	0	0	0	0	0.0	.000

Julio Becquer

BECQUER, JULIO
Born Julio Becquer (Villegas).
B. Dec. 20, 1931, Havana, Cuba.
BL TL 5′11½″ 178 lbs.

Year	Team	Lg	W	L	PCT	ERA	G	GS	CG	IP	H	BB	SO	ShO	Relief W	Relief L	Relief SV	Batting AB	Batting H	Batting HR	BA	PO	A	E	DP	TC/G	FA
1960	WAS	A	0	0	—	9.00	1	0	0	1	1	0	0	0	0	0	0	298	75	4	.252	15	2	0	2	8.5	1.000
1961	MIN	A	0	0	—	20.25	1	0	0	1.1	4	1	0	0	0	0	0	92	20	5	.217	73	5	0	8	2.7	1.000
2 yrs.			0	0		15.43	2	0	0	2.1	5	1	0	0	0	0	0	*				1773	130	14	162	7.7	.993

Phil Bedgood

BEDGOOD, PHILLIP BURLETTE
B. Mar. 8, 1898, Harrison, Ga. D. Nov. 8, 1927, Fort Pierce, Fla.
BR TR 6′ 3″ 218 lbs.

Year	Team	Lg	W	L	PCT	ERA	G	GS	CG	IP	H	BB	SO	ShO	Relief W	Relief L	Relief SV	Batting AB	Batting H	Batting HR	BA	PO	A	E	DP	TC/G	FA
1922	CLE	A	1	0	1.000	4.00	1	1	1	9	7	4	5	0	0	0	0	2	0	0	.000	1	1	0	0	2.0	1.000
1923			0	2	.000	5.30	9	2	0	18.2	16	14	7	0	0	1	0	4	1	0	.250	0	5	0	0	0.6	1.000
2 yrs.			1	2	.333	4.88	10	3	1	27.2	23	18	12	0	0	1	0	6	1	0	.167	1	6	0	0	0.7	1.000

Hugh Bedient

BEDIENT, HUGH CARPENTER
B. Oct. 23, 1889, Gerry, N. Y. D. July 21, 1965, Jamestown, N. Y.
BR TR 6′ 185 lbs.

Year	Team	Lg	W	L	PCT	ERA	G	GS	CG	IP	H	BB	SO	ShO	Relief W	Relief L	Relief SV	Batting AB	Batting H	Batting HR	BA	PO	A	E	DP	TC/G	FA
1912	BOS	A	20	9	.690	2.92	41	28	19	231	206	55	122	0	**6**	0	2	73	14	0	.192	6	67	2	1	1.8	.973
1913			15	14	.517	2.78	43	29	19	259	255	67	122	1	3	1	5	80	10	0	.125	9	55	3	0	1.6	.955
1914			8	12	.400	3.60	42	16	7	177.1	185	45	70	1	3	**5**	2	50	5	0	.100	5	52	5	2	1.5	.919
1915	BUF	F	15	18	.455	3.17	53	30	16	269.1	284	69	106	2	3	1	**10**	83	9	0	.108	5	74	7	2	1.6	.919
4 yrs.			58	53	.523	3.08	179	103	61	936.2	930	236	420	4	15	7	19	286	38	0	.133	25	248	17	5	1.6	.941
WORLD SERIES																											
1912	BOS	A	1	0	1.000	0.50	4	2	1	18	10	7	7	0	0	0	0	6	0	0	.000	0	1	0	0	0.3	1.000

Andy Bednar

BEDNAR, ANDREW JACKSON
B. Aug. 16, 1908, Streator, Ill. D. Nov. 26, 1937, Graham, Tex.
BR TR 5′10½″ 180 lbs.

Year	Team	Lg	W	L	PCT	ERA	G	GS	CG	IP	H	BB	SO	ShO	Relief W	Relief L	Relief SV	Batting AB	Batting H	Batting HR	BA	PO	A	E	DP	TC/G	FA
1930	PIT	N	0	0	—	27.00	2	0	0	1.1	4	1	1	0	0	0	0	0	0	0	—	0	1	0	0	0.5	1.000
1931			0	0	—	11.25	3	0	0	4	10	0	2	0	0	0	0	0	0	0	—	0	1	0	0	0.3	1.000
2 yrs.			0	0		15.19	5	0	0	5.1	14	1	3	0	0	0	0	0	0	0		0	2	0	0	0.4	1.000

Steve Bedrosian

BEDROSIAN, STEPHEN WAYNE (Bedrock)
B. Dec. 6, 1957, Methuen, Mass.
BR TR 6′ 3″ 200 lbs.

Year	Team	Lg	W	L	PCT	ERA	G	GS	CG	IP	H	BB	SO	ShO	Relief W	Relief L	Relief SV	Batting AB	Batting H	Batting HR	BA	PO	A	E	DP	TC/G	FA
1981	ATL	N	1	2	.333	4.50	15	1	0	24	15	15	9	0	1	1	0	2	0	0	.000	1	2	0	1	0.2	1.000
1982			8	6	.571	2.42	64	3	0	137.2	102	57	123	0	7	4	11	26	1	0	.038	12	14	1	2	0.4	.963
1983			9	10	.474	3.60	70	1	0	120	100	51	114	0	9	10	19	19	2	0	.105	4	16	0	2	0.3	1.000
1984			9	6	.600	2.37	40	4	0	83.2	65	33	81	0	6	5	11	17	2	0	.118	1	8	1	0	0.3	.900
1985			7	15	.318	3.83	37	37	0	206.2	198	111	134	0	0	0	0	64	5	0	.078	13	23	4	3	1.1	.900
1986	PHI	N	8	6	.571	3.39	68	0	0	90.1	79	34	82	0	8	6	29	5	1	0	.200	2	10	0	1	0.2	1.000
1987			5	3	.625	2.83	65	0	0	89	79	28	74	0	5	3	**40**	4	0	0	.000	3	7	0	0	0.2	1.000
1988			6	6	.500	3.75	57	0	0	74.1	75	27	61	0	6	6	28	2	0	0	.000	5	9	0	0	0.2	1.000
1989	2 teams	PHI N (28G 2–3) SF N (40G 1–4)																									
"	total		3	7	.300	2.87	68	0	0	84.2	56	39	58	0	3	7	23	6	1	0	.167	2	5	1	1	0.1	.875
1990	SF	N	9	9	.500	4.20	68	0	0	79.1	72	44	43	0	9	**9**	17	4	2	0	.500	9	11	1	1	0.3	.952
1991	MIN	A	5	3	.625	4.42	56	0	0	77.1	70	35	44	0	5	3	6	0	0	0	—	6	5	0	0	0.2	1.000
1993	ATL	N	5	2	.714	1.63	49	0	0	49.2	34	14	33	0	5	2	0	2	0	0	.000	3	5	0	0	0.2	1.000
1994			0	2	.000	3.33	46	0	0	46	41	18	43	0	0	2	0	2	1	0	.500	3	4	1	0	0.2	.875
1995			1	2	.333	6.11	29	0	0	28	40	12	22	0	1	2	0	0	0	0	—	0	3	1	0	0.1	.750
14 yrs.			76	79	.490	3.38	732	46	0	1190.2	1026	518	921	0	65	60	184	153	15	0	.098	64	122	10	11	0.3	.949
LEAGUE CHAMPIONSHIP SERIES																											
1982	ATL	N	0	0	—	18.00	2	0	0	1	3	1	2	0	0	0	0	0	0	0	—	0	0	0	0	0.0	.000
1989	SF	N	0	0	—	2.70	4	0	0	3.1	4	2	2	0	0	0	3	0	0	0	—	0	0	0	0	0.0	.000
1991	MIN	A	0	0	—	0.00	2	0	0	1.1	3	2	2	0	0	0	0	0	0	0	—	0	0	0	0	0.0	.000
3 yrs.			0	0		4.76	8	0	0	5.2	10	5	6	0	0	0	3 **6th**	0	0	0		0	0	0	0	0.0	
WORLD SERIES																											
1989	SF	N	0	0	—	0.00	2	0	0	2.2	0	2	2	0	0	0	0	0	0	0	—	0	0	0	0	0.0	.000
1991	MIN	A	0	0	—	5.40	3	0	0	3.1	3	0	2	0	0	0	0	0	0	0	—	0	1	0	0	0.3	1.000
2 yrs.			0	0		3.00	5	0	0	6	3	2	4	0	0	0	0	0	0	0		0	1	0	0	0.2	1.000

Fred Beebe

BEEBE, FREDERICK LEONARD
B. Dec. 31, 1880, Lincoln, Neb. D. Oct. 30, 1957, Elgin, Ill.
BR TR 6′ 1″ 190 lbs.

Year	Team	W	L	PCT	ERA	G	GS	CG	IP	H	BB	SO	ShO	Relief Pitching W	Relief Pitching L	Relief Pitching SV	Batting AB	Batting H	Batting HR	BA	PO	A	E	DP	TC/G	FA
1906	2 teams CHI N (14G 6–1) STL N (20G 9–9)																									
″	total	15	10	.600	2.93	34	25	20	230.2	171	100	**171**	1	3	0	1	87	13	0	.149	9	54	9	1	2.1	.875
1907	STL N	7	19	.269	2.72	31	29	24	238.1	192	109	141	4	1	0	0	86	11	0	.128	18	62	5	3	2.7	.941
1908		5	13	.278	2.63	29	19	12	174.1	134	66	72	0	0	1	0	56	7	0	.125	9	54	2	5	2.2	.969
1909		15	21	.417	2.82	44	34	18	287.2	256	104	105	1	2	3	1	108	18	0	.167	15	81	7	3	2.3	.932
1910	CIN N	12	15	.444	3.07	35	26	11	214.1	193	94	93	2	3	0	0	73	12	0	.164	9	74	4	1	2.5	.954
1911	PHI N	3	3	.500	4.47	9	8	3	48.1	52	24	20	0	0	0	0	19	5	0	.263	0	18	0	0	2.0	1.000
1916	CLE A	5	3	.625	2.41	20	12	5	100.2	92	37	32	1	0	0	2	28	6	0	.214	8	27	4	1	2.0	.897
7 yrs.		62	84	.425	2.86	202	153	93	1294.1	1090	534	634	9	9	4	4	457	72	0	.158	68	370	31	14	2.3	.934

Harry Beecher

BEECHER, EDWARD HARRY
B. July 2, 1860, Guilford, Conn. D. Sept. 12, 1935, Hartford, Conn.
BL TL 5′10″ 185 lbs.

Year	Team	W	L	PCT	ERA	G	GS	CG	IP	H	BB	SO	ShO	Relief W	Relief L	SV	AB	H	HR	BA	PO	A	E	DP	TC/G	FA
1890	BUF P	0	0	—	12.00	1	0	0	6	10	3	0	0	0	0	0	*				85	12	9	1	2.6	.915

Roy Beecher

BEECHER, LeROY (Colonel)
B. May 10, 1884, Swanton, Ohio D. Oct. 11, 1952, Toledo, Ohio.
BL TR 6′ 2″ 180 lbs.

Year	Team	W	L	PCT	ERA	G	GS	CG	IP	H	BB	SO	ShO	Relief W	Relief L	SV	AB	H	HR	BA	PO	A	E	DP	TC/G	FA
1907	NY N	0	2	.000	2.57	2	2	2	14	17	6	5	0	0	0	0	5	0	0	.000	0	3	1	0	2.0	.750
1908		0	0	—	7.94	2	0	0	5.2	11	3	0	0	0	0	1	3	1	0	.333	1	3	0	0	2.0	1.000
2 yrs.		0	2	.000	4.12	4	2	2	19.2	28	9	5	0	0	0	1	8	1	0	.125	1	6	1	0	2.0	.875

Andy Beene

BEENE, RAMON ANDREW
B. Oct. 13, 1956, Freeport, Tex.
BR TR 6′ 3″ 205 lbs.

Year	Team	W	L	PCT	ERA	G	GS	CG	IP	H	BB	SO	ShO	Relief W	Relief L	SV	AB	H	HR	BA	PO	A	E	DP	TC/G	FA
1983	MIL A	0	0	—	4.50	1	0	0	2	3	1	0	0	0	0	0	0	0	0	—	0	0	0	0	0.0	.000
1984		0	2	.000	11.09	5	3	0	18.2	28	9	11	0	0	0	0	0	0	0	—	1	4	0	1	1.0	1.000
2 yrs.		0	2	.000	10.45	6	3	0	20.2	31	10	11	0	0	0	0	0	0	0		1	4	0	1	0.8	1.000

Fred Beene

BEENE, FREDDY RAY
B. Nov. 24, 1942, Angleton, Tex.
BB TR 5′ 9″ 155 lbs.

Year	Team	W	L	PCT	ERA	G	GS	CG	IP	H	BB	SO	ShO	Relief W	Relief L	SV	AB	H	HR	BA	PO	A	E	DP	TC/G	FA
1968	BAL A	0	0	—	9.00	1	0	0	1	2	1	1	0	0	0	0	0	0	0	—	0	0	0	0	0.0	.000
1969		0	0	—	0.00	2	0	0	2.2	2	1	0	0	0	0	0	0	0	0	—	1	0	0	0	0.5	1.000
1970		0	0	—	6.00	4	0	0	6	8	5	4	0	0	0	0	0	0	0	—	0	0	0	0	0.0	.000
1972	NY A	1	3	.250	2.33	29	1	0	58	55	24	37	0	1	3	3	9	0	0	.000	8	6	1	1	0.5	.933
1973		6	0	1.000	1.68	19	4	0	91	67	27	49	0	4	0	1	0	0	0	—	9	15	0	2	1.3	1.000
1974	2 teams NY A (6G 0–0) CLE A (32G 4–4)																									
″	total	4	4	.500	4.66	38	0	0	83	77	28	45	0	4	4	3	0	0	0		9	17	0	0	0.7	1.000
1975	CLE A	1	0	1.000	6.94	19	1	0	46.2	63	25	20	0	1	0	1	0	0	0	—	3	9	0	0	0.6	1.000
7 yrs.		12	7	.632	3.62	112	6	0	288.1	274	111	156	0	10	7	8	9	0	0	.000	30	47	1	3	0.7	.987

Clarence Beers

BEERS, CLARENCE SCOTT
B. Dec. 9, 1918, El Dorado, Kans.
BR TR 6′ 175 lbs.

Year	Team	W	L	PCT	ERA	G	GS	CG	IP	H	BB	SO	ShO	Relief W	Relief L	SV	AB	H	HR	BA	PO	A	E	DP	TC/G	FA
1948	STL N	0	0	—	13.50	1	0	0	0.2	3	1	0	0	0	0	0	0	0	0	—	0	0	0	0	0.0	.000

Joe Beggs

BEGGS, JOSEPH STANLEY (Fireman)
B. Nov. 4, 1910, Rankin, Pa. D. July 19, 1983, Indianapolis, Ind.
BR TR 6′ 1″ 182 lbs.

Year	Team	W	L	PCT	ERA	G	GS	CG	IP	H	BB	SO	ShO	Relief W	Relief L	SV	AB	H	HR	BA	PO	A	E	DP	TC/G	FA
1938	NY A	3	2	.600	5.40	14	9	4	58.1	69	20	8	0	0	0	0	20	5	0	.250	1	19	0	4	1.4	1.000
1940	CIN N	12	3	.800	2.00	37	1	0	76.2	68	21	25	0	**12**	3	**7**	21	4	0	.190	6	20	0	3	0.7	1.000
1941		4	3	.571	3.79	37	0	0	57	57	27	19	0	4	3	5	10	3	0	.300	3	12	1	1	0.4	.938
1942		6	5	.545	2.13	38	0	0	88.2	65	33	24	0	6	5	8	21	0	0	.000	6	31	0	2	1.0	1.000
1943		7	6	.538	2.34	39	4	4	115.1	120	25	28	2	4	5	6	35	5	0	.143	5	30	0	2	0.9	1.000
1944		1	0	1.000	2.00	1	1	1	9	8	0	2	0	0	0	0	4	0	0	.000	1	2	0	0	3.0	1.000
1946		12	10	.545	2.32	28	22	14	190	175	39	38	2	0	1	1	63	14	0	.222	11	45	1	2	2.0	.982
1947	2 teams CIN N (11G 0–3) NY N (32G 3–3)																									
″	total	3	6	.333	4.58	43	4	0	98.1	123	24	34	0	3	3	2	24	2	0	.083	6	20	0	0	0.6	1.000
1948	NY N	0	0	—	0.00	1	0	0	0.1	2	0	0	0	0	0	0	0	0	0	—	0	0	0	0	0.0	.000
9 yrs.		48	35	.578	2.96	238	41	23	693.2	687	189	178	4	29	20	29	198	33	0	.167	39	179	2	14	0.9	.991
WORLD SERIES																										
1940	CIN N	0	0	—	9.00	1	0	0	1	3	0	1	0	0	0	0	0	0	0	—	0	0	0	0	0.0	.000

Ed Begley

BEGLEY, EDWARD N.
Born Edward N. Bagley.
B. 1863, New York, N. Y. D. July 24, 1919, Waterbury, Conn.

Year	Team	W	L	PCT	ERA	G	GS	CG	IP	H	BB	SO	ShO	Relief W	Relief L	SV	AB	H	HR	BA	PO	A	E	DP	TC/G	FA
1884	NY N	12	18	.400	*4.16*	31	30	30	266	296	99	104	0	0	0	0	121	22	0	.182	16	46	9	2	2.2	.873
1885	NY AA	4	9	.308	*4.93*	15	14	10	115	131	48	44	0	0	0	0	52	9	1	.173	7	25	6	0	2.0	.842
2 yrs.		16	27	.372	4.39	46	44	40	381	427	147	148	0	0	0	0	173	31	1	.179	23	71	15	2	2.1	.862

Petie Behan

BEHAN, CHARLES FREDERICK
B. Dec. 11, 1887, Dallas City, Pa. D. Jan. 22, 1957, Bradford, Pa.
BR TR 5′10″ 160 lbs.

Year	Team	W	L	PCT	ERA	G	GS	CG	IP	H	BB	SO	ShO	Relief W	Relief L	SV	AB	H	HR	BA	PO	A	E	DP	TC/G	FA
1921	PHI N	0	1	.000	5.91	2	2	1	10.2	17	1	3	0	0	0	0	4	0	0	.000	2	1	0	0	1.5	1.000
1922		4	2	.667	2.47	7	5	3	47.1	49	14	13	1	1	0	0	20	5	0	.250	2	6	1	0	1.3	.889
1923		3	12	.200	5.50	31	17	5	131	182	57	27	0	0	1	2	43	8	0	.186	7	27	2	1	1.2	.944
3 yrs.		7	15	.318	4.76	40	24	9	189	248	72	43	1	1	1	2	67	13	0	.194	11	34	3	1	1.2	.938

Rick Behenna

BEHENNA, RICHARD KIPP
B. Mar. 6, 1960, Miami, Fla.
BR TR 6′ 2″ 170 lbs.

Year	Team	W	L	PCT	ERA	G	GS	CG	IP	H	BB	SO	ShO	Relief W	Relief L	SV	AB	H	HR	BA	PO	A	E	DP	TC/G	FA
1983	2 teams ATL N (14G 3–3) CLE A (5G 0–2)																									
″	total	3	5	.375	4.41	19	10	0	63.1	59	26	26	0	0	2	0	12	4	1	.333	5	8	0	1	0.7	1.000
1984	CLE A	0	3	.000	13.97	3	3	0	9.2	17	8	6	0	0	0	0	0	0	0	—	3	0	0	0	1.0	1.000
1985		0	2	.000	7.78	4	4	0	19.2	29	8	4	0	0	0	0	0	0	0	—	0	1	0	0	0.3	1.000
3 yrs.		3	10	.231	6.12	26	17	0	92.2	105	42	36	0	0	2	0	12	4	1	.333	8	9	0	1	0.7	1.000

Mel Behney

BEHNEY, MELVIN BRIAN
B. Sept. 2, 1947, Newark, N. J.
BL TL 6′ 2″ 180 lbs.

Year	Team	W	L	PCT	ERA	G	GS	CG	IP	H	BB	SO	ShO	Relief W	Relief L	SV	AB	H	HR	BA	PO	A	E	DP	TC/G	FA
1970	CIN N	0	2	.000	4.50	5	1	0	10	15	8	2	0	0	1	0	1	0	0	.000	0	1	0	0	0.2	1.000

Hank Behrman

BEHRMAN, HENRY BERNARD BR TR 5′11″ 174 lbs.
B. June 27, 1921, Brooklyn, N. Y. D. Jan. 20, 1987, New York, N. Y.

Year	Team	W	L	PCT	ERA	G	GS	CG	IP	H	BB	SO	ShO	Relief Pitching W	Relief Pitching L	Relief Pitching SV	Batting AB	Batting H	Batting HR	BA	PO	A	E	DP	TC/G	FA
1946	BKN N	11	5	.688	2.93	47	11	2	150.2	138	69	78	0	6	1	4	42	4	0	.095	10	18	2	0	0.6	.933
1947	2 teams PIT N	(10G 0–2)	BKN N	(40G 5–3)																						
″	total	5	5	.500	6.25	50	8	0	116.2	130	65	44	0	1	4	8	32	6	0	.188	2	14	3	0	0.4	.842
1948	BKN N	5	4	.556	4.05	34	4	2	91	95	42	42	1	3	2	7	28	3	0	.107	3	15	0	1	0.5	1.000
1949	NY N	3	3	.500	4.92	43	4	1	71.1	64	52	25	1	2	2	0	13	1	0	.077	6	11	0	0	0.4	1.000
4 yrs.		24	17	.585	4.40	174	27	5	429.2	427	228	189	2	12	9	19	115	14	0	.122	21	58	5	1	0.5	.940
WORLD SERIES																										
1947	BKN N	0	0	—	7.11	5	0	0	6.1	9	5	3	0	0	0	0	0	0	0	—	1	3	0	0	0.8	1.000

Tim Belcher

BELCHER, TIMOTHY WAYNE BR TR 6′ 3″ 210 lbs.
B. Oct. 19, 1961, Mount Gilead, Ohio.

Year	Team	W	L	PCT	ERA	G	GS	CG	IP	H	BB	SO	ShO	Relief Pitching W	Relief Pitching L	Relief Pitching SV	Batting AB	Batting H	Batting HR	BA	PO	A	E	DP	TC/G	FA
1987	LA N	4	2	.667	2.38	6	5	0	34	30	7	23	0	1	0	0	10	2	0	.200	1	5	0	0	1.0	1.000
1988		12	6	.667	2.91	36	27	4	179.2	143	51	152	1	1	0	4	56	4	1	.071	14	19	0	2	0.9	1.000
1989		15	12	.556	2.82	39	30	**10**	230	182	80	200	**8**	1	2	1	70	7	0	.100	21	18	3	3	1.1	.929
1990		9	9	.500	4.00	24	24	5	153	136	48	102	2	0	0	0	43	7	0	.163	11	11	0	1	0.9	1.000
1991		10	9	.526	2.62	33	33	2	209.1	189	75	156	1	0	0	0	67	8	0	.119	11	20	2	2	1.0	.939
1992	CIN N	15	14	.517	3.91	35	34	2	227.2	201	80	149	1	0	1	0	76	8	1	.105	23	27	1	2	1.5	.980
1993	2 teams CIN N	(22G 9–6)	CHI A	(12G 3–5)																						
″	total	12	11	.522	4.44	34	33	5	208.2	198	74	135	3	0	0	0	50	10	0	.200	19	17	2	2	1.1	.947
1994	DET A	7	**15**	.318	5.89	25	**25**	3	162	192	78	76	0	0	0	0	0	0	0	—	19	25	4	4	1.9	.917
1995	SEA A	10	12	.455	4.52	28	28	1	179.1	188	88	96	0	0	0	0	0	0	0	—	22	16	1	5	1.4	.974
9 yrs.		94	90	.511	3.78	260	239	32	1583.2	1459	581	1089	16	3	3	5	372	46	2	.124	141	158	13	21	1.2	.958
DIVISIONAL PLAYOFF SERIES																										
1995	SEA A	0	1	.000	6.23	2	0	0	4.1	4	5	0	0	0	1	0	0	0	0	—	0	1	0	0	0.5	1.000
LEAGUE CHAMPIONSHIP SERIES																										
1988	LA N	2	0	1.000	4.11	2	2	0	15.1	12	4	16	0	0	0	0	8	1	0	.125	1	0	0	0	0.5	1.000
1993	CHI A	1	0	1.000	2.45	1	0	0	3.2	3	3	1	0	1	0	0	0	0	0	—	1	1	0	0	2.0	1.000
1995	SEA A	0	1	.000	6.35	1	1	0	5.2	9	2	1	0	0	0	0	0	0	0	—	1	0	0	0	1.0	1.000
3 yrs.		3	1	.750	4.38	4	3	0	24.2	24	9	18	0	1	0	0	8	1	0	.125	3	1	0	0	1.0	1.000
WORLD SERIES																										
1988	LA N	1	0	1.000	6.23	2	2	0	8.2	10	6	10	0	0	0	0	0	0	0	—	0	0	0	0	0.0	.000

Stan Belinda

BELINDA, STANLEY PETER BR TR 6′ 3″ 185 lbs.
B. Aug. 6, 1966, Huntingdon, Pa.

Year	Team	W	L	PCT	ERA	G	GS	CG	IP	H	BB	SO	ShO	Relief Pitching W	Relief Pitching L	Relief Pitching SV	Batting AB	Batting H	Batting HR	BA	PO	A	E	DP	TC/G	FA
1989	PIT N	0	1	.000	6.10	8	0	0	10.1	13	2	10	0	0	1	0	0	0	0	—	0	0	0	0	0.0	.000
1990		3	4	.429	3.55	55	0	0	58.1	48	29	55	0	3	4	8	5	0	0	.000	2	4	0	0	0.1	1.000
1991		7	5	.583	3.45	60	0	0	78.1	50	35	71	0	7	5	16	7	0	0	.000	5	5	0	1	0.2	1.000
1992		6	4	.600	3.15	59	0	0	71.1	58	29	57	0	6	4	18	3	2	0	.667	4	4	0	1	0.1	1.000
1993	2 teams PIT N	(40G 3–1)	KC A	(23G 1–1)																						
″	total	4	2	.667	3.88	63	0	0	69.2	65	17	55	0	4	2	19	1	0	0	.000	4	5	0	1	0.1	1.000
1994	KC A	2	2	.500	5.14	37	0	0	49	47	24	37	0	2	2	1	0	0	0	—	0	4	0	0	0.1	1.000
1995	BOS A	8	1	.889	3.10	63	0	0	69.2	51	28	57	0	8	1	10	0	0	0	—	3	5	0	0	0.1	1.000
7 yrs.		30	19	.612	3.70	345	0	0	406.2	332	164	342	0	30	19	72	16	2	0	.125	18	27	0	3	0.1	1.000
DIVISIONAL PLAYOFF SERIES																										
1995	BOS A	0	0	—	0.00	1	0	0	0.1	0	0	0	0	0	0	0	0	0	0	—	0	0	0	0	0.0	.000
LEAGUE CHAMPIONSHIP SERIES																										
1990	PIT N	0	0	—	2.45	3	0	0	3.2	3	0	4	0	0	0	0	0	0	0	—	0	0	0	0	0.0	.000
1991		1	0	1.000	0.00	3	0	0	5	0	3	4	0	1	0	0	0	0	0	—	0	2	0	0	0.7	1.000
1992		0	0	—	0.00	2	0	0	1.2	2	1	2	0	0	0	0	0	0	0	—	0	0	0	0	0.0	.000
3 yrs.		1	0	1.000	0.87	8	0	0	10.1	5	4	10	0	1	0	0	0	0	0		0	2	0	0	0.3	1.000

Bo Belinsky

BELINSKY, ROBERT BL TL 6′ 2″ 191 lbs.
B. Dec. 7, 1936, New York, N. Y.

Year	Team	W	L	PCT	ERA	G	GS	CG	IP	H	BB	SO	ShO	Relief Pitching W	Relief Pitching L	Relief Pitching SV	Batting AB	Batting H	Batting HR	BA	PO	A	E	DP	TC/G	FA
1962	LA A	10	11	.476	3.56	33	31	5	187.1	149	**122**	145	3	0	0	1	60	10	0	.167	6	30	4	2	1.2	.900
1963		2	9	.182	5.75	13	13	2	76.2	78	35	60	0	0	0	0	27	2	0	.074	2	16	0	1	1.4	1.000
1964		9	8	.529	2.86	23	22	4	135.1	120	49	91	1	0	0	0	42	4	0	.095	4	17	1	2	1.0	.955
1965	PHI N	4	9	.308	4.84	30	14	3	109.2	103	48	71	0	1	1	1	32	6	0	.188	5	17	4	1	0.9	.846
1966		0	2	.000	2.93	9	1	0	15.1	14	5	8	0	0	2	0	3	1	0	.333	0	3	0	0	0.3	1.000
1967	HOU N	3	9	.250	4.68	27	18	0	115.1	112	54	80	0	0	1	0	39	3	0	.077	3	11	2	0	0.6	.875
1969	PIT N	0	3	.000	4.50	8	3	0	18	17	14	15	0	0	0	0	2	0	0	.000	1	3	0	0	0.5	1.000
1970	CIN N	0	0	—	4.50	3	0	0	8	10	6	6	0	0	0	0	1	1	0	1.000	0	0	0	0	0.0	.000
8 yrs.		28	51	.354	4.10	146	102	14	665.2	603	333	476	4	1	4	2	206	27	0	.131	21	97	11	6	0.9	.915

Bill Bell

BELL, WILLIAM SAMUEL (Ding Dong) BR TR 6′ 3″ 200 lbs.
B. Oct. 24, 1933, Goldsboro, N. C. D. Oct. 11, 1962, Durham, N. C.

Year	Team	W	L	PCT	ERA	G	GS	CG	IP	H	BB	SO	ShO	Relief Pitching W	Relief Pitching L	Relief Pitching SV	Batting AB	Batting H	Batting HR	BA	PO	A	E	DP	TC/G	FA
1952	PIT N	0	1	.000	4.60	4	1	0	15.2	16	13	4	0	0	0	0	4	0	0	.000	1	4	0	1	1.3	1.000
1955		0	0	—	0.00	1	0	0	1	0	1	0	0	0	0	0	0	0	0	—	0	0	0	0	0.0	.000
2 yrs.		0	1	.000	4.32	5	1	0	16.2	16	14	4	0	0	0	0	4	0	0	.000	1	4	0	1	1.0	1.000

Charlie Bell

BELL, CHARLES C. TR
Brother of Frank Bell.
B. Aug. 12, 1868, Cincinnati, Ohio D. Feb. 7, 1937, Cincinnati, Ohio.

Year	Team	W	L	PCT	ERA	G	GS	CG	IP	H	BB	SO	ShO	Relief Pitching W	Relief Pitching L	Relief Pitching SV	Batting AB	Batting H	Batting HR	BA	PO	A	E	DP	TC/G	FA
1889	KC AA	1	0	1.000	1.00	1	1	1	9	4	3	3	0	0	0	0	6	1	0	.167	1	4	1	0	3.0	.833
1891	2 teams LOU AA	(10G 2–6)	CIN AA	(1G 1–0)																						
″	total	3	6	.333	4.19	11	10	9	86	95	23	17	0	0	0	0	32	3	0	.094	5	17	5	0	2.5	.815
2 yrs.		4	6	.400	3.88	12	11	10	95	99	26	20	0	0	0	0	38	4	0	.105	6	21	6	0	2.5	.818

Eric Bell

BELL, ERIC ALVIN BL TL 6′ 165 lbs.
B. Oct. 27, 1963, Modesto, Calif.

Year	Team	W	L	PCT	ERA	G	GS	CG	IP	H	BB	SO	ShO	Relief Pitching W	Relief Pitching L	Relief Pitching SV	Batting AB	Batting H	Batting HR	BA	PO	A	E	DP	TC/G	FA
1985	BAL A	0	0	—	4.76	4	0	0	5.2	4	4	4	0	0	0	0	0	0	0	—	2	1	0	0	0.8	1.000
1986		1	2	.333	5.01	4	4	0	23.1	23	14	18	0	0	0	0	0	0	0	—	1	0	0	0	0.3	1.000
1987		10	13	.435	5.45	33	29	2	165	174	78	111	0	0	0	0	0	0	0	—	8	16	0	2	0.7	1.000

Eric Bell *continued*

Year	Team	W	L	PCT	ERA	G	GS	CG	IP	H	BB	SO	ShO	Relief Pitching W	Relief Pitching L	Relief Pitching SV	Batting AB	Batting H	Batting HR	BA	PO	A	E	DP	TC/G	FA
1991	CLE A	4	0	1.000	0.50	10	0	0	18	5	5	7	0	4	0	0	0	0	0	—	2	1	0	0	0.3	1.000
1992		0	2	.000	7.63	7	1	0	15.1	22	9	10	0	0	1	0	0	0	0	—	0	5	0	0	0.7	1.000
1993	HOU N	0	1	.000	6.14	10	0	0	7.1	10	2	2	0	0	1	0	0	0	0	—	0	0	0	0	0.0	.000
6 yrs.		15	18	.455	5.18	68	34	2	234.2	238	112	152	0	4	2	0	0	0	0		13	23	0	2	0.5	1.000

Gary Bell

BELL, GARY BR TR 6′ 1″ 196 lbs.
B. Nov. 17, 1936, San Antonio, Tex.

Year	Team	W	L	PCT	ERA	G	GS	CG	IP	H	BB	SO	ShO	Relief Pitching W	Relief Pitching L	Relief Pitching SV	Batting AB	Batting H	Batting HR	BA	PO	A	E	DP	TC/G	FA
1958	CLE A	12	10	.545	3.31	33	23	10	182	141	73	110	0	1	2	1	56	11	0	.196	10	15	0	5	0.8	1.000
1959		16	11	.593	4.04	44	28	12	234	208	105	136	1	3	1	5	75	18	0	.240	19	27	2	3	1.1	.958
1960		9	10	.474	4.13	28	23	6	154.2	139	82	109	2	0	0	1	47	7	0	.149	11	26	2	4	1.4	.949
1961		12	16	.429	4.10	34	34	11	228.1	214	100	163	2	0	0	0	81	16	0	.198	26	24	1	1	1.5	.980
1962		10	9	.526	4.26	57	6	1	107.2	104	52	80	0	**9**	6	12	24	5	0	.208	14	9	1	2	0.4	.958
1963		8	5	.615	2.95	58	7	0	119	91	52	98	0	7	1	5	26	3	0	.115	6	20	1	2	0.5	.963
1964		8	6	.571	4.33	56	2	0	106	106	53	89	0	7	5	4	16	6	0	.375	3	14	1	1	0.3	.944
1965		6	5	.545	3.04	60	0	0	103.2	86	50	86	0	6	5	17	16	1	1	.063	5	12	0	0	0.3	1.000
1966		14	15	.483	3.22	40	37	12	254.1	211	79	194	0	1	0	0	76	10	0	.132	8	50	2	3	1.5	.967
1967	2 teams CLE A (9G 1–5) BOS A (29G 12–8)																									
″	total	13	13	.500	3.31	38	33	9	226	193	71	154	0	0	0	3	74	12	0	.162	17	35	1	3	1.4	.981
1968	BOS A	11	11	.500	3.12	35	27	9	199.1	177	68	103	3	1	1	1	59	13	0	.220	16	29	2	4	1.3	.957
1969	2 teams SEA A (13G 2–6) CHI A (23G 0–0)																									
″	total	2	6	.250	5.31	36	13	1	100	124	57	56	1	0	0	2	19	3	0	.158	6	17	2	2	0.7	.920
12 yrs.		121	117	.508	3.68	519	233	71	2015	1794	842	1378	9	35	21	51	569	105	1	.185	141	278	15	30	0.8	.965
WORLD SERIES																										
1967	BOS A	0	1	.000	5.06	3	1	0	5.1	8	1	1	0	0	0	1	0	0	0	—	0	2	0	1	0.7	1.000

George Bell

BELL, GEORGE GLENN (Farmer) BR TR 6′ 195 lbs.
B. Nov. 2, 1874, Greenwood, N. Y. D. Dec. 25, 1941, New York, N. Y.

Year	Team	W	L	PCT	ERA	G	GS	CG	IP	H	BB	SO	ShO	Relief Pitching W	Relief Pitching L	Relief Pitching SV	Batting AB	Batting H	Batting HR	BA	PO	A	E	DP	TC/G	FA
1907	BKN N	8	16	.333	2.25	35	27	20	263.2	222	77	88	3	1	1	1	84	8	0	.095	4	91	6	2	2.9	.941
1908		4	15	.211	3.59	29	21	12	155.1	162	45	63	2	0	1	1	47	8	0	.170	2	51	1	0	1.9	.981
1909		16	15	.516	2.71	33	30	29	256	236	73	95	6	1	0	1	90	15	0	.167	10	81	6	1	2.9	.938
1910		10	**27**	.270	2.64	44	36	25	310	267	82	102	4	0	3	1	97	13	0	.134	8	74	2	2	1.9	.976
1911		5	6	.455	4.28	19	12	6	101	123	28	28	2	1	0	0	33	4	0	.121	2	40	3	0	2.4	.933
5 yrs.		43	79	.352	2.85	160	126	92	1086	1010	305	376	17	3	5	4	351	48	0	.137	26	337	18	5	2.4	.953

Hi Bell

BELL, HERMAN S. BR TR 6′ 185 lbs.
B. July 16, 1897, Mt. Sherman, Ky. D. June 7, 1949, Glendale, Calif.

Year	Team	W	L	PCT	ERA	G	GS	CG	IP	H	BB	SO	ShO	Relief Pitching W	Relief Pitching L	Relief Pitching SV	Batting AB	Batting H	Batting HR	BA	PO	A	E	DP	TC/G	FA
1924	STL N	3	8	.273	4.92	28	10	5	113.1	124	29	29	0	0	1	1	31	2	0	.065	1	31	3	1	1.3	.914
1926		6	6	.500	3.18	27	8	3	85	82	17	27	0	3	2	2	25	3	0	.120	2	17	4	0	0.9	.826
1927		1	3	.250	3.92	25	1	0	57.1	71	22	31	0	1	2	0	11	1	0	.091	0	14	2	0	0.6	.875
1929		0	2	.000	6.92	7	0	0	13	19	4	4	0	0	2	0	3	0	0	.000	0	2	2	0	0.6	.500
1930		4	3	.571	3.90	39	9	2	115.1	143	23	42	0	3	1	**8**	26	2	0	.077	2	28	3	2	0.8	.909
1932	NY N	8	4	.667	3.67	35	10	3	120	132	16	25	0	3	1	2	34	3	0	.088	4	23	1	2	0.8	.964
1933		6	5	.545	2.05	38	7	1	105.1	100	20	24	1	4	2	5	29	4	0	.138	3	19	1	1	0.6	.957
1934		4	3	.571	3.67	22	2	0	54	72	12	9	0	4	2	6	19	2	0	.105	1	8	1	1	0.5	.900
8 yrs.		32	34	.485	3.69	221	47	14	663.1	743	143	191	1	18	13	24	178	17	0	.096	13	142	17	7	0.8	.901
WORLD SERIES																										
1926	STL N	0	0	—	9.00	1	0	0	2	4	1	1	0	0	0	0	0	0	0	—	0	0	0	0	0.0	.000
1930		0	0	—	0.00	1	0	0	1	0	0	0	0	0	0	0	0	0	0	—	0	1	0	0	1.0	1.000
1933	NY N	0	0	—	0.00	1	0	0	1	0	0	0	0	0	0	0	0	0	0	—	0	0	0	0	0.0	.000
3 yrs.		0	0		4.50	3	0	0	4	4	1	1	0	0	0	0	0	0	0		0	1	0	0	0.3	1.000

Jerry Bell

BELL, JERRY HOUSTON BB TR 6′ 4″ 190 lbs.
B. Oct. 6, 1947, Madison, Tenn.

Year	Team	W	L	PCT	ERA	G	GS	CG	IP	H	BB	SO	ShO	Relief Pitching W	Relief Pitching L	Relief Pitching SV	Batting AB	Batting H	Batting HR	BA	PO	A	E	DP	TC/G	FA
1971	MIL A	2	1	.667	3.00	8	0	0	15	10	6	8	0	2	1	0	0	0	0	—	0	1	0	0	0.1	1.000
1972		5	1	.833	1.65	25	3	0	71	50	33	20	0	2	1	0	14	1	0	.071	7	13	0	1	0.8	1.000
1973		9	9	.500	3.97	31	25	8	183.2	185	70	57	0	1	2	1	0	0	0	—	13	34	1	2	1.5	.979
1974		1	0	1.000	2.57	5	0	0	14	17	5	4	0	1	0	0	0	0	0	—	0	3	2	0	1.0	.600
4 yrs.		17	11	.607	3.27	69	28	8	283.2	262	114	89	0	6	4	1	14	1	0	.071	20	51	3	3	1.1	.959

Ralph Bell

BELL, RALPH ALBERT BL TL 5′11½″ 170 lbs.
B. Nov. 6, 1890, Kahoka, Mo. D. Oct. 18, 1959, Burlington, Iowa.

Year	Team	W	L	PCT	ERA	G	GS	CG	IP	H	BB	SO	ShO	Relief Pitching W	Relief Pitching L	Relief Pitching SV	Batting AB	Batting H	Batting HR	BA	PO	A	E	DP	TC/G	FA
1912	CHI A	0	0	—	9.00	3	0	0	6	8	8	5	0	0	0	0	2	0	0	.000	0	3	0	0	1.0	1.000

Chief Bender

BENDER, CHARLES ALBERT BR TR 6′ 2″ 185 lbs.
B. May 5, 1884, Crow Wing County, Minn. D. May 22, 1954, Philadelphia, Pa.
Hall of Fame 1953.

Year	Team	W	L	PCT	ERA	G	GS	CG	IP	H	BB	SO	ShO	Relief Pitching W	Relief Pitching L	Relief Pitching SV	Batting AB	Batting H	Batting HR	BA	PO	A	E	DP	TC/G	FA
1903	PHI A	17	14	.548	3.07	36	33	29	270	239	65	127	2	1	0	0	120	22	0	.183	37	80	10	2	3.2	.921
1904		10	11	.476	2.87	29	20	18	203.2	167	59	149	4	2	0	0	79	18	0	.228	13	48	7	0	2.3	.897
1905		18	11	.621	2.83	35	23	17	229	193	90	142	4	7	1	0	92	20	0	.217	14	77	3	2	2.7	.968
1906		15	10	.600	2.53	36	27	24	238.1	208	48	159	0	1	0	**3**	99	25	3	.253	32	54	8	1	2.3	.915
1907		16	8	.667	2.05	33	24	20	219.1	185	34	112	4	0	2	3	100	23	0	.230	32	57	8	2	2.6	.918
1908		8	9	.471	1.75	18	17	14	138.2	121	21	85	2	0	0	1	50	11	0	.220	25	31	3	1	3.1	.949
1909		18	8	.692	1.66	34	29	24	250	196	45	161	5	0	0	1	93	20	0	.215	13	78	4	1	2.8	.958
1910		23	5	**.821**	1.58	30	28	25	250	182	47	155	3	1	0	0	93	25	0	.269	13	85	3	3	3.4	.970
1911		17	5	**.773**	2.16	31	24	16	216.1	198	58	114	3	2	1	3	79	13	0	.165	11	58	0	4	2.2	1.000
1912		13	8	.619	2.74	27	19	12	171	169	33	90	1	2	3	2	60	9	0	.150	6	36	2	2	1.6	.955
1913		21	10	.677	2.21	48	22	16	236.2	208	59	135	2	6	**5**	**13**	78	12	0	.154	8	55	2	1	1.4	.969
1914		17	3	**.850**	2.26	28	23	14	179	159	55	107	7	1	1	2	62	9	1	.145	7	47	2	0	2.0	.964
1915	BAL F	4	16	.200	3.99	26	23	15	178.1	198	37	89	0	0	1	1	60	16	1	.267	12	45	4	3	2.3	.934

Chief Bender *continued*

Year	Team	W	L	PCT	ERA	G	GS	CG	IP	H	BB	SO	ShO	Relief Pitching W	Relief Pitching L	Relief Pitching SV	Batting AB	Batting H	Batting HR	BA	PO	A	E	DP	TC/G	FA
1916	**PHI N**	7	7	.500	3.74	27	13	4	122.2	137	34	43	0	2	1	3	43	12	0	.279	9	40	2	1	1.8	.961
1917		8	2	.800	1.67	20	10	8	113	84	26	43	4	0	0	2	39	8	1	.205	5	22	1	4	1.4	.964
1925	**CHI A**	0	0	—	18.00	1	0	0	1	1	1	0	0	0	0	0	0	0	0	—	0	0	0	0	0.0	.000
16 yrs.		212	127	.625	2.46	459	335	256	3017	2645	712	1711	41	25	15	34	*				237	813	59	27	2.3	.947
WORLD SERIES																										
1905	**PHI A**	1	1	.500	1.06	2	2	2	17	9	6	13	1	0	0	0	5	0	0	.000	1	6	0	0	3.5	1.000
1910		1	1	.500	1.93	2	2	2	18.2	12	4	14	0	0	0	0	6	2	0	.333	1	2	0	1	1.5	1.000
1911		2	1	.667	1.04	3	3	3	26	16	8	20	0	0	0	0	11	1	0	.091	1	6	0	0	2.3	1.000
1913		2	0	1.000	4.00	2	2	2	18	19	1	9	0	0	0	0	8	0	0	.000	0	5	0	0	2.5	1.000
1914		0	1	.000	10.13	1	1	0	5.1	8	2	3	0	0	0	0	2	0	0	.000	1	3	0	2	4.0	1.000
5 yrs.		6	4	.600	2.44	10	10	9	85	64	21	59	1	0	0	0	*				4	22	0	3	2.6	1.000
		5th					**4th**	**2nd**	**4th**			**6th**														

Alan Benes

BENES, ALAN PAUL BR TR 6′ 5″ 215 lbs.
Brother of Andy Benes.
B. Jan. 21, 1972, Evansville, Ind.

Year	Team	W	L	PCT	ERA	G	GS	CG	IP	H	BB	SO	ShO	Relief W	Relief L	Relief SV	AB	H	HR	BA	PO	A	E	DP	TC/G	FA
1995	**STL N**	1	2	.333	8.44	3	3	0	16	24	4	20	0	0	0	0	6	0	0	.000	1	0	0	0	0.3	1.000

Andy Benes

BENES, ANDREW CHARLES BR TR 6′ 6″ 235 lbs.
Brother of Alan Benes.
B. Aug. 20, 1967, Evansville, Ind.

Year	Team	W	L	PCT	ERA	G	GS	CG	IP	H	BB	SO	ShO	Relief W	Relief L	Relief SV	AB	H	HR	BA	PO	A	E	DP	TC/G	FA
1989	**SD N**	6	3	.667	3.51	10	10	0	66.2	51	31	66	0	0	0	0	24	6	1	.250	4	8	0	1	1.2	1.000
1990		10	11	.476	3.60	32	31	2	192.1	177	69	140	0	0	0	0	60	6	0	.100	15	9	1	1	0.8	.960
1991		15	11	.577	3.03	33	33	4	223	194	59	167	1	0	0	0	62	2	1	.032	8	29	0	3	1.1	1.000
1992		13	14	.481	3.35	34	34	2	231.1	**230**	61	169	2	0	0	0	67	10	1	.149	14	34	1	1	1.4	.980
1993		15	15	.500	3.78	34	34	4	230.2	200	86	179	2	0	0	0	72	9	1	.125	17	14	1	2	0.9	.969
1994		6	**14**	.300	3.86	25	25	2	172.1	155	51	**189**	2	0	0	0	49	8	0	.163	21	19	0	2	1.6	1.000
1995	**2 teams** **SD N** (19G 4–7) **SEA A** (12G 7–2)																									
″	**total**	11	9	.550	4.76	31	31	1	181.2	193	78	171	1	0	0	0	40	6	0	.150	8	15	1	1	0.8	.958
7 yrs.		76	77	.497	3.68	199	198	15	1298	1200	435	1081	8	0	0	0	374	47	4	.126	87	128	4	11	1.1	.982
DIVISIONAL PLAYOFF SERIES																										
1995	**SEA A**	0	0	—	5.40	2	2	0	11.2	10	9	8	0	0	0	0	0	0	0	—	1	0	0	0	0.5	1.000
LEAGUE CHAMPIONSHIP SERIES																										
1995	**SEA A**	0	1	.000	23.14	1	1	0	2.1	6	2	3	0	0	0	0	0	0	0	—	0	0	0	0	0.0	.000

Ray Benge

BENGE, RAYMOND ADELPHIA (Silent Cal) BR TR 5′ 9½″ 160 lbs.
B. Apr. 22, 1902, Jacksonville, Tex.

Year	Team	W	L	PCT	ERA	G	GS	CG	IP	H	BB	SO	ShO	Relief W	Relief L	Relief SV	AB	H	HR	BA	PO	A	E	DP	TC/G	FA
1925	**CLE A**	1	0	1.000	1.54	2	2	1	11.2	9	3	3	1	0	0	0	5	2	0	.400	0	1	0	0	0.5	1.000
1926		1	0	1.000	3.86	8	0	0	11.2	15	4	3	0	1	0	0	3	1	0	.333	0	4	1	0	0.6	.800
1928	**PHI N**	8	18	.308	4.55	40	28	12	201.2	219	88	68	1	2	0	1	58	12	0	.207	4	39	1	3	1.1	.977
1929		11	15	.423	6.29	38	27	9	199	255	77	78	2	0	3	4	74	15	0	.203	2	34	3	0	1.0	.923
1930		11	15	.423	5.70	38	29	14	225.2	305	81	70	0	0	3	1	88	18	0	.205	9	41	4	1	1.4	.926
1931		14	18	.438	3.17	38	31	16	247	251	61	117	2	1	2	2	88	18	0	.205	12	36	2	4	1.3	.960
1932		13	12	.520	4.05	41	28	13	222.1	247	58	89	2	0	0	6	75	13	0	.173	7	41	1	2	1.2	.980
1933	**BKN N**	10	17	.370	3.42	37	30	16	228.2	238	55	74	2	0	1	1	76	14	0	.184	6	37	0	1	1.2	1.000
1934		14	12	.538	4.32	36	32	14	227	252	61	64	1	1	0	0	89	15	0	.169	13	43	1	3	1.6	.982
1935		9	9	.500	4.48	23	17	5	124.2	142	47	39	1	1	1	1	47	9	0	.191	3	19	1	2	1.0	.957
1936	**2 teams** **BOS N** (21G 7–9) **PHI N** (15G 1–4)																									
″	**total**	8	13	.381	5.49	36	25	2	160.2	231	57	45	0	1	0	1	53	6	0	.113	2	20	2	0	0.7	.917
1938	**CIN N**	1	1	.500	4.11	9	0	0	15.1	13	6	5	0	1	1	2	3	1	0	.333	1	2	0	0	0.3	1.000
12 yrs.		101	130	.437	4.52	346	249	102	1875.1	2177	598	655	12	8	11	19	659	124	0	.188	59	317	16	16	1.1	.959

Armando Benitez

BENITEZ, ARMANDO GERMAN BR TR 6′ 4″ 180 lbs.
B. Nov. 3, 1972, Ramon Santana, Dominican Republic.

Year	Team	W	L	PCT	ERA	G	GS	CG	IP	H	BB	SO	ShO	Relief W	Relief L	Relief SV	AB	H	HR	BA	PO	A	E	DP	TC/G	FA
1994	**BAL A**	0	0	—	0.90	3	0	0	10	8	4	14	0	0	0	0	0	0	0	—	0	1	0	0	0.3	1.000
1995		1	5	.167	5.66	44	0	0	47.2	37	37	56	0	1	5	2	0	0	0	—	1	0	1	1	0.0	.500
2 yrs.		1	5	.167	4.84	47	0	0	57.2	45	41	70	0	1	5	2	0	0	0		1	1	1	1	0.1	.667

Henry Benn

BENN, HENRY OMER BR TR 6′ 190 lbs.
B. Jan. 25, 1890, Viola, Wis. D. June 4, 1967, Madison, Wis.

Year	Team	W	L	PCT	ERA	G	GS	CG	IP	H	BB	SO	ShO	Relief W	Relief L	Relief SV	AB	H	HR	BA	PO	A	E	DP	TC/G	FA
1914	**CLE A**	0	0	—	0.00	1	0	0	1	0	0	1	0	0	0	0	0	0	0	—	0	0	0	0	0.0	.000

Bugs Bennett

BENNETT, JOSEPH HARLEY BR TR 5′ 9½″ 163 lbs.
Played as Bugs Morris in 1921.
Born Joseph Harley Morris.
B. Apr. 19, 1892, Kansas City, Mo. D. Nov. 21, 1957, Noel, Mo.

Year	Team	W	L	PCT	ERA	G	GS	CG	IP	H	BB	SO	ShO	Relief W	Relief L	Relief SV	AB	H	HR	BA	PO	A	E	DP	TC/G	FA
1918	**STL A**	0	2	.000	3.48	4	2	0	10.1	12	7	0	0	0	0	0	4	1	0	.250	0	5	0	0	1.3	1.000
1921	**2 teams** **CHI A** (3G 0–3) **STL A** (3G 0–0)																									
″	**total**	0	3	.000	8.10	6	3	1	23.1	30	22	5	0	0	1	0	7	3	0	.429	2	7	0	0	1.5	1.000
2 yrs.		0	5	.000	6.68	10	5	1	33.2	42	29	5	0	0	1	0	11	4	0	.364	2	12	0	0	1.4	1.000

Dave Bennett

BENNETT, DAVID HANS BR TR 6′ 5″ 195 lbs.
Brother of Dennis Bennett.
B. Nov. 7, 1945, Berkeley, Calif.

Year	Team	W	L	PCT	ERA	G	GS	CG	IP	H	BB	SO	ShO	Relief W	Relief L	Relief SV	AB	H	HR	BA	PO	A	E	DP	TC/G	FA
1964	**PHI N**	0	0	—	9.00	1	0	0	1	2	0	1	0	0	0	0	0	0	0	—	0	0	0	0	0.0	.000

Dennis Bennett

BENNETT, DENNIS JOHN BL TL 6′ 3″ 192 lbs.
Brother of Dave Bennett.
B. Oct. 5, 1939, Oakland, Calif.

Year	Team	W	L	PCT	ERA	G	GS	CG	IP	H	BB	SO	ShO	Relief W	Relief L	Relief SV	AB	H	HR	BA	PO	A	E	DP	TC/G	FA
1962	**PHI N**	9	9	.500	3.81	31	24	7	174.2	144	68	149	2	1	0	3	63	8	1	.127	8	24	1	0	1.1	.970
1963		9	5	.643	2.64	23	16	6	119.1	102	33	82	1	1	0	1	40	9	1	.225	6	21	1	3	1.2	.964
1964		12	14	.462	3.68	41	32	7	208	222	58	125	2	1	0	1	66	13	0	.197	11	37	3	1	1.2	.941

Dennis Bennett *continued*

Year	Team	Lg	W	L	PCT	ERA	G	GS	CG	IP	H	BB	SO	ShO	Relief Pitching W	Relief Pitching L	Relief Pitching SV	Batting AB	Batting H	Batting HR	BA	PO	A	E	DP	TC/G	FA
1965	BOS	A	5	7	.417	4.38	34	18	3	141.2	152	53	85	0	1	0	0	39	7	0	.179	11	21	2	1	1.0	.941
1966			3	3	.500	3.24	16	13	0	75	75	23	47	0	0	0	0	23	3	1	.130	0	9	0	0	0.6	1.000
1967	2 teams BOS A (13G 4–3) NY N (8G 1–1)																										
"	total		5	4	.556	4.22	21	17	4	96	109	29	48	1	0	0	0	33	5	1	.152	4	16	2	1	1.0	.909
1968	CAL	A	0	5	.000	3.54	16	7	1	48.1	46	17	36	0	0	1	1	13	1	0	.077	1	10	0	0	0.7	1.000
7 yrs.			43	47	.478	3.69	182	127	28	863	850	281	572	6	4	1	6	277	46	4	.166	41	138	9	6	1.0	.952

Erik Bennett

BENNETT, ERIK HANS BR TR 6′ 2″ 205 lbs.
B. Sept. 13, 1968, Yreka, Calif.

Year	Team	Lg	W	L	PCT	ERA	G	GS	CG	IP	H	BB	SO	ShO	Relief Pitching W	Relief Pitching L	Relief Pitching SV	Batting AB	Batting H	Batting HR	BA	PO	A	E	DP	TC/G	FA
1995	CAL	A	0	0	—	0.00	1	0	0	0.1	0	0	0	0	0	0	0	0	0	0	—	0	0	0	0	0.0	.000

Frank Bennett

BENNETT, FRANCIS ALLEN (Chip) BR TR 5′10½″ 163 lbs.
B. Oct. 27, 1904, Mardela Springs, Md. D. Mar. 18, 1966, New Castle, Del.

Year	Team	Lg	W	L	PCT	ERA	G	GS	CG	IP	H	BB	SO	ShO	Relief Pitching W	Relief Pitching L	Relief Pitching SV	Batting AB	Batting H	Batting HR	BA	PO	A	E	DP	TC/G	FA
1927	BOS	A	0	1	.000	2.92	4	1	0	12.1	15	6	1	0	0	0	0	3	0	0	.000	2	2	0	1	1.0	1.000
1928			0	0	—	0.00	1	0	0	1	1	0	0	0	0	0	0	0	0	0	—	0	1	0	0	1.0	1.000
2 yrs.			0	1	.000	2.70	5	1	0	13.1	16	6	1	0	0	0	0	3	0	0	.000	2	3	0	1	1.0	1.000

Allen Benson

BENSON, ALLEN WILBERT (Bullet Ben) BR TR 6′ 1″ 185 lbs.
B. Mar. 28, 1908, Hurley, S. D.

Year	Team	Lg	W	L	PCT	ERA	G	GS	CG	IP	H	BB	SO	ShO	Relief Pitching W	Relief Pitching L	Relief Pitching SV	Batting AB	Batting H	Batting HR	BA	PO	A	E	DP	TC/G	FA
1934	WAS	A	0	1	.000	12.10	2	2	0	9.2	19	5	4	0	0	0	0	3	0	0	.000	0	0	0	0	0.0	.000

Jack Bentley

BENTLEY, JOHN NEEDLES BL TL 5′11½″ 200 lbs.
B. Mar. 8, 1895, Sandy Spring, Md. D. Oct. 24, 1969, Olney, Md.

Year	Team	Lg	W	L	PCT	ERA	G	GS	CG	IP	H	BB	SO	ShO	Relief Pitching W	Relief Pitching L	Relief Pitching SV	Batting AB	Batting H	Batting HR	BA	PO	A	E	DP	TC/G	FA
1913	WAS	A	1	0	1.000	0.00	3	1	0	11	5	2	5	0	0	0	1	3	0	0	.000	0	5	0	0	1.7	1.000
1914			5	7	.417	2.37	30	12	3	125.1	110	53	55	2	0	1	**4**	40	11	0	.275	9	33	3	1	1.5	.933
1915			0	2	.000	0.79	4	2	0	11.1	8	3	0	0	0	0	0	2	0	0	.000	1	2	1	0	1.0	.750
1916			0	0	—	0.00	2	0	0	1.1	0	1	1	0	0	0	0	0	0	0	—	0	1	0	0	0.5	1.000
1923	NY	N	13	8	.619	4.48	31	26	12	183	198	67	80	1	0	1	3	89	38	1	.427	5	38	1	1	1.4	.977
1924			16	5	.762	3.78	28	24	13	188	196	56	60	1	1	0	1	98	26	0	.265	3	43	1	3	1.7	.979
1925			11	9	.550	5.04	28	22	11	157	200	59	47	0	1	0	0	99	30	3	.303	13	33	3	2	1.5	.939
1926	2 teams PHI N (7G 0–2) NY N (1G 0–0)																										
"	total		0	2	.000	7.57	8	3	0	27.1	37	12	8	0	0	0	0	244	63	2	.258	516	33	4	41	8.6	.993
1927	NY	N	0	0	—	2.79	4	0	0	9.2	7	10	3	0	0	0	0	9	2	1	.222	10	2	1	0	2.2	.923
9 yrs.			46	33	.582	4.01	138	90	39	714	761	263	259	4	2	2	9	*				557	190	14	48	3.8	.982
WORLD SERIES																											
1923	NY	N	0	1	.000	9.45	2	1	0	6.2	10	4	1	0	0	0	0	5	3	0	.600	0	2	0	0	1.0	1.000
1924			1	2	.333	3.18	3	2	1	17	18	8	10	0	0	1	0	7	2	1	.286	1	3	0	0	1.3	1.000
2 yrs.			1	3	.250	4.94	5	3	1	23.2	28	12	11	0	0	1	0	*				1	5	0	0	1.2	1.000

Al Benton

BENTON, JOHN ALTON BR TR 6′ 4″ 215 lbs.
B. Mar. 18, 1911, Noble, Okla. D. Apr. 14, 1968, Lynwood, Calif.

Year	Team	Lg	W	L	PCT	ERA	G	GS	CG	IP	H	BB	SO	ShO	Relief Pitching W	Relief Pitching L	Relief Pitching SV	Batting AB	Batting H	Batting HR	BA	PO	A	E	DP	TC/G	FA
1934	PHI	A	7	9	.438	4.88	32	21	7	155	145	88	58	0	1	1	1	55	6	0	.109	11	28	1	3	1.3	.975
1935			3	4	.429	7.67	27	9	0	78.2	110	47	42	0	3	1	0	25	1	0	.040	2	12	1	0	0.6	.933
1938	DET	A	5	3	.625	3.30	19	10	6	95.1	93	39	33	0	0	0	0	33	4	0	.121	3	25	1	0	1.5	.966
1939			6	8	.429	4.56	37	16	3	150	182	58	67	0	1	3	5	44	4	0	.091	6	27	2	0	0.9	.943
1940			6	10	.375	4.42	42	0	0	79.1	93	36	50	0	6	**10**	**17**	17	0	0	.000	5	11	3	1	0.5	.842
1941			15	6	.714	2.97	38	14	7	157.2	130	65	63	1	6	2	7	50	3	0	.060	9	27	3	4	1.0	.923
1942			7	13	.350	2.90	35	30	9	226.2	210	84	110	1	0	1	2	67	5	0	.075	18	39	5	0	1.8	.919
1945			13	8	.619	2.02	31	27	12	191.2	175	63	76	5	0	1	3	63	4	0	.063	11	44	2	4	1.8	.965
1946			11	7	.611	3.65	28	15	6	140.2	132	58	60	1	1	2	1	49	9	0	.184	16	26	2	0	1.6	.955
1947			6	7	.462	4.40	36	14	4	133	147	61	33	0	1	0	7	39	6	0	.154	6	24	4	1	0.9	.882
1948			2	2	.500	5.68	30	0	0	44.1	45	36	18	0	2	2	3	11	2	0	.182	2	8	1	1	0.4	.909
1949	CLE	A	9	6	.600	2.12	40	11	4	135.2	116	51	41	2	4	0	10	38	5	0	.132	4	17	0	2	0.5	1.000
1950			4	2	.667	3.57	36	0	0	63	57	30	26	0	4	2	4	12	1	0	.083	1	8	0	2	0.3	1.000
1952	BOS	A	4	3	.571	2.39	24	0	0	37.2	37	17	20	0	4	3	6	9	0	0	.000	3	5	1	0	0.4	.889
14 yrs.			98	88	.527	3.66	455	167	58	1688.2	1672	733	697	10	33	28	66	512	50	0	.098	97	301	26	18	0.9	.939
WORLD SERIES																											
1945	DET	A	0	0	—	1.93	3	0	0	4.2	6	0	5	0	0	0	0	0	0	0	—	0	3	0	0	1.0	1.000

Larry Benton

BENTON, LAWRENCE JAMES BR TR 5′11″ 165 lbs.
B. Nov. 20, 1897, St. Louis, Mo. D. Apr. 3, 1953, Amberley, Ohio.

Year	Team	Lg	W	L	PCT	ERA	G	GS	CG	IP	H	BB	SO	ShO	Relief Pitching W	Relief Pitching L	Relief Pitching SV	Batting AB	Batting H	Batting HR	BA	PO	A	E	DP	TC/G	FA
1923	BOS	N	5	9	.357	4.99	35	9	2	128	141	57	42	0	4	**4**	0	31	5	0	.161	5	33	4	2	1.2	.905
1924			5	7	.417	4.15	30	13	4	128	129	64	41	0	1	0	1	33	3	0	.091	3	30	1	2	1.1	.971
1925			14	7	.667	3.09	31	21	16	183.1	170	70	49	2	1	1	1	58	14	0	.241	6	39	3	2	1.5	.938
1926			14	14	.500	3.85	43	27	12	231.2	244	81	103	1	3	2	1	78	12	0	.154	3	43	0	1	1.1	1.000
1927	2 teams BOS N (11G 4–2) NY N (29G 13–5)																										
"	total		17	7	**.708**	4.09	40	33	11	233.1	255	81	90	1	3	1	2	68	12	0	.176	13	43	3	3	1.5	.949
1928	NY	N	**25**	9	**.735**	2.73	42	35	**28**	310.1	299	71	90	2	0	1	4	112	16	0	.143	15	69	1	5	2.0	.988
1929			11	17	.393	4.14	39	30	14	237	276	61	63	3	0	1	3	86	9	1	.105	11	58	3	7	1.8	.958
1930	2 teams NY N (8G 1–3) CIN N (35G 7–12)																										
"	total		8	15	.348	5.50	43	26	10	207.2	288	59	63	0	2	0	2	72	14	1	.194	14	23	1	2	0.9	.974
1931	CIN	N	10	15	.400	3.35	38	23	12	204.1	240	53	35	2	3	1	2	66	11	0	.167	10	48	2	5	1.6	.967
1932			6	13	.316	4.31	35	21	7	179.2	201	27	35	0	1	1	2	54	11	0	.204	6	38	2	1	1.3	.957
1933			10	11	.476	3.71	34	19	7	152.2	160	36	33	2	1	4	2	53	9	0	.170	5	27	2	1	1.0	.941
1934			0	1	.000	6.52	16	1	0	29	53	7	5	0	0	0	2	7	2	0	.286	0	6	0	1	0.4	1.000
1935	BOS	N	2	3	.400	6.88	29	0	0	72	103	24	21	0	2	3	0	20	4	0	.200	2	12	0	1	0.5	1.000
13 yrs.			127	128	.498	4.03	455	258	123	2297	2559	691	670	13	21	19	22	738	122	2	.165	93	469	22	33	1.3	.962

Rube Benton

BENTON, JOHN CLEBON BR TL 6′ 1″ 190 lbs.
B. June 27, 1887, Clinton, N. C. D. Dec. 12, 1937, Dothan, Ala.

Year	Team	Lg	W	L	PCT	ERA	G	GS	CG	IP	H	BB	SO	ShO	Relief Pitching W	Relief Pitching L	Relief Pitching SV	Batting AB	Batting H	Batting HR	BA	PO	A	E	DP	TC/G	FA
1910	CIN	N	1	1	.500	4.74	12	2	0	38	44	23	15	0	0	0	0	11	1	0	.091	1	13	0	1	1.2	1.000
1911			3	3	.500	2.01	6	6	5	44.2	44	23	28	0	0	0	0	14	2	0	.143	1	10	0	0	1.8	1.000

Rube Benton *continued*

Year	Team	W	L	PCT	ERA	G	GS	CG	IP	H	BB	SO	ShO	Relief Pitching W	Relief Pitching L	Relief Pitching SV	Batting AB	Batting H	Batting HR	BA	PO	A	E	DP	TC/G	FA
1912		18	21	.462	3.10	**50**	**39**	22	302	316	118	162	2	3	1	2	104	14	0	.135	13	78	3	2	1.9	.968
1913		11	7	.611	3.49	23	22	9	144.1	140	60	68	1	1	0	0	48	10	0	.208	0	35	4	0	1.7	.897
1914		17	18	.486	2.96	41	31	16	271	223	95	121	5	2	3	2	91	13	0	.143	9	70	5	3	2.0	.940
1915	**2 teams** **CIN N** (35G 9–13) **NY N** (10G 4–5)																									
″	**total**	13	18	.419	3.19	45	28	9	237	222	76	109	2	4	3	**5**	76	16	0	.211	8	72	3	2	1.8	.964
1916	**NY N**	16	8	.667	2.87	38	29	15	238.2	210	58	115	3	2	0	2	78	7	0	.090	6	57	0	3	1.7	1.000
1917		15	9	.625	2.72	35	25	14	215	190	41	70	3	0	2	3	72	12	0	.167	2	58	3	0	1.8	.952
1918		1	2	.333	1.88	3	3	2	24	17	3	9	0	0	0	0	7	1	0	.143	1	7	0	1	2.7	1.000
1919		17	11	.607	2.63	35	28	11	209	181	52	53	1	3	0	2	67	13	1	.194	3	60	0	0	1.8	1.000
1920		9	16	.360	3.03	33	25	12	193.1	222	31	52	4	0	3	2	65	6	0	.092	13	74	2	0	2.7	.978
1921		5	2	.714	2.88	18	9	3	72	72	17	11	1	0	1	0	21	3	0	.143	2	16	1	1	1.1	.947
1923	**CIN N**	14	10	.583	3.66	33	26	15	219	243	57	59	0	0	0	1	80	23	0	.287	7	57	2	2	2.0	.970
1924		7	9	.438	2.77	32	19	6	162.2	166	24	42	1	1	1	1	46	12	0	.261	7	46	4	3	1.8	.930
1925		9	10	.474	4.05	33	16	6	146.2	182	34	36	1	2	2	1	45	9	0	.200	3	31	1	3	1.1	.971
15 yrs.		156	145	.518	3.09	437	308	145	2517.1	2472	712	950	24	18	16	21	825	142	1	.172	76	684	28	21	1.8	.964
WORLD SERIES																										
1917	**NY N**	1	1	.500	0.00	2	2	1	14	9	1	8	1	0	0	0	4	0	0	.000	1	2	0	0	1.5	1.000

Sid Benton

BENTON, SIDNEY WRIGHT BR TR 6′ 1″ 170 lbs.
B. Aug. 4, 1895, Buckner, Ark. D. Mar. 8, 1977, Fayetteville, Ark.

Year	Team	W	L	PCT	ERA	G	GS	CG	IP	H	BB	SO	ShO	Relief Pitching W	Relief Pitching L	Relief Pitching SV	Batting AB	Batting H	Batting HR	BA	PO	A	E	DP	TC/G	FA
1922	**STL N**	0	0	—	0.00	1	0	0		0	2	0	0	0	0	0	0	0	0	—	0	0	0	0	0.0	.000

Joe Benz

BENZ, JOSEPH LOUIS (Blitzen) BR TR 6′ 1½″ 196 lbs.
B. Jan. 21, 1886, New Alsace, Ind. D. Apr. 22, 1957, Chicago, Ill.

Year	Team	W	L	PCT	ERA	G	GS	CG	IP	H	BB	SO	ShO	Relief Pitching W	Relief Pitching L	Relief Pitching SV	Batting AB	Batting H	Batting HR	BA	PO	A	E	DP	TC/G	FA
1911	**CHI A**	3	2	.600	2.26	12	6	2	55.2	52	13	28	0	1	0	0	17	1	0	.059	1	22	5	1	2.3	.821
1912		13	17	.433	2.92	41	31	12	237.2	230	70	96	3	2	2	0	76	10	0	.132	10	77	10	0	2.4	.897
1913		7	10	.412	2.74	33	17	6	151	146	59	79	1	3	0	1	50	9	0	.180	4	66	4	1	2.2	.946
1914		14	**19**	.424	2.26	48	35	16	283.1	245	66	142	4	3	0	2	92	12	0	.130	5	112	11	8	2.7	.914
1915		15	11	.577	2.11	39	28	17	238.1	209	43	81	2	0	2	0	79	10	0	.127	5	86	3	5	2.4	.968
1916		9	5	.643	2.03	28	16	6	142	108	32	57	4	1	1	0	46	3	0	.065	5	46	4	1	2.0	.927
1917		7	3	.700	2.47	19	13	7	94.2	76	23	25	2	0	1	0	30	5	0	.167	3	32	5	0	2.1	.875
1918		8	8	.500	2.51	29	17	10	154	156	28	30	1	1	1	0	51	11	0	.216	4	62	4	2	2.4	.943
1919		0	0	—	0.00	1	0	0	2	2	0	0	0	0	0	0	0	0	0	—	0	1	0	0	1.0	1.000
9 yrs.		76	75	.503	2.42	250	163	76	1358.2	1224	334	538	17	11	7	3	441	61	0	.138	37	504	46	18	2.3	.922

Jason Bere

BERE, JASON PHILLIP BR TR 6′ 3″ 185 lbs.
B. May 26, 1971, Cambridge, Mass.

Year	Team	W	L	PCT	ERA	G	GS	CG	IP	H	BB	SO	ShO	Relief Pitching W	Relief Pitching L	Relief Pitching SV	Batting AB	Batting H	Batting HR	BA	PO	A	E	DP	TC/G	FA
1993	**CHI A**	12	5	.706	3.47	24	24	1	142.2	109	81	129	0	0	0	0	0	0	0	—	11	14	2	1	1.1	.926
1994		12	2	**.857**	3.81	24	24	0	141.2	119	80	127	0	0	0	0	0	0	0	—	9	12	2	1	1.0	.913
1995		8	15	.348	7.19	27	27	1	137.2	151	106	110	0	0	0	0	0	0	0	—	10	19	0	1	1.1	1.000
3 yrs.		32	22	.593	4.80	75	75	2	422	379	267	366	0	0	0	0	0	0	0		30	45	4	3	1.1	.949
LEAGUE CHAMPIONSHIP SERIES																										
1993	**CHI A**	0	0	—	11.57	1	1	0	2.1	5	2	3	0	0	0	0	0	0	0	—	0	0	0	0	0.0	.000

Juan Berenguer

BERENGUER, JUAN BAUTISTA BR TR 5′11″ 186 lbs.
B. Nov. 30, 1954, Aguadulce, Panama.

Year	Team	W	L	PCT	ERA	G	GS	CG	IP	H	BB	SO	ShO	Relief Pitching W	Relief Pitching L	Relief Pitching SV	Batting AB	Batting H	Batting HR	BA	PO	A	E	DP	TC/G	FA
1978	**NY N**	0	2	.000	8.31	5	3	0	13	17	11	8	0	0	0	0	3	0	0	.000	0	2	0	0	0.4	1.000
1979		1	1	.500	2.90	5	5	0	31	28	12	25	0	0	0	0	7	1	0	.143	0	1	1	0	0.4	.500
1980		0	1	.000	6.00	6	0	0	9	9	10	7	0	0	1	0	0	0	0	—	0	2	0	0	0.3	1.000
1981	**2 teams** **KC A** (8G 0–4) **TOR A** (12G 2–9)																									
″	**total**	2	**13**	.133	5.24	20	14	1	91	84	51	49	0	0	2	0	0	0	0		1	9	0	0	0.5	1.000
1982	**DET A**	0	0	—	6.75	2	1	0	6.2	5	9	8	0	0	0	0	0	0	0	—	0	0	0	0	0.0	.000
1983		9	5	.643	3.14	37	19	2	157.2	110	71	129	1	2	0	1	0	0	0	—	10	11	3	1	0.6	.875
1984		11	10	.524	3.48	31	27	2	168.1	146	79	118	1	0	0	0	0	0	0	—	11	15	2	0	0.9	.929
1985		5	6	.455	5.59	31	13	0	95	96	48	82	0	1	1	0	0	0	0	—	11	12	2	1	0.8	.920
1986	**SF N**	2	3	.400	2.70	46	4	0	73.1	64	44	72	0	2	2	4	7	1	0	.143	2	7	1	0	0.2	.900
1987	**MIN A**	8	1	.889	3.94	47	6	0	112	100	47	110	0	6	1	4	0	0	0	—	5	7	1	0	0.3	.923
1988		8	4	.667	3.96	57	1	0	100	74	61	99	0	8	4	2	0	0	0	—	7	10	0	1	0.3	1.000
1989		9	3	.750	3.48	56	0	0	106	96	47	93	0	9	3	3	0	0	0	—	2	11	0	1	0.2	1.000
1990		8	5	.615	3.41	51	0	0	100.1	85	58	77	0	8	5	0	0	0	0	—	3	5	0	0	0.2	1.000
1991	**ATL N**	0	3	.000	2.24	49	0	0	64.1	43	20	53	0	0	3	17	5	0	0	.000	7	5	0	0	0.2	1.000
1992	**2 teams** **ATL N** (28G 3–1) **KC A** (19G 1–4)																									
″	**total**	4	5	.444	5.42	47	2	0	78	77	36	45	0	4	3	1	2	0	0	.000	4	9	1	1	0.3	.929
15 yrs.		67	62	.519	3.90	490	95	5	1205.2	1034	604	975	2	40	25	32	24	2	0	.083	63	106	11	5	0.4	.939
LEAGUE CHAMPIONSHIP SERIES																										
1987	**MIN A**	0	0	—	1.50	4	0	0	6	1	3	6	0	0	0	1	0	0	0	—	0	0	0	0	0.0	.000
WORLD SERIES																										
1987	**MIN A**	0	1	.000	10.38	3	0	0	4.1	10	0	1	0	0	1	0	0	0	0	—	0	0	0	0	0.0	.000

Bruce Berenyi

BERENYI, BRUCE MICHAEL BR TR 6′ 3″ 205 lbs.
B. Aug. 21, 1954, Bryan, Ohio.

Year	Team	W	L	PCT	ERA	G	GS	CG	IP	H	BB	SO	ShO	Relief Pitching W	Relief Pitching L	Relief Pitching SV	Batting AB	Batting H	Batting HR	BA	PO	A	E	DP	TC/G	FA
1980	**CIN N**	2	2	.500	7.71	6	6	0	28	34	23	19	0	0	0	0	7	0	0	.000	0	3	0	0	0.5	1.000
1981		9	6	.600	3.50	21	20	5	126	97	**77**	106	3	0	0	0	42	8	0	.190	7	12	0	2	0.9	1.000
1982		9	**18**	.333	3.36	34	34	4	222.1	208	96	157	1	0	0	0	62	15	0	.242	18	40	2	1	1.8	.967
1983		9	14	.391	3.86	32	31	4	186.1	173	102	151	1	0	0	0	55	12	0	.218	5	41	2	2	1.5	.958
1984	**2 teams** **CIN N** (13G 3–7) **NY N** (19G 9–6)																									
″	**total**	12	13	.480	4.45	32	30	0	166	163	95	134	0	1	0	0	53	10	0	.189	12	17	0	1	0.9	1.000
1985	**NY N**	1	0	1.000	2.63	3	3	0	13.2	8	10	10	0	0	0	0	4	1	0	.250	1	4	0	1	1.7	1.000
1986		2	2	.500	6.35	14	7	0	39.2	47	22	30	0	1	0	0	11	0	0	.000	3	5	0	0	0.6	1.000
7 yrs.		44	55	.444	4.03	142	131	13	782	730	425	607	5	2	0	0	234	46	0	.197	46	122	4	7	1.2	.977

Heinie Berger

BERGER, CHARLES TR 5′ 9½″
B. Jan. 7, 1882, LaSalle, Ill. D. Feb. 10, 1954, Lakewood, Ohio.

Year	Team	W	L	PCT	ERA	G	GS	CG	IP	H	BB	SO	ShO	Relief Pitching W	Relief Pitching L	Relief Pitching SV	Batting AB	Batting H	Batting HR	BA	PO	A	E	DP	TC/G	FA
1907	CLE A	3	3	.500	2.99	14	7	5	87.1	74	20	50	1	1	0	0	28	5	0	.179	2	20	2	0	1.7	.917
1908		13	8	.619	2.12	29	24	16	199.1	152	66	101	0	0	0	0	74	8	0	.108	8	58	1	0	2.3	.985
1909		13	14	.481	2.63	34	29	19	257	221	58	162	4	0	0	1	83	11	0	.133	11	68	6	3	2.5	.929
1910		3	4	.429	3.03	13	8	2	65.1	57	32	24	0	1	1	0	21	3	0	.143	4	20	3	0	2.1	.889
4 yrs.		32	29	.525	2.56	90	68	42	609	504	176	337	5	2	1	1	206	27	0	.131	25	166	12	3	2.3	.941

Sean Bergman

BERGMAN, SEAN FREDERICK BR TR 6′ 4″ 205 lbs.
B. Apr. 11, 1970, Joliet, Ill.

Year	Team	W	L	PCT	ERA	G	GS	CG	IP	H	BB	SO	ShO	Relief Pitching W	Relief Pitching L	Relief Pitching SV	Batting AB	Batting H	Batting HR	BA	PO	A	E	DP	TC/G	FA
1993	DET A	1	4	.200	5.67	9	6	1	39.2	47	23	19	0	1	0	0	0	0	0	—	3	6	0	1	1.0	1.000
1994		2	1	.667	5.60	3	3	0	17.2	22	7	12	0	0	0	0	0	0	0	—	2	1	0	0	1.0	1.000
1995		7	10	.412	5.12	28	28	1	135.1	169	67	86	1	0	0	0	0	0	0	—	9	15	3	0	1.0	.889
3 yrs.		10	15	.400	5.28	40	37	2	192.2	238	97	117	1	1	0	0	0	0	0		14	22	3	1	1.0	.923

Jack Berly

BERLY, JOHN CHAMBERS BR TR 5′11½″ 190 lbs.
B. May 24, 1903, Natchitoches, La. D. June 26, 1977, Houston, Tex.

Year	Team	W	L	PCT	ERA	G	GS	CG	IP	H	BB	SO	ShO	Relief Pitching W	Relief Pitching L	Relief Pitching SV	Batting AB	Batting H	Batting HR	BA	PO	A	E	DP	TC/G	FA
1924	STL N	0	0	—	5.63	4	0	0	8	8	4	2	0	0	0	0	2	0	0	.000	0	4	0	0	1.0	1.000
1931	NY N	7	8	.467	3.88	27	11	4	111.1	114	51	45	1	2	4	0	35	6	0	.171	5	29	0	0	1.3	1.000
1932	PHI N	1	2	.333	7.63	21	1	1	46	61	21	15	0	1	1	2	10	0	0	.000	4	13	1	0	0.9	.944
1933		2	3	.400	5.04	13	6	1	50	62	22	4	1	0	0	0	13	4	0	.308	2	14	0	2	1.2	1.000
4 yrs.		10	13	.435	5.02	65	18	6	215.1	245	98	66	2	3	5	2	60	10	0	.167	11	60	1	2	1.1	.986

Vic Bernal

BERNAL, VICTOR HUGO BR TR 6′ 1″ 175 lbs.
B. Oct. 6, 1953, Los Angeles, Calif.

Year	Team	W	L	PCT	ERA	G	GS	CG	IP	H	BB	SO	ShO	Relief Pitching W	Relief Pitching L	Relief Pitching SV	Batting AB	Batting H	Batting HR	BA	PO	A	E	DP	TC/G	FA
1977	SD N	1	1	.500	5.40	15	0	0	20	23	9	6	0	1	1	0	1	0	0	.000	1	2	1	0	0.3	.750

Dwight Bernard

BERNARD, DWIGHT VERN BR TR 6′ 2″ 170 lbs.
B. May 31, 1952, Mt. Vernon, Ill.

Year	Team	W	L	PCT	ERA	G	GS	CG	IP	H	BB	SO	ShO	Relief Pitching W	Relief Pitching L	Relief Pitching SV	Batting AB	Batting H	Batting HR	BA	PO	A	E	DP	TC/G	FA
1978	NY N	1	4	.200	4.31	30	1	0	48	54	27	26	0	1	4	0	5	1	0	.200	2	7	0	2	0.3	1.000
1979		0	3	.000	4.70	32	1	0	44	59	26	20	0	0	2	0	0	0	0	—	2	8	0	1	0.3	1.000
1981	MIL A	0	0	—	3.60	6	0	0	5	5	6	1	0	0	0	0	0	0	0	—	0	0	0	0	0.0	.000
1982		3	1	.750	3.76	47	0	0	79	78	27	45	0	3	1	6	0	0	0	—	3	8	0	0	0.2	1.000
4 yrs.		4	8	.333	4.14	115	2	0	176	196	86	92	0	4	7	6	5	1	0	.200	7	23	0	3	0.3	1.000
DIVISIONAL PLAYOFF SERIES																										
1981	MIL A	0	0	—	0.00	2	0	0	2.1	0	0	0	0	0	0	0	0	0	0	—	0	0	0	0	0.0	.000
LEAGUE CHAMPIONSHIP SERIES																										
1982	MIL A	0	0	—	0.00	1	0	0	1	0	0	0	0	0	0	0	0	0	0	—	0	0	0	0	0.0	.000
WORLD SERIES																										
1982	MIL A	0	0	—	0.00	1	0	0	1	0	0	1	0	0	0	0	0	0	0	—	0	0	0	0	0.0	.000

Joe Bernard

BERNARD, JOSEPH CARL BR TR 6′ 1″ 175 lbs.
B. Mar. 24, 1882, Brighton, Ill. D. Sept. 22, 1960, Springfield, Ill.

Year	Team	W	L	PCT	ERA	G	GS	CG	IP	H	BB	SO	ShO	Relief Pitching W	Relief Pitching L	Relief Pitching SV	Batting AB	Batting H	Batting HR	BA	PO	A	E	DP	TC/G	FA
1909	STL N	0	0	—	0.00	1	0	0	1	1	2	2	0	0	0	0	0	0	0	—	0	0	0	0	0.0	.000

Bill Bernhard

BERNHARD, WILLIAM HENRY (Bernie) BB TR 6′ 1″ 205 lbs.
B. Mar. 16, 1871, Clarence, N. Y. D. Mar. 30, 1949, San Diego, Calif.

Year	Team	W	L	PCT	ERA	G	GS	CG	IP	H	BB	SO	ShO	Relief Pitching W	Relief Pitching L	Relief Pitching SV	Batting AB	Batting H	Batting HR	BA	PO	A	E	DP	TC/G	FA
1899	PHI N	6	6	.500	2.65	21	12	10	132.1	120	36	23	1	1	1	0	54	13	0	.241	2	34	4	1	1.9	.900
1900		15	10	.600	4.77	32	27	20	218.2	284	74	49	0	2	0	2	91	14	0	.154	5	60	4	7	2.2	.942
1901	PHI A	17	10	.630	4.52	31	27	26	257	328	50	58	1	1	0	0	107	20	0	.187	22	86	4	1	3.5	.964
1902	2 teams PHI A (1G 1–0) CLE A (27G 17–5)																									
″	total	18	5	**.783**	2.15	28	25	23	226	176	37	58	3	1	0	1	94	18	0	.191	5	71	4	2	2.9	.950
1903	CLE A	14	6	.700	2.12	20	19	18	165.2	151	21	60	3	0	1	0	65	12	0	.185	6	56	2	1	3.2	.969
1904		23	13	.639	2.13	38	37	35	320.2	323	55	137	4	1	0	0	124	22	0	.177	8	102	6	2	3.1	.948
1905		7	13	.350	3.36	22	19	17	174.1	185	34	56	0	2	0	0	69	6	0	.087	14	53	3	1	3.2	.957
1906		16	15	.516	2.54	31	30	23	255.1	235	47	85	2	1	0	0	99	21	0	.212	19	83	3	4	3.4	.971
1907		0	4	.000	3.21	8	4	3	42	58	11	19	0	0	0	0	15	3	0	.200	2	16	4	0	2.8	.818
9 yrs.		116	82	.586	3.04	231	200	175	1792	1860	365	545	14	9	2	3	718	129	0	.180	83	561	34	19	2.9	.950

Walter Bernhardt

BERNHARDT, WALTER JACOB (Sarah) BR TR 6′ 2″ 195 lbs.
B. May 20, 1893, Pleasant Village, Pa. D. July 26, 1958, Watertown, N. Y.

Year	Team	W	L	PCT	ERA	G	GS	CG	IP	H	BB	SO	ShO	Relief Pitching W	Relief Pitching L	Relief Pitching SV	Batting AB	Batting H	Batting HR	BA	PO	A	E	DP	TC/G	FA
1918	NY A	0	0	—	0.00	1	0	0	0.2	0	0	0	0	0	0	0	0	0	0	—	0	0	0	0	0.0	.000

Joe Berry

BERRY, JONAS ARTHUR (Jittery Joe) BL TR 5′10½″ 145 lbs.
B. Dec. 16, 1904, Huntsville, Ark. D. Sept. 27, 1958, Anaheim, Calif.

Year	Team	W	L	PCT	ERA	G	GS	CG	IP	H	BB	SO	ShO	Relief Pitching W	Relief Pitching L	Relief Pitching SV	Batting AB	Batting H	Batting HR	BA	PO	A	E	DP	TC/G	FA
1942	CHI N	0	0	—	18.00	2	0	0	2	7	2	1	0	0	0	0	0	0	0	—	0	1	0	0	0.5	1.000
1944	PHI A	10	8	.556	1.94	53	0	0	111.1	78	23	44	0	**10**	**8**	**12**	25	3	0	.120	14	26	2	2	0.8	.952
1945		8	7	.533	2.35	**52**	0	0	130.1	114	38	51	0	**8**	**7**	5	35	5	0	.143	11	30	1	0	0.8	.976
1946	2 teams PHI A (5G 0–1) CLE A (21G 3–6)																									
″	total	3	7	.300	3.22	26	0	0	50.1	47	24	21	0	3	**7**	1	10	3	0	.300	3	6	0	0	0.3	1.000
4 yrs.		21	22	.488	2.45	133	0	0	294	246	87	117	0	21	22	18	70	11	0	.157	28	63	3	2	0.7	.968

Frank Bertaina

BERTAINA, FRANK LOUIS BL TL 5′11″ 177 lbs.
B. Apr. 14, 1944, San Francisco, Calif.

Year	Team	W	L	PCT	ERA	G	GS	CG	IP	H	BB	SO	ShO	Relief Pitching W	Relief Pitching L	Relief Pitching SV	Batting AB	Batting H	Batting HR	BA	PO	A	E	DP	TC/G	FA
1964	BAL A	1	0	1.000	2.77	6	4	1	26	18	13	18	1	0	0	0	5	0	0	.000	0	6	0	0	1.0	1.000
1965		0	0	—	6.00	2	1	0	6	9	4	5	0	0	0	0	1	0	0	.000	0	1	0	0	0.5	1.000
1966		2	5	.286	3.13	16	9	0	63.1	52	36	46	0	1	0	0	19	2	0	.105	2	4	4	0	0.6	.600
1967	2 teams BAL A (5G 1–1) WAS A (18G 6–5)																									
″	total	7	6	.538	2.99	23	19	4	117.1	107	51	86	4	0	0	0	44	3	0	.068	4	16	0	2	0.9	1.000
1968	WAS A	7	13	.350	4.66	27	23	1	127.1	133	69	81	0	0	0	0	38	5	0	.132	9	17	0	2	1.0	1.000
1969	2 teams WAS A (14G 1–3) BAL A (3G 0–0)																									
″	total	1	3	.250	5.62	17	5	0	41.2	44	26	30	0	0	3	0	12	5	1	.417	3	7	2	0	0.7	.833
1970	STL N	1	2	.333	3.19	8	5	0	31	36	15	14	0	0	0	0	7	1	0	.143	0	5	0	0	0.6	1.000
7 yrs.		19	29	.396	3.84	99	66	6	412.2	399	214	280	5	1	3	0	126	16	1	.127	18	56	6	4	0.8	.925

Mike Bertotti

BERTOTTI, MICHAEL DAVID BL TL 6′ 1″ 185 lbs.
B. Jan. 18, 1970, Jersey City, N. J.

Year	Team		W	L	PCT	ERA	G	GS	CG	IP	H	BB	SO	ShO	Relief Pitching W	Relief Pitching L	Relief Pitching SV	Batting AB	Batting H	Batting HR	BA	PO	A	E	DP	TC/G	FA
1995	CHI	A	1	1	.500	12.56	4	4	0	14.1	23	11	15	0	0	0	0	0	0	0	—	0	0	0	0	0.0	.000

Lefty Bertrand

BERTRAND, ROMAN MATHIAS BR TL 6′ 180 lbs.
B. Feb. 28, 1909, Cobden, Minn.

Year	Team		W	L	PCT	ERA	G	GS	CG	IP	H	BB	SO	ShO	Relief Pitching W	Relief Pitching L	Relief Pitching SV	Batting AB	Batting H	Batting HR	BA	PO	A	E	DP	TC/G	FA
1936	PHI	N	0	0	—	9.00	1	0	0	2	3	2	1	0	0	0	0	0	0	0	—	0	0	0	0	0.0	.000

Andres Berumen

BERUMEN, ANDRES BR TR 6′ 2″ 210 lbs.
B. Apr. 5, 1971, Tijuana, Mexico.

Year	Team		W	L	PCT	ERA	G	GS	CG	IP	H	BB	SO	ShO	Relief Pitching W	Relief Pitching L	Relief Pitching SV	Batting AB	Batting H	Batting HR	BA	PO	A	E	DP	TC/G	FA
1995	SD	N	2	3	.400	5.68	37	0	0	44.1	37	36	42	0	2	3	1	1	0	0	.000	4	1	1	0	0.2	.833

Fred Besana

BESANA, FREDERICK CYRIL BR TL 6′ 3½″ 200 lbs.
B. Apr. 5, 1931, Lincoln, Calif.

Year	Team		W	L	PCT	ERA	G	GS	CG	IP	H	BB	SO	ShO	Relief Pitching W	Relief Pitching L	Relief Pitching SV	Batting AB	Batting H	Batting HR	BA	PO	A	E	DP	TC/G	FA
1956	BAL	A	1	0	1.000	5.60	7	2	0	17.2	22	14	7	0	0	0	0	4	0	0	.000	2	5	0	0	1.0	1.000

Herman Besse

BESSE, HERMAN A. (Long Herm) BL TL 6′ 2″ 190 lbs.
B. Aug. 16, 1911, St. Louis, Mo. D. Aug. 13, 1972, Los Angeles, Calif.

Year	Team		W	L	PCT	ERA	G	GS	CG	IP	H	BB	SO	ShO	Relief Pitching W	Relief Pitching L	Relief Pitching SV	Batting AB	Batting H	Batting HR	BA	PO	A	E	DP	TC/G	FA
1940	PHI	A	0	3	.000	8.83	17	5	0	53	70	34	19	0	0	0	0	19	5	0	.263	0	5	0	0	0.3	1.000
1941			2	0	1.000	10.07	6	2	1	19.2	28	12	8	0	1	0	0	5	1	0	.200	1	4	0	1	0.8	1.000
1942			2	9	.182	6.50	30	14	4	133	163	69	78	0	0	1	1	53	12	0	.226	0	18	1	0	0.6	.947
1943			1	1	.500	3.31	5	1	0	16.1	18	4	3	0	0	1	0	8	0	0	.000	0	4	0	0	0.8	1.000
1946			0	2	.000	5.23	7	3	0	20.2	19	9	10	0	0	0	1	5	0	0	.000	0	3	0	0	0.4	1.000
5 yrs.			5	15	.250	6.97	65	25	5	242.2	298	128	118	0	1	2	2	90	18	0	.200	1	34	1	1	0.6	.972

Don Bessent

BESSENT, FRED DONALD (The Weasel) BR TR 6′ 175 lbs.
B. Mar. 13, 1931, Jacksonville, Fla. D. July 7, 1990, Jacksonville, Fla.

Year	Team		W	L	PCT	ERA	G	GS	CG	IP	H	BB	SO	ShO	Relief Pitching W	Relief Pitching L	Relief Pitching SV	Batting AB	Batting H	Batting HR	BA	PO	A	E	DP	TC/G	FA
1955	BKN	N	8	1	.889	2.70	24	2	1	63.1	51	21	29	0	6	1	3	20	2	0	.100	1	11	0	0	0.5	1.000
1956			4	3	.571	2.50	38	0	0	79.1	63	31	52	0	4	3	9	18	2	0	.111	3	8	1	1	0.3	.917
1957			1	3	.250	5.73	27	0	0	44	58	19	24	0	1	3	0	4	1	0	.250	6	4	0	0	0.4	1.000
1958	LA	N	1	0	1.000	3.33	19	0	0	24.1	24	17	13	0	1	0	0	2	0	0	.000	2	6	0	2	0.4	1.000
4 yrs.			14	7	.667	3.33	108	2	1	211	196	88	118	0	12	7	12	44	5	0	.114	12	29	1	3	0.4	.976
WORLD SERIES																											
1955	BKN	N	0	0	—	0.00	3	0	0	3.1	3	1	1	0	0	0	0	1	0	0	.000	0	2	0	0	0.7	1.000
1956			1	0	1.000	1.80	2	0	0	10	8	3	5	0	1	0	0	2	1	0	.500	0	0	0	0	0.0	.000
2 yrs.			1	0	1.000	1.35	5	0	0	13.1	11	4	6	0	1	0	0	3	1	0	.333	0	2	0	0	0.4	1.000

Karl Best

BEST, KARL JON BR TR 6′ 4″ 200 lbs.
B. Mar. 6, 1959, Aberdeen, Wash.

Year	Team		W	L	PCT	ERA	G	GS	CG	IP	H	BB	SO	ShO	Relief Pitching W	Relief Pitching L	Relief Pitching SV	Batting AB	Batting H	Batting HR	BA	PO	A	E	DP	TC/G	FA
1983	SEA	A	0	1	.000	13.50	4	0	0	5.1	14	5	3	0	0	1	0	0	0	0	—	0	0	0	0	0.0	.000
1984			1	1	.500	3.00	5	0	0	6	7	0	6	0	1	1	0	0	0	0	—	0	0	0	0	0.0	.000
1985			2	1	.667	1.95	15	0	0	32.1	25	6	32	0	2	1	4	0	0	0	—	0	3	1	0	0.3	.750
1986			2	3	.400	4.04	26	0	0	35.2	35	21	23	0	2	3	1	0	0	0	—	1	3	0	0	0.2	1.000
1988	MIN	A	0	0	—	6.00	11	0	0	12	15	7	9	0	0	0	0	0	0	0	—	0	1	0	0	0.1	1.000
5 yrs.			5	6	.455	4.04	61	0	0	91.1	96	39	73	0	5	6	5	0	0	0		1	7	1	0	0.1	.889

Jim Bethke

BETHKE, JAMES CHARLES BR TR 6′ 3″ 185 lbs.
B. Nov. 5, 1946, Falls City, Neb.

Year	Team		W	L	PCT	ERA	G	GS	CG	IP	H	BB	SO	ShO	Relief Pitching W	Relief Pitching L	Relief Pitching SV	Batting AB	Batting H	Batting HR	BA	PO	A	E	DP	TC/G	FA
1965	NY	N	2	0	1.000	4.28	25	0	0	40	41	22	19	0	2	0	0	4	0	0	.000	2	12	0	2	0.6	1.000

Jeff Bettendorf

BETTENDORF, JEFFREY ALLEN BR TR 6′ 3″ 180 lbs.
B. Dec. 10, 1960, Lompoc, Calif.

Year	Team		W	L	PCT	ERA	G	GS	CG	IP	H	BB	SO	ShO	Relief Pitching W	Relief Pitching L	Relief Pitching SV	Batting AB	Batting H	Batting HR	BA	PO	A	E	DP	TC/G	FA
1984	OAK	A	0	0	—	4.66	3	0	0	9.2	9	5	5	0	0	0	1	0	0	0	—	0	0	0	0	0.0	.000

Hal Betts

BETTS, HAROLD MATTHEW BR TR 5′10″ 200 lbs.
B. June 19, 1881, Alliance, Ohio D. May 22, 1946, San Antonio, Tex.

Year	Team		W	L	PCT	ERA	G	GS	CG	IP	H	BB	SO	ShO	Relief Pitching W	Relief Pitching L	Relief Pitching SV	Batting AB	Batting H	Batting HR	BA	PO	A	E	DP	TC/G	FA
1903	STL	N	0	1	.000	10.00	1	1	1	9	11	5	2	0	0	0	0	3	0	0	.000	1	1	0	1	2.0	1.000
1913	CIN	N	0	0	—	2.70	1	0	0	3.1	1	3	0	0	0	0	0	1	0	0	.000	0	0	0	0	0.0	.000
2 yrs.			0	1	.000	8.03	2	1	1	12.1	12	8	2	0	0	0	0	4	0	0	.000	1	1	0	1	1.0	1.000

Huck Betts

BETTS, WALTER MARTIN BR TR 5′11″ 170 lbs.
B. Feb. 18, 1897, Millsboro, Del. D. June 16, 1987, Millsboro, Del.

Year	Team		W	L	PCT	ERA	G	GS	CG	IP	H	BB	SO	ShO	Relief Pitching W	Relief Pitching L	Relief Pitching SV	Batting AB	Batting H	Batting HR	BA	PO	A	E	DP	TC/G	FA
1920	PHI	N	1	1	.500	3.57	27	4	1	88.1	86	33	18	0	0	1	0	25	2	0	.080	3	23	1	0	1.0	.963
1921			3	7	.300	4.47	32	2	1	100.2	141	14	28	0	3	5	4	30	8	0	.267	4	27	2	1	1.0	.939
1922			1	0	1.000	9.60	7	0	0	15	23	8	4	0	1	0	0	4	0	0	.000	0	2	0	0	0.3	1.000
1923			2	4	.333	3.09	19	4	3	84.1	100	14	18	0	1	1	1	31	3	0	.097	3	22	1	0	1.4	.962
1924			7	10	.412	4.30	37	9	2	144.1	160	42	46	0	5	**5**	2	45	7	0	.156	5	29	3	0	1.0	.919
1925			4	5	.444	5.55	35	7	1	97.1	146	38	28	0	3	1	1	34	10	0	.294	1	30	2	0	0.9	.939
1932	BOS	N	13	11	.542	2.80	31	27	16	221.2	229	35	32	3	2	0	1	79	19	0	.241	9	40	0	2	1.6	1.000
1933			11	11	.500	2.79	35	26	17	242	225	55	40	2	0	1	4	76	17	0	.224	5	78	1	2	2.4	.988
1934			17	10	.630	4.06	40	27	10	213	258	42	69	2	3	1	3	69	13	0	.188	9	36	2	3	1.2	.957
1935			2	9	.182	5.47	44	19	2	159.2	213	40	40	1	1	2	0	44	7	0	.159	3	40	1	0	1.0	.977
10 yrs.			61	68	.473	3.93	307	125	53	1366.1	1581	321	323	8	19	17	16	437	86	0	.197	42	327	13	8	1.2	.966

Bill Bevens

BEVENS, FLOYD CLIFFORD BR TR 6′ 3½″ 210 lbs.
B. Oct. 21, 1916, Hubbard, Ore. D. Oct. 26, 1991, Salem, Ore.

Year	Team		W	L	PCT	ERA	G	GS	CG	IP	H	BB	SO	ShO	Relief Pitching W	Relief Pitching L	Relief Pitching SV	Batting AB	Batting H	Batting HR	BA	PO	A	E	DP	TC/G	FA
1944	NY	A	4	1	.800	2.68	8	5	3	43.2	44	13	16	0	0	0	0	16	1	0	.063	1	7	0	2	1.0	1.000
1945			13	9	.591	3.67	29	25	14	184	174	68	76	2	0	1	0	63	7	1	.111	10	39	4	5	1.8	.925
1946			16	13	.552	2.23	31	31	18	249.2	213	78	120	3	0	0	0	84	7	2	.083	9	25	5	1	1.3	.872
1947			7	13	.350	3.82	28	23	11	165	167	77	77	1	1	1	0	58	7	0	.121	8	24	0	2	1.1	1.000
4 yrs.			40	36	.526	3.08	96	84	46	642.1	598	236	289	6	1	2	0	221	22	3	.100	28	95	9	10	1.4	.932
WORLD SERIES																											
1947	NY	A	0	1	.000	2.38	2	1	1	11.1	3	11	7	0	0	0	0	4	0	0	.000	0	1	0	0	0.5	1.000

Lou Bevil

BEVIL, LOUIS EUGENE BB TR 5′11½″ 190 lbs.
Born Louis Eugene Bevilacqua.
B. Nov. 27, 1922, Nelson, Ill. D. Feb. 1, 1973, Dixon, Ill.

Year	Team		W	L	PCT	ERA	G	GS	CG	IP	H	BB	SO	ShO	Relief Pitching W	L	SV	Batting AB	H	HR	BA	PO	A	E	DP	TC/G	FA
1942	WAS	A	0	1	.000	6.52	4	1	0	9.2	9	11	2	0	0	0	0	3	0	0	.000	0	1	0	0	0.3	1.000

Charlie Beville

BEVILLE, CLARENCE BENJAMIN (Candy Ben) BR TR 5′ 9″ 190 lbs.
B. Aug. 28, 1877, Colusa, Calif. D. Jan. 5, 1937, Yountville, Calif.

Year	Team		W	L	PCT	ERA	G	GS	CG	IP	H	BB	SO	ShO	Relief Pitching W	L	SV	Batting AB	H	HR	BA	PO	A	E	DP	TC/G	FA
1901	BOS	A	0	2	.000	4.00	2	2	1	9	8	9	1	0	0	0	0	7	2	0	.286	5	2	1	0	2.7	.875

Jim Bibby

BIBBY, JAMES BLAIR BR TR 6′ 5″ 235 lbs.
B. Oct. 29, 1944, Franklinton, N. C.

Year	Team		W	L	PCT	ERA	G	GS	CG	IP	H	BB	SO	ShO	Relief Pitching W	L	SV	Batting AB	H	HR	BA	PO	A	E	DP	TC/G	FA
1972	STL	N	1	3	.250	3.35	6	6	0	40.1	29	19	28	0	0	0	0	8	1	0	.125	2	6	0	0	1.3	1.000
1973	2 teams	STL N	(6G 0–2)		TEX A	(26G 9–10)																					
″	total		9	12	.429	3.77	32	26	11	196	140	123	167	2	0	0	1	2	0	0	.000	5	22	2	1	0.9	.931
1974	TEX	A	19	19	.500	4.74	41	41	11	264	255	113	149	5	0	0	0	0	0	0	—	22	36	3	4	1.5	.951
1975	2 teams	TEX A	(12G 2–6)		CLE A	(24G 5–9)																					
″	total		7	15	.318	3.88	36	24	6	181	172	78	93	1	1	3	1	0	0	0		11	27	2	3	1.1	.950
1976	CLE	A	13	7	.650	3.20	34	21	4	163	162	56	84	3	3	1	1	0	0	0	—	10	19	2	2	0.9	.935
1977			12	13	.480	3.57	37	30	9	207	197	73	141	2	0	1	2	0	0	0	—	14	21	5	0	1.1	.875
1978	PIT	N	8	7	.533	3.53	34	14	3	107	100	39	72	2	3	2	1	31	4	1	.129	3	20	2	0	0.7	.920
1979			12	4	.750	2.80	34	17	4	138	110	47	103	1	2	1	0	45	8	2	.178	5	12	0	1	0.5	1.000
1980			19	6	**.760**	3.33	35	34	6	238	210	88	144	1	1	0	0	77	12	1	.156	9	30	3	1	1.2	.929
1981			6	3	.667	2.49	14	14	2	94	79	26	48	2	0	0	0	28	4	1	.143	2	11	1	3	1.0	.929
1983			5	12	.294	6.69	29	12	0	78	92	51	44	0	3	4	2	18	2	0	.111	4	10	0	1	0.5	1.000
1984	TEX	A	0	0	—	4.41	8	0	0	16.1	19	10	6	0	0	0	0	0	0	0	—	1	2	0	0	0.4	1.000
12 yrs.			111	101	.524	3.76	340	239	56	1722.2	1565	723	1079	19	13	12	8	209	31	5	.148	88	216	20	16	1.0	.938
LEAGUE CHAMPIONSHIP SERIES																											
1979	PIT	N	0	0	—	1.29	1	1	0	7	4	4	5	0	0	0	0	0	0	0	—	0	1	0	0	1.0	1.000
WORLD SERIES																											
1979	PIT	N	0	0	—	2.61	2	2	0	10.1	10	2	10	0	0	0	0	4	0	0	.000	1	0	0	0	0.5	1.000

Vern Bickford

BICKFORD, VERNON EDGELL BR TR 6′ 180 lbs.
B. Aug. 17, 1920, Hellier, Ky. D. May 6, 1960, Concord, Va.

Year	Team		W	L	PCT	ERA	G	GS	CG	IP	H	BB	SO	ShO	Relief Pitching W	L	SV	Batting AB	H	HR	BA	PO	A	E	DP	TC/G	FA
1948	BOS	N	11	5	.688	3.27	33	22	10	146	125	63	60	1	0	1	1	49	10	0	.204	6	22	1	0	0.9	.966
1949			16	11	.593	4.25	37	36	15	230.2	246	106	101	2	0	1	0	81	15	0	.185	7	50	1	3	1.6	.983
1950			19	14	.576	3.47	40	**39**	**27**	**311.2**	293	122	126	2	0	0	0	116	16	0	.138	26	45	2	5	1.8	.973
1951			11	9	.550	3.12	25	20	12	164.2	146	76	76	3	0	2	0	52	6	0	.115	14	38	1	4	2.1	.981
1952			7	12	.368	3.74	26	22	7	161.1	165	64	62	1	0	0	0	51	9	0	.176	12	32	1	4	1.7	.978
1953	MIL	N	2	5	.286	5.28	20	9	2	58	60	35	25	0	1	0	1	15	1	0	.067	3	14	0	3	0.9	1.000
1954	BAL	A	0	1	.000	9.00	1	1	0	4	5	1	0	0	0	0	0	1	0	0	.000	0	1	0	0	1.0	1.000
7 yrs.			66	57	.537	3.71	182	149	73	1076.1	1040	467	450	9	1	4	2	365	57	0	.156	68	202	6	19	1.5	.978
WORLD SERIES																											
1948	BOS	N	0	1	.000	2.70	1	1	0	3.1	4	5	1	0	0	0	0	0	0	0	—	0	0	0	0	0.0	.000

Dan Bickham

BICKHAM, DANIEL DENISON BR TR 5′10″ 160 lbs.
B. Oct. 31, 1864, Dayton, Ohio D. Mar. 3, 1951, Dayton, Ohio.

Year	Team		W	L	PCT	ERA	G	GS	CG	IP	H	BB	SO	ShO	Relief Pitching W	L	SV	Batting AB	H	HR	BA	PO	A	E	DP	TC/G	FA
1886	CIN	AA	1	0	1.000	3.00	1	1	1	9	13	3	6	0	0	0	0	3	1	0	.333	0	3	1	0	4.0	.750

Charlie Bicknell

BICKNELL, CHARLES STEPHEN (Bud) BR TR 5′11″ 170 lbs.
B. July 27, 1928, Plainfield, N. J.

Year	Team		W	L	PCT	ERA	G	GS	CG	IP	H	BB	SO	ShO	Relief Pitching W	L	SV	Batting AB	H	HR	BA	PO	A	E	DP	TC/G	FA
1948	PHI	N	0	1	.000	5.96	17	1	0	25.2	29	17	5	0	0	0	0	5	0	0	.000	2	2	0	1	0.2	1.000
1949			0	0	—	7.62	13	0	0	28.1	32	17	4	0	0	0	0	1	0	0	.000	2	5	1	1	0.6	.875
2 yrs.			0	1	.000	6.83	30	1	0	54	61	34	9	0	0	0	0	6	0	0	.000	4	7	1	2	0.4	.917

Mike Bielecki

BIELECKI, MICHAEL JOSEPH BR TR 6′ 3″ 195 lbs.
B. July 31, 1959, Baltimore, Md.

Year	Team		W	L	PCT	ERA	G	GS	CG	IP	H	BB	SO	ShO	Relief Pitching W	L	SV	Batting AB	H	HR	BA	PO	A	E	DP	TC/G	FA
1984	PIT	N	0	0	—	0.00	4	0	0	4.1	4	0	1	0	0	0	0	0	0	0	—	0	1	0	0	0.3	1.000
1985			2	3	.400	4.53	12	7	0	45.2	45	31	22	0	0	0	0	10	0	0	.000	5	11	0	0	1.3	1.000
1986			6	11	.353	4.66	31	27	0	148.2	149	83	83	0	0	0	0	48	3	0	.063	17	16	1	1	1.1	.971
1987			2	3	.400	4.73	8	8	2	45.2	43	12	25	0	0	0	0	16	1	0	.063	6	5	1	0	1.5	.917
1988	CHI	N	2	2	.500	3.35	19	5	0	48.1	55	16	33	0	1	0	0	10	1	0	.100	4	5	0	0	0.5	1.000
1989			18	7	**.720**	3.14	33	33	4	212.1	187	81	147	3	0	0	0	70	3	0	.043	18	21	1	0	1.2	.975
1990			8	11	.421	4.93	36	29	0	168	188	70	103	0	1	0	1	43	7	0	.163	17	33	3	2	1.5	.943
1991	2 teams	CHI N	(39G 13–11)		ATL N	(2G 0–0)																					
″	total		13	11	.542	4.46	41	25	0	173.2	171	56	75	0	3	3	0	46	3	0	.065	22	24	0	3	1.1	1.000
1992	ATL	N	2	4	.333	2.57	19	14	1	80.2	77	27	62	1	0	0	0	24	3	0	.125	5	14	0	0	1.0	1.000
1993	CLE	A	4	5	.444	5.90	13	13	0	68.2	90	23	38	0	0	0	0	0	0	0	—	5	11	0	1	1.2	1.000
1994	ATL	N	2	0	1.000	4.00	19	1	0	27	28	12	18	0	2	0	0	3	0	0	.000	3	4	0	1	0.4	1.000
1995	CAL	A	4	6	.400	5.97	22	11	0	75.1	80	31	45	0	0	0	0	0	0	0	—	6	7	2	0	0.7	.867
12 yrs.			63	63	.500	4.29	257	173	7	1098.1	1117	442	652	4	7	3	1	270	21	0	.078	108	152	8	8	1.0	.970
LEAGUE CHAMPIONSHIP SERIES																											
1989	CHI	N	0	1	.000	3.65	2	2	0	12.1	7	6	11	0	0	0	0	5	1	0	.200	1	2	0	0	1.5	1.000

Harry Biemiller

BIEMILLER, HARRY LEE BR TR 6′ 1″ 171 lbs.
B. Oct. 9, 1897, Baltimore, Md. D. May 25, 1965, Orlando, Fla.

Year	Team		W	L	PCT	ERA	G	GS	CG	IP	H	BB	SO	ShO	Relief Pitching W	L	SV	Batting AB	H	HR	BA	PO	A	E	DP	TC/G	FA
1920	WAS	A	1	0	1.000	4.76	5	2	1	17	21	13	10	0	0	0	0	4	0	0	.000	1	7	0	0	1.6	1.000
1925	CIN	N	0	1	.000	4.02	23	1	0	47	45	21	9	0	0	0	2	9	0	0	.000	2	19	1	1	1.0	.955
2 yrs.			1	1	.500	4.22	28	3	1	64	66	34	19	0	0	0	2	13	0	0	.000	3	26	1	1	1.1	.967

Lou Bierbauer

BIERBAUER, LOUIS W. BL TR 5′ 8″ 140 lbs.
Also appeared in box score as Bauer.
B. Sept. 28, 1865, Erie, Pa. D. Jan. 31, 1926, Erie, Pa.

Year	Team	W	L	PCT	ERA	G	GS	CG	IP	H	BB	SO	ShO	Relief Pitching W	Relief Pitching L	Relief Pitching SV	Batting AB	Batting H	HR	BA	PO	A	E	DP	TC/G	FA
1886	PHI AA	0	0	—	4.22	2	0	0	10.2	8	5	1	0	0	0	0	522	118	2	.226	406	435	89	55	6.6	.904
1887		0	0	—	0.00	1	0	0	1	0	0	1	0	0	0	1	530	144	1	.272	332	378	61	45	6.1	.921
1888		0	0	—	0.00	1	0	0	3	5	0	3	0	0	0	0	535	143	0	.267	364	423	70	41	6.3	.918
3 yrs.		0	0		3.07	4	0	0	14.2	13	5	5	0	0	0	1	*				3775	4592	585	623	6.4	.935

Lyle Bigbee

BIGBEE, LYLE RANDOLPH (Al) BL TR 6′ 180 lbs.
Brother of Carson Bigbee.
B. Aug. 22, 1893, Sweet Home, Ore. D. Aug. 5, 1942, Portland, Ore.

Year	Team	W	L	PCT	ERA	G	GS	CG	IP	H	BB	SO	ShO	Relief Pitching W	Relief Pitching L	Relief Pitching SV	Batting AB	Batting H	HR	BA	PO	A	E	DP	TC/G	FA
1920	PHI A	0	3	.000	8.00	12	0	0	45	66	25	12	0	0	3	0	70	13	1	.186	23	12	4	0	1.6	.897
1921	PIT N	0	0	—	1.13	5	0	0	8	4	4	1	0	0	0	0	2	0	0	.000	0	2	0	0	0.4	1.000
2 yrs.		0	3	.000	6.96	17	0	0	53	70	29	13	0	0	3	0	*				23	14	4	0	1.4	.902

Charlie Biggs

BIGGS, CHARLES ORVAL BR TR 6′ 1″ 185 lbs.
B. Sept. 15, 1906, French Lick, Ind. D. May 24, 1954, French Lick, Ind.

Year	Team	W	L	PCT	ERA	G	GS	CG	IP	H	BB	SO	ShO	Relief Pitching W	Relief Pitching L	Relief Pitching SV	Batting AB	Batting H	HR	BA	PO	A	E	DP	TC/G	FA
1932	CHI A	1	1	.500	6.93	6	4	0	24.2	32	12	1	0	0	0	0	9	1	0	.111	2	4	0	2	1.0	1.000

Larry Biittner

BIITTNER, LAWRENCE DAVID BL TL 6′ 2″ 205 lbs.
B. July 27, 1945, Pocahontas, Iowa.

Year	Team	W	L	PCT	ERA	G	GS	CG	IP	H	BB	SO	ShO	Relief Pitching W	Relief Pitching L	Relief Pitching SV	Batting AB	Batting H	HR	BA	PO	A	E	DP	TC/G	FA
1977	CHI N	0	0	—	54.00	1	0	0	1	5	1	3	0	0	0	0	*				83	7	6	1	2.2	.938

Jim Bilbrey

BILBREY, JAMES MELVIN BR TR 6′ 2½″ 205 lbs.
B. Apr. 20, 1924, Rickman, Tenn. D. Dec. 26, 1985, Toledo, Ohio.

Year	Team	W	L	PCT	ERA	G	GS	CG	IP	H	BB	SO	ShO	Relief Pitching W	Relief Pitching L	Relief Pitching SV	Batting AB	Batting H	HR	BA	PO	A	E	DP	TC/G	FA
1949	STL A	0	0	—	18.00	1	0	0	1	1	3	0	0	0	0	0	0	0	0	—	0	1	0	0	1.0	1.000

Emil Bildilli

BILDILLI, EMIL (Hill Billy) BR TL 5′10″ 170 lbs.
B. Sept. 16, 1912, Diamond, Ind. D. Sept. 16, 1946, Hartford City, Ind.

Year	Team	W	L	PCT	ERA	G	GS	CG	IP	H	BB	SO	ShO	Relief Pitching W	Relief Pitching L	Relief Pitching SV	Batting AB	Batting H	HR	BA	PO	A	E	DP	TC/G	FA
1937	STL A	0	1	.000	10.13	4	1	0	8	12	3	2	0	0	0	0	2	0	0	.000	0	4	0	0	1.0	1.000
1938		1	2	.333	7.06	5	3	2	21.2	33	11	11	0	0	0	0	8	2	0	.250	0	4	0	0	0.8	1.000
1939		1	1	.500	3.32	2	2	2	19	21	6	8	0	0	0	0	5	0	0	.000	1	4	0	0	2.5	1.000
1940		2	4	.333	5.57	28	11	3	97	113	52	32	0	0	0	1	30	6	0	.200	7	32	2	2	1.5	.951
1941		0	0	—	11.57	2	0	0	2.1	5	3	2	0	0	0	0	0	0	0	—	0	1	0	0	0.5	1.000
5 yrs.		4	8	.333	5.84	41	17	7	148	184	75	55	0	0	0	1	45	8	0	.178	8	45	2	2	1.3	.964

Harry Billiard

BILLIARD, HARRY PREE BR TR 6′ 190 lbs.
B. Nov. 11, 1883, Monroe, Ind. D. June 3, 1923, Wooster, Ohio.

Year	Team	W	L	PCT	ERA	G	GS	CG	IP	H	BB	SO	ShO	Relief Pitching W	Relief Pitching L	Relief Pitching SV	Batting AB	Batting H	HR	BA	PO	A	E	DP	TC/G	FA
1908	NY A	0	0	—	2.57	5	0	0	14	13	13	9	0	0	0	0	5	1	0	.200	1	2	1	0	0.8	.750
1914	IND F	8	7	.533	3.72	32	16	5	125.2	117	63	45	0	4	2	1	38	7	0	.184	2	33	5	0	1.3	.875
1915	NWK F	1	0	1.000	5.72	14	2	0	28.1	32	28	7	0	1	0	0	6	2	0	.333	2	12	0	0	1.0	1.000
3 yrs.		9	7	.563	3.96	51	18	5	168	162	104	61	0	5	2	1	49	10	0	.204	5	47	6	0	1.1	.897

Jack Billingham

BILLINGHAM, JOHN EUGENE BR TR 6′ 4″ 195 lbs.
B. Feb. 21, 1943, Orlando, Fla.

Year	Team	W	L	PCT	ERA	G	GS	CG	IP	H	BB	SO	ShO	Relief Pitching W	Relief Pitching L	Relief Pitching SV	Batting AB	Batting H	HR	BA	PO	A	E	DP	TC/G	FA
1968	LA N	3	0	1.000	2.14	50	1	0	71.1	54	30	46	0	3	0	8	3	0	0	.000	5	15	1	1	0.4	.952
1969	HOU N	6	7	.462	4.23	52	4	1	83	92	29	71	0	0	0	2	14	1	0	.071	3	12	1	1	0.3	.938
1970		13	9	.591	3.97	46	24	8	188	190	63	134	2	2	0	0	58	6	0	.103	13	30	2	1	1.0	.956
1971		10	16	.385	3.39	33	33	8	228	205	68	139	3	0	0	0	73	9	0	.123	20	32	4	3	1.7	.929
1972	CIN N	12	12	.500	3.18	36	31	8	217.2	197	64	137	4	0	0	1	71	5	0	.070	14	28	1	0	1.2	.977
1973		19	10	.655	3.04	40	**40**	16	**293.1**	257	95	155	**7**	0	0	0	93	6	0	.065	18	53	2	3	1.8	.973
1974		19	11	.633	3.95	36	35	8	212	233	64	103	3	1	0	0	67	5	0	.075	14	35	1	1	1.4	.980
1975		15	10	.600	4.11	33	32	5	208	222	76	79	0	0	0	0	65	7	0	.108	8	24	0	5	1.0	1.000
1976		12	10	.545	4.32	34	29	5	177	190	62	76	2	1	1	1	59	14	0	.237	10	25	1	1	1.1	.972
1977		10	10	.500	5.22	36	23	3	162	195	56	76	2	1	2	0	56	9	0	.161	12	34	1	2	1.3	.979
1978	DET A	15	8	.652	3.88	30	30	10	201.2	218	65	59	4	0	0	0	0	0	0	—	9	30	1	0	1.3	.975
1979		10	7	.588	3.30	35	19	2	158	163	60	59	0	3	2	3	0	0	0	—	6	21	2	3	0.8	.931
1980	2 teams DET A (8G 0–0) BOS A (7G 1–3)																									
″	total	1	3	.250	10.45	15	4	0	31	56	18	7	0	0	0	0	0	0	0		1	5	0	0	0.4	1.000
13 yrs.		145	113	.562	3.83	476	305	74	2231	2272	750	1141	27	11	5	15	559	62	0	.111	133	344	17	21	1.0	.966
LEAGUE CHAMPIONSHIP SERIES																										
1972	CIN N	0	0	—	3.86	1	1	0	4.2	5	2	4	0	0	0	0	2	0	0	.000	1	0	0	0	1.0	1.000
1973		0	1	.000	4.50	2	2	0	12	9	4	9	0	0	0	0	3	0	0	.000	0	2	0	0	1.0	1.000
2 yrs.		0	1	.000	4.32	3	3	0	16.2	14	6	13	0	0	0	0	5	0	0	.000	1	2	0	0	1.0	1.000
WORLD SERIES																										
1972	CIN N	1	0	1.000	0.00	3	2	0	13.2	6	4	11	0	0	0	1	5	0	0	.000	1	1	0	0	0.7	1.000
1975		0	0	—	1.00	3	1	0	9	8	5	7	0	0	0	0	2	0	0	.000	0	2	0	1	0.7	1.000
1976		1	0	1.000	0.00	1	0	0	2.2	0	0	1	0	1	0	0	0	0	0	—	1	0	0	0	1.0	1.000
3 yrs.		2	0	1.000 1st	0.36 1st	7	3	0	25.1	14	9	19	0	1	0	1	7	0	0	.000	2	3	0	1	0.7	1.000

Haskell Billings

BILLINGS, HASKELL CLARK BR TR 5′11″ 180 lbs.
B. Sept. 27, 1907, New York, N. Y. D. Dec. 26, 1983, Greenbrae, Calif.

Year	Team	W	L	PCT	ERA	G	GS	CG	IP	H	BB	SO	ShO	Relief Pitching W	Relief Pitching L	Relief Pitching SV	Batting AB	Batting H	HR	BA	PO	A	E	DP	TC/G	FA
1927	DET A	5	4	.556	4.84	10	9	5	67	64	39	18	0	0	1	0	27	7	0	.259	1	15	0	0	1.6	1.000
1928		5	10	.333	5.12	21	16	3	110.2	118	59	48	1	0	0	0	35	10	0	.286	5	22	1	1	1.3	.964
1929		0	1	.000	5.12	8	0	0	19.1	27	9	1	0	0	1	0	6	0	0	.000	2	9	1	0	1.5	.917
3 yrs.		10	15	.400	5.03	39	25	8	197	209	107	67	1	0	2	0	68	17	0	.250	8	46	2	1	1.4	.964

Doug Bird

BIRD, JAMES DOUGLAS BR TR 6′ 4″ 180 lbs.
B. Mar. 5, 1950, Corona, Calif.

Year	Team	W	L	PCT	ERA	G	GS	CG	IP	H	BB	SO	ShO	Relief Pitching W	Relief Pitching L	Relief Pitching SV	Batting AB	Batting H	HR	BA	PO	A	E	DP	TC/G	FA
1973	KC A	4	4	.500	3.00	54	0	0	102	81	30	83	0	4	4	20	0	0	0	—	2	5	0	1	0.1	1.000
1974		7	6	.538	2.74	55	1	1	92	100	27	62	0	7	5	10	0	0	0	—	8	12	0	3	0.4	1.000
1975		9	6	.600	3.25	51	4	0	105.1	100	40	81	0	9	5	11	0	0	0	—	12	8	3	2	0.5	.870
1976		12	10	.545	3.36	39	27	2	198	191	31	107	1	3	0	2	0	0	0	—	14	21	2	1	0.9	.946
1977		11	4	.733	3.89	53	5	0	118	120	29	83	0	11	3	14	0	0	0	—	6	13	0	0	0.4	1.000

Doug Bird *continued*

Year	Team	W	L	PCT	ERA	G	GS	CG	IP	H	BB	SO	ShO	Relief Pitching W	Relief Pitching L	Relief Pitching SV	Batting AB	Batting H	Batting HR	BA	PO	A	E	DP	TC/G	FA
1978		6	6	.500	5.29	40	6	0	98.2	110	31	48	0	5	3	1	0	0	0	—	6	13	0	0	0.5	1.000
1979	PHI N	2	0	1.000	5.16	32	1	1	61	73	16	33	0	1	0	0	6	1	0	.167	4	2	0	0	0.2	1.000
1980	NY A	3	0	1.000	2.65	22	1	0	51	47	14	17	0	2	0	1	0	0	0	—	3	10	0	1	0.6	1.000
1981	2 teams NY A	(17G 5–1)		CHI N	(12G 4–5)																					
"	total	9	6	.600	3.23	29	16	2	128	130	32	62	1	2	0	0	20	2	0	.100	13	14	0	2	0.9	1.000
1982	CHI N	9	14	.391	5.14	35	33	2	191	230	30	71	1	0	0	0	56	8	0	.143	19	19	0	0	1.1	1.000
1983	BOS A	1	4	.200	6.65	22	6	0	67.2	91	16	33	0	0	1	1	0	0	0	—	7	7	0	1	0.6	1.000
11 yrs.		73	60	.549	3.99	432	100	8	1212.2	1273	296	680	3	44	21	60	82	11	0	.134	94	124	5	11	0.5	.978
LEAGUE CHAMPIONSHIP SERIES																										
1976	KC A	1	0	1.000	1.93	1	0	0	4.2	4	0	1	0	1	0	0	0	0	0	—	0	1	1	0	2.0	.500
1977		0	0	—	0.00	3	0	0	2	4	0	1	0	0	0	0	0	0	0	—	0	0	0	0	0.0	.000
1978		0	1	.000	9.00	2	0	0	1	2	0	1	0	0	1	0	0	0	0	—	0	1	0	0	0.5	1.000
3 yrs.		1	1	.500	2.35	6	0	0	7.2	10	0	3	0	1	1	0	0	0	0		0	2	1	0	0.5	.667

Red Bird

BIRD, JAMES EDWARD BL TL 5′11″ 170 lbs.
B. Apr. 25, 1890, Stephenville, Tex. D. Mar. 23, 1972, Murfreesboro, Ark.

Year	Team	W	L	PCT	ERA	G	GS	CG	IP	H	BB	SO	ShO	Relief W	Relief L	Relief SV	AB	H	HR	BA	PO	A	E	DP	TC/G	FA
1921	WAS A	0	0	—	5.40	1	0	0	5	5	1	2	0	0	0	0	1	0	0	.000	0	3	0	0	3.0	1.000

Mike Birkbeck

BIRKBECK, MICHAEL LAWRENCE BR TR 6′ 1″ 180 lbs.
B. Mar. 10, 1961, Orrville, Ohio.

Year	Team	W	L	PCT	ERA	G	GS	CG	IP	H	BB	SO	ShO	Relief W	Relief L	Relief SV	AB	H	HR	BA	PO	A	E	DP	TC/G	FA
1986	MIL A	1	1	.500	4.50	7	4	0	22	24	12	13	0	0	0	0	0	0	0	—	1	2	0	0	0.4	1.000
1987		1	4	.200	6.20	10	10	1	45	63	19	25	0	0	0	0	0	0	0	—	2	13	1	0	1.6	.938
1988		10	8	.556	4.72	23	23	0	124	141	37	64	0	0	0	0	0	0	0	—	21	19	2	2	1.8	.952
1989		0	4	.000	5.44	9	9	1	44.2	57	22	31	0	0	0	0	0	0	0	—	4	5	3	0	1.3	.750
1992	NY N	0	1	.000	9.00	1	1	0	7	12	1	2	0	0	0	0	2	0	0	.000	3	1	1	1	5.0	.800
1995		0	1	.000	1.63	4	4	0	27.2	22	2	14	0	0	0	0	6	2	0	.333	0	5	0	0	1.3	1.000
6 yrs.		12	19	.387	4.86	54	51	2	270.1	319	93	149	0	0	0	0	8	2	0	.250	31	45	7	3	1.5	.916

Ralph Birkofer

BIRKOFER, RALPH JOSEPH (Lefty) BL TL 5′11″ 213 lbs.
B. Nov. 5, 1908, Cincinnati, Ohio D. Mar. 16, 1971, Cincinnati, Ohio.

Year	Team	W	L	PCT	ERA	G	GS	CG	IP	H	BB	SO	ShO	Relief W	Relief L	Relief SV	AB	H	HR	BA	PO	A	E	DP	TC/G	FA
1933	PIT N	4	2	.667	2.31	9	8	3	50.2	43	17	20	1	0	0	0	22	7	0	.318	1	10	0	0	1.2	1.000
1934		11	12	.478	4.10	41	24	11	204	227	66	71	0	2	1	1	75	17	0	.227	2	39	3	1	1.1	.932
1935		9	7	.563	4.07	37	18	8	150.1	173	42	80	1	2	0	1	58	14	0	.241	3	18	4	1	0.7	.840
1936		7	5	.583	4.69	34	13	2	109.1	130	41	44	0	6	2	0	41	9	0	.220	1	14	7	0	0.6	.682
1937	BKN N	0	2	.000	6.67	11	1	0	29.2	45	9	9	0	0	1	0	11	3	0	.273	0	5	0	0	0.5	1.000
5 yrs.		31	28	.525	4.19	132	64	24	544	618	175	224	2	10	4	2	207	50	0	.242	7	86	14	2	0.8	.869

Babe Birrer

BIRRER, WERNER JOSEPH BR TR 6′ 195 lbs.
B. July 4, 1928, Buffalo, N. Y.

Year	Team	W	L	PCT	ERA	G	GS	CG	IP	H	BB	SO	ShO	Relief W	Relief L	Relief SV	AB	H	HR	BA	PO	A	E	DP	TC/G	FA
1955	DET A	4	3	.571	4.15	36	3	1	80.1	77	29	28	0	3	1	3	19	3	2	.158	8	8	0	1	0.4	1.000
1956	BAL A	0	0	—	6.75	4	0	0	5.1	9	1	1	0	0	0	0	1	0	0	.000	0	0	0	0	0.0	.000
1958	LA N	0	0	—	4.50	16	0	0	34	43	7	16	0	0	0	1	7	4	0	.571	0	1	0	0	0.1	1.000
3 yrs.		4	3	.571	4.36	56	3	1	119.2	129	37	45	0	3	1	4	27	7	2	.259	8	9	0	1	0.3	1.000

Tim Birtsas

BIRTSAS, TIMOTHY DEAN BL TL 6′ 7″ 240 lbs.
B. Sept. 5, 1960, Pontiac, Mich.

Year	Team	W	L	PCT	ERA	G	GS	CG	IP	H	BB	SO	ShO	Relief W	Relief L	Relief SV	AB	H	HR	BA	PO	A	E	DP	TC/G	FA
1985	OAK A	10	6	.625	4.01	29	25	2	141.1	124	91	94	0	0	0	0	0	0	0	—	0	11	1	1	0.4	.917
1986		0	0	—	22.50	2	0	0	2	2	4	1	0	0	0	0	0	0	0	—	0	0	0	0	0.0	.000
1988	CIN N	1	3	.250	4.20	36	4	0	64.1	61	24	38	0	1	0	0	10	0	0	.000	2	8	2	0	0.3	.833
1989		2	2	.500	3.75	42	1	0	69.2	68	27	57	0	2	1	1	4	1	1	.250	0	9	1	0	0.2	.900
1990		1	3	.250	3.86	29	0	0	51.1	69	24	41	0	1	3	0	4	0	0	.000	3	8	0	0	0.4	1.000
5 yrs.		14	14	.500	4.08	138	30	2	328.2	324	170	231	0	4	4	1	18	1	1	.056	5	36	4	1	0.3	.911

Frank Biscan

BISCAN, FRANK STEPHEN (Porky) BL TL 5′11″ 190 lbs.
B. Mar. 13, 1920, Mt. Olive, Ill. D. May 22, 1959, St. Louis, Mo.

Year	Team	W	L	PCT	ERA	G	GS	CG	IP	H	BB	SO	ShO	Relief W	Relief L	Relief SV	AB	H	HR	BA	PO	A	E	DP	TC/G	FA
1942	STL A	0	1	.000	2.33	11	0	0	27	13	11	10	0	0	1	1	6	0	0	.000	1	6	0	0	0.6	1.000
1946		1	1	.500	5.16	16	0	0	22.2	28	22	9	0	1	1	1	3	0	0	.000	0	3	0	0	0.2	1.000
1948		6	7	.462	6.11	47	4	1	98.2	129	71	45	0	6	5	2	26	5	0	.192	3	20	3	2	0.6	.885
3 yrs.		7	9	.438	5.28	74	4	1	148.1	170	104	64	0	7	7	4	35	5	0	.143	4	29	3	2	0.5	.917

Bill Bishop

BISHOP, WILLIAM HENRY (Lefty) BL TL 5′ 8″ 170 lbs.
B. Oct. 22, 1900, Houtzdale, Pa. D. Feb. 14, 1956, St. Joseph, Mo.

Year	Team	W	L	PCT	ERA	G	GS	CG	IP	H	BB	SO	ShO	Relief W	Relief L	Relief SV	AB	H	HR	BA	PO	A	E	DP	TC/G	FA
1921	PHI A	0	0	—	9.00	2	0	0	7	8	10	4	0	0	0	0	3	0	0	.000	0	3	0	0	1.5	1.000

Bill Bishop

BISHOP, WILLIAM ROBINSON
B. Dec. 27, 1869, Adamsburg, Pa. D. Dec. 15, 1932, Pittsburgh, Pa.

Year	Team	W	L	PCT	ERA	G	GS	CG	IP	H	BB	SO	ShO	Relief W	Relief L	Relief SV	AB	H	HR	BA	PO	A	E	DP	TC/G	FA
1886	PIT AA	0	1	.000	*3.18*	2	2	2	17	17	11	4	0	0	0	0	7	1	0	.143	0	3	4	0	3.5	.429
1887	PIT N	0	3	.000	13.33	3	3	3	27	45	22	4	0	0	0	0	9	0	0	.000	0	5	1	0	2.0	.833
1889	CHI N	0	0	—	18.00	2	0	0	3	6	6	1	0	0	0	2	1	0	0	.000	0	0	0	0	0.0	.000
3 yrs.		0	4	.000	9.96	7	5	5	47	68	39	9	0	0	0	2	17	1	0	.059	0	8	5	0	1.9	.615

Charlie Bishop

BISHOP, CHARLES TULLER BR TR 6′ 2″ 195 lbs.
B. Jan. 1, 1924, Atlanta, Ga. D. July 5, 1993, Lawrenceville, Ga.

Year	Team	W	L	PCT	ERA	G	GS	CG	IP	H	BB	SO	ShO	Relief W	Relief L	Relief SV	AB	H	HR	BA	PO	A	E	DP	TC/G	FA
1952	PHI A	2	2	.500	6.46	6	5	1	30.2	29	24	17	0	0	0	0	9	1	0	.111	3	7	1	0	1.8	.909
1953		3	14	.176	5.66	39	20	1	160.2	174	86	66	1	2	1	2	56	5	0	.089	5	36	0	3	1.1	1.000
1954		4	6	.400	4.41	20	12	4	96	98	50	34	0	0	0	1	33	4	0	.121	6	9	0	0	0.8	1.000
1955	KC A	1	0	1.000	5.40	4	0	0	6.2	6	8	4	0	1	0	0	2	1	0	.500	0	1	0	0	0.3	1.000
4 yrs.		10	22	.313	5.33	69	37	6	294	307	168	121	1	3	1	3	100	11	0	.110	14	53	1	3	1.0	.985

Jim Bishop

BISHOP, JAMES MORTON BR TR 6′ 185 lbs.
B. Jan. 28, 1898, Montgomery City, Mo. D. Sept. 20, 1973, Montgomery City, Mo.

Year	Team	W	L	PCT	ERA	G	GS	CG	IP	H	BB	SO	ShO	Relief W	Relief L	Relief SV	AB	H	HR	BA	PO	A	E	DP	TC/G	FA
1923	PHI N	0	3	.000	6.34	15	0	0	32.2	48	11	5	0	0	3	1	10	0	0	.000	3	11	0	0	0.9	1.000
1924		0	1	.000	6.48	7	1	0	16.2	24	7	3	0	0	0	0	5	1	0	.200	1	6	0	0	1.0	1.000
2 yrs.		0	4	.000	6.39	22	1	0	49.1	72	18	8	0	0	3	1	15	1	0	.067	4	17	0	0	1.0	1.000

Lloyd Bishop

BISHOP, LLOYD CLIFTON BR TR 6′ 180 lbs.
B. Apr. 25, 1890, Conway Springs, Kans. D. June 18, 1968, Wichita, Kans.

Year	Team	W	L	PCT	ERA	G	GS	CG	IP	H	BB	SO	ShO	Relief W	Relief L	Relief SV	AB	H	HR	BA	PO	A	E	DP	TC/G	FA
1914	CLE A	0	1	.000	5.63	3	1	0	8	14	3	1	0	0	0	0	2	0	0	.000	0	1	0	0	0.3	1.000

Hi Bithorn

BITHORN, HIRAM GABRIEL BR TR 6′ 1″ 200 lbs.
Born Hiram Gabriel Bithorn (Sosa).
B. Mar. 18, 1916, Santurce, Puerto Rico D. Jan. 1, 1952, El Mante, Mexico.

Year	Team	W	L	PCT	ERA	G	GS	CG	IP	H	BB	SO	ShO	Relief W	Relief L	Relief SV	AB	H	HR	BA	PO	A	E	DP	TC/G	FA
1942	CHI N	9	14	.391	3.68	38	16	9	171.1	191	81	65	0	3	5	2	57	7	0	.123	5	35	2	3	1.1	.952
1943		18	12	.600	2.60	39	30	19	249.2	226	65	86	**7**	1	1	2	92	16	0	.174	12	57	1	2	1.8	.986
1946		6	5	.545	3.84	26	7	2	86.2	97	25	34	1	4	2	1	28	5	0	.179	1	17	1	2	0.7	.947
1947	CHI A	1	0	1.000	0.00	2	0	0	2	2	0	0	0	1	0	0	0	0	0	—	0	0	0	0	0.0	.000
4 yrs.		34	31	.523	3.16	105	53	30	509.2	516	171	185	8	9	8	5	177	28	0	.158	18	109	4	7	1.2	.969

Joe Bitker

BITKER, JOSEPH ANTHONY BR TR 6′ 1″ 175 lbs.
B. Feb. 12, 1964, Glendale, Calif.

Year	Team	W	L	PCT	ERA	G	GS	CG	IP	H	BB	SO	ShO	Relief W	Relief L	Relief SV	AB	H	HR	BA	PO	A	E	DP	TC/G	FA
1990	2 teams OAK A (1G 0–0) TEX A (5G 0–0)																									
″	total	0	0		2.25	6	0	0	12	8	4	8	0	0	0	0	0	0	0		1	2	0	1	0.5	1.000
1991	TEX A	1	0	1.000	6.75	9	0	0	14.2	17	8	16	0	1	0	0	0	0	0	—	0	1	0	0	0.1	1.000
2 yrs.		1	0	1.000	4.72	15	0	0	26.2	25	12	24	0	1	0	0	0	0	0		1	3	0	1	0.3	1.000

Jeff Bittiger

BITTIGER, JEFFREY SCOTT BR TR 5′10″ 175 lbs.
B. Apr. 13, 1962, Jersey City, N. J.

Year	Team	W	L	PCT	ERA	G	GS	CG	IP	H	BB	SO	ShO	Relief W	Relief L	Relief SV	AB	H	HR	BA	PO	A	E	DP	TC/G	FA
1986	PHI N	1	1	.500	5.52	3	3	0	14.2	16	7	8	0	0	0	0	3	1	1	.333	2	2	0	0	1.3	1.000
1987	MIN A	1	0	1.000	5.40	3	1	0	8.1	11	0	5	0	0	0	0	0	0	0	—	0	2	0	0	0.7	1.000
1988	CHI A	2	4	.333	4.23	25	7	0	61.2	59	29	33	0	1	0	0	0	0	0	—	1	6	0	0	0.3	1.000
1989		0	1	.000	6.52	2	1	0	9.2	9	6	7	0	0	0	0	0	0	0	—	0	0	0	0	0.0	.000
4 yrs.		4	6	.400	4.77	33	12	0	94.1	95	42	53	0	1	0	0	3	1	1	.333	3	10	0	0	0.4	1.000

Jim Bivin

BIVIN, JAMES NATHANIEL BR TR 6′ 155 lbs.
B. Dec. 11, 1909, Jackson, Miss. D. Nov. 7, 1982, Pueblo, Colo.

Year	Team	W	L	PCT	ERA	G	GS	CG	IP	H	BB	SO	ShO	Relief W	Relief L	Relief SV	AB	H	HR	BA	PO	A	E	DP	TC/G	FA
1935	PHI N	2	9	.182	5.79	47	14	0	161.2	220	65	54	0	2	1	1	48	7	0	.146	4	32	1	1	0.8	.973

Bill Black

BLACK, WILLIAM CARROLL (Bud) BR TR 6′ 3″ 197 lbs.
B. July 9, 1932, St. Louis, Mo.

Year	Team	W	L	PCT	ERA	G	GS	CG	IP	H	BB	SO	ShO	Relief W	Relief L	Relief SV	AB	H	HR	BA	PO	A	E	DP	TC/G	FA
1952	DET A	0	1	.000	10.57	2	2	0	7.2	14	5	0	0	0	0	0	3	0	0	.000	0	1	0	0	0.5	1.000
1955		1	1	.500	1.26	3	2	1	14.1	12	8	7	1	0	1	0	4	1	0	.250	1	3	1	0	1.7	.800
1956		1	1	.500	3.60	5	1	0	10	10	5	7	0	1	0	0	2	0	0	.000	1	2	0	0	0.6	1.000
3 yrs.		2	3	.400	4.22	10	5	1	32	36	18	14	1	1	1	0	9	1	0	.111	2	6	1	0	0.9	.889

Bob Black

BLACK, ROBERT BENJAMIN
B. Dec. 10, 1862, Cincinnati, Ohio D. Mar. 21, 1933, Sioux City, Iowa.

Year	Team	W	L	PCT	ERA	G	GS	CG	IP	H	BB	SO	ShO	Relief W	Relief L	Relief SV	AB	H	HR	BA	PO	A	E	DP	TC/G	FA
1884	KC U	4	9	.308	*3.22*	16	15	13	123	127	17	93	0	0	0	0	*				58	50	20	4	3.0	.844

Bud Black

BLACK, HARRY RALSTON BL TL 6′ 2″ 180 lbs.
B. June 30, 1957, San Mateo, Calif.

Year	Team	W	L	PCT	ERA	G	GS	CG	IP	H	BB	SO	ShO	Relief W	Relief L	Relief SV	AB	H	HR	BA	PO	A	E	DP	TC/G	FA
1981	SEA A	0	0	—	0.00	2	0	0	1	2	3	0	0	0	0	0	0	0	0	—	0	1	0	0	0.5	1.000
1982	KC A	4	6	.400	4.58	22	14	0	88.1	92	34	40	0	0	0	0	0	0	0	—	6	12	1	1	0.9	.947
1983		10	7	.588	3.79	24	24	3	161.1	159	43	58	0	0	0	0	0	0	0	—	7	32	1	5	1.7	.975
1984		17	12	.586	3.12	35	35	8	257	226	64	140	1	0	0	0	0	0	0	—	13	51	2	2	1.9	.970
1985		10	15	.400	4.33	33	33	5	205.2	216	59	122	2	0	0	0	0	0	0	—	6	30	4	0	1.2	.900
1986		5	10	.333	3.20	56	4	0	121	100	43	68	0	4	7	9	0	0	0	—	3	21	0	1	0.4	1.000
1987		8	6	.571	3.60	29	18	0	122.1	126	35	61	0	1	1	1	0	0	0	—	4	19	0	0	0.8	1.000
1988	2 teams KC A (17G 2–1) CLE A (16G 2–3)																									
″	total	4	4	.500	5.00	33	7	0	81	82	34	63	0	3	2	1	0	0	0		5	12	0	0	0.5	1.000
1989	CLE A	12	11	.522	3.36	33	32	6	222.1	213	52	88	3	1	0	0	0	0	0	—	13	33	2	3	1.5	.958
1990	2 teams CLE A (29G 11–10) TOR A (3G 2–1)																									
″	total	13	11	.542	3.57	32	31	5	206.2	181	61	106	2	1	0	0	0	0	0		7	33	1	2	1.3	.976
1991	SF N	12	**16**	.429	3.99	34	34	3	214.1	201	71	104	3	0	0	0	71	13	0	.183	14	38	0	4	1.5	1.000
1992		10	12	.455	3.97	28	28	2	177	178	59	82	1	0	0	0	54	3	0	.056	5	37	0	4	1.5	1.000
1993		8	2	.800	3.56	16	16	0	93.2	89	33	45	0	0	0	0	37	9	0	.243	3	22	2	2	1.7	.926
1994		4	2	.667	4.47	10	10	0	54.1	50	16	28	0	0	0	0	17	1	0	.059	3	7	0	1	1.0	1.000
1995	CLE A	4	2	.667	6.85	11	10	0	47.1	63	16	34	0	0	0	0	0	0	0	—	0	8	0	0	0.7	1.000
15 yrs.		121	116	.511	3.84	398	296	32	2053.1	1978	623	1039	12	10	10	11	179	26	0	.145	89	356	13	25	1.2	.972
LEAGUE CHAMPIONSHIP SERIES																										
1984	KC A	0	1	.000	7.20	1	1	0	5	7	1	3	0	0	0	0	0	0	0	—	1	1	0	0	2.0	1.000
1985		0	0	—	1.69	3	1	0	10.2	11	4	8	0	0	0	0	0	0	0	—	1	2	0	1	1.0	1.000
2 yrs.		0	1	.000	3.45	4	2	0	15.2	18	5	11	0	0	0	0	0	0	0		2	3	0	1	1.3	1.000
WORLD SERIES																										
1985	KC A	0	1	.000	5.06	2	1	0	5.1	4	5	4	0	0	0	0	1	0	0	.000	1	2	1	1	2.0	.750

Dave Black

BLACK, DAVID BL TR 6′ 2″ 175 lbs.
B. Apr. 19, 1892, Chicago, Ill. D. Oct. 27, 1936, Pittsburgh, Pa.

Year	Team	W	L	PCT	ERA	G	GS	CG	IP	H	BB	SO	ShO	Relief W	Relief L	Relief SV	AB	H	HR	BA	PO	A	E	DP	TC/G	FA
1914	CHI F	1	0	1.000	6.12	8	1	1	25	28	4	19	0	0	0	0	12	4	0	.333	6	9	0	0	1.7	1.000
1915	2 teams CHI F (25G 6–7) BAL F (8G 1–3)																									
″	total	7	10	.412	2.72	33	14	3	155.1	136	48	53	0	1	**4**	0	49	7	0	.143	5	57	0	4	1.9	1.000
1923	BOS A	0	0	—	0.00	2	0	0	1	2	0	0	0	0	0	0	0	0	0	—	0	0	0	0	0.0	.000
3 yrs.		8	10	.444	3.18	43	15	4	181.1	166	52	72	0	1	4	0	61	11	0	.180	11	66	0	4	1.8	1.000

Don Black

BLACK, DONALD PAUL BR TR 6′ 185 lbs.
B. July 20, 1916, Salix, Iowa D. Apr. 21, 1959, Cuyahoga Falls, Ohio.

Year	Team	W	L	PCT	ERA	G	GS	CG	IP	H	BB	SO	ShO	Relief Pitching W	L	SV	Batting AB	H	HR	BA	PO	A	E	DP	TC/G	FA
1943	PHI A	6	16	.273	4.20	33	26	12	208	193	110	65	1	1	0	1	69	13	0	.188	15	41	0	3	1.7	1.000
1944		10	12	.455	4.06	29	27	8	177.1	177	75	78	0	0	0	0	59	11	0	.186	7	32	1	3	1.4	.975
1945		5	11	.313	5.17	26	18	8	125.1	154	69	47	0	2	1	0	37	6	0	.162	8	18	1	0	1.0	.963
1946	CLE A	1	2	.333	4.53	18	4	0	43.2	45	21	15	0	0	0	0	10	2	0	.200	4	10	1	1	0.8	.933
1947		10	12	.455	3.92	30	28	8	190.2	177	85	72	3	0	1	0	66	12	0	.182	15	31	1	2	1.6	.979
1948		2	2	.500	5.37	18	10	1	52	57	40	16	0	0	0	0	15	3	0	.200	3	11	0	1	0.8	1.000
6 yrs.		34	55	.382	4.35	154	113	37	797	803	400	293	4	3	2	1	256	47	0	.184	52	143	4	10	1.3	.980

Joe Black

BLACK, JOSEPH BR TR 6′ 2″ 220 lbs.
B. Feb. 8, 1924, Plainfield, N. J.

Year	Team	W	L	PCT	ERA	G	GS	CG	IP	H	BB	SO	ShO	Relief Pitching W	L	SV	Batting AB	H	HR	BA	PO	A	E	DP	TC/G	FA
1952	BKN N	15	4	.789	2.15	56	2	1	142.1	102	41	85	0	14	3	15	36	5	0	.139	7	18	4	2	0.5	.862
1953		6	3	.667	5.33	34	3	0	72.2	74	27	42	0	6	2	5	17	4	0	.235	3	11	1	0	0.4	.933
1954		0	0	—	11.57	5	0	0	7	11	5	3	0	0	0	0	0	0	0	—	0	1	0	0	0.2	1.000
1955	2 teams BKN N	(6G 1–0)		CIN N	(32G 5–2)																					
″	total	6	2	.750	4.05	38	11	1	117.2	121	30	63	0	3	0	3	33	4	0	.121	3	18	2	1	0.6	.913
1956	CIN N	3	2	.600	4.52	32	0	0	61.2	61	25	27	0	3	2	2	10	0	0	.000	5	7	1	2	0.4	.923
1957	WAS A	0	1	.000	7.11	7	0	0	12.2	22	1	2	0	0	1	0	0	0	0	—	1	3	0	0	0.6	1.000
6 yrs.		30	12	.714	3.91	172	16	2	414	391	129	222	0	26	8	25	96	13	0	.135	19	58	8	5	0.5	.906
WORLD SERIES																										
1952	BKN N	1	2	.333	2.53	3	3	1	21.1	15	8	9	0	0	0	0	6	0	0	.000	1	2	0	0	1.0	1.000
1953		0	0	—	9.00	1	0	0	1	1	0	2	0	0	0	0	0	0	0	—	0	0	0	0	0.0	.000
2 yrs.		1	2	.333	2.82	4	3	1	22.1	16	8	11	0	0	0	0	6	0	0	.000	1	2	0	0	0.8	1.000

Babe Blackburn

BLACKBURN, FOSTER EDWIN (Charlie) BR TR 6′ 1″ 165 lbs.
B. Jan. 6, 1895, Chicago, Ill. D. Mar. 9, 1984, New Port Richey, Fla.

Year	Team	W	L	PCT	ERA	G	GS	CG	IP	H	BB	SO	ShO	Relief Pitching W	L	SV	Batting AB	H	HR	BA	PO	A	E	DP	TC/G	FA
1915	KC F	0	1	.000	8.62	7	2	0	15.2	19	13	7	0	0	0	0	4	0	0	.000	1	6	0	0	1.0	1.000
1921	CHI A	0	0	—	0.00	1	0	0	1	0	1	0	0	0	0	0	0	0	0	—	0	0	0	0	0.0	.000
2 yrs.		0	1	.000	8.10	8	2	0	16.2	19	14	7	0	0	0	0	4	0	0	.000	1	6	0	0	0.9	1.000

George Blackburn

BLACKBURN, GEORGE W. TR 5′11″ 184 lbs.
B. Sept. 21, 1871, Ozark, Mo. Deceased.

Year	Team	W	L	PCT	ERA	G	GS	CG	IP	H	BB	SO	ShO	Relief Pitching W	L	SV	Batting AB	H	HR	BA	PO	A	E	DP	TC/G	FA
1897	BAL N	2	2	.500	6.82	5	4	3	33	34	12	1	0	0	0	0	13	1	0	.077	2	7	0	0	1.8	1.000

Jim Blackburn

BLACKBURN, JAMES RAY (Bones) BR TR 6′ 4″ 175 lbs.
B. June 19, 1924, Warsaw, Ky. D. Oct. 26, 1969, Cincinnati, Ohio.

Year	Team	W	L	PCT	ERA	G	GS	CG	IP	H	BB	SO	ShO	Relief Pitching W	L	SV	Batting AB	H	HR	BA	PO	A	E	DP	TC/G	FA
1948	CIN N	0	2	.000	4.18	16	0	0	32.1	38	14	10	0	0	2	0	6	0	0	.000	0	6	0	0	0.4	1.000
1951		0	0	—	17.18	2	0	0	3.2	8	2	1	0	0	0	0	0	0	0	—	0	1	0	0	0.5	1.000
2 yrs.		0	2	.000	5.50	18	0	0	36	46	16	11	0	0	2	0	6	0	0	.000	0	7	0	0	0.4	1.000

Ron Blackburn

BLACKBURN, RONALD HAMILTON BR TR 6′½″ 160 lbs.
B. Apr. 23, 1935, Mt. Airy, N. C.

Year	Team	W	L	PCT	ERA	G	GS	CG	IP	H	BB	SO	ShO	Relief Pitching W	L	SV	Batting AB	H	HR	BA	PO	A	E	DP	TC/G	FA
1958	PIT N	2	1	.667	3.39	38	2	0	63.2	61	27	31	0	2	0	3	7	2	0	.286	3	14	1	3	0.5	.944
1959		1	1	.500	3.65	26	0	0	44.1	50	15	19	0	1	1	1	5	1	1	.200	2	5	2	0	0.3	.778
2 yrs.		3	2	.600	3.50	64	2	0	108	111	42	50	0	3	1	4	12	3	1	.250	5	19	3	3	0.4	.889

Lena Blackburne

BLACKBURNE, RUSSELL AUBREY (Slats) BR TR 5′11″ 160 lbs.
B. Oct. 23, 1886, Clifton Heights, Pa. D. Feb. 29, 1968, Riverside, N. J.
Manager 1928–29.

Year	Team	W	L	PCT	ERA	G	GS	CG	IP	H	BB	SO	ShO	Relief Pitching W	L	SV	Batting AB	H	HR	BA	PO	A	E	DP	TC/G	FA
1929	CHI A	0	0	—	0.00	1	0	0	0.1	1	0	0	0	0	0	0	*				173	265	43	29	6.5	.911

Ewell Blackwell

BLACKWELL, EWELL (The Whip) BR TR 6′ 6″ 195 lbs.
B. Oct. 23, 1922, Fresno, Calif.

Year	Team	W	L	PCT	ERA	G	GS	CG	IP	H	BB	SO	ShO	Relief Pitching W	L	SV	Batting AB	H	HR	BA	PO	A	E	DP	TC/G	FA
1942	CIN N	0	0	—	6.00	2	0	0	3	3	3	1	0	0	0	0	1	0	0	.000	0	2	0	0	1.0	1.000
1946		9	13	.409	2.45	33	25	10	194.1	160	79	100	**6**	0	0	0	56	6	0	.107	7	58	3	7	2.1	.956
1947		**22**	8	.733	2.47	33	33	**23**	273	227	95	**193**	6	0	0	0	106	13	0	.123	10	70	3	2	2.5	.964
1948		7	9	.438	4.54	22	20	4	138.2	134	52	114	1	0	0	1	48	11	0	.229	7	40	1	2	2.2	.979
1949		5	5	.500	4.23	30	4	0	76.2	80	34	55	0	4	3	1	19	4	0	.211	4	18	1	1	0.8	.957
1950		17	15	.531	2.97	40	32	18	261	203	112	188	1	1	1	4	89	13	0	.146	8	54	5	2	1.7	.925
1951		16	15	.516	3.45	38	32	11	232.1	204	97	120	2	2	1	2	82	24	1	.293	6	46	5	5	1.5	.912
1952	2 teams CIN N	(23G 3–12)		NY A	(5G 1–0)																					
″	total	4	12	.250	4.73	28	19	3	118	119	72	55	0	1	1	1	37	6	0	.162	3	20	0	1	0.8	1.000
1953	NY A	2	0	1.000	3.66	8	4	0	19.2	17	13	11	0	0	0	1	5	0	0	.000	1	3	1	0	0.6	.800
1955	KC A	0	1	.000	6.75	2	0	0	4	3	5	2	0	0	1	1	0	0	0	—	0	0	0	0	0.0	.000
10 yrs.		82	78	.512	3.30	236	169	69	1320.2	1150	562	839	16	7	7	11	443	77	1	.174	46	311	19	20	1.6	.949
WORLD SERIES																										
1952	NY A	0	0	—	7.20	1	1	0	5	4	3	4	0	0	0	0	1	0	0	.000	0	1	0	0	1.0	1.000

George Blaeholder

BLAEHOLDER, GEORGE FRANKLIN BR TR 5′11″ 175 lbs.
B. Jan. 26, 1904, Orange, Calif. D. Dec. 29, 1947, Garden Grove, Calif.

Year	Team	W	L	PCT	ERA	G	GS	CG	IP	H	BB	SO	ShO	Relief Pitching W	L	SV	Batting AB	H	HR	BA	PO	A	E	DP	TC/G	FA
1925	STL A	0	0	—	31.50	2	0	0	2	6	1	1	0	0	0	0	0	0	0	—	0	0	0	0	0.0	.000
1927		0	1	.000	5.00	1	1	1	9	8	4	2	0	0	0	0	3	1	0	.333	1	3	0	0	4.0	1.000
1928		10	15	.400	4.37	38	26	9	214.1	235	52	87	1	1	0	3	71	15	2	.211	13	70	6	2	2.3	.933
1929		14	15	.483	4.18	42	24	13	222	237	61	72	**4**	4	3	2	74	9	1	.122	15	74	1	4	2.1	.989
1930		11	13	.458	4.61	37	23	10	191.1	235	46	70	1	1	2	4	65	12	0	.185	19	27	6	4	1.4	.885
1931		11	15	.423	4.53	35	32	13	226.1	280	56	79	1	0	1	0	77	11	0	.143	25	55	4	3	2.4	.952
1932		14	14	.500	4.70	42	36	16	258.1	304	76	80	1	0	1	0	88	12	0	.136	14	53	4	6	1.7	.944
1933		15	19	.441	4.72	38	36	14	255.2	283	69	63	3	2	0	0	77	14	0	.182	15	68	3	4	2.3	.965

George Blaeholder *continued*

Year	Team	Lg	W	L	PCT	ERA	G	GS	CG	IP	H	BB	SO	ShO	Relief Pitching W	Relief Pitching L	Relief Pitching SV	Batting AB	Batting H	Batting HR	BA	PO	A	E	DP	TC/G	FA
1934			14	18	.438	4.22	39	33	14	234.1	**276**	68	66	1	2	1	3	75	7	0	.093	16	43	3	6	1.6	.952
1935	2 teams	STL A	(6G 1–1)		PHI A	(23G 6–10)																					
″	total		7	11	.389	4.32	29	24	10	166.2	198	55	22	1	0	1	0	50	2	0	.040	11	46	7	3	2.2	.891
1936	CLE	A	8	4	.667	5.09	35	16	6	134.1	158	47	30	0	2	0	0	46	6	0	.130	12	30	2	1	1.3	.955
11 yrs.			104	125	.454	4.54	338	251	106	1914.1	2220	535	572	13	12	9	12	626	89	3	.142	141	469	36	33	1.9	.944

Bill Blair

BLAIR, WILLIAM ELLSWORTH BL TL 5′ 8½″ 172 lbs.
B. Sept. 17, 1863, Pittsburgh, Pa. D. Feb. 22, 1890, Pittsburgh, Pa.

Year	Team	Lg	W	L	PCT	ERA	G	GS	CG	IP	H	BB	SO	ShO	Relief Pitching W	Relief Pitching L	Relief Pitching SV	Batting AB	Batting H	Batting HR	BA	PO	A	E	DP	TC/G	FA
1888	PHI	AA	1	3	.250	2.61	4	4	3	31	29	8	16	0	0	0	0	13	4	0	.308	2	12	3	1	3.4	.824

Dennis Blair

BLAIR, DENNIS HERMAN BR TR 6′ 5″ 182 lbs.
B. June 5, 1954, Middletown, Ohio.

Year	Team	Lg	W	L	PCT	ERA	G	GS	CG	IP	H	BB	SO	ShO	Relief Pitching W	Relief Pitching L	Relief Pitching SV	Batting AB	Batting H	Batting HR	BA	PO	A	E	DP	TC/G	FA
1974	MON	N	11	7	.611	3.27	22	22	4	146	113	72	76	1	0	0	0	51	6	0	.118	10	34	4	3	2.2	.917
1975			8	15	.348	3.81	30	27	1	163	150	106	82	0	0	0	0	49	7	0	.143	8	21	1	2	1.0	.967
1976			0	2	.000	4.02	5	4	1	15.2	21	11	9	0	0	0	0	4	0	0	.000	1	2	0	0	0.6	1.000
1980	SD	N	0	1	.000	6.43	5	1	0	14	18	3	11	0	0	1	0	5	1	0	.200	0	0	0	0	0.0	.000
4 yrs.			19	25	.432	3.69	62	54	6	338.2	302	192	178	1	0	1	0	109	14	0	.128	19	57	5	5	1.3	.938

Willie Blair

BLAIR, WILLIAM ALLEN BR TR 6′ 1″ 185 lbs.
B. Dec. 18, 1965, Paintsville, Ky.

Year	Team	Lg	W	L	PCT	ERA	G	GS	CG	IP	H	BB	SO	ShO	Relief Pitching W	Relief Pitching L	Relief Pitching SV	Batting AB	Batting H	Batting HR	BA	PO	A	E	DP	TC/G	FA
1990	TOR	A	3	5	.375	4.06	27	6	0	68.2	66	28	43	0	3	2	0	0	0	0	—	3	6	0	0	0.3	1.000
1991	CLE	A	2	3	.400	6.75	11	5	0	36	58	10	13	0	0	1	0	0	0	0	—	2	5	0	1	0.6	1.000
1992	HOU	N	5	7	.417	4.00	29	8	0	78.2	74	25	48	0	4	2	0	17	1	0	.059	4	7	2	0	0.4	.846
1993	CLR	N	6	10	.375	4.75	46	18	1	146	184	42	84	0	2	0	0	36	4	0	.111	9	16	0	0	0.5	1.000
1994			0	5	.000	5.79	47	1	0	77.2	98	39	68	0	0	4	3	6	0	0	.000	3	7	1	0	0.2	.909
1995	SD	N	7	5	.583	4.34	40	12	0	114	112	45	83	0	3	1	0	24	0	0	.000	6	13	2	1	0.5	.905
6 yrs.			23	35	.397	4.75	200	50	1	521	592	189	339	0	12	10	3	83	5	0	.060	27	54	5	2	0.4	.942

Dick Blaisdell

BLAISDELL, HOWARD CARLETON
B. June 18, 1862, Bradford, Mass. D. Aug. 20, 1886, Malden, Mass.

Year	Team	Lg	W	L	PCT	ERA	G	GS	CG	IP	H	BB	SO	ShO	Relief Pitching W	Relief Pitching L	Relief Pitching SV	Batting AB	Batting H	Batting HR	BA	PO	A	E	DP	TC/G	FA
1884	KC	U	0	3	.000	*8.65*	3	3	3	26	49	4	8	0	0	0	0	16	5	0	.313	3	5	4	0	3.0	.667

Ed Blake

BLAKE, EDWARD JAMES BR TR 5′11″ 175 lbs.
B. Dec. 23, 1925, East St. Louis, Ill.

Year	Team	Lg	W	L	PCT	ERA	G	GS	CG	IP	H	BB	SO	ShO	Relief Pitching W	Relief Pitching L	Relief Pitching SV	Batting AB	Batting H	Batting HR	BA	PO	A	E	DP	TC/G	FA
1951	CIN	N	0	0	—	11.25	3	0	0	4	10	1	1	0	0	0	0	0	0	0	—	1	2	1	1	1.3	.750
1952			0	0	—	0.00	2	0	0	3	3	0	0	0	0	0	0	0	0	0	—	0	2	0	0	1.0	1.000
1953			0	0	—	∞	1	0	0		1	1	0	0	0	0	0	0	0	0	—	0	0	0	0	0.0	.000
1957	KC	A	0	0	—	5.40	2	0	0	1.2	1	2	0	0	0	0	0	0	0	0	—	0	0	0	0	0.0	.000
4 yrs.			0	0		8.31	8	0	0	8.2	15	4	1	0	0	0	0	0	0	0		1	4	1	1	0.8	.833

Sheriff Blake

BLAKE, JOHN FREDERICK BB TR 6′ 180 lbs.
B. Sept. 17, 1899, Ansted, W. Va. D. Oct. 31, 1982, Beckley, W. Va.

Year	Team	Lg	W	L	PCT	ERA	G	GS	CG	IP	H	BB	SO	ShO	Relief Pitching W	Relief Pitching L	Relief Pitching SV	Batting AB	Batting H	Batting HR	BA	PO	A	E	DP	TC/G	FA
1920	PIT	N	0	0	—	8.10	6	0	0	13.1	21	6	7	0	0	0	0	4	1	0	.250	1	2	0	1	0.5	1.000
1924	CHI	N	6	6	.500	4.57	29	11	4	106.1	123	44	42	0	2	2	1	31	9	0	.290	2	30	0	0	1.1	1.000
1925			10	18	.357	4.86	36	31	14	231.1	260	114	93	0	0	1	2	79	12	0	.152	7	52	2	6	1.7	.967
1926			11	12	.478	3.60	39	27	11	197.2	204	**92**	95	4	1	1	1	65	14	0	.215	9	54	1	1	1.6	.984
1927			13	14	.481	3.29	32	27	13	224.1	238	82	64	2	0	3	0	83	16	0	.193	10	64	4	5	2.4	.949
1928			17	11	.607	2.47	34	29	16	240.2	209	101	78	**4**	3	0	1	88	19	0	.216	4	48	3	3	1.6	.945
1929			14	13	.519	4.29	35	30	13	218.1	244	103	70	1	0	0	1	81	14	0	.173	6	43	2	1	1.5	.961
1930			10	14	.417	4.82	34	24	7	186.2	213	99	80	0	2	2	0	66	15	0	.227	7	50	1	4	1.7	.983
1931	2 teams	CHI N	(16G 0–4)		PHI N	(14G 4–5)																					
″	total		4	9	.308	5.43	30	14	1	121	154	61	60	0	0	3	1	41	14	0	.341	6	38	0	3	1.5	1.000
1937	2 teams	STL A	(15G 2–2)		STL N	(14G 0–3)																					
″	total		2	5	.286	5.49	29	3	2	80.1	100	38	32	0	2	3	1	20	4	0	.200	3	20	0	0	0.8	1.000
10 yrs.			87	102	.460	4.13	304	196	81	1620	1766	740	621	11	10	15	8	558	118	0	.211	55	401	13	24	1.5	.972
WORLD SERIES																											
1929	CHI	N	0	1	.000	13.50	2	0	0	1.1	4	0	1	0	0	1	0	1	1	0	1.000	0	2	0	0	1.0	1.000

Al Blanche

BLANCHE, PROSBY ALBERT BR TR 6′ 178 lbs.
Born Prosber Albert Belangio.
B. Sept. 21, 1909, Somerville, Mass.

Year	Team	Lg	W	L	PCT	ERA	G	GS	CG	IP	H	BB	SO	ShO	Relief Pitching W	Relief Pitching L	Relief Pitching SV	Batting AB	Batting H	Batting HR	BA	PO	A	E	DP	TC/G	FA
1935	BOS	N	0	0	—	1.56	6	0	0	17.1	14	5	4	0	0	0	0	6	1	0	.167	0	4	0	0	0.7	1.000
1936			0	1	.000	6.19	11	0	0	16	20	8	4	0	0	1	1	4	1	0	.250	3	7	2	0	1.1	.833
2 yrs.			0	1	.000	3.78	17	0	0	33.1	34	13	8	0	0	1	1	10	2	0	.200	3	11	2	0	0.9	.875

Gil Blanco

BLANCO, GILBERT HENRY BL TL 6′ 5″ 205 lbs.
B. Dec. 15, 1945, Phoenix, Ariz.

Year	Team	Lg	W	L	PCT	ERA	G	GS	CG	IP	H	BB	SO	ShO	Relief Pitching W	Relief Pitching L	Relief Pitching SV	Batting AB	Batting H	Batting HR	BA	PO	A	E	DP	TC/G	FA
1965	NY	A	1	1	.500	3.98	17	1	0	20.1	16	12	14	0	1	0	0	0	0	0	—	0	1	0	0	0.1	1.000
1966	KC	A	2	4	.333	4.70	11	8	0	38.1	31	36	21	0	0	0	0	12	2	0	.167	0	9	1	0	0.9	.900
2 yrs.			3	5	.375	4.45	28	9	0	58.2	47	48	35	0	1	0	0	12	2	0	.167	0	10	1	0	0.4	.909

Fred Blanding

BLANDING, FREDERICK JAMES (Fritz) BR TR 6′ 185 lbs.
B. Feb. 8, 1888, Redlands, Calif. D. July 16, 1950, Salem, Va.

Year	Team	Lg	W	L	PCT	ERA	G	GS	CG	IP	H	BB	SO	ShO	Relief Pitching W	Relief Pitching L	Relief Pitching SV	Batting AB	Batting H	Batting HR	BA	PO	A	E	DP	TC/G	FA
1910	CLE	A	2	2	.500	2.78	6	5	4	45.1	43	12	25	1	0	0	0	18	2	0	.111	0	12	0	0	2.0	1.000
1911			7	11	.389	3.68	29	16	11	176	190	60	80	0	4	1	2	65	17	0	.262	8	49	4	4	2.1	.934
1912			18	14	.563	2.92	39	31	23	262	259	79	75	1	3	0	1	93	21	1	.226	9	77	4	6	2.3	.956
1913			15	10	.600	2.55	41	22	14	215	234	72	63	3	4	1	0	86	21	0	.244	4	58	5	0	1.6	.925
1914			3	9	.250	3.96	29	12	5	116	133	54	35	0	0	1	1	39	4	0	.103	2	43	5	1	1.7	.900
5 yrs.			45	46	.495	3.13	144	86	57	814.1	859	277	278	5	11	3	4	301	65	1	.216	23	239	18	11	1.9	.936

Fred Blank

BLANK, FREDERICK AUGUST BL TL 6′½″ 175 lbs.
B. June 18, 1874, DeSoto, Mo. D. Feb. 5, 1936, St. Louis, Mo.

Year	Team	W	L	PCT	ERA	G	GS	CG	IP	H	BB	SO	ShO	Relief W	Relief L	Relief SV	AB	H	HR	BA	PO	A	E	DP	TC/G	FA
1894	CIN N	0	1	.000	4.50	1	1	1	8	5	9	1	0	0	0	0	3	0	0	.000	0	4	0	0	4.0	1.000

Homer Blankenship

BLANKENSHIP, HOMER (Si) BR TR 6′ 185 lbs.
Brother of Ted Blankenship.
B. Aug. 4, 1902, Bonham, Tex. D. June 22, 1974, Longview, Tex.

Year	Team	W	L	PCT	ERA	G	GS	CG	IP	H	BB	SO	ShO	Relief W	Relief L	Relief SV	AB	H	HR	BA	PO	A	E	DP	TC/G	FA
1922	CHI A	0	0	—	4.85	4	0	0	13	21	5	3	0	0	0	0	4	0	0	.000	1	2	0	0	0.8	1.000
1923		1	1	.500	3.60	4	0	0	5	9	1	1	0	1	1	1	0	0	0	—	0	2	0	0	0.5	1.000
1928	PIT N	0	2	.000	5.82	5	2	1	21.2	27	9	6	0	0	0	0	8	3	0	.375	1	8	0	0	1.8	1.000
3 yrs.		1	3	.250	5.22	13	2	1	39.2	57	15	10	0	1	1	1	12	3	0	.250	2	12	0	0	1.1	1.000

Kevin Blankenship

BLANKENSHIP, KEVIN DeWAYNE BR TR 6′ 180 lbs.
B. Jan. 26, 1963, Anaheim, Calif.

Year	Team	W	L	PCT	ERA	G	GS	CG	IP	H	BB	SO	ShO	Relief W	Relief L	Relief SV	AB	H	HR	BA	PO	A	E	DP	TC/G	FA
1988	2 teams ATL N (2G 0–1) CHI N (1G 1–0)																									
"	total	1	1	.500	4.60	3	3	0	15.2	14	8	9	0	0	0	0	6	0	0	.000	1	0	0	0	0.3	1.000
1989	CHI N	0	0	—	1.69	2	0	0	5.1	4	2	2	0	0	0	0	1	0	0	.000	1	0	0	0	0.5	1.000
1990		0	2	.000	5.84	3	2	0	12.1	13	6	5	0	0	0	0	4	0	0	.000	1	2	1	0	1.3	.750
3 yrs.		1	3	.250	4.59	8	5	0	33.1	31	16	16	0	0	0	0	11	0	0	.000	3	2	1	0	0.8	.833

Ted Blankenship

BLANKENSHIP, THEODORE BR TR 6′ 1″ 170 lbs.
Brother of Homer Blankenship.
B. May 10, 1901, Bonham, Tex. D. Jan. 14, 1945, Atoka, Okla.

Year	Team	W	L	PCT	ERA	G	GS	CG	IP	H	BB	SO	ShO	Relief W	Relief L	Relief SV	AB	H	HR	BA	PO	A	E	DP	TC/G	FA
1922	CHI A	8	10	.444	3.81	24	15	7	127.2	124	47	42	0	3	1	1	41	7	0	.171	3	31	0	4	1.4	1.000
1923		9	14	.391	4.27	44	23	9	208.2	219	100	57	1	3	3	0	76	16	3	.211	10	51	3	1	1.5	.953
1924		7	6	.538	5.17	25	11	7	125.1	167	38	36	0	1	3	1	46	15	1	.326	1	22	1	1	1.0	.958
1925		17	8	.680	3.16	40	23	16	222	218	69	81	3	3	3	1	88	18	2	.205	4	38	2	3	1.1	.955
1926		13	10	.565	3.61	29	26	15	209.1	217	65	66	1	1	0	1	76	10	0	.132	4	42	0	1	1.6	1.000
1927		12	17	.414	5.06	37	34	11	236.2	280	74	51	3	0	0	0	80	15	3	.188	7	48	2	3	1.5	.965
1928		9	11	.450	4.61	27	22	8	158	186	80	36	0	0	0	0	59	10	0	.169	2	31	1	3	1.3	.971
1929		0	2	.000	8.84	8	1	0	18.1	28	9	7	0	0	1	0	4	1	0	.250	1	1	0	0	0.3	1.000
1930		2	1	.667	9.20	7	1	0	14.2	23	7	2	0	2	0	0	5	1	0	.200	0	1	0	0	0.1	1.000
9 yrs.		77	79	.494	4.32	241	156	73	1320.2	1462	489	378	8	13	11	4	475	93	9	.196	32	265	9	16	1.3	.971

Cy Blanton

BLANTON, DARRELL ELIJAH BL TR 5′11½″ 180 lbs.
B. July 6, 1908, Waurika, Okla. D. Sept. 13, 1945, Norman, Okla.

Year	Team	W	L	PCT	ERA	G	GS	CG	IP	H	BB	SO	ShO	Relief W	Relief L	Relief SV	AB	H	HR	BA	PO	A	E	DP	TC/G	FA
1934	PIT N	0	1	.000	3.38	1	1	0	8	5	4	5	0	0	0	0	1	0	0	.000	0	2	0	0	2.0	1.000
1935		18	13	.581	**2.58**	35	31	23	254.1	220	55	142	**4**	1	2	1	97	13	0	.134	10	60	2	1	2.1	.972
1936		13	15	.464	3.51	44	32	15	235.2	235	55	127	**4**	0	5	3	84	13	0	.155	16	50	3	0	1.6	.957
1937		14	12	.538	3.30	36	**34**	14	242.2	250	76	143	4	0	0	0	85	14	0	.165	9	48	5	5	1.7	.919
1938		11	7	.611	3.70	29	26	10	172.2	190	46	80	1	0	0	0	64	13	0	.203	7	42	2	7	1.8	.961
1939		2	3	.400	4.29	10	6	1	42	45	10	11	0	0	0	0	14	4	0	.286	1	9	1	0	1.1	.909
1940	PHI N	4	3	.571	4.32	13	10	5	77	82	21	24	0	0	0	0	24	2	0	.083	4	16	0	0	1.5	1.000
1941		6	13	.316	4.51	28	25	7	163.2	186	57	64	1	0	0	0	51	6	0	.118	3	22	2	0	1.0	.926
1942		0	4	.000	5.64	6	3	0	22.1	30	13	15	0	0	1	0	8	1	0	.125	1	4	0	0	0.8	1.000
9 yrs.		68	71	.489	3.55	202	168	75	1218.1	1243	337	611	14	1	8	4	428	66	0	.154	51	253	15	13	1.6	.953

Wade Blasingame

BLASINGAME, WADE ALLEN BL TL 6′ 1″ 185 lbs.
B. Nov. 22, 1943, Deming, N. M.

Year	Team	W	L	PCT	ERA	G	GS	CG	IP	H	BB	SO	ShO	Relief W	Relief L	Relief SV	AB	H	HR	BA	PO	A	E	DP	TC/G	FA
1963	MIL N	0	0	—	12.00	2	0	0	3	7	2	6	0	0	0	0	0	0	0	—	0	1	0	0	0.5	1.000
1964		9	5	.643	4.24	28	13	3	116.2	113	51	70	1	1	1	2	40	7	1	.175	5	23	0	2	1.0	1.000
1965		16	10	.615	3.77	38	36	10	224.2	200	116	117	1	1	0	1	81	15	1	.185	21	41	0	3	1.6	1.000
1966	ATL N	3	7	.300	5.32	16	12	0	67.2	71	25	34	0	0	0	0	23	5	0	.217	4	10	1	1	0.9	.933
1967	2 teams ATL N (10G 1–0) HOU N (15G 4–7)																									
"	total	5	7	.417	5.63	25	18	0	102.1	118	48	66	0	1	0	0	29	5	0	.172	8	16	0	0	1.0	1.000
1968	HOU N	1	2	.333	4.75	22	2	0	36	45	10	22	0	1	2	1	5	0	0	.000	1	10	0	1	0.5	1.000
1969		0	5	.000	5.37	26	5	0	52	66	33	33	0	0	0	1	12	0	0	.000	5	9	3	0	0.7	.824
1970		3	3	.500	3.46	13	13	1	78	76	23	55	0	0	0	0	24	2	0	.083	2	15	1	0	1.4	.944
1971		9	11	.450	4.61	30	28	2	158	177	45	93	0	0	0	0	49	10	1	.204	8	29	1	1	1.3	.974
1972	2 teams HOU N (10G 0–0) NY A (12G 0–1)																									
"	total	0	1	.000	5.76	22	1	0	25	18	19	16	0	0	0	0	2	0	0	.000	6	6	0	0	0.5	1.000
10 yrs.		46	51	.474	4.52	222	128	16	863.1	891	372	512	2	4	3	5	265	44	3	.166	60	160	6	8	1.0	.973

Steve Blass

BLASS, STEPHEN ROBERT BR TR 6′ 165 lbs.
B. Apr. 18, 1942, Canaan, Conn.

Year	Team	W	L	PCT	ERA	G	GS	CG	IP	H	BB	SO	ShO	Relief W	Relief L	Relief SV	AB	H	HR	BA	PO	A	E	DP	TC/G	FA
1964	PIT N	5	8	.385	4.04	24	13	3	104.2	107	45	67	1	1	1	0	30	2	0	.067	10	18	2	2	1.3	.933
1966		11	7	.611	3.87	34	25	1	155.2	173	46	76	0	2	1	0	52	12	0	.231	6	15	3	1	0.7	.875
1967		6	8	.429	3.55	32	16	2	126.2	126	47	72	0	1	1	0	39	5	0	.128	7	23	1	2	1.0	.968
1968		18	6	**.750**	2.12	33	31	12	220.1	191	57	132	7	0	0	0	80	11	0	.138	22	27	0	1	1.4	1.000
1969		16	10	.615	4.46	38	32	9	210	207	86	147	0	0	0	2	84	21	1	.250	21	41	2	3	1.7	.969
1970		10	12	.455	3.52	31	31	6	197	187	73	120	1	0	0	0	70	8	0	.114	21	26	2	1	1.6	.959
1971		15	8	.652	2.85	33	33	12	240	226	68	136	**5**	0	0	0	83	10	0	.120	27	36	4	2	2.0	.940
1972		19	8	.704	2.49	33	32	11	249.2	227	84	117	2	0	0	0	82	15	0	.183	15	46	2	6	1.9	.968
1973		3	9	.250	9.85	23	18	1	88.2	109	84	27	0	0	0	0	24	10	0	.417	8	18	0	1	1.1	1.000
1974		0	0	—	9.00	1	0	0	5	5	7	2	0	0	0	0	2	0	0	.000	0	1	0	0	1.0	1.000
10 yrs.		103	76	.575	3.63	282	231	57	1597.2	1558	597	896	16	4	3	2	546	94	1	.172	137	251	16	19	1.4	.960
LEAGUE CHAMPIONSHIP SERIES																										
1971	PIT N	0	1	.000	11.57	2	2	0	7	14	2	11	0	0	0	0	1	0	0	.000	1	0	0	0	0.5	1.000
1972		1	0	1.000	1.72	2	2	0	15.2	12	6	5	0	0	0	0	6	0	0	.000	1	3	0	0	2.0	1.000
2 yrs.		1	1	.500	4.76	4	4	0	22.2	26	8	16	0	0	0	0	7	0	0	.000	2	3	0	0	1.3	1.000
WORLD SERIES																										
1971	PIT N	2	0	1.000	1.00	2	2	2	18	7	4	13	0	0	0	0	7	0	0	.000	2	4	0	0	3.0	1.000

Steve Blateric

BLATERIC, STEPHEN LAWRENCE
B. Mar. 20, 1944, Denver, Colo.
BR TR 6′ 3″ 200 lbs.

Year	Team	Lg	W	L	PCT	ERA	G	GS	CG	IP	H	BB	SO	ShO	Relief W	Relief L	Relief SV	Batting AB	Batting H	Batting HR	BA	PO	A	E	DP	TC/G	FA
1971	**CIN**	**N**	0	0	—	12.00	2	0	0	3	5	0	4	0	0	0	0	0	0	0	—	0	1	0	0	0.5	1.000
1972	**NY**	**A**	0	0	—	0.00	1	0	0	4	2	0	4	0	0	0	0	1	0	0	.000	0	1	0	1	1.0	1.000
1975	**CAL**	**A**	0	0	—	6.23	2	0	0	4.1	9	1	5	0	0	0	0	0	0	0	—	0	0	0	0	0.0	.000
3 yrs.			0	0		5.56	5	0	0	11.1	16	1	13	0	0	0	0	1	0	0	.000	0	2	0	1	0.4	1.000

Henry Blauvelt

BLAUVELT, HENRY RUSSELL
B. Apr. 8, 1873, Rochester, N. Y. D. Dec. 28, 1926, Portland, Ore.

Year	Team	Lg	W	L	PCT	ERA	G	GS	CG	IP	H	BB	SO	ShO	Relief W	Relief L	Relief SV	Batting AB	Batting H	Batting HR	BA	PO	A	E	DP	TC/G	FA
1890	**ROC**	**AA**	0	0	—	*10.22*	2	0	0	12.1	19	8	5	0	0	0	0	6	3	0	.500	1	4	1	1	3.0	.833

Bob Blaylock

BLAYLOCK, ROBERT EDWARD
B. June 28, 1935, Chattanooga, Tenn.
BR TR 6′ 1″ 185 lbs.

Year	Team	Lg	W	L	PCT	ERA	G	GS	CG	IP	H	BB	SO	ShO	Relief W	Relief L	Relief SV	Batting AB	Batting H	Batting HR	BA	PO	A	E	DP	TC/G	FA
1956	**STL**	**N**	1	6	.143	6.37	14	6	0	41	45	24	39	0	1	1	0	11	1	0	.091	1	8	0	0	0.6	1.000
1959			0	1	.000	4.00	3	1	0	9	8	3	3	0	0	1	0	1	0	0	.000	0	2	0	0	0.7	1.000
2 yrs.			1	7	.125	5.94	17	7	0	50	53	27	42	0	1	2	0	12	1	0	.083	1	10	0	0	0.6	1.000

Gary Blaylock

BLAYLOCK, GARY NELSON
B. Oct. 11, 1931, Clarkton, Mo.
BR TR 6′ 196 lbs.

Year	Team	Lg	W	L	PCT	ERA	G	GS	CG	IP	H	BB	SO	ShO	Relief W	Relief L	Relief SV	Batting AB	Batting H	Batting HR	BA	PO	A	E	DP	TC/G	FA
1959	**2 teams**	**STL N** (26G 4–5) **NY A** (15G 0–1)																									
″	**total**		4	6	.400	4.80	41	13	3	125.2	147	58	81	0	1	1	0	36	5	2	.139	13	18	2	1	0.8	.939

Ray Blemker

BLEMKER, RAYMOND (Buddy)
B. Aug. 9, 1937, Huntingburg, Ind. D. Feb. 15, 1994, Evansville, Ind.
BR TL 5′11″ 190 lbs.

Year	Team	Lg	W	L	PCT	ERA	G	GS	CG	IP	H	BB	SO	ShO	Relief W	Relief L	Relief SV	Batting AB	Batting H	Batting HR	BA	PO	A	E	DP	TC/G	FA
1960	**KC**	**A**	0	0	—	27.00	1	0	0	1.2	3	2	0	0	0	0	0	0	0	0	—	0	0	0	0	0.0	.000

Clarence Blethen

BLETHEN, CLARENCE WALDO (Climax)
B. July 11, 1893, Dover-Foxcroft, Me. D. Apr. 11, 1973, Frederick, Md.
BL TR 5′11″ 165 lbs.

Year	Team	Lg	W	L	PCT	ERA	G	GS	CG	IP	H	BB	SO	ShO	Relief W	Relief L	Relief SV	Batting AB	Batting H	Batting HR	BA	PO	A	E	DP	TC/G	FA
1923	**BOS**	**A**	0	0	—	7.13	5	0	0	17.2	29	7	2	0	0	0	0	6	0	0	.000	1	1	0	0	0.4	1.000
1929	**BKN**	**N**	0	0	—	9.00	2	0	0	2	4	3	0	0	0	0	0	0	0	0	—	0	2	0	0	1.0	1.000
2 yrs.			0	0		7.32	7	0	0	19.2	33	10	2	0	0	0	0	6	0	0	.000	1	3	0	0	0.6	1.000

Bob Blewett

BLEWETT, ROBERT LAWRENCE
B. June 28, 1877, Fond du Lac, Wis. D. Mar. 17, 1958, Sedro Woolley, Wash.
BL TL 5′11″ 170 lbs.

Year	Team	Lg	W	L	PCT	ERA	G	GS	CG	IP	H	BB	SO	ShO	Relief W	Relief L	Relief SV	Batting AB	Batting H	Batting HR	BA	PO	A	E	DP	TC/G	FA
1902	**NY**	**N**	0	2	.000	4.82	5	3	2	28	39	7	8	0	0	0	0	10	0	0	.000	0	3	3	0	1.2	.500

Elmer Bliss

BLISS, ELMER WARD
B. Mar. 9, 1875, Penfield, Pa. D. Mar. 18, 1962, Bradford, Pa.
BL TR 6′ 180 lbs.

Year	Team	Lg	W	L	PCT	ERA	G	GS	CG	IP	H	BB	SO	ShO	Relief W	Relief L	Relief SV	Batting AB	Batting H	Batting HR	BA	PO	A	E	DP	TC/G	FA
1903	**NY**	**A**	1	0	1.000	0.00	1	0	0	6	4	0	3	0	1	0	0	*				0	0	0	0	0.0	.000

Terry Blocker

BLOCKER, TERRY FENNELL
B. Aug. 18, 1959, Columbia, S. C.
BL TL 6′ 2″ 195 lbs.

Year	Team	Lg	W	L	PCT	ERA	G	GS	CG	IP	H	BB	SO	ShO	Relief W	Relief L	Relief SV	Batting AB	Batting H	Batting HR	BA	PO	A	E	DP	TC/G	FA
1989	**ATL**	**N**	0	0	—	0.00	1	0	0	1	0	2	0	0	0	0	0	*				4	0	0	0	0.8	1.000

Ben Blomdahl

BLOMDAHL, BENJAMIN EARL
B. Dec. 30, 1970, Long Beach, Calif.
BR TR 6′ 2″ 185 lbs.

Year	Team	Lg	W	L	PCT	ERA	G	GS	CG	IP	H	BB	SO	ShO	Relief W	Relief L	Relief SV	Batting AB	Batting H	Batting HR	BA	PO	A	E	DP	TC/G	FA
1995	**DET**	**A**	0	0	—	7.77	14	0	0	24.1	36	13	15	0	0	0	1	0	0	0	—	1	6	0	0	0.5	1.000

Joe Blong

BLONG, JOSEPH MYLES
B. Sept. 17, 1853, St. Louis, Mo. D. Sept. 16, 1892, St. Louis, Mo.
BR TR

Year	Team	Lg	W	L	PCT	ERA	G	GS	CG	IP	H	BB	SO	ShO	Relief W	Relief L	Relief SV	Batting AB	Batting H	Batting HR	BA	PO	A	E	DP	TC/G	FA
1876	**STL**	**N**	0	0	—	0.00	1	0	0	4	2	1	0	0	0	0	0	264	62	0	.235	64	15	9	2	1.4	.898
1877			10	9	.526	2.74	25	21	17	187.1	203	38	51	0	0	0	0	218	47	0	.216	73	30	18	0	1.9	.851
2 yrs.			10	9	.526	2.68	26	21	17	191.1	205	39	51	0	0	0	0	*				137	45	27	2	1.6	.871

Vida Blue

BLUE, VIDA ROCHELLE
B. July 28, 1949, Mansfield, La.
BB TL 6′ 189 lbs.
BL 1969

Year	Team	Lg	W	L	PCT	ERA	G	GS	CG	IP	H	BB	SO	ShO	Relief W	Relief L	Relief SV	Batting AB	Batting H	Batting HR	BA	PO	A	E	DP	TC/G	FA
1969	**OAK**	**A**	1	1	.500	6.21	12	4	0	42	49	18	24	0	0	0	1	10	0	0	.000	1	4	0	0	0.4	1.000
1970			2	0	1.000	2.08	6	6	2	39	20	12	35	2	0	0	0	15	3	1	.200	1	7	0	0	1.3	1.000
1971			24	8	.750	**1.82**	39	39	24	312	209	88	301	**8**	0	0	0	102	12	0	.118	15	24	0	0	1.0	1.000
1972			6	10	.375	2.80	25	23	5	151.1	117	48	111	4	0	1	0	45	2	0	.044	4	17	2	0	0.9	.913
1973			20	9	.690	3.28	37	37	13	263.2	214	105	158	4	0	0	0	1	0	0	.000	9	30	0	0	1.1	1.000
1974			17	15	.531	3.26	40	40	12	282	246	98	174	1	0	0	0	0	0	0	—	10	16	3	0	0.7	.897
1975			22	11	.667	3.01	39	38	13	278	243	99	189	2	0	0	1	0	0	0	—	4	34	1	1	1.0	.974
1976			18	13	.581	2.36	37	37	20	298	268	63	166	6	0	0	0	0	0	0	—	3	34	1	2	1.0	.974
1977			14	**19**	.424	3.83	38	38	16	280	**284**	86	157	1	0	0	0	1	0	0	.000	6	42	3	2	1.3	.941
1978	**SF**	**N**	18	10	.643	2.79	35	35	9	258	233	70	171	4	0	0	0	79	6	1	.076	12	29	0	4	1.2	1.000
1979			14	14	.500	5.01	34	34	10	237	246	111	138	0	0	0	0	83	10	1	.120	10	42	1	5	1.6	.981
1980			14	10	.583	2.97	31	31	10	224	202	61	129	3	0	0	0	68	5	0	.074	14	42	1	4	1.8	.982
1981			8	6	.571	2.45	18	18	1	125	97	54	63	0	0	0	0	35	7	0	.200	11	29	1	1	2.3	.976
1982	**KC**	**A**	13	12	.520	3.78	31	31	6	181	163	80	103	2	0	0	0	0	0	0	—	14	22	2	0	1.2	.947
1983			0	5	.000	6.01	19	14	1	85.1	96	35	53	0	0	0	0	0	0	0	—	3	10	0	1	0.7	1.000
1985	**SF**	**N**	8	8	.500	4.47	33	20	1	131	115	80	103	0	2	1	0	30	4	0	.133	7	21	2	1	0.9	.933
1986			10	10	.500	3.27	28	28	0	156.2	137	77	100	0	0	0	0	43	4	1	.093	3	24	2	0	1.0	.931
17 yrs.			209	161	.565	3.26	502	473	143	3344	2939	1185	2175	37	2	2	2	512	53	4	.104	127	427	19	21	1.1	.967
LEAGUE CHAMPIONSHIP SERIES																											
1971	**OAK**	**A**	0	1	.000	6.43	1	1	0	7	7	2	8	0	0	0	0	3	0	0	.000	0	1	0	0	1.0	1.000
1972			0	0	—	0.00	4	0	0	5.1	4	1	5	0	0	0	1	1	0	0	.000	0	1	0	0	0.3	1.000
1973			0	1	.000	10.29	2	2	0	7	8	5	3	0	0	0	0	0	0	0	—	1	0	0	0	0.5	1.000
1974			1	0	1.000	0.00	1	1	1	9	2	0	7	1	0	0	0	0	0	0	—	0	1	0	0	1.0	1.000
1975			0	0	—	9.00	1	1	0	3	6	0	2	0	0	0	0	0	0	0	—	0	0	0	0	0.0	.000
5 yrs.			1	2	.333	4.60	9	5	1	31.1	27	8	25	1 **1st**	0	0	1	4	0	0	.000	1	3	0	0	0.4	1.000

Vida Blue *continued*

Year	Team	Lg	W	L	PCT	ERA	G	GS	CG	IP	H	BB	SO	ShO	Relief Pitching W	L	SV	Batting AB	H	HR	BA	PO	A	E	DP	TC/G	FA
WORLD SERIES																											
1972	**OAK**	**A**	0	1	.000	4.15	4	1	0	8.2	8	5	5	0	0	0	1	1	0	0	.000	0	1	0	0	0.3	1.000
1973			0	1	.000	4.91	2	2	0	11	10	3	8	0	0	0	0	4	0	0	.000	2	1	0	0	1.5	1.000
1974			0	1	.000	3.29	2	2	0	13.2	10	7	9	0	0	0	0	4	0	0	.000	0	3	0	0	1.5	1.000
3 yrs.			0	3	.000	4.05	8	5	0	33.1	28	15	22	0	0	0	1	9	0	0	.000	2	5	0	0	0.9	1.000

Jim Bluejacket

BLUEJACKET, JAMES
Born James Smith.
B. July 8, 1887, Adair, Okla. D. Mar. 26, 1947, Pekin, Ill.
BR TR 6′ 2½″ 200 lbs.

Year	Team	Lg	W	L	PCT	ERA	G	GS	CG	IP	H	BB	SO	ShO	Relief Pitching W	L	SV	Batting AB	H	HR	BA	PO	A	E	DP	TC/G	FA
1914	**BKN**	**F**	4	5	.444	3.76	17	7	3	67	77	19	29	1	1	1	1	22	3	0	.136	3	24	0	0	1.6	1.000
1915			9	11	.450	3.15	24	21	10	162.2	155	75	48	2	1	0	0	61	8	0	.131	7	35	6	2	2.0	.875
1916	**CIN**	**N**	0	1	.000	7.71	3	2	0	7	12	3	1	0	0	0	0	2	0	0	.000	0	1	0	0	0.3	1.000
3 yrs.			13	17	.433	3.46	44	30	13	236.2	244	97	78	3	2	1	1	85	11	0	.129	10	60	6	2	1.7	.921

Clint Blume

BLUME, CLINTON WILLIS
B. Oct. 17, 1898, Brooklyn, N. Y. D. June 12, 1973, Islip, N. Y.
BR TR 5′11″ 175 lbs.

Year	Team	Lg	W	L	PCT	ERA	G	GS	CG	IP	H	BB	SO	ShO	Relief Pitching W	L	SV	Batting AB	H	HR	BA	PO	A	E	DP	TC/G	FA
1922	**NY**	**N**	1	0	1.000	1.00	1	1	1	9	7	1	2	0	0	0	0	1	1	0	1.000	0	0	1	0	1.0	.000
1923			2	0	1.000	3.75	12	1	0	24	22	20	2	0	2	0	0	5	0	0	.000	0	4	0	0	0.3	1.000
2 yrs.			3	0	1.000	3.00	13	2	1	33	29	21	4	0	2	0	0	6	1	0	.167	0	4	1	0	0.4	.800

Bert Blyleven

BLYLEVEN, RIK AALBERT
B. Apr. 6, 1951, Zeist, Netherlands.
BR TR 6′ 3″ 200 lbs.

Year	Team	Lg	W	L	PCT	ERA	G	GS	CG	IP	H	BB	SO	ShO	Relief Pitching W	L	SV	Batting AB	H	HR	BA	PO	A	E	DP	TC/G	FA
1970	**MIN**	**A**	10	9	.526	3.18	27	25	5	164	143	47	135	1	0	1	0	50	7	0	.140	5	16	1	1	0.8	.955
1971			16	15	.516	2.82	38	38	17	278	267	59	224	5	0	0	0	91	12	0	.132	19	38	2	0	1.6	.966
1972			17	17	.500	2.73	39	38	11	287	247	69	228	3	0	1	0	94	15	0	.160	18	45	3	4	1.7	.955
1973			20	17	.541	2.52	40	40	25	325	296	67	258	**9**	0	0	0	0	0	0	—	21	34	1	0	1.4	.982
1974			17	17	.500	2.66	37	37	19	281	244	77	249	3	0	0	0	0	0	0	—	19	34	3	2	1.5	.946
1975			15	10	.600	3.00	35	35	20	275.2	219	84	233	3	0	0	0	0	0	0	—	16	48	6	5	2.0	.914
1976	**2 teams**	**MIN A**	(12G 4–5)	**TEX A**	(24G 9–11)																						
″	**total**		13	16	.448	2.87	36	36	18	297.2	283	81	219	6	0	0	0	0	0	0		22	44	0	4	1.8	1.000
1977	**TEX**	**A**	14	12	.538	2.72	30	30	15	235	181	69	182	5	0	0	0	0	0	0	—	10	35	1	4	1.5	.978
1978	**PIT**	**N**	14	10	.583	3.02	34	34	11	244	217	66	182	4	0	0	0	85	11	0	.129	11	41	1	4	1.6	.981
1979			12	5	.706	3.61	37	37	4	237	238	92	172	0	0	0	0	70	9	0	.129	14	20	0	0	0.9	1.000
1980			8	13	.381	3.82	34	32	5	217	219	59	168	2	0	0	0	61	5	0	.082	10	30	2	2	1.2	.952
1981	**CLE**	**A**	11	7	.611	2.89	20	20	9	159	145	40	107	1	0	0	0	0	0	0	—	9	16	1	2	1.3	.962
1982			2	2	.500	4.87	4	4	0	20.1	16	11	19	0	0	0	0	0	0	0	—	2	2	0	0	1.0	1.000
1983			7	10	.412	3.91	24	24	5	156.1	160	44	123	0	0	0	0	0	0	0	—	7	26	1	3	1.4	.971
1984			19	7	.731	2.87	33	32	12	245	204	74	170	4	0	0	0	0	0	0	—	21	30	2	2	1.6	.962
1985	**2 teams**	**CLE A**	(23G 9–11)	**MIN A**	(14G 8–5)																						
″	**total**		17	16	.515	3.16	37	**37**	**24**	**293.2**	264	75	**206**	5	0	0	0	0	0	0		17	32	0	2	1.3	1.000
1986	**MIN**	**A**	17	14	.548	4.01	36	36	16	**271.2**	262	58	215	3	0	0	0	0	0	0	—	15	31	0	0	1.3	1.000
1987			15	12	.556	4.01	37	37	8	267	249	101	196	1	0	0	0	0	0	0	—	17	43	4	3	1.7	.938
1988			10	**17**	.370	5.43	33	33	7	207.1	240	51	145	0	0	0	0	0	0	0	—	12	22	1	3	1.1	.971
1989	**CAL**	**A**	17	5	.773	2.73	33	33	8	241	225	44	131	**5**	0	0	0	0	0	0	—	14	38	0	6	1.6	1.000
1990			8	7	.533	5.24	23	23	2	134	163	25	69	0	0	0	0	0	0	0	—	3	24	1	0	1.2	.964
1992			8	12	.400	4.74	25	24	1	133	150	29	70	0	0	0	0	0	0	0	—	5	13	0	1	0.7	1.000
22 yrs.			287	250	.534	3.31	692	685	242	4969.2	4632	1322	3701	60	0	2	0	451	59	0	.131	287	662	30	48	1.4	.969
				10th									**3rd**	**9th**													
LEAGUE CHAMPIONSHIP SERIES																											
1970	**MIN**	**A**	0	0	—	0.00	1	0	0	2	2	0	2	0	0	0	0	0	0	0	—	1	0	0	0	1.0	1.000
1979	**PIT**	**N**	1	0	1.000	1.00	1	1	1	9	8	0	9	0	0	0	0	3	1	0	.333	1	1	0	0	2.0	1.000
1987	**MIN**	**A**	2	0	1.000	4.05	2	2	0	13.1	12	3	9	0	0	0	0	0	0	0	—	0	1	0	0	0.5	1.000
3 yrs.			3	0	1.000	2.59	4	3	1	24.1	22	3	20	0	0	0	0	3	1	0	.333	2	2	0	0	1.0	1.000
WORLD SERIES																											
1979	**PIT**	**N**	1	0	1.000	1.80	2	1	0	10	8	3	4	0	1	0	0	3	0	0	.000	0	1	0	1	0.5	1.000
1987	**MIN**	**A**	1	1	.500	2.77	2	2	0	13	13	2	12	0	0	0	0	1	0	0	.000	0	1	0	0	0.5	1.000
2 yrs.			2	1	.667	2.35	4	3	0	23	21	5	16	0	1	0	0	4	0	0	.000	0	2	0	1	0.5	1.000

Mike Blyzka

BLYZKA, MICHAEL JOHN
B. Dec. 25, 1928, Hamtramck, Mich.
BR TR 5′11½″ 190 lbs.

Year	Team	Lg	W	L	PCT	ERA	G	GS	CG	IP	H	BB	SO	ShO	Relief Pitching W	L	SV	Batting AB	H	HR	BA	PO	A	E	DP	TC/G	FA
1953	**STL**	**A**	2	6	.250	6.39	33	9	2	94.1	110	56	23	0	1	1	0	23	0	0	.000	6	13	0	1	0.6	1.000
1954	**BAL**	**A**	1	5	.167	4.69	37	0	0	86.1	83	51	35	0	1	5	1	15	2	0	.133	4	17	1	0	0.6	.955
2 yrs.			3	11	.214	5.58	70	9	2	180.2	193	107	58	0	2	6	1	38	2	0	.053	10	30	1	1	0.6	.976

Charlie Boardman

BOARDMAN, CHARLES LOUIS
B. Apr. 27, 1893, Seneca Falls, N. Y. D. Aug. 10, 1968, Sacramento, Calif.
BL TL 6′ 2½″ 194 lbs.

Year	Team	Lg	W	L	PCT	ERA	G	GS	CG	IP	H	BB	SO	ShO	Relief Pitching W	L	SV	Batting AB	H	HR	BA	PO	A	E	DP	TC/G	FA
1913	**PHI**	**A**	0	2	.000	2.00	2	2	1	9	10	6	4	0	0	0	0	3	0	0	.000	0	1	0	0	0.5	1.000
1914			0	0	—	4.91	2	0	0	7.1	10	4	2	0	0	0	0	2	0	0	.000	0	2	0	0	1.0	1.000
1915	**STL**	**N**	1	0	1.000	1.42	3	1	1	19	12	15	7	0	0	0	0	7	2	0	.286	0	4	0	0	1.3	1.000
3 yrs.			1	2	.333	2.29	7	3	2	35.1	32	25	13	0	0	0	0	12	2	0	.167	0	7	0	0	1.0	1.000

Doug Bochtler

BOCHTLER, DOUGLAS EUGENE
B. July 5, 1970, West Palm Beach, Fla.
BR TR 6′ 3″ 205 lbs.

Year	Team	Lg	W	L	PCT	ERA	G	GS	CG	IP	H	BB	SO	ShO	Relief Pitching W	L	SV	Batting AB	H	HR	BA	PO	A	E	DP	TC/G	FA
1995	**SD**	**N**	4	4	.500	3.57	34	0	0	45.1	38	19	45	0	4	4	1	2	0	0	.000	1	7	0	1	0.2	1.000

Randy Bockus

BOCKUS, RANDY WALTER
B. Oct. 5, 1960, Canton, Ohio.
BL TR 6′ 2″ 190 lbs.

Year	Team	Lg	W	L	PCT	ERA	G	GS	CG	IP	H	BB	SO	ShO	Relief Pitching W	L	SV	Batting AB	H	HR	BA	PO	A	E	DP	TC/G	FA
1986	**SF**	**N**	0	0	—	2.57	5	0	0	7	7	6	4	0	0	0	0	1	0	0	.000	0	4	0	0	0.7	1.000
1987			1	0	1.000	3.63	12	0	0	17.1	17	4	9	0	1	0	0	1	0	0	.000	0	3	1	0	0.3	.750
1988			1	1	.500	4.78	20	0	0	32	35	13	18	0	1	1	0	6	1	0	.167	2	7	0	0	0.4	1.000
1989	**DET**	**A**	0	0	—	5.06	2	0	0	5.1	7	2	2	0	0	0	0	0	0	0	—	0	0	0	0	0.0	.000
4 yrs.			2	1	.667	4.23	39	0	0	61.2	66	25	33	0	2	1	0	8	1	0	.125	2	14	1	0	0.4	.941

Mike Boddicker

BODDICKER, MICHAEL JAMES BR TR 5′11″ 172 lbs.
B. Aug. 23, 1957, Cedar Rapids, Iowa.

Year	Team		W	L	PCT	ERA	G	GS	CG	IP	H	BB	SO	ShO	Relief Pitching W	Relief Pitching L	Relief Pitching SV	Batting AB	Batting H	Batting HR	BA	PO	A	E	DP	TC/G	FA
1980	**BAL**	**A**	0	1	.000	6.43	1	1	0	7	6	5	4	0	0	0	0	0	0	0	—	0	0	1	0	1.0	.000
1981			0	0	—	4.50	2	0	0	6	6	2	2	0	0	0	0	0	0	0	—	1	0	1	0	1.0	.500
1982			1	0	1.000	3.51	7	0	0	25.2	25	12	20	0	1	0	0	0	0	0	—	5	3	1	0	1.3	.889
1983			16	8	.667	2.77	27	26	10	179	141	52	120	**5**	0	0	0	0	0	0	—	24	32	3	4	2.2	.949
1984			**20**	11	.645	**2.79**	34	34	16	261.1	218	81	128	4	0	0	0	0	0	0	—	49	49	7	6	3.0	.933
1985			12	17	.414	4.07	32	32	9	203.1	227	89	135	2	0	0	0	0	0	0	—	26	46	2	6	2.2	.973
1986			14	12	.538	4.70	33	33	7	218.1	214	74	175	0	0	0	0	0	0	0	—	28	36	3	4	2.0	.955
1987			10	12	.455	4.18	33	33	7	226	212	78	152	2	0	0	0	0	0	0	—	18	46	2	5	2.0	.970
1988	**2 teams**	**BAL A**	(21G 6–12)		**BOS A**	(15G 7–3)																					
″	**total**		13	15	.464	3.39	36	35	5	236	234	77	156	1	0	0	0	0	0	0		22	33	2	1	1.6	.965
1989	**BOS**	**A**	15	11	.577	4.00	34	34	3	211.2	217	71	145	2	0	0	0	0	0	0	—	14	36	3	2	1.6	.943
1990			17	8	.680	3.36	34	34	4	228	225	69	143	0	0	0	0	0	0	0	—	29	27	2	6	1.7	.966
1991	**KC**	**A**	12	12	.500	4.08	30	29	1	180.2	188	59	79	0	1	0	0	0	0	0	—	12	36	2	1	1.7	.960
1992			1	4	.200	4.98	29	8	0	86.2	92	37	47	0	1	0	3	0	0	0	—	12	13	1	1	0.9	.962
1993	**MIL**	**A**	3	5	.375	5.67	10	10	1	54	77	15	24	0	0	0	0	0	0	0	—	5	9	2	1	1.6	.875
14 yrs.			134	116	.536	3.80	342	309	63	2123.2	2082	721	1330	16	3	0	3	0	0	0		245	366	32	37	1.9	.950
LEAGUE CHAMPIONSHIP SERIES																											
1983	**BAL**	**A**	1	0	1.000	0.00	1	1	1	9	5	3	14	1	0	0	0	0	0	0	—	0	1	0	0	1.0	1.000
1988	**BOS**	**A**	0	1	.000	20.25	1	1	0	2.2	8	1	2	0	0	0	0	0	0	0	—	0	0	0	0	0.0	.000
1990			0	1	.000	2.25	1	1	1	8	6	3	7	0	0	0	0	0	0	0	—	0	2	1	0	3.0	.667
3 yrs.			1	2	.333	3.66	3	3	2 **4th**	19.2	19	7	23	1 **1st**	0	0	0	0	0	0		0	3	1	0	1.3	.750
WORLD SERIES																											
1983	**BAL**	**A**	1	0	1.000	0.00	1	1	1	9	3	0	6	0	0	0	0	3	0	0	.000	1	2	0	0	3.0	1.000

George Boehler

BOEHLER, GEORGE HENRY BR TR 6′ 2″ 180 lbs.
B. Jan. 2, 1892, Lawrenceburg, Ind. D. June 23, 1958, Lawrenceburg, Ind.

Year	Team		W	L	PCT	ERA	G	GS	CG	IP	H	BB	SO	ShO	Relief Pitching W	Relief Pitching L	Relief Pitching SV	Batting AB	Batting H	Batting HR	BA	PO	A	E	DP	TC/G	FA
1912	**DET**	**A**	0	2	.000	6.68	4	4	2	31	49	14	13	0	0	0	0	10	1	0	.100	0	15	0	0	3.8	1.000
1913			0	1	.000	6.75	1	1	1	8	11	6	2	0	0	0	0	3	1	0	.333	0	5	0	0	5.0	1.000
1914			2	3	.400	3.57	18	6	2	63	54	48	37	0	0	1	0	17	3	0	.176	3	18	1	1	1.2	.955
1915			1	1	.500	1.80	8	0	0	15	19	4	7	0	1	1	0	4	3	0	.750	0	3	0	1	0.4	1.000
1916			1	1	.500	4.72	5	2	1	13.1	12	9	8	0	0	0	0	3	0	0	.000	0	6	0	0	1.2	1.000
1920	**STL**	**A**	0	1	.000	7.71	3	1	0	7	10	4	2	0	0	0	0	1	0	0	.000	0	3	1	0	1.3	.750
1921			0	0	—	0.00	1	0	0	1	1	0	0	0	0	0	0	0	0	0	—	0	0	0	0	0.0	.000
1923	**PIT**	**N**	1	3	.250	6.04	10	3	1	28.1	33	26	12	0	0	1	0	10	3	0	.300	0	5	0	1	0.5	1.000
1926	**BKN**	**N**	1	0	1.000	4.41	10	1	0	34.2	42	23	10	0	0	0	0	12	3	0	.250	0	7	1	0	0.8	.875
9 yrs.			6	12	.333	4.74	60	18	7	201.1	231	134	91	0	1	3	0	60	14	0	.233	3	62	3	3	1.1	.956

Joe Boehling

BOEHLING, JOHN JOSEPH BL TL 5′11″ 168 lbs.
B. Mar. 20, 1891, Richmond, Va. D. Sept. 8, 1941, Richmond, Va.

Year	Team		W	L	PCT	ERA	G	GS	CG	IP	H	BB	SO	ShO	Relief Pitching W	Relief Pitching L	Relief Pitching SV	Batting AB	Batting H	Batting HR	BA	PO	A	E	DP	TC/G	FA
1912	**WAS**	**A**	0	0	—	7.20	3	0	0	5	4	6	2	0	0	0	0	0	0	0	—	0	3	0	0	1.0	1.000
1913			17	7	.708	2.14	38	25	18	235.1	197	82	110	3	2	0	4	86	19	0	.221	14	86	10	4	2.9	.909
1914			12	8	.600	3.03	27	24	14	196	180	76	91	2	0	1	1	71	17	0	.239	19	60	2	2	3.0	.975
1915			14	13	.519	3.22	40	32	14	229.1	217	119	108	2	0	3	0	75	13	1	.173	10	77	2	0	2.2	.978
1916	**2 teams**	**WAS A**	(27G 9–11)		**CLE A**	(12G 2–4)																					
″	**total**		11	15	.423	2.97	39	28	10	200.1	197	77	70	2	2	2	0	60	12	0	.200	14	77	5	2	2.5	.948
1917	**CLE**	**A**	1	6	.143	4.66	12	7	1	46.1	50	16	11	0	0	1	0	16	3	0	.188	3	12	0	1	1.3	1.000
1920			0	1	.000	4.85	3	2	0	13	16	10	4	0	0	0	0	3	2	0	.667	1	3	0	0	1.3	1.000
7 yrs.			55	50	.524	2.97	162	118	57	925.1	861	386	396	9	4	7	5	311	66	1	.212	61	318	19	9	2.5	.952

Brian Boehringer

BOEHRINGER, BRIAN EDWARD BB TR 6′ 2″ 180 lbs.
B. Jan. 8, 1969, St. Louis, Mo.

Year	Team		W	L	PCT	ERA	G	GS	CG	IP	H	BB	SO	ShO	Relief Pitching W	Relief Pitching L	Relief Pitching SV	Batting AB	Batting H	Batting HR	BA	PO	A	E	DP	TC/G	FA
1995	**NY**	**A**	0	3	.000	13.75	7	3	0	17.2	24	22	10	0	0	0	0	0	0	0	—	1	0	0	0	0.1	1.000

Larry Boerner

BOERNER, LAWRENCE HYER BR TR 6′ 4½″ 175 lbs.
B. Jan. 21, 1905, Staunton, Va. D. Oct. 16, 1969, Staunton, Va.

Year	Team		W	L	PCT	ERA	G	GS	CG	IP	H	BB	SO	ShO	Relief Pitching W	Relief Pitching L	Relief Pitching SV	Batting AB	Batting H	Batting HR	BA	PO	A	E	DP	TC/G	FA
1932	**BOS**	**A**	0	4	.000	5.02	21	5	0	61	71	37	19	0	0	0	0	17	0	0	.000	4	14	0	0	0.9	1.000

Joe Boever

BOEVER, JOSEPH MARTIN BR TR 6′ 1″ 200 lbs.
B. Oct. 4, 1960, Kirkwood, Mo.

Year	Team		W	L	PCT	ERA	G	GS	CG	IP	H	BB	SO	ShO	Relief Pitching W	Relief Pitching L	Relief Pitching SV	Batting AB	Batting H	Batting HR	BA	PO	A	E	DP	TC/G	FA
1985	**STL**	**N**	0	0	—	4.41	13	0	0	16.1	17	4	20	0	0	0	0	0	0	0	—	0	0	0	0	0.0	.000
1986			0	1	.000	1.66	11	0	0	21.2	19	11	8	0	0	1	0	2	1	0	.500	1	2	0	0	0.3	1.000
1987	**ATL**	**N**	1	0	1.000	7.36	14	0	0	18.1	29	12	18	0	1	0	0	0	0	0	—	0	2	0	0	0.1	1.000
1988			0	2	.000	1.77	16	0	0	20.1	12	1	7	0	0	2	1	0	0	0	—	2	3	0	1	0.3	1.000
1989			4	11	.267	3.94	66	0	0	82.1	78	34	68	0	4	**11**	21	1	0	0	.000	7	15	0	0	0.3	1.000
1990	**2 teams**	**ATL N**	(33G 1–3)		**PHI N**	(34G 2–3)																					
″	**total**		3	6	.333	3.36	67	0	0	88.1	77	51	75	0	3	6	14	3	0	0	.000	6	7	2	1	0.2	.867
1991	**PHI**	**N**	3	5	.375	3.84	68	0	0	98.1	90	54	89	0	3	5	0	3	1	0	.333	1	10	0	0	0.2	1.000
1992	**HOU**	**N**	3	6	.333	2.51	**81**	0	0	111.1	103	45	67	0	3	6	2	7	0	0	.000	4	19	2	2	0.3	.920
1993	**2 teams**	**OAK A**	(42G 4–2)		**DET A**	(19G 2–1)																					
″	**total**		6	3	.667	3.61	61	0	0	102.1	101	44	63	0	6	3	3	0	0	0		9	12	1	1	0.4	.955
1994	**DET**	**A**	9	2	.818	3.98	46	0	0	81.1	80	37	49	0	**9**	2	3	0	0	0	—	10	13	1	1	0.5	.958
1995			5	7	.417	6.39	60	0	0	98.2	128	44	71	0	5	7	3	0	0	0	—	4	10	1	0	0.3	.933
11 yrs.			34	43	.442	3.90	503	0	0	739.1	734	337	535	0	34	43	47	16	2	0	.125	44	93	7	6	0.3	.951

John Bogart

BOGART, JOHN RENZIE (Big John) BR TR 6′ 2″ 195 lbs.
B. Sept. 21, 1900, Bloomsburg, Pa. D. Dec. 7, 1986, Clarence, N. Y.

Year	Team		W	L	PCT	ERA	G	GS	CG	IP	H	BB	SO	ShO	Relief Pitching W	Relief Pitching L	Relief Pitching SV	Batting AB	Batting H	Batting HR	BA	PO	A	E	DP	TC/G	FA
1920	**DET**	**A**	2	1	.667	3.04	4	2	0	23.2	16	18	5	0	1	0	0	8	2	0	.250	0	2	0	0	0.5	1.000

Ray Boggs

BOGGS, RAYMOND JOSEPH (Lefty) BL TL 6′½″ 170 lbs.
B. Dec. 12, 1904, Reamsville, Kans. D. Nov. 27, 1989, Grand Junction, Colo.

Year	Team		W	L	PCT	ERA	G	GS	CG	IP	H	BB	SO	ShO	Relief Pitching W	Relief Pitching L	Relief Pitching SV	Batting AB	Batting H	Batting HR	BA	PO	A	E	DP	TC/G	FA
1928	**BOS**	**N**	0	0	—	5.40	4	0	0	5	2	7	0	0	0	0	0	0	0	0	—	0	1	0	0	0.3	1.000

Tommy Boggs

BOGGS, THOMAS WINTON — BR TR 6′ 2″ 195 lbs.
B. Oct. 25, 1955, Poughkeepsie, N. Y.

Year	Team	Lg	W	L	PCT	ERA	G	GS	CG	IP	H	BB	SO	ShO	Relief W	Relief L	Relief SV	AB	H	HR	BA	PO	A	E	DP	TC/G	FA
1976	TEX	A	1	7	.125	3.50	13	13	3	90	87	34	36	0	0	0	0	0	0	0	—	7	10	0	1	1.3	1.000
1977			0	3	.000	6.00	6	6	0	27	40	12	15	0	0	0	0	0	0	0	—	2	2	0	0	0.7	1.000
1978	ATL	N	2	8	.200	6.71	16	12	1	59	80	26	21	1	0	0	0	18	3	1	.167	5	3	3	0	0.7	.727
1979			0	2	.000	6.23	3	3	0	13	21	4	1	0	0	0	0	4	1	0	.250	0	3	0	0	1.0	1.000
1980			12	9	.571	3.42	32	26	4	192	180	46	84	3	0	0	0	63	10	0	.159	17	16	0	0	1.0	1.000
1981			3	13	.188	4.09	25	24	2	143	140	54	81	0	0	1	0	46	7	0	.152	13	20	5	0	1.5	.868
1982			2	2	.500	3.30	10	10	0	46.1	43	22	29	0	0	0	0	17	4	0	.235	3	7	2	0	1.2	.833
1983			0	0	—	5.68	5	0	0	6.1	8	1	5	0	0	0	0	0	0	0	—	0	0	0	0	0.0	.000
1985	TEX	A	0	0	—	11.57	4	0	0	7	13	2	6	0	0	0	0	0	0	0	—	0	2	0	0	0.5	1.000
9 yrs.			20	44	.313	4.23	114	94	10	583.2	612	201	278	4	0	1	0	148	25	1	.169	47	63	10	1	1.1	.917

Warren Bogle

BOGLE, WARREN FREDERICK — BL TL 6′ 4″ 220 lbs.
B. Oct. 19, 1946, Passaic, N. J.

Year	Team	Lg	W	L	PCT	ERA	G	GS	CG	IP	H	BB	SO	ShO	Relief W	Relief L	Relief SV	AB	H	HR	BA	PO	A	E	DP	TC/G	FA
1968	OAK	A	0	0	—	4.30	16	1	0	23	26	8	26	0	0	0	0	5	0	0	.000	2	5	0	0	0.4	1.000

Brian Bohanon

BOHANON, BRIAN EDWARD — BL TL 6′ 2″ 210 lbs.
B. Aug. 1, 1968, Denton, Tex.

Year	Team	Lg	W	L	PCT	ERA	G	GS	CG	IP	H	BB	SO	ShO	Relief W	Relief L	Relief SV	AB	H	HR	BA	PO	A	E	DP	TC/G	FA
1990	TEX	A	0	3	.000	6.62	11	6	0	34	40	18	15	0	0	0	0	0	0	0	—	1	10	0	2	1.0	1.000
1991			4	3	.571	4.84	11	11	1	61.1	66	23	34	0	0	0	0	0	0	0	—	3	6	0	1	0.8	1.000
1992			1	1	.500	6.31	18	7	0	45.2	57	25	29	0	0	0	0	0	0	0	—	5	3	1	0	0.5	.889
1993			4	4	.500	4.76	36	8	0	92.2	107	46	45	0	3	1	0	0	0	0	—	5	18	0	3	0.6	1.000
1994			2	2	.500	7.23	11	5	0	37.1	51	8	26	0	0	0	0	0	0	0	—	3	6	0	0	0.8	1.000
1995	DET	A	1	1	.500	5.54	52	10	0	105.2	121	41	63	0	1	0	1	0	0	0	—	7	13	0	0	0.4	1.000
6 yrs.			12	14	.462	5.59	139	47	1	376.2	442	161	212	0	4	1	1	0	0	0		24	56	1	6	0.6	.988

Pat Bohen

BOHEN, LEO IGNATIUS — BR TR 5′10″ 155 lbs.
B. Sept. 30, 1891, Oakland, Iowa D. Apr. 8, 1942, Napa, Calif.

Year	Team	Lg	W	L	PCT	ERA	G	GS	CG	IP	H	BB	SO	ShO	Relief W	Relief L	Relief SV	AB	H	HR	BA	PO	A	E	DP	TC/G	FA
1913	PHI	A	0	1	.000	1.13	1	1	1	8	3	2	5	0	0	0	0	3	0	0	.000	0	2	0	0	2.0	1.000
1914	PIT	N	0	0	—	18.00	1	0	0	1	2	2	0	0	0	0	0	1	0	0	.000	0	0	0	0	0.0	.000
2 yrs.			0	1	.000	3.00	2	1	1	9	5	4	5	0	0	0	0	4	0	0	.000	0	2	0	0	1.0	1.000

Charlie Bohn

BOHN, CHARLES (Sir Charles) — BR TR 5′ 9″ 165 lbs.
B. 1857, Cleveland, Ohio D. Aug. 1, 1903, Cleveland, Ohio.

Year	Team	Lg	W	L	PCT	ERA	G	GS	CG	IP	H	BB	SO	ShO	Relief W	Relief L	Relief SV	AB	H	HR	BA	PO	A	E	DP	TC/G	FA
1882	LOU	AA	1	1	.500	*3.00*	2	2	2	18	21	3	1	0	0	0	0	*				5	9	4	0	4.5	.778

John Bohnet

BOHNET, JOHN KELLY — BB TL 6′ 180 lbs.
B. Jan. 18, 1961, Pasadena, Calif.

Year	Team	Lg	W	L	PCT	ERA	G	GS	CG	IP	H	BB	SO	ShO	Relief W	Relief L	Relief SV	AB	H	HR	BA	PO	A	E	DP	TC/G	FA
1982	CLE	A	0	0	—	6.94	3	3	0	11.2	11	7	4	0	0	0	0	0	0	0	—	1	2	0	0	1.0	1.000

Danny Boitano

BOITANO, DANNY JON — BR TR 6′ 185 lbs.
B. Mar. 22, 1953, Sacramento, Calif.

Year	Team	Lg	W	L	PCT	ERA	G	GS	CG	IP	H	BB	SO	ShO	Relief W	Relief L	Relief SV	AB	H	HR	BA	PO	A	E	DP	TC/G	FA
1978	PHI	N	0	0	—	0.00	1	0	0	1	0	1	0	0	0	0	0	0	0	0	—	0	0	0	0	0.0	.000
1979	MIL	A	0	0	—	1.50	5	0	0	6	6	3	5	0	0	0	0	0	0	0	—	0	1	0	0	0.2	1.000
1980			0	1	.000	8.00	11	0	0	18	26	6	11	0	0	1	0	0	0	0	—	0	3	0	0	0.3	1.000
1981	NY	N	2	1	.667	5.63	15	0	0	16	21	5	8	0	2	1	0	0	0	0	—	0	3	0	0	0.2	1.000
1982	TEX	A	0	0	—	5.34	19	0	0	30.1	33	13	28	0	0	0	0	0	0	0	—	1	3	0	0	0.2	1.000
5 yrs.			2	2	.500	5.68	51	0	0	71.1	86	28	52	0	2	2	0	0	0	0		1	10	0	0	0.2	1.000

Dick Bokelmann

BOKELMANN, RICHARD WERNER — BR TR 6′½″ 180 lbs.
B. Oct. 26, 1926, Arlington Heights, Ill.

Year	Team	Lg	W	L	PCT	ERA	G	GS	CG	IP	H	BB	SO	ShO	Relief W	Relief L	Relief SV	AB	H	HR	BA	PO	A	E	DP	TC/G	FA
1951	STL	N	3	3	.500	3.78	20	1	0	52.1	49	31	22	0	3	2	3	14	0	0	.000	2	7	2	0	0.6	.818
1952			0	1	.000	9.24	11	0	0	12.2	20	7	5	0	0	1	0	0	0	0	—	3	5	0	0	0.7	1.000
1953			0	0	—	6.00	3	0	0	3	4	0	0	0	0	0	0	0	0	0	—	1	2	0	0	1.0	1.000
3 yrs.			3	4	.429	4.90	34	1	0	68	73	38	27	0	3	3	3	14	0	0	.000	6	14	2	0	0.6	.909

Joe Bokina

BOKINA, JOSEPH — BR TR 6′ 184 lbs.
B. Apr. 4, 1910, Northampton, Mass. D. Oct. 25, 1991, Chattanooga, Tenn.

Year	Team	Lg	W	L	PCT	ERA	G	GS	CG	IP	H	BB	SO	ShO	Relief W	Relief L	Relief SV	AB	H	HR	BA	PO	A	E	DP	TC/G	FA
1936	WAS	A	0	2	.000	8.64	5	1	0	8.1	15	6	5	0	0	1	0	1	0	0	.000	0	1	0	0	0.2	1.000

Bernie Boland

BOLAND, BERNARD ANTHONY — BR TR 5′ 8½″ 168 lbs.
B. Jan. 21, 1892, Rochester, N. Y. D. Sept. 12, 1973, Detroit, Mich.

Year	Team	Lg	W	L	PCT	ERA	G	GS	CG	IP	H	BB	SO	ShO	Relief W	Relief L	Relief SV	AB	H	HR	BA	PO	A	E	DP	TC/G	FA
1915	DET	A	13	7	.650	3.11	45	18	8	202.2	167	75	72	1	4	2	2	63	11	0	.175	12	59	3	5	1.6	.959
1916			10	3	.769	3.94	46	9	5	130.1	111	73	59	1	5	0	3	32	8	0	.250	3	22	1	1	0.6	.962
1917			16	11	.593	2.68	43	28	13	238	192	95	89	3	2	2	6	72	4	0	.056	9	72	2	0	1.9	.976
1918			14	10	.583	2.65	29	25	14	204	176	67	63	4	1	1	0	69	12	0	.174	11	49	2	2	2.1	.968
1919			14	16	.467	3.04	35	30	18	242.2	222	80	71	1	1	1	1	74	8	0	.108	14	57	2	2	2.1	.973
1920			0	2	.000	7.79	4	3	1	17.1	23	14	4	0	0	0	0	7	1	0	.143	5	3	1	0	2.3	.889
1921	STL	A	1	4	.200	8.89	8	6	0	28.1	34	28	6	0	0	0	0	10	1	0	.100	2	6	0	0	1.0	1.000
7 yrs.			68	53	.562	3.24	210	119	59	1063.1	925	432	364	10	13	6	12	327	45	0	.138	56	268	11	10	1.6	.967

Bill Bolden

BOLDEN, WILLIAM HORACE (Big Bill) — BR TR 6′ 4″ 200 lbs.
B. May 9, 1893, Dandridge, Tenn. D. Dec. 8, 1966, Jefferson City, Tenn.

Year	Team	Lg	W	L	PCT	ERA	G	GS	CG	IP	H	BB	SO	ShO	Relief W	Relief L	Relief SV	AB	H	HR	BA	PO	A	E	DP	TC/G	FA
1919	STL	N	0	1	.000	5.25	3	1	0	12	17	4	4	0	0	0	0	3	1	0	.333	0	4	0	1	1.3	1.000

Stew Bolen

BOLEN, STEWART O'NEAL — BL TL 5′11″ 180 lbs.
B. Oct. 12, 1902, Jackson, Ala. D. Aug. 30, 1969, Mobile, Ala.

Year	Team	Lg	W	L	PCT	ERA	G	GS	CG	IP	H	BB	SO	ShO	Relief W	Relief L	Relief SV	AB	H	HR	BA	PO	A	E	DP	TC/G	FA
1926	STL	A	0	0	—	6.14	5	0	0	14.2	21	6	7	0	0	0	0	4	2	0	.500	1	3	1	0	1.0	.800
1927			0	1	.000	8.38	3	1	1	9.2	14	5	7	0	0	0	0	3	1	0	.333	0	2	0	0	0.7	1.000
1931	PHI	N	3	12	.200	6.39	28	16	2	98.2	117	63	55	0	1	2	0	32	5	0	.156	2	23	4	1	1.0	.862
1932			0	0	—	2.81	5	0	0	16	18	10	3	0	0	0	0	7	1	0	.143	0	2	0	0	0.4	1.000
4 yrs.			3	13	.188	6.09	41	17	3	139	170	84	72	0	1	2	0	46	9	0	.196	3	30	5	1	0.9	.868

Bobby Bolin

BOLIN, BOBBY DONALD
B. Jan. 29, 1939, Hickory Grove, S. C.
BR TR 6′ 4″ 185 lbs.

Year	Team	W	L	PCT	ERA	G	GS	CG	IP	H	BB	SO	ShO	Relief Pitching W	Relief Pitching L	Relief Pitching SV	Batting AB	Batting H	Batting HR	BA	PO	A	E	DP	TC/G	FA
1961	SF N	2	2	.500	3.19	37	1	0	48	37	37	48	0	2	2	5	7	2	0	.286	0	4	1	0	0.1	.800
1962		7	3	.700	3.62	41	5	2	92	84	35	74	0	3	2	5	23	6	0	.261	3	10	0	0	0.3	1.000
1963		10	6	.625	3.28	47	12	2	137.1	128	57	134	0	7	2	7	35	5	1	.143	4	11	1	0	0.3	.938
1964		6	9	.400	3.25	38	23	5	174.2	143	77	146	3	1	0	1	50	5	0	.100	13	22	1	4	0.9	.972
1965		14	6	.700	2.76	45	13	2	163	125	56	135	0	8	1	2	54	9	1	.167	9	16	0	1	0.6	1.000
1966		11	10	.524	2.89	36	34	10	224.1	174	70	143	4	0	0	1	76	13	2	.171	13	30	5	0	1.3	.896
1967		6	8	.429	4.88	37	15	0	120	120	50	69	0	4	0	0	33	8	0	.242	12	15	1	0	0.8	.964
1968		10	5	.667	1.99	34	19	6	176.2	128	46	126	3	2	0	0	55	5	0	.091	10	23	2	0	1.0	.943
1969		7	7	.500	4.44	30	22	2	146	149	49	102	0	0	0	0	39	6	1	.154	7	19	0	0	0.9	1.000
1970	2 teams MIL A (32G 5–11) BOS A (6G 2–0)																									
″	total	7	11	.389	4.63	38	20	3	140	133	72	89	0	3	2	3	37	7	1	.189	5	18	1	0	0.6	.958
1971	BOS A	5	3	.625	4.24	52	0	0	70	74	24	51	0	5	3	6	12	3	0	.250	2	7	1	1	0.2	.900
1972		0	1	.000	2.90	21	0	0	31	24	11	27	0	0	1	5	2	0	0	.000	1	4	1	0	0.3	.833
1973		3	4	.429	2.72	39	0	0	53	45	13	31	0	3	4	15	0	0	0	—	8	11	1	0	0.5	.950
13 yrs.		88	75	.540	3.40	495	164	32	1576	1364	597	1175	10	38	17	50	423	69	6	.163	87	190	15	6	0.6	.949
WORLD SERIES																										
1962	SF N	0	0	—	6.75	2	0	0	2.2	4	2	2	0	0	0	0	0	0	0	—	0	0	0	0	0.0	.000

Greg Bollo

BOLLO, GREGORY GENE
B. Nov. 16, 1943, Detroit, Mich.
BR TR 6′ 4″ 183 lbs.

Year	Team	W	L	PCT	ERA	G	GS	CG	IP	H	BB	SO	ShO	Relief Pitching W	Relief Pitching L	Relief Pitching SV	Batting AB	Batting H	Batting HR	BA	PO	A	E	DP	TC/G	FA
1965	CHI A	0	0	—	3.57	15	0	0	22.2	12	9	16	0	0	0	0	0	0	0	—	3	4	0	1	0.5	1.000
1966		0	1	.000	2.57	3	1	0	7	7	3	4	0	0	0	0	1	0	0	.000	0	1	0	0	0.3	1.000
2 yrs.		0	1	.000	3.34	18	1	0	29.2	19	12	20	0	0	0	0	1	0	0	.000	3	5	0	1	0.4	1.000

Rodney Bolton

BOLTON, RODNEY EARL
B. Sept. 23, 1968, Chattanooga, Tenn.
BR TR 6′ 2″ 190 lbs.

Year	Team	W	L	PCT	ERA	G	GS	CG	IP	H	BB	SO	ShO	Relief Pitching W	Relief Pitching L	Relief Pitching SV	Batting AB	Batting H	Batting HR	BA	PO	A	E	DP	TC/G	FA
1993	CHI A	2	6	.250	7.44	9	8	0	42.1	55	16	17	0	1	0	0	0	0	0	—	4	9	0	0	1.4	1.000
1995		0	2	.000	8.18	8	3	0	22	33	14	10	0	0	0	0	0	0	0	—	2	3	0	0	0.6	1.000
2 yrs.		2	8	.200	7.69	17	11	0	64.1	88	30	27	0	1	0	0	0	0	0		6	12	0	0	1.1	1.000

Tom Bolton

BOLTON, THOMAS EDWARD
B. May 6, 1962, Nashville, Tenn.
BL TL 6′ 2″ 172 lbs.

Year	Team	W	L	PCT	ERA	G	GS	CG	IP	H	BB	SO	ShO	Relief Pitching W	Relief Pitching L	Relief Pitching SV	Batting AB	Batting H	Batting HR	BA	PO	A	E	DP	TC/G	FA
1987	BOS A	1	0	1.000	4.38	29	0	0	61.2	83	27	49	0	1	0	0	0	0	0	—	3	9	0	1	0.4	1.000
1988		1	3	.250	4.75	28	0	0	30.1	35	14	21	0	1	3	1	0	0	0	—	1	10	0	0	0.4	1.000
1989		0	4	.000	8.31	4	4	0	17.1	21	10	9	0	0	0	0	0	0	0	—	1	2	0	0	0.8	1.000
1990		10	5	.667	3.38	21	16	3	119.2	111	47	65	0	2	0	0	0	0	0	—	4	21	1	1	1.2	.962
1991		8	9	.471	5.24	25	19	0	110	136	51	64	0	1	0	0	0	0	0	—	1	15	2	3	0.7	.889
1992	2 teams BOS A (21G 1–2) CIN N (16G 3–3)																									
″	total	4	5	.444	4.54	37	9	0	75.1	86	37	50	0	2	1	0	14	0	0	.000	3	14	1	1	0.5	.944
1993	DET A	6	6	.500	4.47	43	8	0	102.2	113	45	66	0	1	4	0	0	0	0	—	6	15	2	2	0.5	.913
1994	BAL A	1	2	.333	5.40	22	0	0	23.1	29	13	12	0	1	2	0	0	0	0	—	3	3	0	1	0.3	1.000
8 yrs.		31	34	.477	4.56	209	56	3	540.1	614	244	336	0	9	10	1	14	0	0	.000	22	89	6	9	0.6	.949
LEAGUE CHAMPIONSHIP SERIES																										
1990	BOS A	0	0	—	0.00	2	0	0	3	2	2	3	0	0	0	0	0	0	0	—	0	0	0	0	0.0	.000

Mark Bomback

BOMBACK, MARK VINCENT
B. Apr. 14, 1953, Portsmouth, Va.
BR TR 5′11″ 170 lbs.

Year	Team	W	L	PCT	ERA	G	GS	CG	IP	H	BB	SO	ShO	Relief Pitching W	Relief Pitching L	Relief Pitching SV	Batting AB	Batting H	Batting HR	BA	PO	A	E	DP	TC/G	FA
1978	MIL A	0	0	—	16.20	2	1	0	1.2	5	1	1	0	0	0	0	0	0	0	—	0	0	0	0	0.0	.000
1980	NY N	10	8	.556	4.09	36	25	2	163	191	49	68	1	2	0	0	43	10	0	.233	20	32	1	2	1.5	.981
1981	TOR A	5	5	.500	3.90	20	11	0	90	84	35	33	0	0	0	0	0	0	0	—	6	16	0	0	1.1	1.000
1982		1	5	.167	6.03	16	8	0	59.2	87	25	22	0	0	0	0	0	0	0	—	6	9	0	0	0.9	1.000
4 yrs.		16	18	.471	4.47	74	45	2	314.1	367	110	124	1	2	0	0	43	10	0	.233	32	57	1	2	1.2	.989

Tommy Bond

BOND, THOMAS HENRY
B. Apr. 2, 1856, Granard, Ireland D. Jan. 24, 1941, Boston, Mass.
Manager 1882.
BR TR 5′ 7½″ 160 lbs.

Year	Team	W	L	PCT	ERA	G	GS	CG	IP	H	BB	SO	ShO	Relief Pitching W	Relief Pitching L	Relief Pitching SV	Batting AB	Batting H	Batting HR	BA	PO	A	E	DP	TC/G	FA
1876	HAR N	31	13	.705	1.68	45	45	45	408	355	13	88	6	0	0	0	182	50	0	.275	25	93	15	0	3.0	.887
1877	BOS N	**40**	17	**.702**	**2.11**	58	58	58	521	530	36	**170**	**6**	0	0	0	259	59	0	.228	30	104	9	2	2.3	.937
1878		**40**	19	**.678**	2.06	**59**	**59**	**57**	**532.2**	**571**	33	**182**	**9**	0	0	0	236	50	0	.212	27	117	9	4	2.5	.941
1879		43	19	.694	**1.96**	64	64	59	555.1	543	24	155	**11**	0	0	0	257	62	0	.241	36	144	9	7	2.7	.952
1880		26	29	.473	2.67	63	57	49	493	559	45	118	3	0	**2**	0	282	62	0	.220	61	153	16	8	2.5	.930
1881		0	3	.000	*4.26*	3	3	2	25.1	40	2	2	0	0	0	0	10	2	0	.200	2	7	0	0	3.0	1.000
1882	WOR N	0	1	.000	4.38	2	2	0	12.1	12	7	2	0	0	0	0	30	4	0	.133	11	1	4	0	1.6	.750
1884	2 teams BOS U (23G 13–9) IND AA (5G 0–5)																									
″	total	13	14	.481	3.49	28	26	24	232	247	18	143	0	1	0	0	185	51	0	.276	27	62	17	3	2.2	.840
8 yrs.		193	115	.627	2.25 9th	322	314	294	2779.2	2857	178	860	35	1	2	0	*				219	681	79	24	2.5	.919

Ricky Bones

BONES, RICARDO
B. Apr. 7, 1969, Salinas, Puerto Rico.
BR TR 5′10″ 175 lbs.

Year	Team	W	L	PCT	ERA	G	GS	CG	IP	H	BB	SO	ShO	Relief Pitching W	Relief Pitching L	Relief Pitching SV	Batting AB	Batting H	Batting HR	BA	PO	A	E	DP	TC/G	FA
1991	SD N	4	6	.400	4.83	11	11	0	54	57	18	31	0	0	0	0	13	1	0	.077	1	2	0	0	0.3	1.000
1992	MIL A	9	10	.474	4.57	31	28	0	163.1	169	48	65	0	0	0	0	0	0	0	—	17	13	2	1	1.0	.938
1993		11	11	.500	4.86	32	31	3	203.2	222	63	63	0	0	0	0	0	0	0	—	26	22	1	2	1.5	.980
1994		10	9	.526	3.43	24	24	4	170.2	166	45	57	1	0	0	0	0	0	0	—	8	14	1	2	1.0	.957
1995		10	12	.455	4.63	32	31	3	200.1	218	83	77	0	0	0	0	0	0	0	—	19	32	0	7	1.6	1.000
5 yrs.		44	48	.478	4.43	130	125	10	792	832	257	293	1	0	0	0	13	1	0	.077	71	83	4	12	1.2	.975

Julio Bonetti

BONETTI, JULIO GIACOMO
B. July 14, 1911, Genoa, Italy D. June 17, 1952, Belmont, Calif.
BR TR 6′ 180 lbs.

Year	Team	W	L	PCT	ERA	G	GS	CG	IP	H	BB	SO	ShO	Relief Pitching W	Relief Pitching L	Relief Pitching SV	Batting AB	Batting H	Batting HR	BA	PO	A	E	DP	TC/G	FA
1937	STL A	4	11	.267	5.84	28	16	7	143.1	190	60	43	0	2	0	1	47	7	0	.149	6	38	4	1	1.7	.917
1938		2	3	.400	6.35	17	0	0	28.1	41	13	7	0	2	3	0	8	0	0	.000	0	7	0	2	0.4	1.000
1940	CHI N	0	0	—	20.25	1	0	0	1.1	3	4	0	0	0	0	0	0	0	0	—	0	0	0	0	0.0	.000
3 yrs.		6	14	.300	6.03	46	16	7	173	234	77	50	0	4	3	1	55	7	0	.127	6	45	4	3	1.2	.927

Hank Boney

BONEY, HENRY TATE BR TR 5′11″ 176 lbs.
B. Oct. 28, 1903, Wallace, N. C.

Year	Team	W	L	PCT	ERA	G	GS	CG	IP	H	BB	SO	ShO	Relief W	Relief L	Relief SV	Batting AB	Batting H	Batting HR	BA	PO	A	E	DP	TC/G	FA
1927	NY N	0	0	—	2.25	3	0	0	4	4	2	0	0	0	0	0	0	0	0	—	0	0	0	0	0.0	.000

Bill Bonham

BONHAM, WILLIAM GORDON BR TR 6′ 3″ 190 lbs.
B. Oct. 1, 1948, Glendale, Calif.

Year	Team	W	L	PCT	ERA	G	GS	CG	IP	H	BB	SO	ShO	Relief W	Relief L	Relief SV	Batting AB	Batting H	Batting HR	BA	PO	A	E	DP	TC/G	FA
1971	CHI N	2	1	.667	4.65	33	2	0	60	63	36	41	0	2	0	0	12	2	0	.167	5	13	0	1	0.5	1.000
1972		1	1	.500	3.10	19	4	0	58	56	25	49	0	0	0	4	14	4	0	.286	3	9	0	0	0.6	1.000
1973		7	5	.583	3.02	44	15	3	152	126	64	121	0	3	0	6	43	4	0	.093	10	40	2	2	1.2	.962
1974		11	**22**	.333	3.85	44	36	10	243	246	109	191	2	1	2	1	84	12	0	.143	20	54	6	4	1.8	.925
1975		13	15	.464	4.72	38	36	7	229	254	109	165	2	0	1	0	82	15	0	.183	15	37	4	3	1.5	.929
1976		9	13	.409	4.27	32	31	3	196	215	96	110	0	0	0	0	65	13	0	.200	8	32	3	2	1.3	.930
1977		10	13	.435	4.35	34	34	1	215	207	82	134	0	0	0	0	65	15	0	.231	20	43	3	4	1.9	.955
1978	CIN N	11	5	.688	3.54	23	23	1	140	151	50	83	0	0	0	0	43	8	0	.186	13	35	3	2	2.2	.941
1979		9	7	.563	3.78	29	29	2	176	173	60	78	0	0	0	0	57	8	0	.140	9	31	4	0	1.5	.909
1980		2	1	.667	4.74	4	4	0	19	21	5	13	0	0	0	0	6	0	0	.000	0	3	1	0	1.0	.750
10 yrs.		75	83	.475	4.00	300	214	27	1488	1512	636	985	4	6	3	11	471	81	0	.172	103	297	26	18	1.4	.939

Ernie Bonham

BONHAM, ERNEST EDWARD (Tiny) BR TR 6′ 2″ 215 lbs.
B. Aug. 16, 1913, Ione, Calif. D. Sept. 15, 1949, Pittsburgh, Pa.

Year	Team	W	L	PCT	ERA	G	GS	CG	IP	H	BB	SO	ShO	Relief W	Relief L	Relief SV	Batting AB	Batting H	Batting HR	BA	PO	A	E	DP	TC/G	FA
1940	NY A	9	3	.750	1.90	12	12	10	99.1	83	13	37	3	0	0	0	37	7	0	.189	6	8	0	0	1.2	1.000
1941		9	6	.600	2.98	23	14	7	126.2	118	31	43	1	1	0	2	50	8	0	.160	6	12	2	1	0.9	.900
1942		21	5	**.808**	2.27	28	27	**22**	226	199	24	71	**6**	1	0	0	74	9	0	.122	11	28	0	2	1.4	1.000
1943		15	8	.652	2.27	28	26	17	225.2	197	52	71	4	0	0	1	76	15	0	.197	8	26	0	1	1.2	1.000
1944		12	9	.571	2.99	26	25	17	213.2	228	41	54	1	0	0	0	75	10	0	.133	8	26	1	5	1.3	.971
1945		8	11	.421	3.29	23	23	12	180.2	186	22	42	0	0	0	0	63	15	0	.238	6	23	0	2	1.3	1.000
1946		5	8	.385	3.70	18	14	6	104.2	97	23	30	2	0	0	3	31	4	0	.129	2	13	2	1	0.9	.882
1947	PIT N	11	8	.579	3.85	33	18	7	149.2	167	35	63	3	3	1	3	45	7	0	.156	7	11	2	1	0.6	.900
1948		6	10	.375	4.31	22	20	7	135.2	145	23	42	0	0	0	0	49	8	0	.163	6	9	1	1	0.7	.938
1949		7	4	.636	4.25	18	14	5	89	81	23	25	1	1	0	0	22	1	0	.045	3	9	0	1	0.7	1.000
10 yrs.		103	72	.589	3.06	231	193	110	1551	1501	287	478	21	6	1	9	522	84	0	.161	63	165	8	15	1.0	.966
WORLD SERIES																										
1941	NY A	1	0	1.000	1.00	1	1	1	9	4	2	2	0	0	0	0	4	0	0	.000	0	1	0	0	1.0	1.000
1942		0	1	.000	4.09	2	1	1	11	9	3	3	0	0	0	0	2	0	0	.000	0	2	0	0	1.0	1.000
1943		0	1	.000	4.50	1	1	0	8	6	3	9	0	0	0	0	2	0	0	.000	0	0	0	0	0.0	.000
3 yrs.		1	2	.333	3.21	4	3	2	28	19	8	14	0	0	0	0	8	0	0	.000	0	3	0	0	0.8	1.000

Joe Bonikowski

BONIKOWSKI, JOSEPH PETER BR TR 6′ 175 lbs.
B. Jan. 16, 1941, Philadelphia, Pa.

Year	Team	W	L	PCT	ERA	G	GS	CG	IP	H	BB	SO	ShO	Relief W	Relief L	Relief SV	Batting AB	Batting H	Batting HR	BA	PO	A	E	DP	TC/G	FA
1962	MIN A	5	7	.417	3.88	30	13	3	99.2	95	38	45	0	2	1	2	27	4	0	.148	7	22	0	1	1.0	1.000

Bill Bonness

BONNESS, WILLIAM JOHN (Lefty) BR TL 6′ 4″ 200 lbs.
B. Dec. 15, 1923, Cleveland, Ohio D. Dec. 3, 1977, Detroit, Mich.

Year	Team	W	L	PCT	ERA	G	GS	CG	IP	H	BB	SO	ShO	Relief W	Relief L	Relief SV	Batting AB	Batting H	Batting HR	BA	PO	A	E	DP	TC/G	FA
1944	CLE A	0	1	.000	7.71	2	1	0	7	11	5	1	0	0	0	0	3	0	0	.000	0	2	0	0	1.0	1.000

Gus Bono

BONO, ADLAI WENDELL BR TR 5′11″ 175 lbs.
B. Aug. 29, 1894, Doe Run, Mo. D. Dec. 3, 1948, Dearborn, Mich.

Year	Team	W	L	PCT	ERA	G	GS	CG	IP	H	BB	SO	ShO	Relief W	Relief L	Relief SV	Batting AB	Batting H	Batting HR	BA	PO	A	E	DP	TC/G	FA
1920	WAS A	0	2	.000	8.76	4	1	0	12.1	17	6	4	0	0	1	0	3	0	0	.000	0	5	1	0	1.5	.833

Greg Booker

BOOKER, GREGORY SCOTT BR TR 6′ 6″ 230 lbs.
B. June 22, 1960, Lynchburg, Va.

Year	Team	W	L	PCT	ERA	G	GS	CG	IP	H	BB	SO	ShO	Relief W	Relief L	Relief SV	Batting AB	Batting H	Batting HR	BA	PO	A	E	DP	TC/G	FA
1983	SD N	0	1	.000	7.71	6	1	0	11.2	18	9	5	0	0	0	0	1	0	0	.000	0	3	0	0	0.5	1.000
1984		1	1	.500	3.30	32	1	0	57.1	67	27	28	0	1	1	0	7	2	0	.286	9	7	1	1	0.5	.941
1985		0	1	.000	6.85	17	0	0	22.1	20	17	7	0	0	1	0	1	0	0	.000	1	3	1	0	0.3	.800
1986		1	0	1.000	1.64	9	0	0	11	10	4	7	0	1	0	0	0	0	0	—	1	1	1	0	0.3	.667
1987		1	1	.500	3.16	44	0	0	68.1	62	30	17	0	1	1	1	6	0	0	.000	8	8	1	1	0.4	.941
1988		2	2	.500	3.39	34	2	0	63.2	68	19	43	0	1	2	0	8	2	0	.250	6	12	0	0	0.5	1.000
1989	2 teams SD N (11G 0–1) MIN A (6G 0–0)																									
″	total	0	1	.000	4.23	17	0	0	27.2	26	12	11	0	0	1	0	0	0	0	—	3	7	0	1	0.6	1.000
1990	SF N	0	0	—	13.50	2	0	0	2	7	0	1	0	0	0	0	0	0	0	—	0	0	0	0	0.0	.000
8 yrs.		5	7	.417	3.89	161	4	0	264	278	118	119	0	4	6	1	23	4	0	.174	28	41	4	3	0.5	.945
LEAGUE CHAMPIONSHIP SERIES																										
1984	SD N	0	0	—	0.00	1	0	0	2	2	1	2	0	0	0	0	0	0	0	—	0	0	0	0	0.0	.000
WORLD SERIES																										
1984	SD N	0	0	—	9.00	1	0	0	1	0	4	0	0	0	0	0	0	0	0	—	0	1	0	0	1.0	1.000

Red Booles

BOOLES, SEABRON JESSE BL TL 5′10″ 150 lbs.
B. July 14, 1880, Bernice, La. D. Mar. 16, 1955, Monroe, La.

Year	Team	W	L	PCT	ERA	G	GS	CG	IP	H	BB	SO	ShO	Relief W	Relief L	Relief SV	Batting AB	Batting H	Batting HR	BA	PO	A	E	DP	TC/G	FA
1909	CLE A	0	1	.000	1.99	4	1	0	22.2	20	8	6	0	0	0	0	6	1	0	.167	0	7	0	0	1.8	1.000

Danny Boone

BOONE, DANIEL HUGH BL TL 5′ 8″ 150 lbs.
B. Jan. 14, 1954, Long Beach, Calif.

Year	Team	W	L	PCT	ERA	G	GS	CG	IP	H	BB	SO	ShO	Relief W	Relief L	Relief SV	Batting AB	Batting H	Batting HR	BA	PO	A	E	DP	TC/G	FA
1981	SD N	1	0	1.000	2.86	37	0	0	63	63	21	43	0	1	0	2	4	2	0	.500	7	14	1	1	0.6	.955
1982	2 teams SD N (10G 1–0) HOU N (10G 0–1)																									
″	total	1	1	.500	4.71	20	0	0	28.2	28	7	12	0	1	1	2	6	1	0	.167	0	7	1	0	0.4	.875
1990	BAL A	0	0	—	2.79	4	1	0	9.2	12	3	2	0	0	0	0	0	0	0	—	0	2	0	0	0.5	1.000
3 yrs.		2	1	.667	3.38	61	1	0	101.1	103	31	57	0	2	1	4	10	3	0	.300	7	23	2	1	0.5	.938

Danny Boone

BOONE, JAMES ALBERT BR TR 6′ 2″ 190 lbs.
Brother of Ike Boone.
B. Jan. 19, 1895, Samantha, Ala. D. June 11, 1968, Tuscaloosa, Ala.

Year	Team	W	L	PCT	ERA	G	GS	CG	IP	H	BB	SO	ShO	Relief W	Relief L	Relief SV	Batting AB	Batting H	Batting HR	BA	PO	A	E	DP	TC/G	FA
1919	PHI A	0	1	.000	6.75	3	2	0	14.2	24	10	1	0	0	0	0	4	0	0	.000	2	7	1	0	3.3	.900
1921	DET A	0	0	—	0.00	1	0	0	2	1	2	0	0	0	0	1	1	0	0	.000	0	1	0	0	1.0	1.000

Danny Boone *continued*

Year	Team	Lg	W	L	PCT	ERA	G	GS	CG	IP	H	BB	SO	ShO	Relief W	Relief L	Relief SV	Batting AB	Batting H	Batting HR	BA	PO	A	E	DP	TC/G	FA
1922	**CLE**	**A**	4	6	.400	4.06	11	10	4	75.1	87	19	9	2	0	1	0	26	5	0	.192	2	25	0	0	2.5	1.000
1923			4	6	.400	6.01	27	4	2	70.1	93	31	15	0	3	3	0	19	4	0	.211	4	30	0	3	1.3	1.000
4 yrs.			8	13	.381	5.10	42	16	6	162.1	205	62	25	2	3	4	1	50	9	0	.180	8	63	1	3	1.7	.986

George Boone

BOONE, GEORGE MORRIS
B. Mar. 1, 1871, Louisville, Ky. D. Sept. 24, 1910, Louisville, Ky.

Year	Team	Lg	W	L	PCT	ERA	G	GS	CG	IP	H	BB	SO	ShO	Relief W	Relief L	Relief SV	Batting AB	Batting H	Batting HR	BA	PO	A	E	DP	TC/G	FA
1891	**LOU**	**AA**	0	0	—	7.80	4	1	0	15	15	9	4	0	0	0	1	6	2	0	.333	0	3	0	0	0.8	1.000

Amos Booth

BOOTH, AMOS SMITH (The Darling) BR TR 5′ 9″ 159 lbs.
B. Sept. 4, 1852, Cincinnati, Ohio D. July 1, 1921, Miamisburg, Ohio.

Year	Team	Lg	W	L	PCT	ERA	G	GS	CG	IP	H	BB	SO	ShO	Relief W	Relief L	Relief SV	Batting AB	Batting H	Batting HR	BA	PO	A	E	DP	TC/G	FA
1876	**CIN**	**N**	0	1	.000	9.31	3	1	0	9.2	22	0	0	0	0	0	0	272	71	0	.261	138	117	76	10	4.4	.770
1877			1	7	.125	3.56	12	8	6	86	114	13	18	0	0	0	0	157	27	0	.172	77	101	36	6	4.2	.832
2 yrs.			1	8	.111	4.14	15	9	6	95.2	136	13	18	0	0	0	0	*				218	221	112	16	4.2	.797

Eddie Booth

BOOTH, EDWARD H.
B. Brooklyn, N. Y. Deceased.

Year	Team	Lg	W	L	PCT	ERA	G	GS	CG	IP	H	BB	SO	ShO	Relief W	Relief L	Relief SV	Batting AB	Batting H	Batting HR	BA	PO	A	E	DP	TC/G	FA
1876	**NY**	**N**	0	0	—	10.80	1	0	0	5	16	0	0	0	0	0	0	*				88	18	31	1	2.3	.774

John Boozer

BOOZER, JOHN MORGAN BR TR 6′ 3″ 205 lbs.
B. July 6, 1938, Columbia, S. C. D. Jan. 24, 1986, Lexington, S. C.

Year	Team	Lg	W	L	PCT	ERA	G	GS	CG	IP	H	BB	SO	ShO	Relief W	Relief L	Relief SV	Batting AB	Batting H	Batting HR	BA	PO	A	E	DP	TC/G	FA
1962	**PHI**	**N**	0	0	—	5.75	9	0	0	20.1	22	10	13	0	0	0	0	1	0	0	.000	0	3	0	1	0.3	1.000
1963			3	4	.429	2.93	26	8	2	83	67	33	69	0	2	0	1	21	3	0	.143	2	7	1	0	0.4	.900
1964			3	4	.429	5.07	22	3	0	60.1	64	18	51	0	2	2	2	13	1	0	.077	5	12	0	1	0.8	1.000
1966			0	0	—	6.75	2	2	0	5.1	8	3	5	0	0	0	0	2	0	0	.000	0	1	0	0	0.5	1.000
1967			5	4	.556	4.10	28	7	1	74.2	86	24	48	0	2	1	1	19	4	0	.211	4	13	0	1	0.6	1.000
1968			2	2	.500	3.67	38	0	0	68.2	76	15	49	0	2	2	5	9	1	0	.111	2	14	0	0	0.4	1.000
1969			1	2	.333	4.28	46	2	0	82	91	36	47	0	1	0	6	9	3	0	.333	3	9	1	1	0.3	.923
7 yrs.			14	16	.467	4.09	171	22	3	394.1	414	139	282	0	9	5	15	74	12	0	.162	16	59	2	4	0.5	.974

Pedro Borbon

BORBON, PEDRO BR TR 6′ 2″ 185 lbs.
Born Pedro Borbon (Rodriguez).
Father of Pedro Borbon.
B. Dec. 2, 1946, Valverde De Mao, Dominican Republic.

Year	Team	Lg	W	L	PCT	ERA	G	GS	CG	IP	H	BB	SO	ShO	Relief W	Relief L	Relief SV	Batting AB	Batting H	Batting HR	BA	PO	A	E	DP	TC/G	FA
1969	**CAL**	**A**	2	3	.400	6.15	22	0	0	41	55	11	20	0	2	3	0	3	0	0	.000	5	4	2	0	0.5	.818
1970	**CIN**	**N**	0	2	.000	6.88	12	1	0	17	21	6	6	0	0	1	0	3	0	0	.000	2	11	0	1	1.1	1.000
1971			0	0	—	4.50	3	0	0	4	3	1	4	0	0	0	0	0	0	0	—	0	0	0	0	0.0	.000
1972			8	3	.727	3.17	62	2	0	122	115	32	48	0	8	3	11	21	1	0	.048	2	20	3	0	0.4	.880
1973			11	4	.733	2.15	80	0	0	121.1	137	35	60	0	11	4	14	15	5	0	.333	9	19	3	1	0.4	.903
1974			10	7	.588	3.24	73	0	0	139	133	32	53	0	10	7	14	26	5	0	.192	7	19	2	2	0.4	.929
1975			9	5	.643	2.95	67	0	0	125	145	21	29	0	9	5	5	24	7	0	.292	6	19	1	1	0.4	.962
1976			4	3	.571	3.35	69	1	0	121	135	31	53	0	4	2	8	18	4	0	.222	6	18	0	0	0.3	1.000
1977			10	5	.667	3.19	73	0	0	127	131	24	48	0	10	5	18	22	4	0	.182	4	14	2	1	0.3	.900
1978			8	2	.800	5.00	62	0	0	99	102	27	35	0	8	2	4	11	2	0	.182	6	15	0	1	0.3	1.000
1979	**2 teams**	**CIN N** (30G 2–2) **SF N** (30G 4–3)																									
″	**total**		6	5	.545	4.17	60	0	0	90.2	104	21	49	0	6	5	5	9	3	0	.333	7	10	2	1	0.3	.895
1980	**STL**	**N**	1	0	1.000	3.79	10	0	0	19	17	10	4	0	1	0	1	4	1	0	.250	0	3	1	0	0.4	.750
12 yrs.			69	39	.639	3.52	593	4	0	1026	1098	251	409	0	69	37	80	156	32	0	.205	54	152	16	8	0.4	.928
LEAGUE CHAMPIONSHIP SERIES																											
1972	**CIN**	**N**	0	0	—	2.08	3	0	0	4.1	2	0	1	0	0	0	0	0	0	0	—	1	0	0	0	0.3	1.000
1973			1	0	1.000	0.00	4	0	0	4.2	3	0	3	0	1	0	1	0	0	0	—	0	2	0	0	0.5	1.000
1975			0	0	—	0.00	1	0	0	1	0	0	1	0	0	0	0	0	0	0	—	0	0	0	0	0.0	.000
1976			0	0	—	0.00	2	0	0	4.1	4	1	0	0	0	0	1	2	0	0	.000	0	0	0	0	0.0	.000
4 yrs.			1	0	1.000	0.63	10	0	0	14.1	9	1	5	0	1	0	2	2	0	0	.000	1	2	0	0	0.3	1.000
WORLD SERIES																											
1972	**CIN**	**N**	0	1	.000	3.86	6	0	0	7	7	2	4	0	0	1	0	0	0	0	—	0	3	0	0	0.5	1.000
1975			0	0	—	6.00	3	0	0	3	3	2	1	0	0	0	0	1	0	0	.000	0	0	0	0	0.0	.000
1976			0	0	—	0.00	1	0	0	1.2	0	0	0	0	0	0	0	0	0	0	—	0	1	0	0	1.0	1.000
3 yrs.			0	1	.000	3.86	10	0	0	11.2	10	4	5	0	0	1	0	1	0	0	.000	0	4	0	0	0.4	1.000

Pedro Borbon

BORBON, PEDRO FELIX BR TL 6′ 1″ 205 lbs.
Born Pedro Felix Borbon (Marte).
Son of Pedro Borbon.
B. Nov. 15, 1967, Mao, Dominican Republic.

Year	Team	Lg	W	L	PCT	ERA	G	GS	CG	IP	H	BB	SO	ShO	Relief W	Relief L	Relief SV	Batting AB	Batting H	Batting HR	BA	PO	A	E	DP	TC/G	FA
1992	**ATL**	**N**	0	1	.000	6.75	2	0	0	1.1	2	1	1	0	0	1	0	0	0	0	—	0	0	0	0	0.0	.000
1993			0	0	—	21.60	3	0	0	1.2	3	3	2	0	0	0	0	0	0	0	—	0	0	0	0	0.0	.000
1995			2	2	.500	3.09	41	0	0	32	29	17	33	0	2	2	2	1	0	0	.000	1	6	0	1	0.2	1.000
3 yrs.			2	3	.400	4.11	46	0	0	35	34	21	36	0	2	3	2	1	0	0	.000	1	6	0	1	0.2	1.000
DIVISIONAL PLAYOFF SERIES																											
1995	**ATL**	**N**	0	0	—	0.00	1	0	0	1	1	0	3	0	0	0	0	0	0	0	—	0	0	0	0	0.0	.000
WORLD SERIES																											
1995	**ATL**	**N**	0	0	—	0.00	1	0	0	1	0	0	2	0	0	0	1	0	0	0	—	0	0	0	0	0.0	.000

George Borchers

BORCHERS, GEORGE BERNARD BB TR 5′10″ 180 lbs.
B. Apr. 18, 1869, Sacramento, Calif. D. Oct. 24, 1938, Sacramento, Calif.

Year	Team	Lg	W	L	PCT	ERA	G	GS	CG	IP	H	BB	SO	ShO	Relief W	Relief L	Relief SV	Batting AB	Batting H	Batting HR	BA	PO	A	E	DP	TC/G	FA
1888	**CHI**	**N**	4	4	.500	3.49	10	10	7	67	67	29	26	1	0	0	0	33	2	0	.061	6	16	7	1	2.2	.759
1895	**LOU**	**N**	0	1	.000	27.00	1	1	0	0.2	1	3	0	0	0	0	0	0	0	0	—	0	0	0	0	0.0	.000
2 yrs.			4	5	.444	3.72	11	11	7	67.2	68	32	26	1	0	0	0	33	2	0	.061	6	16	7	1	2.1	.759

Joe Borden

BORDEN, JOSEPH EMLEY BR TR 5′ 9″ 140 lbs.
Also appeared in box score as Josephs.
B. May 9, 1854, Jacobstown, N. J. D. Oct. 14, 1929, Yeadon, Pa.

Year	Team	Lg	W	L	PCT	ERA	G	GS	CG	IP	H	BB	SO	ShO	Relief W	Relief L	Relief SV	Batting AB	Batting H	Batting HR	BA	PO	A	E	DP	TC/G	FA
1876	**BOS**	**N**	11	12	.478	2.89	29	24	16	218.1	257	**51**	34	2	0	**1**	1	121	25	0	.207	20	34	29	0	1.8	.651

Rich Bordi

BORDI, RICHARD ALBERT BR TR 6′ 7″ 210 lbs.
B. Apr. 18, 1959, San Francisco, Calif.

Year	Team	Lg	W	L	PCT	ERA	G	GS	CG	IP	H	BB	SO	ShO	Relief W	Relief L	Relief SV	AB	Batting H	HR	BA	PO	A	E	DP	TC/G	FA
1980	OAK	A	0	0	—	4.50	1	0	0	2	4	0	0	0	0	0	0	0	0	0	—	0	0	0	0	0.0	.000
1981			0	0	—	0.00	2	0	0	2	1	1	0	0	0	0	0	0	0	0	—	0	0	0	0	0.0	.000
1982	SEA	A	0	2	.000	8.31	7	2	0	13	18	1	10	0	0	0	0	0	0	0	—	1	1	0	0	0.3	1.000
1983	CHI	N	0	2	.000	4.97	11	1	0	25.1	34	12	20	0	0	1	1	4	0	0	.000	3	3	2	1	0.7	.750
1984			5	2	.714	3.46	31	7	0	83.1	78	20	41	0	1	1	4	19	1	0	.053	4	10	2	0	0.5	.875
1985	NY	A	6	8	.429	3.21	51	3	0	98	95	29	64	0	4	7	2	0	0	0	—	2	12	1	1	0.3	.933
1986	BAL	A	6	4	.600	4.46	52	1	0	107	105	41	83	0	6	3	3	0	0	0	—	7	15	1	2	0.4	.957
1987	NY	A	3	1	.750	7.64	16	1	0	33	42	12	23	0	3	0	0	0	0	0	—	2	1	1	0	0.3	.750
1988	OAK	A	0	1	.000	4.70	2	2	0	7.2	6	5	6	0	0	0	0	0	0	0	—	0	0	0	0	0.0	.000
9 yrs.			20	20	.500	4.34	173	17	0	371.1	383	121	247	0	14	12	10	23	1	0	.043	19	42	7	4	0.4	.897

Bill Bordley

BORDLEY, WILLIAM CLARK BL TL 6′ 3″ 195 lbs.
B. Jan. 9, 1958, Rolling Hills Est., Calif.

Year	Team	Lg	W	L	PCT	ERA	G	GS	CG	IP	H	BB	SO	ShO	Relief W	Relief L	Relief SV	AB	Batting H	HR	BA	PO	A	E	DP	TC/G	FA
1980	SF	N	2	3	.400	4.65	8	6	0	31	34	21	11	0	0	0	0	6	1	0	.167	2	9	0	0	1.4	1.000

Paul Boris

BORIS, PAUL STANLEY BR TR 6′ 2″ 200 lbs.
B. Dec. 13, 1955, Irvington, N. J.

Year	Team	Lg	W	L	PCT	ERA	G	GS	CG	IP	H	BB	SO	ShO	Relief W	Relief L	Relief SV	AB	Batting H	HR	BA	PO	A	E	DP	TC/G	FA
1982	MIN	A	1	2	.333	3.99	23	0	0	49.2	46	19	30	0	1	2	0	0	0	0	—	2	4	0	0	0.3	1.000

Frank Bork

BORK, FRANK BERNARD BR TL 6′ 2″ 175 lbs.
B. July 13, 1940, Buffalo, N. Y.

Year	Team	Lg	W	L	PCT	ERA	G	GS	CG	IP	H	BB	SO	ShO	Relief W	Relief L	Relief SV	AB	Batting H	HR	BA	PO	A	E	DP	TC/G	FA
1964	PIT	N	2	2	.500	4.07	33	2	0	42	51	11	31	0	1	1	2	5	1	0	.200	1	10	0	0	0.3	1.000

Toby Borland

BORLAND, TOBY SHAWN BR TR 6′ 6″ 186 lbs.
B. May 29, 1969, Ruston, La.

Year	Team	Lg	W	L	PCT	ERA	G	GS	CG	IP	H	BB	SO	ShO	Relief W	Relief L	Relief SV	AB	Batting H	HR	BA	PO	A	E	DP	TC/G	FA
1994	PHI	N	1	0	1.000	2.36	24	0	0	34.1	31	14	26	0	1	0	1	3	0	0	.000	5	1	0	0	0.3	1.000
1995			1	3	.250	3.77	50	0	0	74	81	37	59	0	1	3	6	5	1	0	.200	2	10	2	0	0.3	.857
2 yrs.			2	3	.400	3.32	74	0	0	108.1	112	51	85	0	2	3	7	8	1	0	.125	7	11	2	0	0.3	.900

Tom Borland

BORLAND, THOMAS BRUCE (Spike) BL TL 6′ 3″ 172 lbs.
B. Feb. 14, 1933, El Dorado, Kans.

Year	Team	Lg	W	L	PCT	ERA	G	GS	CG	IP	H	BB	SO	ShO	Relief W	Relief L	Relief SV	AB	Batting H	HR	BA	PO	A	E	DP	TC/G	FA
1960	BOS	A	0	4	.000	6.53	26	4	0	51	67	23	32	0	0	1	3	13	0	0	.000	5	7	0	0	0.5	1.000
1961			0	0	—	18.00	1	0	0	1	3	0	0	0	0	0	0	0	0	0	—	0	0	0	0	0.0	.000
2 yrs.			0	4	.000	6.75	27	4	0	52	70	23	32	0	0	1	3	13	0	0	.000	5	7	0	0	0.4	1.000

Joe Borowski

BOROWSKI, JOSEPH THOMAS BR TR 6′ 2″ 225 lbs.
B. May 4, 1971, Bayonne, N. J.

Year	Team	Lg	W	L	PCT	ERA	G	GS	CG	IP	H	BB	SO	ShO	Relief W	Relief L	Relief SV	AB	Batting H	HR	BA	PO	A	E	DP	TC/G	FA
1995	BAL	A	0	0	—	1.23	6	0	0	7.1	5	4	3	0	0	0	0	0	0	0	—	1	2	0	0	0.5	1.000

Hank Borowy

BOROWY, HENRY LUDWIG BR TR 6′ 175 lbs.
B. May 12, 1916, Bloomfield, N. J.

Year	Team	Lg	W	L	PCT	ERA	G	GS	CG	IP	H	BB	SO	ShO	Relief W	Relief L	Relief SV	AB	Batting H	HR	BA	PO	A	E	DP	TC/G	FA
1942	NY	A	15	4	.789	2.52	25	21	13	178.1	157	66	85	4	1	0	1	70	11	0	.157	12	38	1	3	2.0	.980
1943			14	9	.609	2.82	29	27	14	217.1	195	72	113	3	1	0	0	74	15	0	.203	12	46	1	4	2.0	.983
1944			17	12	.586	2.64	35	30	19	252.2	224	88	107	3	0	0	2	90	12	0	.133	13	47	1	5	1.7	.984
1945	2 teams	NY A	(18G 10–5)	CHI N	(15G 11–2)																						
″	total		21	7	.750	**2.65**	33	32	18	254.2	212	105	82	2	0	0	1	91	18	0	.198	10	51	0	3	1.8	1.000
1946	CHI	N	12	10	.545	3.76	32	28	8	201	220	61	95	1	1	0	0	72	13	0	.181	9	42	3	1	1.7	.944
1947			8	12	.400	4.38	40	25	7	183	190	63	75	1	1	1	2	56	7	0	.125	7	36	2	2	1.1	.956
1948			5	10	.333	4.89	39	17	2	127	156	49	50	1	1	0	1	36	8	0	.222	6	34	1	3	1.1	.976
1949	PHI	N	12	12	.500	4.19	28	28	12	193.1	188	63	43	2	0	0	0	61	13	0	.213	6	32	0	0	1.4	1.000
1950	3 teams	PHI N	(3G 0–0)	PIT N	(11G 1–3)	DET A	(13G 1–1)																				
″	total		2	4	.333	4.83	27	5	1	63.1	60	29	24	0	2	1	0	13	2	0	.154	8	10	1	0	0.7	.947
1951	DET	A	2	2	.500	6.95	26	1	0	45.1	58	27	16	0	2	2	0	8	0	0	.000	2	14	1	1	0.7	.941
10 yrs.			108	82	.568	3.50	314	214	94	1716	1660	623	690	17	9	4	7	571	99	0	.173	85	350	11	22	1.4	.975
WORLD SERIES																											
1942	NY	A	0	0	—	18.00	1	1	0	3	6	3	1	0	0	0	0	1	0	0	.000	0	1	0	0	1.0	1.000
1943			1	0	1.000	2.25	1	1	0	8	6	3	4	0	0	0	0	2	1	0	.500	2	0	0	0	2.0	1.000
1945	CHI	N	2	2	.500	4.00	4	3	1	18	21	6	8	1	1	0	0	5	1	0	.200	1	2	0	0	0.8	1.000
3 yrs.			3	2	.600	4.97	6	5	1	29	33	12	13	1	1	0	0	8	2	0	.250	3	3	0	0	1.0	1.000

Chris Bosio

BOSIO, CHRISTOPHER LOUIS BR TR 6′ 3″ 220 lbs.
B. Apr. 3, 1963, Carmichael, Calif.

Year	Team	Lg	W	L	PCT	ERA	G	GS	CG	IP	H	BB	SO	ShO	Relief W	Relief L	Relief SV	AB	Batting H	HR	BA	PO	A	E	DP	TC/G	FA
1986	MIL	A	0	4	.000	7.01	10	4	0	34.2	41	13	29	0	0	1	0	0	0	0	—	4	5	1	1	1.0	.900
1987			11	8	.579	5.24	46	19	2	170	187	50	150	1	3	1	2	0	0	0	—	14	24	4	5	0.9	.905
1988			7	15	.318	3.36	38	22	9	182	190	38	84	1	1	3	6	0	0	0	—	22	33	3	7	1.5	.948
1989			15	10	.600	2.95	33	33	8	234.2	225	48	173	2	0	0	0	0	0	0	—	16	35	2	2	1.6	.962
1990			4	9	.308	4.00	20	20	4	132.2	131	38	76	1	0	0	0	0	0	0	—	12	24	1	2	1.9	.973
1991			14	10	.583	3.25	32	32	5	204.2	187	58	117	1	0	0	0	0	0	0	—	20	21	2	4	1.3	.953
1992			16	6	.727	3.62	33	33	4	231.1	223	44	120	2	0	0	0	0	0	0	—	20	26	0	5	1.4	1.000
1993	SEA	A	9	9	.500	3.45	29	24	3	164.1	138	59	119	1	1	0	1	0	0	0	—	13	21	1	2	1.2	.971
1994			4	10	.286	4.32	19	19	4	125	137	40	67	0	0	0	0	0	0	0	—	11	24	0	3	1.8	1.000
1995			10	8	.556	4.92	31	31	0	170	211	69	85	0	0	0	0	0	0	0	—	12	23	1	3	1.2	.972
10 yrs.			90	89	.503	3.89	291	237	39	1649.1	1670	457	1020	9	5	5	9	0	0	0		144	236	15	34	1.4	.962
DIVISIONAL PLAYOFF SERIES																											
1995	SEA	A	0	0	—	10.57	2	2	0	7.2	10	4	2	0	0	0	0	0	0	0	—	1	0	0	0	0.5	1.000
LEAGUE CHAMPIONSHIP SERIES																											
1995	SEA	A	0	1	.000	3.38	1	1	0	5.1	7	2	3	0	0	0	0	0	0	0	—	0	2	0	0	2.0	1.000

Shawn Boskie

BOSKIE, SHAWN KEALOHA BR TR 6′ 3″ 205 lbs.
B. May 28, 1967, Hawthorne, Nev.

Year	Team	Lg	W	L	PCT	ERA	G	GS	CG	IP	H	BB	SO	ShO	Relief W	Relief L	Relief SV	AB	Batting H	HR	BA	PO	A	E	DP	TC/G	FA
1990	CHI	N	5	6	.455	3.69	15	15	1	97.2	99	31	49	0	0	0	0	36	8	0	.222	12	12	0	2	1.6	1.000
1991			4	9	.308	5.23	28	20	0	129	150	52	62	0	1	0	0	41	7	1	.171	14	21	2	0	1.3	.946
1992			5	11	.313	5.01	23	18	0	91.2	96	36	39	0	2	1	0	27	5	0	.185	8	21	1	2	1.3	.967

Shawn Boskie *continued*

Year	Team	W	L	PCT	ERA	G	GS	CG	IP	H	BB	SO	ShO	Relief Pitching W	Relief Pitching L	Relief Pitching SV	Batting AB	Batting H	Batting HR	BA	PO	A	E	DP	TC/G	FA
1993		5	3	.625	3.43	39	2	0	65.2	63	21	39	0	4	2	0	11	3	0	.273	3	5	1	0	0.2	.889
1994	3 teams CHI N (2G 0–0) PHI N (18G 4–6) SEA A (2G 0–1)																									
"	total	4	7	.364	5.06	22	15	1	90.2	92	30	61	0	0	0	0	26	3	0	.115	8	13	1	2	1.0	.955
1995	CAL A	7	7	.500	5.64	20	20	1	111.2	127	25	51	0	0	0	0	0	0	0	—	4	19	0	1	1.1	1.000
6 yrs.		30	43	.411	4.79	147	90	3	586.1	627	195	301	0	7	3	0	141	26	1	.184	49	91	5	7	1.0	.966

Dick Bosman

BOSMAN, RICHARD ALLEN
B. Feb. 17, 1944, Kenosha, Wis.
BR TR 6' 2" 195 lbs.

Year	Team	W	L	PCT	ERA	G	GS	CG	IP	H	BB	SO	ShO	Relief Pitching W	Relief Pitching L	Relief Pitching SV	Batting AB	Batting H	Batting HR	BA	PO	A	E	DP	TC/G	FA
1966	WAS A	2	6	.250	7.62	13	7	0	39	60	12	20	0	0	3	0	12	3	0	.250	1	3	0	0	0.3	1.000
1967		3	1	.750	1.75	7	7	2	51.1	38	10	25	1	0	0	0	15	3	0	.200	4	6	1	0	1.6	.909
1968		2	9	.182	3.69	46	10	0	139	139	35	63	0	1	7	1	30	6	0	.200	8	21	1	2	0.7	.967
1969		14	5	.737	**2.19**	31	26	5	193	156	39	99	2	1	0	1	64	6	0	.094	18	32	1	1	1.6	.980
1970		16	12	.571	3.00	36	34	7	231	212	71	134	3	0	0	0	80	11	0	.138	19	32	0	3	1.4	1.000
1971		12	16	.429	3.72	35	35	7	237	245	71	113	1	0	0	0	75	7	0	.093	21	27	1	1	1.4	.980
1972	TEX A	8	10	.444	3.64	29	29	1	173	183	48	105	1	0	0	0	53	5	0	.094	17	28	1	3	1.6	.978
1973	2 teams TEX A (7G 2–5) CLE A (22G 1–8)																									
"	total	3	13	.188	5.64	29	24	3	137.1	172	46	55	1	0	0	0	0	0	0		8	17	2	0	0.9	.926
1974	CLE A	7	5	.583	4.11	25	18	2	127	126	29	56	1	0	0	0	0	0	0	—	8	8	3	0	0.8	.842
1975	2 teams CLE A (6G 0–2) OAK A (22G 11–4)																									
"	total	11	6	.647	3.63	28	24	2	151.1	145	32	53	0	0	0	0	0	0	0		6	19	0	0	0.9	1.000
1976	OAK A	4	2	.667	4.10	27	15	0	112	118	19	34	0	0	1	0	0	0	0	—	9	19	1	2	1.1	.966
11 yrs.		82	85	.491	3.67	306	229	29	1591	1594	412	757	10	2	11	2	329	41	0	.125	119	212	11	12	1.1	.968
LEAGUE CHAMPIONSHIP SERIES																										
1975	OAK A	0	0	—	0.00	1	0	0	0.1	0	0	0	0	0	0	0	0	0	0	—	0	0	0	0	0.0	.000

Mel Bosser

BOSSER, MELVIN EDWARD
B. Feb. 8, 1920, Johnstown, Pa.
BR TR 6' 173 lbs.

Year	Team	W	L	PCT	ERA	G	GS	CG	IP	H	BB	SO	ShO	Relief Pitching W	Relief Pitching L	Relief Pitching SV	Batting AB	Batting H	Batting HR	BA	PO	A	E	DP	TC/G	FA
1945	CIN N	2	0	1.000	3.31	7	1	0	16.1	9	17	3	0	1	0	0	4	0	0	.000	0	2	0	0	0.3	1.000

Andy Boswell

BOSWELL, ANDREW COTTRELL
B. Sept. 5, 1874, New Gretna, N. J. D. Feb. 3, 1936, Ocean City, N. J.
TR 6' 1" 165 lbs.

Year	Team	W	L	PCT	ERA	G	GS	CG	IP	H	BB	SO	ShO	Relief Pitching W	Relief Pitching L	Relief Pitching SV	Batting AB	Batting H	Batting HR	BA	PO	A	E	DP	TC/G	FA
1895	2 teams NY N (5G 2–2) WAS N (6G 1–2)																									
"	total	3	4	.429	5.91	11	7	6	64	85	41	30	0	0	0	0	30	7	0	.233	14	6	5	0	2.1	.800

Dave Boswell

BOSWELL, DAVID WILSON
B. Jan. 20, 1945, Baltimore, Md.
BR TR 6' 3" 185 lbs.

Year	Team	W	L	PCT	ERA	G	GS	CG	IP	H	BB	SO	ShO	Relief Pitching W	Relief Pitching L	Relief Pitching SV	Batting AB	Batting H	Batting HR	BA	PO	A	E	DP	TC/G	FA
1964	MIN A	2	0	1.000	4.24	4	4	0	23.1	21	12	25	0	0	0	0	9	2	0	.222	2	5	0	0	1.8	1.000
1965		6	5	.545	3.40	27	12	1	106	77	46	85	0	1	2	0	38	12	0	.316	5	14	1	1	0.7	.950
1966		12	5	.706	3.14	28	21	8	169.1	120	65	173	1	0	0	0	63	9	0	.143	10	29	2	0	1.5	.951
1967		14	12	.538	3.27	37	32	11	222.2	162	107	204	3	0	0	0	73	16	1	.219	11	24	0	2	0.9	1.000
1968		10	13	.435	3.32	34	28	7	190	148	87	143	2	0	0	0	60	14	1	.233	17	15	3	1	1.0	.914
1969		20	12	.625	3.23	39	38	10	256.1	215	99	190	0	0	0	0	94	16	2	.170	9	31	2	2	1.1	.952
1970		3	7	.300	6.39	18	15	0	69	80	44	45	0	0	0	0	25	4	0	.160	6	5	0	1	0.6	1.000
1971	2 teams DET A (3G 0–0) BAL A (15G 1–2)																									
"	total	1	2	.333	4.66	18	1	0	29	35	21	17	0	1	1	0	5	1	0	.200	2	6	0	0	0.4	1.000
8 yrs.		68	56	.548	3.52	205	151	37	1065.2	858	481	882	6	2	3	0	367	74	4	.202	62	129	8	7	1.0	.960
LEAGUE CHAMPIONSHIP SERIES																										
1969	MIN A	0	1	.000	0.84	1	1	0	10.2	7	7	4	0	0	0	0	4	0	0	.000	1	4	0	1	5.0	1.000
WORLD SERIES																										
1965	MIN A	0	0	—	3.38	1	0	0	2.2	3	2	3	0	0	0	0	0	0	0	—	0	0	0	0	0.0	.000

Derek Botelho

BOTELHO, DEREK WAYNE
B. Aug. 2, 1956, Long Beach, Calif.
BR TR 6' 2" 160 lbs.

Year	Team	W	L	PCT	ERA	G	GS	CG	IP	H	BB	SO	ShO	Relief Pitching W	Relief Pitching L	Relief Pitching SV	Batting AB	Batting H	Batting HR	BA	PO	A	E	DP	TC/G	FA
1982	KC A	2	1	.667	4.13	8	4	0	24	25	8	12	0	0	0	0	0	0	0	—	1	2	0	0	0.4	1.000
1985	CHI N	1	3	.250	5.32	11	7	1	44	52	23	23	0	0	0	0	14	2	0	.143	2	5	0	0	0.6	1.000
2 yrs.		3	4	.429	4.90	19	11	1	68	77	31	35	0	0	0	0	14	2	0	.143	3	7	0	0	0.5	1.000

Ricky Bottalico

BOTTALICO, RICKY PAUL
B. Aug. 26, 1969, New Britain, Conn.
BL TR 6' 1" 200 lbs.

Year	Team	W	L	PCT	ERA	G	GS	CG	IP	H	BB	SO	ShO	Relief Pitching W	Relief Pitching L	Relief Pitching SV	Batting AB	Batting H	Batting HR	BA	PO	A	E	DP	TC/G	FA
1994	PHI N	0	0	—	0.00	3	0	0	3	3	1	3	0	0	0	0	0	0	0	—	0	0	0	0	0.0	.000
1995		5	3	.625	2.46	62	0	0	87.2	50	42	87	0	5	3	1	5	0	0	.000	6	7	0	1	0.2	1.000
2 yrs.		5	3	.625	2.38	65	0	0	90.2	53	43	90	0	5	3	1	5	0	0	.000	6	7	0	1	0.2	1.000

Kent Bottenfield

BOTTENFIELD, KENT DENNIS
B. Nov. 14, 1968, Portland, Ore.
BB TR 6' 3" 225 lbs.

Year	Team	W	L	PCT	ERA	G	GS	CG	IP	H	BB	SO	ShO	Relief Pitching W	Relief Pitching L	Relief Pitching SV	Batting AB	Batting H	Batting HR	BA	PO	A	E	DP	TC/G	FA
1992	MON N	1	2	.333	2.23	10	4	0	32.1	26	11	14	0	0	1	1	8	3	0	.375	2	2	0	0	0.4	1.000
1993	2 teams MON N (23G 2–5) CLR N (14G 3–5)																									
"	total	5	10	.333	5.07	37	25	1	159.2	179	71	63	0	0	1	0	50	11	0	.220	9	32	2	5	1.2	.953
1994	2 teams CLR N (15G 3–1) SF N (1G 0–0)																									
"	total	3	1	.750	6.15	16	1	0	26.1	33	10	15	0	3	0	1	1	0	0	.000	1	2	1	0	0.3	.750
3 yrs.		9	13	.409	4.78	63	30	1	218.1	238	92	92	0	3	2	2	59	14	0	.237	12	36	3	5	0.8	.941

Ralph Botting

BOTTING, RALPH WAYNE
B. May 12, 1955, Houlton, Me.
BL TL 6' 195 lbs.

Year	Team	W	L	PCT	ERA	G	GS	CG	IP	H	BB	SO	ShO	Relief Pitching W	Relief Pitching L	Relief Pitching SV	Batting AB	Batting H	Batting HR	BA	PO	A	E	DP	TC/G	FA
1979	CAL A	2	0	1.000	8.70	12	1	0	30	46	15	22	0	1	0	0	0	0	0	—	1	4	0	0	0.4	1.000
1980		0	3	.000	5.88	6	6	0	26	40	13	12	0	0	0	0	0	0	0		1	3	1	0	0.8	.800
2 yrs.		2	3	.400	7.39	18	7	0	56	86	28	34	0	1	0	0	0	0	0	—	2	7	1	0	0.6	.900

Bob Botz

BOTZ, ROBERT ALLEN (Butterball)
B. Apr. 28, 1935, Milwaukee, Wis.
BR TR 5'11" 170 lbs.

Year	Team	W	L	PCT	ERA	G	GS	CG	IP	H	BB	SO	ShO	Relief Pitching W	Relief Pitching L	Relief Pitching SV	Batting AB	Batting H	Batting HR	BA	PO	A	E	DP	TC/G	FA
1962	LA A	2	1	.667	3.43	35	0	0	63	71	11	24	0	2	1	2	9	0	0	.000	1	8	0	0	0.3	1.000

Denis Boucher

BOUCHER, DENIS — BR TL 6′ 1″ 195 lbs.
B. Mar. 7, 1968, Montreal, Que., Canada.

Year	Team	W	L	PCT	ERA	G	GS	CG	IP	H	BB	SO	ShO	Relief Pitching W	L	SV	Batting AB	H	HR	BA	PO	A	E	DP	TC/G	FA
1991	2 teams TOR A (7G 0–3) CLE A (5G 1–4)																									
″	total	1	7	.125	6.05	12	12	0	58	74	24	29	0	0	0	0	0	0	0		2	13	2	2	1.4	.882
1992	CLE A	2	2	.500	6.37	8	7	0	41	48	20	17	0	0	0	0	0	0	0	—	3	3	0	0	0.8	1.000
1993	MON N	3	1	.750	1.91	5	5	0	28.1	24	3	14	0	0	0	0	6	1	0	.167	1	4	0	0	1.0	1.000
1994		0	1	.000	6.75	10	2	0	18.2	24	7	17	0	0	0	0	3	1	0	.333	1	3	0	0	0.4	1.000
4 yrs.		6	11	.353	5.42	35	26	0	146	170	54	77	0	0	0	0	9	2	0	.222	7	23	2	2	0.9	.938

Carl Bouldin

BOULDIN, CARL EDWARD — BB TR 6′ 2″ 180 lbs. BL 1961
B. Sept. 17, 1939, Germantown, Ky.

Year	Team	W	L	PCT	ERA	G	GS	CG	IP	H	BB	SO	ShO	Relief Pitching W	L	SV	Batting AB	H	HR	BA	PO	A	E	DP	TC/G	FA
1961	WAS A	0	1	.000	16.20	2	1	0	3.1	9	2	2	0	0	0	0	1	0	0	.000	1	1	0	0	1.0	1.000
1962		1	2	.333	5.85	6	3	1	20	26	9	12	0	0	1	0	7	0	0	.000	1	3	1	0	0.8	.800
1963		2	2	.500	5.79	10	3	0	23.1	31	8	10	0	2	0	0	7	0	0	.000	2	4	1	1	0.7	.857
1964		0	3	.000	5.40	9	3	0	25	30	11	12	0	0	1	0	6	0	0	.000	2	4	1	0	0.8	.857
4 yrs.		3	8	.273	6.15	27	10	1	71.2	96	30	36	0	2	2	0	21	0	0	.000	6	12	3	1	0.8	.857

Jake Boultes

BOULTES, JACOB JOHN — TR 6′ 3″
B. Aug. 6, 1884, St. Louis, Mo. D. Dec. 24, 1955, St. Louis, Mo.

Year	Team	W	L	PCT	ERA	G	GS	CG	IP	H	BB	SO	ShO	Relief Pitching W	L	SV	Batting AB	H	HR	BA	PO	A	E	DP	TC/G	FA
1907	BOS N	5	9	.357	2.71	24	12	11	139.2	140	50	49	0	2	0	0	68	9	0	.132	20	59	4	5	2.9	.952
1908		3	5	.375	3.01	17	5	1	74.2	80	8	28	0	2	2	0	21	3	0	.143	7	17	0	0	1.4	1.000
1909		0	0	—	6.75	1	0	0	8	9	0	1	0	0	0	0	3	1	0	.333	2	1	0	0	3.0	1.000
3 yrs.		8	14	.364	2.96	42	17	12	222.1	229	58	78	0	4	2	0	92	13	0	.141	29	77	4	5	2.3	.964

Jim Bouton

BOUTON, JAMES ALAN (Bulldog) — BR TR 6′ 170 lbs.
B. Mar. 8, 1939, Newark, N. J.

Year	Team	W	L	PCT	ERA	G	GS	CG	IP	H	BB	SO	ShO	Relief Pitching W	L	SV	Batting AB	H	HR	BA	PO	A	E	DP	TC/G	FA
1962	NY A	7	7	.500	3.99	36	16	3	133	124	59	71	1	3	1	2	32	2	0	.063	8	23	0	3	0.9	1.000
1963		21	7	.750	2.53	40	30	12	249.1	191	87	148	6	3	1	1	83	6	0	.072	22	32	2	1	1.4	.964
1964		18	13	.581	3.02	38	**37**	11	271.1	227	60	125	4	0	0	0	100	13	0	.130	31	27	5	1	1.7	.921
1965		4	15	.211	4.82	30	25	2	151.1	158	60	97	0	0	1	0	43	4	0	.093	13	21	0	3	1.1	1.000
1966		3	8	.273	2.69	24	19	3	120.1	117	38	65	0	0	1	1	38	4	0	.105	13	22	3	2	1.6	.921
1967		1	0	1.000	4.67	17	1	0	44.1	47	18	31	0	1	0	0	7	0	0	.000	1	7	0	1	0.5	1.000
1968		1	1	.500	3.68	12	3	1	44	49	9	24	0	0	0	0	7	0	0	.000	7	11	0	1	1.5	1.000
1969	2 teams SEA A (57G 2–1) HOU N (16G 0–2)																									
″	total	2	3	.400	3.95	73	2	1	123	109	50	100	0	2	1	2	13	0	0	.000	10	20	1	1	0.4	.968
1970	HOU N	4	6	.400	5.42	29	6	1	73	84	33	49	0	2	4	0	17	6	0	.353	4	11	3	0	0.6	.833
1978	ATL N	1	3	.250	4.97	5	5	0	29	25	21	10	0	0	0	0	7	0	0	.000	3	3	1	0	1.4	.857
10 yrs.		62	63	.496	3.57	304	144	34	1238.2	1131	435	720	11	11	9	6	347	35	0	.101	112	177	15	13	1.0	.951
WORLD SERIES																										
1963	NY A	0	1	.000	1.29	1	1	0	7	4	5	4	0	0	0	0	2	0	0	.000	1	2	0	0	3.0	1.000
1964		2	0	1.000	1.56	2	2	1	17.1	15	5	7	0	0	0	0	7	1	0	.143	4	0	0	0	2.0	1.000
2 yrs.		2	1	.667	1.48	3	3	1	24.1	19	10	11	0	0	0	0	9	1	0	.111	5	2	0	0	2.3	1.000

Cy Bowen

BOWEN, SUTHERLAND McCOY — BR TR 6′ 175 lbs.
B. Feb. 17, 1871, Kingston, Ind. D. Jan. 25, 1925, Greensburg, Ind.

Year	Team	W	L	PCT	ERA	G	GS	CG	IP	H	BB	SO	ShO	Relief Pitching W	L	SV	Batting AB	H	HR	BA	PO	A	E	DP	TC/G	FA
1896	NY N	0	1	.000	6.00	2	1	1	12	12	9	3	0	0	0	0	3	1	0	.333	0	5	2	0	3.5	.714

Ryan Bowen

BOWEN, RYAN EUGENE — BR TR 6′ 185 lbs.
B. Feb. 10, 1968, Hanford, Calif.

Year	Team	W	L	PCT	ERA	G	GS	CG	IP	H	BB	SO	ShO	Relief Pitching W	L	SV	Batting AB	H	HR	BA	PO	A	E	DP	TC/G	FA
1991	HOU N	6	4	.600	5.15	14	13	0	71.2	73	36	49	0	1	0	0	22	4	0	.182	4	3	2	0	0.6	.778
1992		0	7	.000	10.96	11	9	0	33.2	48	30	22	0	0	0	0	9	1	0	.111	0	3	0	0	0.3	1.000
1993	FLA N	8	12	.400	4.42	27	27	2	156.2	156	87	98	1	0	0	0	51	6	0	.118	7	24	2	0	1.2	.939
1994		1	5	.167	4.94	8	8	1	47.1	50	19	32	0	0	0	0	14	5	0	.357	0	3	1	0	0.5	.750
1995		2	0	1.000	3.78	4	3	0	16.2	23	12	15	0	0	0	0	6	2	0	.333	0	2	0	0	0.5	1.000
5 yrs.		17	28	.378	5.30	64	60	3	326	350	184	216	1	1	0	0	102	18	0	.176	11	35	5	0	0.8	.902

Frank Bowerman

BOWERMAN, FRANK EUGENE (Mike) — BR TR 6′ 2″ 190 lbs.
B. Dec. 5, 1868, Romeo, Mich. D. Nov. 30, 1948, Romeo, Mich.
Manager 1909.

Year	Team	W	L	PCT	ERA	G	GS	CG	IP	H	BB	SO	ShO	Relief Pitching W	L	SV	Batting AB	H	HR	BA	PO	A	E	DP	TC/G	FA
1904	NY N	0	0	—	9.00	1	0	0	1	3	1	0	0	0	0	0	*				2	0	0	0	2.0	1.000

Stew Bowers

BOWERS, STEWART COLE (Doc) — BB TR 6′ 170 lbs.
B. Feb. 26, 1915, New Freedom, Pa.

Year	Team	W	L	PCT	ERA	G	GS	CG	IP	H	BB	SO	ShO	Relief Pitching W	L	SV	Batting AB	H	HR	BA	PO	A	E	DP	TC/G	FA
1935	BOS A	2	1	.667	3.42	10	2	1	23.2	26	17	5	0	1	0	0	5	1	0	.200	0	7	1	0	0.8	.875
1936		0	0	—	9.53	5	0	0	5.2	10	2	0	0	0	0	0	0	0	0	—	0	0	0	0	0.0	.000
2 yrs.		2	1	.667	4.60	15	2	1	29.1	36	19	5	0	1	0	0	5	1	0	.200	0	7	1	0	0.5	.875

Grant Bowler

BOWLER, GRANT TIERNEY (Moose) — BR TR 6′ 190 lbs.
B. Oct. 24, 1907, Denver, Colo. D. June 25, 1968, Denver, Colo.

Year	Team	W	L	PCT	ERA	G	GS	CG	IP	H	BB	SO	ShO	Relief Pitching W	L	SV	Batting AB	H	HR	BA	PO	A	E	DP	TC/G	FA
1931	CHI A	0	1	.000	5.35	13	3	1	35.1	40	24	15	0	0	0	0	10	1	0	.100	2	3	1	0	0.5	.833
1932		0	0	—	15.63	4	0	0	6.1	15	3	2	0	0	0	0	2	0	0	.000	0	2	1	1	0.8	.667
2 yrs.		0	1	.000	6.91	17	3	1	41.2	55	27	17	0	0	0	0	12	1	0	.083	2	5	2	1	0.5	.778

Charlie Bowles

BOWLES, CHARLES JAMES — BR TR 6′ 3″ 180 lbs.
B. Mar. 15, 1917, Norwood, Mass.

Year	Team	W	L	PCT	ERA	G	GS	CG	IP	H	BB	SO	ShO	Relief Pitching W	L	SV	Batting AB	H	HR	BA	PO	A	E	DP	TC/G	FA
1943	PHI A	1	1	.500	3.00	2	2	2	18	17	4	6	0	0	0	0	8	1	0	.125	2	3	1	2	3.0	.833
1945		0	3	.000	5.13	8	4	1	33.1	35	23	11	0	0	1	0	21	5	0	.238	5	6	0	0	1.4	1.000
2 yrs.		1	4	.200	4.38	10	6	3	51.1	52	27	17	0	0	1	0	29	6	0	.207	7	9	1	2	1.7	.941

Emmett Bowles

BOWLES, EMMETT JEROME (Chief) — BR TR 6′ 180 lbs.
B. Aug. 2, 1898, Wanette, Okla. D. Sept. 3, 1959, Flagstaff, Ariz.

Year	Team	W	L	PCT	ERA	G	GS	CG	IP	H	BB	SO	ShO	Relief Pitching W	L	SV	Batting AB	H	HR	BA	PO	A	E	DP	TC/G	FA
1922	CHI A	0	0	—	27.00	1	0	0	1	2	1	0	0	0	0	0	0	0	0	—	0	0	0	0	0.0	.000

Abe Bowman

BOWMAN, ALVAH EDSON BR TR 6′ 1″ 190 lbs.
B. Jan. 25, 1893, Greenup, Ill. D. Oct. 11, 1979, Longview, Tex.

Year	Team	W	L	PCT	ERA	G	GS	CG	IP	H	BB	SO	ShO	Relief Pitching W	L	SV	Batting AB	H	HR	BA	PO	A	E	DP	TC/G	FA
1914	CLE A	2	7	.222	4.46	22	10	2	72.2	74	45	27	1	1	0	0	21	1	0	.048	5	19	3	1	1.2	.889
1915		0	1	.000	20.25	2	1	0	1.1	1	3	0	0	0	0	0	0	0	0	—	0	3	0	0	1.5	1.000
2 yrs.		2	8	.200	4.74	24	11	2	74	75	48	27	1	1	0	0	21	1	0	.048	5	22	3	1	1.3	.900

Bob Bowman

BOWMAN, ROBERT JAMES BR TR 5′10½″ 160 lbs.
B. Oct. 3, 1910, Keystone, W. Va. D. Sept. 4, 1972, Bluefield, W. Va.

Year	Team	W	L	PCT	ERA	G	GS	CG	IP	H	BB	SO	ShO	Relief Pitching W	L	SV	Batting AB	H	HR	BA	PO	A	E	DP	TC/G	FA
1939	STL N	13	5	.722	2.60	51	15	4	169.1	141	60	78	2	7	0	**9**	47	4	0	.085	4	30	2	0	0.7	.944
1940		7	5	.583	4.33	28	17	7	114.1	118	43	43	0	0	2	0	33	2	0	.061	2	23	1	0	0.9	.962
1941	NY N	6	7	.462	5.71	29	6	2	80.1	100	36	25	0	4	4	1	21	1	1	.048	4	20	0	0	0.8	1.000
1942	CHI N	0	0	—	0.00	1	0	0	1	1	0	0	0	0	0	0	0	0	0	—	0	0	0	0	0.0	.000
4 yrs.		26	17	.605	3.82	109	38	13	365	360	139	146	2	11	6	10	101	7	1	.069	10	73	3	0	0.8	.965

Bob Bowman

BOWMAN, ROBERT LEROY BR TR 6′ 1″ 195 lbs.
B. May 10, 1931, Laytonville, Calif.

Year	Team	W	L	PCT	ERA	G	GS	CG	IP	H	BB	SO	ShO	Relief Pitching W	L	SV	Batting AB	H	HR	BA	PO	A	E	DP	TC/G	FA
1959	PHI N	0	1	.000	6.00	5	0	0	6	5	5	0	0	0	1	0	*				3	0	0	0	1.5	1.000

Joe Bowman

BOWMAN, JOSEPH EMIL BL TR 6′ 2″ 190 lbs.
B. June 17, 1910, Argentine, Kans. D. Nov. 22, 1990, Kansas City, Mo.

Year	Team	W	L	PCT	ERA	G	GS	CG	IP	H	BB	SO	ShO	Relief Pitching W	L	SV	Batting AB	H	HR	BA	PO	A	E	DP	TC/G	FA
1932	PHI A	0	1	.000	8.18	7	0	0	11	14	6	4	0	0	1	0	1	1	0	1.000	1	6	1	0	1.1	.875
1934	NY N	5	4	.556	3.61	30	10	3	107.1	119	36	36	0	1	1	3	29	5	0	.172	6	20	0	0	0.9	1.000
1935	PHI N	7	10	.412	4.25	33	17	6	148.1	157	56	58	1	2	3	1	67	13	1	.194	9	28	2	2	1.1	.949
1936		9	20	.310	5.04	40	28	12	203.2	243	53	80	0	1	3	1	77	15	0	.195	7	32	5	4	1.1	.886
1937	PIT N	8	8	.500	4.57	30	19	7	128	161	35	38	0	1	1	1	47	10	0	.213	14	24	0	3	1.3	1.000
1938		3	4	.429	4.65	17	1	0	60	68	20	25	0	3	3	1	21	7	0	.333	2	8	1	2	0.6	.909
1939		10	14	.417	4.48	37	27	10	184.2	217	43	58	1	1	0	1	96	33	0	.344	6	39	0	3	1.2	1.000
1940		9	10	.474	4.46	32	24	10	187.2	209	66	57	0	2	0	2	90	22	1	.244	15	36	1	0	1.6	.981
1941		3	2	.600	2.99	18	7	1	69.1	77	28	22	1	1	1	1	31	8	0	.258	5	13	0	0	1.0	1.000
1944	BOS A	12	8	.600	4.81	26	24	10	168.1	175	64	53	1	0	0	0	100	20	0	.200	9	20	2	3	1.2	.935
1945	2 teams BOS A (3G 0–2) CIN N (25G 11–13)																									
"	total	11	15	.423	3.92	28	27	15	197.1	216	77	71	1	0	0	0	80	7	0	.087	12	28	3	0	1.5	.930
11 yrs.		77	96	.445	4.40	298	184	74	1465.2	1656	484	502	5	12	13	11	*				86	254	15	17	1.2	.958

Roger Bowman

BOWMAN, ROGER CLINTON BR TL 6′ 175 lbs.
B. Aug. 18, 1927, Amsterdam, N. Y.

Year	Team	W	L	PCT	ERA	G	GS	CG	IP	H	BB	SO	ShO	Relief Pitching W	L	SV	Batting AB	H	HR	BA	PO	A	E	DP	TC/G	FA
1949	NY N	0	0	—	4.26	2	2	0	6.1	6	7	4	0	0	0	0	2	0	0	.000	1	3	0	0	2.0	1.000
1951		2	4	.333	6.15	9	5	0	26.1	35	22	24	0	1	1	0	6	0	0	.000	2	1	0	0	0.3	1.000
1952		0	0	—	12.00	2	1	0	3	6	3	3	0	0	0	0	1	0	0	.000	0	0	0	0	0.0	.000
1953	PIT N	0	4	.000	4.82	30	2	0	65.1	65	29	36	0	0	2	0	7	2	0	.286	6	11	0	0	0.6	1.000
1955		0	3	.000	8.64	7	2	0	16.2	25	10	8	0	0	1	0	2	1	0	.500	1	5	0	0	0.9	1.000
5 yrs.		2	11	.154	5.81	50	12	0	117.2	137	71	75	0	1	4	0	18	3	0	.167	10	20	0	0	0.6	1.000

Sumner Bowman

BOWMAN, SUMNER SALLADE BL TL 6′ 160 lbs.
B. Feb. 9, 1867, Millersburg, Pa. D. Jan. 11, 1954, Millersburg, Pa.

Year	Team	W	L	PCT	ERA	G	GS	CG	IP	H	BB	SO	ShO	Relief Pitching W	L	SV	Batting AB	H	HR	BA	PO	A	E	DP	TC/G	FA
1890	2 teams PHI N (1G 0–0) PIT N (9G 2–5)																									
"	total	2	5	.286	6.75	10	8	6	78.2	111	52	24	0	0	0	0	40	12	0	.300	4	14	4	0	1.8	.818
1891	PHI AA	2	5	.286	3.44	8	8	8	68	73	37	22	0	0	0	0	54	13	0	.241	8	14	4	1	1.9	.846
2 yrs.		4	10	.286	5.22	18	16	14	146.2	184	89	46	0	0	0	0	94	25	0	.266	12	28	8	1	1.8	.833

Ted Bowsfield

BOWSFIELD, EDWARD OLIVER BR TL 6′ 1″ 190 lbs.
B. Jan. 10, 1935, Vernon, B. C., Canada.

Year	Team	W	L	PCT	ERA	G	GS	CG	IP	H	BB	SO	ShO	Relief Pitching W	L	SV	Batting AB	H	HR	BA	PO	A	E	DP	TC/G	FA
1958	BOS A	4	2	.667	3.84	16	10	2	65.2	58	36	38	0	1	0	0	26	4	0	.154	5	16	1	1	1.4	.955
1959		0	1	.000	15.00	5	2	0	9	16	9	4	0	0	0	0	1	0	0	.000	1	0	0	0	0.2	1.000
1960	2 teams BOS A (17G 1–2) CLE A (11G 3–4)																									
"	total	4	6	.400	5.11	28	8	1	61.2	67	33	32	1	1	2	2	14	2	0	.143	6	15	1	3	0.8	.955
1961	LA A	11	8	.579	3.73	41	21	4	157	154	63	88	1	2	1	0	51	7	0	.137	4	26	5	1	0.9	.857
1962		9	8	.529	4.40	34	25	1	139	154	40	52	0	1	1	1	37	6	0	.162	12	13	5	0	0.9	.833
1963	KC A	5	7	.417	4.45	41	11	2	111.1	115	47	67	1	2	2	3	23	1	0	.043	12	25	1	2	0.9	.974
1964		4	7	.364	4.10	50	9	2	118.2	135	31	45	1	2	2	0	21	2	0	.095	9	20	2	2	0.6	.935
7 yrs.		37	39	.487	4.35	215	86	12	662.1	699	259	326	4	9	8	6	173	22	0	.127	49	115	15	9	0.8	.916

Gary Boyd

BOYD, GARY LEE BR TR 6′ 4″ 200 lbs.
B. Aug. 22, 1946, Pasadena, Calif.

Year	Team	W	L	PCT	ERA	G	GS	CG	IP	H	BB	SO	ShO	Relief Pitching W	L	SV	Batting AB	H	HR	BA	PO	A	E	DP	TC/G	FA
1969	CLE A	0	2	.000	9.00	8	3	0	11	8	14	9	0	0	0	0	1	0	0	.000	2	0	0	0	0.3	1.000

Jake Boyd

BOYD, JACOB HENRY TL 160 lbs.
B. Jan. 19, 1874, Martinsburg, W. Va. D. Aug. 12, 1932, Gettysburg, Pa.

Year	Team	W	L	PCT	ERA	G	GS	CG	IP	H	BB	SO	ShO	Relief Pitching W	L	SV	Batting AB	H	HR	BA	PO	A	E	DP	TC/G	FA
1894	WAS N	0	3	.000	8.53	3	3	3	19	37	14	3	0	0	0	0	21	3	0	.143	4	8	2	0	2.3	.857
1895		2	11	.154	7.07	14	12	8	85.1	126	35	16	0	0	1	0	157	42	1	.268	50	55	24	5	2.4	.814
1896		1	2	.333	6.75	4	2	2	32	45	15	6	0	1	0	0	13	1	0	.077	1	9	1	0	2.8	.909
3 yrs.		3	16	.158	7.20	21	17	13	136.1	208	64	25	0	1	1	0	*				55	72	27	5	2.4	.825

Oil Can Boyd

BOYD, DENNIS RAY BR TR 6′ 1″ 155 lbs.
B. Oct. 6, 1959, Meridian, Miss.

Year	Team	W	L	PCT	ERA	G	GS	CG	IP	H	BB	SO	ShO	Relief Pitching W	L	SV	Batting AB	H	HR	BA	PO	A	E	DP	TC/G	FA
1982	BOS A	0	1	.000	5.40	3	1	0	8.1	11	2	2	0	0	0	0	0	0	0	—	0	1	0	0	0.3	1.000
1983		4	8	.333	3.28	15	13	5	98.2	103	23	43	0	0	0	0	0	0	0	—	5	10	1	1	1.1	.938
1984		12	12	.500	4.37	29	26	10	197.2	207	53	134	3	0	1	0	0	0	0	—	20	31	2	3	1.8	.962
1985		15	13	.536	3.70	35	35	13	272.1	**273**	67	154	3	0	0	0	0	0	0	—	42	41	1	2	2.4	.988
1986		16	10	.615	3.78	30	30	10	214.1	222	45	129	0	0	0	0	0	0	0	—	24	27	2	4	1.8	.962
1987		1	3	.250	5.89	7	7	0	36.2	47	9	12														
1988		9	7	.563	5.34	23	23	1	129.2	147	41	71	0	0	0	0	0	0	0	—	4	11	0	0	2.1	1.000
1989		3	2	.600	4.42	10	10	0	59	57	19	26	0	0	0	0	0	0	0	—	8	15	2	0	1.1	.920
																					7	10	0	1	1.7	1.000

Oil Can Boyd *continued*

Year	Team	Lg	W	L	PCT	ERA	G	GS	CG	IP	H	BB	SO	ShO	Relief Pitching W	Relief Pitching L	Relief Pitching SV	Batting AB	Batting H	Batting HR	BA	PO	A	E	DP	TC/G	FA
1990	**MON**	**N**	10	6	.625	2.93	31	31	3	190.2	164	52	113	3	0	0	0	59	3	0	.051	7	24	3	1	1.1	.912
1991	**2 teams**		**MON N** (19G 6–8) **TEX A** (12G 2–7)																								
"	**total**		8	15	.348	4.59	31	31	1	182.1	196	57	115	1	0	0	0	36	3	0	.083	11	17	0	1	0.9	1.000
10 yrs.			78	77	.503	4.04	214	207	43	1389.2	1427	368	799	10	0	1	0	95	6	0	.063	128	187	11	13	1.5	.966
LEAGUE CHAMPIONSHIP SERIES																											
1986	**BOS**	**A**	1	1	.500	4.61	2	2	0	13.2	17	3	8	0	0	0	0	0	0	0	—	2	3	0	0	2.5	1.000
WORLD SERIES																											
1986	**BOS**	**A**	0	1	.000	7.71	1	1	0	7	9	1	3	0	0	0	0	0	0	0	—	1	0	0	0	1.0	1.000

Ray Boyd

BOYD, RAYMOND C. BR TR 5′10″ 160 lbs.
B. Feb. 11, 1887, Hortonville, Ind. D. Feb. 11, 1920, Hortonville, Ind.

Year	Team	Lg	W	L	PCT	ERA	G	GS	CG	IP	H	BB	SO	ShO	Relief W	Relief L	Relief SV	AB	H	HR	BA	PO	A	E	DP	TC/G	FA
1910	**STL**	**A**	0	2	.000	4.40	3	2	1	14.1	16	5	6	0	0	0	0	5	1	0	.200	0	2	0	0	0.7	1.000
1911	**CIN**	**N**	3	2	.600	2.66	7	4	3	44	34	19	20	0	1	0	1	12	1	0	.083	4	11	3	0	2.6	.833
2 yrs.			3	4	.429	3.09	10	6	4	58.1	50	24	26	0	1	0	1	17	2	0	.118	4	13	3	0	2.0	.850

Cloyd Boyer

BOYER, CLOYD VICTOR (Junior) BR TR 6′ 1″ 188 lbs.
Brother of Ken Boyer. Brother of Clete Boyer.
B. Sept. 1, 1927, Alba, Mo.

Year	Team	Lg	W	L	PCT	ERA	G	GS	CG	IP	H	BB	SO	ShO	Relief W	Relief L	Relief SV	AB	H	HR	BA	PO	A	E	DP	TC/G	FA
1949	**STL**	**N**	0	0	—	10.80	3	1	0	3.1	5	7	0	0	0	0	0	0	0	0	—	1	0	0	1	0.3	1.000
1950			7	7	.500	3.52	36	14	6	120.1	105	49	82	2	2	1	1	33	6	0	.182	5	22	4	1	0.9	.871
1951			2	5	.286	5.26	19	8	1	63.1	68	46	40	0	1	2	1	20	4	0	.200	1	4	1	0	0.3	.833
1952			6	6	.500	4.24	23	14	4	110.1	108	47	44	2	0	0	0	38	8	0	.211	4	12	2	1	0.8	.889
1955	**KC**	**A**	5	5	.500	6.22	30	11	2	98.1	107	69	32	0	1	1	0	29	2	0	.069	9	13	2	0	0.8	.917
5 yrs.			20	23	.465	4.73	111	48	13	395.2	393	218	198	4	4	4	2	120	20	0	.167	20	51	9	3	0.7	.887

Henry Boyle

BOYLE, HENRY J. (Handsome Henry) TR
B. Sept. 20, 1860, Philadelphia, Pa. D. May 25, 1932, Philadelphia, Pa.

Year	Team	Lg	W	L	PCT	ERA	G	GS	CG	IP	H	BB	SO	ShO	Relief W	Relief L	Relief SV	AB	H	HR	BA	PO	A	E	DP	TC/G	FA
1884	**STL**	**U**	15	3	.833	*1.74*	19	16	16	150	118	10	88	2	1	1	1	262	68	4	.260	85	49	19	7	2.2	.876
1885	**STL**	**N**	16	24	.400	*2.75*	42	39	39	366.2	346	100	133	1	**1**	0	0	258	52	1	.202	94	76	19	4	2.5	.899
1886			9	15	.375	**1.76**	25	24	23	210	183	46	101	2	1	0	0	108	27	1	.250	18	39	9	1	2.1	.864
1887	**IND**	**N**	13	24	.351	3.65	38	38	37	328	356	69	85	0	0	0	0	141	27	2	.191	12	42	10	2	1.5	.844
1888			15	22	.405	3.26	37	37	36	323	315	58	98	3	0	0	0	125	18	1	.144	14	84	7	1	2.8	.933
1889			21	23	.477	3.92	46	45	38	378.2	422	95	97	2	1	0	0	155	38	1	.245	17	51	3	0	1.5	.958
6 yrs.			89	111	.445	3.06	207	199	189	1756.1	1740	378	602	10	4	1	1	*				240	341	67	15	2.1	.897

Harry Boyles

BOYLES, HARRY (Stretch) BR TR 6′ 5″ 185 lbs.
B. Nov. 29, 1911, Granite City, Ill.

Year	Team	Lg	W	L	PCT	ERA	G	GS	CG	IP	H	BB	SO	ShO	Relief W	Relief L	Relief SV	AB	H	HR	BA	PO	A	E	DP	TC/G	FA
1938	**CHI**	**A**	0	4	.000	5.22	9	2	1	29.1	31	25	18	0	0	2	1	8	1	0	.125	1	12	2	0	1.7	.867
1939			0	0	—	10.80	2	0	0	3.1	4	6	1	0	0	0	0	1	0	0	.000	0	0	0	0	0.0	.000
2 yrs.			0	4	.000	5.79	11	2	1	32.2	35	31	19	0	0	2	1	9	1	0	.111	1	12	2	0	1.4	.867

Gene Brabender

BRABENDER, EUGENE MATHEW BR TR 6′ 5½″ 225 lbs.
B. Aug. 14, 1941, Madison, Wis.

Year	Team	Lg	W	L	PCT	ERA	G	GS	CG	IP	H	BB	SO	ShO	Relief W	Relief L	Relief SV	AB	H	HR	BA	PO	A	E	DP	TC/G	FA
1966	**BAL**	**A**	4	3	.571	3.55	31	1	0	71	57	29	62	0	3	3	2	13	1	0	.077	7	12	2	0	0.7	.905
1967			6	4	.600	3.35	14	14	3	94	77	23	71	1	0	0	0	28	2	0	.071	7	13	3	1	1.6	.870
1968			6	7	.462	3.32	37	15	3	124.2	116	48	92	2	1	1	3	35	3	1	.086	6	15	3	1	0.6	.875
1969	**SEA**	**A**	13	14	.481	4.36	40	29	7	202.1	193	103	139	1	0	2	0	70	9	1	.129	13	17	3	1	0.8	.909
1970	**MIL**	**A**	6	15	.286	6.00	29	21	2	129	127	79	76	0	1	1	1	41	4	0	.098	13	17	3	1	1.1	.909
5 yrs.			35	43	.449	4.25	151	80	15	621	570	282	440	4	5	7	6	187	19	2	.102	46	74	14	4	0.9	.896

Jack Bracken

BRACKEN, JOHN JAMES BR TR 5′11″ 175 lbs.
B. Apr. 14, 1881, Cleveland, Ohio D. July 16, 1954, Highland Park, Mich.

Year	Team	Lg	W	L	PCT	ERA	G	GS	CG	IP	H	BB	SO	ShO	Relief W	Relief L	Relief SV	AB	H	HR	BA	PO	A	E	DP	TC/G	FA
1901	**CLE**	**A**	4	8	.333	6.21	12	12	12	100	137	31	18	0	0	0	0	44	10	0	.227	0	25	0	0	2.1	1.000

John Brackenridge

BRACKENRIDGE, JOHN GIVLER BR TR 6′
B. Dec. 24, 1880, Harrisburg, Pa. D. Mar. 20, 1953, Harrisburg, Pa.

Year	Team	Lg	W	L	PCT	ERA	G	GS	CG	IP	H	BB	SO	ShO	Relief W	Relief L	Relief SV	AB	H	HR	BA	PO	A	E	DP	TC/G	FA
1904	**PHI**	**N**	0	1	.000	5.56	7	1	0	34	37	16	11	0	0	0	0	13	2	0	.154	2	19	2	1	3.3	.913

Don Bradey

BRADEY, DONALD EUGENE BR TR 5′ 9″ 180 lbs.
B. Oct. 4, 1934, Charlotte, N. C.

Year	Team	Lg	W	L	PCT	ERA	G	GS	CG	IP	H	BB	SO	ShO	Relief W	Relief L	Relief SV	AB	H	HR	BA	PO	A	E	DP	TC/G	FA
1964	**HOU**	**N**	0	2	.000	19.29	3	1	0	2.1	6	3	2	0	0	1	0	0	0	0	—	0	0	0	0	0.0	.000

Bill Bradford

BRADFORD, WILLIAM D BR TR 6′ 2″ 180 lbs.
B. Aug. 28, 1921, Choctaw, Ark.

Year	Team	Lg	W	L	PCT	ERA	G	GS	CG	IP	H	BB	SO	ShO	Relief W	Relief L	Relief SV	AB	H	HR	BA	PO	A	E	DP	TC/G	FA
1956	**KC**	**A**	0	0	—	9.00	1	0	0	2	2	1	0	0	0	0	0	0	0	0	—	0	1	0	0	1.0	1.000

Larry Bradford

BRADFORD, LARRY BR TL 6′ 1″ 200 lbs.
B. Dec. 21, 1949, Chicago, Ill.

Year	Team	Lg	W	L	PCT	ERA	G	GS	CG	IP	H	BB	SO	ShO	Relief W	Relief L	Relief SV	AB	H	HR	BA	PO	A	E	DP	TC/G	FA
1977	**ATL**	**N**	0	0	—	3.00	2	0	0	3	3	0	1	0	0	0	0	0	0	0	—	0	1	0	0	0.5	1.000
1979			1	0	1.000	0.95	21	0	0	19	11	10	11	0	1	0	2	1	0	0	.000	0	5	1	0	0.3	.833
1980			3	4	.429	2.45	56	0	0	55	49	22	32	0	3	4	4	3	0	0	.000	3	8	0	0	0.2	1.000
1981			2	0	1.000	3.67	25	0	0	27	26	12	14	0	2	0	1	1	1	0	1.000	1	6	0	0	0.3	1.000
4 yrs.			6	4	.600	2.51	104	0	0	104	89	44	58	0	6	4	7	5	1	0	.200	4	20	1	0	0.2	.960

Bert Bradley

BRADLEY, STEVEN BERT BB TR 6′ 1″ 190 lbs.
B. Dec. 23, 1956, Athens, Ga.

Year	Team	Lg	W	L	PCT	ERA	G	GS	CG	IP	H	BB	SO	ShO	Relief W	Relief L	Relief SV	AB	H	HR	BA	PO	A	E	DP	TC/G	FA
1983	**OAK**	**A**	0	0	—	6.48	6	0	0	8.1	14	4	3	0	0	0	0	0	0	0	—	0	3	0	2	0.5	1.000

Bill Bradley

BRADLEY, WILLIAM JOSEPH BR TR 6′ 185 lbs.
B. Feb. 13, 1878, Cleveland, Ohio D. Mar. 11, 1954, Cleveland, Ohio.
Manager 1905, 1914.

Year	Team	Lg	W	L	PCT	ERA	G	GS	CG	IP	H	BB	SO	ShO	Relief W	Relief L	Relief SV	AB	H	HR	BA	PO	A	E	DP	TC/G	FA
1901	**CLE**	**A**	0	0	—	0.00	1	0	0	1	4	0	0	0	0	0	0	*				61	82	23	8	4.7	.861

Foghorn Bradley

BRADLEY, GEORGE H.
B. July 1, 1855, Medford, Mass. D. Apr. 3, 1900, Philadelphia, Pa.
BR TR

Year	Team	Lg	W	L	PCT	ERA	G	GS	CG	IP	H	BB	SO	ShO	Relief Pitching W	Relief Pitching L	Relief Pitching SV	Batting AB	Batting H	Batting HR	BA	PO	A	E	DP	TC/G	FA
1876	BOS	N	9	10	.474	2.49	22	21	16	173.1	201	16	16	1	0	0	1	82	19	0	.232	12	24	3	0	1.5	.923

Fred Bradley

BRADLEY, FREDERICK LANGDON
B. July 31, 1920, Parsons, Kans.
BR TR 6′ 1″ 180 lbs.

Year	Team	Lg	W	L	PCT	ERA	G	GS	CG	IP	H	BB	SO	ShO	Relief Pitching W	Relief Pitching L	Relief Pitching SV	Batting AB	Batting H	Batting HR	BA	PO	A	E	DP	TC/G	FA
1948	CHI	A	0	0	—	4.60	8	0	0	15.2	11	4	2	0	0	0	0	1	0	0	.000	3	3	0	0	0.8	1.000
1949			0	0	—	13.50	1	1	0	2	4	3	0	0	0	0	0	1	0	0	.000	0	1	0	0	1.0	1.000
2 yrs.			0	0		5.60	9	1	0	17.2	15	7	2	0	0	0	0	2	0	0	.000	3	4	0	0	0.8	1.000

George Bradley

BRADLEY, GEORGE WASHINGTON (Grin)
B. July 13, 1852, Reading, Pa. D. Oct. 2, 1931, Philadelphia, Pa.
BR TR 5′10½″ 175 lbs.

Year	Team	Lg	W	L	PCT	ERA	G	GS	CG	IP	H	BB	SO	ShO	Relief Pitching W	Relief Pitching L	Relief Pitching SV	Batting AB	Batting H	Batting HR	BA	PO	A	E	DP	TC/G	FA
1876	STL	N	45	19	.703	**1.23**	64	64	63	573	470	38	103	**16**	0	0	0	265	66	0	.249	50	87	12	4	2.3	.919
1877	CHI	N	18	23	.439	3.31	50	44	35	394	452	39	59	2	1	0	0	214	52	0	.243	48	89	18	2	2.2	.884
1879	TRO	N	13	**40**	.245	2.85	54	54	53	487	590	26	133	3	0	0	0	251	62	0	.247	62	154	33	1	3.9	.867
1880	PRO	N	12	9	.571	1.38	28	20	16	196	158	6	54	4	**3**	1	1	309	70	0	.227	104	214	55	10	4.0	.853
1881	CLE	N	2	4	.333	3.88	6	6	5	51	70	3	6	0	0	0	0	245	60	2	.245	89	106	39	9	3.8	.833
1882			6	10	.375	*3.73*	18	16	15	147	164	22	32	0	0	0	0	115	21	0	.183	82	47	13	8	4.3	.908
1883	PHI	AA	16	7	.696	*3.15*	26	23	22	214.1	215	22	56	0	0	0	0	328	78	1	.238	92	160	68	10	3.7	.788
1884	CIN	U	25	15	.625	*2.71*	41	38	36	342	350	23	168	3	1	1	0	226	43	0	.190	82	94	24	4	3.1	.880
8 yrs.			137	127	.519	2.50	287	265	245	2404.1	2469	179	611	28	5	2	1	*				625	1000	275	50	3.4	.855

Herb Bradley

BRADLEY, HERBERT THEODORE
B. Jan. 3, 1903, Agenda, Kans. D. Oct. 16, 1959, Clay Center, Kans.
BR TR 6′ 170 lbs.

Year	Team	Lg	W	L	PCT	ERA	G	GS	CG	IP	H	BB	SO	ShO	Relief Pitching W	Relief Pitching L	Relief Pitching SV	Batting AB	Batting H	Batting HR	BA	PO	A	E	DP	TC/G	FA
1927	BOS	A	1	1	.500	3.13	6	2	2	23	16	7	6	0	0	0	0	7	3	0	.429	0	5	0	0	0.8	1.000
1928			0	3	.000	7.23	15	5	1	47.1	64	16	14	1	0	0	0	13	2	0	.154	2	17	0	0	1.3	1.000
1929			0	0	—	6.75	3	0	0	4	7	2	0	0	0	0	0	1	0	0	.000	0	2	0	0	0.7	1.000
3 yrs.			1	4	.200	5.93	24	7	3	74.1	87	25	20	1	0	0	0	21	5	0	.238	2	24	0	0	1.1	1.000

Tom Bradley

BRADLEY, THOMAS WILLIAM
B. Mar. 16, 1947, Asheville, N. C.
BR TR 6′ 2½″ 180 lbs.

Year	Team	Lg	W	L	PCT	ERA	G	GS	CG	IP	H	BB	SO	ShO	Relief Pitching W	Relief Pitching L	Relief Pitching SV	Batting AB	Batting H	Batting HR	BA	PO	A	E	DP	TC/G	FA
1969	CAL	A	0	1	.000	27.00	3	0	0	2	9	0	2	0	0	1	0	0	0	0	—	0	1	0	0	0.3	1.000
1970			2	5	.286	4.11	17	11	1	70	71	33	53	1	0	0	0	18	3	0	.167	5	9	1	0	0.9	.933
1971	CHI	A	15	15	.500	2.96	45	39	7	286	273	74	206	6	0	1	2	96	15	1	.156	24	32	2	0	1.3	.966
1972			15	14	.517	2.98	40	40	11	260	225	65	209	2	0	0	0	91	12	0	.132	13	35	2	2	1.3	.960
1973	SF	N	13	12	.520	3.90	35	34	6	223.2	212	69	136	1	0	0	0	77	15	0	.195	12	25	3	0	1.1	.925
1974			8	11	.421	5.17	30	21	2	134	152	52	72	0	0	1	0	40	3	0	.075	10	13	3	2	0.9	.885
1975			2	3	.400	6.21	13	6	0	42	57	18	13	0	0	0	0	10	0	0	.000	1	9	0	0	0.8	1.000
7 yrs.			55	61	.474	3.72	183	151	27	1017.2	999	311	691	10	0	3	2	332	48	1	.145	65	124	11	4	1.1	.945

Joe Bradshaw

BRADSHAW, JOE SIAH
B. Aug. 17, 1897, Ro Ellen, Tenn. D. Jan. 30, 1985, Tavares, Fla.
BR TR 6′ 2½″ 200 lbs.

Year	Team	Lg	W	L	PCT	ERA	G	GS	CG	IP	H	BB	SO	ShO	Relief Pitching W	Relief Pitching L	Relief Pitching SV	Batting AB	Batting H	Batting HR	BA	PO	A	E	DP	TC/G	FA
1929	BKN	N	0	0	—	4.50	2	0	0	4	3	4	1	0	0	0	0	0	0	0	—	0	2	0	1	1.0	1.000

Bill Brady

BRADY, WILLIAM ALOYSIUS
B. Aug. 18, 1889, New York, N. Y. Deceased.
BR TR 6′ 1½″ 180 lbs.

Year	Team	Lg	W	L	PCT	ERA	G	GS	CG	IP	H	BB	SO	ShO	Relief Pitching W	Relief Pitching L	Relief Pitching SV	Batting AB	Batting H	Batting HR	BA	PO	A	E	DP	TC/G	FA
1912	BOS	N	0	0	—	0.00	1	0	0	1	2	0	0	0	0	0	0	0	0	0	—	0	0	0	0	0.0	.000

Jim Brady

BRADY, JAMES JOSEPH (Diamond Jim)
B. Mar. 2, 1936, Jersey City, N. J.
BL TL 6′ 2″ 185 lbs.

Year	Team	Lg	W	L	PCT	ERA	G	GS	CG	IP	H	BB	SO	ShO	Relief Pitching W	Relief Pitching L	Relief Pitching SV	Batting AB	Batting H	Batting HR	BA	PO	A	E	DP	TC/G	FA
1956	DET	A	0	0	—	28.42	6	0	0	6.1	15	11	3	0	0	0	0	0	0	0	—	0	1	0	0	0.2	1.000

King Brady

BRADY, JAMES WARD
B. May 28, 1881, Elmer, N. J. D. Aug. 21, 1947, Albany, N. Y.
BR TR 6′ 190 lbs.

Year	Team	Lg	W	L	PCT	ERA	G	GS	CG	IP	H	BB	SO	ShO	Relief Pitching W	Relief Pitching L	Relief Pitching SV	Batting AB	Batting H	Batting HR	BA	PO	A	E	DP	TC/G	FA
1905	PHI	N	1	1	.500	3.46	2	2	2	13	19	2	3	0	0	0	0	5	1	0	.200	1	3	1	1	2.5	.800
1906	PIT	N	1	1	.500	2.35	3	2	1	23	30	4	14	0	0	1	0	10	1	0	.100	1	3	0	0	1.3	1.000
1907			0	0	—	0.00	1	0	0	2	2	1	0	0	0	0	0	0	0	0	—	0	0	1	0	1.0	.000
1908	BOS	A	1	0	1.000	0.00	1	1	1	9	8	0	3	1	0	0	0	2	0	0	.000	0	1	0	0	1.0	1.000
1912	BOS	N	0	0	—	20.25	1	0	0	2.2	5	3	0	0	0	0	0	1	0	0	.000	0	1	0	0	0.5	1.000
5 yrs.			3	2	.600	3.08	8	5	4	49.2	64	10	20	1	0	1	0	18	2	0	.111	2	8	2	1	1.3	.833

Neal Brady

BRADY, CORNELIUS JOSEPH
B. Mar. 4, 1897, Covington, Ky. D. June 19, 1947, Fort Mitchell, Ky.
BR TR 6′½″ 197 lbs.

Year	Team	Lg	W	L	PCT	ERA	G	GS	CG	IP	H	BB	SO	ShO	Relief Pitching W	Relief Pitching L	Relief Pitching SV	Batting AB	Batting H	Batting HR	BA	PO	A	E	DP	TC/G	FA
1915	NY	A	0	0	—	3.12	2	1	0	8.2	9	7	6	0	0	0	0	4	0	0	.000	0	2	0	0	1.0	1.000
1917			1	0	1.000	2.00	2	1	0	9	6	5	4	0	0	0	0	2	1	0	.500	0	5	0	0	2.5	1.000
1925	CIN	N	1	3	.250	4.66	20	3	2	63.2	73	20	12	0	0	1	1	25	6	0	.240	6	16	2	0	1.2	.917
3 yrs.			2	3	.400	4.20	24	5	2	81.1	88	32	22	0	0	1	1	31	7	0	.226	6	23	2	0	1.3	.935

Dick Braggins

BRAGGINS, RICHARD REALF
B. Dec. 25, 1879, Mercer, Pa. D. Aug. 16, 1963, Lake Wales, Fla.
BR TR 5′11″ 170 lbs.

Year	Team	Lg	W	L	PCT	ERA	G	GS	CG	IP	H	BB	SO	ShO	Relief Pitching W	Relief Pitching L	Relief Pitching SV	Batting AB	Batting H	Batting HR	BA	PO	A	E	DP	TC/G	FA
1901	CLE	A	1	2	.333	4.78	4	3	2	32	44	15	1	0	0	0	0	13	2	0	.154	0	10	0	1	2.5	1.000

Al Braithwood

BRAITHWOOD, ALFRED
B. Feb. 15, 1892, Braceville, Ill. D. Nov. 24, 1960, Rowlesburg, W. Va.
BR TL 6′ 1½″ 145 lbs.

Year	Team	Lg	W	L	PCT	ERA	G	GS	CG	IP	H	BB	SO	ShO	Relief Pitching W	Relief Pitching L	Relief Pitching SV	Batting AB	Batting H	Batting HR	BA	PO	A	E	DP	TC/G	FA
1915	PIT	F	0	0	—	0.00	2	0	0	3	0	0	2	0	0	0	0	0	0	0	—	0	0	0	0	0.0	.000

Erv Brame

BRAME, ERVIN BECKHAM
B. Oct. 12, 1901, Big Rock, Tenn. D. Nov. 22, 1949, Hopkinsville, Ky.
BL TR 6′ 2″ 190 lbs.

Year	Team	Lg	W	L	PCT	ERA	G	GS	CG	IP	H	BB	SO	ShO	Relief Pitching W	Relief Pitching L	Relief Pitching SV	Batting AB	Batting H	Batting HR	BA	PO	A	E	DP	TC/G	FA
1928	PIT	N	7	4	.636	5.08	24	11	6	95.2	110	44	22	0	0	1	0	49	13	1	.265	2	18	1	0	0.9	.952
1929			16	11	.593	4.55	37	28	19	229.2	250	71	68	1	2	0	0	116	36	4	.310	7	36	3	0	1.2	.935
1930			17	8	.680	4.70	32	29	**22**	235.2	291	56	55	0	1	0	1	116	41	3	.353	1	39	2	0	1.3	.952
1931			9	13	.409	4.21	26	21	15	179.2	211	45	33	2	2	1	0	95	26	0	.274	1	34	1	2	1.4	.972
1932			3	1	.750	7.41	23	3	0	51	84	16	10	0	3	0	0	20	5	0	.250	0	9	0	1	0.4	1.000
5 yrs.			52	37	.584	4.76	142	92	62	791.2	946	232	188	3	8	2	1	*				11	136	7	3	1.1	.955

Ralph Branca

BRANCA, RALPH THEODORE JOSEPH (Hawk) BR TR 6′ 3″ 220 lbs.
B. Jan. 6, 1926, Mt. Vernon, N. Y.

Year	Team	W	L	PCT	ERA	G	GS	CG	IP	H	BB	SO	ShO	Relief Pitching W	Relief Pitching L	Relief Pitching SV	Batting AB	Batting H	Batting HR	BA	PO	A	E	DP	TC/G	FA
1944	BKN N	0	2	.000	7.05	21	1	0	44.2	46	32	16	0	0	1	1	6	0	0	.000	2	8	0	0	0.5	1.000
1945		5	6	.455	3.04	16	15	7	109.2	73	79	69	0	0	0	1	40	4	0	.100	7	20	2	1	1.8	.931
1946		3	1	.750	3.88	24	10	2	67.1	62	41	42	2	0	1	3	18	2	0	.111	3	6	1	0	0.4	.900
1947		21	12	.636	2.67	43	**36**	15	280	251	98	148	4	3	1	1	97	12	0	.124	9	35	3	0	1.1	.936
1948		14	9	.609	3.51	36	28	11	215.2	189	80	122	1	1	0	1	74	15	0	.203	10	18	1	0	0.8	.966
1949		13	5	.722	4.39	34	27	9	186.2	181	91	109	2	0	1	1	62	5	0	.081	6	15	2	0	0.7	.913
1950		7	9	.438	4.69	43	15	5	142	152	55	100	0	2	4	7	34	4	2	.118	8	19	0	0	0.6	1.000
1951		13	12	.520	3.26	42	27	13	204	180	85	118	3	1	2	3	63	11	0	.175	12	19	0	1	0.7	1.000
1952		4	2	.667	3.84	16	7	2	61	52	21	26	0	1	0	0	19	3	0	.158	5	7	1	1	0.8	.923
1953	**2 teams**	BKN N	(7G 0–0)	DET A	(17G 4–7)																					
″	**total**	4	7	.364	4.70	24	14	7	113	113	36	55	0	0	0	1	34	4	0	.118	7	12	1	1	0.8	.950
1954	**2 teams**	DET A	(17G 3–3)	NY A	(5G 1–0)																					
″	**total**	4	3	.571	5.12	22	8	0	58	72	43	22	0	2	3	0	17	6	0	.353	3	9	1	1	0.6	.923
1956	BKN N	0	0	—	0.00	1	0	0	2	1	2	2	0	0	0	0	0	0	0	—	0	1	0	0	1.0	1.000
12 yrs.		88	68	.564	3.79	322	188	71	1484	1372	663	829	12	10	13	19	464	66	2	.142	72	169	12	5	0.8	.953
WORLD SERIES																										
1947	BKN N	1	1	.500	8.64	3	1	0	8.1	12	5	8	0	1	0	0	4	0	0	.000	0	1	0	0	0.3	1.000
1949		0	1	.000	4.15	1	1	0	8.2	4	4	6	0	0	0	0	3	0	0	.000	1	0	0	0	1.0	1.000
2 yrs.		1	2	.333	6.35	4	2	0	17	16	9	14	0	1	0	0	7	0	0	.000	1	1	0	0	0.5	1.000

Harvey Branch

BRANCH, HARVEY ALFRED BR TL 6′ 175 lbs.
B. Feb. 8, 1939, Memphis, Tenn.

Year	Team	W	L	PCT	ERA	G	GS	CG	IP	H	BB	SO	ShO	Relief Pitching W	Relief Pitching L	Relief Pitching SV	Batting AB	Batting H	Batting HR	BA	PO	A	E	DP	TC/G	FA
1962	STL N	0	1	.000	5.40	1	1	0	5	5	5	2	0	0	0	0	1	0	0	.000	1	2	0	0	3.0	1.000

Norm Branch

BRANCH, NORMAN DOWNS (Red) BR TR 6′ 3″ 200 lbs.
B. Mar. 22, 1915, Spokane, Wash. D. Nov. 21, 1971, Novasota, Tex.

Year	Team	W	L	PCT	ERA	G	GS	CG	IP	H	BB	SO	ShO	Relief Pitching W	Relief Pitching L	Relief Pitching SV	Batting AB	Batting H	Batting HR	BA	PO	A	E	DP	TC/G	FA
1941	NY A	5	1	.833	2.87	27	0	0	47	37	26	28	0	5	1	2	10	0	0	.000	0	12	0	0	0.4	1.000
1942		0	1	.000	6.32	10	0	0	15.2	18	16	13	0	0	1	2	3	1	0	.333	0	5	0	0	0.5	1.000
2 yrs.		5	2	.714	3.73	37	0	0	62.2	55	42	41	0	5	2	4	13	1	0	.077	0	17	0	0	0.5	1.000

Roy Branch

BRANCH, ROY BR TR 6′ 175 lbs.
B. July 12, 1953, St. Louis, Mo.

Year	Team	W	L	PCT	ERA	G	GS	CG	IP	H	BB	SO	ShO	Relief Pitching W	Relief Pitching L	Relief Pitching SV	Batting AB	Batting H	Batting HR	BA	PO	A	E	DP	TC/G	FA
1979	SEA A	0	1	.000	8.18	2	2	0	11	12	7	6	0	0	0	0	0	0	0	—	0	0	0	0	0.0	.000

Mark Brandenburg

BRANDENBURG, MARK CLAY BR TR 6′ 180 lbs.
B. July 14, 1970, Houston, Tex.

Year	Team	W	L	PCT	ERA	G	GS	CG	IP	H	BB	SO	ShO	Relief Pitching W	Relief Pitching L	Relief Pitching SV	Batting AB	Batting H	Batting HR	BA	PO	A	E	DP	TC/G	FA
1995	TEX A	0	1	.000	5.93	11	0	0	27.1	36	7	21	0	0	1	0	0	0	0	—	1	2	0	0	0.3	1.000

Chick Brandom

BRANDOM, CHESTER MILTON BR TR 5′ 8″ 161 lbs.
B. Mar. 31, 1887, Coldwater, Kans. D. Oct. 7, 1958, Santa Ana, Calif.

Year	Team	W	L	PCT	ERA	G	GS	CG	IP	H	BB	SO	ShO	Relief Pitching W	Relief Pitching L	Relief Pitching SV	Batting AB	Batting H	Batting HR	BA	PO	A	E	DP	TC/G	FA
1908	PIT N	1	0	1.000	0.53	3	1	1	17	13	4	8	0	1	0	0	7	1	0	.143	1	6	0	0	2.3	1.000
1909		1	0	1.000	1.11	13	2	0	40.2	33	10	21	0	1	0	2	10	1	0	.100	1	17	2	0	1.5	.900
1915	NWK F	1	1	.500	3.40	16	1	1	50.1	55	15	15	0	0	1	0	10	2	0	.200	1	20	2	0	1.4	.913
3 yrs.		3	1	.750	2.08	32	4	2	108	101	29	44	0	2	1	2	27	4	0	.148	3	43	4	0	1.6	.920

Darrell Brandon

BRANDON, DARRELL G. (Bucky) BR TR 6′ 2″ 200 lbs.
B. July 8, 1940, Nacogdoches, Tex.

Year	Team	W	L	PCT	ERA	G	GS	CG	IP	H	BB	SO	ShO	Relief Pitching W	Relief Pitching L	Relief Pitching SV	Batting AB	Batting H	Batting HR	BA	PO	A	E	DP	TC/G	FA
1966	BOS A	8	8	.500	3.31	40	17	5	157.2	129	70	101	2	1	1	2	44	8	0	.182	13	26	1	0	1.0	.975
1967		5	11	.313	4.17	39	19	2	157.2	147	59	96	0	2	2	3	43	8	0	.186	11	23	2	2	0.9	.944
1968		0	0	—	6.39	8	0	0	12.2	19	9	10	0	0	0	0	1	0	0	.000	0	2	0	0	0.3	1.000
1969	**2 teams**	SEA A	(8G 0–1)	MIN A	(3G 0–0)																					
″	**total**	0	1	.000	7.36	11	1	0	18.1	20	19	11	0	0	0	0	1	0	0	.000	0	3	2	0	0.5	.600
1971	PHI N	6	6	.500	3.90	52	0	0	83	81	47	44	0	6	6	4	13	2	0	.154	6	10	0	0	0.3	1.000
1972		7	7	.500	3.45	42	6	0	104.1	106	46	67	0	7	4	2	15	1	0	.067	6	7	1	0	0.3	.929
1973		2	4	.333	5.43	36	0	0	56.1	54	25	25	0	2	4	2	5	1	0	.200	5	8	1	1	0.4	.929
7 yrs.		28	37	.431	4.04	228	43	7	590	556	275	354	2	18	17	13	122	20	0	.164	41	79	7	3	0.6	.945

Bill Brandt

BRANDT, WILLIAM GEORGE BR TR 5′ 8½″ 170 lbs.
B. Mar. 21, 1915, Aurora, Ind. D. May 16, 1968, Fort Wayne, Ind.

Year	Team	W	L	PCT	ERA	G	GS	CG	IP	H	BB	SO	ShO	Relief Pitching W	Relief Pitching L	Relief Pitching SV	Batting AB	Batting H	Batting HR	BA	PO	A	E	DP	TC/G	FA
1941	PIT N	0	1	.000	3.86	2	1	0	7	5	3	0	0	0	0	0	1	0	0	.000	0	1	0	0	0.5	1.000
1942		1	1	.500	4.96	3	3	1	16.1	23	5	4	0	0	0	0	7	1	0	.143	0	2	0	0	0.7	1.000
1943		4	1	.800	3.14	29	3	0	57.1	57	19	17	0	3	0	0	7	1	0	.143	1	12	0	0	0.4	1.000
3 yrs.		5	3	.625	3.57	34	7	1	80.2	85	27	21	0	3	0	0	15	2	0	.133	1	15	0	0	0.5	1.000

Ed Brandt

BRANDT, EDWARD ARTHUR BL TL 6′ 1″ 190 lbs.
B. Feb. 17, 1905, Spokane, Wash. D. Nov. 1, 1944, Spokane, Wash.

Year	Team	W	L	PCT	ERA	G	GS	CG	IP	H	BB	SO	ShO	Relief Pitching W	Relief Pitching L	Relief Pitching SV	Batting AB	Batting H	Batting HR	BA	PO	A	E	DP	TC/G	FA
1928	BOS N	9	**21**	.300	5.07	38	31	12	225.1	234	109	84	1	1	2	0	70	17	0	.243	3	61	0	3	1.7	1.000
1929		8	13	.381	5.53	26	21	13	167.2	196	83	50	0	1	1	0	64	15	0	.234	8	47	2	4	2.2	.965
1930		4	11	.267	5.01	41	13	4	147.1	168	59	65	1	2	2	1	50	12	0	.240	6	35	0	2	1.0	1.000
1931		18	11	.621	2.92	33	29	23	250	228	77	112	3	0	1	2	82	21	0	.256	10	64	2	1	2.3	.974
1932		16	16	.500	3.97	35	31	19	254	271	57	79	2	1	2	1	92	19	0	.207	8	63	1	1	2.1	.986
1933		18	14	.563	2.60	41	32	23	287.2	256	77	104	3	1	1	4	97	30	0	.309	14	60	1	2	1.8	.987
1934		16	14	.533	3.53	40	28	20	255	249	83	106	3	2	2	5	96	23	0	.240	12	39	2	0	1.3	.962
1935		5	19	.208	5.00	29	25	12	174.2	224	66	61	0	0	2	0	62	13	0	.210	7	42	3	1	1.8	.942
1936	BKN N	11	13	.458	3.50	38	29	12	234	246	65	104	1	1	1	2	84	16	0	.190	4	40	1	3	1.2	.978
1937	PIT N	11	10	.524	3.11	33	25	7	176.1	177	67	74	3	0	1	2	59	10	0	.169	4	43	1	1	1.5	.979
1938		5	4	.556	3.46	24	13	5	96.1	93	35	38	1	1	1	0	37	11	0	.297	2	18	1	1	0.9	.952
11 yrs.		121	146	.453	3.86	378	277	150	2268.1	2342	778	877	18	10	16	17	793	187	0	.236	78	512	14	19	1.6	.977

Cliff Brantley

BRANTLEY, CLIFFORD
B. Apr. 12, 1968, Staten Island, N. Y.
BR TR 6' 2" 190 lbs.

Year	Team		W	L	PCT	ERA	G	GS	CG	IP	H	BB	SO	ShO	Relief Pitching W	Relief Pitching L	Relief Pitching SV	Batting AB	Batting H	Batting HR	BA	PO	A	E	DP	TC/G	FA
1991	PHI	N	2	2	.500	3.41	6	5	0	31.2	26	19	25	0	0	0	0	8	0	0	.000	2	5	1	0	1.3	.875
1992			2	6	.250	4.60	28	9	0	76.1	71	58	32	0	0	2	0	14	3	0	.214	6	14	3	1	0.8	.870
2 yrs.			4	8	.333	4.25	34	14	0	108	97	77	57	0	0	2	0	22	3	0	.136	8	19	4	1	0.9	.871

Jeff Brantley

BRANTLEY, JEFFREY HOKE
B. Sept. 5, 1963, Florence, Ala.
BR TR 5'11" 180 lbs.

Year	Team		W	L	PCT	ERA	G	GS	CG	IP	H	BB	SO	ShO	Relief Pitching W	Relief Pitching L	Relief Pitching SV	Batting AB	Batting H	Batting HR	BA	PO	A	E	DP	TC/G	FA
1988	SF	N	0	1	.000	5.66	9	1	0	20.2	22	6	11	0	0	0	1	2	1	0	.500	0	7	0	0	0.8	1.000
1989			7	1	.875	4.07	59	1	0	97.1	101	37	69	0	7	0	0	12	1	0	.083	3	16	0	0	0.3	1.000
1990			5	3	.625	1.56	55	0	0	86.2	77	33	61	0	5	3	19	7	2	0	.286	6	11	1	1	0.3	.944
1991			5	2	.714	2.45	67	0	0	95.1	78	52	81	0	5	2	15	3	0	0	.000	4	9	0	1	0.2	1.000
1992			7	7	.500	2.95	56	4	0	91.2	67	45	86	0	4	7	7	9	1	0	.111	4	9	0	0	0.2	1.000
1993			5	6	.455	4.28	53	12	0	113.2	112	46	76	0	2	1	0	28	3	0	.107	6	9	2	0	0.3	.882
1994	CIN	N	6	6	.500	2.48	50	0	0	65.1	46	28	63	0	6	**6**	15	3	0	0	.000	2	10	0	1	0.2	1.000
1995			3	2	.600	2.82	56	0	0	70.1	53	20	62	0	3	2	28	3	0	0	.000	7	4	0	1	0.2	1.000
8 yrs.			38	28	.576	3.12	405	18	0	641	556	267	509	0	32	21	85	67	8	0	.119	32	75	3	4	0.3	.973
DIVISIONAL PLAYOFF SERIES																											
1995	CIN	N	0	0	—	6.00	3	0	0	3	5	0	2	0	0	0	1	0	0	0	—	0	0	0	0	0.0	.000
LEAGUE CHAMPIONSHIP SERIES																											
1989	SF	N	0	0	—	0.00	3	0	0	5	1	2	3	0	0	0	0	0	0	0	—	0	0	0	0	0.0	.000
1995	CIN	N	0	0	—	0.00	2	0	0	2.2	0	2	1	0	0	0	0	0	0	0	—	2	0	0	0	1.0	1.000
2 yrs.			0	0		0.00	5	0	0	7.2	1	4	4	0	0	0	0	0	0	0		2	0	0	0	0.4	1.000
WORLD SERIES																											
1989	SF	N	0	0	—	4.15	3	0	0	4.1	5	3	1	0	0	0	0	0	0	0	—	1	0	0	0	0.3	1.000

Kitty Brashear

BRASHEAR, NORMAN C.
Brother of Roy Brashear.
B. Aug. 27, 1877, Mansfield, Ohio D. Dec. 22, 1934, Los Angeles, Calif.
BR TR 5'11" 205 lbs.

Year	Team		W	L	PCT	ERA	G	GS	CG	IP	H	BB	SO	ShO	Relief Pitching W	Relief Pitching L	Relief Pitching SV	Batting AB	Batting H	Batting HR	BA	PO	A	E	DP	TC/G	FA
1899	LOU	N	1	0	1.000	4.50	3	0	0	8	8	2	5	0	1	0	0	2	1	0	.500	0	3	0	0	1.0	1.000

John Braun

BRAUN, JOHN PAUL
B. Dec. 26, 1939, Madison, Wis.
BR TR 6' 5" 218 lbs.

Year	Team		W	L	PCT	ERA	G	GS	CG	IP	H	BB	SO	ShO	Relief Pitching W	Relief Pitching L	Relief Pitching SV	Batting AB	Batting H	Batting HR	BA	PO	A	E	DP	TC/G	FA
1964	MIL	N	0	0	—	0.00	1	0	0	2	2	1	1	0	0	0	0	0	0	0	—	0	0	0	0	0.0	.000

Garland Braxton

BRAXTON, EDGAR GARLAND
B. June 10, 1900, Snow Camp, N. C. D. Feb. 26, 1966, Norfolk, Va.
BB TL 5'11" 152 lbs.
BR 1921–1922
BB 1925–1926, 1933

Year	Team		W	L	PCT	ERA	G	GS	CG	IP	H	BB	SO	ShO	Relief Pitching W	Relief Pitching L	Relief Pitching SV	Batting AB	Batting H	Batting HR	BA	PO	A	E	DP	TC/G	FA
1921	BOS	N	1	3	.250	4.82	17	2	0	37.1	44	17	16	0	1	1	0	7	0	0	.000	1	13	1	1	0.9	.933
1922			1	2	.333	3.38	25	5	2	66.2	75	24	15	0	0	1	0	16	1	0	.063	3	13	1	0	0.7	.941
1925	NY	A	1	1	.500	6.52	3	2	0	19.1	26	5	11	0	0	0	0	6	2	0	.333	0	5	1	0	2.0	.833
1926			5	1	.833	2.67	37	1	0	67.1	71	19	30	0	5	1	2	20	6	0	.300	3	16	1	1	0.5	.950
1927	WAS	A	10	9	.526	2.95	**58**	2	0	155.1	143	33	95	0	10	**7**	**13**	39	9	0	.231	5	23	2	1	0.5	.933
1928			13	11	.542	**2.51**	38	24	15	218.1	177	44	94	2	1	3	6	72	9	0	.125	9	50	3	2	1.6	.952
1929			12	10	.545	4.85	37	20	9	182	219	51	59	0	4	1	4	54	8	0	.148	8	32	1	2	1.1	.976
1930	2 teams	WAS A (15G 3–2)	CHI A (19G 4–10)																								
"	total		7	12	.368	5.72	34	10	2	118	149	42	51	0	5	4	6	28	2	0	.071	2	15	2	0	0.6	.895
1931	2 teams	CHI A (17G 0–3)	STL A (11G 0–0)																								
"	total		0	3	.000	7.85	28	4	0	65.1	98	33	35	0	0	1	1	14	3	0	.214	4	13	1	0	0.6	.944
1933	STL	A	0	1	.000	9.72	5	1	0	8.1	11	8	5	0	0	0	0	1	0	0	.000	0	1	0	0	0.2	1.000
10 yrs.			50	53	.485	4.13	282	71	28	938	1013	276	411	2	26	19	32	257	40	0	.156	35	181	13	7	0.8	.943

Al Brazle

BRAZLE, ALPHA EUGENE (Cotton)
B. Oct. 19, 1913, Loyal, Okla. D. Oct. 24, 1973, Grand Junction, Colo.
BL TL 6' 2" 185 lbs.

Year	Team		W	L	PCT	ERA	G	GS	CG	IP	H	BB	SO	ShO	Relief Pitching W	Relief Pitching L	Relief Pitching SV	Batting AB	Batting H	Batting HR	BA	PO	A	E	DP	TC/G	FA
1943	STL	N	8	2	.800	1.53	13	9	8	88	74	29	26	1	1	0	0	32	9	0	.281	3	20	0	1	1.8	1.000
1946			11	10	.524	3.29	37	15	6	153.1	152	55	58	2	4	2	0	52	11	0	.212	5	33	2	1	1.1	.950
1947			14	8	.636	2.84	44	19	7	168	186	48	85	0	4	1	4	64	14	0	.219	4	47	1	1	1.2	.981
1948			10	6	.625	3.80	42	23	6	156.1	171	50	55	3	3	0	1	55	8	0	.145	5	45	0	1	1.2	1.000
1949			14	8	.636	3.18	39	25	9	206.1	208	61	75	1	3	0	0	82	11	0	.134	4	39	2	1	1.2	.956
1950			11	9	.550	4.10	46	12	3	164.2	188	80	47	0	5	4	6	61	13	0	.213	6	31	4	3	0.9	.902
1951			6	5	.545	3.09	56	8	5	154.1	139	60	66	0	2	2	7	46	5	0	.109	4	19	2	1	0.4	.920
1952			12	5	.706	2.72	46	6	3	109.1	75	42	55	2	8	3	**16**	32	4	0	.125	5	13	1	0	0.4	.947
1953			6	7	.462	4.21	60	0	0	92	101	43	57	0	6	7	**18**	15	5	0	.333	3	24	0	0	0.4	1.000
1954			5	4	.556	4.16	58	0	0	84.1	93	24	30	0	5	4	8	14	0	0	.000	4	13	1	2	0.3	.944
10 yrs.			97	64	.602	3.31	441	117	47	1376.2	1387	492	554	9	41	23	60	453	80	0	.177	43	284	13	11	0.8	.962
WORLD SERIES																											
1943	STL	N	0	1	.000	3.68	1	1	0	7.1	5	2	4	0	0	0	0	3	0	0	.000	1	2	0	0	3.0	1.000
1946			0	1	.000	5.40	1	0	0	6.2	7	6	4	0	0	1	0	2	0	0	.000	0	1	0	0	1.0	1.000
2 yrs.			0	2	.000	4.50	2	1	0	14	12	8	8	0	0	1	0	5	0	0	.000	1	3	0	0	2.0	1.000

Harry Brecheen

BRECHEEN, HARRY DAVID (The Cat)
B. Oct. 14, 1914, Broken Bow, Okla.
BL TL 5'10" 160 lbs.

Year	Team		W	L	PCT	ERA	G	GS	CG	IP	H	BB	SO	ShO	Relief Pitching W	Relief Pitching L	Relief Pitching SV	Batting AB	Batting H	Batting HR	BA	PO	A	E	DP	TC/G	FA
1940	STL	N	0	0	—	0.00	3	0	0	3.1	2	2	4	0	0	0	0	0	0	0	—	0	2	0	0	0.7	1.000
1943			9	6	.600	2.26	29	13	8	135.1	98	39	68	1	4	1	4	42	8	0	.190	8	28	0	3	1.2	1.000
1944			16	5	.762	2.85	30	22	13	189.1	174	46	88	3	3	0	0	68	11	0	.162	3	36	0	2	1.3	1.000
1945			15	4	**.789**	2.52	24	18	13	157.1	136	44	63	3	2	1	2	57	7	0	.123	6	26	1	2	1.4	.970
1946			15	15	.500	2.49	36	30	14	231.1	212	67	117	5	0	0	3	83	11	0	.133	11	50	1	6	1.7	.984
1947			16	11	.593	3.30	29	28	18	223.1	220	66	89	1	0	0	1	83	20	0	.241	11	47	1	0	2.0	.983
1948			20	7	**.741**	**2.24**	33	30	21	233.1	193	49	**149**	**7**	0	0	1	82	12	0	.146	5	45	0	2	1.5	1.000
1949			14	11	.560	3.35	32	31	14	214.2	207	65	88	2	0	0	1	77	21	0	.273	5	37	3	0	1.4	.933
1950			8	11	.421	3.80	27	23	12	163.1	151	45	80	2	0	2	1	58	14	1	.241	11	25	0	1	1.3	1.000
1951			8	4	.667	3.25	24	16	5	138.2	134	54	57	0	2	0	2	55	12	1	.218	5	25	2	1	1.3	.938

Harry Brecheen *continued*

Year	Team	Lg	W	L	PCT	ERA	G	GS	CG	IP	H	BB	SO	ShO	Relief Pitching W	Relief Pitching L	Relief Pitching SV	Batting AB	Batting H	HR	BA	PO	A	E	DP	TC/G	FA
1952			7	5	.583	3.32	25	13	4	100.1	82	28	54	1	2	1	2	29	6	0	.207	8	26	0	3	1.4	1.000
1953	STL	A	5	13	.278	3.07	26	16	3	117.1	122	31	44	0	2	3	1	39	7	0	.179	5	29	0	2	1.3	1.000
12 yrs.			133	92	.591	2.92	318	240	125	1907.2	1731	536	901	25	15	8	18	673	129	2	.192	78	376	8	22	1.5	.983
WORLD SERIES																											
1943	STL	N	0	1	.000	2.45	3	0	0	3.2	5	3	3	0	0	1	0	0	0	0	—	0	2	0	0	0.7	1.000
1944			1	0	1.000	1.00	1	1	1	9	9	4	4	0	0	0	0	4	0	0	.000	1	3	0	0	4.0	1.000
1946			3	0	1.000	0.45	3	2	2	20	14	5	11	1	1	0	0	8	1	0	.125	0	2	0	1	0.7	1.000
3 yrs.			4	1	.800	0.83 **2nd**	7	3	3	32.2	28	12	18	1	1	1	0	12	1	0	.083	1	7	0	1	1.1	1.000

Bill Breckinridge

BRECKINRIDGE, WILLIAM ROBERTSON BR TR 5′11″ 175 lbs.
B. Oct. 16, 1907, Tulsa, Okla. D. Aug. 23, 1958, Tulsa, Okla.

Year	Team	Lg	W	L	PCT	ERA	G	GS	CG	IP	H	BB	SO	ShO	Relief Pitching W	Relief Pitching L	Relief Pitching SV	Batting AB	Batting H	HR	BA	PO	A	E	DP	TC/G	FA
1929	PHI	A	0	0	—	8.10	3	1	0	10	10	16	2	0	0	0	0	4	0	0	.000	0	0	0	0	0.0	.000

Fred Breining

BREINING, FRED LAWRENCE BR TR 6′ 4″ 185 lbs.
B. Nov. 15, 1955, San Francisco, Calif.

Year	Team	Lg	W	L	PCT	ERA	G	GS	CG	IP	H	BB	SO	ShO	Relief Pitching W	Relief Pitching L	Relief Pitching SV	Batting AB	Batting H	HR	BA	PO	A	E	DP	TC/G	FA
1980	SF	N	0	0	—	5.14	5	0	0	7	8	4	3	0	0	0	0	0	0	0	—	0	1	0	0	0.2	1.000
1981			5	2	.714	2.54	45	1	0	78	66	38	37	0	5	2	1	11	0	0	.000	3	12	0	0	0.3	1.000
1982			11	6	.647	3.08	54	9	2	143.1	146	52	98	0	6	3	0	29	6	0	.207	12	25	4	2	0.8	.902
1983			11	12	.478	3.82	32	32	6	202.2	202	60	117	0	0	0	0	67	10	0	.149	21	24	2	0	1.5	.957
1984	MON	N	0	0	—	1.35	4	0	0	6.2	4	5	5	0	0	0	0	1	0	0	.000	0	0	0	0	0.0	.000
5 yrs.			27	20	.574	3.33	140	42	8	437.2	426	159	260	0	11	5	1	108	16	0	.148	36	62	6	2	0.7	.942

Alonzo Breitenstein

BREITENSTEIN, ALONZO
B. Nov. 9, 1857, Utica, N. Y. D. June 19, 1932, Utica, N. Y.

Year	Team	Lg	W	L	PCT	ERA	G	GS	CG	IP	H	BB	SO	ShO	Relief Pitching W	Relief Pitching L	Relief Pitching SV	Batting AB	Batting H	HR	BA	PO	A	E	DP	TC/G	FA
1883	PHI	N	0	1	.000	*9.00*	1	1	0	5	8	2	0	0	0	0	0	2	0	0	.000	0	1	1	0	2.0	.500

Ted Breitenstein

BREITENSTEIN, THEODORE P. BL TL 5′ 9″ 167 lbs.
B. June 1, 1869, St. Louis, Mo. D. May 3, 1935, St. Louis, Mo.

Year	Team	Lg	W	L	PCT	ERA	G	GS	CG	IP	H	BB	SO	ShO	Relief Pitching W	Relief Pitching L	Relief Pitching SV	Batting AB	Batting H	HR	BA	PO	A	E	DP	TC/G	FA
1891	STL	AA	2	0	1.000	2.20	6	1	1	28.2	15	14	13	1	1	0	1	12	0	0	.000	2	3	0	0	0.7	1.000
1892	STL	N	14	20	.412	4.69	39	32	28	282.1	280	148	126	1	0	0	0	131	16	0	.122	33	69	6	3	2.2	.944
1893			19	20	.487	**3.18**	48	42	38	382.2	359	156	102	1	0	**3**	1	160	29	1	.181	43	82	8	4	2.7	.940
1894			27	25	.519	4.79	**56**	**50**	**46**	**447.1**	**497**	191	140	1	2	0	0	182	40	0	.220	47	83	10	4	2.2	.929
1895			18	**30**	.375	4.44	54	**50**	**46**	429.2	458	**178**	127	1	0	1	1	218	42	0	.193	63	98	17	1	2.5	.904
1896			18	26	.409	4.48	44	43	37	339.2	376	138	114	1	1	0	0	162	42	0	.259	46	89	8	4	2.8	.944
1897	CIN	N	23	12	.657	3.62	40	39	32	320.1	345	91	98	2	0	0	0	124	33	0	.266	16	65	3	3	2.1	.964
1898			20	14	.588	3.42	39	37	32	315.2	313	123	68	3	1	0	0	121	26	0	.215	22	89	4	3	2.8	.965
1899			13	9	.591	3.59	26	24	21	210.2	219	71	59	0	1	0	0	105	37	1	.352	25	50	5	1	2.4	.938
1900			10	10	.500	3.65	24	20	18	192.1	205	79	39	1	1	1	0	126	24	2	.190	29	62	7	0	2.7	.929
1901	STL	N	0	3	.000	6.60	3	3	1	15	24	14	3	0	0	0	0	6	2	0	.333	2	7	0	2	3.0	1.000
11 yrs.			164	169	.492	4.04	379	341	300	2964.1	3091	1203	889	12	7	5	3	*				328	697	68	25	2.5	.938

Ad Brennan

BRENNAN, ADDISON FOSTER BL TL 5′11″ 170 lbs.
B. July 18, 1881, La Harpe, Kans. D. Jan. 7, 1962, Kansas City, Mo.

Year	Team	Lg	W	L	PCT	ERA	G	GS	CG	IP	H	BB	SO	ShO	Relief Pitching W	Relief Pitching L	Relief Pitching SV	Batting AB	Batting H	HR	BA	PO	A	E	DP	TC/G	FA
1910	PHI	N	3	0	1.000	2.33	19	5	2	73.1	72	28	28	0	1	0	0	25	7	0	.280	3	13	1	1	0.9	.941
1911			2	1	.667	3.57	5	3	1	22.2	22	12	12	0	1	0	0	9	2	0	.222	1	8	1	0	2.0	.900
1912			11	9	.550	3.57	27	19	13	174	185	49	78	1	2	1	2	59	15	1	.254	7	53	1	1	2.3	.984
1913			14	12	.538	2.39	40	25	12	207	204	46	94	1	4	1	1	67	11	0	.164	12	53	4	1	1.7	.942
1914	CHI	F	5	4	.556	3.57	16	11	5	85.2	84	21	31	1	0	1	0	32	8	0	.250	1	23	3	2	1.7	.889
1915			3	9	.250	3.74	19	13	7	106	117	30	40	2	0	0	0	27	5	0	.185	2	23	1	0	1.3	.962
1918	2 teams	WAS A (2G 0–0) CLE A (1G 0–0)																									
″	total		0	0		4.32	3	1	0	8.1	10	8	0	0	0	0	0	1	0	0	.000	0	2	0	0	0.7	1.000
7 yrs.			38	35	.521	3.11	129	77	40	677	694	194	283	5	8	3	3	220	48	1	.218	26	175	11	5	1.6	.948

Bill Brennan

BRENNAN, WILLIAM RAYMOND BR TR 6′ 3″ 200 lbs.
B. Jan. 15, 1963, Tampa, Fla.

Year	Team	Lg	W	L	PCT	ERA	G	GS	CG	IP	H	BB	SO	ShO	Relief Pitching W	Relief Pitching L	Relief Pitching SV	Batting AB	Batting H	HR	BA	PO	A	E	DP	TC/G	FA
1988	LA	N	0	1	.000	6.75	4	2	0	9.1	13	6	7	0	0	0	0	2	0	0	.000	2	2	0	0	1.0	1.000
1993	CHI	N	2	1	.667	4.20	8	1	0	15	16	8	11	0	2	0	0	1	0	0	.000	2	2	0	0	0.5	1.000
2 yrs.			2	2	.500	5.18	12	3	0	24.1	29	14	18	0	2	0	0	3	0	0	.000	4	4	0	0	0.7	1.000

Don Brennan

BRENNAN, JAMES DONALD BR TR 6′ 210 lbs.
B. Dec. 2, 1903, Augusta, Me. D. Apr. 26, 1953, Boston, Mass.

Year	Team	Lg	W	L	PCT	ERA	G	GS	CG	IP	H	BB	SO	ShO	Relief Pitching W	Relief Pitching L	Relief Pitching SV	Batting AB	Batting H	HR	BA	PO	A	E	DP	TC/G	FA
1933	NY	A	5	1	.833	4.98	18	10	3	85	92	47	46	0	0	1	3	27	7	0	.259	3	23	2	2	1.6	.929
1934	CIN	N	4	3	.571	3.81	28	7	2	78	89	35	31	0	2	1	2	22	5	0	.227	1	15	1	0	0.6	.941
1935			5	5	.500	3.15	38	5	2	114.1	101	44	48	1	3	3	5	30	3	0	.100	4	14	0	1	0.5	1.000
1936			5	2	.714	4.39	41	4	0	94.1	117	35	40	0	5	2	9	25	2	0	.080	1	19	2	1	0.5	.909
1937	2 teams	CIN N (10G 1–1) NY N (6G 1–0)																									
″	total		2	1	.667	6.75	16	0	0	25.1	37	19	7	0	2	1	0	6	0	0	.000	1	4	0	0	0.3	1.000
5 yrs.			21	12	.636	4.19	141	26	7	397	436	180	172	1	12	8	19	110	17	0	.155	10	75	5	4	0.6	.944
WORLD SERIES																											
1937	NY	N	0	0	—	0.00	2	0	0	3	1	1	1	0	0	0	0	0	0	0	—	0	0	0	0	0.0	.000

Tom Brennan

BRENNAN, THOMAS MARTIN (The Gray Flamingo) BR TR 6′ 1″ 180 lbs.
B. Oct. 30, 1952, Chicago, Ill.

Year	Team	Lg	W	L	PCT	ERA	G	GS	CG	IP	H	BB	SO	ShO	Relief Pitching W	Relief Pitching L	Relief Pitching SV	Batting AB	Batting H	HR	BA	PO	A	E	DP	TC/G	FA
1981	CLE	A	2	2	.500	3.19	7	6	1	48	49	14	15	0	0	0	0	0	0	0	—	5	12	1	2	2.6	.944
1982			4	2	.667	4.27	30	4	0	92.2	112	10	46	0	1	2	2	0	0	0	—	9	13	0	2	0.7	1.000
1983			2	2	.500	3.86	11	5	1	39.2	45	8	21	1	0	0	0	0	0	0	—	4	4	1	0	0.8	.889
1984	CHI	A	0	1	.000	4.05	4	1	0	6.2	8	3	3	0	0	0	0	0	0	0	—	0	3	0	0	0.8	1.000
1985	LA	N	1	3	.250	7.39	12	4	0	31.2	41	11	17	0	1	1	0	8	1	0	.125	3	11	0	1	1.2	1.000
5 yrs.			9	10	.474	4.40	64	20	2	218.2	255	46	102	1	2	3	2	8	1	0	.125	21	43	2	5	1.0	.970

Jim Brenneman

BRENNEMAN, JAMES LeROY BR TR 6′ 2″ 180 lbs.
B. Feb. 13, 1941, San Diego, Calif.

Year	Team		W	L	PCT	ERA	G	GS	CG	IP	H	BB	SO	ShO	Relief Pitching W	L	SV	Batting AB	H	HR	BA	PO	A	E	DP	TC/G	FA
1965	NY	A	0	0	—	18.00	3	0	0	2	5	3	2	0	0	0	0	0	0	0	—	0	0	0	0	0.0	.000

Bert Brenner

BRENNER, DELBERT HENRY (Dutch) BR TR 6′ 175 lbs.
B. July 18, 1887, Minneapolis, Minn. D. Apr. 11, 1971, St. Louis Park, Minn.

Year	Team		W	L	PCT	ERA	G	GS	CG	IP	H	BB	SO	ShO	Relief Pitching W	L	SV	Batting AB	H	HR	BA	PO	A	E	DP	TC/G	FA
1912	CLE	A	1	0	1.000	2.77	2	1	1	13	14	4	3	0	0	0	0	5	0	0	.000	1	5	0	0	3.0	1.000

Lynn Brenton

BRENTON, LYNN DAVIS (Buck, Herb) BR TR 5′10″ 165 lbs.
B. Oct. 7, 1890, Peoria, Ill. D. Oct. 14, 1968, Los Angeles, Calif.

Year	Team		W	L	PCT	ERA	G	GS	CG	IP	H	BB	SO	ShO	Relief Pitching W	L	SV	Batting AB	H	HR	BA	PO	A	E	DP	TC/G	FA
1913	CLE	A	0	0	—	9.00	1	0	0	2	4	0	2	0	0	0	0	0	0	0	—	0	0	0	0	0.0	.000
1915			2	3	.400	3.35	11	5	1	51	60	20	18	1	0	0	0	17	2	0	.118	2	12	1	0	1.4	.933
1920	CIN	N	2	1	.667	4.91	5	1	1	18.1	17	4	13	0	1	1	1	8	2	0	.250	0	12	0	1	2.4	1.000
1921			1	8	.111	4.05	17	9	2	60	80	17	19	0	0	0	1	15	2	0	.133	4	25	1	0	1.8	.967
4 yrs.			5	12	.294	3.97	34	15	4	131.1	161	41	52	1	1	1	2	40	6	0	.150	6	49	2	1	1.7	.965

Roger Bresnahan

BRESNAHAN, ROGER PHILIP (The Duke of Tralee) BR TR 5′ 9″ 200 lbs.
B. June 11, 1879, Toledo, Ohio D. Dec. 4, 1944, Toledo, Ohio.
Manager 1909–12, 1915.
Hall of Fame 1945.

Year	Team		W	L	PCT	ERA	G	GS	CG	IP	H	BB	SO	ShO	Relief Pitching W	L	SV	Batting AB	H	HR	BA	PO	A	E	DP	TC/G	FA
1897	WAS	N	4	0	1.000	3.95	6	5	3	41	52	10	12	1	0	0	0	16	6	0	.375	2	7	0	0	1.3	1.000
1901	BAL	A	0	1	.000	6.00	2	1	0	6	10	4	3	0	0	0	0	295	79	1	.268	0	0	0	0	0.0	.000
1910	STL	N	0	0	—	0.00	1	0	0	3.1	6	1	0	0	0	0	0	234	65	0	.278	219	71	27	4	3.7	.915
3 yrs.			4	1	.800	3.93	9	6	3	50.1	68	15	15	1	0	0	0	*				5136	1414	240	138	4.9	.965

Rube Bressler

BRESSLER, RAYMOND BLOOM BR TL 6′ 187 lbs.
B. Oct. 23, 1894, Coder, Pa. D. Nov. 7, 1966, Mt. Washington, Ohio.

Year	Team		W	L	PCT	ERA	G	GS	CG	IP	H	BB	SO	ShO	Relief Pitching W	L	SV	Batting AB	H	HR	BA	PO	A	E	DP	TC/G	FA
1914	PHI	A	10	4	.714	1.77	29	10	8	147.2	112	56	96	1	3	2	2	51	11	0	.216	6	26	2	2	1.2	.941
1915			4	17	.190	5.20	32	20	7	178.1	183	118	69	1	0	**4**	0	55	8	1	.145	7	56	7	0	2.2	.900
1916			0	2	.000	6.60	4	2	0	15	16	14	8	0	0	0	0	5	1	0	.200	0	2	0	0	0.5	1.000
1917	CIN	N	0	0	—	6.00	2	1	0	9	15	5	2	0	0	0	0	5	1	0	.200	1	1	0	0	1.0	1.000
1918			8	5	.615	2.46	17	13	10	128	124	39	37	0	1	0	0	62	17	0	.274	10	51	1	2	3.1	.984
1919			2	4	.333	3.46	13	4	1	41.2	37	8	13	0	2	1	0	165	34	2	.206	107	19	5	1	2.1	.962
1920			2	0	1.000	1.77	10	2	1	20.1	24	2	4	1	1	0	0	30	8	0	.267	25	7	4	2	2.4	.889
7 yrs.			26	32	.448	3.40	107	52	27	540	511	242	229	3	7	7	2	*				3104	287	85	122	3.2	.976

Herb Brett

BRETT, HERBERT JAMES (Sparky) BR TR 6′ 175 lbs.
B. May 23, 1900, Lawrenceville, Va. D. Nov. 25, 1974, St. Petersburg, Fla.

Year	Team		W	L	PCT	ERA	G	GS	CG	IP	H	BB	SO	ShO	Relief Pitching W	L	SV	Batting AB	H	HR	BA	PO	A	E	DP	TC/G	FA
1924	CHI	N	0	0	—	5.06	1	1	0	5.1	6	7	1	0	0	0	0	2	0	0	.000	0	0	0	0	0.0	.000
1925			1	1	.500	3.63	10	1	0	17.1	12	3	6	0	1	0	0	1	0	0	.000	1	6	0	0	0.7	1.000
2 yrs.			1	1	.500	3.97	11	2	0	22.2	18	10	7	0	1	0	0	3	0	0	.000	1	6	0	0	0.6	1.000

Ken Brett

BRETT, KENNETH ALVEN BL TL 6′ 190 lbs.
Brother of George Brett.
B. Sept. 18, 1948, Brooklyn, N. Y.

Year	Team		W	L	PCT	ERA	G	GS	CG	IP	H	BB	SO	ShO	Relief Pitching W	L	SV	Batting AB	H	HR	BA	PO	A	E	DP	TC/G	FA
1967	BOS	A	0	0	—	4.50	1	0	0	2	3	0	2	0	0	0	0	0	0	0	—	0	0	0	0	0.0	.000
1969			2	3	.400	5.26	8	8	0	39.1	41	22	23	0	0	0	0	10	3	1	.300	2	6	0	0	1.0	1.000
1970			8	9	.471	4.08	41	14	1	139	118	79	155	1	3	5	2	41	13	2	.317	9	20	2	0	0.8	.935
1971			0	3	.000	5.34	29	2	0	59	57	35	57	0	0	2	1	10	2	0	.200	0	8	0	0	0.3	1.000
1972	MIL	A	7	12	.368	4.53	26	22	2	133	121	49	74	1	0	0	0	44	10	0	.227	6	15	3	1	0.9	.875
1973	PHI	N	13	9	.591	3.44	31	25	10	211.2	206	74	111	1	1	1	0	80	20	4	.250	13	39	0	4	1.7	1.000
1974	PIT	N	13	9	.591	3.30	27	27	10	191	192	52	96	3	0	0	0	87	27	2	.310	12	28	0	1	1.5	1.000
1975			9	5	.643	3.36	23	16	4	118	110	43	47	1	1	1	0	52	12	1	.231	13	18	1	0	1.4	.969
1976	2 teams	NY A (2G 0–0) CHI A (27G 10–12)																									
″	total		10	12	.455	3.28	29	26	16	203	173	76	92	1	0	0	2	12	1	0	.083	11	35	3	0	1.7	.939
1977	2 teams	CHI A (13G 6–4) CAL A (21G 7–10)																									
″	total		13	14	.481	4.52	34	34	7	225	258	53	80	0	0	0	0	0	0	0		11	48	2	6	1.8	.967
1978	CAL	A	3	5	.375	4.95	31	10	1	100	100	42	43	1	1	1	1	0	0	0	—	12	20	2	4	1.1	.941
1979	2 teams	MIN A (9G 0–0) LA N (30G 4–3)																									
″	total		4	3	.571	3.75	39	0	0	60	68	18	16	0	4	3	2	11	3	0	.273	10	17	0	1	0.7	1.000
1980	KC	A	0	0	—	0.00	8	0	0	13	8	5	4	0	0	0	1	0	0	0	—	0	3	0	0	0.4	1.000
1981			1	1	.500	4.22	22	0	0	32	35	14	7	0	1	1	2	0	0	0	—	5	6	0	1	0.5	1.000
14 yrs.			83	85	.494	3.93	349	184	51	1526	1490	562	807	9	11	14	11	*				104	263	13	18	1.1	.966
LEAGUE CHAMPIONSHIP SERIES																											
1974	PIT	N	0	0	—	7.71	1	0	0	2.1	3	2	1	0	0	0	0	1	0	0	.000	0	1	0	0	1.0	1.000
1975			0	0	—	0.00	2	0	0	2.1	1	0	1	0	0	0	0	0	0	0	—	0	0	0	0	0.0	.000
2 yrs.			0	0		3.86	3	0	0	4.2	4	2	2	0	0	0	0	*				0	1	0	0	0.3	1.000
WORLD SERIES																											
1967	BOS	A	0	0	—	0.00	2	0	0	1.1	0	1	1	0	0	0	0	*				0	0	0	0	0.0	.000

Marv Breuer

BREUER, MARVIN HOWARD (Baby Face) BR TR 6′ 2″ 185 lbs.
B. Apr. 29, 1914, Rolla, Mo.

Year	Team		W	L	PCT	ERA	G	GS	CG	IP	H	BB	SO	ShO	Relief Pitching W	L	SV	Batting AB	H	HR	BA	PO	A	E	DP	TC/G	FA
1939	NY	A	0	0	—	9.00	1	0	0	1	2	1	0	0	0	0	0	0	0	0	—	0	1	0	0	1.0	1.000
1940			8	9	.471	4.55	27	22	10	164	175	61	71	0	1	0	0	54	2	0	.037	5	26	1	2	1.2	.969
1941			9	7	.563	4.09	26	18	7	141	131	49	77	1	2	1	2	46	4	0	.087	2	23	1	0	1.0	.962
1942			8	9	.471	3.07	27	19	6	164.1	157	37	72	0	2	2	1	54	3	0	.056	12	22	4	2	1.4	.895
1943			0	1	.000	8.36	5	1	0	14	22	6	6	0	0	0	0	3	1	0	.333	0	3	0	0	0.6	1.000
5 yrs.			25	26	.490	4.03	86	60	23	484.1	487	154	226	1	5	3	3	157	10	0	.064	19	75	6	4	1.2	.940
WORLD SERIES																											
1941	NY	A	0	0	—	0.00	1	0	0	3	3	1	2	0	0	0	0	1	0	0	.000	0	1	0	0	1.0	1.000
1942			0	0	—	0.00	1	0	0		2	0	0	0	0	0	0	0	0	0	—	0	0	1	0	1.0	.000
2 yrs.			0	0		0.00	2	0	0	3	5	1	2	0	0	0	0	1	0	0	.000	0	1	1	0	1.0	.500

Billy Brewer — **BREWER, WILLIAM ROBERT** — B. Apr. 15, 1968, Fort Worth, Tex. — BL TL 6′ 1″ 175 lbs.

Year	Team	W	L	PCT	ERA	G	GS	CG	IP	H	BB	SO	ShO	Relief Pitching W	L	SV	Batting AB	H	HR	BA	PO	A	E	DP	TC/G	FA
1993	KC A	2	2	.500	3.46	46	0	0	39	31	20	28	0	2	2	0	0	0	0	—	1	4	2	0	0.2	.714
1994		4	1	.800	2.56	50	0	0	38.2	28	16	25	0	4	1	3	0	0	0	—	2	6	1	0	0.2	.889
1995		2	4	.333	5.56	48	0	0	45.1	54	20	31	0	2	4	0	0	0	0	—	3	4	0	1	0.1	1.000
3 yrs.		8	7	.533	3.95	144	0	0	123	113	56	84	0	8	7	3	0	0	0		6	14	3	1	0.2	.870

Jack Brewer — **BREWER, JOHN HERNDON (Buddy)** — B. July 21, 1919, Los Angeles, Calif. — BR TR 6′ 2″ 170 lbs.

Year	Team	W	L	PCT	ERA	G	GS	CG	IP	H	BB	SO	ShO	Relief Pitching W	L	SV	Batting AB	H	HR	BA	PO	A	E	DP	TC/G	FA
1944	NY N	1	4	.200	5.56	14	7	2	55	66	16	21	0	0	0	0	19	4	0	.211	2	8	2	0	0.9	.833
1945		8	6	.571	3.83	28	21	8	159.2	162	58	49	0	0	1	0	56	10	0	.179	4	21	2	1	1.0	.926
1946		0	0	—	13.50	1	0	0	2	3	2	3	0	0	0	0	0	0	0	—	0	0	0	0	0.0	.000
3 yrs.		9	10	.474	4.36	43	28	10	216.2	231	76	73	0	0	1	0	75	14	0	.187	6	29	4	1	0.9	.897

Jim Brewer — **BREWER, JAMES THOMAS** — B. Nov. 14, 1937, Merced, Calif. D. Nov. 16, 1987, Tyler, Tex. — BL TL 6′ 1″ 186 lbs.

Year	Team	W	L	PCT	ERA	G	GS	CG	IP	H	BB	SO	ShO	Relief Pitching W	L	SV	Batting AB	H	HR	BA	PO	A	E	DP	TC/G	FA
1960	CHI N	0	3	.000	5.82	5	4	0	21.2	25	6	7	0	0	0	0	6	1	0	.167	2	5	1	0	1.6	.875
1961		1	7	.125	5.82	36	11	0	86.2	116	21	57	0	0	1	0	22	4	0	.182	4	8	1	0	0.4	.923
1962		0	1	.000	9.53	6	1	0	5.2	10	3	1	0	0	1	0	0	0	0	—	1	1	0	1	0.3	1.000
1963		3	2	.600	4.89	29	1	0	49.2	59	15	35	0	3	1	0	6	0	0	.000	2	3	1	0	0.2	.833
1964	LA N	4	3	.571	3.00	34	5	1	93	79	25	63	1	2	2	1	22	6	0	.273	3	11	0	0	0.4	1.000
1965		3	2	.600	1.82	19	2	0	49.1	33	28	31	0	3	1	2	10	0	0	.000	1	11	0	1	0.6	1.000
1966		0	2	.000	3.68	13	0	0	22	17	11	8	0	0	2	2	0	0	0	—	1	5	0	1	0.5	1.000
1967		5	4	.556	2.68	30	11	0	100.2	78	31	74	0	1	0	1	22	1	0	.045	1	14	0	0	0.5	1.000
1968		8	3	.727	2.49	54	0	0	76	59	33	75	0	8	3	14	9	2	0	.222	4	11	1	1	0.3	.938
1969		7	6	.538	2.56	59	0	0	88	71	41	92	0	7	6	20	11	1	0	.091	6	13	1	1	0.3	.950
1970		7	6	.538	3.13	58	0	0	89	66	33	91	0	7	6	24	12	1	0	.083	0	14	1	0	0.3	.933
1971		6	5	.545	1.89	55	0	0	81	55	24	66	0	6	5	22	9	3	0	.333	2	15	2	1	0.3	.895
1972		8	7	.533	1.26	51	0	0	78.1	41	25	69	0	8	7	17	1	0	0	.000	1	11	1	1	0.3	.923
1973		6	8	.429	3.01	56	0	0	71.2	58	25	56	0	6	8	20	5	2	0	.400	0	12	1	1	0.2	.923
1974		4	4	.500	2.54	24	0	0	39	29	10	26	0	4	4	0	2	0	0	.000	0	4	0	0	0.2	1.000
1975	2 teams LA N (21G 3–1) CAL A (21G 1–0)																									
″	total	4	1	.800	3.46	42	0	0	67.2	82	23	43	0	4	1	7	3	0	0	.000	0	10	0	2	0.2	1.000
1976	CAL A	3	1	.750	2.70	13	0	0	20	20	6	16	0	3	1	2	0	0	0	—	2	2	0	0	0.3	1.000
17 yrs.		69	65	.515	3.07	584	35	1	1039.1	898	360	810	1	62	49	132	140	21	0	.150	30	150	10	10	0.3	.947
WORLD SERIES																										
1965	LA N	0	0	—	4.50	1	0	0	2	3	0	1	0	0	0	0	0	0	0	—	0	0	0	0	0.0	.000
1966		0	0	—	0.00	1	0	0	1	0	0	1	0	0	0	0	0	0	0	—	0	0	0	0	0.0	.000
1974		0	0	—	0.00	1	0	0	0.1	0	0	1	0	0	0	0	0	0	0	—	0	0	0	0	0.0	.000
3 yrs.		0	0		2.70	3	0	0	3.1	3	0	3	0	0	0	0	0	0	0		0	0	0	0	0.0	

Rod Brewer — **BREWER, RODNEY LEE** — B. Feb. 24, 1966, Eustis, Fla. — BL TL 6′ 3″ 210 lbs.

Year	Team	W	L	PCT	ERA	G	GS	CG	IP	H	BB	SO	ShO	Relief Pitching W	L	SV	Batting AB	H	HR	BA	PO	A	E	DP	TC/G	FA
1993	STL N	0	0	—	45.00	1	0	0	1	3	2	1	0	0	0	0	*				46	6	1	5	5.9	.981

Tom Brewer — **BREWER, THOMAS AUSTIN** — B. Sept. 3, 1931, Wadesboro, N. C. — BR TR 6′ 1″ 175 lbs.

Year	Team	W	L	PCT	ERA	G	GS	CG	IP	H	BB	SO	ShO	Relief Pitching W	L	SV	Batting AB	H	HR	BA	PO	A	E	DP	TC/G	FA
1954	BOS A	10	9	.526	4.65	33	23	7	162.2	152	95	69	0	0	0	0	60	16	0	.267	9	18	3	1	0.9	.900
1955		11	10	.524	4.20	31	28	9	192.2	198	87	91	2	1	0	0	73	11	0	.151	15	44	1	4	1.9	.983
1956		19	9	.679	3.50	32	32	15	244.1	200	112	127	4	0	0	0	94	28	1	.298	28	52	1	2	2.5	.988
1957		16	13	.552	3.85	32	32	15	238.1	225	93	128	2	0	0	0	94	19	0	.202	20	65	3	3	2.8	.966
1958		12	12	.500	3.72	33	32	10	227.1	227	93	124	1	1	0	0	82	16	0	.195	13	57	4	7	2.2	.946
1959		10	12	.455	3.76	36	32	11	215.1	219	88	121	3	0	0	2	72	8	1	.111	23	49	2	1	2.1	.973
1960		10	15	.400	4.82	34	29	8	186.2	220	72	60	1	0	1	1	62	12	1	.194	15	45	2	3	1.8	.968
1961		3	2	.600	3.43	10	9	0	42	37	29	13	0	0	0	0	14	4	0	.286	2	13	0	1	1.5	1.000
8 yrs.		91	82	.526	4.00	241	217	75	1509.1	1478	669	733	13	2	1	3	551	114	3	.207	125	343	16	22	2.0	.967

Jamie Brewington — **BREWINGTON, JAMIE CHANCELLOR** — B. Sept. 28, 1971, Greenville, N. C. — BR TR 6′ 4″ 180 lbs.

Year	Team	W	L	PCT	ERA	G	GS	CG	IP	H	BB	SO	ShO	Relief Pitching W	L	SV	Batting AB	H	HR	BA	PO	A	E	DP	TC/G	FA
1995	SF N	6	4	.600	4.54	13	13	0	75.1	68	45	45	0	0	0	0	23	5	0	.217	3	10	0	1	1.0	1.000

Alan Brice — **BRICE, ALAN HEALEY** — B. Oct. 1, 1937, New York, N. Y. — BR TR 6′ 5″ 215 lbs.

Year	Team	W	L	PCT	ERA	G	GS	CG	IP	H	BB	SO	ShO	Relief Pitching W	L	SV	Batting AB	H	HR	BA	PO	A	E	DP	TC/G	FA
1961	CHI A	0	1	.000	0.00	3	0	0	3.1	4	3	3	0	0	1	0	0	0	0	—	0	0	0	0	0.0	.000

Ralph Brickner — **BRICKNER, RALPH HAROLD (Brick)** — B. May 2, 1925, Cincinnati, Ohio D. May 9, 1994, Bridgetown, Ohio. — BR TR 6′ 3½″ 215 lbs.

Year	Team	W	L	PCT	ERA	G	GS	CG	IP	H	BB	SO	ShO	Relief Pitching W	L	SV	Batting AB	H	HR	BA	PO	A	E	DP	TC/G	FA
1952	BOS A	3	1	.750	2.18	14	1	0	33	32	11	9	0	3	1	1	8	2	0	.250	2	3	0	0	0.4	1.000

Marshall Bridges — **BRIDGES, MARSHALL (Sheriff)** — B. June 2, 1931, Jackson, Miss. D. Sept. 3, 1990, Jackson, Miss. — BB TL 6′ 1″ 165 lbs. BR 1962–1965

Year	Team	W	L	PCT	ERA	G	GS	CG	IP	H	BB	SO	ShO	Relief Pitching W	L	SV	Batting AB	H	HR	BA	PO	A	E	DP	TC/G	FA
1959	STL N	6	3	.667	4.26	27	4	1	76	67	37	76	0	4	2	1	23	5	1	.217	2	3	1	0	0.2	.833
1960	2 teams STL N (20G 2–2) CIN N (14G 4–0)																									
″	total	6	2	.750	2.38	34	1	0	56.2	47	23	53	0	6	1	3	10	1	0	.100	2	5	0	0	0.2	1.000
1961	CIN N	0	1	.000	7.84	13	0	0	20.2	26	11	17	0	0	1	0	2	0	0	.000	0	3	0	0	0.2	1.000
1962	NY A	8	4	.667	3.14	52	0	0	71.2	49	48	66	0	8	4	18	14	0	0	.000	5	18	1	3	0.5	.958
1963		2	0	1.000	3.82	23	0	0	33	27	30	35	0	2	0	1	0	0	0	—	2	11	0	3	0.6	1.000
1964	WAS A	0	3	.000	5.70	17	0	0	30	37	17	16	0	0	3	2	3	0	0	.000	1	5	0	0	0.4	1.000
1965		1	2	.333	2.67	40	0	0	57.1	62	25	39	0	1	2	0	7	1	0	.143	3	9	1	0	0.3	.923
7 yrs.		23	15	.605	3.75	206	5	1	345.1	315	191	302	0	21	13	25	59	7	1	.119	15	54	3	6	0.3	.958
WORLD SERIES																										
1962	NY A	0	0	—	4.91	2	0	0	3.2	4	2	3	0	0	0	0	0	0	0	—	0	1	0	0	0.5	1.000

Tommy Bridges

BRIDGES, THOMAS JEFFERSON DAVIS
B. Dec. 28, 1906, Gordonsville, Tenn. D. Apr. 19, 1968, Nashville, Tenn.
BR TR 5′10½″ 155 lbs.

Year	Team		W	L	PCT	ERA	G	GS	CG	IP	H	BB	SO	ShO	Relief Pitching W	L	SV	Batting AB	H	HR	BA	PO	A	E	DP	TC/G	FA
1930	DET	A	3	2	.600	4.06	8	5	2	37.2	28	23	17	0	0	0	0	10	3	0	.300	0	7	1	0	1.0	.875
1931			8	16	.333	4.99	35	23	15	173	182	108	105	2	1	2	0	54	8	0	.148	5	27	2	0	1.0	.941
1932			14	12	.538	3.36	34	26	10	201	174	119	108	**4**	2	2	1	67	11	0	.164	5	34	2	1	1.2	.951
1933			14	12	.538	3.09	33	28	17	233	192	110	120	2	1	0	2	78	16	0	.205	9	49	3	5	1.8	.951
1934			22	11	.667	3.67	36	**35**	23	275	249	104	151	3	0	0	1	98	12	0	.122	6	42	2	2	1.4	.960
1935			21	10	.677	3.51	36	34	23	274.1	277	113	**163**	4	0	1	1	109	26	0	.239	15	39	2	4	1.6	.964
1936			**23**	11	.676	3.60	39	**38**	26	294.2	289	115	**175**	5	0	0	0	118	25	0	.212	19	51	2	3	1.8	.972
1937			15	12	.556	4.07	34	31	18	245.1	267	91	138	3	1	0	0	96	23	0	.240	14	46	1	2	1.8	.984
1938			13	9	.591	4.59	25	20	13	151	171	58	101	0	1	3	1	54	7	0	.130	8	19	2	0	1.2	.931
1939			17	7	.708	3.50	29	26	16	198	186	61	129	2	0	0	2	71	14	0	.197	8	28	3	2	1.3	.923
1940			12	9	.571	3.37	29	28	12	197.2	171	88	133	2	1	0	0	68	12	0	.176	4	30	2	0	1.2	.944
1941			9	12	.429	3.41	25	22	10	147.2	128	70	90	1	1	0	0	47	4	0	.085	15	30	1	1	1.8	.978
1942			9	7	.563	2.74	23	22	11	174	164	61	97	2	0	0	1	63	6	0	.095	15	32	1	2	2.1	.979
1943			12	7	.632	2.39	25	22	11	191.2	159	61	124	3	0	1	0	64	14	0	.219	18	28	0	1	1.8	1.000
1945			1	0	1.000	3.27	4	1	0	11	14	2	6	0	0	0	0	3	0	0	.000	2	4	0	0	1.5	1.000
1946			1	1	.500	5.91	9	1	0	21.1	24	8	17	0	0	1	1	3	0	0	.000	1	3	0	0	0.4	1.000
16 yrs.			194	138	.584	3.57	424	362	207	2826.1	2675	1192	1674	33	8	10	10	1003	181	0	.180	144	469	24	23	1.5	.962
WORLD SERIES																											
1934	DET	A	1	1	.500	3.63	3	2	1	17.1	21	1	12	0	0	0	0	7	1	0	.143	0	2	0	0	0.7	1.000
1935			2	0	1.000	2.50	2	2	2	18	18	4	9	0	0	0	0	8	1	0	.125	1	5	0	1	3.0	1.000
1940			1	0	1.000	3.00	1	1	1	9	10	1	5	0	0	0	0	3	0	0	.000	0	1	0	0	1.0	1.000
1945			0	0	—	16.20	1	0	0	1.2	3	3	1	0	0	0	0	0	0	0	—	0	0	0	0	0.0	.000
4 yrs.			4	1	.800	3.52	7	5	4	46	52	9	27	0	0	0	0	18	2	0	.111	1	8	0	1	1.3	1.000

Buttons Briggs

BRIGGS, HERBERT THEODORE
B. July 8, 1875, Poughkeepsie, N. Y. D. Feb. 18, 1911, Cleveland, Ohio.
BR TR 6′ 1″ 180 lbs.

Year	Team		W	L	PCT	ERA	G	GS	CG	IP	H	BB	SO	ShO	Relief Pitching W	L	SV	Batting AB	H	HR	BA	PO	A	E	DP	TC/G	FA
1896	CHI	N	12	8	.600	4.31	26	21	19	194	202	108	84	0	0	1	1	78	10	0	.128	6	29	4	0	1.5	.897
1897			4	17	.190	5.26	22	22	21	186.2	246	85	60	0	0	0	0	81	13	0	.160	8	35	1	0	2.0	.977
1898			1	3	.250	5.70	4	4	3	30	38	10	14	0	0	0	0	14	6	0	.429	1	6	2	0	2.3	.778
1904			19	11	.633	2.05	34	30	28	277	252	77	112	3	1	0	2	94	16	1	.170	16	54	0	2	2.1	1.000
1905			8	8	.500	2.14	20	20	13	168	141	52	68	5	0	0	0	57	3	0	.053	11	36	2	0	2.5	.959
5 yrs.			44	47	.484	3.41	106	97	84	855.2	879	332	338	8	1	1	3	324	48	1	.148	42	160	9	2	2.0	.957

Johnny Briggs

BRIGGS, JONATHAN TIFT
B. Jan. 24, 1934, Natoma, Calif.
BR TR 5′10″ 175 lbs.

Year	Team		W	L	PCT	ERA	G	GS	CG	IP	H	BB	SO	ShO	Relief Pitching W	L	SV	Batting AB	H	HR	BA	PO	A	E	DP	TC/G	FA
1956	CHI	N	0	0	—	1.69	3	0	0	5.1	5	4	1	0	0	0	0	0	0	0	—	0	1	0	0	0.3	1.000
1957			0	1	.000	12.46	3	0	0	4.1	7	3	1	0	0	1	0	0	0	0	—	0	0	0	0	0.0	.000
1958			5	5	.500	4.52	20	17	3	95.2	99	45	46	1	0	0	0	35	9	0	.257	7	12	2	0	1.0	.905
1959	CLE	A	0	1	.000	2.13	4	1	0	12.2	12	3	5	0	0	0	0	2	0	0	.000	2	1	0	0	0.8	1.000
1960	2 teams	CLE A (21G 4–2)	KC A (8G 0–2)																								
″	total		4	4	.500	6.42	29	3	0	47.2	51	27	27	0	3	2	1	11	1	0	.091	2	3	1	0	0.2	.833
5 yrs.			9	11	.450	5.00	59	21	3	165.2	174	82	80	1	3	3	1	48	10	0	.208	11	17	3	0	0.5	.903

Nellie Briles

BRILES, NELSON KELLEY
B. Aug. 5, 1943, Dorris, Calif.
BR TR 5′11″ 195 lbs.

Year	Team		W	L	PCT	ERA	G	GS	CG	IP	H	BB	SO	ShO	Relief Pitching W	L	SV	Batting AB	H	HR	BA	PO	A	E	DP	TC/G	FA
1965	STL	N	3	3	.500	3.50	37	2	0	82.1	79	26	52	0	2	2	4	15	2	0	.133	6	8	0	1	0.4	1.000
1966			4	15	.211	3.21	49	17	0	154	162	54	100	0	1	6	6	38	3	0	.079	9	29	1	3	0.8	.974
1967			14	5	.737	2.43	49	14	4	155.1	139	40	94	2	4	3	6	40	6	0	.150	10	18	2	1	0.6	.933
1968			19	11	.633	2.81	33	33	13	243.2	251	55	141	4	0	0	0	80	11	0	.138	15	31	2	1	1.5	.958
1969			15	13	.536	3.51	36	33	10	228	218	63	126	3	0	0	0	76	8	1	.105	13	34	3	3	1.4	.940
1970			6	7	.462	6.22	30	19	1	107	129	36	59	1	1	2	0	39	7	0	.179	6	7	0	0	0.4	1.000
1971	PIT	N	8	4	.667	3.04	37	14	4	136	131	35	76	2	1	2	1	39	10	1	.256	13	13	1	1	0.7	.963
1972			14	11	.560	3.08	28	27	9	195.2	185	43	120	2	1	0	0	70	11	0	.157	11	26	1	1	1.4	.974
1973			14	13	.519	2.84	33	33	7	218.2	201	51	94	1	0	0	0	72	14	1	.194	14	35	1	3	1.5	.980
1974	KC	A	5	7	.417	4.02	18	17	3	103	118	21	41	0	0	0	0	0	0	0	—	8	12	1	1	1.2	.952
1975			6	6	.500	4.26	24	16	3	112	127	25	73	0	1	0	2	0	0	0	—	11	15	1	1	1.1	.963
1976	TEX	A	11	9	.550	3.26	32	31	7	210	224	47	98	1	0	0	1	0	0	0	—	10	18	0	0	0.9	1.000
1977	2 teams	TEX A (30G 6–4)	BAL A (2G 0–0)																								
″	total		6	4	.600	4.17	32	15	2	112.1	119	30	59	1	2	0	2	0	0	0		3	13	0	1	0.5	1.000
1978	BAL	A	4	4	.500	4.64	16	8	1	54.1	58	21	30	0	3	0	0	0	0	0	—	2	4	1	0	0.4	.857
14 yrs.			129	112	.535	3.43	454	279	64	2112.1	2141	547	1163	17	16	15	22	469	72	3	.154	131	263	14	17	0.9	.966
LEAGUE CHAMPIONSHIP SERIES																											
1972	PIT	N	0	0	—	3.00	1	1	0	6	6	1	3	0	0	0	0	2	0	0	.000	1	1	0	0	2.0	1.000
WORLD SERIES																											
1967	STL	N	1	0	1.000	1.64	2	1	1	11	7	1	4	0	0	0	0	3	0	0	.000	0	4	0	0	2.0	1.000
1968			0	1	.000	5.56	2	2	0	11.1	13	4	7	0	0	0	0	4	0	0	.000	0	2	0	0	1.0	1.000
1971	PIT	N	1	0	1.000	0.00	1	1	1	9	2	2	2	1	0	0	0	2	1	0	.500	0	1	0	0	1.0	1.000
3 yrs.			2	1	.667	2.59	5	4	2	31.1	22	7	13	1	0	0	0	9	1	0	.111	0	7	0	0	1.4	1.000

Frank Brill

BRILL, FRANCIS HASBROUCK
Born Francis Hasbrouck Briell.
B. Mar. 28, 1864, Astoria, N. Y. D. Nov. 19, 1944, Flushing, N. Y.
BR TR 5′ 8″ 155 lbs.

Year	Team		W	L	PCT	ERA	G	GS	CG	IP	H	BB	SO	ShO	Relief Pitching W	L	SV	Batting AB	H	HR	BA	PO	A	E	DP	TC/G	FA
1884	DET	N	2	10	.167	*5.50*	12	12	12	103	148	26	18	1	0	0	0	44	6	0	.136	5	14	1	0	1.5	.950

Jim Brillheart

BRILLHEART, JAMES BENSON (Buck)
B. Sept. 28, 1903, Dublin, Va. D. Sept. 2, 1972, Radford, Va.
BR TL 5′11″ 170 lbs.

Year	Team		W	L	PCT	ERA	G	GS	CG	IP	H	BB	SO	ShO	Relief Pitching W	L	SV	Batting AB	H	HR	BA	PO	A	E	DP	TC/G	FA
1922	WAS	A	4	6	.400	3.61	31	10	3	119.2	120	72	47	0	0	2	1	36	3	0	.083	3	22	4	0	0.9	.862
1923			0	1	.000	7.00	12	0	0	18	27	12	8	0	0	1	0	2	0	0	.000	2	6	1	0	0.8	.889
1927	CHI	N	4	2	.667	4.13	32	12	4	128.2	140	38	36	0	0	0	0	44	1	0	.023	1	25	0	3	0.8	1.000
1931	BOS	A	0	0	—	5.49	11	1	0	19.2	27	15	7	0	0	0	0	4	2	1	.500	1	7	0	0	0.7	1.000
4 yrs.			8	9	.471	4.19	86	23	7	286	314	137	98	0	0	3	1	86	6	1	.070	7	60	5	3	0.8	.931

Brad Brink

BRINK, BRADFORD ALBERT BR TR 6′ 2″ 195 lbs.
B. Jan. 20, 1965, Roseville, Calif.

Year	Team	W	L	PCT	ERA	G	GS	CG	IP	H	BB	SO	ShO	Relief Pitching W	Relief Pitching L	Relief Pitching SV	Batting AB	Batting H	Batting HR	BA	PO	A	E	DP	TC/G	FA
1992	PHI N	0	4	.000	4.14	8	7	0	41.1	53	13	16	0	0	0	0	12	1	0	.083	0	2	1	0	0.4	.667
1993		0	0	—	3.00	2	0	0	6	3	3	8	0	0	0	0	1	0	0	.000	0	0	1	0	0.5	.000
1994	SF N	0	0	—	1.08	4	0	0	8.1	4	4	3	0	0	0	0	1	0	0	.000	1	1	0	0	0.5	1.000
3 yrs.		0	4	.000	3.56	14	7	0	55.2	60	20	27	0	0	0	0	14	1	0	.071	1	3	2	0	0.4	.667

John Briscoe

BRISCOE, JOHN ERIC BR TR 6′ 3″ 185 lbs.
B. Sept. 22, 1967, La Grange, Ill.

Year	Team	W	L	PCT	ERA	G	GS	CG	IP	H	BB	SO	ShO	Relief Pitching W	Relief Pitching L	Relief Pitching SV	Batting AB	Batting H	Batting HR	BA	PO	A	E	DP	TC/G	FA
1991	OAK A	0	0	—	7.07	11	0	0	14	12	10	9	0	0	0	0	0	0	0	—	0	1	0	0	0.1	1.000
1992		0	1	.000	6.43	2	2	0	7	12	9	4	0	0	0	0	0	0	0	—	0	1	1	0	1.0	.500
1993		1	0	1.000	8.03	17	0	0	24.2	26	26	24	0	1	0	0	0	0	0	—	1	4	0	0	0.3	1.000
1994		4	2	.667	4.01	37	0	0	49.1	31	39	45	0	4	2	1	0	0	0	—	2	2	0	1	0.1	1.000
1995		0	1	.000	8.35	16	0	0	18.1	25	21	19	0	0	1	0	0	0	0	—	2	2	0	1	0.3	1.000
5 yrs.		5	4	.556	6.11	83	2	0	113.1	106	105	101	0	5	3	1	0	0	0		5	10	1	2	0.2	.938

Lou Brissie

BRISSIE, LELAND VICTOR BL TL 6′ 4½″ 210 lbs.
B. June 5, 1924, Anderson, S. C.

Year	Team	W	L	PCT	ERA	G	GS	CG	IP	H	BB	SO	ShO	Relief Pitching W	Relief Pitching L	Relief Pitching SV	Batting AB	Batting H	Batting HR	BA	PO	A	E	DP	TC/G	FA
1947	PHI A	0	1	.000	6.43	1	1	0	7	9	5	4	0	0	0	0	2	0	0	.000	1	1	0	0	2.0	1.000
1948		14	10	.583	4.13	39	25	11	194	202	95	127	0	4	2	5	76	18	0	.237	8	22	0	1	0.8	1.000
1949		16	11	.593	4.28	34	29	18	229.1	220	118	118	0	1	0	3	90	24	0	.267	6	21	0	3	0.8	1.000
1950		7	19	.269	4.02	46	31	15	246	237	117	101	2	0	1	8	87	15	0	.172	7	41	2	6	1.1	.960
1951	2 teams PHI A (2G 0–2) CLE A (54G 4–3)																									
″	total	4	5	.444	3.58	56	6	1	125.2	110	69	53	0	3	1	9	28	7	0	.250	4	12	2	3	0.3	.889
1952	CLE A	3	2	.600	3.48	42	1	0	82.2	68	34	28	0	3	1	2	12	3	0	.250	3	21	0	0	0.6	1.000
1953		0	0	—	7.62	16	0	0	13	21	13	5	0	0	0	2	0	0	0	—	0	2	0	0	0.1	1.000
7 yrs.		44	48	.478	4.07	234	93	45	897.2	867	451	436	2	11	5	29	295	67	0	.227	29	120	4	13	0.7	.974

John Brittin

BRITTIN, JOHN ALBERT BR TR 5′11″ 175 lbs.
B. Mar. 4, 1924, Athens, Ill. D. Jan. 5, 1994, Springfield, Ill.

Year	Team	W	L	PCT	ERA	G	GS	CG	IP	H	BB	SO	ShO	Relief Pitching W	Relief Pitching L	Relief Pitching SV	Batting AB	Batting H	Batting HR	BA	PO	A	E	DP	TC/G	FA
1950	PHI N	0	0	—	4.50	3	0	0	4	2	3	3	0	0	0	0	0	0	0	—	0	1	0	0	0.3	1.000
1951		0	0	—	9.00	3	0	0	4	5	6	3	0	0	0	0	0	0	0	—	0	1	0	0	0.3	1.000
2 yrs.		0	0		6.75	6	0	0	8	7	9	6	0	0	0	0	0	0	0		0	2	0	0	0.3	1.000

Jim Britton

BRITTON, JAMES ALLAN BR TR 6′ 5″ 225 lbs.
B. Mar. 25, 1944, North Tonawanda, N. Y.

Year	Team	W	L	PCT	ERA	G	GS	CG	IP	H	BB	SO	ShO	Relief Pitching W	Relief Pitching L	Relief Pitching SV	Batting AB	Batting H	Batting HR	BA	PO	A	E	DP	TC/G	FA
1967	ATL N	0	2	.000	6.08	2	2	0	13.1	15	2	4	0	0	0	0	4	0	0	.000	2	1	1	0	2.0	.750
1968		4	6	.400	3.09	34	9	2	90.1	81	34	61	2	2	2	3	21	3	0	.143	2	16	0	1	0.5	1.000
1969		7	5	.583	3.78	24	13	2	88	69	49	60	1	0	0	1	21	4	0	.190	1	12	1	0	0.6	.929
1971	MON N	2	3	.400	5.67	16	6	0	46	49	27	23	0	1	0	0	9	0	0	.000	2	4	0	0	0.4	1.000
4 yrs.		13	16	.448	4.01	76	30	4	237.2	214	112	148	3	3	2	4	55	7	0	.127	7	33	2	1	0.6	.952
LEAGUE CHAMPIONSHIP SERIES																										
1969	ATL N	0	0	—	0.00	1	0	0	0.1	0	1	0	0	0	0	0	0	0	0	—	0	0	0	0	0.0	.000

Tony Brizzolara

BRIZZOLARA, ANTHONY JOHN BR TR 6′ 5″ 215 lbs.
B. Jan. 14, 1957, Santa Monica, Calif.

Year	Team	W	L	PCT	ERA	G	GS	CG	IP	H	BB	SO	ShO	Relief Pitching W	Relief Pitching L	Relief Pitching SV	Batting AB	Batting H	Batting HR	BA	PO	A	E	DP	TC/G	FA
1979	ATL N	6	9	.400	5.30	20	19	2	107	133	33	64	0	0	0	0	35	1	0	.029	7	15	1	1	1.1	.957
1983		1	0	1.000	3.54	14	0	0	20.1	22	6	17	0	1	0	1	0	0	0	—	2	0	0	0	0.1	1.000
1984		1	2	.333	5.28	10	4	0	29	33	13	17	0	0	1	0	7	0	0	.000	4	3	0	0	0.7	1.000
3 yrs.		8	11	.421	5.07	44	23	2	156.1	188	52	98	0	1	1	1	42	1	0	.024	13	18	1	1	0.7	.969

Johnny Broaca

BROACA, JOHN JOSEPH BR TR 5′11″ 190 lbs.
B. Oct. 3, 1909, Lawrence, Mass. D. May 16, 1985, Lawrence, Mass.

Year	Team	W	L	PCT	ERA	G	GS	CG	IP	H	BB	SO	ShO	Relief Pitching W	Relief Pitching L	Relief Pitching SV	Batting AB	Batting H	Batting HR	BA	PO	A	E	DP	TC/G	FA
1934	NY A	12	9	.571	4.16	26	24	13	177.1	203	65	74	1	0	0	0	66	2	0	.030	3	25	1	1	1.1	.966
1935		15	7	.682	3.58	29	27	14	201	199	79	78	2	1	1	0	80	12	0	.150	4	28	2	1	1.2	.941
1936		12	7	.632	4.24	37	27	12	206	235	66	84	1	0	0	3	82	9	0	.110	6	29	0	0	0.9	1.000
1937		1	4	.200	4.70	7	6	3	44	58	17	9	0	0	0	0	14	0	0	.000	1	4	1	0	0.9	.833
1939	CLE A	4	2	.667	4.70	22	2	0	46	53	28	13	0	4	1	0	12	0	0	.000	0	8	1	2	0.4	.889
5 yrs.		44	29	.603	4.08	121	86	42	674.1	748	255	258	4	5	2	3	254	23	0	.091	14	94	5	4	0.9	.956

Pete Broberg

BROBERG, PETER SVEN BR TR 6′ 3″ 205 lbs.
B. Mar. 2, 1950, West Palm Beach, Fla.

Year	Team	W	L	PCT	ERA	G	GS	CG	IP	H	BB	SO	ShO	Relief Pitching W	Relief Pitching L	Relief Pitching SV	Batting AB	Batting H	Batting HR	BA	PO	A	E	DP	TC/G	FA
1971	WAS A	5	9	.357	3.46	18	18	7	125	104	53	89	1	0	0	0	44	5	1	.114	10	12	0	1	1.2	1.000
1972	TEX A	5	12	.294	4.30	39	25	3	175.2	153	85	133	2	0	0	1	51	4	0	.078	16	27	1	2	1.1	.977
1973		5	9	.357	5.60	22	20	6	119	130	66	57	1	0	0	0	0	0	0	—	5	18	1	1	1.1	.958
1974		0	4	.000	8.07	12	2	0	29	29	13	15	0	0	2	0	0	0	0	—	2	4	1	0	0.6	.857
1975	MIL A	14	16	.467	4.13	38	32	7	220.1	219	106	100	2	2	0	0	0	0	0	—	7	36	4	4	1.2	.915
1976		1	7	.125	4.97	20	11	1	92.1	99	72	28	0	0	0	0	0	0	0	—	4	11	1	0	0.8	.938
1977	CHI N	1	2	.333	4.75	22	0	0	36	34	18	20	0	1	2	0	6	0	0	.000	1	7	0	0	0.4	1.000
1978	OAK A	10	12	.455	4.62	35	26	2	165.2	174	65	94	0	2	1	0	0	0	0	—	8	28	0	1	1.0	1.000
8 yrs.		41	71	.366	4.56	206	134	26	963	942	478	536	6	5	5	1	101	9	1	.089	53	143	8	9	1.0	.961

Doug Brocail

BROCAIL, DOUGLAS KEITH BL TR 6′ 5″ 220 lbs.
B. May 16, 1967, Clearfield, Pa.

Year	Team	W	L	PCT	ERA	G	GS	CG	IP	H	BB	SO	ShO	Relief Pitching W	Relief Pitching L	Relief Pitching SV	Batting AB	Batting H	Batting HR	BA	PO	A	E	DP	TC/G	FA
1992	SD N	0	0	—	6.43	3	3	0	14	17	5	15	0	0	0	0	5	1	0	.200	1	1	1	0	1.0	.667
1993		4	13	.235	4.56	24	24	0	128.1	143	42	70	0	0	0	0	33	6	0	.182	8	20	2	1	1.3	.933
1994		0	0	—	5.82	12	0	0	17	21	5	11	0	0	0	0	2	0	0	.000	1	2	1	0	0.3	.750
1995	HOU N	6	4	.600	4.19	36	7	0	77.1	87	22	39	0	4	2	1	16	4	0	.250	11	9	0	0	0.6	1.000
4 yrs.		10	17	.370	4.64	75	34	0	236.2	268	74	135	0	4	2	1	56	11	0	.196	21	32	4	1	0.8	.930

Lew Brockett

BROCKETT, LEWIS ALBERT (King) BR TR 5′10½″ 168 lbs.
B. July 23, 1880, Brownsville, Ill. D. Sept. 19, 1960, Norris City, Ill.

Year	Team	W	L	PCT	ERA	G	GS	CG	IP	H	BB	SO	ShO	Relief Pitching W	Relief Pitching L	Relief Pitching SV	Batting AB	Batting H	Batting HR	BA	PO	A	E	DP	TC/G	FA
1907	NY A	1	2	.333	6.22	8	4	1	46.1	58	26	13	0	0	0	0	22	4	0	.182	2	10	2	1	1.6	.857
1909		10	8	.556	2.37	26	18	10	152	148	59	70	3	2	0	1	60	17	0	.283	10	71	6	4	3.3	.931
1911		2	4	.333	4.66	16	8	2	75.1	73	39	25	0	1	1	0	39	12	0	.308	5	31	3	1	2.1	.923
3 yrs.		13	14	.481	3.65	50	30	13	273.2	279	124	108	3	3	1	1	121	33	0	.273	17	112	11	6	2.6	.921

Dick Brodowski

BRODOWSKI, RICHARD STANLEY
B. July 26, 1932, Bayonne, N. J.
BR TR 6′ 1″ 182 lbs.

Year	Team		W	L	PCT	ERA	G	GS	CG	IP	H	BB	SO	ShO	Relief Pitching W	L	SV	Batting AB	H	HR	BA	PO	A	E	DP	TC/G	FA
1952	BOS	A	5	5	.500	4.40	20	12	4	114.2	111	50	42	0	0	1	0	39	8	1	.205	11	20	1	1	1.6	.969
1955			1	0	1.000	5.63	16	0	0	32	36	25	10	0	1	0	0	10	5	1	.500	5	7	0	0	0.8	1.000
1956	WAS	A	0	3	.000	9.17	7	3	1	17.2	31	12	8	0	0	0	0	5	0	0	.000	2	3	0	0	0.7	1.000
1957			0	1	.000	11.12	6	0	0	11.1	12	10	4	0	0	1	0	1	0	0	.000	1	2	0	0	0.5	1.000
1958	CLE	A	1	0	1.000	0.00	5	0	0	10	3	6	12	0	1	0	0	1	0	0	.000	0	1	0	0	0.2	1.000
1959			2	2	.500	1.80	18	0	0	30	19	21	9	0	2	2	5	6	2	0	.333	4	3	2	0	0.5	.778
6 yrs.			9	11	.450	4.76	72	15	5	215.2	212	124	85	0	4	4	5	62	15	2	.242	23	36	3	1	0.9	.952

Ernie Broglio

BROGLIO, ERNEST GILBERT
B. Aug. 27, 1935, Berkeley, Calif.
BR TR 6′ 2″ 200 lbs.

Year	Team		W	L	PCT	ERA	G	GS	CG	IP	H	BB	SO	ShO	Relief Pitching W	L	SV	Batting AB	H	HR	BA	PO	A	E	DP	TC/G	FA
1959	STL	N	7	12	.368	4.72	35	25	6	181.1	174	89	133	3	0	3	0	61	6	0	.098	11	30	0	2	1.2	1.000
1960			**21**	9	**.700**	2.74	52	24	9	226.1	172	100	188	3	7	2	0	68	14	0	.206	17	35	1	5	1.0	.981
1961			9	12	.429	4.12	29	26	7	174.2	166	75	113	2	0	1	0	62	9	0	.145	13	27	1	0	1.4	.976
1962			12	9	.571	3.00	34	30	11	222.1	193	93	132	4	1	1	0	72	10	0	.139	19	39	2	3	1.8	.967
1963			18	8	.692	2.99	39	35	11	250	202	90	145	5	2	1	0	89	10	0	.112	30	37	4	4	1.8	.944
1964	2 teams	STL N	(11G 3–5)		CHI N	(18G 4–7)																					
″	total		7	12	.368	3.82	29	27	6	169.2	176	56	82	1	0	0	1	56	12	0	.214	12	24	1	0	1.3	.973
1965	CHI	N	1	6	.143	6.93	26	6	0	50.2	63	46	22	0	1	3	0	4	0	0	.000	2	5	0	0	0.3	1.000
1966			2	6	.250	6.35	15	11	2	62.1	70	38	34	0	0	0	1	19	7	0	.368	2	18	0	2	1.3	1.000
8 yrs.			77	74	.510	3.74	259	184	52	1337.1	1216	587	849	18	11	11	2	431	68	0	.158	106	215	9	16	1.3	.973

Ken Brondell

BRONDELL, KENNETH LeROY
B. Oct. 17, 1921, Bradshaw, Neb.
BR TR 6′ 1″ 195 lbs.

Year	Team		W	L	PCT	ERA	G	GS	CG	IP	H	BB	SO	ShO	Relief Pitching W	L	SV	Batting AB	H	HR	BA	PO	A	E	DP	TC/G	FA
1944	NY	N	0	1	.000	8.38	7	2	1	19.1	27	8	1	0	0	0	0	4	0	0	.000	2	1	0	0	0.4	1.000

Jeff Bronkey

BRONKEY, JACOB JEFFREY
B. Sept. 18, 1965, Kabul, Afghanistan.
BR TR 6′ 3″ 215 lbs.

Year	Team		W	L	PCT	ERA	G	GS	CG	IP	H	BB	SO	ShO	Relief Pitching W	L	SV	Batting AB	H	HR	BA	PO	A	E	DP	TC/G	FA
1993	TEX	A	1	1	.500	4.00	21	0	0	36	39	11	18	0	1	1	1	1	0	0	.000	3	10	0	1	0.6	1.000
1994	MIL	A	1	1	.500	4.35	16	0	0	20.2	20	12	13	0	1	1	1	0	0	0	—	1	4	0	0	0.3	1.000
1995			0	0	—	3.65	8	0	0	12.1	15	6	5	0	0	0	0	0	0	0	—	3	0	0	0	0.4	1.000
3 yrs.			2	2	.500	4.04	45	0	0	69	74	29	36	0	2	2	2	1	0	0	.000	7	14	0	1	0.5	1.000

Jim Bronstad

BRONSTAD, JAMES WARREN
B. June 22, 1936, Fort Worth, Tex.
BR TR 6′ 3″ 196 lbs.

Year	Team		W	L	PCT	ERA	G	GS	CG	IP	H	BB	SO	ShO	Relief Pitching W	L	SV	Batting AB	H	HR	BA	PO	A	E	DP	TC/G	FA
1959	NY	A	0	3	.000	5.22	16	3	0	29.1	34	13	14	0	0	1	2	5	0	0	.000	3	6	0	0	0.6	1.000
1963	WAS	A	1	3	.250	5.65	25	0	0	57.1	66	22	22	0	1	3	1	12	0	0	.000	7	14	0	2	0.8	1.000
1964			0	1	.000	5.14	4	0	0	7	10	2	9	0	0	1	0	0	0	0	—	0	0	0	0	0.0	.000
3 yrs.			1	7	.125	5.48	45	3	0	93.2	110	37	45	0	1	5	3	17	0	0	.000	10	20	0	2	0.7	1.000

Ike Brookens

BROOKENS, EDWARD DWAIN
B. Jan. 3, 1949, Chambersburg, Pa.
BR TR 6′ 5″ 170 lbs.

Year	Team		W	L	PCT	ERA	G	GS	CG	IP	H	BB	SO	ShO	Relief Pitching W	L	SV	Batting AB	H	HR	BA	PO	A	E	DP	TC/G	FA
1975	DET	A	0	0	—	5.40	3	0	0	10	11	5	8	0	0	0	0	0	0	0	—	0	2	0	0	0.7	1.000

Harry Brooks

BROOKS, HARRY FRANK
B. Nov. 30, 1865, Philadelphia, Pa. D. Dec. 5, 1945, Philadelphia, Pa.

Year	Team		W	L	PCT	ERA	G	GS	CG	IP	H	BB	SO	ShO	Relief Pitching W	L	SV	Batting AB	H	HR	BA	PO	A	E	DP	TC/G	FA
1886	NY	AA	0	1	.000	*36.00*	1	1	0	2	9	2	0	0	0	0	0	*				1	0	5	0	3.0	.167

Jim Brosnan

BROSNAN, JAMES PATRICK (Professor)
B. Oct. 24, 1929, Cincinnati, Ohio.
BR TR 6′ 4″ 197 lbs.

Year	Team		W	L	PCT	ERA	G	GS	CG	IP	H	BB	SO	ShO	Relief Pitching W	L	SV	Batting AB	H	HR	BA	PO	A	E	DP	TC/G	FA
1954	CHI	N	1	0	1.000	9.45	18	0	0	33.1	44	18	17	0	1	0	0	8	1	0	.125	3	10	1	2	0.8	.929
1956			5	9	.357	3.79	30	10	1	95	95	45	51	1	3	4	1	22	4	0	.182	8	11	0	0	0.6	1.000
1957			5	5	.500	3.38	41	5	1	98.2	79	46	73	0	4	4	0	20	5	0	.250	4	19	1	1	0.6	.958
1958	2 teams	CHI N	(8G 3–4)		STL N	(33G 8–4)																					
″	total		11	8	.579	3.35	41	20	4	166.2	148	79	89	0	4	1	7	50	5	0	.100	12	30	1	3	1.0	.977
1959	2 teams	STL N	(20G 1–3)		CIN N	(26G 8–3)																					
″	total		9	6	.600	3.79	46	10	1	116.1	113	41	74	1	5	3	4	30	3	0	.100	9	23	1	3	0.7	.970
1960	CIN	N	7	2	.778	2.36	57	2	0	99	79	22	62	0	7	2	12	15	3	1	.200	7	14	0	2	0.4	1.000
1961			10	4	.714	3.04	53	0	0	80	77	18	40	0	10	4	16	13	2	0	.154	9	18	3	0	0.6	.900
1962			4	4	.500	3.34	48	0	0	64.2	76	18	51	0	4	4	13	6	0	0	.000	4	8	1	0	0.3	.923
1963	2 teams	CIN N	(6G 0–1)		CHI A	(45G 3–8)																					
″	total		3	9	.250	3.13	51	0	0	77.2	79	25	50	0	3	**9**	14	13	4	0	.308	3	13	0	1	0.3	1.000
9 yrs.			55	47	.539	3.54	385	47	7	831.1	790	312	507	2	41	31	67	177	27	1	.153	59	146	8	12	0.6	.962
WORLD SERIES																											
1961	CIN	N	0	0	—	7.50	3	0	0	6	9	4	5	0	0	0	0	0	0	0	—	0	0	0	0	0.0	.000

Terry Bross

BROSS, TERRANCE PAUL
B. Mar. 30, 1966, El Paso, Tex.
BR TR 6′ 9″ 234 lbs.

Year	Team		W	L	PCT	ERA	G	GS	CG	IP	H	BB	SO	ShO	Relief Pitching W	L	SV	Batting AB	H	HR	BA	PO	A	E	DP	TC/G	FA
1991	NY	N	0	0	—	1.80	8	0	0	10	7	3	5	0	0	0	0	0	0	0	—	0	0	0	0	0.0	.000
1993	SF	N	0	0	—	9.00	2	0	0	2	3	1	1	0	0	0	0	0	0	0	—	0	0	0	0	0.0	.000
2 yrs.			0	0		3.00	10	0	0	12	10	4	6	0	0	0	0	0	0	0		0	0	0	0	0.0	

Frank Brosseau

BROSSEAU, FRANKLIN LEE
B. July 31, 1944, Drayton, N. D.
BR TR 6′ 1″ 180 lbs.

Year	Team		W	L	PCT	ERA	G	GS	CG	IP	H	BB	SO	ShO	Relief Pitching W	L	SV	Batting AB	H	HR	BA	PO	A	E	DP	TC/G	FA
1969	PIT	N	0	0	—	9.00	2	0	0	2	2	2	2	0	0	0	0	0	0	0	—	0	0	0	0	0.0	.000
1971			0	0	—	0.00	1	0	0	2	1	0	0	0	0	0	0	0	0	0	—	1	1	0	0	2.0	1.000
2 yrs.			0	0		4.50	3	0	0	4	3	2	2	0	0	0	0	0	0	0		1	1	0	0	0.7	1.000

Dan Brouthers

BROUTHERS, DENNIS JOSEPH (Big Dan)
B. May 8, 1858, Sylvan Lake, N. Y. D. Aug. 2, 1932, East Orange, N. J.
Hall of Fame 1945.
BL TL 6′ 2″ 207 lbs.

Year	Team		W	L	PCT	ERA	G	GS	CG	IP	H	BB	SO	ShO	Relief Pitching W	L	SV	Batting AB	H	HR	BA	PO	A	E	DP	TC/G	FA
1879	TRO	N	0	2	.000	5.57	3	2	2	21	35	8	6	0	0	0	0	168	46	4	.274	406	7	34	11	11.2	.924
1883	BUF	N	0	0	—	31.50	1	0	0	2	9	3	2	0	0	0	0	425	159	3	.374	25	0	3	1	9.3	.893
2 yrs.			0	2	.000	7.83	4	2	2	23	44	11	8	0	0	0	0	*				16414	667	531	891	10.5	.970

Scott Brow

BROW, SCOTT JOHN BR TR 6′ 3″ 200 lbs.
B. Mar. 17, 1969, Butte, Mont.

Year	Team	W	L	PCT	ERA	G	GS	CG	IP	H	BB	SO	ShO	Relief Pitching W	L	SV	Batting AB	H	HR	BA	PO	A	E	DP	TC/G	FA
1993	TOR A	1	1	.500	6.00	6	3	0	18	19	10	7	0	0	0	0	0	0	0	—	3	8	0	1	1.8	1.000
1994		0	3	.000	5.90	18	0	0	29	34	19	15	0	0	3	2	0	0	0	—	1	4	0	1	0.3	1.000
2 yrs.		1	4	.200	5.94	24	3	0	47	53	29	22	0	0	3	2	0	0	0		4	12	0	2	0.7	1.000

Frank Brower

BROWER, FRANK WILLARD (Turkeyfoot) BL TR 6′ 2″ 180 lbs.
B. Mar. 26, 1893, Gainesville, Va. D. Nov. 20, 1960, Baltimore, Md.

Year	Team	W	L	PCT	ERA	G	GS	CG	IP	H	BB	SO	ShO	Relief Pitching W	L	SV	Batting AB	H	HR	BA	PO	A	E	DP	TC/G	FA
1924	CLE A	0	0	—	0.93	4	0	0	9.2	7	4	0	0	0	0	0	*				131	10	5	7	4.9	.966

Alton Brown

BROWN, ALTON LEO (Deacon) BR TR 6′ 2″ 195 lbs.
B. Apr. 16, 1925, Norfolk, Va.

Year	Team	W	L	PCT	ERA	G	GS	CG	IP	H	BB	SO	ShO	Relief Pitching W	L	SV	Batting AB	H	HR	BA	PO	A	E	DP	TC/G	FA
1951	WAS A	0	0	—	9.26	7	0	0	11.2	14	12	7	0	0	0	0	1	0	0	.000	0	1	0	0	0.1	1.000

Boardwalk Brown

BROWN, CARROLL WILLIAM BR TR 6′ 1½″ 178 lbs.
B. Feb. 20, 1887, Woodbury, N. J. D. Feb. 8, 1977, Burlington, N. J.

Year	Team	W	L	PCT	ERA	G	GS	CG	IP	H	BB	SO	ShO	Relief Pitching W	L	SV	Batting AB	H	HR	BA	PO	A	E	DP	TC/G	FA
1911	PHI A	0	1	.000	4.50	2	1	1	12	12	2	6	0	0	0	0	4	0	0	.000	1	3	0	0	2.0	1.000
1912		13	11	.542	3.66	34	24	16	199	204	87	64	3	2	2	1	76	11	0	.145	10	72	3	2	2.5	.965
1913		17	11	.607	2.94	43	35	11	235.1	200	87	70	3	1	3	1	82	13	1	.159	7	65	5	2	1.8	.935
1914	2 teams	PHI A (15G 1–6)		NY A (20G 5–5)																						
″	total	6	11	.353	3.54	35	22	10	188.1	187	68	77	0	1	1	1	64	8	0	.125	10	69	5	1	2.4	.940
1915	NY A	2	6	.250	4.10	19	10	5	96.2	95	47	34	0	0	0	1	32	6	0	.188	3	28	3	3	1.8	.912
5 yrs.		38	40	.487	3.47	133	92	43	731.1	698	291	251	6	4	6	4	258	38	1	.147	31	237	16	8	2.1	.944

Bob Brown

Playing record listed under Bob Smith.

Bob Brown

BROWN, ROBERT MURRAY BR TR 6′ 1″ 190 lbs.
B. Apr. 1, 1911, Dorchester, Mass. D. Aug. 3, 1990, Pembroke, Mass.

Year	Team	W	L	PCT	ERA	G	GS	CG	IP	H	BB	SO	ShO	Relief Pitching W	L	SV	Batting AB	H	HR	BA	PO	A	E	DP	TC/G	FA
1930	BOS N	0	0	—	10.50	3	0	0	6	10	8	1	0	0	0	0	2	0	0	.000	1	1	0	0	0.7	1.000
1931		0	1	.000	8.53	3	1	0	6.1	9	3	2	0	0	0	0	2	1	0	.500	0	3	0	0	1.0	1.000
1932		14	7	.667	3.30	35	28	9	213	187	104	110	0	3	0	1	67	13	0	.194	6	39	0	2	1.3	1.000
1933		0	0	—	2.70	5	0	0	6.2	6	3	3	0	0	0	0	2	0	0	.000	0	1	0	0	0.2	1.000
1934		1	3	.250	5.71	16	8	2	58.1	59	36	21	1	0	0	0	21	5	0	.238	5	6	1	0	0.8	.917
1935		1	8	.111	6.37	15	10	2	65	79	36	17	1	0	1	0	19	2	0	.105	4	8	1	0	0.9	.923
1936		0	2	.000	5.40	2	2	0	8.1	10	3	5	0	0	0	0	2	0	0	.000	0	3	0	0	1.5	1.000
7 yrs.		16	21	.432	4.48	79	49	13	363.2	360	193	159	2	3	1	1	115	21	0	.183	16	61	2	2	1.0	.975

Buster Brown

BROWN, CHARLES EDWARD BR TR 6′ 180 lbs.
B. Aug. 31, 1881, Boone, Iowa D. Feb. 9, 1914, Sioux City, Iowa.

Year	Team	W	L	PCT	ERA	G	GS	CG	IP	H	BB	SO	ShO	Relief Pitching W	L	SV	Batting AB	H	HR	BA	PO	A	E	DP	TC/G	FA
1905	STL N	8	11	.421	2.97	23	21	17	179	172	62	57	3	0	0	0	65	6	0	.092	12	61	4	3	3.3	.948
1906		8	16	.333	2.64	32	27	21	238.1	208	112	109	0	0	1	0	85	14	1	.165	17	71	7	4	3.0	.926
1907	2 teams	STL N (9G 1–6)		PHI N (21G 9–6)																						
″	total	10	12	.455	2.74	30	24	19	193.2	175	101	55	4	0	0	0	79	17	0	.215	11	60	2	2	2.4	.973
1908	PHI N	0	0	—	2.57	3	0	0	7	9	5	3	0	0	0	0	5	1	0	.200	2	6	0	0	2.7	1.000
1909	2 teams	PHI N (7G 0–0)		BOS N (18G 4–10)																						
″	total	4	10	.286	3.16	25	18	8	148.1	130	72	42	2	0	0	0	57	7	0	.123	11	44	4	1	2.4	.932
1910	BOS N	9	23	.281	2.67	46	29	16	263	251	94	88	1	3	**5**	2	81	16	1	.198	10	80	7	3	2.1	.928
1911		8	18	.308	4.29	42	25	13	241	258	116	76	0	2	1	2	84	21	1	.250	8	67	6	6	1.9	.926
1912		4	15	.211	4.01	31	21	13	168.1	146	66	68	0	0	1	0	61	13	0	.213	4	42	0	1	1.5	1.000
1913		0	0	—	4.72	2	0	0	13.1	19	3	3	0	0	0	0	5	0	0	.000	0	3	0	0	1.5	1.000
9 yrs.		51	105	.327	3.20	234	165	107	1452	1368	631	501	10	5	8	4	522	95	3	.182	75	434	30	20	2.3	.944

Charlie Brown

BROWN, CHARLES E. (Buster, Yank) TL 6′ 180 lbs.
B. 1878, Baltimore, Md. Deceased.

Year	Team	W	L	PCT	ERA	G	GS	CG	IP	H	BB	SO	ShO	Relief Pitching W	L	SV	Batting AB	H	HR	BA	PO	A	E	DP	TC/G	FA
1897	CLE N	1	2	.333	7.77	4	4	2	24.1	30	17	8	0	0	0	0	11	3	0	.273	0	5	0	0	1.3	1.000

Clint Brown

BROWN, CLINTON HAROLD BL TR 6′ 1″ 190 lbs.
B. July 8, 1903, Blackash, Pa. D. Dec. 31, 1955, Rocky River, Ohio.

Year	Team	W	L	PCT	ERA	G	GS	CG	IP	H	BB	SO	ShO	Relief Pitching W	L	SV	Batting AB	H	HR	BA	PO	A	E	DP	TC/G	FA
1928	CLE A	0	1	.000	4.91	2	1	1	11	14	2	2	0	0	0	0	5	1	0	.200	2	3	0	0	2.5	1.000
1929		0	2	.000	3.31	3	1	1	16.1	18	6	1	0	0	1	0	7	0	0	.000	1	9	0	0	3.3	1.000
1930		11	12	.478	4.97	35	31	16	213.2	271	51	54	2	0	0	1	73	18	0	.247	12	54	5	5	2.0	.930
1931		11	15	.423	4.71	39	33	12	233.1	284	55	50	2	0	0	0	87	15	0	.172	9	67	0	3	1.9	1.000
1932		15	12	.556	4.08	37	32	21	262.2	298	50	59	1	0	0	1	100	25	2	.250	15	63	2	2	2.2	.975
1933		11	12	.478	3.41	33	23	10	185	202	34	47	2	1	1	1	62	9	0	.145	11	53	0	3	1.9	1.000
1934		4	3	.571	5.90	17	2	0	50.1	83	14	15	0	4	2	1	17	5	0	.294	0	10	1	0	0.6	.909
1935		4	3	.571	5.14	23	5	1	49	61	14	20	0	3	0	2	10	2	0	.200	5	12	1	1	0.8	.944
1936	CHI A	6	2	.750	4.99	38	2	0	83	106	24	19	0	6	1	5	25	4	0	.160	8	15	1	0	0.6	.958
1937		7	7	.500	3.42	**53**	0	0	100	92	36	51	0	7	**7**	**18**	18	4	0	.222	4	24	1	1	0.5	.966
1938		1	3	.250	4.61	8	0	0	13.2	16	9	2	0	1	3	2	2	1	0	.500	1	7	0	2	1.0	1.000
1939		11	10	.524	3.88	**61**	0	0	118.1	127	27	41	0	**11**	**10**	18	19	4	0	.211	3	29	1	3	0.5	.970
1940		4	6	.400	3.68	37	0	0	66	75	16	23	0	4	6	10	14	1	0	.071	2	14	0	0	0.4	1.000
1941	CLE A	3	3	.500	3.27	41	0	0	74.1	77	28	22	0	3	3	5	17	2	0	.118	2	27	0	3	0.7	1.000
1942		1	1	.500	6.00	7	0	0	9	16	2	4	0	1	1	0	1	0	0	.000	0	0	0	0	0.0	.000
15 yrs.		89	92	.492	4.26	434	130	62	1485.2	1740	368	410	7	41	35	64	457	91	2	.199	75	387	12	23	1.1	.975

Curly Brown

BROWN, CHARLES ROY (Lefty) BL TL 5′10½″ 165 lbs.
B. Dec. 9, 1888, Spring Hill, Kans. D. June 10, 1968, Spring Hill, Kans.

Year	Team	W	L	PCT	ERA	G	GS	CG	IP	H	BB	SO	ShO	Relief Pitching W	L	SV	Batting AB	H	HR	BA	PO	A	E	DP	TC/G	FA
1911	STL A	1	2	.333	2.74	3	2	2	23	22	5	8	0	1	0	0	9	0	0	.000	1	7	2	1	3.3	.800
1912		1	3	.250	4.87	16	5	2	64.2	69	35	28	1	0	1	0	24	5	0	.208	1	7	1	0	0.6	.889
1913		1	1	.500	2.57	2	2	2	14	12	4	3	0	0	0	0	5	2	0	.400	0	4	0	0	2.0	1.000
1915	CIN N	0	2	.000	4.67	7	3	0	27	26	6	13	0	0	0	0	11	4	0	.364	0	1	1	0	0.3	.500
4 yrs.		3	8	.273	4.20	28	12	6	128.2	129	50	52	1	1	1	0	49	11	0	.224	2	19	4	1	0.9	.840

Curt Brown

BROWN, CURTIS STEVEN BR TR 6′ 5″ 200 lbs.
B. Jan. 15, 1960, Ft. Lauderdale, Fla.

Year	Team	Lg	W	L	PCT	ERA	G	GS	CG	IP	H	BB	SO	ShO	Relief W	Relief L	Relief SV	AB	H	HR	BA	PO	A	E	DP	TC/G	FA
1983	CAL	A	1	1	.500	7.31	10	0	0	16	25	4	7	0	1	1	0	0	0	0	—	1	1	0	0	0.2	1.000
1984	NY	A	1	1	.500	2.70	13	0	0	16.2	18	4	10	0	1	1	0	0	0	0	—	2	2	0	0	0.3	1.000
1986	MON	N	0	1	.000	3.00	6	0	0	12	15	2	4	0	0	1	0	1	0	0	.000	1	3	1	0	0.8	.800
1987			0	1	.000	7.71	5	0	0	7	10	4	6	0	0	1	0	0	0	0	—	0	2	1	0	0.6	.667
4 yrs.			2	4	.333	4.88	34	0	0	51.2	68	14	27	0	2	4	0	1	0	0	.000	4	8	2	0	0.4	.857

Ed Brown

BROWN, EDWARD P. TR 178 lbs.
B. Chicago, Ill. Deceased.

Year	Team	Lg	W	L	PCT	ERA	G	GS	CG	IP	H	BB	SO	ShO	Relief W	Relief L	Relief SV	AB	H	HR	BA	PO	A	E	DP	TC/G	FA
1882	STL	AA	0	0	—	*0.00*	1	0	0	2	2	0	1	0	0	0	0	60	11	0	.183	21	6	6	0	1.8	.818
1884	TOL	AA	0	1	.000	*9.00*	1	1	1	9	19	4	1	0	0	0	0	153	27	0	.176	45	56	24	1	2.8	.808
2 yrs.			0	1	.000	7.36	2	1	1	11	21	4	2	0	0	0	0	*				66	62	30	1	2.5	.810

Elmer Brown

BROWN, ELMER YOUNG (Shook) BL TR 5′11½″ 172 lbs.
B. Mar. 25, 1883, Southport, Ind. D. Jan. 23, 1955, Indianapolis, Ind.

Year	Team	Lg	W	L	PCT	ERA	G	GS	CG	IP	H	BB	SO	ShO	Relief W	Relief L	Relief SV	AB	H	HR	BA	PO	A	E	DP	TC/G	FA
1911	STL	A	1	1	.500	6.61	5	3	1	16.1	16	14	5	1	0	0	0	7	1	0	.143	1	7	0	0	1.6	1.000
1912			5	8	.385	2.99	23	11	2	120.1	122	42	45	1	1	2	0	36	6	0	.167	2	31	2	1	1.5	.943
1913	BKN	N	0	0	—	2.08	3	1	0	13	6	10	6	0	0	0	0	4	0	0	.000	0	3	0	0	1.0	1.000
1914			2	2	.500	3.93	11	4	1	36.2	33	23	22	0	2	2	0	12	1	0	.083	2	12	0	0	1.3	1.000
1915			0	0	—	9.00	1	0	0	2	4	3	1	0	0	0	0	0	0	0	—	0	2	0	0	2.0	1.000
5 yrs.			8	11	.421	3.49	43	19	4	188.1	181	92	79	2	3	4	0	59	8	0	.136	5	55	2	1	1.4	.968

Hal Brown

BROWN, HECTOR HAROLD (Skinny) BR TR 6′ 2″ 180 lbs.
B. Dec. 11, 1924, Greensboro, N. C.

Year	Team	Lg	W	L	PCT	ERA	G	GS	CG	IP	H	BB	SO	ShO	Relief W	Relief L	Relief SV	AB	H	HR	BA	PO	A	E	DP	TC/G	FA
1951	CHI	A	0	0	—	9.35	3	0	0	8.2	15	4	4	0	0	0	1	2	2	0	1.000	1	2	0	0	1.0	1.000
1952			2	3	.400	4.23	24	8	1	72.1	82	21	31	0	0	0	0	19	3	1	.158	5	11	0	1	0.7	1.000
1953	BOS	A	11	6	.647	4.65	30	25	6	166.1	177	57	62	1	0	1	0	58	17	1	.293	8	27	1	2	1.2	.972
1954			1	8	.111	4.12	40	5	1	118	126	41	66	0	1	4	0	24	3	0	.125	4	23	2	4	0.7	.931
1955	2 teams	BOS A (2G 1–0) BAL A (15G 0–4)																									
″	total		1	4	.200	3.98	17	5	1	61	53	28	28	0	1	1	0	17	1	0	.059	3	7	2	1	0.7	.833
1956	BAL	A	9	7	.563	4.04	35	14	4	151.2	142	37	57	1	3	2	2	42	8	0	.190	7	25	1	4	0.9	.970
1957			7	8	.467	3.90	25	20	7	150	132	37	62	2	0	0	1	48	10	0	.208	12	19	0	4	1.2	1.000
1958			7	5	.583	3.07	19	17	4	96.2	96	20	44	2	0	0	1	27	4	0	.148	6	14	0	1	1.0	1.000
1959			11	9	.550	3.79	31	21	2	164	158	32	81	0	1	0	3	42	2	0	.048	9	25	1	2	1.1	.971
1960			12	5	.706	3.06	30	20	6	159	155	22	66	1	4	1	0	44	8	0	.182	9	20	1	2	1.0	.967
1961			10	6	.625	3.19	27	23	6	166.2	153	33	61	3	0	1	1	50	7	0	.140	16	25	0	1	1.5	1.000
1962	2 teams	BAL A (22G 6–4) NY A (2G 0–1)																									
″	total		6	5	.545	4.29	24	12	0	92.1	97	23	27	0	2	2	1	29	8	0	.276	6	10	0	1	0.7	1.000
1963	HOU	N	5	11	.313	3.31	26	20	6	141.1	137	8	68	3	1	0	0	43	4	0	.093	3	15	0	0	0.7	1.000
1964			3	15	.167	3.95	27	21	3	132	154	26	53	0	1	0	1	39	5	0	.128	4	20	0	0	0.9	1.000
14 yrs.			85	92	.480	3.81	358	211	47	1680	1677	389	710	13	14	12	11	484	82	2	.169	93	243	8	23	1.0	.977

Jackie Brown

BROWN, JACKIE GENE BR TR 6′ 1″ 195 lbs.
Brother of Paul Brown.
B. May 31, 1943, Holdenville, Okla.

Year	Team	Lg	W	L	PCT	ERA	G	GS	CG	IP	H	BB	SO	ShO	Relief W	Relief L	Relief SV	AB	H	HR	BA	PO	A	E	DP	TC/G	FA
1970	WAS	A	2	2	.500	3.95	24	5	1	57	49	37	47	0	1	0	0	13	2	0	.154	4	2	0	0	0.3	1.000
1971			3	4	.429	5.94	14	9	0	47	60	27	21	0	0	0	0	15	2	0	.133	6	9	0	0	1.1	1.000
1973	TEX	A	5	5	.500	3.90	25	3	2	67	82	25	45	1	3	5	2	0	0	0	—	3	4	0	3	0.3	1.000
1974			13	12	.520	3.57	35	26	9	217	219	74	134	2	1	2	0	0	0	0	—	17	24	2	4	1.2	.953
1975	2 teams	TEX A (17G 5–5) CLE A (25G 1–2)																									
″	total		6	7	.462	4.25	42	10	3	139.2	142	64	76	1	3	4	1	0	0	0		8	12	3	1	0.5	.870
1976	CLE	A	9	11	.450	4.25	32	27	5	180	193	55	104	2	2	0	0	0	0	0	—	13	21	1	2	1.1	.971
1977	MON	N	9	12	.429	4.50	42	25	6	186	189	71	89	2	1	0	0	56	7	0	.125	9	21	2	2	0.8	.938
7 yrs.			47	53	.470	4.18	214	105	26	893.2	934	353	516	8	11	11	3	84	11	0	.131	60	93	8	12	0.8	.950

Jim Brown

BROWN, JAMES W. H.
B. Dec. 12, 1860, Clinton County, Pa. D. Apr. 6, 1908, Williamsport, Pa.

Year	Team	Lg	W	L	PCT	ERA	G	GS	CG	IP	H	BB	SO	ShO	Relief W	Relief L	Relief SV	AB	H	HR	BA	PO	A	E	DP	TC/G	FA
1884	3 teams	ALT U (11G 1–9) NY N (1G 0–1) STP U (6G 1–4)																									
″	total		2	14	.125	4.84	18	18	12	119	152	58	61	1	0	0	0	107	27	1	.252	33	34	24	3	2.7	.736
1886	PHI	AA	0	1	.000	3.24	1	1	1	8.1	9	3	4	0	0	0	0	3	0	0	.000	0	1	0	0	1.0	1.000
2 yrs.			2	15	.118	4.74	19	19	13	127.1	161	61	65	1	0	0	0	110	27	1	.245	33	35	24	3	2.6	.739

Joe Brown

BROWN, JOSEPH E. 5′10″ 162 lbs.
B. Apr. 4, 1859, Warren, Pa. D. June 28, 1888, Warren, Pa.

Year	Team	Lg	W	L	PCT	ERA	G	GS	CG	IP	H	BB	SO	ShO	Relief W	Relief L	Relief SV	AB	H	HR	BA	PO	A	E	DP	TC/G	FA
1884	CHI	N	4	2	.667	*4.68*	7	6	5	50	56	7	27	0	0	0	0	61	13	0	.213	11	13	4	0	1.6	.857
1885	BAL	AA	0	4	.000	*5.68*	4	4	4	38	52	4	9	0	0	0	0	19	3	0	.158	5	8	0	2	2.6	1.000
2 yrs.			4	6	.400	5.11	11	10	9	88	108	11	36	0	0	0	0	*				16	21	4	2	1.8	.902

Joe Brown

BROWN, JOSEPH HENRY (Smokey, Bullet) BR TR 6′ 176 lbs.
B. July 3, 1900, Little Rock, Ark. D. Mar. 7, 1950, Los Angeles, Calif.

Year	Team	Lg	W	L	PCT	ERA	G	GS	CG	IP	H	BB	SO	ShO	Relief W	Relief L	Relief SV	AB	H	HR	BA	PO	A	E	DP	TC/G	FA
1927	CHI	A	0	0	—	∞	1	0	0		2	1	0	0	0	0	0	0	0	0	—	0	0	0	0	0.0	.000

John Brown

BROWN, JOHN J.
B. Trenton, N. J. Deceased.

Year	Team	Lg	W	L	PCT	ERA	G	GS	CG	IP	H	BB	SO	ShO	Relief W	Relief L	Relief SV	AB	H	HR	BA	PO	A	E	DP	TC/G	FA
1897	BKN	N	0	1	.000	7.20	1	1	0	5	7	4	0	0	0	0	0	2	1	0	.500	0	3	0	0	3.0	1.000

Jophrey Brown

BROWN, JOPHREY CLIFFORD BL TR 6′ 2″ 190 lbs.
B. Jan. 22, 1945, Grambling, La.

Year	Team	Lg	W	L	PCT	ERA	G	GS	CG	IP	H	BB	SO	ShO	Relief W	Relief L	Relief SV	AB	H	HR	BA	PO	A	E	DP	TC/G	FA
1968	CHI	N	0	0	—	4.50	1	0	0	2	2	1	0	0	0	0	0	0	0	0	—	1	1	0	0	2.0	1.000

Jumbo Brown

BROWN, WALTER GEORGE BR TR 6′ 4″ 295 lbs.
B. Apr. 30, 1907, Greene, R. I. D. Oct. 2, 1966, Freeport, N. Y.

Year	Team	Lg	W	L	PCT	ERA	G	GS	CG	IP	H	BB	SO	ShO	Relief W	Relief L	Relief SV	AB	H	HR	BA	PO	A	E	DP	TC/G	FA
1925	CHI	N	0	0	—	3.00	2	0	0	6	5	4	0	0	0	0	0	1	0	0	.000	0	2	0	0	1.0	1.000
1927	CLE	A	0	2	.000	6.27	8	0	0	18.2	19	26	8	0	0	2	0	3	2	0	.667	1	5	1	1	0.9	.857

Jumbo Brown *continued*

Year	Team	W	L	PCT	ERA	G	GS	CG	IP	H	BB	SO	ShO	Relief Pitching W	L	SV	Batting AB	H	HR	BA	PO	A	E	DP	TC/G	FA
1928		0	1	.000	6.75	5	0	0	14.2	19	15	12	0	0	1	0	3	2	0	.667	1	1	0	0	0.4	1.000
1932	**NY A**	5	2	.714	4.45	19	3	3	56.2	58	30	31	1	2	2	1	23	4	0	.174	5	16	0	1	1.1	1.000
1933		7	5	.583	5.23	21	8	1	74	78	52	55	0	3	3	0	28	5	0	.179	0	14	1	1	0.7	.933
1935		6	5	.545	3.61	20	8	3	87.1	94	37	41	0	2	1	0	32	10	0	.313	8	16	1	1	1.3	.960
1936		1	4	.200	5.91	20	3	0	64	93	29	19	0	1	2	1	19	0	0	.000	1	17	1	1	0.9	.947
1937	**2 teams CIN N** (4G 1–0) **NY N** (4G 1–0)																									
"	**total**	2	0	1.000	4.91	8	1	0	18.1	21	8	8	0	1	0	0	2	0	0	.000	0	6	0	0	0.8	1.000
1938	**NY N**	5	3	.625	1.80	43	0	0	90	65	28	42	0	5	3	5	16	3	0	.188	5	11	2	1	0.4	.889
1939		4	0	1.000	4.15	31	0	0	56.1	69	25	24	0	4	0	7	11	4	0	.364	0	12	0	1	0.4	1.000
1940		2	4	.333	3.42	41	0	0	55.1	49	25	31	0	2	4	**7**	10	1	0	.100	0	7	0	0	0.2	1.000
1941		1	5	.167	3.32	31	0	0	57	49	21	30	0	1	**5**	**8**	9	1	0	.111	0	8	0	0	0.3	1.000
12 yrs.		33	31	.516	4.06	249	23	7	598.1	619	300	301	1	21	23	29	157	32	0	.204	21	115	6	7	0.6	.958

Keith Brown

BROWN, KEITH EDWARD
B. Feb. 14, 1964, Flagstaff, Ariz.
BB TR 6′ 4″ 215 lbs.

Year	Team	W	L	PCT	ERA	G	GS	CG	IP	H	BB	SO	ShO	Relief Pitching W	L	SV	Batting AB	H	HR	BA	PO	A	E	DP	TC/G	FA
1988	**CIN N**	2	1	.667	2.76	4	3	0	16.1	14	4	6	0	0	0	0	4	0	0	.000	0	3	0	1	0.8	1.000
1990		0	0	—	4.76	8	0	0	11.1	12	3	8	0	0	0	0	0	0	0	—	1	2	0	0	0.4	1.000
1991		0	0	—	2.25	11	0	0	12	15	6	4	0	0	0	0	0	0	0	—	2	2	1	0	0.5	.800
1992		0	1	.000	4.50	2	2	0	8	10	5	5	0	0	0	0	2	0	0	.000	0	1	1	0	1.0	.500
4 yrs.		2	2	.500	3.40	25	5	0	47.2	51	18	23	0	0	0	0	6	0	0	.000	3	8	2	1	0.5	.846

Kevin Brown

BROWN, JAMES KEVIN
B. Mar. 14, 1965, Milledgeville, Ga.
BR TR 6′ 4″ 195 lbs.

Year	Team	W	L	PCT	ERA	G	GS	CG	IP	H	BB	SO	ShO	Relief Pitching W	L	SV	Batting AB	H	HR	BA	PO	A	E	DP	TC/G	FA
1986	**TEX A**	1	0	1.000	3.60	1	1	0	5	6	0	4	0	0	0	0	0	0	0	—	0	1	0	0	1.0	1.000
1988		1	1	.500	4.24	4	4	1	23.1	33	8	12	0	0	0	0	0	0	0	—	1	2	0	0	0.8	1.000
1989		12	9	.571	3.35	28	28	7	191	167	70	104	0	0	0	0	0	0	0	—	15	41	2	6	2.1	.966
1990		12	10	.545	3.60	26	26	6	180	175	60	88	2	0	0	0	1	0	0	.000	15	24	3	0	1.6	.929
1991		9	12	.429	4.40	33	33	0	210.2	233	90	96	0	0	0	0	0	0	0	—	18	32	2	3	1.6	.962
1992		**21**	11	.656	3.32	35	35	11	**265.2**	**262**	76	173	1	0	0	0	0	0	0	—	37	36	8	4	2.3	.901
1993		15	12	.556	3.59	34	34	12	233	228	74	142	3	0	0	0	0	0	0	—	28	42	3	2	2.1	.959
1994		7	9	.438	4.82	26	**25**	3	170	**218**	50	123	0	0	1	0	0	0	0	—	20	29	4	2	2.0	.925
1995	**BAL A**	10	9	.526	3.60	26	26	3	172.1	155	48	117	1	0	0	0	0	0	0	—	41	41	2	3	3.2	.976
9 yrs.		88	73	.547	3.78	213	212	43	1451	1477	476	859	7	0	1	0	1	0	0	.000	175	248	24	20	2.1	.946

Kevin Brown

BROWN, KEVIN DEWAYNE
B. Mar. 14, 1966, Oroville, Calif.
BL TL 6′ 1″ 185 lbs.

Year	Team	W	L	PCT	ERA	G	GS	CG	IP	H	BB	SO	ShO	Relief Pitching W	L	SV	Batting AB	H	HR	BA	PO	A	E	DP	TC/G	FA
1990	**2 teams NY N** (2G 0–0) **MIL A** (5G 1–1)																									
"	**total**	1	1	.500	2.35	7	3	0	23	16	8	12	0	0	0	0	0	0	0		2	6	0	0	1.1	1.000
1991	**MIL A**	2	4	.333	5.51	15	10	0	63.2	66	34	30	0	0	1	0	0	0	0	—	6	11	1	0	1.2	.944
1992	**SEA A**	0	0	—	9.00	2	0	0	3	4	3	2	0	0	0	0	0	0	0	—	0	1	0	0	0.5	1.000
3 yrs.		3	5	.375	4.82	24	13	0	89.2	86	45	44	0	0	1	0	0	0	0		8	18	1	0	1.1	.963

Lew Brown

BROWN, LEWIS J. (Blower)
B. Feb. 1, 1858, Leominster, Mass. D. Jan. 16, 1889, Boston, Mass.
BR TR 5′10½″ 185 lbs.

Year	Team	W	L	PCT	ERA	G	GS	CG	IP	H	BB	SO	ShO	Relief Pitching W	L	SV	Batting AB	H	HR	BA	PO	A	E	DP	TC/G	FA
1878	**PRO N**	0	0	—	18.00	1	0	0	1	0	4	0	0	0	0	0	243	74	1	.305	193	45	40	4	6.0	.856
1884	**BOS U**	0	0	—	*36.00*	1	0	0	1	6	1	0	0	0	0	1	325	75	1	.231	387	67	49	5	8.5	.903
2 yrs.		0	0		27.00	2	0	0	2	6	5	0	0	0	0	1	*				2683	411	324	89	8.7	.905

Lloyd Brown

BROWN, LLOYD ANDREW (Gimpy)
B. Dec. 25, 1904, Beeville, Tex. D. Jan. 14, 1974, Opa-Locka, Fla.
BL TL 5′ 9″ 170 lbs.

Year	Team	W	L	PCT	ERA	G	GS	CG	IP	H	BB	SO	ShO	Relief Pitching W	L	SV	Batting AB	H	HR	BA	PO	A	E	DP	TC/G	FA
1925	**BKN N**	0	3	.000	4.12	17	5	1	63.1	79	25	23	0	0	0	0	23	2	0	.087	3	15	0	1	1.1	1.000
1928	**WAS A**	4	4	.500	4.04	27	10	2	107	112	40	38	0	2	0	1	31	5	0	.161	10	36	0	2	1.7	1.000
1929		8	7	.533	4.18	40	15	7	168	186	69	48	1	4	4	0	50	11	0	.220	8	43	0	2	1.3	1.000
1930		16	12	.571	4.25	38	22	10	197	220	65	59	1	6	2	0	65	14	1	.215	9	56	3	5	1.8	.956
1931		15	14	.517	3.20	42	32	15	258.2	256	79	79	1	1	2	0	96	22	0	.229	13	59	1	2	1.7	.986
1932		15	12	.556	4.44	46	24	10	202.2	239	55	53	2	4	2	5	70	7	0	.100	10	50	4	1	1.4	.938
1933	**2 teams STL A** (8G 1–6) **BOS A** (33G 8–11)																									
"	**total**	9	17	.346	4.63	41	27	9	202.1	237	81	44	2	0	3	1	68	19	2	.279	16	66	3	4	2.1	.965
1934	**CLE A**	5	10	.333	3.85	38	15	5	117	116	51	39	0	3	1	6	30	7	0	.233	5	32	1	3	1.0	.974
1935		8	7	.533	3.61	42	8	4	122	123	37	45	2	5	3	4	37	4	0	.108	7	28	1	1	0.9	.972
1936		8	10	.444	4.17	24	16	12	140.1	166	45	34	1	1	1	1	45	10	1	.222	6	29	0	2	1.5	1.000
1937		2	6	.250	6.55	31	5	2	77	107	27	32	0	1	2	0	24	4	0	.167	7	15	2	1	0.8	.917
1940	**PHI N**	1	3	.250	6.21	18	2	0	37.2	58	16	16	0	0	3	3	13	1	0	.077	5	7	2	0	0.8	.857
12 yrs.		91	105	.464	4.20	404	181	77	1693	1899	590	510	10	27	23	21	552	106	4	.192	99	436	17	24	1.4	.969

Mace Brown

BROWN, MACE STANLEY
B. May 21, 1909, North English, Iowa.
BR TR 6′ 1″ 190 lbs.

Year	Team	W	L	PCT	ERA	G	GS	CG	IP	H	BB	SO	ShO	Relief Pitching W	L	SV	Batting AB	H	HR	BA	PO	A	E	DP	TC/G	FA
1935	**PIT N**	4	1	.800	3.59	18	5	2	72.2	84	22	28	0	1	0	0	24	4	0	.167	4	23	1	1	1.6	.964
1936		10	11	.476	3.87	47	12	3	165	178	55	56	0	**7**	5	3	60	10	0	.167	4	41	0	4	1.0	1.000
1937		7	2	.778	4.18	50	2	0	107.2	109	45	60	0	6	1	**7**	30	9	0	.300	5	17	0	0	0.4	1.000
1938		15	9	.625	3.80	**51**	2	0	132.2	155	44	55	0	**15**	**8**	5	38	5	0	.132	3	28	2	1	0.6	.939
1939		9	13	.409	3.37	47	19	8	200.1	232	52	71	1	2	3	7	64	7	0	.109	8	42	1	3	1.1	.980
1940		10	9	.526	3.49	48	17	5	172.2	181	49	73	2	5	2	**7**	52	6	0	.115	10	40	2	1	1.1	.962
1941	**2 teams PIT N** (1G 0–0) **BKN N** (24G 3–2)																									
"	**total**	3	2	.600	3.07	25	0	0	44	33	26	22	0	3	2	3	8	0	0	.000	4	14	1	1	0.8	.947
1942	**BOS A**	9	3	.750	3.43	34	0	0	60.1	56	28	20	0	**9**	3	6	15	1	0	.067	0	17	0	1	0.5	1.000
1943		6	6	.500	2.12	**49**	0	0	93.1	71	51	40	0	6	6	9	17	1	0	.059	4	20	2	3	0.5	.923
1946		3	1	.750	2.05	18	0	0	26.1	26	16	10	0	3	1	1	5	0	0	.000	0	9	1	0	0.6	.900
10 yrs.		76	57	.571	3.47	387	57	18	1075	1125	388	435	3	57	31	48	313	43	0	.137	42	251	10	15	0.8	.967
WORLD SERIES																										
1946	**BOS A**	0	0	—	27.00	1	0	0	1	4	1	0	0	0	0	0	0	0	0	—	0	0	0	0	0.0	.000

Mark Brown

BROWN, MARK ANTHONY BB TR 6′ 2″ 190 lbs.
B. July 13, 1959, Bellows Falls, Vt.

Year	Team	W	L	PCT	ERA	G	GS	CG	IP	H	BB	SO	ShO	Relief Pitching W	Relief Pitching L	Relief Pitching SV	Batting AB	Batting H	HR	BA	PO	A	E	DP	TC/G	FA
1984	BAL A	1	2	.333	3.91	9	0	0	23	22	7	10	0	1	2	0	0	0	0	—	0	2	0	0	0.2	1.000
1985	MIN A	0	0	—	6.89	6	0	0	15.2	21	7	5	0	0	0	0	0	0	0	—	1	1	0	0	0.3	1.000
2 yrs.		1	2	.333	5.12	15	0	0	38.2	43	14	15	0	1	2	0	0	0	0		1	3	0	0	0.3	1.000

Mike Brown

BROWN, MICHAEL GARY BR TR 6′ 2″ 195 lbs.
B. Mar. 24, 1959, Camden County, N. J.

Year	Team	W	L	PCT	ERA	G	GS	CG	IP	H	BB	SO	ShO	Relief Pitching W	Relief Pitching L	Relief Pitching SV	Batting AB	Batting H	HR	BA	PO	A	E	DP	TC/G	FA
1982	BOS A	1	0	1.000	0.00	3	0	0	6	7	1	4	0	1	0	0	0	0	0	—	0	0	0	0	0.0	.000
1983		6	6	.500	4.67	19	18	3	104	110	43	35	1	0	0	0	0	0	0	—	11	11	2	0	1.3	.917
1984		1	8	.111	6.85	15	11	0	67	104	19	32	0	0	0	0	0	0	0	—	11	8	2	1	1.4	.905
1985		0	0	—	21.60	2	1	0	3.1	9	3	3	0	0	0	0	0	0	0	—	0	0	0	0	0.0	.000
1986	2 teams BOS A	(15G 4–4)		SEA A	(6G 0–2)																					
″	total	4	6	.400	5.79	21	12	0	73	91	36	41	0	0	0	0	0	0	0		7	12	0	0	0.9	1.000
1987	SEA A	0	0	—	54.00	1	0	0	0.1	3	0	0	0	0	0	0	0	0	0	—	0	0	0	0	0.0	.000
6 yrs.		12	20	.375	5.75	61	42	3	253.2	324	102	115	1	1	0	0	0	0	0		29	31	4	1	1.0	.938

Myrl Brown

BROWN, MYRL LINCOLN (Brainie) BR TR 5′11″ 172 lbs.
B. Oct. 10, 1894, Waynesboro, Pa. D. Feb. 23, 1981, Harrisburg, Pa.

Year	Team	W	L	PCT	ERA	G	GS	CG	IP	H	BB	SO	ShO	Relief Pitching W	Relief Pitching L	Relief Pitching SV	Batting AB	Batting H	HR	BA	PO	A	E	DP	TC/G	FA
1922	PIT N	3	1	.750	5.97	7	5	2	34.2	42	13	9	0	0	1	0	11	3	0	.273	0	11	1	1	1.7	.917

Norm Brown

BROWN, NORMAN LADELLE BB TR 6′ 3″ 180 lbs.
B. Feb. 1, 1919, Evergreen, N. C. D. May 31, 1995, Bennettsville, S. C.

Year	Team	W	L	PCT	ERA	G	GS	CG	IP	H	BB	SO	ShO	Relief Pitching W	Relief Pitching L	Relief Pitching SV	Batting AB	Batting H	HR	BA	PO	A	E	DP	TC/G	FA
1943	PHI A	0	0	—	0.00	1	1	0	7	5	0	1	0	0	0	0	3	0	0	.000	1	3	0	0	4.0	1.000
1946		0	1	.000	6.14	4	0	0	7.1	8	6	3	0	0	1	0	0	0	0	—	0	1	0	0	0.3	1.000
2 yrs.		0	1	.000	3.14	5	1	0	14.1	13	6	4	0	0	1	0	3	0	0	.000	1	4	0	0	1.0	1.000

Paul Brown

BROWN, PAUL DWAYNE BR TR 6′ 1″ 190 lbs.
Brother of Jackie Brown.
B. June 18, 1941, Fort Smith, Ark.

Year	Team	W	L	PCT	ERA	G	GS	CG	IP	H	BB	SO	ShO	Relief Pitching W	Relief Pitching L	Relief Pitching SV	Batting AB	Batting H	HR	BA	PO	A	E	DP	TC/G	FA
1961	PHI N	0	1	.000	8.10	5	1	0	10	13	8	1	0	0	0	0	2	1	0	.500	0	2	0	0	0.4	1.000
1962		0	6	.000	5.94	23	9	0	63.2	74	33	29	0	0	0	1	13	2	0	.154	7	8	2	1	0.7	.882
1963		0	1	.000	4.11	6	2	0	15.1	15	5	11	0	0	0	0	2	1	0	.500	0	5	0	0	0.8	1.000
1968		0	0	—	9.00	2	0	0	4	6	1	4	0	0	0	0	0	0	0	—	0	0	0	0	0.0	.000
4 yrs.		0	8	.000	6.00	36	12	0	93	108	47	45	0	0	0	1	17	4	0	.235	7	15	2	1	0.7	.917

Ray Brown

BROWN, PAUL PERCIVAL BR TR 6′ 1″ 172 lbs.
B. Jan. 31, 1889, Chicago, Ill. D. May 29, 1955, Los Angeles, Calif.

Year	Team	W	L	PCT	ERA	G	GS	CG	IP	H	BB	SO	ShO	Relief Pitching W	Relief Pitching L	Relief Pitching SV	Batting AB	Batting H	HR	BA	PO	A	E	DP	TC/G	FA
1909	CHI N	1	0	1.000	2.00	1	1	1	9	5	4	2	0	0	0	0	3	0	0	.000	0	1	0	0	1.0	1.000

Scott Brown

BROWN, SCOTT EDWARD BR TR 6′ 2″ 220 lbs.
B. Aug. 30, 1956, DeQuincy, La.

Year	Team	W	L	PCT	ERA	G	GS	CG	IP	H	BB	SO	ShO	Relief Pitching W	Relief Pitching L	Relief Pitching SV	Batting AB	Batting H	HR	BA	PO	A	E	DP	TC/G	FA
1981	CIN N	1	0	1.000	2.77	10	0	0	13	16	1	7	0	1	0	0	1	0	0	.000	0	2	0	0	0.2	1.000

Steve Brown

BROWN, STEVEN ELBERT BR TR 6′ 5″ 200 lbs.
B. Feb. 12, 1957, San Francisco, Calif.

Year	Team	W	L	PCT	ERA	G	GS	CG	IP	H	BB	SO	ShO	Relief Pitching W	Relief Pitching L	Relief Pitching SV	Batting AB	Batting H	HR	BA	PO	A	E	DP	TC/G	FA
1983	CAL A	2	3	.400	3.52	12	4	2	46	45	16	23	1	1	1	0	0	0	0	—	4	5	0	1	0.8	1.000
1984		0	1	.000	9.00	3	3	0	11	16	9	5	0	0	0	0	0	0	0	—	0	1	0	0	0.3	1.000
2 yrs.		2	4	.333	4.58	15	7	2	57	61	25	28	1	1	1	0	0	0	0		4	6	0	1	0.7	1.000

Stub Brown

BROWN, RICHARD P. TL 6′ 2″ 220 lbs.
B. Aug. 3, 1870, Baltimore, Md. D. Mar. 11, 1948, Baltimore, Md.

Year	Team	W	L	PCT	ERA	G	GS	CG	IP	H	BB	SO	ShO	Relief Pitching W	Relief Pitching L	Relief Pitching SV	Batting AB	Batting H	HR	BA	PO	A	E	DP	TC/G	FA
1893	BAL N	0	0	—	6.00	2	0	0	9	13	5	0	0	0	0	0	5	1	0	.200	0	0	0	0	0.0	.000
1894		4	0	1.000	4.89	9	6	3	49.2	59	24	8	0	0	0	0	23	2	0	.087	0	7	1	1	0.9	.875
1897	CIN N	0	1	.000	4.15	2	1	1	13	17	8	2	0	0	0	0	5	0	0	.000	0	3	0	0	1.5	1.000
3 yrs.		4	1	.800	4.90	13	7	4	71.2	89	37	10	0	0	0	0	33	3	0	.091	0	10	1	1	0.8	.909

Three Finger Brown

BROWN, MORDECAI PETER CENTENNIAL (Miner) BB TR 5′10″ 175 lbs.
B. Oct. 19, 1876, Nyesville, Ind. D. Feb. 14, 1948, Terre Haute, Ind.
Manager 1914.
Hall of Fame 1949.

Year	Team	W	L	PCT	ERA	G	GS	CG	IP	H	BB	SO	ShO	Relief Pitching W	Relief Pitching L	Relief Pitching SV	Batting AB	Batting H	HR	BA	PO	A	E	DP	TC/G	FA
1903	STL N	9	13	.409	2.60	26	24	19	201	231	59	83	1	0	0	0	77	15	0	.195	5	60	3	7	2.6	.956
1904	CHI N	15	10	.600	1.86	26	23	21	212.1	155	50	81	4	**2**	0	1	89	19	0	.213	20	50	5	2	2.7	.933
1905		18	12	.600	2.17	30	24	24	249	219	44	89	4	2	2	0	93	13	1	.140	18	66	4	3	2.9	.955
1906		26	6	.813	**1.04**	36	32	27	277.1	198	61	144	**9**	1	0	3	98	20	0	.204	18	81	2	4	2.8	.980
1907		20	6	.769	1.39	34	27	20	233	180	40	107	6	1	0	3	85	13	1	.153	21	75	1	5	2.8	.990
1908		29	9	.763	1.47	44	31	27	312.1	214	49	123	9	**4**	1	**5**	121	25	0	.207	35	73	0	3	2.5	1.000
1909		**27**	9	.750	1.31	**50**	34	**32**	**342.2**	246	53	172	8	1	1	**7**	125	22	0	.176	18	83	3	6	2.1	.971
1910		25	13	.658	1.86	46	31	**27**	295.1	256	64	143	**7**	2	2	**7**	103	18	0	.175	10	92	4	3	2.3	.962
1911		21	11	.656	2.80	**53**	27	21	270	267	55	129	0	5	3	**13**	91	23	0	.253	8	53	1	0	1.2	.984
1912		5	6	.455	2.64	15	8	5	88.2	92	20	34	2	2	3	0	31	9	0	.290	1	15	1	1	1.1	.941
1913	CIN N	11	12	.478	2.91	39	16	11	173.1	174	44	41	1	4	3	6	54	11	0	.204	5	40	4	3	1.3	.918
1914	2 teams STL F	(26G 12–6)		BKN F	(9G 2–5)																					
″	total	14	11	.560	3.52	35	26	18	232.2	235	61	113	2	1	2	0	78	19	0	.244	6	56	3	1	1.9	.954
1915	CHI F	17	8	.680	2.09	35	25	17	236.1	189	64	95	3	3	2	3	82	24	0	.293	7	87	5	5	2.8	.949
1916	CHI N	2	3	.400	3.91	12	4	2	48.1	52	9	21	0	1	0	0	16	4	0	.250	1	12	0	0	1.1	1.000
14 yrs.		239	129	.649	2.06	481	332	271	3172.1	2708	673	1375	56	29	19	48	1143	235	2	.206	173	843	36	43	2.2	.966
					3rd																					
WORLD SERIES																										
1906	CHI N	1	2	.333	3.66	3	3	2	19.2	14	4	12	1	0	0	0	6	2	0	.333	2	12	1	0	5.0	.933
1907		1	0	1.000	0.00	1	1	1	9	7	1	4	1	0	0	0	3	0	0	.000	1	1	0	0	2.0	1.000
1908		2	0	1.000	0.00	2	1	1	11	6	1	5	1	1	0	0	4	0	0	.000	0	6	0	1	3.0	1.000
1910		1	2	.333	5.00	3	2	1	18	23	7	14	0	1	0	0	7	0	0	.000	0	10	1	0	3.7	.909
4 yrs.		5	4	.556	2.81	9	7	5	57.2	50	13	35	3	2	0	0	20	2	0	.100	3	29	2	1	3.8	.941
		8th											**2nd**													

Tom Brown

BROWN, THOMAS DALE — BR TR 6′ 1″ 170 lbs.
B. Aug. 10, 1949, Lafayette, La.

Year	Team	Lg	W	L	PCT	ERA	G	GS	CG	IP	H	BB	SO	ShO	Relief W	Relief L	Relief SV	Batting AB	Batting H	Batting HR	BA	PO	A	E	DP	TC/G	FA
1978	SEA	A	0	0	—	4.15	6	0	0	13	14	4	8	0	0	0	0	0	0	0	—	2	2	0	0	0.7	1.000

Tom Brown

BROWN, THOMAS TARLTON (Handsome) — BL TR 5′10″ 168 lbs.
B. Sept. 21, 1860, Liverpool, England D. Oct. 25, 1927, Washington, D. C.
Manager 1897–98.

Year	Team	Lg	W	L	PCT	ERA	G	GS	CG	IP	H	BB	SO	ShO	Relief W	Relief L	Relief SV	Batting AB	Batting H	Batting HR	BA	PO	A	E	DP	TC/G	FA
1882	BAL	AA	0	0	—	1.08	2	0	0	8.1	13	6	2	0	0	0	0	181	55	1	.304	59	16	28	1	2.2	.728
1883	COL	AA	0	1	.000	*5.79*	3	1	1	14	14	10	6	0	0	0	0	420	115	5	.274	153	22	49	3	2.3	.781
1884			2	1	.667	*7.11*	4	0	0	19	27	7	5	0	2	**1**	0	451	123	5	.273	165	18	35	5	2.0	.839
1885	PIT	AA	0	0	—	*3.00*	2	0	0	6	0	3	2	0	0	0	0	437	134	4	.307	186	21	44	2	2.3	.825
1886			0	0	—	*9.00*	1	0	0	2	2	5	1	0	0	0	0	460	131	1	.285	185	32	42	12	2.2	.838
5 yrs.			2	2	.500	5.29	12	1	1	49.1	56	31	16	0	2	1	0	*				3626	350	501	85	2.5	.888

Walter Brown

BROWN, WALTER IRVING — BR TR 5′11″ 175 lbs.
B. Apr. 23, 1915, Jamestown, N. Y. D. Feb. 3, 1991, Westfield, N. Y.

Year	Team	Lg	W	L	PCT	ERA	G	GS	CG	IP	H	BB	SO	ShO	Relief W	Relief L	Relief SV	Batting AB	Batting H	Batting HR	BA	PO	A	E	DP	TC/G	FA
1947	STL	A	1	0	1.000	4.89	19	0	0	46	50	28	10	0	1	0	0	11	0	0	.000	0	9	0	0	0.5	1.000

Cal Browning

BROWNING, CALVIN DUANE — BL TL 5′11″ 190 lbs.
B. Mar. 16, 1938, Burns Flat, Okla.

Year	Team	Lg	W	L	PCT	ERA	G	GS	CG	IP	H	BB	SO	ShO	Relief W	Relief L	Relief SV	Batting AB	Batting H	Batting HR	BA	PO	A	E	DP	TC/G	FA
1960	STL	N	0	0	—	40.50	1	0	0	0.2	5	1	0	0	0	0	0	0	0	0	—	0	0	0	0	0.0	.000

Frank Browning

BROWNING, FRANK — BR TR 5′ 5″ 145 lbs.
B. Oct. 29, 1882, Falmouth, Ky. D. May 19, 1948, San Antonio, Tex.

Year	Team	Lg	W	L	PCT	ERA	G	GS	CG	IP	H	BB	SO	ShO	Relief W	Relief L	Relief SV	Batting AB	Batting H	Batting HR	BA	PO	A	E	DP	TC/G	FA
1910	DET	A	2	2	.500	3.00	11	6	2	42	51	10	16	0	0	1	3	14	0	0	.000	3	21	1	1	2.3	.960

Pete Browning

BROWNING, LOUIS ROGERS (The Louisville Slugger, The Gladiator) — BR TR 6′ 180 lbs.
B. June 17, 1861, Louisville, Ky. D. Sept. 10, 1905, Louisville, Ky.

Year	Team	Lg	W	L	PCT	ERA	G	GS	CG	IP	H	BB	SO	ShO	Relief W	Relief L	Relief SV	Batting AB	Batting H	Batting HR	BA	PO	A	E	DP	TC/G	FA
1884	LOU	AA	0	1	.000	*54.00*	1	1	0	0.1	2	2	0	0	0	0	0	*				200	221	63	31	6.6	.870

Tom Browning

BROWNING, THOMAS LEO — BL TL 6′ 1″ 190 lbs.
B. Apr. 28, 1960, Casper, Wyo.

Year	Team	Lg	W	L	PCT	ERA	G	GS	CG	IP	H	BB	SO	ShO	Relief W	Relief L	Relief SV	Batting AB	Batting H	Batting HR	BA	PO	A	E	DP	TC/G	FA
1984	CIN	N	1	0	1.000	1.54	3	3	0	23.1	27	5	14	0	0	0	0	7	1	0	.143	1	3	0	0	1.3	1.000
1985			20	9	.690	3.55	38	38	6	261.1	242	73	155	4	0	0	0	88	17	0	.193	12	34	2	1	1.3	.958
1986			14	13	.519	3.81	39	**39**	4	243.1	225	70	147	2	0	0	0	86	14	0	.163	11	26	3	5	1.0	.925
1987			10	13	.435	5.02	32	31	2	183	201	61	117	0	0	0	0	52	8	0	.154	5	23	3	1	1.0	.903
1988			18	5	.783	3.41	36	**36**	5	250.2	205	64	124	2	0	0	0	83	12	0	.145	8	30	3	3	1.1	.927
1989			15	12	.556	3.39	37	**37**	9	249.2	241	64	118	2	0	0	0	78	7	0	.090	8	35	0	3	1.2	1.000
1990			15	9	.625	3.80	35	**35**	2	227.2	235	52	99	1	0	0	0	75	7	0	.093	8	27	3	1	1.1	.921
1991			14	14	.500	4.18	36	36	1	230.1	241	56	115	0	0	0	0	70	12	1	.171	8	24	5	2	1.0	.865
1992			6	5	.545	5.07	16	16	0	87	108	28	33	0	0	0	0	31	7	0	.226	6	14	1	3	1.3	.952
1993			7	7	.500	4.74	21	20	0	114	159	20	53	0	0	0	0	37	8	1	.216	10	21	0	2	1.5	1.000
1994			3	1	.750	4.20	7	7	2	40.2	34	13	22	1	0	0	0	14	2	0	.143	1	6	0	0	1.0	1.000
1995	KC	A	0	2	.000	8.10	2	2	0	10	13	5	3	0	0	0	0	0	0	0	—	0	2	0	0	1.0	1.000
12 yrs.			123	90	.577	3.94	302	300	31	1921	1931	511	1000	12	0	0	0	621	95	2	.153	78	245	20	21	1.1	.942
LEAGUE CHAMPIONSHIP SERIES																											
1990	CIN	N	1	1	.500	3.27	2	2	0	11	9	6	5	0	0	0	0	3	0	0	.000	1	1	0	0	1.0	1.000
WORLD SERIES																											
1990	CIN	N	1	0	1.000	4.50	1	1	0	6	6	2	2	0	0	0	0	0	0	0	—	0	0	0	0	0.0	.000

Bruce Brubaker

BRUBAKER, BRUCE ELLSWORTH — BR TR 6′ 1″ 198 lbs.
B. Dec. 29, 1941, Harrisburg, Pa.

Year	Team	Lg	W	L	PCT	ERA	G	GS	CG	IP	H	BB	SO	ShO	Relief W	Relief L	Relief SV	Batting AB	Batting H	Batting HR	BA	PO	A	E	DP	TC/G	FA
1967	LA	N	0	0	—	20.25	1	0	0	1.1	3	0	2	0	0	0	0	0	0	0	—	0	1	0	0	1.0	1.000
1970	MIL	A	0	0	—	9.00	1	0	0	2	2	1	0	0	0	0	0	0	0	0	—	0	0	0	0	0.0	.000
2 yrs.			0	0		13.50	2	0	0	3.1	5	1	2	0	0	0	0	0	0	0		0	1	0	0	0.5	1.000

Bob Bruce

BRUCE, ROBERT JAMES — BR TR 6′ 3″ 200 lbs.
B. May 16, 1933, Detroit, Mich.

Year	Team	Lg	W	L	PCT	ERA	G	GS	CG	IP	H	BB	SO	ShO	Relief W	Relief L	Relief SV	Batting AB	Batting H	Batting HR	BA	PO	A	E	DP	TC/G	FA
1959	DET	A	0	1	.000	9.00	2	1	0	2	2	3	1	0	0	0	0	0	0	0	—	0	0	0	0	0.0	.000
1960			4	7	.364	3.74	34	15	1	130	127	56	76	0	0	2	0	39	7	0	.179	9	23	1	2	1.0	.970
1961			1	2	.333	4.43	14	6	0	44.2	57	24	25	0	0	1	0	9	1	0	.111	5	1	1	0	0.5	.857
1962	HOU	N	10	9	.526	4.06	32	27	6	175	164	82	135	0	1	0	0	55	11	0	.200	14	26	1	2	1.3	.976
1963			5	9	.357	3.59	30	25	1	170.1	162	60	123	1	0	0	0	55	7	0	.127	13	21	1	1	1.2	.971
1964			15	9	.625	2.76	35	29	9	202.1	191	33	135	4	1	0	0	63	12	0	.190	11	35	1	0	1.3	.979
1965			9	18	.333	3.72	35	34	7	229.2	241	38	145	1	0	0	0	74	9	0	.122	25	36	3	1	1.8	.953
1966			3	13	.188	5.34	25	23	1	129.2	160	29	71	0	0	1	0	39	3	0	.077	15	18	0	1	1.3	1.000
1967	ATL	N	2	3	.400	4.89	12	7	1	38.2	42	15	22	0	0	1	1	12	2	0	.167	3	4	0	0	0.6	1.000
9 yrs.			49	71	.408	3.85	219	167	26	1122.1	1146	340	733	6	2	5	1	346	52	0	.150	95	164	8	7	1.2	.970

Lou Bruce

BRUCE, LOUIS R. — BL TR 5′ 5″ 145 lbs.
B. Jan. 16, 1877, St. Regis, N. Y. D. Feb. 9, 1968, Ilion, N. Y.

Year	Team	Lg	W	L	PCT	ERA	G	GS	CG	IP	H	BB	SO	ShO	Relief W	Relief L	Relief SV	Batting AB	Batting H	Batting HR	BA	PO	A	E	DP	TC/G	FA
1904	PHI	A	0	0	—	4.91	2	0	0	11	11	2	2	0	0	0	0	*				30	11	3	2	1.5	.932

Fred Bruckbauer

BRUCKBAUER, FREDERICK JOHN — BR TR 6′ 1″ 185 lbs.
B. May 27, 1938, New Ulm, Minn.

Year	Team	Lg	W	L	PCT	ERA	G	GS	CG	IP	H	BB	SO	ShO	Relief W	Relief L	Relief SV	Batting AB	Batting H	Batting HR	BA	PO	A	E	DP	TC/G	FA
1961	MIN	A	0	0	—	∞	1	0	0		3	1	0	0	0	0	0	0	0	0	—	0	0	0	0	0.0	.000

Andy Bruckmiller

BRUCKMILLER, ANDREW — BR TR 5′11″ 175 lbs.
B. Jan. 1, 1882, Pittsburgh, Pa. D. Jan. 12, 1970, McKeesport, Pa.

Year	Team	Lg	W	L	PCT	ERA	G	GS	CG	IP	H	BB	SO	ShO	Relief W	Relief L	Relief SV	Batting AB	Batting H	Batting HR	BA	PO	A	E	DP	TC/G	FA
1905	DET	A	0	0	—	27.00	1	0	0	1	4	1	1	0	0	0	0	1	0	0	.000	0	0	0	0	0.0	.000

Mike Bruhert

BRUHERT, MICHAEL EDWIN — BR TR 6′ 6″ 220 lbs.
B. June 24, 1951, Jamaica, N. Y.

Year	Team	Lg	W	L	PCT	ERA	G	GS	CG	IP	H	BB	SO	ShO	Relief W	Relief L	Relief SV	Batting AB	Batting H	Batting HR	BA	PO	A	E	DP	TC/G	FA
1978	NY	N	4	11	.267	4.77	27	22	1	134	171	34	56	1	0	0	0	40	3	0	.075	11	22	5	1	1.4	.868

Duff Brumley

BRUMLEY, DUFF LECHAUN — B. Aug. 25, 1970, Cleveland, Tenn. — BR TR 6′ 4″ 195 lbs.

Year	Team	W	L	PCT	ERA	G	GS	CG	IP	H	BB	SO	ShO	Relief Pitching W	Relief Pitching L	Relief Pitching SV	Batting AB	Batting H	HR	BA	PO	A	E	DP	TC/G	FA
1994	TEX A	0	0	—	16.20	2	0	0	3.1	6	5	4	0	0	0	0	0	0	0	—	0	0	0	0	0.0	.000

Greg Brummett

BRUMMETT, GREGORY SCOTT — B. Apr. 20, 1967, Wichita, Kans. — BR TR 6′ 185 lbs.

Year	Team	W	L	PCT	ERA	G	GS	CG	IP	H	BB	SO	ShO	Relief Pitching W	Relief Pitching L	Relief Pitching SV	Batting AB	Batting H	HR	BA	PO	A	E	DP	TC/G	FA
1993	2 teams SF N (8G 2–3) MIN A (5G 2–1)																									
″	total	4	4	.500	5.08	13	13	0	72.2	82	28	30	0	0	0	0	15	0	0	.000	5	8	0	0	1.0	1.000

Jack Bruner

BRUNER, JACK RAYMOND (Pappy) — B. July 1, 1924, Waterloo, Iowa. — BL TL 6′ 1″ 185 lbs.

Year	Team	W	L	PCT	ERA	G	GS	CG	IP	H	BB	SO	ShO	Relief Pitching W	Relief Pitching L	Relief Pitching SV	Batting AB	Batting H	HR	BA	PO	A	E	DP	TC/G	FA
1949	CHI A	1	2	.333	8.22	4	2	0	7.2	10	8	4	0	1	0	0	1	0	0	.000	0	0	0	0	0.0	.000
1950	2 teams CHI A (9G 0–0) STL A (13G 1–2)																									
″	total	1	2	.333	4.37	22	1	0	47.1	43	37	24	0	1	1	1	10	0	0	.000	2	4	3	0	0.4	.667
2 yrs.		2	4	.333	4.91	26	3	0	55	53	45	28	0	2	1	1	11	0	0	.000	2	4	3	0	0.3	.667

Roy Bruner

BRUNER, WALTER ROY — B. Feb. 10, 1917, Cecilia, Ky. D. Nov. 30, 1986, St. Matthews, Ky. — BR TR 6′ 165 lbs.

Year	Team	W	L	PCT	ERA	G	GS	CG	IP	H	BB	SO	ShO	Relief Pitching W	Relief Pitching L	Relief Pitching SV	Batting AB	Batting H	HR	BA	PO	A	E	DP	TC/G	FA
1939	PHI N	0	4	.000	6.67	4	4	2	27	38	13	11	0	0	0	0	9	1	0	.111	1	3	0	0	1.0	1.000
1940		0	0	—	5.68	2	0	0	6.1	5	6	4	0	0	0	0	2	1	0	.500	0	2	0	0	1.0	1.000
1941		0	3	.000	4.91	13	1	0	29.1	37	25	13	0	0	2	0	6	0	0	.000	0	4	0	0	0.3	1.000
3 yrs.		0	7	.000	5.74	19	5	2	62.2	80	44	28	0	0	2	0	17	2	0	.118	1	9	0	0	0.5	1.000

George Brunet

BRUNET, GEORGE STUART (Lefty) — B. June 8, 1935, Houghton, Mich. D. Oct. 25, 1991, Poza Rica, Mexico. — BR TL 6′ 1″ 195 lbs.

Year	Team	W	L	PCT	ERA	G	GS	CG	IP	H	BB	SO	ShO	Relief Pitching W	Relief Pitching L	Relief Pitching SV	Batting AB	Batting H	HR	BA	PO	A	E	DP	TC/G	FA
1956	KC A	0	0	—	7.00	6	1	0	9	10	11	5	0	0	0	0	2	0	0	.000	0	3	0	0	0.5	1.000
1957		0	1	.000	5.56	4	2	0	11.1	13	4	3	0	0	0	0	2	0	0	.000	0	2	0	0	0.5	1.000
1959		0	0	—	11.57	2	0	0	4.2	10	7	7	0	0	0	0	0	0	0	—	0	4	1	0	2.5	.800
1960	2 teams KC A (3G 0–2) MIL N (17G 2–0)																									
″	total	2	2	.500	4.95	20	8	0	60	65	32	43	0	1	0	0	14	1	0	.071	2	16	0	0	0.9	1.000
1961	MIL N	0	0	—	5.40	5	0	0	5	7	2	0	0	0	0	0	0	0	0	—	0	3	0	0	0.6	1.000
1962	HOU N	2	4	.333	4.50	17	11	2	54	62	21	36	0	0	0	0	17	1	0	.059	4	12	2	2	1.1	.889
1963	2 teams HOU N (5G 0–3) BAL A (16G 0–1)																									
″	total	0	4	.000	6.06	21	2	0	32.2	49	15	24	0	0	2	1	4	0	0	.000	3	5	0	2	0.4	1.000
1964	LA A	2	2	.500	3.61	10	7	0	42.1	38	25	36	0	0	0	0	11	2	0	.182	3	5	0	0	0.8	1.000
1965	CAL A	9	11	.450	2.56	41	26	8	197	149	69	141	3	1	1	2	56	3	0	.054	6	29	2	1	0.9	.946
1966		13	13	.500	3.31	41	32	8	212	183	106	148	2	1	2	0	68	7	1	.103	11	33	1	2	1.1	.978
1967		11	**19**	.367	3.31	40	37	7	250	203	90	165	2	0	1	1	78	6	0	.077	5	36	1	0	1.0	.976
1968		13	**17**	.433	2.86	39	36	8	245.1	191	68	132	5	0	1	0	74	6	0	.081	5	31	1	1	0.9	.973
1969	2 teams CAL A (23G 6–7) SEA A (12G 2–5)																									
″	total	8	12	.400	4.44	35	30	4	164.1	168	67	93	2	0	0	0	47	4	1	.085	5	27	1	1	0.9	.970
1970	2 teams WAS A (24G 8–6) PIT N (12G 1–1)																									
″	total	9	7	.563	4.20	36	21	2	135	143	57	84	1	2	2	0	42	6	1	.143	2	19	2	2	0.6	.913
1971	STL N	0	1	.000	6.00	7	0	0	9	12	7	4	0	0	1	0	3	1	0	.333	0	0	0	0	0.0	.000
15 yrs.		69	93	.426	3.62	324	213	39	1431.2	1303	581	921	15	5	10	4	418	37	3	.089	46	225	11	11	0.9	.961

Tom Bruno

BRUNO, THOMAS MICHAEL — B. Jan. 26, 1953, Chicago, Ill. — BR TR 6′ 5″ 210 lbs.

Year	Team	W	L	PCT	ERA	G	GS	CG	IP	H	BB	SO	ShO	Relief Pitching W	Relief Pitching L	Relief Pitching SV	Batting AB	Batting H	HR	BA	PO	A	E	DP	TC/G	FA
1976	KC A	1	0	1.000	6.88	12	0	0	17	20	9	11	0	1	0	0	0	0	0	—	0	1	0	0	0.1	1.000
1977	TOR A	0	1	.000	8.00	12	0	0	18	30	13	9	0	0	1	0	0	0	0	—	2	3	1	0	0.5	.833
1978	STL N	4	3	.571	1.98	18	3	0	50	38	17	33	0	3	2	1	12	1	0	.083	2	4	0	1	0.3	1.000
1979		2	3	.400	4.26	27	1	0	38	37	22	27	0	2	2	0	5	1	0	.200	2	5	0	0	0.3	1.000
4 yrs.		7	7	.500	4.24	69	4	0	123	125	61	80	0	6	5	1	17	2	0	.118	6	13	1	1	0.3	.950

Jim Bruske

BRUSKE, JAMES SCOTT — B. Oct. 7, 1964, East St. Louis, Ill. — BR TR 6′ 1″ 185 lbs.

Year	Team	W	L	PCT	ERA	G	GS	CG	IP	H	BB	SO	ShO	Relief Pitching W	Relief Pitching L	Relief Pitching SV	Batting AB	Batting H	HR	BA	PO	A	E	DP	TC/G	FA
1995	LA N	0	0	—	4.50	9	0	0	10	12	4	5	0	0	0	1	0	0	0	—	1	0	0	0	0.1	1.000

Warren Brusstar

BRUSSTAR, WARREN SCOTT — B. Feb. 2, 1952, Oakland, Calif. — BR TR 6′ 3″ 200 lbs.

Year	Team	W	L	PCT	ERA	G	GS	CG	IP	H	BB	SO	ShO	Relief Pitching W	Relief Pitching L	Relief Pitching SV	Batting AB	Batting H	HR	BA	PO	A	E	DP	TC/G	FA
1977	PHI N	7	2	.778	2.66	46	0	0	71	64	24	46	0	7	2	3	6	0	0	.000	3	16	0	1	0.4	1.000
1978		6	3	.667	2.33	58	0	0	89	74	30	60	0	6	3	0	7	1	0	.143	5	22	0	4	0.5	1.000
1979		1	0	1.000	7.07	13	0	0	14	23	4	3	0	1	0	1	0	0	0	—	1	2	0	0	0.2	1.000
1980		2	2	.500	3.69	26	0	0	39	42	13	21	0	2	2	0	1	0	0	.000	2	7	1	0	0.4	.900
1981		0	1	.000	4.50	14	0	0	12	12	10	8	0	0	1	0	0	0	0	—	2	1	0	0	0.2	1.000
1982	2 teams PHI N (22G 2–3) CHI A (10G 2–0)																									
″	total	4	3	.571	4.17	32	0	0	41	50	8	19	0	4	3	2	2	0	0	.000	2	9	0	1	0.3	1.000
1983	CHI N	3	1	.750	2.35	59	0	0	80.1	67	37	46	0	3	1	1	4	0	0	.000	7	12	0	1	0.3	1.000
1984		1	1	.500	3.11	41	0	0	63.2	57	21	36	0	1	1	3	5	1	0	.200	8	7	0	0	0.4	1.000
1985		4	3	.571	6.05	51	0	0	74.1	87	36	34	0	4	3	4	7	1	0	.143	6	3	2	0	0.2	.818
9 yrs.		28	16	.636	3.51	340	0	0	484.1	476	183	273	0	28	16	14	32	3	0	.094	36	79	3	7	0.3	.975
DIVISIONAL PLAYOFF SERIES																										
1981	PHI N	0	0	—	4.91	2	0	0	3.2	5	1	3	0	0	0	0	0	0	0	—	0	0	0	0	0.0	.000
LEAGUE CHAMPIONSHIP SERIES																										
1977	PHI N	0	0	—	3.38	2	0	0	2.2	2	1	2	0	0	0	0	0	0	0	—	0	0	0	0	0.0	.000
1978		0	0	—	0.00	3	0	0	2.2	2	1	0	0	0	0	0	0	0	0	—	0	0	0	0	0.0	.000
1980		1	0	1.000	3.38	2	0	0	2.2	1	1	0	0	1	0	0	1	0	0	.000	0	0	0	0	0.0	.000
1984	CHI N	0	0	—	0.00	3	0	0	4.2	6	0	1	0	0	0	0	1	0	0	.000	0	1	0	0	0.3	1.000
4 yrs.		1	0	1.000	1.42	10	0	0	12.2	11	3	3	0	1	0	0	2	0	0	.000	0	1	0	0	0.1	1.000
WORLD SERIES																										
1980	PHI N	0	0	—	0.00	1	0	0	2.1	0	1	0	0	0	0	0	0	0	0	—	0	0	0	0	0.0	.000

Clay Bryant

BRYANT, CLAIBORNE HENRY BR TR 6′ 2½″ 195 lbs.
B. Nov. 26, 1911, Madison Heights, Va.

Year	Team	Lg	W	L	PCT	ERA	G	GS	CG	IP	H	BB	SO	ShO	Relief W	Relief L	Relief SV	AB	H	HR	BA	PO	A	E	DP	TC/G	FA
1935	CHI	N	1	2	.333	5.16	9	1	0	22.2	34	7	13	0	1	2	2	6	2	1	.333	2	3	0	0	0.6	1.000
1936			1	2	.333	3.30	26	0	0	57.1	57	24	35	0	1	2	0	12	5	0	.417	6	13	2	0	0.8	.905
1937			9	3	.750	4.26	38	9	4	135.1	117	78	75	1	7	0	3	45	14	1	.311	4	13	2	3	0.5	.895
1938			19	11	.633	3.10	44	30	17	270.1	235	**125**	**135**	3	4	1	2	106	24	3	.226	9	38	2	4	1.1	.959
1939			2	1	.667	5.74	4	4	2	31.1	42	14	9	0	0	0	0	14	3	0	.214	7	2	1	0	2.0	.900
1940			0	1	.000	4.78	8	0	0	26.1	26	14	5	0	0	1	0	9	3	0	.333	3	5	0	0	1.0	1.000
6 yrs.			32	20	.615	3.73	129	44	23	543.1	511	262	272	4	13	6	7	192	51	5	.266	31	74	7	7	0.9	.938
WORLD SERIES																											
1938	CHI	N	0	1	.000	6.75	1	1	0	5.1	6	5	3	0	0	0	0	2	0	0	.000	0	0	0	0	0.0	.000

Ron Bryant

BRYANT, RONALD RAYMOND (Bear) BB TL 6′ 190 lbs.
B. Nov. 12, 1947, Redlands, Calif.

Year	Team	Lg	W	L	PCT	ERA	G	GS	CG	IP	H	BB	SO	ShO	Relief W	Relief L	Relief SV	AB	H	HR	BA	PO	A	E	DP	TC/G	FA
1967	SF	N	0	0	—	4.50	1	0	0	4	3	0	2	0	0	0	0	1	0	0	.000	0	0	0	0	0.0	.000
1969			4	3	.571	4.34	16	8	0	58	60	25	30	0	0	0	1	16	3	0	.188	1	11	1	1	0.8	.923
1970			5	8	.385	4.78	34	11	1	96	103	38	66	0	3	2	0	27	3	0	.111	4	20	0	0	0.7	1.000
1971			7	10	.412	3.79	27	22	3	140	146	49	79	2	1	0	0	50	10	0	.200	1	26	2	1	1.1	.931
1972			14	7	.667	2.90	35	28	11	214	176	77	107	4	0	1	0	70	12	0	.171	3	15	3	2	0.6	.857
1973			**24**	12	.667	3.54	41	39	8	269.2	240	115	143	0	1	0	0	95	16	0	.168	9	45	1	1	1.3	.982
1974			3	15	.167	5.60	41	23	0	127	142	68	75	0	0	1	0	31	4	0	.129	5	18	1	1	0.6	.958
1975	STL	N	0	1	.000	16.00	10	1	0	9	20	7	7	0	0	0	0	1	0	0	.000	1	2	0	0	0.3	1.000
8 yrs.			57	56	.504	4.02	205	132	23	917.2	890	379	509	6	5	4	1	291	48	0	.165	24	137	8	6	0.8	.953
LEAGUE CHAMPIONSHIP SERIES																											
1971	SF	N	0	0	—	4.50	1	0	0	2	1	1	2	0	0	0	0	0	0	0	—	0	0	0	0	0.0	.000

T. R. Bryden

BRYDEN, THOMAS RAY BR TR 6′ 4″ 190 lbs.
B. Jan. 17, 1959, Moses Lake, Wash.

Year	Team	Lg	W	L	PCT	ERA	G	GS	CG	IP	H	BB	SO	ShO	Relief W	Relief L	Relief SV	AB	H	HR	BA	PO	A	E	DP	TC/G	FA
1986	CAL	A	2	1	.667	6.55	16	0	0	34.1	38	21	25	0	2	1	0	0	0	0	—	2	4	0	1	0.4	1.000

Charlie Brynan

BRYNAN, CHARLES RULEY (Tod) BR TR
B. July 1863, Philadelphia, Pa. D. May 10, 1925, Philadelphia, Pa.

Year	Team	Lg	W	L	PCT	ERA	G	GS	CG	IP	H	BB	SO	ShO	Relief W	Relief L	Relief SV	AB	H	HR	BA	PO	A	E	DP	TC/G	FA
1888	CHI	N	2	1	.667	6.48	3	3	2	25	29	7	11	0	0	0	0	11	2	0	.182	1	3	1	0	1.3	.800
1891	BOS	N	0	1	.000	54.00	1	1	0	1	4	3	0	0	0	0	0	0	0	0	—	0	0	0	0	0.0	.000
2 yrs.			2	2	.500	8.31	4	4	2	26	33	10	11	0	0	0	0	11	2	0	.182	1	3	1	0	1.0	.800

Bob Buchanan

BUCHANAN, ROBERT GORDON BL TL 6′ 1″ 185 lbs.
B. May 3, 1961, Ridley Park, Pa.

Year	Team	Lg	W	L	PCT	ERA	G	GS	CG	IP	H	BB	SO	ShO	Relief W	Relief L	Relief SV	AB	H	HR	BA	PO	A	E	DP	TC/G	FA
1985	CIN	N	1	0	1.000	8.44	14	0	0	16	25	9	3	0	1	0	0	1	0	0	.000	1	3	0	0	0.3	1.000
1989	KC	A	0	0	—	16.20	2	0	0	3.1	5	3	3	0	0	0	0	0	0	0	—	0	0	0	0	0.0	.000
2 yrs.			1	0	1.000	9.78	16	0	0	19.1	30	12	6	0	1	0	0	1	0	0	.000	1	3	0	0	0.3	1.000

Jim Buchanan

BUCHANAN, JAMES FORREST (Buck) BL TR 5′10½″ 170 lbs.
B. July 1, 1876, Chatham Hill, Va. D. June 15, 1949, Norfolk, Neb.

Year	Team	Lg	W	L	PCT	ERA	G	GS	CG	IP	H	BB	SO	ShO	Relief W	Relief L	Relief SV	AB	H	HR	BA	PO	A	E	DP	TC/G	FA
1905	STL	A	5	9	.357	3.50	22	15	12	141.1	149	27	54	1	0	0	**2**	46	7	0	.152	8	47	8	1	2.9	.873

Gary Buckels

BUCKELS, GARY SCOTT BR TR 6′ 185 lbs.
B. July 22, 1965, La Mirada, Calif.

Year	Team	Lg	W	L	PCT	ERA	G	GS	CG	IP	H	BB	SO	ShO	Relief W	Relief L	Relief SV	AB	H	HR	BA	PO	A	E	DP	TC/G	FA
1994	STL	N	0	1	.000	2.25	10	0	0	12	8	7	9	0	0	1	0	1	0	0	.000	2	2	0	0	0.4	1.000

Garland Buckeye

BUCKEYE, GARLAND MAIERS (Gob) BB TL 6′ 260 lbs.
B. Oct. 16, 1897, Heron Lake, Minn. D. Nov. 14, 1975, Stone Lake, Wis.

Year	Team	Lg	W	L	PCT	ERA	G	GS	CG	IP	H	BB	SO	ShO	Relief W	Relief L	Relief SV	AB	H	HR	BA	PO	A	E	DP	TC/G	FA
1918	WAS	A	0	0	—	18.00	1	0	0	2	3	6	2	0	0	0	0	0	0	0	—	1	1	0	0	2.0	1.000
1925	CLE	A	13	8	.619	3.65	30	18	11	153	161	58	49	1	3	2	0	62	14	3	.226	8	31	0	2	1.3	1.000
1926			6	9	.400	3.10	32	18	5	165.2	160	69	36	1	2	1	0	60	12	2	.200	7	35	3	5	1.4	.933
1927			10	17	.370	3.96	35	25	13	204.2	231	74	38	2	1	3	1	71	19	0	.268	7	50	3	4	1.7	.950
1928	2 teams	CLE A (9G 1–5) NY N (1G 0–0)																									
″	total		1	5	.167	7.32	10	6	0	39.1	67	7	9	0	0	1	0	11	2	0	.182	1	8	0	1	0.9	1.000
5 yrs.			30	39	.435	3.90	108	67	29	564.2	622	214	134	4	6	7	1	204	47	5	.230	24	125	6	12	1.4	.961

Ed Buckingham

BUCKINGHAM, EDWARD TAYLOR
B. May 22, 1874, Metuchen, N. J. D. July 30, 1942, Bridgeport, Conn.

Year	Team	Lg	W	L	PCT	ERA	G	GS	CG	IP	H	BB	SO	ShO	Relief W	Relief L	Relief SV	AB	H	HR	BA	PO	A	E	DP	TC/G	FA
1895	WAS	N	0	0	—	6.00	1	1	0	3	6	2	1	0	0	0	0	1	0	0	.000	0	1	0	0	1.0	1.000

Jess Buckles

BUCKLES, JESSE ROBERT (Jim) BL TL 6′ 2½″ 205 lbs.
B. May 20, 1890, LaVerne, Calif. D. Aug. 2, 1975, Westminster, Calif.

Year	Team	Lg	W	L	PCT	ERA	G	GS	CG	IP	H	BB	SO	ShO	Relief W	Relief L	Relief SV	AB	H	HR	BA	PO	A	E	DP	TC/G	FA
1916	NY	A	0	0	—	2.25	2	0	0	4	3	1	2	0	0	0	0	1	0	0	.000	0	1	1	0	1.0	.500

John Buckley

BUCKLEY, JOHN EDWARD BL TR 6′ 1″ 200 lbs.
B. Mar. 20, 1870, Marlboro, Mass. D. May 3, 1942, Westboro, Mass.

Year	Team	Lg	W	L	PCT	ERA	G	GS	CG	IP	H	BB	SO	ShO	Relief W	Relief L	Relief SV	AB	H	HR	BA	PO	A	E	DP	TC/G	FA
1890	BUF	P	1	3	.250	7.68	4	4	4	34	49	16	4	0	0	0	0	15	0	0	.000	1	11	0	0	3.0	1.000

Mike Budnick

BUDNICK, MICHAEL JOE BR TR 6′ 1″ 200 lbs.
B. Sept. 15, 1919, Astoria, Ore.

Year	Team	Lg	W	L	PCT	ERA	G	GS	CG	IP	H	BB	SO	ShO	Relief W	Relief L	Relief SV	AB	H	HR	BA	PO	A	E	DP	TC/G	FA
1946	NY	N	2	3	.400	3.16	35	7	1	88.1	75	48	36	1	2	3	3	20	6	1	.300	5	21	2	0	0.8	.929
1947			0	0	—	10.50	7	1	0	12	16	10	6	0	0	0	0	4	1	0	.250	3	3	0	0	0.9	1.000
2 yrs.			2	3	.400	4.04	42	8	1	100.1	91	58	42	1	2	3	3	24	7	1	.292	8	24	2	0	0.8	.941

Charlie Buffinton

BUFFINTON, CHARLES G. BR TR 6′ 1″ 180 lbs.
B. June 14, 1861, Fall River, Mass. D. Sept. 23, 1907, Fall River, Mass.
Manager 1890.

Year	Team	Lg	W	L	PCT	ERA	G	GS	CG	IP	H	BB	SO	ShO	Relief W	Relief L	Relief SV	AB	H	HR	BA	PO	A	E	DP	TC/G	FA
1882	BOS	N	2	3	.400	*4.07*	5	5	4	42	53	14	17	1	0	0	0	50	13	0	.260	34	12	7	0	3.3	.868
1883			25	14	.641	*3.03*	43	41	34	333	346	51	188	**5**	1	0	1	341	81	1	.238	84	69	33	6	1.9	.823
1884			48	16	.750	*2.15*	67	67	63	587	506	76	417	8	0	0	0	352	94	1	.267	146	118	24	6	3.2	.917
1885			22	27	.449	*2.88*	51	50	49	434.1	425	112	242	6	0	0	0	338	81	1	.240	196	121	27	11	4.1	.922
1886			7	10	.412	4.59	18	17	16	151	203	39	47	0	0	0	0	176	51	1	.290	181	35	11	8	6.1	.952

Charlie Buffinton *continued*

Year	Team	Lg	W	L	PCT	ERA	G	GS	CG	IP	H	BB	SO	ShO	Relief W	Relief L	Relief SV	Batting AB	Batting H	HR	BA	PO	A	E	DP	TC/G	FA
1887	PHI	N	21	17	.553	3.66	40	38	35	332.1	352	92	160	1	1	0	0	269	72	1	.268	124	93	23	8	3.3	.904
1888			28	17	.622	1.91	46	46	43	400.1	324	59	199	6	0	0	0	160	29	0	.181	31	122	10	3	3.5	.939
1889			28	16	.636	3.24	47	43	37	380	390	121	153	2	**3**	0	0	154	32	0	.208	18	80	9	4	2.2	.916
1890	PHI	P	19	15	.559	3.81	36	33	28	283.1	312	126	89	0	1	0	1	150	41	1	.273	50	81	16	6	3.3	.891
1891	BOS	AA	29	9	**.763**	2.55	48	43	33	363.2	303	120	158	2	2	0	1	181	34	1	.188	43	119	13	5	2.8	.926
1892	BAL	N	4	8	.333	4.92	13	13	9	97	130	46	30	0	0	0	0	43	15	0	.349	3	30	4	1	2.8	.892
11 yrs.			233	152	.605	2.96	414	396	351	3404	3344	856	1700	31	8	0	3	*				910	880	177	58	3.2	.910

Bob Buhl

BUHL, ROBERT RAY
B. Aug. 12, 1928, Saginaw, Mich.

BR TR 6′ 2″ 180 lbs.
BB 1958–1960, 1966

Year	Team	Lg	W	L	PCT	ERA	G	GS	CG	IP	H	BB	SO	ShO	Relief W	Relief L	Relief SV	Batting AB	Batting H	HR	BA	PO	A	E	DP	TC/G	FA
1953	MIL	N	13	8	.619	2.97	30	18	8	154.1	133	73	83	3	4	2	0	53	6	0	.113	14	25	1	3	1.3	.975
1954			2	7	.222	4.00	31	14	2	110.1	117	65	57	1	0	2	3	31	1	0	.032	5	18	1	1	0.8	.958
1955			13	11	.542	3.21	38	27	11	201.2	168	109	117	1	1	1	1	57	6	0	.105	12	30	2	1	1.2	.955
1956			18	8	.692	3.32	38	33	13	216.2	190	105	86	2	1	0	0	73	7	0	.096	19	35	1	2	1.4	.982
1957			18	7	**.720**	2.74	34	31	14	216.2	191	121	117	2	0	0	0	73	6	0	.082	14	25	2	2	1.2	.951
1958			5	2	.714	3.45	11	10	3	73	74	30	27	0	0	0	1	25	5	0	.200	5	19	2	0	2.4	.923
1959			15	9	.625	2.86	31	25	12	198	181	74	105	**4**	0	1	0	70	4	0	.057	21	43	1	4	2.1	.985
1960			16	9	.640	3.09	36	33	11	238.2	202	**103**	121	2	1	0	0	89	14	0	.157	26	50	1	3	2.1	.987
1961			9	10	.474	4.11	32	28	9	188.1	180	98	77	1	0	0	0	60	4	0	.067	16	37	1	1	1.7	.981
1962	2 teams	MIL N (1G 0–1)	CHI N (34G 12–13)																								
″	total		12	14	.462	3.87	35	31	8	214	210	98	110	1	0	0	0	70	0	0	.000	15	29	3	2	1.3	.936
1963	CHI	N	11	14	.440	3.38	37	34	6	226	219	62	108	0	0	0	0	74	8	0	.108	12	44	0	5	1.5	1.000
1964			15	14	.517	3.83	36	35	11	227.2	208	68	107	3	0	0	0	73	7	0	.096	22	48	0	4	1.9	1.000
1965			13	11	.542	4.39	32	31	2	184.1	207	57	92	0	0	0	0	67	4	0	.060	14	34	2	0	1.6	.960
1966	2 teams	CHI N (1G 0–0)	PHI N (32G 6–8)																								
″	total		6	8	.429	4.96	33	19	1	134.1	160	40	60	0	2	2	1	42	4	0	.095	16	23	1	3	1.2	.975
1967	PHI	N	0	0	—	13.50	3	0	0	2.2	6	2	1	0	0	0	0	0	0	0	—	0	1	0	1	0.3	1.000
15 yrs.			166	132	.557	3.55	457	369	111	2586.2	2446	1105	1268	20	9	8	6	857	76	0	.089	211	461	18	32	1.5	.974
WORLD SERIES																											
1957	MIL	N	0	1	.000	10.80	2	2	0	3.1	6	6	4	0	0	0	0	1	0	0	.000	0	2	1	0	1.5	.667

DeWayne Buice

BUICE, DeWAYNE ALLISON
B. Aug. 20, 1957, Lynwood, Calif.

BR TR 6′ 170 lbs.

Year	Team	Lg	W	L	PCT	ERA	G	GS	CG	IP	H	BB	SO	ShO	Relief W	Relief L	Relief SV	Batting AB	Batting H	HR	BA	PO	A	E	DP	TC/G	FA
1987	CAL	A	6	7	.462	3.39	57	0	0	114	87	40	109	0	6	7	17	0	0	0	—	3	15	1	2	0.3	.947
1988			2	4	.333	5.88	32	0	0	41.1	45	19	38	0	2	4	3	0	0	0	—	4	6	0	0	0.3	1.000
1989	TOR	A	1	0	1.000	5.82	7	0	0	17	13	13	10	0	1	0	0	0	0	0	—	0	3	0	0	0.4	1.000
3 yrs.			9	11	.450	4.23	96	0	0	172.1	145	72	157	0	9	11	20	0	0	0		7	24	1	2	0.3	.969

Cy Buker

BUKER, CYRIL OWEN
B. Feb. 5, 1919, Greenwood, Wis.

BL TR 5′11″ 190 lbs.

Year	Team	Lg	W	L	PCT	ERA	G	GS	CG	IP	H	BB	SO	ShO	Relief W	Relief L	Relief SV	Batting AB	Batting H	HR	BA	PO	A	E	DP	TC/G	FA
1945	BKN	N	7	2	.778	3.30	42	4	0	87.1	90	45	48	0	5	2	5	16	3	0	.188	3	11	1	1	0.4	.933

Jim Bullinger

BULLINGER, JAMES ERIC
B. Aug. 21, 1965, New Orleans, La.

BR TR 6′ 2″ 185 lbs.

Year	Team	Lg	W	L	PCT	ERA	G	GS	CG	IP	H	BB	SO	ShO	Relief W	Relief L	Relief SV	Batting AB	Batting H	HR	BA	PO	A	E	DP	TC/G	FA
1992	CHI	N	2	8	.200	4.66	39	9	1	85	72	54	36	0	1	2	7	20	5	1	.250	17	17	0	2	0.9	1.000
1993			1	0	1.000	4.32	15	0	0	16.2	18	9	10	0	1	0	1	1	0	0	.000	1	1	0	0	0.1	1.000
1994			6	2	.750	3.60	33	10	1	100	87	34	72	0	2	0	2	22	3	0	.136	6	11	0	0	0.5	1.000
1995			12	8	.600	4.14	24	24	1	150	152	65	93	1	0	0	0	47	6	0	.128	20	20	0	2	1.7	1.000
4 yrs.			21	18	.538	4.12	111	43	3	351.2	329	162	211	1	4	2	10	90	14	1	.156	44	49	0	4	0.8	1.000

Red Bullock

BULLOCK, MALTON JOSEPH
B. Oct. 12, 1911, Biloxi, Miss. D. June 27, 1988, Pascagoula, Miss.

BL TL 6′ 1″ 192 lbs.

Year	Team	Lg	W	L	PCT	ERA	G	GS	CG	IP	H	BB	SO	ShO	Relief W	Relief L	Relief SV	Batting AB	Batting H	HR	BA	PO	A	E	DP	TC/G	FA
1936	PHI	A	0	2	.000	14.04	12	2	0	16.2	19	37	7	0	0	1	0	4	0	0	.000	3	3	0	0	0.5	1.000

Melvin Bunch

BUNCH, MELVIN LYNN, JR.
B. Nov. 4, 1971, Texarkana, Tex.

BR TR 6′ 1″ 165 lbs.

Year	Team	Lg	W	L	PCT	ERA	G	GS	CG	IP	H	BB	SO	ShO	Relief W	Relief L	Relief SV	Batting AB	Batting H	HR	BA	PO	A	E	DP	TC/G	FA
1995	KC	A	1	3	.250	5.63	13	5	0	40	42	14	19	0	0	0	0	0	0	0	—	2	3	1	0	0.5	.833

Wally Bunker

BUNKER, WALLACE EDWARD
B. Jan. 25, 1945, Seattle, Wash.

BR TR 6′ 2″ 197 lbs.

Year	Team	Lg	W	L	PCT	ERA	G	GS	CG	IP	H	BB	SO	ShO	Relief W	Relief L	Relief SV	Batting AB	Batting H	HR	BA	PO	A	E	DP	TC/G	FA
1963	BAL	A	0	1	.000	13.50	1	1	0	4	10	3	1	0	0	0	0	2	1	0	.500	0	0	0	0	0.0	.000
1964			19	5	**.792**	2.69	29	29	12	214	161	62	96	1	0	0	0	72	5	0	.069	20	34	1	3	1.9	.982
1965			10	8	.556	3.38	34	27	4	189	170	58	84	1	0	0	2	55	4	0	.073	8	32	1	0	1.2	.976
1966			10	6	.625	4.29	29	24	3	142.2	151	48	89	0	0	1	0	48	5	0	.104	8	19	0	3	0.9	1.000
1967			3	7	.300	4.09	29	9	1	88	83	31	51	0	1	2	1	26	2	0	.077	4	20	0	1	0.8	1.000
1968			2	0	1.000	2.41	18	10	2	71	59	14	44	1	0	0	0	18	2	0	.111	5	9	1	0	0.8	.933
1969	KC	A	12	11	.522	3.23	35	31	10	222.2	198	62	130	1	1	0	2	70	10	0	.143	19	43	2	6	1.8	.969
1970			2	11	.154	4.20	24	15	2	122	109	50	59	1	0	1	0	31	2	0	.065	5	17	3	0	1.0	.880
1971			2	3	.400	5.06	7	6	0	32	35	6	15	0	0	0	0	9	0	0	.000	1	5	0	0	0.9	1.000
9 yrs.			60	52	.536	3.51	206	152	34	1085.1	976	334	569	5	2	4	5	331	31	0	.094	70	179	8	13	1.2	.969
WORLD SERIES																											
1966	BAL	A	1	0	1.000	0.00	1	1	1	9	6	1	6	1	0	0	0	2	0	0	.000	0	3	0	0	3.0	1.000

Jim Bunning

BUNNING, JAMES PAUL DAVID
B. Oct. 23, 1931, Southgate, Ky.
Hall of Fame 1996.

BR TR 6′ 3″ 190 lbs.

Year	Team	Lg	W	L	PCT	ERA	G	GS	CG	IP	H	BB	SO	ShO	Relief W	Relief L	Relief SV	Batting AB	Batting H	HR	BA	PO	A	E	DP	TC/G	FA
1955	DET	A	3	5	.375	6.35	15	8	0	51	59	32	37	0	2	0	1	15	3	0	.200	4	8	1	1	0.9	.923
1956			5	1	.833	3.71	15	3	0	53.1	55	28	34	0	4	0	1	18	6	0	.333	2	6	0	0	0.5	1.000
1957			**20**	8	.714	2.69	45	30	14	**267.1**	214	72	182	1	2	1	1	94	20	1	.213	12	19	0	0	0.7	1.000
1958			14	12	.538	3.52	35	34	10	219.2	188	79	177	3	0	0	0	75	14	0	.187	9	16	0	0	0.7	1.000
1959			17	13	.567	3.89	40	35	14	249.2	220	75	**201**	1	0	1	1	89	17	1	.191	11	16	3	1	0.8	.900

Jim Bunning *continued*

Year	Team	Lg	W	L	PCT	ERA	G	GS	CG	IP	H	BB	SO	ShO	Relief Pitching W	Relief Pitching L	Relief Pitching SV	Batting AB	Batting H	Batting HR	BA	PO	A	E	DP	TC/G	FA
1960			11	14	.440	2.79	36	34	10	252	217	64	**201**	3	0	0	0	81	13	0	.160	11	31	0	0	1.2	1.000
1961			17	11	.607	3.19	38	37	12	268	232	71	194	4	0	0	1	100	13	0	.130	21	29	3	6	1.4	.943
1962			19	10	.655	3.59	41	35	12	258	**262**	74	184	2	0	0	6	95	23	1	.242	17	13	0	1	0.7	1.000
1963			12	13	.480	3.88	39	35	6	248.1	245	69	196	2	0	0	1	84	13	0	.155	18	25	1	1	1.1	.977
1964	PHI	N	19	8	.704	2.63	41	39	13	284.1	248	46	219	5	0	0	2	99	12	0	.121	10	31	3	2	1.1	.932
1965			19	9	.679	2.60	39	39	15	291	253	62	268	7	0	0	0	103	22	1	.214	29	40	3	2	1.8	.958
1966			19	14	.576	2.41	43	**41**	16	314	260	55	252	**5**	1	0	1	106	19	0	.179	18	30	2	0	1.2	.960
1967			17	15	.531	2.29	40	**40**	16	**302.1**	241	73	**253**	**6**	0	0	0	104	17	2	.163	16	33	1	1	1.3	.980
1968	PIT	N	4	14	.222	3.88	27	26	3	160	168	48	95	1	0	0	0	51	5	0	.098	6	17	2	1	0.9	.920
1969	2 teams	PIT N (25G 10–9)	LA N (9G 3–1)																								
"	total		13	10	.565	3.69	34	34	5	212.1	212	59	157	0	0	0	0	65	4	0	.062	5	15	1	2	0.6	.952
1970	PHI	N	10	15	.400	4.11	34	33	4	219	233	56	147	0	0	0	0	71	9	0	.127	12	27	2	1	1.2	.951
1971			5	12	.294	5.48	29	16	1	110	126	37	58	0	0	2	1	25	3	1	.120	5	16	1	1	0.8	.955
17 yrs.			224	184	.549	3.27	591	519	151	3760.1	3433	1000	2855	40	9	4	16	1275	213	7	.167	206	372	23	20	1.0	.962

Dave Burba

BURBA, DAVID ALLEN BR TR 6′ 4″ 220 lbs.
B. July 7, 1966, Dayton, Ohio.

Year	Team	Lg	W	L	PCT	ERA	G	GS	CG	IP	H	BB	SO	ShO	Relief Pitching W	Relief Pitching L	Relief Pitching SV	Batting AB	Batting H	Batting HR	BA	PO	A	E	DP	TC/G	FA
1990	SEA	A	0	0	—	4.50	6	0	0	8	8	2	4	0	0	0	0	0	0	0	—	1	2	1	0	0.7	.750
1991			2	2	.500	3.68	22	2	0	36.2	34	14	16	0	1	1	1	0	0	0	—	2	4	0	0	0.3	1.000
1992	SF	N	2	7	.222	4.97	23	11	0	70.2	80	31	47	0	1	1	0	15	1	0	.067	3	8	0	0	0.5	1.000
1993			10	3	.769	4.25	54	5	0	95.1	95	37	88	0	7	2	0	17	5	0	.294	7	12	1	0	0.4	.950
1994			3	6	.333	4.38	57	0	0	74	59	45	84	0	3	**6**	0	3	0	0	.000	3	5	0	1	0.1	1.000
1995	2 teams	SF N (37G 4–2)	CIN N (15G 6–2)																								
"	total		10	4	.714	3.97	52	9	1	106.2	90	51	96	1	6	2	0	15	1	0	.067	10	7	0	0	0.3	1.000
6 yrs.			27	22	.551	4.28	214	27	1	391.1	366	180	335	1	18	12	1	50	7	0	.140	26	38	2	1	0.3	.970
DIVISIONAL PLAYOFF SERIES																											
1995	CIN	N	1	0	1.000	0.00	1	0	0	1	2	1	0	0	1	0	0	0	0	0	—	0	0	0	0	0.0	.000
LEAGUE CHAMPIONSHIP SERIES																											
1995	CIN	N	0	0	—	0.00	2	0	0	3.2	3	4	0	0	0	0	0	0	0	0	—	0	0	0	0	0.0	.000

Bill Burbach

BURBACH, WILLIAM DAVID BR TR 6′ 4″ 215 lbs.
B. Aug. 22, 1947, Dickeyville, Wis.

Year	Team	Lg	W	L	PCT	ERA	G	GS	CG	IP	H	BB	SO	ShO	Relief Pitching W	Relief Pitching L	Relief Pitching SV	Batting AB	Batting H	Batting HR	BA	PO	A	E	DP	TC/G	FA
1969	NY	A	6	8	.429	3.65	31	24	2	140.2	112	102	82	1	1	0	0	40	4	0	.100	10	16	0	1	0.8	1.000
1970			0	2	.000	10.06	4	4	0	17	23	9	10	0	0	0	0	5	0	0	.000	0	2	1	0	0.8	.667
1971			0	1	.000	12.00	2	0	0	3	6	5	3	0	0	1	0	2	0	0	.000	0	0	1	0	0.5	.000
3 yrs.			6	11	.353	4.48	37	28	2	160.2	141	116	95	1	1	1	0	47	4	0	.085	10	18	2	1	0.8	.933

Larry Burchart

BURCHART, LARRY WAYNE BR TR 6′ 3″ 205 lbs.
B. Feb. 8, 1946, Tulsa, Okla.

Year	Team	Lg	W	L	PCT	ERA	G	GS	CG	IP	H	BB	SO	ShO	Relief Pitching W	Relief Pitching L	Relief Pitching SV	Batting AB	Batting H	Batting HR	BA	PO	A	E	DP	TC/G	FA
1969	CLE	A	0	2	.000	4.25	29	0	0	42.1	42	24	26	0	0	2	0	0	0	0	—	1	5	2	0	0.3	.750

Fred Burchell

BURCHELL, FREDERICK DUFF BL TL 5′11″ 190 lbs.
B. July 14, 1879, Perth Amboy, N. J. D. Nov. 20, 1951, Jordan, N. Y.

Year	Team	Lg	W	L	PCT	ERA	G	GS	CG	IP	H	BB	SO	ShO	Relief Pitching W	Relief Pitching L	Relief Pitching SV	Batting AB	Batting H	Batting HR	BA	PO	A	E	DP	TC/G	FA
1903	PHI	N	0	3	.000	2.86	6	3	2	44	48	14	12	0	0	0	0	16	3	0	.188	0	13	3	0	2.7	.813
1907	BOS	A	0	1	.000	2.70	2	1	0	10	8	2	6	0	0	0	0	5	1	0	.200	0	2	0	0	1.0	1.000
1908			10	8	.556	2.96	31	19	9	179.2	161	65	94	0	1	1	0	69	17	0	.246	5	48	8	0	2.0	.869
1909			3	3	.500	2.94	10	5	1	52	51	11	12	0	1	0	0	19	3	0	.158	1	21	3	1	2.5	.880
4 yrs.			13	15	.464	2.93	49	28	12	285.2	268	92	124	0	2	1	0	109	24	0	.220	6	84	14	1	2.1	.865

Freddie Burdette

BURDETTE, FREDDIE THOMASON BR TR 6′ 1″ 170 lbs.
B. Sept. 15, 1936, Moultrie, Ga.

Year	Team	Lg	W	L	PCT	ERA	G	GS	CG	IP	H	BB	SO	ShO	Relief Pitching W	Relief Pitching L	Relief Pitching SV	Batting AB	Batting H	Batting HR	BA	PO	A	E	DP	TC/G	FA
1962	CHI	N	0	0	—	3.72	8	0	0	9.2	5	8	5	0	0	0	1	1	0	0	.000	0	2	1	0	0.4	.667
1963			0	0	—	3.86	4	0	0	4.2	5	2	1	0	0	0	0	0	0	0	—	0	2	0	1	0.5	1.000
1964			1	0	1.000	3.15	18	0	0	20	17	10	4	0	1	0	0	1	1	0	1.000	3	2	0	0	0.3	1.000
3 yrs.			1	0	1.000	3.41	30	0	0	34.1	27	20	10	0	1	0	1	2	1	0	.500	3	6	1	1	0.3	.900

Lew Burdette

BURDETTE, SELVA LEWIS BR TR 6′ 2″ 180 lbs.
B. Nov. 22, 1926, Nitro, W. Va.

Year	Team	Lg	W	L	PCT	ERA	G	GS	CG	IP	H	BB	SO	ShO	Relief Pitching W	Relief Pitching L	Relief Pitching SV	Batting AB	Batting H	Batting HR	BA	PO	A	E	DP	TC/G	FA
1950	NY	A	0	0	—	6.75	2	0	0	1.1	3	0	0	0	0	0	0	0	0	0	—	0	1	0	1	0.5	1.000
1951	BOS	N	0	0	—	6.23	3	0	0	4.1	6	5	1	0	0	0	0	1	0	0	.000	0	1	0	0	0.3	1.000
1952			6	11	.353	3.61	45	9	5	137	138	47	47	0	2	8	7	35	4	0	.114	9	29	1	3	0.9	.974
1953	MIL	N	15	5	.750	3.24	46	13	6	175	177	56	58	1	8	0	8	53	9	0	.170	11	37	1	6	1.1	.980
1954			15	14	.517	2.76	38	32	13	238	224	62	79	4	1	1	0	79	7	0	.089	17	49	4	4	1.8	.943
1955			13	8	.619	4.03	42	33	11	230	253	73	70	2	2	1	0	86	20	0	.233	18	47	2	6	1.6	.970
1956			19	10	.655	**2.70**	39	35	16	256.1	234	52	110	**6**	0	0	1	86	16	0	.186	19	48	1	4	1.7	.985
1957			17	9	.654	3.72	37	33	14	256.2	260	59	78	1	2	1	0	88	13	2	.148	22	53	4	3	2.1	.949
1958			20	10	**.667**	2.91	40	36	19	275.1	279	50	113	3	2	0	0	99	24	3	.242	27	53	1	4	2.0	.988
1959			**21**	15	.583	4.07	41	**39**	20	289.2	**312**	38	105	**4**	0	0	1	104	21	0	.202	21	47	1	6	1.7	.986
1960			19	13	.594	3.36	45	32	**18**	275.2	**277**	35	83	4	3	2	4	91	16	2	.176	31	68	2	6	2.2	.980
1961			18	11	.621	4.00	40	36	14	**272.1**	**295**	33	92	3	2	0	0	103	21	3	.204	27	60	1	2	2.2	.989
1962			10	9	.526	4.89	37	19	6	143.2	172	23	59	1	3	1	2	51	9	0	.176	8	33	2	1	1.2	.953
1963	2 teams	MIL N (15G 6–5)	STL N (21G 3–8)																								
"	total		9	13	.409	3.70	36	27	7	182.2	177	40	73	1	1	2	2	57	4	0	.070	11	27	5	3	1.2	.884
1964	2 teams	STL N (8G 1–0)	CHI N (28G 9–9)																								
"	total		10	9	.526	4.66	36	17	8	141	162	22	43	2	2	1	0	44	12	2	.273	10	36	0	3	1.3	1.000
1965	2 teams	CHI N (7G 0–2)	PHI N (19G 3–3)																								
"	total		3	5	.375	5.44	26	12	1	91	121	21	28	1	0	0	0	26	8	0	.308	6	17	0	3	0.9	1.000
1966	CAL	A	7	2	.778	3.39	54	0	0	79.2	80	12	27	0	7	2	5	8	1	0	.125	8	11	2	0	0.4	.905
1967			1	0	1.000	4.91	19	0	0	18.1	16	0	8	0	1	0	1	0	0	0	—	0	5	0	0	0.3	1.000
18 yrs.			203	144	.585	3.66	626	373	158	3068	3186	628	1074	33	36	19	31	1011	185	12	.183	245	622	27	55	1.4	.970

Lew Burdette *continued*

Year	Team	Lg	W	L	PCT	ERA	G	GS	CG	IP	H	BB	SO	ShO	Relief Pitching W	Relief Pitching L	Relief Pitching SV	Batting AB	Batting H	Batting HR	BA	PO	A	E	DP	TC/G	FA
WORLD SERIES																											
1957	MIL	N	3	0	1.000	0.67	3	3	3	27	21	4	13	2	0	0	0	8	0	0	.000	0	9	0	0	3.0	1.000
1958			1	2	.333	5.64	3	3	1	22.1	22	4	12	0	0	0	0	9	1	1	.111	2	2	0	0	1.3	1.000
2 yrs.			4	2	.667	2.92	6	6	4	49.1	43	8	25	2 4th	0	0	0	17	1	1	.059	2	11	0	0	2.2	1.000

Bill Burdick

BURDICK, WILLIAM BYRON BR TR
B. Oct. 11, 1859, Austin, Minn. D. Oct. 23, 1949, Spokane, Wash.

Year	Team	Lg	W	L	PCT	ERA	G	GS	CG	IP	H	BB	SO	ShO	Relief Pitching W	Relief Pitching L	Relief Pitching SV	Batting AB	Batting H	Batting HR	BA	PO	A	E	DP	TC/G	FA
1888	IND	N	10	10	.500	2.81	20	20	20	176	168	43	55	0	0	0	0	68	10	0	.147	14	34	6	0	2.6	.889
1889			2	4	.333	4.53	10	4	2	45.2	58	13	16	0	0	**2**	1	17	2	0	.118	2	8	0	0	1.0	1.000
2 yrs.			12	14	.462	3.17	30	24	22	221.2	226	56	71	0	0	2	1	85	12	0	.141	16	42	6	0	2.1	.906

Tom Burgmeier

BURGMEIER, THOMAS HENRY (Bugs) BL TL 5′11″ 185 lbs.
B. Aug. 2, 1943, St. Paul, Minn.

Year	Team	Lg	W	L	PCT	ERA	G	GS	CG	IP	H	BB	SO	ShO	Relief Pitching W	Relief Pitching L	Relief Pitching SV	Batting AB	Batting H	Batting HR	BA	PO	A	E	DP	TC/G	FA
1968	CAL	A	1	4	.200	4.33	56	2	0	72.2	65	24	33	0	1	2	5	2	0	0	.000	11	23	1	7	0.6	.971
1969	KC	A	3	1	.750	4.17	31	0	0	54	67	21	23	0	3	1	0	18	3	0	.167	9	15	0	1	0.8	1.000
1970			6	6	.500	3.18	41	0	0	68	59	23	43	0	6	6	1	14	2	0	.143	3	20	2	0	0.6	.920
1971			9	7	.563	1.74	67	0	0	88	71	30	44	0	9	7	17	20	5	0	.250	7	28	1	3	0.5	.972
1972			6	2	.750	4.25	51	0	0	55	67	33	18	0	6	2	9	12	4	0	.333	6	13	1	0	0.4	.950
1973			0	0	—	5.40	6	0	0	10	13	4	4	0	0	0	1	0	0	0	—	1	0	0	0	0.2	1.000
1974	MIN	A	5	3	.625	4.52	50	0	0	91.2	92	26	34	0	5	3	4	0	0	0	—	11	25	1	0	0.7	.973
1975			5	8	.385	3.09	46	0	0	75.2	76	23	41	0	5	8	11	0	0	0	—	6	12	0	1	0.4	1.000
1976			8	1	.889	2.50	57	0	0	115.1	95	29	45	0	8	1	1	0	0	0	—	8	26	0	2	0.6	1.000
1977			6	4	.600	5.10	61	0	0	97	113	33	35	0	6	4	7	0	0	0	—	11	18	1	1	0.5	.967
1978	BOS	A	2	1	.667	4.40	35	1	0	61.1	74	23	24	0	2	1	4	0	0	0	—	5	13	2	3	0.6	.900
1979			3	2	.600	2.73	44	0	0	89	89	16	60	0	3	2	4	0	0	0	—	5	14	0	3	0.4	1.000
1980			5	4	.556	2.00	62	0	0	99	87	20	54	0	5	4	24	0	0	0	—	7	27	0	5	0.5	1.000
1981			4	5	.444	2.85	32	0	0	60	61	17	35	0	4	5	6	0	0	0	—	7	13	0	3	0.6	1.000
1982			7	0	1.000	2.29	40	0	0	102.1	98	22	44	0	7	0	2	0	0	0	—	17	20	1	4	0.9	.974
1983	OAK	A	6	7	.462	2.81	49	0	0	96	89	32	39	0	6	7	4	0	0	0	—	7	23	3	2	0.6	.909
1984			3	0	1.000	2.35	17	0	0	23	15	8	8	0	3	0	2	0	0	0	—	3	3	0	1	0.4	1.000
17 yrs.			79	55	.590	3.23	745	3	0	1258	1231	384	584	0	79	53	102	66	14	0	.212	124	293	13	36	0.6	.970

Enrique Burgos

BURGOS, ENRIQUE BL TL 6′ 4″ 195 lbs.
Born Enrique Burgos (Calles).
B. Oct. 7, 1965, Chorrera, Panama.

Year	Team	Lg	W	L	PCT	ERA	G	GS	CG	IP	H	BB	SO	ShO	Relief Pitching W	Relief Pitching L	Relief Pitching SV	Batting AB	Batting H	Batting HR	BA	PO	A	E	DP	TC/G	FA
1993	KC	A	0	1	.000	9.00	5	0	0	5	5	6	6	0	0	1	0	0	0	0	—	0	1	0	0	0.2	1.000
1995	SF	N	0	0	—	8.64	5	0	0	8.1	14	6	12	0	0	0	0	0	0	0	—	0	0	0	0	0.0	.000
2 yrs.			0	1	.000	8.77	10	0	0	13.1	19	12	18	0	0	1	0	0	0	0		0	1	0	0	0.1	1.000

Sandy Burk

BURK, CHARLES SANFORD BR TR 5′ 8″ 155 lbs.
B. Apr. 22, 1887, Columbus, Ohio D. Oct. 11, 1934, Brooklyn, N. Y.

Year	Team	Lg	W	L	PCT	ERA	G	GS	CG	IP	H	BB	SO	ShO	Relief Pitching W	Relief Pitching L	Relief Pitching SV	Batting AB	Batting H	Batting HR	BA	PO	A	E	DP	TC/G	FA
1910	BKN	N	0	3	.000	6.05	4	3	1	19.1	17	27	14	0	0	0	0	5	0	0	.000	1	6	3	0	2.5	.700
1911			1	3	.250	5.12	13	7	1	58	54	47	15	0	0	0	0	19	2	0	.105	1	19	2	0	1.7	.909
1912	2 teams	BKN N (2G 0–0)	STL N (12G 1–3)																								
″	total		1	3	.250	2.55	14	4	2	53	46	15	19	0	0	1	1	15	1	0	.067	2	9	1	0	0.9	.917
1913	STL	N	1	2	.333	5.14	19	5	0	70	81	33	29	0	0	2	1	22	2	0	.091	1	16	0	0	0.9	1.000
1915	PIT	F	2	0	1.000	1.00	2	2	1	18	8	11	9	0	0	0	0	6	1	0	.167	2	2	0	0	2.0	1.000
5 yrs.			5	11	.313	4.25	52	21	5	218.1	206	133	86	0	0	3	2	67	6	0	.090	7	52	6	0	1.3	.908

Elmer Burkart

BURKART, ELMER ROBERT (Swede) BR TR 6′ 2″ 190 lbs.
B. Feb. 1, 1917, Torresdale, Pa. D. Feb. 6, 1995, Baltimore, Md.

Year	Team	Lg	W	L	PCT	ERA	G	GS	CG	IP	H	BB	SO	ShO	Relief Pitching W	Relief Pitching L	Relief Pitching SV	Batting AB	Batting H	Batting HR	BA	PO	A	E	DP	TC/G	FA
1936	PHI	N	0	0	—	3.52	2	2	0	7.2	4	12	2	0	0	0	0	2	0	0	.000	0	2	0	1	1.0	1.000
1937			0	0	—	6.19	7	0	0	16	20	9	4	0	0	0	0	6	0	0	.000	0	4	0	0	0.6	1.000
1938			0	1	.000	4.50	2	1	1	10	12	3	1	0	0	0	0	3	0	0	.000	1	1	1	0	1.5	.667
1939			1	0	1.000	4.32	5	0	0	8.1	11	2	2	0	1	0	0	1	1	0	1.000	0	1	0	0	0.2	1.000
4 yrs.			1	1	.500	4.93	16	3	1	42	47	26	9	0	1	0	0	12	1	0	.083	1	8	1	1	0.6	.900

Billy Burke

BURKE, WILLIAM IGNATIUS BL TL 5′10″ 165 lbs.
B. July 11, 1889, Clinton, Mass. D. Feb. 9, 1967, Worcester, Mass.

Year	Team	Lg	W	L	PCT	ERA	G	GS	CG	IP	H	BB	SO	ShO	Relief Pitching W	Relief Pitching L	Relief Pitching SV	Batting AB	Batting H	Batting HR	BA	PO	A	E	DP	TC/G	FA
1910	BOS	N	1	0	1.000	4.08	19	1	1	64	68	29	22	0	0	0	0	21	4	0	.190	6	11	2	0	1.0	.895
1911			0	1	.000	18.90	2	1	0	3.1	6	5	1	0	0	0	0	1	1	0	1.000	0	0	1	0	0.5	.000
2 yrs.			1	1	.500	4.81	21	2	1	67.1	74	34	23	0	0	0	0	22	5	0	.227	6	11	3	0	1.0	.850

Bobby Burke

BURKE, ROBERT JAMES (Lefty) BL TL 6′½″ 150 lbs.
B. Jan. 23, 1907, Joliet, Ill. D. Feb. 8, 1971, Joliet, Ill.

Year	Team	Lg	W	L	PCT	ERA	G	GS	CG	IP	H	BB	SO	ShO	Relief Pitching W	Relief Pitching L	Relief Pitching SV	Batting AB	Batting H	Batting HR	BA	PO	A	E	DP	TC/G	FA
1927	WAS	A	3	2	.600	3.96	36	6	1	100	92	32	21	0	1	0	0	24	3	0	.125	6	24	0	1	0.8	1.000
1928			2	4	.333	3.90	26	7	2	85.1	87	18	27	1	0	1	0	20	5	0	.250	5	19	1	1	1.0	.960
1929			6	8	.429	4.79	37	17	4	141	154	55	51	0	1	1	0	43	6	0	.140	4	20	0	1	0.6	1.000
1930			3	4	.429	3.63	24	4	2	74.1	62	29	35	0	1	2	3	23	4	0	.174	6	8	3	0	0.7	.824
1931			8	3	.727	4.27	30	13	3	128.2	124	50	38	1	3	0	2	47	10	0	.213	4	29	1	1	1.1	.971
1932			3	6	.333	5.14	22	10	2	91	98	44	32	0	1	0	0	25	5	0	.200	3	14	0	0	0.8	1.000
1933			4	3	.571	3.23	25	6	4	64	64	31	28	1	0	1	0	17	4	0	.235	0	17	3	1	0.8	.850
1934			8	8	.500	3.21	37	15	7	168	155	72	52	1	2	2	0	57	13	0	.228	8	36	2	1	1.2	.957
1935			1	8	.111	7.46	15	10	2	66.1	90	27	16	0	0	0	0	22	4	0	.182	4	16	0	0	1.3	1.000
1937	PHI	N	0	0	—	∞	2	0	0		1	2	0	0	0	0	0	0	0	0	—	0	0	0	0	0.0	.000
10 yrs.			38	46	.452	4.29	254	88	27	918.2	927	360	300	4	9	7	5	278	54	0	.194	40	183	10	6	0.9	.957

James Burke

BURKE, JAMES
B. Attleboro, Mass. Deceased.

Year	Team	W	L	PCT	ERA	G	GS	CG	IP	H	BB	SO	ShO	Relief Pitching W	Relief Pitching L	Relief Pitching SV	Batting AB	Batting H	Batting HR	BA	PO	A	E	DP	TC/G	FA
1882	BUF N	0	1	.000	*11.25*	1	1	0	4	10	0	0	0	0	0	0	4	0	0	.000	2	4	0	0	3.0	1.000
1883		0	0	—	5.63	1	1	0	8	9	3	1	0	0	0	0	5	1	0	.200	0	1	0	0	0.5	1.000
1884	BOS U	19	15	.559	*2.85*	38	36	34	322	326	31	255	0	1	0	0	184	41	0	.223	20	50	17	3	1.7	.805
3 yrs.		19	16	.543	3.02	40	38	34	334	345	34	256	0	1	0	0	193	42	0	.218	22	55	17	3	1.7	.819

John Burke

BURKE, JOHN PATRICK BR TR
B. Jan. 27, 1877, Hazleton, Pa. D. Aug. 4, 1950, Jersey City, N. J.

Year	Team	W	L	PCT	ERA	G	GS	CG	IP	H	BB	SO	ShO	Relief Pitching W	Relief Pitching L	Relief Pitching SV	Batting AB	Batting H	Batting HR	BA	PO	A	E	DP	TC/G	FA
1902	NY N	0	1	.000	5.79	2	1	1	14	21	3	3	0	0	0	0	*				5	3	0	0	2.0	1.000

Steve Burke

BURKE, STEVEN MICHAEL BB TR 6′ 2″ 200 lbs.
B. Mar. 5, 1955, Stockton, Calif.

Year	Team	W	L	PCT	ERA	G	GS	CG	IP	H	BB	SO	ShO	Relief Pitching W	Relief Pitching L	Relief Pitching SV	Batting AB	Batting H	Batting HR	BA	PO	A	E	DP	TC/G	FA
1977	SEA A	0	1	.000	2.81	6	0	0	16	12	7	6	0	0	1	0	0	0	0	—	2	3	1	0	1.0	.833
1978		0	1	.000	3.49	18	0	0	49	46	24	16	0	0	1	0	0	0	0	—	2	8	2	3	0.7	.833
2 yrs.		0	2	.000	3.32	24	0	0	65	58	31	22	0	0	2	0	0	0	0		4	11	3	3	0.8	.833

Tim Burke

BURKE, TIMOTHY PHILIP BR TR 6′ 3″ 205 lbs.
B. Feb. 19, 1959, Omaha, Neb.

Year	Team	W	L	PCT	ERA	G	GS	CG	IP	H	BB	SO	ShO	Relief Pitching W	Relief Pitching L	Relief Pitching SV	Batting AB	Batting H	Batting HR	BA	PO	A	E	DP	TC/G	FA
1985	MON N	9	4	.692	2.39	**78**	0	0	120.1	86	44	87	0	9	4	8	10	1	0	.100	5	21	1	2	0.3	.963
1986		9	7	.563	2.93	68	2	0	101.1	103	46	82	0	8	7	4	7	0	0	.000	4	22	1	1	0.4	.963
1987		7	0	1.000	1.19	55	0	0	91	64	17	58	0	7	0	18	10	0	0	.000	6	17	0	0	0.4	1.000
1988		3	5	.375	3.40	61	0	0	82	84	25	42	0	3	5	18	2	0	0	.000	8	14	0	0	0.4	1.000
1989		9	3	.750	2.55	68	0	0	84.2	68	22	54	0	9	3	28	3	0	0	.000	4	16	0	0	0.3	1.000
1990		3	3	.500	2.52	58	0	0	75	71	21	47	0	3	3	20	6	1	0	.167	3	20	0	1	0.4	1.000
1991	2 teams MON N (37G 3–4) NY N (35G 3–3)																									
″	total	6	7	.462	3.36	72	0	0	101.2	96	26	59	0	6	7	6	6	0	0	.000	3	21	2	1	0.4	.923
1992	2 teams NY N (15G 1–2) NY A (23G 2–2)																									
″	total	3	4	.429	4.15	38	0	0	43.1	52	18	15	0	3	4	0	0	0	0		3	12	1	0	0.4	.938
8 yrs.		49	33	.598	2.72	498	2	0	699.1	624	219	444	0	48	33	102	44	2	0	.045	36	143	5	5	0.4	.973

Turk Burke

BURKE, WILLIAM R. 6′ 200 lbs.
B. Nov. 1865, Cincinnati, Ohio D. Mar. 17, 1939, Atchison, Kans.

Year	Team	W	L	PCT	ERA	G	GS	CG	IP	H	BB	SO	ShO	Relief Pitching W	Relief Pitching L	Relief Pitching SV	Batting AB	Batting H	Batting HR	BA	PO	A	E	DP	TC/G	FA
1887	DET N	0	1	.000	6.00	2	2	1	15	21	5	3	0	0	0	0	8	2	0	.250	0	3	1	0	1.3	.750

Jesse Burkett

BURKETT, JESSE CAIL (The Crab) BL TL 5′ 8″ 155 lbs.
B. Dec. 4, 1868, Wheeling, W. Va. D. May 27, 1953, Worcester, Mass.
Hall of Fame 1946.

Year	Team	W	L	PCT	ERA	G	GS	CG	IP	H	BB	SO	ShO	Relief Pitching W	Relief Pitching L	Relief Pitching SV	Batting AB	Batting H	Batting HR	BA	PO	A	E	DP	TC/G	FA
1890	NY N	3	10	.231	5.57	21	12	6	118	134	92	82	0	**2**	0	0	401	124	4	.309	111	56	36	5	1.8	.823
1894	CLE N	0	0	—	4.50	1	0	0	4	6	1	0	0	0	0	0	523	187	8	.358	53	5	7	1	1.5	.892
1902	STL A	0	1	.000	9.00	1	0	0	1	4	1	2	0	0	1	0	549	168	5	.306	271	20	31	7	2.2	.904
3 yrs.		3	11	.214	5.56	23	12	6	123	144	94	84	0	2	1	0	*				3967	309	393	64	2.2	.916

John Burkett

BURKETT, JOHN DAVID BR TR 6′ 2″ 175 lbs.
B. Nov. 28, 1964, New Brighton, Pa.

Year	Team	W	L	PCT	ERA	G	GS	CG	IP	H	BB	SO	ShO	Relief Pitching W	Relief Pitching L	Relief Pitching SV	Batting AB	Batting H	Batting HR	BA	PO	A	E	DP	TC/G	FA
1987	SF N	0	0	—	4.50	3	0	0	6	7	3	5	0	0	0	0	1	0	0	.000	0	1	0	1	0.3	1.000
1990		14	7	.667	3.79	33	32	2	204	201	61	118	0	0	0	1	63	3	0	.048	11	25	1	4	1.1	.973
1991		12	11	.522	4.18	36	34	3	206.2	223	60	131	1	0	0	0	55	5	0	.091	13	25	1	2	1.1	.974
1992		13	9	.591	3.84	32	32	3	189.2	194	45	107	1	0	0	0	55	1	0	.018	11	18	1	0	0.9	.967
1993		**22**	7	.759	3.65	34	34	2	231.2	224	40	145	1	0	0	0	76	9	0	.118	21	36	0	2	1.7	1.000
1994		6	8	.429	3.62	25	25	0	159.1	176	36	85	0	0	0	0	51	3	0	.059	14	23	0	1	1.5	1.000
1995	FLA N	14	14	.500	4.30	30	30	4	188.1	208	57	126	0	0	0	0	66	7	0	.106	17	26	0	0	1.4	1.000
7 yrs.		81	56	.591	3.90	193	187	14	1185.2	1233	302	717	3	0	0	1	367	28	0	.076	87	154	3	10	1.3	.988

Ken Burkhart

BURKHART, KENNETH WILLIAM BR TR 6′ 1″ 190 lbs.
Born Kenneth William Burkhardt.
B. Nov. 18, 1916, Knoxville, Tenn.

Year	Team	W	L	PCT	ERA	G	GS	CG	IP	H	BB	SO	ShO	Relief Pitching W	Relief Pitching L	Relief Pitching SV	Batting AB	Batting H	Batting HR	BA	PO	A	E	DP	TC/G	FA
1945	STL N	18	8	.692	2.90	42	22	12	217.1	206	66	67	4	6	1	2	72	13	0	.181	6	41	2	0	1.2	.959
1946		6	3	.667	2.88	25	13	5	100	111	36	32	2	1	1	2	34	5	0	.147	1	15	2	1	0.7	.889
1947		3	6	.333	5.21	34	6	1	95	108	23	44	0	1	3	1	24	3	0	.125	6	20	0	0	0.8	1.000
1948	2 teams STL N (20G 0–0) CIN N (16G 0–3)																									
″	total	0	3	.000	6.27	36	0	0	79	92	30	30	0	0	3	1	13	4	1	.308	7	14	1	1	0.6	.955
1949	CIN N	0	0	—	3.18	11	0	0	28.1	29	10	8	0	0	0	1	7	2	0	.286	1	6	0	1	0.6	1.000
5 yrs.		27	20	.574	3.84	148	41	18	519.2	546	165	181	6	8	8	7	150	27	1	.180	21	96	5	3	0.8	.959

Wally Burnette

BURNETTE, WALLACE HARPER BR TR 6′½″ 178 lbs.
B. June 20, 1929, Blairs, Va.

Year	Team	W	L	PCT	ERA	G	GS	CG	IP	H	BB	SO	ShO	Relief Pitching W	Relief Pitching L	Relief Pitching SV	Batting AB	Batting H	Batting HR	BA	PO	A	E	DP	TC/G	FA
1956	KC A	6	8	.429	2.89	18	14	4	121.1	115	39	54	1	2	1	0	39	2	0	.051	6	16	1	2	1.3	.957
1957		7	12	.368	4.30	38	9	1	113	115	44	57	0	5	6	1	32	8	0	.250	10	25	0	6	0.9	1.000
1958		1	1	.500	3.49	12	4	0	28.1	29	14	11	0	0	0	0	6	1	0	.167	0	3	0	0	0.3	1.000
3 yrs.		14	21	.400	3.56	68	27	5	262.2	259	97	122	1	7	7	1	77	11	0	.143	16	44	1	8	0.9	.984

Bill Burns

BURNS, WILLIAM THOMAS (Sleepy Bill) BB TL 6′ 2″ 195 lbs.
B. Jan. 29, 1880, San Saba, Tex. D. June 6, 1953, Ramona, Calif.

Year	Team	W	L	PCT	ERA	G	GS	CG	IP	H	BB	SO	ShO	Relief Pitching W	Relief Pitching L	Relief Pitching SV	Batting AB	Batting H	Batting HR	BA	PO	A	E	DP	TC/G	FA
1908	WAS A	6	11	.353	1.69	23	19	11	165	135	18	55	2	0	1	0	54	8	0	.148	2	69	6	2	3.3	.922
1909	2 teams WAS A (6G 1–1) CHI A (22G 7–13)																									
″	total	8	14	.364	1.86	28	23	9	203.2	194	42	65	3	1	1	0	69	12	0	.174	6	74	7	0	3.1	.920
1910	2 teams CHI A (1G 0–0) CIN N (31G 8–13)																									
″	total	8	13	.381	3.47	32	21	13	179	183	50	57	2	0	3	0	61	16	0	.262	3	57	6	2	2.1	.909
1911	2 teams CIN N (6G 1–0) PHI N (21G 6–10)																									
″	total	7	10	.412	3.38	27	17	8	138.2	149	29	52	3	1	2	1	47	9	0	.191	6	46	3	3	2.0	.945
1912	DET A	1	4	.200	5.35	6	5	2	38.2	52	9	6	0	0	0	0	13	3	0	.231	1	12	2	1	2.5	.867
5 yrs.		30	52	.366	2.69	116	85	43	725	713	148	235	10	2	7	1	244	48	0	.197	18	258	24	8	2.6	.920

Britt Burns

BURNS, ROBERT BRITT BL TL 6′ 5″ 215 lbs.
B. June 8, 1959, Houston, Tex.

Year	Team	Lg	W	L	PCT	ERA	G	GS	CG	IP	H	BB	SO	ShO	Relief W	Relief L	Relief SV	Batting AB	Batting H	HR	BA	PO	A	E	DP	TC/G	FA
1978	**CHI**	**A**	0	2	.000	12.91	2	2	0	7.2	14	3	3	0	0	0	0	0	0	0	—	0	2	0	0	1.0	1.000
1979			0	0	—	5.40	6	0	0	5	10	1	2	0	0	0	0	0	0	0	—	0	0	0	0	0.0	.000
1980			15	13	.536	2.84	34	32	11	238	213	63	133	1	1	0	0	0	0	0	—	6	34	1	0	1.2	.976
1981			10	6	.625	2.64	24	23	5	157	139	49	108	1	0	0	0	0	0	0	—	0	8	1	0	0.4	.889
1982			13	5	.722	4.04	28	28	5	169.1	168	67	116	1	0	0	0	0	0	0	—	2	14	2	0	0.6	.889
1983			10	11	.476	3.58	29	26	8	173.2	165	55	115	4	1	0	0	0	0	0	—	1	15	1	1	0.6	.941
1984			4	12	.250	5.00	34	16	2	117	130	45	85	0	1	2	3	0	0	0	—	2	17	2	0	0.6	.905
1985			18	11	.621	3.96	36	34	8	227	206	79	172	4	1	0	0	0	0	0	—	6	27	2	0	1.0	.943
8 yrs.			70	60	.538	3.66	193	161	39	1094.2	1045	362	734	11	4	2	3	0	0	0		17	117	9	1	0.7	.937
LEAGUE CHAMPIONSHIP SERIES																											
1983	**CHI**	**A**	0	1	.000	0.96	1	1	0	9.1	6	5	8	0	0	0	0	0	0	0	—	0	2	0	0	2.0	1.000

Denny Burns

BURNS, DENNIS BR TR 5′10″ 180 lbs.
B. May 24, 1898, Tiff City, Mo. D. May 21, 1969, Tulsa, Okla.

Year	Team	Lg	W	L	PCT	ERA	G	GS	CG	IP	H	BB	SO	ShO	Relief W	Relief L	Relief SV	Batting AB	Batting H	HR	BA	PO	A	E	DP	TC/G	FA
1923	**PHI**	**A**	2	1	.667	2.00	4	3	2	27	21	7	8	0	0	0	0	9	1	0	.111	0	6	0	0	1.5	1.000
1924			6	8	.429	5.08	37	17	7	154	191	68	26	0	0	1	1	42	6	0	.143	4	37	1	4	1.1	.976
2 yrs.			8	9	.471	4.62	41	20	9	181	212	75	34	0	0	1	1	51	7	0	.137	4	43	1	4	1.2	.979

Dick Burns

BURNS, RICHARD SIMON BB TL 5′ 7″ 140 lbs.
B. Dec. 26, 1863, Holyoke, Mass. D. Nov. 16, 1937, Holyoke, Mass.

Year	Team	Lg	W	L	PCT	ERA	G	GS	CG	IP	H	BB	SO	ShO	Relief W	Relief L	Relief SV	Batting AB	Batting H	HR	BA	PO	A	E	DP	TC/G	FA
1883	**DET**	**N**	2	12	.143	*4.51*	17	13	13	127.2	172	33	30	0	0	1	0	140	26	0	.186	22	32	14	2	1.7	.794
1884	**CIN**	**U**	23	15	.605	*2.46*	40	40	34	329.2	298	47	167	1	0	0	0	350	107	4	.306	87	81	26	1	2.3	.866
1885	**STL**	**N**	0	0	—	9.00	1	0	0	3	3	0	2	0	0	0	0	54	12	0	.222	13	5	7	1	1.7	.720
3 yrs.			25	27	.481	3.07	58	53	47	460.1	473	80	199	1	0	1	0	*				122	118	47	4	2.0	.836

Farmer Burns

BURNS, JAMES (Slab) TR 5′ 7″ 168 lbs.
B. Ashtabula, Ohio Deceased.

Year	Team	Lg	W	L	PCT	ERA	G	GS	CG	IP	H	BB	SO	ShO	Relief W	Relief L	Relief SV	Batting AB	Batting H	HR	BA	PO	A	E	DP	TC/G	FA
1901	**STL**	**N**	0	0	—	9.00	1	0	0	1	2	1	0	0	0	0	0	0	0	0	—	0	0	0	0	0.0	.000

Oyster Burns

BURNS, THOMAS P. BR TR 5′ 8″ 183 lbs.
B. Sept. 6, 1864, Philadelphia, Pa. D. Nov. 11, 1928, Brooklyn, N. Y.

Year	Team	Lg	W	L	PCT	ERA	G	GS	CG	IP	H	BB	SO	ShO	Relief W	Relief L	Relief SV	Batting AB	Batting H	HR	BA	PO	A	E	DP	TC/G	FA
1884	**BAL**	**AA**	0	0	—	*3.00*	2	0	0	9	12	2	6	0	0	0	**1**	138	40	6	.290	51	41	15	2	2.7	.860
1885			7	4	.636	*3.58*	15	11	10	105.2	112	21	30	1	0	0	**3**	321	74	5	.231	121	83	27	12	2.8	.883
1887			1	0	1.000	*9.53*	3	0	0	11.1	16	4	2	0	**1**	0	0	551	188	9	.341	205	326	101	23	4.4	.840
1888			0	1	.000	4.26	5	0	0	12.2	12	3	2	0	0	**1**	0	529	155	6	.293	226	182	69	16	3.4	.855
4 yrs.			8	5	.615	4.09	25	11	10	138.2	152	30	40	1	1	1	4	*				1736	870	336	91	2.4	.886

Todd Burns

BURNS, TODD EDWARD BR TR 6′ 2″ 186 lbs.
B. July 6, 1963, Maywood, Calif.

Year	Team	Lg	W	L	PCT	ERA	G	GS	CG	IP	H	BB	SO	ShO	Relief W	Relief L	Relief SV	Batting AB	Batting H	HR	BA	PO	A	E	DP	TC/G	FA
1988	**OAK**	**A**	8	2	.800	3.16	17	14	2	102.2	93	34	57	0	1	0	1	0	0	0	—	3	11	0	1	0.8	1.000
1989			6	5	.545	2.24	50	2	0	96.1	66	28	49	0	5	5	8	0	0	0	—	9	9	3	1	0.4	.857
1990			3	3	.500	2.97	43	2	0	78.2	78	32	43	0	2	3	3	0	0	0	—	2	7	0	1	0.2	1.000
1991			1	0	1.000	3.38	9	0	0	13.1	10	8	3	0	1	0	0	0	0	0	—	3	2	0	0	0.6	1.000
1992	**TEX**	**A**	3	5	.375	3.84	35	10	0	103	97	32	55	0	1	1	1	0	0	0	—	5	8	1	1	0.4	.929
1993	**2 teams**	**TEX A**	(25G 0–4)		**STL N**	(24G 0–4)																					
″	**total**		0	8	.000	5.08	49	5	0	95.2	95	41	45	0	0	4	0	3	0	0	.000	7	5	2	1	0.3	.857
6 yrs.			21	23	.477	3.47	203	33	2	489.2	439	175	252	0	10	13	13	3	0	0	.000	29	42	6	5	0.4	.922
WORLD SERIES																											
1988	**OAK**	**A**	0	0	—	0.00	1	0	0	0.1	0	0	0	0	0	0	0	0	0	0	—	0	0	0	0	0.0	.000
1989			0	0	—	0.00	2	0	0	1.2	1	1	0	0	0	0	0	0	0	0	—	0	0	0	0	0.0	.000
1990			0	0	—	16.20	2	0	0	1.2	5	2	0	0	0	0	0	0	0	0	—	0	0	0	0	0.0	.000
3 yrs.			0	0		7.36	5	0	0	3.2	6	3	0	0	0	0	0	0	0	0		0	0	0	0	0.0	

Tom Burns

BURNS, THOMAS EVERETT BR TR 5′ 7″ 152 lbs.
B. Mar. 30, 1857, Honesdale, Pa. D. Mar. 19, 1902, Jersey City, N. J.
Manager 1892, 1898–99.

Year	Team	Lg	W	L	PCT	ERA	G	GS	CG	IP	H	BB	SO	ShO	Relief W	Relief L	Relief SV	Batting AB	Batting H	HR	BA	PO	A	E	DP	TC/G	FA
1880	**CHI**	**N**	0	0	—	0.00	1	0	0	1.1	2	2	1	0	0	0	0	*				73	202	46	9	3.5	.857

Pete Burnside

BURNSIDE, PETER WILLITS BR TL 6′ 2″ 180 lbs.
B. July 2, 1930, Evanston, Ill.

Year	Team	Lg	W	L	PCT	ERA	G	GS	CG	IP	H	BB	SO	ShO	Relief W	Relief L	Relief SV	Batting AB	Batting H	HR	BA	PO	A	E	DP	TC/G	FA
1955	**NY**	**N**	1	0	1.000	2.84	2	2	1	12.2	10	9	2	0	0	0	0	5	1	0	.200	0	2	0	1	1.0	1.000
1957			1	4	.200	8.80	10	9	1	30.2	47	13	18	1	0	1	0	9	0	0	.000	1	5	1	0	0.7	.857
1958	**SF**	**N**	0	0	—	6.75	6	1	0	10.2	20	5	4	0	0	0	0	0	0	0	—	0	2	0	0	0.3	1.000
1959	**DET**	**A**	1	3	.250	3.77	30	0	0	62	55	25	49	0	1	3	1	10	0	0	.000	3	11	0	1	0.5	1.000
1960			7	7	.500	4.28	31	15	2	113.2	122	50	71	0	3	1	2	27	4	0	.148	3	14	1	1	0.6	.944
1961	**WAS**	**A**	4	9	.308	4.53	33	16	4	113.1	106	51	56	2	0	0	2	34	2	0	.059	2	17	2	1	0.6	.905
1962			5	11	.313	4.45	40	20	6	149.2	152	51	74	0	0	1	2	35	2	0	.057	11	16	2	0	0.7	.931
1963	**2 teams**	**BAL A**	(6G 0–1)		**WAS A**	(38G 0–1)																					
″	**total**		0	2	.000	6.03	44	1	0	74.2	95	26	29	0	0	1	0	12	1	0	.083	1	7	1	1	0.2	.889
8 yrs.			19	36	.345	4.81	196	64	14	567.1	607	230	303	3	4	7	7	132	10	0	.076	21	74	7	5	0.5	.931

Sheldon Burnside

BURNSIDE, SHELDON JOHN BR TL 6′ 5″ 200 lbs.
B. Dec. 22, 1954, South Bend, Ind.

Year	Team	Lg	W	L	PCT	ERA	G	GS	CG	IP	H	BB	SO	ShO	Relief W	Relief L	Relief SV	Batting AB	Batting H	HR	BA	PO	A	E	DP	TC/G	FA
1978	**DET**	**A**	0	0	—	9.00	2	0	0	4	4	2	3	0	0	0	0	0	0	0	—	0	0	0	0	0.0	.000
1979			1	1	.500	6.43	10	0	0	21	28	8	13	0	1	1	0	0	0	0	—	0	4	0	1	0.4	1.000
1980	**CIN**	**N**	1	0	1.000	1.80	7	0	0	5	6	1	2	0	1	0	0	1	0	0	.000	0	4	0	0	0.6	1.000
3 yrs.			2	1	.667	6.00	19	0	0	30	38	11	18	0	2	1	0	1	0	0	.000	0	8	0	1	0.4	1.000

George Burpo

BURPO, GEORGE HARVIE BR TL 6′ 195 lbs.
B. June 19, 1922, Jenkins, Ky.

Year	Team	Lg	W	L	PCT	ERA	G	GS	CG	IP	H	BB	SO	ShO	Relief W	Relief L	Relief SV	Batting AB	Batting H	HR	BA	PO	A	E	DP	TC/G	FA
1946	**CIN**	**N**	0	0	—	15.43	2	0	0	2.1	4	5	1	0	0	0	0	0	0	0	—	0	0	0	0	0.0	.000

Harry Burrell

BURRELL, HARRY J.
B. May 26, 1869, Bethel, Vt. D. Dec. 11, 1914, Omaha, Neb.

Year	Team	Lg	W	L	PCT	ERA	G	GS	CG	IP	H	BB	SO	ShO	Relief Pitching W	L	SV	Batting AB	H	HR	BA	PO	A	E	DP	TC/G	FA
1891	STL	AA	4	2	.667	4.81	7	4	3	43	51	21	19	0	2	0	1	20	4	0	.200	3	10	2	0	1.9	.867

Al Burris

BURRIS, ALVA BURTON BR TR
B. Jan. 28, 1874, Warwick, Md. D. Mar. 24, 1938, Salisbury, Md.

Year	Team	Lg	W	L	PCT	ERA	G	GS	CG	IP	H	BB	SO	ShO	Relief Pitching W	L	SV	Batting AB	H	HR	BA	PO	A	E	DP	TC/G	FA
1894	PHI	N	0	0	—	18.00	1	0	0	5	14	2	0	0	0	0	0	4	2	0	.500	0	1	0	0	1.0	1.000

Ray Burris

BURRIS, BERTRAM RAY BR TR 6′ 5″ 200 lbs.
B. Aug. 22, 1950, Idabel, Okla.

Year	Team	Lg	W	L	PCT	ERA	G	GS	CG	IP	H	BB	SO	ShO	Relief Pitching W	L	SV	Batting AB	H	HR	BA	PO	A	E	DP	TC/G	FA
1973	CHI	N	1	1	.500	2.91	31	1	0	65	65	27	57	0	0	1	0	7	1	0	.143	0	14	1	2	0.5	.933
1974			3	5	.375	6.60	40	5	0	75	91	26	40	0	3	1	1	13	1	0	.077	4	9	0	0	0.3	1.000
1975			15	10	.600	4.12	36	35	8	238	259	73	108	2	0	0	0	82	15	0	.183	16	16	2	0	0.9	.941
1976			15	13	.536	3.11	37	36	10	249	251	70	112	4	0	0	0	81	9	0	.111	15	42	5	3	1.7	.919
1977			14	16	.467	4.72	39	39	5	221	270	67	105	1	0	0	0	69	12	1	.174	16	46	1	1	1.6	.984
1978			7	13	.350	4.75	40	32	4	199	210	79	94	1	1	1	1	61	7	0	.115	23	38	4	2	1.6	.938
1979	3 teams	CHI N (14G 0–0) NY A (15G 1–3) NY N (4G 0–2)																									
″	total		1	5	.167	5.30	33	4	0	71.1	84	31	43	0	1	3	0	7	1	0	.143	9	10	1	0	0.6	.950
1980	NY	N	7	13	.350	4.02	29	29	1	170	181	54	83	0	0	0	0	51	5	0	.098	13	22	2	1	1.3	.946
1981	MON	N	9	7	.563	3.04	22	21	4	136	117	41	52	0	0	0	0	37	7	0	.189	8	17	3	2	1.3	.893
1982			4	14	.222	4.73	37	15	2	123.2	143	53	55	0	4	3	2	28	5	0	.179	11	16	2	1	0.8	.931
1983			4	7	.364	3.68	40	17	2	154	139	56	100	1	1	2	0	39	9	0	.231	12	23	0	1	0.9	1.000
1984	OAK	A	13	10	.565	3.15	34	28	5	211.2	193	90	93	1	1	0	0	0	0	0	—	5	16	0	2	0.6	1.000
1985	MIL	A	9	13	.409	4.81	29	28	6	170.1	182	53	81	0	0	0	0	0	0	0	—	18	19	2	0	1.3	.949
1986	STL	N	4	5	.444	5.60	23	10	0	82	92	32	34	0	0	1	0	27	4	0	.148	4	9	0	1	0.6	1.000
1987	MIL	A	2	2	.500	5.87	10	2	0	23	33	12	8	0	1	1	0	0	0	0	—	3	3	0	0	0.6	1.000
15 yrs.			108	134	.446	4.17	480	302	47	2189	2310	764	1065	10	12	13	4	502	76	1	.151	157	300	23	16	1.0	.952
DIVISIONAL PLAYOFF SERIES																											
1981	MON	N	0	1	.000	5.06	1	1	0	5.1	7	4	4	0	0	0	0	2	0	0	.000	0	0	0	0	0.0	.000
LEAGUE CHAMPIONSHIP SERIES																											
1981	MON	N	1	0	1.000	0.53	2	2	1	17	10	3	4	1 1st	0	0	0	6	0	0	.000	0	1	0	0	0.5	1.000

John Burrows

BURROWS, JOHN BR TL 5′10″ 200 lbs.
B. Oct. 30, 1913, Winnfield, La. D. Apr. 27, 1987, Coal Run, Ohio.

Year	Team	Lg	W	L	PCT	ERA	G	GS	CG	IP	H	BB	SO	ShO	Relief Pitching W	L	SV	Batting AB	H	HR	BA	PO	A	E	DP	TC/G	FA
1943	2 teams	PHI A (4G 0–1) CHI N (23G 0–2)																									
″	total		0	3	.000	4.69	27	2	0	40.1	33	25	21	0	0	1	2	4	2	0	.500	0	9	1	2	0.4	.900
1944	CHI	N	0	0	—	18.00	3	0	0	3	7	3	1	0	0	0	0	0	0	0	—	0	1	1	0	0.7	.500
2 yrs.			0	3	.000	5.61	30	2	0	43.1	40	28	22	0	0	1	2	4	2	0	.500	0	10	2	2	0.4	.833

Terry Burrows

BURROWS, TERRY DALE BL TL 6′ 1″ 185 lbs.
B. Nov. 28, 1968, Lake Charles, La.

Year	Team	Lg	W	L	PCT	ERA	G	GS	CG	IP	H	BB	SO	ShO	Relief Pitching W	L	SV	Batting AB	H	HR	BA	PO	A	E	DP	TC/G	FA
1994	TEX	A	0	0	—	9.00	1	0	0	1	1	1	0	0	0	0	0	0	0	0	—	0	0	0	0	0.0	.000
1995			2	2	.500	6.45	28	3	0	44.2	60	19	22	0	2	2	1	0	0	0	—	3	4	0	0	0.3	1.000
2 yrs.			2	2	.500	6.50	29	3	0	45.2	61	20	22	0	2	2	1	0	0	0		3	4	0	0	0.2	1.000

Jim Burton

BURTON, JIM SCOTT BR TL 6′ 3″ 195 lbs.
B. Oct. 27, 1949, Royal Oak, Mich.

Year	Team	Lg	W	L	PCT	ERA	G	GS	CG	IP	H	BB	SO	ShO	Relief Pitching W	L	SV	Batting AB	H	HR	BA	PO	A	E	DP	TC/G	FA
1975	BOS	A	1	2	.333	2.89	29	4	0	53	58	19	39	0	1	0	1	0	0	0	—	2	7	0	1	0.3	1.000
1977			0	0	—	0.00	1	0	0	2.2	2	1	3	0	0	0	0	0	0	0	—	0	0	0	0	0.0	.000
2 yrs.			1	2	.333	2.75	30	4	0	55.2	60	20	42	0	1	0	1	0	0	0		2	7	0	1	0.3	1.000
WORLD SERIES																											
1975	BOS	A	0	1	.000	9.00	2	0	0	1	1	3	0	0	0	1	0	0	0	0	—	0	0	0	0	0.0	.000

Moe Burtschy

BURTSCHY, EDWARD FRANK BR TR 6′ 3″ 208 lbs.
B. Apr. 18, 1922, Cincinnati, Ohio.

Year	Team	Lg	W	L	PCT	ERA	G	GS	CG	IP	H	BB	SO	ShO	Relief Pitching W	L	SV	Batting AB	H	HR	BA	PO	A	E	DP	TC/G	FA
1950	PHI	A	0	1	.000	7.11	9	1	0	19	22	21	12	0	0	0	0	5	0	0	.000	3	2	0	0	0.6	1.000
1951			0	0	—	5.29	7	0	0	17	18	12	4	0	0	0	0	3	1	0	.333	3	2	0	0	0.7	1.000
1954			5	4	.556	3.80	46	0	0	94.2	80	53	54	0	5	4	4	17	2	0	.118	7	15	3	2	0.5	.880
1955	KC	A	2	0	1.000	10.32	7	0	0	11.1	17	10	9	0	2	0	0	3	1	0	.333	0	0	0	0	0.0	.000
1956			3	1	.750	3.95	21	0	0	43.1	41	30	18	0	3	1	0	8	1	0	.125	2	15	0	2	0.8	1.000
5 yrs.			10	6	.625	4.71	90	1	0	185.1	178	126	97	0	10	5	4	36	5	0	.139	15	34	3	4	0.6	.942

Dennis Burtt

BURTT, DENNIS ALLEN BB TR 6′ 187 lbs.
B. Nov. 29, 1957, San Diego, Calif.

Year	Team	Lg	W	L	PCT	ERA	G	GS	CG	IP	H	BB	SO	ShO	Relief Pitching W	L	SV	Batting AB	H	HR	BA	PO	A	E	DP	TC/G	FA
1985	MIN	A	2	2	.500	3.81	5	2	0	28.1	20	7	9	0	0	2	0	0	0	0	—	1	5	0	1	1.2	1.000
1986			0	0	—	31.50	3	0	0	2	7	3	1	0	0	0	0	0	0	0	—	0	0	0	0	0.0	.000
2 yrs.			2	2	.500	5.64	8	2	0	30.1	27	10	10	0	0	2	0	0	0	0		1	5	0	1	0.8	1.000

Bill Burwell

BURWELL, WILLIAM EDWIN BL TR 5′11″ 175 lbs.
B. Mar. 27, 1895, Jarbalo, Kans. D. June 11, 1973, Ormond Beach, Fla.
Manager 1947.

Year	Team	Lg	W	L	PCT	ERA	G	GS	CG	IP	H	BB	SO	ShO	Relief Pitching W	L	SV	Batting AB	H	HR	BA	PO	A	E	DP	TC/G	FA
1920	STL	A	6	4	.600	3.65	33	2	0	113.1	133	42	30	0	**6**	3	4	42	7	0	.167	14	24	2	1	1.2	.950
1921			2	4	.333	5.12	33	3	1	84.1	102	29	17	0	1	3	2	25	6	0	.240	3	20	3	0	0.8	.885
1928	PIT	N	1	0	1.000	5.23	4	1	0	20.2	18	8	2	0	1	0	0	9	2	0	.222	1	8	1	0	2.5	.900
3 yrs.			9	8	.529	4.37	70	6	1	218.1	253	79	49	0	8	6	6	76	15	0	.197	18	52	6	1	1.1	.921

Dick Burwell

BURWELL, RICHARD MATTHEW BR TR 6′ 1″ 190 lbs.
B. Jan. 23, 1940, Alton, Ill.

Year	Team	Lg	W	L	PCT	ERA	G	GS	CG	IP	H	BB	SO	ShO	Relief Pitching W	L	SV	Batting AB	H	HR	BA	PO	A	E	DP	TC/G	FA
1960	CHI	N	0	0	—	5.59	3	1	0	9.2	11	7	1	0	0	0	0	3	1	0	.333	1	1	0	1	0.7	1.000
1961			0	0	—	9.00	2	0	0	4	6	4	0	0	0	0	0	1	0	0	.000	0	2	0	0	1.0	1.000
2 yrs.			0	0		6.59	5	1	0	13.2	17	11	1	0	0	0	0	4	1	0	.250	1	3	0	1	0.8	1.000

Steve Busby

BUSBY, STEVEN LEE
B. Sept. 29, 1949, Burbank, Calif.
BR TR 6′ 2″ 205 lbs.

Year	Team	W	L	PCT	ERA	G	GS	CG	IP	H	BB	SO	ShO	Relief Pitching W	Relief Pitching L	Relief Pitching SV	Batting AB	Batting H	HR	BA	PO	A	E	DP	TC/G	FA
1972	KC A	3	1	.750	1.58	5	5	3	40	28	8	31	0	0	0	0	15	3	0	.200	1	4	1	0	1.2	.833
1973		16	15	.516	4.24	37	37	7	238	246	105	174	1	0	0	0	0	0	0	—	10	47	6	3	1.7	.905
1974		22	14	.611	3.39	38	38	20	292.1	284	92	198	3	0	0	0	0	0	0	—	24	53	8	2	2.2	.906
1975		18	12	.600	3.08	34	34	18	260.1	233	81	160	3	0	0	0	0	0	0	—	22	52	3	2	2.3	.961
1976		3	3	.500	4.38	13	13	1	72	58	49	29	0	0	0	0	0	0	0	—	10	9	3	0	1.7	.864
1978		1	0	1.000	7.59	7	5	0	21.1	24	15	10	0	0	0	0	0	0	0	—	0	5	1	0	0.9	.833
1979		6	6	.500	3.64	22	12	4	94	71	64	45	0	1	2	0	0	0	0	—	4	24	0	1	1.3	1.000
1980		1	3	.250	6.21	11	6	0	42	59	19	12	0	0	0	0	0	0	0	—	5	4	1	0	0.9	.900
8 yrs.		70	54	.565	3.72	167	150	53	1060	1003	433	659	7	1	2	0	15	3	0	.200	76	198	23	8	1.8	.923

Don Buschhorn

BUSCHHORN, DONALD LEE
B. Apr. 29, 1946, Independence, Mo.
BL TR 6′ 170 lbs.

Year	Team	W	L	PCT	ERA	G	GS	CG	IP	H	BB	SO	ShO	Relief Pitching W	Relief Pitching L	Relief Pitching SV	Batting AB	Batting H	HR	BA	PO	A	E	DP	TC/G	FA
1965	KC A	0	1	.000	4.35	12	3	0	31	36	8	9	0	0	0	0	4	2	0	.500	2	5	0	0	0.6	1.000

Guy Bush

BUSH, GUY TERRELL (The Mississippi Mudcat)
B. Aug. 23, 1901, Aberdeen, Miss. D. July 2, 1985, Shannon, Miss.
BR TR 6′ 175 lbs.

Year	Team	W	L	PCT	ERA	G	GS	CG	IP	H	BB	SO	ShO	Relief Pitching W	Relief Pitching L	Relief Pitching SV	Batting AB	Batting H	HR	BA	PO	A	E	DP	TC/G	FA
1923	CHI N	0	0	—	0.00	1	0	0	1	1	0	2	0	0	0	0	0	0	0	—	0	0	0	0	0.0	.000
1924		2	5	.286	4.02	16	8	4	80.2	91	24	36	0	0	1	0	26	4	0	.154	1	9	1	1	0.7	.909
1925		6	13	.316	4.30	42	15	5	182	213	52	76	0	4	2	**4**	57	11	0	.193	2	61	4	3	1.6	.940
1926		13	9	.591	2.86	35	16	7	157.1	149	42	32	2	**6**	2	2	48	8	0	.167	4	39	2	1	1.3	.956
1927		10	10	.500	3.03	36	22	9	193.1	177	79	62	1	3	0	2	65	8	0	.123	9	41	1	4	1.4	.980
1928		15	6	.714	3.83	42	24	9	204.1	229	86	61	2	4	0	2	73	6	0	.082	5	46	2	2	1.3	.962
1929		18	7	.720	3.66	**50**	29	18	270.2	277	107	82	2	2	1	**8**	91	15	0	.165	10	60	1	6	1.4	.986
1930		15	10	.600	6.20	46	25	11	225	291	86	75	0	3	2	3	78	22	0	.282	21	46	1	3	1.5	.985
1931		16	8	.667	4.49	39	24	14	180.1	190	66	54	1	4	0	2	57	7	0	.123	10	55	4	7	1.8	.942
1932		19	11	.633	3.21	40	30	15	238.2	262	70	73	1	4	2	0	84	15	0	.179	22	50	3	10	1.9	.960
1933		20	12	.625	2.75	41	32	20	258.2	261	68	84	4	1	1	2	88	11	0	.125	18	72	1	2	2.2	.989
1934		18	10	.643	3.83	40	27	15	209.1	213	54	75	1	3	1	2	70	16	0	.229	13	46	1	3	1.5	.983
1935	PIT N	11	11	.500	4.32	41	25	8	204.1	237	40	42	1	**5**	1	2	63	8	0	.127	9	41	0	2	1.2	1.000
1936	2 teams PIT N (16G 1–3) BOS N (15G 4–5)																									
″	total	5	8	.385	4.10	31	11	5	125	147	31	38	0	2	3	2	34	6	0	.176	6	32	0	2	1.2	1.000
1937	BOS N	8	15	.348	3.54	32	20	11	180.2	201	48	56	1	2	3	1	54	6	0	.111	8	45	0	1	1.7	1.000
1938	STL N	0	1	.000	5.06	6	0	0	5.1	6	3	1	0	0	1	1	0	0	0	—	0	0	0	0	0.0	.000
1945	CIN N	0	0	—	8.31	4	0	0	4.1	5	3	1	0	0	0	1	0	0	0	—	0	0	0	0	0.0	.000
17 yrs.		176	136	.564	3.86	542	308	151	2721	2950	859	850	16	43	20	34	888	143	0	.161	138	643	21	47	1.5	.974
WORLD SERIES																										
1929	CHI N	1	0	1.000	0.82	2	1	1	11	12	2	4	0	0	0	0	3	0	0	.000	0	3	0	0	1.5	1.000
1932		0	1	.000	14.29	2	2	0	5.2	5	6	2	0	0	0	0	1	0	0	.000	0	2	0	0	1.0	1.000
2 yrs.		1	1	.500	5.40	4	3	1	16.2	17	8	6	0	0	0	0	4	0	0	.000	0	5	0	0	1.3	1.000

Joe Bush

BUSH, LESLIE AMBROSE (Bullet Joe)
B. Nov. 27, 1892, Brainerd, Minn. D. Nov. 1, 1974, Ft. Lauderdale, Fla.
BR TR 5′ 9″ 173 lbs.

Year	Team	W	L	PCT	ERA	G	GS	CG	IP	H	BB	SO	ShO	Relief Pitching W	Relief Pitching L	Relief Pitching SV	Batting AB	Batting H	HR	BA	PO	A	E	DP	TC/G	FA
1912	PHI A	0	0	—	7.88	1	1	0	8	14	4	3	0	0	0	0	4	2	0	.500	1	1	1	1	3.0	.667
1913		15	6	.714	3.82	39	15	5	200.1	199	66	81	1	**8**	1	3	70	11	0	.157	15	75	2	4	2.4	.978
1914		16	12	.571	3.06	38	22	14	206	184	81	109	2	4	2	3	74	14	1	.189	8	55	3	1	1.7	.955
1915		5	15	.250	4.14	25	18	8	145.2	137	89	89	0	1	3	0	49	7	0	.143	7	39	3	3	2.0	.939
1916		15	**24**	.385	2.57	40	33	25	286.2	222	130	157	8	1	5	0	100	14	0	.140	19	94	6	8	3.0	.950
1917		11	17	.393	2.47	37	31	17	233.1	207	111	121	4	1	0	2	80	16	0	.200	20	61	6	0	2.4	.931
1918	BOS A	15	15	.500	2.11	36	31	26	272.2	241	91	125	7	0	0	2	98	27	0	.276	16	81	2	5	2.8	.980
1919		0	0	—	5.00	3	2	0	9	11	4	3	0	0	0	0	5	2	0	.400	0	2	0	1	0.7	1.000
1920		15	15	.500	4.25	35	32	18	243.2	287	94	88	0	1	0	1	102	25	0	.245	25	66	4	7	2.6	.958
1921		16	9	.640	3.50	37	32	20	254.1	244	93	96	3	0	0	1	120	39	0	.325	15	64	1	0	2.0	.988
1922	NY A	26	7	**.788**	3.31	39	30	20	255.1	240	85	92	0	4	1	3	95	31	0	.326	16	61	0	4	2.0	1.000
1923		19	15	.559	3.43	37	30	23	275.2	263	117	125	3	2	2	0	113	31	2	.274	15	74	3	3	2.5	.967
1924		17	16	.515	3.57	39	31	19	252	262	**109**	80	3	1	**5**	1	124	42	1	.339	24	60	1	4	2.2	.988
1925	STL A	14	14	.500	4.97	33	30	15	213.2	239	91	63	2	2	1	0	102	26	2	.255	17	54	0	5	2.1	1.000
1926	2 teams WAS A (12G 1–8) PIT N (19G 6–6)																									
″	total	7	14	.333	4.45	31	22	12	182	180	70	65	2	0	1	3	79	20	1	.253	9	39	2	3	1.6	.960
1927	2 teams PIT N (5G 1–2) NY N (3G 1–1)																									
″	total	2	3	.400	9.64	8	5	1	18.2	32	10	7	0	1	0	0	9	5	0	.556	0	4	0	0	0.5	1.000
1928	PHI A	2	1	.667	5.09	11	2	1	35.1	39	18	15	0	1	0	1	15	1	0	.067	5	10	0	1	1.3	1.000
17 yrs.		195	183	.516	3.51	489	367	224	3092.1	3001	1263	1319	35	27	21	20	*				212	840	34	50	2.2	.969
WORLD SERIES																										
1913	PHI A	1	0	1.000	1.00	1	1	1	9	5	4	3	0	0	0	0	4	1	0	.250	0	1	0	1	1.0	1.000
1914		0	1	.000	3.27	1	1	1	11	9	4	4	0	0	0	0	5	0	0	.000	0	5	1	0	6.0	.833
1918	BOS A	0	1	.000	3.00	2	1	1	9	7	3	0	0	0	0	1	2	0	0	.000	0	3	0	0	1.5	1.000
1922	NY A	0	2	.000	4.80	2	2	1	15	21	5	6	0	0	0	0	6	1	0	.167	1	3	0	2	2.0	1.000
1923		1	1	.500	1.08	3	1	1	16.2	7	4	5	0	0	1	0	7	3	0	.429	2	3	0	0	1.7	1.000
5 yrs.		2	5 (2nd)	.286	2.67	9	6	5	60.2	49	20	18	0	0	1	1	*				3	15	1	3	2.1	.947

Jack Bushelman

BUSHELMAN, JOHN FRANCIS
B. Aug. 29, 1885, Cincinnati, Ohio D. Oct. 26, 1955, Roanoke, Va.
BR TR 6′ 2″ 175 lbs.

Year	Team	W	L	PCT	ERA	G	GS	CG	IP	H	BB	SO	ShO	Relief Pitching W	Relief Pitching L	Relief Pitching SV	Batting AB	Batting H	HR	BA	PO	A	E	DP	TC/G	FA
1909	CIN N	0	1	.000	2.57	1	1	1	7	7	4	3	0	0	0	0	1	0	0	.000	0	0	0	0	0.0	.000
1911	BOS A	0	1	.000	3.00	3	1	1	12	8	10	5	0	0	0	0	3	0	0	.000	1	2	1	0	1.3	.750
1912		1	0	1.000	4.70	3	0	0	7.2	9	5	5	0	1	0	0	3	0	0	.000	0	4	1	0	1.7	.800
3 yrs.		1	2	.333	3.38	7	2	2	26.2	24	19	13	0	1	0	0	7	0	0	.000	1	6	2	0	1.3	.778

Frank Bushey

BUSHEY, FRANCIS CLYDE BR TR 6′ 180 lbs.
B. Aug. 1, 1906, Wheaton, Kans. D. Mar. 18, 1972, Topeka, Kans.

Year	Team	W	L	PCT	ERA	G	GS	CG	IP	H	BB	SO	ShO	Relief Pitching W	Relief Pitching L	Relief Pitching SV	Batting AB	Batting H	Batting HR	BA	PO	A	E	DP	TC/G	FA
1927	BOS A	0	0	—	6.75	1	0	0	1.1	2	2	0	0	0	0	0	0	0	0	—	0	0	0	0	0.0	.000
1930		0	1	.000	6.30	11	0	0	30	34	15	4	0	0	1	0	9	1	0	.111	4	6	1	1	1.0	.909
2 yrs.		0	1	.000	6.32	12	0	0	31.1	36	17	4	0	0	1	0	9	1	0	.111	4	6	1	1	0.9	.909

Chris Bushing

BUSHING, CHRISTOPHER SHAUN BR TR 6′ 183 lbs.
B. Nov. 4, 1967, Rockville Centre, N. Y.

Year	Team	W	L	PCT	ERA	G	GS	CG	IP	H	BB	SO	ShO	Relief Pitching W	Relief Pitching L	Relief Pitching SV	Batting AB	Batting H	Batting HR	BA	PO	A	E	DP	TC/G	FA
1993	CIN N	0	0	—	12.46	6	0	0	4.1	9	4	3	0	0	0	0	0	0	0	—	0	0	0	0	0.0	.000

Tom Buskey

BUSKEY, THOMAS WILLIAM BR TR 6′ 3″ 200 lbs.
B. Feb. 20, 1947, Harrisburg, Pa.

Year	Team	W	L	PCT	ERA	G	GS	CG	IP	H	BB	SO	ShO	Relief Pitching W	Relief Pitching L	Relief Pitching SV	Batting AB	Batting H	Batting HR	BA	PO	A	E	DP	TC/G	FA
1973	NY A	0	1	.000	5.40	8	0	0	16.2	18	4	8	0	0	1	1	0	0	0	—	0	2	0	1	0.3	1.000
1974	2 teams NY A (4G 0–1) CLE A (51G 2–6)																									
″	total	2	7	.222	3.38	55	0	0	98.2	103	36	43	0	2	7	18	0	0	0		7	18	1	0	0.5	.962
1975	CLE A	5	3	.625	2.57	50	0	0	77	69	29	29	0	5	3	7	0	0	0	—	9	19	1	2	0.6	.966
1976		5	4	.556	3.64	39	0	0	94	88	34	32	0	5	4	1	0	0	0	—	4	18	0	2	0.6	1.000
1977		0	0	—	5.29	21	0	0	34	45	8	15	0	0	0	0	0	0	0	—	4	3	0	0	0.3	1.000
1978	TOR A	0	1	.000	3.38	8	0	0	13.1	14	4	7	0	0	1	0	0	0	0	—	0	5	0	0	0.6	1.000
1979		6	10	.375	3.42	44	0	0	79	74	25	44	0	6	10	7	0	0	0	—	5	19	1	1	0.6	.960
1980		3	1	.750	4.43	33	0	0	67	68	26	34	0	3	1	0	0	0	0	—	5	10	0	1	0.5	1.000
8 yrs.		21	27	.438	3.66	258	0	0	479.2	479	166	212	0	21	27	34	0	0	0		34	94	3	7	0.5	.977

John Butcher

BUTCHER, JOHN DANIEL BR TR 6′ 4″ 185 lbs.
B. Mar. 8, 1957, Glendale, Calif.

Year	Team	W	L	PCT	ERA	G	GS	CG	IP	H	BB	SO	ShO	Relief Pitching W	Relief Pitching L	Relief Pitching SV	Batting AB	Batting H	Batting HR	BA	PO	A	E	DP	TC/G	FA
1980	TEX A	3	3	.500	4.11	6	6	1	35	34	13	27	0	0	0	0	0	0	0	—	1	6	1	0	1.3	.875
1981		1	2	.333	1.61	5	3	1	28	18	8	19	1	0	0	0	0	0	0	—	3	5	0	0	1.6	1.000
1982		1	5	.167	4.87	18	13	2	94.1	102	34	39	0	0	0	1	0	0	0	—	7	19	0	3	1.4	1.000
1983		6	6	.500	3.51	36	6	1	123	128	41	58	1	3	4	5	0	0	0	—	11	17	0	0	0.8	1.000
1984	MIN A	13	11	.542	3.44	34	34	8	225	242	53	83	1	0	0	0	0	0	0	—	25	20	3	5	1.4	.938
1985		11	14	.440	4.98	34	33	8	207.2	239	43	92	2	0	0	0	0	0	0	—	24	27	2	2	1.6	.962
1986	2 teams MIN A (16G 0–3) CLE A (13G 1–5)																									
″	total	1	8	.111	6.56	29	18	2	120.2	168	37	45	1	0	1	0	0	0	0		9	15	3	2	0.9	.889
7 yrs.		36	49	.424	4.42	162	113	23	833.2	931	229	363	6	3	5	6	0	0	0		80	109	9	12	1.2	.955

Max Butcher

BUTCHER, ALBERT MAXWELL BR TR 6′ 2″ 220 lbs.
B. Sept. 21, 1910, Holden, W. Va. D. Sept. 15, 1957, Man, W. Va.

Year	Team	W	L	PCT	ERA	G	GS	CG	IP	H	BB	SO	ShO	Relief Pitching W	Relief Pitching L	Relief Pitching SV	Batting AB	Batting H	Batting HR	BA	PO	A	E	DP	TC/G	FA
1936	BKN N	6	6	.500	3.96	38	15	5	147.2	154	59	55	0	2	0	2	48	6	0	.125	5	25	2	1	0.8	.938
1937		11	15	.423	4.27	39	24	8	191.2	203	75	57	1	5	0	0	62	10	0	.161	17	53	1	4	1.8	.986
1938	2 teams BKN N (24G 5–4) PHI N (12G 4–8)																									
″	total	9	12	.429	4.47	36	20	14	171	198	70	50	1	1	2	2	60	13	1	.217	9	40	2	5	1.4	.961
1939	2 teams PHI N (19G 2–13) PIT N (14G 4–4)																									
″	total	6	**17**	.261	4.62	33	28	8	191	235	74	48	2	0	1	0	69	10	0	.145	3	41	0	2	1.3	1.000
1940	PIT N	8	9	.471	6.01	35	24	6	136.1	161	46	40	2	0	0	2	50	15	0	.300	5	34	2	2	1.2	.951
1941		17	12	.586	3.05	33	32	19	236	249	66	61	0	0	1	0	82	15	0	.183	17	48	0	2	2.0	1.000
1942		5	8	.385	2.93	24	18	9	150.2	144	44	49	0	0	0	1	49	7	0	.143	11	33	1	0	1.9	.978
1943		10	8	.556	2.60	33	21	10	193.2	191	57	45	2	1	0	1	61	10	0	.164	11	40	2	4	1.6	.962
1944		13	11	.542	3.12	35	27	13	199	216	46	43	5	1	0	1	63	12	0	.190	12	51	2	3	1.9	.969
1945		10	8	.556	3.03	28	20	12	169.1	184	46	37	2	2	0	0	54	12	0	.222	8	37	1	2	1.6	.978
10 yrs.		95	106	.473	3.73	334	229	104	1786.1	1935	583	485	15	12	4	9	598	110	1	.184	98	402	13	25	1.5	.975

Mike Butcher

BUTCHER, MICHAEL DANA BR TR 6′ 1″ 200 lbs.
B. May 10, 1965, Davenport, Iowa.

Year	Team	W	L	PCT	ERA	G	GS	CG	IP	H	BB	SO	ShO	Relief Pitching W	Relief Pitching L	Relief Pitching SV	Batting AB	Batting H	Batting HR	BA	PO	A	E	DP	TC/G	FA
1992	CAL A	2	2	.500	3.25	19	0	0	27.2	29	13	24	0	2	2	0	0	0	0	—	0	3	0	0	0.2	1.000
1993		1	0	1.000	2.86	23	0	0	28.1	21	15	24	0	1	0	8	0	0	0	—	1	1	0	0	0.1	1.000
1994		2	1	.667	6.67	33	0	0	29.2	31	23	19	0	2	1	1	0	0	0	—	2	9	0	3	0.3	1.000
1995		6	1	.857	4.73	40	0	0	51.1	49	31	29	0	6	1	0	0	0	0	—	4	3	0	1	0.2	1.000
4 yrs.		11	4	.733	4.47	115	0	0	137	130	82	96	0	11	4	9	0	0	0		7	16	0	4	0.2	1.000

Sal Butera

BUTERA, SALVATORE PHILIP BR TR 6′ 190 lbs.
B. Sept. 25, 1952, Richmond Hill, N. Y.

Year	Team	W	L	PCT	ERA	G	GS	CG	IP	H	BB	SO	ShO	Relief Pitching W	Relief Pitching L	Relief Pitching SV	Batting AB	Batting H	Batting HR	BA	PO	A	E	DP	TC/G	FA
1985	MON N	0	0	—	0.00	1	0	0	1	0	0	0	0	0	0	0	120	24	3	.200	106	9	6	0	3.6	.950
1986	CIN N	0	0	—	0.00	1	0	0	1	0	1	1	0	0	0	0	113	27	2	.239	215	17	5	2	4.4	.979
2 yrs.		0	0		0.00	2	0	0	2	0	1	1	0	0	0	0	*				1384	149	35	16	4.4	.978

Bill Butland

BUTLAND, WILBURN RUE BR TR 6′ 5″ 185 lbs.
B. Mar. 22, 1918, Terre Haute, Ind.

Year	Team	W	L	PCT	ERA	G	GS	CG	IP	H	BB	SO	ShO	Relief Pitching W	Relief Pitching L	Relief Pitching SV	Batting AB	Batting H	Batting HR	BA	PO	A	E	DP	TC/G	FA
1940	BOS A	1	2	.333	5.57	3	3	1	21	27	10	5	0	0	0	0	7	0	0	.000	1	7	0	0	2.7	1.000
1942		7	1	.875	2.51	23	10	6	111.1	85	33	46	2	0	0	1	28	1	0	.036	14	20	0	0	1.5	1.000
1946		1	0	1.000	11.02	5	2	0	16.1	23	13	10	0	0	0	0	4	1	0	.250	0	4	0	0	0.8	1.000
1947		0	0	—	4.50	1	0	0	2	3	0	1	0	0	0	0	0	0	0	—	0	0	0	0	0.0	.000
4 yrs.		9	3	.750	3.88	32	15	7	150.2	138	56	62	2	0	0	1	39	2	0	.051	15	31	0	0	1.4	1.000

Bill Butler

BUTLER, WILLIAM FRANKLIN BL TL 6′ 2″ 210 lbs.
B. Mar. 12, 1947, Hyattsville, Md.

Year	Team	W	L	PCT	ERA	G	GS	CG	IP	H	BB	SO	ShO	Relief Pitching W	Relief Pitching L	Relief Pitching SV	Batting AB	Batting H	Batting HR	BA	PO	A	E	DP	TC/G	FA
1969	KC A	9	10	.474	3.90	34	29	5	193.2	174	91	156	4	0	0	0	60	3	0	.050	4	16	1	1	0.6	.952
1970		4	12	.250	3.77	25	25	2	141	117	87	75	1	0	0	0	44	2	0	.045	3	13	1	1	0.7	.941
1971		1	2	.333	3.48	14	6	0	44	45	18	32	0	0	0	0	12	1	0	.083	0	7	1	0	0.6	.875
1972	CLE A	0	0	—	1.50	6	2	0	12	9	10	6	0	0	0	0	1	0	0	.000	0	1	0	0	0.2	1.000
1974	MIN A	4	6	.400	4.09	26	12	2	99	91	56	79	0	1	0	1	0	0	0	—	1	6	0	0	0.3	1.000
1975		5	4	.556	5.95	23	8	1	81.2	100	35	55	0	2	2	0	0	0	0	—	4	11	2	0	0.7	.882
1977		0	1	.000	6.86	6	4	0	21	19	15	5	0	0	0	0	0	0	0	—	0	1	0	0	0.2	1.000
7 yrs.		23	35	.397	4.21	134	86	10	592.1	555	312	408	5	3	2	1	117	6	0	.051	12	55	5	2	0.5	.931

Cecil Butler

BUTLER, CECIL DEAN (Slewfoot)
B. Oct. 23, 1937, Dallas, Ga.
BR TR 6′ 4″ 195 lbs.

Year	Team	Lg	W	L	PCT	ERA	G	GS	CG	IP	H	BB	SO	ShO	Relief W	Relief L	SV	AB	H	HR	BA	PO	A	E	DP	TC/G	FA
1962	MIL	N	2	0	1.000	2.61	9	2	1	31	26	9	22	0	1	0	0	8	0	0	.000	0	7	0	0	0.8	1.000
1964			0	0	—	8.31	2	0	0	4.1	7	0	2	0	0	0	0	0	0	0	—	0	1	0	0	0.5	1.000
2 yrs.			2	0	1.000	3.31	11	2	1	35.1	33	9	24	0	1	0	0	8	0	0	.000	0	8	0	0	0.7	1.000

Charlie Butler

BUTLER, CHARLES THOMAS (Lefty)
B. May 12, 1906, Green Cove Springs, Fla. D. May 10, 1964, Brunswick, Ga.
BR TL 6′ 1½″ 210 lbs.

Year	Team	Lg	W	L	PCT	ERA	G	GS	CG	IP	H	BB	SO	ShO	Relief W	Relief L	SV	AB	H	HR	BA	PO	A	E	DP	TC/G	FA
1933	PHI	N	0	0	—	9.00	1	0	0	1	1	2	0	0	0	0	0	0	0	0	—	0	0	0	0	0.0	.000

Ike Butler

BUTLER, ISAAC BURR
B. Aug. 22, 1873, Langston, Mich. D. Mar. 17, 1948, Oakland, Calif.
TR 6′ 175 lbs.

Year	Team	Lg	W	L	PCT	ERA	G	GS	CG	IP	H	BB	SO	ShO	Relief W	Relief L	SV	AB	H	HR	BA	PO	A	E	DP	TC/G	FA
1902	BAL	A	1	10	.091	5.34	16	14	12	116.1	168	45	13	0	0	0	0	53	6	0	.113	5	34	6	0	2.4	.867

Tom Butters

BUTTERS, THOMAS ARDEN
B. Apr. 8, 1938, Delaware, Ohio.
BR TR 6′ 2″ 195 lbs.

Year	Team	Lg	W	L	PCT	ERA	G	GS	CG	IP	H	BB	SO	ShO	Relief W	Relief L	SV	AB	H	HR	BA	PO	A	E	DP	TC/G	FA
1962	PIT	N	0	0	—	1.50	4	0	0	6	5	6	10	0	0	0	0	0	0	0	—	0	1	0	0	0.3	1.000
1963			0	0	—	4.41	6	1	0	16.1	15	8	11	0	0	0	0	3	1	0	.333	1	1	0	1	0.3	1.000
1964			2	2	.500	2.38	28	4	0	64.1	52	37	58	0	0	0	0	11	2	0	.182	0	9	1	1	0.4	.900
1965			0	1	.000	7.00	5	0	0	9	9	5	6	0	0	1	0	1	0	0	.000	3	1	0	0	0.8	1.000
4 yrs.			2	3	.400	3.10	43	5	0	95.2	81	56	85	0	0	1	0	15	3	0	.200	4	12	1	2	0.4	.941

Ralph Buxton

BUXTON, RALPH STANLEY (Buck)
B. June 7, 1911, Wayburn, Sask., Canada D. Jan. 6, 1988, San Leandro, Calif.
BR TR 5′11½″ 163 lbs.

Year	Team	Lg	W	L	PCT	ERA	G	GS	CG	IP	H	BB	SO	ShO	Relief W	Relief L	SV	AB	H	HR	BA	PO	A	E	DP	TC/G	FA
1938	PHI	A	0	1	.000	4.82	5	0	0	9.1	12	5	9	0	0	1	0	1	0	0	.000	0	1	0	0	0.2	1.000
1949	NY	A	0	1	.000	4.05	14	0	0	26.2	22	16	14	0	0	1	2	3	0	0	.000	2	3	0	0	0.4	1.000
2 yrs.			0	2	.000	4.25	19	0	0	36	34	21	23	0	0	2	2	4	0	0	.000	2	4	0	0	0.3	1.000

John Buzhardt

BUZHARDT, JOHN WILLIAM
B. Aug. 17, 1936, Prosperity, S. C.
BR TR 6′ 2½″ 195 lbs.

Year	Team	Lg	W	L	PCT	ERA	G	GS	CG	IP	H	BB	SO	ShO	Relief W	Relief L	SV	AB	H	HR	BA	PO	A	E	DP	TC/G	FA
1958	CHI	N	3	0	1.000	1.85	6	2	1	24.1	16	7	9	1	1	0	0	8	1	0	.125	2	7	0	0	1.5	1.000
1959			4	5	.444	4.97	31	10	1	101.1	107	29	33	1	1	2	0	29	2	0	.069	7	22	3	1	1.0	.906
1960	PHI	N	5	16	.238	3.86	30	29	5	200.1	198	68	73	0	0	0	0	62	10	0	.161	19	30	1	4	1.7	.980
1961			6	18	.250	4.49	41	27	6	202.1	200	65	92	1	0	2	0	57	6	0	.105	20	34	3	4	1.4	.947
1962	CHI	A	8	12	.400	4.19	28	25	8	152.1	156	59	64	2	1	0	0	51	6	0	.118	12	32	0	3	1.6	1.000
1963			9	4	.692	2.42	19	18	6	126.1	100	31	59	3	0	0	0	48	4	0	.083	12	25	1	1	2.0	.974
1964			10	8	.556	2.98	31	25	8	160	150	35	97	3	0	0	0	54	11	0	.204	10	27	1	2	1.2	.974
1965			13	8	.619	3.01	32	30	4	188.2	167	56	108	1	0	1	1	56	7	0	.125	15	26	2	4	1.3	.953
1966			6	11	.353	3.83	33	22	5	150.1	144	30	66	4	1	2	1	43	5	0	.116	19	34	1	1	1.6	.981
1967	3 teams	CHI A (28G 3–9)			BAL A (7G 0–1)		HOU N (1G 0–0)																				
″	total		3	10	.231	4.01	36	8	0	101	114	42	40	0	1	5	0	21	4	0	.190	9	21	1	1	0.9	.968
1968	HOU	N	4	4	.500	3.12	39	4	0	83.2	73	35	37	0	3	3	5	16	4	0	.250	8	17	0	1	0.6	1.000
11 yrs.			71	96	.425	3.66	326	200	44	1490.2	1425	457	678	15	8	15	7	445	60	0	.135	133	275	13	22	1.3	.969

Bud Byerly

BYERLY, ELDRED WILLIAM
B. Oct. 26, 1920, Webster Groves, Mo.
BR TR 6′ 2½″ 185 lbs.

Year	Team	Lg	W	L	PCT	ERA	G	GS	CG	IP	H	BB	SO	ShO	Relief W	Relief L	SV	AB	H	HR	BA	PO	A	E	DP	TC/G	FA
1943	STL	N	1	0	1.000	3.46	2	2	0	13	14	5	6	0	0	0	0	3	0	0	.000	0	2	0	0	1.0	1.000
1944			2	2	.500	3.40	9	4	2	42.1	37	20	13	0	1	0	0	12	2	0	.167	2	11	0	0	1.4	1.000
1945			4	5	.444	4.74	33	8	2	95	111	41	39	0	2	1	0	23	5	0	.217	10	25	0	3	1.1	1.000
1950	CIN	N	0	1	.000	2.45	4	1	0	14.2	12	4	5	0	0	0	0	3	0	0	.000	1	1	0	0	0.5	1.000
1951			2	1	.667	3.27	40	0	0	66	69	25	28	0	2	1	0	6	0	0	.000	4	16	2	0	0.6	.909
1952			0	1	.000	5.11	12	2	0	24.2	29	7	14	0	0	0	1	5	1	0	.200	0	5	0	0	0.4	1.000
1956	WAS	A	2	4	.333	2.96	25	0	0	51.2	45	14	19	0	2	4	4	11	1	0	.091	3	10	0	0	0.5	1.000
1957			6	6	.500	3.13	47	0	0	95	94	22	39	0	6	6	6	15	1	0	.067	5	22	1	0	0.6	.964
1958	2 teams	WAS A (17G 2–0)			BOS A (18G 1–2)																						
″	total		3	2	.600	3.98	35	0	0	54.1	65	18	29	0	3	2	1	6	0	0	.000	8	6	1	0	0.4	.933
1959	SF	N	1	0	1.000	1.38	11	0	0	13	11	5	4	0	1	0	0	0	0	0	—	1	5	0	0	0.5	1.000
1960			1	0	1.000	5.32	19	0	0	22	32	6	13	0	1	0	2	1	0	0	.000	0	3	0	0	0.2	1.000
11 yrs.			22	22	.500	3.70	237	17	4	491.2	519	167	209	0	18	14	14	85	10	0	.118	34	106	4	3	0.6	.972
WORLD SERIES																											
1944	STL	N	0	0	—	0.00	1	0	0	1.1	0	0	1	0	0	0	0	0	0	0	—	0	0	0	0	0.0	.000

Harry Byrd

BYRD, HARRY GLADWIN
B. Feb. 3, 1925, Darlington, S. C. D. May 14, 1985, Darlington, S. C.
BR TR 6′ 1″ 188 lbs.
BB 1955

Year	Team	Lg	W	L	PCT	ERA	G	GS	CG	IP	H	BB	SO	ShO	Relief W	Relief L	SV	AB	H	HR	BA	PO	A	E	DP	TC/G	FA
1950	PHI	A	0	0	—	16.88	6	0	0	10.2	25	9	2	0	0	0	0	2	0	0	.000	0	2	0	0	0.3	1.000
1952			15	15	.500	3.31	37	28	15	228.1	244	98	116	3	0	2	2	75	10	0	.133	26	32	4	5	1.7	.935
1953			11	**20**	.355	5.51	40	**37**	11	236.2	279	115	122	2	0	1	0	81	18	0	.222	6	35	2	1	1.1	.953
1954	NY	A	9	7	.563	2.99	25	21	5	132.1	131	43	52	1	0	0	0	46	9	0	.196	5	21	2	2	1.1	.929
1955	2 teams	BAL A (14G 3–2)			CHI A (25G 4–6)																						
″	total		7	8	.467	4.61	39	20	2	156.1	149	58	69	2	1	1	2	49	5	0	.102	9	24	1	0	0.9	.971
1956	CHI	A	0	1	.000	10.38	3	1	0	4.1	9	4	0	0	0	0	0	1	0	0	.000	0	2	0	0	0.7	1.000
1957	DET	A	4	3	.571	3.36	37	1	0	59	53	28	20	0	4	3	5	8	0	0	.000	0	10	0	0	0.3	1.000
7 yrs.			46	54	.460	4.35	187	108	33	827.2	890	355	381	8	5	7	9	262	42	0	.160	46	126	9	8	1.0	.950

Jeff Byrd

BYRD, JEFFREY ALAN
B. Nov. 11, 1956, La Mesa, Calif.
BR TR 6′ 3″ 195 lbs.

Year	Team	Lg	W	L	PCT	ERA	G	GS	CG	IP	H	BB	SO	ShO	Relief W	Relief L	SV	AB	H	HR	BA	PO	A	E	DP	TC/G	FA
1977	TOR	A	2	13	.133	6.21	17	17	1	87	98	68	40	0	0	0	0	0	0	0	—	9	15	2	1	1.5	.923

Paul Byrd

BYRD, PAUL GREGORY
B. Dec. 3, 1970, Louisville, Ky.
BR TR 6′ 1″ 185 lbs.

Year	Team	Lg	W	L	PCT	ERA	G	GS	CG	IP	H	BB	SO	ShO	Relief W	Relief L	SV	AB	H	HR	BA	PO	A	E	DP	TC/G	FA
1995	NY	N	2	0	1.000	2.05	17	0	0	22	18	7	26	0	2	0	0	1	1	0	1.000	1	3	1	0	0.3	.800

Jerry Byrne

BYRNE, GERALD WILFORD BR TR 6′ 170 lbs.
B. Feb. 2, 1907, Parnell, Mich. D. Aug. 11, 1955, Lansing, Mich.

Year	Team	W	L	PCT	ERA	G	GS	CG	IP	H	BB	SO	ShO	Relief Pitching W	Relief Pitching L	Relief Pitching SV	Batting AB	Batting H	Batting HR	BA	PO	A	E	DP	TC/G	FA
1929	CHI A	0	1	.000	7.36	3	1	0	7.1	11	6	1	0	0	0	0	2	0	0	.000	0	0	0	0	0.0	.000

Tommy Byrne

BYRNE, THOMAS JOSEPH BL TL 6′ 1″ 182 lbs.
B. Dec. 31, 1919, Baltimore, Md.

Year	Team	W	L	PCT	ERA	G	GS	CG	IP	H	BB	SO	ShO	Relief Pitching W	Relief Pitching L	Relief Pitching SV	Batting AB	Batting H	Batting HR	BA	PO	A	E	DP	TC/G	FA
1943	NY A	2	1	.667	6.54	11	2	0	31.2	28	35	22	0	2	0	0	11	1	0	.091	2	8	1	0	1.0	.909
1946		0	1	.000	5.79	4	1	0	9.1	7	8	5	0	0	0	0	9	2	0	.222	1	2	0	0	0.8	1.000
1947		0	0	—	4.15	4	1	0	4.1	5	6	2	0	0	0	0	0	0	0	—	0	1	0	0	0.3	1.000
1948		8	5	.615	3.30	31	11	5	133.2	79	101	93	1	2	1	2	46	15	1	.326	2	17	0	2	0.6	1.000
1949		15	7	.682	3.72	32	30	12	196	125	**179**	129	3	0	1	0	83	16	0	.193	7	19	3	4	0.9	.897
1950		15	9	.625	4.74	31	31	10	203.1	188	**160**	118	2	0	0	0	81	22	2	.272	9	23	0	2	1.0	1.000
1951	2 teams NY A (9G 2–1) STL A (19G 4–10)																									
″	total	6	11	.353	4.26	28	20	7	143.2	120	**150**	71	2	2	0	0	66	18	2	.273	6	20	1	2	1.0	.963
1952	STL A	7	14	.333	4.68	29	24	14	196	182	112	91	0	1	0	0	84	21	1	.250	10	15	2	1	0.9	.926
1953	2 teams CHI A (6G 2–0) WAS A (6G 0–5)																									
″	total	2	5	.286	6.16	12	11	2	49.2	53	48	26	0	0	1	0	35	4	1	.114	4	11	2	0	1.4	.882
1954	NY A	3	2	.600	2.70	5	5	4	40	36	19	24	1	0	0	0	19	7	0	.368	0	8	1	1	1.8	.889
1955		16	5	**.762**	3.15	27	22	9	160	137	87	76	3	1	0	2	78	16	1	.205	4	22	2	3	1.0	.929
1956		7	3	.700	3.36	37	8	1	109.2	108	72	52	0	6	2	6	52	14	3	.269	8	18	1	4	0.7	.963
1957		4	6	.400	4.36	30	4	1	84.2	70	60	57	0	4	4	2	37	7	3	.189	6	9	1	0	0.5	.938
13 yrs.		85	69	.552	4.11	281	170	65	1362	1138	1037	766	12	18	9	12	*				59	173	14	19	0.9	.943
WORLD SERIES																										
1949	NY A	0	0	—	2.70	1	1	0	3.1	2	2	1	0	0	0	0	1	1	0	1.000	0	0	0	0	0.0	.000
1955		1	1	.500	1.88	2	2	1	14.1	8	8	8	0	0	0	0	6	1	0	.167	0	2	0	0	1.0	1.000
1956		0	0	—	0.00	1	0	0	0.1	1	0	1	0	0	0	0	1	0	0	.000	0	0	0	0	0.0	.000
1957		0	0	—	5.40	2	0	0	3.1	1	2	1	0	0	0	0	2	1	0	.500	0	0	0	0	0.0	.000
4 yrs.		1	1	.500	2.53	6	3	1	21.1	12	12	11	0	0	0	0	*				0	2	0	0	0.3	1.000

Marty Bystrom

BYSTROM, MARTIN EUGENE BR TR 6′ 5″ 200 lbs.
B. July 26, 1958, Coral Gables, Fla.

Year	Team	W	L	PCT	ERA	G	GS	CG	IP	H	BB	SO	ShO	Relief Pitching W	Relief Pitching L	Relief Pitching SV	Batting AB	Batting H	Batting HR	BA	PO	A	E	DP	TC/G	FA
1980	PHI N	5	0	1.000	1.50	6	5	1	36	26	9	21	1	1	0	0	14	1	0	.071	4	10	0	1	2.3	1.000
1981		4	3	.571	3.33	9	9	1	54	55	16	24	0	0	0	0	17	2	0	.118	3	13	2	0	2.0	.889
1982		5	6	.455	4.85	19	16	1	89	93	35	50	0	0	0	0	24	3	0	.125	6	8	2	1	0.8	.875
1983		6	9	.400	4.60	24	23	1	119.1	136	44	87	1	0	0	0	38	9	0	.237	10	10	1	0	0.9	.952
1984	2 teams PHI N (11G 4–4) NY A (7G 2–2)																									
″	total	6	6	.500	4.22	18	18	0	96	100	35	60	0	0	0	0	19	3	0	.158	8	8	0	0	0.9	1.000
1985	NY A	3	2	.600	5.71	8	8	0	41	44	19	16	0	0	0	0	0	0	0	—	1	9	1	0	1.4	.909
6 yrs.		29	26	.527	4.26	84	79	4	435.1	454	158	258	2	1	0	0	112	18	0	.161	32	58	6	2	1.1	.938
LEAGUE CHAMPIONSHIP SERIES																										
1980	PHI N	0	0	—	1.69	1	1	0	5.1	7	2	1	0	0	0	0	2	0	0	.000	0	0	0	0	0.0	.000
WORLD SERIES																										
1980	PHI N	0	0	—	5.40	1	1	0	5	10	1	4	0	0	0	0	0	0	0	—	1	1	0	0	2.0	1.000
1983		0	0	—	0.00	1	0	0	1	0	0	1	0	0	0	0	0	0	0	—	0	0	0	0	0.0	.000
2 yrs.		0	0		4.50	2	1	0	6	10	1	5	0	0	0	0	0	0	0		1	1	0	0	1.0	1.000

Greg Cadaret

CADARET, GREGORY JAMES BL TL 6′ 3″ 200 lbs.
B. Feb. 27, 1962, Detroit, Mich.

Year	Team	W	L	PCT	ERA	G	GS	CG	IP	H	BB	SO	ShO	Relief Pitching W	Relief Pitching L	Relief Pitching SV	Batting AB	Batting H	Batting HR	BA	PO	A	E	DP	TC/G	FA
1987	OAK A	6	2	.750	4.54	29	0	0	39.2	37	24	30	0	6	2	0	0	0	0	—	6	6	0	1	0.4	1.000
1988		5	2	.714	2.89	58	0	0	71.2	60	36	64	0	5	2	3	0	0	0	—	3	9	0	1	0.2	1.000
1989	2 teams OAK A (26G 0–0) NY A (20G 5–5)																									
″	total	5	5	.500	4.05	46	13	3	120	130	57	80	1	1	0	0	0	0	0		9	21	2	2	0.7	.938
1990	NY A	5	4	.556	4.15	54	6	0	121.1	120	64	80	0	4	1	3	0	0	0	—	7	27	1	1	0.6	.971
1991		8	6	.571	3.62	68	5	0	121.2	110	59	105	0	5	5	3	0	0	0	—	5	17	1	5	0.3	.957
1992		4	8	.333	4.25	46	11	1	103.2	104	74	73	1	1	3	1	0	0	0	—	5	18	0	2	0.5	1.000
1993	2 teams CIN N (34G 2–1) KC A (13G 1–1)																									
″	total	3	2	.600	4.31	47	0	0	48	54	30	25	0	3	2	1	2	0	0	.000	4	6	0	0	0.2	1.000
1994	2 teams TOR A (21G 0–1) DET A (17G 1–0)																									
″	total	1	1	.500	4.72	38	0	0	40	41	33	29	0	1	1	2	0	0	0		2	7	0	1	0.2	1.000
8 yrs.		37	30	.552	3.99	386	35	4	666	656	377	486	2	26	16	13	2	0	0	.000	41	111	4	13	0.4	.974
LEAGUE CHAMPIONSHIP SERIES																										
1988	OAK A	0	0	—	27.00	1	0	0	0.1	1	0	0	0	0	0	0	0	0	0	—	0	0	0	0	0.0	.000
WORLD SERIES																										
1988	OAK A	0	0	—	0.00	3	0	0	2	2	0	3	0	0	0	0	0	0	0	—	0	0	0	0	0.0	.000

Leon Cadore

CADORE, LEON JOSEPH BR TR 6′ 1″ 190 lbs.
B. Nov. 20, 1890, Chicago, Ill. D. Mar. 16, 1958, Spokane, Wash.

Year	Team	W	L	PCT	ERA	G	GS	CG	IP	H	BB	SO	ShO	Relief Pitching W	Relief Pitching L	Relief Pitching SV	Batting AB	Batting H	Batting HR	BA	PO	A	E	DP	TC/G	FA
1915	BKN N	0	2	.000	5.57	7	2	1	21	28	8	12	0	0	0	0	6	0	0	.000	0	6	1	0	1.0	.857
1916		0	0	—	4.50	1	0	0	6	10	0	2	0	0	0	0	3	0	0	.000	0	4	0	0	4.0	1.000
1917		13	13	.500	2.45	37	30	21	264	231	63	115	1	0	0	3	92	24	0	.261	16	62	4	3	2.2	.951
1918		1	0	1.000	0.53	2	2	1	17	6	2	5	1	0	0	0	4	0	0	.000	1	5	0	0	3.0	1.000
1919		14	12	.538	2.37	35	27	16	250.2	228	39	94	3	2	0	0	87	14	0	.161	15	53	6	2	2.1	.919
1920		15	14	.517	2.62	35	30	16	254.1	256	56	79	4	1	1	0	91	20	2	.220	9	77	2	4	2.5	.977
1921		13	14	.481	4.17	35	30	12	211.2	243	46	79	1	1	2	0	75	14	1	.187	7	49	0	0	1.6	1.000
1922		8	15	.348	4.35	29	21	13	190.1	224	57	49	0	4	0	0	71	19	2	.268	8	30	1	3	1.3	.974
1923	2 teams BKN N (8G 4–1) CHI A (1G 0–1)																									
″	total	4	2	.667	4.46	9	5	3	38.1	45	15	8	0	1	0	0	13	1	0	.077	1	5	1	0	0.8	.857
1924	NY N	0	0	—	0.00	2	0	0	4	2	3	2	0	0	0	0	0	0	0	—	0	1	0	0	0.5	1.000
10 yrs.		68	72	.486	3.14	192	147	83	1257.1	1273	289	445	10	9	3	3	442	92	5	.208	57	292	15	12	1.9	.959
WORLD SERIES																										
1920	BKN N	0	1	.000	9.00	2	1	0	2	4	1	1	0	0	0	0	0	0	0	—	1	1	0	0	1.0	1.000

Charlie Cady

CADY, CHARLES B. 5′11″ 180 lbs.
B. Dec. 1865, Chicago, Ill. D. June 7, 1909, Kankakee, Ill.

Year	Team	W	L	PCT	ERA	G	GS	CG	IP	H	BB	SO	ShO	Relief W	Relief L	Relief SV	AB	H	HR	BA	PO	A	E	DP	TC/G	FA
1883	CLE N	0	1	.000	7.88	1	1	1	8	13	4	5	0	0	0	0	11	0	0	.000	1	1	0	0	0.7	1.000
1884	CHI U	3	1	.750	2.83	4	4	4	35	37	13	15	0	0	0	0	23	2	0	.087	7	8	7	0	2.8	.682
2 yrs.		3	2	.600	3.77	5	5	5	43	50	17	20	0	0	0	0	*				8	9	7	0	2.2	.708

John Cahill

CAHILL, JOHN PATRICK PARNELL (Patsy) BR TR 5′ 7½″ 168 lbs.
B. Apr. 30, 1865, San Francisco, Calif. D. Oct. 31, 1901, Pleasanton, Calif.

Year	Team	W	L	PCT	ERA	G	GS	CG	IP	H	BB	SO	ShO	Relief W	Relief L	Relief SV	AB	H	HR	BA	PO	A	E	DP	TC/G	FA
1884	COL AA	1	0	1.000	*5.06*	2	1	1	16	15	4	1	0	0	0	0	210	46	0	.219	71	28	19	2	1.9	.839
1886	STL N	1	0	1.000	3.00	2	0	0	12	11	3	2	0	1	0	0	463	92	1	.199	166	39	36	5	1.9	.851
1887	IND N	0	2	.000	14.32	6	1	1	22	40	19	5	0	0	1	0	263	54	0	.205	90	28	28	3	2.0	.808
3 yrs.		2	2	.500	8.64	10	2	2	50	66	26	8	0	1	1	0	*				327	95	83	10	1.9	.836

Bob Cain

CAIN, ROBERT MAX (Sugar) BL TL 6′ 165 lbs.
B. Oct. 16, 1924, Longford, Kans.

Year	Team	W	L	PCT	ERA	G	GS	CG	IP	H	BB	SO	ShO	Relief W	Relief L	Relief SV	AB	H	HR	BA	PO	A	E	DP	TC/G	FA
1949	CHI A	0	0	—	2.45	6	0	0	11	7	5	5	0	0	0	1	3	0	0	.000	1	0	0	0	0.2	1.000
1950		9	12	.429	3.93	34	23	11	171.2	153	109	77	1	1	1	2	61	12	0	.197	7	31	1	1	1.1	.974
1951	2 teams CHI A (4G 1–2) DET A (35G 11–10)																									
″	total	12	12	.500	4.56	39	26	7	175.2	160	95	61	1	2	2	2	62	16	0	.258	9	30	1	2	1.0	.975
1952	STL A	12	10	.545	4.13	29	27	8	170	169	62	70	1	0	0	2	58	8	0	.138	7	21	1	1	1.0	.966
1953		4	10	.286	6.23	32	13	1	99.2	129	45	36	0	0	4	1	30	6	0	.200	4	9	0	1	0.4	1.000
5 yrs.		37	44	.457	4.50	140	89	27	628	618	316	249	3	3	7	8	214	42	0	.196	28	91	3	5	0.9	.975

Les Cain

CAIN, LESLIE BL TL 6′ 1″ 200 lbs.
B. Jan. 13, 1948, San Luis Obispo, Calif.

Year	Team	W	L	PCT	ERA	G	GS	CG	IP	H	BB	SO	ShO	Relief W	Relief L	Relief SV	AB	H	HR	BA	PO	A	E	DP	TC/G	FA
1968	DET A	1	0	1.000	3.00	8	4	0	24	25	20	13	0	0	0	0	7	1	0	.143	0	6	0	0	0.8	1.000
1970		12	7	.632	3.83	29	29	5	181	167	98	156	0	0	0	0	68	11	1	.162	8	24	2	0	1.2	.941
1971		10	9	.526	4.34	26	26	3	145	121	91	118	1	0	0	0	55	8	1	.145	5	19	1	2	1.0	.960
1972		0	3	.000	3.75	5	5	0	24	18	16	16	0	0	0	0	7	1	0	.143	0	3	2	0	1.0	.600
4 yrs.		23	19	.548	3.97	68	64	8	374	331	225	303	1	0	0	0	137	21	2	.153	13	52	5	2	1.0	.929

Sugar Cain

CAIN, MERRITT PATRICK BL TR 5′11″ 190 lbs.
B. Apr. 5, 1907, Macon, Ga. D. Apr. 3, 1975, Atlanta, Ga. BB 1932–1933

Year	Team	W	L	PCT	ERA	G	GS	CG	IP	H	BB	SO	ShO	Relief W	Relief L	Relief SV	AB	H	HR	BA	PO	A	E	DP	TC/G	FA
1932	PHI A	3	4	.429	5.00	10	6	3	45	42	28	24	0	1	0	0	12	3	0	.250	1	8	0	0	0.9	1.000
1933		13	12	.520	4.25	38	32	16	218	244	137	43	1	0	1	1	80	16	0	.200	6	45	2	5	1.4	.962
1934		9	17	.346	4.41	36	32	15	230.2	235	128	66	0	1	1	0	82	13	0	.159	5	47	5	2	1.6	.912
1935	2 teams PHI A (6G 0–5) STL A (31G 9–8)																									
″	total	9	13	.409	5.44	37	29	8	193.2	236	**123**	73	0	0	1	0	65	11	0	.169	2	26	3	4	0.8	.903
1936	2 teams STL A (4G 1–1) CHI A (30G 14–10)																									
″	total	15	11	.577	4.89	34	29	15	211.2	248	84	50	1	1	1	0	75	9	0	.120	3	28	3	3	1.0	.912
1937	CHI A	4	2	.667	6.16	18	6	1	68.2	88	51	17	0	3	0	0	22	4	0	.182	0	14	0	1	0.8	1.000
1938		0	1	.000	4.58	5	3	0	19.2	26	18	6	0	0	0	0	8	0	0	.000	1	0	1	0	0.4	.500
7 yrs.		53	60	.469	4.83	178	137	58	987.1	1119	569	279	2	6	4	1	344	56	0	.163	18	168	14	15	1.1	.930

Charlie Caldwell

CALDWELL, CHARLES WILLIAM BR TR 5′10″ 180 lbs.
B. Aug. 2, 1901, Bristol, Va. D. Nov. 1, 1957, Princeton, N. J.

Year	Team	W	L	PCT	ERA	G	GS	CG	IP	H	BB	SO	ShO	Relief W	Relief L	Relief SV	AB	H	HR	BA	PO	A	E	DP	TC/G	FA
1925	NY A	0	0	—	16.88	3	0	0	2.2	7	3	1	0	0	0	0	1	0	0	.000	0	0	0	0	0.0	.000

Earl Caldwell

CALDWELL, EARL WELTON (Teach) BR TR 6′ 1″ 178 lbs.
B. Apr. 9, 1905, Sparks, Tex. D. Sept. 15, 1981, Mission, Tex.

Year	Team	W	L	PCT	ERA	G	GS	CG	IP	H	BB	SO	ShO	Relief W	Relief L	Relief SV	AB	H	HR	BA	PO	A	E	DP	TC/G	FA
1928	PHI N	1	4	.200	5.71	5	5	1	34.2	46	17	6	1	0	0	0	9	1	0	.111	0	10	0	0	2.0	1.000
1935	STL A	3	2	.600	3.68	6	5	2	36.2	34	17	5	1	0	0	0	11	2	0	.182	3	13	0	0	2.7	1.000
1936		7	16	.304	6.00	41	25	10	189	252	83	59	2	0	2	2	58	11	1	.190	6	32	5	3	1.0	.884
1937		0	0	—	6.83	9	2	0	29	39	13	8	0	0	0	0	9	2	0	.222	0	6	0	0	0.7	1.000
1945	CHI A	6	7	.462	3.59	27	11	5	105.1	108	37	45	1	1	3	4	37	8	0	.216	8	34	1	3	1.6	.977
1946		13	4	.765	2.08	39	0	0	90.2	60	29	42	0	**13**	4	8	18	3	0	.167	5	19	0	0	0.6	1.000
1947		1	4	.200	3.64	40	0	0	54.1	53	30	22	0	1	4	8	7	0	0	.000	1	6	1	0	0.2	.875
1948	2 teams CHI A (25G 1–5) BOS A (8G 1–1)																									
″	total	2	6	.250	6.75	33	1	0	48	64	33	15	0	2	5	3	8	1	0	.125	2	5	0	0	0.2	1.000
8 yrs.		33	43	.434	4.69	200	49	18	587.2	656	259	202	5	17	18	25	157	28	1	.178	25	125	7	6	0.8	.955

Mike Caldwell

CALDWELL, RALPH MICHAEL BR TL 6′ 185 lbs.
B. Jan. 22, 1949, Tarboro, N. C.

Year	Team	W	L	PCT	ERA	G	GS	CG	IP	H	BB	SO	ShO	Relief W	Relief L	Relief SV	AB	H	HR	BA	PO	A	E	DP	TC/G	FA
1971	SD N	1	0	1.000	0.00	6	0	0	7	4	3	5	0	1	0	0	1	1	0	1.000	1	2	0	0	0.5	1.000
1972		7	11	.389	4.01	42	20	4	163.2	183	49	102	2	2	2	2	50	7	0	.140	9	47	2	3	1.4	.966
1973		5	14	.263	3.74	55	13	3	149	146	53	86	1	2	5	10	35	5	0	.143	12	29	2	1	0.8	.953
1974	SF N	14	5	.737	2.95	31	27	6	189	176	63	83	2	1	0	0	63	9	0	.143	11	48	0	7	1.9	1.000
1975		7	13	.350	4.80	38	21	4	163	194	48	57	0	1	2	1	44	7	0	.159	10	33	1	2	1.2	.977
1976		1	7	.125	4.86	50	9	0	107.1	145	20	55	0	1	3	2	19	3	0	.158	8	22	1	2	0.6	.968
1977	2 teams CIN N (14G 0–0) MIL A (21G 5–8)																									
″	total	5	8	.385	4.46	35	12	2	119	126	44	49	0	2	0	1	4	2	0	.500	7	31	0	3	1.1	1.000
1978	MIL A	22	9	.710	2.36	37	34	**23**	293.1	258	54	131	6	0	0	1	0	0	0	—	14	50	0	2	1.7	1.000
1979		16	6	**.727**	3.29	30	30	16	235	252	39	89	4	0	0	0	0	0	0	—	7	64	2	3	2.4	.973
1980		13	11	.542	4.04	34	33	11	225	248	56	74	2	0	0	1	0	0	0	—	8	37	1	5	1.4	.978
1981		11	9	.550	3.94	24	23	3	144	151	38	41	0	0	0	0	0	0	0	—	5	26	0	0	1.3	1.000
1982		17	13	.567	3.91	35	34	12	258	269	58	75	3	0	0	0	0	0	0	—	13	48	1	5	1.8	.984
1983		12	11	.522	4.53	32	32	10	228.1	269	51	58	2	0	0	0	0	0	0	—	4	38	2	4	1.4	.955
1984		6	13	.316	4.64	26	19	4	126	160	21	34	1	0	2	0	0	0	0	—	7	24	3	2	1.3	.912
14 yrs.		137	130	.513	3.81	475	307	98	2407.2	2581	597	939	23	10	14	18	216	34	0	.157	116	499	15	39	1.3	.976
DIVISIONAL PLAYOFF SERIES																										
1981	MIL A	0	1	.000	4.32	2	1	0	8.1	9	0	4	0	0	0	0	0	0	0	—	0	0	0	0	0.0	.000
LEAGUE CHAMPIONSHIP SERIES																										
1982	MIL A	0	1	.000	15.00	1	1	0	3	7	1	2	0	0	0	0	0	0	0	—	2	0	1	0	3.0	.667

Mike Caldwell *continued*

Year	Team	Lg	W	L	PCT	ERA	G	GS	CG	IP	H	BB	SO	ShO	Relief Pitching W	L	SV	Batting AB	H	HR	BA	PO	A	E	DP	TC/G	FA
WORLD SERIES																											
1982	MIL	A	2	0	1.000	2.04	3	2	1	17.2	19	3	6	1	0	0	0	0	0	0	—	4	2	0	0	2.0	1.000

Ralph Caldwell

CALDWELL, RALPH GRANT (Lefty) BL TL 5′ 9″ 155 lbs.
B. Jan. 18, 1884, Philadelphia, Pa. D. Aug. 5, 1969, West Trenton, N. J.

Year	Team	Lg	W	L	PCT	ERA	G	GS	CG	IP	H	BB	SO	ShO	Relief W	Relief L	SV	AB	H	HR	BA	PO	A	E	DP	TC/G	FA
1904	PHI	N	2	2	.500	4.17	6	5	5	41	40	15	30	0	0	0	0	18	8	0	.444	4	9	0	0	2.2	1.000
1905			1	2	.333	4.24	7	2	1	34	44	7	29	0	0	1	1	15	0	0	.000	1	4	2	0	1.0	.714
2 yrs.			3	4	.429	4.20	13	7	6	75	84	22	59	0	0	1	1	33	8	0	.242	5	13	2	0	1.5	.900

Ray Caldwell

CALDWELL, RAYMOND BENJAMIN (Slim) BL TR 6′ 2″ 190 lbs.
B. Apr. 26, 1888, Croydon, Pa. D. Aug. 17, 1967, Salamanca, N. Y.

Year	Team	Lg	W	L	PCT	ERA	G	GS	CG	IP	H	BB	SO	ShO	Relief W	Relief L	SV	AB	H	HR	BA	PO	A	E	DP	TC/G	FA
1910	NY	A	1	0	1.000	3.72	6	2	1	19.1	19	9	17	0	0	0	1	6	0	0	.000	1	4	0	0	0.8	1.000
1911			14	14	.500	3.35	41	27	19	255	240	79	145	1	4	2	1	147	40	0	.272	27	56	6	2	1.7	.933
1912			8	16	.333	4.47	30	26	13	183.1	196	67	95	3	0	1	0	76	18	0	.237	2	59	4	2	2.2	.938
1913			9	8	.529	2.41	27	16	15	164.1	131	60	87	2	0	1	1	97	28	0	.289	8	42	0	1	1.7	1.000
1914			17	9	.654	1.94	31	23	22	213	153	51	92	5	2	1	1	113	22	0	.195	56	46	6	3	2.9	.944
1915			19	16	.543	2.89	36	35	31	305	266	107	130	3	0	1	0	144	35	4	.243	12	72	1	5	2.4	.988
1916			5	12	.294	2.99	21	18	14	165.2	142	65	76	1	0	1	0	93	19	0	.204	4	45	3	2	2.2	.942
1917			13	16	.448	2.86	32	29	21	236	199	76	102	1	3	0	0	124	32	2	.258	23	60	2	1	2.1	.976
1918			9	8	.529	3.06	24	21	14	176.2	173	62	59	1	0	1	1	151	44	1	.291	52	38	3	2	2.2	.968
1919	2 teams	BOS A (18G 7–4)	CLE A (6G 5–1)																								
″	total		12	5	.706	2.98	24	18	10	139	121	49	46	2	1	1	0	71	21	0	.296	6	26	2	0	1.3	.941
1920	CLE	A	20	10	.667	3.86	34	33	20	237.2	286	63	80	0	0	0	0	89	19	0	.213	6	49	5	0	1.8	.917
1921			6	6	.500	4.90	37	13	5	147	159	49	76	1	2	3	4	53	11	1	.208	5	35	3	1	1.2	.930
12 yrs.			133	120	.526	3.21	343	261	185	2242	2085	737	1005	20	12	12	9	*				202	532	35	19	1.9	.954
WORLD SERIES																											
1920	CLE	A	0	1	.000	27.00	1	1	0	0.1	2	1	0	0	0	0	0	*				0	0	0	0	0.0	.000

Jeff Calhoun

CALHOUN, JEFFREY WILTON BL TL 6′ 2″ 190 lbs.
B. Apr. 11, 1958, LaGrange, Ga.

Year	Team	Lg	W	L	PCT	ERA	G	GS	CG	IP	H	BB	SO	ShO	Relief W	Relief L	SV	AB	H	HR	BA	PO	A	E	DP	TC/G	FA
1984	HOU	N	0	1	.000	1.17	9	0	0	15.1	5	2	11	0	0	1	0	0	0	0	—	1	1	0	0	0.2	1.000
1985			2	5	.286	2.54	44	0	0	63.2	56	24	47	0	2	5	4	5	0	0	.000	5	10	2	2	0.4	.882
1986			1	0	1.000	3.71	20	0	0	26.2	28	12	14	0	1	0	0	0	0	0	—	2	1	0	0	0.2	1.000
1987	PHI	N	3	1	.750	1.48	42	0	0	42.2	25	26	31	0	3	1	1	1	0	0	.000	4	8	0	0	0.3	1.000
1988			0	0	—	15.43	3	0	0	2.1	6	1	1	0	0	0	0	0	0	0	—	0	0	0	0	0.0	.000
5 yrs.			6	7	.462	2.51	118	0	0	150.2	120	65	104	0	6	7	5	6	0	0	.000	12	20	2	2	0.3	.941
LEAGUE CHAMPIONSHIP SERIES																											
1986	HOU	N	0	0	—	9.00	1	0	0	1	1	1	0	0	0	0	0	0	0	0	—	0	0	0	0	0.0	.000

Fred Caligiuri

CALIGIURI, FREDERICK JOHN BR TR 6′ 190 lbs.
B. Oct. 22, 1918, West Hickory, Pa.

Year	Team	Lg	W	L	PCT	ERA	G	GS	CG	IP	H	BB	SO	ShO	Relief W	Relief L	SV	AB	H	HR	BA	PO	A	E	DP	TC/G	FA
1941	PHI	A	2	2	.500	2.93	5	5	4	43	45	14	7	0	0	0	0	20	4	0	.200	2	8	0	0	2.0	1.000
1942			0	3	.000	6.38	13	2	0	36.2	45	18	20	0	0	1	1	12	1	0	.083	0	8	1	0	0.7	.889
2 yrs.			2	5	.286	4.52	18	7	4	79.2	90	32	27	0	0	1	1	32	5	0	.156	2	16	1	0	1.1	.947

Ben Callahan

CALLAHAN, BENJAMIN FRANKLIN III BR TR 6′ 7″ 230 lbs.
B. May 19, 1957, Mt. Airy, N. C.

Year	Team	Lg	W	L	PCT	ERA	G	GS	CG	IP	H	BB	SO	ShO	Relief W	Relief L	SV	AB	H	HR	BA	PO	A	E	DP	TC/G	FA
1983	OAK	A	1	2	.333	12.54	4	2	0	9.1	18	5	2	0	0	1	0	0	0	0	—	0	3	0	0	0.8	1.000

Jim Callahan

CALLAHAN, JAMES W.
B. Moberly, Mo. Deceased.

Year	Team	Lg	W	L	PCT	ERA	G	GS	CG	IP	H	BB	SO	ShO	Relief W	Relief L	SV	AB	H	HR	BA	PO	A	E	DP	TC/G	FA
1898	STL	N	0	2	.000	16.20	2	2	1	8.1	18	7	2	0	0	0	0	4	0	0	.000	0	2	0	0	1.0	1.000

Joe Callahan

CALLAHAN, JOSEPH THOMAS BR TR 6′ 2″ 170 lbs.
B. Oct. 8, 1916, East Boston, Mass. D. May 24, 1949, South Boston, Mass.

Year	Team	Lg	W	L	PCT	ERA	G	GS	CG	IP	H	BB	SO	ShO	Relief W	Relief L	SV	AB	H	HR	BA	PO	A	E	DP	TC/G	FA
1939	BOS	N	1	0	1.000	3.12	4	1	1	17.1	17	3	8	0	0	0	0	4	0	0	.000	3	3	0	0	1.5	1.000
1940			0	2	.000	10.20	6	2	0	15	20	13	3	0	0	0	0	5	0	0	.000	0	6	0	1	1.0	1.000
2 yrs.			1	2	.333	6.40	10	3	1	32.1	37	16	11	0	0	0	0	9	0	0	.000	3	9	0	1	1.2	1.000

Nixey Callahan

CALLAHAN, JAMES JOSEPH (Cal) BR TR 5′10½″ 180 lbs.
B. Mar. 18, 1874, Fitchburg, Mass. D. Oct. 4, 1934, Boston, Mass.
Manager 1903–04, 1912–14, 1916–17.

Year	Team	Lg	W	L	PCT	ERA	G	GS	CG	IP	H	BB	SO	ShO	Relief W	Relief L	SV	AB	H	HR	BA	PO	A	E	DP	TC/G	FA
1894	PHI	N	1	2	.333	9.89	9	2	1	33.2	64	17	9	0	1	0	2	21	5	0	.238	4	8	1	0	1.4	.923
1897	CHI	N	12	9	.571	4.03	23	22	21	189.2	221	55	52	1	0	1	0	360	105	3	.292	147	201	42	25	4.1	.892
1898			20	10	.667	2.46	31	31	30	274.1	267	71	73	2	0	0	0	164	43	0	.262	42	67	11	3	2.8	.908
1899			21	12	.636	3.06	35	34	33	294.1	327	76	77	3	1	0	0	150	39	0	.260	40	103	14	4	3.3	.911
1900			13	16	.448	3.82	32	32	32	285.1	347	74	77	2	0	0	0	115	27	0	.235	21	94	3	2	3.7	.975
1901	CHI	A	15	8	.652	2.42	27	22	20	215.1	195	50	70	1	1	2	0	118	39	1	.331	27	93	10	5	3.7	.923
1902			16	14	.533	3.60	35	31	29	282.1	287	89	75	2	1	0	0	218	51	0	.234	57	108	9	7	2.9	.948
1903			1	2	.333	4.50	3	3	3	28	40	5	12	0	0	0	0	439	128	2	.292	131	216	38	5	3.4	.901
8 yrs.			99	73	.576	3.39	195	177	169	1603	1748	437	445	11	4	3	2	*				1137	992	166	58	2.6	.928

Ray Callahan

CALLAHAN, RAYMOND JAMES (Pat) BL TL 5′10½″ 170 lbs.
B. Aug. 29, 1891, Ashland, Wis. D. Jan. 23, 1973, Olympia, Wash.

Year	Team	Lg	W	L	PCT	ERA	G	GS	CG	IP	H	BB	SO	ShO	Relief W	Relief L	SV	AB	H	HR	BA	PO	A	E	DP	TC/G	FA
1915	CIN	N	0	0	—	8.53	3	0	0	6.1	12	1	4	0	0	0	0	3	1	0	.333	0	0	0	0	0.0	.000

Will Callahan

CALLAHAN, WILLIAM T. 5′ 8″ 150 lbs.
B. 1867, Oswego, N. Y. D. Dec. 20, 1917, Rochester, N. Y.

Year	Team	Lg	W	L	PCT	ERA	G	GS	CG	IP	H	BB	SO	ShO	Relief W	Relief L	SV	AB	H	HR	BA	PO	A	E	DP	TC/G	FA
1890	ROC	AA	18	15	.545	*3.28*	37	36	31	296.1	276	125	127	0	0	0	0	159	23	1	.145	33	74	11	6	2.4	.907
1891	PHI	AA	6	6	.500	6.43	13	11	11	112	151	47	28	0	1	0	0	56	11	0	.196	9	38	2	1	3.3	.959
2 yrs.			24	21	.533	4.14	50	47	42	408.1	427	172	155	0	1	0	0	215	34	1	.158	42	112	13	7	2.6	.922

Dick Calmus

CALMUS, RICHARD LEE
B. Jan. 7, 1944, Los Angeles, Calif.
BR TR 6′ 4″ 187 lbs.

Year	Team	Lg	W	L	PCT	ERA	G	GS	CG	IP	H	BB	SO	ShO	Relief Pitching W	Relief Pitching L	Relief Pitching SV	Batting AB	Batting H	Batting HR	BA	PO	A	E	DP	TC/G	FA
1963	LA	N	3	1	.750	2.66	21	1	0	44	32	16	25	0	3	0	0	6	0	0	.000	1	6	0	0	0.3	1.000
1967	CHI	N	0	0	—	8.31	1	1	0	4.1	5	0	1	0	0	0	0	2	1	0	.500	0	1	0	0	1.0	1.000
2 yrs.			3	1	.750	3.17	22	2	0	48.1	37	16	26	0	3	0	0	8	1	0	.125	1	7	0	0	0.4	1.000

Mark Calvert

CALVERT, MARK
B. Sept. 29, 1956, Tulsa, Okla.
BR TR 6′ 1″ 195 lbs.

Year	Team	Lg	W	L	PCT	ERA	G	GS	CG	IP	H	BB	SO	ShO	Relief Pitching W	Relief Pitching L	Relief Pitching SV	Batting AB	Batting H	Batting HR	BA	PO	A	E	DP	TC/G	FA
1983	SF	N	1	4	.200	6.27	18	4	0	37.1	46	34	14	0	0	2	0	8	0	0	.000	5	7	0	0	0.7	1.000
1984			2	4	.333	5.06	10	5	1	32	40	9	5	0	0	1	0	8	0	0	.000	2	8	0	0	1.0	1.000
2 yrs.			3	8	.273	5.71	28	9	1	69.1	86	43	19	0	0	3	0	16	0	0	.000	7	15	0	0	0.8	1.000

Paul Calvert

CALVERT, PAUL LEO EMILE
B. Oct. 6, 1917, Montreal, Que., Canada.
BR TR 6′ 175 lbs.

Year	Team	Lg	W	L	PCT	ERA	G	GS	CG	IP	H	BB	SO	ShO	Relief Pitching W	Relief Pitching L	Relief Pitching SV	Batting AB	Batting H	Batting HR	BA	PO	A	E	DP	TC/G	FA
1942	CLE	A	0	0	—	0.00	1	0	0	2	0	2	2	0	0	0	0	0	0	0	—	0	0	0	0	0.0	.000
1943			0	0	—	4.32	5	0	0	8.1	6	6	2	0	0	0	0	1	0	0	.000	0	2	0	0	0.4	1.000
1944			1	3	.250	4.56	35	4	0	77	89	38	31	0	0	2	0	15	4	0	.267	9	21	3	2	0.9	.909
1945			0	0	—	13.50	1	0	0	1.1	3	1	1	0	0	0	0	0	0	0	—	0	0	0	0	0.0	.000
1949	WAS	A	6	**17**	.261	5.43	34	23	5	160.2	175	86	52	0	1	2	1	51	7	0	.137	15	40	0	2	1.6	1.000
1950	DET	A	2	2	.500	6.31	32	0	0	51.1	71	25	14	0	2	2	4	7	0	0	.000	5	12	1	0	0.6	.944
1951			0	0	—	0.00	1	0	0	1	1	0	0	0	0	0	0	0	0	0	—	0	1	0	0	1.0	1.000
7 yrs.			9	22	.290	5.31	109	27	5	301.2	345	158	102	0	3	6	5	74	11	0	.149	29	76	4	4	1.0	.963

Ernie Camacho

CAMACHO, ERNEST CARLOS
B. Feb. 1, 1955, Salinas, Calif.
BR TR 6′ 1″ 180 lbs.

Year	Team	Lg	W	L	PCT	ERA	G	GS	CG	IP	H	BB	SO	ShO	Relief Pitching W	Relief Pitching L	Relief Pitching SV	Batting AB	Batting H	Batting HR	BA	PO	A	E	DP	TC/G	FA
1980	OAK	A	0	0	—	6.75	5	0	0	12	20	5	9	0	0	0	0	0	0	0	—	0	0	0	0	0.0	.000
1981	PIT	N	0	1	.000	4.91	7	3	0	22	23	15	11	0	0	0	0	4	0	0	.000	0	3	0	1	0.4	1.000
1983	CLE	A	0	1	.000	5.06	4	0	0	5.1	5	2	2	0	0	1	0	0	0	0	—	0	0	0	0	0.0	.000
1984			5	9	.357	2.43	69	0	0	100	83	37	48	0	5	9	23	0	0	0	—	1	15	0	0	0.2	1.000
1985			0	1	.000	8.10	2	0	0	3.1	4	1	2	0	0	1	0	0	0	0	—	0	1	0	0	0.5	1.000
1986			2	4	.333	4.08	51	0	0	57.1	60	31	36	0	2	4	20	0	0	0	—	5	11	1	0	0.3	.941
1987			0	1	.000	9.22	15	0	0	13.2	21	5	9	0	0	1	1	0	0	0	—	1	5	0	0	0.4	1.000
1988	HOU	N	0	3	.000	7.64	13	0	0	17.2	25	12	13	0	0	3	1	1	0	0	.000	1	3	0	0	0.3	1.000
1989	SF	N	3	0	1.000	2.76	13	0	0	16.1	10	11	14	0	3	0	0	1	0	0	.000	2	5	0	0	0.5	1.000
1990	2 teams SF N (8G 0–0) STL N (6G 0–0)																										
″	total		0	0		5.17	14	0	0	15.2	17	9	15	0	0	0	0	0	0	0		0	1	0	0	0.1	1.000
10 yrs.			10	20	.333	4.20	193	3	0	263.1	268	128	159	0	10	19	45	6	0	0	.000	10	44	1	1	0.3	.982

Fred Cambria

CAMBRIA, FREDERICK DENNIS
B. Jan. 22, 1948, Cambria Heights, N. Y.
BR TR 6′ 2″ 195 lbs.

Year	Team	Lg	W	L	PCT	ERA	G	GS	CG	IP	H	BB	SO	ShO	Relief Pitching W	Relief Pitching L	Relief Pitching SV	Batting AB	Batting H	Batting HR	BA	PO	A	E	DP	TC/G	FA
1970	PIT	N	1	2	.333	3.55	6	5	0	33	37	12	14	0	0	0	0	10	2	0	.200	1	6	0	1	1.2	1.000

John Cameron

CAMERON, JOHN S. (Happy Jack)
B. Sept. 1884, Nova Scotia, Canada D. Aug. 17, 1951, Boston, Mass.

Year	Team	Lg	W	L	PCT	ERA	G	GS	CG	IP	H	BB	SO	ShO	Relief Pitching W	Relief Pitching L	Relief Pitching SV	Batting AB	Batting H	Batting HR	BA	PO	A	E	DP	TC/G	FA
1906	BOS	N	0	0	—	0.00	2	1	0	6	4	6	2	0	0	0	0	*				20	5	4	1	1.6	.862

Harry Camnitz

CAMNITZ, HENRY RICHARDSON
Brother of Howie Camnitz.
B. Oct. 26, 1884, McKinney, Ky. D. Jan. 6, 1951, Louisville, Ky.
BR TR 6′ 1″ 168 lbs.

Year	Team	Lg	W	L	PCT	ERA	G	GS	CG	IP	H	BB	SO	ShO	Relief Pitching W	Relief Pitching L	Relief Pitching SV	Batting AB	Batting H	Batting HR	BA	PO	A	E	DP	TC/G	FA
1909	PIT	N	0	0	—	4.50	1	0	0	4	6	1	1	0	0	0	0	2	0	0	.000	0	3	0	0	3.0	1.000
1911	STL	N	1	0	1.000	0.00	2	0	0	2	0	1	2	0	1	0	0	0	0	0	—	0	0	0	0	0.0	.000
2 yrs.			1	0	1.000	3.00	3	0	0	6	6	2	3	0	1	0	0	2	0	0	.000	0	3	0	0	1.0	1.000

Howie Camnitz

CAMNITZ, SAMUEL HOWARD (Red)
Brother of Harry Camnitz.
B. Aug. 22, 1881, Covington, Ky. D. Mar. 2, 1960, Louisville, Ky.
BR TR 5′ 9″ 169 lbs.

Year	Team	Lg	W	L	PCT	ERA	G	GS	CG	IP	H	BB	SO	ShO	Relief Pitching W	Relief Pitching L	Relief Pitching SV	Batting AB	Batting H	Batting HR	BA	PO	A	E	DP	TC/G	FA
1904	PIT	N	1	3	.250	4.22	10	2	2	49	48	20	21	0	1	1	0	16	1	0	.063	2	9	0	0	1.1	1.000
1906			1	0	1.000	2.00	2	1	1	9	6	5	5	1	0	0	0	3	0	0	.000	1	1	0	0	1.0	1.000
1907			13	8	.619	2.15	31	19	15	180	135	59	85	4	3	2	1	60	3	0	.050	8	46	1	1	1.8	.982
1908			16	9	.640	1.56	38	26	17	236.2	182	69	118	3	0	0	2	72	6	0	.083	7	64	6	0	2.0	.922
1909			25	6	**.806**	1.62	41	30	20	283	207	68	133	6	**7**	0	3	87	12	0	.138	9	63	2	3	1.8	.973
1910			12	13	.480	3.22	38	31	16	260	246	61	120	1	2	0	2	88	11	1	.125	14	57	2	1	1.9	.973
1911			20	15	.571	3.13	40	33	18	267.2	245	84	139	1	3	2	0	84	12	0	.143	4	59	5	1	1.7	.926
1912			22	12	.647	2.83	41	32	22	276.2	256	82	121	2	5	0	2	98	23	0	.235	4	59	4	1	1.6	.940
1913	2 teams PIT N (36G 6–17) PHI N (9G 3–3)																										
″	total		9	20	.310	3.73	45	27	6	241.1	252	107	85	1	3	5	3	75	10	0	.133	5	64	4	1	1.6	.945
1914	PIT	F	14	18	.438	3.23	36	34	20	262	256	90	82	1	0	1	1	87	14	0	.161	9	61	7	0	2.1	.909
1915			0	2	.000	4.50	4	2	0	20	19	11	6	0	0	1	0	7	0	0	.000	0	3	0	0	0.8	1.000
11 yrs.			133	106	.556	2.75	326	237	137	2085.1	1852	656	915	20	24	12	14	677	92	1	.136	63	486	31	8	1.8	.947
WORLD SERIES																											
1909	PIT	N	0	1	.000	12.27	2	1	0	3.2	8	2	2	0	0	0	0	1	0	0	.000	0	2	0	0	1.0	1.000

Kid Camp

CAMP, WINFIELD SCOTT
Brother of Llewellan Camp.
B. 1870, Columbus, Ohio D. Mar. 2, 1895, Omaha, Neb.
TR 6′ 160 lbs.

Year	Team	Lg	W	L	PCT	ERA	G	GS	CG	IP	H	BB	SO	ShO	Relief Pitching W	Relief Pitching L	Relief Pitching SV	Batting AB	Batting H	Batting HR	BA	PO	A	E	DP	TC/G	FA
1892	PIT	N	0	1	.000	6.26	4	1	1	23	31	9	6	0	0	0	0	11	1	0	.091	2	0	2	0	1.0	.500
1894	CHI	N	0	1	.000	6.55	3	2	2	22	34	12	6	0	0	0	0	11	0	0	.000	0	6	0	0	2.0	1.000
2 yrs.			0	2	.000	6.40	7	3	3	45	65	21	12	0	0	0	0	22	1	0	.045	2	6	2	0	1.4	.800

Rick Camp

CAMP, RICK LAMAR
B. June 10, 1953, Trion, Ga.
BR TR 6′ 1″ 195 lbs.

Year	Team	Lg	W	L	PCT	ERA	G	GS	CG	IP	H	BB	SO	ShO	Relief Pitching W	Relief Pitching L	Relief Pitching SV	Batting AB	Batting H	Batting HR	BA	PO	A	E	DP	TC/G	FA
1976	ATL	N	0	1	.000	6.55	5	1	0	11	13	2	6	0	0	0	0	2	0	0	.000	3	5	1	0	1.8	.889
1977			6	3	.667	3.99	54	0	0	79	89	47	51	0	6	3	10	6	0	0	.000	4	10	2	1	0.3	.875
1978			2	4	.333	3.77	42	4	0	74	99	32	23	0	0	4	0	8	0	0	.000	8	12	3	0	0.5	.870

Rick Camp *continued*

Year	Team	Lg	W	L	PCT	ERA	G	GS	CG	IP	H	BB	SO	ShO	Relief Pitching W	Relief Pitching L	Relief Pitching SV	Batting AB	Batting H	Batting HR	BA	PO	A	E	DP	TC/G	FA
1980			6	4	.600	1.92	77	0	0	108	92	29	33	0	6	4	22	9	1	0	.111	9	34	1	2	0.6	.977
1981			9	3	.750	1.78	48	0	0	76	68	12	47	0	**9**	3	17	12	0	0	.000	11	9	0	1	0.4	1.000
1982			11	13	.458	3.65	51	21	3	177.1	199	52	68	0	4	3	5	41	1	0	.024	18	30	3	2	1.0	.941
1983			10	9	.526	3.79	40	16	1	140	146	38	61	0	4	2	0	39	3	0	.077	14	23	5	1	1.0	.881
1984			8	6	.571	3.27	31	21	1	148.2	134	63	69	0	1	0	0	45	5	0	.111	12	24	1	0	1.2	.973
1985			4	6	.400	3.95	66	2	0	127.2	130	61	49	0	3	5	3	13	3	1	.231	7	13	4	3	0.4	.833
9 yrs.			56	49	.533	3.37	414	65	5	941.2	970	336	407	0	33	24	57	175	13	1	.074	86	160	20	10	0.6	.925
LEAGUE CHAMPIONSHIP SERIES																											
1982	ATL	N	0	1	.000	36.00	1	1	0	1	4	1	0	0	0	0	0	0	0	0	—	0	0	0	0	0.0	.000

Bert Campaneris

CAMPANERIS, DAGOBERTO (Campy) BR TR 5′10″ 160 lbs.
Born Dagoberto Campaneris (Blanco).
B. Mar. 9, 1942, Pueblo Nuevo, Cuba.

Year	Team	Lg	W	L	PCT	ERA	G	GS	CG	IP	H	BB	SO	ShO	Relief Pitching W	Relief Pitching L	Relief Pitching SV	Batting AB	Batting H	Batting HR	BA	PO	A	E	DP	TC/G	FA
1965	KC	A	0	0	—	9.00	1	0	0	1	1	2	1	0	0	0	0	*				102	108	8	16	3.1	.963

Archie Campbell

CAMPBELL, ARCHIBALD STEWART (Iron Man) BR TR 6′ 1″ 180 lbs.
B. Oct. 20, 1903, Maplewood, N. J. D. Dec. 22, 1989, Sparks, Nev.

Year	Team	Lg	W	L	PCT	ERA	G	GS	CG	IP	H	BB	SO	ShO	Relief Pitching W	Relief Pitching L	Relief Pitching SV	Batting AB	Batting H	Batting HR	BA	PO	A	E	DP	TC/G	FA
1928	NY	A	0	1	.000	5.25	13	1	0	24	30	11	9	0	0	1	2	4	1	0	.250	1	4	2	0	0.5	.714
1929	WAS	A	0	1	.000	15.75	4	0	0	4	10	5	1	0	0	1	0	0	0	0	—	0	2	0	1	0.5	1.000
1930	CIN	N	2	4	.333	5.43	23	3	1	58	71	31	19	0	1	2	4	15	4	0	.267	4	22	1	1	1.2	.963
3 yrs.			2	6	.250	5.86	40	4	1	86	111	47	29	0	1	4	6	19	5	0	.263	5	28	3	2	0.9	.917

Bill Campbell

CAMPBELL, WILLIAM RICHARD BL TR 6′ 3″ 185 lbs.
B. Aug. 9, 1948, Highland Park, Mich.

Year	Team	Lg	W	L	PCT	ERA	G	GS	CG	IP	H	BB	SO	ShO	Relief Pitching W	Relief Pitching L	Relief Pitching SV	Batting AB	Batting H	Batting HR	BA	PO	A	E	DP	TC/G	FA
1973	MIN	A	3	3	.500	3.14	28	2	0	51.2	44	20	42	0	3	2	7	0	0	0	—	2	8	1	0	0.4	.909
1974			8	7	.533	2.63	63	0	0	120	109	55	89	0	8	7	19	0	0	0	—	10	16	2	3	0.4	.929
1975			4	6	.400	3.79	47	7	2	121	119	46	76	1	1	4	5	1	0	0	.000	12	18	1	2	0.7	.968
1976			17	5	**.773**	3.01	**78**	0	0	167.2	145	62	115	0	**17**	5	20	0	0	0	—	12	20	1	1	0.4	.970
1977	BOS	A	13	9	.591	2.96	69	0	0	140	112	60	114	0	13	9	**31**	0	0	0	—	19	20	1	2	0.6	.975
1978			7	5	.583	3.91	29	0	0	50.2	62	17	47	0	7	5	4	0	0	0	—	10	6	1	0	0.6	.941
1979			3	4	.429	4.25	41	0	0	55	55	23	25	0	3	4	9	0	0	0	—	10	11	0	1	0.5	1.000
1980			4	0	1.000	4.83	23	0	0	41	44	22	17	0	4	0	0	0	0	0	—	3	2	0	0	0.2	1.000
1981			1	1	.500	3.19	30	0	0	48	45	20	37	0	1	1	7	0	0	0	—	4	7	1	0	0.4	.917
1982	CHI	N	3	6	.333	3.69	62	0	0	100	89	40	71	0	3	6	8	7	1	0	.143	10	23	0	1	0.5	1.000
1983			6	8	.429	4.49	**82**	0	0	122.1	128	49	97	0	6	8	8	10	1	0	.100	15	24	2	0	0.5	.951
1984	PHI	N	6	5	.545	3.43	57	0	0	81.1	68	35	52	0	6	5	1	1	0	0	.000	6	5	0	0	0.2	1.000
1985	STL	N	5	3	.625	3.50	50	0	0	64.1	55	21	41	0	5	3	4	6	2	0	.333	0	6	1	0	0.1	.857
1986	DET	A	3	6	.333	3.88	34	0	0	55.2	46	21	37	0	3	6	3	0	0	0	—	6	4	2	1	0.4	.833
1987	MON	N	0	0	—	8.10	7	0	0	10	18	4	4	0	0	0	0	1	0	0	.000	0	2	0	0	0.3	1.000
15 yrs.			83	68	.550	3.55	700	9	2	1228.2	1139	495	864	1	80	65	126	26	4	0	.154	119	172	13	11	0.4	.957
LEAGUE CHAMPIONSHIP SERIES																											
1985	STL	N	0	0	—	0.00	3	0	0	2.1	3	0	2	0	0	0	0	0	0	0	—	0	0	0	0	0.0	.000
WORLD SERIES																											
1985	STL	N	0	0	—	2.25	3	0	0	4	4	2	5	0	0	0	0	0	0	0	—	1	0	0	0	0.3	1.000

Billy Campbell

CAMPBELL, WILLIAM JAMES BL TL 5′10″ 165 lbs.
B. Nov. 5, 1873, Pittsburgh, Pa. D. Oct. 6, 1957, Cincinnati, Ohio.

Year	Team	Lg	W	L	PCT	ERA	G	GS	CG	IP	H	BB	SO	ShO	Relief Pitching W	Relief Pitching L	Relief Pitching SV	Batting AB	Batting H	Batting HR	BA	PO	A	E	DP	TC/G	FA
1905	STL	N	1	1	.500	7.41	2	2	2	17	27	7	2	0	0	0	0	7	1	0	.143	2	9	0	0	5.5	1.000
1907	CIN	N	3	0	1.000	2.14	3	3	3	21	19	3	4	0	0	0	0	8	2	0	.250	4	7	0	0	3.7	1.000
1908			12	13	.480	2.60	35	24	19	221.1	203	44	73	2	2	1	1	72	6	0	.083	10	87	7	1	3.0	.933
1909			7	11	.389	2.67	30	15	7	148.1	162	39	37	0	1	4	2	43	6	0	.140	3	55	1	2	2.0	.983
4 yrs.			23	25	.479	2.80	70	44	31	407.2	411	93	116	2	3	5	3	130	15	0	.115	19	158	8	3	2.6	.957

Dave Campbell

CAMPBELL, DAVID ALAN BR TR 6′ 3″ 210 lbs.
B. Sept. 3, 1951, Princeton, Ind.

Year	Team	Lg	W	L	PCT	ERA	G	GS	CG	IP	H	BB	SO	ShO	Relief Pitching W	Relief Pitching L	Relief Pitching SV	Batting AB	Batting H	Batting HR	BA	PO	A	E	DP	TC/G	FA
1977	ATL	N	0	6	.000	3.03	65	0	0	89	78	33	42	0	0	6	13	12	1	0	.083	0	9	1	0	0.2	.900
1978			4	4	.500	4.83	53	0	0	69	67	49	45	0	4	4	1	0	0	0	—	6	9	1	1	0.3	.938
2 yrs.			4	10	.286	3.82	118	0	0	158	145	82	87	0	4	10	14	12	1	0	.083	6	18	2	1	0.2	.923

Jim Campbell

CAMPBELL, JAMES MARCUS BL TL 5′11″ 175 lbs.
B. May 19, 1966, Santa Monica, Calif.

Year	Team	Lg	W	L	PCT	ERA	G	GS	CG	IP	H	BB	SO	ShO	Relief Pitching W	Relief Pitching L	Relief Pitching SV	Batting AB	Batting H	Batting HR	BA	PO	A	E	DP	TC/G	FA
1990	KC	A	1	0	1.000	8.38	2	2	0	9.2	15	1	2	0	0	0	0	0	0	0	—	1	0	0	0	0.5	1.000

John Campbell

CAMPBELL, JOHN MILLARD BR TR 6′ 1½″ 184 lbs.
B. Sept. 13, 1907, Washington, D. C. D. Apr. 24, 1995, Daytona Beach, Fla.

Year	Team	Lg	W	L	PCT	ERA	G	GS	CG	IP	H	BB	SO	ShO	Relief Pitching W	Relief Pitching L	Relief Pitching SV	Batting AB	Batting H	Batting HR	BA	PO	A	E	DP	TC/G	FA
1933	WAS	A	0	0	—	0.00	1	0	0	1	1	1	0	0	0	0	0	0	0	0	—	0	0	0	0	0.0	.000

Kevin Campbell

CAMPBELL, KEVIN WADE BR TR 6′ 2″ 225 lbs.
B. Dec. 6, 1964, Marianna, Ark.

Year	Team	Lg	W	L	PCT	ERA	G	GS	CG	IP	H	BB	SO	ShO	Relief Pitching W	Relief Pitching L	Relief Pitching SV	Batting AB	Batting H	Batting HR	BA	PO	A	E	DP	TC/G	FA
1991	OAK	A	1	0	1.000	2.74	14	0	0	23	13	14	16	0	1	0	0	0	0	0	—	3	2	0	0	0.4	1.000
1992			2	3	.400	5.12	32	5	0	65	66	45	38	0	1	2	1	0	0	0	—	1	6	0	0	0.2	1.000
1993			0	0	—	7.31	11	0	0	16	20	11	9	0	0	0	0	0	0	0	—	0	1	0	0	0.1	1.000
1994	MIN	A	1	0	1.000	2.92	14	0	0	24.2	20	5	15	0	1	0	0	0	0	0	—	0	7	0	0	0.5	1.000
1995			0	0	—	4.66	6	0	0	9.2	8	5	5	0	0	0	0	0	0	0	—	2	0	0	0	0.3	1.000
5 yrs.			4	3	.571	4.55	77	5	0	138.1	127	80	83	0	3	2	1	0	0	0		6	16	0	0	0.3	1.000

Mike Campbell

CAMPBELL, MICHAEL THOMAS BR TR 6′ 3″ 210 lbs.
B. Feb. 17, 1964, Seattle, Wash.

Year	Team	Lg	W	L	PCT	ERA	G	GS	CG	IP	H	BB	SO	ShO	Relief Pitching W	Relief Pitching L	Relief Pitching SV	Batting AB	Batting H	Batting HR	BA	PO	A	E	DP	TC/G	FA
1987	SEA	A	1	4	.200	4.74	9	9	1	49.1	41	25	35	0	0	0	0	0	0	0	—	6	5	0	0	1.2	1.000
1988			6	10	.375	5.89	20	20	2	114.2	128	43	63	0	0	0	0	0	0	0	—	7	13	3	1	1.1	.870
1989			1	2	.333	7.29	5	5	0	21	28	10	6	0	0	0	0	0	0	0	—	2	1	0	0	0.6	1.000

Mike Campbell *continued*

Year	Team	Lg	W	L	PCT	ERA	G	GS	CG	IP	H	BB	SO	ShO	Relief Pitching W	Relief Pitching L	Relief Pitching SV	Batting AB	Batting H	Batting HR	BA	PO	A	E	DP	TC/G	FA
1992	TEX	A	0	1	.000	9.82	1	0	0	3.2	3	2	2	0	0	1	0	0	0	0	—	0	0	0	0	0.0	.000
1994	SD	N	1	1	.500	12.96	3	2	0	8.1	13	5	10	0	1	0	0	3	1	0	.333	0	0	0	0	0.0	.000
5 yrs.			9	18	.333	6.12	38	36	3	197	213	85	116	0	1	1	0	3	1	0	.333	15	19	3	1	1.0	.919

Card Camper

CAMPER, CARDELL
B. July 6, 1952, Boley, Okla.
BR TR 6′ 3″ 208 lbs.

Year	Team	Lg	W	L	PCT	ERA	G	GS	CG	IP	H	BB	SO	ShO	Relief Pitching W	Relief Pitching L	Relief Pitching SV	Batting AB	Batting H	Batting HR	BA	PO	A	E	DP	TC/G	FA
1977	CLE	A	1	0	1.000	4.00	3	1	0	9	7	4	9	0	0	0	0	0	0	0	—	0	0	0	0	0.0	.000

Sal Campfield

CAMPFIELD, WILLIAM HOLTON
B. Feb. 19, 1868, Meadville, Pa. D. May 16, 1952, Meadville, Pa.
BR TR 6′½″

Year	Team	Lg	W	L	PCT	ERA	G	GS	CG	IP	H	BB	SO	ShO	Relief Pitching W	Relief Pitching L	Relief Pitching SV	Batting AB	Batting H	Batting HR	BA	PO	A	E	DP	TC/G	FA
1896	NY	N	1	1	.500	4.00	6	2	2	27	31	6	6	0	0	0	0	12	2	0	.167	0	5	1	0	1.0	.833

Sal Campisi

CAMPISI, SALVATORE JOHN
B. Aug. 11, 1942, Brooklyn, N. Y.
BR TR 6′ 2″ 210 lbs.

Year	Team	Lg	W	L	PCT	ERA	G	GS	CG	IP	H	BB	SO	ShO	Relief Pitching W	Relief Pitching L	Relief Pitching SV	Batting AB	Batting H	Batting HR	BA	PO	A	E	DP	TC/G	FA
1969	STL	N	1	0	1.000	0.90	7	0	0	10	4	6	7	0	1	0	0	0	0	0	—	0	4	2	0	0.9	.667
1970			2	2	.500	2.94	37	0	0	49	53	37	26	0	2	2	4	1	0	0	.000	1	8	0	0	0.2	1.000
1971	MIN	A	0	0	—	4.50	6	0	0	4	5	4	2	0	0	0	0	0	0	0	—	0	1	0	0	0.2	1.000
3 yrs.			3	2	.600	2.71	50	0	0	63	62	47	35	0	3	2	4	1	0	0	.000	1	13	2	0	0.3	.875

Hugh Canavan

CANAVAN, HUGH EDWARD (Hugo)
B. May 13, 1897, Worcester, Mass. D. Sept. 4, 1967, Boston, Mass.
BL TL 5′ 8″ 160 lbs.

Year	Team	Lg	W	L	PCT	ERA	G	GS	CG	IP	H	BB	SO	ShO	Relief Pitching W	Relief Pitching L	Relief Pitching SV	Batting AB	Batting H	Batting HR	BA	PO	A	E	DP	TC/G	FA
1918	BOS	N	0	4	.000	6.36	11	3	3	46.2	70	15	18	0	0	1	0	21	2	0	.095	3	20	2	0	1.9	.920

John Candelaria

CANDELARIA, JOHN ROBERT (The Candy Man)
B. Nov. 6, 1953, New York, N. Y.
BR TL 6′ 7″ 205 lbs.
BL 1975–1981
BB 1982–1986

Year	Team	Lg	W	L	PCT	ERA	G	GS	CG	IP	H	BB	SO	ShO	Relief Pitching W	Relief Pitching L	Relief Pitching SV	Batting AB	Batting H	Batting HR	BA	PO	A	E	DP	TC/G	FA
1975	PIT	N	8	6	.571	2.75	18	18	4	121	95	36	95	1	0	0	0	43	6	0	.140	3	13	4	0	1.1	.800
1976			16	7	.696	3.15	32	31	11	220	173	60	138	4	0	0	1	76	14	0	.184	3	31	0	2	1.1	1.000
1977			20	5	**.800**	**2.34**	33	33	6	231	197	50	133	1	0	0	0	80	18	0	.225	6	30	1	3	1.1	.973
1978			12	11	.522	3.24	30	29	3	189	191	49	94	1	0	0	1	52	9	0	.173	4	25	0	0	1.0	1.000
1979			14	9	.609	3.22	33	30	8	207	201	41	101	0	0	1	0	68	9	0	.132	2	36	0	3	1.2	1.000
1980			11	14	.440	4.02	35	34	7	233	246	50	97	0	0	0	1	77	15	0	.195	8	38	2	3	1.4	.958
1981			2	2	.500	3.51	6	6	0	41	42	11	14	0	0	0	0	13	3	0	.231	1	7	0	1	1.3	1.000
1982			12	7	.632	2.94	31	30	1	174.2	166	37	133	1	0	0	1	54	12	0	.222	1	23	1	1	0.8	.960
1983			15	8	.652	3.23	33	32	2	197.2	191	45	157	0	0	0	1	65	9	0	.138	5	20	0	1	0.8	1.000
1984			12	11	.522	2.72	33	28	3	185.1	179	34	133	1	0	1	2	62	8	1	.129	3	21	0	1	0.7	1.000
1985	2 teams PIT N (37G 2–4) CAL A (13G 7–3)																										
″	total		9	7	.563	3.73	50	13	1	125.1	127	38	100	1	2	4	9	1	0	0	.000	3	16	2	0	0.4	.905
1986	CAL	A	10	2	.833	2.55	16	16	1	91.2	68	26	81	1	0	0	0	0	0	0	—	3	10	0	0	0.8	1.000
1987	2 teams CAL A (20G 8–6) NY N (3G 2–0)																										
″	total		10	6	.625	4.81	23	23	0	129	144	23	84	0	0	0	0	5	1	0	.200	6	24	0	1	1.3	1.000
1988	NY	A	13	7	.650	3.38	25	24	6	157	150	23	121	2	0	0	1	0	0	0	—	4	22	0	0	1.0	1.000
1989	2 teams NY A (10G 3–3) MON N (12G 0–2)																										
″	total		3	5	.375	4.68	22	6	1	65.1	66	16	51	0	0	3	0	0	0	0		2	7	1	0	0.5	.900
1990	2 teams MIN A (34G 7–3) TOR A (13G 0–3)																										
″	total		7	6	.538	3.95	47	3	0	79.2	87	20	63	0	7	3	5	0	0	0		4	9	0	0	0.3	1.000
1991	LA	N	1	1	.500	3.74	59	0	0	33.2	31	11	38	0	1	1	2	0	0	0	—	0	2	0	0	0.0	1.000
1992			2	5	.286	2.84	50	0	0	25.1	20	13	23	0	2	5	5	0	0	0	—	0	5	0	0	0.1	1.000
1993	PIT	N	0	3	.000	8.24	24	0	0	19.2	25	9	17	0	0	3	1	0	0	0	—	0	0	0	0	0.0	.000
19 yrs.			177	122	.592	3.33	600	356	54	2526.1	2399	592	1673	13	12	21	29	596	104	1	.174	58	339	11	16	0.7	.973
LEAGUE CHAMPIONSHIP SERIES																											
1975	PIT	N	0	0	—	3.52	1	1	0	7.2	3	2	14	0	0	0	0	3	0	0	.000	0	0	0	0	0.0	.000
1979			0	0	—	2.57	1	1	0	7	5	1	4	0	0	0	0	3	0	0	.000	0	0	0	0	0.0	.000
1986	CAL	A	1	1	.500	0.84	2	2	0	10.2	11	6	7	0	0	0	0	0	0	0	—	0	1	0	0	0.5	1.000
3 yrs.			1	1	.500	2.13	4	4	0	25.1	19	9	25	0	0	0	0	6	0	0	.000	0	1	0	0	0.3	1.000
WORLD SERIES																											
1979	PIT	N	1	1	.500	5.00	2	2	0	9	14	2	4	0	0	0	0	3	1	0	.333	0	1	0	0	0.5	1.000

Milo Candini

CANDINI, MARIO CAIN
B. Aug. 3, 1917, Manteca, Calif.
BR TR 6′ 187 lbs.

Year	Team	Lg	W	L	PCT	ERA	G	GS	CG	IP	H	BB	SO	ShO	Relief Pitching W	Relief Pitching L	Relief Pitching SV	Batting AB	Batting H	Batting HR	BA	PO	A	E	DP	TC/G	FA
1943	WAS	A	11	7	.611	2.49	28	21	8	166	144	65	67	3	2	0	1	56	9	1	.161	9	36	0	2	1.6	1.000
1944			6	7	.462	4.11	28	10	4	103	110	49	31	2	1	4	1	32	10	0	.313	4	17	0	4	0.8	1.000
1946			2	0	1.000	2.08	9	0	0	21.2	15	4	6	0	2	0	1	6	2	0	.333	0	3	0	0	0.3	1.000
1947			3	4	.429	5.17	38	2	0	87	96	35	31	0	3	2	1	18	3	0	.167	6	15	0	1	0.6	1.000
1948			2	3	.400	5.15	35	4	1	94.1	96	63	23	0	2	1	3	22	8	0	.364	9	16	2	0	0.8	.926
1949			0	0	—	4.76	3	0	0	5.2	4	1	1	0	0	0	1	1	1	0	1.000	1	0	0	0	0.3	1.000
1950	PHI	N	1	0	1.000	2.70	18	0	0	30	32	15	10	0	1	0	0	6	1	0	.167	3	7	0	1	0.6	1.000
1951			1	0	1.000	6.00	15	0	0	30	33	18	14	0	1	0	0	3	1	0	.333	1	7	1	1	0.6	.889
8 yrs.			26	21	.553	3.92	174	37	13	537.2	530	250	183	5	12	7	8	144	35	1	.243	33	101	3	9	0.8	.978

Tom Candiotti

CANDIOTTI, THOMAS CAESAR
B. Aug. 31, 1957, Walnut Creek, Calif.
BR TR 6′ 3″ 205 lbs.

Year	Team	Lg	W	L	PCT	ERA	G	GS	CG	IP	H	BB	SO	ShO	Relief Pitching W	Relief Pitching L	Relief Pitching SV	Batting AB	Batting H	Batting HR	BA	PO	A	E	DP	TC/G	FA
1983	MIL	A	4	4	.500	3.23	10	8	2	55.2	62	16	21	1	0	0	0	0	0	0	—	4	5	0	1	0.9	1.000
1984			2	2	.500	5.29	8	6	0	32.1	38	10	23	0	0	0	0	0	0	0	—	3	1	0	0	0.5	1.000
1986	CLE	A	16	12	.571	3.57	36	34	**17**	252.1	234	106	167	3	0	0	0	0	0	0	—	27	41	3	7	2.0	.958
1987			7	18	.280	4.78	32	32	7	201.2	193	93	111	2	0	0	0	0	0	0	—	17	29	1	1	1.5	.979
1988			14	8	.636	3.28	31	31	11	216.2	225	53	137	1	0	0	0	0	0	0	—	17	36	1	2	1.7	.981
1989			13	10	.565	3.10	31	31	4	206	188	55	124	0	0	0	0	0	0	0	—	28	41	1	1	2.3	.986
1990			15	11	.577	3.65	31	29	3	202	207	55	128	1	0	0	0	0	0	0	—	22	37	2	1	2.0	.967
1991	2 teams CLE A (15G 7–6) TOR A (19G 6–7)																										
″	total		13	13	.500	2.65	34	34	6	238	202	73	167	0	0	0	0	0	0	0		19	28	1	1	1.4	.979
1992	LA	N	11	**15**	.423	3.00	32	30	6	203.2	177	63	152	2	1	0	0	56	6	0	.107	16	32	1	3	1.5	.980
1993			8	10	.444	3.12	33	32	2	213.2	192	71	155	0	0	0	0	60	8	0	.133	10	30	3	3	1.3	.930

Tom Candiotti *continued*

Year	Team	W	L	PCT	ERA	G	GS	CG	IP	H	BB	SO	ShO	Relief Pitching W	Relief L	Relief SV	Batting AB	Batting H	HR	BA	PO	A	E	DP	TC/G	FA
1994		7	7	.500	4.12	23	22	5	153	149	54	102	0	0	0	0	50	7	0	.140	14	22	0	1	1.6	1.000
1995		7	14	.333	3.50	30	30	1	190.1	187	58	141	1	0	0	0	55	6	0	.109	15	24	1	0	1.3	.975
12 yrs.		117	124	.485	3.47	331	319	64	2165.1	2054	707	1428	11	1	0	0	221	27	0	.122	192	326	14	21	1.6	.974
LEAGUE CHAMPIONSHIP SERIES																										
1991	TOR A	0	1	.000	8.22	2	2	0	7.2	17	2	5	0	0	0	0	0	0	0	—	0	2	0	1	1.0	1.000

John Caneira

CANEIRA, JOHN CASCAES BR TR 6′ 3″ 180 lbs.
B. Oct. 7, 1952, Waterbury, Conn.

Year	Team	W	L	PCT	ERA	G	GS	CG	IP	H	BB	SO	ShO	Relief Pitching W	Relief L	Relief SV	Batting AB	Batting H	HR	BA	PO	A	E	DP	TC/G	FA
1977	CAL A	2	2	.500	4.08	6	4	0	28.2	27	16	17	0	0	0	0	0	0	0	—	1	2	1	0	0.7	.750
1978		0	0	—	7.04	2	2	0	7.2	8	3	0	0	0	0	0	0	0	0	—	0	0	1	0	0.5	.000
2 yrs.		2	2	.500	4.71	8	6	0	36.1	35	19	17	0	0	0	0	0	0	0		1	2	2	0	0.6	.600

John Cangelosi

CANGELOSI, JOHN ANTHONY BB TL 5′ 8″ 150 lbs.
B. Mar. 10, 1963, Brooklyn, N. Y.

Year	Team	W	L	PCT	ERA	G	GS	CG	IP	H	BB	SO	ShO	Relief Pitching W	Relief L	Relief SV	Batting AB	Batting H	HR	BA	PO	A	E	DP	TC/G	FA
1988	PIT N	0	0	—	0.00	1	0	0	2	1	0	0	0	0	0	0	118	30	0	.254	1	0	0	0	0.2	1.000
1995	HOU N	0	0	—	0.00	1	0	0	1	0	1	0	0	0	0	0	201	64	2	.318	276	7	9	1	2.2	.969
2 yrs.		0	0		0.00	2	0	0	3	1	1	0	0	0	0	0	*				730	24	24	3	1.7	.969

Jose Cano

CANO, JOSELITO BR TR 6′ 3″ 175 lbs.
Born Joselito Cano (Soriano).
B. Mar. 7, 1962, Boca de Soco, Dominican Republic.

Year	Team	W	L	PCT	ERA	G	GS	CG	IP	H	BB	SO	ShO	Relief Pitching W	Relief L	Relief SV	Batting AB	Batting H	HR	BA	PO	A	E	DP	TC/G	FA
1989	HOU N	1	1	.500	5.09	6	3	1	23	24	7	8	0	0	0	0	6	0	0	.000	2	2	1	1	0.8	.800

Jose Canseco

CANSECO, JOSE BR TR 6′ 3″ 185 lbs.
Born Jose Canseco (Capas).
Brother of Ozzie Canseco.
B. July 2, 1964, Havana, Cuba.

Year	Team	W	L	PCT	ERA	G	GS	CG	IP	H	BB	SO	ShO	Relief Pitching W	Relief L	Relief SV	Batting AB	Batting H	HR	BA	PO	A	E	DP	TC/G	FA
1993	TEX A	0	0	—	27.00	1	0	0	1	2	3	0	0	0	0	0	*				56	2	3	1	2.3	.951

Guy Cantrell

CANTRELL, GUY DEWEY (Gunner) BR TR 6′ 190 lbs.
B. Apr. 9, 1904, Clarita, Okla. D. Jan. 31, 1961, McAlester, Okla.

Year	Team	W	L	PCT	ERA	G	GS	CG	IP	H	BB	SO	ShO	Relief Pitching W	Relief L	Relief SV	Batting AB	Batting H	HR	BA	PO	A	E	DP	TC/G	FA
1925	BKN N	1	0	1.000	3.00	14	3	1	36	42	14	13	0	0	0	0	9	0	0	.000	3	13	1	1	1.2	.941
1927	**2 teams** **BKN N** (6G 0–0) **PHI A** (2G 0–2)																									
″	**total**	0	2	.000	4.18	8	2	2	28	35	13	12	0	0	0	0	9	2	0	.222	1	8	0	0	1.1	1.000
1930	DET A	1	5	.167	5.66	16	2	1	35	38	20	20	0	1	3	0	9	0	0	.000	1	10	0	0	0.7	1.000
3 yrs.		2	7	.222	4.27	38	7	4	99	115	47	45	0	1	3	0	27	2	0	.074	5	31	1	1	1.0	.973

Ben Cantwell

CANTWELL, BENJAMIN CALDWELL BR TR 6′ 1″ 168 lbs.
B. Apr. 13, 1902, Milan, Tenn. D. Dec. 4, 1962, Salem, Mo.

Year	Team	W	L	PCT	ERA	G	GS	CG	IP	H	BB	SO	ShO	Relief Pitching W	Relief L	Relief SV	Batting AB	Batting H	HR	BA	PO	A	E	DP	TC/G	FA
1927	NY N	1	1	.500	4.12	5	2	1	19.2	26	2	6	0	0	0	0	8	2	0	.250	2	2	0	0	0.8	1.000
1928	**2 teams** **NY N** (7G 1–0) **BOS N** (22G 3–3)																									
″	**total**	4	3	.571	4.98	29	10	3	108.1	132	40	18	0	1	0	1	33	7	0	.212	7	34	3	1	1.5	.932
1929	BOS N	4	13	.235	4.47	27	20	8	157	171	52	25	0	1	0	2	50	9	0	.180	12	53	4	5	2.6	.942
1930		9	15	.375	4.88	31	21	10	173.1	213	45	43	0	4	1	2	63	19	0	.302	13	50	1	9	2.1	.984
1931		7	9	.438	3.63	33	16	9	156.1	160	34	32	2	1	1	2	57	13	0	.228	7	49	3	2	1.8	.949
1932		13	11	.542	2.96	37	9	3	146	133	33	33	1	**12**	**8**	5	50	14	0	.280	12	43	1	6	1.5	.982
1933		20	10	**.667**	2.62	40	29	18	254.2	242	54	57	2	4	1	2	85	12	0	.141	12	77	1	2	2.3	.989
1934		5	11	.313	4.33	27	19	6	143.1	163	34	45	1	1	0	5	43	12	0	.279	8	40	3	1	1.9	.941
1935		4	**25**	.138	4.61	39	24	13	210.2	235	44	34	0	1	**5**	0	67	19	0	.284	12	54	1	4	1.7	.985
1936		9	9	.500	3.04	34	12	4	133.1	127	35	42	0	6	3	2	41	8	0	.195	9	44	2	2	1.6	.964
1937	**2 teams** **NY N** (1G 0–1) **BKN N** (13G 0–0)																									
″	**total**	0	1	.000	5.17	14	1	0	31.1	38	9	13	0	0	0	0	6	1	0	.167	1	17	0	0	1.3	1.000
11 yrs.		76	108	.413	3.91	316	163	75	1534	1640	382	348	6	31	19	21	503	116	0	.231	95	463	19	32	1.8	.967

Mike Cantwell

CANTWELL, MICHAEL JOSEPH BL TL 6′ 160 lbs.
Brother of Tom Cantwell.
B. Jan. 15, 1896, Washington, D. C. D. Jan. 5, 1953, Oteen, N. C.

Year	Team	W	L	PCT	ERA	G	GS	CG	IP	H	BB	SO	ShO	Relief Pitching W	Relief L	Relief SV	Batting AB	Batting H	HR	BA	PO	A	E	DP	TC/G	FA
1916	NY A	0	0	—	0.00	1	0	0	2	0	2	0	0	0	0	0	0	0	0	—	0	0	0	0	0.0	.000
1919	PHI N	1	3	.250	5.60	5	3	2	27.1	36	9	6	0	0	1	0	9	2	0	.222	1	4	0	0	1.0	1.000
1920		0	3	.000	3.86	5	1	0	23.1	25	15	8	0	0	2	0	7	1	0	.143	1	8	0	0	1.8	1.000
3 yrs.		1	6	.143	4.61	11	4	2	52.2	61	26	14	0	0	3	0	16	3	0	.188	2	12	0	0	1.3	1.000

Tom Cantwell

CANTWELL, THOMAS ALOYSIUS BR TR 6′ 1″ 175 lbs.
Brother of Mike Cantwell.
B. Dec. 23, 1888, Washington, D. C. D. Apr. 1, 1968, Washington, D. C.

Year	Team	W	L	PCT	ERA	G	GS	CG	IP	H	BB	SO	ShO	Relief Pitching W	Relief L	Relief SV	Batting AB	Batting H	HR	BA	PO	A	E	DP	TC/G	FA
1909	CIN N	1	0	1.000	1.66	6	1	1	21.2	16	7	7	0	1	0	0	5	3	0	.600	1	5	0	0	1.0	1.000
1910		0	0	—	13.50	2	0	0	1.1	2	3	0	0	0	0	0	0	0	0	—	0	0	0	0	0.0	.000
2 yrs.		1	0	1.000	2.35	8	1	1	23	18	10	7	0	1	0	0	5	3	0	.600	1	5	0	0	0.8	1.000

Mike Capel

CAPEL, MICHAEL LEE BR TR 6′ 1″ 175 lbs.
B. Oct. 13, 1961, Marshall, Tex.

Year	Team	W	L	PCT	ERA	G	GS	CG	IP	H	BB	SO	ShO	Relief Pitching W	Relief L	Relief SV	Batting AB	Batting H	HR	BA	PO	A	E	DP	TC/G	FA
1988	CHI N	2	1	.667	4.91	22	0	0	29.1	34	13	19	0	2	1	0	2	0	0	.000	4	3	1	0	0.4	.875
1990	MIL A	0	0	—	135.00	2	0	0	0.1	6	1	1	0	0	0	0	0	0	0	—	0	0	0	0	0.0	.000
1991	HOU N	1	3	.250	3.03	25	0	0	32.2	33	15	23	0	1	3	3	0	0	0	—	3	4	0	1	0.3	1.000
3 yrs.		3	4	.429	4.62	49	0	0	62.1	73	29	43	0	3	4	3	2	0	0	.000	7	7	1	1	0.3	.933

Doug Capilla

CAPILLA, DOUGLAS EDMUND BL TL 5′11″ 160 lbs.
B. Jan. 7, 1952, Honolulu, Hawaii.

Year	Team	W	L	PCT	ERA	G	GS	CG	IP	H	BB	SO	ShO	Relief Pitching W	Relief L	Relief SV	Batting AB	Batting H	HR	BA	PO	A	E	DP	TC/G	FA
1976	STL N	1	0	1.000	5.40	7	0	0	8.1	8	4	5	0	1	0	0	0	0	0	—	1	1	0	0	0.3	1.000
1977	**2 teams** **STL N** (2G 0–0) **CIN N** (22G 7–8)																									
″	**total**	7	8	.467	4.47	24	16	1	108.2	96	61	75	0	0	0	0	34	2	0	.059	6	13	3	0	0.9	.864
1978	CIN N	0	1	.000	9.82	6	3	0	11	14	11	9	0	0	0	0	2	0	0	.000	0	1	0	0	0.2	1.000

Doug Capilla *continued*

Year	Team	Lg	W	L	PCT	ERA	G	GS	CG	IP	H	BB	SO	ShO	Relief Pitching W	Relief L	Relief SV	Batting AB	Batting H	Batting HR	BA	PO	A	E	DP	TC/G	FA
1979	**2 teams**	**CIN N**	(5G 1–0)	**CHI N**	(13G 0–1)																						
″	**total**		1	1	.500	4.18	18	1	0	23.2	21	12	10	0	1	0	0	1	1	0	1.000	0	7	1	0	0.4	.875
1980	**CHI**	**N**	2	8	.200	4.10	39	11	0	90	82	51	51	0	1	0	0	21	4	0	.190	6	19	3	0	0.7	.893
1981			1	0	1.000	3.18	42	0	0	51	52	34	28	0	1	0	0	3	0	0	.000	0	10	1	0	0.3	.909
6 yrs.			12	18	.400	4.34	136	31	1	292.2	273	173	178	0	4	0	0	61	7	0	.115	13	51	8	0	0.5	.889

George Cappuzzello

CAPPUZZELLO, GEORGE ANGELO
B. Jan. 15, 1954, Youngstown, Ohio.
BR TL 6′ 175 lbs.

Year	Team	Lg	W	L	PCT	ERA	G	GS	CG	IP	H	BB	SO	ShO	Relief Pitching W	Relief L	Relief SV	Batting AB	Batting H	Batting HR	BA	PO	A	E	DP	TC/G	FA
1981	**DET**	**A**	1	1	.500	3.44	18	3	0	34	28	18	19	0	1	0	1	0	0	0	—	0	5	0	1	0.3	1.000
1982	**HOU**	**N**	0	1	.000	2.79	17	0	0	19.1	16	7	13	0	0	1	0	1	0	0	.000	1	4	0	1	0.3	1.000
2 yrs.			1	2	.333	3.21	35	3	0	53.1	44	25	32	0	1	1	1	1	0	0	.000	1	9	0	2	0.3	1.000

Buzz Capra

CAPRA, LEE WILLIAM
B. Oct. 1, 1947, Chicago, Ill.
BR TR 5′10″ 168 lbs.

Year	Team	Lg	W	L	PCT	ERA	G	GS	CG	IP	H	BB	SO	ShO	Relief Pitching W	Relief L	Relief SV	Batting AB	Batting H	Batting HR	BA	PO	A	E	DP	TC/G	FA
1971	**NY**	**N**	0	1	.000	9.00	3	0	0	5	3	5	6	0	0	1	0	1	0	0	.000	0	1	0	0	0.3	1.000
1972			3	2	.600	4.58	14	6	0	53	50	27	45	0	0	0	0	12	3	0	.250	5	10	0	2	1.1	1.000
1973			2	7	.222	3.86	24	0	0	42	35	28	35	0	2	7	4	2	0	0	.000	1	7	0	0	0.3	1.000
1974	**ATL**	**N**	16	8	.667	**2.28**	39	27	11	217	163	84	137	5	1	2	1	67	11	0	.164	13	19	3	2	0.9	.914
1975			4	7	.364	4.27	12	12	5	78	77	28	35	0	0	0	0	23	1	0	.043	6	13	0	1	1.6	1.000
1976			0	1	.000	9.00	5	0	0	9	9	6	4	0	0	1	0	0	0	0	—	0	3	0	0	0.6	1.000
1977			6	11	.353	5.37	45	16	0	139	142	80	100	0	4	3	0	36	4	0	.111	6	18	1	1	0.6	.960
7 yrs.			31	37	.456	3.88	142	61	16	543	479	258	362	5	7	14	5	141	19	0	.135	31	71	4	6	0.7	.962

Pat Caraway

CARAWAY, CECIL BRADFORD PATRICK
B. Sept. 26, 1906, Erath County, Tex. D. June 9, 1974, El Paso, Tex.
BL TL 6′ 4″ 175 lbs.

Year	Team	Lg	W	L	PCT	ERA	G	GS	CG	IP	H	BB	SO	ShO	Relief Pitching W	Relief L	Relief SV	Batting AB	Batting H	Batting HR	BA	PO	A	E	DP	TC/G	FA
1930	**CHI**	**A**	10	10	.500	3.86	38	21	9	193.1	194	57	83	1	2	1	1	64	11	0	.172	7	53	3	2	1.7	.952
1931			10	**24**	.294	6.22	51	32	11	220	268	101	55	1	1	3	2	72	14	0	.194	11	40	1	0	1.0	.981
1932			2	6	.250	6.82	19	9	1	64.2	80	37	13	0	0	1	0	21	3	0	.143	3	15	2	2	1.1	.900
3 yrs.			22	40	.355	5.35	108	62	21	478	542	195	151	2	3	5	3	157	28	0	.178	21	108	6	4	1.3	.956

John Carden

CARDEN, JOHN BRUTON
B. May 19, 1921, Killeen, Tex. D. Feb. 8, 1949, Mexia, Tex.
BR TR 6′ 5″ 210 lbs.

Year	Team	Lg	W	L	PCT	ERA	G	GS	CG	IP	H	BB	SO	ShO	Relief Pitching W	Relief L	Relief SV	Batting AB	Batting H	Batting HR	BA	PO	A	E	DP	TC/G	FA
1946	**NY**	**N**	0	0	—	22.50	1	0	0	2	4	4	1	0	0	0	0	0	0	0	—	0	0	1	0	1.0	.000

Conrad Cardinal

CARDINAL, CONRAD SETH
B. Mar. 30, 1942, Brooklyn, N. Y.
BR TR 6′ 1″ 190 lbs.

Year	Team	Lg	W	L	PCT	ERA	G	GS	CG	IP	H	BB	SO	ShO	Relief Pitching W	Relief L	Relief SV	Batting AB	Batting H	Batting HR	BA	PO	A	E	DP	TC/G	FA
1963	**HOU**	**N**	0	1	.000	6.08	6	1	0	13.1	15	7	7	0	0	0	0	2	0	0	.000	0	4	0	0	0.7	1.000

Ben Cardoni

CARDONI, ARMAND JOSEPH (Big Ben)
B. Aug. 21, 1920, Jessup, Pa. D. Apr. 2, 1969, Jessup, Pa.
BR TR 6′ 3″ 195 lbs.

Year	Team	Lg	W	L	PCT	ERA	G	GS	CG	IP	H	BB	SO	ShO	Relief Pitching W	Relief L	Relief SV	Batting AB	Batting H	Batting HR	BA	PO	A	E	DP	TC/G	FA
1943	**BOS**	**N**	0	0	—	6.43	11	0	0	28	38	14	5	0	0	0	1	7	0	0	.000	1	7	0	0	0.7	1.000
1944			0	6	.000	3.93	22	5	1	75.2	83	37	24	0	0	2	0	17	4	0	.235	2	12	2	1	0.7	.875
1945			0	0	—	9.00	3	0	0	4	6	3	5	0	0	0	0	0	0	0	—	0	0	0	0	0.0	.000
3 yrs.			0	6	.000	4.76	36	5	1	107.2	127	54	34	0	0	2	1	24	4	0	.167	3	19	2	1	0.7	.917

Don Cardwell

CARDWELL, DONALD EUGENE
B. Dec. 7, 1935, Winston-Salem, N. C.
BR TR 6′ 4″ 210 lbs.

Year	Team	Lg	W	L	PCT	ERA	G	GS	CG	IP	H	BB	SO	ShO	Relief Pitching W	Relief L	Relief SV	Batting AB	Batting H	Batting HR	BA	PO	A	E	DP	TC/G	FA
1957	**PHI**	**N**	4	8	.333	4.91	30	19	5	128.1	122	42	92	1	0	0	1	35	7	1	.200	12	18	2	0	1.1	.938
1958			3	6	.333	4.51	16	14	3	107.2	99	37	77	0	0	0	0	38	8	0	.211	11	13	0	2	1.5	1.000
1959			9	10	.474	4.06	25	22	5	153	135	65	106	1	0	1	0	55	3	1	.055	4	13	3	2	0.8	.850
1960	**2 teams**	**PHI N**	(5G 1–2)	**CHI N**	(31G 8–14)																						
″	**total**		9	16	.360	4.38	36	30	6	205.1	194	79	150	1	1	2	0	77	16	5	.208	13	24	2	0	1.1	.949
1961	**CHI**	**N**	15	14	.517	3.82	39	**38**	13	259.1	243	88	156	3	0	1	0	95	10	3	.105	18	54	2	3	1.9	.973
1962			7	16	.304	4.92	41	29	6	195.2	205	60	104	1	1	0	4	61	9	0	.148	15	37	1	2	1.3	.981
1963	**PIT**	**N**	13	15	.464	3.07	33	32	7	213.2	195	52	112	2	1	0	0	71	6	0	.085	16	35	5	1	1.7	.911
1964			1	2	.333	2.79	4	4	1	19.1	15	7	10	1	0	0	0	7	1	0	.143	0	6	1	1	1.8	.857
1965			13	10	.565	3.18	37	34	12	240.1	214	59	107	2	0	0	0	74	12	2	.162	23	51	2	6	2.1	.974
1966			6	6	.500	4.60	32	14	1	101.2	112	27	60	0	3	1	1	29	3	0	.103	13	24	2	2	1.2	.949
1967	**NY**	**N**	5	9	.357	3.57	26	16	3	118.1	112	39	71	3	1	0	0	38	6	1	.158	13	27	0	3	1.5	1.000
1968			7	13	.350	2.95	29	25	5	180	156	50	82	1	0	0	1	61	3	1	.049	16	39	1	1	1.9	.982
1969			8	10	.444	3.01	30	21	4	152.1	145	47	60	0	1	1	0	47	8	1	.170	9	41	3	0	1.8	.943
1970	**2 teams**	**NY N**	(16G 0–2)	**ATL N**	(16G 2–1)																						
″	**total**		2	3	.400	7.69	32	3	1	48	62	19	24	1	1	1	0	10	2	0	.200	1	12	1	2	0.4	.929
14 yrs.			102	138	.425	3.92	410	301	72	2123	2009	671	1211	17	9	7	7	698	94	15	.135	164	394	25	25	1.4	.957
WORLD SERIES																											
1969	**NY**	**N**	0	0	—	0.00	1	0	0	1	0	0	0	0	0	0	0	0	0	0	—	0	0	0	0	0.0	.000

Tex Carleton

CARLETON, JAMES OTTO
B. Aug. 19, 1906, Comanche, Tex. D. Jan. 11, 1977, Fort Worth, Tex.
BB TR 6′ 1½″ 180 lbs.

Year	Team	Lg	W	L	PCT	ERA	G	GS	CG	IP	H	BB	SO	ShO	Relief Pitching W	Relief L	Relief SV	Batting AB	Batting H	Batting HR	BA	PO	A	E	DP	TC/G	FA
1932	**STL**	**N**	10	13	.435	4.08	44	22	9	196.1	198	70	113	3	3	2	0	60	9	1	.150	11	48	3	3	1.4	.952
1933			17	11	.607	3.38	44	33	15	277	263	97	147	4	1	1	3	91	17	1	.187	13	50	2	1	1.5	.969
1934			16	11	.593	4.26	40	31	16	240.2	260	52	103	0	0	1	2	88	17	1	.193	21	44	3	4	1.7	.956
1935	**CHI**	**N**	11	8	.579	3.89	31	22	8	171	169	60	84	0	2	2	1	62	8	0	.129	14	42	1	2	1.8	.982
1936			14	10	.583	3.65	35	26	12	197.1	204	67	88	**4**	2	1	1	60	14	3	.233	10	47	0	7	1.6	1.000
1937			16	8	.667	3.15	32	27	18	208.1	183	94	105	4	0	1	0	71	12	0	.169	13	49	3	2	2.0	.954
1938			10	9	.526	5.42	33	24	9	167.2	213	74	80	0	2	1	0	65	15	0	.231	8	32	2	2	1.3	.952
1940	**BKN**	**N**	6	6	.500	3.81	34	17	4	149	140	47	88	1	2	1	2	43	8	0	.186	3	22	0	2	0.7	1.000
8 yrs.			100	76	.568	3.91	293	202	91	1607.1	1630	561	808	16	12	10	9	540	100	6	.185	93	334	14	23	1.5	.968

Tex Carleton *continued*

Year	Team	W	L	PCT	ERA	G	GS	CG	IP	H	BB	SO	ShO	Relief Pitching W	Relief Pitching L	Relief Pitching SV	Batting AB	Batting H	Batting HR	BA	PO	A	E	DP	TC/G	FA
WORLD SERIES																										
1934	**STL N**	0	0	—	7.36	2	1	0	3.2	5	2	2	0	0	0	0	1	0	0	.000	0	0	0	0	0.0	.000
1935	**CHI N**	0	1	.000	1.29	1	1	0	7	6	7	4	0	0	0	0	1	0	0	.000	0	2	0	0	2.0	1.000
1938		0	0	—	∞	1	0	0		1	2	0	0	0	0	0	0	0	0	—	0	0	0	0	0.0	.000
3 yrs.		0	1	.000	5.06	4	2	0	10.2	12	11	6	0	0	0	0	2	0	0	.000	0	2	0	0	0.5	1.000

Cisco Carlos

CARLOS, FRANCISCO MANUEL
B. Sept. 17, 1940, Monrovia, Calif.
BR TR 6′ 3″ 205 lbs.

Year	Team	W	L	PCT	ERA	G	GS	CG	IP	H	BB	SO	ShO	Relief Pitching W	Relief Pitching L	Relief Pitching SV	Batting AB	Batting H	Batting HR	BA	PO	A	E	DP	TC/G	FA
1967	**CHI A**	2	0	1.000	0.86	8	7	1	41.2	23	9	27	1	0	0	0	16	1	0	.063	4	8	1	0	1.6	.923
1968		4	14	.222	3.90	29	21	0	122.1	121	37	57	0	0	0	0	31	2	0	.065	15	26	2	3	1.5	.953
1969	**2 teams CHI A** (25G 4–3) **WAS A** (6G 1–1)																									
″	**total**	5	4	.556	5.37	31	8	0	67	75	29	33	0	3	2	0	15	1	0	.067	4	17	2	0	0.7	.913
1970	**WAS A**	0	0	—	1.50	5	0	0	6	3	4	2	0	0	0	0	0	0	0	—	1	1	0	0	0.4	1.000
4 yrs.		11	18	.379	3.72	73	36	1	237	222	79	119	1	3	2	0	62	4	0	.065	24	52	5	3	1.1	.938

Don Carlsen

CARLSEN, DONALD HERBERT
B. Oct. 15, 1926, Chicago, Ill.
BR TR 6′ 1″ 175 lbs.

Year	Team	W	L	PCT	ERA	G	GS	CG	IP	H	BB	SO	ShO	Relief Pitching W	Relief Pitching L	Relief Pitching SV	Batting AB	Batting H	Batting HR	BA	PO	A	E	DP	TC/G	FA
1948	**CHI N**	0	0	—	36.00	1	0	0	1	5	2	1	0	0	0	0	0	0	0	—	0	0	0	0	0.0	.000
1951	**PIT N**	2	3	.400	4.19	7	6	2	43	50	14	20	0	0	0	0	16	4	0	.250	1	6	2	1	1.3	.778
1952		0	1	.000	10.80	5	1	0	10	20	5	2	0	0	0	0	3	1	0	.333	0	6	0	1	1.2	1.000
3 yrs.		2	4	.333	6.00	13	7	2	54	75	21	23	0	0	0	0	19	5	0	.263	1	12	2	2	1.2	.867

Hal Carlson

CARLSON, HAROLD GUST
B. May 17, 1892, Rockford, Ill. D. May 28, 1930, Chicago, Ill.
BR TR 6′ 180 lbs.

Year	Team	W	L	PCT	ERA	G	GS	CG	IP	H	BB	SO	ShO	Relief Pitching W	Relief Pitching L	Relief Pitching SV	Batting AB	Batting H	Batting HR	BA	PO	A	E	DP	TC/G	FA
1917	**PIT N**	7	11	.389	2.90	34	17	9	161.1	140	49	68	1	3	2	1	49	6	0	.122	6	53	1	3	1.8	.983
1918		0	1	.000	3.75	3	2	0	12	12	5	5	0	0	0	0	5	1	0	.200	1	2	1	0	1.3	.750
1919		8	10	.444	2.23	22	14	7	141	114	39	49	1	3	1	0	43	7	0	.163	8	44	2	0	2.5	.963
1920		14	13	.519	3.36	39	31	16	246.2	262	63	62	3	1	0	3	85	23	0	.271	10	47	4	2	1.6	.934
1921		4	8	.333	4.27	31	10	3	109.2	121	23	37	0	1	3	4	34	10	0	.294	4	32	1	1	1.2	.973
1922		9	12	.429	5.70	39	18	6	145.1	193	58	64	0	2	4	2	56	15	1	.268	5	44	2	1	1.3	.961
1923		0	0	—	4.72	4	0	0	13.1	19	2	4	0	0	0	0	5	0	0	.000	0	5	0	0	1.3	1.000
1924	**PHI N**	8	17	.320	4.86	38	23	12	203.2	267	55	66	1	1	3	2	76	21	2	.276	6	52	0	1	1.5	1.000
1925		13	14	.481	4.23	35	32	18	234	281	52	80	**4**	0	1	0	93	17	2	.183	7	48	1	3	1.6	.982
1926		17	12	.586	3.23	35	34	20	267.1	293	47	55	3	0	0	0	96	23	0	.240	9	49	3	4	1.7	.951
1927	**2 teams PHI N** (11G 4–5) **CHI N** (27G 12–8)																									
″	**total**	16	13	.552	3.70	38	31	19	248	281	45	40	2	1	0	1	92	17	0	.185	9	54	0	1	1.7	1.000
1928	**CHI N**	3	2	.600	5.91	20	5	2	56.1	74	15	11	0	1	0	4	19	5	0	.263	1	16	1	0	0.9	.944
1929		11	5	.688	5.16	31	14	6	111.2	131	31	35	2	2	2	2	39	9	0	.231	6	33	0	1	1.3	1.000
1930		4	2	.667	5.05	8	6	3	51.2	68	14	14	0	1	0	0	20	5	0	.250	2	18	1	1	2.6	.952
14 yrs.		114	120	.487	3.97	377	237	121	2002	2256	498	590	17	16	16	19	712	159	5	.223	74	497	17	18	1.6	.971
WORLD SERIES																										
1929	**CHI N**	0	0	—	6.75	2	0	0	4	7	1	3	0	0	0	0	0	0	0	—	0	0	0	0	0.0	.000

Leon Carlson

CARLSON, LEON ALTON (Swede)
B. Feb. 17, 1895, Jamestown, N. Y. D. Sept. 15, 1961, Jamestown, N. Y.
BR TR 6′ 3″ 195 lbs.

Year	Team	W	L	PCT	ERA	G	GS	CG	IP	H	BB	SO	ShO	Relief Pitching W	Relief Pitching L	Relief Pitching SV	Batting AB	Batting H	Batting HR	BA	PO	A	E	DP	TC/G	FA
1920	**WAS A**	0	0	—	3.65	3	0	0	12.1	14	2	3	0	0	0	0	6	1	0	.167	0	2	0	0	0.7	1.000

Steve Carlton

CARLTON, STEVEN NORMAN (Lefty)
B. Dec. 22, 1944, Miami, Fla.
Hall of Fame 1994.
BL TL 6′ 4″ 210 lbs.

Year	Team	W	L	PCT	ERA	G	GS	CG	IP	H	BB	SO	ShO	Relief Pitching W	Relief Pitching L	Relief Pitching SV	Batting AB	Batting H	Batting HR	BA	PO	A	E	DP	TC/G	FA
1965	**STL N**	0	0	—	2.52	15	2	0	25	27	8	21	0	0	0	0	2	0	0	.000	1	6	0	1	0.5	1.000
1966		3	3	.500	3.12	9	9	2	52	56	18	25	1	0	0	0	15	4	0	.267	2	10	0	2	1.3	1.000
1967		14	9	.609	2.98	30	28	11	193	173	62	168	2	0	1	1	72	11	0	.153	8	30	2	3	1.3	.950
1968		13	11	.542	2.99	34	33	10	232	214	61	162	5	0	1	0	73	12	2	.164	4	39	3	1	1.4	.935
1969		17	11	.607	2.17	31	31	12	236	185	93	210	2	0	0	0	80	17	1	.212	1	34	3	1	1.2	.921
1970		10	**19**	.345	3.72	34	33	13	254	239	109	193	2	0	0	0	80	16	0	.200	6	38	4	1	1.4	.917
1971		20	9	.690	3.56	37	36	18	273	275	98	172	4	0	0	0	96	17	0	.177	11	40	0	3	1.4	1.000
1972	**PHI N**	**27**	10	.730	**1.97**	41	**41**	**30**	**346.1**	**257**	87	**310**	8	0	0	0	117	23	1	.197	8	37	2	3	1.1	.957
1973		13	**20**	.394	3.90	40	**40**	**18**	**293.1**	**293**	113	223	3	0	0	0	100	16	2	.160	4	42	5	3	1.3	.902
1974		16	13	.552	3.22	39	39	17	291	249	**136**	**240**	1	0	0	0	102	25	0	.245	6	42	4	1	1.3	.923
1975		15	14	.517	3.56	37	37	14	255	217	104	192	3	0	0	0	90	14	0	.156	10	32	1	4	1.2	.977
1976		20	7	**.741**	3.13	35	35	13	252.2	224	72	195	2	0	0	0	92	20	0	.217	4	19	0	2	0.7	1.000
1977		**23**	10	.697	2.64	36	36	17	283	229	89	198	2	0	0	0	97	26	3	.268	4	52	1	2	1.6	.982
1978		16	13	.552	2.84	34	34	12	247	228	63	161	3	0	0	0	86	25	0	.291	5	46	3	1	1.6	.944
1979		18	11	.621	3.62	35	35	13	251	202	89	213	4	0	0	0	94	21	0	.223	3	32	5	0	1.1	.875
1980		**24**	9	.727	2.34	38	**38**	13	**304**	243	90	**286**	3	0	0	0	101	19	0	.188	2	42	0	1	1.2	1.000
1981		13	4	.765	2.42	24	24	10	190	152	62	179	1	0	0	0	67	9	0	.134	3	22	0	0	1.0	1.000
1982		**23**	11	.676	3.10	38	**38**	**19**	**295.2**	**253**	86	**286**	**6**	0	0	0	101	22	2	.218	6	37	4	2	1.2	.915
1983		15	16	.484	3.11	37	37	8	**283.2**	**277**	84	**275**	3	0	0	0	97	19	0	.196	4	37	4	0	1.2	.911
1984		13	7	.650	3.58	33	33	1	229	214	79	163	0	0	0	0	84	16	1	.190	7	22	0	0	0.9	1.000
1985		1	8	.111	3.33	16	16	0	92	84	53	48	0	0	0	0	28	5	0	.179	3	18	0	1	1.3	1.000
1986	**3 teams PHI N** (16G 4–8) **SF N** (6G 1–3) **CHI A** (10G 4–3)																									
″	**total**	9	14	.391	5.10	32	32	0	176.1	196	86	120	0	0	0	0	45	9	1	.200	4	23	0	2	0.8	1.000
1987	**2 teams CLE A** (23G 5–9) **MIN A** (9G 1–5)																									
″	**total**	6	14	.300	5.74	32	21	3	152	165	86	91	0	2	2	1	0	0	0		3	23	1	2	0.8	.963
1988	**MIN A**	0	1	.000	16.76	4	1	0	9.2	20	5	5	0	0	0	0	0	0	0	—	0	1	0	0	0.3	1.000
24 yrs.		329 **9th**	244	.574	3.22	741	709	254	5216.2 **9th**	4672	1833 **2nd**	4136 **2nd**	55	2	4	2	1719	346	13	.201	109	724	42	36	1.2	.952
DIVISIONAL PLAYOFF SERIES																										
1981	**PHI N**	0	2	.000	3.86	2	2	0	14	14	8	13	0	0	0	0	4	1	0	.250	0	0	0	0	0.0	.000

Steve Carlton *continued*

LEAGUE CHAMPIONSHIP SERIES

Year	Team		W	L	PCT	ERA	G	GS	CG	IP	H	BB	SO	ShO	Relief W	Relief L	Relief SV	Batting AB	Batting H	Batting HR	BA	PO	A	E	DP	TC/G	FA
1976	PHI	N	0	1	.000	5.14	1	1	0	7	8	5	6	0	0	0	0	2	0	0	.000	0	0	0	0	0.0	.000
1977			0	1	.000	6.94	2	2	0	11.2	13	8	6	0	0	0	0	4	2	0	.500	0	0	0	0	0.0	.000
1978			1	0	1.000	4.00	1	1	1	9	8	2	8	0	0	0	0	4	2	1	.500	0	0	0	0	0.0	.000
1980			1	0	1.000	2.19	2	2	0	12.1	11	8	6	0	0	0	0	4	0	0	.000	0	1	0	0	0.5	1.000
1983			2	0	1.000	0.66	2	2	0	13.2	13	5	13	0	0	0	0	5	1	0	.200	1	3	0	0	2.0	1.000
5 yrs.			4	2	.667	3.52	8	8	1	53.2	53	28	39	0	0	0	0	19	5	1	.263	1	4	0	0	0.6	1.000
			3rd					**3rd**		**4th**		**1st**	**4th**														

WORLD SERIES

Year	Team		W	L	PCT	ERA	G	GS	CG	IP	H	BB	SO	ShO	Relief W	Relief L	Relief SV	Batting AB	Batting H	Batting HR	BA	PO	A	E	DP	TC/G	FA
1967	STL	N	0	1	.000	0.00	1	1	0	6	3	2	5	0	0	0	0	1	0	0	.000	0	0	0	0	0.0	.000
1968			0	0	—	6.75	2	0	0	4	7	1	3	0	0	0	0	0	0	0	—	1	1	0	0	1.0	1.000
1980	PHI	N	2	0	1.000	2.40	2	2	0	15	14	9	17	0	0	0	0	0	0	0	—	0	3	0	0	1.5	1.000
1983			0	1	.000	2.70	1	1	0	6.2	5	3	7	0	0	0	0	3	0	0	.000	0	0	0	0	0.0	.000
4 yrs.			2	2	.500	2.56	6	4	0	31.2	29	15	32	0	0	0	0	4	0	0	.000	1	4	0	0	0.8	1.000

Don Carman

CARMAN, DONALD WAYNE
B. Aug. 14, 1959, Oklahoma City, Okla.
BL TL 6′ 3″ 195 lbs.

Year	Team		W	L	PCT	ERA	G	GS	CG	IP	H	BB	SO	ShO	Relief W	Relief L	Relief SV	Batting AB	Batting H	Batting HR	BA	PO	A	E	DP	TC/G	FA
1983	PHI	N	0	0	—	0.00	1	0	0	1	0	0	0	0	0	0	1	0	0	0	—	1	0	0	0	1.0	1.000
1984			0	1	.000	5.40	11	0	0	13.1	14	6	16	0	0	1	0	1	0	0	.000	0	0	0	0	0.0	.000
1985			9	4	.692	2.08	71	0	0	86.1	52	38	87	0	9	4	7	3	0	0	.000	5	11	2	2	0.3	.889
1986			10	5	.667	3.22	50	14	2	134.1	113	52	98	1	3	2	1	31	0	0	.000	4	30	0	2	0.7	1.000
1987			13	11	.542	4.22	35	35	3	211	194	69	125	2	0	0	0	61	5	0	.082	7	21	0	0	0.8	1.000
1988			10	14	.417	4.29	36	32	2	201.1	211	70	116	0	0	0	0	63	3	0	.048	9	19	0	0	0.8	1.000
1989			5	**15**	.250	5.24	49	20	0	149.1	152	86	81	0	2	2	0	34	1	0	.029	4	20	1	0	0.5	.960
1990			6	2	.750	4.15	59	1	0	86.2	69	38	58	0	6	1	1	11	3	0	.273	5	12	1	1	0.3	.944
1991	CIN	N	0	2	.000	5.25	28	0	0	36	40	19	15	0	0	2	1	5	0	0	.000	1	8	0	1	0.3	1.000
1992	TEX	A	0	0	—	7.71	2	0	0	2.1	4	0	2	0	0	0	0	0	0	0	—	0	0	0	0	0.0	.000
10 yrs.			53	54	.495	4.11	342	102	7	921.2	849	378	598	3	20	12	11	209	12	0	.057	36	121	4	6	0.5	.975

Chet Carmichael

CARMICHAEL, CHESTER KELLER
B. Jan. 9, 1888, Muncie, Ind. D. Aug. 22, 1960, Rochester, N. Y.
BR TR 5′11½″ 200 lbs.

Year	Team		W	L	PCT	ERA	G	GS	CG	IP	H	BB	SO	ShO	Relief W	Relief L	Relief SV	Batting AB	Batting H	Batting HR	BA	PO	A	E	DP	TC/G	FA
1909	CIN	N	0	0	—	0.00	2	0	0	7	9	3	2	0	0	0	0	2	0	0	.000	0	1	2	0	1.5	.333

Rafael Carmona

CARMONA, RAFAEL
B. Oct. 2, 1972, Rio Piedras, Puerto Rico.
BL TR 6′ 2″ 185 lbs.

Year	Team		W	L	PCT	ERA	G	GS	CG	IP	H	BB	SO	ShO	Relief W	Relief L	Relief SV	Batting AB	Batting H	Batting HR	BA	PO	A	E	DP	TC/G	FA
1995	SEA	A	2	4	.333	5.66	15	3	0	47.2	55	34	28	0	2	2	1	0	0	0	—	9	5	1	1	1.0	.933

Eddie Carnett

CARNETT, EDWIN ELLIOTT (Lefty)
B. Oct. 21, 1916, Springfield, Mo.
BL TL 6′ 185 lbs.

Year	Team		W	L	PCT	ERA	G	GS	CG	IP	H	BB	SO	ShO	Relief W	Relief L	Relief SV	Batting AB	Batting H	Batting HR	BA	PO	A	E	DP	TC/G	FA
1941	BOS	N	0	0	—	20.25	2	0	0	1.1	4	3	2	0	0	0	0	0	0	0	—	0	0	0	0	0.0	.000
1944	CHI	A	0	0	—	9.00	2	0	0	2	3	0	1	0	0	0	0	457	126	1	.276	425	17	12	16	3.9	.974
1945	CLE	A	0	0	—	0.00	2	0	0	2	0	0	1	0	0	0	0	73	16	0	.219	33	1	1	1	1.9	.971
3 yrs.			0	0		8.44	6	0	0	5.1	7	3	4	0	0	0	0	*				458	18	13	17	3.6	.973

Pat Carney

CARNEY, PATRICK JOSEPH (Doc)
B. Aug. 7, 1876, Holyoke, Mass. D. Jan. 9, 1953, Worcester, Mass.
BL TL 6′ 200 lbs.

Year	Team		W	L	PCT	ERA	G	GS	CG	IP	H	BB	SO	ShO	Relief W	Relief L	Relief SV	Batting AB	Batting H	Batting HR	BA	PO	A	E	DP	TC/G	FA
1902	BOS	N	0	1	.000	9.00	2	0	0	5	6	3	3	0	0	1	0	522	141	2	.270	14	0	1	0	1.2	.933
1903			4	5	.444	4.04	10	9	9	78	93	31	29	0	1	0	0	392	94	1	.240	116	29	7	4	1.5	.954
1904			0	3	.000	5.81	4	3	1	26.1	40	12	5	0	0	**2**	0	279	57	0	.204	92	18	5	5	1.5	.957
3 yrs.			4	9	.308	4.69	16	12	10	109.1	139	46	37	0	1	3	0	*				375	66	26	16	1.4	.944

Bob Carpenter

CARPENTER, ROBERT LOUIS
B. Dec. 12, 1917, Chicago, Ill.
BR TR 6′ 3″ 195 lbs.

Year	Team		W	L	PCT	ERA	G	GS	CG	IP	H	BB	SO	ShO	Relief W	Relief L	Relief SV	Batting AB	Batting H	Batting HR	BA	PO	A	E	DP	TC/G	FA
1940	NY	N	2	0	1.000	2.73	5	3	2	33	29	14	25	0	0	0	0	10	1	0	.100	2	5	0	0	1.4	1.000
1941			11	6	.647	3.83	29	19	8	131.2	138	42	42	1	1	0	2	45	7	0	.156	3	17	2	2	0.8	.909
1942			11	10	.524	3.15	28	25	12	185.2	192	51	53	2	1	1	0	65	12	0	.185	14	23	0	0	1.3	1.000
1946			1	3	.250	4.85	12	6	1	39	37	18	13	1	0	0	0	10	1	0	.100	2	6	1	0	0.8	.889
1947	2 teams	NY N (2G 0–0)	CHI N (4G 0–1)																								
″	total		0	1	.000	6.97	6	1	0	10.1	15	7	1	0	0	0	0	1	1	0	1.000	0	3	0	0	0.5	1.000
5 yrs.			25	20	.556	3.60	80	54	23	399.2	411	132	134	4	2	1	2	131	22	0	.168	21	54	3	2	1.0	.962

Cris Carpenter

CARPENTER, CRIS HOWELL
B. Apr. 5, 1965, St. Augustine, Fla.
BR TR 6′ 1″ 195 lbs.

Year	Team		W	L	PCT	ERA	G	GS	CG	IP	H	BB	SO	ShO	Relief W	Relief L	Relief SV	Batting AB	Batting H	Batting HR	BA	PO	A	E	DP	TC/G	FA
1988	STL	N	2	3	.400	4.72	8	8	1	47.2	56	9	24	0	0	0	0	14	2	0	.143	6	4	0	1	1.3	1.000
1989			4	4	.500	3.18	36	5	0	68	70	26	35	0	3	2	0	9	4	0	.444	3	10	0	1	0.4	1.000
1990			0	0	—	4.50	4	0	0	8	5	2	6	0	0	0	0	1	0	0	.000	0	0	1	0	0.3	.000
1991			10	4	.714	4.23	59	0	0	66	53	20	47	0	10	4	0	3	1	0	.333	4	8	0	0	0.2	1.000
1992			5	4	.556	2.97	73	0	0	88	69	27	46	0	5	4	1	3	1	0	.333	7	10	0	1	0.2	1.000
1993	2 teams	FLA N (29G 0–1)	TEX A (27G 4–1)																								
″	total		4	2	.667	3.50	56	0	0	69.1	64	25	53	0	4	2	1	0	0	0		3	12	0	1	0.3	1.000
1994	TEX	A	2	5	.286	5.03	47	0	0	59	69	20	39	0	2	5	5	0	0	0	—	2	8	1	1	0.2	.909
7 yrs.			27	22	.551	3.83	283	13	1	406	386	129	250	0	24	17	7	30	8	0	.267	25	52	2	5	0.3	.975

Lew Carpenter

CARPENTER, LEWIS EMMETT
B. Aug. 16, 1913, Woodstock, Ga. D. Apr. 25, 1979, Marietta, Ga.
BR TR 6′ 2″ 195 lbs.

Year	Team		W	L	PCT	ERA	G	GS	CG	IP	H	BB	SO	ShO	Relief W	Relief L	Relief SV	Batting AB	Batting H	Batting HR	BA	PO	A	E	DP	TC/G	FA
1943	WAS	A	0	0	—	0.00	4	0	0	3.1	1	4	1	0	0	0	0	0	0	0	—	0	0	0	0	0.0	.000

Paul Carpenter

CARPENTER, PAUL CALVIN
B. Aug. 12, 1894, Granville, Ohio D. Mar. 14, 1968, Newark, Ohio.
BR TR 5′11″ 165 lbs.

Year	Team		W	L	PCT	ERA	G	GS	CG	IP	H	BB	SO	ShO	Relief W	Relief L	Relief SV	Batting AB	Batting H	Batting HR	BA	PO	A	E	DP	TC/G	FA
1916	PIT	N	0	0	—	1.17	5	0	0	7.2	8	4	5	0	0	0	0	2	0	0	.000	0	2	0	0	0.4	1.000

Frank Carpin

CARPIN, FRANK DOMINIC BL TL 5′10″ 172 lbs.
B. Sept. 14, 1938, Brooklyn, N. Y.

Year	Team	W	L	PCT	ERA	G	GS	CG	IP	H	BB	SO	ShO	Relief Pitching W	Relief Pitching L	Relief Pitching SV	Batting AB	Batting H	Batting HR	BA	PO	A	E	DP	TC/G	FA
1965	PIT N	3	1	.750	3.18	39	0	0	39.2	35	24	27	0	3	1	4	1	0	0	.000	2	13	0	1	0.4	1.000
1966	HOU N	1	0	1.000	7.50	10	0	0	6	9	6	2	0	1	0	0	0	0	0	—	0	0	1	0	0.1	.000
2 yrs.		4	1	.800	3.74	49	0	0	45.2	44	30	29	0	4	1	4	1	0	0	.000	2	13	1	1	0.3	.938

Giovanni Carrara

CARRARA, GIOVANNI BR TR 6′ 2″ 225 lbs.
Born Giovanni Carrara (Jimenez).
B. Mar. 4, 1968, Edo Anzoategui, Venezuela.

Year	Team	W	L	PCT	ERA	G	GS	CG	IP	H	BB	SO	ShO	Relief Pitching W	Relief Pitching L	Relief Pitching SV	Batting AB	Batting H	Batting HR	BA	PO	A	E	DP	TC/G	FA
1995	TOR A	2	4	.333	7.21	12	7	1	48.2	64	25	27	0	1	0	0	0	0	0	—	1	3	0	0	0.3	1.000

Hector Carrasco

CARRASCO, HECTOR BR TR 6′ 2″ 175 lbs.
Born Hector Carrasco (Pacheco).
B. Oct. 22, 1969, San Pedro de Macoris, Dominican Republic.

Year	Team	W	L	PCT	ERA	G	GS	CG	IP	H	BB	SO	ShO	Relief Pitching W	Relief Pitching L	Relief Pitching SV	Batting AB	Batting H	Batting HR	BA	PO	A	E	DP	TC/G	FA
1994	CIN N	5	6	.455	2.24	45	0	0	56.1	42	30	41	0	5	**6**	6	6	0	0	.000	3	7	1	0	0.2	.909
1995		2	7	.222	4.12	64	0	0	87.1	86	46	64	0	2	7	5	7	0	0	.000	4	9	2	1	0.2	.867
2 yrs.		7	13	.350	3.38	109	0	0	143.2	128	76	105	0	7	13	11	13	0	0	.000	7	16	3	1	0.2	.885
LEAGUE CHAMPIONSHIP SERIES																										
1995	CIN N	0	0	—	0.00	1	0	0	1.1	1	0	3	0	0	0	0	0	0	0	—	0	0	0	0	0.0	.000

Alex Carrasquel

CARRASQUEL, ALEJANDRO APARICIO BR TR 6′ 1″ 182 lbs.
Born Alejandro Aparicio Eloy (Carrasquel).
B. July 24, 1912, Caracas, Venezuela D. Aug. 19, 1969, Caracas, Venezuela.

Year	Team	W	L	PCT	ERA	G	GS	CG	IP	H	BB	SO	ShO	Relief Pitching W	Relief Pitching L	Relief Pitching SV	Batting AB	Batting H	Batting HR	BA	PO	A	E	DP	TC/G	FA
1939	WAS A	5	9	.357	4.69	40	17	7	159.1	165	68	41	0	1	1	2	42	7	1	.167	5	30	1	3	0.9	.972
1940		6	2	.750	4.88	28	0	0	48	42	29	19	0	6	2	0	7	0	0	.000	1	10	0	2	0.4	1.000
1941		6	2	.750	3.44	35	5	4	96.2	103	49	30	0	4	1	2	21	2	0	.095	13	29	0	7	1.2	1.000
1942		7	7	.500	3.43	35	15	7	152.1	161	53	40	1	1	2	4	44	6	0	.136	6	39	2	3	1.3	.957
1943		11	7	.611	3.68	39	13	4	144.1	160	54	48	1	5	3	5	43	8	0	.186	4	36	1	1	1.1	.976
1944		8	7	.533	3.43	43	7	3	134	143	50	35	0	5	3	2	36	7	0	.194	7	32	3	3	1.0	.929
1945		7	5	.583	2.71	35	7	5	122.2	105	40	38	2	4	3	1	36	3	0	.083	6	26	3	1	1.0	.914
1949	CHI A	0	0	—	14.73	3	0	0	3.2	8	4	1	0	0	0	0	0	0	0	—	0	1	0	0	0.3	1.000
8 yrs.		50	39	.562	3.73	258	64	30	861	887	347	252	4	26	15	16	229	33	1	.144	42	203	10	20	1.0	.961

Amalio Carreno

CARRENO, AMALIO RAFAEL BR TR 6′ 170 lbs.
Born Amalio Rafael Carreno (Adrian).
B. Apr. 11, 1964, Chacachacare, Venezuela.

Year	Team	W	L	PCT	ERA	G	GS	CG	IP	H	BB	SO	ShO	Relief Pitching W	Relief Pitching L	Relief Pitching SV	Batting AB	Batting H	Batting HR	BA	PO	A	E	DP	TC/G	FA
1991	PHI N	0	0	—	16.20	3	0	0	3.1	5	3	2	0	0	0	0	1	0	0	.000	0	0	0	0	0.0	.000

Bill Carrick

CARRICK, WILLIAM MARTIN (Can't Win) TR
B. Sept. 5, 1873, Erie, Pa. D. Mar. 7, 1932, Philadelphia, Pa.

Year	Team	W	L	PCT	ERA	G	GS	CG	IP	H	BB	SO	ShO	Relief Pitching W	Relief Pitching L	Relief Pitching SV	Batting AB	Batting H	Batting HR	BA	PO	A	E	DP	TC/G	FA
1898	NY N	3	1	.750	3.40	5	4	4	39.2	39	21	10	0	0	0	0	18	3	0	.167	5	10	0	1	3.0	1.000
1899		16	27	.372	4.65	44	**43**	**40**	361.2	**485**	122	60	3	0	1	0	130	18	0	.138	15	99	12	7	2.9	.905
1900		19	**21**	.475	3.53	**45**	**41**	32	341.2	**415**	92	63	1	2	1	0	115	20	0	.174	16	84	11	2	2.5	.901
1901	WAS A	14	23	.378	3.75	42	37	34	324	367	93	70	0	1	0	0	126	20	0	.159	9	94	8	3	2.6	.928
1902		11	17	.393	4.86	31	30	28	257.2	344	72	36	0	0	0	0	108	20	0	.185	10	66	9	5	2.6	.894
5 yrs.		63	89	.414	4.14	167	155	138	1324.2	1650	400	239	4	3	2	0	497	81	0	.163	55	353	40	18	2.7	.911

Don Carrithers

CARRITHERS, DONALD GEORGE BR TR 6′ 2″ 180 lbs.
B. Sept. 15, 1949, Lynwood, Calif.

Year	Team	W	L	PCT	ERA	G	GS	CG	IP	H	BB	SO	ShO	Relief Pitching W	Relief Pitching L	Relief Pitching SV	Batting AB	Batting H	Batting HR	BA	PO	A	E	DP	TC/G	FA
1970	SF N	2	1	.667	7.36	11	2	0	22	31	14	14	0	2	0	0	6	0	0	.000	1	3	0	0	0.4	1.000
1971		5	3	.625	4.05	22	12	2	80	77	37	41	1	1	0	1	17	3	0	.176	3	12	3	1	0.8	.833
1972		4	8	.333	5.80	25	14	2	90	108	42	42	1	0	1	1	29	6	0	.207	7	13	1	1	0.8	.952
1973		1	2	.333	4.81	25	3	0	58	64	35	36	0	1	0	0	16	4	0	.250	7	13	0	1	0.8	1.000
1974	MON N	5	2	.714	3.00	22	3	0	60	56	17	31	0	4	0	1	14	4	0	.286	4	14	2	0	0.9	.900
1975		5	3	.625	3.30	19	14	5	101	90	38	37	2	0	0	0	34	6	0	.176	7	24	0	2	1.6	1.000
1976		6	12	.333	4.43	34	19	2	140.1	153	78	71	0	1	1	0	37	4	0	.108	13	23	1	5	1.1	.973
1977	MIN A	0	1	.000	7.07	7	0	0	14	16	6	3	0	0	1	0	0	0	0	—	3	2	0	0	0.7	1.000
8 yrs.		28	32	.467	4.46	165	67	11	565.1	595	267	275	4	9	3	3	153	27	0	.176	45	104	7	10	0.9	.955
LEAGUE CHAMPIONSHIP SERIES																										
1971	SF N	0	0	—	∞	1	0	0		3	0	0	0	0	0	0	0	0	0	—	0	0	0	0	0.0	.000

Clay Carroll

CARROLL, CLAY PALMER (Hawk) BR TR 6′ 1″ 178 lbs.
B. May 2, 1941, Clanton, Ala.

Year	Team	W	L	PCT	ERA	G	GS	CG	IP	H	BB	SO	ShO	Relief Pitching W	Relief Pitching L	Relief Pitching SV	Batting AB	Batting H	Batting HR	BA	PO	A	E	DP	TC/G	FA
1964	MIL N	2	0	1.000	1.77	11	1	0	20.1	15	3	17	0	2	0	1	2	0	0	.000	2	7	0	0	0.8	1.000
1965		0	1	.000	4.41	19	1	0	34.2	35	13	16	0	0	1	1	5	0	0	.000	3	5	1	1	0.5	.889
1966	ATL N	8	7	.533	2.37	**73**	3	0	144.1	127	29	67	0	8	6	11	30	3	0	.100	6	31	0	2	0.5	1.000
1967		6	12	.333	5.52	42	7	1	93	111	29	35	0	3	**8**	0	16	1	0	.063	3	22	0	4	0.6	1.000
1968	2 teams ATL N (10G 0–1) CIN N (58G 7–7)																									
″	total	7	8	.467	2.69	68	1	0	144	128	38	71	0	7	**8**	17	29	6	0	.207	4	36	1	1	0.6	.976
1969	CIN N	12	6	.667	3.52	71	4	0	151	149	78	90	0	11	6	7	29	6	1	.207	6	39	1	3	0.6	.978
1970		9	4	.692	2.60	65	0	0	104	104	27	63	0	**9**	4	16	14	1	0	.071	8	22	2	1	0.5	.938
1971		10	4	.714	2.49	61	0	0	94	78	42	64	0	10	4	15	10	1	0	.100	8	29	1	3	0.6	.974
1972		6	4	.600	2.25	**65**	0	0	96	89	32	51	0	6	4	**37**	11	2	0	.182	4	21	1	1	0.4	.962
1973		8	8	.500	3.69	53	5	0	92.2	111	34	41	0	6	7	14	14	3	0	.214	4	20	1	0	0.5	.960
1974		12	5	.706	2.14	57	3	0	101	96	30	46	0	10	4	6	18	3	0	.167	4	25	2	3	0.5	.935
1975		7	5	.583	2.63	56	2	0	96	93	32	44	0	7	5	7	19	0	0	.000	2	14	0	0	0.3	1.000
1976	CHI A	4	4	.500	2.57	29	0	0	77	67	24	38	0	4	4	6	0	0	0	—	0	15	0	2	0.5	1.000
1977	2 teams CHI A (8G 1–3) STL N (51G 4–2)																									
″	total	5	5	.500	2.76	59	1	0	101	91	28	38	0	5	5	5	11	1	0	.091	6	22	1	3	0.5	.966
1978	PIT N	0	0	—	2.25	2	0	0	4	2	3	0	0	0	0	0	0	0	0	—	0	2	0	0	1.0	1.000
15 yrs.		96	73	.568	2.94	731	28	1	1353	1296	442	681	0	88	66	143	208	27	1	.130	60	310	11	24	0.5	.971
LEAGUE CHAMPIONSHIP SERIES																										
1970	CIN N	0	0	—	0.00	2	0	0	1.1	2	0	2	0	0	0	1	0	0	0	—	0	0	0	0	0.0	.000
1972		1	1	.500	3.38	2	0	0	2.2	2	3	0	0	1	1	0	0	0	0	—	0	1	0	0	0.5	1.000

Clay Carroll *continued*

Year	Team		W	L	PCT	ERA	G	GS	CG	IP	H	BB	SO	ShO	Relief W	Relief L	Relief SV	AB	H	HR	BA	PO	A	E	DP	TC/G	FA
1973			1	0	1.000	1.29	3	0	0	7	5	1	2	0	1	0	0	0	0	0	—	0	2	0	0	0.7	1.000
1975			0	0	—	0.00	1	0	0	1	0	1	1	0	0	0	0	0	0	0	—	0	1	0	0	1.0	1.000
4 yrs.			2	1	.667	1.50	8	0	0	12	9	5	5	0	2	1	1	0	0	0		0	4	0	0	0.5	1.000
WORLD SERIES																											
1970	CIN	N	1	0	1.000	0.00	4	0	0	9	5	2	11	0	1	0	0	1	0	0	.000	0	0	0	0	0.0	.000
1972			0	1	.000	1.59	5	0	0	5.2	6	4	3	0	0	1	1	0	0	0	—	1	3	0	0	0.8	1.000
1975			1	0	1.000	3.18	5	0	0	5.2	4	2	3	0	1	0	0	0	0	0	—	2	0	0	0	0.4	1.000
3 yrs.			2	1	.667	1.33	14 5th	0	0	20.1	15	8	17	0	2	1	1	1	0	0	.000	3	3	0	0	0.4	1.000

Dick Carroll

CARROLL, RICHARD THOMAS (Shadow) BR TR 6′ 2″
B. July 21, 1884, Cleveland, Ohio D. Nov. 22, 1945, Cleveland, Ohio.

Year	Team		W	L	PCT	ERA	G	GS	CG	IP	H	BB	SO	ShO	Relief W	Relief L	Relief SV	AB	H	HR	BA	PO	A	E	DP	TC/G	FA
1909	NY	A	0	0	—	3.60	2	1	0	5	7	1	1	0	0	0	0	2	1	0	.500	0	1	1	0	1.0	.500

Ed Carroll

CARROLL, EDGAR FLEISCHER BR TR 6′ 3″ 185 lbs.
B. July 27, 1907, Baltimore, Md. D. Oct. 13, 1984, Rossville, Md.

Year	Team		W	L	PCT	ERA	G	GS	CG	IP	H	BB	SO	ShO	Relief W	Relief L	Relief SV	AB	H	HR	BA	PO	A	E	DP	TC/G	FA
1929	BOS	A	1	0	1.000	5.61	24	3	0	67.1	77	20	13	0	0	0	0	16	1	0	.063	2	17	0	1	0.8	1.000

Ownie Carroll

CARROLL, OWEN THOMAS BR TR 5′10½″ 165 lbs.
B. Nov. 11, 1902, Kearny, N. J. D. June 8, 1975, Orange, N. J.

Year	Team		W	L	PCT	ERA	G	GS	CG	IP	H	BB	SO	ShO	Relief W	Relief L	Relief SV	AB	H	HR	BA	PO	A	E	DP	TC/G	FA
1925	DET	A	3	1	.750	3.76	10	4	1	40.2	46	28	12	0	1	0	0	16	6	0	.375	1	4	2	0	0.6	.714
1927			10	6	.625	3.98	31	15	8	172	186	73	41	0	3	0	0	69	12	0	.174	10	49	1	4	1.9	.983
1928			16	12	.571	3.27	34	28	19	231	219	87	51	2	2	2	2	98	19	0	.194	17	59	5	2	2.1	.938
1929			9	17	.346	4.63	34	26	12	202	249	86	54	0	2	3	1	74	17	0	.230	10	56	5	2	2.1	.930
1930	3 teams	DET A (6G 0–5)	NY A (10G 0–1)	CIN N (3G 0–1)																							
″	total		0	7	.000	7.39	19	6	1	67	96	30	12	0	0	3	0	22	4	0	.182	5	17	1	3	1.2	.957
1931	CIN	N	3	9	.250	5.53	29	12	4	107.1	135	51	24	0	1	2	0	34	7	0	.206	7	26	2	5	1.2	.943
1932			10	**19**	.345	4.50	32	26	15	210	245	44	55	0	2	1	1	77	16	0	.208	13	39	1	3	1.7	.981
1933	BKN	N	13	15	.464	3.78	33	31	11	226.1	248	54	45	0	0	0	0	74	11	0	.149	13	64	2	4	2.4	.975
1934			1	3	.250	6.42	26	5	0	74.1	108	33	17	0	1	0	1	25	6	0	.240	5	28	1	1	1.3	.971
9 yrs.			65	89	.422	4.43	248	153	71	1330.2	1532	486	311	2	12	11	5	489	98	0	.200	81	342	20	24	1.7	.955

Tom Carroll

CARROLL, THOMAS MICHAEL BL TR 6′ 3″ 190 lbs.
B. Nov. 5, 1952, Oriskany, N. Y.

Year	Team		W	L	PCT	ERA	G	GS	CG	IP	H	BB	SO	ShO	Relief W	Relief L	Relief SV	AB	H	HR	BA	PO	A	E	DP	TC/G	FA
1974	CIN	N	4	3	.571	3.69	16	13	0	78	68	44	37	0	0	0	0	26	4	0	.154	5	7	1	0	0.8	.923
1975			4	1	.800	4.98	12	7	0	47	52	26	14	0	1	0	0	14	0	0	.000	1	4	0	1	0.4	1.000
2 yrs.			8	4	.667	4.18	28	20	0	125	120	70	51	0	1	0	0	40	4	0	.100	6	11	1	1	0.6	.944

Kid Carsey

CARSEY, WILFRED BL TR 5′ 7″ 168 lbs.
B. Oct. 22, 1870, New York, N. Y. D. Mar. 29, 1960, Miami, Fla.

Year	Team		W	L	PCT	ERA	G	GS	CG	IP	H	BB	SO	ShO	Relief W	Relief L	Relief SV	AB	H	HR	BA	PO	A	E	DP	TC/G	FA
1891	WAS	AA	14	**37**	.275	4.99	54	53	46	415	**513**	161	174	1	1	0	0	187	28	0	.150	25	126	14	5	2.6	.915
1892	PHI	N	19	16	.543	3.12	43	36	30	317.2	320	104	76	1	2	0	1	131	20	1	.153	20	85	14	3	2.6	.882
1893			20	15	.571	4.81	39	35	30	318.1	375	124	50	1	1	2	0	145	27	0	.186	17	81	8	1	2.7	.925
1894			18	12	.600	5.56	35	31	26	277	349	102	41	0	0	1	0	125	34	0	.272	15	59	5	4	2.3	.937
1895			24	16	.600	4.92	44	40	35	342.1	**460**	118	64	0	1	1	1	141	41	0	.291	9	77	12	2	2.2	.878
1896			11	11	.500	5.62	27	21	18	187.1	273	72	36	1	2	0	1	81	18	0	.222	9	50	6	3	2.4	.908
1897	2 teams	PHI N (4G 2–1)	STL N (12G 3–8)																								
″	total		5	9	.357	5.81	16	15	13	127	168	47	15	0	0	0	0	56	16	0	.286	8	32	3	0	2.7	.930
1898	STL	N	2	12	.143	6.33	20	13	10	123.2	177	37	10	0	0	1	0	105	21	1	.200	29	65	13	3	2.8	.879
1899	2 teams	CLE N (10G 1–8)	WAS N (4G 1–2)																								
″	total		2	10	.167	5.15	14	12	10	106.2	136	28	14	0	1	0	0	65	16	0	.246	18	53	10	4	4.1	.877
1901	BKN	N	1	0	1.000	10.29	2	0	0	7	9	3	4	0	1	0	0	2	0	0	.000	0	1	0	0	0.5	1.000
10 yrs.			116	138	.457	4.95	294	256	218	2222	2780	796	484	4	9	5	3	*				150	629	85	25	2.6	.902

Al Carson

CARSON, ALBERT JAMES (Soldier) TR
B. Aug. 22, 1882, Chicago, Ill. D. Nov. 26, 1962, San Diego, Calif.

Year	Team		W	L	PCT	ERA	G	GS	CG	IP	H	BB	SO	ShO	Relief W	Relief L	Relief SV	AB	H	HR	BA	PO	A	E	DP	TC/G	FA
1910	CHI	N	0	0	—	4.05	2	0	0	6.2	6	1	2	0	0	0	0	1	0	0	.000	0	2	0	0	1.0	1.000

Andy Carter

CARTER, ANDREW GODFREY BL TL 6′ 5″ 200 lbs.
B. Nov. 9, 1968, Philadelphia, Pa.

Year	Team		W	L	PCT	ERA	G	GS	CG	IP	H	BB	SO	ShO	Relief W	Relief L	Relief SV	AB	H	HR	BA	PO	A	E	DP	TC/G	FA
1994	PHI	N	0	2	.000	4.46	20	0	0	34.1	34	12	18	0	0	2	0	6	0	0	.000	1	2	0	0	0.2	1.000
1995			0	0	—	6.14	4	0	0	7.1	4	2	6	0	0	0	0	1	1	0	1.000	0	0	0	0	0.0	.000
2 yrs.			0	2	.000	4.75	24	0	0	41.2	38	14	24	0	0	2	0	7	1	0	.143	1	2	0	0	0.1	1.000

Arnold Carter

CARTER, ARNOLD LEE (Lefty) BL TL 5′10″ 170 lbs.
B. Mar. 14, 1918, Rainelle, W. Va. D. Apr. 12, 1989, Louisville, Ky.

Year	Team		W	L	PCT	ERA	G	GS	CG	IP	H	BB	SO	ShO	Relief W	Relief L	Relief SV	AB	H	HR	BA	PO	A	E	DP	TC/G	FA
1944	CIN	N	11	7	.611	2.61	33	18	9	148.1	143	40	33	3	1	1	3	48	12	2	.250	5	37	2	0	1.3	.955
1945			2	4	.333	3.09	13	6	2	46.2	54	13	4	1	1	0	0	17	3	0	.176	6	9	0	1	1.2	1.000
2 yrs.			13	11	.542	2.72	46	24	11	195	197	53	37	4	2	1	3	65	15	2	.231	11	46	2	1	1.3	.966

Jeff Carter

CARTER, JEFFREY ALLEN BR TR 6′ 3″ 195 lbs.
B. Dec. 3, 1964, Tampa, Fla.

Year	Team		W	L	PCT	ERA	G	GS	CG	IP	H	BB	SO	ShO	Relief W	Relief L	Relief SV	AB	H	HR	BA	PO	A	E	DP	TC/G	FA
1991	CHI	A	0	1	.000	5.25	5	2	0	12	8	5	2	0	0	0	0	0	0	0	—	0	1	0	0	0.2	1.000

Larry Carter

CARTER, LARRY GENE BR TR 6′ 5″ 195 lbs.
B. May 22, 1965, Charleston, W. Va.

Year	Team		W	L	PCT	ERA	G	GS	CG	IP	H	BB	SO	ShO	Relief W	Relief L	Relief SV	AB	H	HR	BA	PO	A	E	DP	TC/G	FA
1992	SF	N	1	5	.167	4.64	6	6	0	33	34	18	21	0	0	0	0	10	2	0	.200	4	1	0	0	0.8	1.000

Nick Carter

CARTER, CONRAD POWELL BL TR 5′ 8″ 140 lbs.
B. May 19, 1879, Oatlands, Va. D. Nov. 23, 1961, Grasonville, Md.

Year	Team		W	L	PCT	ERA	G	GS	CG	IP	H	BB	SO	ShO	Relief W	Relief L	Relief SV	AB	H	HR	BA	PO	A	E	DP	TC/G	FA
1908	PHI	A	2	5	.286	2.97	14	6	2	60.2	58	17	17	0	2	1	0	20	2	0	.100	7	22	1	1	2.1	.967

Paul Carter

CARTER, PAUL WARREN (Nick) BL TR 6′ 3″ 175 lbs.
B. May 1, 1894, Lake Park, Ga. D. Sept. 11, 1984, Lake Park, Ga.

Year	Team	W	L	PCT	ERA	G	GS	CG	IP	H	BB	SO	ShO	Relief Pitching W	L	SV	Batting AB	H	HR	BA	PO	A	E	DP	TC/G	FA
1914	CLE A	1	3	.250	2.92	5	4	1	24.2	35	5	9	0	0	0	0	7	0	0	.000	0	7	1	0	1.6	.875
1915		1	1	.500	3.21	11	2	2	42	44	18	14	0	0	0	0	14	3	0	.214	0	16	0	0	1.5	1.000
1916	CHI N	2	2	.500	2.75	8	5	2	36	26	17	14	0	0	0	0	12	2	0	.167	0	16	0	2	2.0	1.000
1917		5	8	.385	3.26	23	13	6	113.1	115	19	34	0	1	2	2	33	6	0	.182	2	30	2	1	1.5	.941
1918		4	1	.800	2.71	21	4	1	73	78	19	13	0	3	0	1	25	6	0	.240	4	29	0	3	1.6	1.000
1919		5	4	.556	2.65	28	7	2	85	81	28	17	0	3	0	1	26	7	0	.269	2	26	2	1	1.1	.933
1920		3	6	.333	4.67	31	8	2	106	131	36	14	0	1	2	2	35	6	0	.171	0	25	3	1	0.9	.893
7 yrs.		21	25	.457	3.32	127	43	16	480	510	142	115	0	8	4	6	152	30	0	.197	8	149	8	8	1.3	.952

Sol Carter

CARTER, SOLOMON MOBLEY (Buck) BR TR 6′ 178 lbs.
B. Dec. 23, 1908, Picayune, Miss.

Year	Team	W	L	PCT	ERA	G	GS	CG	IP	H	BB	SO	ShO	Relief Pitching W	L	SV	Batting AB	H	HR	BA	PO	A	E	DP	TC/G	FA
1931	PHI A	0	0	—	19.29	2	0	0	2.1	1	4	1	0	0	0	0	0	0	0	—	0	3	0	0	1.5	1.000

Bob Caruthers

CARUTHERS, ROBERT LEE (Parisian Bob) BL TR 5′ 7″ 138 lbs.
B. Jan. 5, 1864, Memphis, Tenn. D. Aug. 5, 1911, Peoria, Ill.
Manager 1892.

Year	Team	W	L	PCT	ERA	G	GS	CG	IP	H	BB	SO	ShO	Relief Pitching W	L	SV	Batting AB	H	HR	BA	PO	A	E	DP	TC/G	FA
1884	STL AA	7	2	.778	*2.61*	13	7	7	82.2	61	15	58	0	**3**	0	0	82	21	2	.256	14	10	5	0	1.0	.828
1885		**40**	13	**.755**	***2.07***	53	53	53	482.1	430	57	190	6	0	0	0	222	50	1	.225	33	86	15	4	2.2	.888
1886		30	14	.682	*2.32*	44	43	42	387.1	323	86	166	2	1	0	0	317	106	4	.334	72	76	19	5	1.9	.886
1887		29	9	**.763**	*3.30*	39	39	39	341	337	61	74	2	0	0	0	364	130	8	.357	182	105	18	4	3.0	.941
1888	BKN AA	29	15	.659	2.39	44	43	42	391.2	337	53	140	4	**1**	0	0	335	77	5	.230	127	97	26	5	2.6	.896
1889		**40**	11	**.784**	3.13	56	50	46	445	444	104	118	**7**	**4**	0	1	172	43	2	.250	33	95	6	4	2.2	.955
1890	BKN N	23	11	.676	3.09	37	33	30	300	292	87	64	2	1	0	0	238	63	1	.265	65	83	20	2	2.2	.881
1891		18	14	.563	3.12	38	32	29	297	323	107	69	2	1	0	1	171	48	2	.281	29	69	11	2	1.9	.899
1892	STL N	2	8	.200	5.84	16	10	10	101.2	131	27	21	0	0	2	1	513	142	3	.277	209	61	29	10	2.0	.903
9 yrs.		218	97	.692	2.83	340	310	298	2828.2	2678	597	900	25	11	2	3	*				788	683	153	36	2.2	.906
				1st																						

Chuck Cary

CARY, CHARLES DOUGLAS BL TL 6′ 4″ 210 lbs.
B. Mar. 3, 1960, Whittier, Calif.

Year	Team	W	L	PCT	ERA	G	GS	CG	IP	H	BB	SO	ShO	Relief Pitching W	L	SV	Batting AB	H	HR	BA	PO	A	E	DP	TC/G	FA
1985	DET A	0	1	.000	3.42	16	0	0	23.2	16	8	22	0	0	1	2	0	0	0	—	0	2	0	0	0.1	1.000
1986		1	2	.333	3.41	22	0	0	31.2	33	15	21	0	1	2	0	0	0	0	—	4	1	0	0	0.2	1.000
1987	ATL N	1	1	.500	3.78	13	0	0	16.2	17	4	15	0	1	1	1	1	0	0	.000	1	3	0	0	0.3	1.000
1988		0	0	—	6.48	7	0	0	8.1	8	4	7	0	0	0	0	0	0	0	—	0	1	0	0	0.1	1.000
1989	NY A	4	4	.500	3.26	22	11	2	99.1	78	29	79	0	0	1	0	0	0	0	—	4	4	2	0	0.5	.800
1990		6	12	.333	4.19	28	27	2	156.2	155	55	134	0	0	0	0	0	0	0	—	8	13	1	1	0.8	.955
1991		1	6	.143	5.91	10	9	0	53.1	61	32	34	0	0	0	0	0	0	0	—	0	7	2	4	0.9	.778
1993	CHI A	1	0	1.000	5.23	16	0	0	20.2	22	11	10	0	1	0	0	0	0	0	—	1	4	0	0	0.3	1.000
8 yrs.		14	26	.350	4.17	134	47	4	410.1	390	158	322	0	3	5	3	1	0	0	.000	18	35	5	5	0.4	.914

Scott Cary

CARY, SCOTT RUSSELL (Red) BL TL 5′11½″ 168 lbs.
B. Apr. 11, 1923, Kendallville, Ind.

Year	Team	W	L	PCT	ERA	G	GS	CG	IP	H	BB	SO	ShO	Relief Pitching W	L	SV	Batting AB	H	HR	BA	PO	A	E	DP	TC/G	FA
1947	WAS A	3	1	.750	5.93	23	3	1	54.2	73	20	25	0	1	0	0	13	1	0	.077	2	6	0	0	0.3	1.000

Jerry Casale

CASALE, JERRY JOSEPH BR TR 6′ 2″ 200 lbs.
B. Sept. 27, 1933, Brooklyn, N. Y.

Year	Team	W	L	PCT	ERA	G	GS	CG	IP	H	BB	SO	ShO	Relief Pitching W	L	SV	Batting AB	H	HR	BA	PO	A	E	DP	TC/G	FA
1958	BOS A	0	0	—	0.00	2	0	0	3	1	2	3	0	0	0	0	0	0	0	—	1	0	0	0	0.5	1.000
1959		13	8	.619	4.31	31	26	9	179.2	162	89	93	3	1	0	0	59	10	3	.169	8	12	3	1	0.7	.870
1960		2	9	.182	6.17	29	14	1	96.1	113	67	54	0	0	0	0	33	9	0	.273	5	13	0	0	0.6	1.000
1961	2 teams LA A (13G 1–5) DET A (3G 0–0)																									
″	total	1	5	.167	6.26	16	8	0	54.2	67	28	41	0	0	0	1	16	6	1	.375	6	6	3	2	0.9	.800
1962	DET A	1	2	.333	4.66	18	1	0	36.2	33	18	16	0	1	2	0	8	0	0	.000	4	6	0	0	0.6	1.000
5 yrs.		17	24	.415	5.08	96	49	10	370.1	376	204	207	3	2	2	1	116	25	4	.216	24	37	6	3	0.7	.910

Joe Cascarella

CASCARELLA, JOSEPH THOMAS (Crooning Joe) BR TR 5′10½″ 175 lbs.
B. June 28, 1907, Philadelphia, Pa.

Year	Team	W	L	PCT	ERA	G	GS	CG	IP	H	BB	SO	ShO	Relief Pitching W	L	SV	Batting AB	H	HR	BA	PO	A	E	DP	TC/G	FA
1934	PHI A	12	15	.444	4.68	42	22	9	194.1	214	104	71	2	**7**	3	1	64	6	0	.094	9	46	4	3	1.4	.932
1935	2 teams PHI A (9G 1–6) BOS A (6G 0–3)																									
″	total	1	9	.100	5.84	15	7	1	49.1	54	33	24	0	1	3	0	10	1	0	.100	1	18	1	0	1.3	.950
1936	2 teams BOS A (10G 0–2) WAS A (22G 9–8)																									
″	total	9	10	.474	4.44	32	17	7	160	174	63	41	1	2	3	1	53	7	0	.132	6	19	0	0	0.8	1.000
1937	2 teams WAS A (10G 0–5) CIN N (11G 1–2)																									
″	total	1	7	.125	5.68	21	7	3	76	94	45	26	0	0	1	2	20	3	0	.150	6	16	2	2	1.1	.917
1938	CIN N	4	7	.364	4.57	33	1	0	61	66	22	30	0	4	6	4	18	3	0	.167	5	9	0	0	0.4	1.000
5 yrs.		27	48	.360	4.84	143	54	20	540.2	602	267	192	3	14	16	8	165	20	0	.121	27	108	7	5	1.0	.951

Charlie Case

CASE, CHARLES EMMETT BR TR 6′ 170 lbs.
B. Sept. 7, 1879, Smith's Landing, Ohio D. Apr. 16, 1964, Clermont, Ohio.

Year	Team	W	L	PCT	ERA	G	GS	CG	IP	H	BB	SO	ShO	Relief Pitching W	L	SV	Batting AB	H	HR	BA	PO	A	E	DP	TC/G	FA
1901	CIN N	1	2	.333	4.67	3	3	3	27	34	6	5	0	0	0	0	10	1	0	.100	0	9	3	0	4.0	.750
1904	PIT N	10	5	.667	2.94	18	17	14	141	129	31	49	3	0	0	0	53	9	0	.170	13	39	3	0	3.1	.945
1905		12	10	.545	2.57	31	24	18	217	202	66	57	3	1	0	1	68	7	0	.103	9	48	3	1	1.9	.950
1906		1	1	.500	5.73	2	2	1	11	8	5	3	0	0	0	0	2	1	0	.500	2	4	1	1	3.5	.857
4 yrs.		24	18	.571	2.93	54	46	36	396	373	108	114	6	1	0	1	133	18	0	.135	24	100	10	2	2.5	.925

Bill Casey

CASEY, WILLIAM B.
B. St. Louis, Mo. Deceased.

Year	Team	W	L	PCT	ERA	G	GS	CG	IP	H	BB	SO	ShO	Relief Pitching W	L	SV	Batting AB	H	HR	BA	PO	A	E	DP	TC/G	FA
1887	PHI AA	0	0	—	*18.00*	1	0	0	1	4	1	0	0	0	0	0	0	0	0	—	0	0	0	0	0.0	.000

Dan Casey

CASEY, DANIEL MAURICE BR TL 6′ 180 lbs.
Brother of Dennis Casey.
B. Nov. 20, 1862, Binghamton, N. Y. D. Feb. 8, 1943, Washington, D. C.

Year	Team	W	L	PCT	ERA	G	GS	CG	IP	H	BB	SO	ShO	Relief Pitching W	L	SV	Batting AB	H	HR	BA	PO	A	E	DP	TC/G	FA
1884	WIL U	1	1	.500	1.00	2	2	2	18	23	4	10	0	0	0	0	6	1	0	.167	0	3	0	0	1.5	1.000
1885	DET N	4	8	.333	*3.29*	12	12	12	104	105	35	79	1	0	0	0	43	5	0	.116	3	24	1	0	2.3	.964

Dan Casey *continued*

Year	Team	W	L	PCT	ERA	G	GS	CG	IP	H	BB	SO	ShO	Relief W	Relief L	Relief SV	AB	H	HR	BA	PO	A	E	DP	TC/G	FA
1886	PHI N	24	18	.571	*2.41*	44	44	39	369	326	104	193	4	0	0	0	151	23	0	.152	18	70	9	0	2.0	.907
1887		28	13	.683	**2.86**	45	45	43	390.1	377	115	119	**4**	0	0	0	164	27	1	.165	11	66	9	0	1.9	.895
1888		14	18	.438	3.15	33	33	31	285.2	298	48	108	2	0	0	0	118	18	0	.153	11	66	10	2	2.6	.885
1889		6	10	.375	3.77	20	20	15	152.2	170	72	65	1	0	0	0	68	15	0	.221	5	32	6	2	2.2	.860
1890	SYR AA	19	22	.463	*4.14*	45	42	40	360.2	365	165	169	2	0	0	0	160	26	0	.163	22	78	14	4	2.5	.877
7 yrs.		96	90	.516	3.18	201	198	182	1680.1	1664	543	743	14	0	0	0	710	115	1	.162	70	339	49	8	2.2	.893

Hugh Casey

CASEY, HUGH THOMAS
B. Oct. 14, 1913, Atlanta, Ga. D. July 3, 1951, Atlanta, Ga.
BR TR 6′ 1″ 207 lbs.

Year	Team	W	L	PCT	ERA	G	GS	CG	IP	H	BB	SO	ShO	Relief W	Relief L	Relief SV	AB	H	HR	BA	PO	A	E	DP	TC/G	FA
1935	CHI N	0	0	—	3.86	13	0	0	25.2	29	14	10	0	0	0	0	6	1	0	.167	3	5	0	1	0.6	1.000
1939	BKN N	15	10	.600	2.93	40	25	15	227.1	228	54	79	0	2	1	1	74	15	0	.203	14	53	0	5	1.7	1.000
1940		11	8	.579	3.62	44	10	5	154	136	51	53	2	6	5	2	36	9	0	.250	5	40	1	1	1.0	.978
1941		14	11	.560	3.89	45	18	4	162	155	57	61	1	**8**	4	7	50	6	0	.120	10	41	1	6	1.2	.981
1942		6	3	.667	2.25	50	2	0	112	91	44	54	0	6	2	**13**	27	4	0	.148	7	18	2	2	0.5	.926
1946		11	5	.688	1.99	46	1	0	99.2	101	33	31	0	**11**	4	5	22	3	0	.136	9	32	2	4	0.9	.953
1947		10	4	.714	3.99	46	0	0	76.2	75	29	40	0	**10**	4	**18**	18	1	0	.056	4	13	0	2	0.4	1.000
1948		3	0	1.000	8.00	22	0	0	36	59	17	7	0	3	0	4	7	0	0	.000	1	7	0	1	0.4	1.000
1949	2 teams PIT N (33G 4–1) NY A (4G 1–0)																									
″	total	5	1	.833	5.24	37	0	0	46.1	61	22	14	0	5	1	5	4	1	0	.250	1	1	0	0	0.1	1.000
9 yrs.		75	42	.641	3.45	343	56	24	939.2	935	321	349	3	51	21	55	244	40	0	.164	54	210	6	22	0.8	.978
WORLD SERIES																										
1941	BKN N	0	2	.000	3.38	3	0	0	5.1	9	2	1	0	0	2	0	2	1	0	.500	0	3	0	0	1.0	1.000
1947		2	0	1.000	0.87	6	0	0	10.1	5	1	3	0	2	0	1	1	0	0	.000	2	3	0	1	0.8	1.000
2 yrs.		2	2	.500	1.72	9	0	0	15.2	14	3	4	0	2	2	1	3	1	0	.333	2	6	0	1	0.9	1.000

Jay Cashion

CASHION, JAY CARL
B. June 6, 1891, Mecklenburg, N. C. D. Nov. 17, 1935, Lake Millicent, Wis.
BL TR 6′ 2″ 200 lbs.

Year	Team	W	L	PCT	ERA	G	GS	CG	IP	H	BB	SO	ShO	Relief W	Relief L	Relief SV	AB	H	HR	BA	PO	A	E	DP	TC/G	FA
1911	WAS A	1	5	.167	4.16	11	9	5	71.1	67	47	26	0	0	0	0	37	12	0	.324	3	22	0	0	2.3	1.000
1912		10	6	.625	3.17	26	17	13	170.1	150	103	84	1	1	0	1	103	22	2	.214	27	41	1	1	2.0	.986
1913		1	1	.500	6.23	4	3	0	8.2	7	14	3	0	0	0	0	12	3	0	.250	4	5	2	1	1.6	.818
1914		0	1	.000	10.80	2	1	0	5	4	6	1	0	0	0	0	1	0	0	.000	1	3	1	1	2.5	.800
4 yrs.		12	13	.480	3.70	43	30	18	255.1	228	170	114	1	1	0	1	*				35	71	4	3	2.0	.964

Larry Casian

CASIAN, LAWRENCE PAUL
B. Oct. 28, 1965, Lynwood, Calif.
BR TL 6′ 1″ 170 lbs.

Year	Team	W	L	PCT	ERA	G	GS	CG	IP	H	BB	SO	ShO	Relief W	Relief L	Relief SV	AB	H	HR	BA	PO	A	E	DP	TC/G	FA
1990	MIN A	2	1	.667	3.22	5	3	0	22.1	26	4	11	0	1	0	0	0	0	0	—	0	3	0	1	0.6	1.000
1991		0	0	—	7.36	15	0	0	18.1	28	7	6	0	0	0	0	0	0	0	—	3	4	0	0	0.5	1.000
1992		1	0	1.000	2.70	6	0	0	6.2	7	1	2	0	1	0	0	0	0	0	—	1	1	0	1	0.3	1.000
1993		5	3	.625	3.02	54	0	0	56.2	59	14	31	0	5	3	1	0	0	0	—	4	4	0	0	0.1	1.000
1994	2 teams MIN A (33G 1–3) CLE A (7G 0–2)																									
″	total	1	5	.167	7.35	40	0	0	49	73	16	20	0	1	5	1	0	0	0		2	14	0	0	0.4	1.000
1995	CHI N	1	0	1.000	1.93	42	0	0	23.1	23	15	11	0	1	0	0	2	0	0	.000	2	4	0	0	0.1	1.000
6 yrs.		10	9	.526	4.54	162	3	0	176.1	216	57	81	0	9	8	2	2	0	0	.000	12	30	0	2	0.3	1.000

Craig Caskey

CASKEY, CRAIG DOUGLAS
B. Dec. 11, 1949, Visalia, Calif.
BB TL 5′11″ 185 lbs.

Year	Team	W	L	PCT	ERA	G	GS	CG	IP	H	BB	SO	ShO	Relief W	Relief L	Relief SV	AB	H	HR	BA	PO	A	E	DP	TC/G	FA
1973	MON N	0	0	—	5.65	9	1	0	14.1	15	4	6	0	0	0	0	1	0	0	.000	1	3	1	0	0.6	.800

Ed Cassian

CASSIAN, EDWIN
B. Conn. Deceased.
5′ 8″ 160 lbs.

Year	Team	W	L	PCT	ERA	G	GS	CG	IP	H	BB	SO	ShO	Relief W	Relief L	Relief SV	AB	H	HR	BA	PO	A	E	DP	TC/G	FA
1891	2 teams PHI N (6G 1–3) WAS AA (7G 2–4)																									
″	total	3	7	.300	4.45	13	9	8	91	113	51	24	0	1	0	0	43	11	0	.256	0	27	4	2	2.4	.871

John Cassidy

CASSIDY, JOHN P.
B. 1855, Brooklyn, N. Y. D. July 3, 1891, Brooklyn, N. Y.
BR TL 5′ 8″ 168 lbs.

Year	Team	W	L	PCT	ERA	G	GS	CG	IP	H	BB	SO	ShO	Relief W	Relief L	Relief SV	AB	H	HR	BA	PO	A	E	DP	TC/G	FA
1877	HAR N	1	1	.500	5.00	2	2	2	18	24	1	2	0	0	0	0	*				41	4	2	3	3.9	.957

George Caster

CASTER, GEORGE JASPER
B. Aug. 4, 1907, Colton, Calif. D. Dec. 18, 1955, Lakewood, Calif.
BR TR 6′ 1½″ 180 lbs.

Year	Team	W	L	PCT	ERA	G	GS	CG	IP	H	BB	SO	ShO	Relief W	Relief L	Relief SV	AB	H	HR	BA	PO	A	E	DP	TC/G	FA
1934	PHI A	3	2	.600	3.41	5	3	2	37	32	14	15	0	1	1	0	15	4	0	.267	5	9	1	1	3.0	.933
1935		1	4	.200	6.25	25	1	0	63.1	86	37	24	0	1	3	1	22	5	0	.227	4	19	1	1	1.0	.958
1937		12	19	.387	4.43	34	33	19	231.2	227	107	100	3	0	0	0	90	19	0	.211	8	44	4	2	1.6	.929
1938		16	**20**	.444	4.37	42	**40**	20	280.1	310	117	112	2	0	0	1	101	20	0	.198	12	44	4	1	1.4	.933
1939		9	9	.500	4.90	28	17	7	136	144	45	59	1	2	0	0	43	9	0	.209	9	21	1	4	1.1	.968
1940		4	**19**	.174	6.56	36	24	11	178.1	234	69	75	0	1	1	2	62	8	0	.129	10	27	2	2	1.1	.949
1941	STL A	3	7	.300	5.00	32	9	3	104.1	105	37	36	0	0	1	3	29	3	0	.103	11	20	1	3	1.0	.969
1942		8	2	.800	2.81	39	0	0	80	62	39	34	0	8	2	5	15	1	0	.067	8	17	1	1	0.7	.962
1943		6	8	.429	2.12	35	0	0	76.1	69	41	43	0	6	**8**	8	22	3	0	.136	2	17	0	1	0.5	1.000
1944		6	6	.500	2.44	42	0	0	81	91	33	46	0	6	6	**12**	20	5	0	.250	2	13	0	1	0.4	1.000
1945	2 teams STL A (10G 1–2) DET A (22G 5–1)																									
″	total	6	3	.667	4.57	32	0	0	67	67	34	32	0	6	3	3	14	3	0	.214	4	11	0	0	0.5	1.000
1946	DET A	2	1	.667	5.66	26	0	0	41.1	42	24	19	0	2	1	4	7	1	0	.143	0	11	1	1	0.5	.917
12 yrs.		76	100	.432	4.54	376	127	62	1376.2	1469	597	595	6	33	26	39	440	81	0	.184	75	253	16	18	0.9	.953
WORLD SERIES																										
1945	DET A	0	0	—	0.00	1	0	0	0.2	0	0	1	0	0	0	0	0	0	0	—	0	0	0	0	0.0	.000

Bobby Castillo

CASTILLO, ROBERT ERNIE
B. Apr. 18, 1955, Los Angeles, Calif.
BR TR 5′10″ 170 lbs.

Year	Team	W	L	PCT	ERA	G	GS	CG	IP	H	BB	SO	ShO	Relief W	Relief L	Relief SV	AB	H	HR	BA	PO	A	E	DP	TC/G	FA
1977	LA N	1	0	1.000	4.09	6	1	0	11	12	2	7	0	1	0	0	1	0	0	.000	1	3	0	0	0.7	1.000
1978		0	4	.000	3.97	18	0	0	34	28	33	30	0	0	4	1	7	0	0	.000	1	6	1	0	0.4	.875
1979		2	0	1.000	1.13	19	0	0	24	26	13	25	0	2	0	7	3	0	0	.000	1	3	0	0	0.2	1.000
1980		8	6	.571	2.76	61	0	0	98	70	45	60	0	8	6	5	9	1	0	.111	10	16	1	1	0.4	.963
1981		2	4	.333	5.29	34	1	0	51	50	24	35	0	2	4	5	9	4	0	.444	3	4	0	1	0.2	1.000

Bobby Castillo *continued*

Year	Team	W	L	PCT	ERA	G	GS	CG	IP	H	BB	SO	ShO	Relief Pitching W	L	SV	Batting AB	H	HR	BA	PO	A	E	DP	TC/G	FA
1982	MIN A	13	11	.542	3.66	40	25	6	218.2	194	85	123	1	2	1	0	0	0	0	—	20	19	3	1	1.0	.929
1983		8	12	.400	4.77	27	25	3	158.1	170	65	90	0	0	0	0	0	0	0	—	13	22	1	1	1.3	.972
1984		2	1	.667	1.78	10	2	0	25.1	14	19	7	0	1	0	0	0	0	0	—	2	2	0	1	0.4	1.000
1985	LA N	2	2	.500	5.43	35	5	0	68	59	41	57	0	0	1	0	10	1	0	.100	5	11	1	1	0.5	.941
9 yrs.		38	40	.487	3.95	250	59	9	688.1	623	327	434	1	16	16	18	39	6	0	.154	56	86	7	6	0.6	.953
LEAGUE CHAMPIONSHIP SERIES																										
1981	LA N	0	0	—	0.00	1	0	0	1	0	0	1	0	0	0	0	0	0	0	—	0	1	0	0	1.0	1.000
1985		0	0	—	3.38	1	0	0	5.1	4	2	4	0	0	0	0	2	0	0	.000	1	3	0	1	4.0	1.000
2 yrs.		0	0		2.84	2	0	0	6.1	4	2	5	0	0	0	0	2	0	0	.000	1	4	0	1	2.5	1.000
WORLD SERIES																										
1981	LA N	0	0	—	9.00	1	0	0	1	0	5	0	0	0	0	0	0	0	0	—	0	2	0	0	2.0	1.000

Frank Castillo

CASTILLO, FRANK ANTHONY
B. Apr. 1, 1969, El Paso, Tex.
BR TR 6′ 1″ 180 lbs.

Year	Team	W	L	PCT	ERA	G	GS	CG	IP	H	BB	SO	ShO	Relief Pitching W	L	SV	Batting AB	H	HR	BA	PO	A	E	DP	TC/G	FA
1991	CHI N	6	7	.462	4.35	18	18	4	111.2	107	33	73	0	0	0	0	35	5	0	.143	6	16	0	0	1.2	1.000
1992		10	11	.476	3.46	33	33	0	205.1	179	63	135	0	0	0	0	65	6	0	.092	10	28	1	2	1.2	.974
1993		5	8	.385	4.84	29	25	2	141.1	162	39	84	0	0	0	0	43	7	0	.163	7	34	1	1	1.4	.976
1994		2	1	.667	4.30	4	4	1	23	25	5	19	0	0	0	0	9	0	0	.000	1	3	2	0	1.5	.667
1995		11	10	.524	3.21	29	29	2	188	179	52	135	2	0	0	0	59	6	0	.102	11	24	2	0	1.3	.946
5 yrs.		34	37	.479	3.86	113	109	9	669.1	652	192	446	2	0	0	0	211	24	0	.114	35	105	6	3	1.3	.959

Juan Castillo

CASTILLO, JUAN FRANCISCO
B. June 23, 1970, Caracas, Venezuela.
BR TR 6′ 5″ 205 lbs.

Year	Team	W	L	PCT	ERA	G	GS	CG	IP	H	BB	SO	ShO	Relief Pitching W	L	SV	Batting AB	H	HR	BA	PO	A	E	DP	TC/G	FA
1994	NY N	0	0	—	6.94	2	2	0	11.2	17	5	1	0	0	0	0	5	1	0	.200	3	6	0	1	4.5	1.000

Manny Castillo

CASTILLO, ESTEBAN MANUEL ANTONIO
Born Esteban Manuel Antonio Castillo (Cabrera).
B. Apr. 1, 1957, Santo Domingo, Dominican Republic.
BB TR 5′ 9″ 160 lbs.

Year	Team	W	L	PCT	ERA	G	GS	CG	IP	H	BB	SO	ShO	Relief Pitching W	L	SV	Batting AB	H	HR	BA	PO	A	E	DP	TC/G	FA
1983	SEA A	0	0	—	23.63	1	0	0	2.2	8	3	2	0	0	0	0	*				2	8	0	0	1.7	1.000

Tony Castillo

CASTILLO, ANTONIO JOSE
Born Antonio Jose Castillo (Jimenez).
B. Mar. 1, 1963, Quibor, Venezuela.
BL TL 5′10″ 177 lbs.

Year	Team	W	L	PCT	ERA	G	GS	CG	IP	H	BB	SO	ShO	Relief Pitching W	L	SV	Batting AB	H	HR	BA	PO	A	E	DP	TC/G	FA
1988	TOR A	1	0	1.000	3.00	14	0	0	15	10	2	14	0	1	0	0	0	0	0	—	0	3	0	0	0.2	1.000
1989	2 teams TOR A (17G 1–1) ATL N (12G 0–1)																									
″	total	1	2	.333	5.67	29	0	0	27	31	14	15	0	1	2	1	1	0	0	.000	2	3	0	0	0.2	1.000
1990	ATL N	5	1	.833	4.23	52	3	0	76.2	93	20	64	0	3	1	1	7	1	0	.143	5	13	0	1	0.3	1.000
1991	2 teams ATL N (7G 1–1) NY N (10G 1–0)																									
″	total	2	1	.667	3.34	17	3	0	32.1	40	11	18	0	1	1	0	4	0	0	.000	3	6	0	0	0.5	1.000
1993	TOR A	3	2	.600	3.38	51	0	0	50.2	44	22	28	0	3	2	0	0	0	0	—	3	9	1	1	0.3	.923
1994		5	2	.714	2.51	41	0	0	68	66	28	43	0	5	2	1	0	0	0	—	4	16	1	0	0.5	.952
1995		1	5	.167	3.22	55	0	0	72.2	64	24	38	0	1	5	13	0	0	0	—	3	10	0	0	0.2	1.000
7 yrs.		18	13	.581	3.52	259	6	0	342.1	348	121	220	0	15	13	16	12	1	0	.083	20	60	2	2	0.3	.976
LEAGUE CHAMPIONSHIP SERIES																										
1993	TOR A	0	0	—	0.00	2	0	0	2	0	1	1	0	0	0	0	0	0	0	—	0	1	0	0	0.5	1.000
WORLD SERIES																										
1993	TOR A	1	0	1.000	8.10	2	0	0	3.1	6	3	1	0	1	0	0	1	0	0	.000	0	0	0	0	0.0	.000

Slick Castleman

CASTLEMAN, CLYDELL
B. Sept. 8, 1913, Donelson, Tenn.
BR TR 6′ 185 lbs.

Year	Team	W	L	PCT	ERA	G	GS	CG	IP	H	BB	SO	ShO	Relief Pitching W	L	SV	Batting AB	H	HR	BA	PO	A	E	DP	TC/G	FA
1934	NY N	1	0	1.000	5.40	7	1	0	16.2	18	10	5	0	1	0	0	4	1	0	.250	1	6	0	0	1.0	1.000
1935		15	6	.714	4.09	29	25	9	173.2	186	64	64	1	2	0	0	67	12	1	.179	12	42	4	3	2.0	.931
1936		4	7	.364	5.64	29	12	2	111.2	148	56	54	1	3	0	1	39	5	1	.128	5	26	2	2	1.1	.939
1937		11	6	.647	3.31	23	23	10	160.1	148	33	78	2	0	0	0	57	4	0	.070	8	20	2	3	1.3	.933
1938		4	5	.444	4.17	21	14	4	90.2	108	37	18	0	0	0	0	31	3	0	.097	4	14	0	2	0.9	1.000
1939		1	2	.333	4.54	12	4	0	33.2	36	23	6	0	1	0	0	9	3	0	.333	2	4	0	0	0.5	1.000
6 yrs.		36	26	.581	4.25	121	79	25	586.2	644	223	225	4	7	0	1	207	28	2	.135	32	112	8	10	1.3	.947
WORLD SERIES																										
1936	NY N	0	0	—	2.08	1	0	0	4.1	3	2	5	0	0	0	0	2	1	0	.500	0	0	0	0	0.0	.000

Roy Castleton

CASTLETON, ROYAL EUGENE
B. July 26, 1885, Salt Lake City, Utah D. June 24, 1967, Los Angeles, Calif.
BL TL 5′11″ 167 lbs.

Year	Team	W	L	PCT	ERA	G	GS	CG	IP	H	BB	SO	ShO	Relief Pitching W	L	SV	Batting AB	H	HR	BA	PO	A	E	DP	TC/G	FA
1907	NY A	1	1	.500	2.81	3	2	1	16	11	3	3	0	0	0	0	5	0	0	.000	0	5	0	0	1.7	1.000
1909	CIN N	1	1	.500	1.93	4	1	1	14	14	6	5	0	0	1	0	3	2	0	.667	0	5	0	1	1.3	1.000
1910		1	2	.333	3.29	4	2	1	13.2	15	6	5	0	0	2	0	5	0	0	.000	0	4	0	0	1.0	1.000
3 yrs.		3	4	.429	2.68	11	5	3	43.2	40	15	13	0	0	3	0	13	2	0	.154	0	14	0	1	1.3	1.000

Paul Castner

CASTNER, PAUL HENRY (Lefty)
B. Feb. 16, 1897, St. Paul, Minn. D. Mar. 3, 1986, St. Paul, Minn.
BL TL 5′11″ 187 lbs.

Year	Team	W	L	PCT	ERA	G	GS	CG	IP	H	BB	SO	ShO	Relief Pitching W	L	SV	Batting AB	H	HR	BA	PO	A	E	DP	TC/G	FA
1923	CHI A	0	0	—	6.30	6	0	0	10	14	5	0	0	0	0	0	3	0	0	.000	0	4	0	0	0.7	1.000

Bill Castro

CASTRO, WILLIAM RADHAMES
Born William Radhames Castro (Checo).
B. Dec. 13, 1953, Santiago, Dominican Republic.
BR TR 5′11″ 170 lbs.

Year	Team	W	L	PCT	ERA	G	GS	CG	IP	H	BB	SO	ShO	Relief Pitching W	L	SV	Batting AB	H	HR	BA	PO	A	E	DP	TC/G	FA
1974	MIL A	0	0	—	4.50	8	0	0	18	19	5	10	0	0	0	0	0	0	0	—	4	1	0	0	0.6	1.000
1975		3	2	.600	2.52	18	5	0	75	78	17	25	0	1	0	1	0	0	0	—	9	11	1	1	1.2	.952
1976		4	6	.400	3.45	39	0	0	70.1	70	19	23	0	4	6	8	0	0	0	—	0	11	0	2	0.3	1.000
1977		8	6	.571	4.17	51	0	0	69	76	23	28	0	8	6	13	0	0	0	—	7	16	3	0	0.5	.885
1978		5	4	.556	1.81	42	0	0	49.2	43	14	17	0	5	4	8	0	0	0	—	3	10	1	0	0.3	.929
1979		3	1	.750	2.05	39	0	0	44	40	13	10	0	3	1	6	0	0	0	—	1	7	1	1	0.2	.889
1980		2	4	.333	2.79	56	0	0	84	89	17	32	0	2	4	8	0	0	0	—	7	15	3	3	0.4	.880
1981	NY A	1	1	.500	3.79	11	0	0	19	26	5	4	0	1	1	0	0	0	0	—	0	3	0	0	0.3	1.000

Bill Castro *continued*

Year	Team	W	L	PCT	ERA	G	GS	CG	IP	H	BB	SO	ShO	Relief Pitching W	Relief Pitching L	Relief Pitching SV	Batting AB	Batting H	Batting HR	BA	PO	A	E	DP	TC/G	FA
1982	KC A	3	2	.600	3.45	21	4	0	75.2	72	20	37	0	1	1	1	0	0	0	—	6	4	0	0	0.5	1.000
1983		2	0	1.000	6.64	18	0	0	40.2	51	12	17	0	2	0	0	0	0	0	—	5	7	3	0	0.8	.800
10 yrs.		31	26	.544	3.33	303	9	0	545.1	564	145	203	0	27	23	45	0	0	0		42	85	12	7	0.5	.914

Eli Cates

CATES, ELI ELDO BR TR 5′9½″ 175 lbs.
B. Jan. 26, 1877, Greensfork, Ind. D. May 29, 1964, Anderson, Ind.

Year	Team	W	L	PCT	ERA	G	GS	CG	IP	H	BB	SO	ShO	Relief Pitching W	Relief Pitching L	Relief Pitching SV	Batting AB	Batting H	Batting HR	BA	PO	A	E	DP	TC/G	FA
1908	WAS A	4	8	.333	2.51	19	10	7	114.2	112	32	33	0	1	2	0	*				8	38	5	1	2.3	.902

Ted Cather

CATHER, THEODORE PHYSICK BR TR 5′10½″ 178 lbs.
B. May 20, 1889, Chester, Pa. D. Apr. 9, 1945, Elkton, Md.

Year	Team	W	L	PCT	ERA	G	GS	CG	IP	H	BB	SO	ShO	Relief Pitching W	Relief Pitching L	Relief Pitching SV	Batting AB	Batting H	Batting HR	BA	PO	A	E	DP	TC/G	FA
1913	STL N	0	0	—	54.00	1	0	0	0.1	1	2	0	0	0	0	0	*				15	2	1	0	3.6	.944

Hardin Cathey

CATHEY, HARDIN (Abner) BR TR 6′ 190 lbs.
B. July 6, 1919, Burns, Tenn.

Year	Team	W	L	PCT	ERA	G	GS	CG	IP	H	BB	SO	ShO	Relief Pitching W	Relief Pitching L	Relief Pitching SV	Batting AB	Batting H	Batting HR	BA	PO	A	E	DP	TC/G	FA
1942	WAS A	1	1	.500	7.42	12	2	0	30.1	44	16	8	0	0	1	0	8	3	0	.375	0	5	0	0	0.4	1.000

Keefe Cato

CATO, JOHN KEEFE BR TR 6′1″ 180 lbs.
B. May 6, 1958, Yonkers, N. Y.

Year	Team	W	L	PCT	ERA	G	GS	CG	IP	H	BB	SO	ShO	Relief Pitching W	Relief Pitching L	Relief Pitching SV	Batting AB	Batting H	Batting HR	BA	PO	A	E	DP	TC/G	FA
1983	CIN N	1	0	1.000	2.45	4	0	0	3.2	2	1	3	0	1	0	0	0	0	0	—	0	0	0	0	0.0	.000
1984		0	1	.000	8.04	8	0	0	15.2	22	4	12	0	0	1	1	4	2	0	.500	2	3	0	1	0.6	1.000
2 yrs.		1	1	.500	6.98	12	0	0	19.1	24	5	15	0	1	1	1	4	2	0	.500	2	3	0	1	0.4	1.000

John Cattanach

CATTANACH, JOHN LECKIE 5′10″ 190 lbs.
B. May 10, 1863, Providence, R. I. D. Nov. 10, 1926, Providence, R. I.

Year	Team	W	L	PCT	ERA	G	GS	CG	IP	H	BB	SO	ShO	Relief Pitching W	Relief Pitching L	Relief Pitching SV	Batting AB	Batting H	Batting HR	BA	PO	A	E	DP	TC/G	FA
1884	2 teams PRO N (1G 0–0) STL U (2G 1–1)																									
″	total	1	1	.500	3.68	3	3	2	22	14	8	15	0	0	0	0	11	0	0	.000	0	5	2	0	1.8	.714

Bill Caudill

CAUDILL, WILLIAM HOLLAND BR TR 6′1″ 190 lbs.
B. July 13, 1956, Santa Monica, Calif.

Year	Team	W	L	PCT	ERA	G	GS	CG	IP	H	BB	SO	ShO	Relief Pitching W	Relief Pitching L	Relief Pitching SV	Batting AB	Batting H	Batting HR	BA	PO	A	E	DP	TC/G	FA
1979	CHI N	1	7	.125	4.80	29	12	0	90	89	41	104	0	1	0	0	17	1	0	.059	5	11	0	1	0.6	1.000
1980		4	6	.400	2.18	72	2	0	128	100	59	112	0	4	6	1	9	2	0	.222	7	11	0	0	0.3	1.000
1981		1	5	.167	5.83	30	10	0	71	87	31	45	0	0	0	0	14	2	0	.143	4	8	1	0	0.4	.923
1982	SEA A	12	9	.571	2.35	70	0	0	95.2	65	35	111	0	12	9	26	0	0	0	—	3	5	0	1	0.1	1.000
1983		2	8	.200	4.71	63	0	0	72.2	70	38	73	0	2	8	26	0	0	0	—	2	5	2	0	0.1	.778
1984	OAK A	9	7	.563	2.71	68	0	0	96.1	77	31	89	0	9	7	36	1	0	0	.000	4	4	0	0	0.1	1.000
1985	TOR A	4	6	.400	2.99	67	0	0	69.1	53	35	46	0	4	6	14	0	0	0	—	2	6	0	0	0.1	1.000
1986		2	4	.333	6.19	40	0	0	36.1	36	17	32	0	2	4	2	0	0	0	—	1	2	0	0	0.1	1.000
1987	OAK A	0	0	—	9.00	6	0	0	8	10	1	8	0	0	0	1	0	0	0	—	0	0	0	0	0.0	.000
9 yrs.		35	52	.402	3.68	445	24	0	667.1	587	288	620	0	34	40	106	41	5	0	.122	28	52	3	2	0.2	.964

Red Causey

CAUSEY, CECIL ALGERTON BR TR 6′1″ 160 lbs.
B. Aug. 11, 1893, Georgetown, Fla. D. Nov. 11, 1960, Avon Park, Fla.

Year	Team	W	L	PCT	ERA	G	GS	CG	IP	H	BB	SO	ShO	Relief Pitching W	Relief Pitching L	Relief Pitching SV	Batting AB	Batting H	Batting HR	BA	PO	A	E	DP	TC/G	FA
1918	NY N	11	6	.647	2.79	29	18	10	158.1	143	42	48	2	2	2	2	48	6	0	.125	3	45	2	0	1.7	.960
1919	2 teams NY N (19G 9–3) BOS N (10G 4–5)																									
″	total	13	8	.619	4.03	29	26	9	174	180	58	39	0	1	0	0	59	7	0	.119	6	50	3	1	2.0	.949
1920	PHI N	7	14	.333	4.32	35	26	11	181.1	203	79	30	1	0	2	3	59	11	0	.186	5	45	2	2	1.5	.962
1921	2 teams PHI N (7G 3–3) NY N (7G 1–1)																									
″	total	4	4	.500	2.76	14	8	4	65.1	71	17	9	0	0	1	0	23	4	0	.174	3	16	2	1	1.5	.905
1922	NY N	4	3	.571	3.18	24	2	1	70.2	69	34	13	0	3	2	1	21	5	0	.238	5	19	2	1	1.1	.923
5 yrs.		39	35	.527	3.59	131	80	35	649.2	666	230	139	3	6	7	6	210	33	0	.157	22	175	11	5	1.6	.947

Pug Cavet

CAVET, TILLER H. BL TL 6′3″ 176 lbs.
B. Dec. 26, 1889, McGregor, Tex. D. Aug. 4, 1966, San Luis Obispo, Calif.

Year	Team	W	L	PCT	ERA	G	GS	CG	IP	H	BB	SO	ShO	Relief Pitching W	Relief Pitching L	Relief Pitching SV	Batting AB	Batting H	Batting HR	BA	PO	A	E	DP	TC/G	FA
1911	DET A	0	0	—	4.50	1	1	0	4	6	1	1	0	0	0	0	1	0	0	.000	0	1	0	0	1.0	1.000
1914		7	7	.500	2.44	31	14	6	151.1	129	44	51	1	2	0	2	47	5	0	.106	0	54	6	1	1.9	.900
1915		4	2	.667	4.06	17	7	2	71	83	22	26	0	1	1	1	24	6	0	.250	4	21	3	1	1.6	.893
3 yrs.		11	9	.550	2.98	49	22	8	226.1	218	67	78	1	3	1	3	72	11	0	.153	4	76	9	2	1.8	.899

Art Ceccarelli

CECCARELLI, ARTHUR EDWARD (Chic) BR TL 6′ 190 lbs.
B. Apr. 2, 1930, New Haven, Conn. BB 1957

Year	Team	W	L	PCT	ERA	G	GS	CG	IP	H	BB	SO	ShO	Relief Pitching W	Relief Pitching L	Relief Pitching SV	Batting AB	Batting H	Batting HR	BA	PO	A	E	DP	TC/G	FA
1955	KC A	4	7	.364	5.31	31	16	3	123.2	123	71	68	1	1	0	0	38	3	0	.079	3	14	0	0	0.5	1.000
1956		0	1	.000	7.20	3	2	0	10	13	4	2	0	0	0	0	3	0	0	.000	0	5	0	0	1.7	1.000
1957	BAL A	0	5	.000	4.50	20	8	1	58	62	31	30	0	0	0	0	14	0	0	.000	2	7	1	0	0.5	.900
1959	CHI N	5	5	.500	4.76	18	15	4	102	95	37	56	2	0	0	0	33	3	0	.091	2	15	1	1	1.0	.944
1960		0	0	—	5.54	7	1	0	13	16	4	10	0	0	0	0	0	0	0	—	0	2	0	0	0.3	1.000
5 yrs.		9	18	.333	5.05	79	42	8	306.2	309	147	166	3	1	0	0	88	6	0	.068	7	43	2	1	0.7	.962

Jose Cecena

CECENA, JOSE ISABEL BR TR 5′11″ 180 lbs.
Born Jose Isabel Cecena (Lugo).
B. Aug. 20, 1963, Ciudad Obregon, Mexico.

Year	Team	W	L	PCT	ERA	G	GS	CG	IP	H	BB	SO	ShO	Relief Pitching W	Relief Pitching L	Relief Pitching SV	Batting AB	Batting H	Batting HR	BA	PO	A	E	DP	TC/G	FA
1988	TEX A	0	0	—	4.78	22	0	0	26.1	20	23	27	0	0	0	1	0	0	0	—	1	2	0	0	0.1	1.000

Rex Cecil

CECIL, REX ROLSTON BL TR 6′3″ 195 lbs.
B. Oct. 8, 1916, Lindsay, Okla. D. Oct. 30, 1966, Long Beach, Calif.

Year	Team	W	L	PCT	ERA	G	GS	CG	IP	H	BB	SO	ShO	Relief Pitching W	Relief Pitching L	Relief Pitching SV	Batting AB	Batting H	Batting HR	BA	PO	A	E	DP	TC/G	FA
1944	BOS A	4	5	.444	5.16	11	9	4	61	72	33	33	0	1	0	0	18	5	0	.278	0	11	1	0	1.1	.917
1945		2	5	.286	5.20	7	7	1	45	46	27	30	0	0	0	0	20	6	0	.300	5	12	1	0	2.6	.944
2 yrs.		6	10	.375	5.18	18	16	5	106	118	60	63	0	1	0	0	38	11	0	.289	5	23	2	0	1.7	.933

Pete Center

CENTER, MARVIN EARL BR TR 6′4″ 190 lbs.
B. Apr. 22, 1912, Hazel Green, Ky.

Year	Team	W	L	PCT	ERA	G	GS	CG	IP	H	BB	SO	ShO	Relief Pitching W	Relief Pitching L	Relief Pitching SV	Batting AB	Batting H	Batting HR	BA	PO	A	E	DP	TC/G	FA
1942	CLE A	0	0	—	16.20	1	0	0	3.1	7	4	0	0	0	0	0	1	0	0	.000	0	0	0	0	0.0	.000
1943		1	2	.333	2.76	24	1	0	42.1	29	18	10	0	1	2	1	5	0	0	.000	1	8	1	0	0.4	.900

Pete Center *continued*

Year	Team	W	L	PCT	ERA	G	GS	CG	IP	H	BB	SO	ShO	Relief Pitching W	Relief Pitching L	Relief Pitching SV	Batting AB	Batting H	Batting HR	BA	PO	A	E	DP	TC/G	FA
1945		6	3	.667	3.99	31	8	2	85.2	89	28	34	0	3	2	1	22	2	0	.091	4	7	0	1	0.4	1.000
1946		0	2	.000	4.97	21	0	0	29	29	20	6	0	0	2	1	3	0	0	.000	0	6	1	0	0.3	.857
4 yrs.		7	7	.500	4.10	77	9	2	160.1	154	70	50	0	4	6	3	31	2	0	.065	5	21	2	1	0.4	.929

Rick Cerone

CERONE, RICHARD ALDO BR TR 5′11″ 192 lbs.
B. May 19, 1954, Newark, N. J.

Year	Team	W	L	PCT	ERA	G	GS	CG	IP	H	BB	SO	ShO	Relief Pitching W	Relief Pitching L	Relief Pitching SV	Batting AB	Batting H	Batting HR	BA	PO	A	E	DP	TC/G	FA
1987	NY A	0	0	—	0.00	2	0	0	2	0	1	1	0	0	0	0	*				18	1	0	0	2.7	1.000

John Cerutti

CERUTTI, JOHN JOSEPH BL TL 6′ 2″ 190 lbs.
B. Apr. 28, 1960, Albany, N. Y.

Year	Team	W	L	PCT	ERA	G	GS	CG	IP	H	BB	SO	ShO	Relief Pitching W	Relief Pitching L	Relief Pitching SV	Batting AB	Batting H	Batting HR	BA	PO	A	E	DP	TC/G	FA
1985	TOR A	0	2	.000	5.40	4	1	0	6.2	10	4	5	0	0	1	0	0	0	0	—	0	1	0	0	0.3	1.000
1986		9	4	.692	4.15	34	20	2	145.1	150	47	89	1	2	0	1	0	0	0	—	8	21	0	2	0.9	1.000
1987		11	4	.733	4.40	44	21	2	151.1	144	59	92	0	2	0	0	0	0	0	—	5	15	1	1	0.5	.952
1988		6	7	.462	3.13	46	12	0	123.2	120	42	65	0	1	3	1	0	0	0	—	13	27	0	2	0.9	1.000
1989		11	11	.500	3.07	33	31	3	205.1	214	53	69	1	0	0	0	0	0	0	—	16	45	1	3	1.9	.984
1990		9	9	.500	4.76	30	23	0	140	162	49	49	0	1	0	0	0	0	0	—	11	18	0	2	1.0	1.000
1991	DET A	3	6	.333	4.57	38	8	1	88.2	94	37	29	0	2	2	2	0	0	0	—	1	20	3	0	0.6	.875
7 yrs.		49	43	.533	3.94	229	116	8	861	894	291	398	2	8	6	4	0	0	0		54	147	5	10	0.9	.976
LEAGUE CHAMPIONSHIP SERIES																										
1989	TOR A	0	0	—	0.00	2	0	0	2.2	0	3	1	0	0	0	0	0	0	0	—	0	2	0	0	1.0	1.000

Ray Chadwick

CHADWICK, RAY CHARLES BB TR 6′ 2″ 180 lbs.
B. Nov. 17, 1962, Durham, N. C.

Year	Team	W	L	PCT	ERA	G	GS	CG	IP	H	BB	SO	ShO	Relief Pitching W	Relief Pitching L	Relief Pitching SV	Batting AB	Batting H	Batting HR	BA	PO	A	E	DP	TC/G	FA
1986	CAL A	0	5	.000	7.24	7	7	0	27.1	39	15	9	0	0	0	0	0	0	0	—	3	4	0	0	1.0	1.000

Leon Chagnon

CHAGNON, LEON WILBUR (Shag) BR TR 6′ 182 lbs.
B. Sept. 28, 1902, Pittsfield, N. H. D. July 30, 1953, Amesbury, Mass.

Year	Team	W	L	PCT	ERA	G	GS	CG	IP	H	BB	SO	ShO	Relief Pitching W	Relief Pitching L	Relief Pitching SV	Batting AB	Batting H	Batting HR	BA	PO	A	E	DP	TC/G	FA
1929	PIT N	0	0	—	9.00	1	1	0	7	11	1	4	0	0	0	0	2	0	0	.000	0	3	0	0	3.0	1.000
1930		0	3	.000	6.82	18	4	3	62	92	23	27	0	0	0	0	20	4	0	.200	4	12	0	0	0.9	1.000
1932		9	6	.600	3.94	30	10	4	128	140	34	52	1	5	1	0	40	9	0	.225	3	21	2	0	0.9	.923
1933		6	4	.600	3.69	39	5	1	100	100	17	35	0	5	2	1	21	1	0	.048	6	17	3	1	0.7	.885
1934		4	1	.800	4.81	33	1	0	58	68	24	19	0	4	1	1	13	3	0	.231	3	18	0	0	0.6	1.000
1935	NY N	0	2	.000	3.52	14	1	0	38.1	32	5	16	0	0	1	1	9	0	0	.000	4	7	0	1	0.8	1.000
6 yrs.		19	16	.543	4.51	135	22	8	393.1	443	104	153	1	14	5	3	105	17	0	.162	20	78	5	2	0.8	.951

Bob Chakales

CHAKALES, ROBERT EDWARD (Chick) BR TR 6′ 1″ 185 lbs.
B. Aug. 10, 1927, Asheville, N. C.

Year	Team	W	L	PCT	ERA	G	GS	CG	IP	H	BB	SO	ShO	Relief Pitching W	Relief Pitching L	Relief Pitching SV	Batting AB	Batting H	Batting HR	BA	PO	A	E	DP	TC/G	FA
1951	CLE A	3	4	.429	4.74	17	10	2	68.1	80	43	32	1	0	0	0	20	7	1	.350	1	11	0	0	0.7	1.000
1952		1	2	.333	9.75	5	1	0	12	19	8	7	0	0	2	0	4	2	0	.500	0	0	0	0	0.0	.000
1953		0	2	.000	2.67	7	3	1	27	28	10	6	0	0	0	0	7	2	0	.286	2	5	1	1	1.1	.875
1954	2 teams CLE A (3G 2–0) BAL A (38G 3–7)																									
″	total	5	7	.417	3.43	41	6	0	99.2	85	55	47	0	5	4	3	25	9	0	.360	5	16	3	1	0.6	.875
1955	2 teams CHI A (7G 0–0) WAS A (29G 2–3)																									
″	total	2	3	.400	4.57	36	0	0	67	66	31	34	0	2	3	0	10	0	0	.000	3	14	1	1	0.5	.944
1956	WAS A	4	4	.500	4.03	43	1	0	96	94	57	33	0	4	4	4	20	3	0	.150	1	25	1	2	0.6	.963
1957	2 teams WAS A (4G 0–1) BOS A (18G 0–2)																									
″	total	0	3	.000	7.15	22	2	0	50.1	73	21	28	0	0	3	3	10	3	0	.300	2	8	1	1	0.5	.909
7 yrs.		15	25	.375	4.54	171	23	3	420.1	445	225	187	1	11	16	10	96	26	1	.271	14	79	7	6	0.6	.930

George Chalmers

CHALMERS, GEORGE W. (Dut) BR TR 6′ 1″ 189 lbs.
B. June 7, 1888, Edinburgh, Scotland D. Aug. 5, 1960, Bronx, N. Y.

Year	Team	W	L	PCT	ERA	G	GS	CG	IP	H	BB	SO	ShO	Relief Pitching W	Relief Pitching L	Relief Pitching SV	Batting AB	Batting H	Batting HR	BA	PO	A	E	DP	TC/G	FA
1910	PHI N	1	1	.500	5.32	4	3	2	22	21	11	12	0	0	0	0	7	1	0	.143	3	11	1	0	3.8	.933
1911		13	10	.565	3.11	38	22	11	208.2	196	101	101	3	4	1	4	73	13	0	.178	11	50	5	2	1.7	.924
1912		3	4	.429	3.28	12	8	3	57.2	64	37	22	0	0	1	0	16	3	0	.188	2	6	1	0	0.8	.889
1913		3	10	.231	4.81	26	13	4	116	133	51	46	0	1	2	1	33	7	0	.212	3	35	1	0	1.5	.974
1914		0	3	.000	5.50	3	2	1	18	23	15	6	0	0	1	0	6	0	0	.000	1	5	1	0	2.3	.857
1915		8	9	.471	2.48	26	20	13	170.1	159	45	82	1	0	1	1	59	10	0	.169	8	49	1	1	2.2	.983
1916		1	4	.200	3.19	12	8	2	53.2	49	19	21	0	0	0	0	15	0	0	.000	4	15	1	0	1.7	.950
7 yrs.		29	41	.414	3.41	121	76	36	646.1	645	279	290	4	5	6	6	209	34	0	.163	32	171	11	3	1.8	.949
WORLD SERIES																										
1915	PHI N	0	1	.000	2.25	1	1	1	8	8	3	6	0	0	0	0	3	1	0	.333	0	4	0	1	4.0	1.000

Bill Chamberlain

CHAMBERLAIN, WILLIAM VINCENT BR TL 5′10½″ 173 lbs.
B. Apr. 21, 1909, Stoughton, Mass. D. Feb. 6, 1994, Brockton, Mass.

Year	Team	W	L	PCT	ERA	G	GS	CG	IP	H	BB	SO	ShO	Relief Pitching W	Relief Pitching L	Relief Pitching SV	Batting AB	Batting H	Batting HR	BA	PO	A	E	DP	TC/G	FA
1932	CHI A	0	5	.000	4.57	12	5	0	41.1	39	25	11	0	0	0	0	10	1	0	.100	0	5	0	1	0.4	1.000

Craig Chamberlain

CHAMBERLAIN, CRAIG PHILLIP BR TR 6′ 1″ 190 lbs.
B. Feb. 2, 1957, Hollywood, Calif.

Year	Team	W	L	PCT	ERA	G	GS	CG	IP	H	BB	SO	ShO	Relief Pitching W	Relief Pitching L	Relief Pitching SV	Batting AB	Batting H	Batting HR	BA	PO	A	E	DP	TC/G	FA
1979	KC A	4	4	.500	3.73	10	10	4	70	68	18	30	0	0	0	0	0	0	0	—	5	2	0	0	0.7	1.000
1980		0	1	.000	7.00	5	0	0	9	10	5	3	0	0	1	0	0	0	0	—	0	2	0	0	0.4	1.000
2 yrs.		4	5	.444	4.10	15	10	4	79	78	23	33	0	0	1	0	0	0	0		5	4	0	0	0.6	1.000

Icebox Chamberlain

CHAMBERLAIN, ELTON P. BR TR 5′ 9″ 168 lbs.
B. Nov. 5, 1867, Buffalo, N. Y. D. Sept. 22, 1929, Baltimore, Md.

Year	Team	W	L	PCT	ERA	G	GS	CG	IP	H	BB	SO	ShO	Relief Pitching W	Relief Pitching L	Relief Pitching SV	Batting AB	Batting H	Batting HR	BA	PO	A	E	DP	TC/G	FA
1886	LOU AA	0	3	.000	*6.61*	4	4	4	31.1	39	17	18	0	0	0	0	19	3	0	.158	4	4	4	0	2.0	.667
1887		18	16	.529	*3.79*	36	36	35	309	340	117	118	1	0	0	0	131	26	1	.198	16	73	11	2	2.6	.890
1888	2 teams LOU AA (24G 14–9) STL AA (14G 11–2)																									
″	total	25	11	.694	2.19	38	38	34	308	238	86	176	2	0	0	0	144	23	1	.160	19	62	3	0	2.0	.964
1889	STL AA	32	15	.681	2.97	53	51	44	421.2	376	165	202	3	0	0	1	171	34	2	.199	15	67	7	0	1.6	.921
1890	2 teams STL AA (5G 3–1) COL AA (25G 12–6)																									
″	total	15	7	.682	2.83	30	26	22	210	175	96	128	6	0	0	0	80	17	0	.213	8	32	5	0	1.5	.889

Icebox Chamberlain *continued*

Year	Team	Lg	W	L	PCT	ERA	G	GS	CG	IP	H	BB	SO	ShO	Relief Pitching W	Relief Pitching L	Relief Pitching SV	Batting AB	Batting H	Batting HR	BA	PO	A	E	DP	TC/G	FA
1891	PHI	AA	22	23	.489	4.22	49	46	44	405.2	397	206	204	0	1	0	0	176	33	2	.188	22	92	11	3	2.3	.912
1892	CIN	N	19	23	.452	3.39	52	49	43	406.1	391	170	169	2	0	1	0	160	36	2	.225	19	67	9	0	1.8	.905
1893			16	12	.571	3.73	34	27	19	241	248	112	59	1	3	1	0	97	19	0	.196	8	46	5	0	1.7	.915
1894			10	9	.526	5.77	23	21	18	177.2	220	91	57	1	0	0	0	70	22	1	.314	6	28	3	1	1.6	.919
1896	CLE	N	0	1	.000	7.36	2	2	1	11	21	5	2	0	0	0	0	3	0	0	.000	0	1	0	0	0.5	1.000
10 yrs.			157	120	.567	3.57	321	300	264	2521.2	2445	1065	1133	16	4	2	1	1051	213	9	.203	117	472	58	6	1.9	.910

Bill Chambers

CHAMBERS, WILLIAM CHRISTOPHER BR TR 5′ 9″ 185 lbs.
B. Sept. 13, 1889, Cameron, W. Va. D. Mar. 27, 1962, Fort Wayne, Ind.

Year	Team	Lg	W	L	PCT	ERA	G	GS	CG	IP	H	BB	SO	ShO	Relief Pitching W	Relief Pitching L	Relief Pitching SV	Batting AB	Batting H	Batting HR	BA	PO	A	E	DP	TC/G	FA
1910	STL	N	0	0	—	0.00	1	0	0	1	1	0	0	0	0	0	0	0	0	0	—	1	0	1	0	2.0	.500

Cliff Chambers

CHAMBERS, CLIFFORD DAY (Lefty) BL TL 6′ 3″ 208 lbs.
B. Jan. 10, 1922, Portland, Ore.

Year	Team	Lg	W	L	PCT	ERA	G	GS	CG	IP	H	BB	SO	ShO	Relief Pitching W	Relief Pitching L	Relief Pitching SV	Batting AB	Batting H	Batting HR	BA	PO	A	E	DP	TC/G	FA
1948	CHI	N	2	9	.182	4.43	29	12	3	103.2	100	48	51	1	0	2	0	30	4	0	.133	5	20	0	1	0.9	1.000
1949	PIT	N	13	7	.650	3.96	34	21	10	177.1	186	58	93	1	1	0	0	55	13	0	.236	6	33	0	2	1.1	1.000
1950			12	15	.444	4.30	37	33	11	249.1	262	92	93	2	1	2	0	90	26	2	.289	9	37	2	1	1.3	.958
1951	2 teams	PIT N (10G 3–6) STL N (21G 11–6)																									
″	total		14	12	.538	4.38	31	26	11	189	184	87	64	2	1	2	0	70	15	1	.214	5	24	3	0	1.0	.906
1952	STL	N	4	4	.500	4.12	26	13	2	98.1	110	33	47	1	0	0	1	32	9	0	.281	10	16	1	3	1.0	.963
1953			3	6	.333	4.86	32	8	0	79.2	82	43	26	0	2	2	0	17	2	0	.118	3	16	1	1	0.6	.950
6 yrs.			48	53	.475	4.29	189	113	37	897.1	924	361	374	7	5	8	1	294	69	3	.235	38	146	7	8	1.0	.963

John Chambers

CHAMBERS, JOHNNIE MONROE BL TR 6′ 185 lbs.
B. Sept. 10, 1911, Copperhill, Tenn. D. May 11, 1977, Palatka, Fla.

Year	Team	Lg	W	L	PCT	ERA	G	GS	CG	IP	H	BB	SO	ShO	Relief Pitching W	Relief Pitching L	Relief Pitching SV	Batting AB	Batting H	Batting HR	BA	PO	A	E	DP	TC/G	FA
1937	STL	N	0	0	—	18.00	2	0	0	2	5	2	1	0	0	0	0	0	0	0	—	0	0	0	0	0.0	.000

Rome Chambers

CHAMBERS, RICHARD JEROME BL TL 6′ 2″ 173 lbs.
B. Aug. 31, 1875, Weaverville, N. C. D. Aug. 30, 1902, Weaverville, N. C.

Year	Team	Lg	W	L	PCT	ERA	G	GS	CG	IP	H	BB	SO	ShO	Relief Pitching W	Relief Pitching L	Relief Pitching SV	Batting AB	Batting H	Batting HR	BA	PO	A	E	DP	TC/G	FA
1900	BOS	N	0	0	—	11.25	1	0	0	4	5	5	2	0	0	0	1	1	0	0	.000	0	0	0	0	0.0	.000

Billy Champion

CHAMPION, BUFORD BILLY BR TR 6′ 4″ 188 lbs.
B. Sept. 18, 1947, Shelby, N. C.

Year	Team	Lg	W	L	PCT	ERA	G	GS	CG	IP	H	BB	SO	ShO	Relief Pitching W	Relief Pitching L	Relief Pitching SV	Batting AB	Batting H	Batting HR	BA	PO	A	E	DP	TC/G	FA
1969	PHI	N	5	10	.333	5.00	23	20	4	117	130	63	70	2	0	0	1	35	6	0	.171	10	22	1	2	1.4	.970
1970			0	2	.000	9.00	7	1	0	14	21	10	12	0	0	1	0	3	0	0	.000	0	3	0	0	0.4	1.000
1971			3	5	.375	4.38	37	9	0	109	100	48	49	0	0	0	0	27	3	0	.111	12	19	1	1	0.9	.969
1972			4	14	.222	5.09	30	22	2	132.2	155	54	54	0	0	1	0	34	5	1	.147	9	22	1	2	1.1	.969
1973	MIL	A	5	8	.385	3.70	37	11	2	136.1	139	62	67	0	4	3	1	0	0	0	—	7	30	1	1	1.0	.974
1974			11	4	.733	3.61	31	23	2	162	168	49	60	0	0	0	0	0	0	0	—	16	16	3	2	1.1	.914
1975			6	6	.500	5.89	27	13	3	110	125	55	40	1	1	1	0	0	0	0	—	8	19	2	2	1.1	.931
1976			0	1	.000	7.13	10	3	0	24	35	13	8	0	0	0	0	0	0	0	—	2	6	0	0	0.8	1.000
8 yrs.			34	50	.405	4.68	202	102	13	805	873	354	360	3	5	6	2	99	14	1	.141	64	137	9	10	1.0	.957

Dean Chance

CHANCE, WILMER DEAN BR TR 6′ 3″ 200 lbs.
B. June 1, 1941, Wayne, Ohio.

Year	Team	Lg	W	L	PCT	ERA	G	GS	CG	IP	H	BB	SO	ShO	Relief Pitching W	Relief Pitching L	Relief Pitching SV	Batting AB	Batting H	Batting HR	BA	PO	A	E	DP	TC/G	FA
1961	LA	A	0	2	.000	6.87	5	4	0	18.1	33	5	11	0	0	0	0	5	0	0	.000	1	6	0	1	1.4	1.000
1962			14	10	.583	2.96	50	24	6	206.2	195	66	127	2	5	2	8	65	4	0	.062	12	37	1	2	1.0	.980
1963			13	18	.419	3.19	45	35	6	248	229	90	168	2	2	1	3	80	12	0	.150	15	46	6	2	1.5	.910
1964			**20**	9	.690	**1.65**	46	35	**15**	**278.1**	194	86	207	**11**	2	1	4	89	7	0	.079	10	33	1	1	1.0	.977
1965	CAL	A	15	10	.600	3.15	36	33	10	225.2	197	101	164	4	0	2	0	75	7	0	.093	14	49	1	6	1.8	.984
1966			12	17	.414	3.08	41	37	11	259.2	206	**114**	180	2	0	2	1	76	2	0	.026	17	48	4	7	1.7	.942
1967	MIN	A	20	14	.588	2.73	41	**39**	**18**	**283.2**	244	68	220	5	0	0	1	92	3	0	.033	15	51	7	6	1.8	.904
1968			16	16	.500	2.53	43	39	15	292	224	63	234	6	0	0	1	93	5	0	.054	15	57	5	3	1.8	.935
1969			5	4	.556	2.95	20	15	1	88.1	76	35	50	0	1	0	0	24	1	0	.042	3	9	0	1	0.6	1.000
1970	2 teams	CLE A (45G 9–8) NY N (3G 0–1)																									
″	total		9	9	.500	4.36	48	19	1	157	175	61	109	1	4	2	5	42	3	0	.071	3	21	2	2	0.5	.923
1971	DET	A	4	6	.400	3.50	31	14	0	90	91	50	64	0	3	0	0	21	0	0	.000	6	16	6	0	0.9	.786
11 yrs.			128	115	.527	2.92	406	294	83	2147.2	1864	739	1534	33	17	10	23	662	44	0	.066	111	373	33	31	1.3	.936
LEAGUE CHAMPIONSHIP SERIES																											
1969	MIN	A	0	0	—	13.50	1	0	0	2	4	0	2	0	0	0	0	0	0	0	—	0	0	0	0	0.0	.000

Ed Chandler

CHANDLER, EDWARD OLIVER BR TR 6′ 2″ 190 lbs.
B. Feb. 17, 1922, Pinson, Ala.

Year	Team	Lg	W	L	PCT	ERA	G	GS	CG	IP	H	BB	SO	ShO	Relief Pitching W	Relief Pitching L	Relief Pitching SV	Batting AB	Batting H	Batting HR	BA	PO	A	E	DP	TC/G	FA
1947	BKN	N	0	1	.000	6.37	15	1	0	29.2	31	12	8	0	0	0	1	2	0	0	.000	2	7	1	0	0.7	.900

Spud Chandler

CHANDLER, SPURGEON FERDINAND BR TR 6′ 181 lbs.
B. Sept. 12, 1907, Commerce, Ga. D. Jan. 9, 1990, South Pasadena, Fla.

Year	Team	Lg	W	L	PCT	ERA	G	GS	CG	IP	H	BB	SO	ShO	Relief Pitching W	Relief Pitching L	Relief Pitching SV	Batting AB	Batting H	Batting HR	BA	PO	A	E	DP	TC/G	FA
1937	NY	A	7	4	.636	2.84	12	10	6	82.1	79	20	31	2	0	1	0	30	4	0	.133	9	23	0	1	2.7	1.000
1938			14	5	.737	4.03	23	23	14	172	183	47	36	2	0	0	0	69	14	3	.203	18	50	0	3	3.0	1.000
1939			3	0	1.000	2.84	11	0	0	19	26	9	4	0	3	0	0	5	2	0	.400	1	7	0	0	0.7	1.000
1940			8	7	.533	4.60	27	24	6	172	184	60	56	1	0	0	0	60	9	2	.150	4	50	2	3	2.1	.964
1941			10	4	.714	3.19	28	20	11	163.2	146	60	60	4	0	0	4	60	11	0	.183	15	42	1	1	2.1	.983
1942			16	5	.762	2.38	24	24	17	200.2	176	74	74	3	0	0	0	71	15	0	.211	25	46	2	8	3.0	.973
1943			**20**	4	**.833**	**1.64**	30	30	**20**	253	197	54	134	**5**	0	0	0	97	25	2	.258	10	63	3	4	2.5	.961
1944			0	0	—	4.50	1	1	0	6	6	1	1	0	0	0	0	1	0	0	.000	0	3	0	0	3.0	1.000
1945			2	1	.667	4.65	4	4	2	31	30	7	12	1	0	0	0	12	4	0	.333	5	5	0	0	2.5	1.000
1946			20	8	.714	2.10	34	32	20	257.1	200	90	138	6	0	0	2	94	14	0	.149	13	60	1	7	2.2	.986
1947			9	5	.643	**2.46**	17	16	13	128	100	41	68	2	0	0	0	49	12	2	.245	6	36	1	1	2.5	.977
11 yrs.			109	43	.717	2.84	211	184	109	1485	1327	463	614	26	3	1	6	548	110	9	.201	106	385	10	28	2.4	.980
WORLD SERIES																											
1941	NY	A	0	1	.000	3.60	1	1	0	5	4	2	2	0	0	0	0	2	1	0	.500	0	0	0	0	0.0	.000
1942			0	1	.000	1.08	2	1	0	8.1	5	1	3	0	0	0	1	2	0	0	.000	2	2	0	0	2.0	1.000

Spud Chandler *continued*

Year	Team	W	L	PCT	ERA	G	GS	CG	IP	H	BB	SO	ShO	Relief Pitching W	Relief Pitching L	Relief Pitching SV	Batting AB	Batting H	Batting HR	BA	PO	A	E	DP	TC/G	FA
1943		2	0	1.000	0.50	2	2	2	18	17	3	10	1	0	0	0	6	1	0	.167	0	4	0	0	2.0	1.000
1947		0	0	—	9.00	1	0	0	2	2	3	1	0	0	0	0	0	0	0	—	0	0	0	0	0.0	.000
4 yrs.		2	2	.500	1.62	6	4	2	33.1	28	9	16	1	0	0	1	10	2	0	.200	2	6	0	0	1.3	1.000

Esty Chaney

CHANEY, ESTY CLYON BR TR 5′11″ 170 lbs.
B. Jan. 29, 1891, Hadley, Pa. D. Feb. 5, 1952, Cleveland, Ohio.

Year	Team	W	L	PCT	ERA	G	GS	CG	IP	H	BB	SO	ShO	Relief Pitching W	Relief Pitching L	Relief Pitching SV	Batting AB	Batting H	Batting HR	BA	PO	A	E	DP	TC/G	FA
1913	BOS A	0	0	—	9.00	1	0	0	1	1	2	0	0	0	0	0	0	0	0	—	0	0	0	0	0.0	.000
1914	BKN F	0	0	—	6.75	1	0	0	4	7	2	1	0	0	0	0	1	0	0	.000	0	1	0	0	1.0	1.000
2 yrs.		0	0		7.20	2	0	0	5	8	4	1	0	0	0	0	1	0	0	.000	0	1	0	0	0.5	1.000

Darrin Chapin

CHAPIN, DARRIN JOHN BR TR 6′ 170 lbs.
B. Jan. 5, 966 , Warren, Ohio.

Year	Team	W	L	PCT	ERA	G	GS	CG	IP	H	BB	SO	ShO	Relief Pitching W	Relief Pitching L	Relief Pitching SV	Batting AB	Batting H	Batting HR	BA	PO	A	E	DP	TC/G	FA
1991	NY A	0	1	.000	5.06	3	0	0	5.1	3	6	5	0	0	1	0	0	0	0	—	0	1	0	0	0.3	1.000
1992	PHI N	0	0	—	9.00	1	0	0	2	2	0	1	0	0	0	0	0	0	0	—	0	0	0	0	0.0	.000
2 yrs.		0	1	.000	6.14	4	0	0	7.1	5	6	6	0	0	1	0	0	0	0		0	1	0	0	0.3	1.000

Tiny Chaplin

CHAPLIN, JAMES BAILEY BR TR 6′ 1″ 195 lbs.
B. July 13, 1905, Los Angeles, Calif. D. Mar. 25, 1939, National City, Calif.

Year	Team	W	L	PCT	ERA	G	GS	CG	IP	H	BB	SO	ShO	Relief Pitching W	Relief Pitching L	Relief Pitching SV	Batting AB	Batting H	Batting HR	BA	PO	A	E	DP	TC/G	FA
1928	NY N	0	2	.000	4.50	12	1	0	24	27	8	5	0	0	2	0	5	0	0	.000	2	3	0	0	0.4	1.000
1930		2	6	.250	5.18	19	8	3	73	89	16	20	0	0	2	1	19	2	1	.105	8	14	0	0	1.2	1.000
1931		2	1	.667	3.19	16	3	1	42.1	39	16	7	0	0	0	1	11	2	0	.182	4	4	0	0	0.5	1.000
1936	BOS N	10	15	.400	4.12	40	31	14	231.1	273	62	86	0	1	0	2	84	17	0	.202	13	57	3	2	1.8	.959
4 yrs.		14	24	.368	4.25	87	43	18	370.2	428	102	118	0	1	4	4	119	21	1	.176	27	78	3	2	1.2	.972

Ben Chapman

CHAPMAN, WILLIAM BENJAMIN BR TR 6′ 190 lbs.
B. Dec. 25, 1908, Nashville, Tenn. D. July 7, 1993, Hoover, Ala.
Manager 1945–48.

Year	Team	W	L	PCT	ERA	G	GS	CG	IP	H	BB	SO	ShO	Relief Pitching W	Relief Pitching L	Relief Pitching SV	Batting AB	Batting H	Batting HR	BA	PO	A	E	DP	TC/G	FA
1944	BKN N	5	3	.625	3.40	11	9	6	79.1	75	33	37	0	0	1	0	38	14	0	.368	232	295	42	47	4.2	.926
1945	2 teams BKN N (10G 3–3) PHI N (3G 0–0)																									
″	total	3	3	.500	5.79	13	7	2	60.2	71	38	27	0	1	0	0	73	19	0	.260	17	21	4	3	1.6	.905
1946	PHI N	0	0	—	0.00	1	0	0	1.1	1	0	1	0	0	0	0	1	0	0	.000	0	0	0	0	0.0	.000
3 yrs.		8	6	.571	4.39	25	16	8	141.1	147	71	65	0	1	1	0	*				3740	514	173	85	2.6	.961

Ed Chapman

CHAPMAN, EDWIN VOLNEY BB TR 6′ 1″ 185 lbs.
B. Nov. 28, 1905, Courtland, Miss.

Year	Team	W	L	PCT	ERA	G	GS	CG	IP	H	BB	SO	ShO	Relief Pitching W	Relief Pitching L	Relief Pitching SV	Batting AB	Batting H	Batting HR	BA	PO	A	E	DP	TC/G	FA
1933	WAS A	0	0	—	8.00	6	1	0	9	10	2	4	0	0	0	0	3	0	0	.000	0	1	0	0	0.2	1.000

Fred Chapman

CHAPMAN, FREDERICK JOSEPH BR TR 5′ 8″ 165 lbs.
B. Nov. 24, 1872, Little Cooley, Pa. D. Dec. 14, 1957, Union City, Pa.

Year	Team	W	L	PCT	ERA	G	GS	CG	IP	H	BB	SO	ShO	Relief Pitching W	Relief Pitching L	Relief Pitching SV	Batting AB	Batting H	Batting HR	BA	PO	A	E	DP	TC/G	FA
1887	PHI AA	0	0	—	*7.20*	1	1	1	5	8	2	4	0	0	0	0	2	0	0	.000	0	0	0	0	0.0	.000

Bill Chappelle

CHAPPELLE, WILLIAM HOGAN (Big Bill) BR TR 6′ 2″ 206 lbs.
B. Mar. 22, 1884, Waterloo, N. Y. D. Dec. 31, 1944, Mineola, N. Y.

Year	Team	W	L	PCT	ERA	G	GS	CG	IP	H	BB	SO	ShO	Relief Pitching W	Relief Pitching L	Relief Pitching SV	Batting AB	Batting H	Batting HR	BA	PO	A	E	DP	TC/G	FA
1908	BOS N	2	4	.333	1.79	13	7	3	70.1	60	17	23	1	0	0	0	21	1	0	.048	3	25	1	0	2.2	.966
1909	2 teams BOS N (5G 1–1) CIN N (1G 0–0)																									
″	total	1	1	.500	1.91	6	3	2	33	36	13	8	0	0	0	1	12	4	1	.333	3	15	1	1	3.2	.947
1914	BKN F	4	2	.667	3.15	16	6	4	74.1	71	29	31	0	0	1	0	23	0	0	.000	2	17	2	1	1.3	.905
3 yrs.		7	7	.500	2.38	35	16	9	177.2	167	59	62	1	0	1	1	56	5	1	.089	8	57	4	2	2.0	.942

Norm Charlton

CHARLTON, NORMAN WOOD BB TL 6′ 3″ 195 lbs.
B. Jan. 6, 1963, Fort Polk, La.

Year	Team	W	L	PCT	ERA	G	GS	CG	IP	H	BB	SO	ShO	Relief Pitching W	Relief Pitching L	Relief Pitching SV	Batting AB	Batting H	Batting HR	BA	PO	A	E	DP	TC/G	FA
1988	CIN N	4	5	.444	3.96	10	10	0	61.1	60	20	39	0	0	0	0	15	0	0	.000	1	9	0	0	1.0	1.000
1989		8	3	.727	2.93	69	0	0	95.1	67	40	98	0	8	3	0	5	0	0	.000	3	13	3	0	0.3	.842
1990		12	9	.571	2.74	56	16	1	154.1	131	70	117	1	6	4	2	37	5	0	.135	6	23	1	3	0.5	.967
1991		3	5	.375	2.91	39	11	0	108.1	92	34	77	0	0	0	1	23	1	0	.043	4	20	1	1	0.6	.960
1992		4	2	.667	2.99	64	0	0	81.1	79	26	90	0	4	2	26	5	1	0	.200	3	8	3	1	0.2	.786
1993	SEA A	1	3	.250	2.34	34	0	0	34.2	22	17	48	0	1	3	18	0	0	0	—	0	2	0	1	0.1	1.000
1995	2 teams PHI N (25G 2–5) SEA A (30G 2–1)																									
″	total	4	6	.400	3.36	55	0	0	69.2	46	31	70	0	4	6	14	1	1	0	1.000	2	6	0	0	0.1	1.000
7 yrs.		36	33	.522	3.00	327	37	1	605	497	238	539	1	23	18	61	86	8	0	.093	19	81	8	6	0.3	.926
DIVISIONAL PLAYOFF SERIES																										
1995	SEA A	1	0	1.000	2.45	4	0	0	7.1	4	3	9	0	1	0	1	0	0	0	—	0	0	0	0	0.0	.000
LEAGUE CHAMPIONSHIP SERIES																										
1990	CIN N	1	1	.500	1.80	4	0	0	5	4	3	3	0	1	1	0	0	0	0	—	1	0	0	1	0.3	1.000
1995	SEA A	1	0	1.000	0.00	3	0	0	6	1	1	5	0	1	0	1	0	0	0	—	0	0	0	0	0.0	.000
2 yrs.		2	1	.667	0.82	7	0	0	11	5	4	8	0	2	1	1	0	0	0		1	0	0	1	0.1	1.000
WORLD SERIES																										
1990	CIN N	0	0	—	0.00	1	0	0	1	1	0	0	0	0	0	0	0	0	0	—	0	0	0	0	0.0	.000

Pete Charton

CHARTON, FRANK LANE BL TR 6′ 2″ 190 lbs.
B. Dec. 21, 1942, Jackson, Tenn.

Year	Team	W	L	PCT	ERA	G	GS	CG	IP	H	BB	SO	ShO	Relief Pitching W	Relief Pitching L	Relief Pitching SV	Batting AB	Batting H	Batting HR	BA	PO	A	E	DP	TC/G	FA
1964	BOS A	0	2	.000	5.26	25	5	0	65	67	24	37	0	0	0	0	10	1	0	.100	7	16	0	2	0.9	1.000

Hal Chase

CHASE, HAROLD HOMER (Prince Hal) BR TL 6′ 175 lbs.
B. Feb. 13, 1883, Los Gatos, Calif. D. May 18, 1947, Colusa, Calif.
Manager 1910–11.

Year	Team	W	L	PCT	ERA	G	GS	CG	IP	H	BB	SO	ShO	Relief Pitching W	Relief Pitching L	Relief Pitching SV	Batting AB	Batting H	Batting HR	BA	PO	A	E	DP	TC/G	FA
1908	NY A	0	0	—	0.00	1	0	0	0.1	0	0	0	0	0	0	0	*				1175	62	32	63	10.2	.975

Ken Chase

CHASE, KENDALL FAY (Lefty) BL TL 6′ 2″ 210 lbs.
B. Oct. 6, 1913, Oneonta, N. Y. D. Jan. 16, 1985, Oneonta, N. Y.

Year	Team	W	L	PCT	ERA	G	GS	CG	IP	H	BB	SO	ShO	Relief Pitching W	Relief Pitching L	Relief Pitching SV	Batting AB	Batting H	Batting HR	BA	PO	A	E	DP	TC/G	FA
1936	WAS A	0	0	—	11.57	1	0	0	2.1	2	4	1	0	0	0	0	1	1	0	1.000	0	0	0	0	0.0	.000
1937		4	3	.571	4.13	14	9	4	76.1	74	60	43	0	0	0	0	29	1	0	.034	1	13	2	1	1.1	.875
1938		9	10	.474	5.58	32	21	7	150	151	113	64	0	2	1	1	48	10	0	.208	4	36	6	0	1.4	.870

Ken Chase *continued*

Year	Team	Lg	W	L	PCT	ERA	G	GS	CG	IP	H	BB	SO	ShO	Relief Pitching W	Relief Pitching L	Relief Pitching SV	Batting AB	Batting H	Batting HR	BA	PO	A	E	DP	TC/G	FA
1939			10	19	.345	3.80	32	31	15	232	215	114	118	1	1	0	0	89	15	0	.169	11	39	3	2	1.7	.943
1940			15	17	.469	3.23	35	34	20	261.2	260	**143**	129	1	0	1	0	92	15	1	.163	7	44	3	1	1.5	.944
1941			6	18	.250	5.08	33	30	8	205.2	228	115	98	1	1	0	0	74	11	0	.149	8	43	2	3	1.6	.962
1942	BOS	A	5	1	.833	3.81	13	10	4	80.1	82	41	34	0	0	0	0	33	6	0	.182	4	12	2	1	1.4	.889
1943	2 teams	BOS A (7G 0–4) NY N (21G 4–12)																									
"	total		4	16	.200	4.60	28	25	4	156.2	176	104	95	1	0	0	0	53	10	0	.189	2	31	3	0	1.3	.917
8 yrs.			53	84	.387	4.27	188	160	62	1165	1188	694	582	4	4	2	1	419	69	1	.165	37	218	21	8	1.5	.924

Jim Chatterton

CHATTERTON, JAMES M.
B. Oct. 14, 1864, Brooklyn, N. Y. D. Dec. 15, 1944, Tewksbury, Mass.

Year	Team	Lg	W	L	PCT	ERA	G	GS	CG	IP	H	BB	SO	ShO	Relief Pitching W	Relief Pitching L	Relief Pitching SV	Batting AB	Batting H	Batting HR	BA	PO	A	E	DP	TC/G	FA
1884	KC	U	0	1	.000	3.60	1	1	0	5	11	2	2	0	0	0	0	*				25	3	2	2	6.0	.933

Nestor Chavez

CHAVEZ, NESTOR ISAIS
Born Nestor Isais Chavez (Silva).
B. July 6, 1947, Chacao, Venezuela D. Mar. 16, 1969, Maracaibo, Venezuela.
BR TR 6′ 170 lbs.

Year	Team	Lg	W	L	PCT	ERA	G	GS	CG	IP	H	BB	SO	ShO	Relief Pitching W	Relief Pitching L	Relief Pitching SV	Batting AB	Batting H	Batting HR	BA	PO	A	E	DP	TC/G	FA
1967	SF	N	1	0	1.000	0.00	2	0	0	5	4	3	3	0	1	0	0	1	0	0	.000	1	2	1	0	2.0	.750

Dave Cheadle

CHEADLE, DAVID BAIRD
B. Feb. 19, 1952, Greensboro, N. C.
BL TL 6′ 2″ 203 lbs.

Year	Team	Lg	W	L	PCT	ERA	G	GS	CG	IP	H	BB	SO	ShO	Relief Pitching W	Relief Pitching L	Relief Pitching SV	Batting AB	Batting H	Batting HR	BA	PO	A	E	DP	TC/G	FA
1973	ATL	N	0	1	.000	18.00	2	0	0	2	2	3	2	0	0	1	0	0	0	0	—	0	0	0	0	0.0	.000

Charlie Chech

CHECH, CHARLES WILLIAM
B. Apr. 27, 1878, Madison, Wis. D. Jan. 31, 1938, Los Angeles, Calif.
BR TR 5′11½″ 190 lbs.

Year	Team	Lg	W	L	PCT	ERA	G	GS	CG	IP	H	BB	SO	ShO	Relief Pitching W	Relief Pitching L	Relief Pitching SV	Batting AB	Batting H	Batting HR	BA	PO	A	E	DP	TC/G	FA
1905	CIN	N	14	15	.483	2.89	39	25	20	268	300	77	79	1	2	**3**	0	89	17	0	.191	11	74	6	7	2.3	.934
1906			1	4	.200	2.32	11	5	5	66	59	24	17	0	0	0	3	25	5	0	.200	2	21	2	0	2.3	.920
1908	CLE	A	11	7	.611	1.74	27	20	14	165.2	136	34	51	4	0	0	0	48	5	0	.104	7	60	1	2	2.5	.985
1909	BOS	A	7	5	.583	2.95	17	13	6	106.2	107	27	40	1	2	1	0	36	3	0	.083	4	33	2	0	2.3	.949
4 yrs.			33	31	.516	2.52	94	63	45	606.1	602	162	187	6	4	4	3	198	30	0	.152	24	188	11	9	2.4	.951

Virgil Cheeves

CHEEVES, VIRGIL EARL (Chief)
B. Feb. 12, 1901, Oklahoma City, Okla. D. May 5, 1979, Dallas, Tex.
BR TR 6′ 195 lbs.

Year	Team	Lg	W	L	PCT	ERA	G	GS	CG	IP	H	BB	SO	ShO	Relief Pitching W	Relief Pitching L	Relief Pitching SV	Batting AB	Batting H	Batting HR	BA	PO	A	E	DP	TC/G	FA
1920	CHI	N	0	0	—	3.50	5	2	0	18	16	7	3	0	0	0	0	4	0	0	.000	0	2	0	0	0.4	1.000
1921			11	12	.478	4.64	37	22	9	163	192	47	39	1	3	1	0	48	8	0	.167	4	33	4	0	1.1	.902
1922			12	11	.522	4.09	39	22	9	182.2	195	76	40	1	3	3	2	62	13	1	.210	3	38	0	3	1.1	1.000
1923			3	4	.429	6.18	19	8	0	71.1	89	37	13	0	3	1	0	23	4	0	.174	2	13	0	1	0.8	1.000
1924	CLE	A	0	0	—	7.79	8	1	0	17.1	26	17	2	0	0	0	0	4	1	0	.250	0	5	0	0	0.6	1.000
1927	NY	N	0	0	—	4.26	3	0	0	6.1	8	4	1	0	0	0	0	0	0	0	—	1	2	0	0	1.0	1.000
6 yrs.			26	27	.491	4.73	111	55	18	458.2	526	188	98	2	9	5	2	141	26	1	.184	10	93	4	4	1.0	.963

Italo Chelini

CHELINI, ITALO VINCENT (Lefty)
B. Oct. 10, 1914, San Francisco, Calif. D. Aug. 25, 1972, San Francisco, Calif.
BL TL 5′10½″ 175 lbs.

Year	Team	Lg	W	L	PCT	ERA	G	GS	CG	IP	H	BB	SO	ShO	Relief Pitching W	Relief Pitching L	Relief Pitching SV	Batting AB	Batting H	Batting HR	BA	PO	A	E	DP	TC/G	FA
1935	CHI	A	0	0	—	12.60	2	0	0	5	7	4	1	0	0	0	0	2	1	0	.500	0	1	0	0	0.5	1.000
1936			4	3	.571	4.95	18	6	5	83.2	100	30	16	0	1	0	0	32	5	0	.156	8	9	1	0	1.0	.944
1937			0	1	.000	10.38	4	0	0	8.2	15	0	3	0	0	1	0	1	0	0	.000	0	1	0	0	0.3	1.000
3 yrs.			4	4	.500	5.83	24	6	5	97.1	122	34	20	0	1	1	0	35	6	0	.171	8	11	1	0	0.8	.950

Larry Cheney

CHENEY, LAURANCE RUSSELL
B. May 2, 1886, Belleville, Kans. D. Jan. 6, 1969, Daytona Beach, Fla.
BR TR 6′ 1½″ 185 lbs.

Year	Team	Lg	W	L	PCT	ERA	G	GS	CG	IP	H	BB	SO	ShO	Relief Pitching W	Relief Pitching L	Relief Pitching SV	Batting AB	Batting H	Batting HR	BA	PO	A	E	DP	TC/G	FA
1911	CHI	N	1	0	1.000	0.00	3	1	0	10	8	3	11	0	0	0	0	4	1	0	.250	0	5	0	0	1.7	1.000
1912			**26**	10	.722	2.85	42	37	28	303.1	262	111	140	4	2	0	0	106	24	1	.226	4	67	3	0	1.8	.959
1913			21	14	.600	2.57	**54**	36	25	305	271	98	136	2	4	0	**11**	104	20	0	.192	4	82	9	1	1.8	.905
1914			20	18	.526	2.54	**50**	**40**	21	311.1	239	**140**	157	6	3	0	5	100	18	0	.180	7	84	6	4	1.9	.938
1915	2 teams	CHI N (25G 8–9) BKN N (5G 0–2)																									
"	total		8	11	.421	3.24	30	22	7	158.1	136	72	79	2	2	2	0	47	7	0	.149	13	52	8	0	2.4	.890
1916	BKN	N	18	12	.600	1.92	41	32	15	253	178	105	166	5	2	3	0	79	9	0	.114	7	61	7	2	1.8	.907
1917			8	12	.400	2.35	35	24	14	210.1	185	73	102	1	1	0	2	68	14	0	.206	4	56	4	0	1.8	.938
1918			11	13	.458	3.00	32	21	15	200.2	177	74	83	0	3	2	1	66	16	0	.242	8	63	6	0	2.3	.922
1919	3 teams	BKN N (9G 1–3) BOS N (8G 0–2) PHI N (9G 2–5)																									
"	total		3	10	.231	4.18	26	12	7	129.1	149	57	52	0	1	1	0	43	6	0	.140	8	31	3	1	1.6	.929
9 yrs.			116	100	.537	2.70	313	225	132	1881.1	1605	733	926	20	18	8	19	617	115	1	.186	55	501	46	8	1.9	.924
WORLD SERIES																											
1916	BKN	N	0	0	—	3.00	1	0	0	3	4	1	5	0	0	0	0	0	0	0	—	0	0	1	0	1.0	.000

Tom Cheney

CHENEY, THOMAS EDGAR
B. Oct. 14, 1934, Morgan, Ga.
BR TR 5′11″ 170 lbs.

Year	Team	Lg	W	L	PCT	ERA	G	GS	CG	IP	H	BB	SO	ShO	Relief Pitching W	Relief Pitching L	Relief Pitching SV	Batting AB	Batting H	Batting HR	BA	PO	A	E	DP	TC/G	FA
1957	STL	N	0	1	.000	5.00	4	3	0	9	6	15	10	0	0	0	0	2	0	0	.000	1	2	0	1	0.8	1.000
1959			0	1	.000	6.94	11	2	0	11.2	17	11	8	0	0	1	0	0	0	0	—	0	2	0	0	0.2	1.000
1960	PIT	N	2	2	.500	3.98	11	8	1	52	44	33	35	1	0	0	0	17	3	0	.176	2	3	2	0	0.6	.714
1961	2 teams	PIT N (1G 0–0) WAS A (10G 1–3)																									
"	total		1	3	.250	10.01	11	7	0	29.2	33	30	20	0	0	0	0	8	4	0	.500	1	3	1	0	0.5	.800
1962	WAS	A	7	9	.438	3.17	37	23	4	173.1	134	97	147	3	0	1	1	48	3	0	.063	9	26	1	1	1.0	.972
1963			8	9	.471	2.71	23	21	7	136.1	99	40	97	4	0	0	0	46	5	0	.109	9	10	3	1	1.0	.864
1964			1	3	.250	3.70	15	6	1	48.2	45	13	25	0	0	0	1	12	3	0	.250	1	7	0	0	0.5	1.000
1966			0	1	.000	5.06	3	1	0	5.1	4	6	3	0	0	0	0	0	0	0	—	0	2	0	1	0.7	1.000
8 yrs.			19	29	.396	3.77	115	71	13	466	382	245	345	8	0	2	2	133	18	0	.135	23	55	7	4	0.7	.918
WORLD SERIES																											
1960	PIT	N	0	0	—	4.50	3	0	0	4	4	1	6	0	0	0	0	0	0	0	—	0	1	0	0	0.3	1.000

Jack Chesbro

CHESBRO, JOHN DWIGHT (Happy Jack) BR TR 5′ 9″ 180 lbs.
B. June 5, 1874, North Adams, Mass. D. Nov. 6, 1931, Conway, Mass.
Hall of Fame 1946.

Year	Team	W	L	PCT	ERA	G	GS	CG	IP	H	BB	SO	ShO	Relief Pitching W	L	SV	Batting AB	H	HR	BA	PO	A	E	DP	TC/G	FA
1899	PIT N	6	9	.400	4.11	19	17	15	149	165	59	28	0	0	0	0	58	9	0	.155	5	26	3	0	1.8	.912
1900		15	13	.536	3.67	32	26	20	215.2	220	79	56	3	1	1	1	85	15	0	.176	4	44	7	3	1.7	.873
1901		21	10	**.677**	2.38	36	28	26	287.2	261	52	129	**6**	2	1	1	116	25	1	.216	12	57	5	2	2.1	.932
1902		**28**	6	**.824**	2.17	35	33	31	286.1	242	62	136	**8**	1	0	1	112	20	0	.179	11	60	4	2	2.1	.947
1903	NY A	21	15	.583	2.77	40	36	33	324.2	300	74	147	1	0	1	0	124	23	2	.185	13	103	2	2	3.0	.983
1904		**41**[1]	12	**.774**	1.82	**55**	**51**	**48**	**454.2**	338	88	239	6	**3**	0	0	174	41	1	.236	24	166	12	7	3.7	.941
1905		19	15	.559	2.20	41	38	24	303.1	262	71	156	3	1	1	0	112	21	0	.188	11	97	7	5	2.8	.939
1906		23	17	.575	2.96	**49**	**42**	24	325	314	75	152	4	3	0	1	125	26	1	.208	11	95	5	3	2.3	.955
1907		10	10	.500	2.53	30	25	17	206	192	46	78	1	0	0	0	72	15	0	.208	3	66	5	2	2.5	.932
1908		14	20	.412	2.93	45	31	21	289	271	67	124	3	3	0	1	102	18	0	.176	6	94	6	2	2.4	.943
1909	2 teams NY A (9G 0–4) BOS A (1G 0–1)																									
"	total	0	5	.000	6.14	10	5	2	55.2	77	17	20	0	0	0	0	19	4	0	.211	2	21	0	0	2.3	1.000
11 yrs.		198	132	.600	2.68	392	332	261	2897	2642	690	1265	35	14	4	5	1099	217	5	.197	102	829	56	28	2.5	.943

Bob Chesnes

CHESNES, ROBERT VINCENT BB TR 6′ 180 lbs.
B. May 6, 1921, Oakland, Calif. D. May 23, 1979, Everett, Wash.

Year	Team	W	L	PCT	ERA	G	GS	CG	IP	H	BB	SO	ShO	Relief Pitching W	L	SV	Batting AB	H	HR	BA	PO	A	E	DP	TC/G	FA
1948	PIT N	14	6	.700	3.57	25	23	15	194.1	180	90	69	0	0	0	0	91	25	1	.275	21	45	3	5	2.8	.957
1949		7	13	.350	5.88	27	25	8	145.1	153	82	49	1	0	0	1	68	17	1	.250	13	35	2	4	1.9	.960
1950		3	3	.500	5.54	9	7	2	39	44	17	12	0	1	0	0	13	2	0	.154	3	15	0	3	2.0	1.000
3 yrs.		24	22	.522	4.66	61	55	25	378.2	377	189	130	1	1	0	1	172	44	2	.256	37	95	5	12	2.2	.964

Mitch Chetkovich

CHETKOVICH, MITCHELL BR TR 6′ 3½″ 208 lbs.
B. July 21, 1917, Fairpoint, Ohio D. Aug. 24, 1971, Grass Valley, Calif.

Year	Team	W	L	PCT	ERA	G	GS	CG	IP	H	BB	SO	ShO	Relief Pitching W	L	SV	Batting AB	H	HR	BA	PO	A	E	DP	TC/G	FA
1945	PHI N	0	0	—	0.00	4	0	0	3	2	3	0	0	0	0	0	0	0	0	—	0	0	1	0	0.3	.000

Tony Chevez

CHEVEZ, SILVIO ANTONIO BR TR 5′11″ 177 lbs.
Born Silvio Antonio Aquilera (Chevez).
B. June 20, 1954, Telica, Nicaragua.

Year	Team	W	L	PCT	ERA	G	GS	CG	IP	H	BB	SO	ShO	Relief Pitching W	L	SV	Batting AB	H	HR	BA	PO	A	E	DP	TC/G	FA
1977	BAL A	0	0	—	12.38	4	0	0	8	10	8	7	0	0	0	0	0	0	0	—	0	1	1	0	0.5	.500

Scott Chiamparino

CHIAMPARINO, SCOTT MICHAEL BR TR 6′ 2″ 190 lbs.
B. Aug. 22, 1966, San Mateo, Calif.

Year	Team	W	L	PCT	ERA	G	GS	CG	IP	H	BB	SO	ShO	Relief Pitching W	L	SV	Batting AB	H	HR	BA	PO	A	E	DP	TC/G	FA
1990	TEX A	1	2	.333	2.63	6	6	0	37.2	36	12	19	0	0	0	0	0	0	0	—	3	1	0	0	0.7	1.000
1991		1	0	1.000	4.03	5	5	0	22.1	26	12	8	0	0	0	0	0	0	0	—	1	1	0	0	0.4	1.000
1992		0	4	.000	3.55	4	4	0	25.1	25	5	13	0	0	0	0	0	0	0	—	1	2	2	0	1.3	.600
3 yrs.		2	6	.250	3.27	15	15	0	85.1	87	29	40	0	0	0	0	0	0	0		5	4	2	0	0.7	.818

Floyd Chiffer

CHIFFER, FLOYD JOHN BR TR 6′ 2″ 185 lbs.
B. Apr. 20, 1956, Glen Cove, N. Y.

Year	Team	W	L	PCT	ERA	G	GS	CG	IP	H	BB	SO	ShO	Relief Pitching W	L	SV	Batting AB	H	HR	BA	PO	A	E	DP	TC/G	FA
1982	SD N	4	3	.571	2.95	51	0	0	79.1	73	34	48	0	4	3	4	8	0	0	.000	5	10	0	0	0.3	1.000
1983		0	2	.000	3.18	15	0	0	22.2	17	10	15	0	0	2	1	1	0	0	.000	3	4	0	0	0.5	1.000
1984		1	0	1.000	7.71	15	1	0	28	42	16	20	0	1	0	0	3	0	0	.000	0	2	0	0	0.1	1.000
3 yrs.		5	5	.500	4.02	81	1	0	130	132	60	83	0	5	5	5	12	0	0	.000	8	16	0	0	0.3	1.000

Harry Child

CHILD, HARRY STEPHEN PATRICK BB TR 5′11″ 175 lbs.
Born Harry Stephen Patrick Chesley.
B. May 23, 1905, Baltimore, Md. D. Nov. 8, 1972, Alexandria, Va.

Year	Team	W	L	PCT	ERA	G	GS	CG	IP	H	BB	SO	ShO	Relief Pitching W	L	SV	Batting AB	H	HR	BA	PO	A	E	DP	TC/G	FA
1930	WAS A	0	0	—	6.30	5	0	0	10	10	5	5	0	0	0	0	4	1	0	.250	0	2	0	0	0.4	1.000

Bill Childers

CHILDERS, WILLIAM
B. St. Louis, Mo. Deceased.

Year	Team	W	L	PCT	ERA	G	GS	CG	IP	H	BB	SO	ShO	Relief Pitching W	L	SV	Batting AB	H	HR	BA	PO	A	E	DP	TC/G	FA
1895	LOU N	0	0	—	∞	1	0	0		2	5	0	0	0	0	0	0	0	0	—	0	0	0	0	0.0	.000

Rocky Childress

CHILDRESS, RODNEY OSBORNE BR TR 6′ 2″ 185 lbs.
B. Feb. 18, 1962, Santa Rosa, Calif.

Year	Team	W	L	PCT	ERA	G	GS	CG	IP	H	BB	SO	ShO	Relief Pitching W	L	SV	Batting AB	H	HR	BA	PO	A	E	DP	TC/G	FA
1985	PHI N	0	1	.000	6.21	16	1	0	33.1	45	9	14	0	0	0	0	6	1	0	.167	1	4	0	0	0.3	1.000
1986		0	0	—	6.75	2	0	0	2.2	4	1	1	0	0	0	0	0	0	0	—	0	0	0	0	0.0	.000
1987	HOU N	1	2	.333	2.98	32	0	0	48.1	46	18	26	0	1	2	0	2	0	0	.000	2	6	0	0	0.3	1.000
1988		1	0	1.000	6.17	11	0	0	23.1	26	9	24	0	1	0	0	4	1	0	.250	0	1	1	1	0.2	.500
4 yrs.		2	3	.400	4.76	61	1	0	107.2	121	37	65	0	2	2	0	12	2	0	.167	3	11	1	1	0.2	.933

Bob Chipman

CHIPMAN, ROBERT HOWARD (Mr. Chips) BL TL 6′ 2″ 190 lbs.
B. Oct. 11, 1918, Brooklyn, N. Y. D. Nov. 8, 1973, Huntington, N. Y.

Year	Team	W	L	PCT	ERA	G	GS	CG	IP	H	BB	SO	ShO	Relief Pitching W	L	SV	Batting AB	H	HR	BA	PO	A	E	DP	TC/G	FA
1941	BKN N	1	0	1.000	0.00	1	0	0	5	3	1	3	0	1	0	0	3	0	0	.000	1	0	0	0	1.0	1.000
1942		0	0	—	0.00	2	0	0	1.1	1	2	1	0	0	0	0	0	0	0	—	0	0	0	0	0.0	.000
1943		0	0	—	0.00	1	0	0	1.2	2	2	0	0	0	0	0	0	0	0	—	0	0	0	0	0.0	.000
1944	2 teams BKN N (11G 3–1) CHI N (26G 9–9)																									
"	total	12	10	.545	3.65	37	24	9	165.1	185	64	61	1	2	3	2	59	7	0	.119	5	32	2	2	1.1	.949
1945	CHI N	4	5	.444	3.50	25	10	3	72	63	34	29	1	0	1	0	17	3	0	.176	4	16	1	1	0.8	.952
1946		6	5	.545	3.13	34	10	5	109.1	103	54	42	3	1	0	2	33	2	0	.061	10	15	1	3	0.8	.962
1947		7	6	.538	3.68	32	17	5	134.2	135	66	51	1	1	0	0	44	4	0	.091	5	32	0	2	1.2	1.000
1948		2	1	.667	3.58	34	3	0	60.1	73	24	16	0	2	0	4	16	4	0	.250	2	18	0	0	0.6	1.000
1949		7	8	.467	3.97	38	11	3	113.1	110	63	46	1	3	2	1	24	3	0	.125	9	12	0	1	0.6	1.000
1950	BOS N	7	7	.500	4.43	27	12	4	124	127	37	40	0	2	1	1	39	6	0	.154	5	12	2	0	0.7	.895
1951		4	3	.571	4.85	33	0	0	52	59	19	17	0	4	3	4	10	1	0	.100	9	5	0	1	0.4	1.000
1952		1	1	.500	2.81	29	0	0	41.2	28	20	16	0	1	1	0	5	2	0	.400	3	8	1	1	0.4	.917
12 yrs.		51	46	.526	3.72	293	87	29	880.2	889	386	322	7	17	11	14	250	32	0	.128	53	150	7	11	0.7	.967
WORLD SERIES																										
1945	CHI N	0	0	—	0.00	1	0	0	0.1	0	1	0	0	0	0	0	0	0	0	—	0	0	0	0	0.0	.000

Steve Chitren

CHITREN, STEPHEN VINCENT BR TR 6′ 180 lbs.
B. June 8, 1967, Tokyo, Japan.

Year	Team		W	L	PCT	ERA	G	GS	CG	IP	H	BB	SO	ShO	Relief Pitching W	Relief Pitching L	Relief Pitching SV	Batting AB	Batting H	Batting HR	BA	PO	A	E	DP	TC/G	FA
1990	OAK	A	1	0	1.000	1.02	8	0	0	17.2	7	4	19	0	1	0	0	0	0	0	—	1	2	0	0	0.4	1.000
1991			1	4	.200	4.33	56	0	0	60.1	59	32	47	0	1	4	4	0	0	0	—	1	8	0	1	0.2	1.000
2 yrs.			2	4	.333	3.58	64	0	0	78	66	36	66	0	2	4	4	0	0	0		2	10	0	1	0.2	1.000

Nels Chittum

CHITTUM, NELSON BOYD BR TR 6′ 1″ 180 lbs.
B. Mar. 25, 1933, Harrisonburg, Va.

Year	Team		W	L	PCT	ERA	G	GS	CG	IP	H	BB	SO	ShO	Relief Pitching W	Relief Pitching L	Relief Pitching SV	Batting AB	Batting H	Batting HR	BA	PO	A	E	DP	TC/G	FA
1958	STL	N	0	1	.000	6.44	13	2	0	29.1	31	7	13	0	0	0	0	4	1	0	.250	4	4	0	0	0.6	1.000
1959	BOS	A	3	0	1.000	1.19	21	0	0	30.1	29	11	12	0	3	0	0	5	1	0	.200	1	9	0	0	0.5	1.000
1960			0	0	—	4.32	6	0	0	8.1	8	6	5	0	0	0	0	1	0	0	.000	1	1	0	0	0.3	1.000
3 yrs.			3	1	.750	3.84	40	2	0	68	68	24	30	0	3	0	0	10	2	0	.200	6	14	0	0	0.5	1.000

Bob Chlupsa

CHLUPSA, ROBERT JOSEPH BR TR 6′ 7″ 215 lbs.
B. Sept. 16, 1945, New York, N. Y.

Year	Team		W	L	PCT	ERA	G	GS	CG	IP	H	BB	SO	ShO	Relief Pitching W	Relief Pitching L	Relief Pitching SV	Batting AB	Batting H	Batting HR	BA	PO	A	E	DP	TC/G	FA
1970	STL	N	0	2	.000	9.00	14	0	0	16	26	9	10	0	0	2	0	0	0	0	—	1	5	0	1	0.4	1.000
1971			0	0	—	9.00	1	0	0	2	3	0	1	0	0	0	0	0	0	0	—	0	1	0	0	1.0	1.000
2 yrs.			0	2	.000	9.00	15	0	0	18	29	9	11	0	0	2	0	0	0	0		1	6	0	1	0.5	1.000

Don Choate

CHOATE, DONALD LEON BR TR 6′ 185 lbs.
B. July 2, 1938, Potosi, Mo.

Year	Team		W	L	PCT	ERA	G	GS	CG	IP	H	BB	SO	ShO	Relief Pitching W	Relief Pitching L	Relief Pitching SV	Batting AB	Batting H	Batting HR	BA	PO	A	E	DP	TC/G	FA
1960	SF	N	0	0	—	2.25	4	0	0	8	7	4	7	0	0	0	0	0	0	0	—	0	3	0	1	0.8	1.000

Chief Chouneau

CHOUNEAU, WILLIAM BR TR 5′ 9″ 150 lbs.
Born William Cadreau.
B. Sept. 2, 1889, Cloquet, Minn. D. Sept. 17, 1948, Cloquet, Minn.

Year	Team		W	L	PCT	ERA	G	GS	CG	IP	H	BB	SO	ShO	Relief Pitching W	Relief Pitching L	Relief Pitching SV	Batting AB	Batting H	Batting HR	BA	PO	A	E	DP	TC/G	FA
1910	CHI	A	0	1	.000	3.38	1	1	0	5.1	7	0	1	0	0	0	0	1	0	0	.000	0	0	0	0	0.0	.000

Mike Chris

CHRIS, MICHAEL BL TL 6′ 3″ 180 lbs.
B. Oct. 8, 1957, Santa Monica, Calif.

Year	Team		W	L	PCT	ERA	G	GS	CG	IP	H	BB	SO	ShO	Relief Pitching W	Relief Pitching L	Relief Pitching SV	Batting AB	Batting H	Batting HR	BA	PO	A	E	DP	TC/G	FA
1979	DET	A	3	3	.500	6.92	13	8	0	39	46	21	31	0	0	0	0	0	0	0	—	1	8	0	0	0.7	1.000
1982	SF	N	0	2	.000	4.85	9	6	0	26	23	26	10	0	0	0	0	7	1	0	.143	2	10	0	0	1.3	1.000
1983			0	0	—	8.10	7	0	0	13.1	16	16	5	0	0	0	0	2	0	0	.000	0	1	1	0	0.3	.500
3 yrs.			3	5	.375	6.43	29	14	0	78.1	85	63	46	0	0	0	0	9	1	0	.111	3	19	1	0	0.8	.957

Gary Christenson

CHRISTENSON, GARY RICHARD BL TL 6′ 5″ 200 lbs.
B. May 5, 1953, Mineola, N. Y.

Year	Team		W	L	PCT	ERA	G	GS	CG	IP	H	BB	SO	ShO	Relief Pitching W	Relief Pitching L	Relief Pitching SV	Batting AB	Batting H	Batting HR	BA	PO	A	E	DP	TC/G	FA
1979	KC	A	0	0	—	3.27	6	0	0	11	10	2	4	0	0	0	0	0	0	0	—	2	1	0	1	0.5	1.000
1980			3	0	1.000	5.23	24	0	0	31	35	18	16	0	3	0	1	0	0	0	—	0	8	0	0	0.3	1.000
2 yrs.			3	0	1.000	4.71	30	0	0	42	45	20	20	0	3	0	1	0	0	0		2	9	0	1	0.4	1.000

Larry Christenson

CHRISTENSON, LARRY RICHARD BR TR 6′ 4″ 215 lbs.
B. Nov. 10, 1953, Everett, Wash.

Year	Team		W	L	PCT	ERA	G	GS	CG	IP	H	BB	SO	ShO	Relief Pitching W	Relief Pitching L	Relief Pitching SV	Batting AB	Batting H	Batting HR	BA	PO	A	E	DP	TC/G	FA
1973	PHI	N	1	4	.200	6.55	10	9	1	34.1	53	20	11	0	0	0	0	10	0	0	.000	2	5	0	0	0.7	1.000
1974			1	1	.500	4.30	10	1	0	23	20	15	18	0	1	0	2	4	0	0	.000	1	2	0	0	0.3	1.000
1975			11	6	.647	3.66	29	26	5	172	149	45	88	2	0	0	1	57	14	2	.246	14	12	2	1	1.0	.929
1976			13	8	.619	3.68	32	29	2	168.2	199	42	54	0	0	0	0	51	10	2	.196	9	14	3	1	0.8	.885
1977			19	6	.760	4.07	34	34	5	219	229	69	118	1	0	0	0	74	10	3	.135	14	28	8	1	1.5	.840
1978			13	14	.481	3.24	33	33	9	228	209	47	131	3	0	0	0	67	5	1	.075	8	37	3	1	1.5	.938
1979			5	10	.333	4.50	19	17	2	106	118	30	53	0	0	0	0	31	9	1	.290	4	15	0	0	1.0	1.000
1980			5	1	.833	4.01	14	14	0	74	62	27	49	0	0	0	0	19	7	1	.368	5	16	3	0	1.7	.875
1981			4	7	.364	3.53	20	15	0	107	108	30	70	0	1	1	1	30	3	0	.100	8	13	2	0	1.1	.913
1982			9	10	.474	3.47	33	33	3	223	212	53	145	0	0	0	0	67	5	1	.075	16	26	2	2	1.3	.955
1983			2	4	.333	3.91	9	9	0	48.1	42	17	44	0	0	0	0	17	1	0	.059	4	9	1	0	1.6	.929
11 yrs.			83	71	.539	3.79	243	220	27	1403.1	1401	395	781	6	2	1	4	427	64	11	.150	85	177	24	6	1.2	.916
DIVISIONAL PLAYOFF SERIES																											
1981	PHI	N	1	0	1.000	1.50	1	1	0	6	4	1	8	0	0	0	0	2	0	0	.000	0	0	0	0	0.0	.000
LEAGUE CHAMPIONSHIP SERIES																											
1977	PHI	N	0	0	—	8.10	1	1	0	3.1	7	0	2	0	0	0	0	0	0	0	—	0	0	0	0	0.0	.000
1978			0	1	.000	12.46	1	1	0	4.1	7	1	3	0	0	0	0	1	0	0	.000	0	0	0	0	0.0	.000
1980			0	0	—	4.05	2	1	0	6.2	5	5	2	0	0	0	0	2	0	0	.000	0	1	1	0	1.0	.500
3 yrs.			0	1	.000	7.53	4	3	0	14.1	19	6	7	0	0	0	0	3	0	0	.000	0	1	1	0	0.5	.500
WORLD SERIES																											
1980	PHI	N	0	1	.000	108.00	1	1	0	0.1	5	0	0	0	0	0	0	0	0	0	—	0	0	1	0	1.0	.000

Clay Christiansen

CHRISTIANSEN, CLAY C. BR TR 6′ 5″ 215 lbs.
B. June 28, 1958, Wichita, Kans.

Year	Team		W	L	PCT	ERA	G	GS	CG	IP	H	BB	SO	ShO	Relief Pitching W	Relief Pitching L	Relief Pitching SV	Batting AB	Batting H	Batting HR	BA	PO	A	E	DP	TC/G	FA
1984	NY	A	2	4	.333	6.05	24	1	0	38.2	50	12	27	0	2	3	2	0	0	0	—	5	3	1	0	0.4	.889

Jason Christiansen

CHRISTIANSEN, JASON SAMUEL BR TL 6′ 5″ 230 lbs.
B. Sept. 21, 1969, Omaha, Neb.

Year	Team		W	L	PCT	ERA	G	GS	CG	IP	H	BB	SO	ShO	Relief Pitching W	Relief Pitching L	Relief Pitching SV	Batting AB	Batting H	Batting HR	BA	PO	A	E	DP	TC/G	FA
1995	PIT	N	1	3	.250	4.15	63	0	0	56.1	49	34	53	0	1	3	0	1	0	0	.000	2	8	2	0	0.2	.833

Mike Christopher

CHRISTOPHER, MICHAEL WAYNE BR TR 6′ 5″ 205 lbs.
B. Nov. 3, 1963, Petersburg, Va.

Year	Team		W	L	PCT	ERA	G	GS	CG	IP	H	BB	SO	ShO	Relief Pitching W	Relief Pitching L	Relief Pitching SV	Batting AB	Batting H	Batting HR	BA	PO	A	E	DP	TC/G	FA
1991	LA	N	0	0	—	0.00	3	0	0	4	2	3	2	0	0	0	0	0	0	0	—	0	1	0	0	0.3	1.000
1992	CLE	A	0	0	—	3.00	10	0	0	18	17	10	13	0	0	0	0	0	0	0	—	1	2	0	0	0.3	1.000
1993			0	0	—	3.86	9	0	0	11.2	14	2	8	0	0	0	0	0	0	0	—	0	1	0	0	0.1	1.000
1995	DET	A	4	0	1.000	3.82	36	0	0	61.1	71	14	34	0	4	0	1	0	0	0	—	4	8	0	0	0.3	1.000
4 yrs.			4	0	1.000	3.51	58	0	0	95	104	29	57	0	4	0	1	0	0	0		5	12	0	0	0.3	1.000

Russ Christopher

CHRISTOPHER, RUSSELL ORMAND BR TR 6′ 3½″ 170 lbs.
Brother of Loyd Christopher.
B. Sept. 12, 1917, Richmond, Calif. D. Dec. 5, 1954, Richmond, Calif.

Year	Team		W	L	PCT	ERA	G	GS	CG	IP	H	BB	SO	ShO	Relief Pitching W	Relief Pitching L	Relief Pitching SV	Batting AB	Batting H	Batting HR	BA	PO	A	E	DP	TC/G	FA
1942	PHI	A	4	13	.235	3.82	30	18	10	165	154	99	58	0	0	1	1	56	5	0	.089	10	60	2	5	2.4	.972
1943			5	8	.385	3.45	24	15	5	133	120	58	56	0	1	3	2	45	7	0	.156	11	61	1	5	3.0	.986
1944			14	14	.500	2.97	35	24	13	215.1	200	63	84	1	2	2	1	81	18	1	.222	27	58	3	5	2.5	.966
1945			13	13	.500	3.17	33	27	17	227.1	213	75	100	2	1	0	2	76	13	1	.171	26	71	1	4	3.0	.990
1946			5	7	.417	4.30	30	13	1	119.1	119	44	79	0	0	1	0	36	5	0	.139	7	38	1	1	1.5	.978
1947			10	7	.588	2.90	44	0	0	80.2	70	33	33	0	10	**7**	12	16	2	0	.125	10	13	1	0	0.5	.958
1948	CLE	A	3	2	.600	2.90	45	0	0	59	55	27	14	0	3	2	**17**	6	0	0	.000	2	13	0	0	0.3	1.000
7 yrs.			54	64	.458	3.37	241	97	46	999.2	931	399	424	3	17	16	35	316	50	2	.158	93	314	9	20	1.7	.978
WORLD SERIES																											
1948	CLE	A	0	0	—	∞	1	0	0		2	0	0	0	0	0	0	0	0	0	—	0	0	0	0	0.0	.000

Bubba Church

CHURCH, EMORY NICHOLAS BR TR 6′ 180 lbs.
B. Sept. 12, 1924, Birmingham, Ala.

Year	Team		W	L	PCT	ERA	G	GS	CG	IP	H	BB	SO	ShO	Relief Pitching W	Relief Pitching L	Relief Pitching SV	Batting AB	Batting H	Batting HR	BA	PO	A	E	DP	TC/G	FA
1950	PHI	N	8	6	.571	2.73	31	18	8	142	113	56	50	2	0	0	1	44	8	0	.182	7	24	1	5	1.0	.969
1951			15	11	.577	3.53	38	33	15	247	246	90	104	4	1	1	1	86	22	1	.256	14	34	1	3	1.3	.980
1952	2 teams	PHI N	(2G 0–0)	CIN N	(29G 5–9)																						
″	total		5	9	.357	4.55	31	23	5	158.1	184	49	50	1	0	0	0	51	12	1	.235	14	24	1	3	1.3	.974
1953	2 teams	CIN N	(11G 3–3)	CHI N	(27G 4–5)																						
″	total		7	8	.467	5.29	38	18	3	148	170	68	59	0	2	2	1	48	11	1	.229	6	24	5	2	0.9	.857
1954	CHI	N	1	3	.250	9.82	7	3	1	14.2	21	13	8	0	0	1	0	5	0	0	.000	2	2	0	0	0.6	1.000
1955			0	0	—	5.40	2	0	0	3.1	4	1	3	0	0	0	1	1	0	0	.000	0	0	0	0	0.0	.000
6 yrs.			36	37	.493	4.10	147	95	32	713.1	738	277	274	7	3	4	4	235	53	3	.226	43	108	8	13	1.1	.950

Len Church

CHURCH, LEONARD BB TR 6′ 190 lbs.
B. Mar. 21, 1942, Chicago, Ill. D. Apr. 22, 1988, Richardson, Tex.

Year	Team		W	L	PCT	ERA	G	GS	CG	IP	H	BB	SO	ShO	Relief Pitching W	Relief Pitching L	Relief Pitching SV	Batting AB	Batting H	Batting HR	BA	PO	A	E	DP	TC/G	FA
1966	CHI	N	0	1	.000	7.50	4	0	0	6	10	7	3	0	0	1	0	1	0	0	.000	0	1	0	0	0.3	1.000

Chuck Churn

CHURN, CLARENCE NOTTINGHAM BR TR 6′ 3″ 205 lbs.
B. Feb. 1, 1930, Bridgetown, Va.

Year	Team		W	L	PCT	ERA	G	GS	CG	IP	H	BB	SO	ShO	Relief Pitching W	Relief Pitching L	Relief Pitching SV	Batting AB	Batting H	Batting HR	BA	PO	A	E	DP	TC/G	FA
1957	PIT	N	0	0	—	4.32	5	0	0	8.1	9	4	4	0	0	0	0	1	0	0	.000	2	4	0	1	1.2	1.000
1958	CLE	A	0	0	—	6.23	6	0	0	8.2	12	5	4	0	0	0	0	0	0	0	—	1	1	0	0	0.3	1.000
1959	LA	N	3	2	.600	4.99	14	0	0	30.2	28	10	24	0	3	2	1	6	1	0	.167	1	7	0	0	0.6	1.000
3 yrs.			3	2	.600	5.10	25	0	0	47.2	49	19	32	0	3	2	1	7	1	0	.143	4	12	0	1	0.6	1.000
WORLD SERIES																											
1959	LA	N	0	0	—	27.00	1	0	0	0.2	5	0	0	0	0	0	0	0	0	0	—	0	1	0	0	1.0	1.000

Mark Ciardi

CIARDI, MARK THOMAS BR TR 6′ 180 lbs.
B. Aug. 19, 1961, New Brunswick, N. J.

Year	Team		W	L	PCT	ERA	G	GS	CG	IP	H	BB	SO	ShO	Relief Pitching W	Relief Pitching L	Relief Pitching SV	Batting AB	Batting H	Batting HR	BA	PO	A	E	DP	TC/G	FA
1987	MIL	A	1	1	.500	9.37	4	3	0	16.1	26	9	8	0	0	0	0	0	0	0	—	0	3	0	0	0.8	1.000

Al Cicotte

CICOTTE, ALVA WARREN (Bozo) BR TR 6′ 3″ 185 lbs.
B. Dec. 23, 1929, Melvindale, Mich. D. Nov. 29, 1982, Westland, Mich.

Year	Team		W	L	PCT	ERA	G	GS	CG	IP	H	BB	SO	ShO	Relief Pitching W	Relief Pitching L	Relief Pitching SV	Batting AB	Batting H	Batting HR	BA	PO	A	E	DP	TC/G	FA
1957	NY	A	2	2	.500	3.03	20	2	0	65.1	57	30	36	0	2	0	2	20	3	0	.150	6	10	0	0	0.8	1.000
1958	2 teams	WAS A	(8G 0–3)	DET A	(14G 3–1)																						
″	total		3	4	.429	4.06	22	6	0	71	86	29	35	0	2	1	0	27	5	0	.185	6	15	2	0	1.0	.913
1959	CLE	A	3	1	.750	5.32	26	1	0	44	46	25	23	0	3	1	1	3	1	0	.333	3	8	0	0	0.4	1.000
1961	STL	N	2	6	.250	5.28	29	7	0	75	83	34	51	0	2	3	1	21	6	0	.286	7	12	0	1	0.7	1.000
1962	HOU	N	0	0	—	3.86	5	0	0	4.2	8	1	4	0	0	0	0	0	0	0	—	1	0	0	0	0.2	1.000
5 yrs.			10	13	.435	4.36	102	16	0	260	280	119	149	0	9	5	4	71	15	0	.211	23	45	2	1	0.7	.971

Eddie Cicotte

CICOTTE, EDWARD VICTOR BB TR 5′ 9″ 175 lbs.
B. June 19, 1884, Springwells, Mich. D. May 5, 1969, Detroit, Mich.

Year	Team		W	L	PCT	ERA	G	GS	CG	IP	H	BB	SO	ShO	Relief Pitching W	Relief Pitching L	Relief Pitching SV	Batting AB	Batting H	Batting HR	BA	PO	A	E	DP	TC/G	FA
1905	DET	A	1	1	.500	3.50	3	1	1	18	25	5	6	0	0	1	0	7	3	0	.429	1	2	0	0	1.0	1.000
1908	BOS	A	11	12	.478	2.43	39	24	17	207.1	198	59	95	2	1	2	2	72	17	0	.236	12	65	8	0	2.2	.906
1909			13	5	.722	1.97	27	17	10	159.2	117	56	82	1	**4**	0	2	49	11	0	.224	4	50	8	2	2.3	.871
1910			15	11	.577	2.74	36	30	20	250	213	86	104	3	1	0	0	85	12	0	.141	9	98	6	1	3.1	.947
1911			11	15	.423	2.81	35	25	16	221	236	73	106	1	2	2	0	71	10	0	.141	11	62	7	2	2.3	.912
1912	2 teams	BOS A	(9G 1–3)	CHI A	(20G 9–7)																						
″	total		10	10	.500	3.50	29	24	15	198	217	52	90	1	0	1	0	69	15	0	.217	10	69	6	6	2.9	.929
1913	CHI	A	18	12	.600	1.58	41	30	18	268	224	73	121	3	2	0	1	91	13	0	.143	10	109	3	9	3.0	.975
1914			11	16	.407	2.04	45	29	15	269.1	220	72	122	4	1	0	3	86	14	0	.163	8	110	6	4	2.8	.952
1915			13	12	.520	3.02	39	26	15	223.1	216	48	106	1	0	2	3	67	14	0	.209	5	68	3	2	1.9	.961
1916			15	7	**.682**	1.78	44	19	11	187	138	70	91	2	3	2	5	57	12	0	.211	9	55	6	4	1.6	.914
1917			**28**	12	.700	**1.53**	49	35	29	**346.2**	246	70	150	7	5	1	4	112	20	0	.179	14	94	5	2	2.3	.956
1918			12	**19**	.387	2.64	38	30	24	266	275	40	104	1	3	1	2	86	14	0	.163	9	71	4	0	2.2	.952
1919			**29**	7	**.806**	1.82	40	35	**30**	**306.2**	256	49	110	5	2	1	1	99	20	0	.202	13	64	3	1	2.0	.963
1920			21	10	.677	3.26	37	35	28	303.1	316	74	87	4	0	0	2	112	22	0	.196	13	81	5	3	2.7	.949
14 yrs.			208	149	.583	2.37	502	360	249	3224.1	2897	827	1374	35	24	13	25	1063	197	0	.185	128	998	70	36	2.4	.941
WORLD SERIES																											
1917	CHI	A	1	1	.500	1.96	3	2	2	23	23	2	13	0	0	0	0	7	1	0	.143	0	7	1	0	2.7	.875
1919			1	2	.333	2.91	3	3	2	21.2	19	5	7	0	0	0	0	8	0	0	.000	0	7	2	1	3.0	.778
2 yrs.			2	3	.400	2.42	6	5	4	44.2	42	7	20	0	0	0	0	15	1	0	.067	0	14	3	1	2.8	.824

Pete Cimino

CIMINO, PETER WILLIAM BR TR 6′ 2″ 195 lbs.
B. Oct. 17, 1942, Philadelphia, Pa.

Year	Team		W	L	PCT	ERA	G	GS	CG	IP	H	BB	SO	ShO	Relief Pitching W	Relief Pitching L	Relief Pitching SV	Batting AB	Batting H	Batting HR	BA	PO	A	E	DP	TC/G	FA
1965	MIN	A	0	0	—	0.00	1	0	0	1	0	0	0	0	0	0	0	0	0	0	—	0	0	0	0	0.0	.000
1966			2	5	.286	2.92	35	0	0	64.2	53	30	57	0	2	5	4	6	0	0	.000	0	8	1	1	0.3	.889
1967	CAL	A	3	3	.500	3.26	46	1	0	88.1	73	31	80	0	3	3	1	12	5	0	.417	4	6	1	0	0.2	.909
1968			0	0	—	2.57	4	0	0	7	7	4	2	0	0	0	0	0	0	0	—	0	0	0	0	0.0	.000
4 yrs.			5	8	.385	3.07	86	1	0	161	133	65	139	0	5	8	5	18	5	0	.278	4	14	2	1	0.2	.900

Frank Cimorelli

CIMORELLI, FRANK THOMAS BR TR 6′ 175 lbs.
B. Aug. 2, 1968, Poughkeepsie, N. Y.

Year	Team	Lg	W	L	PCT	ERA	G	GS	CG	IP	H	BB	SO	ShO	Relief W	Relief L	Relief SV	Batting AB	Batting H	Batting HR	BA	PO	A	E	DP	TC/G	FA
1994	STL	N	0	0	—	8.78	11	0	0	13.1	20	10	1	0	0	0	1	2	0	0	.000	1	1	2	0	0.4	.500

Lou Ciola

CIOLA, LOUIS ALEXANDER BR TR 5′ 9″ 165 lbs.
B. Sept. 6, 1922, Norfolk, Va. D. Oct. 18, 1981, Austin, Minn.

Year	Team	Lg	W	L	PCT	ERA	G	GS	CG	IP	H	BB	SO	ShO	Relief W	Relief L	Relief SV	Batting AB	Batting H	Batting HR	BA	PO	A	E	DP	TC/G	FA
1943	PHI	A	1	3	.250	5.56	12	3	2	43.2	48	22	7	0	0	1	0	18	3	0	.167	2	9	2	0	1.1	.846

Galen Cisco

CISCO, GALEN BERNARD BR TR 6′ 200 lbs.
B. Mar. 7, 1936, St. Marys, Ohio.

Year	Team	Lg	W	L	PCT	ERA	G	GS	CG	IP	H	BB	SO	ShO	Relief W	Relief L	Relief SV	Batting AB	Batting H	Batting HR	BA	PO	A	E	DP	TC/G	FA
1961	BOS	A	2	4	.333	6.71	17	8	0	52.1	67	28	26	0	1	0	0	10	1	0	.100	3	7	0	1	0.6	1.000
1962	2 teams	BOS A (23G 4–7)			NY N (4G 1–1)																						
″	total		5	8	.385	6.07	27	11	2	102.1	110	61	56	0	1	1	0	32	2	0	.063	6	22	1	3	1.1	.966
1963	NY	N	7	15	.318	4.34	51	17	1	155.2	165	64	81	0	5	3	0	38	5	0	.132	9	26	1	0	0.7	.972
1964			6	19	.240	3.62	36	25	5	191.2	182	54	78	2	0	3	0	54	6	0	.111	15	42	2	6	1.6	.966
1965			4	8	.333	4.49	35	17	1	112.1	119	51	58	1	0	0	0	27	7	0	.259	7	12	2	3	0.6	.905
1967	BOS	A	0	1	.000	3.63	11	0	0	22.1	21	8	8	0	0	1	1	3	0	0	.000	1	4	0	0	0.5	1.000
1969	KC	A	1	1	.500	3.63	15	0	0	22.1	17	15	18	0	1	1	1	0	0	0	—	2	5	1	0	0.5	.875
7 yrs.			25	56	.309	4.56	192	78	9	659	681	281	325	3	8	9	2	164	21	0	.128	43	118	7	13	0.9	.958

Ralph Citarella

CITARELLA, RALPH ALEXANDER BR TR 6′ 175 lbs.
B. Feb. 7, 1958, East Orange, N. J.

Year	Team	Lg	W	L	PCT	ERA	G	GS	CG	IP	H	BB	SO	ShO	Relief W	Relief L	Relief SV	Batting AB	Batting H	Batting HR	BA	PO	A	E	DP	TC/G	FA
1983	STL	N	0	0	—	1.64	6	0	0	11	8	3	4	0	0	0	0	1	0	0	.000	1	1	0	0	0.3	1.000
1984			0	1	.000	3.63	10	2	0	22.1	20	7	15	0	0	0	0	4	1	0	.250	0	6	0	0	0.6	1.000
1987	CHI	A	0	0	—	7.36	5	0	0	11	13	4	9	0	0	0	0	0	0	0	—	0	1	0	0	0.2	1.000
3 yrs.			0	1	.000	4.06	21	2	0	44.1	41	14	28	0	0	0	0	5	1	0	.200	1	8	0	0	0.4	1.000

Bobby Clack

CLACK, ROBERT S. (Gentlemanly Bobby) BR TR 5′ 9″ 153 lbs.
Born Robert S. Clark.
B. June 1850, England D. Oct. 22, 1933, Danvers, Mass.

Year	Team	Lg	W	L	PCT	ERA	G	GS	CG	IP	H	BB	SO	ShO	Relief W	Relief L	Relief SV	Batting AB	Batting H	Batting HR	BA	PO	A	E	DP	TC/G	FA
1876	CIN	N	0	0	—	4.50	1	0	0	2	2	0	0	0	0	0	0	*				105	33	26	1	4.8	.841

Jim Clancy

CLANCY, JAMES BR TR 6′ 4″ 220 lbs.
B. Dec. 18, 1955, Chicago, Ill.

Year	Team	Lg	W	L	PCT	ERA	G	GS	CG	IP	H	BB	SO	ShO	Relief W	Relief L	Relief SV	Batting AB	Batting H	Batting HR	BA	PO	A	E	DP	TC/G	FA
1977	TOR	A	4	9	.308	5.03	13	13	4	77	80	47	44	1	0	0	0	0	0	0	—	6	14	3	4	1.8	.870
1978			10	12	.455	4.09	31	30	7	193.2	199	91	106	0	0	0	0	0	0	0	—	14	30	2	3	1.5	.957
1979			2	7	.222	5.48	12	11	2	64	65	31	33	0	0	0	0	0	0	0	—	1	11	0	0	1.0	1.000
1980			13	16	.448	3.30	34	34	15	251	217	**128**	152	2	0	0	0	0	0	0	—	14	35	2	2	1.5	.961
1981			6	12	.333	4.90	22	22	2	125	126	64	56	0	0	0	0	0	0	0	—	2	10	0	0	0.5	1.000
1982			16	14	.533	3.71	40	**40**	11	266.2	251	77	139	3	0	0	0	0	0	0	—	14	27	2	2	1.1	.953
1983			15	11	.577	3.91	34	34	11	223	238	61	99	1	0	0	0	0	0	0	—	23	17	1	1	1.2	.976
1984			13	15	.464	5.12	36	**36**	5	219.2	249	88	118	0	0	0	0	0	0	0	—	15	30	1	4	1.3	.978
1985			9	6	.600	3.78	23	23	1	128.2	117	37	66	0	0	0	0	0	0	0	—	6	15	1	1	1.0	.955
1986			14	14	.500	3.94	34	34	6	219.1	202	63	126	3	0	0	0	0	0	0	—	34	23	1	2	1.7	.983
1987			15	11	.577	3.54	37	37	5	241.1	234	80	180	1	0	0	0	0	0	0	—	25	36	2	4	1.7	.968
1988			11	13	.458	4.49	36	31	4	196.1	207	47	118	0	0	0	1	0	0	0	—	15	21	3	4	1.1	.923
1989	HOU	N	7	14	.333	5.08	33	26	1	147	155	66	91	0	1	1	0	41	6	0	.146	9	10	7	2	0.8	.731
1990			2	8	.200	6.51	33	10	0	76	100	33	44	0	0	1	1	14	3	0	.214	4	13	0	1	0.5	1.000
1991	2 teams	HOU N (30G 0–3)			ATL N (24G 3–2)																						
″	total		3	5	.375	3.91	54	0	0	89.2	73	34	50	0	3	5	8	6	0	0	.000	3	9	1	0	0.2	.923
15 yrs.			140	167	.456	4.22	472	381	74	2518.1	2513	947	1422	11	4	7	10	61	9	0	.148	185	301	26	30	1.1	.949
LEAGUE CHAMPIONSHIP SERIES																											
1985	TOR	A	0	1	.000	9.00	1	0	0	1	2	1	0	0	0	1	0	0	0	0	—	0	1	0	0	1.0	1.000
1991	ATL	N	0	0	—	0.00	1	0	0	0.1	0	0	0	0	0	0	0	0	0	0	—	0	0	0	0	0.0	.000
2 yrs.			0	1	.000	6.75	2	0	0	1.1	2	1	0	0	0	1	0	0	0	0		0	1	0	0	0.5	1.000
WORLD SERIES																											
1991	ATL	N	1	0	1.000	4.15	3	0	0	4.1	3	4	2	0	1	0	0	1	0	0	.000	0	0	0	0	0.0	.000

Bill Clark

CLARK, WILLIAM WINFIELD (Win) BR TR 5′10″ 175 lbs.
B. Apr. 11, 1875, Circleville, Ohio D. Apr. 15, 1959, Los Angeles, Calif.

Year	Team	Lg	W	L	PCT	ERA	G	GS	CG	IP	H	BB	SO	ShO	Relief W	Relief L	Relief SV	Batting AB	Batting H	Batting HR	BA	PO	A	E	DP	TC/G	FA
1897	LOU	N	0	0	—	0.00	0	0	0		0	0	0	0	0	0	0	*				12	16	6	1	4.9	.824

Bob Clark

CLARK, ROBERT WILLIAM BR TR 6′ 3″ 188 lbs.
B. Aug. 22, 1897, Newport, Pa. D. May 18, 1944, Carlsbad, N. M.

Year	Team	Lg	W	L	PCT	ERA	G	GS	CG	IP	H	BB	SO	ShO	Relief W	Relief L	Relief SV	Batting AB	Batting H	Batting HR	BA	PO	A	E	DP	TC/G	FA
1920	CLE	A	1	2	.333	3.43	11	2	2	42	59	13	8	1	0	1	0	10	2	0	.200	0	10	0	0	0.9	1.000
1921			0	0	—	14.46	5	0	0	9.1	23	6	2	0	0	0	0	3	0	0	.000	0	2	0	0	0.4	1.000
2 yrs.			1	2	.333	5.44	16	2	2	51.1	82	19	10	1	0	1	0	13	2	0	.154	0	12	0	0	0.8	1.000

Bryan Clark

CLARK, BRYAN DONALD BL TL 6′ 2″ 185 lbs.
B. July 12, 1956, Madera, Calif.

Year	Team	Lg	W	L	PCT	ERA	G	GS	CG	IP	H	BB	SO	ShO	Relief W	Relief L	Relief SV	Batting AB	Batting H	Batting HR	BA	PO	A	E	DP	TC/G	FA
1981	SEA	A	2	5	.286	4.35	29	9	1	93	92	55	52	0	2	1	2	0	0	0	—	0	22	1	0	0.8	.957
1982			5	2	.714	2.75	37	5	1	114.2	104	58	70	1	2	1	0	0	0	0	—	7	20	0	3	0.7	1.000
1983			7	10	.412	3.94	41	17	2	162.1	160	72	76	0	4	2	0	0	0	0	—	8	38	3	4	1.2	.939
1984	TOR	A	1	2	.333	5.91	20	3	0	45.2	66	22	21	0	1	1	0	0	0	0	—	1	13	0	0	0.7	1.000
1985	CLE	A	3	4	.429	6.32	31	3	0	62.2	78	34	24	0	3	2	2	0	0	0	—	7	13	1	2	0.7	.952
1986	CHI	A	0	0	—	4.50	5	0	0	8	8	2	5	0	0	0	0	0	0	0	—	2	0	0	0	0.4	1.000
1987			0	0	—	2.41	11	0	0	18.2	19	8	8	0	0	0	0	0	0	0	—	0	1	0	0	0.1	1.000
1990	SEA	A	2	0	1.000	3.27	12	0	0	11	9	10	3	0	2	0	0	0	0	0	—	1	3	0	1	0.3	1.000
8 yrs.			20	23	.465	4.15	186	37	4	516	536	261	259	1	14	7	4	0	0	0		26	110	5	10	0.8	.965

Ed Clark

CLARK, EDWARD C.
B. Cincinnati, Ohio Deceased.

Year	Team	Lg	W	L	PCT	ERA	G	GS	CG	IP	H	BB	SO	ShO	Relief Pitching W	Relief Pitching L	Relief Pitching SV	Batting AB	Batting H	HR	BA	PO	A	E	DP	TC/G	FA
1886	PHI	AA	0	1	.000	6.75	1	1	1	8	10	2	2	0	0	0	0	2	0	0	.000	0	0	0	0	0.0	.000
1891	COL	AA	0	0	—	0.00	1	0	0	2	2	0	1	0	0	0	0	1	0	0	.000	0	1	0	1	1.0	1.000
2 yrs.			0	1	.000	5.40	2	1	1	10	12	2	3	0	0	0	0	3	0	0	.000	0	1	0	1	0.5	1.000

George Clark

CLARK, GEORGE MYRON BR TL 6′ 190 lbs.
B. May 19, 1891, Smithland, Iowa D. Nov. 14, 1940, Sioux City, Iowa.

Year	Team	Lg	W	L	PCT	ERA	G	GS	CG	IP	H	BB	SO	ShO	Relief Pitching W	Relief Pitching L	Relief Pitching SV	Batting AB	Batting H	HR	BA	PO	A	E	DP	TC/G	FA
1913	NY	A	0	1	.000	9.00	11	1	0	19	22	19	5	0	0	0	0	4	2	0	.500	0	6	1	0	0.6	.857

Ginger Clark

CLARK, HARVEY DANIEL BR TR 5′11″ 165 lbs.
B. Mar. 7, 1879, Wooster, Ohio D. May 10, 1943, Lake Charles, La.

Year	Team	Lg	W	L	PCT	ERA	G	GS	CG	IP	H	BB	SO	ShO	Relief Pitching W	Relief Pitching L	Relief Pitching SV	Batting AB	Batting H	HR	BA	PO	A	E	DP	TC/G	FA
1902	CLE	A	1	0	1.000	6.00	1	0	0	6	10	3	1	0	1	0	0	4	2	0	.500	0	3	0	0	3.0	1.000

Mark Clark

CLARK, MARK WILLARD BR TR 6′ 5″ 225 lbs.
B. May 12, 1968, Bath, Ill.

Year	Team	Lg	W	L	PCT	ERA	G	GS	CG	IP	H	BB	SO	ShO	Relief Pitching W	Relief Pitching L	Relief Pitching SV	Batting AB	Batting H	HR	BA	PO	A	E	DP	TC/G	FA
1991	STL	N	1	1	.500	4.03	7	2	0	22.1	17	11	13	0	1	1	0	7	0	0	.000	2	1	0	0	0.4	1.000
1992			3	10	.231	4.45	20	20	1	113.1	117	36	44	1	0	0	0	36	5	0	.139	2	13	1	0	0.8	.938
1993	CLE	A	7	5	.583	4.28	26	15	1	109.1	119	25	57	0	0	0	0	0	0	0	—	4	10	2	0	0.6	.875
1994			11	3	.786	3.82	20	20	4	127.1	133	40	60	1	0	0	0	0	0	0	—	5	23	0	3	1.4	1.000
1995			9	7	.563	5.27	22	21	2	124.2	143	42	68	0	1	0	0	0	0	0	—	8	15	0	3	1.0	1.000
5 yrs.			31	26	.544	4.44	95	78	8	497	529	154	242	2	2	1	0	43	5	0	.116	21	62	3	6	0.9	.965

Mike Clark

CLARK, MICHAEL JOHN BR TR 6′ 4″ 190 lbs.
B. Feb. 12, 1922, Camden, N. J.

Year	Team	Lg	W	L	PCT	ERA	G	GS	CG	IP	H	BB	SO	ShO	Relief Pitching W	Relief Pitching L	Relief Pitching SV	Batting AB	Batting H	HR	BA	PO	A	E	DP	TC/G	FA
1952	STL	N	2	0	1.000	6.04	12	4	0	25.1	32	14	10	0	2	0	0	5	0	0	.000	3	5	1	1	0.8	.889
1953			1	0	1.000	4.79	23	2	0	35.2	46	21	17	0	0	0	1	6	0	0	.000	3	9	3	1	0.7	.800
2 yrs.			3	0	1.000	5.31	35	6	0	61	78	35	27	0	2	0	1	11	0	0	.000	6	14	4	2	0.7	.833

Otie Clark

CLARK, WILLIAM OTIS BL TR 6′ 1½″ 190 lbs.
B. May 22, 1918, Boscobel, Wis.

Year	Team	Lg	W	L	PCT	ERA	G	GS	CG	IP	H	BB	SO	ShO	Relief Pitching W	Relief Pitching L	Relief Pitching SV	Batting AB	Batting H	HR	BA	PO	A	E	DP	TC/G	FA
1945	BOS	A	4	4	.500	3.06	12	9	4	82.1	86	19	20	1	0	0	0	24	5	0	.208	4	7	0	0	0.9	1.000

Phil Clark

CLARK, PHILIP JAMES BR TR 6′ 3″ 210 lbs.
B. Oct. 3, 1932, Albany, Ga.

Year	Team	Lg	W	L	PCT	ERA	G	GS	CG	IP	H	BB	SO	ShO	Relief Pitching W	Relief Pitching L	Relief Pitching SV	Batting AB	Batting H	HR	BA	PO	A	E	DP	TC/G	FA
1958	STL	N	0	1	.000	3.52	7	0	0	7.2	11	3	1	0	0	1	1	1	0	0	.000	0	0	0	0	0.0	.000
1959			0	1	.000	12.86	7	0	0	7	8	8	5	0	0	1	0	0	0	0	—	0	3	0	0	0.4	1.000
2 yrs.			0	2	.000	7.98	14	0	0	14.2	19	11	6	0	0	2	1	1	0	0	.000	0	3	0	0	0.2	1.000

Rickey Clark

CLARK, RICKEY CHARLES BR TR 6′ 2″ 170 lbs.
B. Mar. 21, 1946, Mt. Clemens, Mich.

Year	Team	Lg	W	L	PCT	ERA	G	GS	CG	IP	H	BB	SO	ShO	Relief Pitching W	Relief Pitching L	Relief Pitching SV	Batting AB	Batting H	HR	BA	PO	A	E	DP	TC/G	FA
1967	CAL	A	12	11	.522	2.59	32	30	1	174	144	69	81	1	1	0	0	50	2	0	.040	16	34	6	2	1.8	.893
1968			1	11	.083	3.53	21	17	0	94.1	74	54	60	0	0	0	0	28	3	0	.107	5	18	3	1	1.2	.885
1969			0	0	—	5.59	6	1	0	9.2	12	7	6	0	0	0	0	2	1	0	.500	0	0	1	0	0.2	.000
1971			2	1	.667	2.86	11	7	1	44	36	28	28	1	0	0	1	15	4	0	.267	2	5	1	0	0.7	.875
1972			4	9	.308	4.50	26	15	2	110	105	55	61	0	0	1	1	31	3	0	.097	7	20	1	1	1.1	.964
5 yrs.			19	32	.373	3.38	96	70	4	432	371	213	236	2	1	1	2	126	13	0	.103	30	77	12	4	1.2	.899

Spider Clark

CLARK, OWEN F. TR 5′10″ 150 lbs.
B. Sept. 16, 1867, Brooklyn, N. Y. D. Feb. 8, 1892, Brooklyn, N. Y.

Year	Team	Lg	W	L	PCT	ERA	G	GS	CG	IP	H	BB	SO	ShO	Relief Pitching W	Relief Pitching L	Relief Pitching SV	Batting AB	Batting H	HR	BA	PO	A	E	DP	TC/G	FA
1890	BUF	P	0	0	—	6.75	1	0	0	4	8	2	2	0	0	0	0	*				101	75	26	10	5.1	.871

Terry Clark

CLARK, TERRY LEE BR TR 6′ 2″ 190 lbs.
B. Oct. 18, 1960, Los Angeles, Calif.

Year	Team	Lg	W	L	PCT	ERA	G	GS	CG	IP	H	BB	SO	ShO	Relief Pitching W	Relief Pitching L	Relief Pitching SV	Batting AB	Batting H	HR	BA	PO	A	E	DP	TC/G	FA
1988	CAL	A	6	6	.500	5.07	15	15	2	94	120	31	39	1	0	0	0	0	0	0	—	8	13	0	0	1.4	1.000
1989			0	2	.000	4.91	4	2	0	11	13	3	7	0	0	0	0	0	0	0	—	0	2	0	0	0.5	1.000
1990	HOU	N	0	0	—	13.50	1	1	0	4	9	3	2	0	0	0	0	2	1	0	.500	0	0	0	0	0.0	.000
1995	2 teams	ATL N (3G 0–0) BAL A (38G 2–5)																									
″	total		2	5	.286	3.59	41	0	0	42.2	43	20	20	0	2	5	1	0	0	0	—	2	3	1	1	0.1	.833
4 yrs.			8	13	.381	4.87	61	18	2	151.2	185	57	68	1	2	5	1	2	1	0	.500	10	18	1	1	0.5	.966

Watty Clark

CLARK, WILLIAM WATSON BL TL 6′½″ 175 lbs.
B. May 16, 1902, St. Joseph, La. D. Mar. 4, 1972, Clearwater, Fla.

Year	Team	Lg	W	L	PCT	ERA	G	GS	CG	IP	H	BB	SO	ShO	Relief Pitching W	Relief Pitching L	Relief Pitching SV	Batting AB	Batting H	HR	BA	PO	A	E	DP	TC/G	FA
1924	CLE	A	1	3	.250	7.01	12	1	0	25.2	38	14	6	0	1	2	0	9	2	0	.222	1	5	0	0	0.5	1.000
1927	BKN	N	7	2	.778	2.32	27	3	1	73.2	74	19	32	0	5	2	2	21	3	0	.143	3	17	1	0	0.8	.952
1928			12	9	.571	2.68	40	19	10	194.2	193	50	85	2	2	4	3	66	10	0	.152	1	49	1	1	1.3	.980
1929			16	**19**	.457	3.74	41	**36**	19	**279**	**295**	71	140	3	0	3	1	97	16	0	.165	8	57	2	3	1.6	.970
1930			13	13	.500	4.18	44	24	9	200	209	38	81	1	4	1	6	68	14	1	.206	4	43	1	2	1.1	.979
1931			14	10	.583	3.20	34	28	16	233.1	243	52	96	3	1	0	1	84	21	0	.250	3	37	0	1	1.2	1.000
1932			20	12	.625	3.49	40	**36**	19	273	282	49	99	2	1	0	0	97	21	0	.216	9	63	3	1	1.9	.960
1933	2 teams	BKN N (11G 2–4) NY N (16G 3–4)																									
″	total		5	8	.385	4.75	27	13	4	94.2	119	17	25	1	2	1	1	24	5	0	.208	2	24	0	0	1.0	1.000
1934	2 teams	NY N (5G 1–2) BKN N (17G 2–0)																									
″	total		3	2	.600	5.93	22	5	1	44	63	14	16	0	1	0	0	14	2	0	.143	5	7	0	0	0.5	1.000
1935	BKN	N	13	8	.619	3.30	33	25	11	207	215	28	35	1	4	0	0	79	14	0	.177	11	54	2	3	2.0	.970
1936			7	11	.389	4.42	33	16	1	120	162	28	28	1	3	2	2	39	9	0	.231	6	27	1	1	1.0	.971
1937			0	0	—	7.71	2	0	0	2.1	4	3	0	0	0	0	0	0	0	0	—	1	1	0	0	1.0	1.000
12 yrs.			111	97	.534	3.66	355	206	91	1747.1	1897	383	643	14	24	15	16	598	117	1	.196	54	384	11	12	1.3	.976

Alan Clarke

CLARKE, ALAN THOMAS (Lefty) BB TL 5′11″ 180 lbs.
B. Mar. 8, 1896, Clarksville, Md. D. Mar. 11, 1975, Cheverly, Md.

Year	Team	Lg	W	L	PCT	ERA	G	GS	CG	IP	H	BB	SO	ShO	Relief Pitching W	Relief Pitching L	Relief Pitching SV	Batting AB	Batting H	Batting HR	BA	PO	A	E	DP	TC/G	FA
1921	**CIN**	**N**	0	1	.000	5.40	1	1	1	5	7	2	1	0	0	0	0	1	0	0	.000	0	0	0	0	0.0	.000

Dad Clarke

CLARKE, WILLIAM H. BB TR
B. Jan. 7, 1865, Oswego, N. Y. D. June 3, 1911, Lorain, Ohio.

Year	Team	Lg	W	L	PCT	ERA	G	GS	CG	IP	H	BB	SO	ShO	Relief Pitching W	Relief Pitching L	Relief Pitching SV	Batting AB	Batting H	Batting HR	BA	PO	A	E	DP	TC/G	FA
1888	**CHI**	**N**	2	1	.667	4.54	5	4	3	37.2	53	7	7	0	0	0	0	7	2	1	.286	5	9	2	1	2.7	.875
1891	**COL**	**AA**	1	2	.333	6.86	4	3	2	21	30	16	2	0	0	0	0	9	1	0	.111	0	5	0	0	1.3	1.000
1894	**NY**	**N**	3	4	.429	4.93	15	6	5	84	114	26	15	0	0	1	1	37	8	0	.216	6	15	2	1	1.5	.913
1895			18	15	.545	3.39	37	30	27	281.2	336	60	67	1	1	**4**	1	121	29	0	.240	13	49	7	6	1.9	.899
1896			17	24	.415	4.26	48	40	33	351	431	60	66	1	2	0	1	147	30	0	.204	12	72	8	1	1.9	.913
1897	**2 teams**	**NY N** (6G 2–1)	**LOU N** (4G 1–3)																								
″	**total**		3	4	.429	4.92	10	8	6	64	87	20	16	0	0	0	0	30	5	0	.167	18	13	3	0	3.1	.912
1898	**LOU**	**N**	0	1	.000	5.00	1	1	1	9	10	2	1	0	0	0	0	3	0	0	.000	0	2	0	0	2.0	1.000
7 yrs.			44	51	.463	4.17	120	92	77	848.1	1061	191	174	2	3	5	3	354	75	1	.212	54	165	22	9	2.0	.909

Henry Clarke

CLARKE, HENRY TEFFT BR TR
B. Aug. 28, 1875, Bellevue, Neb. D. Mar. 28, 1950, Colorado Springs, Colo.

Year	Team	Lg	W	L	PCT	ERA	G	GS	CG	IP	H	BB	SO	ShO	Relief Pitching W	Relief Pitching L	Relief Pitching SV	Batting AB	Batting H	Batting HR	BA	PO	A	E	DP	TC/G	FA
1897	**CLE**	**N**	0	4	.000	5.87	5	4	3	30.2	32	12	3	0	0	0	0	25	7	0	.280	3	5	4	0	1.7	.667
1898	**CHI**	**N**	1	0	1.000	2.00	1	1	1	9	8	5	1	0	0	0	0	4	1	0	.250	0	1	0	0	0.5	1.000
2 yrs.			1	4	.200	4.99	6	5	4	39.2	40	17	4	0	0	0	0	29	8	0	.276	3	6	4	0	1.4	.692

Rufe Clarke

CLARKE, RUFUS RIVERS BR TR 6′ 1″ 203 lbs.
Brother of Sumpter Clarke.
B. Apr. 13, 1900, Estill, S. C. D. Feb. 8, 1983, Columbia, S. C.

Year	Team	Lg	W	L	PCT	ERA	G	GS	CG	IP	H	BB	SO	ShO	Relief Pitching W	Relief Pitching L	Relief Pitching SV	Batting AB	Batting H	Batting HR	BA	PO	A	E	DP	TC/G	FA
1923	**DET**	**A**	1	1	.500	4.50	5	0	0	6	6	6	2	0	1	1	0	0	0	0	—	1	2	0	0	0.6	1.000
1924			0	0	—	3.38	2	0	0	5.1	3	5	1	0	0	0	0	1	0	0	.000	2	0	0	0	1.0	1.000
2 yrs.			1	1	.500	3.97	7	0	0	11.1	9	11	3	0	1	1	0	1	0	0	.000	3	2	0	0	0.7	1.000

Stan Clarke

CLARKE, STANLEY MARTEN BR TL 6′ 1″ 180 lbs.
B. Aug. 9, 1960, Toledo, Ohio.

Year	Team	Lg	W	L	PCT	ERA	G	GS	CG	IP	H	BB	SO	ShO	Relief Pitching W	Relief Pitching L	Relief Pitching SV	Batting AB	Batting H	Batting HR	BA	PO	A	E	DP	TC/G	FA
1983	**TOR**	**A**	1	1	.500	3.27	10	0	0	11	10	5	7	0	1	1	0	0	0	0	—	0	2	0	0	0.2	1.000
1985			0	0	—	4.50	4	0	0	4	3	2	2	0	0	0	0	0	0	0	—	0	1	0	0	0.3	1.000
1986			0	1	.000	9.24	10	0	0	12.2	18	10	9	0	0	1	0	0	0	0	—	0	3	0	0	0.3	1.000
1987	**SEA**	**A**	2	2	.500	5.48	22	0	0	23	31	10	13	0	2	2	0	0	0	0	—	1	2	0	0	0.1	1.000
1989	**KC**	**A**	0	2	.000	15.43	2	2	0	7	14	4	2	0	0	0	0	0	0	0	—	0	1	0	0	0.5	1.000
1990	**STL**	**N**	0	0	—	2.70	2	0	0	3.1	2	0	3	0	0	0	0	0	0	0	—	0	0	0	0	0.0	.000
6 yrs.			3	6	.333	6.79	50	2	0	61	78	31	36	0	3	4	0	0	0	0		1	9	0	0	0.2	1.000

Webbo Clarke

CLARKE, VIBERT ERNESTO BL TL 6′ 165 lbs.
B. June 8, 1928, Colon, Panama D. June 14, 1970, Cristobal, Canal Zone.

Year	Team	Lg	W	L	PCT	ERA	G	GS	CG	IP	H	BB	SO	ShO	Relief Pitching W	Relief Pitching L	Relief Pitching SV	Batting AB	Batting H	Batting HR	BA	PO	A	E	DP	TC/G	FA
1955	**WAS**	**A**	0	0	—	4.64	7	2	0	21.1	17	14	9	0	0	0	0	6	1	0	.167	1	4	0	0	0.7	1.000

Bill Clarkson

CLARKSON, WILLIAM HENRY (Blackie) BR TR 6′ 165 lbs.
B. Sept. 27, 1898, Portsmouth, Va. D. Aug. 27, 1971, Raleigh, N. C.

Year	Team	Lg	W	L	PCT	ERA	G	GS	CG	IP	H	BB	SO	ShO	Relief Pitching W	Relief Pitching L	Relief Pitching SV	Batting AB	Batting H	Batting HR	BA	PO	A	E	DP	TC/G	FA
1927	**NY**	**N**	3	9	.250	4.36	26	7	2	86.2	92	52	28	0	3	2	2	20	1	0	.050	2	20	0	0	0.8	1.000
1928	**2 teams**	**NY N** (4G 0–0)	**BOS N** (19G 0–2)																								
″	**total**		0	2	.000	6.92	23	1	0	40.1	63	23	11	0	0	1	0	3	0	0	.000	2	15	1	1	0.8	.944
1929	**BOS**	**N**	0	1	.000	10.29	2	1	0	7	16	4	0	0	0	0	0	2	1	0	.500	1	2	1	0	2.0	.750
3 yrs.			3	12	.200	5.44	51	9	2	134	171	79	39	0	3	3	2	25	2	0	.080	5	37	2	1	0.9	.955

Dad Clarkson

CLARKSON, ARTHUR HAMILTON BR TR 5′10″ 165 lbs.
Brother of Walter Clarkson. Brother of John Clarkson.
B. Aug. 31, 1866, Cambridge, Mass. D. Feb. 5, 1911, Somerville, Mass.

Year	Team	Lg	W	L	PCT	ERA	G	GS	CG	IP	H	BB	SO	ShO	Relief Pitching W	Relief Pitching L	Relief Pitching SV	Batting AB	Batting H	Batting HR	BA	PO	A	E	DP	TC/G	FA
1891	**NY**	**N**	1	2	.333	2.89	5	2	1	28	24	18	11	0	1	0	0	9	4	0	.444	2	6	2	0	2.0	.800
1892	**BOS**	**N**	1	0	1.000	1.29	1	1	1	7	5	3	0	0	0	0	0	3	0	0	.000	1	1	0	0	2.0	1.000
1893	**STL**	**N**	12	9	.571	3.48	24	21	17	186.1	194	79	37	1	1	0	0	75	10	0	.133	11	47	8	1	2.6	.879
1894			8	17	.320	6.36	32	32	24	233.1	318	117	46	1	0	0	0	88	16	0	.182	11	46	5	5	1.9	.919
1895	**2 teams**	**STL N** (7G 1–6)	**BAL N** (20G 12–3)																								
″	**total**		13	9	.591	4.92	27	21	17	203	260	90	32	0	2	1	0	80	9	1	.112	6	51	4	1	2.3	.934
1896	**BAL**	**N**	4	2	.667	4.98	7	4	3	47	72	18	7	0	2	0	0	18	5	0	.278	0	11	1	0	1.7	.917
6 yrs.			39	39	.500	4.90	96	81	63	704.2	873	325	133	2	6	1	0	273	44	1	.161	31	162	20	7	2.2	.906

John Clarkson

CLARKSON, JOHN GIBSON BR TR 5′10″ 155 lbs.
Brother of Walter Clarkson. Brother of Dad Clarkson.
B. July 1, 1861, Cambridge, Mass. D. Feb. 4, 1909, Belmont, Mass.
Hall of Fame 1963.

Year	Team	Lg	W	L	PCT	ERA	G	GS	CG	IP	H	BB	SO	ShO	Relief Pitching W	Relief Pitching L	Relief Pitching SV	Batting AB	Batting H	Batting HR	BA	PO	A	E	DP	TC/G	FA
1882	**WOR**	**N**	1	2	.333	*4.50*	3	3	2	24	49	2	3	0	0	0	0	11	4	0	.364	1	6	1	0	2.0	.875
1884	**CHI**	**N**	10	3	.769	*2.14*	14	13	12	118	94	25	102	0	0	0	0	84	22	3	.262	14	45	20	6	3.2	.747
1885			**53**	16	.768	*1.85*	**70**	**70**	**68**	**623**	497	97	**308**	**10**	0	0	0	283	61	4	.216	27	175	20	8	3.0	.910
1886			35	17	.673	2.41	55	55	50	466.2	419	86	313	3	0	0	0	210	49	3	.233	20	114	19	3	2.5	.876
1887			**38**	21	.644	3.08	**60**	**59**	**56**	**523**	**513**	92	**237**	2	1	0	0	215	52	6	.242	39	125	8	5	2.6	.953
1888	**BOS**	**N**	33	20	.623	2.76	54	54	53	**483.1**	448	**119**	223	3	0	0	0	205	40	1	.195	23	117	21	3	2.9	.870
1889			**49**	19	**.721**	**2.73**	**73**	**72**	**68**	**620**	**589**	**203**	**284**	**8**	0	0	1	262	54	2	.206	37	172	27	8	3.1	.886
1890			25	18	.581	3.27	44	44	43	383	370	140	138	2	0	0	0	173	43	2	.249	22	72	17	3	2.5	.847
1891			33	19	.635	2.79	55	51	47	460.2	435	154	141	3	0	1	**3**	187	42	0	.225	27	114	13	2	2.8	.916
1892	**2 teams**	**BOS N** (16G 8–6)	**CLE N** (29G 17–10)																								
″	**total**		25	16	.610	2.48	45	44	42	389	350	132	139	5	0	0	1	158	27	1	.171	11	87	15	4	2.5	.867
1893	**CLE**	**N**	16	17	.485	4.45	36	35	31	295	358	95	62	0	0	1	0	131	27	1	.206	15	82	8	1	2.8	.924
1894			8	9	.471	4.42	22	18	13	150.2	173	46	28	1	0	2	0	55	11	1	.200	3	42	9	2	2.5	.833
12 yrs.			326 **10th**	177	.648	2.81	531	518	485 **8th**	4536.1	4295	1191	1978	37	1	4	5	*				239	1151	178	45	2.8	.886

Walter Clarkson

CLARKSON, WALTER HAMILTON BR TR 5′10″ 150 lbs.
Brother of John Clarkson. Brother of Dad Clarkson.
B. Nov. 3, 1878, Cambridge, Mass. D. Oct. 10, 1946, Cambridge, Mass.

Year	Team	W	L	PCT	ERA	G	GS	CG	IP	H	BB	SO	ShO	Relief Pitching W	Relief Pitching L	Relief Pitching SV	Batting AB	Batting H	Batting HR	BA	PO	A	E	DP	TC/G	FA
1904	NY A	1	2	.333	5.02	13	4	2	66.1	63	25	43	0	1	0	1	26	7	0	.269	2	14	1	0	1.3	.941
1905		3	3	.500	3.91	9	4	3	46	40	13	35	0	2	1	0	19	1	0	.053	1	11	2	0	1.6	.857
1906		9	4	.692	2.32	32	16	9	151	135	55	64	3	1	0	0	51	8	0	.157	3	39	1	1	1.3	.977
1907	2 teams NY A (5G 1–1) CLE A (17G 4–6)																									
″	total	5	7	.417	2.67	22	12	9	108	96	37	35	1	1	0	0	35	3	0	.086	10	30	3	3	2.0	.930
1908	CLE A	0	0	—	10.80	2	1	0	3.1	6	2	1	0	0	0	0	1	1	0	1.000	0	0	0	0	0.0	.000
5 yrs.		18	16	.529	3.17	78	37	23	374.2	340	132	178	4	5	1	1	132	20	0	.152	16	94	7	4	1.5	.940

Marty Clary

CLARY, MARTIN KEITH BR TR 6′ 4″ 190 lbs.
B. Apr. 3, 1962, Detroit, Mich.

Year	Team	W	L	PCT	ERA	G	GS	CG	IP	H	BB	SO	ShO	Relief Pitching W	Relief Pitching L	Relief Pitching SV	Batting AB	Batting H	Batting HR	BA	PO	A	E	DP	TC/G	FA
1987	ATL N	0	1	.000	6.14	7	1	0	14.2	20	4	7	0	0	0	0	1	0	0	.000	0	2	0	0	0.3	1.000
1989		4	3	.571	3.15	18	17	2	108.2	103	31	30	1	0	0	0	31	5	0	.161	10	18	0	1	1.6	1.000
1990		1	10	.091	5.67	33	14	0	101.2	128	39	44	0	0	1	0	28	0	0	.000	6	20	1	0	0.8	.963
3 yrs.		5	14	.263	4.48	58	32	2	225	251	74	81	1	0	1	0	60	5	0	.083	16	40	1	1	1.0	.982

Gowell Claset

CLASET, GOWELL SYLVESTER (Lefty) BB TL 6′ 3½″ 210 lbs.
B. Nov. 26, 1907, Battle Creek, Mich. D. Mar. 8, 1981, St. Petersburg, Fla.

Year	Team	W	L	PCT	ERA	G	GS	CG	IP	H	BB	SO	ShO	Relief Pitching W	Relief Pitching L	Relief Pitching SV	Batting AB	Batting H	Batting HR	BA	PO	A	E	DP	TC/G	FA
1933	PHI A	2	0	1.000	9.53	8	1	0	11.1	23	11	1	0	2	0	0	2	1	0	.500	0	4	0	0	0.5	1.000

Fritz Clausen

CLAUSEN, FREDERICK WILLIAM BR TL 5′11″ 190 lbs.
B. Apr. 26, 1869, New York, N. Y. D. Feb. 11, 1960, Memphis, Tenn.

Year	Team	W	L	PCT	ERA	G	GS	CG	IP	H	BB	SO	ShO	Relief Pitching W	Relief Pitching L	Relief Pitching SV	Batting AB	Batting H	Batting HR	BA	PO	A	E	DP	TC/G	FA
1892	LOU N	9	13	.409	3.06	24	24	24	200	181	87	94	2	0	0	0	84	13	0	.155	11	37	6	0	2.3	.889
1893	2 teams LOU N (5G 1–4) CHI N (10G 6–2)																									
″	total	7	6	.538	3.96	15	14	11	109	112	61	35	0	0	0	1	47	7	0	.149	5	24	1	1	2.0	.967
1894	CHI N	0	1	.000	10.38	1	1	0	4.1	5	3	1	0	0	0	0	1	0	0	.000	0	2	0	0	2.0	1.000
1896	LOU N	0	2	.000	6.55	2	2	1	11	17	6	4	0	0	0	0	4	0	0	.000	1	4	1	0	3.0	.833
4 yrs.		16	22	.421	3.58	42	41	36	324.1	315	157	134	2	0	0	1	136	20	0	.147	17	67	8	1	2.2	.913

Al Clauss

CLAUSS, ALBERT STANLEY (Lefty) BR TL 5′10½″ 178 lbs.
B. June 24, 1891, New Haven, Conn. D. Sept. 13, 1952, New Haven, Conn.

Year	Team	W	L	PCT	ERA	G	GS	CG	IP	H	BB	SO	ShO	Relief Pitching W	Relief Pitching L	Relief Pitching SV	Batting AB	Batting H	Batting HR	BA	PO	A	E	DP	TC/G	FA
1913	DET A	0	1	.000	4.72	5	1	0	13.1	11	12	1	0	0	0	0	4	0	0	.000	0	3	0	1	0.6	1.000

Danny Clay

CLAY, DANNY BRUCE BR TR 6′ 1″ 190 lbs.
B. Oct. 24, 1961, Sun Valley, Calif.

Year	Team	W	L	PCT	ERA	G	GS	CG	IP	H	BB	SO	ShO	Relief Pitching W	Relief Pitching L	Relief Pitching SV	Batting AB	Batting H	Batting HR	BA	PO	A	E	DP	TC/G	FA
1988	PHI N	0	1	.000	6.00	17	0	0	24	27	21	12	0	0	1	0	2	0	0	.000	1	2	1	0	0.2	.750

Ken Clay

CLAY, KENNETH EARL BR TR 6′ 3″ 185 lbs.
B. Apr. 6, 1954, Lynchburg, Va.

Year	Team	W	L	PCT	ERA	G	GS	CG	IP	H	BB	SO	ShO	Relief Pitching W	Relief Pitching L	Relief Pitching SV	Batting AB	Batting H	Batting HR	BA	PO	A	E	DP	TC/G	FA
1977	NY A	2	3	.400	4.34	21	3	0	56	53	24	20	0	2	1	1	0	0	0	—	8	7	0	0	0.7	1.000
1978		3	4	.429	4.28	28	6	0	75.2	89	21	32	0	1	4	0	0	0	0	—	6	9	2	1	0.6	.882
1979		1	7	.125	5.42	32	5	0	78	88	25	28	0	1	3	2	0	0	0	—	8	12	1	0	0.7	.952
1980	TEX A	2	3	.400	4.60	8	8	0	43	43	29	17	0	0	0	0	0	0	0	—	3	4	1	0	1.0	.875
1981	SEA A	2	7	.222	4.63	22	14	0	101	116	42	32	0	0	1	0	0	0	0	—	6	10	1	1	0.8	.941
5 yrs.		10	24	.294	4.68	111	36	0	353.2	389	141	129	0	4	9	3	0	0	0		31	42	5	2	0.7	.936
LEAGUE CHAMPIONSHIP SERIES																										
1978	NY A	0	0	—	0.00	1	0	0	3.2	0	3	2	0	0	0	1	0	0	0	—	0	0	0	0	0.0	.000
WORLD SERIES																										
1977	NY A	0	0	—	2.45	2	0	0	3.2	2	1	0	0	0	0	0	0	0	0	—	1	1	0	0	1.0	1.000
1978		0	0	—	11.57	1	0	0	2.1	4	2	2	0	0	0	0	0	0	0	—	0	0	0	0	0.0	.000
2 yrs.		0	0		6.00	3	0	0	6	6	3	2	0	0	0	0	0	0	0		1	1	0	0	0.7	1.000

Mark Clear

CLEAR, MARK ALAN BR TR 6′ 4″ 200 lbs.
B. May 27, 1956, Los Angeles, Calif.

Year	Team	W	L	PCT	ERA	G	GS	CG	IP	H	BB	SO	ShO	Relief Pitching W	Relief Pitching L	Relief Pitching SV	Batting AB	Batting H	Batting HR	BA	PO	A	E	DP	TC/G	FA
1979	CAL A	11	5	.688	3.63	52	0	0	109	87	68	98	0	11	5	14	0	0	0	—	4	10	2	0	0.3	.875
1980		11	11	.500	3.31	58	0	0	106	82	65	105	0	11	**11**	9	0	0	0	—	3	10	0	0	0.2	1.000
1981	BOS A	8	3	.727	4.09	34	0	0	77	69	51	82	0	8	3	9	0	0	0	—	5	4	0	0	0.3	1.000
1982		14	9	.609	3.00	55	0	0	105	92	61	109	0	**14**	9	14	0	0	0	—	7	11	3	0	0.4	.857
1983		4	5	.444	6.28	48	0	0	96	101	68	81	0	4	5	4	0	0	0	—	8	5	1	0	0.3	.929
1984		8	3	.727	4.03	47	0	0	67	47	70	76	0	8	3	8	0	0	0	—	4	8	0	0	0.3	1.000
1985		1	3	.250	3.72	41	0	0	55.2	45	50	55	0	1	3	3	0	0	0	—	4	12	2	0	0.4	.889
1986	MIL A	5	5	.500	2.20	59	0	0	73.2	53	36	85	0	5	5	16	0	0	0	—	4	6	1	0	0.2	.909
1987		8	5	.615	4.48	58	1	0	78.1	70	55	81	0	8	4	6	0	0	0	—	8	12	1	0	0.4	.952
1988		1	0	1.000	2.79	25	0	0	29	23	21	26	0	1	0	0	0	0	0	—	2	1	0	0	0.1	1.000
1990	CAL A	0	0	—	5.87	4	0	0	7.2	5	9	6	0	0	0	0	0	0	0	—	0	0	0	0	0.0	.000
11 yrs.		71	49	.592	3.85	481	1	0	804.1	674	554	804	0	71	48	83	0	0	0		49	79	10	0	0.3	.928
LEAGUE CHAMPIONSHIP SERIES																										
1979	CAL A	0	0	—	4.76	1	0	0	5.2	4	2	3	0	0	0	0	0	0	0	—	0	0	0	0	0.0	.000

Joe Cleary

CLEARY, JOSEPH CHRISTOPHER (Fire) BR TR 5′ 9″ 145 lbs.
B. Dec. 3, 1918, Cork, Ireland

Year	Team	W	L	PCT	ERA	G	GS	CG	IP	H	BB	SO	ShO	Relief Pitching W	Relief Pitching L	Relief Pitching SV	Batting AB	Batting H	Batting HR	BA	PO	A	E	DP	TC/G	FA
1945	WAS A	0	0	—	189.00	1	0	0	0.1	5	3	1	0	0	0	0	0	0	0	—	0	0	0	0	0.0	.000

Roger Clemens

CLEMENS, WILLIAM ROGER (Rocket Man) BR TR 6′ 4″ 205 lbs.
B. Aug. 4, 1962, Dayton, Ohio.

Year	Team	W	L	PCT	ERA	G	GS	CG	IP	H	BB	SO	ShO	Relief Pitching W	Relief Pitching L	Relief Pitching SV	Batting AB	Batting H	Batting HR	BA	PO	A	E	DP	TC/G	FA
1984	BOS A	9	4	.692	4.32	21	20	5	133.1	146	29	126	1	0	0	0	0	0	0	—	11	14	0	0	1.2	1.000
1985		7	5	.583	3.29	15	15	3	98.1	83	37	74	1	0	0	0	0	0	0	—	12	9	0	1	1.4	1.000
1986		**24**	4	**.857**	**2.48**	33	33	10	254	179	67	238	1	0	0	0	0	0	0	—	27	21	4	0	1.6	.923
1987		**20**	9	**.690**	2.97	36	36	**18**	281.2	248	83	256	**7**	0	0	0	0	0	0	—	15	25	0	1	1.1	1.000
1988		18	12	.600	2.93	35	35	**14**	264	217	62	**291**	**8**	0	0	0	0	0	0	—	17	17	1	1	1.0	.971
1989		17	11	.607	3.13	35	35	8	253.1	215	93	230	3	0	0	0	0	0	0	—	17	27	0	1	1.3	1.000
1990		21	6	.778	**1.93**	31	31	7	228.1	193	54	209	**4**	0	0	0	0	0	0	—	23	26	2	1	1.6	.961
1991		18	10	.643	**2.62**	35	**35**	13	**271.1**	219	65	**241**	**4**	0	0	0	0	0	0	—	31	30	1	1	1.8	.984

Roger Clemens *continued*

Year	Team		W	L	PCT	ERA	G	GS	CG	IP	H	BB	SO	ShO	Relief Pitching W	Relief Pitching L	Relief Pitching SV	Batting AB	Batting H	Batting HR	BA	PO	A	E	DP	TC/G	FA
1992			18	11	.621	**2.41**	32	32	11	246.2	203	62	208	**5**	0	0	0	0	0	0	—	19	25	1	0	1.4	.978
1993			11	14	.440	4.46	29	29	2	191.2	175	67	160	1	0	0	0	0	0	0	—	11	20	1	1	1.1	.969
1994			9	7	.563	2.85	24	24	3	170.2	124	71	168	1	0	0	0	0	0	0	—	8	19	2	2	1.2	.931
1995			10	5	.667	4.18	23	23	0	140	141	60	132	0	0	0	0	0	0	0	—	13	19	1	1	1.4	.970
12 yrs.			182	98	.650	3.00	349	348	94	2533.1	2143	750	2333	36	0	0	0	0	0	0		204	252	13	10	1.3	.972
DIVISIONAL PLAYOFF SERIES																											
1995	**BOS**	**A**	0	0	—	3.86	1	1	0	7	5	1	5	0	0	0	0	0	0	0	—	0	0	0	0	0.0	.000
LEAGUE CHAMPIONSHIP SERIES																											
1986	**BOS**	**A**	1	1	.500	4.37	3	3	0	22.2	22	7	17	0	0	0	0	0	0	0	—	1	2	0	0	1.0	1.000
1988			0	0	—	3.86	1	1	0	7	6	0	8	0	0	0	0	0	0	0	—	0	0	1	0	1.0	.000
1990			0	1	.000	3.52	2	2	0	7.2	7	5	4	0	0	0	0	0	0	0	—	0	1	0	0	0.5	1.000
3 yrs.			1	2	.333	4.10	6	6	0	37.1	35	12	29	0	0	0	0	0	0	0		1	3	1	0	0.8	.800
WORLD SERIES																											
1986	**BOS**	**A**	0	0	—	3.18	2	2	0	11.1	9	6	11	0	0	0	0	4	0	0	.000	1	2	0	0	1.5	1.000

Bill Clemensen

CLEMENSEN, WILLIAM MELVILLE BR TR 6′ 1″ 193 lbs.
B. June 20, 1919, New Brunswick, N. J. D. Feb. 18, 1994, Alta, California.

Year	Team		W	L	PCT	ERA	G	GS	CG	IP	H	BB	SO	ShO	Relief Pitching W	Relief Pitching L	Relief Pitching SV	Batting AB	Batting H	Batting HR	BA	PO	A	E	DP	TC/G	FA
1939	**PIT**	**N**	0	1	.000	7.33	12	1	0	27	32	20	73	0	0	0	0	6	2	0	.333	3	11	1	1	1.3	.933
1941			1	0	1.000	2.77	2	1	1	13	7	7	4	0	0	0	0	4	0	0	.000	1	1	1	0	1.5	.667
1946			0	0	—	0.00	1	0	0	2	0	0	2	0	0	0	0	0	0	0	—	0	0	0	0	0.0	.000
3 yrs.			1	1	.500	5.57	15	2	1	42	39	27	79	0	0	0	0	10	2	0	.200	4	12	2	1	1.2	.889

Pat Clements

CLEMENTS, PATRICK BRIAN BR TL 6′ 175 lbs.
B. Feb. 2, 1962, McCloud, Calif.

Year	Team		W	L	PCT	ERA	G	GS	CG	IP	H	BB	SO	ShO	Relief Pitching W	Relief Pitching L	Relief Pitching SV	Batting AB	Batting H	Batting HR	BA	PO	A	E	DP	TC/G	FA
1985	**2 teams**	**CAL A** (41G 5–0) **PIT N** (27G 0–2)																									
″	**total**		5	2	.714	3.46	68	0	0	96.1	86	40	36	0	5	2	3	3	1	0	.333	2	18	1	2	0.3	.952
1986	**PIT**	**N**	0	4	.000	2.80	65	0	0	61	53	32	31	0	0	4	2	6	0	0	.000	7	11	0	1	0.3	1.000
1987	**NY**	**A**	3	3	.500	4.95	55	0	0	80	91	30	36	0	3	3	7	0	0	0	—	5	15	0	2	0.4	1.000
1988			0	0	—	6.48	6	1	0	8.1	12	4	3	0	0	0	0	0	0	0	—	1	1	0	0	0.3	1.000
1989	**SD**	**N**	4	1	.800	3.92	23	1	0	39	39	15	18	0	4	0	0	6	0	0	.000	1	8	0	1	0.4	1.000
1990			0	0	—	4.15	9	0	0	13	20	7	6	0	0	0	0	0	0	0	—	3	2	0	0	0.6	1.000
1991			1	0	1.000	3.77	12	0	0	14.1	13	9	8	0	1	0	0	1	0	0	.000	0	3	0	1	0.3	1.000
1992	**2 teams**	**SD N** (27G 2–1) **BAL A** (23G 2–0)																									
″	**total**		4	1	.800	2.98	50	0	0	48.1	48	23	20	0	4	1	0	1	0	0	.000	3	14	0	2	0.3	1.000
8 yrs.			17	11	.607	3.77	288	2	0	360.1	362	160	158	0	17	10	12	17	1	0	.059	22	72	1	9	0.3	.989

Lance Clemons

CLEMONS, LANCE LEVIS BL TL 6′ 2″ 205 lbs.
B. July 6, 1947, Philadelphia, Pa.

Year	Team		W	L	PCT	ERA	G	GS	CG	IP	H	BB	SO	ShO	Relief Pitching W	Relief Pitching L	Relief Pitching SV	Batting AB	Batting H	Batting HR	BA	PO	A	E	DP	TC/G	FA
1971	**KC**	**A**	1	0	1.000	4.13	10	3	0	24	26	12	20	0	1	0	0	7	2	1	.286	1	4	1	0	0.6	.833
1972	**STL**	**N**	0	1	.000	10.13	3	1	0	5.1	8	5	2	0	0	0	0	1	0	0	.000	0	1	0	0	0.3	1.000
1974	**BOS**	**A**	1	0	1.000	10.50	6	0	0	6	8	4	1	0	1	0	0	0	0	0	—	1	1	0	1	0.3	1.000
3 yrs.			2	1	.667	6.11	19	4	0	35.1	42	21	23	0	2	0	0	8	2	1	.250	2	6	1	1	0.5	.889

Reggie Cleveland

CLEVELAND, REGINALD LESLIE BR TR 6′ 1″ 195 lbs.
B. May 23, 1948, Swift Current, Sask., Canada.

Year	Team		W	L	PCT	ERA	G	GS	CG	IP	H	BB	SO	ShO	Relief Pitching W	Relief Pitching L	Relief Pitching SV	Batting AB	Batting H	Batting HR	BA	PO	A	E	DP	TC/G	FA
1969	**STL**	**N**	0	0	—	9.00	1	1	0	4	7	1	3	0	0	0	0	1	0	0	.000	0	0	0	0	0.0	.000
1970			0	4	.000	7.62	16	1	0	26	31	18	22	0	0	3	0	4	1	0	.250	1	1	1	0	0.2	.667
1971			12	12	.500	4.01	34	34	10	222	238	53	148	2	0	0	0	82	14	0	.171	15	30	1	1	1.4	.978
1972			14	15	.483	3.94	33	33	11	230.2	229	60	153	3	0	0	0	71	17	0	.239	17	25	4	0	1.4	.913
1973			14	10	.583	3.01	32	32	6	224	211	61	122	3	0	0	0	74	17	0	.230	11	24	3	2	1.2	.921
1974	**BOS**	**A**	12	14	.462	4.32	41	27	10	221	234	69	103	0	2	1	0	0	0	0	—	12	38	2	0	1.3	.962
1975			13	9	.591	4.43	31	20	3	170.2	173	52	78	1	3	2	0	0	0	0	—	12	25	2	1	1.3	.949
1976			10	9	.526	3.07	41	14	3	170	159	61	76	0	5	3	2	0	0	0	—	10	25	4	4	1.0	.897
1977			11	8	.579	4.26	36	27	9	190.1	211	43	85	1	0	0	2	0	0	0	—	18	20	3	3	1.1	.927
1978	**2 teams**	**BOS A** (1G 0–1) **TEX A** (53G 5–7)																									
″	**total**		5	8	.385	3.08	54	0	0	76	66	23	46	0	5	8	12	0	0	0		3	13	1	0	0.3	.941
1979	**MIL**	**A**	1	5	.167	6.71	29	1	0	55	77	23	22	0	1	4	4	0	0	0	—	2	5	2	1	0.3	.778
1980			11	9	.550	3.74	45	13	5	154	150	49	54	2	7	4	4	0	0	0	—	17	16	0	1	0.7	1.000
1981			2	3	.400	5.12	35	0	0	65	57	30	18	0	2	3	1	0	0	0	—	3	5	1	1	0.3	.889
13 yrs.			105	106	.498	4.02	428	203	57	1808.2	1843	543	930	12	25	28	25	232	49	0	.211	121	227	24	14	0.9	.935
LEAGUE CHAMPIONSHIP SERIES																											
1975	**BOS**	**A**	0	0	—	5.40	1	1	0	5	7	1	2	0	0	0	0	0	0	0	—	0	1	0	0	1.0	1.000
WORLD SERIES																											
1975	**BOS**	**A**	0	1	.000	6.75	3	1	0	6.2	7	3	5	0	0	0	0	2	0	0	.000	0	0	0	0	0.0	.000

Tex Clevenger

CLEVENGER, TRUMAN EUGENE BR TR 6′ 1″ 180 lbs.
B. July 9, 1932, Visalia, Calif.

Year	Team		W	L	PCT	ERA	G	GS	CG	IP	H	BB	SO	ShO	Relief Pitching W	Relief Pitching L	Relief Pitching SV	Batting AB	Batting H	Batting HR	BA	PO	A	E	DP	TC/G	FA
1954	**BOS**	**A**	2	4	.333	4.79	23	8	1	67.2	67	29	43	0	1	0	0	14	3	0	.214	6	11	2	0	0.8	.895
1956	**WAS**	**A**	0	0	—	5.40	20	1	0	31.2	33	21	17	0	0	0	0	2	0	0	.000	4	4	1	0	0.4	.889
1957			7	6	.538	4.19	52	9	2	139.2	139	47	75	0	5	4	8	33	7	0	.212	10	27	3	6	0.8	.925
1958			9	9	.500	4.35	**55**	4	0	124	119	50	70	0	9	6	6	22	3	0	.136	8	31	1	4	0.7	.975
1959			8	5	.615	3.91	50	7	2	117.1	114	51	71	2	5	2	8	23	4	0	.174	10	35	1	3	0.9	.978
1960			5	11	.313	4.20	53	11	1	128.2	150	49	49	0	3	4	7	22	2	0	.091	3	21	0	3	0.5	1.000
1961	**2 teams**	**LA A** (12G 2–1) **NY A** (21G 1–1)																									
″	**total**		3	2	.600	3.78	33	0	0	47.2	48	34	25	0	3	2	1	7	1	0	.143	5	12	0	1	0.5	1.000
1962	**NY**	**A**	2	0	1.000	2.84	21	0	0	38	36	17	11	0	2	0	0	4	0	0	.000	4	5	0	3	0.4	1.000
8 yrs.			36	37	.493	4.18	307	40	6	694.2	706	298	361	2	28	18	30	127	20	0	.157	50	146	8	20	0.7	.961

Stewart Cliburn

CLIBURN, STEWART WALKER BR TR 6′ 195 lbs.
Brother of Stan Cliburn.
B. Dec. 19, 1956, Jackson, Miss.

Year	Team	Lg	W	L	PCT	ERA	G	GS	CG	IP	H	BB	SO	ShO	Relief Pitching W	Relief Pitching L	Relief Pitching SV	Batting AB	Batting H	Batting HR	BA	PO	A	E	DP	TC/G	FA
1984	CAL	A	0	0	—	13.50	1	0	0	2	3	1	1	0	0	0	0	0	0	0	—	1	1	0	0	2.0	1.000
1985			9	3	.750	2.09	44	0	0	99	87	26	48	0	9	3	6	0	0	0	—	8	17	0	3	0.6	1.000
1988			4	2	.667	4.07	40	1	0	84	83	32	42	0	4	1	0	0	0	0	—	6	12	0	2	0.4	1.000
3 yrs.			13	5	.722	3.11	85	1	0	185	173	59	91	0	13	4	6	0	0	0		15	30	0	5	0.5	1.000

Jim Clinton

CLINTON, JAMES LAWRENCE (Big Jim) BR TR 5′ 8½″ 174 lbs.
B. Aug. 10, 1850, New York, N. Y. D. Sept. 3, 1921, Brooklyn, N. Y.

Year	Team	Lg	W	L	PCT	ERA	G	GS	CG	IP	H	BB	SO	ShO	Relief Pitching W	Relief Pitching L	Relief Pitching SV	Batting AB	Batting H	Batting HR	BA	PO	A	E	DP	TC/G	FA
1876	LOU	N	0	1	.000	6.00	1	1	1	9	12	0	1	0	0	0	0	*				20	7	7	1	2.1	.794

Tony Cloninger

CLONINGER, TONY LEE BR TR 6′ 210 lbs.
B. Aug. 13, 1940, Lincoln, N. C.

Year	Team	Lg	W	L	PCT	ERA	G	GS	CG	IP	H	BB	SO	ShO	Relief Pitching W	Relief Pitching L	Relief Pitching SV	Batting AB	Batting H	Batting HR	BA	PO	A	E	DP	TC/G	FA
1961	MIL	N	7	2	.778	5.25	19	10	3	84	84	33	51	0	2	0	0	30	5	0	.167	11	16	0	0	1.4	1.000
1962			8	3	.727	4.30	24	15	4	111	113	46	69	1	0	0	0	39	4	0	.103	10	18	1	3	1.2	.966
1963			9	11	.450	3.78	41	18	4	145.1	131	63	100	2	2	4	1	37	5	0	.135	8	17	1	0	0.6	.962
1964			19	14	.576	3.56	38	34	15	242.2	206	82	163	3	1	0	2	87	21	0	.241	14	41	2	1	1.5	.965
1965			24	11	.686	3.29	40	38	16	279	247	**119**	211	1	0	0	1	105	17	1	.162	15	41	6	2	1.5	.903
1966	ATL	N	14	11	.560	4.12	39	38	11	257.2	253	**116**	178	1	0	0	1	111	26	5	.234	14	43	8	1	1.7	.877
1967			4	7	.364	5.17	16	16	1	76.2	85	31	55	0	0	0	0	25	5	0	.200	3	11	0	1	0.9	1.000
1968	2 teams	ATL N	(8G 1–3)		CIN N	(17G 4–3)																					
″	total		5	6	.455	4.08	25	18	2	110.1	96	59	72	2	1	2	0	38	7	2	.184	12	15	1	0	1.1	.964
1969	CIN	N	11	17	.393	5.02	35	34	6	190	184	103	103	2	0	0	0	72	12	1	.167	9	23	3	3	1.0	.914
1970			9	7	.563	3.83	30	18	0	148	136	78	56	0	1	1	1	47	10	2	.213	13	31	2	5	1.5	.957
1971			3	6	.333	3.90	28	8	1	97	79	49	51	1	0	2	0	27	7	0	.259	4	16	2	3	0.8	.909
1972	STL	N	0	2	.000	5.19	17	0	0	26	29	19	11	0	0	2	0	3	0	0	.000	1	7	0	1	0.5	1.000
12 yrs.			113	97	.538	4.07	352	247	63	1767.2	1643	798	1120	13	7	11	6	621	119	11	.192	114	279	26	20	1.2	.938
LEAGUE CHAMPIONSHIP SERIES																											
1970	CIN	N	0	0	—	3.60	1	1	0	5	7	4	1	0	0	0	0	1	0	0	.000	0	2	0	0	2.0	1.000
WORLD SERIES																											
1970	CIN	N	0	1	.000	7.36	2	1	0	7.1	10	5	4	0	0	0	0	2	0	0	.000	0	1	0	0	0.5	1.000

Brad Clontz

CLONTZ, JOHN BRADLEY BR TR 6′ 1″ 180 lbs.
B. Apr. 25, 1971, Stuart, Va.

Year	Team	Lg	W	L	PCT	ERA	G	GS	CG	IP	H	BB	SO	ShO	Relief Pitching W	Relief Pitching L	Relief Pitching SV	Batting AB	Batting H	Batting HR	BA	PO	A	E	DP	TC/G	FA
1995	ATL	N	8	1	.889	3.65	59	0	0	69	71	22	55	0	**8**	1	4	2	0	0	.000	7	8	0	1	0.3	1.000
DIVISIONAL PLAYOFF SERIES																											
1995	ATL	N	0	0	—	0.00	1	0	0	1.1	0	0	2	0	0	0	0	0	0	0	—	0	1	0	0	1.0	1.000
LEAGUE CHAMPIONSHIP SERIES																											
1995	ATL	N	0	0	—	0.00	1	0	0	0.1	1	0	0	0	0	0	0	0	0	0	—	0	0	0	0	0.0	.000
WORLD SERIES																											
1995	ATL	N	0	0	—	2.70	2	0	0	3.1	2	0	2	0	0	0	0	0	0	0	—	0	0	0	0	0.0	.000

Al Closter

CLOSTER, ALAN EDWARD BL TL 6′ 2″ 190 lbs.
B. June 15, 1943, Creighton, Neb.

Year	Team	Lg	W	L	PCT	ERA	G	GS	CG	IP	H	BB	SO	ShO	Relief Pitching W	Relief Pitching L	Relief Pitching SV	Batting AB	Batting H	Batting HR	BA	PO	A	E	DP	TC/G	FA
1966	WAS	A	0	0	—	0.00	1	0	0	0.1	1	2	0	0	0	0	0	0	0	0	—	0	0	0	0	0.0	.000
1971	NY	A	2	2	.500	5.14	14	1	0	28	33	13	22	0	2	1	0	6	0	0	.000	0	8	1	0	0.6	.889
1972			0	0	—	13.50	2	0	0	2	2	4	2	0	0	0	0	1	0	0	.000	0	1	0	0	0.5	1.000
1973	ATL	N	0	0	—	15.75	4	0	0	4	7	4	2	0	0	0	0	0	0	0	—	1	1	0	0	0.5	1.000
4 yrs.			2	2	.500	6.82	21	1	0	34.1	43	23	26	0	2	1	0	7	0	0	.000	1	10	1	0	0.6	.917

Ed Clough

CLOUGH, EDGAR GEORGE (Spec) BL TL 6′ 188 lbs.
B. Oct. 28, 1906, Wiconisco, Pa. D. Jan. 30, 1944, Harrisburg, Pa.

Year	Team	Lg	W	L	PCT	ERA	G	GS	CG	IP	H	BB	SO	ShO	Relief Pitching W	Relief Pitching L	Relief Pitching SV	Batting AB	Batting H	Batting HR	BA	PO	A	E	DP	TC/G	FA
1925	STL	N	0	1	.000	8.10	3	1	0	10	11	5	3	0	0	0	0	4	1	0	.250	12	1	0	0	2.2	1.000
1926			0	0	—	22.50	1	0	0	2	5	3	0	0	0	0	0	1	0	0	.000	0	0	0	0	0.0	.000
2 yrs.			0	1	.000	10.50	4	1	0	12	16	8	3	0	0	0	0	*				13	2	0	0	1.5	1.000

Bill Clowers

CLOWERS, WILLIAM PERRY BL TL 5′11″ 175 lbs.
B. Aug. 14, 1898, San Marcos, Tex. D. Jan. 13, 1978, Sweeney, Tex.

Year	Team	Lg	W	L	PCT	ERA	G	GS	CG	IP	H	BB	SO	ShO	Relief Pitching W	Relief Pitching L	Relief Pitching SV	Batting AB	Batting H	Batting HR	BA	PO	A	E	DP	TC/G	FA
1926	BOS	A	0	0	—	0.00	2	0	0	1.2	2	0	0	0	0	0	0	0	0	0	—	1	0	0	0	0.5	1.000

Bryan Clutterbuck

CLUTTERBUCK, BRYAN RICHARD BR TR 6′ 4″ 223 lbs.
B. Dec. 17, 1959, Detroit, Mich.

Year	Team	Lg	W	L	PCT	ERA	G	GS	CG	IP	H	BB	SO	ShO	Relief Pitching W	Relief Pitching L	Relief Pitching SV	Batting AB	Batting H	Batting HR	BA	PO	A	E	DP	TC/G	FA
1986	MIL	A	0	1	.000	4.29	20	0	0	56.2	68	16	38	0	0	1	0	0	0	0	—	7	5	0	0	0.6	1.000
1989			2	5	.286	4.14	14	11	1	67.1	73	16	29	0	0	0	0	0	0	0	—	2	3	0	0	0.4	1.000
2 yrs.			2	6	.250	4.21	34	11	1	124	141	32	67	0	0	1	0	0	0	0		9	8	0	0	0.5	1.000

David Clyde

CLYDE, DAVID EUGENE BL TL 6′ 1½″ 180 lbs.
B. Apr. 22, 1955, Kansas City, Kans.

Year	Team	Lg	W	L	PCT	ERA	G	GS	CG	IP	H	BB	SO	ShO	Relief Pitching W	Relief Pitching L	Relief Pitching SV	Batting AB	Batting H	Batting HR	BA	PO	A	E	DP	TC/G	FA
1973	TEX	A	4	8	.333	5.03	18	18	0	93	106	54	74	0	0	0	0	0	0	0	—	3	12	2	2	0.9	.882
1974			3	9	.250	4.38	28	21	4	117	129	47	52	0	0	0	0	0	0	0	—	2	12	2	1	0.6	.875
1975			0	1	.000	2.57	1	1	0	7	6	6	2	0	0	0	0	0	0	0	—	0	1	1	0	2.0	.500
1978	CLE	A	8	11	.421	4.28	28	25	5	153.1	166	60	83	0	0	0	0	0	0	0	—	9	18	1	0	1.0	.964
1979			3	4	.429	5.87	9	8	1	46	50	13	17	0	0	0	0	0	0	0	—	2	6	1	0	1.0	.889
5 yrs.			18	33	.353	4.63	84	73	10	416.1	457	180	228	0	0	0	0	0	0	0		16	49	7	3	0.9	.903

Tom Clyde

CLYDE, THOMAS KNOX BR TR 6′ 3″ 195 lbs.
B. Aug. 17, 1923, Wachapreague, Va.

Year	Team	Lg	W	L	PCT	ERA	G	GS	CG	IP	H	BB	SO	ShO	Relief Pitching W	Relief Pitching L	Relief Pitching SV	Batting AB	Batting H	Batting HR	BA	PO	A	E	DP	TC/G	FA
1943	PHI	A	0	0	—	9.00	4	0	0	6	7	4	0	0	0	0	0	2	0	0	.000	0	1	2	0	0.8	.333

Andy Coakley

COAKLEY, ANDREW JAMES BL TR 6′ 165 lbs.
Played as Jack McAllister in 1902.
B. Nov. 20, 1882, Providence, R. I. D. Sept. 27, 1963, New York, N. Y.

Year	Team	W	L	PCT	ERA	G	GS	CG	IP	H	BB	SO	ShO	Relief Pitching W	Relief Pitching L	Relief Pitching SV	Batting AB	Batting H	Batting HR	BA	PO	A	E	DP	TC/G	FA
1902	PHI A	2	1	.667	2.67	3	3	3	27	25	9	9	0	0	0	0	8	3	0	.375	3	9	2	1	4.7	.857
1903		0	3	.000	5.50	6	3	2	37.2	48	11	20	0	0	0	0	15	3	0	.200	1	11	2	0	2.3	.857
1904		4	3	.571	2.03	8	8	7	62	50	23	33	2	0	0	0	23	2	0	.087	1	18	0	0	2.4	1.000
1905		18	8	.692	1.84	35	31	22	255	227	73	145	3	1	0	0	90	13	0	.144	10	68	8	2	2.5	.907
1906		7	8	.467	3.14	22	16	10	149	144	44	59	0	1	0	0	49	7	0	.143	8	32	3	0	2.0	.930
1907	CIN N	17	16	.515	2.34	37	30	21	265.1	269	79	89	1	**4**	1	1	84	6	0	.071	12	58	2	2	1.9	.972
1908	2 teams CIN N (32G 8–18) CHI N (4G 2–0)																									
″	total	10	18	.357	1.78	36	31	22	262.2	233	70	68	5	0	1	2	82	7	0	.085	8	56	4	0	1.9	.941
1909	CHI N	0	1	.000	18.00	1	1	0	2	7	3	1	0	0	0	0	0	0	0	—	0	1	0	0	1.0	1.000
1911	NY A	0	1	.000	5.40	2	1	1	11.2	20	2	4	0	0	0	0	4	1	0	.250	1	3	0	0	2.0	1.000
9 yrs.		58	59	.496	2.36	150	124	88	1072.1	1023	314	428	11	6	2	3	355	42	0	.118	44	256	21	5	2.1	.935
WORLD SERIES																										
1905	PHI A	0	1	.000	2.00	1	1	1	9	9	5	2	0	0	0	0	2	0	0	.000	0	2	0	1	2.0	1.000

Jim Coates

COATES, JAMES ALTON BR TR 6′ 4″ 192 lbs.
B. Aug. 4, 1932, Farnham, Va.

Year	Team	W	L	PCT	ERA	G	GS	CG	IP	H	BB	SO	ShO	Relief Pitching W	Relief Pitching L	Relief Pitching SV	Batting AB	Batting H	Batting HR	BA	PO	A	E	DP	TC/G	FA
1956	NY A	0	0	—	13.50	2	0	0	2	1	4	0	0	0	0	0	0	0	0	—	0	1	0	0	0.5	1.000
1959		6	1	.857	2.87	37	4	2	100.1	89	36	64	0	4	1	3	21	2	0	.095	7	17	2	0	0.7	.923
1960		13	3	.813	4.28	35	18	6	149.1	139	66	73	2	4	0	1	48	12	0	.250	9	15	4	1	0.8	.857
1961		11	5	.688	3.44	43	11	4	141.1	128	53	80	1	6	2	5	35	1	0	.029	12	19	2	2	0.8	.939
1962		7	6	.538	4.44	50	6	0	117.2	119	50	67	0	7	5	6	32	4	0	.125	6	12	2	2	0.4	.900
1963	2 teams WAS A (20G 2–4) CIN N (9G 0–0)																									
″	total	2	4	.333	5.34	29	2	0	60.2	72	28	42	0	2	4	0	9	0	0	.000	2	10	0	2	0.4	1.000
1965	CAL A	2	0	1.000	3.54	17	0	0	28	23	16	15	0	2	0	3	1	0	0	.000	1	6	2	0	0.5	.778
1966		1	1	.500	3.98	9	4	1	31.2	32	10	16	1	0	0	0	11	1	0	.091	3	3	0	0	0.7	1.000
1967		1	2	.333	4.30	25	1	0	52.1	47	23	39	0	1	1	0	3	1	0	.333	4	8	0	2	0.5	1.000
9 yrs.		43	22	.662	4.00	247	46	13	683.1	650	286	396	4	26	13	18	160	21	0	.131	44	91	12	9	0.6	.918
WORLD SERIES																										
1960	NY A	0	0	—	5.68	3	0	0	6.1	6	1	3	0	0	0	0	1	0	0	.000	1	1	0	0	0.7	1.000
1961		0	0	—	0.00	1	0	0	4	1	1	2	0	0	0	1	1	0	0	.000	0	0	0	0	0.0	.000
1962		0	1	.000	6.75	2	0	0	2.2	1	1	3	0	0	1	0	0	0	0	—	0	0	0	0	0.0	.000
3 yrs.		0	1	.000	4.15	6	0	0	13	8	3	8	0	0	1	1	2	0	0	.000	1	1	0	0	0.3	1.000

George Cobb

COBB, GEORGE WOODWORTH 6′ 168 lbs.
B. Sept. 25, 1865, Independence, Iowa D. Aug. 19, 1926, Pomona, Calif.

Year	Team	W	L	PCT	ERA	G	GS	CG	IP	H	BB	SO	ShO	Relief Pitching W	Relief Pitching L	Relief Pitching SV	Batting AB	Batting H	Batting HR	BA	PO	A	E	DP	TC/G	FA
1892	BAL N	10	**37**	.213	4.86	53	47	42	394.1	495	140	159	0	1	1	0	172	36	1	.209	16	96	14	0	2.1	.889

Herb Cobb

COBB, HERBERT EDWARD BR TR 5′11″ 150 lbs.
B. Aug. 6, 1904, Pinetops, N. C. D. Jan. 8, 1980, Tarboro, N. C.

Year	Team	W	L	PCT	ERA	G	GS	CG	IP	H	BB	SO	ShO	Relief Pitching W	Relief Pitching L	Relief Pitching SV	Batting AB	Batting H	Batting HR	BA	PO	A	E	DP	TC/G	FA
1929	STL A	0	0	—	36.00	1	0	0	1	3	1	0	0	0	0	0	0	0	0	—	0	0	0	0	0.0	.000

Ty Cobb

COBB, TYRUS RAYMOND (The Georgia Peach) BL TR 6′ 1″ 175 lbs.
B. Dec. 18, 1886, Narrows, Ga. D. July 17, 1961, Atlanta, Ga.
Manager 1921–26.
Hall of Fame 1936.

Year	Team	W	L	PCT	ERA	G	GS	CG	IP	H	BB	SO	ShO	Relief Pitching W	Relief Pitching L	Relief Pitching SV	Batting AB	Batting H	Batting HR	BA	PO	A	E	DP	TC/G	FA
1918	DET A	0	0	—	4.50	2	0	0	4	6	2	0	0	0	0	0	421	161	3	.382	85	6	4	1	2.3	.958
1925		0	0	—	0.00	1	0	0	1	0	0	0	0	0	0	1	415	157	12	.378	208	14	9	4	2.4	.961
2 yrs.		0	0		3.60	3	0	0	5	6	2	0	0	0	0	1	*				6507	410	278	113	2.4	.961

Jaime Cocanower

COCANOWER, JAMES STANLEY BR TR 6′ 4″ 200 lbs.
Born James Stanley Cocanower (Geiser).
B. Feb. 14, 1957, San Juan, Puerto Rico

Year	Team	W	L	PCT	ERA	G	GS	CG	IP	H	BB	SO	ShO	Relief Pitching W	Relief Pitching L	Relief Pitching SV	Batting AB	Batting H	Batting HR	BA	PO	A	E	DP	TC/G	FA
1983	MIL A	2	0	1.000	1.80	5	3	1	30	21	12	8	0	0	0	0	0	0	0	—	4	6	1	0	2.2	.909
1984		8	16	.333	4.02	33	27	1	174.2	188	78	65	0	0	2	0	0	0	0	—	15	32	6	0	1.6	.887
1985		6	8	.429	4.33	24	15	3	116.1	122	73	44	1	1	0	0	0	0	0	—	7	20	4	1	1.3	.871
1986		0	1	.000	4.43	17	2	0	44.2	40	38	22	0	0	0	0	0	0	0	—	7	11	3	3	1.2	.857
4 yrs.		16	25	.390	3.99	79	47	5	365.2	371	201	139	1	1	2	0	0	0	0		33	69	14	4	1.5	.879

Al Cochran

COCHRAN, ALVAH JACKSON (Goat) BR TR 5′10″ 175 lbs.
B. Jan. 31, 1891, Concord, Ga. D. May 23, 1947, Atlanta, Ga.

Year	Team	W	L	PCT	ERA	G	GS	CG	IP	H	BB	SO	ShO	Relief Pitching W	Relief Pitching L	Relief Pitching SV	Batting AB	Batting H	Batting HR	BA	PO	A	E	DP	TC/G	FA
1915	CIN N	0	0	—	9.00	1	0	0	2	5	0	1	0	0	0	0	0	0	0	—	0	0	0	0	0.0	.000

Gene Cocreham

COCREHAM, EUGENE BR TR 6′ 3½″ 192 lbs.
B. Nov. 14, 1884, Luling, Tex. D. Dec. 27, 1945, Luling, Tex.

Year	Team	W	L	PCT	ERA	G	GS	CG	IP	H	BB	SO	ShO	Relief Pitching W	Relief Pitching L	Relief Pitching SV	Batting AB	Batting H	Batting HR	BA	PO	A	E	DP	TC/G	FA
1913	BOS N	0	1	.000	7.56	1	1	0	8.1	13	4	3	0	0	0	0	4	0	0	.000	2	1	0	0	3.0	1.000
1914		3	4	.429	4.84	15	3	1	44.2	48	27	15	0	2	2	0	10	1	0	.100	1	6	1	0	0.5	.875
1915		0	0	—	5.40	1	0	0	1.2	3	0	0	0	0	0	0	0	0	0	—	0	0	0	0	0.0	.000
3 yrs.		3	5	.375	5.27	17	4	1	54.2	64	31	18	0	2	2	0	14	1	0	.071	3	7	1	0	0.6	.909

Chris Codiroli

CODIROLI, CHRISTOPHER ALLEN BR TR 6′ 1″ 160 lbs.
B. Mar. 26, 1958, Oxnard, Calif.

Year	Team	W	L	PCT	ERA	G	GS	CG	IP	H	BB	SO	ShO	Relief Pitching W	Relief Pitching L	Relief Pitching SV	Batting AB	Batting H	Batting HR	BA	PO	A	E	DP	TC/G	FA
1982	OAK A	1	2	.333	4.32	3	3	0	16.2	16	4	5	0	0	0	0	0	0	0	—	3	3	0	0	2.0	1.000
1983		12	12	.500	4.46	37	31	7	205.2	208	72	85	2	1	1	1	0	0	0	—	14	21	4	1	1.1	.897
1984		6	4	.600	5.84	28	14	1	89.1	111	34	44	0	0	0	1	0	0	0	—	5	11	1	1	0.6	.941
1985		14	14	.500	4.46	37	**37**	4	226	228	78	111	0	0	0	0	0	0	0	—	18	27	4	1	1.3	.918
1986		5	8	.385	4.03	16	16	1	91.2	91	38	43	0	0	0	0	0	0	0	—	13	15	5	2	2.1	.848
1987		0	2	.000	8.74	3	3	0	11.1	12	8	4	0	0	0	0	0	0	0	—	1	1	0	0	0.7	1.000
1988	CLE A	0	4	.000	9.31	14	2	0	19.1	32	10	12	0	0	2	1	0	0	0	—	3	2	0	1	0.4	1.000
1990	KC A	0	1	.000	9.58	6	2	0	10.1	13	17	8	0	0	0	0	0	0	0	—	1	0	0	0	0.2	1.000
8 yrs.		38	47	.447	4.87	144	108	13	670.1	711	261	312	2	1	3	3	0	0	0		58	80	14	6	1.1	.908

Dick Coffman

COFFMAN, SAMUEL RICHARD BR TR 6′ 2″ 195 lbs.
Brother of Slick Coffman.
B. Dec. 18, 1906, Veto, Ala. D. Mar. 24, 1972, Athens, Ala.

Year	Team	W	L	PCT	ERA	G	GS	CG	IP	H	BB	SO	ShO	Relief Pitching W	Relief Pitching L	Relief Pitching SV	Batting AB	Batting H	HR	BA	PO	A	E	DP	TC/G	FA
1927	WAS A	0	1	.000	3.38	5	2	0	16	20	2	5	0	0	0	0	3	1	0	.333	3	4	0	0	1.4	1.000
1928	STL A	4	5	.444	6.09	29	7	3	85.2	122	37	25	0	1	1	1	23	1	0	.043	4	21	1	1	0.9	.962
1929		1	1	.500	5.98	27	3	1	52.2	61	14	11	1	0	1	1	7	0	0	.000	3	12	0	0	0.6	1.000
1930		8	18	.308	5.14	38	30	12	196	250	69	54	1	1	1	1	66	9	0	.136	6	43	0	0	1.3	1.000
1931		9	13	.409	3.88	32	17	11	169.1	159	51	39	2	2	4	1	51	4	0	.078	15	24	1	1	1.3	.975
1932	2 teams STL A (9G 5–3) WAS A (22G 1–6)																									
″	total	6	9	.400	4.06	31	15	5	137.1	158	52	31	2	1	1	0	44	3	0	.068	11	19	0	1	1.0	1.000
1933	STL A	3	7	.300	5.89	21	13	3	81	114	39	19	1	0	1	1	27	1	0	.037	5	19	1	0	1.2	.960
1934		9	10	.474	4.53	40	21	6	173	212	59	55	1	2	0	3	51	11	0	.216	7	36	4	1	1.2	.915
1935		5	11	.313	6.14	41	18	5	143.2	206	46	34	0	1	3	2	41	6	0	.146	5	27	5	0	0.9	.865
1936	NY N	7	5	.583	3.90	42	2	0	101.2	119	23	26	0	**7**	3	7	20	4	0	.200	11	26	1	1	0.9	.974
1937		8	3	.727	3.04	42	1	0	80	93	31	30	0	**8**	3	3	19	7	0	.368	2	20	1	2	0.5	.957
1938		8	4	.667	3.48	**51**	3	1	111.1	116	21	21	1	7	2	**12**	28	2	0	.071	3	18	3	1	0.5	.875
1939		1	2	.333	3.08	28	0	0	38	50	6	9	0	1	2	3	4	0	0	.000	3	6	2	0	0.4	.818
1940	BOS N	1	5	.167	5.40	31	0	0	48.1	63	11	11	0	1	5	3	12	1	0	.083	4	7	0	0	0.4	1.000
1945	PHI N	2	1	.667	5.13	14	0	0	26.1	39	2	2	0	2	1	0	4	1	0	.250	0	11	0	2	0.8	1.000
15 yrs.		72	95	.431	4.65	472	132	47	1460.1	1782	463	372	9	34	28	38	400	51	0	.127	82	293	19	10	0.8	.952
WORLD SERIES																										
1936	NY N	0	0	—	32.40	2	0	0	1.2	5	1	1	0	0	0	0	0	0	0	—	0	1	0	0	0.5	1.000
1937		0	0	—	4.15	2	0	0	4.1	2	5	1	0	0	0	0	1	0	0	.000	0	1	0	0	0.5	1.000
2 yrs.		0	0		12.00	4	0	0	6	7	6	2	0	0	0	0	1	0	0	.000	0	2	0	0	0.5	1.000

Kevin Coffman

COFFMAN, KEVIN REESE BR TR 6′ 2″ 175 lbs.
B. Jan. 19, 1965, Austin, Tex.

Year	Team	W	L	PCT	ERA	G	GS	CG	IP	H	BB	SO	ShO	Relief Pitching W	Relief Pitching L	Relief Pitching SV	Batting AB	Batting H	HR	BA	PO	A	E	DP	TC/G	FA
1987	ATL N	2	3	.400	4.62	5	5	0	25.1	31	22	14	0	0	0	0	10	1	0	.100	1	9	0	1	2.0	1.000
1988		2	6	.250	5.78	18	11	0	67	62	54	24	0	0	0	0	22	5	0	.227	9	12	2	1	1.3	.913
1990	CHI N	0	2	.000	11.29	8	2	0	18.1	26	19	9	0	0	0	0	5	1	0	.200	3	4	0	0	0.9	1.000
3 yrs.		4	11	.267	6.42	31	18	0	110.2	119	95	47	0	0	0	0	37	7	0	.189	13	25	2	2	1.3	.950

Slick Coffman

COFFMAN, GEORGE DAVID BR TR 6′ 155 lbs.
Brother of Dick Coffman.
B. Dec. 11, 1910, Veto, Ala.

Year	Team	W	L	PCT	ERA	G	GS	CG	IP	H	BB	SO	ShO	Relief Pitching W	Relief Pitching L	Relief Pitching SV	Batting AB	Batting H	HR	BA	PO	A	E	DP	TC/G	FA
1937	DET A	7	5	.583	4.37	28	5	1	101	121	39	22	0	5	3	0	29	5	0	.172	4	16	1	1	0.8	.952
1938		4	4	.500	6.02	39	6	1	95.2	120	48	31	0	3	1	2	24	4	0	.167	1	16	0	0	0.4	1.000
1939		2	1	.667	6.38	23	1	0	42.1	51	22	10	0	2	1	0	5	0	0	.000	1	8	0	0	0.4	1.000
1940	STL A	2	2	.500	6.27	31	4	1	74.2	108	23	26	0	1	0	1	15	3	0	.200	3	19	0	0	0.7	1.000
4 yrs.		15	12	.556	5.60	121	16	3	313.2	400	132	89	0	11	5	3	73	12	0	.164	9	59	1	1	0.6	.986

Dick Cogan

COGAN, RICHARD HENRY BR TR 5′ 7″ 150 lbs.
B. Dec. 5, 1871, Paterson, N. J. D. May 2, 1948, Paterson, N. J.

Year	Team	W	L	PCT	ERA	G	GS	CG	IP	H	BB	SO	ShO	Relief Pitching W	Relief Pitching L	Relief Pitching SV	Batting AB	Batting H	HR	BA	PO	A	E	DP	TC/G	FA
1897	BAL N	0	0	—	13.50	1	0	0	2	4	2	0	0	0	0	0	1	0	0	.000	0	0	0	0	0.0	.000
1899	CHI N	2	3	.400	4.30	5	5	5	44	54	24	9	0	0	0	0	25	5	0	.200	5	8	4	0	2.1	.765
1900	NY N	0	0	—	6.75	2	0	0	8	10	6	1	0	0	0	0	8	1	0	.125	3	6	1	2	3.3	.900
3 yrs.		2	3	.400	5.00	8	5	5	54	68	32	10	0	0	0	0	34	6	0	.176	8	14	5	2	2.3	.815

Hy Cohen

COHEN, HYMAN BR TR 6′ 5″ 215 lbs.
B. Jan. 29, 1931, Brooklyn, N. Y.

Year	Team	W	L	PCT	ERA	G	GS	CG	IP	H	BB	SO	ShO	Relief Pitching W	Relief Pitching L	Relief Pitching SV	Batting AB	Batting H	HR	BA	PO	A	E	DP	TC/G	FA
1955	CHI N	0	0	—	7.94	7	1	0	17	28	10	4	0	0	0	0	3	0	0	.000	0	2	0	0	0.3	1.000

Syd Cohen

COHEN, SYDNEY HARRY BB TL 5′11″ 180 lbs.
Brother of Andy Cohen.
B. May 7, 1906, Baltimore, Md. D. Apr. 9, 1988, El Paso, Tex.

Year	Team	W	L	PCT	ERA	G	GS	CG	IP	H	BB	SO	ShO	Relief Pitching W	Relief Pitching L	Relief Pitching SV	Batting AB	Batting H	HR	BA	PO	A	E	DP	TC/G	FA
1934	WAS A	1	1	.500	7.50	3	2	2	18	25	6	6	0	0	0	0	11	3	0	.273	6	8	0	1	3.5	1.000
1936		0	2	.000	5.25	19	1	0	36	44	14	21	0	0	1	1	8	0	0	.000	2	16	0	0	0.9	1.000
1937		2	4	.333	3.11	33	0	0	55	64	17	22	0	2	4	4	14	2	0	.143	3	17	1	2	0.6	.952
3 yrs.		3	7	.300	4.54	55	3	2	109	133	37	49	0	2	5	5	33	5	0	.152	11	41	1	3	0.9	.981

Rocky Colavito

COLAVITO, ROCCO DOMENICO BR TR 6′ 3″ 190 lbs.
B. Aug. 10, 1933, New York, N. Y.

Year	Team	W	L	PCT	ERA	G	GS	CG	IP	H	BB	SO	ShO	Relief Pitching W	Relief Pitching L	Relief Pitching SV	Batting AB	Batting H	HR	BA	PO	A	E	DP	TC/G	FA
1958	CLE A	0	0	—	0.00	1	0	0	3	0	3	1	0	0	0	0	489	148	41	.303	7	1	0	1	4.0	1.000
1968	NY A	1	0	1.000	0.00	1	0	0	2.2	1	2	1	0	1	0	0	204	43	8	.211	177	6	6	0	1.9	.968
2 yrs.		1	0	1.000	0.00	2	0	0	5.2	1	5	2	0	1	0	0	*				3407	124	74	31	2.0	.979

Vince Colbert

COLBERT, VINCENT NORMAN BR TR 6′ 4″ 200 lbs.
B. Dec. 20, 1945, Washington, D. C.

Year	Team	W	L	PCT	ERA	G	GS	CG	IP	H	BB	SO	ShO	Relief Pitching W	Relief Pitching L	Relief Pitching SV	Batting AB	Batting H	HR	BA	PO	A	E	DP	TC/G	FA
1970	CLE A	1	1	.500	7.26	23	0	0	31	37	16	17	0	1	1	2	2	0	0	.000	2	6	1	0	0.4	.889
1971		7	6	.538	3.97	50	10	2	143	140	71	74	0	2	1	2	29	4	0	.138	11	26	4	0	0.8	.902
1972		1	7	.125	4.56	22	11	1	75	74	38	36	1	0	0	0	20	4	0	.200	1	15	0	2	0.7	1.000
3 yrs.		9	14	.391	4.55	95	21	3	249	251	125	127	1	3	2	4	51	8	0	.157	14	47	5	2	0.7	.924

Jim Colborn

COLBORN, JAMES WILLIAM BR TR 6′ 185 lbs.
B. May 22, 1946, Santa Paula, Calif.

Year	Team	W	L	PCT	ERA	G	GS	CG	IP	H	BB	SO	ShO	Relief Pitching W	Relief Pitching L	Relief Pitching SV	Batting AB	Batting H	HR	BA	PO	A	E	DP	TC/G	FA
1969	CHI N	1	0	1.000	3.00	6	2	0	15	15	9	4	0	0	0	0	3	0	0	.000	1	4	0	1	0.8	1.000
1970		3	1	.750	3.58	34	5	0	73	88	23	50	0	2	1	4	15	1	0	.067	4	13	1	1	0.5	.944
1971		0	1	.000	7.20	14	0	0	10	18	3	2	0	0	1	0	0	0	0	—	0	4	0	0	0.3	1.000
1972	MIL A	7	7	.500	3.10	39	12	4	148	135	43	97	1	2	0	0	37	3	0	.081	8	17	1	1	0.7	.962
1973		20	12	.625	3.18	43	36	22	314.1	297	87	135	4	2	0	1	0	0	0	—	19	55	0	4	1.7	1.000
1974		10	13	.435	4.06	33	31	10	224	230	60	83	1	1	0	0	0	0	0	—	19	35	4	0	1.8	.931
1975		11	13	.458	4.27	36	29	8	206.1	215	65	79	1	0	1	2	0	0	0	—	15	36	2	2	1.5	.962
1976		9	15	.375	3.71	32	32	7	225.2	232	54	101	0	0	0	0	0	0	0	—	11	32	1	4	1.4	.977

Jim Colborn *continued*

Year	Team	Lg	W	L	PCT	ERA	G	GS	CG	IP	H	BB	SO	ShO	Relief Pitching W	Relief Pitching L	Relief Pitching SV	Batting AB	Batting H	Batting HR	BA	PO	A	E	DP	TC/G	FA
1977	**KC**	**A**	18	14	.563	3.62	36	35	6	239	233	81	103	1	0	0	0	0	0	0	—	27	39	5	3	2.0	.930
1978	**2 teams** **KC A** (8G 1–2) **SEA A** (20G 3–10)																										
"	**total**		4	12	.250	5.26	28	22	3	142	156	50	34	0	1	0	0	0	0	0		10	39	3	2	1.9	.942
10 yrs.			83	88	.485	3.80	301	204	60	1597.1	1619	475	688	8	8	3	7	55	4	0	.073	114	274	17	18	1.3	.958

Tom Colcolough

COLCOLOUGH, THOMAS BERNARD BR TR 5′10½″ 180 lbs.
B. Oct. 8, 1870, Charleston, S. C. D. Dec. 10, 1919, Charleston, S. C.

Year	Team	Lg	W	L	PCT	ERA	G	GS	CG	IP	H	BB	SO	ShO	Relief Pitching W	Relief Pitching L	Relief Pitching SV	Batting AB	Batting H	Batting HR	BA	PO	A	E	DP	TC/G	FA
1893	**PIT**	**N**	1	0	1.000	4.22	8	3	1	42.2	45	32	7	0	0	0	**2**	14	2	0	.143	3	7	1	0	1.4	.909
1894			8	5	.615	7.08	22	14	11	148.2	207	70	29	0	1	0	0	70	14	0	.200	7	30	3	1	1.8	.925
1895			1	1	.500	5.60	6	5	2	35.1	38	21	15	0	0	0	0	15	5	0	.333	1	5	1	0	1.2	.857
1899	**NY**	**N**	4	5	.444	3.97	11	8	7	81.2	85	41	14	0	1	0	0	37	10	0	.270	6	24	2	0	2.7	.938
4 yrs.			14	11	.560	5.69	47	30	21	308.1	375	164	65	0	2	0	2	136	31	0	.228	17	66	7	1	1.9	.922

Bert Cole

COLE, ALBERT GEORGE BL TL 6′ 1″ 180 lbs.
B. July 1, 1896, San Francisco, Calif. D. May 30, 1975, San Mateo, Calif.

Year	Team	Lg	W	L	PCT	ERA	G	GS	CG	IP	H	BB	SO	ShO	Relief Pitching W	Relief Pitching L	Relief Pitching SV	Batting AB	Batting H	Batting HR	BA	PO	A	E	DP	TC/G	FA
1921	**DET**	**A**	7	4	.636	4.27	20	11	7	109.2	134	36	22	1	1	0	1	46	13	0	.283	3	28	0	0	1.5	1.000
1922			1	6	.143	4.88	23	5	2	79.1	105	39	21	1	0	3	0	25	4	0	.160	9	21	2	1	1.3	.938
1923			13	5	.722	4.14	52	13	5	163	183	61	32	1	5	2	5	55	14	1	.255	9	37	1	1	0.9	.979
1924			3	9	.250	4.69	28	12	2	109.1	135	35	16	1	1	2	2	37	10	0	.270	13	28	1	0	1.4	.976
1925	**2 teams** **DET A** (14G 2–3) **CLE A** (13G 1–1)																										
"	**total**		3	4	.429	6.03	27	4	1	77.2	99	40	16	0	2	2	2	24	5	0	.208	6	22	2	0	1.1	.933
1927	**CHI**	**A**	1	4	.200	4.72	27	2	0	66.2	79	19	12	0	1	3	0	18	3	0	.167	1	27	2	1	1.1	.933
6 yrs.			28	32	.467	4.67	177	47	17	605.2	735	230	119	4	10	12	10	205	49	1	.239	41	163	8	3	1.2	.962

Dave Cole

COLE, DAVID BRUCE BR TR 6′ 2″ 175 lbs.
B. Aug. 29, 1930, Williamsport, Md.

Year	Team	Lg	W	L	PCT	ERA	G	GS	CG	IP	H	BB	SO	ShO	Relief Pitching W	Relief Pitching L	Relief Pitching SV	Batting AB	Batting H	Batting HR	BA	PO	A	E	DP	TC/G	FA
1950	**BOS**	**N**	0	1	.000	1.13	4	0	0	8	7	3	8	0	0	1	0	1	0	0	.000	1	0	0	0	0.3	1.000
1951			2	4	.333	4.26	23	7	1	67.2	64	64	33	0	0	2	0	17	6	1	.353	4	13	1	2	0.8	.944
1952			1	1	.500	4.03	22	3	0	44.2	38	42	22	0	0	0	0	8	0	0	.000	1	9	0	1	0.5	1.000
1953	**MIL**	**N**	0	1	.000	8.59	10	0	0	14.2	17	14	13	0	0	1	0	2	1	1	.500	1	4	0	0	0.5	1.000
1954	**CHI**	**N**	3	8	.273	5.36	18	14	2	84	74	62	37	1	0	0	0	28	6	1	.214	9	11	1	0	1.2	.952
1955	**PHI**	**N**	0	3	.000	6.38	7	3	0	18.1	21	14	6	0	0	0	0	5	1	0	.200	0	6	1	1	1.0	.857
6 yrs.			6	18	.250	4.93	84	27	3	237.1	221	199	119	1	0	4	0	61	14	3	.230	16	43	3	4	0.7	.952

Ed Cole

COLE, EDWARD WILLIAM BR TR 5′11″ 170 lbs.
Born Edward William Kisleauskas.
B. Mar. 22, 1909, Wilkes-Barre, Pa.

Year	Team	Lg	W	L	PCT	ERA	G	GS	CG	IP	H	BB	SO	ShO	Relief Pitching W	Relief Pitching L	Relief Pitching SV	Batting AB	Batting H	Batting HR	BA	PO	A	E	DP	TC/G	FA
1938	**STL**	**A**	1	5	.167	5.18	36	6	1	88.2	116	48	26	0	0	2	3	21	3	0	.143	0	15	2	0	0.5	.882
1939			0	2	.000	7.11	6	0	0	6.1	8	6	5	0	0	2	0	1	0	0	.000	0	1	0	0	0.2	1.000
2 yrs.			1	7	.125	5.31	42	6	1	95	124	54	31	0	0	4	3	22	3	0	.136	0	16	2	0	0.4	.889

King Cole

COLE, LEONARD LESLIE BR TR 6′ 1″ 170 lbs.
B. Apr. 15, 1886, Toledo, Iowa D. Jan. 6, 1916, Bay City, Mich.

Year	Team	Lg	W	L	PCT	ERA	G	GS	CG	IP	H	BB	SO	ShO	Relief Pitching W	Relief Pitching L	Relief Pitching SV	Batting AB	Batting H	Batting HR	BA	PO	A	E	DP	TC/G	FA
1909	**CHI**	**N**	1	0	1.000	0.00	1	1	1	9	6	3	1	1	0	0	0	4	3	0	.750	0	1	0	0	1.0	1.000
1910			20	4	**.833**	1.80	33	29	21	239.2	174	130	114	4	2	0	0	91	21	0	.231	3	65	7	3	2.3	.907
1911			18	7	.720	3.13	32	27	13	221.1	188	99	101	2	1	1	0	79	12	0	.152	3	52	5	5	1.9	.917
1912	**2 teams** **CHI N** (8G 1–2) **PIT N** (12G 2–2)																										
"	**total**		3	4	.429	7.68	20	7	2	68	97	26	20	0	1	1	0	20	4	0	.200	1	21	3	0	1.3	.880
1914	**NY**	**A**	11	9	.550	3.30	33	15	8	141.2	151	51	43	2	5	2	0	42	2	0	.048	4	29	3	1	1.1	.917
1915			3	3	.500	3.18	10	6	2	51	41	22	19	0	1	0	1	13	1	0	.077	1	16	4	1	2.1	.810
6 yrs.			56	27	.675	3.12	129	85	47	730.2	657	331	298	9	10	4	1	249	43	0	.173	12	184	22	10	1.7	.899
WORLD SERIES																											
1910	**CHI**	**N**	0	0	—	3.38	1	1	0	8	10	3	5	0	0	0	0	2	0	0	.000	1	3	0	1	4.0	1.000

Victor Cole

COLE, VICTOR ALEXANDER BR TR 5′10″ 160 lbs.
B. Jan. 23, 1968, Leningrad, Russia.

Year	Team	Lg	W	L	PCT	ERA	G	GS	CG	IP	H	BB	SO	ShO	Relief Pitching W	Relief Pitching L	Relief Pitching SV	Batting AB	Batting H	Batting HR	BA	PO	A	E	DP	TC/G	FA
1992	**PIT**	**N**	0	2	.000	5.48	8	4	0	23	23	14	12	0	0	0	0	4	0	0	.000	3	3	0	0	0.8	1.000

Joe Coleman

COLEMAN, JOSEPH HOWARD BR TR 6′ 3″ 175 lbs.
Son of Joe Coleman.
B. Feb. 3, 1947, Boston, Mass.

Year	Team	Lg	W	L	PCT	ERA	G	GS	CG	IP	H	BB	SO	ShO	Relief Pitching W	Relief Pitching L	Relief Pitching SV	Batting AB	Batting H	Batting HR	BA	PO	A	E	DP	TC/G	FA
1965	**WAS**	**A**	2	0	1.000	1.50	2	2	2	18	9	8	7	0	0	0	0	6	0	0	.000	0	6	0	1	3.0	1.000
1966			1	0	1.000	2.00	1	1	1	9	6	2	4	0	0	0	0	3	0	0	.000	2	2	0	1	4.0	1.000
1967			8	9	.471	4.63	28	22	3	134	154	47	77	0	0	1	0	36	2	0	.056	9	14	1	0	0.9	.958
1968			12	16	.429	3.27	33	33	12	223	212	51	139	2	0	0	0	70	9	0	.129	30	20	3	0	1.6	.943
1969			12	13	.480	3.27	40	36	12	247.2	222	100	182	4	0	0	1	84	9	0	.107	21	35	2	3	1.5	.966
1970			8	12	.400	3.58	39	29	6	219	190	89	152	1	0	0	0	67	8	0	.119	16	30	0	3	1.2	1.000
1971	**DET**	**A**	20	9	.690	3.15	39	38	16	286	241	96	236	3	0	0	0	96	9	0	.094	18	32	3	2	1.4	.943
1972			19	14	.576	2.80	40	39	9	279.2	216	110	222	3	0	0	0	82	9	0	.110	6	39	1	2	1.1	.978
1973			23	15	.605	3.53	40	40	13	288	283	93	202	2	0	0	0	0	0	0	—	23	37	2	1	1.5	.968
1974			14	12	.538	4.31	41	41	11	286	272	158	177	2	0	0	0	0	0	0	—	21	47	3	4	1.7	.958
1975			10	18	.357	5.55	31	31	6	201	234	85	125	1	0	0	0	0	0	0	—	6	32	2	1	1.3	.950
1976	**2 teams** **DET A** (12G 2–5) **CHI N** (39G 2–8)																										
"	**total**		4	13	.235	4.44	51	16	1	146	152	69	104	0	2	5	4	13	2	0	.154	8	31	4	2	0.8	.907
1977	**OAK**	**A**	4	4	.500	2.95	43	12	2	128	114	49	55	0	0	0	2	0	0	0	—	13	17	3	2	0.8	.909
1978	**2 teams** **OAK A** (10G 3–0) **TOR A** (31G 2–0)																										
"	**total**		5	0	1.000	3.78	41	0	0	81	79	35	32	0	5	0	0	0	0	0		5	9	0	0	0.3	1.000
1979	**2 teams** **SF N** (5G 0–0) **PIT N** (10G 0–0)																										
"	**total**		0	0		5.18	15	0	0	24.1	32	11	14	0	0	0	0	5	1	0	.200	1	0	1	0	0.1	.500
15 yrs.			142	135	.513	3.69	484	340	94	2570.2	2416	1003	1728	18	7	6	7	462	49	0	.106	179	351	25	22	1.1	.955

Joe Coleman *continued*

LEAGUE CHAMPIONSHIP SERIES

Year	Team	W	L	PCT	ERA	G	GS	CG	IP	H	BB	SO	ShO	Relief Pitching W	Relief Pitching L	Relief Pitching SV	Batting AB	Batting H	Batting HR	BA	PO	A	E	DP	TC/G	FA
1972	DET A	1	0	1.000	0.00	1	1	1	9	7	3	14	1 1st	0	0	0	2	1	0	.500	0	0	0	0	0.0	.000

Joe Coleman

COLEMAN, JOSEPH PATRICK BR TR 6′ 2½″ 200 lbs.
Father of Joe Coleman.
B. July 30, 1922, Medford, Mass.

Year	Team	W	L	PCT	ERA	G	GS	CG	IP	H	BB	SO	ShO	Relief Pitching W	Relief Pitching L	Relief Pitching SV	Batting AB	Batting H	Batting HR	BA	PO	A	E	DP	TC/G	FA
1942	PHI A	0	1	.000	3.00	1	0	0	6	8	1	0	0	0	1	0	4	0	0	.000	0	1	0	0	1.0	1.000
1946		0	2	.000	5.54	4	2	0	13	19	8	8	0	0	0	0	5	2	0	.400	0	1	0	0	0.3	1.000
1947		6	12	.333	4.32	32	21	9	160.1	171	62	65	2	1	0	1	48	7	0	.146	5	16	1	0	0.7	.955
1948		14	13	.519	4.09	33	29	13	215.2	224	90	86	3	0	1	0	74	9	0	.122	6	33	3	3	1.3	.929
1949		13	14	.481	3.86	33	30	18	240.1	249	127	109	1	1	0	1	79	14	1	.177	7	23	2	3	1.0	.938
1950		0	5	.000	8.50	15	6	2	54	74	50	12	0	0	0	0	17	1	1	.059	0	3	0	0	0.2	1.000
1951		1	6	.143	5.98	28	9	1	96.1	117	59	34	0	0	2	1	27	7	0	.259	7	9	1	1	0.6	.941
1953		3	4	.429	4.00	21	9	2	90	85	49	18	1	0	0	0	28	8	0	.286	1	10	0	0	0.5	1.000
1954	BAL A	13	17	.433	3.50	33	32	15	221.1	184	96	103	4	0	1	0	74	13	2	.176	15	41	3	5	1.8	.949
1955	2 teams	BAL A (6G 0–1)		DET A (17G 2–1)																						
″	total	2	2	.500	5.59	23	2	0	37	41	24	9	0	2	1	3	7	5	0	.714	3	8	0	0	0.5	1.000
10 yrs.		52	76	.406	4.38	223	140	60	1134	1172	566	444	11	4	6	6	363	66	4	.182	44	145	10	12	0.9	.950

John Coleman

COLEMAN, JOHN TL 5′10″ 174 lbs.
B. 1874, Lee's Summit, Mo. Deceased.

Year	Team	W	L	PCT	ERA	G	GS	CG	IP	H	BB	SO	ShO	Relief Pitching W	Relief Pitching L	Relief Pitching SV	Batting AB	Batting H	Batting HR	BA	PO	A	E	DP	TC/G	FA
1895	STL N	0	1	.000	13.50	1	1	1	8	12	8	5	0	0	0	0	5	1	0	.200	0	2	1	0	3.0	.667

John Coleman

COLEMAN, JOHN TR
B. Bristol, Pa. Deceased.

Year	Team	W	L	PCT	ERA	G	GS	CG	IP	H	BB	SO	ShO	Relief Pitching W	Relief Pitching L	Relief Pitching SV	Batting AB	Batting H	Batting HR	BA	PO	A	E	DP	TC/G	FA
1890	PHI N	0	1	.000	21.60	1	1	0	1.2	4	3	2	0	0	0	0	0	0	0	—	0	0	0	0	0.0	.000

John Coleman

COLEMAN, JOHN FRANCIS BL TR 5′ 9½″ 170 lbs.
B. Mar. 6, 1863, Saratoga Springs, N. Y. D. May 31, 1922, Detroit, Mich. BB 1887

Year	Team	W	L	PCT	ERA	G	GS	CG	IP	H	BB	SO	ShO	Relief Pitching W	Relief Pitching L	Relief Pitching SV	Batting AB	Batting H	Batting HR	BA	PO	A	E	DP	TC/G	FA
1883	PHI N	12	**48**	.200	*4.87*	65	61	59	538.1	**772**	48	159	3	0	1	0	354	83	0	.234	91	132	31	6	2.6	.878
1884	2 teams	PHI N (21G 5–15)		PHI AA (3G 0–2)																						
″	total	5	17	.227	4.72	24	21	16	175.1	244	24	42	1	**1**	0	0	278	64	2	.230	106	55	24	3	2.3	.870
1885	PHI AA	2	2	.500	*3.43*	8	3	3	60.1	82	5	12	0	**1**	0	0	398	119	2	.299	130	32	28	5	1.9	.853
1886		1	1	.500	*2.61*	3	1	1	20.2	18	5	2	0	0	**1**	0	535	136	0	.254	235	32	36	9	2.2	.881
1889		3	2	.600	2.91	5	5	4	34	38	14	6	0	0	0	0	19	1	0	.053	226	17	28	3	2.3	.897
1890	PIT N	0	2	.000	9.64	2	2	1	14	28	6	3	0	0	0	0	11	2	0	.182	2	1	0	0	0.8	1.000
6 yrs.		23	72	.242	4.68	107	93	84	842.2	1182	102	224	4	2	2	0	*				1188	303	169	40	2.5	.898

Percy Coleman

COLEMAN, PIERCE D. TR
B. Oct. 15, 1876, Mason, Ohio D. Feb. 16, 1948, Van Nuys, Calif.

Year	Team	W	L	PCT	ERA	G	GS	CG	IP	H	BB	SO	ShO	Relief Pitching W	Relief Pitching L	Relief Pitching SV	Batting AB	Batting H	Batting HR	BA	PO	A	E	DP	TC/G	FA
1897	STL N	1	2	.333	8.16	12	4	2	57.1	99	32	10	0	0	0	0	28	6	0	.214	5	15	2	0	1.8	.909
1898	CIN N	0	1	.000	3.00	1	1	1	9	13	3	2	0	0	0	0	3	0	0	.000	0	1	1	0	2.0	.500
2 yrs.		1	3	.250	7.46	13	5	3	66.1	112	35	12	0	0	0	0	31	6	0	.194	5	16	3	0	1.8	.875

Rip Coleman

COLEMAN, WALTER GARY BL TL 6′ 2″ 185 lbs.
B. July 31, 1931, Troy, N. Y.

Year	Team	W	L	PCT	ERA	G	GS	CG	IP	H	BB	SO	ShO	Relief Pitching W	Relief Pitching L	Relief Pitching SV	Batting AB	Batting H	Batting HR	BA	PO	A	E	DP	TC/G	FA
1955	NY A	2	1	.667	5.28	10	6	0	29	40	16	15	0	0	0	1	10	2	0	.200	2	5	0	0	0.7	1.000
1956		3	5	.375	3.67	29	9	0	88.1	97	42	42	0	1	3	2	24	1	0	.042	10	14	2	0	0.9	.923
1957	KC A	0	7	.000	5.93	19	6	1	41	53	25	15	1	0	4	0	9	0	0	.000	1	9	1	1	0.6	.909
1959	2 teams	KC A (29G 2–10)		BAL A (3G 0–0)																						
″	total	2	10	.167	4.34	32	11	2	85	89	36	58	0	0	4	2	25	2	0	.080	1	18	2	3	0.7	.905
1960	BAL A	0	2	.000	11.25	5	1	0	4	8	5	0	0	0	1	0	1	0	0	.000	1	2	0	0	0.6	1.000
5 yrs.		7	25	.219	4.58	95	33	3	247.1	287	124	130	1	1	12	5	69	5	0	.072	15	48	5	4	0.7	.926

WORLD SERIES

Year	Team	W	L	PCT	ERA	G	GS	CG	IP	H	BB	SO	ShO	Relief Pitching W	Relief Pitching L	Relief Pitching SV	Batting AB	Batting H	Batting HR	BA	PO	A	E	DP	TC/G	FA
1955	NY A	0	0	—	9.00	1	0	0	1	5	0	1	0	0	0	0	0	0	0	—	0	0	0	0	0.0	.000

Allan Collamore

COLLAMORE, ALLAN EDWARD BR TR 6′ 170 lbs.
B. June 5, 1887, Worcester, Mass. D. Aug. 8, 1980, Battle Creek, Mich.

Year	Team	W	L	PCT	ERA	G	GS	CG	IP	H	BB	SO	ShO	Relief Pitching W	Relief Pitching L	Relief Pitching SV	Batting AB	Batting H	Batting HR	BA	PO	A	E	DP	TC/G	FA
1911	PHI A	0	1	.000	36.00	2	0	0	2	6	3	1	0	0	1	0	0	0	0	—	0	0	0	0	0.0	.000
1914	CLE A	3	7	.300	3.25	27	8	3	105.1	100	49	32	0	1	1	0	32	3	0	.094	5	28	3	2	1.3	.917
1915		2	5	.286	2.38	11	6	5	64.1	52	22	15	2	0	1	0	23	4	0	.174	4	22	1	1	2.5	.963
3 yrs.		5	13	.278	3.30	40	14	8	171.2	158	74	48	2	1	3	0	55	7	0	.127	9	50	4	3	1.6	.937

Hap Collard

COLLARD, EARL CLINTON BR TR 6′ 170 lbs.
B. Aug. 29, 1898, Williams, Ariz. D. July 9, 1968, Jamestown, Calif.

Year	Team	W	L	PCT	ERA	G	GS	CG	IP	H	BB	SO	ShO	Relief Pitching W	Relief Pitching L	Relief Pitching SV	Batting AB	Batting H	Batting HR	BA	PO	A	E	DP	TC/G	FA
1927	CLE A	0	0	—	5.06	4	0	0	5.1	8	3	2	0	0	0	0	0	0	0	—	0	3	1	0	1.0	.750
1928		0	0	—	2.25	1	0	0	4	4	4	1	0	0	0	0	1	1	0	1.000	0	0	0	0	0.0	.000
1930	PHI N	6	12	.333	6.80	30	15	4	127	188	39	25	0	2	2	0	44	9	0	.205	8	32	1	2	1.4	.976
3 yrs.		6	12	.333	6.60	35	15	4	136.1	200	46	28	0	2	2	0	45	10	0	.222	8	35	2	2	1.3	.956

Orlin Collier

COLLIER, ORLIN EDWARD BR TR 5′11½″ 180 lbs.
B. Feb. 17, 1907, East Prairie, Mo. D. Sept. 9, 1944, Memphis, Tenn.

Year	Team	W	L	PCT	ERA	G	GS	CG	IP	H	BB	SO	ShO	Relief Pitching W	Relief Pitching L	Relief Pitching SV	Batting AB	Batting H	Batting HR	BA	PO	A	E	DP	TC/G	FA
1931	DET A	0	1	.000	7.84	2	2	0	10.1	17	7	3	0	0	0	0	3	0	0	.000	0	1	0	0	0.5	1.000

Harry Colliflower

COLLIFLOWER, JAMES HARRY (Collie) BL TL 5′11½″ 175 lbs.
B. Mar. 11, 1869, Petersville, Md. D. Aug. 12, 1961, Washington, D. C.

Year	Team	W	L	PCT	ERA	G	GS	CG	IP	H	BB	SO	ShO	Relief Pitching W	Relief Pitching L	Relief Pitching SV	Batting AB	Batting H	Batting HR	BA	PO	A	E	DP	TC/G	FA
1899	CLE N	1	11	.083	8.17	14	12	11	98	152	41	8	0	0	0	0	76	23	0	.303	36	26	8	3	2.9	.886

Don Collins

COLLINS, DONALD EDWARD BR TL 6′ 2″ 195 lbs.
B. Sept. 15, 1952, Lyons, Ga.

Year	Team	Lg	W	L	PCT	ERA	G	GS	CG	IP	H	BB	SO	ShO	Relief W	Relief L	Relief SV	Batting AB	Batting H	HR	BA	PO	A	E	DP	TC/G	FA
1977	ATL	N	3	9	.250	5.07	40	6	0	71	82	41	27	0	3	4	2	11	0	0	.000	1	7	0	0	0.2	1.000
1980	CLE	A	0	0	—	7.50	4	0	0	6	9	7	0	0	0	0	0	0	0	0	—	0	1	0	0	0.3	1.000
2 yrs.			3	9	.250	5.26	44	6	0	77	91	48	27	0	3	4	2	11	0	0	.000	1	8	0	0	0.2	1.000

Orth Collins

COLLINS, ORTH STEIN (Buck) BL TR 6′ 150 lbs.
B. Apr. 27, 1880, Lafayette, Ind. D. Dec. 13, 1949, Fort Lauderdale, Fla.

Year	Team	Lg	W	L	PCT	ERA	G	GS	CG	IP	H	BB	SO	ShO	Relief W	Relief L	Relief SV	Batting AB	Batting H	HR	BA	PO	A	E	DP	TC/G	FA
1909	WAS	A	0	0	—	0.00	1	0	0	1	0	0	1	0	0	0	0	*				4	5	0	0	1.8	1.000

Phil Collins

COLLINS, PHILIP EUGENE (Fidgety Phil) BR TR 5′11″ 175 lbs.
B. Aug. 27, 1901, Chicago, Ill. D. Aug. 14, 1948, Chicago, Ill.

Year	Team	Lg	W	L	PCT	ERA	G	GS	CG	IP	H	BB	SO	ShO	Relief W	Relief L	Relief SV	Batting AB	Batting H	HR	BA	PO	A	E	DP	TC/G	FA
1923	CHI	N	1	0	1.000	3.60	1	1	0	5	8	1	2	0	0	0	0	2	0	0	.000	0	3	0	1	3.0	1.000
1929	PHI	N	9	7	.563	5.75	43	11	3	153.1	172	83	61	0	7	2	5	58	11	1	.190	7	27	1	0	0.8	.971
1930			16	11	.593	4.78	47	25	17	239	287	86	87	1	3	1	3	87	22	3	.253	12	39	5	0	1.2	.911
1931			12	16	.429	3.86	42	27	16	240.1	268	83	73	2	0	2	4	95	16	0	.168	17	51	5	2	1.7	.932
1932			14	12	.538	5.27	43	21	6	184.1	231	65	66	0	5	3	3	68	18	0	.265	7	41	9	3	1.3	.842
1933			8	13	.381	4.11	42	13	5	151	178	57	40	1	3	**6**	**6**	53	7	0	.132	8	25	2	3	0.8	.943
1934			13	18	.419	4.18	45	32	15	254	277	87	72	0	4	1	1	88	15	0	.170	7	40	3	2	1.1	.940
1935	2 teams	PHI N (3G 0–2)	STL N (26G 7–6)																								
″	total		7	8	.467	5.64	29	11	2	97.1	120	35	22	0	3	2	2	31	4	0	.129	7	17	1	1	0.9	.960
8 yrs.			80	85	.485	4.66	292	141	64	1324.1	1541	497	423	4	25	17	24	482	93	4	.193	65	243	26	12	1.1	.922

Ray Collins

COLLINS, RAYMOND WILLISTON BL TL 6′ 1″ 185 lbs.
B. Feb. 11, 1887, Colchester, Vt. D. Jan. 9, 1970, Burlington, Vt.

Year	Team	Lg	W	L	PCT	ERA	G	GS	CG	IP	H	BB	SO	ShO	Relief W	Relief L	Relief SV	Batting AB	Batting H	HR	BA	PO	A	E	DP	TC/G	FA
1909	BOS	A	4	3	.571	2.81	12	8	4	73.2	70	18	31	2	0	0	0	23	3	0	.130	6	26	2	0	2.8	.941
1910			13	11	.542	1.62	35	26	18	244.2	205	41	109	4	1	0	1	84	15	0	.179	8	62	2	1	2.1	.972
1911			11	12	.478	2.39	31	24	14	203.2	189	46	88	0	2	1	1	60	9	0	.150	5	39	4	1	1.5	.917
1912			13	8	.619	2.53	27	23	17	199.1	192	42	82	4	0	0	0	65	11	0	.169	3	45	2	0	1.9	.960
1913			19	8	.704	2.63	30	30	19	246.2	242	37	88	3	0	0	0	80	12	1	.150	6	54	1	1	2.0	.984
1914			20	13	.606	2.51	39	30	16	272.1	252	56	72	6	5	1	0	79	11	0	.139	8	57	3	2	1.7	.956
1915			4	7	.364	4.30	25	9	2	104.2	101	31	43	0	2	2	2	28	8	0	.286	2	16	1	2	0.8	.947
7 yrs.			84	62	.575	2.51	199	150	90	1345	1251	271	513	19	10	4	4	419	69	1	.165	38	299	15	7	1.8	.957
WORLD SERIES																											
1912	BOS	A	0	0	—	1.88	2	1	0	14.1	14	0	6	0	0	0	0	5	0	0	.000	0	3	0	3	1.5	1.000

Rip Collins

COLLINS, HARRY WARREN BR TR 6′ 1″ 205 lbs.
B. Feb. 26, 1896, Weatherford, Tex. D. May 27, 1968, Bryan, Tex.
BB 1920–1923

Year	Team	Lg	W	L	PCT	ERA	G	GS	CG	IP	H	BB	SO	ShO	Relief W	Relief L	Relief SV	Batting AB	Batting H	HR	BA	PO	A	E	DP	TC/G	FA
1920	NY	A	14	8	.636	3.17	36	20	12	187.1	171	79	66	3	4	0	1	62	8	0	.129	7	44	2	3	1.5	.962
1921			11	5	.688	5.44	28	16	7	137.1	158	78	64	2	1	2	0	56	11	0	.196	3	29	2	1	1.2	.941
1922	BOS	A	14	11	.560	3.76	32	29	15	210.2	219	**103**	69	3	0	0	0	76	12	0	.158	16	45	1	2	1.9	.984
1923	DET	A	3	7	.300	4.87	17	13	3	92.1	104	32	25	1	0	0	0	27	3	0	.111	8	24	2	0	2.0	.941
1924			14	7	.667	3.21	34	30	11	216	199	63	75	1	0	0	0	76	11	0	.145	11	50	3	2	1.8	.953
1925			6	11	.353	4.56	26	20	5	140	149	52	33	0	0	0	0	42	5	0	.119	7	53	1	0	2.3	.984
1926			8	8	.500	2.73	30	13	5	122	128	44	44	3	2	3	1	39	6	0	.154	5	37	5	2	1.6	.894
1927			13	7	.650	4.69	30	25	10	172.2	207	59	37	1	1	0	0	54	11	0	.204	11	64	1	6	2.5	.987
1929	STL	A	11	6	.647	4.00	26	20	10	155.1	162	73	47	1	1	1	1	62	17	1	.274	7	34	0	1	1.6	1.000
1930			9	7	.563	4.35	35	20	6	171.2	168	63	75	1	0	0	2	54	7	0	.130	11	29	0	1	1.1	1.000
1931			5	5	.500	3.79	17	14	2	107	130	38	34	0	0	1	0	34	5	0	.147	4	28	1	2	1.9	.970
11 yrs.			108	82	.568	3.99	311	220	86	1712.1	1795	684	569	16	9	7	5	582	96	1	.165	90	437	18	20	1.7	.967
WORLD SERIES																											
1921	NY	A	0	0	—	54.00	1	0	0	0.2	4	1	0	0	0	0	0	0	0	0	—	0	0	0	0	0.0	.000

Jackie Collum

COLLUM, JACK DEAN BL TL 5′ 7½″ 160 lbs.
B. June 21, 1927, Victor, Iowa.

Year	Team	Lg	W	L	PCT	ERA	G	GS	CG	IP	H	BB	SO	ShO	Relief W	Relief L	Relief SV	Batting AB	Batting H	HR	BA	PO	A	E	DP	TC/G	FA
1951	STL	N	2	1	.667	1.59	3	2	1	17	11	10	5	1	0	1	0	7	3	0	.429	2	4	0	0	2.0	1.000
1952			0	0	—	0.00	2	0	0	3	2	1	0	0	0	0	0	0	0	0	—	0	2	0	0	1.0	1.000
1953	2 teams	STL N (7G 0–0)	CIN N (30G 7–11)																								
″	total		7	11	.389	3.97	37	12	4	136	138	43	56	1	3	3	3	39	10	0	.256	4	33	0	3	1.0	1.000
1954	CIN	N	7	3	.700	3.74	36	2	1	79.1	86	32	28	0	7	2	0	13	3	1	.231	11	24	1	0	1.0	.972
1955			9	8	.529	3.63	32	17	5	134	128	37	49	0	2	1	1	40	10	0	.250	6	24	3	0	1.0	.909
1956	STL	N	6	2	.750	4.20	38	1	0	60	63	27	17	0	6	2	7	14	3	0	.214	4	16	2	1	0.6	.909
1957	2 teams	CHI N (9G 1–1)	BKN N (3G 0–0)																								
″	total		1	1	.500	7.20	12	0	0	15	15	10	10	0	1	1	1	0	0	0		2	1	0	0	0.3	1.000
1958	LA	N	0	0	—	8.10	2	0	0	3.1	4	2	0	0	0	0	0	1	0	0	.000	0	1	0	1	0.5	1.000
1962	2 teams	MIN A (8G 0–2)	CLE A (1G 0–0)																								
″	total		0	2	.000	11.34	9	3	0	16.2	33	11	6	0	0	0	0	4	0	0	.000	1	4	1	0	0.7	.833
9 yrs.			32	28	.533	4.15	171	37	11	464.1	480	173	171	2	19	10	12	118	29	1	.246	30	109	7	5	0.9	.952

Dick Colpaert

COLPAERT, RICHARD CHARLES BR TR 5′10″ 182 lbs.
B. Jan. 3, 1944, Fraser, Mich.

Year	Team	Lg	W	L	PCT	ERA	G	GS	CG	IP	H	BB	SO	ShO	Relief W	Relief L	Relief SV	Batting AB	Batting H	HR	BA	PO	A	E	DP	TC/G	FA
1970	PIT	N	1	0	1.000	5.73	8	0	0	11	9	8	6	0	1	0	0	0	0	0	—	2	0	0	0	0.3	1.000

Loyd Colson

COLSON, LOYD ALBERT BR TR 6′ 1″ 190 lbs.
B. Nov. 4, 1947, Wellington, Tex.

Year	Team	Lg	W	L	PCT	ERA	G	GS	CG	IP	H	BB	SO	ShO	Relief W	Relief L	Relief SV	Batting AB	Batting H	HR	BA	PO	A	E	DP	TC/G	FA
1970	NY	A	0	0	—	4.50	1	0	0	2	3	0	3	0	0	0	0	0	0	0	—	0	0	0	0	0.0	.000

Larry Colton

COLTON, LAWRENCE ROBERT BL TR 6′ 3″ 200 lbs.
B. June 8, 1942, Los Angeles, Calif.

Year	Team	Lg	W	L	PCT	ERA	G	GS	CG	IP	H	BB	SO	ShO	Relief W	Relief L	Relief SV	Batting AB	Batting H	HR	BA	PO	A	E	DP	TC/G	FA
1968	PHI	N	0	0	—	4.50	1	0	0	2	3	0	2	0	0	0	0	0	0	0	—	0	0	0	0	0.0	.000

Jeff Combe

COMBE, GEOFFREY WADE BR TR 6' 2" 185 lbs.
B. Feb. 1, 1956, Melrose, Mass.

Year	Team		W	L	PCT	ERA	G	GS	CG	IP	H	BB	SO	ShO	Relief W	Relief L	Relief SV	Batting AB	Batting H	Batting HR	BA	PO	A	E	DP	TC/G	FA
1980	CIN	N	0	0	—	10.29	4	0	0	7	9	4	10	0	0	0	0	0	0	0	—	0	1	0	0	0.3	1.000
1981			1	0	1.000	7.50	14	0	0	18	27	10	9	0	1	0	0	0	0	0	—	0	2	0	0	0.1	1.000
2 yrs.			1	0	1.000	8.28	18	0	0	25	36	14	19	0	1	0	0	0	0	0		0	3	0	0	0.2	1.000

Pat Combs

COMBS, PATRICK DENNIS BL TL 6' 3" 200 lbs.
B. Oct. 29, 1966, Newport, R. I.

Year	Team		W	L	PCT	ERA	G	GS	CG	IP	H	BB	SO	ShO	Relief W	Relief L	Relief SV	Batting AB	Batting H	Batting HR	BA	PO	A	E	DP	TC/G	FA
1989	PHI	N	4	0	1.000	2.09	6	6	1	38.2	36	6	30	1	0	0	0	12	2	0	.167	1	3	0	0	0.7	1.000
1990			10	10	.500	4.07	32	31	3	183.1	179	86	108	2	0	0	0	60	9	0	.150	10	25	0	1	1.1	1.000
1991			2	6	.250	4.90	14	13	1	64.1	64	43	41	0	0	0	0	15	2	0	.133	2	9	0	0	0.8	1.000
1992			1	1	.500	7.71	4	4	0	18.2	20	12	11	0	0	0	0	8	1	0	.125	0	6	0	0	1.5	1.000
4 yrs.			17	17	.500	4.22	56	54	5	305	299	147	190	3	0	0	0	95	14	0	.147	13	43	0	1	1.0	1.000

Jorge Comellas

COMELLAS, JORGE (Pancho) BR TR 6' 185 lbs.
Born Jorge Comellas (Pous).
B. Dec. 7, 1916, Havana, Cuba/

Year	Team		W	L	PCT	ERA	G	GS	CG	IP	H	BB	SO	ShO	Relief W	Relief L	Relief SV	Batting AB	Batting H	Batting HR	BA	PO	A	E	DP	TC/G	FA
1945	CHI	N	0	2	.000	4.50	7	1	0	12	11	6	6	0	0	1	0	3	0	0	.000	0	9	0	1	1.3	1.000

Steve Comer

COMER, STEPHEN MICHAEL BB TR 6' 3" 195 lbs.
B. Jan. 13, 1954, Minneapolis, Minn.

Year	Team		W	L	PCT	ERA	G	GS	CG	IP	H	BB	SO	ShO	Relief W	Relief L	Relief SV	Batting AB	Batting H	Batting HR	BA	PO	A	E	DP	TC/G	FA
1978	TEX	A	11	5	.688	2.30	30	11	3	117.1	107	37	65	2	5	2	1	0	0	0	—	8	20	1	0	1.0	.966
1979			17	12	.586	3.68	36	36	6	242	230	84	86	1	0	0	0	0	0	0	—	19	38	4	0	1.7	.934
1980			2	4	.333	7.93	12	11	0	42	65	22	9	0	0	0	0	0	0	0	—	6	5	1	1	1.0	.917
1981			8	2	.800	2.57	36	1	0	77	70	31	22	0	8	1	6	0	0	0	—	5	18	1	2	0.7	.958
1982			1	6	.143	5.10	37	3	1	97	133	36	23	0	0	4	6	0	0	0	—	3	15	1	1	0.5	.947
1983	PHI	N	1	0	1.000	5.19	3	1	0	8.2	11	3	1	0	0	0	0	1	0	0	.000	2	0	0	0	0.7	1.000
1984	CLE	A	4	8	.333	5.68	22	20	1	117.1	146	39	39	0	0	0	0	0	0	0	—	7	20	1	1	1.3	.964
7 yrs.			44	37	.543	4.13	176	83	11	701.1	762	252	245	3	13	7	13	1	0	0	.000	50	116	9	5	1.0	.949

Charlie Comiskey

COMISKEY, CHARLES ALBERT (Commy, The Old Roman) BR TR 6' 180 lbs.
B. Aug. 15, 1859, Chicago, Ill. D. Oct. 26, 1931, Eagle River, Wis.
Manager 1883–94.
Hall of Fame 1939.

Year	Team		W	L	PCT	ERA	G	GS	CG	IP	H	BB	SO	ShO	Relief W	Relief L	Relief SV	Batting AB	Batting H	Batting HR	BA	PO	A	E	DP	TC/G	FA
1882	STL	AA	0	1	.000	0.00	2	1	1	8	12	3	2	0	0	0	0	329	80	1	.243	861	16	30	25	11.5	.967
1884			0	0	—	*2.25*	1	0	0	4	1	0	4	0	0	0	0	460	110	2	.239	1085	20	43	49	11.8	.963
1889			0	0	—	0.00	1	0	0	0.1	0	0	0	0	0	0	0	587	168	3	.286	1193	38	40	56	11.6	.969
3 yrs.			0	1	.000	0.73	4	1	1	12.1	13	3	6	0	0	0	0	*				13874	568	417	746	10.6	.972

Clint Compton

COMPTON, ROBERT CLINTON BL TL 5'11" 185 lbs.
B. Nov. 1, 1950, Montgomery, Ala.

Year	Team		W	L	PCT	ERA	G	GS	CG	IP	H	BB	SO	ShO	Relief W	Relief L	Relief SV	Batting AB	Batting H	Batting HR	BA	PO	A	E	DP	TC/G	FA
1972	CHI	N	0	0	—	9.00	1	0	0	2	2	2	0	0	0	0	0	0	0	0	—	0	0	0	0	0.0	.000

Jack Compton

COMPTON, HARRY LEROY BR TR 5' 9" 157 lbs.
B. Mar. 9, 1882, Lancaster, Ohio D. July 4, 1974, Lancaster, Ohio.

Year	Team		W	L	PCT	ERA	G	GS	CG	IP	H	BB	SO	ShO	Relief W	Relief L	Relief SV	Batting AB	Batting H	Batting HR	BA	PO	A	E	DP	TC/G	FA
1911	CIN	N	0	1	.000	3.91	8	3	0	25.1	19	15	6	0	0	1	1	6	2	0	.333	0	7	1	0	1.0	.875

Keith Comstock

COMSTOCK, KEITH MARTIN BL TL 6' 174 lbs.
B. Dec. 23, 1955, San Francisco, Calif.

Year	Team		W	L	PCT	ERA	G	GS	CG	IP	H	BB	SO	ShO	Relief W	Relief L	Relief SV	Batting AB	Batting H	Batting HR	BA	PO	A	E	DP	TC/G	FA
1984	MIN	A	0	0	—	8.53	4	0	0	6.1	6	4	2	0	0	0	0	0	0	0	—	1	2	0	0	0.8	1.000
1987	2 teams SF N (15G 2–0) SD N (26G 0–1)																										
"	total		2	1	.667	4.61	41	0	0	56.2	52	31	59	0	2	1	1	2	0	0	.000	2	4	0	1	0.1	1.000
1988	SD	N	0	0	—	6.75	7	0	0	8	8	3	9	0	0	0	0	0	0	0	—	1	1	0	0	0.3	1.000
1989	SEA	A	1	2	.333	2.81	31	0	0	25.2	26	10	22	0	1	2	0	0	0	0	—	0	4	1	0	0.2	.800
1990			7	4	.636	2.89	60	0	0	56	40	26	50	0	7	4	2	0	0	0	—	2	11	1	0	0.2	.929
1991			0	0	—	54.00	1	0	0	0.1	2	1	0	0	0	0	0	0	0	0	—	0	0	0	0	0.0	.000
6 yrs.			10	7	.588	4.06	144	0	0	153	134	75	142	0	10	7	3	2	0	0	.000	6	22	2	1	0.2	.933

Ralph Comstock

COMSTOCK, RALPH REMICK (Commy) BR TR 5'10" 168 lbs.
B. Nov. 24, 1890, Sylvania, Ohio D. Sept. 13, 1966, Toledo, Ohio.

Year	Team		W	L	PCT	ERA	G	GS	CG	IP	H	BB	SO	ShO	Relief W	Relief L	Relief SV	Batting AB	Batting H	Batting HR	BA	PO	A	E	DP	TC/G	FA
1913	DET	A	2	5	.286	5.37	10	7	1	60.1	90	16	37	0	0	0	1	22	5	0	.227	3	17	1	1	2.1	.952
1915	2 teams BOS A (3G 1–0) PIT F (12G 3–3)																										
"	total		4	3	.571	3.06	15	7	3	61.2	54	9	19	0	1	0	2	18	0	0	.000	2	18	2	0	1.5	.909
1918	PIT	N	5	6	.455	3.00	15	8	6	81	78	14	44	0	2	1	1	26	5	0	.192	2	22	1	1	1.7	.960
3 yrs.			11	14	.440	3.72	40	22	10	203	222	39	100	0	3	1	4	66	10	0	.152	7	57	4	2	1.7	.941

Dave Concepcion

CONCEPCION, DAVID ISMAEL BR TR 6' 2" 155 lbs.
Born David Ismael Concepcion (Benitez).
B. June 17, 1948, Aragua, Venezuela.

Year	Team		W	L	PCT	ERA	G	GS	CG	IP	H	BB	SO	ShO	Relief W	Relief L	Relief SV	Batting AB	Batting H	Batting HR	BA	PO	A	E	DP	TC/G	FA
1988	CIN	N	0	0	—	0.00	1	0	0	1.1	2	0	1	0	0	0	0	*				144	247	22	51	4.3	.947

Bob Cone

CONE, ROBERT EARL (Ike) BR TR 6' 2" 172 lbs.
B. Feb. 27, 1894, Galveston, Tex. D. May 24, 1955, Galveston, Tex.

Year	Team		W	L	PCT	ERA	G	GS	CG	IP	H	BB	SO	ShO	Relief W	Relief L	Relief SV	Batting AB	Batting H	Batting HR	BA	PO	A	E	DP	TC/G	FA
1915	PHI	A	0	0	—	40.50	1	1	0	0.2	5	0	0	0	0	0	0	0	0	0	—	0	0	0	0	0.0	.000

David Cone

CONE, DAVID BRIAN BL TR 6' 1" 180 lbs.
B. Jan. 2, 1963, Kansas City, Mo.

Year	Team		W	L	PCT	ERA	G	GS	CG	IP	H	BB	SO	ShO	Relief W	Relief L	Relief SV	Batting AB	Batting H	Batting HR	BA	PO	A	E	DP	TC/G	FA
1986	KC	A	0	0	—	5.56	11	0	0	22.2	29	13	21	0	0	0	0	0	0	0	—	4	0	0	0	0.4	1.000
1987	NY	N	5	6	.455	3.71	21	13	1	99.1	87	44	68	0	1	1	1	31	2	0	.065	12	10	1	0	1.1	.957
1988			20	3	**.870**	2.22	35	28	8	231.1	178	80	213	4	2	0	0	80	12	0	.150	17	23	1	0	1.2	.976
1989			14	8	.636	3.52	34	33	7	219.2	183	74	190	2	0	0	0	77	18	0	.234	21	14	1	0	1.1	.972
1990			14	10	.583	3.23	31	30	6	211.2	177	65	**233**	2	0	0	0	70	14	0	.200	17	20	3	1	1.3	.925
1991			14	14	.500	3.29	34	34	5	232.2	204	73	**241**	2	0	0	0	72	9	0	.125	18	26	4	2	1.4	.917
1992	2 teams NY N (27G 13–7) TOR A (8G 4–3)																										
"	total		17	10	.630	2.81	35	34	7	249.2	201	**111**	261	5	0	0	0	65	6	0	.092	18	22	2	1	1.2	.952

David Cone *continued*

Year	Team	Lg	W	L	PCT	ERA	G	GS	CG	IP	H	BB	SO	ShO	Relief Pitching W	Relief Pitching L	Relief Pitching SV	Batting AB	Batting H	Batting HR	BA	PO	A	E	DP	TC/G	FA
1993	KC	A	11	14	.440	3.33	34	34	6	254	205	114	191	1	0	0	0	0	0	0	—	24	24	1	3	1.4	.980
1994			16	5	.762	2.94	23	23	4	171.2	130	54	132	3	0	0	0	0	0	0	—	20	18	3	3	1.8	.927
1995	2 teams	TOR A (17G 9–6)	NY A (13G 9–2)																								
"	total		18	8	.692	3.57	30	30	6	229.1	195	88	191	2	0	0	0	0	0	0	—	12	27	3	2	1.4	.929
10 yrs.			129	78	.623	3.17	288	259	50	1922	1589	716	1741	21	3	1	1	395	61	0	.154	163	184	19	12	1.3	.948
DIVISIONAL PLAYOFF SERIES																											
1995	NY	A	1	0	1.000	4.60	2	2	0	15.2	15	9	14	0	0	0	0	0	0	0	—	1	0	0	0	0.5	1.000
LEAGUE CHAMPIONSHIP SERIES																											
1988	NY	N	1	1	.500	4.50	3	2	1	12	10	5	9	0	0	0	0	4	0	0	.000	1	0	0	0	0.3	1.000
1992	TOR	A	1	1	.500	3.00	2	2	0	12	11	5	9	0	0	0	0	0	0	0	—	0	1	1	0	1.0	.500
2 yrs.			2	2	.500	3.75	5	4	1	24	21	10	18	0	0	0	0	4	0	0	.000	1	1	1	0	0.6	.667
WORLD SERIES																											
1992	TOR	A	0	0	—	3.48	2	2	0	10.1	9	8	8	0	0	0	0	4	2	0	.500	0	0	0	0	0.0	.000

Dick Conger

CONGER, RICHARD BR TR 6′ 185 lbs.
B. Apr. 3, 1921, Los Angeles, Calif. D. Feb. 16, 1970, Los Angeles, Calif.

Year	Team	Lg	W	L	PCT	ERA	G	GS	CG	IP	H	BB	SO	ShO	Relief Pitching W	Relief Pitching L	Relief Pitching SV	Batting AB	Batting H	Batting HR	BA	PO	A	E	DP	TC/G	FA
1940	DET	A	1	0	1.000	3.00	2	0	0	3	2	3	1	0	1	0	0	0	0	0	—	0	0	0	0	0.0	.000
1941	PIT	N	0	0	—	0.00	2	1	0	4	3	3	2	0	0	0	0	0	0	0	—	0	0	0	0	0.0	.000
1942			0	0	—	2.16	2	1	0	8.1	9	5	3	0	0	0	0	3	0	0	.000	0	5	1	0	3.0	.833
1943	PHI	N	2	7	.222	6.09	13	10	2	54.2	72	24	18	0	0	0	0	16	1	0	.063	1	12	1	0	1.1	.929
4 yrs.			3	7	.300	5.14	19	12	2	70	86	35	24	0	1	0	0	19	1	0	.053	1	17	2	0	1.1	.900

Red Conkwright

CONKWRIGHT, ALLEN HOWARD (Red) BR TR 5′10″ 170 lbs.
B. Dec. 4, 1896, Sedalia, Mo. D. July 30, 1991, La Mesa, Calif.

Year	Team	Lg	W	L	PCT	ERA	G	GS	CG	IP	H	BB	SO	ShO	Relief Pitching W	Relief Pitching L	Relief Pitching SV	Batting AB	Batting H	Batting HR	BA	PO	A	E	DP	TC/G	FA
1920	DET	A	2	1	.667	6.98	5	3	0	19.1	29	16	4	0	2	0	1	4	1	0	.250	5	4	0	0	1.8	1.000

Bob Conley

CONLEY, ROBERT BURNS BR TR 6′ 1″ 188 lbs.
B. Feb. 1, 1934, Mousie, Ky.

Year	Team	Lg	W	L	PCT	ERA	G	GS	CG	IP	H	BB	SO	ShO	Relief Pitching W	Relief Pitching L	Relief Pitching SV	Batting AB	Batting H	Batting HR	BA	PO	A	E	DP	TC/G	FA
1958	PHI	N	0	0	—	7.56	2	2	0	8.1	9	1	0	0	0	0	0	1	0	0	.000	0	1	0	0	0.5	1.000

Ed Conley

CONLEY, EDWARD J. 5′ 8″ 142 lbs.
B. July 10, 1864, Sandwich, Mass. D. Oct. 16, 1894, Cumberland, R. I.

Year	Team	Lg	W	L	PCT	ERA	G	GS	CG	IP	H	BB	SO	ShO	Relief Pitching W	Relief Pitching L	Relief Pitching SV	Batting AB	Batting H	Batting HR	BA	PO	A	E	DP	TC/G	FA
1884	PRO	N	4	4	.500	*2.15*	8	8	8	71	63	22	33	1	0	0	0	28	4	0	.143	1	9	0	0	1.3	1.000

Gene Conley

CONLEY, DONALD EUGENE BR TR 6′ 8″ 225 lbs.
B. Nov. 10, 1930, Muskogee, Okla.

Year	Team	Lg	W	L	PCT	ERA	G	GS	CG	IP	H	BB	SO	ShO	Relief Pitching W	Relief Pitching L	Relief Pitching SV	Batting AB	Batting H	Batting HR	BA	PO	A	E	DP	TC/G	FA
1952	BOS	N	0	3	.000	7.82	4	3	0	12.2	23	9	6	0	0	0	0	5	2	0	.400	1	2	0	0	0.8	1.000
1954	MIL	N	14	9	.609	2.96	28	27	12	194.1	171	79	113	2	1	0	0	77	12	0	.156	10	29	1	3	1.4	.975
1955			11	7	.611	4.16	22	21	10	158	152	52	107	0	0	1	0	54	11	0	.204	7	24	0	0	1.4	1.000
1956			8	9	.471	3.13	31	19	5	158.1	169	52	68	1	1	2	3	45	7	0	.156	8	25	2	3	1.1	.943
1957			9	9	.500	3.16	35	18	6	148	133	64	61	1	4	1	1	46	9	0	.196	5	27	1	3	0.9	.970
1958			0	6	.000	4.88	26	7	0	72	89	17	53	0	0	3	2	16	3	1	.188	1	12	0	0	0.5	1.000
1959	PHI	N	12	7	.632	3.00	25	22	12	180	159	42	102	3	0	0	1	67	16	0	.239	9	29	2	2	1.6	.950
1960			8	14	.364	3.68	29	25	9	183.1	192	42	117	2	1	0	0	63	8	1	.127	6	26	5	2	1.3	.865
1961	BOS	A	11	14	.440	4.91	33	30	6	199.2	229	65	113	2	0	1	1	73	16	2	.219	12	28	2	2	1.3	.952
1962			15	14	.517	3.95	34	33	9	241.2	238	68	134	2	0	0	1	87	18	1	.207	17	35	5	2	1.7	.912
1963			3	4	.429	6.64	9	9	0	40.2	51	21	14	0	0	0	0	15	3	0	.200	2	4	1	0	0.8	.857
11 yrs.			91	96	.487	3.82	276	214	69	1588.2	1606	511	888	13	7	8	9	548	105	5	.192	78	241	19	17	1.2	.944
WORLD SERIES																											
1957	MIL	N	0	0	—	10.80	1	0	0	1.2	2	1	0	0	0	0	0	0	0	0	—	1	0	0	0	1.0	1.000

Snipe Conley

CONLEY, JAMES PATRICK BR TR 5′11½″ 179 lbs.
B. Apr. 25, 1894, Cressona, Pa. D. Jan. 7, 1978, DeSoto, Tex.

Year	Team	Lg	W	L	PCT	ERA	G	GS	CG	IP	H	BB	SO	ShO	Relief Pitching W	Relief Pitching L	Relief Pitching SV	Batting AB	Batting H	Batting HR	BA	PO	A	E	DP	TC/G	FA
1914	BAL	F	4	6	.400	2.52	35	11	4	125	112	47	86	2	1	3	0	35	4	0	.114	5	28	2	2	1.0	.943
1915			1	4	.200	4.29	25	6	4	86	97	32	40	0	0	1	0	24	6	0	.250	4	22	1	0	1.1	.963
1918	CIN	N	2	0	1.000	5.27	5	0	0	13.2	17	5	2	0	2	0	1	4	1	0	.250	2	4	0	1	1.2	1.000
3 yrs.			7	10	.412	3.36	65	17	8	224.2	226	84	128	2	3	4	1	63	11	0	.175	11	54	3	3	1.0	.956

Bert Conn

CONN, ALBERT THOMAS TR
B. Sept. 22, 1879, Philadelphia, Pa. D. Nov. 2, 1944, Philadelphia, Pa.

Year	Team	Lg	W	L	PCT	ERA	G	GS	CG	IP	H	BB	SO	ShO	Relief Pitching W	Relief Pitching L	Relief Pitching SV	Batting AB	Batting H	Batting HR	BA	PO	A	E	DP	TC/G	FA
1898	PHI	N	0	1	.000	6.43	1	1	0	7	13	2	3	0	0	0	0	3	1	0	.333	0	1	0	0	1.0	1.000
1900			0	2	.000	8.31	4	1	1	17.1	29	16	2	0	0	1	0	9	3	0	.333	3	1	2	0	1.5	.667
2 yrs.			0	3	.000	7.77	5	2	1	24.1	42	18	5	0	0	1	0	*				12	15	5	0	3.2	.844

Sarge Connally

CONNALLY, GEORGE WALTER BR TR 5′11″ 170 lbs.
B. Aug. 31, 1898, McGregor, Tex. D. Jan. 27, 1978, Temple, Tex.

Year	Team	Lg	W	L	PCT	ERA	G	GS	CG	IP	H	BB	SO	ShO	Relief Pitching W	Relief Pitching L	Relief Pitching SV	Batting AB	Batting H	Batting HR	BA	PO	A	E	DP	TC/G	FA
1921	CHI	A	0	1	.000	6.45	5	2	0	22.1	29	10	6	0	0	0	0	8	4	0	.500	1	5	0	1	1.2	1.000
1923			0	0	—	6.23	3	0	0	8.2	7	12	3	0	0	0	0	3	1	0	.333	0	2	0	0	0.7	1.000
1924			7	13	.350	4.05	44	13	6	160	177	68	55	0	5	**5**	6	50	11	0	.220	10	50	3	4	1.4	.952
1925			6	7	.462	4.64	40	2	0	104.2	122	58	45	0	5	**6**	8	28	7	0	.250	3	39	1	0	1.1	.977
1926			6	5	.545	3.16	31	8	5	108.1	128	35	47	0	2	4	3	32	5	0	.156	7	32	1	3	1.3	.975
1927			10	15	.400	4.08	43	18	11	198.1	217	83	58	1	5	3	5	67	22	0	.328	10	50	1	5	1.4	.984
1928			2	5	.286	4.84	28	5	1	74.1	89	29	28	0	1	4	2	19	2	0	.105	3	15	2	1	0.7	.900
1929			0	0	—	4.76	11	0	0	11.1	13	8	3	0	0	0	1	0	0	0	—	1	1	1	1	0.3	.667
1931	CLE	A	5	5	.500	4.20	17	9	5	85.2	87	50	37	0	2	0	1	27	5	0	.185	4	17	4	0	1.5	.840
1932			8	6	.571	4.33	35	7	4	112.1	119	42	32	1	4	4	3	40	7	1	.175	5	24	3	2	0.9	.906
1933			5	3	.625	4.89	41	3	1	103	112	49	30	0	4	2	1	26	6	0	.231	5	11	2	1	0.4	.889
1934			0	0	—	5.06	5	0	0	5.1	4	5	1	0	0	0	1	1	0	0	.000	1	2	0	1	0.6	1.000
12 yrs.			49	60	.450	4.30	303	67	33	994.1	1104	449	345	2	28	28	31	301	70	1	.233	50	248	18	19	1.0	.943

Bill Connelly

CONNELLY, WILLIAM WIRT (Wild Bill) BL TR 6′ 175 lbs.
B. June 29, 1925, Alberta, Va. D. Nov. 27, 1980, Richmond, Va.

Year	Team	W	L	PCT	ERA	G	GS	CG	IP	H	BB	SO	ShO	Relief W	Relief L	Relief SV	AB	H	HR	BA	PO	A	E	DP	TC/G	FA
1945	PHI A	1	1	.500	4.50	2	1	0	8	7	8	0	0	1	0	0	1	0	0	.000	1	0	1	0	1.0	.500
1950	2 teams	CHI A (2G 0–0)	DET A (2G 0–0)																							
″	total	0	0		8.53	4	0	0	6.1	9	3	1	0	0	0	0	1	0	0	.000	0	1	0	1	0.3	1.000
1952	NY N	5	0	1.000	4.55	11	4	0	31.2	22	25	22	0	2	0	0	11	4	0	.364	3	7	0	0	0.9	1.000
1953		0	1	.000	11.07	8	2	0	20.1	33	17	11	0	0	0	0	6	0	0	.000	0	2	0	0	0.3	1.000
4 yrs.		6	2	.750	6.92	25	7	0	66.1	71	53	34	0	3	0	0	19	4	0	.211	4	10	1	1	0.6	.933

Ed Connolly

CONNOLLY, EDWARD JOSEPH, JR. BL TL 6′ 1″ 190 lbs.
Son of Ed Connolly.
B. Dec. 3, 1939, Brooklyn, N. Y.

Year	Team	W	L	PCT	ERA	G	GS	CG	IP	H	BB	SO	ShO	Relief W	Relief L	Relief SV	AB	H	HR	BA	PO	A	E	DP	TC/G	FA
1964	BOS A	4	11	.267	4.91	27	15	1	80.2	80	64	73	1	0	1	0	18	3	0	.167	4	6	2	0	0.4	.833
1967	CLE A	2	1	.667	7.48	15	4	0	49.1	63	34	45	0	1	0	0	11	2	0	.182	0	7	0	0	0.5	1.000
2 yrs.		6	12	.333	5.88	42	19	1	130	143	98	118	1	1	1	0	29	5	0	.172	4	13	2	0	0.5	.895

John Connor

CONNOR, JOHN
B. Aug. 1854, Scotland D. Oct. 13, 1932, Boston, Mass.

Year	Team	W	L	PCT	ERA	G	GS	CG	IP	H	BB	SO	ShO	Relief W	Relief L	Relief SV	AB	H	HR	BA	PO	A	E	DP	TC/G	FA
1884	BOS N	1	4	.200	*3.15*	7	7	7	60	70	18	29	0	0	0	0	25	2	0	.080	2	15	3	0	2.9	.850
1885	2 teams	BUF N (1G 0–1)	LOU AA (4G 1–3)																							
″	total	1	4	.200	4.70	5	5	5	44	57	14	19	0	0	0	0	17	2	0	.118	1	0	0	0	0.2	1.000
2 yrs.		2	8	.200	3.81	12	12	12	104	127	32	48	0	0	0	0	42	4	0	.095	3	15	3	0	1.8	.857

Bill Connors

CONNORS, WILLIAM JOSEPH BR TR 6′ 1″ 180 lbs.
B. Nov. 2, 1941, Schenectady, N. Y.

Year	Team	W	L	PCT	ERA	G	GS	CG	IP	H	BB	SO	ShO	Relief W	Relief L	Relief SV	AB	H	HR	BA	PO	A	E	DP	TC/G	FA
1966	CHI N	0	1	.000	7.31	11	0	0	16	20	7	3	0	0	1	0	0	0	0	—	0	3	0	0	0.3	1.000
1967	NY N	0	0	—	6.23	6	1	0	13	8	5	13	0	0	0	0	1	0	0	.000	0	0	0	0	0.0	.000
1968		0	1	.000	9.00	9	0	0	14	21	7	8	0	0	1	0	1	1	0	1.000	3	2	0	0	0.6	1.000
3 yrs.		0	2	.000	7.53	26	1	0	43	49	19	24	0	0	2	0	2	1	0	.500	3	5	0	0	0.3	1.000

Joe Connors

CONNORS, JOSEPH P.
B. Paterson, N. J. Deceased.

Year	Team	W	L	PCT	ERA	G	GS	CG	IP	H	BB	SO	ShO	Relief W	Relief L	Relief SV	AB	H	HR	BA	PO	A	E	DP	TC/G	FA
1884	2 teams	ALT U (1G 0–1)	KC U (2G 0–1)																							
″	total	0	2	.000	5.57	3	2	2	21	42	5	1	0	0	0	0	*				8	7	3	0	2.6	.833

Ted Conovar

CONOVAR, THEODORE BR TR 5′10½″ 165 lbs.
B. Mar. 10, 1868, Lexington, Ky. D. July 27, 1910, Paris, Ky.

Year	Team	W	L	PCT	ERA	G	GS	CG	IP	H	BB	SO	ShO	Relief W	Relief L	Relief SV	AB	H	HR	BA	PO	A	E	DP	TC/G	FA
1889	CIN AA	0	0	—	13.50	1	0	0	2	4	2	1	0	0	0	1	0	0	0	—	0	0	0	0	0.0	.000

Tim Conroy

CONROY, TIMOTHY JAMES BL TL 6′ 178 lbs.
B. Apr. 3, 1960, McKeesport, Pa.

Year	Team	W	L	PCT	ERA	G	GS	CG	IP	H	BB	SO	ShO	Relief W	Relief L	Relief SV	AB	H	HR	BA	PO	A	E	DP	TC/G	FA
1978	OAK A	0	0	—	7.71	2	2	0	4.2	3	9	0	0	0	0	0	0	0	0	—	0	0	1	0	0.5	.000
1982		2	2	.500	3.55	5	5	1	25.1	20	18	17	0	0	0	0	0	0	0	—	1	3	2	0	1.2	.667
1983		7	10	.412	3.94	39	18	3	162.1	141	98	112	1	2	0	0	0	0	0	—	7	11	2	0	0.5	.900
1984		1	6	.143	5.23	38	14	0	93	82	63	69	0	0	0	0	0	0	0	—	0	7	0	1	0.2	1.000
1985		0	1	.000	4.26	16	2	0	25.1	22	15	8	0	0	0	0	0	0	0	—	0	3	1	0	0.3	.750
1986	STL N	5	11	.313	5.23	25	21	1	115.1	122	56	79	0	1	0	0	29	4	0	.138	3	16	5	0	1.0	.792
1987		3	2	.600	5.53	10	9	0	40.2	48	25	22	0	0	0	0	15	0	0	.000	3	4	1	1	0.8	.875
7 yrs.		18	32	.360	4.69	135	71	5	466.2	438	284	307	1	3	0	0	44	4	0	.091	14	44	12	2	0.5	.829

Jim Constable

CONSTABLE, JIMMY LEE (Sheriff) BB TL 6′ 1″ 185 lbs.
B. June 14, 1933, Jonesboro, Tenn.

Year	Team	W	L	PCT	ERA	G	GS	CG	IP	H	BB	SO	ShO	Relief W	Relief L	Relief SV	AB	H	HR	BA	PO	A	E	DP	TC/G	FA
1956	NY N	0	0	—	14.54	3	0	0	4.1	9	7	1	0	0	0	0	0	0	0	—	1	0	0	0	0.3	1.000
1957		1	1	.500	2.86	16	0	0	28.1	27	7	13	0	1	1	0	5	0	0	.000	3	2	0	0	0.3	1.000
1958	3 teams	SF N (9G 1–0)	CLE A (6G 0–1)	WAS A (15G 0–1)																						
″	total	1	2	.333	6.40	30	4	0	45	56	22	32	0	1	1	1	7	4	0	.571	2	7	1	1	0.3	.900
1962	MIL N	1	1	.500	2.00	3	2	1	18	14	4	12	1	0	0	1	5	0	0	.000	2	0	0	0	0.7	1.000
1963	SF N	0	0	—	3.86	4	0	0	2.1	3	1	1	0	0	0	0	0	0	0	—	0	1	0	0	0.3	1.000
5 yrs.		3	4	.429	4.87	56	6	1	98	109	41	59	1	2	2	2	17	4	0	.235	8	10	1	1	0.3	.947

Sandy Consuegra

CONSUEGRA, SANDALIO SIMEON BR TR 5′11″ 165 lbs.
Born Sandalio Simeon Consuegra (Castello).
B. Sept. 3, 1920, Potrerillos, Cuba.

Year	Team	W	L	PCT	ERA	G	GS	CG	IP	H	BB	SO	ShO	Relief W	Relief L	Relief SV	AB	H	HR	BA	PO	A	E	DP	TC/G	FA
1950	WAS A	7	8	.467	4.40	21	18	8	124.2	132	57	38	2	0	0	2	40	7	0	.175	6	24	2	2	1.5	.938
1951		7	8	.467	4.01	40	12	5	146	140	63	31	0	2	5	3	43	10	0	.233	5	31	0	2	0.9	1.000
1952		6	0	1.000	3.05	30	2	0	73.2	80	27	19	0	5	0	5	17	3	0	.176	2	11	0	1	0.4	1.000
1953	2 teams	WAS A (4G 0–0)	CHI A (29G 7–5)																							
″	total	7	5	.583	2.86	33	13	5	129	131	32	30	1	3	0	3	35	2	0	.057	11	36	1	1	1.5	.979
1954	CHI A	16	3	**.842**	2.69	39	17	3	154	142	35	31	2	**8**	0	3	48	11	0	.229	8	34	1	1	1.1	.977
1955		6	5	.545	2.64	44	7	3	126.1	120	18	35	0	3	3	7	29	3	0	.103	5	23	2	1	0.7	.933
1956	2 teams	CHI A (28G 1–2)	BAL A (4G 1–1)																							
″	total	2	3	.400	4.98	32	2	0	47	55	13	8	0	1	2	3	6	1	0	.167	1	9	1	0	0.3	.909
1957	2 teams	BAL A (5G 0–0)	NY N (4G 0–0)																							
″	total	0	0		2.08	9	0	0	8.2	11	1	1	0	0	0	0	0	0	0		0	2	0	0	0.2	1.000
8 yrs.		51	32	.614	3.37	248	71	24	809.1	811	246	193	5	22	10	26	218	37	0	.170	38	170	7	8	0.9	.967

Nardi Contreras

CONTRERAS, ARNALDO JUAN BB TR 6′ 2″ 193 lbs.
B. Sept. 19, 1951, Tampa, Fla.

Year	Team	W	L	PCT	ERA	G	GS	CG	IP	H	BB	SO	ShO	Relief W	Relief L	Relief SV	AB	H	HR	BA	PO	A	E	DP	TC/G	FA
1980	CHI A	0	0	—	5.79	8	0	0	14	18	7	8	0	0	0	0	0	0	0	—	1	4	2	1	0.9	.714

Jim Converse

CONVERSE, JAMES DANIEL BL TR 5′ 9″ 180 lbs.
B. Aug. 17, 1971, San Francisco, Calif.

Year	Team	Lg	W	L	PCT	ERA	G	GS	CG	IP	H	BB	SO	ShO	Relief W	Relief L	Relief SV	Batting AB	Batting H	HR	BA	PO	A	E	DP	TC/G	FA
1993	SEA	A	1	3	.250	5.31	4	4	0	20.1	23	14	10	0	0	0	0	0	0	0	—	2	6	0	0	2.0	1.000
1994			0	5	.000	8.69	13	8	0	48.2	73	40	39	0	0	0	0	0	0	0	—	3	6	1	0	0.8	.900
1995	2 teams SEA A (6G 0–3) KC A (9G 1–0)																										
″	total		1	3	.250	6.56	15	1	0	23.1	28	16	14	0	1	2	1	0	0	0	—	1	4	0	0	0.3	1.000
3 yrs.			2	11	.154	7.41	32	13	0	92.1	124	70	63	0	1	2	1	0	0	0		6	16	1	0	0.7	.957

Dick Conway

CONWAY, RICHARD BUTLER BL TR 5′ 7½″ 140 lbs.
Brother of Bill Conway.
B. Apr. 25, 1866, Lowell, Mass. D. Sept. 9, 1926, Lowell, Mass.

Year	Team	Lg	W	L	PCT	ERA	G	GS	CG	IP	H	BB	SO	ShO	Relief W	Relief L	Relief SV	Batting AB	Batting H	HR	BA	PO	A	E	DP	TC/G	FA
1886	BAL	AA	2	7	.222	*6.81*	9	9	8	76.2	106	43	64	0	0	0	0	34	7	0	.206	1	21	2	0	2.4	.917
1887	BOS	N	9	15	.375	4.66	26	26	25	222.1	249	86	45	0	0	0	0	145	36	0	.248	25	53	13	0	2.2	.857
1888			4	2	.667	2.38	6	6	6	53	49	8	12	0	0	0	0	25	4	0	.160	4	9	0	0	1.9	1.000
3 yrs.			15	24	.385	4.78	41	41	39	352	404	137	121	0	0	0	0	204	47	0	.230	30	83	15	0	2.2	.883

Jim Conway

CONWAY, JAMES P. TR
Brother of Pete Conway.
B. Oct. 8, 1858, Clifton Heights, Pa. Deceased.

Year	Team	Lg	W	L	PCT	ERA	G	GS	CG	IP	H	BB	SO	ShO	Relief W	Relief L	Relief SV	Batting AB	Batting H	HR	BA	PO	A	E	DP	TC/G	FA
1884	BKN	AA	3	9	.250	*4.44*	13	13	10	105.1	132	15	25	0	0	0	0	47	6	0	.128	5	18	12	0	2.1	.657
1885	PHI	AA	0	1	.000	7.30	2	2	1	12.1	19	2	0	0	0	0	0	6	0	0	.000	0	2	0	0	0.7	1.000
1889	KC	AA	19	19	.500	3.25	41	37	33	335	334	90	115	0	1	0	0	149	31	0	.208	10	85	7	2	2.5	.931
3 yrs.			22	29	.431	3.64	56	52	44	452.2	485	107	140	0	1	0	0	202	37	0	.183	15	105	19	2	2.3	.863

Pat Conway

CONWAY, JEROME PATRICK BL TL 6′ 2″ 190 lbs.
B. June 7, 1901, Holyoke, Mass. D. Apr. 16, 1980, Holyoke, Mass.

Year	Team	Lg	W	L	PCT	ERA	G	GS	CG	IP	H	BB	SO	ShO	Relief W	Relief L	Relief SV	Batting AB	Batting H	HR	BA	PO	A	E	DP	TC/G	FA
1920	WAS	A	0	0	—	0.00	1	0	0	2	1	1	0	0	0	0	0	0	0	0	—	0	0	0	0	0.0	.000

Pete Conway

CONWAY, PETER J. BR TR 5′10½″ 162 lbs.
Brother of Jim Conway.
B. Oct. 30, 1866, Burmont, Pa. D. Jan. 13, 1903, Clifton Heights, Pa.

Year	Team	Lg	W	L	PCT	ERA	G	GS	CG	IP	H	BB	SO	ShO	Relief W	Relief L	Relief SV	Batting AB	Batting H	HR	BA	PO	A	E	DP	TC/G	FA
1885	BUF	N	10	17	.370	*4.67*	27	27	26	210	256	44	94	1	0	0	0	90	10	1	.111	7	54	10	0	2.3	.859
1886	2 teams KC N (23G 5–15) DET N (11G 6–5)																										
″	total		11	20	.355	4.95	34	31	30	271	329	86	116	0	0	0	0	237	55	3	.232	60	58	22	3	2.1	.843
1887	DET	N	8	9	.471	2.90	17	17	16	146	132	47	40	0	0	0	0	95	22	1	.232	26	37	5	0	2.7	.926
1888			30	14	.682	2.26	45	45	43	391	315	57	176	4	0	0	0	167	46	3	.275	10	96	7	4	2.5	.938
1889	PIT	N	2	1	.667	4.91	3	3	2	22	26	16	2	0	0	0	0	10	1	1	.100	1	6	1	0	2.0	.875
5 yrs.			61	61	.500	3.59	126	123	117	1040	1058	250	428	5	0	0	0	*				104	251	45	7	2.3	.887

Joe Conzelman

CONZELMAN, JOSEPH HARRISON BR TR 6′ 170 lbs.
B. July 14, 1885, Bristol, Conn. D. Apr. 17, 1979, Mountain Brook, Ala.

Year	Team	Lg	W	L	PCT	ERA	G	GS	CG	IP	H	BB	SO	ShO	Relief W	Relief L	Relief SV	Batting AB	Batting H	HR	BA	PO	A	E	DP	TC/G	FA
1913	PIT	N	0	1	.000	1.20	3	2	1	15	13	5	9	0	0	0	0	4	0	0	.000	0	4	0	0	1.3	1.000
1914			5	6	.455	2.94	33	9	4	101	88	40	39	1	2	2	1	27	3	0	.111	4	33	0	1	1.1	1.000
1915			1	1	.500	3.42	18	1	0	47.1	41	20	22	0	1	0	0	11	1	0	.091	0	16	1	0	0.9	.941
3 yrs.			6	8	.429	2.92	54	12	5	163.1	142	65	70	1	3	2	1	42	4	0	.095	4	53	1	1	1.1	.983

Andy Cook

COOK, ANDREW BERNARD BR TR 6′ 5″ 205 lbs.
B. Aug. 30, 1967, Memphis, Tenn.

Year	Team	Lg	W	L	PCT	ERA	G	GS	CG	IP	H	BB	SO	ShO	Relief W	Relief L	Relief SV	Batting AB	Batting H	HR	BA	PO	A	E	DP	TC/G	FA
1993	NY	A	0	1	.000	5.06	4	0	0	5.1	4	7	4	0	0	1	0	0	0	0	—	0	1	0	0	0.3	1.000

Dennis Cook

COOK, DENNIS BRYAN BL TL 6′ 3″ 185 lbs.
B. Oct. 4, 1962, LaMarque, Tex.

Year	Team	Lg	W	L	PCT	ERA	G	GS	CG	IP	H	BB	SO	ShO	Relief W	Relief L	Relief SV	Batting AB	Batting H	HR	BA	PO	A	E	DP	TC/G	FA
1988	SF	N	2	1	.667	2.86	4	4	1	22	9	11	13	1	0	0	0	4	0	0	.000	0	1	0	0	0.3	1.000
1989	2 teams SF N (2G 1–0) PHI N (21G 6–8)																										
″	total		7	8	.467	3.72	23	18	2	121	110	38	67	1	1	0	0	42	9	0	.214	4	16	3	0	1.0	.870
1990	2 teams PHI N (42G 8–3) LA N (5G 1–1)																										
″	total		9	4	.692	3.92	47	16	2	156	155	56	64	1	3	1	1	49	15	1	.306	10	22	0	1	0.7	1.000
1991	LA	N	1	0	1.000	0.51	20	1	0	17.2	12	7	8	0	0	0	0	1	0	0	.000	0	4	0	0	0.2	1.000
1992	CLE	A	5	7	.417	3.82	32	25	1	158	156	50	96	0	0	1	0	0	0	0	—	3	15	1	2	0.6	.947
1993			5	5	.500	5.67	25	6	0	54	62	16	34	0	4	2	0	0	0	0	—	2	6	2	1	0.4	.800
1994	CHI	A	3	1	.750	3.55	38	0	0	33	29	14	26	0	3	1	0	0	0	0	—	2	2	0	0	0.1	1.000
1995	2 teams CLE A (11G 0–0) TEX A (35G 0–2)																										
″	total		0	2	.000	4.53	46	1	0	57.2	63	26	53	0	0	1	2	0	0	0	—	0	6	0	0	0.1	1.000
8 yrs.			32	28	.533	3.91	235	71	6	619.1	596	218	361	3	11	6	3	96	24	1	.250	21	72	6	4	0.4	.939

Earl Cook

COOK, EARL DAVIS BR TR 6′ 195 lbs.
B. Dec. 10, 1908, Stouffville, Ont., Canada.

Year	Team	Lg	W	L	PCT	ERA	G	GS	CG	IP	H	BB	SO	ShO	Relief W	Relief L	Relief SV	Batting AB	Batting H	HR	BA	PO	A	E	DP	TC/G	FA
1941	DET	A	0	0	—	4.50	1	0	0	2	4	0	1	0	0	0	0	0	0	0	—	0	0	0	0	0.0	.000

Glen Cook

COOK, GLEN PATRICK BR TR 5′11″ 180 lbs.
B. Sept. 8, 1959, Buffalo, N. Y.

Year	Team	Lg	W	L	PCT	ERA	G	GS	CG	IP	H	BB	SO	ShO	Relief W	Relief L	Relief SV	Batting AB	Batting H	HR	BA	PO	A	E	DP	TC/G	FA
1985	TEX	A	2	3	.400	9.45	9	7	0	40	53	18	19	0	0	0	0	0	0	0	—	3	2	1	1	0.7	.833

Mike Cook

COOK, MICHAEL HORACE BR TR 6′ 3″ 200 lbs.
B. Aug. 14, 1963, Charleston, S. C.

Year	Team	Lg	W	L	PCT	ERA	G	GS	CG	IP	H	BB	SO	ShO	Relief W	Relief L	Relief SV	Batting AB	Batting H	HR	BA	PO	A	E	DP	TC/G	FA
1986	CAL	A	0	2	.000	9.00	5	1	0	9	13	7	6	0	0	1	0	0	0	0	—	0	2	0	0	0.4	1.000
1987			1	2	.333	5.50	16	1	0	34.1	34	18	27	0	1	1	0	0	0	0	—	4	8	0	1	0.8	1.000
1988			0	1	.000	4.91	3	0	0	3.2	4	1	2	0	0	1	0	0	0	0	—	0	0	0	0	0.0	.000
1989	MIN	A	0	1	.000	5.06	15	0	0	21.1	22	17	15	0	0	1	0	0	0	0	—	2	0	0	0	0.1	1.000
1993	BAL	A	0	0	—	0.00	2	0	0	3	1	2	3	0	0	0	0	0	0	0	—	0	0	0	0	0.0	.000
5 yrs.			1	6	.143	5.55	41	2	0	71.1	74	45	53	0	1	4	0	0	0	0		6	10	0	1	0.4	1.000

Rollin Cook

COOK, ROLLIN EDWARD BR TR 5′ 9″ 160 lbs.
B. Oct. 5, 1890, Toledo, Ohio D. Aug. 11, 1975, Toledo, Ohio.

Year	Team	Lg	W	L	PCT	ERA	G	GS	CG	IP	H	BB	SO	ShO	Relief W	Relief L	Relief SV	Batting AB	Batting H	HR	BA	PO	A	E	DP	TC/G	FA
1915	STL	A	0	0	—	7.24	5	0	0	13.2	16	9	7	0	0	0	0	4	1	0	.250	0	6	0	0	1.2	1.000

Ron Cook

COOK, RONALD WAYNE BL TL 6′ 1″ 175 lbs.
B. July 11, 1947, Jefferson, Tex.

Year	Team	Lg	W	L	PCT	ERA	G	GS	CG	IP	H	BB	SO	ShO	Relief W	Relief L	Relief SV	Batting AB	Batting H	Batting HR	BA	PO	A	E	DP	TC/G	FA
1970	HOU	N	4	4	.500	3.73	41	7	0	82	80	42	50	0	3	1	2	17	4	0	.235	3	13	2	1	0.4	.889
1971			0	4	.000	4.85	5	4	0	26	23	8	10	0	0	0	0	8	2	0	.250	1	5	1	0	1.4	.857
2 yrs.			4	8	.333	4.00	46	11	0	108	103	50	60	0	3	1	2	25	6	0	.240	4	18	3	1	0.5	.880

Steve Cooke

COOKE, STEVEN MONTAGUE BR TL 6′ 6″ 220 lbs.
B. Jan. 14, 1970, Lihue, Hawaii.

Year	Team	Lg	W	L	PCT	ERA	G	GS	CG	IP	H	BB	SO	ShO	Relief W	Relief L	Relief SV	Batting AB	Batting H	Batting HR	BA	PO	A	E	DP	TC/G	FA
1992	PIT	N	2	0	1.000	3.52	11	0	0	23	22	4	10	0	2	0	1	3	1	0	.333	0	3	0	0	0.3	1.000
1993			10	10	.500	3.89	32	32	3	210.2	207	59	132	1	0	0	0	71	11	0	.155	7	23	3	0	1.0	.909
1994			4	11	.267	5.02	25	23	2	134.1	157	46	74	0	1	0	0	42	8	0	.190	3	16	1	1	0.8	.950
3 yrs.			16	21	.432	4.28	68	55	5	368	386	109	216	1	3	0	1	116	20	0	.172	10	42	4	1	0.8	.929

Bobby Coombs

COOMBS, RAYMOND FRANKLIN BR TR 5′ 9½″ 160 lbs.
B. Feb. 2, 1908, Goodwins Mills, Me. D. Oct. 21, 1991, Ogunquit, Me.

Year	Team	Lg	W	L	PCT	ERA	G	GS	CG	IP	H	BB	SO	ShO	Relief W	Relief L	Relief SV	Batting AB	Batting H	Batting HR	BA	PO	A	E	DP	TC/G	FA
1933	PHI	A	0	1	.000	7.47	21	0	0	31.1	47	20	8	0	0	1	2	5	2	0	.400	2	5	0	0	0.3	1.000
1943	NY	N	0	1	.000	12.94	9	0	0	16	33	8	5	0	0	1	0	2	0	0	.000	0	6	1	0	0.8	.857
2 yrs.			0	2	.000	9.32	30	0	0	47.1	80	28	13	0	0	2	2	7	2	0	.286	2	11	1	0	0.5	.929

Danny Coombs

COOMBS, DANIEL BERNARD BR TL 6′ 4″ 200 lbs.
B. Mar. 23, 1942, Lincoln, Me. BL 1967

Year	Team	Lg	W	L	PCT	ERA	G	GS	CG	IP	H	BB	SO	ShO	Relief W	Relief L	Relief SV	Batting AB	Batting H	Batting HR	BA	PO	A	E	DP	TC/G	FA
1963	HOU	N	0	0	—	27.00	1	0	0	0.1	3	0	0	0	0	0	0	0	0	0	—	0	1	0	0	1.0	1.000
1964			1	1	.500	5.00	7	1	0	18	21	10	14	0	0	1	0	4	0	0	.000	0	2	0	0	0.3	1.000
1965			0	2	.000	4.79	26	3	0	47	54	23	35	0	0	0	0	9	1	0	.111	4	10	1	1	0.6	.933
1966			0	0	—	3.38	2	0	0	2.2	4	0	3	0	0	0	0	1	0	0	.000	0	0	0	0	0.0	.000
1967			3	0	1.000	3.33	6	2	0	24.1	21	9	23	0	3	0	0	8	1	0	.125	0	6	0	0	1.0	1.000
1968			4	3	.571	3.28	40	2	0	46.2	52	17	29	0	3	2	2	10	4	0	.400	2	11	1	1	0.3	.929
1969			0	1	.000	6.75	8	0	0	8	12	2	3	0	0	1	0	2	0	0	.000	0	0	0	0	0.0	.000
1970	SD	N	10	14	.417	3.30	35	27	5	188	185	76	105	1	2	1	0	52	5	0	.096	4	20	0	1	0.7	1.000
1971			1	6	.143	6.21	19	7	0	58	81	25	37	0	0	2	0	14	3	0	.214	2	15	0	1	0.9	1.000
9 yrs.			19	27	.413	4.08	144	42	5	393	433	162	249	1	8	7	2	100	14	0	.140	12	65	2	4	0.5	.975

Jack Coombs

COOMBS, JOHN WESLEY (Cy) BB TR 6′ 185 lbs.
B. Nov. 18, 1882, LeGrand, Iowa D. Apr. 15, 1957, Palestine, Tex.
Manager 1919.

Year	Team	Lg	W	L	PCT	ERA	G	GS	CG	IP	H	BB	SO	ShO	Relief W	Relief L	Relief SV	Batting AB	Batting H	Batting HR	BA	PO	A	E	DP	TC/G	FA
1906	PHI	A	10	10	.500	2.50	23	18	13	173	144	68	90	1	2	**2**	0	67	16	0	.239	16	44	2	4	2.7	.968
1907			6	9	.400	3.12	23	17	10	132.2	109	64	73	2	0	0	2	48	8	1	.167	9	37	1	2	2.0	.979
1908			7	5	.583	2.00	26	18	10	153	130	64	80	4	1	0	0	220	56	1	.255	102	48	4	4	2.1	.974
1909			12	11	.522	2.32	31	24	19	205.2	156	73	97	6	0	**3**	1	83	14	0	.169	12	60	2	2	2.4	.973
1910			**31**	9	.775	1.30	**45**	38	35	353	248	115	224	**13**	4	1	1	132	29	0	.220	19	77	1	2	2.2	.990
1911			**28**	12	.700	3.53	47	**40**	26	336.2	**360**	119	185	1	3	1	2	141	45	2	.319	24	71	9	3	2.2	.913
1912			21	10	.677	3.29	40	32	23	262.1	227	94	120	1	3	0	2	110	28	0	.255	16	66	0	4	2.0	1.000
1913			0	0	—	10.13	2	2	0	5.1	5	6	0	0	0	0	0	3	1	0	.333	1	0	1	0	1.0	.500
1914			0	1	.000	4.50	2	2	0	8	8	3	1	0	0	0	0	11	3	0	.273	4	1	0	0	1.3	1.000
1915	BKN	N	15	10	.600	2.58	29	24	17	195.2	166	91	56	2	2	1	0	75	21	0	.280	17	31	1	2	1.7	.980
1916			13	8	.619	2.66	27	20	10	159	136	44	47	3	2	0	0	61	11	0	.180	7	15	0	1	0.8	1.000
1917			7	11	.389	3.96	31	14	9	141	147	49	34	0	3	2	0	44	10	0	.227	8	26	1	1	1.1	.971
1918			8	14	.364	3.81	27	20	16	189	191	49	44	2	1	0	0	113	19	0	.168	20	41	3	0	1.6	.953
1920	DET	A	0	0	—	3.18	2	0	0	5.2	7	2	1	0	0	0	0	2	0	0	.000	0	1	0	0	0.5	1.000
14 yrs.			158	110	.590	2.78	355	269	188	2320	2034	841	1052	35	21	10	8	*				255	518	25	25	1.9	.969
WORLD SERIES																											
1910	PHI	A	3	0	1.000	3.33	3	3	3	27	23	14	17	0	0	0	0	13	5	0	.385	1	4	2	0	2.3	.714
1911			1	0	1.000	1.35	2	2	1	20	11	6	16	0	0	0	0	8	2	0	.250	1	2	0	0	1.5	1.000
1916	BKN	N	1	0	1.000	4.26	1	1	0	6.1	7	1	1	0	0	0	0	3	1	0	.333	0	2	0	0	2.0	1.000
3 yrs.			5	0	1.000	2.70	6	6	4	53.1	41	21	34	0	0	0	0	*				2	8	2	0	2.0	.833
			8th		**1st**																						

William Coon

COON, WILLIAM K.
B. Mar. 21, 1855, Philadelphia, Pa. D. Aug. 30, 1915, Burlington, N. J.

Year	Team	Lg	W	L	PCT	ERA	G	GS	CG	IP	H	BB	SO	ShO	Relief W	Relief L	Relief SV	Batting AB	Batting H	Batting HR	BA	PO	A	E	DP	TC/G	FA
1876	PHI	N	0	0	—	5.14	2	0	0	7	9	0	0	0	0	0	0	*				106	31	60	2	3.5	.695

Bill Cooney

COONEY, WILLIAM A. TR
B. Apr. 7, 1883, Boston, Mass. D. Nov. 6, 1928, Roxbury, Mass.

Year	Team	Lg	W	L	PCT	ERA	G	GS	CG	IP	H	BB	SO	ShO	Relief W	Relief L	Relief SV	Batting AB	Batting H	Batting HR	BA	PO	A	E	DP	TC/G	FA
1909	BOS	N	0	0	—	1.42	3	0	0	6.1	4	2	3	0	0	0	0	*				2	6	1	0	1.8	.889

Bob Cooney

COONEY, ROBERT DANIEL BR TR 5′11″ 160 lbs.
B. July 12, 1907, Glens Falls, N. Y. D. May 4, 1976, Glens Falls, N. Y.

Year	Team	Lg	W	L	PCT	ERA	G	GS	CG	IP	H	BB	SO	ShO	Relief W	Relief L	Relief SV	Batting AB	Batting H	Batting HR	BA	PO	A	E	DP	TC/G	FA
1931	STL	A	0	3	.000	4.12	5	4	1	39.1	46	20	13	0	0	0	0	13	5	0	.385	2	6	0	0	1.6	1.000
1932			1	2	.333	6.97	23	3	1	71	94	36	23	0	0	0	1	22	0	0	.000	3	5	0	1	0.3	1.000
2 yrs.			1	5	.167	5.95	28	7	2	110.1	140	56	36	0	0	0	1	35	5	0	.143	5	11	0	1	0.6	1.000

Johnny Cooney

COONEY, JOHN WALTER BR TL 5′10″ 165 lbs.
Son of Jimmy Cooney. Brother of Jimmy Cooney.
B. Mar. 18, 1901, Cranston, R. I. D. July 8, 1986, Sarasota, Fla.
Manager 1949.

Year	Team	Lg	W	L	PCT	ERA	G	GS	CG	IP	H	BB	SO	ShO	Relief W	Relief L	Relief SV	Batting AB	Batting H	Batting HR	BA	PO	A	E	DP	TC/G	FA
1921	BOS	N	0	1	.000	3.92	8	1	0	20.2	19	10	9	0	0	0	0	5	1	0	.200	2	5	0	0	0.9	1.000
1922			1	2	.333	2.16	4	3	1	25	19	6	7	0	0	0	0	8	0	0	.000	1	6	0	1	1.8	1.000
1923			3	5	.375	3.31	23	8	5	98	92	22	23	2	0	0	0	66	25	0	.379	34	17	0	1	1.5	1.000
1924			8	9	.471	3.18	34	19	12	181	176	50	67	2	0	0	2	130	33	0	.254	70	33	5	3	2.2	.954
1925			14	14	.500	3.48	31	29	20	245.2	267	50	65	2	2	0	0	103	33	0	.320	32	61	5	10	2.8	.949
1926			3	3	.500	4.00	19	8	3	83.1	106	29	23	1	1	1	0	126	38	0	.302	251	45	3	28	5.8	.990
1928			3	7	.300	4.32	24	6	2	89.2	106	31	18	0	2	2	1	41	7	0	.171	29	32	1	5	2.1	.984
1929			2	3	.400	5.00	14	2	1	45	57	22	11	0	1	3	3	72	23	0	.319	49	16	1	2	2.2	.985
1930			0	0	—	18.00	2	0	0	7	16	3	1	0	0	0	0	3	0	0	.000	0	4	0	0	2.0	1.000
9 yrs.			34	44	.436	3.72	159	76	44	795.1	858	223	224	7	6	6	6	*				2534	291	35	90	2.7	.988

Cal Cooper

COOPER, CALVIN ASA BR TR 6′ 2½″ 180 lbs.
B. Aug. 11, 1922, Great Falls, S. C.

Year	Team	Lg	W	L	PCT	ERA	G	GS	CG	IP	H	BB	SO	ShO	Relief W	Relief L	Relief SV	AB	H	HR	BA	PO	A	E	DP	TC/G	FA
1948	WAS	A	0	0	—	45.00	1	0	0	1	5	1	0	0	0	0	0	0	0	0	—	0	0	0	0	0.0	.000

Don Cooper

COOPER, DONALD JAMES BR TR 6′ 1″ 185 lbs.
B. Feb. 15, 1956, New York, N. Y.

Year	Team	Lg	W	L	PCT	ERA	G	GS	CG	IP	H	BB	SO	ShO	Relief W	Relief L	Relief SV	AB	H	HR	BA	PO	A	E	DP	TC/G	FA
1981	MIN	A	1	5	.167	4.27	27	2	0	59	61	32	33	0	1	3	0	0	0	0	—	1	6	0	0	0.3	1.000
1982			0	1	.000	9.53	6	1	0	11.1	14	11	5	0	0	0	0	0	0	0	—	1	1	0	0	0.3	1.000
1983	TOR	A	0	0	—	6.75	4	0	0	5.1	8	0	5	0	0	0	0	0	0	0	—	0	0	0	0	0.0	.000
1985	NY	A	0	0	—	5.40	7	0	0	10	12	3	4	0	0	0	0	0	0	0	—	0	0	0	0	0.0	.000
4 yrs.			1	6	.143	5.25	44	3	0	85.2	95	46	47	0	1	3	0	0	0	0		2	7	0	0	0.2	1.000

Guy Cooper

COOPER, GUY EVANS (Rebel) BB TR 6′ 1″ 185 lbs.
B. Jan. 28, 1893, Rome, Ga. D. Aug. 2, 1951, Santa Monica, Calif.

Year	Team	Lg	W	L	PCT	ERA	G	GS	CG	IP	H	BB	SO	ShO	Relief W	Relief L	Relief SV	AB	H	HR	BA	PO	A	E	DP	TC/G	FA
1914	2 teams	NY A (1G 0–0) BOS A (9G 1–0)																									
″	total		1	0	1.000	5.76	10	1	0	25	26	11	8	0	0	0	0	8	0	0	.000	0	4	0	0	0.4	1.000
1915	BOS	A	0	0	—	0.00	1	0	0	2	0	2	0	0	0	0	0	0	0	0	—	1	0	0	0	1.0	1.000
2 yrs.			1	0	1.000	5.33	11	1	0	27	26	13	8	0	0	0	0	8	0	0	.000	1	4	0	0	0.5	1.000

Mort Cooper

COOPER, MORTON CECIL BR TR 6′ 2″ 210 lbs.
Brother of Walker Cooper.
B. Mar. 2, 1913, Atherton, Mo. D. Nov. 17, 1958, Little Rock, Ark.

Year	Team	Lg	W	L	PCT	ERA	G	GS	CG	IP	H	BB	SO	ShO	Relief W	Relief L	Relief SV	AB	H	HR	BA	PO	A	E	DP	TC/G	FA
1938	STL	N	2	1	.667	3.04	4	3	1	23.2	17	12	11	0	0	0	1	9	2	0	.222	2	8	1	0	2.8	.909
1939			12	6	.667	3.25	45	26	7	210.2	208	97	130	2	2	0	4	69	16	2	.232	7	25	3	0	0.8	.914
1940			11	12	.478	3.63	38	29	16	230.2	225	86	95	3	1	0	3	83	13	0	.157	4	38	2	1	1.2	.955
1941			13	9	.591	3.91	29	25	12	186.2	175	69	118	0	1	0	0	70	13	0	.186	6	32	1	3	1.3	.974
1942			**22**	7	.759	**1.78**	37	35	22	278.2	207	68	152	**10**	0	1	0	103	19	0	.184	6	44	2	3	1.4	.962
1943			**21**	8	**.724**	2.30	37	32	24	274	228	79	141	6	1	1	3	100	17	1	.170	7	46	3	3	1.5	.946
1944			22	7	.759	2.46	34	33	22	252.1	227	60	97	**7**	0	0	1	94	19	0	.202	4	28	0	1	0.9	1.000
1945	2 teams	STL N (4G 2–0) BOS N (20G 7–4)																									
″	total		9	4	.692	2.92	24	14	5	101.2	97	34	59	1	3	2	1	32	8	1	.250	3	17	2	3	0.9	.909
1946	BOS	N	13	11	.542	3.12	28	27	15	199	181	39	83	4	0	0	1	67	14	1	.209	6	25	2	3	1.2	.939
1947	2 teams	BOS N (10G 2–5) NY N (8G 1–5)																									
″	total		3	10	.231	5.40	18	15	4	83.1	99	26	27	0	1	0	0	27	6	1	.222	5	7	0	0	0.7	1.000
1949	CHI	N	0	0	—	∞	1	0	0		2	1	0	0	0	0	0	0	0	0	—	0	0	0	0	0.0	.000
11 yrs.			128	75	.631	2.97	295	239	128	1840.2	1666	571	913	33	9	4	14	654	127	6	.194	50	270	16	17	1.1	.952
WORLD SERIES																											
1942	STL	N	0	1	.000	5.54	2	2	0	13	17	4	9	0	0	0	0	5	1	0	.200	0	1	0	0	0.5	1.000
1943			1	1	.500	2.81	2	2	1	16	11	3	10	0	0	0	0	5	0	0	.000	0	1	0	0	0.5	1.000
1944			1	1	.500	1.13	2	2	1	16	9	5	16	1	0	0	0	4	0	0	.000	0	6	0	0	3.0	1.000
3 yrs.			2	3	.400	3.00	6	6	2	45	37	12	35	1	0	0	0	14	1	0	.071	0	8	0	0	1.3	1.000

Pat Cooper

COOPER, ORGE PATTERSON BR TR 6′ 3″ 180 lbs.
B. Nov. 26, 1917, Albermarle, N. C. D. Mar. 15, 1993, Charlotte, N. C.

Year	Team	Lg	W	L	PCT	ERA	G	GS	CG	IP	H	BB	SO	ShO	Relief W	Relief L	Relief SV	AB	H	HR	BA	PO	A	E	DP	TC/G	FA
1946	PHI	A	0	0	—	0.00	1	0	0	1	1	1	0	0	0	0	0	*				0	1	0	0	1.0	1.000

Wilbur Cooper

COOPER, ARLEY WILBUR BR TL 5′11″ 175 lbs.
B. Feb. 24, 1892, Bearsville, W. Va. D. Aug. 7, 1973, Encino, Calif.

Year	Team	Lg	W	L	PCT	ERA	G	GS	CG	IP	H	BB	SO	ShO	Relief W	Relief L	Relief SV	AB	H	HR	BA	PO	A	E	DP	TC/G	FA
1912	PIT	N	3	0	1.000	1.66	6	4	3	38	32	15	30	2	0	0	0	13	2	0	.154	0	8	0	0	1.3	1.000
1913			5	3	.625	3.29	30	9	3	93	98	45	39	1	3	1	0	26	2	0	.077	0	18	2	1	0.7	.900
1914			16	15	.516	2.13	40	34	19	266.2	246	79	102	0	0	1	0	92	19	0	.207	12	72	8	2	2.3	.913
1915			5	16	.238	3.30	38	21	11	185.2	180	52	71	1	1	0	4	60	7	0	.117	6	58	6	0	1.8	.914
1916			12	11	.522	1.87	42	23	16	246	189	74	111	2	4	0	2	79	17	0	.215	15	58	5	2	1.8	.936
1917			17	11	.607	2.36	40	34	23	297.2	276	54	99	7	1	0	1	103	21	0	.204	11	71	4	4	2.1	.953
1918			19	14	.576	2.11	38	29	26	273.1	219	65	117	3	4	1	**3**	95	23	0	.242	4	68	0	0	1.9	1.000
1919			19	13	.594	2.67	35	32	**27**	286.2	229	74	106	4	1	0	1	101	29	0	.287	4	63	5	0	2.1	.931
1920			24	15	.615	2.39	44	37	28	327	307	52	114	3	2	1	2	113	25	0	.221	11	75	1	2	2.0	.989
1921			**22**	14	.611	3.25	38	**38**	29	**327**	**341**	80	134	2	0	0	0	122	31	0	.254	10	68	3	4	2.1	.963
1922			23	14	.622	3.18	41	36	**27**	294.2	330	61	129	4	0	1	0	108	29	4	.269	7	55	0	5	1.5	1.000
1923			17	**19**	.472	3.57	39	**38**	26	294.2	331	71	77	1	1	0	0	107	28	0	.262	11	63	2	2	1.9	.974
1924			20	14	.588	3.28	38	35	25	268.2	296	40	62	**4**	1	0	1	104	36	0	.346	6	51	4	4	1.6	.934
1925	CHI	N	12	14	.462	4.28	32	26	13	212.1	249	61	41	0	3	1	0	82	17	2	.207	4	42	1	1	1.5	.979
1926	2 teams	CHI N (8G 2–1) DET A (8G 0–4)																									
″	total		2	5	.286	5.77	16	11	3	68.2	92	30	20	2	0	1	0	22	7	0	.318	1	15	1	0	1.1	.941
15 yrs.			216	178	.548	2.89	517	407	279	3480	3415	853	1252	36	21	7	14	1227	293	6	.239	102	785	42	27	1.8	.955

Mays Copeland

COPELAND, MAYS BR TR 6′ 180 lbs.
B. Aug. 31, 1913, Mountain View, Ark. D. Nov. 29, 1982, Indio, Calif.

Year	Team	Lg	W	L	PCT	ERA	G	GS	CG	IP	H	BB	SO	ShO	Relief W	Relief L	Relief SV	AB	H	HR	BA	PO	A	E	DP	TC/G	FA
1935	STL	N	0	0	—	13.50	1	0	0	0.2	2	0	0	0	0	0	0	0	0	0	—	0	1	1	0	2.0	.500

Henry Coppola

COPPOLA, HENRY PETER BR TR 5′11″ 175 lbs.
B. Aug. 6, 1912, East Douglas, Mass. D. July 10, 1990, Norfolk, Mass.

Year	Team	Lg	W	L	PCT	ERA	G	GS	CG	IP	H	BB	SO	ShO	Relief W	Relief L	Relief SV	AB	H	HR	BA	PO	A	E	DP	TC/G	FA
1935	WAS	A	3	4	.429	5.92	19	5	2	59.1	72	29	19	1	1	2	0	14	1	0	.071	2	11	1	0	0.7	.929
1936			0	0	—	4.50	6	0	0	14	17	12	2	0	0	0	1	3	1	0	.333	1	4	0	0	0.8	1.000
2 yrs.			3	4	.429	5.65	25	5	2	73.1	89	41	21	1	1	2	1	17	2	0	.118	3	15	1	0	0.8	.947

Doug Corbett

CORBETT, DOUGLAS MITCHELL BR TR 6′ 1″ 185 lbs.
B. Nov. 4, 1952, Sarasota, Fla.

Year	Team	Lg	W	L	PCT	ERA	G	GS	CG	IP	H	BB	SO	ShO	Relief W	Relief L	Relief SV	AB	H	HR	BA	PO	A	E	DP	TC/G	FA
1980	MIN	A	8	6	.571	1.99	73	0	0	136	102	42	89	0	8	6	23	0	0	0	—	13	31	1	1	0.6	.978
1981			2	6	.250	2.56	**54**	0	0	88	80	34	60	0	2	6	17	0	0	0	—	7	22	2	0	0.6	.935
1982	2 teams	MIN A (10G 0–2) CAL A (33G 1–7)																									
″	total		1	9	.100	5.13	43	0	0	79	73	35	52	0	1	9	11	0	0	0		13	12	1	0	0.6	.962
1983	CAL	A	1	1	.500	3.63	11	0	0	17.1	26	4	18	0	1	1	0	0	0	0	—	0	1	0	0	0.1	1.000
1984			5	1	.833	2.12	45	1	0	85	76	30	48	0	4	1	4	0	0	0	—	4	13	0	0	0.4	1.000

Doug Corbett *continued*

Year	Team	Lg	W	L	PCT	ERA	G	GS	CG	IP	H	BB	SO	ShO	Relief W	Relief L	Relief SV	Batting AB	Batting H	HR	BA	PO	A	E	DP	TC/G	FA
1985			3	3	.500	4.89	30	0	0	46	49	20	24	0	3	3	0	0	0	0	—	1	9	1	0	0.4	.909
1986			4	2	.667	3.66	46	0	0	78.2	66	22	36	0	4	2	10	0	0	0	—	8	15	0	3	0.5	1.000
1987	**BAL**	**A**	0	2	.000	7.83	11	0	0	23	25	13	16	0	0	2	1	0	0	0	—	2	5	0	2	0.6	1.000
8 yrs.			24	30	.444	3.32	313	1	0	553	497	200	343	0	23	30	66	0	0	0		48	108	5	6	0.5	.969
LEAGUE CHAMPIONSHIP SERIES																											
1986	**CAL**	**A**	1	0	1.000	5.40	3	0	0	6.2	9	2	2	0	1	0	0	0	0	0	—	0	1	0	0	0.3	1.000

Joe Corbett

CORBETT, JOSEPH A. BR TR 5′10″
B. Dec. 4, 1875, San Francisco, Calif. D. May 2, 1945, San Francisco, Calif.

Year	Team	Lg	W	L	PCT	ERA	G	GS	CG	IP	H	BB	SO	ShO	Relief W	Relief L	Relief SV	Batting AB	Batting H	HR	BA	PO	A	E	DP	TC/G	FA
1895	**WAS**	**N**	0	2	.000	5.68	3	3	3	19	26	9	3	0	0	0	0	15	2	0	.133	4	7	4	0	2.1	.733
1896	**BAL**	**N**	3	0	1.000	2.20	8	3	3	41	31	17	28	0	0	0	1	22	6	0	.273	4	5	1	0	1.1	.900
1897			24	8	.750	3.11	37	37	34	313	330	115	149	1	0	0	0	150	37	0	.247	21	76	17	1	2.9	.851
1904	**STL**	**N**	5	9	.357	4.39	14	14	12	108.2	110	51	68	0	0	0	0	43	9	0	.209	9	28	5	2	3.0	.881
4 yrs.			32	19	.627	3.42	62	57	52	481.2	497	192	248	1	0	0	1	230	54	0	.235	38	116	27	3	2.6	.851

Sherman Corbett

CORBETT, SHERMAN STANLEY BL TL 6′ 4″ 205 lbs.
B. Nov. 3, 1962, New Braunfels, Tex.

Year	Team	Lg	W	L	PCT	ERA	G	GS	CG	IP	H	BB	SO	ShO	Relief W	Relief L	Relief SV	Batting AB	Batting H	HR	BA	PO	A	E	DP	TC/G	FA
1988	**CAL**	**A**	2	1	.667	4.14	34	0	0	45.2	47	23	28	0	2	1	1	0	0	0	—	1	7	1	0	0.3	.889
1989			0	0	—	3.38	4	0	0	5.1	3	1	3	0	0	0	0	0	0	0	—	0	0	0	0	0.0	.000
1990			0	0	—	9.00	4	0	0	5	8	3	2	0	0	0	0	0	0	0	—	0	0	0	0	0.0	.000
3 yrs.			2	1	.667	4.50	42	0	0	56	58	27	33	0	2	1	1	0	0	0		1	7	1	0	0.2	.889

Archie Corbin

CORBIN, ARCHIE RAY BR TR 6′ 4″ 190 lbs.
B. Dec. 30, 1967, Beaumont, Tex.

Year	Team	Lg	W	L	PCT	ERA	G	GS	CG	IP	H	BB	SO	ShO	Relief W	Relief L	Relief SV	Batting AB	Batting H	HR	BA	PO	A	E	DP	TC/G	FA
1991	**KC**	**A**	0	0	—	3.86	2	0	0	2.1	3	2	1	0	0	0	0	0	0	0	—	0	0	0	0	0.0	.000

Ray Corbin

CORBIN, ALTON RAY BR TR 6′ 2″ 200 lbs.
B. Feb. 12, 1949, Live Oak, Fla.

Year	Team	Lg	W	L	PCT	ERA	G	GS	CG	IP	H	BB	SO	ShO	Relief W	Relief L	Relief SV	Batting AB	Batting H	HR	BA	PO	A	E	DP	TC/G	FA
1971	**MIN**	**A**	8	11	.421	4.11	52	11	2	140	141	70	83	0	6	4	3	34	7	0	.206	7	30	2	0	0.8	.949
1972			8	9	.471	2.61	31	19	5	162	135	53	83	3	2	0	0	49	4	0	.082	12	16	4	1	1.0	.875
1973			8	5	.615	3.03	51	7	1	148.1	124	60	83	0	4	5	14	0	0	0	—	13	16	2	0	0.6	.935
1974			7	6	.538	5.30	29	15	1	112	133	40	50	0	3	1	0	0	0	0	—	11	21	3	1	1.2	.914
1975			5	7	.417	5.12	18	11	3	89.2	105	38	49	0	2	0	0	0	0	0	—	6	16	2	2	1.3	.917
5 yrs.			36	38	.486	3.84	181	63	12	652	638	261	348	3	17	10	17	83	11	0	.133	49	99	13	4	0.9	.919

John Corcoran

CORCORAN, JOHN H.
B. 1860, Lowell, Mass. Deceased.

Year	Team	Lg	W	L	PCT	ERA	G	GS	CG	IP	H	BB	SO	ShO	Relief W	Relief L	Relief SV	Batting AB	Batting H	HR	BA	PO	A	E	DP	TC/G	FA
1884	**BKN**	**AA**	0	0	—	0.00	1	0	0	1	0	1	0	0	0	0	0	*				205	77	42	5	6.0	.870

Larry Corcoran

CORCORAN, LAWRENCE J. BL TR 120 lbs.
Brother of Mike Corcoran.
B. Aug. 10, 1859, Brooklyn, N. Y. D. Oct. 14, 1891, Newark, N. J.

Year	Team	Lg	W	L	PCT	ERA	G	GS	CG	IP	H	BB	SO	ShO	Relief W	Relief L	Relief SV	Batting AB	Batting H	HR	BA	PO	A	E	DP	TC/G	FA
1880	**CHI**	**N**	43	14	.754	1.95	63	60	57	536.1	404	**99**	**268**	4	0	0	2	286	66	0	.231	42	146	13	4	2.5	.935
1881			**31**	14	.689	2.31	45	44	43	396.2	380	78	150	4	**1**	0	0	189	42	0	.222	31	70	11	0	2.3	.902
1882			27	12	**.692**	**1.95**	39	39	38	355.2	281	63	170	3	0	0	0	169	35	1	.207	22	64	8	1	2.3	.915
1883			34	20	.630	*2.49*	56	53	51	473.2	483	82	216	3	1	0	0	263	55	0	.209	56	94	21	4	2.3	.877
1884			35	23	.603	*2.40*	60	59	57	516.2	473	116	272	7	0	**1**	0	251	61	1	.243	51	142	25	5	3.3	.885
1885	**2 teams**	**CHI N** (7G 5–2) **NY N** (3G 2–1)																									
″	**total**		7	3	.700	3.42	10	10	8	84.1	87	35	20	1	0	0	0	36	11	0	.306	6	24	2	2	2.9	.938
1886	**WAS**	**N**	0	1	.000	5.79	2	1	1	14	16	4	3	0	0	0	0	85	15	0	.176	21	33	22	4	3.3	.711
1887	**IND**	**N**	0	2	.000	12.60	2	2	1	15	23	19	4	0	0	0	0	10	2	0	.200	3	4	0	0	1.8	1.000
8 yrs.			177	89	.665	2.36	277	268	256	2392.1	2147	496	1103	22	2	1	2	*				232	577	102	20	2.6	.888
					6th																						

Mike Corcoran

CORCORAN, MICHAEL
Brother of Larry Corcoran.
B. Brooklyn, N. Y. Deceased.

Year	Team	Lg	W	L	PCT	ERA	G	GS	CG	IP	H	BB	SO	ShO	Relief W	Relief L	Relief SV	Batting AB	Batting H	HR	BA	PO	A	E	DP	TC/G	FA
1884	**CHI**	**N**	0	1	.000	4.00	1	1	1	9	16	7	2	0	0	0	0	3	0	0	.000	2	0	0	0	2.0	1.000

Ed Corey

COREY, EDWARD NORMAN BR TR 6′ 170 lbs.
Born Abraham Simon Cohen.
B. July 13, 1899, Chicago, Ill. D. Sept. 17, 1970, Kenosha, Wis.

Year	Team	Lg	W	L	PCT	ERA	G	GS	CG	IP	H	BB	SO	ShO	Relief W	Relief L	Relief SV	Batting AB	Batting H	HR	BA	PO	A	E	DP	TC/G	FA
1918	**CHI**	**A**	0	0	—	4.50	1	0	0	2	2	1	0	0	0	0	0	1	0	0	.000	0	1	0	0	1.0	1.000

Fred Corey

COREY, FREDERICK HARRISON BR TR
B. 1857, S. Kingston, R. I. D. Nov. 27, 1912, Providence, R. I.

Year	Team	Lg	W	L	PCT	ERA	G	GS	CG	IP	H	BB	SO	ShO	Relief W	Relief L	Relief SV	Batting AB	Batting H	HR	BA	PO	A	E	DP	TC/G	FA
1878	**PRO**	**N**	1	2	.333	2.35	5	5	2	23	22	7	7	0	0	0	0	21	3	0	.143	11	11	1	1	2.9	.957
1880	**WOR**	**N**	8	9	.471	2.43	25	17	9	148.1	131	16	47	2	0	1	2	138	24	0	.174	29	24	15	2	1.2	.779
1881			6	15	.286	*3.72*	23	21	20	188.2	231	31	33	1	0	0	0	203	45	0	.222	55	71	15	3	2.6	.894
1882			1	13	.071	*3.56*	21	14	12	139	180	19	36	0	0	**1**	0	255	63	0	.247	98	117	35	6	3.4	.860
1883	**PHI**	**AA**	10	7	.588	*3.40*	18	16	15	148.1	182	24	42	0	0	**1**	0	298	77	1	.258	86	150	57	7	3.8	.805
1885			1	0	1.000	7.00	1	1	1	9	18	1	3	0	0	0	0	384	94	1	.245	121	209	42	10	3.6	.887
6 yrs.			27	46	.370	3.32	93	74	59	656.1	764	98	168	3	0	3	2	*				505	771	208	44	3.2	.860

Pop Corkhill

CORKHILL, JOHN STEWART BL TR 5′10″ 180 lbs.
B. Apr. 11, 1858, Parkesburg, Pa. D. Apr. 4, 1921, Pennsauken, N. J.

Year	Team	Lg	W	L	PCT	ERA	G	GS	CG	IP	H	BB	SO	ShO	Relief W	Relief L	Relief SV	Batting AB	Batting H	HR	BA	PO	A	E	DP	TC/G	FA
1884	**CIN**	**AA**	1	0	1.000	*1.80*	1	0	0	5	1	2	4	0	1	0	0	452	124	4	.274	172	21	14	0	2.3	.932
1885			1	4	.200	*3.65*	8	1	0	37	36	10	12	0	**1**	**3**	1	440	111	1	.252	234	44	17	6	2.4	.942
1886			0	0	—	*13.50*	1	0	0	0.2	1	0	1	0	0	0	0	540	143	4	.265	228	62	29	8	2.4	.909
1887			1	0	1.000	*5.52*	5	0	0	14.2	22	5	3	0	**1**	0	0	541	168	5	.311	310	31	17	7	2.7	.953
1888			0	0	—	10.80	2	0	0	5	8	0	1	0	0	0	**1**	561	160	2	.285	316	26	13	5	2.6	.963
5 yrs.			3	4	.429	4.62	17	1	0	62.1	68	17	21	0	3	3	2	*				2402	328	157	55	2.6	.946

Mike Corkins

CORKINS, MICHAEL PATRICK BR TR 6′ 1″ 190 lbs.
B. May 25, 1946, Riverside, Calif.

Year	Team	Lg	W	L	PCT	ERA	G	GS	CG	IP	H	BB	SO	ShO	Relief Pitching W	Relief Pitching L	Relief Pitching SV	Batting AB	Batting H	Batting HR	BA	PO	A	E	DP	TC/G	FA
1969	SD	N	1	3	.250	8.47	6	4	0	17	27	8	13	0	0	0	0	3	0	0	.000	1	3	0	0	0.7	1.000
1970			5	6	.455	4.62	24	18	1	111	109	79	75	0	0	0	0	37	8	1	.216	8	10	3	1	0.9	.857
1971			0	0	—	3.46	8	0	0	13	14	6	16	0	0	0	0	0	0	0	—	2	0	0	0	0.3	1.000
1972			6	9	.400	3.54	47	9	2	140	125	62	108	1	4	3	6	38	9	1	.237	8	22	2	0	0.7	.938
1973			5	8	.385	4.50	47	11	2	122	130	61	82	0	2	3	3	33	7	3	.212	8	8	4	0	0.4	.800
1974			2	2	.500	4.82	25	2	0	56	53	32	41	0	2	1	0	8	0	0	.000	1	5	0	0	0.2	1.000
6 yrs.			19	28	.404	4.39	157	44	5	459	458	248	335	1	8	7	9	119	24	5	.202	28	48	9	1	0.5	.894

Rheal Cormier

CORMIER, RHEAL PAUL BL TL 5′10″ 185 lbs.
B. Apr. 23, 1967, Moncton, N. B., Canada.

Year	Team	Lg	W	L	PCT	ERA	G	GS	CG	IP	H	BB	SO	ShO	Relief Pitching W	Relief Pitching L	Relief Pitching SV	Batting AB	Batting H	Batting HR	BA	PO	A	E	DP	TC/G	FA
1991	STL	N	4	5	.444	4.12	11	10	2	67.2	74	8	38	0	0	0	0	21	5	0	.238	3	8	0	0	1.0	1.000
1992			10	10	.500	3.68	31	30	3	186	194	33	117	0	0	0	0	59	6	0	.102	9	34	0	2	1.4	1.000
1993			7	6	.538	4.33	38	21	1	145.1	163	27	75	0	1	1	0	47	11	0	.234	8	27	3	2	1.0	.921
1994			3	2	.600	5.45	7	7	0	39.2	40	7	26	0	0	0	0	14	4	0	.286	1	3	1	0	0.7	.800
1995	BOS	A	7	5	.583	4.07	48	12	0	115	131	31	69	0	3	2	0	0	0	0	—	7	21	2	3	0.6	.933
5 yrs.			31	28	.525	4.11	135	80	6	553.2	602	106	325	0	4	3	0	141	26	0	.184	28	93	6	7	0.9	.953
DIVISIONAL PLAYOFF SERIES																											
1995	BOS	A	0	0	—	13.50	2	0	0	0.2	2	1	2	0	0	0	0	0	0	0	—	0	0	0	0	0.0	.000

Mardie Cornejo

CORNEJO, NIEVES MARDIE BR TR 6′ 3″ 200 lbs.
B. Aug. 5, 1951, Wellington, Kans.

Year	Team	Lg	W	L	PCT	ERA	G	GS	CG	IP	H	BB	SO	ShO	Relief Pitching W	Relief Pitching L	Relief Pitching SV	Batting AB	Batting H	Batting HR	BA	PO	A	E	DP	TC/G	FA
1978	NY	N	4	2	.667	2.43	25	0	0	37	37	14	17	0	4	2	3	0	0	0	—	2	4	0	0	0.2	1.000

Reid Cornelius

CORNELIUS, JONATHAN REID BR TR 6′ 200 lbs.
B. June 2, 1970, Thomasville, Ala.

Year	Team	Lg	W	L	PCT	ERA	G	GS	CG	IP	H	BB	SO	ShO	Relief Pitching W	Relief Pitching L	Relief Pitching SV	Batting AB	Batting H	Batting HR	BA	PO	A	E	DP	TC/G	FA
1995	2 teams	MON N	(8G 0–0)		NY N	(10G 3–7)																					
″	total		3	7	.300	5.53	18	10	0	66.2	75	30	39	0	0	0	0	20	2	0	.100	7	12	1	2	1.1	.950

Jeff Cornell

CORNELL, JEFFREY RAY BB TR 6′ 170 lbs.
B. Feb. 10, 1957, Kansas City, Mo.

Year	Team	Lg	W	L	PCT	ERA	G	GS	CG	IP	H	BB	SO	ShO	Relief Pitching W	Relief Pitching L	Relief Pitching SV	Batting AB	Batting H	Batting HR	BA	PO	A	E	DP	TC/G	FA
1984	SF	N	1	3	.250	6.10	23	0	0	38.1	51	22	19	0	1	3	0	4	0	0	.000	0	4	0	1	0.2	1.000

Brad Cornett

CORNETT, BRAD BYRON BR TR 6′ 3″ 190 lbs.
B. Feb. 4, 1969, LaMesa, Tex.

Year	Team	Lg	W	L	PCT	ERA	G	GS	CG	IP	H	BB	SO	ShO	Relief Pitching W	Relief Pitching L	Relief Pitching SV	Batting AB	Batting H	Batting HR	BA	PO	A	E	DP	TC/G	FA
1994	TOR	A	1	3	.250	6.68	9	4	0	31	40	11	22	0	0	0	0	0	0	0	—	0	5	0	0	0.6	1.000
1995			0	0	—	9.00	5	0	0	5	9	3	4	0	0	0	0	0	0	0	—	0	2	0	0	0.4	1.000
2 yrs.			1	3	.250	7.00	14	4	0	36	49	14	26	0	0	0	0	0	0	0		0	7	0	0	0.5	1.000

Terry Cornutt

CORNUTT, TERRY STANTON BR TR 6′ 2″ 195 lbs.
B. Oct. 2, 1952, Roseburg, Ore.

Year	Team	Lg	W	L	PCT	ERA	G	GS	CG	IP	H	BB	SO	ShO	Relief Pitching W	Relief Pitching L	Relief Pitching SV	Batting AB	Batting H	Batting HR	BA	PO	A	E	DP	TC/G	FA
1977	SF	N	1	2	.333	3.89	28	1	0	44	38	22	23	0	1	1	0	1	0	0	.000	1	3	2	0	0.2	.667
1978			0	0	—	0.00	1	0	0	3	1	0	0	0	0	0	0	0	0	0	—	0	0	0	0	0.0	.000
2 yrs.			1	2	.333	3.64	29	1	0	47	39	22	23	0	1	1	0	1	0	0	.000	1	3	2	0	0.2	.667

Ed Correa

CORREA, EDWIN JOSUE BR TR 6′ 2″ 190 lbs.
Born Edwin Josue Correa (Andino).
B. Apr. 29, 1966, Hato Rey, Puerto Rico.

Year	Team	Lg	W	L	PCT	ERA	G	GS	CG	IP	H	BB	SO	ShO	Relief Pitching W	Relief Pitching L	Relief Pitching SV	Batting AB	Batting H	Batting HR	BA	PO	A	E	DP	TC/G	FA
1985	CHI	A	1	0	1.000	6.97	5	1	0	10.1	11	11	10	0	0	0	0	0	0	0	—	0	0	0	0	0.0	.000
1986	TEX	A	12	14	.462	4.23	32	32	4	202.1	167	126	189	2	0	0	0	0	0	0	—	20	34	3	0	1.8	.947
1987			3	5	.375	7.59	15	15	0	70	83	52	61	0	0	0	0	0	0	0	—	5	9	3	1	1.1	.824
3 yrs.			16	19	.457	5.16	52	48	4	282.2	261	189	260	2	0	0	0	0	0	0		25	43	6	1	1.4	.919

Frank Corridon

CORRIDON, FRANK J. (Fiddler) BR TR 6′ 170 lbs.
B. Nov. 25, 1880, Newport, R. I. D. Feb. 21, 1941, Syracuse, N. Y.

Year	Team	Lg	W	L	PCT	ERA	G	GS	CG	IP	H	BB	SO	ShO	Relief Pitching W	Relief Pitching L	Relief Pitching SV	Batting AB	Batting H	Batting HR	BA	PO	A	E	DP	TC/G	FA
1904	2 teams	CHI N	(12G 5–5)		PHI N	(12G 6–5)																					
″	total		11	10	.524	2.64	24	21	20	194.2	176	65	78	1	1	1	0	93	19	0	.204	37	79	6	5	3.9	.951
1905	PHI	N	10	13	.435	3.48	35	26	18	212	203	57	79	1	1	1	1	72	15	1	.208	13	72	8	2	2.7	.914
1907			18	14	.563	2.46	37	32	23	274	228	89	131	3	0	1	1	97	16	0	.165	18	99	9	3	3.3	.929
1908			14	10	.583	2.51	27	24	18	208.1	178	48	50	2	0	0	1	73	9	0	.123	13	78	5	0	3.6	.948
1909			11	7	.611	2.11	27	19	11	171	147	61	69	3	1	1	0	59	11	0	.186	8	70	4	0	3.0	.951
1910	STL	N	6	14	.300	3.81	30	18	9	156	168	55	51	0	1	2	2	51	10	0	.196	10	56	3	2	2.3	.957
6 yrs.			70	68	.507	2.80	180	140	99	1216	1100	375	458	10	4	6	5	445	80	1	.180	99	454	35	12	3.1	.940

Jim Corsi

CORSI, JAMES BERNARD BR TR 6′ 1″ 210 lbs.
B. Sept. 9, 1961, Newton, Mass.

Year	Team	Lg	W	L	PCT	ERA	G	GS	CG	IP	H	BB	SO	ShO	Relief Pitching W	Relief Pitching L	Relief Pitching SV	Batting AB	Batting H	Batting HR	BA	PO	A	E	DP	TC/G	FA
1988	OAK	A	0	1	.000	3.80	11	1	0	21.1	20	6	10	0	0	1	0	0	0	0	—	0	3	1	0	0.4	.750
1989			1	2	.333	1.88	22	0	0	38.1	26	10	21	0	1	2	0	0	0	0	—	3	5	0	0	0.4	1.000
1991	HOU	N	0	5	.000	3.71	47	0	0	77.2	76	23	53	0	0	5	0	1	0	0	.000	6	15	1	1	0.5	.955
1992	OAK	A	4	2	.667	1.43	32	0	0	44	44	18	19	0	4	2	0	0	0	0	—	6	10	0	0	0.5	1.000
1993	FLA	N	0	2	.000	6.64	15	0	0	20.1	28	10	7	0	0	2	0	0	0	0	—	1	4	0	0	0.3	1.000
1995	OAK	A	2	4	.333	2.20	38	0	0	45	31	26	26	0	2	4	2	0	0	0	—	3	9	0	1	0.3	1.000
6 yrs.			7	16	.304	2.99	165	1	0	246.2	225	93	136	0	7	16	2	1	0	0	.000	19	46	2	2	0.4	.970
LEAGUE CHAMPIONSHIP SERIES																											
1992	OAK	A	0	0	—	0.00	3	0	0	2	2	3	0	0	0	0	0	0	0	0	—	0	0	0	0	0.0	.000

Barry Cort

CORT, BARRY LEE BR TR 6′ 5″ 210 lbs.
B. Apr. 15, 1956, Toronto, Ont., Canada.

Year	Team	Lg	W	L	PCT	ERA	G	GS	CG	IP	H	BB	SO	ShO	Relief Pitching W	Relief Pitching L	Relief Pitching SV	Batting AB	Batting H	Batting HR	BA	PO	A	E	DP	TC/G	FA
1977	MIL	A	1	1	.500	3.38	7	3	1	24	25	9	17	0	0	0	0	0	0	0	—	1	4	0	0	0.7	1.000

Al Corwin

CORWIN, ELMER NATHAN BR TR 6′ 1″ 170 lbs.
B. Dec. 3, 1926, Newburgh, N. Y.

Year	Team	W	L	PCT	ERA	G	GS	CG	IP	H	BB	SO	ShO	Relief Pitching W	Relief Pitching L	Relief Pitching SV	Batting AB	Batting H	HR	BA	PO	A	E	DP	TC/G	FA
1951	NY N	5	1	.833	3.66	15	8	3	59	49	21	30	1	1	0	1	20	1	0	.050	0	1	1	0	0.1	.500
1952		6	1	.857	2.66	21	7	1	67.2	58	36	36	0	3	0	2	21	2	0	.095	3	6	0	1	0.4	1.000
1953		6	4	.600	4.98	48	7	2	106.2	122	68	49	1	4	2	2	32	9	2	.281	5	13	0	1	0.4	1.000
1954		1	3	.250	4.02	20	0	0	31.1	35	14	14	0	1	3	0	3	0	0	.000	1	3	0	0	0.2	1.000
1955		0	1	.000	4.01	13	0	0	24.2	25	17	13	0	0	1	0	3	0	0	.000	0	3	1	1	0.3	.750
5 yrs.		18	10	.643	3.98	117	22	6	289.1	289	156	142	2	9	6	5	79	12	2	.152	9	26	2	3	0.3	.946
WORLD SERIES																										
1951	NY N	0	0	—	0.00	1	0	0	1.2	1	0	1	0	0	0	0	0	0	0	—	1	0	0	0	1.0	1.000

Mike Cosgrove

COSGROVE, MICHAEL JOHN BL TL 6′ 1″ 170 lbs.
B. Feb. 17, 1951, Phoenix, Ariz.

Year	Team	W	L	PCT	ERA	G	GS	CG	IP	H	BB	SO	ShO	Relief Pitching W	Relief Pitching L	Relief Pitching SV	Batting AB	Batting H	HR	BA	PO	A	E	DP	TC/G	FA
1972	HOU N	0	1	.000	4.61	7	1	0	13.2	16	3	7	0	0	0	1	2	0	0	.000	0	0	0	0	0.0	.000
1973		1	1	.500	1.80	13	0	0	10	11	8	2	0	1	1	0	0	0	0	—	0	0	0	0	0.0	.000
1974		7	3	.700	3.49	45	0	0	90.1	76	39	47	0	7	3	2	18	1	0	.056	1	13	1	2	0.3	.933
1975		1	2	.333	3.04	32	3	1	71	62	37	32	0	0	1	5	13	2	0	.154	2	12	1	1	0.5	.933
1976		3	4	.429	5.50	22	16	1	90	106	58	34	1	0	0	0	23	2	0	.087	2	14	0	2	0.7	1.000
5 yrs.		12	11	.522	4.03	119	20	2	275	271	145	122	1	8	5	8	56	5	0	.089	5	39	2	5	0.4	.957

Jim Cosman

COSMAN, JAMES HENRY BR TR 6′ 4½″ 211 lbs.
B. Feb. 19, 1943, Brockport, N. Y.

Year	Team	W	L	PCT	ERA	G	GS	CG	IP	H	BB	SO	ShO	Relief Pitching W	Relief Pitching L	Relief Pitching SV	Batting AB	Batting H	HR	BA	PO	A	E	DP	TC/G	FA
1966	STL N	1	0	1.000	0.00	1	1	1	9	2	2	5	1	0	0	0	3	0	0	.000	1	0	0	0	1.0	1.000
1967		1	0	1.000	3.16	10	5	0	31.1	21	24	11	0	0	0	0	8	1	0	.125	5	2	0	0	0.7	1.000
1970	CHI N	0	0	—	27.00	1	0	0	1	3	1	0	0	0	0	0	0	0	0	—	0	0	0	0	0.0	.000
3 yrs.		2	0	1.000	3.05	12	6	1	41.1	26	27	16	1	0	0	0	11	1	0	.091	6	2	0	0	0.7	1.000

John Costello

COSTELLO, JOHN REILLY BR TR 6′ 1″ 190 lbs.
B. Dec. 24, 1960, Bronx, N. Y.

Year	Team	W	L	PCT	ERA	G	GS	CG	IP	H	BB	SO	ShO	Relief Pitching W	Relief Pitching L	Relief Pitching SV	Batting AB	Batting H	HR	BA	PO	A	E	DP	TC/G	FA
1988	STL N	5	2	.714	1.81	36	0	0	49.2	44	25	38	0	5	2	1	5	0	0	.000	3	3	0	0	0.2	1.000
1989		5	4	.556	3.32	48	0	0	62.1	48	20	40	0	5	4	3	6	0	0	.000	3	4	0	0	0.1	1.000
1990	2 teams STL N (4G 0–0) MON N (4G 0–0)																									
″	total	0	0		5.91	8	0	0	10.2	12	2	2	0	0	0	0	0	0	0		0	0	0	0	0.0	
1991	SD N	1	0	1.000	3.09	27	0	0	35	37	17	24	0	1	0	0	1	0	0	.000	0	5	0	0	0.2	1.000
4 yrs.		11	6	.647	2.97	119	0	0	157.2	141	64	104	0	11	6	4	12	0	0	.000	6	12	0	0	0.2	1.000

Dan Cotter

COTTER, DANIEL JOSEPH BR TR
B. Apr. 14, 1867, Boston, Mass. D. Sept. 14, 1935, Dorchester, Mass.

Year	Team	W	L	PCT	ERA	G	GS	CG	IP	H	BB	SO	ShO	Relief Pitching W	Relief Pitching L	Relief Pitching SV	Batting AB	Batting H	HR	BA	PO	A	E	DP	TC/G	FA
1890	BUF P	0	1	.000	14.00	1	1	1	9	18	7	0	0	0	0	0	4	0	0	.000	1	1	1	0	3.0	.667

Ensign Cottrell

COTTRELL, ENSIGN STOVER BL TL 5′ 9½″ 173 lbs.
B. Aug. 29, 1888, Hoosick Falls, N. Y. D. Feb. 27, 1947, Syracuse, N. Y.

Year	Team	W	L	PCT	ERA	G	GS	CG	IP	H	BB	SO	ShO	Relief Pitching W	Relief Pitching L	Relief Pitching SV	Batting AB	Batting H	HR	BA	PO	A	E	DP	TC/G	FA
1911	PIT N	0	0	—	9.00	1	0	0	1	4	1	0	0	0	0	0	0	0	0	—	0	0	0	0	0.0	.000
1912	CHI N	0	0	—	9.00	1	0	0	4	8	1	1	0	0	0	0	1	0	0	.000	0	0	0	0	0.0	.000
1913	PHI A	1	0	1.000	5.40	2	1	1	10	15	2	3	0	0	0	0	4	1	0	.250	0	1	0	1	0.5	1.000
1914	BOS N	0	1	.000	9.00	1	1	0	1	2	3	1	0	0	0	0	0	0	0	—	0	0	0	0	0.0	.000
1915	NY A	0	1	.000	3.38	7	0	0	21.1	29	7	7	0	0	1	0	7	0	0	.000	2	8	1	1	1.6	.909
5 yrs.		1	2	.333	4.82	12	2	1	37.1	58	14	12	0	0	1	0	12	1	0	.083	2	9	1	2	1.0	.917

Johnny Couch

COUCH, JOHN DANIEL BL TR 6′ 180 lbs.
B. Mar. 31, 1891, Vaughn, Mont. D. Dec. 8, 1975, San Mateo, Calif.

Year	Team	W	L	PCT	ERA	G	GS	CG	IP	H	BB	SO	ShO	Relief Pitching W	Relief Pitching L	Relief Pitching SV	Batting AB	Batting H	HR	BA	PO	A	E	DP	TC/G	FA
1917	DET A	0	0	—	2.70	3	0	0	13.1	13	1	1	0	0	0	0	4	0	0	.000	1	6	1	0	2.7	.875
1922	CIN N	16	9	.640	3.89	43	33	18	264	301	56	45	2	1	0	1	91	12	0	.132	9	65	0	3	1.7	1.000
1923	2 teams CIN N (19G 2–7) PHI N (11G 2–4)																									
″	total	4	11	.267	5.63	30	15	3	134.1	189	36	32	0	0	1	0	47	10	0	.213	8	26	4	1	1.3	.895
1924	PHI N	4	8	.333	4.73	37	7	3	137	170	39	23	0	4	3	3	49	10	2	.204	3	40	2	1	1.2	.956
1925		5	6	.455	5.44	34	7	2	94.1	112	39	11	1	4	0	2	31	5	1	.161	3	30	2	2	1.0	.943
5 yrs.		29	34	.460	4.63	147	62	26	643	785	171	112	3	9	4	6	222	37	3	.167	24	167	9	7	1.4	.955

Mike Couchee

COUCHEE, MICHAEL EUGENE BR TR 6′ 190 lbs.
B. Dec. 4, 1957, San Jose, Calif.

Year	Team	W	L	PCT	ERA	G	GS	CG	IP	H	BB	SO	ShO	Relief Pitching W	Relief Pitching L	Relief Pitching SV	Batting AB	Batting H	HR	BA	PO	A	E	DP	TC/G	FA
1983	SD N	0	1	.000	5.14	8	0	0	14	12	6	5	0	0	1	0	2	1	0	.500	1	1	0	0	0.3	1.000

Ed Coughlin

COUGHLIN, EDWARD E.
B. Aug. 5, 1861, Hartford, Conn. D. Dec. 25, 1952, Hartford, Conn.

Year	Team	W	L	PCT	ERA	G	GS	CG	IP	H	BB	SO	ShO	Relief Pitching W	Relief Pitching L	Relief Pitching SV	Batting AB	Batting H	HR	BA	PO	A	E	DP	TC/G	FA
1884	BUF N	0	0	—	∞	1	0	0		3	0	0	0	0	0	0	*				3	0	1	0	2.0	.750

Roscoe Coughlin

COUGHLIN, WILLIAM EDWARD TR 5′10″ 160 lbs.
B. Mar. 15, 1868, Walpole, Mass. D. Mar. 20, 1951, Chelsea, Mass.

Year	Team	W	L	PCT	ERA	G	GS	CG	IP	H	BB	SO	ShO	Relief Pitching W	Relief Pitching L	Relief Pitching SV	Batting AB	Batting H	HR	BA	PO	A	E	DP	TC/G	FA
1890	CHI N	4	6	.400	4.26	11	10	10	95	102	40	29	0	0	0	0	39	10	0	.256	6	25	2	1	3.0	.939
1891	NY N	3	4	.429	3.84	8	7	6	61	74	23	22	0	0	0	0	23	3	0	.130	7	14	0	1	2.6	1.000
2 yrs.		7	10	.412	4.10	19	17	16	156	176	63	51	0	0	0	0	62	13	0	.210	13	39	2	2	2.8	.963

Fritz Coumbe

COUMBE, FREDERICK NICHOLAS BL TL 6′ 152 lbs.
B. Dec. 13, 1889, Antrim, Pa. D. Mar. 21, 1978, Paradise, Calif.

Year	Team	W	L	PCT	ERA	G	GS	CG	IP	H	BB	SO	ShO	Relief Pitching W	Relief Pitching L	Relief Pitching SV	Batting AB	Batting H	HR	BA	PO	A	E	DP	TC/G	FA
1914	2 teams BOS A (17G 1–2) CLE A (14G 1–5)																									
″	total	2	7	.222	2.29	31	10	3	117.2	108	32	39	0	1	1	1	41	8	0	.195	11	39	6	1	1.8	.893
1915	CLE A	4	7	.364	3.47	30	12	4	114	123	37	37	1	1	0	2	37	10	0	.270	11	49	9	1	2.3	.870
1916		7	5	.583	2.02	29	13	7	120.1	121	27	39	2	2	0	0	35	2	0	.057	10	56	2	6	2.3	.971
1917		8	6	.571	2.14	34	10	4	134.1	119	35	30	1	3	1	5	39	6	0	.154	6	56	7	2	2.0	.899
1918		13	7	.650	3.00	30	17	9	150	164	52	41	0	3	2	3	56	12	0	.214	9	66	1	1	2.5	.987
1919		1	1	.500	5.32	8	2	0	23.2	32	9	7	0	0	1	1	6	3	0	.500	0	9	2	0	1.4	.818
1920	CIN N	0	1	.000	4.91	3	0	0	14.2	17	4	7	0	0	1	0	13	3	1	.231	2	6	0	0	1.6	1.000
1921		3	4	.429	3.22	28	6	3	86.2	89	21	12	0	1	1	1	25	8	0	.320	7	35	1	1	1.5	.977
8 yrs.		38	38	.500	2.79	193	70	30	761.1	773	217	212	4	11	7	13	252	52	1	.206	56	316	28	12	2.0	.930

Henry Courtney

COURTNEY, HENRY SEYMOUR BL TL 6′ 4″ 185 lbs.
B. Nov. 19, 1898, Asheville, N. C. D. Dec. 11, 1954, Lyme, Calif.

Year	Team	Lg	W	L	PCT	ERA	G	GS	CG	IP	H	BB	SO	ShO	Relief Pitching W	Relief Pitching L	Relief Pitching SV	Batting AB	Batting H	Batting HR	BA	PO	A	E	DP	TC/G	FA
1919	**WAS**	**A**	3	0	1.000	2.73	4	3	3	26.1	25	19	6	1	0	0	0	10	2	0	.200	2	1	0	0	0.8	1.000
1920			8	11	.421	4.74	37	24	10	188	223	77	48	1	0	2	0	69	16	1	.232	3	36	7	3	1.2	.848
1921			6	9	.400	5.63	30	15	3	132.2	159	71	26	0	1	1	1	47	14	0	.298	5	36	3	1	1.5	.932
1922	**2 teams**	**WAS A** (5G 0–0)	**CHI A** (18G 5–6)																								
″	**total**		5	6	.455	4.81	23	11	5	97.1	111	46	32	0	1	0	0	37	9	0	.243	0	22	0	2	1.0	1.000
4 yrs.			22	26	.458	4.90	94	53	21	444.1	518	213	112	2	2	3	1	163	41	1	.252	10	95	10	6	1.2	.913

John Courtright

COURTRIGHT, JOHN CHARLES BL TL 6′ 2″ 185 lbs.
B. May 30, 1970, Marion, Ohio.

Year	Team	Lg	W	L	PCT	ERA	G	GS	CG	IP	H	BB	SO	ShO	Relief W	Relief L	SV	AB	H	HR	BA	PO	A	E	DP	TC/G	FA
1995	**CIN**	**N**	0	0	—	9.00	1	0	0	1	2	0	0	0	0	0	0	0	0	0	—	0	0	0	0	0.0	.000

Harry Coveleski

COVELESKI, HARRY FRANK (The Giant Killer) BB TL 6′ 180 lbs.
Born Harry Frank Kowalewski.
Brother of Stan Coveleski.
B. Apr. 23, 1886, Shamokin, Pa. D. Aug. 4, 1950, Shamokin, Pa.

Year	Team	Lg	W	L	PCT	ERA	G	GS	CG	IP	H	BB	SO	ShO	Relief W	Relief L	SV	AB	H	HR	BA	PO	A	E	DP	TC/G	FA
1907	**PHI**	**N**	1	0	1.000	0.00	4	0	0	20	10	3	6	0	1	0	0	8	0	0	.000	0	6	1	0	1.8	.857
1908			4	1	.800	1.24	6	5	5	43.2	29	12	22	2	0	0	0	15	2	0	.133	3	15	0	0	3.0	1.000
1909			6	10	.375	2.74	24	17	8	121.2	109	49	56	2	1	0	1	37	4	0	.108	6	39	2	1	2.0	.957
1910	**CIN**	**N**	1	1	.500	5.26	7	4	2	39.1	35	42	27	0	0	0	0	16	1	0	.063	1	14	0	0	2.1	1.000
1914	**DET**	**A**	22	12	.647	2.49	44	36	23	303.1	251	100	124	5	2	1	2	95	23	0	.242	12	123	5	4	3.2	.964
1915			22	13	.629	2.45	**50**	38	20	312.2	**271**	87	150	1	4	2	4	103	18	0	.175	16	109	11	5	2.7	.919
1916			21	11	.656	1.97	44	39	22	324.1	278	63	108	3	1	1	2	118	25	0	.212	4	119	5	5	2.9	.961
1917			4	6	.400	2.61	16	11	2	69	70	14	15	0	1	0	0	22	5	0	.227	3	30	4	1	2.3	.892
1918			0	1	.000	3.86	3	1	1	14	17	6	3	0	0	0	0	4	1	0	.250	1	6	0	0	2.3	1.000
9 yrs.			81	55	.596	2.39	198	151	83	1248	1070	376	511	13	10	4	9	418	79	0	.189	46	461	28	16	2.7	.948

Stan Coveleski

COVELESKI, STANLEY ANTHONY BR TR 5′11″ 166 lbs.
Born Stanley Anthony Kowalewski.
Brother of Harry Coveleski.
B. July 13, 1889, Shamokin, Pa. D. Mar. 20, 1984, South Bend, Ind.
Hall of Fame 1969.

Year	Team	Lg	W	L	PCT	ERA	G	GS	CG	IP	H	BB	SO	ShO	Relief W	Relief L	SV	AB	H	HR	BA	PO	A	E	DP	TC/G	FA
1912	**PHI**	**A**	2	1	.667	3.43	5	2	2	21	18	4	9	1	1	0	0	7	1	0	.143	1	4	1	0	1.2	.833
1916	**CLE**	**A**	15	13	.536	3.41	45	27	11	232	247	58	76	1	2	4	3	75	13	1	.173	19	72	1	3	2.0	.989
1917			19	14	.576	1.81	45	36	24	298.1	202	94	133	**9**	1	2	4	97	13	0	.134	12	66	4	3	1.8	.951
1918			22	13	.629	1.82	38	33	25	311	261	76	87	2	1	1	1	110	21	0	.191	14	83	4	4	2.7	.960
1919			24	12	.667	2.52	43	34	24	296	**286**	60	118	4	1	**4**	4	94	20	0	.213	15	88	3	2	2.5	.972
1920			24	14	.632	2.49	41	37	26	315	284	65	**133**	3	1	0	2	111	25	0	.225	17	90	3	6	2.7	.973
1921			23	13	.639	3.36	43	**40**	29	315.2	341	84	99	2	0	0	2	116	18	0	.155	23	108	1	3	3.1	.992
1922			17	14	.548	3.32	35	33	21	276.2	292	64	98	3	0	0	2	99	10	0	.101	14	69	3	4	2.5	.965
1923			13	14	.481	**2.76**	33	31	17	228	251	42	54	**5**	0	0	2	79	7	0	.089	18	70	1	5	2.7	.989
1924			15	16	.484	4.04	37	33	18	240.1	286	73	58	2	2	1	0	82	11	0	.134	21	49	1	2	1.9	.986
1925	**WAS**	**A**	20	5	**.800**	**2.84**	32	32	15	241	230	73	58	3	0	0	0	81	9	0	.111	10	61	3	7	2.3	.959
1926			14	11	.560	3.12	36	34	11	245.1	272	81	50	3	0	0	1	82	17	0	.207	8	69	2	6	2.2	.975
1927			2	1	.667	3.14	5	4	0	14.1	13	8	3	0	0	0	0	6	2	0	.333	0	3	1	0	0.8	.750
1928	**NY**	**A**	5	1	.833	5.74	12	8	2	58	72	20	5	0	0	0	0	19	1	0	.053	2	19	1	0	1.8	.955
14 yrs.			215	142	.602	2.88	450	384	225	3092.2	3055	802	981	38	9	12	21	1058	168	1	.159	174	851	29	45	2.3	.972
WORLD SERIES																											
1920	**CLE**	**A**	3	0	1.000	0.67	3	3	3	27	15	2	8	1	0	0	0	10	1	0	.100	1	5	1	0	2.3	.857
1925	**WAS**	**A**	0	2	.000	3.77	2	2	1	14.1	16	5	3	0	0	0	0	3	0	0	.000	0	4	0	1	2.0	1.000
2 yrs.			3	2	.600	1.74	5	5	4	41.1	31	7	11	1	0	0	0	13	1	0	.077	1	9	1	1	2.2	.909

Chet Covington

COVINGTON, CHESTER ROGERS (Chesty) BB TL 6′ 2″ 225 lbs.
B. Nov. 6, 1910, Cairo, Ill. D. June 11, 1976, Pembroke Park, Fla.

Year	Team	Lg	W	L	PCT	ERA	G	GS	CG	IP	H	BB	SO	ShO	Relief W	Relief L	SV	AB	H	HR	BA	PO	A	E	DP	TC/G	FA
1944	**PHI**	**N**	1	1	.500	4.66	19	0	0	38.2	46	8	13	0	1	1	0	6	0	0	.000	2	6	0	0	0.4	1.000

Tex Covington

COVINGTON, WILLIAM WILKES BL TR 6′ 1″ 175 lbs.
Brother of Sam Covington.
B. Mar. 19, 1887, Henryville, Tenn. D. Dec. 10, 1931, Denison, Tex.

Year	Team	Lg	W	L	PCT	ERA	G	GS	CG	IP	H	BB	SO	ShO	Relief W	Relief L	SV	AB	H	HR	BA	PO	A	E	DP	TC/G	FA
1911	**DET**	**A**	7	1	.875	4.09	17	6	5	83.2	94	33	29	0	2	0	0	32	6	0	.188	3	17	0	2	1.2	1.000
1912			3	4	.429	4.12	14	9	2	63.1	58	30	19	1	0	0	0	15	2	0	.133	0	19	3	0	1.6	.864
2 yrs.			10	5	.667	4.10	31	15	7	147	152	63	48	1	2	0	0	47	8	0	.170	3	36	3	2	1.4	.929

Joe Cowley

COWLEY, JOSEPH ALAN BR TR 6′ 5″ 205 lbs.
B. Aug. 15, 1958, Lexington, Ky.

Year	Team	Lg	W	L	PCT	ERA	G	GS	CG	IP	H	BB	SO	ShO	Relief W	Relief L	SV	AB	H	HR	BA	PO	A	E	DP	TC/G	FA
1982	**ATL**	**N**	1	2	.333	4.47	17	8	0	52.1	53	16	27	0	1	0	0	15	3	0	.200	6	6	0	1	0.7	1.000
1984	**NY**	**A**	9	2	.818	3.56	16	11	3	83.1	75	31	71	1	1	2	0	0	0	0	—	7	12	2	0	1.3	.905
1985			12	6	.667	3.95	30	26	1	159.2	132	85	97	0	1	0	0	0	0	0	—	6	22	3	1	1.0	.903
1986	**CHI**	**A**	11	11	.500	3.88	27	27	4	162.1	133	83	132	0	0	0	0	0	0	0	—	16	16	4	0	1.3	.889
1987	**PHI**	**N**	0	4	.000	15.43	5	4	0	11.2	21	17	5	0	0	0	0	3	1	0	.333	1	0	1	0	0.4	.500
5 yrs.			33	25	.569	4.20	95	76	8	469.1	414	232	332	1	3	2	0	18	4	0	.222	36	56	10	2	1.1	.902

Bill Cox

COX, WILLIAM DONALD BR TR 6′ 1″ 185 lbs.
B. June 23, 1913, Ashmore, Ill. D. Feb. 16, 1988, Charleston, Ill.

Year	Team	Lg	W	L	PCT	ERA	G	GS	CG	IP	H	BB	SO	ShO	Relief W	Relief L	SV	AB	H	HR	BA	PO	A	E	DP	TC/G	FA
1936	**STL**	**N**	0	0	—	6.75	2	0	0	2.2	4	1	1	0	0	0	0	0	0	0	—	0	0	1	0	0.5	.000
1937	**CHI**	**A**	1	0	1.000	0.71	3	2	1	12.2	9	5	8	0	0	0	0	4	1	0	.250	0	1	0	0	0.3	1.000
1938	**2 teams**	**CHI A** (7G 0–2)	**STL A** (22G 1–4)																								
″	**total**		1	6	.143	6.99	29	8	1	74.2	92	48	21	0	0	1	0	19	1	0	.053	4	15	1	1	0.7	.950
1939	**STL**	**A**	0	2	.000	9.64	4	2	1	9.1	10	8	8	0	0	0	0	1	0	0	.000	2	4	0	0	1.5	1.000
1940			0	1	.000	7.27	12	0	0	17.1	23	12	7	0	0	1	0	1	0	0	.000	1	4	0	0	0.4	1.000
5 yrs.			2	9	.182	6.56	50	12	3	116.2	138	74	45	0	0	2	0	25	2	0	.080	7	24	2	1	0.7	.939

Year	Team		W	L	PCT	ERA	G	GS	CG	IP	H	BB	SO	ShO	Relief Pitching W	Relief Pitching L	Relief Pitching SV	Batting AB	Batting H	Batting HR	BA	PO	A	E	DP	TC/G	FA

Casey Cox

COX, JOSEPH CASEY BR TR 6′ 5″ 200 lbs.
B. July 3, 1941, Long Beach, Calif.

1966	WAS	A	4	5	.444	3.50	66	0	0	113	104	35	46	0	4	5	7	8	0	0	.000	2	24	1	1	0.4	.963
1967			7	4	.636	2.96	54	0	0	73	67	21	32	0	7	4	1	3	0	0	.000	4	14	0	0	0.3	1.000
1968			0	1	.000	2.35	4	0	0	7.2	7	0	4	0	0	1	0	0	0	0	—	1	0	0	0	0.3	1.000
1969			12	7	.632	2.78	52	13	4	171.2	161	64	73	0	7	3	0	47	5	0	.106	11	21	0	3	0.6	1.000
1970			8	12	.400	4.45	37	30	1	192	211	44	68	0	0	0	1	58	7	0	.121	13	24	2	0	1.1	.949
1971			5	7	.417	3.99	54	11	0	124	131	40	43	0	5	4	7	26	2	0	.077	5	20	1	2	0.5	.962
1972	2 teams	TEX A	(35G 3–5)		NY A	(5G 0–1)																					
″	total		3	6	.333	4.44	40	5	0	77	86	29	31	0	2	2	4	9	1	0	.111	5	11	0	0	0.4	1.000
1973	NY	A	0	0	—	6.00	1	0	0	3	5	1	0	0	0	0	0	0	0	0	—	0	1	0	0	1.0	1.000
8 yrs.			39	42	.481	3.70	308	59	5	761.1	772	234	297	0	25	19	20	151	15	0	.099	41	115	4	6	0.5	.975

Danny Cox

COX, DANNY BRADFORD BR TR 6′ 4″ 220 lbs.
B. Sept. 21, 1959, Northampton, England.

1983	STL	N	3	6	.333	3.25	12	12	0	83	92	23	36	0	0	0	0	27	2	0	.074	9	16	2	1	2.3	.926
1984			9	11	.450	4.03	29	27	1	156.1	171	54	70	1	1	0	0	53	7	0	.132	11	27	1	4	1.3	.974
1985			18	9	.667	2.88	35	35	10	241	226	64	131	4	0	0	0	79	12	0	.152	22	31	2	1	1.6	.964
1986			12	13	.480	2.90	32	32	8	220	189	60	108	0	0	0	0	65	5	0	.077	22	10	5	0	1.2	.865
1987			11	9	.550	3.88	31	31	2	199.1	224	71	101	0	0	0	0	69	8	0	.116	23	24	1	1	1.5	.979
1988			3	8	.273	3.98	13	13	0	86	89	25	47	0	0	0	0	23	1	0	.043	10	12	0	2	1.7	1.000
1991	PHI	N	4	6	.400	4.57	23	17	0	102.1	98	39	46	0	0	0	0	29	3	0	.103	10	11	0	1	0.9	1.000
1992	2 teams	PHI N	(9G 2–2)		PIT N	(16G 3–1)																					
″	total		5	3	.625	4.60	25	7	0	62.2	66	27	48	0	3	1	3	14	1	0	.071	8	9	2	1	0.8	.895
1993	TOR	A	7	6	.538	3.12	44	0	0	83.2	73	29	84	0	7	6	2	0	0	0	—	4	4	1	1	0.2	.889
1994			1	1	.500	1.45	10	0	0	18.2	7	7	14	0	1	1	3	0	0	0	—	2	1	0	0	0.3	1.000
1995			1	3	.250	7.40	24	0	0	45	57	33	38	0	1	3	0	0	0	0	—	2	6	2	1	0.4	.800
11 yrs.			74	75	.497	3.64	278	174	21	1298	1292	432	723	5	13	11	8	359	39	0	.109	123	151	16	13	1.0	.945
LEAGUE CHAMPIONSHIP SERIES																											
1985	STL	N	1	0	1.000	3.00	1	1	0	6	4	5	4	0	0	0	0	2	0	0	.000	0	3	0	0	3.0	1.000
1987			1	1	.500	2.12	2	2	2	17	17	3	11	1	0	0	0	6	2	0	.333	4	5	0	2	4.5	1.000
1992	PIT	N	0	0	—	0.00	2	0	0	1.1	1	1	1	0	0	0	0	0	0	0	—	0	0	0	0	0.0	.000
1993	TOR	A	0	0	—	0.00	2	0	0	5	3	2	5	0	0	0	0	0	0	0	—	0	1	0	0	0.5	1.000
4 yrs.			2	1	.667	1.84 **4th**	7	3	2 **4th**	29.1	25	11	21	1 **1st**	0	0	0	8	2	0	.250	4	9	0	2	1.9	1.000
WORLD SERIES																											
1985	STL	N	0	0	—	1.29	2	2	0	14	14	4	13	0	0	0	0	4	0	0	.000	1	2	0	1	1.5	1.000
1987			1	2	.333	7.71	3	2	0	11.2	13	8	9	0	0	1	0	2	0	0	.000	1	1	0	0	0.7	1.000
1993	TOR	A	0	0	—	8.10	3	0	0	3.1	6	5	6	0	0	0	0	1	0	0	.000	1	0	0	1	0.3	1.000
3 yrs.			1	2	.333	4.66	8	4	0	29	33	17	28	0	0	1	0	7	0	0	.000	3	3	0	2	0.8	1.000

Ernie Cox

COX, ERNEST THOMPSON (Elmer) BL TR 6′ 1″ 180 lbs.
B. Feb. 19, 1894, Birmingham, Ala. D. Apr. 29, 1974, Birmingham, Ala.

1922	CHI	A	0	0	—	18.00	1	0	0	1	1	2	0	0	0	0	0	0	0	0	—	0	0	0	0	0.0	.000

George Cox

COX, GEORGE MELVIN BR TR 6′ 1″ 170 lbs.
B. Nov. 15, 1904, Sherman, Tex.

1928	CHI	A	1	2	.333	5.26	26	2	0	89	110	39	22	0	1	1	0	26	2	0	.077	0	29	0	2	1.1	1.000

Glenn Cox

COX, GLENN MELVIN (Jingles) BR TR 6′ 2″ 210 lbs.
B. Feb. 3, 1931, Montebello, Calif.

1955	KC	A	0	2	.000	30.86	2	2	0	2.1	11	1	2	0	0	0	0	1	0	0	.000	0	2	0	0	1.0	1.000
1956			0	2	.000	4.24	3	3	1	23.1	15	22	6	0	0	0	0	7	0	0	.000	0	0	0	0	0.0	.000
1957			1	0	1.000	5.02	10	0	0	14.1	18	9	8	0	1	0	0	2	0	0	.000	0	3	0	0	0.3	1.000
1958			0	0	—	9.82	2	0	0	3.2	6	3	1	0	0	0	0	0	0	0	—	0	0	0	0	0.0	.000
4 yrs.			1	4	.200	6.39	17	5	1	43.2	50	35	17	0	1	0	0	10	0	0	.000	0	5	0	0	0.3	1.000

Les Cox

COX, LESLIE WARREN BR TR 6′ 164 lbs.
B. Aug. 14, 1905, Junction, Tex. D. Oct. 14, 1934, San Angelo, Tex.

1926	CHI	A	0	1	.000	5.40	2	0	0	5	6	5	3	0	0	1	0	2	1	0	.500	0	1	0	0	0.5	1.000

Red Cox

COX, PLATEAU REX BL TR 6′ 2″ 190 lbs.
B. Feb. 16, 1895, Laurel Springs, N. C. D. Oct. 15, 1984, Roanoke, Va.

1920	DET	A	0	0	—	5.40	3	0	0	5	9	3	1	0	0	0	0	1	0	0	.000	0	2	2	0	1.3	.500

Terry Cox

COX, TERRY LEE BR TR 6′ 5″ 215 lbs.
B. Mar. 30, 1949, Odessa, Tex.

1970	CAL	A	0	0	—	4.50	3	0	0	2	4	0	3	0	0	0	0	0	0	0	—	0	0	0	0	0.0	.000

Bill Coyle

COYLE, WILLIAM CLAUDE TR
B. Pittsburgh, Pa. Deceased.

1893	BOS	N	0	1	.000	9.00	2	1	0	8	14	3	2	0	0	0	0	4	0	0	.000	0	2	0	0	1.0	1.000

Charlie Cozart

COZART, CHARLES RHUBIN BR TL 6′ 190 lbs.
B. Oct. 17, 1919, Lenoir, N. C.

1945	BOS	N	1	0	1.000	10.13	5	0	0	8	10	15	4	0	1	0	0	2	0	0	.000	0	7	0	0	1.4	1.000

Jim Crabb

CRABB, JAMES ROY BR TR 5′11″ 160 lbs.
B. Aug. 23, 1890, Monticello, Iowa D. Mar. 30, 1940, Lewistown, Mont.

1912	2 teams	CHI A	(2G 0–1)		PHI A	(7G 2–4)																					
″	total		2	5	.286	3.29	9	8	3	52	54	21	15	0	0	0	0	19	0	0	.000	3	17	2	1	2.4	.909

Year	Team		W	L	PCT	ERA	G	GS	CG	IP	H	BB	SO	ShO	Relief Pitching W	Relief Pitching L	Relief Pitching SV	Batting AB	Batting H	Batting HR	BA	PO	A	E	DP	TC/G	FA

George Crable

CRABLE, GEORGE E. BL TL 6′ 1″ 190 lbs.
B. Dec. 1885, Nebraska Deceased.

Year	Team		W	L	PCT	ERA	G	GS	CG	IP	H	BB	SO	ShO	W	L	SV	AB	H	HR	BA	PO	A	E	DP	TC/G	FA
1910	BKN	N	0	0	—	4.91	2	1	1	7.1	5	5	3	0	0	0	0	2	0	0	.000	0	2	0	0	1.0	1.000

Tim Crabtree

CRABTREE, TIMOTHY LYLE BR TR 6′ 4″ 205 lbs.
B. Oct. 13, 1969, Jackson, Mich.

Year	Team		W	L	PCT	ERA	G	GS	CG	IP	H	BB	SO	ShO	W	L	SV	AB	H	HR	BA	PO	A	E	DP	TC/G	FA
1995	TOR	A	0	2	.000	3.09	31	0	0	32	30	13	21	0	0	2	0	0	0	0	—	2	8	0	1	0.3	1.000

Walter Craddock

CRADDOCK, WALTER ANDERSON BR TL 5′11½″ 176 lbs.
B. Mar. 25, 1932, Pax, W. Va. D. July 6, 1980, Parma Heights, Ohio.

Year	Team		W	L	PCT	ERA	G	GS	CG	IP	H	BB	SO	ShO	W	L	SV	AB	H	HR	BA	PO	A	E	DP	TC/G	FA
1955	KC	A	0	2	.000	7.80	4	2	0	15	18	10	9	0	0	1	0	5	0	0	.000	0	2	0	0	0.5	1.000
1956			0	2	.000	6.75	2	2	0	9.1	9	10	8	0	0	0	0	2	0	0	.000	0	1	0	0	0.5	1.000
1958			0	3	.000	5.89	23	1	0	36.2	41	20	22	0	0	2	0	2	0	0	.000	1	8	0	1	0.4	1.000
3 yrs.			0	7	.000	6.49	29	5	0	61	68	40	39	0	0	3	0	9	0	0	.000	1	11	0	1	0.4	1.000

Molly Craft

CRAFT, MAURICE MONTAGUE BR TR 6′ 2″ 165 lbs.
B. Nov. 28, 1895, Portsmouth, Va. D. Oct. 25, 1978, Los Angeles, Calif.

Year	Team		W	L	PCT	ERA	G	GS	CG	IP	H	BB	SO	ShO	W	L	SV	AB	H	HR	BA	PO	A	E	DP	TC/G	FA
1916	WAS	A	0	1	.000	3.27	2	1	1	11	12	6	9	0	0	0	0	4	0	0	.000	2	4	1	0	2.3	.857
1917			0	0	—	3.86	8	0	0	14	17	8	2	0	0	0	1	2	1	0	.500	1	5	0	1	0.8	1.000
1918			0	0	—	1.29	3	0	0	7	5	1	5	0	0	0	0	2	0	0	.000	1	2	0	0	1.0	1.000
1919			0	3	.000	3.88	16	2	0	48.2	59	18	17	0	0	2	0	18	2	0	.111	2	13	1	0	1.0	.938
4 yrs.			0	4	.000	3.57	29	3	1	80.2	93	33	33	0	0	2	1	26	3	0	.115	6	24	2	1	1.1	.938

Howard Craghead

CRAGHEAD, HOWARD OLIVER (Judge) BR TR 6′ 2″ 200 lbs.
B. May 25, 1908, Selma, Calif. D. July 15, 1962, San Diego, Calif.

Year	Team		W	L	PCT	ERA	G	GS	CG	IP	H	BB	SO	ShO	W	L	SV	AB	H	HR	BA	PO	A	E	DP	TC/G	FA
1931	CLE	A	0	0	—	6.35	4	0	0	5.2	8	2	2	0	0	0	0	0	0	0	—	0	2	0	0	0.5	1.000
1933			0	0	—	6.23	11	0	0	17.1	19	10	2	0	0	0	0	3	0	0	.000	1	5	1	0	0.6	.857
2 yrs.			0	0		6.26	15	0	0	23	27	12	4	0	0	0	0	3	0	0	.000	1	7	1	0	0.6	.889

George Craig

CRAIG, GEORGE McCARTHY (Lefty) TL
B. Nov. 15, 1887, Philadelphia, Pa. D. Apr. 23, 1911, Indianapolis, Ind.

Year	Team		W	L	PCT	ERA	G	GS	CG	IP	H	BB	SO	ShO	W	L	SV	AB	H	HR	BA	PO	A	E	DP	TC/G	FA
1907	PHI	A	0	0	—	10.80	2	0	0	1.2	2	3	0	0	0	0	0	1	0	0	.000	0	0	0	0	0.0	.000

Pete Craig

CRAIG, PETER JOEL BL TR 6′ 5″ 220 lbs.
B. July 10, 1940, La Salle, Ont., Canada.

Year	Team		W	L	PCT	ERA	G	GS	CG	IP	H	BB	SO	ShO	W	L	SV	AB	H	HR	BA	PO	A	E	DP	TC/G	FA
1964	WAS	A	0	0	—	48.60	2	1	0	1.2	8	4	0	0	0	0	0	0	0	0	—	0	0	0	0	0.0	.000
1965			0	3	.000	8.16	3	3	0	14.1	18	8	2	0	0	0	0	3	2	0	.667	6	3	0	0	3.0	1.000
1966			0	0	—	4.50	1	0	0	2	2	1	1	0	0	0	0	0	0	0	—	0	0	1	0	1.0	.000
3 yrs.			0	3	.000	11.50	6	4	0	18	28	13	3	0	0	0	0	3	2	0	.667	6	3	1	0	1.7	.900

Roger Craig

CRAIG, ROGER LEE BR TR 6′ 4″ 185 lbs.
B. Feb. 17, 1930, Durham, N. C.
Manager 1978–79, 1985–92.

Year	Team		W	L	PCT	ERA	G	GS	CG	IP	H	BB	SO	ShO	W	L	SV	AB	H	HR	BA	PO	A	E	DP	TC/G	FA
1955	BKN	N	5	3	.625	2.78	21	10	3	90.2	81	43	48	0	0	1	2	26	2	0	.077	6	11	1	1	0.9	.944
1956			12	11	.522	3.71	35	32	8	199	169	87	109	2	0	2	1	61	1	0	.016	10	22	0	1	0.9	1.000
1957			6	9	.400	4.61	32	13	1	111.1	102	47	69	0	4	2	0	29	4	0	.138	11	19	0	4	0.9	1.000
1958	LA	N	2	1	.667	4.50	9	2	1	32	30	12	16	0	0	1	0	9	0	0	.000	0	3	1	0	0.4	.750
1959			11	5	.688	2.06	29	17	7	152.2	122	45	76	**4**	2	0	0	52	3	0	.058	19	18	1	2	1.3	.974
1960			8	3	.727	3.27	21	15	6	115.2	99	43	69	1	1	0	0	36	2	0	.056	10	16	0	2	1.2	1.000
1961			5	6	.455	6.15	40	14	2	112.2	130	52	63	0	2	1	2	27	4	0	.148	5	15	1	1	0.5	.952
1962	NY	N	10	**24**	.294	4.51	42	33	13	233.1	261	70	118	0	4	2	3	76	4	0	.053	23	54	4	4	1.9	.951
1963			5	**22**	.185	3.78	46	31	14	236	249	58	108	0	0	1	2	69	6	0	.087	18	60	8	4	1.9	.907
1964	STL	N	7	9	.438	3.25	39	19	3	166	180	35	84	0	2	1	5	48	10	0	.208	13	37	1	2	1.3	.980
1965	CIN	N	1	4	.200	3.64	40	0	0	64.1	74	25	30	0	1	4	3	11	2	0	.182	2	13	1	0	0.4	.938
1966	PHI	N	2	1	.667	5.56	14	0	0	22.2	31	5	13	0	2	1	1	4	0	0	.000	3	6	0	0	0.6	1.000
12 yrs.			74	98	.430	3.83	368	186	58	1536.1	1528	522	803	7	18	16	19	448	38	0	.085	120	274	18	21	1.1	.956
WORLD SERIES																											
1955	BKN	N	1	0	1.000	3.00	1	1	0	6	4	5	4	0	0	0	0	0	0	0	—	0	1	0	0	1.0	1.000
1956			0	1	.000	12.00	2	1	0	6	10	3	4	0	0	0	0	2	1	0	.500	1	1	0	1	1.0	1.000
1959	LA	N	0	1	.000	8.68	2	2	0	9.1	15	5	8	0	0	0	0	3	0	0	.000	0	2	0	0	1.0	1.000
1964	STL	N	1	0	1.000	0.00	2	0	0	5	2	3	9	0	1	0	0	1	0	0	.000	0	2	0	0	1.0	1.000
4 yrs.			2	2	.500	6.49	7	4	0	26.1	31	16	25	0	1	0	0	6	1	0	.167	1	6	0	1	1.0	1.000

Jerry Cram

CRAM, GERALD ALLEN BR TR 6′ 180 lbs.
B. Dec. 9, 1947, Los Angeles, Calif.

Year	Team		W	L	PCT	ERA	G	GS	CG	IP	H	BB	SO	ShO	W	L	SV	AB	H	HR	BA	PO	A	E	DP	TC/G	FA
1969	KC	A	0	1	.000	3.24	5	2	0	16.2	15	6	10	0	0	0	0	3	0	0	.000	2	1	0	0	0.6	1.000
1974	NY	N	0	1	.000	1.64	10	0	0	22	22	4	8	0	0	1	0	3	1	0	.333	1	4	0	1	0.5	1.000
1975			0	1	.000	5.40	4	0	0	5	7	2	2	0	0	1	0	0	0	0	—	0	1	0	0	0.3	1.000
1976	KC	A	0	0	—	6.75	4	0	0	4	8	1	2	0	0	0	0	0	0	0	—	2	0	0	0	0.5	1.000
4 yrs.			0	3	.000	3.02	23	2	0	47.2	52	13	22	0	0	2	0	6	1	0	.167	5	6	0	1	0.5	1.000

Bill Cramer

CRAMER, WILLIAM WENDELL BR TR 6′ 175 lbs.
B. May 21, 1891, Bedford, Ind. D. Sept. 11, 1966, Fort Wayne, Ind.

Year	Team		W	L	PCT	ERA	G	GS	CG	IP	H	BB	SO	ShO	W	L	SV	AB	H	HR	BA	PO	A	E	DP	TC/G	FA
1912	CIN	N	0	0	—	0.00	1	0	0	2.1	6	0	2	0	0	0	0	1	0	0	.000	0	1	4	0	5.0	.200

Doc Cramer

CRAMER, ROGER MAXWELL (Flit) BL TR 6′ 2″ 185 lbs.
B. July 22, 1905, Beach Haven, N. J. D. Sept. 9, 1990, Manahawkin, N. J.

Year	Team		W	L	PCT	ERA	G	GS	CG	IP	H	BB	SO	ShO	W	L	SV	AB	H	HR	BA	PO	A	E	DP	TC/G	FA
1938	BOS	A	0	0	—	4.50	1	0	0	4	3	3	1	0	0	0	0	*				6	0	0	0	6.0	1.000

Doc Crandall

CRANDALL, JAMES OTIS BR TR 5′10½″ 180 lbs.
B. Oct. 8, 1887, Wadena, Ind. D. Aug. 17, 1951, Bell, Calif.

Year	Team		W	L	PCT	ERA	G	GS	CG	IP	H	BB	SO	ShO	W	L	SV	AB	H	HR	BA	PO	A	E	DP	TC/G	FA
1908	NY	N	12	12	.500	2.93	32	24	13	214.2	198	59	77	0	2	1	0	72	16	2	.222	15	52	1	2	2.1	.985
1909			6	4	.600	2.88	30	8	4	122	117	33	55	0	5	1	4	41	10	1	.244	9	39	3	4	1.7	.941
1910			17	4	.810	2.56	42	18	13	207.2	194	43	73	2	**7**	1	4	73	25	1	.342	12	49	1	3	1.4	.984
1911			15	5	.750	2.63	41	15	9	198.2	199	51	94	2	**7**	0	5	113	27	2	.239	17	76	6	3	2.0	.939
1912			13	7	.650	3.61	37	10	7	162	181	35	60	0	**6**	**5**	2	80	25	0	.313	9	44	2	0	1.4	.964

Doc Crandall *continued*

Year	Team	Lg	W	L	PCT	ERA	G	GS	CG	IP	H	BB	SO	ShO	Relief Pitching W	Relief Pitching L	Relief Pitching SV	Batting AB	Batting H	Batting HR	BA	PO	A	E	DP	TC/G	FA
1913			4	4	.500	2.86	35	3	2	97.2	102	24	42	0	3	3	6	49	15	0	.306	4	34	0	1	1.1	1.000
1914	**STL**	**F**	13	9	.591	3.54	27	21	18	196	194	52	84	1	1	0	0	278	86	2	.309	106	204	25	12	3.6	.925
1915			21	15	.583	2.59	51	33	22	312.2	**307**	77	117	4	**6**	3	0	141	40	1	.284	15	99	5	3	2.3	.958
1916	**STL**	**A**	0	0	—	27.00	2	0	0	1.1	7	1	0	0	0	0	0	12	1	0	.083	0	0	1	0	0.5	.000
1918	**BOS**	**N**	1	2	.333	2.38	5	3	3	34	39	4	4	0	0	0	0	28	8	0	.286	7	10	0	1	2.1	1.000
10 yrs.			102	62	.622	2.92	302	135	91	1546.2	1538	379	606	9	37	14	21	*				194	607	44	29	2.2	.948
WORLD SERIES																											
1911	**NY**	**N**	1	0	1.000	0.00	2	0	0	4	2	0	2	0	1	0	0	2	1	0	.500	0	2	0	0	1.0	1.000
1912			0	0	—	0.00	1	0	0	2	1	0	2	0	0	0	0	1	0	0	.000	0	1	0	0	1.0	1.000
1913			0	0	—	3.86	2	0	0	4.2	4	0	2	0	0	0	0	4	0	0	.000	0	2	0	0	1.0	1.000
3 yrs.			1	0	1.000	1.69	5	0	0	10.2	7	0	6	0	1	0	0	*				0	5	0	0	1.0	1.000

Cannonball Crane

CRANE, EDWARD NICHOLAS BR TR 5′10½″ 204 lbs.
B. May 27, 1862, Boston, Mass. D. Sept. 19, 1896, Rochester, N. Y.

Year	Team	Lg	W	L	PCT	ERA	G	GS	CG	IP	H	BB	SO	ShO	Relief Pitching W	Relief Pitching L	Relief Pitching SV	Batting AB	Batting H	Batting HR	BA	PO	A	E	DP	TC/G	FA
1884	**BOS**	**U**	0	2	.000	*4.00*	4	2	1	18	17	6	13	0	0	0	0	428	122	12	.285	364	102	88	6	5.1	.841
1886	**WAS**	**N**	1	7	.125	*7.20*	10	8	7	70	91	53	39	1	0	0	0	292	50	0	.171	20	1	7	0	2.0	.750
1888	**NY**	**N**	5	6	.455	2.43	12	11	11	92.2	70	40	58	2	0	0	1	37	6	1	.162	3	23	4	0	2.5	.867
1889			14	10	.583	3.68	29	25	23	230	221	136	130	0	1	1	0	103	21	2	.204	12	24	11	1	1.6	.766
1890	**NY**	**P**	16	19	.457	4.63	43	35	28	330.1	323	210	117	0	0	1	1	146	46	0	.315	17	71	16	0	2.4	.846
1891	**2 teams**	**CIN AA** (32G 14–14) **CIN N** (15G 4–8)																									
″	**total**		18	22	.450	**2.97**	47	44	36	366.2	350	203	173	2	0	0	0	156	22	1	.141	13	81	17	2	2.2	.847
1892	**NY**	**N**	16	24	.400	3.80	47	42	35	364.1	350	189	174	2	0	1	1	163	40	0	.245	28	69	23	4	2.5	.808
1893	**2 teams**	**NY N** (10G 2–4) **BKN N** (2G 0–2)																									
″	**total**		2	6	.250	6.89	12	9	5	78.1	103	50	16	0	0	0	0	31	14	0	.452	3	14	3	0	1.3	.850
8 yrs.			72	96	.429	3.99	204	176	146	1550.1	1525	887	720	7	1	3	3	*				576	420	189	18	2.9	.841

Jim Crawford

CRAWFORD, JAMES FREDERICK (Catfish) BL TL 6′ 3″ 200 lbs.
B. Sept. 29, 1950, Chicago, Ill.

Year	Team	Lg	W	L	PCT	ERA	G	GS	CG	IP	H	BB	SO	ShO	Relief Pitching W	Relief Pitching L	Relief Pitching SV	Batting AB	Batting H	Batting HR	BA	PO	A	E	DP	TC/G	FA
1973	**HOU**	**N**	2	4	.333	4.50	48	0	0	70	69	33	56	0	2	4	6	13	3	0	.231	3	14	1	0	0.4	.944
1975			3	5	.375	3.62	44	2	0	87	92	37	37	0	3	3	4	17	5	0	.294	8	13	2	2	0.5	.913
1976	**DET**	**A**	1	8	.111	4.53	32	5	1	109.1	115	43	68	0	0	5	2	0	0	0	—	1	40	1	2	1.3	.976
1977			7	8	.467	4.79	37	7	0	126	156	50	91	0	5	4	1	0	0	0	—	1	24	0	0	0.7	1.000
1978			2	3	.400	4.35	20	0	0	39.1	45	19	24	0	2	3	0	0	0	0	—	1	4	0	2	0.3	1.000
5 yrs.			15	28	.349	4.40	181	14	1	431.2	477	182	276	0	12	19	13	30	8	0	.267	14	95	4	6	0.6	.965

Larry Crawford

CRAWFORD, CHARLES LOWRIE BL TL 6′ 1″ 165 lbs.
B. Apr. 27, 1914, Swissvale, Pa. D. Dec. 20, 1994, Hanover, Pa.

Year	Team	Lg	W	L	PCT	ERA	G	GS	CG	IP	H	BB	SO	ShO	Relief Pitching W	Relief Pitching L	Relief Pitching SV	Batting AB	Batting H	Batting HR	BA	PO	A	E	DP	TC/G	FA
1937	**PHI**	**N**	0	0	—	15.00	6	0	0	6	12	1	2	0	0	0	0	0	0	0	—	1	0	0	0	0.2	1.000

Steve Crawford

CRAWFORD, STEVEN RAY BR TR 6′ 5″ 225 lbs.
B. Apr. 29, 1958, Pryor, Okla.

Year	Team	Lg	W	L	PCT	ERA	G	GS	CG	IP	H	BB	SO	ShO	Relief Pitching W	Relief Pitching L	Relief Pitching SV	Batting AB	Batting H	Batting HR	BA	PO	A	E	DP	TC/G	FA
1980	**BOS**	**A**	2	0	1.000	3.66	6	4	2	32	41	8	10	0	0	0	0	0	0	0	—	4	2	0	0	1.0	1.000
1981			0	5	.000	4.97	14	11	0	58	69	18	29	0	0	0	0	0	0	0	—	8	8	0	1	1.1	1.000
1982			1	0	1.000	2.00	5	0	0	9	14	0	2	0	1	0	0	0	0	0	—	0	1	0	0	0.2	1.000
1984			5	0	1.000	3.34	35	0	0	62	69	21	21	0	5	0	1	0	0	0	—	4	8	0	1	0.3	1.000
1985			6	5	.545	3.76	44	1	0	91	103	28	58	0	5	5	12	0	0	0	—	7	15	3	2	0.6	.880
1986			0	2	.000	3.92	40	0	0	57.1	69	19	32	0	0	2	4	0	0	0	—	4	7	1	2	0.3	.917
1987			5	4	.556	5.33	29	0	0	72.2	91	32	43	0	5	4	0	0	0	0	—	8	10	0	2	0.6	1.000
1989	**KC**	**A**	3	1	.750	2.83	25	0	0	54	48	19	33	0	3	1	0	0	0	0	—	7	13	0	1	0.8	1.000
1990			5	4	.556	4.16	46	0	0	80	79	23	54	0	5	4	1	0	0	0	—	8	13	0	0	0.5	1.000
1991			3	2	.600	5.98	33	0	0	46.2	60	18	38	0	3	2	1	0	0	0	—	4	5	0	0	0.3	1.000
10 yrs.			30	23	.566	4.17	277	16	2	562.2	643	186	320	0	27	18	19	0	0	0		54	82	4	9	0.5	.971
LEAGUE CHAMPIONSHIP SERIES																											
1986	**BOS**	**A**	1	0	1.000	0.00	1	0	0	1.2	1	2	1	0	1	0	0	0	0	0	—	1	0	0	0	1.0	1.000
WORLD SERIES																											
1986	**BOS**	**A**	1	0	1.000	6.23	3	0	0	4.1	5	0	4	0	1	0	0	1	0	0	.000	0	0	0	0	0.0	.000

Doug Creek

CREEK, PAUL DOUGLAS BL TL 5′10″ 205 lbs.
B. Mar. 1, 1969, Winchester, Va.

Year	Team	Lg	W	L	PCT	ERA	G	GS	CG	IP	H	BB	SO	ShO	Relief Pitching W	Relief Pitching L	Relief Pitching SV	Batting AB	Batting H	Batting HR	BA	PO	A	E	DP	TC/G	FA
1995	**STL**	**N**	0	0	—	0.00	6	0	0	6.2	2	3	10	0	0	0	0	0	0	0	—	0	0	0	0	0.0	.000

Jack Creel

CREEL, JACK DALTON (Tex) BR TR 6′ 165 lbs.
B. Apr. 23, 1916, Kyle, Tex.

Year	Team	Lg	W	L	PCT	ERA	G	GS	CG	IP	H	BB	SO	ShO	Relief Pitching W	Relief Pitching L	Relief Pitching SV	Batting AB	Batting H	Batting HR	BA	PO	A	E	DP	TC/G	FA
1945	**STL**	**N**	5	4	.556	4.14	26	8	2	87	78	45	34	0	2	0	2	26	2	0	.077	3	19	1	0	0.9	.957

Keith Creel

CREEL, STEVEN KEITH BR TR 6′ 2″ 180 lbs.
B. Feb. 4, 1959, Dallas, Tex.

Year	Team	Lg	W	L	PCT	ERA	G	GS	CG	IP	H	BB	SO	ShO	Relief Pitching W	Relief Pitching L	Relief Pitching SV	Batting AB	Batting H	Batting HR	BA	PO	A	E	DP	TC/G	FA
1982	**KC**	**A**	1	4	.200	5.40	9	6	0	41.2	43	25	13	0	0	0	0	0	0	0	—	1	8	0	1	1.0	1.000
1983			2	5	.286	6.35	25	10	1	89.1	116	35	31	0	0	1	0	0	0	0	—	6	8	0	0	0.6	1.000
1985	**CLE**	**A**	2	5	.286	4.79	15	8	0	62	73	23	31	0	0	1	0	0	0	0	—	4	2	0	1	0.4	1.000
1987	**TEX**	**A**	0	0	—	4.66	6	0	0	9.2	12	5	5	0	0	0	0	0	0	0	—	1	3	0	0	0.7	1.000
4 yrs.			5	14	.263	5.60	55	24	1	202.2	244	88	80	0	0	2	0	0	0	0		12	21	0	2	0.6	1.000

Bob Cremins

CREMINS, ROBERT ANTHONY (Crooked Arm) BL TL 5′11″ 178 lbs.
B. Feb. 15, 1906, Pelham Manor, N. Y.

Year	Team	Lg	W	L	PCT	ERA	G	GS	CG	IP	H	BB	SO	ShO	Relief Pitching W	Relief Pitching L	Relief Pitching SV	Batting AB	Batting H	Batting HR	BA	PO	A	E	DP	TC/G	FA
1927	**BOS**	**A**	0	0	—	5.06	4	0	0	5.1	5	3	0	0	0	0	0	0	0	0	—	0	2	1	0	0.8	.667

Walker Cress

CRESS, WALKER JAMES (Foots) BR TR 6′ 5″ 205 lbs.
B. Mar. 16, 1917, Ben Hur, Va.

Year	Team	Lg	W	L	PCT	ERA	G	GS	CG	IP	H	BB	SO	ShO	Relief Pitching W	Relief Pitching L	Relief Pitching SV	Batting AB	Batting H	Batting HR	BA	PO	A	E	DP	TC/G	FA
1948	**CIN**	**N**	0	1	.000	4.50	30	2	1	60	60	42	33	0	0	0	0	8	4	0	.500	0	8	2	0	0.3	.800
1949			0	0	—	0.00	3	0	0	2	2	3	0	0	0	0	0	0	0	0	—	0	0	1	0	0.3	.000
2 yrs.			0	1	.000	4.35	33	2	1	62	62	45	33	0	0	0	0	8	4	0	.500	0	8	3	0	0.3	.727

Tim Crews

CREWS, STANLEY TIMOTHY
B. Apr. 3, 1961, Tampa, Fla. D. Mar. 23, 1993, Orlando, Fla.
BR TR 6′ 180 lbs.

Year	Team	W	L	PCT	ERA	G	GS	CG	IP	H	BB	SO	ShO	Relief W	Relief L	Relief SV	AB	H	HR	BA	PO	A	E	DP	TC/G	FA
1987	LA N	1	1	.500	2.48	20	0	0	29	30	8	20	0	1	1	3	2	0	0	.000	2	5	0	0	0.3	1.000
1988		4	0	1.000	3.14	42	0	0	71.2	77	16	45	0	4	0	0	5	1	0	.200	6	4	1	1	0.3	.909
1989		0	1	.000	3.21	44	0	0	61.2	69	23	56	0	0	1	1	0	0	0	—	3	7	0	0	0.2	1.000
1990		4	5	.444	2.77	66	2	0	107.1	98	24	76	0	3	4	5	7	0	0	.000	8	7	1	0	0.2	.938
1991		2	3	.400	3.43	60	0	0	76	75	19	53	0	2	3	6	1	0	0	.000	7	10	1	0	0.3	.944
1992		0	3	.000	5.19	49	2	0	78	95	20	43	0	0	2	0	7	2	0	.286	5	10	1	0	0.3	.938
6 yrs.		11	13	.458	3.44	281	4	0	423.2	444	110	293	0	10	11	15	22	3	0	.136	31	43	4	1	0.3	.949

Jerry Crider

CRIDER, JERRY STEPHEN
B. Sept. 2, 1941, Sioux Falls, S. D.
BR TR 6′ 2″ 200 lbs.

Year	Team	W	L	PCT	ERA	G	GS	CG	IP	H	BB	SO	ShO	Relief W	Relief L	Relief SV	AB	H	HR	BA	PO	A	E	DP	TC/G	FA
1969	MIN A	1	0	1.000	4.71	21	1	0	28.2	31	15	16	0	1	0	1	9	4	0	.444	2	4	0	1	0.3	1.000
1970	CHI A	4	7	.364	4.45	32	8	0	91	101	34	40	0	2	2	4	24	2	0	.083	3	7	1	0	0.3	.909
2 yrs.		5	7	.417	4.51	53	9	0	119.2	132	49	56	0	3	2	5	33	6	0	.182	5	11	1	1	0.3	.941

Chuck Crim

CRIM, CHARLES ROBERT
B. July 23, 1961, Van Nuys, Calif.
BR TR 6′ 175 lbs.

Year	Team	W	L	PCT	ERA	G	GS	CG	IP	H	BB	SO	ShO	Relief W	Relief L	Relief SV	AB	H	HR	BA	PO	A	E	DP	TC/G	FA
1987	MIL A	6	8	.429	3.67	53	5	0	130	133	39	56	0	5	4	12	0	0	0	—	14	17	4	3	0.7	.886
1988		7	6	.538	2.91	**70**	0	0	105	95	28	58	0	7	6	9	0	0	0	—	12	13	3	1	0.4	.893
1989		9	7	.563	2.83	**76**	0	0	117.2	114	36	59	0	9	7	7	0	0	0	—	5	13	1	2	0.2	.947
1990		3	5	.375	3.47	67	0	0	85.2	88	23	39	0	3	5	11	0	0	0	—	10	12	1	1	0.3	.957
1991		8	5	.615	4.63	66	0	0	91.1	115	25	39	0	8	5	3	0	0	0	—	8	14	1	0	0.3	.957
1992	CAL A	7	6	.538	5.17	57	0	0	87	100	29	30	0	7	6	1	0	0	0	—	7	12	1	0	0.4	.950
1993		2	2	.500	5.87	11	0	0	15.1	17	5	10	0	2	2	0	0	0	0	—	0	5	0	0	0.5	1.000
1994	CHI N	5	4	.556	4.48	49	1	0	64.1	69	24	43	0	4	4	2	2	0	0	.000	6	8	0	1	0.3	1.000
8 yrs.		47	43	.522	3.83	449	6	0	696.1	731	209	334	0	45	39	45	2	0	0	.000	62	94	11	8	0.4	.934

Jack Crimian

CRIMIAN, JOHN MELVIN
B. Feb. 17, 1926, Philadelphia, Pa.
BR TR 5′10″ 180 lbs.

Year	Team	W	L	PCT	ERA	G	GS	CG	IP	H	BB	SO	ShO	Relief W	Relief L	Relief SV	AB	H	HR	BA	PO	A	E	DP	TC/G	FA
1951	STL N	1	0	1.000	9.00	11	0	0	17	24	8	5	0	1	0	1	3	1	0	.333	1	1	0	0	0.2	1.000
1952		0	0	—	9.72	5	0	0	8.1	15	4	4	0	0	0	0	1	0	0	.000	0	1	0	0	0.2	1.000
1956	KC A	4	8	.333	5.51	54	7	0	129	129	49	59	0	3	3	3	22	5	0	.227	3	22	1	1	0.5	.962
1957	DET A	0	1	.000	12.71	4	0	0	5.2	9	4	1	0	0	1	0	0	0	0	—	0	1	0	0	0.3	1.000
4 yrs.		5	9	.357	6.36	74	7	0	160	177	65	69	0	4	4	4	26	6	0	.231	4	25	1	1	0.4	.967

Dode Criss

CRISS, DODE
B. Mar. 12, 1885, Sherman, Miss. D. Sept. 8, 1955, Sherman, Miss.
BL TR 6′ 2″ 200 lbs.

Year	Team	W	L	PCT	ERA	G	GS	CG	IP	H	BB	SO	ShO	Relief W	Relief L	Relief SV	AB	H	HR	BA	PO	A	E	DP	TC/G	FA
1908	STL A	0	1	.000	6.50	9	1	0	18	15	13	9	0	0	1	0	82	28	0	.341	21	4	2	0	1.3	.926
1909		1	5	.167	3.42	11	6	3	55.1	53	32	43	0	0	1	0	48	14	0	.292	2	10	0	0	1.1	1.000
1910		2	1	.667	1.40	6	0	0	19.1	12	9	9	0	2	1	0	91	21	1	.231	114	10	2	5	7.0	.984
1911		0	2	.000	8.35	4	2	0	18.1	24	10	9	0	0	0	0	83	21	2	.253	124	12	6	5	7.9	.958
4 yrs.		3	9	.250	4.38	30	9	3	111	104	64	70	0	2	3	0	*				261	36	10	10	4.5	.967

Bill Cristall

CRISTALL, WILLIAM ARTHUR (Lefty)
B. Sept. 12, 1878, Odessa, Russia D. Jan. 28, 1939, Buffalo, N. Y.
BL TL 5′ 7″ 147 lbs.

Year	Team	W	L	PCT	ERA	G	GS	CG	IP	H	BB	SO	ShO	Relief W	Relief L	Relief SV	AB	H	HR	BA	PO	A	E	DP	TC/G	FA
1901	CLE A	1	5	.167	4.84	6	6	5	48.1	54	30	12	1	0	0	0	20	7	0	.350	3	19	1	3	3.8	.957

Leo Cristante

CRISTANTE, DANTE LEO
B. Dec. 10, 1926, Detroit, Mich. D. Aug. 24, 1977, Dearborn, Mich.
BR TR 6′ 1″ 195 lbs.

Year	Team	W	L	PCT	ERA	G	GS	CG	IP	H	BB	SO	ShO	Relief W	Relief L	Relief SV	AB	H	HR	BA	PO	A	E	DP	TC/G	FA
1951	PHI N	1	1	.500	4.91	10	1	0	22	28	9	6	0	1	0	0	6	1	0	.167	1	5	0	0	0.6	1.000
1955	DET A	0	1	.000	3.19	20	1	0	36.2	37	14	9	0	0	1	0	7	0	0	.000	1	1	1	0	0.2	.667
2 yrs.		1	2	.333	3.84	30	2	0	58.2	65	23	15	0	1	1	0	13	1	0	.077	2	6	1	0	0.3	.889

Morrie Critchley

CRITCHLEY, MORRIS ARTHUR
B. Mar. 26, 1850, New London, Conn. D. Mar. 6, 1910, Pittsburgh, Pa.
6′ 1″ 190 lbs.

Year	Team	W	L	PCT	ERA	G	GS	CG	IP	H	BB	SO	ShO	Relief W	Relief L	Relief SV	AB	H	HR	BA	PO	A	E	DP	TC/G	FA
1882	2 teams	PIT AA (1G 1–0)	STL AA (4G 0–4)																							
″	total	1	4	.200	3.35	5	5	5	43	50	8	5	1	0	0	0	19	3	0	.158	2	9	1	0	2.4	.917

Claude Crocker

CROCKER, CLAUDE ARTHUR
B. July 20, 1924, Caroleen, N. C.
BR TR 6′ 2″ 185 lbs.

Year	Team	W	L	PCT	ERA	G	GS	CG	IP	H	BB	SO	ShO	Relief W	Relief L	Relief SV	AB	H	HR	BA	PO	A	E	DP	TC/G	FA
1944	BKN N	0	0	—	10.80	2	0	0	3.1	6	5	1	0	0	0	0	1	1	0	1.000	0	1	0	0	0.5	1.000
1945		0	0	—	0.00	1	0	0	2	2	1	1	0	0	0	1	0	0	0	—	0	0	0	0	0.0	.000
2 yrs.		0	0		6.75	3	0	0	5.1	8	6	2	0	0	0	1	1	1	0	1.000	0	1	0	0	0.3	1.000

Ray Crone

CRONE, RAYMOND HAYES
B. Aug. 7, 1931, Memphis, Tenn.
BR TR 6′ 2″ 165 lbs.

Year	Team	W	L	PCT	ERA	G	GS	CG	IP	H	BB	SO	ShO	Relief W	Relief L	Relief SV	AB	H	HR	BA	PO	A	E	DP	TC/G	FA
1954	MIL N	1	0	1.000	2.02	19	2	1	49	44	19	33	0	0	0	1	10	2	0	.200	1	7	0	0	0.4	1.000
1955		10	9	.526	3.46	33	15	6	140.1	117	42	76	1	5	2	0	44	7	0	.159	11	19	0	5	0.9	1.000
1956		11	10	.524	3.87	35	21	6	169.2	173	44	73	0	1	2	2	49	6	0	.122	15	23	1	2	1.1	.974
1957	2 teams	MIL N (11G 3–1)	NY N (25G 4–8)																							
″	total	7	9	.438	4.36	36	22	4	163	185	55	71	0	0	1	1	51	3	0	.059	11	42	0	4	1.5	1.000
1958	SF N	1	2	.333	6.75	14	1	0	24	35	13	7	0	1	2	0	2	0	0	.000	0	4	0	0	0.3	1.000
5 yrs.		30	30	.500	3.87	137	61	17	546	554	173	260	1	7	7	4	156	18	0	.115	38	95	1	11	1.0	.993

John Cronin

CRONIN, JOHN J.
B. May 26, 1874, West New Brighton, N. Y. D. July 13, 1929, Middletown, N. Y.
BR TR 6′ 200 lbs.

Year	Team	W	L	PCT	ERA	G	GS	CG	IP	H	BB	SO	ShO	Relief W	Relief L	Relief SV	AB	H	HR	BA	PO	A	E	DP	TC/G	FA
1895	BKN N	0	0	—	10.80	2	0	0	5	10	3	1	0	0	0	2	2	1	0	.500	0	0	0	0	0.0	.000
1898	PIT N	2	2	.500	3.54	4	4	2	28	35	8	9	1	0	0	0	10	1	0	.100	2	8	1	0	2.8	.909
1899	CIN N	2	2	.500	5.49	5	5	5	41	56	16	9	0	0	0	0	17	2	0	.118	1	7	3	0	2.2	.727
1901	DET A	13	15	.464	3.89	30	28	21	219.2	261	42	62	1	1	0	0	85	21	0	.247	13	51	12	3	2.5	.842
1902	3 teams	DET A (4G 0–0)	BAL A (10G 3–5)	NY N (13G 5–6)																						
″	total	8	11	.421	3.09	27	20	19	207	197	50	77	0	0	0	0	99	15	0	.152	26	69	6	2	3.0	.941

John Cronin *continued*

Year	Team	Lg	W	L	PCT	ERA	G	GS	CG	IP	H	BB	SO	ShO	Relief W	Relief L	Relief SV	Batting AB	Batting H	HR	BA	PO	A	E	DP	TC/G	FA
1903	NY	N	6	4	.600	3.81	20	11	8	115.2	130	37	50	0	1	0	1	46	9	0	.196	9	29	3	1	2.0	.927
1904	BKN	N	12	23	.343	2.70	40	34	33	307	284	79	110	4	1	1	0	108	17	0	.157	18	84	8	3	2.8	.927
7 yrs.			43	57	.430	3.40	128	102	88	923.1	973	235	318	6	3	1	3	367	66	0	.180	69	248	33	9	2.6	.906

George Crosby

CROSBY, GEORGE WASHINGTON
B. 1860, Chicago, Ill. D. Jan. 9, 1913, San Francisco, Calif.

Year	Team	Lg	W	L	PCT	ERA	G	GS	CG	IP	H	BB	SO	ShO	Relief W	Relief L	Relief SV	Batting AB	Batting H	HR	BA	PO	A	E	DP	TC/G	FA
1884	CHI	N	1	2	.333	*3.54*	3	3	3	28	27	12	11	0	0	0	0	13	4	1	.308	2	8	0	0	3.3	1.000

Ken Crosby

CROSBY, KENNETH STEWART BR TR 6′ 2″ 179 lbs.
B. Dec. 15, 1947, New Denver, B. C., Canada.

Year	Team	Lg	W	L	PCT	ERA	G	GS	CG	IP	H	BB	SO	ShO	Relief W	Relief L	Relief SV	Batting AB	Batting H	HR	BA	PO	A	E	DP	TC/G	FA
1975	CHI	N	1	0	1.000	3.38	9	0	0	8	10	7	6	0	1	0	0	0	0	0	—	0	3	0	0	0.3	1.000
1976			0	0	—	12.00	7	1	0	12	20	8	5	0	0	0	0	2	1	0	.500	1	2	0	0	0.4	1.000
2 yrs.			1	0	1.000	8.55	16	1	0	20	30	15	11	0	1	0	0	2	1	0	.500	1	5	0	0	0.4	1.000

Lem Cross

CROSS, GEORGE LEWIS TR 5′ 9″ 155 lbs.
B. Jan. 9, 1872, Sanbornton, N. H. D. Oct. 9, 1930, Manchester, N. H.

Year	Team	Lg	W	L	PCT	ERA	G	GS	CG	IP	H	BB	SO	ShO	Relief W	Relief L	Relief SV	Batting AB	Batting H	HR	BA	PO	A	E	DP	TC/G	FA
1893	CIN	N	0	2	.000	5.57	3	3	2	21	24	9	7	0	0	0	0	6	2	0	.333	1	6	0	0	2.3	1.000
1894			3	4	.429	8.49	8	7	3	53	94	21	11	0	0	1	0	26	6	0	.231	1	8	1	0	1.3	.900
2 yrs.			3	6	.333	7.66	11	10	5	74	118	30	18	0	0	1	0	32	8	0	.250	2	14	1	0	1.5	.941

Dug Crothers

CROTHERS, DOUGLASS BR TR
B. Nov. 16, 1859, Natchez, Miss. D. Mar. 29, 1907, St. Louis, Mo.

Year	Team	Lg	W	L	PCT	ERA	G	GS	CG	IP	H	BB	SO	ShO	Relief W	Relief L	Relief SV	Batting AB	Batting H	HR	BA	PO	A	E	DP	TC/G	FA
1884	KC	U	1	2	.333	*1.80*	3	3	3	25	26	6	11	0	0	0	0	15	2	0	.133	0	6	6	0	3.0	.500
1885	NY	AA	7	11	.389	*5.08*	18	18	18	154	192	49	40	1	0	0	0	51	8	0	.157	5	30	7	1	2.3	.833
2 yrs.			8	13	.381	4.63	21	21	21	179	218	55	51	1	0	0	0	66	10	0	.152	5	36	13	1	2.5	.759

Bill Crouch

CROUCH, WILLIAM HENRY (Skip) BL TL 6′ 1″ 210 lbs.
Father of Bill Crouch.
B. Dec. 3, 1886, Marshallton, Del. D. Dec. 22, 1945, Highland Park, Mich.

Year	Team	Lg	W	L	PCT	ERA	G	GS	CG	IP	H	BB	SO	ShO	Relief W	Relief L	Relief SV	Batting AB	Batting H	HR	BA	PO	A	E	DP	TC/G	FA
1910	STL	A	0	0	—	3.38	1	1	1	8	6	7	2	0	0	0	0	3	0	0	.000	2	1	0	0	3.0	1.000

Bill Crouch

CROUCH, WILMER ELMER BB TR 6′ 1″ 180 lbs.
Son of Bill Crouch.
B. Aug. 20, 1910, Wilmington, Del. D. Dec. 26, 1980, Howell, Mich.

Year	Team	Lg	W	L	PCT	ERA	G	GS	CG	IP	H	BB	SO	ShO	Relief W	Relief L	Relief SV	Batting AB	Batting H	HR	BA	PO	A	E	DP	TC/G	FA
1939	BKN	N	4	0	1.000	2.58	6	3	3	38.1	37	14	10	0	1	0	0	15	2	0	.133	3	4	0	0	1.2	1.000
1941	2 teams	PHI N (20G 2–3) STL N (18G 1–2)																									
″	total		3	5	.375	3.81	38	9	1	104	110	31	41	0	0	2	7	24	1	0	.042	3	26	1	1	0.8	.967
1945	STL	N	1	0	1.000	3.38	6	0	0	13.1	12	7	4	0	1	0	0	2	0	0	.000	1	3	0	0	0.7	1.000
3 yrs.			8	5	.615	3.47	50	12	4	155.2	159	52	55	0	2	2	7	41	3	0	.073	7	33	1	1	0.8	.976

Zach Crouch

CROUCH, ZACHARY QUINN BL TL 6′ 3″ 190 lbs.
B. Oct. 26, 1965, Folsom, Calif.

Year	Team	Lg	W	L	PCT	ERA	G	GS	CG	IP	H	BB	SO	ShO	Relief W	Relief L	Relief SV	Batting AB	Batting H	HR	BA	PO	A	E	DP	TC/G	FA
1988	BOS	A	0	0	—	6.75	3	0	0	1.1	4	2	0	0	0	0	0	0	0	0	—	0	0	0	0	0.0	.000

General Crowder

CROWDER, ALVIN FLOYD BL TR 5′10″ 170 lbs.
B. Jan. 11, 1899, Winston-Salem, N. C. D. Apr. 3, 1972, Winston-Salem, N. C.

Year	Team	Lg	W	L	PCT	ERA	G	GS	CG	IP	H	BB	SO	ShO	Relief W	Relief L	Relief SV	Batting AB	Batting H	HR	BA	PO	A	E	DP	TC/G	FA
1926	WAS	A	7	4	.636	3.96	19	12	6	100	97	60	26	0	1	0	1	38	9	0	.237	5	13	1	0	1.0	.947
1927	2 teams	WAS A (15G 4–7) STL A (21G 3–5)																									
″	total		7	12	.368	4.79	36	19	6	141	129	84	52	3	2	1	3	45	9	0	.200	4	24	0	1	0.8	1.000
1928	STL	A	21	5	**.808**	3.69	41	31	19	244	238	91	99	1	0	0	2	80	15	0	.188	4	33	2	3	1.0	.949
1929			17	15	.531	3.92	40	34	19	266.2	272	93	79	**4**	1	0	4	96	18	0	.188	6	50	1	1	1.4	.982
1930	2 teams	STL A (13G 3–7) WAS A (27G 15–9)																									
″	total		18	16	.529	3.89	40	35	25	279.2	276	96	107	1	0	0	2	101	17	0	.168	8	42	1	3	1.3	.980
1931	WAS	A	18	11	.621	3.88	44	26	13	234.1	255	72	85	1	4	2	2	88	19	0	.216	5	34	1	1	0.9	.975
1932			**26**	13	.667	3.33	50	**39**	21	**327**	**319**	77	103	3	5	0	1	122	27	0	.221	7	53	1	5	1.2	.984
1933			**24**	15	.615	3.97	**52**	35	17	299.1	**311**	81	110	0	4	4	4	102	19	0	.186	0	53	0	2	1.0	1.000
1934	2 teams	WAS A (29G 4–10) DET A (9G 5–1)																									
″	total		9	11	.450	5.75	38	22	7	167.1	223	58	69	1	1	4	3	62	11	0	.177	5	25	0	0	0.8	1.000
1935	DET	A	16	10	.615	4.26	33	32	16	241	269	67	59	2	0	0	0	93	17	0	.183	10	31	0	5	1.2	1.000
1936			4	3	.571	8.39	9	7	1	44	64	21	10	0	1	0	0	20	3	0	.150	4	6	0	1	1.1	1.000
11 yrs.			167	115	.592	4.12	402	292	150	2344.1	2453	800	799	16	19	11	22	847	164	0	.194	58	364	7	22	1.1	.984
WORLD SERIES																											
1933	WAS	A	0	1	.000	7.36	2	2	0	11	16	5	7	0	0	0	0	4	1	0	.250	0	3	0	0	1.5	1.000
1934	DET	A	0	1	.000	1.50	2	1	0	6	6	1	2	0	0	0	0	1	0	0	.000	0	0	0	0	0.0	.000
1935			1	0	1.000	1.00	1	1	1	9	5	3	5	0	0	0	0	3	1	0	.333	2	1	0	0	3.0	1.000
3 yrs.			1	2	.333	3.81	5	4	1	26	27	9	14	0	0	0	0	8	2	0	.250	2	4	0	0	1.2	1.000

Billy Crowell

CROWELL, WILLIAM THEODORE BR TR 5′ 8½″ 160 lbs.
B. Nov. 6, 1865, Cincinnati, Ohio D. July 24, 1935, Fort Worth, Tex.

Year	Team	Lg	W	L	PCT	ERA	G	GS	CG	IP	H	BB	SO	ShO	Relief W	Relief L	Relief SV	Batting AB	Batting H	HR	BA	PO	A	E	DP	TC/G	FA
1887	CLE	AA	14	31	.311	*4.88*	45	45	45	389.1	541	138	72	1	0	0	0	156	22	0	.141	5	65	5	4	1.7	.933
1888	2 teams	CLE AA (18G 5–13) LOU AA (1G 0–1)																									
″	total		5	14	.263	5.81	19	19	17	159.2	224	67	66	0	0	0	0	61	5	0	.082	2	35	3	1	2.0	.925
2 yrs.			19	45	.297	5.15	64	64	62	549	765	205	138	1	0	0	0	217	27	0	.124	7	100	8	5	1.8	.930

Cap Crowell

CROWELL, MINOT JOY BR TR 6′ 1″ 178 lbs.
B. Sept. 5, 1892, Roxbury, Mass. D. Sept. 30, 1962, Central Falls, R. I.

Year	Team	Lg	W	L	PCT	ERA	G	GS	CG	IP	H	BB	SO	ShO	Relief W	Relief L	Relief SV	Batting AB	Batting H	HR	BA	PO	A	E	DP	TC/G	FA
1915	PHI	A	2	6	.250	5.47	10	8	4	54.1	56	47	15	0	0	0	0	22	5	0	.227	1	15	0	0	1.6	1.000
1916			0	5	.000	4.76	9	6	1	39.2	43	34	15	0	0	0	0	12	0	0	.000	2	8	1	0	1.2	.909
2 yrs.			2	11	.154	5.17	19	14	5	94	99	81	30	0	0	0	0	34	5	0	.147	3	23	1	0	1.4	.963

Woody Crowson

CROWSON, THOMAS WOODROW BR TR 6′ 2″ 185 lbs.
B. Sept. 9, 1918, Fuquay Springs, N. C. D. Aug. 14, 1947, Mayodan, N. C.

Year	Team	Lg	W	L	PCT	ERA	G	GS	CG	IP	H	BB	SO	ShO	Relief Pitching W	Relief Pitching L	Relief Pitching SV	Batting AB	Batting H	Batting HR	BA	PO	A	E	DP	TC/G	FA
1945	PHI	A	0	0	—	6.00	1	0	0	3	2	3	2	0	0	0	0	1	0	0	.000	0	2	0	0	2.0	1.000

Cal Crum

CRUM, CALVIN N. BR TR 6′ 1″ 175 lbs.
B. July 27, 1890, Cooks Mills, Ill. D. Dec. 7, 1945, Tulsa, Okla.

Year	Team	Lg	W	L	PCT	ERA	G	GS	CG	IP	H	BB	SO	ShO	Relief Pitching W	Relief Pitching L	Relief Pitching SV	Batting AB	Batting H	Batting HR	BA	PO	A	E	DP	TC/G	FA
1917	BOS	N	0	0	—	0.00	1	0	0	1	1	1	0	0	0	0	0	0	0	0	—	0	2	0	0	2.0	1.000
1918			0	1	.000	15.43	1	1	0	2.1	6	3	0	0	0	0	0	1	0	0	.000	0	2	0	0	2.0	1.000
2 yrs.			0	1	.000	10.80	2	1	0	3.1	7	4	0	0	0	0	0	1	0	0	.000	0	4	0	0	2.0	1.000

Roy Crumpler

CRUMPLER, ROY MAXTON BL TL 6′ 1″ 195 lbs.
B. July 8, 1896, Clinton, N. C. D. Oct. 6, 1969, Fayetteville, N. C.

Year	Team	Lg	W	L	PCT	ERA	G	GS	CG	IP	H	BB	SO	ShO	Relief Pitching W	Relief Pitching L	Relief Pitching SV	Batting AB	Batting H	Batting HR	BA	PO	A	E	DP	TC/G	FA
1920	DET	A	1	0	1.000	5.54	3	2	1	13	17	11	2	0	0	0	0	9	3	0	.333	0	2	1	0	1.0	.667
1925	PHI	N	0	0	—	7.71	3	1	0	4.2	8	2	1	0	0	0	0	2	0	0	.000	0	3	0	0	1.0	1.000
2 yrs.			1	0	1.000	6.11	6	3	1	17.2	25	13	3	0	0	0	0	11	3	0	.273	0	5	1	0	1.0	.833

Dick Crutcher

CRUTCHER, RICHARD LOUIS BR TR 5′ 9″ 148 lbs.
B. Nov. 25, 1889, Frankfort, Ky. D. June 19, 1952, Frankfort, Ky.

Year	Team	Lg	W	L	PCT	ERA	G	GS	CG	IP	H	BB	SO	ShO	Relief Pitching W	Relief Pitching L	Relief Pitching SV	Batting AB	Batting H	Batting HR	BA	PO	A	E	DP	TC/G	FA
1914	BOS	N	5	7	.417	3.46	33	15	5	158.2	169	66	48	1	2	2	0	54	8	0	.148	3	48	1	0	1.6	.981
1915			2	2	.500	4.33	14	4	1	43.2	50	16	17	0	1	0	2	13	3	0	.231	4	14	3	0	1.5	.857
2 yrs.			7	9	.438	3.65	47	19	6	202.1	219	82	65	1	3	2	2	67	11	0	.164	7	62	4	0	1.6	.945

Todd Cruz

CRUZ, TODD RUBEN BR TR 6′ 175 lbs.
B. Nov. 23, 1955, Highland Park, Mich.

Year	Team	Lg	W	L	PCT	ERA	G	GS	CG	IP	H	BB	SO	ShO	Relief Pitching W	Relief Pitching L	Relief Pitching SV	Batting AB	Batting H	Batting HR	BA	PO	A	E	DP	TC/G	FA
1984	BAL	A	0	0	—	0.00	1	0	0	1	0	0	0	0	0	0	0	*				1	6	0	0	3.5	1.000

Victor Cruz

CRUZ, VICTOR MANUEL BR TR 5′ 9″ 174 lbs.
Born Victor Manuel De La Cruz (Gil).
B. Dec. 24, 1957, Ranch Viejo la Vega, Dominican Republic.

Year	Team	Lg	W	L	PCT	ERA	G	GS	CG	IP	H	BB	SO	ShO	Relief Pitching W	Relief Pitching L	Relief Pitching SV	Batting AB	Batting H	Batting HR	BA	PO	A	E	DP	TC/G	FA
1978	TOR	A	7	3	.700	1.71	32	0	0	47.1	28	36	51	0	7	3	9	0	0	0	—	1	5	0	0	0.2	1.000
1979	CLE	A	3	9	.250	4.22	61	0	0	79	70	44	63	0	3	9	10	0	0	0	—	1	4	2	0	0.1	.714
1980			6	7	.462	3.45	55	0	0	86	71	27	88	0	6	7	12	0	0	0	—	1	5	1	1	0.1	.857
1981	PIT	N	1	1	.500	2.65	22	0	0	34	33	15	28	0	1	1	1	4	0	0	.000	1	5	0	1	0.3	1.000
1983	TEX	A	1	3	.250	1.44	17	0	0	25	16	10	18	0	1	3	5	0	0	0	—	1	2	1	0	0.2	.750
5 yrs.			18	23	.439	3.08	187	0	0	271.1	218	132	248	0	18	23	37	4	0	0	.000	5	21	4	2	0.2	.867

Cookie Cuccurullo

CUCCURULLO, ARTHUR JOSEPH BL TL 5′10″ 168 lbs.
B. Feb. 8, 1918, Asbury Park, N. J. D. Jan. 23, 1983, West Orange, N. J.

Year	Team	Lg	W	L	PCT	ERA	G	GS	CG	IP	H	BB	SO	ShO	Relief Pitching W	Relief Pitching L	Relief Pitching SV	Batting AB	Batting H	Batting HR	BA	PO	A	E	DP	TC/G	FA
1943	PIT	N	0	1	.000	6.43	1	1	0	7	10	3	3	0	0	0	0	0	0	0	—	1	2	1	1	4.0	.750
1944			2	1	.667	4.06	32	4	0	106.1	110	44	31	0	2	1	4	38	14	0	.368	9	23	2	2	1.1	.941
1945			1	3	.250	5.24	29	4	0	56.2	68	34	17	0	1	1	1	14	3	0	.214	2	12	1	0	0.5	.933
3 yrs.			3	5	.375	4.55	62	9	0	170	188	81	51	0	3	2	5	52	17	0	.327	12	37	4	3	0.9	.925

Jim Cudworth

CUDWORTH, JAMES ALARIC BR TR 6′ 165 lbs.
B. Aug. 22, 1858, Fairhaven, Mass. D. Dec. 21, 1943, Middleboro, Mass.

Year	Team	Lg	W	L	PCT	ERA	G	GS	CG	IP	H	BB	SO	ShO	Relief Pitching W	Relief Pitching L	Relief Pitching SV	Batting AB	Batting H	Batting HR	BA	PO	A	E	DP	TC/G	FA
1884	KC	U	0	0	—	4.24	2	1	1	17	19	3	6	0	0	0	0	*				202	9	8	10	6.6	.963

Bobby Cuellar

CUELLAR, ROBERT BR TR 5′11″ 188 lbs.
B. Aug. 20, 1952, Alice, Tex.

Year	Team	Lg	W	L	PCT	ERA	G	GS	CG	IP	H	BB	SO	ShO	Relief Pitching W	Relief Pitching L	Relief Pitching SV	Batting AB	Batting H	Batting HR	BA	PO	A	E	DP	TC/G	FA
1977	TEX	A	0	0	—	1.29	4	0	0	7	4	2	3	0	0	0	0	0	0	0	—	0	0	0	0	0.0	.000

Charlie Cuellar

CUELLAR, JESUS PATRACIS BR TR 5′11″ 183 lbs.
B. Sept. 24, 1917, Ybor City, Fla. D. Oct. 11, 1994, Tampa, Fla.

Year	Team	Lg	W	L	PCT	ERA	G	GS	CG	IP	H	BB	SO	ShO	Relief Pitching W	Relief Pitching L	Relief Pitching SV	Batting AB	Batting H	Batting HR	BA	PO	A	E	DP	TC/G	FA
1950	CHI	A	0	0	—	33.75	2	0	0	1.1	6	3	1	0	0	0	0	0	0	0	—	0	0	0	0	0.0	.000

Mike Cuellar

CUELLAR, MIGUEL ANGEL BL TL 6′ 165 lbs.
Born Miguel Angel Cuellar (Santana).
B. May 8, 1937, Las Villas, Cuba.

Year	Team	Lg	W	L	PCT	ERA	G	GS	CG	IP	H	BB	SO	ShO	Relief Pitching W	Relief Pitching L	Relief Pitching SV	Batting AB	Batting H	Batting HR	BA	PO	A	E	DP	TC/G	FA
1959	CIN	N	0	0	—	15.75	2	0	0	4	7	4	5	0	0	0	0	1	0	0	.000	0	0	0	0	0.0	.000
1964	STL	N	5	5	.500	4.50	32	7	1	72	80	33	56	0	3	0	4	18	0	0	.000	4	18	3	1	0.8	.880
1965	HOU	N	1	4	.200	3.54	25	4	0	56	55	21	46	0	1	1	2	12	0	0	.000	2	10	1	1	0.5	.923
1966			12	10	.545	2.22	38	28	11	227.1	193	52	175	1	3	1	2	71	8	1	.113	5	38	2	4	1.2	.956
1967			16	11	.593	3.03	36	32	16	246.1	233	63	203	3	1	0	1	93	13	0	.140	15	35	2	1	1.4	.962
1968			8	11	.421	2.74	28	24	11	170.2	152	45	133	2	0	1	1	57	11	1	.193	13	24	4	1	1.5	.902
1969	BAL	A	23	11	.676	2.38	39	39	18	290.2	213	79	182	5	0	0	0	103	12	0	.117	9	45	2	7	1.4	.964
1970			**24**	8	**.750**	3.47	40	**40**	**21**	298	273	69	190	4	0	0	0	112	10	2	.089	9	34	2	1	1.1	.956
1971			20	9	.690	3.08	38	38	21	292	250	78	124	4	0	0	0	107	11	1	.103	14	53	2	5	1.8	.971
1972			18	12	.600	2.57	35	35	17	248.1	197	71	132	4	0	0	0	87	11	2	.126	10	43	5	5	1.7	.914
1973			18	13	.581	3.27	38	38	17	267	265	84	140	2	0	0	0	0	0	0	—	9	47	3	2	1.6	.949
1974			22	10	**.688**	3.11	38	38	20	269	253	86	106	5	0	0	0	0	0	0	—	5	35	1	1	1.1	.976
1975			14	12	.538	3.66	36	36	17	256	229	84	105	5	0	0	0	0	0	0	—	14	55	2	3	1.9	.972
1976			4	13	.235	4.96	26	19	2	107	129	50	32	1	0	2	1	0	0	0	—	2	18	1	1	0.8	.952
1977	CAL	A	0	1	.000	18.90	2	1	0	3.1	9	3	3	0	0	0	0	0	0	0	—	0	0	0	0	0.0	.000
15 yrs.			185	130	.587	3.14	453	379	172	2807.2	2538	822	1632	36	8	5	11	661	76	7	.115	111	455	30	33	1.3	.950
LEAGUE CHAMPIONSHIP SERIES																											
1969	BAL	A	0	0	—	2.25	1	1	0	8	3	1	7	0	0	0	0	2	0	0	.000	0	0	0	0	0.0	.000
1970			0	0	—	12.46	1	1	0	4.1	10	1	2	0	0	0	0	2	1	1	.500	1	3	0	0	4.0	1.000
1971			1	0	1.000	1.00	1	1	1	9	6	1	2	0	0	0	0	3	1	0	.333	0	2	0	0	2.0	1.000
1973			0	1	.000	1.80	1	1	1	10	4	3	11	0	0	0	0	0	0	0	—	0	2	0	0	2.0	1.000
1974			1	1	.500	2.84	2	2	0	12.2	9	13	6	0	0	0	0	0	0	0	—	0	5	0	0	2.5	1.000
5 yrs.			2	2	.500	3.07	6	6	2	44	32	19	28	0	0	0	0	7	2	1	.286	1	12	0	0	2.2	1.000
								9th	**4th**	**10th**		**4th**															

Mike Cuellar *continued*

Year	Team	W	L	PCT	ERA	G	GS	CG	IP	H	BB	SO	ShO	Relief Pitching W	Relief Pitching L	Relief Pitching SV	Batting AB	Batting H	Batting HR	BA	PO	A	E	DP	TC/G	FA
WORLD SERIES																										
1969	BAL A	1	0	1.000	1.13	2	2	1	16	13	4	13	0	0	0	0	5	2	0	.400	0	1	0	0	0.5	1.000
1970		1	0	1.000	3.18	2	2	1	11.1	10	2	5	0	0	0	0	4	0	0	.000	0	1	0	1	0.5	1.000
1971		0	2	.000	3.86	2	2	0	14	11	6	10	0	0	0	0	3	0	0	.000	0	3	1	0	2.0	.750
3 yrs.		2	2	.500	2.61	6	6	2	41.1	34	12	28	0	0	0	0	12	2	0	.167	0	5	1	1	1.0	.833

Berto Cueto

CUETO, DAGOBERTO BR TR 6′ 4″ 170 lbs.
Born Dagoberto Cueto (Concepcion).
B. Aug. 14, 1937, San Luis Pinar, Cuba.

Year	Team	W	L	PCT	ERA	G	GS	CG	IP	H	BB	SO	ShO	Relief Pitching W	Relief Pitching L	Relief Pitching SV	Batting AB	Batting H	Batting HR	BA	PO	A	E	DP	TC/G	FA
1961	MIN A	1	3	.250	7.17	7	5	0	21.1	27	10	5	0	1	1	0	5	0	0	.000	2	4	1	0	1.0	.857

Jack Cullen

CULLEN, JOHN PATRICK BR TR 5′11″ 170 lbs.
B. Oct. 6, 1939, Newark, N. J.

Year	Team	W	L	PCT	ERA	G	GS	CG	IP	H	BB	SO	ShO	Relief Pitching W	Relief Pitching L	Relief Pitching SV	Batting AB	Batting H	Batting HR	BA	PO	A	E	DP	TC/G	FA
1962	NY A	0	0	—	0.00	2	0	0	3	2	2	2	0	0	0	1	0	0	0	—	0	0	0	0	0.0	.000
1965		3	4	.429	3.05	12	9	2	59	59	21	25	1	0	0	0	20	3	0	.150	2	16	2	0	1.7	.900
1966		1	0	1.000	3.97	5	0	0	11.1	11	5	7	0	1	0	0	3	0	0	.000	1	0	1	0	0.4	.500
3 yrs.		4	4	.500	3.07	19	9	2	73.1	72	28	34	1	1	0	1	23	3	0	.130	3	16	3	0	1.2	.864

Nick Cullop

CULLOP, HENRY NICHOLAS (Tomato Face) BR TR 6′ 200 lbs.
Born Heinrich Nicholas Kolop.
B. Oct. 16, 1900, St. Louis, Mo. D. Dec. 8, 1978, Gahanna, Ohio.

Year	Team	W	L	PCT	ERA	G	GS	CG	IP	H	BB	SO	ShO	Relief Pitching W	Relief Pitching L	Relief Pitching SV	Batting AB	Batting H	Batting HR	BA	PO	A	E	DP	TC/G	FA
1927	CLE A	0	0	—	9.00	1	0	0	1	3	0	0	0	0	0	0	*				59	4	1	0	2.4	.984

Nick Cullop

CULLOP, NORMAN ANDREW BL TL 5′11½″ 172 lbs.
B. Sept. 17, 1887, Chilhowie, Va. D. Apr. 15, 1961, Tazewell, Va.

Year	Team	W	L	PCT	ERA	G	GS	CG	IP	H	BB	SO	ShO	Relief Pitching W	Relief Pitching L	Relief Pitching SV	Batting AB	Batting H	Batting HR	BA	PO	A	E	DP	TC/G	FA
1913	CLE A	3	7	.300	4.42	23	8	4	97.2	105	35	30	0	1	3	0	31	4	0	.129	7	32	1	0	1.7	.975
1914	2 teams CLE A (1G 0–1) KC F (44G 14–17)																									
″	total	14	18	.438	2.35	45	36	22	299	260	88	152	4	1	2	1	100	14	0	.140	9	92	9	3	2.4	.918
1915	KC F	22	11	.667	2.44	44	36	22	302.1	278	67	111	3	2	0	2	96	18	0	.188	12	121	5	3	3.1	.964
1916	NY A	13	6	.684	2.05	28	22	9	167	151	32	77	0	2	0	1	55	6	0	.109	8	24	1	0	1.2	.970
1917		5	9	.357	3.32	30	18	5	146.1	161	31	27	2	1	1	1	44	7	0	.159	5	44	1	2	1.7	.980
1921	STL A	0	2	.000	8.49	4	1	0	11.2	18	6	3	0	0	1	0	3	0	0	.000	3	2	0	0	1.3	1.000
6 yrs.		57	53	.518	2.73	174	121	62	1024	973	259	400	9	7	7	5	329	49	0	.149	44	315	17	8	2.2	.955

Bud Culloton

CULLOTON, BERNARD ALOYSIUS BR TR 5′11″ 180 lbs.
B. May 19, 1896, Kingston, N. Y. D. Nov. 9, 1976, Kingston, N. Y.

Year	Team	W	L	PCT	ERA	G	GS	CG	IP	H	BB	SO	ShO	Relief Pitching W	Relief Pitching L	Relief Pitching SV	Batting AB	Batting H	Batting HR	BA	PO	A	E	DP	TC/G	FA
1925	PIT N	0	1	.000	2.57	9	1	0	21	19	1	3	0	0	0	0	3	0	0	.000	0	4	0	0	0.4	1.000
1926		0	0	—	7.36	4	0	0	3.2	3	6	1	0	0	0	0	0	0	0	—	0	1	0	0	0.3	1.000
2 yrs.		0	1	.000	3.28	13	1	0	24.2	22	7	4	0	0	0	0	3	0	0	.000	0	5	0	0	0.4	1.000

Bill Culp

CULP, WILLIAM EDWARD BB TR 6′ 1½″ 165 lbs.
B. June 11, 1887, Bellaire, Ohio D. Sept. 3, 1969, Arnold, Pa.

Year	Team	W	L	PCT	ERA	G	GS	CG	IP	H	BB	SO	ShO	Relief Pitching W	Relief Pitching L	Relief Pitching SV	Batting AB	Batting H	Batting HR	BA	PO	A	E	DP	TC/G	FA
1910	PHI N	0	0	—	8.10	4	0	0	6.2	8	4	4	0	0	0	1	2	0	0	.000	1	5	0	1	1.5	1.000

Ray Culp

CULP, RAYMOND LEONARD BR TR 6′ 200 lbs.
B. Aug. 6, 1941, Elgin, Tex.

Year	Team	W	L	PCT	ERA	G	GS	CG	IP	H	BB	SO	ShO	Relief Pitching W	Relief Pitching L	Relief Pitching SV	Batting AB	Batting H	Batting HR	BA	PO	A	E	DP	TC/G	FA
1963	PHI N	14	11	.560	2.97	34	30	10	203.1	148	**102**	176	5	2	1	0	66	9	0	.136	13	27	0	3	1.2	1.000
1964		8	7	.533	4.13	30	19	3	135	139	56	96	1	1	0	0	44	5	0	.114	10	20	2	0	1.1	.938
1965		14	10	.583	3.22	33	30	11	204.1	188	78	134	2	1	1	0	68	6	0	.088	19	24	0	2	1.3	1.000
1966		7	4	.636	5.04	34	12	1	110.2	106	53	100	0	4	0	1	26	2	0	.077	3	14	2	0	0.6	.895
1967	CHI N	8	11	.421	3.89	30	22	4	152.2	138	59	111	1	1	1	0	51	5	0	.098	7	21	1	2	1.0	.966
1968	BOS A	16	6	.727	2.91	35	30	11	216.1	166	82	190	6	0	0	0	70	8	0	.114	15	23	0	1	1.1	1.000
1969		17	8	.680	3.81	32	32	9	227	195	79	172	2	0	0	0	79	12	1	.152	20	31	8	1	1.8	.864
1970		17	14	.548	3.05	33	33	15	251	211	91	197	1	0	0	0	97	12	0	.124	22	24	5	4	1.5	.902
1971		14	16	.467	3.61	35	35	12	242	236	67	151	3	0	0	0	68	8	0	.118	8	32	3	1	1.2	.930
1972		5	8	.385	4.46	16	16	4	105	104	53	52	1	0	0	0	33	7	0	.212	12	14	0	1	1.6	1.000
1973		2	6	.250	4.50	10	9	0	50	46	32	32	0	0	0	0	0	0	0	—	6	7	1	0	1.4	.929
11 yrs.		122	101	.547	3.58	322	268	80	1897.1	1677	752	1411	22	9	3	1	602	74	1	.123	135	237	22	15	1.2	.944

George Culver

CULVER, GEORGE RAYMOND BR TR 6′ 2″ 185 lbs.
B. July 8, 1943, Salinas, Calif.

Year	Team	W	L	PCT	ERA	G	GS	CG	IP	H	BB	SO	ShO	Relief Pitching W	Relief Pitching L	Relief Pitching SV	Batting AB	Batting H	Batting HR	BA	PO	A	E	DP	TC/G	FA
1966	CLE A	0	2	.000	8.38	5	1	0	9.2	15	7	6	0	0	1	0	2	0	0	.000	1	3	0	1	0.8	1.000
1967		7	3	.700	3.96	53	1	0	75	71	31	41	0	7	2	3	4	1	0	.250	6	16	1	1	0.4	.957
1968	CIN N	11	16	.407	3.23	42	35	5	226	229	84	114	2	2	0	2	66	8	0	.121	23	45	2	2	1.7	.971
1969		5	7	.417	4.28	32	13	0	101	117	52	58	0	0	0	4	31	3	0	.097	10	23	1	1	1.1	.971
1970	2 teams STL N (11G 3–3) HOU N (32G 3–3)																									
″	total	6	6	.500	3.98	43	7	2	101.2	108	45	54	0	3	6	3	21	4	0	.190	8	19	2	2	0.7	.931
1971	HOU N	5	8	.385	2.65	59	0	0	95	89	38	57	0	5	8	7	11	1	0	.091	7	17	3	3	0.5	.889
1972		6	2	.750	3.05	45	0	0	97.1	73	43	82	0	6	2	2	19	3	0	.158	6	12	2	1	0.4	.900
1973	2 teams LA N (28G 4–4) PHI N (14G 3–1)																									
″	total	7	5	.583	3.56	42	0	0	60.2	71	36	30	0	7	5	2	4	0	0	.000	6	18	0	2	0.6	1.000
1974	PHI N	1	0	1.000	6.55	14	0	0	22	20	16	9	0	1	0	0	3	0	0	.000	0	3	2	0	0.4	.600
9 yrs.		48	49	.495	3.62	335	57	7	788.1	793	352	451	2	31	24	23	161	20	0	.124	67	156	13	13	0.7	.945

John Cumberland

CUMBERLAND, JOHN SHELDON BR TL 6′ 185 lbs.
B. May 10, 1947, Westbrook, Me.

Year	Team	W	L	PCT	ERA	G	GS	CG	IP	H	BB	SO	ShO	Relief Pitching W	Relief Pitching L	Relief Pitching SV	Batting AB	Batting H	Batting HR	BA	PO	A	E	DP	TC/G	FA
1968	NY A	0	0	—	9.00	1	0	0	2	3	1	1	0	0	0	0	0	0	0	—	1	2	0	0	3.0	1.000
1969		0	0	—	4.50	2	0	0	4	3	4	0	0	0	0	0	0	0	0	—	0	1	0	0	0.5	1.000
1970	2 teams NY A (15G 3–4) SF N (7G 2–0)																									
″	total	5	4	.556	3.48	22	8	1	75	68	19	44	0	3	0	0	18	1	0	.056	2	8	0	0	0.5	1.000

John Cumberland *continued*

Year	Team	Lg	W	L	PCT	ERA	G	GS	CG	IP	H	BB	SO	ShO	Relief Pitching W	Relief Pitching L	Relief Pitching SV	Batting AB	Batting H	Batting HR	BA	PO	A	E	DP	TC/G	FA
1971	**SF**	**N**	9	6	.600	2.92	45	21	5	185	153	55	65	2	2	0	2	59	7	0	.119	7	20	3	1	0.7	.900
1972	**2 teams** **SF N** (9G 0–4) **STL N** (14G 1–1)																										
″	**total**		1	5	.167	7.71	23	7	0	46.2	61	14	15	0	1	0	0	14	1	0	.071	1	0	2	0	0.1	.333
1974	**CAL**	**A**	0	1	.000	3.68	17	0	0	22	24	10	12	0	0	1	0	0	0	0	—	0	2	1	0	0.2	.667
6 yrs.			15	16	.484	3.82	110	36	6	334.2	312	103	137	2	6	1	2	91	9	0	.099	11	33	6	1	0.5	.880
LEAGUE CHAMPIONSHIP SERIES																											
1971	**SF**	**N**	0	1	.000	9.00	1	1	0	3	7	0	4	0	0	0	0	0	0	0	—	0	0	0	0	0.0	.000

Candy Cummings

CUMMINGS, WILLIAM ARTHUR BR TR 5′ 9″ 120 lbs.
B. Oct. 18, 1848, Ware, Mass. D. May 16, 1924, Toledo, Ohio.
Hall of Fame 1939.

Year	Team	Lg	W	L	PCT	ERA	G	GS	CG	IP	H	BB	SO	ShO	Relief Pitching W	Relief Pitching L	Relief Pitching SV	Batting AB	Batting H	Batting HR	BA	PO	A	E	DP	TC/G	FA
1876	**HAR**	**N**	16	8	.667	1.67	24	24	24	216	215	14	26	5	0	0	0	105	17	0	.162	9	27	2	0	1.6	.947
1877	**CIN**	**N**	5	14	.263	4.34	19	19	16	155.2	219	13	11	0	0	0	0	70	14	0	.200	11	32	4	0	2.1	.915
2 yrs.			21	22	.488	2.78	43	43	40	371.2	434	27	37	5	0	0	0	175	31	0	.177	20	59	6	0	1.8	.929

John Cummings

CUMMINGS, JOHN RUSSELL BL TL 6′ 3″ 200 lbs.
B. May 10, 1969, Torrance, Calif.

Year	Team	Lg	W	L	PCT	ERA	G	GS	CG	IP	H	BB	SO	ShO	Relief Pitching W	Relief Pitching L	Relief Pitching SV	Batting AB	Batting H	Batting HR	BA	PO	A	E	DP	TC/G	FA
1993	**SEA**	**A**	0	6	.000	6.02	10	8	1	46.1	59	16	19	0	0	0	0	0	0	0	—	3	6	2	0	1.1	.818
1994			2	4	.333	5.63	17	8	0	64	66	37	33	0	1	0	0	0	0	0	—	2	5	0	0	0.4	1.000
1995	**2 teams** **SEA A** (4G 0–0) **LA N** (35G 3–1)																										
″	**total**		3	1	.750	4.06	39	0	0	44.1	46	17	25	0	3	1	0	3	0	0	.000	4	5	0	2	0.2	1.000
3 yrs.			5	11	.313	5.30	66	16	1	154.2	171	70	77	0	4	1	0	3	0	0	.000	9	16	2	2	0.4	.926
DIVISIONAL PLAYOFF SERIES																											
1995	**LA**	**N**	0	0	—	20.25	2	0	0	1.1	3	2	3	0	0	0	0	0	0	0	—	0	0	0	0	0.0	.000

Steve Cummings

CUMMINGS, STEVEN BRENT BB TR 6′ 2″ 200 lbs.
B. July 15, 1964, Houston, Tex.

Year	Team	Lg	W	L	PCT	ERA	G	GS	CG	IP	H	BB	SO	ShO	Relief Pitching W	Relief Pitching L	Relief Pitching SV	Batting AB	Batting H	Batting HR	BA	PO	A	E	DP	TC/G	FA
1989	**TOR**	**A**	2	0	1.000	3.00	5	2	0	21	18	11	8	0	1	0	0	0	0	0	—	0	4	1	0	1.0	.800
1990			0	0	—	5.11	6	2	0	12.1	22	5	4	0	0	0	0	0	0	0	—	1	1	0	0	0.3	1.000
2 yrs.			2	0	1.000	3.78	11	4	0	33.1	40	16	12	0	1	0	0	0	0	0		1	5	1	0	0.6	.857

Bert Cunningham

CUNNINGHAM, ELLSWORTH ELMER BR TR 187 lbs.
B. Nov. 25, 1865, Wilmington, Del. D. May 14, 1952, Cragmere, Del.

Year	Team	Lg	W	L	PCT	ERA	G	GS	CG	IP	H	BB	SO	ShO	Relief Pitching W	Relief Pitching L	Relief Pitching SV	Batting AB	Batting H	Batting HR	BA	PO	A	E	DP	TC/G	FA
1887	**BKN**	**AA**	0	2	.000	*5.09*	3	3	3	23	26	13	8	0	0	0	0	8	0	0	.000	1	4	1	0	2.0	.833
1888	**BAL**	**AA**	22	29	.431	3.39	51	51	50	453.1	412	**157**	186	0	0	0	0	177	33	1	.186	20	106	25	3	2.9	.834
1889			16	19	.457	4.87	39	33	29	279.1	306	141	140	0	2	0	1	131	27	0	.206	9	62	12	0	2.0	.855
1890	**2 teams** **PHI P** (14G 3–9) **BUF P** (25G 9–15)																										
″	**total**		12	24	.333	5.63	39	36	35	319.2	384	201	111	2	0	1	0	153	29	0	.190	18	86	23	5	3.0	.819
1891	**BAL**	**AA**	11	14	.440	4.01	30	25	21	237.2	241	138	59	0	1	0	0	100	15	1	.150	11	69	7	3	2.6	.920
1895	**LOU**	**N**	11	16	.407	4.75	31	28	24	231	299	104	49	1	0	0	0	100	30	0	.300	19	56	10	3	2.7	.882
1896			7	14	.333	5.09	27	20	17	189.1	242	74	37	0	0	1	1	88	22	2	.250	26	50	10	3	3.1	.884
1897			14	13	.519	4.14	29	27	25	234.2	286	72	49	0	2	0	0	93	22	2	.237	27	58	7	0	3.0	.924
1898			28	15	.651	3.16	44	42	41	362	387	65	34	0	0	1	0	140	32	1	.229	29	81	13	5	2.8	.894
1899			17	17	.500	3.84	39	37	33	323.2	385	75	36	1	0	1	0	154	40	2	.260	40	103	9	2	3.5	.941
1900	**CHI**	**N**	4	3	.571	4.36	8	7	7	64	84	21	7	0	0	0	0	27	4	0	.148	8	9	1	1	2.3	.944
1901			0	1	.000	5.00	1	1	1	9	11	3	2	0	0	0	0	1	0	0	.000	2	5	0	0	7.0	1.000
12 yrs.			142	167	.460	4.22	341	310	286	2726.2	3063	1064	718	4	5	4	2	1172	254	9	.217	210	689	118	25	2.8	.884

Bruce Cunningham

CUNNINGHAM, BRUCE LEE BR TR 5′10½″ 165 lbs.
B. Sept. 29, 1905, San Francisco, Calif. D. Mar. 8, 1984, Hayward, Calif.

Year	Team	Lg	W	L	PCT	ERA	G	GS	CG	IP	H	BB	SO	ShO	Relief Pitching W	Relief Pitching L	Relief Pitching SV	Batting AB	Batting H	Batting HR	BA	PO	A	E	DP	TC/G	FA
1929	**BOS**	**N**	4	6	.400	4.52	17	8	4	91.2	100	32	22	0	1	1	1	27	4	0	.148	5	27	1	0	1.9	.970
1930			5	6	.455	5.48	36	6	2	106.2	121	41	28	0	3	2	0	31	6	0	.194	4	35	0	3	1.1	1.000
1931			3	12	.200	4.48	33	16	6	136.2	157	54	32	1	0	3	1	42	3	0	.071	6	50	1	4	1.7	.982
1932			1	0	1.000	3.45	18	3	0	47	50	19	21	0	1	0	0	9	2	0	.222	1	12	0	5	0.7	1.000
4 yrs.			13	24	.351	4.64	104	33	12	382	428	146	103	1	5	6	2	109	15	0	.138	16	124	2	12	1.4	.986

George Cunningham

CUNNINGHAM, GEORGE HAROLD BR TR 5′11″ 185 lbs.
B. July 13, 1894, Sturgeon Lake, Minn. D. Mar. 10, 1972, Chattanooga, Tenn.

Year	Team	Lg	W	L	PCT	ERA	G	GS	CG	IP	H	BB	SO	ShO	Relief Pitching W	Relief Pitching L	Relief Pitching SV	Batting AB	Batting H	Batting HR	BA	PO	A	E	DP	TC/G	FA
1916	**DET**	**A**	7	10	.412	2.75	35	14	5	150.1	146	74	68	0	2	1	2	41	11	0	.268	6	46	2	2	1.5	.963
1917			2	7	.222	2.91	44	8	4	139	113	51	49	0	2	1	4	34	6	1	.176	4	43	4	3	1.2	.922
1918			6	7	.462	3.15	27	14	10	140	131	38	39	0	2	0	1	112	25	0	.223	21	35	5	1	1.3	.918
1919			1	1	.500	4.91	17	0	0	47.2	54	15	11	0	1	1	1	23	5	0	.217	2	16	3	1	1.2	.857
4 yrs.			16	25	.390	3.13	123	36	19	477	444	178	167	0	7	3	8	*				34	140	14	7	1.3	.926

Mike Cunningham

CUNNINGHAM, MODY BR TR 5′10½″ 175 lbs.
B. June 14, 1882, Lancaster, S. C. D. Dec. 10, 1969, Lancaster, S. C.

Year	Team	Lg	W	L	PCT	ERA	G	GS	CG	IP	H	BB	SO	ShO	Relief Pitching W	Relief Pitching L	Relief Pitching SV	Batting AB	Batting H	Batting HR	BA	PO	A	E	DP	TC/G	FA
1906	**PHI**	**A**	1	0	1.000	3.21	5	1	1	28	29	9	15	0	0	0	0	12	4	0	.333	2	6	0	0	1.6	1.000

Nig Cuppy

CUPPY, GEORGE JOSEPH BR TR 5′ 7″ 160 lbs.
Born George Maceo Koppe.
B. July 3, 1869, Logansport, Ind. D. July 27, 1922, Elkhart, Ind.

Year	Team	Lg	W	L	PCT	ERA	G	GS	CG	IP	H	BB	SO	ShO	Relief Pitching W	Relief Pitching L	Relief Pitching SV	Batting AB	Batting H	Batting HR	BA	PO	A	E	DP	TC/G	FA
1892	**CLE**	**N**	28	13	.683	2.51	47	42	38	376	333	121	103	1	0	0	1	168	36	0	.214	12	103	6	3	2.4	.950
1893			17	10	.630	4.47	31	30	24	243.2	316	75	39	0	0	0	0	109	27	0	.248	15	48	5	1	2.1	.926
1894			24	15	.615	4.56	43	33	29	316	381	128	65	**3**	**8**	0	0	135	35	0	.259	19	60	2	5	1.8	.975
1895			26	14	.650	3.54	47	40	36	353	384	95	91	1	3	0	2	140	40	0	.286	30	90	4	2	2.6	.968
1896			25	14	.641	3.12	46	40	35	358	388	75	86	1	2	0	1	141	38	1	.270	16	106	6	3	2.7	.953
1897			10	6	.625	3.18	19	17	13	138.2	150	26	23	1	0	0	0	55	8	0	.145	1	32	2	0	1.8	.943
1898			9	8	.529	3.30	18	15	13	128	147	25	27	1	1	**2**	0	48	5	0	.104	3	24	2	1	1.6	.931
1899	**STL**	**N**	11	8	.579	3.15	21	21	18	171.2	203	26	25	1	0	0	0	70	13	0	.186	4	47	5	1	2.7	.911
1900	**BOS**	**N**	8	4	.667	3.08	17	13	9	105.1	107	24	23	0	1	0	1	42	11	0	.262	0	22	2	0	1.4	.917
1901	**BOS**	**A**	4	6	.400	4.15	13	11	9	93.1	111	14	22	0	0	0	0	49	10	0	.204	3	20	2	0	1.5	.920
10 yrs.			162	98	.623	3.48	302	262	224	2283.2	2520	609	504	9	15	2	5	957	223	1	.233	103	552	36	16	2.2	.948

Sam Curran

CURRAN, SIMON FRANCIS TL
B. Oct. 30, 1874, Dorchester, Mass. D. May 19, 1936, Dorchester, Mass.

Year	Team	Lg	W	L	PCT	ERA	G	GS	CG	IP	H	BB	SO	ShO	Relief W	Relief L	SV	AB	H	HR	BA	PO	A	E	DP	TC/G	FA
1902	BOS	N	0	0	—	1.35	1	0	0	6.2	6	0	3	0	0	0	0	2	0	0	.000	0	0	0	0	0.0	.000

Lafayette Currence

CURRENCE, DELANCEY LAFAYETTE BB TL 5′11″ 175 lbs.
B. Dec. 3, 1951, Rock Hill, S. C.

Year	Team	Lg	W	L	PCT	ERA	G	GS	CG	IP	H	BB	SO	ShO	Relief W	Relief L	SV	AB	H	HR	BA	PO	A	E	DP	TC/G	FA
1975	MIL	A	0	2	.000	7.71	8	1	0	18.2	25	14	7	0	0	1	0	0	0	0	—	0	1	0	0	0.1	1.000

Bill Currie

CURRIE, WILLIAM CLEVELAND BR TR 6′ 175 lbs.
B. Nov. 29, 1928, Leary, Ga.

Year	Team	Lg	W	L	PCT	ERA	G	GS	CG	IP	H	BB	SO	ShO	Relief W	Relief L	SV	AB	H	HR	BA	PO	A	E	DP	TC/G	FA
1955	WAS	A	0	0	—	12.46	3	0	0	4.1	7	2	2	0	0	0	0	0	0	0	—	0	2	0	0	0.7	1.000

Clarence Currie

CURRIE, CLARENCE FRANKLIN BR TR
B. Dec. 30, 1878, Glencoe, Ont., Canada. D. July 15, 1941, Little Chute, Wis.

Year	Team	Lg	W	L	PCT	ERA	G	GS	CG	IP	H	BB	SO	ShO	Relief W	Relief L	SV	AB	H	HR	BA	PO	A	E	DP	TC/G	FA
1902	2 teams	CIN N (10G 3–4) STL N (16G 7–5)																									
″	total		10	9	.526	2.95	26	19	16	192	195	52	50	3	0	0	0	70	11	0	.157	8	64	4	3	2.9	.947
1903	2 teams	STL N (22G 4–12) CHI N (6G 1–2)																									
″	total		5	14	.263	3.82	28	19	15	181.1	190	69	61	1	**2**	1	2	59	9	0	.153	9	74	8	3	3.3	.912
2 yrs.			15	23	.395	3.38	54	38	31	373.1	385	121	111	4	2	1	2	129	20	0	.155	17	138	12	6	3.1	.928

Murphy Currie

CURRIE, ARCHIBALD MURPHY BR TR 5′11½″ 185 lbs.
B. Aug. 31, 1893, Fayetteville, N. C. D. June 22, 1939, Asheboro, N. C.

Year	Team	Lg	W	L	PCT	ERA	G	GS	CG	IP	H	BB	SO	ShO	Relief W	Relief L	SV	AB	H	HR	BA	PO	A	E	DP	TC/G	FA
1916	STL	N	0	0	—	1.88	6	0	0	14.1	7	9	8	0	0	0	0	3	0	0	.000	0	1	1	0	0.3	.500

George Curry

CURRY, GEORGE JAMES (Soldier Boy) BR TR 6′ 185 lbs.
B. Dec. 21, 1888, Bridgeport, Conn. D. Oct. 5, 1963, West Haven, Conn.

Year	Team	Lg	W	L	PCT	ERA	G	GS	CG	IP	H	BB	SO	ShO	Relief W	Relief L	SV	AB	H	HR	BA	PO	A	E	DP	TC/G	FA
1911	STL	A	0	3	.000	7.47	3	3	0	15.2	19	24	2	0	0	0	0	5	0	0	.000	0	4	0	0	1.3	1.000

Steve Curry

CURRY, STEPHEN THOMAS BR TR 6′ 6″ 217 lbs.
B. Sept. 13, 1965, Winter Park, Fla.

Year	Team	Lg	W	L	PCT	ERA	G	GS	CG	IP	H	BB	SO	ShO	Relief W	Relief L	SV	AB	H	HR	BA	PO	A	E	DP	TC/G	FA
1988	BOS	A	0	1	.000	8.18	3	3	0	11	15	14	4	0	0	0	0	0	0	0	—	0	3	0	0	1.0	1.000

Wes Curry

CURRY, WESLEY
B. Apr. 1, 1860, Wilmington, Del. D. May 19, 1933, Philadelphia, Pa.

Year	Team	Lg	W	L	PCT	ERA	G	GS	CG	IP	H	BB	SO	ShO	Relief W	Relief L	SV	AB	H	HR	BA	PO	A	E	DP	TC/G	FA
1884	RIC	AA	0	2	.000	*5.06*	2	2	2	16	15	3	1	0	0	0	0	8	2	0	.250	0	4	4	0	4.0	.500

Cliff Curtis

CURTIS, CLIFTON GARFIELD BR TR 6′ 2″ 180 lbs.
B. July 3, 1883, Delaware, Ohio D. Apr. 23, 1943, Utica, Ohio.

Year	Team	Lg	W	L	PCT	ERA	G	GS	CG	IP	H	BB	SO	ShO	Relief W	Relief L	SV	AB	H	HR	BA	PO	A	E	DP	TC/G	FA
1909	BOS	N	4	5	.444	1.41	10	9	8	83	53	30	22	2	0	1	0	29	1	0	.034	3	28	5	1	3.6	.861
1910			6	24	.200	3.55	43	37	12	251	251	124	75	2	0	1	2	82	12	0	.146	9	102	5	1	2.7	.957
1911	3 teams	BOS N (12G 1–8) CHI N (4G 1–2) PHI N (8G 2–1)																									
″	total		4	11	.267	3.77	24	15	8	129	131	54	40	1	1	2	1	45	12	0	.267	7	37	5	1	2.0	.898
1912	2 teams	PHI N (10G 2–5) BKN N (19G 4–7)																									
″	total		6	12	.333	3.67	29	17	5	130	127	54	42	0	1	2	0	41	8	0	.195	3	37	2	1	1.4	.952
1913	BKN	N	8	9	.471	3.26	30	16	5	151.2	145	55	57	0	3	1	1	49	6	0	.122	11	44	1	0	1.9	.982
5 yrs.			28	61	.315	3.31	136	94	38	744.2	707	317	236	5	5	7	4	246	39	0	.159	33	248	18	4	2.2	.940

Jack Curtis

CURTIS, JACK PATRICK BL TL 5′10″ 175 lbs.
B. Jan. 11, 1937, Rhodhiss, N. C.

Year	Team	Lg	W	L	PCT	ERA	G	GS	CG	IP	H	BB	SO	ShO	Relief W	Relief L	SV	AB	H	HR	BA	PO	A	E	DP	TC/G	FA
1961	CHI	N	10	13	.435	4.89	31	27	6	180.1	220	51	57	0	0	0	0	60	10	2	.167	5	42	3	1	1.6	.940
1962	2 teams	CHI N (4G 0–2) MIL N (30G 4–4)																									
″	total		4	6	.400	4.04	34	8	0	93.2	100	33	48	0	4	3	1	22	5	0	.227	6	11	1	1	0.5	.944
1963	CLE	A	0	0	—	18.00	4	0	0	5	8	5	3	0	0	0	0	0	0	0	—	0	2	0	0	0.5	1.000
3 yrs.			14	19	.424	4.84	69	35	6	279	328	89	108	0	4	3	1	82	15	2	.183	11	55	4	2	1.0	.943

John Curtis

CURTIS, JOHN DUFFIELD II BL TL 6′ 1″ 175 lbs.
B. Mar. 9, 1948, Newton, Mass.

Year	Team	Lg	W	L	PCT	ERA	G	GS	CG	IP	H	BB	SO	ShO	Relief W	Relief L	SV	AB	H	HR	BA	PO	A	E	DP	TC/G	FA
1970	BOS	A	0	0	—	13.50	1	0	0	2	4	1	1	0	0	0	0	0	0	0	—	0	2	0	0	2.0	1.000
1971			2	2	.500	3.12	5	3	1	26	30	6	19	0	1	0	0	9	1	0	.111	0	1	0	0	0.2	1.000
1972			11	8	.579	3.73	26	21	8	154.1	161	50	106	3	1	0	0	53	5	0	.094	4	23	2	4	1.1	.931
1973			13	13	.500	3.58	35	30	10	221	225	83	101	4	0	0	0	0	0	0	—	9	33	2	1	1.3	.955
1974	STL	N	10	14	.417	3.78	33	29	5	195	199	83	89	2	0	1	1	63	10	0	.159	10	31	0	2	1.2	1.000
1975			8	9	.471	3.43	39	18	4	147	151	65	67	0	0	1	1	38	8	0	.211	7	31	1	3	1.0	.974
1976			6	11	.353	4.50	37	15	3	134	139	65	52	1	0	4	1	35	7	0	.200	7	22	0	1	0.8	1.000
1977	SF	N	3	3	.500	5.49	43	9	1	77	95	48	47	1	1	1	1	13	3	0	.231	9	14	0	3	0.5	1.000
1978			4	3	.571	3.71	46	0	0	63	60	29	38	0	4	3	1	2	0	0	.000	6	9	2	1	0.4	.882
1979			10	9	.526	4.17	27	18	3	121	121	42	85	2	1	2	0	34	5	0	.147	4	13	0	1	0.6	1.000
1980	SD	N	10	8	.556	3.51	30	27	6	187	184	67	71	0	0	0	0	62	12	0	.194	5	37	1	2	1.4	.977
1981			2	6	.250	5.10	28	8	0	67	70	30	31	0	2	4	0	13	1	0	.077	0	12	1	1	0.5	.923
1982	2 teams	SD N (26G 8–6) CAL A (8G 0–1)																									
″	total		8	7	.533	4.28	34	18	1	128.1	137	49	64	1	1	2	1	37	11	0	.297	2	18	2	1	0.6	.909
1983	CAL	A	1	2	.333	3.80	37	3	0	90	89	40	36	0	1	1	5	0	0	0	—	1	10	1	1	0.3	.917
1984			1	2	.333	4.40	17	0	0	28.2	30	11	18	0	1	2	0	0	0	0	—	2	4	0	0	0.4	1.000
15 yrs.			89	97	.478	3.96	438	199	42	1641.1	1695	669	825	14	13	21	11	359	63	0	.175	66	260	12	21	0.8	.964

Vern Curtis

CURTIS, VERNON EUGENE (Turk) BR TR 6′ 170 lbs.
B. May 24, 1920, Cairo, Ill. D. June 24, 1992, Cairo, Ill.

Year	Team	Lg	W	L	PCT	ERA	G	GS	CG	IP	H	BB	SO	ShO	Relief W	Relief L	SV	AB	H	HR	BA	PO	A	E	DP	TC/G	FA
1943	WAS	A	0	0	—	6.75	2	0	0	4	3	6	1	0	0	0	0	0	0	0	—	1	0	0	0	0.5	1.000
1944			0	1	.000	2.79	3	1	0	9.2	8	3	2	0	0	0	0	2	0	0	.000	2	1	0	0	1.0	1.000
1946			0	0	—	7.16	11	0	0	16.1	19	10	7	0	0	0	0	2	0	0	.000	3	2	0	0	0.5	1.000
3 yrs.			0	1	.000	5.70	16	1	0	30	30	19	10	0	0	0	0	4	0	0	.000	6	3	0	0	0.6	1.000

Ed Cushman

CUSHMAN, EDGAR LEANDER BR TL 6′ 177 lbs.
B. Mar. 27, 1852, Eagleville, Ohio D. Sept. 26, 1915, Erie, Pa.

Year	Team		W	L	PCT	ERA	G	GS	CG	IP	H	BB	SO	ShO	Relief W	Relief L	Relief SV	Batting AB	Batting H	Batting HR	BA	PO	A	E	DP	TC/G	FA
1883	BUF	N	3	3	.500	*3.93*	7	7	5	50.1	61	17	34	0	0	0	0	23	5	0	.217	1	8	3	0	1.5	.750
1884	MIL	U	4	0	1.000	*1.00*	4	4	4	36	10	3	47	2	0	0	0	11	1	0	.091	0	4	1	0	1.3	.800
1885	2 teams	PHI AA (10G 3–7)	NY AA (22G 8–14)																								
″	total		11	21	.344	3.01	32	32	32	278	259	50	170	0	0	0	0	106	17	0	.160	5	32	10	0	1.5	.787
1886	NY	AA	17	20	.459	*3.12*	38	38	37	325.2	278	99	167	2	0	0	0	126	19	0	.151	5	59	9	2	1.9	.877
1887			10	14	.417	*5.97*	26	26	25	220	310	83	64	0	0	0	0	93	23	0	.247	4	42	7	2	2.0	.868
1890	TOL	AA	17	21	.447	*4.19*	40	38	34	315.2	346	107	125	0	0	1	1	130	13	0	.100	1	46	7	1	1.4	.870
6 yrs.			62	79	.440	3.86	147	145	137	1225.2	1264	359	607	4	0	1	1	489	78	0	.160	16	191	37	5	1.6	.848

Harv Cushman

CUSHMAN, HARVEY BARNES
B. July 10, 1877, Rockland, Me. D. Dec. 27, 1920, Ensworth, Pa.

Year	Team		W	L	PCT	ERA	G	GS	CG	IP	H	BB	SO	ShO	Relief W	Relief L	Relief SV	Batting AB	Batting H	Batting HR	BA	PO	A	E	DP	TC/G	FA
1902	PIT	N	0	4	.000	7.36	4	4	3	25.2	30	31	12	0	0	0	0	10	2	0	.200	1	4	2	0	1.8	.714

Mike Cvengros

CVENGROS, MICHAEL JOHN BL TL 5′ 8″ 159 lbs.
B. Dec. 1, 1901, Pana, Ill. D. Aug. 2, 1970, Hot Springs, Ark.

Year	Team		W	L	PCT	ERA	G	GS	CG	IP	H	BB	SO	ShO	Relief W	Relief L	Relief SV	Batting AB	Batting H	Batting HR	BA	PO	A	E	DP	TC/G	FA
1922	NY	N	0	1	.000	4.00	1	1	1	9	6	3	3	0	0	0	0	3	0	0	.000	1	2	0	0	3.0	1.000
1923	CHI	A	12	13	.480	4.39	41	26	14	215.1	216	107	86	0	2	1	3	74	15	0	.203	9	53	2	4	1.6	.969
1924			3	12	.200	5.88	26	15	2	105.2	119	67	36	0	1	3	0	30	6	0	.200	2	26	1	1	1.1	.966
1925			3	9	.250	4.30	22	11	4	104.2	109	55	32	0	1	2	0	33	5	0	.152	2	27	3	2	1.5	.906
1927	PIT	N	2	1	.667	3.35	23	4	0	53.2	55	24	21	0	2	0	1	19	3	0	.158	3	16	0	0	0.8	1.000
1929	CHI	N	5	4	.556	4.64	32	2	0	64	82	29	23	0	5	4	2	15	6	0	.400	2	14	0	1	0.5	1.000
6 yrs.			25	40	.385	4.58	145	59	21	552.1	587	285	201	0	11	10	6	174	35	0	.201	19	138	6	8	1.1	.963
WORLD SERIES																											
1927	PIT	N	0	0	—	3.86	2	0	0	2.1	3	0	2	0	0	0	0	0	0	0	—	0	0	0	0	0.0	.000

Jim Czajkowski

CZAJKOWSKI, JAMES MARK BB TR 6′ 4″ 215 lbs.
B. Dec. 18, 1963, Parma, Ohio.

Year	Team		W	L	PCT	ERA	G	GS	CG	IP	H	BB	SO	ShO	Relief W	Relief L	Relief SV	Batting AB	Batting H	Batting HR	BA	PO	A	E	DP	TC/G	FA
1994	CLR	N	0	0	—	4.15	5	0	0	8.2	9	6	2	0	0	0	0	0	0	0	—	1	3	0	0	0.8	1.000

Omar Daal

DAAL, OMAR JESUS BL TL 6′ 3″ 160 lbs.
Born Omar Jesus Daal (Cordero).
B. Mar. 1, 1972, Maracaibo, Venezuela.

Year	Team		W	L	PCT	ERA	G	GS	CG	IP	H	BB	SO	ShO	Relief W	Relief L	Relief SV	Batting AB	Batting H	Batting HR	BA	PO	A	E	DP	TC/G	FA
1993	LA	N	2	3	.400	5.09	47	0	0	35.1	36	21	19	0	2	3	0	0	0	0	—	5	6	0	0	0.2	1.000
1994			0	0	—	3.29	24	0	0	13.2	12	5	9	0	0	0	0	0	0	0	—	1	2	1	0	0.2	.750
1995			4	0	1.000	7.20	28	0	0	20	29	15	11	0	4	0	0	0	0	0	—	0	2	0	0	0.1	1.000
3 yrs.			6	3	.667	5.35	99	0	0	69	77	41	39	0	6	3	0	0	0	0		6	10	1	0	0.2	.941

John D'Acquisto

D'ACQUISTO, JOHN FRANCIS BR TR 6′ 2″ 205 lbs.
B. Dec. 24, 1951, San Diego, Calif.

Year	Team		W	L	PCT	ERA	G	GS	CG	IP	H	BB	SO	ShO	Relief W	Relief L	Relief SV	Batting AB	Batting H	Batting HR	BA	PO	A	E	DP	TC/G	FA
1973	SF	N	1	1	.500	3.54	7	3	1	28	23	19	29	0	0	0	0	9	0	0	.000	0	2	0	0	0.3	1.000
1974			12	14	.462	3.77	38	36	5	215	182	124	167	1	0	0	0	71	8	1	.113	11	12	2	1	0.7	.920
1975			2	4	.333	10.29	10	6	0	28	29	34	22	0	1	0	0	7	0	0	.000	1	2	2	1	0.5	.600
1976			3	8	.273	5.35	28	19	0	106	93	102	53	0	0	0	0	26	7	0	.269	5	17	2	0	0.9	.917
1977	2 teams	STL N (3G 0–0)	SD N (17G 1–2)																								
″	total		1	2	.333	6.54	20	14	0	52.1	54	57	54	0	1	0	0	8	0	0	.000	4	6	2	3	0.6	.833
1978	SD	N	4	3	.571	2.13	45	3	0	93	60	56	104	0	3	2	10	21	4	0	.190	3	6	0	0	0.2	1.000
1979			9	13	.409	4.90	51	11	1	134	140	86	97	1	5	7	2	31	4	0	.129	3	9	1	0	0.3	.923
1980	2 teams	SD N (39G 2–3)	MON N (11G 0–2)																								
″	total		2	5	.286	3.38	50	0	0	88	81	45	59	0	2	5	3	8	0	0	.000	1	12	0	1	0.3	1.000
1981	CAL	A	0	0	—	10.89	6	0	0	19	26	12	8	0	0	0	0	0	0	0	—	1	1	0	0	0.3	1.000
1982	OAK	A	0	1	.000	5.29	11	0	0	17	20	9	7	0	0	1	0	0	0	0	—	0	2	0	2	0.2	1.000
10 yrs.			34	51	.400	4.56	266	92	7	780.1	708	544	600	2	12	15	15	181	23	1	.127	29	69	9	8	0.4	.916

John Dagenhard

DAGENHARD, JOHN DOUGLAS BR TR 6′ 2″ 195 lbs.
B. Apr. 25, 1917, Magnolia, Ohio.

Year	Team		W	L	PCT	ERA	G	GS	CG	IP	H	BB	SO	ShO	Relief W	Relief L	Relief SV	Batting AB	Batting H	Batting HR	BA	PO	A	E	DP	TC/G	FA
1943	BOS	N	1	0	1.000	0.00	2	1	1	11	9	4	2	0	0	0	0	3	0	0	.000	1	4	0	0	2.5	1.000

Pete Daglia

DAGLIA, PETER GEORGE BR TR 6′ 1″ 200 lbs.
B. Feb. 28, 1906, Napa, Calif. D. Mar. 11, 1952, Willits, Calif.

Year	Team		W	L	PCT	ERA	G	GS	CG	IP	H	BB	SO	ShO	Relief W	Relief L	Relief SV	Batting AB	Batting H	Batting HR	BA	PO	A	E	DP	TC/G	FA
1932	CHI	A	2	4	.333	5.76	12	5	2	50	67	20	16	0	1	0	0	13	1	0	.077	4	5	0	1	0.8	1.000

Jay Dahl

DAHL, JAY STEVEN BB TL 5′10″ 183 lbs.
B. Dec. 6, 1945, San Bernardino, Calif. D. June 20, 1965, Salisbury, N. C.

Year	Team		W	L	PCT	ERA	G	GS	CG	IP	H	BB	SO	ShO	Relief W	Relief L	Relief SV	Batting AB	Batting H	Batting HR	BA	PO	A	E	DP	TC/G	FA
1963	HOU	N	0	1	.000	16.88	1	1	0	2.2	7	0	0	0	0	0	0	0	0	0	—	0	0	0	0	0.0	.000

Jerry Dahlke

DAHLKE, JEROME ALEXANDER (Joe) BR TR 6′ 180 lbs.
B. June 8, 1930, Marathon, Wis.

Year	Team		W	L	PCT	ERA	G	GS	CG	IP	H	BB	SO	ShO	Relief W	Relief L	Relief SV	Batting AB	Batting H	Batting HR	BA	PO	A	E	DP	TC/G	FA
1956	CHI	A	0	0	—	19.29	5	0	0	2.1	5	6	1	0	0	0	0	0	0	0	—	0	1	0	0	0.2	1.000

Bill Dailey

DAILEY, WILLIAM GARLAND BR TR 6′ 3″ 185 lbs.
B. May 13, 1935, Arlington, Va.

Year	Team		W	L	PCT	ERA	G	GS	CG	IP	H	BB	SO	ShO	Relief W	Relief L	Relief SV	Batting AB	Batting H	Batting HR	BA	PO	A	E	DP	TC/G	FA
1961	CLE	A	1	0	1.000	0.95	12	0	0	19	16	6	7	0	1	0	0	2	0	0	.000	2	5	0	0	0.6	1.000
1962			2	2	.500	3.59	27	0	0	42.2	43	17	24	0	2	2	1	3	0	0	.000	4	6	1	0	0.4	.909
1963	MIN	A	6	3	.667	1.99	66	0	0	108.2	80	19	72	0	6	3	21	21	5	1	.238	4	32	4	0	0.6	.900
1964			1	2	.333	8.22	14	0	0	15.1	23	17	6	0	1	2	0	0	0	0	—	0	4	0	1	0.3	1.000
4 yrs.			10	7	.588	2.76	119	0	0	185.2	162	59	109	0	10	7	22	26	5	1	.192	10	47	5	1	0.5	.919

Sam Dailey

DAILEY, SAMUEL LAWRENCE BL TR 5′11″ 168 lbs.
B. Mar. 31, 1904, Oakford, Ill. D. Dec. 2, 1979, Columbia, Mo.

Year	Team		W	L	PCT	ERA	G	GS	CG	IP	H	BB	SO	ShO	Relief W	Relief L	Relief SV	Batting AB	Batting H	Batting HR	BA	PO	A	E	DP	TC/G	FA
1929	PHI	N	2	2	.500	7.54	20	5	0	51.1	74	23	18	0	2	0	0	17	1	0	.059	4	3	0	0	0.3	1.000

Vince Dailey

DAILEY, VINCENT PERRY 6′ 200 lbs.
B. Dec. 25, 1864, Osceola, Pa. D. Nov. 14, 1919, Hornell, N. Y.

Year	Team	W	L	PCT	ERA	G	GS	CG	IP	H	BB	SO	ShO	Relief W	Relief L	Relief SV	AB	H	HR	BA	PO	A	E	DP	TC/G	FA
1890	CLE N	0	1	.000	7.71	2	1	0	7	12	7	0	0	0	0	0	*				103	13	19	2	2.0	.859

Ed Daily

DAILY, EDWARD M. BR TR 5′10½″ 174 lbs.
Brother of Con Daily.
B. Sept. 7, 1862, Providence, R. I. D. Oct. 21, 1891, Washington, D. C.

Year	Team	W	L	PCT	ERA	G	GS	CG	IP	H	BB	SO	ShO	Relief W	Relief L	Relief SV	AB	H	HR	BA	PO	A	E	DP	TC/G	FA
1885	PHI N	26	23	.531	2.21	50	50	49	440	370	90	140	4	0	0	0	184	38	1	.207	11	87	12	2	2.2	.891
1886		16	9	.640	3.06	27	23	22	218	211	59	95	1	**3**	0	0	309	70	4	.227	98	70	27	3	2.3	.862
1887	2 teams PHI N (6G 0–4) WAS N (1G 0–1)																									
″	total	0	5	.000	7.26	7	6	5	48.1	57	31	10	0	0	0	0	417	108	3	.259	144	25	35	1	1.9	.828
1888	WAS N	2	7	.222	4.89	9	8	8	73.2	88	19	20	0	0	1	0	453	102	8	.225	196	37	22	5	2.3	.914
1889	COL AA	0	0	—	21.60	2	0	0	1.2	1	4	2	0	0	0	1	578	148	3	.256	212	27	41	4	2.0	.854
1890	3 teams BKN AA (27G 10–15) NY N (2G 2–0) LOU AA (12G 6–3)																									
″	total	18	18	.500	3.33	41	38	37	343.2	341	129	113	1	2	0	0	489	116	1	.237	147	106	26	6	2.3	.907
1891	LOU AA	4	8	.333	5.74	15	14	11	111.1	149	48	27	0	0	0	0	143	34	0	.238	43	31	17	2	2.1	.813
7 yrs.		66	70	.485	3.37	151	139	132	1236.2	1217	380	407	6	5	1	1	*				851	383	180	23	2.2	.873

One Arm Daily

DAILY, HUGH IGNATIUS BR TR 6′ 2″ 180 lbs.
Born Harry Criss.
B. 1857, Baltimore, Md. Deceased.

Year	Team	W	L	PCT	ERA	G	GS	CG	IP	H	BB	SO	ShO	Relief W	Relief L	Relief SV	AB	H	HR	BA	PO	A	E	DP	TC/G	FA
1882	BUF N	15	14	.517	*2.99*	29	29	29	255.2	246	70	116	0	0	0	0	110	18	0	.164	1	28	4	0	1.1	.879
1883	CLE N	23	19	.548	*2.42*	45	43	40	378.2	360	**99**	171	4	0	1	1	142	18	0	.127	6	71	5	1	1.8	.939
1884	3 teams CHI U (46G 22–23) PIT U (10G 5–4) WAS U (2G 1–1)																									
″	total	28	28	.500	2.44	58	58	56	500.2	446	72	**483**	4	0	0	0	201	43	0	.214	15	110	23	3	2.3	.845
1885	STL N	3	8	.273	*3.94*	11	11	10	91.1	92	44	31	1	0	0	0	35	3	0	.086	0	21	1	1	2.0	.955
1886	WAS N	0	6	.000	7.35	6	6	6	49	69	40	15	0	0	0	0	16	2	0	.125	2	10	1	0	2.2	.923
1887	CLE AA	4	12	.250	3.67	16	16	16	139.2	181	44	30	0	0	0	0	58	4	0	.069	0	26	3	0	1.8	.897
6 yrs.		73	87	.456	2.93	165	163	157	1415	1394	369	846	9	0	1	1	562	88	0	.157	24	266	37	5	1.9	.887

Bruce Dal Canton

DAL CANTON, JOHN BRUCE BR TR 6′ 2″ 205 lbs.
B. June 15, 1942, California, Pa.

Year	Team	W	L	PCT	ERA	G	GS	CG	IP	H	BB	SO	ShO	Relief W	Relief L	Relief SV	AB	H	HR	BA	PO	A	E	DP	TC/G	FA
1967	PIT N	2	1	.667	1.88	8	2	1	24	19	10	13	0	2	0	0	6	2	0	.333	1	2	0	0	0.4	1.000
1968		1	1	.500	2.12	7	0	0	17	7	6	8	0	1	1	2	3	0	0	.000	0	1	0	0	0.1	1.000
1969		8	2	.800	3.35	57	0	0	86	79	49	56	0	8	2	5	10	3	0	.300	7	12	1	1	0.4	.950
1970		9	4	.692	4.55	41	6	1	85	94	39	53	0	6	3	1	16	0	0	.000	3	10	0	2	0.3	1.000
1971	KC A	8	6	.571	3.45	25	22	2	141	144	44	58	0	0	0	0	46	4	0	.087	11	16	2	0	1.2	.931
1972		6	6	.500	3.40	35	16	1	132.1	135	29	75	0	2	2	2	41	4	0	.098	5	14	1	1	0.6	.950
1973		4	3	.571	4.82	32	3	1	97	108	46	38	0	3	1	3	0	0	0	—	5	17	1	1	0.7	.957
1974		8	10	.444	3.14	31	22	9	175	135	82	96	2	2	2	0	0	0	0	—	14	25	1	2	1.3	.975
1975	2 teams KC A (4G 0–2) ATL N (26G 2–7)																									
″	total	2	9	.182	4.76	30	11	0	75.2	86	31	43	0	2	2	3	19	2	0	.105	7	13	0	1	0.7	1.000
1976	ATL N	3	5	.375	3.58	42	1	0	73	67	42	36	0	3	4	1	9	2	0	.222	4	17	2	0	0.5	.913
1977	CHI A	0	2	.000	3.75	8	0	0	24	20	13	9	0	0	2	2	0	0	0	—	1	1	0	0	0.3	1.000
11 yrs.		51	49	.510	3.68	316	83	15	930	894	391	485	2	29	19	19	150	17	0	.113	58	128	8	8	0.6	.959

Gene Dale

DALE, EMMETT EUGENE BR TR 6′ 3″ 179 lbs.
B. June 16, 1889, St. Louis, Mo. D. Mar. 20, 1958, St. Louis, Mo.

Year	Team	W	L	PCT	ERA	G	GS	CG	IP	H	BB	SO	ShO	Relief W	Relief L	Relief SV	AB	H	HR	BA	PO	A	E	DP	TC/G	FA
1911	STL N	0	2	.000	6.75	5	2	0	14.2	13	16	13	0	0	0	0	5	2	0	.400	2	2	0	1	0.8	1.000
1912		0	5	.000	6.57	19	3	1	61.2	76	51	37	0	0	2	0	22	6	0	.273	3	10	2	1	0.8	.867
1915	CIN N	18	17	.514	2.46	49	35	20	296.2	256	**107**	104	4	3	2	3	91	20	0	.220	8	76	6	4	1.8	.933
1916		3	4	.429	5.17	17	5	2	69.2	80	33	23	0	2	1	0	21	3	0	.143	3	26	0	0	1.7	1.000
4 yrs.		21	28	.429	3.60	90	45	23	442.2	425	207	177	4	5	5	3	139	31	0	.223	16	114	8	6	1.5	.942

Bill Daley

DALEY, WILLIAM TL
B. June 27, 1868, Poughkeepsie, N. Y. D. May 4, 1922, Poughkeepsie, N. Y.

Year	Team	W	L	PCT	ERA	G	GS	CG	IP	H	BB	SO	ShO	Relief W	Relief L	Relief SV	AB	H	HR	BA	PO	A	E	DP	TC/G	FA
1889	BOS N	3	3	.500	4.31	9	7	4	48	34	43	40	0	0	0	0	20	3	0	.150	3	20	1	3	2.7	.958
1890	BOS P	18	7	**.720**	3.60	34	25	19	235	246	167	110	2	**4**	0	2	110	17	2	.155	22	47	7	2	2.1	.908
1891	BOS AA	8	6	.571	2.98	19	11	10	126.2	119	81	68	0	1	**2**	2	59	10	0	.169	7	32	4	1	2.0	.907
3 yrs.		29	16	.644	3.49	62	43	33	409.2	399	291	218	2	5	2	4	189	30	2	.159	32	99	12	6	2.1	.916

Bud Daley

DALEY, LEAVITT LEO BL TL 6′ 1″ 185 lbs.
B. Oct. 7, 1932, Orange, Calif.

Year	Team	W	L	PCT	ERA	G	GS	CG	IP	H	BB	SO	ShO	Relief W	Relief L	Relief SV	AB	H	HR	BA	PO	A	E	DP	TC/G	FA
1955	CLE A	0	1	.000	6.43	2	1	0	7	10	1	2	0	0	0	0	2	0	0	.000	0	3	1	0	2.0	.750
1956		1	0	1.000	6.20	14	0	0	20.1	21	14	13	0	1	0	0	2	0	0	.000	4	6	0	0	0.7	1.000
1957		2	8	.200	4.43	34	10	1	87.1	99	40	54	0	0	2	2	20	4	0	.200	6	22	5	2	1.0	.848
1958	KC A	3	2	.600	3.31	26	5	1	70.2	67	19	39	0	2	0	0	16	2	0	.125	3	16	1	2	0.8	.950
1959		16	13	.552	3.16	39	29	12	216.1	212	62	125	2	1	2	1	78	23	0	.295	10	35	2	2	1.2	.957
1960		16	16	.500	4.56	37	35	13	231	234	96	126	1	1	1	0	75	12	0	.160	19	36	1	4	1.5	.982
1961	2 teams KC A (16G 4–8) NY A (23G 8–9)																									
″	total	12	17	.414	4.28	39	27	9	193.1	211	73	119	0	1	3	1	63	8	0	.127	16	28	4	3	1.2	.917
1962	NY A	7	5	.583	3.59	43	6	0	105.1	105	21	55	0	5	3	4	27	5	0	.185	9	17	2	0	0.7	.929
1963		0	0	—	0.00	1	0	0	1	2	0	0	0	0	0	1	0	0	0	—	0	0	0	0	0.0	.000
1964		3	2	.600	4.63	13	3	0	35	37	25	16	0	0	2	1	8	2	0	.250	2	9	0	0	0.8	1.000
10 yrs.		60	64	.484	4.03	248	116	36	967.1	998	351	549	3	11	13	10	291	56	0	.192	69	172	16	13	1.0	.938
WORLD SERIES																										
1961	NY A	1	0	1.000	0.00	2	0	0	7	5	0	3	0	1	0	0	1	0	0	.000	0	0	1	0	0.5	.000
1962		0	0	—	0.00	1	0	0	1	1	1	0	0	0	0	0	0	0	0	—	0	0	0	0	0.0	.000
2 yrs.		1	0	1.000	0.00	3	0	0	8	6	1	3	0	1	0	0	1	0	0	.000	0	0	1	0	0.3	.000

Mike Dalton

DALTON, MICHAEL EDWARD BL TL 6′ 215 lbs.
B. Mar. 27, 1963, Palo Alto, Calif.

Year	Team	W	L	PCT	ERA	G	GS	CG	IP	H	BB	SO	ShO	Relief W	Relief L	Relief SV	AB	H	HR	BA	PO	A	E	DP	TC/G	FA
1991	DET A	0	0	—	3.38	4	0	0	8	12	2	4	0	0	0	0	0	0	0	—	0	1	0	1	0.3	1.000

George Daly

DALY, GEORGE JOSEPHS (Pecks) BR TR 5′10½″ 175 lbs.
B. July 28, 1887, Buffalo, N. Y. D. Dec. 12, 1957, Buffalo, N. Y.

Year	Team		W	L	PCT	ERA	G	GS	CG	IP	H	BB	SO	ShO	Relief Pitching W	Relief Pitching L	Relief Pitching SV	Batting AB	Batting H	Batting HR	BA	PO	A	E	DP	TC/G	FA
1909	NY	N	0	3	.000	6.00	3	3	3	21	31	8	8	0	0	0	0	9	1	0	.111	0	0	0	0	0.0	.000

Bill Dammann

DAMMANN, WILLIAM HENRY (Wee Willie) BL TL 5′ 7″ 155 lbs.
B. Aug. 9, 1872, Chicago, Ill. D. Dec. 6, 1948, Lynnhaven, Va.

Year	Team		W	L	PCT	ERA	G	GS	CG	IP	H	BB	SO	ShO	Relief Pitching W	Relief Pitching L	Relief Pitching SV	Batting AB	Batting H	Batting HR	BA	PO	A	E	DP	TC/G	FA
1897	CIN	N	6	4	.600	4.74	16	11	7	95	122	37	21	1	1	1	0	31	5	0	.161	4	26	2	0	2.0	.938
1898			16	10	.615	3.61	35	22	16	224.2	277	67	51	2	**4**	**2**	2	82	16	0	.195	9	44	7	1	1.7	.883
1899			2	1	.667	4.88	9	5	3	48	74	11	2	1	0	0	1	18	1	0	.056	3	13	2	1	2.0	.889
3 yrs.			24	15	.615	4.06	60	38	26	367.2	473	115	74	4	5	3	3	131	22	0	.168	16	83	11	2	1.8	.900

Lee Daney

DANEY, ARTHUR LEE BR TR 5′11″ 165 lbs.
B. July 9, 1904, Talihina, Okla. D. Mar. 11, 1988, Phoenix, Ariz.

Year	Team		W	L	PCT	ERA	G	GS	CG	IP	H	BB	SO	ShO	Relief Pitching W	Relief Pitching L	Relief Pitching SV	Batting AB	Batting H	Batting HR	BA	PO	A	E	DP	TC/G	FA
1928	PHI	A	0	0	—	0.00	1	0	0	1	1	0	0	0	0	0	0	0	0	0	—	0	1	0	0	1.0	1.000

Dave Danforth

DANFORTH, DAVID CHARLES (Dauntless Dave) BL TL 6′ 167 lbs.
B. Mar. 7, 1890, Granger, Tex. D. Sept. 19, 1970, Baltimore, Md.

Year	Team		W	L	PCT	ERA	G	GS	CG	IP	H	BB	SO	ShO	Relief Pitching W	Relief Pitching L	Relief Pitching SV	Batting AB	Batting H	Batting HR	BA	PO	A	E	DP	TC/G	FA
1911	PHI	A	4	1	.800	3.74	14	2	1	33.2	29	17	21	0	3	0	1	6	1	0	.167	3	7	0	0	0.7	1.000
1912			0	0	—	3.98	3	0	0	20.1	26	12	8	0	0	0	0	8	2	0	.250	1	6	0	1	2.3	1.000
1916	CHI	A	6	5	.545	3.27	28	8	1	93.2	87	37	49	0	5	0	2	23	2	0	.087	2	32	3	0	1.3	.919
1917			11	6	.647	2.65	**50**	9	1	173	155	74	79	1	**6**	3	**9**	46	6	0	.130	0	42	4	0	0.9	.913
1918			6	15	.286	3.43	39	13	5	139	148	40	48	0	**6**	6	2	42	6	0	.143	7	39	2	1	1.2	.958
1919			1	2	.333	7.78	15	1	0	41.2	58	20	17	0	1	1	1	9	1	0	.111	1	10	0	0	0.7	1.000
1922	STL	A	5	2	.714	3.28	20	10	3	79.2	93	38	48	0	0	0	1	23	2	0	.087	6	11	0	2	0.9	1.000
1923			16	14	.533	3.94	38	29	16	226.1	221	87	96	1	1	2	1	71	15	0	.211	7	40	0	2	1.2	1.000
1924			15	12	.556	4.51	41	27	12	219.2	246	69	65	1	3	2	4	76	13	0	.171	4	40	2	2	1.1	.957
1925			7	9	.438	4.36	38	15	5	159	172	61	53	0	3	2	2	46	8	0	.174	4	21	2	0	0.7	.926
10 yrs.			71	66	.518	3.89	286	114	44	1186	1235	455	484	3	28	16	23	350	56	0	.160	35	248	13	8	1.0	.956
WORLD SERIES																											
1917	CHI	A	0	0	—	18.00	1	0	0	1	3	0	2	0	0	0	0	0	0	0	—	0	1	0	0	1.0	1.000

Chuck Daniel

DANIEL, CHARLES EDWARD BR TR 6′ 2″ 195 lbs.
B. Sept. 17, 1933, Bluffton, Ark.

Year	Team		W	L	PCT	ERA	G	GS	CG	IP	H	BB	SO	ShO	Relief Pitching W	Relief Pitching L	Relief Pitching SV	Batting AB	Batting H	Batting HR	BA	PO	A	E	DP	TC/G	FA
1957	DET	A	0	0	—	7.71	1	0	0	2.1	3	0	2	0	0	0	0	0	0	0	—	0	0	0	0	0.0	.000

Bennie Daniels

DANIELS, BENNIE BL TR 6′ 1½″ 193 lbs.
B. June 17, 1932, Tuscaloosa, Ala.

Year	Team		W	L	PCT	ERA	G	GS	CG	IP	H	BB	SO	ShO	Relief Pitching W	Relief Pitching L	Relief Pitching SV	Batting AB	Batting H	Batting HR	BA	PO	A	E	DP	TC/G	FA
1957	PIT	N	0	1	.000	1.29	1	1	0	7	5	3	2	0	0	0	0	2	0	0	.000	1	4	1	0	6.0	.833
1958			0	3	.000	5.53	8	5	1	27.2	31	15	7	0	0	0	0	8	1	0	.125	4	10	2	1	2.0	.875
1959			7	9	.438	5.45	34	12	0	100.2	115	39	67	0	4	3	1	29	9	1	.310	6	14	2	0	0.6	.909
1960			1	3	.250	7.81	10	6	0	40.1	52	17	16	0	0	0	0	16	3	0	.188	4	11	0	0	1.5	1.000
1961	WAS	A	12	11	.522	3.44	32	28	12	212	184	80	110	1	0	1	0	76	15	2	.197	18	38	3	1	1.8	.949
1962			7	16	.304	4.85	44	21	3	161.1	172	68	66	1	3	3	2	46	6	1	.130	24	45	3	2	1.6	.958
1963			5	10	.333	4.38	35	24	6	168.2	163	58	88	1	0	0	1	46	7	0	.152	16	41	5	0	1.7	.919
1964			8	10	.444	3.70	33	24	3	163	147	64	73	2	1	0	0	47	6	1	.128	10	39	3	4	1.6	.942
1965			5	13	.278	4.72	33	18	1	116.1	135	39	42	0	2	1	1	30	4	0	.133	3	22	0	1	0.8	1.000
9 yrs.			45	76	.372	4.44	230	139	26	997	1004	383	471	5	10	8	5	300	51	5	.170	86	224	19	9	1.4	.942

Charlie Daniels

DANIELS, CHARLES L.
B. July 1, 1861, Roxbury, Mass. D. Feb. 9, 1938, Boston, Mass.

Year	Team		W	L	PCT	ERA	G	GS	CG	IP	H	BB	SO	ShO	Relief Pitching W	Relief Pitching L	Relief Pitching SV	Batting AB	Batting H	Batting HR	BA	PO	A	E	DP	TC/G	FA
1884	BOS	U	0	2	.000	*4.32*	2	2	2	16.2	20	2	12	0	0	0	0	11	3	0	.273	1	3	3	0	2.3	.571

Pete Daniels

DANIELS, PETER J. BL TL
B. Apr. 8, 1864, County Cavan, Ireland D. Feb. 13, 1928, Indianapolis, Ind.

Year	Team		W	L	PCT	ERA	G	GS	CG	IP	H	BB	SO	ShO	Relief Pitching W	Relief Pitching L	Relief Pitching SV	Batting AB	Batting H	Batting HR	BA	PO	A	E	DP	TC/G	FA
1890	PIT	N	1	2	.333	7.07	4	4	3	28	40	12	8	0	0	0	0	12	4	0	.333	1	5	2	0	2.0	.750
1898	STL	N	1	6	.143	3.62	10	6	3	54.2	62	14	13	0	1	0	0	17	3	0	.176	2	14	4	1	2.0	.800
2 yrs.			2	8	.200	4.79	14	10	6	82.2	102	26	21	0	1	0	0	29	7	0	.241	3	19	6	1	2.0	.786

George Darby

DARBY, GEORGE WILLIAM (Deek) BL TR 5′10½″ 160 lbs.
B. Feb. 6, 1869, Kansas City, Mo. D. Feb. 25, 1937, Sacramento, Calif.

Year	Team		W	L	PCT	ERA	G	GS	CG	IP	H	BB	SO	ShO	Relief Pitching W	Relief Pitching L	Relief Pitching SV	Batting AB	Batting H	Batting HR	BA	PO	A	E	DP	TC/G	FA
1893	CIN	N	1	1	.500	7.76	4	3	2	29	41	18	6	0	0	0	0	10	3	0	.300	0	13	0	0	3.3	1.000

Pat Darcy

DARCY, PATRICK LEONARD BR TR 6′ 3″ 175 lbs.
B. May 12, 1950, Troy, Ohio.

Year	Team		W	L	PCT	ERA	G	GS	CG	IP	H	BB	SO	ShO	Relief Pitching W	Relief Pitching L	Relief Pitching SV	Batting AB	Batting H	Batting HR	BA	PO	A	E	DP	TC/G	FA
1974	CIN	N	1	0	1.000	3.71	6	2	0	17	17	8	14	0	0	0	0	3	1	0	.333	0	2	0	0	0.3	1.000
1975			11	5	.688	3.57	27	22	1	131	134	59	46	0	2	0	1	47	4	0	.085	8	21	2	0	1.1	.935
1976			2	3	.400	6.23	11	4	0	39	41	22	15	0	0	1	2	11	2	0	.182	1	5	1	0	0.6	.857
3 yrs.			14	8	.636	4.14	44	28	1	187	192	89	75	0	2	1	3	61	7	0	.115	9	28	3	0	0.9	.925
WORLD SERIES																											
1975	CIN	N	0	1	.000	4.50	2	0	0	4	3	2	1	0	0	1	0	1	0	0	.000	0	1	0	0	0.5	1.000

Alvin Dark

DARK, ALVIN RALPH (Blackie) BR TR 5′11″ 185 lbs.
B. Jan. 7, 1922, Comanche, Okla.
Manager 1961–64, 1966–71, 1974–75, 1977.

Year	Team		W	L	PCT	ERA	G	GS	CG	IP	H	BB	SO	ShO	Relief Pitching W	Relief Pitching L	Relief Pitching SV	Batting AB	Batting H	Batting HR	BA	PO	A	E	DP	TC/G	FA
1953	NY	N	0	0	—	18.00	1	1	0	1	1	1	0	0	0	0	0	*				6	14	2	2	1.7	.909

Ron Darling

DARLING, RONALD MAURICE, JR. BR TR 6′ 3″ 205 lbs.
B. Aug. 19, 1960, Honolulu, Hawaii.

Year	Team		W	L	PCT	ERA	G	GS	CG	IP	H	BB	SO	ShO	Relief Pitching W	Relief Pitching L	Relief Pitching SV	Batting AB	Batting H	Batting HR	BA	PO	A	E	DP	TC/G	FA
1983	NY	N	1	3	.250	2.80	5	5	1	35.1	31	17	23	0	0	0	0	10	1	0	.100	2	6	0	1	1.6	1.000
1984			12	9	.571	3.81	33	33	2	205.2	179	104	136	2	0	0	0	67	10	0	.149	17	38	3	3	1.8	.948
1985			16	6	.727	2.90	36	35	4	248	214	**114**	167	2	0	0	0	76	13	0	.171	24	47	2	5	2.0	.973
1986			15	6	.714	2.81	34	34	4	237	203	81	184	2	0	0	0	81	8	0	.099	24	47	7	7	2.3	.910
1987			12	8	.600	4.29	32	32	2	207.2	183	96	167	0	0	0	0	65	8	0	.123	17	43	3	5	2.0	.952
1988			17	9	.654	3.25	34	34	7	240.2	218	60	161	4	0	0	0	82	18	0	.220	17	35	3	4	1.6	.945
1989			14	14	.500	3.52	33	33	4	217.1	214	70	153	0	0	0	0	73	9	2	.123	15	37	4	5	1.7	.929

Ron Darling *continued*

Year	Team	W	L	PCT	ERA	G	GS	CG	IP	H	BB	SO	ShO	Relief Pitching W	Relief Pitching L	Relief Pitching SV	Batting AB	Batting H	Batting HR	BA	PO	A	E	DP	TC/G	FA
1990		7	9	.438	4.50	33	18	1	126	135	44	99	0	1	2	0	31	4	0	.129	7	22	2	0	0.9	.935
1991	**3 teams**	**NY N** (17G 5–6)		**MON N**	(3G 0–2)	**OAK A**	(12G 3–7)																			
″	**total**	8	15	.348	4.26	32	32	0	194.1	185	71	129	0	0	0	0	40	5	0	.125	18	27	6	2	1.6	.882
1992	**OAK A**	15	10	.600	3.66	33	33	4	206.1	198	72	99	3	0	0	0	0	0	0	—	11	26	4	2	1.2	.902
1993		5	9	.357	5.16	31	29	3	178	198	72	95	0	0	0	0	0	0	0	—	12	17	1	0	1.0	.967
1994		10	11	.476	4.50	25	**25**	4	160	162	59	108	0	0	0	0	1	0	0	.000	3	27	2	1	1.3	.938
1995		4	7	.364	6.23	21	21	1	104	124	46	69	0	0	0	0	0	0	0	—	10	20	0	2	1.4	1.000
13 yrs.		136	116	.540	3.87	382	364	37	2360.1	2244	906	1590	13	1	2	0	526	76	2	.144	177	392	37	37	1.6	.939
LEAGUE CHAMPIONSHIP SERIES																										
1986	**NY N**	0	0	—	7.20	1	1	0	5	6	2	5	0	0	0	0	1	0	0	.000	1	2	0	0	3.0	1.000
1988		0	1	.000	7.71	2	2	0	7	11	4	7	0	0	0	0	3	0	0	.000	1	3	0	0	2.0	1.000
1992	**OAK A**	0	1	.000	3.00	1	1	0	6	4	2	3	0	0	0	0	0	0	0	—	1	0	0	0	1.0	1.000
3 yrs.		0	2	.000	6.00	4	4	0	18	21	8	15	0	0	0	0	4	0	0	.000	3	5	0	0	2.0	1.000
WORLD SERIES																										
1986	**NY N**	1	1	.500	1.53	3	3	0	17.2	13	10	12	0	0	0	0	3	0	0	.000	0	4	0	0	1.3	1.000

Bob Darnell

DARNELL, ROBERT JACK BR TR 5′10″ 175 lbs.
B. Nov. 6, 1930, Wewoka, Okla.

Year	Team	W	L	PCT	ERA	G	GS	CG	IP	H	BB	SO	ShO	Relief Pitching W	Relief Pitching L	Relief Pitching SV	Batting AB	Batting H	Batting HR	BA	PO	A	E	DP	TC/G	FA
1954	**BKN N**	0	0	—	3.14	6	1	0	14.1	15	7	5	0	0	0	0	2	0	0	.000	0	5	0	0	0.8	1.000
1956		0	0	—	0.00	1	0	0	1.1	1	0	0	0	0	0	0	0	0	0	—	0	0	0	0	0.0	.000
2 yrs.		0	0		2.87	7	1	0	15.2	16	7	5	0	0	0	0	2	0	0	.000	0	5	0	0	0.7	1.000

Mike Darr

DARR, MICHAEL EDWARD BR TR 6′ 4″ 190 lbs.
B. Mar. 23, 1956, Pomona, Calif.

Year	Team	W	L	PCT	ERA	G	GS	CG	IP	H	BB	SO	ShO	Relief Pitching W	Relief Pitching L	Relief Pitching SV	Batting AB	Batting H	Batting HR	BA	PO	A	E	DP	TC/G	FA
1977	**TOR A**	0	1	.000	45.00	1	1	0	1	3	4	1	0	0	0	0	0	0	0	—	0	0	0	0	0.0	.000

George Darrow

DARROW, GEORGE OLIVER BL TL 6′ 180 lbs.
B. July 12, 1903, Beloit, Kans. D. Mar. 24, 1983, Sun City, Ariz.

Year	Team	W	L	PCT	ERA	G	GS	CG	IP	H	BB	SO	ShO	Relief Pitching W	Relief Pitching L	Relief Pitching SV	Batting AB	Batting H	Batting HR	BA	PO	A	E	DP	TC/G	FA
1934	**PHI N**	2	6	.250	5.51	17	8	2	49	57	28	14	0	1	1	1	15	2	0	.133	2	12	2	1	0.9	.875

Bobby Darwin

DARWIN, ARTHUR BOBBY LEE BR TR 6′ 2″ 190 lbs.
B. Feb. 16, 1943, Los Angeles, Calif.

Year	Team	W	L	PCT	ERA	G	GS	CG	IP	H	BB	SO	ShO	Relief Pitching W	Relief Pitching L	Relief Pitching SV	Batting AB	Batting H	Batting HR	BA	PO	A	E	DP	TC/G	FA
1962	**LA A**	0	1	.000	10.80	1	1	0	3.1	8	4	6	0	0	0	0	1	0	0	.000	0	0	1	0	1.0	.000
1969	**LA N**	0	0	—	9.00	3	0	0	4	4	5	0	0	0	0	0	0	0	0	—	0	0	0	0	0.0	.000
2 yrs.		0	1	.000	9.82	4	1	0	7.1	12	9	6	0	0	0	0	*				964	39	26	4	1.7	.975

Danny Darwin

DARWIN, DANIEL WAYNE BR TR 6′ 3″ 185 lbs.
Brother of Jeff Darwin.
B. Oct. 25, 1955, Bonham, Tex.

Year	Team	W	L	PCT	ERA	G	GS	CG	IP	H	BB	SO	ShO	Relief Pitching W	Relief Pitching L	Relief Pitching SV	Batting AB	Batting H	Batting HR	BA	PO	A	E	DP	TC/G	FA
1978	**TEX A**	1	0	1.000	4.15	3	1	0	8.2	11	1	8	0	0	0	0	0	0	0	—	0	0	0	0	0.0	.000
1979		4	4	.500	4.04	20	6	1	78	50	30	58	0	1	3	0	0	0	0	—	2	6	0	0	0.4	1.000
1980		13	4	.765	2.62	53	2	0	110	98	50	104	0	12	3	8	0	0	0	—	7	11	0	1	0.3	1.000
1981		9	9	.500	3.64	22	22	6	146	115	57	98	2	0	0	0	0	0	0	—	8	16	2	3	1.2	.923
1982		10	8	.556	3.44	56	1	0	89	95	37	61	0	10	7	7	0	0	0	—	5	19	0	0	0.4	1.000
1983		8	13	.381	3.49	28	26	9	183	175	62	92	2	0	0	0	0	0	0	—	20	18	3	1	1.5	.927
1984		8	12	.400	3.94	35	32	5	223.2	249	54	123	1	0	0	0	0	0	0	—	13	21	3	2	1.1	.919
1985	**MIL A**	8	18	.308	3.80	39	29	11	217.2	212	65	125	1	1	2	2	0	0	0	—	15	16	2	1	0.8	.939
1986	**2 teams**	**MIL A** (27G 6–8)		**HOU N**	(12G 5–2)																					
″	**total**	11	10	.524	3.17	39	22	6	184.2	170	44	120	1	3	1	0	16	1	0	.063	10	27	3	2	1.0	.925
1987	**HOU N**	9	10	.474	3.59	33	30	3	195.2	184	69	134	1	0	0	0	66	12	0	.182	10	22	2	0	1.0	.941
1988		8	13	.381	3.84	44	20	3	192	189	48	129	0	4	3	3	56	4	1	.071	14	37	1	2	1.2	.981
1989		11	4	.733	2.36	68	0	0	122	92	33	104	0	11	4	7	17	2	0	.118	2	12	2	2	0.2	.875
1990		11	4	.733	**2.21**	48	17	3	162.2	136	31	109	0	2	1	2	38	5	0	.132	11	15	1	1	0.6	.963
1991	**BOS A**	3	6	.333	5.16	12	12	0	68	71	15	42	0	0	0	0	0	0	0	—	6	9	0	0	1.3	1.000
1992		9	9	.500	3.96	51	15	2	161.1	159	53	124	0	5	4	3	0	0	0	—	9	13	1	2	0.5	.957
1993		15	11	.577	3.26	34	34	2	229.1	196	49	130	1	0	0	0	0	0	0	—	14	31	2	2	1.4	.957
1994		7	5	.583	6.30	13	13	0	75.2	101	24	54	0	0	0	0	0	0	0	—	5	8	0	0	1.0	1.000
1995	**2 teams**	**TOR A** (13G 1–8)		**TEX A**	(7G 2–2)																					
″	**total**	3	10	.231	7.45	20	15	1	99	131	31	58	0	0	0	0	0	0	0	—	3	7	2	1	0.6	.833
18 yrs.		148	150	.497	3.71	618	297	52	2546.1	2434	753	1673	9	49	28	32	193	24	1	.124	154	288	24	20	0.8	.948

Jeff Darwin

DARWIN, JEFFREY SCOTT BR TR 6′ 3″ 180 lbs.
Brother of Danny Darwin.
B. July 6, 1969, Sherman, Tex.

Year	Team	W	L	PCT	ERA	G	GS	CG	IP	H	BB	SO	ShO	Relief Pitching W	Relief Pitching L	Relief Pitching SV	Batting AB	Batting H	Batting HR	BA	PO	A	E	DP	TC/G	FA
1994	**SEA A**	0	0	—	13.50	2	0	0	4	7	3	1	0	0	0	0	0	0	0	—	0	0	0	0	0.0	.000

Doug Dascenzo

DASCENZO, DOUGLAS CRAIG BB TL 5′ 7″ 150 lbs.
B. June 30, 1964, Cleveland, Ohio.

Year	Team	W	L	PCT	ERA	G	GS	CG	IP	H	BB	SO	ShO	Relief Pitching W	Relief Pitching L	Relief Pitching SV	Batting AB	Batting H	Batting HR	BA	PO	A	E	DP	TC/G	FA
1990	**CHI N**	0	0	—	0.00	1	0	0	1	1	0	0	0	0	0	0	241	61	1	.253	55	1	0	0	2.8	1.000
1991		0	0	—	0.00	3	0	0	4	2	2	2	0	0	0	0	239	61	1	.255	134	0	2	0	1.5	.985
2 yrs.		0	0		0.00	4	0	0	5	3	2	2	0	0	0	0	*				771	10	8	3	1.7	.990

Lee Dashner

DASHNER, LEE CLAIRE (Lefty) BB TL 5′11½″ 192 lbs.
B. Apr. 25, 1887, Renault, Ill. D. Dec. 16, 1959, El Dorado, Kans.

Year	Team	W	L	PCT	ERA	G	GS	CG	IP	H	BB	SO	ShO	Relief Pitching W	Relief Pitching L	Relief Pitching SV	Batting AB	Batting H	Batting HR	BA	PO	A	E	DP	TC/G	FA
1913	**CLE A**	0	0	—	5.40	1	0	0	1.2	0	0	2	0	0	0	0	0	0	0	—	0	0	0	0	0.0	.000

Frank Dasso

DASSO, FRANCIS JOSEPH NICHOLAS BR TR 5′11½″ 185 lbs.
B. Aug. 31, 1917, Chicago, Ill.

Year	Team	W	L	PCT	ERA	G	GS	CG	IP	H	BB	SO	ShO	Relief Pitching W	Relief Pitching L	Relief Pitching SV	Batting AB	Batting H	Batting HR	BA	PO	A	E	DP	TC/G	FA
1945	**CIN N**	4	5	.444	3.67	16	12	6	95.2	89	53	39	0	1	1	0	31	5	0	.161	6	19	0	1	1.6	1.000
1946		0	0	—	27.00	2	0	0	1	2	2	1	0	0	0	0	0	0	0	—	0	0	0	0	0.0	.000
2 yrs.		4	5	.444	3.91	18	12	6	96.2	91	55	40	0	1	1	0	31	5	0	.161	6	19	0	1	1.4	1.000

Dan Daub

DAUB, DANIEL WILLIAM (Mickey) BR TR 5′10″ 160 lbs.
B. Jan. 12, 1868, Middletown, Ohio D. Mar. 25, 1951, Bradenton, Fla.

Year	Team		W	L	PCT	ERA	G	GS	CG	IP	H	BB	SO	ShO	Relief W	Relief L	Relief SV	Bat AB	Bat H	HR	BA	PO	A	E	DP	TC/G	FA
1892	CIN	N	1	2	.333	2.88	4	3	2	25	23	13	7	0	0	0	0	7	0	0	.000	1	6	1	0	2.0	.875
1893	BKN	N	6	6	.500	3.84	12	12	12	103	104	61	25	0	0	0	0	42	8	0	.190	7	35	2	1	3.7	.955
1894			9	12	.429	6.32	33	26	14	215	283	90	45	0	0	0	0	92	16	0	.174	4	42	7	0	1.6	.868
1895			10	10	.500	4.29	25	21	16	184.2	212	51	36	0	1	0	0	71	14	0	.197	3	54	3	3	2.4	.950
1896			12	11	.522	3.60	32	24	18	225	255	63	53	0	2	0	0	84	19	0	.226	8	74	2	1	2.6	.976
1897			6	11	.353	6.08	19	16	11	137.2	180	48	19	0	2	1	0	49	11	0	.224	5	32	4	2	2.2	.902
6 yrs.			44	52	.458	4.79	125	102	73	890.1	1057	326	185	0	5	1	0	345	68	0	.197	28	243	19	7	2.3	.934

Hooks Dauss

DAUSS, GEORGE AUGUST BR TR 5′10½″ 168 lbs.
Born George August Daus.
B. Sept. 22, 1889, Indianapolis, Ind. D. July 27, 1963, St. Louis, Mo.

Year	Team		W	L	PCT	ERA	G	GS	CG	IP	H	BB	SO	ShO	Relief W	Relief L	Relief SV	Bat AB	Bat H	HR	BA	PO	A	E	DP	TC/G	FA
1912	DET	A	1	1	.500	3.18	2	2	2	17	11	9	7	0	0	0	0	4	1	0	.250	0	8	0	0	4.0	1.000
1913			13	12	.520	2.68	33	29	22	225	188	82	107	2	0	1	1	79	14	0	.177	8	64	9	2	2.5	.889
1914			18	15	.545	2.86	45	35	22	302	286	87	150	3	1	2	**4**	97	21	1	.216	9	89	4	1	2.3	.961
1915			24	13	.649	2.50	46	35	27	309.2	261	112	132	1	3	2	2	103	15	0	.146	11	137	5	3	3.3	.967
1916			19	12	.613	3.21	39	29	18	238.2	220	90	95	1	4	0	4	72	16	1	.222	5	85	6	2	2.5	.938
1917			17	14	.548	2.43	37	31	22	270.2	243	87	102	6	1	0	2	87	11	0	.126	10	100	4	2	3.0	.965
1918			12	16	.429	2.99	33	26	21	249.2	243	58	73	1	1	3	3	77	14	0	.182	6	79	4	1	2.7	.955
1919			21	9	.700	3.55	34	32	22	256.1	262	63	73	2	1	0	0	97	14	0	.144	5	101	2	6	3.2	.981
1920			13	21	.382	3.56	38	32	18	270.1	308	84	82	0	1	3	0	83	14	0	.169	7	114	2	0	3.2	.984
1921			10	15	.400	4.33	32	28	16	233	275	81	68	0	1	1	1	88	23	1	.261	10	84	1	2	3.0	.989
1922			13	13	.500	4.20	39	25	12	218.2	251	59	78	1	5	1	4	72	15	1	.208	5	61	2	1	1.7	.971
1923			21	13	.618	3.62	50	39	22	316	331	78	105	4	1	0	3	104	24	0	.231	6	92	1	2	2.0	.990
1924			12	11	.522	4.59	40	10	5	131.1	155	40	44	0	8	**5**	6	38	5	0	.132	4	32	0	1	0.9	1.000
1925			16	11	.593	3.16	35	30	16	228	238	85	58	1	2	1	1	81	15	1	.185	7	52	1	2	1.7	.983
1926			12	6	.667	4.20	35	5	0	124.1	135	49	27	0	**11**	4	9	42	10	1	.238	7	30	1	0	1.1	.974
15 yrs.			222	182	.550	3.32	538	388	245	3390.2	3407	1064	1201	22	40	23	40	1124	212	6	.189	100	1128	42	25	2.4	.967

Vic Davalillo

DAVALILLO, VICTOR JOSE BL TL 5′ 7″ 150 lbs.
Born Victor Jose Davalillo (Romero).
Brother of Yo-Yo Davalillo.
B. July 31, 1936, Cabimas, Venezuela.

Year	Team		W	L	PCT	ERA	G	GS	CG	IP	H	BB	SO	ShO	Relief W	Relief L	Relief SV	Bat AB	Bat H	HR	BA	PO	A	E	DP	TC/G	FA
1969	STL	N	0	0	—	∞	2	0	0		2	2	0	0	0	0	0	*				247	10	3	0	2.9	.988

Claude Davenport

DAVENPORT, CLAUDE EDWIN BR TR 6′ 6″ 193 lbs.
Brother of Dave Davenport.
B. May 28, 1898, Runge, Tex. D. June 13, 1976, Corpus Christi, Tex.

Year	Team		W	L	PCT	ERA	G	GS	CG	IP	H	BB	SO	ShO	Relief W	Relief L	Relief SV	Bat AB	Bat H	HR	BA	PO	A	E	DP	TC/G	FA
1920	NY	N	0	0	—	4.50	1	0	0	2	2	1	0	0	0	0	0	1	0	0	.000	0	0	0	0	0.0	.000

Dave Davenport

DAVENPORT, DAVID W. (Big Dave) BR TR 6′ 6″ 220 lbs.
Brother of Claude Davenport.
B. Feb. 20, 1890, DeRidder, La. D. Oct. 16, 1954, El Dorado, Ark.

Year	Team		W	L	PCT	ERA	G	GS	CG	IP	H	BB	SO	ShO	Relief W	Relief L	Relief SV	Bat AB	Bat H	HR	BA	PO	A	E	DP	TC/G	FA
1914	**2 teams**	**CIN N**	(10G 2–2)		**STL F**	(33G 8–13)																					
″	**total**		10	15	.400	3.27	43	32	16	269.2	242	110	164	3	0	4	6	86	8	0	.093	10	76	3	3	2.1	.966
1915	STL	F	22	18	.550	2.20	**55**	**46**	**30**	**392.2**	300	96	**229**	**10**	0	2	1	130	12	0	.092	1	79	4	2	1.5	.952
1916	STL	A	12	11	.522	2.85	**59**	31	13	290.2	267	100	129	1	2	3	2	73	10	0	.137	2	72	5	2	1.3	.937
1917			17	17	.500	3.08	47	**39**	19	280.2	273	105	100	2	0	0	2	92	9	0	.098	4	83	6	0	2.0	.935
1918			10	11	.476	3.25	31	22	12	180	182	69	60	2	0	0	1	52	7	1	.135	3	61	7	2	2.3	.901
1919			2	11	.154	3.94	24	16	5	123.1	135	41	37	0	0	1	0	39	3	0	.077	5	36	1	2	1.8	.976
6 yrs.			73	83	.468	2.93	259	186	95	1537	1399	521	719	18	2	10	12	472	49	1	.104	25	407	26	11	1.8	.943

Lum Davenport

DAVENPORT, JOUBERT LUM BL TL 6′ 1″ 165 lbs.
B. June 27, 1900, Tucson, Ariz. D. Apr. 21, 1961, Dallas, Tex.

Year	Team		W	L	PCT	ERA	G	GS	CG	IP	H	BB	SO	ShO	Relief W	Relief L	Relief SV	Bat AB	Bat H	HR	BA	PO	A	E	DP	TC/G	FA
1921	CHI	A	0	3	.000	6.88	13	2	0	35.1	41	32	9	0	0	2	0	17	7	0	.412	0	9	2	1	0.8	.818
1922			1	1	.500	10.80	9	1	0	16.2	14	13	9	0	0	1	0	3	0	0	.000	0	6	0	0	0.7	1.000
1923			0	0	—	6.23	2	0	0	4.1	7	4	1	0	0	0	0	1	1	0	1.000	0	1	0	0	0.5	1.000
1924			0	0	—	0.00	1	0	0	2	1	2	1	0	0	0	0	0	0	0	—	0	0	1	0	1.0	.000
4 yrs.			1	4	.200	7.71	25	3	0	58.1	63	51	20	0	0	3	0	21	8	0	.381	0	16	3	1	0.8	.842

Mike Davey

DAVEY, MICHAEL GERARD BR TL 6′ 2″ 190 lbs.
B. June 2, 1952, Spokane, Wash.

Year	Team		W	L	PCT	ERA	G	GS	CG	IP	H	BB	SO	ShO	Relief W	Relief L	Relief SV	Bat AB	Bat H	HR	BA	PO	A	E	DP	TC/G	FA
1977	ATL	N	0	0	—	5.06	16	0	0	16	19	9	7	0	0	0	2	1	0	0	.000	3	1	0	0	0.3	1.000
1978			0	0	—	0.00	3	0	0	3	1	1	0	0	0	0	0	0	0	0	—	0	0	0	0	0.0	.000
2 yrs.			0	0		4.26	19	0	0	19	20	10	7	0	0	0	2	1	0	0	.000	3	1	0	0	0.2	1.000

Ray Daviault

DAVIAULT, RAYMOND JOSEPH ROBERT BR TR 6′ 1″ 170 lbs.
B. May 27, 1934, Montreal, Que., Canada.

Year	Team		W	L	PCT	ERA	G	GS	CG	IP	H	BB	SO	ShO	Relief W	Relief L	Relief SV	Bat AB	Bat H	HR	BA	PO	A	E	DP	TC/G	FA
1962	NY	N	1	5	.167	6.22	36	3	0	81	92	48	51	0	1	3	0	15	1	0	.067	9	6	0	0	0.4	1.000

Bobby Davidson

DAVIDSON, ROBERT BANKS BR TR 6′ 185 lbs.
B. Jan. 6, 1963, Bad Kurznach, W. Germany.

Year	Team		W	L	PCT	ERA	G	GS	CG	IP	H	BB	SO	ShO	Relief W	Relief L	Relief SV	Bat AB	Bat H	HR	BA	PO	A	E	DP	TC/G	FA
1989	NY	A	0	0	—	18.00	1	0	0	1	1	1	0	0	0	0	0	0	0	0	—	0	0	0	0	0.0	.000

Ted Davidson

DAVIDSON, THOMAS EUGENE BR TL 6′ 192 lbs.
B. Oct. 4, 1939, Las Vegas, Nev.

Year	Team		W	L	PCT	ERA	G	GS	CG	IP	H	BB	SO	ShO	Relief W	Relief L	Relief SV	Bat AB	Bat H	HR	BA	PO	A	E	DP	TC/G	FA
1965	CIN	N	4	3	.571	2.23	24	1	0	68.2	57	17	54	0	3	3	1	17	0	0	.000	1	14	1	1	0.7	.938
1966			5	4	.556	3.90	54	0	0	85.1	82	23	54	0	5	4	4	12	0	0	.000	3	14	1	0	0.3	.944
1967			1	0	1.000	4.15	9	0	0	13	13	3	6	0	1	0	0	0	0	0	—	0	4	0	0	0.4	1.000
1968	**2 teams**	**CIN N**	(23G 1–0)		**ATL N**	(4G 0–0)																					
″	**total**		1	0	1.000	6.35	27	0	0	28.1	37	11	10	0	1	0	0	2	0	0	.000	0	7	0	0	0.3	1.000
4 yrs.			11	7	.611	3.69	114	1	0	195.1	189	54	124	0	10	7	5	31	0	0	.000	4	39	2	1	0.4	.956

Jerry Davie

DAVIE, GERALD LEE — BR TR 6′ 180 lbs.
B. Feb. 10, 1933, Detroit, Mich.

Year	Team		W	L	PCT	ERA	G	GS	CG	IP	H	BB	SO	ShO	Relief W	Relief L	Relief SV	AB	H	HR	BA	PO	A	E	DP	TC/G	FA
1959	DET	A	2	2	.500	4.17	11	5	1	36.2	40	17	20	0	0	0	0	10	4	0	.400	4	9	0	0	1.2	1.000

Chick Davies

DAVIES, LLOYD GARRISON — BL TL 5′ 8″ 145 lbs.
B. Mar. 6, 1892, Peabody, Mass. D. Sept. 5, 1973, Middletown, Conn.

Year	Team		W	L	PCT	ERA	G	GS	CG	IP	H	BB	SO	ShO	Relief W	Relief L	Relief SV	AB	H	HR	BA	PO	A	E	DP	TC/G	FA
1914	PHI	A	1	0	1.000	1.00	1	1	1	9	8	3	4	0	0	0	0	46	11	0	.239	25	3	3	2	2.8	.903
1915			1	2	.333	8.80	4	2	0	15.1	20	12	2	0	1	0	0	132	24	0	.182	67	14	2	1	2.3	.976
1925	NY	N	0	0	—	6.14	2	1	0	7.1	13	4	5	0	0	0	0	6	0	0	.000	3	3	0	0	2.0	1.000
1926			2	4	.333	3.94	38	1	0	89	96	35	27	0	2	3	**6**	18	4	0	.222	4	26	2	2	0.8	.938
4 yrs.			4	6	.400	4.48	45	5	1	120.2	137	54	38	0	3	3	6	*				99	46	7	5	1.7	.954

George Davies

DAVIES, GEORGE WASHINGTON — 180 lbs.
B. Feb. 22, 1868, Portage, Wis. D. Sept. 22, 1906, Waterloo, Wis.

Year	Team		W	L	PCT	ERA	G	GS	CG	IP	H	BB	SO	ShO	Relief W	Relief L	Relief SV	AB	H	HR	BA	PO	A	E	DP	TC/G	FA
1891	MIL	AA	7	5	.583	2.66	12	12	12	101.2	94	35	61	1	0	0	0	37	9	0	.243	2	18	2	0	1.8	.909
1892	CLE	N	10	16	.385	2.59	26	26	23	215.2	201	69	95	0	0	0	0	87	12	0	.138	8	61	9	2	3.0	.885
1893	2 teams	CLE N (3G 0–2) NY N (5G 1–1)																									
″	total		1	3	.250	7.71	8	4	2	51.1	69	23	10	0	0	1	0	18	6	0	.333	3	16	3	0	2.8	.864
3 yrs.			18	24	.429	3.32	46	42	37	368.2	364	127	166	1	0	1	0	142	27	0	.190	13	95	14	2	2.7	.885

Bob Davis

DAVIS, ROBERT EDWARD — BR TR 6′ 170 lbs.
B. Sept. 11, 1933, New York, N. Y.

Year	Team		W	L	PCT	ERA	G	GS	CG	IP	H	BB	SO	ShO	Relief W	Relief L	Relief SV	AB	H	HR	BA	PO	A	E	DP	TC/G	FA
1958	KC	A	0	4	.000	7.84	8	4	0	31	45	12	22	0	0	0	0	6	1	0	.167	0	7	1	1	1.0	.875
1960			0	0	—	3.66	21	0	0	32	31	22	28	0	0	0	1	4	1	0	.250	7	7	0	1	0.7	1.000
2 yrs.			0	4	.000	5.71	29	4	0	63	76	34	50	0	0	0	1	10	2	0	.200	7	14	1	2	0.8	.955

Bud Davis

DAVIS, JOHN WILBUR (Country) — BL TR 6′ 207 lbs.
B. July 7, 1896, Merry Point, Va. D. May 26, 1967, Williamsburg, Va.

Year	Team		W	L	PCT	ERA	G	GS	CG	IP	H	BB	SO	ShO	Relief W	Relief L	Relief SV	AB	H	HR	BA	PO	A	E	DP	TC/G	FA
1915	PHI	A	0	2	.000	4.05	18	2	2	66.2	65	59	18	0	0	0	0	26	8	0	.308	0	20	4	1	1.3	.833

Chili Davis

DAVIS, CHARLES THEODORE — BB TR 6′ 3″ 195 lbs.
B. Jan. 17, 1960, Kingston, Jamaica.

Year	Team		W	L	PCT	ERA	G	GS	CG	IP	H	BB	SO	ShO	Relief W	Relief L	Relief SV	AB	H	HR	BA	PO	A	E	DP	TC/G	FA
1993	CAL	A	0	0	—	0.00	1	0	0	2	0	0	0	0	0	0	0	*				7	0	0	0	1.2	1.000

Curt Davis

DAVIS, CURTIS BENTON (Coonskin) — BR TR 6′ 2″ 185 lbs.
B. Sept. 7, 1903, Greenfield, Mo. D. Oct. 13, 1965, Covina, Calif.

Year	Team		W	L	PCT	ERA	G	GS	CG	IP	H	BB	SO	ShO	Relief W	Relief L	Relief SV	AB	H	HR	BA	PO	A	E	DP	TC/G	FA
1934	PHI	N	19	17	.528	2.95	**51**	31	18	274.1	283	60	99	3	6	2	5	95	20	1	.211	21	95	8	12	2.4	.935
1935			16	14	.533	3.66	44	27	19	231	264	47	74	3	2	2	2	75	13	1	.173	21	50	2	4	1.7	.973
1936	2 teams	PHI N (10G 2–4) CHI N (24G 11–9)																									
″	total		13	13	.500	3.46	34	28	13	213.1	217	50	70	0	1	2	1	79	12	0	.152	21	53	3	5	2.3	.961
1937	CHI	N	10	5	.667	4.08	28	14	8	123.2	138	30	32	0	1	1	1	40	12	1	.300	10	34	1	1	1.6	.978
1938	STL	N	12	8	.600	3.63	40	21	8	173.1	187	27	36	2	4	0	3	57	13	3	.228	9	38	0	2	1.2	1.000
1939			22	16	.579	3.63	49	31	13	248	279	48	70	3	3	**5**	7	105	40	1	.381	7	59	1	2	1.4	.985
1940	2 teams	STL N (14G 0–4) BKN N (22G 8–7)																									
″	total		8	11	.421	4.19	36	25	9	191	208	38	58	0	1	1	3	66	6	1	.091	18	48	2	1	1.9	.971
1941	BKN	N	13	7	.650	2.97	28	16	10	154.1	141	27	50	5	2	3	2	59	11	2	.186	3	55	1	0	2.1	.983
1942			15	6	.714	2.36	32	26	13	206	179	51	60	5	2	0	2	68	12	0	.176	6	61	0	7	2.1	1.000
1943			10	13	.435	3.78	31	21	8	164.1	182	39	47	2	3	1	3	55	9	0	.164	13	43	1	2	1.8	.982
1944			10	11	.476	3.34	31	23	12	194	207	39	49	1	1	0	4	63	10	0	.159	9	47	1	1	1.8	.982
1945			10	10	.500	3.25	24	18	10	149.2	171	21	39	0	0	2	0	51	7	1	.137	8	32	1	0	1.7	.976
1946			0	0	—	13.50	1	0	0	2	3	2	0	0	0	0	0	0	0	0	—	0	1	0	0	1.0	1.000
13 yrs.			158	131	.547	3.42	429	281	141	2325	2459	479	684	24	26	19	33	813	165	11	.203	146	616	21	37	1.8	.973
WORLD SERIES																											
1941	BKN	N	0	1	.000	5.06	1	1	0	5.1	6	3	1	0	0	0	0	2	0	0	.000	1	0	0	0	1.0	1.000

Daisy Davis

DAVIS, JOHN HENRY ALBERT — TR
B. May 17, 1858, Boston, Mass. D. Nov. 5, 1902, Lynn, Mass.

Year	Team		W	L	PCT	ERA	G	GS	CG	IP	H	BB	SO	ShO	Relief W	Relief L	Relief SV	AB	H	HR	BA	PO	A	E	DP	TC/G	FA
1884	2 teams	STL AA (25G 10–12) BOS N (4G 1–3)																									
″	total		11	15	.423	3.57	29	28	23	229.1	246	43	156	1	0	0	0	103	15	0	.146	14	40	14	1	2.0	.794
1885	BOS	N	5	6	.455	*4.29*	11	11	10	94.1	110	28	30	1	0	0	0	37	7	0	.189	1	16	1	0	1.6	.944
2 yrs.			16	21	.432	3.78	40	39	33	323.2	356	71	186	2	0	0	0	140	22	0	.157	15	56	15	1	1.9	.826

Dixie Davis

DAVIS, FRANK TALMADGE — BR TR 5′11″ 155 lbs.
B. Oct. 12, 1890, Wilson Mills, N. C. D. Feb. 4, 1944, Raleigh, N. C.

Year	Team		W	L	PCT	ERA	G	GS	CG	IP	H	BB	SO	ShO	Relief W	Relief L	Relief SV	AB	H	HR	BA	PO	A	E	DP	TC/G	FA
1912	CIN	N	0	1	.000	2.70	7	0	0	26.2	25	16	12	0	0	1	0	10	2	0	.200	0	4	0	0	0.6	1.000
1915	CHI	A	0	0	—	0.00	2	0	0	3	2	2	2	0	0	0	0	0	0	0	—	0	1	0	0	0.5	1.000
1918	PHI	N	0	2	.000	3.06	17	2	1	47	43	30	18	0	0	0	0	9	0	0	.000	4	7	2	0	0.8	.846
1920	STL	A	18	12	.600	3.17	38	31	22	269.1	250	**149**	85	0	1	0	0	94	25	0	.266	13	47	3	3	1.7	.952
1921			16	16	.500	4.44	40	36	20	265.1	279	**123**	100	2	0	0	0	95	20	0	.211	19	54	1	3	1.9	.986
1922			11	6	.647	4.08	25	25	7	174.1	162	87	65	2	0	0	0	59	8	0	.136	8	40	2	2	2.0	.960
1923			4	6	.400	3.62	19	17	5	109.1	106	63	36	1	0	0	0	40	10	0	.250	5	18	2	2	1.3	.920
1924			11	13	.458	4.10	29	24	11	160.1	159	72	45	5	1	0	0	46	7	0	.152	10	29	2	7	1.4	.951
1925			12	7	.632	4.59	35	22	9	180.1	192	106	58	0	2	1	1	64	11	0	.172	8	49	4	3	1.7	.934
1926			3	8	.273	4.66	27	7	2	83	93	40	39	0	3	3	1	24	4	0	.167	2	19	1	0	0.8	.955
10 yrs.			75	71	.514	3.97	239	164	77	1318.2	1311	688	460	10	7	5	2	441	87	0	.197	69	268	17	20	1.5	.952

George Davis

DAVIS, GEORGE ALLEN (Iron) — BB TR 5′10½″ 175 lbs.
B. Mar. 9, 1890, Lancaster, N. Y. D. June 4, 1961, Buffalo, N. Y.

Year	Team		W	L	PCT	ERA	G	GS	CG	IP	H	BB	SO	ShO	Relief W	Relief L	Relief SV	AB	H	HR	BA	PO	A	E	DP	TC/G	FA
1912	NY	A	1	4	.200	6.50	10	7	5	54	61	28	22	0	0	0	0	18	2	0	.111	0	9	0	0	0.9	1.000
1913	BOS	N	0	0	—	4.50	2	0	0	8	7	5	3	0	0	0	0	2	0	0	.000	0	1	1	0	1.0	.500
1914			3	3	.500	3.40	9	6	4	55.2	42	26	26	1	0	0	0	18	3	0	.167	1	7	0	0	0.9	1.000
1915			3	3	.500	3.80	15	9	4	73.1	85	19	26	0	0	0	0	23	6	0	.261	2	21	1	1	1.6	.958
4 yrs.			7	10	.412	4.48	36	22	13	191	195	78	77	1	0	0	0	61	11	0	.180	3	38	2	1	1.2	.953

George Davis

DAVIS, GEORGE STACEY BB TR 5′ 9″ 180 lbs.
B. Aug. 23, 1870, Cohoes, N. Y. D. Oct. 17, 1940, Philadelphia, Pa.
Manager 1895, 1900–01.

Year	Team	W	L	PCT	ERA	G	GS	CG	IP	H	BB	SO	ShO	Relief Pitching W	Relief Pitching L	Relief Pitching SV	Batting AB	Batting H	Batting HR	BA	PO	A	E	DP	TC/G	FA
1891	CLE N	0	1	.000	15.75	3	0	0	4	8	3	4	0	0	1	1	*				288	38	18	10	2.5	.948

Jim Davis

DAVIS, JAMES BENNETT BB TL 6′ 180 lbs.
B. Sept. 15, 1924, Red Bluff, Calif. D. Dec. 6, 1995, San Mateo, Calif.

Year	Team	W	L	PCT	ERA	G	GS	CG	IP	H	BB	SO	ShO	Relief Pitching W	Relief Pitching L	Relief Pitching SV	Batting AB	Batting H	Batting HR	BA	PO	A	E	DP	TC/G	FA
1954	CHI N	11	7	.611	3.52	46	12	2	127.2	114	51	58	0	6	2	4	32	2	0	.063	13	24	1	0	0.8	.974
1955		7	11	.389	4.44	42	16	0	133.2	122	58	62	0	5	3	3	37	1	0	.027	5	22	1	0	0.7	.964
1956		5	7	.417	3.66	46	11	2	120.1	116	59	66	1	3	2	2	28	5	0	.179	2	23	0	3	0.5	1.000
1957	2 teams STL N (10G 0–1) NY N (10G 1–0)																									
″	total	1	1	.500	5.84	20	0	0	24.2	31	11	11	0	1	1	1	2	1	0	.500	0	6	1	1	0.3	.857
4 yrs.		24	26	.480	4.01	154	39	4	406.1	383	179	197	1	15	8	10	99	9	0	.091	20	75	3	4	0.6	.969

Joel Davis

DAVIS, JOEL CLARK BL TR 6′ 5″ 205 lbs.
B. Jan. 30, 1965, Jacksonville, Fla.

Year	Team	W	L	PCT	ERA	G	GS	CG	IP	H	BB	SO	ShO	Relief Pitching W	Relief Pitching L	Relief Pitching SV	Batting AB	Batting H	Batting HR	BA	PO	A	E	DP	TC/G	FA
1985	CHI A	3	3	.500	4.16	12	11	1	71.1	71	26	37	0	0	0	0	0	0	0	—	4	3	1	1	0.7	.875
1986		4	5	.444	4.70	19	19	1	105.1	115	51	54	0	0	0	0	0	0	0	—	7	18	2	1	1.4	.926
1987		1	5	.167	5.73	13	9	1	55	56	29	25	0	0	1	0	0	0	0	—	5	1	1	1	0.5	.857
1988		0	1	.000	6.75	5	2	0	16	21	5	10	0	0	0	0	0	0	0	—	1	1	0	0	0.4	1.000
4 yrs.		8	14	.364	4.91	49	41	3	247.2	263	111	126	0	0	1	0	0	0	0		17	23	4	3	0.9	.909

John Davis

DAVIS, JOHN KIRK BR TR 6′ 7″ 215 lbs.
B. Jan. 5, 1963, Chicago, Ill.

Year	Team	W	L	PCT	ERA	G	GS	CG	IP	H	BB	SO	ShO	Relief Pitching W	Relief Pitching L	Relief Pitching SV	Batting AB	Batting H	Batting HR	BA	PO	A	E	DP	TC/G	FA
1987	KC A	5	2	.714	2.27	27	0	0	43.2	29	26	24	0	5	2	2	0	0	0	—	5	7	1	1	0.5	.923
1988	CHI A	2	5	.286	6.64	34	1	0	63.2	77	50	37	0	2	4	1	0	0	0	—	5	7	1	1	0.4	.923
1989		0	1	.000	4.50	4	0	0	6	5	2	5	0	0	1	1	0	0	0	—	0	1	0	0	0.3	1.000
1990	SD N	0	1	.000	5.79	6	0	0	9.1	9	4	7	0	0	1	0	1	0	0	.000	0	1	0	0	0.2	1.000
4 yrs.		7	9	.438	4.92	71	1	0	122.2	120	82	73	0	7	8	4	1	0	0	.000	10	16	2	2	0.4	.929

Mark Davis

DAVIS, MARK WILLIAM BL TL 6′ 3″ 180 lbs.
B. Oct. 19, 1960, Livermore, Calif.

Year	Team	W	L	PCT	ERA	G	GS	CG	IP	H	BB	SO	ShO	Relief Pitching W	Relief Pitching L	Relief Pitching SV	Batting AB	Batting H	Batting HR	BA	PO	A	E	DP	TC/G	FA
1980	PHI N	0	0	—	2.57	2	1	0	7	4	5	5	0	0	0	0	2	1	0	.500	0	0	0	0	0.0	.000
1981		1	4	.200	7.74	9	9	0	43	49	24	29	0	0	0	0	11	1	0	.091	0	6	0	0	0.7	1.000
1983	SF N	6	4	.600	3.49	20	20	2	111	93	50	83	2	0	0	0	30	4	0	.133	4	13	0	0	0.9	1.000
1984		5	17	.227	5.36	46	27	1	174.2	201	54	124	0	3	4	0	46	6	0	.130	1	22	3	1	0.6	.885
1985		5	12	.294	3.54	77	1	0	114.1	89	41	131	0	5	**11**	7	12	3	0	.250	2	12	0	0	0.2	1.000
1986		5	7	.417	2.99	67	2	0	84.1	63	34	90	0	5	6	4	8	1	0	.125	3	11	3	1	0.3	.824
1987	2 teams SF N (20G 4–5) SD N (43G 5–3)																									
″	total	9	8	.529	3.99	63	11	1	133	123	59	98	0	5	3	2	30	7	0	.233	4	20	2	3	0.4	.923
1988	SD N	5	10	.333	2.01	62	0	0	98.1	70	42	102	0	5	**10**	28	10	2	1	.200	4	21	1	2	0.4	.962
1989		4	3	.571	1.85	70	0	0	92.2	66	31	92	0	4	3	**44**	13	0	0	.000	1	11	3	0	0.2	.800
1990	KC A	2	7	.222	5.11	53	3	0	68.2	71	52	73	0	2	5	6	0	0	0	—	1	6	1	0	0.2	.875
1991		6	3	.667	4.45	29	5	0	62.2	55	39	47	0	3	2	1	0	0	0	—	1	7	0	1	0.3	1.000
1992	2 teams KC A (13G 1–3) ATL N (14G 1–0)																									
″	total	2	3	.400	7.13	27	6	0	53	64	41	34	0	1	0	0	1	0	0	.000	3	6	1	0	0.4	.900
1993	2 teams PHI N (25G 1–2) SD N (35G 0–3)																									
″	total	1	5	.167	4.26	60	0	0	69.2	79	44	70	0	1	5	4	4	1	0	.250	3	8	2	1	0.2	.846
1994	SD N	0	1	.000	8.82	20	0	0	16.1	20	13	15	0	0	1	0	0	0	0	—	0	3	0	0	0.2	1.000
14 yrs.		51	84	.378	4.15	605	85	4	1128.2	1047	529	993	2	34	50	96	167	26	1	.156	27	146	16	9	0.3	.915

Peaches Davis

DAVIS, ROY THOMAS BL TR 6′ 3½″ 190 lbs.
B. May 31, 1905, Glen Rose, Tex. D. Apr. 28, 1995, Duncan, Oklahoma.

Year	Team	W	L	PCT	ERA	G	GS	CG	IP	H	BB	SO	ShO	Relief Pitching W	Relief Pitching L	Relief Pitching SV	Batting AB	Batting H	Batting HR	BA	PO	A	E	DP	TC/G	FA
1936	CIN N	8	8	.500	3.58	26	15	5	125.2	139	36	32	0	2	1	5	43	7	0	.163	14	26	3	0	1.7	.930
1937		11	13	.458	3.59	42	24	11	218	252	51	59	1	1	3	3	78	10	0	.128	21	31	5	2	1.4	.912
1938		7	12	.368	3.97	29	19	11	167.2	193	40	28	1	1	2	1	61	15	0	.246	1	23	1	2	0.9	.960
1939		1	0	1.000	6.46	20	0	0	30.2	43	11	4	0	1	0	2	3	1	0	.333	2	8	0	0	0.5	1.000
4 yrs.		27	33	.450	3.87	117	58	27	542	627	138	123	2	5	6	11	185	33	0	.178	38	88	9	4	1.2	.933

Ron Davis

DAVIS, RONALD GENE BR TR 6′ 4″ 205 lbs.
B. Aug. 6, 1955, Houston, Tex.

Year	Team	W	L	PCT	ERA	G	GS	CG	IP	H	BB	SO	ShO	Relief Pitching W	Relief Pitching L	Relief Pitching SV	Batting AB	Batting H	Batting HR	BA	PO	A	E	DP	TC/G	FA
1978	NY A	0	0	—	11.57	4	0	0	2.1	3	3	0	0	0	0	0	0	0	0	—	1	0	0	0	0.3	1.000
1979		14	2	.875	2.86	44	0	0	85	84	28	43	0	**14**	2	9	1	0	0	.000	5	15	0	2	0.5	1.000
1980		9	3	.750	2.95	53	0	0	131	121	32	65	0	9	3	7	1	0	0	.000	4	23	1	0	0.5	.964
1981		4	5	.444	2.71	43	0	0	73	47	25	83	0	4	5	6	0	0	0	—	4	5	0	0	0.2	1.000
1982	MIN A	3	9	.250	4.42	63	0	0	106	106	47	89	0	3	9	22	0	0	0	—	6	10	0	1	0.3	1.000
1983		5	8	.385	3.34	66	0	0	89	89	33	84	0	5	8	30	0	0	0	—	0	4	1	0	0.1	.800
1984		7	11	.389	4.55	64	0	0	83	79	41	74	0	7	**11**	29	0	0	0	—	4	8	0	0	0.2	1.000
1985		2	6	.250	3.48	57	0	0	64.2	55	35	72	0	2	6	25	0	0	0	—	3	5	0	1	0.1	1.000
1986	2 teams MIN A (36G 2–6) CHI N (17G 0–2)																									
″	total	2	8	.200	8.59	53	0	0	58.2	86	32	40	0	2	8	2	2	0	0	.000	6	6	1	0	0.2	.923
1987	2 teams CHI N (21G 0–0) LA N (4G 0–0)																									
″	total	0	0		5.94	25	0	0	36.1	50	18	32	0	0	0	0	0	0	0		1	3	0	2	0.2	1.000
1988	SF N	1	1	.500	4.67	9	0	0	17.1	15	6	15	0	1	1	0	2	0	0	.000	1	4	1	0	0.7	.833
11 yrs.		47	53	.470	4.05	481	0	0	746.1	735	300	597	0	47	53	130	6	0	0	.000	35	83	4	6	0.3	.967
DIVISIONAL PLAYOFF SERIES																										
1981	NY A	1	0	1.000	0.00	3	0	0	6	1	2	6	0	1	0	0	0	0	0	—	0	0	0	0	0.0	.000
LEAGUE CHAMPIONSHIP SERIES																										
1980	NY A	0	0	—	2.25	1	0	0	4	3	1	3	0	0	0	0	0	0	0	—	0	2	0	0	2.0	1.000
1981		0	0	—	0.00	2	0	0	3.1	0	2	4	0	0	0	0	0	0	0	—	0	0	0	0	0.0	.000
2 yrs.		0	0		1.23	3	0	0	7.1	3	3	7	0	0	0	0	0	0	0		0	2	0	0	0.7	1.000
WORLD SERIES																										
1981	NY A	0	0	—	23.14	4	0	0	2.1	4	5	4	0	0	0	0	0	0	0	—	0	0	0	0	0.0	.000

Steve Davis

DAVIS, STEVEN KENNON BL TL 6′ 1″ 183 lbs.
B. Aug. 4, 1960, San Antonio, Tex.

Year	Team	Lg	W	L	PCT	ERA	G	GS	CG	IP	H	BB	SO	ShO	Relief Pitching W	Relief Pitching L	Relief Pitching SV	Batting AB	Batting H	Batting HR	BA	PO	A	E	DP	TC/G	FA
1985	TOR	A	2	1	.667	3.54	10	5	0	28	23	13	22	0	1	0	0	0	0	0	—	0	4	0	0	0.4	1.000
1986			0	0	—	17.18	3	0	0	3.2	8	5	5	0	0	0	0	0	0	0	—	0	0	0	0	0.0	.000
1989	CLE	A	1	1	.500	8.06	12	2	0	25.2	34	14	12	0	0	0	0	0	0	0	—	1	3	0	0	0.3	1.000
3 yrs.			3	2	.600	6.44	25	7	0	57.1	65	32	39	0	1	0	0	0	0	0		1	7	0	0	0.3	1.000

Storm Davis

DAVIS, GEORGE EARL BR TR 6′ 4″ 210 lbs.
B. Dec. 26, 1961, Dallas, Tex.

Year	Team	Lg	W	L	PCT	ERA	G	GS	CG	IP	H	BB	SO	ShO	Relief Pitching W	Relief Pitching L	Relief Pitching SV	Batting AB	Batting H	Batting HR	BA	PO	A	E	DP	TC/G	FA
1982	BAL	A	8	4	.667	3.49	29	8	1	100.2	96	28	67	0	3	2	0	0	0	0	—	6	12	1	0	0.7	.947
1983			13	7	.650	3.59	34	29	6	200.1	180	64	125	1	0	0	0	0	0	0	—	14	19	3	1	1.1	.917
1984			14	9	.609	3.12	35	31	10	225	205	71	105	2	0	1	1	0	0	0	—	15	18	2	1	1.0	.943
1985			10	8	.556	4.53	31	28	8	175	172	70	93	1	0	0	0	0	0	0	—	15	20	0	0	1.1	1.000
1986			9	12	.429	3.62	25	25	2	154	166	49	96	0	0	0	0	0	0	0	—	22	21	1	3	1.8	.977
1987	2 teams	SD N (21G 2–7)	OAK A (5G 1–1)																								
″	total		3	8	.273	5.23	26	15	0	93	98	47	65	0	0	1	0	16	1	0	.063	8	9	1	0	0.7	.944
1988	OAK	A	16	7	.696	3.70	33	33	1	201.2	211	91	127	0	0	0	0	0	0	0	—	6	21	1	2	0.8	.964
1989			19	7	.731	4.36	31	31	1	169.1	187	68	91	0	0	0	0	0	0	0	—	12	17	2	0	1.0	.935
1990	KC	A	7	10	.412	4.74	21	20	0	112	129	35	62	0	0	0	0	0	0	0	—	4	10	1	3	0.7	.933
1991			3	9	.250	4.96	51	9	1	114.1	140	46	53	1	1	4	2	0	0	0	—	5	12	0	0	0.3	1.000
1992	BAL	A	7	3	.700	3.43	48	2	0	89.1	79	36	53	0	7	3	4	0	0	0	—	3	14	0	3	0.4	1.000
1993	2 teams	OAK A (19G 2–6)	DET A (24G 0–2)																								
″	total		2	8	.200	5.05	43	8	0	98	93	48	73	0	1	4	4	0	0	0		5	14	1	1	0.5	.950
1994	DET	A	2	4	.333	3.56	35	0	0	48	36	34	38	0	2	4	0	0	0	0	—	6	9	0	1	0.4	1.000
13 yrs.			113	96	.541	4.02	442	239	30	1780.2	1792	687	1048	5	14	19	11	16	1	0	.063	121	196	13	15	0.7	.961
LEAGUE CHAMPIONSHIP SERIES																											
1983	BAL	A	0	0	—	0.00	1	1	0	6	5	2	2	0	0	0	0	0	0	0	—	0	0	0	0	0.0	.000
1988	OAK	A	0	0	—	0.00	1	1	0	6.1	2	5	4	0	0	0	0	0	0	0	—	0	2	0	0	2.0	1.000
1989			0	1	.000	7.11	1	1	0	6.1	5	2	3	0	0	0	0	0	0	0	—	0	0	0	0	0.0	.000
3 yrs.			0	1	.000	2.41	3	3	0	18.2	12	9	9	0	0	0	0	0	0	0		0	2	0	0	0.7	1.000
WORLD SERIES																											
1983	BAL	A	1	0	1.000	5.40	1	1	0	5	6	1	3	0	0	0	0	2	0	0	.000	0	1	0	0	1.0	1.000
1988	OAK	A	0	2	.000	11.25	2	2	0	8	14	1	7	0	0	0	0	1	0	0	.000	2	1	0	0	1.5	1.000
2 yrs.			1	2	.333	9.00	3	3	0	13	20	2	10	0	0	0	0	3	0	0	.000	2	2	0	0	1.3	1.000

Tim Davis

DAVIS, TIMOTHY HOWARD BL TL 5′11″ 165 lbs.
B. July 14, 1970, Marianna, Fla.

Year	Team	Lg	W	L	PCT	ERA	G	GS	CG	IP	H	BB	SO	ShO	Relief Pitching W	Relief Pitching L	Relief Pitching SV	Batting AB	Batting H	Batting HR	BA	PO	A	E	DP	TC/G	FA
1994	SEA	A	2	2	.500	4.01	42	1	0	49.1	57	25	28	0	1	2	2	0	0	0	—	2	8	0	0	0.2	1.000
1995			2	1	.667	6.38	5	5	0	24	30	18	19	0	0	0	0	0	0	0	—	1	7	0	0	1.6	1.000
2 yrs.			4	3	.571	4.79	47	6	0	73.1	87	43	47	0	1	2	2	0	0	0		3	15	0	0	0.4	1.000

Wiley Davis

DAVIS, WILEY ANDERSON BR TR 5′10″ 165 lbs.
B. Aug. 1, 1875, Seymour, Tenn. D. Sept. 22, 1942, Detroit, Mich.

Year	Team	Lg	W	L	PCT	ERA	G	GS	CG	IP	H	BB	SO	ShO	Relief Pitching W	Relief Pitching L	Relief Pitching SV	Batting AB	Batting H	Batting HR	BA	PO	A	E	DP	TC/G	FA
1896	CIN	N	1	1	.500	8.31	2	0	0	4.1	8	2	1	0	1	1	0	1	0	0	.000	0	4	0	0	2.0	1.000

Woody Davis

DAVIS, WOODROW WILSON (Babe) BL TR 6′ 1″ 200 lbs.
B. Apr. 25, 1913, Nicholas, Ga.

Year	Team	Lg	W	L	PCT	ERA	G	GS	CG	IP	H	BB	SO	ShO	Relief Pitching W	Relief Pitching L	Relief Pitching SV	Batting AB	Batting H	Batting HR	BA	PO	A	E	DP	TC/G	FA
1938	DET	A	0	0	—	1.50	2	0	0	6	3	4	1	0	0	0	0	1	0	0	.000	1	0	1	0	1.0	.500

Mike Davison

DAVISON, MICHAEL LYNN BL TL 6′ 1″ 170 lbs.
B. Aug. 4, 1945, Galesburg, Ill.

Year	Team	Lg	W	L	PCT	ERA	G	GS	CG	IP	H	BB	SO	ShO	Relief Pitching W	Relief Pitching L	Relief Pitching SV	Batting AB	Batting H	Batting HR	BA	PO	A	E	DP	TC/G	FA
1969	SF	N	0	0	—	4.50	1	0	0	2	2	0	2	0	0	0	0	0	0	0	—	0	0	0	0	0.0	.000
1970			3	5	.375	6.50	31	0	0	36	46	22	21	0	3	5	1	1	0	0	.000	4	9	0	1	0.4	1.000
2 yrs.			3	5	.375	6.39	32	0	0	38	48	22	23	0	3	5	1	1	0	0	.000	4	9	0	1	0.4	1.000

Scott Davison

DAVISON, SCOTTY RAY BR TR 6′ 190 lbs.
B. Oct. 16, 1970, Inglewood, Calif.

Year	Team	Lg	W	L	PCT	ERA	G	GS	CG	IP	H	BB	SO	ShO	Relief Pitching W	Relief Pitching L	Relief Pitching SV	Batting AB	Batting H	Batting HR	BA	PO	A	E	DP	TC/G	FA
1995	SEA	A	0	0	—	6.23	3	0	0	4.1	7	1	3	0	0	0	0	0	0	0	—	0	1	0	0	0.3	1.000

Bill Dawley

DAWLEY, WILLIAM CHESTER BR TR 6′ 5″ 235 lbs.
B. Feb. 6, 1958, Norwich, Conn.

Year	Team	Lg	W	L	PCT	ERA	G	GS	CG	IP	H	BB	SO	ShO	Relief Pitching W	Relief Pitching L	Relief Pitching SV	Batting AB	Batting H	Batting HR	BA	PO	A	E	DP	TC/G	FA
1983	HOU	N	6	6	.500	2.82	48	0	0	79.2	51	22	60	0	6	6	14	9	2	0	.222	2	5	0	1	0.1	1.000
1984			11	4	.733	1.93	60	0	0	98	82	35	47	0	**11**	4	5	9	3	0	.333	6	11	1	0	0.3	.944
1985			5	3	.625	3.56	49	0	0	81	76	37	48	0	5	3	2	10	2	0	.200	6	13	1	2	0.4	.950
1986	CHI	A	0	7	.000	3.32	46	0	0	97.2	91	28	66	0	0	7	2	2	0	0	.000	8	8	1	0	0.4	.941
1987	STL	N	5	8	.385	4.47	60	0	0	96.2	93	38	65	0	5	8	2	12	2	0	.167	10	17	0	2	0.4	1.000
1988	PHI	N	0	2	.000	13.50	8	0	0	8.2	16	4	3	0	0	2	0	0	0	0	—	0	1	0	0	0.1	1.000
1989	OAK	A	0	0	—	4.00	4	0	0	9	11	2	3	0	0	0	0	0	0	0	—	0	1	0	0	0.3	1.000
7 yrs.			27	30	.474	3.42	275	0	0	470.2	420	166	292	0	27	30	25	42	9	0	.214	32	56	3	5	0.3	.967

Joe Dawson

DAWSON, RALPH FENTON BR TR 5′11″ 182 lbs.
Brother of Rex Dawson.
B. Mar. 9, 1897, Bow, Wash. D. Jan. 4, 1978, Longview, Tex.

Year	Team	Lg	W	L	PCT	ERA	G	GS	CG	IP	H	BB	SO	ShO	Relief Pitching W	Relief Pitching L	Relief Pitching SV	Batting AB	Batting H	Batting HR	BA	PO	A	E	DP	TC/G	FA
1924	CLE	A	1	2	.333	6.64	4	4	0	20.1	24	21	7	0	0	0	0	7	2	0	.286	1	8	0	0	2.3	1.000
1927	PIT	N	3	7	.300	4.46	20	7	4	80.2	80	32	17	0	2	2	0	25	5	0	.200	1	18	2	0	1.0	.905
1928			7	7	.500	3.29	31	7	1	128.2	116	56	36	0	5	2	3	43	12	0	.279	6	15	0	0	0.7	1.000
1929			0	1	.000	8.31	4	0	0	8.2	13	3	2	0	0	1	0	2	1	0	.500	0	2	0	0	0.5	1.000
4 yrs.			11	17	.393	4.15	59	18	5	238.1	233	112	62	0	7	5	3	77	20	0	.260	8	43	2	0	0.9	.962
WORLD SERIES																											
1927	PIT	N	0	0	—	0.00	1	0	0	1	0	0	0	0	0	0	0	0	0	0	—	0	0	0	0	0.0	.000

Rex Dawson

DAWSON, REXFORD PAUL BL TR 6′ 185 lbs.
Brother of Joe Dawson.
B. Feb. 10, 1889, Skagit County, Wash. D. Oct. 20, 1958, Indianapolis, Ind.

Year	Team	Lg	W	L	PCT	ERA	G	GS	CG	IP	H	BB	SO	ShO	Relief Pitching W	Relief Pitching L	Relief Pitching SV	Batting AB	Batting H	Batting HR	BA	PO	A	E	DP	TC/G	FA
1913	WAS	A	0	0	—	0.00	1	0	0	1	1	0	0	0	0	0	0	0	0	0	—	0	0	0	0	0.0	.000

Bill Day

DAY, WILLIAM M. TR 5′ 8″ 150 lbs.
B. July 28, 1867, Wilmington, Del. D. Aug. 16, 1923, Wilmington, Del.

Year	Team	W	L	PCT	ERA	G	GS	CG	IP	H	BB	SO	ShO	Relief Pitching W	Relief Pitching L	Relief Pitching SV	Batting AB	Batting H	Batting HR	BA	PO	A	E	DP	TC/G	FA
1889	PHI N	0	3	.000	5.21	4	3	2	19	16	23	20	0	0	0	0	10	0	0	.000	1	3	2	0	1.5	.667
1890	2 teams PHI N (4G 1–1) PIT N (6G 0–6)																									
″	total	1	7	.125	4.52	10	8	8	73.2	92	36	19	0	0	0	0	33	2	0	.061	1	24	2	0	2.7	.926
2 yrs.		1	10	.091	4.66	14	11	10	92.2	108	59	39	0	0	0	0	43	2	0	.047	2	27	4	0	2.4	.879

Pea Ridge Day

DAY, CLYDE HENRY BR TR 6′ 190 lbs.
B. Aug. 26, 1899, Pea Ridge, Ark. D. Mar. 21, 1934, Kansas City, Mo.

Year	Team	W	L	PCT	ERA	G	GS	CG	IP	H	BB	SO	ShO	Relief Pitching W	Relief Pitching L	Relief Pitching SV	Batting AB	Batting H	Batting HR	BA	PO	A	E	DP	TC/G	FA
1924	STL N	1	1	.500	4.58	3	3	1	17.2	22	6	3	0	0	0	0	8	1	0	.125	0	3	0	0	1.0	1.000
1925		2	4	.333	6.30	17	4	1	40	53	7	13	0	1	1	1	13	2	0	.154	0	6	0	0	0.4	1.000
1926	CIN N	0	0	—	7.36	4	0	0	7.1	13	2	2	0	0	0	0	2	0	0	.000	0	0	0	0	0.0	.000
1931	BKN N	2	2	.500	4.55	22	2	1	57.1	75	13	30	0	2	0	1	18	4	0	.222	0	9	2	0	0.5	.818
4 yrs.		5	7	.417	5.30	46	9	3	122.1	163	28	48	0	3	1	2	41	7	0	.171	0	18	2	0	0.4	.900

Ken Dayley

DAYLEY, KENNETH GRANT BL TL 6′ 178 lbs.
B. Feb. 25, 1959, Jerome, Ida.

Year	Team	W	L	PCT	ERA	G	GS	CG	IP	H	BB	SO	ShO	Relief Pitching W	Relief Pitching L	Relief Pitching SV	Batting AB	Batting H	Batting HR	BA	PO	A	E	DP	TC/G	FA
1982	ATL N	5	6	.455	4.54	20	11	0	71.1	79	25	34	0	2	0	0	20	5	0	.250	3	5	0	0	0.4	1.000
1983		5	8	.385	4.30	24	16	0	104.2	100	39	70	0	1	2	0	32	7	0	.219	0	7	0	0	0.3	1.000
1984	2 teams ATL N (4G 0–3) STL N (3G 0–2)																									
″	total	0	5	.000	7.99	7	6	0	23.2	44	11	10	0	0	0	0	4	2	0	.500	1	4	0	0	0.7	1.000
1985	STL N	4	4	.500	2.76	57	0	0	65.1	65	18	62	0	4	4	11	5	2	0	.400	5	15	0	0	0.4	1.000
1986		0	3	.000	3.26	31	0	0	38.2	42	11	33	0	0	3	5	5	1	0	.200	1	7	0	0	0.3	1.000
1987		9	5	.643	2.66	53	0	0	61	52	33	63	0	9	5	4	0	0	0	—	3	4	0	1	0.1	1.000
1988		2	7	.222	2.77	54	0	0	55.1	48	19	38	0	2	7	5	4	0	0	.000	2	7	0	0	0.2	1.000
1989		4	3	.571	2.87	71	0	0	75.1	63	30	40	0	4	3	12	5	0	0	.000	2	5	1	0	0.1	.875
1990		4	4	.500	3.56	58	0	0	73.1	63	30	51	0	4	4	2	6	0	0	.000	5	8	1	1	0.2	.929
1991	TOR A	0	0	—	6.23	8	0	0	4.1	7	5	3	0	0	0	0	0	0	0	—	1	1	0	0	0.3	1.000
1993		0	0	—	0.00	2	0	0	0.2	1	4	2	0	0	0	0	0	0	0	—	0	0	0	0	0.0	.000
11 yrs.		33	45	.423	3.64	385	33	0	573.2	564	225	406	0	26	28	39	81	17	0	.210	23	63	2	2	0.2	.977
LEAGUE CHAMPIONSHIP SERIES																										
1985	STL N	0	0	—	0.00	5	0	0	6	2	1	3	0	0	0	2	2	1	0	.500	0	1	0	0	0.2	1.000
1987		0	0	—	0.00	3	0	0	4	1	2	4	0	0	0	2	0	0	0	—	0	0	0	0	0.0	.000
2 yrs.		0	0		0.00	8	0	0	10	3	3	7	0	0	0	4 3rd	2	1	0	.500	0	1	0	0	0.1	1.000
WORLD SERIES																										
1985	STL N	1	0	1.000	0.00	4	0	0	6	1	3	5	0	1	0	0	0	0	0	—	0	0	0	0	0.0	.000
1987		0	0	—	1.93	4	0	0	4.2	2	0	3	0	0	0	1	1	0	0	.000	0	0	0	0	0.0	.000
2 yrs.		1	0	1.000	0.84	8	0	0	10.2	3	3	8	0	1	0	1	1	0	0	.000	0	0	0	0	0.0	

Ren Deagle

DEAGLE, LORENZO BURROUGHS BR TR 5′ 9″ 190 lbs.
B. June 26, 1858, New York, N. Y. D. Dec. 24, 1936, Kansas City, Mo.

Year	Team	W	L	PCT	ERA	G	GS	CG	IP	H	BB	SO	ShO	Relief Pitching W	Relief Pitching L	Relief Pitching SV	Batting AB	Batting H	Batting HR	BA	PO	A	E	DP	TC/G	FA
1883	CIN AA	10	8	.556	*2.31*	18	18	17	148	136	34	46	1	0	0	0	70	9	0	.129	4	28	10	0	2.1	.762
1884	2 teams CIN AA (4G 3–1) LOU AA (12G 4–6)																									
″	total	7	7	.500	3.26	16	16	12	121.1	119	22	35	1	0	0	0	58	6	0	.103	5	28	3	0	1.9	.917
2 yrs.		17	15	.531	2.74	34	34	29	269.1	255	56	81	2	0	0	0	128	15	0	.117	9	56	13	0	2.0	.833

Cot Deal

DEAL, ELLIS FERGUSON BB TR 5′10½″ 185 lbs.
B. Jan. 23, 1923, Arapaho, Okla. BL 1947–1948

Year	Team	W	L	PCT	ERA	G	GS	CG	IP	H	BB	SO	ShO	Relief Pitching W	Relief Pitching L	Relief Pitching SV	Batting AB	Batting H	Batting HR	BA	PO	A	E	DP	TC/G	FA
1947	BOS A	0	1	.000	9.24	5	2	0	12.2	20	7	6	0	0	0	0	4	2	0	.500	1	2	0	0	0.6	1.000
1948		1	0	1.000	0.00	4	0	0	4	3	3	2	0	1	0	0	0	0	0	—	0	1	0	0	0.3	1.000
1950	STL N	0	0	—	18.00	3	0	0	1	3	2	1	0	0	0	0	0	0	0	—	0	0	1	0	0.3	.000
1954		2	3	.400	6.28	33	0	0	71.2	85	36	25	0	2	3	1	20	2	1	.100	5	12	0	1	0.5	1.000
4 yrs.		3	4	.429	6.55	45	2	0	89.1	111	48	34	0	3	3	1	24	4	1	.167	6	15	1	1	0.5	.955

Chubby Dean

DEAN, ALFRED LOVELL BL TL 5′11″ 181 lbs.
B. Aug. 24, 1916, Mt. Airy, N. C. D. Dec. 21, 1970, Riverside, Calif.

Year	Team	W	L	PCT	ERA	G	GS	CG	IP	H	BB	SO	ShO	Relief Pitching W	Relief Pitching L	Relief Pitching SV	Batting AB	Batting H	Batting HR	BA	PO	A	E	DP	TC/G	FA
1937	PHI A	1	0	1.000	4.00	2	1	0	9	7	6	4	0	0	0	0	309	81	2	.262	680	37	8	62	9.4	.989
1938		2	1	.667	3.52	6	1	0	23	22	15	3	0	2	0	0	20	6	0	.300	0	8	0	0	1.3	1.000
1939		5	8	.385	5.25	54	1	0	116.2	132	80	39	0	5	7	7	77	27	0	.351	3	36	2	4	0.8	.951
1940		6	13	.316	6.61	30	19	8	159.1	220	63	38	1	1	3	1	90	26	0	.289	12	36	1	2	1.6	.980
1941	2 teams PHI A (18G 2–4) CLE A (8G 1–4)																									
″	total	3	8	.273	5.44	26	15	4	129	147	59	36	0	1	0	0	62	13	0	.210	7	28	0	1	1.3	1.000
1942	CLE A	8	11	.421	3.81	27	22	8	172.2	170	66	46	0	2	0	1	101	27	0	.267	7	24	2	0	1.2	.939
1943		5	5	.500	4.50	17	9	3	76	83	34	29	0	1	2	0	46	9	0	.196	2	11	1	1	0.8	.929
7 yrs.		30	46	.395	5.08	162	68	23	685.2	781	323	195	1	12	12	9	*				1417	220	21	125	5.2	.987

Dizzy Dean

DEAN, JAY HANNA BR TR 6′ 2″ 182 lbs.
Brother of Paul Dean.
B. Jan. 16, 1910, Lucas, Ark. D. July 17, 1974, Reno, Nev.
Hall of Fame 1953.

Year	Team	W	L	PCT	ERA	G	GS	CG	IP	H	BB	SO	ShO	Relief Pitching W	Relief Pitching L	Relief Pitching SV	Batting AB	Batting H	Batting HR	BA	PO	A	E	DP	TC/G	FA
1930	STL N	1	0	1.000	1.00	1	1	1	9	3	3	5	0	0	0	0	3	1	0	.333	1	4	0	0	5.0	1.000
1932		18	15	.545	3.30	46	33	16	**286**	280	102	**191**	**4**	0	3	2	97	25	2	.258	9	46	3	7	1.3	.948
1933		20	18	.526	3.04	**48**	34	**26**	293	279	64	**199**	3	1	3	4	105	19	1	.181	9	35	5	1	1.0	.898
1934		**30**	7	**.811**	2.66	50	33	**24**	311.2	288	75	**195**	**7**	4	2	7	118	29	2	.246	18	46	2	1	1.3	.970
1935		**28**	12	.700	3.04	50	**36**	**29**	**325.1**	**324**	77	**190**	3	4	3	5	128	30	2	.234	13	42	2	0	1.1	.965
1936		24	13	.649	3.17	**51**	34	**28**	**315**	310	53	195	2	2	3	**11**	121	27	0	.223	10	44	1	3	1.1	.982
1937		13	10	.565	2.69	27	25	17	197.1	206	33	120	4	0	1	1	66	15	1	.227	4	24	1	3	1.1	.966
1938	CHI N	7	1	.875	1.81	13	10	3	74.2	63	8	22	1	0	0	0	26	5	0	.192	2	11	0	0	1.0	1.000
1939		6	4	.600	3.36	19	13	7	96.1	98	17	27	2	0	1	0	34	5	0	.147	5	16	0	0	1.1	1.000
1940		3	3	.500	5.17	10	9	3	54	68	20	18	0	0	0	0	18	4	0	.222	5	15	1	0	2.1	.952
1941		0	0	—	18.00	1	1	0	1	3	0	1	0	0	0	0	0	0	0	—	0	0	0	0	0.0	.000
1947	STL A	0	0	—	0.00	1	1	0	4	3	1	0	0	0	0	0	1	1	0	1.000	0	0	0	0	0.0	.000
12 yrs.		150	83	.644	3.02	317	230	154	1967.1	1925	453	1163	26	11	16	30	717	161	8	.225	76	283	15	15	1.2	.960

Dizzy Dean *continued*

Year	Team	Lg	W	L	PCT	ERA	G	GS	CG	IP	H	BB	SO	ShO	Relief W	Relief L	Relief SV	AB	H	HR	BA	PO	A	E	DP	TC/G	FA
WORLD SERIES																											
1934	STL	N	2	1	.667	1.73	3	3	2	26	20	5	17	1	0	0	0	12	3	0	.250	2	2	0	0	1.3	1.000
1938	CHI	N	0	1	.000	6.48	2	1	0	8.1	8	1	2	0	0	0	0	3	2	0	.667	0	2	0	0	1.0	1.000
2 yrs.			2	2	.500	2.88	5	4	2	34.1	28	6	19	1	0	0	0	15	5	0	.333	2	4	0	0	1.2	1.000

Dory Dean

DEAN, CHARLES WILSON BR TR 5′ 9″ 160 lbs.
B. Nov. 6, 1852, Cincinnati, Ohio D. May 4, 1935, Nashville, Tenn.

Year	Team	Lg	W	L	PCT	ERA	G	GS	CG	IP	H	BB	SO	ShO	Relief W	Relief L	Relief SV	AB	H	HR	BA	PO	A	E	DP	TC/G	FA
1876	CIN	N	4	26	.133	3.73	30	30	26	262.2	397	24	22	0	0	0	0	138	36	0	.261	26	38	15	2	2.1	.810

Harry Dean

DEAN, JAMES HARRY BR TR 6′ 4″ 185 lbs.
B. May 12, 1915, Rockmart, Ga. D. June 1, 1960, Rockmart, Ga.

Year	Team	Lg	W	L	PCT	ERA	G	GS	CG	IP	H	BB	SO	ShO	Relief W	Relief L	Relief SV	AB	H	HR	BA	PO	A	E	DP	TC/G	FA
1941	WAS	A	0	0	—	4.50	2	0	0	2	2	3	0	0	0	0	0	0	0	0	—	0	0	1	0	0.5	.000

Paul Dean

DEAN, PAUL DEE (Daffy) BR TR 6′ 175 lbs.
Brother of Dizzy Dean.
B. Aug. 14, 1913, Lucas, Ark. D. Mar. 17, 1981, Springdale, Ark.

Year	Team	Lg	W	L	PCT	ERA	G	GS	CG	IP	H	BB	SO	ShO	Relief W	Relief L	Relief SV	AB	H	HR	BA	PO	A	E	DP	TC/G	FA
1934	STL	N	19	11	.633	3.43	39	26	16	233.1	225	52	150	5	2	4	2	83	20	0	.241	3	20	4	0	0.7	.852
1935			19	12	.613	3.37	46	33	19	269.2	261	55	143	2	3	1	5	90	12	0	.133	6	27	3	2	0.8	.917
1936			5	5	.500	4.60	17	14	5	92	113	20	28	0	0	1	1	34	2	0	.059	2	7	1	0	0.6	.900
1937			0	0	—	∞	1	0	0		1	2	0	0	0	0	0	0	0	0	—	0	0	0	0	0.0	.000
1938			3	1	.750	2.61	5	4	2	31	37	5	14	1	0	0	0	11	2	0	.182	1	3	0	0	0.8	1.000
1939			0	1	.000	6.07	16	2	0	43	54	10	16	0	0	0	0	9	1	0	.111	1	8	2	0	0.7	.818
1940	NY	N	4	4	.500	3.90	27	7	2	99.1	110	29	32	0	2	3	0	26	3	0	.115	3	14	0	0	0.6	1.000
1941			0	0	—	3.18	5	0	0	5.2	8	3	3	0	0	0	0	0	0	0	—	0	1	0	0	0.2	1.000
1943	STL	A	0	0	—	3.38	3	1	0	13.1	16	3	1	0	0	0	0	3	0	0	.000	0	2	0	0	0.7	1.000
9 yrs.			50	34	.595	3.75	159	87	44	787.1	825	179	387	8	7	9	8	256	40	0	.156	16	82	10	2	0.7	.907
WORLD SERIES																											
1934	STL	N	2	0	1.000	1.00	2	2	2	18	15	7	11	0	0	0	0	6	1	0	.167	0	0	1	0	0.5	.000

Wayland Dean

DEAN, WAYLAND OGDEN BB TR 6′ 2″ 178 lbs.
B. June 20, 1902, Richwood, W. Va. D. Apr. 10, 1930, Huntington, W. Va.

Year	Team	Lg	W	L	PCT	ERA	G	GS	CG	IP	H	BB	SO	ShO	Relief W	Relief L	Relief SV	AB	H	HR	BA	PO	A	E	DP	TC/G	FA
1924	NY	N	6	12	.333	5.01	26	20	6	125.2	139	45	39	0	1	2	0	40	8	2	.200	12	41	3	2	2.2	.946
1925			10	7	.588	4.64	33	14	6	151.1	169	50	53	1	5	1	1	51	12	1	.235	10	36	6	1	1.6	.885
1926	PHI	N	8	16	.333	6.10	33	26	15	163.2	245	89	52	1	0	2	0	102	27	3	.265	6	44	3	3	1.6	.943
1927	2 teams PHI N (2G 0–1) CHI N (2G 0–0)																										
″	total		0	1	.000	7.20	4	0	0	5	6	4	3	0	0	1	0	3	2	0	.667	0	2	0	1	0.5	1.000
4 yrs.			24	36	.400	5.31	96	60	27	445.2	559	188	147	2	6	6	1	*				28	123	12	7	1.7	.926
WORLD SERIES																											
1924	NY	N	0	0	—	4.50	1	0	0	2	3	0	2	0	0	0	0	*				0	0	0	0	0.0	.000

Denny DeBarr

DeBARR, DENNIS LEE BL TL 6′ 2″ 190 lbs.
B. Jan. 16, 1953, Cheyenne, Wyo.

Year	Team	Lg	W	L	PCT	ERA	G	GS	CG	IP	H	BB	SO	ShO	Relief W	Relief L	Relief SV	AB	H	HR	BA	PO	A	E	DP	TC/G	FA
1977	TOR	A	0	1	.000	6.00	14	0	0	21	29	8	10	0	0	1	0	0	0	0	—	1	3	0	0	0.3	1.000

Joe DeBerry

DeBERRY, JOSEPH GADDY BL TR 6′ 1″ 175 lbs.
B. Nov. 29, 1896, Mt. Gilead, N. C. D. Oct. 9, 1944, Southern Pines, N. C.

Year	Team	Lg	W	L	PCT	ERA	G	GS	CG	IP	H	BB	SO	ShO	Relief W	Relief L	Relief SV	AB	H	HR	BA	PO	A	E	DP	TC/G	FA
1920	STL	A	2	4	.333	4.94	10	7	3	54.2	65	20	12	1	0	1	0	18	3	0	.167	7	14	1	0	2.2	.955
1921			0	1	.000	6.57	10	1	0	12.1	15	10	1	0	0	0	0	2	0	0	.000	1	3	0	0	0.4	1.000
2 yrs.			2	5	.286	5.24	20	8	3	67	80	30	13	1	0	1	0	20	3	0	.150	8	17	1	0	1.3	.962

Dave DeBusschere

DeBUSSCHERE, DAVID ALBERT BR TR 6′ 6″ 225 lbs.
B. Oct. 16, 1940, Detroit, Mich.

Year	Team	Lg	W	L	PCT	ERA	G	GS	CG	IP	H	BB	SO	ShO	Relief W	Relief L	Relief SV	AB	H	HR	BA	PO	A	E	DP	TC/G	FA
1962	CHI	A	0	0	—	2.00	12	0	0	18	5	23	8	0	0	0	0	0	0	0	—	1	3	0	0	0.3	1.000
1963			3	4	.429	3.09	24	10	1	84.1	80	34	53	1	0	0	0	22	1	0	.045	8	13	1	2	0.9	.955
2 yrs.			3	4	.429	2.90	36	10	1	102.1	85	57	61	1	0	0	0	22	1	0	.045	9	16	1	2	0.7	.962

Art Decatur

DECATUR, ARTHUR RUE BR TR 6′ 1″ 190 lbs.
B. Jan. 14, 1894, Cleveland, Ohio D. Apr. 25, 1966, Talladega, Ala.

Year	Team	Lg	W	L	PCT	ERA	G	GS	CG	IP	H	BB	SO	ShO	Relief W	Relief L	Relief SV	AB	H	HR	BA	PO	A	E	DP	TC/G	FA
1922	BKN	N	3	4	.429	2.77	29	3	1	87.2	87	29	31	0	3	3	1	25	2	0	.080	1	14	1	0	0.6	.938
1923			3	3	.500	2.67	36	5	2	104.2	115	34	27	0	2	0	3	21	0	0	.000	3	17	2	0	0.6	.909
1924			10	9	.526	4.07	31	10	4	128.1	158	28	39	0	**7**	2	1	44	5	0	.114	3	21	2	3	0.8	.923
1925	2 teams BKN N (1G 0–0) PHI N (25G 4–13)																										
″	total		4	13	.235	5.37	26	15	4	129	173	35	31	0	0	4	2	41	2	0	.049	3	21	0	1	0.9	1.000
1926	PHI	N	0	0	—	6.00	2	1	0	3	6	2	0	0	0	0	0	1	0	0	.000	0	0	0	0	0.0	.000
1927			3	5	.375	7.26	29	3	0	96.2	130	20	27	0	3	3	0	27	6	0	.222	2	11	1	0	0.5	.929
6 yrs.			23	34	.404	4.47	153	37	11	549.1	669	148	155	0	15	12	7	159	15	0	.094	12	84	6	4	0.7	.941

Joe Decker

DECKER, GEORGE HENRY BR TR 6′ 183 lbs.
B. June 16, 1947, Storm Lake, Iowa.

Year	Team	Lg	W	L	PCT	ERA	G	GS	CG	IP	H	BB	SO	ShO	Relief W	Relief L	Relief SV	AB	H	HR	BA	PO	A	E	DP	TC/G	FA
1969	CHI	N	1	0	1.000	3.00	4	1	0	12	10	6	13	0	0	0	0	2	0	0	.000	1	0	0	0	0.3	1.000
1970			2	7	.222	4.62	24	17	1	109	108	56	79	0	0	0	0	34	6	1	.176	4	14	3	0	0.9	.857
1971			3	2	.600	4.70	21	4	0	46	62	25	37	0	2	0	0	8	2	0	.250	0	11	0	0	0.5	1.000
1972			1	0	1.000	2.08	5	1	0	13	9	4	7	0	0	0	0	2	0	0	.000	1	0	0	0	0.2	1.000
1973	MIN	A	10	10	.500	4.17	29	24	6	170.1	167	88	109	3	0	0	0	0	0	0	—	24	20	3	0	1.6	.936
1974			16	14	.533	3.29	37	37	11	249	234	97	158	1	0	0	0	0	0	0	—	19	20	1	2	1.1	.975
1975			1	3	.250	8.54	10	7	1	26.1	25	36	8	0	0	0	0	0	0	0	—	1	3	0	0	0.4	1.000
1976			2	7	.222	5.28	13	12	0	58	60	51	35	0	0	0	0	0	0	0	—	4	13	0	0	1.3	1.000
1979	SEA	A	0	1	.000	4.33	9	2	0	27	27	14	12	0	0	0	0	0	0	0	—	4	6	1	1	1.2	.909
9 yrs.			36	44	.450	4.17	152	105	19	710.2	702	377	458	4	2	0	0	46	8	1	.174	58	87	8	3	1.0	.948

Marty Decker

DECKER, DEE MARTIN BR TR 5′11″ 170 lbs.
B. June 7, 1957, Upland, Calif.

Year	Team	Lg	W	L	PCT	ERA	G	GS	CG	IP	H	BB	SO	ShO	Relief Pitching W	Relief Pitching L	Relief Pitching SV	Batting AB	Batting H	Batting HR	BA	PO	A	E	DP	TC/G	FA
1983	SD	N	0	0	—	2.08	4	0	0	8.2	5	3	9	0	0	0	0	0	0	0	—	0	2	1	0	0.8	.667

Jeff Dedmon

DEDMON, JEFFREY LINDEN BL TR 6′ 3″ 185 lbs.
B. Mar. 4, 1960, Torrance, Calif.

Year	Team	Lg	W	L	PCT	ERA	G	GS	CG	IP	H	BB	SO	ShO	Relief Pitching W	Relief Pitching L	Relief Pitching SV	Batting AB	Batting H	Batting HR	BA	PO	A	E	DP	TC/G	FA
1983	ATL	N	0	0	—	13.50	5	0	0	4	10	0	3	0	0	0	0	0	0	0	—	1	1	0	0	0.4	1.000
1984			4	3	.571	3.78	54	0	0	81	86	35	51	0	4	3	4	6	0	0	.000	2	22	2	1	0.5	.923
1985			6	3	.667	4.08	60	0	0	86	84	49	41	0	6	3	0	9	1	0	.111	9	27	2	4	0.6	.947
1986			6	6	.500	2.98	57	0	0	99.2	90	39	58	0	6	6	3	16	2	0	.125	9	22	2	1	0.6	.939
1987			3	4	.429	3.91	53	3	0	89.2	82	42	40	0	3	3	4	16	4	0	.250	10	17	0	1	0.5	1.000
1988	CLE	A	1	0	1.000	4.54	21	0	0	33.2	35	21	17	0	1	0	1	0	0	0	—	4	9	0	2	0.6	1.000
6 yrs.			20	16	.556	3.84	250	3	0	394	387	186	210	0	20	15	12	47	7	0	.149	35	98	6	9	0.6	.957

Jim Dedrick

DEDRICK, JAMES MICHAEL BB TR 6′ 185 lbs.
B. Apr. 4, 1968, Los Angeles, Calif.

Year	Team	Lg	W	L	PCT	ERA	G	GS	CG	IP	H	BB	SO	ShO	Relief Pitching W	Relief Pitching L	Relief Pitching SV	Batting AB	Batting H	Batting HR	BA	PO	A	E	DP	TC/G	FA
1995	BAL	A	0	0	—	2.35	6	0	0	7.2	8	6	3	0	0	0	0	0	0	0	—	1	1	0	0	0.3	1.000

Dummy Deegan

DEEGAN, WILLIAM JOHN
B. Nov. 16, 1874, Bronx, N. Y. D. May 17, 1957, Bronx, N. Y.

Year	Team	Lg	W	L	PCT	ERA	G	GS	CG	IP	H	BB	SO	ShO	Relief Pitching W	Relief Pitching L	Relief Pitching SV	Batting AB	Batting H	Batting HR	BA	PO	A	E	DP	TC/G	FA
1901	NY	N	0	2	.000	6.35	2	1	1	17	27	6	8	0	0	1	0	5	0	0	.000	0	5	0	0	2.5	1.000

John Deering

DEERING, JOHN THOMAS BR TR 6′ 180 lbs.
B. June 25, 1878, Lynn, Mass. D. Feb. 15, 1943, Beverly, Mass.

Year	Team	Lg	W	L	PCT	ERA	G	GS	CG	IP	H	BB	SO	ShO	Relief Pitching W	Relief Pitching L	Relief Pitching SV	Batting AB	Batting H	Batting HR	BA	PO	A	E	DP	TC/G	FA
1903	2 teams	DET A (10G 3–4)	NY A (9G 3–3)																								
"	total		6	7	.462	3.80	19	15	11	120.2	136	42	28	1	0	0	0	47	9	0	.191	6	30	3	0	2.1	.923

Mike DeGerick

DeGERICK, MICHAEL ARTHUR BR TR 6′ 2″ 178 lbs.
B. Apr. 1, 1943, New York, N. Y.

Year	Team	Lg	W	L	PCT	ERA	G	GS	CG	IP	H	BB	SO	ShO	Relief Pitching W	Relief Pitching L	Relief Pitching SV	Batting AB	Batting H	Batting HR	BA	PO	A	E	DP	TC/G	FA
1961	CHI	A	0	0	—	5.40	1	0	0	1.2	2	1	0	0	0	0	0	0	0	0	—	0	1	0	0	1.0	1.000
1962			0	0	—	0.00	1	0	0	1	1	1	0	0	0	0	0	0	0	0	—	0	1	0	0	1.0	1.000
2 yrs.			0	0		3.38	2	0	0	2.2	3	2	0	0	0	0	0	0	0	0		0	2	0	0	1.0	1.000

Pep Deininger

DEININGER, OTTO CHARLES BL TL 5′ 8½″ 180 lbs.
B. Oct. 10, 1877, Wasseralfingen, Germany D. Sept. 25, 1950, Boston, Mass.

Year	Team	Lg	W	L	PCT	ERA	G	GS	CG	IP	H	BB	SO	ShO	Relief Pitching W	Relief Pitching L	Relief Pitching SV	Batting AB	Batting H	Batting HR	BA	PO	A	E	DP	TC/G	FA
1902	BOS	A	0	0	—	9.75	2	1	0	12	19	9	2	0	0	0	0	*				0	1	0	1	0.5	1.000

Jose DeJesus

DeJESUS, JOSE LUIS BR TR 6′ 5″ 175 lbs.
B. Jan. 6, 1965, Brooklyn, N. Y.

Year	Team	Lg	W	L	PCT	ERA	G	GS	CG	IP	H	BB	SO	ShO	Relief Pitching W	Relief Pitching L	Relief Pitching SV	Batting AB	Batting H	Batting HR	BA	PO	A	E	DP	TC/G	FA
1988	KC	A	0	1	.000	27.00	2	1	0	2.2	6	5	2	0	0	0	0	0	0	0	—	0	0	0	0	0.0	.000
1989			0	0	—	4.50	3	1	0	8	7	8	2	0	0	0	0	0	0	0	—	0	1	0	0	0.3	1.000
1990	PHI	N	7	8	.467	3.74	22	22	3	130	97	73	87	1	0	0	0	38	3	0	.079	9	14	2	1	1.1	.920
1991			10	9	.526	3.42	31	29	3	181.2	147	**128**	118	0	0	0	1	62	8	0	.129	4	18	1	0	0.7	.957
1994	KC	A	3	1	.750	4.72	5	4	0	26.2	27	13	12	0	0	0	0	0	0	0	—	2	1	0	0	0.6	1.000
5 yrs.			20	19	.513	3.84	63	57	6	349	284	227	221	1	0	0	1	100	11	0	.110	15	34	3	1	0.8	.942

Tommy de la Cruz

de la CRUZ, TOMAS BR TR 6′ 1″ 168 lbs.
Born Tomas de la Cruz (Rivero).
B. Sept. 18, 1911, Marianao, Cuba D. Sept. 6, 1958, Havana, Cuba.

Year	Team	Lg	W	L	PCT	ERA	G	GS	CG	IP	H	BB	SO	ShO	Relief Pitching W	Relief Pitching L	Relief Pitching SV	Batting AB	Batting H	Batting HR	BA	PO	A	E	DP	TC/G	FA
1944	CIN	N	9	9	.500	3.25	34	20	9	191.1	170	45	65	0	2	1	1	58	9	0	.155	6	37	1	0	1.3	.977

Jim Delahanty

DELAHANTY, JAMES CHRISTOPHER BR TR 5′10½″ 170 lbs.
Brother of Tom Delahanty. Brother of Joe Delahanty.
Brother of Frank Delahanty. Brother of Ed Delahanty.
B. June 20, 1879, Cleveland, Ohio D. Oct. 17, 1953, Cleveland, Ohio.

Year	Team	Lg	W	L	PCT	ERA	G	GS	CG	IP	H	BB	SO	ShO	Relief Pitching W	Relief Pitching L	Relief Pitching SV	Batting AB	Batting H	Batting HR	BA	PO	A	E	DP	TC/G	FA
1904	BOS	N	0	0	—	0.00	1	0	0	3.1	5	1	0	0	0	0	0	499	142	3	.285	21	29	7	2	3.2	.877
1905			0	0	—	4.50	1	1	0	2	5	0	0	0	0	0	0	461	119	5	.258	186	17	8	1	1.7	.962
2 yrs.			0	0		1.69	2	1	0	5.1	10	1	0	0	0	0	0	*				2786	2067	315	222	4.5	.939

Art Delaney

DELANEY, ARTHUR DEWEY (Swede) BR TR 5′10½″ 178 lbs.
Born Arthur Dewey Helenius.
B. Jan. 5, 1897, Chicago, Ill. D. May 2, 1970, Hayward, Calif.

Year	Team	Lg	W	L	PCT	ERA	G	GS	CG	IP	H	BB	SO	ShO	Relief Pitching W	Relief Pitching L	Relief Pitching SV	Batting AB	Batting H	Batting HR	BA	PO	A	E	DP	TC/G	FA
1924	STL	N	1	0	1.000	1.80	8	1	1	20	19	6	2	0	0	0	0	7	2	0	.286	1	7	0	0	1.0	1.000
1928	BOS	N	9	17	.346	3.79	39	22	8	192.1	197	56	45	0	4	3	2	63	9	0	.143	13	47	2	3	1.6	.968
1929			3	5	.375	6.12	20	8	3	75	103	35	17	1	1	1	0	21	3	1	.143	3	14	2	0	0.9	.895
3 yrs.			13	22	.371	4.26	67	31	12	287.1	319	97	64	1	5	4	2	91	14	1	.154	17	68	4	3	1.3	.955

Francisco de la Rosa

de la ROSA, FRANCISCO BB TR 5′11″ 185 lbs.
Born Francisco de la Rosa (Jimenez).
B. Mar. 3, 1966, La Romana, Dominican Republic.

Year	Team	Lg	W	L	PCT	ERA	G	GS	CG	IP	H	BB	SO	ShO	Relief Pitching W	Relief Pitching L	Relief Pitching SV	Batting AB	Batting H	Batting HR	BA	PO	A	E	DP	TC/G	FA
1991	BAL	A	0	0	—	4.50	2	0	0	4	6	2	1	0	0	0	0	0	0	0	—	0	0	0	0	0.0	.000

Jose DeLeon

DeLEON, JOSE BR TR 6′ 3″ 195 lbs.
Born Jose DeLeon (Chestaro).
B. Dec. 20, 1960, La Vega, Dominican Republic.

Year	Team	Lg	W	L	PCT	ERA	G	GS	CG	IP	H	BB	SO	ShO	Relief Pitching W	Relief Pitching L	Relief Pitching SV	Batting AB	Batting H	Batting HR	BA	PO	A	E	DP	TC/G	FA
1983	PIT	N	7	3	.700	2.83	15	15	3	108	75	47	118	2	0	0	0	34	2	0	.059	6	9	1	0	1.1	.938
1984			7	13	.350	3.74	30	28	5	192.1	147	92	153	1	1	0	0	59	5	0	.085	6	16	2	1	0.8	.917
1985			2	**19**	.095	4.70	31	25	1	162.2	138	89	149	0	0	1	3	36	2	0	.056	9	16	1	1	0.8	.962
1986	2 teams	PIT N (9G 1–3)	CHI A (13G 4–5)																								
"	total		5	8	.385	3.87	22	14	1	95.1	66	59	79	0	1	2	1	1	0	0	.000	6	14	1	2	1.0	.952
1987	CHI	A	11	12	.478	4.02	33	31	2	206	177	97	153	0	0	0	0	0	0	0	—	10	14	3	0	0.8	.889
1988	STL	N	13	10	.565	3.67	34	34	3	225.1	198	86	208	1	0	0	0	72	10	0	.139	11	21	0	0	0.9	1.000
1989			16	12	.571	3.05	36	36	5	244.2	173	80	**201**	3	0	0	0	83	8	0	.096	9	16	5	0	0.8	.833
1990			7	**19**	.269	4.43	32	32	0	182.2	168	86	164	0	0	0	0	56	6	0	.107	8	15	2	0	0.8	.920
1991			5	9	.357	2.71	28	28	1	162.2	144	61	118	0	0	0	0	46	2	0	.043	5	17	0	0	0.8	1.000
1992	2 teams	STL N (29G 2–7)	PHI N (3G 0–1)																								
"	total		2	8	.200	4.37	32	18	0	117.1	111	48	79	0	0	0	0	26	3	0	.115	7	10	0	0	0.5	1.000

Year	Team	Lg	W	L	PCT	ERA	G	GS	CG	IP	H	BB	SO	ShO	Relief Pitching W	Relief Pitching L	Relief Pitching SV	Batting AB	Batting H	Batting HR	BA	PO	A	E	DP	TC/G	FA

Jose DeLeon *continued*

Year	Team	Lg	W	L	PCT	ERA	G	GS	CG	IP	H	BB	SO	ShO	W	L	SV	AB	H	HR	BA	PO	A	E	DP	TC/G	FA
1993	2 teams PHI N (24G 3–0) CHI A (11G 0–0)																										
"	total		3	0	1.000	2.98	35	3	0	57.1	44	30	40	0	3	0	0	6	0	0	.000	2	3	0	0	0.1	1.000
1994	CHI	A	3	2	.600	3.36	42	0	0	67	48	31	67	0	3	2	2	0	0	0	—	1	6	0	0	0.2	1.000
1995	2 teams CHI A (38G 5–3) MON N (7G 0–1)																										
"	total		5	4	.556	5.45	45	0	0	76	67	35	65	0	5	4	0	0	0	0	—	0	4	1	0	0.1	.800
13 yrs.			86	119	.420	3.76	415	264	21	1897.1	1556	841	1594	7	13	9	6	419	38	0	.091	80	161	16	4	0.6	.938
LEAGUE CHAMPIONSHIP SERIES																											
1993	CHI	A	0	0	—	1.93	2	0	0	4.2	7	1	6	0	0	0	0	0	0	0	—	0	0	0	0	0.0	.000

Luis DeLeon

DeLEON, LUIS ANTONIO BR TR 6′ 1″ 153 lbs.
Born Luis Antonio DeLeon (Tricoche).
B. Aug. 19, 1958, Ponce, Puerto Rico.

Year	Team	Lg	W	L	PCT	ERA	G	GS	CG	IP	H	BB	SO	ShO	W	L	SV	AB	H	HR	BA	PO	A	E	DP	TC/G	FA
1981	STL	N	0	1	.000	2.40	10	0	0	15	11	3	8	0	0	1	0	1	0	0	.000	0	2	0	0	0.2	1.000
1982	SD	N	9	5	.643	2.03	61	0	0	102	77	16	60	0	9	5	15	11	1	0	.091	13	18	3	1	0.6	.912
1983			6	6	.500	2.68	63	0	0	111	89	27	90	0	6	6	13	14	2	0	.143	2	9	1	1	0.2	.917
1984			2	2	.500	5.48	32	0	0	42.2	44	12	44	0	2	2	0	4	0	0	.000	4	4	1	1	0.3	.889
1985			0	3	.000	4.19	29	0	0	38.2	39	10	31	0	0	3	3	5	1	0	.200	1	5	0	0	0.2	1.000
1987	BAL	A	0	2	.000	4.79	11	0	0	20.2	19	8	13	0	0	2	1	0	0	0	—	2	0	0	0	0.2	1.000
1989	SEA	A	0	0	—	2.25	1	1	0	4	5	1	2	0	0	0	0	0	0	0	—	0	0	0	0	0.0	.000
7 yrs.			17	19	.472	3.13	207	1	0	334	284	77	248	0	17	19	32	35	4	0	.114	22	38	5	3	0.3	.923

Flame Delhi

DELHI, LEE WILLIAM BR TR 6′ 2½″ 198 lbs.
B. Nov. 5, 1892, Harqua Hala, Ariz. D. May 9, 1966, San Rafael, Calif.

Year	Team	Lg	W	L	PCT	ERA	G	GS	CG	IP	H	BB	SO	ShO	W	L	SV	AB	H	HR	BA	PO	A	E	DP	TC/G	FA
1912	CHI	A	0	0	—	9.00	1	0	0	3	7	3	2	0	0	0	0	0	0	0	—	1	2	0	0	3.0	1.000

Wheezer Dell

DELL, WILLIAM GEORGE BR TR 6′ 4″ 210 lbs.
B. June 11, 1887, Tuscarora, Nev. D. Aug. 24, 1966, Independence, Calif.

Year	Team	Lg	W	L	PCT	ERA	G	GS	CG	IP	H	BB	SO	ShO	W	L	SV	AB	H	HR	BA	PO	A	E	DP	TC/G	FA
1912	STL	N	0	0	—	11.57	3	0	0	2.1	3	3	0	0	0	0	0	0	0	0	—	0	0	0	0	0.0	.000
1915	BKN	N	11	10	.524	2.34	40	24	12	215	166	100	94	4	2	0	1	66	10	0	.152	3	60	1	2	1.6	.984
1916			8	9	.471	2.26	32	16	9	155	143	43	76	2	2	1	1	44	4	0	.091	6	32	1	2	1.2	.974
1917			0	4	.000	3.72	17	4	0	58	55	25	28	0	0	1	1	16	1	0	.063	1	13	3	0	1.0	.824
4 yrs.			19	23	.452	2.55	92	44	21	430.1	367	171	198	6	4	2	3	126	15	0	.119	10	105	5	4	1.3	.958
WORLD SERIES																											
1916	BKN	N	0	0	—	0.00	1	0	0	1	1	0	0	0	0	0	0	0	0	0	—	0	0	0	0	0.0	.000

Ike Delock

DELOCK, IVAN MARTIN BR TR 5′11″ 175 lbs.
B. Nov. 11, 1929, Highland Park, Mich.

Year	Team	Lg	W	L	PCT	ERA	G	GS	CG	IP	H	BB	SO	ShO	W	L	SV	AB	H	HR	BA	PO	A	E	DP	TC/G	FA
1952	BOS	A	4	9	.308	4.26	39	7	1	95	88	50	46	1	2	5	5	22	1	0	.045	1	16	0	1	0.4	1.000
1953			3	1	.750	4.44	23	1	0	48.2	60	20	22	0	2	1	1	10	1	0	.100	1	5	0	0	0.3	1.000
1955			9	7	.563	3.76	29	18	6	143.2	136	61	88	0	1	1	3	49	7	0	.143	6	19	1	1	0.9	.962
1956			13	7	.650	4.21	48	8	1	128.1	122	80	105	0	**11**	2	9	29	3	0	.103	10	18	2	1	0.6	.933
1957			9	8	.529	3.83	49	2	0	94	80	45	62	0	9	6	11	21	1	0	.048	3	12	0	1	0.3	1.000
1958			14	8	.636	3.38	31	19	9	160	155	56	82	1	4	0	2	48	3	0	.063	9	22	1	1	1.0	.969
1959			11	6	.647	2.95	28	17	4	134.1	120	62	55	0	5	0	0	47	3	1	.064	8	15	1	1	0.9	.958
1960			9	10	.474	4.73	24	23	3	129.1	145	52	49	1	0	0	0	43	5	0	.116	10	16	2	3	1.2	.929
1961			6	9	.400	4.90	28	28	3	156	185	52	80	1	0	0	0	48	5	0	.104	13	17	4	1	1.2	.882
1962			4	5	.444	3.75	17	13	4	86.1	89	24	49	2	0	0	0	23	2	0	.087	3	12	0	0	0.9	1.000
1963	2 teams BOS A (6G 1–2) BAL A (7G 1–3)																										
"	total		2	5	.286	4.76	13	11	1	62.1	56	28	34	0	0	0	0	21	0	0	.000	8	8	1	0	1.3	.941
11 yrs.			84	75	.528	4.03	329	147	32	1238	1236	530	672	6	34	15	31	361	31	1	.086	72	160	12	10	0.7	.951

Ramon de los Santos

de los SANTOS, RAMON BL TL 6′ 175 lbs.
Born Ramon de los Santos (Genero).
B. Jan. 19, 1949, Santo Domingo, Dominican Republic.

Year	Team	Lg	W	L	PCT	ERA	G	GS	CG	IP	H	BB	SO	ShO	W	L	SV	AB	H	HR	BA	PO	A	E	DP	TC/G	FA
1974	HOU	N	1	1	.500	2.25	12	0	0	12	11	9	7	0	1	1	0	0	0	0	—	1	1	0	1	0.2	1.000

Rich DeLucia

DeLUCIA, RICHARD ANTHONY BR TR 6′ 185 lbs.
B. Oct. 7, 1964, Reading, Pa.

Year	Team	Lg	W	L	PCT	ERA	G	GS	CG	IP	H	BB	SO	ShO	W	L	SV	AB	H	HR	BA	PO	A	E	DP	TC/G	FA
1990	SEA	A	1	2	.333	2.00	5	5	1	36	30	9	20	0	0	0	0	0	0	0	—	3	2	1	0	1.2	.833
1991			12	13	.480	5.09	32	31	0	182	176	78	98	0	1	0	0	0	0	0	—	8	19	0	1	0.8	1.000
1992			3	6	.333	5.49	30	11	0	83.2	100	35	66	0	0	0	1	0	0	0	—	8	6	1	0	0.5	.933
1993			3	6	.333	4.64	30	1	0	42.2	46	23	48	0	3	5	0	0	0	0	—	2	7	0	0	0.3	1.000
1994	CIN	N	0	0	—	4.22	8	0	0	10.2	9	5	15	0	0	0	0	0	0	0	—	1	0	0	0	0.1	1.000
1995	STL	N	8	7	.533	3.39	56	1	0	82.1	63	36	76	0	**8**	6	0	10	2	0	.200	3	14	2	1	0.3	.895
6 yrs.			27	34	.443	4.53	161	49	1	437.1	424	186	323	0	12	11	1	10	2	0	.200	25	48	4	2	0.5	.948

Fred Demarais

DEMARAIS, FRED TR 5′ 9″ 168 lbs.
B. Nov. 1, 1866 D. Mar. 6, 1919, Stamford, Conn.

Year	Team	Lg	W	L	PCT	ERA	G	GS	CG	IP	H	BB	SO	ShO	W	L	SV	AB	H	HR	BA	PO	A	E	DP	TC/G	FA
1890	CHI	N	0	0	—	0.00	1	0	0	2	1	1	1	0	0	0	0	2	0	0	.000	0	0	0	0	0.0	.000

Al Demaree

DEMAREE, ALBERT WENTWORTH BL TR 6′ 170 lbs.
B. Sept. 8, 1884, Quincy, Ill. D. Apr. 30, 1962, Los Angeles, Calif.

Year	Team	Lg	W	L	PCT	ERA	G	GS	CG	IP	H	BB	SO	ShO	W	L	SV	AB	H	HR	BA	PO	A	E	DP	TC/G	FA
1912	NY	N	1	0	1.000	1.69	2	2	1	16	17	2	11	1	0	0	0	5	0	0	.000	1	4	0	0	2.5	1.000
1913			13	4	.765	2.21	31	24	11	199.2	176	38	76	3	0	1	2	66	7	0	.106	1	38	1	1	1.3	.975
1914			10	17	.370	3.09	38	30	13	224	219	77	89	2	0	2	0	68	9	0	.132	3	58	2	0	1.7	.968
1915	PHI	N	14	11	.560	3.05	32	26	13	209.2	201	58	69	3	0	1	1	68	12	0	.176	8	35	0	0	1.3	1.000
1916			19	14	.576	2.62	39	35	25	285	252	48	130	4	2	0	1	101	11	0	.109	2	47	3	0	1.3	.942
1917	2 teams CHI N (24G 5–9) NY N (15G 4–5)																										
"	total		9	14	.391	2.58	39	29	7	219.2	195	54	66	1	2	0	1	59	7	0	.119	4	68	0	1	1.8	1.000
1918	NY	N	8	6	.571	2.47	26	14	8	142	143	25	39	2	0	1	1	47	6	0	.128	4	40	1	1	1.7	.978
1919	BOS	N	6	6	.500	3.80	25	13	6	128	147	35	34	0	2	1	3	42	2	0	.048	5	27	0	2	1.3	1.000
8 yrs.			80	72	.526	2.77	232	173	84	1424	1350	337	514	16	6	6	9	456	54	0	.118	28	317	7	5	1.5	.980

Al Demaree *continued*

Year	Team	Lg	W	L	PCT	ERA	G	GS	CG	IP	H	BB	SO	ShO	Relief Pitching W	Relief Pitching L	Relief Pitching SV	Batting AB	Batting H	Batting HR	BA	PO	A	E	DP	TC/G	FA
WORLD SERIES																											
1913	**NY**	**N**	0	1	.000	4.50	1	1	0	4	7	1	0	0	0	0	0	1	0	0	.000	0	2	0	0	2.0	1.000

Larry Demery

DEMERY, LAWRENCE CALVIN BR TR 6′ 170 lbs.
B. June 4, 1953, Bakersfield, Calif.

Year	Team	Lg	W	L	PCT	ERA	G	GS	CG	IP	H	BB	SO	ShO	Relief Pitching W	Relief Pitching L	Relief Pitching SV	Batting AB	Batting H	Batting HR	BA	PO	A	E	DP	TC/G	FA
1974	**PIT**	**N**	6	6	.500	4.26	19	15	2	95	95	51	51	0	0	0	0	33	5	0	.152	6	10	1	0	0.9	.941
1975			7	5	.583	2.90	45	8	1	115	95	43	59	0	4	3	4	24	3	0	.125	7	13	1	1	0.5	.952
1976			10	7	.588	3.17	36	15	4	145	123	58	72	1	4	1	2	40	5	0	.125	9	21	2	2	0.9	.938
1977			6	5	.545	5.10	39	8	0	90	100	47	35	0	3	2	1	20	3	0	.150	5	14	2	0	0.5	.905
4 yrs.			29	23	.558	3.72	139	46	7	445	413	199	217	1	11	6	7	117	16	0	.137	27	58	6	3	0.7	.934
LEAGUE CHAMPIONSHIP SERIES																											
1974	**PIT**	**N**	0	0	—	27.00	2	0	0	1	3	2	0	0	0	0	0	0	0	0	—	0	1	0	0	0.5	1.000
1975			0	0	—	18.00	1	0	0	2	4	1	1	0	0	0	0	0	0	0	—	0	0	0	0	0.0	.000
2 yrs.			0	0		21.00	3	0	0	3	7	3	1	0	0	0	0	0	0	0		0	1	0	0	0.3	1.000

Harry DeMiller

DeMILLER, HARRY BR TL
B. Nov. 12, 1867, Wooster, Ohio D. Oct. 19, 1928, Santa Ana, Calif.

Year	Team	Lg	W	L	PCT	ERA	G	GS	CG	IP	H	BB	SO	ShO	Relief Pitching W	Relief Pitching L	Relief Pitching SV	Batting AB	Batting H	Batting HR	BA	PO	A	E	DP	TC/G	FA
1892	**CHI**	**N**	1	1	.500	6.38	4	2	2	24	29	16	15	0	0	0	0	10	3	0	.300	1	6	1	0	2.0	.875

Don DeMola

DeMOLA, DONALD JOHN BR TR 6′ 2″ 185 lbs.
B. July 5, 1952, Glen Cove, N. Y.

Year	Team	Lg	W	L	PCT	ERA	G	GS	CG	IP	H	BB	SO	ShO	Relief Pitching W	Relief Pitching L	Relief Pitching SV	Batting AB	Batting H	Batting HR	BA	PO	A	E	DP	TC/G	FA
1974	**MON**	**N**	1	0	1.000	3.10	25	1	0	58	46	21	47	0	1	0	0	4	0	0	.000	2	5	0	1	0.3	1.000
1975			4	7	.364	4.13	60	0	0	98	92	42	63	0	4	7	1	8	0	0	.000	1	3	1	0	0.1	.800
2 yrs.			5	7	.417	3.75	85	1	0	156	138	63	110	0	5	7	1	12	0	0	.000	3	8	1	1	0.1	.917

Ben DeMott

DeMOTT, BENYEW HARRISON BR TR 6′ 192 lbs.
B. Apr. 2, 1889, Green Village, N. J. D. July 5, 1963, Somerville, N. J.

Year	Team	Lg	W	L	PCT	ERA	G	GS	CG	IP	H	BB	SO	ShO	Relief Pitching W	Relief Pitching L	Relief Pitching SV	Batting AB	Batting H	Batting HR	BA	PO	A	E	DP	TC/G	FA
1910	**CLE**	**A**	0	3	.000	5.40	6	4	1	28.1	90	8	13	0	0	0	0	14	3	0	.214	2	10	0	0	2.0	1.000
1911			0	1	.000	12.27	1	1	0	3.2	10	2	2	0	0	0	0	4	0	0	.000	1	3	0	0	2.0	1.000
2 yrs.			0	4	.000	6.19	7	5	1	32	100	10	15	0	0	0	0	18	3	0	.167	3	13	0	0	2.0	1.000

Con Dempsey

DEMPSEY, CORNELIUS FRANCIS BR TR 6′ 4″ 190 lbs.
B. Sept. 16, 1923, San Francisco, Calif.

Year	Team	Lg	W	L	PCT	ERA	G	GS	CG	IP	H	BB	SO	ShO	Relief Pitching W	Relief Pitching L	Relief Pitching SV	Batting AB	Batting H	Batting HR	BA	PO	A	E	DP	TC/G	FA
1951	**PIT**	**N**	0	2	.000	9.00	3	2	0	7	11	4	3	0	0	0	0	1	0	0	.000	0	2	0	0	0.7	1.000

Mark Dempsey

DEMPSEY, MARK STEVEN BR TR 6′ 6″ 220 lbs.
B. Dec. 17, 1957, Dayton, Ohio.

Year	Team	Lg	W	L	PCT	ERA	G	GS	CG	IP	H	BB	SO	ShO	Relief Pitching W	Relief Pitching L	Relief Pitching SV	Batting AB	Batting H	Batting HR	BA	PO	A	E	DP	TC/G	FA
1982	**SF**	**N**	0	0	—	7.94	3	1	0	5.2	11	2	4	0	0	0	0	1	0	0	.000	0	1	0	0	0.3	1.000

Rick Dempsey

DEMPSEY, JOHN RIKARD BR TR 6′ 180 lbs.
B. Sept. 13, 1949, Fayetteville, Tenn.

Year	Team	Lg	W	L	PCT	ERA	G	GS	CG	IP	H	BB	SO	ShO	Relief Pitching W	Relief Pitching L	Relief Pitching SV	Batting AB	Batting H	Batting HR	BA	PO	A	E	DP	TC/G	FA
1991	**MIL**	**A**	0	0	—	4.50	2	0	0	2	3	1	0	0	0	0	0	*				5	0	1	0	2.0	.833

Bill Denehy

DENEHY, WILLIAM FRANCIS BB TR 6′ 3″ 200 lbs.
B. Mar. 31, 1946, Middletown, Conn. BL 1971

Year	Team	Lg	W	L	PCT	ERA	G	GS	CG	IP	H	BB	SO	ShO	Relief Pitching W	Relief Pitching L	Relief Pitching SV	Batting AB	Batting H	Batting HR	BA	PO	A	E	DP	TC/G	FA
1967	**NY**	**N**	1	7	.125	4.70	15	8	0	53.2	51	29	35	0	0	0	0	9	0	0	.000	3	7	1	0	0.7	.909
1968	**WAS**	**A**	0	0	—	9.00	3	0	0	2	4	4	1	0	0	0	0	0	0	0	—	1	0	0	0	0.3	1.000
1971	**DET**	**A**	0	3	.000	4.22	31	1	0	49	47	28	27	0	0	2	1	2	0	0	.000	4	6	0	0	0.3	1.000
3 yrs.			1	10	.091	4.56	49	9	0	104.2	102	61	63	0	0	2	1	11	0	0	.000	8	13	1	0	0.4	.955

Brian Denman

DENMAN, BRIAN JOHN BR TR 6′ 4″ 215 lbs.
B. Feb. 12, 1956, Minneapolis, Minn.

Year	Team	Lg	W	L	PCT	ERA	G	GS	CG	IP	H	BB	SO	ShO	Relief Pitching W	Relief Pitching L	Relief Pitching SV	Batting AB	Batting H	Batting HR	BA	PO	A	E	DP	TC/G	FA
1982	**BOS**	**A**	3	4	.429	4.78	9	9	2	49	55	9	9	1	0	0	0	0	0	0	—	6	5	0	0	1.2	1.000

Don Dennis

DENNIS, DONALD RAY BR TR 6′ 2″ 190 lbs.
B. Mar. 3, 1942, Uniontown, Kans.

Year	Team	Lg	W	L	PCT	ERA	G	GS	CG	IP	H	BB	SO	ShO	Relief Pitching W	Relief Pitching L	Relief Pitching SV	Batting AB	Batting H	Batting HR	BA	PO	A	E	DP	TC/G	FA
1965	**STL**	**N**	2	3	.400	2.29	41	0	0	55	47	16	29	0	2	3	6	5	2	0	.400	6	16	0	1	0.5	1.000
1966			4	2	.667	4.98	38	1	0	59.2	73	17	25	0	4	2	2	12	1	0	.083	5	24	1	0	0.8	.967
2 yrs.			6	5	.545	3.69	79	1	0	114.2	120	33	54	0	6	5	8	17	3	0	.176	11	40	1	1	0.7	.981

Jerry Denny

DENNY, JEREMIAH DENNIS BR TR 5′11½″ 180 lbs.
Born Jeremiah Dennis Eldridge.
B. Mar. 16, 1859, New York, N. Y. D. Aug. 16, 1927, Houston, Tex.

Year	Team	Lg	W	L	PCT	ERA	G	GS	CG	IP	H	BB	SO	ShO	Relief Pitching W	Relief Pitching L	Relief Pitching SV	Batting AB	Batting H	Batting HR	BA	PO	A	E	DP	TC/G	FA
1888	**IND**	**N**	0	0	—	9.00	1	0	0	4	5	4	1	0	0	0	0	*				144	181	62	12	4.6	.840

John Denny

DENNY, JOHN ALLEN BR TR 6′ 3″ 185 lbs.
B. Nov. 8, 1952, Prescott, Ariz.

Year	Team	Lg	W	L	PCT	ERA	G	GS	CG	IP	H	BB	SO	ShO	Relief Pitching W	Relief Pitching L	Relief Pitching SV	Batting AB	Batting H	Batting HR	BA	PO	A	E	DP	TC/G	FA
1974	**STL**	**N**	0	0	—	0.00	2	0	0	2	3	0	1	0	0	0	0	0	0	0	—	0	0	0	0	0.0	.000
1975			10	7	.588	3.97	25	24	3	136	149	51	72	2	0	0	0	44	10	0	.227	11	30	4	2	1.8	.911
1976			11	9	.550	**2.52**	30	30	8	207	189	74	74	3	0	0	0	67	15	0	.224	24	34	4	3	2.1	.935
1977			8	8	.500	4.50	26	26	3	150	165	62	60	1	0	0	0	51	5	0	.098	9	37	3	3	1.9	.939
1978			14	11	.560	2.96	33	33	11	234	200	74	103	2	0	0	0	73	13	0	.178	17	73	4	8	2.8	.957
1979			8	11	.421	4.85	31	31	5	206	206	100	99	2	0	0	0	70	9	0	.129	16	36	2	4	1.7	.963
1980	**CLE**	**A**	8	6	.571	4.38	16	16	4	109	116	47	59	1	0	0	0	0	0	0	—	8	18	1	2	1.7	.963
1981			10	6	.625	3.14	19	19	6	146	139	66	94	3	0	0	0	0	0	0	—	14	40	3	7	3.0	.947
1982	**2 teams**	**CLE A**	(21G 6–11)			**PHI N**	(4G 0–2)																				
″	**total**		6	13	.316	4.87	25	25	5	160.2	144	83	113	0	0	0	0	6	1	0	.167	13	26	0	3	1.6	1.000
1983	**PHI**	**N**	**19**	6	**.760**	2.37	36	36	7	242.2	229	53	139	1	0	0	0	77	13	0	.169	16	42	8	6	1.8	.879
1984			7	7	.500	2.45	22	22	2	154.1	122	29	94	0	0	0	0	47	9	0	.191	20	36	1	2	2.6	.982
1985			11	14	.440	3.82	33	33	6	230.2	252	83	123	2	0	0	0	81	10	0	.123	15	39	0	4	1.6	1.000
1986	**CIN**	**N**	11	10	.524	4.20	27	27	2	171.1	179	56	115	1	0	0	0	54	12	0	.222	16	40	2	2	2.1	.966
13 yrs.			123	108	.532	3.58	325	322	62	2149.2	2093	778	1146	18	0	0	0	570	97	0	.170	179	451	32	46	2.0	.952

John Denny *continued*

Year	Team		W	L	PCT	ERA	G	GS	CG	IP	H	BB	SO	ShO	Relief Pitching W	Relief Pitching L	Relief Pitching SV	Batting AB	Batting H	Batting HR	BA	PO	A	E	DP	TC/G	FA
LEAGUE CHAMPIONSHIP SERIES																											
1983	**PHI**	**N**	0	1	.000	0.00	1	1	0	6	5	3	3	0	0	0	0	1	0	0	.000	0	0	0	0	0.0	.000
WORLD SERIES																											
1983	**PHI**	**N**	1	1	.500	3.46	2	2	0	13	12	3	9	0	0	0	0	5	1	0	.200	3	1	0	0	2.0	1.000

Eddie Dent

DENT, ELLIOTT ESTILL BR TR 6′ 1″ 190 lbs.
B. Dec. 8, 1887, Baltimore, Md. D. Nov. 25, 1974, Birmingham, Ala.

Year	Team		W	L	PCT	ERA	G	GS	CG	IP	H	BB	SO	ShO	Relief W	Relief L	Relief SV	AB	H	HR	BA	PO	A	E	DP	TC/G	FA
1909	**BKN**	**N**	2	4	.333	4.29	6	5	4	42	47	15	17	0	0	1	0	15	1	0	.067	0	9	0	0	1.5	1.000
1911			2	1	.667	3.69	5	3	1	31.2	30	10	3	0	0	0	0	10	1	0	.100	2	11	0	0	2.6	1.000
1912			0	0	—	36.00	1	0	0	1	4	1	1	0	0	0	0	1	0	0	.000	1	0	0	0	1.0	1.000
3 yrs.			4	5	.444	4.46	12	8	5	74.2	81	26	21	0	0	1	0	26	2	0	.077	3	20	0	0	1.9	1.000

Roger Denzer

DENZER, ROGER (Peaceful Valley) BL TR 6′ 180 lbs.
B. Oct. 5, 1871, LeSueur, Minn. D. Sept. 18, 1949, LeSueur, Minn.

Year	Team		W	L	PCT	ERA	G	GS	CG	IP	H	BB	SO	ShO	Relief W	Relief L	Relief SV	AB	H	HR	BA	PO	A	E	DP	TC/G	FA
1897	**CHI**	**N**	2	8	.200	5.13	12	10	8	94.2	125	34	17	0	1	1	0	39	6	0	.154	8	17	0	0	2.1	1.000
1901	**NY**	**N**	2	5	.286	3.36	11	9	3	61.2	69	5	22	1	0	0	0	22	2	0	.091	0	9	2	1	1.0	.818
2 yrs.			4	13	.235	4.43	23	19	11	156.1	194	39	39	1	1	1	0	61	8	0	.131	8	26	2	1	1.6	.944

George Derby

DERBY, GEORGE H. BL TR 6′ 175 lbs.
B. July 6, 1857, Webster, Mass. D. July 4, 1925, Philadelphia, Pa.

Year	Team		W	L	PCT	ERA	G	GS	CG	IP	H	BB	SO	ShO	Relief W	Relief L	Relief SV	AB	H	HR	BA	PO	A	E	DP	TC/G	FA
1881	**DET**	**N**	29	26	.527	2.20	56	55	55	494.2	505	86	**212**	**9**	0	0	0	236	44	0	.186	32	98	12	4	2.4	.915
1882			17	20	.459	3.26	40	39	38	362	386	81	182	3	0	0	0	149	29	0	.195	20	69	4	1	2.2	.957
1883	**BUF**	**N**	2	10	.167	*5.85*	14	13	12	107.2	173	15	34	0	0	0	1	59	14	0	.237	7	26	4	1	2.2	.892
3 yrs.			48	56	.462	3.01	110	107	105	964.1	1064	182	428	12	0	0	1	444	87	0	.196	59	193	20	6	2.3	.926

Paul Derringer

DERRINGER, SAMUEL PAUL ('Oom Paul, Duke) BR TR 6′ 3½″ 205 lbs.
B. Oct. 17, 1906, Springfield, Ky. D. Nov. 17, 1987, Sarasota, Fla.

Year	Team		W	L	PCT	ERA	G	GS	CG	IP	H	BB	SO	ShO	Relief W	Relief L	Relief SV	AB	H	HR	BA	PO	A	E	DP	TC/G	FA
1931	**STL**	**N**	18	8	**.692**	3.36	35	23	15	211.2	225	65	134	4	4	0	2	72	7	0	.097	9	38	2	3	1.4	.959
1932			11	14	.440	4.05	39	30	14	233.1	296	67	78	1	1	1	0	73	13	0	.178	9	43	3	0	1.4	.945
1933	**2 teams**	**STL N** (3G 0–2) **CIN N** (33G 7–25)																									
″	**total**		7	**27**	.206	3.30	36	33	17	248	264	60	89	2	0	1	1	81	14	0	.173	4	61	1	1	1.8	.985
1934	**CIN**	**N**	15	21	.417	3.59	47	31	18	261	297	59	122	1	2	4	4	92	18	0	.196	11	44	1	2	1.2	.982
1935			22	13	.629	3.51	45	33	20	276.2	295	49	120	3	3	2	2	93	13	0	.140	9	69	1	5	1.8	.987
1936			19	19	.500	4.02	**51**	**37**	13	282.1	**331**	42	121	2	1	3	5	90	18	0	.200	19	53	2	5	1.5	.973
1937			10	14	.417	4.04	43	26	12	222.2	240	55	94	1	1	4	1	80	16	0	.200	17	50	4	3	1.7	.944
1938			21	14	.600	2.93	41	**37**	**26**	**307**	**315**	49	132	4	0	0	3	119	21	2	.176	13	51	1	3	1.6	.985
1939			25	7	**.781**	2.93	38	35	28	301	**321**	35	128	5	1	0	0	110	23	0	.209	11	48	3	1	1.6	.952
1940			20	12	.625	3.06	37	**37**	26	296.2	280	48	115	3	0	0	0	108	18	0	.167	8	47	3	0	1.6	.948
1941			12	14	.462	3.31	29	28	17	228.1	233	54	76	2	0	0	1	84	13	0	.155	10	42	1	2	1.8	.981
1942			10	11	.476	3.06	29	27	13	208.2	203	49	68	1	0	0	0	68	9	0	.132	8	28	1	1	1.3	.973
1943	**CHI**	**N**	10	14	.417	3.57	32	22	10	174	184	39	75	2	1	2	3	58	13	0	.224	3	20	1	0	0.8	.958
1944			7	13	.350	4.15	42	16	7	180	205	39	69	0	2	5	3	57	9	0	.158	7	30	1	3	0.9	.974
1945			16	11	.593	3.45	35	30	15	213.2	223	51	86	1	1	0	4	75	15	0	.200	9	32	1	0	1.2	.976
15 yrs.			223	212	.513	3.46	579	445	251	3645	3912	761	1507	32	17	22	29	1260	220	2	.175	147	656	26	29	1.4	.969
WORLD SERIES																											
1931	**STL**	**N**	0	2	.000	4.26	3	2	0	12.2	14	7	14	0	0	0	0	2	0	0	.000	0	2	0	0	0.7	1.000
1939	**CIN**	**N**	0	1	.000	2.35	2	2	1	15.1	9	3	9	0	0	0	0	5	1	0	.200	2	0	0	0	1.0	1.000
1940			2	1	.667	2.79	3	3	2	19.1	17	10	6	0	0	0	0	7	0	0	.000	0	5	0	1	1.7	1.000
1945	**CHI**	**N**	0	0	—	6.75	3	0	0	5.1	5	7	1	0	0	0	0	0	0	0	—	0	0	0	0	0.0	.000
4 yrs.			2	4	.333	3.42	11	7	3	52.2	45	27	30	0	0	0	0	14	1	0	.071	2	7	0	1	0.8	1.000
							10th					**6th**															

Jim Derrington

DERRINGTON, CHARLES JAMES (Blackie) BL TL 6′ 3″ 190 lbs.
B. Nov. 29, 1939, Compton, Calif.

Year	Team		W	L	PCT	ERA	G	GS	CG	IP	H	BB	SO	ShO	Relief W	Relief L	Relief SV	AB	H	HR	BA	PO	A	E	DP	TC/G	FA
1956	**CHI**	**A**	0	1	.000	7.50	1	1	0	6	9	6	3	0	0	0	0	2	1	0	.500	0	0	0	0	0.0	.000
1957			0	1	.000	4.86	20	5	0	37	29	29	14	0	0	0	0	4	0	0	.000	3	1	1	0	0.3	.800
2 yrs.			0	2	.000	5.23	21	6	0	43	38	35	17	0	0	0	0	6	1	0	.167	3	1	1	0	0.2	.800

Jim Deshaies

DESHAIES, JAMES JOSEPH BL TL 6′ 4″ 222 lbs.
B. June 23, 1960, Massena, N. Y.

Year	Team		W	L	PCT	ERA	G	GS	CG	IP	H	BB	SO	ShO	Relief W	Relief L	Relief SV	AB	H	HR	BA	PO	A	E	DP	TC/G	FA
1984	**NY**	**A**	0	1	.000	11.57	2	2	0	7	14	7	5	0	0	0	0	0	0	0	—	0	1	0	0	0.5	1.000
1985	**HOU**	**N**	0	0	—	0.00	2	0	0	3	1	0	2	0	0	0	0	0	0	0	—	0	0	0	0	0.0	.000
1986			12	5	.706	3.25	26	26	1	144	124	59	128	1	0	0	0	43	2	0	.047	9	13	2	0	0.9	.917
1987			11	6	.647	4.62	26	25	1	152	149	57	104	0	0	0	0	53	5	0	.094	5	22	1	0	1.1	.964
1988			11	14	.440	3.00	31	31	3	207	164	72	127	2	0	0	0	63	3	0	.048	7	25	2	1	1.1	.941
1989			15	10	.600	2.91	34	34	6	225.2	180	79	153	3	0	0	0	75	9	0	.120	8	31	3	2	1.2	.929
1990			7	12	.368	3.78	34	34	2	209.1	186	84	119	0	0	0	0	63	4	0	.063	3	32	2	1	1.1	.946
1991			5	12	.294	4.98	28	28	1	161	156	72	98	0	0	0	0	41	4	0	.098	4	18	3	1	0.9	.880
1992	**SD**	**N**	4	7	.364	3.28	15	15	0	96	92	33	46	0	0	0	0	29	6	0	.207	2	22	0	1	1.6	1.000
1993	**2 teams**	**MIN A** (27G 11–13) **SF N** (5G 2–2)																									
″	**total**		13	15	.464	4.39	32	31	1	184.1	183	57	85	0	0	0	0	5	0	0	.000	4	25	0	0	0.9	1.000
1994	**MIN**	**A**	6	12	.333	7.39	25	**25**	0	130.1	170	54	78	0	0	0	0	0	0	0	—	3	15	1	1	0.8	.947
1995	**PHI**	**N**	0	1	.000	20.25	2	2	0	5.1	15	1	6	0	0	0	0	1	0	0	.000	0	0	0	0	0.0	.000
12 yrs.			84	95	.469	4.14	257	253	15	1525	1434	575	951	6	0	0	0	373	33	0	.088	45	204	14	7	1.0	.947

Jimmie DeShong

DeSHONG, JAMES BROOKLYN BR TR 5′11″ 165 lbs.
B. Nov. 30, 1909, Harrisburg, Pa. D. Oct. 16, 1993, Dauphin County, Pa.

Year	Team		W	L	PCT	ERA	G	GS	CG	IP	H	BB	SO	ShO	Relief W	Relief L	Relief SV	AB	H	HR	BA	PO	A	E	DP	TC/G	FA
1932	**PHI**	**A**	0	0	—	11.70	6	0	0	10	17	9	5	0	0	0	0	3	0	0	.000	0	3	0	0	0.5	1.000
1934	**NY**	**A**	6	7	.462	4.11	31	12	6	133.2	126	56	40	0	0	2	3	42	8	0	.190	4	28	1	0	1.1	.970
1935			4	1	.800	3.26	29	3	0	69	64	33	30	0	3	1	3	14	1	0	.071	4	22	1	0	0.9	.963
1936	**WAS**	**A**	18	10	.643	4.63	34	31	16	223.2	255	96	59	2	0	1	2	79	15	0	.190	4	34	2	6	1.2	.950
1937			14	15	.483	4.90	37	34	20	264.1	290	124	86	0	1	0	1	94	19	0	.202	15	52	2	2	1.9	.971

Jimmie DeShong *continued*

Year	Team	Lg	W	L	PCT	ERA	G	GS	CG	IP	H	BB	SO	ShO	Relief Pitching W	Relief L	Relief SV	Batting AB	Batting H	HR	BA	PO	A	E	DP	TC/G	FA
1938			5	8	.385	6.58	31	14	1	131.1	160	83	41	0	1	2	0	46	12	0	.261	8	26	3	4	1.2	.919
1939			0	3	.000	8.63	7	6	1	40.2	56	31	12	0	0	0	0	15	3	0	.200	1	14	1	0	2.3	.938
7 yrs.			47	44	.516	5.08	175	100	44	872.2	968	432	273	2	5	6	9	293	58	0	.198	36	179	10	12	1.3	.956

John DeSilva

DeSILVA, JOHN REED BR TR 6′ 195 lbs.
B. Sept. 30, 1967, Fort Bragg, Calif.

Year	Team	Lg	W	L	PCT	ERA	G	GS	CG	IP	H	BB	SO	ShO	Relief Pitching W	Relief L	Relief SV	Batting AB	Batting H	HR	BA	PO	A	E	DP	TC/G	FA
1993	**2 teams**	**DET A** (1G 0–0) **LA N** (3G 0–0)																									
″	**total**		0	0		7.11	4	0	0	6.1	8	1	6	0	0	0	0	0	0	0		0	0	0	0	0.0	
1995	**BAL**	**A**	1	0	1.000	7.27	2	2	0	8.2	8	7	1	0	0	0	0	0	0	0	—	0	2	0	1	1.0	1.000
2 yrs.			1	0	1.000	7.20	6	2	0	15	16	8	7	0	0	0	0	0	0	0		0	2	0	1	0.3	1.000

Shorty Des Jardien

DES JARDIEN, PAUL RAYMOND BR TR 6′ 4½″ 205 lbs.
B. Aug. 24, 1893, Coffeyville, Kans. D. Mar. 7, 1956, Monrovia, Calif.

Year	Team	Lg	W	L	PCT	ERA	G	GS	CG	IP	H	BB	SO	ShO	Relief Pitching W	Relief L	Relief SV	Batting AB	Batting H	HR	BA	PO	A	E	DP	TC/G	FA
1916	**CLE**	**A**	0	0	—	18.00	1	0	0	1	1	1	0	0	0	0	0	0	0	0	—	0	0	0	0	0.0	.000

Rube Dessau

DESSAU, FRANK ROLLAND BB TR 5′11″ 175 lbs.
B. Mar. 29, 1883, New Galilee, Pa. D. May 6, 1952, York, Pa.

Year	Team	Lg	W	L	PCT	ERA	G	GS	CG	IP	H	BB	SO	ShO	Relief Pitching W	Relief L	Relief SV	Batting AB	Batting H	HR	BA	PO	A	E	DP	TC/G	FA
1907	**BOS**	**N**	0	1	.000	10.61	2	2	1	9.1	13	10	1	0	0	0	0	4	0	0	.000	1	2	2	0	2.5	.600
1910	**BKN**	**N**	2	3	.400	5.79	19	0	0	51.1	67	29	24	0	2	3	0	15	1	0	.067	0	9	2	0	0.6	.818
2 yrs.			2	4	.333	6.53	21	2	1	60.2	80	39	25	0	2	3	0	19	1	0	.053	1	11	4	0	0.8	.750

John Dettmer

DETTMER, JOHN FRANKLIN BR TR 6′ 185 lbs.
B. Mar. 4, 1970, Centerville, Ill.

Year	Team	Lg	W	L	PCT	ERA	G	GS	CG	IP	H	BB	SO	ShO	Relief Pitching W	Relief L	Relief SV	Batting AB	Batting H	HR	BA	PO	A	E	DP	TC/G	FA
1994	**TEX**	**A**	0	6	.000	4.33	11	9	0	54	63	20	27	0	0	0	0	0	0	0	—	5	6	0	0	1.0	1.000
1995			0	0	—	27.00	1	0	0	0.1	2	0	0	0	0	0	0	0	0	0	—	0	0	0	0	0.0	.000
2 yrs.			0	6	.000	4.47	12	9	0	54.1	65	20	27	0	0	0	0	0	0	0		5	6	0	0	0.9	1.000

Tom Dettore

DETTORE, THOMAS ANTHONY BL TR 6′ 4″ 200 lbs.
B. Nov. 17, 1947, Canonsburg, Pa.

Year	Team	Lg	W	L	PCT	ERA	G	GS	CG	IP	H	BB	SO	ShO	Relief Pitching W	Relief L	Relief SV	Batting AB	Batting H	HR	BA	PO	A	E	DP	TC/G	FA
1973	**PIT**	**N**	0	1	.000	5.96	12	1	0	22.2	33	14	13	0	0	0	0	4	0	0	.000	2	1	0	0	0.3	1.000
1974	**CHI**	**N**	3	5	.375	4.15	16	9	0	65	64	31	43	0	1	0	0	20	5	0	.250	10	8	0	1	1.1	1.000
1975			5	4	.556	5.40	36	5	0	85	88	31	46	0	4	2	0	24	6	0	.250	6	14	2	2	0.6	.909
1976			0	1	.000	10.29	4	0	0	7	11	2	4	0	0	1	0	0	0	0	—	2	0	0	0	0.5	1.000
4 yrs.			8	11	.421	5.21	68	15	0	179.2	196	78	106	0	5	3	0	48	11	0	.229	20	23	2	3	0.7	.956

Mel Deutsch

DEUTSCH, MELVIN ELLIOTT BR TR 6′ 4″ 215 lbs.
B. July 26, 1915, Caldwell, Tex.

Year	Team	Lg	W	L	PCT	ERA	G	GS	CG	IP	H	BB	SO	ShO	Relief Pitching W	Relief L	Relief SV	Batting AB	Batting H	HR	BA	PO	A	E	DP	TC/G	FA
1946	**BOS**	**A**	0	0	—	5.68	3	0	0	6.1	7	3	2	0	0	0	0	2	0	0	.000	0	1	1	0	0.7	.500

Charlie Devens

DEVENS, CHARLES BR TR 6′ 1″ 180 lbs.
B. Jan. 1, 1910, Milton, Mass.

Year	Team	Lg	W	L	PCT	ERA	G	GS	CG	IP	H	BB	SO	ShO	Relief Pitching W	Relief L	Relief SV	Batting AB	Batting H	HR	BA	PO	A	E	DP	TC/G	FA
1932	**NY**	**A**	1	0	1.000	2.00	1	1	1	9	6	7	4	0	0	0	0	2	0	0	.000	0	1	0	0	1.0	1.000
1933			3	3	.500	4.35	14	8	2	62	59	50	23	0	1	1	0	21	2	0	.095	3	9	1	1	0.9	.923
1934			1	0	1.000	1.64	1	1	1	11	9	5	4	0	0	0	0	2	1	0	.500	0	3	0	1	3.0	1.000
3 yrs.			5	3	.625	3.73	16	10	4	82	74	62	31	0	1	1	0	25	3	0	.120	3	13	1	2	1.1	.941

Adrian Devine

DEVINE, PAUL ADRIAN BR TR 6′ 4″ 185 lbs.
B. Dec. 2, 1951, Galveston, Tex.

Year	Team	Lg	W	L	PCT	ERA	G	GS	CG	IP	H	BB	SO	ShO	Relief Pitching W	Relief L	Relief SV	Batting AB	Batting H	HR	BA	PO	A	E	DP	TC/G	FA
1973	**ATL**	**N**	2	3	.400	6.47	24	1	0	32	45	12	15	0	2	2	4	4	1	0	.250	2	2	0	0	0.2	1.000
1975			1	0	1.000	4.50	5	2	0	16	19	7	8	0	0	0	0	5	0	0	.000	1	1	0	0	0.4	1.000
1976			5	6	.455	3.21	48	1	0	73	72	26	48	0	5	6	9	14	0	0	.000	3	8	1	0	0.3	.917
1977	**TEX**	**A**	11	6	.647	3.57	56	2	0	106	102	31	67	0	10	6	15	0	0	0	—	12	24	0	1	0.6	1.000
1978	**ATL**	**N**	5	4	.556	5.95	31	6	0	65	84	25	26	0	2	2	3	11	1	0	.091	10	9	1	1	0.6	.950
1979			1	2	.333	3.22	40	0	0	67	84	25	22	0	1	2	0	7	0	0	.000	1	12	4	1	0.4	.765
1980	**TEX**	**A**	1	1	.500	4.82	13	0	0	28	49	9	8	0	1	1	0	0	0	0	—	2	3	1	0	0.5	.833
7 yrs.			26	22	.542	4.21	217	12	0	387	455	135	194	0	21	19	31	41	2	0	.049	31	59	7	3	0.4	.928

Jim Devine

DEVINE, WALTER JAMES TL
B. Oct. 5, 1858, Brooklyn, N. Y. D. Jan. 11, 1905, Syracuse, N. Y.

Year	Team	Lg	W	L	PCT	ERA	G	GS	CG	IP	H	BB	SO	ShO	Relief Pitching W	Relief L	Relief SV	Batting AB	Batting H	HR	BA	PO	A	E	DP	TC/G	FA
1883	**BAL**	**AA**	1	1	.500	*7.36*	2	2	1	11	15	1	3	0	0	0	0	*				1	0	1	0	0.7	.500

Hal Deviney

DEVINEY, HAROLD JOHN BR TR
B. Apr. 11, 1893, Newton, Mass. D. Jan. 4, 1933, Westwood, Mass.

Year	Team	Lg	W	L	PCT	ERA	G	GS	CG	IP	H	BB	SO	ShO	Relief Pitching W	Relief L	Relief SV	Batting AB	Batting H	HR	BA	PO	A	E	DP	TC/G	FA
1920	**BOS**	**A**	0	0	—	15.00	1	0	0	3	7	2	0	0	0	0	0	2	2	0	1.000	0	0	0	0	0.0	.000

Jim Devlin

DEVLIN, JAMES ALEXANDER BR TR 5′11″ 175 lbs.
B. 1849, Philadelphia, Pa. D. Oct. 10, 1883, Philadelphia, Pa.

Year	Team	Lg	W	L	PCT	ERA	G	GS	CG	IP	H	BB	SO	ShO	Relief Pitching W	Relief L	Relief SV	Batting AB	Batting H	HR	BA	PO	A	E	DP	TC/G	FA
1876	**LOU**	**N**	30	**35**	.462	1.56	**68**	**68**	**66**	**622**	566	37	**122**	5	0	0	0	298	94	0	.315	52	101	10	5	2.4	.939
1877			35	**25**	.583	2.25	**61**	**61**	**61**	**559**	**617**	41	141	4	0	0	0	268	72	1	.269	30	110	10	2	2.5	.933
2 yrs.			65	60	.520	1.89	129	129	127	1181	1183	78	263	9	0	0	0	566	166	1	.293	82	211	20	7	2.4	.936

Jim Devlin

DEVLIN, JAMES H. TL 5′ 7″ 135 lbs.
B. Apr. 16, 1866, Troy, N. Y. D. Dec. 14, 1900, Troy, N. Y.

Year	Team	Lg	W	L	PCT	ERA	G	GS	CG	IP	H	BB	SO	ShO	Relief Pitching W	Relief L	Relief SV	Batting AB	Batting H	HR	BA	PO	A	E	DP	TC/G	FA
1886	**NY**	**N**	0	0	—	18.00	1	0	0	2	3	4	2	0	0	0	1	1	0	0	.000	1	1	0	0	2.0	1.000
1887	**PHI**	**N**	0	2	.000	6.00	2	2	2	18	20	10	6	0	0	0	0	6	2	0	.333	0	5	0	0	2.5	1.000
1888	**STL**	**AA**	6	5	.545	3.19	11	11	10	90.1	82	20	45	0	0	0	0	37	11	0	.297	3	22	4	0	2.6	.862
1889			5	3	.625	2.40	9	8	5	60	56	24	37	0	1	0	0	26	5	0	.192	0	18	3	0	2.3	.857
4 yrs.			11	10	.524	3.38	23	21	17	170.1	161	58	90	0	1	0	1	70	18	0	.257	4	46	7	0	2.5	.877

Charlie Dewald

DEWALD, CHARLES H. TL
B. Sept. 1867, Newark, N. J. D. Aug. 22, 1904, Cleveland, Ohio.

Year	Team	Lg	W	L	PCT	ERA	G	GS	CG	IP	H	BB	SO	ShO	Relief Pitching W	Relief L	Relief SV	Batting AB	Batting H	HR	BA	PO	A	E	DP	TC/G	FA
1890	**CLE**	**P**	2	0	1.000	0.64	2	2	2	14	13	5	6	0	0	0	0	8	3	0	.375	0	2	1	0	1.5	.667

Mark Dewey

DEWEY, MARK ALAN BR TR 6′ 185 lbs.
B. Jan. 3, 1965, Grand Rapids, Mich.

Year	Team	Lg	W	L	PCT	ERA	G	GS	CG	IP	H	BB	SO	ShO	Relief W	Relief L	Relief SV	AB	H	HR	BA	PO	A	E	DP	TC/G	FA
1990	SF	N	1	1	.500	2.78	14	0	0	22.2	22	5	11	0	1	1	0	1	0	0	.000	2	2	0	1	0.3	1.000
1992	NY	N	1	0	1.000	4.32	20	0	0	33.1	37	10	24	0	1	0	0	1	0	0	.000	3	5	0	0	0.4	1.000
1993	PIT	N	1	2	.333	2.36	21	0	0	26.2	14	10	14	0	1	2	7	0	0	0	—	2	6	0	0	0.4	1.000
1994			2	1	.667	3.68	45	0	0	51.1	61	19	30	0	2	1	1	1	1	0	1.000	4	4	1	1	0.2	.889
1995	SF	N	1	0	1.000	3.13	27	0	0	31.2	30	17	32	0	1	0	0	1	0	0	.000	1	3	1	1	0.2	.800
5 yrs.			6	4	.600	3.37	127	0	0	165.2	164	61	111	0	6	4	8	4	1	0	.250	12	20	2	3	0.3	.941

Carlos Diaz

DIAZ, CARLOS ANTONIO BR TL 6′ 161 lbs.
B. Jan. 7, 1958, Kaneohe, Hawaii.

Year	Team	Lg	W	L	PCT	ERA	G	GS	CG	IP	H	BB	SO	ShO	Relief W	Relief L	Relief SV	AB	H	HR	BA	PO	A	E	DP	TC/G	FA
1982	2 teams	ATL N	(19G 3–2)		NY N	(4G 0–0)																					
″	total		3	2	.600	4.03	23	0	0	29	37	13	16	0	3	2	1	3	0	0	.000	5	4	0	0	0.4	1.000
1983	NY	N	3	1	.750	2.05	54	0	0	83.1	62	35	64	0	3	1	2	5	0	0	.000	8	13	0	2	0.4	1.000
1984	LA	N	1	0	1.000	5.49	37	0	0	41	47	24	36	0	1	0	1	1	0	0	.000	2	2	0	0	0.1	1.000
1985			6	3	.667	2.61	46	0	0	79.1	70	18	73	0	6	3	0	4	0	0	.000	1	8	0	0	0.2	1.000
1986			0	0	—	4.26	19	0	0	25.1	33	7	18	0	0	0	0	1	0	0	.000	1	6	1	0	0.4	.875
5 yrs.			13	6	.684	3.21	179	0	0	258	249	97	207	0	13	6	4	14	0	0	.000	17	33	1	2	0.3	.980
LEAGUE CHAMPIONSHIP SERIES																											
1985	LA	N	0	0	—	3.00	2	0	0	3	5	1	2	0	0	0	0	0	0	0	—	1	0	0	0	0.5	1.000

Rob Dibble

DIBBLE, ROBERT KEITH BL TR 6′ 4″ 230 lbs.
B. Jan. 24, 1964, Bridgeport, Conn.

Year	Team	Lg	W	L	PCT	ERA	G	GS	CG	IP	H	BB	SO	ShO	Relief W	Relief L	Relief SV	AB	H	HR	BA	PO	A	E	DP	TC/G	FA
1988	CIN	N	1	1	.500	1.82	37	0	0	59.1	43	21	59	0	1	1	0	2	0	0	.000	1	3	0	0	0.1	1.000
1989			10	5	.667	2.09	74	0	0	99	62	39	141	0	10	5	2	8	0	0	.000	3	5	1	0	0.1	.889
1990			8	3	.727	1.74	68	0	0	98	62	34	136	0	8	3	11	7	0	0	.000	5	8	0	0	0.2	1.000
1991			3	5	.375	3.17	67	0	0	82.1	67	25	124	0	3	5	31	2	0	0	.000	4	7	1	0	0.2	.917
1992			3	5	.375	3.07	63	0	0	70.1	48	31	110	0	3	5	25	5	2	0	.400	5	3	1	0	0.1	.889
1993			1	4	.200	6.48	45	0	0	41.2	34	42	49	0	1	4	19	1	1	0	1.000	5	4	0	2	0.2	1.000
1995	2 teams	CHI A	(16G 0–1)		MIL A	(15G 1–1)																					
″	total		1	2	.333	7.18	31	0	0	26.1	16	46	26	0	1	2	1	0	0	0	—	0	2	0	0	0.1	1.000
7 yrs.			27	25	.519	2.98	385	0	0	477	332	238	645	0	27	25	89	25	3	0	.120	23	32	3	2	0.2	.948
LEAGUE CHAMPIONSHIP SERIES																											
1990	CIN	N	0	0	—	0.00	4	0	0	5	0	1	10	0	0	0	1	2	0	0	.000	0	0	0	0	0.0	.000
WORLD SERIES																											
1990	CIN	N	1	0	1.000	0.00	3	0	0	4.2	3	1	4	0	1	0	0	0	0	0	—	0	0	0	0	0.0	.000

Pedro Dibut

DIBUT, PEDRO BR TR 5′ 8″ 190 lbs.
Born Pedro Dibut (Villafana).
B. Nov. 18, 1892, Cienfuegos, Cuba D. Dec. 4, 1979, Hialeah, Fla.

Year	Team	Lg	W	L	PCT	ERA	G	GS	CG	IP	H	BB	SO	ShO	Relief W	Relief L	Relief SV	AB	H	HR	BA	PO	A	E	DP	TC/G	FA
1924	CIN	N	3	0	1.000	2.21	7	2	2	36.2	24	12	15	0	1	0	0	11	3	0	.273	2	12	0	0	2.0	1.000
1925			0	0	—	∞	1	0	0		3	0	0	0	0	0	0	0	0	0	—	0	0	0	0	0.0	.000
2 yrs.			3	0	1.000	2.70	8	2	2	36.2	27	12	15	0	1	0	0	11	3	0	.273	2	12	0	0	1.8	1.000

Leo Dickerman

DICKERMAN, LEO LOUIS BR TR 6′ 4″ 192 lbs.
B. Oct. 31, 1896, DeSoto, Mo. D. Apr. 30, 1982, Atkins, Ark.

Year	Team	Lg	W	L	PCT	ERA	G	GS	CG	IP	H	BB	SO	ShO	Relief W	Relief L	Relief SV	AB	H	HR	BA	PO	A	E	DP	TC/G	FA
1923	BKN	N	8	12	.400	3.59	35	20	7	165.2	185	71	57	1	2	1	0	52	13	2	.250	2	50	4	3	1.6	.929
1924	2 teams	BKN N	(7G 0–0)		STL N	(18G 7–4)																					
″	total		7	4	.636	2.84	25	15	8	139.1	128	67	37	1	0	0	0	45	10	0	.222	5	36	2	4	1.7	.953
1925	STL	N	4	11	.267	5.58	29	18	7	130.2	135	79	40	2	0	0	1	44	5	0	.114	6	47	0	1	1.8	1.000
3 yrs.			19	27	.413	3.95	89	53	22	435.2	448	217	134	4	2	1	1	141	28	2	.199	13	133	6	8	1.7	.961

George Dickerson

DICKERSON, GEORGE CLARK BR TR 6′ 1″ 170 lbs.
B. Dec. 1, 1892, Renner, Tex. D. July 9, 1938, Los Angeles, Calif.

Year	Team	Lg	W	L	PCT	ERA	G	GS	CG	IP	H	BB	SO	ShO	Relief W	Relief L	Relief SV	AB	H	HR	BA	PO	A	E	DP	TC/G	FA
1917	CLE	A	0	0	—	0.00	1	0	0	1	0	0	0	0	0	0	0	0	0	0	—	0	0	0	0	0.0	.000

Emerson Dickman

DICKMAN, GEORGE EMERSON BR TR 6′ 2″ 175 lbs.
B. Nov. 12, 1914, Buffalo, N. Y. D. Apr. 27, 1981, New York, N. Y.

Year	Team	Lg	W	L	PCT	ERA	G	GS	CG	IP	H	BB	SO	ShO	Relief W	Relief L	Relief SV	AB	H	HR	BA	PO	A	E	DP	TC/G	FA
1936	BOS	A	0	0	—	9.00	1	0	0	1	2	1	2	0	0	0	0	0	0	0	—	0	0	0	0	0.0	.000
1938			5	5	.500	5.28	32	11	3	104	117	54	22	1	2	0	0	35	10	1	.286	4	18	0	2	0.7	1.000
1939			8	3	.727	4.43	48	1	0	113.2	126	43	46	0	8	3	5	36	2	0	.056	4	33	2	3	0.8	.949
1940			8	6	.571	6.03	35	9	2	100	121	38	40	0	5	1	3	28	3	0	.107	5	29	3	5	1.1	.919
1941			1	1	.500	6.39	9	3	1	31	37	17	16	0	0	0	0	11	1	0	.091	1	1	1	0	0.3	.667
5 yrs.			22	15	.595	5.33	125	24	6	349.2	403	153	126	1	15	4	8	110	16	1	.145	14	81	6	10	0.8	.941

Jim Dickson

DICKSON, JAMES EDWARD BL TR 6′ 1″ 185 lbs.
B. Apr. 20, 1938, Portland, Ore.

Year	Team	Lg	W	L	PCT	ERA	G	GS	CG	IP	H	BB	SO	ShO	Relief W	Relief L	Relief SV	AB	H	HR	BA	PO	A	E	DP	TC/G	FA
1963	HOU	N	0	1	.000	6.14	13	0	0	14.2	22	2	6	0	0	1	2	1	0	0	.000	0	2	0	0	0.2	1.000
1964	CIN	N	1	0	1.000	7.20	4	0	0	5	8	5	6	0	1	0	0	0	0	0	—	0	1	0	0	0.3	1.000
1965	KC	A	3	2	.600	3.47	68	0	0	85.2	68	47	54	0	3	2	0	2	0	0	.000	2	12	1	0	0.2	.933
1966			1	0	1.000	5.35	24	1	0	37	37	23	20	0	1	0	1	4	1	0	.250	0	7	1	0	0.3	.875
4 yrs.			5	3	.625	4.36	109	1	0	142.1	135	77	86	0	5	3	3	7	1	0	.143	2	22	2	0	0.2	.923

Lance Dickson

DICKSON, LANCE MICHAEL BR TL 6′ 185 lbs.
B. Oct. 19, 1969, Fullerton, Calif.

Year	Team	Lg	W	L	PCT	ERA	G	GS	CG	IP	H	BB	SO	ShO	Relief W	Relief L	Relief SV	AB	H	HR	BA	PO	A	E	DP	TC/G	FA
1990	CHI	N	0	3	.000	7.24	3	3	0	13.2	20	4	4	0	0	0	0	3	0	0	.000	1	6	0	1	2.3	1.000

Murry Dickson

DICKSON, MURRY MONROE BR TR 5′10½″ 157 lbs.
B. Aug. 21, 1916, Tracy, Mo. D. Sept. 21, 1989, Kansas City, Kans.

Year	Team	Lg	W	L	PCT	ERA	G	GS	CG	IP	H	BB	SO	ShO	Relief W	Relief L	Relief SV	AB	H	HR	BA	PO	A	E	DP	TC/G	FA
1939	STL	N	0	0	—	0.00	1	0	0	3.2	1	1	2	0	0	0	0	1	0	0	.000	0	2	0	0	2.0	1.000
1940			0	0	—	16.20	1	1	0	1.2	5	1	0	0	0	0	0	0	0	0	—	0	0	1	0	1.0	.000
1942			6	3	.667	2.91	36	7	2	120.2	91	61	66	0	4	1	2	42	8	0	.190	10	27	0	2	1.0	1.000
1943			8	2	.800	3.58	31	7	2	115.2	114	49	44	0	2	2	0	34	9	0	.265	6	21	2	3	0.9	.931
1946			15	6	**.714**	2.88	47	19	12	184.1	160	56	82	2	4	2	1	65	18	0	.277	13	52	1	5	1.4	.985

Murry Dickson *continued*

Year	Team	W	L	PCT	ERA	G	GS	CG	IP	H	BB	SO	ShO	Relief Pitching W	Relief Pitching L	Relief Pitching SV	Batting AB	Batting H	Batting HR	BA	PO	A	E	DP	TC/G	FA
1947		13	16	.448	3.07	47	25	11	231.2	211	88	111	4	3	2	3	80	17	0	.212	13	47	4	3	1.4	.938
1948		12	16	.429	4.14	42	29	11	252.1	257	85	113	1	2	4	1	96	27	0	.281	12	51	0	0	1.5	1.000
1949	**PIT N**	12	14	.462	3.29	44	20	11	224.1	216	80	89	2	3	5	0	84	17	0	.202	26	52	3	8	1.8	.963
1950		10	15	.400	3.80	51	22	8	225	227	83	76	0	5	3	3	82	21	0	.256	20	45	1	6	1.3	.985
1951		20	16	.556	4.02	45	35	19	288.2	**294**	101	112	3	4	2	2	110	30	1	.273	19	70	3	3	2.0	.967
1952		14	**21**	.400	3.57	43	34	21	277.2	278	76	112	2	2	0	2	107	24	0	.224	29	62	4	7	2.2	.958
1953		10	**19**	.345	4.53	45	26	10	200.2	240	58	88	1	2	4	4	61	7	0	.115	14	34	4	2	1.2	.923
1954	**PHI N**	10	**20**	.333	3.78	40	31	12	226.1	256	73	64	4	1	1	3	79	15	0	.190	12	55	3	3	1.8	.957
1955		12	11	.522	3.50	36	28	12	216	190	82	92	4	1	1	0	82	18	1	.220	17	39	1	4	1.6	.982
1956	**2 teams PHI N** (3G 0–3) **STL N** (28G 13–8)																									
"	**total**	13	11	.542	3.28	31	30	12	219.1	195	69	110	3	0	1	0	86	22	0	.256	24	51	1	5	2.5	.987
1957	**STL N**	5	3	.625	4.14	14	13	3	74	87	25	29	1	0	0	0	27	6	0	.222	11	20	1	0	2.3	.969
1958	**2 teams KC A** (27G 9–5) **NY A** (6G 1–2)																									
"	**total**	10	7	.588	3.70	33	11	3	119.1	117	43	55	0	7	3	2	42	11	1	.262	9	27	0	3	1.1	1.000
1959	**KC A**	2	1	.667	4.94	38	0	0	71	85	27	36	0	2	1	0	17	3	0	.176	1	13	1	0	0.4	.933
18 yrs.		172	181	.487	3.66	625	338	149	3052.1	3024	1058	1281	27	42	32	23	1095	253	3	.231	236	668	30	54	1.5	.968
WORLD SERIES																										
1943	**STL N**	0	0	—	0.00	1	0	0	0.2	0	1	0	0	0	0	0	0	0	0	—	1	0	0	0	1.0	1.000
1946		0	1	.000	3.86	2	2	0	14	11	4	7	0	0	0	0	5	2	0	.400	0	3	0	0	1.5	1.000
1958	**NY A**	0	0	—	4.50	2	0	0	4	4	0	1	0	0	0	0	0	0	0	—	0	0	0	0	0.0	.000
3 yrs.		0	1	.000	3.86	5	2	0	18.2	15	5	8	0	0	0	0	5	2	0	.400	1	3	0	0	0.8	1.000

Walt Dickson

DICKSON, WALTER R. (Hickory) BR TR 5′11½″ 175 lbs.
B. Dec. 3, 1878, New Summerfield, Tex. D. Dec. 9, 1918, Ardmore, Okla.

Year	Team	W	L	PCT	ERA	G	GS	CG	IP	H	BB	SO	ShO	Relief Pitching W	Relief Pitching L	Relief Pitching SV	Batting AB	Batting H	Batting HR	BA	PO	A	E	DP	TC/G	FA
1910	**NY N**	1	0	1.000	5.46	12	1	0	29.2	31	9	9	0	1	0	0	4	1	0	.250	0	6	1	0	0.6	.857
1912	**BOS N**	3	19	.136	3.86	36	20	9	189	233	61	47	1	2	4	0	60	10	0	.167	4	63	6	1	2.0	.918
1913		6	7	.462	3.23	19	15	8	128	118	45	47	0	0	1	0	45	8	0	.178	6	26	1	1	1.7	.970
1914	**PIT F**	9	**21**	.300	3.16	40	32	19	256.2	262	74	63	3	0	2	1	83	7	0	.084	8	81	3	3	2.3	.967
1915		6	5	.545	4.19	27	11	4	96.2	115	33	36	0	2	2	0	31	4	0	.129	3	32	1	0	1.3	.972
5 yrs.		25	52	.325	3.60	134	79	40	700	759	222	202	4	5	9	1	223	30	0	.135	21	208	12	5	1.8	.950

George Diehl

DIEHL, GEORGE KRAUSE BR TR 6′ 2″ 196 lbs.
B. Feb. 25, 1918, Emmaus, Pa. D. Aug. 24, 1986, Kingsport, Tenn.

Year	Team	W	L	PCT	ERA	G	GS	CG	IP	H	BB	SO	ShO	Relief Pitching W	Relief Pitching L	Relief Pitching SV	Batting AB	Batting H	Batting HR	BA	PO	A	E	DP	TC/G	FA
1942	**BOS N**	0	0	—	2.45	1	0	0	3.2	2	2	0	0	0	0	0	1	0	0	.000	0	1	0	0	1.0	1.000
1943		0	0	—	4.50	1	0	0	4	4	3	1	0	0	0	0	1	0	0	.000	0	5	0	0	5.0	1.000
2 yrs.		0	0		3.52	2	0	0	7.2	6	5	1	0	0	0	0	2	0	0	.000	0	6	0	0	3.0	1.000

Larry Dierker

DIERKER, LAWRENCE EDWARD BR TR 6′ 4″ 215 lbs.
B. Sept. 22, 1946, Hollywood, Calif.

Year	Team	W	L	PCT	ERA	G	GS	CG	IP	H	BB	SO	ShO	Relief Pitching W	Relief Pitching L	Relief Pitching SV	Batting AB	Batting H	Batting HR	BA	PO	A	E	DP	TC/G	FA
1964	**HOU N**	0	1	.000	2.00	3	1	0	9	7	3	5	0	0	0	0	3	0	0	.000	0	0	1	0	0.3	.000
1965		7	8	.467	3.50	26	19	1	146.2	135	37	109	0	1	0	0	50	5	1	.100	10	17	4	0	1.2	.871
1966		10	8	.556	3.18	29	28	8	187	173	45	108	2	0	0	0	67	10	1	.149	13	26	2	1	1.4	.951
1967		6	5	.545	3.36	15	15	4	99	95	25	68	0	0	0	0	31	7	0	.226	7	10	2	0	1.3	.895
1968		12	15	.444	3.31	32	32	10	233.2	206	89	161	1	0	0	0	73	5	0	.068	13	28	1	2	1.3	.976
1969		20	13	.606	2.33	39	37	20	305	240	72	232	4	0	0	0	118	17	1	.144	14	42	3	5	1.5	.949
1970		16	12	.571	3.87	37	36	17	270	263	82	191	2	0	0	1	92	16	0	.174	19	31	3	3	1.4	.943
1971		12	6	.667	2.72	24	23	6	159	150	33	91	2	0	0	0	54	4	0	.074	16	23	1	0	1.7	.975
1972		15	8	.652	3.40	31	31	12	214.2	209	51	115	5	0	0	0	78	13	0	.167	16	19	0	1	1.1	1.000
1973		1	1	.500	4.33	14	3	0	27	27	13	18	0	1	0	0	4	0	0	.000	0	3	0	0	0.2	1.000
1974		11	10	.524	2.89	33	33	7	224	189	82	150	3	0	0	0	71	14	0	.197	10	34	1	1	1.4	.978
1975		14	16	.467	4.00	34	34	14	232	225	91	127	2	0	0	0	76	7	0	.092	15	31	3	1	1.4	.939
1976		13	14	.481	3.69	28	28	7	188	171	72	112	4	0	0	0	64	9	1	.141	17	18	2	2	1.3	.946
1977	**STL N**	2	6	.250	4.62	11	9	0	39	40	16	6	0	0	0	0	8	0	0	.000	2	5	0	0	0.6	1.000
14 yrs.		139	123	.531	3.30	356	329	106	2334	2130	711	1493	25	2	0	1	789	107	4	.136	152	287	23	16	1.3	.950

Bill Dietrich

DIETRICH, WILLIAM JOHN (Bullfrog) BR TR 6′ 185 lbs.
B. Mar. 29, 1910, Philadelphia, Pa. D. June 20, 1978, Philadelphia, Pa.

Year	Team	W	L	PCT	ERA	G	GS	CG	IP	H	BB	SO	ShO	Relief Pitching W	Relief Pitching L	Relief Pitching SV	Batting AB	Batting H	Batting HR	BA	PO	A	E	DP	TC/G	FA
1933	**PHI A**	0	1	.000	5.82	8	1	0	17	13	19	4	0	0	0	0	3	1	0	.333	0	5	0	1	0.6	1.000
1934		11	12	.478	4.68	39	23	14	207.2	201	114	88	4	0	2	3	72	15	1	.208	12	31	3	0	1.2	.935
1935		7	13	.350	5.39	43	15	8	185.1	203	101	59	1	4	3	3	60	5	0	.083	10	34	3	0	1.1	.936
1936	**3 teams PHI A** (21G 4–6) **WAS A** (5G 0–1) **CHI A** (14G 4–4)																									
"	**total**	8	11	.421	5.75	40	15	6	162.2	197	82	77	1	4	3	3	57	11	0	.193	5	34	3	3	1.0	.929
1937	**CHI A**	8	10	.444	4.90	29	20	7	143.1	162	72	62	1	1	0	1	44	8	0	.182	3	31	1	1	1.2	.971
1938		2	4	.333	5.44	8	7	1	48	49	31	11	0	0	0	0	16	1	0	.063	3	7	0	0	1.3	1.000
1939		7	8	.467	5.22	25	19	2	127.2	134	56	43	0	1	0	0	37	8	1	.216	5	19	2	2	1.0	.923
1940		10	6	.625	4.03	23	17	6	149.2	154	65	43	1	1	0	0	50	12	1	.240	8	20	1	2	1.3	.966
1941		5	8	.385	5.35	19	15	4	109.1	114	50	26	1	0	1	0	34	3	0	.088	10	13	2	1	1.3	.920
1942		6	11	.353	4.89	26	23	6	160	173	70	39	0	0	0	0	48	5	0	.104	7	32	0	2	1.5	1.000
1943		12	10	.545	2.80	26	26	12	186.2	180	53	52	2	0	0	0	56	8	1	.143	10	46	1	3	2.2	.982
1944		16	**17**	.485	3.62	36	36	15	246	269	68	70	2	0	0	0	77	9	1	.117	10	46	3	0	1.6	.949
1945		7	10	.412	4.19	18	16	6	122.1	136	36	43	4	0	2	0	36	6	0	.167	9	23	1	2	1.8	.970
1946		3	3	.500	2.61	11	9	3	62	63	24	20	0	0	0	1	19	1	0	.053	2	17	0	2	1.7	1.000
1947	**PHI A**	5	2	.714	3.12	11	9	2	60.2	48	40	18	1	1	0	0	16	1	0	.063	1	8	4	3	1.2	.692
1948		1	2	.333	5.87	4	2	0	15.1	21	9	5	0	1	0	0	2	0	0	.000	0	3	0	0	0.8	1.000
16 yrs.		108	128	.458	4.48	366	253	92	2003.2	2117	890	660	18	13	11	11	627	94	5	.150	95	369	24	22	1.3	.951

Dutch Dietz

DIETZ, LLOYD ARTHUR BR TR 5′11½″ 180 lbs.
B. Feb. 12, 1912, Cincinnati, Ohio D. Oct. 29, 1972, Beaumont, Tex.

Year	Team	W	L	PCT	ERA	G	GS	CG	IP	H	BB	SO	ShO	Relief Pitching W	Relief Pitching L	Relief Pitching SV	Batting AB	Batting H	Batting HR	BA	PO	A	E	DP	TC/G	FA
1940	**PIT N**	0	1	.000	5.87	4	2	0	15.1	22	4	8	0	0	0	0	7	1	0	.143	0	2	1	1	0.8	.667
1941		7	2	.778	2.33	33	6	4	100.1	88	33	22	1	4	0	1	25	4	0	.160	13	18	1	1	1.0	.969

Dutch Dietz *continued*

Year	Team	W	L	PCT	ERA	G	GS	CG	IP	H	BB	SO	ShO	Relief Pitching W	Relief Pitching L	Relief Pitching SV	Batting AB	Batting H	Batting HR	BA	PO	A	E	DP	TC/G	FA
1942		6	9	.400	3.95	40	13	3	134.1	139	57	35	0	2	2	3	35	7	0	.200	7	21	1	1	0.7	.966
1943	2 teams PIT N (8G 0–3) PHI N (21G 1–1)																									
"	total	1	4	.200	6.40	29	0	0	45	54	19	14	0	1	4	2	6	1	0	.167	0	12	0	0	0.4	1.000
4 yrs.		14	16	.467	3.87	106	21	7	295	303	113	79	1	7	6	6	73	13	0	.178	20	53	3	3	0.7	.961

Reese Diggs

DIGGS, REESE WILSON (Diggsy) — BB TR 6′ 2″ 180 lbs.
B. Sept. 22, 1915, Mathews, Va. D. Oct. 30, 1978, Baltimore, Md.

Year	Team	W	L	PCT	ERA	G	GS	CG	IP	H	BB	SO	ShO	Relief W	Relief L	SV	AB	H	HR	BA	PO	A	E	DP	TC/G	FA
1934	WAS A	1	2	.333	6.75	4	3	2	21.1	26	15	2	0	0	0	0	8	2	0	.250	0	4	0	0	1.0	1.000

Jack DiLauro

DiLAURO, JACK EDWARD — BB TL 6′ 2″ 185 lbs.
B. May 3, 1943, Akron, Ohio.

Year	Team	W	L	PCT	ERA	G	GS	CG	IP	H	BB	SO	ShO	Relief W	Relief L	SV	AB	H	HR	BA	PO	A	E	DP	TC/G	FA
1969	NY N	1	4	.200	2.40	23	4	0	63.2	50	18	27	0	1	1	1	12	0	0	.000	6	10	0	0	0.7	1.000
1970	HOU N	1	3	.250	4.24	42	0	0	34	34	17	23	0	1	3	3	2	0	0	.000	2	4	2	0	0.2	.750
2 yrs.		2	7	.222	3.04	65	4	0	97.2	84	35	50	0	2	4	4	14	0	0	.000	8	14	2	0	0.4	.917

Gordon Dillard

DILLARD, GORDON LEE — BL TL 6′ 1″ 180 lbs.
B. May 20, 1964, Salinas, Calif.

Year	Team	W	L	PCT	ERA	G	GS	CG	IP	H	BB	SO	ShO	Relief W	Relief L	SV	AB	H	HR	BA	PO	A	E	DP	TC/G	FA
1988	BAL A	0	0	—	6.00	2	1	0	3	3	4	2	0	0	0	0	0	0	0	—	0	1	0	0	0.5	1.000
1989	PHI N	0	0	—	6.75	5	0	0	4	7	0	2	0	0	0	0	0	0	0	—	0	1	0	0	0.2	1.000
2 yrs.		0	0		6.43	7	1	0	7	10	4	4	0	0	0	0	0	0	0		0	2	0	0	0.3	1.000

Harley Dillinger

DILLINGER, HARLEY HUGH (Hoke, Lefty) — BR TL 5′11″ 175 lbs.
B. Oct. 30, 1894, Pomeroy, Ohio D. Jan. 8, 1959, Cleveland, Ohio.

Year	Team	W	L	PCT	ERA	G	GS	CG	IP	H	BB	SO	ShO	Relief W	Relief L	SV	AB	H	HR	BA	PO	A	E	DP	TC/G	FA
1914	CLE A	0	1	.000	4.54	11	2	1	33.2	41	25	11	0	0	0	0	10	0	0	.000	0	8	1	0	0.8	.889

Bill Dillman

DILLMAN, WILLIAM HOWARD — BR TR 6′ 2″ 180 lbs.
B. May 25, 1945, Trenton, N. J.

Year	Team	W	L	PCT	ERA	G	GS	CG	IP	H	BB	SO	ShO	Relief W	Relief L	SV	AB	H	HR	BA	PO	A	E	DP	TC/G	FA
1967	BAL A	5	9	.357	4.35	32	15	2	124	115	33	69	1	2	0	3	31	5	0	.161	7	15	0	1	0.7	1.000
1970	MON N	2	3	.400	5.23	18	0	0	31	28	18	17	0	2	3	0	2	0	0	.000	3	6	0	0	0.5	1.000
2 yrs.		7	12	.368	4.53	50	15	2	155	143	51	86	1	4	3	3	33	5	0	.152	10	21	0	1	0.6	1.000

Steve Dillon

DILLON, STEPHEN EDWARD — BL TL 5′10″ 160 lbs.
B. Mar. 20, 1943, Yonkers, N. Y.

Year	Team	W	L	PCT	ERA	G	GS	CG	IP	H	BB	SO	ShO	Relief W	Relief L	SV	AB	H	HR	BA	PO	A	E	DP	TC/G	FA
1963	NY N	0	0	—	10.80	1	0	0	1.2	3	0	1	0	0	0	0	0	0	0	—	1	0	0	0	1.0	1.000
1964		0	0	—	9.00	2	0	0	3	4	2	2	0	0	0	0	0	0	0	—	0	0	0	0	0.0	.000
2 yrs.		0	0		9.64	3	0	0	4.2	7	2	3	0	0	0	0	0	0	0		1	0	0	0	0.3	1.000

Frank DiMichele

DiMICHELE, FRANK LAWRENCE — BR TL 6′ 3″ 205 lbs.
B. Feb. 16, 1965, Philadelphia, Pa.

Year	Team	W	L	PCT	ERA	G	GS	CG	IP	H	BB	SO	ShO	Relief W	Relief L	SV	AB	H	HR	BA	PO	A	E	DP	TC/G	FA
1988	CAL A	0	0	—	9.64	4	0	0	4.2	5	2	1	0	0	0	0	0	0	0	—	0	0	0	0	0.0	.000

Bill Dinneen

DINNEEN, WILLIAM HENRY (Big Bill) — BR TR 6′ 1″ 190 lbs.
B. Apr. 5, 1876, Syracuse, N. Y. D. Jan. 13, 1955, Syracuse, N. Y.

Year	Team	W	L	PCT	ERA	G	GS	CG	IP	H	BB	SO	ShO	Relief W	Relief L	SV	AB	H	HR	BA	PO	A	E	DP	TC/G	FA
1898	WAS N	9	16	.360	4.00	29	27	22	218.1	238	88	83	0	1	0	0	80	8	0	.100	6	50	5	1	2.0	.918
1899		14	20	.412	3.93	37	35	30	291	350	106	91	0	0	2	0	119	36	0	.303	16	85	10	1	2.9	.910
1900	BOS N	20	14	.588	3.12	40	37	33	320.2	304	105	107	1	0	0	0	125	35	0	.280	25	80	6	0	2.8	.946
1901		15	18	.455	2.94	37	34	31	309.1	295	77	141	0	1	0	0	147	31	1	.211	39	72	9	2	2.9	.925
1902	BOS A	21	**21**	.500	2.93	42	42	39	371.1	348	99	136	2	0	0	0	141	18	0	.128	9	77	6	1	2.1	.935
1903		21	13	.618	2.26	37	34	32	299	255	66	148	6	0	1	**2**	106	17	0	.160	11	79	2	4	2.5	.978
1904		23	14	.622	2.20	37	37	37	335.2	283	63	153	5	0	0	0	120	25	0	.208	19	98	4	3	3.3	.967
1905		12	14	.462	3.73	31	29	23	243.2	235	50	97	2	1	0	1	88	13	0	.148	11	77	6	3	3.0	.936
1906		8	19	.296	2.92	28	27	22	218.2	209	52	60	1	0	0	0	63	7	0	.111	10	58	7	1	2.7	.907
1907	2 teams BOS A (5G 0–4) STL A (24G 7–10)																									
"	total	7	14	.333	2.92	29	21	18	188	195	41	46	2	0	1	**4**	59	10	0	.169	5	46	3	1	1.9	.944
1908	STL A	14	7	.667	2.10	27	16	11	167	133	53	39	2	4	1	0	59	12	0	.203	3	44	1	1	1.8	.979
1909		6	7	.462	3.46	17	13	8	112	112	29	26	3	1	0	0	36	7	0	.194	6	34	1	1	2.4	.976
12 yrs.		170	177	.490	3.01	391	352	306	3074.2	2957	829	1127	24	8	5	7	*				160	800	60	19	2.5	.941
WORLD SERIES																										
1903	BOS A	3	1	.750	2.06	4	4	4	35	29	8	28	2 **4th**	0	0	0	*				1	9	0	0	2.5	1.000

Ron Diorio

DIORIO, RONALD MICHAEL — BR TR 6′ 6″ 212 lbs.
B. July 15, 1946, Waterbury, Conn.

Year	Team	W	L	PCT	ERA	G	GS	CG	IP	H	BB	SO	ShO	Relief W	Relief L	SV	AB	H	HR	BA	PO	A	E	DP	TC/G	FA
1973	PHI N	0	0	—	2.33	23	0	0	19.1	18	6	11	0	0	0	1	0	0	0	—	0	2	0	1	0.1	1.000
1974		0	0	—	18.00	2	0	0	1	2	1	0	0	0	0	0	0	0	0	—	0	1	0	0	0.5	1.000
2 yrs.		0	0		3.10	25	0	0	20.1	20	7	11	0	0	0	1	0	0	0		0	3	0	1	0.1	1.000

Frank DiPino

DiPINO, FRANK MICHAEL — BL TL 5′10″ 175 lbs.
B. Oct. 22, 1956, Syracuse, N. Y.

Year	Team	W	L	PCT	ERA	G	GS	CG	IP	H	BB	SO	ShO	Relief W	Relief L	SV	AB	H	HR	BA	PO	A	E	DP	TC/G	FA
1981	MIL A	0	0	—	0.00	2	0	0	2	0	3	3	0	0	0	0	0	0	0	—	0	0	0	0	0.0	.000
1982	HOU N	2	2	.500	6.04	6	6	0	28.1	32	11	25	0	0	0	0	8	0	0	.000	0	2	0	0	0.3	1.000
1983		3	4	.429	2.65	53	0	0	71.1	52	20	67	0	3	4	20	6	1	0	.167	5	11	0	1	0.3	1.000
1984		4	9	.308	3.35	57	0	0	75.1	74	36	65	0	4	9	14	10	0	0	.000	3	12	0	0	0.3	1.000
1985		3	7	.300	4.03	54	0	0	76	69	43	49	0	3	7	6	12	2	0	.167	3	5	1	0	0.2	.889
1986	2 teams HOU N (31G 1–3) CHI N (30G 2–4)																									
"	total	3	7	.300	4.37	61	0	0	80.1	74	30	70	0	3	7	3	6	1	0	.167	8	17	1	1	0.4	.962
1987	CHI N	3	3	.500	3.15	69	0	0	80	75	34	61	0	3	3	4	2	1	0	.500	2	16	1	2	0.3	.947
1988		2	3	.400	4.98	63	0	0	90.1	102	32	69	0	2	3	6	10	1	0	.100	3	12	0	0	0.2	1.000
1989	STL N	9	0	1.000	2.45	67	0	0	88.1	73	20	44	0	9	0	0	13	1	0	.077	6	13	0	0	0.3	1.000
1990		5	2	.714	4.56	62	0	0	81	92	31	49	0	5	2	3	4	1	0	.250	2	15	0	1	0.3	1.000
1992		0	0	—	1.64	9	0	0	11	9	3	8	0	0	0	0	1	1	0	1.000	1	3	0	0	0.4	1.000
1993	KC A	1	1	.500	6.89	11	0	0	15.2	21	6	5	0	1	1	0	0	0	0	—	0	3	0	0	0.3	1.000
12 yrs.		35	38	.479	3.83	514	6	0	699.2	673	269	515	0	33	36	56	72	9	0	.125	33	109	3	5	0.3	.979

Jerry DiPoto

DiPOTO, GERALD PETER III — BR TR 6′ 2″ 203 lbs.
B. May 24, 1968, Jersey City, N. J.

Year	Team	Lg	W	L	PCT	ERA	G	GS	CG	IP	H	BB	SO	ShO	Relief Pitching W	Relief Pitching L	Relief Pitching SV	Batting AB	Batting H	Batting HR	BA	PO	A	E	DP	TC/G	FA
1993	**CLE**	**A**	4	4	.500	2.40	46	0	0	56.1	57	30	41	0	4	4	11	0	0	0	—	4	10	2	1	0.3	.875
1994			0	0	—	8.04	7	0	0	15.2	26	10	9	0	0	0	0	0	0	0	—	0	1	0	0	0.1	1.000
1995	**NY**	**N**	4	6	.400	3.78	58	0	0	78.2	77	29	49	0	4	6	2	5	0	0	.000	4	16	3	1	0.4	.870
3 yrs.			8	10	.444	3.70	111	0	0	150.2	160	69	99	0	8	10	13	5	0	0	.000	8	27	5	2	0.4	.875

George Disch

DISCH, GEORGE CHARLES — 5′11″
B. Mar. 15, 1879, Lincoln, Mo. D. Aug. 25, 1950, Rapid City, S. D.

Year	Team	Lg	W	L	PCT	ERA	G	GS	CG	IP	H	BB	SO	ShO	Relief Pitching W	Relief Pitching L	Relief Pitching SV	Batting AB	Batting H	Batting HR	BA	PO	A	E	DP	TC/G	FA
1905	**DET**	**A**	0	2	.000	2.64	8	3	1	47.2	43	8	14	0	0	1	0	19	2	0	.105	2	14	0	2	2.0	1.000

Glenn Dishman

DISHMAN, GLENELG EDWARD — BR TL 6′ 1″ 195 lbs.
B. Nov. 5, 1970, Baltimore, Md.

Year	Team	Lg	W	L	PCT	ERA	G	GS	CG	IP	H	BB	SO	ShO	Relief Pitching W	Relief Pitching L	Relief Pitching SV	Batting AB	Batting H	Batting HR	BA	PO	A	E	DP	TC/G	FA
1995	**SD**	**N**	4	8	.333	5.01	19	16	0	97	104	34	43	0	0	0	0	30	6	0	.200	4	13	0	1	0.9	1.000

Alec Distaso

DISTASO, ALEC JOHN — BR TR 6′ 2″ 200 lbs.
B. Dec. 23, 1948, Los Angeles, Calif.

Year	Team	Lg	W	L	PCT	ERA	G	GS	CG	IP	H	BB	SO	ShO	Relief Pitching W	Relief Pitching L	Relief Pitching SV	Batting AB	Batting H	Batting HR	BA	PO	A	E	DP	TC/G	FA
1969	**CHI**	**N**	0	0	—	3.60	2	0	0	5	6	1	1	0	0	0	0	0	0	0	—	0	2	0	0	1.0	1.000

Art Ditmar

DITMAR, ARTHUR JOHN — BR TR 6′ 2″ 185 lbs.
B. Apr. 3, 1929, Winthrop, Mass.

Year	Team	Lg	W	L	PCT	ERA	G	GS	CG	IP	H	BB	SO	ShO	Relief Pitching W	Relief Pitching L	Relief Pitching SV	Batting AB	Batting H	Batting HR	BA	PO	A	E	DP	TC/G	FA
1954	**PHI**	**A**	1	4	.200	6.41	14	5	0	39.1	50	36	14	0	0	2	0	8	1	0	.125	4	5	1	1	0.7	.900
1955	**KC**	**A**	12	12	.500	5.03	35	22	7	175.1	180	86	79	1	3	2	1	62	13	0	.210	15	29	1	3	1.3	.978
1956			12	**22**	.353	4.42	44	34	14	254.1	254	108	126	2	3	1	1	91	13	1	.143	20	33	2	3	1.3	.964
1957	**NY**	**A**	8	3	.727	3.25	46	11	0	127.1	128	35	64	0	6	1	6	35	7	0	.200	8	19	4	0	0.7	.871
1958			9	8	.529	3.42	38	13	4	139.2	124	38	52	0	4	4	4	44	11	0	.250	6	15	0	1	0.6	1.000
1959			13	9	.591	2.90	38	25	7	202	156	52	96	1	1	1	1	76	15	1	.197	21	25	3	2	1.3	.939
1960			15	9	.625	3.06	34	28	8	200	195	56	65	1	1	2	0	69	11	0	.159	18	24	1	3	1.3	.977
1961	**2 teams**	**NY A**	(12G 2–3)	**KC A**	(20G 0–5)																						
″	**total**		2	8	.200	5.15	32	13	1	108.1	119	37	43	0	0	2	1	31	3	0	.097	9	19	1	0	0.9	.966
1962	**KC**	**A**	0	2	.000	6.65	6	5	0	21.2	31	13	13	0	0	0	0	6	1	0	.167	2	3	0	0	0.8	1.000
9 yrs.			72	77	.483	3.98	287	156	41	1268	1237	461	552	5	18	15	14	422	75	2	.178	103	172	13	13	1.0	.955
WORLD SERIES																											
1957	**NY**	**A**	0	0	—	0.00	2	0	0	6	2	0	2	0	0	0	0	1	0	0	.000	0	0	0	0	0.0	.000
1958			0	0	—	0.00	1	0	0	3.2	2	0	2	0	0	0	0	1	0	0	.000	1	0	1	0	2.0	.500
1960			0	2	.000	21.60	2	2	0	1.2	6	1	0	0	0	0	0	0	0	0	—	0	0	0	0	0.0	.000
3 yrs.			0	2	.000	3.18	5	2	0	11.1	10	1	4	0	0	0	0	2	0	0	.000	1	0	1	0	0.4	.500

Ken Dixon

DIXON, KENNETH JOHN — BB TR 5′10″ 175 lbs.
B. Oct. 17, 1960, Monroe, Va.

Year	Team	Lg	W	L	PCT	ERA	G	GS	CG	IP	H	BB	SO	ShO	Relief Pitching W	Relief Pitching L	Relief Pitching SV	Batting AB	Batting H	Batting HR	BA	PO	A	E	DP	TC/G	FA
1984	**BAL**	**A**	0	1	.000	4.15	2	2	0	13	14	4	8	0	0	0	0	0	0	0	—	2	2	0	0	2.0	1.000
1985			8	4	.667	3.67	34	18	3	162	144	64	108	1	0	1	1	0	0	0	—	13	17	4	0	0.9	.882
1986			11	13	.458	4.58	35	33	2	202.1	194	83	170	0	0	0	0	0	0	0	—	12	21	2	1	1.0	.943
1987			7	10	.412	6.43	34	15	0	105	128	27	91	0	2	4	5	0	0	0	—	17	7	1	1	0.7	.960
4 yrs.			26	28	.481	4.66	105	68	5	482.1	480	178	377	1	2	5	6	0	0	0		44	47	7	2	0.9	.929

Sonny Dixon

DIXON, JOHN CRAIG — BB TR 6′ 2½″ 205 lbs.
B. Nov. 5, 1924, Charlotte, N. C.

Year	Team	Lg	W	L	PCT	ERA	G	GS	CG	IP	H	BB	SO	ShO	Relief Pitching W	Relief Pitching L	Relief Pitching SV	Batting AB	Batting H	Batting HR	BA	PO	A	E	DP	TC/G	FA
1953	**WAS**	**A**	5	8	.385	3.75	43	6	3	120	123	31	40	0	2	5	3	26	4	0	.154	6	31	0	0	0.9	1.000
1954	**2 teams**	**WAS A**	(16G 1–2)	**PHI A**	(38G 5–7)																						
″	**total**		6	9	.400	4.47	**54**	6	1	137	162	39	49	0	4	6	5	34	7	0	.206	11	39	1	1	0.9	.980
1955	**KC**	**A**	0	0	—	16.20	2	0	0	1.2	6	0	0	0	0	0	0	0	0	0	—	1	0	0	0	0.5	1.000
1956	**NY**	**A**	0	1	.000	2.08	3	0	0	4.1	5	5	1	0	0	1	1	1	0	0	.000	0	2	0	0	0.7	1.000
4 yrs.			11	18	.379	4.17	102	12	4	263	296	75	90	0	6	12	9	61	11	0	.180	18	72	1	1	0.9	.989

Steve Dixon

DIXON, STEVEN ROSS — BL TL 6′ 190 lbs.
B. Aug. 3, 1969, Cincinnati, Ohio.

Year	Team	Lg	W	L	PCT	ERA	G	GS	CG	IP	H	BB	SO	ShO	Relief Pitching W	Relief Pitching L	Relief Pitching SV	Batting AB	Batting H	Batting HR	BA	PO	A	E	DP	TC/G	FA
1993	**STL**	**N**	0	0	—	33.75	4	0	0	2.2	7	5	2	0	0	0	0	0	0	0	—	0	1	0	0	0.3	1.000
1994			0	0	—	23.14	2	0	0	2.1	3	8	1	0	0	0	0	0	0	0	—	0	0	0	0	0.0	.000
2 yrs.			0	0		28.80	6	0	0	5	10	13	3	0	0	0	0	0	0	0		0	1	0	0	0.2	1.000

Tom Dixon

DIXON, THOMAS EARL — BR TR 5′11″ 175 lbs.
B. Apr. 23, 1955, Orlando, Fla.

Year	Team	Lg	W	L	PCT	ERA	G	GS	CG	IP	H	BB	SO	ShO	Relief Pitching W	Relief Pitching L	Relief Pitching SV	Batting AB	Batting H	Batting HR	BA	PO	A	E	DP	TC/G	FA
1977	**HOU**	**N**	1	0	1.000	3.30	9	4	1	30	40	7	15	0	0	0	0	7	0	0	.000	2	6	2	0	1.1	.800
1978			7	11	.389	3.99	30	19	3	140	140	40	66	2	2	0	1	40	4	0	.100	12	16	1	1	1.0	.966
1979			1	2	.333	6.58	19	1	0	26	39	15	9	0	1	2	0	1	1	0	1.000	3	6	0	1	0.5	1.000
1983	**MON**	**N**	0	1	.000	9.82	4	0	0	3.2	6	1	4	0	0	1	0	0	0	0	—	0	0	0	0	0.0	.000
4 yrs.			9	14	.391	4.33	62	24	4	199.2	225	63	94	2	3	3	1	48	5	0	.104	17	28	3	2	0.8	.938

Bill Doak

DOAK, WILLIAM LEOPOLD (Spittin' Bill) — BR TR 6′½″ 165 lbs.
B. Jan. 28, 1891, Pittsburgh, Pa. D. Nov. 26, 1954, Bradenton, Fla.

Year	Team	Lg	W	L	PCT	ERA	G	GS	CG	IP	H	BB	SO	ShO	Relief Pitching W	Relief Pitching L	Relief Pitching SV	Batting AB	Batting H	Batting HR	BA	PO	A	E	DP	TC/G	FA
1912	**CIN**	**N**	0	0	—	4.50	1	1	0	2	4	1	0	0	0	0	0	0	0	0	—	0	0	0	0	0.0	.000
1913	**STL**	**N**	2	8	.200	3.10	15	12	5	93	79	39	51	1	0	0	1	31	1	0	.032	7	26	2	1	2.3	.943
1914			20	6	.769	**1.72**	36	33	16	256	193	87	118	7	1	0	0	85	10	0	.118	9	93	8	1	3.1	.927
1915			16	18	.471	2.64	38	36	19	276	263	85	124	3	0	0	1	86	15	0	.174	10	108	3	3	3.2	.975
1916			12	8	.600	2.63	29	26	11	192	177	55	82	3	0	0	0	62	8	0	.129	6	64	4	1	2.6	.946
1917			16	20	.444	3.10	44	37	16	281.1	257	85	111	3	2	1	2	95	12	0	.126	10	103	3	2	2.6	.974
1918			9	15	.375	2.43	31	23	16	211	191	60	74	1	0	2	1	66	12	0	.182	7	88	2	0	3.1	.979
1919			13	14	.481	3.11	31	29	13	202.2	182	55	69	3	1	0	0	64	7	0	.109	11	78	3	2	3.0	.967
1920			20	12	.625	2.53	39	37	20	270	256	80	90	5	0	0	1	88	10	0	.114	17	71	3	5	2.3	.967
1921			15	6	**.714**	**2.59**	32	29	13	208.2	224	37	83	1	1	0	1	70	10	0	.143	7	62	4	4	2.3	.945
1922			11	13	.458	5.54	37	29	8	180.1	222	69	73	2	1	1	2	54	7	0	.130	3	43	2	2	1.3	.958
1923			8	13	.381	3.26	30	26	7	185	199	69	53	3	0	3	0	67	3	0	.045	1	62	3	3	2.2	.955
1924	**2 teams**	**STL N**	(11G 2–1)	**BKN N**	(21G 11–5)																						
″	**total**		13	6	.684	3.10	32	17	8	171.1	155	49	39	2	4	2	3	61	11	1	.180	7	57	2	6	2.1	.970

Bill Doak *continued*

Year	Team		W	L	PCT	ERA	G	GS	CG	IP	H	BB	SO	ShO	Relief Pitching W	Relief Pitching L	Relief Pitching SV	Batting AB	Batting H	Batting HR	BA	PO	A	E	DP	TC/G	FA
1927	**BKN**	**N**	11	8	.579	3.48	27	20	6	145	153	40	32	1	3	0	0	47	6	0	.128	5	40	1	1	1.7	.978
1928			3	8	.273	3.26	28	12	4	99.1	104	35	12	1	1	2	3	27	3	0	.111	3	38	2	2	1.5	.953
1929	**STL**	**N**	1	2	.333	12.00	3	2	0	9	17	5	3	0	0	1	0	2	0	0	.000	0	1	1	0	0.7	.500
16 yrs.			170	157	.520	2.98	453	369	162	2782.2	2676	851	1014	36	14	12	15	905	115	1	.127	103	934	43	33	2.4	.960

Walt Doane

DOANE, WALTER RUDOLPH BL TR 6' 165 lbs.
B. Mar. 12, 1887, Bellevue, Ida. D. Oct. 19, 1935, West Brandywine, Pa.

Year	Team		W	L	PCT	ERA	G	GS	CG	IP	H	BB	SO	ShO	Relief W	Relief L	Relief SV	AB	H	HR	BA	PO	A	E	DP	TC/G	FA
1909	**CLE**	**A**	0	1	.000	5.40	1	1	0	5	10	1	2	0	0	0	0	9	1	0	.111	6	2	2	0	3.3	.800
1910			0	0	—	5.60	6	0	0	17.2	31	8	7	0	0	0	0	7	2	0	.286	1	2	1	0	0.7	.750
2 yrs.			0	1	.000	5.56	7	1	0	22.2	41	9	9	0	0	0	0	16	3	0	.188	7	4	3	0	1.6	.786

John Dobb

DOBB, JOHN KENNETH (Lefty) BR TL 6' 2" 180 lbs.
B. Nov. 15, 1901, Muskegon, Mich. D. July 13, 1991, Muskegon, Mich.

Year	Team		W	L	PCT	ERA	G	GS	CG	IP	H	BB	SO	ShO	Relief W	Relief L	Relief SV	AB	H	HR	BA	PO	A	E	DP	TC/G	FA
1924	**CHI**	**A**	0	0	—	9.00	2	0	0	2	4	1	2	0	0	0	0	0	0	0	—	0	0	0	0	0.0	.000

Ray Dobens

DOBENS, RAYMOND JOSEPH (Lefty) BL TL 5' 8" 175 lbs.
B. July 28, 1906, Nashua, N. H. D. Apr. 21, 1980, Stuart, Fla.

Year	Team		W	L	PCT	ERA	G	GS	CG	IP	H	BB	SO	ShO	Relief W	Relief L	Relief SV	AB	H	HR	BA	PO	A	E	DP	TC/G	FA
1929	**BOS**	**A**	0	0	—	3.81	11	2	0	28.1	32	9	4	0	0	0	0	8	3	0	.375	2	2	1	0	0.5	.800

Jess Dobernic

DOBERNIC, ANDREW JOSEPH BR TR 5'10" 170 lbs.
B. Nov. 20, 1917, Mt. Olive, Ill.

Year	Team		W	L	PCT	ERA	G	GS	CG	IP	H	BB	SO	ShO	Relief W	Relief L	Relief SV	AB	H	HR	BA	PO	A	E	DP	TC/G	FA
1939	**CHI**	**A**	0	1	.000	13.50	4	0	0	3.1	3	6	1	0	0	1	0	1	0	0	.000	0	1	0	0	0.3	1.000
1948	**CHI**	**N**	7	2	.778	3.15	54	0	0	85.2	67	40	48	0	7	2	1	10	2	0	.200	6	6	2	0	0.3	.857
1949	**2 teams**	**CHI N** (4G 0–0)		**CIN N** (14G 0–0)																							
"	**total**		0	0		11.57	18	0	0	23.1	37	20	6	0	0	0	0	2	0	0	.000	2	3	0	0	0.3	1.000
3 yrs.			7	3	.700	5.21	76	0	0	112.1	107	66	55	0	7	3	1	13	2	0	.154	8	10	2	0	0.3	.900

Chuck Dobson

DOBSON, CHARLES THOMAS BR TR 6' 4" 200 lbs.
B. Jan. 10, 1944, Kansas City, Mo.

Year	Team		W	L	PCT	ERA	G	GS	CG	IP	H	BB	SO	ShO	Relief W	Relief L	Relief SV	AB	H	HR	BA	PO	A	E	DP	TC/G	FA
1966	**KC**	**A**	4	6	.400	4.09	14	14	1	83.2	71	50	61	0	0	0	0	26	3	0	.115	6	18	0	2	1.7	1.000
1967			10	10	.500	3.69	32	29	4	197.2	172	75	110	1	0	0	0	72	13	0	.181	8	33	0	2	1.3	1.000
1968	**OAK**	**A**	12	14	.462	3.00	35	34	11	225.1	197	80	168	3	0	0	0	75	15	0	.200	11	40	1	3	1.5	.981
1969			15	13	.536	3.86	35	35	11	235.1	244	80	137	1	0	0	0	79	8	0	.101	7	29	2	4	1.1	.947
1970			16	15	.516	3.74	41	**40**	13	267	230	92	149	**5**	0	1	0	93	11	0	.118	19	28	1	3	1.2	.979
1971			15	5	.750	3.81	30	30	7	189	185	71	100	1	0	0	0	66	13	0	.197	15	30	0	2	1.5	1.000
1973			0	1	.000	7.71	1	1	0	2.1	6	2	3	0	0	0	0	0	0	0	—	0	1	0	0	1.0	1.000
1974	**CAL**	**A**	2	3	.400	5.70	5	5	2	30	39	13	16	0	0	0	0	0	0	0	—	4	3	1	0	1.6	.875
1975			0	2	.000	6.75	9	2	0	28	30	13	14	0	0	1	0	0	0	0	—	0	2	0	0	0.2	1.000
9 yrs.			74	69	.517	3.78	202	190	49	1258.1	1174	476	758	11	0	2	0	411	63	0	.153	70	184	5	16	1.3	.981

Joe Dobson

DOBSON, JOSEPH GORDON (Burrhead) BR TR 6' 2" 197 lbs.
B. Jan. 20, 1917, Durant, Okla. D. June 23, 1994, Jacksonville, Fla.

Year	Team		W	L	PCT	ERA	G	GS	CG	IP	H	BB	SO	ShO	Relief W	Relief L	Relief SV	AB	H	HR	BA	PO	A	E	DP	TC/G	FA
1939	**CLE**	**A**	2	3	.400	5.88	35	3	0	78	87	51	27	0	2	1	1	18	1	0	.056	3	16	0	0	0.5	1.000
1940			3	7	.300	4.95	40	7	2	100	101	48	57	1	2	2	3	24	3	0	.125	6	15	0	1	0.5	1.000
1941	**BOS**	**A**	12	5	.706	4.49	27	18	7	134.1	136	67	69	1	2	1	0	47	7	1	.149	10	13	0	0	0.9	1.000
1942			11	9	.550	3.30	30	23	10	182.2	155	68	72	3	1	1	0	69	10	0	.145	17	42	0	2	2.0	1.000
1943			7	11	.389	3.12	25	20	9	164.1	144	57	63	3	0	1	0	52	5	0	.096	9	22	1	2	1.3	.969
1946			13	7	.650	3.24	32	24	9	166.2	148	68	91	1	2	0	0	50	5	0	.100	18	33	1	1	1.6	.981
1947			18	8	.692	2.95	33	31	15	228.2	203	73	110	1	0	0	1	77	16	0	.208	13	25	0	1	1.2	1.000
1948			16	10	.615	3.56	38	32	16	245.1	237	92	116	5	0	2	2	84	17	1	.202	10	36	2	3	1.3	.958
1949			14	12	.538	3.85	33	27	12	212.2	219	97	87	2	2	1	2	68	10	0	.147	12	30	0	3	1.3	1.000
1950			15	10	.600	4.18	39	27	12	206.2	217	81	81	1	2	0	4	70	15	0	.214	8	44	3	4	1.4	.945
1951	**CHI**	**A**	7	6	.538	3.62	28	21	6	146.2	136	51	67	0	0	0	3	46	3	0	.065	6	25	1	5	1.1	.969
1952			14	10	.583	2.51	29	25	11	200.2	164	60	101	3	1	1	1	63	12	0	.190	7	26	1	2	1.2	.971
1953			5	5	.500	3.67	23	15	3	100.2	96	37	50	1	0	0	1	29	2	0	.069	6	14	2	0	1.0	.909
1954	**BOS**	**A**	0	0	—	6.75	2	0	0	2.2	5	1	1	0	0	0	0	0	0	0	—	1	0	0	0	0.5	1.000
14 yrs.			137	103	.571	3.62	414	273	112	2170	2048	851	992	22	14	10	18	697	106	2	.152	126	341	11	24	1.2	.977
WORLD SERIES																											
1946	**BOS**	**A**	1	0	1.000	0.00	3	1	1	12.2	4	3	10	0	0	0	0	3	0	0	.000	0	2	0	0	0.7	1.000

Pat Dobson

DOBSON, PATRICK EDWARD BR TR 6' 3" 190 lbs.
B. Feb. 12, 1942, Depew, N. Y.

Year	Team		W	L	PCT	ERA	G	GS	CG	IP	H	BB	SO	ShO	Relief W	Relief L	Relief SV	AB	H	HR	BA	PO	A	E	DP	TC/G	FA
1967	**DET**	**A**	1	2	.333	2.92	28	1	0	49.1	38	27	34	0	1	1	0	5	0	0	.000	4	4	0	0	0.3	1.000
1968			5	8	.385	2.66	47	10	2	125	89	48	93	1	3	3	7	28	4	0	.143	12	22	1	0	0.7	.971
1969			5	10	.333	3.60	49	9	1	105	100	39	64	0	3	6	9	22	2	0	.091	8	16	1	1	0.5	.960
1970	**SD**	**N**	14	15	.483	3.76	40	34	8	251	257	78	185	1	0	0	1	71	10	0	.141	17	31	0	2	1.2	1.000
1971	**BAL**	**A**	20	8	.714	2.90	38	37	18	282	248	63	187	4	0	0	1	91	10	0	.110	11	42	2	1	1.4	.964
1972			16	**18**	.471	2.65	38	36	13	268.1	220	69	161	3	0	0	0	85	12	0	.141	15	33	2	2	1.3	.960
1973	**2 teams**	**ATL N** (12G 3–7)		**NY A** (22G 9–8)																							
"	**total**		12	15	.444	4.40	34	31	7	200.1	223	53	93	2	2	0	0	15	1	0	.067	16	32	4	1	1.5	.923
1974	**NY**	**A**	19	15	.559	3.07	39	39	12	281	282	75	157	2	0	0	0	0	0	0	—	22	32	3	4	1.5	.947
1975			11	14	.440	4.07	33	30	7	207.2	205	83	129	1	0	0	0	0	0	0	—	14	27	1	0	1.3	.976
1976	**CLE**	**A**	16	12	.571	3.48	35	35	6	217	226	65	117	0	0	0	0	0	0	0	—	14	28	3	3	1.3	.933
1977			3	12	.200	6.16	33	17	0	133	155	65	81	0	1	2	1	0	0	0	—	9	22	2	0	1.0	.939
11 yrs.			122	129	.486	3.54	414	279	74	2119.2	2043	665	1301	14	10	12	19	317	39	0	.123	142	289	19	14	1.1	.958
WORLD SERIES																											
1968	**DET**	**A**	0	0	—	3.86	3	0	0	4.2	5	1	0	0	0	0	0	0	0	0	—	1	0	0	0	0.3	1.000
1971	**BAL**	**A**	0	0	—	4.05	3	1	0	6.2	13	4	6	0	0	0	0	2	0	0	.000	0	3	0	0	1.0	1.000
2 yrs.			0	0		3.97	6	1	0	11.1	18	5	6	0	0	0	0	2	0	0	.000	1	3	0	0	0.7	1.000

George Dockins

DOCKINS, GEORGE WOODROW (Lefty) BL TL 6′ 175 lbs.
B. May 5, 1917, Clyde, Kans.

Year	Team	Lg	W	L	PCT	ERA	G	GS	CG	IP	H	BB	SO	ShO	Relief Pitching W	Relief Pitching L	Relief Pitching SV	Batting AB	Batting H	Batting HR	BA	PO	A	E	DP	TC/G	FA
1945	STL	N	8	6	.571	3.21	31	12	5	126.1	132	38	33	2	3	4	0	34	6	0	.176	5	24	1	0	1.0	.967
1947	BKN	N	0	0	—	11.81	4	0	0	5.1	10	2	1	0	0	0	0	1	0	0	.000	0	2	0	0	0.5	1.000
2 yrs.			8	6	.571	3.55	35	12	5	131.2	142	40	34	2	3	4	0	35	6	0	.171	5	26	1	0	0.9	.969

Sam Dodge

DODGE, SAMUEL EDWARD BR TR 6′ 1″ 170 lbs.
B. Dec. 9, 1899, Neath, Pa. D. Apr. 5, 1966, Utica, N. Y.

Year	Team	Lg	W	L	PCT	ERA	G	GS	CG	IP	H	BB	SO	ShO	Relief Pitching W	Relief Pitching L	Relief Pitching SV	Batting AB	Batting H	Batting HR	BA	PO	A	E	DP	TC/G	FA
1921	BOS	A	0	0	—	9.00	1	0	0	1	1	1	0	0	0	0	0	0	0	0	—	0	0	0	0	0.0	.000
1922			0	0	—	4.50	3	0	0	6	11	3	3	0	0	0	0	2	0	0	.000	0	3	0	0	1.0	1.000
2 yrs.			0	0		5.14	4	0	0	7	12	4	3	0	0	0	0	2	0	0	.000	0	3	0	0	0.8	1.000

Al Doe

DOE, ALFRED GEORGE (Count) BR TR 5′10″ 165 lbs.
B. Apr. 18, 1864, Gloucester, Mass. D. Oct. 4, 1938, Quincy, Mass.

Year	Team	Lg	W	L	PCT	ERA	G	GS	CG	IP	H	BB	SO	ShO	Relief Pitching W	Relief Pitching L	Relief Pitching SV	Batting AB	Batting H	Batting HR	BA	PO	A	E	DP	TC/G	FA
1890	2 teams BUF P (1G 0–1) PIT P (1G 0–0)																										
″	total		0	1	.000	9.00	2	1	1	10	14	9	4	0	0	0	0	4	1	0	.250	0	2	0	0	1.0	1.000

Ed Doheny

DOHENY, EDWIN RICHARD BL TL 5′10½″ 165 lbs.
B. Nov. 24, 1873, Northfield, Vt. D. Dec. 29, 1916, Worcester, Mass.

Year	Team	Lg	W	L	PCT	ERA	G	GS	CG	IP	H	BB	SO	ShO	Relief Pitching W	Relief Pitching L	Relief Pitching SV	Batting AB	Batting H	Batting HR	BA	PO	A	E	DP	TC/G	FA
1895	NY	N	0	3	.000	6.66	3	3	3	25.2	37	19	9	0	0	0	0	10	1	0	.100	2	4	3	1	3.0	.667
1896			6	7	.462	4.49	17	15	9	108.1	112	59	39	0	0	0	0	40	6	0	.150	5	23	5	2	1.9	.848
1897			4	4	.500	2.12	10	10	10	85	69	45	37	0	0	0	0	35	7	0	.200	4	31	4	3	3.9	.897
1898			7	19	.269	3.68	28	27	23	213	238	101	96	0	0	1	0	86	14	2	.163	14	62	10	2	3.1	.884
1899			14	17	.452	4.51	35	33	30	265.1	282	156	115	1	0	0	0	112	27	0	.241	15	87	16	1	3.4	.864
1900			4	14	.222	5.45	20	18	12	133.2	148	96	44	0	1	0	0	54	12	0	.222	4	43	10	1	2.8	.825
1901	2 teams NY N (10G 2–5) PIT N (11G 6–2)																										
″	total		8	7	.533	3.23	21	16	12	150.2	156	39	64	1	0	1	0	55	13	0	.236	2	37	8	0	2.2	.830
1902	PIT	N	16	4	.800	2.53	22	21	19	188.1	161	61	88	2	0	0	0	77	12	1	.156	9	43	5	1	2.6	.912
1903			16	8	.667	3.19	27	25	22	222.2	209	89	75	2	0	0	2	91	19	0	.209	17	86	10	0	4.2	.912
9 yrs.			75	83	.475	3.75	183	168	140	1392.2	1412	665	567	6	1	2	2	560	111	3	.198	72	416	71	11	3.1	.873

John Doherty

DOHERTY, JOHN HAROLD BR TR 6′ 4″ 190 lbs.
B. June 11, 1967, Bronx, N. Y.

Year	Team	Lg	W	L	PCT	ERA	G	GS	CG	IP	H	BB	SO	ShO	Relief Pitching W	Relief Pitching L	Relief Pitching SV	Batting AB	Batting H	Batting HR	BA	PO	A	E	DP	TC/G	FA
1992	DET	A	7	4	.636	3.88	47	11	0	116	131	25	37	0	2	2	3	0	0	0	—	10	19	1	4	0.6	.967
1993			14	11	.560	4.44	32	31	3	184.2	205	48	63	2	0	0	0	0	0	0	—	14	20	5	1	1.2	.872
1994			6	7	.462	6.48	18	17	2	101.1	139	26	28	0	0	0	0	0	0	0	—	6	25	0	4	1.7	1.000
1995			5	9	.357	5.10	48	2	0	113	130	37	46	0	5	**7**	6	0	0	0	—	12	17	0	1	0.6	1.000
4 yrs.			32	31	.508	4.86	145	61	5	515	605	136	174	2	7	9	9	0	0	0		42	81	6	10	0.9	.953

Cozy Dolan

DOLAN, PATRICK HENRY BL TL 5′10″ 160 lbs.
B. Dec. 3, 1872, Cambridge, Mass. D. Mar. 29, 1907, Louisville, Ky.

Year	Team	Lg	W	L	PCT	ERA	G	GS	CG	IP	H	BB	SO	ShO	Relief Pitching W	Relief Pitching L	Relief Pitching SV	Batting AB	Batting H	Batting HR	BA	PO	A	E	DP	TC/G	FA
1895	BOS	N	11	7	.611	4.27	25	21	18	198.1	215	67	47	3	0	0	1	83	20	0	.241	14	62	5	2	3.1	.938
1896			1	4	.200	4.83	6	5	3	41	55	27	14	0	0	0	0	14	2	0	.143	5	8	4	0	2.8	.765
1905			0	1	.000	9.00	2	0	0	4	7	1	1	0	0	1	0	510	137	3	.269	18	1	4	0	1.8	.826
1906			0	1	.000	4.50	2	0	0	12	12	6	7	0	0	1	0	549	136	0	.248	221	43	22	5	1.9	.923
4 yrs.			12	13	.480	4.44	35	26	21	255.1	289	101	69	3	0	2	1	*				1734	226	122	42	2.5	.941

John Dolan

DOLAN, JOHN TR 5′10″ 170 lbs.
B. Sept. 12, 1867, Newport, Ky. D. May 8, 1948, Springfield, Ohio.

Year	Team	Lg	W	L	PCT	ERA	G	GS	CG	IP	H	BB	SO	ShO	Relief Pitching W	Relief Pitching L	Relief Pitching SV	Batting AB	Batting H	Batting HR	BA	PO	A	E	DP	TC/G	FA
1890	CIN	N	1	1	.500	4.50	2	2	2	18	17	10	9	0	0	0	0	8	1	0	.125	0	2	0	0	1.0	1.000
1891	COL	AA	12	11	.522	4.16	27	24	19	203.1	216	84	68	0	0	0	0	78	7	1	.090	8	40	6	1	1.9	.889
1892	WAS	N	2	2	.500	4.38	5	4	3	37	39	15	8	0	0	1	0	13	3	0	.231	1	6	0	0	1.4	1.000
1893	STL	N	0	2	.000	4.15	3	1	1	17.1	26	7	1	0	0	0	1	7	1	1	.143	4	1	1	0	2.0	.833
1895	CHI	N	0	1	.000	6.55	2	2	1	11	16	6	1	0	0	0	0	3	0	0	.000	1	4	0	0	2.5	1.000
5 yrs.			15	17	.469	4.30	39	33	26	286.2	314	122	87	0	0	1	1	109	12	2	.110	14	53	7	1	1.9	.905

Tom Dolan

DOLAN, THOMAS J. BR TR
B. Jan. 10, 1859, New York, N. Y. D. Jan. 16, 1913, St. Louis, Mo.

Year	Team	Lg	W	L	PCT	ERA	G	GS	CG	IP	H	BB	SO	ShO	Relief Pitching W	Relief Pitching L	Relief Pitching SV	Batting AB	Batting H	Batting HR	BA	PO	A	E	DP	TC/G	FA
1883	STL	AA	0	0	—	4.50	1	0	0	4	4	0	0	0	0	0	0	*				6	2	0	0	8.0	1.000

Art Doll

DOLL, ARTHUR JAMES (Moose) BR TR 6′ 1″ 190 lbs.
B. May 7, 1913, Chicago, Ill. D. Apr. 28, 1978, Calumet City, Ill.

Year	Team	Lg	W	L	PCT	ERA	G	GS	CG	IP	H	BB	SO	ShO	Relief Pitching W	Relief Pitching L	Relief Pitching SV	Batting AB	Batting H	Batting HR	BA	PO	A	E	DP	TC/G	FA
1936	BOS	N	0	1	.000	3.38	1	1	0	8	11	2	2	0	0	0	0	2	0	0	.000	11	2	2	0	5.0	.867
1938			0	0	—	2.25	3	0	0	4	4	3	1	0	0	0	0	1	1	0	1.000	0	2	0	0	0.7	1.000
2 yrs.			0	1	.000	3.00	4	1	0	12	15	5	3	0	0	0	0	13	2	0	.154	11	5	2	1	2.6	.889

Deacon Donahue

DONAHUE, JOHN STEPHEN MICHAEL BR TR 6′ 175 lbs.
B. June 23, 1920, Chicago, Ill.

Year	Team	Lg	W	L	PCT	ERA	G	GS	CG	IP	H	BB	SO	ShO	Relief Pitching W	Relief Pitching L	Relief Pitching SV	Batting AB	Batting H	Batting HR	BA	PO	A	E	DP	TC/G	FA
1943	PHI	N	0	0	—	4.50	2	0	0	4	4	1	1	0	0	0	0	0	0	0	—	0	1	0	0	0.5	1.000
1944			0	2	.000	7.71	6	0	0	9.1	18	2	2	0	0	2	0	1	0	0	.000	0	3	0	1	0.5	1.000
2 yrs.			0	2	.000	6.75	8	0	0	13.1	22	3	3	0	0	2	0	1	0	0	.000	0	4	0	1	0.5	1.000

Red Donahue

DONAHUE, FRANCIS ROSTELL BR TR 6′ 187 lbs.
B. Jan. 23, 1873, Waterbury, Conn. D. Aug. 25, 1913, Philadelphia, Pa.

Year	Team	Lg	W	L	PCT	ERA	G	GS	CG	IP	H	BB	SO	ShO	Relief Pitching W	Relief Pitching L	Relief Pitching SV	Batting AB	Batting H	Batting HR	BA	PO	A	E	DP	TC/G	FA
1893	NY	N	0	0	—	9.00	2	0	0	5	8	3	1	0	0	0	1	2	0	0	.000	0	1	0	0	0.5	1.000
1895	STL	N	0	1	.000	6.75	1	1	1	8	9	3	2	0	0	0	0	3	0	0	.000	0	2	0	0	2.0	1.000
1896			7	24	.226	5.80	32	32	28	267	376	98	70	0	0	0	0	107	17	0	.159	14	59	7	4	2.4	.913
1897			10	**35**[1]	.222	6.13	**46**	**42**	**38**	348	**484**	106	64	1	1	2	1	155	33	1	.213	33	97	4	1	2.7	.970
1898	PHI	N	17	17	.500	3.55	35	35	33	284.1	327	80	57	1	0	0	0	112	16	0	.143	12	87	9	4	3.1	.917
1899			21	8	.724	3.39	35	31	27	279	292	63	51	4	1	1	0	111	20	0	.180	10	82	4	0	2.7	.958
1900			15	10	.600	3.60	32	24	21	240	299	50	41	2	3	1	0	90	20	0	.222	9	58	2	0	2.2	.971
1901			21	13	.618	2.60	35	33	34	304.1	307	60	89	1	1	0	0	117	11	0	.094	8	75	4	0	2.5	.954
1902	STL	A	22	11	.667	2.76	35	34	33	316.1	322	65	63	2	1	0	0	118	11	0	.093	15	130	8	3	4.4	.948
1903	2 teams STL A (16G 8–7) CLE A (16G 7–9)																										
″	total		15	16	.484	2.59	32	30	28	267.2	287	34	96	4	1	1	0	104	16	0	.154	11	93	9	2	3.5	.920

Red Donahue *continued*

Year	Team	Lg	W	L	PCT	ERA	G	GS	CG	IP	H	BB	SO	ShO	Relief Pitching W	Relief Pitching L	Relief Pitching SV	Batting AB	Batting H	Batting HR	BA	PO	A	E	DP	TC/G	FA
1904	CLE	A	19	14	.576	2.40	35	32	30	277	281	49	127	6	1	1	0	101	17	0	.168	6	101	2	2	3.1	.982
1905			6	12	.333	3.40	20	18	13	137.2	132	25	45	1	0	0	0	53	4	0	.075	9	48	0	2	2.8	1.000
1906	DET	A	13	14	.481	2.73	28	28	26	241	260	54	82	3	0	0	0	81	10	0	.123	10	73	4	4	3.0	.954
13 yrs.			166	175	.487	3.61	368	340	312	2975.1	3384	690	788	25	9	6	2	1154	175	1	.152	137	906	53	22	2.9	.952

Atley Donald

DONALD, RICHARD ATLEY (Swampy) BL TR 6′ 1″ 186 lbs.
B. Aug. 19, 1910, Morton, Miss. D. Oct. 19, 1992, West Monroe, La.

Year	Team	Lg	W	L	PCT	ERA	G	GS	CG	IP	H	BB	SO	ShO	Relief Pitching W	Relief Pitching L	Relief Pitching SV	Batting AB	Batting H	Batting HR	BA	PO	A	E	DP	TC/G	FA
1938	NY	A	0	1	.000	5.25	2	2	0	12	7	14	6	0	0	0	0	6	1	0	.167	1	4	0	0	2.5	1.000
1939			13	3	.813	3.71	24	20	11	153	144	60	55	2	1	0	1	60	15	0	.250	3	22	0	2	1.0	1.000
1940			8	3	.727	3.03	24	11	6	118.2	113	59	60	1	2	0	0	41	6	0	.146	2	12	4	0	0.8	.778
1941			9	5	.643	3.57	22	20	10	159	141	69	71	0	0	0	0	62	5	0	.081	8	28	2	2	1.7	.947
1942			11	3	.786	3.11	20	19	10	147.2	133	45	53	1	0	0	0	61	9	0	.148	7	21	2	1	1.5	.933
1943			6	4	.600	4.60	22	15	2	119.1	134	38	57	0	2	0	0	47	6	0	.128	3	15	0	0	0.8	1.000
1944			13	10	.565	3.34	30	19	9	159	173	59	48	0	3	4	0	55	10	0	.182	4	24	0	4	0.9	1.000
1945			5	4	.556	2.97	9	9	6	63.2	62	25	19	2	0	0	0	24	5	1	.208	1	7	3	0	1.2	.727
8 yrs.			65	33	.663	3.52	153	115	54	932.1	907	369	369	6	8	4	1	356	57	1	.160	29	133	11	9	1.1	.936
WORLD SERIES																											
1941	NY	A	0	0	—	9.00	1	1	0	4	6	3	2	0	0	0	0	2	0	0	.000	0	1	0	0	1.0	1.000
1942			0	1	.000	6.00	1	0	0	3	3	2	1	0	0	1	0	2	0	0	.000	0	0	0	0	0.0	.000
2 yrs.			0	1	.000	7.71	2	1	0	7	9	5	3	0	0	1	0	4	0	0	.000	0	1	0	0	0.5	1.000

Ed Donalds

DONALDS, EDWARD ALEXANDER (Skipper) BR TR 5′11″ 180 lbs.
B. June 22, 1885, Bidwell, Ohio D. July 3, 1950, Columbus, Ohio.

Year	Team	Lg	W	L	PCT	ERA	G	GS	CG	IP	H	BB	SO	ShO	Relief Pitching W	Relief Pitching L	Relief Pitching SV	Batting AB	Batting H	Batting HR	BA	PO	A	E	DP	TC/G	FA
1912	CIN	N	1	0	1.000	4.50	1	0	0	4	7	0	1	0	1	0	0	1	0	0	.000	0	1	0	0	1.0	1.000

Mike Donlin

DONLIN, MICHAEL JOSEPH (Highlonesome) BL TL 5′ 9″ 170 lbs.
B. May 30, 1878, Peoria, Ill. D. Sept. 24, 1933, Hollywood, Calif.

Year	Team	Lg	W	L	PCT	ERA	G	GS	CG	IP	H	BB	SO	ShO	Relief Pitching W	Relief Pitching L	Relief Pitching SV	Batting AB	Batting H	Batting HR	BA	PO	A	E	DP	TC/G	FA
1899	STL	N	0	1	.000	7.63	3	1	0	15.1	15	14	6	0	0	0	0	266	86	6	.323	215	25	29	7	3.8	.892
1902	CIN	N	0	0	—	0.00	1	0	0	1	1	0	0	0	0	0	0	143	42	0	.294	308	11	21	14	5.0	.938
2 yrs.			0	1	.000	7.16	4	1	0	16.1	16	14	6	0	0	0	0	*				2416	165	176	60	2.8	.936

Blix Donnelly

DONNELLY, SYLVESTER URBAN BR TR 5′10″ 166 lbs.
B. Jan. 21, 1914, Olivia, Minn. D. June 20, 1976, Olivia, Minn.

Year	Team	Lg	W	L	PCT	ERA	G	GS	CG	IP	H	BB	SO	ShO	Relief Pitching W	Relief Pitching L	Relief Pitching SV	Batting AB	Batting H	Batting HR	BA	PO	A	E	DP	TC/G	FA
1944	STL	N	2	1	.667	2.12	27	4	2	76.1	61	34	45	1	0	1	2	16	1	0	.063	3	17	1	0	0.8	.952
1945			8	10	.444	3.52	31	23	9	166.1	157	87	76	4	0	1	2	54	7	0	.130	4	17	2	0	0.7	.913
1946	2 teams	STL N (13G 1–2) PHI N (12G 3–4)																									
″	total		4	6	.400	3.10	25	8	2	90	81	34	49	0	1	2	1	25	7	0	.280	3	11	0	0	0.6	1.000
1947	PHI	N	4	6	.400	2.98	38	10	5	120.2	113	46	31	1	0	3	5	32	2	0	.063	2	24	2	2	0.7	.929
1948			5	7	.417	3.69	26	19	8	131.2	125	49	46	1	0	0	2	45	10	0	.222	2	15	2	0	0.7	.895
1949			2	1	.667	5.06	23	10	1	78.1	84	40	36	0	1	0	0	23	4	0	.174	0	7	1	0	0.3	.875
1950			2	4	.333	4.29	14	1	0	21	30	10	10	0	2	3	0	5	1	0	.200	0	6	0	0	0.4	1.000
1951	BOS	N	0	1	.000	7.36	6	0	0	7.1	8	6	3	0	0	1	0	1	0	0	.000	1	2	0	0	0.5	1.000
8 yrs.			27	36	.429	3.49	190	75	27	691.2	659	306	296	7	4	11	12	201	32	0	.159	15	99	8	2	0.6	.934
WORLD SERIES																											
1944	STL	N	1	0	1.000	0.00	2	0	0	6	2	1	9	0	1	0	0	1	0	0	.000	0	2	0	0	1.0	1.000

Ed Donnelly

DONNELLY, EDWARD BR TR 6′ 1″ 205 lbs.
Born Edward O'Donnell.
B. July 29, 1880, Hampton, N. Y. D. Nov. 28, 1957, Rutland, Vt.

Year	Team	Lg	W	L	PCT	ERA	G	GS	CG	IP	H	BB	SO	ShO	Relief Pitching W	Relief Pitching L	Relief Pitching SV	Batting AB	Batting H	Batting HR	BA	PO	A	E	DP	TC/G	FA
1911	BOS	N	3	2	.600	2.45	5	4	4	36.2	33	9	16	1	0	1	0	14	1	0	.071	3	9	1	0	2.6	.923
1912			5	10	.333	4.35	37	18	10	184.1	225	72	67	0	0	1	0	69	19	0	.275	7	51	4	1	1.7	.935
2 yrs.			8	12	.400	4.03	42	22	14	221	258	81	83	1	0	2	0	83	20	0	.241	10	60	5	1	1.8	.933

Ed Donnelly

DONNELLY, EDWARD VINCENT BR TR 6′ 175 lbs.
B. Dec. 10, 1934, Allen, Mich.

Year	Team	Lg	W	L	PCT	ERA	G	GS	CG	IP	H	BB	SO	ShO	Relief Pitching W	Relief Pitching L	Relief Pitching SV	Batting AB	Batting H	Batting HR	BA	PO	A	E	DP	TC/G	FA
1959	CHI	N	1	1	.500	3.14	9	0	0	14.1	18	9	6	0	1	1	0	0	0	0	—	0	3	0	0	0.3	1.000

Frank Donnelly

DONNELLY, FRANKLIN MARION 5′ 6″ 180 lbs.
B. Oct. 7, 1869, Tamaroa, Ill. D. Feb. 3, 1953, Canton, Ill.

Year	Team	Lg	W	L	PCT	ERA	G	GS	CG	IP	H	BB	SO	ShO	Relief Pitching W	Relief Pitching L	Relief Pitching SV	Batting AB	Batting H	Batting HR	BA	PO	A	E	DP	TC/G	FA
1893	CHI	N	3	1	.750	5.36	7	5	3	42	51	17	6	0	0	0	**2**	18	8	0	.444	7	8	4	0	2.7	.789

Jim Donohue

DONOHUE, JAMES THOMAS BR TR 6′ 4″ 190 lbs.
B. Oct. 31, 1938, St. Louis, Mo.

Year	Team	Lg	W	L	PCT	ERA	G	GS	CG	IP	H	BB	SO	ShO	Relief Pitching W	Relief Pitching L	Relief Pitching SV	Batting AB	Batting H	Batting HR	BA	PO	A	E	DP	TC/G	FA
1961	2 teams	DET A (14G 1–1) LA A (38G 4–6)																									
″	total		5	7	.417	4.18	52	7	0	120.2	116	65	99	0	5	5	6	28	4	0	.143	8	13	0	1	0.4	1.000
1962	2 teams	LA A (12G 1–0) MIN A (6G 0–1)																									
″	total		1	1	.500	4.67	18	2	0	34.2	36	17	17	0	1	1	1	6	1	0	.167	0	5	1	0	0.3	.833
2 yrs.			6	8	.429	4.29	70	9	0	155.1	152	82	116	0	6	6	7	34	5	0	.147	8	18	1	1	0.4	.963

Pete Donohue

DONOHUE, PETER JOSEPH BR TR 6′ 2″ 185 lbs.
B. Nov. 5, 1900, Athens, Tex. D. Feb. 23, 1988, Fort Worth, Tex.

Year	Team	Lg	W	L	PCT	ERA	G	GS	CG	IP	H	BB	SO	ShO	Relief Pitching W	Relief Pitching L	Relief Pitching SV	Batting AB	Batting H	Batting HR	BA	PO	A	E	DP	TC/G	FA
1921	CIN	N	7	6	.538	3.35	21	11	7	118.1	117	26	44	0	1	2	1	38	8	1	.211	4	41	2	0	2.2	.957
1922			18	9	**.667**	3.12	33	30	18	242	257	43	66	2	0	1	1	88	16	0	.182	7	62	3	2	2.2	.958
1923			21	15	.583	3.38	42	36	19	274.1	304	68	84	2	2	0	3	96	24	1	.250	9	70	8	4	2.1	.908
1924			16	9	.640	3.60	35	31	16	222.1	248	36	72	3	0	1	0	73	14	1	.192	8	46	0	3	1.5	1.000
1925			21	14	.600	3.08	42	**38**	**27**	**301**	310	49	78	3	1	0	2	109	32	1	.294	6	62	4	2	1.7	.944
1926			**20**	14	.588	3.37	47	**38**	17	**285.2**	**298**	39	73	**5**	4	0	2	106	33	0	.311	6	60	4	2	1.5	.943
1927			6	16	.273	4.11	33	24	12	190.2	253	32	48	1	0	1	1	64	16	0	.250	11	42	2	4	1.7	.964
1928			7	11	.389	4.74	23	18	8	150	180	32	37	0	1	0	0	48	7	1	.146	8	42	1	0	2.2	.980
1929			10	13	.435	5.42	32	24	7	177.2	243	51	30	0	2	0	0	60	20	0	.333	7	44	4	4	1.7	.927
1930	2 teams	CIN N (8G 1–3) NY N (18G 7–6)																									
″	total		8	9	.471	6.17	26	16	6	121	188	31	30	0	1	2	2	43	10	1	.233	4	23	1	2	1.1	.964

Pete Donohue *continued*

Year	Team		W	L	PCT	ERA	G	GS	CG	IP	H	BB	SO	ShO	Relief Pitching W	Relief Pitching L	Relief Pitching SV	Batting AB	Batting H	Batting HR	BA	PO	A	E	DP	TC/G	FA
1931	2 teams	NY N (4G 0–1)	CLE A (2G 0–0)																								
"	total		0	1	.000	6.48	6	1	0	16.2	23	9	8	0	0	0	0	4	0	0	.000	0	2	0	0	0.3	1.000
1932	BOS	A	0	1	.000	7.82	4	2	0	12.2	18	6	1	0	0	0	0	3	0	0	.000	1	5	0	0	1.5	1.000
12 yrs.			134	118	.532	3.87	344	269	137	2112.1	2439	422	571	16	12	7	12	732	180	6	.246	71	499	29	23	1.7	.952

Lino Donoso

DONOSO, LINO BL TL 5′11″ 160 lbs.
Born Lino Donoso (Galeta).
B. Sept. 23, 1922, Havana, Cuba D. Oct. 13, 1990, Veracruz, Mexico.

Year	Team		W	L	PCT	ERA	G	GS	CG	IP	H	BB	SO	ShO	Relief Pitching W	Relief Pitching L	Relief Pitching SV	Batting AB	Batting H	Batting HR	BA	PO	A	E	DP	TC/G	FA
1955	PIT	N	4	6	.400	5.31	25	9	3	95	106	35	38	0	1	2	1	27	5	0	.185	6	18	2	1	1.0	.923
1956			0	0	—	0.00	3	0	0	1.2	2	1	1	0	0	0	0	0	0	0	—	0	1	0	0	0.3	1.000
2 yrs.			4	6	.400	5.21	28	9	3	96.2	108	36	39	0	1	2	1	27	5	0	.185	6	19	2	1	1.0	.926

Bill Donovan

DONOVAN, WILLARD EARL BR TL 6′ 2″ 198 lbs.
B. July 6, 1916, Maywood, Ill.

Year	Team		W	L	PCT	ERA	G	GS	CG	IP	H	BB	SO	ShO	Relief Pitching W	Relief Pitching L	Relief Pitching SV	Batting AB	Batting H	Batting HR	BA	PO	A	E	DP	TC/G	FA
1942	BOS	N	3	6	.333	3.43	31	10	2	89.1	97	32	23	1	1	1	0	25	6	0	.240	5	32	2	0	1.3	.949
1943			1	0	1.000	1.84	7	0	0	14.2	17	9	1	0	1	0	0	3	1	0	.333	0	9	0	0	1.3	1.000
2 yrs.			4	6	.400	3.20	38	10	2	104	114	41	24	1	2	1	0	28	7	0	.250	5	41	2	0	1.3	.958

Dick Donovan

DONOVAN, RICHARD EDWARD BL TR 6′ 3″ 190 lbs.
B. Dec. 7, 1927, Boston, Mass.

Year	Team		W	L	PCT	ERA	G	GS	CG	IP	H	BB	SO	ShO	Relief Pitching W	Relief Pitching L	Relief Pitching SV	Batting AB	Batting H	Batting HR	BA	PO	A	E	DP	TC/G	FA
1950	BOS	N	0	2	.000	8.19	10	3	0	29.2	28	34	9	0	0	0	0	6	1	0	.167	1	5	0	1	0.6	1.000
1951			0	0	—	5.27	8	2	0	13.2	17	11	4	0	0	0	0	3	1	0	.333	1	4	0	0	0.6	1.000
1952			0	2	.000	5.54	7	2	0	13	18	12	6	0	0	0	1	3	0	0	.000	0	6	1	0	1.0	.857
1954	DET	A	0	0	—	10.50	2	0	0	6	9	5	2	0	0	0	0	1	0	0	.000	0	1	0	0	0.5	1.000
1955	CHI	A	15	9	.625	3.32	29	24	11	187	186	48	88	5	2	1	0	76	17	1	.224	11	33	0	2	1.5	1.000
1956			12	10	.545	3.64	34	31	14	234.2	212	59	120	3	0	0	0	90	20	3	.222	11	46	1	4	1.7	.983
1957			16	6	**.727**	2.77	28	28	**16**	220.2	203	45	88	2	0	0	0	83	12	3	.145	18	37	0	3	2.0	1.000
1958			15	14	.517	3.01	34	34	16	248	240	53	127	4	0	0	0	80	9	0	.113	16	34	2	3	1.5	.962
1959			9	10	.474	3.66	31	29	5	179.2	171	58	71	1	0	0	0	61	8	1	.131	11	26	4	1	1.3	.902
1960			6	1	.857	5.38	33	8	0	78.2	87	25	30	0	5	0	3	23	3	0	.130	6	19	1	0	0.8	.962
1961	WAS	A	10	10	.500	**2.40**	23	22	11	168.2	138	35	62	2	0	0	0	56	10	1	.179	15	26	4	1	2.0	.911
1962	CLE	A	20	10	.667	3.59	34	34	16	250.2	255	47	94	**5**	0	0	0	89	16	4	.180	23	36	3	6	1.8	.952
1963			11	13	.458	4.24	30	30	7	206	211	28	84	3	0	0	0	69	9	1	.130	20	29	2	1	1.7	.961
1964			7	9	.438	4.55	30	23	5	158.1	181	29	83	0	0	0	1	48	7	1	.146	9	30	1	3	1.3	.975
1965			1	3	.250	5.96	12	3	0	22.2	32	6	12	0	0	1	0	6	0	0	.000	2	4	1	0	0.6	.857
15 yrs.			122	99	.552	3.67	345	273	101	2017.1	1988	495	880	25	7	2	5	694	113	15	.163	144	336	20	25	1.4	.960
WORLD SERIES																											
1959	CHI	A	0	1	.000	5.40	3	1	0	8.1	4	3	5	0	0	0	1	3	1	0	.333	1	1	0	0	0.7	1.000

Tom Donovan

DONOVAN, THOMAS JOSEPH BR TR 6′ 2″ 168 lbs.
B. Jan. 1, 1873, West Troy, N. Y. D. Mar. 25, 1933, Watervliet, N. Y.

Year	Team		W	L	PCT	ERA	G	GS	CG	IP	H	BB	SO	ShO	Relief Pitching W	Relief Pitching L	Relief Pitching SV	Batting AB	Batting H	Batting HR	BA	PO	A	E	DP	TC/G	FA
1901	CLE	A	0	0	—	5.14	1	0	0	7	16	3	0	0	0	0	0	*				21	6	4	0	1.6	.871

Wild Bill Donovan

DONOVAN, WILLIAM EDWARD BB TR 5′11″ 190 lbs.
B. Oct. 13, 1876, Lawrence, Mass. D. Dec. 9, 1923, Forsyth, N. Y.
Manager 1915–17, 1921.

Year	Team		W	L	PCT	ERA	G	GS	CG	IP	H	BB	SO	ShO	Relief Pitching W	Relief Pitching L	Relief Pitching SV	Batting AB	Batting H	Batting HR	BA	PO	A	E	DP	TC/G	FA
1898	WAS	N	1	6	.143	4.30	17	7	6	88	88	69	36	0	0	0	0	103	17	1	.165	45	22	8	6	1.9	.893
1899	BKN	N	1	2	.333	4.32	5	2	2	25	35	13	11	0	0	1	1	13	3	0	.231	1	5	1	0	1.4	.857
1900			1	2	.333	6.68	5	4	2	31	36	18	13	0	0	0	0	13	0	0	.000	0	12	0	0	2.4	1.000
1901			**25**	15	.625	2.77	**45**	38	36	351	324	**152**	226	2	**4**	0	1	135	23	2	.170	14	75	7	5	2.1	.927
1902			17	15	.531	2.78	35	33	30	297.2	250	111	170	4	0	0	1	161	27	1	.168	117	81	7	5	4.3	.966
1903	DET	A	17	16	.515	2.29	35	34	**34**	307	247	95	187	4	0	0	0	124	30	0	.242	26	71	8	3	2.7	.924
1904			17	16	.515	2.46	34	34	30	293	251	94	137	3	0	0	0	140	38	1	.271	80	89	7	3	4.1	.960
1905			18	15	.545	2.60	34	32	27	280.2	236	101	135	5	1	1	0	130	25	0	.192	28	73	7	3	2.5	.935
1906			9	15	.375	3.15	25	25	22	211.2	221	72	85	0	0	0	0	91	11	0	.121	17	65	5	1	3.0	.943
1907			25	4	**.862**	2.19	32	28	27	271	222	82	123	3	2	0	1	109	29	0	.266	13	56	4	0	2.3	.945
1908			18	7	.720	2.08	29	28	25	242.2	210	53	141	6	0	0	0	82	13	0	.159	16	39	5	0	2.1	.917
1909			8	7	.533	2.31	21	17	13	140.1	121	60	76	4	0	0	2	45	9	0	.200	9	29	1	1	1.9	.974
1910			17	7	.708	2.42	26	23	20	208.2	184	61	107	3	1	0	0	69	10	0	.145	9	33	2	2	1.7	.955
1911			10	9	.526	3.31	20	19	15	168.1	160	64	81	1	1	0	0	60	12	1	.200	4	25	2	0	1.5	.935
1912			1	0	1.000	0.90	3	1	0	10	5	2	6	0	0	0	0	13	1	0	.077	5	1	1	0	1.0	.857
1915	NY	A	0	3	.000	4.81	9	1	0	33.2	35	10	17	0	0	2	0	12	1	0	.083	1	7	0	0	0.9	1.000
1916			0	0	—	0.00	1	0	0	1	1	1	0	0	0	0	0	0	0	0	—	0	0	0	0	0.0	.000
1918	DET	A	1	0	1.000	1.50	2	1	0	6	5	1	1	0	0	0	0	2	1	0	.500	0	1	0	0	0.5	1.000
18 yrs.			186	139	.572	2.69	378	327	289	2966.2	2631	1059	1552	35	9	4	6	*				385	684	65	29	2.6	.943
WORLD SERIES																											
1907	DET	A	0	1	.000	1.29	2	2	2	21	17	5	16	0	0	0	0	8	0	0	.000	3	3	0	0	3.0	1.000
1908			0	2	.000	4.24	2	2	2	17	17	4	10	0	0	0	0	4	0	0	.000	1	2	1	0	2.0	.750
1909			1	1	.500	3.00	2	2	1	12	7	8	7	0	0	0	0	4	0	0	.000	0	5	1	0	3.0	.833
3 yrs.			1	4	.200	2.70	6	6	5	50	41	17	33	0	0	0	0	*				4	10	2	0	2.7	.875

John Dopson

DOPSON, JOHN ROBERT, JR. BL TR 6′ 4″ 205 lbs.
B. July 14, 1963, Baltimore, Md.

Year	Team		W	L	PCT	ERA	G	GS	CG	IP	H	BB	SO	ShO	Relief Pitching W	Relief Pitching L	Relief Pitching SV	Batting AB	Batting H	Batting HR	BA	PO	A	E	DP	TC/G	FA
1985	MON	N	0	2	.000	11.08	4	3	0	13	25	4	4	0	0	0	0	4	0	0	.000	0	2	0	0	0.5	1.000
1988			3	11	.214	3.04	26	26	1	168.2	150	58	101	0	0	0	0	51	3	0	.059	10	15	2	1	1.0	.926
1989	BOS	A	12	8	.600	3.99	29	28	2	169.1	166	69	95	0	1	0	0	0	0	0	—	20	34	1	1	1.9	.982
1990			0	0	—	2.04	4	4	0	17.2	13	9	9	0	0	0	0	0	0	0	—	1	5	0	0	1.5	1.000
1991			0	0	—	18.00	1	0	0	1	2	1	0	0	0	0	0	0	0	0	—	0	1	0	0	1.0	1.000

John Dopson *continued*

Year	Team	W	L	PCT	ERA	G	GS	CG	IP	H	BB	SO	ShO	Relief W	Relief L	Relief SV	AB	H	HR	BA	PO	A	E	DP	TC/G	FA
1992		7	11	.389	4.08	25	25	0	141.1	159	38	55	0	0	0	0	0	0	0	—	19	18	1	1	1.5	.974
1993		7	11	.389	4.97	34	28	1	155.2	170	59	89	1	0	2	0	0	0	0	—	17	22	0	0	1.1	1.000
1994	CAL A	1	4	.200	6.14	21	5	0	58.2	67	26	33	0	0	1	1	0	0	0	—	3	10	0	0	0.6	1.000
8 yrs.		30	47	.390	4.27	144	119	4	725.1	752	264	386	1	1	3	1	55	3	0	.055	70	107	4	3	1.3	.978

John Doran

DORAN, JOHN F. TL 5′ 4″ 160 lbs.
B. 1867, Chicago, Ill. Deceased.

Year	Team	W	L	PCT	ERA	G	GS	CG	IP	H	BB	SO	ShO	Relief W	Relief L	Relief SV	AB	H	HR	BA	PO	A	E	DP	TC/G	FA
1891	LOU AA	5	10	.333	5.43	15	14	12	126	160	75	55	1	0	1	0	53	10	0	.189	4	29	6	1	2.6	.846

Mike Dorgan

DORGAN, MICHAEL CORNELIUS BR TR 5′ 9″ 180 lbs.
Brother of Jerry Dorgan.
B. Oct. 2, 1853, Middletown, Conn. D. Apr. 26, 1909, Hartford, Conn.
Manager 1879–81.

Year	Team	W	L	PCT	ERA	G	GS	CG	IP	H	BB	SO	ShO	Relief W	Relief L	Relief SV	AB	H	HR	BA	PO	A	E	DP	TC/G	FA
1879	SYR N	0	0	—	2.25	2	0	0	12	13	2	8	0	0	0	0	270	72	1	.267	118	21	29	3	2.5	.827
1880	PRO N	0	0	—	1.13	1	0	0	8	4	0	2	0	0	0	0	321	79	0	.246	98	28	24	4	1.9	.840
1883	NY N	0	1	.000	3.86	1	1	1	7	8	6	3	0	0	0	0	261	61	0	.234	367	25	26	13	7.1	.938
1884		8	6	.571	*3.50*	14	14	12	113	98	51	90	0	0	0	0	341	94	1	.276	153	52	49	4	2.9	.807
4 yrs.		8	7	.533	3.28	18	15	13	140	123	59	103	0	0	0	0	*				1626	233	259	48	2.9	.878

Harry Dorish

DORISH, HARRY (Fritz) BR TR 5′11″ 204 lbs.
B. July 13, 1921, Swoyersville, Pa.

Year	Team	W	L	PCT	ERA	G	GS	CG	IP	H	BB	SO	ShO	Relief W	Relief L	Relief SV	AB	H	HR	BA	PO	A	E	DP	TC/G	FA
1947	BOS A	7	8	.467	4.70	41	9	2	136	149	54	50	0	4	3	2	35	5	0	.143	10	27	4	0	1.0	.902
1948		0	1	.000	5.65	9	0	0	14.1	18	6	5	0	0	1	0	4	1	0	.250	1	2	0	0	0.3	1.000
1949		0	0	—	2.35	5	0	0	7.2	7	1	5	0	0	0	0	0	0	0	—	1	2	0	0	0.6	1.000
1950	STL A	4	9	.308	6.44	29	13	4	109	162	36	36	0	1	2	0	31	5	0	.161	5	14	1	3	0.7	.950
1951	CHI A	5	6	.455	3.54	32	4	2	96.2	101	31	29	1	3	5	0	31	8	0	.258	3	20	1	1	0.7	.958
1952		8	4	.667	2.47	39	1	1	91	66	42	47	0	7	4	**11**	22	2	0	.091	4	23	0	3	0.7	1.000
1953		10	6	.625	3.40	55	6	2	145.2	140	52	69	0	7	4	18	41	7	0	.171	15	31	0	0	0.8	1.000
1954		6	4	.600	2.72	37	6	2	109	88	29	48	1	2	2	6	27	3	0	.111	6	14	0	0	0.5	1.000
1955	2 teams CHI A (13G 2–0) BAL A (35G 3–3)																									
"	total	5	3	.625	2.83	48	1	0	82.2	74	37	28	0	5	2	7	13	1	0	.077	5	26	0	1	0.6	1.000
1956	2 teams BAL A (13G 0–0) BOS A (15G 0–2)																									
"	total	0	2	.000	3.83	28	0	0	42.1	45	13	15	0	0	2	0	0	0	0	—	6	15	0	1	0.8	1.000
10 yrs.		45	43	.511	3.83	323	40	13	834.1	850	301	332	2	29	25	44	204	32	0	.157	56	174	6	9	0.7	.975

Gus Dorner

DORNER, AUGUSTUS BR TR 5′10″ 176 lbs.
B. Aug. 18, 1876, Chambersburg, Pa. D. May 4, 1956, Chambersburg, Pa.

Year	Team	W	L	PCT	ERA	G	GS	CG	IP	H	BB	SO	ShO	Relief W	Relief L	Relief SV	AB	H	HR	BA	PO	A	E	DP	TC/G	FA
1902	CLE A	3	1	.750	1.25	4	4	4	36	33	13	5	1	0	0	0	13	5	0	.385	2	10	0	0	3.0	1.000
1903		4	5	.444	3.30	12	8	4	73.2	83	24	28	2	1	1	0	25	2	0	.080	1	25	0	0	2.2	1.000
1906	2 teams CIN N (2G 1–1) BOS N (34G 8–25)																									
"	total	9	**26**	.257	3.73	36	33	30	272.1	280	107	109	0	1	1	0	105	14	0	.133	19	92	10	5	3.4	.917
1907	BOS N	12	16	.429	3.12	36	31	24	271.1	253	92	85	2	1	0	0	92	12	0	.130	17	58	0	3	2.1	1.000
1908		8	19	.296	3.54	38	28	14	216.1	176	77	41	3	2	0	0	67	12	0	.179	8	77	5	2	2.4	.944
1909		1	2	.333	2.55	5	2	0	24.2	17	17	7	0	0	1	1	6	1	0	.167	1	6	2	0	1.8	.778
6 yrs.		37	69	.349	3.33	131	106	76	894.1	842	330	275	8	5	3	1	308	46	0	.149	48	268	17	10	2.5	.949

Bert Dorr

DORR, CHARLES ALBERT
B. Feb. 2, 1862, New York, N. Y. D. June 16, 1914, Dickinson, N. Y.

Year	Team	W	L	PCT	ERA	G	GS	CG	IP	H	BB	SO	ShO	Relief W	Relief L	Relief SV	AB	H	HR	BA	PO	A	E	DP	TC/G	FA
1882	STL AA	2	6	.250	*2.59*	8	8	8	66	53	1	34	0	0	0	0	26	4	0	.154	5	22	2	0	3.6	.931

Cal Dorsett

DORSETT, CALVIN LEAVELLE (Preacher) BR TR 6′ 180 lbs.
B. June 10, 1913, Long Oak, Tex. D. Oct. 22, 1970, Elk City, Okla.

Year	Team	W	L	PCT	ERA	G	GS	CG	IP	H	BB	SO	ShO	Relief W	Relief L	Relief SV	AB	H	HR	BA	PO	A	E	DP	TC/G	FA
1940	CLE A	0	0	—	9.00	1	0	0	1	1	0	0	0	0	0	0	0	0	0	—	0	0	0	0	0.0	.000
1941		0	1	.000	10.32	5	2	0	11.1	21	10	5	0	0	0	0	2	0	0	.000	0	2	0	0	0.4	1.000
1947		0	0	—	27.00	2	0	0	1.1	3	3	1	0	0	0	0	0	0	0	—	0	0	0	0	0.0	.000
3 yrs.		0	1	.000	11.85	8	2	0	13.2	25	13	6	0	0	0	0	2	0	0	.000	0	2	0	0	0.3	1.000

Jerry Dorsey

DORSEY, MICHAEL JEREMIAH
B. 1854 D. Nov. 3, 1938, Auburn, N. Y.

Year	Team	W	L	PCT	ERA	G	GS	CG	IP	H	BB	SO	ShO	Relief W	Relief L	Relief SV	AB	H	HR	BA	PO	A	E	DP	TC/G	FA
1884	BAL U	0	1	.000	*9.00*	1	1	0	4	7	0	3	0	0	0	0	*				0	1	0	0	0.5	1.000

Jim Dorsey

DORSEY, JAMES EDWARD BR TR 6′ 7″ 190 lbs.
B. Aug. 2, 1955, Chicago, Ill.

Year	Team	W	L	PCT	ERA	G	GS	CG	IP	H	BB	SO	ShO	Relief W	Relief L	Relief SV	AB	H	HR	BA	PO	A	E	DP	TC/G	FA
1980	CAL A	1	2	.333	9.00	4	4	0	16	25	8	8	0	0	0	0	0	0	0	—	1	2	0	0	0.8	1.000
1984	BOS A	0	0	—	10.13	2	0	0	2.2	6	2	4	0	0	0	0	0	0	0	—	0	1	0	0	0.5	1.000
1985		0	1	.000	20.25	2	1	0	5.1	12	10	2	0	0	0	0	0	0	0	—	0	0	1	0	0.5	.000
3 yrs.		1	3	.250	11.63	8	5	0	24	43	20	14	0	0	0	0	0	0	0	—	1	3	1	0	0.6	.800

Jack Doscher

DOSCHER, JOHN HENRY, JR. BL TL 6′ 1″ 205 lbs.
Son of Herm Doscher.
B. July 27, 1880, Troy, N. Y. D. May 27, 1971, Park Ridge, N. J.

Year	Team	W	L	PCT	ERA	G	GS	CG	IP	H	BB	SO	ShO	Relief W	Relief L	Relief SV	AB	H	HR	BA	PO	A	E	DP	TC/G	FA
1903	2 teams CHI N (1G 0–1) BKN N (3G 0–0)																									
"	total	0	1	.000	9.00	4	1	0	10	14	11	9	0	0	0	0	4	0	0	.000	1	1	0	0	0.5	1.000
1904	BKN N	0	1	.000	0.00	2	0	0	6.1	1	1	2	0	0	1	0	2	1	0	.500	0	1	0	0	0.5	1.000
1905		1	5	.167	3.17	12	7	6	71	60	30	33	0	0	0	0	24	2	0	.083	2	13	3	0	1.5	.833
1906		0	1	.000	1.29	2	1	1	14	12	4	10	0	0	0	0	5	0	0	.000	1	2	0	0	1.5	1.000
1908	CIN N	1	3	.250	1.83	7	4	3	44.1	31	22	7	0	0	0	0	15	2	0	.133	1	13	2	0	2.3	.875
5 yrs.		2	11	.154	2.84	27	13	10	145.2	118	68	61	0	0	1	0	50	5	0	.100	5	30	5	0	1.5	.875

Richard Dotson

DOTSON, RICHARD ELLIOTT BR TR 6′ 1″ 190 lbs.
B. Jan. 10, 1959, Cincinnati, Ohio.

Year	Team	W	L	PCT	ERA	G	GS	CG	IP	H	BB	SO	ShO	Relief W	Relief L	Relief SV	AB	H	HR	BA	PO	A	E	DP	TC/G	FA
1979	CHI A	2	0	1.000	3.75	5	5	1	24	28	6	13	1	0	0	0	0	0	0	—	1	4	0	0	1.0	1.000
1980		12	10	.545	4.27	33	32	8	198	185	87	109	0	0	0	0	0	0	0	—	13	33	1	0	1.4	.979

Richard Dotson *continued*

Year	Team	Lg	W	L	PCT	ERA	G	GS	CG	IP	H	BB	SO	ShO	Relief Pitching W	Relief Pitching L	Relief Pitching SV	Batting AB	Batting H	Batting HR	BA	PO	A	E	DP	TC/G	FA
1981			9	8	.529	3.77	24	24	5	141	145	49	73	**4**	0	0	0	0	0	0	—	7	20	0	4	1.1	1.000
1982			11	15	.423	3.84	34	31	3	196.2	219	73	109	1	0	0	0	0	0	0	—	13	24	1	1	1.1	.974
1983			22	7	**.759**	3.23	35	35	8	240	209	**106**	137	1	0	0	0	0	0	0	—	20	48	1	8	2.0	.986
1984			14	15	.483	3.59	32	32	14	245.2	216	103	120	1	0	0	0	0	0	0	—	8	36	1	3	1.4	.978
1985			3	4	.429	4.47	9	9	0	52.1	53	17	33	0	0	0	0	0	0	0	—	3	5	0	0	0.9	1.000
1986			10	**17**	.370	5.48	34	34	3	197	226	69	110	1	0	0	0	0	0	0	—	13	23	3	0	1.1	.923
1987			11	12	.478	4.17	31	31	7	211.1	201	86	114	2	0	0	0	0	0	0	—	14	38	2	4	1.7	.963
1988	**NY**	**A**	12	9	.571	5.00	32	29	4	171	178	72	77	0	0	0	0	0	0	0	—	17	14	0	1	1.0	1.000
1989	**2 teams**	**NY A** (11G 2–5)			**CHI A** (17G 3–7)																						
″	**total**		5	12	.294	4.46	28	26	2	151.1	181	58	69	0	0	0	0	0	0	0		5	21	2	3	1.0	.929
1990	**KC**	**A**	0	4	.000	8.48	8	7	0	28.2	43	14	9	0	0	0	0	0	0	0	—	2	3	0	1	0.6	1.000
12 yrs.			111	113	.496	4.23	305	295	55	1857	1884	740	973	11	0	0	0	0	0	0		116	269	11	25	1.3	.972
LEAGUE CHAMPIONSHIP SERIES																											
1983	**CHI**	**A**	0	1	.000	10.80	1	1	0	5	6	3	3	0	0	0	0	0	0	0	—	1	1	0	0	2.0	1.000

Gary Dotter

DOTTER, GARY RICHARD BL TL 6′ 1″ 180 lbs.
B. Aug. 7, 1942, St. Louis, Mo.

Year	Team	Lg	W	L	PCT	ERA	G	GS	CG	IP	H	BB	SO	ShO	Relief Pitching W	Relief Pitching L	Relief Pitching SV	Batting AB	Batting H	Batting HR	BA	PO	A	E	DP	TC/G	FA
1961	**MIN**	**A**	0	0	—	9.00	2	0	0	6	6	4	2	0	0	0	0	1	0	0	.000	1	1	0	0	1.0	1.000
1963			0	0	—	0.00	2	0	0	2	0	0	2	0	0	0	0	0	0	0	—	0	1	0	0	0.5	1.000
1964			0	0	—	2.08	3	0	0	4.1	3	3	6	0	0	0	0	0	0	0	—	0	0	0	0	0.0	.000
3 yrs.			0	0		5.11	7	0	0	12.1	9	7	10	0	0	0	0	1	0	0	.000	1	2	0	0	0.4	1.000

Babe Doty

DOTY, ELMER L. BL TR 6′ 160 lbs.
B. Dec. 17, 1867, Genoa, Ohio D. Nov. 20, 1929, Toledo, Ohio.

Year	Team	Lg	W	L	PCT	ERA	G	GS	CG	IP	H	BB	SO	ShO	Relief Pitching W	Relief Pitching L	Relief Pitching SV	Batting AB	Batting H	Batting HR	BA	PO	A	E	DP	TC/G	FA
1890	**TOL**	**AA**	1	0	1.000	*1.00*	1	1	1	9	9	1	4	0	0	0	0	3	0	0	.000	0	0	0	0	0.0	.000

Jim Dougherty

DOUGHERTY, JAMES E. BR TR 6′ 210 lbs.
B. Mar. 8, 1968, Brentwood, N. Y.

Year	Team	Lg	W	L	PCT	ERA	G	GS	CG	IP	H	BB	SO	ShO	Relief Pitching W	Relief Pitching L	Relief Pitching SV	Batting AB	Batting H	Batting HR	BA	PO	A	E	DP	TC/G	FA
1995	**HOU**	**N**	8	4	.667	4.92	56	0	0	67.2	76	25	49	0	**8**	4	0	8	1	0	.125	4	14	0	4	0.3	1.000

Tom Dougherty

DOUGHERTY, THOMAS JAMES (Sugar Boy) BL TR 195 lbs.
B. May 30, 1881, Chicago, Ill. D. Nov. 6, 1953, Milwaukee, Wis.

Year	Team	Lg	W	L	PCT	ERA	G	GS	CG	IP	H	BB	SO	ShO	Relief Pitching W	Relief Pitching L	Relief Pitching SV	Batting AB	Batting H	Batting HR	BA	PO	A	E	DP	TC/G	FA
1904	**CHI**	**A**	1	0	1.000	0.00	1	0	0	2	0	0	0	0	1	0	0	1	0	0	.000	1	1	0	0	2.0	1.000

Larry Douglas

DOUGLAS, LAWRENCE HOWARD (Doug) BR TR 6′ 3″ 175 lbs.
B. June 5, 1890, Jellico, Tenn. D. Nov. 4, 1949, Jellico, Tenn.

Year	Team	Lg	W	L	PCT	ERA	G	GS	CG	IP	H	BB	SO	ShO	Relief Pitching W	Relief Pitching L	Relief Pitching SV	Batting AB	Batting H	Batting HR	BA	PO	A	E	DP	TC/G	FA
1915	**BAL**	**F**	0	0	—	3.00	2	0	0	3	3	2	1	0	0	0	0	0	0	0	—	0	1	0	0	0.5	1.000

Phil Douglas

DOUGLAS, PHILLIP BROOKS (Shufflin' Phil) BR TR 6′ 3″ 190 lbs.
B. June 17, 1890, Cedartown, Ga. D. Aug. 1, 1952, Sequatchie Valley, Tenn.

Year	Team	Lg	W	L	PCT	ERA	G	GS	CG	IP	H	BB	SO	ShO	Relief Pitching W	Relief Pitching L	Relief Pitching SV	Batting AB	Batting H	Batting HR	BA	PO	A	E	DP	TC/G	FA
1912	**CHI**	**A**	0	1	.000	7.30	3	1	0	12.1	21	6	7	0	0	0	0	2	0	0	.000	0	5	1	0	2.0	.833
1914	**CIN**	**N**	11	18	.379	2.56	45	25	13	239.1	186	92	121	0	4	4	1	73	10	0	.137	7	54	6	0	1.5	.910
1915	**3 teams**	**CIN N** (8G 1–5)			**BKN N** (20G 5–5)		**CHI N** (4G 1–1)																				
″	**total**		7	11	.389	3.25	32	24	7	188.1	174	47	110	2	0	0	0	64	8	0	.125	5	51	4	3	1.9	.933
1917	**CHI**	**N**	14	20	.412	2.55	**51**	37	20	293.1	269	50	151	5	3	0	1	89	11	0	.124	9	102	7	3	2.3	.941
1918			9	9	.500	2.13	25	19	11	156.2	145	31	51	2	1	1	2	55	14	0	.255	4	61	2	3	2.7	.970
1919	**2 teams**	**CHI N** (25G 10–6)			**NY N** (8G 2–4)																						
″	**total**		12	10	.545	2.03	33	25	12	213	186	40	84	4	2	0	0	66	8	0	.121	7	83	2	1	2.8	.978
1920	**NY**	**N**	14	10	.583	2.71	46	21	10	226	225	55	71	3	4	5	2	73	11	0	.151	11	65	3	3	1.7	.962
1921			15	10	.600	4.22	40	27	13	221.2	266	55	55	**3**	2	1	2	81	16	1	.198	5	64	3	3	1.8	.958
1922			11	4	.733	2.63	24	21	9	157.2	154	35	33	1	1	0	0	58	12	1	.207	13	36	4	2	2.2	.925
9 yrs.			93	93	.500	2.80	299	200	95	1708.1	1626	411	683	20	17	11	8	561	90	2	.160	61	521	32	18	2.1	.948
WORLD SERIES																											
1918	**CHI**	**N**	0	1	.000	0.00	1	0	0	1	1	0	0	0	0	1	0	0	0	0	—	0	0	1	0	1.0	.000
1921	**NY**	**N**	2	1	.667	2.08	3	3	2	26	24	5	17	0	0	0	0	7	0	0	.000	2	10	0	0	4.0	1.000
2 yrs.			2	2	.500	2.00	4	3	2	27	25	5	17	0	0	1	0	7	0	0	.000	2	10	1	0	3.3	.923

Whammy Douglas

DOUGLAS, CHARLES WILLIAM BR TR 6′ 2″ 185 lbs.
B. Feb. 17, 1935, Carrboro, N. C.

Year	Team	Lg	W	L	PCT	ERA	G	GS	CG	IP	H	BB	SO	ShO	Relief Pitching W	Relief Pitching L	Relief Pitching SV	Batting AB	Batting H	Batting HR	BA	PO	A	E	DP	TC/G	FA
1957	**PIT**	**N**	3	3	.500	3.26	11	8	0	47	48	30	28	0	0	0	0	16	1	0	.063	4	6	1	0	1.0	.909

Skip Dowd

DOWD, JAMES JOSEPH BR TR 5′10½″ 160 lbs.
B. Feb. 16, 1889, Holyoke, Mass. D. Dec. 20, 1960, Holyoke, Mass.

Year	Team	Lg	W	L	PCT	ERA	G	GS	CG	IP	H	BB	SO	ShO	Relief Pitching W	Relief Pitching L	Relief Pitching SV	Batting AB	Batting H	Batting HR	BA	PO	A	E	DP	TC/G	FA
1910	**PIT**	**N**	0	0	—	0.00	1	0	0	2	4	2	1	0	0	0	0	0	0	0	—	0	0	0	0	0.0	.000

Dave Dowling

DOWLING, DAVID BARCLAY BR TL 6′ 2″ 181 lbs.
B. Aug. 23, 1942, Baton Rouge, La.

Year	Team	Lg	W	L	PCT	ERA	G	GS	CG	IP	H	BB	SO	ShO	Relief Pitching W	Relief Pitching L	Relief Pitching SV	Batting AB	Batting H	Batting HR	BA	PO	A	E	DP	TC/G	FA
1964	**STL**	**N**	0	0	—	0.00	1	0	0	1	2	0	0	0	0	0	0	0	0	0	—	0	0	0	0	0.0	.000
1966	**CHI**	**N**	1	0	1.000	2.00	1	1	1	9	10	0	3	0	0	0	0	2	0	0	.000	1	0	0	0	1.0	1.000
2 yrs.			1	0	1.000	1.80	2	1	1	10	12	0	3	0	0	0	0	2	0	0	.000	1	0	0	0	0.5	1.000

Pete Dowling

DOWLING, HENRY PETER TL 5′11″
B. St. Louis, Mo. D. June 30, 1905, Hot Lake, Ore.

Year	Team	Lg	W	L	PCT	ERA	G	GS	CG	IP	H	BB	SO	ShO	Relief Pitching W	Relief Pitching L	Relief Pitching SV	Batting AB	Batting H	Batting HR	BA	PO	A	E	DP	TC/G	FA
1897	**LOU**	**N**	1	2	.333	5.88	4	4	2	26	39	8	3	0	0	0	0	10	2	0	.200	4	3	0	1	1.8	1.000
1898			13	20	.394	4.16	36	32	30	285.2	284	120	84	0	1	1	0	107	21	0	.196	11	68	12	2	2.5	.868
1899			13	17	.433	3.11	34	32	29	289.2	321	93	88	0	1	0	0	116	27	0	.233	5	73	11	2	2.6	.876
1901	**2 teams**	**MIL A** (10G 1–4)			**CLE A** (33G 11–22)																						
″	**total**		12	**26**	.316	4.15	43	34	31	306	340	118	124	2	0	**4**	1	118	20	1	.169	10	84	7	2	2.3	.931
4 yrs.			39	65	.375	3.87	117	102	92	907.1	984	339	299	2	2	5	1	351	70	1	.199	30	228	30	7	2.5	.896

Al Downing

DOWNING, ALPHONSO ERWIN BR TL 5′11″ 175 lbs.
B. June 28, 1941, Trenton, N. J.

Year	Team	W	L	PCT	ERA	G	GS	CG	IP	H	BB	SO	ShO	Relief Pitching W	Relief Pitching L	Relief Pitching SV	Batting AB	Batting H	Batting HR	BA	PO	A	E	DP	TC/G	FA
1961	NY A	0	1	.000	8.00	5	1	0	9	7	12	12	0	0	0	0	1	0	0	.000	0	2	0	0	0.4	1.000
1962		0	0	—	0.00	1	0	0	1	0	0	1	0	0	0	0	0	0	0	—	0	0	0	0	0.0	.000
1963		13	5	.722	2.56	24	22	10	175.2	114	80	171	4	0	1	0	58	6	0	.103	7	18	1	1	1.1	.962
1964		13	8	.619	3.47	37	35	11	244	201	**120**	**217**	1	0	0	2	85	15	0	.176	6	39	0	0	1.2	1.000
1965		12	14	.462	3.40	35	32	8	212	185	105	179	2	0	0	0	74	8	1	.108	6	36	2	4	1.3	.955
1966		10	11	.476	3.56	30	30	1	200	178	79	152	0	0	0	0	70	7	0	.100	4	16	3	2	0.8	.870
1967		14	10	.583	2.63	31	28	10	201.2	158	61	171	4	2	0	0	66	8	1	.121	9	27	1	2	1.2	.973
1968		3	3	.500	3.52	15	12	1	61.1	54	20	40	0	0	0	0	17	3	0	.176	2	9	0	0	0.7	1.000
1969		7	5	.583	3.38	30	15	5	130.2	117	49	85	1	1	1	0	44	6	0	.136	3	14	1	1	0.6	.944
1970	2 teams OAK A (10G 3–3) MIL A (17G 2–10)																									
″	total	5	13	.278	3.52	27	22	2	135.1	118	81	79	0	0	0	0	35	4	0	.114	9	30	3	2	1.6	.929
1971	LA N	20	9	.690	2.68	37	36	12	262	245	84	136	**5**	0	0	0	92	16	0	.174	7	40	1	2	1.3	.979
1972		9	9	.500	2.98	31	30	7	202.2	196	67	117	4	0	0	0	66	8	0	.121	5	54	1	5	1.9	.983
1973		9	9	.500	3.31	30	28	5	193	155	68	124	2	1	0	0	57	5	0	.088	8	34	3	1	1.5	.933
1974		5	6	.455	3.67	21	16	1	98	94	45	63	1	0	0	0	29	5	0	.172	2	20	1	2	1.1	.957
1975		2	1	.667	2.88	22	6	0	75	59	28	39	0	2	1	1	16	0	0	.000	4	17	0	0	1.0	1.000
1976		1	2	.333	3.86	17	3	0	46.2	43	18	30	0	1	1	0	6	0	0	.000	0	9	0	1	0.5	1.000
1977		0	1	.000	6.75	12	1	0	20	22	16	23	0	0	1	0	1	0	0	.000	0	3	1	0	0.3	.750
17 yrs.		123	107	.535	3.22	405	317	73	2268	1946	933	1639	24	7	5	3	717	91	2	.127	72	368	18	23	1.1	.961
LEAGUE CHAMPIONSHIP SERIES																										
1974	LA N	0	0	—	0.00	1	0	0	4	1	1	0	0	0	0	0	1	0	0	.000	0	0	1	0	1.0	.000
WORLD SERIES																										
1963	NY A	0	1	.000	5.40	1	1	0	5	7	1	6	0	0	0	0	1	0	0	.000	0	1	0	0	1.0	1.000
1964		0	1	.000	8.22	3	1	0	7.2	9	2	5	0	0	0	0	2	0	0	.000	0	1	0	0	0.3	1.000
1974	LA N	0	1	.000	2.45	1	1	0	3.2	4	4	3	0	0	0	0	1	0	0	.000	0	3	0	0	3.0	1.000
3 yrs.		0	3	.000	6.06	5	3	0	16.1	20	7	14	0	0	0	0	4	0	0	.000	0	5	0	0	1.0	1.000

Dave Downs

DOWNS, DAVID RALPH BR TR 6′ 5″ 220 lbs.
Brother of Kelly Downs.
B. June 21, 1952, Logan, Utah.

Year	Team	W	L	PCT	ERA	G	GS	CG	IP	H	BB	SO	ShO	Relief Pitching W	Relief Pitching L	Relief Pitching SV	Batting AB	Batting H	Batting HR	BA	PO	A	E	DP	TC/G	FA
1972	PHI N	1	1	.500	2.74	4	4	1	23	25	3	5	1	0	0	0	8	2	0	.250	0	5	0	0	1.3	1.000

Kelly Downs

DOWNS, KELLY ROBERT BR TR 6′ 4″ 195 lbs.
Brother of Dave Downs.
B. Oct. 25, 1960, Ogden, Utah.

Year	Team	W	L	PCT	ERA	G	GS	CG	IP	H	BB	SO	ShO	Relief Pitching W	Relief Pitching L	Relief Pitching SV	Batting AB	Batting H	Batting HR	BA	PO	A	E	DP	TC/G	FA
1986	SF N	4	4	.500	2.75	14	14	1	88.1	78	30	64	0	0	0	0	29	5	0	.172	6	13	1	0	1.4	.950
1987		12	9	.571	3.63	41	28	4	186	185	67	137	3	1	1	1	56	8	0	.143	11	10	3	0	0.6	.875
1988		13	9	.591	3.32	27	26	6	168	140	47	118	3	0	0	0	54	9	0	.167	15	22	1	2	1.4	.974
1989		4	8	.333	4.79	18	15	0	82.2	82	26	49	0	0	0	0	22	2	0	.091	7	8	1	1	0.9	.938
1990		3	2	.600	3.43	13	9	0	63	56	20	31	0	0	0	0	13	0	0	.000	6	12	1	0	1.5	.947
1991		10	4	.714	4.19	45	11	0	111.2	99	53	62	0	7	0	0	23	2	0	.087	9	19	1	1	0.6	.966
1992	2 teams SF N (19G 1–2) OAK A (18G 5–5)																									
″	total	6	7	.462	3.37	37	20	0	144.1	137	70	71	0	2	0	0	14	0	0	.000	9	11	1	0	0.6	.952
1993	OAK A	5	10	.333	5.64	42	12	0	119.2	135	60	66	0	5	4	0	0	0	0	—	3	10	0	2	0.3	1.000
8 yrs.		57	53	.518	3.86	237	135	11	963.2	912	373	598	6	15	5	1	211	26	0	.123	66	105	9	6	0.8	.950
LEAGUE CHAMPIONSHIP SERIES																										
1987	SF N	0	0	—	0.00	1	0	0	1.1	1	0	0	0	0	0	0	0	0	0	—	0	0	0	0	0.0	.000
1989		1	0	1.000	3.12	2	0	0	8.2	8	6	6	0	1	0	0	3	0	0	.000	0	1	0	1	0.5	1.000
1992	OAK A	0	1	.000	3.86	2	0	0	2.1	3	1	0	0	0	1	0	0	0	0	—	0	0	0	0	0.0	.000
3 yrs.		1	1	.500	2.92	5	0	0	12.1	12	7	6	0	1	1	0	3	0	0	.000	0	1	0	1	0.2	1.000
WORLD SERIES																										
1989	SF N	0	0	—	7.71	3	0	0	4.2	3	2	4	0	0	0	0	0	0	0	—	0	0	0	0	0.0	.000

Tom Dowse

DOWSE, THOMAS JOSEPH BR TR 5′11″ 175 lbs.
B. Aug. 12, 1866, Ireland D. Dec. 14, 1946, Riverside, Calif.

Year	Team	W	L	PCT	ERA	G	GS	CG	IP	H	BB	SO	ShO	Relief Pitching W	Relief Pitching L	Relief Pitching SV	Batting AB	Batting H	Batting HR	BA	PO	A	E	DP	TC/G	FA
1890	CLE N	0	0	—	5.40	1	0	0	5	6	1	0	0	0	0	0	*				151	14	11	10	4.4	.938

Carl Doyle

DOYLE, WILLIAM CARL BR TR 6′ 1″ 185 lbs.
B. July 30, 1912, Knoxville, Tenn. D. Sept. 4, 1951, Knoxville, Tenn.

Year	Team	W	L	PCT	ERA	G	GS	CG	IP	H	BB	SO	ShO	Relief Pitching W	Relief Pitching L	Relief Pitching SV	Batting AB	Batting H	Batting HR	BA	PO	A	E	DP	TC/G	FA
1935	PHI A	2	7	.222	5.99	14	9	3	79.2	86	72	34	0	0	1	0	30	4	0	.133	5	17	0	3	1.6	1.000
1936		0	3	.000	10.94	8	6	1	38.2	66	29	12	0	0	0	0	15	4	0	.267	1	2	1	0	0.5	.750
1939	BKN N	1	2	.333	1.02	5	1	1	17.2	8	7	7	1	0	2	1	6	1	0	.167	1	4	0	0	1.0	1.000
1940	2 teams BKN N (3G 0–0) STL N (21G 3–3)																									
″	total	3	3	.500	7.27	24	5	1	86.2	117	47	48	0	2	2	1	31	7	1	.226	5	15	0	2	0.8	1.000
4 yrs.		6	15	.286	6.95	51	21	6	222.2	277	155	101	1	2	5	2	82	16	1	.195	12	38	1	5	1.0	.980

Jess Doyle

DOYLE, JESSE HERBERT BR TR 5′11″ 175 lbs.
B. Apr. 14, 1898, Knoxville, Tenn. D. Apr. 15, 1961, Belleville, Ill.

Year	Team	W	L	PCT	ERA	G	GS	CG	IP	H	BB	SO	ShO	Relief Pitching W	Relief Pitching L	Relief Pitching SV	Batting AB	Batting H	Batting HR	BA	PO	A	E	DP	TC/G	FA
1925	DET A	4	7	.364	5.93	45	3	0	118.1	158	50	31	0	4	5	8	33	8	2	.242	4	27	0	0	0.7	1.000
1926		0	0	—	4.15	2	0	0	4.1	6	1	2	0	0	0	1	1	1	0	1.000	0	1	1	0	1.0	.500
1927		0	0	—	8.03	7	0	0	12.1	16	5	5	0	0	0	0	3	1	0	.333	0	3	0	1	0.4	1.000
1931	STL A	0	0	—	27.00	1	0	0	1	3	1	0	0	0	0	0	0	0	0	—	0	0	0	0	0.0	.000
4 yrs.		4	7	.364	6.22	55	3	0	136	183	57	38	0	4	5	9	37	10	2	.270	4	31	1	1	0.7	.972

John Doyle

DOYLE, JOHN ALOYSIUS
B. 1858, Nova Scotia, Canada D. Dec. 24, 1915, Providence, R. I.

Year	Team	W	L	PCT	ERA	G	GS	CG	IP	H	BB	SO	ShO	Relief Pitching W	Relief Pitching L	Relief Pitching SV	Batting AB	Batting H	Batting HR	BA	PO	A	E	DP	TC/G	FA
1882	STL AA	0	3	.000	2.63	3	3	3	24	41	3	5	0	0	0	0	11	2	0	.182	1	5	0	0	2.0	1.000

Paul Doyle

DOYLE, PAUL SINNOTT BL TL 5′11″ 172 lbs.
B. Oct. 2, 1939, Philadelphia, Pa.

Year	Team	Lg	W	L	PCT	ERA	G	GS	CG	IP	H	BB	SO	ShO	Relief W	Relief L	Relief SV	Batting AB	Batting H	Batting HR	BA	PO	A	E	DP	TC/G	FA
1969	ATL	N	2	0	1.000	2.08	36	0	0	39	31	16	25	0	2	0	4	3	0	0	.000	2	10	0	0	0.3	1.000
1970	2 teams	CAL A (40G 3–1) SD N (9G 0–2)																									
″	total		3	3	.500	5.33	49	0	0	49	52	27	36	0	3	3	7	4	0	0	.000	1	16	0	2	0.3	1.000
1972	CAL	A	0	0	—	0.00	2	0	0	2	2	3	4	0	0	0	0	0	0	0	—	0	1	0	0	0.5	1.000
3 yrs.			5	3	.625	3.80	87	0	0	90	85	46	65	0	5	3	11	7	0	0	.000	3	27	0	2	0.3	1.000
LEAGUE CHAMPIONSHIP SERIES																											
1969	ATL	N	0	0	—	0.00	1	0	0	1	2	1	3	0	0	0	0	0	0	0	—	0	0	0	0	0.0	.000

Slow Joe Doyle

DOYLE, JUDD BRUCE BL TR 5′ 8″ 150 lbs.
B. Sept. 15, 1881, Clay Center, Kans. D. Nov. 21, 1947, Tannersville, N. Y.

Year	Team	Lg	W	L	PCT	ERA	G	GS	CG	IP	H	BB	SO	ShO	Relief W	Relief L	Relief SV	Batting AB	Batting H	Batting HR	BA	PO	A	E	DP	TC/G	FA
1906	NY	A	2	1	.667	2.38	9	6	3	45.1	34	13	28	2	0	0	0	14	3	0	.214	4	13	0	0	1.9	1.000
1907			11	11	.500	2.65	29	23	15	193.2	169	67	94	1	1	0	1	58	8	0	.138	5	45	3	2	1.8	.943
1908			1	1	.500	2.63	12	4	2	48	42	14	20	1	0	0	0	14	3	0	.214	1	8	2	1	0.9	.818
1909			8	6	.571	2.58	17	15	8	125.2	103	37	57	3	0	0	0	42	7	0	.167	5	23	1	0	1.7	.966
1910	2 teams	NY A (3G 0–2) CIN N (5G 0–0)																									
″	total		0	2	.000	7.23	8	2	1	23.2	35	16	10	0	0	0	0	7	1	0	.143	0	9	3	0	1.5	.750
5 yrs.			22	21	.512	2.85	75	50	29	436.1	383	147	209	7	1	0	1	135	22	0	.163	15	98	9	3	1.6	.926

Buzz Dozier

DOZIER, WILLIAM JOSEPH BR TR 6′ 3″ 185 lbs.
B. Aug. 31, 1927, Waco, Tex.

Year	Team	Lg	W	L	PCT	ERA	G	GS	CG	IP	H	BB	SO	ShO	Relief W	Relief L	Relief SV	Batting AB	Batting H	Batting HR	BA	PO	A	E	DP	TC/G	FA
1947	WAS	A	0	0	—	0.00	2	0	0	4.2	2	1	2	0	0	0	0	1	0	0	.000	0	1	0	0	0.5	1.000
1949			0	0	—	11.37	2	0	0	6.1	12	6	1	0	0	0	0	2	0	0	.000	0	0	0	0	0.0	.000
2 yrs.			0	0		6.55	4	0	0	11	14	7	3	0	0	0	0	3	0	0	.000	0	1	0	0	0.3	1.000

Tom Dozier

DOZIER, THOMAS DEAN BR TR 6′ 2″ 190 lbs.
B. Sept. 5, 1961, San Pablo, Calif.

Year	Team	Lg	W	L	PCT	ERA	G	GS	CG	IP	H	BB	SO	ShO	Relief W	Relief L	Relief SV	Batting AB	Batting H	Batting HR	BA	PO	A	E	DP	TC/G	FA
1986	OAK	A	0	0	—	5.68	4	0	0	6.1	6	5	4	0	0	0	0	0	0	0	—	1	0	0	0	0.3	1.000

Doug Drabek

DRABEK, DOUGLAS DEAN BR TR 6′ 1″ 185 lbs.
B. July 25, 1962, Victoria, Tex.

Year	Team	Lg	W	L	PCT	ERA	G	GS	CG	IP	H	BB	SO	ShO	Relief W	Relief L	Relief SV	Batting AB	Batting H	Batting HR	BA	PO	A	E	DP	TC/G	FA
1986	NY	A	7	8	.467	4.10	27	21	0	131.2	126	50	76	0	0	0	0	0	0	0	—	5	13	0	0	0.7	1.000
1987	PIT	N	11	12	.478	3.88	29	28	1	176.1	165	46	120	1	0	0	0	59	7	0	.119	24	23	2	0	1.7	.959
1988			15	7	.682	3.08	33	32	3	219.1	194	50	127	1	0	0	0	76	13	0	.171	29	21	6	6	1.7	.893
1989			14	12	.538	2.80	35	34	8	244.1	215	69	123	5	1	0	0	77	8	0	.104	24	34	2	0	1.7	.967
1990			**22**	6	**.786**	2.76	33	33	9	231.1	190	56	131	3	0	0	0	84	18	1	.214	25	36	1	1	1.9	.984
1991			15	14	.517	3.07	35	35	5	234.2	245	62	142	2	0	0	0	84	15	0	.179	27	41	5	1	2.1	.932
1992			15	11	.577	2.77	34	34	10	256.2	218	54	177	4	0	0	0	89	14	0	.157	29	36	3	4	2.0	.956
1993	HOU	N	9	**18**	.333	3.79	34	34	7	237.2	242	60	157	2	0	0	0	71	6	1	.085	19	32	0	2	1.5	1.000
1994			12	6	.667	2.84	23	23	6	164.2	132	45	121	2	0	0	0	58	14	0	.241	21	28	3	2	2.3	.942
1995			10	9	.526	4.77	31	**31**	2	185	205	54	143	1	0	0	0	60	14	0	.233	24	20	2	3	1.5	.957
10 yrs.			130	103	.558	3.32	314	305	51	2081.2	1932	546	1317	21	1	0	0	658	109	2	.166	227	284	24	19	1.7	.955
LEAGUE CHAMPIONSHIP SERIES																											
1990	PIT	N	1	1	.500	1.65	2	2	1	16.1	12	3	13	0	0	0	0	6	1	0	.167	1	6	1	0	4.0	.875
1991			1	1	.500	0.60	2	2	1	15	10	5	10	0	0	0	0	5	1	0	.200	3	0	0	0	1.5	1.000
1992			0	3	.000	3.71	3	3	0	17	18	6	10	0	0	0	0	6	0	0	.000	0	0	0	0	0.0	.000
3 yrs.			2	5	.286	2.05	7	7	2	48.1	40	14	33	0	0	0	0	17	2	0	.118	4	6	1	0	1.6	.909
				2nd				**4th**	**4th**	**8th**			**9th**														

Moe Drabowsky

DRABOWSKY, MYRON WALTER BR TR 6′ 3″ 190 lbs.
B. July 21, 1935, Ozanna, Poland.

Year	Team	Lg	W	L	PCT	ERA	G	GS	CG	IP	H	BB	SO	ShO	Relief W	Relief L	Relief SV	Batting AB	Batting H	Batting HR	BA	PO	A	E	DP	TC/G	FA
1956	CHI	N	2	4	.333	2.47	9	7	3	51	37	39	36	0	0	0	0	16	4	0	.250	2	7	0	0	1.0	1.000
1957			13	15	.464	3.53	36	33	12	239.2	214	94	170	2	0	0	0	82	15	1	.183	19	35	0	1	1.5	1.000
1958			9	11	.450	4.51	22	20	4	125.2	118	73	77	1	1	1	0	45	7	0	.156	12	16	1	2	1.3	.966
1959			5	10	.333	4.13	31	23	3	141.2	138	75	70	1	0	0	0	45	5	0	.111	12	21	2	1	1.1	.943
1960			3	1	.750	6.44	32	7	0	50.1	71	23	26	0	2	0	1	6	0	0	.000	1	6	0	0	0.2	1.000
1961	MIL	N	0	2	.000	4.62	16	0	0	25.1	26	18	5	0	0	2	2	4	1	0	.250	1	7	1	0	0.6	.889
1962	2 teams	CIN N (23G 2–6) KC A (10G 1–1)																									
″	total		3	7	.300	5.03	33	13	1	111	113	41	75	0	1	1	1	23	1	0	.043	9	12	2	2	0.7	.913
1963	KC	A	7	13	.350	3.05	26	22	9	174.1	135	64	109	2	0	0	0	62	10	2	.161	11	19	1	1	1.2	.968
1964			5	13	.278	5.29	53	21	1	168.1	176	72	119	0	1	2	1	43	1	0	.023	11	26	1	4	0.7	.974
1965			1	5	.167	4.42	14	5	0	38.2	44	18	25	0	1	2	0	11	1	0	.091	2	5	0	1	0.5	1.000
1966	BAL	A	6	0	1.000	2.81	44	3	0	96	62	29	98	0	5	0	7	22	8	0	.364	1	12	0	0	0.3	1.000
1967			7	5	.583	1.60	43	0	0	95.1	66	25	96	0	7	5	12	20	7	0	.350	4	15	0	1	0.4	1.000
1968			4	4	.500	1.91	45	0	0	61.1	35	25	46	0	4	4	7	7	2	0	.286	2	8	2	1	0.3	.833
1969	KC	A	11	9	.550	2.94	52	0	0	98	68	30	76	0	**11**	9	11	17	4	0	.235	6	19	0	0	0.5	1.000
1970	2 teams	KC A (24G 1–2) BAL A (21G 4–2)																									
″	total		5	4	.556	3.52	45	0	0	69	58	27	59	0	5	4	3	9	1	0	.111	3	8	0	0	0.2	1.000
1971	STL	N	6	1	.857	3.45	51	0	0	60	45	33	49	0	6	1	8	6	1	0	.167	2	5	0	0	0.1	1.000
1972	2 teams	STL N (30G 1–1) CHI A (7G 0–0)																									
″	total		1	1	.500	2.57	37	0	0	35	35	16	26	0	1	1	2	2	0	0	.000	2	1	3	0	0.2	.500
17 yrs.			88	105	.456	3.71	589	154	33	1640.2	1441	702	1162	6	45	32	55	420	68	3	.162	100	222	13	14	0.6	.961
WORLD SERIES																											
1966	BAL	A	1	0	1.000	0.00	1	0	0	6.2	1	2	11	0	1	0	0	2	0	0	.000	0	0	0	0	0.0	.000
1970			0	0	—	2.70	2	0	0	3.1	2	1	1	0	0	0	0	1	0	0	.000	1	0	0	0	0.5	1.000
2 yrs.			1	0	1.000	0.90	3	0	0	10	3	3	12	0	1	0	0	3	0	0	.000	1	0	0	0	0.3	1.000

Dick Drago

DRAGO, RICHARD ANTHONY BR TR 6′ 1″ 190 lbs.
B. June 25, 1945, Toledo, Ohio.

Year	Team	Lg	W	L	PCT	ERA	G	GS	CG	IP	H	BB	SO	ShO	Relief W	Relief L	Relief SV	Batting AB	Batting H	Batting HR	BA	PO	A	E	DP	TC/G	FA
1969	KC	A	11	13	.458	3.77	41	26	10	200.2	190	65	108	2	0	1	1	52	3	0	.058	25	32	1	6	1.4	.983
1970			9	15	.375	3.75	35	34	7	240	239	72	127	1	0	0	0	76	4	0	.053	10	33	1	5	1.3	.977
1971			17	11	.607	2.99	35	34	15	241	251	46	109	4	0	0	0	77	10	0	.130	7	42	2	9	1.5	.961
1972			12	17	.414	3.01	34	33	11	239.1	230	51	135	2	0	0	0	68	4	0	.059	4	28	2	5	1.0	.941
1973			12	14	.462	4.23	37	33	10	212.2	252	76	98	1	0	1	0	0	0	0	—	14	38	3	3	1.5	.945

Dick Drago *continued*

Year	Team	W	L	PCT	ERA	G	GS	CG	IP	H	BB	SO	ShO	Relief Pitching W	Relief Pitching L	Relief Pitching SV	Batting AB	Batting H	Batting HR	BA	PO	A	E	DP	TC/G	FA
1974	**BOS A**	7	10	.412	3.48	33	18	8	176	165	56	90	0	3	0	3	0	0	0	—	3	21	0	1	0.7	1.000
1975		2	2	.500	3.84	40	2	0	72.2	69	31	43	0	2	2	15	0	0	0	—	3	12	0	0	0.4	1.000
1976	**CAL A**	7	8	.467	4.42	43	0	0	79.1	80	31	43	0	7	8	6	0	0	0	—	3	4	1	0	0.2	.875
1977	**2 teams** **CAL A** (13G 0–1) **BAL A** (36G 6–3)																									
"	**total**	6	4	.600	3.41	49	0	0	60.2	71	18	35	0	6	4	5	0	0	0		0	9	1	0	0.2	.900
1978	**BOS A**	4	4	.500	3.03	37	1	0	77.1	71	32	42	0	3	4	7	0	0	0	—	2	10	1	0	0.4	.923
1979		10	6	.625	3.03	53	1	0	89	85	21	67	0	10	6	13	0	0	0	—	5	11	1	2	0.3	.941
1980		7	7	.500	4.13	43	7	1	133	127	44	63	0	4	4	3	1	0	0	.000	6	17	0	1	0.5	1.000
1981	**SEA A**	4	6	.400	5.50	39	0	0	54	71	15	27	0	4	6	5	0	0	0	—	1	11	0	1	0.3	1.000
13 yrs.		108	117	.480	3.62	519	189	62	1875.2	1901	558	987	10	39	36	58	274	21	0	.077	83	268	13	33	0.7	.964
LEAGUE CHAMPIONSHIP SERIES																										
1975	**BOS A**	0	0	—	0.00	2	0	0	4.2	2	1	2	0	0	0	2	0	0	0	—	1	1	0	0	1.0	1.000
WORLD SERIES																										
1975	**BOS A**	0	1	.000	2.25	2	0	0	4	3	1	1	0	0	1	0	0	0	0	—	0	0	0	0	0.0	.000

Brian Drahman

DRAHMAN, BRIAN STACY BR TR 6′ 3″ 205 lbs.
B. Nov. 7, 1966, Kenton, Ky.

Year	Team	W	L	PCT	ERA	G	GS	CG	IP	H	BB	SO	ShO	Relief Pitching W	Relief Pitching L	Relief Pitching SV	Batting AB	Batting H	Batting HR	BA	PO	A	E	DP	TC/G	FA
1991	**CHI A**	3	2	.600	3.23	28	0	0	30.2	21	13	18	0	3	2	0	0	0	0	—	1	5	1	0	0.3	.857
1992		0	0	—	2.57	5	0	0	7	6	2	1	0	0	0	0	0	0	0	—	1	0	1	0	0.4	.500
1993		0	0	—	0.00	5	0	0	5.1	7	2	3	0	0	0	1	0	0	0	—	0	1	0	0	0.2	1.000
1994	**FLA N**	0	0	—	6.23	9	0	0	13	15	6	7	0	0	0	0	0	0	0	—	1	2	0	1	0.3	1.000
4 yrs.		3	2	.600	3.54	47	0	0	56	49	23	29	0	3	2	1	0	0	0		3	8	2	1	0.3	.846

Logan Drake

DRAKE, LOGAN GAFFNEY BR TR 5′10½″ 165 lbs.
B. Dec. 26, 1900, Spartanburg, S. C. D. June 1, 1940, Columbia, S. C.

Year	Team	W	L	PCT	ERA	G	GS	CG	IP	H	BB	SO	ShO	Relief Pitching W	Relief Pitching L	Relief Pitching SV	Batting AB	Batting H	Batting HR	BA	PO	A	E	DP	TC/G	FA
1922	**CLE A**	0	0	—	3.00	1	0	0	3	4	2	1	0	0	0	0	1	0	0	.000	0	0	0	0	0.0	.000
1923		0	0	—	4.15	4	0	0	4.1	2	5	2	0	0	0	0	0	0	0	—	0	0	0	0	0.0	.000
1924		0	1	.000	10.32	5	1	0	11.1	18	10	8	0	0	0	0	1	0	0	.000	0	2	1	0	0.6	.667
3 yrs.		0	1	.000	7.71	10	1	0	18.2	24	17	11	0	0	0	0	2	0	0	.000	0	2	1	0	0.3	.667

Tom Drake

DRAKE, THOMAS KENDALL BR TR 6′ 1″ 185 lbs.
B. Aug. 7, 1912, Birmingham, Ala. D. July 2, 1988, Birmingham, Ala.

Year	Team	W	L	PCT	ERA	G	GS	CG	IP	H	BB	SO	ShO	Relief Pitching W	Relief Pitching L	Relief Pitching SV	Batting AB	Batting H	Batting HR	BA	PO	A	E	DP	TC/G	FA
1939	**CLE A**	0	1	.000	9.00	8	1	0	15	23	19	1	0	0	1	0	2	0	0	.000	2	4	1	0	0.9	.857
1941	**BKN N**	1	1	.500	4.38	10	2	0	24.2	26	9	12	0	0	0	0	5	2	0	.400	3	3	0	0	0.5	1.000
2 yrs.		1	2	.333	6.13	18	3	0	39.2	49	28	13	0	0	1	0	7	2	0	.286	5	7	1	0	0.7	.923

Mike Draper

DRAPER, MICHAEL ANTHONY BR TR 6′ 2″ 180 lbs.
B. Sept. 14, 1966, Hagerstown, Md.

Year	Team	W	L	PCT	ERA	G	GS	CG	IP	H	BB	SO	ShO	Relief Pitching W	Relief Pitching L	Relief Pitching SV	Batting AB	Batting H	Batting HR	BA	PO	A	E	DP	TC/G	FA
1993	**NY N**	1	1	.500	4.25	29	1	0	42.1	53	14	16	0	1	1	0	3	2	0	.667	2	8	1	0	0.4	.909

Dave Dravecky

DRAVECKY, DAVID FRANCIS BR TL 6′ 1″ 195 lbs.
B. Feb. 14, 1956, Youngstown, Ohio.

Year	Team	W	L	PCT	ERA	G	GS	CG	IP	H	BB	SO	ShO	Relief Pitching W	Relief Pitching L	Relief Pitching SV	Batting AB	Batting H	Batting HR	BA	PO	A	E	DP	TC/G	FA
1982	**SD N**	5	3	.625	2.57	31	10	0	105	86	33	59	0	1	1	2	23	3	0	.130	7	24	0	3	1.0	1.000
1983		14	10	.583	3.58	28	28	9	183.2	181	44	74	1	0	0	0	61	6	0	.098	7	35	1	3	1.5	.977
1984		9	8	.529	2.93	50	14	3	156.2	125	51	71	2	4	4	8	41	4	0	.098	5	19	1	1	0.5	.960
1985		13	11	.542	2.93	34	31	7	214.2	200	57	105	2	0	1	0	69	8	0	.116	13	30	3	2	1.4	.935
1986		9	11	.450	3.07	26	26	3	161.1	149	54	87	1	0	0	0	50	7	1	.140	10	27	1	0	1.5	.974
1987	**2 teams** **SD N** (30G 3–7) **SF N** (18G 7–5)																									
"	**total**	10	12	.455	3.43	48	28	5	191.1	186	64	138	3	0	4	0	56	8	0	.143	16	30	2	2	1.0	.958
1988	**SF N**	2	2	.500	3.16	7	7	1	37	33	8	19	0	0	0	0	10	1	0	.100	0	8	2	0	1.4	.800
1989		2	0	1.000	3.46	2	2	0	13	8	4	5	0	0	0	0	3	1	0	.333	0	3	0	0	1.5	1.000
8 yrs.		64	57	.529	3.13	226	146	28	1062.2	968	315	558	9	5	10	10	313	38	1	.121	58	176	10	11	1.1	.959
LEAGUE CHAMPIONSHIP SERIES																										
1984	**SD N**	0	0	—	0.00	3	0	0	6	2	0	5	0	0	0	0	0	0	0	—	1	1	0	0	0.7	1.000
1987	**SF N**	1	1	.500	0.60	2	2	1	15	7	4	14	1	0	0	0	6	1	0	.167	0	2	0	0	1.0	1.000
2 yrs.		1	1	.500	0.43	5	2	1	21	9	4	19	1 **1st**	0	0	0	6	1	0	.167	1	3	0	0	0.8	1.000
WORLD SERIES																										
1984	**SD N**	0	0	—	0.00	2	0	0	4.2	3	1	5	0	0	0	0	0	0	0	—	0	0	0	0	0.0	.000

Tom Drees

DREES, THOMAS KENT BB TL 6′ 6″ 210 lbs.
B. June 16, 1963, Des Moines, Iowa.

Year	Team	W	L	PCT	ERA	G	GS	CG	IP	H	BB	SO	ShO	Relief Pitching W	Relief Pitching L	Relief Pitching SV	Batting AB	Batting H	Batting HR	BA	PO	A	E	DP	TC/G	FA
1991	**CHI A**	0	0	—	12.27	4	0	0	7.1	10	6	2	0	0	0	0	0	0	0	—	2	0	0	0	0.5	1.000

Darren Dreifort

DREIFORT, DARREN JAMES BR TR 6′ 2″ 205 lbs.
B. May 18, 1972, Wichita, Kans.

Year	Team	W	L	PCT	ERA	G	GS	CG	IP	H	BB	SO	ShO	Relief Pitching W	Relief Pitching L	Relief Pitching SV	Batting AB	Batting H	Batting HR	BA	PO	A	E	DP	TC/G	FA
1994	**LA N**	0	5	.000	6.21	27	0	0	29	45	15	22	0	0	5	6	1	1	0	1.000	2	8	2	0	0.4	.833

Clem Dreisewerd

DREISEWERD, CLEMENT JOHN (Steamboat) BL TL 6′ 1½″ 195 lbs.
B. Jan. 24, 1916, Old Monroe, Mo.

Year	Team	W	L	PCT	ERA	G	GS	CG	IP	H	BB	SO	ShO	Relief Pitching W	Relief Pitching L	Relief Pitching SV	Batting AB	Batting H	Batting HR	BA	PO	A	E	DP	TC/G	FA
1944	**BOS A**	2	4	.333	4.07	7	7	3	48.2	52	9	9	0	0	0	0	16	3	0	.188	1	7	1	0	1.3	.889
1945		0	1	.000	4.66	2	2	0	9.2	13	2	3	0	0	0	0	3	0	0	.000	0	0	0	0	0.0	.000
1946		4	1	.800	4.18	20	1	0	47.1	50	15	19	0	3	1	0	10	0	0	.000	1	15	1	0	0.9	.941
1948	**2 teams** **STL A** (13G 0–2) **NY N** (4G 0–0)																									
"	**total**	0	2	.000	5.66	17	0	0	35	45	13	8	0	0	2	2	9	1	0	.111	1	4	0	1	0.3	1.000
4 yrs.		6	8	.429	4.54	46	10	3	140.2	160	39	39	0	3	3	2	38	4	0	.105	3	26	2	1	0.7	.935
WORLD SERIES																										
1946	**BOS A**	0	0	—	0.00	1	0	0	0.1	0	0	0	0	0	0	0	0	0	0	—	0	0	0	0	0.0	.000

Kirk Dressendorfer

DRESSENDORFER, KIRK RICHARD BR TR 5′11″ 180 lbs.
B. Apr. 8, 1969, Houston, Tex.

Year	Team	W	L	PCT	ERA	G	GS	CG	IP	H	BB	SO	ShO	Relief Pitching W	Relief Pitching L	Relief Pitching SV	Batting AB	Batting H	Batting HR	BA	PO	A	E	DP	TC/G	FA
1991	**OAK A**	3	3	.500	5.45	7	7	0	34.2	33	21	17	0	0	0	0	0	0	0	—	2	3	0	0	0.7	1.000

Bob Dresser

DRESSER, ROBERT NICHOLSON BL TL
B. Oct. 4, 1878, Newton, Mass. D. July 27, 1924, Duxbury, Mass.

Year	Team	Lg	W	L	PCT	ERA	G	GS	CG	IP	H	BB	SO	ShO	Relief W	Relief L	Relief SV	AB	H	HR	BA	PO	A	E	DP	TC/G	FA
1902	BOS	N	0	1	.000	3.00	1	1	1	9	12	0	8	0	0	0	0	4	1	0	.250	0	1	1	0	2.0	.500

Rob Dressler

DRESSLER, ROBERT ANTHONY BR TR 6′ 3″ 180 lbs.
B. Feb. 2, 1954, Portland, Ore.

Year	Team	Lg	W	L	PCT	ERA	G	GS	CG	IP	H	BB	SO	ShO	Relief W	Relief L	Relief SV	AB	H	HR	BA	PO	A	E	DP	TC/G	FA
1975	SF	N	1	0	1.000	1.13	3	2	1	16	17	4	6	0	0	0	0	4	0	0	.000	2	4	0	0	2.0	1.000
1976			3	10	.231	4.43	25	19	0	107.2	125	35	33	0	1	0	0	31	4	0	.129	13	19	4	1	1.4	.889
1978	STL	N	0	1	.000	2.08	3	2	0	13	12	4	4	0	0	0	0	3	0	0	.000	0	2	0	0	0.7	1.000
1979	SEA	A	3	2	.600	4.93	21	11	2	104	134	22	36	0	0	0	0	0	0	0	—	4	16	0	1	1.0	1.000
1980			4	10	.286	3.99	30	14	3	149	161	33	50	0	0	3	0	0	0	0	—	8	30	3	3	1.4	.927
5 yrs.			11	23	.324	4.18	82	48	6	389.2	449	98	129	0	1	3	0	38	4	0	.105	27	71	7	5	1.3	.933

Dave Drew

DREW, DAVID
Deceased.

Year	Team	Lg	W	L	PCT	ERA	G	GS	CG	IP	H	BB	SO	ShO	Relief W	Relief L	Relief SV	AB	H	HR	BA	PO	A	E	DP	TC/G	FA
1884	PHI	U	0	1	.000	*3.86*	1	0	0	7	7	0	2	0	0	1	0	*				62	30	12	4	6.1	.885

Karl Drews

DREWS, KARL AUGUST BR TR 6′ 4½″ 192 lbs.
B. Feb. 22, 1920, Staten Island, N. Y. D. Aug. 13, 1963, Dania, Fla.

Year	Team	Lg	W	L	PCT	ERA	G	GS	CG	IP	H	BB	SO	ShO	Relief W	Relief L	Relief SV	AB	H	HR	BA	PO	A	E	DP	TC/G	FA
1946	NY	A	0	1	.000	8.53	3	1	0	6.1	6	6	4	0	0	0	0	1	0	0	.000	0	1	1	0	0.7	.500
1947			6	6	.500	4.91	30	10	0	91.2	92	55	45	0	4	0	1	27	1	0	.037	4	17	1	1	0.7	.955
1948	2 teams	NY A (19G 2–3)	STL A (20G 3–2)																								
″	total		5	5	.500	5.92	39	4	0	76	78	69	22	0	4	4	3	15	0	0	.000	3	20	0	1	0.6	1.000
1949	STL	A	4	12	.250	6.64	31	23	3	139.2	180	66	35	1	0	1	0	46	0	0	.000	5	23	0	1	0.9	1.000
1951	PHI	N	1	0	1.000	6.26	5	3	1	23	29	7	13	0	0	0	0	8	2	0	.250	3	4	0	0	1.4	1.000
1952			14	15	.483	2.72	33	30	15	228.2	213	52	96	5	1	0	0	82	9	0	.110	15	44	3	3	1.9	.952
1953			9	10	.474	4.52	47	27	6	185.1	218	50	72	0	0	1	3	59	7	0	.119	13	38	1	3	1.1	.981
1954	2 teams	PHI N (8G 1–0)	CIN N (22G 4–4)																								
″	total		5	4	.556	5.92	30	9	1	76	97	27	35	1	2	1	0	16	2	0	.125	3	15	0	1	0.6	1.000
8 yrs.			44	53	.454	4.76	218	107	26	826.2	913	332	322	7	11	7	7	254	21	0	.083	46	162	6	10	1.0	.972
WORLD SERIES																											
1947	NY	A	0	0	—	3.00	2	0	0	3	2	1	0	0	0	0	0	2	0	0	.000	0	3	0	0	1.5	1.000

Steve Dreyer

DREYER, STEVEN WILLIAM BR TR 6′ 3″ 185 lbs.
B. Nov. 19, 1969, Ames, Iowa.

Year	Team	Lg	W	L	PCT	ERA	G	GS	CG	IP	H	BB	SO	ShO	Relief W	Relief L	Relief SV	AB	H	HR	BA	PO	A	E	DP	TC/G	FA
1993	TEX	A	3	3	.500	5.71	10	6	0	41	48	20	23	0	0	0	0	0	0	0	—	2	4	0	0	0.6	1.000
1994			1	1	.500	5.71	5	3	0	17.1	19	8	11	0	0	0	0	0	0	0	—	2	0	0	0	0.4	1.000
2 yrs.			4	4	.500	5.71	15	9	0	58.1	67	28	34	0	0	0	0	0	0	0		4	4	0	0	0.5	1.000

Denny Driscoll

DRISCOLL, JOHN F. BL TL 5′10½″ 160 lbs.
B. Nov. 19, 1855, Lowell, Mass. D. July 11, 1886, Lowell, Mass.

Year	Team	Lg	W	L	PCT	ERA	G	GS	CG	IP	H	BB	SO	ShO	Relief W	Relief L	Relief SV	AB	H	HR	BA	PO	A	E	DP	TC/G	FA
1880	BUF	N	1	3	.250	3.89	6	4	4	41.2	48	9	17	0	0	0	0	65	10	0	.154	18	10	4	2	1.6	.875
1882	PIT	AA	13	9	.591	***1.21***	23	23	23	201	162	12	59	0	0	0	0	80	11	1	.138	4	50	7	1	2.7	.885
1883			18	21	.462	*3.99*	41	40	35	336.1	427	39	79	1	0	0	0	148	27	0	.182	14	99	14	2	2.8	.890
1884	LOU	AA	6	6	.500	*3.44*	13	13	10	102	110	7	16	0	0	0	0	48	9	0	.188	3	37	9	2	3.3	.816
4 yrs.			38	39	.494	3.08	83	80	72	681	747	67	171	1	0	0	0	*				51	207	43	8	2.7	.857

Mike Driscoll

DRISCOLL, MICHAEL COLUMBUS BR TR 6′ 1″ 160 lbs.
B. Oct. 19, 1892, Rockland, Mass. D. Mar. 22, 1953, Foxboro, Mass.

Year	Team	Lg	W	L	PCT	ERA	G	GS	CG	IP	H	BB	SO	ShO	Relief W	Relief L	Relief SV	AB	H	HR	BA	PO	A	E	DP	TC/G	FA
1916	PHI	A	0	1	.000	5.40	1	0	0	5	6	2	0	0	0	1	0	2	0	0	.000	0	4	0	0	4.0	1.000

Tom Drohan

DROHAN, THOMAS F. BR TR 5′10″ 175 lbs.
B. Aug. 26, 1887, Fall River, Mass. D. Sept. 17, 1926, Kewanee, Ill.

Year	Team	Lg	W	L	PCT	ERA	G	GS	CG	IP	H	BB	SO	ShO	Relief W	Relief L	Relief SV	AB	H	HR	BA	PO	A	E	DP	TC/G	FA
1913	WAS	A	0	0	—	9.00	2	0	0	2	5	0	2	0	0	0	0	0	0	0	—	0	1	0	0	0.5	1.000

Dick Drott

DROTT, RICHARD FRED (Hummer) BR TR 6′ 185 lbs.
B. July 1, 1936, Cincinnati, Ohio D. Aug. 16, 1985, Glendale Heights, Ill.

Year	Team	Lg	W	L	PCT	ERA	G	GS	CG	IP	H	BB	SO	ShO	Relief W	Relief L	Relief SV	AB	H	HR	BA	PO	A	E	DP	TC/G	FA
1957	CHI	N	15	11	.577	3.58	38	32	7	229	200	**129**	170	3	2	0	0	80	8	0	.100	7	33	1	2	1.1	.976
1958			7	11	.389	5.43	39	31	4	167.1	156	99	127	0	0	0	0	55	15	0	.273	9	27	1	0	0.9	.973
1959			1	2	.333	5.93	8	6	1	27.1	25	26	15	1	0	0	0	8	1	0	.125	0	4	1	0	0.6	.800
1960			0	6	.000	7.16	23	9	0	55.1	63	42	32	0	0	0	0	10	1	0	.100	4	7	0	0	0.5	1.000
1961			1	4	.200	4.22	35	8	0	98	75	51	48	0	1	1	0	22	6	0	.273	1	11	1	0	0.4	.923
1962	HOU	N	1	0	1.000	7.62	6	1	0	13	12	9	10	0	0	0	0	4	0	0	.000	1	1	1	0	0.5	.667
1963			2	12	.143	4.98	27	14	2	97.2	95	49	58	1	0	2	0	23	3	0	.130	2	13	1	0	0.6	.938
7 yrs.			27	46	.370	4.78	176	101	14	687.2	626	405	460	5	3	3	0	202	34	0	.168	24	96	6	2	0.7	.952

Louis Drucke

DRUCKE, LOUIS FRANK BR TR 6′ 1″ 188 lbs.
B. Dec. 3, 1888, Waco, Tex. D. Sept. 22, 1955, Waco, Tex.

Year	Team	Lg	W	L	PCT	ERA	G	GS	CG	IP	H	BB	SO	ShO	Relief W	Relief L	Relief SV	AB	H	HR	BA	PO	A	E	DP	TC/G	FA
1909	NY	N	2	1	.667	2.25	3	3	2	24	20	13	8	0	0	0	0	8	1	0	.125	0	5	0	0	1.7	1.000
1910			12	10	.545	2.47	34	27	15	215.1	174	82	151	0	1	0	0	70	15	1	.214	11	59	8	5	2.3	.897
1911			4	4	.500	4.04	15	10	4	75.2	83	41	42	0	0	0	0	23	2	0	.087	4	23	1	1	1.9	.964
1912			0	0	—	13.50	1	0	0	2	5	1	0	0	0	0	1	0	0	0	—	0	0	0	0	0.0	.000
4 yrs.			18	15	.545	2.90	53	40	21	317	282	137	201	0	1	0	1	101	18	1	.178	15	87	9	6	2.1	.919

Carl Druhot

DRUHOT, CARL A. BL TL 5′ 7″ 150 lbs.
B. Sept. 1, 1882, Ohio D. Feb. 11, 1918, Portland, Ore.

Year	Team	Lg	W	L	PCT	ERA	G	GS	CG	IP	H	BB	SO	ShO	Relief W	Relief L	Relief SV	AB	H	HR	BA	PO	A	E	DP	TC/G	FA
1906	2 teams	CIN N (4G 2–2)	STL N (15G 6–7)																								
″	total		8	9	.471	2.90	19	16	13	155.1	144	53	59	1	2	0	0	65	15	0	.231	9	39	1	4	2.6	.980
1907	STL	N	0	1	.000	15.43	1	1	0	2.1	3	4	1	0	0	0	0	0	0	0	—	0	1	0	0	1.0	1.000
2 yrs.			8	10	.444	3.08	20	17	13	157.2	147	57	60	1	2	0	0	65	15	0	.231	9	40	1	4	2.5	.980

Tim Drummond

DRUMMOND, TIMOTHY DARNELL
B. Dec. 24, 1964, La Plata, Md.
BR TR 6′ 3″ 170 lbs.

Year	Team	W	L	PCT	ERA	G	GS	CG	IP	H	BB	SO	ShO	Relief W	Relief L	Relief SV	AB	H	HR	BA	PO	A	E	DP	TC/G	FA
1987	PIT N	0	0	—	4.50	6	0	0	6	5	3	5	0	0	0	0	1	0	0	.000	0	2	0	0	0.3	1.000
1989	MIN A	0	0	—	3.86	8	0	0	16.1	16	8	9	0	0	0	1	0	0	0	—	0	1	0	0	0.1	1.000
1990		3	5	.375	4.35	35	4	0	91	104	36	49	0	3	2	1	0	0	0	—	6	7	1	1	0.4	.929
3 yrs.		3	5	.375	4.29	49	4	0	113.1	125	47	63	0	3	2	2	1	0	0	.000	6	10	1	1	0.3	.941

Don Drysdale

DRYSDALE, DONALD SCOTT (Big D)
B. July 23, 1936, Van Nuys, Calif. D. July 3, 1993, Montreal, Que., Canada.
Hall of Fame 1984.
BR TR 6′ 5″ 190 lbs.

Year	Team	W	L	PCT	ERA	G	GS	CG	IP	H	BB	SO	ShO	Relief W	Relief L	Relief SV	AB	H	HR	BA	PO	A	E	DP	TC/G	FA
1956	BKN N	5	5	.500	2.64	25	12	2	99	95	31	55	0	1	0	0	26	5	1	.192	8	20	2	1	1.2	.933
1957		17	9	.654	2.69	34	29	9	221	197	61	148	4	2	1	0	73	9	2	.123	15	60	2	4	2.3	.974
1958	LA N	12	13	.480	4.17	44	29	6	211.2	214	72	131	1	1	1	0	66	15	7	.227	15	45	6	10	1.5	.909
1959		17	13	.567	3.46	44	36	15	270.2	237	93	**242**	**4**	1	2	2	91	15	4	.165	18	48	3	4	1.6	.957
1960		15	14	.517	2.84	41	36	15	269	214	72	**246**	5	1	1	2	83	13	0	.157	18	60	3	3	2.0	.963
1961		13	10	.565	3.69	40	37	10	244	236	83	182	3	0	0	0	83	16	5	.193	13	36	3	3	1.3	.942
1962		**25**	9	.735	2.83	43	**41**	19	**314.1**	272	78	**232**	2	0	1	1	111	22	0	.198	10	60	7	5	1.8	.909
1963		19	17	.528	2.63	42	**42**	17	315.1	**287**	57	251	3	0	0	0	96	16	0	.167	19	62	4	7	2.0	.953
1964		18	16	.529	2.18	40	**40**	21	**321.1**	242	68	237	5	0	0	0	110	19	1	.173	13	68	3	5	2.1	.964
1965		23	12	.657	2.77	44	**42**	20	308.1	**270**	66	210	7	0	0	1	130	39	7	.300	22	55	9	4	2.0	.895
1966		13	16	.448	3.42	40	40	11	273.2	279	45	177	3	0	0	0	106	20	2	.189	10	45	7	1	1.5	.887
1967		13	16	.448	2.74	38	38	9	282	269	60	196	3	0	0	0	93	12	0	.129	11	64	5	3	2.1	.938
1968		14	12	.538	2.15	31	31	12	239	201	56	155	8	0	0	0	79	14	0	.177	15	50	5	4	2.3	.929
1969		5	4	.556	4.43	12	12	1	63	71	13	24	1	0	0	0	22	3	0	.136	1	13	0	1	1.2	1.000
14 yrs.		209	166	.557	2.95	518	465	167	3432.1	3084	855	2486	49	6	6	6	1169	218	29	.186	188	686	59	55	1.8	.937
WORLD SERIES																										
1956	BKN N	0	0	—	9.00	1	0	0	2	2	1	1	0	0	0	0	0	0	0	—	0	0	0	0	0.0	.000
1959	LA N	1	0	1.000	1.29	1	1	0	7	11	4	5	0	0	0	0	2	0	0	.000	1	1	0	0	2.0	1.000
1963		1	0	1.000	0.00	1	1	1	9	3	1	9	1	0	0	0	1	0	0	.000	1	3	0	0	4.0	1.000
1965		1	1	.500	3.86	2	2	1	11.2	12	3	15	0	0	0	0	5	0	0	.000	0	2	0	0	1.0	1.000
1966		0	2	.000	4.50	2	2	1	10	8	3	6	0	0	0	0	2	0	0	.000	0	3	0	0	1.5	1.000
5 yrs.		3	3	.500	2.95	7	6	3	39.2	36	12	36	1	0	0	0	10	0	0	.000	2	9	0	0	1.6	1.000

Monk Dubiel

DUBIEL, WALTER JOHN
B. Feb. 12, 1918, Hartford, Conn. D. Oct. 23, 1969, Hartford, Conn.
BR TR 6′ 190 lbs.

Year	Team	W	L	PCT	ERA	G	GS	CG	IP	H	BB	SO	ShO	Relief W	Relief L	Relief SV	AB	H	HR	BA	PO	A	E	DP	TC/G	FA
1944	NY A	13	13	.500	3.38	30	28	19	232	217	86	79	3	1	0	0	83	15	0	.181	13	45	2	2	2.0	.967
1945		10	9	.526	4.64	26	20	9	151.1	157	62	45	1	1	1	0	58	16	1	.276	9	21	1	2	1.2	.968
1948	PHI N	9	10	.474	3.89	37	17	6	150.1	139	58	42	2	1	3	4	42	7	0	.167	12	18	1	1	0.8	.968
1949	CHI N	6	9	.400	4.14	32	20	3	147.2	142	54	52	1	1	1	4	35	10	0	.286	13	31	4	3	1.5	.917
1950		6	10	.375	4.16	39	12	4	142.2	152	67	51	2	3	3	2	45	9	0	.200	10	34	1	2	1.2	.978
1951		2	2	.500	2.30	22	0	0	54.2	46	22	19	0	2	2	1	12	0	0	.000	7	8	0	1	0.7	1.000
1952		0	0	—	0.00	1	0	0	0.2	1	0	1	0	0	0	0	0	0	0	—	0	0	0	0	0.0	.000
7 yrs.		46	53	.465	3.87	187	97	41	879.1	854	349	289	9	9	10	11	275	57	1	.207	64	157	9	11	1.2	.961

Brian Dubois

DUBOIS, BRIAN ANDREW
B. Apr. 18, 1967, Joliet, Ill.
BL TL 5′10″ 165 lbs.

Year	Team	W	L	PCT	ERA	G	GS	CG	IP	H	BB	SO	ShO	Relief W	Relief L	Relief SV	AB	H	HR	BA	PO	A	E	DP	TC/G	FA
1989	DET A	0	4	.000	1.75	6	5	0	36	29	17	13	0	0	0	1	0	0	0	—	2	5	0	0	1.2	1.000
1990		3	5	.375	5.09	12	11	0	58.1	70	22	34	0	0	0	0	0	0	0	—	1	3	1	1	0.4	.800
2 yrs.		3	9	.250	3.82	18	16	0	94.1	99	39	47	0	0	0	1	0	0	0		3	8	1	1	0.7	.917

Jean Dubuc

DUBUC, JEAN JOSEPH OCTAVE (Chauncey)
Born Jean Baptiste Arthur Dubuc.
B. Sept. 15, 1888, St. Johnsbury, Vt. D. Aug. 28, 1958, Ft. Myers, Fla.
BR TR 5′10½″ 185 lbs.

Year	Team	W	L	PCT	ERA	G	GS	CG	IP	H	BB	SO	ShO	Relief W	Relief L	Relief SV	AB	H	HR	BA	PO	A	E	DP	TC/G	FA
1908	CIN N	5	6	.455	2.74	15	9	7	85.1	62	41	32	1	2	0	0	29	4	0	.138	6	26	2	0	2.3	.941
1909		3	5	.375	3.66	19	5	2	71.1	72	46	19	0	2	2	2	18	3	0	.167	4	23	5	0	1.7	.844
1912	DET A	17	10	.630	2.77	37	26	23	250	217	109	97	2	1	1	3	108	29	1	.269	12	94	4	5	2.8	.964
1913		15	14	.517	2.89	36	28	22	242.2	228	91	73	1	0	2	2	135	36	2	.267	16	110	6	7	3.4	.955
1914		13	14	.481	3.46	36	27	15	224	216	76	70	2	2	0	1	124	28	1	.226	14	83	6	3	2.9	.942
1915		17	12	.586	3.21	39	33	22	258	231	88	74	5	0	2	2	112	23	0	.205	9	86	3	2	2.5	.969
1916		10	10	.500	2.96	36	16	8	170.1	134	84	40	1	5	2	1	78	20	0	.256	7	73	4	5	2.3	.952
1918	BOS A	0	1	.000	4.22	2	1	1	10.2	11	5	1	0	0	0	0	6	1	0	.167	2	2	0	0	2.0	1.000
1919	NY N	6	4	.600	2.66	36	5	1	132	119	37	32	0	**6**	**4**	3	42	6	0	.143	8	46	2	1	1.6	.964
9 yrs.		86	76	.531	3.04	256	150	101	1444.1	1290	577	438	12	18	13	14	*				78	543	32	23	2.5	.951

Jim Duckworth

DUCKWORTH, JAMES RAYMOND
B. May 24, 1939, National City, Calif.
BR TR 6′ 4″ 194 lbs.

Year	Team	W	L	PCT	ERA	G	GS	CG	IP	H	BB	SO	ShO	Relief W	Relief L	Relief SV	AB	H	HR	BA	PO	A	E	DP	TC/G	FA
1963	WAS A	4	12	.250	6.04	37	15	2	120.2	131	67	66	0	2	3	0	27	0	0	.000	6	18	4	0	0.8	.857
1964		1	6	.143	4.34	30	2	0	56	52	25	56	0	1	4	3	9	2	0	.222	1	9	1	2	0.4	.909
1965		2	2	.500	3.94	17	8	0	64	45	36	74	0	0	0	0	18	0	0	.000	3	5	0	0	0.5	1.000
1966	**2 teams** **WAS A** (5G 0–3) **KC A** (8G 0–2)																									
"	**total**	0	5	.000	6.84	13	4	0	26.1	28	20	24	0	0	2	1	5	0	0	.000	1	2	0	0	0.2	1.000
4 yrs.		7	25	.219	5.26	97	29	2	267	256	148	220	0	3	9	4	59	2	0	.034	11	34	5	2	0.5	.900

Clise Dudley

DUDLEY, ELZIE CLISE
B. Aug. 8, 1903, Graham, N. C. D. Jan. 12, 1989, Moncks Corner, S. C.
BL TR 6′ 1″ 195 lbs.

Year	Team	W	L	PCT	ERA	G	GS	CG	IP	H	BB	SO	ShO	Relief W	Relief L	Relief SV	AB	H	HR	BA	PO	A	E	DP	TC/G	FA
1929	BKN N	6	14	.300	5.69	35	21	8	156.2	202	64	33	1	1	2	0	51	5	2	.098	8	48	4	2	1.7	.933
1930		2	4	.333	6.34	21	7	2	66.2	103	27	18	0	0	0	1	24	5	0	.208	2	17	1	2	1.0	.950
1931	PHI N	8	14	.364	3.52	30	24	8	179	206	56	50	0	0	0	0	84	18	0	.214	12	41	0	1	1.8	1.000
1932		1	1	.500	7.13	13	0	0	17.2	23	8	5	0	1	1	1	14	4	1	.286	0	6	0	0	0.5	1.000
1933	PIT N	0	0	—	135.00	1	0	0	0.1	6	1	0	0	0	0	0	0	0	0	—	0	0	0	0	0.0	.000
5 yrs.		17	33	.340	5.03	100	52	18	420.1	540	156	106	1	2	3	2	173	32	3	.185	22	112	5	5	1.4	.964

Hal Dues

DUES, HAL JOSEPH BR TR 6′ 3″ 180 lbs.
B. Sept. 22, 1954, LaMarque, Tex.

Year	Team	Lg	W	L	PCT	ERA	G	GS	CG	IP	H	BB	SO	ShO	Relief Pitching W	Relief Pitching L	Relief Pitching SV	Batting AB	Batting H	HR	BA	PO	A	E	DP	TC/G	FA
1977	**MON**	**N**	1	1	.500	4.30	6	4	0	23	26	9	9	0	0	0	0	5	0	0	.000	2	5	0	0	1.2	1.000
1978			5	6	.455	2.36	25	12	1	99	85	42	36	0	1	1	1	31	6	0	.194	5	16	2	0	0.9	.913
1980			0	1	.000	6.75	6	1	0	12	17	4	2	0	0	1	0	3	0	0	.000	0	4	0	0	0.7	1.000
3 yrs.			6	8	.429	3.09	37	17	1	134	128	55	47	0	1	2	1	39	6	0	.154	7	25	2	0	0.9	.941

Larry Duff

DUFF, CECIL ELBA BL TR 6′ 1″ 175 lbs.
B. May 6, 1895, Radersburg, Mont. D. Nov. 10, 1969, Bend, Ore.

Year	Team	Lg	W	L	PCT	ERA	G	GS	CG	IP	H	BB	SO	ShO	Relief Pitching W	Relief Pitching L	Relief Pitching SV	Batting AB	Batting H	HR	BA	PO	A	E	DP	TC/G	FA
1922	**CHI**	**A**	1	1	.500	4.97	3	1	0	12.2	16	3	7	0	1	0	0	5	2	0	.400	0	1	0	0	0.3	1.000

Jim Duffalo

DUFFALO, JAMES FRANCIS BR TR 6′ 1″ 175 lbs.
B. Nov. 25, 1935, Helvetia, Pa.

Year	Team	Lg	W	L	PCT	ERA	G	GS	CG	IP	H	BB	SO	ShO	Relief Pitching W	Relief Pitching L	Relief Pitching SV	Batting AB	Batting H	HR	BA	PO	A	E	DP	TC/G	FA
1961	**SF**	**N**	5	1	.833	4.23	24	4	1	61.2	59	32	37	0	3	0	1	17	5	1	.294	2	9	0	0	0.5	1.000
1962			1	2	.333	3.64	24	2	0	42	42	23	29	0	1	1	0	6	0	0	.000	1	5	1	1	0.3	.857
1963			4	2	.667	2.87	34	5	0	75.1	56	37	55	0	3	0	2	18	2	0	.111	7	15	1	0	0.7	.957
1964			5	1	.833	2.92	35	3	1	74	57	31	55	0	4	1	3	14	1	0	.071	4	9	1	0	0.4	.929
1965	**2 teams** **SF N** (2G 0–1) **CIN N** (22G 0–1)																										
″	**total**		0	2	.000	3.63	24	0	0	44.2	34	32	34	0	0	2	0	8	0	0	.000	5	8	0	1	0.5	1.000
5 yrs.			15	8	.652	3.39	141	14	2	297.2	248	155	210	0	11	4	6	63	8	1	.127	19	46	3	2	0.5	.956

John Duffie

DUFFIE, JOHN BROWN BR TR 6′ 7″ 210 lbs.
B. Oct. 4, 1945, Greenwood, S. C.

Year	Team	Lg	W	L	PCT	ERA	G	GS	CG	IP	H	BB	SO	ShO	Relief Pitching W	Relief Pitching L	Relief Pitching SV	Batting AB	Batting H	HR	BA	PO	A	E	DP	TC/G	FA
1967	**LA**	**N**	0	2	.000	2.79	2	2	0	9.2	11	4	6	0	0	0	0	2	0	0	.000	1	2	2	0	2.5	.600

Bernie Duffy

DUFFY, BERNARD ALLEN BR TR 5′11″ 180 lbs.
B. Aug. 18, 1893, Vinson, Okla. D. Feb. 9, 1962, Abilene, Tex.

Year	Team	Lg	W	L	PCT	ERA	G	GS	CG	IP	H	BB	SO	ShO	Relief Pitching W	Relief Pitching L	Relief Pitching SV	Batting AB	Batting H	HR	BA	PO	A	E	DP	TC/G	FA
1913	**PIT**	**N**	0	0	—	5.56	3	2	0	11.1	18	3	8	0	0	0	0	4	1	0	.250	0	4	0	0	1.3	1.000

Dan Dugan

DUGAN, DANIEL PHILLIP BL TL 6′ 1½″ 187 lbs.
B. Feb. 22, 1907, Plainfield, N. J. D. June 25, 1968, Greenbrook, N. J.

Year	Team	Lg	W	L	PCT	ERA	G	GS	CG	IP	H	BB	SO	ShO	Relief Pitching W	Relief Pitching L	Relief Pitching SV	Batting AB	Batting H	HR	BA	PO	A	E	DP	TC/G	FA
1928	**CHI**	**A**	0	0	—	0.00	1	0	0	0.1	0	0	0	0	0	0	0	0	0	0	—	0	0	0	0	0.0	.000
1929			1	4	.200	6.65	19	2	0	65	77	19	15	0	1	2	1	20	3	0	.150	2	6	0	0	0.4	1.000
2 yrs.			1	4	.200	6.61	20	2	0	65.1	77	19	15	0	1	2	1	20	3	0	.150	2	6	0	0	0.4	1.000

Ed Dugan

DUGAN, EDWARD JOHN
Brother of Bill Dugan.
B. 1864, Brooklyn, N. Y. Deceased.

Year	Team	Lg	W	L	PCT	ERA	G	GS	CG	IP	H	BB	SO	ShO	Relief Pitching W	Relief Pitching L	Relief Pitching SV	Batting AB	Batting H	HR	BA	PO	A	E	DP	TC/G	FA
1884	**RIC**	**AA**	5	14	.263	*4.49*	20	20	20	166.1	196	15	60	0	0	0	0	70	8	0	.114	17	27	15	2	2.7	.746

Bill Duggleby

DUGGLEBY, WILLIAM JAMES (Frosty Bill) TR
B. Mar. 16, 1874, Utica, N. Y. D. Aug. 30, 1944, Redfield, N. Y.

Year	Team	Lg	W	L	PCT	ERA	G	GS	CG	IP	H	BB	SO	ShO	Relief Pitching W	Relief Pitching L	Relief Pitching SV	Batting AB	Batting H	HR	BA	PO	A	E	DP	TC/G	FA
1898	**PHI**	**N**	3	3	.500	5.50	9	5	4	54	70	18	12	0	1	0	0	21	5	1	.238	4	16	1	1	2.3	.952
1901			19	12	.613	2.87	34	29	25	275.2	294	40	94	5	1	1	0	111	19	0	.171	20	94	8	2	3.6	.934
1902	**2 teams** **PHI A** (2G 1–1) **PHI N** (33G 11–17)																										
″	**total**		12	18	.400	3.36	35	29	27	275.2	301	61	64	0	1	0	0	105	17	0	.162	14	89	7	3	3.1	.936
1903	**PHI**	**N**	13	18	.419	3.75	36	30	28	264.1	318	79	57	3	1	0	1	104	24	0	.231	13	80	9	2	2.8	.912
1904			12	13	.480	3.78	32	27	22	223.2	265	53	55	2	1	1	1	82	14	2	.171	9	69	8	1	2.7	.907
1905			18	17	.514	2.46	38	36	27	289	270	83	75	1	1	1	0	101	11	1	.109	8	77	4	4	2.3	.955
1906			13	19	.406	2.25	42	30	22	280.1	241	66	83	5	1	2	2	99	14	2	.141	14	86	5	1	2.5	.952
1907	**2 teams** **PHI N** (5G 0–2) **PIT N** (9G 2–2)																										
″	**total**		2	4	.333	4.67	14	5	3	69.1	77	23	12	1	1	0	0	22	3	0	.136	4	30	1	1	2.5	.971
8 yrs.			92	104	.469	3.19	240	191	158	1732	1836	423	452	17	8	5	4	645	107	6	.166	86	541	43	15	2.8	.936

Martin Duke

DUKE, MARTIN F. TL
Born Martin F. Duck.
B. 1867, Zanesville, Ohio D. Dec. 31, 1898, Minneapolis, Minn.

Year	Team	Lg	W	L	PCT	ERA	G	GS	CG	IP	H	BB	SO	ShO	Relief Pitching W	Relief Pitching L	Relief Pitching SV	Batting AB	Batting H	HR	BA	PO	A	E	DP	TC/G	FA
1891	**WAS**	**AA**	0	3	.000	7.43	4	3	2	23	36	19	5	0	0	0	0	9	1	0	.111	0	6	2	1	2.0	.750

Jan Dukes

DUKES, NOBLE JAN BL TL 5′11″ 175 lbs.
B. Aug. 16, 1945, Cheyenne, Wyo.

Year	Team	Lg	W	L	PCT	ERA	G	GS	CG	IP	H	BB	SO	ShO	Relief Pitching W	Relief Pitching L	Relief Pitching SV	Batting AB	Batting H	HR	BA	PO	A	E	DP	TC/G	FA
1969	**WAS**	**A**	0	2	.000	2.45	8	0	0	11	8	4	3	0	0	2	0	1	0	0	.000	0	0	0	0	0.0	.000
1970			0	0	—	2.57	5	0	0	7	6	1	4	0	0	0	0	1	0	0	.000	1	1	0	0	0.4	1.000
1972	**TEX**	**A**	0	0	—	4.50	3	0	0	2	1	5	0	0	0	0	0	0	0	0	—	0	1	0	0	0.3	1.000
3 yrs.			0	2	.000	2.70	16	0	0	20	15	10	7	0	0	2	0	2	0	0	.000	1	2	0	0	0.2	1.000

Tom Dukes

DUKES, THOMAS EARL BR TR 6′ 2″ 185 lbs.
B. Aug. 31, 1942, Knoxville, Tenn.

Year	Team	Lg	W	L	PCT	ERA	G	GS	CG	IP	H	BB	SO	ShO	Relief Pitching W	Relief Pitching L	Relief Pitching SV	Batting AB	Batting H	HR	BA	PO	A	E	DP	TC/G	FA
1967	**HOU**	**N**	0	2	.000	5.32	17	0	0	23.2	25	11	23	0	0	2	1	2	1	0	.500	1	2	0	0	0.2	1.000
1968			2	2	.500	4.27	43	0	0	52.2	62	28	37	0	2	2	4	4	0	0	.000	1	11	1	0	0.3	.923
1969	**SD**	**N**	1	0	1.000	7.36	13	0	0	22	26	10	15	0	1	0	1	1	0	0	.000	0	4	0	0	0.3	1.000
1970			1	6	.143	4.04	53	0	0	69	62	25	56	0	1	6	10	7	0	0	.000	2	8	1	1	0.2	.909
1971	**BAL**	**A**	1	5	.167	3.55	28	0	0	38	40	8	30	0	1	5	4	7	1	0	.143	1	3	0	0	0.1	1.000
1972	**CAL**	**A**	0	1	.000	1.64	7	0	0	11	11	0	8	0	0	1	1	0	0	0	—	0	0	1	0	0.1	.000
6 yrs.			5	16	.238	4.37	161	0	0	216.1	226	82	169	0	5	16	21	21	2	0	.095	5	28	3	1	0.2	.917
WORLD SERIES																											
1971	**BAL**	**A**	0	0	—	0.00	2	0	0	4	2	0	1	0	0	0	0	0	0	0	—	0	0	0	0	0.0	.000

Bob Duliba

DULIBA, ROBERT JOHN BR TR 5′10″ 180 lbs.
B. Jan. 9, 1935, Glen Lyon, Pa.

Year	Team	Lg	W	L	PCT	ERA	G	GS	CG	IP	H	BB	SO	ShO	Relief Pitching W	Relief Pitching L	Relief Pitching SV	Batting AB	Batting H	HR	BA	PO	A	E	DP	TC/G	FA
1959	**STL**	**N**	0	1	.000	2.78	11	0	0	22.2	19	12	14	0	0	1	1	4	0	0	.000	4	7	0	0	1.0	1.000
1960			4	4	.500	4.20	27	0	0	40.2	49	16	23	0	4	4	0	5	1	0	.200	3	5	0	0	0.3	1.000
1962			2	0	1.000	2.06	28	0	0	39.1	33	17	22	0	2	0	2	4	0	0	.000	3	7	0	0	0.4	1.000
1963	**LA**	**A**	1	1	.500	1.17	6	0	0	7.2	3	6	4	0	1	1	1	1	0	0	.000	0	0	0	0	0.0	.000
1964			6	4	.600	3.59	58	0	0	72.2	80	22	33	0	6	4	9	5	0	0	.000	5	14	0	2	0.3	1.000

Bob Duliba *continued*

Year	Team		W	L	PCT	ERA	G	GS	CG	IP	H	BB	SO	ShO	Relief Pitching W	L	SV	Batting AB	H	HR	BA	PO	A	E	DP	TC/G	FA
1965	BOS	A	4	2	.667	3.78	39	0	0	64.1	60	22	27	0	4	2	1	7	0	0	.000	2	12	2	1	0.4	.875
1967	KC	A	0	0	—	6.52	7	0	0	9.2	13	1	6	0	0	0	0	0	0	0	—	0	1	0	0	0.1	1.000
7 yrs.			17	12	.586	3.47	176	0	0	257	257	96	129	0	17	12	14	26	1	0	.038	17	46	2	3	0.4	.969

George Dumont

DUMONT, GEORGE HENRY (Pea Soup) BR TR 5′11″ 163 lbs.
B. Nov. 13, 1895, Minneapolis, Minn. D. Oct. 13, 1956, Minneapolis, Minn.

1915	WAS	A	2	1	.667	2.02	6	4	3	40	23	12	18	2	0	0	0	12	2	0	.167	3	7	1	0	1.8	.909
1916			2	3	.400	3.06	17	5	2	53	37	17	21	0	0	1	1	14	1	0	.071	1	11	2	0	0.8	.857
1917			5	14	.263	2.55	37	23	8	204.2	171	76	65	2	2	1	2	58	2	0	.034	11	46	8	2	1.8	.877
1918			1	1	.500	5.14	4	1	1	14	18	6	12	0	1	0	0	3	1	0	.333	0	4	0	0	1.0	1.000
1919	BOS	A	0	4	.000	4.33	13	2	0	35.1	45	19	12	0	0	3	0	7	0	0	.000	4	11	2	0	1.3	.882
5 yrs.			10	23	.303	2.85	77	35	14	347	294	130	128	4	3	5	3	94	6	0	.064	19	79	13	2	1.4	.883

Dan Dumoulin

DUMOULIN, DANIEL LYNN BR TR 6′ 175 lbs.
B. Aug. 20, 1953, Kokomo, Ind.

1977	CIN	N	0	0	—	14.40	5	0	0	5	12	3	5	0	0	0	0	0	0	0	—	1	1	0	0	0.4	1.000
1978			1	0	1.000	1.80	3	0	0	5	7	3	2	0	1	0	0	0	0	0	—	0	2	0	0	0.7	1.000
2 yrs.			1	0	1.000	8.10	8	0	0	10	19	6	7	0	1	0	0	0	0	0		1	3	0	0	0.5	1.000

Nick Dumovich

DUMOVICH, NICHOLAS BL TL 6′ 170 lbs.
B. Jan. 2, 1902, Sacramento, Calif. D. Dec. 12, 1979, Laguna Hills, Calif.

1923	CHI	N	3	5	.375	4.60	28	8	1	94	118	45	23	0	2	1	1	29	7	0	.241	4	27	0	0	1.1	1.000

Matt Dunbar

DUNBAR, MATTHEW MARSHALL BL TL 6′ 170 lbs.
B. Oct. 15, 1968, Tallahassee, Fla.

1995	FLA	N	0	1	.000	11.57	8	0	0	7	12	11	5	0	0	1	0	0	0	0	—	0	3	0	1	0.4	1.000

Ed Dundon

DUNDON, EDWARD JOSEPH (Dummy) TR
B. July 10, 1859, Columbus, Ohio D. Aug. 18, 1893, Columbus, Ohio.

1883	COL	AA	3	16	.158	*4.48*	20	19	16	166.2	213	38	31	0	0	0	0	93	15	0	.161	24	37	12	3	2.4	.836
1884			6	4	.600	*3.78*	11	9	7	81	85	15	37	0	1	0	0	86	12	0	.140	60	22	5	3	2.9	.943
2 yrs.			9	20	.310	4.25	31	28	23	247.2	298	53	68	0	1	0	0	*				84	59	17	6	2.7	.894

Jim Dunegan

DUNEGAN, JAMES WILLIAM, JR. BR TR 6′1″ 205 lbs.
B. Aug. 6, 1947, Burlington, Iowa.

1970	CHI	N	0	2	.000	4.85	7	0	0	13	13	12	3	0	0	2	0	4	1	0	.250	1	4	0	0	0.7	1.000

Wiley Dunham

DUNHAM, HENRY HUSTON 6′1″ 180 lbs.
B. Jan. 30, 1877, Piketon, Ohio D. Jan. 16, 1934, Cleveland, Ohio.

1902	STL	N	2	3	.400	5.68	7	5	3	38	47	13	15	0	0	0	1	12	1	0	.083	1	8	1	0	1.4	.900

Davey Dunkle

DUNKLE, EDWARD PERKS BB TR 6′2″ 220 lbs.
B. Aug. 30, 1872, Philipsburg, Pa. D. Nov. 19, 1941, Lock Haven, Pa.

1897	PHI	N	5	2	.714	3.48	7	7	7	62	72	23	9	0	0	0	0	23	4	0	.174	2	14	5	1	3.0	.762
1898			1	4	.200	6.98	12	7	4	68.1	83	38	21	0	0	0	0	28	6	0	.214	1	11	2	0	1.2	.857
1899	WAS	N	0	2	.000	10.04	4	2	2	26	46	14	9	0	0	0	0	11	3	0	.273	1	5	2	0	2.0	.750
1903	2 teams	CHI A	(12G 4–4)	WAS A	(14G 5–9)																						
″	total		9	13	.409	4.16	26	20	16	190.1	207	64	77	0	**2**	0	1	74	14	0	.189	5	41	7	0	2.0	.868
1904	WAS	A	2	9	.182	4.96	12	11	7	74.1	95	23	23	0	0	0	0	28	4	0	.143	3	23	0	1	2.2	1.000
5 yrs.			17	30	.362	5.02	61	47	36	421	503	162	139	0	2	0	1	164	31	0	.189	12	94	16	2	2.0	.869

Fred Dunlap

DUNLAP, FREDERICK C. (Sure Shot) BR TR 5′8″ 165 lbs.
B. May 21, 1859, Philadelphia, Pa. D. Dec. 1, 1902, Philadelphia, Pa.
Manager 1882, 1884–85, 1889.

1884	STL	U	0	0	—	*13.50*	1	0	0	0.2	2	0	1	0	0	0	1	449	185	13	.412	252	290	53	44	7.0	.911
1887	DET	N	0	0	—	4.50	1	0	0	2	4	0	1	0	0	0	0	272	72	5	.265	258	255	52	41	7.1	.908
2 yrs.			0	0		6.75	2	0	0	2.2	6	0	2	0	0	0	1	*				2912	3171	499	513	6.8	.924

Jack Dunleavy

DUNLEAVY, JOHN FRANCIS TL 5′6″ 167 lbs.
B. Sept. 14, 1879, Harrison, N. J. D. Apr. 11, 1944, South Norwalk, Conn.

1903	STL	N	6	8	.429	4.06	14	13	9	102	101	57	51	0	1	0	0	193	48	0	.249	58	43	3	5	2.0	.971
1904			1	4	.200	4.42	7	5	5	55	63	23	28	0	0	0	0	172	40	1	.233	77	20	2	2	1.9	.980
2 yrs.			7	12	.368	4.18	21	18	14	157	164	80	79	0	1	0	0	*				312	91	13	14	1.9	.969

Jack Dunn

DUNN, JOHN JOSEPH (Handyman) BR TR 5′9″
B. Oct. 6, 1872, Meadville, Pa. D. Oct. 22, 1928, Towson, Md.

1897	BKN	N	14	9	.609	4.57	25	21	21	216.2	251	66	26	0	1	1	0	131	29	0	.221	31	74	14	3	3.3	.882
1898			16	21	.432	3.60	41	37	31	322.2	352	82	66	0	2	0	0	167	41	0	.246	42	91	12	6	2.8	.917
1899			23	13	.639	3.70	41	34	29	299.1	323	86	48	2	2	1	2	122	30	0	.246	21	83	4	1	2.6	.963
1900	2 teams	BKN N	(10G 3–4)	PHI N	(10G 5–5)																						
″	total		8	9	.471	5.16	20	16	14	143	175	57	18	1	1	1	0	59	16	0	.271	7	40	3	0	2.5	.940
1901	2 teams	PHI N	(2G 0–1)	BAL A	(9G 3–3)																						
″	total		3	4	.429	4.90	11	8	6	64.1	85	28	6	0	0	0	0	363	91	0	.251	157	207	53	14	4.2	.873
1902	NY	N	0	3	.000	3.71	3	2	2	26.2	28	12	6	0	0	1	0	342	72	0	.211	154	153	23	17	3.2	.930
1904			0	0	—	4.50	1	0	0	4	3	3	1	0	0	0	1	181	56	1	.309	101	173	26	24	4.2	.913
7 yrs.			64	59	.520	4.11	142	118	103	1076.2	1217	334	171	3	6	4	3	*				574	910	150	72	3.4	.908

Jim Dunn

DUNN, JAMES WILLIAM (Bill) BR TR 6′½″ 185 lbs.
B. Feb. 25, 1931, Valdosta, Ga.

1952	PIT	N	0	0	—	3.38	3	0	0	5.1	4	3	2	0	0	0	0	1	0	0	.000	2	0	0	0	0.7	1.000

Mike Dunne

DUNNE, MICHAEL DENNIS BR TR 6′ 4″ 190 lbs.
B. Oct. 27, 1962, South Bend, Ind.

Year	Team	Lg	W	L	PCT	ERA	G	GS	CG	IP	H	BB	SO	ShO	Relief Pitching W	Relief Pitching L	Relief Pitching SV	Batting AB	Batting H	Batting HR	BA	PO	A	E	DP	TC/G	FA
1987	PIT	N	13	6	.684	3.03	23	23	5	163.1	143	68	72	1	0	0	0	53	5	0	.094	18	32	1	3	2.2	.980
1988			7	11	.389	3.92	30	28	1	170	163	88	70	0	0	0	0	46	5	0	.109	18	27	1	0	1.5	.978
1989	2 teams	PIT N (3G 1–1)	SEA A (15G 2–9)																								
″	total		3	10	.231	5.60	18	18	1	99.2	125	46	42	0	0	0	0	4	1	0	.250	7	17	1	2	1.4	.960
1990	SD	N	0	3	.000	5.65	10	6	0	28.2	28	17	15	0	0	0	0	6	0	0	.000	4	5	0	1	0.9	1.000
1992	CHI	A	2	0	1.000	4.26	4	1	0	12.2	12	6	6	0	2	0	0	0	0	0	—	1	2	0	1	0.8	1.000
5 yrs.			25	30	.455	4.08	85	76	7	474.1	471	225	205	1	2	0	0	109	11	0	.101	48	83	3	7	1.6	.978

Andy Dunning

DUNNING, ANDREW JACKSON BR TR 6′ 175 lbs.
B. Aug. 12, 1871, New York, N. Y. D. June 21, 1952, New York, N. Y.

Year	Team	Lg	W	L	PCT	ERA	G	GS	CG	IP	H	BB	SO	ShO	Relief Pitching W	Relief Pitching L	Relief Pitching SV	Batting AB	Batting H	Batting HR	BA	PO	A	E	DP	TC/G	FA
1889	PIT	N	0	2	.000	7.00	2	2	2	18	20	16	4	0	0	0	0	7	0	0	.000	2	4	0	0	3.0	1.000
1891	NY	N	0	1	.000	4.50	1	1	0	2	3	3	2	0	0	0	0	0	0	0	—	0	0	0	0	0.0	.000
2 yrs.			0	3	.000	6.75	3	3	2	20	23	19	6	0	0	0	0	7	0	0	.000	2	4	0	0	2.0	1.000

Steve Dunning

DUNNING, STEVEN JOHN BR TR 6′ 2″ 205 lbs.
B. May 15, 1949, Denver, Colo.

Year	Team	Lg	W	L	PCT	ERA	G	GS	CG	IP	H	BB	SO	ShO	Relief Pitching W	Relief Pitching L	Relief Pitching SV	Batting AB	Batting H	Batting HR	BA	PO	A	E	DP	TC/G	FA
1970	CLE	A	4	9	.308	4.98	19	17	0	94	93	54	77	0	0	0	0	31	5	0	.161	7	17	2	2	1.4	.923
1971			8	14	.364	4.50	31	29	3	184	173	109	132	1	0	0	1	55	10	1	.182	13	38	2	0	1.7	.962
1972			6	4	.600	3.26	16	16	1	105	98	43	52	0	0	0	0	33	9	3	.273	2	16	2	0	1.3	.900
1973	2 teams	CLE A (4G 0–2)	TEX A (23G 2–6)																								
″	total		2	8	.200	5.53	27	15	2	112.1	118	65	48	0	0	0	0	0	0	0		9	17	3	0	1.1	.897
1974	TEX	A	0	0	—	22.50	1	0	0	2	3	3	1	0	0	0	0	0	0	0	—	1	0	0	0	1.0	1.000
1976	2 teams	CAL A (4G 0–0)	MON N (32G 2–6)																								
″	total		2	6	.250	4.35	36	7	1	97.1	102	39	76	0	0	2	0	15	2	0	.133	8	14	3	0	0.7	.880
1977	OAK	A	1	0	1.000	4.00	6	0	0	18	17	10	4	0	1	0	0	0	0	0	—	1	3	0	1	0.7	1.000
7 yrs.			23	41	.359	4.57	136	84	7	612.2	604	323	390	1	1	2	1	134	26	4	.194	41	105	12	3	1.2	.924

Frank Dupee

DUPEE, FRANK OLIVER TL 6′ 1″ 200 lbs.
B. Apr. 29, 1877, Monkton, Vt. D. Aug. 14, 1956, Portland, Me.

Year	Team	Lg	W	L	PCT	ERA	G	GS	CG	IP	H	BB	SO	ShO	Relief Pitching W	Relief Pitching L	Relief Pitching SV	Batting AB	Batting H	Batting HR	BA	PO	A	E	DP	TC/G	FA
1901	CHI	A	0	1	.000	∞	1	1	0		0	3	0	0	0	0	0	0	0	0	—	0	0	0	0	0.0	.000

Mike Dupree

DUPREE, MICHAEL DENNIS BR TR 6′ 1″ 185 lbs.
B. May 29, 1953, Kansas City, Kans.

Year	Team	Lg	W	L	PCT	ERA	G	GS	CG	IP	H	BB	SO	ShO	Relief Pitching W	Relief Pitching L	Relief Pitching SV	Batting AB	Batting H	Batting HR	BA	PO	A	E	DP	TC/G	FA
1976	SD	N	0	0	—	9.19	12	0	0	15.2	18	7	5	0	0	0	0	1	1	0	1.000	1	4	0	0	0.4	1.000

Kid Durbin

DURBIN, BLAINE ALPHONSUS BL TL 5′ 8″ 155 lbs.
B. Sept. 10, 1886, Lamar, Mo. D. Sept. 11, 1943, Kirkwood, Mo.

Year	Team	Lg	W	L	PCT	ERA	G	GS	CG	IP	H	BB	SO	ShO	Relief Pitching W	Relief Pitching L	Relief Pitching SV	Batting AB	Batting H	Batting HR	BA	PO	A	E	DP	TC/G	FA
1907	CHI	N	0	1	.000	5.40	5	1	1	16.2	14	10	5	0	0	0	1	*				4	7	0	0	1.1	1.000

Ryne Duren

DUREN, RINOLD GEORGE BR TR 6′ 2″ 190 lbs.
B. Feb. 22, 1929, Cazenovia, Wis.

Year	Team	Lg	W	L	PCT	ERA	G	GS	CG	IP	H	BB	SO	ShO	Relief Pitching W	Relief Pitching L	Relief Pitching SV	Batting AB	Batting H	Batting HR	BA	PO	A	E	DP	TC/G	FA
1954	BAL	A	0	0	—	9.00	1	0	0	2	3	1	2	0	0	0	0	0	0	0	—	0	0	0	0	0.0	.000
1957	KC	A	0	3	.000	5.27	14	6	0	42.2	37	30	37	0	0	0	1	14	1	0	.071	3	8	0	0	0.8	1.000
1958	NY	A	6	4	.600	2.02	44	1	0	75.2	40	43	87	0	6	4	**20**	13	1	0	.077	1	11	1	2	0.3	.923
1959			3	6	.333	1.88	41	0	0	76.2	49	43	96	0	3	6	14	14	0	0	.000	1	9	0	2	0.2	1.000
1960			3	4	.429	4.96	42	1	0	49	27	49	67	0	3	4	9	6	0	0	.000	2	9	0	0	0.3	1.000
1961	2 teams	NY A (4G 0–1)	LA A (40G 6–12)																								
″	total		6	13	.316	5.19	44	14	1	104	89	79	115	1	4	9	2	25	1	0	.040	6	6	2	0	0.3	.857
1962	LA	A	2	9	.182	4.42	42	3	0	71.1	53	57	74	0	2	8	8	15	1	0	.067	0	8	1	0	0.2	.889
1963	PHI	N	6	2	.750	3.30	33	7	1	87.1	65	52	84	0	3	1	2	21	3	0	.143	3	7	0	0	0.3	1.000
1964	2 teams	PHI N (2G 0–0)	CIN N (26G 0–2)																								
″	total		0	2	.000	3.09	28	0	0	46.2	46	16	44	0	0	2	1	5	0	0	.000	1	4	2	0	0.3	.714
1965	2 teams	PHI N (6G 0–0)	WAS A (16G 1–1)																								
″	total		1	1	.500	5.56	22	0	0	34	34	22	24	0	1	1	0	1	0	0	.000	0	6	0	0	0.3	1.000
10 yrs.			27	44	.380	3.83	311	32	2	589.1	443	392	630	1	22	35	57	114	7	0	.061	17	68	6	4	0.3	.934
WORLD SERIES																											
1958	NY	A	1	1	.500	1.93	3	0	0	9.1	7	6	14	0	1	1	1	3	0	0	.000	0	1	0	1	0.3	1.000
1960			0	0	—	2.25	2	0	0	4	2	1	5	0	0	0	0	0	0	0	—	0	2	0	0	1.0	1.000
2 yrs.			1	1	.500	2.03	5	0	0	13.1	9	7	19	0	1	1	1	3	0	0	.000	0	3	0	1	0.6	1.000

Bull Durham

DURHAM, LOUIS STAUB (Judge, Whitey) BR TR 5′10″
Born Louis Raphael Staub.
B. June 27, 1877, New Oxford, Pa. D. June 28, 1960, Bentley, Kans.

Year	Team	Lg	W	L	PCT	ERA	G	GS	CG	IP	H	BB	SO	ShO	Relief Pitching W	Relief Pitching L	Relief Pitching SV	Batting AB	Batting H	Batting HR	BA	PO	A	E	DP	TC/G	FA
1904	BKN	N	1	0	1.000	3.27	2	2	1	11	10	5	1	0	0	0	0	4	1	0	.250	0	2	1	0	1.5	.667
1907	WAS	A	0	0	—	12.60	2	0	0	5	10	4	1	0	0	0	0	1	0	0	.000	0	1	0	0	0.5	1.000
1908	NY	N	0	0	—	9.00	1	0	0	2	2	1	2	0	0	0	0	0	0	0	—	0	0	0	0	0.0	.000
1909			0	0	—	3.27	4	0	0	11	15	2	2	0	0	0	1	2	0	0	.000	0	3	1	0	1.0	.750
4 yrs.			1	0	1.000	5.28	9	2	1	29	37	12	6	0	0	0	1	7	1	0	.143	0	6	2	0	0.9	.750

Don Durham

DURHAM, DONALD GARY (Bull) BR TR 6′ 170 lbs.
B. Mar. 21, 1949, Yosemite, Ky.

Year	Team	Lg	W	L	PCT	ERA	G	GS	CG	IP	H	BB	SO	ShO	Relief Pitching W	Relief Pitching L	Relief Pitching SV	Batting AB	Batting H	Batting HR	BA	PO	A	E	DP	TC/G	FA
1972	STL	N	2	7	.222	4.34	10	8	1	47.2	42	22	35	0	0	1	0	14	7	2	.500	1	4	0	0	0.5	1.000
1973	TEX	A	0	4	.000	7.65	15	4	0	40	49	23	23	0	0	0	1	0	0	0	—	4	2	0	1	0.4	1.000
2 yrs.			2	11	.154	5.85	25	12	1	87.2	91	45	58	0	0	1	1	14	7	2	.500	5	6	0	1	0.4	1.000

Ed Durham

DURHAM, EDWARD FANT (Bull) BL TR 5′11″ 170 lbs.
B. Aug. 17, 1908, Chester, S. C. D. Apr. 27, 1976, Chester, S. C.

Year	Team	Lg	W	L	PCT	ERA	G	GS	CG	IP	H	BB	SO	ShO	Relief Pitching W	Relief Pitching L	Relief Pitching SV	Batting AB	Batting H	Batting HR	BA	PO	A	E	DP	TC/G	FA
1929	BOS	A	1	0	1.000	9.27	14	1	0	22.1	34	14	6	0	0	0	0	4	0	0	.000	2	4	1	0	0.5	.857
1930			4	15	.211	4.69	33	12	6	140	144	43	28	1	2	5	1	41	4	0	.098	0	30	1	2	0.9	.968
1931			8	10	.444	4.25	38	15	7	165.1	175	50	53	2	2	3	0	54	3	0	.056	7	24	3	0	0.9	.912
1932			6	13	.316	3.80	34	22	4	175.1	187	49	52	0	2	1	0	57	7	0	.123	14	37	1	4	1.5	.981
1933	CHI	A	10	6	.625	4.48	24	21	6	138.2	137	46	65	0	1	0	0	46	10	0	.217	1	25	0	0	1.1	1.000
5 yrs.			29	44	.397	4.45	143	71	23	641.2	677	202	204	3	7	9	1	202	24	0	.119	24	120	6	6	1.0	.960

Jimmy Durham

DURHAM, JAMES GARFIELD BR TR 6′ 175 lbs.
B. Oct. 7, 1881, Douglass, Kans. D. May 7, 1949, Coffeyville, Kans.

Year	Team		W	L	PCT	ERA	G	GS	CG	IP	H	BB	SO	ShO	Relief Pitching W	L	SV	Batting AB	H	HR	BA	PO	A	E	DP	TC/G	FA
1902	**CHI**	**A**	1	1	.500	5.85	3	3	3	20	21	16	3	0	0	0	0	15	1	0	.067	3	6	1	1	2.0	.900

Dick Durning

DURNING, RICHARD KNOTT BL TL 6′ 2″ 178 lbs.
B. Oct. 10, 1892, Louisville, Ky. D. Sept. 23, 1948, Castle Point, N. Y.

Year	Team		W	L	PCT	ERA	G	GS	CG	IP	H	BB	SO	ShO	Relief Pitching W	L	SV	Batting AB	H	HR	BA	PO	A	E	DP	TC/G	FA
1917	**BKN**	**N**	0	0	—	0.00	1	0	0	1	0	0	0	0	0	0	0	0	0	0	—	0	0	0	0	0.0	.000
1918			0	0	—	13.50	1	0	0	2	3	4	0	0	0	0	0	0	0	0	—	0	1	0	0	1.0	1.000
2 yrs.			0	0		9.00	2	0	0	3	3	4	0	0	0	0	0	0	0	0		0	1	0	0	0.5	1.000

Jesse Duryea

DURYEA, JAMES NEWTON (Cyclone Jim) BR TR 5′10″ 175 lbs.
B. Sept. 7, 1859, Osage, Iowa D. Aug. 19, 1942, Algona, Iowa.

Year	Team		W	L	PCT	ERA	G	GS	CG	IP	H	BB	SO	ShO	Relief Pitching W	L	SV	Batting AB	H	HR	BA	PO	A	E	DP	TC/G	FA
1889	**CIN**	**AA**	32	19	.627	2.56	53	48	38	401	372	127	183	2	2	**2**	1	162	44	0	.272	17	80	11	1	1.9	.898
1890	**CIN**	**N**	16	12	.571	2.92	33	32	29	274	270	60	108	2	0	0	0	99	15	1	.152	7	59	10	4	2.2	.868
1891	**2 teams**	**CIN N**	(10G 1–9)		**STL AA**	(3G 1–1)																					
″	**total**		2	10	.167	4.90	13	13	10	101	120	35	36	0	0	0	0	43	5	0	.116	5	21	4	0	2.3	.867
1892	**2 teams**	**CIN N**	(9G 2–5)		**WAS N**	(18G 3–10)																					
″	**total**		5	15	.250	2.82	27	22	18	195	157	71	69	1	1	1	2	77	9	0	.117	16	63	7	0	3.2	.919
1893	**WAS**	**N**	4	10	.286	7.54	17	15	9	117	182	56	20	0	0	1	0	47	13	0	.277	4	29	2	0	2.1	.943
5 yrs.			59	66	.472	3.45	143	130	104	1088	1101	349	416	5	3	4	3	428	86	1	.201	49	252	34	5	2.3	.899

Erv Dusak

DUSAK, ERVIN FRANK (Four Sack) BR TR 6′ 2″ 185 lbs.
B. July 29, 1920, Chicago, Ill. D. Nov. 6, 1994, Glendale Heights, Ill.

Year	Team		W	L	PCT	ERA	G	GS	CG	IP	H	BB	SO	ShO	Relief Pitching W	L	SV	Batting AB	H	HR	BA	PO	A	E	DP	TC/G	FA
1948	**STL**	**N**	0	0	—	0.00	1	0	0	1	0	1	0	0	0	0	0	311	65	6	.209	10	0	0	0	2.5	1.000
1950			0	2	.000	3.72	14	2	0	36.1	27	27	16	0	0	0	1	12	1	0	.083	14	5	0	1	2.1	1.000
1951	**2 teams**	**STL N**	(5G 0–0)		**PIT N**	(3G 0–1)																					
″	**total**		0	1	.000	9.18	8	1	0	16.2	24	16	10	0	0	0	0	41	13	2	.317	13	4	1	1	0.8	.944
3 yrs.			0	3	.000	5.33	23	3	0	54	51	44	26	0	0	0	1	*				568	154	16	26	2.1	.978

Carl Duser

DUSER, CARL ROBERT BL TL 6′ 1″ 175 lbs.
B. July 22, 1932, Hazleton, Pa.

Year	Team		W	L	PCT	ERA	G	GS	CG	IP	H	BB	SO	ShO	Relief Pitching W	L	SV	Batting AB	H	HR	BA	PO	A	E	DP	TC/G	FA
1956	**KC**	**A**	1	1	.500	9.00	2	2	0	6	14	2	5	0	0	0	0	3	0	0	.000	0	2	0	0	1.0	1.000
1958			0	0	—	4.50	1	0	0	2	5	1	0	0	0	0	0	0	0	0	—	0	0	0	0	0.0	.000
2 yrs.			1	1	.500	7.88	3	2	0	8	19	3	5	0	0	0	0	3	0	0	.000	0	2	0	0	0.7	1.000

Bob Dustal

DUSTAL, ROBERT ANDREW BR TR 6′ 172 lbs.
B. Sept. 28, 1935, Sayreville, N. J.

Year	Team		W	L	PCT	ERA	G	GS	CG	IP	H	BB	SO	ShO	Relief Pitching W	L	SV	Batting AB	H	HR	BA	PO	A	E	DP	TC/G	FA
1963	**DET**	**A**	0	1	.000	9.00	7	0	0	6	10	5	4	0	0	1	0	0	0	0	—	1	4	0	0	0.7	1.000

Bill Duzen

DUZEN, WILLIAM GEORGE BR TR 5′11″ 165 lbs.
B. Feb. 21, 1870, Buffalo, N. Y. D. Mar. 11, 1944, Buffalo, N. Y.

Year	Team		W	L	PCT	ERA	G	GS	CG	IP	H	BB	SO	ShO	Relief Pitching W	L	SV	Batting AB	H	HR	BA	PO	A	E	DP	TC/G	FA
1890	**BUF**	**P**	0	2	.000	13.85	2	2	2	13	20	14	5	0	0	0	0	4	1	0	.250	0	2	0	0	1.0	1.000

Frank Dwyer

DWYER, JOHN FRANCIS BR TR 5′ 8″ 145 lbs.
B. Mar. 25, 1868, Lee, Mass. D. Feb. 4, 1943, Pittsfield, Mass.
Manager 1902.

Year	Team		W	L	PCT	ERA	G	GS	CG	IP	H	BB	SO	ShO	Relief Pitching W	L	SV	Batting AB	H	HR	BA	PO	A	E	DP	TC/G	FA
1888	**CHI**	**N**	4	1	.800	1.07	5	5	5	42	32	9	17	1	0	0	0	21	4	0	.190	2	10	2	0	2.8	.857
1889			16	13	.552	3.59	32	30	27	276	307	72	63	0	1	0	0	135	27	1	.200	32	49	8	5	2.4	.910
1890	**CHI**	**P**	3	6	.333	6.23	12	6	6	69.1	98	25	17	0	2	1	1	53	14	0	.264	6	24	4	0	2.1	.882
1891	**2 teams**	**CIN AA**	(35G 13–19)		**MIL AA**	(10G 6–4)																					
″	**total**		19	23	.452	3.99	45	41	39	374.2	424	145	128	1	0	1	0	181	49	0	.271	31	97	11	1	2.7	.921
1892	**2 teams**	**STL N**	(10G 2–8)		**CIN N**	(33G 19–10)																					
″	**total**		21	18	.538	2.98	43	38	30	323.1	341	73	61	3	2	1	1	154	23	0	.149	23	70	5	3	2.0	.949
1893	**CIN**	**N**	18	15	.545	4.13	37	31	28	287.1	332	93	53	1	2	2	**2**	120	24	1	.200	47	66	2	7	2.9	.983
1894			19	22	.463	5.07	45	40	34	348	471	106	49	1	1	1	1	172	46	2	.267	37	67	7	2	1.9	.937
1895			18	15	.545	4.24	37	31	23	280.1	355	74	46	2	2	3	0	113	30	1	.265	26	54	4	6	2.3	.952
1896			24	11	.686	3.15	36	34	30	288.2	321	60	57	3	1	0	1	110	29	0	.264	24	52	6	5	2.3	.927
1897			18	13	.581	3.78	37	31	22	247.1	315	56	41	0	3	1	0	94	25	0	.266	11	42	4	0	1.5	.930
1898			16	10	.615	3.04	31	28	24	240	257	42	29	0	1	0	0	85	12	0	.141	11	52	6	3	2.2	.913
1899			0	5	.000	5.51	5	5	2	32.2	48	9	2	0	0	0	0	11	4	0	.364	1	8	0	1	1.8	1.000
12 yrs.			176	152	.537	3.85	365	320	270	2809.2	3301	764	563	12	15	10	6	*				251	591	59	33	2.3	.935

Ben Dyer

DYER, BENJAMIN FRANKLIN BR TR 5′10″ 170 lbs.
B. Feb. 13, 1893, Chicago, Ill. D. Aug. 7, 1959, Kenosha, Wis.

Year	Team		W	L	PCT	ERA	G	GS	CG	IP	H	BB	SO	ShO	Relief Pitching W	L	SV	Batting AB	H	HR	BA	PO	A	E	DP	TC/G	FA
1918	**DET**	**A**	0	0	—	0.00	2	0	0	1.2	0	0	0	0	0	0	0	*				2	5	1	1	1.1	.875

Eddie Dyer

DYER, EDWIN HAWLEY BL TL 5′11½″ 168 lbs.
B. Oct. 11, 1900, Morgan City, La. D. Apr. 20, 1964, Houston, Tex.
Manager 1946–50.

Year	Team		W	L	PCT	ERA	G	GS	CG	IP	H	BB	SO	ShO	Relief Pitching W	L	SV	Batting AB	H	HR	BA	PO	A	E	DP	TC/G	FA
1922	**STL**	**N**	0	0	—	2.45	2	0	0	3.2	7	0	3	0	0	0	0	3	1	0	.333	3	0	0	0	1.5	1.000
1923			2	1	.667	4.09	4	3	2	22	30	5	7	1	0	0	0	45	12	2	.267	18	4	0	0	1.8	1.000
1924			8	11	.421	4.61	29	15	7	136.2	174	51	23	1	3	2	0	76	18	0	.237	10	40	5	1	1.8	.909
1925			4	3	.571	4.15	27	5	1	82.1	93	24	25	0	3	2	3	31	3	0	.097	0	22	2	1	0.9	.917
1926			1	0	1.000	11.57	6	0	0	9.1	7	14	4	0	1	0	0	2	1	0	.500	0	3	0	0	0.5	1.000
1927			0	0	—	18.00	1	0	0	2	5	2	1	0	0	0	0	0	0	0	—	0	0	0	0	0.0	.000
6 yrs.			15	15	.500	4.75	69	23	10	256	316	96	63	2	7	4	3	*				31	69	7	2	1.4	.935

Mike Dyer

DYER, MICHAEL LAWRENCE BR TR 6′ 3″ 195 lbs.
B. Sept. 8, 1966, Upland, Calif.

Year	Team		W	L	PCT	ERA	G	GS	CG	IP	H	BB	SO	ShO	Relief Pitching W	L	SV	Batting AB	H	HR	BA	PO	A	E	DP	TC/G	FA
1989	**MIN**	**A**	4	7	.364	4.82	16	12	1	71	74	37	37	0	0	1	0	0	0	0	—	6	3	0	1	0.6	1.000
1994	**PIT**	**N**	1	1	.500	5.87	14	0	0	15.1	15	12	13	0	1	1	4	1	0	0	.000	0	1	0	0	0.1	1.000
1995			4	5	.444	4.34	55	0	0	74.2	81	30	53	0	4	5	0	7	4	0	.571	3	13	0	2	0.3	1.000
3 yrs.			9	13	.409	4.70	85	12	1	161	170	79	103	0	5	7	4	8	4	0	.500	9	17	0	3	0.3	1.000

Jimmy Dygert

DYGERT, JAMES HENRY (Sunny Jim) BR TR 5′10″ 185 lbs.
B. July 5, 1884, Utica, N. Y. D. Feb. 8, 1936, New Orleans, La.

Year	Team	W	L	PCT	ERA	G	GS	CG	IP	H	BB	SO	ShO	Relief Pitching W	Relief Pitching L	Relief Pitching SV	Batting AB	Batting H	Batting HR	BA	PO	A	E	DP	TC/G	FA
1905	PHI A	1	4	.200	4.33	6	3	2	35.1	41	11	24	0	1	1	0	15	4	0	.267	1	18	1	1	3.3	.950
1906		11	13	.458	2.70	35	25	15	213.2	175	91	106	4	2	**2**	0	74	13	1	.176	3	68	2	1	2.1	.973
1907		21	8	.724	2.34	42	28	18	261.2	200	85	151	5	3	2	1	94	12	0	.128	13	74	9	2	2.3	.906
1908		11	15	.423	2.87	41	27	15	238.2	184	**97**	164	5	2	1	1	75	6	0	.080	8	79	2	0	2.2	.978
1909		9	5	.643	2.42	32	13	6	137.1	117	50	79	1	3	1	0	42	9	0	.214	1	34	2	1	1.2	.946
1910		4	4	.500	2.54	19	8	6	99.1	81	49	59	1	0	0	0	36	3	0	.083	1	20	1	1	1.2	.955
6 yrs.		57	49	.538	2.65	175	104	62	986	798	383	583	16	11	7	2	336	47	1	.140	27	293	17	6	1.9	.950

Jimmy Dykes

DYKES, JAMES JOSEPH BR TR 5′ 9″ 185 lbs.
B. Nov. 10, 1896, Philadelphia, Pa. D. June 15, 1976, Philadelphia, Pa.
Manager 1934–46, 1951–54, 1958–61.

Year	Team	W	L	PCT	ERA	G	GS	CG	IP	H	BB	SO	ShO	Relief Pitching W	Relief Pitching L	Relief Pitching SV	Batting AB	Batting H	Batting HR	BA	PO	A	E	DP	TC/G	FA
1927	PHI A	0	0	—	4.50	2	0	0	2	2	1	0	0	0	0	0	*				139	190	21	33	6.1	.940

Arnold Earley

EARLEY, ARNOLD CARL BL TL 6′ 1″ 195 lbs.
B. June 4, 1933, Lincoln Park, Mich.

Year	Team	W	L	PCT	ERA	G	GS	CG	IP	H	BB	SO	ShO	Relief Pitching W	Relief Pitching L	Relief Pitching SV	Batting AB	Batting H	Batting HR	BA	PO	A	E	DP	TC/G	FA
1960	BOS A	0	1	.000	15.75	2	0	0	4	9	4	5	0	0	1	0	1	0	0	.000	0	0	0	0	0.0	.000
1961		2	4	.333	3.99	33	0	0	49.2	42	34	44	0	2	4	7	6	0	0	.000	1	9	2	0	0.4	.833
1962		4	5	.444	5.80	38	3	0	68.1	76	46	59	0	3	3	5	10	2	0	.200	4	14	2	0	0.5	.900
1963		3	7	.300	4.75	53	4	0	115.2	124	43	97	0	1	5	1	18	5	0	.278	11	16	3	1	0.6	.900
1964		1	1	.500	2.68	25	3	1	50.1	51	18	45	0	0	0	1	9	1	0	.111	4	9	0	1	0.5	1.000
1965		0	1	.000	3.63	57	0	0	74.1	79	29	47	0	0	1	0	6	0	0	.000	4	13	3	1	0.4	.850
1966	CHI N	2	1	.667	3.57	13	0	0	17.2	14	9	12	0	2	1	0	1	0	0	.000	0	0	1	0	0.1	.000
1967	HOU N	0	0	—	27.00	2	0	0	1.1	5	1	1	0	0	0	0	0	0	0	—	0	1	0	0	0.5	1.000
8 yrs.		12	20	.375	4.48	223	10	1	381.1	400	184	310	0	8	15	14	51	8	0	.157	24	62	11	3	0.4	.887

Bill Earley

EARLEY, WILLIAM ALBERT BR TL 6′ 4″ 200 lbs.
B. Jan. 30, 1956, Cincinnati, Ohio.

Year	Team	W	L	PCT	ERA	G	GS	CG	IP	H	BB	SO	ShO	Relief Pitching W	Relief Pitching L	Relief Pitching SV	Batting AB	Batting H	Batting HR	BA	PO	A	E	DP	TC/G	FA
1986	STL N	0	0	—	0.00	3	0	0	3	0	2	2	0	0	0	0	0	0	0	—	0	0	0	0	0.0	.000

Tom Earley

EARLEY, THOMAS FRANCIS ALOYSIUS (Chick) BR TR 6′ 180 lbs.
B. Feb. 19, 1917, Roxbury, Mass. D. Apr. 5, 1988, Nantucket, Mass.

Year	Team	W	L	PCT	ERA	G	GS	CG	IP	H	BB	SO	ShO	Relief Pitching W	Relief Pitching L	Relief Pitching SV	Batting AB	Batting H	Batting HR	BA	PO	A	E	DP	TC/G	FA
1938	BOS N	1	0	1.000	3.27	2	1	1	11	8	1	4	0	0	0	0	4	0	0	.000	0	2	0	0	1.0	1.000
1939		1	4	.200	4.72	14	2	0	40	49	19	9	0	0	3	1	10	3	0	.300	1	11	0	0	0.9	1.000
1940		2	0	1.000	3.86	4	1	1	16.1	16	3	5	1	1	0	0	5	2	0	.400	2	1	0	0	0.8	1.000
1941		6	8	.429	2.53	33	13	6	138.2	120	46	54	1	1	1	3	47	11	0	.234	5	24	2	6	0.9	.935
1942		6	11	.353	4.71	27	18	6	112.2	120	55	28	0	1	1	1	34	4	0	.118	3	29	1	0	1.2	.970
1945		2	1	.667	4.61	11	2	1	41	36	19	4	0	1	1	0	14	3	0	.214	2	9	0	0	1.0	1.000
6 yrs.		18	24	.429	3.78	91	37	15	359.2	349	143	104	2	4	6	5	114	23	0	.202	13	76	3	6	1.0	.967

George Earnshaw

EARNSHAW, GEORGE LIVINGSTON (Moose) BR TR 6′ 4″ 210 lbs.
B. Feb. 15, 1900, New York, N. Y. D. Dec. 1, 1976, Little Rock, Ark.

Year	Team	W	L	PCT	ERA	G	GS	CG	IP	H	BB	SO	ShO	Relief Pitching W	Relief Pitching L	Relief Pitching SV	Batting AB	Batting H	Batting HR	BA	PO	A	E	DP	TC/G	FA
1928	PHI A	7	7	.500	3.81	26	22	7	158.1	143	100	117	3	0	0	1	57	14	0	.246	6	27	4	0	1.4	.892
1929		**24**	8	.750	3.29	44	33	13	254.2	233	**125**	149	3	3	0	1	87	15	1	.172	12	38	6	1	1.3	.893
1930		22	13	.629	4.44	49	**39**	20	296	299	**139**	193	**3**	2	2	2	114	26	0	.228	8	53	5	2	1.3	.924
1931		21	7	.750	3.67	43	30	23	281.2	255	75	152	3	1	0	6	114	30	2	.263	15	52	5	4	1.7	.931
1932		19	13	.594	4.77	36	33	21	245.1	262	94	109	1	1	1	0	91	26	0	.286	7	54	3	3	1.8	.953
1933		5	10	.333	5.97	21	18	4	117.2	153	58	37	0	1	0	0	44	8	0	.182	6	30	0	2	1.7	1.000
1934	CHI A	14	11	.560	4.52	33	30	16	227	242	104	97	2	0	1	0	79	16	0	.203	4	45	4	0	1.6	.925
1935	2 teams	CHI A	(3G 1–2)		BKN N	(25G 8–12)																				
″	total	9	14	.391	4.60	28	25	6	184	201	64	80	2	1	1	0	67	15	0	.224	5	38	1	3	1.6	.977
1936	2 teams	BKN N	(19G 4–9)		STL N	(20G 2–1)																				
″	total	6	10	.375	5.73	39	19	5	150.2	193	50	71	1	3	0	2	51	12	0	.235	8	34	2	2	1.1	.955
9 yrs.		127	93	.577	4.38	319	249	115	1915.1	1981	809	1005	18	12	5	12	704	162	3	.230	71	371	30	17	1.5	.936
WORLD SERIES																										
1929	PHI A	1	1	.500	2.63	2	2	1	13.2	14	6	17	0	0	0	0	5	0	0	.000	0	2	0	0	1.0	1.000
1930		2	0	1.000	0.72	3	3	2	25	13	7	19	0	0	0	0	9	0	0	.000	1	6	0	0	2.3	1.000
1931		1	2	.333	1.88	3	3	2	24	12	4	20	1	0	0	0	8	0	0	.000	1	7	0	0	2.7	1.000
3 yrs.		4	3	.571	1.58	8	8	5	62.2	39	17	56	1	0	0	0	22	0	0	.000	2	15	0	0	2.1	1.000
							10th		**10th**			**7th**														

Logan Easley

EASLEY, KENNETH LOGAN BR TR 6′ 1″ 185 lbs.
B. Nov. 4, 1961, Salt Lake City, Utah.

Year	Team	W	L	PCT	ERA	G	GS	CG	IP	H	BB	SO	ShO	Relief Pitching W	Relief Pitching L	Relief Pitching SV	Batting AB	Batting H	Batting HR	BA	PO	A	E	DP	TC/G	FA
1987	PIT N	1	1	.500	5.47	17	0	0	26.1	23	17	21	0	1	1	1	2	0	0	.000	2	8	0	1	0.6	1.000
1989		1	0	1.000	4.38	10	0	0	12.1	8	7	6	0	1	0	1	1	0	0	.000	0	2	1	0	0.3	.667
2 yrs.		2	1	.667	5.12	27	0	0	38.2	31	24	27	0	2	1	2	3	0	0	.000	2	10	1	1	0.5	.923

Mal Eason

EASON, MALCOLM WAYNE (Kid) BR TR 6′ 175 lbs.
B. Mar. 13, 1879, Brookville, Pa. D. Apr. 16, 1970, Douglas, Ariz.

Year	Team	W	L	PCT	ERA	G	GS	CG	IP	H	BB	SO	ShO	Relief Pitching W	Relief Pitching L	Relief Pitching SV	Batting AB	Batting H	Batting HR	BA	PO	A	E	DP	TC/G	FA
1900	CHI N	1	0	1.000	1.00	1	1	1	9	9	3	2	0	0	0	0	3	0	0	.000	0	1	0	0	1.0	1.000
1901		8	17	.320	3.59	27	25	23	220.2	246	60	68	1	0	0	0	87	12	0	.138	13	51	6	0	2.6	.914
1902	2 teams	CHI N	(2G 1–1)		BOS N	(27G 9–11)																				
″	total	10	12	.455	2.61	29	29	22	224.1	258	61	54	2	0	0	0	77	7	0	.091	11	60	6	0	2.7	.922
1903	DET A	2	5	.286	3.36	7	6	6	56.1	60	19	21	1	0	1	0	20	2	0	.100	2	24	1	0	3.9	.963
1905	BKN N	5	21	.192	4.30	27	27	20	207	230	72	64	3	0	0	0	81	14	0	.173	7	69	6	1	2.8	.927
1906		10	17	.370	3.25	34	26	18	227	212	74	64	3	1	0	0	88	8	0	.091	16	72	2	3	2.5	.978
6 yrs.		36	72	.333	3.39	125	114	90	944.1	1015	289	273	10	1	1	0	356	43	0	.121	49	277	21	4	2.7	.939

Carl East

EAST, CARLTON WILLIAM BL TR 6′ 2″ 178 lbs.
B. Aug. 27, 1894, Marietta, Ga. D. Jan. 15, 1953, Whitesburg, Ga.

Year	Team	W	L	PCT	ERA	G	GS	CG	IP	H	BB	SO	ShO	Relief Pitching W	Relief Pitching L	Relief Pitching SV	Batting AB	Batting H	Batting HR	BA	PO	A	E	DP	TC/G	FA
1915	STL A	0	0	—	16.20	1	1	0	3.1	6	2	1	0	0	0	0	*				0	0	0	0	0.0	.000

Hugh East

EAST, GORDON HUGH BR TR 6′ 2″ 185 lbs.
B. July 7, 1919, Birmingham, Ala. D. Nov. 2, 1981, Charleston, S. C.

Year	Team	W	L	PCT	ERA	G	GS	CG	IP	H	BB	SO	ShO	Relief W	Relief L	Relief SV	AB	H	HR	BA	PO	A	E	DP	TC/G	FA
1941	NY N	1	1	.500	3.45	2	2	0	15.2	19	9	4	0	0	0	0	9	2	0	.222	2	3	1	0	3.0	.833
1942		0	2	.000	9.82	4	1	0	7.1	15	7	2	0	0	1	0	2	1	1	.500	0	2	0	0	0.5	1.000
1943		1	3	.250	5.36	13	5	1	40.1	51	25	21	0	0	0	0	13	1	0	.077	0	5	0	0	0.4	1.000
3 yrs.		2	6	.250	5.40	19	8	1	63.1	85	41	27	0	0	1	0	24	4	1	.167	2	10	1	0	0.7	.923

Jamie Easterly

EASTERLY, JAMES MORRIS BL TL 5′ 9″ 180 lbs.
B. Feb. 17, 1953, Houston, Tex. BB 1974–1976

Year	Team	W	L	PCT	ERA	G	GS	CG	IP	H	BB	SO	ShO	Relief W	Relief L	Relief SV	AB	H	HR	BA	PO	A	E	DP	TC/G	FA
1974	ATL N	0	0	—	15.00	3	0	0	3	6	4	0	0	0	0	0	0	0	0	—	0	1	0	0	0.3	1.000
1975		2	9	.182	4.96	21	13	0	69	73	42	34	0	0	0	0	18	1	0	.056	1	9	0	1	0.5	1.000
1976		1	1	.500	4.91	4	4	0	22	23	13	11	0	0	0	0	9	1	0	.111	1	4	0	0	1.3	1.000
1977		2	4	.333	6.10	22	5	0	59	72	30	37	0	0	2	1	15	4	0	.267	2	3	1	0	0.3	.833
1978		3	6	.333	5.65	37	6	0	78	91	45	42	0	3	3	1	19	4	0	.211	2	14	1	1	0.5	.941
1979		0	0	—	12.00	4	0	0	3	7	3	3	0	0	0	0	0	0	0	—	0	1	0	0	0.3	1.000
1981	MIL A	3	3	.500	3.19	44	0	0	62	46	34	31	0	3	3	4	0	0	0	—	7	10	0	0	0.4	1.000
1982		0	2	.000	4.70	28	0	0	30.2	39	15	16	0	0	2	2	0	0	0	—	3	7	0	0	0.4	1.000
1983	2 teams MIL A (12G 0–1) CLE A (41G 4–2)																									
″	total	4	3	.571	3.67	53	0	0	68.2	83	32	45	0	4	3	4	1	0	0	.000	5	10	0	0	0.3	1.000
1984	CLE A	3	1	.750	3.38	26	1	0	69.1	74	23	42	0	3	1	2	0	0	0	—	6	10	0	0	0.6	1.000
1985		4	1	.800	3.92	50	7	0	98.2	96	53	58	0	2	0	0	0	0	0	—	11	10	0	1	0.4	1.000
1986		0	2	.000	7.64	13	0	0	17.2	27	12	9	0	0	2	0	0	0	0	—	2	1	0	0	0.2	1.000
1987		1	1	.500	4.55	16	0	0	31.2	26	13	22	0	1	1	0	0	0	0	—	3	4	0	0	0.4	1.000
13 yrs.		23	33	.411	4.61	321	36	0	612.2	663	319	350	0	16	17	14	62	10	0	.161	43	84	2	3	0.4	.984
DIVISIONAL PLAYOFF SERIES																										
1981	MIL A	0	0	—	6.75	2	0	0	1.1	2	0	1	0	0	0	0	0	0	0	—	0	0	0	0	0.0	.000

John Easton

EASTON, JOHN S.
B. Feb. 28, 1867, Bridgeport, Ohio D. Nov. 28, 1903, Steubenville, Ohio.

Year	Team	W	L	PCT	ERA	G	GS	CG	IP	H	BB	SO	ShO	Relief W	Relief L	Relief SV	AB	H	HR	BA	PO	A	E	DP	TC/G	FA
1889	COL AA	1	0	1.000	3.50	4	1	1	18	13	21	7	0	0	0	1	7	0	0	.000	1	4	3	0	2.0	.625
1890		15	14	.517	*3.52*	37	29	23	255.2	213	125	147	0	2	1	1	107	19	0	.178	13	54	13	3	1.9	.837
1891	2 teams COL AA (20G 5–12) STL AA (7G 3–2)																									
″	total	8	14	.364	4.59	27	24	19	198	208	86	87	0	0	0	0	102	20	0	.196	13	42	5	1	1.8	.917
1892	STL N	2	0	1.000	6.39	5	2	2	31	38	26	4	0	0	0	0	17	3	0	.176	4	8	1	0	2.2	.923
1894	PIT N	0	1	.000	4.12	3	1	1	19.2	26	4	1	0	0	0	0	5	0	0	.000	1	1	2	0	1.3	.500
5 yrs.		26	29	.473	4.12	76	57	46	522.1	498	262	246	0	2	1	2	238	42	0	.176	32	109	24	4	1.9	.855

Rawly Eastwick

EASTWICK, RAWLINS JACKSON III BR TR 6′ 3″ 180 lbs.
B. Oct. 24, 1950, Camden, N. J.

Year	Team	W	L	PCT	ERA	G	GS	CG	IP	H	BB	SO	ShO	Relief W	Relief L	Relief SV	AB	H	HR	BA	PO	A	E	DP	TC/G	FA
1974	CIN N	0	0	—	2.00	8	0	0	18	12	5	14	0	0	0	2	1	0	0	.000	1	1	0	0	0.3	1.000
1975		5	3	.625	2.60	58	0	0	90	77	25	61	0	5	3	**22**	15	1	0	.067	5	5	0	1	0.2	1.000
1976		11	5	.688	2.08	71	0	0	108	93	27	70	0	11	5	**26**	17	0	0	.000	3	9	0	0	0.2	1.000
1977	2 teams CIN N (23G 2–2) STL N (41G 3–7)																									
″	total	5	9	.357	3.90	64	1	0	97	114	29	47	0	5	8	11	11	3	0	.273	5	6	0	0	0.2	1.000
1978	2 teams NY A (8G 2–1) PHI N (22G 2–1)																									
″	total	4	2	.667	3.76	30	0	0	64.2	53	22	27	0	4	2	0	3	0	0	.000	3	7	0	0	0.3	1.000
1979	PHI N	3	6	.333	4.88	51	0	0	83	90	25	47	0	3	6	6	7	0	0	.000	4	4	0	0	0.2	1.000
1980	KC A	0	1	.000	5.32	14	0	0	22	37	8	5	0	0	1	0	0	0	0	—	3	6	1	0	0.7	.900
1981	CHI N	0	1	.000	2.30	30	0	0	43	43	15	24	0	0	1	1	2	0	0	.000	4	8	1	0	0.4	.923
8 yrs.		28	27	.509	3.30	326	1	0	525.2	519	156	295	0	28	26	68	56	4	0	.071	28	46	2	1	0.2	.974
LEAGUE CHAMPIONSHIP SERIES																										
1975	CIN N	1	0	1.000	0.00	2	0	0	3.2	2	2	1	0	1	0	1	0	0	0	—	1	0	0	0	0.5	1.000
1976		1	0	1.000	12.00	2	0	0	3	7	2	1	0	1	0	0	0	0	0	—	0	1	0	0	0.5	1.000
1978	PHI N	0	0	—	9.00	1	0	0	1	3	0	1	0	0	0	0	0	0	0	—	0	0	0	0	0.0	.000
3 yrs.		2	0	1.000	5.87	5	0	0	7.2	12	4	3	0	2	0	1	0	0	0		1	1	0	0	0.4	1.000
WORLD SERIES																										
1975	CIN N	2	0	1.000	2.25	5	0	0	8	6	3	4	0	2	0	1	1	0	0	.000	0	0	0	0	0.0	.000

Craig Eaton

EATON, CRAIG BR TR 5′11″ 175 lbs.
B. Sept. 7, 1954, Cincinnati, Ohio.

Year	Team	W	L	PCT	ERA	G	GS	CG	IP	H	BB	SO	ShO	Relief W	Relief L	Relief SV	AB	H	HR	BA	PO	A	E	DP	TC/G	FA
1979	KC A	0	0	—	2.70	5	0	0	10	8	3	4	0	0	0	0	0	0	0	—	1	1	0	1	0.4	1.000

Zeb Eaton

EATON, ZEBULON VANCE (Red) BR TR 5′10″ 185 lbs.
B. Feb. 2, 1920, Cooleemee, N. C. D. Dec. 17, 1989, West Palm Beach, Fla.

Year	Team	W	L	PCT	ERA	G	GS	CG	IP	H	BB	SO	ShO	Relief W	Relief L	Relief SV	AB	H	HR	BA	PO	A	E	DP	TC/G	FA
1944	DET A	0	0	—	5.74	6	0	0	15.2	19	8	4	0	0	0	0	10	1	0	.100	1	2	0	0	0.5	1.000
1945		4	2	.667	4.05	17	3	0	53.1	48	40	15	0	3	0	0	32	8	2	.250	4	11	2	0	1.0	.882
2 yrs.		4	2	.667	4.43	23	3	0	69	67	48	19	0	3	0	0	42	9	2	.214	5	13	2	0	0.9	.900

Gary Eave

EAVE, GARY LOUIS BR TR 6′ 4″ 200 lbs.
B. July 22, 1963, Monroe, La.

Year	Team	W	L	PCT	ERA	G	GS	CG	IP	H	BB	SO	ShO	Relief W	Relief L	Relief SV	AB	H	HR	BA	PO	A	E	DP	TC/G	FA
1988	ATL N	0	0	—	9.00	5	0	0	5	7	3	0	0	0	0	0	0	0	0	—	0	0	0	0	0.0	.000
1989		2	0	1.000	1.31	3	3	0	20.2	15	12	9	0	0	0	0	6	0	0	.000	1	0	0	0	0.3	1.000
1990	SEA A	0	3	.000	4.20	8	5	0	30	27	20	16	0	0	1	0	0	0	0	—	1	5	0	1	0.8	1.000
3 yrs.		2	3	.400	3.56	16	8	0	55.2	49	35	25	0	0	1	0	6	0	0	.000	2	5	0	1	0.4	1.000

Vallie Eaves

EAVES, VALLIE ENNIS (Chief) BR TR 6′ 2½″ 180 lbs.
B. Sept. 6, 1911, Allen, Okla. D. Apr. 19, 1960, Norman, Okla.

Year	Team	W	L	PCT	ERA	G	GS	CG	IP	H	BB	SO	ShO	Relief W	Relief L	Relief SV	AB	H	HR	BA	PO	A	E	DP	TC/G	FA
1935	PHI A	1	2	.333	5.14	3	3	1	14	12	15	6	0	0	0	0	4	0	0	.000	0	2	0	0	0.7	1.000
1939	CHI A	0	1	.000	4.63	2	1	1	11.2	11	8	5	0	0	0	0	6	2	0	.333	0	2	0	0	1.0	1.000
1940		0	2	.000	6.75	5	3	0	18.2	22	24	11	0	0	0	0	5	0	0	.000	0	0	0	0	0.0	.000
1941	CHI N	3	3	.500	3.53	12	7	4	58.2	56	21	24	0	1	0	0	20	2	0	.100	0	6	0	0	0.5	1.000
1942		0	0	—	9.00	2	0	0	3	4	2	0	0	0	0	0	0	0	0	—	0	0	1	0	0.5	.000
5 yrs.		4	8	.333	4.58	24	14	6	106	105	70	46	0	1	0	0	35	4	0	.114	0	10	1	0	0.5	.909

Eddie Eayrs

EAYRS, EDWIN BL TL 5′ 7″ 160 lbs.
B. Nov. 10, 1890, Blackstone, Mass. D. Nov. 30, 1969, Warwick, R. I.

Year	Team	Lg	W	L	PCT	ERA	G	GS	CG	IP	H	BB	SO	ShO	Relief Pitching W	Relief Pitching L	Relief Pitching SV	Batting AB	Batting H	Batting HR	BA	PO	A	E	DP	TC/G	FA
1913	PIT	N	0	0	—	2.25	2	0	0	8	8	6	5	0	0	0	0	6	1	0	.167	0	2	1	0	1.5	.667
1920	BOS	N	1	2	.333	5.47	7	3	0	26.1	36	12	7	0	0	0	0	244	80	1	.328	109	18	6	2	1.9	.955
1921			0	0	—	17.36	2	0	0	4.2	9	9	1	0	0	0	0	21	2	0	.095	0	0	0	0	0.0	
3 yrs.			1	2	.333	6.23	11	3	0	39	53	27	13	0	0	0	0	*				109	20	7	2	1.8	.949

Harry Eccles

ECCLES, HARRY JOSIAH (Buggs) BL TL 6′ 2″ 170 lbs.
B. July 9, 1893, Kennedy, N. Y. D. June 2, 1955, Jamestown, N. Y.

Year	Team	Lg	W	L	PCT	ERA	G	GS	CG	IP	H	BB	SO	ShO	Relief Pitching W	Relief Pitching L	Relief Pitching SV	Batting AB	Batting H	Batting HR	BA	PO	A	E	DP	TC/G	FA
1915	PHI	A	0	1	.000	6.86	5	1	0	21	18	6	13	0	0	0	1	6	1	0	.167	1	3	2	0	1.2	.667

Dennis Eckersley

ECKERSLEY, DENNIS LEE (The Eck) BR TR 6′ 2″ 190 lbs.
B. Oct. 3, 1954, Oakland, Calif.

Year	Team	Lg	W	L	PCT	ERA	G	GS	CG	IP	H	BB	SO	ShO	Relief Pitching W	Relief Pitching L	Relief Pitching SV	Batting AB	Batting H	Batting HR	BA	PO	A	E	DP	TC/G	FA
1975	CLE	A	13	7	.650	2.60	34	24	6	186.2	147	90	152	2	1	0	2	0	0	0	—	7	12	1	0	0.6	.950
1976			13	12	.520	3.44	36	30	9	199	155	78	200	3	1	0	1	0	0	0	—	9	20	1	1	0.8	.967
1977			14	13	.519	3.53	33	33	12	247	214	54	191	3	0	0	0	0	0	0	—	6	22	2	1	0.9	.933
1978	BOS	A	20	8	.714	2.99	35	35	16	268.1	258	71	162	3	0	0	0	0	0	0	—	19	29	0	1	1.4	1.000
1979			17	10	.630	2.99	33	33	17	247	234	59	150	2	0	0	0	0	0	0	—	12	42	6	3	1.8	.900
1980			12	14	.462	4.27	30	30	8	198	188	44	121	0	0	0	0	0	0	0	—	10	24	3	0	1.2	.919
1981			9	8	.529	4.27	23	23	8	154	160	35	79	2	0	0	0	0	0	0	—	12	19	1	1	1.4	.969
1982			13	13	.500	3.73	33	33	11	224.1	228	43	127	3	0	0	0	0	0	0	—	21	21	1	2	1.3	.977
1983			9	13	.409	5.61	28	28	2	176.1	223	39	77	0	0	0	0	0	0	0	—	19	18	1	0	1.4	.974
1984	2 teams	BOS A (9G 4–4)	CHI N (24G 10–8)																								
″	total		14	12	.538	3.60	33	33	4	225	223	49	114	0	0	0	0	55	6	0	.109	27	38	5	3	2.1	.929
1985	CHI	N	11	7	.611	3.08	25	25	6	169.1	145	19	117	2	0	0	0	56	7	1	.125	10	26	3	1	1.6	.923
1986			6	11	.353	4.57	33	32	1	201	226	43	137	0	0	0	0	69	11	2	.159	16	28	3	3	1.4	.936
1987	OAK	A	6	8	.429	3.03	54	2	0	115.2	99	17	113	0	6	6	16	0	0	0	—	4	13	1	0	0.3	.944
1988			4	2	.667	2.35	60	0	0	72.2	52	11	70	0	4	2	**45**	0	0	0	—	7	3	0	0	0.2	1.000
1989			4	0	1.000	1.56	51	0	0	57.2	32	3	55	0	4	0	33	0	0	0	—	4	4	0	1	0.2	1.000
1990			4	2	.667	0.61	63	0	0	73.1	41	4	73	0	4	2	48	0	0	0	—	3	1	0	0	0.1	1.000
1991			5	4	.556	2.96	67	0	0	76	60	9	87	0	5	4	43	0	0	0	—	6	9	0	0	0.2	1.000
1992			7	1	.875	1.91	69	0	0	80	62	11	93	0	7	1	**51**	0	0	0	—	3	10	0	1	0.2	1.000
1993			2	4	.333	4.16	64	0	0	67	67	13	80	0	2	4	36	0	0	0	—	0	5	0	0	0.1	1.000
1994			5	4	.556	4.26	45	0	0	44.1	49	13	47	0	5	4	19	0	0	0	—	2	1	0	0	0.1	1.000
1995			4	6	.400	4.83	52	0	0	50.1	53	11	40	0	4	6	29	0	0	0	—	3	5	1	2	0.2	.889
21 yrs.			192	159	.547	3.48	901	361	100	3133	2916	716	2285	20	43	29	323	180	24	3	.133	200	350	29	20	0.6	.950
							9th										**4th**										

LEAGUE CHAMPIONSHIP SERIES

Year	Team	Lg	W	L	PCT	ERA	G	GS	CG	IP	H	BB	SO	ShO	Relief Pitching W	Relief Pitching L	Relief Pitching SV	Batting AB	Batting H	Batting HR	BA	PO	A	E	DP	TC/G	FA
1984	CHI	N	0	1	.000	8.44	1	1	0	5.1	9	0	0	0	0	0	0	2	0	0	.000	0	0	0	0	0.0	.000
1988	OAK	A	0	0	—	0.00	4	0	0	6	1	2	5	0	0	0	4	0	0	0	—	2	0	0	0	0.5	1.000
1989			0	0	—	1.59	4	0	0	5.2	4	0	2	0	0	0	3	0	0	0	—	0	1	0	0	0.3	1.000
1990			0	0	—	0.00	3	0	0	3.1	2	0	3	0	0	0	2	0	0	0	—	0	0	0	0	0.0	.000
1992			0	0	—	6.00	3	0	0	3	8	0	2	0	0	0	1	0	0	0	—	0	0	0	0	0.0	.000
5 yrs.			0	1	.000	3.09	15	1	0	23.1	24	2	12	0	0	0	10	2	0	0	.000	2	1	0	0	0.2	1.000
							1st										**1st**										

WORLD SERIES

Year	Team	Lg	W	L	PCT	ERA	G	GS	CG	IP	H	BB	SO	ShO	Relief Pitching W	Relief Pitching L	Relief Pitching SV	Batting AB	Batting H	Batting HR	BA	PO	A	E	DP	TC/G	FA
1988	OAK	A	0	1	.000	10.80	2	0	0	1.2	2	1	2	0	0	1	0	0	0	0	—	0	0	0	0	0.0	.000
1989			0	0	—	0.00	2	0	0	1.2	0	0	0	0	0	0	1	0	0	0	—	1	0	0	0	0.5	1.000
1990			0	1	.000	6.75	2	0	0	1.1	3	0	1	0	0	1	0	0	0	0	—	0	0	0	0	0.0	.000
3 yrs.			0	2	.000	5.79	6	0	0	4.2	5	1	3	0	0	2	1	0	0	0		1	0	0	0	0.1	1.000

Al Eckert

ECKERT, ALBERT GEORGE (Obbie) BL TL 5′10″ 174 lbs.
B. May 17, 1906, Milwaukee, Wis. D. Apr. 20, 1974, Milwaukee, Wis.

Year	Team	Lg	W	L	PCT	ERA	G	GS	CG	IP	H	BB	SO	ShO	Relief Pitching W	Relief Pitching L	Relief Pitching SV	Batting AB	Batting H	Batting HR	BA	PO	A	E	DP	TC/G	FA
1930	CIN	N	0	1	.000	7.20	2	1	0	5	7	4	1	0	0	0	0	1	0	0	.000	0	2	0	0	1.0	1.000
1931			0	1	.000	9.16	14	1	0	18.2	26	9	5	0	0	0	0	3	1	0	.333	0	3	0	2	0.2	1.000
1935	STL	N	0	0	—	12.00	2	0	0	3	7	1	1	0	0	0	0	0	0	0	—	0	0	0	0	0.0	.000
3 yrs.			0	2	.000	9.11	18	2	0	26.2	40	14	7	0	0	0	0	4	1	0	.250	0	5	0	2	0.3	1.000

Charlie Eckert

ECKERT, CHARLES WILLIAM (Buzz) BR TR 5′10½″ 165 lbs.
B. Aug. 8, 1897, Philadelphia, Pa. D. Aug. 22, 1986, Trevose, Pa.

Year	Team	Lg	W	L	PCT	ERA	G	GS	CG	IP	H	BB	SO	ShO	Relief Pitching W	Relief Pitching L	Relief Pitching SV	Batting AB	Batting H	Batting HR	BA	PO	A	E	DP	TC/G	FA
1919	PHI	A	0	1	.000	3.94	2	1	1	16	17	3	6	0	0	0	0	6	1	0	.167	2	4	0	0	3.0	1.000
1920			0	0	—	4.76	2	0	0	5.2	8	1	1	0	0	0	0	1	0	0	.000	0	0	1	0	0.5	.000
1922			0	2	.000	4.68	21	0	0	50	61	23	15	0	0	2	0	11	1	0	.091	1	20	0	0	1.0	1.000
3 yrs.			0	3	.000	4.52	25	1	1	71.2	86	27	22	0	0	2	0	18	2	0	.111	3	24	1	0	1.1	.964

Chris Eddy

EDDY, CHRISTOPHER MARK BL TL 6′ 3″ 200 lbs.
B. Nov. 27, 1969, Dallas, Tex.

Year	Team	Lg	W	L	PCT	ERA	G	GS	CG	IP	H	BB	SO	ShO	Relief Pitching W	Relief Pitching L	Relief Pitching SV	Batting AB	Batting H	Batting HR	BA	PO	A	E	DP	TC/G	FA
1995	OAK	A	0	0	—	7.36	6	0	0	3.2	7	2	2	0	0	0	0	0	0	0	—	0	1	0	0	0.2	1.000

Don Eddy

EDDY, DONALD EUGENE BR TL 5′11″ 170 lbs.
B. Oct. 25, 1946, Mason City, Iowa.

Year	Team	Lg	W	L	PCT	ERA	G	GS	CG	IP	H	BB	SO	ShO	Relief Pitching W	Relief Pitching L	Relief Pitching SV	Batting AB	Batting H	Batting HR	BA	PO	A	E	DP	TC/G	FA
1970	CHI	A	0	0	—	2.25	7	0	0	12	10	6	9	0	0	0	0	0	0	0	—	2	1	0	0	0.4	1.000
1971			0	2	.000	2.35	22	0	0	23	19	19	14	0	0	2	0	1	1	0	1.000	1	2	1	0	0.2	.750
2 yrs.			0	2	.000	2.31	29	0	0	35	29	25	23	0	0	2	0	1	1	0	1.000	3	3	1	0	0.2	.857

Steve Eddy

EDDY, STEVEN ALLEN BR TR 6′ 2″ 185 lbs.
B. Aug. 21, 1957, Sterling, Ill.

Year	Team	Lg	W	L	PCT	ERA	G	GS	CG	IP	H	BB	SO	ShO	Relief Pitching W	Relief Pitching L	Relief Pitching SV	Batting AB	Batting H	Batting HR	BA	PO	A	E	DP	TC/G	FA
1979	CAL	A	1	1	.500	4.78	7	4	0	32	36	20	7	0	0	0	0	0	0	0	—	5	7	2	0	2.0	.857

Ed Edelen

EDELEN, EDWARD JOSEPH (Doc) BR TR 6′ 191 lbs.
B. Mar. 16, 1912, Bryantown, Md. D. Feb. 1, 1982, La Plata, Md.

Year	Team	Lg	W	L	PCT	ERA	G	GS	CG	IP	H	BB	SO	ShO	Relief Pitching W	Relief Pitching L	Relief Pitching SV	Batting AB	Batting H	Batting HR	BA	PO	A	E	DP	TC/G	FA
1932	WAS	A	0	0	—	20.25	2	0	0	1.1	0	6	0	0	0	0	0	0	0	0	—	0	0	0	0	0.0	.000

Joe Edelen

EDELEN, BENNY JOE BR TR 6′ 165 lbs.
B. Sept. 16, 1955, Durant, Okla.

Year	Team	W	L	PCT	ERA	G	GS	CG	IP	H	BB	SO	ShO	Relief W	Relief L	Relief SV	Batting AB	Batting H	HR	BA	PO	A	E	DP	TC/G	FA
1981	2 teams STL N (13G 1–0) CIN N (5G 1–0)																									
″	total	2	0	1.000	5.70	18	0	0	30	34	3	15	0	2	0	0	5	1	0	.200	1	2	0	0	0.2	1.000
1982	CIN N	0	0	—	8.80	9	0	0	15.1	22	8	11	0	0	0	0	2	1	0	.500	2	1	0	0	0.3	1.000
2 yrs.		2	0	1.000	6.75	27	0	0	45.1	56	11	26	0	2	0	0	7	2	0	.286	3	3	0	0	0.2	1.000

John Edelman

EDELMAN, JOHN ROGERS BR TR 6′ 3″ 185 lbs.
B. July 27, 1935, Philadelphia, Pa.

Year	Team	W	L	PCT	ERA	G	GS	CG	IP	H	BB	SO	ShO	Relief W	Relief L	Relief SV	Batting AB	Batting H	HR	BA	PO	A	E	DP	TC/G	FA
1955	MIL N	0	0	—	11.12	5	0	0	5.2	7	8	3	0	0	0	0	0	0	0	—	0	1	0	0	0.2	1.000

Charlie Eden

EDEN, CHARLES M. BL TL 168 lbs.
B. Jan. 18, 1855, Lexington, Ky. D. Sept. 17, 1920, Cincinnati, Ohio.

Year	Team	W	L	PCT	ERA	G	GS	CG	IP	H	BB	SO	ShO	Relief W	Relief L	Relief SV	Batting AB	Batting H	HR	BA	PO	A	E	DP	TC/G	FA
1884	PIT AA	0	1	.000	*6.00*	2	1	1	12	12	3	3	0	0	0	0	122	33	1	.270	17	2	9	1	1.9	.679
1885		1	2	.333	*5.17*	4	1	0	15.2	22	3	5	0	1	1	0	405	103	0	.254	113	10	32	2	1.5	.794
2 yrs.		1	3	.250	5.53	6	2	1	27.2	34	6	8	0	1	1	0	*				284	38	87	6	1.7	.787

Ken Edenfield

EDENFIELD, KENNETH EDWARD BR TR 6′ 1″ 165 lbs.
B. Mar. 18, 1967, Jessup, Ga.

Year	Team	W	L	PCT	ERA	G	GS	CG	IP	H	BB	SO	ShO	Relief W	Relief L	Relief SV	Batting AB	Batting H	HR	BA	PO	A	E	DP	TC/G	FA
1995	CAL A	0	0	—	4.26	7	0	0	12.2	15	5	6	0	0	0	0	0	0	0	—	0	2	0	0	0.3	1.000

Tom Edens

EDENS, THOMAS PATRICK BR TR 6′ 3″ 185 lbs.
B. June 9, 1961, Ontario, Ore.

Year	Team	W	L	PCT	ERA	G	GS	CG	IP	H	BB	SO	ShO	Relief W	Relief L	Relief SV	Batting AB	Batting H	HR	BA	PO	A	E	DP	TC/G	FA
1987	NY N	0	0	—	6.75	2	2	0	8	15	4	4	0	0	0	0	3	0	0	.000	0	4	1	0	2.5	.800
1990	MIL A	4	5	.444	4.45	35	6	0	89	89	33	40	0	2	3	2	0	0	0	—	7	10	3	0	0.6	.850
1991	MIN A	2	2	.500	4.09	8	6	0	33	34	10	19	0	0	0	0	0	0	0	—	5	5	0	0	1.3	1.000
1992		6	3	.667	2.83	52	0	0	76.1	65	36	57	0	6	3	3	0	0	0	—	8	4	0	0	0.2	1.000
1993	HOU N	1	1	.500	3.12	38	0	0	49	47	19	21	0	1	1	0	1	0	0	.000	3	10	1	0	0.4	.929
1994	2 teams HOU N (39G 4–1) PHI N (3G 1–0)																									
″	total	5	1	.833	4.33	42	0	0	54	59	18	39	0	5	1	1	2	0	0	.000	6	13	0	1	0.5	1.000
1995	CHI N	1	0	1.000	6.00	5	0	0	3	6	3	2	0	1	0	0	0	0	0	—	1	0	0	0	0.2	1.000
7 yrs.		19	12	.613	3.86	182	14	0	312.1	315	123	182	0	15	8	6	6	0	0	.000	30	46	5	1	0.4	.938

Butch Edge

EDGE, CLAUDE LEE, JR. BR TR 6′ 3″ 203 lbs.
B. July 18, 1956, Houston, Tex.

Year	Team	W	L	PCT	ERA	G	GS	CG	IP	H	BB	SO	ShO	Relief W	Relief L	Relief SV	Batting AB	Batting H	HR	BA	PO	A	E	DP	TC/G	FA
1979	TOR A	3	4	.429	5.19	9	9	1	52	60	24	19	0	0	0	0	0	0	0	—	1	7	0	0	0.9	1.000

Bill Edgerton

EDGERTON, WILLIAM ALBERT BL TL 6′ 2″ 185 lbs.
B. Aug. 16, 1941, South Bend, Ind.

Year	Team	W	L	PCT	ERA	G	GS	CG	IP	H	BB	SO	ShO	Relief W	Relief L	Relief SV	Batting AB	Batting H	HR	BA	PO	A	E	DP	TC/G	FA
1966	KC A	0	1	.000	3.24	6	1	0	8.1	10	7	3	0	0	1	0	0	0	0	—	0	3	0	0	0.5	1.000
1967		1	0	1.000	2.16	7	0	0	8.1	11	3	6	0	1	0	0	0	0	0	—	0	2	0	0	0.3	1.000
1969	SEA A	0	1	.000	13.50	4	0	0	4	10	0	2	0	0	1	0	0	0	0	—	0	1	0	1	0.3	1.000
3 yrs.		1	2	.333	4.79	17	1	0	20.2	31	10	11	0	1	2	0	0	0	0		0	6	0	1	0.4	1.000

George Edmondson

EDMONDSON, GEORGE HENDERSON (Big Ed) BR TR 6′ 1″ 179 lbs.
B. May 18, 1896, Waxahachie, Tex. D. July 11, 1973, Waco, Tex.

Year	Team	W	L	PCT	ERA	G	GS	CG	IP	H	BB	SO	ShO	Relief W	Relief L	Relief SV	Batting AB	Batting H	HR	BA	PO	A	E	DP	TC/G	FA
1922	CLE A	0	0	—	9.00	2	0	0	2	4	0	0	0	0	0	0	0	0	0	—	0	1	0	0	0.5	1.000
1923		0	0	—	11.25	1	0	0	4	8	3	0	0	0	0	0	1	0	0	.000	0	2	0	1	2.0	1.000
1924		0	0	—	9.00	5	1	0	8	10	5	3	0	0	0	0	3	1	0	.333	0	0	0	0	0.0	.000
3 yrs.		0	0		9.64	8	1	0	14	22	8	3	0	0	0	0	4	1	0	.250	0	3	0	1	0.4	1.000

Paul Edmondson

EDMONDSON, PAUL MICHAEL BR TR 6′ 5″ 195 lbs.
B. Feb. 12, 1943, Kansas City, Kans. D. Feb. 13, 1970, Santa Barbara, Calif.

Year	Team	W	L	PCT	ERA	G	GS	CG	IP	H	BB	SO	ShO	Relief W	Relief L	Relief SV	Batting AB	Batting H	HR	BA	PO	A	E	DP	TC/G	FA
1969	CHI A	1	6	.143	3.70	14	13	1	87.2	72	39	46	0	0	1	0	29	5	0	.172	6	27	1	1	2.4	.971

Sam Edmonston

EDMONSTON, SAMUEL SHERWOOD BL TL 5′11½″ 185 lbs.
B. Aug. 30, 1883, Washington, D. C. D. Apr. 12, 1979, Corpus Christi, Tex.

Year	Team	W	L	PCT	ERA	G	GS	CG	IP	H	BB	SO	ShO	Relief W	Relief L	Relief SV	Batting AB	Batting H	HR	BA	PO	A	E	DP	TC/G	FA
1906	WAS A	0	1	.000	4.50	2	1	1	10	10	2	0	0	0	0	0	3	1	0	.333	0	5	0	0	2.5	1.000
1907		0	0	—	9.00	1	0	0	3	8	1	0	0	0	0	0	2	0	0	.000	0	2	0	0	2.0	1.000
2 yrs.		0	1	.000	5.54	3	1	1	13	18	3	0	0	0	0	0	5	1	0	.200	0	7	0	0	2.3	1.000

Foster Edwards

EDWARDS, FOSTER HAMILTON (Eddie) BR TR 6′ 3″ 175 lbs.
B. Sept. 1, 1903, Holstein, Iowa D. Jan. 4, 1980, Orleans, Mass.

Year	Team	W	L	PCT	ERA	G	GS	CG	IP	H	BB	SO	ShO	Relief W	Relief L	Relief SV	Batting AB	Batting H	HR	BA	PO	A	E	DP	TC/G	FA
1925	BOS N	0	0	—	9.00	1	0	0	2	6	1	1	0	0	0	0	0	0	0	—	0	0	0	0	0.0	.000
1926		2	0	1.000	0.72	3	3	1	25	20	13	4	0	0	0	0	9	0	0	.000	2	5	0	1	2.3	1.000
1927		2	8	.200	4.99	29	11	1	92	95	45	37	0	1	0	0	22	1	0	.045	1	17	2	1	0.7	.900
1928		2	1	.667	5.66	21	3	2	49.1	67	23	17	0	0	0	0	11	1	0	.091	3	10	0	1	0.6	1.000
1930	NY A	0	0	—	21.60	2	0	0	1.2	5	2	1	0	0	0	0	0	0	0	—	0	0	0	0	0.0	.000
5 yrs.		6	9	.400	4.76	56	17	4	170	193	84	60	0	1	0	0	42	2	0	.048	6	32	2	3	0.7	.950

Jim Joe Edwards

EDWARDS, JAMES CORBETTE BR TL 6′ 2″ 185 lbs.
B. Dec. 14, 1894, Banner, Miss. D. Jan. 19, 1965, Serepta, Miss.

Year	Team	W	L	PCT	ERA	G	GS	CG	IP	H	BB	SO	ShO	Relief W	Relief L	Relief SV	Batting AB	Batting H	HR	BA	PO	A	E	DP	TC/G	FA
1922	CLE A	3	8	.273	4.70	25	7	0	88	113	40	44	0	2	3	0	23	2	0	.087	4	19	2	1	1.0	.920
1923		10	10	.500	3.71	38	21	7	179.1	200	75	68	1	0	3	1	59	7	0	.119	8	42	1	1	1.3	.980
1924		4	3	.571	2.84	10	7	5	57	64	34	15	1	0	0	0	20	3	0	.150	2	14	1	0	1.7	.941
1925	2 teams CLE A (13G 0–3) CHI A (9G 1–2)																									
″	total	1	5	.167	5.86	22	7	2	81.1	106	46	32	1	0	2	0	26	4	0	.154	2	29	1	0	1.5	.969
1926	CHI A	6	9	.400	4.18	32	16	8	142	140	63	41	3	2	3	1	46	5	0	.109	6	31	0	0	1.2	1.000
1928	CIN N	2	2	.500	7.59	18	1	0	32	43	20	11	0	1	2	2	10	3	0	.300	1	4	1	0	0.3	.833
6 yrs.		26	37	.413	4.41	145	59	22	579.2	666	278	211	6	5	13	4	184	24	0	.130	23	139	6	2	1.2	.964

Sherman Edwards

EDWARDS, SHERMAN STANLEY BR TR 6′ 165 lbs.
B. July 25, 1909, Mt. Ida, Ark. D. Mar. 8, 1992, El Dorado, Ark.

Year	Team	W	L	PCT	ERA	G	GS	CG	IP	H	BB	SO	ShO	Relief W	Relief L	Relief SV	Batting AB	Batting H	HR	BA	PO	A	E	DP	TC/G	FA
1934	CIN N	0	0	—	3.00	1	0	0	3	4	1	1	0	0	0	0	1	0	0	.000	0	1	0	0	1.0	1.000

Year	Team		W	L	PCT	ERA	G	GS	CG	IP	H	BB	SO	ShO	Relief Pitching W	L	SV	Batting AB	H	HR	BA	PO	A	E	DP	TC/G	FA

Wayne Edwards

EDWARDS, WAYNE MAURICE BL TL 6′ 5″ 185 lbs.
B. Mar. 7, 1964, Burbank, Calif.

1989	CHI	A	0	0	—	3.68	7	0	0	7.1	7	3	9	0	0	0	0	0	0	0	—	0	1	0	1	0.1	1.000
1990			5	3	.625	3.22	42	5	0	95	81	41	63	0	2	2	2	0	0	0	—	6	14	1	1	0.5	.952
1991			0	2	.000	3.86	13	0	0	23.1	22	17	12	0	0	2	0	0	0	0	—	1	2	0	0	0.2	1.000
3 yrs.			5	5	.500	3.37	62	5	0	125.2	110	61	84	0	2	4	2	0	0	0		7	17	1	2	0.4	.960

Harry Eells

EELLS, HARRY ARCHIBALD BR TR 6′ 1″ 195 lbs.
B. Feb. 14, 1881, Ida Grove, Iowa D. Oct. 15, 1940, Los Angeles, Calif.

1906	CLE	A	4	5	.444	2.61	14	8	6	86.1	77	48	35	1	0	1	0	32	6	0	.188	8	26	1	2	2.5	.971

Dick Egan

EGAN, RICHARD WALLIS BL TL 6′ 4″ 193 lbs.
B. Mar. 24, 1937, Berkeley, Calif.

1963	DET	A	0	1	.000	5.14	20	0	0	21	25	3	16	0	0	1	0	0	0	0	—	2	3	0	0	0.3	1.000
1964			0	0	—	4.46	23	0	0	34.1	33	17	21	0	0	0	2	3	0	0	.000	2	8	1	1	0.5	.909
1966	CAL	A	0	0	—	4.40	11	0	0	14.1	17	6	11	0	0	0	0	1	0	0	.000	2	1	0	0	0.3	1.000
1967	LA	N	1	1	.500	6.25	20	0	0	31.2	34	15	20	0	1	1	0	1	0	0	.000	3	4	3	0	0.5	.700
4 yrs.			1	2	.333	5.15	74	0	0	101.1	109	41	68	0	1	2	2	5	0	0	.000	9	16	4	1	0.4	.862

Jim Egan

EGAN, JAMES K. (Troy Terrier) TL
B. 1858, Derby, Conn. D. Sept. 26, 1884, New Haven, Conn.

1882	TRO	N	4	6	.400	*4.14*	12	10	10	100	133	24	20	0	0	0	0	*				36	15	20	3	2.2	.718

Rip Egan

EGAN, JOHN JOSEPH TR 5′11″ 168 lbs.
B. July 9, 1871, Philadelphia, Pa. D. Dec. 22, 1950, Cranston, R. I.

1894	WAS	N	0	0	—	10.80	1	0	0	5	8	2	2	0	0	0	0	3	0	0	.000	0	1	0	0	1.0	1.000

Wish Egan

EGAN, ALOYSIUS JEROME BR TR 6′ 3″ 185 lbs.
B. June 16, 1881, Evart, Mich. D. Apr. 13, 1951, Detroit, Mich.

1902	DET	A	0	2	.000	2.86	3	3	2	22	23	6	0	0	0	0	0	8	2	0	.250	1	9	0	2	3.3	1.000
1905	STL	N	6	15	.286	3.58	23	19	18	171	189	39	29	0	0	2	0	59	6	0	.102	15	72	3	1	3.9	.967
1906			2	9	.182	4.59	16	12	7	86.1	97	27	23	0	0	1	0	29	2	0	.069	4	30	1	1	2.2	.971
3 yrs.			8	26	.235	3.83	42	34	27	279.1	309	72	52	0	0	3	0	96	10	0	.104	20	111	4	4	3.2	.970

Bruce Egloff

EGLOFF, BRUCE EDWARD BR TR 6′ 2″ 215 lbs.
B. Apr. 10, 1965, Denver, Colo.

1991	CLE	A	0	0	—	4.76	6	0	0	5.2	8	4	8	0	0	0	0	0	0	0	—	2	1	0	0	0.5	1.000

Howard Ehmke

EHMKE, HOWARD JONATHAN (Bob) BR TR 6′ 3″ 190 lbs.
B. Apr. 24, 1894, Silver Creek, N. Y. D. Mar. 17, 1959, Philadelphia, Pa. BB 1923

1915	BUF	F	0	2	.000	5.53	18	2	0	53.2	69	25	18	0	0	0	0	12	0	0	.000	2	25	3	2	1.7	.900
1916	DET	A	3	1	.750	3.13	5	4	4	37.1	34	15	15	0	0	0	0	14	2	0	.143	10	15	1	0	5.2	.962
1917			10	15	.400	2.97	35	25	13	206	174	88	90	4	0	1	2	69	17	0	.246	14	68	4	1	2.5	.953
1919			17	10	.630	3.18	33	31	20	248.2	255	**107**	79	2	1	0	0	91	23	0	.253	9	86	3	3	3.0	.969
1920			15	18	.455	3.29	38	33	23	268.1	250	124	98	2	0	1	3	105	25	0	.238	20	93	4	2	3.1	.966
1921			13	14	.481	4.54	30	22	13	196.1	220	81	68	1	3	2	0	74	21	0	.284	9	55	2	3	2.2	.970
1922			17	17	.500	4.22	45	29	16	279.2	299	101	108	1	7	1	1	102	16	0	.157	11	75	2	2	2.0	.977
1923	BOS	A	20	17	.541	3.78	43	39	28	316.2	318	119	121	2	0	0	3	112	25	0	.223	18	101	3	8	2.8	.975
1924			19	**17**	.528	3.46	45	36	26	**315**	324	81	119	4	2	1	4	126	28	0	.222	15	78	3	1	2.1	.969
1925			9	20	.310	3.73	34	31	**22**	260.2	285	85	95	0	0	1	1	88	13	0	.148	6	88	6	4	2.9	.940
1926	2 teams	BOS A	(14G 3–10)		PHI A	(20G 12–4)																					
"	total		15	14	.517	3.86	34	32	17	244.2	240	95	93	2	1	0	0	80	12	0	.150	10	66	7	5	2.4	.916
1927	PHI	A	12	10	.545	4.22	30	27	10	189.2	200	60	68	1	1	0	0	68	14	0	.206	13	57	4	1	2.5	.946
1928			9	8	.529	3.62	23	18	5	139.1	135	44	34	1	0	2	0	46	11	0	.239	6	35	2	2	1.9	.953
1929			7	2	.778	3.29	11	8	2	54.2	48	15	20	0	2	0	0	19	2	0	.105	7	10	1	0	1.6	.944
1930			0	1	.000	11.70	3	1	0	10	22	2	4	0	0	0	0	3	1	0	.333	0	3	0	1	1.0	1.000
15 yrs.			166	166	.500	3.75	427	338	199	2820.2	2873	1042	1030	20	17	9	14	1009	210	0	.208	150	855	45	35	2.5	.957
WORLD SERIES																											
1929	PHI	A	1	0	1.000	1.42	2	2	1	12.2	14	3	13	0	0	0	0	5	1	0	.200	0	4	0	0	2.0	1.000

Red Ehret

EHRET, PHILIP SYDNEY BR TR 6′ 175 lbs.
B. Aug. 31, 1868, Louisville, Ky. D. July 28, 1940, Cincinnati, Ohio.

1888	KC	AA	3	2	.600	3.98	7	6	5	52	58	22	12	0	0	0	0	63	12	0	.190	24	18	6	0	2.5	.875
1889	LOU	AA	10	29	.256	4.80	45	38	35	364	441	115	135	1	0	**2**	0	258	65	1	.252	43	109	29	4	2.6	.840
1890			25	14	.641	*2.53*	43	38	35	359	351	79	174	4	1	1	2	146	31	0	.212	9	64	12	2	2.0	.859
1891			13	13	.500	3.47	26	24	23	220.2	225	70	76	2	0	**2**	0	91	22	0	.242	4	57	9	4	2.7	.871
1892	PIT	N	16	20	.444	2.65	39	36	32	316	290	83	101	0	0	1	0	132	34	0	.258	14	57	12	1	2.1	.855
1893			18	18	.500	3.44	39	35	32	314.1	322	115	70	**4**	1	2	0	136	24	1	.176	12	80	11	0	2.6	.893
1894			19	21	.475	5.14	46	38	31	346.2	441	128	102	1	5	0	0	135	23	0	.170	12	61	12	2	1.8	.859
1895	STL	N	6	19	.240	6.02	37	32	18	231.2	360	88	55	0	1	0	0	96	21	1	.219	11	56	12	0	2.1	.848
1896	CIN	N	18	14	.563	3.42	34	33	29	276.2	298	74	60	2	1	0	0	102	20	1	.196	15	69	7	3	2.6	.923
1897			8	10	.444	4.78	34	19	11	184.1	256	47	43	0	2	1	2	66	13	0	.197	12	33	2	4	1.4	.957
1898	LOU	N	3	7	.300	5.76	12	10	9	89	130	20	20	0	0	0	0	40	9	0	.225	3	17	5	0	2.1	.800
11 yrs.			139	167	.454	4.02	362	309	260	2754.1	3172	841	848	14	11	9	4	*				159	621	117	20	2.2	.870

Rube Ehrhardt

EHRHARDT, WELTON CLAUDE BR TR 6′ 2″ 190 lbs.
B. Nov. 20, 1894, Beecher, Ill. D. Apr. 27, 1980, Chicago Heights, Ill.

1924	BKN	N	5	3	.625	2.26	15	9	6	83.2	71	17	13	2	0	0	0	29	4	0	.138	3	12	1	0	1.1	.938
1925			10	14	.417	5.03	36	25	12	207.2	239	62	47	0	1	3	1	71	15	1	.211	13	67	4	4	2.3	.952
1926			2	5	.286	3.90	44	1	0	97	101	35	25	0	2	**4**	4	24	6	0	.250	1	18	1	0	0.5	.950
1927			3	7	.300	3.57	46	3	2	95.2	90	37	22	0	2	6	2	24	6	0	.250	5	36	3	1	1.0	.932
1928			1	3	.250	4.67	28	2	1	54	74	27	12	0	0	2	2	14	4	0	.286	1	18	4	2	0.8	.826
1929	CIN	N	1	2	.333	4.74	24	1	1	49.1	58	22	9	1	0	2	1	11	2	0	.182	0	15	0	1	0.6	1.000
6 yrs.			22	34	.393	4.15	193	41	22	587.1	633	200	128	3	5	17	10	173	37	1	.214	23	166	13	8	1.0	.936

Hack Eibel

EIBEL, HENRY HACK — BL TL 5′11″ 220 lbs.
B. Dec. 6, 1893, Brooklyn, N. Y. D. Oct. 16, 1945, Macon, Ga.

Year	Team	Lg	W	L	PCT	ERA	G	GS	CG	IP	H	BB	SO	ShO	Relief Pitching W	Relief Pitching L	Relief Pitching SV	Batting AB	Batting H	HR	BA	PO	A	E	DP	TC/G	FA
1920	BOS	A	0	0	—	3.48	3	0	0	10.1	10	3	5	0	0	0	0	*				0	0	0	0	0.0	.000

Juan Eichelberger

EICHELBERGER, JUAN TYRONE — BR TR 6′ 2″ 195 lbs.
B. Oct. 21, 1953, St. Louis, Mo.

Year	Team	Lg	W	L	PCT	ERA	G	GS	CG	IP	H	BB	SO	ShO	Relief Pitching W	Relief Pitching L	Relief Pitching SV	Batting AB	Batting H	HR	BA	PO	A	E	DP	TC/G	FA
1978	SD	N	0	0	—	12.00	3	0	0	3	4	2	2	0	0	0	0	0	0	0	—	1	0	0	0	0.3	1.000
1979			1	1	.500	3.43	3	3	1	21	15	11	12	0	0	0	0	5	2	0	.400	0	2	0	0	0.7	1.000
1980			4	2	.667	3.64	15	13	0	89	73	55	43	0	1	0	0	27	3	0	.111	2	10	3	0	1.0	.800
1981			8	8	.500	3.51	25	24	3	141	136	74	81	1	0	0	0	46	4	0	.087	10	28	7	4	1.8	.844
1982			7	14	.333	4.20	31	24	8	177.2	171	72	74	0	0	2	0	55	5	0	.091	9	25	1	0	1.1	.971
1983	CLE	A	4	11	.267	4.90	28	15	2	134	132	59	56	0	1	0	0	0	0	0	—	9	14	0	3	0.8	1.000
1988	ATL	N	2	0	1.000	3.86	20	0	0	37.1	44	10	13	0	2	0	0	3	0	0	.000	4	8	1	1	0.6	.923
7 yrs.			26	36	.419	4.10	125	79	14	603	575	283	281	1	4	2	0	136	14	0	.103	35	87	12	8	1.1	.910

Mark Eichhorn

EICHHORN, MARK ANTHONY — BR TR 6′ 4″ 200 lbs.
B. Nov. 21, 1960, San Jose, Calif.

Year	Team	Lg	W	L	PCT	ERA	G	GS	CG	IP	H	BB	SO	ShO	Relief Pitching W	Relief Pitching L	Relief Pitching SV	Batting AB	Batting H	HR	BA	PO	A	E	DP	TC/G	FA
1982	TOR	A	0	3	.000	5.45	7	7	0	38	40	14	16	0	0	0	0	0	0	0	—	1	3	0	0	0.6	1.000
1986			14	6	.700	1.72	69	0	0	157	105	45	166	0	**14**	6	10	0	0	0	—	16	21	0	1	0.5	1.000
1987			10	6	.625	3.17	**89**	0	0	127.2	110	52	96	0	10	6	4	0	0	0	—	2	30	1	2	0.4	.970
1988			0	3	.000	4.18	37	0	0	66.2	79	27	28	0	0	3	1	0	0	0	—	5	13	0	1	0.5	1.000
1989	ATL	N	5	5	.500	4.35	45	0	0	68.1	70	19	49	0	5	5	0	2	0	0	.000	9	17	0	1	0.6	1.000
1990	CAL	A	2	5	.286	3.08	60	0	0	84.2	98	23	69	0	2	5	13	0	0	0	—	7	16	0	0	0.4	1.000
1991			3	3	.500	1.98	70	0	0	81.2	63	13	49	0	3	3	1	0	0	0	—	4	18	0	2	0.3	1.000
1992	2 teams	CAL A	(42G 2–4)		TOR A	(23G 2–0)																					
″	total		4	4	.500	3.08	65	0	0	87.2	86	25	61	0	4	4	2	0	0	0		5	19	1	0	0.4	.960
1993	TOR	A	3	1	.750	2.72	54	0	0	72.2	76	22	47	0	3	1	0	0	0	0	—	7	18	0	1	0.5	1.000
1994	BAL	A	6	5	.545	2.15	43	0	0	71	62	19	35	0	6	5	1	0	0	0	—	3	19	0	1	0.5	1.000
10 yrs.			47	41	.534	2.93	539	7	0	855.1	789	259	616	0	47	38	32	2	0	0	.000	59	174	2	9	0.4	.991
LEAGUE CHAMPIONSHIP SERIES																											
1992	TOR	A	0	0	—	0.00	1	0	0	1	0	0	0	0	0	0	0	0	0	0	—	0	0	0	0	0.0	.000
1993			0	0	—	0.00	1	0	0	2	1	1	1	0	0	0	0	0	0	0	—	0	0	0	0	0.0	.000
2 yrs.			0	0		0.00	2	0	0	3	1	1	1	0	0	0	0	0	0	0		0	0	0	0	0.0	
WORLD SERIES																											
1992	TOR	A	0	0	—	0.00	1	0	0	1	0	0	1	0	0	0	0	0	0	0	—	0	0	0	0	0.0	.000
1993			0	0	—	0.00	1	0	0	0.1	1	1	0	0	0	0	0	0	0	0	—	0	0	0	0	0.0	.000
2 yrs.			0	0		0.00	2	0	0	1.1	1	1	1	0	0	0	0	0	0	0		0	0	0	0	0.0	

Dave Eiland

EILAND, DAVID WILLIAM — BR TR 6′ 3″ 210 lbs.
B. July 5, 1966, Dade City, Fla.

Year	Team	Lg	W	L	PCT	ERA	G	GS	CG	IP	H	BB	SO	ShO	Relief Pitching W	Relief Pitching L	Relief Pitching SV	Batting AB	Batting H	HR	BA	PO	A	E	DP	TC/G	FA
1988	NY	A	0	0	—	6.39	3	3	0	12.2	15	4	7	0	0	0	0	0	0	0	—	1	3	0	0	1.3	1.000
1989			1	3	.250	5.77	6	6	0	34.1	44	13	11	0	0	0	0	0	0	0	—	2	2	0	0	0.7	1.000
1990			2	1	.667	3.56	5	5	0	30.1	31	5	16	0	0	0	0	0	0	0	—	1	3	0	0	0.8	1.000
1991			2	5	.286	5.33	18	13	0	72.2	87	23	18	0	0	0	0	0	0	0	—	6	2	0	0	0.4	1.000
1992	SD	N	0	2	.000	5.67	7	7	0	27	33	5	10	0	0	0	0	9	1	1	.111	1	5	0	0	0.9	1.000
1993			0	3	.000	5.21	10	9	0	48.1	58	17	14	0	0	0	0	12	1	0	.083	4	8	1	2	1.3	.923
1995	NY	A	1	1	.500	6.30	4	1	0	10	16	3	6	0	0	1	0	0	0	0	—	3	1	0	0	1.0	1.000
7 yrs.			6	15	.286	5.28	53	44	0	235.1	284	70	82	0	0	1	0	21	2	1	.095	18	24	1	2	0.8	.977

Dave Eilers

EILERS, DAVID LOUIS — BR TR 5′11″ 188 lbs.
B. Dec. 3, 1936, Oldenberg, Tex.

Year	Team	Lg	W	L	PCT	ERA	G	GS	CG	IP	H	BB	SO	ShO	Relief Pitching W	Relief Pitching L	Relief Pitching SV	Batting AB	Batting H	HR	BA	PO	A	E	DP	TC/G	FA
1964	MIL	N	0	0	—	4.70	6	0	0	7.2	11	1	1	0	0	0	0	0	0	0	—	1	0	0	0	0.2	1.000
1965	2 teams	MIL N	(6G 0–0)		NY N	(11G 1–1)																					
″	total		1	1	.500	5.40	17	0	0	21.2	28	4	10	0	1	1	2	1	1	0	1.000	2	3	0	0	0.3	1.000
1966	NY	N	1	1	.500	4.67	23	0	0	34.2	39	7	14	0	1	1	0	1	0	0	.000	2	8	0	1	0.4	1.000
1967	HOU	N	6	4	.600	3.94	35	0	0	59.1	68	17	27	0	6	4	1	7	0	0	.000	3	10	0	1	0.4	1.000
4 yrs.			8	6	.571	4.45	81	0	0	123.1	146	29	52	0	8	6	3	9	1	0	.111	8	21	0	2	0.4	1.000

Joey Eischen

EISCHEN, JOSEPH RAYMOND — BL TL 6′ 1″ 190 lbs.
B. May 25, 1970, West Covina, Calif.

Year	Team	Lg	W	L	PCT	ERA	G	GS	CG	IP	H	BB	SO	ShO	Relief Pitching W	Relief Pitching L	Relief Pitching SV	Batting AB	Batting H	HR	BA	PO	A	E	DP	TC/G	FA
1994	MON	N	0	0	—	54.00	1	0	0	0.2	4	0	1	0	0	0	0	0	0	0	—	0	0	0	0	0.0	.000
1995	LA	N	0	0	—	3.10	17	0	0	20.1	19	11	15	0	0	0	0	1	0	0	.000	3	1	0	0	0.2	1.000
2 yrs.			0	0		4.71	18	0	0	21	23	11	16	0	0	0	0	1	0	0	.000	3	1	0	0	0.2	1.000

Jake Eisenhart

EISENHART, JACOB HENRY (Hank) — BL TL 6′ 3½″ 195 lbs.
B. Oct. 3, 1922, Perkasie, Pa. D. Dec. 20, 1987, Huntingdon, Pa.

Year	Team	Lg	W	L	PCT	ERA	G	GS	CG	IP	H	BB	SO	ShO	Relief Pitching W	Relief Pitching L	Relief Pitching SV	Batting AB	Batting H	HR	BA	PO	A	E	DP	TC/G	FA
1944	CIN	N	0	0	—	0.00	1	0	0	0.1	0	1	0	0	0	0	0	0	0	0	—	0	0	0	0	0.0	.000

Harry Eisenstat

EISENSTAT, HARRY — BL TL 5′11″ 185 lbs.
B. Oct. 10, 1915, Brooklyn, N. Y.

Year	Team	Lg	W	L	PCT	ERA	G	GS	CG	IP	H	BB	SO	ShO	Relief Pitching W	Relief Pitching L	Relief Pitching SV	Batting AB	Batting H	HR	BA	PO	A	E	DP	TC/G	FA
1935	BKN	N	0	1	.000	13.50	2	0	0	4.2	9	2	2	0	0	1	0	1	0	0	.000	0	4	0	0	2.0	1.000
1936			1	2	.333	5.65	5	2	1	14.1	22	6	5	0	0	1	0	3	1	0	.333	1	4	0	0	1.0	1.000
1937			3	3	.500	3.97	13	5	0	47.2	61	11	12	0	2	1	0	11	0	0	.000	2	15	1	0	1.4	.944
1938	DET	A	9	6	.600	3.73	32	9	5	125.1	131	29	37	0	6	**5**	4	36	5	0	.139	6	27	2	2	1.1	.943
1939	2 teams	DET A	(10G 2–2)		CLE A	(26G 6–7)																					
″	total		8	9	.471	4.12	36	13	5	133.1	148	32	44	1	4	2	2	40	11	0	.275	4	22	0	1	0.7	1.000
1940	CLE	A	1	4	.200	3.14	27	3	0	71.2	78	12	27	0	1	2	4	22	6	0	.273	2	12	0	1	0.5	1.000
1941			1	1	.500	4.24	21	0	0	34	43	16	11	0	1	1	2	6	2	0	.333	0	3	0	0	0.1	1.000
1942			2	1	.667	2.45	29	1	0	47.2	58	6	19	0	2	0	2	4	1	0	.250	2	8	0	1	0.3	1.000
8 yrs.			25	27	.481	3.84	165	33	11	478.2	550	114	157	1	16	13	14	123	26	0	.211	17	95	3	5	0.7	.974

Ed Eiteljorge

EITELJORGE, EDWARD HENRY BR TR 6′ 2″ 190 lbs.
B. Oct. 14, 1871, Berlin, Germany D. Dec. 5, 1942, Greencastle, Ind.

Year	Team	Lg	W	L	PCT	ERA	G	GS	CG	IP	H	BB	SO	ShO	Relief Pitching W	Relief Pitching L	Relief Pitching SV	Batting AB	Batting H	Batting HR	BA	PO	A	E	DP	TC/G	FA
1890	CHI	N	0	1	.000	22.50	1	1	0	2	5	1	1	0	0	0	0	1	0	0	.000	0	0	0	0	0.0	.000
1891	WAS	AA	1	5	.167	6.16	8	7	6	61.1	79	41	23	0	0	0	0	26	5	0	.192	3	20	1	2	3.0	.958
2 yrs.			1	6	.143	6.68	9	8	6	63.1	84	42	24	0	0	0	0	27	5	0	.185	3	20	1	2	2.7	.958

Heinie Elder

ELDER, HENRY KNOX BL TL 6′ 2″ 200 lbs.
B. Aug. 23, 1890, Seattle, Wash. D. Nov. 13, 1958, Long Beach, Calif.

Year	Team	Lg	W	L	PCT	ERA	G	GS	CG	IP	H	BB	SO	ShO	Relief Pitching W	Relief Pitching L	Relief Pitching SV	Batting AB	Batting H	Batting HR	BA	PO	A	E	DP	TC/G	FA
1913	DET	A	0	0	—	8.10	1	0	0	3.1	4	5	0	0	0	0	0	1	0	0	.000	0	0	0	0	0.0	.000

Cal Eldred

ELDRED, CALVIN JOHN BR TR 6′ 4″ 215 lbs.
B. Nov. 24, 1967, Cedar Rapids, Iowa.

Year	Team	Lg	W	L	PCT	ERA	G	GS	CG	IP	H	BB	SO	ShO	Relief Pitching W	Relief Pitching L	Relief Pitching SV	Batting AB	Batting H	Batting HR	BA	PO	A	E	DP	TC/G	FA
1991	MIL	A	2	0	1.000	4.50	3	3	0	16	20	6	10	0	0	0	0	0	0	0	—	2	1	0	0	1.0	1.000
1992			11	2	.846	1.79	14	14	2	100.1	76	23	62	1	0	0	0	0	0	0	—	4	12	1	0	1.2	.941
1993			16	16	.500	4.01	36	**36**	8	**258**	232	91	180	1	0	0	0	0	0	0	—	26	27	2	4	1.5	.964
1994			11	11	.500	4.68	25	**25**	6	179	158	84	98	0	0	0	0	0	0	0	—	20	23	0	2	1.7	1.000
1995			1	1	.500	3.42	4	4	0	23.2	24	10	18	0	0	0	0	0	0	0	—	2	2	1	0	1.3	.800
5 yrs.			41	30	.577	3.82	82	82	16	577	510	214	368	2	0	0	0	0	0	0		54	65	4	6	1.5	.967

Hod Eller

ELLER, HORACE OWEN BR TR 5′11½″ 185 lbs.
B. July 5, 1894, Muncie, Ind. D. July 18, 1961, Indianapolis, Ind.

Year	Team	Lg	W	L	PCT	ERA	G	GS	CG	IP	H	BB	SO	ShO	Relief Pitching W	Relief Pitching L	Relief Pitching SV	Batting AB	Batting H	Batting HR	BA	PO	A	E	DP	TC/G	FA
1917	CIN	N	10	5	.667	2.36	37	11	7	152.1	131	37	77	1	4	1	1	45	6	0	.133	5	33	0	0	1.0	1.000
1918			16	12	.571	2.36	37	22	14	217.2	205	59	84	0	**7**	1	1	70	11	0	.157	4	39	0	3	1.2	1.000
1919			20	9	.690	2.39	38	30	16	248.1	216	50	137	7	3	0	2	93	26	1	.280	3	52	2	2	1.5	.965
1920			13	12	.520	2.95	35	23	15	210.1	208	52	76	2	2	1	0	87	22	0	.253	19	51	2	2	1.9	.972
1921			2	2	.500	4.98	13	3	0	34.1	46	15	7	0	0	2	1	13	3	0	.231	1	4	1	0	0.5	.833
5 yrs.			61	40	.604	2.62	160	89	52	863	806	213	381	10	16	5	5	308	68	1	.221	32	179	5	7	1.3	.977
WORLD SERIES																											
1919	CIN	N	2	0	1.000	2.00	2	2	2	18	13	2	15	1	0	0	0	7	2	0	.286	0	2	0	0	1.0	1.000

Joe Ellick

ELLICK, JOSEPH J. 5′10″ 162 lbs.
B. Apr. 3, 1854, Cincinnati, Ohio D. Apr. 21, 1923, Kansas City, Mo.
Manager 1884.

Year	Team	Lg	W	L	PCT	ERA	G	GS	CG	IP	H	BB	SO	ShO	Relief Pitching W	Relief Pitching L	Relief Pitching SV	Batting AB	Batting H	Batting HR	BA	PO	A	E	DP	TC/G	FA
1878	MIL	N	0	1	.000	3.00	1	0	0	3	1	1	0	0	0	**1**	0	*				8	3	3	1	3.5	.786

Bruce Ellingsen

ELLINGSEN, HAROLD BRUCE (Little Pod) BL TL 6′ 180 lbs.
B. Apr. 26, 1949, Pocatello, Ida.

Year	Team	Lg	W	L	PCT	ERA	G	GS	CG	IP	H	BB	SO	ShO	Relief Pitching W	Relief Pitching L	Relief Pitching SV	Batting AB	Batting H	Batting HR	BA	PO	A	E	DP	TC/G	FA
1974	CLE	A	1	1	.500	3.21	16	2	0	42	45	17	16	0	1	0	0	0	0	0	—	1	7	1	0	0.6	.889

Claude Elliott

ELLIOTT, CLAUDE JUDSON (Chaucer, Old Pardee) BR TR 6′ 190 lbs.
B. Nov. 17, 1879, Pardeeville, Wis. D. June 21, 1923, Pardeeville, Wis.

Year	Team	Lg	W	L	PCT	ERA	G	GS	CG	IP	H	BB	SO	ShO	Relief Pitching W	Relief Pitching L	Relief Pitching SV	Batting AB	Batting H	Batting HR	BA	PO	A	E	DP	TC/G	FA
1904	**2 teams**	**CIN N** (9G 3–1) **NY N** (3G 0–2)																									
″	**total**		3	3	.500	2.97	12	7	5	72.2	74	26	27	1	0	0	0	29	6	1	.207	2	19	2	0	1.9	.913
1905	NY	N	0	1	.000	4.03	10	2	2	38	41	12	20	0	0	0	**6**	16	3	0	.188	3	11	0	1	1.4	1.000
2 yrs.			3	4	.429	3.33	22	9	7	110.2	115	38	47	1	0	0	6	45	9	1	.200	5	30	2	1	1.7	.946

Donnie Elliott

ELLIOTT, DONALD GLENN BR TR 6′ 4″ 190 lbs.
B. Sept. 20, 1968, Pasadena, Tex.

Year	Team	Lg	W	L	PCT	ERA	G	GS	CG	IP	H	BB	SO	ShO	Relief Pitching W	Relief Pitching L	Relief Pitching SV	Batting AB	Batting H	Batting HR	BA	PO	A	E	DP	TC/G	FA
1994	SD	N	0	1	.000	3.27	30	1	0	33	31	21	24	0	0	1	0	1	0	0	.000	4	2	0	1	0.2	1.000
1995			0	0	—	0.00	1	0	0	2	2	1	3	0	0	0	0	0	0	0	—	0	0	0	0	0.0	.000
2 yrs.			0	1	.000	3.09	31	1	0	35	33	22	27	0	0	1	0	1	0	0	.000	4	2	0	1	0.2	1.000

Glenn Elliott

ELLIOTT, HERBERT GLENN (Lefty) BB TL 5′11″ 175 lbs.
B. Nov. 11, 1919, Sapulpa, Okla. D. July 27, 1969, Portland, Ore.

Year	Team	Lg	W	L	PCT	ERA	G	GS	CG	IP	H	BB	SO	ShO	Relief Pitching W	Relief Pitching L	Relief Pitching SV	Batting AB	Batting H	Batting HR	BA	PO	A	E	DP	TC/G	FA
1947	BOS	N	0	1	.000	4.74	11	0	0	19	18	11	8	0	0	1	1	2	1	0	.500	0	5	0	1	0.5	1.000
1948			1	0	1.000	3.00	1	1	0	3	5	1	2	0	0	0	0	2	0	0	.000	0	0	0	0	0.0	.000
1949			3	4	.429	3.95	22	6	1	68.1	70	27	15	0	2	0	0	17	1	0	.059	2	16	0	1	0.8	1.000
3 yrs.			4	5	.444	4.08	34	7	1	90.1	93	39	25	0	2	1	1	21	2	0	.095	2	21	0	2	0.7	1.000

Hal Elliott

ELLIOTT, HAROLD WILLIAM (Ace) BR TR 6′ 1½″ 170 lbs.
B. May 29, 1899, Mt. Clemens, Mich. D. Apr. 25, 1963, Honolulu, Hawaii.

Year	Team	Lg	W	L	PCT	ERA	G	GS	CG	IP	H	BB	SO	ShO	Relief Pitching W	Relief Pitching L	Relief Pitching SV	Batting AB	Batting H	Batting HR	BA	PO	A	E	DP	TC/G	FA
1929	PHI	N	3	7	.300	6.06	40	8	2	114.1	146	59	32	0	2	2	2	30	5	0	.167	9	29	0	2	0.9	1.000
1930			6	11	.353	7.67	**48**	11	2	117.1	191	58	37	0	5	2	0	32	3	0	.094	2	34	3	0	0.8	.923
1931			0	2	.000	9.55	16	4	0	33	46	19	8	0	0	1	2	9	1	0	.111	2	8	0	0	0.6	1.000
1932			2	4	.333	5.77	16	7	0	57.2	70	38	13	0	1	1	0	18	3	0	.167	1	8	0	0	0.6	1.000
4 yrs.			11	24	.314	6.95	120	30	4	322.1	453	174	90	0	8	6	4	89	12	0	.135	14	79	3	2	0.8	.969

Jumbo Elliott

ELLIOTT, JAMES THOMAS BR TL 6′ 3″ 235 lbs.
B. Oct. 22, 1900, St. Louis, Mo. D. Jan. 7, 1970, Terre Haute, Ind.

Year	Team	Lg	W	L	PCT	ERA	G	GS	CG	IP	H	BB	SO	ShO	Relief Pitching W	Relief Pitching L	Relief Pitching SV	Batting AB	Batting H	Batting HR	BA	PO	A	E	DP	TC/G	FA
1923	STL	A	0	0	—	27.00	1	0	0	1	1	3	0	0	0	0	0	0	0	0	—	0	0	0	0	0.0	.000
1925	BKN	N	0	2	.000	8.44	3	1	0	10.2	17	9	3	0	0	1	0	4	0	0	.000	0	1	0	0	0.3	1.000
1927			6	13	.316	3.30	30	21	12	188.1	188	60	99	2	0	2	3	64	9	0	.141	6	19	1	1	0.9	.962
1928			9	14	.391	3.89	41	21	7	192	194	64	74	2	2	4	1	68	12	3	.176	2	34	4	0	1.0	.900
1929			1	2	.333	6.63	6	3	0	19	21	16	7	0	0	0	0	4	1	0	.250	0	2	0	1	0.3	1.000
1930			10	7	.588	3.95	35	21	6	198.1	204	70	59	2	3	0	1	68	10	1	.147	4	29	0	2	0.9	1.000
1931	PHI	N	**19**	14	.576	4.27	**52**	30	12	249	288	83	99	2	3	0	5	90	11	0	.122	8	25	1	3	0.7	.971
1932			11	10	.524	5.42	39	22	8	166	210	47	62	0	2	3	0	61	12	0	.197	4	28	5	2	0.9	.865
1933			6	10	.375	3.84	35	21	6	161.2	188	49	43	0	1	0	2	52	12	0	.231	8	19	4	1	0.9	.871
1934	**2 teams**	**PHI N** (3G 0–1) **BOS N** (7G 1–1)																									
″	**total**		1	2	.333	6.97	10	4	0	20.2	27	13	7	0	0	1	0	5	1	0	.200	0	3	1	0	0.4	.750
10 yrs.			63	74	.460	4.24	252	144	51	1206.2	1338	414	453	8	11	11	12	416	68	4	.163	32	160	16	10	0.8	.923

Dock Ellis

ELLIS, DOCK PHILLIP BB TR 6′ 3″ 205 lbs.
B. Mar. 11, 1945, Los Angeles, Calif.

Year	Team	Lg	W	L	PCT	ERA	G	GS	CG	IP	H	BB	SO	ShO	Relief Pitching W	Relief Pitching L	Relief Pitching SV	Batting AB	Batting H	Batting HR	BA	PO	A	E	DP	TC/G	FA
1968	PIT	N	6	5	.545	2.50	26	10	2	104.1	82	38	52	0	1	2	0	29	2	0	.069	5	18	0	2	0.9	1.000
1969			11	17	.393	3.58	35	33	8	219	206	76	173	2	0	0	0	68	6	0	.088	15	35	3	2	1.5	.943

Dock Ellis *continued*

Year	Team	W	L	PCT	ERA	G	GS	CG	IP	H	BB	SO	ShO	Relief Pitching W	Relief Pitching L	Relief Pitching SV	Batting AB	Batting H	Batting HR	BA	PO	A	E	DP	TC/G	FA
1970		13	10	.565	3.21	30	30	9	202	194	87	128	4	0	0	0	70	7	0	.100	21	34	2	3	1.9	.965
1971		19	9	.679	3.05	31	31	11	227	207	63	137	2	0	0	0	79	16	0	.203	22	32	2	1	1.8	.964
1972		15	7	.682	2.70	25	25	4	163.1	156	33	96	1	0	0	0	59	9	0	.153	16	15	0	2	1.2	1.000
1973		12	14	.462	3.05	28	28	3	192	176	55	122	1	0	0	0	65	7	0	.108	16	30	1	3	1.7	.979
1974		12	9	.571	3.15	26	26	9	177	163	41	91	0	0	0	0	56	12	0	.214	14	22	4	2	1.5	.900
1975		8	9	.471	3.79	27	24	5	140	163	43	69	2	0	0	0	36	4	0	.111	8	16	2	4	1.0	.923
1976	NY A	17	8	.680	3.19	32	32	8	211.2	195	76	65	1	0	0	0	0	0	0	—	19	20	3	0	1.3	.929
1977	3 teams NY A (3G 1–1) OAK A (7G 1–5) TEX A (23G 10–6)																									
″	total	12	12	.500	3.64	33	32	8	212.2	211	64	106	1	0	0	1	0	0	0		17	21	3	4	1.2	.927
1978	TEX A	9	7	.563	4.20	22	22	3	141.1	131	46	45	0	0	0	0	0	0	0	—	11	22	2	2	1.6	.943
1979	3 teams TEX A (10G 1–5) NY N (17G 3–7) PIT N (3G 0–0)																									
″	total	4	12	.250	5.83	30	24	1	139	183	52	52	0	1	0	0	27	2	0	.074	9	22	1	1	1.1	.969
12 yrs.		138	119	.537	3.45	345	317	71	2129.1	2067	674	1136	14	2	2	1	489	65	0	.133	173	287	23	26	1.4	.952
LEAGUE CHAMPIONSHIP SERIES																										
1970	PIT N	0	1	.000	2.79	1	1	0	9.2	9	4	1	0	0	0	0	2	0	0	.000	0	3	0	0	3.0	1.000
1971		1	0	1.000	3.60	1	1	0	5	6	4	1	0	0	0	0	3	0	0	.000	0	0	0	0	0.0	.000
1972		0	1	.000	0.00	1	1	0	5	5	1	3	0	0	0	0	1	0	0	.000	0	0	0	0	0.0	.000
1975		0	0	—	0.00	1	0	0	2	2	0	2	0	0	0	0	0	0	0	—	0	0	0	0	0.0	.000
1976	NY A	1	0	1.000	3.38	1	1	0	8	6	2	5	0	0	0	0	0	0	0	—	1	0	0	0	1.0	1.000
5 yrs.		2	2	.500	2.43	5	4	0	29.2	28	11	12	0	0	0	0	6	0	0	.000	1	3	0	0	0.8	1.000
WORLD SERIES																										
1971	PIT N	0	1	.000	15.43	1	1	0	2.1	4	1	1	0	0	0	0	1	0	0	.000	1	0	0	0	1.0	1.000
1976	NY A	0	1	.000	10.80	1	1	0	3.1	7	0	1	0	0	0	0	0	0	0	—	0	0	0	0	0.0	.000
2 yrs.		0	2	.000	12.71	2	2	0	5.2	11	1	2	0	0	0	0	1	0	0	.000	1	0	0	0	0.5	1.000

Jim Ellis

ELLIS, JAMES RUSSELL BR TL 6′ 2″ 185 lbs.
B. Mar. 25, 1945, Tulare, Calif.

Year	Team	W	L	PCT	ERA	G	GS	CG	IP	H	BB	SO	ShO	Relief Pitching W	Relief Pitching L	Relief Pitching SV	Batting AB	Batting H	Batting HR	BA	PO	A	E	DP	TC/G	FA
1967	CHI N	1	1	.500	3.24	8	1	0	16.2	20	9	8	0	0	1	0	5	1	0	.200	2	1	0	0	0.4	1.000
1969	STL N	0	0	—	1.80	2	1	0	5	7	3	0	0	0	0	0	0	0	0	—	0	0	0	0	0.0	.000
2 yrs.		1	1	.500	2.91	10	2	0	21.2	27	12	8	0	0	1	0	5	1	0	.200	2	1	0	0	0.3	1.000

Sammy Ellis

ELLIS, SAMUEL JOSEPH BL TR 6′ 1″ 175 lbs.
B. Feb. 11, 1941, Youngstown, Ohio.

Year	Team	W	L	PCT	ERA	G	GS	CG	IP	H	BB	SO	ShO	Relief Pitching W	Relief Pitching L	Relief Pitching SV	Batting AB	Batting H	Batting HR	BA	PO	A	E	DP	TC/G	FA
1962	CIN N	2	2	.500	6.75	8	4	0	28	29	29	27	0	0	0	0	10	2	0	.200	1	3	2	1	0.8	.667
1964		10	3	.769	2.57	52	5	2	122.1	101	28	125	0	7	2	14	24	2	0	.083	8	18	1	3	0.5	.963
1965		22	10	.688	3.79	44	39	15	263.2	222	104	183	2	2	0	2	96	12	0	.125	15	32	5	1	1.2	.904
1966		12	19	.387	5.29	41	36	7	221	226	78	154	0	1	0	0	70	8	0	.114	8	23	1	1	0.8	.969
1967		8	11	.421	3.84	32	27	8	175.2	197	67	80	1	0	0	0	49	4	0	.082	9	27	2	1	1.2	.947
1968	CAL A	9	10	.474	3.95	42	24	3	164	150	56	93	0	1	1	2	44	2	0	.045	12	14	2	0	0.7	.929
1969	CHI A	0	3	.000	5.83	10	5	0	29.1	42	16	15	0	0	1	0	6	1	0	.167	3	6	0	0	0.9	1.000
7 yrs.		63	58	.521	4.15	229	140	35	1004	967	378	677	3	11	4	18	299	31	0	.104	56	123	13	7	0.8	.932

George Ellison

ELLISON, GEORGE RUSSELL BR TR 6′ 3″ 185 lbs.
B. Jan. 24, 1895, California D. Jan. 20, 1978, San Francisco, Calif.

Year	Team	W	L	PCT	ERA	G	GS	CG	IP	H	BB	SO	ShO	Relief Pitching W	Relief Pitching L	Relief Pitching SV	Batting AB	Batting H	Batting HR	BA	PO	A	E	DP	TC/G	FA
1920	CLE A	0	0	—	0.00	1	0	0	1	0	2	1	0	0	0	0	0	0	0	—	0	1	0	0	1.0	1.000

Dick Ellsworth

ELLSWORTH, RICHARD CLARK BL TL 6′ 3½″ 180 lbs.
Father of Steve Ellsworth.
B. Mar. 22, 1940, Lusk, Wyo.

Year	Team	W	L	PCT	ERA	G	GS	CG	IP	H	BB	SO	ShO	Relief Pitching W	Relief Pitching L	Relief Pitching SV	Batting AB	Batting H	Batting HR	BA	PO	A	E	DP	TC/G	FA
1958	CHI N	0	1	.000	15.43	1	1	0	2.1	4	3	0	0	0	0	0	1	0	0	.000	0	0	0	0	0.0	.000
1960		7	13	.350	3.72	31	27	6	176.2	170	72	94	0	0	0	0	48	2	0	.042	12	29	0	1	1.3	1.000
1961		10	11	.476	3.86	37	31	7	186.2	213	48	91	1	1	0	0	56	2	0	.036	8	49	2	7	1.6	.966
1962		9	20	.310	5.09	37	33	6	208.2	241	77	113	0	1	1	1	62	7	0	.113	7	41	3	3	1.4	.941
1963		22	10	.688	2.11	37	37	19	290.2	223	75	185	4	0	0	0	94	9	0	.096	15	60	3	3	2.1	.962
1964		14	18	.438	3.75	37	36	16	256.2	**267**	71	148	1	0	1	0	87	4	0	.046	13	58	6	2	2.1	.922
1965		14	15	.483	3.81	36	34	8	222.1	227	57	130	0	1	0	1	73	7	0	.096	8	50	2	3	1.7	.967
1966		8	**22**	.267	3.98	38	37	9	269.1	**321**	51	144	0	0	0	0	90	14	0	.156	19	53	5	3	2.0	.935
1967	PHI N	6	7	.462	4.38	32	21	3	125.1	152	36	45	1	0	0	0	37	4	0	.108	8	31	2	1	1.3	.951
1968	BOS A	16	7	.696	3.03	31	28	10	196	196	37	106	1	1	0	0	72	4	0	.056	10	30	1	2	1.3	.976
1969	2 teams BOS A (2G 0–0) CLE A (34G 6–9)																									
″	total	6	9	.400	4.10	36	24	3	147	178	44	52	1	0	0	0	48	6	0	.125	15	21	1	3	1.0	.973
1970	2 teams CLE A (29G 3–3) MIL A (14G 0–0)																									
″	total	3	3	.500	3.79	43	1	0	59.1	60	17	22	0	3	2	3	4	0	0	.000	4	14	0	1	0.4	1.000
1971	MIL A	0	1	.000	4.80	11	0	0	15	22	7	10	0	0	1	0	1	0	0	.000	1	1	0	0	0.2	1.000
13 yrs.		115	137	.456	3.72	407	310	87	2156	2274	595	1140	9	7	5	5	673	59	0	.088	120	437	25	29	1.4	.957

Steve Ellsworth

ELLSWORTH, STEVEN CLARK BR TR 6′ 8″ 220 lbs.
Son of Dick Ellsworth.
B. July 30, 1960, Chicago, Ill.

Year	Team	W	L	PCT	ERA	G	GS	CG	IP	H	BB	SO	ShO	Relief Pitching W	Relief Pitching L	Relief Pitching SV	Batting AB	Batting H	Batting HR	BA	PO	A	E	DP	TC/G	FA
1988	BOS A	1	6	.143	6.75	8	7	0	36	47	16	16	0	0	1	0	0	0	0	—	4	2	0	0	0.8	1.000

Don Elston

ELSTON, DONALD RAY BR TR 6′ 165 lbs.
B. Apr. 6, 1929, Campbellstown, Ohio D. Jan. 2, 1995, Evanston, Ill.

Year	Team	W	L	PCT	ERA	G	GS	CG	IP	H	BB	SO	ShO	Relief Pitching W	Relief Pitching L	Relief Pitching SV	Batting AB	Batting H	Batting HR	BA	PO	A	E	DP	TC/G	FA
1953	CHI N	0	1	.000	14.40	2	1	0	5	11	0	2	0	0	0	0	1	0	0	.000	1	0	0	0	0.5	1.000
1957	2 teams BKN N (1G 0–0) CHI N (39G 6–7)																									
″	total	6	7	.462	3.54	40	14	2	145	140	55	103	0	3	1	8	37	4	0	.108	9	23	2	1	0.9	.941
1958	CHI N	9	8	.529	2.88	**69**	0	0	97	75	39	84	0	**9**	8	10	14	5	0	.357	7	19	0	1	0.4	1.000
1959		10	8	.556	3.32	**65**	0	0	97.2	77	46	82	0	10	8	13	19	4	0	.211	3	14	2	1	0.3	.895
1960		8	9	.471	3.40	60	0	0	127	109	55	85	0	8	**9**	11	24	3	0	.125	10	13	4	1	0.4	.852
1961		6	7	.462	5.59	58	0	0	93.1	108	45	59	0	6	7	8	11	2	0	.182	4	18	0	1	0.4	1.000
1962		4	8	.333	2.44	57	0	0	66.1	57	32	37	0	4	8	8	8	0	0	.000	5	16	0	2	0.4	1.000

Don Elston *continued*

Year	Team	Lg	W	L	PCT	ERA	G	GS	CG	IP	H	BB	SO	ShO	Relief Pitching W	Relief Pitching L	Relief Pitching SV	Batting AB	Batting H	Batting HR	BA	PO	A	E	DP	TC/G	FA
1963			4	1	.800	2.83	51	0	0	70	57	21	41	0	4	1	4	4	0	0	.000	4	9	0	1	0.3	1.000
1964			2	5	.286	5.30	48	0	0	54.1	68	34	26	0	2	5	1	6	1	0	.167	3	16	3	4	0.5	.864
9 yrs.			49	54	.476	3.69	450	15	2	755.2	702	327	519	0	46	47	63	124	19	0	.153	46	128	11	12	0.4	.941

Narciso Elvira

ELVIRA, NARCISO CHICHO BL TL 5′10″ 160 lbs.
Born Narciso Chicho Elvira (Delgado).
B. Oct. 29, 1967, Veracruz, Mexico.

Year	Team	Lg	W	L	PCT	ERA	G	GS	CG	IP	H	BB	SO	ShO	Relief Pitching W	Relief Pitching L	Relief Pitching SV	Batting AB	Batting H	Batting HR	BA	PO	A	E	DP	TC/G	FA
1990	MIL	A	0	0	—	5.40	4	0	0	5	6	5	6	0	0	0	0	0	0	0	—	0	1	0	0	0.3	1.000

Bones Ely

ELY, WILLIAM FREDERICK BR TR 6′ 1″ 155 lbs.
B. June 7, 1863, North Girard, Pa. D. Jan. 10, 1952, Imola, Calif.

Year	Team	Lg	W	L	PCT	ERA	G	GS	CG	IP	H	BB	SO	ShO	Relief Pitching W	Relief Pitching L	Relief Pitching SV	Batting AB	Batting H	Batting HR	BA	PO	A	E	DP	TC/G	FA
1884	BUF	N	0	1	.000	*14.40*	1	1	0	5	17	5	4	0	0	0	0	4	0	0	.000	0	1	1	0	1.0	.500
1886	LOU	AA	0	4	.000	*5.32*	6	4	4	44	53	26	28	0	0	0	**1**	32	5	0	.156	9	8	1	0	1.6	.944
1890	SYR	AA	0	0	—	22.50	1	0	0	2	7	0	0	0	0	0	0	496	130	0	.262	298	143	33	20	3.9	.930
1894	STL	N	0	0	—	0.00	1	0	0	1	0	3	0	0	0	0	0	510	156	12	.306	58	117	26	9	6.5	.871
4 yrs.			0	5	.000	6.75	9	5	4	52	77	34	32	0	0	0	1	*				2829	4396	606	481	5.8	.923

Harry Ely

ELY, HARRY
Deceased.

Year	Team	Lg	W	L	PCT	ERA	G	GS	CG	IP	H	BB	SO	ShO	Relief Pitching W	Relief Pitching L	Relief Pitching SV	Batting AB	Batting H	Batting HR	BA	PO	A	E	DP	TC/G	FA
1892	BAL	N	0	1	.000	7.71	1	1	1	7	14	7	0	0	0	0	0	3	0	0	.000	1	1	1	0	3.0	.667

Alan Embree

EMBREE, ALAN DUANE BL TL 6′ 2″ 185 lbs.
B. Jan. 23, 1970, Vancouver, Wash.

Year	Team	Lg	W	L	PCT	ERA	G	GS	CG	IP	H	BB	SO	ShO	Relief Pitching W	Relief Pitching L	Relief Pitching SV	Batting AB	Batting H	Batting HR	BA	PO	A	E	DP	TC/G	FA
1992	CLE	A	0	2	.000	7.00	4	4	0	18	19	8	12	0	0	0	0	0	0	0	—	1	0	1	0	0.5	.500
1995			3	2	.600	5.11	23	0	0	24.2	23	16	23	0	3	2	1	0	0	0	—	0	3	0	0	0.1	1.000
2 yrs.			3	4	.429	5.91	27	4	0	42.2	42	24	35	0	3	2	1	0	0	0		1	3	1	0	0.2	.800
LEAGUE CHAMPIONSHIP SERIES																											
1995	CLE	A	0	0	—	0.00	1	0	0	0.1	0	0	1	0	0	0	0	0	0	0	—	0	0	0	0	0.0	.000
WORLD SERIES																											
1995	CLE	A	0	0	—	2.70	4	0	0	3.1	2	2	2	0	0	0	0	0	0	0	—	0	1	0	0	0.3	1.000

Red Embree

EMBREE, CHARLES WILLARD BR TR 6′ 165 lbs.
B. Aug. 30, 1917, El Monte, Calif.

Year	Team	Lg	W	L	PCT	ERA	G	GS	CG	IP	H	BB	SO	ShO	Relief Pitching W	Relief Pitching L	Relief Pitching SV	Batting AB	Batting H	Batting HR	BA	PO	A	E	DP	TC/G	FA
1941	CLE	A	0	1	.000	6.75	1	1	0	4	7	3	4	0	0	0	0	1	0	0	.000	0	0	0	0	0.0	.000
1942			3	4	.429	3.86	19	6	2	63	58	31	44	0	2	1	0	15	2	0	.133	1	11	1	1	0.7	.923
1944			0	1	.000	13.50	3	1	0	3.1	2	5	4	0	0	0	0	0	0	0	—	0	1	0	0	0.3	1.000
1945			4	4	.500	1.93	8	8	5	70	56	26	42	1	0	0	0	21	3	0	.143	5	15	0	0	2.5	1.000
1946			8	12	.400	3.46	28	26	8	200	170	79	87	0	1	0	0	70	13	0	.186	11	29	3	3	1.5	.930
1947			8	10	.444	3.15	27	21	6	162.2	137	67	56	0	2	0	0	52	9	0	.173	6	30	1	4	1.4	.973
1948	NY	A	5	3	.625	3.76	20	8	4	76.2	77	30	25	0	0	1	0	27	4	0	.148	2	9	0	0	0.6	1.000
1949	STL	A	3	13	.188	5.37	35	19	4	127.1	146	89	24	0	0	1	1	37	6	0	.162	2	24	1	3	0.8	.963
8 yrs.			31	48	.392	3.72	141	90	29	707	653	330	286	1	5	3	1	223	37	0	.166	27	119	6	11	1.1	.961

Slim Embrey

EMBREY, CHARLES AKIN BR TR 6′ 2″ 184 lbs.
B. Aug. 17, 1901, Columbia, Tenn. D. Oct. 10, 1947, Nashville, Tenn.

Year	Team	Lg	W	L	PCT	ERA	G	GS	CG	IP	H	BB	SO	ShO	Relief Pitching W	Relief Pitching L	Relief Pitching SV	Batting AB	Batting H	Batting HR	BA	PO	A	E	DP	TC/G	FA
1923	CHI	A	0	0	—	10.13	1	0	0	2.2	7	2	1	0	0	0	0	0	0	0	—	1	1	0	0	2.0	1.000

Charlie Emig

EMIG, CHARLES HENRY TL
B. Apr. 5, 1875, Cincinnati, Ohio D. Oct. 2, 1975, Oklahoma City, Okla.

Year	Team	Lg	W	L	PCT	ERA	G	GS	CG	IP	H	BB	SO	ShO	Relief Pitching W	Relief Pitching L	Relief Pitching SV	Batting AB	Batting H	Batting HR	BA	PO	A	E	DP	TC/G	FA
1896	LOU	N	0	1	.000	7.88	1	1	1	8	12	7	1	0	0	0	0	3	0	0	.000	0	5	1	0	6.0	.833

Slim Emmerich

EMMERICH, WILLIAM PETER BR TR 6′ 1″ 170 lbs.
B. Sept. 29, 1919, Allentown, Pa.

Year	Team	Lg	W	L	PCT	ERA	G	GS	CG	IP	H	BB	SO	ShO	Relief Pitching W	Relief Pitching L	Relief Pitching SV	Batting AB	Batting H	Batting HR	BA	PO	A	E	DP	TC/G	FA
1945	NY	N	4	4	.500	4.86	31	7	1	100	111	33	27	0	3	0	0	25	3	0	.120	3	19	0	0	0.7	1.000
1946			0	0	—	4.50	2	0	0	4	6	0	1	0	0	0	0	0	0	0	—	1	1	0	0	1.0	1.000
2 yrs.			4	4	.500	4.85	33	7	1	104	117	33	28	0	3	0	0	25	3	0	.120	4	20	0	0	0.7	1.000

Bob Emslie

EMSLIE, ROBERT DANIEL BR TR 5′11″
B. Jan. 27, 1859, Guelph, Ont., Canada
D. Apr. 26, 1943, St. Thomas, Ont., Canada.

Year	Team	Lg	W	L	PCT	ERA	G	GS	CG	IP	H	BB	SO	ShO	Relief Pitching W	Relief Pitching L	Relief Pitching SV	Batting AB	Batting H	Batting HR	BA	PO	A	E	DP	TC/G	FA
1883	BAL	AA	9	13	.409	*3.17*	24	23	21	201.1	188	41	62	1	0	0	0	97	16	0	.165	17	50	14	1	2.8	.827
1884			32	17	.653	*2.75*	50	50	50	455.1	419	88	264	4	0	0	0	195	37	0	.190	28	84	22	0	2.6	.836
1885	**2 teams** **BAL AA** (13G 3–10) **PHI AA** (4G 0–4)																										
"	**total**		3	14	.176	4.71	17	17	14	135.2	168	36	36	0	0	0	0	63	13	0	.206	6	23	9	0	1.9	.763
3 yrs.			44	44	.500	3.19	91	90	85	792.1	775	165	362	5	0	0	0	355	66	0	.186	51	157	45	1	2.5	.822

Luis Encarnacion

ENCARNACION, LUIS MARTIN BR TR 5′10″ 178 lbs.
Born Luis Martin Lora (Encarnacion).
B. Oct. 20, 1963, Santo Domingo, Dominican Republic.

Year	Team	Lg	W	L	PCT	ERA	G	GS	CG	IP	H	BB	SO	ShO	Relief Pitching W	Relief Pitching L	Relief Pitching SV	Batting AB	Batting H	Batting HR	BA	PO	A	E	DP	TC/G	FA
1990	KC	A	0	0	—	7.84	4	0	0	10.1	14	4	8	0	0	0	0	0	0	0	—	1	0	0	0	0.3	1.000

Joe Engel

ENGEL, JOSEPH WILLIAM BR TL 6′ 1½″ 183 lbs.
B. Mar. 12, 1893, Washington, D. C. D. June 12, 1969, Chattanooga, Tenn.

Year	Team	Lg	W	L	PCT	ERA	G	GS	CG	IP	H	BB	SO	ShO	Relief Pitching W	Relief Pitching L	Relief Pitching SV	Batting AB	Batting H	Batting HR	BA	PO	A	E	DP	TC/G	FA
1912	WAS	A	2	5	.286	3.96	17	10	2	75	70	50	29	0	1	0	1	17	1	0	.059	0	28	1	1	1.7	.966
1913			8	9	.471	3.06	36	23	6	164.2	124	85	70	2	1	0	0	49	3	0	.061	2	52	7	0	1.7	.885
1914			7	5	.583	2.97	35	15	1	124.1	108	75	41	0	2	1	3	28	3	0	.107	4	39	6	0	1.4	.878
1915			0	3	.000	3.21	11	3	0	33.2	30	19	9	0	0	0	0	6	0	0	.000	1	13	1	1	1.4	.933
1917	CIN	N	0	1	.000	5.63	1	1	1	8	12	6	2	0	0	0	0	3	0	0	.000	1	3	1	0	5.0	.800
1919	CLE	A	0	0	—	∞	1	0	0		0	3	0	0	0	0	0	0	0	0	—	0	0	0	0	0.0	.000
1920	WAS	A	0	0	—	21.60	1	0	0	1.2	0	4	0	0	0	0	0	1	0	0	.000	0	0	0	0	0.0	.000
7 yrs.			17	23	.425	3.38	102	52	10	407.1	344	242	151	2	4	1	4	104	7	0	.067	8	135	16	2	1.6	.899

Steve Engel

ENGEL, STEVEN MICHAEL BR TL 6′ 3″ 210 lbs.
B. Dec. 31, 1961, Cincinnati, Ohio.

Year	Team	W	L	PCT	ERA	G	GS	CG	IP	H	BB	SO	ShO	Relief Pitching W	Relief Pitching L	Relief Pitching SV	Batting AB	Batting H	Batting HR	BA	PO	A	E	DP	TC/G	FA
1985	CHI N	1	5	.167	5.57	11	8	1	51.2	61	26	29	0	0	0	1	16	3	1	.188	2	8	0	0	0.9	1.000

Rick Engle

ENGLE, RICHARD DOUGLAS BR TL 5′11½″ 181 lbs.
B. Apr. 7, 1957, Corbin, Ky.

Year	Team	W	L	PCT	ERA	G	GS	CG	IP	H	BB	SO	ShO	Relief Pitching W	Relief Pitching L	Relief Pitching SV	Batting AB	Batting H	Batting HR	BA	PO	A	E	DP	TC/G	FA
1981	MON N	0	0	—	18.00	1	0	0	2	6	1	2	0	0	0	0	0	0	0	—	0	0	0	0	0.0	.000

Jack Enright

ENRIGHT, JACKSON PERCY BR TR 5′11″ 177 lbs.
B. Nov. 29, 1895, Fort Worth, Tex. D. Aug. 17, 1975, Pompano Beach, Fla.

Year	Team	W	L	PCT	ERA	G	GS	CG	IP	H	BB	SO	ShO	Relief Pitching W	Relief Pitching L	Relief Pitching SV	Batting AB	Batting H	Batting HR	BA	PO	A	E	DP	TC/G	FA
1917	NY A	0	1	.000	5.40	1	1	0	5	5	3	1	0	0	0	0	1	0	0	.000	1	5	0	0	6.0	1.000

Terry Enyart

ENYART, TERRY GENE BR TL 6′ 2″ 190 lbs.
B. Oct. 10, 1950, Ironton, Ohio.

Year	Team	W	L	PCT	ERA	G	GS	CG	IP	H	BB	SO	ShO	Relief Pitching W	Relief Pitching L	Relief Pitching SV	Batting AB	Batting H	Batting HR	BA	PO	A	E	DP	TC/G	FA
1974	MON N	0	0	—	13.50	2	0	0	2	4	4	2	0	0	0	0	0	0	0	—	0	0	1	0	0.5	.000

Johnny Enzmann

ENZMANN, JOHN (Gentleman John) BR TR 5′10″ 165 lbs.
B. Mar. 4, 1890, Brooklyn, N. Y. D. Mar. 14, 1984, Riverhead, N. Y.

Year	Team	W	L	PCT	ERA	G	GS	CG	IP	H	BB	SO	ShO	Relief Pitching W	Relief Pitching L	Relief Pitching SV	Batting AB	Batting H	Batting HR	BA	PO	A	E	DP	TC/G	FA
1914	BKN N	1	0	1.000	4.74	7	1	0	19	21	8	5	0	0	0	0	6	0	0	.000	0	9	1	1	1.4	.900
1918	CLE A	5	7	.417	2.37	30	14	8	136.2	130	29	38	0	1	1	2	47	7	0	.149	7	39	1	0	1.6	.979
1919		3	2	.600	2.28	14	4	2	55.1	67	8	13	0	1	1	0	15	2	0	.133	0	14	0	2	1.0	1.000
1920	PHI N	2	3	.400	3.84	16	2	1	58.2	79	16	35	0	1	2	0	24	4	0	.167	3	14	0	0	1.0	1.000
4 yrs.		11	12	.478	2.84	67	21	11	269.2	297	61	91	0	3	4	2	92	13	0	.141	10	76	2	3	1.3	.977

Al Epperly

EPPERLY, ALBERT PAUL (Pard) BL TR 6′ 2″ 194 lbs.
B. May 7, 1918, Glidden, Iowa.

Year	Team	W	L	PCT	ERA	G	GS	CG	IP	H	BB	SO	ShO	Relief Pitching W	Relief Pitching L	Relief Pitching SV	Batting AB	Batting H	Batting HR	BA	PO	A	E	DP	TC/G	FA
1938	CHI N	2	0	1.000	3.67	9	4	1	27	28	15	10	0	0	0	0	8	2	0	.250	1	6	0	0	0.8	1.000
1950	BKN N	0	0	—	5.00	5	0	0	9	14	5	3	0	0	0	0	0	0	0	—	0	1	0	0	0.2	1.000
2 yrs.		2	0	1.000	4.00	14	4	1	36	42	20	13	0	0	0	0	8	2	0	.250	1	7	0	0	0.6	1.000

Joe Erardi

ERARDI, JOSEPH GREGORY BR TR 6′ 1″ 190 lbs.
B. May 31, 1954, Syracuse, N. Y.

Year	Team	W	L	PCT	ERA	G	GS	CG	IP	H	BB	SO	ShO	Relief Pitching W	Relief Pitching L	Relief Pitching SV	Batting AB	Batting H	Batting HR	BA	PO	A	E	DP	TC/G	FA
1977	SEA A	0	1	.000	6.00	5	0	0	9	12	6	5	0	0	1	0	0	0	0	—	0	1	0	0	0.2	1.000

Eddie Erautt

ERAUTT, EDWARD LORENZ SEBASTIAN BR TR 5′11½″ 185 lbs.
Brother of Joe Erautt.
B. Sept. 26, 1924, Portland, Ore.

Year	Team	W	L	PCT	ERA	G	GS	CG	IP	H	BB	SO	ShO	Relief Pitching W	Relief Pitching L	Relief Pitching SV	Batting AB	Batting H	Batting HR	BA	PO	A	E	DP	TC/G	FA
1947	CIN N	4	9	.308	5.07	36	10	2	119	146	53	43	0	3	2	0	29	2	0	.069	7	26	2	2	1.0	.943
1948		0	0	—	6.00	2	0	0	3	3	1	0	0	0	0	0	0	0	0	—	0	0	0	0	0.0	.000
1949		4	11	.267	3.36	39	9	1	112.2	99	61	43	0	3	5	1	23	4	0	.174	3	18	1	0	0.6	.955
1950		4	2	.667	5.65	33	2	1	65.1	82	22	35	0	3	1	1	13	2	0	.154	4	9	0	0	0.4	1.000
1951		0	0	—	5.72	30	0	0	39.1	50	23	20	0	0	0	0	3	0	0	.000	2	4	0	1	0.2	1.000
1953	2 teams CIN N (4G 0–0) STL N (20G 3–1)																									
″	total	3	1	.750	6.25	24	1	0	40.1	54	19	16	0	3	0	0	7	1	0	.143	1	9	0	2	0.4	1.000
6 yrs.		15	23	.395	4.86	164	22	4	379.2	434	179	157	0	12	8	2	75	9	0	.120	17	66	3	5	0.5	.965

John Ericks

ERICKS, JOHN EDWARD III BR TR 6′ 7″ 220 lbs.
B. Sept. 16, 1967, Tinley Park, Ill.

Year	Team	W	L	PCT	ERA	G	GS	CG	IP	H	BB	SO	ShO	Relief Pitching W	Relief Pitching L	Relief Pitching SV	Batting AB	Batting H	Batting HR	BA	PO	A	E	DP	TC/G	FA
1995	PIT N	3	9	.250	4.58	19	18	1	106	108	50	80	0	0	0	0	31	3	0	.097	7	10	3	0	1.1	.850

Don Erickson

ERICKSON, DON LEE BR TR 6′ 175 lbs.
B. Dec. 13, 1931, Springfield, Ill.

Year	Team	W	L	PCT	ERA	G	GS	CG	IP	H	BB	SO	ShO	Relief Pitching W	Relief Pitching L	Relief Pitching SV	Batting AB	Batting H	Batting HR	BA	PO	A	E	DP	TC/G	FA
1958	PHI N	0	1	.000	4.63	9	0	0	11.2	11	9	9	0	0	1	1	1	0	0	.000	0	0	0	0	0.0	.000

Eric Erickson

ERICKSON, ERIC GEORGE ADOLPH BR TR 6′ 2″ 190 lbs.
B. Mar. 13, 1895, Goteborg, Sweden D. May 19, 1965, Jamestown, N. Y.

Year	Team	W	L	PCT	ERA	G	GS	CG	IP	H	BB	SO	ShO	Relief Pitching W	Relief Pitching L	Relief Pitching SV	Batting AB	Batting H	Batting HR	BA	PO	A	E	DP	TC/G	FA
1914	NY N	0	1	.000	0.00	1	1	0	5	8	3	3	0	0	0	0	1	0	0	.000	0	0	0	0	0.0	.000
1916	DET A	0	0	—	2.81	8	0	0	16	13	8	7	0	0	0	0	4	0	0	.000	0	3	3	0	0.8	.500
1918		4	5	.444	2.48	12	9	8	94.1	81	29	48	0	0	1	1	33	4	0	.121	0	13	1	0	1.2	.929
1919	2 teams DET A (3G 0–2) WAS A (20G 6–11)																									
″	total	6	13	.316	4.23	23	17	7	146.2	147	73	90	1	1	1	0	53	8	0	.151	3	25	1	0	1.3	.966
1920	WAS A	12	16	.429	3.84	39	28	12	239.1	231	128	87	0	2	3	1	83	23	1	.277	9	44	4	0	1.5	.930
1921		8	10	.444	3.62	32	22	9	179	181	65	71	3	0	1	0	60	9	0	.150	5	32	2	0	1.2	.949
1922		4	12	.250	4.96	30	17	6	141.2	144	73	61	2	0	1	2	45	6	0	.133	6	23	4	2	1.1	.879
7 yrs.		34	57	.374	3.85	145	94	42	822	805	379	367	6	3	7	4	279	50	1	.179	23	140	15	2	1.2	.916

Hal Erickson

ERICKSON, HAROLD JAMES BR TR 6′ 5″ 230 lbs.
B. July 17, 1919, Portland, Ore.

Year	Team	W	L	PCT	ERA	G	GS	CG	IP	H	BB	SO	ShO	Relief Pitching W	Relief Pitching L	Relief Pitching SV	Batting AB	Batting H	Batting HR	BA	PO	A	E	DP	TC/G	FA
1953	DET A	0	1	.000	4.73	18	0	0	32.1	43	10	19	0	0	1	1	4	0	0	.000	3	3	0	0	0.3	1.000

Paul Erickson

ERICKSON, PAUL WALFORD (Li'l Abner) BR TR 6′2½″ 200 lbs.
B. Dec. 14, 1915, Zion, Ill.

Year	Team	W	L	PCT	ERA	G	GS	CG	IP	H	BB	SO	ShO	Relief Pitching W	Relief Pitching L	Relief Pitching SV	Batting AB	Batting H	Batting HR	BA	PO	A	E	DP	TC/G	FA
1941	CHI N	5	7	.417	3.70	32	15	7	141	126	64	85	1	0	0	1	46	7	1	.152	2	21	1	0	0.8	.958
1942		1	6	.143	5.43	18	7	1	63	70	41	26	0	1	0	0	21	3	0	.143	5	12	0	2	0.9	1.000
1943		1	3	.250	6.12	15	4	0	42.2	47	22	24	0	0	1	0	15	3	0	.200	1	6	0	0	0.5	1.000
1944		5	9	.357	3.55	33	15	5	124.1	113	67	82	3	1	2	1	36	2	1	.056	7	30	2	1	1.2	.949
1945		7	4	.636	3.32	28	9	3	108.1	94	48	53	0	2	2	3	32	5	0	.156	2	19	0	0	0.8	1.000
1946		9	7	.563	2.43	32	14	5	137	119	65	70	1	2	0	0	40	2	0	.050	5	22	0	0	0.8	1.000
1947		7	12	.368	4.34	40	20	6	174	179	93	82	0	3	1	1	60	15	1	.250	8	33	1	3	1.0	.976
1948	3 teams CHI N (3G 0–0) PHI N (4G 2–0) NY N (2G 0–0)																									
″	total	2	0	1.000	5.25	9	2	0	24	26	25	10	0	0	0	0	8	1	0	.125	3	5	0	0	0.9	1.000
8 yrs.		37	48	.435	3.86	207	86	27	814.1	774	425	432	5	9	6	6	258	38	3	.147	33	148	4	6	0.9	.978
WORLD SERIES																										
1945	CHI N	0	0	—	3.86	4	0	0	7	8	3	5	0	0	0	0	0	0	0	—	0	1	0	0	0.3	1.000

Ralph Erickson

ERICKSON, RALPH LIEF BL TL 6′ 1″ 175 lbs.
B. June 25, 1902, Dubois, Ida.

Year	Team		W	L	PCT	ERA	G	GS	CG	IP	H	BB	SO	ShO	Relief Pitching W	Relief Pitching L	Relief Pitching SV	Batting AB	Batting H	HR	BA	PO	A	E	DP	TC/G	FA
1929	**PIT**	**N**	0	0	—	27.00	1	0	0	1	2	2	0	0	0	0	0	0	0	0	—	0	0	0	0	0.0	.000
1930			1	0	1.000	7.07	7	0	0	14	21	10	2	0	1	0	0	4	1	0	.250	1	3	0	0	0.6	1.000
2 yrs.			1	0	1.000	8.40	8	0	0	15	23	12	2	0	1	0	0	4	1	0	.250	1	3	0	0	0.5	1.000

Roger Erickson

ERICKSON, ROGER FARRELL BR TR 6′ 3″ 180 lbs.
B. Aug. 30, 1956, Springfield, Ill.

Year	Team		W	L	PCT	ERA	G	GS	CG	IP	H	BB	SO	ShO	Relief Pitching W	Relief Pitching L	Relief Pitching SV	Batting AB	Batting H	HR	BA	PO	A	E	DP	TC/G	FA
1978	**MIN**	**A**	14	13	.519	3.96	37	37	14	265.2	268	79	121	0	0	0	0	0	0	0	—	13	44	5	3	1.7	.919
1979			3	10	.231	5.63	24	21	0	123	154	48	47	0	0	1	0	0	0	0	—	9	17	2	1	1.2	.929
1980			7	13	.350	3.25	32	27	7	191	198	56	97	0	0	0	0	0	0	0	—	8	28	1	4	1.2	.973
1981			3	8	.273	3.86	14	14	1	91	93	31	44	0	0	0	0	0	0	0	—	8	13	2	1	1.6	.913
1982	**2 teams** **MIN A** (7G 4–3) **NY A** (16G 4–5)																										
″	**total**		8	8	.500	4.61	23	18	2	111.1	142	29	49	0	0	0	1	0	0	0		6	14	1	0	0.9	.952
1983	**NY**	**A**	0	1	.000	4.32	5	0	0	16.2	13	8	7	0	0	1	0	0	0	0	—	4	2	0	0	1.2	1.000
6 yrs.			35	53	.398	4.14	135	117	24	798.2	868	251	365	0	0	2	1	0	0	0		48	118	11	9	1.3	.938

Scott Erickson

ERICKSON, SCOTT GAVIN BR TR 6′ 4″ 220 lbs.
B. Feb. 2, 1968, Long Beach, Calif.

Year	Team		W	L	PCT	ERA	G	GS	CG	IP	H	BB	SO	ShO	Relief Pitching W	Relief Pitching L	Relief Pitching SV	Batting AB	Batting H	HR	BA	PO	A	E	DP	TC/G	FA
1990	**MIN**	**A**	8	4	.667	2.87	19	17	1	113	108	51	53	0	0	0	0	0	0	0	—	10	13	0	0	1.2	1.000
1991			**20**	8	**.714**	3.18	32	32	5	204	189	71	108	3	0	0	0	0	0	0	—	19	31	1	3	1.6	.980
1992			13	12	.520	3.40	32	32	5	212	197	83	101	3	0	0	0	0	0	0	—	18	34	1	3	1.7	.981
1993			8	**19**	.296	5.19	34	34	1	218.2	**266**	71	116	0	0	0	0	0	0	0	—	18	34	3	3	1.6	.945
1994			8	11	.421	5.44	23	23	2	144	173	59	104	1	0	0	0	0	0	0	—	9	23	4	4	1.6	.889
1995	**2 teams** **MIN A** (15G 4–6) **BAL A** (17G 9–4)																										
″	**total**		13	10	.565	4.81	32	31	7	196.1	213	67	106	2	0	0	0	0	0	0	—	26	40	1	2	2.1	.985
6 yrs.			70	64	.522	4.19	172	169	21	1088	1146	402	588	9	0	0	0	0	0	0		100	175	10	15	1.7	.965
LEAGUE CHAMPIONSHIP SERIES																											
1991	**MIN**	**A**	0	0	—	4.50	1	1	0	4	3	5	2	0	0	0	0	0	0	0	—	1	1	0	0	2.0	1.000
WORLD SERIES																											
1991	**MIN**	**A**	0	0	—	5.06	2	2	0	10.2	10	4	5	0	0	0	0	1	0	0	.000	1	0	0	0	0.5	1.000

Dick Errickson

ERRICKSON, RICHARD MERRIWELL (Leif) BL TR 6′ 1″ 175 lbs.
B. Mar. 4, 1914, Vineland, N. J.

Year	Team		W	L	PCT	ERA	G	GS	CG	IP	H	BB	SO	ShO	Relief Pitching W	Relief Pitching L	Relief Pitching SV	Batting AB	Batting H	HR	BA	PO	A	E	DP	TC/G	FA
1938	**BOS**	**N**	9	7	.563	3.15	34	10	6	122.2	113	56	40	1	3	3	6	35	4	0	.114	6	34	2	0	1.2	.952
1939			6	9	.400	4.00	28	11	3	128.1	143	54	33	0	1	3	1	44	10	0	.227	5	36	2	0	1.5	.953
1940			12	13	.480	3.16	34	29	17	236.1	241	90	34	3	0	0	4	83	13	0	.157	9	58	2	5	2.0	.971
1941			6	12	.333	4.78	38	23	5	165.2	192	62	45	2	1	1	1	45	8	0	.178	7	39	1	0	1.2	.979
1942	**2 teams** **BOS N** (21G 2–5) **CHI N** (13G 1–1)																										
″	**total**		3	6	.333	4.75	34	4	0	83.1	115	28	24	0	1	5	1	21	2	0	.095	2	18	0	1	0.6	1.000
5 yrs.			36	47	.434	3.85	168	77	31	736.1	804	290	176	6	6	12	13	228	37	0	.162	29	185	7	6	1.3	.968

Carl Erskine

ERSKINE, CARL DANIEL (Oisk) BR TR 5′10″ 165 lbs.
B. Dec. 13, 1926, Anderson, Ind.

Year	Team		W	L	PCT	ERA	G	GS	CG	IP	H	BB	SO	ShO	Relief Pitching W	Relief Pitching L	Relief Pitching SV	Batting AB	Batting H	HR	BA	PO	A	E	DP	TC/G	FA
1948	**BKN**	**N**	6	3	.667	3.23	17	9	3	64	51	35	29	0	3	1	0	21	2	0	.095	2	6	1	2	0.5	.889
1949			8	1	.889	4.63	22	3	2	79.2	68	51	49	0	6	1	0	26	3	0	.115	3	13	1	2	0.8	.941
1950			7	6	.538	4.72	22	13	3	103	109	35	50	0	1	0	1	37	9	0	.243	10	12	2	2	1.1	.917
1951			16	12	.571	4.46	46	19	7	189.2	206	78	95	0	9	7	4	61	8	0	.131	13	32	2	1	1.0	.957
1952			14	6	.700	2.70	33	26	10	206.2	167	71	131	4	1	1	2	66	10	0	.152	16	45	3	4	1.9	.953
1953			20	6	**.769**	3.54	39	33	16	246.2	213	95	187	4	1	0	3	93	20	0	.215	15	30	4	0	1.3	.918
1954			18	15	.545	4.15	38	37	12	260.1	239	92	166	2	0	0	1	88	14	0	.159	14	41	2	2	1.5	.965
1955			11	8	.579	3.79	31	29	7	194.2	185	64	84	2	1	0	1	74	15	1	.203	6	26	3	1	1.1	.914
1956			13	11	.542	4.25	31	28	8	186.1	189	57	95	1	2	1	0	66	8	0	.121	9	34	1	2	1.4	.977
1957			5	3	.625	3.55	15	7	1	66	62	20	26	0	1	0	0	22	2	0	.091	6	5	0	0	0.7	1.000
1958	**LA**	**N**	4	4	.500	5.13	31	9	2	98.1	115	35	54	1	1	1	0	27	1	0	.037	10	15	1	4	0.8	.962
1959			0	3	.000	7.71	10	3	0	23.1	33	13	15	0	0	0	1	7	0	0	.000	1	3	0	0	0.4	1.000
12 yrs.			122	78	.610	4.00	335	216	71	1718.2	1637	646	981	14	26	12	13	588	92	1	.156	105	262	20	20	1.2	.948
WORLD SERIES																											
1949	**BKN**	**N**	0	0	—	16.20	2	0	0	1.2	3	1	0	0	0	0	0	0	0	0	—	0	0	0	0	0.0	.000
1952			1	1	.500	4.50	3	2	1	18	12	10	10	0	0	0	0	6	0	0	.000	0	2	0	0	0.7	1.000
1953			1	0	1.000	5.79	3	3	1	14	14	9	16	0	0	0	0	4	1	0	.250	1	2	1	0	1.3	.750
1955			0	0	—	9.00	1	1	0	3	3	2	3	0	0	0	0	1	0	0	.000	0	1	0	0	1.0	1.000
1956			0	1	.000	5.40	2	1	0	5	4	2	2	0	0	0	0	1	0	0	.000	1	2	0	0	1.5	1.000
5 yrs.			2	2	.500	5.83	11 **10th**	7	2	41.2	36	24	31	0	0	0	0	12	1	0	.083	2	7	1	0	0.9	.900

Ernesto Escarrega

ESCARREGA, ERNESTO (Chico) BR TR 5′11″ 185 lbs.
Born Ernesto Escarrega (Acosta).
B. Dec. 27, 1949, Los Mochis, Mexico.

Year	Team		W	L	PCT	ERA	G	GS	CG	IP	H	BB	SO	ShO	Relief Pitching W	Relief Pitching L	Relief Pitching SV	Batting AB	Batting H	HR	BA	PO	A	E	DP	TC/G	FA
1982	**CHI**	**A**	1	3	.250	3.67	38	2	0	73.2	73	16	33	0	1	1	1	0	0	0	—	6	7	0	1	0.3	1.000

Vaughn Eshelman

ESHELMAN, VAUGHN MICHAEL BL TL 6′ 3″ 205 lbs.
B. May 22, 1969, Philadelphia, Pa.

Year	Team		W	L	PCT	ERA	G	GS	CG	IP	H	BB	SO	ShO	Relief Pitching W	Relief Pitching L	Relief Pitching SV	Batting AB	Batting H	HR	BA	PO	A	E	DP	TC/G	FA
1995	**BOS**	**A**	6	3	.667	4.85	23	14	0	81.2	86	36	41	0	1	0	0	0	0	0	—	6	8	1	1	0.7	.933

Duke Esper

ESPER, CHARLES H. TL 5′11½″ 185 lbs.
B. July 28, 1868, Salem, N. J. D. Aug. 31, 1910, Philadelphia, Pa.

Year	Team		W	L	PCT	ERA	G	GS	CG	IP	H	BB	SO	ShO	Relief Pitching W	Relief Pitching L	Relief Pitching SV	Batting AB	Batting H	HR	BA	PO	A	E	DP	TC/G	FA
1890	**3 teams** **PHI AA** (18G 8–9) **PIT N** (2G 0–2) **PHI N** (5G 5–0)																										
″	**total**		13	11	.542	4.55	25	23	20	201.2	234	93	88	1	1	0	0	87	22	0	.253	12	43	3	3	2.3	.948
1891	**PHI**	**N**	20	15	.571	3.56	39	36	25	296	302	121	108	1	1	0	1	123	27	0	.220	4	67	4	2	1.9	.947
1892	**2 teams** **PHI N** (21G 11–6) **PIT N** (3G 2–0)																										
″	**total**		13	6	.684	3.63	24	21	15	178.2	189	70	50	0	1	0	1	79	17	1	.215	8	37	1	1	1.8	.978
1893	**WAS**	**N**	12	**28**	.300	4.71	42	36	34	334.1	442	156	78	0	2	2	0	143	41	0	.287	14	79	9	0	2.4	.912
1894	**2 teams** **WAS N** (19G 5–10) **BAL N** (16G 10–2)																										
″	**total**		15	12	.556	5.86	35	24	15	224.1	298	76	52	0	3	2	2	102	26	1	.255	14	43	1	2	1.6	.983

Duke Esper *continued*

Year	Team	Lg	W	L	PCT	ERA	G	GS	CG	IP	H	BB	SO	ShO	Relief Pitching W	L	SV	Batting AB	H	HR	BA	PO	A	E	DP	TC/G	FA
1895	BAL	N	10	12	.455	3.92	34	25	16	218.1	248	79	39	1	1	**4**	1	90	16	0	.178	5	43	6	0	1.6	.889
1896			14	5	.737	3.58	20	18	14	155.2	168	39	19	1	2	0	0	66	13	0	.197	4	32	1	0	1.9	.973
1897	STL	N	1	6	.143	5.28	8	8	7	61.1	95	12	8	0	0	0	0	25	8	0	.320	5	19	0	0	3.0	1.000
1898			3	5	.375	5.98	10	8	6	64.2	86	22	14	0	0	0	0	27	10	0	.370	2	17	1	0	2.0	.950
9 yrs.			101	100	.502	4.40	237	199	152	1735	2062	668	456	4	11	8	5	742	180	2	.243	68	380	26	8	2.0	.945

Nino Espinosa

ESPINOSA, ARNULFO BR TR 6′ 1″ 165 lbs.
Born Arnulfo Acevedo (Espinosa).
B. Aug. 15, 1953, Villa Altagracia, Dominican Republic
D. Dec. 24, 1987, Santo Domingo, Dominican Republic.

Year	Team	Lg	W	L	PCT	ERA	G	GS	CG	IP	H	BB	SO	ShO	Relief Pitching W	L	SV	Batting AB	H	HR	BA	PO	A	E	DP	TC/G	FA
1974	NY	N	0	0	—	5.00	2	1	0	9	12	0	2	0	0	0	0	2	1	0	.500	0	2	0	0	1.0	1.000
1975			0	1	.000	18.00	2	0	0	3	8	1	2	0	0	1	0	0	0	0	—	0	0	0	0	0.0	.000
1976			4	4	.500	3.64	12	5	0	42	41	13	30	0	2	2	0	9	0	0	.000	0	3	0	0	0.3	1.000
1977			10	13	.435	3.42	32	29	7	200	188	55	105	1	1	0	0	62	8	0	.129	16	25	0	4	1.3	1.000
1978			11	15	.423	4.72	32	32	6	204	230	75	76	1	0	0	0	67	14	0	.209	10	47	1	2	1.8	.983
1979	PHI	N	14	12	.538	3.65	33	33	8	212	211	65	88	3	0	0	0	72	14	0	.194	11	34	2	2	1.4	.957
1980			3	5	.375	3.79	12	12	1	76	73	19	13	0	0	0	0	26	3	0	.115	8	10	1	0	1.6	.947
1981	2 teams	PHI N	(14G 2–5)		TOR A	(1G 0–0)																					
″	total		2	5	.286	6.12	15	14	2	75	102	24	22	0	0	0	0	20	4	0	.200	6	8	0	0	0.9	1.000
8 yrs.			44	55	.444	4.17	140	126	24	821	865	252	338	5	3	3	0	258	44	0	.171	51	129	4	8	1.3	.978

Alvaro Espinoza

ESPINOZA, ALVARO ALBERTO BR TR 6′ 160 lbs.
Born Alvaro Alberto Espinoza (Ramirez).
B. Feb. 19, 1962, Valencia, Venezuela.

Year	Team	Lg	W	L	PCT	ERA	G	GS	CG	IP	H	BB	SO	ShO	Relief Pitching W	L	SV	Batting AB	H	HR	BA	PO	A	E	DP	TC/G	FA
1991	NY	A	0	0	—	0.00	1	0	0	0.2	0	0	0	0	0	0	0	*				0	0	0	0	0.0	.000

Mark Esser

ESSER, MARK GERALD BR TL 6′ 1″ 190 lbs.
B. Apr. 1, 1956, Erie, Pa.

Year	Team	Lg	W	L	PCT	ERA	G	GS	CG	IP	H	BB	SO	ShO	Relief Pitching W	L	SV	Batting AB	H	HR	BA	PO	A	E	DP	TC/G	FA
1979	CHI	A	0	0	—	13.50	2	0	0	2	2	4	1	0	0	0	0	0	0	0	—	0	0	0	0	0.0	.000

Bill Essick

ESSICK, WILLIAM EARL (Vinegar Bill) TR 5′10″ 175 lbs.
B. Dec. 18, 1881, Grand Ridge, Ill. D. Oct. 12, 1951, Los Angeles, Calif.

Year	Team	Lg	W	L	PCT	ERA	G	GS	CG	IP	H	BB	SO	ShO	Relief Pitching W	L	SV	Batting AB	H	HR	BA	PO	A	E	DP	TC/G	FA
1906	CIN	N	2	1	.667	2.97	6	4	3	39.1	39	16	16	0	0	0	0	13	1	0	.077	2	5	0	0	1.2	1.000
1907			0	2	.000	2.91	3	2	2	21.2	23	8	7	0	0	0	0	8	0	0	.000	0	11	1	0	4.0	.917
2 yrs.			2	3	.400	2.95	9	6	5	61	62	24	23	0	0	0	0	21	1	0	.048	2	16	1	0	2.1	.947

Dick Estelle

ESTELLE, RICHARD HENRY BB TL 6′ 2″ 170 lbs.
B. Jan. 18, 1942, Lakewood, N. J.

Year	Team	Lg	W	L	PCT	ERA	G	GS	CG	IP	H	BB	SO	ShO	Relief Pitching W	L	SV	Batting AB	H	HR	BA	PO	A	E	DP	TC/G	FA
1964	SF	N	1	2	.333	3.02	6	6	0	41.2	39	23	23	0	0	0	0	15	1	0	.067	2	3	0	0	0.8	1.000
1965			0	0	—	3.97	6	1	0	11.1	12	8	6	0	0	0	0	1	0	0	.000	1	3	1	0	0.8	.800
2 yrs.			1	2	.333	3.23	12	7	0	53	51	31	29	0	0	0	0	16	1	0	.063	3	6	1	0	0.8	.900

Shawn Estes

ESTES, AARON SHAWN BB TL 6′ 2″ 185 lbs.
B. Feb. 18, 1973, San Bernardino, Calif.

Year	Team	Lg	W	L	PCT	ERA	G	GS	CG	IP	H	BB	SO	ShO	Relief Pitching W	L	SV	Batting AB	H	HR	BA	PO	A	E	DP	TC/G	FA
1995	SF	N	0	3	.000	6.75	3	3	0	17.1	16	5	14	0	0	0	0	5	0	0	.000	0	1	0	0	0.3	1.000

George Estock

ESTOCK, GEORGE JOHN BR TR 6′ 185 lbs.
B. Nov. 2, 1924, Stirling, N. J.

Year	Team	Lg	W	L	PCT	ERA	G	GS	CG	IP	H	BB	SO	ShO	Relief Pitching W	L	SV	Batting AB	H	HR	BA	PO	A	E	DP	TC/G	FA
1951	BOS	N	0	1	.000	4.33	37	1	0	60.1	56	37	11	0	0	0	3	7	2	0	.286	4	13	1	1	0.5	.944

Chuck Estrada

ESTRADA, CHARLES LEONARD BR TR 6′ 1″ 185 lbs.
B. Feb. 15, 1938, San Luis Obispo, Calif.

Year	Team	Lg	W	L	PCT	ERA	G	GS	CG	IP	H	BB	SO	ShO	Relief Pitching W	L	SV	Batting AB	H	HR	BA	PO	A	E	DP	TC/G	FA
1960	BAL	A	**18**	11	.621	3.58	36	25	12	208.2	162	101	144	1	5	2	2	64	9	0	.141	8	29	0	4	1.0	1.000
1961			15	9	.625	3.69	33	31	6	212	159	**132**	160	1	0	0	0	70	8	0	.114	19	17	1	1	1.1	.973
1962			9	**17**	.346	3.83	34	33	6	223.1	199	121	165	0	0	0	0	66	10	1	.152	7	24	2	1	1.0	.939
1963			3	2	.600	4.60	8	7	0	31.1	26	19	16	0	0	0	0	10	1	0	.100	3	2	0	0	0.6	1.000
1964			3	2	.600	5.27	17	6	0	54.2	62	21	32	0	1	2	0	14	2	0	.143	2	3	0	0	0.3	1.000
1966	CHI	N	1	1	.500	7.30	9	1	0	12.1	16	5	3	0	1	1	0	3	0	0	.000	0	1	0	0	0.1	1.000
1967	NY	N	1	2	.333	9.41	9	2	0	22	28	17	15	0	1	0	0	5	0	0	.000	2	2	0	0	0.4	1.000
7 yrs.			50	44	.532	4.07	146	105	24	764.1	652	416	535	2	8	5	2	232	30	1	.129	41	78	3	6	0.8	.975

Oscar Estrada

ESTRADA, OSCAR BL TL 5′ 8″ 160 lbs.
B. Feb. 15, 1904, Havana, Cuba D. Jan. 2, 1978, Havana, Cuba.

Year	Team	Lg	W	L	PCT	ERA	G	GS	CG	IP	H	BB	SO	ShO	Relief Pitching W	L	SV	Batting AB	H	HR	BA	PO	A	E	DP	TC/G	FA
1929	STL	A	0	0	—	0.00	1	0	0	1	1	1	0	0	0	0	0	0	0	0	—	0	1	0	0	1.0	1.000

Mark Ettles

ETTLES, MARK EDWARD BR TR 6′ 178 lbs.
B. Oct. 30, 1966, Perth, Australia.

Year	Team	Lg	W	L	PCT	ERA	G	GS	CG	IP	H	BB	SO	ShO	Relief Pitching W	L	SV	Batting AB	H	HR	BA	PO	A	E	DP	TC/G	FA
1993	SD	N	1	0	1.000	6.50	14	0	0	18	23	4	9	0	1	0	0	2	0	0	.000	0	4	0	0	0.3	1.000

John Eubank

EUBANK, JOHN FRANKLIN (Honest John) BR TR 6′ 2″ 215 lbs.
B. Sept. 9, 1872, Servia, Ind. D. Nov. 3, 1958, Bellevue, Mich.

Year	Team	Lg	W	L	PCT	ERA	G	GS	CG	IP	H	BB	SO	ShO	Relief Pitching W	L	SV	Batting AB	H	HR	BA	PO	A	E	DP	TC/G	FA
1905	DET	A	1	0	1.000	2.08	3	2	0	17.1	13	3	1	0	1	0	0	11	4	0	.364	3	4	1	0	2.0	.875
1906			4	10	.286	3.53	24	12	7	135	147	35	38	1	1	1	2	60	12	0	.200	9	50	3	0	2.3	.952
1907			3	3	.500	2.67	15	8	4	81	88	20	17	1	0	0	0	31	4	0	.129	3	32	2	0	2.5	.946
3 yrs.			8	13	.381	3.12	42	22	11	233.1	248	58	56	2	2	1	2	102	20	0	.196	15	86	6	0	2.3	.944

Uel Eubanks

EUBANKS, UEL MELVIN (Poss) BR TR 6′ 3″ 175 lbs.
B. Feb. 14, 1903, Quinlan, Tex. D. Nov. 21, 1954, Dallas, Tex.

Year	Team	Lg	W	L	PCT	ERA	G	GS	CG	IP	H	BB	SO	ShO	Relief Pitching W	L	SV	Batting AB	H	HR	BA	PO	A	E	DP	TC/G	FA
1922	CHI	N	0	0	—	27.00	2	0	0	1.2	5	4	1	0	0	0	0	1	1	0	1.000	0	1	0	0	0.5	1.000

Frank Eufemia

EUFEMIA, FRANK ANTHONY BR TR 5′11″ 185 lbs.
B. Dec. 23, 1959, Bronx, N. Y.

Year	Team	Lg	W	L	PCT	ERA	G	GS	CG	IP	H	BB	SO	ShO	Relief Pitching W	L	SV	Batting AB	H	HR	BA	PO	A	E	DP	TC/G	FA
1985	MIN	A	4	2	.667	3.79	39	0	0	61.2	56	21	30	0	4	2	2	0	0	0	—	4	12	0	1	0.4	1.000

Art Evans

EVANS, WILLIAM ARTHUR BB TL 6′ 1½″ 181 lbs.
B. Aug. 3, 1911, Elvins, Mo. D. Jan. 8, 1952, Wichita, Kans.

Year	Team		W	L	PCT	ERA	G	GS	CG	IP	H	BB	SO	ShO	Relief Pitching W	Relief Pitching L	Relief Pitching SV	Batting AB	Batting H	Batting HR	BA	PO	A	E	DP	TC/G	FA
1932	CHI	A	0	0	—	3.00	7	0	0	18	19	10	6	0	0	0	0	5	0	0	.000	4	4	0	1	1.1	1.000

Bill Evans

EVANS, WILLIAM JAMES BR TR 6′ 175 lbs.
B. Feb. 10, 1894, Reidsville, N. C. D. Dec. 21, 1946, Burlington, N. C.

Year	Team		W	L	PCT	ERA	G	GS	CG	IP	H	BB	SO	ShO	Relief Pitching W	Relief Pitching L	Relief Pitching SV	Batting AB	Batting H	Batting HR	BA	PO	A	E	DP	TC/G	FA
1916	PIT	N	2	5	.286	3.00	13	7	3	63	57	16	21	0	1	0	0	20	3	0	.150	5	23	1	4	2.2	.966
1917			0	4	.000	3.38	8	2	1	26.2	24	14	5	0	0	2	0	9	1	0	.111	1	7	0	0	1.0	1.000
1919			0	4	.000	5.65	7	3	2	36.2	41	18	15	0	0	1	0	11	0	0	.000	6	11	0	0	2.4	1.000
3 yrs.			2	13	.133	3.85	28	12	6	126.1	122	48	41	0	1	3	0	40	4	0	.100	12	41	1	4	1.9	.981

Bill Evans

EVANS, WILLIAM LAWRENCE BR TR 6′ 2″ 180 lbs.
B. Mar. 25, 1919, Quanah, Tex. D. Nov. 30, 1983, Grand Junction, Colo.

Year	Team		W	L	PCT	ERA	G	GS	CG	IP	H	BB	SO	ShO	Relief Pitching W	Relief Pitching L	Relief Pitching SV	Batting AB	Batting H	Batting HR	BA	PO	A	E	DP	TC/G	FA
1949	CHI	A	0	1	.000	7.11	4	0	0	6.1	6	8	1	0	0	1	0	1	0	0	.000	0	0	0	0	0.0	.000
1951	BOS	A	0	0	—	4.11	9	0	0	15.1	15	8	3	0	0	0	0	4	0	0	.000	1	2	0	0	0.3	1.000
2 yrs.			0	1	.000	4.98	13	0	0	21.2	21	16	4	0	0	1	0	5	0	0	.000	1	2	0	0	0.2	1.000

Chick Evans

EVANS, CHARLES FRANKLIN BR TR
B. Oct. 15, 1889, Arlington, Vt. D. Sept. 2, 1916, Schenectady, N. Y.

Year	Team		W	L	PCT	ERA	G	GS	CG	IP	H	BB	SO	ShO	Relief Pitching W	Relief Pitching L	Relief Pitching SV	Batting AB	Batting H	Batting HR	BA	PO	A	E	DP	TC/G	FA
1909	BOS	N	0	3	.000	4.57	4	3	1	21.2	25	14	11	0	0	0	0	9	0	0	.000	0	7	3	0	2.5	.700
1910			1	1	.500	5.23	13	1	0	31	28	27	12	0	1	0	0	10	1	0	.100	0	10	0	1	0.8	1.000
2 yrs.			1	4	.200	4.96	17	4	1	52.2	53	41	23	0	1	0	0	19	1	0	.053	0	17	3	1	1.2	.850

Jake Evans

EVANS, URIAH L.P. (Bloody Jake) TR 5′ 8″ 154 lbs.
B. Sept. 1856, Baltimore, Md. D. Jan. 16, 1907, Baltimore, Md.

Year	Team		W	L	PCT	ERA	G	GS	CG	IP	H	BB	SO	ShO	Relief Pitching W	Relief Pitching L	Relief Pitching SV	Batting AB	Batting H	Batting HR	BA	PO	A	E	DP	TC/G	FA
1880	TRO	N	0	0	—	13.50	1	0	0	4	11	0	0	0	0	0	0	180	46	0	.256	153	30	24	4	2.9	.884
1882	WOR	N	0	1	.000	*5.63*	1	1	1	8	13	0	2	0	0	0	0	334	71	0	.213	69	11	8	4	1.8	.909
1883	CLE	N	0	0	—	0.00	1	0	0	3	0	0	1	0	0	0	0	332	79	0	.238	133	43	20	2	2.1	.898
3 yrs.			0	1	.000	6.60	3	1	1	15	24	0	3	0	0	0	0	*				829	233	114	31	2.4	.903

Red Evans

EVANS, RUSSELL EDISON BR TR 5′11″ 168 lbs.
B. Nov. 12, 1906, Chicago, Ill. D. June 14, 1982, Lakeview, Ark.

Year	Team		W	L	PCT	ERA	G	GS	CG	IP	H	BB	SO	ShO	Relief Pitching W	Relief Pitching L	Relief Pitching SV	Batting AB	Batting H	Batting HR	BA	PO	A	E	DP	TC/G	FA
1936	CHI	A	0	3	.000	7.61	17	0	0	47.1	70	22	19	0	0	3	1	15	2	0	.133	3	15	1	0	1.1	.947
1939	BKN	N	1	8	.111	5.18	24	6	0	64.1	74	26	28	0	1	2	1	13	4	0	.308	5	18	1	0	1.0	.958
2 yrs.			1	11	.083	6.21	41	6	0	111.2	144	48	47	0	1	5	2	28	6	0	.214	8	33	2	0	1.0	.953

Roy Evans

EVANS, ROY BR TR 6′ 180 lbs.
B. Mar. 19, 1874, Knoxville, Tenn. D. Aug. 15, 1915, Galveston, Tex.

Year	Team		W	L	PCT	ERA	G	GS	CG	IP	H	BB	SO	ShO	Relief Pitching W	Relief Pitching L	Relief Pitching SV	Batting AB	Batting H	Batting HR	BA	PO	A	E	DP	TC/G	FA
1897	**2 teams**	**STL N** (3G 0–0) **LOU N** (9G 5–4)																									
″	**total**		5	4	.556	5.10	12	8	6	72.1	99	37	24	0	0	1	0	26	3	0	.115	1	11	2	0	1.2	.857
1898	WAS	N	3	3	.500	3.38	7	6	4	50.2	50	25	11	0	0	0	0	19	1	0	.053	1	8	2	0	1.6	.818
1899			3	4	.429	5.67	7	7	6	54	60	25	27	0	0	0	0	20	4	0	.200	2	12	2	0	2.3	.875
1902	**2 teams**	**NY N** (23G 8–13) **BKN N** (13G 5–6)																									
″	**total**		13	19	.406	3.00	36	28	28	273.1	277	91	83	2	**2**	**3**	0	88	17	0	.193	16	62	7	3	2.4	.918
1903	**2 teams**	**BKN N** (15G 4–8) **STL A** (7G 0–4)																									
″	**total**		4	12	.250	3.57	22	19	13	164	187	55	66	0	1	1	0	48	7	0	.146	4	40	4	1	2.2	.917
5 yrs.			28	42	.400	3.66	84	68	57	614.1	673	233	211	2	3	5	0	201	32	0	.159	24	133	17	4	2.1	.902

Leon Everitt

EVERITT, EDWARD LEON BL TR 6′ 1½″ 195 lbs.
B. Jan. 12, 1947, Marshall, Tex.

Year	Team		W	L	PCT	ERA	G	GS	CG	IP	H	BB	SO	ShO	Relief Pitching W	Relief Pitching L	Relief Pitching SV	Batting AB	Batting H	Batting HR	BA	PO	A	E	DP	TC/G	FA
1969	SD	N	0	1	.000	7.88	5	0	0	16	18	12	11	0	0	1	0	3	0	0	.000	0	5	0	0	1.0	1.000

Bryan Eversgerd

EVERSGERD, BRYAN DAVID BR TL 6′ 1″ 190 lbs.
B. Feb. 11, 1969, Centralia, Ill.

Year	Team		W	L	PCT	ERA	G	GS	CG	IP	H	BB	SO	ShO	Relief Pitching W	Relief Pitching L	Relief Pitching SV	Batting AB	Batting H	Batting HR	BA	PO	A	E	DP	TC/G	FA
1994	STL	N	2	3	.400	4.52	40	1	0	67.2	75	20	47	0	1	3	0	6	0	0	.000	5	13	0	2	0.4	1.000
1995	MON	N	0	0	—	5.14	25	0	0	21	22	9	8	0	0	0	0	1	0	0	.000	2	2	1	0	0.2	.800
2 yrs.			2	3	.400	4.67	65	1	0	88.2	97	29	55	0	1	3	0	7	0	0	.000	7	15	1	2	0.4	.957

Bob Ewing

EWING, GEORGE LEMUEL (Long Bob) BR TR 6′ 1½″ 170 lbs.
B. Apr. 24, 1873, New Hampshire, Ohio D. June 20, 1947, Wapakoneta, Ohio.

Year	Team		W	L	PCT	ERA	G	GS	CG	IP	H	BB	SO	ShO	Relief Pitching W	Relief Pitching L	Relief Pitching SV	Batting AB	Batting H	Batting HR	BA	PO	A	E	DP	TC/G	FA
1902	CIN	N	6	6	.500	2.98	15	12	10	117.2	126	47	44	0	0	0	0	71	12	0	.169	11	29	2	0	2.1	.952
1903			14	13	.519	2.77	29	28	27	246.2	254	64	104	1	0	0	1	95	24	0	.253	15	80	5	3	3.1	.950
1904			11	13	.458	2.46	26	24	22	212	198	58	99	0	1	0	0	97	25	1	.258	14	50	2	3	2.2	.970
1905			20	11	.645	2.51	40	34	30	312	284	79	164	4	3	0	0	122	32	0	.262	10	70	5	1	2.0	.941
1906			13	14	.481	2.38	33	32	26	287.2	248	60	145	2	0	1	0	101	14	1	.139	19	76	1	3	2.9	.990
1907			17	19	.472	1.73	41	37	32	332.2	279	85	147	2	1	1	0	123	19	1	.154	15	61	3	2	1.8	.962
1908			17	15	.531	2.21	37	32	23	293.2	247	57	95	4	1	1	3	94	14	0	.149	11	69	3	0	2.2	.964
1909			11	12	.478	2.43	31	29	14	218.1	195	63	86	2	0	1	0	73	8	0	.110	7	42	8	1	1.8	.860
1910	PHI	N	16	14	.533	3.00	34	32	20	255.1	235	86	102	4	0	1	0	90	20	0	.222	5	60	2	2	2.0	.970
1911			0	1	.000	7.88	4	3	1	24	29	14	12	0	0	0	0	6	2	0	.333	1	5	0	0	1.5	1.000
1912	STL	N	0	0	—	0.00	1	1	0	1.1	2	1	0	0	0	0	0	0	0	0	—	1	0	0	0	1.0	1.000
11 yrs.			125	118	.514	2.49	291	264	205	2301.1	2097	614	998	19	6	5	4	872	170	3	.195	109	542	31	15	2.2	.955

Buck Ewing

EWING, WILLIAM BR TR 5′10″ 188 lbs.
Brother of John Ewing.
B. Oct. 17, 1859, Hoagland, Ohio D. Oct. 20, 1906, Cincinnati, Ohio.
Manager 1890, 1895–00.
Hall of Fame 1939.

Year	Team		W	L	PCT	ERA	G	GS	CG	IP	H	BB	SO	ShO	Relief Pitching W	Relief Pitching L	Relief Pitching SV	Batting AB	Batting H	Batting HR	BA	PO	A	E	DP	TC/G	FA
1882	TRO	N	0	0	—	9.00	1	0	0	1	2	1	0	0	0	0	0	328	89	2	.271	48	7	11	0	4.7	.833
1884	NY	N	0	1	.000	1.13	1	1	1	8	7	4	3	0	0	0	0	382	106	3	.277	254	185	43	18	7.0	.911
1885			0	1	.000	4.50	1	0	0	2	4	3	0	0	0	**1**	0	342	104	6	.304	377	119	47	9	6.2	.913
1888			0	0	—	2.57	2	0	0	7	8	4	6	0	0	0	1	415	127	6	.306	311	97	36	4	5.9	.919
1889			2	0	1.000	4.05	3	2	2	20	23	8	12	0	0	0	0	407	133	4	.327	525	152	47	10	7.2	.935
1890	NY	P	0	1	.000	4.00	1	1	1	9	11	3	2	0	0	0	0	352	119	8	.338	374	113	28	8	6.2	.946
6 yrs.			2	3	.400	3.45	9	4	4	47	55	23	23	0	0	1	1	*				6353	1782	572	282	6.5	.934

John Ewing

EWING, JOHN TR
Brother of Buck Ewing.
B. June 1, 1863, Cincinnati, Ohio D. Apr. 23, 1895, Denver, Colo.

Year	Team		W	L	PCT	ERA	G	GS	CG	IP	H	BB	SO	ShO	Relief Pitching W	L	SV	Batting AB	H	HR	BA	PO	A	E	DP	TC/G	FA
1888	LOU	AA	8	13	.381	2.83	21	21	21	191	175	34	87	2	0	0	0	79	16	0	.203	1	0	2	0	3.0	.333
1889			6	30	.167	4.87	40	39	37	331	407	147	155	1	0	0	0	134	23	0	.172	12	73	4	3	2.2	.955
1890	NY	P	18	12	.600	4.24	35	31	27	267.1	293	104	145	1	1	0	2	114	24	2	.211	14	61	4	1	2.3	.949
1891	NY	N	21	8	**.724**	**2.27**	33	30	28	269.1	237	105	138	5	1	0	0	113	23	0	.204	17	49	6	3	2.2	.917
4 yrs.			53	63	.457	3.68	129	121	113	1058.2	1112	390	525	9	2	0	2	454	87	2	.192	50	228	23	7	2.3	.924

George Eyrich

EYRICH, GEORGE LINCOLN BR TR 5′11″ 175 lbs.
B. Mar. 3, 1925, Reading, Pa.

Year	Team		W	L	PCT	ERA	G	GS	CG	IP	H	BB	SO	ShO	Relief Pitching W	L	SV	Batting AB	H	HR	BA	PO	A	E	DP	TC/G	FA
1943	PHI	N	0	0	—	3.38	9	0	0	18.2	23	9	5	0	0	0	0	2	0	0	.000	1	3	0	0	0.4	1.000

Red Faber

FABER, URBAN CHARLES BB TR 6′ 2″ 180 lbs.
B. Sept. 6, 1888, Cascade, Iowa D. Sept. 25, 1976, Chicago, Ill. BR 1925
Hall of Fame 1964.

Year	Team		W	L	PCT	ERA	G	GS	CG	IP	H	BB	SO	ShO	Relief Pitching W	L	SV	Batting AB	H	HR	BA	PO	A	E	DP	TC/G	FA
1914	CHI	A	10	9	.526	2.68	40	20	11	181.1	154	64	88	2	2	2	**4**	55	8	0	.145	7	58	2	3	1.7	.970
1915			24	14	.632	2.55	**50**	32	22	299.2	264	99	182	3	**5**	**4**	2	84	11	0	.131	7	85	8	4	2.0	.920
1916			17	9	.654	2.02	35	25	15	205.1	167	61	87	3	2	1	1	63	6	0	.095	3	71	5	1	2.3	.937
1917			16	13	.552	1.92	41	29	16	248	224	85	84	3	2	3	3	69	4	0	.058	13	84	8	0	2.6	.924
1918			4	1	.800	1.23	11	9	5	80.2	70	23	26	1	0	0	1	24	1	0	.042	1	29	1	1	2.8	.968
1919			11	9	.550	3.83	25	20	9	162.1	185	45	45	0	3	0	0	54	10	0	.185	6	48	5	1	2.4	.915
1920			23	13	.639	2.99	40	**39**	28	319	332	88	108	2	0	0	1	104	11	0	.106	15	78	10	5	2.6	.903
1921			25	15	.625	**2.48**	43	39	**32**	330.2	293	87	124	4	1	1	1	108	16	0	.148	10	90	5	3	2.4	.952
1922			21	17	.553	**2.80**	43	38	**31**	**353**	334	83	148	4	1	1	2	125	25	0	.200	4	94	4	1	2.4	.961
1923			14	11	.560	3.41	32	31	15	232.1	233	62	91	2	0	1	0	69	15	1	.217	8	70	4	3	2.6	.951
1924			9	11	.450	3.85	21	20	9	161.1	173	58	47	0	0	1	0	54	8	0	.148	4	31	1	1	1.7	.972
1925			12	11	.522	3.78	34	32	16	238	266	59	71	1	1	1	0	77	8	0	.104	13	67	4	1	2.5	.952
1926			15	9	.625	3.56	27	25	13	184.2	203	57	65	1	0	2	0	60	9	0	.150	1	33	2	1	1.3	.944
1927			4	7	.364	4.55	18	15	6	110.2	131	41	39	0	0	0	0	37	10	0	.270	5	37	0	1	2.3	1.000
1928			13	9	.591	3.75	27	27	16	201.1	223	68	43	2	0	0	0	70	8	1	.114	11	52	1	2	2.4	.984
1929			13	13	.500	3.88	31	31	15	234	241	61	68	1	0	0	0	78	10	1	.128	7	61	2	1	2.3	.971
1930			8	13	.381	4.21	29	26	10	169	188	49	62	0	0	0	1	49	2	0	.041	3	47	1	2	1.8	.980
1931			10	14	.417	3.82	44	19	5	184	210	57	49	1	5	2	1	53	4	0	.075	6	33	3	0	1.0	.929
1932			2	11	.154	3.74	42	5	0	106	123	38	26	0	2	6	6	18	4	0	.222	3	21	1	1	0.6	.960
1933			3	4	.429	3.44	36	2	0	86.1	92	28	18	0	3	2	5	18	0	0	.000	3	19	4	1	0.7	.846
20 yrs.			254	213	.544	3.15	669	484	274	4087.2	4106	1213	1471	30	27	27	28	1269	170	3	.134	130	1108	71	33	2.0	.946
WORLD SERIES																											
1917	CHI	A	3	1	.750	2.33	4	3	2	27	21	3	9	0	1	0	0	7	1	0	.143	1	9	0	2	2.5	1.000

Roy Face

FACE, ELROY LEON BR TR 5′ 8″ 155 lbs.
B. Feb. 20, 1928, Stephentown, N. Y. BB 1960–1969

Year	Team		W	L	PCT	ERA	G	GS	CG	IP	H	BB	SO	ShO	Relief Pitching W	L	SV	Batting AB	H	HR	BA	PO	A	E	DP	TC/G	FA
1953	PIT	N	6	8	.429	6.58	41	13	2	119	145	30	56	0	3	2	0	30	4	0	.133	11	12	0	1	0.6	1.000
1955			5	7	.417	3.58	42	10	4	125.2	128	40	84	0	1	1	5	26	3	0	.115	14	13	1	1	0.7	.964
1956			12	13	.480	3.52	**68**	3	0	135.1	131	42	96	0	11	**12**	6	26	5	0	.192	10	25	1	2	0.5	.972
1957			4	6	.400	3.07	59	1	0	93.2	97	24	53	0	4	6	10	16	2	0	.125	4	9	0	0	0.2	1.000
1958			5	2	.714	2.89	57	0	0	84	77	22	47	0	5	2	**20**	7	0	0	.000	6	18	0	0	0.4	1.000
1959			18	1	**.947**[1]	2.70	57	0	0	93.1	91	25	69	0	**18**[1]	1	10	13	3	0	.231	7	12	1	0	0.4	.950
1960			10	8	.556	2.90	**68**	0	0	114.2	93	29	72	0	10	8	24	17	7	0	.412	12	21	0	1	0.5	1.000
1961			6	12	.333	3.82	62	0	0	92	94	10	55	0	6	**12**	**17**	11	3	0	.273	13	22	3	2	0.6	.921
1962			8	7	.533	1.88	63	0	0	91	74	18	45	0	8	7	**28**	12	1	0	.083	4	12	2	3	0.3	.889
1963			3	9	.250	3.23	56	0	0	69.2	75	19	41	0	3	**9**	16	8	2	0	.250	6	17	3	1	0.5	.885
1964			3	3	.500	5.20	55	0	0	79.2	82	27	63	0	3	3	4	4	0	0	.000	8	11	0	1	0.3	1.000
1965			5	2	.714	2.66	16	0	0	20.1	20	7	19	0	5	2	0	1	0	0	.000	0	1	0	0	0.1	1.000
1966			6	6	.500	2.70	54	0	0	70	68	24	67	0	6	6	18	11	0	0	.000	2	15	2	1	0.4	.895
1967			7	5	.583	2.42	61	0	0	74.1	62	22	41	0	7	5	17	6	0	0	.000	2	10	0	1	0.2	1.000
1968	**2 teams**	**PIT N** (43G 2–4)	**DET A** (2G 0–0)																								
″	**total**		2	4	.333	2.55	45	0	0	53	48	8	35	0	2	4	13	4	0	0	.000	2	7	1	1	0.2	.900
1969	MON	N	4	2	.667	3.94	44	0	0	59.1	62	15	34	0	4	2	5	2	1	0	.500	3	7	0	0	0.2	1.000
16 yrs.			104	95	.523	3.48	848	27	6	1375	1347	362	877	0	96 **6th**	82	193	194	31	0	.160	104	212	14	15	0.4	.958
WORLD SERIES																											
1960	PIT	N	0	0	—	5.23	4	0	0	10.1	9	2	4	0	0	0	3 **4th**	3	0	0	.000	0	2	0	0	0.5	1.000

Tony Faeth

FAETH, ANTHONY JOSEPH BR TR 6′ 180 lbs.
B. July 9, 1893, Aberdeen, S. D. D. Dec. 22, 1982, St. Paul, Minn.

Year	Team		W	L	PCT	ERA	G	GS	CG	IP	H	BB	SO	ShO	Relief Pitching W	L	SV	Batting AB	H	HR	BA	PO	A	E	DP	TC/G	FA
1919	CLE	A	0	0	—	0.49	6	0	0	18.1	13	10	7	0	0	0	0	4	0	0	.000	0	4	0	0	0.7	1.000
1920			0	0	—	4.32	13	0	0	25	31	20	14	0	0	0	0	5	0	0	.000	0	6	0	0	0.5	1.000
2 yrs.			0	0		2.70	19	0	0	43.1	44	30	21	0	0	0	0	9	0	0	.000	0	10	0	0	0.5	1.000

Bill Fagan

FAGAN, WILLIAM A. (Clinkers) TL 5′11″ 165 lbs.
B. Feb. 15, 1869, Troy, N. Y. D. Mar. 21, 1930, Troy, N. Y.

Year	Team		W	L	PCT	ERA	G	GS	CG	IP	H	BB	SO	ShO	Relief Pitching W	L	SV	Batting AB	H	HR	BA	PO	A	E	DP	TC/G	FA
1887	NY	AA	1	4	.200	*4.00*	6	6	6	45	55	24	12	0	0	0	0	21	3	0	.143	1	11	2	0	2.3	.857
1888	KC	AA	5	11	.313	5.69	17	17	15	142.1	179	75	49	0	0	0	0	65	14	0	.215	7	37	8	2	2.7	.846
2 yrs.			6	15	.286	5.28	23	23	21	187.1	234	99	61	0	0	0	0	86	17	0	.198	8	48	10	2	2.6	.848

Everett Fagan

FAGAN, EVERETT JOSEPH BR TR 6′ 195 lbs.
B. Jan. 13, 1918, Pottersville, N. J. D. Feb. 16, 1983, Morristown, N. J.

Year	Team		W	L	PCT	ERA	G	GS	CG	IP	H	BB	SO	ShO	Relief Pitching W	L	SV	Batting AB	H	HR	BA	PO	A	E	DP	TC/G	FA
1943	PHI	A	2	6	.250	6.27	18	2	0	37.1	41	14	9	0	2	4	3	7	0	0	.000	2	10	1	0	0.7	.923
1946			0	1	.000	4.80	20	0	0	45	47	24	12	0	0	1	0	14	4	0	.286	2	7	1	0	0.5	.900
2 yrs.			2	7	.222	5.47	38	2	0	82.1	88	38	21	0	2	5	3	21	4	0	.190	4	17	2	0	0.6	.913

Frank Fahey

FAHEY, FRANCIS RAYMOND BB TR 6′ 1″ 190 lbs.
B. Jan. 22, 1896, Milford, Mass. D. Mar. 19, 1954, Boston, Mass.

Year	Team		W	L	PCT	ERA	G	GS	CG	IP	H	BB	SO	ShO	Relief W	Relief L	Relief SV	Batting AB	Batting H	Batting HR	BA	PO	A	E	DP	TC/G	FA
1918	PHI	A	0	0	—	6.00	3	0	0	9	5	14	1	0	0	0	0					4	0	0	0	0.5	1.000

Red Fahr

FAHR, GERALD WARREN BR TR 6′ 5″ 185 lbs.
B. Dec. 9, 1924, Marmaduke, Ark.

Year	Team		W	L	PCT	ERA	G	GS	CG	IP	H	BB	SO	ShO	Relief W	Relief L	Relief SV	Batting AB	Batting H	Batting HR	BA	PO	A	E	DP	TC/G	FA
1951	CLE	A	0	0	—	4.76	5	0	0	5.2	11	2	0	0	0	0	0	0	0	0	—	0	1	0	0	0.2	1.000

Pete Fahrer

FAHRER, CLARENCE WILLIE BL TR 6′ 190 lbs.
B. Mar. 10, 1890, Holgate, Ohio D. June 10, 1967, Fremont, Mich.

Year	Team		W	L	PCT	ERA	G	GS	CG	IP	H	BB	SO	ShO	Relief W	Relief L	Relief SV	Batting AB	Batting H	Batting HR	BA	PO	A	E	DP	TC/G	FA
1914	CIN	N	0	0	—	1.13	5	0	0	8	8	4	2	0	0	0	0	1	0	0	.000	1	3	0	1	0.8	1.000

Jim Fairbank

FAIRBANK, JAMES LEE (Lee, Smoky) BR TR 5′10″ 185 lbs.
B. Mar. 17, 1881, Deansboro, N. Y. D. Dec. 27, 1955, Utica, N. Y.

Year	Team		W	L	PCT	ERA	G	GS	CG	IP	H	BB	SO	ShO	Relief W	Relief L	Relief SV	Batting AB	Batting H	Batting HR	BA	PO	A	E	DP	TC/G	FA
1903	PHI	A	1	1	.500	4.88	4	1	1	24	33	12	10	0	0	1	0	10	1	0	.100	4	10	0	0	3.5	1.000
1904			0	1	.000	6.35	3	1	1	17	19	13	6	0	0	0	0	6	0	0	.000	0	10	0	0	3.3	1.000
2 yrs.			1	2	.333	5.49	7	2	2	41	52	25	16	0	0	1	0	16	1	0	.063	4	20	0	0	3.4	1.000

Rags Faircloth

FAIRCLOTH, JAMES LAMAR BR TR 5′11″ 160 lbs.
B. Aug. 19, 1892, Kenton, Tenn. D. Oct. 5, 1953, Tucson, Ariz.

Year	Team		W	L	PCT	ERA	G	GS	CG	IP	H	BB	SO	ShO	Relief W	Relief L	Relief SV	Batting AB	Batting H	Batting HR	BA	PO	A	E	DP	TC/G	FA
1919	PHI	N	0	0	—	9.00	2	0	0	2	5	0	0	0	0	0	0	0	0	0	—	0	1	0	0	0.5	1.000

Hector Fajardo

FAJARDO, HECTOR BR TR 6′ 4″ 185 lbs.
Born Hector Fajardo (Nabaratte).
B. Nov. 16, 1970, Sahuayo, Mexico.

Year	Team		W	L	PCT	ERA	G	GS	CG	IP	H	BB	SO	ShO	Relief W	Relief L	Relief SV	Batting AB	Batting H	Batting HR	BA	PO	A	E	DP	TC/G	FA
1991	**2 teams**	**PIT N** (2G 0–0)	**TEX A** (4G 0–2)																								
″	**total**		0	2	.000	6.75	6	5	0	25.1	35	11	23	0	0	0	0	3	0	0	.000	1	1	0	0	0.3	1.000
1993	TEX	A	0	0	—	0.00	1	0	0	0.2	0	0	1	0	0	0	0	0	0	0	—	0	0	0	0	0.0	.000
1994			5	7	.417	6.91	18	12	0	83.1	95	26	45	0	0	0	0	0	0	0	—	3	11	0	0	0.8	1.000
1995			0	0	—	7.80	5	0	0	15	19	5	9	0	0	0	0	0	0	0	—	0	3	0	0	0.8	1.000
4 yrs.			5	9	.357	6.95	30	17	0	124.1	149	42	78	0	0	0	0	3	0	0	.000	4	15	0	0	0.7	1.000

Pete Falcone

FALCONE, PETER BL TL 6′ 2″ 185 lbs.
B. Oct. 1, 1953, Brooklyn, N. Y.

Year	Team		W	L	PCT	ERA	G	GS	CG	IP	H	BB	SO	ShO	Relief W	Relief L	Relief SV	Batting AB	Batting H	Batting HR	BA	PO	A	E	DP	TC/G	FA
1975	SF	N	12	11	.522	4.17	34	32	3	190	171	111	131	1	0	0	0	65	4	0	.062	2	29	2	0	1.0	.939
1976	STL	N	12	16	.429	3.23	32	32	9	212	173	93	138	2	0	0	0	62	8	0	.129	3	14	0	0	0.5	1.000
1977			4	8	.333	5.44	27	22	1	124	130	61	75	1	0	1	1	41	10	0	.244	4	15	0	1	0.7	1.000
1978			2	7	.222	5.76	19	14	0	75	94	48	28	0	0	0	0	21	5	0	.238	0	7	2	0	0.5	.778
1979	NY	N	6	14	.300	4.16	33	31	1	184	194	76	113	1	0	0	0	52	9	0	.173	3	14	1	1	0.5	.944
1980			7	10	.412	4.53	37	23	1	157	163	58	109	0	1	1	1	41	6	0	.146	1	12	0	0	0.4	1.000
1981			5	3	.625	2.56	35	9	3	95	84	36	56	1	2	1	1	22	4	1	.182	2	9	1	0	0.3	.917
1982			8	10	.444	3.84	40	23	3	171	159	71	101	0	1	1	2	53	6	0	.113	2	16	0	1	0.4	1.000
1983	ATL	N	9	4	.692	3.63	33	15	2	106.2	102	60	59	0	3	1	0	26	3	0	.115	1	11	0	0	0.4	1.000
1984			5	7	.417	4.13	35	16	2	120	115	57	55	1	1	0	2	33	7	0	.212	0	17	1	0	0.5	.944
10 yrs.			70	90	.438	4.07	325	217	25	1434.2	1385	671	865	7	8	5	7	416	62	1	.149	18	144	7	3	0.5	.959

Chet Falk

FALK, CHESTER EMANUEL (Spot) BL TL 6′ 2″ 170 lbs.
Brother of Bibb Falk.
B. May 15, 1905, Austin, Tex. D. Jan. 7, 1982, Austin, Tex.

Year	Team		W	L	PCT	ERA	G	GS	CG	IP	H	BB	SO	ShO	Relief W	Relief L	Relief SV	Batting AB	Batting H	Batting HR	BA	PO	A	E	DP	TC/G	FA
1925	STL	A	0	0	—	8.28	13	0	0	25	38	17	7	0	0	0	0	8	5	0	.625	0	8	0	0	0.6	1.000
1926			4	4	.500	5.35	18	8	3	74	95	27	7	0	1	0	0	31	6	0	.194	3	16	1	4	1.1	.950
1927			1	0	1.000	5.74	9	0	0	15.2	25	10	2	0	1	0	0	5	1	0	.200	2	5	0	0	0.8	1.000
3 yrs.			5	4	.556	6.04	40	8	3	114.2	158	54	16	0	2	0	0	44	12	0	.273	5	29	1	4	0.9	.971

Cy Falkenberg

FALKENBERG, FREDERICK PETER BR TR 6′5″ 180 lbs.
B. Dec. 17, 1880, Chicago, Ill. D. Apr. 14, 1961, San Francisco, Calif.

Year	Team		W	L	PCT	ERA	G	GS	CG	IP	H	BB	SO	ShO	Relief W	Relief L	Relief SV	Batting AB	Batting H	Batting HR	BA	PO	A	E	DP	TC/G	FA
1903	PIT	N	2	4	.333	3.86	10	6	3	56	65	32	24	0	0	0	0	21	4	0	.190	7	21	3	0	3.1	.903
1905	WAS	A	7	2	.778	3.82	12	10	6	75.1	71	31	35	2	1	0	0	32	4	0	.125	6	17	2	1	2.1	.920
1906			14	20	.412	2.86	40	36	30	298.2	277	**108**	178	2	0	0	1	106	18	1	.170	12	92	8	3	2.8	.929
1907			6	17	.261	2.35	32	24	17	233.2	195	77	108	1	0	2	0	86	12	0	.140	10	82	6	2	3.1	.939
1908	**2 teams**	**WAS A** (17G 6–2)	**CLE A** (8G 2–4)																								
″	**total**		8	6	.571	2.65	25	15	7	129	122	31	51	1	1	0	0	44	8	0	.182	3	42	1	0	1.8	.978
1909	CLE	A	10	9	.526	2.40	24	18	13	165	135	50	82	2	0	1	0	52	9	0	.173	12	61	4	1	3.2	.948
1910			14	13	.519	2.95	37	29	18	256.2	246	75	107	3	3	0	1	82	15	0	.183	14	97	4	3	3.1	.965
1911			8	5	.615	3.29	15	13	7	106.2	117	24	46	0	0	1	1	40	7	0	.175	4	33	3	1	2.7	.925
1913			23	10	.697	2.22	39	36	23	276	238	88	166	6	0	0	0	84	10	0	.119	8	69	7	1	2.2	.917
1914	IND	F	25	16	.610	2.22	**49**	**43**	33	**377.1**	332	89	**236**	**9**	0	2	3	125	21	0	.168	20	113	5	5	2.8	.964
1915	**2 teams**	**NWK F** (25G 9–11)	**BKN F** (7G 3–3)																								
″	**total**		12	14	.462	2.86	32	28	19	220	206	59	96	1	1	0	1	72	4	0	.056	6	71	4	4	2.5	.951
1917	PHI	A	2	6	.250	3.35	15	8	4	80.2	86	26	35	0	0	1	0	27	5	0	.185	2	30	5	5	2.5	.865
12 yrs.			131	122	.518	2.68	330	266	180	2275	2090	690	1164	27	6	7	7	771	117	1	.152	104	728	52	26	2.7	.941

Ed Fallenstin

FALLENSTIN, EDWARD JOSEPH (Jack) BR TR 6′ 3″ 180 lbs.
Born Edward Joseph Valestin.
B. Dec. 22, 1908, Newark, N. J. D. Nov. 24, 1971, Orange, N. J.

Year	Team		W	L	PCT	ERA	G	GS	CG	IP	H	BB	SO	ShO	Relief W	Relief L	Relief SV	Batting AB	Batting H	Batting HR	BA	PO	A	E	DP	TC/G	FA
1931	PHI	N	0	0	—	7.13	24	0	0	41.2	56	26	15	0	0	0	0	5	1	0	.200	3	9	1	0	0.5	.923
1933	BOS	N	2	1	.667	3.60	9	4	1	35	43	13	5	1	0	0	0	8	3	0	.375	1	7	1	0	1.0	.889
2 yrs.			2	1	.667	5.52	33	4	1	76.2	99	39	20	1	0	0	0	13	4	0	.308	4	16	2	0	0.7	.909

Bob Fallon

FALLON, ROBERT JOSEPH BL TL 6′ 3″ 200 lbs.
B. Feb. 18, 1960, Bronx, N. Y.

Year	Team		W	L	PCT	ERA	G	GS	CG	IP	H	BB	SO	ShO	Relief W	Relief L	Relief SV	Batting AB	Batting H	Batting HR	BA	PO	A	E	DP	TC/G	FA
1984	CHI	A	0	0	—	3.68	3	3	0	14.2	12	11	10	0	0	0	0	0	0	0	—	1	3	0	0	1.3	1.000
1985			0	0	—	6.19	10	0	0	16	25	9	17	0	0	0	0	0	0	0	—	2	3	0	1	0.5	1.000
2 yrs.			0	0		4.99	13	3	0	30.2	37	20	27	0	0	0	0	0	0	0		3	6	0	1	0.7	1.000

Cliff Fannin

FANNIN, CLIFFORD BRYSON (Mule) BL TR 6′ 170 lbs.
B. May 13, 1924, Louisa, Ky. D. Dec. 11, 1966, Sandusky, Ohio.

Year	Team	W	L	PCT	ERA	G	GS	CG	IP	H	BB	SO	ShO	Relief W	Relief L	Relief SV	AB	H	HR	BA	PO	A	E	DP	TC/G	FA
1945	STL A	0	0	—	2.61	5	0	0	10.1	8	5	5	0	0	0	0	1	0	0	.000	0	1	0	1	0.2	1.000
1946		5	2	.714	3.01	27	7	4	86.2	76	42	52	1	0	0	2	31	5	0	.161	3	13	0	1	0.6	1.000
1947		6	8	.429	3.58	26	18	6	145.2	134	77	77	2	0	0	1	46	9	0	.196	10	23	2	1	1.3	.943
1948		10	14	.417	4.17	34	29	10	213.2	198	104	102	3	0	0	1	65	11	0	.169	10	24	2	3	1.1	.944
1949		8	14	.364	6.17	30	25	5	143	177	93	57	0	0	2	1	55	9	0	.164	4	15	0	0	0.6	1.000
1950		5	9	.357	6.53	25	16	3	102	116	58	42	0	2	1	1	34	6	0	.176	3	17	2	2	0.9	.909
1951		0	2	.000	6.46	7	1	0	15.1	20	5	11	0	0	2	0	4	1	0	.250	2	2	0	0	0.6	1.000
1952		0	2	.000	12.67	10	2	0	16.1	34	9	6	0	0	0	0	1	0	0	.000	0	1	0	0	0.1	1.000
8 yrs.		34	51	.400	4.85	164	98	28	733	763	393	352	6	2	5	6	237	41	0	.173	32	96	6	8	0.8	.955

Jack Fanning

FANNING, JOHN JACOB TR 5′ 9″ 163 lbs.
B. 1863, South Orange, N. J. D. June 10, 1917, Aberdeen, Wash.

Year	Team	W	L	PCT	ERA	G	GS	CG	IP	H	BB	SO	ShO	Relief W	Relief L	Relief SV	AB	H	HR	BA	PO	A	E	DP	TC/G	FA
1889	IND N	0	1	.000	18.00	1	1	0	1	3	2	0	0	0	0	0	1	0	0	.000	0	1	0	0	1.0	1.000
1894	PHI N	1	3	.250	8.07	5	4	2	32.1	45	20	7	0	0	0	0	13	2	0	.154	1	6	2	0	1.8	.778
2 yrs.		1	4	.200	8.37	6	5	2	33.1	48	22	7	0	0	0	0	14	2	0	.143	1	7	2	0	1.7	.800

Harry Fanok

FANOK, HARRY MICHAEL (The Flame Thrower) BB TR 6′ 180 lbs.
B. May 11, 1940, Whippany, N. J.

Year	Team	W	L	PCT	ERA	G	GS	CG	IP	H	BB	SO	ShO	Relief W	Relief L	Relief SV	AB	H	HR	BA	PO	A	E	DP	TC/G	FA
1963	STL N	2	1	.667	5.26	12	0	0	25.2	24	21	25	0	2	1	1	5	2	0	.400	2	3	1	0	0.5	.833
1964		0	0	—	5.87	4	0	0	7.2	5	3	10	0	0	0	0	1	0	0	.000	0	1	1	0	0.5	.500
2 yrs.		2	1	.667	5.40	16	0	0	33.1	29	24	35	0	2	1	1	6	2	0	.333	2	4	2	0	0.5	.750

Frank Fanovich

FANOVICH, FRANK JOSEPH (Lefty) BL TL 5′11″ 180 lbs.
B. Jan. 11, 1922, New York, N. Y.

Year	Team	W	L	PCT	ERA	G	GS	CG	IP	H	BB	SO	ShO	Relief W	Relief L	Relief SV	AB	H	HR	BA	PO	A	E	DP	TC/G	FA
1949	CIN N	0	2	.000	5.40	29	1	0	43.1	44	28	27	0	0	1	0	4	0	0	.000	1	9	2	1	0.4	.833
1953	PHI A	0	3	.000	5.55	26	3	0	61.2	62	37	37	0	0	1	0	11	2	0	.182	2	8	2	0	0.5	.833
2 yrs.		0	5	.000	5.49	55	4	0	105	106	65	64	0	0	2	0	15	2	0	.133	3	17	4	1	0.4	.833

Stan Fansler

FANSLER, STANLEY ROBERT BR TR 5′11″ 180 lbs.
B. Feb. 12, 1965, Elkins, W. Va.

Year	Team	W	L	PCT	ERA	G	GS	CG	IP	H	BB	SO	ShO	Relief W	Relief L	Relief SV	AB	H	HR	BA	PO	A	E	DP	TC/G	FA
1986	PIT N	0	3	.000	3.75	5	5	0	24	20	15	13	0	0	0	0	6	1	0	.167	5	1	0	1	1.2	1.000

Harry Fanwell

FANWELL, HARRY CLAYTON BB TR 6′ 175 lbs.
B. Oct. 16, 1886, Patapsco, Md. D. July 15, 1965, Baltimore, Md.

Year	Team	W	L	PCT	ERA	G	GS	CG	IP	H	BB	SO	ShO	Relief W	Relief L	Relief SV	AB	H	HR	BA	PO	A	E	DP	TC/G	FA
1910	CLE A	2	9	.182	3.62	17	11	5	92	87	38	30	1	1	0	0	30	1	0	.033	2	36	0	0	2.2	1.000

Ed Farmer

FARMER, EDWARD JOSEPH BR TR 6′ 5″ 200 lbs.
B. Oct. 18, 1949, Evergreen Park, Ill.

Year	Team	W	L	PCT	ERA	G	GS	CG	IP	H	BB	SO	ShO	Relief W	Relief L	Relief SV	AB	H	HR	BA	PO	A	E	DP	TC/G	FA
1971	CLE A	5	4	.556	4.33	43	4	0	79	77	41	48	0	5	2	4	14	1	0	.071	2	12	0	2	0.3	1.000
1972		2	5	.286	4.43	46	1	0	61	51	27	33	0	2	4	7	7	1	0	.143	4	12	1	0	0.4	.941
1973	2 teams CLE A (16G 0–2) DET A (24G 3–0)																									
″	total	3	2	.600	4.91	40	0	0	62.1	77	32	38	0	3	2	3	0	0	0		4	3	0	1	0.2	1.000
1974	PHI N	2	1	.667	8.42	14	3	0	31	41	27	20	0	1	0	0	9	1	0	.111	0	4	1	0	0.4	.800
1977	BAL A	0	0	—	∞	1	0	0		1	1	0	0	0	0	0	0	0	0	—	0	0	0	0	0.0	.000
1978	MIL A	1	0	1.000	0.82	3	0	0	11	7	4	6	0	1	0	1	0	0	0	—	1	1	0	0	0.7	1.000
1979	2 teams TEX A (11G 2–0) CHI A (42G 3–7)																									
″	total	5	7	.417	3.00	53	5	0	114	96	53	73	0	5	7	14	0	0	0		9	15	0	1	0.5	1.000
1980	CHI A	7	9	.438	3.33	64	0	0	100	92	56	54	0	7	9	30	0	0	0	—	5	17	0	4	0.3	1.000
1981		3	3	.500	4.58	42	0	0	53	53	34	42	0	3	3	10	0	0	0	—	5	9	1	1	0.4	.933
1982	PHI N	2	6	.250	4.86	47	4	0	76	66	50	58	0	1	4	6	11	0	0	.000	1	12	0	1	0.3	1.000
1983	2 teams PHI N (12G 0–6) OAK A (5G 0–0)																									
″	total	0	6	.000	5.35	17	4	0	37	50	20	23	0	0	3	0	6	1	0	.167	3	5	0	0	0.5	1.000
11 yrs.		30	43	.411	4.30	370	21	0	624.1	611	345	395	0	28	34	75	47	4	0	.085	34	90	3	10	0.3	.976

Howard Farmer

FARMER, HOWARD EARL BR TR 6′ 3″ 185 lbs.
B. Jan. 18, 1966, Gary, Ind.

Year	Team	W	L	PCT	ERA	G	GS	CG	IP	H	BB	SO	ShO	Relief W	Relief L	Relief SV	AB	H	HR	BA	PO	A	E	DP	TC/G	FA
1990	MON N	0	3	.000	7.04	6	4	0	23	26	10	14	0	0	1	0	5	2	0	.400	1	7	0	1	1.3	1.000

Jimmy Farr

FARR, JAMES ALFRED BR TR 6′ 1″ 195 lbs.
B. May 18, 1956, Waverly, N. Y.

Year	Team	W	L	PCT	ERA	G	GS	CG	IP	H	BB	SO	ShO	Relief W	Relief L	Relief SV	AB	H	HR	BA	PO	A	E	DP	TC/G	FA
1982	TEX A	0	0	—	2.50	5	0	0	18	20	7	6	0	0	0	0	0	0	0	—	0	2	0	0	0.4	1.000

Steve Farr

FARR, STEVEN MICHAEL BR TR 5′10″ 190 lbs.
B. Dec. 12, 1956, Cheverly, Md.

Year	Team	W	L	PCT	ERA	G	GS	CG	IP	H	BB	SO	ShO	Relief W	Relief L	Relief SV	AB	H	HR	BA	PO	A	E	DP	TC/G	FA
1984	CLE A	3	11	.214	4.58	31	16	0	116	106	46	83	0	1	2	1	0	0	0	—	7	18	2	1	0.9	.926
1985	KC A	2	1	.667	3.11	16	3	0	37.2	34	20	36	0	1	0	1	0	0	0	—	3	6	0	0	0.6	1.000
1986		8	4	.667	3.13	56	0	0	109.1	90	39	83	0	8	4	8	0	0	0	—	8	16	0	1	0.4	1.000
1987		4	3	.571	4.15	47	0	0	91	97	44	88	0	4	3	1	0	0	0	—	3	6	2	0	0.2	.818
1988		5	4	.556	2.50	62	1	0	82.2	74	30	72	0	4	4	20	0	0	0	—	3	7	0	0	0.2	1.000
1989		2	5	.286	4.12	51	2	0	63.1	75	22	56	0	1	5	18	0	0	0	—	7	4	0	0	0.2	1.000
1990		13	7	.650	1.98	57	6	1	127	99	48	94	1	8	6	1	0	0	0	—	7	18	2	1	0.5	.926
1991	NY A	5	5	.500	2.19	60	0	0	70	57	20	60	0	5	5	23	0	0	0	—	7	11	0	1	0.3	1.000
1992		2	2	.500	1.56	50	0	0	52	34	19	37	0	2	2	30	0	0	0	—	2	4	2	0	0.2	.750
1993		2	2	.500	4.21	49	0	0	47	44	28	39	0	2	2	25	0	0	0	—	6	10	0	0	0.3	1.000
1994	2 teams CLE A (19G 1–1) BOS A (11G 1–0)																									
″	total	2	1	.667	5.72	30	0	0	28.1	41	18	20	0	2	1	4	0	0	0		2	2	1	0	0.2	.800
11 yrs.		48	45	.516	3.25	509	28	1	824.1	751	334	668	1	38	34	132	0	0	0		55	102	9	4	0.3	.946
LEAGUE CHAMPIONSHIP SERIES																										
1985	KC A	1	0	1.000	1.42	2	0	0	6.1	4	1	3	0	1	0	0	0	0	0	—	0	1	0	1	0.5	1.000

Dick Farrell

FARRELL, RICHARD JOSEPH (Turk) BR TR 6′ 4″ 215 lbs.
B. Apr. 8, 1934, Boston, Mass. D. June 10, 1977, Great Yarmouth, England.

Year	Team	Lg	W	L	PCT	ERA	G	GS	CG	IP	H	BB	SO	ShO	Relief Pitching W	Relief Pitching L	Relief Pitching SV	Batting AB	Batting H	Batting HR	BA	PO	A	E	DP	TC/G	FA
1956	PHI	N	0	1	.000	12.46	1	1	0	4.1	6	3	0	0	0	0	0	1	0	0	.000	0	3	0	0	3.0	1.000
1957			10	2	.833	2.38	52	0	0	83.1	74	36	54	0	**10**	2	10	9	1	1	.111	3	16	1	0	0.4	.950
1958			8	9	.471	3.35	54	0	0	94	84	40	73	0	8	**9**	11	24	5	0	.208	2	8	2	0	0.2	.833
1959			1	6	.143	4.74	38	0	0	57	61	25	31	0	1	6	6	6	1	0	.167	2	8	0	0	0.3	1.000
1960			10	6	.625	2.70	59	0	0	103.1	88	29	70	0	10	6	11	15	3	0	.200	6	13	2	1	0.4	.905
1961	2 teams	PHI N (5G 2–1)	LA N (50G 6–6)																								
″	total		8	7	.533	5.20	55	0	0	98.2	117	49	90	0	8	7	10	20	1	0	.050	2	7	0	0	0.2	1.000
1962	HOU	N	10	20	.333	3.02	43	29	11	241.2	210	55	203	2	2	4	4	78	14	2	.179	10	28	2	1	0.9	.950
1963			14	13	.519	3.02	34	26	12	202.1	161	35	141	0	3	1	1	63	9	0	.143	9	27	0	1	1.1	1.000
1964			11	10	.524	3.27	32	27	7	198.1	196	52	117	0	0	1	0	69	5	0	.072	5	31	0	2	1.1	1.000
1965			11	11	.500	3.50	33	29	8	208.1	202	35	122	3	1	0	1	74	10	0	.135	9	30	3	3	1.3	.929
1966			6	10	.375	4.60	32	21	3	152.2	167	28	101	0	2	0	2	48	7	1	.146	11	13	2	1	0.8	.923
1967	2 teams	HOU N (7G 1–0)	PHI N (50G 9–6)																								
″	total		10	6	.625	2.34	57	1	0	103.2	87	22	78	0	**10**	5	12	20	2	0	.100	3	12	1	0	0.3	.938
1968	PHI	N	4	6	.400	3.48	54	0	0	82.2	83	32	57	0	4	6	12	6	1	0	.167	0	14	1	0	0.3	.933
1969			3	4	.429	4.01	46	0	0	74	92	27	40	0	3	4	3	3	0	0	.000	2	2	0	0	0.1	1.000
14 yrs.			106	111	.488	3.45	590	134	41	1704.1	1628	468	1177	5	62	51	83	436	59	4	.135	64	212	14	9	0.5	.952

John Farrell

FARRELL, JOHN EDWARD BR TR 6′ 4″ 210 lbs.
B. Aug. 4, 1962, Monmouth Beach, N. J.

Year	Team	Lg	W	L	PCT	ERA	G	GS	CG	IP	H	BB	SO	ShO	Relief Pitching W	Relief Pitching L	Relief Pitching SV	Batting AB	Batting H	Batting HR	BA	PO	A	E	DP	TC/G	FA
1987	CLE	A	5	1	.833	3.39	10	9	1	69	68	22	28	0	1	0	0	0	0	0	—	8	7	2	1	1.7	.882
1988			14	10	.583	4.24	31	30	4	210.1	216	67	92	0	0	0	0	0	0	0	—	21	23	0	2	1.4	1.000
1989			9	14	.391	3.63	31	31	7	208	196	71	132	2	0	0	0	0	0	0	—	18	20	2	1	1.3	.950
1990			4	5	.444	4.28	17	17	1	96.2	108	33	44	0	0	0	0	0	0	0	—	8	12	2	1	1.3	.909
1993	CAL	A	3	12	.200	7.35	21	17	0	90.2	110	44	45	0	0	1	0	0	0	0	—	5	11	0	0	0.8	1.000
1994			1	2	.333	9.00	3	3	0	13	16	8	10	0	0	0	0	0	0	0	—	1	6	1	1	2.7	.875
1995	CLE	A	0	0	—	3.86	1	0	0	4.2	7	0	4	0	0	0	0	0	0	0	—	1	0	1	1	2.0	.500
7 yrs.			36	44	.450	4.47	114	107	13	692.1	721	245	355	2	1	1	0	0	0	0		62	79	8	7	1.3	.946

Kerby Farrell

FARRELL, MAJOR KERBY BL TL 5′11″ 172 lbs.
B. Sept. 3, 1913, Leapwood, Tenn. D. Dec. 17, 1975, Nashville, Tenn.
Manager 1957.

Year	Team	Lg	W	L	PCT	ERA	G	GS	CG	IP	H	BB	SO	ShO	Relief Pitching W	Relief Pitching L	Relief Pitching SV	Batting AB	Batting H	Batting HR	BA	PO	A	E	DP	TC/G	FA
1943	BOS	N	0	1	.000	4.30	5	0	0	23	24	9	4	0	0	1	0	*				740	55	4	62	10.8	.995

Jeff Fassero

FASSERO, JEFFREY JOSEPH BL TL 6′ 1″ 180 lbs.
B. Jan. 15, 1963, Springfield, Ill.

Year	Team	Lg	W	L	PCT	ERA	G	GS	CG	IP	H	BB	SO	ShO	Relief Pitching W	Relief Pitching L	Relief Pitching SV	Batting AB	Batting H	Batting HR	BA	PO	A	E	DP	TC/G	FA
1991	MON	N	2	5	.286	2.44	51	0	0	55.1	39	17	42	0	2	5	8	3	0	0	.000	3	11	1	1	0.3	.933
1992			8	7	.533	2.84	70	0	0	85.2	81	34	63	0	8	7	1	7	1	0	.143	1	15	0	0	0.2	1.000
1993			12	5	.706	2.29	56	15	1	149.2	119	54	140	0	5	1	1	32	2	0	.063	5	22	3	0	0.5	.900
1994			8	6	.571	2.99	21	21	1	138.2	119	40	119	0	0	0	0	44	3	0	.068	9	33	0	1	2.0	1.000
1995			13	14	.481	4.33	30	30	1	189	207	74	164	0	0	0	0	57	4	0	.070	7	35	4	1	1.5	.913
5 yrs.			43	37	.538	3.16	228	66	3	618.1	565	219	528	0	15	13	10	143	10	0	.070	25	116	8	3	0.7	.946

Fast

FAST
B. Milwaukee, Wis. Deceased.

Year	Team	Lg	W	L	PCT	ERA	G	GS	CG	IP	H	BB	SO	ShO	Relief Pitching W	Relief Pitching L	Relief Pitching SV	Batting AB	Batting H	Batting HR	BA	PO	A	E	DP	TC/G	FA
1887	IND	N	0	1	.000	10.34	4	2	1	15.2	25	8	0	0	0	0	**1**	11	2	0	.182	1	5	0	0	1.2	1.000

Darcy Fast

FAST, DARCY RAE BL TL 6′ 3″ 195 lbs.
B. Mar. 10, 1947, Dallas, Ore.

Year	Team	Lg	W	L	PCT	ERA	G	GS	CG	IP	H	BB	SO	ShO	Relief Pitching W	Relief Pitching L	Relief Pitching SV	Batting AB	Batting H	Batting HR	BA	PO	A	E	DP	TC/G	FA
1968	CHI	N	0	1	.000	5.40	8	1	0	10	8	8	10	0	0	1	0	3	0	0	.000	1	1	0	0	0.3	1.000

Jack Faszholz

FASZHOLZ, JOHN EDWARD (Preacher) BR TR 6′ 3″ 205 lbs.
B. Apr. 11, 1927, St. Louis, Mo.

Year	Team	Lg	W	L	PCT	ERA	G	GS	CG	IP	H	BB	SO	ShO	Relief Pitching W	Relief Pitching L	Relief Pitching SV	Batting AB	Batting H	Batting HR	BA	PO	A	E	DP	TC/G	FA
1953	STL	N	0	0	—	6.94	4	1	0	11.2	16	1	7	0	0	0	0	3	0	0	.000	0	0	0	0	0.0	.000

Bill Faul

FAUL, WILLIAM ALVAN BR TR 5′10″ 184 lbs.
B. Apr. 21, 1940, Cincinnati, Ohio.

Year	Team	Lg	W	L	PCT	ERA	G	GS	CG	IP	H	BB	SO	ShO	Relief Pitching W	Relief Pitching L	Relief Pitching SV	Batting AB	Batting H	Batting HR	BA	PO	A	E	DP	TC/G	FA
1962	DET	A	0	0	—	32.40	1	0	0	1.2	4	3	2	0	0	0	0	0	0	0	—	0	0	0	0	0.0	.000
1963			5	6	.455	4.64	28	10	2	97	93	48	64	0	1	1	1	27	4	0	.148	3	6	0	0	0.3	1.000
1964			0	0	—	10.80	1	1	0	5	5	2	1	0	0	0	0	2	0	0	.000	0	0	0	0	0.0	.000
1965	CHI	N	6	6	.500	3.54	17	16	5	96.2	83	18	59	3	0	0	0	30	3	0	.100	5	10	3	0	1.1	.833
1966			1	4	.200	5.08	17	6	1	51.1	47	18	32	0	0	0	0	13	0	0	.000	5	4	1	0	0.6	.900
1970	SF	N	0	0	—	7.20	7	0	0	10	15	6	6	0	0	0	1	0	0	0	—	0	0	0	0	0.0	.000
6 yrs.			12	16	.429	4.71	71	33	8	261.2	247	95	164	3	1	1	2	72	7	0	.097	13	20	4	0	0.5	.892

Jim Faulkner

FAULKNER, JAMES LeROY (Lefty) BB TL 6′ 3″ 190 lbs.
B. July 27, 1899, Beatrice, Neb. D. June 1, 1962, West Palm Beach, Fla. BL 1927

Year	Team	Lg	W	L	PCT	ERA	G	GS	CG	IP	H	BB	SO	ShO	Relief Pitching W	Relief Pitching L	Relief Pitching SV	Batting AB	Batting H	Batting HR	BA	PO	A	E	DP	TC/G	FA
1927	NY	N	1	0	1.000	3.72	3	1	0	9.2	13	5	2	0	0	0	0	2	1	0	.500	1	1	0	0	0.7	1.000
1928			9	8	.529	3.53	38	8	3	117.1	131	41	32	0	**7**	6	2	39	9	0	.231	3	31	1	3	0.9	.971
1930	BKN	N	0	0	—	81.00	2	1	0	0.1	2	1	0	0	0	0	1	0	0	0	—	0	1	0	0	0.5	1.000
3 yrs.			10	8	.556	3.75	43	10	3	127.1	146	47	34	0	7	6	3	41	10	0	.244	4	33	1	3	0.9	.974

Buck Fausett

FAUSETT, ROBERT SHAW (Leaky) BL TR 5′10″ 170 lbs.
B. Apr. 8, 1908, Sheridan, Ark. D. May 2, 1994, College Station, Tex.

Year	Team	Lg	W	L	PCT	ERA	G	GS	CG	IP	H	BB	SO	ShO	Relief Pitching W	Relief Pitching L	Relief Pitching SV	Batting AB	Batting H	Batting HR	BA	PO	A	E	DP	TC/G	FA
1944	CIN	N	0	0	—	5.91	2	0	0	10.2	13	7	3	0	0	0	0	*				6	23	1	1	3.8	.967

Charlie Faust

FAUST, CHARLES VICTOR (Victory) BR TR 6′ 2″
B. Oct. 9, 1880, Marion, Kans. D. June 18, 1915, Fort Steilacoom, Wash.

Year	Team	Lg	W	L	PCT	ERA	G	GS	CG	IP	H	BB	SO	ShO	Relief Pitching W	Relief Pitching L	Relief Pitching SV	Batting AB	Batting H	Batting HR	BA	PO	A	E	DP	TC/G	FA
1911	NY	N	0	0	—	4.50	2	0	0	2	2	0	0	0	0	0	0	0	0	0	—	0	2	0	0	1.0	1.000

Clay Fauver

FAUVER, CLAYTON KING (Pop) BB TR 5′10″
B. Aug. 1, 1872, North Eaton, Ohio D. Mar. 3, 1942, Chatsworth, Ga.

Year	Team	Lg	W	L	PCT	ERA	G	GS	CG	IP	H	BB	SO	ShO	Relief Pitching W	Relief Pitching L	Relief Pitching SV	Batting AB	Batting H	Batting HR	BA	PO	A	E	DP	TC/G	FA
1899	LOU	N	1	0	1.000	0.00	1	1	1	9	11	2	1	0	0	0	0	4	0	0	.000	0	2	0	0	2.0	1.000

Vern Fear

FEAR, LUVERN CARL BB TR 6′ 170 lbs.
B. Aug. 21, 1924, Everly, Iowa D. Sept. 6, 1976, Spencer, Iowa.

Year	Team	Lg	W	L	PCT	ERA	G	GS	CG	IP	H	BB	SO	ShO	Relief Pitching W	Relief Pitching L	Relief Pitching SV	Batting AB	Batting H	Batting HR	BA	PO	A	E	DP	TC/G	FA
1952	**CHI**	**N**	0	0	—	7.88	4	0	0	8	9	3	4	0	0	0	0	1	0	0	.000	0	1	0	0	0.3	1.000

Jack Fee

FEE, JOHN
B. Dec. 23, 1867, Carbondale, Pa. D. Mar. 3, 1913, Carbondale, Pa.

Year	Team	Lg	W	L	PCT	ERA	G	GS	CG	IP	H	BB	SO	ShO	Relief Pitching W	Relief Pitching L	Relief Pitching SV	Batting AB	Batting H	Batting HR	BA	PO	A	E	DP	TC/G	FA
1889	**IND**	**N**	2	2	.500	4.28	7	3	2	40	39	31	10	0	1	0	0	21	3	0	.143	2	11	1	0	2.0	.929

Harry Feldman

FELDMAN, HARRY BR TR 6′ 175 lbs.
B. Nov. 10, 1919, New York, N. Y. D. Mar. 16, 1962, Ft. Smith, Ark.

Year	Team	Lg	W	L	PCT	ERA	G	GS	CG	IP	H	BB	SO	ShO	Relief Pitching W	Relief Pitching L	Relief Pitching SV	Batting AB	Batting H	Batting HR	BA	PO	A	E	DP	TC/G	FA
1941	**NY**	**N**	1	1	.500	3.98	3	3	1	20.1	21	6	9	1	0	0	0	6	1	0	.167	0	3	1	0	1.3	.750
1942			7	1	.875	3.16	31	6	2	114	100	73	49	1	5	0	0	39	11	1	.282	4	22	1	3	0.9	.963
1943			4	5	.444	4.30	31	10	1	104.2	114	58	49	0	2	0	0	30	4	0	.133	5	20	1	4	0.8	.962
1944			11	13	.458	4.16	40	27	8	205.1	214	91	70	1	2	2	2	73	15	0	.205	9	29	7	3	1.1	.844
1945			12	13	.480	3.27	35	30	10	217.2	213	69	74	3	0	2	1	72	7	1	.097	12	31	1	0	1.3	.977
1946			0	2	.000	18.00	3	2	0	4	9	3	3	0	0	0	0	1	0	0	.000	0	0	0	0	0.0	.000
6 yrs.			35	35	.500	3.80	143	78	22	666	671	300	254	6	9	4	3	221	38	2	.172	30	105	11	10	1.0	.925

Harry Felix

FELIX, HARRY BR TR 5′ 7½″ 160 lbs.
B. 1870, Brooklyn, N. Y. D. Oct. 17, 1961, Miami, Fla.

Year	Team	Lg	W	L	PCT	ERA	G	GS	CG	IP	H	BB	SO	ShO	Relief Pitching W	Relief Pitching L	Relief Pitching SV	Batting AB	Batting H	Batting HR	BA	PO	A	E	DP	TC/G	FA
1901	**NY**	**N**	0	0	—	0.00	1	0	0	2	3	0	0	0	0	0	0	1	0	0	.000	0	0	0	0	0.0	.000
1902	**PHI**	**N**	1	3	.250	5.60	9	5	3	45	61	11	10	0	0	0	0	37	5	0	.135	7	28	7	1	2.6	.833
2 yrs.			1	3	.250	5.36	10	5	3	47	64	11	10	0	0	0	0	38	5	0	.132	7	28	7	1	2.5	.833

Bob Feller

FELLER, ROBERT WILLIAM ANDREW (Rapid Robert) BR TR 6′ 185 lbs.
B. Nov. 3, 1918, Van Meter, Iowa
Hall of Fame 1962.

Year	Team	Lg	W	L	PCT	ERA	G	GS	CG	IP	H	BB	SO	ShO	Relief Pitching W	Relief Pitching L	Relief Pitching SV	Batting AB	Batting H	Batting HR	BA	PO	A	E	DP	TC/G	FA
1936	**CLE**	**A**	5	3	.625	3.34	14	8	5	62	52	47	76	0	0	0	1	22	3	0	.136	0	5	0	0	0.4	1.000
1937			9	7	.563	3.39	26	19	9	148.2	116	106	150	0	2	0	1	53	9	0	.170	0	27	2	1	1.1	.931
1938			17	11	.607	4.08	39	36	20	277.2	225	**208**	**240**	2	0	1	1	94	17	0	.181	8	37	3	1	1.2	.938
1939			**24**	9	.727	2.85	39	35	**24**	**296.2**	227	**142**	**246**	4	1	0	1	99	21	0	.212	8	44	3	2	1.4	.945
1940			**27**	11	.711	**2.61**	**43**	**37**	**31**	**320.1**	245	118	**261**	**4**	1	1	4	115	18	2	.157	5	34	2	2	1.0	.951
1941			**25**	13	.658	3.15	**44**	**40**	28	**343**	**284**	**194**	**260**	**6**	0	1	2	120	18	1	.150	12	50	1	1	1.4	.984
1945			5	3	.625	2.50	9	9	7	72	50	35	59	1	0	0	0	25	4	0	.160	7	4	0	0	1.2	1.000
1946			**26**	15	.634	2.18	**48**	**42**	**36**	**371.1**	**277**	**153**	**348**	**10**	0	0	4	124	16	0	.129	13	47	1	2	1.3	.984
1947			**20**	11	.645	2.68	42	**37**	20	**299**	230	127	**196**	**5**	0	1	3	98	18	0	.184	17	50	1	2	1.6	.985
1948			19	15	.559	3.56	44	**38**	18	280.1	**255**	116	**164**	3	0	1	3	95	9	0	.095	16	39	2	1	1.3	.965
1949			15	14	.517	3.75	36	28	15	211	198	84	108	0	1	0	0	72	17	2	.236	12	19	1	2	0.9	.969
1950			16	11	.593	3.43	35	34	16	247	230	103	119	3	0	1	0	83	10	2	.120	8	23	0	2	0.9	1.000
1951			**22**	8	**.733**	3.50	33	32	16	249.2	239	95	111	4	0	1	0	81	10	0	.123	6	32	2	2	1.2	.950
1952			9	13	.409	4.74	30	30	11	191.2	219	83	81	1	0	0	0	60	7	1	.117	13	34	3	1	1.7	.940
1953			10	7	.588	3.59	25	25	10	175.2	163	60	60	1	0	0	0	56	6	0	.107	10	31	0	5	1.6	1.000
1954			13	3	.813	3.09	19	19	9	140	127	39	59	1	0	0	0	48	9	0	.188	7	15	0	2	1.2	1.000
1955			4	4	.500	3.47	25	11	2	83	71	31	25	1	1	0	0	21	1	0	.048	2	11	3	2	0.6	.813
1956			0	4	.000	4.97	19	4	2	58	63	23	18	0	0	1	1	16	0	0	.000	2	8	1	0	0.6	.909
18 yrs.			266	162	.621	3.25	570	484	279	3827	3271	1764 **5th**	2581	46	6	8	21	1282	193	8	.151	146	510	25	28	1.2	.963
WORLD SERIES																											
1948	**CLE**	**A**	0	2	.000	5.02	2	2	1	14.1	10	5	7	0	0	0	0	4	0	0	.000	2	4	0	0	3.0	1.000

Terry Felton

FELTON, TERRY LANE BR TR 6′ 1″ 180 lbs.
B. Oct. 29, 1957, Texarkana, Tex.

Year	Team	Lg	W	L	PCT	ERA	G	GS	CG	IP	H	BB	SO	ShO	Relief Pitching W	Relief Pitching L	Relief Pitching SV	Batting AB	Batting H	Batting HR	BA	PO	A	E	DP	TC/G	FA
1979	**MIN**	**A**	0	0	—	0.00	1	0	0	2	0	0	1	0	0	0	0	0	0	0	—	0	0	0	0	0.0	.000
1980			0	3	.000	7.00	5	4	0	18	20	9	14	0	0	0	0	0	0	0	—	0	2	1	0	0.6	.667
1981			0	0	—	54.00	1	0	0	1	4	2	1	0	0	0	0	0	0	0	—	0	0	0	0	0.0	.000
1982			0	13	.000	4.99	48	6	0	117.1	99	76	92	0	0	9	3	0	0	0	—	5	5	1	0	0.2	.909
4 yrs.			0	16	.000	5.53	55	10	0	138.1	123	87	108	0	0	9	3	0	0	0		5	7	2	0	0.3	.857

Hod Fenner

FENNER, HORACE ALFRED BR TR 5′10½″ 165 lbs.
B. July 12, 1897, Martin, Mich. D. Nov. 20, 1954, Detroit, Mich.

Year	Team	Lg	W	L	PCT	ERA	G	GS	CG	IP	H	BB	SO	ShO	Relief Pitching W	Relief Pitching L	Relief Pitching SV	Batting AB	Batting H	Batting HR	BA	PO	A	E	DP	TC/G	FA
1921	**CHI**	**A**	0	0	—	7.71	2	1	0	7	14	3	1	0	0	0	0	2	0	0	.000	0	0	0	0	0.0	.000

Stan Ferens

FERENS, STANLEY (Lefty) BB TL 5′11″ 170 lbs.
B. Mar. 5, 1915, Wendel, Pa. D. Oct. 7, 1994, Westmoreland County, Pa.

Year	Team	Lg	W	L	PCT	ERA	G	GS	CG	IP	H	BB	SO	ShO	Relief Pitching W	Relief Pitching L	Relief Pitching SV	Batting AB	Batting H	Batting HR	BA	PO	A	E	DP	TC/G	FA
1942	**STL**	**A**	3	4	.429	3.78	19	3	1	69	76	21	23	0	2	3	0	21	3	0	.143	5	13	1	1	1.0	.947
1946			2	9	.182	4.50	34	6	1	88	100	38	28	0	1	5	0	24	4	0	.167	4	14	3	1	0.6	.857
2 yrs.			5	13	.278	4.18	53	9	2	157	176	59	51	0	3	8	0	45	7	0	.156	9	27	4	2	0.8	.900

Alex Ferguson

FERGUSON, JAMES ALEXANDER BR TR 6′ 180 lbs.
B. Feb. 16, 1897, Montclair, N. J. D. Apr. 26, 1976, Sepulveda, Calif.

Year	Team	Lg	W	L	PCT	ERA	G	GS	CG	IP	H	BB	SO	ShO	Relief Pitching W	Relief Pitching L	Relief Pitching SV	Batting AB	Batting H	Batting HR	BA	PO	A	E	DP	TC/G	FA
1918	**NY**	**A**	0	0	—	0.00	1	0	0	1.2	2	2	1	0	0	0	0	1	0	0	.000	0	0	0	0	0.0	.000
1921			3	1	.750	5.91	17	4	1	56.1	64	27	9	0	1	0	1	19	4	0	.211	2	15	1	0	1.1	.944
1922	**BOS**	**A**	9	16	.360	4.31	39	27	10	198.1	201	62	44	1	3	0	2	65	6	0	.092	10	43	2	4	1.4	.964
1923			9	13	.409	4.04	34	27	11	198.1	229	67	72	0	1	0	0	62	6	0	.097	5	45	4	5	1.6	.926
1924			14	**17**	.452	3.79	40	32	15	235	257	107	78	0	3	1	2	85	11	0	.129	12	60	1	1	1.8	.986
1925	**3 teams**	**BOS A** (5G 0–2) **NY A** (21G 4–2) **WAS A** (7G 5–1)																									
″	**total**		9	5	.643	6.18	33	16	3	125.1	157	70	49	0	3	2	2	39	3	0	.077	4	26	1	2	0.9	.968
1926	**WAS**	**A**	3	4	.429	7.74	19	4	0	47.2	69	18	16	0	2	2	1	11	2	0	.182	2	14	1	1	0.9	.941
1927	**PHI**	**N**	8	16	.333	4.84	31	31	16	227	280	65	73	0	0	0	0	70	7	0	.100	12	49	5	3	2.1	.924
1928			5	10	.333	5.88	34	19	5	134.2	168	52	51	1	1	0	2	39	1	0	.026	9	35	0	0	1.3	1.000
1929	**2 teams**	**PHI N** (5G 1–2) **BKN N** (3G 0–1)																									
″	**total**		1	3	.250	13.50	8	7	1	14.2	26	11	4	0	0	0	0	5	1	0	.200	1	6	0	0	0.9	1.000
10 yrs.			61	85	.418	4.93	256	167	62	1239	1453	481	397	2	14	5	10	396	41	0	.104	57	293	15	16	1.4	.959
WORLD SERIES																											
1925	**WAS**	**A**	1	1	.500	3.21	2	2	2	14	13	6	11	0	0	0	0	4	0	0	.000	0	0	0	0	0.0	.000

Bob Ferguson

FERGUSON, ROBERT LESTER BR TR 6′ 1½″ 180 lbs.
B. Apr. 18, 1919, Birmingham, Ala.

Year	Team	Lg	W	L	PCT	ERA	G	GS	CG	IP	H	BB	SO	ShO	Relief Pitching W	Relief Pitching L	Relief Pitching SV	Batting AB	Batting H	Batting HR	BA	PO	A	E	DP	TC/G	FA
1944	CIN	N	0	3	.000	9.00	9	2	0	16	24	10	9	0	0	3	1	3	1	0	.333	1	3	1	0	0.6	.800

Bob Ferguson

FERGUSON, ROBERT VAVASOUR (Death to Flying Things) BB TR 5′ 9½″ 149 lbs.
B. Jan. 31, 1845, Brooklyn, N. Y. D. May 3, 1894, Brooklyn, N. Y.
Manager 1876–84, 1886–87.

Year	Team	Lg	W	L	PCT	ERA	G	GS	CG	IP	H	BB	SO	ShO	Relief Pitching W	Relief Pitching L	Relief Pitching SV	Batting AB	Batting H	Batting HR	BA	PO	A	E	DP	TC/G	FA
1877	HAR	N	1	1	.500	3.96	3	2	2	25	38	2	1	0	0	0	0	254	65	0	.256	124	133	54	5	4.5	.826
1883	PHI	N	0	0	—	9.00	1	0	0	1	2	0	0	0	0	0	0	329	85	0	.258	113	159	51	6	5.5	.842
2 yrs.			1	1	.500	4.15	4	2	2	26	40	2	1	0	0	0	0	*				1488	1635	433	198	6.3	.878

Charlie Ferguson

FERGUSON, CHARLES AUGUSTUS TR 5′11″
B. May 10, 1875, Okemos, Mich. D. May 17, 1931, Sault Ste. Marie, Mich.

Year	Team	Lg	W	L	PCT	ERA	G	GS	CG	IP	H	BB	SO	ShO	Relief Pitching W	Relief Pitching L	Relief Pitching SV	Batting AB	Batting H	Batting HR	BA	PO	A	E	DP	TC/G	FA
1901	CHI	N	0	0	—	0.00	1	0	0	2	1	2	0	0	0	0	0	1	0	0	.000	0	0	0	0	0.0	.000

Charlie Ferguson

FERGUSON, CHARLES J. BB TR 6′ 165 lbs.
B. Apr. 17, 1863, Charlottesville, Va. D. Apr. 29, 1888, Philadelphia, Pa.

Year	Team	Lg	W	L	PCT	ERA	G	GS	CG	IP	H	BB	SO	ShO	Relief Pitching W	Relief Pitching L	Relief Pitching SV	Batting AB	Batting H	Batting HR	BA	PO	A	E	DP	TC/G	FA
1884	PHI	N	21	25	.457	*3.54*	50	47	46	416.2	443	93	194	2	0	0	1	203	50	0	.246	35	73	13	4	2.2	.893
1885			26	20	.565	*2.22*	48	45	45	405	345	81	197	5	**1**	**1**	0	235	72	1	.306	56	89	15	3	2.5	.906
1886			30	9	.769	*1.98*	48	45	43	395.2	317	69	212	4	0	0	**2**	261	66	2	.253	72	101	14	1	2.5	.925
1887			22	10	.688	3.00	37	33	31	297.1	297	47	125	2	1	0	**1**	264	89	3	.337	93	130	22	11	3.3	.910
4 yrs.			99	64	.607	2.67	183	170	165	1514.2	1402	290	728	13	2	1	4	*				256	393	64	19	2.7	.910

George Ferguson

FERGUSON, GEORGE CECIL BR TR 5′10″ 165 lbs.
B. Aug. 19, 1886, Ellsworth, Kans. D. Sept. 5, 1943, Orlando, Fla.

Year	Team	Lg	W	L	PCT	ERA	G	GS	CG	IP	H	BB	SO	ShO	Relief Pitching W	Relief Pitching L	Relief Pitching SV	Batting AB	Batting H	Batting HR	BA	PO	A	E	DP	TC/G	FA
1906	NY	N	2	1	.667	2.58	22	1	1	52.1	43	24	32	1	2	1	**6**	15	5	0	.333	3	18	1	1	1.0	.955
1907			3	1	.750	2.11	15	5	4	64	63	20	37	0	0	1	1	18	1	0	.056	8	12	1	0	1.4	.952
1908	BOS	N	12	11	.522	2.47	37	20	13	208	168	84	98	3	3	2	0	65	11	0	.169	9	45	6	1	1.6	.900
1909			5	**23**	.179	3.73	36	30	19	226.2	235	83	87	3	0	0	0	73	15	0	.205	10	63	5	1	2.2	.936
1910			8	7	.533	3.80	26	14	10	123	110	58	40	1	2	2	0	40	7	1	.175	6	33	3	1	1.6	.929
1911			1	3	.250	9.75	6	3	0	24	40	12	4	0	1	0	0	7	2	0	.286	0	8	2	0	1.7	.800
6 yrs.			31	46	.403	3.34	142	73	47	698	659	281	298	8	8	6	7	218	41	1	.188	36	179	18	4	1.6	.923

Ramon Fermin

FERMIN, RAMON ANTONIO BR TR 6′ 3″ 180 lbs.
Born Ramon Antonio Fermin (Ventura).
B. Nov. 25, 1972, San Francisco de Macoris, Dominican Republic.

Year	Team	Lg	W	L	PCT	ERA	G	GS	CG	IP	H	BB	SO	ShO	Relief Pitching W	Relief Pitching L	Relief Pitching SV	Batting AB	Batting H	Batting HR	BA	PO	A	E	DP	TC/G	FA
1995	OAK	A	0	0	—	13.50	1	0	0	1.1	4	1	0	0	0	0	0	0	0	0	—	0	0	0	0	0.0	.000

Alex Fernandez

FERNANDEZ, ALEXANDER BR TR 6′ 2″ 200 lbs.
B. Aug. 13, 1969, Miami, Fla.

Year	Team	Lg	W	L	PCT	ERA	G	GS	CG	IP	H	BB	SO	ShO	Relief Pitching W	Relief Pitching L	Relief Pitching SV	Batting AB	Batting H	Batting HR	BA	PO	A	E	DP	TC/G	FA
1990	CHI	A	5	5	.500	3.80	13	13	3	87.2	89	34	61	0	0	0	0	0	0	0	—	3	12	2	0	1.3	.882
1991			9	13	.409	4.51	34	32	2	191.2	186	88	145	0	0	0	0	0	0	0	—	7	31	3	2	1.2	.927
1992			8	11	.421	4.27	29	29	4	187.2	199	50	95	2	0	0	0	0	0	0	—	10	33	2	5	1.6	.956
1993			18	9	.667	3.13	34	34	3	247.1	221	67	169	1	0	0	0	0	0	0	—	18	38	0	2	1.6	1.000
1994			11	7	.611	3.86	24	24	4	170.1	163	50	122	3	0	0	0	0	0	0	—	16	39	1	4	2.3	.982
1995			12	8	.600	3.80	30	30	5	203.2	200	65	159	2	0	0	0	0	0	0	—	11	26	3	5	1.3	.925
6 yrs.			63	53	.543	3.86	164	162	21	1088.1	1058	354	751	8	0	0	0	0	0	0		65	179	11	18	1.6	.957
LEAGUE CHAMPIONSHIP SERIES																											
1993	CHI	A	0	2	.000	1.80	2	2	0	15	15	6	10	0	0	0	0	0	0	0	—	2	1	0	1	1.5	1.000

Sid Fernandez

FERNANDEZ, CHARLES SIDNEY (El Sid) BL TL 6′ 1″ 220 lbs.
B. Oct. 12, 1962, Honolulu, Hawaii.

Year	Team	Lg	W	L	PCT	ERA	G	GS	CG	IP	H	BB	SO	ShO	Relief Pitching W	Relief Pitching L	Relief Pitching SV	Batting AB	Batting H	Batting HR	BA	PO	A	E	DP	TC/G	FA
1983	LA	N	0	1	.000	6.00	2	1	0	6	7	7	9	0	0	0	0	1	1	0	1.000	1	1	0	0	1.0	1.000
1984	NY	N	6	6	.500	3.50	15	15	0	90	74	34	62	0	0	0	0	28	5	0	.179	0	6	0	0	0.4	1.000
1985			9	9	.500	2.80	26	26	3	170.1	108	80	180	0	0	0	0	52	11	0	.212	1	23	0	0	0.9	1.000
1986			16	6	.727	3.52	32	31	2	204.1	161	91	200	1	0	0	1	68	11	0	.162	3	18	1	1	0.7	.955
1987			12	8	.600	3.81	28	27	3	156	130	67	134	1	0	0	0	43	7	0	.163	4	12	1	0	0.6	.941
1988			12	10	.545	3.03	31	31	1	187	127	70	189	1	0	0	0	56	14	0	.250	2	13	0	0	0.5	1.000
1989			14	5	.737	2.83	35	32	6	219.1	157	75	198	2	0	0	0	71	15	1	.211	4	13	0	2	0.5	1.000
1990			9	14	.391	3.46	30	30	2	179.1	130	67	181	1	0	0	0	58	11	0	.190	1	16	2	0	0.6	.895
1991			1	3	.250	2.86	8	8	0	44	36	9	31	0	0	0	0	13	2	0	.154	1	11	0	0	1.5	1.000
1992			14	11	.560	2.73	32	32	5	214.2	162	67	193	2	0	0	0	74	15	0	.203	4	21	1	1	0.8	.962
1993			5	6	.455	2.93	18	18	1	119.2	82	36	81	1	0	0	0	32	3	0	.094	2	10	0	1	0.7	1.000
1994	BAL	A	6	6	.500	5.15	19	19	2	115.1	109	46	95	0	0	0	0	0	0	0	—	1	9	0	0	0.5	1.000
1995	2 teams	BAL A	(8G 0–4)		PHI N	(11G 6–1)																					
″	total		6	5	.545	4.56	19	18	0	92.2	84	38	110	0	0	0	0	23	1	0	.043	0	3	1	0	0.2	.750
13 yrs.			110	90	.550	3.35	295	288	25	1798.2	1367	687	1663	9	0	0	1	519	96	1	.185	24	156	6	5	0.6	.968
LEAGUE CHAMPIONSHIP SERIES																											
1986	NY	N	0	1	.000	4.50	1	1	0	6	3	1	5	0	0	0	0	1	0	0	.000	0	0	0	0	0.0	.000
1988			0	1	.000	13.50	1	1	0	4	7	1	5	0	0	0	0	1	0	0	.000	0	0	0	0	0.0	.000
2 yrs.			0	2	.000	8.10	2	2	0	10	10	2	10	0	0	0	0	2	0	0	.000	0	0	0	0	0.0	
WORLD SERIES																											
1986	NY	N	0	0	—	1.35	3	0	0	6.2	6	1	10	0	0	0	0	0	0	0	—	0	0	0	0	0.0	.000

Don Ferrarese

FERRARESE, DONALD HUGH (Midget) BR TL 5′ 9″ 170 lbs.
B. June 19, 1929, Oakland, Calif.

Year	Team	Lg	W	L	PCT	ERA	G	GS	CG	IP	H	BB	SO	ShO	Relief Pitching W	Relief Pitching L	Relief Pitching SV	Batting AB	Batting H	Batting HR	BA	PO	A	E	DP	TC/G	FA
1955	BAL	A	0	0	—	3.00	6	0	0	9	8	11	5	0	0	0	0	1	0	0	.000	0	1	0	0	0.2	1.000
1956			4	10	.286	5.03	36	14	3	102	86	64	81	1	2	2	2	28	1	0	.036	10	14	1	2	0.7	.960
1957			1	1	.500	4.74	8	2	0	19	14	12	13	0	1	0	0	3	0	0	.000	1	4	0	0	0.6	1.000
1958	CLE	A	3	4	.429	3.71	28	10	2	94.2	91	46	62	0	2	1	1	26	3	0	.115	2	13	3	1	0.6	.833
1959			5	3	.625	3.20	15	10	4	76	58	51	45	0	0	0	0	27	7	0	.259	0	15	0	2	1.0	1.000

Don Ferrarese *continued*

Year	Team	Lg	W	L	PCT	ERA	G	GS	CG	IP	H	BB	SO	ShO	Relief Pitching W	Relief Pitching L	Relief Pitching SV	Batting AB	Batting H	Batting HR	BA	PO	A	E	DP	TC/G	FA
1960	**CHI**	**A**	0	1	.000	18.00	5	0	0	4	8	9	4	0	0	1	0	2	1	0	.500	0	0	0	0	0.0	.000
1961	**PHI**	**N**	5	12	.294	3.76	42	14	3	138.2	120	68	89	1	2	3	1	35	6	0	.171	8	12	1	1	0.5	.952
1962	**2 teams**	**PHI N** (5G 0–1)	**STL N** (38G 1–4)																								
″	**total**		1	5	.167	3.27	43	0	0	63.1	64	34	51	0	1	5	1	6	2	1	.333	4	15	0	3	0.4	1.000
8 yrs.			19	36	.345	4.00	183	50	12	506.2	449	295	350	2	8	12	5	128	20	1	.156	25	74	5	9	0.6	.952

Bill Ferrazzi

FERRAZZI, WILLIAM JOSEPH BR TR 6′ 2½″ 200 lbs.
B. Apr. 19, 1907, West Quincy, Mass. D. Aug. 10, 1993, Gainesville, Fla.

Year	Team	Lg	W	L	PCT	ERA	G	GS	CG	IP	H	BB	SO	ShO	Relief Pitching W	Relief Pitching L	Relief Pitching SV	Batting AB	Batting H	Batting HR	BA	PO	A	E	DP	TC/G	FA
1935	**PHI**	**A**	1	2	.333	5.14	3	2	0	7	7	5	0	0	1	0	0	1	0	0	.000	1	2	0	0	1.0	1.000

Tony Ferreira

FERREIRA, ANTHONY ROSS BL TL 6′ 1″ 160 lbs.
B. Oct. 4, 1962, Riverside, Calif.

Year	Team	Lg	W	L	PCT	ERA	G	GS	CG	IP	H	BB	SO	ShO	Relief Pitching W	Relief Pitching L	Relief Pitching SV	Batting AB	Batting H	Batting HR	BA	PO	A	E	DP	TC/G	FA
1985	**KC**	**A**	0	0	—	7.94	2	0	0	5.2	6	2	5	0	0	0	0	0	0	0	—	0	2	0	1	1.0	1.000

Wes Ferrell

FERRELL, WESLEY CHEEK BR TR 6′ 2″ 195 lbs.
Brother of Rick Ferrell.
B. Feb. 2, 1908, Greensboro, N. C. D. Dec. 9, 1976, Sarasota, Fla.

Year	Team	Lg	W	L	PCT	ERA	G	GS	CG	IP	H	BB	SO	ShO	Relief Pitching W	Relief Pitching L	Relief Pitching SV	Batting AB	Batting H	Batting HR	BA	PO	A	E	DP	TC/G	FA
1927	**CLE**	**A**	0	0	—	27.00	1	0	0	1	3	2	0	0	0	0	0	0	0	0	—	0	0	0	0	0.0	.000
1928			0	2	.000	2.25	2	2	1	16	15	5	4	0	0	0	0	4	1	0	.250	1	4	0	0	2.5	1.000
1929			21	10	.677	3.60	43	25	18	242.2	256	109	100	1	4	2	5	93	22	1	.237	10	63	2	3	1.7	.973
1930			25	13	.658	3.31	43	35	25	296.2	303	106	143	1	2	1	3	118	35	0	.297	19	39	2	0	1.4	.967
1931			22	12	.647	3.75	40	35	**27**	276.1	276	**130**	123	2	1	1	3	116	37	9	.319	19	74	3	3	2.4	.969
1932			23	13	.639	3.66	38	34	26	287.2	299	104	105	3	1	2	1	128	31	2	.242	14	59	1	5	1.9	.986
1933			11	12	.478	4.21	28	26	16	201	225	70	41	1	0	0	0	140	38	7	.271	43	49	0	5	2.2	1.000
1934	**BOS**	**A**	14	5	.737	3.63	26	23	17	181	205	49	67	3	1	0	1	78	22	4	.282	8	23	1	2	1.2	.969
1935			**25**	14	.641	3.52	41	**38**	**31**	**322.1**	**336**	108	110	3	0	3	0	150	52	7	.347	9	76	2	1	2.1	.977
1936			20	15	.571	4.19	39	**38**	**28**	**301**	**330**	119	106	3	0	0	0	135	36	5	.267	9	42	2	2	1.4	.962
1937	**2 teams**	**BOS A** (12G 3–6)	**WAS A** (25G 11–13)																								
″	**total**		14	19	.424	4.90	37	35	**26**	**281**	**325**	122	123	0	0	0	0	139	39	1	.281	11	55	2	4	1.8	.971
1938	**2 teams**	**WAS A** (23G 13–8)	**NY A** (5G 2–2)																								
″	**total**		15	10	.600	6.28	28	26	10	179	245	86	43	0	1	0	0	61	13	1	.213	10	41	2	6	1.9	.962
1939	**NY**	**A**	1	2	.333	4.66	3	3	1	19.1	14	17	6	0	0	0	0	8	1	0	.125	0	4	0	0	1.3	1.000
1940	**BKN**	**N**	0	0	—	6.75	1	0	0	4	4	4	4	0	0	0	0	2	0	0	.000	0	3	0	0	3.0	1.000
1941	**BOS**	**N**	2	1	.667	5.14	4	3	1	14	13	9	10	0	1	0	0	4	2	1	.500	0	1	0	0	0.3	1.000
15 yrs.			193	128	.601	4.04	374	323	227	2623	2849	1040	985	17	11	9	13	*				153	533	17	31	1.8	.976

Tom Ferrick

FERRICK, THOMAS JEROME BR TR 6′ 2½″ 220 lbs.
B. Jan. 6, 1915, New York, N. Y.

Year	Team	Lg	W	L	PCT	ERA	G	GS	CG	IP	H	BB	SO	ShO	Relief Pitching W	Relief Pitching L	Relief Pitching SV	Batting AB	Batting H	Batting HR	BA	PO	A	E	DP	TC/G	FA
1941	**PHI**	**A**	8	10	.444	3.77	36	4	2	119.1	130	33	30	1	7	**8**	7	44	9	0	.205	12	31	1	4	1.2	.977
1942	**CLE**	**A**	3	2	.600	1.99	31	2	2	81.1	56	32	28	0	2	1	3	19	4	0	.211	7	24	1	4	1.0	.969
1946	**2 teams**	**CLE A** (9G 0–0)	**STL A** (25G 4–1)																								
″	**total**		4	1	.800	3.58	34	1	0	50.1	51	9	22	0	4	1	6	7	2	0	.286	2	12	3	1	0.5	.824
1947	**WAS**	**A**	1	7	.125	3.15	31	0	0	60	57	20	23	0	1	**7**	9	10	1	0	.100	7	15	0	1	0.7	1.000
1948			2	5	.286	4.15	37	0	0	73.2	75	38	34	0	2	5	10	15	1	0	.067	8	17	2	1	0.7	.926
1949	**STL**	**A**	6	4	.600	3.88	50	0	0	104.1	102	41	34	0	6	4	6	21	3	0	.143	6	26	1	2	0.7	.970
1950	**2 teams**	**STL A** (16G 1–3)	**NY A** (30G 8–4)																								
″	**total**		9	7	.563	3.79	46	0	0	80.2	73	29	26	0	**9**	7	11	18	3	0	.167	4	22	1	0	0.6	.963
1951	**2 teams**	**NY A** (9G 1–1)	**WAS A** (22G 2–0)																								
″	**total**		3	1	.750	3.52	31	0	0	53.2	57	14	20	0	3	1	3	8	3	0	.375	5	8	1	2	0.5	.929
1952	**WAS**	**A**	4	3	.571	3.02	27	0	0	50.2	53	11	28	0	4	3	1	5	1	0	.200	4	13	1	0	0.7	.944
9 yrs.			40	40	.500	3.47	323	7	4	674	654	227	245	1	38	37	56	147	27	0	.184	55	168	11	15	0.7	.953
WORLD SERIES																											
1950	**NY**	**A**	1	0	1.000	0.00	1	0	0	1	1	1	0	0	1	0	0	0	0	0	—	0	0	0	0	0.0	.000

Bob Ferris

FERRIS, ROBERT EUGENE BR TR 6′ 6″ 225 lbs.
B. May 7, 1955, Arlington, Va.

Year	Team	Lg	W	L	PCT	ERA	G	GS	CG	IP	H	BB	SO	ShO	Relief Pitching W	Relief Pitching L	Relief Pitching SV	Batting AB	Batting H	Batting HR	BA	PO	A	E	DP	TC/G	FA
1979	**CAL**	**A**	0	0	—	1.50	2	0	0	6	5	3	2	0	0	0	0	0	0	0	—	0	2	0	0	1.0	1.000
1980			0	2	.000	6.00	5	3	0	15	23	9	4	0	0	0	0	0	0	0	—	0	3	0	0	0.6	1.000
2 yrs.			0	2	.000	4.71	7	3	0	21	28	12	6	0	0	0	0	0	0	0		0	5	0	0	0.7	1.000

Boo Ferriss

FERRISS, DAVID MEADOW BL TR 6′ 2″ 208 lbs.
B. Dec. 5, 1921, Shaw, Miss.

Year	Team	Lg	W	L	PCT	ERA	G	GS	CG	IP	H	BB	SO	ShO	Relief Pitching W	Relief Pitching L	Relief Pitching SV	Batting AB	Batting H	Batting HR	BA	PO	A	E	DP	TC/G	FA
1945	**BOS**	**A**	21	10	.677	2.96	35	31	26	264.2	**263**	85	94	5	1	0	2	120	32	1	.267	22	67	2	10	2.6	.978
1946			25	6	**.806**	3.25	40	35	26	274	274	71	106	6	1	0	3	115	24	0	.209	25	43	1	5	1.7	.986
1947			12	11	.522	4.04	33	28	14	218.1	241	92	64	1	0	1	0	99	27	0	.273	13	33	2	2	1.5	.958
1948			7	3	.700	5.23	31	9	1	115.1	127	61	30	0	5	1	3	37	9	0	.243	10	21	0	1	1.0	1.000
1949			0	0	—	4.05	4	0	0	6.2	7	4	1	0	0	0	0	1	1	0	1.000	1	0	0	0	0.3	1.000
1950			0	0	—	18.00	1	0	0	1	2	1	1	0	0	0	0	0	0	0	—	0	0	0	0	0.0	.000
6 yrs.			65	30	.684	3.64	144	103	67	880	914	314	296	12	7	2	8	*				71	164	5	18	1.7	.979
WORLD SERIES																											
1946	**BOS**	**A**	1	0	1.000	2.02	2	2	1	13.1	13	2	4	1	0	0	0	*				0	3	0	0	1.5	1.000

Cy Ferry

FERRY, ALFRED JOSEPH BR TR 6′ 1″ 170 lbs.
Brother of Jack Ferry.
B. Sept. 27, 1878, Hudson, N. Y. D. Sept. 27, 1938, Pittsfield, Mass.

Year	Team	Lg	W	L	PCT	ERA	G	GS	CG	IP	H	BB	SO	ShO	Relief Pitching W	Relief Pitching L	Relief Pitching SV	Batting AB	Batting H	Batting HR	BA	PO	A	E	DP	TC/G	FA
1904	**DET**	**A**	0	1	.000	6.23	3	1	1	13	12	11	4	0	0	0	0	6	2	0	.333	0	4	0	1	1.3	1.000
1905	**CLE**	**A**	0	0	—	13.50	1	1	0	2	3	0	2	0	0	0	0	1	0	0	.000	0	1	0	0	1.0	1.000
2 yrs.			0	1	.000	7.20	4	2	1	15	15	11	6	0	0	0	0	7	2	0	.286	0	5	0	1	1.3	1.000

Jack Ferry

FERRY, JOHN FRANCIS — BR TR 5′11″ 175 lbs.
Brother of Cy Ferry.
B. Apr. 7, 1887, Pittsfield, Mass. D. Aug. 29, 1954, Pittsfield, Mass.

Year	Team	W	L	PCT	ERA	G	GS	CG	IP	H	BB	SO	ShO	Relief W	Relief L	Relief SV	Batting AB	Batting H	HR	BA	PO	A	E	DP	TC/G	FA
1910	PIT N	1	2	.333	2.32	6	3	2	31	26	8	12	0	0	0	0	9	3	0	.333	1	9	0	0	1.7	1.000
1911		6	4	.600	3.15	26	8	4	85.2	83	27	32	1	2	4	3	29	9	0	.310	2	17	3	0	0.8	.864
1912		2	0	1.000	3.00	11	3	1	39	33	23	10	1	0	0	1	13	1	0	.077	0	14	1	0	1.4	.933
1913		1	0	1.000	5.40	4	0	0	5	4	2	2	0	1	0	0	0	0	0	—	0	2	0	0	0.5	1.000
4 yrs.		10	6	.625	3.02	47	14	7	160.2	146	60	56	2	3	4	4	51	13	0	.255	3	42	4	0	1.0	.918

Alex Ferson

FERSON, ALEXANDER (Colonel) — BR TR 5′9″ 165 lbs.
B. July 14, 1866, Philadelphia, Pa. D. Dec. 5, 1957, Boston, Mass.

Year	Team	W	L	PCT	ERA	G	GS	CG	IP	H	BB	SO	ShO	Relief W	Relief L	Relief SV	Batting AB	Batting H	HR	BA	PO	A	E	DP	TC/G	FA
1889	WAS N	17	17	.500	3.90	36	33	28	288.1	319	105	85	1	1	0	0	114	13	0	.114	4	50	8	1	1.7	.871
1890	BUF P	1	7	.125	5.45	10	10	7	71	88	40	13	0	0	0	0	32	7	0	.219	1	19	0	0	1.8	1.000
1892	BAL N	0	1	.000	11.00	2	1	1	9	17	6	8	0	0	0	0	4	0	0	.000	0	0	0	0	0.0	.000
3 yrs.		18	25	.419	4.37	48	44	36	368.1	424	151	106	1	1	0	0	150	20	0	.133	5	69	8	1	1.7	.902

Lou Fette

FETTE, LOUIS HENRY WILLIAM — BR TR 6′ 1½″ 200 lbs.
B. Mar. 15, 1907, Alma, Mo. D. Jan. 3, 1981, Warrensburg, Mo.

Year	Team	W	L	PCT	ERA	G	GS	CG	IP	H	BB	SO	ShO	Relief W	Relief L	Relief SV	Batting AB	Batting H	HR	BA	PO	A	E	DP	TC/G	FA
1937	BOS N	20	10	.667	2.88	35	33	23	259	243	81	70	**5**	0	1	0	92	22	0	.239	8	63	3	3	2.1	.959
1938		11	13	.458	3.15	33	32	17	239.2	235	79	83	3	0	0	1	85	16	0	.188	10	56	0	4	2.0	1.000
1939		10	10	.500	2.96	27	26	11	146	123	61	35	**6**	0	0	0	49	3	0	.061	5	46	3	0	2.0	.944
1940	2 teams BOS N (7G 0–5) BKN N (2G 0–0)																									
″	total	0	5	.000	5.09	9	5	0	35.1	41	20	2	0	0	0	0	8	3	0	.375	1	4	0	0	0.6	1.000
1945	BOS N	0	2	.000	5.73	5	1	0	11	16	7	4	0	0	1	0	2	0	0	.000	0	3	0	0	0.6	1.000
5 yrs.		41	40	.506	3.15	109	97	51	691	658	248	194	14	0	2	1	236	44	0	.186	24	172	6	7	1.9	.970

Mike Fetters

FETTERS, MICHAEL LEE — BR TR 6′ 4″ 200 lbs.
B. Dec. 19, 1964, Van Nuys, Calif.

Year	Team	W	L	PCT	ERA	G	GS	CG	IP	H	BB	SO	ShO	Relief W	Relief L	Relief SV	Batting AB	Batting H	HR	BA	PO	A	E	DP	TC/G	FA
1989	CAL A	0	0	—	8.10	1	0	0	3.1	5	1	4	0	0	0	0	0	0	0	—	0	1	0	0	1.0	1.000
1990		1	1	.500	4.12	26	2	0	67.2	77	20	35	0	1	1	1	0	0	0	—	9	11	1	0	0.8	.952
1991		2	5	.286	4.84	19	4	0	44.2	53	28	24	0	2	1	0	0	0	0	—	2	4	1	0	0.4	.857
1992	MIL A	5	1	.833	1.87	50	0	0	62.2	38	24	43	0	5	1	2	0	0	0	—	3	11	0	1	0.3	1.000
1993		3	3	.500	3.34	45	0	0	59.1	59	22	23	0	3	3	0	0	0	0	—	5	7	1	4	0.3	.923
1994		1	4	.200	2.54	42	0	0	46	41	27	31	0	1	4	17	0	0	0	—	3	5	1	1	0.2	.889
1995		0	3	.000	3.38	40	0	0	34.2	40	20	33	0	0	3	22	0	0	0	—	2	1	1	0	0.1	.750
7 yrs.		12	17	.414	3.36	223	6	0	318.1	313	142	193	0	12	13	42	0	0	0		24	40	5	6	0.3	.928

John Fick

FICK, JOHN RALPH — BL TL 5′10″ 150 lbs.
B. May 18, 1921, Baltimore, Md. D. June 9, 1958, Somers Point, N. J.

Year	Team	W	L	PCT	ERA	G	GS	CG	IP	H	BB	SO	ShO	Relief W	Relief L	Relief SV	Batting AB	Batting H	HR	BA	PO	A	E	DP	TC/G	FA
1944	PHI N	0	0	—	3.38	4	0	0	5.1	3	3	2	0	0	0	0	0	0	0	—	0	1	1	0	0.5	.500

Mark Fidrych

FIDRYCH, MARK STEVEN (The Bird) — BR TR 6′ 3″ 175 lbs.
B. Aug. 14, 1954, Worcester, Mass.

Year	Team	W	L	PCT	ERA	G	GS	CG	IP	H	BB	SO	ShO	Relief W	Relief L	Relief SV	Batting AB	Batting H	HR	BA	PO	A	E	DP	TC/G	FA
1976	DET A	19	9	.679	**2.34**	31	29	**24**	250	217	53	97	4	0	0	0	0	0	0	—	19	59	0	4	2.5	1.000
1977		6	4	.600	2.89	11	11	7	81	82	12	42	1	0	0	0	0	0	0	—	7	6	1	0	1.3	.929
1978		2	0	1.000	2.45	3	3	2	22	17	5	10	0	0	0	0	0	0	0	—	4	7	0	0	3.7	1.000
1979		0	3	.000	10.20	4	4	0	15	23	9	5	0	0	0	0	0	0	0	—	2	1	0	0	0.8	1.000
1980		2	3	.400	5.73	9	9	1	44	58	20	16	0	0	0	0	0	0	0	—	5	9	0	0	1.6	1.000
5 yrs.		29	19	.604	3.10	58	56	34	412	397	99	170	5	0	0	0	0	0	0		37	82	1	4	2.1	.992

Clarence Fieber

FIEBER, CLARENCE THOMAS (Lefty) — BL TL 6′ 4″ 187 lbs.
B. Sept. 4, 1913, San Francisco, Calif. D. Aug. 20, 1985, Redwood City, Calif.

Year	Team	W	L	PCT	ERA	G	GS	CG	IP	H	BB	SO	ShO	Relief W	Relief L	Relief SV	Batting AB	Batting H	HR	BA	PO	A	E	DP	TC/G	FA
1932	CHI A	1	0	1.000	1.69	3	0	0	5.1	6	3	1	0	1	0	0	0	0	0	—	0	2	0	0	0.7	1.000

Jim Field

FIELD, JAMES C. — 6′ 1″ 170 lbs.
B. Apr. 24, 1863, Philadelphia, Pa. D. May 13, 1953, Atlantic City, N. J.

Year	Team	W	L	PCT	ERA	G	GS	CG	IP	H	BB	SO	ShO	Relief W	Relief L	Relief SV	Batting AB	Batting H	HR	BA	PO	A	E	DP	TC/G	FA
1890	ROC AA	1	0	1.000	*2.79*	2	1	1	9.2	7	4	2	0	0	0	1	*				781	10	52	44	11.1	.938

Jocko Fields

FIELDS, JOHN JOSEPH — BR TR 5′10″ 160 lbs.
B. Oct. 20, 1864, Cork, Ireland D. Oct. 14, 1950, Jersey City, N. J.

Year	Team	W	L	PCT	ERA	G	GS	CG	IP	H	BB	SO	ShO	Relief W	Relief L	Relief SV	Batting AB	Batting H	HR	BA	PO	A	E	DP	TC/G	FA
1887	PIT N	0	0	—	0.00	1	0	0	1	0	2	0	0	0	0	0	*				141	29	18	2	4.1	.904

Lou Fiene

FIENE, LOUIS HENRY (Big Finn) — BR TR 6′ 175 lbs.
B. Dec. 29, 1884, Fort Dodge, Iowa D. Dec. 22, 1964, Chicago, Ill.

Year	Team	W	L	PCT	ERA	G	GS	CG	IP	H	BB	SO	ShO	Relief W	Relief L	Relief SV	Batting AB	Batting H	HR	BA	PO	A	E	DP	TC/G	FA
1906	CHI A	1	1	.500	2.90	6	2	1	31	35	9	12	0	0	0	0	10	2	0	.200	3	9	1	0	2.2	.923
1907		0	1	.000	4.15	6	1	1	26	30	7	15	0	0	0	1	11	2	0	.182	4	7	0	0	1.8	1.000
1908		0	1	.000	4.00	1	1	1	9	9	1	3	0	0	0	0	3	0	0	.000	0	5	0	0	5.0	1.000
1909		2	5	.286	4.13	13	6	4	72	75	18	24	0	1	0	0	29	2	0	.069	3	30	5	1	2.9	.868
4 yrs.		3	8	.273	3.85	26	10	7	138	149	35	54	0	1	0	1	53	6	0	.113	10	51	6	1	2.6	.910

Dan Fife

FIFE, DANNY WAYNE — BR TR 6′ 3″ 175 lbs.
B. Oct. 5, 1949, Harrisburg, Ill.

Year	Team	W	L	PCT	ERA	G	GS	CG	IP	H	BB	SO	ShO	Relief W	Relief L	Relief SV	Batting AB	Batting H	HR	BA	PO	A	E	DP	TC/G	FA
1973	MIN A	3	2	.600	4.35	10	7	1	51.2	54	29	18	0	0	1	0	0	0	0	—	4	7	0	0	1.1	1.000
1974		0	0	—	17.36	4	0	0	4.2	10	4	3	0	0	0	0	0	0	0	—	0	0	0	0	0.0	.000
2 yrs.		3	2	.600	5.43	14	7	1	56.1	64	33	21	0	0	1	0	0	0	0		4	7	0	0	0.8	1.000

Jack Fifield

FIFIELD, JOHN PROCTOR — BR TR 5′11″ 160 lbs.
B. Oct. 5, 1871, Enfield, N. H. D. Nov. 27, 1939, Syracuse, N. Y.

Year	Team	W	L	PCT	ERA	G	GS	CG	IP	H	BB	SO	ShO	Relief W	Relief L	Relief SV	Batting AB	Batting H	HR	BA	PO	A	E	DP	TC/G	FA
1897	PHI N	5	18	.217	5.51	27	26	21	210.2	263	80	38	0	0	0	0	77	18	2	.234	12	49	2	1	2.3	.968
1898		11	9	.550	3.31	21	21	18	171.1	170	60	31	2	0	0	0	64	7	0	.109	5	29	3	2	1.8	.919
1899	2 teams PHI N (14G 3–8) WAS N (6G 2–4)																									
″	total	5	12	.294	4.77	20	17	15	139.2	183	53	20	1	0	0	1	55	13	0	.236	6	36	5	0	2.2	.894
3 yrs.		21	39	.350	4.59	68	64	54	521.2	616	193	89	3	0	0	1	196	38	2	.194	23	114	10	3	2.1	.932

Frank Figgemeier

FIGGEMEIER, FRANK Y.
B. Apr. 22, 1873, St. Louis, Mo. D. Apr. 15, 1915, St. Louis, Mo.

Year	Team		W	L	PCT	ERA	G	GS	CG	IP	H	BB	SO	ShO	Relief W	Relief L	Relief SV	Batting AB	Batting H	HR	BA	PO	A	E	DP	TC/G	FA
1894	PHI	N	0	1	.000	11.25	1	1	1	8	12	4	2	0	0	0	0	3	1	0	.333	1	2	0	0	3.0	1.000

Ed Figueroa

FIGUEROA, EDUARDO (Figgy) BR TR 6′ 1″ 190 lbs.
Born Eduardo Figueroa (Padilla).
B. Oct. 14, 1948, Ciales, Puerto Rico.

Year	Team		W	L	PCT	ERA	G	GS	CG	IP	H	BB	SO	ShO	Relief W	Relief L	Relief SV	Batting AB	Batting H	HR	BA	PO	A	E	DP	TC/G	FA
1974	CAL	A	2	8	.200	3.69	25	12	5	105	119	36	49	1	0	0	0	0	0	0	—	4	17	1	1	0.9	.955
1975			16	13	.552	2.91	33	32	16	244.2	213	84	139	2	0	0	0	0	0	0	—	11	42	6	5	1.8	.898
1976	NY	A	19	10	.655	3.02	34	34	14	256.2	237	94	119	4	0	0	0	0	0	0	—	16	23	1	0	1.2	.975
1977			16	11	.593	3.58	32	32	12	239	228	75	104	2	0	0	0	0	0	0	—	18	29	2	2	1.5	.959
1978			20	9	.690	2.99	35	35	12	253	233	77	92	2	0	0	0	0	0	0	—	17	37	1	2	1.6	.982
1979			4	6	.400	4.11	16	16	4	105	109	35	42	1	0	0	0	0	0	0	—	9	16	2	1	1.7	.926
1980	2 teams	NY A	(15G 3–3)	TEX A	(8G 0–7)																						
″	total		3	10	.231	6.52	23	17	0	98	152	36	25	0	0	0	1	0	0	0		13	17	3	4	1.4	.909
1981	OAK	A	0	0	—	5.63	2	1	0	8	8	6	1	0	0	0	0	0	0	0	—	1	1	0	0	1.0	1.000
8 yrs.			80	67	.544	3.51	200	179	63	1309.1	1299	443	571	12	0	0	1	0	0	0		89	182	16	15	1.4	.944
LEAGUE CHAMPIONSHIP SERIES																											
1976	NY	A	0	1	.000	5.84	2	2	0	12.1	14	2	5	0	0	0	0	0	0	0	—	0	2	0	0	1.0	1.000
1977			0	0	—	10.80	1	1	0	3.1	5	2	3	0	0	0	0	0	0	0	—	0	0	0	0	0.0	.000
1978			0	1	.000	27.00	1	1	0	1	5	0	0	0	0	0	0	0	0	0	—	0	0	0	0	0.0	.000
3 yrs.			0	2	.000	8.10	4	4	0	16.2	24	4	8	0	0	0	0	0	0	0		0	2	0	0	0.5	1.000
WORLD SERIES																											
1976	NY	A	0	1	.000	5.63	1	1	0	8	6	5	2	0	0	0	0	0	0	0	—	0	1	0	0	1.0	1.000
1978			0	1	.000	8.10	2	2	0	6.2	9	5	2	0	0	0	0	0	0	0	—	0	0	0	0	0.0	.000
2 yrs.			0	2	.000	6.75	3	3	0	14.2	15	10	4	0	0	0	0	0	0	0		0	1	0	0	0.3	1.000

Tom Filer

FILER, THOMAS CARSON BR TR 6′ 1″ 195 lbs.
B. Dec. 1, 1956, Philadelphia, Pa.

Year	Team		W	L	PCT	ERA	G	GS	CG	IP	H	BB	SO	ShO	Relief W	Relief L	Relief SV	Batting AB	Batting H	HR	BA	PO	A	E	DP	TC/G	FA
1982	CHI	N	1	2	.333	5.53	8	8	0	40.2	50	18	15	0	0	0	0	12	1	0	.083	13	10	0	2	2.9	1.000
1985	TOR	A	7	0	1.000	3.88	11	9	0	48.2	38	18	24	0	0	0	0	0	0	0	—	1	5	0	1	0.5	1.000
1988	MIL	A	5	8	.385	4.43	19	16	2	101.2	108	33	39	1	0	1	0	0	0	0	—	24	17	0	4	2.2	1.000
1989			7	3	.700	3.61	13	13	0	72.1	74	23	20	0	0	0	0	0	0	0	—	4	16	2	4	1.6	.909
1990			2	3	.400	6.14	7	4	0	22	26	9	8	0	0	1	0	0	0	0	—	1	1	0	0	0.3	1.000
1992	NY	N	0	1	.000	2.05	9	1	0	22	18	6	9	0	0	1	0	3	0	0	.000	3	4	1	0	0.9	.875
6 yrs.			22	17	.564	4.25	67	51	2	307.1	314	107	115	1	0	3	0	15	1	0	.067	46	53	3	11	1.5	.971

Eddie Files

FILES, CHARLES EDWARD BR TR
B. May 19, 1883, Portland, Me. D. May 10, 1954, Cornish, Me.

Year	Team		W	L	PCT	ERA	G	GS	CG	IP	H	BB	SO	ShO	Relief W	Relief L	Relief SV	Batting AB	Batting H	HR	BA	PO	A	E	DP	TC/G	FA
1908	PHI	A	0	0	—	6.00	2	0	0	9	8	3	6	0	0	0	0	3	0	0	.000	0	1	0	0	0.5	1.000

Marc Filley

FILLEY, MARCUS LUCIUS BR TR 5′11″ 172 lbs.
B. Feb. 28, 1912, Lansingburg, N. Y. D. Jan. 20, 1995, Yarmouth, Me.

Year	Team		W	L	PCT	ERA	G	GS	CG	IP	H	BB	SO	ShO	Relief W	Relief L	Relief SV	Batting AB	Batting H	HR	BA	PO	A	E	DP	TC/G	FA
1934	WAS	A	0	0	—	27.00	1	0	0	0.1	2	0	0	0	0	0	0	0	0	0	—	0	0	0	0	0.0	.000

Dana Fillingim

FILLINGIM, DANA BL TR 5′10″ 175 lbs.
B. Nov. 6, 1893, Columbus, Ga. D. Feb. 3, 1961, Tuskegee, Ala.

Year	Team		W	L	PCT	ERA	G	GS	CG	IP	H	BB	SO	ShO	Relief W	Relief L	Relief SV	Batting AB	Batting H	HR	BA	PO	A	E	DP	TC/G	FA
1915	PHI	A	0	5	.000	3.43	8	4	1	39.1	42	32	17	0	0	1	0	12	2	0	.167	0	10	0	0	1.3	1.000
1918	BOS	N	7	6	.538	2.23	14	13	10	113	99	28	29	4	0	0	0	42	9	0	.214	1	34	0	1	2.5	1.000
1919			6	13	.316	3.38	32	18	9	186.1	185	39	50	0	2	0	2	65	16	0	.246	4	67	2	2	2.3	.973
1920			12	21	.364	3.11	37	31	22	272	292	79	66	2	1	2	0	92	16	0	.174	6	104	2	6	3.0	.982
1921			15	10	.600	3.45	44	23	11	239.2	249	56	54	**3**	4	1	1	85	21	2	.247	2	62	2	2	1.5	.970
1922			5	9	.357	4.54	25	12	5	117	143	37	25	1	1	3	2	38	6	0	.158	2	24	0	1	1.0	1.000
1923			1	9	.100	5.20	35	12	1	100.1	141	36	27	0	1	1	0	31	7	0	.226	0	25	0	0	0.7	1.000
1925	PHI	N	1	0	1.000	10.38	5	1	0	8.2	19	6	2	0	1	0	0	3	0	0	.000	1	2	0	1	0.6	1.000
8 yrs.			47	73	.392	3.56	200	114	59	1076.1	1170	313	270	10	10	8	5	368	77	2	.209	16	328	6	13	1.8	.983

Pete Filson

FILSON, WILLIAM PETER BB TL 6′ 2″ 195 lbs.
B. Sept. 28, 1958, Darby, Pa.

Year	Team		W	L	PCT	ERA	G	GS	CG	IP	H	BB	SO	ShO	Relief W	Relief L	Relief SV	Batting AB	Batting H	HR	BA	PO	A	E	DP	TC/G	FA
1982	MIN	A	0	2	.000	8.76	5	3	0	12.1	17	8	10	0	0	0	0	0	0	0	—	0	0	0	0	0.0	.000
1983			4	1	.800	3.40	26	8	0	90	87	29	49	0	1	0	1	0	0	0	—	2	6	1	0	0.3	.889
1984			6	5	.545	4.10	55	7	0	118.2	106	54	59	0	4	3	1	0	0	0	—	2	13	1	0	0.3	.938
1985			4	5	.444	3.67	40	6	1	95.2	93	30	42	0	3	0	2	0	0	0	—	3	13	2	0	0.4	.889
1986	2 teams	MIN A	(4G 0–0)	CHI A	(3G 0–1)																						
″	total		0	1	.000	6.00	7	1	0	18	27	7	8	0	0	0	0	0	0	0		1	0	0	0	0.1	1.000
1987	NY	A	1	0	1.000	3.27	7	2	0	22	26	9	10	0	0	0	0	0	0	0	—	1	7	0	0	1.1	1.000
1990	KC	A	0	4	.000	5.91	8	7	0	35	42	13	9	0	0	0	0	0	0	0	—	2	3	0	0	0.6	1.000
7 yrs.			15	18	.455	4.18	148	34	1	391.2	398	150	187	0	8	3	4	0	0	0		11	42	4	0	0.4	.930

Joel Finch

FINCH, JOEL D. BR TR 6′ 2″ 175 lbs.
B. Aug. 20, 1956, South Bend, Ind.

Year	Team		W	L	PCT	ERA	G	GS	CG	IP	H	BB	SO	ShO	Relief W	Relief L	Relief SV	Batting AB	Batting H	HR	BA	PO	A	E	DP	TC/G	FA
1979	BOS	A	0	3	.000	4.89	15	7	0	57	65	25	25	0	0	0	0	1	0	0	.000	10	10	1	1	1.4	.952

Bill Fincher

FINCHER, WILLIAM ALLEN BR TR 6′ 1″ 180 lbs.
B. May 26, 1894, Atlanta, Ga. D. May 7, 1946, Shreveport, La.

Year	Team		W	L	PCT	ERA	G	GS	CG	IP	H	BB	SO	ShO	Relief W	Relief L	Relief SV	Batting AB	Batting H	HR	BA	PO	A	E	DP	TC/G	FA
1916	STL	A	0	1	.000	2.14	12	1	0	21	22	7	5	0	0	0	0	4	1	0	.250	1	12	0	0	1.1	1.000

Tom Fine

FINE, THOMAS MORGAN BB TR 6′ 180 lbs.
B. Oct. 10, 1914, Cleburne, Tex.

Year	Team		W	L	PCT	ERA	G	GS	CG	IP	H	BB	SO	ShO	Relief W	Relief L	Relief SV	Batting AB	Batting H	HR	BA	PO	A	E	DP	TC/G	FA
1947	BOS	A	1	2	.333	5.50	9	7	1	36	41	19	10	0	0	0	0	9	3	0	.333	4	12	0	1	1.8	1.000
1950	STL	A	0	1	.000	8.10	14	0	0	36.2	53	25	6	0	0	1	0	12	4	0	.333	1	6	0	2	0.5	1.000
2 yrs.			1	3	.250	6.81	23	7	1	72.2	94	44	16	0	0	1	0	21	7	0	.333	5	18	0	3	1.0	1.000

Rollie Fingers

FINGERS, ROLAND GLEN
B. Aug. 25, 1946, Steubenville, Ohio.
Hall of Fame 1992.
BR TR 6′ 4″ 190 lbs.

Year	Team	Lg	W	L	PCT	ERA	G	GS	CG	IP	H	BB	SO	ShO	Relief Pitching W	Relief Pitching L	Relief Pitching SV	Batting AB	Batting H	Batting HR	BA	PO	A	E	DP	TC/G	FA
1968	**OAK**	**A**	0	0	—	27.00	1	0	0	1.1	4	1	0	0	0	0	0	0	0	0	—	0	0	0	0	0.0	.000
1969			6	7	.462	3.71	60	8	1	119	116	41	61	1	4	3	12	25	5	0	.200	9	30	3	3	0.7	.929
1970			7	9	.438	3.65	45	19	1	148	137	48	79	0	3	1	2	39	4	1	.103	7	26	2	3	0.8	.943
1971			4	6	.400	3.00	48	8	2	129	94	30	98	1	3	3	17	33	7	0	.212	14	24	0	4	0.8	1.000
1972			11	9	.550	2.51	65	0	0	111.1	85	32	113	0	**11**	**9**	21	19	6	1	.316	7	11	0	1	0.3	1.000
1973			7	8	.467	1.92	62	2	0	126.2	107	39	110	0	7	6	22	1	0	0	.000	3	14	1	0	0.3	.944
1974			9	5	.643	2.65	**76**	0	0	119	104	29	95	0	9	5	18	0	0	0	—	9	21	0	4	0.4	1.000
1975			10	6	.625	2.98	**75**	0	0	126.2	95	33	115	0	**10**	6	24	1	0	0	.000	8	14	0	2	0.3	1.000
1976			13	11	.542	2.47	70	0	0	135	118	40	113	0	13	11	20	0	0	0	—	4	26	1	0	0.4	.968
1977	**SD**	**N**	8	9	.471	3.00	**78**	0	0	132	123	36	113	0	8	9	**35**	20	1	0	.050	5	19	3	1	0.3	.889
1978			6	13	.316	2.52	67	0	0	107	84	29	72	0	6	**13**	**37**	12	2	0	.167	14	12	1	1	0.4	.963
1979			9	9	.500	4.50	54	0	0	84	91	37	65	0	9	9	13	12	1	0	.083	3	9	1	0	0.2	.923
1980			11	9	.550	2.80	66	0	0	103	101	32	69	0	**11**	9	23	18	5	0	.278	9	11	1	0	0.3	.952
1981	**MIL**	**A**	6	3	.667	1.04	47	0	0	78	55	13	61	0	6	3	**28**	0	0	0	—	2	13	1	1	0.3	.938
1982			5	6	.455	2.60	50	0	0	79.2	63	20	71	0	5	6	29	0	0	0	—	4	10	0	1	0.3	1.000
1984			1	2	.333	1.96	33	0	0	46	38	13	40	0	1	2	23	0	0	0	—	3	3	0	0	0.2	1.000
1985			1	6	.143	5.04	47	0	0	55.1	59	19	24	0	1	6	17	0	0	0	—	7	10	0	1	0.4	1.000
17 yrs.			114	118	.491	2.90	944	37	4	1701	1474	492	1299	2	107	101	341	180	31	2	.172	108	253	14	22	0.4	.963
							5th								**4th**		**3rd**										
DIVISIONAL PLAYOFF SERIES																											
1981	**MIL**	**A**	1	0	1.000	3.86	3	0	0	4.2	7	1	5	0	1	0	1	0	0	0	—	0	0	0	0	0.0	.000
LEAGUE CHAMPIONSHIP SERIES																											
1971	**OAK**	**A**	0	0	—	7.71	2	0	0	2.1	2	1	2	0	0	0	0	0	0	0	—	0	0	0	0	0.0	.000
1972			1	0	1.000	1.69	3	0	0	5.1	4	1	3	0	1	0	0	1	0	0	.000	0	0	0	0	0.0	.000
1973			0	1	.000	1.93	3	0	0	4.2	4	2	4	0	0	1	1	0	0	0	—	0	0	0	0	0.0	.000
1974			0	0	—	3.00	2	0	0	3	3	1	3	0	0	0	1	0	0	0	—	0	0	0	0	0.0	.000
1975			0	1	.000	6.75	1	0	0	4	5	1	3	0	0	1	0	0	0	0	—	1	0	0	0	1.0	1.000
5 yrs.			1	2	.333	3.72	11	0	0	19.1	18	6	15	0	1	2	2	1	0	0	.000	1	0	0	0	0.1	1.000
							9th																				
WORLD SERIES																											
1972	**OAK**	**A**	1	1	.500	1.74	6	0	0	10.1	4	4	11	0	1	1	2	1	0	0	.000	0	2	0	0	0.3	1.000
1973			0	1	.000	0.66	6	0	0	13.2	13	4	8	0	0	1	2	3	1	0	.333	0	2	0	0	0.3	1.000
1974			1	0	1.000	1.93	4	0	0	9.1	8	2	6	0	1	0	2	2	0	0	.000	0	1	0	0	0.3	1.000
3 yrs.			2	2	.500	1.35	16	0	0	33.1	25	10	25	0	2	2	6	6	1	0	.167	0	5	0	0	0.3	1.000
							2nd										**1st**										

Herman Fink

FINK, HERMAN ADAM
B. Aug. 22, 1911, Concord, N. C. D. Aug. 24, 1980, Salisbury, N. C.
BR TR 6′ 2″ 198 lbs.

Year	Team	Lg	W	L	PCT	ERA	G	GS	CG	IP	H	BB	SO	ShO	Relief Pitching W	Relief Pitching L	Relief Pitching SV	Batting AB	Batting H	Batting HR	BA	PO	A	E	DP	TC/G	FA
1935	**PHI**	**A**	0	3	.000	9.19	5	3	0	15.2	18	10	2	0	0	0	0	5	1	0	.200	2	3	1	1	1.2	.833
1936			8	16	.333	5.39	34	24	9	188.2	222	78	53	0	0	2	3	64	8	0	.125	3	28	3	0	1.0	.912
1937			2	1	.667	4.05	28	3	1	80	82	35	18	0	2	0	1	24	5	0	.208	0	16	0	1	0.6	1.000
3 yrs.			10	20	.333	5.22	67	30	10	284.1	322	123	73	0	2	2	4	93	14	0	.151	5	47	4	2	0.8	.929

Pembroke Finlayson

FINLAYSON, PEMBROKE
B. July 31, 1888, Cheraw, S. C. D. Mar. 6, 1912, Brooklyn, N. Y.
BR TR

Year	Team	Lg	W	L	PCT	ERA	G	GS	CG	IP	H	BB	SO	ShO	Relief Pitching W	Relief Pitching L	Relief Pitching SV	Batting AB	Batting H	Batting HR	BA	PO	A	E	DP	TC/G	FA
1908	**BKN**	**N**	0	0	—	135.00	1	0	0	0.1	0	4	0	0	0	0	0	0	0	0	—	0	0	0	0	0.0	.000
1909			0	0	—	5.14	1	0	0	7	7	4	2	0	0	0	0	3	0	0	.000	0	1	0	0	1.0	1.000
2 yrs.			0	0		11.05	2	0	0	7.1	7	8	2	0	0	0	0	3	0	0	.000	0	1	0	0	0.5	1.000

Chuck Finley

FINLEY, CHARLES EDWARD
B. Nov. 26, 1962, Monroe, La.
BL TL 6′ 6″ 220 lbs.

Year	Team	Lg	W	L	PCT	ERA	G	GS	CG	IP	H	BB	SO	ShO	Relief Pitching W	Relief Pitching L	Relief Pitching SV	Batting AB	Batting H	Batting HR	BA	PO	A	E	DP	TC/G	FA
1986	**CAL**	**A**	3	1	.750	3.30	25	0	0	46.1	40	23	37	0	3	1	0	0	0	0	—	8	8	0	1	0.6	1.000
1987			2	7	.222	4.67	35	3	0	90.2	102	43	63	0	2	6	0	0	0	0	—	6	11	1	1	0.5	.944
1988			9	15	.375	4.17	31	31	2	194.1	191	82	111	0	0	0	0	0	0	0	—	5	24	1	1	1.0	.967
1989			16	9	.640	2.57	29	29	9	199.2	171	82	156	1	0	0	0	0	0	0	—	4	16	2	0	0.8	.909
1990			18	9	.667	2.40	32	32	7	236	210	81	177	2	0	0	0	0	0	0	—	14	21	5	2	1.3	.875
1991			18	9	.667	3.80	34	34	4	227.1	205	101	171	2	0	0	0	0	0	0	—	11	16	2	3	0.9	.931
1992			7	12	.368	3.96	31	31	4	204.1	212	98	124	1	0	0	0	0	0	0	—	3	17	3	1	0.7	.870
1993			16	14	.533	3.15	35	35	**13**	251.1	243	82	187	2	0	0	0	0	0	0	—	10	26	5	0	1.2	.878
1994			10	10	.500	4.32	25	**25**	7	**183.1**	178	71	148	2	0	0	0	0	0	0	—	9	17	4	1	1.2	.867
1995			15	12	.556	4.21	32	32	2	203	192	93	195	1	0	0	0	0	0	0	—	4	18	4	4	0.8	.846
10 yrs.			114	98	.538	3.58	309	252	48	1836.1	1744	756	1369	11	5	7	0	0	0	0		74	174	27	14	0.9	.902
LEAGUE CHAMPIONSHIP SERIES																											
1986	**CAL**	**A**	0	0	—	0.00	3	0	0	2	1	0	1	0	0	0	0	0	0	0	—	0	0	0	0	0.0	.000

Happy Finneran

FINNERAN, JOSEPH IGNATIUS (Smokey Joe)
B. Oct. 29, 1891, East Orange, N. J. D. Feb. 3, 1942, Orange, N. J.
BR TR 5′10½″ 169 lbs.

Year	Team	Lg	W	L	PCT	ERA	G	GS	CG	IP	H	BB	SO	ShO	Relief Pitching W	Relief Pitching L	Relief Pitching SV	Batting AB	Batting H	Batting HR	BA	PO	A	E	DP	TC/G	FA
1912	**PHI**	**N**	0	2	.000	2.53	14	4	0	46.1	50	10	10	0	0	1	1	10	2	0	.200	3	11	0	0	1.0	1.000
1913			0	0	—	7.20	3	0	0	5	12	2	0	0	0	0	0	3	2	0	.667	0	0	0	0	0.0	.000
1914	**BKN**	**F**	12	11	.522	3.18	27	23	13	175.1	153	60	54	2	1	0	1	55	7	0	.127	8	48	2	1	2.1	.966
1915			12	13	.480	2.80	37	24	12	215.1	197	87	68	1	3	2	0	74	11	0	.149	15	61	2	1	2.1	.974
1918	**2 teams**	**DET A**	(5G 0–2)		**NY A**	(23G 3–6)																					
″	**total**		3	8	.273	4.43	28	15	4	128	156	43	36	0	1	0	1	42	9	0	.214	4	35	0	1	1.4	1.000
5 yrs.			27	34	.443	3.30	109	66	29	570	568	202	168	3	5	3	3	184	31	0	.168	30	155	4	3	1.7	.979

Gar Finnvold

FINNVOLD, ANDERS GAR
B. Mar. 11, 1968, Boynton Beach, Fla.
BR TR 6′ 5″ 195 lbs.

Year	Team	Lg	W	L	PCT	ERA	G	GS	CG	IP	H	BB	SO	ShO	Relief Pitching W	Relief Pitching L	Relief Pitching SV	Batting AB	Batting H	Batting HR	BA	PO	A	E	DP	TC/G	FA
1994	**BOS**	**A**	0	4	.000	5.94	8	8	0	36.1	45	15	17	0	0	0	0	0	0	0	—	3	2	1	0	0.8	.833

Year	Team		W	L	PCT	ERA	G	GS	CG	IP	H	BB	SO	ShO	Relief Pitching W	Relief Pitching L	Relief Pitching SV	Batting AB	Batting H	Batting HR	BA	PO	A	E	DP	TC/G	FA

Steve Fireovid

FIREOVID, STEPHEN JOHN BB TR 6′ 2″ 195 lbs.
B. June 6, 1957, Bryan, Ohio.

1981	SD	N	0	1	.000	2.77	5	4	0	26	30	7	11	0	0	0	0	7	1	0	.143	0	5	0	0	1.0	1.000
1983			0	0	—	1.80	3	0	0	5	4	2	1	0	0	0	0	0	0	0	—	0	1	0	0	0.3	1.000
1984	PHI	N	0	0	—	1.59	6	0	0	5.2	4	0	3	0	0	0	0	0	0	0	—	3	1	0	1	0.7	1.000
1985	CHI	A	0	0	—	5.14	4	0	0	7	17	2	2	0	0	0	0	0	0	0	—	0	0	0	0	0.0	.000
1986	SEA	A	2	0	1.000	4.29	10	1	0	21	28	4	10	0	2	0	0	0	0	0	—	3	2	1	0	0.6	.833
1992	TEX	A	1	0	1.000	4.05	3	0	0	6.2	10	4	0	0	1	0	0	0	0	0	—	1	2	0	2	1.0	1.000
6 yrs.			3	1	.750	3.41	31	5	0	71.1	93	19	27	0	3	0	0	7	1	0	.143	7	11	1	3	0.6	.947

Ted Firth

FIRTH, THEODORE JOHN
B. 1856, Philadelphia, Pa. D. Apr. 18, 1885, Marshalltown, Iowa.

1884	RIC	AA	0	1	.000	*8.00*	1	1	1	9	14	5	0	0	0	0	0	3	1	0	.333	1	1	0	0	2.0	1.000

Bill Fischer

FISCHER, WILLIAM CHARLES BR TR 6′ 190 lbs.
B. Oct. 11, 1930, Wausau, Wis.

1956	CHI	A	0	0	—	21.60	3	0	0	1.2	6	1	2	0	0	0	0	0	0	0	—	1	0	0	0	0.3	1.000
1957			7	8	.467	3.48	33	11	3	124	139	35	48	1	3	4	1	40	6	0	.150	6	20	1	0	0.8	.963
1958	3 teams		CHI A (17G 2–3)			DET A (22G 2–4)				WAS A (3G 0–3)																	
″	total		4	10	.286	6.34	42	6	0	88	113	31	42	0	2	6	2	13	2	0	.154	4	23	0	2	0.6	1.000
1959	WAS	A	9	11	.450	4.28	34	29	6	187.1	211	43	62	1	0	0	0	54	7	0	.130	21	48	1	2	2.1	.986
1960	2 teams		WAS A (20G 3–5)			DET A (20G 5–3)																					
″	total		8	8	.500	4.30	40	13	2	132	135	35	55	0	2	1	0	30	7	1	.233	8	28	0	4	0.9	1.000
1961	2 teams		DET A (26G 3–2)			KC A (15G 1–0)																					
″	total		4	2	.667	4.66	41	1	0	67.2	80	23	30	0	4	1	5	9	0	0	.000	7	9	0	0	0.4	1.000
1962	KC	A	4	12	.250	3.95	34	16	5	127.2	150	8	38	0	1	0	2	38	4	0	.105	15	16	0	1	0.9	1.000
1963			9	6	.600	3.57	45	2	0	95.2	86	29	34	0	9	6	3	15	1	0	.067	3	14	1	1	0.4	.944
1964	MIN	A	0	1	.000	7.36	9	0	0	7.1	16	5	2	0	0	1	0	0	0	0	—	0	3	0	0	0.3	1.000
9 yrs.			45	58	.437	4.34	281	78	16	831.1	936	210	313	2	21	19	13	199	27	1	.136	65	161	3	10	0.8	.987

Carl Fischer

FISCHER, CHARLES WILLIAM BR TL 6′ 180 lbs.
B. Nov. 5, 1905, Medina, N. Y. D. Dec. 10, 1963, Medina, N. Y.

1930	WAS	A	1	1	.500	4.86	8	4	1	33.1	37	18	21	0	0	0	1	9	0	0	.000	1	9	1	0	1.4	.909
1931			13	9	.591	4.38	46	23	7	191	207	80	96	0	2	0	3	66	8	0	.121	1	23	2	0	0.6	.923
1932	2 teams		WAS A (12G 3–2)			STL A (24G 3–7)																					
″	total		6	9	.400	5.36	36	18	5	147.2	179	76	58	1	1	0	1	49	12	0	.245	5	15	1	1	0.6	.952
1933	DET	A	11	15	.423	3.55	35	22	9	182.2	176	84	93	0	5	1	3	62	9	0	.145	1	29	1	1	0.9	.968
1934			6	4	.600	4.37	20	15	4	94.2	107	38	39	1	1	1	1	31	2	0	.065	3	8	0	0	0.6	1.000
1935	2 teams		DET A (3G 0–1)			CHI A (24G 5–5)																					
″	total		5	6	.455	6.17	27	12	3	100.2	118	44	38	1	2	1	0	23	4	0	.174	5	13	1	0	0.7	.947
1937	2 teams		CLE A (2G 0–1)			WAS A (17G 4–5)																					
″	total		4	6	.400	4.58	19	11	2	72.2	76	32	31	0	0	2	2	22	3	0	.136	1	5	1	0	0.4	.857
7 yrs.			46	50	.479	4.63	191	105	31	822.2	900	372	376	3	11	5	11	262	38	0	.145	17	102	7	2	0.7	.944

Hank Fischer

FISCHER, HENRY WILLIAM (Bulldog) BR TR 6′ 190 lbs.
B. Jan. 11, 1940, Yonkers, N. Y.

1962	MIL	N	2	3	.400	5.30	29	0	0	37.1	43	20	29	0	2	3	4	4	0	0	.000	3	5	0	0	0.3	1.000
1963			4	3	.571	4.96	31	6	1	74.1	74	28	72	0	1	3	0	19	2	0	.105	4	9	1	0	0.5	.929
1964			11	10	.524	4.01	37	28	9	168.1	177	39	99	5	0	0	2	52	8	0	.154	14	23	2	0	1.1	.949
1965			8	9	.471	3.89	31	19	2	122.2	126	39	79	0	1	0	0	37	4	0	.108	10	11	3	0	0.8	.875
1966	3 teams		ATL N (14G 2–3)			CIN N (11G 0–6)				BOS A (6G 2–3)																	
″	total		4	12	.250	4.53	31	22	1	117.1	143	40	72	0	0	0	0	33	3	0	.091	2	15	2	0	0.6	.895
1967	BOS	A	1	2	.333	2.36	9	2	1	26.2	24	8	18	0	0	1	1	7	1	0	.143	1	4	0	0	0.6	1.000
6 yrs.			30	39	.435	4.23	168	77	14	546.2	587	174	369	5	4	7	7	152	18	0	.118	34	67	8	0	0.6	.927

Jeff Fischer

FISCHER, JEFFREY THOMAS BR TR 6′ 3″ 185 lbs.
B. Aug. 17, 1963, West Palm Beach, Fla.

1987	MON	N	0	1	.000	8.56	4	2	0	13.2	21	5	6	0	0	0	0	5	1	0	.200	1	2	0	0	0.8	1.000
1989	LA	N	0	0	—	13.50	2	0	0	3.1	7	0	2	0	0	0	0	0	0	0	—	0	0	0	0	0.0	.000
2 yrs.			0	1	.000	9.53	6	2	0	17	28	5	8	0	0	0	0	5	1	0	.200	1	2	0	0	0.5	1.000

Rube Fischer

FISCHER, REUBEN WALTER BR TR 6′ 4″ 190 lbs.
B. Sept. 19, 1916, Carlock, S. D.

1941	NY	N	1	0	1.000	2.45	2	1	1	11	10	6	9	0	0	0	0	3	1	0	.333	1	1	0	0	1.0	1.000
1943			5	10	.333	4.61	22	17	4	130.2	140	59	47	0	1	0	1	43	11	1	.256	2	18	1	2	1.0	.952
1944			6	14	.300	5.18	38	18	2	128.2	128	87	39	1	3	4	2	40	5	0	.125	2	17	0	0	0.5	1.000
1945			3	8	.273	5.63	31	4	0	76.2	90	49	27	0	2	5	1	19	4	1	.211	5	10	1	1	0.5	.938
1946			1	2	.333	6.31	15	1	0	35.2	48	21	14	0	1	2	0	9	1	0	.111	0	9	3	0	0.8	.750
5 yrs.			16	34	.320	5.10	108	41	7	382.2	416	222	136	1	7	11	4	114	22	2	.193	10	55	5	3	0.6	.929

Todd Fischer

FISCHER, TODD RICHARD BR TR 5′10″ 170 lbs.
B. Sept. 15, 1960, Columbus, Ohio.

1986	CAL	A	0	0	—	4.24	9	0	0	17	18	8	7	0	0	0	0	0	0	0	—	0	2	0	1	0.2	1.000

Leo Fishel

FISHEL, LEO BR TR 6′ 175 lbs.
B. Dec. 13, 1877, Babylon, N. Y. D. May 19, 1960, Hempstead, N. Y.

1899	NY	N	0	1	.000	6.00	1	1	1	9	9	6	6	0	0	0	0	4	1	0	.250	1	2	0	0	3.0	1.000

Fisher

FISHER
B. Johnstown, Pa. Deceased.

1884	PHI	U	1	7	.125	*3.57*	8	8	8	70.2	76	13	42	0	0	0	0	36	8	0	.222	23	15	15	1	5.3	.717

Fisher

FISHER
B. Philadelphia, Pa. Deceased.

1885	BUF	N	0	1	.000	5.00	1	1	1	9	10	2	4	0	0	0	0	4	0	0	.000	1	3	0	0	4.0	1.000

Year	Team	Lg	W	L	PCT	ERA	G	GS	CG	IP	H	BB	SO	ShO	Relief Pitching W	Relief Pitching L	Relief Pitching SV	Batting AB	Batting H	Batting HR	BA	PO	A	E	DP	TC/G	FA

Brian Fisher

FISHER, BRIAN KEVIN BR TR 6′ 4″ 210 lbs.
B. Mar. 18, 1962, Honolulu, Hawaii.

Year	Team	Lg	W	L	PCT	ERA	G	GS	CG	IP	H	BB	SO	ShO	Relief W	Relief L	Relief SV	AB	H	HR	BA	PO	A	E	DP	TC/G	FA
1985	NY	A	4	4	.500	2.38	55	0	0	98.1	77	29	85	0	4	4	14	0	0	0	—	4	13	1	1	0.3	.944
1986			9	5	.643	4.93	62	0	0	96.2	105	37	67	0	9	5	6	0	0	0	—	3	7	1	1	0.2	.909
1987	PIT	N	11	9	.550	4.52	37	26	6	185.1	185	72	117	3	0	0	0	58	11	2	.190	13	20	1	1	0.9	.971
1988			8	10	.444	4.61	33	22	1	146.1	157	57	66	1	2	0	1	42	2	0	.048	6	17	3	2	0.8	.885
1989			0	3	.000	7.94	9	3	0	17	25	10	8	0	0	1	1	5	0	0	.000	2	1	0	0	0.3	1.000
1990	HOU	N	0	0	—	7.20	4	0	0	5	9	0	1	0	0	0	0	0	0	0	—	0	0	0	0	0.0	.000
1992	SEA	A	4	3	.571	4.53	22	14	0	91.1	80	47	26	0	0	0	1	0	0	0	—	5	13	1	0	0.9	.947
7 yrs.			36	34	.514	4.39	222	65	7	640	638	252	370	4	15	10	23	105	13	2	.124	33	71	7	5	0.5	.937

Chauncey Fisher

FISHER, CHAUNCEY BURR (Peach) BR TR 5′11″ 175 lbs.
Brother of Tom Fisher.
B. Jan. 8, 1872, Anderson, Ind. D. Apr. 27, 1939, Los Angeles, Calif.

Year	Team	Lg	W	L	PCT	ERA	G	GS	CG	IP	H	BB	SO	ShO	Relief W	Relief L	Relief SV	AB	H	HR	BA	PO	A	E	DP	TC/G	FA
1893	CLE	N	0	2	.000	5.50	2	2	2	18	26	9	9	0	0	0	0	8	2	0	.250	3	3	0	0	3.0	1.000
1894	2 teams	CLE N (3G 0–2)	CIN N (11G 2–8)																								
″	total		2	10	.167	7.76	14	13	10	102	156	49	14	0	0	0	0	47	10	1	.213	3	17	2	1	1.6	.909
1896	CIN	N	10	7	.588	4.45	27	15	13	159.2	199	36	25	2	2	2	2	57	14	0	.246	10	37	4	2	1.9	.922
1897	BKN	N	9	7	.563	4.23	20	13	11	149	184	43	31	1	2	1	1	59	12	0	.203	4	26	0	2	1.5	1.000
1901	2 teams	NY N (1G 0–1)	STL N (1G 0–0)																								
″	total		0	1	.000	15.43	2	1	0	7	18	3	1	0	0	0	0	3	0	0	.000	0	2	0	0	1.0	1.000
5 yrs.			21	27	.438	5.37	65	44	36	435.2	583	140	80	3	4	3	3	174	38	1	.218	20	85	6	5	1.7	.946

Cherokee Fisher

FISHER, WILLIAM CHARLES BR TR 5′ 9″ 164 lbs.
B. Dec. 1845, Philadelphia, Pa. D. Sept. 26, 1912, New York, N. Y.

Year	Team	Lg	W	L	PCT	ERA	G	GS	CG	IP	H	BB	SO	ShO	Relief W	Relief L	Relief SV	AB	H	HR	BA	PO	A	E	DP	TC/G	FA
1876	CIN	N	4	20	.167	3.02	28	24	22	229.1	294	6	29	0	0	0	0	129	32	0	.248	38	29	15	0	2.0	.817
1878	PRO	N	0	1	.000	4.00	1	1	1	9	14	0	2	0	0	0	0	3	0	0	.000	0	2	1	0	3.0	.667
2 yrs.			4	21	.160	3.06	29	25	23	238.1	308	6	31	0	0	0	0	136	32	0	.235	40	32	16	0	2.0	.818

Clarence Fisher

FISHER, CLARENCE HENRY BR TR 6′ 174 lbs.
B. Aug. 27, 1898, Letart, W. Va. D. Nov. 2, 1965, Point Pleasant, W. Va.

Year	Team	Lg	W	L	PCT	ERA	G	GS	CG	IP	H	BB	SO	ShO	Relief W	Relief L	Relief SV	AB	H	HR	BA	PO	A	E	DP	TC/G	FA
1919	WAS	A	0	0	—	13.50	2	0	0	4	8	3	1	0	0	0	0	0	0	0	—	0	1	0	0	0.5	1.000
1920			0	1	.000	9.82	2	0	0	3.2	5	5	0	0	0	1	0	1	0	0	.000	0	4	0	0	2.0	1.000
2 yrs.			0	1	.000	11.74	4	0	0	7.2	13	8	1	0	0	1	0	1	0	0	.000	0	5	0	0	1.3	1.000

Don Fisher

FISHER, DONALD RAYMOND BR TR 6′ 210 lbs.
B. Feb. 6, 1916, Cleveland, Ohio D. July 29, 1973, Mayfield Heights, Ohio.

Year	Team	Lg	W	L	PCT	ERA	G	GS	CG	IP	H	BB	SO	ShO	Relief W	Relief L	Relief SV	AB	H	HR	BA	PO	A	E	DP	TC/G	FA
1945	NY	N	1	0	1.000	2.00	2	1	1	18	12	7	4	1	0	0	0	7	1	0	.143	0	4	1	0	2.5	.800

Ed Fisher

FISHER, EDWARD FREDRICK BR TR 6′ 2″ 200 lbs.
B. Oct. 31, 1876, Wayne, Mich. D. July 24, 1951, Spokane, Wash.

Year	Team	Lg	W	L	PCT	ERA	G	GS	CG	IP	H	BB	SO	ShO	Relief W	Relief L	Relief SV	AB	H	HR	BA	PO	A	E	DP	TC/G	FA
1902	DET	A	0	0	—	0.00	1	0	0	4	4	1	0	0	0	0	0	2	0	0	.000	0	0	0	0	0.0	.000

Eddie Fisher

FISHER, EDDIE GENE BR TR 6′ 2½″ 200 lbs.
B. July 16, 1936, Shreveport, La.

Year	Team	Lg	W	L	PCT	ERA	G	GS	CG	IP	H	BB	SO	ShO	Relief W	Relief L	Relief SV	AB	H	HR	BA	PO	A	E	DP	TC/G	FA
1959	SF	N	2	6	.250	7.88	17	5	0	40	57	8	15	0	0	4	1	8	0	0	.000	5	3	0	0	0.5	1.000
1960			1	0	1.000	3.55	3	1	1	12.2	11	2	7	0	0	0	0	5	3	0	.600	1	2	0	0	1.0	1.000
1961			0	2	.000	5.35	15	1	0	33.2	36	9	16	0	0	2	1	7	1	0	.143	3	6	1	0	0.7	.900
1962	CHI	A	9	5	.643	3.10	57	12	2	182.2	169	45	88	1	4	3	5	46	6	0	.130	16	30	3	3	0.9	.939
1963			9	8	.529	3.95	33	15	2	120.2	114	28	67	1	2	3	0	36	5	0	.139	10	24	2	0	1.1	.944
1964			6	3	.667	3.02	59	2	0	125	86	32	74	0	6	3	9	18	3	0	.167	7	20	0	1	0.5	1.000
1965			15	7	.682	2.40	**82**	0	0	165.1	118	43	90	0	**15**	7	24	29	4	0	.138	9	35	1	3	0.5	.978
1966	2 teams	CHI A (23G 1–3)	BAL A (44G 5–3)																								
″	total		6	6	.500	2.52	**67**	0	0	107	87	36	57	0	6	6	19	15	2	0	.133	7	19	3	0	0.4	.897
1967	BAL	A	4	3	.571	3.61	46	0	0	89.2	82	26	53	0	4	3	1	5	1	0	.200	4	12	1	1	0.4	.941
1968	CLE	A	4	2	.667	2.85	54	0	0	94.2	87	17	42	0	4	2	4	12	0	0	.000	9	18	0	1	0.5	1.000
1969	CAL	A	3	2	.600	3.63	52	1	0	96.2	100	28	47	0	2	2	2	13	0	0	.000	6	16	2	3	0.5	.917
1970			4	4	.500	3.05	67	2	0	130	117	35	74	0	4	4	8	11	1	0	.091	11	25	1	1	0.6	.973
1971			10	8	.556	2.72	57	3	0	119	92	50	82	0	9	6	3	16	1	0	.063	6	17	0	0	0.4	1.000
1972	2 teams	CAL A (43G 4–5)	CHI A (6G 0–1)																								
″	total		4	6	.400	3.91	49	5	0	103.2	104	40	42	0	4	3	4	24	2	0	.083	6	17	2	1	0.5	.920
1973	2 teams	CHI A (26G 6–7)	STL N (6G 2–1)																								
″	total		8	8	.500	4.67	32	16	2	117.2	138	39	58	0	2	1	0	1	1	0	1.000	7	18	1	3	0.8	.962
15 yrs.			85	70	.548	3.41	690	63	7	1538.1	1398	438	812	2	62	49	81	246	30	0	.122	107	262	17	17	0.6	.956

Fritz Fisher

FISHER, FREDERICK BROWN BL TL 6′ 1″ 180 lbs.
B. Nov. 28, 1941, Adrian, Mich.

Year	Team	Lg	W	L	PCT	ERA	G	GS	CG	IP	H	BB	SO	ShO	Relief W	Relief L	Relief SV	AB	H	HR	BA	PO	A	E	DP	TC/G	FA
1964	DET	A	0	0	—	108.00	1	0	0	0.1	2	2	1	0	0	0	0	0	0	0	—	0	0	0	0	0.0	.000

Harry Fisher

FISHER, HARRY DEVERAUX BL TR 6′ 180 lbs.
B. Jan. 3, 1926, Newbury, Ont., Canada D. Sept. 20, 1981, Waterloo, Ont., Canada.

Year	Team	Lg	W	L	PCT	ERA	G	GS	CG	IP	H	BB	SO	ShO	Relief W	Relief L	Relief SV	AB	H	HR	BA	PO	A	E	DP	TC/G	FA
1952	PIT	N	1	2	.333	6.87	8	3	0	18.1	17	13	5	0	0	0	0	*				1	1	0	0	0.3	1.000

Jack Fisher

FISHER, JOHN HOWARD (Fat Jack) BR TR 6′ 2″ 215 lbs.
B. Mar. 4, 1939, Frostburg, Md.

Year	Team	Lg	W	L	PCT	ERA	G	GS	CG	IP	H	BB	SO	ShO	Relief W	Relief L	Relief SV	AB	H	HR	BA	PO	A	E	DP	TC/G	FA
1959	BAL	A	1	6	.143	3.05	27	7	1	88.2	76	38	52	1	0	2	2	23	3	0	.130	2	11	1	0	0.5	.929
1960			12	11	.522	3.41	40	20	8	197.2	174	78	99	3	6	3	2	60	11	1	.183	11	33	1	1	1.1	.978
1961			10	13	.435	3.90	36	25	10	196	205	75	118	1	0	4	1	56	5	0	.089	8	22	2	1	0.9	.938
1962			7	9	.438	5.09	32	25	4	152	173	56	81	0	0	1	1	49	5	0	.102	18	18	0	1	1.1	1.000
1963	SF	N	6	10	.375	4.58	36	12	2	116	132	38	57	0	3	2	1	29	3	0	.103	10	19	0	0	0.8	1.000
1964	NY	N	10	17	.370	4.23	40	34	8	227.2	256	56	115	1	0	2	0	76	12	0	.158	18	34	3	5	1.4	.945
1965			8	**24**	.250	3.94	43	36	10	253.2	252	68	116	0	0	2	1	78	12	0	.154	27	49	1	4	1.8	.987
1966			11	14	.440	3.68	38	33	10	230	229	54	127	2	1	0	0	67	6	0	.090	26	45	3	3	1.9	.959

Jack Fisher *continued*

Year	Team	Lg	W	L	PCT	ERA	G	GS	CG	IP	H	BB	SO	ShO	Relief Pitching W	Relief Pitching L	Relief Pitching SV	Batting AB	Batting H	Batting HR	BA	PO	A	E	DP	TC/G	FA
1967			9	**18**	.333	4.70	39	30	7	220.1	251	64	117	1	1	1	0	70	7	0	.100	15	43	1	1	1.5	.983
1968	**CHI**	**A**	8	13	.381	2.99	35	28	2	180.2	176	48	80	0	0	1	0	53	6	0	.113	18	24	1	2	1.2	.977
1969	**CIN**	**N**	4	4	.500	5.50	34	15	0	113	137	30	55	0	1	0	1	33	4	0	.121	4	14	2	0	0.6	.900
11 yrs.			86	139	.382	4.06	400	265	62	1975.2	2061	605	1017	9	12	18	9	594	74	1	.125	157	312	15	18	1.2	.969

Maury Fisher

FISHER, MAURICE WAYNE BR TR 6′ 5″ 210 lbs.
B. Feb. 16, 1931, Uniondale, Ind.

Year	Team	Lg	W	L	PCT	ERA	G	GS	CG	IP	H	BB	SO	ShO	Relief Pitching W	Relief Pitching L	Relief Pitching SV	Batting AB	Batting H	Batting HR	BA	PO	A	E	DP	TC/G	FA
1955	**CIN**	**N**	0	0	—	6.75	1	0	0	2.2	5	2	1	0	0	0	0	1	0	0	.000	0	0	0	0	0.0	.000

Ray Fisher

FISHER, RAY LYLE BR TR 5′11½″ 180 lbs.
B. Oct. 4, 1887, Middlebury, Vt. D. Nov. 3, 1982, Ann Arbor, Mich.

Year	Team	Lg	W	L	PCT	ERA	G	GS	CG	IP	H	BB	SO	ShO	Relief Pitching W	Relief Pitching L	Relief Pitching SV	Batting AB	Batting H	Batting HR	BA	PO	A	E	DP	TC/G	FA
1910	**NY**	**A**	5	3	.625	2.92	17	7	3	92.1	95	18	42	0	1	0	1	29	3	0	.103	2	37	3	0	2.5	.929
1911			10	11	.476	3.25	29	22	8	171.2	178	55	99	2	2	1	0	59	7	1	.119	6	67	5	1	2.7	.936
1912			2	8	.200	5.88	17	13	5	90.1	107	32	47	0	1	0	0	31	2	0	.065	3	38	4	0	2.6	.911
1913			12	16	.429	3.18	43	31	14	246.1	244	71	92	1	0	1	1	79	22	0	.278	12	85	7	0	2.4	.933
1914			10	12	.455	2.28	29	26	17	209	177	61	86	2	0	0	1	65	9	0	.138	8	77	4	4	3.1	.955
1915			18	11	.621	2.11	30	28	20	247.2	219	62	97	4	2	0	0	83	9	0	.108	9	76	6	0	3.0	.934
1916			11	8	.579	3.17	31	21	9	179	191	51	56	1	2	1	2	62	11	0	.177	6	51	3	1	1.9	.950
1917			8	9	.471	2.19	23	18	12	144	126	43	64	3	0	0	0	50	9	1	.180	12	42	2	5	2.4	.964
1919	**CIN**	**N**	14	5	.737	2.17	26	20	12	174.1	141	38	41	5	1	0	1	59	16	0	.271	8	68	2	1	3.0	.974
1920			10	11	.476	2.73	33	21	10	201	189	50	56	1	1	0	1	70	17	0	.243	6	69	3	1	2.4	.962
10 yrs.			100	94	.515	2.82	278	207	110	1755.2	1667	481	680	19	10	3	7	587	105	2	.179	72	610	39	13	2.6	.946
WORLD SERIES																											
1919	**CIN**	**N**	0	1	.000	2.35	2	1	0	7.2	7	2	2	0	0	0	0	2	1	0	.500	0	6	1	0	3.5	.857

Tom Fisher

FISHER, THOMAS CHALMERS (Red) BR TR 5′10½″ 185 lbs.
Brother of Chauncey Fisher.
B. Nov. 1, 1880, Anderson, Ind. D. Sept. 3, 1972, Anderson, Ind.

Year	Team	Lg	W	L	PCT	ERA	G	GS	CG	IP	H	BB	SO	ShO	Relief Pitching W	Relief Pitching L	Relief Pitching SV	Batting AB	Batting H	Batting HR	BA	PO	A	E	DP	TC/G	FA
1904	**BOS**	**N**	6	15	.286	4.25	31	21	19	214	257	82	84	3	0	1	0	99	21	2	.212	26	34	7	0	1.8	.896

Tom Fisher

FISHER, THOMAS GENE BR TR 6′ 180 lbs.
B. Apr. 4, 1942, Cleveland, Ohio.

Year	Team	Lg	W	L	PCT	ERA	G	GS	CG	IP	H	BB	SO	ShO	Relief Pitching W	Relief Pitching L	Relief Pitching SV	Batting AB	Batting H	Batting HR	BA	PO	A	E	DP	TC/G	FA
1967	**BAL**	**A**	0	0	—	0.00	2	0	0	3.1	2	2	1	0	0	0	0	0	0	0	—	0	0	0	0	0.0	.000

Max Fiske

FISKE, MAXIMILIAN PATRICK (Mox Ski) BR TR 5′11″ 185 lbs.
B. Oct. 12, 1888, Chicago, Ill. D. May 15, 1928, Chicago, Ill.

Year	Team	Lg	W	L	PCT	ERA	G	GS	CG	IP	H	BB	SO	ShO	Relief Pitching W	Relief Pitching L	Relief Pitching SV	Batting AB	Batting H	Batting HR	BA	PO	A	E	DP	TC/G	FA
1914	**CHI**	**F**	12	9	.571	3.14	38	22	7	198	161	59	87	0	4	1	0	68	16	0	.235	0	63	3	1	1.7	.955

Paul Fittery

FITTERY, PAUL CLARENCE BB TL 5′ 8″ 168 lbs.
B. Oct. 10, 1887, Lebanon, Pa. D. Jan. 28, 1974, Cartersville, Ga.

Year	Team	Lg	W	L	PCT	ERA	G	GS	CG	IP	H	BB	SO	ShO	Relief Pitching W	Relief Pitching L	Relief Pitching SV	Batting AB	Batting H	Batting HR	BA	PO	A	E	DP	TC/G	FA
1914	**CIN**	**N**	0	2	.000	3.09	8	4	2	43.2	41	12	21	0	0	0	0	17	1	0	.059	3	13	3	0	2.1	.842
1917	**PHI**	**N**	1	1	.500	4.53	17	2	1	55.2	69	27	13	0	0	0	0	22	2	0	.091	6	23	0	2	1.5	1.000
2 yrs.			1	3	.250	3.90	25	6	3	99.1	110	39	34	0	0	0	0	39	3	0	.077	9	36	3	2	1.7	.938

John Fitzgerald

FITZGERALD, JOHN FRANCIS BL TL 6′ 3″ 190 lbs.
B. Sept. 15, 1933, Brooklyn, N. Y.

Year	Team	Lg	W	L	PCT	ERA	G	GS	CG	IP	H	BB	SO	ShO	Relief Pitching W	Relief Pitching L	Relief Pitching SV	Batting AB	Batting H	Batting HR	BA	PO	A	E	DP	TC/G	FA
1958	**SF**	**N**	0	0	—	3.00	1	1	0	3	1	1	3	0	0	0	0	1	0	0	.000	1	1	0	0	2.0	1.000

John Fitzgerald

FITZGERALD, JOHN H.
B. May 30, 1870, Natick, Mass. D. Mar. 31, 1921, Boston, Mass.

Year	Team	Lg	W	L	PCT	ERA	G	GS	CG	IP	H	BB	SO	ShO	Relief Pitching W	Relief Pitching L	Relief Pitching SV	Batting AB	Batting H	Batting HR	BA	PO	A	E	DP	TC/G	FA
1891	**BOS**	**AA**	1	1	.500	5.63	6	3	2	32	49	11	16	0	0	0	1	14	1	0	.071	0	8	1	0	1.5	.889

John Fitzgerald

FITZGERALD, JOHN J.
Deceased.

Year	Team	Lg	W	L	PCT	ERA	G	GS	CG	IP	H	BB	SO	ShO	Relief Pitching W	Relief Pitching L	Relief Pitching SV	Batting AB	Batting H	Batting HR	BA	PO	A	E	DP	TC/G	FA
1890	**ROC**	**AA**	3	8	.273	4.04	11	11	8	78	77	45	35	1	0	0	0	31	6	0	.194	3	21	1	0	2.3	.960

John Fitzgerald

FITZGERALD, JOHN T.
B. Leadville, Colo. Deceased.

Year	Team	Lg	W	L	PCT	ERA	G	GS	CG	IP	H	BB	SO	ShO	Relief Pitching W	Relief Pitching L	Relief Pitching SV	Batting AB	Batting H	Batting HR	BA	PO	A	E	DP	TC/G	FA
1891	**LOU**	**AA**	14	17	.452	3.44	31	30	27	267	265	89	110	3	0	1	0	108	19	1	.176	13	45	4	2	1.9	.935
1892	**LOU**	**N**	1	3	.250	4.24	4	4	4	34	45	11	3	0	0	0	0	15	2	0	.133	0	6	0	0	1.5	1.000
2 yrs.			15	20	.429	3.53	35	34	31	301	310	100	113	3	0	1	0	123	21	1	.171	13	51	4	2	1.9	.941

Paul Fitzke

FITZKE, PAUL FREDERICK HERMAN (Bob) BR TR 5′11½″ 185 lbs.
B. July 30, 1900, LaCrosse, Wis. D. June 30, 1950, Sacramento, Calif.

Year	Team	Lg	W	L	PCT	ERA	G	GS	CG	IP	H	BB	SO	ShO	Relief Pitching W	Relief Pitching L	Relief Pitching SV	Batting AB	Batting H	Batting HR	BA	PO	A	E	DP	TC/G	FA
1924	**CLE**	**A**	0	0	—	4.50	1	0	0	4	5	3	1	0	0	0	0	1	0	0	.000	0	0	0	0	0.0	.000

Al Fitzmorris

FITZMORRIS, ALAN JAMES BB TR 6′ 2″ 190 lbs.
B. Mar. 21, 1946, Buffalo, N. Y.

Year	Team	Lg	W	L	PCT	ERA	G	GS	CG	IP	H	BB	SO	ShO	Relief Pitching W	Relief Pitching L	Relief Pitching SV	Batting AB	Batting H	Batting HR	BA	PO	A	E	DP	TC/G	FA
1969	**KC**	**A**	1	1	.500	4.22	7	0	0	10.2	9	4	3	0	1	1	2	1	0	0	.000	1	1	0	0	0.3	1.000
1970			8	5	.615	4.42	43	11	2	118	112	52	47	0	4	1	1	31	9	0	.290	12	21	1	1	0.8	.971
1971			7	5	.583	4.18	36	15	2	127	112	55	53	1	0	0	0	44	11	0	.250	15	25	2	4	1.2	.952
1972			2	5	.286	3.74	38	2	0	101	99	28	51	0	2	3	3	23	4	0	.174	7	22	0	3	0.8	1.000
1973			8	3	.727	2.83	15	13	3	89	88	25	26	1	1	0	0	0	0	0	—	9	20	0	1	1.9	1.000
1974			13	6	.684	2.79	34	27	9	190	189	63	53	4	0	0	1	0	0	0	—	20	39	0	4	1.7	1.000
1975			16	12	.571	3.57	35	35	11	242	239	76	78	3	0	0	0	0	0	0	—	26	37	1	1	1.8	.984
1976			15	11	.577	3.07	35	33	8	220	227	56	80	2	0	0	0	0	0	0	—	19	49	3	4	2.0	.958
1977	**CLE**	**A**	6	10	.375	5.41	29	21	1	133	164	53	54	0	1	0	0	0	0	0	—	7	22	1	1	1.0	.967
1978	**2 teams**	**CLE A** (7G 0–1) **CAL A** (9G 1–0)																									
″	**total**		1	1	.500	3.13	16	2	0	46	45	21	13	0	0	1	0	0	0	0		3	6	1	0	0.6	.900
10 yrs.			77	59	.566	3.65	288	159	36	1276.2	1284	433	458	11	9	6	7	99	24	0	.242	119	242	9	19	1.3	.976

Freddie Fitzsimmons

FITZSIMMONS, FREDERICK LANDIS (Fat Freddie) BR TR 5′11″ 185 lbs.
B. July 26, 1901, Mishawaka, Ind. D. Nov. 18, 1979, Yucca Valley, Calif.
Manager 1943–45.

Year	Team	W	L	PCT	ERA	G	GS	CG	IP	H	BB	SO	ShO	Relief Pitching W	Relief Pitching L	Relief Pitching SV	Batting AB	Batting H	Batting HR	BA	PO	A	E	DP	TC/G	FA
1925	NY N	6	3	.667	2.65	10	8	6	74.2	70	18	17	1	1	0	0	29	9	0	.310	3	27	0	0	3.0	1.000
1926		14	10	.583	2.88	37	26	12	219	224	58	48	0	1	2	0	86	11	0	.128	20	62	0	5	2.2	1.000
1927		17	10	.630	3.72	42	31	14	244.2	260	67	78	1	2	1	3	87	18	0	.207	19	59	2	3	1.9	.975
1928		20	9	.690	3.68	40	32	16	261.1	264	65	67	1	4	0	1	94	18	0	.191	23	63	0	4	2.2	1.000
1929		15	11	.577	4.10	37	31	14	221.2	242	66	55	4	1	0	1	82	15	0	.183	13	70	4	7	2.4	.954
1930		19	7	**.731**	4.25	41	29	17	224.1	230	59	76	1	3	0	1	83	22	2	.265	22	70	2	6	2.3	.979
1931		18	11	.621	3.05	35	33	19	253.2	242	62	78	4	0	1	0	92	21	4	.228	13	89	4	9	3.0	.962
1932		11	11	.500	4.43	35	31	11	237.2	287	83	65	0	0	0	0	86	19	2	.221	16	78	2	10	2.7	.979
1933		16	11	.593	2.90	36	**35**	13	251.2	243	72	65	1	0	0	0	95	19	2	.200	12	83	4	6	2.8	.960
1934		18	14	.563	3.04	38	37	14	263.1	266	51	73	3	0	0	1	95	22	2	.232	24	71	3	10	2.6	.969
1935		4	8	.333	4.02	18	15	6	94	104	22	23	**4**	0	0	0	31	8	0	.258	8	24	0	1	1.8	1.000
1936		10	7	.588	3.32	28	17	7	141	147	39	35	0	1	2	2	47	7	0	.149	11	31	3	5	1.6	.933
1937	2 teams NY N (6G 2–2) BKN N (13G 4–8)																									
″	total	6	10	.375	4.35	19	17	5	118	119	40	42	1	1	0	0	40	8	1	.200	5	28	0	1	1.7	1.000
1938	BKN N	11	8	.579	3.02	27	26	12	202.2	205	43	38	3	0	0	0	70	12	0	.171	13	66	1	7	3.0	.988
1939		7	9	.438	3.87	27	20	5	151.1	178	28	44	0	1	1	3	47	11	1	.234	13	52	0	1	2.4	1.000
1940		16	2	**.889**	2.81	20	18	11	134.1	120	25	35	4	1	0	1	47	5	0	.106	15	28	2	2	2.3	.956
1941		6	1	.857	2.07	13	12	3	82.2	78	26	19	1	1	0	0	28	4	0	.143	3	30	0	1	2.5	1.000
1942		0	0	—	15.00	1	1	0	3	6	1	0	0	0	0	0	2	1	0	.500	0	1	0	0	1.0	1.000
1943		3	4	.429	5.44	9	7	1	44.2	50	21	12	0	0	1	0	14	1	0	.071	4	10	1	1	1.7	.933
19 yrs.		217	146	.598	3.51	513	426	186	3223.2	3335	846	870	29	17	8	13	1155	231	14	.200	237	942	28	79	2.4	.977
WORLD SERIES																										
1933	NY N	0	1	.000	5.14	1	1	0	7	9	0	2	0	0	0	0	2	1	0	.500	0	1	0	0	1.0	1.000
1936		0	2	.000	5.40	2	2	1	11.2	13	2	6	0	0	0	0	4	2	0	.500	1	2	0	0	1.5	1.000
1941	BKN N	0	0	—	0.00	1	1	0	7	4	3	1	0	0	0	0	2	0	0	.000	0	2	0	0	2.0	1.000
3 yrs.		0	3	.000	3.86	4	4	1	25.2	26	5	9	0	0	0	0	8	3	0	.375	1	5	0	0	1.5	1.000

Patsy Flaherty

FLAHERTY, PATRICK JOSEPH BL TL 5′ 8″ 165 lbs.
B. June 29, 1876, Mansfield, Pa. D. Jan. 23, 1968, Alexandria, La.

Year	Team	W	L	PCT	ERA	G	GS	CG	IP	H	BB	SO	ShO	Relief Pitching W	Relief Pitching L	Relief Pitching SV	Batting AB	Batting H	Batting HR	BA	PO	A	E	DP	TC/G	FA
1899	LOU N	2	3	.400	2.31	5	4	4	39	41	5	5	0	1	0	0	24	5	0	.208	4	8	5	0	2.4	.706
1900	PIT N	0	0	—	6.14	4	1	0	22	30	9	5	0	0	0	0	9	1	0	.111	0	10	0	0	2.5	1.000
1903	CHI A	11	**25**	.306	3.74	40	34	29	293.2	**338**	50	65	2	**2**	1	1	102	14	0	.137	21	107	12	5	3.5	.914
1904	2 teams CHI A (5G 1–2) PIT N (29G 19–9)																									
″	total	20	11	.645	2.05	34	33	32	285	246	69	68	5	0	0	0	116	26	2	.224	34	105	7	3	4.1	.952
1905	PIT N	9	10	.474	3.49	27	20	15	188	197	49	44	0	0	1	1	76	15	0	.197	9	70	9	1	3.0	.898
1907	BOS N	12	15	.444	2.70	27	25	23	217	197	59	34	0	1	1	0	115	22	2	.191	26	78	9	8	3.2	.920
1908		12	18	.400	3.25	31	31	21	244	221	81	50	0	0	0	0	86	12	0	.140	20	79	4	3	3.3	.961
1910	PHI N	0	0	—	0.00	1	0	0	0.1	1	1	0	0	0	0	0	2	1	0	.500	1	0	0	0	0.5	1.000
1911	BOS N	0	2	.000	7.07	4	2	1	14	21	8	0	0	0	0	0	94	27	2	.287	26	6	4	0	1.6	.889
9 yrs.		66	84	.440	3.10	173	150	125	1303	1292	331	271	7	4	3	2	*				141	463	50	20	3.2	.924

Mike Flanagan

FLANAGAN, MICHAEL KENDALL BL TL 6′ 180 lbs.
B. Dec. 16, 1951, Manchester, N. H.

Year	Team	W	L	PCT	ERA	G	GS	CG	IP	H	BB	SO	ShO	Relief Pitching W	Relief Pitching L	Relief Pitching SV	Batting AB	Batting H	Batting HR	BA	PO	A	E	DP	TC/G	FA
1975	BAL A	0	1	.000	2.79	2	1	0	9.2	9	6	7	0	0	0	0	0	0	0	—	0	2	0	0	1.0	1.000
1976		3	5	.375	4.13	20	10	4	85	83	33	56	0	0	3	0	0	0	0	—	4	13	0	0	0.9	1.000
1977		15	10	.600	3.64	36	33	15	235	235	70	149	2	0	1	1	0	0	0	—	7	36	0	3	1.2	1.000
1978		19	15	.559	4.03	40	**40**	17	281.1	271	87	167	2	0	0	0	0	0	0	—	6	38	2	1	1.1	.957
1979		**23**	9	.719	3.08	39	38	16	266	245	70	190	**5**	0	0	0	0	0	0	—	4	41	2	2	1.2	.957
1980		16	13	.552	4.12	37	37	12	251	**278**	71	128	2	0	0	0	0	0	0	—	6	42	1	2	1.3	.980
1981		9	6	.600	4.19	20	20	3	116	108	37	72	2	0	0	0	0	0	0	—	4	24	1	1	1.5	.966
1982		15	11	.577	3.97	36	35	11	236	233	76	103	1	0	0	0	0	0	0	—	7	38	0	1	1.3	1.000
1983		12	4	.750	3.30	20	20	3	125.1	135	31	50	1	0	0	0	0	0	0	—	6	15	2	1	1.1	.913
1984		13	13	.500	3.53	34	34	10	226.2	213	81	115	2	0	0	0	0	0	0	—	3	33	0	2	1.1	1.000
1985		4	5	.444	5.13	15	15	1	86	101	28	42	0	0	0	0	0	0	0	—	4	11	0	0	1.0	1.000
1986		7	11	.389	4.24	29	28	2	172	179	66	96	0	0	0	0	0	0	0	—	4	17	0	1	0.7	1.000
1987	2 teams BAL A (16G 3–6) TOR A (7G 3–2)																									
″	total	6	8	.429	4.06	23	23	4	144	148	51	93	0	0	0	0	0	0	0		8	17	1	2	1.1	.962
1988	TOR A	13	13	.500	4.18	34	34	2	211	220	80	99	1	0	0	0	0	0	0	—	6	35	0	2	1.2	1.000
1989		8	10	.444	3.93	30	30	1	171.2	186	47	47	1	0	0	0	0	0	0	—	8	33	0	4	1.4	1.000
1990		2	2	.500	5.31	5	5	0	20.1	28	8	5	0	0	0	0	0	0	0	—	0	6	1	0	1.4	.857
1991	BAL A	2	7	.222	2.38	64	1	0	98.1	84	25	55	0	2	6	3	0	0	0	—	6	23	0	2	0.5	1.000
1992		0	0	—	8.05	42	0	0	34.2	50	23	17	0	0	0	0	0	0	0	—	6	6	1	2	0.3	.923
18 yrs.		167	143	.539	3.90	526	404	101	2770	2806	890	1491	19	2	10	4	0	0	0		89	430	11	26	1.0	.979
LEAGUE CHAMPIONSHIP SERIES																										
1979	BAL A	1	0	1.000	5.14	1	1	0	7	6	1	2	0	0	0	0	0	0	0	—	0	0	0	0	0.0	.000
1983		1	0	1.000	1.80	1	1	0	5	5	0	1	0	0	0	0	0	0	0	—	0	0	0	0	0.0	.000
1989	TOR A	0	1	.000	10.38	1	1	0	4.1	7	1	3	0	0	0	0	0	0	0	—	2	3	0	2	5.0	1.000
3 yrs.		2	1	.667	5.51	3	3	0	16.1	18	2	6	0	0	0	0	0	0	0		2	3	0	2	1.7	1.000
WORLD SERIES																										
1979	BAL A	1	1	.500	3.00	3	2	1	15	18	2	13	0	0	0	0	5	0	0	.000	0	4	0	0	1.3	1.000
1983		0	0	—	4.50	1	1	0	4	6	1	1	0	0	0	0	1	0	0	.000	0	0	0	0	0.0	.000
2 yrs.		1	1	.500	3.32	4	3	1	19	24	3	14	0	0	0	0	6	0	0	.000	0	4	0	0	1.0	1.000

Ray Flanigan

FLANIGAN, RAYMOND ARTHUR BR TR 6′ 190 lbs.
B. Jan. 8, 1923, Morgantown, W. Va. D. Mar. 28, 1993, Baltimore, Md.

Year	Team	Lg	W	L	PCT	ERA	G	GS	CG	IP	H	BB	SO	ShO	Relief Pitching W	Relief Pitching L	Relief Pitching SV	Batting AB	Batting H	Batting HR	BA	PO	A	E	DP	TC/G	FA
1946	CLE	A	0	1	.000	11.00	3	1	0	9	11	8	2	0	0	0	0	2	1	0	.500	0	3	0	0	1.0	1.000

Tom Flanigan

FLANIGAN, THOMAS ANTHONY BR TL 6′ 3″ 175 lbs.
B. Sept. 6, 1934, Cincinnati, Ohio.

Year	Team	Lg	W	L	PCT	ERA	G	GS	CG	IP	H	BB	SO	ShO	Relief Pitching W	Relief Pitching L	Relief Pitching SV	Batting AB	Batting H	Batting HR	BA	PO	A	E	DP	TC/G	FA
1954	CHI	A	0	0	—	0.00	2	0	0	1.2	1	1	0	0	0	0	0	0	0	0	—	0	1	0	0	0.5	1.000
1958	STL	N	0	0	—	9.00	1	0	0	1	2	1	0	0	0	0	0	0	0	0	—	0	0	0	0	0.0	.000
2 yrs.			0	0		3.38	3	0	0	2.2	3	2	0	0	0	0	0	0	0	0		0	1	0	0	0.3	1.000

Jack Flater

FLATER, JOHN WILLIAM BR TR 5′10″ 175 lbs.
B. Sept. 22, 1880, Sandymount, Md. D. Mar. 20, 1970, Westminster, Md.

Year	Team	Lg	W	L	PCT	ERA	G	GS	CG	IP	H	BB	SO	ShO	Relief Pitching W	Relief Pitching L	Relief Pitching SV	Batting AB	Batting H	Batting HR	BA	PO	A	E	DP	TC/G	FA
1908	PHI	A	1	3	.250	2.06	5	3	3	39.1	35	12	8	0	1	0	0	15	2	0	.133	6	19	3	2	5.6	.893

John Flavin

FLAVIN, JOHN THOMAS BL TL 6′ 2″ 208 lbs.
B. May 7, 1942, Albany, Calif.

Year	Team	Lg	W	L	PCT	ERA	G	GS	CG	IP	H	BB	SO	ShO	Relief Pitching W	Relief Pitching L	Relief Pitching SV	Batting AB	Batting H	Batting HR	BA	PO	A	E	DP	TC/G	FA
1964	CHI	N	0	1	.000	13.50	5	1	0	4.2	11	3	5	0	0	0	0	1	0	0	.000	0	0	0	0	0.0	.000

Bill Fleming

FLEMING, LESLIE FLETCHARD BR TR 6′ 190 lbs.
B. July 31, 1913, Rowland, Calif.

Year	Team	Lg	W	L	PCT	ERA	G	GS	CG	IP	H	BB	SO	ShO	Relief Pitching W	Relief Pitching L	Relief Pitching SV	Batting AB	Batting H	Batting HR	BA	PO	A	E	DP	TC/G	FA
1940	BOS	A	1	2	.333	4.86	10	6	1	46.1	53	20	24	0	0	1	0	13	0	0	.000	1	5	0	0	0.6	1.000
1941			1	1	.500	3.92	16	1	0	41.1	32	24	20	0	1	1	1	9	2	0	.222	2	10	0	0	0.8	1.000
1942	CHI	N	5	6	.455	3.01	33	14	4	134.1	117	63	59	2	1	0	2	39	2	0	.051	5	24	2	2	0.9	.935
1943			0	1	.000	6.40	11	0	0	32.1	40	12	12	0	0	1	0	8	0	0	.000	3	10	0	0	1.2	1.000
1944			9	10	.474	3.13	39	18	9	158.1	163	62	42	1	1	2	0	53	9	0	.170	8	39	3	0	1.3	.940
1946			0	1	.000	6.14	14	1	0	29.1	37	12	10	0	0	0	0	3	0	0	.000	0	7	0	0	0.5	1.000
6 yrs.			16	21	.432	3.79	123	40	14	442	442	193	167	3	3	5	3	125	13	0	.104	19	95	5	2	1.0	.958

Dave Fleming

FLEMING, DAVID ANTHONY BL TL 6′ 3″ 200 lbs.
B. Nov. 7, 1969, Jackson Heights, N. Y.

Year	Team	Lg	W	L	PCT	ERA	G	GS	CG	IP	H	BB	SO	ShO	Relief Pitching W	Relief Pitching L	Relief Pitching SV	Batting AB	Batting H	Batting HR	BA	PO	A	E	DP	TC/G	FA
1991	SEA	A	1	0	1.000	6.62	9	3	0	17.2	19	3	11	0	0	0	0	0	0	0	—	3	6	0	2	1.0	1.000
1992			17	10	.630	3.39	33	33	7	228.1	225	60	112	4	0	0	0	0	0	0	—	4	33	1	4	1.2	.974
1993			12	5	.706	4.36	26	26	1	167.1	189	67	75	1	0	0	0	0	0	0	—	9	28	0	1	1.4	1.000
1994			7	11	.389	6.46	23	23	0	117	152	65	65	0	0	0	0	0	0	0	—	8	15	1	1	1.0	.958
1995	2 teams	SEA A (16G 1–5)	KC A (9G 0–1)																								
″	total		1	6	.143	5.96	25	12	1	80	84	53	40	0	0	1	0	0	0	0	—	5	13	0	1	0.7	1.000
5 yrs.			38	32	.543	4.67	116	97	9	610.1	669	248	303	5	0	1	0	0	0	0		29	95	2	9	1.1	.984

Huck Flener

FLENER, GREGORY ALAN BB TL 5′11″ 175 lbs.
B. Feb. 25, 1969, Austin, Tex.

Year	Team	Lg	W	L	PCT	ERA	G	GS	CG	IP	H	BB	SO	ShO	Relief Pitching W	Relief Pitching L	Relief Pitching SV	Batting AB	Batting H	Batting HR	BA	PO	A	E	DP	TC/G	FA
1993	TOR	A	0	0	—	4.05	6	0	0	6.2	7	4	2	0	0	0	0	0	0	0	—	2	2	0	0	0.7	1.000

Paul Fletcher

FLETCHER, EDWARD PAUL BR TR 6′ 1″ 190 lbs.
B. Jan. 14, 1967, Gallipolis, Ohio.

Year	Team	Lg	W	L	PCT	ERA	G	GS	CG	IP	H	BB	SO	ShO	Relief Pitching W	Relief Pitching L	Relief Pitching SV	Batting AB	Batting H	Batting HR	BA	PO	A	E	DP	TC/G	FA
1993	PHI	N	0	0	—	0.00	1	0	0	0.1	0	0	0	0	0	0	0	0	0	0	—	0	0	0	0	0.0	.000
1995			1	0	1.000	5.40	10	0	0	13.1	15	9	10	0	1	0	0	0	0	0	—	0	1	0	0	0.1	1.000
2 yrs.			1	0	1.000	5.27	11	0	0	13.2	15	9	10	0	1	0	0	0	0	0		0	1	0	0	0.1	1.000

Sam Fletcher

FLETCHER, SAMUEL S. TR 6′ 2″ 210 lbs.
B. Altoona, Pa.

Year	Team	Lg	W	L	PCT	ERA	G	GS	CG	IP	H	BB	SO	ShO	Relief Pitching W	Relief Pitching L	Relief Pitching SV	Batting AB	Batting H	Batting HR	BA	PO	A	E	DP	TC/G	FA
1909	BKN	N	0	1	.000	8.00	1	1	1	9	13	2	5	0	0	0	0	3	0	0	.000	0	2	0	0	2.0	1.000
1912	CIN	N	0	0	—	12.10	2	0	0	9.2	15	11	3	0	0	0	0	4	2	0	.500	0	3	0	0	1.5	1.000
2 yrs.			0	1	.000	10.13	3	1	1	18.2	28	13	8	0	0	0	0	7	2	0	.286	0	5	0	0	1.7	1.000

Tom Fletcher

FLETCHER, THOMAS WAYNE BB TL 6′ 170 lbs.
Father of Darrin Fletcher.
B. June 28, 1942, Elmira, N. Y.

Year	Team	Lg	W	L	PCT	ERA	G	GS	CG	IP	H	BB	SO	ShO	Relief Pitching W	Relief Pitching L	Relief Pitching SV	Batting AB	Batting H	Batting HR	BA	PO	A	E	DP	TC/G	FA
1962	DET	A	0	0	—	0.00	1	0	0	2	2	2	1	0	0	0	0	0	0	0	—	1	0	0	0	1.0	1.000

Van Fletcher

FLETCHER, ALFRED VANOIDE BR TR 6′ 2″ 185 lbs.
B. Aug. 6, 1924, East Bend, N. C.

Year	Team	Lg	W	L	PCT	ERA	G	GS	CG	IP	H	BB	SO	ShO	Relief Pitching W	Relief Pitching L	Relief Pitching SV	Batting AB	Batting H	Batting HR	BA	PO	A	E	DP	TC/G	FA
1955	DET	A	0	0	—	3.00	9	0	0	12	13	2	4	0	0	0	0	0	0	0	—	1	1	1	0	0.3	.667

John Flinn

FLINN, JOHN RICHARD BR TR 6′ 175 lbs.
B. Sept. 2, 1954, Merced, Calif.

Year	Team	Lg	W	L	PCT	ERA	G	GS	CG	IP	H	BB	SO	ShO	Relief Pitching W	Relief Pitching L	Relief Pitching SV	Batting AB	Batting H	Batting HR	BA	PO	A	E	DP	TC/G	FA
1978	BAL	A	1	1	.500	8.04	13	0	0	15.2	24	13	8	0	1	1	0	0	0	0	—	1	3	1	0	0.4	.800
1979			0	0	—	0.00	4	0	0	3	2	1	0	0	0	0	0	0	0	0	—	1	0	0	0	0.3	1.000
1980	MIL	A	2	1	.667	3.89	20	1	0	37	31	20	15	0	2	1	2	0	0	0	—	6	3	0	0	0.4	1.000
1982	BAL	A	2	0	1.000	1.32	5	0	0	13.2	13	3	13	0	2	0	0	0	0	0	—	2	0	0	0	0.4	1.000
4 yrs.			5	2	.714	4.15	42	1	0	69.1	70	37	36	0	5	2	2	0	0	0		10	6	1	0	0.4	.941

Hilly Flitcraft

FLITCRAFT, HILDRETH MILTON BL TL 6′ 2″ 180 lbs.
B. Aug. 21, 1923, Woodstown, N. J.

Year	Team	Lg	W	L	PCT	ERA	G	GS	CG	IP	H	BB	SO	ShO	Relief Pitching W	Relief Pitching L	Relief Pitching SV	Batting AB	Batting H	Batting HR	BA	PO	A	E	DP	TC/G	FA
1942	PHI	N	0	0	—	8.10	3	0	0	3.1	6	2	1	0	0	0	0	0	0	0	—	0	1	0	0	0.3	1.000

Mort Flohr

FLOHR, MORITZ HERMAN (Dutch) BL TL 6′ 173 lbs.
B. Aug. 15, 1911, Canisteo, N. Y. D. Jan. 2, 1994, Hornell, N. Y.

Year	Team	Lg	W	L	PCT	ERA	G	GS	CG	IP	H	BB	SO	ShO	Relief Pitching W	Relief Pitching L	Relief Pitching SV	Batting AB	Batting H	Batting HR	BA	PO	A	E	DP	TC/G	FA
1934	PHI	A	0	2	.000	5.87	14	3	0	30.2	34	33	6	0	0	0	0	12	4	0	.333	1	12	1	0	1.0	.929

Don Florence

FLORENCE, DONALD EMERY BR TL 6′ 195 lbs.
B. Mar. 16, 1967, Manchester, N. H.

Year	Team	Lg	W	L	PCT	ERA	G	GS	CG	IP	H	BB	SO	ShO	Relief Pitching W	Relief Pitching L	Relief Pitching SV	Batting AB	Batting H	Batting HR	BA	PO	A	E	DP	TC/G	FA
1995	NY	N	3	0	1.000	1.50	14	0	0	12	17	6	5	0	3	0	0	1	0	0	.000	0	4	0	0	0.3	1.000

Jesse Flores

FLORES, JESSE BR TR 5′10″ 175 lbs.
Born Jesse Flores (Sandoval).
B. Nov. 2, 1914, Guadalajara, Mexico D. Dec. 17, 1991, Orange, Calif.

Year	Team	Lg	W	L	PCT	ERA	G	GS	CG	IP	H	BB	SO	ShO	Relief W	Relief L	Relief SV	Batting AB	Batting H	Batting HR	BA	PO	A	E	DP	TC/G	FA
1942	CHI	N	0	1	.000	3.38	4	0	0	5.1	5	2	6	0	0	1	0	0	0	0	—	0	2	1	0	0.8	.667
1943	PHI	A	12	14	.462	3.11	31	27	13	231.1	208	70	113	0	1	2	0	80	14	0	.175	11	50	3	5	2.1	.953
1944			9	11	.450	3.39	27	25	11	185.2	172	49	65	2	0	0	0	64	11	0	.172	9	33	1	0	1.6	.977
1945			7	10	.412	3.43	29	24	9	191.1	180	63	52	4	0	2	1	61	9	0	.148	14	23	4	3	1.4	.902
1946			9	7	.563	2.32	29	15	8	155	147	38	48	4	1	0	1	44	11	0	.250	8	18	3	1	1.0	.897
1947			4	13	.235	3.39	28	20	4	151.1	139	59	41	0	1	0	0	44	10	0	.227	12	19	3	3	1.2	.912
1950	CLE	A	3	3	.500	3.74	28	2	1	53	53	25	27	1	2	3	4	11	0	0	.000	2	2	3	0	0.3	.571
7 yrs.			44	59	.427	3.18	176	113	46	973	904	306	352	11	5	8	6	304	55	0	.181	56	147	18	12	1.3	.919

Bryce Florie

FLORIE, BRYCE BETTENCOURT BR TR 6′ 185 lbs.
B. May 21, 1970, Charleston, S. C.

Year	Team	Lg	W	L	PCT	ERA	G	GS	CG	IP	H	BB	SO	ShO	Relief W	Relief L	Relief SV	Batting AB	Batting H	Batting HR	BA	PO	A	E	DP	TC/G	FA
1994	SD	N	0	0	—	0.96	9	0	0	9.1	8	3	8	0	0	0	0	0	0	0	—	2	3	0	0	0.6	1.000
1995			2	2	.500	3.01	47	0	0	68.2	49	38	68	0	2	2	1	2	0	0	.000	4	10	1	0	0.3	.933
2 yrs.			2	2	.500	2.77	56	0	0	78	57	41	76	0	2	2	1	2	0	0	.000	6	13	1	0	0.4	.950

Ben Flowers

FLOWERS, BENNETT BR TR 6′ 4″ 195 lbs.
B. June 15, 1927, Wilson, N. C.

Year	Team	Lg	W	L	PCT	ERA	G	GS	CG	IP	H	BB	SO	ShO	Relief W	Relief L	Relief SV	Batting AB	Batting H	Batting HR	BA	PO	A	E	DP	TC/G	FA
1951	BOS	A	0	0	—	0.00	1	0	0	3	2	1	2	0	0	0	0	1	0	0	.000	0	0	0	0	0.0	.000
1953			1	4	.200	3.86	32	6	1	79.1	87	24	36	1	0	0	3	19	3	0	.158	4	15	1	2	0.6	.950
1955	2 teams DET A (4G 0–0) STL N (4G 1–0)																										
″	total		1	0	1.000	4.05	8	4	0	33.1	32	14	21	0	0	0	0	11	1	0	.091	2	5	2	1	1.1	.778
1956	2 teams STL N (3G 1–1) PHI N (32G 0–2)																										
″	total		1	3	.250	5.98	35	3	0	52.2	69	15	27	0	0	2	0	5	0	0	.000	2	13	1	1	0.5	.938
4 yrs.			3	7	.300	4.49	76	13	1	168.1	190	54	86	1	0	2	3	36	4	0	.111	8	33	4	4	0.6	.911

Wes Flowers

FLOWERS, CHARLES WESLEY BL TL 6′ 1½″ 190 lbs.
B. Aug. 13, 1913, Vanndale, Ark.

Year	Team	Lg	W	L	PCT	ERA	G	GS	CG	IP	H	BB	SO	ShO	Relief W	Relief L	Relief SV	Batting AB	Batting H	Batting HR	BA	PO	A	E	DP	TC/G	FA
1940	BKN	N	1	1	.500	3.43	5	2	0	21	23	10	8	0	1	0	0	5	1	0	.200	0	5	0	0	1.0	1.000
1944			1	1	.500	7.79	9	1	0	17.1	26	13	3	0	0	1	0	5	3	0	.600	1	3	0	0	0.4	1.000
2 yrs.			2	2	.500	5.40	14	3	0	38.1	49	23	11	0	1	1	0	10	4	0	.400	1	8	0	0	0.6	1.000

Carney Flynn

FLYNN, CORNELIUS FRANCIS XAVIER BL TL 5′11″ 165 lbs.
B. Jan. 23, 1875, Cincinnati, Ohio D. Feb. 10, 1947, Cincinnati, Ohio.

Year	Team	Lg	W	L	PCT	ERA	G	GS	CG	IP	H	BB	SO	ShO	Relief W	Relief L	Relief SV	Batting AB	Batting H	Batting HR	BA	PO	A	E	DP	TC/G	FA
1894	CIN	N	0	2	.000	17.61	2	1	0	7.2	16	10	4	0	0	1	0	3	0	0	.000	0	0	0	0	0.0	.000
1896	2 teams NY N (3G 0–2) WAS N (4G 0–1)																										
″	total		0	3	.000	9.68	7	3	2	30.2	61	18	7	0	0	0	0	12	4	1	.333	5	3	2	0	1.4	.800
2 yrs.			0	5	.000	11.27	9	4	2	38.1	77	28	11	0	0	1	0	15	4	1	.267	5	3	2	0	1.1	.800

Jocko Flynn

FLYNN, JOHN A. TR 5′ 6½″ 143 lbs.
B. June 30, 1864, Lawrence, Mass. D. Dec. 30, 1907, Lawrence, Mass.

Year	Team	Lg	W	L	PCT	ERA	G	GS	CG	IP	H	BB	SO	ShO	Relief W	Relief L	Relief SV	Batting AB	Batting H	Batting HR	BA	PO	A	E	DP	TC/G	FA
1886	CHI	N	24	6	**.800**	2.24	32	29	28	257	207	63	146	2	1	0	1	*				34	59	9	2	1.7	.912

Stu Flythe

FLYTHE, STUART McGUIRE BR TR 6′ 2″ 175 lbs.
B. Dec. 5, 1911, Conway, N. C. D. Oct. 18, 1963, Durham, N. C.

Year	Team	Lg	W	L	PCT	ERA	G	GS	CG	IP	H	BB	SO	ShO	Relief W	Relief L	Relief SV	Batting AB	Batting H	Batting HR	BA	PO	A	E	DP	TC/G	FA
1936	PHI	A	0	0	—	13.04	17	3	0	39.1	49	61	14	0	0	0	0	15	4	0	.267	1	7	0	0	0.5	1.000

Gene Fodge

FODGE, EUGENE ARLAN (Suds) BR TR 6′ 175 lbs.
B. July 9, 1931, South Bend, Ind.

Year	Team	Lg	W	L	PCT	ERA	G	GS	CG	IP	H	BB	SO	ShO	Relief W	Relief L	Relief SV	Batting AB	Batting H	Batting HR	BA	PO	A	E	DP	TC/G	FA
1958	CHI	N	1	1	.500	4.76	16	4	1	39.2	47	11	15	0	0	0	0	7	0	0	.000	1	7	0	1	0.5	1.000

Jim Fogarty

FOGARTY, JAMES G. BR TR 5′10½″ 180 lbs.
Brother of Joe Fogarty.
B. Feb. 12, 1864, San Francisco, Calif. D. May 20, 1891, Philadelphia, Pa.
Manager 1890.

Year	Team	Lg	W	L	PCT	ERA	G	GS	CG	IP	H	BB	SO	ShO	Relief W	Relief L	Relief SV	Batting AB	Batting H	Batting HR	BA	PO	A	E	DP	TC/G	FA
1884	PHI	N	0	0	—	0.00	1	0	0	1	2	0	1	0	0	0	0	378	80	1	.212	229	43	34	5	3.1	.889
1886			0	1	.000	0.00	1	0	0	6	7	0	4	0	0	**1**	0	280	82	3	.293	273	92	29	12	3.5	.926
1887			0	0	—	9.00	1	0	0	3	3	1	0	0	0	0	0	495	129	8	.261	274	47	29	10	2.7	.917
1889			0	0	—	9.00	4	0	0	4	4	2	0	0	0	0	0	499	129	3	.259	251	35	25	11	2.5	.920
4 yrs.			0	1	.000	4.50	7	0	0	14	16	3	5	0	0	1	0	*				1673	328	162	57	2.8	.925

Curry Foley

FOLEY, CHARLES JOSEPH TL 5′10″ 160 lbs.
B. Jan. 14, 1856, Milltown, Ireland D. Oct. 20, 1898, New York, N. Y.

Year	Team	Lg	W	L	PCT	ERA	G	GS	CG	IP	H	BB	SO	ShO	Relief W	Relief L	Relief SV	Batting AB	Batting H	Batting HR	BA	PO	A	E	DP	TC/G	FA
1879	BOS	N	9	9	.500	2.51	21	16	16	161.2	175	15	57	1	2	0	**1**	146	46	0	.315	29	29	13	0	1.8	.817
1880			14	14	.500	3.89	36	28	21	238	264	40	68	1	1	1	0	332	97	2	.292	276	63	25	10	3.8	.931
1881	BUF	N	2	4	.333	*5.27*	10	6	2	41	70	5	2	0	**1**	0	0	375	96	1	.256	372	32	38	14	4.8	.914
1882			0	0	—	18.00	1	0	0	1	2	0	0	0	0	0	0	341	104	3	.305	118	22	28	7	2.0	.833
1883			1	0	1.000	0.00	1	0	0	1	0	4	0	0	1	0	0	111	30	0	.270	44	2	6	0	2.2	.885
5 yrs.			26	27	.491	3.54	69	50	39	442.2	511	64	127	2	5	1	1	*				839	148	110	31	3.3	.900

John Foley

FOLEY, JOHN J. TL
B. Mar. 1860, England Deceased.

Year	Team	Lg	W	L	PCT	ERA	G	GS	CG	IP	H	BB	SO	ShO	Relief W	Relief L	Relief SV	Batting AB	Batting H	Batting HR	BA	PO	A	E	DP	TC/G	FA
1885	PRO	N	0	1	.000	*4.50*	1	1	1	8	6	5	2	0	0	0	0	2	0	0	.000	0	2	0	0	2.0	1.000

Tom Foley

FOLEY, THOMAS MICHAEL BL TR 6′ 1″ 160 lbs.
B. Sept. 9, 1959, Fort Benning, Ga.

Year	Team	Lg	W	L	PCT	ERA	G	GS	CG	IP	H	BB	SO	ShO	Relief W	Relief L	Relief SV	Batting AB	Batting H	Batting HR	BA	PO	A	E	DP	TC/G	FA
1989	MON	N	0	0	—	27.00	1	0	0	0.1	1	0	0	0	0	0	0	*				54	76	2	16	3.1	.985

Rich Folkers

FOLKERS, RICHARD NEVIN BL TL 6′ 2″ 180 lbs.
B. Oct. 17, 1946, Waterloo, Iowa.

Year	Team	Lg	W	L	PCT	ERA	G	GS	CG	IP	H	BB	SO	ShO	Relief W	Relief L	Relief SV	Batting AB	Batting H	Batting HR	BA	PO	A	E	DP	TC/G	FA
1970	NY	N	0	2	.000	6.52	16	1	0	29	36	25	15	0	0	1	2	6	2	0	.333	0	10	0	2	0.6	1.000
1972	STL	N	1	0	1.000	3.38	9	0	0	13.1	12	5	7	0	1	0	0	1	0	0	.000	0	2	0	0	0.2	1.000
1973			4	4	.500	3.61	34	9	1	82.1	74	34	44	0	1	0	3	20	2	0	.100	4	11	1	1	0.5	.938
1974			6	2	.750	3.00	55	0	0	90	65	38	57	0	6	2	2	10	1	0	.100	3	7	1	2	0.2	.909
1975	SD	N	6	11	.353	4.18	45	15	4	142	155	39	87	0	1	3	0	36	6	0	.167	10	20	3	0	0.7	.909

Rich Folkers *continued*

Year	Team	Lg	W	L	PCT	ERA	G	GS	CG	IP	H	BB	SO	ShO	Relief Pitching W	Relief Pitching L	Relief Pitching SV	Batting AB	Batting H	Batting HR	BA	PO	A	E	DP	TC/G	FA
1976			2	3	.400	5.28	33	3	0	59.2	67	25	26	0	2	0	0	4	0	0	.000	4	8	0	0	0.4	1.000
1977	MIL	A	0	1	.000	4.50	3	0	0	6	7	4	6	0	0	1	0	0	0	0	—	0	1	0	0	0.3	1.000
7 yrs.			19	23	.452	4.11	195	28	5	422.1	416	170	242	0	11	7	7	77	11	0	.143	21	59	5	5	0.4	.941

Lew Fonseca

FONSECA, LEWIS ALBERT BR TR 5′10½″ 180 lbs.
B. Jan. 21, 1899, Oakland, Calif. D. Nov. 26, 1989, Ely, Iowa.
Manager 1932–34.

Year	Team	Lg	W	L	PCT	ERA	G	GS	CG	IP	H	BB	SO	ShO	Relief Pitching W	Relief Pitching L	Relief Pitching SV	Batting AB	Batting H	Batting HR	BA	PO	A	E	DP	TC/G	FA
1932	CHI	A	0	0	—	0.00	1	0	0	1	0	0	0	0	0	0	0	*				307	155	14	30	5.8	.971

Ray Fontenot

FONTENOT, SILTON RAY BL TL 6′ 175 lbs.
B. Aug. 8, 1957, Lake Charles, La.

Year	Team	Lg	W	L	PCT	ERA	G	GS	CG	IP	H	BB	SO	ShO	Relief Pitching W	Relief Pitching L	Relief Pitching SV	Batting AB	Batting H	Batting HR	BA	PO	A	E	DP	TC/G	FA
1983	NY	A	8	2	.800	3.33	15	15	3	97.1	101	25	27	1	0	0	0	0	0	0	—	3	19	1	1	1.5	.957
1984			8	9	.471	3.61	33	24	0	169.1	189	58	85	0	1	0	0	0	0	0	—	6	28	3	1	1.1	.919
1985	CHI	N	6	10	.375	4.36	38	23	0	154.2	177	45	70	0	0	1	0	41	2	0	.049	6	35	1	3	1.1	.976
1986	2 teams	CHI N	(42G 3–5)		MIN A	(15G 0–0)																					
″	total		3	5	.375	5.23	57	0	0	72.1	84	25	34	0	3	5	2	7	1	0	.143	4	13	5	0	0.4	.773
4 yrs.			25	26	.490	4.03	143	62	3	493.2	551	153	216	1	4	6	2	48	3	0	.063	19	95	10	5	0.9	.919

Jim Foor

FOOR, JAMES EMERSON BL TL 6′ 2″ 170 lbs.
B. Jan. 13, 1949, St. Louis, Mo.

Year	Team	Lg	W	L	PCT	ERA	G	GS	CG	IP	H	BB	SO	ShO	Relief Pitching W	Relief Pitching L	Relief Pitching SV	Batting AB	Batting H	Batting HR	BA	PO	A	E	DP	TC/G	FA
1971	DET	A	0	0	—	18.00	3	0	0	1	2	4	2	0	0	0	0	0	0	0	—	0	0	0	0	0.0	.000
1972			1	0	1.000	13.50	7	0	0	4	6	6	2	0	1	0	0	0	0	0	—	0	1	0	0	0.1	1.000
1973	PIT	N	0	0	—	0.00	3	0	0	1.1	2	1	1	0	0	0	0	0	0	0	—	0	1	0	0	0.3	1.000
3 yrs.			1	0	1.000	11.37	13	0	0	6.1	10	11	5	0	1	0	0	0	0	0		0	2	0	0	0.2	1.000

Dave Ford

FORD, DAVID ALAN BR TR 6′ 4″ 190 lbs.
B. Dec. 29, 1956, Cleveland, Ohio.

Year	Team	Lg	W	L	PCT	ERA	G	GS	CG	IP	H	BB	SO	ShO	Relief Pitching W	Relief Pitching L	Relief Pitching SV	Batting AB	Batting H	Batting HR	BA	PO	A	E	DP	TC/G	FA
1978	BAL	A	1	0	1.000	0.00	2	1	0	15	10	2	5	0	0	0	0	0	0	0	—	2	1	0	0	1.5	1.000
1979			2	1	.667	2.10	9	2	0	30	23	7	7	0	1	1	2	0	0	0	—	0	7	0	0	0.8	1.000
1980			1	3	.250	4.24	25	3	1	70	66	13	22	0	0	1	1	0	0	0	—	4	8	0	0	0.5	1.000
1981			1	2	.333	6.53	15	2	0	40	61	10	12	0	1	1	0	0	0	0	—	2	5	0	0	0.5	1.000
4 yrs.			5	6	.455	4.01	51	8	1	155	160	32	46	0	2	3	3	0	0	0		8	21	0	0	0.6	1.000

Gene Ford

FORD, EUGENE MATTHEW BR TR 6′ 2″ 195 lbs.
B. June 23, 1912, Fort Dodge, Iowa D. Sept. 7, 1970, Emmetsburg, Iowa.

Year	Team	Lg	W	L	PCT	ERA	G	GS	CG	IP	H	BB	SO	ShO	Relief Pitching W	Relief Pitching L	Relief Pitching SV	Batting AB	Batting H	Batting HR	BA	PO	A	E	DP	TC/G	FA
1936	BOS	N	0	0	—	13.50	2	1	0	2	2	3	0	0	0	0	0	0	0	0	—	0	1	0	0	0.5	1.000
1938	CHI	A	0	0	—	10.29	4	0	0	14	21	12	2	0	0	0	0	6	1	0	.167	2	2	0	0	1.0	1.000
2 yrs.			0	0		10.69	6	1	0	16	23	15	2	0	0	0	0	6	1	0	.167	2	3	0	0	0.8	1.000

Gene Ford

FORD, EUGENE WYMAN BR TR 6′ 170 lbs.
Brother of Russ Ford.
B. Apr. 16, 1881, Milton, Nova Scotia, Canada D. Aug. 23, 1973, Dunedin, Fla.

Year	Team	Lg	W	L	PCT	ERA	G	GS	CG	IP	H	BB	SO	ShO	Relief Pitching W	Relief Pitching L	Relief Pitching SV	Batting AB	Batting H	Batting HR	BA	PO	A	E	DP	TC/G	FA
1905	DET	A	0	1	.000	5.66	7	1	1	35	51	14	20	0	0	0	0	10	0	0	.000	1	12	3	0	2.3	.813

Russ Ford

FORD, RUSSELL WILLIAM BR TR 5′11″ 175 lbs.
Brother of Gene Ford.
B. Apr. 25, 1883, Brandon, Man., Canada D. Jan. 24, 1960, Rockingham, N. C.

Year	Team	Lg	W	L	PCT	ERA	G	GS	CG	IP	H	BB	SO	ShO	Relief Pitching W	Relief Pitching L	Relief Pitching SV	Batting AB	Batting H	Batting HR	BA	PO	A	E	DP	TC/G	FA
1909	NY	A	0	0	—	9.00	1	0	0	3	4	4	2	0	0	0	0	1	0	0	.000	1	2	1	1	4.0	.750
1910			26	6	.813	1.65	36	33	29	299.2	194	70	209	8	0	0	1	96	20	0	.208	7	75	7	4	2.5	.921
1911			22	11	.667	2.27	37	33	26	281.1	251	76	158	1	2	1	0	102	20	0	.196	16	70	5	0	2.5	.945
1912			13	**21**	.382	3.55	36	35	30	291.2	317	79	112	0	0	0	0	112	32	1	.286	18	99	7	6	3.1	.944
1913			12	18	.400	2.66	33	28	15	237	244	58	72	1	3	0	2	74	12	0	.162	11	56	8	1	2.3	.893
1914	BUF	F	20	6	**.769**	1.82	35	26	19	247.1	190	41	123	5	0	2	**6**	78	10	0	.128	9	72	1	2	2.3	.988
1915			5	9	.357	4.52	21	15	7	127.1	140	48	34	0	0	1	0	43	12	0	.279	2	40	0	1	2.0	1.000
7 yrs.			98	71	.580	2.59	199	170	126	1487.1	1340	376	710	15	5	4	9	506	106	1	.209	64	414	29	15	2.5	.943

Tom Ford

FORD, THOMAS WALTER 5′10½″ 155 lbs.
B. 1866, Chattanooga, Tenn. D. May 27, 1917, Chattanooga, Tenn.

Year	Team	Lg	W	L	PCT	ERA	G	GS	CG	IP	H	BB	SO	ShO	Relief Pitching W	Relief Pitching L	Relief Pitching SV	Batting AB	Batting H	Batting HR	BA	PO	A	E	DP	TC/G	FA
1890	2 teams	COL AA	(1G 0–0)		BKN AA	(7G 0–6)																					
″	total		0	6	.000	6.71	8	6	6	51	70	35	12	0	0	0	0	31	1	0	.032	3	21	8	0	2.7	.750

Wenty Ford

FORD, PERCIVAL EDMUND WENTWORTH BR TR 5′11″ 165 lbs.
B. Nov. 25, 1946, Nassau, Bahamas D. July 8, 1980, Nassau, Bahamas.

Year	Team	Lg	W	L	PCT	ERA	G	GS	CG	IP	H	BB	SO	ShO	Relief Pitching W	Relief Pitching L	Relief Pitching SV	Batting AB	Batting H	Batting HR	BA	PO	A	E	DP	TC/G	FA
1973	ATL	N	1	2	.333	5.63	4	2	1	16	17	8	4	0	0	1	0	5	2	0	.400	1	3	0	0	1.0	1.000

Whitey Ford

FORD, EDWARD CHARLES (The Chairman of the Board) BL TL 5′10″ 178 lbs.
B. Oct. 21, 1926, New York, N. Y.
Hall of Fame 1974.

Year	Team	Lg	W	L	PCT	ERA	G	GS	CG	IP	H	BB	SO	ShO	Relief Pitching W	Relief Pitching L	Relief Pitching SV	Batting AB	Batting H	Batting HR	BA	PO	A	E	DP	TC/G	FA
1950	NY	A	9	1	.900	2.81	20	12	7	112	87	52	59	2	0	1	1	36	7	0	.194	7	17	0	1	1.2	1.000
1953			18	6	.750	3.00	32	30	11	207	187	110	110	3	0	0	0	75	20	0	.267	8	35	1	3	1.4	.977
1954			16	8	.667	2.82	34	28	11	210.2	170	101	125	3	2	2	1	62	10	0	.161	7	39	2	3	1.4	.958
1955			**18**	7	.720	2.63	39	33	**18**	253.2	188	113	137	5	0	1	2	86	14	1	.163	10	41	1	1	1.3	.981
1956			19	6	**.760**	**2.47**	31	30	18	225.2	187	84	141	2	0	0	1	78	17	0	.218	9	57	1	6	2.2	.985
1957			11	5	.688	2.57	24	17	5	129.1	114	53	84	0	3	0	0	42	6	0	.143	6	28	2	5	1.5	.944
1958			14	7	.667	**2.01**	30	29	15	219.1	174	62	145	**7**	0	0	1	73	15	0	.205	7	44	6	2	1.9	.895
1959			16	10	.615	3.04	35	29	9	204	194	89	114	2	2	2	1	65	15	1	.231	15	49	1	5	1.9	.985
1960			12	9	.571	3.08	33	29	8	192.2	168	65	85	**4**	0	0	0	53	8	0	.151	12	38	1	2	1.5	.980
1961			**25**	4	**.862**	3.21	39	**39**	11	**283**	242	92	209	3	0	0	0	96	17	0	.177	12	45	5	5	1.6	.919
1962			17	8	.680	2.90	38	37	7	257.2	243	69	160	0	0	0	0	85	10	0	.118	25	58	3	4	2.3	.965
1963			**24**	7	**.774**	2.74	38	**37**	13	**269.1**	240	56	189	3	0	0	1	92	13	1	.141	20	38	5	3	1.7	.921
1964			17	6	.739	2.13	39	36	12	244.2	212	57	172	8	0	0	1	67	8	0	.119	18	47	1	2	1.7	.985

Whitey Ford *continued*

Year	Team	W	L	PCT	ERA	G	GS	CG	IP	H	BB	SO	ShO	Relief Pitching W	Relief Pitching L	Relief Pitching SV	Batting AB	Batting H	Batting HR	BA	PO	A	E	DP	TC/G	FA
1965		16	13	.552	3.24	37	36	9	244.1	241	50	162	2	0	0	1	82	15	0	.183	7	53	0	4	1.6	1.000
1966		2	5	.286	2.47	22	9	0	73	79	24	43	0	2	1	0	18	0	0	.000	7	26	4	2	1.7	.892
1967		2	4	.333	1.64	7	7	2	44	40	9	21	1	0	0	0	13	2	0	.154	3	15	0	1	2.6	1.000
16 yrs.		236	106	.690 **3rd**	2.75	498	438	156	3170.1	2766	1086	1956	45	9	7	10	1023	177	3	.173	173	630	33	49	1.7	.961
WORLD SERIES																										
1950	**NY A**	1	0	1.000	0.00	1	1	0	8.2	7	1	7	0	0	0	0	3	0	0	.000	1	0	0	0	1.0	1.000
1953		0	1	.000	4.50	2	2	0	8	9	2	7	0	0	0	0	3	1	0	.333	0	1	0	0	0.5	1.000
1955		2	0	1.000	2.12	2	2	1	17	13	8	10	0	0	0	0	6	0	0	.000	1	4	0	0	2.5	1.000
1956		1	1	.500	5.25	2	2	1	12	14	2	8	0	0	0	0	4	0	0	.000	1	0	0	0	0.5	1.000
1957		1	1	.500	1.13	2	2	1	16	11	5	7	0	0	0	0	5	0	0	.000	1	1	0	0	1.0	1.000
1958		0	1	.000	4.11	3	3	0	15.1	19	5	16	0	0	0	0	4	0	0	.000	1	1	0	0	0.7	1.000
1960		2	0	1.000	0.00	2	2	2	18	11	2	8	2	0	0	0	8	2	0	.250	3	5	0	1	4.0	1.000
1961		2	0	1.000	0.00	2	2	1	14	6	1	7	1	0	0	0	5	0	0	.000	0	1	0	0	0.5	1.000
1962		1	1	.500	4.12	3	3	1	19.2	24	4	12	0	0	0	0	7	0	0	.000	0	4	1	0	1.7	.800
1963		0	2	.000	4.50	2	2	0	12	10	3	8	0	0	0	0	3	0	0	.000	3	2	0	0	2.5	1.000
1964		0	1	.000	8.44	1	1	0	5.1	8	1	4	0	0	0	0	1	1	0	1.000	0	1	0	0	1.0	1.000
11 yrs.		10 **1st**	8 **1st**	.556	2.71	22 **1st**	22 **1st**	7 **4th**	146 **1st**	132	34 **1st**	94 **1st**	3 **2nd**	0	0	0	49	4	0	.082	11	20	1	1	1.5	.969

Brownie Foreman

FOREMAN, JOHN DAVIS BL TL 5′ 8″ 150 lbs.
Brother of Frank Foreman.
B. Aug. 6, 1875, Baltimore, Md. D. Oct. 10, 1926, Baltimore, Md.

Year	Team	W	L	PCT	ERA	G	GS	CG	IP	H	BB	SO	ShO	Relief Pitching W	Relief Pitching L	Relief Pitching SV	Batting AB	Batting H	Batting HR	BA	PO	A	E	DP	TC/G	FA
1895	**PIT N**	8	6	.571	3.22	19	16	12	139.2	131	64	54	0	0	0	2	46	3	0	.065	3	43	5	1	2.7	.902
1896	**2 teams** **PIT N** (9G 3–3) **CIN N** (4G 0–4)																									
″	**total**	3	7	.300	8.81	13	12	7	79.2	112	51	22	0	0	1	0	28	4	0	.143	2	22	1	1	1.9	.960
2 yrs.		11	13	.458	5.25	32	28	19	219.1	243	115	76	0	0	1	2	74	7	0	.095	5	65	6	2	2.4	.921

Frank Foreman

FOREMAN, FRANCIS ISAIAH (Monk) BL TL 6′ 160 lbs.
Brother of Brownie Foreman.
B. May 1, 1863, Baltimore, Md. D. Nov. 19, 1957, Baltimore, Md.

Year	Team	W	L	PCT	ERA	G	GS	CG	IP	H	BB	SO	ShO	Relief Pitching W	Relief Pitching L	Relief Pitching SV	Batting AB	Batting H	Batting HR	BA	PO	A	E	DP	TC/G	FA
1884	**2 teams** **CHI U** (3G 1–2) **KC U** (1G 0–1)																									
″	**total**	1	3	.250	4.50	4	4	2	26	40	4	15	0	0	0	0	14	1	0	.071	9	6	2	0	2.8	.882
1885	**BAL AA**	2	1	.667	*6.00*	3	3	2	27	33	9	11	0	0	0	0	14	4	0	.286	0	4	1	0	1.3	.800
1889		23	21	.523	3.52	51	48	43	414	364	137	180	5	0	0	0	181	26	1	.144	11	72	14	1	1.8	.856
1890	**CIN N**	13	10	.565	3.95	25	24	20	198.1	201	89	57	0	0	0	0	75	10	1	.133	10	23	6	0	1.5	.846
1891	**WAS AA**	18	20	.474	3.73	43	41	39	345.1	381	142	170	1	0	0	1	157	35	4	.223	23	69	6	4	1.9	.939
1892	**2 teams** **WAS N** (11G 2–4) **BAL N** (4G 0–3)																									
″	**total**	2	7	.222	4.34	15	10	6	85	93	48	21	0	0	0	0	51	17	1	.333	10	18	10	0	1.9	.737
1893	**NY N**	0	1	.000	27.00	2	1	0	5.2	19	10	0	0	0	0	0	3	0	0	.000	0	1	0	0	0.5	1.000
1895	**CIN N**	11	14	.440	4.11	32	27	19	219	253	92	55	0	0	1	1	94	29	2	.309	11	34	6	1	1.6	.882
1896		15	6	.714	3.68	27	23	18	190.2	214	62	38	1	1	1	1	76	19	0	.250	8	45	4	2	2.1	.930
1901	**2 teams** **BOS A** (1G 0–1) **BAL A** (24G 12–6)																									
″	**total**	12	7	.632	3.88	25	23	19	199.1	233	60	42	1	0	0	1	84	26	0	.310	4	45	6	0	2.2	.891
1902	**BAL A**	0	2	.000	6.06	2	2	2	16.1	28	6	2	0	0	0	0	7	3	0	.429	0	9	2	0	5.5	.818
11 yrs.		97	92	.513	3.94	229	206	170	1726.2	1859	659	591	8	1	2	4	756	170	9	.225	86	326	57	8	1.9	.878

Happy Foreman

FOREMAN, AUGUST BL TL 5′ 7″ 160 lbs.
B. July 20, 1897, Memphis, Tenn. D. Feb. 13, 1953, New York, N. Y.

Year	Team	W	L	PCT	ERA	G	GS	CG	IP	H	BB	SO	ShO	Relief Pitching W	Relief Pitching L	Relief Pitching SV	Batting AB	Batting H	Batting HR	BA	PO	A	E	DP	TC/G	FA
1924	**CHI A**	0	0	—	2.25	3	0	0	4	7	4	1	0	0	0	0	2	0	0	.000	0	0	0	0	0.0	.000
1926	**BOS A**	0	0	—	3.68	3	0	0	7.1	3	5	3	0	0	0	0	2	0	0	.000	0	5	0	0	1.7	1.000
2 yrs.		0	0		3.18	6	0	0	11.1	10	9	4	0	0	0	0	4	0	0	.000	0	5	0	0	0.8	1.000

Bill Forman

FORMAN, WILLIAM ORANGE BB TR 5′11″ 180 lbs.
B. Oct. 10, 1886, Venango, Pa. D. Oct. 3, 1958, Uniontown, Pa.

Year	Team	W	L	PCT	ERA	G	GS	CG	IP	H	BB	SO	ShO	Relief Pitching W	Relief Pitching L	Relief Pitching SV	Batting AB	Batting H	Batting HR	BA	PO	A	E	DP	TC/G	FA
1909	**WAS A**	0	2	.000	4.91	2	2	1	11	8	7	2	0	0	0	0	3	1	0	.333	0	7	1	1	4.0	.875
1910		0	0	—	13.50	1	0	0	0.2	1	0	0	0	0	0	0	0	0	0	—	0	0	0	0	0.0	.000
2 yrs.		0	2	.000	5.40	3	2	1	11.2	9	7	2	0	0	0	0	3	1	0	.333	0	7	1	1	2.7	.875

Mike Fornieles

FORNIELES, JOSE MIGUEL BR TR 5′11″ 155 lbs.
Born Jose Miguel Fornieles (Torres).
B. Jan. 18, 1932, Havana, Cuba.

Year	Team	W	L	PCT	ERA	G	GS	CG	IP	H	BB	SO	ShO	Relief Pitching W	Relief Pitching L	Relief Pitching SV	Batting AB	Batting H	Batting HR	BA	PO	A	E	DP	TC/G	FA
1952	**WAS A**	2	2	.500	1.37	4	2	2	26.1	13	11	12	1	1	1	0	10	0	0	.000	1	4	0	0	1.3	1.000
1953	**CHI A**	8	7	.533	3.59	39	16	5	153	160	61	72	0	4	1	3	41	4	0	.098	16	30	2	2	1.2	.958
1954		1	2	.333	4.29	15	6	0	42	41	14	18	0	1	1	1	11	3	0	.273	1	11	2	1	0.9	.857
1955		6	3	.667	3.86	26	9	2	86.1	84	29	23	0	3	1	2	29	3	0	.103	1	18	1	2	0.8	.950
1956	**2 teams** **CHI A** (6G 0–1) **BAL A** (30G 4–7)																									
″	**total**	4	8	.333	4.05	36	11	1	126.2	131	31	59	1	3	2	1	35	6	0	.171	5	30	0	3	1.0	1.000
1957	**2 teams** **BAL A** (15G 2–6) **BOS A** (25G 8–7)																									
″	**total**	10	13	.435	3.75	40	22	8	182.1	193	55	107	2	3	3	2	62	11	0	.177	14	25	3	2	1.0	.929
1958	**BOS A**	4	6	.400	4.96	37	7	1	110.2	123	33	49	0	3	3	1	29	6	0	.207	5	18	1	1	0.6	.958
1959		5	3	.625	3.07	46	0	0	82	77	29	54	0	5	3	11	19	3	0	.158	5	13	1	0	0.4	.947
1960		10	5	.667	2.64	**70**	0	0	109	86	49	64	0	10	5	**14**	15	6	0	.400	7	19	3	3	0.4	.897
1961		9	8	.529	4.68	57	2	1	119.1	121	54	70	0	8	7	15	32	5	1	.156	12	25	1	2	0.7	.974
1962		3	6	.333	5.36	42	1	0	82.1	96	37	36	0	3	5	5	16	3	0	.188	5	14	1	1	0.5	.950
1963	**2 teams** **BOS A** (9G 0–0) **MIN A** (11G 1–1)																									
″	**total**	1	1	.500	5.40	20	0	0	36.2	40	18	12	0	1	1	0	9	2	0	.222	3	2	0	0	0.3	1.000
12 yrs.		63	64	.496	3.96	432	76	20	1156.2	1165	421	576	4	45	33	55	308	52	1	.169	75	209	15	17	0.7	.950

Bob Forsch

FORSCH, ROBERT HERBERT BR TR 6′ 4″ 200 lbs.
Brother of Ken Forsch.
B. Jan. 13, 1950, Sacramento, Calif.

Year	Team	W	L	PCT	ERA	G	GS	CG	IP	H	BB	SO	ShO	Relief Pitching W	Relief Pitching L	Relief Pitching SV	Batting AB	Batting H	Batting HR	BA	PO	A	E	DP	TC/G	FA
1974	**STL N**	7	4	.636	2.97	19	14	5	100	84	34	39	2	0	0	0	29	7	0	.241	10	13	0	0	1.2	1.000
1975		15	10	.600	2.86	34	34	7	230	213	70	108	4	0	0	0	78	24	1	.308	18	37	1	7	1.6	.982
1976		8	10	.444	3.94	33	32	2	194	209	71	76	0	0	1	0	62	11	1	.177	24	28	4	2	1.7	.929
1977		20	7	.741	3.48	35	35	8	217	210	69	95	2	0	0	0	72	12	0	.167	12	29	2	2	1.2	.953
1978		11	17	.393	3.69	34	34	7	234	205	97	114	3	0	0	0	83	15	1	.181	18	37	0	4	1.6	1.000
1979		11	11	.500	3.82	33	32	7	219	215	52	92	1	0	0	0	73	8	0	.110	25	31	1	3	1.7	.982
1980		11	10	.524	3.77	31	31	8	215	225	33	87	0	0	0	0	78	23	3	.295	11	44	2	5	1.8	.965
1981		10	5	.667	3.19	20	20	1	124	106	29	41	0	0	0	0	41	5	0	.122	14	20	0	1	1.7	1.000
1982		15	9	.625	3.48	36	34	6	233	238	54	69	2	0	0	1	73	15	0	.205	21	30	2	1	1.5	.962
1983		10	12	.455	4.28	34	30	6	187	190	54	56	2	1	0	0	54	13	1	.241	14	29	1	1	1.3	.977
1984		2	5	.286	6.02	16	11	1	52.1	64	19	21	0	1	0	0	16	4	0	.250	8	8	0	0	1.0	1.000
1985		9	6	.600	3.90	34	19	3	136	132	47	48	1	1	0	2	45	11	1	.244	12	20	1	0	1.0	.970
1986		14	10	.583	3.25	33	33	3	230	211	68	104	0	0	0	0	76	13	2	.171	17	32	0	5	1.5	1.000
1987		11	7	.611	4.32	33	30	2	179	189	45	89	1	0	0	0	57	17	2	.298	9	25	0	2	1.0	1.000
1988	**2 teams STL N** (30G 9–4) **HOU N** (6G 1–4)																									
″	**total**	10	8	.556	4.29	36	18	1	136.1	153	44	54	1	4	2	0	32	8	0	.250	8	13	3	1	0.7	.875
1989	**HOU N**	4	5	.444	5.32	37	15	0	108.1	133	46	40	0	1	1	0	24	4	0	.167	13	9	1	1	0.6	.957
16 yrs.		168	136	.553	3.76	498	422	67	2795	2777	832	1133	19	8	4	3	893	190	12	.213	234	405	18	35	1.3	.973
LEAGUE CHAMPIONSHIP SERIES																										
1982	**STL N**	1	0	1.000	0.00	1	1	1	9	3	0	6	1	0	0	0	3	2	0	.667	0	2	0	0	2.0	1.000
1985		0	0	—	5.40	1	1	0	3.1	3	2	0	0	0	0	0	0	0	0	—	0	1	0	0	1.0	1.000
1987		1	1	.500	12.00	3	0	0	3	4	1	3	0	1	1	0	0	0	0	—	0	1	0	0	0.3	1.000
3 yrs.		2	1	.667	3.52	5	2	1	15.1	10	3	9	1	1	1	0	3	2	0	.667	0	4	0	0	0.8	1.000
													1st													
WORLD SERIES																										
1982	**STL N**	0	2	.000	4.97	2	2	0	12.2	18	3	4	0	0	0	0	0	0	0	—	1	0	1	0	1.0	.500
1985		0	1	.000	12.00	2	1	0	3	6	1	3	0	0	0	0	0	0	0	—	0	0	0	0	0.0	.000
1987		1	0	1.000	9.95	3	0	0	6.1	8	5	3	0	1	0	0	2	0	0	.000	1	0	0	1	0.3	1.000
3 yrs.		1	3	.250	7.36	7	3	0	22	32	9	10	0	1	0	0	2	0	0	.000	2	0	1	1	0.4	.667

Ken Forsch

FORSCH, KENNETH ROTH BR TR 6′4″ 195 lbs.
Brother of Bob Forsch.
B. Sept. 8, 1946, Sacramento, Calif.

Year	Team	W	L	PCT	ERA	G	GS	CG	IP	H	BB	SO	ShO	Relief Pitching W	Relief Pitching L	Relief Pitching SV	Batting AB	Batting H	Batting HR	BA	PO	A	E	DP	TC/G	FA
1970	**HOU N**	1	2	.333	5.63	4	4	1	24	28	5	13	0	0	0	0	6	0	0	.000	2	2	0	1	1.0	1.000
1971		8	8	.500	2.54	33	23	7	188	162	53	131	2	0	0	0	59	8	0	.136	8	19	2	1	0.9	.931
1972		6	8	.429	3.91	30	24	1	156.1	163	62	113	0	0	0	0	41	6	0	.146	9	9	2	1	0.7	.900
1973		9	12	.429	4.20	46	26	5	201.1	197	74	149	0	1	3	4	62	4	0	.065	15	16	0	1	0.7	1.000
1974		8	7	.533	2.80	70	0	0	103	98	37	48	0	8	7	10	7	0	0	.000	9	14	2	1	0.4	.920
1975		4	8	.333	3.22	34	9	2	109	114	30	54	0	2	3	2	22	1	0	.045	6	14	2	3	0.6	.909
1976		4	3	.571	2.15	52	0	0	92	76	26	49	0	4	3	19	11	1	0	.091	4	17	0	0	0.4	1.000
1977		5	8	.385	2.72	42	5	0	86	80	28	45	0	5	5	8	13	1	0	.077	10	15	1	1	0.6	.962
1978		10	6	.625	2.71	52	6	4	133	136	37	71	2	6	4	7	27	5	0	.185	9	24	2	0	0.7	.943
1979		11	6	.647	3.03	26	24	10	178	155	35	58	2	1	0	0	58	8	0	.138	10	37	1	5	1.8	.979
1980		12	13	.480	3.20	32	32	6	222	230	41	84	3	0	0	0	77	18	0	.234	11	45	3	2	1.8	.949
1981	**CAL A**	11	7	.611	2.88	20	20	10	153	143	27	55	**4**	0	0	0	0	0	0	—	18	24	2	2	2.2	.955
1982		13	11	.542	3.87	37	35	12	228	225	57	73	4	2	0	0	0	0	0	—	13	29	5	2	1.3	.894
1983		11	12	.478	4.06	31	31	11	219.1	226	61	81	1	0	0	0	0	0	0	—	9	31	3	2	1.4	.930
1984		1	1	.500	2.20	2	2	1	16.1	14	3	10	0	0	0	0	0	0	0	—	1	6	0	1	3.5	1.000
1986		0	1	.000	9.53	10	0	0	17	24	10	13	0	0	1	1	0	0	0	—	0	3	1	1	0.4	.750
16 yrs.		114	113	.502	3.37	521	241	70	2126.1	2071	586	1047	18	29	26	51	383	52	0	.136	134	305	26	24	0.9	.944
LEAGUE CHAMPIONSHIP SERIES																										
1980	**HOU N**	0	1	.000	4.15	2	1	1	8.2	10	1	6	0	0	0	0	2	2	0	1.000	1	0	0	0	0.5	1.000

Terry Forster

FORSTER, TERRY JAY BL TL 6′ 3″ 200 lbs.
B. Jan. 14, 1952, Sioux Falls, S. D.

Year	Team	W	L	PCT	ERA	G	GS	CG	IP	H	BB	SO	ShO	Relief Pitching W	Relief Pitching L	Relief Pitching SV	Batting AB	Batting H	Batting HR	BA	PO	A	E	DP	TC/G	FA
1971	**CHI A**	2	3	.400	3.96	45	3	0	50	46	23	48	0	2	2	1	5	2	0	.400	4	6	0	0	0.2	1.000
1972		6	5	.545	2.25	62	0	0	100	75	44	104	0	6	5	29	19	10	0	.526	1	21	2	0	0.4	.917
1973		6	11	.353	3.23	51	12	4	172.2	174	78	120	0	3	4	16	1	0	0	.000	8	45	2	8	1.1	.964
1974		7	8	.467	3.63	59	1	0	134	120	48	105	0	7	7	**24**	0	0	0	—	6	33	1	4	0.7	.975
1975		3	3	.500	2.19	17	1	0	37	30	24	32	0	3	3	4	0	0	0	—	2	14	1	1	1.0	.941
1976		2	12	.143	4.38	29	16	1	111	126	41	70	0	0	5	1	0	0	0	—	5	26	2	0	1.1	.939
1977	**PIT N**	6	4	.600	4.45	33	6	0	87	90	32	58	0	4	1	1	26	9	0	.346	4	13	1	1	0.5	.944
1978	**LA N**	5	4	.556	1.94	47	0	0	65	56	23	46	0	5	4	22	8	4	0	.500	2	10	2	0	0.3	.857
1979		1	2	.333	5.63	17	0	0	16	18	11	8	0	1	2	2	0	0	0	—	1	5	0	0	0.4	1.000
1980		0	0	—	3.00	9	0	0	12	10	4	2	0	0	0	0	0	0	0	—	2	4	1	0	0.8	.857
1981		0	1	.000	4.06	21	0	0	31	37	15	17	0	0	1	0	2	0	0	.000	0	11	0	0	0.5	1.000
1982		5	6	.455	3.04	56	0	0	83	66	31	52	0	5	6	3	2	0	0	.000	4	18	1	0	0.4	.957
1983	**ATL N**	3	2	.600	2.16	56	0	0	79.1	60	31	54	0	3	2	13	8	4	0	.500	3	15	1	1	0.3	.947
1984		2	0	1.000	2.70	25	0	0	26.2	30	7	10	0	2	0	5	3	2	0	.667	2	4	0	1	0.2	1.000
1985		2	3	.400	2.28	46	0	0	59.1	49	28	37	0	2	3	1	4	0	0	.000	2	7	1	0	0.2	.900
1986	**CAL A**	4	1	.800	3.51	41	0	0	41	47	17	28	0	4	1	5	0	0	0	—	2	11	0	2	0.3	1.000
16 yrs.		54	65	.454	3.23	614	39	5	1105	1034	457	791	0	47	46	127	78	31	0	.397	48	243	15	18	0.5	.951
DIVISIONAL PLAYOFF SERIES																										
1981	**LA N**	0	0	—	0.00	1	0	0	0.1	0	0	0	0	0	0	0	0	0	0	—	0	0	0	0	0.0	.000
LEAGUE CHAMPIONSHIP SERIES																										
1978	**LA N**	1	0	1.000	0.00	1	0	0	1	1	0	2	0	1	0	0	0	0	0	—	0	0	0	0	0.0	.000
1981		0	0	—	0.00	1	0	0	0.1	0	0	1	0	0	0	0	0	0	0	—	0	0	0	0	0.0	.000
2 yrs.		1	0	1.000	0.00	2	0	0	1.1	1	0	3	0	1	0	0	0	0	0		0	0	0	0	0.0	

Terry Forster *continued*

Year	Team	Lg	W	L	PCT	ERA	G	GS	CG	IP	H	BB	SO	ShO	Relief Pitching W	Relief Pitching L	Relief Pitching SV	Batting AB	Batting H	Batting HR	BA	PO	A	E	DP	TC/G	FA
WORLD SERIES																											
1978	LA	N	0	0	—	0.00	3	0	0	4	5	1	6	0	0	0	0	0	0	0	—	0	1	0	0	0.3	1.000
1981			0	0	—	0.00	2	0	0	2	1	3	0	0	0	0	0	0	0	0	—	0	1	0	0	0.5	1.000
2 yrs.			0	0		0.00	5	0	0	6	6	4	6	0	0	0	0	0	0	0		0	2	0	0	0.4	1.000

Tim Fortugno

FORTUGNO, TIMOTHY SHAWN BL TL 6′ 1″ 195 lbs.
B. Apr. 11, 1962, Clinton, Mass.

Year	Team	Lg	W	L	PCT	ERA	G	GS	CG	IP	H	BB	SO	ShO	Relief Pitching W	Relief Pitching L	Relief Pitching SV	Batting AB	Batting H	Batting HR	BA	PO	A	E	DP	TC/G	FA
1992	CAL	A	1	1	.500	5.18	14	5	1	41.2	37	19	31	1	0	0	1	0	0	0	—	0	4	0	0	0.3	1.000
1994	CIN	N	1	0	1.000	4.20	25	0	0	30	32	14	29	0	1	0	0	3	1	0	.333	2	6	0	1	0.3	1.000
1995	CHI	A	1	3	.250	5.59	37	0	0	38.2	30	19	24	0	1	3	0	0	0	0	—	1	7	2	0	0.3	.800
3 yrs.			3	4	.429	5.06	76	5	1	110.1	99	52	84	1	2	3	1	3	1	0	.333	3	17	2	1	0.3	.909

Gary Fortune

FORTUNE, GARRETT REESE BB TR 5′11½″ 176 lbs.
B. Oct. 11, 1894, High Point, N. C. D. Sept. 23, 1955, Washington, D. C.

Year	Team	Lg	W	L	PCT	ERA	G	GS	CG	IP	H	BB	SO	ShO	Relief Pitching W	Relief Pitching L	Relief Pitching SV	Batting AB	Batting H	Batting HR	BA	PO	A	E	DP	TC/G	FA
1916	PHI	N	0	1	.000	3.60	1	1	0	5	2	4	3	0	0	0	0	2	0	0	.000	0	0	0	0	0.0	.000
1918			0	2	.000	8.13	5	2	1	31	41	19	10	0	0	0	0	10	2	0	.200	1	8	1	0	2.0	.900
1920	BOS	A	0	2	.000	5.83	14	3	1	41.2	46	23	10	0	0	1	0	12	2	0	.167	1	9	0	0	0.7	1.000
3 yrs.			0	5	.000	6.61	20	6	2	77.2	89	46	23	0	0	1	0	24	4	0	.167	2	17	1	0	1.0	.950

Jerry Fosnow

FOSNOW, GERALD EUGENE BR TL 6′ 4″ 195 lbs.
B. Sept. 21, 1940, Deshler, Ohio.

Year	Team	Lg	W	L	PCT	ERA	G	GS	CG	IP	H	BB	SO	ShO	Relief Pitching W	Relief Pitching L	Relief Pitching SV	Batting AB	Batting H	Batting HR	BA	PO	A	E	DP	TC/G	FA
1964	MIN	A	0	1	.000	10.97	7	0	0	10.2	13	8	9	0	0	1	0	0	0	0	—	0	1	1	0	0.3	.500
1965			3	3	.500	4.44	29	0	0	46.2	33	25	35	0	3	3	2	5	0	0	.000	1	12	3	0	0.6	.813
2 yrs.			3	4	.429	5.65	36	0	0	57.1	46	33	44	0	3	4	2	5	0	0	.000	1	13	4	0	0.5	.778

Larry Foss

FOSS, LARRY CURTIS BR TR 6′ 2″ 187 lbs.
B. Apr. 18, 1936, Castleton, Kans.

Year	Team	Lg	W	L	PCT	ERA	G	GS	CG	IP	H	BB	SO	ShO	Relief Pitching W	Relief Pitching L	Relief Pitching SV	Batting AB	Batting H	Batting HR	BA	PO	A	E	DP	TC/G	FA
1961	PIT	N	1	1	.500	5.87	3	3	0	15.1	15	11	9	0	0	0	0	6	1	0	.167	1	2	1	0	1.3	.750
1962	NY	N	0	1	.000	4.63	5	1	0	11.2	17	7	3	0	0	0	0	1	0	0	.000	2	1	0	0	0.6	1.000
2 yrs.			1	2	.333	5.33	8	4	0	27	32	18	12	0	0	0	0	7	1	0	.143	3	3	1	0	0.9	.857

Tony Fossas

FOSSAS, EMILIO ANTONIO BL TL 6′ 195 lbs.
Born Emilio Antonio Fossas (Morejon).
B. Sept. 23, 1957, Havana, Cuba.

Year	Team	Lg	W	L	PCT	ERA	G	GS	CG	IP	H	BB	SO	ShO	Relief Pitching W	Relief Pitching L	Relief Pitching SV	Batting AB	Batting H	Batting HR	BA	PO	A	E	DP	TC/G	FA
1988	TEX	A	0	0	—	4.76	5	0	0	5.2	11	2	0	0	0	0	0	0	0	0	—	1	1	0	1	0.4	1.000
1989	MIL	A	2	2	.500	3.54	51	0	0	61	57	22	42	0	2	2	1	0	0	0	—	1	12	2	0	0.3	.867
1990			2	3	.400	6.44	32	0	0	29.1	44	10	24	0	2	3	0	0	0	0	—	1	4	3	0	0.3	.625
1991	BOS	A	3	2	.600	3.47	64	0	0	57	49	28	29	0	3	2	1	0	0	0	—	6	12	2	2	0.3	.900
1992			1	2	.333	2.43	60	0	0	29.2	31	14	19	0	1	2	2	0	0	0	—	2	6	0	0	0.1	1.000
1993			1	1	.500	5.17	71	0	0	40	38	15	39	0	1	1	0	0	0	0	—	1	6	1	0	0.1	.875
1994			2	0	1.000	4.76	44	0	0	34	35	15	31	0	2	0	1	0	0	0	—	0	5	2	0	0.2	.714
1995	STL	N	3	0	1.000	1.47	58	0	0	36.2	28	10	40	0	3	0	0	0	0	0	—	1	3	1	0	0.1	.800
8 yrs.			14	10	.583	3.84	385	0	0	293.1	293	116	224	0	14	10	5	0	0	0		13	49	11	3	0.2	.849

Alan Foster

FOSTER, ALAN BENTON BR TR 6′ 180 lbs.
B. Dec. 8, 1946, Pasadena, Calif.

Year	Team	Lg	W	L	PCT	ERA	G	GS	CG	IP	H	BB	SO	ShO	Relief Pitching W	Relief Pitching L	Relief Pitching SV	Batting AB	Batting H	Batting HR	BA	PO	A	E	DP	TC/G	FA
1967	LA	N	0	1	.000	2.16	4	2	0	16.2	10	3	15	0	0	0	0	4	0	0	.000	3	3	0	0	1.5	1.000
1968			1	1	.500	1.72	3	3	0	15.2	11	2	10	0	0	0	0	4	1	0	.250	0	2	0	0	0.7	1.000
1969			3	9	.250	4.37	24	15	2	103	119	29	59	2	0	0	0	27	2	0	.074	2	18	1	0	0.9	.952
1970			10	13	.435	4.25	33	33	7	199	200	81	83	1	0	0	0	64	7	0	.109	17	23	2	4	1.3	.952
1971	CLE	A	8	12	.400	4.15	36	26	3	182	158	82	97	0	1	0	0	51	2	0	.039	10	9	2	0	0.6	.905
1972	CAL	A	0	1	.000	4.85	8	0	0	13	12	6	11	0	0	1	0	0	0	0	—	2	2	0	0	0.5	1.000
1973	STL	N	13	9	.591	3.14	35	29	6	203.2	195	63	106	2	0	2	0	68	13	0	.191	17	21	3	1	1.2	.927
1974			7	10	.412	3.89	31	25	5	162	167	61	78	1	0	0	0	48	8	0	.167	14	20	4	1	1.2	.895
1975	SD	N	3	1	.750	2.40	17	4	1	45	41	21	20	0	1	0	0	11	1	0	.091	4	8	2	0	0.8	.857
1976			3	6	.333	3.22	26	11	2	86.2	75	35	22	0	0	0	0	18	1	0	.056	9	9	0	1	0.7	1.000
10 yrs.			48	63	.432	3.73	217	148	26	1026.2	988	383	501	6	2	3	0	295	35	0	.119	78	115	14	7	0.9	.932

Kevin Foster

FOSTER, KEVIN CHRISTOPHER BR TR 6′ 1″ 160 lbs.
B. Jan. 13, 1969, Evanston, Ill.

Year	Team	Lg	W	L	PCT	ERA	G	GS	CG	IP	H	BB	SO	ShO	Relief Pitching W	Relief Pitching L	Relief Pitching SV	Batting AB	Batting H	Batting HR	BA	PO	A	E	DP	TC/G	FA
1993	PHI	N	0	1	.000	14.85	2	1	0	6.2	13	7	6	0	0	0	0	2	0	0	.000	1	0	0	0	0.5	1.000
1994	CHI	N	3	4	.429	2.89	13	13	0	81	70	35	75	0	0	0	0	27	2	0	.074	4	5	0	0	0.7	1.000
1995			12	11	.522	4.51	30	28	0	167.2	149	65	146	0	0	0	0	60	15	1	.250	7	14	0	0	0.7	1.000
3 yrs.			15	16	.484	4.27	45	42	0	255.1	232	107	227	0	0	0	0	89	17	1	.191	12	19	0	0	0.7	1.000

Larry Foster

FOSTER, LARRY LYNN BL TR 6′ 185 lbs.
B. Dec. 24, 1937, Lansing, Mich.

Year	Team	Lg	W	L	PCT	ERA	G	GS	CG	IP	H	BB	SO	ShO	Relief Pitching W	Relief Pitching L	Relief Pitching SV	Batting AB	Batting H	Batting HR	BA	PO	A	E	DP	TC/G	FA
1963	DET	A	0	0	—	13.50	1	0	0	2	4	1	1	0	0	0	0	0	0	0	—	0	1	0	0	1.0	1.000

Rube Foster

FOSTER, GEORGE BR TR 5′ 7½″ 170 lbs.
B. Jan. 5, 1888, Lehigh, Okla. D. Mar. 1, 1976, Bokoshe, Okla.

Year	Team	Lg	W	L	PCT	ERA	G	GS	CG	IP	H	BB	SO	ShO	Relief Pitching W	Relief Pitching L	Relief Pitching SV	Batting AB	Batting H	Batting HR	BA	PO	A	E	DP	TC/G	FA
1913	BOS	A	3	4	.429	3.16	19	8	4	68.1	64	28	36	1	0	0	0	21	2	0	.095	5	21	1	0	1.4	.963
1914			14	8	.636	1.65	32	27	17	212.2	162	52	92	5	0	0	0	63	11	0	.175	18	58	4	1	2.5	.950
1915			19	8	.704	2.11	37	33	22	255.1	217	86	82	5	0	0	1	83	23	1	.277	18	77	2	0	2.6	.979
1916			14	7	.667	3.06	33	19	9	182.1	173	86	53	3	4	0	2	62	11	0	.177	16	57	1	5	2.2	.986
1917			8	7	.533	2.53	17	16	9	124.2	108	53	34	1	0	1	0	41	11	0	.268	14	38	2	1	3.2	.963
5 yrs.			58	34	.630	2.35	138	103	61	843.1	724	305	297	15	4	1	3	270	58	1	.215	71	251	10	7	2.4	.970
WORLD SERIES																											
1915	BOS	A	2	0	1.000	2.00	2	2	2	18	12	2	13	0	0	0	0	8	4	0	.500	4	3	0	1	3.5	1.000
1916			0	0	—	0.00	1	0	0	3	3	0	1	0	0	0	0	1	0	0	.000	1	2	0	0	3.0	1.000
2 yrs.			2	0	1.000	1.71	3	2	2	21	15	2	14	0	0	0	0	9	4	0	.444	5	5	0	1	3.3	1.000

Slim Foster

FOSTER, EDWARD LEE BR TR 6′ 1″
B. 1885, Ga. D. Mar. 1, 1929, Montgomery, Ala.

Year	Team	Lg	W	L	PCT	ERA	G	GS	CG	IP	H	BB	SO	ShO	Relief W	Relief L	Relief SV	Batting AB	Batting H	HR	BA	PO	A	E	DP	TC/G	FA
1908	**CLE**	**A**	1	0	1.000	2.14	6	1	1	21	16	12	11	0	0	0	2	6	0	0	.000	0	2	0	0	0.3	1.000

Steve Foster

FOSTER, STEVEN EUGENE BR TR 6′ 180 lbs.
B. Aug. 16, 1964, Dallas, Tex.

Year	Team	Lg	W	L	PCT	ERA	G	GS	CG	IP	H	BB	SO	ShO	Relief W	Relief L	Relief SV	Batting AB	Batting H	HR	BA	PO	A	E	DP	TC/G	FA
1991	**CIN**	**N**	0	0	—	1.93	11	0	0	14	7	4	11	0	0	0	0	0	0	0	—	2	1	0	0	0.3	1.000
1992			1	1	.500	2.88	31	1	0	50	52	13	34	0	1	0	2	5	1	0	.200	5	11	0	0	0.5	1.000
1993			2	2	.500	1.75	17	0	0	25.2	23	5	16	0	2	2	0	0	0	0	—	0	2	0	0	0.1	1.000
3 yrs.			3	3	.500	2.41	59	1	0	89.2	82	22	61	0	3	2	2	5	1	0	.200	7	14	0	0	0.4	1.000

Steve Foucault

FOUCAULT, STEVEN RAYMOND BL TR 6′ 205 lbs.
B. Oct. 3, 1949, Duluth, Minn.

Year	Team	Lg	W	L	PCT	ERA	G	GS	CG	IP	H	BB	SO	ShO	Relief W	Relief L	Relief SV	Batting AB	Batting H	HR	BA	PO	A	E	DP	TC/G	FA
1973	**TEX**	**A**	2	4	.333	3.86	32	0	0	56	54	31	28	0	2	4	8	0	0	0	—	4	10	0	1	0.4	1.000
1974			8	9	.471	2.25	69	0	0	144	123	40	106	0	8	9	12	0	0	0	—	11	19	2	3	0.5	.938
1975			8	4	.667	4.12	59	0	0	107	96	55	56	0	8	4	10	0	0	0	—	5	13	1	3	0.3	.947
1976			8	8	.500	3.32	46	0	0	76	68	25	41	0	8	8	5	0	0	0	—	4	20	0	3	0.5	1.000
1977	**DET**	**A**	7	7	.500	3.16	44	0	0	74	64	17	58	0	7	7	13	0	0	0	—	3	8	0	0	0.3	1.000
1978	**2 teams**	**DET A** (24G 2–4)	**KC A** (3G 0–0)																								
″	**total**		2	4	.333	3.23	27	0	0	39	53	22	18	0	2	4	4	0	0	0		2	5	2	0	0.3	.778
6 yrs.			35	36	.493	3.21	277	0	0	496	458	190	307	0	35	36	52	0	0	0		29	75	5	10	0.4	.954

Henry Fournier

FOURNIER, JULIUS HENRY (Frenchy) TL
B. Aug. 8, 1865, Syracuse, N. Y. D. Dec. 8, 1945, Eloise, Mich.

Year	Team	Lg	W	L	PCT	ERA	G	GS	CG	IP	H	BB	SO	ShO	Relief W	Relief L	Relief SV	Batting AB	Batting H	HR	BA	PO	A	E	DP	TC/G	FA
1894	**CIN**	**N**	1	3	.250	5.40	6	4	4	45	71	20	5	0	0	0	0	19	2	0	.105	0	11	1	1	2.0	.917

Jack Fournier

FOURNIER, JOHN FRANK BL TR 6′ 195 lbs.
B. Sept. 28, 1889, Au Sable, Mich. D. Sept. 5, 1973, Tacoma, Wash.

Year	Team	Lg	W	L	PCT	ERA	G	GS	CG	IP	H	BB	SO	ShO	Relief W	Relief L	Relief SV	Batting AB	Batting H	HR	BA	PO	A	E	DP	TC/G	FA
1922	**STL**	**N**	0	0	—	0.00	1	0	0	1	0	0	0	0	0	0	0	*				154	16	2	4	10.1	.988

Dave Foutz

FOUTZ, DAVID LUTHER (Scissors) BR TR 6′ 2″ 161 lbs.
Brother of Frank Foutz.
B. Sept. 7, 1856, Carroll County, Md. D. Mar. 5, 1897, Waverly, Md.
Manager 1893–96.

Year	Team	Lg	W	L	PCT	ERA	G	GS	CG	IP	H	BB	SO	ShO	Relief W	Relief L	Relief SV	Batting AB	Batting H	HR	BA	PO	A	E	DP	TC/G	FA
1884	**STL**	**AA**	15	6	.714	*2.18*	25	25	19	206.2	167	36	95	2	0	0	0	119	27	0	.227	26	45	6	6	2.0	.922
1885			33	14	.702	*2.63*	47	46	46	407.2	351	92	147	2	**1**	0	0	238	59	0	.248	189	109	23	15	4.9	.928
1886			**41**	16	**.719**	***2.11***	59	57	55	504	418	144	283	11	1	0	**1**	414	116	3	.280	211	86	19	7	3.0	.940
1887			25	12	.676	*3.87*	40	38	36	339.1	369	90	94	1	0	0	0	423	151	4	.357	282	65	23	11	3.5	.938
1888	**BKN**	**AA**	12	7	.632	2.51	23	19	19	176	146	35	73	0	0	0	0	563	156	3	.277	588	71	28	28	4.8	.959
1889			3	0	1.000	4.37	12	4	3	59.2	70	19	21	0	0	0	0	553	153	7	.277	1376	48	31	66	10.0	.979
1890	**BKN**	**N**	2	1	.667	1.86	5	2	2	29	29	6	4	0	1	0	**2**	509	154	5	.303	1222	44	30	64	9.9	.977
1891			3	2	.600	3.29	6	5	5	52	51	16	14	0	0	0	0	521	134	2	.257	1246	60	31	52	10.2	.977
1892			13	8	.619	3.41	27	20	17	203	210	63	56	0	0	2	1	220	41	1	.186	109	62	16	5	3.0	.914
1893			0	0	—	7.50	6	0	0	18	28	8	3	0	0	0	0	557	137	7	.246	735	36	27	22	5.8	.966
1894			0	0	—	13.50	1	0	0	2	4	1	0	0	0	0	0	293	90	0	.307	658	33	17	37	9.7	.976
11 yrs.			147	66	.690 **2nd**	2.84	251	216	202	1997.1	1843	510	790	16	3	2	4	*				6758	664	261	317	6.6	.966

Art Fowler

FOWLER, JOHN ARTHUR BR TR 5′11″ 180 lbs.
Brother of Jesse Fowler.
B. July 3, 1922, Converse, S. C.

Year	Team	Lg	W	L	PCT	ERA	G	GS	CG	IP	H	BB	SO	ShO	Relief W	Relief L	Relief SV	Batting AB	Batting H	HR	BA	PO	A	E	DP	TC/G	FA
1954	**CIN**	**N**	12	10	.545	3.83	40	29	8	227.2	256	85	93	1	1	2	0	60	6	0	.100	10	35	2	4	1.2	.957
1955			11	10	.524	3.90	46	28	8	207.2	198	63	94	3	1	0	2	60	12	0	.200	12	30	0	1	0.9	1.000
1956			11	11	.500	4.05	45	23	8	177.2	191	35	86	0	3	1	1	48	7	0	.146	12	35	1	0	1.1	.979
1957			3	0	1.000	6.47	33	7	1	87.2	111	24	45	0	1	0	0	17	3	0	.176	5	15	0	0	0.6	1.000
1959	**LA**	**N**	3	4	.429	5.31	36	0	0	61	70	23	47	0	3	4	2	12	1	0	.083	2	12	1	0	0.4	.933
1961	**LA**	**A**	5	8	.385	3.64	53	3	0	89	68	29	78	0	5	6	11	13	1	0	.077	4	7	0	0	0.2	1.000
1962			4	3	.571	2.81	48	0	0	77	67	25	38	0	4	3	5	11	3	0	.273	5	12	0	0	0.4	1.000
1963			5	3	.625	2.42	57	0	0	89.1	70	19	53	0	5	3	10	9	2	0	.222	4	9	1	0	0.2	.929
1964			0	2	.000	10.29	4	0	0	7	8	5	5	0	0	2	0	1	0	0	.000	1	2	0	1	0.8	1.000
9 yrs.			54	51	.514	4.03	362	90	25	1024	1039	308	539	4	23	21	32	231	35	0	.152	55	157	5	6	0.6	.977

Dick Fowler

FOWLER, RICHARD JOHN BR TR 6′ 4½″ 215 lbs.
B. Mar. 30, 1921, Toronto, Ont., Canada D. May 22, 1972, Oneonta, N. Y.

Year	Team	Lg	W	L	PCT	ERA	G	GS	CG	IP	H	BB	SO	ShO	Relief W	Relief L	Relief SV	Batting AB	Batting H	HR	BA	PO	A	E	DP	TC/G	FA
1941	**PHI**	**A**	1	2	.333	3.38	4	3	1	24	26	8	8	0	0	1	0	9	0	0	.000	0	4	0	1	1.0	1.000
1942			6	11	.353	4.95	31	17	4	140	159	45	38	0	2	2	1	50	8	0	.160	8	18	3	2	0.9	.897
1945			1	2	.333	4.82	7	3	2	37.1	41	18	21	1	0	1	0	18	8	0	.444	1	4	0	0	0.7	1.000
1946			9	**16**	.360	3.28	32	28	14	205.2	213	75	89	1	0	0	0	71	13	0	.183	13	29	3	2	1.4	.933
1947			12	11	.522	2.81	36	31	16	227.1	210	85	75	3	1	1	0	82	14	0	.171	14	29	2	1	1.3	.956
1948			15	8	.652	3.78	29	26	16	204.2	221	76	50	2	0	0	2	82	14	1	.171	10	30	1	4	1.4	.976
1949			15	11	.577	3.75	31	28	15	213.2	210	115	43	4	1	0	1	77	18	0	.234	15	46	1	5	2.0	.984
1950			1	5	.167	6.48	11	9	2	66.2	75	56	15	0	0	0	0	26	5	0	.192	6	11	1	2	1.6	.944
1951			5	11	.313	5.62	22	22	4	125	141	72	29	0	0	0	0	42	8	0	.190	11	16	2	3	1.3	.931
1952			1	2	.333	6.44	18	3	1	58.2	71	28	14	0	0	0	0	15	0	0	.000	5	14	0	0	1.1	1.000
10 yrs.			66	79	.455	4.11	221	170	75	1303	1367	578	382	11	4	5	4	472	88	1	.186	83	201	13	20	1.3	.956

Jesse Fowler

FOWLER, JESSE PETER BR TL 5′10½″ 158 lbs.
Brother of Art Fowler.
B. Oct. 30, 1898, Spartanburg, S. C. D. Sept. 23, 1973, Columbia, S. C.

Year	Team	Lg	W	L	PCT	ERA	G	GS	CG	IP	H	BB	SO	ShO	Relief W	Relief L	Relief SV	Batting AB	Batting H	HR	BA	PO	A	E	DP	TC/G	FA
1924	**STL**	**N**	1	1	.500	4.41	13	3	0	32.2	28	18	5	0	1	0	0	9	2	0	.222	0	5	1	0	0.5	.833

Alan Fowlkes

FOWLKES, ALAN KIM BR TR 6′ 2″ 190 lbs.
B. Aug. 8, 1958, Brawley, Calif.

Year	Team	Lg	W	L	PCT	ERA	G	GS	CG	IP	H	BB	SO	ShO	Relief Pitching W	Relief Pitching L	Relief Pitching SV	Batting AB	Batting H	Batting HR	BA	PO	A	E	DP	TC/G	FA
1982	SF	N	4	2	.667	5.19	21	15	1	85	111	24	50	0	0	0	0	26	3	0	.115	4	13	2	0	0.9	.895
1985	CAL	A	0	0	—	9.00	2	0	0	7	8	4	5	0	0	0	0	0	0	0	—	1	1	0	0	1.0	1.000
2 yrs.			4	2	.667	5.48	23	15	1	92	119	28	55	0	0	0	0	26	3	0	.115	5	14	2	0	0.9	.905

Henry Fox

FOX, HENRY
Born Henry Fuchs.
B. Nov. 18, 1874, Scranton, Pa. D. June 6, 1927, Scranton, Pa.

Year	Team	Lg	W	L	PCT	ERA	G	GS	CG	IP	H	BB	SO	ShO	Relief Pitching W	Relief Pitching L	Relief Pitching SV	Batting AB	Batting H	Batting HR	BA	PO	A	E	DP	TC/G	FA
1902	PHI	N	0	0	—	18.00	1	0	0	1	2	1	1	0	0	0	1	0	0	0	—	0	0	0	0	0.0	.000

Howie Fox

FOX, HOWARD FRANCIS BR TR 6′ 3″ 210 lbs.
B. Mar. 1, 1921, Coburg, Ore. D. Oct. 9, 1955, San Antonio, Tex.

Year	Team	Lg	W	L	PCT	ERA	G	GS	CG	IP	H	BB	SO	ShO	Relief Pitching W	Relief Pitching L	Relief Pitching SV	Batting AB	Batting H	Batting HR	BA	PO	A	E	DP	TC/G	FA
1944	CIN	N	0	0	—	0.00	2	0	0	2.1	2	0	0	0	0	0	0	1	0	0	.000	0	0	0	0	0.0	.000
1945			8	13	.381	4.93	45	15	7	164.1	169	77	54	0	4	2	0	46	13	0	.283	9	52	1	0	1.4	.984
1946			0	0	—	18.00	4	0	0	5	12	5	1	0	0	0	0	0	0	0	—	1	1	0	0	0.5	1.000
1948			6	9	.400	4.53	34	24	5	171	185	62	63	0	0	0	1	60	12	0	.200	14	33	2	5	1.4	.959
1949			6	**19**	.240	3.98	38	30	9	215	221	77	60	0	1	0	0	72	17	0	.236	14	65	3	7	2.2	.963
1950			11	8	.579	4.33	34	22	10	187	196	85	64	1	0	0	1	63	11	1	.175	8	52	3	1	1.9	.952
1951			9	14	.391	3.83	40	30	9	228	239	69	57	4	1	1	2	70	8	1	.114	8	49	2	3	1.5	.966
1952	PHI	N	2	7	.222	5.08	13	11	2	62	70	26	16	0	0	2	0	21	1	0	.048	3	19	1	2	1.8	.957
1954	BAL	A	1	2	.333	3.67	38	0	0	73.2	80	34	27	0	1	2	2	16	4	0	.250	3	19	0	3	0.6	1.000
9 yrs.			43	72	.374	4.33	248	132	42	1108.1	1174	435	342	5	7	7	6	349	66	2	.189	60	290	12	21	1.5	.967

John Fox

FOX, JOHN JOSEPH
B. Feb. 7, 1859, Roxbury, Mass. D. Apr. 18, 1893, Boston, Mass.

Year	Team	Lg	W	L	PCT	ERA	G	GS	CG	IP	H	BB	SO	ShO	Relief Pitching W	Relief Pitching L	Relief Pitching SV	Batting AB	Batting H	Batting HR	BA	PO	A	E	DP	TC/G	FA
1881	BOS	N	6	8	.429	*3.33*	17	16	12	124.1	144	39	30	0	0	0	0	118	21	0	.178	68	29	10	4	3.1	.907
1883	BAL	AA	6	13	.316	*4.03*	20	19	18	165.1	209	32	49	0	0	0	0	92	14	0	.152	27	34	21	2	3.3	.744
1884	PIT	AA	1	6	.143	*5.64*	7	7	7	59	76	16	22	0	0	0	0	25	6	0	.240	2	15	2	1	2.4	.895
1886	WAS	N	0	1	.000	*9.00*	1	1	1	8	11	11	3	0	0	0	0	3	1	0	.333	0	2	0	0	2.0	1.000
4 yrs.			13	28	.317	4.16	45	43	38	356.2	440	98	104	0	0	0	0	238	42	0	.176	97	80	33	7	3.0	.843

Terry Fox

FOX, TERRENCE EDWARD BR TR 6′ 175 lbs.
B. July 31, 1935, Chicago, Ill.

Year	Team	Lg	W	L	PCT	ERA	G	GS	CG	IP	H	BB	SO	ShO	Relief Pitching W	Relief Pitching L	Relief Pitching SV	Batting AB	Batting H	Batting HR	BA	PO	A	E	DP	TC/G	FA
1960	MIL	N	0	0	—	4.32	5	0	0	8.1	6	6	5	0	0	0	0	1	0	0	.000	0	1	0	0	0.2	1.000
1961	DET	A	5	2	.714	1.41	39	0	0	57.1	42	16	32	0	5	2	12	12	2	0	.167	6	12	1	1	0.5	.947
1962			3	1	.750	1.71	44	0	0	58	48	16	23	0	3	1	16	8	2	0	.250	2	13	1	1	0.4	.938
1963			8	6	.571	3.59	46	0	0	80.1	81	20	35	0	8	6	11	11	1	0	.091	7	16	3	0	0.6	.885
1964			4	3	.571	3.39	32	0	0	61	77	16	28	0	4	3	5	12	3	0	.250	5	11	1	3	0.5	.941
1965			6	4	.600	2.78	42	0	0	77.2	59	31	34	0	6	4	10	15	0	0	.000	6	22	1	2	0.7	.966
1966	2 teams	DET A (4G 0–1)	PHI N (36G 3–2)																								
″	total		3	3	.500	4.80	40	0	0	54.1	66	19	28	0	3	3	5	6	0	0	.000	1	11	0	0	0.3	1.000
7 yrs.			29	19	.604	2.99	248	0	0	397	379	124	185	0	29	19	59	65	8	0	.123	27	86	7	7	0.5	.942

Bill Foxen

FOXEN, WILLIAM ALOYSIUS BL TL 5′11½″ 165 lbs.
B. May 31, 1884, Tenafly, N. J. D. Apr. 17, 1937, Brooklyn, N. Y.

Year	Team	Lg	W	L	PCT	ERA	G	GS	CG	IP	H	BB	SO	ShO	Relief Pitching W	Relief Pitching L	Relief Pitching SV	Batting AB	Batting H	Batting HR	BA	PO	A	E	DP	TC/G	FA
1908	PHI	N	7	7	.500	1.95	22	16	10	147.1	126	53	52	2	0	0	0	53	5	0	.094	9	51	3	0	2.9	.952
1909			3	7	.300	3.35	18	7	5	83.1	65	32	37	1	0	3	0	24	5	1	.208	6	42	2	0	2.8	.960
1910	2 teams	PHI N (16G 5–5)	CHI N (2G 0–0)																								
″	total		5	5	.500	2.94	18	9	5	82.2	80	43	35	0	2	0	0	25	4	0	.160	1	30	2	3	1.8	.939
1911	CHI	N	1	1	.500	2.08	3	1	0	13	12	12	6	0	0	1	0	4	1	0	.250	2	6	0	0	2.7	1.000
4 yrs.			16	20	.444	2.56	61	33	20	326.1	283	140	130	3	2	4	0	106	15	1	.142	18	129	7	3	2.5	.955

Jimmie Foxx

FOXX, JAMES EMORY (Double X, The Beast) BR TR 6′ 195 lbs.
B. Oct. 22, 1907, Sudlersville, Md. D. July 21, 1967, Miami, Fla.
Hall of Fame 1951.

Year	Team	Lg	W	L	PCT	ERA	G	GS	CG	IP	H	BB	SO	ShO	Relief Pitching W	Relief Pitching L	Relief Pitching SV	Batting AB	Batting H	Batting HR	BA	PO	A	E	DP	TC/G	FA
1939	BOS	A	0	0	—	0.00	1	0	0	1	0	0	1	0	0	0	0	467	168	35	.360	0	0	0	0	0.0	.000
1945	PHI	N	1	0	1.000	1.59	9	2	0	22.2	13	14	10	0	0	0	0	224	60	7	.268	19	5	0	0	1.6	1.000
2 yrs.			1	0	1.000	1.52	10	2	0	23.2	13	14	11	0	0	0	0	*				17786	1561	192	1553	8.9	.990

Paul Foytack

FOYTACK, PAUL EUGENE BR TR 5′11″ 175 lbs.
B. Nov. 16, 1930, Scranton, Pa.

Year	Team	Lg	W	L	PCT	ERA	G	GS	CG	IP	H	BB	SO	ShO	Relief Pitching W	Relief Pitching L	Relief Pitching SV	Batting AB	Batting H	Batting HR	BA	PO	A	E	DP	TC/G	FA
1953	DET	A	0	0	—	11.17	6	0	0	9.2	15	9	7	0	0	0	0	1	0	0	.000	0	1	0	0	0.2	1.000
1955			0	1	.000	5.26	22	1	0	49.2	48	36	38	0	0	0	0	11	1	0	.091	2	7	0	0	0.4	1.000
1956			15	13	.536	3.59	43	33	16	256	211	**142**	184	1	1	0	1	90	11	0	.122	11	33	3	5	1.1	.936
1957			14	11	.560	3.14	38	27	8	212	175	104	118	1	3	2	1	63	14	0	.222	3	30	4	1	1.0	.892
1958			15	13	.536	3.44	39	33	16	230	198	77	135	2	0	0	1	75	18	0	.240	12	25	0	3	0.9	1.000
1959			14	14	.500	4.64	39	**37**	11	240.1	239	64	110	2	0	0	1	81	9	0	.111	9	36	1	0	1.2	.978
1960			2	11	.154	6.14	28	13	1	96.2	108	49	38	0	0	4	2	25	7	0	.280	7	7	0	0	0.5	1.000
1961			11	10	.524	3.93	32	20	6	169.2	152	56	89	0	3	2	0	54	12	1	.222	8	13	0	2	0.7	1.000
1962			10	7	.588	4.39	29	21	5	143.2	145	86	63	1	2	0	0	42	6	0	.143	13	25	0	1	1.3	1.000
1963	2 teams	DET A (9G 0–1)	LA A (25G 5–5)																								
″	total		5	6	.455	4.70	34	8	0	88	86	37	44	0	2	2	1	19	4	0	.211	6	11	2	0	0.6	.895
1964	LA	A	0	1	.000	15.43	2	0	0	2.1	4	2	1	0	0	1	0	0	0	0	—	0	0	0	0	0.0	.000
11 yrs.			86	87	.497	4.14	312	193	63	1498	1381	662	827	7	11	11	7	461	82	1	.178	71	188	10	12	0.9	.963

Ken Frailing

FRAILING, KENNETH DOUGLAS BL TL 6′ 190 lbs.
B. Jan. 19, 1948, Madison, Wis.

Year	Team	Lg	W	L	PCT	ERA	G	GS	CG	IP	H	BB	SO	ShO	Relief Pitching W	Relief Pitching L	Relief Pitching SV	Batting AB	Batting H	Batting HR	BA	PO	A	E	DP	TC/G	FA
1972	CHI	A	1	0	1.000	3.00	4	0	0	3	3	1	1	0	1	0	0	0	0	0	—	0	1	0	0	0.3	1.000
1973			0	0	—	1.96	10	0	0	18.1	18	7	15	0	0	0	0	0	0	0	—	2	2	1	0	0.5	.800
1974	CHI	N	6	9	.400	3.89	55	16	1	125	150	43	71	0	1	2	1	31	8	0	.258	8	19	1	0	0.5	.964
1975			2	5	.286	5.43	41	0	0	53	61	26	39	0	2	5	1	7	1	0	.143	7	15	0	0	0.5	1.000
1976			1	2	.333	2.37	6	3	0	19	20	5	10	0	1	0	0	3	0	0	.000	1	3	0	0	0.7	1.000
5 yrs.			10	16	.385	3.96	116	19	1	218.1	252	82	136	0	5	7	2	41	9	0	.220	18	40	2	0	0.5	.967

Ossie France

FRANCE, OSMAN BEVERLY BL TL 5′ 8″ 155 lbs.
B. Oct. 4, 1858, Greensburg, Ohio D. May 2, 1947, Akron, Ohio.

Year	Team		W	L	PCT	ERA	G	GS	CG	IP	H	BB	SO	ShO	Relief W	Relief L	Relief SV	Batting AB	Batting H	Batting HR	BA	PO	A	E	DP	TC/G	FA
1890	CHI	N	0	0	—	13.50	1	0	0	2	3	2	0	0	0	0	0	1	0	0	.000	0	0	0	0	0.0	.000

Earl Francis

FRANCIS, EARL COLEMAN BR TR 6′ 2″ 210 lbs.
B. July 14, 1935, Slab Fork, W. Va.

Year	Team		W	L	PCT	ERA	G	GS	CG	IP	H	BB	SO	ShO	Relief W	Relief L	Relief SV	Batting AB	Batting H	Batting HR	BA	PO	A	E	DP	TC/G	FA
1960	PIT	N	1	0	1.000	2.00	7	0	0	18	14	4	8	0	1	0	0	5	0	0	.000	1	2	0	1	0.4	1.000
1961			2	8	.200	4.21	23	15	0	102.2	110	47	53	0	0	1	0	28	3	0	.107	8	20	1	1	1.3	.966
1962			9	8	.529	3.07	36	23	5	176	153	83	121	1	2	0	0	61	10	1	.164	12	33	1	3	1.3	.978
1963			4	6	.400	4.53	33	13	0	97.1	107	43	72	0	2	0	0	26	8	0	.308	4	19	4	3	0.8	.852
1964			0	1	.000	8.53	2	1	0	6.1	7	1	6	0	0	0	0	1	0	0	.000	0	0	0	0	0.0	.000
1965	STL	N	0	0	—	5.06	2	0	0	5.1	7	3	3	0	0	0	0	1	0	0	.000	0	0	1	0	0.5	.000
6 yrs.			16	23	.410	3.77	103	52	5	405.2	398	181	263	1	5	1	0	122	21	1	.172	25	74	7	8	1.0	.934

Ray Francis

FRANCIS, RAY JAMES BL TL 6′ 1½″ 182 lbs.
B. Mar. 8, 1893, Sherman, Tex. D. July 6, 1934, Atlanta, Ga.

Year	Team		W	L	PCT	ERA	G	GS	CG	IP	H	BB	SO	ShO	Relief W	Relief L	Relief SV	Batting AB	Batting H	Batting HR	BA	PO	A	E	DP	TC/G	FA
1922	WAS	A	7	18	.280	4.28	39	26	15	225	265	66	64	2	0	3	2	78	13	0	.167	10	54	5	2	1.8	.928
1923	DET	A	5	8	.385	4.42	33	6	0	79.1	95	28	27	0	1	3	1	21	3	0	.143	2	19	0	1	0.6	1.000
1925	2 teams	NY A (4G 0–0)	BOS A (6G 0–2)																								
″	total		0	2	.000	7.71	10	4	0	32.2	49	16	5	0	0	0	0	8	1	0	.125	2	8	0	0	1.0	1.000
3 yrs.			12	28	.300	4.65	82	36	15	337	409	110	96	2	1	6	3	107	17	0	.159	14	81	5	3	1.2	.950

John Franco

FRANCO, JOHN ANTHONY BL TL 5′10″ 175 lbs.
B. Sept. 17, 1960, Brooklyn, N. Y.

Year	Team		W	L	PCT	ERA	G	GS	CG	IP	H	BB	SO	ShO	Relief W	Relief L	Relief SV	Batting AB	Batting H	Batting HR	BA	PO	A	E	DP	TC/G	FA
1984	CIN	N	6	2	.750	2.61	54	0	0	79.1	74	36	55	0	6	2	4	3	0	0	.000	5	15	0	0	0.4	1.000
1985			12	3	.800	2.18	67	0	0	99	83	40	61	0	**12**	3	12	6	2	0	.333	9	21	1	1	0.5	.968
1986			6	6	.500	2.94	74	0	0	101	90	44	84	0	6	6	29	4	0	0	.000	6	22	4	2	0.4	.875
1987			8	5	.615	2.52	68	0	0	82	76	27	61	0	8	5	32	2	0	0	.000	4	7	0	0	0.2	1.000
1988			6	6	.500	1.57	70	0	0	86	60	27	46	0	6	6	**39**	1	0	0	.000	3	18	1	1	0.3	.955
1989			4	8	.333	3.12	60	0	0	80.2	77	36	60	0	4	8	32	3	1	0	.333	2	19	1	1	0.4	.955
1990	NY	N	5	3	.625	2.53	55	0	0	67.2	66	21	56	0	5	3	**33**	5	0	0	.000	4	13	1	0	0.3	.944
1991			5	9	.357	2.93	52	0	0	55.1	61	18	45	0	5	**9**	30	1	0	0	.000	3	10	1	1	0.3	.929
1992			6	2	.750	1.64	31	0	0	33	24	11	20	0	6	2	15	1	0	0	.000	2	12	0	2	0.5	1.000
1993			4	3	.571	5.20	35	0	0	36.1	46	19	29	0	4	3	10	1	0	0	.000	3	9	0	0	0.3	1.000
1994			1	4	.200	2.70	47	0	0	50	47	19	42	0	1	4	**30**	3	0	0	.000	4	7	0	1	0.2	1.000
1995			5	3	.625	2.44	48	0	0	51.2	48	17	41	0	5	3	29	0	0	0	—	2	9	0	1	0.2	1.000
12 yrs.			68	54	.557	2.62	661	0	0	822	752	315	600	0	68	54	295 **8th**	30	3	0	.100	47	162	9	10	0.3	.959

Terry Francona

FRANCONA, TERRY JON BL TL 6′ 1″ 190 lbs.
Son of Tito Francona.
B. Apr. 22, 1959, Aberdeen, S. D.

Year	Team		W	L	PCT	ERA	G	GS	CG	IP	H	BB	SO	ShO	Relief W	Relief L	Relief SV	Batting AB	Batting H	Batting HR	BA	PO	A	E	DP	TC/G	FA
1989	MIL	A	0	0	—	0.00	1	0	0	1	0	0	1	0	0	0	0	*				41	5	0	0	1.7	1.000

Charlie Frank

FRANK, CHARLES 5′10″ 170 lbs.
B. May 30, 1870, Mobile, Ala. D. May 24, 1922, Memphis, Tenn.

Year	Team		W	L	PCT	ERA	G	GS	CG	IP	H	BB	SO	ShO	Relief W	Relief L	Relief SV	Batting AB	Batting H	Batting HR	BA	PO	A	E	DP	TC/G	FA
1894	STL	N	0	0	—	15.00	2	0	0	3	6	7	1	0	0	0	0	*				84	9	7	1	2.5	.930

Fred Frankhouse

FRANKHOUSE, FREDERICK MELOY BR TR 5′11″ 175 lbs.
B. Apr. 9, 1904, Port Royal, Pa. D. Aug. 17, 1989, Port Royal, Pa.

Year	Team		W	L	PCT	ERA	G	GS	CG	IP	H	BB	SO	ShO	Relief W	Relief L	Relief SV	Batting AB	Batting H	Batting HR	BA	PO	A	E	DP	TC/G	FA
1927	STL	N	5	1	.833	2.70	6	6	5	50	41	16	20	1	0	0	0	20	5	0	.250	3	6	2	0	1.8	.818
1928			3	2	.600	3.96	21	10	1	84	91	36	29	0	0	0	1	27	5	0	.185	2	23	1	4	1.2	.962
1929			7	2	.778	4.12	30	12	6	133.1	149	43	37	0	1	0	1	52	15	1	.288	5	41	1	5	1.6	.979
1930	2 teams	STL N (8G 2–3)	BOS N (27G 7–6)																								
″	total		9	9	.500	5.87	35	12	3	130.1	169	54	34	1	5	3	0	44	14	0	.318	8	27	1	1	1.0	.972
1931	BOS	N	8	8	.500	4.03	26	15	6	127.1	125	43	50	0	0	1	1	40	6	0	.150	7	29	3	3	1.5	.923
1932			4	6	.400	3.56	37	6	3	108.2	113	45	35	0	2	3	0	30	3	0	.100	7	41	4	1	1.4	.923
1933			16	15	.516	3.16	43	30	14	244.2	249	77	83	2	2	2	2	80	19	0	.237	12	71	1	6	2.0	.988
1934			17	9	.654	3.20	37	31	13	233.2	239	77	78	2	0	0	1	85	17	0	.200	9	48	1	2	1.6	.983
1935			11	15	.423	4.76	40	29	10	230.2	278	81	64	1	0	0	0	76	20	0	.263	15	63	2	2	2.0	.975
1936	BKN	N	13	10	.565	3.65	41	31	9	234.1	236	89	84	1	1	1	2	91	13	0	.143	15	52	1	3	1.7	.985
1937			10	13	.435	4.27	33	25	9	179.1	214	78	64	1	2	1	0	58	11	0	.190	20	48	5	2	2.2	.932
1938			3	5	.375	4.04	30	8	2	93.2	92	44	32	1	2	1	0	26	4	0	.154	5	24	2	1	1.0	.935
1939	BOS	N	0	2	.000	2.61	23	0	0	38	37	18	12	0	0	2	4	7	0	0	.000	0	4	0	0	0.2	1.000
13 yrs.			106	97	.522	3.92	402	215	81	1888	2033	701	622	10	15	14	12	636	132	1	.208	108	477	24	30	1.5	.961

Jack Franklin

FRANKLIN, JACK WILFORD BR TR 5′11½″ 170 lbs.
B. Oct. 20, 1919, Paris, Ill. D. Nov. 15, 1991, Panama City, Fla.

Year	Team		W	L	PCT	ERA	G	GS	CG	IP	H	BB	SO	ShO	Relief W	Relief L	Relief SV	Batting AB	Batting H	Batting HR	BA	PO	A	E	DP	TC/G	FA
1944	BKN	N	0	0	—	13.50	1	0	0	2	2	4	0	0	0	0	0	0	0	0	—	0	0	0	0	0.0	.000

Jay Franklin

FRANKLIN, JOHN WILLIAM BR TR 6′ 2″ 180 lbs.
B. Mar. 16, 1953, Arlington, Va.

Year	Team		W	L	PCT	ERA	G	GS	CG	IP	H	BB	SO	ShO	Relief W	Relief L	Relief SV	Batting AB	Batting H	Batting HR	BA	PO	A	E	DP	TC/G	FA
1971	SD	N	0	1	.000	6.00	3	1	0	6	5	4	4	0	0	0	0	1	0	0	.000	0	2	0	0	0.7	1.000

John Frascatore

FRASCATORE, JOHN VINCENT BR TR 6′ 1″ 200 lbs.
B. Feb. 4, 1970, Ozone Park, N. Y.

Year	Team		W	L	PCT	ERA	G	GS	CG	IP	H	BB	SO	ShO	Relief W	Relief L	Relief SV	Batting AB	Batting H	Batting HR	BA	PO	A	E	DP	TC/G	FA
1994	STL	N	0	1	.000	16.20	1	1	0	3.1	7	2	2	0	0	0	0	1	0	0	.000	0	1	0	0	1.0	1.000
1995			1	1	.500	4.41	14	4	0	32.2	39	16	21	0	0	0	0	7	0	0	.000	3	2	0	0	0.4	1.000
2 yrs.			1	2	.333	5.50	15	5	0	36	46	18	23	0	0	0	0	8	0	0	.000	3	3	0	0	0.4	1.000

Chick Fraser

FRASER, CHARLES CARROLTON BR TR 5′10½″ 188 lbs.
B. Mar. 17, 1871, Chicago, Ill. D. May 8, 1940, Wendell, Ida.

Year	Team		W	L	PCT	ERA	G	GS	CG	IP	H	BB	SO	ShO	Relief W	Relief L	Relief SV	Batting AB	Batting H	Batting HR	BA	PO	A	E	DP	TC/G	FA
1896	LOU	N	12	27	.308	4.87	43	38	36	349.1	396	**166**	91	0	0	2	1	146	22	0	.151	43	96	27	5	3.7	.837
1897			15	19	.441	4.09	35	34	32	286.1	332	133	70	0	1	0	0	112	18	2	.161	33	84	12	5	3.6	.907

Chick Fraser *continued*

Year	Team	W	L	PCT	ERA	G	GS	CG	IP	H	BB	SO	ShO	Relief W	Relief L	SV	AB	H	HR	BA	PO	A	E	DP	TC/G	FA
1898	2 teams LOU N (26G 7–17) CLE N (6G 2–3)																									
″	total	9	20	.310	5.36	32	32	26	245	279	112	77	1	0	0	0	94	17	0	.181	20	73	3	1	3.0	.969
1899	PHI N	21	12	.636	3.36	35	33	29	270.2	278	85	68	4	0	1	0	117	21	0	.179	29	78	11	3	3.0	.907
1900		16	10	.615	3.14	29	26	22	223.1	250	93	58	1	0	0	0	85	22	0	.259	27	63	4	2	3.2	.957
1901	PHI A	22	16	.579	3.81	40	37	35	331	344	**132**	110	2	1	0	0	139	26	0	.187	37	92	7	4	3.2	.949
1902	PHI N	12	13	.480	3.42	27	26	24	224	238	74	97	3	0	1	0	86	15	0	.174	15	51	4	1	2.6	.943
1903		12	17	.414	4.50	31	29	26	250	260	97	104	1	0	1	1	93	19	1	.204	15	70	3	2	2.8	.966
1904		14	24	.368	3.25	42	36	32	302	287	100	127	2	**2**	1	1	110	17	0	.155	38	87	10	3	3.1	.926
1905	BOS N	14	22	.389	3.29	39	37	35	334	320	**149**	130	2	0	0	0	156	35	0	.224	71	82	9	1	3.6	.944
1906	CIN N	10	20	.333	2.67	31	28	25	236	221	80	58	2	1	2	0	82	14	0	.171	23	70	4	3	3.1	.959
1907	CHI N	8	5	.615	2.28	22	15	9	138.1	112	46	41	2	**4**	0	0	45	3	0	.067	7	42	3	0	2.4	.942
1908		11	9	.550	2.27	26	17	11	162.2	141	61	66	2	3	0	2	50	6	0	.120	14	61	1	2	2.9	.987
1909		0	0	—	0.00	1	0	0	3	2	4	1	0	0	0	0	1	0	0	.000	0	0	0	0	0.0	.000
14 yrs.		176	214	.451	3.68	433	388	342	3355.2	3460	1332	1098	22	12	8	5	1316	235	3	.179	372	949	98	32	3.1	.931

Willie Fraser

FRASER, WILLIAM PATRICK
B. May 26, 1964, New York, N.Y.
BR TR 6′ 1″ 200 lbs.

Year	Team	W	L	PCT	ERA	G	GS	CG	IP	H	BB	SO	ShO	Relief W	Relief L	SV	AB	H	HR	BA	PO	A	E	DP	TC/G	FA
1986	CAL A	0	0	—	8.31	1	1	0	4.1	6	1	2	0	0	0	0	0	0	0	—	0	0	0	0	0.0	.000
1987		10	10	.500	3.92	36	23	5	176.2	160	63	106	1	3	1	1	0	0	0	—	6	15	1	0	0.6	.955
1988		12	13	.480	5.41	34	32	2	194.2	203	80	86	0	1	0	0	0	0	0	—	21	20	3	3	1.3	.932
1989		4	7	.364	3.24	44	0	0	91.2	80	23	46	0	4	7	2	0	0	0	—	6	14	0	1	0.5	1.000
1990		5	4	.556	3.08	45	0	0	76	69	24	32	0	5	4	2	0	0	0	—	2	6	0	0	0.2	1.000
1991	2 teams TOR A (13G 0–2) STL N (35G 3–3)																									
″	total	3	5	.375	5.35	48	1	0	75.2	77	32	37	0	3	4	0	2	0	0	.000	3	6	0	0	0.2	1.000
1994	FLA N	2	0	1.000	5.84	9	0	0	12.1	20	6	7	0	2	0	0	0	0	0	—	0	1	0	0	0.1	1.000
1995	MON N	2	1	.667	5.61	22	0	0	25.2	25	9	12	0	2	1	2	2	0	0	.000	1	4	0	0	0.2	1.000
8 yrs.		38	40	.487	4.47	239	57	7	657	640	238	328	1	20	17	7	4	0	0	.000	39	66	4	4	0.5	.963

Vic Frasier

FRASIER, VICTOR PATRICK
B. Aug. 5, 1904, Ruston, La. D. Jan. 10, 1977, Jacksonville, Tex.
BR TR 6′ 182 lbs.

Year	Team	W	L	PCT	ERA	G	GS	CG	IP	H	BB	SO	ShO	Relief W	Relief L	SV	AB	H	HR	BA	PO	A	E	DP	TC/G	FA
1931	CHI A	13	15	.464	4.46	46	29	13	254	258	127	87	2	1	1	4	86	18	0	.209	6	50	6	2	1.3	.903
1932		3	13	.188	6.23	29	21	4	146	180	70	33	0	0	1	0	44	4	0	.091	5	42	1	1	1.7	.979
1933	2 teams CHI A (10G 1–1) DET A (20G 5–5)																									
″	total	6	6	.500	7.00	30	15	4	124.2	161	70	30	0	0	2	0	41	7	0	.171	4	35	0	2	1.3	1.000
1934	DET A	1	3	.250	5.96	8	2	0	22.2	30	12	11	0	1	2	0	7	2	0	.286	1	13	2	0	2.0	.875
1937	BOS N	0	0	—	5.63	3	0	0	8	12	1	2	0	0	0	0	1	0	0	.000	1	2	0	0	1.0	1.000
1939	CHI A	0	1	.000	10.27	10	1	0	23.2	45	11	7	0	0	0	0	7	2	0	.286	0	5	0	0	0.5	1.000
6 yrs.		23	38	.377	5.77	126	68	21	579	686	291	170	2	2	6	4	186	33	0	.177	17	147	9	5	1.4	.948

George Frazier

FRAZIER, GEORGE ALLEN
B. Oct. 13, 1954, Oklahoma City, Okla.
BR TR 6′ 5″ 205 lbs.

Year	Team	W	L	PCT	ERA	G	GS	CG	IP	H	BB	SO	ShO	Relief W	Relief L	SV	AB	H	HR	BA	PO	A	E	DP	TC/G	FA
1978	STL N	0	3	.000	4.09	14	0	0	22	22	6	8	0	0	3	0	3	1	0	.333	0	5	1	0	0.4	.833
1979		2	4	.333	4.50	25	0	0	32	35	12	14	0	2	4	0	1	0	0	.000	4	4	1	0	0.4	.889
1980		1	4	.200	2.74	22	0	0	23	24	7	11	0	1	4	3	0	0	0	—	1	4	0	0	0.2	1.000
1981	NY A	0	1	.000	1.61	16	0	0	28	26	11	17	0	0	1	3	0	0	0	—	1	4	1	0	0.4	.833
1982		4	4	.500	3.47	63	0	0	111.2	103	39	69	0	4	4	1	0	0	0	—	6	17	3	2	0.4	.885
1983		4	4	.500	3.43	61	0	0	115.1	94	45	78	0	4	4	8	0	0	0	—	5	17	2	0	0.4	.917
1984	2 teams CLE A (22G 3–2) CHI N (37G 6–3)																									
″	total	9	5	.643	3.92	59	0	0	108	98	40	82	0	9	5	4	7	2	0	.286	7	9	3	0	0.3	.842
1985	CHI N	7	8	.467	6.39	51	0	0	76	88	52	46	0	7	8	2	6	0	0	.000	5	9	1	2	0.3	.933
1986	2 teams CHI N (35G 2–4) MIN A (15G 1–1)																									
″	total	3	5	.375	5.06	50	0	0	78.1	86	50	66	0	3	5	6	4	0	0	.000	3	6	0	0	0.2	1.000
1987	MIN A	5	5	.500	4.98	54	0	0	81.1	77	51	58	0	5	5	2	0	0	0	—	2	8	1	0	0.2	.909
10 yrs.		35	43	.449	4.20	415	0	0	675.2	653	313	449	0	35	43	29	21	3	0	.143	34	83	13	4	0.3	.900
LEAGUE CHAMPIONSHIP SERIES																										
1981	NY A	1	0	1.000	0.00	1	0	0	5.2	5	1	5	0	1	0	0	0	0	0	—	0	2	0	1	2.0	1.000
1984	CHI N	0	0	—	10.80	1	0	0	1.2	2	0	1	0	0	0	0	0	0	0	—	0	0	0	0	0.0	.000
2 yrs.		1	0	1.000	2.45	2	0	0	7.1	7	1	6	0	1	0	0	0	0	0		0	2	0	1	1.0	1.000
WORLD SERIES																										
1981	NY A	0	3	.000	17.18	3	0	0	3.2	9	3	2	0	0	3	0	2	0	0	.000	0	0	0	0	0.0	.000
1987	MIN A	0	0	—	0.00	1	0	0	2	1	0	2	0	0	0	0	0	0	0	—	0	1	0	0	1.0	1.000
2 yrs.		0	3	.000	11.12	4	0	0	5.2	10	3	4	0	0	3	0	2	0	0	.000	0	1	0	0	0.3	1.000

Scott Fredrickson

FREDRICKSON, SCOTT ERIC
B. Aug. 19, 1967, Manchester, N. H.
BR TR 6′ 3″ 220 lbs.

Year	Team	W	L	PCT	ERA	G	GS	CG	IP	H	BB	SO	ShO	Relief W	Relief L	SV	AB	H	HR	BA	PO	A	E	DP	TC/G	FA
1993	CLR N	0	1	.000	6.21	25	0	0	29	33	17	20	0	0	1	0	3	0	0	.000	4	1	0	0	0.2	1.000

Buck Freeman

FREEMAN, ALEXANDER VERNON
B. July 5, 1896, Mart, Tex. D. Feb. 21, 1953, Fort Sam Houston, Tex.
BB TR 5′10″ 167 lbs.
BR 1922

Year	Team	W	L	PCT	ERA	G	GS	CG	IP	H	BB	SO	ShO	Relief W	Relief L	SV	AB	H	HR	BA	PO	A	E	DP	TC/G	FA
1921	CHI N	9	10	.474	4.11	38	20	6	177.1	189	70	42	0	4	2	3	53	11	0	.208	3	43	3	2	1.3	.939
1922		0	1	.000	8.77	11	1	0	25.2	47	10	10	0	0	0	1	8	1	0	.125	0	11	2	2	1.2	.846
2 yrs.		9	11	.450	4.70	49	21	6	203	236	80	52	0	4	2	4	61	12	0	.197	3	54	5	4	1.3	.919

Buck Freeman

FREEMAN, JOHN FRANK
B. Oct. 30, 1871, Catasauqua, Pa. D. June 25, 1949, Wilkes-Barre, Pa.
BL TL 5′ 9″ 169 lbs.

Year	Team	W	L	PCT	ERA	G	GS	CG	IP	H	BB	SO	ShO	Relief W	Relief L	SV	AB	H	HR	BA	PO	A	E	DP	TC/G	FA
1891	WAS AA	3	2	.600	3.89	5	4	4	44	35	33	28	0	1	0	0	18	4	0	.222	0	10	3	0	2.6	.769
1899	WAS N	0	0	—	7.71	2	0	0	7	15	3	0	0	0	0	0	588	187	25	.318	39	5	1	2	1.6	.978
2 yrs.		3	2	.600	4.41	7	4	4	51	50	36	28	0	1	0	0	*				3576	224	137	134	3.6	.965

Harvey Freeman

FREEMAN, HARVEY BAYARD (Buck)
B. Dec. 22, 1897, Mottville, Mich. D. Jan. 10, 1970, Kalamazoo, Mich.
BR TR 5′10″ 145 lbs.

Year	Team	W	L	PCT	ERA	G	GS	CG	IP	H	BB	SO	ShO	Relief W	Relief L	SV	AB	H	HR	BA	PO	A	E	DP	TC/G	FA
1921	PHI A	1	4	.200	7.24	18	4	2	51	65	35	5	0	0	1	0	12	1	0	.083	0	19	0	0	1.1	1.000

Hersh Freeman

FREEMAN, HERSHELL BASKIN (Buster) BR TR 6′ 3″ 220 lbs.
B. July 1, 1928, Gadsden, Ala.

Year	Team	Lg	W	L	PCT	ERA	G	GS	CG	IP	H	BB	SO	ShO	Relief Pitching W	Relief Pitching L	Relief Pitching SV	Batting AB	Batting H	HR	BA	PO	A	E	DP	TC/G	FA
1952	BOS	A	1	0	1.000	3.29	4	1	1	13.2	13	5	5	0	0	0	0	4	2	0	.500	0	4	0	0	1.0	1.000
1953			1	4	.200	5.54	18	2	0	39	50	17	15	0	1	2	0	11	1	0	.091	0	7	0	0	0.4	1.000
1955	2 teams	BOS A (2G 0–0)	CIN N (52G 7–4)																								
″	total		7	4	.636	2.12	54	0	0	93.1	95	31	38	0	7	4	11	18	3	1	.167	4	20	0	4	0.4	1.000
1956	CIN	N	14	5	.737	3.40	64	0	0	108.2	112	34	50	0	**14**	5	18	18	1	0	.056	8	15	0	2	0.4	1.000
1957			7	2	.778	4.52	52	0	0	83.2	90	14	36	0	7	2	8	10	2	0	.200	5	12	0	1	0.3	1.000
1958	2 teams	CIN N (3G 0–0)	CHI N (9G 0–1)																								
″	total		0	1	.000	6.53	12	0	0	20.2	27	8	14	0	0	1	0	2	0	0	.000	2	5	0	0	0.6	1.000
6 yrs.			30	16	.652	3.74	204	3	1	359	387	109	158	0	29	14	37	63	9	1	.143	19	63	0	7	0.4	1.000

Jimmy Freeman

FREEMAN, JIMMY LEE BL TL 6′ 4″ 180 lbs.
B. June 29, 1951, Carlsbad, N. M.

Year	Team	Lg	W	L	PCT	ERA	G	GS	CG	IP	H	BB	SO	ShO	Relief Pitching W	Relief Pitching L	Relief Pitching SV	Batting AB	Batting H	HR	BA	PO	A	E	DP	TC/G	FA
1972	ATL	N	2	2	.500	6.00	6	6	1	36	40	22	18	0	0	0	0	13	1	0	.077	1	2	1	0	0.7	.750
1973			0	2	.000	7.78	13	5	0	37	50	25	20	0	0	1	1	13	2	0	.154	1	3	0	0	0.3	1.000
2 yrs.			2	4	.333	6.90	19	11	1	73	90	47	38	0	0	1	1	26	3	0	.115	2	5	1	0	0.4	.875

Julie Freeman

FREEMAN, JULIUS BENJAMIN BR
B. Nov. 7, 1868, Missouri D. June 10, 1921, St. Louis, Mo.

Year	Team	Lg	W	L	PCT	ERA	G	GS	CG	IP	H	BB	SO	ShO	Relief Pitching W	Relief Pitching L	Relief Pitching SV	Batting AB	Batting H	HR	BA	PO	A	E	DP	TC/G	FA
1888	STL	AA	0	1	.000	4.26	1	1	0	6.1	7	4	1	0	0	0	0	3	1	0	.333	0	1	0	0	1.0	1.000

Mark Freeman

FREEMAN, MARK PRICE BR TR 6′ 4″ 220 lbs.
B. Dec. 7, 1930, Memphis, Tenn.

Year	Team	Lg	W	L	PCT	ERA	G	GS	CG	IP	H	BB	SO	ShO	Relief Pitching W	Relief Pitching L	Relief Pitching SV	Batting AB	Batting H	HR	BA	PO	A	E	DP	TC/G	FA
1959	2 teams	NY A (1G 0–0)	KC A (3G 0–0)																								
″	total		0	0		5.06	4	1	0	10.2	12	5	5	0	0	0	0	2	0	0	.000	0	1	0	0	0.3	1.000
1960	CHI	N	3	3	.500	5.63	30	8	1	76.2	70	33	50	0	1	2	1	20	3	0	.150	3	6	1	0	0.3	.900
2 yrs.			3	3	.500	5.56	34	9	1	87.1	82	38	55	0	1	2	1	22	3	0	.136	3	7	1	0	0.3	.909

Marvin Freeman

FREEMAN, MARVIN (Starvin' Marvin) BR TR 6′ 7″ 200 lbs.
B. Apr. 10, 1963, Chicago, Ill.

Year	Team	Lg	W	L	PCT	ERA	G	GS	CG	IP	H	BB	SO	ShO	Relief Pitching W	Relief Pitching L	Relief Pitching SV	Batting AB	Batting H	HR	BA	PO	A	E	DP	TC/G	FA
1986	PHI	N	2	0	1.000	2.25	3	3	0	16	6	10	8	0	0	0	0	6	0	0	.000	0	1	0	0	0.3	1.000
1988			2	3	.400	6.10	11	11	0	51.2	55	43	37	0	0	0	0	14	3	0	.214	2	9	0	0	1.0	1.000
1989			0	0	—	6.00	1	1	0	3	2	5	0	0	0	0	0	2	0	0	.000	0	0	0	0	0.0	.000
1990	2 teams	PHI N (16G 0–2)	ATL N (9G 1–0)																								
″	total		1	2	.333	4.31	25	3	0	48	41	17	38	0	1	1	1	7	0	0	.000	1	6	1	1	0.3	.875
1991	ATL	N	1	0	1.000	3.00	34	0	0	48	37	13	34	0	1	0	1	7	0	0	.000	3	4	0	0	0.2	1.000
1992			7	5	.583	3.22	58	0	0	64.1	61	29	41	0	7	5	3	4	2	0	.500	4	5	2	0	0.2	.818
1993			2	0	1.000	6.08	21	0	0	23.2	24	10	25	0	2	0	0	0	0	0	—	1	0	0	0	0.0	1.000
1994	COL	N	10	2	.833	2.80	19	18	0	112.2	113	23	67	0	1	0	0	36	4	1	.111	8	20	0	0	1.5	1.000
1995			3	7	.300	5.89	22	18	0	94.2	122	41	61	0	0	0	0	23	2	1	.087	9	11	3	0	1.0	.870
9 yrs.			28	19	.596	4.21	194	54	0	462	461	191	311	0	12	6	5	99	11	2	.111	28	56	6	1	0.5	.933
LEAGUE CHAMPIONSHIP SERIES																											
1992	ATL	N	0	0	—	14.73	3	0	0	3.2	8	2	1	0	0	0	0	0	0	0	—	0	2	0	0	0.7	1.000

Jake Freeze

FREEZE, CARL ALEXANDER BR TR 5′ 8″ 150 lbs.
B. Apr. 25, 1900, Huntington, Ark. D. Apr. 9, 1983, San Angelo, Tex.

Year	Team	Lg	W	L	PCT	ERA	G	GS	CG	IP	H	BB	SO	ShO	Relief Pitching W	Relief Pitching L	Relief Pitching SV	Batting AB	Batting H	HR	BA	PO	A	E	DP	TC/G	FA
1925	CHI	A	0	0	—	2.45	2	0	0	3.2	5	3	1	0	0	0	0	1	0	0	.000	0	0	0	0	0.0	.000

Dave Freisleben

FREISLEBEN, DAVID JAMES BR TR 5′11″ 195 lbs.
B. Oct. 31, 1951, Coraopolis, Pa.

Year	Team	Lg	W	L	PCT	ERA	G	GS	CG	IP	H	BB	SO	ShO	Relief Pitching W	Relief Pitching L	Relief Pitching SV	Batting AB	Batting H	HR	BA	PO	A	E	DP	TC/G	FA
1974	SD	N	9	14	.391	3.65	33	31	6	212	194	112	130	2	0	0	0	64	11	0	.172	12	28	1	3	1.2	.976
1975			5	14	.263	4.28	36	27	4	181	206	82	77	1	0	0	0	48	4	0	.083	15	26	1	2	1.2	.976
1976			10	13	.435	3.51	34	24	6	172	163	66	81	3	2	1	1	37	7	0	.189	16	33	2	2	1.5	.961
1977			7	9	.438	4.60	33	23	1	139	140	71	72	0	1	1	0	37	5	0	.135	6	11	1	2	0.5	.944
1978	2 teams	SD N (12G 0–3)	CLE A (12G 1–4)																								
″	total		1	7	.125	6.69	24	14	0	71.1	93	46	35	0	0	1	0	6	0	0	.000	7	8	2	0	0.7	.882
1979	TOR	A	2	3	.400	4.95	42	2	0	91	101	53	35	0	2	2	3	0	0	0	—	3	13	1	1	0.4	.941
6 yrs.			34	60	.362	4.29	202	121	17	866.1	897	430	430	6	5	5	4	192	27	0	.141	59	119	8	10	0.9	.957

Tony Freitas

FREITAS, ANTONIO BR TL 5′ 8″ 161 lbs.
B. May 5, 1908, Mill Valley, Calif. D. Mar. 13, 1994, Orangevale, Calif.

Year	Team	Lg	W	L	PCT	ERA	G	GS	CG	IP	H	BB	SO	ShO	Relief Pitching W	Relief Pitching L	Relief Pitching SV	Batting AB	Batting H	HR	BA	PO	A	E	DP	TC/G	FA
1932	PHI	A	12	5	.706	3.83	23	18	10	150.1	150	48	31	1	1	2	0	54	8	0	.148	16	32	0	2	2.1	1.000
1933			2	4	.333	7.27	19	9	2	64.1	90	24	15	0	0	1	1	16	1	0	.063	8	12	2	2	1.2	.909
1934	CIN	N	6	12	.333	4.01	30	18	5	152.2	194	25	37	0	1	2	1	47	9	0	.191	10	42	2	4	1.8	.963
1935			5	10	.333	4.57	31	18	5	143.2	174	38	51	0	0	1	2	46	6	0	.130	15	27	1	5	1.4	.977
1936			0	2	.000	1.29	4	0	0	7	6	2	1	0	0	2	0	2	0	0	.000	1	1	0	0	0.5	1.000
5 yrs.			25	33	.431	4.48	107	63	22	518	614	137	135	1	2	8	4	165	24	0	.145	50	114	5	13	1.6	.970

Larry French

FRENCH, LAWRENCE HERBERT BR TL 6′ 1″ 195 lbs.
B. Nov. 1, 1907, Visalia, Calif. D. Feb. 9, 1987, San Diego, Calif. BB 1934, 1940–1942

Year	Team	Lg	W	L	PCT	ERA	G	GS	CG	IP	H	BB	SO	ShO	Relief Pitching W	Relief Pitching L	Relief Pitching SV	Batting AB	Batting H	HR	BA	PO	A	E	DP	TC/G	FA
1929	PIT	N	7	5	.583	4.90	30	13	6	123	130	62	49	0	2	1	1	42	8	0	.190	3	35	2	1	1.3	.950
1930			17	**18**	.486	4.36	42	35	21	274.2	325	89	90	3	1	1	1	91	22	0	.242	5	53	3	3	1.5	.951
1931			15	13	.536	3.26	39	33	20	275.2	**301**	70	73	1	1	0	1	95	17	0	.179	7	56	3	6	1.7	.955
1932			18	16	.529	3.02	**47**	33	20	274.1	**301**	62	72	3	2	2	4	92	19	0	.207	8	45	7	3	1.3	.883
1933			18	13	.581	2.72	47	**35**	21	291.1	**290**	55	88	5	1	2	1	101	15	0	.149	12	45	3	4	1.3	.950
1934			12	18	.400	3.58	49	35	16	263.2	299	59	103	3	1	4	1	84	16	0	.190	10	40	3	4	1.1	.943
1935	CHI	N	17	10	.630	2.96	42	30	16	246.1	279	44	90	**4**	1	3	2	85	12	0	.141	16	55	2	5	1.7	.973
1936			18	9	.667	3.39	43	28	16	252.1	262	54	104	**4**	3	2	3	85	18	0	.212	14	37	3	3	1.3	.944
1937			16	10	.615	3.98	42	28	11	208	229	65	100	4	3	1	0	71	9	0	.127	10	55	4	4	1.6	.942
1938			10	19	.345	3.80	43	27	10	201.1	210	62	83	3	2	4	0	62	13	0	.210	19	41	1	1	1.4	.984
1939			15	8	.652	3.29	36	21	10	194	205	50	98	2	4	0	1	73	14	1	.192	5	47	2	3	1.5	.963
1940			14	14	.500	3.29	40	33	18	246	240	64	107	3	1	1	2	85	14	0	.165	7	63	2	2	1.8	.972

Larry French *continued*

Year	Team	W	L	PCT	ERA	G	GS	CG	IP	H	BB	SO	ShO	Relief Pitching W	Relief Pitching L	Relief Pitching SV	Batting AB	Batting H	Batting HR	BA	PO	A	E	DP	TC/G	FA
1941	**2 teams** **CHI N** (26G 5–14) **BKN N** (6G 0–0)																									
″	**total**	5	14	.263	4.51	32	19	6	153.2	177	47	68	1	1	0	0	51	10	0	.196	1	29	2	0	1.0	.938
1942	**BKN N**	15	4	**.789**	1.83	38	14	8	147.2	127	36	62	4	7	1	0	40	12	0	.300	7	27	2	1	0.9	.944
14 yrs.		197	171	.535	3.44	570	384	199	3152	3375	819	1187	40	30	22	17	1057	199	1	.188	124	628	39	40	1.4	.951
WORLD SERIES																										
1935	**CHI N**	0	2	.000	3.38	2	1	1	10.2	15	2	8	0	0	1	0	4	1	0	.250	1	2	0	0	1.5	1.000
1938		0	0	—	2.70	3	0	0	3.1	1	1	2	0	0	0	0	0	0	0	—	0	2	0	0	0.7	1.000
1941	**BKN N**	0	0	—	0.00	2	0	0	1	0	0	0	0	0	0	0	0	0	0	—	0	0	0	0	0.0	.000
3 yrs.		0	2	.000	3.00	7	1	1	15	16	3	10	0	0	1	0	4	1	0	.250	1	4	0	0	0.7	1.000

Benny Frey

FREY, BENJAMIN RUDOLPH BR TR 5′10″ 165 lbs.
B. Apr. 6, 1906, Dexter, Mich. D. Nov. 1, 1937, Spring Arbor, Mich.

Year	Team	W	L	PCT	ERA	G	GS	CG	IP	H	BB	SO	ShO	Relief Pitching W	Relief Pitching L	Relief Pitching SV	Batting AB	Batting H	Batting HR	BA	PO	A	E	DP	TC/G	FA
1929	**CIN N**	1	2	.333	4.13	3	3	2	24	29	8	1	0	0	0	0	8	3	0	.375	2	11	3	2	5.3	.813
1930		11	**18**	.379	4.70	44	28	14	245	295	62	43	2	2	2	1	88	25	0	.284	10	79	1	7	2.0	.989
1931		8	12	.400	4.92	34	17	7	133.2	166	36	19	1	3	0	2	44	14	0	.318	4	48	1	5	1.6	.981
1932	**2 teams** **STL N** (2G 0–2) **CIN N** (28G 4–10)																									
″	**total**	4	12	.250	4.49	30	15	5	134.1	165	32	27	0	1	2	0	45	9	0	.200	7	39	0	3	1.5	1.000
1933	**CIN N**	6	4	.600	3.82	37	9	1	132	144	21	12	1	4	0	0	42	11	0	.262	11	36	3	3	1.4	.940
1934		11	16	.407	3.52	39	30	12	245.1	288	42	33	2	1	1	2	82	14	0	.171	8	74	1	6	2.1	.988
1935		6	10	.375	6.85	38	13	3	114.1	164	32	24	1	3	2	2	32	11	0	.344	6	34	1	5	1.1	.976
1936		10	8	.556	4.25	31	12	5	131.1	164	30	20	0	4	2	0	44	11	0	.250	6	33	5	2	1.4	.886
8 yrs.		57	82	.410	4.50	256	127	49	1160	1415	263	179	7	18	9	7	385	98	0	.255	54	354	15	33	1.7	.965

Steve Frey

FREY, STEVEN FRANCIS BR TL 5′9″ 170 lbs.
B. July 29, 1963, Meadowbrook, Pa.

Year	Team	W	L	PCT	ERA	G	GS	CG	IP	H	BB	SO	ShO	Relief Pitching W	Relief Pitching L	Relief Pitching SV	Batting AB	Batting H	Batting HR	BA	PO	A	E	DP	TC/G	FA
1989	**MON N**	3	2	.600	5.48	20	0	0	21.1	29	11	15	0	3	2	0	0	0	0	—	1	2	0	0	0.2	1.000
1990		8	2	.800	2.10	51	0	0	55.2	44	29	29	0	8	2	9	1	0	0	.000	4	7	1	0	0.2	.917
1991		0	1	.000	4.99	31	0	0	39.2	43	23	21	0	0	1	1	2	0	0	.000	1	4	0	0	0.2	1.000
1992	**CAL A**	4	2	.667	3.57	51	0	0	45.1	39	22	24	0	4	2	4	0	0	0	—	4	5	0	1	0.2	1.000
1993		2	3	.400	2.98	55	0	0	48.1	41	26	22	0	2	3	13	0	0	0	—	2	6	0	0	0.1	1.000
1994	**SF N**	1	0	1.000	4.94	44	0	0	31	37	15	20	0	1	0	0	0	0	0	—	2	4	0	0	0.1	1.000
1995	**3 teams** **SF N** (9G 0–1) **SEA A** (13G 0–3) **PHI N** (9G 0–0)																									
″	**total**	0	4	.000	3.18	31	0	0	28.1	26	10	14	0	0	4	1	1	0	0	.000	1	6	1	0	0.3	.875
7 yrs.		18	14	.563	3.64	283	0	0	269.2	259	136	145	0	18	14	28	4	0	0	.000	15	34	2	1	0.2	.961

Barney Friberg

FRIBERG, GUSTAF BERNHARD BR TR 5′11″ 178 lbs.
B. Aug. 18, 1899, Manchester, N. H. D. Dec. 8, 1958, Lynn, Mass.

Year	Team	W	L	PCT	ERA	G	GS	CG	IP	H	BB	SO	ShO	Relief Pitching W	Relief Pitching L	Relief Pitching SV	Batting AB	Batting H	Batting HR	BA	PO	A	E	DP	TC/G	FA
1925	**PHI N**	0	0	—	4.50	1	0	0	4	4	3	1	0	0	0	0	*				13	0	0	0	1.9	1.000

Marion Fricano

FRICANO, MARION JOHN BR TR 6′ 170 lbs.
B. July 15, 1923, Brant, N. Y. D. May 18, 1976, Tijuana, Mexico.

Year	Team	W	L	PCT	ERA	G	GS	CG	IP	H	BB	SO	ShO	Relief Pitching W	Relief Pitching L	Relief Pitching SV	Batting AB	Batting H	Batting HR	BA	PO	A	E	DP	TC/G	FA
1952	**PHI A**	1	0	1.000	1.80	2	0	0	5	5	1	0	0	1	0	0	0	0	0	—	0	1	0	0	0.5	1.000
1953		9	12	.429	3.88	39	23	10	211	206	90	67	0	1	0	0	69	10	0	.145	8	28	0	2	0.9	1.000
1954		5	11	.313	5.16	37	20	4	151.2	163	64	43	0	1	0	1	41	4	0	.098	9	20	3	2	0.9	.906
1955	**KC A**	0	0	—	3.15	10	0	0	20	19	9	5	0	0	0	0	3	2	0	.667	5	4	1	0	1.0	.900
4 yrs.		15	23	.395	4.32	88	43	14	387.2	393	164	115	0	3	0	1	113	16	0	.142	22	53	4	4	0.9	.949

Skipper Friday

FRIDAY, GRIER WILLIAM BR TR 5′11″ 170 lbs.
B. Oct. 26, 1897, Gastonia, N. C. D. Aug. 25, 1962, Gastonia, N. C.

Year	Team	W	L	PCT	ERA	G	GS	CG	IP	H	BB	SO	ShO	Relief Pitching W	Relief Pitching L	Relief Pitching SV	Batting AB	Batting H	Batting HR	BA	PO	A	E	DP	TC/G	FA
1923	**WAS A**	0	1	.000	6.90	7	2	1	30	35	22	9	0	0	0	0	9	2	0	.222	1	12	0	1	1.9	1.000

Cy Fried

FRIED, ARTHUR EDWIN BL TL 5′11½″ 150 lbs.
B. July 23, 1897, San Antonio, Tex. D. Oct. 10, 1970, San Antonio, Tex.

Year	Team	W	L	PCT	ERA	G	GS	CG	IP	H	BB	SO	ShO	Relief Pitching W	Relief Pitching L	Relief Pitching SV	Batting AB	Batting H	Batting HR	BA	PO	A	E	DP	TC/G	FA
1920	**DET A**	0	0	—	16.20	2	0	0	1.2	3	4	0	0	0	0	0	0	0	0	—	0	1	0	0	0.5	1.000

Bob Friedrichs

FRIEDRICHS, ROBERT GEORGE BR TR 5′11½″ 165 lbs.
B. Aug. 30, 1906, Cincinnati, Ohio.

Year	Team	W	L	PCT	ERA	G	GS	CG	IP	H	BB	SO	ShO	Relief Pitching W	Relief Pitching L	Relief Pitching SV	Batting AB	Batting H	Batting HR	BA	PO	A	E	DP	TC/G	FA
1932	**WAS A**	0	0	—	11.25	2	0	0	4	4	7	2	0	0	0	0	1	0	0	.000	0	0	0	0	0.0	.000

Bill Friel

FRIEL, WILLIAM EDWARD BL TR 5′10″ 165 lbs.
Brother of Pat Friel.
B. Apr. 1, 1876, Renovo, Pa. D. Dec. 24, 1959, St. Louis, Mo.

Year	Team	W	L	PCT	ERA	G	GS	CG	IP	H	BB	SO	ShO	Relief Pitching W	Relief Pitching L	Relief Pitching SV	Batting AB	Batting H	Batting HR	BA	PO	A	E	DP	TC/G	FA
1902	**STL A**	0	0	—	4.50	1	0	0	4	4	0	0	0	0	0	0	*				142	183	46	16	3.6	.876

Bob Friend

FRIEND, ROBERT BARTMESS (Warrior) BR TR 6′ 190 lbs.
B. Nov. 24, 1930, Lafayette, Ind.

Year	Team	W	L	PCT	ERA	G	GS	CG	IP	H	BB	SO	ShO	Relief Pitching W	Relief Pitching L	Relief Pitching SV	Batting AB	Batting H	Batting HR	BA	PO	A	E	DP	TC/G	FA
1951	**PIT N**	6	10	.375	4.27	34	22	3	149.2	173	68	41	1	0	1	0	44	4	0	.091	10	29	1	1	1.2	.975
1952		7	17	.292	4.18	35	23	6	185	186	84	75	1	2	2	0	52	3	0	.058	10	37	2	3	1.4	.959
1953		8	11	.421	4.90	32	24	8	170.2	193	57	66	0	0	1	0	52	7	0	.135	7	36	3	2	1.4	.935
1954		7	12	.368	5.07	35	20	4	170.1	204	58	73	2	1	1	2	51	14	1	.275	7	27	1	1	1.0	.971
1955		14	9	.609	**2.83**	44	20	9	200.1	178	52	98	2	5	1	2	61	10	0	.164	7	50	2	6	1.3	.966
1956		17	17	.500	3.46	49	**42**	19	**314.1**	310	85	166	4	0	0	3	97	16	1	.165	14	49	2	1	1.3	.969
1957		14	18	.438	3.38	40	**38**	17	**277**	**273**	68	143	3	0	1	0	87	16	0	.184	18	38	1	3	1.4	.982
1958		**22**	14	.611	3.68	38	**38**	16	274	**299**	61	135	1	0	0	0	94	10	0	.106	7	47	1	4	1.4	.982
1959		8	**19**	.296	4.03	35	35	7	234.2	267	52	104	2	0	0	0	73	12	0	.164	24	37	1	2	1.8	.984
1960		18	12	.600	3.00	38	37	16	275.2	266	45	183	4	0	0	1	88	6	0	.068	24	43	1	1	1.8	.985
1961		14	**19**	.424	3.85	41	35	10	236	271	45	108	1	1	1	1	79	11	0	.139	19	37	3	3	1.4	.949
1962		18	14	.563	3.06	39	36	13	261.2	280	53	144	**5**	0	0	1	91	11	0	.121	18	43	1	3	1.6	.984
1963		17	16	.515	2.34	39	38	12	268.2	236	44	144	4	1	0	0	86	9	0	.105	23	41	2	2	1.7	.970

Bob Friend *continued*

Year	Team	Lg	W	L	PCT	ERA	G	GS	CG	IP	H	BB	SO	ShO	Relief Pitching W	Relief Pitching L	Relief Pitching SV	Batting AB	Batting H	Batting HR	BA	PO	A	E	DP	TC/G	FA
1964			13	18	.419	3.33	35	35	13	240.1	253	50	128	3	0	0	0	71	5	0	.070	12	55	2	3	2.0	.971
1965			8	12	.400	3.24	34	34	8	222	221	47	74	2	0	0	0	71	3	0	.042	21	39	1	5	1.8	.984
1966	2 teams	NY A (12G 1–4) NY N (22G 5–8)																									
″	total		6	12	.333	4.55	34	20	2	130.2	162	25	52	1	1	4	1	40	1	0	.025	7	22	3	0	0.9	.906
16 yrs.			197	230	.461	3.58	602	497	163	3611	3772	894	1734	36	11	12	11	1137	138	2	.121	228	630	27	40	1.5	.969
WORLD SERIES																											
1960	PIT	N	0	2	.000	13.50	3	2	0	6	13	3	7	0	0	0	0	1	0	0	.000	1	3	0	0	1.3	1.000

Danny Friend

FRIEND, DANIEL SEBASTIAN TL 5′ 9″ 175 lbs.
B. Apr. 8, 1873, Cincinnati, Ohio D. June 1, 1942, Chillicothe, Ohio.

Year	Team	Lg	W	L	PCT	ERA	G	GS	CG	IP	H	BB	SO	ShO	Relief Pitching W	Relief Pitching L	Relief Pitching SV	Batting AB	Batting H	Batting HR	BA	PO	A	E	DP	TC/G	FA
1895	CHI	N	2	2	.500	5.27	5	5	5	41	50	14	10	0	0	0	0	17	4	0	.235	3	8	0	0	2.2	1.000
1896			18	14	.563	4.74	36	33	28	290.2	298	139	86	1	1	1	0	126	30	1	.238	20	59	10	3	2.4	.888
1897			12	11	.522	4.52	24	24	23	203	244	86	58	0	0	0	0	88	25	0	.284	19	32	7	6	2.3	.879
1898			0	2	.000	5.29	2	2	2	17	20	10	4	0	0	0	0	7	2	0	.286	3	13	0	0	8.0	1.000
4 yrs.			32	29	.525	4.71	67	64	58	551.2	612	249	158	1	1	1	0	238	61	1	.256	45	112	17	9	2.5	.902

Pete Fries

FRIES, PETER MARTIN BL TL 5′ 8″ 160 lbs.
B. Oct. 30, 1857, Scranton, Pa. D. July 30, 1937, Chicago, Ill.

Year	Team	Lg	W	L	PCT	ERA	G	GS	CG	IP	H	BB	SO	ShO	Relief Pitching W	Relief Pitching L	Relief Pitching SV	Batting AB	Batting H	Batting HR	BA	PO	A	E	DP	TC/G	FA
1883	COL	AA	0	3	.000	*6.48*	3	3	3	25	34	14	7	0	0	0	0	10	3	0	.300	1	5	1	0	2.3	.857

John Frill

FRILL, JOHN EDMOND BR TL 5′10½″ 170 lbs.
B. Apr. 3, 1879, Reading, Pa. D. Sept. 28, 1918, Westerly, R. I.

Year	Team	Lg	W	L	PCT	ERA	G	GS	CG	IP	H	BB	SO	ShO	Relief Pitching W	Relief Pitching L	Relief Pitching SV	Batting AB	Batting H	Batting HR	BA	PO	A	E	DP	TC/G	FA
1910	NY	A	2	2	.500	4.47	10	5	3	48.1	55	5	27	1	0	0	1	18	2	0	.111	2	16	2	0	2.0	.900
1912	2 teams	STL A (3G 0–1) CIN N (3G 1–0)																									
″	total		1	1	.500	9.31	6	5	0	19.1	35	2	6	0	0	0	0	6	2	0	.333	0	6	0	0	1.0	1.000
2 yrs.			3	3	.500	5.85	16	10	3	67.2	90	7	33	1	0	0	1	24	4	0	.167	2	22	2	0	1.6	.923

Danny Frisella

FRISELLA, DANIEL VINCENT (Bear) BL TR 6′ 185 lbs.
B. Mar. 4, 1946, San Francisco, Calif. D. Jan. 1, 1977, Phoenix, Ariz.

Year	Team	Lg	W	L	PCT	ERA	G	GS	CG	IP	H	BB	SO	ShO	Relief Pitching W	Relief Pitching L	Relief Pitching SV	Batting AB	Batting H	Batting HR	BA	PO	A	E	DP	TC/G	FA
1967	NY	N	1	6	.143	3.41	14	11	0	74	68	33	51	0	0	0	0	23	2	0	.087	3	12	2	0	1.2	.882
1968			2	4	.333	3.91	19	4	0	50.2	53	17	47	0	0	2	2	12	1	0	.083	3	8	0	0	0.6	1.000
1969			0	0	—	7.71	3	0	0	4.2	8	3	5	0	0	0	0	1	0	0	.000	0	0	0	0	0.0	.000
1970			8	3	.727	3.00	30	1	0	66	49	34	54	0	7	3	1	13	4	0	.308	3	8	0	1	0.4	1.000
1971			8	5	.615	1.98	53	0	0	91	76	30	93	0	8	5	12	13	3	0	.231	7	13	0	0	0.4	1.000
1972			5	8	.385	3.34	39	0	0	67.1	63	20	46	0	5	8	9	7	2	0	.286	5	15	1	0	0.5	.952
1973	ATL	N	1	2	.333	4.20	42	0	0	45	40	23	27	0	1	2	8	2	1	0	.500	4	6	1	0	0.3	.909
1974			3	4	.429	5.14	36	1	0	42	37	28	27	0	3	4	6	1	0	0	.000	5	2	0	2	0.2	1.000
1975	SD	N	1	6	.143	3.12	65	0	0	98	86	51	67	0	1	6	9	5	1	0	.200	6	13	2	0	0.3	.905
1976	2 teams	STL N (18G 0–0) MIL A (32G 5–2)																									
″	total		5	2	.714	3.13	50	0	0	72	49	47	54	0	5	2	10	1	0	0	.000	3	10	0	0	0.3	1.000
10 yrs.			34	40	.459	3.32	351	17	0	610.2	529	286	471	0	30	32	57	78	14	0	.179	39	87	6	3	0.4	.955

Emil Frisk

FRISK, JOHN EMIL BL TR 6′ 1″ 190 lbs.
B. Oct. 15, 1874, Kalkaska, Mich. D. Jan. 27, 1922, Seattle, Wash.

Year	Team	Lg	W	L	PCT	ERA	G	GS	CG	IP	H	BB	SO	ShO	Relief Pitching W	Relief Pitching L	Relief Pitching SV	Batting AB	Batting H	Batting HR	BA	PO	A	E	DP	TC/G	FA
1899	CIN	N	3	6	.333	3.95	9	9	9	68.1	81	17	17	0	0	0	0	25	7	0	.280	4	15	1	0	2.2	.950
1901	DET	A	5	4	.556	4.34	11	7	6	74.2	94	26	22	0	2	0	0	48	15	1	.313	7	36	8	0	3.9	.843
2 yrs.			8	10	.444	4.15	20	16	15	143	175	43	39	0	2	0	0	*				128	66	20	2	1.6	.907

Charlie Fritz

FRITZ, CHARLES CORNELIUS TL
B. June 18, 1882, Mobile, Ala. D. July 30, 1943, Mobile, Ala.

Year	Team	Lg	W	L	PCT	ERA	G	GS	CG	IP	H	BB	SO	ShO	Relief Pitching W	Relief Pitching L	Relief Pitching SV	Batting AB	Batting H	Batting HR	BA	PO	A	E	DP	TC/G	FA
1907	PHI	A	0	0	—	3.38	1	1	0	2.2	0	3	1	0	0	0	0	1	0	0	.000	0	0	0	0	0.0	.000

Bill Froats

FROATS, WILLIAM JOHN BL TL 6′ 180 lbs.
B. Oct. 20, 1930, New York, N. Y.

Year	Team	Lg	W	L	PCT	ERA	G	GS	CG	IP	H	BB	SO	ShO	Relief Pitching W	Relief Pitching L	Relief Pitching SV	Batting AB	Batting H	Batting HR	BA	PO	A	E	DP	TC/G	FA
1955	DET	A	0	0	—	0.00	1	0	0	2	0	2	0	0	0	0	0	0	0	0	—	0	1	0	0	1.0	1.000

Sam Frock

FROCK, SAMUEL WILLIAM BR TR 6′ 168 lbs.
B. Dec. 23, 1882, Baltimore, Md. D. Nov. 3, 1925, Baltimore, Md.

Year	Team	Lg	W	L	PCT	ERA	G	GS	CG	IP	H	BB	SO	ShO	Relief Pitching W	Relief Pitching L	Relief Pitching SV	Batting AB	Batting H	Batting HR	BA	PO	A	E	DP	TC/G	FA
1907	BOS	N	1	2	.333	2.97	5	3	3	33.1	28	11	12	1	0	0	0	14	1	0	.071	0	2	0	0	0.4	1.000
1909	PIT	N	2	1	.667	2.48	8	4	4	36.1	44	4	11	0	1	0	0	14	2	0	.143	0	12	0	0	1.5	1.000
1910	2 teams	PIT N (1G 0–1) BOS N (45G 11–19)																									
″	total		11	20	.355	3.22	46	29	15	257.1	247	93	171	2	5	2	2	84	16	0	.190	7	71	2	3	1.7	.975
1911	BOS	N	0	1	.000	5.63	4	1	1	16	29	5	8	0	0	0	0	5	1	0	.200	1	4	0	0	1.3	1.000
4 yrs.			14	24	.368	3.23	63	37	23	343	348	113	202	3	6	2	2	117	20	0	.171	8	89	2	3	1.6	.980

Todd Frohwirth

FROHWIRTH, TODD GERARD BR TR 6′ 4″ 190 lbs.
B. Sept. 28, 1962, Milwaukee, Wis.

Year	Team	Lg	W	L	PCT	ERA	G	GS	CG	IP	H	BB	SO	ShO	Relief Pitching W	Relief Pitching L	Relief Pitching SV	Batting AB	Batting H	Batting HR	BA	PO	A	E	DP	TC/G	FA
1987	PHI	N	1	0	1.000	0.00	10	0	0	11	12	2	9	0	1	0	0	1	0	0	.000	1	1	0	1	0.2	1.000
1988			1	2	.333	8.25	12	0	0	12	16	11	11	0	1	2	0	0	0	0	—	0	5	0	0	0.4	1.000
1989			1	0	1.000	3.59	45	0	0	62.2	56	18	39	0	1	0	0	1	0	0	.000	5	8	0	0	0.3	1.000
1990			0	1	.000	18.00	5	0	0	1	3	6	1	0	0	1	0	0	0	0	—	0	1	1	0	0.4	.500
1991	BAL	A	7	3	.700	1.87	51	0	0	96.1	64	29	77	0	7	3	3	0	0	0	—	14	24	3	3	0.8	.927
1992			4	3	.571	2.46	65	0	0	106	97	41	58	0	4	3	4	0	0	0	—	8	24	1	4	0.5	.970
1993			6	7	.462	3.83	70	0	0	96.1	91	44	50	0	6	**7**	3	0	0	0	—	8	21	1	3	0.4	.967
1994	BOS	A	0	3	.000	10.80	22	0	0	26.2	40	17	13	0	0	3	1	0	0	0	—	1	8	1	0	0.5	.900
8 yrs.			20	19	.513	3.50	280	0	0	412	379	168	258	0	20	19	11	2	0	0	.000	37	92	7	11	0.5	.949

Art Fromme

FROMME, ARTHUR HENRY BR TR 6′ 178 lbs.
B. Sept. 3, 1883, Quincy, Ill. D. Aug. 24, 1956, Los Angeles, Calif.

Year	Team	Lg	W	L	PCT	ERA	G	GS	CG	IP	H	BB	SO	ShO	Relief Pitching W	Relief Pitching L	Relief Pitching SV	Batting AB	Batting H	Batting HR	BA	PO	A	E	DP	TC/G	FA
1906	STL	N	1	2	.333	1.44	3	3	3	25	19	10	11	1	0	0	0	9	2	0	.222	0	12	3	0	5.0	.800
1907			5	13	.278	2.90	23	16	13	145.2	138	67	67	2	1	1	0	55	10	0	.182	9	39	3	1	2.2	.941
1908			5	13	.278	2.72	20	14	9	116	102	50	62	2	1	**3**	0	36	5	0	.139	3	30	0	1	1.6	1.000
1909	CIN	N	19	13	.594	1.90	37	34	22	279.1	195	101	126	4	1	0	2	94	18	0	.191	7	89	8	1	2.8	.923
1910			3	4	.429	2.92	11	5	1	49.1	44	39	10	0	2	1	0	15	2	0	.133	1	16	1	0	1.6	.944

Art Fromme *continued*

Year	Team	W	L	PCT	ERA	G	GS	CG	IP	H	BB	SO	ShO	Relief Pitching W	Relief Pitching L	Relief Pitching SV	Batting AB	Batting H	Batting HR	BA	PO	A	E	DP	TC/G	FA
1911		10	11	.476	3.46	38	26	11	208	190	79	107	1	0	0	0	74	14	0	.189	8	56	3	3	1.8	.955
1912		16	18	.471	2.74	43	37	23	296	285	88	120	3	0	1	0	103	9	0	.087	7	76	9	3	2.1	.902
1913	**2 teams** **CIN N** (9G 1–4) **NY N** (26G 11–6)																									
"	**total**	12	10	.545	4.06	35	19	5	168.1	167	50	74	0	**6**	1	0	56	9	0	.161	7	44	0	1	1.5	1.000
1914	**NY N**	9	5	.643	3.20	38	12	3	138	142	44	57	1	4	0	2	31	7	0	.226	6	53	2	0	1.6	.967
1915		0	1	.000	5.84	4	1	0	12.1	15	2	4	0	0	1	0	3	1	0	.333	0	4	1	0	1.3	.800
10 yrs.		80	90	.471	2.90	252	167	90	1438	1297	530	638	14	15	8	4	476	77	0	.162	48	419	30	10	2.0	.940

Dave Frost

FROST, CARL DAVID BR TR 6′ 6″ 235 lbs.
B. Nov. 17, 1952, Long Beach, Calif.

Year	Team	W	L	PCT	ERA	G	GS	CG	IP	H	BB	SO	ShO	Relief Pitching W	Relief Pitching L	Relief Pitching SV	Batting AB	Batting H	Batting HR	BA	PO	A	E	DP	TC/G	FA
1977	**CHI A**	1	1	.500	3.00	4	3	0	24	30	3	15	0	0	0	0	0	0	0	—	2	3	0	0	1.3	1.000
1978	**CAL A**	5	4	.556	2.58	11	10	2	80.1	71	24	30	1	0	0	0	0	0	0	—	5	19	1	0	2.3	.960
1979		16	10	.615	3.58	36	33	12	239	226	77	107	2	0	1	1	0	0	0	—	8	34	2	2	1.2	.955
1980		4	8	.333	5.31	15	15	2	78	97	21	28	0	0	0	0	0	0	0	—	2	7	1	1	0.7	.900
1981		1	8	.111	5.55	12	9	0	47	44	19	16	0	0	1	0	0	0	0	—	1	9	0	0	0.8	1.000
1982	**KC A**	6	6	.500	5.51	21	14	0	81.2	103	30	26	0	3	0	0	0	0	0	—	5	6	1	1	0.6	.917
6 yrs.		33	37	.471	4.11	99	84	16	550	571	174	222	3	3	2	1	0	0	0		23	78	5	4	1.1	.953
LEAGUE CHAMPIONSHIP SERIES																										
1979	**CAL A**	0	1	.000	18.69	2	1	0	4.1	8	5	1	0	0	0	0	0	0	0	—	0	0	0	0	0.0	.000

Jay Fry

FRY, JOHNSON BR TR 6′ 1″ 150 lbs.
B. Nov. 21, 1901, Huntington, W. Va. D. Apr. 7, 1959, Carmi, Ill.

Year	Team	W	L	PCT	ERA	G	GS	CG	IP	H	BB	SO	ShO	Relief Pitching W	Relief Pitching L	Relief Pitching SV	Batting AB	Batting H	Batting HR	BA	PO	A	E	DP	TC/G	FA
1923	**CLE A**	0	0	—	12.27	1	0	0	3.2	6	4	0	0	0	0	0	1	1	0	1.000	0	1	0	0	1.0	1.000

Charlie Frye

FRYE, CHARLES ANDREW BR TR 6′ 1″ 175 lbs.
B. July 17, 1914, Hickory, N. C. D. May 25, 1945, Hickory, N. C.

Year	Team	W	L	PCT	ERA	G	GS	CG	IP	H	BB	SO	ShO	Relief Pitching W	Relief Pitching L	Relief Pitching SV	Batting AB	Batting H	Batting HR	BA	PO	A	E	DP	TC/G	FA
1940	**PHI N**	0	6	.000	4.65	15	5	1	50.1	58	26	18	0	0	1	0	19	5	1	.263	0	7	0	1	0.5	1.000

Woodie Fryman

FRYMAN, WOODROW THOMPSON BR TL 6′ 3″ 197 lbs.
B. Apr. 12, 1940, Ewing, Ky.

Year	Team	W	L	PCT	ERA	G	GS	CG	IP	H	BB	SO	ShO	Relief Pitching W	Relief Pitching L	Relief Pitching SV	Batting AB	Batting H	Batting HR	BA	PO	A	E	DP	TC/G	FA
1966	**PIT N**	12	9	.571	3.81	36	28	9	181.2	182	47	105	3	1	0	1	63	10	0	.159	6	21	0	1	0.8	1.000
1967		3	8	.273	4.05	28	18	3	113.1	121	44	74	1	0	0	1	34	4	0	.118	6	26	0	3	1.1	1.000
1968	**PHI N**	12	14	.462	2.78	34	32	10	213.2	198	64	151	5	0	0	0	71	6	0	.085	3	31	1	2	1.0	.971
1969		12	15	.444	4.42	36	35	10	228	243	89	150	1	0	0	0	76	9	1	.118	3	38	0	1	1.1	1.000
1970		8	6	.571	4.08	27	20	4	128	122	43	97	3	1	0	0	39	5	0	.128	5	17	0	1	0.8	1.000
1971		10	7	.588	3.38	37	17	3	149	133	46	104	2	3	2	2	37	7	0	.189	6	35	1	1	1.1	.976
1972	**2 teams** **PHI N** (23G 4–10) **DET A** (16G 10–3)																									
"	**total**	14	13	.519	3.24	39	31	9	233.2	224	70	141	3	0	0	1	73	10	1	.137	11	34	1	0	1.2	.978
1973	**DET A**	6	13	.316	5.35	34	29	1	170	200	64	119	0	0	0	0	0	0	0	—	11	28	1	2	1.2	.975
1974		6	9	.400	4.31	27	22	4	142	120	67	92	1	0	0	0	0	0	0	—	8	15	0	1	0.9	1.000
1975	**MON N**	9	12	.429	3.32	38	20	7	157	141	68	118	3	2	4	3	49	10	0	.204	6	26	0	4	0.8	1.000
1976		13	13	.500	3.37	34	32	4	216.1	218	76	123	2	0	0	2	64	7	0	.109	9	30	0	2	1.1	1.000
1977	**CIN N**	5	5	.500	5.40	17	12	0	75	83	45	57	0	0	1	1	22	7	0	.318	3	14	0	0	1.0	1.000
1978	**2 teams** **CHI N** (13G 2–4) **MON N** (19G 5–7)																									
"	**total**	7	11	.389	4.19	32	26	4	150.1	157	74	81	3	1	0	1	50	3	0	.060	8	27	0	2	1.1	1.000
1979	**MON N**	3	6	.333	2.79	44	0	0	58	52	22	44	0	3	6	10	7	0	0	.000	3	11	0	1	0.3	1.000
1980		7	4	.636	2.25	61	0	0	80	61	30	59	0	7	4	17	12	2	0	.167	1	10	1	1	0.2	.917
1981		5	3	.625	1.88	35	0	0	43	38	14	25	0	5	3	7	3	2	0	.667	2	8	0	1	0.3	1.000
1982		9	4	.692	3.75	60	0	0	69.2	66	26	46	0	9	4	12	9	2	0	.222	6	16	1	2	0.4	.957
1983		0	3	.000	21.00	6	0	0	3	8	1	1	0	0	3	0	0	0	0	—	0	2	0	0	0.3	1.000
18 yrs.		141	155	.476	3.77	625	322	68	2411.2	2367	890	1587	27	32	27	58	609	84	2	.138	97	389	6	25	0.8	.988
DIVISIONAL PLAYOFF SERIES																										
1981	**MON N**	0	0	—	6.75	1	0	0	1.1	3	1	0	0	0	0	0	0	0	0	—	0	0	0	0	0.0	.000
LEAGUE CHAMPIONSHIP SERIES																										
1972	**DET A**	0	2	.000	3.65	2	2	0	12.1	11	2	8	0	0	0	0	3	0	0	.000	0	3	0	0	1.5	1.000
1981	**MON N**	0	0	—	36.00	1	0	0	1	3	1	1	0	0	0	0	0	0	0	—	0	0	0	0	0.0	.000
2 yrs.		0	2	.000	6.07	3	2	0	13.1	14	3	9	0	0	0	0	3	0	0	.000	0	3	0	0	1.0	1.000

Charlie Fuchs

FUCHS, CHARLES THOMAS BB TR 5′10″ 178 lbs.
B. Nov. 18, 1913, Union City, N. J. D. June 10, 1969, Weehawken, N. J.

Year	Team	W	L	PCT	ERA	G	GS	CG	IP	H	BB	SO	ShO	Relief Pitching W	Relief Pitching L	Relief Pitching SV	Batting AB	Batting H	Batting HR	BA	PO	A	E	DP	TC/G	FA
1942	**DET A**	3	3	.500	6.63	9	4	1	36.2	43	19	15	1	0	2	0	13	1	0	.077	3	12	0	0	1.7	1.000
1943	**2 teams** **PHI N** (17G 2–7) **STL A** (13G 0–0)																									
"	**total**	2	7	.222	4.21	30	9	4	113.1	118	45	21	1	0	1	1	29	2	0	.069	10	18	2	1	1.0	.933
1944	**BKN N**	1	0	1.000	5.74	8	0	0	15.2	25	9	5	0	1	0	0	1	0	0	.000	2	5	0	0	0.9	1.000
3 yrs.		6	10	.375	4.89	47	13	5	165.2	186	73	41	2	1	3	1	43	3	0	.070	15	35	2	1	1.1	.962

Mickey Fuentes

FUENTES, MIGUEL BR TR 6′ 160 lbs.
Born Miguel Fuentes (Pinet).
B. May 10, 1946, Loiza Aldea, Puerto Rico
D. Jan. 29, 1970, Loiza Aldea, Puerto Rico.

Year	Team	W	L	PCT	ERA	G	GS	CG	IP	H	BB	SO	ShO	Relief Pitching W	Relief Pitching L	Relief Pitching SV	Batting AB	Batting H	Batting HR	BA	PO	A	E	DP	TC/G	FA
1969	**SEA A**	1	3	.250	5.19	8	4	1	26	29	16	14	0	0	0	0	6	2	0	.333	1	2	1	0	0.5	.750

Oscar Fuhr

FUHR, OSCAR LAWRENCE BR TL 5′10″ 170 lbs.
B. Aug. 22, 1893, Defiance, Mo. D. Mar. 27, 1975, Dallas, Tex.

Year	Team	W	L	PCT	ERA	G	GS	CG	IP	H	BB	SO	ShO	Relief Pitching W	Relief Pitching L	Relief Pitching SV	Batting AB	Batting H	Batting HR	BA	PO	A	E	DP	TC/G	FA
1921	**CHI N**	0	0	—	9.00	1	0	0	4	11	0	2	0	0	0	0	1	0	0	.000	0	1	0	0	1.0	1.000
1924	**BOS A**	3	6	.333	5.94	23	10	4	80.1	100	39	30	1	0	2	0	22	4	0	.182	4	23	1	0	1.2	.964
1925		0	6	.000	6.60	39	5	0	91.1	138	30	27	0	0	2	0	20	5	0	.250	6	25	1	3	0.8	.969
3 yrs.		3	12	.200	6.35	63	15	4	175.2	249	69	59	1	0	4	0	43	9	0	.209	10	49	2	3	1.0	.967

John Fulgham

FULGHAM, JOHN THOMAS
B. June 9, 1956, St. Louis, Mo.
BR TR 6′ 2″ 205 lbs.

Year	Team	Lg	W	L	PCT	ERA	G	GS	CG	IP	H	BB	SO	ShO	Relief Pitching W	Relief Pitching L	Relief Pitching SV	Batting AB	Batting H	Batting HR	BA	PO	A	E	DP	TC/G	FA
1979	STL	N	10	6	.625	2.53	20	19	10	146	123	26	75	2	0	0	0	42	6	0	.143	7	12	2	1	1.0	.905
1980			4	6	.400	3.39	15	14	4	85	66	32	48	1	0	0	0	27	0	0	.000	7	11	1	1	1.3	.947
2 yrs.			14	12	.538	2.84	35	33	14	231	189	58	123	3	0	0	0	69	6	0	.087	14	23	3	2	1.1	.925

Ed Fuller

FULLER, EDWARD ASTON WHITE
B. Mar. 22, 1869, Washington, D. C. D. Mar. 15, 1935, Hyattsville, Md.
BR TR 6′ 158 lbs.

Year	Team	Lg	W	L	PCT	ERA	G	GS	CG	IP	H	BB	SO	ShO	Relief Pitching W	Relief Pitching L	Relief Pitching SV	Batting AB	Batting H	Batting HR	BA	PO	A	E	DP	TC/G	FA
1886	WAS	N	0	1	.000	6.92	2	1	1	13	15	5	3	0	0	0	0	7	1	0	.143	0	3	1	0	1.3	.750

Curt Fullerton

FULLERTON, CURTIS HOOPER
B. Sept. 13, 1898, Ellsworth, Me. D. Jan. 2, 1975, Winthrop, Mass.
BL TR 6′ 162 lbs.

Year	Team	Lg	W	L	PCT	ERA	G	GS	CG	IP	H	BB	SO	ShO	Relief Pitching W	Relief Pitching L	Relief Pitching SV	Batting AB	Batting H	Batting HR	BA	PO	A	E	DP	TC/G	FA
1921	BOS	A	0	1	.000	8.80	4	1	1	15.1	22	10	4	0	0	0	0	4	0	0	.000	2	1	1	0	1.0	.750
1922			1	4	.200	5.46	31	3	0	64.1	70	35	17	0	1	2	0	8	2	0	.250	3	22	0	0	0.8	1.000
1923			2	15	.118	5.09	37	16	7	143.1	167	71	37	0	1	1	1	37	11	0	.297	5	31	3	1	1.1	.923
1924			7	12	.368	4.32	33	20	9	152	166	73	33	0	1	0	2	42	3	0	.071	1	38	2	1	1.2	.951
1925			0	3	.000	3.18	4	2	0	22.2	22	9	3	0	0	1	0	10	2	0	.200	2	8	1	1	2.8	.909
1933			0	2	.000	8.53	6	2	2	25.1	36	13	10	0	0	0	0	9	2	0	.222	0	2	0	1	0.3	1.000
6 yrs.			10	37	.213	5.11	115	44	19	423	483	211	104	0	3	4	3	110	20	0	.182	13	102	7	4	1.1	.943

Chris Fulmer

FULMER, CHRISTOPHER
B. July 4, 1858, Tamaqua, Pa. D. Nov. 9, 1931, Tamaqua, Pa.
BR TR 5′ 8″ 165 lbs.

Year	Team	Lg	W	L	PCT	ERA	G	GS	CG	IP	H	BB	SO	ShO	Relief Pitching W	Relief Pitching L	Relief Pitching SV	Batting AB	Batting H	Batting HR	BA	PO	A	E	DP	TC/G	FA
1886	BAL	AA	0	0	—	*4.50*	1	0	0	2	2	1	0	0	0	0	0	*				267	45	18	4	6.0	.945

Bill Fulton

FULTON, WILLIAM DAVID
B. Oct. 22, 1963, Pittsburgh, Pa.
BR TR 6′ 3″ 195 lbs.

Year	Team	Lg	W	L	PCT	ERA	G	GS	CG	IP	H	BB	SO	ShO	Relief Pitching W	Relief Pitching L	Relief Pitching SV	Batting AB	Batting H	Batting HR	BA	PO	A	E	DP	TC/G	FA
1987	NY	A	1	0	1.000	11.57	3	0	0	4.2	9	1	2	0	1	0	0	0	0	0	—	0	1	0	0	0.3	1.000

Frank Funk

FUNK, FRANKLIN RAY
B. Aug. 30, 1935, Washington, D. C.
BR TR 6′ 175 lbs.

Year	Team	Lg	W	L	PCT	ERA	G	GS	CG	IP	H	BB	SO	ShO	Relief Pitching W	Relief Pitching L	Relief Pitching SV	Batting AB	Batting H	Batting HR	BA	PO	A	E	DP	TC/G	FA
1960	CLE	A	4	2	.667	1.99	9	0	0	31.2	27	9	18	0	4	2	1	9	1	0	.111	2	5	0	1	0.8	1.000
1961			11	11	.500	3.31	56	0	0	92.1	79	31	64	0	11	**11**	11	17	1	0	.059	14	11	2	0	0.5	.926
1962			2	1	.667	3.24	47	0	0	80.2	62	32	49	0	2	1	6	15	1	0	.067	5	11	0	1	0.3	1.000
1963	MIL	N	3	3	.500	2.68	25	0	0	43.2	42	13	19	0	3	3	0	4	0	0	.000	3	3	1	0	0.3	.857
4 yrs.			20	17	.541	3.01	137	0	0	248.1	210	85	150	0	20	17	18	45	3	0	.067	24	30	3	2	0.4	.947

Tom Funk

FUNK, THOMAS JAMES
B. Mar. 13, 1962, Kansas City, Mo.
BL TL 6′ 2″ 210 lbs.

Year	Team	Lg	W	L	PCT	ERA	G	GS	CG	IP	H	BB	SO	ShO	Relief Pitching W	Relief Pitching L	Relief Pitching SV	Batting AB	Batting H	Batting HR	BA	PO	A	E	DP	TC/G	FA
1986	HOU	N	0	0	—	6.48	8	0	0	8.1	10	6	2	0	0	0	0	1	0	0	.000	1	1	0	0	0.3	1.000

Ed Fusselbach

FUSSELBACH, EDWARD L.
B. July 4, 1858, Philadelphia, Pa. D. Apr. 14, 1926, Philadelphia, Pa.
BR 5′ 6″ 156 lbs.

Year	Team	Lg	W	L	PCT	ERA	G	GS	CG	IP	H	BB	SO	ShO	Relief Pitching W	Relief Pitching L	Relief Pitching SV	Batting AB	Batting H	Batting HR	BA	PO	A	E	DP	TC/G	FA
1882	STL	AA	1	2	.333	*4.70*	4	2	2	23	34	2	3	0	**1**	0	**1**	*				92	54	25	4	4.5	.854

Fred Fussell

FUSSELL, FREDERICK MORRIS (Moonlight Ace)
B. Oct. 7, 1895, Sheridan, Mo. D. Oct. 23, 1966, Syracuse, N. Y.
BL TL 5′10″ 155 lbs.

Year	Team	Lg	W	L	PCT	ERA	G	GS	CG	IP	H	BB	SO	ShO	Relief Pitching W	Relief Pitching L	Relief Pitching SV	Batting AB	Batting H	Batting HR	BA	PO	A	E	DP	TC/G	FA
1922	CHI	N	1	1	.500	4.74	3	2	1	19	24	8	4	0	0	0	0	6	0	0	.000	0	6	0	0	2.0	1.000
1923			3	5	.375	5.54	28	2	1	76.1	90	31	38	0	3	3	3	20	4	0	.200	2	19	3	2	0.9	.875
1928	PIT	N	8	9	.471	3.61	28	20	9	159.2	183	41	43	2	1	1	1	58	7	0	.121	4	25	2	1	1.1	.935
1929			2	2	.500	8.62	21	3	0	39.2	68	8	18	0	1	1	1	16	4	2	.250	4	7	0	0	0.5	1.000
4 yrs.			14	17	.452	4.86	80	27	11	294.2	365	88	103	2	5	5	5	100	15	2	.150	10	57	5	3	0.9	.931

Frank Gabler

GABLER, FRANK HAROLD (The Great Gabbo)
B. Nov. 6, 1911, East Highlands, Calif. D. Nov. 1, 1967, Long Beach, Calif.
BR TR 6′ 1″ 175 lbs.

Year	Team	Lg	W	L	PCT	ERA	G	GS	CG	IP	H	BB	SO	ShO	Relief Pitching W	Relief Pitching L	Relief Pitching SV	Batting AB	Batting H	Batting HR	BA	PO	A	E	DP	TC/G	FA
1935	NY	N	2	1	.667	5.70	26	1	0	60	79	20	24	0	2	0	0	16	2	0	.125	3	13	1	0	0.7	.941
1936			9	8	.529	3.12	43	14	5	161.2	170	34	46	0	3	2	6	48	10	0	.208	5	31	1	4	0.9	.973
1937	2 teams	NY N (6G 0–0)	BOS N (19G 4–7)																								
″	total		4	7	.364	5.61	25	9	2	85	104	18	22	1	2	2	2	22	4	0	.182	6	17	1	1	1.0	.958
1938	2 teams	BOS N (1G 0–0)	CHI A (18G 1–7)																								
″	total		1	7	.125	9.43	19	7	3	69.2	104	35	17	0	0	3	0	21	5	0	.238	2	9	0	1	0.6	1.000
4 yrs.			16	23	.410	5.26	113	31	10	376.1	457	107	109	1	7	7	8	107	21	0	.196	16	70	3	6	0.8	.966
WORLD SERIES																											
1936	NY	N	0	0	—	7.20	2	0	0	5	7	4	0	0	0	0	0	0	0	0	—	1	0	0	0	0.5	1.000

John Gabler

GABLER, JOHN RICHARD (Gabe)
B. Oct. 2, 1930, Kansas City, Mo.
BB TR 6′ 2″ 165 lbs.
BB 1960

Year	Team	Lg	W	L	PCT	ERA	G	GS	CG	IP	H	BB	SO	ShO	Relief Pitching W	Relief Pitching L	Relief Pitching SV	Batting AB	Batting H	Batting HR	BA	PO	A	E	DP	TC/G	FA
1959	NY	A	1	1	.500	2.79	3	1	0	19.1	21	10	11	0	1	0	0	6	0	0	.000	1	3	0	1	1.3	1.000
1960			3	3	.500	4.15	21	4	0	52	46	32	19	0	2	1	1	11	1	0	.091	4	9	1	0	0.7	.929
1961	WAS	A	3	8	.273	4.86	29	9	0	92.2	104	37	33	0	2	2	4	25	5	0	.200	11	20	1	1	1.1	.969
3 yrs.			7	12	.368	4.39	53	14	0	164	171	79	63	0	5	3	5	42	6	0	.143	16	32	2	2	0.9	.960

Ken Gables

GABLES, KENNETH HARLIN
B. Jan. 31, 1919, Walnut Grove, Mo. D. Jan. 2, 1960, Walnut Grove, Mo.
BR TR 5′11″ 210 lbs.

Year	Team	Lg	W	L	PCT	ERA	G	GS	CG	IP	H	BB	SO	ShO	Relief Pitching W	Relief Pitching L	Relief Pitching SV	Batting AB	Batting H	Batting HR	BA	PO	A	E	DP	TC/G	FA
1945	PIT	N	11	7	.611	4.15	29	16	6	138.2	139	46	49	0	5	1	1	39	4	0	.103	5	17	0	0	0.8	1.000
1946			2	4	.333	5.27	32	7	0	100.2	113	52	39	0	1	0	1	24	6	0	.250	3	12	1	0	0.5	.938
1947			0	0	—	54.00	1	0	0	0.1	3	0	0	0	0	0	0	0	0	0	—	0	0	0	0	0.0	.000
3 yrs.			13	11	.542	4.69	62	23	6	239.2	255	98	88	0	6	1	2	63	10	0	.159	8	29	1	0	0.6	.974

John Gaddy

GADDY, JOHN WILSON (Sheriff)
B. Feb. 5, 1914, Wadesboro, N. C. D. May 3, 1966, Albermarle, N. C.
BR TR 6′½″ 182 lbs.

Year	Team	Lg	W	L	PCT	ERA	G	GS	CG	IP	H	BB	SO	ShO	Relief Pitching W	Relief Pitching L	Relief Pitching SV	Batting AB	Batting H	Batting HR	BA	PO	A	E	DP	TC/G	FA
1938	BKN	N	2	0	1.000	0.69	2	2	1	13	13	4	3	0	0	0	0	6	0	0	.000	0	2	0	0	1.0	1.000

Brent Gaff

GAFF, BRENT ALLEN BR TR 6′ 2″ 200 lbs.
B. Oct. 5, 1958, Fort Wayne, Ind.

Year	Team		W	L	PCT	ERA	G	GS	CG	IP	H	BB	SO	ShO	Relief Pitching W	Relief Pitching L	Relief Pitching SV	Batting AB	Batting H	Batting HR	BA	PO	A	E	DP	TC/G	FA
1982	NY	N	0	3	.000	4.55	7	5	0	31.2	41	10	14	0	0	0	0	8	0	0	.000	2	5	2	1	1.3	.778
1983			1	0	1.000	6.10	4	0	0	10.1	18	1	4	0	1	0	0	3	0	0	.000	1	2	2	0	1.3	.600
1984			3	2	.600	3.63	47	0	0	84.1	77	36	42	0	3	2	1	6	0	0	.000	11	12	1	0	0.5	.958
3 yrs.			4	5	.444	4.06	58	5	0	126.1	136	47	60	0	4	2	1	17	0	0	.000	14	19	5	1	0.7	.868

Nemo Gaines

GAINES, WILLARD ROLAND BL TL 6′ 180 lbs.
B. Dec. 23, 1897, Alexandria, Va. D. Jan. 28, 1979, Warrentown, Va.

Year	Team		W	L	PCT	ERA	G	GS	CG	IP	H	BB	SO	ShO	Relief Pitching W	Relief Pitching L	Relief Pitching SV	Batting AB	Batting H	Batting HR	BA	PO	A	E	DP	TC/G	FA
1921	WAS	A	0	0	—	0.00	4	0	0	4.2	5	2	1	0	0	0	0	1	0	0	.000	0	0	0	0	0.0	.000

Fred Gaiser

GAISER, FREDERICK JACOB
B. Aug. 31, 1885, Stuttgart, Germany D. Oct. 9, 1918, Trenton, N. J.

Year	Team		W	L	PCT	ERA	G	GS	CG	IP	H	BB	SO	ShO	Relief Pitching W	Relief Pitching L	Relief Pitching SV	Batting AB	Batting H	Batting HR	BA	PO	A	E	DP	TC/G	FA
1908	STL	N	0	0	—	7.71	1	0	0	2.1	4	3	2	0	0	0	0	1	0	0	.000	0	1	0	0	1.0	1.000

Dan Gakeler

GAKELER, DANIEL MICHAEL BR TR 6′ 6″ 215 lbs.
B. May 1, 1964, Mt. Holly, N. J.

Year	Team		W	L	PCT	ERA	G	GS	CG	IP	H	BB	SO	ShO	Relief Pitching W	Relief Pitching L	Relief Pitching SV	Batting AB	Batting H	Batting HR	BA	PO	A	E	DP	TC/G	FA
1991	DET	A	1	4	.200	5.74	31	7	0	73.2	73	39	43	0	0	1	2	0	0	0	—	5	12	0	0	0.5	1.000

Bob Galasso

GALASSO, ROBERT JOSEPH BL TR 6′ 1″ 205 lbs.
B. Jan. 13, 1952, Connellsville, Pa.

Year	Team		W	L	PCT	ERA	G	GS	CG	IP	H	BB	SO	ShO	Relief Pitching W	Relief Pitching L	Relief Pitching SV	Batting AB	Batting H	Batting HR	BA	PO	A	E	DP	TC/G	FA
1977	SEA	A	0	6	.000	9.00	11	7	0	35	57	8	21	0	0	1	0	0	0	0	—	1	4	0	0	0.5	1.000
1979	MIL	A	3	1	.750	4.41	31	0	0	51	64	26	28	0	3	1	3	0	0	0	—	0	7	0	0	0.2	1.000
1981	SEA	A	1	1	.500	4.78	13	1	0	32	32	13	14	0	1	0	1	0	0	0	—	3	4	0	0	0.5	1.000
3 yrs.			4	8	.333	5.87	55	8	0	118	153	47	63	0	4	2	4	0	0	0		4	15	0	0	0.3	1.000

Milt Galatzer

GALATZER, MILTON BL TL 5′10″ 168 lbs.
B. May 4, 1907, Chicago, Ill. D. Jan. 29, 1976, San Francisco, Calif.

Year	Team		W	L	PCT	ERA	G	GS	CG	IP	H	BB	SO	ShO	Relief Pitching W	Relief Pitching L	Relief Pitching SV	Batting AB	Batting H	Batting HR	BA	PO	A	E	DP	TC/G	FA
1936	CLE	A	0	0	—	4.50	1	0	0	6	7	5	3	0	0	0	0	*				104	7	2	2	2.5	.982

Rich Gale

GALE, RICHARD BLACKWELL BR TR 6′ 7″ 225 lbs.
B. Jan. 19, 1954, Littleton, N. H.

Year	Team		W	L	PCT	ERA	G	GS	CG	IP	H	BB	SO	ShO	Relief Pitching W	Relief Pitching L	Relief Pitching SV	Batting AB	Batting H	Batting HR	BA	PO	A	E	DP	TC/G	FA
1978	KC	A	14	8	.636	3.09	31	30	9	192.1	171	100	88	3	0	0	0	0	0	0	—	3	26	4	1	1.1	.879
1979			9	10	.474	5.64	34	31	2	182	197	99	103	1	0	0	0	0	0	0	—	9	25	4	3	1.1	.895
1980			13	9	.591	3.91	32	28	6	191	169	78	97	1	0	2	1	0	0	0	—	10	26	1	1	1.2	.973
1981			6	6	.500	5.38	19	15	2	102	107	38	47	0	1	0	0	0	0	0	—	6	8	1	1	0.8	.933
1982	SF	N	7	14	.333	4.23	33	29	2	170.1	193	81	102	0	1	2	0	48	6	1	.125	10	31	1	1	1.3	.976
1983	CIN	N	4	6	.400	5.82	33	7	0	89.2	103	43	53	0	2	1	1	20	3	1	.150	7	10	2	0	0.6	.895
1984	BOS	A	2	3	.400	5.56	13	4	0	43.2	57	18	28	0	1	2	0	0	0	0	—	4	3	0	0	0.5	1.000
7 yrs.			55	56	.495	4.53	195	144	21	971	997	457	518	5	5	7	2	68	9	2	.132	49	129	13	7	1.0	.932
WORLD SERIES																											
1980	KC	A	0	1	.000	4.26	2	2	0	6.1	11	4	4	0	0	0	0	0	0	0	—	0	1	0	0	0.5	1.000

Denny Galehouse

GALEHOUSE, DENNIS WARD BR TR 6′ 1″ 195 lbs.
B. Dec. 7, 1911, Marshallville, Ohio.

Year	Team		W	L	PCT	ERA	G	GS	CG	IP	H	BB	SO	ShO	Relief Pitching W	Relief Pitching L	Relief Pitching SV	Batting AB	Batting H	Batting HR	BA	PO	A	E	DP	TC/G	FA
1934	CLE	A	0	0	—	18.00	1	0	0	1	2	1	0	0	0	0	0	0	0	0	—	0	0	1	0	1.0	.000
1935			1	0	1.000	9.00	5	1	1	13	16	9	8	0	0	0	0	4	1	0	.250	1	3	0	0	0.8	1.000
1936			8	7	.533	4.85	36	15	11	148.1	161	68	71	0	2	1	1	47	8	0	.170	6	15	1	0	0.6	.955
1937			9	14	.391	4.57	36	29	7	200.2	238	83	78	0	2	0	3	72	15	0	.208	6	42	2	3	1.4	.960
1938			7	8	.467	4.34	36	12	5	114	119	65	66	1	4	**5**	3	39	6	0	.154	4	21	0	2	0.7	1.000
1939	BOS	A	9	10	.474	4.54	30	18	6	146.2	160	52	68	1	3	1	0	47	3	0	.064	11	24	3	2	1.3	.921
1940			6	6	.500	5.17	25	20	5	120	155	41	53	0	0	0	0	39	3	0	.077	11	22	0	2	1.3	1.000
1941	STL	A	9	10	.474	3.64	30	24	11	190.1	183	68	61	2	1	0	0	68	13	0	.191	15	35	0	3	1.7	1.000
1942			12	12	.500	3.62	32	28	12	191.1	193	79	75	3	0	0	1	72	14	0	.194	15	41	2	3	1.8	.966
1943			11	11	.500	2.77	31	28	14	224	217	74	114	2	0	1	1	72	9	0	.125	7	33	2	0	1.4	.952
1944			9	10	.474	3.12	24	19	6	153	162	44	80	2	1	1	0	48	3	0	.063	3	21	3	0	1.1	.889
1946			8	12	.400	3.65	30	24	11	180	194	52	90	2	0	0	0	55	5	0	.091	11	17	1	1	1.0	.966
1947	2 teams	STL A	(9G 1–3)		BOS A	(21G 11–7)																					
″	total		12	10	.545	3.82	30	25	11	181.1	192	50	49	3	0	0	1	60	5	0	.083	8	28	1	2	1.2	.973
1948	BOS	A	8	8	.500	4.00	27	15	6	137.1	152	46	38	1	4	1	3	42	7	0	.167	6	17	2	2	0.9	.920
1949			0	0	—	13.50	2	0	0	2	4	3	0	0	0	0	0	0	0	0	—	0	1	0	0	0.5	1.000
15 yrs.			109	118	.480	3.98	375	258	106	2003	2148	735	851	17	17	10	13	665	92	0	.138	104	320	18	20	1.2	.959
WORLD SERIES																											
1944	STL	A	1	1	.500	1.50	2	2	2	18	13	5	15	0	0	0	0	5	1	0	.200	0	5	0	0	2.5	1.000

Bill Gallagher

GALLAGHER, WILLIAM JOHN TL
B. Philadelphia, Pa. Deceased.

Year	Team		W	L	PCT	ERA	G	GS	CG	IP	H	BB	SO	ShO	Relief Pitching W	Relief Pitching L	Relief Pitching SV	Batting AB	Batting H	Batting HR	BA	PO	A	E	DP	TC/G	FA
1883	BAL	AA	0	5	.000	*5.40*	7	5	4	51.2	79	6	19	0	0	0	0	69	10	0	.145	21	13	9	1	2.0	.791
1884	PHI	U	1	2	.333	*3.24*	3	3	3	25	32	4	12	0	0	0	0	11	1	0	.091	2	6	2	0	3.3	.800
2 yrs.			1	7	.125	4.70	10	8	7	76.2	111	10	31	0	0	0	0	*				23	19	11	1	2.1	.792

Doug Gallagher

GALLAGHER, DOUGLAS EUGENE BR TL 6′ 3½″ 195 lbs.
B. Feb. 21, 1940, Fremont, Ohio

Year	Team		W	L	PCT	ERA	G	GS	CG	IP	H	BB	SO	ShO	Relief Pitching W	Relief Pitching L	Relief Pitching SV	Batting AB	Batting H	Batting HR	BA	PO	A	E	DP	TC/G	FA
1962	DET	A	0	4	.000	4.68	9	2	0	25	31	15	14	0	0	2	1	6	2	0	.333	3	4	1	1	0.9	.875

Ed Gallagher

GALLAGHER, EDWARD MICHAEL (Lefty) BB TL 6′ 2″ 197 lbs.
B. Nov. 28, 1910, Dorchester, Mass. D. Dec. 22, 1981, Hyannis, Mass.

Year	Team		W	L	PCT	ERA	G	GS	CG	IP	H	BB	SO	ShO	Relief Pitching W	Relief Pitching L	Relief Pitching SV	Batting AB	Batting H	Batting HR	BA	PO	A	E	DP	TC/G	FA
1932	BOS	A	0	3	.000	12.55	9	3	0	23.2	30	28	6	0	0	0	0	5	0	0	.000	2	5	1	0	0.9	.875

Bert Gallia

GALLIA, MELVIN ALLYS BR TR 6′ 165 lbs.
B. Oct. 14, 1891, Beeville, Tex. D. Mar. 19, 1976, Devine, Tex.

Year	Team		W	L	PCT	ERA	G	GS	CG	IP	H	BB	SO	ShO	Relief Pitching W	Relief Pitching L	Relief Pitching SV	Batting AB	Batting H	Batting HR	BA	PO	A	E	DP	TC/G	FA
1912	WAS	A	0	0	—	0.00	2	0	0	2	0	3	0	0	0	0	0	0	0	0	—	0	0	0	0	0.0	.000
1913			1	5	.167	4.13	31	4	0	96	85	46	46	0	1	2	3	23	2	0	.087	5	39	3	0	1.5	.936
1914			0	0	—	4.50	2	0	0	6	3	4	4	0	0	0	0	2	0	0	.000	0	1	2	0	1.5	.333
1915			17	11	.607	2.29	43	29	14	259.2	220	64	130	3	4	1	1	85	14	0	.165	11	66	3	2	1.9	.963
1916			17	12	.586	2.76	49	31	13	283.2	278	99	120	1	4	3	2	93	18	0	.194	9	65	3	2	1.6	.961

Year	Team	Lg	W	L	PCT	ERA	G	GS	CG	IP	H	BB	SO	ShO	Relief Pitching W	Relief Pitching L	Relief Pitching SV	Batting AB	Batting H	Batting HR	BA	PO	A	E	DP	TC/G	FA

Bert Gallia *continued*

Year	Team	Lg	W	L	PCT	ERA	G	GS	CG	IP	H	BB	SO	ShO	Relief W	Relief L	SV	AB	H	HR	BA	PO	A	E	DP	TC/G	FA
1917			9	13	.409	2.99	42	23	9	207.2	191	93	84	1	3	4	1	67	14	0	.209	5	54	3	3	1.5	.952
1918	STL	A	8	6	.571	3.48	19	17	10	124	126	61	48	1	0	0	0	46	6	0	.130	1	38	3	0	2.2	.929
1919			12	14	.462	3.60	34	25	14	222.1	220	92	83	1	2	1	1	72	11	1	.153	18	63	2	4	2.4	.976
1920	2 teams	STL A (2G 0–1)	PHI N (18G 2–6)																								
"	total		2	7	.222	4.64	20	6	1	75.2	87	32	35	0	2	1	2	24	4	0	.167	5	15	1	0	1.0	.952
9 yrs.			66	68	.493	3.14	242	135	61	1277	1210	494	550	7	16	12	10	412	69	1	.167	54	341	20	11	1.7	.952

Phil Gallivan

GALLIVAN, PHILIP JOSEPH BR TR 6′ 180 lbs.
B. May 29, 1907, Seattle, Wash. D. Nov. 24, 1969, St. Paul, Minn.

Year	Team	Lg	W	L	PCT	ERA	G	GS	CG	IP	H	BB	SO	ShO	Relief W	Relief L	SV	AB	H	HR	BA	PO	A	E	DP	TC/G	FA
1931	BKN	N	0	1	.000	5.28	6	1	0	15.1	23	7	1	0	0	0	0	3	0	0	.000	3	6	0	1	1.5	1.000
1932	CHI	A	1	3	.250	7.56	13	3	1	33.1	49	24	12	0	1	0	0	8	3	0	.375	2	5	0	0	0.5	1.000
1934			4	7	.364	5.61	35	7	3	126.2	155	64	55	0	4	4	1	40	9	0	.225	5	20	2	0	0.8	.926
3 yrs.			5	11	.313	5.95	54	11	4	175.1	227	95	68	0	5	4	1	51	12	0	.235	10	31	2	1	0.8	.953

Balvino Galvez

GALVEZ, BALVINO BR TR 6′ 170 lbs.
Born Balvino Galvez (Jerez).
B. Mar. 31, 1964, San Pedro de Macoris, Dominican Republic.

Year	Team	Lg	W	L	PCT	ERA	G	GS	CG	IP	H	BB	SO	ShO	Relief W	Relief L	SV	AB	H	HR	BA	PO	A	E	DP	TC/G	FA
1986	LA	N	0	1	.000	3.92	10	0	0	20.2	19	12	11	0	0	1	0	2	0	0	.000	3	3	1	1	0.7	.857

Lou Galvin

GALVIN, LOUIS J.
B. Apr. 1862, St. Paul, Minn. Deceased.

Year	Team	Lg	W	L	PCT	ERA	G	GS	CG	IP	H	BB	SO	ShO	Relief W	Relief L	SV	AB	H	HR	BA	PO	A	E	DP	TC/G	FA
1884	STP	U	0	2	.000	*2.88*	3	3	3	25	21	10	17	0	0	0	0	9	2	0	.222	1	1	1	0	1.0	.667

Pud Galvin

GALVIN, JAMES FRANCIS (Gentle Jeems, The Little Steam Engine) BR TR 5′ 8″ 190 lbs.
B. Dec. 25, 1856, St. Louis, Mo. D. Mar. 7, 1902, Pittsburgh, Pa.
Manager 1885.
Hall of Fame 1965.

Year	Team	Lg	W	L	PCT	ERA	G	GS	CG	IP	H	BB	SO	ShO	Relief W	Relief L	SV	AB	H	HR	BA	PO	A	E	DP	TC/G	FA
1879	BUF	N	37	27	.578	2.28	66	66	65	593	585	31	136	6	0	0	0	265	66	0	.249	36	143	27	8	3.1	.869
1880			20	35	.364	2.71	58	54	46	458.2	528	32	128	5	0	**2**	0	241	51	0	.212	44	100	21	1	2.1	.873
1881			29	24	.547	*2.37*	56	53	48	474	546	46	136	5	0	0	0	236	50	0	.212	52	126	22	7	2.8	.890
1882			28	23	.549	*3.17*	52	51	48	445.1	476	40	162	3	0	0	0	206	44	0	.214	22	87	9	1	2.0	.924
1883			46	29	.613	*2.72*	**76**	**75**	**72**	**656.1**	676	50	279	**5**	1	0	0	322	71	1	.220	45	130	13	4	2.2	.931
1884			46	22	.676	*1.99*	72	72	71	636.1	**566**	63	369	**12**	0	0	0	274	49	0	.179	32	154	7	3	2.6	.964
1885	2 teams	BUF N (33G 13–19)	PIT AA (11G 3–7)																								
"	total		16	26	.381	3.99	44	43	40	372.1	453	44	120	3	0	0	1	160	27	1	.169	21	98	17	3	3.0	.875
1886	PIT	AA	29	21	.580	*2.67*	50	50	49	434.2	457	75	72	2	0	0	0	194	49	0	.253	22	101	8	3	2.6	.939
1887	PIT	N	28	21	.571	3.29	49	48	47	440.2	490	67	76	3	1	0	0	193	41	2	.212	22	123	11	2	3.1	.929
1888			23	25	.479	2.63	50	50	49	437.1	446	53	107	6	0	0	0	175	25	1	.143	23	113	10	2	2.9	.932
1889			23	16	.590	4.17	41	40	38	341	392	78	77	4	0	0	0	150	28	0	.187	20	72	11	6	2.5	.893
1890	PIT	P	12	13	.480	4.35	26	25	23	217	275	49	35	1	1	0	0	97	20	0	.206	22	71	7	1	3.8	.930
1891	PIT	N	14	13	.519	2.88	33	30	23	246.2	256	62	46	2	0	0	0	109	18	0	.165	20	52	8	1	2.4	.900
1892	2 teams	PIT N (12G 5–6)	STL N (12G 5–7)																								
"	total		10	13	.435	2.92	24	24	20	188	206	54	56	0	0	0	0	80	7	0	.087	7	35	7	1	2.0	.857
14 yrs.			361	308	.540	2.87	697	681	639	5941.1	6352	744	1799	57	3	2	1	*				388	1405	178	43	2.6	.910
			6th	**2nd**					**2nd**	**2nd**																	

Bob Gamble

GAMBLE, ROBERT J. TR 5′10″ 155 lbs.
B. Feb. 1867, Hazleton, Pa. Deceased.

Year	Team	Lg	W	L	PCT	ERA	G	GS	CG	IP	H	BB	SO	ShO	Relief W	Relief L	SV	AB	H	HR	BA	PO	A	E	DP	TC/G	FA
1888	PHI	AA	0	1	.000	8.00	1	1	1	9	10	3	2	0	0	0	0	3	1	0	.333	2	2	2	0	6.0	.667

Gussie Gannon

GANNON, JAMES EDWARD BL TL 5′11″ 154 lbs.
B. Nov. 26, 1873, Erie, Pa. D. Apr. 12, 1966, Erie, Pa.

Year	Team	Lg	W	L	PCT	ERA	G	GS	CG	IP	H	BB	SO	ShO	Relief W	Relief L	SV	AB	H	HR	BA	PO	A	E	DP	TC/G	FA
1895	PIT	N	0	0	—	1.80	1	0	0	5	7	2	0	0	0	0	0	2	0	0	.000	0	0	0	0	0.0	.000

Joe Gannon

GANNON, JOSEPH
B. St. Louis, Mo. Deceased.

Year	Team	Lg	W	L	PCT	ERA	G	GS	CG	IP	H	BB	SO	ShO	Relief W	Relief L	SV	AB	H	HR	BA	PO	A	E	DP	TC/G	FA
1898	STL	N	0	1	.000	11.00	1	1	1	9	13	5	2	0	0	0	0	3	0	0	.000	0	2	0	0	2.0	1.000

Jim Gantner

GANTNER, JAMES ELMER BL TR 6′ 180 lbs.
B. Jan. 5, 1953, Fond du Lac, Wis.

Year	Team	Lg	W	L	PCT	ERA	G	GS	CG	IP	H	BB	SO	ShO	Relief W	Relief L	SV	AB	H	HR	BA	PO	A	E	DP	TC/G	FA
1979	MIL	A	0	0	—	0.00	1	0	0	1	2	0	0	0	0	0	0	*				17	37	1	3	2.1	.982

John Ganzel

GANZEL, JOHN HENRY BR TR 6′½″ 195 lbs.
Brother of Charlie Ganzel.
B. Apr. 7, 1874, Kalamazoo, Mich. D. Jan. 14, 1959, Orlando, Fla.
Manager 1908, 1915.

Year	Team	Lg	W	L	PCT	ERA	G	GS	CG	IP	H	BB	SO	ShO	Relief W	Relief L	SV	AB	H	HR	BA	PO	A	E	DP	TC/G	FA
1898	PIT	N	0	0	—	0.00	1	0	0		0	0	0	0	0	0	0	*				102	3	4	5	8.4	.963

Keith Garagozzo

GARAGOZZO, KEITH JOHN BL TL 6′ 170 lbs.
B. Oct. 25, 1969, Camden, N. J.

Year	Team	Lg	W	L	PCT	ERA	G	GS	CG	IP	H	BB	SO	ShO	Relief W	Relief L	SV	AB	H	HR	BA	PO	A	E	DP	TC/G	FA
1994	MIN	A	0	0	—	9.64	7	0	0	9.1	9	13	3	0	0	0	0	0	0	0	—	0	2	0	0	0.3	1.000

Gene Garber

GARBER, HENRY EUGENE BR TR 5′10″ 175 lbs.
B. Nov. 13, 1947, Lancaster, Pa.

Year	Team	Lg	W	L	PCT	ERA	G	GS	CG	IP	H	BB	SO	ShO	Relief W	Relief L	SV	AB	H	HR	BA	PO	A	E	DP	TC/G	FA
1969	PIT	N	0	0	—	5.40	2	1	0	5	6	1	3	0	0	0	0	1	0	0	.000	0	0	0	0	0.0	.000
1970			0	3	.000	5.32	14	0	0	22	22	10	7	0	0	3	0	3	2	0	.667	2	7	0	2	0.6	1.000
1972			0	0	—	7.50	4	0	0	6	7	3	3	0	0	0	0	1	0	0	.000	1	1	0	0	0.5	1.000
1973	KC	A	9	9	.500	4.24	48	8	4	153	164	49	60	0	7	4	11	0	0	0	—	14	26	2	3	0.9	.952
1974	2 teams	KC A (17G 1–2)	PHI N (34G 4–0)																								
"	total		5	2	.714	3.08	51	0	0	76	74	44	41	0	5	2	5	3	0	0	.000	8	12	3	0	0.5	.870
1975	PHI	N	10	12	.455	3.60	**71**	0	0	110	103	27	69	0	10	12	14	12	2	0	.167	13	12	0	0	0.4	1.000
1976			9	3	.750	2.82	59	0	0	92.2	78	30	92	0	9	3	11	7	2	0	.286	13	14	1	0	0.5	.964
1977			8	6	.571	2.36	64	0	0	103	82	23	78	0	8	6	19	10	0	0	.000	12	20	1	3	0.5	.970

Gene Garber *continued*

Year	Team	W	L	PCT	ERA	G	GS	CG	IP	H	BB	SO	ShO	Relief Pitching W	L	SV	Batting AB	H	HR	BA	PO	A	E	DP	TC/G	FA
1978	**2 teams** **PHI N** (22G 2–1) **ATL N** (43G 4–4)																									
″	**total**	6	5	.545	2.15	65	0	0	117	84	24	85	0	6	5	25	14	1	0	.071	16	15	0	0	0.5	1.000
1979	**ATL N**	6	16	.273	4.33	68	0	0	106	121	24	56	0	6	**16**	25	10	3	0	.300	14	16	1	1	0.5	.968
1980		5	5	.500	3.84	68	0	0	82	95	24	51	0	5	5	7	2	1	0	.500	8	18	0	1	0.4	1.000
1981		4	6	.400	2.59	35	0	0	59	49	20	34	0	4	6	2	5	0	0	.000	8	17	1	1	0.7	.962
1982		8	10	.444	2.34	69	0	0	119.1	100	32	68	0	8	**10**	30	15	2	0	.133	13	27	4	5	0.6	.909
1983		4	5	.444	4.60	43	0	0	60.2	72	23	45	0	4	5	9	3	0	0	.000	4	17	0	1	0.5	1.000
1984		3	6	.333	3.06	62	0	0	106	103	24	55	0	3	6	11	14	2	0	.143	6	19	0	1	0.4	1.000
1985		6	6	.500	3.61	59	0	0	97.1	98	25	66	0	6	6	1	5	1	0	.200	11	17	0	1	0.5	1.000
1986		5	5	.500	2.54	61	0	0	78	76	20	56	0	5	5	24	6	1	0	.167	7	14	0	1	0.3	1.000
1987	**2 teams** **ATL N** (49G 8–10) **KC A** (13G 0–0)																									
″	**total**	8	10	.444	4.09	62	0	0	83.2	100	29	51	0	8	**10**	18	4	0	0	.000	6	22	1	2	0.5	.966
1988	**KC A**	0	4	.000	3.58	26	0	0	32.2	29	13	20	0	0	4	6	0	0	0	—	3	6	1	1	0.4	.900
19 yrs.		96	113	.459	3.34	931	9	4	1509.1	1463	445	940	0	94	108	218	115	17	0	.148	159	280	15	23	0.5	.967
						7th								**7th**												
LEAGUE CHAMPIONSHIP SERIES																										
1976	**PHI N**	0	1	.000	13.50	2	0	0	0.2	2	1	0	0	0	1	0	0	0	0	—	0	0	0	0	0.0	.000
1977		1	1	.500	3.38	3	0	0	5.1	4	0	3	0	1	1	0	0	0	0	—	0	2	1	0	1.0	.667
1982	**ATL N**	0	1	.000	8.10	2	0	0	3.1	4	1	3	0	0	1	0	1	0	0	.000	0	1	0	0	0.5	1.000
3 yrs.		1	3	.250	5.79	7	0	0	9.1	10	2	6	0	1	3	0	1	0	0	.000	0	3	1	0	0.6	.750
			5th																							

Mike Garber

GARBER, ROBERT MITCHELL BR TR 6′ 1″ 190 lbs.
B. Sept. 10, 1928, Hunker, Pa.

Year	Team	W	L	PCT	ERA	G	GS	CG	IP	H	BB	SO	ShO	Relief Pitching W	L	SV	Batting AB	H	HR	BA	PO	A	E	DP	TC/G	FA
1956	**PIT N**	0	0	—	2.25	2	0	0	4	3	3	3	0	0	0	0	0	0	0	—	0	0	1	0	0.5	.000

Rich Garces

GARCES, RICHARD ARON BR TR 6′ 187 lbs.
Born Richard Aron Garces (Mendoza).
B. May 18, 1971, Maracay, Venezuela.

Year	Team	W	L	PCT	ERA	G	GS	CG	IP	H	BB	SO	ShO	Relief Pitching W	L	SV	Batting AB	H	HR	BA	PO	A	E	DP	TC/G	FA
1990	**MIN A**	0	0	—	1.59	5	0	0	5.2	4	4	1	0	0	0	2	0	0	0	—	0	1	0	0	0.2	1.000
1993		0	0	—	0.00	3	0	0	4	4	2	3	0	0	0	0	0	0	0	—	0	0	0	0	0.0	.000
1995	**2 teams** **CHI N** (7G 0–0) **FLA N** (11G 0–2)																									
″	**total**	0	2	.000	4.44	18	0	0	24.1	25	11	22	0	0	2	0	1	0	0	.000	2	1	0	0	0.2	1.000
3 yrs.		0	2	.000	3.44	26	0	0	34	33	17	26	0	0	2	2	1	0	0	.000	2	2	0	0	0.2	1.000

Miguel Garcia

GARCIA, MIGUEL ANGEL BL TL 5′11″ 173 lbs.
Born Miguel Angel Garcia (Sifontes).
B. Apr. 3, 1967, Caracas, Venezuela.

Year	Team	W	L	PCT	ERA	G	GS	CG	IP	H	BB	SO	ShO	Relief Pitching W	L	SV	Batting AB	H	HR	BA	PO	A	E	DP	TC/G	FA
1987	**2 teams** **CAL A** (1G 0–0) **PIT N** (1G 0–0)																									
″	**total**	0	0		11.57	2	0	0	2.1	3	3	0	0	0	0	0	0	0	0		0	1	0	0	0.5	1.000
1988	**PIT N**	0	0	—	4.50	1	0	0	2	3	2	2	0	0	0	0	0	0	0	—	0	0	0	0	0.0	.000
1989		0	2	.000	8.44	11	0	0	16	25	7	9	0	0	2	0	1	1	0	1.000	1	3	0	0	0.4	1.000
3 yrs.		0	2	.000	8.41	14	0	0	20.1	31	12	11	0	0	2	0	1	1	0	1.000	1	4	0	0	0.4	1.000

Mike Garcia

GARCIA, EDWARD MIGUEL (The Big Bear) BR TR 6′ 1″ 195 lbs.
B. Nov. 17, 1923, San Gabriel, Calif. D. Jan. 13, 1986, Fairview Park, Ohio.

Year	Team	W	L	PCT	ERA	G	GS	CG	IP	H	BB	SO	ShO	Relief Pitching W	L	SV	Batting AB	H	HR	BA	PO	A	E	DP	TC/G	FA
1948	**CLE A**	0	0	—	0.00	1	0	0	2	3	0	1	0	0	0	0	0	0	0	—	0	2	0	0	2.0	1.000
1949		14	5	.737	2.36	41	20	8	175.2	154	60	94	5	3	1	2	51	12	1	.235	11	34	1	4	1.1	.978
1950		11	11	.500	3.86	33	29	11	184	191	74	76	0	0	0	0	65	13	0	.200	10	42	1	2	1.6	.981
1951		20	13	.606	3.15	47	30	15	254	239	82	118	1	3	2	6	85	18	1	.212	18	46	2	4	1.4	.970
1952		22	11	.667	2.37	46	**36**	19	292.1	**284**	87	143	**6**	1	2	4	95	13	0	.137	17	59	3	4	1.7	.962
1953		18	9	.667	3.25	38	35	21	271.2	260	81	134	3	0	1	0	96	24	0	.250	14	39	0	4	1.4	1.000
1954		19	8	.704	**2.64**	45	34	13	258.2	220	71	129	**5**	0	0	5	81	11	0	.136	20	41	1	2	1.4	.984
1955		11	13	.458	4.02	38	31	6	210.2	230	56	120	2	0	2	3	69	15	0	.217	12	29	1	0	1.1	.976
1956		11	12	.478	3.78	35	30	8	197.2	213	74	119	4	0	1	0	61	7	0	.115	13	27	0	2	1.1	1.000
1957		12	8	.600	3.75	38	27	9	211.1	221	73	110	1	1	0	0	75	12	0	.160	12	22	1	5	0.9	.971
1958		1	0	1.000	9.00	6	1	0	8	15	7	2	0	1	0	0	1	0	0	.000	0	2	0	0	0.3	1.000
1959		3	6	.333	4.00	29	8	1	72	72	31	49	0	3	3	1	14	1	0	.071	6	11	1	0	0.6	.944
1960	**CHI A**	0	0	—	4.58	15	0	0	17.2	23	10	8	0	0	0	2	3	1	0	.333	1	4	0	0	0.3	1.000
1961	**WAS A**	0	1	.000	4.74	16	0	0	19	23	13	14	0	0	1	0	0	0	0	—	0	1	3	0	0.3	.250
14 yrs.		142	97	.594	3.27	428	281	111	2174.2	2148	719	1117	27	12	13	23	696	127	2	.182	134	359	14	27	1.2	.972
WORLD SERIES																										
1954	**CLE A**	0	1	.000	5.40	2	1	0	5	6	4	4	0	0	0	0	0	0	0	—	0	2	1	0	1.5	.667

Ralph Garcia

GARCIA, RALPH BR TR 6′ 195 lbs.
B. Dec. 14, 1948, Los Angeles, Calif.

Year	Team	W	L	PCT	ERA	G	GS	CG	IP	H	BB	SO	ShO	Relief Pitching W	L	SV	Batting AB	H	HR	BA	PO	A	E	DP	TC/G	FA
1972	**SD N**	0	0	—	1.80	3	0	0	5	4	3	3	0	0	0	0	0	0	0	—	0	2	0	0	0.7	1.000
1974		0	0	—	6.30	8	0	0	10	15	7	9	0	0	0	0	0	0	0	—	1	2	0	0	0.4	1.000
2 yrs.		0	0		4.80	11	0	0	15	19	10	12	0	0	0	0	0	0	0		1	4	0	0	0.5	1.000

Ramon Garcia

GARCIA, RAMON BR TR 5′10″ 170 lbs.
Born Ramon Garcia (Garcia).
B. Mar. 5, 1924, La Esperanza, Cuba.

Year	Team	W	L	PCT	ERA	G	GS	CG	IP	H	BB	SO	ShO	Relief Pitching W	L	SV	Batting AB	H	HR	BA	PO	A	E	DP	TC/G	FA
1948	**WAS A**	0	0	—	17.18	4	0	0	3.2	11	4	2	0	0	0	0	1	1	0	1.000	0	1	0	0	0.3	1.000

Ramon Garcia

GARCIA, RAMON ANTONIO BR TR 6′ 2″ 200 lbs.
Born Ramon Antonio Garcia (Fortunato).
B. Feb. 9, 1969, Guanare, Venezuela.

Year	Team	W	L	PCT	ERA	G	GS	CG	IP	H	BB	SO	ShO	Relief Pitching W	L	SV	Batting AB	H	HR	BA	PO	A	E	DP	TC/G	FA
1991	**CHI A**	4	4	.500	5.40	16	15	0	78.1	79	31	40	0	0	0	0	0	0	0	—	9	12	1	2	1.4	.955

Art Gardiner

GARDINER, ARTHUR CECIL BR TR
B. Dec. 26, 1899, Brooklyn, N. Y. D. Oct. 21, 1954, Copaigue, N. Y.

Year	Team	Lg	W	L	PCT	ERA	G	GS	CG	IP	H	BB	SO	ShO	Relief W	Relief L	Relief SV	Batting AB	Batting H	Batting HR	BA	PO	A	E	DP	TC/G	FA
1923	PHI	N	0	0	—	0.00	1	0	0		1	1	0	0	0	0	0	0	0	0	—	0	0	0	0	0.0	.000

Mike Gardiner

GARDINER, MICHAEL JAMES BB TR 6′ 185 lbs.
B. Oct. 19, 1965, Sarina, Ont., Canada.

Year	Team	Lg	W	L	PCT	ERA	G	GS	CG	IP	H	BB	SO	ShO	Relief W	Relief L	Relief SV	Batting AB	Batting H	Batting HR	BA	PO	A	E	DP	TC/G	FA
1990	SEA	A	0	2	.000	10.66	5	3	0	12.2	22	5	6	0	0	0	0	0	0	0	—	1	2	0	0	0.6	1.000
1991	BOS	A	9	10	.474	4.85	22	22	0	130	140	47	91	0	0	0	0	0	0	0	—	12	13	1	2	1.2	.962
1992			4	10	.286	4.75	28	18	0	130.2	126	58	79	0	2	2	0	0	0	0	—	13	15	1	2	1.0	.966
1993	2 teams	MON N	(24G 2–3)		DET A	(10G 0–0)																					
″	total		2	3	.400	4.93	34	2	0	49.1	52	26	25	0	1	2	0	4	0	0	.000	1	7	0	0	0.2	1.000
1994	DET	A	2	2	.500	4.14	38	1	0	58.2	53	23	31	0	2	2	5	0	0	0	—	6	2	0	0	0.2	1.000
1995			0	0	—	14.59	9	0	0	12.1	27	2	7	0	0	0	0	0	0	0	—	2	1	0	0	0.3	1.000
6 yrs.			17	27	.386	5.21	136	46	0	393.2	420	161	239	0	5	6	5	4	0	0	.000	35	40	2	4	0.6	.974

Bill Gardner

GARDNER, WILLIAM A.
B. Sept. 1868, Baltimore, Mass. Deceased.

Year	Team	Lg	W	L	PCT	ERA	G	GS	CG	IP	H	BB	SO	ShO	Relief W	Relief L	Relief SV	Batting AB	Batting H	Batting HR	BA	PO	A	E	DP	TC/G	FA
1887	BAL	AA	0	1	.000	11.08	3	2	1	13	23	10	3	0	0	0	0	11	3	0	.273	2	2	1	1	1.0	.800

Chris Gardner

GARDNER, CHRISTOPHER JOHN BR TR 6′ 175 lbs.
B. Mar. 30, 1969, Long Beach, Calif.

Year	Team	Lg	W	L	PCT	ERA	G	GS	CG	IP	H	BB	SO	ShO	Relief W	Relief L	Relief SV	Batting AB	Batting H	Batting HR	BA	PO	A	E	DP	TC/G	FA
1991	HOU	N	1	2	.333	4.01	5	4	0	24.2	19	14	12	0	0	0	0	5	0	0	.000	3	6	1	1	2.0	.900

Gid Gardner

GARDNER, FRANKLIN WASHINGTON 165 lbs.
B. June 9, 1859, Attleboro, Mass. D. Aug. 1, 1914, Cambridge, Mass.

Year	Team	Lg	W	L	PCT	ERA	G	GS	CG	IP	H	BB	SO	ShO	Relief W	Relief L	Relief SV	Batting AB	Batting H	Batting HR	BA	PO	A	E	DP	TC/G	FA
1879	TRO	N	0	2	.000	5.79	2	2	2	14	27	0	3	0	0	0	0	6	1	0	.167	1	2	4	0	3.5	.429
1880	CLE	N	1	8	.111	2.57	9	9	9	77	80	20	21	0	0	0	0	32	6	0	.188	0	17	3	0	2.0	.850
1883	BAL	AA	1	0	1.000	*5.14*	2	0	0	7	9	1	2	0	**1**	0	0	161	44	1	.273	74	25	22	0	2.8	.818
1884	CHI	U	0	1	.000	6.00	1	1	0	6	10	1	4	0	0	0	0	326	76	2	.233	125	34	21	6	2.2	.883
1885	BAL	AA	0	1	.000	10.00	1	1	1	9	16	6	3	0	0	0	0	170	37	0	.218	129	135	35	17	6.5	.883
5 yrs.			2	12	.143	3.90	15	13	12	113	142	28	33	0	1	0	0	*				361	241	92	24	3.4	.867

Glenn Gardner

GARDNER, MILES GLENN BR TR 5′11″ 180 lbs.
B. Jan. 25, 1916, Burnsville, N. C. D. July 7, 1964, Rochester, N. Y.

Year	Team	Lg	W	L	PCT	ERA	G	GS	CG	IP	H	BB	SO	ShO	Relief W	Relief L	Relief SV	Batting AB	Batting H	Batting HR	BA	PO	A	E	DP	TC/G	FA
1945	STL	N	3	1	.750	3.29	17	4	2	54.2	50	27	20	1	1	1	1	21	7	0	.333	2	8	0	0	0.6	1.000

Harry Gardner

GARDNER, HARRY RAY BB TR 6′ 2″ 180 lbs.
B. Sept. 20, 1888, Portland, Ore. D. Aug. 2, 1961, Barlow, Ore.

Year	Team	Lg	W	L	PCT	ERA	G	GS	CG	IP	H	BB	SO	ShO	Relief W	Relief L	Relief SV	Batting AB	Batting H	Batting HR	BA	PO	A	E	DP	TC/G	FA
1911	PIT	N	1	1	.500	4.50	13	3	2	42	39	20	24	0	0	0	2	14	3	0	.214	0	7	0	0	0.5	1.000
1912			0	0	—	0.00	1	0	0	0.1	3	1	0	0	0	0	0	0	0	0	—	1	0	0	0	1.0	1.000
2 yrs.			1	1	.500	4.46	14	3	2	42.1	42	21	24	0	0	0	2	14	3	0	.214	1	7	0	0	0.6	1.000

Jim Gardner

GARDNER, JAMES ANDERSON TR
B. Oct. 4, 1874, Pittsburgh, Pa. D. Apr. 24, 1905, Pittsburgh, Pa.

Year	Team	Lg	W	L	PCT	ERA	G	GS	CG	IP	H	BB	SO	ShO	Relief W	Relief L	Relief SV	Batting AB	Batting H	Batting HR	BA	PO	A	E	DP	TC/G	FA
1895	PIT	N	8	2	.800	2.64	11	10	8	85.1	99	27	31	0	0	0	0	34	9	0	.265	3	16	2	1	1.9	.905
1897			5	5	.500	5.19	14	11	8	95.1	115	32	35	0	1	0	0	76	12	1	.158	17	29	10	0	2.1	.821
1898			10	13	.435	3.21	25	22	19	185.1	179	48	41	1	0	1	0	91	14	0	.154	26	50	5	1	2.4	.938
1899			1	0	1.000	7.52	6	3	0	32.1	52	13	2	0	0	0	0	13	3	0	.231	3	0	1	0	0.7	.750
1902	CHI	N	1	2	.333	2.88	3	3	2	25	23	10	6	0	0	0	0	10	2	0	.200	2	7	0	0	3.0	1.000
5 yrs.			25	22	.532	3.85	59	49	37	423.1	468	130	115	1	1	1	0	224	40	1	.179	51	102	18	2	2.1	.895

Mark Gardner

GARDNER, MARK ALLAN BR TR 6′ 1″ 190 lbs.
B. Mar. 1, 1962, Los Angeles, Calif.

Year	Team	Lg	W	L	PCT	ERA	G	GS	CG	IP	H	BB	SO	ShO	Relief W	Relief L	Relief SV	Batting AB	Batting H	Batting HR	BA	PO	A	E	DP	TC/G	FA
1989	MON	N	0	3	.000	5.13	7	4	0	26.1	26	11	21	0	0	0	0	6	1	0	.167	1	3	0	0	0.6	1.000
1990			7	9	.438	3.42	27	26	3	152.2	129	61	135	3	0	1	0	44	5	0	.114	9	25	0	4	1.3	1.000
1991			9	11	.450	3.85	27	27	0	168.1	139	75	107	0	0	0	0	55	5	0	.091	12	15	1	1	1.0	.964
1992			12	10	.545	4.36	33	30	0	179.2	179	60	132	0	1	0	0	50	7	0	.140	14	22	2	0	1.2	.947
1993	KC	A	4	6	.400	6.19	17	16	0	91.2	92	36	54	0	0	0	0	0	0	0	—	6	5	1	1	0.7	.917
1994	FLA	N	4	4	.500	4.87	20	14	0	92.1	97	30	57	0	0	0	0	25	1	0	.040	8	8	0	0	0.8	1.000
1995			5	5	.500	4.49	39	11	1	102.1	109	43	87	1	1	1	1	21	4	0	.190	3	10	2	1	0.4	.867
7 yrs.			41	48	.461	4.38	170	128	4	813.1	771	316	593	4	2	2	1	201	23	0	.114	53	88	6	7	0.9	.959

Rob Gardner

GARDNER, RICHARD FRANK BR TL 6′ 1″ 176 lbs.
B. Dec. 19, 1944, Binghamton, N. Y.

Year	Team	Lg	W	L	PCT	ERA	G	GS	CG	IP	H	BB	SO	ShO	Relief W	Relief L	Relief SV	Batting AB	Batting H	Batting HR	BA	PO	A	E	DP	TC/G	FA
1965	NY	N	0	2	.000	3.21	5	4	0	28	23	7	19	0	0	0	0	7	0	0	.000	2	5	0	1	1.4	1.000
1966			4	8	.333	5.12	41	17	3	133.2	147	64	74	0	1	1	1	41	7	0	.171	4	24	1	1	0.7	.966
1967	CHI	N	0	2	.000	3.98	18	5	0	31.2	33	6	16	0	0	0	0	6	0	0	.000	1	6	0	0	0.4	1.000
1968	CLE	A	0	0	—	6.75	5	0	0	2.2	5	2	6	0	0	0	0	0	0	0	—	0	0	0	0	0.0	.000
1970	NY	A	1	0	1.000	5.14	1	1	0	7	8	4	6	0	0	0	0	3	1	0	.333	0	1	0	0	1.0	1.000
1971	2 teams	OAK A	(4G 0–0)		NY A	(2G 0–0)																					
″	total		0	0		2.53	6	1	0	10.2	11	5	7	0	0	0	0	2	1	0	.500	1	2	0	0	0.5	1.000
1972	NY	A	8	5	.615	3.06	20	14	1	97	91	28	58	0	0	1	0	28	3	0	.107	2	13	0	1	0.8	1.000
1973	2 teams	MIL A	(10G 1–1)		OAK A	(3G 0–0)																					
″	total		1	1	.500	8.10	13	0	0	20	27	17	7	0	1	1	1	0	0	0		1	3	0	1	0.3	1.000
8 yrs.			14	18	.438	4.35	109	42	4	330.2	345	133	193	0	2	3	2	87	12	0	.138	11	54	1	4	0.6	.985

Wes Gardner

GARDNER, WESLEY BRIAN BR TR 6′ 4″ 195 lbs.
B. Apr. 29, 1961, Benton, Ark.

Year	Team	Lg	W	L	PCT	ERA	G	GS	CG	IP	H	BB	SO	ShO	Relief W	Relief L	Relief SV	Batting AB	Batting H	Batting HR	BA	PO	A	E	DP	TC/G	FA
1984	NY	N	1	1	.500	6.39	21	0	0	25.1	34	8	19	0	1	1	1	1	0	0	.000	1	3	0	0	0.2	1.000
1985			0	2	.000	5.25	9	0	0	12	18	8	11	0	0	2	0	0	0	0	—	0	4	0	0	0.4	1.000
1986	BOS	A	0	0	—	9.00	1	0	0	1	1	0	1	0	0	0	0	0	0	0	—	0	0	0	0	0.0	.000
1987			3	6	.333	5.42	49	1	0	89.2	98	42	70	0	3	6	10	0	0	0	—	2	7	0	0	0.2	1.000
1988			8	6	.571	3.50	36	18	1	149	119	64	106	0	1	1	2	0	0	0	—	15	14	0	0	0.8	1.000

Wes Gardner *continued*

Year	Team	W	L	PCT	ERA	G	GS	CG	IP	H	BB	SO	ShO	Relief Pitching W	Relief Pitching L	Relief Pitching SV	Batting AB	Batting H	Batting HR	BA	PO	A	E	DP	TC/G	FA
1989		3	7	.300	5.97	22	16	0	86	97	47	81	0	1	0	0	0	0	0	—	3	8	1	1	0.5	.917
1990		3	7	.300	4.89	34	9	0	77.1	77	35	58	0	1	3	0	0	0	0	—	8	7	1	1	0.5	.938
1991	**2 teams** **SD N** (14G 0–1) **KC A** (3G 0–0)																									
"	**total**	0	1	.000	5.88	17	0	0	26	32	14	12	0	0	1	1	2	0	0	.000	1	5	0	0	0.4	1.000
8 yrs.		18	30	.375	4.90	189	44	1	466.1	476	218	358	0	7	14	14	3	0	0	.000	30	48	2	2	0.4	.975
LEAGUE CHAMPIONSHIP SERIES																										
1988	**BOS A**	0	0	—	5.79	1	0	0	4.2	6	2	8	0	0	0	0	0	0	0	—	0	0	0	0	0.0	.000

Bill Garfield

GARFIELD, WILLIAM MILTON BR TR 5′11½″ 160 lbs.
B. Oct. 26, 1867, Sheffield, Ohio D. Dec. 16, 1941, Danville, Ill.

Year	Team	W	L	PCT	ERA	G	GS	CG	IP	H	BB	SO	ShO	Relief Pitching W	Relief Pitching L	Relief Pitching SV	Batting AB	Batting H	Batting HR	BA	PO	A	E	DP	TC/G	FA
1889	**PIT N**	0	2	.000	7.76	4	2	2	29	45	17	4	0	0	0	0	13	0	0	.000	2	6	1	1	2.3	.889
1890	**CLE N**	1	7	.125	4.89	9	8	7	70	91	35	16	0	0	0	0	26	4	0	.154	4	13	1	0	2.0	.944
2 yrs.		1	9	.100	5.73	13	10	9	99	136	52	20	0	0	0	0	39	4	0	.103	6	19	2	1	2.1	.926

Bob Garibaldi

GARIBALDI, ROBERT ROY BL TR 6′ 4″ 210 lbs.
B. Mar. 3, 1942, Stockton, Calif.

Year	Team	W	L	PCT	ERA	G	GS	CG	IP	H	BB	SO	ShO	Relief Pitching W	Relief Pitching L	Relief Pitching SV	Batting AB	Batting H	Batting HR	BA	PO	A	E	DP	TC/G	FA
1962	**SF N**	0	0	—	5.11	9	0	0	12.1	13	5	9	0	0	0	1	1	0	0	.000	2	3	1	0	0.7	.833
1963		0	1	.000	1.13	4	0	0	8	8	4	4	0	0	1	1	1	0	0	.000	0	2	1	1	0.8	.667
1966		0	0	—	0.00	1	0	0	1	1	0	0	0	0	0	0	0	0	0	—	0	0	0	0	0.0	.000
1969		0	1	.000	1.80	1	1	0	5	6	2	1	0	0	0	0	2	0	0	.000	0	1	0	0	1.0	1.000
4 yrs.		0	2	.000	3.08	15	1	0	26.1	28	11	14	0	0	1	2	4	0	0	.000	2	6	2	1	0.7	.800

Lou Garland

GARLAND, LOUIS LYMAN BR TR 6′ 2½″ 200 lbs.
B. July 16, 1905, Archie, Mo. D. Aug. 30, 1990, Idaho Falls, Ida.

Year	Team	W	L	PCT	ERA	G	GS	CG	IP	H	BB	SO	ShO	Relief Pitching W	Relief Pitching L	Relief Pitching SV	Batting AB	Batting H	Batting HR	BA	PO	A	E	DP	TC/G	FA
1931	**CHI A**	0	2	.000	10.26	7	2	0	16.2	30	14	4	0	0	2	0	3	0	0	.000	1	7	1	0	1.3	.889

Wayne Garland

GARLAND, MARCUS WAYNE BR TR 6′ 195 lbs.
B. Oct. 26, 1950, Nashville, Tenn.

Year	Team	W	L	PCT	ERA	G	GS	CG	IP	H	BB	SO	ShO	Relief Pitching W	Relief Pitching L	Relief Pitching SV	Batting AB	Batting H	Batting HR	BA	PO	A	E	DP	TC/G	FA
1973	**BAL A**	0	1	.000	3.94	4	1	0	16	14	7	10	0	0	0	0	0	0	0	—	1	1	0	0	0.5	1.000
1974		5	5	.500	2.97	20	6	0	91	68	26	40	0	3	1	1	0	0	0	—	5	11	2	1	0.9	.889
1975		2	5	.286	3.71	29	1	0	87.1	80	31	46	0	2	5	4	0	0	0	—	6	11	0	0	0.6	1.000
1976		20	7	.741	2.68	38	25	14	232	224	64	113	4	4	0	1	0	0	0	—	27	37	3	2	1.8	.955
1977	**CLE A**	13	**19**	.406	3.59	38	38	21	283	281	88	118	1	0	0	0	0	0	0	—	24	42	3	3	1.8	.957
1978		2	3	.400	7.89	6	6	0	29.2	43	16	13	0	0	0	0	0	0	0	—	1	5	0	0	1.0	1.000
1979		4	10	.286	5.21	18	14	2	95	120	34	40	0	1	1	0	0	0	0	—	11	8	3	0	1.2	.864
1980		6	9	.400	4.62	25	20	4	150	163	48	55	1	0	0	0	0	0	0	—	14	16	0	0	1.2	1.000
1981		3	7	.300	5.79	12	10	2	56	89	14	15	1	0	0	0	0	0	0	—	4	11	0	0	1.3	1.000
9 yrs.		55	66	.455	3.89	190	121	43	1040	1082	328	450	7	10	7	6	0	0	0		93	142	11	6	1.3	.955
LEAGUE CHAMPIONSHIP SERIES																										
1974	**BAL A**	0	0	—	0.00	1	0	0	0.2	1	1	0	0	0	0	0	0	0	0	—	0	0	0	0	0.0	.000

Mike Garman

GARMAN, MICHAEL DOUGLAS BR TR 6′ 3″ 195 lbs.
B. Sept. 16, 1949, Caldwell, Ida.

Year	Team	W	L	PCT	ERA	G	GS	CG	IP	H	BB	SO	ShO	Relief Pitching W	Relief Pitching L	Relief Pitching SV	Batting AB	Batting H	Batting HR	BA	PO	A	E	DP	TC/G	FA
1969	**BOS A**	1	0	1.000	4.38	2	2	0	12.1	13	10	10	0	0	0	0	5	2	0	.400	3	1	0	0	2.0	1.000
1971		1	1	.500	3.79	3	3	0	19	15	9	6	0	0	0	0	6	2	0	.333	0	0	0	0	0.0	.000
1972		0	1	.000	12.00	3	1	0	3	4	2	1	0	0	0	0	0	0	0	—	0	0	0	0	0.0	.000
1973		0	0	—	5.32	12	0	0	22	32	15	9	0	0	0	0	0	0	0	—	1	3	1	0	0.4	.800
1974	**STL N**	7	2	.778	2.63	64	0	0	82	66	27	45	0	7	2	6	10	1	0	.100	2	14	2	4	0.3	.889
1975		3	8	.273	2.39	66	0	0	79	73	48	48	0	3	8	10	2	0	0	.000	3	9	4	0	0.2	.750
1976	**CHI N**	2	4	.333	4.97	47	2	0	76	79	35	37	0	2	2	1	7	0	0	.000	3	14	0	1	0.4	1.000
1977	**LA N**	4	4	.500	2.71	49	0	0	63	60	22	29	0	4	4	12	7	0	0	.000	3	8	1	1	0.2	.917
1978	**2 teams** **LA N** (10G 0–1) **MON N** (47G 4–6)																									
"	**total**	4	7	.364	4.40	57	0	0	77.2	69	34	28	0	4	7	13	5	0	0	.000	4	10	1	1	0.3	.933
9 yrs.		22	27	.449	3.63	303	8	0	434	411	202	213	0	20	23	42	42	5	0	.119	19	59	9	7	0.3	.897
LEAGUE CHAMPIONSHIP SERIES																										
1977	**LA N**	0	0	—	0.00	2	0	0	1.1	0	0	1	0	0	0	1	0	0	0	—	0	0	0	0	0.0	.000
WORLD SERIES																										
1977	**LA N**	0	0	—	0.00	2	0	0	4	2	1	3	0	0	0	0	0	0	0	—	0	0	0	0	0.0	.000

Willie Garoni

GARONI, WILLIAM BR TR 6′ 1″ 165 lbs.
B. July 28, 1877, Fort Lee, N. J. D. Sept. 9, 1914, Fort Lee, N. J.

Year	Team	W	L	PCT	ERA	G	GS	CG	IP	H	BB	SO	ShO	Relief Pitching W	Relief Pitching L	Relief Pitching SV	Batting AB	Batting H	Batting HR	BA	PO	A	E	DP	TC/G	FA
1899	**NY N**	0	1	.000	4.50	3	1	1	10	12	2	2	0	0	0	0	4	0	0	.000	0	4	1	1	1.7	.800

Scott Garrelts

GARRELTS, SCOTT WILLIAM BR TR 6′ 4″ 200 lbs.
B. Oct. 30, 1961, Champaign, Ill.

Year	Team	W	L	PCT	ERA	G	GS	CG	IP	H	BB	SO	ShO	Relief Pitching W	Relief Pitching L	Relief Pitching SV	Batting AB	Batting H	Batting HR	BA	PO	A	E	DP	TC/G	FA
1982	**SF N**	0	0	—	13.50	1	0	0	2	3	2	4	0	0	0	0	0	0	0	—	0	0	0	0	0.0	.000
1983		2	2	.500	2.52	5	5	1	35.2	33	19	16	1	0	0	0	9	2	0	.222	1	7	0	1	1.6	1.000
1984		2	3	.400	5.65	21	3	0	43	45	34	32	0	2	3	0	10	1	0	.100	2	4	0	0	0.3	1.000
1985		9	6	.600	2.30	74	0	0	105.2	76	58	106	0	9	6	13	9	2	0	.222	7	22	2	0	0.4	.935
1986		13	9	.591	3.11	53	18	2	173.2	144	74	125	0	8	2	10	45	8	1	.178	9	37	2	2	0.9	.958
1987		11	7	.611	3.22	64	0	0	106.1	70	55	127	0	**11**	7	12	10	2	0	.200	5	10	1	1	0.3	.938
1988		5	9	.357	3.58	65	0	0	98	80	46	86	0	5	9	13	13	1	0	.077	5	12	2	0	0.3	.895
1989		14	5	.737	**2.28**	30	29	2	193.1	149	46	119	1	0	0	0	66	9	0	.136	18	24	1	0	1.4	.977
1990		12	11	.522	4.15	31	31	4	182	190	70	80	2	0	0	0	66	4	0	.061	5	26	3	0	1.1	.912
1991		1	1	.500	6.41	8	3	0	19.2	25	9	8	0	0	0	0	4	0	0	.000	4	1	0	1	0.6	1.000
10 yrs.		69	53	.566	3.29	352	89	9	959.1	815	413	703	4	35	27	48	232	29	1	.125	56	143	11	5	0.6	.948
LEAGUE CHAMPIONSHIP SERIES																										
1987	**SF N**	0	0	—	6.75	2	0	0	2.2	2	4	4	0	0	0	0	0	0	0	—	1	0	0	0	0.5	1.000
1989		1	0	1.000	5.40	2	2	0	11.2	16	2	8	0	0	0	0	4	0	0	.000	0	1	0	0	0.5	1.000
2 yrs.		1	0	1.000	5.65	4	2	0	14.1	18	6	12	0	0	0	0	4	0	0	.000	1	1	0	0	0.5	1.000
WORLD SERIES																										
1989	**SF N**	0	2	.000	9.82	2	2	0	7.1	13	1	8	0	0	0	0	1	0	0	.000	0	2	0	0	1.0	1.000

Clarence Garrett

GARRETT, CLARENCE RAYMOND (Laz) BR TR 6′ 5½″ 185 lbs.
B. Mar. 6, 1891, Reader, W. Va. D. Feb. 11, 1977, Moundsville, W. Va.

Year	Team	W	L	PCT	ERA	G	GS	CG	IP	H	BB	SO	ShO	Relief Pitching W	L	SV	Batting AB	H	HR	BA	PO	A	E	DP	TC/G	FA
1915	CLE A	2	2	.500	2.31	4	4	2	23.1	19	6	5	0	0	0	0	8	0	0	.000	1	12	1	0	3.5	.929

Greg Garrett

GARRETT, GREGORY BB TL 6′ 200 lbs.
B. Mar. 12, 1948, Atascadero, Calif.

Year	Team	W	L	PCT	ERA	G	GS	CG	IP	H	BB	SO	ShO	Relief Pitching W	L	SV	Batting AB	H	HR	BA	PO	A	E	DP	TC/G	FA
1970	CAL A	5	6	.455	2.64	32	7	0	75	48	44	53	0	4	2	0	15	1	0	.067	0	12	0	0	0.4	1.000
1971	CIN N	0	1	.000	1.00	2	1	0	9	7	10	2	0	0	1	0	3	1	0	.333	0	1	0	0	0.5	1.000
2 yrs.		5	7	.417	2.46	34	8	0	84	55	54	55	0	4	3	0	18	2	0	.111	0	13	0	0	0.4	1.000

Cliff Garrison

GARRISON, CLIFFORD WILLIAM BR TR 6′ 195 lbs.
B. Aug. 13, 1906, Belmont, Okla. D. Aug. 25, 1994, Woodland, Calif.

Year	Team	W	L	PCT	ERA	G	GS	CG	IP	H	BB	SO	ShO	Relief Pitching W	L	SV	Batting AB	H	HR	BA	PO	A	E	DP	TC/G	FA
1928	BOS A	0	0	—	7.88	6	0	0	16	22	6	0	0	0	0	0	3	0	0	.000	1	7	0	0	1.3	1.000

Jim Garry

GARRY, JAMES THOMAS TL
B. Sept. 21, 1869, Great Barrington, Mass. D. Jan. 15, 1917, Pittsfield, Mass.

Year	Team	W	L	PCT	ERA	G	GS	CG	IP	H	BB	SO	ShO	Relief Pitching W	L	SV	Batting AB	H	HR	BA	PO	A	E	DP	TC/G	FA
1893	BOS N	0	1	.000	63.00	1	0	0	1	5	4	2	0	0	1	0	1	0	0	.000	0	0	0	0	0.0	.000

Ned Garver

GARVER, NED FRANKLIN BR TR 5′10½″ 180 lbs.
B. Dec. 25, 1925, Ney, Ohio.

Year	Team	W	L	PCT	ERA	G	GS	CG	IP	H	BB	SO	ShO	Relief Pitching W	L	SV	Batting AB	H	HR	BA	PO	A	E	DP	TC/G	FA
1948	STL A	7	11	.389	3.41	38	24	7	198	200	95	75	0	1	0	5	66	19	1	.288	19	34	1	3	1.4	.981
1949		12	**17**	.414	3.98	41	32	16	223.2	245	102	70	1	3	0	3	75	14	0	.187	15	42	5	3	1.5	.919
1950		13	18	.419	3.39	37	31	**22**	260	264	108	85	2	1	2	0	91	26	1	.286	28	52	5	4	2.2	.941
1951		20	12	.625	3.73	33	30	**24**	246	237	96	84	1	2	1	0	95	29	1	.305	26	42	3	6	2.2	.958
1952	2 teams STL A (21G 7–10) DET A (1G 1–0)																									
″	total	8	10	.444	3.60	22	22	8	157.2	139	58	63	2	0	0	0	51	9	0	.176	12	26	1	7	1.8	.974
1953	DET A	11	11	.500	4.45	30	26	13	198.1	228	66	69	0	1	0	1	72	11	1	.153	13	39	1	0	1.8	.981
1954		14	11	.560	2.81	35	32	16	246.1	216	62	93	3	0	0	1	79	13	0	.165	21	48	2	2	2.0	.972
1955		12	16	.429	3.98	33	32	16	230.2	**251**	67	83	1	0	0	0	76	17	1	.224	17	40	3	4	1.8	.950
1956		0	2	.000	4.08	6	3	1	17.2	15	13	6	0	0	0	0	5	0	0	.000	1	5	0	1	1.0	1.000
1957	KC A	6	13	.316	3.84	24	23	6	145.1	120	55	61	1	0	0	0	44	8	0	.182	13	21	1	2	1.5	.971
1958		12	11	.522	4.03	31	28	10	201	192	66	72	3	0	0	1	69	12	0	.174	18	57	2	4	2.5	.974
1959		10	13	.435	3.71	32	30	9	201.1	214	42	61	2	0	0	1	71	20	2	.282	10	35	1	3	1.4	.978
1960		4	9	.308	3.83	28	15	5	122.1	110	35	50	2	0	0	0	27	2	0	.074	9	18	2	2	1.0	.931
1961	LA A	0	3	.000	5.59	12	2	0	29	40	16	9	0	0	1	0	6	0	0	.000	1	11	0	0	1.0	1.000
14 yrs.		129	157	.451	3.73	402	330	153	2477.1	2471	881	881	18	8	4	12	827	180	7	.218	203	470	27	41	1.7	.961

Jerry Garvin

GARVIN, THEODORE JARED BL TL 6′ 3″ 195 lbs.
B. Oct. 21, 1955, Oakland, Calif.

Year	Team	W	L	PCT	ERA	G	GS	CG	IP	H	BB	SO	ShO	Relief Pitching W	L	SV	Batting AB	H	HR	BA	PO	A	E	DP	TC/G	FA
1977	TOR A	10	18	.357	4.19	34	34	12	245	247	85	127	1	0	0	0	0	0	0	—	12	66	3	1	2.4	.963
1978		4	12	.250	5.54	26	22	3	144.2	189	48	67	0	0	0	0	0	0	0	—	9	28	0	1	1.4	1.000
1979		0	1	.000	2.74	8	1	0	23	15	10	14	0	0	1	0	0	0	0	—	1	1	0	1	0.3	1.000
1980		4	7	.364	2.28	61	0	0	83	70	27	52	0	4	7	8	0	0	0	—	5	14	0	1	0.3	1.000
1981		1	2	.333	3.40	35	4	0	53	46	23	25	0	1	1	0	0	0	0	—	1	9	0	2	0.3	1.000
1982		1	1	.500	7.25	32	4	0	58.1	81	26	35	0	1	1	0	0	0	0	—	5	17	0	0	0.7	1.000
6 yrs.		20	41	.328	4.42	196	65	15	607	648	219	320	1	6	10	8	0	0	0		33	135	3	6	0.9	.982

Ned Garvin

GARVIN, VIRGIL LEE TR 6′ 3½″ 160 lbs.
B. Jan. 1, 1874, Navasota, Tex. D. June 16, 1908, Fresno, Calif.

Year	Team	W	L	PCT	ERA	G	GS	CG	IP	H	BB	SO	ShO	Relief Pitching W	L	SV	Batting AB	H	HR	BA	PO	A	E	DP	TC/G	FA
1896	PHI N	0	1	.000	7.62	2	1	1	13	19	7	4	0	0	0	0	6	0	0	.000	0	1	0	0	0.5	1.000
1899	CHI N	9	13	.409	2.85	24	23	22	199	202	42	69	4	0	0	0	71	11	0	.155	7	51	3	1	2.5	.951
1900		10	18	.357	2.41	30	28	25	246.1	225	63	107	1	0	1	0	91	14	0	.154	5	78	6	1	3.0	.933
1901	MIL A	7	20	.259	3.46	37	27	22	257.1	258	90	122	1	0	0	2	93	10	0	.108	14	83	7	2	2.8	.933
1902	2 teams CHI A (23G 10–10) BKN N (2G 1–1)																									
″	total	11	11	.500	2.09	25	21	18	193.1	184	47	62	3	1	0	0	66	10	0	.152	4	73	4	3	3.2	.951
1903	BKN N	15	18	.455	3.08	38	34	30	298	277	84	154	2	0	1	2	106	8	0	.075	7	117	11	3	3.6	.919
1904	2 teams BKN N (23G 5–15) NY A (2G 0–1)																									
″	total	5	16	.238	1.72	25	24	16	193.2	155	80	94	2	0	0	0	67	8	0	.119	18	73	11	5	4.1	.892
7 yrs.		57	97	.370	2.72	181	158	134	1400.2	1320	413	612	13	1	2	4	500	61	0	.122	55	476	42	15	3.2	.927

Harry Gaspar

GASPAR, HARRY LAMBERT BR TR 6′ 180 lbs.
B. Apr. 28, 1883, Kingsley, Iowa D. May 14, 1940, Orange, Calif.

Year	Team	W	L	PCT	ERA	G	GS	CG	IP	H	BB	SO	ShO	Relief Pitching W	L	SV	Batting AB	H	HR	BA	PO	A	E	DP	TC/G	FA
1909	CIN N	18	11	.621	2.01	44	29	19	260	228	57	65	4	2	2	2	82	10	0	.122	2	56	3	2	1.4	.951
1910		15	17	.469	2.59	48	31	16	275	257	75	74	4	1	1	5	87	10	0	.115	6	73	6	2	1.8	.929
1911		10	17	.370	3.30	44	32	11	253.2	272	69	76	2	2	2	3	85	13	0	.153	7	66	7	5	1.8	.912
1912		1	3	.250	4.17	7	6	2	36.2	38	16	13	1	0	1	0	12	3	0	.250	1	10	1	0	1.7	.917
4 yrs.		44	48	.478	2.69	143	98	48	825.1	795	217	228	11	5	6	10	266	36	0	.135	16	205	17	9	1.7	.929

Charlie Gassaway

GASSAWAY, CHARLES CASON (Sheriff) BL TL 6′ 2½″ 210 lbs.
B. Aug. 12, 1918, Gassaway, Ga. D. Jan. 15, 1992, Miami, Fla.

Year	Team	W	L	PCT	ERA	G	GS	CG	IP	H	BB	SO	ShO	Relief Pitching W	L	SV	Batting AB	H	HR	BA	PO	A	E	DP	TC/G	FA
1944	CHI N	0	1	.000	7.71	2	2	0	11.2	20	10	7	0	0	0	0	4	1	0	.250	0	1	0	0	0.5	1.000
1945	PHI A	4	7	.364	3.74	24	11	4	118	114	55	50	0	0	0	0	39	6	0	.154	3	20	6	1	1.2	.793
1946	CLE A	1	1	.500	3.91	13	6	0	50.2	54	26	23	0	0	0	0	15	1	0	.067	5	7	0	1	0.9	1.000
3 yrs.		5	9	.357	4.04	39	19	4	180.1	188	91	80	0	0	0	0	58	8	0	.138	8	28	6	2	1.1	.857

Milt Gaston

GASTON, NATHANIEL MILTON BR TR 6′ 1″ 185 lbs.
Brother of Alex Gaston. BB 1933
B. Jan. 27, 1896, Ridgefield Park, N. J.

Year	Team	W	L	PCT	ERA	G	GS	CG	IP	H	BB	SO	ShO	Relief Pitching W	L	SV	Batting AB	H	HR	BA	PO	A	E	DP	TC/G	FA
1924	NY A	5	3	.625	4.50	29	2	0	86	92	44	24	0	5	1	1	27	6	0	.222	2	14	0	1	0.6	1.000
1925	STL A	15	14	.517	4.41	42	29	16	238.2	284	101	84	0	3	3	1	80	21	1	.263	10	49	0	2	1.4	1.000
1926		10	**18**	.357	4.33	32	28	14	214.1	227	101	39	1	0	2	0	78	13	1	.167	16	47	2	2	2.0	.969
1927		13	17	.433	5.00	37	30	21	254	275	100	77	0	0	2	1	96	25	3	.260	18	58	4	9	2.2	.950
1928	WAS A	6	12	.333	5.51	28	22	8	148.2	179	53	45	3	0	1	0	49	7	0	.143	9	38	3	1	1.8	.940

Milt Gaston *continued*

Year	Team	W	L	PCT	ERA	G	GS	CG	IP	H	BB	SO	ShO	Relief Pitching W	Relief Pitching L	Relief Pitching SV	Batting AB	Batting H	Batting HR	BA	PO	A	E	DP	TC/G	FA
1929	**BOS A**	12	19	.387	3.73	39	29	20	243.2	265	81	83	1	2	3	2	78	15	1	.192	13	42	2	4	1.5	.965
1930		13	**20**	.394	3.92	38	34	20	273	272	98	99	2	0	1	2	98	20	0	.204	15	58	4	4	2.0	.948
1931		2	13	.133	4.46	23	18	4	119	137	41	33	0	0	0	0	38	6	0	.158	4	24	3	3	1.3	.903
1932	**CHI A**	7	17	.292	4.00	28	25	7	166.2	183	73	44	1	0	1	1	60	14	0	.233	6	42	4	7	1.9	.923
1933		8	12	.400	4.85	30	25	7	167	177	60	39	1	0	0	0	52	8	0	.154	4	36	3	1	1.4	.930
1934		6	19	.240	5.85	29	28	10	194	247	84	48	1	0	0	0	68	10	0	.147	9	52	1	2	2.1	.984
11 yrs.		97	164	.372	4.55	355	270	127	2105	2338	836	615	10	10	14	8	724	145	6	.200	106	460	26	36	1.7	.956

Welcome Gaston

GASTON, WELCOME THORNBURG TL
B. Dec. 19, 1872, Guernsey County, Ohio D. Dec. 13, 1944, Columbus, Ohio.

Year	Team	W	L	PCT	ERA	G	GS	CG	IP	H	BB	SO	ShO	Relief Pitching W	Relief Pitching L	Relief Pitching SV	Batting AB	Batting H	Batting HR	BA	PO	A	E	DP	TC/G	FA
1898	**BKN N**	1	1	.500	2.81	2	2	2	16	17	9	0	0	0	0	0	8	1	0	.125	1	3	1	1	2.5	.800
1899		0	0	—	3.00	1	0	0	3	3	4	0	0	0	0	0	1	1	0	1.000	0	1	0	0	1.0	1.000
2 yrs.		1	1	.500	2.84	3	2	2	19	20	13	0	0	0	0	0	9	2	0	.222	1	4	1	1	2.0	.833

Hank Gastright

GASTRIGHT, HENRY CARL BR TR 6′ 2″ 190 lbs.
Born Henry Carl Gastreich.
B. Mar. 29, 1865, Covington, Ky. D. Oct. 9, 1937, Cold Springs, Ky.

Year	Team	W	L	PCT	ERA	G	GS	CG	IP	H	BB	SO	ShO	Relief Pitching W	Relief Pitching L	Relief Pitching SV	Batting AB	Batting H	Batting HR	BA	PO	A	E	DP	TC/G	FA
1889	**COL AA**	10	16	.385	4.57	32	26	21	222.2	255	104	115	0	0	1	0	94	17	0	.181	6	47	5	1	1.8	.914
1890		30	14	.682	*2.94*	48	45	41	401.1	312	135	199	4	**3**	0	0	169	36	0	.213	12	55	5	2	1.5	.931
1891		12	19	.387	3.78	35	33	28	283.2	280	136	109	1	0	1	0	117	23	0	.197	11	73	5	2	2.5	.944
1892	**WAS N**	3	3	.500	5.08	11	8	6	79.2	94	38	32	0	0	0	0	29	4	0	.138	1	10	1	2	1.1	.917
1893	**2 teams PIT N** (9G 3–1) **BOS N** (19G 12–4)																									
″	**total**	15	5	**.750**	5.44	28	23	19	215	253	115	39	0	2	0	0	92	14	0	.152	4	46	3	1	1.8	.943
1894	**BKN N**	2	6	.250	6.39	16	8	6	93	135	55	20	1	0	2	2	41	7	0	.171	5	14	2	0	1.3	.905
1896	**CIN N**	0	0	—	4.50	1	0	0	6	8	1	0	0	0	0	0	2	0	0	.000	0	1	0	0	1.0	1.000
7 yrs.		72	63	.533	4.20	171	143	121	1301.1	1337	584	514	6	5	4	2	544	101	0	.186	39	246	21	8	1.8	.931

Aubrey Gatewood

GATEWOOD, AUBREY LEE BR TR 6′ 1″ 170 lbs.
B. Nov. 17, 1938, Little Rock, Ark.

Year	Team	W	L	PCT	ERA	G	GS	CG	IP	H	BB	SO	ShO	Relief Pitching W	Relief Pitching L	Relief Pitching SV	Batting AB	Batting H	Batting HR	BA	PO	A	E	DP	TC/G	FA
1963	**LA A**	1	1	.500	1.50	4	3	1	24	12	16	13	0	0	0	0	8	0	0	.000	0	4	0	0	1.0	1.000
1964		3	3	.500	2.24	15	7	0	60.1	59	12	25	0	1	1	0	20	2	0	.100	8	6	0	0	0.9	1.000
1965	**CAL A**	4	5	.444	3.42	46	3	0	92	91	37	37	0	4	3	0	14	3	0	.214	6	15	1	0	0.5	.955
1970	**ATL N**	0	0	—	4.50	3	0	0	2	4	2	0	0	0	0	0	0	0	0	—	1	1	0	0	0.7	1.000
4 yrs.		8	9	.471	2.78	68	13	1	178.1	166	67	75	0	5	4	0	42	5	0	.119	15	26	1	0	0.6	.976

Chippy Gaw

GAW, GEORGE JOSEPH BR TR 5′11″ 180 lbs.
B. Mar. 13, 1892, West Newton, Mass. D. May 26, 1968, Boston, Mass.

Year	Team	W	L	PCT	ERA	G	GS	CG	IP	H	BB	SO	ShO	Relief Pitching W	Relief Pitching L	Relief Pitching SV	Batting AB	Batting H	Batting HR	BA	PO	A	E	DP	TC/G	FA
1920	**CHI N**	1	1	.500	4.85	6	1	0	13	16	3	4	0	1	0	0	4	1	0	.250	0	3	0	0	0.5	1.000

Dale Gear

GEAR, DALE DUDLEY BR TR 5′11″ 165 lbs.
B. Feb. 2, 1872, Lone Elm, Kans. D. Sept. 23, 1951, Topeka, Kans.

Year	Team	W	L	PCT	ERA	G	GS	CG	IP	H	BB	SO	ShO	Relief Pitching W	Relief Pitching L	Relief Pitching SV	Batting AB	Batting H	Batting HR	BA	PO	A	E	DP	TC/G	FA
1896	**CLE N**	0	2	.000	5.48	3	2	2	23	35	6	6	0	0	0	0	15	6	0	.400	9	4	2	1	3.8	.867
1901	**WAS A**	4	11	.267	4.03	24	16	14	163	199	22	35	1	1	1	0	199	47	0	.236	9	3	4	0	2.7	.750
2 yrs.		4	13	.235	4.21	27	18	16	186	234	28	41	1	1	1	0	*				74	66	12	4	2.2	.921

Dinty Gearin

GEARIN, DENNIS JOHN BL TL 5′ 4″ 148 lbs.
B. Oct. 15, 1897, Providence, R. I. D. Mar. 11, 1959, Providence, R. I.

Year	Team	W	L	PCT	ERA	G	GS	CG	IP	H	BB	SO	ShO	Relief Pitching W	Relief Pitching L	Relief Pitching SV	Batting AB	Batting H	Batting HR	BA	PO	A	E	DP	TC/G	FA
1923	**NY N**	1	1	.500	3.38	6	2	1	24	23	10	9	0	1	0	0	7	2	0	.286	0	5	1	0	1.0	.833
1924	**2 teams NY N** (6G 1–2) **BOS N** (1G 0–1)																									
″	**total**	1	3	.250	4.03	7	4	2	29	33	18	4	0	0	1	0	9	3	0	.333	0	7	1	0	1.1	.875
2 yrs.		2	4	.333	3.74	13	6	3	53	56	28	13	0	1	1	0	16	5	0	.313	0	12	2	0	1.1	.857

Bob Geary

GEARY, ROBERT NORTON (Speed) BR TR 5′11″ 168 lbs.
B. May 10, 1891, Cincinnati, Ohio D. Jan. 3, 1980, Cincinnati, Ohio.

Year	Team	W	L	PCT	ERA	G	GS	CG	IP	H	BB	SO	ShO	Relief Pitching W	Relief Pitching L	Relief Pitching SV	Batting AB	Batting H	Batting HR	BA	PO	A	E	DP	TC/G	FA
1918	**PHI A**	2	5	.286	2.69	16	7	6	87	94	31	22	2	0	0	4	27	4	0	.148	1	21	0	0	1.4	1.000
1919		0	3	.000	4.73	9	2	1	32.1	32	18	9	0	0	1	0	10	5	0	.500	2	11	2	0	1.7	.867
1921	**CIN N**	1	1	.500	4.34	10	1	0	29	38	2	10	0	0	1	0	8	2	0	.250	1	6	1	0	0.8	.875
3 yrs.		3	9	.250	3.46	35	10	7	148.1	164	51	41	2	0	2	4	45	11	0	.244	4	38	3	0	1.3	.933

Bob Gebhard

GEBHARD, ROBERT HENRY BR TR 6′ 2″ 210 lbs.
B. Jan. 3, 1943, Lamberton, Minn.

Year	Team	W	L	PCT	ERA	G	GS	CG	IP	H	BB	SO	ShO	Relief Pitching W	Relief Pitching L	Relief Pitching SV	Batting AB	Batting H	Batting HR	BA	PO	A	E	DP	TC/G	FA
1971	**MIN A**	1	2	.333	3.00	17	0	0	18	17	11	13	0	1	2	0	0	0	0	—	0	7	0	0	0.4	1.000
1972		0	1	.000	8.57	13	0	0	21	36	13	13	0	0	1	1	0	0	0	—	2	5	0	1	0.5	1.000
1974	**MON N**	0	0	—	4.50	1	0	0	2	5	0	0	0	0	0	0	0	0	0	—	0	1	0	0	1.0	1.000
3 yrs.		1	3	.250	5.93	31	0	0	41	58	24	26	0	1	3	1	0	0	0		2	13	0	1	0.5	1.000

Pete Gebrian

GEBRIAN, PETER (Gabe) BR TR 6′ 170 lbs.
B. Aug. 10, 1923, Bayonne, N. J.

Year	Team	W	L	PCT	ERA	G	GS	CG	IP	H	BB	SO	ShO	Relief Pitching W	Relief Pitching L	Relief Pitching SV	Batting AB	Batting H	Batting HR	BA	PO	A	E	DP	TC/G	FA
1947	**CHI A**	2	3	.400	4.48	27	4	0	66.1	61	33	17	0	2	0	5	13	0	0	.000	2	9	1	0	0.4	.917

Jim Geddes

GEDDES, JAMES LEE BR TR 6′ 2″ 200 lbs.
B. Mar. 23, 1949, Columbus, Ohio.

Year	Team	W	L	PCT	ERA	G	GS	CG	IP	H	BB	SO	ShO	Relief Pitching W	Relief Pitching L	Relief Pitching SV	Batting AB	Batting H	Batting HR	BA	PO	A	E	DP	TC/G	FA
1972	**CHI A**	0	0	—	6.97	5	1	0	10.1	12	10	3	0	0	0	0	1	0	0	.000	0	1	1	1	0.4	.500
1973		0	0	—	2.87	6	1	0	15.2	14	14	7	0	0	0	0	0	0	0	—	1	3	0	1	0.7	1.000
2 yrs.		0	0		4.50	11	2	0	26	26	24	10	0	0	0	0	1	0	0	.000	1	4	1	2	0.5	.833

Joe Gedeon

GEDEON, ELMER JOSEPH BR TR 6′ 167 lbs.
B. Dec. 5, 1893, Sacramento, Calif. D. May 19, 1941, San Francisco, Calif.

Year	Team	W	L	PCT	ERA	G	GS	CG	IP	H	BB	SO	ShO	Relief Pitching W	Relief Pitching L	Relief Pitching SV	Batting AB	Batting H	Batting HR	BA	PO	A	E	DP	TC/G	FA
1913	**WAS A**	0	0	—	0.00	1	0	0		0	0	0	0	0	0	1	*				32	16	3	2	2.0	.941

Johnny Gee

GEE, JOHN ALEXANDER (Whiz) BL TL 6′ 9″ 225 lbs.
B. Dec. 7, 1915, Syracuse, N. Y. D. Jan. 23, 1988, Cortland, N. Y.

Year	Team		W	L	PCT	ERA	G	GS	CG	IP	H	BB	SO	ShO	Relief Pitching W	L	SV	Batting AB	H	HR	BA	PO	A	E	DP	TC/G	FA
1939	PIT	N	1	2	.333	4.12	3	3	1	19.2	20	10	16	0	0	0	0	6	0	0	.000	1	6	1	0	2.7	.875
1941			0	2	.000	6.14	3	2	0	7.1	10	5	2	0	0	0	0	3	1	0	.333	0	1	0	0	0.3	1.000
1943			4	4	.500	4.28	15	10	2	82	89	27	18	0	2	0	0	26	3	0	.115	2	5	1	0	0.5	.875
1944	2 teams	PIT N (4G 0–0) NY N (4G 0–0)																									
″	total		0	0		4.96	8	0	0	16.1	25	5	6	0	0	0	0	2	1	0	.500	0	5	0	0	0.6	1.000
1945	NY	N	0	0	—	9.00	2	0	0	3	5	2	1	0	0	0	1	1	0	0	.000	1	0	0	0	0.5	1.000
1946			2	4	.333	3.99	13	6	1	47.1	60	15	22	0	0	0	0	13	3	0	.231	1	7	1	0	0.7	.889
6 yrs.			7	12	.368	4.41	44	21	4	175.2	209	64	65	0	2	0	1	51	8	0	.157	5	24	3	0	0.7	.906

Billy Geer

GEER, WILLIAM HENRY HARRISON TR 5′ 8″ 160 lbs.
Born George Harrison Geer.
B. Aug. 13, 1849, Syracuse, N. Y. D. Jan. 5, 1922, Syracuse, N. Y.

Year	Team		W	L	PCT	ERA	G	GS	CG	IP	H	BB	SO	ShO	Relief Pitching W	L	SV	Batting AB	H	HR	BA	PO	A	E	DP	TC/G	FA
1884	BKN	AA	0	0	—	*12.60*	2	0	0	5	14	3	1	0	0	0	0	*				62	181	38	15	4.5	.865

Charlie Geggus

GEGGUS, CHARLES FREDERICK
B. Mar. 25, 1862, San Francisco, Calif. D. Jan. 16, 1917, San Francisco, Calif.

Year	Team		W	L	PCT	ERA	G	GS	CG	IP	H	BB	SO	ShO	Relief Pitching W	L	SV	Batting AB	H	HR	BA	PO	A	E	DP	TC/G	FA
1884	WAS	U	10	9	.526	*2.54*	23	21	19	177.1	143	38	156	0	0	0	0	*				50	49	23	1	2.5	.811

Henry Gehring

GEHRING, HENRY BR TR
B. Jan. 24, 1881, St. Paul, Minn. D. Apr. 18, 1912, Kansas City, Mo.

Year	Team		W	L	PCT	ERA	G	GS	CG	IP	H	BB	SO	ShO	Relief Pitching W	L	SV	Batting AB	H	HR	BA	PO	A	E	DP	TC/G	FA
1907	WAS	A	3	7	.300	3.31	15	9	8	87	92	14	31	2	0	1	0	44	9	1	.205	3	19	1	2	1.5	.957
1908			0	1	.000	14.40	3	1	0	5	9	2	0	0	0	0	0	4	2	0	.500	0	2	0	0	0.7	1.000
2 yrs.			3	8	.273	3.91	18	10	8	92	101	16	31	2	0	1	0	48	11	1	.229	3	21	1	2	1.4	.960

Paul Gehrman

GEHRMAN, PAUL ARTHUR (Dutch) BR TR 6′ 195 lbs.
B. May 3, 1912, Marquam, Ore. D. Oct. 23, 1986, Bend, Ore.

Year	Team		W	L	PCT	ERA	G	GS	CG	IP	H	BB	SO	ShO	Relief Pitching W	L	SV	Batting AB	H	HR	BA	PO	A	E	DP	TC/G	FA
1937	CIN	N	0	1	.000	2.89	2	1	0	9.1	11	5	1	0	0	0	0	3	0	0	.000	0	3	1	1	2.0	.750

Gary Geiger

GEIGER, GARY MERLE BL TR 6′ 168 lbs.
B. Apr. 4, 1937, Sand Ridge, Ill.

Year	Team		W	L	PCT	ERA	G	GS	CG	IP	H	BB	SO	ShO	Relief Pitching W	L	SV	Batting AB	H	HR	BA	PO	A	E	DP	TC/G	FA
1958	CLE	A	0	0	—	9.00	1	0	0	2	2	1	2	0	0	0	0	*				133	7	4	2	2.6	.972

Emil Geis

GEIS, EMIL MICHAEL BR TR 5′11″ 170 lbs.
B. Mar. 1861, Villmer, Germany Deceased.

Year	Team		W	L	PCT	ERA	G	GS	CG	IP	H	BB	SO	ShO	Relief Pitching W	L	SV	Batting AB	H	HR	BA	PO	A	E	DP	TC/G	FA
1882	BAL	AA	4	9	.308	4.80	13	13	10	95.2	84	22	10	1	0	0	0	41	6	0	.146	8	23	11	0	2.5	.738

Dave Geisel

GEISEL, JOHN DAVID BL TL 6′ 3″ 210 lbs.
B. Jan. 18, 1955, Windber, Pa.

Year	Team		W	L	PCT	ERA	G	GS	CG	IP	H	BB	SO	ShO	Relief Pitching W	L	SV	Batting AB	H	HR	BA	PO	A	E	DP	TC/G	FA
1978	CHI	N	1	0	1.000	4.30	18	1	0	23	27	11	15	0	1	0	0	3	0	0	.000	1	2	0	0	0.2	1.000
1979			0	0	—	0.60	7	0	0	15	10	4	5	0	0	0	0	1	0	0	.000	2	0	0	0	0.3	1.000
1981			2	0	1.000	0.56	11	2	0	16	11	10	7	0	2	0	0	3	0	0	.000	2	1	0	0	0.3	1.000
1982	TOR	A	1	1	.500	3.98	16	2	0	31.2	32	17	22	0	1	0	0	0	0	0	—	0	3	0	0	0.2	1.000
1983			0	3	.000	4.64	47	0	0	52.1	47	31	50	0	0	3	5	0	0	0	—	0	4	0	0	0.1	1.000
1984	SEA	A	1	1	.500	4.15	20	3	0	43.1	47	9	28	0	1	0	3	0	0	0	—	2	2	0	0	0.2	1.000
1985			0	0	—	6.33	12	0	0	27	35	15	17	0	0	0	0	0	0	0	—	0	3	0	1	0.3	1.000
7 yrs.			5	5	.500	4.02	131	8	0	208.1	209	97	144	0	5	3	8	7	0	0	.000	7	15	0	1	0.2	1.000

Vern Geishert

GEISHERT, VERNON WILLIAM BR TR 6′ 1″ 215 lbs.
B. Jan. 10, 1946, Madison, Wis.

Year	Team		W	L	PCT	ERA	G	GS	CG	IP	H	BB	SO	ShO	Relief Pitching W	L	SV	Batting AB	H	HR	BA	PO	A	E	DP	TC/G	FA
1969	CAL	A	1	1	.500	4.65	11	3	0	31	32	7	18	0	1	0	1	9	0	0	.000	1	6	1	1	0.7	.875

Bill Geiss

GEISS, WILLIAM J. 5′10″ 164 lbs.
Brother of Emil Geiss.
B. July 15, 1858, Chicago, Ill. D. Sept. 18, 1924, Chicago, Ill.

Year	Team		W	L	PCT	ERA	G	GS	CG	IP	H	BB	SO	ShO	Relief Pitching W	L	SV	Batting AB	H	HR	BA	PO	A	E	DP	TC/G	FA
1884	DET	N	0	0	—	*14.40*	1	0	0	5	14	2	1	0	0	0	0	*				203	218	65	28	6.4	.866

Emil Geiss

GEISS, EMIL AUGUST BR TR 5′11″ 170 lbs.
Brother of Bill Geiss.
B. Mar. 20, 1867, Chicago, Ill. D. Oct. 4, 1911, Chicago, Ill.

Year	Team		W	L	PCT	ERA	G	GS	CG	IP	H	BB	SO	ShO	Relief Pitching W	L	SV	Batting AB	H	HR	BA	PO	A	E	DP	TC/G	FA
1887	CHI	N	0	1	.000	8.00	1	1	1	9	17	3	4	0	0	0	0	*				13	4	3	0	6.7	.850

Charley Gelbert

GELBERT, CHARLES MAGNUS BR TR 5′11″ 170 lbs.
B. Jan. 26, 1906, Scranton, Pa. D. Jan. 13, 1967, Easton, Pa.

Year	Team		W	L	PCT	ERA	G	GS	CG	IP	H	BB	SO	ShO	Relief Pitching W	L	SV	Batting AB	H	HR	BA	PO	A	E	DP	TC/G	FA
1940	WAS	A	0	0	—	9.00	2	0	0	4	5	3	1	0	0	0	0	*				338	499	46	95	6.0	.948

John Gelnar

GELNAR, JOHN RICHARD BR TR 6′ 2″ 185 lbs.
B. June 25, 1943, Granite, Okla.

Year	Team		W	L	PCT	ERA	G	GS	CG	IP	H	BB	SO	ShO	Relief Pitching W	L	SV	Batting AB	H	HR	BA	PO	A	E	DP	TC/G	FA
1964	PIT	N	0	0	—	5.00	7	0	0	9	11	1	4	0	0	0	0	0	0	0	—	1	1	1	0	0.4	.667
1967			0	1	.000	8.05	10	1	0	19	30	11	5	0	0	0	0	6	1	0	.167	0	5	0	0	0.5	1.000
1969	SEA	A	3	10	.231	3.31	39	10	0	108.2	103	26	69	0	2	3	3	19	1	0	.053	7	14	0	0	0.5	1.000
1970	MIL	A	4	3	.571	4.21	53	0	0	92	98	23	48	0	4	3	4	12	1	0	.083	6	20	1	2	0.5	.963
1971			0	0	—	18.00	2	0	0	1	3	1	0	0	0	0	0	0	0	0	—	0	1	0	0	0.5	1.000
5 yrs.			7	14	.333	4.19	111	11	0	229.2	245	62	126	0	6	6	7	37	3	0	.081	14	41	2	2	0.5	.965

Joe Genewich

GENEWICH, JOSEPH EDWARD BR TR 6′ 174 lbs.
B. Jan. 15, 1897, Elmira, N. Y. D. Dec. 21, 1985, Lockport, N. Y.

Year	Team		W	L	PCT	ERA	G	GS	CG	IP	H	BB	SO	ShO	Relief Pitching W	L	SV	Batting AB	H	HR	BA	PO	A	E	DP	TC/G	FA
1922	BOS	N	0	2	.000	7.04	6	2	1	23	29	11	4	0	0	0	0	6	1	0	.167	0	5	0	0	0.8	1.000
1923			13	14	.481	3.72	43	24	12	227.1	272	46	54	1	1	**4**	1	77	19	0	.247	17	58	2	1	1.8	.974
1924			10	19	.345	5.21	34	27	11	200.1	258	65	43	2	2	1	1	60	10	0	.167	3	50	0	4	1.6	1.000
1925			12	10	.545	3.99	34	21	10	169	185	41	34	0	3	2	0	55	15	0	.273	8	36	4	5	1.4	.917
1926			8	16	.333	3.88	37	26	12	216	239	63	59	2	1	1	2	67	11	0	.164	15	53	2	4	1.9	.971

Joe Genewich *continued*

Year	Team	Lg	W	L	PCT	ERA	G	GS	CG	IP	H	BB	SO	ShO	Relief Pitching W	Relief Pitching L	Relief Pitching SV	Batting AB	Batting H	Batting HR	BA	PO	A	E	DP	TC/G	FA
1927			11	8	.579	3.83	40	19	7	181	199	54	38	0	5	0	1	57	11	0	.193	8	40	0	2	1.2	1.000
1928	2 teams	BOS N	(13G 3–7)		NY N	(26G 11–4)																					
″	total		14	11	.560	3.50	39	29	14	239	224	72	52	2	1	1	3	90	14	0	.156	8	65	1	3	1.9	.986
1929	NY	N	3	7	.300	6.78	21	9	1	85	133	30	19	0	2	3	1	32	12	0	.375	6	19	2	1	1.3	.926
1930			2	5	.286	5.61	18	9	3	61	71	20	13	0	0	0	3	20	3	0	.150	4	23	1	2	1.6	.964
9 yrs.			73	92	.442	4.29	272	166	71	1401.2	1610	402	316	7	15	12	12	464	96	0	.207	69	349	12	22	1.6	.972

Gary Gentry

GENTRY, GARY EDWARD BR TR 6′ 170 lbs.
B. Oct. 6, 1946, Phoenix, Ariz.

Year	Team	Lg	W	L	PCT	ERA	G	GS	CG	IP	H	BB	SO	ShO	Relief Pitching W	Relief Pitching L	Relief Pitching SV	Batting AB	Batting H	Batting HR	BA	PO	A	E	DP	TC/G	FA
1969	NY	N	13	12	.520	3.43	35	35	6	233.2	192	81	154	3	0	0	0	74	6	0	.081	13	41	0	4	1.5	1.000
1970			9	9	.500	3.69	32	29	5	188	155	86	134	2	0	1	1	59	4	0	.068	15	17	1	1	1.0	.970
1971			12	11	.522	3.24	32	31	8	203	167	82	155	3	0	0	0	68	5	0	.074	10	22	0	3	1.0	1.000
1972			7	10	.412	4.01	32	26	3	164	153	75	120	0	0	0	0	48	5	0	.104	15	27	0	1	1.3	1.000
1973	ATL	N	4	6	.400	3.41	16	14	3	87	74	35	42	0	0	0	1	30	7	0	.233	9	7	0	0	1.0	1.000
1974			0	0	—	1.29	3	1	0	7	4	2	0	0	0	0	0	1	0	0	.000	0	1	0	0	0.3	1.000
1975			1	1	.500	4.95	7	2	0	20	25	8	10	0	1	0	0	5	0	0	.000	0	4	0	0	0.6	1.000
7 yrs.			46	49	.484	3.56	157	138	25	902.2	770	369	615	8	1	1	2	285	27	0	.095	62	119	1	9	1.2	.995
LEAGUE CHAMPIONSHIP SERIES																											
1969	NY	N	0	0	—	9.00	1	1	0	2	5	1	1	0	0	0	0	0	0	0	—	0	0	0	0	0.0	.000
WORLD SERIES																											
1969	NY	N	1	0	1.000	0.00	1	1	0	6.2	3	5	4	0	0	0	0	3	1	0	.333	0	0	0	0	0.0	.000

Rufe Gentry

GENTRY, JAMES RUFFUS BR TR 6′ 1″ 180 lbs.
B. May 18, 1918, Daisy Station, N. C.

Year	Team	Lg	W	L	PCT	ERA	G	GS	CG	IP	H	BB	SO	ShO	Relief Pitching W	Relief Pitching L	Relief Pitching SV	Batting AB	Batting H	Batting HR	BA	PO	A	E	DP	TC/G	FA
1943	DET	A	1	3	.250	3.68	4	4	2	29.1	30	12	8	0	0	0	0	10	0	0	.000	1	6	0	0	1.8	1.000
1944			12	14	.462	4.24	37	30	10	203.2	211	**108**	68	4	2	0	0	76	15	0	.197	5	43	1	6	1.3	.980
1946			0	0	—	15.00	2	0	0	3	4	7	1	0	0	0	0	0	0	0	—	0	0	0	0	0.0	.000
1947			0	0	—	81.00	1	0	0	0.1	1	2	0	0	0	0	0	0	0	0	—	0	0	0	0	0.0	.000
1948			0	0	—	2.70	4	0	0	6.2	5	5	1	0	0	0	0	1	1	0	1.000	2	0	0	0	0.5	1.000
5 yrs.			13	17	.433	4.37	48	34	12	243	251	134	78	4	2	0	0	87	16	0	.184	8	49	1	6	1.2	.983

Bill George

GEORGE, WILLIAM M. BR TL 5′ 8″ 165 lbs.
B. Jan. 27, 1865, Bellaire, Ohio D. Aug. 23, 1916, Wheeling, W. Va.

Year	Team	Lg	W	L	PCT	ERA	G	GS	CG	IP	H	BB	SO	ShO	Relief Pitching W	Relief Pitching L	Relief Pitching SV	Batting AB	Batting H	Batting HR	BA	PO	A	E	DP	TC/G	FA
1887	NY	N	3	9	.250	5.25	13	13	11	108	126	89	49	0	0	0	0	53	9	0	.170	8	27	6	0	2.9	.854
1888			2	1	.667	1.34	4	3	3	33.2	18	11	26	1	0	0	1	39	9	1	.231	4	6	1	0	1.1	.909
1889	COL	AA	0	0	—	7.88	2	0	0	8	11	3	3	0	0	0	0	32	8	0	.250	12	1	3	1	1.8	.813
3 yrs.			5	10	.333	4.51	19	16	14	149.2	155	103	78	1	0	0	1	124	26	1	.210	24	34	10	1	2.1	.853

Chris George

GEORGE, CHRISTOPHER SEAN BR TR 6′ 2″ 200 lbs.
B. Sept. 24, 1966, Pittsburgh, Pa.

Year	Team	Lg	W	L	PCT	ERA	G	GS	CG	IP	H	BB	SO	ShO	Relief Pitching W	Relief Pitching L	Relief Pitching SV	Batting AB	Batting H	Batting HR	BA	PO	A	E	DP	TC/G	FA
1991	MIL	A	0	0	—	3.00	2	1	0	6	8	0	2	0	0	0	0	0	0	0	—	0	0	0	0	0.0	.000

Lefty George

GEORGE, THOMAS EDWARD BL TL 6′ 155 lbs.
B. Aug. 13, 1886, Pittsburgh, Pa. D. May 13, 1955, York, Pa.

Year	Team	Lg	W	L	PCT	ERA	G	GS	CG	IP	H	BB	SO	ShO	Relief Pitching W	Relief Pitching L	Relief Pitching SV	Batting AB	Batting H	Batting HR	BA	PO	A	E	DP	TC/G	FA
1911	STL	A	4	9	.308	4.18	27	13	6	116.1	136	51	23	1	2	1	0	44	5	0	.114	5	30	5	2	1.5	.875
1912	CLE	A	0	5	.000	4.87	11	5	2	44.1	69	18	18	0	0	0	0	14	3	0	.214	0	15	2	0	1.5	.882
1915	CIN	N	2	2	.500	3.86	5	3	2	28	24	8	11	1	1	0	0	12	4	0	.333	0	11	0	0	2.2	1.000
1918	BOS	N	1	5	.167	2.32	9	5	4	54.1	56	21	22	0	0	1	0	22	2	0	.091	2	23	0	1	2.8	1.000
4 yrs.			7	21	.250	3.85	52	26	14	243	285	98	74	2	3	2	0	92	14	0	.152	7	79	7	3	1.8	.925

Oscar Georgy

GEORGY, OSCAR JOHN BR TR 6′ 3½″ 180 lbs.
B. Nov. 25, 1916, New Orleans, La.

Year	Team	Lg	W	L	PCT	ERA	G	GS	CG	IP	H	BB	SO	ShO	Relief Pitching W	Relief Pitching L	Relief Pitching SV	Batting AB	Batting H	Batting HR	BA	PO	A	E	DP	TC/G	FA
1938	NY	N	0	0	—	18.00	1	0	0	1	2	1	0	0	0	0	0	0	0	0	—	0	0	0	0	0.0	.000

Dave Gerard

GERARD, DAVID FREDERICK BR TR 6′ 2″ 205 lbs.
B. Aug. 6, 1936, New York, N. Y.

Year	Team	Lg	W	L	PCT	ERA	G	GS	CG	IP	H	BB	SO	ShO	Relief Pitching W	Relief Pitching L	Relief Pitching SV	Batting AB	Batting H	Batting HR	BA	PO	A	E	DP	TC/G	FA
1962	CHI	N	2	3	.400	4.91	39	0	0	58.2	67	28	30	0	2	3	3	8	3	0	.375	4	9	2	0	0.4	.867

George Gerberman

GERBERMAN, GEORGE ALOIS BR TR 6′ 180 lbs.
B. Mar. 8, 1942, El Campo, Tex.

Year	Team	Lg	W	L	PCT	ERA	G	GS	CG	IP	H	BB	SO	ShO	Relief Pitching W	Relief Pitching L	Relief Pitching SV	Batting AB	Batting H	Batting HR	BA	PO	A	E	DP	TC/G	FA
1962	CHI	N	0	0	—	1.69	1	1	0	5.1	3	5	1	0	0	0	0	1	0	0	.000	0	1	1	0	2.0	.500

Allen Gerhardt

GERHARDT, ALLEN RUSSELL (Rusty) BB TL 5′ 9″ 175 lbs.
B. Aug. 13, 1950, Baltimore, Md.

Year	Team	Lg	W	L	PCT	ERA	G	GS	CG	IP	H	BB	SO	ShO	Relief Pitching W	Relief Pitching L	Relief Pitching SV	Batting AB	Batting H	Batting HR	BA	PO	A	E	DP	TC/G	FA
1974	SD	N	2	1	.667	7.00	23	1	0	36	44	17	22	0	1	1	1	6	1	0	.167	0	4	1	1	0.2	.800

Al Gerheauser

GERHEAUSER, ALBERT (Lefty) BL TL 6′ 3″ 190 lbs.
B. June 24, 1917, St. Louis, Mo. D. May 28, 1972, Springfield, Mo.

Year	Team	Lg	W	L	PCT	ERA	G	GS	CG	IP	H	BB	SO	ShO	Relief Pitching W	Relief Pitching L	Relief Pitching SV	Batting AB	Batting H	Batting HR	BA	PO	A	E	DP	TC/G	FA
1943	PHI	N	10	19	.345	3.60	38	31	11	215	222	70	92	2	1	1	0	71	8	0	.113	9	36	2	3	1.2	.957
1944			8	16	.333	4.58	30	29	10	182.2	210	65	66	2	0	0	0	65	15	1	.231	6	29	1	1	1.2	.972
1945	PIT	N	5	10	.333	3.91	32	14	5	140.1	170	54	55	0	2	3	1	48	12	0	.250	9	33	2	0	1.4	.955
1946			2	2	.500	3.97	35	3	1	81.2	92	25	32	0	2	1	0	21	7	0	.333	3	21	0	2	0.7	1.000
1948	STL	A	0	3	.000	7.33	14	2	0	23.1	32	10	10	0	0	1	0	6	2	0	.333	1	3	0	0	0.3	1.000
5 yrs.			25	50	.333	4.13	149	79	27	643	726	224	255	4	5	6	1	211	44	1	.209	28	122	5	6	1.0	.968

Steve Gerkin

GERKIN, STEPHEN PAUL (Splinter) BR TR 6′ 1″ 162 lbs.
B. Nov. 19, 1912, Grafton, W. Va. D. Nov. 8, 1978, Bay Pines, Fla.

Year	Team	Lg	W	L	PCT	ERA	G	GS	CG	IP	H	BB	SO	ShO	Relief Pitching W	Relief Pitching L	Relief Pitching SV	Batting AB	Batting H	Batting HR	BA	PO	A	E	DP	TC/G	FA
1945	PHI	A	0	12	.000	3.62	21	12	3	102	112	27	25	0	0	3	0	34	2	0	.059	5	24	3	1	1.5	.906

Les German

GERMAN, LESTER STANLEY BR TR 5′ 8″ 165 lbs.
B. June 1, 1869, Baltimore, Md. D. June 10, 1934, Germantown, Md.

Year	Team	Lg	W	L	PCT	ERA	G	GS	CG	IP	H	BB	SO	ShO	Relief Pitching W	Relief Pitching L	Relief Pitching SV	Batting AB	Batting H	Batting HR	BA	PO	A	E	DP	TC/G	FA
1890	BAL	AA	5	11	.313	4.84	17	16	15	132	147	54	37	0	1	0	0	51	6	0	.118	3	21	4	0	1.6	.857
1893	NY	N	8	8	.500	4.14	20	18	14	152	162	70	35	0	1	1	0	74	23	0	.311	11	31	8	0	2.3	.840

Les German *continued*

Year	Team		W	L	PCT	ERA	G	GS	CG	IP	H	BB	SO	ShO	Relief Pitching W	L	SV	Batting AB	H	HR	BA	PO	A	E	DP	TC/G	FA
1894			9	8	.529	5.78	23	15	10	134	178	66	17	0	2	2	1	57	17	0	.298	9	36	3	1	2.1	.938
1895			7	11	.389	5.96	25	18	16	178.1	243	78	36	0	0	2	0	111	29	2	.261	17	52	10	6	2.2	.873
1896	**2 teams**	**NY N**	(1G 0–0)		**WAS N**	(28G 2–20)																					
"	**total**		2	20	.091	6.43	29	20	14	169.1	249	75	20	0	1	**3**	1	71	16	1	.225	13	46	7	1	2.1	.894
1897	**WAS**	**N**	3	5	.375	5.59	15	5	4	83.2	117	33	2	0	2	1	0	44	15	0	.341	8	17	2	0	1.5	.926
6 yrs.			34	63	.351	5.49	129	92	73	849.1	1096	376	147	0	7	9	2	408	106	3	.260	61	203	34	8	2.0	.886

Ed Gerner

GERNER, EDWIN FREDERICK (Lefty) BL TL 5′ 8½″ 175 lbs.
B. July 22, 1897, Philadelphia, Pa. D. May 15, 1970, Philadelphia, Pa.

Year	Team		W	L	PCT	ERA	G	GS	CG	IP	H	BB	SO	ShO	Relief Pitching W	L	SV	Batting AB	H	HR	BA	PO	A	E	DP	TC/G	FA
1919	**CIN**	**N**	1	0	1.000	3.18	5	1	0	17	22	3	2	0	0	0	0	6	1	0	.167	1	7	0	1	1.6	1.000

Lefty Gervais

GERVAIS, LUCIEN EDWARD BL TL 5′10″ 165 lbs.
B. July 6, 1890, Grover, Wis. D. Oct. 19, 1950, Los Angeles, Calif.

Year	Team		W	L	PCT	ERA	G	GS	CG	IP	H	BB	SO	ShO	Relief Pitching W	L	SV	Batting AB	H	HR	BA	PO	A	E	DP	TC/G	FA
1913	**BOS**	**N**	0	1	.000	5.74	5	2	1	15.2	18	4	1	0	0	0	0	5	0	0	.000	0	4	1	0	1.0	.800

Charlie Gessner

GESSNER, CHARLES J.
B. Philadelphia, Pa. Deceased.

Year	Team		W	L	PCT	ERA	G	GS	CG	IP	H	BB	SO	ShO	Relief Pitching W	L	SV	Batting AB	H	HR	BA	PO	A	E	DP	TC/G	FA
1886	**PHI**	**AA**	0	1	.000	*9.00*	1	1	1	8	13	5	0	0	0	0	0	4	1	0	.250	0	1	2	0	3.0	.333

Al Gettel

GETTEL, ALLEN JONES BR TR 6′ 3½″ 200 lbs.
B. Sept. 17, 1917, Norfolk, Va.

Year	Team		W	L	PCT	ERA	G	GS	CG	IP	H	BB	SO	ShO	Relief Pitching W	L	SV	Batting AB	H	HR	BA	PO	A	E	DP	TC/G	FA
1945	**NY**	**A**	9	8	.529	3.90	27	17	9	154.2	141	53	67	0	0	0	3	57	16	0	.281	4	24	1	3	1.1	.966
1946			6	7	.462	2.97	26	11	5	103	89	40	54	2	3	0	0	32	4	0	.125	5	18	0	2	0.9	1.000
1947	**CLE**	**A**	11	10	.524	3.20	31	21	9	149	122	62	64	2	1	2	0	51	15	0	.294	7	28	0	1	1.1	1.000
1948	**2 teams**	**CLE A**	(5G 0–1)		**CHI A**	(22G 8–10)																					
"	**total**		8	11	.421	4.68	27	21	7	155.2	169	70	53	0	0	2	1	57	13	0	.228	5	26	0	3	1.0	1.000
1949	**2 teams**	**CHI A**	(19G 2–5)		**WAS A**	(16G 0–2)																					
"	**total**		2	7	.222	6.08	35	8	1	97.2	112	50	29	1	1	4	2	26	3	0	.115	5	18	0	1	0.7	1.000
1951	**NY**	**N**	1	2	.333	4.87	30	1	0	57.1	52	25	36	0	1	2	0	12	1	0	.083	4	13	1	0	0.6	.944
1955	**STL**	**N**	1	0	1.000	9.00	8	0	0	17	26	10	7	0	1	0	0	6	3	0	.500	1	1	2	0	0.5	.500
7 yrs.			38	45	.458	4.28	184	79	31	734.1	711	310	310	5	7	10	6	241	55	0	.228	31	128	4	10	0.9	.975

Charlie Gettig

GETTIG, CHARLES HENRY BR 5′10″ 172 lbs.
B. Dec. 1870, Baltimore, Md. D. Apr. 11, 1935, Baltimore, Md.

Year	Team		W	L	PCT	ERA	G	GS	CG	IP	H	BB	SO	ShO	Relief Pitching W	L	SV	Batting AB	H	HR	BA	PO	A	E	DP	TC/G	FA
1896	**NY**	**N**	1	0	1.000	9.64	4	1	1	14	20	8	5	0	0	0	1	9	3	0	.333	0	5	0	0	1.3	1.000
1897			1	1	.500	5.21	3	2	2	19	23	9	7	0	0	0	0	75	15	0	.200	19	26	16	1	2.8	.738
1898			6	3	.667	3.83	17	8	7	115	141	39	14	0	1	1	0	196	49	0	.250	70	103	21	6	2.9	.892
1899			7	8	.467	4.43	18	15	12	128	161	54	25	0	0	0	0	97	24	0	.247	27	59	16	0	3.1	.843
4 yrs.			15	12	.556	4.50	42	26	22	276	345	110	51	0	1	1	1	*				116	193	53	7	2.9	.854

Tom Gettinger

GETTINGER, LEWIS THOMAS LEYTON BL TL 5′10″ 180 lbs.
Born Lewis Thomas Leyton Gittinger.
B. Dec. 11, 1868, Frederick, Md. D. July 26, 1943, Pensacola, Fla.

Year	Team		W	L	PCT	ERA	G	GS	CG	IP	H	BB	SO	ShO	Relief Pitching W	L	SV	Batting AB	H	HR	BA	PO	A	E	DP	TC/G	FA
1895	**LOU**	**N**	0	0	—	7.11	2	0	0	6.1	13	1	0	0	0	0	0	*				6	0	2	0	2.0	.750

Charlie Getzien

GETZIEN, CHARLES H. (Pretzels) BR TR 5′10″ 172 lbs.
B. Feb. 14, 1864, Germany D. June 19, 1932, Chicago, Ill.

Year	Team		W	L	PCT	ERA	G	GS	CG	IP	H	BB	SO	ShO	Relief Pitching W	L	SV	Batting AB	H	HR	BA	PO	A	E	DP	TC/G	FA
1884	**DET**	**N**	5	12	.294	*1.95*	17	17	17	147.1	118	25	107	1	0	0	0	55	6	0	.109	3	22	7	1	1.9	.781
1885			12	25	.324	*3.03*	37	37	37	330	360	92	110	1	0	0	0	137	29	0	.212	18	66	10	0	2.4	.894
1886			30	11	.732	*3.03*	43	43	42	386.2	388	85	172	1	0	0	0	165	29	0	.176	17	65	1	3	1.9	.988
1887			29	13	**.690**	3.73	43	42	41	366.2	373	106	135	2	1	0	0	156	29	1	.186	23	58	3	1	1.9	.964
1888			19	25	.432	3.05	46	46	45	404	411	54	202	2	0	0	0	167	41	1	.246	29	70	16	5	2.5	.861
1889	**IND**	**N**	18	22	.450	4.54	45	44	36	349	395	100	139	0	0	0	1	139	25	2	.180	22	53	11	0	1.9	.872
1890	**BOS**	**N**	23	17	.575	3.19	40	40	39	350	342	82	140	4	0	0	0	147	34	2	.231	15	63	20	2	2.4	.796
1891	**2 teams**	**BOS N**	(11G 4–5)		**CLE N**	(1G 0–1)																					
"	**total**		4	6	.400	4.22	12	10	8	98	124	27	33	0	0	0	0	45	7	1	.156	6	22	3	1	2.1	.903
1892	**STL**	**N**	5	8	.385	5.67	13	13	12	108	159	31	32	0	0	0	0	45	9	1	.200	7	18	2	0	2.1	.926
9 yrs.			145	139	.511	3.46	296	292	277	2539.2	2670	602	1070	11	1	0	1	1056	209	8	.198	140	437	73	13	2.1	.888

Rube Geyer

GEYER, JACOB BOWMAN BR TR 5′10″ 170 lbs.
B. Mar. 22, 1884, Allegheny, Pa. D. Oct. 12, 1962, Wahkon, Minn.

Year	Team		W	L	PCT	ERA	G	GS	CG	IP	H	BB	SO	ShO	Relief Pitching W	L	SV	Batting AB	H	HR	BA	PO	A	E	DP	TC/G	FA
1910	**STL**	**N**	0	1	.000	4.50	4	0	0	4	5	3	5	0	0	1	0	1	0	0	.000	0	0	1	0	0.3	.000
1911			9	6	.600	3.27	29	11	7	148.2	141	56	46	1	3	2	0	57	13	0	.228	5	35	4	2	1.5	.909
1912			7	14	.333	3.28	41	18	6	181	191	84	61	0	4	3	0	53	11	0	.208	7	49	5	1	1.5	.918
1913			1	5	.167	5.26	30	4	2	78.2	83	38	21	0	0	2	1	22	2	0	.091	2	19	4	3	0.8	.840
4 yrs.			17	26	.395	3.67	104	33	15	412.1	420	181	133	1	7	8	1	133	26	0	.195	14	103	14	6	1.3	.893

Tony Ghelfi

GHELFI, ANTHONY PAUL BR TR 6′ 3″ 185 lbs.
B. Aug. 23, 1961, La Crosse, Wis.

Year	Team		W	L	PCT	ERA	G	GS	CG	IP	H	BB	SO	ShO	Relief Pitching W	L	SV	Batting AB	H	HR	BA	PO	A	E	DP	TC/G	FA
1983	**PHI**	**N**	1	1	.500	3.14	3	3	0	14.1	15	6	14	0	0	0	0	4	1	0	.250	0	5	0	0	1.7	1.000

Bob Giallombardo

GIALLOMBARDO, ROBERT PAUL BL TL 6′ 175 lbs.
B. May 20, 1937, Brooklyn, N. Y.

Year	Team		W	L	PCT	ERA	G	GS	CG	IP	H	BB	SO	ShO	Relief Pitching W	L	SV	Batting AB	H	HR	BA	PO	A	E	DP	TC/G	FA
1958	**LA**	**N**	1	1	.500	3.76	6	5	0	26.1	29	15	14	0	0	0	0	6	1	0	.167	2	7	3	1	2.0	.750

Joe Giard

GIARD, JOSEPH OSCAR (Peco) BL TL 5′10½″ 170 lbs.
B. Oct. 7, 1898, Ware, Mass. D. July 10, 1956, Worcester, Mass.

Year	Team		W	L	PCT	ERA	G	GS	CG	IP	H	BB	SO	ShO	Relief Pitching W	L	SV	Batting AB	H	HR	BA	PO	A	E	DP	TC/G	FA
1925	**STL**	**A**	10	5	.667	5.04	30	21	9	160.2	179	87	43	4	0	0	0	53	3	0	.057	18	44	4	3	2.2	.939
1926			3	10	.231	7.00	22	16	2	90	113	67	18	0	0	1	0	29	8	0	.276	6	18	2	2	1.2	.923
1927	**NY**	**A**	0	0	—	8.00	16	0	0	27	38	19	10	0	0	0	0	7	2	0	.286	2	5	1	0	0.5	.875
3 yrs.			13	15	.464	5.96	68	37	11	277.2	330	173	71	4	0	1	0	89	13	0	.146	26	67	7	5	1.5	.930

Joe Gibbon

GIBBON, JOSEPH CHARLES
B. Apr. 10, 1935, Hickory, Miss.

BR TL 6′ 4″ 210 lbs.
BB 1967–1968

Year	Team	W	L	PCT	ERA	G	GS	CG	IP	H	BB	SO	ShO	Relief W	Relief L	Relief SV	AB	H	HR	BA	PO	A	E	DP	TC/G	FA
1960	PIT N	4	2	.667	4.03	27	9	0	80.1	87	31	60	0	3	0	0	19	4	0	.211	2	15	1	1	0.7	.944
1961		13	10	.565	3.32	30	29	7	195.1	185	57	145	3	0	0	0	59	8	0	.136	3	35	0	2	1.3	1.000
1962		3	4	.429	3.63	19	8	0	57	53	24	26	0	1	1	0	17	3	0	.176	2	16	2	1	1.1	.900
1963		5	12	.294	3.30	37	22	5	147.1	147	54	110	0	1	1	1	43	4	0	.093	7	30	3	4	1.1	.925
1964		10	7	.588	3.68	28	24	3	146.2	145	54	97	0	1	0	0	47	12	0	.255	5	34	6	2	1.6	.867
1965		4	9	.308	4.51	31	15	1	105.2	85	34	63	0	3	1	1	26	3	0	.115	3	23	1	0	0.9	.963
1966	SF N	4	6	.400	3.67	37	10	1	81	86	16	48	0	1	3	1	15	3	0	.200	3	21	2	1	0.7	.923
1967		6	2	.750	3.07	28	10	3	82	65	33	63	1	1	0	1	24	1	0	.042	5	23	0	0	1.0	1.000
1968		1	2	.333	1.58	29	0	0	40	33	19	22	0	1	2	1	1	0	0	.000	2	7	0	0	0.3	1.000
1969	2 teams SF N (16G 1–3) PIT N (35G 5–1)																									
″	total	6	4	.600	2.40	51	0	0	71.1	53	30	44	0	6	4	11	8	0	0	.000	0	22	2	2	0.5	.917
1970	PIT N	0	1	.000	4.83	41	0	0	41	44	24	26	0	0	1	5	3	0	0	.000	3	7	1	0	0.3	.909
1971	CIN N	5	6	.455	2.95	50	0	0	64	54	32	34	0	5	6	11	1	0	0	.000	1	18	2	1	0.4	.905
1972	2 teams CIN N (2G 0–0) HOU N (9G 0–0)																									
″	total	0	0		11.74	11	0	0	7.2	16	6	5	0	0	0	0	0	0	0		2	3	0	0	0.5	1.000
13 yrs.		61	65	.484	3.52	419	127	20	1119.1	1053	414	743	4	23	19	32	263	38	0	.144	38	254	20	14	0.7	.936
LEAGUE CHAMPIONSHIP SERIES																										
1970	PIT N	0	0	—	0.00	2	0	0	0.1	1	0	1	0	0	0	0	0	0	0	—	0	0	0	0	0.0	.000
WORLD SERIES																										
1960	PIT N	0	0	—	9.00	2	0	0	3	4	1	2	0	0	0	0	0	0	0	—	1	0	0	0	0.5	1.000

Bob Gibson

GIBSON, PACK ROBERT (Hoot)
B. Nov. 9, 1935, Omaha, Neb.
Hall of Fame 1981.

BR TR 6′ 1″ 189 lbs.

Year	Team	W	L	PCT	ERA	G	GS	CG	IP	H	BB	SO	ShO	Relief W	Relief L	Relief SV	AB	H	HR	BA	PO	A	E	DP	TC/G	FA
1959	STL N	3	5	.375	3.33	13	9	2	75.2	77	39	48	1	1	0	0	26	3	0	.115	6	10	2	2	1.4	.889
1960		3	6	.333	5.61	27	12	2	86.2	97	48	69	0	1	0	0	28	5	0	.179	7	14	0	3	0.8	1.000
1961		13	12	.520	3.24	35	27	10	211.1	186	**119**	166	2	0	1	1	66	13	1	.197	14	35	2	4	1.5	.961
1962		15	13	.536	2.85	32	30	15	233.2	174	95	208	**5**	1	0	1	76	20	2	.263	18	35	3	6	1.8	.946
1963		18	9	.667	3.39	36	33	14	254.2	224	96	204	2	1	0	0	87	18	3	.207	27	28	5	0	1.7	.917
1964		19	12	.613	3.01	40	36	17	287.1	250	86	245	2	1	1	1	96	15	0	.156	24	36	6	4	1.6	.909
1965		20	12	.625	3.07	38	36	20	299	243	103	270	6	0	0	1	104	25	5	.240	27	33	3	1	1.7	.952
1966		21	12	.636	2.44	35	35	20	280.1	210	78	225	**5**	0	0	0	100	20	1	.200	26	28	2	4	1.6	.964
1967		13	7	.650	2.98	24	24	10	175.1	151	40	147	2	0	0	0	60	8	0	.133	19	23	0	0	1.8	1.000
1968		22	9	.710	**1.12**	34	34	28	304.2	198	62	**268**	**13**	0	0	0	94	16	0	.170	21	28	1	2	1.5	.980
1969		20	13	.606	2.18	35	35	**28**	314	251	95	269	4	0	0	0	118	29	1	.246	21	32	3	5	1.6	.946
1970		**23**	7	**.767**	3.12	34	34	23	294	262	88	274	3	0	0	0	109	33	2	.303	22	32	4	3	1.7	.931
1971		16	13	.552	3.04	31	31	20	246	215	76	185	**5**	0	0	0	87	15	2	.172	10	39	3	1	1.7	.942
1972		19	11	.633	2.46	34	34	23	278	226	88	208	4	0	0	0	103	20	5	.194	12	46	1	3	1.7	.983
1973		12	10	.545	2.77	25	25	13	195	159	57	142	1	0	0	0	65	12	2	.185	11	24	2	2	1.5	.946
1974		11	13	.458	3.83	33	33	9	240	236	104	129	1	0	0	0	81	17	0	.210	20	26	2	4	1.5	.958
1975		3	10	.231	5.04	22	14	1	109	120	62	60	0	1	2	2	28	5	0	.179	6	15	3	2	1.1	.875
17 yrs.		251	174	.591	2.91	528	482	255	3884.2	3279	1336	3117	56	6	4	6	1328	274	24	.206	291	484	42	46	1.5	.949
												10th														
WORLD SERIES																										
1964	STL N	2	1	.667	3.00	3	3	2	27	23	8	31	0	0	0	0	9	2	0	.222	1	2	0	0	1.0	1.000
1967		3	0	1.000	1.00	3	3	3	27	14	5	26	1	0	0	0	11	1	1	.091	2	3	0	0	1.7	1.000
1968		2	1	.667	1.67	3	3	3	27	18	4	35	1	0	0	0	8	1	1	.125	2	0	0	0	0.7	1.000
3 yrs.		7	2	.778	1.89	9	9	8	81	55	17	92	2	0	0	0	28	4	2	.143	5	5	0	0	1.1	1.000
		2nd					**6th**	**3rd**	**6th**			**2nd**	**4th**													

Bob Gibson

GIBSON, ROBERT LOUIS
B. June 19, 1957, Philadelphia, Pa.

BR TR 6′ 195 lbs.

Year	Team	W	L	PCT	ERA	G	GS	CG	IP	H	BB	SO	ShO	Relief W	Relief L	Relief SV	AB	H	HR	BA	PO	A	E	DP	TC/G	FA
1983	MIL A	3	4	.429	3.90	27	7	0	80.2	71	46	46	0	1	2	2	0	0	0	—	6	8	2	0	0.6	.875
1984		2	5	.286	4.96	18	9	1	69	61	47	54	1	0	0	0	0	0	0	—	11	7	0	0	1.0	1.000
1985		6	7	.462	3.90	41	1	0	92.1	86	49	53	0	6	6	11	0	0	0	—	8	10	0	2	0.4	1.000
1986		1	2	.333	4.72	11	1	0	26.2	23	23	11	0	1	1	0	0	0	0	—	4	1	0	0	0.5	1.000
1987	NY N	0	0	—	0.00	1	0	0	1	0	1	2	0	0	0	0	0	0	0	—	1	0	0	0	1.0	1.000
5 yrs.		12	18	.400	4.24	98	18	1	269.2	241	166	166	1	8	9	13	0	0	0		30	26	2	2	0.6	.966

Bob Gibson

GIBSON, ROBERT MURRAY
B. Aug. 20, 1869, Duncansville, Pa. D. Dec. 19, 1949, Pittsburgh, Pa.

BR TR 6′ 3″ 185 lbs.

Year	Team	W	L	PCT	ERA	G	GS	CG	IP	H	BB	SO	ShO	Relief W	Relief L	Relief SV	AB	H	HR	BA	PO	A	E	DP	TC/G	FA
1890	2 teams CHI N (1G 1–0) PIT N (3G 0–3)																									
″	total	1	3	.250	9.86	4	4	3	21	30	25	4	0	0	0	0	17	3	0	.176	1	4	5	0	1.7	.500

Norwood Gibson

GIBSON, NORWOOD RINGOLD
B. Mar. 11, 1877, Peoria, Ill. D. July 7, 1959, Peoria, Ill.

BR TR 5′10″ 165 lbs.

Year	Team	W	L	PCT	ERA	G	GS	CG	IP	H	BB	SO	ShO	Relief W	Relief L	Relief SV	AB	H	HR	BA	PO	A	E	DP	TC/G	FA
1903	BOS A	13	9	.591	3.19	24	21	17	183.1	166	65	76	2	1	0	0	64	17	0	.266	10	55	4	2	2.9	.942
1904		17	14	.548	2.21	33	32	29	273	216	81	112	1	0	0	0	92	6	0	.065	5	83	6	2	2.8	.936
1905		4	7	.364	3.69	23	17	9	134	118	55	67	0	0	1	0	45	4	0	.089	11	28	3	2	1.8	.929
1906		0	2	.000	5.30	5	2	1	18.2	25	7	3	0	0	0	0	5	1	0	.200	0	5	0	0	1.0	1.000
4 yrs.		34	32	.515	2.93	85	72	56	609	525	208	258	3	1	1	0	206	28	0	.136	26	171	13	6	2.5	.938

Paul Gibson

GIBSON, PAUL MARSHALL
B. Jan. 4, 1960, Southampton, N. Y.

BR TL 6′ 165 lbs.

Year	Team	W	L	PCT	ERA	G	GS	CG	IP	H	BB	SO	ShO	Relief W	Relief L	Relief SV	AB	H	HR	BA	PO	A	E	DP	TC/G	FA
1988	DET A	4	2	.667	2.93	40	1	0	92	83	34	50	0	3	2	0	0	0	0	—	7	11	0	2	0.4	1.000
1989		4	8	.333	4.64	45	13	0	132	129	57	77	0	3	3	0	0	0	0	—	6	20	2	0	0.6	.929
1990		5	4	.556	3.05	61	0	0	97.1	99	44	56	0	5	4	3	0	0	0	—	9	11	0	1	0.3	1.000
1991		5	7	.417	4.59	68	0	0	96	112	48	52	0	5	**7**	8	0	0	0	—	6	13	0	0	0.3	1.000
1992	NY N	0	1	.000	5.23	43	1	0	62	70	25	49	0	0	1	0	6	0	0	.000	2	6	0	0	0.2	1.000

Paul Gibson *continued*

Year	Team	W	L	PCT	ERA	G	GS	CG	IP	H	BB	SO	ShO	Relief Pitching W	Relief Pitching L	Relief Pitching SV	Batting AB	Batting H	Batting HR	BA	PO	A	E	DP	TC/G	FA
1993	2 teams NY N (8G 1–1) NY A (20G 2–0)																									
"	total	3	1	.750	3.48	28	0	0	44	45	11	37	0	3	1	0	0	0	0		3	5	0	1	0.3	1.000
1994	NY A	1	1	.500	4.97	30	0	0	29	26	17	21	0	1	1	0	0	0	0	—	2	4	0	0	0.2	1.000
7 yrs.		22	24	.478	4.06	315	15	0	552.1	564	236	342	0	20	19	11	6	0	0	.000	35	70	2	4	0.3	.981

Sam Gibson

GIBSON, SAMUEL BRAXTON
B. Aug. 5, 1899, King, N. C. D. Jan. 31, 1983, High Point, N. C.
BL TR 6′ 2″ 198 lbs.

Year	Team	W	L	PCT	ERA	G	GS	CG	IP	H	BB	SO	ShO	Relief Pitching W	Relief Pitching L	Relief Pitching SV	Batting AB	Batting H	Batting HR	BA	PO	A	E	DP	TC/G	FA
1926	DET A	12	9	.571	3.48	35	24	16	196.1	199	75	61	2	1	0	2	72	18	0	.250	4	50	1	3	1.6	.982
1927		11	12	.478	3.69	33	26	11	190.1	201	86	76	0	0	2	0	66	14	0	.212	7	38	3	0	1.5	.938
1928		5	8	.385	5.42	20	18	5	119.2	155	52	29	1	0	0	0	42	12	0	.286	7	24	1	2	1.6	.969
1930	NY A	0	1	.000	15.00	2	2	0	6	14	6	3	0	0	0	0	3	1	0	.333	1	1	0	0	1.0	1.000
1932	NY N	4	8	.333	4.85	41	5	1	81.2	107	30	39	1	2	5	3	19	5	0	.263	2	13	0	0	0.4	1.000
5 yrs.		32	38	.457	4.24	131	75	33	594	676	249	208	4	3	7	5	202	50	0	.248	21	126	5	5	1.2	.967

George Gick

GICK, GEORGE EDWARD
B. Oct. 18, 1915, Dunnington, Ind.
BB TR 6′ 190 lbs.

Year	Team	W	L	PCT	ERA	G	GS	CG	IP	H	BB	SO	ShO	Relief Pitching W	Relief Pitching L	Relief Pitching SV	Batting AB	Batting H	Batting HR	BA	PO	A	E	DP	TC/G	FA
1937	CHI A	0	0	—	0.00	1	0	0	2	0	0	1	0	0	0	1	0	0	0	—	0	0	0	0	0.0	.000
1938		0	0	—	0.00	1	0	0	1	0	0	1	0	0	0	0	0	0	0	—	0	0	0	0	0.0	.000
2 yrs.		0	0		0.00	2	0	0	3	0	0	2	0	0	0	1	0	0	0		0	0	0	0	0.0	

Brett Gideon

GIDEON, BYRON BRETT
B. Aug. 8, 1963, Ozona, Tex.
BR TR 6′ 2″ 200 lbs.

Year	Team	W	L	PCT	ERA	G	GS	CG	IP	H	BB	SO	ShO	Relief Pitching W	Relief Pitching L	Relief Pitching SV	Batting AB	Batting H	Batting HR	BA	PO	A	E	DP	TC/G	FA
1987	PIT N	1	5	.167	4.66	29	0	0	36.2	34	10	31	0	1	5	3	1	1	0	1.000	1	5	0	0	0.2	1.000
1989	MON N	0	0	—	1.93	4	0	0	4.2	5	5	2	0	0	0	0	0	0	0	—	0	0	0	0	0.0	.000
1990		0	0	—	9.00	1	0	0	1	2	4	0	0	0	0	0	0	0	0	—	0	1	0	0	1.0	1.000
3 yrs.		1	5	.167	4.46	34	0	0	42.1	41	19	33	0	1	5	3	1	1	0	1.000	1	6	0	0	0.2	1.000

Jim Gideon

GIDEON, JAMES LESLIE
B. Sept. 26, 1953, Taylor, Tex.
BR TR 6′ 3″ 190 lbs.

Year	Team	W	L	PCT	ERA	G	GS	CG	IP	H	BB	SO	ShO	Relief Pitching W	Relief Pitching L	Relief Pitching SV	Batting AB	Batting H	Batting HR	BA	PO	A	E	DP	TC/G	FA
1975	TEX A	0	0	—	7.94	1	1	0	5.2	7	5	2	0	0	0	0	0	0	0	—	0	0	0	0	0.0	.000

Floyd Giebell

GIEBELL, FLOYD GEORGE
B. Dec. 10, 1909, Pennsboro, W. Va.
BL TR 6′ 2½″ 172 lbs.

Year	Team	W	L	PCT	ERA	G	GS	CG	IP	H	BB	SO	ShO	Relief Pitching W	Relief Pitching L	Relief Pitching SV	Batting AB	Batting H	Batting HR	BA	PO	A	E	DP	TC/G	FA
1939	DET A	1	1	.500	2.93	9	0	0	15.1	19	12	9	0	1	1	0	2	0	0	.000	1	1	1	0	0.3	.667
1940		2	0	1.000	1.00	2	2	2	18	14	4	11	1	0	0	0	6	0	0	.000	2	2	0	0	2.0	1.000
1941		0	0	—	6.03	17	2	0	34.1	45	26	10	0	0	0	0	6	2	0	.333	1	7	1	0	0.5	.889
3 yrs.		3	1	.750	3.99	28	4	2	67.2	78	42	30	1	1	1	0	14	2	0	.143	4	10	2	0	0.6	.875

Paul Giel

GIEL, PAUL ROBERT
B. Sept. 29, 1932, Winona, Minn.
BR TR 5′11″ 185 lbs.

Year	Team	W	L	PCT	ERA	G	GS	CG	IP	H	BB	SO	ShO	Relief Pitching W	Relief Pitching L	Relief Pitching SV	Batting AB	Batting H	Batting HR	BA	PO	A	E	DP	TC/G	FA
1954	NY N	0	0	—	8.31	6	0	0	4.1	8	2	4	0	0	0	0	0	0	0	—	0	0	0	0	0.0	.000
1955		4	4	.500	3.39	34	2	0	82.1	70	50	47	0	4	3	0	19	1	0	.053	4	10	0	1	0.4	1.000
1958	SF N	4	5	.444	4.70	29	9	0	92	89	55	55	0	2	0	0	27	2	0	.074	8	18	0	2	0.9	1.000
1959	PIT N	0	0	—	14.09	4	0	0	7.2	17	6	3	0	0	0	0	0	0	0	—	0	2	0	0	0.5	1.000
1960		2	0	1.000	5.73	16	0	0	33	35	15	21	0	2	0	0	7	0	0	.000	2	3	1	0	0.4	.833
1961	2 teams MIN A (12G 1–0) KC A (1G 0–0)																									
"	total	1	0	1.000	12.00	13	0	0	21	30	20	15	0	1	0	0	2	1	0	.500	1	5	2	0	0.6	.750
6 yrs.		11	9	.550	5.39	102	11	0	240.1	249	148	145	0	9	3	0	55	4	0	.073	15	38	3	3	0.5	.946

Bob Giggie

GIGGIE, ROBERT THOMAS
B. Aug. 13, 1933, Dorchester, Mass.
BR TR 6′ 1″ 200 lbs.

Year	Team	W	L	PCT	ERA	G	GS	CG	IP	H	BB	SO	ShO	Relief Pitching W	Relief Pitching L	Relief Pitching SV	Batting AB	Batting H	Batting HR	BA	PO	A	E	DP	TC/G	FA
1959	MIL N	1	0	1.000	4.05	13	0	0	20	24	10	15	0	1	0	1	1	0	0	.000	0	8	0	0	0.6	1.000
1960	2 teams MIL N (3G 0–0) KC A (10G 1–0)																									
"	total	1	0	1.000	5.48	13	0	0	23	29	19	13	0	1	0	0	2	0	0	.000	1	4	0	0	0.4	1.000
1962	KC A	1	1	.500	6.28	4	2	0	14.1	17	3	4	0	0	0	0	4	0	0	.000	1	0	0	0	0.3	1.000
3 yrs.		3	1	.750	5.18	30	2	0	57.1	70	32	32	0	2	0	1	7	0	0	.000	2	12	0	0	0.5	1.000

Bill Gilbert

GILBERT, ALFRED GIDEON
B. Mar. 13, 1868, Havre de Grace, Md. Deceased.
6′ 180 lbs.

Year	Team	W	L	PCT	ERA	G	GS	CG	IP	H	BB	SO	ShO	Relief Pitching W	Relief Pitching L	Relief Pitching SV	Batting AB	Batting H	Batting HR	BA	PO	A	E	DP	TC/G	FA
1892	BAL N	0	1	.000	5.79	2	1	1	14	14	17	5	0	0	0	0	6	2	0	.333	0	0	1	0	0.5	.000

Joe Gilbert

GILBERT, JOE DENNIS
B. Apr. 20, 1952, Jasper, Tex.
BR TL 6′ 1″ 167 lbs.

Year	Team	W	L	PCT	ERA	G	GS	CG	IP	H	BB	SO	ShO	Relief Pitching W	Relief Pitching L	Relief Pitching SV	Batting AB	Batting H	Batting HR	BA	PO	A	E	DP	TC/G	FA
1972	MON N	0	1	.000	8.45	22	0	0	33	41	18	25	0	0	1	0	3	0	0	.000	0	3	0	0	0.1	1.000
1973		1	2	.333	4.97	21	0	0	29	30	19	17	0	1	2	1	2	0	0	.000	1	5	0	0	0.3	1.000
2 yrs.		1	3	.250	6.82	43	0	0	62	71	37	42	0	1	3	1	5	0	0	.000	1	8	0	0	0.2	1.000

Bill Gilbreth

GILBRETH, WILLIAM FREEMAN
B. Sept. 3, 1947, Abilene, Tex.
BL TL 6′ 180 lbs.

Year	Team	W	L	PCT	ERA	G	GS	CG	IP	H	BB	SO	ShO	Relief Pitching W	Relief Pitching L	Relief Pitching SV	Batting AB	Batting H	Batting HR	BA	PO	A	E	DP	TC/G	FA
1971	DET A	2	1	.667	4.80	9	5	2	30	28	21	14	0	0	0	0	11	2	0	.182	1	7	0	0	0.9	1.000
1972		0	0	—	16.20	2	0	0	5	10	4	2	0	0	0	0	1	0	0	.000	0	1	0	0	0.5	1.000
1974	CAL A	0	0	—	13.50	3	0	0	1.1	2	1	0	0	0	0	0	0	0	0	—	0	0	0	0	0.0	.000
3 yrs.		2	1	.667	6.69	14	5	2	36.1	40	26	16	0	0	0	0	12	2	0	.167	1	8	0	0	0.6	1.000

Bob Gilks

GILKS, ROBERT JAMES
B. July 2, 1864, Cincinnati, Ohio D. Aug. 21, 1944, Brunswick, Ga.
BR TR 5′ 8″ 178 lbs.

Year	Team	W	L	PCT	ERA	G	GS	CG	IP	H	BB	SO	ShO	Relief Pitching W	Relief Pitching L	Relief Pitching SV	Batting AB	Batting H	Batting HR	BA	PO	A	E	DP	TC/G	FA
1887	CLE AA	7	5	.583	*3.08*	13	13	12	108	104	42	28	1	0	0	0	83	26	0	.313	65	33	7	6	4.6	.933
1888		0	2	.000	8.14	4	2	2	21	26	8	3	0	0	0	**1**	484	111	1	.229	172	94	38	12	2.5	.875
1890	CLE N	2	2	.500	4.26	4	3	3	31.2	34	9	5	0	1	0	0	544	116	0	.213	172	54	9	9	4.4	.962
3 yrs.		9	9	.500	3.98	21	18	17	160.2	164	59	36	1	1	0	1	*				684	225	75	33	2.8	.924

Ed Gill

GILL, EDWARD JAMES
B. Aug. 7, 1895, Somerville, Mass. D. Oct. 10, 1995, Brockton, Mass.
BL TR 5′10″ 165 lbs.

Year	Team	W	L	PCT	ERA	G	GS	CG	IP	H	BB	SO	ShO	Relief Pitching W	Relief Pitching L	Relief Pitching SV	Batting AB	Batting H	Batting HR	BA	PO	A	E	DP	TC/G	FA
1919	WAS A	1	1	.500	4.82	16	2	0	37.1	38	21	7	0	0	1	0	7	0	0	.000	1	8	1	0	0.6	.900

George Gill

GILL, GEORGE LLOYD BR TR 6′ 1″ 185 lbs.
B. Feb. 13, 1909, Catchings, Miss.

Year	Team	W	L	PCT	ERA	G	GS	CG	IP	H	BB	SO	ShO	Relief W	Relief L	Relief SV	AB	H	HR	BA	PO	A	E	DP	TC/G	FA
1937	DET A	11	4	.733	4.51	31	10	4	127.2	146	42	40	1	7	1	1	50	7	0	.140	3	32	2	3	1.2	.946
1938		12	9	.571	4.12	24	23	13	164	195	50	30	1	0	0	0	57	6	0	.105	3	32	1	10	1.5	.972
1939	2 teams DET A (3G 0–1) STL A (27G 1–12)																									
"	total	1	13	.071	7.21	30	12	5	103.2	153	37	25	0	0	4	0	28	4	0	.143	2	15	2	2	0.6	.895
3 yrs.		24	26	.480	5.05	85	45	22	395.1	494	129	95	2	7	5	1	135	17	0	.126	8	79	5	15	1.1	.946

Haddie Gill

GILL, HAROLD EDWARD BL TL 5′11″ 165 lbs.
B. Jan. 23, 1899, Brockton, Mass. D. Aug. 1, 1932, Brockton, Mass.

Year	Team	W	L	PCT	ERA	G	GS	CG	IP	H	BB	SO	ShO	Relief W	Relief L	Relief SV	AB	H	HR	BA	PO	A	E	DP	TC/G	FA
1923	CIN N	0	0	—	0.00	1	0	0	1	1	1	1	0	0	0	0	0	0	0	—	0	0	0	0	0.0	.000

Claral Gillenwater

GILLENWATER, CLARAL LEWIS BR TR 6′ 187 lbs.
B. May 20, 1900, Sims, Ind. D. Feb. 26, 1978, Bradenton, Fla.

Year	Team	W	L	PCT	ERA	G	GS	CG	IP	H	BB	SO	ShO	Relief W	Relief L	Relief SV	AB	H	HR	BA	PO	A	E	DP	TC/G	FA
1923	CHI A	1	3	.250	5.48	5	3	1	21.1	28	6	2	1	1	1	0	6	0	0	.000	0	7	1	0	1.6	.875

Tom Gilles

GILLES, THOMAS BRADFORD BR TR 6′ 1″ 185 lbs.
B. July 2, 1962, Peoria, Ill.

Year	Team	W	L	PCT	ERA	G	GS	CG	IP	H	BB	SO	ShO	Relief W	Relief L	Relief SV	AB	H	HR	BA	PO	A	E	DP	TC/G	FA
1990	TOR A	1	0	1.000	6.75	2	0	0	1.1	2	0	1	0	1	0	0	0	0	0	—	0	1	0	0	0.5	1.000

Bob Gillespie

GILLESPIE, ROBERT WILLIAM (Bunch) BR TR 6′ 4″ 187 lbs.
B. Oct. 8, 1918, Columbus, Ohio.

Year	Team	W	L	PCT	ERA	G	GS	CG	IP	H	BB	SO	ShO	Relief W	Relief L	Relief SV	AB	H	HR	BA	PO	A	E	DP	TC/G	FA
1944	DET A	0	1	.000	6.55	7	0	0	11	7	12	4	0	0	1	0	2	0	0	.000	0	3	0	0	0.4	1.000
1947	CHI A	5	8	.385	4.73	25	17	1	118	133	53	36	0	0	0	0	33	2	0	.061	4	35	1	0	1.6	.975
1948		0	4	.000	5.13	25	6	1	72	81	33	19	0	0	0	0	16	0	0	.000	3	13	0	0	0.6	1.000
1950	BOS A	0	0	—	20.25	1	0	0	1.1	2	4	0	0	0	0	0	0	0	0	—	0	0	0	0	0.0	.000
4 yrs.		5	13	.278	5.07	58	23	2	202.1	223	102	59	0	0	1	0	51	2	0	.039	7	51	1	0	1.0	.983

John Gillespie

GILLESPIE, JOHN PATRICK (Silent John) BR TR 5′11½″ 172 lbs.
B. Feb. 25, 1900, Oakland, Calif. D. Feb. 15, 1954, Vallejo, Calif.

Year	Team	W	L	PCT	ERA	G	GS	CG	IP	H	BB	SO	ShO	Relief W	Relief L	Relief SV	AB	H	HR	BA	PO	A	E	DP	TC/G	FA
1922	CIN N	3	3	.500	4.52	31	4	1	77.2	84	29	21	0	2	2	0	15	2	0	.133	4	20	0	0	0.8	1.000

Paul Gilliford

GILLIFORD, PAUL GANT (Gorilla) BR TL 5′11″ 210 lbs.
B. Jan. 12, 1945, Bryn Mawr, Pa.

Year	Team	W	L	PCT	ERA	G	GS	CG	IP	H	BB	SO	ShO	Relief W	Relief L	Relief SV	AB	H	HR	BA	PO	A	E	DP	TC/G	FA
1967	BAL A	0	0	—	12.00	2	0	0	3	6	1	2	0	0	0	0	0	0	0	—	0	2	0	0	1.0	1.000

Jack Gilligan

GILLIGAN, JOHN PATRICK BB TR 6′ 190 lbs.
B. Oct. 18, 1885, Chicago, Ill. D. Nov. 19, 1980, Modesto, Calif.

Year	Team	W	L	PCT	ERA	G	GS	CG	IP	H	BB	SO	ShO	Relief W	Relief L	Relief SV	AB	H	HR	BA	PO	A	E	DP	TC/G	FA
1909	STL A	1	2	.333	5.48	3	3	3	23	28	9	4	0	0	0	0	9	1	0	.111	0	5	0	0	1.7	1.000
1910		0	3	.000	3.66	9	5	2	39.1	37	28	10	0	0	1	0	15	3	0	.200	1	17	5	1	2.6	.783
2 yrs.		1	5	.167	4.33	12	8	5	62.1	65	37	14	0	0	1	0	24	4	0	.167	1	22	5	1	2.3	.821

George Gillpatrick

GILLPATRICK, GEORGE F.
B. Feb. 28, 1875, Holden, Mo. D. Dec. 15, 1941, Kansas City, Mo.

Year	Team	W	L	PCT	ERA	G	GS	CG	IP	H	BB	SO	ShO	Relief W	Relief L	Relief SV	AB	H	HR	BA	PO	A	E	DP	TC/G	FA
1898	STL N	0	2	.000	6.94	7	3	1	35	42	19	12	0	0	0	0	16	2	0	.125	2	6	4	0	1.7	.667

Frank Gilmore

GILMORE, FRANK T. BR
B. Apr. 27, 1864, Webster, Mass. D. July 21, 1929, Hartford, Conn.

Year	Team	W	L	PCT	ERA	G	GS	CG	IP	H	BB	SO	ShO	Relief W	Relief L	Relief SV	AB	H	HR	BA	PO	A	E	DP	TC/G	FA
1886	WAS N	4	4	.500	2.52	9	9	9	75	57	22	75	1	0	0	0	29	0	0	.000	2	8	0	0	1.1	1.000
1887		7	20	.259	3.87	28	27	27	234.2	247	92	114	1	0	0	0	93	6	0	.065	3	28	2	0	1.2	.939
1888		1	9	.100	6.59	12	11	10	95.2	131	29	23	0	0	0	0	41	1	0	.024	4	12	4	1	1.4	.800
3 yrs.		12	33	.267	4.26	49	47	46	405.1	435	143	212	2	0	0	0	163	7	0	.043	9	48	6	1	1.2	.905

Len Gilmore

GILMORE, LEONARD PRESTON (Meow) BR TR 6′ 3″ 175 lbs.
B. Nov. 3, 1917, Fairview Park, Ind.

Year	Team	W	L	PCT	ERA	G	GS	CG	IP	H	BB	SO	ShO	Relief W	Relief L	Relief SV	AB	H	HR	BA	PO	A	E	DP	TC/G	FA
1944	PIT N	0	1	.000	7.88	1	1	1	8	13	0	0	0	0	0	0	2	0	0	.000	2	4	1	0	7.0	.857

John Gilroy

GILROY, JOHN M.
B. Oct. 26, 1869, Washington, D. C. D. Aug. 4, 1897, Norfolk, Va.

Year	Team	W	L	PCT	ERA	G	GS	CG	IP	H	BB	SO	ShO	Relief W	Relief L	Relief SV	AB	H	HR	BA	PO	A	E	DP	TC/G	FA
1895	WAS N	1	4	.200	6.53	8	4	2	41.1	63	24	2	0	0	1	0	29	7	0	.241	10	10	1	0	1.8	.952
1896		0	0	—	0.00	1	0	0	2	0	1	0	0	0	0	0	1	0	0	.000	1	0	0	0	1.0	1.000
2 yrs.		1	4	.200	6.23	9	4	2	43.1	63	25	2	0	0	1	0	30	7	0	.233	11	10	1	0	1.7	.955

Hal Gilson

GILSON, HAROLD (Lefty) BR TL 6′ 5″ 195 lbs.
B. Feb. 9, 1942, Los Angeles, Calif.

Year	Team	W	L	PCT	ERA	G	GS	CG	IP	H	BB	SO	ShO	Relief W	Relief L	Relief SV	AB	H	HR	BA	PO	A	E	DP	TC/G	FA
1968	2 teams STL N (13G 0–2) HOU N (2G 0–0)																									
"	total	0	2	.000	4.97	15	0	0	25.1	34	12	20	0	0	2	2	4	0	0	.000	1	1	0	0	0.1	1.000

Billy Ging

GING, WILLIAM JOSEPH BR TR 5′10″ 170 lbs.
B. Nov. 7, 1872, Elmira, N. Y. D. Sept. 14, 1950, Elmira, N. Y.

Year	Team	W	L	PCT	ERA	G	GS	CG	IP	H	BB	SO	ShO	Relief W	Relief L	Relief SV	AB	H	HR	BA	PO	A	E	DP	TC/G	FA
1899	BOS N	1	0	1.000	1.13	1	1	1	8	5	5	2	0	0	0	0	2	0	0	.000	0	0	0	0	0.0	.000

Joe Gingras

GINGRAS, JOSEPH JOHN BR TR 6′ 2″ 188 lbs.
B. Jan. 10, 1893, New York, N. Y. D. Sept. 6, 1947, Jersey City, N. J.

Year	Team	W	L	PCT	ERA	G	GS	CG	IP	H	BB	SO	ShO	Relief W	Relief L	Relief SV	AB	H	HR	BA	PO	A	E	DP	TC/G	FA
1915	KC F	0	0	—	6.75	2	0	0	4	6	1	2	0	0	0	0	1	0	0	.000	0	1	0	0	0.5	1.000

Charlie Girard

GIRARD, CHARLES AUGUST BR TR 5′10″ 175 lbs.
B. Dec. 16, 1884, Brooklyn, N. Y. D. Aug. 6, 1936, Brooklyn, N. Y.

Year	Team	W	L	PCT	ERA	G	GS	CG	IP	H	BB	SO	ShO	Relief W	Relief L	Relief SV	AB	H	HR	BA	PO	A	E	DP	TC/G	FA
1910	PHI N	0	2	.000	6.41	7	1	0	26.2	33	12	11	0	0	1	0	8	1	0	.125	2	2	2	0	0.9	.667

Dave Giusti

GIUSTI, DAVID JOHN BR TR 5′11″ 190 lbs.
B. Nov. 27, 1939, Seneca Falls, N. Y.

Year	Team	W	L	PCT	ERA	G	GS	CG	IP	H	BB	SO	ShO	Relief W	Relief L	Relief SV	AB	H	HR	BA	PO	A	E	DP	TC/G	FA
1962	HOU N	2	3	.400	5.62	22	5	0	73.2	82	30	43	0	2	0	0	24	7	0	.292	8	13	1	2	1.0	.955
1964		0	0	—	3.16	8	0	0	25.2	24	8	16	0	0	0	0	7	2	0	.286	6	7	1	0	1.8	.929
1965		8	7	.533	4.32	38	13	4	131.1	132	46	92	1	4	3	3	35	6	1	.171	17	24	1	0	1.1	.976
1966		15	14	.517	4.20	34	33	9	210	215	54	131	4	0	0	0	74	17	0	.230	18	24	1	0	1.3	.977
1967		11	15	.423	4.18	37	33	8	221.2	231	58	157	1	0	1	1	84	13	3	.155	14	26	1	0	1.1	.976

Dave Giusti *continued*

Year	Team		W	L	PCT	ERA	G	GS	CG	IP	H	BB	SO	ShO	Relief Pitching W	Relief Pitching L	Relief Pitching SV	Batting AB	Batting H	Batting HR	BA	PO	A	E	DP	TC/G	FA
1968			11	14	.440	3.19	37	34	12	251	226	67	186	2	0	0	1	82	15	0	.183	20	51	2	3	2.0	.973
1969	STL	N	3	7	.300	3.60	22	12	2	100	96	37	62	1	0	0	0	25	5	0	.200	5	20	1	1	1.2	.962
1970	PIT	N	9	3	.750	3.06	66	1	0	103	98	39	85	0	**9**	3	26	16	3	0	.188	5	14	0	1	0.3	1.000
1971			5	6	.455	2.93	58	0	0	86	79	31	55	0	5	6	**30**	17	1	0	.059	6	7	1	1	0.2	.929
1972			7	4	.636	1.93	54	0	0	74.2	59	20	54	0	7	4	22	10	0	0	.000	1	15	1	0	0.3	.941
1973			9	2	.818	2.37	67	0	0	98.2	89	37	64	0	9	2	20	13	4	0	.308	10	4	1	0	0.2	.933
1974			7	5	.583	3.31	64	2	0	106	101	40	53	0	6	5	12	9	1	0	.111	8	21	0	1	0.5	1.000
1975			5	4	.556	2.93	61	0	0	92	79	42	38	0	5	4	17	10	3	0	.300	4	17	3	0	0.4	.875
1976			5	4	.556	4.32	40	0	0	58.1	59	27	24	0	5	4	6	4	0	0	.000	4	11	1	0	0.4	.938
1977	**2 teams**	**CHI N**	(20G 0–2)		**OAK A**	(40G 3–3)																					
″	**total**		3	5	.375	3.92	60	0	0	85	84	34	43	0	3	5	7	2	0	0	.000	8	10	0	2	0.3	1.000
15 yrs.			100	93	.518	3.60	668	133	35	1717	1654	570	1103	9	55	37	145	412	77	4	.187	134	264	15	11	0.6	.964
LEAGUE CHAMPIONSHIP SERIES																											
1970	PIT	N	0	0	—	3.86	2	0	0	2.1	3	1	1	0	0	0	0	0	0	0	—	1	0	0	0	0.5	1.000
1971			0	0	—	0.00	4	0	0	5.1	1	2	3	0	0	0	3	1	0	0	.000	0	1	0	0	0.3	1.000
1972			0	1	.000	6.75	3	0	0	2.2	5	0	3	0	0	1	1	1	0	0	.000	1	0	0	0	0.3	1.000
1974			0	1	.000	21.60	3	0	0	3.1	13	5	1	0	0	1	0	0	0	0	—	1	2	0	0	1.0	1.000
1975			0	0	—	0.00	1	1	0	1.1	0	0	1	0	0	0	0	0	0	0	—	0	0	0	0	0.0	.000
5 yrs.			0	2	.000	6.60	13 **5th**	1	0	15	22	8	9	0	0	2	4 **3rd**	2	0	0	.000	3	3	0	0	0.5	1.000
WORLD SERIES																											
1971	PIT	N	0	0	—	0.00	3	0	0	5.1	3	2	4	0	0	0	1	0	0	0	—	0	0	0	0	0.0	.000

Brian Givens

GIVENS, BRIAN ALLEN BR TL 6′ 6″ 220 lbs.
B. Nov. 6, 1965, Lompoc, Calif.

Year	Team		W	L	PCT	ERA	G	GS	CG	IP	H	BB	SO	ShO	Relief W	Relief L	SV	AB	H	HR	BA	PO	A	E	DP	TC/G	FA
1995	MIL	A	5	7	.417	4.95	19	19	0	107.1	116	54	73	0	0	0	0	0	0	0	—	4	10	2	2	0.8	.875

Dan Gladden

GLADDEN, CLINTON DANIEL III BR TR 5′11″ 175 lbs.
B. July 7, 1957, San Jose, Calif.

Year	Team		W	L	PCT	ERA	G	GS	CG	IP	H	BB	SO	ShO	Relief W	Relief L	SV	AB	H	HR	BA	PO	A	E	DP	TC/G	FA
1988	MIN	A	0	0	—	0.00	1	0	0	1	0	0	0	0	0	0	0	576	155	11	.269	53	0	0	0	2.9	1.000
1989			0	0	—	9.00	1	0	0	1	2	1	0	0	0	0	0	461	136	8	.295	245	8	9	3	2.2	.966
2 yrs.			0	0		4.50	2	0	0	2	2	1	0	0	0	0	0	*				2520	81	43	20	2.3	.984

Fred Gladding

GLADDING, FRED EARL BL TR 6′ 1″ 220 lbs.
B. June 28, 1936, Flat Rock, Mich.

Year	Team		W	L	PCT	ERA	G	GS	CG	IP	H	BB	SO	ShO	Relief W	Relief L	SV	AB	H	HR	BA	PO	A	E	DP	TC/G	FA
1961	DET	A	1	0	1.000	3.31	8	0	0	16.1	18	11	11	0	1	0	0	3	0	0	.000	1	1	1	0	0.4	.667
1962			0	0	—	0.00	6	0	0	5	3	2	4	0	0	0	0	0	0	0	—	0	2	0	0	0.3	1.000
1963			1	1	.500	1.98	22	0	0	27.1	19	14	24	0	1	1	7	1	0	0	.000	1	6	0	0	0.3	1.000
1964			7	4	.636	3.07	42	0	0	67.1	57	27	59	0	7	4	7	9	0	0	.000	5	12	0	0	0.4	1.000
1965			6	2	.750	2.83	46	0	0	70	63	29	43	0	6	2	5	7	0	0	.000	2	9	1	0	0.3	.917
1966			5	0	1.000	3.28	51	0	0	74	62	29	57	0	5	0	2	2	0	0	.000	1	11	2	0	0.3	.857
1967			6	4	.600	1.99	42	1	0	77	62	19	64	0	6	4	12	18	0	0	.000	5	9	1	1	0.4	.933
1968	HOU	N	0	0	—	14.54	7	0	0	4.1	8	3	2	0	0	0	2	0	0	0	—	1	0	0	0	0.1	1.000
1969			4	8	.333	4.19	57	0	0	73	83	27	40	0	4	8	**29**	10	1	0	.100	5	12	0	0	0.3	1.000
1970			7	4	.636	4.06	63	0	0	71	84	24	46	0	7	4	18	6	0	0	.000	7	15	1	1	0.4	.957
1971			4	5	.444	2.12	48	0	0	51	51	22	17	0	4	5	12	2	0	0	.000	3	3	2	0	0.2	.750
1972			5	6	.455	2.77	42	0	0	48.2	38	12	18	0	5	6	14	5	0	0	.000	1	4	1	0	0.1	.833
1973			2	0	1.000	4.50	16	0	0	16	18	4	9	0	2	0	1	0	0	0	—	1	3	0	0	0.3	1.000
13 yrs.			48	34	.585	3.13	450	1	0	601	566	223	394	0	48	34	109	63	1	0	.016	33	87	9	2	0.3	.930

Fred Glade

GLADE, FREDERICK MONROE BR TR 5′10″ 175 lbs.
B. Jan. 25, 1876, Dubuque, Iowa D. Nov. 21, 1934, Grand Island, Neb.

Year	Team		W	L	PCT	ERA	G	GS	CG	IP	H	BB	SO	ShO	Relief W	Relief L	SV	AB	H	HR	BA	PO	A	E	DP	TC/G	FA
1902	CHI	N	0	1	.000	9.00	1	1	1	8	13	3	3	0	0	0	0	3	1	0	.333	1	2	0	0	3.0	1.000
1904	STL	A	18	15	.545	2.27	35	34	30	289	248	58	156	6	0	0	1	102	19	0	.186	14	100	9	2	3.5	.927
1905			6	**25**	.194	2.81	32	32	28	275	257	58	127	2	0	0	0	98	9	0	.092	13	102	4	2	3.7	.966
1906			15	14	.517	2.36	35	32	28	266.2	215	59	96	4	0	0	1	95	13	0	.137	5	73	6	4	2.4	.929
1907			13	9	.591	2.67	24	22	18	202	187	45	71	2	0	1	0	73	15	0	.205	3	45	4	3	2.2	.923
1908	NY	A	0	4	.000	4.22	5	5	2	32	30	14	11	0	0	0	0	10	0	0	.000	1	7	1	0	1.8	.889
6 yrs.			52	68	.433	2.62	132	126	107	1072.2	950	237	464	14	0	1	2	381	57	0	.150	37	329	24	11	3.0	.938

John Glaiser

GLAISER, JOHN BURKE (Bert) BR TR 5′ 8″ 165 lbs.
B. July 28, 1894, Yoakum, Tex. D. Mar. 7, 1959, Houston, Tex.

Year	Team		W	L	PCT	ERA	G	GS	CG	IP	H	BB	SO	ShO	Relief W	Relief L	SV	AB	H	HR	BA	PO	A	E	DP	TC/G	FA
1920	DET	A	0	0	—	6.35	9	1	0	17	23	8	3	0	0	0	1	3	0	0	.000	1	11	0	0	1.3	1.000

Tom Glass

GLASS, THOMAS JOSEPH BR TR 6′ 3″ 170 lbs.
B. Apr. 29, 1898, Greensboro, N. C. D. Dec. 15, 1981, Greensboro, N. C.

Year	Team		W	L	PCT	ERA	G	GS	CG	IP	H	BB	SO	ShO	Relief W	Relief L	SV	AB	H	HR	BA	PO	A	E	DP	TC/G	FA
1925	PHI	A	1	0	1.000	5.40	2	0	0	5	9	0	2	0	1	0	0	2	0	0	.000	0	1	1	0	1.0	.500

Jack Glasscock

GLASSCOCK, JOHN WESLEY (Old Battle Ax) BR TR 5′ 8″ 160 lbs.
B. July 22, 1859, Wheeling, W. Va. D. Feb. 24, 1947, Wheeling, W. Va.
Manager 1889, 1892.

Year	Team		W	L	PCT	ERA	G	GS	CG	IP	H	BB	SO	ShO	Relief W	Relief L	SV	AB	H	HR	BA	PO	A	E	DP	TC/G	FA
1884	CLE	N	0	0	—	*5.40*	2	0	0	5	8	2	1	0	0	0	0	453	142	3	.313	233	238	43	18	6.4	.916
1887	IND	N	0	0	—	0.00	1	0	0	1	0	0	1	0	0	0	0	483	142	0	.294	107	252	44	21	5.2	.891
1888			0	0	—	54.00	1	0	0	0.1	1	2	1	0	0	0	0	442	119	1	.269	209	347	61	39	5.4	.901
1889			0	0	—	0.00	1	0	0	0.2	3	3	0	0	0	0	0	582	205	7	.352	249	485	68	61	5.9	.915
4 yrs.			0	0		6.43	5	0	0	7	12	7	3	0	0	0	0	*				3163	5949	895	656	5.8	.911

Luke Glavenich

GLAVENICH, LUKE FRANK BR TR 5′ 9½″ 189 lbs.
B. Jan. 17, 1893, Jackson, Calif. D. May 22, 1935, Stockton, Calif.

Year	Team		W	L	PCT	ERA	G	GS	CG	IP	H	BB	SO	ShO	Relief W	Relief L	SV	AB	H	HR	BA	PO	A	E	DP	TC/G	FA
1913	CLE	A	0	0	—	9.00	1	0	0	1	3	3	1	0	0	0	0	0	0	0	—	0	0	1	0	1.0	.000

Tom Glavine

GLAVINE, THOMAS MICHAEL BL TL 6′ 175 lbs.
B. Mar. 25, 1966, Concord, Mass.

Year	Team	W	L	PCT	ERA	G	GS	CG	IP	H	BB	SO	ShO	Relief W	Relief L	Relief SV	Batting AB	Batting H	Batting HR	BA	PO	A	E	DP	TC/G	FA
1987	ATL N	2	4	.333	5.54	9	9	0	50.1	55	33	20	0	0	0	0	16	2	0	.125	1	13	1	0	1.7	.933
1988		7	**17**	.292	4.56	34	34	1	195.1	201	63	84	0	0	0	0	60	11	0	.183	12	41	4	3	1.7	.930
1989		14	8	.636	3.68	29	29	6	186	172	40	90	4	0	0	0	67	10	0	.149	7	37	4	4	1.7	.917
1990		10	12	.455	4.28	33	33	1	214.1	232	78	129	0	0	0	0	62	7	0	.113	19	33	1	1	1.6	.981
1991		**20**	11	.645	2.55	34	34	**9**	246.2	201	69	192	1	0	0	0	74	17	0	.230	16	45	0	4	1.8	1.000
1992		**20**	8	.714	2.76	33	33	7	225	197	70	129	**5**	0	0	0	77	19	0	.247	18	31	0	2	1.5	1.000
1993		**22**	6	.786	3.20	36	**36**	4	239.1	236	90	120	2	0	0	0	81	14	0	.173	17	36	2	4	1.5	.964
1994		13	9	.591	3.97	25	25	2	165.1	173	70	140	0	0	0	0	56	10	0	.179	11	33	1	1	1.8	.978
1995		16	7	.696	3.08	29	29	3	198.2	182	66	127	1	0	0	0	63	14	1	.222	14	42	1	6	2.0	.982
9 yrs.		124	82	.602	3.52	262	262	33	1721	1649	579	1031	13	0	0	0	556	104	1	.187	115	311	14	25	1.7	.968
DIVISIONAL PLAYOFF SERIES																										
1995	ATL N	0	0	—	2.57	1	1	0	7	5	1	3	0	0	0	0	3	1	0	.333	1	1	0	0	2.0	1.000
LEAGUE CHAMPIONSHIP SERIES																										
1991	ATL N	0	2	.000	3.21	2	2	0	14	12	6	11	0	0	0	0	4	1	0	.250	1	3	0	0	2.0	1.000
1992		0	2	.000	12.27	2	2	0	7.1	13	3	2	0	0	0	0	2	0	0	.000	1	2	0	0	1.5	1.000
1993		1	0	1.000	2.57	1	1	0	7	6	0	5	0	0	0	0	3	0	0	.000	0	3	0	0	3.0	1.000
1995		0	0	—	1.29	1	1	0	7	7	2	5	0	0	0	0	1	0	0	.000	0	1	0	1	1.0	1.000
4 yrs.		1	4 3rd	.200	4.58	6	6	0	35.1	38	11	23	0	0	0	0	10	1	0	.100	2	9	0	1	1.8	1.000
WORLD SERIES																										
1991	ATL N	1	1	.500	2.70	2	2	1	13.1	8	7	8	0	0	0	0	2	0	0	.000	0	3	0	1	1.5	1.000
1992		1	1	.500	1.59	2	2	2	17	10	4	8	0	0	0	0	2	0	0	.000	0	2	0	0	1.0	1.000
1995		2	0	1.000	1.29	2	2	0	14	4	6	11	0	0	0	0	4	0	0	.000	1	3	0	0	2.0	1.000
3 yrs.		4	2	.667	1.83	6	6	3	44.1	22	17	27	0	0	0	0	8	0	0	.000	1	8	0	1	1.5	1.000

Ralph Glaze

GLAZE, DANIEL RALPH BR TR 5′ 9″ 165 lbs.
B. Mar. 13, 1882, Denver, Colo. D. Oct. 31, 1968, Atascadero, Calif.

Year	Team	W	L	PCT	ERA	G	GS	CG	IP	H	BB	SO	ShO	Relief W	Relief L	Relief SV	Batting AB	Batting H	Batting HR	BA	PO	A	E	DP	TC/G	FA
1906	BOS A	4	6	.400	3.59	19	10	7	123	110	32	56	0	0	0	0	55	10	0	.182	14	35	4	2	2.7	.925
1907		9	13	.409	2.32	32	21	11	182.1	150	48	68	1	0	2	0	61	11	1	.180	8	40	2	1	1.6	.960
1908		2	2	.500	3.38	10	3	2	34.2	43	5	13	0	0	1	0	13	1	0	.077	1	7	0	0	0.8	1.000
3 yrs.		15	21	.417	2.89	61	34	20	340	303	85	137	1	0	3	0	129	22	1	.171	23	82	6	3	1.8	.946

Whitey Glazner

GLAZNER, CHARLES FRANKLIN BR TR 5′ 9″ 165 lbs.
B. Sept. 17, 1893, Sycamore, Ala. D. June 6, 1989, Orlando, Fla.

Year	Team	W	L	PCT	ERA	G	GS	CG	IP	H	BB	SO	ShO	Relief W	Relief L	Relief SV	Batting AB	Batting H	Batting HR	BA	PO	A	E	DP	TC/G	FA
1920	PIT N	0	0	—	3.12	2	0	0	8.2	9	2	1	0	0	0	0	3	0	0	.000	0	1	0	0	0.5	1.000
1921		14	5	.737	2.77	36	25	15	234	214	58	88	0	0	1	1	76	10	0	.132	10	43	6	2	1.6	.898
1922		11	12	.478	4.38	34	26	10	193	238	52	77	1	1	0	1	65	16	1	.246	8	43	1	2	1.5	.981
1923	2 teams PIT N (7G 2–1) PHI N (28G 7–14)																									
″	total	9	15	.375	4.47	35	27	13	191.1	224	74	59	3	0	1	2	65	13	1	.200	6	43	3	6	1.5	.942
1924	PHI N	7	16	.304	5.92	35	24	8	156.2	210	63	41	2	2	2	0	51	8	0	.157	5	43	2	5	1.4	.960
5 yrs.		41	48	.461	4.21	142	102	46	783.2	895	249	266	6	3	4	4	260	47	2	.181	29	173	12	15	1.5	.944

Bill Gleason

GLEASON, WILLIAM
B. 1868, Cleveland, Ohio D. Dec. 2, 1893, Cleveland, Ohio.

Year	Team	W	L	PCT	ERA	G	GS	CG	IP	H	BB	SO	ShO	Relief W	Relief L	Relief SV	Batting AB	Batting H	Batting HR	BA	PO	A	E	DP	TC/G	FA
1890	CLE P	0	1	.000	27.00	1	1	0	4	14	6	0	0	0	0	0	2	0	0	.000	0	0	0	0	0.0	.000

Joe Gleason

GLEASON, JOSEPH PAUL BR TR 5′10½″ 175 lbs.
B. July 9, 1895, Phelps, N. Y. D. Sept. 8, 1990, Phelps, N. Y.

Year	Team	W	L	PCT	ERA	G	GS	CG	IP	H	BB	SO	ShO	Relief W	Relief L	Relief SV	Batting AB	Batting H	Batting HR	BA	PO	A	E	DP	TC/G	FA
1920	WAS A	0	0	—	13.50	3	0	0	8	14	6	2	0	0	0	0	2	0	0	.000	0	3	0	0	1.0	1.000
1922		2	3	.400	4.65	8	5	3	40.2	53	18	12	0	0	1	0	14	2	0	.143	3	9	1	0	1.6	.923
2 yrs.		2	3	.400	6.10	11	5	3	48.2	67	24	14	0	0	1	0	16	2	0	.125	3	12	1	0	1.5	.938

Kid Gleason

GLEASON, WILLIAM J. (Youngster) BB TR 5′ 7″ 158 lbs.
Brother of Harry Gleason.
B. Oct. 26, 1866, Camden, N. J. D. Jan. 2, 1933, Philadelphia, Pa.
Manager 1919–23.

Year	Team	W	L	PCT	ERA	G	GS	CG	IP	H	BB	SO	ShO	Relief W	Relief L	Relief SV	Batting AB	Batting H	Batting HR	BA	PO	A	E	DP	TC/G	FA
1888	PHI N	7	16	.304	2.84	24	23	23	199.2	199	53	89	0	0	0	0	83	17	0	.205	6	31	7	1	1.8	.841
1889		9	15	.375	5.58	29	21	15	205	242	97	64	0	2	**2**	1	99	25	0	.253	19	52	10	1	2.5	.877
1890		38	17	.691	2.63	60	55	54	506	479	167	222	6	1	0	**2**	224	47	0	.210	26	102	11	4	2.2	.921
1891		24	22	.522	3.51	53	44	40	418	431	165	100	1	1	2	1	214	53	0	.248	47	78	15	3	2.1	.893
1892	STL N	16	24	.400	3.33	47	45	43	400	389	151	133	2	0	0	0	233	50	3	.215	0	0	0	0	0.0	
1893		21	25	.457	4.61	48	45	37	380.1	436	187	86	1	1	1	1	199	51	0	.256	53	91	16	3	2.7	.900
1894	2 teams STL N (8G 2–6) BAL N (21G 15–5)																									
″	total	17	11	.607	4.85	29	28	25	230	299	65	44	0	0	0	0	114	37	0	.325	41	38	7	2	2.8	.919
1895	BAL N	2	4	.333	6.97	9	5	3	50.1	77	21	6	0	1	2	1	421	130	0	.309	234	277	61	33	5.2	.893
8 yrs.		134	134	.500	3.79	299	266	240	2389.1	2552	906	744	10	6	7	6	*				4155	5195	659	604	5.1	.934

Jerry Don Gleaton

GLEATON, JERRY DON BL TL 6′ 3″ 205 lbs.
B. Sept. 14, 1957, Brownwood, Tex.

Year	Team	W	L	PCT	ERA	G	GS	CG	IP	H	BB	SO	ShO	Relief W	Relief L	Relief SV	Batting AB	Batting H	Batting HR	BA	PO	A	E	DP	TC/G	FA
1979	TEX A	0	1	.000	6.30	5	2	0	10	15	2	2	0	0	0	0	0	0	0	—	0	4	0	0	0.8	1.000
1980		0	0	—	2.57	5	0	0	7	5	4	2	0	0	0	0	0	0	0	—	1	2	0	0	0.6	1.000
1981	SEA A	4	7	.364	4.76	20	13	1	85	88	38	31	0	0	0	0	0	0	0	—	5	12	1	0	0.9	.944
1982		0	0	—	13.50	3	0	0	4.2	7	2	1	0	0	0	0	0	0	0	—	1	0	0	0	0.3	1.000
1984	CHI A	1	2	.333	3.44	11	1	0	18.1	20	6	4	0	1	1	2	0	0	0	—	1	1	1	0	0.3	.667
1985		1	0	1.000	5.76	31	0	0	29.2	37	13	22	0	1	0	1	0	0	0	—	0	4	0	0	0.1	1.000
1987	KC A	4	4	.500	4.26	48	0	0	50.2	38	28	44	0	4	4	5	0	0	0	—	2	12	1	1	0.3	.933
1988		0	4	.000	3.55	42	0	0	38	33	17	29	0	0	4	3	0	0	0	—	3	3	0	0	0.1	1.000
1989		0	0	—	5.65	15	0	0	14.1	20	6	9	0	0	0	0	0	0	0	—	0	2	0	0	0.1	1.000
1990	DET A	1	3	.250	2.94	57	0	0	82.2	62	25	56	0	1	3	13	0	0	0	—	1	11	1	0	0.2	.923
1991		3	2	.600	4.06	47	0	0	75.1	74	39	47	0	3	2	2	0	0	0	—	4	11	0	1	0.3	1.000
1992	PIT N	1	0	1.000	4.26	23	0	0	31.2	34	19	18	0	1	0	0	2	0	0	.000	0	6	0	0	0.3	1.000
12 yrs.		15	23	.395	4.25	307	16	1	447.1	433	199	265	0	11	14	26	2	0	0	.000	18	68	4	2	0.3	.956

Martin Glendon

GLENDON, MARTIN J. 5′11″ 180 lbs.
B. Feb. 8, 1877, Milwaukee, Wis. D. Nov. 6, 1950, Chicago, Ill.

Year	Team		W	L	PCT	ERA	G	GS	CG	IP	H	BB	SO	ShO	Relief Pitching W	Relief Pitching L	Relief Pitching SV	Batting AB	Batting H	Batting HR	BA	PO	A	E	DP	TC/G	FA
1902	CIN	N	0	1	.000	12.00	1	1	0	3	5	4	0	0	0	0	0	1	0	0	.000	0	2	1	0	3.0	.667
1903	CLE	A	1	2	.333	0.98	3	3	3	27.2	20	7	9	0	0	0	0	8	0	0	.000	3	11	0	0	4.7	1.000
2 yrs.			1	3	.250	2.05	4	4	3	30.2	25	11	9	0	0	0	0	9	0	0	.000	3	13	1	0	4.3	.941

Bob Glenn

GLENN, BURDETTE
B. June 16, 1894, West Sunbury, Pa. D. June 3, 1977, Richmond, Calif.

Year	Team		W	L	PCT	ERA	G	GS	CG	IP	H	BB	SO	ShO	Relief Pitching W	Relief Pitching L	Relief Pitching SV	Batting AB	Batting H	Batting HR	BA	PO	A	E	DP	TC/G	FA
1920	STL	N	0	0	—	0.00	2	0	0	2	2	0	0	0	0	0	0	0	0	0	—	1	0	0	0	0.5	1.000

Sal Gliatto

GLIATTO, SALVADOR MICHAEL BB TR 5′ 8½″ 150 lbs.
B. May 7, 1902, Chicago, Ill. D. Nov. 2, 1995, Tyler, Tex.

Year	Team		W	L	PCT	ERA	G	GS	CG	IP	H	BB	SO	ShO	Relief Pitching W	Relief Pitching L	Relief Pitching SV	Batting AB	Batting H	Batting HR	BA	PO	A	E	DP	TC/G	FA
1930	CLE	A	0	0	—	6.60	8	0	0	15	21	9	7	0	0	0	2	2	0	0	.000	0	2	2	0	0.5	.500

George Glinatsis

GLINATSIS, GEORGE, JR. BR TR 6′ 4″ 195 lbs.
B. June 29, 1969, Youngstown, Ohio.

Year	Team		W	L	PCT	ERA	G	GS	CG	IP	H	BB	SO	ShO	Relief Pitching W	Relief Pitching L	Relief Pitching SV	Batting AB	Batting H	Batting HR	BA	PO	A	E	DP	TC/G	FA
1994	SEA	A	0	1	.000	13.50	2	2	0	5.1	9	6	1	0	0	0	0	0	0	0	—	0	0	0	0	0.0	.000

Ed Glynn

GLYNN, EDWARD PAUL (The Flushing Flash) BR TL 6′ 2″ 180 lbs.
B. June 3, 1953, New York, N. Y.

Year	Team		W	L	PCT	ERA	G	GS	CG	IP	H	BB	SO	ShO	Relief Pitching W	Relief Pitching L	Relief Pitching SV	Batting AB	Batting H	Batting HR	BA	PO	A	E	DP	TC/G	FA
1975	DET	A	0	2	.000	4.30	3	1	0	14.2	11	8	8	0	0	1	0	0	0	0	—	1	3	1	1	1.7	.800
1976			1	3	.250	6.00	5	4	1	24	22	20	17	0	0	0	0	0	0	0	—	0	1	0	0	0.2	1.000
1977			2	1	.667	5.33	8	3	0	27	36	12	13	0	1	0	0	0	0	0	—	0	3	0	0	0.4	1.000
1978			0	0	—	3.07	10	0	0	14.2	11	4	9	0	0	0	0	0	0	0	—	0	6	0	0	0.6	1.000
1979	NY	N	1	4	.200	3.00	46	0	0	60	57	40	32	0	1	4	7	4	0	0	.000	5	3	0	0	0.2	1.000
1980			3	3	.500	4.15	38	0	0	52	49	23	32	0	3	3	1	6	0	0	.000	0	12	0	0	0.3	1.000
1981	CLE	A	0	0	—	1.13	4	0	0	8	5	4	4	0	0	0	0	0	0	0	—	0	0	0	0	0.0	.000
1982			5	2	.714	4.17	47	0	0	49.2	43	30	54	0	5	2	4	0	0	0	—	1	4	0	0	0.1	1.000
1983			0	2	.000	5.84	11	0	0	12.1	22	6	13	0	0	2	0	0	0	0	—	0	1	1	0	0.2	.500
1985	MON	N	0	0	—	19.29	3	0	0	2.1	5	4	2	0	0	0	0	0	0	0	—	0	0	0	0	0.0	.000
10 yrs.			12	17	.414	4.25	175	8	1	264.2	261	151	184	0	10	12	12	10	0	0	.000	7	33	2	1	0.2	.952

Jot Goar

GOAR, JOSHUA MERCER BR TR 5′ 9″ 160 lbs.
B. Jan. 31, 1870, New Lisbon, Ind. D. Apr. 4, 1947, New Castle, Ind.

Year	Team		W	L	PCT	ERA	G	GS	CG	IP	H	BB	SO	ShO	Relief Pitching W	Relief Pitching L	Relief Pitching SV	Batting AB	Batting H	Batting HR	BA	PO	A	E	DP	TC/G	FA
1896	PIT	N	0	1	.000	16.88	3	0	0	13.1	36	8	3	0	0	1	0	6	1	0	.167	0	2	2	0	1.3	.500
1898	CIN	N	0	0	—	9.00	1	0	0	2	4	1	0	0	0	0	0	0	0	0	—	0	1	0	0	1.0	1.000
2 yrs.			0	1	.000	15.85	4	0	0	15.1	40	9	3	0	0	1	0	6	1	0	.167	0	3	2	0	1.3	.600

George Goetz

GOETZ, GEORGE BURT 6′ 2″ 180 lbs.
B. 1865, Greencastle, Pa. Deceased.

Year	Team		W	L	PCT	ERA	G	GS	CG	IP	H	BB	SO	ShO	Relief Pitching W	Relief Pitching L	Relief Pitching SV	Batting AB	Batting H	Batting HR	BA	PO	A	E	DP	TC/G	FA
1889	BAL	AA	1	0	1.000	4.00	1	1	0	9	12	0	2	0	0	0	0	4	0	0	.000	0	4	1	0	5.0	.800

John Goetz

GOETZ, JOHN HARDY BR TR 6′ 185 lbs.
B. Oct. 24, 1937, Goetzville, Mich.

Year	Team		W	L	PCT	ERA	G	GS	CG	IP	H	BB	SO	ShO	Relief Pitching W	Relief Pitching L	Relief Pitching SV	Batting AB	Batting H	Batting HR	BA	PO	A	E	DP	TC/G	FA
1960	CHI	N	0	0	—	12.79	4	0	0	6.1	10	4	6	0	0	0	0	1	0	0	.000	0	1	0	0	0.3	1.000

Bill Gogolewski

GOGOLEWSKI, WILLIAM JOSEPH BL TR 6′ 4″ 190 lbs.
B. Oct. 26, 1947, Oshkosh, Wis.

Year	Team		W	L	PCT	ERA	G	GS	CG	IP	H	BB	SO	ShO	Relief Pitching W	Relief Pitching L	Relief Pitching SV	Batting AB	Batting H	Batting HR	BA	PO	A	E	DP	TC/G	FA
1970	WAS	A	2	2	.500	4.76	8	5	0	34	33	25	19	0	0	0	0	7	0	0	.000	1	9	0	1	1.3	1.000
1971			6	5	.545	2.76	27	17	4	124	112	39	70	1	0	0	0	32	5	0	.156	10	18	1	1	1.1	.966
1972	TEX	A	4	11	.267	4.23	36	21	2	151	136	58	95	1	0	1	2	40	5	0	.125	7	21	0	2	0.8	1.000
1973			3	6	.333	4.21	49	1	0	124	139	48	77	0	3	6	6	0	0	0	—	9	28	2	2	0.8	.949
1974	CLE	A	0	0	—	4.50	5	0	0	14	15	2	3	0	0	0	0	0	0	0	—	1	8	0	1	1.8	1.000
1975	CHI	A	0	0	—	5.24	19	0	0	55	61	28	37	0	0	0	2	0	0	0	—	4	11	1	2	0.8	.938
6 yrs.			15	24	.385	4.02	144	44	6	502	496	200	301	2	3	7	10	79	10	0	.127	32	95	4	9	0.9	.969

Greg Gohr

GOHR, GREGORY JAMES BR TR 6′ 3″ 205 lbs.
B. Oct. 29, 1967, Santa Clara, Calif.

Year	Team		W	L	PCT	ERA	G	GS	CG	IP	H	BB	SO	ShO	Relief Pitching W	Relief Pitching L	Relief Pitching SV	Batting AB	Batting H	Batting HR	BA	PO	A	E	DP	TC/G	FA
1993	DET	A	0	0	—	5.96	16	0	0	22.2	26	14	23	0	0	0	0	0	0	0	—	1	1	0	1	0.1	1.000
1994			2	2	.500	4.50	8	6	0	34	36	21	21	0	1	0	0	0	0	0	—	2	1	0	0	0.4	1.000
1995			1	0	1.000	0.87	10	0	0	10.1	9	3	12	0	1	0	0	0	0	0	—	0	1	0	0	0.1	1.000
3 yrs.			3	2	.600	4.43	34	6	0	67	71	38	56	0	2	0	0	0	0	0		3	3	0	1	0.2	1.000

Jim Golden

GOLDEN, JAMES EDWARD BL TR 6′ 175 lbs.
B. Mar. 20, 1936, Eldon, Mo.

Year	Team		W	L	PCT	ERA	G	GS	CG	IP	H	BB	SO	ShO	Relief Pitching W	Relief Pitching L	Relief Pitching SV	Batting AB	Batting H	Batting HR	BA	PO	A	E	DP	TC/G	FA
1960	LA	N	1	0	1.000	6.43	1	1	0	7	6	4	4	0	0	0	0	3	1	0	.333	0	1	0	0	1.0	1.000
1961			1	1	.500	5.79	28	0	0	42	52	20	18	0	1	1	0	3	0	0	.000	1	8	0	0	0.3	1.000
1962	HOU	N	7	11	.389	4.07	37	18	5	152.2	163	50	88	2	2	1	1	54	12	0	.222	10	29	2	1	1.1	.951
1963			0	1	.000	5.68	3	1	0	6.1	12	2	5	0	0	0	0	0	0	0	—	0	1	0	0	0.3	1.000
4 yrs.			9	13	.409	4.54	69	20	5	208	233	76	115	2	3	2	1	60	13	0	.217	11	39	2	1	0.8	.962

Mike Golden

GOLDEN, MICHAEL HENRY BR TR 5′ 7″ 166 lbs.
B. Sept. 11, 1851, Shirley, Mass. D. Jan. 11, 1929, Rockford, Ill.

Year	Team		W	L	PCT	ERA	G	GS	CG	IP	H	BB	SO	ShO	Relief Pitching W	Relief Pitching L	Relief Pitching SV	Batting AB	Batting H	Batting HR	BA	PO	A	E	DP	TC/G	FA
1878	MIL	N	3	13	.188	4.14	22	18	15	161	217	33	52	0	0	0	0	*				75	45	22	2	2.3	.845

Roy Golden

GOLDEN, ROY KRAMER BR TR 6′ 1″ 195 lbs.
B. July 12, 1888, Madisonville, Ohio D. Oct. 4, 1961, Norwood, Ohio.

Year	Team		W	L	PCT	ERA	G	GS	CG	IP	H	BB	SO	ShO	Relief Pitching W	Relief Pitching L	Relief Pitching SV	Batting AB	Batting H	Batting HR	BA	PO	A	E	DP	TC/G	FA
1910	STL	N	2	3	.400	4.43	7	6	3	42.2	44	33	31	0	0	0	0	15	4	0	.267	3	14	3	2	2.9	.850
1911			4	9	.308	5.02	30	25	6	148.2	127	129	81	0	0	0	0	44	5	0	.114	5	39	5	0	1.6	.898
2 yrs.			6	12	.333	4.89	37	31	9	191.1	171	162	112	0	0	0	0	59	9	0	.153	8	53	8	2	1.9	.884

Fred Goldsmith

GOLDSMITH, FRED ERNEST BR TR 6′ 1″ 195 lbs.
B. May 15, 1852, New Haven, Conn. D. Mar. 28, 1939, Berkley, Mich.

Year	Team		W	L	PCT	ERA	G	GS	CG	IP	H	BB	SO	ShO	Relief Pitching W	Relief Pitching L	Relief Pitching SV	Batting AB	Batting H	Batting HR	BA	PO	A	E	DP	TC/G	FA
1879	TRO	N	2	4	.333	1.57	8	7	7	63	61	1	31	0	0	0	0	38	9	0	.237	9	14	5	1	2.5	.821
1880	CHI	N	21	3	**.875**	1.75	26	24	22	210.1	189	18	90	4	0	0	1	142	37	0	.261	55	53	11	0	3.0	.908
1881			24	13	.649	2.59	39	39	37	330	328	44	76	5	0	0	0	158	38	0	.241	21	97	21	2	3.3	.849

Fred Goldsmith *continued*

Year	Team	W	L	PCT	ERA	G	GS	CG	IP	H	BB	SO	ShO	Relief Pitching W	Relief Pitching L	Relief Pitching SV	Batting AB	Batting H	Batting HR	BA	PO	A	E	DP	TC/G	FA
1882		28	17	.622	*2.42*	45	45	45	405	377	38	109	4	0	0	0	183	42	0	.230	33	67	7	0	2.4	.935
1883		25	19	.568	*3.15*	46	45	40	383.1	456	39	82	2	0	0	0	235	52	1	.221	55	89	24	3	2.6	.857
1884	**2 teams** **CHI N** (21G 9–11) **BAL AA** (4G 3–1)																									
"	**total**	12	12	.500	4.05	25	25	23	218	274	31	45	1	0	0	0	95	13	2	.137	17	42	14	0	2.6	.808
6 yrs.		112	68	.622	2.73	189	185	174	1609.2	1685	171	433	16	0	0	1	*				190	362	82	6	2.8	.871

Hal Goldsmith

GOLDSMITH, HAROLD EUGENE BR TR 6′ 174 lbs.
B. Aug. 18, 1898, Peconic, N. Y. D. Oct. 20, 1985, Riverhead, N. Y.

Year	Team	W	L	PCT	ERA	G	GS	CG	IP	H	BB	SO	ShO	Relief Pitching W	Relief Pitching L	Relief Pitching SV	Batting AB	Batting H	Batting HR	BA	PO	A	E	DP	TC/G	FA
1926	**BOS N**	5	7	.417	4.37	19	15	5	101	135	28	16	0	1	1	0	38	8	0	.211	8	28	1	2	1.9	.973
1927		1	3	.250	3.52	22	5	1	71.2	83	26	13	0	0	1	1	21	5	0	.238	4	16	1	2	1.0	.952
1928		0	0	—	3.24	4	0	0	8.1	14	1	1	0	0	0	0	2	0	0	.000	1	4	1	0	1.5	.833
1929	**STL N**	0	0	—	6.75	2	0	0	4	3	1	0	0	0	0	0	1	0	0	.000	0	0	0	0	0.0	.000
4 yrs.		6	10	.375	4.04	47	20	6	185	235	56	30	0	1	2	1	62	13	0	.210	13	48	3	4	1.4	.953

Izzy Goldstein

GOLDSTEIN, ISIDORE BB TR 6′ 160 lbs.
B. June 6, 1908, Odessa, Russia D. Sept. 24, 1993, Delray Beach, Fla.

Year	Team	W	L	PCT	ERA	G	GS	CG	IP	H	BB	SO	ShO	Relief Pitching W	Relief Pitching L	Relief Pitching SV	Batting AB	Batting H	Batting HR	BA	PO	A	E	DP	TC/G	FA
1932	**DET A**	3	2	.600	4.47	16	6	2	56.1	63	41	14	0	0	0	0	17	5	0	.294	2	13	2	0	1.1	.882

Dave Goltz

GOLTZ, DAVID ALLAN BR TR 6′ 4″ 200 lbs.
B. June 23, 1949, Pelican Rapids, Minn.

Year	Team	W	L	PCT	ERA	G	GS	CG	IP	H	BB	SO	ShO	Relief Pitching W	Relief Pitching L	Relief Pitching SV	Batting AB	Batting H	Batting HR	BA	PO	A	E	DP	TC/G	FA
1972	**MIN A**	3	3	.500	2.67	15	11	2	91	75	26	38	0	0	0	1	29	3	0	.103	8	14	1	0	1.5	.957
1973		6	4	.600	5.25	32	10	1	106.1	138	32	66	0	3	0	1	0	0	0	—	7	17	1	4	0.8	.960
1974		10	10	.500	3.26	28	24	5	174	192	45	89	1	1	0	1	0	0	0	—	14	27	2	3	1.5	.953
1975		14	14	.500	3.67	32	32	15	243	235	72	128	1	0	0	0	0	0	0	—	20	38	3	4	1.9	.951
1976		14	14	.500	3.36	36	35	13	249.1	239	91	133	4	0	0	0	0	0	0	—	18	35	3	3	1.6	.946
1977		**20**	11	.645	3.36	39	**39**	19	303	**284**	91	186	2	0	0	0	0	0	0	—	20	41	5	4	1.6	.924
1978		15	10	.600	2.49	29	29	13	220.1	209	67	116	2	0	0	0	0	0	0	—	24	28	2	2	1.9	.963
1979		14	13	.519	4.16	36	35	12	251	**282**	69	132	1	0	0	0	0	0	0	—	16	34	2	3	1.4	.962
1980	**LA N**	7	11	.389	4.32	35	27	2	171	198	59	91	2	0	0	1	47	6	0	.128	11	24	1	1	1.0	.972
1981		2	7	.222	4.09	26	8	0	77	83	25	48	0	1	3	1	17	1	0	.059	6	14	0	1	0.8	1.000
1982	**2 teams** **LA N** (2G 0–1) **CAL A** (28G 8–5)																									
"	**total**	8	6	.571	4.12	30	8	1	89.2	88	32	52	0	4	4	3	1	0	0	.000	4	7	0	0	0.4	1.000
1983	**CAL A**	0	6	.000	6.22	15	6	0	63.2	81	37	27	0	0	2	0	0	0	0	—	4	8	1	1	0.9	.923
12 yrs.		113	109	.509	3.69	353	264	83	2039.1	2104	646	1106	13	9	9	8	94	10	0	.106	152	287	21	26	1.3	.954
LEAGUE CHAMPIONSHIP SERIES																										
1982	**CAL A**	0	0	—	7.36	1	0	0	3.2	4	2	2	0	0	0	0	0	0	0	—	0	0	0	0	0.0	.000
WORLD SERIES																										
1981	**LA N**	0	0	—	5.40	2	0	0	3.1	4	1	2	0	0	0	0	0	0	0	—	0	0	0	0	0.0	.000

Lefty Gomez

GOMEZ, VERNON LOUIS (Goofy, The Gay Castillion) BL TL 6′ 2″ 173 lbs.
B. Nov. 26, 1908, Rodeo, Calif. D. Feb. 17, 1989, Greenbrae, Calif.
Hall of Fame 1972.

Year	Team	W	L	PCT	ERA	G	GS	CG	IP	H	BB	SO	ShO	Relief Pitching W	Relief Pitching L	Relief Pitching SV	Batting AB	Batting H	Batting HR	BA	PO	A	E	DP	TC/G	FA
1930	**NY A**	2	5	.286	5.55	15	6	2	60	66	28	22	0	0	2	1	20	3	0	.150	1	18	0	0	1.3	1.000
1931		21	9	.700	2.63	40	26	17	243	206	85	150	1	3	2	3	83	11	0	.133	6	43	1	1	1.3	.980
1932		24	7	.774	4.21	37	31	21	265.1	266	105	176	1	1	2	1	104	18	0	.173	2	36	2	3	1.1	.950
1933		16	10	.615	3.18	35	30	14	234.2	218	106	**163**	4	0	2	2	80	9	0	.113	4	30	4	0	1.1	.895
1934		**26**	5	**.839**	**2.33**	38	33	**25**	**281.2**	223	96	**158**	**6**	1	2	1	99	13	0	.131	7	42	1	2	1.3	.980
1935		12	15	.444	3.18	34	30	15	246	223	86	138	2	0	1	1	83	10	0	.120	6	49	2	2	1.7	.965
1936		13	7	.650	4.39	31	30	10	188.2	184	122	105	0	0	0	0	69	10	0	.145	4	29	1	3	1.1	.971
1937		**21**	11	.656	**2.33**	34	34	25	278.1	233	93	**194**	**6**	0	0	0	105	21	0	.200	3	36	3	1	1.2	.929
1938		18	12	.600	3.35	32	32	20	239	239	99	129	**4**	0	0	0	86	13	0	.151	12	51	1	5	2.0	.984
1939		12	8	.600	3.41	26	26	14	198	173	84	102	2	0	0	0	73	11	0	.151	2	33	1	0	1.4	.972
1940		3	3	.500	6.59	9	5	0	27.1	37	18	14	0	0	1	0	9	0	0	.000	1	2	0	0	0.3	1.000
1941		15	5	**.750**	3.74	23	23	8	156.1	151	103	76	2	0	0	0	59	9	0	.153	6	11	2	2	0.8	.895
1942		6	4	.600	4.28	13	13	2	80	67	65	41	0	0	0	0	33	5	0	.152	2	9	1	0	0.9	.917
1943	**WAS A**	0	1	.000	5.79	1	1	0	4.2	4	5	0	0	0	0	0	1	0	0	.000	0	4	1	1	5.0	.800
14 yrs.		189	102	.649	3.34	368	320	173	2503	2290	1095	1468	28	5	12	9	904	133	0	.147	56	393	20	20	1.3	.957
WORLD SERIES																										
1932	**NY A**	1	0	1.000	1.00	1	1	1	9	9	1	8	0	0	0	0	3	0	0	.000	0	3	0	0	3.0	1.000
1936		2	0	1.000	4.70	2	2	1	15.1	14	11	9	0	0	0	0	8	2	0	.250	0	3	0	0	1.5	1.000
1937		2	0	1.000	1.50	2	2	2	18	16	2	8	0	0	0	0	6	1	0	.167	1	3	0	0	2.0	1.000
1938		1	0	1.000	3.86	1	1	0	7	9	1	5	0	0	0	0	2	0	0	.000	0	1	0	0	1.0	1.000
1939		0	0	—	9.00	1	1	0	1	3	0	1	0	0	0	0	1	0	0	.000	0	0	0	0	0.0	.000
5 yrs.		6	0	1.000	2.86	7	7	4	50.1	51	15	31	0	0	0	0	20	3	0	.150	1	10	0	0	1.6	1.000
		5th		**1st**																						

Luis Gomez

GOMEZ, LUIS BR TR 5′ 9″ 150 lbs.
Born Luis Gomez (Sanchez).
B. Aug. 19, 1951, Guadalajara, Mexico.

Year	Team	W	L	PCT	ERA	G	GS	CG	IP	H	BB	SO	ShO	Relief Pitching W	Relief Pitching L	Relief Pitching SV	Batting AB	Batting H	Batting HR	BA	PO	A	E	DP	TC/G	FA
1981	**ATL N**	0	0	—	27.00	1	0	0	1	3	2	0	0	0	0	0	*				97	194	12	37	3.9	.960

Pat Gomez

GOMEZ, PATRICK ALEXANDER BL TL 6′ 190 lbs.
B. Mar. 17, 1968, Roseville, Calif.

Year	Team	W	L	PCT	ERA	G	GS	CG	IP	H	BB	SO	ShO	Relief Pitching W	Relief Pitching L	Relief Pitching SV	Batting AB	Batting H	Batting HR	BA	PO	A	E	DP	TC/G	FA
1993	**SD N**	1	2	.333	5.12	27	1	0	31.2	35	19	26	0	1	1	0	5	0	0	.000	0	3	1	0	0.1	.750
1994	**SF N**	0	1	.000	3.78	26	0	0	33.1	23	20	14	0	0	1	0	2	0	0	.000	3	2	1	0	0.2	.833
1995		0	0	—	5.14	18	0	0	14	16	12	15	0	0	0	0	1	0	0	.000	1	1	0	0	0.1	1.000
3 yrs.		1	3	.250	4.56	71	1	0	79	74	51	55	0	1	2	0	8	0	0	.000	4	6	2	0	0.2	.833

Ruben Gomez

GOMEZ, RUBEN BR TR 6′ 170 lbs.
Born Ruben Gomez (Colon).
B. July 13, 1927, Arroyo, Puerto Rico.

Year	Team	W	L	PCT	ERA	G	GS	CG	IP	H	BB	SO	ShO	Relief Pitching W	Relief Pitching L	Relief Pitching SV	Batting AB	Batting H	Batting HR	BA	PO	A	E	DP	TC/G	FA
1953	**NY N**	13	11	.542	3.40	29	26	13	204	166	101	113	3	0	0	0	72	15	0	.208	20	39	3	1	2.1	.952
1954		17	9	.654	2.88	37	32	10	221.2	202	**109**	106	4	0	2	0	81	14	2	.173	13	47	4	3	1.7	.938

Ruben Gomez *continued*

Year	Team	Lg	W	L	PCT	ERA	G	GS	CG	IP	H	BB	SO	ShO	Relief Pitching W	Relief Pitching L	Relief Pitching SV	Batting AB	Batting H	Batting HR	BA	PO	A	E	DP	TC/G	FA
1955			9	10	.474	4.56	33	31	9	185.1	207	63	79	3	0	1	1	60	18	0	.300	22	39	2	4	1.9	.968
1956			7	17	.292	4.58	40	31	4	196.1	191	77	76	2	1	0	0	60	11	0	.183	19	40	1	4	1.5	.983
1957			15	13	.536	3.78	38	36	16	238.1	233	71	92	1	0	0	0	87	16	1	.184	14	51	2	3	1.7	.970
1958	SF	N	10	12	.455	4.38	42	30	8	207.2	204	77	112	1	0	2	1	70	14	0	.200	21	39	2	3	1.5	.968
1959	PHI	N	3	8	.273	6.10	20	12	2	72.1	90	24	37	1	1	1	1	17	3	0	.176	7	18	2	3	1.4	.926
1960			0	3	.000	5.33	22	1	0	52.1	68	9	24	0	0	3	1	12	1	0	.083	5	6	2	0	0.6	.846
1962	2 teams	CLE A (15G 1–2)		MIN A (6G 1–1)																							
"	total		2	3	.400	4.45	21	6	1	64.2	67	36	29	0	0	1	1	18	3	0	.167	5	13	1	2	0.9	.947
1967	PHI	N	0	0	—	3.97	7	0	0	11.1	8	7	9	0	0	0	0	0	0	0	—	1	5	0	1	0.9	1.000
10 yrs.			76	86	.469	4.09	289	205	63	1454	1436	574	677	15	2	10	5	477	95	3	.199	127	297	19	24	1.5	.957
WORLD SERIES																											
1954	NY	N	1	0	1.000	2.45	1	1	0	7.1	4	3	2	0	0	0	0	4	0	0	.000	1	2	0	0	3.0	1.000

Joe Gonzales

GONZALES, JOE MADRID BR TR 5′ 9″ 175 lbs.
B. Mar. 19, 1915, San Francisco, Calif.

Year	Team	Lg	W	L	PCT	ERA	G	GS	CG	IP	H	BB	SO	ShO	Relief Pitching W	Relief Pitching L	Relief Pitching SV	Batting AB	Batting H	Batting HR	BA	PO	A	E	DP	TC/G	FA
1937	BOS	A	1	2	.333	4.35	8	2	2	31	37	11	11	0	1	0	0	10	0	0	.000	0	6	0	1	0.8	1.000

Rene Gonzales

GONZALES, RENE ADRIAN BR TR 6′ 3″ 180 lbs.
B. Sept. 23, 1960, Austin, Tex.

Year	Team	Lg	W	L	PCT	ERA	G	GS	CG	IP	H	BB	SO	ShO	Relief Pitching W	Relief Pitching L	Relief Pitching SV	Batting AB	Batting H	Batting HR	BA	PO	A	E	DP	TC/G	FA
1993	CAL	A	0	0	—	0.00	1	0	0	1	0	0	0	0	0	0	0	*				17	28	2	5	1.7	.957

Vince Gonzales

GONZALES, WENCESLAO BL TL 6′ 1″ 165 lbs.
Born Wenceslao Gonzales (O'Reilly).
B. Sept. 28, 1925, Quivican, Cuba D. Mar. 11, 1981, Ciudad del Carmen, Mexico.

Year	Team	Lg	W	L	PCT	ERA	G	GS	CG	IP	H	BB	SO	ShO	Relief Pitching W	Relief Pitching L	Relief Pitching SV	Batting AB	Batting H	Batting HR	BA	PO	A	E	DP	TC/G	FA
1955	WAS	A	0	0	—	27.00	1	0	0	2	6	3	1	0	0	0	0	0	0	0	—	0	0	0	0	0.0	.000

German Gonzalez

GONZALEZ, GERMAN JOSE BR TR 6′ 170 lbs.
Born German Jose Gonzalez (Caraballo).
B. Mar. 7, 1962, Rio Caribe, Venezuela.

Year	Team	Lg	W	L	PCT	ERA	G	GS	CG	IP	H	BB	SO	ShO	Relief Pitching W	Relief Pitching L	Relief Pitching SV	Batting AB	Batting H	Batting HR	BA	PO	A	E	DP	TC/G	FA
1988	MIN	A	0	0	—	3.38	16	0	0	21.1	20	8	19	0	0	0	1	0	0	0	—	3	2	0	0	0.3	1.000
1989			3	2	.600	4.66	22	0	0	29	32	11	25	0	3	2	0	0	0	0	—	4	2	0	0	0.3	1.000
2 yrs.			3	2	.600	4.11	38	0	0	50.1	52	19	44	0	3	2	1	0	0	0		7	4	0	0	0.3	1.000

Julio Gonzalez

GONZALEZ, JULIO ENRIQUE BR TR 5′11″ 150 lbs.
Born Julio Enrique Gonzalez (Herrera).
B. Dec. 20, 1920, Banes, Cuba D. Feb. 15, 1991, Banes, Cuba.

Year	Team	Lg	W	L	PCT	ERA	G	GS	CG	IP	H	BB	SO	ShO	Relief Pitching W	Relief Pitching L	Relief Pitching SV	Batting AB	Batting H	Batting HR	BA	PO	A	E	DP	TC/G	FA
1949	WAS	A	0	0	—	4.72	13	0	0	34.1	33	27	5	0	0	0	0	5	1	0	.200	2	6	0	0	0.6	1.000

Ralph Good

GOOD, RALPH NELSON BR TR 6′ 165 lbs.
B. Apr. 25, 1886, Monticello, Me. D. Nov. 24, 1965, Waterville, Me.

Year	Team	Lg	W	L	PCT	ERA	G	GS	CG	IP	H	BB	SO	ShO	Relief Pitching W	Relief Pitching L	Relief Pitching SV	Batting AB	Batting H	Batting HR	BA	PO	A	E	DP	TC/G	FA
1910	BOS	N	0	0	—	2.00	2	0	0	9	6	2	4	0	0	0	0	3	0	0	.000	0	4	0	1	2.0	1.000

Wilbur Good

GOOD, WILBUR DAVID (Lefty) BL TL 5′ 6″ 165 lbs.
B. Sept. 28, 1885, Punxsutawney, Pa. D. Dec. 30, 1963, Brooksville, Fla.

Year	Team	Lg	W	L	PCT	ERA	G	GS	CG	IP	H	BB	SO	ShO	Relief Pitching W	Relief Pitching L	Relief Pitching SV	Batting AB	Batting H	Batting HR	BA	PO	A	E	DP	TC/G	FA
1905	NY	A	0	2	.000	4.74	5	2	0	19	18	14	13	0	0	0	0	*				1	7	1	0	1.8	.889

Herb Goodall

GOODALL, HERBERT FRANK BR TR 5′ 9″ 180 lbs.
B. Mar. 10, 1870, Mansfield, Pa. D. Jan. 20, 1938, Mansfield, Pa.

Year	Team	Lg	W	L	PCT	ERA	G	GS	CG	IP	H	BB	SO	ShO	Relief Pitching W	Relief Pitching L	Relief Pitching SV	Batting AB	Batting H	Batting HR	BA	PO	A	E	DP	TC/G	FA
1890	LOU	AA	8	5	.615	*3.39*	18	13	8	109	94	51	46	1	0	0	**4**	45	19	0	.422	7	25	3	0	1.8	.914

John Goodell

GOODELL, JOHN HENRY WILLIAM (Lefty) BR TL 5′10″ 165 lbs.
B. Apr. 5, 1907, Muskogee, Okla. D. Sept. 21, 1993, Mesquite, Tex.

Year	Team	Lg	W	L	PCT	ERA	G	GS	CG	IP	H	BB	SO	ShO	Relief Pitching W	Relief Pitching L	Relief Pitching SV	Batting AB	Batting H	Batting HR	BA	PO	A	E	DP	TC/G	FA
1928	CHI	A	0	0	—	18.00	2	0	0	3	6	2	0	0	0	0	0	0	0	0	—	0	1	0	0	0.5	1.000

Dwight Gooden

GOODEN, DWIGHT EUGENE (Doc) BR TR 6′ 2″ 190 lbs.
B. Nov. 16, 1964, Tampa, Fla.

Year	Team	Lg	W	L	PCT	ERA	G	GS	CG	IP	H	BB	SO	ShO	Relief Pitching W	Relief Pitching L	Relief Pitching SV	Batting AB	Batting H	Batting HR	BA	PO	A	E	DP	TC/G	FA
1984	NY	N	17	9	.654	2.60	31	31	7	218	161	73	**276**	3	0	0	0	70	14	0	.200	21	22	2	0	1.5	.956
1985			**24**	4	.857	**1.53**	35	35	**16**	**276.2**	198	69	**268**	8	0	0	0	93	21	1	.226	25	38	2	6	1.9	.969
1986			17	6	.739	2.84	33	33	12	250	197	80	200	2	0	0	0	81	7	0	.086	36	36	2	5	2.2	.973
1987			15	7	**.682**	3.21	25	25	7	179.2	162	53	148	3	0	0	0	64	14	0	.219	15	22	3	3	1.6	.925
1988			18	9	.667	3.19	34	34	10	248.1	242	57	175	3	0	0	0	90	16	1	.178	27	56	5	3	2.6	.943
1989			9	4	.692	2.89	19	17	0	118.1	93	47	101	0	0	0	1	40	8	0	.200	8	16	3	0	1.4	.889
1990			19	7	.731	3.83	34	34	2	232.2	229	70	223	1	0	0	0	75	14	1	.187	15	35	4	5	1.6	.926
1991			13	7	.650	3.60	27	27	3	190	185	56	150	1	0	0	0	63	15	1	.238	15	28	2	3	1.7	.956
1992			10	13	.435	3.67	31	31	3	206	197	70	145	0	0	0	0	72	19	1	.264	9	40	6	1	1.8	.891
1993			12	15	.444	3.45	29	29	7	208.2	188	61	149	2	0	0	0	70	14	2	.200	19	24	2	1	1.6	.956
1994			3	4	.429	6.31	7	7	0	41.1	46	15	40	0	0	0	0	12	2	0	.167	1	11	1	1	1.9	.923
11 yrs.			157	85	.649	3.10	305	303	67	2169.2	1898	651	1875	23	0	0	1	730	144	7	.197	191	328	32	28	1.8	.942
LEAGUE CHAMPIONSHIP SERIES																											
1986	NY	N	0	1	.000	1.06	2	2	0	17	16	5	9	0	0	0	0	5	0	0	.000	3	2	0	0	2.5	1.000
1988			0	0	—	2.95	3	2	0	18.1	10	8	20	0	0	0	0	5	1	0	.200	1	3	0	0	1.3	1.000
2 yrs.			0	1	.000	2.04 **10th**	5	4	0	35.1	26	13	29	0	0	0	0	10	1	0	.100	4	5	0	0	1.8	1.000
WORLD SERIES																											
1986	NY	N	0	2	.000	8.00	2	2	0	9	17	4	9	0	0	0	0	2	1	0	.500	1	2	0	0	1.5	1.000

Art Goodwin

GOODWIN, ARTHUR INGRAM TR 5′ 8″ 195 lbs.
B. Feb. 27, 1876, Greene County, Pa. D. June 19, 1943, Greene County, Pa.

Year	Team	Lg	W	L	PCT	ERA	G	GS	CG	IP	H	BB	SO	ShO	Relief Pitching W	Relief Pitching L	Relief Pitching SV	Batting AB	Batting H	Batting HR	BA	PO	A	E	DP	TC/G	FA
1905	NY	A	0	0	—	81.00	1	0	0	0.1	2	2	0	0	0	0	0	0	0	0	—	0	0	0	0	0.0	.000

Clyde Goodwin

GOODWIN, CLYDE SAMUEL BR TR 5′11″ 145 lbs.
B. Nov. 12, 1886, Shade, Ohio D. Oct. 12, 1963, Dayton, Ohio.

Year	Team		W	L	PCT	ERA	G	GS	CG	IP	H	BB	SO	ShO	Relief Pitching W	Relief Pitching L	Relief Pitching SV	Batting AB	Batting H	Batting HR	BA	PO	A	E	DP	TC/G	FA
1906	WAS	A	0	2	.000	4.43	4	3	1	22.1	20	13	9	0	0	0	0	5	1	0	.200	0	4	0	0	1.0	1.000

Jim Goodwin

GOODWIN, JAMES PATRICK BL TL 6′ 1″ 170 lbs.
B. Aug. 15, 1926, St. Louis, Mo.

Year	Team		W	L	PCT	ERA	G	GS	CG	IP	H	BB	SO	ShO	Relief Pitching W	Relief Pitching L	Relief Pitching SV	Batting AB	Batting H	Batting HR	BA	PO	A	E	DP	TC/G	FA
1948	CHI	A	0	0	—	8.71	8	1	0	10.1	9	12	3	0	0	0	1	2	1	0	.500	1	2	0	0	0.4	1.000

Marv Goodwin

GOODWIN, MARVIN MARDO BR TR 5′11″ 168 lbs.
B. Jan. 16, 1891, Gordonsville, Va. D. Oct. 22, 1925, Houston, Tex.

Year	Team		W	L	PCT	ERA	G	GS	CG	IP	H	BB	SO	ShO	Relief Pitching W	Relief Pitching L	Relief Pitching SV	Batting AB	Batting H	Batting HR	BA	PO	A	E	DP	TC/G	FA
1916	WAS	A	0	0	—	3.18	3	0	0	5.2	5	3	1	0	0	0	0	1	0	0	.000	0	1	0	0	0.3	1.000
1917	STL	N	6	4	.600	2.21	14	12	6	85.1	70	19	38	3	0	1	0	23	4	0	.174	3	33	0	1	2.6	1.000
1919			11	9	.550	2.51	33	17	7	179	163	33	48	0	3	3	0	60	12	0	.200	3	52	4	1	1.8	.932
1920			3	8	.273	4.95	32	12	3	116.1	153	28	23	0	1	1	1	35	7	0	.200	3	25	6	0	1.1	.824
1921			1	2	.333	3.72	14	4	1	36.1	47	9	7	0	0	0	1	6	0	0	.000	2	11	1	1	1.0	.929
1922			0	0	—	2.25	2	0	0	4	3	3	0	0	0	0	0	0	0	0	—	1	2	1	1	2.0	.750
1925	CIN	N	0	2	.000	4.79	4	3	2	20.2	26	5	4	0	0	0	0	4	1	0	.250	2	9	0	1	2.8	1.000
7 yrs.			21	25	.457	3.30	102	48	19	447.1	467	100	121	3	4	5	2	129	24	0	.186	14	133	12	5	1.6	.925

Ray Gordinier

GORDINIER, RAYMOND CORNELIUS BB TR 5′ 8½″ 170 lbs.
B. Apr. 11, 1892, Rochester, N. Y. D. Nov. 15, 1960, Rochester, N. Y. BB 1922

Year	Team		W	L	PCT	ERA	G	GS	CG	IP	H	BB	SO	ShO	Relief Pitching W	Relief Pitching L	Relief Pitching SV	Batting AB	Batting H	Batting HR	BA	PO	A	E	DP	TC/G	FA
1921	BKN	N	1	0	1.000	5.25	3	3	0	12	10	8	4	0	0	0	0	4	1	0	.250	0	4	1	1	1.7	.800
1922			0	0	—	8.74	5	0	0	11.1	13	8	5	0	0	0	0	2	0	0	.000	1	2	1	0	0.8	.750
2 yrs.			1	0	1.000	6.94	8	3	0	23.1	23	16	9	0	0	0	0	6	1	0	.167	1	6	2	1	1.1	.778

Don Gordon

GORDON, DONALD THOMAS BR TR 6′ 1″ 175 lbs.
B. Oct. 10, 1959, New York, N. Y.

Year	Team		W	L	PCT	ERA	G	GS	CG	IP	H	BB	SO	ShO	Relief Pitching W	Relief Pitching L	Relief Pitching SV	Batting AB	Batting H	Batting HR	BA	PO	A	E	DP	TC/G	FA
1986	TOR	A	0	1	.000	7.06	14	0	0	21.2	28	8	13	0	0	1	1	0	0	0	—	1	2	2	0	0.4	.600
1987	2 teams	TOR A	(5G 0–0)	CLE A	(21G 0–3)																						
"	total		0	3	.000	4.09	26	0	0	50.2	57	15	23	0	0	3	1	0	0	0		3	11	2	1	0.6	.875
1988	CLE	A	3	4	.429	4.40	38	0	0	59.1	65	19	20	0	3	4	1	0	0	0	—	4	12	1	0	0.4	.941
3 yrs.			3	8	.273	4.72	78	0	0	131.2	150	42	56	0	3	8	3	0	0	0		8	25	5	1	0.5	.868

Tom Gordon

GORDON, THOMAS (Flash) BR TR 5′ 9″ 160 lbs.
B. Nov. 18, 1967, Sebring, Fla.

Year	Team		W	L	PCT	ERA	G	GS	CG	IP	H	BB	SO	ShO	Relief Pitching W	Relief Pitching L	Relief Pitching SV	Batting AB	Batting H	Batting HR	BA	PO	A	E	DP	TC/G	FA
1988	KC	A	0	2	.000	5.17	5	2	0	15.2	16	7	18	0	0	0	0	0	0	0	—	2	2	0	0	0.8	1.000
1989			17	9	.654	3.64	49	16	1	163	122	86	153	1	10	2	1	0	0	0	—	15	26	0	7	0.8	1.000
1990			12	11	.522	3.73	32	32	6	195.1	192	99	175	1	0	0	0	0	0	0	—	17	24	1	1	1.3	.976
1991			9	14	.391	3.87	45	14	1	158	129	87	167	0	4	**7**	1	0	0	0	—	12	17	2	1	0.7	.935
1992			6	10	.375	4.59	40	11	0	117.2	116	55	98	0	6	5	0	0	0	0	—	11	14	1	1	0.6	.962
1993			12	6	.667	3.58	48	14	2	155.2	125	77	143	0	4	2	1	0	0	0	—	18	21	2	1	0.9	.951
1994			11	7	.611	4.35	24	24	0	155.1	136	87	126	0	0	0	0	0	0	0	—	12	25	2	3	1.6	.949
1995			12	12	.500	4.43	31	31	2	189	204	89	119	0	0	0	0	0	0	0	—	25	26	2	3	1.7	.962
8 yrs.			79	71	.527	4.02	274	144	12	1149.2	1040	587	999	2	24	16	3	0	0	0		112	155	10	17	1.0	.964

Charlie Gorin

GORIN, CHARLES PERRY BL TL 5′10″ 165 lbs.
B. Feb. 6, 1928, Waco, Tex.

Year	Team		W	L	PCT	ERA	G	GS	CG	IP	H	BB	SO	ShO	Relief Pitching W	Relief Pitching L	Relief Pitching SV	Batting AB	Batting H	Batting HR	BA	PO	A	E	DP	TC/G	FA
1954	MIL	N	0	1	.000	1.86	5	0	0	9.2	5	6	12	0	0	1	0	3	0	0	.000	1	0	0	0	0.2	1.000
1955			0	0	—	54.00	2	0	0	0.1	1	3	0	0	0	0	0	0	0	0	—	0	0	0	0	0.0	.000
2 yrs.			0	1	.000	3.60	7	0	0	10	6	9	12	0	0	1	0	3	0	0	.000	1	0	0	0	0.1	1.000

Jack Gorman

GORMAN, JOHN F. (Stooping Jack)
B. 1859, St. Louis, Mo. D. Sept. 9, 1889, St. Louis, Mo.

Year	Team		W	L	PCT	ERA	G	GS	CG	IP	H	BB	SO	ShO	Relief Pitching W	Relief Pitching L	Relief Pitching SV	Batting AB	Batting H	Batting HR	BA	PO	A	E	DP	TC/G	FA
1884	PIT	AA	1	2	.333	*4.68*	3	3	3	25	22	5	10	0	0	0	0	*				1	1	1	0	3.0	.667

Tom Gorman

GORMAN, THOMAS ALOYSIUS BR TR 6′ 1″ 190 lbs.
B. Jan. 4, 1925, New York, N. Y. D. Dec. 26, 1992, Valley Stream, N. Y.

Year	Team		W	L	PCT	ERA	G	GS	CG	IP	H	BB	SO	ShO	Relief Pitching W	Relief Pitching L	Relief Pitching SV	Batting AB	Batting H	Batting HR	BA	PO	A	E	DP	TC/G	FA
1952	NY	A	6	2	.750	4.60	12	6	1	60.2	63	22	31	1	3	0	1	23	2	0	.087	2	11	3	0	1.3	.813
1953			4	5	.444	3.39	40	1	0	77	65	32	38	0	4	4	6	15	2	0	.133	5	11	1	0	0.4	.941
1954			0	0	—	2.21	23	0	0	36.2	30	14	31	0	0	0	2	4	0	0	.000	2	6	0	1	0.3	1.000
1955	KC	A	7	6	.538	3.55	57	0	0	109	98	36	46	0	7	6	18	24	2	0	.083	8	13	3	1	0.4	.875
1956			9	10	.474	3.83	52	13	1	171.1	168	68	56	0	6	3	3	39	2	0	.051	11	29	3	1	0.8	.930
1957			5	9	.357	3.83	38	12	3	124.2	125	33	66	1	1	5	3	33	4	0	.121	10	19	2	0	0.8	.935
1958			4	4	.500	3.51	50	1	0	89.2	86	20	44	0	4	3	8	17	2	0	.118	2	11	0	0	0.3	1.000
1959			1	0	1.000	7.08	17	0	0	20.1	24	14	9	0	1	0	1	0	0	0	—	0	0	1	0	0.1	.000
8 yrs.			36	36	.500	3.77	289	33	5	689.1	659	239	321	2	26	21	42	155	14	0	.090	40	100	13	3	0.5	.915
WORLD SERIES																											
1952	NY	A	0	0	—	0.00	1	0	0	0.2	1	0	0	0	0	0	0	0	0	0	—	0	0	0	0	0.0	.000
1953			0	0	—	3.00	1	0	0	3	4	0	1	0	0	0	0	1	0	0	.000	1	0	0	0	1.0	1.000
2 yrs.			0	0		2.45	2	0	0	3.2	5	0	1	0	0	0	0	1	0	0	.000	1	0	0	0	0.5	1.000

Tom Gorman

GORMAN, THOMAS DAVID (Big Tom) BR TL 6′ 2″ 200 lbs.
B. Mar. 16, 1916, New York, N. Y. D. Aug. 11, 1986, Closter, N. J.

Year	Team		W	L	PCT	ERA	G	GS	CG	IP	H	BB	SO	ShO	Relief Pitching W	Relief Pitching L	Relief Pitching SV	Batting AB	Batting H	Batting HR	BA	PO	A	E	DP	TC/G	FA
1939	NY	N	0	0	—	7.20	4	0	0	5	7	1	2	0	0	0	0	1	0	0	.000	0	2	0	0	0.5	1.000

Tom Gorman

GORMAN, THOMAS PATRICK BL TL 6′ 4″ 194 lbs.
B. Dec. 16, 1957, Portland, Ore.

Year	Team		W	L	PCT	ERA	G	GS	CG	IP	H	BB	SO	ShO	Relief Pitching W	Relief Pitching L	Relief Pitching SV	Batting AB	Batting H	Batting HR	BA	PO	A	E	DP	TC/G	FA
1981	MON	N	0	0	—	4.20	9	0	0	15	12	6	13	0	0	0	0	0	0	0	—	0	6	0	0	0.7	1.000
1982	2 teams	MON N	(5G 1–0)	NY N	(3G 0–1)																						
"	total		1	1	.500	2.76	8	1	0	16.1	16	4	13	0	1	0	0	1	0	0	.000	2	2	0	0	0.5	1.000
1983	NY	N	1	4	.200	4.93	25	4	0	49.1	45	15	30	0	1	0	0	4	1	0	.250	3	7	0	2	0.4	1.000
1984			6	0	1.000	2.97	36	0	0	57.2	51	13	40	0	6	0	0	3	0	0	.000	2	9	0	0	0.3	1.000
1985			4	4	.500	5.13	34	2	0	52.2	56	18	32	0	3	3	0	5	0	0	.000	3	14	0	1	0.5	1.000

Tom Gorman *continued*

Year	Team	Lg	W	L	PCT	ERA	G	GS	CG	IP	H	BB	SO	ShO	Relief Pitching W	Relief Pitching L	Relief Pitching SV	Batting AB	Batting H	Batting HR	BA	PO	A	E	DP	TC/G	FA
1986	**PHI**	**N**	0	1	.000	7.71	8	0	0	11.2	21	5	8	0	0	1	0	1	0	0	.000	2	2	0	0	0.5	1.000
1987	**SD**	**N**	0	0	—	4.09	6	0	0	11	11	5	8	0	0	0	0	0	0	0	—	0	0	0	0	0.0	.000
7 yrs.			12	10	.545	4.34	126	7	0	213.2	212	66	144	0	11	4	0	14	1	0	.071	12	40	0	3	0.4	1.000

Joe Gormley

GORMLEY, JOSEPH BL TL
B. Dec. 20, 1866, Summit Hill, Pa. D. July 2, 1950, Summit Hill, Pa.

Year	Team	Lg	W	L	PCT	ERA	G	GS	CG	IP	H	BB	SO	ShO	Relief Pitching W	Relief Pitching L	Relief Pitching SV	Batting AB	Batting H	Batting HR	BA	PO	A	E	DP	TC/G	FA
1891	**PHI**	**N**	0	1	.000	5.63	1	1	1	8	10	5	2	0	0	0	0	4	0	0	.000	0	3	0	0	3.0	1.000

Hank Gornicki

GORNICKI, HENRY FRANK BR TR 6′ 145 lbs.
B. Jan. 14, 1911, Niagara Falls, N. Y.

Year	Team	Lg	W	L	PCT	ERA	G	GS	CG	IP	H	BB	SO	ShO	Relief Pitching W	Relief Pitching L	Relief Pitching SV	Batting AB	Batting H	Batting HR	BA	PO	A	E	DP	TC/G	FA
1941	**2 teams**	**STL N** (4G 1–0)	**CHI N** (1G 0–0)																								
″	**total**		1	0	1.000	3.38	5	1	1	13.1	9	9	8	1	0	0	0	4	1	0	.250	0	3	0	1	0.6	1.000
1942	**PIT**	**N**	5	6	.455	2.57	25	14	7	112	89	40	48	2	0	0	2	35	4	1	.114	6	18	2	0	1.0	.923
1943			9	13	.409	3.98	42	18	4	147	165	47	63	1	3	3	4	40	7	0	.175	7	25	2	1	0.8	.941
1946			0	0	—	3.55	7	0	0	12.2	12	11	4	0	0	0	0	3	0	0	.000	0	2	0	0	0.3	1.000
4 yrs.			15	19	.441	3.38	79	33	12	285	275	107	123	4	3	3	6	82	12	1	.146	13	48	4	2	0.8	.938

Johnny Gorsica

GORSICA, JOHN JOSEPH PERRY BR TR 6′ 2″ 180 lbs.
Born John Joseph Perry Gorczyca.
B. Mar. 29, 1915, Bayonne, N. J.

Year	Team	Lg	W	L	PCT	ERA	G	GS	CG	IP	H	BB	SO	ShO	Relief Pitching W	Relief Pitching L	Relief Pitching SV	Batting AB	Batting H	Batting HR	BA	PO	A	E	DP	TC/G	FA
1940	**DET**	**A**	7	7	.500	4.33	29	20	5	160	170	57	68	2	0	0	0	62	12	1	.194	15	53	4	2	2.5	.944
1941			9	11	.450	4.47	33	21	8	171	193	55	59	1	4	1	2	57	17	0	.298	10	52	2	3	1.9	.969
1942			3	2	.600	4.75	28	0	0	53	63	26	19	0	3	2	4	10	1	0	.100	5	29	1	0	1.3	.971
1943			4	5	.444	3.36	35	4	1	96.1	88	40	45	0	4	3	5	23	4	0	.174	10	30	0	3	1.1	1.000
1944			6	14	.300	4.11	34	19	8	162	192	32	47	1	1	2	4	52	7	0	.135	17	42	2	5	1.8	.967
1946			0	0	—	4.56	14	0	0	23.2	28	11	14	0	0	0	1	3	2	0	.667	2	2	1	0	0.4	.800
1947			2	0	1.000	3.75	31	0	0	57.2	44	26	20	0	2	0	1	10	2	0	.200	9	12	0	1	0.7	1.000
7 yrs.			31	39	.443	4.18	204	64	22	723.2	778	247	272	4	14	8	17	217	45	1	.207	68	220	10	14	1.5	.966
WORLD SERIES																											
1940	**DET**	**A**	0	0	—	0.79	2	0	0	11.1	6	4	4	0	0	0	0	4	0	0	.000	0	6	0	1	3.0	1.000

Goose Gossage

GOSSAGE, RICHARD MICHAEL BR TR 6′ 3″ 180 lbs.
B. July 5, 1951, Colorado Springs, Colo.

Year	Team	Lg	W	L	PCT	ERA	G	GS	CG	IP	H	BB	SO	ShO	Relief Pitching W	Relief Pitching L	Relief Pitching SV	Batting AB	Batting H	Batting HR	BA	PO	A	E	DP	TC/G	FA
1972	**CHI**	**A**	7	1	.875	4.28	36	1	0	80	72	44	57	0	7	0	2	16	0	0	.000	3	10	1	1	0.4	.929
1973			0	4	.000	7.43	20	4	1	49.2	57	37	33	0	0	0	0	0	0	0	—	5	5	1	0	0.6	.909
1974			4	6	.400	4.15	39	3	0	89	92	47	64	0	4	5	1	0	0	0	—	3	14	2	1	0.5	.895
1975			9	8	.529	1.84	62	0	0	141.2	99	70	130	0	9	8	**26**	0	0	0	—	3	25	3	3	0.5	.903
1976			9	17	.346	3.94	31	29	15	224	214	90	135	0	0	1	1	0	0	0	—	18	27	3	1	1.5	.938
1977	**PIT**	**N**	11	9	.550	1.62	72	0	0	133	78	49	151	0	**11**	9	26	23	5	0	.217	4	10	1	0	0.2	.933
1978	**NY**	**A**	10	11	.476	2.01	63	0	0	134.1	87	59	122	0	10	11	**27**	0	0	0	—	6	12	3	0	0.3	.857
1979			5	3	.625	2.64	36	0	0	58	48	19	41	0	5	3	18	0	0	0	—	1	4	0	0	0.1	1.000
1980			6	2	.750	2.27	64	0	0	99	74	37	103	0	6	2	**33**	0	0	0	—	1	10	2	0	0.2	.846
1981			3	2	.600	0.77	32	0	0	47	22	14	48	0	3	2	20	0	0	0	—	2	7	1	1	0.3	.900
1982			4	5	.444	2.23	56	0	0	93	63	28	102	0	4	5	30	0	0	0	—	2	6	0	1	0.1	1.000
1983			13	5	.722	2.27	57	0	0	87.1	82	25	90	0	13	5	22	0	0	0	—	2	3	1	0	0.1	.833
1984	**SD**	**N**	10	6	.625	2.90	62	0	0	102.1	75	36	84	0	10	6	25	22	4	0	.182	5	8	0	0	0.2	1.000
1985			5	3	.625	1.82	50	0	0	79	64	17	52	0	5	3	26	11	0	0	.000	0	7	0	1	0.1	1.000
1986			5	7	.417	4.45	45	0	0	64.2	69	20	63	0	5	7	21	7	0	0	.000	2	5	0	0	0.2	1.000
1987			5	4	.556	3.12	40	0	0	52	47	19	44	0	5	4	11	4	0	0	.000	2	5	0	0	0.2	1.000
1988	**CHI**	**N**	4	4	.500	4.33	46	0	0	43.2	50	15	30	0	4	4	13	1	0	0	.000	1	7	0	0	0.2	1.000
1989	**2 teams**	**SF N** (31G 2–1)	**NY A** (11G 1–0)																								
″	**total**		3	1	.750	2.95	42	0	0	58	46	30	30	0	3	1	5	1	0	0	.000	7	4	1	1	0.3	.917
1991	**TEX**	**A**	4	2	.667	3.57	44	0	0	40.1	33	16	28	0	4	2	1	0	0	0	—	2	2	1	0	0.1	.800
1992	**OAK**	**A**	0	2	.000	2.84	30	0	0	38	32	19	26	0	0	2	0	0	0	0	—	2	4	0	0	0.2	1.000
1993			4	5	.444	4.53	39	0	0	47.2	49	26	40	0	4	5	1	0	0	0	—	5	3	1	0	0.2	.889
1994	**SEA**	**A**	3	0	1.000	4.18	36	0	0	47.1	44	15	29	0	3	0	1	0	0	0	—	2	2	0	1	0.1	1.000
22 yrs.			124	107	.537	3.01	1002 **3rd**	37	16	1809	1497	732	1502	0	115 **3rd**	85	310 **6th**	85	9	0	.106	78	180	21	11	0.3	.925
DIVISIONAL PLAYOFF SERIES																											
1981	**NY**	**A**	0	0	—	0.00	3	0	0	6.2	3	2	8	0	0	0	3	0	0	0	—	0	0	0	0	0.0	.000
LEAGUE CHAMPIONSHIP SERIES																											
1978	**NY**	**A**	1	0	1.000	4.50	2	0	0	4	3	0	3	0	1	0	1	0	0	0	—	0	1	0	0	0.5	1.000
1980			0	1	.000	54.00	1	0	0	0.1	3	0	0	0	0	1	0	0	0	0	—	0	0	0	0	0.0	.000
1981			0	0	—	0.00	2	0	0	2.2	1	0	2	0	0	0	1	0	0	0	—	0	0	0	0	0.0	.000
1984	**SD**	**N**	0	0	—	4.50	3	0	0	4	5	1	5	0	0	0	1	0	0	0	—	0	0	0	0	0.0	.000
4 yrs.			1	1	.500	4.91	8	0	0	11	12	1	10	0	1	1	3 **6th**	0	0	0		0	1	0	0	0.1	1.000
WORLD SERIES																											
1978	**NY**	**A**	1	0	1.000	0.00	3	0	0	6	1	1	4	0	1	0	0	0	0	0	—	0	0	0	0	0.0	.000
1981			0	0	—	0.00	3	0	0	5	2	2	5	0	0	0	2	1	0	0	.000	0	0	0	0	0.0	.000
1984	**SD**	**N**	0	0	—	13.50	2	0	0	2.2	3	1	2	0	0	0	0	0	0	0	—	0	1	0	0	0.5	1.000
3 yrs.			1	0	1.000	2.63	8	0	0	13.2	6	4	11	0	1	0	2	1	0	0	.000	0	1	0	0	0.1	1.000

Jim Gott

GOTT, JAMES WILLIAM BR TR 6′ 4″ 200 lbs.
B. Aug. 3, 1959, Hollywood, Calif.

Year	Team	Lg	W	L	PCT	ERA	G	GS	CG	IP	H	BB	SO	ShO	Relief Pitching W	Relief Pitching L	Relief Pitching SV	Batting AB	Batting H	Batting HR	BA	PO	A	E	DP	TC/G	FA
1982	**TOR**	**A**	5	10	.333	4.43	30	23	1	136	134	66	82	1	0	0	0	0	0	0	—	6	18	1	2	0.8	.960
1983			9	14	.391	4.74	34	30	6	176.2	195	68	121	1	0	1	0	0	0	0	—	9	20	1	2	0.9	.967
1984			7	6	.538	4.02	35	12	1	109.2	93	49	73	1	2	1	2	0	0	0	—	6	9	1	0	0.5	.938
1985	**SF**	**N**	7	10	.412	3.88	26	26	2	148.1	144	51	78	0	0	0	0	51	10	3	.196	9	28	0	0	1.4	1.000
1986			0	0	—	7.62	9	2	0	13	16	13	9	0	0	0	1	3	0	0	.000	0	2	0	0	0.2	1.000

Jim Gott *continued*

Year	Team	Lg	W	L	PCT	ERA	G	GS	CG	IP	H	BB	SO	ShO	Relief Pitching W	L	SV	Batting AB	H	HR	BA	PO	A	E	DP	TC/G	FA
1987	2 teams	SF N	(30G 1–0)		PIT N	(25G 0–2)																					
"	total		1	2	.333	3.41	55	3	0	87	81	40	90	0	1	2	13	11	1	1	.091	5	10	1	0	0.3	.938
1988	PIT	N	6	6	.500	3.49	67	0	0	77.1	68	22	76	0	6	6	34	1	0	0	.000	4	8	0	0	0.2	1.000
1989			0	0	—	0.00	1	0	0	0.2	1	1	1	0	0	0	0	0	0	0	—	0	0	0	0	0.0	.000
1990	LA	N	3	5	.375	2.90	50	0	0	62	59	34	44	0	3	5	3	1	0	0	.000	6	5	0	0	0.2	1.000
1991			4	3	.571	2.96	55	0	0	76	63	32	73	0	4	3	2	2	1	0	.500	10	9	0	1	0.3	1.000
1992			3	3	.500	2.45	68	0	0	88	72	41	75	0	3	3	6	2	1	0	.500	11	15	0	0	0.4	1.000
1993			4	8	.333	2.32	62	0	0	77.2	71	17	67	0	4	8	25	1	0	0	.000	8	8	0	1	0.3	1.000
1994			5	3	.625	5.94	37	0	0	36.1	46	20	29	0	5	3	2	0	0	0	—	3	6	2	1	0.3	.818
1995	PIT	N	2	4	.333	6.03	25	0	0	31.1	38	12	19	0	2	4	3	1	0	0	.000	2	7	1	0	0.4	.900
14 yrs.			56	74	.431	3.87	554	96	10	1120	1081	466	837	3	30	36	91	73	13	4	.178	79	145	7	7	0.4	.970

Ted Goulait

GOULAIT, THEODORE LEE (Snooze) BR TR 5′ 9½″ 172 lbs.
B. Aug. 12, 1889, St. Clair, Mich. D. July 15, 1936, St. Clair, Mich.

Year	Team	Lg	W	L	PCT	ERA	G	GS	CG	IP	H	BB	SO	ShO	Relief W	L	SV	AB	H	HR	BA	PO	A	E	DP	TC/G	FA
1912	NY	N	0	0	—	6.43	1	1	1	7	11	4	6	0	0	0	0	2	1	0	.500	1	1	0	0	2.0	1.000

Al Gould

GOULD, ALBERT FRANK (Pudgy) BR TR 5′ 6½″ 160 lbs.
B. Jan. 20, 1893, Muscatine, Iowa D. Aug. 8, 1982, San Jose, Calif.

Year	Team	Lg	W	L	PCT	ERA	G	GS	CG	IP	H	BB	SO	ShO	Relief W	L	SV	AB	H	HR	BA	PO	A	E	DP	TC/G	FA
1916	CLE	A	5	7	.417	2.53	30	9	6	106.2	101	40	41	1	0	3	1	29	3	0	.103	3	29	2	0	1.1	.941
1917			4	4	.500	3.64	27	7	1	94	95	52	24	0	2	1	0	24	5	0	.208	3	37	1	0	1.5	.976
2 yrs.			9	11	.450	3.05	57	16	7	200.2	196	92	65	1	2	4	1	53	8	0	.151	6	66	3	0	1.3	.960

Charlie Gould

GOULD, CHARLES HARVEY BR TR 6′ 172 lbs.
B. Aug. 21, 1847, Cincinnati, Ohio D. Apr. 10, 1917, Flushing, N. Y.
Manager 1876.

Year	Team	Lg	W	L	PCT	ERA	G	GS	CG	IP	H	BB	SO	ShO	Relief W	L	SV	AB	H	HR	BA	PO	A	E	DP	TC/G	FA
1876	CIN	N	0	0	—	0.00	2	0	0	4.1	10	0	0	0	0	0	0	*				584	14	40	28	10.1	.937

Larry Gowell

GOWELL, LAWRENCE CLYDE BR TR 6′ 2″ 182 lbs.
B. May 2, 1948, Lewiston, Me.

Year	Team	Lg	W	L	PCT	ERA	G	GS	CG	IP	H	BB	SO	ShO	Relief W	L	SV	AB	H	HR	BA	PO	A	E	DP	TC/G	FA
1972	NY	A	0	1	.000	1.29	2	1	0	7	3	2	7	0	0	0	0	1	1	0	1.000	0	1	0	0	0.5	1.000

Mauro Gozzo

GOZZO, MAURO PAUL (Goose) BR TR 6′ 2″ 210 lbs.
B. Mar. 7, 1966, New Britain, Conn.

Year	Team	Lg	W	L	PCT	ERA	G	GS	CG	IP	H	BB	SO	ShO	Relief W	L	SV	AB	H	HR	BA	PO	A	E	DP	TC/G	FA
1989	TOR	A	4	1	.800	4.83	9	3	0	31.2	35	9	10	0	1	1	0	0	0	0	—	3	3	0	0	0.7	1.000
1990	CLE	A	0	0	—	0.00	2	0	0	3	2	2	2	0	0	0	0	0	0	0	—	0	0	0	0	0.0	.000
1991			0	0	—	19.29	2	2	0	4.2	9	7	3	0	0	0	0	0	0	0	—	0	0	0	0	0.0	.000
1992	MIN	A	0	0	—	27.00	2	0	0	1.2	7	0	1	0	0	0	0	0	0	0	—	0	0	0	0	0.0	.000
1993	NY	N	0	1	.000	2.57	10	0	0	14	11	5	6	0	0	1	1	0	0	0	—	0	0	0	0	0.0	.000
1994			3	5	.375	4.83	23	8	0	69	86	28	33	0	1	2	0	16	4	0	.250	3	9	0	0	0.5	1.000
6 yrs.			7	7	.500	5.30	48	13	0	124	150	51	55	0	2	4	1	16	4	0	.250	6	12	0	0	0.4	1.000

Al Grabowski

GRABOWSKI, ALFONS FRANCIS (Hook) BL TL 5′11½″ 175 lbs.
Brother of Reggie Grabowski.
B. Sept. 4, 1901, Syracuse, N. Y. D. Oct. 29, 1966, Memphis, Tenn.

Year	Team	Lg	W	L	PCT	ERA	G	GS	CG	IP	H	BB	SO	ShO	Relief W	L	SV	AB	H	HR	BA	PO	A	E	DP	TC/G	FA
1929	STL	N	3	2	.600	2.52	6	6	4	50	44	8	22	2	0	0	0	16	4	0	.250	6	8	0	0	2.3	1.000
1930			6	4	.600	4.84	33	8	1	106	121	50	45	0	2	3	1	33	12	0	.364	4	21	2	0	0.8	.926
2 yrs.			9	6	.600	4.10	39	14	5	156	165	58	67	2	2	3	1	49	16	0	.327	10	29	2	0	1.1	.951

Reggie Grabowski

GRABOWSKI, REGINALD JOHN BR TR 6′½″ 185 lbs.
Brother of Al Grabowski.
B. July 16, 1907, Syracuse, N. Y. D. Apr. 2, 1955, Syracuse, N. Y.

Year	Team	Lg	W	L	PCT	ERA	G	GS	CG	IP	H	BB	SO	ShO	Relief W	L	SV	AB	H	HR	BA	PO	A	E	DP	TC/G	FA
1932	PHI	N	2	2	.500	3.67	14	2	0	34.1	38	22	15	0	2	1	0	6	0	0	.000	1	5	1	0	0.5	.857
1933			1	3	.250	2.44	10	5	4	48	38	10	9	1	0	0	0	16	2	0	.125	4	5	0	0	0.9	1.000
1934			1	3	.250	9.23	27	5	0	65.1	114	23	13	0	1	0	0	18	1	0	.056	5	6	0	2	0.4	1.000
3 yrs.			4	8	.333	5.73	51	12	4	147.2	190	55	37	1	3	1	0	40	3	0	.075	10	16	1	2	0.5	.963

Mike Grace

GRACE, MICHAEL JAMES BR TR 6′ 4″ 210 lbs.
B. June 20, 1970, Joliet, Ill.

Year	Team	Lg	W	L	PCT	ERA	G	GS	CG	IP	H	BB	SO	ShO	Relief W	L	SV	AB	H	HR	BA	PO	A	E	DP	TC/G	FA
1995	PHI	N	1	1	.500	3.18	2	2	0	11.1	10	4	7	0	0	0	0	2	0	0	.000	1	2	0	0	1.5	1.000

John Graff

GRAFF, JOHN F.
B. Philadelphia, Pa. Deceased.

Year	Team	Lg	W	L	PCT	ERA	G	GS	CG	IP	H	BB	SO	ShO	Relief W	L	SV	AB	H	HR	BA	PO	A	E	DP	TC/G	FA
1893	WAS	N	0	1	.000	11.25	2	1	1	12	21	13	4	0	0	0	0	5	1	0	.200	0	2	0	0	1.0	1.000

Bill Graham

GRAHAM, WILLIAM ALBERT BR TR 6′ 3″ 217 lbs.
B. Jan. 21, 1937, Flemingsburg, Ky.

Year	Team	Lg	W	L	PCT	ERA	G	GS	CG	IP	H	BB	SO	ShO	Relief W	L	SV	AB	H	HR	BA	PO	A	E	DP	TC/G	FA
1966	DET	A	0	0	—	0.00	1	0	0	2	2	0	2	0	0	0	0	0	0	0	—	0	0	0	0	0.0	.000
1967	NY	N	1	2	.333	2.63	5	3	1	27.1	20	11	14	0	0	0	0	8	1	0	.125	1	1	1	0	0.6	.667
2 yrs.			1	2	.333	2.45	6	3	1	29.1	22	11	16	0	0	0	0	8	1	0	.125	1	1	1	0	0.5	.667

Kyle Graham

GRAHAM, KYLE (Skinny) BR TR 6′ 2″ 172 lbs.
B. Aug. 14, 1899, Oak Grove, Ala. D. Dec. 1, 1973, Oak Grove, Ala.

Year	Team	Lg	W	L	PCT	ERA	G	GS	CG	IP	H	BB	SO	ShO	Relief W	L	SV	AB	H	HR	BA	PO	A	E	DP	TC/G	FA
1924	BOS	N	0	4	.000	3.82	5	4	1	33	33	11	15	0	0	0	0	7	0	0	.000	1	6	0	1	1.4	1.000
1925			7	12	.368	4.41	34	23	5	157	177	62	32	0	1	1	1	44	6	0	.136	4	28	1	1	1.0	.970
1926			3	3	.500	7.93	15	4	1	36.1	54	19	7	0	2	2	0	12	2	0	.167	1	11	0	0	0.8	1.000
1929	DET	A	1	3	.250	5.57	13	6	2	51.2	70	33	7	0	0	1	1	19	2	1	.105	0	9	0	1	0.7	1.000
4 yrs.			11	22	.333	5.02	67	37	9	278	334	125	61	0	3	4	2	82	10	1	.122	6	54	1	3	0.9	.984

Oscar Graham

GRAHAM, OSCAR M. BL TL 6′½″
B. July 20, 1878, Plattsmouth, Neb. D. Oct. 15, 1931, Moline, Ill.

Year	Team	Lg	W	L	PCT	ERA	G	GS	CG	IP	H	BB	SO	ShO	Relief W	L	SV	AB	H	HR	BA	PO	A	E	DP	TC/G	FA
1907	WAS	A	4	9	.308	3.98	20	14	6	104	116	29	44	0	0	1	0	48	11	1	.229	4	25	3	0	1.5	.906

Peaches Graham

GRAHAM, GEORGE FREDERICK BR TR 5′ 9″ 180 lbs.
Father of Jack Graham.
B. Mar. 23, 1877, Aledo, Ill. D. July 25, 1939, Long Beach, Calif.

Year	Team	Lg	W	L	PCT	ERA	G	GS	CG	IP	H	BB	SO	ShO	Relief Pitching W	Relief Pitching L	Relief Pitching SV	Batting AB	Batting H	Batting HR	BA	PO	A	E	DP	TC/G	FA
1903	CHI	N	0	1	.000	5.40	1	1	0	5	9	3	4	0	0	0	0	*				2	5	0	0	7.0	1.000

Bill Grahame

GRAHAME, WILLIAM JAMES TL 6′
B. July 22, 1883, Owosso, Mich. D. Feb. 15, 1936, Holt, Mich.

Year	Team	Lg	W	L	PCT	ERA	G	GS	CG	IP	H	BB	SO	ShO	Relief Pitching W	Relief Pitching L	Relief Pitching SV	Batting AB	Batting H	Batting HR	BA	PO	A	E	DP	TC/G	FA
1908	STL	A	6	7	.462	2.30	21	13	7	117.1	104	32	47	0	3	1	0	42	5	0	.119	6	35	2	2	2.0	.953
1909			8	14	.364	3.12	34	21	13	187.1	171	60	82	3	2	2	1	63	10	0	.159	9	58	4	5	2.1	.944
1910			0	8	.000	3.56	9	6	1	43	46	13	12	0	0	2	0	13	2	0	.154	1	8	4	0	1.4	.692
3 yrs.			14	29	.326	2.90	64	40	21	347.2	321	105	141	3	5	5	1	118	17	0	.144	16	101	10	7	2.0	.921

Joe Grahe

GRAHE, JOSEPH MILTON BR TR 6′ 1″ 196 lbs.
B. Aug. 14, 1967, West Palm Beach, Fla.

Year	Team	Lg	W	L	PCT	ERA	G	GS	CG	IP	H	BB	SO	ShO	Relief Pitching W	Relief Pitching L	Relief Pitching SV	Batting AB	Batting H	Batting HR	BA	PO	A	E	DP	TC/G	FA
1990	CAL	A	3	4	.429	4.98	8	8	0	43.1	51	23	25	0	0	0	0	0	0	0	—	2	11	0	2	1.6	1.000
1991			3	7	.300	4.81	18	10	1	73	84	33	40	0	1	0	0	0	0	0	—	4	11	1	0	0.9	.938
1992			5	6	.455	3.52	46	7	0	94.2	85	39	39	0	3	3	21	0	0	0	—	12	13	3	1	0.6	.893
1993			4	1	.800	2.86	45	0	0	56.2	54	25	31	0	4	1	11	0	0	0	—	3	13	0	1	0.4	1.000
1994			2	5	.286	6.65	40	0	0	43.1	68	18	26	0	2	5	13	0	0	0	—	3	8	0	0	0.3	1.000
1995	CLR	N	4	3	.571	5.08	17	9	0	56.2	69	27	27	0	0	1	0	12	5	0	.417	5	12	1	1	1.1	.944
6 yrs.			21	26	.447	4.46	174	34	1	367.2	411	165	188	0	10	10	45	12	5	0	.417	29	68	5	5	0.6	.951

Tommy Gramly

GRAMLY, BERT THOMAS BR TR 6′ 3″ 175 lbs.
B. Apr. 19, 1945, Dallas, Tex.

Year	Team	Lg	W	L	PCT	ERA	G	GS	CG	IP	H	BB	SO	ShO	Relief Pitching W	Relief Pitching L	Relief Pitching SV	Batting AB	Batting H	Batting HR	BA	PO	A	E	DP	TC/G	FA
1968	CLE	A	0	1	.000	2.70	3	0	0	3.1	3	2	1	0	0	1	0	0	0	0	—	0	0	0	0	0.0	.000

Henry Grampp

GRAMPP, HENRY ERCHARDT BR TR 6′ 1″ 185 lbs.
B. Sept. 28, 1903, New York, N. Y. D. Mar. 24, 1986, New York, N. Y.

Year	Team	Lg	W	L	PCT	ERA	G	GS	CG	IP	H	BB	SO	ShO	Relief Pitching W	Relief Pitching L	Relief Pitching SV	Batting AB	Batting H	Batting HR	BA	PO	A	E	DP	TC/G	FA
1927	CHI	N	0	0	—	9.00	2	0	0	3	4	1	3	0	0	0	0	0	0	0	—	0	1	0	0	0.5	1.000
1929			0	1	.000	27.00	1	1	0	2	4	3	0	0	0	0	0	0	0	0	—	0	0	0	0	0.0	.000
2 yrs.			0	1	.000	16.20	3	1	0	5	8	4	3	0	0	0	0	0	0	0		0	1	0	0	0.3	1.000

Jack Graney

GRANEY, JOHN GLADSTONE BL TL 5′ 9″ 180 lbs.
B. June 10, 1886, St. Thomas, Ont., Canada D. Apr. 20, 1978, Louisiana, Mo.

Year	Team	Lg	W	L	PCT	ERA	G	GS	CG	IP	H	BB	SO	ShO	Relief Pitching W	Relief Pitching L	Relief Pitching SV	Batting AB	Batting H	Batting HR	BA	PO	A	E	DP	TC/G	FA
1908	CLE	A	0	0	—	5.40	2	0	0	3.1	6	1	0	0	0	0	0	*				0	0	0	0	0.0	.000

Jeff Granger

GRANGER, JEFFREY ADAM BR TL 6′ 4″ 200 lbs.
B. Dec. 16, 1971, San Pedro, Calif.

Year	Team	Lg	W	L	PCT	ERA	G	GS	CG	IP	H	BB	SO	ShO	Relief Pitching W	Relief Pitching L	Relief Pitching SV	Batting AB	Batting H	Batting HR	BA	PO	A	E	DP	TC/G	FA
1993	KC	A	0	0	—	27.00	1	0	0	1	3	2	1	0	0	0	0	0	0	0	—	0	0	0	0	0.0	.000
1994			0	1	.000	6.75	2	2	0	9.1	13	6	3	0	0	0	0	0	0	0	—	0	2	0	0	1.0	1.000
2 yrs.			0	1	.000	8.71	3	2	0	10.1	16	8	4	0	0	0	0	0	0	0		0	2	0	0	0.7	1.000

Wayne Granger

GRANGER, WAYNE ALLAN BR TR 6′ 2″ 165 lbs.
B. Mar. 15, 1944, Springfield, Mass.

Year	Team	Lg	W	L	PCT	ERA	G	GS	CG	IP	H	BB	SO	ShO	Relief Pitching W	Relief Pitching L	Relief Pitching SV	Batting AB	Batting H	Batting HR	BA	PO	A	E	DP	TC/G	FA
1968	STL	N	4	2	.667	2.25	34	0	0	44	40	12	27	0	4	2	4	5	1	0	.200	6	14	2	1	0.6	.909
1969	CIN	N	9	6	.600	2.79	**90**	0	0	145	143	40	68	0	9	6	27	21	2	0	.095	14	29	2	3	0.5	.956
1970			6	5	.545	2.65	67	0	0	85	79	27	38	0	6	5	**35**	10	1	0	.100	8	22	4	4	0.5	.882
1971			7	6	.538	3.33	**70**	0	0	100	94	28	51	0	7	6	11	7	1	1	.143	9	29	0	1	0.5	1.000
1972	MIN	A	4	6	.400	3.00	63	0	0	90	83	28	45	0	4	6	19	10	2	0	.200	5	14	2	0	0.3	.905
1973	2 teams	STL N (33G 2–4) NY A (7G 0–1)																									
″	total		2	5	.286	3.63	40	0	0	62	69	24	24	0	2	5	5	3	0	0	.000	4	8	3	0	0.4	.800
1974	CHI	A	0	0	—	7.88	5	0	0	8	16	3	4	0	0	0	0	0	0	0	—	1	2	0	1	0.6	1.000
1975	HOU	N	2	5	.286	3.65	55	0	0	74	76	23	30	0	2	5	5	9	0	0	.000	2	18	3	1	0.4	.870
1976	MON	N	1	0	1.000	3.66	27	0	0	32	32	16	16	0	1	0	2	3	0	0	.000	1	5	1	0	0.3	.857
9 yrs.			35	35	.500	3.14	451	0	0	640	632	201	303	0	35	35	108	68	7	1	.103	50	141	17	11	0.5	.918
LEAGUE CHAMPIONSHIP SERIES																											
1970	CIN	N	0	0	—	0.00	1	0	0	0.2	1	0	0	0	0	0	0	0	0	0	—	0	0	0	0	0.0	.000
WORLD SERIES																											
1968	STL	N	0	0	—	0.00	1	0	0	2	0	1	1	0	0	0	0	0	0	0	—	0	1	0	1	1.0	1.000
1970	CIN	N	0	0	—	33.75	2	0	0	1.1	7	1	1	0	0	0	0	0	0	0	—	0	1	0	0	0.5	1.000
2 yrs.			0	0		13.50	3	0	0	3.1	7	2	2	0	0	0	0	0	0	0		0	2	0	1	0.7	1.000

George Grant

GRANT, GEORGE ADDISON BR TR 5′11½″ 175 lbs.
B. Jan. 6, 1903, East Tallassee, Ala. D. Mar. 25, 1986, Montgomery, Ala.

Year	Team	Lg	W	L	PCT	ERA	G	GS	CG	IP	H	BB	SO	ShO	Relief Pitching W	Relief Pitching L	Relief Pitching SV	Batting AB	Batting H	Batting HR	BA	PO	A	E	DP	TC/G	FA
1923	STL	A	0	0	—	5.19	4	0	0	8.2	15	3	2	0	0	0	0	2	0	0	.000	0	4	0	0	1.0	1.000
1924			1	2	.333	6.26	21	2	0	50.1	67	25	11	0	1	0	0	13	0	0	.000	5	8	0	0	0.6	1.000
1925			0	2	.000	6.06	12	0	0	16.1	26	8	7	0	0	2	0	4	1	0	.250	1	5	1	1	0.6	.857
1927	CLE	A	4	6	.400	4.46	25	3	2	74.2	85	40	19	0	3	4	1	21	2	0	.095	6	19	0	0	1.0	1.000
1928			10	8	.556	5.04	28	18	6	155.1	196	76	39	1	2	1	0	60	11	0	.183	9	46	0	2	2.0	1.000
1929			0	2	.000	10.50	12	0	0	24	41	23	5	0	0	2	0	2	0	0	.000	0	7	0	0	0.6	1.000
1931	PIT	N	0	0	—	7.41	11	0	0	17	28	7	6	0	0	0	0	2	0	0	.000	2	4	1	1	0.6	.857
7 yrs.			15	20	.429	5.64	113	23	8	346.1	458	182	89	1	6	9	1	104	14	0	.135	23	93	2	4	1.0	.983

Jim Grant

GRANT, JAMES RONALD BR TL 5′11″ 180 lbs.
B. Aug. 4, 1894, Coalville, Iowa D. Nov. 30, 1985, Des Moines, Iowa.

Year	Team	Lg	W	L	PCT	ERA	G	GS	CG	IP	H	BB	SO	ShO	Relief Pitching W	Relief Pitching L	Relief Pitching SV	Batting AB	Batting H	Batting HR	BA	PO	A	E	DP	TC/G	FA
1923	PHI	N	0	0	—	13.50	2	0	0	4	10	4	0	0	0	0	0	1	0	0	.000	0	1	0	0	0.5	1.000

Mark Grant

GRANT, MARK ANDREW BR TR 6′ 2″ 205 lbs.
B. Oct. 24, 1963, Aurora, Ill.

Year	Team	Lg	W	L	PCT	ERA	G	GS	CG	IP	H	BB	SO	ShO	Relief Pitching W	Relief Pitching L	Relief Pitching SV	Batting AB	Batting H	Batting HR	BA	PO	A	E	DP	TC/G	FA
1984	SF	N	1	4	.200	6.37	11	10	0	53.2	56	19	32	0	0	0	1	17	0	0	.000	6	6	1	0	1.2	.923
1986			0	1	.000	3.60	4	1	0	10	6	5	5	0	0	0	0	1	0	0	.000	0	1	0	1	0.3	1.000
1987	2 teams	SF N (16G 1–2) SD N (17G 6–7)																									
″	total		7	9	.438	4.24	33	25	2	163.1	170	73	90	1	1	1	1	44	4	0	.091	10	21	4	0	1.1	.886
1988	SD	N	2	8	.200	3.69	33	11	0	97.2	97	36	61	0	1	3	0	16	0	0	.000	4	16	0	1	0.6	1.000
1989			8	2	.800	3.33	50	0	0	116.1	105	32	69	0	8	2	2	20	1	0	.050	9	14	1	1	0.5	.958

Mark Grant *continued*

Year	Team	W	L	PCT	ERA	G	GS	CG	IP	H	BB	SO	ShO	Relief Pitching W	Relief Pitching L	Relief Pitching SV	Batting AB	Batting H	Batting HR	BA	PO	A	E	DP	TC/G	FA
1990	**2 teams** **SD N** (26G 1–1) **ATL N** (33G 1–2)																									
″	**total**	2	3	.400	4.73	59	1	0	91.1	108	37	69	0	2	3	3	6	2	0	.333	6	14	1	1	0.4	.952
1992	**SEA A**	2	4	.333	3.89	23	10	0	81	100	22	42	0	0	0	0	0	0	0	—	6	7	3	0	0.7	.813
1993	**2 teams** **HOU N** (6G 0–0) **CLR N** (14G 0–1)																									
″	**total**	0	1	.000	7.46	20	0	0	25.1	34	11	14	0	0	1	1	0	0	0		1	6	0	1	0.3	1.000
8 yrs.		22	32	.407	4.31	233	58	2	638.2	676	235	382	1	12	10	8	104	7	0	.067	42	85	10	5	0.6	.927

Mudcat Grant

GRANT, JAMES TIMOTHY BR TR 6′ 1″ 186 lbs.
B. Aug. 13, 1935, Lacoochee, Fla.

Year	Team	W	L	PCT	ERA	G	GS	CG	IP	H	BB	SO	ShO	Relief Pitching W	Relief Pitching L	Relief Pitching SV	Batting AB	Batting H	Batting HR	BA	PO	A	E	DP	TC/G	FA
1958	**CLE A**	10	11	.476	3.84	44	28	11	204	173	104	111	1	2	2	4	66	5	0	.076	7	28	3	2	0.9	.921
1959		10	7	.588	4.14	38	19	6	165.1	140	81	85	1	1	1	3	55	11	1	.200	14	25	2	3	1.1	.951
1960		9	8	.529	4.40	33	19	5	159.2	147	78	75	0	1	3	0	57	16	0	.281	25	15	2	1	1.3	.952
1961		15	9	.625	3.86	35	35	11	244.2	207	109	146	3	0	0	0	88	15	1	.170	25	36	2	4	1.8	.968
1962		7	10	.412	4.27	26	23	6	149.2	128	81	90	1	0	0	0	53	8	0	.151	5	23	0	3	1.1	1.000
1963		13	14	.481	3.69	38	32	10	229.1	213	87	157	2	1	0	1	69	13	1	.188	11	21	3	1	0.9	.914
1964	**2 teams** **CLE A** (13G 3–4) **MIN A** (26G 11–9)																									
″	**total**	14	13	.519	3.67	39	32	11	228	244	61	118	1	1	0	1	82	16	2	.195	19	35	0	6	1.4	1.000
1965	**MIN A**	**21**	7	**.750**	3.30	41	39	14	270.1	252	61	142	**6**	0	1	0	97	15	0	.155	16	50	2	6	1.7	.971
1966		13	13	.500	3.25	35	35	10	249	248	49	110	3	0	0	0	78	15	0	.192	9	55	3	6	1.9	.955
1967		5	6	.455	4.72	27	14	2	95.1	121	17	50	0	0	0	0	28	5	0	.179	3	7	1	3	0.4	.909
1968	**LA N**	6	4	.600	2.08	37	4	1	95	77	19	35	0	5	2	3	31	4	1	.129	4	21	0	0	0.7	1.000
1969	**2 teams** **MON N** (11G 1–6) **STL N** (30G 7–5)																									
″	**total**	8	11	.421	4.42	41	13	2	114	126	36	55	0	6	3	7	33	7	0	.212	9	16	1	0	0.6	.962
1970	**2 teams** **OAK A** (72G 6–2) **PIT N** (8G 2–1)																									
″	**total**	8	3	.727	1.87	80	0	0	135	112	32	58	0	8	3	24	11	2	0	.182	10	24	0	3	0.4	1.000
1971	**2 teams** **PIT N** (42G 5–3) **OAK A** (15G 1–0)																									
″	**total**	6	3	.667	3.18	57	0	0	102	104	34	35	0	6	3	10	11	3	0	.273	5	20	0	0	0.4	1.000
14 yrs.		145	119	.549	3.63	571	293	89	2441.1	2292	849	1267	18	31	18	53	759	135	6	.178	162	376	19	38	1.0	.966
LEAGUE CHAMPIONSHIP SERIES																										
1971	**OAK A**	0	0	—	0.00	1	0	0	2	3	0	2	0	0	0	0	0	0	0	—	0	1	0	0	1.0	1.000
WORLD SERIES																										
1965	**MIN A**	2	1	.667	2.74	3	3	2	23	22	2	12	0	0	0	0	8	2	1	.250	0	1	0	0	0.3	1.000

Dick Grapenthin

GRAPENTHIN, RICHARD RAY BR TR 6′ 2″ 190 lbs.
B. Apr. 16, 1958, Linn Grove, Iowa.

Year	Team	W	L	PCT	ERA	G	GS	CG	IP	H	BB	SO	ShO	Relief Pitching W	Relief Pitching L	Relief Pitching SV	Batting AB	Batting H	Batting HR	BA	PO	A	E	DP	TC/G	FA
1983	**MON N**	0	1	.000	9.00	1	0	0	4	4	1	3	0	0	1	0	1	0	0	.000	0	1	0	0	1.0	1.000
1984		1	2	.333	3.52	13	1	0	23	19	7	9	0	1	1	2	5	1	0	.200	2	4	0	0	0.5	1.000
1985		0	0	—	14.14	5	0	0	7	13	8	4	0	0	0	0	1	1	0	1.000	0	1	0	0	0.2	1.000
3 yrs.		1	3	.250	6.35	19	1	0	34	36	16	16	0	1	2	2	7	2	0	.286	2	6	0	0	0.4	1.000

Lou Grasmick

GRASMICK, LOUIS JUNIOR BR TR 6′ 195 lbs.
B. Sept. 11, 1924, Baltimore, Md.

Year	Team	W	L	PCT	ERA	G	GS	CG	IP	H	BB	SO	ShO	Relief Pitching W	Relief Pitching L	Relief Pitching SV	Batting AB	Batting H	Batting HR	BA	PO	A	E	DP	TC/G	FA
1948	**PHI N**	0	0	—	7.20	2	0	0	5	3	8	2	0	0	0	0	1	1	0	1.000	1	1	0	0	1.0	1.000

Don Grate

GRATE, DONALD (Buckeye) BR TR 6′ 2½″ 180 lbs.
B. Aug. 27, 1923, Greenfield, Ohio.

Year	Team	W	L	PCT	ERA	G	GS	CG	IP	H	BB	SO	ShO	Relief Pitching W	Relief Pitching L	Relief Pitching SV	Batting AB	Batting H	Batting HR	BA	PO	A	E	DP	TC/G	FA
1945	**PHI N**	0	1	.000	17.28	4	2	0	8.1	18	12	6	0	0	0	0	3	0	0	.000	0	0	0	0	0.0	.000
1946		1	0	1.000	1.13	3	0	0	8	4	2	2	0	1	0	0	1	0	0	.000	0	0	0	0	0.0	.000
2 yrs.		1	1	.500	9.37	7	2	0	16.1	22	14	8	0	1	0	0	4	0	0	.000	0	0	0	0	0.0	

Mark Grater

GRATER, MARK ANTHONY BR TR 5′10″ 205 lbs.
B. Jan. 19, 1964, Rochester, Pa.

Year	Team	W	L	PCT	ERA	G	GS	CG	IP	H	BB	SO	ShO	Relief Pitching W	Relief Pitching L	Relief Pitching SV	Batting AB	Batting H	Batting HR	BA	PO	A	E	DP	TC/G	FA
1991	**STL N**	0	0	—	0.00	3	0	0	3	5	2	0	0	0	0	0	0	0	0	—	1	0	1	0	0.7	.500
1993	**DET A**	0	0	—	5.40	6	0	0	5	6	4	4	0	0	0	0	0	0	0	—	0	0	0	0	0.0	.000
2 yrs.		0	0		3.38	9	0	0	8	11	6	4	0	0	0	0	0	0	0		1	0	1	0	0.2	.500

Frank Graves

GRAVES, FRANK M. 6′ 163 lbs.
B. Nov. 2, 1860, Cincinnati, Ohio Deceased.

Year	Team	W	L	PCT	ERA	G	GS	CG	IP	H	BB	SO	ShO	Relief Pitching W	Relief Pitching L	Relief Pitching SV	Batting AB	Batting H	Batting HR	BA	PO	A	E	DP	TC/G	FA
1886	**STL N**	0	0	—	9.00	1	0	0	7	10	1	2	0	0	0	0	*				227	77	41	3	7.7	.881

Charlie Gray

GRAY, CHARLES
B. 1867, Indianapolis, Ind. Deceased.

Year	Team	W	L	PCT	ERA	G	GS	CG	IP	H	BB	SO	ShO	Relief Pitching W	Relief Pitching L	Relief Pitching SV	Batting AB	Batting H	Batting HR	BA	PO	A	E	DP	TC/G	FA
1890	**PIT N**	1	4	.200	7.55	5	4	3	31	48	24	10	0	1	0	0	15	3	0	.200	0	3	0	1	0.6	1.000

Chummy Gray

GRAY, GEORGE EDWARD TR 5′11½″ 163 lbs.
B. July 17, 1873, Rockland, Me. D. Aug. 14, 1913, Rockland, Me.

Year	Team	W	L	PCT	ERA	G	GS	CG	IP	H	BB	SO	ShO	Relief Pitching W	Relief Pitching L	Relief Pitching SV	Batting AB	Batting H	Batting HR	BA	PO	A	E	DP	TC/G	FA
1899	**PIT N**	3	3	.500	3.44	9	7	6	70.2	85	24	9	0	0	0	0	26	1	0	.038	1	26	0	0	3.0	1.000

Dave Gray

GRAY, DAVID ALEXANDER BR TR 6′ 1″ 190 lbs.
B. Jan. 7, 1943, Ogden, Utah.

Year	Team	W	L	PCT	ERA	G	GS	CG	IP	H	BB	SO	ShO	Relief Pitching W	Relief Pitching L	Relief Pitching SV	Batting AB	Batting H	Batting HR	BA	PO	A	E	DP	TC/G	FA
1964	**BOS A**	0	0	—	9.00	9	1	0	13	18	20	17	0	0	0	0	1	1	0	1.000	0	3	0	0	0.3	1.000

Dolly Gray

GRAY, WILLIAM DENTON BL TL 6′ 2″ 160 lbs.
B. Dec. 3, 1878, Houghton, Mich. D. Apr. 4, 1956, Yuba City, Calif.

Year	Team	W	L	PCT	ERA	G	GS	CG	IP	H	BB	SO	ShO	Relief Pitching W	Relief Pitching L	Relief Pitching SV	Batting AB	Batting H	Batting HR	BA	PO	A	E	DP	TC/G	FA
1909	**WAS A**	5	19	.208	3.59	36	26	19	218	210	77	87	0	0	0	0	89	13	0	.146	4	65	4	2	2.0	.945
1910		8	19	.296	2.63	34	29	21	229	216	64	84	3	0	2	0	85	21	0	.247	15	82	9	2	3.1	.915
1911		2	13	.133	5.06	28	15	6	121	160	40	42	0	0	3	0	44	10	0	.227	4	42	6	1	1.9	.885
3 yrs.		15	51	.227	3.52	98	70	46	568	586	181	213	3	0	5	0	218	44	0	.202	23	189	19	5	2.3	.918

Jeff Gray

GRAY, JEFFREY EDWARD
B. Apr. 10, 1963, Richmond, Va.

BR TR 6′ 1″ 175 lbs.

Year	Team	Lg	W	L	PCT	ERA	G	GS	CG	IP	H	BB	SO	ShO	Relief Pitching W	Relief Pitching L	Relief Pitching SV	Batting AB	Batting H	Batting HR	BA	PO	A	E	DP	TC/G	FA
1988	**CIN**	**N**	0	0	—	3.86	5	0	0	9.1	12	4	5	0	0	0	0	1	0	0	.000	1	3	0	0	0.8	1.000
1990	**BOS**	**A**	2	4	.333	4.44	41	0	0	50.2	53	15	50	0	2	4	9	0	0	0	—	2	5	0	1	0.2	1.000
1991			2	3	.400	2.34	50	0	0	61.2	39	10	41	0	2	3	1	0	0	0	—	7	10	1	0	0.4	.944
3 yrs.			4	7	.364	3.33	96	0	0	121.2	104	29	96	0	4	7	10	1	0	0	.000	10	18	1	1	0.3	.966
LEAGUE CHAMPIONSHIP SERIES																											
1990	**BOS**	**A**	0	0	—	2.70	2	0	0	3.1	4	1	2	0	0	0	0	0	0	0	—	0	0	1	0	0.5	.000

John Gray

GRAY, JOHN LEONARD
B. Dec. 11, 1927, West Palm Beach, Fla.

BR TR 6′ 4″ 226 lbs.

Year	Team	Lg	W	L	PCT	ERA	G	GS	CG	IP	H	BB	SO	ShO	Relief Pitching W	Relief Pitching L	Relief Pitching SV	Batting AB	Batting H	Batting HR	BA	PO	A	E	DP	TC/G	FA
1954	**PHI**	**A**	3	12	.200	6.51	18	16	5	105	111	91	51	0	0	0	0	34	1	0	.029	11	14	1	2	1.4	.962
1955	**KC**	**A**	0	3	.000	6.41	8	5	0	26.2	28	24	11	0	0	0	0	8	1	0	.125	2	1	0	0	0.4	1.000
1957	**CLE**	**A**	1	3	.250	5.85	7	3	1	20	21	13	3	1	0	1	0	4	0	0	.000	3	3	1	0	1.0	.857
1958	**PHI**	**N**	0	0	—	4.15	15	0	0	17.1	12	14	10	0	0	0	0	1	0	0	.000	0	3	0	0	0.2	1.000
4 yrs.			4	18	.182	6.18	48	24	6	169	172	142	75	1	0	1	0	47	2	0	.043	16	21	2	2	0.8	.949

Sam Gray

GRAY, SAMUEL DAVID (Sad Sam)
B. Oct. 15, 1897, Van Alstyne, Tex. D. Apr. 16, 1953, McKinney, Tex.

BR TR 5′10″ 175 lbs.

Year	Team	Lg	W	L	PCT	ERA	G	GS	CG	IP	H	BB	SO	ShO	Relief Pitching W	Relief Pitching L	Relief Pitching SV	Batting AB	Batting H	Batting HR	BA	PO	A	E	DP	TC/G	FA
1924	**PHI**	**A**	8	7	.533	3.98	34	19	8	151.2	169	89	54	2	1	0	2	57	10	0	.175	5	31	1	2	1.1	.973
1925			16	8	.667	3.40	32	28	14	195.2	199	63	80	4	0	0	3	67	12	0	.179	8	37	3	1	1.5	.938
1926			11	12	.478	3.64	38	18	5	150.2	164	50	82	0	4	3	0	51	11	0	.216	5	29	7	2	1.1	.829
1927			9	6	.600	4.60	37	13	3	141	162	53	54	1	2	2	3	42	8	0	.190	8	32	3	2	1.2	.930
1928	**STL**	**A**	20	12	.625	3.19	35	31	21	262.2	256	86	102	2	1	0	3	101	19	1	.188	20	67	2	6	2.5	.978
1929			18	15	.545	3.72	43	**37**	23	**305**	**336**	96	109	**4**	1	0	1	103	19	0	.184	9	61	3	4	1.7	.959
1930			4	15	.211	6.28	27	24	7	167.2	215	52	51	0	0	1	0	54	11	0	.204	3	33	5	2	1.5	.878
1931			11	**24**	.314	5.09	43	**37**	13	258	**323**	54	88	0	1	1	2	79	14	1	.177	11	49	8	0	1.6	.882
1932			8	12	.400	4.53	52	18	7	206.2	250	53	79	3	2	1	4	62	13	0	.210	9	39	4	1	1.0	.923
1933			7	4	.636	4.10	38	6	0	112	131	45	36	0	4	4	4	32	7	0	.219	3	21	2	2	0.7	.923
10 yrs.			112	115	.493	4.20	379	231	101	1951	2205	641	735	16	16	12	22	648	124	2	.191	81	399	38	22	1.4	.927

Ted Gray

GRAY, TED GLENN
B. Dec. 31, 1924, Detroit, Mich.

BB TL 5′11″ 175 lbs.
BR 1946

Year	Team	Lg	W	L	PCT	ERA	G	GS	CG	IP	H	BB	SO	ShO	Relief Pitching W	Relief Pitching L	Relief Pitching SV	Batting AB	Batting H	Batting HR	BA	PO	A	E	DP	TC/G	FA
1946	**DET**	**A**	0	2	.000	8.49	3	2	0	11.2	17	5	5	0	0	0	1	3	0	0	.000	1	1	0	0	0.7	1.000
1948			6	2	.750	4.22	26	11	3	85.1	73	72	60	1	0	0	0	29	7	0	.241	3	11	0	1	0.5	1.000
1949			10	10	.500	3.51	34	27	8	195	163	103	96	3	0	0	1	63	8	0	.127	9	37	0	3	1.4	1.000
1950			10	7	.588	4.40	27	21	7	149.1	139	72	102	0	1	0	1	50	7	0	.140	5	16	1	0	0.8	.955
1951			7	**14**	.333	4.06	34	28	9	197.1	194	95	131	1	0	1	1	63	9	0	.143	10	25	3	2	1.1	.921
1952			12	17	.414	4.14	35	32	13	224	212	101	138	2	0	0	0	76	13	0	.171	14	40	2	3	1.6	.964
1953			10	15	.400	4.60	30	28	8	176	166	76	115	0	0	0	0	61	14	0	.230	9	22	2	0	1.1	.939
1954			3	5	.375	5.38	19	10	2	72	70	56	29	0	0	0	0	22	1	0	.045	0	9	1	1	0.5	.900
1955	**4 teams**	**CHI A** (2G 0–0) **CLE A** (2G 0–0) **NY A** (1G 0–0) **BAL A** (9G 1–2)																									
″	**total**		1	2	.333	9.64	14	3	0	23.1	38	15	11	0	1	1	0	3	0	0	.000	1	7	0	1	0.6	1.000
9 yrs.			59	74	.444	4.37	222	162	50	1134	1072	595	687	7	2	2	4	370	59	0	.159	52	168	9	11	1.0	.961

Eli Grba

GRBA, ELI
B. Aug. 9, 1934, Chicago, Ill.

BR TR 6′ 2″ 205 lbs.

Year	Team	Lg	W	L	PCT	ERA	G	GS	CG	IP	H	BB	SO	ShO	Relief Pitching W	Relief Pitching L	Relief Pitching SV	Batting AB	Batting H	Batting HR	BA	PO	A	E	DP	TC/G	FA
1959	**NY**	**A**	2	5	.286	6.44	19	6	0	50.1	52	39	23	0	1	1	0	14	3	0	.214	3	9	1	0	0.7	.923
1960			6	4	.600	3.68	24	9	1	80.2	65	46	32	0	5	0	1	21	5	1	.238	9	9	1	1	0.8	.947
1961	**LA**	**A**	11	13	.458	4.25	40	30	8	211.2	197	114	105	0	2	1	2	64	15	2	.234	11	31	2	2	1.1	.955
1962			8	9	.471	4.54	40	29	1	176.1	185	75	90	0	0	0	1	58	12	1	.207	9	37	7	3	1.3	.868
1963			1	2	.333	4.67	12	1	0	17.1	14	10	5	0	1	1	0	3	0	0	.000	2	3	0	1	0.4	1.000
5 yrs.			28	33	.459	4.48	135	75	10	536.1	513	284	255	0	9	3	4	160	35	4	.219	34	89	11	7	1.0	.918

Bill Greason

GREASON, WILLIAM HENRY (Booster)
B. Sept. 3, 1924, Atlanta, Ga.

BR TR 5′10″ 170 lbs.

Year	Team	Lg	W	L	PCT	ERA	G	GS	CG	IP	H	BB	SO	ShO	Relief Pitching W	Relief Pitching L	Relief Pitching SV	Batting AB	Batting H	Batting HR	BA	PO	A	E	DP	TC/G	FA
1954	**STL**	**N**	0	1	.000	13.50	3	2	0	4	8	4	2	0	0	0	0	1	0	0	.000	0	1	0	0	0.3	1.000

Chris Green

GREEN, CHRISTOPHER DeWAYNE
B. Sept. 5, 1960, Los Angeles, Calif.

BL TL 6′ 2″ 180 lbs.

Year	Team	Lg	W	L	PCT	ERA	G	GS	CG	IP	H	BB	SO	ShO	Relief Pitching W	Relief Pitching L	Relief Pitching SV	Batting AB	Batting H	Batting HR	BA	PO	A	E	DP	TC/G	FA
1984	**PIT**	**N**	0	0	—	6.00	4	0	0	3	5	1	3	0	0	0	0	0	0	0	—	0	1	0	0	0.3	1.000

Dallas Green

GREEN, GEORGE DALLAS
B. Aug. 4, 1934, Newport, Del.
Manager 1979–81, 1989, 1993–95.

BL TR 6′ 5″ 210 lbs.

Year	Team	Lg	W	L	PCT	ERA	G	GS	CG	IP	H	BB	SO	ShO	Relief Pitching W	Relief Pitching L	Relief Pitching SV	Batting AB	Batting H	Batting HR	BA	PO	A	E	DP	TC/G	FA
1960	**PHI**	**N**	3	6	.333	4.06	23	10	5	108.2	100	44	51	1	0	1	0	34	7	0	.206	11	15	0	0	1.1	1.000
1961			2	4	.333	4.85	42	10	1	128	160	47	51	1	1	1	1	33	5	0	.152	14	22	1	2	0.9	.973
1962			6	6	.500	3.83	37	10	2	129.1	145	43	58	0	3	1	1	32	2	0	.063	17	28	0	1	1.2	1.000
1963			7	5	.583	3.23	40	14	4	120	134	38	68	0	3	0	2	35	3	0	.086	11	26	1	1	0.9	.974
1964			2	1	.667	5.79	25	0	0	42	63	14	21	0	2	1	0	3	0	0	.000	0	8	3	0	0.4	.727
1965	**WAS**	**A**	0	0	—	3.14	6	2	0	14.1	14	3	6	0	0	0	0	4	0	0	.000	3	3	0	0	1.0	1.000
1966	**NY**	**N**	0	0	—	5.40	4	0	0	5	6	2	1	0	0	0	0	0	0	0	—	0	2	0	0	0.5	1.000
1967	**PHI**	**N**	0	0	—	9.00	8	0	0	15	25	6	12	0	0	0	0	1	0	0	.000	0	5	0	0	0.6	1.000
8 yrs.			20	22	.476	4.26	185	46	12	562.1	647	197	268	2	9	4	4	142	17	0	.120	56	109	5	4	0.9	.971

Ed Green

GREEN, EDWARD M.
B. 1850, Philadelphia, Pa. Deceased.

Year	Team	Lg	W	L	PCT	ERA	G	GS	CG	IP	H	BB	SO	ShO	Relief Pitching W	Relief Pitching L	Relief Pitching SV	Batting AB	Batting H	Batting HR	BA	PO	A	E	DP	TC/G	FA
1890	**PHI**	**AA**	7	15	.318	*5.80*	25	22	20	191	267	94	56	1	0	0	1	126	15	0	.119	33	84	14	2	3.3	.893

Freddie Green

GREEN, FRED ALLEN
Father of Gary Green.
B. Sept. 14, 1933, Titusville, N. J.

BR TL 6′ 4″ 190 lbs.

Year	Team	Lg	W	L	PCT	ERA	G	GS	CG	IP	H	BB	SO	ShO	Relief Pitching W	Relief Pitching L	Relief Pitching SV	Batting AB	Batting H	Batting HR	BA	PO	A	E	DP	TC/G	FA
1959	**PIT**	**N**	1	2	.333	3.13	17	1	0	37.1	37	15	20	0	1	1	1	6	0	0	.000	2	8	0	0	0.6	1.000
1960			8	4	.667	3.21	45	0	0	70	61	33	49	0	8	4	3	8	3	2	.375	4	9	1	0	0.3	.929
1961			0	0	—	4.79	13	0	0	20.2	27	9	4	0	0	0	0	3	0	0	.000	1	7	0	1	0.6	1.000

Freddie Green *continued*

Year	Team	Lg	W	L	PCT	ERA	G	GS	CG	IP	H	BB	SO	ShO	Relief W	Relief L	Relief SV	AB	H	HR	BA	PO	A	E	DP	TC/G	FA
1962	WAS	A	0	1	.000	6.43	5	0	0	7	7	6	2	0	0	1	0	0	0	0	—	0	2	0	0	0.4	1.000
1964	PIT	N	0	0	—	1.23	8	0	0	7.1	10	0	2	0	0	0	0	0	0	0	—	0	0	1	0	0.1	.000
5 yrs.			9	7	.563	3.48	88	1	0	142.1	142	63	77	0	9	6	4	17	3	2	.176	7	26	2	1	0.4	.943
WORLD SERIES																											
1960	PIT	N	0	0	—	22.50	3	0	0	4	11	1	3	0	0	0	0	1	0	0	.000	0	0	0	0	0.0	.000

Harvey Green

GREEN, HARVEY GEORGE (Buck) BB TR 6′ 2½″ 185 lbs.
B. Feb. 9, 1915, Kenosha, Wis. D. July 24, 1970, Franklin, La.

Year	Team	Lg	W	L	PCT	ERA	G	GS	CG	IP	H	BB	SO	ShO	Relief W	Relief L	Relief SV	AB	H	HR	BA	PO	A	E	DP	TC/G	FA
1935	BKN	N	0	0	—	9.00	2	0	0	1	2	3	0	0	0	0	0	0	0	0	—	0	0	0	0	0.0	.000

Tyler Green

GREEN, TYLER SCOTT BR TR 6′ 5″ 185 lbs.
B. Feb. 18, 1970, Springfield, Ohio.

Year	Team	Lg	W	L	PCT	ERA	G	GS	CG	IP	H	BB	SO	ShO	Relief W	Relief L	Relief SV	AB	H	HR	BA	PO	A	E	DP	TC/G	FA
1993	PHI	N	0	0	—	7.36	3	2	0	7.1	16	5	7	0	0	0	0	2	0	0	.000	0	0	1	0	0.3	.000
1995			8	9	.471	5.31	26	25	4	140.2	157	66	85	2	0	0	0	44	8	1	.182	9	17	1	2	1.0	.963
2 yrs.			8	9	.471	5.41	29	27	4	148	173	71	92	2	0	0	0	46	8	1	.174	9	17	2	2	1.0	.929

June Greene

GREENE, JULIUS FOUST BL TR 6′ 2½″ 185 lbs.
B. June 25, 1899, Ramseur, N. C. D. Mar. 19, 1974, Glendora, Calif.

Year	Team	Lg	W	L	PCT	ERA	G	GS	CG	IP	H	BB	SO	ShO	Relief W	Relief L	Relief SV	AB	H	HR	BA	PO	A	E	DP	TC/G	FA
1928	PHI	N	0	0	—	9.00	1	0	0	2	5	0	0	0	0	0	0	6	3	0	.500	0	2	0	0	2.0	1.000
1929			0	0	—	19.76	5	0	0	13.2	33	9	4	0	0	0	0	19	4	0	.211	1	4	0	0	1.0	1.000
2 yrs.			0	0		18.38	6	0	0	15.2	38	9	4	0	0	0	0	*				1	6	0	0	1.2	1.000

Nelson Greene

GREENE, NELSON GEORGE (Lefty) BL TL 6′ 185 lbs.
B. Sept. 20, 1900, Philadelphia, Pa. D. Apr. 6, 1983, Lebanon, Pa.

Year	Team	Lg	W	L	PCT	ERA	G	GS	CG	IP	H	BB	SO	ShO	Relief W	Relief L	Relief SV	AB	H	HR	BA	PO	A	E	DP	TC/G	FA
1924	BKN	N	0	1	.000	4.00	4	1	0	9	14	2	3	0	0	0	0	1	0	0	.000	1	4	1	0	1.5	.833
1925			2	0	1.000	10.64	11	0	0	22	45	7	4	0	2	0	1	7	2	0	.286	0	6	0	1	0.5	1.000
2 yrs.			2	1	.667	8.71	15	1	0	31	59	9	7	0	2	0	1	8	2	0	.250	1	10	1	1	0.8	.917

Tommy Greene

GREENE, IRA THOMAS BR TR 6′ 5″ 225 lbs.
B. Apr. 6, 1967, Lumberton, N. C.

Year	Team	Lg	W	L	PCT	ERA	G	GS	CG	IP	H	BB	SO	ShO	Relief W	Relief L	Relief SV	AB	H	HR	BA	PO	A	E	DP	TC/G	FA
1989	ATL	N	1	2	.333	4.10	4	4	1	26.1	22	6	17	1	0	0	0	10	1	0	.100	2	2	0	0	1.0	1.000
1990	2 teams	ATL N (5G 1–0)	PHI N (10G 2–3)																								
″	total		3	3	.500	5.08	15	9	0	51.1	50	26	21	0	0	0	0	12	2	0	.167	3	6	1	0	0.7	.900
1991	PHI	N	13	7	.650	3.38	36	27	3	207.2	177	66	154	2	1	0	0	71	19	2	.268	14	16	1	0	0.9	.968
1992			3	3	.500	5.32	13	12	0	64.1	75	34	39	0	0	0	0	24	3	0	.125	3	7	3	0	1.0	.769
1993			16	4	.800	3.42	31	30	7	200	175	62	167	2	0	0	0	72	16	2	.222	5	23	1	3	0.9	.966
1994			2	0	1.000	4.54	7	7	0	35.2	37	22	28	0	0	0	0	13	5	0	.385	1	4	0	2	0.7	1.000
1995			0	5	.000	8.29	11	6	0	33.2	45	20	24	0	0	0	0	8	0	0	.000	3	3	0	0	0.5	1.000
7 yrs.			38	24	.613	4.10	117	95	11	619	581	236	450	5	1	0	0	210	46	4	.219	31	61	6	5	0.8	.939
LEAGUE CHAMPIONSHIP SERIES																											
1993	PHI	N	1	1	.500	9.64	2	2	0	9.1	12	7	7	0	0	0	0	0	0	0	—	0	3	0	0	1.5	1.000
WORLD SERIES																											
1993	PHI	N	0	0	—	27.00	1	1	0	2.1	7	4	1	0	0	0	0	1	1	0	1.000	0	0	0	0	0.0	.000

Kent Greenfield

GREENFIELD, KENT BR TR 6′ 1″ 180 lbs.
B. July 1, 1902, Guthrie, Ky. D. Mar. 14, 1978, Guthrie, Ky.

Year	Team	Lg	W	L	PCT	ERA	G	GS	CG	IP	H	BB	SO	ShO	Relief W	Relief L	Relief SV	AB	H	HR	BA	PO	A	E	DP	TC/G	FA
1924	NY	N	0	1	.000	15.00	1	1	0	3	9	1	1	0	0	0	0	0	0	0	—	0	0	0	0	0.0	.000
1925			12	8	.600	3.88	29	20	12	171.2	195	64	66	0	1	0	0	62	5	0	.081	4	43	2	2	1.7	.959
1926			13	12	.520	3.96	39	28	8	222.2	206	82	74	1	2	3	1	65	6	0	.092	6	46	3	1	1.4	.945
1927	2 teams	NY N (12G 2–2)	BOS N (27G 11–14)																								
″	total		13	16	.448	4.37	39	27	11	210	242	72	63	1	2	2	0	66	11	0	.167	5	47	1	1	1.4	.981
1928	BOS	N	3	11	.214	5.32	32	23	5	143.2	173	60	30	0	0	0	0	38	2	0	.053	8	37	2	2	1.5	.957
1929	2 teams	BOS N (6G 0–0)	BKN N (6G 0–0)																								
″	total		0	0		9.99	12	2	0	24.1	46	18	8	0	0	0	0	6	0	0	.000	1	10	0	0	0.9	1.000
6 yrs.			41	48	.461	4.54	152	101	36	775.1	871	297	242	2	5	5	1	237	24	0	.101	24	183	8	6	1.4	.963

John Greening

GREENING, JOHN A.
Born John A. Greenig.
B. Philadelphia, Pa. Deceased.

Year	Team	Lg	W	L	PCT	ERA	G	GS	CG	IP	H	BB	SO	ShO	Relief W	Relief L	Relief SV	AB	H	HR	BA	PO	A	E	DP	TC/G	FA
1888	WAS	N	0	1	.000	11.00	1	1	1	9	17	4	2	0	0	0	0	3	0	0	.000	0	1	0	0	1.0	1.000

Bob Greenwood

GREENWOOD, ROBERT CHANDLER (Greenie) BR TR 6′ 5″ 200 lbs.
B. Mar. 13, 1928, Cananea, Mexico.

Year	Team	Lg	W	L	PCT	ERA	G	GS	CG	IP	H	BB	SO	ShO	Relief W	Relief L	Relief SV	AB	H	HR	BA	PO	A	E	DP	TC/G	FA
1954	PHI	N	1	2	.333	3.19	11	4	0	36.2	28	18	9	0	0	0	0	9	0	0	.000	3	7	0	1	0.9	1.000
1955			0	0	—	15.43	1	0	0	2.1	7	0	0	0	0	0	0	1	0	0	.000	0	0	0	0	0.0	.000
2 yrs.			1	2	.333	3.92	12	4	0	39	35	18	9	0	0	0	0	10	0	0	.000	3	7	0	1	0.8	1.000

Kenny Greer

GREER, KENNETH WILLIAM BR TR 6′ 3″ 210 lbs.
B. May 12, 1967, Boston, Mass.

Year	Team	Lg	W	L	PCT	ERA	G	GS	CG	IP	H	BB	SO	ShO	Relief W	Relief L	Relief SV	AB	H	HR	BA	PO	A	E	DP	TC/G	FA
1993	NY	N	1	0	1.000	0.00	1	0	0	1	0	0	2	0	1	0	0	0	0	0	—	0	0	0	0	0.0	.000
1995	SF	N	0	2	.000	5.25	8	0	0	12	15	5	7	0	0	2	0	1	0	0	.000	0	3	1	0	0.5	.750
2 yrs.			1	2	.333	4.85	9	0	0	13	15	5	9	0	1	2	0	1	0	0	.000	0	3	1	0	0.4	.750

Dave Gregg

GREGG, DAVID CHARLES (Highpockets) BR TR 6′ 1″ 185 lbs.
Brother of Vean Gregg.
B. Mar. 14, 1891, Chehalis, Wash. D. Nov. 12, 1965, Clarkston, Wash.

Year	Team	Lg	W	L	PCT	ERA	G	GS	CG	IP	H	BB	SO	ShO	Relief W	Relief L	Relief SV	AB	H	HR	BA	PO	A	E	DP	TC/G	FA
1913	CLE	A	0	0	—	18.00	1	0	0	1	2	0	0	0	0	0	0	0	0	0	—	0	1	0	0	1.0	1.000

Hal Gregg

GREGG, HAROLD DANA BR TR 6′ 3½″ 195 lbs.
B. July 11, 1921, Anaheim, Calif. D. May 13, 1991, Bishop, Calif.

Year	Team	Lg	W	L	PCT	ERA	G	GS	CG	IP	H	BB	SO	ShO	Relief W	Relief L	Relief SV	AB	H	HR	BA	PO	A	E	DP	TC/G	FA
1943	BKN	N	0	3	.000	9.64	5	4	0	18.2	21	21	7	0	0	0	0	2	0	0	.000	1	3	0	0	0.8	1.000
1944			9	16	.360	5.46	39	31	6	197.2	201	**137**	92	0	1	0	2	68	14	0	.206	13	36	5	3	1.4	.907
1945			18	13	.581	3.47	42	34	13	254.1	221	**120**	139	2	1	2	2	91	20	1	.220	8	47	4	4	1.4	.932

Hal Gregg *continued*

Year	Team	W	L	PCT	ERA	G	GS	CG	IP	H	BB	SO	ShO	Relief Pitching W	Relief Pitching L	Relief Pitching SV	Batting AB	Batting H	Batting HR	BA	PO	A	E	DP	TC/G	FA
1946		6	4	.600	2.99	26	16	4	117.1	103	44	54	2	1	1	2	32	4	0	.125	6	16	2	0	0.9	.917
1947		4	5	.444	5.87	37	16	2	104.1	115	55	59	1	1	0	1	34	9	0	.265	9	17	2	2	0.8	.929
1948	PIT N	2	4	.333	4.60	22	8	1	74.1	72	34	25	0	0	2	1	22	6	1	.273	7	10	0	1	0.8	1.000
1949		1	1	.500	3.38	8	1	0	18.2	20	8	9	0	1	0	0	5	0	0	.000	1	1	0	1	0.3	1.000
1950		0	1	.000	13.50	5	1	0	5.1	10	7	3	0	0	0	0	1	0	0	.000	0	1	0	0	0.2	1.000
1952	NY N	0	1	.000	4.71	16	4	1	36.1	42	17	13	0	0	0	1	8	1	0	.125	1	3	0	1	0.3	1.000
9 yrs.		40	48	.455	4.54	200	115	27	827	805	443	401	5	5	5	9	263	54	2	.205	46	134	13	12	1.0	.933
WORLD SERIES																										
1947	BKN N	0	1	.000	3.55	3	1	0	12.2	9	8	10	0	0	0	0	3	0	0	.000	1	3	0	1	1.3	1.000

Vean Gregg

GREGG, SYLVEANUS AUGUSTUS BR TL 6′ 1″ 185 lbs.
Brother of Dave Gregg.
B. Apr. 13, 1885, Chehalis, Wash. D. July 29, 1964, Aberdeen, Wash.

Year	Team	W	L	PCT	ERA	G	GS	CG	IP	H	BB	SO	ShO	Relief Pitching W	Relief Pitching L	Relief Pitching SV	Batting AB	Batting H	Batting HR	BA	PO	A	E	DP	TC/G	FA
1911	CLE A	23	7	.767	**1.81**	34	26	22	244	172	86	125	5	5	0	0	85	14	0	.165	7	67	4	4	2.3	.949
1912		20	13	.606	2.59	37	34	26	271.1	242	90	184	1	0	1	2	97	17	0	.175	10	61	7	2	2.1	.910
1913		20	13	.606	2.24	44	34	23	285.2	258	**124**	166	3	2	0	3	99	13	0	.131	9	70	8	2	2.0	.908
1914	2 teams CLE A (17G 9–3) BOS A (12G 3–4)																									
″	total	12	7	.632	3.44	29	21	10	165	159	85	80	1	2	0	0	52	10	0	.192	5	40	3	5	1.7	.938
1915	BOS A	4	2	.667	3.36	18	9	3	75	71	32	43	1	0	0	3	20	7	0	.350	2	22	0	0	1.3	1.000
1916		2	5	.286	3.01	21	7	3	77.2	71	30	41	0	1	1	0	18	2	0	.111	5	19	0	0	1.1	1.000
1918	PHI A	9	14	.391	3.12	30	25	17	199.1	180	67	63	3	0	0	2	71	12	0	.169	9	48	1	2	1.9	.983
1925	WAS A	2	2	.500	4.12	26	5	1	74.1	87	38	18	0	1	1	2	14	3	0	.214	3	16	3	0	0.8	.864
8 yrs.		92	63	.594	2.70	239	161	105	1392.1	1240	552	720	14	11	3	12	456	78	0	.171	50	343	26	15	1.8	.938

Frank Gregory

GREGORY, FRANK ERNEST BR TR 5′11″ 185 lbs.
B. July 25, 1888, Spring Valley, Wis. D. Nov. 5, 1955, Beloit, Wis.

Year	Team	W	L	PCT	ERA	G	GS	CG	IP	H	BB	SO	ShO	Relief Pitching W	Relief Pitching L	Relief Pitching SV	Batting AB	Batting H	Batting HR	BA	PO	A	E	DP	TC/G	FA
1912	CIN N	2	0	1.000	4.60	4	2	1	15.2	19	7	4	0	1	0	0	5	1	0	.200	0	1	0	0	0.3	1.000

Howie Gregory

GREGORY, HOWARD WATTERSON BL TR 6′ 175 lbs.
B. Nov. 18, 1886, Hannibal, Mo. D. May 30, 1970, Tulsa, Okla.

Year	Team	W	L	PCT	ERA	G	GS	CG	IP	H	BB	SO	ShO	Relief Pitching W	Relief Pitching L	Relief Pitching SV	Batting AB	Batting H	Batting HR	BA	PO	A	E	DP	TC/G	FA
1911	STL A	0	1	.000	5.14	3	1	0	7	11	4	1	0	0	0	0	2	0	0	.000	0	2	0	0	0.7	1.000

Lee Gregory

GREGORY, GROVER LeROY BL TL 6′ 1″ 180 lbs.
B. June 2, 1938, Bakersfield, Calif.

Year	Team	W	L	PCT	ERA	G	GS	CG	IP	H	BB	SO	ShO	Relief Pitching W	Relief Pitching L	Relief Pitching SV	Batting AB	Batting H	Batting HR	BA	PO	A	E	DP	TC/G	FA
1964	CHI N	0	0	—	3.50	11	0	0	18	23	5	8	0	0	0	0	13	1	0	.077	0	5	0	0	0.5	1.000

Paul Gregory

GREGORY, PAUL EDWIN (Pop) BR TR 6′ 2″ 180 lbs.
B. July 9, 1908, Tomnolen, Miss.

Year	Team	W	L	PCT	ERA	G	GS	CG	IP	H	BB	SO	ShO	Relief Pitching W	Relief Pitching L	Relief Pitching SV	Batting AB	Batting H	Batting HR	BA	PO	A	E	DP	TC/G	FA
1932	CHI A	5	3	.625	4.51	33	9	3	117.2	125	51	39	0	2	0	0	38	3	0	.079	5	38	2	2	1.4	.956
1933		4	11	.267	4.95	23	17	5	103.2	124	47	18	0	0	0	0	35	5	0	.143	6	30	0	0	1.6	1.000
2 yrs.		9	14	.391	4.72	56	26	8	221.1	249	98	57	0	2	0	0	73	8	0	.110	11	68	2	2	1.4	.975

Bill Greif

GREIF, WILLIAM BRILEY BR TR 6′ 4″ 196 lbs.
B. Apr. 25, 1950, Fort Stockton, Tex.

Year	Team	W	L	PCT	ERA	G	GS	CG	IP	H	BB	SO	ShO	Relief Pitching W	Relief Pitching L	Relief Pitching SV	Batting AB	Batting H	Batting HR	BA	PO	A	E	DP	TC/G	FA
1971	HOU N	1	1	.500	5.06	7	3	0	16	18	8	14	0	1	0	0	3	1	0	.333	0	3	0	0	0.4	1.000
1972	SD N	5	16	.238	5.60	34	22	2	125.1	143	47	91	1	1	0	2	33	1	0	.030	5	12	4	0	0.6	.810
1973		10	17	.370	3.21	36	31	9	199.1	181	62	120	3	0	0	1	61	6	0	.098	11	24	1	0	1.0	.972
1974		9	19	.321	4.66	43	35	7	226	244	95	137	1	0	0	1	56	4	0	.071	13	33	3	4	1.1	.939
1975		4	6	.400	3.88	59	1	0	72	74	38	43	0	4	6	9	1	0	0	.000	0	5	1	0	0.1	.833
1976	2 teams SD N (5G 1–3) STL N (47G 1–5)																									
″	total	2	8	.200	5.26	52	5	0	77	87	37	37	0	1	5	6	12	0	0	.000	6	9	0	0	0.3	1.000
6 yrs.		31	67	.316	4.41	231	97	18	715.2	747	287	442	5	7	11	19	166	12	0	.072	35	86	9	4	0.6	.931

Bill Grevell

GREVELL, WILLIAM J. BR TR 5′11″ 170 lbs.
B. Mar. 5, 1898, Williamstown, N. J. D. June 21, 1923, Philadelphia, Pa.

Year	Team	W	L	PCT	ERA	G	GS	CG	IP	H	BB	SO	ShO	Relief Pitching W	Relief Pitching L	Relief Pitching SV	Batting AB	Batting H	Batting HR	BA	PO	A	E	DP	TC/G	FA
1919	PHI A	0	0	—	14.25	5	2	0	12	15	18	3	0	0	0	0	5	0	0	.000	0	6	0	0	1.2	1.000

Lee Griffeth

GRIFFETH, LEON CLIFFORD BB TL 5′11½″ 180 lbs.
B. May 20, 1925, Carmel, N. Y.

Year	Team	W	L	PCT	ERA	G	GS	CG	IP	H	BB	SO	ShO	Relief Pitching W	Relief Pitching L	Relief Pitching SV	Batting AB	Batting H	Batting HR	BA	PO	A	E	DP	TC/G	FA
1946	PHI A	0	0	—	2.93	10	0	0	15.1	13	6	4	0	0	0	0	1	0	0	.000	2	1	0	0	0.3	1.000

Hank Griffin

GRIFFIN, JAMES LINTON (Pepper) BR TR 6′ 170 lbs.
B. July 11, 1886, Whitehouse, Tex. D. Feb. 11, 1950, Terrell, Tex.

Year	Team	W	L	PCT	ERA	G	GS	CG	IP	H	BB	SO	ShO	Relief Pitching W	Relief Pitching L	Relief Pitching SV	Batting AB	Batting H	Batting HR	BA	PO	A	E	DP	TC/G	FA
1911	2 teams CHI N (1G 0–0) BOS N (15G 0–6)																									
″	total	0	6	.000	5.38	16	7	1	83.2	97	37	31	0	0	1	0	30	7	0	.233	3	24	2	0	1.8	.931
1912	BOS N	0	0	—	27.00	3	0	0	1.2	3	3	0	0	0	0	0	0	0	0	—	0	0	0	0	0.0	.000
2 yrs.		0	6	.000	5.80	19	7	1	85.1	100	40	31	0	0	1	0	30	7	0	.233	3	24	2	0	1.5	.931

Marty Griffin

GRIFFIN, MARTIN JOHN BR TR 6′ 2″ 200 lbs.
B. Sept. 2, 1901, San Francisco, Calif. D. Nov. 19, 1951, Los Angeles, Calif.

Year	Team	W	L	PCT	ERA	G	GS	CG	IP	H	BB	SO	ShO	Relief Pitching W	Relief Pitching L	Relief Pitching SV	Batting AB	Batting H	Batting HR	BA	PO	A	E	DP	TC/G	FA
1928	BOS A	0	3	.000	5.02	11	3	0	37.2	42	17	9	0	0	0	0	13	4	0	.308	1	8	0	0	0.8	1.000

Mike Griffin

GRIFFIN, MICHAEL LEROY BR TR 6′ 4″ 195 lbs.
B. June 26, 1957, Colusa, Calif.

Year	Team	W	L	PCT	ERA	G	GS	CG	IP	H	BB	SO	ShO	Relief Pitching W	Relief Pitching L	Relief Pitching SV	Batting AB	Batting H	Batting HR	BA	PO	A	E	DP	TC/G	FA
1979	NY A	0	0	—	4.50	3	0	0	4	5	2	5	0	0	0	1	0	0	0	—	0	0	0	0	0.0	.000
1980		2	4	.333	4.83	13	9	0	54	64	23	25	0	0	1	0	0	0	0	—	6	7	1	0	1.1	.929
1981	2 teams NY A (2G 0–0) CHI N (16G 2–5)																									
″	total	2	5	.286	4.34	18	9	0	56	69	9	24	0	0	0	1	13	2	0	.154	1	13	0	0	0.8	1.000
1982	SD N	0	1	.000	3.48	7	0	0	10.1	9	3	4	0	0	1	0	1	0	0	.000	0	1	0	0	0.1	1.000
1987	BAL A	3	5	.375	4.36	23	6	1	74.1	78	33	42	0	0	2	1	0	0	0	—	6	8	2	0	0.7	.875
1989	CIN N	0	0	—	12.46	3	0	0	4.1	10	3	1	0	0	0	0	1	1	0	1.000	0	1	0	0	0.3	1.000
6 yrs.		7	15	.318	4.61	67	24	1	203	235	73	101	0	0	4	3	15	3	0	.200	13	30	3	0	0.7	.935

Pat Griffin

GRIFFIN, PATRICK RICHARD BR TR 6′ 2″ 180 lbs.
B. May 6, 1893, Niles, Ohio D. June 7, 1927, Youngstown, Ohio.

Year	Team		W	L	PCT	ERA	G	GS	CG	IP	H	BB	SO	ShO	Relief Pitching W	Relief Pitching L	Relief Pitching SV	Batting AB	Batting H	Batting HR	BA	PO	A	E	DP	TC/G	FA
1914	CIN	N	0	0	—	9.00	1	0	0	1	3	2	0	0	0	0	0	0	0	0	—	0	2	0	0	2.0	1.000

Tom Griffin

GRIFFIN, THOMAS JAMES BR TR 6′ 3″ 210 lbs.
B. Feb. 22, 1948, Los Angeles, Calif.

Year	Team		W	L	PCT	ERA	G	GS	CG	IP	H	BB	SO	ShO	Relief Pitching W	Relief Pitching L	Relief Pitching SV	Batting AB	Batting H	Batting HR	BA	PO	A	E	DP	TC/G	FA
1969	HOU	N	11	10	.524	3.54	31	31	6	188	156	93	200	3	0	0	0	62	9	2	.145	8	16	2	1	0.8	.923
1970			3	13	.188	5.76	23	20	2	111	118	72	72	1	0	0	0	33	2	0	.061	8	10	1	0	0.8	.947
1971			0	6	.000	4.74	10	6	0	38	44	20	29	0	0	2	0	9	1	0	.111	0	10	0	0	1.0	1.000
1972			5	4	.556	3.24	39	5	1	94.1	92	38	83	1	4	1	3	25	7	1	.280	3	11	2	0	0.4	.875
1973			4	6	.400	4.15	25	12	4	99.2	83	46	69	0	0	1	0	28	3	1	.107	7	14	0	0	0.8	1.000
1974			14	10	.583	3.54	34	34	8	211	202	89	110	3	0	0	0	68	20	2	.294	19	35	8	2	1.8	.871
1975			3	8	.273	5.35	17	13	3	79	89	46	56	1	0	0	0	22	3	0	.136	5	14	1	2	1.2	.950
1976	2 teams	HOU N (20G 5–3) SD N (11G 4–3)																									
″	total		9	6	.600	4.10	31	13	2	112	100	79	69	0	5	1	0	31	2	0	.065	6	16	3	1	0.8	.880
1977	SD	N	6	9	.400	4.47	38	20	0	151	144	88	79	0	2	1	0	45	6	2	.133	6	16	3	2	0.7	.880
1978	CAL	A	3	4	.429	4.02	24	4	0	56	63	31	35	0	3	1	0	0	0	0	—	3	12	2	0	0.7	.882
1979	SF	N	5	6	.455	3.93	59	3	0	94	83	46	82	0	5	3	2	14	1	0	.071	5	19	1	1	0.4	.960
1980			5	1	.833	2.75	42	4	0	108	80	49	79	0	3	1	0	18	2	1	.111	6	17	0	1	0.5	1.000
1981			8	8	.500	3.77	22	22	3	129	121	57	83	1	0	0	0	41	8	1	.195	9	29	3	0	1.9	.927
1982	PIT	N	1	3	.250	8.87	6	4	0	22.1	32	15	8	0	0	0	0	9	2	0	.222	0	6	1	0	1.2	.857
14 yrs.			77	94	.450	4.07	401	191	29	1493.1	1407	769	1054	10	22	11	5	405	66	10	.163	85	225	27	10	0.8	.920

Clark Griffith

GRIFFITH, CLARK CALVIN (General, Griff) BR TR 5′ 6½″ 156 lbs.
B. Nov. 20, 1869, Clear Creek, Mo. D. Oct. 27, 1955, Washington, D. C.
Manager 1901–20.
Hall of Fame 1946.

Year	Team		W	L	PCT	ERA	G	GS	CG	IP	H	BB	SO	ShO	Relief Pitching W	Relief Pitching L	Relief Pitching SV	Batting AB	Batting H	Batting HR	BA	PO	A	E	DP	TC/G	FA
1891	2 teams	STL AA (27G 11–8) BOS AA (7G 3–1)																									
″	total		14	9	.609	3.74	34	21	15	226.1	242	73	88	0	**5**	0	2	100	16	2	.160	12	51	6	1	1.9	.913
1893	CHI	N	1	2	.333	5.03	4	2	2	19.2	24	5	9	0	0	1	0	11	2	0	.182	2	6	0	0	2.0	1.000
1894			21	14	.600	4.92	36	31	28	261.1	328	85	71	0	3	3	0	142	33	0	.232	27	46	10	1	1.9	.880
1895			26	14	.650	3.93	42	41	39	353	434	91	79	0	1	0	0	144	46	1	.319	28	81	9	2	2.7	.924
1896			23	11	.676	3.54	36	35	35	317.2	370	70	81	0	0	0	0	135	36	1	.267	20	79	9	3	3.0	.917
1897			21	18	.538	3.72	41	38	**38**	343.2	410	86	102	1	1	0	1	162	38	0	.235	31	96	12	4	3.0	.914
1898			24	10	.706	**1.88**	38	38	36	325.2	305	64	97	4	0	0	0	122	20	0	.164	18	82	5	2	2.8	.952
1899			22	14	.611	2.79	38	38	35	319.2	329	65	73	0	0	0	0	120	31	0	.258	18	110	11	3	3.6	.921
1900			14	13	.519	3.05	30	30	27	248	245	51	61	**4**	0	0	0	95	24	1	.253	9	57	6	0	2.4	.917
1901	CHI	A	24	7	**.774**	2.67	35	30	26	266.2	275	50	67	**5**	**3**	0	1	89	27	2	.303	9	78	5	3	2.6	.946
1902			15	9	.625	4.19	28	24	20	212.2	247	47	51	3	2	0	0	92	20	0	.217	13	55	0	1	2.2	1.000
1903	NY	A	14	11	.560	2.70	25	24	22	213	201	33	69	3	1	0	0	69	11	1	.159	8	50	1	1	2.4	.983
1904			7	5	.583	2.87	16	11	8	100.1	91	16	36	1	1	0	0	42	6	0	.143	3	32	2	0	2.3	.946
1905			9	6	.600	1.67	25	7	4	102.2	82	15	46	2	6	**3**	1	32	7	0	.219	1	23	1	0	1.0	.960
1906			2	2	.500	3.02	17	2	1	59.2	58	15	16	0	1	**2**	2	18	2	0	.111	1	23	0	2	1.4	1.000
1907			0	0	—	8.64	4	0	0	8.1	15	6	5	0	0	0	0	2	0	0	.000	0	4	1	0	1.3	.800
1909	CIN	N	0	1	.000	6.00	1	1	1	6	11	2	3	0	0	0	0	2	0	0	.000	1	4	0	0	5.0	1.000
1912	WAS	A	0	0	—	∞	1	0	0		1	0	0	0	0	0	0	1	0	0	.000	0	2	0	0	1.0	1.000
1913			0	0	—	0.00	1	0	0	1	1	0	0	0	0	0	0	1	1	0	1.000	0	0	0	0	0.0	
1914			0	0	—	0.00	1	0	0	1	1	0	1	0	0	0	1	1	1	0	1.000	0	0	0	0	0.0	.000
20 yrs.			237	146	.619	3.31	453	373	337	3386.1	3670	774	955	23	24	9	8	*				201	879	78	23	2.4	.933

Frank Griffith

GRIFFITH, FRANK WESLEY BL TL 150 lbs.
B. Nov. 18, 1872, Gilman, Ill. D. Dec. 13, 1908

Year	Team		W	L	PCT	ERA	G	GS	CG	IP	H	BB	SO	ShO	Relief Pitching W	Relief Pitching L	Relief Pitching SV	Batting AB	Batting H	Batting HR	BA	PO	A	E	DP	TC/G	FA
1892	CHI	N	0	1	.000	11.25	1	1	0	4	3	6	3	0	0	0	0	1	0	0	.000	0	0	0	0	0.0	.000
1894	CLE	N	1	2	.333	9.99	7	6	3	42.1	64	37	15	0	0	0	0	24	8	0	.333	1	8	2	0	1.4	.818
2 yrs.			1	3	.250	10.10	8	7	3	46.1	67	43	18	0	0	0	0	25	8	0	.320	1	8	2	0	1.2	.818

Hal Griggs

GRIGGS, HAROLD LLOYD BR TR 6′ 170 lbs.
B. Aug. 24, 1928, Shannon, Ga.

Year	Team		W	L	PCT	ERA	G	GS	CG	IP	H	BB	SO	ShO	Relief Pitching W	Relief Pitching L	Relief Pitching SV	Batting AB	Batting H	Batting HR	BA	PO	A	E	DP	TC/G	FA
1956	WAS	A	1	6	.143	6.02	34	12	1	98.2	120	76	48	0	0	0	1	16	0	0	.000	10	19	1	4	0.9	.967
1957			0	1	.000	3.29	2	2	0	13.2	11	7	12	0	0	0	0	4	1	0	.250	0	3	0	1	1.5	1.000
1958			3	11	.214	5.52	32	21	3	137	138	74	69	0	0	0	0	41	5	0	.122	6	22	2	3	0.9	.933
1959			2	8	.200	5.25	37	10	2	97.2	103	52	43	1	0	2	2	18	1	0	.056	1	18	1	1	0.5	.950
4 yrs.			6	26	.188	5.50	105	45	6	347	372	209	172	1	0	2	3	79	7	0	.089	17	62	4	9	0.8	.952

Guido Grilli

GRILLI, GUIDO JOHN BL TL 6′ 188 lbs.
B. Jan. 9, 1939, Memphis, Tenn.

Year	Team		W	L	PCT	ERA	G	GS	CG	IP	H	BB	SO	ShO	Relief Pitching W	Relief Pitching L	Relief Pitching SV	Batting AB	Batting H	Batting HR	BA	PO	A	E	DP	TC/G	FA
1966	2 teams	BOS A (6G 0–1) KC A (16G 0–1)																									
″	total		0	2	.000	7.08	22	0	0	20.1	24	20	12	0	0	2	1	2	1	0	.500	1	2	2	0	0.2	.600

Steve Grilli

GRILLI, STEPHEN JOSEPH BR TR 6′ 2″ 170 lbs.
B. May 2, 1949, Brooklyn, N. Y.

Year	Team		W	L	PCT	ERA	G	GS	CG	IP	H	BB	SO	ShO	Relief Pitching W	Relief Pitching L	Relief Pitching SV	Batting AB	Batting H	Batting HR	BA	PO	A	E	DP	TC/G	FA
1975	DET	A	0	0	—	1.35	3	0	0	6.2	3	6	5	0	0	0	0	0	0	0	—	1	0	0	0	0.3	1.000
1976			3	1	.750	4.64	36	0	0	66	63	41	36	0	3	1	3	0	0	0	—	5	18	1	1	0.7	.958
1977			1	2	.333	4.81	30	2	0	73	71	49	49	0	1	1	0	0	0	0	—	2	7	0	0	0.3	1.000
1979	TOR	A	0	0	—	0.00	1	0	0	2	1	0	1	0	0	0	0	0	0	0	—	0	0	0	0	0.0	.000
4 yrs.			4	3	.571	4.51	70	2	0	147.2	138	96	91	0	4	2	3	0	0	0		8	25	1	1	0.5	.971

Bob Grim

GRIM, ROBERT ANTON BR TR 6′ 1″ 175 lbs.
B. Mar. 8, 1930, New York, N. Y.

Year	Team		W	L	PCT	ERA	G	GS	CG	IP	H	BB	SO	ShO	Relief Pitching W	Relief Pitching L	Relief Pitching SV	Batting AB	Batting H	Batting HR	BA	PO	A	E	DP	TC/G	FA
1954	NY	A	20	6	.769	3.26	37	20	8	199	175	85	108	1	**8**	0	0	70	10	1	.143	11	26	1	4	1.0	.974
1955			7	5	.583	4.19	26	11	1	92.1	81	42	63	1	3	3	4	25	3	0	.120	5	14	1	1	0.8	.950
1956			6	1	.857	2.77	26	6	1	74.2	64	31	48	0	3	0	5	16	1	0	.063	4	8	1	2	0.5	.923
1957			12	8	.600	2.63	46	0	0	72	60	36	52	0	**12**	**8**	**19**	9	1	1	.111	7	10	0	1	0.4	1.000
1958	2 teams	NY A (11G 0–1) KC A (26G 7–6)																									
″	total		7	7	.500	3.81	37	14	5	130	130	51	65	1	0	3	0	33	6	0	.182	3	19	2	0	0.6	.917

Bob Grim *continued*

Year	Team	Lg	W	L	PCT	ERA	G	GS	CG	IP	H	BB	SO	ShO	Relief Pitching W	Relief Pitching L	Relief Pitching SV	Batting AB	Batting H	Batting HR	BA	PO	A	E	DP	TC/G	FA
1959	**KC**	**A**	6	10	.375	4.09	40	9	3	125.1	124	57	65	1	2	6	4	32	3	1	.094	7	13	1	1	0.5	.952
1960	**3 teams**	**CLE A** (3G 0–1) **CIN N** (26G 2–2) **STL N** (15G 1–0)																									
"	**total**		3	3	.500	4.22	44	0	0	53.1	60	20	39	0	3	3	2	2	0	0	.000	1	9	1	1	0.3	.909
1962	**KC**	**A**	0	1	.000	6.23	12	0	0	13	14	8	3	0	0	1	3	2	0	0	.000	1	5	0	0	0.5	1.000
8 yrs.			61	41	.598	3.61	268	60	18	759.2	708	330	443	4	31	24	37	189	24	3	.127	39	104	7	10	0.6	.953
WORLD SERIES																											
1955	**NY**	**A**	0	1	.000	4.15	3	1	0	8.2	8	5	8	0	0	0	1	2	0	0	.000	1	1	0	0	0.7	1.000
1957			0	1	.000	7.71	2	0	0	2.1	3	0	2	0	0	1	0	0	0	0	—	0	0	0	0	0.0	.000
2 yrs.			0	2	.000	4.91	5	1	0	11	11	5	10	0	0	1	1	2	0	0	.000	1	1	0	0	0.4	1.000

John Grim

GRIM, JOHN HELM BR TR 6′ 2″ 175 lbs.
B. Aug. 9, 1867, Lebanon, Ky. D. July 28, 1961, Indianapolis, Ind.

Year	Team	Lg	W	L	PCT	ERA	G	GS	CG	IP	H	BB	SO	ShO	Relief Pitching W	Relief Pitching L	Relief Pitching SV	Batting AB	Batting H	Batting HR	BA	PO	A	E	DP	TC/G	FA
1890	**ROC**	**AA**	0	0	—	0.00	1	0	0	3.1	3	4	3	0	0	0	0	*				1	4	2	0	3.5	.714

Burleigh Grimes

GRIMES, BURLEIGH ARLAND (Ol' Stubblebeard) BR TR 5′10″ 175 lbs.
B. Aug. 18, 1893, Emerald, Wis. D. Dec. 6, 1985, Clear Lake, Wis.
Manager 1937–38.
Hall of Fame 1964.

Year	Team	Lg	W	L	PCT	ERA	G	GS	CG	IP	H	BB	SO	ShO	Relief Pitching W	Relief Pitching L	Relief Pitching SV	Batting AB	Batting H	Batting HR	BA	PO	A	E	DP	TC/G	FA
1916	**PIT**	**N**	2	3	.400	2.36	6	5	4	45.2	40	10	20	0	1	0	0	17	3	0	.176	1	16	3	1	3.3	.850
1917			3	16	.158	3.53	37	17	8	194	186	70	72	1	1	**4**	0	69	16	0	.232	9	62	6	3	2.1	.922
1918	**BKN**	**N**	19	9	.679	2.14	**41**	30	19	269.2	210	76	113	7	1	1	1	90	18	0	.200	12	94	5	1	2.7	.955
1919			10	11	.476	3.47	25	21	13	181.1	179	60	82	1	1	1	0	69	17	0	.246	12	50	3	3	2.6	.954
1920			23	11	**.676**	2.22	40	33	25	303.2	271	67	131	5	2	1	2	111	34	0	.306	17	95	7	2	3.0	.941
1921			**22**	13	.629	2.83	37	35	**30**	302.1	313	76	**136**	2	0	1	0	114	27	1	.237	17	89	2	5	2.9	.981
1922			17	14	.548	4.76	36	34	18	259	324	84	99	1	1	0	1	93	22	0	.237	12	79	6	2	2.7	.938
1923			21	18	.538	3.58	39	**38**	**33**	**327**	**356**	100	119	2	0	1	0	126	30	0	.238	16	101	10	6	3.3	.921
1924			22	13	.629	3.82	38	**36**	**30**	**310.2**	**351**	91	135	1	0	0	1	124	37	0	.298	25	91	4	5	3.2	.967
1925			12	**19**	.387	5.04	33	31	19	246.2	305	102	73	0	1	0	0	96	24	1	.250	18	92	7	11	3.5	.940
1926			12	13	.480	3.71	30	29	18	225.1	238	88	64	1	0	0	0	81	18	0	.222	4	72	3	1	2.6	.962
1927	**NY**	**N**	19	8	.704	3.54	39	34	15	259.2	274	87	102	2	1	0	2	96	18	0	.188	16	71	0	9	2.2	1.000
1928	**PIT**	**N**	**25**	14	.641	2.99	**48**	**37**	**28**	**330.2**	311	77	97	**4**	4	1	3	131	42	0	.321	9	106	4	6	2.5	.966
1929			17	7	.708	3.13	33	29	18	232.2	245	70	62	2	0	1	2	91	26	0	.286	10	65	3	5	2.4	.962
1930	**2 teams**	**BOS N** (11G 3–5) **STL N** (22G 13–6)																									
"	**total**		16	11	.593	4.07	33	28	11	201.1	246	65	73	1	2	2	0	73	18	0	.247	8	47	1	3	1.7	.982
1931	**STL**	**N**	17	9	.654	3.65	29	28	17	212.1	240	59	67	3	1	0	0	76	14	0	.184	16	57	4	3	2.7	.948
1932	**CHI**	**N**	6	11	.353	4.78	30	18	5	141.1	174	50	36	1	0	2	1	44	11	0	.250	12	33	2	4	1.6	.957
1933	**2 teams**	**CHI N** (17G 3–6) **STL N** (4G 0–1)																									
"	**total**		3	7	.300	3.78	21	10	3	83.1	86	37	16	1	1	1	4	25	4	0	.160	6	16	1	2	1.1	.957
1934	**3 teams**	**STL N** (4G 2–1) **PIT N** (8G 1–2) **NY A** (10G 1–2)																									
"	**total**		4	5	.444	6.11	22	4	0	53	63	26	15	0	4	3	1	9	1	0	.111	5	16	0	2	1.0	1.000
19 yrs.			270	212	.560	3.53	617	497	314	4179.2	4412	1295	1512	35	21	19	18	1535	380	2	.248	225	1252	71	74	2.5	.954
WORLD SERIES																											
1920	**BKN**	**N**	1	2	.333	4.19	3	3	1	19.1	23	9	4	1	0	0	0	6	2	0	.333	1	7	1	0	3.0	.889
1930	**STL**	**N**	0	2	.000	3.71	2	2	2	17	10	6	13	0	0	0	0	5	2	0	.400	0	3	0	0	1.5	1.000
1931			2	0	1.000	2.04	2	2	1	17.2	9	9	11	0	0	0	0	7	2	0	.286	0	3	0	0	1.5	1.000
1932	**CHI**	**N**	0	0	—	23.63	2	0	0	2.2	7	2	0	0	0	0	0	1	0	0	.000	0	0	0	0	0.0	.000
4 yrs.			3	4	.429	4.29	9	7	4	56.2	49	26 **8th**	28	1	0	0	0	19	6	0	.316	1	13	1	0	1.7	.933

John Grimes

GRIMES, JOHN THOMAS BR TR 5′11″ 160 lbs.
B. Apr. 17, 1869, Woodstock, Md. D. Jan. 17, 1964, San Francisco, Calif.

Year	Team	Lg	W	L	PCT	ERA	G	GS	CG	IP	H	BB	SO	ShO	Relief Pitching W	Relief Pitching L	Relief Pitching SV	Batting AB	Batting H	Batting HR	BA	PO	A	E	DP	TC/G	FA
1897	**STL**	**N**	0	2	.000	5.95	3	1	1	19.2	24	8	4	0	0	1	0	7	2	0	.286	0	12	1	0	4.3	.923

Jason Grimsley

GRIMSLEY, JASON ALAN BR TR 6′ 3″ 180 lbs.
B. Aug. 7, 1967, Cleveland, Tex.

Year	Team	Lg	W	L	PCT	ERA	G	GS	CG	IP	H	BB	SO	ShO	Relief Pitching W	Relief Pitching L	Relief Pitching SV	Batting AB	Batting H	Batting HR	BA	PO	A	E	DP	TC/G	FA
1989	**PHI**	**N**	1	3	.250	5.89	4	4	0	18.1	19	19	7	0	0	0	0	5	0	0	.000	1	4	1	1	1.5	.833
1990			3	2	.600	3.30	11	11	0	57.1	47	43	41	0	0	0	0	16	3	0	.188	13	8	1	2	2.0	.955
1991			1	7	.125	4.87	12	12	0	61	54	41	42	0	0	0	0	17	1	0	.059	2	14	1	3	1.4	.941
1993	**CLE**	**A**	3	4	.429	5.31	10	6	0	42.1	52	20	27	0	1	2	0	0	0	0	—	4	4	0	0	0.8	1.000
1994			5	2	.714	4.57	14	13	1	82.2	91	34	59	0	0	0	0	0	0	0	—	6	9	0	1	1.1	1.000
1995			0	0	—	6.09	15	2	0	34	37	32	25	0	0	0	1	0	0	0	—	0	8	0	1	0.5	1.000
6 yrs.			13	18	.419	4.75	66	48	1	295.2	300	189	201	0	1	2	1	38	4	0	.105	26	47	3	8	1.2	.961

Ross Grimsley

GRIMSLEY, ROSS ALBERT, SR. (Lefty) BL TL 6′ 175 lbs.
Father of Ross Grimsley.
B. June 4, 1922, Americus, Kans. D. Feb. 6, 1994, Memphis, Tenn.

Year	Team	Lg	W	L	PCT	ERA	G	GS	CG	IP	H	BB	SO	ShO	Relief Pitching W	Relief Pitching L	Relief Pitching SV	Batting AB	Batting H	Batting HR	BA	PO	A	E	DP	TC/G	FA
1951	**CHI**	**A**	0	0	—	3.86	7	0	0	14	12	10	8	0	0	0	0	2	0	0	.000	0	0	0	0	0.0	.000

Ross Grimsley

GRIMSLEY, ROSS ALBERT II BL TL 6′ 3″ 195 lbs.
Son of Ross Grimsley.
B. Jan. 7, 1950, Topeka, Kans.

Year	Team	Lg	W	L	PCT	ERA	G	GS	CG	IP	H	BB	SO	ShO	Relief Pitching W	Relief Pitching L	Relief Pitching SV	Batting AB	Batting H	Batting HR	BA	PO	A	E	DP	TC/G	FA
1971	**CIN**	**N**	10	7	.588	3.58	26	26	6	161	151	43	67	3	0	0	0	51	6	0	.118	5	25	0	0	1.2	1.000
1972			14	8	.636	3.05	30	28	4	197.2	194	50	79	1	0	0	1	66	8	0	.121	3	34	0	0	1.2	1.000
1973			13	10	.565	3.23	38	36	8	242.1	245	68	90	1	0	0	1	82	5	0	.061	11	33	0	3	1.2	1.000
1974	**BAL**	**A**	18	13	.581	3.07	40	39	17	296	267	76	158	4	0	0	1	0	0	0	—	3	51	2	1	1.4	.964
1975			10	13	.435	4.07	35	32	8	197	210	47	89	1	0	0	0	0	0	0	—	6	33	0	2	1.1	1.000
1976			8	7	.533	3.94	28	19	2	137	143	35	41	0	0	0	0	0	0	0	—	8	19	1	0	1.0	.964
1977			14	10	.583	3.96	34	34	11	218	230	74	53	2	0	0	0	0	0	0	—	8	52	3	4	1.9	.952
1978	**MON**	**N**	20	11	.645	3.05	36	36	19	263	237	67	84	3	0	0	0	90	13	0	.144	9	53	2	3	1.8	.969

Ross Grimsley *continued*

Year	Team	W	L	PCT	ERA	G	GS	CG	IP	H	BB	SO	ShO	Relief W	Relief L	Relief SV	Batting AB	Batting H	Batting HR	BA	PO	A	E	DP	TC/G	FA
1979		10	9	.526	5.36	32	27	2	151	199	41	42	0	0	1	0	55	11	0	.200	3	27	3	0	1.0	.909
1980	2 teams	MON N (11G 2–4)		CLE A (14G 4–5)																						
"	total	6	9	.400	6.59	25	18	2	116	164	36	29	0	0	0	0	9	2	0	.222	2	19	1	0	0.9	.955
1982	BAL A	1	2	.333	5.25	21	0	0	60	65	22	18	0	1	2	0	0	0	0	—	2	11	1	1	0.7	.929
11 yrs.		124	99	.556	3.81	345	295	79	2039	2105	559	750	15	1	3	3	353	45	0	.127	60	357	13	14	1.2	.970
LEAGUE CHAMPIONSHIP SERIES																										
1972	CIN N	1	0	1.000	1.00	1	1	1	9	2	0	5	0	0	0	0	4	2	0	.500	0	0	0	0	0.0	.000
1973		0	1	.000	12.27	2	1	0	3.2	7	2	3	0	0	0	0	0	0	0	—	1	0	0	0	0.5	1.000
1974	BAL A	0	0	—	1.69	2	0	0	5.1	1	2	2	0	0	0	0	0	0	0	—	0	1	0	0	0.5	1.000
3 yrs.		1	1	.500	3.50	5	2	1	18	10	4	10	0	0	0	0	4	2	0	.500	1	1	0	0	0.4	1.000
WORLD SERIES																										
1972	CIN N	2	1	.667	2.57	4	1	0	7	7	3	2	0	2	0	0	2	0	0	.000	0	2	0	0	0.5	1.000

Dan Griner

GRINER, DONALD DEXTER (Rusty) BL TR 6′ 1½″ 200 lbs.
B. Mar. 7, 1888, Centerville, Tenn. D. June 3, 1950, Bishopville, S. C.

Year	Team	W	L	PCT	ERA	G	GS	CG	IP	H	BB	SO	ShO	Relief W	Relief L	Relief SV	Batting AB	Batting H	Batting HR	BA	PO	A	E	DP	TC/G	FA
1912	STL N	3	4	.429	3.17	12	7	2	54	59	15	20	0	0	0	0	13	1	0	.077	1	8	0	0	0.8	1.000
1913		10	**22**	.313	5.08	34	34	18	225	279	66	79	1	0	0	0	81	21	0	.259	7	69	2	0	2.3	.974
1914		9	13	.409	2.51	37	18	11	179	163	57	74	2	1	1	2	55	14	0	.255	7	41	1	0	1.3	.980
1915		5	11	.313	2.81	37	18	9	150.1	137	46	46	3	0	3	3	52	14	0	.269	3	35	1	1	1.1	.974
1916		0	0	—	4.09	4	0	0	11	15	3	3	0	0	0	1	4	1	0	.250	0	3	0	0	0.8	1.000
1918	BKN N	1	5	.167	2.15	11	6	3	54.1	47	15	22	1	0	0	0	14	1	0	.071	0	17	0	0	1.4	1.000
6 yrs.		28	55	.337	3.49	135	83	43	673.2	700	202	244	7	1	4	6	219	52	0	.237	18	173	4	1	1.4	.979

Lee Grissom

GRISSOM, LEE THEO (Lefty) BB TL 6′ 3″ 200 lbs.
Brother of Marv Grissom. BR 1934, 1937
B. Oct. 23, 1907, Sherman, Tex.

Year	Team	W	L	PCT	ERA	G	GS	CG	IP	H	BB	SO	ShO	Relief W	Relief L	Relief SV	Batting AB	Batting H	Batting HR	BA	PO	A	E	DP	TC/G	FA
1934	CIN N	0	1	.000	15.43	4	1	0	7	13	7	4	0	0	0	0	1	0	0	.000	0	1	0	0	0.3	1.000
1935		1	1	.500	3.86	3	3	1	21	31	4	13	0	0	0	0	7	0	0	.000	1	6	0	0	2.3	1.000
1936		1	1	.500	6.29	6	4	0	24.1	33	9	13	0	0	0	0	9	0	0	.000	2	4	0	0	1.0	1.000
1937		12	17	.414	3.26	50	30	14	223.2	193	93	149	**5**	1	1	6	64	7	0	.109	5	34	1	1	0.8	.975
1938		2	3	.400	5.29	14	7	0	51	60	22	16	0	0	0	0	16	3	0	.188	2	11	2	0	1.1	.867
1939		9	7	.563	4.10	33	21	3	153.2	145	56	53	0	1	1	0	47	4	0	.085	2	24	1	3	0.8	.963
1940	2 teams	NY A (5G 0–0)		BKN N (14G 2–5)																						
"	total	2	5	.286	2.64	19	10	3	78.1	63	36	52	1	0	0	0	23	5	0	.217	3	11	2	1	0.8	.875
1941	2 teams	BKN N (4G 0–0)		PHI N (29G 2–13)																						
"	total	2	13	.133	3.85	33	19	2	142.2	130	78	79	0	0	0	1	38	7	0	.184	1	26	2	0	0.9	.931
8 yrs.		29	48	.377	3.89	162	95	23	701.2	668	305	379	6	2	2	7	205	26	0	.127	16	117	8	5	0.9	.943
WORLD SERIES																										
1939	CIN N	0	0	—	0.00	1	0	0	1.1	0	1	0	0	0	0	0	0	0	0	—	0	0	0	0	0.0	.000

Marv Grissom

GRISSOM, MARVIN EDWARD BR TR 6′ 3″ 190 lbs.
Brother of Lee Grissom.
B. Mar. 31, 1918, Los Molinos, Calif.

Year	Team	W	L	PCT	ERA	G	GS	CG	IP	H	BB	SO	ShO	Relief W	Relief L	Relief SV	Batting AB	Batting H	Batting HR	BA	PO	A	E	DP	TC/G	FA
1946	NY N	0	2	.000	4.34	4	3	0	18.2	17	13	9	0	0	0	0	5	1	0	.200	1	6	0	0	1.8	1.000
1949	DET A	2	4	.333	6.41	27	2	0	39.1	56	34	17	0	2	3	0	9	2	0	.222	1	8	1	0	0.4	.900
1952	CHI A	12	10	.545	3.74	28	24	7	166	156	79	97	1	0	1	0	53	8	0	.151	4	23	1	0	1.0	.964
1953	2 teams	BOS A (13G 2–6)		NY N (21G 4–2)																						
"	total	6	8	.429	4.26	34	18	4	143.2	144	61	77	1	0	1	0	45	2	0	.044	9	23	1	3	1.0	.970
1954	NY N	10	7	.588	2.35	56	3	1	122.1	100	50	64	1	9	7	19	32	5	0	.156	7	18	2	3	0.5	.926
1955		5	4	.556	2.92	55	0	0	89.1	76	41	49	0	5	4	8	13	2	0	.154	3	16	0	0	0.3	1.000
1956		1	1	.500	1.56	43	2	0	80.2	71	16	49	0	1	1	7	11	1	0	.091	1	12	0	0	0.3	1.000
1957		4	4	.500	2.61	55	0	0	82.2	74	23	51	0	4	4	14	12	2	0	.167	1	20	0	1	0.4	1.000
1958	SF N	7	5	.583	3.99	51	0	0	65.1	71	26	46	0	7	5	10	9	0	0	.000	1	12	0	1	0.3	1.000
1959	STL N	0	0	—	22.50	3	0	0	2	6	0	0	0	0	0	0	0	0	0	—	0	1	0	0	0.3	1.000
10 yrs.		47	45	.511	3.41	356	52	12	810	771	343	459	3	28	26	58	189	23	0	.122	28	139	5	8	0.5	.971
WORLD SERIES																										
1954	NY N	1	0	1.000	0.00	1	0	0	2.2	1	3	2	0	1	0	0	1	0	0	.000	0	0	0	0	0.0	.000

Connie Grob

GROB, CONRAD GEORGE BL TR 6′½″ 180 lbs.
B. Nov. 9, 1932, Cross Plains, Wis.

Year	Team	W	L	PCT	ERA	G	GS	CG	IP	H	BB	SO	ShO	Relief W	Relief L	Relief SV	Batting AB	Batting H	Batting HR	BA	PO	A	E	DP	TC/G	FA
1956	WAS A	4	5	.444	7.83	37	1	0	79.1	121	26	27	0	4	5	1	18	6	0	.333	6	18	2	1	0.7	.923

Johnny Grodzicki

GRODZICKI, JOHN BR TR 6′ 2″ 200 lbs.
B. Feb. 26, 1917, Nanticoke, Pa.

Year	Team	W	L	PCT	ERA	G	GS	CG	IP	H	BB	SO	ShO	Relief W	Relief L	Relief SV	Batting AB	Batting H	Batting HR	BA	PO	A	E	DP	TC/G	FA
1941	STL N	2	1	.667	1.35	5	1	0	13.1	6	11	10	0	2	0	0	2	0	0	.000	0	2	0	0	0.4	1.000
1946		0	0	—	9.00	3	0	0	4	4	4	2	0	0	0	0	0	0	0	—	0	2	1	0	1.0	.667
1947		0	1	.000	5.40	16	0	0	23.1	21	19	8	0	0	1	0	1	0	0	.000	1	6	0	0	0.4	1.000
3 yrs.		2	2	.500	4.43	24	1	0	40.2	31	34	20	0	2	1	0	3	0	0	.000	1	10	1	0	0.5	.917

Steve Gromek

GROMEK, STEPHEN JOSEPH BB TR 6′ 2″ 180 lbs.
B. Jan. 15, 1920, Hamtramck, Mich.

Year	Team	W	L	PCT	ERA	G	GS	CG	IP	H	BB	SO	ShO	Relief W	Relief L	Relief SV	Batting AB	Batting H	Batting HR	BA	PO	A	E	DP	TC/G	FA
1941	CLE A	1	1	.500	4.24	9	2	1	23.1	25	11	19	0	0	0	2	6	1	0	.167	0	0	0	0	0.0	.000
1942		2	0	1.000	3.65	14	0	0	44.1	46	23	14	0	2	0	0	15	5	0	.333	2	6	2	1	0.7	.800
1943		0	0	—	9.00	3	0	0	4	6	0	4	0	0	0	0	2	2	0	1.000	0	0	0	0	0.0	.000
1944		10	9	.526	2.56	35	21	12	203.2	160	70	115	2	0	1	1	73	19	0	.260	10	22	2	3	1.0	.941
1945		19	9	.679	2.55	33	30	21	251	229	66	101	3	0	1	1	91	21	0	.231	15	31	2	1	1.5	.958
1946		5	15	.250	4.33	29	21	5	153.2	159	47	75	2	0	2	4	56	11	0	.196	10	21	1	2	1.1	.969
1947		3	5	.375	3.74	29	7	0	84.1	77	36	39	0	1	3	4	22	7	0	.318	2	13	1	0	0.6	.938
1948		9	3	.750	2.84	38	9	4	130	109	51	50	1	3	1	2	41	6	0	.146	8	17	2	3	0.7	.926
1949		4	6	.400	3.33	27	12	3	92	86	40	22	0	1	2	0	24	4	0	.167	8	18	1	0	1.0	.963
1950		10	7	.588	3.65	31	13	4	113.1	94	36	43	1	4	0	0	38	6	0	.158	11	14	0	3	0.8	1.000

Steve Gromek *continued*

Year	Team	W	L	PCT	ERA	G	GS	CG	IP	H	BB	SO	ShO	Relief Pitching W	Relief Pitching L	Relief Pitching SV	Batting AB	Batting H	Batting HR	BA	PO	A	E	DP	TC/G	FA
1951		7	4	.636	2.77	27	8	4	107.1	98	29	40	0	3	2	1	27	8	0	.296	13	18	0	3	1.1	1.000
1952		7	7	.500	3.67	29	13	3	122.2	109	28	65	1	1	1	1	30	3	0	.100	7	9	0	0	0.6	1.000
1953	2 teams CLE A (5G 1–1) DET A (19G 6–8)																									
"	total	7	9	.438	4.41	24	18	6	136.2	149	39	67	1	1	0	1	43	3	0	.070	10	13	0	1	1.0	1.000
1954	DET A	18	16	.529	2.74	36	32	17	252.2	236	57	102	4	2	0	1	79	15	0	.190	16	26	1	1	1.2	.977
1955		13	10	.565	3.98	28	25	8	181	183	37	73	2	2	0	0	54	9	0	.167	12	22	1	2	1.3	.971
1956		8	6	.571	4.28	40	13	4	141	142	47	64	0	3	0	4	27	4	0	.148	1	16	0	0	0.4	1.000
1957		0	1	.000	6.08	15	1	0	23.2	32	13	11	0	0	1	1	2	0	0	.000	1	2	0	0	0.2	1.000
17 yrs.		123	108	.532	3.41	447	225	92	2064.2	1940	630	904	17	23	14	23	630	124	0	.197	126	248	13	20	0.9	.966
WORLD SERIES																										
1948	CLE A	1	0	1.000	1.00	1	1	1	9	7	1	2	0	0	0	0	3	0	0	.000	1	1	0	1	2.0	1.000

Bob Groom

GROOM, ROBERT BR TR 6′ 2″ 175 lbs.
B. Sept. 12, 1884, Belleville, Ill. D. Feb. 19, 1948, Belleville, Ill.

Year	Team	W	L	PCT	ERA	G	GS	CG	IP	H	BB	SO	ShO	Relief Pitching W	Relief Pitching L	Relief Pitching SV	Batting AB	Batting H	Batting HR	BA	PO	A	E	DP	TC/G	FA
1909	WAS A	7	**26**	.212	2.87	44	31	17	260.2	218	**105**	131	1	2	1	0	88	8	0	.091	10	98	12	3	2.6	.900
1910		12	17	.414	2.76	34	30	22	257.2	255	77	98	3	0	2	0	92	11	0	.120	10	77	6	0	2.7	.935
1911		13	17	.433	3.82	37	32	20	254.2	280	67	135	2	1	0	2	82	11	0	.134	8	73	5	0	2.3	.942
1912		24	13	.649	2.62	43	40	28	316	287	94	179	2	0	2	1	103	12	0	.117	13	77	9	2	2.3	.909
1913		16	16	.500	3.23	37	36	17	264.1	258	81	156	4	0	1	0	92	15	0	.163	14	75	5	3	2.5	.947
1914	STL F	13	20	.394	3.24	42	34	23	280.2	281	75	167	1	0	3	1	94	15	0	.160	18	74	6	3	2.3	.939
1915		11	11	.500	3.27	37	26	11	209	200	73	111	4	2	0	1	66	10	0	.152	5	63	2	2	1.9	.971
1916	STL A	13	9	.591	2.57	41	26	8	217.1	174	98	92	1	2	1	4	63	7	0	.111	10	72	6	2	2.1	.932
1917		8	**19**	.296	2.94	38	28	11	232.2	193	95	82	4	1	1	3	72	8	0	.111	9	59	1	3	1.8	.986
1918	CLE A	2	2	.500	7.06	14	5	0	43.1	70	18	8	0	1	0	0	12	1	0	.083	0	14	0	0	1.0	1.000
10 yrs.		119	150	.442	3.10	367	288	157	2336.1	2216	783	1159	22	9	11	12	764	98	0	.128	97	682	52	18	2.3	.937

Buddy Groom

GROOM, WEDSEL GARY BL TL 6′ 2″ 200 lbs.
B. July 10, 1965, Dallas, Tex.

Year	Team	W	L	PCT	ERA	G	GS	CG	IP	H	BB	SO	ShO	Relief Pitching W	Relief Pitching L	Relief Pitching SV	Batting AB	Batting H	Batting HR	BA	PO	A	E	DP	TC/G	FA
1992	DET A	0	5	.000	5.82	12	7	0	38.2	48	22	15	0	0	0	1	0	0	0	—	0	6	0	0	0.5	1.000
1993		0	2	.000	6.14	19	3	0	36.2	48	13	15	0	0	1	0	0	0	0	—	1	7	1	0	0.5	.889
1994		0	1	.000	3.94	40	0	0	32	31	13	27	0	0	1	1	0	0	0	—	0	0	0	0	0.0	.000
1995	2 teams DET A (23G 1–3) FLA N (14G 1–2)																									
"	total	2	5	.286	7.44	37	4	0	55.2	81	32	35	0	1	4	1	0	0	0	—	2	6	1	0	0.2	.889
4 yrs.		2	13	.133	6.07	108	14	0	163	208	80	92	0	1	6	3	0	0	0		3	19	2	0	0.2	.917

Don Gross

GROSS, DONALD JOHN BL TL 5′11″ 186 lbs.
B. June 30, 1931, Weidman, Mich.

Year	Team	W	L	PCT	ERA	G	GS	CG	IP	H	BB	SO	ShO	Relief Pitching W	Relief Pitching L	Relief Pitching SV	Batting AB	Batting H	Batting HR	BA	PO	A	E	DP	TC/G	FA
1955	CIN N	4	5	.444	4.14	17	11	2	67.1	79	16	33	1	0	2	0	19	3	0	.158	3	12	2	1	1.0	.882
1956		3	0	1.000	1.95	19	7	2	69.1	69	20	47	0	0	0	0	19	2	0	.105	6	13	0	3	1.0	1.000
1957		7	9	.438	4.31	43	16	5	148.1	152	33	73	0	1	4	1	46	5	0	.109	14	22	0	1	0.8	1.000
1958	PIT N	5	7	.417	3.98	40	3	0	74.2	67	38	59	0	5	5	7	18	1	0	.056	5	14	0	1	0.5	1.000
1959		1	1	.500	3.55	21	0	0	33	28	10	15	0	1	1	2	2	0	0	.000	1	11	0	0	0.6	1.000
1960		0	0	—	3.38	5	0	0	5.1	5	0	3	0	0	0	0	0	0	0	—	0	0	0	0	0.0	.000
6 yrs.		20	22	.476	3.73	145	37	9	398	400	117	230	1	7	12	10	104	11	0	.106	29	72	2	6	0.7	.981

Greg Gross

GROSS, GREGORY EUGENE BL TL 5′10″ 160 lbs.
B. Aug. 1, 1952, York, Pa.

Year	Team	W	L	PCT	ERA	G	GS	CG	IP	H	BB	SO	ShO	Relief Pitching W	Relief Pitching L	Relief Pitching SV	Batting AB	Batting H	Batting HR	BA	PO	A	E	DP	TC/G	FA
1986	PHI N	0	0	—	0.00	1	0	0	0.2	1	1	2	0	0	0	0	101	25	0	.248	13	2	0	0	1.7	1.000
1989	HOU N	0	0	—	18.00	1	0	0	1	3	1	1	0	0	0	0	75	15	0	.200	296	15	2	4	2.1	.994
2 yrs.		0	0		10.80	2	0	0	1.2	4	2	3	0	0	0	0	*				1882	108	33	43	1.6	.984

Kevin Gross

GROSS, KEVIN FRANK BR TR 6′ 5″ 200 lbs.
B. June 8, 1961, Downey, Calif.

Year	Team	W	L	PCT	ERA	G	GS	CG	IP	H	BB	SO	ShO	Relief Pitching W	Relief Pitching L	Relief Pitching SV	Batting AB	Batting H	Batting HR	BA	PO	A	E	DP	TC/G	FA
1983	PHI N	4	6	.400	3.56	17	17	1	96	100	35	66	1	0	0	0	33	3	0	.091	11	13	0	0	1.4	1.000
1984		8	5	.615	4.12	44	14	1	129	140	44	84	0	4	0	1	30	2	0	.067	9	22	2	3	0.8	.939
1985		15	13	.536	3.41	38	31	6	205.2	194	81	151	2	1	2	0	65	9	1	.138	18	34	3	0	1.4	.945
1986		12	12	.500	4.02	37	36	7	241.2	240	94	154	2	0	0	0	80	15	1	.188	25	28	2	2	1.5	.964
1987		9	16	.360	4.35	34	33	3	200.2	205	87	110	1	1	0	0	63	12	1	.190	13	23	3	1	1.1	.923
1988		12	14	.462	3.69	33	33	5	231.2	209	**89**	162	1	0	0	0	75	13	0	.173	13	34	2	2	1.5	.959
1989	MON N	11	12	.478	4.38	31	31	4	201.1	188	88	158	3	0	0	0	64	9	0	.141	15	25	2	1	1.4	.952
1990		9	12	.429	4.57	31	26	2	163.1	171	65	111	1	1	0	0	50	10	1	.200	6	13	1	0	0.6	.950
1991	LA N	10	11	.476	3.58	46	10	0	115.2	123	50	95	0	6	6	3	25	7	0	.280	9	14	1	0	0.5	.958
1992		8	13	.381	3.17	34	30	4	204.2	182	77	158	3	0	0	0	63	6	0	.095	11	25	1	2	1.1	.973
1993		13	13	.500	4.14	33	32	3	202.1	224	74	150	0	0	1	0	64	13	1	.203	11	40	0	1	1.5	1.000
1994		9	7	.563	3.60	25	23	1	157.1	162	43	124	0	0	0	1	47	7	1	.149	14	29	1	1	1.8	.977
1995	TEX A	9	15	.375	5.54	31	30	4	183.2	200	89	106	0	0	0	0	0	0	0	—	15	20	2	5	1.2	.946
13 yrs.		129	149	.464	4.02	434	346	41	2333	2338	916	1629	14	13	9	5	659	106	6	.161	170	320	20	18	1.2	.961

Kip Gross

GROSS, KIP LEE BR TR 6′ 2″ 195 lbs.
B. Aug. 24, 1964, Scottsbluff, Neb.

Year	Team	W	L	PCT	ERA	G	GS	CG	IP	H	BB	SO	ShO	Relief Pitching W	Relief Pitching L	Relief Pitching SV	Batting AB	Batting H	Batting HR	BA	PO	A	E	DP	TC/G	FA
1990	CIN N	0	0	—	4.26	5	0	0	6.1	6	2	3	0	0	0	0	0	0	0	—	0	0	0	0	0.0	.000
1991		6	4	.600	3.47	29	9	1	85.2	93	40	40	0	2	0	0	22	2	0	.091	5	15	2	0	0.8	.909
1992	LA N	1	1	.500	4.18	16	1	0	23.2	32	10	14	0	0	1	0	2	2	0	1.000	1	7	0	0	0.5	1.000
1993		0	0	—	0.60	10	0	0	15	13	4	12	0	0	0	0	0	0	0	—	0	3	0	0	0.3	1.000
4 yrs.		7	5	.583	3.31	60	10	1	130.2	144	56	69	0	2	1	0	24	4	0	.167	6	25	2	0	0.6	.939

Wayne Gross

GROSS, WAYNE DALE BL TR 6′ 2″ 210 lbs.
B. Jan. 14, 1952, Riverside, Calif.

Year	Team	W	L	PCT	ERA	G	GS	CG	IP	H	BB	SO	ShO	Relief Pitching W	Relief Pitching L	Relief Pitching SV	Batting AB	Batting H	Batting HR	BA	PO	A	E	DP	TC/G	FA
1983	OAK A	0	0	—	0.00	1	0	0	2.1	2	1	0	0	0	0	0	*				30	1	1	2	4.0	.969

Harley Grossman

GROSSMAN, HARLEY JOSEPH BR TR 6′ 170 lbs.
B. May 5, 1930, Evansville, Ind.

Year	Team	Lg	W	L	PCT	ERA	G	GS	CG	IP	H	BB	SO	ShO	Relief W	Relief L	Relief SV	Batting AB	Batting H	HR	BA	PO	A	E	DP	TC/G	FA
1952	WAS	A	0	0	—	54.00	1	0	0	0.1	2	0	0	0	0	0	0	0	0	0	—	1	0	0	0	1.0	1.000

Ernie Groth

GROTH, ERNEST JOHN BR TR 5′11″ 175 lbs.
B. Dec. 24, 1884, Cedarburg, Wis. D. May 23, 1950, Milwaukee, Wis.

Year	Team	Lg	W	L	PCT	ERA	G	GS	CG	IP	H	BB	SO	ShO	Relief W	Relief L	Relief SV	Batting AB	Batting H	HR	BA	PO	A	E	DP	TC/G	FA
1904	CHI	N	0	2	.000	5.63	3	2	2	16	22	6	9	0	0	0	1	6	0	0	.000	0	2	0	1	0.7	1.000

Ernie Groth

GROTH, ERNEST WILLIAM BR TR 5′ 9″ 185 lbs.
B. May 3, 1922, Beaver Falls, Pa.

Year	Team	Lg	W	L	PCT	ERA	G	GS	CG	IP	H	BB	SO	ShO	Relief W	Relief L	Relief SV	Batting AB	Batting H	HR	BA	PO	A	E	DP	TC/G	FA
1947	CLE	A	0	0	—	0.00	2	0	0	1.1	0	1	1	0	0	0	0	0	0	0	—	0	0	0	0	0.0	.000
1948			0	0	—	9.00	1	0	0	1	1	2	0	0	0	0	0	0	0	0	—	0	0	0	0	0.0	.000
1949	CHI	A	0	1	.000	5.40	3	0	0	5	2	3	1	0	0	1	0	0	0	0	—	1	0	1	0	0.7	.500
3 yrs.			0	1	.000	4.91	6	0	0	7.1	3	6	2	0	0	1	0	0	0	0		1	0	1	0	0.3	.500

Matt Grott

GROTT, MATTHEW ALLEN BL TL 6′ 1″ 210 lbs.
B. Dec. 5, 1967, LaPorte, Ind.

Year	Team	Lg	W	L	PCT	ERA	G	GS	CG	IP	H	BB	SO	ShO	Relief W	Relief L	Relief SV	Batting AB	Batting H	HR	BA	PO	A	E	DP	TC/G	FA
1995	CIN	N	0	0	—	21.60	2	0	0	1.2	6	0	2	0	0	0	0	0	0	0	—	0	1	0	0	0.5	1.000

Lefty Grove

GROVE, ROBERT MOSES (Mose) BL TL 6′ 3″ 190 lbs.
B. Mar. 6, 1900, Lonaconing, Md. D. May 22, 1975, Norwalk, Ohio.
Hall of Fame 1947.

Year	Team	Lg	W	L	PCT	ERA	G	GS	CG	IP	H	BB	SO	ShO	Relief W	Relief L	Relief SV	Batting AB	Batting H	HR	BA	PO	A	E	DP	TC/G	FA
1925	PHI	A	10	12	.455	4.75	45	18	5	197	207	**131**	**116**	0	5	3	1	65	8	0	.123	6	55	2	3	1.4	.968
1926			13	13	.500	**2.51**	45	33	20	258	227	101	**194**	1	1	1	6	81	8	0	.099	6	53	3	3	1.4	.952
1927			20	13	.606	3.19	51	28	14	262.1	251	79	**174**	1	3	5	9	80	10	2	.125	8	55	9	2	1.4	.875
1928			**24**	8	.750	2.58	39	31	24	261.2	228	64	**183**	4	1	0	4	88	15	1	.170	6	40	1	0	1.2	.979
1929			20	6	**.769**	**2.81**	42	**37**	21	275.1	278	81	**170**	2	0	0	4	102	22	1	.216	3	44	2	0	1.2	.959
1930			**28**	5	**.848**	**2.54**	**50**	32	22	291	273	60	**209**	2	5	2	**9**	110	22	2	.200	6	53	2	1	1.2	.967
1931			**31**	4	**.886**	**2.06**	41	30	**27**	288.2	249	62	**175**	**4**	4	1	5	115	23	0	.200	2	47	0	1	1.2	1.000
1932			25	10	.714	**2.84**	44	30	**27**	291.2	269	79	188	**4**	3	2	7	107	18	4	.168	3	46	1	1	1.1	.980
1933			**24**	8	**.750**	3.20	45	28	**21**	275.1	280	83	114	2	6	2	6	105	9	1	.086	9	58	2	5	1.5	.971
1934	BOS	A	8	8	.500	6.50	22	11	5	109.1	149	32	43	0	3	3	0	37	6	1	.162	3	18	2	1	1.0	.913
1935			20	12	.625	**2.70**	35	30	23	273	269	65	121	2	2	1	1	89	7	1	.079	1	63	2	6	1.9	.970
1936			17	12	.586	**2.81**	35	30	22	253.1	237	65	130	**6**	0	2	2	80	11	0	.138	3	49	2	0	1.5	.963
1937			17	9	.654	3.02	32	32	21	262	269	83	153	3	0	0	0	91	13	0	.143	6	43	1	1	1.6	.980
1938			14	4	.778	**3.08**	24	21	12	163.2	169	52	99	1	0	0	1	54	8	0	.148	0	29	0	0	1.2	1.000
1939			15	4	**.789**	**2.54**	23	23	17	191	180	58	81	2	0	0	0	67	9	1	.134	0	21	3	2	1.0	.875
1940			7	6	.538	3.99	22	21	9	153.1	159	50	62	1	0	0	0	53	8	1	.151	1	34	3	0	1.7	.921
1941			7	7	.500	4.37	21	21	10	134	155	42	54	0	0	0	0	45	5	0	.111	2	17	3	0	1.0	.864
17 yrs.			300	141	.680 **4th**	3.06	616	456	300	3940.2	3849	1187	2266	35	33	22	55	1369	202	15	.148	65	725	38	26	1.3	.954
WORLD SERIES																											
1929	PHI	A	0	0	—	0.00	2	0	0	6.1	3	1	10	0	0	0	2	2	0	0	.000	0	1	0	0	0.5	1.000
1930			2	1	.667	1.42	3	2	2	19	15	3	10	0	1	0	0	6	0	0	.000	0	1	0	0	0.3	1.000
1931			2	1	.667	2.42	3	3	2	26	28	2	16	0	0	0	0	10	0	0	.000	0	0	0	0	0.0	.000
3 yrs.			4	2	.667	1.75	8	5	4	51.1	46	6	36	0	1	0	2	18	0	0	.000	0	2	0	0	0.3	1.000

Orval Grove

GROVE, ORVAL LeROY BR TR 6′ 3″ 196 lbs.
B. Aug. 29, 1919, Mineral, Kans. D. Apr. 20, 1992, Carmichael, Calif.

Year	Team	Lg	W	L	PCT	ERA	G	GS	CG	IP	H	BB	SO	ShO	Relief W	Relief L	Relief SV	Batting AB	Batting H	HR	BA	PO	A	E	DP	TC/G	FA
1940	CHI	A	0	0	—	3.00	3	0	0	6	4	4	1	0	0	0	0	1	0	0	.000	1	0	0	0	0.3	1.000
1941			0	0	—	10.29	2	0	0	7	9	5	5	0	0	0	0	2	0	0	.000	0	3	0	0	1.5	1.000
1942			4	6	.400	5.16	12	8	4	66.1	77	33	21	0	1	1	0	22	5	1	.227	8	16	1	1	2.1	.960
1943			15	9	.625	2.75	32	25	18	216.1	192	72	76	3	1	0	2	66	12	0	.182	21	43	1	0	2.0	.985
1944			14	15	.483	3.72	34	33	11	234.2	237	71	105	2	1	0	0	77	8	0	.104	6	64	3	3	2.1	.959
1945			14	12	.538	3.44	33	30	16	217	233	68	54	4	0	0	1	71	7	0	.099	12	55	5	3	2.2	.931
1946			8	13	.381	3.02	33	26	10	205.1	213	78	60	1	0	0	0	65	7	0	.108	8	49	4	5	1.8	.934
1947			6	8	.429	4.44	25	19	6	135.2	158	70	33	1	0	0	0	48	7	0	.146	11	19	1	1	1.2	.968
1948			2	10	.167	6.16	32	11	1	87.2	110	42	18	0	1	2	1	21	2	0	.095	5	26	3	1	1.1	.912
1949			0	0	—	54.00	1	0	0	0.2	4	1	1	0	0	0	0	0	0	0	—	0	0	0	0	0.0	.000
10 yrs.			63	73	.463	3.78	207	152	66	1176.2	1237	444	374	11	4	3	4	373	48	1	.129	72	275	18	14	1.8	.951

Charlie Grover

GROVER, CHARLES BYRD (Bugs) BL TR 6′ 1½″ 185 lbs.
B. June 20, 1890, Huntington Twp., Ohio D. May 24, 1971, Emmett, Mich.

Year	Team	Lg	W	L	PCT	ERA	G	GS	CG	IP	H	BB	SO	ShO	Relief W	Relief L	Relief SV	Batting AB	Batting H	HR	BA	PO	A	E	DP	TC/G	FA
1913	DET	A	0	0	—	3.38	2	1	0	10.2	9	7	2	0	0	0	0	3	0	0	.000	1	3	0	0	2.0	1.000

Tom Grubbs

GRUBBS, THOMAS DILLARD (Judge) BR TR 6′ 2″ 165 lbs.
B. Feb. 22, 1894, Mt. Sterling, Ky. D. Jan. 28, 1986, Lexington, Ky.

Year	Team	Lg	W	L	PCT	ERA	G	GS	CG	IP	H	BB	SO	ShO	Relief W	Relief L	Relief SV	Batting AB	Batting H	HR	BA	PO	A	E	DP	TC/G	FA
1920	NY	N	0	1	.000	7.20	1	1	0	5	9	0	0	0	0	0	0	1	0	0	.000	0	0	0	0	0.0	.000

Henry Gruber

GRUBER, HENRY JOHN (Hen) BR TL 5′ 9″ 155 lbs.
B. Dec. 14, 1863, Hamden, Conn. D. Sept. 26, 1932, New Haven, Conn.

Year	Team	Lg	W	L	PCT	ERA	G	GS	CG	IP	H	BB	SO	ShO	Relief W	Relief L	Relief SV	Batting AB	Batting H	HR	BA	PO	A	E	DP	TC/G	FA
1887	DET	N	4	3	.571	2.74	7	7	7	62.1	63	21	12	0	0	0	0	24	4	0	.167	0	7	1	0	1.1	.875
1888			11	14	.440	2.29	27	25	25	240	196	41	71	3	1	1	0	92	13	0	.141	4	61	8	2	2.7	.890
1889	CLE	N	7	16	.304	3.64	25	23	23	205	198	94	74	0	1	0	1	69	7	0	.101	6	40	6	2	2.1	.885
1890	CLE	P	22	23	.489	4.27	48	44	39	383.1	464	204	110	1	0	0	1	163	36	0	.221	9	111	15	3	2.6	.889
1891	CLE	N	17	22	.436	4.13	44	40	35	348.2	407	119	79	1	2	1	0	141	23	1	.163	9	90	10	5	2.4	.908
5 yrs.			61	78	.439	3.67	151	139	129	1239.1	1328	479	346	5	4	2	2	489	83	1	.170	28	309	40	12	2.4	.894

Al Grunwald

GRUNWALD, ALFRED HENRY (Stretch) BL TL 6′ 4″ 210 lbs.
B. Feb. 13, 1930, Los Angeles, Calif.

Year	Team	Lg	W	L	PCT	ERA	G	GS	CG	IP	H	BB	SO	ShO	Relief W	Relief L	Relief SV	Batting AB	Batting H	HR	BA	PO	A	E	DP	TC/G	FA
1955	PIT	N	0	0	—	4.70	3	0	0	7.2	7	7	2	0	0	0	0	4	2	0	.500	2	0	0	0	0.7	1.000
1959	KC	A	0	1	.000	7.94	6	1	0	11.1	18	11	9	0	0	0	1	4	0	0	.000	0	2	1	1	0.5	.667
2 yrs.			0	1	.000	6.63	9	1	0	19	25	18	11	0	0	0	1	8	2	0	.250	2	2	1	1	0.6	.800

Joe Grzenda

GRZENDA, JOSEPH CHARLES BR TL 6′ 2″ 180 lbs.
B. June 8, 1937, Scranton, Pa.

Year	Team	W	L	PCT	ERA	G	GS	CG	IP	H	BB	SO	ShO	Relief Pitching W	Relief Pitching L	Relief Pitching SV	Batting AB	Batting H	Batting HR	BA	PO	A	E	DP	TC/G	FA
1961	**DET A**	1	0	1.000	7.94	4	0	0	5.2	9	2	0	0	1	0	0	1	1	0	1.000	1	2	0	0	0.8	1.000
1964	**KC A**	0	2	.000	5.40	20	0	0	25	34	13	17	0	0	2	0	2	0	0	.000	0	10	0	0	0.5	1.000
1966		0	2	.000	3.27	21	0	0	22	28	12	14	0	0	2	0	1	0	0	.000	0	6	0	1	0.3	1.000
1967	**NY N**	0	0	—	2.16	11	0	0	16.2	14	8	9	0	0	0	0	1	0	0	.000	0	1	0	0	0.1	1.000
1969	**MIN A**	4	1	.800	3.88	38	0	0	48.2	52	17	24	0	4	1	3	5	0	0	.000	0	14	0	1	0.4	1.000
1970	**WAS A**	3	6	.333	4.98	49	3	0	85	86	34	38	0	2	5	6	12	0	0	.000	3	16	0	1	0.4	1.000
1971		5	2	.714	1.93	46	0	0	70	54	17	56	0	5	2	5	7	1	0	.143	0	11	0	0	0.2	1.000
1972	**STL N**	1	0	1.000	5.71	30	0	0	34.2	46	17	15	0	1	0	0	1	0	0	.000	2	6	0	0	0.3	1.000
8 yrs.		14	13	.519	4.01	219	3	0	307.2	323	120	173	0	13	12	14	30	2	0	.067	6	66	0	3	0.3	1.000
LEAGUE CHAMPIONSHIP SERIES																										
1969	**MIN A**	0	0	—	0.00	1	0	0	0.2	0	0	0	0	0	0	0	0	0	0	—	0	0	0	0	0.0	.000

Cecilio Guante

GUANTE, CECILIO BR TR 6′ 3″ 200 lbs.
Born Cecilio Guante (Magallane).
B. Feb. 1, 1960, Villa Mella, Dominican Republic.

Year	Team	W	L	PCT	ERA	G	GS	CG	IP	H	BB	SO	ShO	Relief Pitching W	Relief Pitching L	Relief Pitching SV	Batting AB	Batting H	Batting HR	BA	PO	A	E	DP	TC/G	FA
1982	**PIT N**	0	0	—	3.33	10	0	0	27	28	5	26	0	0	0	0	5	0	0	.000	1	2	0	0	0.3	1.000
1983		2	6	.250	3.32	49	0	0	100.1	90	46	82	0	2	6	9	22	2	0	.091	5	9	2	0	0.3	.875
1984		2	3	.400	2.61	27	0	0	41.1	32	16	30	0	2	3	2	4	0	0	.000	2	3	0	0	0.2	1.000
1985		4	6	.400	2.72	63	0	0	109	84	40	92	0	4	6	5	17	1	0	.059	6	13	1	0	0.3	.950
1986		5	2	.714	3.35	52	0	0	78	65	29	63	0	5	2	4	1	0	0	.000	1	5	1	0	0.1	.857
1987	**NY A**	3	2	.600	5.73	23	0	0	44	42	20	46	0	3	2	1	0	0	0	—	1	2	1	0	0.2	.750
1988	**2 teams NY A** (56G 5–6) **TEX A** (7G 0–0)																									
″	**total**	5	6	.455	2.82	63	0	0	79.2	67	26	65	0	5	6	12	0	0	0		2	3	1	0	0.1	.833
1989	**TEX A**	6	6	.500	3.91	50	0	0	69	66	36	69	0	6	6	2	0	0	0	—	4	5	0	0	0.2	1.000
1990	**CLE A**	2	3	.400	5.01	26	1	0	46.2	38	18	30	0	2	2	0	0	0	0	—	3	5	0	2	0.3	1.000
9 yrs.		29	34	.460	3.48	363	1	0	595	512	236	503	0	29	33	35	49	3	0	.061	25	47	6	2	0.2	.923

Eddie Guardado

GUARDADO, EDWARD ADRIAN BR TL 6′ 195 lbs.
B. Oct. 2, 1970, Stockton, Calif.

Year	Team	W	L	PCT	ERA	G	GS	CG	IP	H	BB	SO	ShO	Relief Pitching W	Relief Pitching L	Relief Pitching SV	Batting AB	Batting H	Batting HR	BA	PO	A	E	DP	TC/G	FA
1993	**MIN A**	3	8	.273	6.18	19	16	0	94.2	123	36	46	0	0	0	0	0	0	0	—	6	9	0	1	0.8	1.000
1994		0	2	.000	8.47	4	4	0	17	26	4	8	0	0	0	0	0	0	0	—	0	0	0	0	0.0	.000
1995		4	9	.308	5.12	51	5	0	91.1	99	45	71	0	4	4	2	0	0	0	—	4	8	1	0	0.3	.923
3 yrs.		7	19	.269	5.90	74	25	0	203	248	85	125	0	4	4	2	0	0	0		10	17	1	1	0.4	.964

Mark Gubicza

GUBICZA, MARK STEVEN BR TR 6′ 6″ 215 lbs.
B. Aug. 14, 1962, Philadelphia, Pa.

Year	Team	W	L	PCT	ERA	G	GS	CG	IP	H	BB	SO	ShO	Relief Pitching W	Relief Pitching L	Relief Pitching SV	Batting AB	Batting H	Batting HR	BA	PO	A	E	DP	TC/G	FA
1984	**KC A**	10	14	.417	4.05	29	29	4	189	172	75	111	2	0	0	0	0	0	0	—	19	31	2	1	1.8	.962
1985		14	10	.583	4.06	29	28	0	177.1	160	77	99	0	1	0	0	0	0	0	—	23	26	0	4	1.7	1.000
1986		12	6	.667	3.64	35	24	3	180.2	155	84	118	2	1	1	0	0	0	0	—	17	32	0	3	1.4	1.000
1987		13	18	.419	3.98	35	35	10	241.2	231	120	166	2	0	0	0	0	0	0	—	32	40	2	7	2.1	.973
1988		20	8	.714	2.70	35	35	8	269.2	237	83	183	4	0	0	0	0	0	0	—	29	44	1	3	2.1	.986
1989		15	11	.577	3.04	36	**36**	8	255	252	63	173	2	0	0	0	0	0	0	—	18	49	5	0	2.0	.931
1990		4	7	.364	4.50	16	16	2	94	101	38	71	0	0	0	0	0	0	0	—	9	10	1	3	1.3	.950
1991		9	12	.429	5.68	26	26	0	133	168	42	89	0	0	0	0	0	0	0	—	8	29	3	5	1.5	.925
1992		7	6	.538	3.72	18	18	2	111.1	110	36	81	1	0	0	0	0	0	0	—	10	12	0	2	1.2	1.000
1993		5	8	.385	4.66	49	6	0	104.1	128	43	80	0	5	4	2	0	0	0	—	11	7	1	0	0.4	.947
1994		7	9	.438	4.50	22	22	0	130	158	26	59	0	0	0	0	0	0	0	—	17	20	3	1	1.8	.925
1995		12	14	.462	3.75	33	33	3	213.1	222	62	81	2	0	0	0	0	0	0	—	28	36	0	2	1.9	1.000
12 yrs.		128	123	.510	3.85	363	308	40	2099.1	2094	749	1311	15	7	5	2	0	0	0		221	336	18	31	1.6	.969
LEAGUE CHAMPIONSHIP SERIES																										
1985	**KC A**	1	0	1.000	3.24	2	1	0	8.1	4	4	4	0	0	0	0	0	0	0	—	0	1	0	0	0.5	1.000

Marv Gudat

GUDAT, MARVIN JOHN BL TL 5′11″ 162 lbs.
B. Aug. 27, 1905, Goliad, Tex. D. Mar. 1, 1954, Los Angeles, Calif.

Year	Team	W	L	PCT	ERA	G	GS	CG	IP	H	BB	SO	ShO	Relief Pitching W	Relief Pitching L	Relief Pitching SV	Batting AB	Batting H	Batting HR	BA	PO	A	E	DP	TC/G	FA
1929	**CIN N**	1	1	.500	3.38	7	2	2	26.2	29	4	0	0	0	0	0	10	2	0	.200	0	4	1	0	0.7	.800
1932	**CHI N**	0	0	—	0.00	1	0	0	1	1	0	2	0	0	0	0	94	24	1	.255	77	4	2	4	3.6	.976
2 yrs.		1	1	.500	3.25	8	2	2	27.2	30	4	2	0	0	0	0	*				77	8	3	4	2.9	.966

Whitey Guese

GUESE, THEODORE BR TR 6′½″ 200 lbs.
B. Jan. 24, 1872, New Bremen, Ohio D. Apr. 8, 1951, Wapakoneta, Ohio.

Year	Team	W	L	PCT	ERA	G	GS	CG	IP	H	BB	SO	ShO	Relief Pitching W	Relief Pitching L	Relief Pitching SV	Batting AB	Batting H	Batting HR	BA	PO	A	E	DP	TC/G	FA
1901	**CIN N**	1	4	.200	6.09	6	5	4	44.1	62	14	11	0	0	0	0	15	3	0	.200	1	6	3	0	1.7	.700

Lee Guetterman

GUETTERMAN, ARTHUR LEE BL TL 6′ 8″ 225 lbs.
B. Nov. 22, 1958, Chattanooga, Tenn.

Year	Team	W	L	PCT	ERA	G	GS	CG	IP	H	BB	SO	ShO	Relief Pitching W	Relief Pitching L	Relief Pitching SV	Batting AB	Batting H	Batting HR	BA	PO	A	E	DP	TC/G	FA
1984	**SEA A**	0	0	—	4.15	3	0	0	4.1	9	2	2	0	0	0	0	0	0	0	—	0	1	0	1	0.3	1.000
1986		0	4	.000	7.34	41	4	1	76	108	30	38	0	0	2	0	0	0	0	—	5	12	2	1	0.5	.895
1987		11	4	.733	3.81	25	17	2	113.1	117	35	42	1	1	0	0	0	0	0	—	7	22	0	3	1.2	1.000
1988	**NY A**	1	2	.333	4.65	20	2	0	40.2	49	14	15	0	1	0	0	0	0	0	—	2	5	0	0	0.3	1.000
1989		5	5	.500	2.45	70	0	0	103	98	26	51	0	5	5	13	0	0	0	—	6	24	3	4	0.5	.909
1990		11	7	.611	3.39	64	0	0	93	80	26	48	0	**11**	7	2	0	0	0	—	6	19	2	1	0.4	.926
1991		3	4	.429	3.68	64	0	0	88	91	25	35	0	3	4	6	0	0	0	—	9	13	3	1	0.4	.880
1992	**2 teams NY A** (15G 1–1) **NY N** (43G 3–4)																									
″	**total**	4	5	.444	7.09	58	0	0	66	92	27	20	0	4	5	2	2	0	0	.000	4	8	0	1	0.2	1.000
1993	**STL N**	3	3	.500	2.93	40	0	0	46	41	16	19	0	3	3	1	2	1	0	.500	1	4	2	0	0.2	.714
1995	**SEA A**	0	0	—	6.88	23	0	0	17	21	11	11	0	0	0	1	0	0	0	—	2	5	0	1	0.3	1.000
10 yrs.		38	34	.528	4.34	408	23	3	647.1	706	212	281	1	28	26	25	4	1	0	.250	42	113	12	13	0.4	.928

Ron Guidry

GUIDRY, RONALD AMES (Gator, Louisiana Lightning) BL TL 5′11″ 161 lbs.
B. Aug. 28, 1950, Lafayette, La.

Year	Team	W	L	PCT	ERA	G	GS	CG	IP	H	BB	SO	ShO	Relief Pitching W	Relief Pitching L	Relief Pitching SV	Batting AB	Batting H	Batting HR	BA	PO	A	E	DP	TC/G	FA
1975	**NY A**	0	1	.000	3.45	10	1	0	15.2	15	9	15	0	0	0	0	0	0	0	—	0	0	0	0	0.0	.000
1976		0	0	—	5.63	7	0	0	16	20	4	12	0	0	0	0	0	0	0	—	0	4	0	0	0.6	1.000
1977		16	7	.696	2.82	31	25	9	211	174	65	176	5	1	0	1	0	0	0	—	7	27	1	2	1.1	.971

Ron Guidry *continued*

Year	Team	W	L	PCT	ERA	G	GS	CG	IP	H	BB	SO	ShO	Relief Pitching W	L	SV	Batting AB	H	HR	BA	PO	A	E	DP	TC/G	FA
1978		**25**	3	**.893**	**1.74**	35	35	16	273.2	187	72	248	**9**	0	0	0	0	0	0	—	14	44	2	1	1.7	.967
1979		18	8	.692	**2.78**	33	30	15	236	203	71	201	2	1	0	2	0	0	0	—	11	29	1	1	1.2	.976
1980		17	10	.630	3.56	37	29	5	220	215	80	166	3	1	1	1	0	0	0	—	16	36	2	4	1.5	.963
1981		11	5	.688	2.76	23	21	0	127	100	26	104	0	0	0	0	0	0	0	—	13	17	0	1	1.3	1.000
1982		14	8	.636	3.81	34	33	6	222	216	69	162	1	0	0	0	0	0	0	—	7	19	0	1	0.8	1.000
1983		21	9	.700	3.42	31	31	**21**	250.1	232	60	156	3	0	0	0	0	0	0	—	9	33	0	2	1.3	1.000
1984		10	11	.476	4.51	29	28	5	195.2	223	44	127	1	0	0	0	0	0	0	—	8	24	0	3	1.1	1.000
1985		**22**	6	**.786**	3.27	34	33	11	259	243	42	143	2	0	0	0	0	0	0	—	6	34	1	3	1.2	.976
1986		9	12	.429	3.98	30	30	5	192.1	202	38	140	0	0	0	0	0	0	0	—	9	21	1	0	1.0	.968
1987		5	8	.385	3.67	22	17	2	117.2	111	38	96	0	0	1	0	0	0	0	—	4	14	0	1	0.8	1.000
1988		2	3	.400	4.18	12	10	0	56	57	15	32	0	0	0	0	0	0	0	—	3	5	0	0	0.7	1.000
14 yrs.		170	91	.651	3.29	368	323	95	2392.1	2198	633	1778	26	3	2	4	0	0	0		107	307	8	19	1.1	.981
DIVISIONAL PLAYOFF SERIES																										
1981	**NY A**	0	0	—	5.40	2	2	0	8.1	11	3	8	0	0	0	0	0	0	0	—	0	0	0	0	0.0	.000
LEAGUE CHAMPIONSHIP SERIES																										
1977	**NY A**	1	0	1.000	3.97	2	2	1	11.1	9	3	8	0	0	0	0	0	0	0	—	2	0	0	0	1.0	1.000
1978		1	0	1.000	1.13	1	1	0	8	7	1	7	0	0	0	0	0	0	0	—	0	0	0	0	0.0	.000
1980		0	1	.000	12.00	1	1	0	3	5	4	2	0	0	0	0	0	0	0	—	0	1	0	0	1.0	1.000
3 yrs.		2	1	.667	4.03	4	4	1	22.1	21	8	17	0	0	0	0	0	0	0		2	1	0	0	0.8	1.000
WORLD SERIES																										
1977	**NY A**	1	0	1.000	2.00	1	1	1	9	4	3	7	0	0	0	0	2	0	0	.000	0	0	0	0	0.0	.000
1978		1	0	1.000	1.00	1	1	1	9	8	7	4	0	0	0	0	0	0	0	—	1	1	0	0	2.0	1.000
1981		1	1	.500	1.93	2	2	0	14	8	4	15	0	0	0	0	5	0	0	.000	0	0	0	0	0.0	.000
3 yrs.		3	1	.750	1.69	4	4	2	32	20	14	26	0	0	0	0	7	0	0	.000	1	1	0	0	0.5	1.000

Skip Guinn

GUINN, DRANNON EUGENE BR TL 5′10″ 180 lbs.
B. Oct. 25, 1944, St. Charles, Mo.

Year	Team	W	L	PCT	ERA	G	GS	CG	IP	H	BB	SO	ShO	Relief Pitching W	L	SV	Batting AB	H	HR	BA	PO	A	E	DP	TC/G	FA
1968	**ATL N**	0	0	—	3.60	3	0	0	5	3	3	4	0	0	0	0	0	0	0	—	0	0	0	0	0.0	.000
1969	**HOU N**	1	2	.333	6.67	28	0	0	27	34	21	33	0	1	2	0	3	0	0	.000	1	3	0	0	0.1	1.000
1971		0	0	—	0.00	4	0	0	5	1	3	3	0	0	0	1	0	0	0	—	1	0	0	0	0.3	1.000
3 yrs.		1	2	.333	5.35	35	0	0	37	38	27	40	0	1	2	1	3	0	0	.000	2	3	0	0	0.1	1.000

Witt Guise

GUISE, WITT ORISON (Lefty) BL TL 6′ 2″ 172 lbs.
B. Sept. 18, 1909, Driggs, Ark. D. Aug. 13, 1968, Little Rock, Ark.

Year	Team	W	L	PCT	ERA	G	GS	CG	IP	H	BB	SO	ShO	Relief Pitching W	L	SV	Batting AB	H	HR	BA	PO	A	E	DP	TC/G	FA
1940	**CIN N**	0	0	—	1.17	2	0	0	7.2	8	5	1	0	0	0	0	3	1	0	.333	0	3	0	0	1.5	1.000

Don Gullett

GULLETT, DONALD EDWARD BR TL 6′ 190 lbs.
B. Jan. 6, 1951, Lynn, Ky.

Year	Team	W	L	PCT	ERA	G	GS	CG	IP	H	BB	SO	ShO	Relief Pitching W	L	SV	Batting AB	H	HR	BA	PO	A	E	DP	TC/G	FA
1970	**CIN N**	5	2	.714	2.42	44	2	0	78	54	44	76	0	4	1	6	19	4	0	.211	2	5	0	1	0.2	1.000
1971		16	6	**.727**	2.64	35	31	4	218	196	64	107	3	0	0	0	75	9	0	.120	6	25	1	2	0.9	.969
1972		9	10	.474	3.94	31	16	2	134.2	127	43	96	0	3	2	2	38	8	0	.211	4	11	1	0	0.5	.938
1973		18	8	.692	3.51	45	30	7	228.1	198	69	153	4	5	1	2	64	12	0	.188	12	31	0	2	1.0	1.000
1974		17	11	.607	3.04	36	35	10	243	201	88	183	3	0	1	0	80	19	0	.237	8	36	1	0	1.3	.978
1975		15	4	**.789**	2.42	22	22	8	160	127	56	98	3	0	0	0	62	14	0	.226	2	22	0	0	1.1	1.000
1976		11	3	.786	3.00	23	20	4	126	119	48	64	0	1	0	1	44	8	0	.182	4	20	0	1	1.0	1.000
1977	**NY A**	14	4	.778	3.59	22	22	7	158	137	69	116	1	0	0	0	0	0	0	—	9	15	1	1	1.1	.960
1978		4	2	.667	3.63	8	8	2	44.2	46	20	28	0	0	0	0	0	0	0	—	2	8	2	0	1.5	.833
9 yrs.		109	50	.686	3.11	266	186	44	1390.2	1205	501	921	14	13	5	11	382	74	0	.194	49	173	6	7	0.9	.974
LEAGUE CHAMPIONSHIP SERIES																										
1970	**CIN N**	0	0	—	0.00	2	0	0	3.2	1	2	3	0	0	0	2	1	0	0	.000	0	0	0	0	0.0	.000
1972		0	1	.000	8.00	2	2	0	9	12	0	5	0	0	0	0	2	1	0	.500	0	0	0	0	0.0	.000
1973		0	1	.000	2.00	3	1	0	9	4	3	6	0	0	0	0	1	0	0	.000	1	0	0	0	0.3	1.000
1975		1	0	1.000	3.00	1	1	1	9	8	2	5	0	0	0	0	4	2	1	.500	4	1	0	0	5.0	1.000
1976		1	0	1.000	1.13	1	1	0	8	2	3	4	0	0	0	0	4	2	0	.500	0	0	0	0	0.0	.000
1977	**NY A**	0	1	.000	18.00	1	1	0	2	4	2	0	0	0	0	0	0	0	0	—	0	0	0	0	0.0	.000
6 yrs.		2	3	.400	3.98	10	6	1	40.2	31	12	23	0	0	0	2	12	5	1	.417	5	1	0	0	0.6	1.000
			5th				**9th**																			
WORLD SERIES																										
1970	**CIN N**	0	0	—	1.35	3	0	0	6.2	5	4	4	0	0	0	0	1	0	0	.000	0	0	0	0	0.0	.000
1972		0	0	—	1.29	1	1	0	7	5	2	4	0	0	0	0	2	0	0	.000	0	1	0	0	1.0	1.000
1975		1	1	.500	4.34	3	3	0	18.2	19	10	15	0	0	0	0	7	2	0	.286	0	0	0	0	0.0	.000
1976		1	0	1.000	1.23	1	1	0	7.1	5	3	4	0	0	0	0	0	0	0	—	0	1	0	0	1.0	1.000
1977	**NY A**	0	1	.000	6.39	2	2	0	12.2	13	7	10	0	0	0	0	2	0	0	.000	1	2	0	0	1.5	1.000
5 yrs.		2	2	.500	3.61	10	7	0	52.1	47	26	37	0	0	0	0	12	2	0	.167	1	4	0	0	0.5	1.000
											8th															

Bill Gullickson

GULLICKSON, WILLIAM LEE BR TR 6′ 3″ 200 lbs.
B. Feb. 20, 1959, Marshall, Minn.

Year	Team	W	L	PCT	ERA	G	GS	CG	IP	H	BB	SO	ShO	Relief Pitching W	L	SV	Batting AB	H	HR	BA	PO	A	E	DP	TC/G	FA
1979	**MON N**	0	0	—	0.00	1	0	0	1	2	0	0	0	0	0	0	0	0	0	—	0	0	0	0	0.0	.000
1980		10	5	.667	3.00	24	19	5	141	127	50	120	2	0	1	0	40	7	0	.175	4	21	1	2	1.1	.962
1981		7	9	.438	2.81	22	22	3	157	142	34	115	2	0	0	0	46	7	0	.152	12	16	1	2	1.3	.966
1982		12	14	.462	3.57	34	34	6	236.2	231	61	155	0	0	0	0	82	10	0	.122	16	18	3	1	1.1	.919
1983		17	12	.586	3.75	34	34	10	242.1	230	59	120	1	0	0	0	82	11	1	.134	27	25	1	3	1.6	.981
1984		12	9	.571	3.61	32	32	3	226.2	230	37	100	0	0	0	0	73	8	0	.110	14	19	4	2	1.2	.892
1985		14	12	.538	3.52	29	29	4	181.1	187	47	68	1	0	0	0	64	12	0	.188	10	26	1	0	1.3	.973
1986	**CIN N**	15	12	.556	3.38	37	37	6	244.2	245	60	121	2	0	0	0	79	6	0	.076	14	32	3	3	1.3	.939
1987	**2 teams CIN N**	(27G 10–11)	**NY A**	(8G 4–2)																						
″	**total**	14	13	.519	4.86	35	35	4	213	218	50	117	1	0	0	0	53	11	1	.208	16	21	0	0	1.1	1.000
1990	**HOU N**	10	14	.417	3.82	32	32	2	193.1	221	61	73	1	0	0	0	57	9	1	.158	11	13	0	1	0.8	1.000
1991	**DET A**	**20**	9	.690	3.90	35	**35**	4	226.1	256	44	91	0	0	0	0	0	0	0	—	14	21	0	0	1.0	1.000
1992		14	13	.519	4.34	34	34	4	221.2	228	50	64	1	0	0	0	0	0	0	—	21	26	1	3	1.4	.979

Bill Gullickson *continued*

Year	Team	Lg	W	L	PCT	ERA	G	GS	CG	IP	H	BB	SO	ShO	Relief Pitching W	Relief Pitching L	Relief Pitching SV	Batting AB	Batting H	Batting HR	BA	PO	A	E	DP	TC/G	FA
1993			13	9	.591	5.37	28	28	2	159.1	186	44	70	0	0	0	0	0	0	0	—	11	24	0	1	1.3	1.000
1994			4	5	.444	5.93	21	19	1	115.1	156	25	65	0	0	0	0	0	0	0	—	15	14	1	0	1.4	.967
14 yrs.			162	136	.544	3.93	398	390	54	2559.2	2659	622	1279	11	0	1	0	576	81	3	.141	185	276	16	18	1.2	.966
DIVISIONAL PLAYOFF SERIES																											
1981	**MON**	**N**	1	0	1.000	1.17	1	1	0	7.2	6	1	3	0	0	0	0	3	0	0	.000	0	0	0	0	0.0	.000
LEAGUE CHAMPIONSHIP SERIES																											
1981	**MON**	**N**	0	2	.000	2.51	2	2	0	14.1	12	6	12	0	0	0	0	3	0	0	.000	0	2	0	0	1.0	1.000

Ad Gumbert

GUMBERT, ADDISON COURTNEY BR TR 5′10″ 200 lbs.
Brother of Billy Gumbert.
B. Oct. 10, 1868, Pittsburgh, Pa. D. Apr. 23, 1925, Pittsburgh, Pa.

Year	Team	Lg	W	L	PCT	ERA	G	GS	CG	IP	H	BB	SO	ShO	Relief Pitching W	Relief Pitching L	Relief Pitching SV	Batting AB	Batting H	Batting HR	BA	PO	A	E	DP	TC/G	FA
1888	**CHI**	**N**	3	3	.500	3.14	6	6	5	48.2	44	10	16	0	0	0	0	24	8	0	.333	4	8	1	0	1.6	.923
1889			16	13	.552	3.62	31	28	25	246.1	258	76	91	2	2	0	0	153	44	7	.288	48	44	15	1	2.4	.860
1890	**BOS**	**P**	23	12	.657	3.96	39	33	27	277.1	338	86	81	1	3	1	0	145	35	3	.241	24	83	14	0	2.6	.884
1891	**CHI**	**N**	17	11	.607	3.58	32	31	24	256.1	282	90	73	1	0	0	0	105	32	0	.305	19	56	8	4	2.4	.904
1892			22	19	.537	3.41	46	45	39	382.2	399	107	118	0	0	0	0	178	42	1	.236	20	97	11	1	2.4	.914
1893	**PIT**	**N**	11	7	.611	5.15	22	20	16	162.2	207	78	40	2	1	0	0	95	21	0	.221	19	24	1	3	1.5	.977
1894			15	14	.517	6.02	37	31	26	269	372	84	65	0	1	0	0	113	33	1	.292	18	49	4	3	1.9	.944
1895	**BKN**	**N**	11	16	.407	5.08	33	26	20	234	288	69	45	0	1	1	1	97	35	2	.361	15	48	5	0	2.0	.926
1896	**2 teams**	**BKN N** (5G 0–4) **PHI N** (11G 5–3)																									
″	**total**		5	7	.417	4.32	16	14	9	108.1	133	34	17	1	0	0	0	45	11	1	.244	5	28	2	1	2.2	.943
9 yrs.			123	102	.547	4.27	262	234	191	1985.1	2321	634	546	7	8	2	1	*				172	437	61	13	2.2	.909

Billy Gumbert

GUMBERT, WILLIAM SKEEN BR TR 6′ 1½″ 200 lbs.
Brother of Ad Gumbert.
B. Aug. 8, 1865, Pittsburgh, Pa. D. Apr. 13, 1946, Pittsburgh, Pa.

Year	Team	Lg	W	L	PCT	ERA	G	GS	CG	IP	H	BB	SO	ShO	Relief Pitching W	Relief Pitching L	Relief Pitching SV	Batting AB	Batting H	Batting HR	BA	PO	A	E	DP	TC/G	FA
1890	**PIT**	**N**	4	6	.400	5.22	10	10	8	79.1	96	31	18	0	0	0	0	37	9	1	.243	14	18	4	2	3.3	.889
1892			3	2	.600	1.36	6	3	2	39.2	30	23	3	0	1	1	0	18	2	0	.111	1	7	6	0	2.0	.571
1893	**LOU**	**N**	0	0	—	27.00	1	1	0	0.2	2	5	0	0	0	0	0	1	1	0	1.000	0	0	0	0	0.0	.000
3 yrs.			7	8	.467	4.06	17	14	10	119.2	128	59	21	0	1	1	0	56	12	1	.214	15	25	10	2	2.6	.800

Harry Gumbert

GUMBERT, HARRY EDWARD (Gunboat) BR TR 6′ 2″ 185 lbs.
B. Nov. 5, 1909, Elizabeth, Pa. D. Jan. 4, 1995, Wimberly, Tex.

Year	Team	Lg	W	L	PCT	ERA	G	GS	CG	IP	H	BB	SO	ShO	Relief Pitching W	Relief Pitching L	Relief Pitching SV	Batting AB	Batting H	Batting HR	BA	PO	A	E	DP	TC/G	FA
1935	**NY**	**N**	1	2	.333	6.08	6	3	1	23.2	35	10	11	0	0	0	0	8	0	0	.000	1	4	1	1	1.0	.833
1936			11	3	.786	3.90	39	15	1	140.2	157	54	52	0	4	0	0	44	11	0	.250	12	44	1	1	1.5	.982
1937			10	11	.476	3.68	34	24	10	200.1	194	62	65	1	0	0	1	72	13	1	.181	16	80	2	2	2.9	.980
1938			15	13	.536	4.01	38	33	14	235.2	238	84	84	1	0	0	0	84	13	0	.155	8	85	1	7	2.5	.989
1939			18	11	.621	4.32	36	34	14	243.2	257	81	81	2	0	1	0	90	18	0	.200	18	76	3	4	2.7	.969
1940			12	14	.462	3.76	35	30	14	237	230	81	77	2	2	0	2	87	17	1	.195	11	65	0	4	2.2	1.000
1941	**2 teams**	**NY N** (5G 1–1) **STL N** (33G 11–5)																									
″	**total**		12	6	.667	3.06	38	22	9	176.2	173	48	62	3	4	0	1	65	19	2	.292	13	57	3	3	1.9	.959
1942	**STL**	**N**	9	5	.643	3.26	38	19	5	163	156	59	52	0	4	0	5	54	6	0	.111	6	60	0	2	1.7	1.000
1943			10	5	.667	2.84	21	19	7	133	115	32	40	2	0	0	0	45	7	0	.156	10	35	1	0	2.2	.978
1944	**2 teams**	**STL N** (10G 4–2) **CIN N** (24G 10–8)																									
″	**total**		14	10	.583	3.07	34	26	14	216.2	217	59	56	2	1	2	3	73	9	0	.123	20	52	3	9	2.2	.960
1946	**CIN**	**N**	6	8	.429	3.24	36	10	5	119.1	112	42	44	0	4	0	4	32	8	0	.250	5	29	0	2	0.9	1.000
1947			10	10	.500	3.89	46	0	0	90.1	88	47	43	0	**10**	**10**	10	22	6	0	.273	2	17	1	3	0.4	.950
1948			10	8	.556	3.47	**61**	0	0	106.1	123	34	25	0	**10**	**8**	**17**	25	1	1	.040	4	40	1	3	0.7	.978
1949	**2 teams**	**CIN N** (29G 4–3) **PIT N** (16G 1–4)																									
″	**total**		5	7	.417	5.64	45	0	0	68.2	88	26	17	0	5	7	5	6	1	0	.167	3	24	0	1	0.6	1.000
1950	**PIT**	**N**	0	0	—	5.40	1	0	0	1.2	3	2	0	0	0	0	0	1	1	0	1.000	0	2	0	0	2.0	1.000
15 yrs.			143	113	.559	3.68	508	235	94	2156.2	2186	721	709	13	44	28	48	708	130	5	.184	129	670	17	42	1.6	.979
WORLD SERIES																											
1936	**NY**	**N**	0	0	—	36.00	2	0	0	2	7	4	2	0	0	0	0	0	0	0	—	0	0	0	0	0.0	.000
1937			0	0	—	27.00	2	0	0	1.1	4	1	1	0	0	0	0	0	0	0	—	0	0	0	0	0.0	.000
1942	**STL**	**N**	0	0	—	0.00	2	0	0	0.2	1	0	0	0	0	0	0	0	0	0	—	0	1	0	0	0.5	1.000
3 yrs.			0	0		27.00	6	0	0	4	12	5	3	0	0	0	0	0	0	0		0	1	0	0	0.2	1.000

Dave Gumpert

GUMPERT, DAVID LAWRENCE BR TR 6′ 1″ 190 lbs.
B. May 5, 1958, South Haven, Mich.

Year	Team	Lg	W	L	PCT	ERA	G	GS	CG	IP	H	BB	SO	ShO	Relief Pitching W	Relief Pitching L	Relief Pitching SV	Batting AB	Batting H	Batting HR	BA	PO	A	E	DP	TC/G	FA
1982	**DET**	**A**	0	0	—	27.00	5	1	0	2	7	2	0	0	0	0	1	0	0	0	—	0	0	0	0	0.0	.000
1983			0	2	.000	2.64	26	0	0	44.1	43	7	14	0	0	2	2	0	0	0	—	2	3	0	0	0.2	1.000
1985	**CHI**	**N**	1	0	1.000	3.48	9	0	0	10.1	12	7	4	0	1	0	0	1	0	0	.000	0	0	0	0	0.0	.000
1986			2	0	1.000	4.37	38	0	0	59.2	60	28	45	0	2	0	2	5	0	0	.000	3	4	0	0	0.2	1.000
1987	**KC**	**A**	0	0	—	6.05	8	0	0	19.1	27	6	13	0	0	0	0	0	0	0	—	1	4	0	1	0.6	1.000
5 yrs.			3	2	.600	4.31	86	1	0	135.2	149	50	76	0	3	2	5	6	0	0	.000	6	11	0	1	0.2	1.000

Randy Gumpert

GUMPERT, RANDALL PENNINGTON BR TR 6′ 3″ 185 lbs.
B. Jan. 23, 1918, Monocacy, Pa.

Year	Team	Lg	W	L	PCT	ERA	G	GS	CG	IP	H	BB	SO	ShO	Relief Pitching W	Relief Pitching L	Relief Pitching SV	Batting AB	Batting H	Batting HR	BA	PO	A	E	DP	TC/G	FA
1936	**PHI**	**A**	1	2	.333	4.76	22	3	2	62.1	74	32	9	0	0	0	2	22	6	0	.273	0	9	0	0	0.4	1.000
1937			0	0	—	12.00	10	1	0	12	16	15	5	0	0	0	0	3	1	0	.333	1	3	0	0	0.4	1.000
1938			0	2	.000	10.95	4	2	0	12.1	24	10	1	0	0	0	0	4	1	0	.250	1	5	0	0	1.5	1.000
1946	**NY**	**A**	11	3	.786	2.31	33	12	4	132.2	113	32	63	0	3	0	1	47	6	0	.128	4	21	3	4	0.8	.893
1947			4	1	.800	5.43	24	6	2	56.1	71	28	25	0	1	0	0	14	1	0	.071	2	9	0	1	0.5	1.000
1948	**2 teams**	**NY A** (15G 1–0) **CHI A** (16G 2–6)																									
″	**total**		3	6	.333	3.60	31	11	6	122.1	130	19	43	1	1	3	0	29	4	0	.138	3	18	1	1	0.7	.955
1949	**CHI**	**A**	13	16	.448	3.81	34	32	18	234	223	83	78	3	0	0	1	84	16	0	.190	15	43	1	6	1.7	.983
1950			5	12	.294	4.75	40	17	6	155.1	165	58	48	1	2	2	0	42	3	0	.071	10	24	1	3	0.9	.971
1951			9	8	.529	4.32	33	16	7	141.2	156	34	45	1	2	3	2	45	15	0	.333	2	16	3	1	0.6	.857
1952	**2 teams**	**BOS A** (10G 1–0) **WAS A** (20G 4–9)																									
″	**total**		5	9	.357	4.22	30	13	2	123.2	127	35	35	0	2	2	1	39	7	0	.179	6	21	2	1	1.0	.931
10 yrs.			51	59	.464	4.17	261	113	47	1052.2	1099	346	352	6	11	10	7	329	60	0	.182	44	169	11	17	0.9	.951

Eric Gunderson

GUNDERSON, ERIC ANDREW — BR TL 6′ 175 lbs.
B. Mar. 29, 1966, Portland, Ore.

Year	Team	Lg	W	L	PCT	ERA	G	GS	CG	IP	H	BB	SO	ShO	Relief W	Relief L	Relief SV	Batting AB	Batting H	Batting HR	BA	PO	A	E	DP	TC/G	FA
1990	SF	N	1	2	.333	5.49	7	4	0	19.2	24	11	14	0	0	0	0	6	0	0	.000	0	4	0	0	0.6	1.000
1991			0	0	—	5.40	2	0	0	3.1	6	1	2	0	0	0	1	0	0	0	—	0	1	0	0	0.5	1.000
1992	SEA	A	2	1	.667	8.68	9	0	0	9.1	12	5	2	0	2	1	0	0	0	0	—	1	2	0	0	0.3	1.000
1994	NY	N	0	0	—	0.00	14	0	0	9	5	4	4	0	0	0	0	0	0	0	—	0	1	0	0	0.1	1.000
1995	2 teams NY N (30G 1–1) BOS A (19G 2–1)																										
″	total		3	2	.600	4.17	49	0	0	36.2	38	17	28	0	3	2	0	0	0	0	—	3	8	0	0	0.2	1.000
5 yrs.			6	5	.545	4.62	81	4	0	78	85	38	50	0	5	3	1	6	0	0	.000	4	16	0	0	0.2	1.000

Red Gunkel

GUNKEL, WOODWARD WILLIAM — BB TR 5′ 8″ 158 lbs.
B. Apr. 15, 1894, Sheffield, Ill. D. Apr. 19, 1954, Chicago, Ill.

Year	Team	Lg	W	L	PCT	ERA	G	GS	CG	IP	H	BB	SO	ShO	Relief W	Relief L	Relief SV	Batting AB	Batting H	Batting HR	BA	PO	A	E	DP	TC/G	FA
1916	CLE	A	0	0	—	0.00	1	0	0	1	0	1	1	0	0	0	0	0	0	0	—	0	0	0	0	0.0	.000

Larry Gura

GURA, LAWRENCE CYRIL — BB TL 6′ 170 lbs.
B. Nov. 26, 1947, Joliet, Ill. — BR 1970–1972

Year	Team	Lg	W	L	PCT	ERA	G	GS	CG	IP	H	BB	SO	ShO	Relief W	Relief L	Relief SV	Batting AB	Batting H	Batting HR	BA	PO	A	E	DP	TC/G	FA
1970	CHI	N	1	3	.250	3.79	20	3	1	38	35	23	21	0	0	1	1	10	0	0	.000	1	6	0	1	0.3	1.000
1971			0	0	—	6.00	6	0	0	3	6	1	2	0	0	0	1	1	0	0	.000	0	0	0	0	0.0	.000
1972			0	0	—	3.75	7	0	0	12	11	3	13	0	0	0	0	1	0	0	.000	0	3	0	0	0.4	1.000
1973			2	4	.333	4.85	21	7	0	65	79	11	43	0	0	1	0	15	3	0	.200	7	13	0	0	1.0	1.000
1974	NY	A	5	1	.833	2.41	8	8	4	56	54	12	17	0	0	0	0	0	0	0	—	4	8	0	0	1.5	1.000
1975			7	8	.467	3.51	26	20	5	151.1	173	41	65	0	0	0	0	0	0	0	—	8	21	0	2	1.1	1.000
1976	KC	A	4	0	1.000	2.29	20	2	1	63	47	20	22	1	3	0	1	0	0	0	—	4	12	0	2	0.8	1.000
1977			8	5	.615	3.14	52	6	1	106	108	28	46	1	5	3	10	0	0	0	—	6	18	2	1	0.5	.923
1978			16	4	.800	2.72	35	26	8	221.2	183	60	81	2	2	0	0	0	0	0	—	13	44	1	2	1.7	.983
1979			13	12	.520	4.46	39	33	7	234	226	73	85	1	1	0	0	0	0	0	—	15	38	2	5	1.4	.964
1980			18	10	.643	2.96	36	36	16	283	272	76	113	4	0	0	0	0	0	0	—	9	50	0	3	1.6	1.000
1981			11	8	.579	2.72	23	23	12	172	139	35	61	2	0	0	0	0	0	0	—	9	30	0	4	1.7	1.000
1982			18	12	.600	4.03	37	37	8	248	251	64	98	3	0	0	0	0	0	0	—	7	50	2	6	1.6	.966
1983			11	**18**	.379	4.90	34	31	5	200.1	220	76	57	0	1	0	0	0	0	0	—	12	42	0	5	1.5	1.000
1984			12	9	.571	5.18	31	25	3	168.2	175	67	68	0	1	0	0	0	0	0	—	6	30	0	1	1.2	1.000
1985	2 teams KC A (3G 0–0) CHI N (5G 0–3)																										
″	total		0	3	.000	9.12	8	4	0	24.2	41	10	9	0	0	0	1	6	0	0	.000	6	4	0	0	1.3	1.000
16 yrs.			126	97	.565	3.76	403	261	71	2046.2	2020	600	801	14	13	5	14	33	3	0	.091	107	369	7	32	1.2	.986
DIVISIONAL PLAYOFF SERIES																											
1981	KC	A	0	1	.000	7.36	1	1	0	3.2	7	3	3	0	0	0	0	0	0	0	—	0	0	0	0	0.0	.000
LEAGUE CHAMPIONSHIP SERIES																											
1976	KC	A	0	1	.000	4.22	2	2	0	10.2	18	1	4	0	0	0	0	0	0	0	—	0	0	0	0	0.0	.000
1977			0	1	.000	18.00	2	1	0	2	7	1	2	0	0	0	0	0	0	0	—	0	0	0	0	0.0	.000
1978			1	0	1.000	2.84	1	1	0	6.1	8	2	2	0	0	0	0	0	0	0	—	1	4	0	0	5.0	1.000
1980			1	0	1.000	2.00	1	1	1	9	10	1	4	0	0	0	0	0	0	0	—	0	1	0	0	1.0	1.000
4 yrs.			2	2	.500	4.18	6	5	1	28	43	5	12	0	0	0	0	0	0	0		1	5	0	0	1.0	1.000
WORLD SERIES																											
1980	KC	A	0	0	—	2.19	2	2	0	12.1	8	3	4	0	0	0	0	0	0	0	—	2	4	0	2	3.0	1.000

Charlie Guth

GUTH, CHARLES J.
B. 1856, Chicago, Ill. D. July 5, 1883, Cambridge, Mass.

Year	Team	Lg	W	L	PCT	ERA	G	GS	CG	IP	H	BB	SO	ShO	Relief W	Relief L	Relief SV	Batting AB	Batting H	Batting HR	BA	PO	A	E	DP	TC/G	FA
1880	CHI	N	1	0	1.000	5.00	1	1	1	9	12	1	7	0	0	0	0	4	1	0	.250	0	0	0	0	0.0	.000

Mark Guthrie

GUTHRIE, MARK ANDREW — BB TR 6′ 4″ 192 lbs.
B. Sept. 22, 1965, Buffalo, N. Y.

Year	Team	Lg	W	L	PCT	ERA	G	GS	CG	IP	H	BB	SO	ShO	Relief W	Relief L	Relief SV	Batting AB	Batting H	Batting HR	BA	PO	A	E	DP	TC/G	FA
1989	MIN	A	2	4	.333	4.55	13	8	0	57.1	66	21	38	0	0	0	0	0	0	0	—	2	8	0	0	0.8	1.000
1990			7	9	.438	3.79	24	21	3	144.2	154	39	101	1	1	0	0	0	0	0	—	5	23	1	0	1.2	.966
1991			7	5	.583	4.32	41	12	0	98	116	41	72	0	2	1	2	0	0	0	—	5	10	1	0	0.4	.938
1992			2	3	.400	2.88	54	0	0	75	59	23	76	0	2	3	5	0	0	0	—	4	6	1	0	0.2	.909
1993			2	1	.667	4.71	22	0	0	21	20	16	15	0	2	1	0	0	0	0	—	0	5	0	0	0.2	1.000
1994			4	2	.667	6.14	50	2	0	51.1	65	18	38	0	4	1	1	0	0	0	—	3	8	0	0	0.2	1.000
1995	2 teams MIN A (36G 5–3) LA N (24G 0–2)																										
″	total		5	5	.500	4.21	60	0	0	62	66	25	67	0	5	5	0	1	0	0	.000	0	5	2	0	0.1	.714
7 yrs.			29	29	.500	4.17	264	43	3	509.1	546	183	407	1	16	11	8	1	0	0	.000	19	65	5	0	0.3	.944
DIVISIONAL PLAYOFF SERIES																											
1995	LA	N	0	0	—	6.75	3	0	0	1.1	2	1	1	0	0	0	0	0	0	0	—	0	0	0	0	0.0	.000
LEAGUE CHAMPIONSHIP SERIES																											
1991	MIN	A	1	0	1.000	0.00	2	0	0	2.2	0	0	0	0	1	0	0	0	0	0	—	0	1	0	0	0.5	1.000
WORLD SERIES																											
1991	MIN	A	0	1	.000	2.25	4	0	0	4	3	4	3	0	0	1	0	0	0	0	—	0	1	0	0	0.3	1.000

Johnny Guzman

GUZMAN, DIONINI RAMON — BR TL 5′10″ 155 lbs.
Born Dionini Ramon Guzman (Estrella).
B. Jan. 21, 1971, Hatillo Palma, Dominican Republic.

Year	Team	Lg	W	L	PCT	ERA	G	GS	CG	IP	H	BB	SO	ShO	Relief W	Relief L	Relief SV	Batting AB	Batting H	Batting HR	BA	PO	A	E	DP	TC/G	FA
1991	OAK	A	1	0	1.000	9.00	5	0	0	5	11	2	3	0	1	0	0	0	0	0	—	0	1	0	1	0.2	1.000
1992			0	0	—	12.00	2	0	0	3	8	0	0	0	0	0	0	0	0	0	—	0	0	0	0	0.0	.000
2 yrs.			1	0	1.000	10.13	7	0	0	8	19	2	3	0	1	0	0	0	0	0		0	1	0	1	0.1	1.000

Jose Guzman

GUZMAN, JOSE ALBERTO — BR TR 6′ 2″ 172 lbs.
Born Jose Alberto Guzman (Mirabel).
B. Apr. 9, 1963, Santa Isabel, Puerto Rico.

Year	Team	Lg	W	L	PCT	ERA	G	GS	CG	IP	H	BB	SO	ShO	Relief W	Relief L	Relief SV	Batting AB	Batting H	Batting HR	BA	PO	A	E	DP	TC/G	FA
1985	TEX	A	3	2	.600	2.76	5	5	0	32.2	27	14	24	0	0	0	0	0	0	0	—	0	5	0	0	1.0	1.000
1986			9	15	.375	4.54	29	29	2	172.1	199	60	87	0	0	0	0	0	0	0	—	13	24	0	0	1.3	1.000
1987			14	14	.500	4.67	37	30	6	208.1	196	82	143	0	3	0	0	0	0	0	—	14	34	2	3	1.4	.960
1988			11	13	.458	3.70	30	30	6	206.2	180	82	157	2	0	0	0	0	0	0	—	15	24	3	1	1.4	.929
1991			13	7	.650	3.08	25	25	5	169.2	152	84	125	1	0	0	0	0	0	0	—	12	32	1	2	1.8	.978

Jose Guzman *continued*

Year	Team	W	L	PCT	ERA	G	GS	CG	IP	H	BB	SO	ShO	Relief Pitching W	L	SV	Batting AB	H	HR	BA	PO	A	E	DP	TC/G	FA
1992		16	11	.593	3.66	33	33	5	224	229	73	179	0	0	0	0	0	0	0	—	16	22	1	3	1.2	.974
1993	CHI N	12	10	.545	4.34	30	30	2	191	188	74	163	1	0	0	0	63	7	0	.111	12	28	5	1	1.5	.889
1994		2	2	.500	9.15	4	4	0	19.2	22	13	11	0	0	0	0	8	0	0	.000	1	1	0	0	0.5	1.000
8 yrs.		80	74	.519	4.05	193	186	26	1224.1	1193	482	889	4	3	0	0	71	7	0	.099	83	170	12	10	1.4	.955

Juan Guzman

GUZMAN, JUAN ANDRES BR TR 5′11″ 190 lbs.
Born Juan Andres Guzman (Correa).
B. Oct. 28, 1966, Santo Domingo, Dominican Republic.

Year	Team	W	L	PCT	ERA	G	GS	CG	IP	H	BB	SO	ShO	Relief Pitching W	L	SV	Batting AB	H	HR	BA	PO	A	E	DP	TC/G	FA
1991	TOR A	10	3	.769	2.99	23	23	1	138.2	98	66	123	0	0	0	0	0	0	0	—	5	9	3	1	0.7	.824
1992		16	5	.762	2.64	28	28	1	180.2	135	72	165	0	0	0	0	0	0	0	—	12	11	0	0	0.8	1.000
1993		14	3	.824	3.99	33	33	2	221	211	110	194	1	0	0	0	0	0	0	—	11	16	1	0	0.8	.964
1994		12	11	.522	5.68	25	**25**	2	147.1	165	76	124	0	0	0	0	0	0	0	—	5	12	2	1	0.8	.895
1995		4	14	.222	6.32	24	24	3	135.1	151	73	94	0	0	0	0	0	0	0	—	7	12	2	0	0.9	.905
5 yrs.		56	36	.609	4.21	133	133	9	823	760	397	700	1	0	0	0	0	0	0		40	60	8	2	0.8	.926
LEAGUE CHAMPIONSHIP SERIES																										
1991	TOR A	1	0	1.000	3.18	1	1	0	5.2	4	4	2	0	0	0	0	0	0	0	—	0	0	0	0	0.0	.000
1992		2	0	1.000	2.08	2	2	0	13	12	5	11	0	0	0	0	0	0	0	—	0	0	0	0	0.0	.000
1993		2	0	1.000	2.08	2	2	0	13	8	9	9	0	0	0	0	0	0	0	—	0	4	0	0	2.0	1.000
3 yrs.		5	0	1.000	2.27	5	5	0	31.2	24	18	22	0	0	0	0	0	0	0		0	4	0	0	0.8	1.000
		2nd		**1st**							**7th**															
WORLD SERIES																										
1992	TOR A	0	0	—	1.13	1	1	0	8	8	1	7	0	0	0	0	0	0	0	—	2	0	0	0	2.0	1.000
1993		0	1	.000	3.75	2	2	0	12	10	8	12	0	0	0	0	2	0	0	.000	0	1	0	0	0.5	1.000
2 yrs.		0	1	.000	2.70	3	3	0	20	18	9	19	0	0	0	0	2	0	0	.000	2	1	0	0	1.0	1.000

Santiago Guzman

GUZMAN, SANTIAGO BR TR 6′ 2″ 180 lbs.
Born Santiago Donovan (Guzman).
B. July 25, 1949, San Pedro de Macoris, Dominican Republic.

Year	Team	W	L	PCT	ERA	G	GS	CG	IP	H	BB	SO	ShO	Relief Pitching W	L	SV	Batting AB	H	HR	BA	PO	A	E	DP	TC/G	FA
1969	STL N	0	1	.000	5.14	1	1	0	7	9	3	7	0	0	0	0	3	1	0	.333	1	0	0	0	1.0	1.000
1970		1	1	.500	7.07	8	3	1	14	14	13	9	0	0	1	0	5	1	0	.200	0	2	0	1	0.3	1.000
1971		0	0	—	0.00	2	1	0	10	6	2	13	0	0	0	0	1	0	0	.000	0	0	0	0	0.0	.000
1972		0	0	—	9.00	1	0	0	1	1	0	0	0	0	0	0	0	0	0	—	0	0	0	0	0.0	.000
4 yrs.		1	2	.333	4.50	12	5	1	32	30	18	29	0	0	1	0	9	2	0	.222	1	2	0	1	0.3	1.000

Bruno Haas

HAAS, BRUNO PHILIP (Boon) BB TL 5′10″ 180 lbs.
B. May 5, 1891, Worcester, Mass. D. June 5, 1952, Sarasota, Fla.

Year	Team	W	L	PCT	ERA	G	GS	CG	IP	H	BB	SO	ShO	Relief Pitching W	L	SV	Batting AB	H	HR	BA	PO	A	E	DP	TC/G	FA
1915	PHI A	0	1	.000	11.93	6	2	1	14.1	23	28	7	0	0	0	0	*				9	6	1	0	1.8	.938

Dave Haas

HAAS, ROBERT DAVID BR TR 6′ 1″ 200 lbs.
B. Oct. 19, 1965, Independence, Mo.

Year	Team	W	L	PCT	ERA	G	GS	CG	IP	H	BB	SO	ShO	Relief Pitching W	L	SV	Batting AB	H	HR	BA	PO	A	E	DP	TC/G	FA
1991	DET A	1	0	1.000	6.75	11	0	0	10.2	8	12	6	0	1	0	0	0	0	0	—	0	0	0	0	0.0	.000
1992		5	3	.625	3.94	12	11	1	61.2	68	16	29	1	0	0	0	0	0	0	—	3	8	0	0	0.9	1.000
1993		1	2	.333	6.11	20	0	0	28	45	8	17	0	1	2	0	0	0	0	—	2	5	0	1	0.3	1.000
3 yrs.		7	5	.583	4.84	43	11	1	100.1	121	36	52	1	2	2	0	0	0	0		5	13	0	1	0.4	1.000

Moose Haas

HAAS, BRYAN EDMUND BR TR 6′ 180 lbs.
B. Apr. 22, 1956, Baltimore, Md.

Year	Team	W	L	PCT	ERA	G	GS	CG	IP	H	BB	SO	ShO	Relief Pitching W	L	SV	Batting AB	H	HR	BA	PO	A	E	DP	TC/G	FA
1976	MIL A	0	1	.000	3.94	5	2	0	16	12	12	9	0	0	0	0	0	0	0	—	2	5	1	1	1.6	.875
1977		10	12	.455	4.32	32	32	6	198	195	84	113	0	0	0	0	0	0	0	—	20	13	2	3	1.1	.943
1978		2	3	.400	6.16	7	6	2	30.2	33	8	32	0	0	0	1	0	0	0	—	4	2	1	0	1.0	.857
1979		11	11	.500	4.77	29	28	8	185	198	59	95	1	0	0	0	0	0	0	—	14	21	1	3	1.2	.972
1980		16	15	.516	3.11	33	33	14	252	246	56	146	3	0	0	0	0	0	0	—	19	31	3	6	1.6	.943
1981		11	7	.611	4.47	24	22	5	137	146	40	64	0	1	0	0	0	0	0	—	16	15	1	1	1.3	.969
1982		11	8	.579	4.47	32	27	3	193.1	232	39	104	0	1	0	1	0	0	0	—	14	18	0	1	1.0	1.000
1983		13	3	.813	3.27	25	25	7	179	170	42	75	3	0	0	0	0	0	0	—	12	22	0	1	1.3	1.000
1984		9	11	.450	3.99	31	30	4	189.1	205	43	84	0	0	0	0	0	0	0	—	19	36	0	2	1.8	1.000
1985		8	8	.500	3.84	27	26	6	161.2	165	25	78	1	0	0	0	0	0	0	—	17	15	4	1	1.3	.889
1986	OAK A	7	2	.778	2.74	12	12	1	72.1	58	19	40	0	0	0	0	0	0	0	—	4	8	0	2	1.0	1.000
1987		2	2	.500	5.75	9	9	0	40.2	57	9	13	0	0	0	0	0	0	0	—	2	5	0	0	0.8	1.000
12 yrs.		100	83	.546	4.01	266	252	56	1655	1717	436	853	8	2	0	2	0	0	0		143	191	13	21	1.3	.963
DIVISIONAL PLAYOFF SERIES																										
1981	MIL A	0	2	.000	9.45	2	2	0	6.2	13	1	1	0	0	0	0	0	0	0	—	0	0	0	0	0.0	.000
LEAGUE CHAMPIONSHIP SERIES																										
1982	MIL A	1	0	1.000	4.91	1	1	0	7.1	5	5	7	0	0	0	0	0	0	0	—	0	0	0	0	0.0	.000
WORLD SERIES																										
1982	MIL A	0	0	—	7.36	2	1	0	7.1	8	3	4	0	0	0	0	0	0	0	—	1	2	0	0	1.5	1.000

Bob Habenicht

HABENICHT, ROBERT JULIUS (Hobby) BR TR 6′ 2″ 185 lbs.
B. Feb. 13, 1926, St. Louis, Mo. D. Dec. 24, 1980, Richmond, Va.

Year	Team	W	L	PCT	ERA	G	GS	CG	IP	H	BB	SO	ShO	Relief Pitching W	L	SV	Batting AB	H	HR	BA	PO	A	E	DP	TC/G	FA
1951	STL N	0	0	—	7.20	3	0	0	5	5	9	1	0	0	0	0	1	0	0	.000	1	1	0	1	0.7	1.000
1953	STL A	0	0	—	5.40	1	0	0	1.2	1	1	1	0	0	0	0	0	0	0	—	0	0	0	0	0.0	.000
2 yrs.		0	0		6.75	4	0	0	6.2	6	10	2	0	0	0	0	1	0	0	.000	1	1	0	1	0.5	1.000

John Habyan

HABYAN, JOHN GABRIEL BR TR 6′ 1″ 195 lbs.
B. Jan. 29, 1964, Bay Shore, N. Y.

Year	Team	W	L	PCT	ERA	G	GS	CG	IP	H	BB	SO	ShO	Relief Pitching W	L	SV	Batting AB	H	HR	BA	PO	A	E	DP	TC/G	FA
1985	BAL A	1	0	1.000	0.00	2	0	0	2.2	3	0	2	0	1	0	0	0	0	0	—	1	0	0	0	0.5	1.000
1986		1	3	.250	4.44	6	5	0	26.1	24	18	14	0	0	0	0	0	0	0	—	1	3	0	0	0.7	1.000
1987		6	7	.462	4.80	27	13	0	116.1	110	40	64	0	4	0	1	0	0	0	—	15	17	0	2	1.2	1.000
1988		1	0	1.000	4.30	7	0	0	14.2	22	4	4	0	1	0	0	0	0	0	—	5	1	0	0	0.9	1.000
1990	NY A	0	0	—	2.08	6	0	0	8.2	10	2	4	0	0	0	0	0	0	0	—	2	0	0	0	0.3	1.000
1991		4	2	.667	2.30	66	0	0	90	73	20	70	0	4	2	2	0	0	0	—	6	12	0	0	0.3	1.000
1992		5	6	.455	3.84	56	0	0	72.2	84	21	44	0	5	6	7	0	0	0	—	3	15	0	1	0.3	1.000

John Habyan *continued*

Year	Team	Lg	W	L	PCT	ERA	G	GS	CG	IP	H	BB	SO	ShO	Relief Pitching W	Relief Pitching L	Relief Pitching SV	Batting AB	Batting H	Batting HR	BA	PO	A	E	DP	TC/G	FA
1993	**2 teams**	**NY A** (36G 2–1) **KC A** (12G 0–0)																									
″	**total**		2	1	.667	4.15	48	0	0	56.1	59	20	39	0	2	1	1	0	0	0		5	7	0	0	0.3	1.000
1994	**STL**	**N**	1	0	1.000	3.23	52	0	0	47.1	50	20	46	0	1	0	1	0	0	0	—	4	8	1	0	0.3	.923
1995	**2 teams**	**STL N** (31G 3–2) **CAL A** (28G 1–2)																									
″	**total**		4	4	.500	3.44	59	0	0	73.1	68	27	60	0	4	4	0	2	0	0	.000	4	8	0	0	0.2	1.000
10 yrs.			25	23	.521	3.70	329	18	0	508.1	503	172	347	0	22	13	12	2	0	0	.000	46	71	1	3	0.4	.992

Warren Hacker

HACKER, WARREN LOUIS BR TR 6′ 1″ 185 lbs.
B. Nov. 21, 1924, Marissa, Ill.

Year	Team	Lg	W	L	PCT	ERA	G	GS	CG	IP	H	BB	SO	ShO	Relief Pitching W	Relief Pitching L	Relief Pitching SV	Batting AB	Batting H	Batting HR	BA	PO	A	E	DP	TC/G	FA
1948	**CHI**	**N**	0	1	.000	21.00	3	1	0	3	7	3	0	0	0	0	0	0	0	0	—	0	1	0	0	0.3	1.000
1949			5	8	.385	4.23	30	12	3	125.2	141	53	40	0	3	1	0	38	7	0	.184	10	25	3	0	1.3	.921
1950			0	1	.000	5.28	5	3	1	15.1	20	8	5	0	0	0	1	5	0	0	.000	0	7	0	0	1.4	1.000
1951			0	0	—	13.50	2	0	0	1.1	3	0	2	0	0	0	0	0	0	0	—	0	0	0	0	0.0	.000
1952			15	9	.625	2.58	33	20	12	185	144	31	84	5	2	2	1	58	7	0	.121	7	19	0	0	0.8	1.000
1953			12	**19**	.387	4.38	39	32	9	221.2	225	54	106	0	1	2	2	78	17	0	.218	10	27	2	0	1.0	.949
1954			6	13	.316	4.25	39	18	4	158.2	157	37	80	1	1	6	2	55	13	0	.236	10	20	0	2	0.8	1.000
1955			11	15	.423	4.27	35	30	13	213	202	43	80	0	1	0	3	72	18	0	.250	14	20	3	0	1.1	.919
1956			3	13	.188	4.66	34	24	4	168	190	44	65	0	0	0	0	54	8	0	.148	5	18	0	2	0.7	1.000
1957	**2 teams**	**CIN N** (15G 3–2) **PHI N** (20G 4–4)																									
″	**total**		7	6	.538	4.76	35	16	1	117.1	122	31	51	0	1	0	0	31	7	0	.226	7	13	0	1	0.6	1.000
1958	**PHI**	**N**	0	1	.000	7.41	9	1	0	17	24	8	4	0	0	0	0	1	0	0	.000	0	2	0	0	0.2	1.000
1961	**CHI**	**A**	3	3	.500	3.77	42	0	0	57.1	62	8	40	0	3	3	8	9	1	0	.111	1	4	0	0	0.1	1.000
12 yrs.			62	89	.411	4.21	306	157	47	1283.1	1297	320	557	6	12	14	17	401	78	0	.195	64	156	8	5	0.7	.965

Jim Hackett

HACKETT, JAMES JOSEPH (Sunny Jim) BR TR 6′ 2″ 185 lbs.
B. Oct. 1, 1877, Jacksonville, Ill. D. Mar. 28, 1961, Douglas, Mich.

Year	Team	Lg	W	L	PCT	ERA	G	GS	CG	IP	H	BB	SO	ShO	Relief Pitching W	Relief Pitching L	Relief Pitching SV	Batting AB	Batting H	Batting HR	BA	PO	A	E	DP	TC/G	FA
1902	**STL**	**N**	0	3	.000	6.23	4	3	3	30.1	46	16	7	0	0	0	0	21	6	0	.286	6	7	3	0	2.7	.813
1903			1	4	.200	3.72	7	6	5	48.1	47	18	21	0	0	0	1	351	80	0	.228	949	53	29	63	10.7	.972
2 yrs.			1	7	.125	4.69	11	9	8	78.2	93	34	28	0	0	0	1	*				955	60	32	63	10.3	.969

Harvey Haddix

HADDIX, HARVEY (The Kitten) BL TL 5′ 9½″ 170 lbs.
B. Sept. 18, 1925, Medway, Ohio D. Jan. 8, 1994, Springfield, Ohio.

Year	Team	Lg	W	L	PCT	ERA	G	GS	CG	IP	H	BB	SO	ShO	Relief Pitching W	Relief Pitching L	Relief Pitching SV	Batting AB	Batting H	Batting HR	BA	PO	A	E	DP	TC/G	FA
1952	**STL**	**N**	2	2	.500	2.79	7	6	3	42	31	10	31	0	0	0	0	14	3	0	.214	0	5	1	0	0.8	.833
1953			20	9	.690	3.06	36	33	19	253	220	69	163	**6**	0	0	1	97	28	1	.289	15	43	2	5	1.7	.967
1954			18	13	.581	3.57	43	35	13	259.2	247	77	184	3	1	1	4	93	18	0	.194	14	39	3	3	1.3	.946
1955			12	16	.429	4.46	37	30	9	208	216	62	150	2	1	1	1	73	12	1	.164	14	38	4	2	1.5	.929
1956	**2 teams**	**STL N** (4G 1–0) **PHI N** (31G 12–8)																									
″	**total**		13	8	.619	3.67	35	30	12	230.1	224	65	170	3	0	0	2	102	24	0	.235	10	31	1	1	1.2	.976
1957	**PHI**	**N**	10	13	.435	4.06	27	25	8	170.2	176	39	136	1	1	0	0	68	21	0	.309	10	15	2	0	1.0	.926
1958	**CIN**	**N**	8	7	.533	3.52	29	26	8	184	191	43	110	1	0	0	0	61	11	1	.180	10	26	1	1	1.3	.973
1959	**PIT**	**N**	12	12	.500	3.13	31	29	14	224.1	189	49	149	2	0	0	0	83	12	0	.145	8	35	0	3	1.4	1.000
1960			11	10	.524	3.97	29	28	4	172.1	189	38	101	0	0	0	1	67	17	0	.254	9	46	1	2	1.9	.982
1961			10	6	.625	4.10	29	22	5	156	159	41	99	2	3	0	0	56	8	0	.143	5	29	2	4	1.2	.944
1962			9	6	.600	4.20	28	20	4	141.1	146	42	101	0	2	1	0	52	13	1	.250	10	19	2	2	1.1	.935
1963			3	4	.429	3.34	49	1	0	70	67	20	70	0	3	4	1	11	2	0	.182	5	10	1	0	0.3	.938
1964	**BAL**	**A**	5	5	.500	2.31	49	0	0	89.2	68	23	90	0	5	5	10	19	0	0	.000	4	16	0	1	0.4	1.000
1965			3	2	.600	3.48	24	0	0	33.2	31	23	21	0	3	2	1	2	0	0	.000	1	6	1	0	0.3	.875
14 yrs.			136	113	.546	3.63	453	285	99	2235	2154	601	1575	20	19	14	21	*				115	358	21	24	1.1	.957
WORLD SERIES																											
1960	**PIT**	**N**	2	0	1.000	2.45	2	1	0	7.1	6	2	6	0	1	0	0	*				1	1	0	0	1.0	1.000

George Haddock

HADDOCK, GEORGE SILAS (Gentleman George) BR TR 5′11″ 155 lbs.
B. Dec. 25, 1866, Portsmouth, N. H. D. Apr. 18, 1926, Boston, Mass.

Year	Team	Lg	W	L	PCT	ERA	G	GS	CG	IP	H	BB	SO	ShO	Relief Pitching W	Relief Pitching L	Relief Pitching SV	Batting AB	Batting H	Batting HR	BA	PO	A	E	DP	TC/G	FA
1888	**WAS**	**N**	0	2	.000	2.25	2	2	2	16	9	2	3	0	0	0	0	5	1	0	.200	2	8	1	0	5.5	.909
1889			11	19	.367	4.20	33	31	30	276.1	299	123	106	0	0	0	0	112	25	2	.223	14	55	9	3	2.2	.885
1890	**BUF**	**P**	9	**26**	.257	5.76	35	34	31	290.2	366	149	123	0	1	0	0	146	36	0	.247	26	88	9	2	2.9	.927
1891	**BOS**	**AA**	34	11	.756	2.49	51	47	37	379.2	330	137	169	**5**	2	0	1	185	45	3	.243	27	116	14	2	2.7	.911
1892	**BKN**	**N**	29	13	.690	3.14	46	44	39	381.1	340	163	153	3	0	0	1	158	28	0	.177	23	81	12	5	2.5	.897
1893			8	9	.471	5.60	23	20	12	151	193	89	37	0	1	0	0	85	24	1	.282	13	19	10	0	1.4	.762
1894	**2 teams**	**PHI N** (10G 4–3) **WAS N** (4G 0–4)																									
″	**total**		4	7	.364	6.78	14	11	9	85	113	51	8	0	0	0	0	45	8	0	.178	6	20	1	0	1.8	.963
7 yrs.			95	87	.522	4.07	204	189	160	1580	1650	714	599	8	4	0	2	*				111	387	56	12	2.4	.899

Bump Hadley

HADLEY, IRVING DARIUS BR TR 5′11″ 190 lbs.
B. July 5, 1904, Lynn, Mass. D. Feb. 15, 1963, Lynn, Mass.

Year	Team	Lg	W	L	PCT	ERA	G	GS	CG	IP	H	BB	SO	ShO	Relief Pitching W	Relief Pitching L	Relief Pitching SV	Batting AB	Batting H	Batting HR	BA	PO	A	E	DP	TC/G	FA
1926	**WAS**	**A**	0	0	—	12.00	1	0	0	3	6	2	0	0	0	0	0	0	0	0	—	0	0	0	0	0.0	.000
1927			14	6	.700	2.85	30	27	13	198.2	177	86	60	0	0	0	0	70	19	0	.271	9	50	2	0	2.0	.967
1928			12	13	.480	3.54	33	31	16	231.2	236	100	80	3	0	0	0	81	17	0	.210	8	52	2	2	1.9	.968
1929			6	16	.273	5.65	37	27	6	194.1	196	85	98	1	0	4	0	62	6	0	.097	9	41	2	3	1.4	.962
1930			15	11	.577	3.73	42	34	15	260.1	242	105	162	1	1	1	2	93	21	0	.226	9	43	2	2	1.3	.963
1931			11	10	.524	3.06	**55**	11	2	179.2	145	92	124	1	**8**	**5**	8	54	9	0	.167	6	39	1	5	0.8	.978
1932	**2 teams**	**CHI A** (3G 1–1) **STL A** (40G 13–20)																									
″	**total**		14	**21**	.400	5.40	43	35	13	248.1	261	**171**	145	1	0	3	2	84	23	0	.274	15	29	2	0	1.1	.957
1933	**STL**	**A**	15	20	.429	3.92	45	36	19	**316.2**	309	**141**	149	2	2	1	3	109	17	0	.156	12	51	2	0	1.4	.969
1934			10	16	.385	4.35	39	32	7	213	212	127	79	2	0	2	1	64	13	0	.203	9	40	2	1	1.3	.961
1935	**WAS**	**A**	10	15	.400	4.92	35	32	13	230.1	268	102	77	0	0	0	0	77	15	0	.195	13	47	3	3	1.8	.952
1936	**NY**	**A**	14	4	.778	4.35	31	17	8	173.2	194	89	74	1	3	1	1	68	16	0	.235	13	32	0	4	1.5	1.000
1937			11	8	.579	5.30	29	25	6	178.1	199	83	70	0	0	1	0	65	11	0	.169	7	37	4	3	1.7	.917
1938			9	8	.529	3.60	29	17	8	167.1	165	66	61	1	1	1	1	54	5	0	.093	17	40	0	3	2.0	1.000

Bump Hadley *continued*

Year	Team	W	L	PCT	ERA	G	GS	CG	IP	H	BB	SO	ShO	Relief Pitching W	Relief Pitching L	Relief Pitching SV	Batting AB	Batting H	HR	BA	PO	A	E	DP	TC/G	FA
1939		12	6	.667	2.98	26	18	7	154	132	85	65	1	2	0	2	62	11	0	.177	8	35	4	4	1.8	.915
1940		3	5	.375	5.74	25	2	0	80	88	52	39	0	3	3	2	27	3	0	.111	2	16	0	0	0.7	1.000
1941	**2 teams** **NY N** (3G 1–0) **PHI A** (25G 4–6)																									
″	**total**	5	6	.455	5.15	28	11	1	115.1	150	56	35	0	1	1	3	34	4	0	.118	3	21	2	0	0.9	.923
16 yrs.		161	165	.494	4.25	528	355	134	2944.2	2980	1442	1318	14	21	23	25	1004	190	0	.189	140	573	28	30	1.4	.962
WORLD SERIES																										
1936	**NY A**	1	0	1.000	1.13	1	1	0	8	10	1	2	0	0	0	0	2	0	0	.000	0	3	0	0	3.0	1.000
1937		0	1	.000	33.75	1	1	0	1.1	6	0	0	0	0	0	0	0	0	0	—	0	0	0	0	0.0	.000
1939		1	0	1.000	2.25	1	0	0	8	7	3	2	0	1	0	0	3	0	0	.000	1	1	1	0	3.0	.667
3 yrs.		2	1	.667	4.15	3	2	0	17.1	23	4	4	0	1	0	0	5	0	0	.000	1	4	1	0	2.0	.833

Mickey Haefner

HAEFNER, MILTON ARNOLD BL TL 5′ 8″ 160 lbs.
B. Oct. 9, 1912, Lenzburg, Ill. D. Jan. 3, 1995, New Athens, Ill.

Year	Team	W	L	PCT	ERA	G	GS	CG	IP	H	BB	SO	ShO	Relief Pitching W	Relief Pitching L	Relief Pitching SV	Batting AB	Batting H	HR	BA	PO	A	E	DP	TC/G	FA
1943	**WAS A**	11	5	.688	2.29	36	13	8	165.1	126	60	65	1	3	1	6	45	6	0	.133	7	31	0	3	1.1	1.000
1944		12	15	.444	3.04	31	28	18	228	221	71	86	3	0	1	1	70	11	0	.157	8	45	1	5	1.7	.981
1945		16	14	.533	3.47	37	28	19	238.1	226	69	83	1	2	0	3	82	20	0	.244	10	53	3	1	1.8	.955
1946		14	11	.560	2.85	33	27	17	227.2	220	80	85	2	0	1	1	74	15	0	.203	13	36	3	2	1.6	.942
1947		10	14	.417	3.64	31	28	14	193	195	85	77	4	0	0	1	59	8	0	.136	7	27	0	3	1.1	1.000
1948		5	13	.278	4.02	28	20	4	147.2	151	61	45	0	1	1	0	43	7	0	.163	4	38	1	2	1.5	.977
1949	**2 teams** **WAS A** (19G 5–5) **CHI A** (14G 4–6)																									
″	**total**	9	11	.450	4.40	33	24	8	172	169	94	40	2	0	1	1	48	11	0	.229	2	43	3	3	1.5	.938
1950	**2 teams** **CHI A** (24G 1–6) **BOS N** (8G 0–2)																									
″	**total**	1	8	.111	5.70	32	11	3	94.2	106	57	27	0	0	0	0	27	6	0	.222	2	14	0	3	0.5	1.000
8 yrs.		78	91	.462	3.50	261	179	91	1466.2	1414	577	508	13	6	5	13	448	84	0	.188	53	287	11	22	1.3	.969

Bud Hafey

HAFEY, DANIEL ALBERT BR TR 6′ 185 lbs.
Brother of Tom Hafey.
B. Aug. 6, 1912, Berkeley, Calif. D. July 27, 1986, Sacramento, Calif.

Year	Team	W	L	PCT	ERA	G	GS	CG	IP	H	BB	SO	ShO	Relief Pitching W	Relief Pitching L	Relief Pitching SV	Batting AB	Batting H	HR	BA	PO	A	E	DP	TC/G	FA
1939	**PHI N**	0	0	—	33.75	2	0	0	1.1	7	1	1	0	0	0	0	*				125	5	4	3	2.9	.970

Leo Hafford

HAFFORD, LEO EDGAR TR 6′ 170 lbs.
B. Sept. 17, 1883, Somerville, Mass. D. Oct. 2, 1911, Willimantic, Conn.

Year	Team	W	L	PCT	ERA	G	GS	CG	IP	H	BB	SO	ShO	Relief Pitching W	Relief Pitching L	Relief Pitching SV	Batting AB	Batting H	HR	BA	PO	A	E	DP	TC/G	FA
1906	**CIN N**	1	1	.500	0.95	3	1	1	19	13	11	5	0	0	1	0	9	2	0	.222	1	2	0	0	1.0	1.000

Frank Hafner

HAFNER, FRANCIS R. TR
B. Aug. 14, 1867, Hannibal, Mo. D. Mar. 2, 1957, Hannibal, Mo.

Year	Team	W	L	PCT	ERA	G	GS	CG	IP	H	BB	SO	ShO	Relief Pitching W	Relief Pitching L	Relief Pitching SV	Batting AB	Batting H	HR	BA	PO	A	E	DP	TC/G	FA
1888	**KC AA**	0	2	.000	7.00	2	2	2	18	24	16	5	0	0	0	0	6	0	0	.000	2	2	0	0	2.0	1.000

Art Hagan

HAGAN, ARTHUR CHARLES TR
B. Mar. 17, 1863, Providence, R. I. D. Mar. 25, 1936, Providence, R. I.

Year	Team	W	L	PCT	ERA	G	GS	CG	IP	H	BB	SO	ShO	Relief Pitching W	Relief Pitching L	Relief Pitching SV	Batting AB	Batting H	HR	BA	PO	A	E	DP	TC/G	FA
1883	**2 teams** **PHI N** (17G 1–14) **BUF N** (2G 0–2)																									
″	**total**	1	16	.059	5.27	19	18	16	152	224	39	46	0	0	0	0	66	6	0	.091	12	25	9	2	2.3	.804
1884	**BUF N**	1	2	.333	*5.88*	3	3	3	26	53	4	4	0	0	0	0	13	4	0	.308	0	3	2	0	1.7	.600
2 yrs.		2	18	.100	5.36	22	21	19	178	277	43	50	0	0	0	0	79	10	0	.127	12	28	11	2	2.2	.784

Casey Hageman

HAGEMAN, KURT MORITZ BR TR 5′10½″ 186 lbs.
B. May 12, 1887, Mt. Oliver, Pa. D. Apr. 1, 1964, New Bedford, Pa.

Year	Team	W	L	PCT	ERA	G	GS	CG	IP	H	BB	SO	ShO	Relief Pitching W	Relief Pitching L	Relief Pitching SV	Batting AB	Batting H	HR	BA	PO	A	E	DP	TC/G	FA
1911	**BOS A**	0	2	.000	2.12	2	2	2	17	16	5	8	0	0	0	0	4	0	0	.000	0	0	1	0	0.5	.000
1912		0	0	—	27.00	2	1	0	1.1	5	3	1	0	0	0	0	0	0	0	—	0	0	0	0	0.0	.000
1914	**2 teams** **STL N** (12G 1–4) **CHI N** (16G 2–1)																									
″	**total**	3	5	.375	2.91	28	8	1	102	87	32	38	0	2	1	1	31	9	0	.290	2	27	2	1	1.1	.935
3 yrs.		3	7	.300	3.07	32	11	3	120.1	108	40	47	0	2	1	1	35	9	0	.257	2	27	3	1	1.0	.906

Kevin Hagen

HAGEN, KEVIN EUGENE BR TR 6′ 2″ 180 lbs.
B. Mar. 8, 1960, Renton, Wash.

Year	Team	W	L	PCT	ERA	G	GS	CG	IP	H	BB	SO	ShO	Relief Pitching W	Relief Pitching L	Relief Pitching SV	Batting AB	Batting H	HR	BA	PO	A	E	DP	TC/G	FA
1983	**STL N**	2	2	.500	4.84	9	4	0	22.1	34	7	7	0	0	1	0	5	0	0	.000	2	4	0	0	0.7	1.000
1984		1	0	1.000	2.45	4	0	0	7.1	9	1	2	0	1	0	0	0	0	0	—	0	1	1	0	0.5	.500
2 yrs.		3	2	.600	4.25	13	4	0	29.2	43	8	9	0	1	1	0	5	0	0	.000	2	5	1	0	0.6	.875

Rip Hagerman

HAGERMAN, ZERIAH ZEQUIEL BR TR 6′ 2″ 200 lbs.
B. June 20, 1888, Lyndon, Kans. D. Jan. 30, 1930, Albuquerque, N. M.

Year	Team	W	L	PCT	ERA	G	GS	CG	IP	H	BB	SO	ShO	Relief Pitching W	Relief Pitching L	Relief Pitching SV	Batting AB	Batting H	HR	BA	PO	A	E	DP	TC/G	FA
1909	**CHI N**	4	4	.500	1.82	13	7	4	79	64	28	32	1	1	0	0	23	3	0	.130	4	19	0	1	1.8	1.000
1914	**CLE A**	9	15	.375	3.09	37	26	12	198	189	118	112	3	1	2	0	61	1	0	.016	3	42	6	3	1.4	.882
1915		6	14	.300	3.52	29	22	7	151	156	77	69	0	1	1	0	38	4	0	.105	3	31	3	0	1.3	.919
1916		0	0	—	12.27	2	0	0	3.2	5	2	1	0	0	0	0	1	0	0	.000	0	1	0	0	0.5	1.000
4 yrs.		19	33	.365	3.09	81	55	23	431.2	414	225	214	4	3	3	0	123	8	0	.065	10	93	9	4	1.4	.920

Fred Hahn

HAHN, FREDERICK ALOYS BR TL 6′ 3″ 174 lbs.
B. Feb. 16, 1929, Nyack, N. Y. D. Aug. 16, 1984, Valhalla, N. Y.

Year	Team	W	L	PCT	ERA	G	GS	CG	IP	H	BB	SO	ShO	Relief Pitching W	Relief Pitching L	Relief Pitching SV	Batting AB	Batting H	HR	BA	PO	A	E	DP	TC/G	FA
1952	**STL N**	0	0	—	0.00	1	0	0	2	2	1	0	0	0	0	0	0	0	0	—	0	1	0	0	1.0	1.000

Noodles Hahn

HAHN, FRANK GEORGE BL TL 5′ 9″ 160 lbs.
B. Apr. 29, 1879, Nashville, Tenn. D. Feb. 6, 1960, Candler, N. C.

Year	Team	W	L	PCT	ERA	G	GS	CG	IP	H	BB	SO	ShO	Relief Pitching W	Relief Pitching L	Relief Pitching SV	Batting AB	Batting H	HR	BA	PO	A	E	DP	TC/G	FA
1899	**CIN N**	23	8	.742	2.68	38	34	32	309	280	68	**145**	4	1	0	0	109	16	0	.147	12	51	13	3	2.0	.829
1900		16	19	.457	3.29	38	36	28	303.1	296	88	127	**4**	0	1	0	111	23	2	.207	9	74	6	1	2.3	.933
1901		22	19	.537	2.71	42	42	**41**	**375.1**	370	69	**239**	2	0	0	0	141	24	0	.170	14	85	6	4	2.5	.943
1902		23	12	.657	1.77	37	36	35	321	282	58	142	6	0	0	0	119	22	0	.185	22	69	10	1	2.6	.901
1903		22	12	.647	2.52	34	34	34	296	297	47	127	5	0	0	0	112	18	0	.161	26	67	7	3	2.9	.930
1904		16	18	.471	2.06	35	34	33	297.2	258	35	98	2	1	0	0	99	17	0	.172	21	80	9	4	3.1	.918
1905		5	3	.625	2.81	13	8	5	77	85	9	17	1	1	0	0	24	4	0	.167	2	12	2	0	1.2	.875
1906	**NY A**	3	2	.600	3.86	6	6	3	42	38	6	17	1	0	0	0	12	4	0	.333	3	9	1	0	2.2	.923
8 yrs.		130	93	.583	2.55	243	230	211	2021.1	1906	380	912	25	3	1	0	727	128	2	.176	109	447	54	16	2.5	.911

Hal Haid

HAID, HAROLD AUGUSTINE BR TR 5′10½″ 150 lbs.
B. Dec. 21, 1897, Barberton, Ohio D. Aug. 13, 1952, Los Angeles, Calif.

Year	Team	W	L	PCT	ERA	G	GS	CG	IP	H	BB	SO	ShO	Relief Pitching W	Relief Pitching L	Relief Pitching SV	Batting AB	Batting H	Batting HR	BA	PO	A	E	DP	TC/G	FA
1919	STL A	0	0	—	18.00	1	0	0	2	5	3	1	0	0	0	0	0	0	0	—	0	1	1	0	2.0	.500
1928	STL N	2	2	.500	2.30	27	0	0	47	39	11	21	0	2	2	**5**	8	3	0	.375	2	11	0	0	0.5	1.000
1929		9	9	.500	4.07	38	12	8	154.2	171	66	41	0	4	3	4	49	4	0	.082	3	32	4	5	1.0	.897
1930		3	2	.600	4.09	20	0	0	33	38	14	13	0	3	2	2	3	0	0	.000	3	9	1	2	0.6	.923
1931	BOS N	0	2	.000	4.50	27	0	0	56	59	16	20	0	0	2	1	8	1	0	.125	5	21	1	0	1.0	.963
1933	CHI A	0	0	—	7.98	6	0	0	14.2	18	13	7	0	0	0	0	4	1	0	.250	1	4	0	0	0.8	1.000
6 yrs.		14	15	.483	4.16	119	12	8	307.1	330	123	103	0	9	9	12	72	9	0	.125	14	78	7	7	0.8	.929

Jesse Haines

HAINES, JESSE JOSEPH (Pop) BR TR 6′ 190 lbs.
B. July 22, 1893, Clayton, Ohio D. Aug. 5, 1978, Dayton, Ohio.
Hall of Fame 1970.

Year	Team	W	L	PCT	ERA	G	GS	CG	IP	H	BB	SO	ShO	Relief Pitching W	Relief Pitching L	Relief Pitching SV	Batting AB	Batting H	Batting HR	BA	PO	A	E	DP	TC/G	FA
1918	CIN N	0	0	—	1.80	1	0	0	5	5	1	2	0	0	0	0	1	1	0	1.000	1	1	0	0	2.0	1.000
1920	STL N	13	20	.394	2.98	**47**	37	19	301.2	303	80	120	4	2	2	2	108	19	1	.176	13	57	4	1	1.6	.946
1921		18	12	.600	3.50	37	29	14	244.1	261	56	84	**3**	3	0	0	94	17	0	.181	7	72	4	5	2.2	.952
1922		11	9	.550	3.84	29	26	11	183	207	45	62	2	0	1	0	72	12	0	.167	12	42	2	2	1.9	.964
1923		20	13	.606	3.11	37	36	23	266	283	75	73	1	1	0	0	99	20	0	.202	13	64	3	1	2.2	.963
1924		8	19	.296	4.41	35	31	16	222.2	275	66	69	1	0	1	0	74	14	0	.189	3	52	3	3	1.7	.948
1925		13	14	.481	4.57	29	25	15	207	234	52	63	0	1	1	0	74	13	0	.176	9	43	2	1	1.9	.963
1926		13	4	.765	3.25	33	21	14	183	186	48	46	3	0	0	1	61	13	0	.213	4	32	2	1	1.2	.947
1927		24	10	.706	2.72	38	36	**25**	300.2	273	77	89	**6**	1	0	1	114	23	0	.202	5	72	1	3	2.1	.987
1928		20	8	.714	3.18	33	28	20	240.1	238	72	77	1	1	1	0	87	16	0	.184	3	43	0	2	1.4	1.000
1929		13	10	.565	5.71	28	25	12	179.2	230	73	59	0	0	0	0	69	11	1	.159	4	20	0	3	0.9	1.000
1930		13	8	.619	4.30	29	24	14	182	215	54	68	0	0	0	1	65	16	0	.246	6	22	1	3	1.0	.966
1931		12	3	.800	3.02	19	17	8	122.1	134	28	27	2	1	0	0	45	6	0	.133	5	21	1	0	1.4	.963
1932		3	5	.375	4.75	20	10	4	85.1	116	16	27	1	0	1	0	27	5	1	.185	2	14	0	2	0.8	1.000
1933		9	6	.600	2.50	32	10	5	115.1	113	37	37	0	5	2	1	30	2	0	.067	3	19	1	0	0.7	.957
1934		4	4	.500	3.50	37	6	0	90	86	19	17	0	4	2	1	19	3	0	.158	7	27	0	3	0.9	1.000
1935		6	5	.545	3.59	30	12	3	115.1	110	28	24	0	1	2	2	33	9	0	.273	6	16	1	2	0.8	.957
1936		7	5	.583	3.90	25	9	4	99.1	110	21	19	0	4	1	1	30	5	0	.167	3	24	2	0	1.2	.931
1937		3	3	.500	4.52	16	6	2	65.2	81	23	18	0	1	0	0	22	4	0	.182	2	10	0	0	0.8	1.000
19 yrs.		210	158	.571	3.64	555	388	209	3208.2	3460	871	981	24	25	14	10	1124	209	3	.186	108	651	27	32	1.4	.966
WORLD SERIES																										
1926	STL N	2	0	1.000	1.08	3	2	1	16.2	13	9	5	1	0	0	0	5	3	1	.600	0	6	0	0	2.0	1.000
1928		0	1	.000	4.50	1	1	0	6	6	3	3	0	0	0	0	2	0	0	.000	0	1	0	0	1.0	1.000
1930		1	0	1.000	1.00	1	1	1	9	4	4	2	0	0	0	0	2	1	0	.500	0	1	0	0	1.0	1.000
1934		0	0	—	0.00	1	0	0	0.2	1	0	2	0	0	0	0	0	0	0	—	0	0	0	0	0.0	.000
4 yrs.		3	1	.750	1.67	6	4	2	32.1	24	16	12	1	0	0	0	9	4	1	.444	0	8	0	0	1.3	1.000

Jim Haislip

HAISLIP, JAMES CLIFTON BR TR 6′3″ 186 lbs.
B. Aug. 4, 1891, Farmersville, Tex. D. Jan. 22, 1970, Dallas, Tex.

Year	Team	W	L	PCT	ERA	G	GS	CG	IP	H	BB	SO	ShO	Relief Pitching W	Relief Pitching L	Relief Pitching SV	Batting AB	Batting H	Batting HR	BA	PO	A	E	DP	TC/G	FA
1913	PHI N	0	0	—	6.00	1	0	0	3	4	3	0	0	0	0	0	1	0	0	.000	0	0	0	0	0.0	.000

Ed Halbriter

HALBRITER, EDWARD L.
B. Feb. 2, 1860, Auburn, N. Y. D. Aug. 9, 1936, Los Angeles, Calif.

Year	Team	W	L	PCT	ERA	G	GS	CG	IP	H	BB	SO	ShO	Relief Pitching W	Relief Pitching L	Relief Pitching SV	Batting AB	Batting H	Batting HR	BA	PO	A	E	DP	TC/G	FA
1882	PHI AA	0	1	.000	*7.88*	1	1	1	8	17	4	4	0	0	0	0	4	0	0	.000	1	1	2	0	4.0	.500

Dad Hale

HALE, RAY LUTHER BR TR 5′10″ 180 lbs.
B. Feb. 18, 1880, Allegan, Mich. D. Feb. 1, 1946, Allegan, Mich.

Year	Team	W	L	PCT	ERA	G	GS	CG	IP	H	BB	SO	ShO	Relief Pitching W	Relief Pitching L	Relief Pitching SV	Batting AB	Batting H	Batting HR	BA	PO	A	E	DP	TC/G	FA
1902	**2 teams** **BOS N** (8G 1–4) **BAL A** (3G 0–1)																									
″	**total**	1	5	.167	5.90	11	8	4	61	90	24	18	0	0	0	0	20	0	0	.000	1	15	5	0	1.9	.762

Ed Halicki

HALICKI, EDWARD LOUIS BR TR 6′7″ 220 lbs.
B. Oct. 4, 1950, Kearny, N. J.

Year	Team	W	L	PCT	ERA	G	GS	CG	IP	H	BB	SO	ShO	Relief Pitching W	Relief Pitching L	Relief Pitching SV	Batting AB	Batting H	Batting HR	BA	PO	A	E	DP	TC/G	FA
1974	SF N	1	8	.111	4.26	16	11	2	74	84	31	40	0	0	0	0	25	6	1	.240	7	8	4	0	1.2	.789
1975		9	13	.409	3.49	24	23	7	160	143	59	153	2	0	1	0	53	6	0	.113	7	20	5	0	1.3	.844
1976		12	14	.462	3.62	32	31	8	186.1	171	61	130	4	1	0	0	53	9	0	.170	16	22	5	3	1.3	.884
1977		16	12	.571	3.31	37	37	7	258	241	70	168	2	0	0	0	85	15	2	.176	15	24	3	1	1.1	.929
1978		9	10	.474	2.85	29	28	9	199	166	45	105	4	0	0	1	66	9	0	.136	13	22	5	1	1.4	.875
1979		5	8	.385	4.57	33	19	3	126	134	47	81	1	0	0	0	34	7	0	.206	9	19	4	1	1.0	.875
1980	**2 teams** **SF N** (11G 0–0) **CAL A** (10G 3–1)																									
″	**total**	3	1	.750	5.10	21	8	0	60	68	21	30	0	0	0	0	6	1	0	.167	4	5	0	1	0.4	1.000
7 yrs.		55	66	.455	3.62	192	157	36	1063.1	1007	334	707	13	1	1	1	322	53	3	.165	71	120	26	7	1.1	.880

Bert Hall

HALL, HERBERT ERNEST BR TR 5′10″ 178 lbs.
B. Oct. 15, 1888, Portland, Ore. D. July 18, 1948, Seattle, Wash.

Year	Team	W	L	PCT	ERA	G	GS	CG	IP	H	BB	SO	ShO	Relief Pitching W	Relief Pitching L	Relief Pitching SV	Batting AB	Batting H	Batting HR	BA	PO	A	E	DP	TC/G	FA
1911	PHI N	0	1	.000	4.00	7	1	0	18	19	13	8	0	0	1	0	3	1	0	.333	0	2	0	0	0.3	1.000

Bill Hall

HALL, WILLIAM BERNARD (Beanie) BR TR 6′2″ 250 lbs.
B. Feb. 22, 1894, Charleston, W. Va. D. Aug. 15, 1947, Newport, Ky.

Year	Team	W	L	PCT	ERA	G	GS	CG	IP	H	BB	SO	ShO	Relief Pitching W	Relief Pitching L	Relief Pitching SV	Batting AB	Batting H	Batting HR	BA	PO	A	E	DP	TC/G	FA
1913	BKN N	0	0	—	5.79	3	0	0	4.2	4	5	3	0	0	0	0	1	0	0	.000	0	1	0	0	0.3	1.000

Bob Hall

HALL, ROBERT LEWIS BR TR 6′2″ 195 lbs.
B. Dec. 22, 1923, Swissvale, Pa. D. Mar. 12, 1983, St. Petersburg, Fla.

Year	Team	W	L	PCT	ERA	G	GS	CG	IP	H	BB	SO	ShO	Relief Pitching W	Relief Pitching L	Relief Pitching SV	Batting AB	Batting H	Batting HR	BA	PO	A	E	DP	TC/G	FA
1949	BOS N	6	4	.600	4.36	31	6	2	74.1	77	41	43	0	5	0	0	22	8	0	.364	3	3	2	0	0.3	.750
1950		0	2	.000	6.97	21	4	0	50.1	58	33	22	0	0	1	0	12	1	0	.083	4	7	1	0	0.6	.917
1953	PIT N	3	12	.200	5.39	37	17	6	152	172	72	68	1	0	1	1	38	6	1	.158	10	23	4	2	1.0	.892
3 yrs.		9	18	.333	5.40	89	27	8	276.2	307	146	133	1	5	2	1	72	15	1	.208	17	33	7	2	0.6	.877

Charley Hall

HALL, CHARLES LOUIS (Sea Lion) BL TR 6′ 1″ 187 lbs.
Born Carlos Clolo.
B. July 27, 1885, Ventura, Calif. D. Dec. 6, 1943, Ventura, Calif.

Year	Team	Lg	W	L	PCT	ERA	G	GS	CG	IP	H	BB	SO	ShO	Relief Pitching W	Relief Pitching L	Relief Pitching SV	Batting AB	Batting H	Batting HR	BA	PO	A	E	DP	TC/G	FA
1906	CIN	N	4	6	.400	3.32	14	9	9	95	86	50	49	1	0	1	1	47	6	0	.128	17	29	4	3	3.1	.920
1907			4	2	.667	2.51	11	8	5	68	51	43	25	0	1	0	0	26	7	0	.269	3	14	1	0	1.6	.944
1909	BOS	A	6	4	.600	2.56	11	7	3	59.2	59	17	27	0	3	0	0	19	3	0	.158	5	16	1	2	2.0	.955
1910			12	9	.571	1.91	35	16	13	188.2	142	73	95	0	**6**	1	2	82	17	0	.207	9	62	4	0	2.0	.947
1911			8	7	.533	3.73	32	10	6	147.1	149	72	83	0	4	3	**4**	64	9	1	.141	4	30	2	0	1.1	.944
1912			15	8	.652	3.02	34	21	9	191	178	70	83	2	**6**	0	2	75	20	1	.267	9	59	3	0	2.1	.958
1913			5	4	.556	3.43	35	4	2	105	97	46	48	0	5	0	2	42	9	0	.214	6	27	2	1	1.0	.943
1916	STL	N	0	4	.000	5.48	10	5	2	42.2	45	14	15	0	0	0	1	14	2	0	.143	1	13	2	2	1.6	.875
1918	DET	A	0	1	.000	6.75	6	1	0	13.1	14	6	2	0	0	0	0	2	0	0	.000	1	1	1	1	0.5	.667
9 yrs.			54	45	.545	3.08	188	81	49	910.2	821	391	427	3	25	5	12	*				55	251	20	9	1.7	.939
WORLD SERIES																											
1912	BOS	A	0	0	—	3.38	2	0	0	10.2	11	9	1	0	0	0	0	*				0	5	1	0	3.0	.833

Darren Hall

HALL, MICHAEL DARREN BR TR 6′ 3″ 205 lbs.
B. July 14, 1964, Marysville, Ohio.

Year	Team	Lg	W	L	PCT	ERA	G	GS	CG	IP	H	BB	SO	ShO	Relief Pitching W	Relief Pitching L	Relief Pitching SV	Batting AB	Batting H	Batting HR	BA	PO	A	E	DP	TC/G	FA
1994	TOR	A	2	3	.400	3.41	30	0	0	31.2	26	14	28	0	2	3	17	0	0	0	—	2	6	0	2	0.3	1.000
1995			0	2	.000	4.41	17	0	0	16.1	21	9	11	0	0	2	3	0	0	0	—	2	1	0	0	0.2	1.000
2 yrs.			2	5	.286	3.75	47	0	0	48	47	23	39	0	2	5	20	0	0	0		4	7	0	2	0.2	1.000

Dick Hall

HALL, RICHARD WALLACE BR TR 6′ 6″ 200 lbs.
B. Sept. 27, 1930, St. Louis, Mo.

Year	Team	Lg	W	L	PCT	ERA	G	GS	CG	IP	H	BB	SO	ShO	Relief Pitching W	Relief Pitching L	Relief Pitching SV	Batting AB	Batting H	Batting HR	BA	PO	A	E	DP	TC/G	FA
1955	PIT	N	6	6	.500	3.91	15	13	4	94.1	92	28	46	0	0	0	1	40	7	1	.175	44	11	1	0	2.9	.982
1956			0	7	.000	4.76	19	9	1	62.1	64	21	27	0	0	1	1	29	10	0	.345	6	7	0	0	0.6	1.000
1957			0	0	—	10.80	8	0	0	10	17	5	7	0	0	0	0	1	0	0	.000	0	0	0	0	0.0	.000
1959			0	0	—	3.12	2	1	0	8.2	12	1	3	0	0	0	0	2	0	0	.000	0	1	0	0	0.5	1.000
1960	KC	A	8	13	.381	4.05	29	28	9	182.1	183	38	79	1	0	1	0	56	6	0	.107	9	28	3	1	1.4	.925
1961	BAL	A	7	5	.583	3.09	29	13	4	122.1	102	30	92	2	2	1	4	36	5	0	.139	9	23	1	1	1.1	.970
1962			6	6	.500	2.28	43	6	1	118.1	102	19	71	0	4	3	6	24	4	0	.167	9	17	0	1	0.6	1.000
1963			5	5	.500	2.98	47	3	0	111.2	91	16	74	0	5	2	12	28	13	1	.464	7	21	0	1	0.6	1.000
1964			9	1	.900	1.85	45	0	0	87.2	58	16	52	0	9	1	7	16	2	0	.125	7	12	0	1	0.4	1.000
1965			11	8	.579	3.07	48	0	0	93.2	84	11	79	0	11	8	12	15	5	0	.333	4	8	1	2	0.3	.923
1966			6	2	.750	3.95	32	0	0	66	59	8	44	0	6	2	7	12	2	0	.167	4	10	0	0	0.4	1.000
1967	PHI	N	10	8	.556	2.20	48	1	1	86	83	12	49	0	9	**8**	8	14	1	0	.071	2	21	0	1	0.5	1.000
1968			4	1	.800	4.89	32	0	0	46	53	5	31	0	4	1	0	3	1	0	.333	2	6	0	0	0.3	1.000
1969	BAL	A	5	2	.714	1.92	39	0	0	65.2	49	9	31	0	5	2	6	7	2	0	.286	4	6	0	2	0.3	1.000
1970			10	5	.667	3.10	32	0	0	61	51	6	30	0	**10**	5	3	12	1	0	.083	3	3	0	0	0.2	1.000
1971			6	6	.500	5.02	27	0	0	43	52	11	26	0	6	6	1	5	2	0	.400	1	3	1	0	0.2	.800
16 yrs.			93	75	.554	3.32	495	74	20	1259	1152	236	741	3	71	41	68	*				376	211	19	17	1.0	.969
LEAGUE CHAMPIONSHIP SERIES																											
1969	BAL	A	1	0	1.000	0.00	1	0	0	0.2	0	0	1	0	1	0	0	0	0	0	—	0	0	0	0	0.0	.000
1970			1	0	1.000	0.00	1	0	0	4.2	1	0	3	0	1	0	0	2	1	0	.500	0	0	0	0	0.0	.000
2 yrs.			2	0	1.000	0.00	2	0	0	5.1	1	0	4	0	2	0	0	*				0	0	0	0	0.0	
WORLD SERIES																											
1969	BAL	A	0	1	.000	0.00	1	0	0		1	1	0	0	0	1	0	0	0	0	—	0	0	0	0	0.0	.000
1970			0	0	—	0.00	1	0	0	2.1	0	0	0	0	0	0	1	1	0	0	.000	0	0	0	0	0.0	.000
1971			0	0	—	0.00	1	0	0	1	1	0	0	0	0	0	1	0	0	0	—	1	0	0	0	1.0	1.000
3 yrs.			0	1	.000	0.00	3	0	0	3.1	2	1	0	0	0	1	2	*				1	0	0	0	0.3	1.000

Drew Hall

HALL, ANDREW CLARK BL TL 6′ 4″ 220 lbs.
B. Mar. 27, 1963, Louisville, Ky.

Year	Team	Lg	W	L	PCT	ERA	G	GS	CG	IP	H	BB	SO	ShO	Relief Pitching W	Relief Pitching L	Relief Pitching SV	Batting AB	Batting H	Batting HR	BA	PO	A	E	DP	TC/G	FA
1986	CHI	N	1	2	.333	4.56	5	4	1	23.2	24	10	21	0	0	0	1	7	1	0	.143	0	2	0	0	0.4	1.000
1987			1	1	.500	6.89	21	0	0	32.2	40	14	20	0	1	1	0	4	0	0	.000	3	3	0	0	0.3	1.000
1988			1	1	.500	7.66	19	0	0	22.1	26	9	22	0	1	1	1	1	0	0	.000	0	4	0	0	0.2	1.000
1989	TEX	A	2	1	.667	3.70	38	0	0	58.1	42	33	45	0	2	1	0	0	0	0	—	2	8	0	1	0.3	1.000
1990	MON	N	4	7	.364	5.09	42	0	0	58.1	52	29	40	0	4	7	3	4	0	0	.000	2	11	1	1	0.3	.929
5 yrs.			9	12	.429	5.21	125	4	1	195.1	184	95	148	0	8	10	5	16	1	0	.063	7	28	1	2	0.3	.972

Herb Hall

HALL, HERBERT SILAS (Iron Duke) BB TR 6′ 4″ 220 lbs.
B. June 5, 1893, Steeleville, Ill. D. July 1, 1970, Fresno, Calif.

Year	Team	Lg	W	L	PCT	ERA	G	GS	CG	IP	H	BB	SO	ShO	Relief Pitching W	Relief Pitching L	Relief Pitching SV	Batting AB	Batting H	Batting HR	BA	PO	A	E	DP	TC/G	FA
1918	DET	A	0	0	—	15.00	3	0	0	6	12	7	1	0	0	0	0	1	0	0	.000	0	2	0	0	0.7	1.000

Johnny Hall

HALL, JOHN SYLVESTER BR TR 6′ 2½″ 170 lbs.
B. Jan. 9, 1924, Muskogee, Okla. D. Jan. 17, 1995, Midwest City, Okla.

Year	Team	Lg	W	L	PCT	ERA	G	GS	CG	IP	H	BB	SO	ShO	Relief Pitching W	Relief Pitching L	Relief Pitching SV	Batting AB	Batting H	Batting HR	BA	PO	A	E	DP	TC/G	FA
1948	BKN	N	0	0	—	6.23	3	0	0	4.1	4	2	2	0	0	0	0	0	0	0	—	0	1	0	0	0.3	1.000

Marc Hall

HALL, MARCUS BR TR 6′ 1½″ 190 lbs.
B. Aug. 12, 1887, Joplin, Mo. D. Feb. 24, 1915, Joplin, Mo.

Year	Team	Lg	W	L	PCT	ERA	G	GS	CG	IP	H	BB	SO	ShO	Relief Pitching W	Relief Pitching L	Relief Pitching SV	Batting AB	Batting H	Batting HR	BA	PO	A	E	DP	TC/G	FA
1910	STL	A	1	7	.125	4.27	8	7	5	46.1	50	31	25	0	1	0	0	15	1	0	.067	3	18	3	1	3.0	.875
1913	DET	A	10	12	.455	3.27	30	21	8	165	154	79	69	1	2	3	0	45	4	0	.089	7	48	1	2	1.9	.982
1914			4	6	.400	2.69	25	8	1	90.1	88	27	18	0	0	3	0	23	1	0	.043	4	29	0	0	1.3	1.000
3 yrs.			15	25	.375	3.25	63	36	14	301.2	292	137	112	1	3	6	0	83	6	0	.072	14	95	4	3	1.8	.965

Tom Hall

HALL, TOM EDWARD (The Blade) BL TL 6′ 150 lbs.
B. Nov. 23, 1947, Thomasville, N. C.

Year	Team	Lg	W	L	PCT	ERA	G	GS	CG	IP	H	BB	SO	ShO	Relief Pitching W	Relief Pitching L	Relief Pitching SV	Batting AB	Batting H	Batting HR	BA	PO	A	E	DP	TC/G	FA
1968	MIN	A	2	1	.667	2.43	8	4	0	29.2	27	12	18	0	1	0	0	9	0	0	.000	1	4	1	0	0.8	.833
1969			8	7	.533	3.33	31	18	5	140.2	129	50	92	2	0	2	0	43	8	0	.186	1	13	0	0	0.5	1.000
1970			11	6	.647	2.55	52	11	1	155	94	66	184	0	4	2	4	44	8	0	.182	2	9	2	1	0.3	.846
1971			4	7	.364	3.32	48	11	0	130	104	58	137	0	3	3	9	34	9	0	.265	8	19	1	0	0.6	.964
1972	CIN	N	10	1	.909	2.61	47	7	1	124.1	77	56	134	1	7	1	8	30	3	0	.100	0	10	2	0	0.3	.833
1973			8	5	.615	3.47	54	7	0	103.2	74	48	96	0	7	4	8	22	1	0	.045	3	6	0	0	0.2	1.000
1974			3	1	.750	4.08	40	1	0	64	54	30	48	0	2	1	1	5	0	0	.000	1	9	0	0	0.3	1.000

Tom Hall *continued*

Year	Team	Lg	W	L	PCT	ERA	G	GS	CG	IP	H	BB	SO	ShO	Relief W	Relief L	SV	AB	H	HR	BA	PO	A	E	DP	TC/G	FA
1975	**2 teams**	**CIN N** (2G 0–0) **NY N** (34G 4–3)																									
"	**total**		4	3	.571	4.57	36	4	0	63	60	33	51	0	2	2	1	5	2	0	.400	2	7	0	0	0.3	1.000
1976	**2 teams**	**NY N** (5G 1–1) **KC A** (31G 1–1)																									
"	**total**		2	2	.500	4.63	36	0	0	35	33	23	27	0	2	2	1	0	0	0		1	9	1	0	0.3	.909
1977	**KC**	**A**	0	0	—	3.38	6	0	0	8	4	6	10	0	0	0	0	0	0	0	—	0	2	0	0	0.3	1.000
10 yrs.			52	33	.612	3.27	358	63	7	853.1	656	382	797	3	28	17	32	192	31	0	.161	19	88	7	1	0.3	.939
LEAGUE CHAMPIONSHIP SERIES																											
1969	**MIN**	**A**	0	0	—	0.00	1	0	0	0.2	0	0	0	0	0	0	0	0	0	0	—	0	0	0	0	0.0	.000
1970			0	1	.000	6.75	2	1	0	5.1	6	4	6	0	0	0	0	1	0	0	.000	0	0	0	0	0.0	.000
1972	**CIN**	**N**	1	0	1.000	1.23	2	0	0	7.1	3	3	8	0	1	0	0	1	0	0	.000	1	0	0	0	0.5	1.000
1973			0	0	—	67.50	3	0	0	0.2	3	4	1	0	0	0	0	0	0	0	—	1	0	0	0	0.3	1.000
1976	**KC**	**A**	0	0	—	0.00	1	0	0	0.1	1	0	0	0	0	0	0	0	0	0	—	0	0	0	0	0.0	.000
5 yrs.			1	1	.500	6.28	9	1	0	14.1	13	11	15	0	1	0	0	2	0	0	.000	2	0	0	0	0.2	1.000
WORLD SERIES																											
1972	**CIN**	**N**	0	0	—	0.00	4	0	0	8.1	6	2	7	0	0	0	1	2	0	0	.000	0	2	0	0	0.5	1.000

John Halla

HALLA, JOHN ARTHUR BL TL 5′11″ 175 lbs.
B. May 13, 1884, St. Louis, Mo. D. Sept. 30, 1947, El Segundo, Calif.

Year	Team	Lg	W	L	PCT	ERA	G	GS	CG	IP	H	BB	SO	ShO	Relief W	Relief L	SV	AB	H	HR	BA	PO	A	E	DP	TC/G	FA
1905	**CLE**	**A**	0	0	—	2.84	3	0	0	12.2	12	0	4	0	0	0	0	4	1	0	.250	0	4	0	0	1.3	1.000

Bill Hallahan

HALLAHAN, WILLIAM ANTHONY (Wild Bill) BR TL 5′10½″ 170 lbs.
B. Aug. 4, 1902, Binghamton, N. Y. D. July 8, 1981, Binghamton, N. Y.

Year	Team	Lg	W	L	PCT	ERA	G	GS	CG	IP	H	BB	SO	ShO	Relief W	Relief L	SV	AB	H	HR	BA	PO	A	E	DP	TC/G	FA
1925	**STL**	**N**	1	0	1.000	3.52	6	0	0	15.1	14	11	8	0	1	0	0	3	1	0	.333	1	5	1	0	1.2	.857
1926			1	4	.200	3.65	19	3	0	56.2	45	32	28	0	1	2	0	16	4	0	.250	1	12	4	1	0.9	.765
1929			4	4	.500	4.42	20	12	5	93.2	94	60	52	0	0	0	0	26	4	0	.154	2	25	1	0	1.4	.964
1930			15	9	.625	4.66	35	32	13	237.1	233	**126**	**177**	2	0	0	2	81	10	0	.123	8	41	3	2	1.5	.942
1931			**19**	9	.679	3.29	37	30	16	248.2	242	**112**	**159**	3	1	1	4	81	8	0	.099	10	34	1	3	1.2	.978
1932			12	7	.632	3.11	25	22	13	176.1	169	69	108	1	1	0	1	56	12	0	.214	7	27	2	10	1.4	.944
1933			16	13	.552	3.50	36	32	16	244.1	245	**98**	93	2	1	1	0	80	12	0	.150	11	39	6	2	1.6	.893
1934			8	12	.400	4.26	32	26	10	162.2	195	66	70	2	0	0	0	55	10	0	.182	5	34	4	2	1.3	.907
1935			15	8	.652	3.42	40	23	8	181.1	196	57	73	2	3	2	1	56	8	1	.143	9	34	4	4	1.2	.915
1936	**2 teams**	**STL N** (9G 2–2) **CIN N** (23G 5–9)																									
"	**total**		7	11	.389	4.76	32	25	6	172	178	77	48	2	0	2	0	56	14	1	.250	10	42	2	2	1.7	.963
1937	**CIN**	**N**	3	9	.250	6.14	21	9	2	63	90	29	18	0	1	3	0	21	2	0	.095	1	18	3	1	1.0	.864
1938	**PHI**	**N**	1	8	.111	5.46	21	10	1	89	107	45	22	0	0	3	0	26	5	0	.192	2	19	1	1	1.0	.955
12 yrs.			102	94	.520	4.03	324	224	90	1740.1	1808	782	856	14	9	14	8	557	90	2	.162	67	330	32	28	1.3	.925
WORLD SERIES																											
1926	**STL**	**N**	0	0	—	4.50	1	0	0	2	2	3	1	0	0	0	0	0	0	0	—	1	0	0	0	1.0	1.000
1930			1	1	.500	1.64	2	2	1	11	9	8	8	1	0	0	0	2	0	0	.000	0	1	0	0	0.5	1.000
1931			2	0	1.000	0.49	3	2	2	18.1	12	8	12	1	0	0	1	6	0	0	.000	0	0	0	0	0.0	.000
1934			0	0	—	2.16	1	1	0	8.1	6	4	6	0	0	0	0	3	0	0	.000	1	3	1	0	5.0	.800
4 yrs.			3	1	.750	1.36	7	5	3	39.2	29	23	27	2 **4th**	0	0	1	11	0	0	.000	2	4	1	0	1.0	.857

Jack Hallett

HALLETT, JACK PRICE BR TR 6′ 4″ 215 lbs.
B. Nov. 13, 1914, Toledo, Ohio D. June 11, 1982, Toledo, Ohio.

Year	Team	Lg	W	L	PCT	ERA	G	GS	CG	IP	H	BB	SO	ShO	Relief W	Relief L	SV	AB	H	HR	BA	PO	A	E	DP	TC/G	FA
1940	**CHI**	**A**	1	1	.500	6.43	2	2	1	14	15	6	9	0	0	0	0	5	2	0	.400	1	2	0	0	1.5	1.000
1941			5	5	.500	6.03	22	6	3	74.2	96	38	25	0	3	1	0	26	4	0	.154	2	14	0	2	0.7	1.000
1942	**PIT**	**N**	0	1	.000	4.84	3	3	2	22.1	23	8	16	0	0	0	0	8	3	1	.375	0	5	0	1	1.7	1.000
1943			1	2	.333	1.70	9	4	2	47.2	36	11	11	1	0	1	0	14	4	0	.286	3	5	0	1	0.9	1.000
1946			5	7	.417	3.29	35	9	3	115	107	39	64	1	3	2	0	26	6	0	.231	8	20	0	0	0.8	1.000
1948	**NY**	**N**	0	0	—	4.50	2	0	0	4	3	4	3	0	0	0	0	1	0	0	.000	0	0	0	0	0.0	.000
6 yrs.			12	16	.429	4.05	73	24	11	277.2	280	106	128	2	6	4	0	80	19	1	.237	14	46	0	4	0.8	1.000

Bill Hallman

HALLMAN, WILLIAM WILSON BR TR 5′ 8″
B. Mar. 31, 1867, Pittsburgh, Pa. D. Sept. 11, 1920, Philadelphia, Pa.
Manager 1897.

Year	Team	Lg	W	L	PCT	ERA	G	GS	CG	IP	H	BB	SO	ShO	Relief W	Relief L	SV	AB	H	HR	BA	PO	A	E	DP	TC/G	FA
1896	**PHI**	**N**	0	0	—	18.00	1	0	0	2	4	2	0	0	0	0	0	*				54	24	12	2	4.7	.867

Charlie Hallstrom

HALLSTROM, CHARLES E. (Swedish Wonder)
B. Jan. 22, 1864, Jonkoping, Sweden D. May 6, 1949, Chicago, Ill.

Year	Team	Lg	W	L	PCT	ERA	G	GS	CG	IP	H	BB	SO	ShO	Relief W	Relief L	SV	AB	H	HR	BA	PO	A	E	DP	TC/G	FA
1885	**PRO**	**N**	0	1	.000	11.00	1	1	1	9	18	6	0	0	0	0	0	4	0	0	.000	0	1	1	0	2.0	.500

Doc Hamann

HAMANN, ELMER JOSEPH BR TR 6′ 1″ 180 lbs.
B. Dec. 21, 1900, New Ulm, Minn. D. Jan. 11, 1973, Milwaukee, Wis.

Year	Team	Lg	W	L	PCT	ERA	G	GS	CG	IP	H	BB	SO	ShO	Relief W	Relief L	SV	AB	H	HR	BA	PO	A	E	DP	TC/G	FA
1922	**CLE**	**A**	0	0	—	∞	1	0	0		3	3	0	0	0	0	0	0	0	0	—	0	0	0	0	0.0	.000

Roger Hambright

HAMBRIGHT, ROGER DEE BR TR 5′10″ 180 lbs.
B. Mar. 26, 1949, Sunnywise, Wash.

Year	Team	Lg	W	L	PCT	ERA	G	GS	CG	IP	H	BB	SO	ShO	Relief W	Relief L	SV	AB	H	HR	BA	PO	A	E	DP	TC/G	FA
1971	**NY**	**A**	3	1	.750	4.33	18	0	0	27	22	10	14	0	3	1	2	2	1	0	.500	1	5	0	0	0.3	1.000

John Hamill

HAMILL, JOHN ALEXANDER CHARLES BR TR 5′ 8″ 158 lbs.
B. Dec. 18, 1860, New York, N. Y. D. Dec. 6, 1911, Bristol, R. I.

Year	Team	Lg	W	L	PCT	ERA	G	GS	CG	IP	H	BB	SO	ShO	Relief W	Relief L	SV	AB	H	HR	BA	PO	A	E	DP	TC/G	FA
1884	**WAS**	**AA**	2	17	.105	*4.48*	19	19	18	156.2	197	43	50	1	0	0	0	71	7	0	.099	15	31	21	0	3.0	.687

Dave Hamilton

HAMILTON, DAVID EDWARD BL TL 6′ 180 lbs.
B. Dec. 13, 1947, Seattle, Wash.

Year	Team	Lg	W	L	PCT	ERA	G	GS	CG	IP	H	BB	SO	ShO	Relief W	Relief L	SV	AB	H	HR	BA	PO	A	E	DP	TC/G	FA
1972	**OAK**	**A**	6	6	.500	2.93	25	14	1	101.1	94	31	55	0	0	1	0	26	4	0	.154	4	17	1	0	0.9	.955
1973			6	4	.600	4.39	16	11	1	69.2	74	24	34	0	1	0	0	0	0	0	—	2	7	0	0	0.6	1.000
1974			7	4	.636	3.15	29	18	1	117	104	48	69	1	1	0	0	0	0	0	—	3	17	2	1	0.8	.909
1975	**2 teams**	**OAK A** (11G 1–2) **CHI A** (30G 6–5)																									
"	**total**		7	7	.500	3.25	41	5	0	105.1	105	47	71	0	7	4	6	0	0	0		3	15	0	3	0.4	1.000
1976	**CHI**	**A**	6	6	.500	3.60	45	1	0	90	81	45	62	0	6	5	10	0	0	0	—	4	9	1	1	0.3	.929

Dave Hamilton *continued*

Year	Team	Lg	W	L	PCT	ERA	G	GS	CG	IP	H	BB	SO	ShO	Relief W	Relief L	Relief SV	Batting AB	Batting H	HR	BA	PO	A	E	DP	TC/G	FA
1977			4	5	.444	3.63	55	0	0	67	71	33	45	0	4	5	9	0	0	0	—	4	10	1	1	0.3	.933
1978	2 teams	STL N (13G 0–0)	PIT N (16G 0–2)																								
″	total		0	2	.000	4.46	29	0	0	40.1	39	18	23	0	0	2	1	7	0	0	.000	3	5	0	0	0.3	1.000
1979	OAK	A	3	4	.429	3.69	40	7	1	83	80	43	52	0	2	0	5	0	0	0	—	3	15	0	0	0.4	1.000
1980			0	3	.000	11.40	21	1	0	30	44	28	23	0	0	3	0	0	0	0	—	2	3	0	0	0.2	1.000
9 yrs.			39	41	.488	3.85	301	57	4	703.2	692	317	434	1	21	20	31	33	4	0	.121	28	98	5	6	0.4	.962
LEAGUE CHAMPIONSHIP SERIES																											
1972	OAK	A	0	0	—	0.00	1	0	0		1	1	0	0	0	0	0	0	0	0	—	0	0	0	0	0.0	.000
WORLD SERIES																											
1972	OAK	A	0	0	—	27.00	2	0	0	1.1	3	1	1	0	0	0	0	0	0	0	—	0	0	0	0	0.0	.000

Earl Hamilton

HAMILTON, EARL ANDREW BL TL 5′ 8″ 160 lbs.
B. July 19, 1891, Gibson City, Ill. D. Nov. 17, 1968, Anaheim, Calif.

Year	Team	Lg	W	L	PCT	ERA	G	GS	CG	IP	H	BB	SO	ShO	Relief W	Relief L	Relief SV	Batting AB	Batting H	HR	BA	PO	A	E	DP	TC/G	FA
1911	STL	A	5	12	.294	3.97	32	17	10	177	191	69	55	1	1	1	0	56	6	0	.107	13	51	2	2	2.1	.970
1912			11	14	.440	3.24	41	26	17	249.2	228	86	139	1	1	1	2	73	13	0	.178	9	57	5	2	1.7	.930
1913			13	12	.520	2.57	31	24	19	217.1	197	83	101	3	0	2	1	74	10	0	.135	15	53	4	2	2.3	.944
1914			17	18	.486	2.50	44	35	20	302.1	265	100	111	5	1	2	2	85	15	0	.176	16	64	3	3	1.9	.964
1915			9	17	.346	2.87	35	27	13	204	203	69	63	1	0	1	0	62	7	0	.113	7	50	2	3	1.7	.966
1916	3 teams	STL A (1G 0–0)	DET A (5G 1–2)	STL A (22G 5–7)																							
″	total		6	9	.400	3.12	28	17	6	132.2	135	52	32	0	2	2	0	37	1	0	.027	3	40	2	1	1.6	.956
1917	STL	A	0	9	.000	3.14	27	8	2	83	86	41	19	0	0	3	1	19	7	0	.368	8	18	0	1	1.0	1.000
1918	PIT	N	6	0	1.000	0.83	6	6	6	54	47	13	20	1	0	0	0	21	6	0	.286	4	13	1	2	3.0	.944
1919			8	11	.421	3.31	28	19	10	160.1	167	49	39	1	1	0	1	52	7	0	.135	11	51	3	6	2.3	.954
1920			10	13	.435	3.24	39	23	12	230.2	223	69	74	0	3	2	3	67	10	0	.149	10	62	1	0	1.9	.986
1921			13	15	.464	3.36	35	30	12	225	237	58	59	2	0	3	0	75	12	0	.160	15	74	3	4	2.6	.967
1922			11	7	.611	3.99	33	14	9	160	183	40	34	1	3	3	2	58	9	0	.155	4	35	0	1	1.2	1.000
1923			7	9	.438	3.77	28	15	5	141	148	42	42	0	2	3	1	52	9	0	.173	9	42	1	2	1.9	.981
1924	PHI	N	0	1	.000	10.50	3	0	0	6	9	2	2	0	0	1	0	2	0	0	.000	0	2	0	0	0.7	1.000
14 yrs.			116	147	.441	3.16	410	261	141	2343	2319	773	790	16	14	24	13	733	112	0	.153	124	612	27	29	1.9	.965

Jack Hamilton

HAMILTON, JACK EDWIN (Hairbreadth Harry) BR TR 6′ 200 lbs.
B. Dec. 25, 1938, Burlington, Iowa

Year	Team	Lg	W	L	PCT	ERA	G	GS	CG	IP	H	BB	SO	ShO	Relief W	Relief L	Relief SV	Batting AB	Batting H	HR	BA	PO	A	E	DP	TC/G	FA
1962	PHI	N	9	12	.429	5.09	41	26	4	182	185	**107**	101	1	2	0	2	54	3	0	.056	16	39	3	6	1.4	.948
1963			2	1	.667	5.40	19	1	0	30	22	17	23	0	2	0	1	3	0	0	.000	1	8	0	0	0.5	1.000
1964	DET	A	0	1	.000	8.40	5	1	0	15	24	8	5	0	0	0	0	3	0	0	.000	1	5	0	0	1.2	1.000
1965			1	1	.500	14.54	4	1	0	4.1	6	4	3	0	1	0	0	0	0	0	—	1	2	0	0	0.8	1.000
1966	NY	N	6	13	.316	3.93	57	13	3	148.2	138	88	93	1	2	6	13	38	5	0	.132	16	25	2	2	0.8	.953
1967	2 teams	NY N (17G 2–0)	CAL A (26G 9–6)																								
″	total		11	6	.647	3.35	43	21	0	150.2	128	79	96	0	3	0	1	43	7	1	.163	5	24	2	1	0.7	.935
1968	CAL	A	3	1	.750	3.32	21	2	1	38	34	15	18	0	2	0	2	7	1	0	.143	4	4	0	1	0.4	1.000
1969	2 teams	CLE A (20G 0–2)	CHI A (8G 0–3)																								
″	total		0	5	.000	6.49	28	0	0	43	60	30	18	0	0	5	1	2	0	0	.000	1	6	0	0	0.3	1.000
8 yrs.			32	40	.444	4.53	218	65	8	611.2	597	348	357	2	12	11	20	150	16	1	.107	45	113	7	10	0.8	.958

Jeff Hamilton

HAMILTON, JEFFREY ROBERT BR TR 6′ 3″ 190 lbs.
B. Mar. 19, 1964, Flint, Mich.

Year	Team	Lg	W	L	PCT	ERA	G	GS	CG	IP	H	BB	SO	ShO	Relief W	Relief L	Relief SV	Batting AB	Batting H	HR	BA	PO	A	E	DP	TC/G	FA
1989	LA	N	0	1	.000	5.40	1	0	0	1.2	2	1	2	0	0	1	0	*				40	87	4	6	1.9	.969

Joey Hamilton

HAMILTON, JOHNS JOSEPH BR TR 6′ 4″ 220 lbs.
B. Sept. 9, 1970, Statesboro, Ga.

Year	Team	Lg	W	L	PCT	ERA	G	GS	CG	IP	H	BB	SO	ShO	Relief W	Relief L	Relief SV	Batting AB	Batting H	HR	BA	PO	A	E	DP	TC/G	FA
1994	SD	N	9	6	.600	2.98	16	16	1	108.2	98	29	61	1	0	0	0	40	0	0	.000	7	16	1	3	1.5	.958
1995			6	9	.400	3.08	31	30	2	204.1	189	56	123	2	0	0	0	65	7	0	.108	12	30	6	1	1.5	.875
2 yrs.			15	15	.500	3.05	47	46	3	313	287	85	184	3	0	0	0	105	7	0	.067	19	46	7	4	1.5	.903

Steve Hamilton

HAMILTON, STEVE ABSHER BL TL 6′ 6″ 190 lbs.
B. Nov. 30, 1935, Columbia, Ky.

Year	Team	Lg	W	L	PCT	ERA	G	GS	CG	IP	H	BB	SO	ShO	Relief W	Relief L	Relief SV	Batting AB	Batting H	HR	BA	PO	A	E	DP	TC/G	FA
1961	CLE	A	0	0	—	2.70	2	0	0	3.1	2	3	4	0	0	0	0	1	1	0	1.000	1	1	0	0	1.0	1.000
1962	WAS	A	3	8	.273	3.77	41	10	1	107.1	103	39	83	0	2	4	2	26	2	0	.077	8	22	2	0	0.8	.938
1963	2 teams	WAS A (3G 0–1)	NY A (34G 5–1)																								
″	total		5	2	.714	2.94	37	0	0	64.1	54	26	64	0	5	2	5	14	4	0	.286	3	13	0	0	0.4	1.000
1964	NY	A	7	2	.778	3.28	30	3	1	60.1	55	15	49	0	5	2	3	20	4	0	.200	3	9	0	1	0.4	1.000
1965			3	1	.750	1.39	46	1	0	58.1	47	16	51	0	3	1	5	6	1	0	.167	0	3	1	0	0.1	.750
1966			8	3	.727	3.00	44	3	1	90	69	22	57	1	7	2	3	19	1	0	.053	2	12	2	0	0.4	.875
1967			2	4	.333	3.48	44	0	0	62	57	23	55	0	2	4	4	9	1	0	.111	0	12	0	0	0.3	1.000
1968			2	2	.500	2.13	40	0	0	50.2	37	13	42	0	2	2	11	3	0	0	.000	2	9	0	1	0.3	1.000
1969			3	4	.429	3.32	38	0	0	57	39	21	39	0	3	4	2	5	0	0	.000	0	4	0	0	0.1	1.000
1970	2 teams	NY A (35G 4–3)	CHI A (3G 0–0)																								
″	total		4	3	.571	2.98	38	0	0	48.1	40	17	36	0	4	3	3	6	0	0	.000	0	11	1	0	0.3	.917
1971	SF	N	2	2	.500	3.00	39	0	0	45	29	11	38	0	2	2	4	2	0	0	.000	3	4	0	0	0.2	1.000
1972	CHI	N	1	0	1.000	4.76	22	0	0	17	24	8	13	0	1	0	0	1	0	0	.000	0	2	0	0	0.1	1.000
12 yrs.			40	31	.563	3.05	421	17	3	663.2	556	214	531	1	36	26	42	112	14	0	.125	22	102	6	2	0.3	.954
LEAGUE CHAMPIONSHIP SERIES																											
1971	SF	N	0	0	—	9.00	1	0	0	1	1	0	3	0	0	0	0	0	0	0	—	0	0	0	0	0.0	.000
WORLD SERIES																											
1963	NY	A	0	0	—	0.00	1	0	0	1	0	0	1	0	0	0	0	0	0	0	—	0	0	0	0	0.0	.000
1964			0	0	—	4.50	2	0	0	2	3	0	2	0	0	0	1	0	0	0	—	0	0	0	0	0.0	.000
2 yrs.			0	0		3.00	3	0	0	3	3	0	3	0	0	0	1	0	0	0		0	0	0	0	0.0	

Luke Hamlin

HAMLIN, LUKE DANIEL (Hot Potato) BL TR 6′ 2″ 168 lbs.
B. July 3, 1904, Ferris Center, Mich. D. Feb. 18, 1978, Clare, Mich.

Year	Team	Lg	W	L	PCT	ERA	G	GS	CG	IP	H	BB	SO	ShO	Relief W	Relief L	Relief SV	Batting AB	Batting H	HR	BA	PO	A	E	DP	TC/G	FA
1933	DET	A	1	0	1.000	4.86	3	3	0	16.2	20	10	10	0	0	0	0	5	2	0	.400	1	0	2	0	1.0	.333
1934			2	3	.400	5.38	20	5	1	75.1	87	44	30	0	0	3	1	26	6	0	.231	4	12	0	0	0.8	1.000

Luke Hamlin *continued*

Year	Team	Lg	W	L	PCT	ERA	G	GS	CG	IP	H	BB	SO	ShO	Relief Pitching W	Relief L	Relief SV	Batting AB	Batting H	Batting HR	BA	PO	A	E	DP	TC/G	FA
1937	**BKN**	**N**	11	13	.458	3.59	39	25	11	185.2	183	48	93	1	2	2	1	59	11	0	.186	7	26	6	1	1.0	.846
1938			12	15	.444	3.68	44	30	10	237.1	243	65	97	3	1	1	6	78	11	0	.141	8	29	2	1	0.9	.949
1939			20	13	.606	3.64	40	**36**	19	269.2	255	54	88	2	2	0	0	103	13	1	.126	13	33	1	1	1.2	.979
1940			9	8	.529	3.06	33	25	9	182.1	183	34	91	2	0	0	0	58	5	0	.086	5	19	2	3	0.8	.923
1941			8	8	.500	4.24	30	20	5	136	139	41	58	1	1	0	1	41	6	0	.146	9	18	0	2	0.9	1.000
1942	**PIT**	**N**	4	4	.500	3.94	23	14	6	112	128	19	38	1	0	0	0	37	9	0	.243	4	15	2	0	0.9	.905
1944	**PHI**	**A**	6	12	.333	3.74	29	23	9	190	204	38	58	2	0	1	0	56	13	0	.232	1	19	4	0	0.8	.833
9 yrs.			73	76	.490	3.77	261	181	70	1405	1442	353	563	12	6	7	9	463	76	1	.164	52	171	19	8	0.9	.921

Pete Hamm

HAMM, PETER WHITFIELD BR TR 6′ 5″ 210 lbs.
B. Sept. 20, 1947, Buffalo, N. Y.

Year	Team	Lg	W	L	PCT	ERA	G	GS	CG	IP	H	BB	SO	ShO	Relief Pitching W	Relief L	Relief SV	Batting AB	Batting H	Batting HR	BA	PO	A	E	DP	TC/G	FA
1970	**MIN**	**A**	0	2	.000	5.63	10	0	0	16	17	7	3	0	0	2	0	1	0	0	.000	1	0	0	0	0.1	1.000
1971			2	4	.333	6.75	13	8	1	44	55	18	16	0	0	1	0	11	3	0	.273	6	7	0	0	1.0	1.000
2 yrs.			2	6	.250	6.45	23	8	1	60	72	25	19	0	0	3	0	12	3	0	.250	7	7	0	0	0.6	1.000

Atlee Hammaker

HAMMAKER, CHARLTON ATLEE BB TL 6′ 3″ 200 lbs.
B. Jan. 24, 1958, Carmel, Calif.

Year	Team	Lg	W	L	PCT	ERA	G	GS	CG	IP	H	BB	SO	ShO	Relief Pitching W	Relief L	Relief SV	Batting AB	Batting H	Batting HR	BA	PO	A	E	DP	TC/G	FA
1981	**KC**	**A**	1	3	.250	5.54	10	6	0	39	44	12	11	0	0	0	0	0	0	0	—	1	4	0	1	0.5	1.000
1982	**SF**	**N**	12	8	.600	4.11	29	27	4	175	189	28	102	1	0	0	0	59	4	0	.068	5	35	1	0	1.4	.976
1983			10	9	.526	**2.25**	23	23	8	172.1	147	32	127	3	0	0	0	59	6	0	.102	3	31	3	2	1.6	.919
1984			2	0	1.000	2.18	6	6	0	33	32	9	24	0	0	0	0	11	2	0	.182	0	6	0	0	1.0	1.000
1985			5	12	.294	3.74	29	29	1	170.2	161	47	100	1	0	0	0	47	4	0	.085	6	32	1	1	1.3	.974
1987			10	10	.500	3.58	31	27	2	168.1	159	57	107	0	1	0	0	57	7	0	.123	7	23	0	1	1.0	1.000
1988			9	9	.500	3.73	43	17	3	144.2	136	41	65	1	4	2	5	33	4	0	.121	7	33	0	3	0.9	1.000
1989			6	6	.500	3.76	28	9	0	76.2	78	23	30	0	3	3	0	19	7	0	.368	3	9	1	0	0.5	.923
1990	**2 teams**	**SF N** (25G 4–5) **SD N** (9G 0–4)																									
″	**total**		4	9	.308	4.36	34	7	0	86.2	85	27	44	0	1	6	0	19	2	0	.105	6	7	0	2	0.4	1.000
1991	**SD**	**N**	0	1	.000	5.79	1	1	0	4.2	8	3	1	0	0	0	0	1	0	0	.000	0	1	0	0	1.0	1.000
1994	**CHI**	**A**	0	0	—	0.00	2	0	0	1.1	1	0	1	0	0	0	0	0	0	0	—	0	0	0	0	0.0	.000
1995			0	0	—	12.79	13	0	0	6.1	11	8	3	0	0	0	0	0	0	0	—	0	2	0	0	0.2	1.000
12 yrs.			59	67	.468	3.66	249	152	18	1078.2	1051	287	615	6	9	11	5	305	36	0	.118	38	183	6	10	0.9	.974
LEAGUE CHAMPIONSHIP SERIES																											
1987	**SF**	**N**	0	1	.000	7.88	2	2	0	8	12	0	7	0	0	0	0	3	0	0	.000	0	1	0	0	0.5	1.000
1989			0	0	—	0.00	1	0	0	1	1	0	0	0	0	0	0	0	0	0	—	0	0	0	0	0.0	.000
2 yrs.			0	1	.000	7.00	3	2	0	9	13	0	7	0	0	0	0	3	0	0	.000	0	1	0	0	0.3	1.000
WORLD SERIES																											
1989	**SF**	**N**	0	0	—	15.43	2	0	0	2.1	8	0	2	0	0	0	0	0	0	0	—	0	1	0	0	0.5	1.000

Chris Hammond

HAMMOND, CHRISTOPHER ANDREW BL TL 6′ 1″ 190 lbs.
B. Jan. 21, 1966, Atlanta, Ga.

Year	Team	Lg	W	L	PCT	ERA	G	GS	CG	IP	H	BB	SO	ShO	Relief Pitching W	Relief L	Relief SV	Batting AB	Batting H	Batting HR	BA	PO	A	E	DP	TC/G	FA
1990	**CIN**	**N**	0	2	.000	6.35	3	3	0	11.1	13	12	4	0	0	0	0	3	0	0	.000	0	3	2	0	1.7	.600
1991			7	7	.500	4.06	20	18	0	99.2	92	48	50	0	0	0	0	34	12	0	.353	6	18	2	1	1.3	.923
1992			7	10	.412	4.21	28	26	0	147.1	149	55	79	0	0	0	0	44	6	1	.136	9	22	2	1	1.2	.939
1993	**FLA**	**N**	11	12	.478	4.66	32	32	1	191	207	66	108	0	0	0	0	63	12	2	.190	8	32	4	1	1.4	.909
1994			4	4	.500	3.07	13	13	1	73.1	79	23	40	1	0	0	0	22	3	0	.136	1	6	1	0	0.6	.875
1995			9	6	.600	3.80	25	24	3	161	157	47	126	2	0	0	0	48	13	1	.271	8	21	1	2	1.2	.967
6 yrs.			38	41	.481	4.13	121	116	5	683.2	697	251	407	3	0	0	0	214	46	4	.215	32	102	12	5	1.2	.918

Granny Hamner

HAMNER, GRANVILLE WILBUR BR TR 5′10″ 163 lbs.
Brother of Garvin Hamner.
B. Apr. 26, 1927, Richmond, Va. D. Sept. 12, 1993, Philadelphia, Pa.

Year	Team	Lg	W	L	PCT	ERA	G	GS	CG	IP	H	BB	SO	ShO	Relief Pitching W	Relief L	Relief SV	Batting AB	Batting H	Batting HR	BA	PO	A	E	DP	TC/G	FA
1956	**PHI**	**N**	0	1	.000	4.32	3	1	0	8.1	10	2	4	0	0	0	0	401	90	4	.224	27	98	9	17	6.4	.933
1957			0	0	—	0.00	1	0	0	1	1	0	1	0	0	0	0	502	114	10	.227	264	291	21	55	4.4	.964
1962	**KC**	**A**	0	1	.000	9.00	3	0	0	4	10	6	0	0	0	1	0	0	0	0	—	44	79	3	11	3.5	.976
3 yrs.			0	2	.000	5.40	7	1	0	13.1	21	8	5	0	0	1	0	*				2811	4304	334	888	4.8	.955

Ralph Hamner

HAMNER, RALPH CONANT (Bruz) BR TR 6′ 3″ 165 lbs.
B. Sept. 12, 1916, Gibsland, La.

Year	Team	Lg	W	L	PCT	ERA	G	GS	CG	IP	H	BB	SO	ShO	Relief Pitching W	Relief L	Relief SV	Batting AB	Batting H	Batting HR	BA	PO	A	E	DP	TC/G	FA
1946	**CHI**	**A**	2	7	.222	4.42	25	7	1	71.1	80	39	29	0	1	1	1	18	3	0	.167	3	10	1	0	0.6	.929
1947	**CHI**	**N**	1	2	.333	2.52	3	3	2	25	24	16	14	0	0	0	0	8	1	0	.125	2	2	1	0	1.7	.800
1948			5	9	.357	4.69	27	17	5	111.1	110	69	53	0	0	1	0	33	6	1	.182	7	26	1	3	1.3	.971
1949			0	2	.000	8.76	6	1	0	12.1	22	8	3	0	0	1	0	2	0	0	.000	3	6	0	0	1.5	1.000
4 yrs.			8	20	.286	4.58	61	28	8	220	236	132	99	0	1	3	1	61	10	1	.164	15	44	3	3	1.0	.952

Mike Hampton

HAMPTON, MICHAEL WILLIAM BR TL 5′10″ 185 lbs.
B. Sept. 9, 1972, Brooksville, Fla.

Year	Team	Lg	W	L	PCT	ERA	G	GS	CG	IP	H	BB	SO	ShO	Relief Pitching W	Relief L	Relief SV	Batting AB	Batting H	Batting HR	BA	PO	A	E	DP	TC/G	FA
1993	**SEA**	**A**	1	3	.250	9.53	13	3	0	17	28	17	8	0	1	0	1	0	0	0	—	0	2	1	0	0.2	.667
1994	**HOU**	**N**	2	1	.667	3.70	44	0	0	41.1	46	16	24	0	2	1	0	1	0	0	.000	6	11	0	2	0.4	1.000
1995			9	8	.529	3.35	24	24	0	150.2	141	49	115	0	0	0	0	48	7	0	.146	10	24	3	2	1.5	.919
3 yrs.			12	12	.500	3.92	81	27	0	209	215	82	147	0	3	1	1	49	7	0	.143	16	37	4	4	0.7	.930

Garry Hancock

HANCOCK, RONALD GARRY BL TL 6′ 175 lbs.
B. Jan. 23, 1954, Tampa, Fla.

Year	Team	Lg	W	L	PCT	ERA	G	GS	CG	IP	H	BB	SO	ShO	Relief Pitching W	Relief L	Relief SV	Batting AB	Batting H	Batting HR	BA	PO	A	E	DP	TC/G	FA
1984	**OAK**	**A**	0	0	—	0.00	1	0	0	1.1	0	0	0	0	0	0	0	*				29	3	0	1	1.0	1.000

Lee Hancock

HANCOCK, LELAND DAVID BL TL 6′ 4″ 215 lbs.
B. June 27, 1967, North Hollywood, Calif.

Year	Team	Lg	W	L	PCT	ERA	G	GS	CG	IP	H	BB	SO	ShO	Relief Pitching W	Relief L	Relief SV	Batting AB	Batting H	Batting HR	BA	PO	A	E	DP	TC/G	FA
1995	**PIT**	**N**	0	0	—	1.93	11	0	0	14	10	2	6	0	0	0	0	0	0	0	—	1	1	0	1	0.2	1.000

Rich Hand

HAND, RICHARD ALLEN BR TR 6′ 1″ 185 lbs.
B. July 10, 1948, Bellevue, Wash.

Year	Team	Lg	W	L	PCT	ERA	G	GS	CG	IP	H	BB	SO	ShO	Relief W	Relief L	Relief SV	AB	H	HR	BA	PO	A	E	DP	TC/G	FA
1970	CLE	A	6	13	.316	3.83	35	25	3	160	132	69	110	1	0	1	3	41	6	0	.146	11	22	2	2	1.0	.943
1971			2	6	.250	5.75	15	12	0	61	74	38	26	0	0	1	0	16	2	0	.125	4	5	0	0	0.6	1.000
1972	TEX	A	10	14	.417	3.32	30	28	2	170.2	139	103	109	1	0	0	0	52	8	0	.154	10	25	3	2	1.3	.921
1973	2 teams	TEX A (8G 2–3) CAL A (16G 4–3)																									
″	total		6	6	.500	4.39	24	13	1	96.1	107	40	33	0	2	0	0	0	0	0		8	16	2	0	1.1	.923
4 yrs.			24	39	.381	4.00	104	78	6	488	452	250	278	2	2	2	3	109	16	0	.147	33	68	7	4	1.0	.935

Jim Handiboe

HANDIBOE, JAMES EDWARD (Nick) BR TR 5′11″ 160 lbs.
B. July 17, 1866, Columbus, Ohio D. Nov. 8, 1942, Columbus, Ohio.

Year	Team	Lg	W	L	PCT	ERA	G	GS	CG	IP	H	BB	SO	ShO	Relief W	Relief L	Relief SV	AB	H	HR	BA	PO	A	E	DP	TC/G	FA
1886	PIT	AA	7	7	.500	*3.32*	14	14	12	114	82	33	83	1	0	0	0	44	5	0	.114	5	17	6	0	1.8	.786

Vern Handrahan

HANDRAHAN, JAMES VERNON BL TR 6′ 2″ 185 lbs.
B. Nov. 27, 1938, Charlottetown, P. E. I., Canada.

Year	Team	Lg	W	L	PCT	ERA	G	GS	CG	IP	H	BB	SO	ShO	Relief W	Relief L	Relief SV	AB	H	HR	BA	PO	A	E	DP	TC/G	FA
1964	KC	A	0	1	.000	6.06	18	1	0	35.2	33	25	18	0	0	0	0	9	2	0	.222	1	6	0	1	0.4	1.000
1966			0	1	.000	4.26	16	1	0	25.1	20	15	18	0	0	0	1	3	0	0	.000	2	4	0	1	0.4	1.000
2 yrs.			0	2	.000	5.31	34	2	0	61	53	40	36	0	0	0	1	12	2	0	.167	3	10	0	2	0.4	1.000

Bill Hands

HANDS, WILLIAM ALFRED BR TR 6′ 2″ 185 lbs.
B. May 6, 1940, Hackensack, N. J.

Year	Team	Lg	W	L	PCT	ERA	G	GS	CG	IP	H	BB	SO	ShO	Relief W	Relief L	Relief SV	AB	H	HR	BA	PO	A	E	DP	TC/G	FA
1965	SF	N	0	2	.000	16.50	4	2	0	6	13	6	5	0	0	0	0	1	0	0	.000	0	2	0	0	0.5	1.000
1966	CHI	N	8	13	.381	4.58	41	26	0	159	168	59	93	0	4	0	2	49	2	0	.041	12	33	4	1	1.2	.918
1967			7	8	.467	2.46	49	11	3	150	134	48	84	1	3	6	6	38	4	0	.105	11	24	1	1	0.7	.972
1968			16	10	.615	2.89	38	34	11	258.2	221	36	148	4	0	1	0	82	5	0	.061	21	39	1	0	1.6	.984
1969			20	14	.588	2.49	41	41	18	300	268	73	181	3	0	0	0	98	9	0	.092	16	56	3	2	1.8	.960
1970			18	15	.545	3.70	39	38	12	265	278	76	170	2	0	0	1	75	10	0	.133	22	42	3	2	1.7	.955
1971			12	18	.400	3.42	36	35	14	242	248	50	128	1	0	0	0	72	6	0	.083	21	32	2	2	1.5	.964
1972			11	8	.579	2.99	32	28	6	189.1	168	47	96	3	0	1	0	57	1	0	.018	12	21	5	1	1.2	.868
1973	MIN	A	7	10	.412	3.49	39	15	3	142	138	41	78	1	2	3	2	0	0	0	—	4	20	2	2	0.7	.923
1974	2 teams	MIN A (35G 4–5) TEX A (2G 2–0)																									
″	total		6	5	.545	4.19	37	12	1	129	141	28	78	1	2	0	3	0	0	0		10	12	0	0	0.6	1.000
1975	TEX	A	6	7	.462	4.02	18	18	4	109.2	118	28	67	1	0	0	0	0	0	0	—	11	16	3	1	1.7	.900
11 yrs.			111	110	.502	3.35	374	260	72	1950.2	1895	492	1128	17	11	11	14	472	37	0	.078	140	297	24	12	1.2	.948

Chris Haney

HANEY, CHRISTOPHER DEANE BL TL 6′ 3″ 185 lbs.
Son of Larry Haney.
B. Nov. 16, 1968, Baltimore, Md.

Year	Team	Lg	W	L	PCT	ERA	G	GS	CG	IP	H	BB	SO	ShO	Relief W	Relief L	Relief SV	AB	H	HR	BA	PO	A	E	DP	TC/G	FA
1991	MON	N	3	7	.300	4.04	16	16	0	84.2	94	43	51	0	0	0	0	27	2	0	.074	6	18	2	1	1.6	.923
1992	2 teams	MON N (9G 2–3) KC A (7G 2–3)																									
″	total		4	6	.400	4.61	16	13	2	80	75	26	54	2	0	0	0	9	2	0	.222	2	6	0	0	0.5	1.000
1993	KC	A	9	9	.500	6.02	23	23	1	124	141	53	65	1	0	0	0	0	0	0	—	7	19	0	0	1.1	1.000
1994			2	2	.500	7.31	6	6	0	28.1	36	11	18	0	0	0	0	0	0	0	—	3	5	0	2	1.3	1.000
1995			3	4	.429	3.65	16	13	1	81.1	78	33	31	0	0	0	0	0	0	0	—	1	15	0	0	1.0	1.000
5 yrs.			21	28	.429	4.93	77	71	4	398.1	424	166	219	3	0	0	0	36	4	0	.111	19	63	2	3	1.1	.976

Don Hankins

HANKINS, DONALD WAYNE BR TR 6′ 3″ 183 lbs.
B. Feb. 9, 1902, Pendleton, Ind. D. May 16, 1963, Winston-Salem, N. C.

Year	Team	Lg	W	L	PCT	ERA	G	GS	CG	IP	H	BB	SO	ShO	Relief W	Relief L	Relief SV	AB	H	HR	BA	PO	A	E	DP	TC/G	FA
1927	DET	A	2	1	.667	6.48	20	1	0	41.2	67	13	10	0	2	0	2	7	1	0	.143	4	10	0	0	0.7	1.000

Frank Hankinson

HANKINSON, FRANK EDWARD BR TR 5′11″ 168 lbs.
B. Apr. 29, 1856, New York, N. Y. D. Apr. 5, 1911, Palisades Park, N. J.

Year	Team	Lg	W	L	PCT	ERA	G	GS	CG	IP	H	BB	SO	ShO	Relief W	Relief L	Relief SV	AB	H	HR	BA	PO	A	E	DP	TC/G	FA
1878	CHI	N	0	1	.000	6.00	1	1	1	9	11	0	4	0	0	0	0	240	64	1	.267	95	138	33	9	4.6	.876
1879			15	10	.600	2.50	26	25	25	230.2	248	27	69	2	1	0	0	171	31	0	.181	42	87	14	1	3.2	.902
1880	CLE	N	1	1	.500	1.08	4	2	2	25	20	3	8	0	0	0	1	263	55	1	.209	79	101	29	7	2.9	.861
1885	NY	AA	0	0	—	4.50	1	0	0	2	2	1	0	0	0	0	0	362	81	2	.224	152	170	34	22	4.2	.904
4 yrs.			16	12	.571	2.50	32	28	28	266.2	281	31	81	2	1	0	1	*				1146	1732	393	129	3.8	.880

Jim Hanley

HANLEY, JAMES PATRICK BR TL 5′11″ 165 lbs.
B. Oct. 13, 1885, Providence, R. I. D. May 1, 1961, Elmhurst, N. Y.

Year	Team	Lg	W	L	PCT	ERA	G	GS	CG	IP	H	BB	SO	ShO	Relief W	Relief L	Relief SV	AB	H	HR	BA	PO	A	E	DP	TC/G	FA
1913	NY	A	0	0	—	6.75	1	0	0	4	5	4	2	0	0	0	0	1	0	0	.000	2	0	0	0	2.0	1.000

Preston Hanna

HANNA, PRESTON LEE BR TR 6′ 1″ 195 lbs.
B. Sept. 10, 1954, Pensacola, Fla.

Year	Team	Lg	W	L	PCT	ERA	G	GS	CG	IP	H	BB	SO	ShO	Relief W	Relief L	Relief SV	AB	H	HR	BA	PO	A	E	DP	TC/G	FA
1975	ATL	N	0	0	—	1.50	4	0	0	6	7	5	2	0	0	0	0	0	0	0	—	0	0	0	0	0.0	.000
1976			0	0	—	4.50	5	0	0	8	11	4	3	0	0	0	0	1	0	0	.000	1	0	0	0	0.2	1.000
1977			2	6	.250	4.95	17	9	1	60	69	34	37	0	0	0	1	14	1	0	.071	2	18	3	0	1.4	.870
1978			7	13	.350	5.14	29	28	0	140	132	93	90	0	0	0	0	49	9	1	.184	10	18	0	1	1.0	1.000
1979			1	1	.500	3.00	6	4	0	24	27	15	15	0	0	0	0	6	0	0	.000	0	8	0	1	1.3	1.000
1980			2	0	1.000	3.19	32	2	0	79	63	44	35	0	1	0	0	14	2	0	.143	6	8	0	0	0.4	1.000
1981			2	1	.667	6.43	20	1	0	35	45	23	22	0	2	0	0	4	1	0	.250	3	12	0	2	0.8	1.000
1982	2 teams	ATL N (20G 3–0) OAK A (23G 0–4)																									
″	total		3	4	.429	4.80	43	3	1	84.1	90	61	49	0	3	2	0	5	2	0	.400	2	8	1	1	0.3	.909
8 yrs.			17	25	.405	4.62	156	47	2	436.1	444	279	253	0	6	2	1	93	15	1	.161	24	72	4	5	0.6	.960

Gerald Hannahs

HANNAHS, GERALD ELLIS BL TL 6′ 3″ 210 lbs.
B. Mar. 6, 1953, Binghamton, N. Y.

Year	Team	Lg	W	L	PCT	ERA	G	GS	CG	IP	H	BB	SO	ShO	Relief W	Relief L	Relief SV	AB	H	HR	BA	PO	A	E	DP	TC/G	FA
1976	MON	N	2	0	1.000	6.75	3	3	0	16	20	12	10	0	0	0	0	8	3	0	.375	0	2	0	0	0.7	1.000
1977			1	5	.167	4.86	8	7	0	37	43	17	21	0	0	0	0	7	0	0	.000	1	6	2	0	1.1	.778
1978	LA	N	0	0	—	9.00	1	0	0	2	3	0	5	0	0	0	0	0	0	0	—	0	0	0	0	0.0	.000
1979			0	2	.000	3.38	4	2	0	16	10	13	6	0	0	0	1	4	1	0	.250	0	3	0	0	0.8	1.000
4 yrs.			3	7	.300	5.07	16	12	0	71	76	42	42	0	0	0	1	19	4	0	.211	1	11	2	0	0.9	.857

Jim Hannan

HANNAN, JAMES JOHN BR TR 6′ 3″ 205 lbs.
B. Jan. 7, 1940, Jersey City, N. J.

Year	Team	Lg	W	L	PCT	ERA	G	GS	CG	IP	H	BB	SO	ShO	Relief Pitching W	Relief L	Relief SV	Batting AB	Batting H	HR	BA	PO	A	E	DP	TC/G	FA
1962	WAS	A	2	4	.333	3.31	42	3	0	68	56	49	39	0	1	2	4	11	1	0	.091	5	12	1	0	0.4	.944
1963			2	2	.500	4.88	13	2	0	27.2	23	17	14	0	1	1	0	6	0	0	.000	1	7	1	0	0.7	.889
1964			4	7	.364	4.16	49	7	0	106	108	45	67	0	4	2	3	20	3	0	.150	4	15	0	0	0.4	1.000
1965			1	1	.500	4.91	4	1	1	14.2	18	6	5	1	0	1	0	3	0	0	.000	1	0	0	0	0.3	1.000
1966			3	9	.250	4.26	30	18	2	114	125	59	68	0	0	1	0	30	2	0	.067	7	18	1	0	0.9	.962
1967			1	1	.500	5.40	8	2	0	21.2	28	7	14	0	1	0	0	4	0	0	.000	2	4	1	0	0.9	.857
1968			10	6	.625	3.01	25	22	4	140.1	147	50	75	1	0	0	0	47	3	0	.064	8	20	1	2	1.2	.966
1969			7	6	.538	3.64	35	28	1	158.1	138	91	72	1	0	0	0	52	6	0	.115	11	21	0	2	0.9	1.000
1970			9	11	.450	4.01	42	17	1	128	119	54	61	1	4	3	0	31	4	0	.129	7	25	1	0	0.8	.970
1971	2 teams	DET A (7G 1–0) MIL A (21G 1–1)																									
″	total		2	1	.667	4.57	28	1	0	43.1	45	28	23	0	2	0	0	5	0	0	.000	4	8	1	1	0.5	.923
10 yrs.			41	48	.461	3.88	276	101	9	822	807	406	438	4	13	10	7	209	19	0	.091	50	130	7	5	0.7	.963

Loy Hanning

HANNING, LOY VERNON BR TR 6′ 2″ 175 lbs.
B. Oct. 18, 1917, Bunker, Mo. D. June 24, 1986, Anaconda, Mo.

Year	Team	Lg	W	L	PCT	ERA	G	GS	CG	IP	H	BB	SO	ShO	Relief Pitching W	Relief L	Relief SV	Batting AB	Batting H	HR	BA	PO	A	E	DP	TC/G	FA
1939	STL	A	0	1	.000	3.60	4	1	0	10	6	4	8	0	0	0	0	1	0	0	.000	1	1	0	0	0.5	1.000
1942			1	1	.500	7.79	11	0	0	17.1	26	12	9	0	1	1	0	4	1	0	.250	0	6	0	1	0.5	1.000
2 yrs.			1	2	.333	6.26	15	1	0	27.1	32	16	17	0	1	1	0	5	1	0	.200	1	7	0	1	0.5	1.000

Greg Hansell

HANSELL, GREGORY MICHAEL BR TR 6′ 5″ 213 lbs.
B. Mar. 12, 1971, Bellflower, Calif.

Year	Team	Lg	W	L	PCT	ERA	G	GS	CG	IP	H	BB	SO	ShO	Relief Pitching W	Relief L	Relief SV	Batting AB	Batting H	HR	BA	PO	A	E	DP	TC/G	FA
1995	LA	N	0	1	.000	7.45	20	0	0	19.1	29	6	13	0	0	1	0	0	0	0	—	2	1	0	0	0.2	1.000

Andy Hansen

HANSEN, ANDREW VIGGO (Swede) BR TR 6′ 3″ 185 lbs.
B. Nov. 12, 1924, Lake Worth, Fla.

Year	Team	Lg	W	L	PCT	ERA	G	GS	CG	IP	H	BB	SO	ShO	Relief Pitching W	Relief L	Relief SV	Batting AB	Batting H	HR	BA	PO	A	E	DP	TC/G	FA
1944	NY	N	3	3	.500	6.49	23	4	0	52.2	63	32	15	0	3	0	1	12	2	0	.167	4	14	0	2	0.8	1.000
1945			4	3	.571	4.66	23	13	4	92.2	98	28	37	0	0	0	3	25	0	0	.000	2	26	0	1	1.2	1.000
1947			1	5	.167	4.37	27	9	1	82.1	78	38	18	0	0	1	0	21	4	0	.190	7	18	0	1	0.9	1.000
1948			5	3	.625	2.97	36	9	3	100	96	36	27	0	2	0	1	20	1	0	.050	7	13	0	0	0.6	1.000
1949			2	6	.250	4.61	33	2	0	66.1	58	28	26	0	2	5	1	12	0	0	.000	6	11	0	2	0.5	1.000
1950			0	1	.000	5.53	31	1	0	57	64	26	19	0	0	0	3	7	0	0	.000	6	8	0	1	0.5	1.000
1951	PHI	N	3	1	.750	2.54	24	0	0	39	34	7	11	0	3	1	0	3	1	0	.333	5	10	0	1	0.6	1.000
1952			5	6	.455	3.26	43	0	0	77.1	76	27	18	0	5	6	4	11	2	0	.182	6	19	1	2	0.6	.962
1953			0	2	.000	4.03	30	1	0	51.1	60	24	17	0	0	1	3	7	2	0	.286	4	11	1	2	0.5	.938
9 yrs.			23	30	.434	4.22	270	39	8	618.2	627	246	188	0	15	14	16	118	12	0	.102	47	130	2	12	0.7	.989

Roy Hansen

HANSEN, ROY INGLOF (Ing) BR TR 6′ 165 lbs.
B. Mar. 6, 1898, Beloit, Wis. D. Feb. 9, 1977, Beloit, Wis.

Year	Team	Lg	W	L	PCT	ERA	G	GS	CG	IP	H	BB	SO	ShO	Relief Pitching W	Relief L	Relief SV	Batting AB	Batting H	HR	BA	PO	A	E	DP	TC/G	FA
1918	WAS	A	1	0	1.000	3.00	5	0	0	9	10	3	2	0	1	0	0	0	0	0	—	0	4	0	0	0.8	1.000

Snipe Hansen

HANSEN, ROY EMIL FREDERICK BB TL 6′ 3″ 195 lbs.
B. Feb. 21, 1907, Chicago, Ill. D. Sept. 11, 1978, Chicago, Ill. BL 1930

Year	Team	Lg	W	L	PCT	ERA	G	GS	CG	IP	H	BB	SO	ShO	Relief Pitching W	Relief L	Relief SV	Batting AB	Batting H	HR	BA	PO	A	E	DP	TC/G	FA
1930	PHI	N	0	7	.000	6.72	22	9	1	84.1	123	38	25	0	0	1	0	27	3	0	.111	2	16	2	0	0.9	.900
1932			10	10	.500	3.72	39	23	5	191	215	51	56	0	0	0	2	63	8	0	.127	9	32	1	0	1.1	.976
1933			6	14	.300	4.44	32	22	8	168.1	199	30	47	0	0	1	1	58	9	0	.155	5	34	4	1	1.3	.907
1934			6	12	.333	5.42	50	16	5	151	194	61	40	2	2	4	3	43	10	0	.233	2	39	0	3	0.8	1.000
1935	2 teams	PHI N (2G 0–1) STL A (10G 0–1)																									
″	total		0	2	.000	9.29	12	1	0	31	52	14	8	0	0	1	0	9	1	0	.111	0	5	1	0	0.5	.833
5 yrs.			22	45	.328	5.01	155	71	19	625.2	783	194	176	2	2	7	6	200	31	0	.155	18	126	8	4	1.0	.947

F. C. Hansford

HANSFORD, F. C. TL 6′ 180 lbs.
Deceased.

Year	Team	Lg	W	L	PCT	ERA	G	GS	CG	IP	H	BB	SO	ShO	Relief Pitching W	Relief L	Relief SV	Batting AB	Batting H	HR	BA	PO	A	E	DP	TC/G	FA
1898	BKN	N	0	0	—	3.86	1	0	0	7	10	5	0	0	0	0	0	3	0	0	.000	0	0	0	0	0.0	.000

Don Hanski

HANSKI, DONALD THOMAS BL TL 5′11″ 180 lbs.
Born Donald Thomas Hanyzewski.
B. Feb. 27, 1916, LaPorte, Ind. D. Sept. 2, 1957, Worth, Ill.

Year	Team	Lg	W	L	PCT	ERA	G	GS	CG	IP	H	BB	SO	ShO	Relief Pitching W	Relief L	Relief SV	Batting AB	Batting H	HR	BA	PO	A	E	DP	TC/G	FA
1943	CHI	A	0	0	—	0.00	1	0	0	1	1	1	0	0	0	0	0	21	5	0	.238	37	3	2	5	7.0	.952
1944			0	0	—	12.00	2	0	0	3	5	2	0	0	0	0	0	1	0	0	.000	0	0	0	0	0.0	.000
2 yrs.			0	0		9.00	3	0	0	4	6	3	0	0	0	0	0	*				37	3	2	5	5.3	.952

Erik Hanson

HANSON, ERIK BRIAN BR TR 6′ 6″ 210 lbs.
B. May 18, 1965, Kinnelon, N. J.

Year	Team	Lg	W	L	PCT	ERA	G	GS	CG	IP	H	BB	SO	ShO	Relief Pitching W	Relief L	Relief SV	Batting AB	Batting H	HR	BA	PO	A	E	DP	TC/G	FA
1988	SEA	A	2	3	.400	3.24	6	6	0	41.2	35	12	36	0	0	0	0	0	0	0	—	0	4	0	1	0.7	1.000
1989			9	5	.643	3.18	17	17	1	113.1	103	32	75	0	0	0	0	0	0	0	—	8	16	0	0	1.4	1.000
1990			18	9	.667	3.24	33	33	5	236	205	68	211	1	0	0	0	0	0	0	—	30	20	4	0	1.6	.926
1991			8	8	.500	3.81	27	27	2	174.2	182	56	143	1	0	0	0	0	0	0	—	14	16	1	0	1.1	.968
1992			8	**17**	.320	4.82	31	30	6	186.2	209	57	112	1	1	0	0	0	0	0	—	14	23	1	2	1.2	.974
1993			11	12	.478	3.47	31	30	7	215	215	60	163	0	0	1	0	0	0	0	—	25	25	3	3	1.7	.943
1994	CIN	N	5	5	.500	4.11	22	21	0	122.2	137	23	101	0	0	0	0	39	6	0	.154	11	16	0	0	1.2	1.000
1995	BOS	A	15	5	.750	4.24	29	29	1	186.2	187	59	139	1	0	0	0	0	0	0	—	17	21	2	1	1.4	.950
8 yrs.			76	64	.543	3.81	196	193	22	1276.2	1273	367	980	4	1	1	0	39	6	0	.154	119	141	11	7	1.4	.959
DIVISIONAL PLAYOFF SERIES																											
1995	BOS	A	0	1	.000	4.50	1	1	1	8	4	4	5	0	0	0	0	0	0	0	—	1	3	0	0	4.0	1.000

Ollie Hanson

HANSON, EARL SYLVESTER BR TR 5′11″ 178 lbs.
B. Jan. 19, 1896, Holbrook, Mass. D. Aug. 19, 1951, Clifton, N. J.

Year	Team	Lg	W	L	PCT	ERA	G	GS	CG	IP	H	BB	SO	ShO	Relief Pitching W	Relief L	Relief SV	Batting AB	Batting H	HR	BA	PO	A	E	DP	TC/G	FA
1921	CHI	N	0	2	.000	7.00	2	2	1	9	9	6	2	0	0	0	0	3	0	0	.000	0	4	0	0	2.0	1.000

Ed Hanyzewski

HANYZEWSKI, EDWARD MICHAEL BR TR 6′ 1″ 200 lbs.
B. Sept. 18, 1920, Union Mills, Ind. D. Oct. 8, 1991, Fargo, N. D.

Year	Team	Lg	W	L	PCT	ERA	G	GS	CG	IP	H	BB	SO	ShO	Relief Pitching W	Relief L	Relief SV	Batting AB	Batting H	HR	BA	PO	A	E	DP	TC/G	FA
1942	CHI	N	1	1	.500	3.79	6	1	0	19	17	8	6	0	1	0	0	5	1	0	.200	1	5	0	0	1.0	1.000
1943			8	7	.533	2.56	33	16	3	130	120	45	55	0	4	0	0	41	2	0	.049	10	33	1	1	1.3	.977

Ed Hanyzewski *continued*

Year	Team	W	L	PCT	ERA	G	GS	CG	IP	H	BB	SO	ShO	Relief W	Relief L	Relief SV	Batting AB	Batting H	HR	BA	PO	A	E	DP	TC/G	FA
1944		2	5	.286	4.47	14	7	3	58.1	61	20	19	0	0	1	0	17	1	0	.059	2	26	0	1	2.0	1.000
1945		0	0	—	5.79	2	1	0	4.2	7	1	0	0	0	0	0	1	0	0	.000	0	2	1	0	1.5	.667
1946		1	0	1.000	4.50	3	0	0	6	8	5	1	0	1	0	0	1	0	0	.000	2	1	0	0	1.0	1.000
5 yrs.		12	13	.480	3.30	58	25	6	218	213	79	81	0	6	1	0	65	4	0	.062	15	67	2	2	1.4	.976

Mel Harder

HARDER, MELVIN LeROY (Chief, Wimpy) BR TR 6′ 1″ 195 lbs.
B. Oct. 15, 1909, Beemer, Neb.
Manager 1961–62.

Year	Team	W	L	PCT	ERA	G	GS	CG	IP	H	BB	SO	ShO	Relief W	Relief L	Relief SV	Batting AB	Batting H	HR	BA	PO	A	E	DP	TC/G	FA
1928	CLE A	0	2	.000	6.61	23	1	0	49	64	32	15	0	0	1	1	8	0	0	.000	0	8	2	0	0.4	.800
1929		1	0	1.000	5.60	11	0	0	17.2	24	5	4	0	1	0	0	1	0	0	.000	0	3	1	0	0.4	.750
1930		11	10	.524	4.21	36	19	7	175.1	205	68	44	0	3	3	2	63	9	0	.143	9	32	7	3	1.3	.854
1931		13	14	.481	4.36	40	24	9	194	229	72	63	0	3	2	1	75	19	0	.253	14	38	4	4	1.4	.929
1932		15	13	.536	3.75	39	32	17	254.2	277	68	90	1	0	2	0	94	17	0	.181	18	65	2	0	2.2	.976
1933		15	17	.469	2.95	43	31	14	253	254	67	81	2	3	1	4	84	16	1	.190	22	87	3	4	2.6	.973
1934		20	12	.625	2.61	44	29	17	255.1	246	81	91	**6**	4	2	4	87	14	0	.161	10	61	7	2	1.8	.910
1935		22	11	.667	3.29	42	35	17	287.1	313	53	95	4	2	0	2	102	21	2	.206	18	81	4	0	2.5	.961
1936		15	15	.500	5.17	36	30	13	224.2	294	71	84	0	3	0	1	80	11	0	.138	13	38	3	3	1.5	.944
1937		15	12	.556	4.28	38	30	13	233.2	269	86	95	0	2	2	2	86	15	0	.174	12	48	1	3	1.6	.984
1938		17	10	.630	3.83	38	29	15	240	257	62	102	2	1	0	4	88	10	0	.114	21	49	1	2	1.9	.986
1939		15	9	.625	3.50	29	26	12	208	213	64	67	1	0	1	1	72	10	1	.139	14	26	1	1	1.4	.976
1940		12	11	.522	4.06	31	25	5	186.1	200	59	76	0	1	1	0	62	11	0	.177	9	38	2	4	1.6	.959
1941		5	4	.556	5.24	15	10	1	68.2	76	37	21	0	0	0	1	25	2	0	.080	7	16	1	0	1.6	.958
1942		13	14	.481	3.44	29	29	13	198.2	179	82	74	4	0	0	0	67	8	0	.119	14	44	3	5	2.1	.951
1943		8	7	.533	3.06	19	18	6	135.1	126	61	40	1	0	0	0	47	10	0	.213	6	27	0	2	1.7	1.000
1944		12	10	.545	3.71	30	27	12	196.1	211	69	64	2	0	0	0	74	16	0	.216	11	34	2	3	1.6	.957
1945		3	7	.300	3.67	11	11	2	76	93	23	16	0	0	0	0	25	2	0	.080	6	19	0	1	2.3	1.000
1946		5	4	.556	3.41	13	12	4	92.1	85	31	21	1	0	1	0	35	3	0	.086	5	9	0	1	1.1	1.000
1947		6	4	.600	4.50	15	15	4	80	91	27	17	1	0	0	0	28	5	0	.179	0	11	1	0	0.8	.917
20 yrs.		223	186	.545	3.80	582	433	181	3426.1	3706	1118	1160	25	23	16	23	1203	199	4	.165	209	734	45	38	1.7	.954

Jim Hardin

HARDIN, JAMES WARREN BR TR 6′ 175 lbs.
B. Aug. 6, 1943, Morris Chapel, Tenn. D. Mar. 9, 1991, Key West, Fla.

Year	Team	W	L	PCT	ERA	G	GS	CG	IP	H	BB	SO	ShO	Relief W	Relief L	Relief SV	Batting AB	Batting H	HR	BA	PO	A	E	DP	TC/G	FA
1967	BAL A	8	3	.727	2.27	19	14	5	111	85	27	64	2	0	0	0	37	5	0	.135	13	9	0	1	1.2	1.000
1968		18	13	.581	2.51	35	35	16	244	188	70	160	2	0	0	0	82	7	0	.085	19	32	1	2	1.5	.981
1969		6	7	.462	3.60	30	20	3	137.2	128	43	64	1	1	1	1	45	7	2	.156	12	16	2	1	1.0	.933
1970		6	5	.545	3.54	36	19	3	145	150	26	78	2	3	0	1	45	3	0	.067	9	14	0	0	0.6	1.000
1971	2 teams BAL A (6G 0–0) NY A (12G 0–2)																									
"	total	0	2	.000	5.03	18	3	0	34	47	12	17	0	0	1	0	4	0	0	.000	4	4	0	0	0.4	1.000
1972	ATL N	5	2	.714	4.39	26	9	1	80	93	24	25	0	2	0	2	21	2	1	.095	3	10	0	1	0.5	1.000
6 yrs.		43	32	.573	3.18	164	100	28	751.2	691	202	408	7	6	2	4	234	24	3	.103	60	85	3	5	0.9	.980

Charlie Harding

HARDING, CHARLES HAROLD (Slim) BR TR 6′ 2½″ 172 lbs.
B. Jan. 3, 1891, Nashville, Tenn. D. Oct. 30, 1971, Bold Springs, Tenn.

Year	Team	W	L	PCT	ERA	G	GS	CG	IP	H	BB	SO	ShO	Relief W	Relief L	Relief SV	Batting AB	Batting H	HR	BA	PO	A	E	DP	TC/G	FA
1913	DET A	0	0	—	4.50	1	0	0	2	3	1	0	0	0	0	0	0	0	0	—	0	1	0	0	1.0	1.000

Alex Hardy

HARDY, DAVID ALEXANDER TL
B. Sept. 29, 1877, Toronto, Ont., Canada D. Apr. 22, 1940, Toronto, Ont., Canada.

Year	Team	W	L	PCT	ERA	G	GS	CG	IP	H	BB	SO	ShO	Relief W	Relief L	Relief SV	Batting AB	Batting H	HR	BA	PO	A	E	DP	TC/G	FA
1902	CHI N	2	2	.500	3.60	4	4	4	35	29	12	12	1	0	0	0	14	3	0	.214	1	6	1	0	2.0	.875
1903		2	1	.667	6.39	3	3	1	12.2	21	7	4	0	0	0	0	6	1	0	.167	0	6	0	0	2.0	1.000
2 yrs.		4	3	.571	4.34	7	7	5	47.2	50	19	16	1	0	0	0	20	4	0	.200	1	12	1	0	2.0	.929

Harry Hardy

HARDY, HARRY BL TL 5′ 6″ 155 lbs.
B. Nov. 5, 1875, Steubenville, Ohio D. Sept. 4, 1943, Steubenville, Ohio.

Year	Team	W	L	PCT	ERA	G	GS	CG	IP	H	BB	SO	ShO	Relief W	Relief L	Relief SV	Batting AB	Batting H	HR	BA	PO	A	E	DP	TC/G	FA
1905	WAS A	1	1	.500	1.88	3	2	2	24	20	6	10	0	0	0	0	9	1	0	.111	0	1	0	0	0.3	1.000
1906		0	3	.000	9.00	5	3	2	20	35	12	4	0	0	0	0	6	0	0	.000	2	11	0	0	2.6	1.000
2 yrs.		1	4	.200	5.11	8	5	4	44	55	18	14	0	0	0	0	15	1	0	.067	2	12	0	0	1.8	1.000

Jack Hardy

HARDY, JOHN GRAYDON BR TR 6′ 2″ 175 lbs.
B. Dec. 8, 1959, St. Petersburg, Fla.

Year	Team	W	L	PCT	ERA	G	GS	CG	IP	H	BB	SO	ShO	Relief W	Relief L	Relief SV	Batting AB	Batting H	HR	BA	PO	A	E	DP	TC/G	FA
1989	CHI A	0	0	—	6.57	5	0	0	12.1	14	5	4	0	0	0	0	0	0	0	—	3	4	0	1	1.4	1.000

Larry Hardy

HARDY, HOWARD LAWRENCE BR TR 5′10″ 180 lbs.
B. Jan. 10, 1948, Goose Creek, Tex.

Year	Team	W	L	PCT	ERA	G	GS	CG	IP	H	BB	SO	ShO	Relief W	Relief L	Relief SV	Batting AB	Batting H	HR	BA	PO	A	E	DP	TC/G	FA
1974	SD N	9	4	.692	4.68	76	1	0	102	129	44	57	0	9	3	2	10	0	0	.000	6	22	2	2	0.4	.933
1975		0	0	—	12.00	3	0	0	3	8	2	3	0	0	0	0	0	0	0	—	0	0	1	0	0.3	.000
1976	HOU N	0	0	—	6.95	15	0	0	22	34	10	10	0	0	0	3	2	0	0	.000	0	4	0	1	0.3	1.000
3 yrs.		9	4	.692	5.24	94	1	0	127	171	56	70	0	9	3	5	12	0	0	.000	6	26	3	3	0.4	.914

Red Hardy

HARDY, FRANCIS JOSEPH BR TR 5′11″ 175 lbs.
B. Jan. 6, 1923, Marmarth, N. D.

Year	Team	W	L	PCT	ERA	G	GS	CG	IP	H	BB	SO	ShO	Relief W	Relief L	Relief SV	Batting AB	Batting H	HR	BA	PO	A	E	DP	TC/G	FA
1951	NY N	0	0	—	6.75	2	0	0	1.1	4	1	0	0	0	0	0	0	0	0	—	0	1	0	0	0.5	1.000

Steve Hargan

HARGAN, STEVEN LOWELL BR TR 6′ 3″ 170 lbs.
B. Sept. 8, 1942, Fort Wayne, Ind.

Year	Team	W	L	PCT	ERA	G	GS	CG	IP	H	BB	SO	ShO	Relief W	Relief L	Relief SV	Batting AB	Batting H	HR	BA	PO	A	E	DP	TC/G	FA
1965	CLE A	4	3	.571	3.43	17	8	1	60.1	55	28	37	0	2	0	2	19	1	0	.053	5	12	2	0	1.1	.895
1966		13	10	.565	2.48	38	21	7	192	173	45	132	3	2	2	0	58	7	0	.121	9	35	3	0	1.2	.936
1967		14	13	.519	2.62	30	29	15	223	180	72	141	**6**	0	1	0	67	11	1	.164	21	37	3	6	2.0	.951
1968		8	15	.348	4.15	32	27	4	158.1	139	81	78	2	1	1	0	51	9	0	.176	14	16	3	1	1.0	.909
1969		5	14	.263	5.70	32	23	1	143.2	145	81	76	1	0	1	0	44	7	0	.159	13	26	1	4	1.3	.975
1970		11	3	.786	2.90	23	19	8	143	101	53	72	1	0	0	0	45	5	0	.111	13	24	0	3	1.6	1.000
1971		1	13	.071	6.21	37	16	1	113	138	56	52	0	0	1	1	32	2	0	.063	7	12	1	0	0.5	.950
1972		0	3	.000	5.85	12	1	0	20	23	15	10	0	0	2	0	3	0	0	.000	3	5	0	2	0.7	1.000

Steve Hargan *continued*

Year	Team		W	L	PCT	ERA	G	GS	CG	IP	H	BB	SO	ShO	Relief Pitching W	L	SV	Batting AB	H	HR	BA	PO	A	E	DP	TC/G	FA
1974	TEX	A	12	9	.571	3.95	37	27	8	187	202	48	98	2	1	0	0	0	0	0	—	16	33	5	3	1.5	.907
1975			9	10	.474	3.80	33	26	8	189.1	203	62	93	1	1	0	0	0	0	0	—	19	36	5	4	1.8	.917
1976			8	8	.500	3.63	35	8	2	124	127	38	63	1	4	4	1	0	0	0	—	6	18	2	1	0.7	.923
1977	3 teams	TOR A	(6G 1–3)		TEX A	(6G 1–0)		ATL N	(16G 0–3)																		
″	total		2	6	.250	6.52	28	10	1	78.2	107	35	39	0	2	2	0	6	0	0	.000	4	18	2	1	0.9	.917
12 yrs.			87	107	.448	3.92	354	215	56	1632.1	1593	614	891	17	13	14	4	325	42	1	.129	130	272	27	25	1.2	.937

Alan Hargesheimer

HARGESHEIMER, ALAN ROBERT BR TR 6′ 3″ 195 lbs.
B. Nov. 21, 1956, Chicago, Ill.

Year	Team		W	L	PCT	ERA	G	GS	CG	IP	H	BB	SO	ShO	Relief W	L	SV	AB	H	HR	BA	PO	A	E	DP	TC/G	FA
1980	SF	N	4	6	.400	4.32	15	13	0	75	82	32	40	0	0	0	0	22	4	0	.182	2	10	0	0	0.8	1.000
1981			1	2	.333	4.26	6	3	0	19	20	9	6	0	0	0	0	5	1	0	.200	2	5	0	0	1.2	1.000
1983	CHI	N	0	0	—	9.00	5	0	0	4	6	2	5	0	0	0	0	0	0	0	—	0	0	0	0	0.0	.000
1986	KC	A	0	1	.000	6.23	5	1	0	13	18	7	4	0	0	1	0	0	0	0	—	0	1	0	0	0.2	1.000
4 yrs.			5	9	.357	4.70	31	17	0	111	126	50	55	0	0	1	0	27	5	0	.185	4	16	0	0	0.6	1.000

Tim Harikkala

HARIKKALA, TIMOTHY ALLAN BR TR 6′ 2″ 185 lbs.
B. July 15, 1971, West Palm Beach, Fla.

Year	Team		W	L	PCT	ERA	G	GS	CG	IP	H	BB	SO	ShO	Relief W	L	SV	AB	H	HR	BA	PO	A	E	DP	TC/G	FA
1995	SEA	A	0	0	—	16.20	1	0	0	3.1	7	1	1	0	0	0	0	0	0	0	—	0	0	0	0	0.0	.000

Mike Harkey

HARKEY, MICHAEL ANTHONY BR TR 6′ 5″ 220 lbs.
B. Oct. 25, 1966, San Diego, Calif.

Year	Team		W	L	PCT	ERA	G	GS	CG	IP	H	BB	SO	ShO	Relief W	L	SV	AB	H	HR	BA	PO	A	E	DP	TC/G	FA
1988	CHI	N	0	3	.000	2.60	5	5	0	34.2	33	15	18	0	0	0	0	11	1	0	.091	2	3	2	0	1.4	.714
1990			12	6	.667	3.26	27	27	2	173.2	153	59	94	1	0	0	0	56	14	0	.250	19	16	1	0	1.3	.972
1991			0	2	.000	5.30	4	4	0	18.2	21	6	15	0	0	0	0	5	2	0	.400	1	3	0	0	1.0	1.000
1992			4	0	1.000	1.89	7	7	0	38	34	15	21	0	0	0	0	15	4	0	.267	1	6	0	1	1.0	1.000
1993			10	10	.500	5.26	28	28	1	157.1	187	43	67	0	0	0	0	54	5	0	.093	9	20	5	2	1.2	.853
1994	CLR	N	1	6	.143	5.79	24	13	0	91.2	125	35	39	0	1	0	0	22	4	0	.182	10	15	0	3	1.0	1.000
1995	2 teams	OAK A	(14G 4–6)		CAL A	(12G 4–3)																					
″	total		8	9	.471	5.44	26	20	1	127.1	155	47	56	0	1	1	0	0	0	0	—	7	17	0	2	0.9	1.000
7 yrs.			35	36	.493	4.49	121	104	4	641.1	708	220	310	1	2	1	0	163	30	0	.184	49	80	8	8	1.1	.942

John Harkins

HARKINS, JOHN JOSEPH (Pa) BR TR 6′ 1″ 205 lbs.
B. Apr. 12, 1859, New Brunswick, N. J. D. Nov. 18, 1940, New Brunswick, N. J.

Year	Team		W	L	PCT	ERA	G	GS	CG	IP	H	BB	SO	ShO	Relief W	L	SV	AB	H	HR	BA	PO	A	E	DP	TC/G	FA
1884	CLE	N	12	**32**	.273	*3.68*	46	45	42	391	399	108	192	3	0	0	0	229	47	0	.205	43	85	25	3	2.4	.837
1885	BKN	AA	14	20	.412	*3.75*	34	34	33	293	303	56	141	1	0	0	0	159	42	1	.264	45	63	21	0	2.9	.837
1886			15	16	.484	*3.60*	34	33	33	292.1	286	114	118	0	0	0	0	142	32	1	.225	29	61	11	2	2.4	.891
1887			10	14	.417	*6.02*	24	24	22	199	262	77	36	0	0	0	0	98	23	0	.235	13	37	6	2	1.9	.893
1888	BAL	AA	0	1	.000	6.75	1	1	1	8	12	3	2	0	0	0	0	3	0	0	.000	0	4	0	0	4.0	1.000
5 yrs.			51	83	.381	4.09	139	137	131	1183.1	1262	358	489	4	0	0	0	*				130	250	63	7	2.4	.858

Specs Harkness

HARKNESS, FREDERICK HARVEY BR TR 5′11″ 180 lbs.
B. Dec. 13, 1887, Los Angeles, Calif. D. May 18, 1952, Compton, Calif.

Year	Team		W	L	PCT	ERA	G	GS	CG	IP	H	BB	SO	ShO	Relief W	L	SV	AB	H	HR	BA	PO	A	E	DP	TC/G	FA
1910	CLE	A	10	7	.588	3.04	26	16	6	136.1	132	55	60	1	5	0	1	50	7	0	.140	5	39	2	1	1.8	.957
1911			2	2	.500	4.30	12	6	3	52.1	62	21	25	0	0	0	0	19	6	0	.316	0	6	0	0	0.5	1.000
2 yrs.			12	9	.571	3.39	38	22	9	188.2	194	76	85	1	5	0	1	69	13	0	.188	5	45	2	1	1.4	.962

Dick Harley

HARLEY, HENRY RISK BR TR
B. Aug. 18, 1874, Springfield, Ohio D. May 16, 1961, Springfield, Ohio.

Year	Team		W	L	PCT	ERA	G	GS	CG	IP	H	BB	SO	ShO	Relief W	L	SV	AB	H	HR	BA	PO	A	E	DP	TC/G	FA
1905	BOS	N	2	5	.286	4.64	9	4	4	66	72	19	19	1	0	**3**	0	22	1	0	.045	8	24	1	1	3.7	.970

Larry Harlow

HARLOW, LARRY DUANE BL TL 6′ 2″ 185 lbs.
B. Nov. 13, 1951, Colorado Springs, Colo.

Year	Team		W	L	PCT	ERA	G	GS	CG	IP	H	BB	SO	ShO	Relief W	L	SV	AB	H	HR	BA	PO	A	E	DP	TC/G	FA
1978	BAL	A	0	0	—	67.50	1	0	0	0.2	2	4	1	0	0	0	0	*				2	0	0	0	0.5	1.000

Bill Harman

HARMAN, WILLIAM BELL BR TR 6′ 4″ 200 lbs.
B. Jan. 2, 1919, Bridgewater, Va.

Year	Team		W	L	PCT	ERA	G	GS	CG	IP	H	BB	SO	ShO	Relief W	L	SV	AB	H	HR	BA	PO	A	E	DP	TC/G	FA
1941	PHI	N	0	0	—	4.85	5	0	0	13	15	8	3	0	0	0	0	*				4	4	0	0	0.8	1.000

Bob Harmon

HARMON, ROBERT GREEN (Hickory Bob) BB TR 6′ 187 lbs.
B. Oct. 15, 1887, Liberal, Mo. D. Nov. 27, 1961, Monroe, La.

Year	Team		W	L	PCT	ERA	G	GS	CG	IP	H	BB	SO	ShO	Relief W	L	SV	AB	H	HR	BA	PO	A	E	DP	TC/G	FA
1909	STL	N	6	11	.353	3.68	21	17	10	159	155	65	48	0	1	1	0	51	13	0	.255	6	45	3	1	2.6	.944
1910			13	15	.464	4.46	43	33	15	236	227	**133**	87	0	3	1	2	76	14	0	.184	11	74	7	4	2.1	.924
1911			23	16	.590	3.13	51	**41**	28	348	290	**181**	144	2	1	1	4	111	17	0	.153	11	98	3	4	2.2	.973
1912			18	18	.500	3.93	43	34	15	268	284	116	73	3	3	2	0	99	23	0	.232	11	87	3	3	2.3	.970
1913			8	21	.276	3.92	42	27	16	273.1	**291**	99	66	1	3	**6**	1	92	24	0	.261	22	75	3	3	2.4	.970
1914	PIT	N	13	17	.433	2.53	37	30	19	245	226	55	61	2	1	0	3	86	12	1	.140	11	59	1	1	1.9	.986
1915			16	17	.485	2.50	37	32	25	269.2	242	62	86	5	0	1	1	95	14	0	.147	9	92	4	2	2.8	.962
1916			8	11	.421	2.81	31	17	10	172.2	175	39	62	2	1	3	0	55	6	0	.109	4	64	2	2	2.3	.971
1918			2	7	.222	2.62	16	9	5	82.1	76	12	7	0	0	1	0	27	4	0	.148	3	26	0	2	1.8	1.000
9 yrs.			107	133	.446	3.33	321	240	143	2054	1966	762	634	15	13	16	11	692	127	1	.184	88	620	26	22	2.3	.965

Pete Harnisch

HARNISCH, PETER THOMAS BB TR 6′ 1″ 195 lbs.
B. Sept. 23, 1966, Commack, N. Y.

Year	Team		W	L	PCT	ERA	G	GS	CG	IP	H	BB	SO	ShO	Relief W	L	SV	AB	H	HR	BA	PO	A	E	DP	TC/G	FA
1988	BAL	A	0	2	.000	5.54	2	2	0	13	13	9	10	0	0	0	0	0	0	0	—	2	2	0	0	2.0	1.000
1989			5	9	.357	4.62	18	17	2	103.1	97	64	70	0	0	0	0	0	0	0	—	7	9	0	2	0.9	1.000
1990			11	11	.500	4.34	31	31	3	188.2	189	86	122	0	0	0	0	0	0	0	—	12	14	1	0	0.9	.963
1991	HOU	N	12	9	.571	2.70	33	33	4	216.2	169	83	172	2	0	0	0	62	6	0	.097	7	18	1	0	0.8	.962
1992			9	10	.474	3.70	34	34	0	206.2	182	64	164	0	0	0	0	67	11	0	.164	16	15	2	1	1.0	.939
1993			16	9	.640	2.98	33	33	5	217.2	171	79	185	**4**	0	0	0	67	7	0	.104	3	15	2	0	0.6	.900
1994			8	5	.615	5.40	17	17	1	95	100	39	62	0	0	0	0	35	6	0	.171	11	8	0	0	1.1	1.000
1995	NY	N	2	8	.200	3.68	18	18	0	110	111	24	82	0	0	0	0	33	3	0	.091	9	12	2	1	1.3	.913
8 yrs.			63	63	.500	3.72	186	185	15	1151	1032	448	867	6	0	0	0	264	33	0	.125	67	93	8	4	0.9	.952

Bill Harper

HARPER, WILLIAM HOMER (Blue Sleeve) BB TR 6′ 1″ 180 lbs.
B. June 14, 1889, Bertrand, Mo. D. June 17, 1951, Somerville, Tenn.

Year	Team		W	L	PCT	ERA	G	GS	CG	IP	H	BB	SO	ShO	Relief W	Relief L	Relief SV	Batting AB	Batting H	HR	BA	PO	A	E	DP	TC/G	FA
1911	STL	A	0	0	—	6.75	2	0	0	8	9	4	6	0	0	0	0	3	0	0	.000	0	2	0	0	1.0	1.000

George Harper

HARPER, GEORGE B. BR TR 5′10″ 165 lbs.
B. Aug. 17, 1866, Milwaukee, Wis. D. Dec. 11, 1931, Stockton, Calif.

Year	Team		W	L	PCT	ERA	G	GS	CG	IP	H	BB	SO	ShO	Relief W	Relief L	Relief SV	Batting AB	Batting H	HR	BA	PO	A	E	DP	TC/G	FA
1894	PHI	N	6	6	.500	5.32	12	9	7	86.1	128	49	24	0	1	2	0	40	6	0	.150	4	12	1	1	1.4	.941
1896	BKN	N	4	8	.333	5.55	16	11	7	86	106	39	22	0	1	1	0	37	6	0	.162	5	24	1	0	1.9	.967
2 yrs.			10	14	.417	5.43	28	20	14	172.1	234	88	46	0	2	3	0	77	12	0	.156	9	36	2	1	1.7	.957

Harry Harper

HARPER, HARRY CLAYTON BL TL 6′ 2″ 165 lbs.
B. Apr. 24, 1895, Hackensack, N. J. D. Apr. 23, 1963, Layton, N. J.

Year	Team		W	L	PCT	ERA	G	GS	CG	IP	H	BB	SO	ShO	Relief W	Relief L	Relief SV	Batting AB	Batting H	HR	BA	PO	A	E	DP	TC/G	FA
1913	WAS	A	0	0	—	3.55	4	0	0	12.2	10	5	9	0	0	0	0	4	1	0	.250	1	4	2	1	1.8	.714
1914			2	1	.667	3.47	23	3	1	57	45	35	50	0	1	0	2	12	3	0	.250	0	11	3	0	0.6	.786
1915			4	4	.500	1.77	19	10	5	86.1	66	40	54	2	0	0	2	25	0	0	.000	0	15	2	0	0.9	.882
1916			14	10	.583	2.45	36	34	12	249.2	209	101	149	2	0	0	0	87	18	0	.207	8	46	4	4	1.6	.931
1917			11	12	.478	3.01	31	31	10	179.1	145	106	99	4	0	0	0	60	7	0	.117	6	37	9	5	1.7	.827
1918			11	10	.524	2.18	35	32	14	244	182	104	78	3	0	0	1	82	11	0	.134	9	45	3	1	1.6	.947
1919			6	**21**	.222	3.72	35	30	8	208	220	97	87	0	0	0	0	65	11	0	.169	10	47	3	2	1.7	.950
1920	BOS	A	5	14	.263	3.04	27	22	11	162.2	163	66	71	1	0	0	0	50	6	0	.120	1	31	3	1	1.3	.914
1921	NY	A	4	3	.571	3.76	8	7	4	52.2	52	25	22	0	0	0	0	16	2	0	.125	5	4	0	0	1.1	1.000
1923	BKN	N	0	1	.000	14.73	1	1	0	3.2	8	3	4	0	0	0	0	1	0	0	.000	0	0	0	0	0.0	.000
10 yrs.			57	76	.429	2.87	219	170	65	1256	1100	582	623	12	1	0	5	402	59	0	.147	40	240	29	14	1.4	.906
WORLD SERIES																											
1921	NY	A	0	0	—	20.25	1	1	0	1.1	3	2	1	0	0	0	0	0	0	0	—	0	0	0	0	0.0	.000

Jack Harper

HARPER, CHARLES WILLIAM BR TR 6′ 178 lbs.
B. Apr. 2, 1878, Galloway, Pa. D. Sept. 30, 1950, Jamestown, N. Y.

Year	Team		W	L	PCT	ERA	G	GS	CG	IP	H	BB	SO	ShO	Relief W	Relief L	Relief SV	Batting AB	Batting H	HR	BA	PO	A	E	DP	TC/G	FA
1899	CLE	N	1	4	.200	3.89	5	5	5	37	44	12	14	0	0	0	0	11	2	0	.182	1	7	0	0	1.6	1.000
1900	STL	N	0	1	.000	12.00	1	1	0	3	4	2	0	0	0	0	0	1	0	0	.000	0	1	0	0	1.0	1.000
1901			23	13	.639	3.62	39	37	28	308.2	294	99	128	1	1	0	0	116	20	1	.172	13	82	4	3	2.5	.960
1902	STL	A	15	11	.577	4.13	29	26	20	222.1	224	81	74	2	1	1	0	83	17	0	.205	8	70	6	3	2.9	.929
1903	CIN	N	6	8	.429	4.33	17	15	13	135	143	70	45	0	0	**2**	0	56	14	0	.250	7	43	4	2	3.2	.926
1904			23	9	.719	2.37	35	35	31	284.2	262	85	125	6	0	0	0	113	18	0	.159	12	58	5	1	2.1	.933
1905			10	13	.435	3.87	26	23	15	179	189	69	70	1	1	0	0	60	10	0	.167	6	49	4	1	2.3	.932
1906	2 teams	CIN N (5G 1–4)	CHI N (1G 0–0)																								
″	total		1	4	.200	4.06	6	6	3	37.2	38	20	10	0	0	0	0	11	3	0	.273	2	7	1	0	1.7	.900
8 yrs.			79	63	.556	3.58	158	148	115	1207.1	1198	438	466	10	3	3	0	451	84	1	.186	49	317	24	10	2.5	.938

Jack Harper

HARPER, JOHN WESLEY BR TR 5′11″ 180 lbs.
B. Aug. 5, 1893, Hendricks, W. Va. D. June 18, 1927, Halstead, Kans.

Year	Team		W	L	PCT	ERA	G	GS	CG	IP	H	BB	SO	ShO	Relief W	Relief L	Relief SV	Batting AB	Batting H	HR	BA	PO	A	E	DP	TC/G	FA
1915	PHI	A	0	0	—	3.12	3	0	0	8.2	5	1	3	0	0	0	0	2	0	0	.000	0	4	0	0	1.3	1.000

Ray Harrell

HARRELL, RAYMOND JAMES (Cowboy) BR TR 6′ 1″ 185 lbs.
B. Feb. 16, 1912, Petrolia, Tex. D. Jan. 28, 1984, Alexandria, La.

Year	Team		W	L	PCT	ERA	G	GS	CG	IP	H	BB	SO	ShO	Relief W	Relief L	Relief SV	Batting AB	Batting H	HR	BA	PO	A	E	DP	TC/G	FA
1935	STL	N	1	1	.500	6.67	11	1	0	29.2	39	11	13	0	1	1	0	4	0	0	.000	2	5	0	0	0.6	1.000
1937			3	7	.300	5.87	35	15	1	96.2	99	59	41	1	1	0	1	22	1	0	.045	3	17	3	1	0.7	.870
1938			2	3	.400	4.86	32	3	1	63	78	29	32	0	1	3	2	10	0	0	.000	0	14	0	2	0.4	1.000
1939	2 teams	CHI N (4G 0–2)	PHI N (22G 3–7)																								
″	total		3	9	.250	5.87	26	12	4	112	127	62	40	0	1	0	0	31	3	0	.097	4	11	3	0	0.7	.833
1940	PIT	N	0	0	—	8.10	3	0	0	3.1	5	2	3	0	0	0	0	0	0	0	—	0	0	0	0	0.0	.000
1945	NY	N	0	0	—	4.97	12	0	0	25.1	34	14	7	0	0	0	0	5	1	0	.200	2	6	0	1	0.7	1.000
6 yrs.			9	20	.310	5.70	119	31	6	330	382	177	136	1	4	4	3	72	5	0	.069	11	53	6	4	0.6	.914

Slim Harrell

HARRELL, OSCAR MARTIN BR TR 6′ 3″ 180 lbs.
B. July 31, 1890, Grandview, Tex. D. Apr. 30, 1971, Hillsboro, Tex.

Year	Team		W	L	PCT	ERA	G	GS	CG	IP	H	BB	SO	ShO	Relief W	Relief L	Relief SV	Batting AB	Batting H	HR	BA	PO	A	E	DP	TC/G	FA
1912	PHI	A	0	0	—	0.00	1	0	0	3	4	0	1	0	0	0	0	1	0	0	.000	0	0	0	0	0.0	.000

Bill Harrelson

HARRELSON, WILLIAM CHARLES BB TR 6′ 5″ 215 lbs.
B. Nov. 17, 1945, Tahlequah, Okla.

Year	Team		W	L	PCT	ERA	G	GS	CG	IP	H	BB	SO	ShO	Relief W	Relief L	Relief SV	Batting AB	Batting H	HR	BA	PO	A	E	DP	TC/G	FA
1968	CAL	A	1	6	.143	5.08	10	5	1	33.2	28	26	22	0	0	2	0	10	1	0	.100	1	3	0	1	0.4	1.000

Andy Harrington

HARRINGTON, ANDREW FRANCIS BR TR 6′ 193 lbs.
B. Nov. 13, 1888, Wakefield, Mass. D. Nov. 12, 1938, Malden, Mass.

Year	Team		W	L	PCT	ERA	G	GS	CG	IP	H	BB	SO	ShO	Relief W	Relief L	Relief SV	Batting AB	Batting H	HR	BA	PO	A	E	DP	TC/G	FA
1913	CIN	N	0	0	—	9.00	1	0	0	4	6	1	1	0	0	0	0	2	1	0	.500	1	0	0	0	1.0	1.000

Bill Harrington

HARRINGTON, WILLIAM WOMBLE BR TR 5′11″ 160 lbs.
B. Oct. 3, 1927, Sanford, N. C.

Year	Team		W	L	PCT	ERA	G	GS	CG	IP	H	BB	SO	ShO	Relief W	Relief L	Relief SV	Batting AB	Batting H	HR	BA	PO	A	E	DP	TC/G	FA
1953	PHI	A	0	0	—	13.50	1	0	0	2	5	0	0	0	0	0	0	0	0	0	—	0	0	0	0	0.0	.000
1955	KC	A	3	3	.500	4.11	34	1	0	76.2	69	41	26	0	3	2	2	17	2	0	.118	4	11	0	0	0.4	1.000
1956			2	2	.500	6.45	23	1	0	37.2	40	26	14	0	2	2	1	7	0	0	.000	3	5	0	1	0.3	1.000
3 yrs.			5	5	.500	5.03	58	2	0	116.1	114	67	40	0	5	4	3	24	2	0	.083	7	16	0	1	0.4	1.000

Ben Harris

HARRIS, BEN FRANKLIN BR TR 6′ 220 lbs.
B. Dec. 17, 1889, Donelson, Tenn. D. Apr. 1, 1927, St. Louis, Mo.

Year	Team		W	L	PCT	ERA	G	GS	CG	IP	H	BB	SO	ShO	Relief W	Relief L	Relief SV	Batting AB	Batting H	HR	BA	PO	A	E	DP	TC/G	FA
1914	KC	F	7	8	.467	4.09	31	14	5	154	179	41	40	0	2	1	1	45	9	0	.200	12	51	1	0	2.1	.984
1915			0	0	—	0.00	1	0	0	2	1	0	0	0	0	0	0	0	0	0	—	0	2	0	0	2.0	1.000
2 yrs.			7	8	.467	4.04	32	14	5	156	180	41	40	0	2	1	1	45	9	0	.200	12	53	1	0	2.1	.985

Bill Harris

HARRIS, WILLIAM MILTON BR TR 6′ 1½″ 180 lbs.
B. June 23, 1900, Wylie, Tex. D. Aug. 21, 1965, Indian Trail, N. C.

Year	Team		W	L	PCT	ERA	G	GS	CG	IP	H	BB	SO	ShO	Relief W	Relief L	Relief SV	Batting AB	Batting H	HR	BA	PO	A	E	DP	TC/G	FA
1923	CIN	N	3	2	.600	5.17	22	3	1	69.2	79	18	18	0	2	0	0	17	6	0	.353	4	17	2	0	1.0	.913
1924			0	0	—	9.00	3	0	0	7	10	2	5	0	0	0	0	1	1	0	1.000	0	3	1	0	1.3	.750
1931	PIT	N	2	2	.500	0.87	4	4	3	31	21	9	10	1	0	0	0	11	1	0	.091	2	7	0	0	2.3	1.000
1932			10	9	.526	3.64	37	17	4	168	178	38	63	0	7	1	2	55	10	0	.182	2	30	1	0	0.9	.970
1933			4	4	.500	3.22	31	0	0	58.2	68	14	19	0	4	4	5	9	0	0	.000	3	9	0	1	0.4	1.000

Bill Harris *continued*

Year	Team	W	L	PCT	ERA	G	GS	CG	IP	H	BB	SO	ShO	Relief Pitching W	Relief Pitching L	Relief Pitching SV	Batting AB	Batting H	HR	BA	PO	A	E	DP	TC/G	FA
1934		0	0	—	6.63	11	2	0	19	28	7	8	0	0	0	0	2	1	0	.500	1	5	0	0	0.5	1.000
1938	BOS A	5	5	.500	4.03	13	11	5	80.1	83	21	26	1	0	0	1	28	6	0	.214	2	14	0	2	1.2	1.000
7 yrs.		24	22	.522	3.92	121	37	13	433.2	467	109	149	2	13	5	8	123	25	0	.203	14	85	4	3	0.9	.961

Bill Harris

HARRIS, WILLIAM THOMAS (Billy)
B. Dec. 3, 1931, Duguayville, N. B., Canada.
BL TR 5′ 8″ 187 lbs.

Year	Team	W	L	PCT	ERA	G	GS	CG	IP	H	BB	SO	ShO	Relief Pitching W	Relief Pitching L	Relief Pitching SV	Batting AB	Batting H	HR	BA	PO	A	E	DP	TC/G	FA
1957	BKN N	0	1	.000	3.86	1	1	0	7	9	1	3	0	0	0	0	2	1	0	.500	0	2	0	0	2.0	1.000
1959	LA N	0	0	—	0.00	1	0	0	1.2	0	3	0	0	0	0	0	0	0	0	—	0	1	0	0	1.0	1.000
2 yrs.		0	1	.000	3.12	2	1	0	8.2	9	4	3	0	0	0	0	2	1	0	.500	0	3	0	0	1.5	1.000

Bob Harris

HARRIS, ROBERT ARTHUR
B. May 1, 1917, Gillette, Wyo. D. Aug. 9, 1989, North Platte, Neb.
BR TR 6′ 185 lbs.

Year	Team	W	L	PCT	ERA	G	GS	CG	IP	H	BB	SO	ShO	Relief Pitching W	Relief Pitching L	Relief Pitching SV	Batting AB	Batting H	HR	BA	PO	A	E	DP	TC/G	FA
1938	DET A	1	0	1.000	7.20	3	1	1	10	14	4	7	0	0	0	0	3	1	0	.333	2	3	0	0	1.7	1.000
1939	2 teams DET A (5G 1–1) STL A (28G 3–12)																									
″	total	4	13	.235	5.50	33	17	6	144	180	79	57	0	2	1	0	42	9	0	.214	8	35	2	5	1.4	.956
1940	STL A	11	15	.423	4.93	35	28	8	193.2	225	85	49	1	2	1	1	60	15	0	.250	10	36	1	1	1.3	.979
1941		12	14	.462	5.21	34	29	9	186.2	237	85	57	2	1	1	1	61	7	0	.115	10	27	1	2	1.1	.974
1942	2 teams STL A (6G 1–5) PHI A (16G 1–5)																									
″	total	2	10	.167	3.71	22	14	2	111.2	114	41	35	1	0	2	0	36	7	0	.194	5	31	0	0	1.6	1.000
5 yrs.		30	52	.366	4.96	127	89	26	646	770	294	205	4	5	5	2	202	39	0	.193	35	132	4	8	1.3	.977

Buddy Harris

HARRIS, WALTER FRANCIS, JR.
B. Dec. 5, 1948, Philadelphia, Pa.
BR TR 6′ 7″ 245 lbs.

Year	Team	W	L	PCT	ERA	G	GS	CG	IP	H	BB	SO	ShO	Relief Pitching W	Relief Pitching L	Relief Pitching SV	Batting AB	Batting H	HR	BA	PO	A	E	DP	TC/G	FA
1970	HOU N	0	0	—	6.00	2	0	0	6	6	0	2	0	0	0	0	1	0	0	.000	1	0	0	0	0.5	1.000
1971		1	1	.500	6.39	20	0	0	31	33	16	21	0	1	1	0	2	0	0	.000	0	2	0	0	0.1	1.000
2 yrs.		1	1	.500	6.32	22	0	0	37	39	16	23	0	1	1	0	3	0	0	.000	1	2	0	0	0.1	1.000

Charlie Harris

HARRIS, CHARLES (Bubba)
B. Feb. 15, 1926, Sulligent, Ala.
BR TR 6′ 4″ 204 lbs.

Year	Team	W	L	PCT	ERA	G	GS	CG	IP	H	BB	SO	ShO	Relief Pitching W	Relief Pitching L	Relief Pitching SV	Batting AB	Batting H	HR	BA	PO	A	E	DP	TC/G	FA
1948	PHI A	5	2	.714	4.13	45	0	0	93.2	89	35	32	0	5	2	5	24	3	0	.125	4	15	1	1	0.4	.950
1949		1	1	.500	5.44	37	0	0	84.1	92	42	18	0	1	1	3	24	3	0	.125	3	27	0	3	0.8	1.000
1951	2 teams PHI A (3G 0–0) CLE A (2G 0–0)																									
″	total	0	0		6.75	5	0	0	8	9	9	3	0	0	0	0	0	0	0		0	3	0	0	0.6	1.000
3 yrs.		6	3	.667	4.84	87	0	0	186	190	86	53	0	6	3	8	48	6	0	.125	7	45	1	4	0.6	.981

Gene Harris

HARRIS, TYRONE EUGENE
B. Dec. 5, 1964, Sebring, Fla.
BR TR 5′11″ 190 lbs.

Year	Team	W	L	PCT	ERA	G	GS	CG	IP	H	BB	SO	ShO	Relief Pitching W	Relief Pitching L	Relief Pitching SV	Batting AB	Batting H	HR	BA	PO	A	E	DP	TC/G	FA
1989	2 teams MON N (11G 1–1) SEA A (10G 1–4)																									
″	total	2	5	.286	5.91	21	6	0	53.1	63	25	25	0	1	2	1	1	0	0	.000	2	13	0	0	0.7	1.000
1990	SEA A	1	2	.333	4.74	25	0	0	38	31	30	43	0	1	2	0	0	0	0	—	4	2	0	1	0.2	1.000
1991		0	0	—	4.05	8	0	0	13.1	15	10	6	0	0	0	1	0	0	0	—	0	2	0	0	0.3	1.000
1992	2 teams SEA A (8G 0–0) SD N (14G 0–2)																									
″	total	0	2	.000	4.15	22	1	0	30.1	23	15	25	0	0	2	0	3	1	0	.333	1	4	3	0	0.4	.625
1993	SD N	6	6	.500	3.03	59	0	0	59.1	57	37	39	0	6	6	23	1	0	0	.000	5	10	0	0	0.3	1.000
1994	2 teams SD N (13G 1–1) DET A (11G 0–0)																									
″	total	1	1	.500	7.61	24	0	0	23.2	34	12	19	0	1	1	1	1	0	0	.000	1	2	0	0	0.1	1.000
1995	2 teams PHI N (21G 2–2) BAL A (3G 0–0)																									
″	total	2	2	.500	4.30	24	0	0	23	23	9	13	0	2	2	0	0	0	0	—	4	5	0	0	0.4	1.000
7 yrs.		12	18	.400	4.71	183	7	0	241	246	138	170	0	11	15	26	6	1	0	.167	17	38	3	1	0.3	.948

Greg Harris

HARRIS, GREG ALLEN
B. Nov. 2, 1955, Lynwood, Calif.
BB TR 6′ 165 lbs.

Year	Team	W	L	PCT	ERA	G	GS	CG	IP	H	BB	SO	ShO	Relief Pitching W	Relief Pitching L	Relief Pitching SV	Batting AB	Batting H	HR	BA	PO	A	E	DP	TC/G	FA
1981	NY N	3	5	.375	4.43	16	14	0	69	65	28	54	0	0	0	1	22	4	0	.182	3	7	1	2	0.7	.909
1982	CIN N	2	6	.250	4.83	34	10	1	91.1	96	37	67	0	0	1	1	18	3	0	.167	8	13	2	2	0.7	.913
1983		0	0	—	27.00	1	0	0	1	2	3	1	0	0	0	0	1	0	0	.000	0	1	0	0	1.0	1.000
1984	2 teams MON N (15G 0–1) SD N (19G 2–1)																									
″	total	2	2	.500	2.48	34	1	0	54.1	38	25	45	0	1	2	3	9	3	0	.333	3	7	1	0	0.3	.909
1985	TEX A	5	4	.556	2.47	58	0	0	113	74	43	111	0	5	4	11	0	0	0	—	8	16	1	4	0.4	.960
1986		10	8	.556	2.83	73	0	0	111.1	103	42	95	0	10	8	20	0	0	0	—	7	18	2	2	0.4	.926
1987		5	10	.333	4.86	42	19	0	140.2	157	56	106	0	1	4	0	0	0	0	—	14	20	5	1	0.9	.872
1988	PHI N	4	6	.400	2.36	66	1	0	107	80	52	71	0	4	5	1	9	3	0	.333	5	17	3	0	0.4	.880
1989	2 teams PHI N (44G 2–2) BOS A (15G 2–2)																									
″	total	4	4	.500	3.31	59	0	0	103.1	85	58	76	0	4	4	1	6	1	0	.167	4	20	3	0	0.5	.889
1990	BOS A	13	9	.591	4.00	34	30	1	184.1	186	77	117	0	1	0	0	0	0	0	—	23	36	4	1	1.9	.937
1991		11	12	.478	3.85	53	21	1	173	157	69	127	0	4	2	2	0	0	0	—	11	32	2	0	0.8	.956
1992		4	9	.308	2.51	70	2	1	107.2	82	60	73	0	4	**8**	4	0	0	0	—	3	16	2	0	0.3	.905
1993		6	7	.462	3.77	**80**	0	0	112.1	95	60	103	0	6	**7**	8	0	0	0	—	8	13	3	1	0.3	.875
1994	2 teams BOS A (35G 3–4) NY A (3G 0–1)																									
″	total	3	5	.375	7.99	38	0	0	50.2	64	26	48	0	3	5	2	0	0	0		1	7	1	1	0.2	.889
1995	MON N	2	3	.400	2.61	45	0	0	48.1	45	16	47	0	2	3	0	3	1	0	.333	3	5	2	0	0.2	.800
15 yrs.		74	90	.451	3.69	703	98	4	1467.1	1329	652	1141	0	45	53	54	68	15	0	.221	101	228	32	14	0.5	.911
LEAGUE CHAMPIONSHIP SERIES																										
1984	SD N	0	0	—	31.50	1	0	0	2	9	3	2	0	0	0	0	0	0	0	—	0	0	0	0	0.0	.000
1990	BOS A	0	1	.000	27.00	1	0	0	0.1	3	0	0	0	0	1	0	0	0	0	—	0	0	0	0	0.0	.000
2 yrs.		0	1	.000	30.86	2	0	0	2.1	12	3	2	0	0	1	0	0	0	0		0	0	0	0	0.0	
WORLD SERIES																										
1984	SD N	0	0	—	0.00	1	0	0	5.1	3	3	5	0	0	0	0	0	0	0	—	0	0	0	0	0.0	.000

Greg Harris

HARRIS, GREGORY WADE
B. Dec. 1, 1963, Greensboro, N. C.
BR TR 6′ 3″ 190 lbs.

Year	Team	W	L	PCT	ERA	G	GS	CG	IP	H	BB	SO	ShO	Relief Pitching W	Relief Pitching L	Relief Pitching SV	Batting AB	Batting H	HR	BA	PO	A	E	DP	TC/G	FA
1988	SD N	2	0	1.000	1.50	3	1	1	18	13	3	15	0	1	0	0	7	0	0	.000	0	2	0	1	0.7	1.000
1989		8	9	.471	2.60	56	8	0	135	106	52	106	0	5	5	6	19	1	0	.053	12	21	0	2	0.6	1.000
1990		8	8	.500	2.30	73	0	0	117.1	92	49	97	0	8	8	9	12	1	0	.083	4	17	0	1	0.3	1.000

Greg Harris *continued*

Year	Team	Lg	W	L	PCT	ERA	G	GS	CG	IP	H	BB	SO	ShO	Relief Pitching W	Relief Pitching L	Relief Pitching SV	Batting AB	Batting H	Batting HR	BA	PO	A	E	DP	TC/G	FA
1991			9	5	.643	2.23	20	20	3	133	116	27	95	2	0	0	0	36	3	0	.083	10	14	1	0	1.3	.960
1992			4	8	.333	4.12	20	20	1	118	113	35	66	0	0	0	0	31	4	0	.129	10	21	5	0	1.8	.861
1993	**2 teams**	**SD N** (22G 10–9)	**CLR N** (13G 1–8)																								
″	**total**		11	17	.393	4.59	35	35	4	225.1	239	69	123	0	0	0	0	73	10	0	.137	17	37	3	3	1.6	.947
1994	**CLR**	**N**	3	12	.200	6.65	29	19	1	130	154	52	82	0	0	1	1	40	7	0	.175	8	22	2	1	1.1	.938
1995	**MIN**	**A**	0	5	.000	8.82	7	6	0	32.2	50	16	21	0	0	1	0	0	0	0	—	7	3	0	0	1.4	1.000
8 yrs.			45	64	.413	3.98	243	109	10	909.1	883	303	605	2	14	15	16	218	26	0	.119	68	137	11	8	0.9	.949

Herb Harris

HARRIS, HERBERT BENJAMIN BL TL 6′ 1″ 175 lbs.
B. Apr. 24, 1913, Chicago, Ill.

Year	Team	Lg	W	L	PCT	ERA	G	GS	CG	IP	H	BB	SO	ShO	Relief Pitching W	Relief Pitching L	Relief Pitching SV	Batting AB	Batting H	Batting HR	BA	PO	A	E	DP	TC/G	FA
1936	**PHI**	**N**	0	0	—	10.29	4	0	0	7	14	5	0	0	0	0	0	1	0	0	.000	0	3	0	0	0.8	1.000

Joe Harris

HARRIS, JOSEPH WHITE BR TR 6′ 1″ 198 lbs.
B. Feb. 1, 1882, Melrose, Mass. D. Apr. 12, 1966, Melrose, Mass.

Year	Team	Lg	W	L	PCT	ERA	G	GS	CG	IP	H	BB	SO	ShO	Relief Pitching W	Relief Pitching L	Relief Pitching SV	Batting AB	Batting H	Batting HR	BA	PO	A	E	DP	TC/G	FA
1905	**BOS**	**A**	1	2	.333	2.35	3	3	3	23	16	8	14	0	0	0	0	9	1	0	.111	2	4	0	0	2.0	1.000
1906			2	**21**	.087	3.52	30	24	20	235	211	67	99	1	0	0	2	81	13	0	.160	11	103	9	1	4.1	.927
1907			0	7	.000	3.05	12	5	3	59	57	13	24	0	0	**3**	0	21	4	0	.190	1	21	3	2	2.1	.880
3 yrs.			3	30	.091	3.35	45	32	26	317	284	88	137	1	0	3	2	111	18	0	.162	14	128	12	3	3.4	.922

Lum Harris

HARRIS, CHALMER LUMAN BR TR 6′ 1″ 180 lbs.
B. Jan. 17, 1915, New Castle, Ala.
Manager 1961, 1964–65, 1968–72.

Year	Team	Lg	W	L	PCT	ERA	G	GS	CG	IP	H	BB	SO	ShO	Relief Pitching W	Relief Pitching L	Relief Pitching SV	Batting AB	Batting H	Batting HR	BA	PO	A	E	DP	TC/G	FA
1941	**PHI**	**A**	4	4	.500	4.78	33	10	5	131.2	134	51	49	0	2	0	2	40	11	0	.275	9	17	1	0	0.8	.963
1942			11	15	.423	3.74	26	20	10	166	146	70	60	1	3	3	0	62	10	0	.161	7	31	1	3	1.5	.974
1943			7	**21**	.250	4.20	32	27	15	216.1	241	63	55	1	1	2	1	70	12	0	.171	9	45	2	6	1.8	.964
1944			10	9	.526	3.30	23	22	12	174.1	193	26	33	2	0	0	0	59	10	0	.169	8	33	1	1	1.8	.976
1946			3	14	.176	5.24	34	12	4	125.1	153	48	33	0	2	3	0	36	8	1	.222	10	36	1	2	1.4	.979
1947	**WAS**	**A**	0	0	—	2.84	3	0	0	6.1	7	7	2	0	0	0	0	1	0	0	.000	0	4	0	0	1.3	1.000
6 yrs.			35	63	.357	4.16	151	91	46	820	874	265	232	4	8	8	3	268	51	1	.190	43	166	6	12	1.4	.972

Mickey Harris

HARRIS, MAURICE CHARLES BL TL 6′ 195 lbs.
B. Jan. 30, 1917, New York, N. Y. D. Apr. 15, 1971, Farmington, Mich.

Year	Team	Lg	W	L	PCT	ERA	G	GS	CG	IP	H	BB	SO	ShO	Relief Pitching W	Relief Pitching L	Relief Pitching SV	Batting AB	Batting H	Batting HR	BA	PO	A	E	DP	TC/G	FA
1940	**BOS**	**A**	4	2	.667	5.00	13	9	3	68.1	83	26	36	0	0	0	0	22	6	0	.273	5	13	0	0	1.4	1.000
1941			8	14	.364	3.25	35	22	11	194	189	86	111	1	2	1	1	55	6	0	.109	5	32	1	0	1.1	.974
1946			17	9	.654	3.64	34	30	15	222.2	236	76	131	0	0	1	0	78	18	0	.231	11	29	1	2	1.2	.976
1947			5	4	.556	2.44	15	6	1	51.2	42	23	35	0	2	2	0	12	5	0	.417	2	8	0	0	0.7	1.000
1948			7	10	.412	5.30	20	17	6	113.2	120	59	42	1	2	0	0	32	2	0	.063	2	14	2	1	0.9	.889
1949	**2 teams**	**BOS A** (7G 2–3)	**WAS A** (23G 2–12)																								
″	**total**		4	15	.211	5.13	30	25	6	166.2	204	75	68	0	0	1	0	51	9	0	.176	8	22	1	3	1.0	.968
1950	**WAS**	**A**	5	9	.357	4.78	**53**	0	0	98	93	46	41	0	5	**9**	**15**	17	4	0	.235	4	11	1	0	0.3	.938
1951			6	8	.429	3.81	41	0	0	87.1	87	43	47	0	6	**8**	4	16	3	0	.188	1	14	2	0	0.4	.882
1952	**2 teams**	**WAS A** (1G 0–0)	**CLE A** (29G 3–0)																								
″	**total**		3	0	1.000	4.72	30	0	0	47.2	43	21	23	0	3	0	1	5	1	0	.200	2	8	0	1	0.3	1.000
9 yrs.			59	71	.454	4.18	271	109	42	1050	1097	455	534	2	20	22	21	288	54	0	.188	40	151	8	7	0.7	.960
WORLD SERIES																											
1946	**BOS**	**A**	0	2	.000	3.72	2	2	0	9.2	11	4	5	0	0	0	0	3	1	0	.333	1	0	0	0	0.5	1.000

Reggie Harris

HARRIS, REGINALD ALLEN BR TR 6′ 1″ 180 lbs.
B. Aug. 12, 1968, Waynesboro, Va.

Year	Team	Lg	W	L	PCT	ERA	G	GS	CG	IP	H	BB	SO	ShO	Relief Pitching W	Relief Pitching L	Relief Pitching SV	Batting AB	Batting H	Batting HR	BA	PO	A	E	DP	TC/G	FA
1990	**OAK**	**A**	1	0	1.000	3.48	16	1	0	41.1	25	21	31	0	1	0	0	0	0	0	—	2	3	0	1	0.3	1.000
1991			0	0	—	12.00	2	0	0	3	5	3	2	0	0	0	0	0	0	0	—	0	0	0	0	0.0	.000
2 yrs.			1	0	1.000	4.06	18	1	0	44.1	30	24	33	0	1	0	0	0	0	0		2	3	0	1	0.3	1.000

Bob Harrison

HARRISON, ROBERT LEE BL TR 5′11″ 178 lbs.
B. Sept. 22, 1930, St. Louis, Mo.

Year	Team	Lg	W	L	PCT	ERA	G	GS	CG	IP	H	BB	SO	ShO	Relief Pitching W	Relief Pitching L	Relief Pitching SV	Batting AB	Batting H	Batting HR	BA	PO	A	E	DP	TC/G	FA
1955	**BAL**	**A**	0	0	—	9.00	1	0	0	2	3	4	0	0	0	0	0	0	0	0	—	0	0	0	0	0.0	.000
1956			0	0	—	16.20	1	1	0	1.2	3	5	0	0	0	0	0	0	0	0	—	0	0	0	0	0.0	.000
2 yrs.			0	0		12.27	2	1	0	3.2	6	9	0	0	0	0	0	0	0	0		0	0	0	0	0.0	

Roric Harrison

HARRISON, RORIC EDWARD BR TR 6′ 3″ 195 lbs.
B. Sept. 20, 1946, Los Angeles, Calif.

Year	Team	Lg	W	L	PCT	ERA	G	GS	CG	IP	H	BB	SO	ShO	Relief Pitching W	Relief Pitching L	Relief Pitching SV	Batting AB	Batting H	Batting HR	BA	PO	A	E	DP	TC/G	FA
1972	**BAL**	**A**	3	4	.429	2.30	39	2	0	94	68	34	62	0	2	3	4	17	2	1	.118	8	10	0	0	0.5	1.000
1973	**ATL**	**N**	11	8	.579	4.16	38	22	3	177.1	161	98	130	0	0	3	5	54	3	2	.056	13	18	2	0	0.9	.939
1974			6	11	.353	4.71	20	20	3	126	148	49	46	0	0	0	0	38	7	3	.184	7	13	1	1	1.0	.952
1975	**2 teams**	**ATL N** (15G 3–4)	**CLE A** (19G 7–7)																								
″	**total**		10	11	.476	4.77	34	26	6	181	195	65	74	0	0	0	1	15	3	0	.200	10	22	2	2	1.0	.941
1978	**MIN**	**A**	0	1	.000	7.50	9	0	0	12	18	11	7	0	0	1	0	0	0	0	—	0	0	0	0	0.0	.000
5 yrs.			30	35	.462	4.24	140	70	12	590.1	590	257	319	0	2	7	10	124	15	6	.121	38	63	5	3	0.8	.953

Tom Harrison

HARRISON, THOMAS JAMES BR TR 6′ 3″ 200 lbs.
B. Jan. 18, 1945, Trail, B. C., Canada.

Year	Team	Lg	W	L	PCT	ERA	G	GS	CG	IP	H	BB	SO	ShO	Relief Pitching W	Relief Pitching L	Relief Pitching SV	Batting AB	Batting H	Batting HR	BA	PO	A	E	DP	TC/G	FA
1965	**KC**	**A**	0	0	—	13.50	1	0	0	0.2	2	1	0	0	0	0	0	*				0	0	0	0	0.0	.000

Slim Harriss

HARRISS, WILLIAM JENNINGS BRYAN BR TR 6′ 6″ 180 lbs.
B. Dec. 11, 1896, Brownwood, Tex. D. Sept. 19, 1963, Temple, Tex.

Year	Team	Lg	W	L	PCT	ERA	G	GS	CG	IP	H	BB	SO	ShO	Relief Pitching W	Relief Pitching L	Relief Pitching SV	Batting AB	Batting H	Batting HR	BA	PO	A	E	DP	TC/G	FA
1920	**PHI**	**A**	9	14	.391	4.08	31	25	11	192	226	57	60	0	0	0	0	66	7	0	.106	5	64	5	3	2.4	.932
1921			11	16	.407	4.27	39	28	14	227.2	258	73	92	0	1	2	2	81	12	0	.148	4	56	4	1	1.6	.938
1922			9	**20**	.310	5.02	47	32	13	229.2	262	94	102	0	1	**6**	3	74	13	0	.176	3	60	4	1	1.4	.940
1923			10	16	.385	4.00	46	28	9	209.1	221	95	89	0	3	1	6	61	4	0	.066	3	78	2	3	1.8	.976
1924			6	10	.375	4.68	36	12	4	123	138	62	45	1	3	3	2	42	7	0	.167	4	48	2	4	1.5	.963
1925			19	12	.613	3.50	46	**33**	15	252.1	263	95	95	2	3	3	1	88	18	1	.205	5	82	3	4	2.0	.967
1926	**2 teams**	**PHI A** (12G 3–5)	**BOS A** (21G 6–10)																								
″	**total**		9	15	.375	4.34	33	28	8	170	201	55	47	1	1	0	0	51	8	0	.157	5	51	2	1	1.8	.966

Slim Harriss *continued*

Year	Team	Lg	W	L	PCT	ERA	G	GS	CG	IP	H	BB	SO	ShO	Relief Pitching W	Relief Pitching L	Relief Pitching SV	Batting AB	Batting H	Batting HR	BA	PO	A	E	DP	TC/G	FA
1927	BOS	A	14	**21**	.400	4.18	44	27	11	217.2	253	66	77	1	4	5	1	66	8	0	.121	2	60	4	3	1.5	.939
1928			8	11	.421	4.63	27	15	4	128.1	141	33	37	1	4	0	1	36	5	0	.139	4	22	0	0	1.0	1.000
9 yrs.			95	135	.413	4.25	349	228	89	1750	1963	630	644	6	20	20	16	565	82	1	.145	35	521	26	20	1.7	.955

Earl Harrist

HARRIST, EARL (Irish) BR TR 6′ 175 lbs.
B. Apr. 20, 1919, Dubach, La.

1945	CIN	N	2	4	.333	3.61	14	5	1	62.1	60	27	15	0	1	0	0	15	0	0	.000	1	9	0	0	0.7	1.000
1947	CHI	A	3	8	.273	3.56	33	4	0	93.2	85	49	55	0	3	5	5	24	5	0	.208	3	18	1	1	0.7	.955
1948	2 teams	CHI A (11G 1–3)	WAS A (23G 3–3)																								
″	total		4	6	.400	4.93	34	5	0	84	93	50	35	0	4	3	0	22	3	0	.136	6	9	0	0	0.4	1.000
1952	STL	A	2	8	.200	4.01	36	9	1	116.2	119	47	49	0	2	2	5	31	3	0	.097	3	25	1	4	0.8	.966
1953	2 teams	CHI A (7G 1–0)	DET A (8G 0–2)																								
″	total		1	2	.333	8.33	15	1	0	27	34	20	8	0	1	1	0	4	0	0	.000	1	8	1	0	0.7	.900
5 yrs.			12	28	.300	4.34	132	24	2	383.2	391	193	162	0	11	11	10	96	11	0	.115	14	69	3	5	0.7	.965

Jack Harshman

HARSHMAN, JOHN ELVIN BL TL 6′ 2″ 178 lbs.
B. July 12, 1927, San Diego, Calif.

1952	NY	N	0	2	.000	14.21	2	2	0	6.1	12	6	6	0	0	0	0	2	0	0	.000	17	1	0	2	6.0	1.000
1954	CHI	A	14	8	.636	2.95	35	21	9	177	157	96	134	4	1	3	1	56	8	2	.143	5	27	1	1	0.9	.970
1955			11	7	.611	3.36	32	23	9	179.1	144	97	116	0	0	0	0	60	11	2	.183	3	29	1	1	1.0	.970
1956			15	11	.577	3.10	34	30	15	226.2	183	102	143	4	0	0	0	71	12	6	.169	2	29	4	3	1.0	.886
1957			8	8	.500	4.10	30	26	6	151.1	142	82	83	0	0	2	1	45	10	2	.222	3	15	1	1	0.6	.947
1958	BAL	A	12	15	.444	2.89	34	29	17	236.1	204	75	161	3	1	0	4	82	16	6	.195	5	43	1	1	1.4	.980
1959	3 teams	BAL A (14G 0–6)	BOS A (8G 2–3)	CLE A (13G 5–1)																							
″	total		7	10	.412	4.76	35	16	5	138	133	51	73	1	2	4	1	51	10	1	.196	8	25	0	2	0.9	1.000
1960	CLE	A	2	4	.333	3.98	15	8	0	54.1	50	30	25	0	0	0	0	17	3	0	.176	2	5	0	1	0.5	1.000
8 yrs.			69	65	.515	3.50	217	155	61	1169.1	1025	539	741	12	4	9	7	*				128	183	9	19	1.4	.972

Oscar Harstad

HARSTAD, OSCAR THEANDER BR TR 6′ 174 lbs.
B. May 24, 1892, Parkland, Wash. D. Nov. 14, 1985, Corvallis, Ore.

1915	CLE	A	3	5	.375	3.40	32	7	4	82	81	35	35	0	1	0	1	16	2	0	.125	4	34	2	2	1.3	.950

Bill Hart

HART, WILLIAM FRANKLIN (Uncle Billy) TR 5′10″ 163 lbs.
B. July 19, 1865, Louisville, Ky. D. Sept. 19, 1936, Cincinnati, Ohio.

1886	PHI	AA	9	13	.409	*3.19*	22	22	22	186	183	66	78	2	0	0	0	73	10	0	.137	7	40	5	1	2.4	.904
1887			1	2	.333	4.50	3	3	3	26	28	17	4	0	0	0	0	13	1	0	.077	0	8	5	0	4.3	.615
1892	BKN	N	9	12	.429	3.28	28	23	16	195	188	96	65	2	1	1	1	125	24	2	.192	31	59	9	1	2.5	.909
1895	PIT	N	14	17	.452	4.75	36	29	24	261.2	293	135	85	0	1	1	1	106	25	0	.236	12	84	5	4	2.8	.950
1896	STL	N	12	**29**	.293	5.12	42	41	37	336	411	141	65	0	0	1	0	161	30	0	.186	38	106	8	3	3.0	.947
1897			9	27	.250	6.26	39	38	31	294.2	395	148	67	0	0	0	0	156	39	2	.250	31	76	10	4	2.5	.915
1898	PIT	N	5	9	.357	4.82	16	15	13	125	141	44	19	1	0	0	1	50	12	0	.240	3	34	6	3	2.7	.860
1901	CLE	A	7	11	.389	3.77	20	19	16	157.2	180	57	48	0	0	0	0	64	14	0	.219	5	55	3	2	3.2	.952
8 yrs.			66	120	.355	4.65	206	190	162	1582	1819	704	431	5	2	3	3	*				127	462	51	18	2.7	.920

Bob Hart

HART, ROBERT LEE (Billy) 5′ 8″
B. May 1866, Palmyra, Mo. D. May 14, 1944, Hannibal, Mo.

1890	STL	AA	12	8	.600	*3.67*	26	24	20	201.1	188	66	95	0	1	0	0	78	15	1	.192	8	24	2	0	1.3	.941

Chuck Hartenstein

HARTENSTEIN, CHARLES OSCAR (Twiggy) BR TR 5′11″ 165 lbs.
B. May 26, 1942, Seguin, Tex.

1966	CHI	N	0	0	—	1.93	5	0	0	9.1	8	3	4	0	0	0	0	0	0	0	—	2	2	0	0	0.8	1.000
1967			9	5	.643	3.08	45	0	0	73	74	17	20	0	9	5	10	16	1	0	.063	5	14	1	0	0.4	.950
1968			2	4	.333	4.54	28	0	0	35.2	41	11	17	0	2	4	1	2	0	0	.000	4	5	2	1	0.4	.818
1969	PIT	N	5	4	.556	3.94	56	0	0	96	84	27	44	0	5	4	10	14	1	0	.071	8	22	0	1	0.5	1.000
1970	3 teams	PIT N (17G 1–1)	STL N (6G 0–0)	BOS A (17G 0–3)																							
″	total		1	4	.200	6.75	40	0	0	56	70	25	35	0	1	4	2	5	0	0	.000	2	11	1	1	0.3	.929
1977	TOR	A	0	2	.000	6.67	13	0	0	27	40	6	15	0	0	2	0	0	0	0	—	1	4	0	0	0.4	1.000
6 yrs.			17	19	.472	4.52	187	0	0	297	317	89	135	0	17	19	23	37	2	0	.054	22	58	4	3	0.4	.952

Frank Harter

HARTER, FRANKLIN PIERCE (Chief) BR TR 5′11″ 165 lbs.
B. Sept. 19, 1886, Keyesport, Ill. D. Apr. 14, 1959, Breese, Ill.

1912	CIN	N	1	2	.333	3.07	6	3	1	29.1	25	11	12	0	0	0	0	11	1	0	.091	0	3	0	0	0.5	1.000
1913			1	1	.500	3.86	17	2	0	46.2	47	19	10	0	1	0	0	14	2	0	.143	0	10	1	0	0.6	.909
1914	IND	F	1	2	.333	4.01	6	1	1	24.2	33	7	8	0	0	2	0	8	0	0	.000	1	6	0	0	1.2	1.000
3 yrs.			3	5	.375	3.67	29	6	2	100.2	105	37	30	0	1	2	0	33	3	0	.091	1	19	1	0	0.7	.952

Dean Hartgraves

HARTGRAVES, DEAN CHARLES BR TL 6′ 185 lbs.
B. Aug. 12, 1966, Bakersfield, Calif.

1995	HOU	N	2	0	1.000	3.22	40	0	0	36.1	30	16	24	0	2	0	0	2	0	0	.000	3	5	0	0	0.2	1.000

Mike Hartley

HARTLEY, MICHAEL EDWARD BR TR 6′ 1″ 192 lbs.
B. Aug. 31, 1961, Hawthorne, Calif.

1989	LA	N	0	1	.000	1.50	5	0	0	6	2	0	4	0	0	1	0	1	0	0	.000	2	0	0	0	0.4	1.000
1990			6	3	.667	2.95	32	6	1	79.1	58	30	76	1	3	1	1	13	1	0	.077	3	8	1	1	0.4	.917
1991	2 teams	LA N (40G 2–0)	PHI N (18G 2–1)																								
″	total		4	1	.800	4.21	58	0	0	83.1	74	47	63	0	4	1	2	5	0	0	.000	10	6	1	2	0.3	.941
1992	PHI	N	7	6	.538	3.44	46	0	0	55	54	23	53	0	7	6	0	4	0	0	.000	2	6	1	0	0.2	.889
1993	MIN	A	1	2	.333	4.00	53	0	0	81	86	36	57	0	1	2	1	0	0	0	—	7	2	1	0	0.2	.900
1995	2 teams	BOS A (5G 0–0)	BAL A (3G 1–0)																								
″	total		1	0	1.000	5.14	8	0	0	14	13	3	6	0	1	0	0	0	0	0	—	0	3	0	0	0.4	1.000
6 yrs.			19	13	.594	3.70	202	6	1	318.2	287	139	259	1	16	11	4	23	1	0	.043	24	25	4	3	0.3	.925

Bob Hartman

HARTMAN, ROBERT LOUIS BR TL 5′11″ 185 lbs.
B. Aug. 28, 1937, Kenosha, Wis.

Year	Team	Lg	W	L	PCT	ERA	G	GS	CG	IP	H	BB	SO	ShO	Relief W	Relief L	SV	AB	H	HR	BA	PO	A	E	DP	TC/G	FA
1959	MIL	N	0	0	—	27.00	3	0	0	1.2	6	2	1	0	0	0	0	0	0	0	—	0	0	0	0	0.0	.000
1962	CLE	A	0	1	.000	3.12	8	2	0	17.1	14	8	11	0	0	0	0	7	0	0	.000	1	1	0	0	0.3	1.000
2 yrs.			0	1	.000	5.21	11	2	0	19	20	10	12	0	0	0	0	7	0	0	.000	1	1	0	0	0.2	1.000

Charlie Hartman

HARTMAN, CHARLES OTTO
B. Aug. 10, 1888, Los Angeles, Calif. D. Oct. 22, 1960, Los Angeles, Calif.

Year	Team	Lg	W	L	PCT	ERA	G	GS	CG	IP	H	BB	SO	ShO	Relief W	Relief L	SV	AB	H	HR	BA	PO	A	E	DP	TC/G	FA
1908	BOS	A	0	0	—	4.50	1	0	0	2	1	2	1	0	0	0	0	0	0	0	—	1	2	0	0	3.0	1.000

Ray Hartranft

HARTRANFT, RAYMOND JOSEPH BL TL 6′ 1″ 195 lbs.
B. Sept. 19, 1890, Quakertown, Pa. D. Feb. 10, 1955, Spring City, Pa.

Year	Team	Lg	W	L	PCT	ERA	G	GS	CG	IP	H	BB	SO	ShO	Relief W	Relief L	SV	AB	H	HR	BA	PO	A	E	DP	TC/G	FA
1913	PHI	N	0	0	—	9.00	1	0	0	1	3	1	1	0	0	0	0	0	0	0	—	0	0	0	0	0.0	.000

Jeff Hartsock

HARTSOCK, JEFFREY ROGER BR TR 6′ 190 lbs.
B. Nov. 19, 1966, Fairfield, Ohio.

Year	Team	Lg	W	L	PCT	ERA	G	GS	CG	IP	H	BB	SO	ShO	Relief W	Relief L	SV	AB	H	HR	BA	PO	A	E	DP	TC/G	FA
1992	CHI	N	0	0	—	6.75	4	0	0	9.1	15	4	6	0	0	0	0	2	0	0	.000	0	2	0	0	0.5	1.000

Clint Hartung

HARTUNG, CLINTON CLARENCE (Floppy, The Hondo Hurricane) BR TR 6′ 5″ 210 lbs.
B. Aug. 10, 1922, Hondo, Tex.

Year	Team	Lg	W	L	PCT	ERA	G	GS	CG	IP	H	BB	SO	ShO	Relief W	Relief L	SV	AB	H	HR	BA	PO	A	E	DP	TC/G	FA
1947	NY	N	9	7	.563	4.57	23	20	8	138	140	69	54	1	0	0	0	94	29	4	.309	15	22	2	0	1.3	.949
1948			8	8	.500	4.75	36	19	6	153.1	146	72	42	2	2	2	1	56	10	0	.179	6	29	0	1	1.0	1.000
1949			9	11	.450	5.00	33	25	8	154.2	156	86	48	0	1	0	0	63	12	4	.190	9	36	2	1	1.4	.957
1950			3	3	.500	6.61	20	8	1	65.1	87	44	23	0	2	0	0	43	13	3	.302	14	23	2	0	1.7	.949
4 yrs.			29	29	.500	5.02	112	72	23	511.1	529	271	167	3	5	2	1	*				93	114	9	3	1.4	.958

Paul Hartzell

HARTZELL, PAUL FRANKLIN BR TR 6′ 5″ 200 lbs.
B. Nov. 2, 1953, Bloomsburg, Pa.

Year	Team	Lg	W	L	PCT	ERA	G	GS	CG	IP	H	BB	SO	ShO	Relief W	Relief L	SV	AB	H	HR	BA	PO	A	E	DP	TC/G	FA
1976	CAL	A	7	4	.636	2.77	37	15	7	166	166	43	51	2	0	2	2	0	0	0	—	13	32	3	1	1.3	.938
1977			8	12	.400	3.57	41	23	6	189.1	200	38	79	0	2	3	4	0	0	0	—	23	30	5	1	1.4	.914
1978			6	10	.375	3.44	54	12	5	157	168	41	55	0	1	5	6	0	0	0	—	15	27	0	2	0.8	1.000
1979	MIN	A	6	10	.375	5.36	28	26	4	163	193	44	44	0	0	0	0	0	0	0	—	14	30	3	1	1.7	.936
1980	BAL	A	0	2	.000	6.50	6	0	0	18	22	9	5	0	0	2	0	0	0	0	—	0	1	0	0	0.2	1.000
1984	MIL	A	0	1	.000	7.84	4	1	0	10.1	17	6	3	0	0	0	0	0	0	0	—	0	2	0	0	0.5	1.000
6 yrs.			27	39	.409	3.90	170	77	22	703.2	766	181	237	2	3	12	12	0	0	0		65	122	11	5	1.2	.944

Bryan Harvey

HARVEY, BRYAN STANLEY BR TR 6′ 3″ 235 lbs.
B. June 2, 1963, Chattanooga, Tenn.

Year	Team	Lg	W	L	PCT	ERA	G	GS	CG	IP	H	BB	SO	ShO	Relief W	Relief L	SV	AB	H	HR	BA	PO	A	E	DP	TC/G	FA
1987	CAL	A	0	0	—	0.00	3	0	0	5	6	2	3	0	0	0	0	0	0	0	—	0	0	0	0	0.0	.000
1988			7	5	.583	2.13	50	0	0	76	59	20	67	0	7	5	17	0	0	0	—	4	2	1	0	0.1	.857
1989			3	3	.500	3.44	51	0	0	55	36	41	78	0	3	3	25	0	0	0	—	1	7	1	0	0.2	.889
1990			4	4	.500	3.22	54	0	0	64.1	45	35	82	0	4	4	25	0	0	0	—	3	4	0	1	0.1	1.000
1991			2	4	.333	1.60	67	0	0	78.2	51	17	101	0	2	4	**46**	0	0	0	—	2	8	2	0	0.2	.833
1992			0	4	.000	2.83	25	0	0	28.2	22	11	34	0	0	4	13	0	0	0	—	0	1	0	0	0.0	1.000
1993	FLA	N	1	5	.167	1.70	59	0	0	69	45	13	73	0	1	5	45	0	0	0	—	3	5	0	0	0.1	1.000
1994			0	0	—	5.23	12	0	0	10.1	12	4	10	0	0	0	6	0	0	0	—	1	1	0	0	0.2	1.000
1995			0	0	—	∞	1	0	0		2	1	0	0	0	0	0	0	0	0	—	0	0	0	0	0.0	.000
9 yrs.			17	25	.405	2.49	322	0	0	387	278	144	448	0	17	25	177	0	0	0		14	28	4	1	0.1	.913

Ervin Harvey

HARVEY, ERVIN KING (Zaza) BL TL 6′ 190 lbs.
B. Jan. 5, 1879, Saratoga, Calif. D. June 3, 1954, Santa Monica, Calif.

Year	Team	Lg	W	L	PCT	ERA	G	GS	CG	IP	H	BB	SO	ShO	Relief W	Relief L	SV	AB	H	HR	BA	PO	A	E	DP	TC/G	FA
1900	CHI	N	0	0	—	0.00	1	0	0	4	3	1	0	0	0	0	0	3	0	0	.000	1	0	0	0	1.0	1.000
1901	CHI	A	3	6	.333	3.62	16	9	5	92	91	34	27	0	2	0	1	210	70	1	.333	87	42	14	6	2.3	.902
2 yrs.			3	6	.333	3.47	17	9	5	96	94	35	27	0	2	0	1	*				104	44	14	7	2.2	.914

Herb Hash

HASH, HERBERT HOWARD BR TR 6′ 1″ 180 lbs.
B. Feb. 13, 1911, Woolwine, Va.

Year	Team	Lg	W	L	PCT	ERA	G	GS	CG	IP	H	BB	SO	ShO	Relief W	Relief L	SV	AB	H	HR	BA	PO	A	E	DP	TC/G	FA
1940	BOS	A	7	7	.500	4.95	34	12	3	120	123	84	36	1	4	3	3	40	7	0	.175	12	26	2	0	1.2	.950
1941			1	0	1.000	5.40	4	0	0	8.1	7	7	3	0	1	0	1	2	0	0	.000	1	2	0	0	0.8	1.000
2 yrs.			8	7	.533	4.98	38	12	3	128.1	130	91	39	1	5	3	4	42	7	0	.167	13	28	2	0	1.1	.953

Andy Hassler

HASSLER, ANDREW EARL BL TL 6′ 5″ 220 lbs.
B. Oct. 18, 1951, Texas City, Tex.

Year	Team	Lg	W	L	PCT	ERA	G	GS	CG	IP	H	BB	SO	ShO	Relief W	Relief L	SV	AB	H	HR	BA	PO	A	E	DP	TC/G	FA
1971	CAL	A	0	3	.000	3.79	6	4	0	19	25	15	13	0	0	0	0	5	0	0	.000	1	3	0	2	0.7	1.000
1973			0	4	.000	3.69	7	4	1	31.2	33	19	19	0	0	0	0	0	0	0	—	1	4	0	0	0.7	1.000
1974			7	11	.389	2.61	23	22	10	162	132	79	76	2	0	0	1	0	0	0	—	1	29	1	2	1.3	.968
1975			3	12	.200	5.94	30	18	6	133.1	158	53	82	1	0	0	0	0	0	0	—	6	23	1	1	1.0	.967
1976	2 teams	CAL A (14G 0–6)	KC A (19G 5–6)																								
″	total		5	12	.294	3.61	33	18	4	147	139	56	61	1	0	3	0	0	0	0		4	27	1	3	1.0	.969
1977	KC	A	9	6	.600	4.21	29	27	3	156	166	75	83	1	0	0	0	0	0	0	—	6	28	3	2	1.3	.919
1978	2 teams	KC A (11G 1–4)	BOS A (13G 2–1)																								
″	total		3	5	.375	3.89	24	11	1	88	114	37	49	0	2	1	1	0	0	0		3	11	2	1	0.7	.875
1979	2 teams	BOS A (8G 1–2)	NY N (29G 4–5)																								
″	total		5	7	.417	4.55	37	8	1	95	97	49	60	0	2	3	4	22	0	0	.000	3	16	1	0	0.5	.950
1980	2 teams	PIT N (6G 0–0)	CAL A (41G 5–1)																								
″	total		5	1	.833	2.65	47	0	0	95	76	41	79	0	5	1	10	2	0	0	.000	5	12	0	0	0.4	1.000
1981	CAL	A	4	3	.571	3.20	42	0	0	76	72	33	44	0	4	3	5	0	0	0	—	4	14	0	1	0.4	1.000
1982			2	1	.667	2.78	54	0	0	71.1	58	40	38	0	2	1	4	0	0	0	—	2	19	1	2	0.4	.955
1983			0	5	.000	5.45	42	0	0	36.1	42	17	20	0	0	5	4	0	0	0	—	3	8	1	2	0.3	.917
1984	STL	N	1	0	1.000	11.57	3	0	0	2.1	4	2	1	0	1	0	0	0	0	0	—	0	1	0	0	0.3	1.000
1985			0	1	.000	1.80	10	0	0	10	9	4	5	0	0	1	0	0	0	0	—	2	0	1	0	0.3	.667
14 yrs.			44	71	.383	3.83	387	112	26	1123	1125	520	630	5	16	18	29	29	0	0	.000	41	195	12	16	0.6	.952

Andy Hassler *continued*

Year	Team	Lg	W	L	PCT	ERA	G	GS	CG	IP	H	BB	SO	ShO	Relief Pitching W	Relief Pitching L	Relief Pitching SV	Batting AB	Batting H	Batting HR	BA	PO	A	E	DP	TC/G	FA
LEAGUE CHAMPIONSHIP SERIES																											
1976	**KC**	**A**	0	1	.000	6.14	2	1	0	7.1	8	6	4	0	0	0	0	0	0	0	—	0	0	0	0	0.0	.000
1977			0	1	.000	4.76	1	1	0	5.2	5	0	3	0	0	0	0	0	0	0	—	1	0	0	0	1.0	1.000
1982	**CAL**	**A**	0	0	—	0.00	2	0	0	2.2	0	0	2	0	0	0	0	0	0	0	—	0	1	0	0	0.5	1.000
3 yrs.			0	2	.000	4.60	5	2	0	15.2	13	6	9	0	0	0	0	0	0	0		1	1	0	0	0.4	1.000

Charlie Hastings

HASTINGS, CHARLES MORTON 5′11″ 179 lbs.
B. Nov. 11, 1870, Ironton, Ohio D. Aug. 3, 1934, Parkersburg, W. Va.

Year	Team	Lg	W	L	PCT	ERA	G	GS	CG	IP	H	BB	SO	ShO	Relief W	Relief L	Relief SV	AB	H	HR	BA	PO	A	E	DP	TC/G	FA
1893	**CLE**	**N**	4	5	.444	4.70	15	9	6	92	128	33	14	0	1	1	1	39	7	0	.179	4	14	2	0	1.3	.900
1896	**PIT**	**N**	5	10	.333	5.88	17	13	9	104	126	44	19	0	1	1	1	37	8	0	.216	8	29	5	3	2.5	.881
1897			5	4	.556	4.58	16	10	9	118	138	47	42	0	0	1	0	43	10	1	.233	10	17	0	1	1.7	1.000
1898			4	10	.286	3.41	19	13	12	137.1	142	52	40	0	0	**2**	0	43	10	0	.233	6	37	3	2	2.4	.935
4 yrs.			18	29	.383	4.55	67	45	36	451.1	534	176	115	0	2	5	2	162	35	1	.216	28	97	10	6	2.0	.926

Bob Hasty

HASTY, ROBERT KELLER BR TR 6′ 3″ 210 lbs.
B. May 3, 1896, Canton, Ga. D. May 28, 1972, Dallas, Ga.

Year	Team	Lg	W	L	PCT	ERA	G	GS	CG	IP	H	BB	SO	ShO	Relief W	Relief L	Relief SV	AB	H	HR	BA	PO	A	E	DP	TC/G	FA
1919	**PHI**	**A**	0	2	.000	5.25	2	2	1	12	15	4	5	0	0	0	0	3	1	0	.333	1	0	1	0	1.0	.500
1920			1	3	.250	5.02	19	4	1	71.2	91	28	12	0	0	0	0	24	6	0	.250	3	27	1	0	1.6	.968
1921			5	16	.238	4.87	35	22	9	179.1	238	40	46	0	1	0	0	68	20	0	.294	3	53	5	2	1.7	.918
1922			9	14	.391	4.25	28	26	14	192.2	225	41	33	1	0	0	0	75	15	1	.200	8	41	7	1	2.0	.875
1923			13	15	.464	4.44	44	36	10	243.1	274	72	56	1	2	1	1	88	17	0	.193	9	61	6	4	1.7	.921
1924			1	3	.250	5.64	18	4	0	52.2	57	30	15	0	1	0	0	13	1	0	.077	5	19	2	3	1.4	.923
6 yrs.			29	53	.354	4.65	146	94	35	751.2	900	215	167	2	4	1	1	271	60	1	.221	29	201	22	10	1.7	.913

Mickey Hatcher

HATCHER, MICHAEL VAUGHN, JR. BR TR 6′ 2″ 200 lbs.
B. Mar. 15, 1955, Cleveland, Ohio.

Year	Team	Lg	W	L	PCT	ERA	G	GS	CG	IP	H	BB	SO	ShO	Relief W	Relief L	Relief SV	AB	H	HR	BA	PO	A	E	DP	TC/G	FA
1989	**LA**	**N**	0	0	—	9.00	1	0	0	1	0	3	0	0	0	0	0	*				47	24	5	0	2.1	.934

Gil Hatfield

HATFIELD, GILBERT TR 5′ 9″ 168 lbs.
Brother of John Hatfield.
B. Jan. 27, 1855, Hoboken, N. J. D. May 27, 1921, Hoboken, N. J.

Year	Team	Lg	W	L	PCT	ERA	G	GS	CG	IP	H	BB	SO	ShO	Relief W	Relief L	Relief SV	AB	H	HR	BA	PO	A	E	DP	TC/G	FA
1889	**NY**	**N**	2	4	.333	3.98	6	5	5	52	53	25	28	0	1	0	0	125	23	1	.184	10	23	6	0	3.5	.846
1890	**NY**	**P**	1	1	.500	3.52	3	0	0	7.2	8	4	3	0	1	1	1	287	80	1	.279	81	156	55	13	4.0	.812
1891	**WAS**	**AA**	0	0	—	11.00	4	0	0	18	29	14	3	0	0	0	0	500	128	1	.256	268	396	98	43	5.5	.871
3 yrs.			3	5	.375	5.56	13	5	5	77.2	90	43	34	0	2	1	1	*				499	797	222	70	4.7	.854

Hilly Hathaway

HATHAWAY, HILLARY HOUSTON BL TL 6′ 4″ 195 lbs.
B. Sept. 12, 1969, Jacksonville, Fla.

Year	Team	Lg	W	L	PCT	ERA	G	GS	CG	IP	H	BB	SO	ShO	Relief W	Relief L	Relief SV	AB	H	HR	BA	PO	A	E	DP	TC/G	FA
1992	**CAL**	**A**	0	0	—	7.94	2	1	0	5.2	8	3	1	0	0	0	0	0	0	0	—	0	0	0	0	0.0	.000
1993			4	3	.571	5.02	11	11	0	57.1	71	26	11	0	0	0	0	0	0	0	—	4	10	0	4	1.3	1.000
2 yrs.			4	3	.571	5.29	13	12	0	63	79	29	12	0	0	0	0	0	0	0		4	10	0	4	1.1	1.000

Ray Hathaway

HATHAWAY, RAY WILSON BR TR 6′ 165 lbs.
B. Oct. 13, 1916, Greenville, Ohio

Year	Team	Lg	W	L	PCT	ERA	G	GS	CG	IP	H	BB	SO	ShO	Relief W	Relief L	Relief SV	AB	H	HR	BA	PO	A	E	DP	TC/G	FA
1945	**BKN**	**N**	0	1	.000	4.00	4	1	0	9	11	6	3	0	0	0	0	2	0	0	.000	3	3	1	0	1.8	.857

Joe Hatten

HATTEN, JOSEPH HILARIAN BR TL 6′ 176 lbs.
B. Nov. 7, 1916, Bancroft, Iowa D. Dec. 16, 1988, Redding, Calif.

Year	Team	Lg	W	L	PCT	ERA	G	GS	CG	IP	H	BB	SO	ShO	Relief W	Relief L	Relief SV	AB	H	HR	BA	PO	A	E	DP	TC/G	FA
1946	**BKN**	**N**	14	11	.560	2.84	42	30	13	222	207	110	85	1	1	1	2	79	6	0	.076	13	36	6	4	1.3	.891
1947			17	8	.680	3.63	42	32	11	225.1	211	105	76	3	2	0	0	83	17	0	.205	15	52	0	4	1.6	1.000
1948			13	10	.565	3.58	42	30	11	208.2	228	94	73	1	0	1	0	63	13	0	.206	11	57	3	5	1.7	.958
1949			12	8	.600	4.18	37	29	11	187.1	194	69	58	2	2	0	2	67	12	0	.179	12	32	2	5	1.2	.957
1950			2	2	.500	4.59	23	8	2	68.2	82	31	29	1	0	0	0	18	2	0	.111	5	10	1	0	0.7	.938
1951	**2 teams**	**BKN N** (11G 1–0) **CHI N** (23G 2–6)																									
″	**total**		3	6	.333	4.91	34	12	1	124.2	137	58	45	0	2	1	0	32	6	0	.188	11	23	1	4	1.0	.971
1952	**CHI**	**N**	4	4	.500	6.08	13	8	2	50.1	65	25	15	0	2	0	0	15	1	0	.067	3	14	0	3	1.3	1.000
7 yrs.			65	49	.570	3.87	233	149	51	1087	1124	492	381	8	9	3	4	357	57	0	.160	70	224	13	25	1.3	.958
WORLD SERIES																											
1947	**BKN**	**N**	0	0	—	7.00	4	1	0	9	12	7	5	0	0	0	0	3	1	0	.333	0	0	0	0	0.0	.000
1949			0	0	—	16.20	2	0	0	1.2	4	2	0	0	0	0	0	0	0	0	—	0	0	0	0	0.0	.000
2 yrs.			0	0		8.44	6	1	0	10.2	16	9	5	0	0	0	0	3	1	0	.333	0	0	0	0	0.0	

Clyde Hatter

HATTER, CLYDE MELNO (Mad) BR TL 5′11″ 170 lbs.
B. Aug. 7, 1908, Poplar Hill, Ky. D. Oct. 16, 1937, Yosemite, Ky.

Year	Team	Lg	W	L	PCT	ERA	G	GS	CG	IP	H	BB	SO	ShO	Relief W	Relief L	Relief SV	AB	H	HR	BA	PO	A	E	DP	TC/G	FA
1935	**DET**	**A**	0	0	—	7.56	8	2	0	33.1	44	30	15	0	0	0	0	10	3	0	.300	1	2	1	0	0.5	.750
1937			1	0	1.000	11.57	3	0	0	9.1	17	11	4	0	1	0	0	3	0	0	.000	0	1	0	0	0.3	1.000
2 yrs.			1	0	1.000	8.44	11	2	0	42.2	61	41	19	0	1	0	0	13	3	0	.231	1	3	1	0	0.5	.800

Chris Haughey

HAUGHEY, CHRISTOPHER FRANCIS (Bud) BR TR 6′ 1″ 180 lbs.
B. Oct. 3, 1925, Astoria, N. Y.

Year	Team	Lg	W	L	PCT	ERA	G	GS	CG	IP	H	BB	SO	ShO	Relief W	Relief L	Relief SV	AB	H	HR	BA	PO	A	E	DP	TC/G	FA
1943	**BKN**	**N**	0	1	.000	3.86	1	0	0	7	5	10	0	0	0	1	0	3	0	0	.000	0	2	1	0	3.0	.667

Phil Haugstad

HAUGSTAD, PHILIP DONALD BR TR 6′ 2″ 165 lbs.
B. Feb. 23, 1924, Black River Falls, Wis.

Year	Team	Lg	W	L	PCT	ERA	G	GS	CG	IP	H	BB	SO	ShO	Relief W	Relief L	Relief SV	AB	H	HR	BA	PO	A	E	DP	TC/G	FA
1947	**BKN**	**N**	1	0	1.000	2.84	6	1	0	12.2	14	4	4	0	1	0	0	2	0	0	.000	0	2	0	0	0.3	1.000
1948			0	0	—	0.00	1	0	0	1	1	0	0	0	0	0	0	0	0	0	—	0	2	0	0	2.0	1.000
1951			0	1	.000	6.46	21	1	0	30.2	28	24	22	0	0	1	0	1	0	0	.000	1	7	0	0	0.4	1.000
1952	**CIN**	**N**	0	0	—	6.75	9	0	0	12	8	13	2	0	0	0	0	1	0	0	.000	0	4	1	0	0.6	.800
4 yrs.			1	1	.500	5.59	37	2	0	56.1	51	41	28	0	1	1	0	4	0	0	.000	1	15	1	0	0.5	.941

Tom Hausman

HAUSMAN, THOMAS MATTHEW BR TR 6′ 4″ 190 lbs.
B. Mar. 31, 1953, Mobridge, S. D.

Year	Team	W	L	PCT	ERA	G	GS	CG	IP	H	BB	SO	ShO	Relief Pitching W	Relief Pitching L	Relief Pitching SV	Batting AB	Batting H	Batting HR	BA	PO	A	E	DP	TC/G	FA
1975	**MIL A**	3	6	.333	4.10	29	9	1	112	110	47	46	0	3	1	0	0	0	0	—	8	19	0	1	0.9	1.000
1976		0	0	—	5.40	3	0	0	3.1	3	3	1	0	0	0	0	0	0	0	—	1	2	0	0	1.0	1.000
1978	**NY N**	3	3	.500	4.67	10	10	0	52	58	9	16	0	0	0	0	17	3	0	.176	6	8	1	0	1.5	.933
1979		2	6	.250	2.73	19	10	1	79	65	19	33	0	0	2	2	26	3	0	.115	10	11	0	0	1.1	1.000
1980		6	5	.545	3.98	55	4	0	122	125	26	53	0	4	4	1	16	1	0	.063	11	23	3	4	0.7	.919
1981		0	1	.000	2.18	20	0	0	33	28	7	13	0	0	1	0	2	0	0	.000	2	6	0	0	0.4	1.000
1982	**2 teams NY N** (21G 1–2) **ATL N** (3G 0–0)																									
″	**total**	1	2	.333	4.46	24	0	0	40.1	50	10	18	0	1	2	0	2	0	0	.000	4	5	1	1	0.4	.900
7 yrs.		15	23	.395	3.79	160	33	2	441.2	439	121	180	0	8	10	3	63	7	0	.111	42	74	5	6	0.8	.959

Clem Hausmann

HAUSMANN, CLEMENS RAYMOND BR TR 5′ 9″ 165 lbs.
B. Aug. 17, 1919, Houston, Tex. D. Aug. 29, 1972, Baytown, Tex.

Year	Team	W	L	PCT	ERA	G	GS	CG	IP	H	BB	SO	ShO	Relief Pitching W	Relief Pitching L	Relief Pitching SV	Batting AB	Batting H	Batting HR	BA	PO	A	E	DP	TC/G	FA
1944	**BOS A**	4	7	.364	3.42	32	12	3	137	139	69	43	0	1	2	2	38	3	0	.079	8	25	0	0	1.0	1.000
1945		5	7	.417	5.04	31	13	4	125	131	60	30	2	1	0	2	39	4	0	.103	13	30	1	2	1.4	.977
1949	**PHI A**	0	0	—	9.00	1	0	0	1	0	2	0	0	0	0	0	0	0	0	—	0	1	0	1	1.0	1.000
3 yrs.		9	14	.391	4.21	64	25	7	263	270	131	73	2	2	2	4	77	7	0	.091	21	56	1	3	1.2	.987

Brad Havens

HAVENS, BRADLEY DAVID BL TL 6′ 1″ 180 lbs.
B. Nov. 17, 1959, Highland Park, Mich.

Year	Team	W	L	PCT	ERA	G	GS	CG	IP	H	BB	SO	ShO	Relief Pitching W	Relief Pitching L	Relief Pitching SV	Batting AB	Batting H	Batting HR	BA	PO	A	E	DP	TC/G	FA
1981	**MIN A**	3	6	.333	3.58	14	12	1	78	76	24	43	1	0	0	0	0	0	0	—	1	11	0	1	0.9	1.000
1982		10	14	.417	4.31	33	32	4	208.2	201	80	129	1	0	1	0	0	0	0	—	4	18	0	0	0.7	1.000
1983		5	8	.385	8.18	16	14	1	80.1	110	38	40	0	0	1	0	0	0	0	—	0	2	0	0	0.1	1.000
1985	**BAL A**	0	1	.000	8.79	8	1	0	14.1	20	10	19	0	0	0	0	0	0	0	—	0	1	0	0	0.1	1.000
1986		3	3	.500	4.56	46	0	0	71	64	29	57	0	3	3	1	0	0	0	—	4	13	1	0	0.4	.944
1987	**LA N**	0	0	—	4.33	31	1	0	35.1	30	23	23	0	0	0	1	2	0	0	.000	1	3	0	0	0.1	1.000
1988	**2 teams LA N** (9G 0–0) **CLE A** (28G 2–3)																									
″	**total**	2	3	.400	3.36	37	0	0	67	77	21	38	0	2	3	1	1	0	0	.000	7	10	0	0	0.5	1.000
1989	**2 teams CLE A** (7G 0–0) **DET A** (13G 1–2)																									
″	**total**	1	2	.333	5.00	20	1	0	36	46	21	21	0	1	1	0	0	0	0		4	7	0	3	0.6	1.000
8 yrs.		24	37	.393	4.81	205	61	6	590.2	624	246	370	2	6	9	3	3	0	0	.000	21	65	1	4	0.4	.989

Ed Hawk

HAWK, EDWARD BL TR 5′11″ 175 lbs.
B. May 11, 1890, Neosho, Mo. D. Mar. 26, 1936, Neosho, Mo.

Year	Team	W	L	PCT	ERA	G	GS	CG	IP	H	BB	SO	ShO	Relief Pitching W	Relief Pitching L	Relief Pitching SV	Batting AB	Batting H	Batting HR	BA	PO	A	E	DP	TC/G	FA
1911	**STL A**	0	4	.000	3.35	5	4	4	37.2	38	8	14	0	0	0	0	13	2	0	.154	0	12	1	1	2.6	.923

Bill Hawke

HAWKE, WILLIAM VICTOR (Dick) BR TR 5′ 8½″ 169 lbs.
B. Apr. 28, 1870, Elsmere, Del. D. Dec. 11, 1902, Wilmington, Del.

Year	Team	W	L	PCT	ERA	G	GS	CG	IP	H	BB	SO	ShO	Relief Pitching W	Relief Pitching L	Relief Pitching SV	Batting AB	Batting H	Batting HR	BA	PO	A	E	DP	TC/G	FA
1892	**STL N**	4	5	.444	3.70	14	11	10	97.1	108	45	55	1	0	1	0	45	4	0	.089	9	18	0	0	1.8	1.000
1893	**2 teams STL N** (1G 0–1) **BAL N** (29G 11–16)																									
″	**total**	11	17	.393	4.77	30	30	22	230.1	257	111	70	1	0	0	0	96	17	1	.177	18	48	10	0	2.5	.868
1894	**BAL N**	16	9	.640	5.84	32	25	17	205	264	78	68	0	2	0	3	92	28	1	.304	9	41	5	3	1.7	.909
3 yrs.		31	31	.500	4.98	76	66	49	532.2	629	234	193	2	2	1	3	233	49	2	.210	36	107	15	3	2.1	.905

Andy Hawkins

HAWKINS, MELTON ANDREW BR TR 6′ 4″ 200 lbs.
B. Jan. 21, 1960, Waco, Tex.

Year	Team	W	L	PCT	ERA	G	GS	CG	IP	H	BB	SO	ShO	Relief Pitching W	Relief Pitching L	Relief Pitching SV	Batting AB	Batting H	Batting HR	BA	PO	A	E	DP	TC/G	FA
1982	**SD N**	2	5	.286	4.10	15	10	1	63.2	66	27	25	0	0	0	0	15	0	0	.000	6	6	1	0	0.9	.923
1983		5	7	.417	2.93	21	19	4	119.2	106	48	59	1	0	0	0	31	2	0	.065	13	18	1	2	1.5	.969
1984		8	9	.471	4.68	36	22	2	146	143	72	77	1	2	1	0	41	8	0	.195	10	16	2	1	0.8	.929
1985		18	8	.692	3.15	33	33	5	228.2	229	65	69	2	0	0	0	77	6	0	.078	21	30	1	3	1.6	.981
1986		10	8	.556	4.30	37	35	3	209.1	218	75	117	1	1	0	0	67	10	0	.149	7	28	0	0	0.9	1.000
1987		3	10	.231	5.05	24	20	0	117.2	131	49	51	0	0	0	0	32	5	0	.156	8	18	0	3	1.1	1.000
1988		14	11	.560	3.35	33	33	4	217.2	196	76	91	2	0	0	0	62	7	0	.113	14	23	2	4	1.2	.949
1989	**NY A**	15	15	.500	4.80	34	34	5	208.1	238	76	98	2	0	0	0	0	0	0	—	8	20	2	1	0.9	.933
1990		5	12	.294	5.37	28	26	2	157.2	156	82	74	1	0	0	0	0	0	0	—	12	9	0	3	0.8	1.000
1991	**2 teams NY A** (4G 0–2) **OAK A** (15G 4–4)																									
″	**total**	4	6	.400	5.52	19	17	1	89.2	91	42	45	0	0	0	0	0	0	0		6	18	0	2	1.3	1.000
10 yrs.		84	91	.480	4.22	280	249	27	1558.1	1574	612	706	10	3	1	0	325	38	0	.117	105	186	9	19	1.1	.970
LEAGUE CHAMPIONSHIP SERIES																										
1984	**SD N**	0	0	—	0.00	3	0	0	3.2	0	2	1	0	0	0	0	0	0	0	—	0	1	0	1	0.3	1.000
WORLD SERIES																										
1984	**SD N**	1	1	.500	0.75	3	0	0	12	4	6	4	0	1	1	0	0	0	0	—	0	1	0	0	0.3	1.000

LaTroy Hawkins

HAWKINS, LaTROY BR TR 6′ 5″ 195 lbs.
B. Dec. 21, 1972, Gary, Ind.

Year	Team	W	L	PCT	ERA	G	GS	CG	IP	H	BB	SO	ShO	Relief Pitching W	Relief Pitching L	Relief Pitching SV	Batting AB	Batting H	Batting HR	BA	PO	A	E	DP	TC/G	FA
1995	**MIN A**	2	3	.400	8.67	6	6	1	27	39	12	9	0	0	0	0	0	0	0	—	3	3	0	1	1.0	1.000

Wynn Hawkins

HAWKINS, WYNN FIRTH (Hawk) BR TR 6′ 3″ 195 lbs.
B. Feb. 20, 1936, E. Palestine, Ohio.

Year	Team	W	L	PCT	ERA	G	GS	CG	IP	H	BB	SO	ShO	Relief Pitching W	Relief Pitching L	Relief Pitching SV	Batting AB	Batting H	Batting HR	BA	PO	A	E	DP	TC/G	FA
1960	**CLE A**	4	4	.500	4.23	15	9	1	66	68	39	39	0	0	0	0	20	2	0	.100	9	11	0	1	1.3	1.000
1961		7	9	.438	4.06	30	21	3	133	139	59	51	1	3	0	1	37	4	0	.108	11	18	3	1	1.1	.906
1962		1	0	1.000	7.36	3	0	0	3.2	9	1	0	0	1	0	0	0	0	0	—	0	0	0	0	0.0	.000
3 yrs.		12	13	.480	4.17	48	30	4	202.2	216	99	90	1	4	0	1	57	6	0	.105	20	29	3	2	1.1	.942

Marv Hawley

HAWLEY, MARVIN HIRAM
B. Painesville, Ohio D. Apr. 28, 1904, Alliance, Ohio.

Year	Team	W	L	PCT	ERA	G	GS	CG	IP	H	BB	SO	ShO	Relief Pitching W	Relief Pitching L	Relief Pitching SV	Batting AB	Batting H	Batting HR	BA	PO	A	E	DP	TC/G	FA
1894	**BOS N**	0	1	.000	7.71	1	1	1	7	10	7	1	0	0	0	0	3	0	0	.000	1	2	0	1	3.0	1.000

Pink Hawley

HAWLEY, EMERSON P. BL TR 5′10″ 185 lbs.
B. Dec. 5, 1872, Beaver Dam, Wis. D. Sept. 19, 1938, Beaver Dam, Wis.

Year	Team	W	L	PCT	ERA	G	GS	CG	IP	H	BB	SO	ShO	Relief Pitching W	Relief Pitching L	Relief Pitching SV	Batting AB	Batting H	Batting HR	BA	PO	A	E	DP	TC/G	FA
1892	**STL N**	6	14	.300	3.19	20	20	18	166.1	160	63	63	0	0	0	0	71	12	1	.169	9	26	4	1	2.0	.897
1893		5	17	.227	4.60	31	24	21	227	249	103	73	0	0	0	1	91	26	0	.286	8	40	10	1	1.9	.828
1894		19	**26**	.422	4.90	53	41	36	392.2	481	149	120	0	2	**5**	0	163	43	2	.264	29	77	12	2	2.2	.898
1895	**PIT N**	31	22	.585	3.18	**56**	**50**	44	**444.1**	449	122	142	**4**	3	2	1	185	57	5	.308	16	110	13	2	2.5	.906
1896		22	21	.512	3.57	49	43	37	378	382	157	137	2	**3**	1	0	163	39	1	.239	12	108	10	2	2.7	.923

Pink Hawley *continued*

Year	Team	Lg	W	L	PCT	ERA	G	GS	CG	IP	H	BB	SO	ShO	Relief W	Relief L	Relief SV	Bat AB	Bat H	Bat HR	BA	PO	A	E	DP	TC/G	FA
1897			18	18	.500	4.80	40	39	33	311.1	362	94	88	0	0	0	0	130	30	0	.231	11	69	4	3	2.1	.952
1898	CIN	N	27	11	.711	3.37	43	37	32	331	357	91	69	3	**4**	0	0	130	24	1	.185	11	58	4	0	1.7	.945
1899			14	17	.452	4.24	34	29	25	250.1	289	65	46	0	1	3	1	101	22	0	.218	13	50	5	2	2.0	.926
1900	NY	N	18	18	.500	3.53	41	38	**34**	329.1	377	89	80	1	0	1	0	123	25	1	.203	14	95	4	5	2.8	.965
1901	MIL	A	7	14	.333	4.59	26	23	17	182.1	228	41	50	0	0	0	0	73	19	0	.260	7	55	4	1	2.4	.939
10 yrs.			167	178	.484	3.96	393	344	297	3012.2	3334	974	868	10	13	12	3	1230	297	11	.241	130	688	70	19	2.2	.921

Hal Haydel

HAYDEL, JOHN HAROLD BR TR 6′ 190 lbs.
B. July 9, 1944, Houma, La.

Year	Team	Lg	W	L	PCT	ERA	G	GS	CG	IP	H	BB	SO	ShO	Relief W	Relief L	Relief SV	Bat AB	Bat H	Bat HR	BA	PO	A	E	DP	TC/G	FA
1970	MIN	A	2	0	1.000	3.00	4	0	0	9	7	4	4	0	2	0	0	3	2	1	.667	0	1	0	0	0.3	1.000
1971			4	2	.667	4.28	31	0	0	40	33	20	29	0	4	2	1	3	1	0	.333	1	7	1	0	0.3	.889
2 yrs.			6	2	.750	4.04	35	0	0	49	40	24	33	0	6	2	1	6	3	1	.500	1	8	1	0	0.3	.900

Gene Hayden

HAYDEN, EUGENE FRANKLIN (Lefty) BL TL 6′ 2″ 175 lbs.
B. Apr. 14, 1935, San Francisco, Calif.

Year	Team	Lg	W	L	PCT	ERA	G	GS	CG	IP	H	BB	SO	ShO	Relief W	Relief L	Relief SV	Bat AB	Bat H	Bat HR	BA	PO	A	E	DP	TC/G	FA
1958	CIN	N	0	0	—	4.91	3	0	0	3.2	5	1	3	0	0	0	0	0	0	0	—	0	0	0	0	0.0	.000

Ben Hayes

HAYES, BEN JOSEPH BR TR 6′ 1″ 180 lbs.
B. Aug. 4, 1957, Niagara Falls, N. Y.

Year	Team	Lg	W	L	PCT	ERA	G	GS	CG	IP	H	BB	SO	ShO	Relief W	Relief L	Relief SV	Bat AB	Bat H	Bat HR	BA	PO	A	E	DP	TC/G	FA
1982	CIN	N	2	0	1.000	1.97	26	0	0	45.2	37	22	38	0	2	0	2	4	0	0	.000	1	4	0	0	0.2	1.000
1983			4	6	.400	6.49	60	0	0	69.1	82	37	44	0	4	6	7	5	0	0	.000	3	11	0	0	0.2	1.000
2 yrs.			6	6	.500	4.70	86	0	0	115	119	59	82	0	6	6	9	9	0	0	.000	4	15	0	0	0.2	1.000

Jim Hayes

HAYES, JAMES MILLARD (Whitey) BL TR 6′ 1″ 168 lbs.
B. Feb. 11, 1913, Montevallo, Ala. D. Nov. 27, 1993, Decatur, Ga.

Year	Team	Lg	W	L	PCT	ERA	G	GS	CG	IP	H	BB	SO	ShO	Relief W	Relief L	Relief SV	Bat AB	Bat H	Bat HR	BA	PO	A	E	DP	TC/G	FA
1935	WAS	A	2	4	.333	8.36	7	4	1	28	38	23	9	0	1	1	0	8	2	0	.250	1	2	1	0	0.6	.750

Heath Haynes

HAYNES, HEATH BURNETT BR TR 6′ 175 lbs.
B. Nov. 30, 1968, Wheeling, W. Va.

Year	Team	Lg	W	L	PCT	ERA	G	GS	CG	IP	H	BB	SO	ShO	Relief W	Relief L	Relief SV	Bat AB	Bat H	Bat HR	BA	PO	A	E	DP	TC/G	FA
1994	MON	N	0	0	—	0.00	4	0	0	3.2	3	3	1	0	0	0	0	0	0	0	—	0	0	0	0	0.0	.000

Jimmy Haynes

HAYNES, JIMMY WAYNE BR TR 6′ 4″ 185 lbs.
B. Sept. 5, 1972, La Grange, Ga.

Year	Team	Lg	W	L	PCT	ERA	G	GS	CG	IP	H	BB	SO	ShO	Relief W	Relief L	Relief SV	Bat AB	Bat H	Bat HR	BA	PO	A	E	DP	TC/G	FA
1995	BAL	A	2	1	.667	2.25	4	3	0	24	11	12	22	0	0	0	0	0	0	0	—	0	3	0	0	0.8	1.000

Joe Haynes

HAYNES, JOSEPH WALTON BR TR 6′ 2½″ 190 lbs.
B. Sept. 21, 1917, Lincolnton, Ga. D. Jan. 6, 1967, Hopkins, Minn.

Year	Team	Lg	W	L	PCT	ERA	G	GS	CG	IP	H	BB	SO	ShO	Relief W	Relief L	Relief SV	Bat AB	Bat H	Bat HR	BA	PO	A	E	DP	TC/G	FA
1939	WAS	A	8	12	.400	5.36	27	20	10	173	186	78	64	1	2	0	0	67	14	0	.209	10	23	1	1	1.3	.971
1940			3	6	.333	6.54	22	7	1	63.1	85	34	23	0	2	3	0	19	2	0	.105	2	9	2	1	0.6	.846
1941	CHI	A	0	0	—	3.86	8	0	0	28	30	11	18	0	0	0	0	11	3	0	.273	1	3	0	0	0.5	1.000
1942			8	5	.615	2.62	**40**	1	1	103	88	47	35	0	8	4	6	28	5	0	.179	6	22	0	0	0.7	1.000
1943			7	2	.778	2.96	35	2	1	109.1	114	32	37	0	5	2	3	34	9	0	.265	4	21	1	0	0.7	.962
1944			5	6	.455	2.57	33	12	8	154.1	148	43	44	0	2	0	2	50	10	0	.200	10	31	3	2	1.3	.932
1945			5	5	.500	3.55	14	13	8	104	92	29	34	1	0	0	1	40	7	0	.175	8	23	0	0	2.2	1.000
1946			7	9	.438	3.76	32	23	9	177.1	203	60	60	0	0	0	2	57	14	0	.246	4	39	0	1	1.3	1.000
1947			14	6	.700	2.42	29	22	7	182	174	61	50	2	3	0	0	65	17	0	.262	12	29	2	5	1.5	.953
1948			9	10	.474	3.97	27	22	6	149.2	167	52	40	0	1	0	0	50	8	0	.160	6	19	2	1	1.0	.926
1949	WAS	A	2	9	.182	6.26	37	10	0	96.1	106	55	19	0	0	5	2	25	6	0	.240	6	23	1	0	0.8	.967
1950			7	5	.583	5.84	27	10	1	101.2	124	46	15	1	3	1	0	35	7	0	.200	9	20	1	1	1.1	.967
1951			1	4	.200	4.56	26	3	1	73	85	37	18	0	1	3	2	21	7	1	.333	2	11	0	0	0.5	1.000
1952			0	3	.000	4.50	22	2	0	66	70	35	18	0	0	1	3	19	2	0	.105	3	10	0	0	0.6	1.000
14 yrs.			76	82	.481	4.01	379	147	53	1581	1672	620	475	5	27	19	21	521	111	1	.213	83	283	13	12	1.0	.966

Ray Hayward

HAYWARD, RAYMOND ALTON BL TL 6′ 1″ 190 lbs.
B. Apr. 27, 1961, Enid, Okla.

Year	Team	Lg	W	L	PCT	ERA	G	GS	CG	IP	H	BB	SO	ShO	Relief W	Relief L	Relief SV	Bat AB	Bat H	Bat HR	BA	PO	A	E	DP	TC/G	FA
1986	SD	N	0	2	.000	9.00	3	3	0	10	16	4	6	0	0	0	0	4	0	0	.000	0	1	1	0	0.7	.500
1987			0	0	—	16.50	4	0	0	6	12	3	2	0	0	0	0	1	0	0	.000	1	3	0	1	1.0	1.000
1988	TEX	A	4	6	.400	5.46	12	12	1	62.2	63	35	37	1	0	0	0	0	0	0	—	5	12	2	3	1.6	.895
3 yrs.			4	8	.333	6.75	19	15	1	78.2	91	42	45	1	0	0	0	5	0	0	.000	6	16	3	4	1.3	.880

Bill Haywood

HAYWOOD, WILLIAM KIERNAN BR TR 6′ 3″ 205 lbs.
B. Apr. 21, 1937, Colon, Panama.

Year	Team	Lg	W	L	PCT	ERA	G	GS	CG	IP	H	BB	SO	ShO	Relief W	Relief L	Relief SV	Bat AB	Bat H	Bat HR	BA	PO	A	E	DP	TC/G	FA
1968	WAS	A	0	0	—	4.63	14	0	0	23.1	27	12	10	0	0	0	0	0	0	0	—	0	4	0	0	0.3	1.000

Ed Head

HEAD, EDWARD MARVIN BR TR 6′ 1″ 175 lbs.
B. Jan. 25, 1918, Selma, La. D. Jan. 31, 1980, Bastrop, La.

Year	Team	Lg	W	L	PCT	ERA	G	GS	CG	IP	H	BB	SO	ShO	Relief W	Relief L	Relief SV	Bat AB	Bat H	Bat HR	BA	PO	A	E	DP	TC/G	FA
1940	BKN	N	1	2	.333	4.12	13	5	2	39.1	40	18	13	0	0	0	0	11	2	0	.182	0	3	0	0	0.2	1.000
1942			10	6	.625	3.56	36	15	5	136.2	118	47	78	1	3	1	4	39	13	0	.333	9	29	3	1	1.1	.927
1943			9	10	.474	3.66	47	18	7	169.2	166	66	83	3	2	3	6	46	7	0	.152	6	40	3	2	1.0	.939
1944			4	3	.571	2.70	9	8	5	63.1	54	19	17	0	0	0	0	19	5	0	.263	4	6	0	0	1.1	1.000
1946			3	2	.600	3.21	13	7	3	56	56	24	17	1	0	0	1	16	5	0	.313	2	9	1	1	0.9	.917
5 yrs.			27	23	.540	3.48	118	53	22	465	434	174	208	5	5	4	11	131	32	0	.244	21	87	7	4	1.0	.939

Ralph Head

HEAD, RALPH BR TR 5′10″ 175 lbs.
B. Aug. 30, 1893, Tallapoosa, Ga. D. Oct. 8, 1962, Muscadine, Ala.

Year	Team	Lg	W	L	PCT	ERA	G	GS	CG	IP	H	BB	SO	ShO	Relief W	Relief L	Relief SV	Bat AB	Bat H	Bat HR	BA	PO	A	E	DP	TC/G	FA
1923	PHI	N	2	9	.182	6.66	35	13	5	132.1	185	57	24	0	1	0	0	42	3	0	.071	2	30	0	1	0.9	1.000

Tom Healey

HEALEY, THOMAS F. TR
B. 1853, Cranston, R. I. D. Feb. 6, 1891, Lewiston, Me.

1878 **2 teams** **PRO N** (3G 0–3) **IND N** (11G 6–4)

Year	Team	Lg	W	L	PCT	ERA	G	GS	CG	IP	H	BB	SO	ShO	Relief W	Relief L	Relief SV	Bat AB	Bat H	Bat HR	BA	PO	A	E	DP	TC/G	FA
″	**total**		6	7	.462	2.39	14	13	12	113	125	20	20	0	0	0	**1**	54	10	0	.185	6	25	7	0	2.2	.816

Egyptian Healy

HEALY, JOHN J. (Long John) BR TR 6′ 2″ 158 lbs.
B. Oct. 27, 1866, Cairo, Ill. D. Mar. 16, 1899, St. Louis, Mo.

Year	Team	Lg	W	L	PCT	ERA	G	GS	CG	IP	H	BB	SO	ShO	Relief Pitching W	Relief Pitching L	Relief Pitching SV	Batting AB	Batting H	Batting HR	BA	PO	A	E	DP	TC/G	FA
1885	STL	N	1	7	.125	*3.00*	8	8	8	66	54	20	32	0	0	0	0	24	1	0	.042	6	16	4	1	3.3	.846
1886			17	23	.425	*2.88*	43	41	39	353.2	315	118	213	3	1	0	0	145	14	0	.097	6	62	4	2	1.7	.944
1887	IND	N	12	**29**	.293	5.17	41	41	40	341	415	108	75	3	0	0	0	138	24	3	.174	7	51	12	0	1.7	.829
1888			12	24	.333	3.89	37	37	36	321.1	347	87	124	1	0	0	0	131	30	0	.229	5	79	15	3	2.6	.848
1889	2 teams	WAS N (13G 1–11)	CHI N (5G 1–4)																								
"	total		2	15	.118	5.69	18	17	15	147	187	56	71	0	0	0	0	65	12	1	.185	6	36	6	0	2.7	.875
1890	TOL	AA	22	21	.512	*2.89*	46	46	44	389	326	127	225	2	0	0	0	156	34	1	.218	50	62	14	4	2.6	.889
1891	BAL	AA	8	10	.444	3.75	23	22	19	170.1	179	57	54	0	0	0	0	64	9	0	.141	0	17	2	1	0.8	.895
1892	2 teams	BAL N (9G 3–6)	LOU N (2G 1–1)																								
"	total		4	7	.364	4.15	11	10	7	86.2	97	26	28	0	1	0	0	34	8	0	.235	3	17	4	1	2.2	.833
8 yrs.			78	136	.364	3.84	227	222	208	1875	1920	599	822	9	2	0	0	757	132	5	.174	83	340	61	12	2.1	.874

Charlie Heard

HEARD, CHARLES BR TR 6′ 2″ 190 lbs.
B. Jan. 30, 1872, Philadelphia, Pa. D. Feb. 20, 1945, Philadelphia, Pa.

Year	Team	Lg	W	L	PCT	ERA	G	GS	CG	IP	H	BB	SO	ShO	Relief Pitching W	Relief Pitching L	Relief Pitching SV	Batting AB	Batting H	Batting HR	BA	PO	A	E	DP	TC/G	FA
1890	PIT	N	0	6	.000	8.39	6	6	5	44	75	32	13	0	0	0	0	*				7	6	6	1	1.6	.684

Jay Heard

HEARD, JEHOSIE BL TL 5′ 7″ 155 lbs.
B. Jan. 17, 1920, Atlanta, Ga.

Year	Team	Lg	W	L	PCT	ERA	G	GS	CG	IP	H	BB	SO	ShO	Relief Pitching W	Relief Pitching L	Relief Pitching SV	Batting AB	Batting H	Batting HR	BA	PO	A	E	DP	TC/G	FA
1954	BAL	A	0	0	—	13.50	2	0	0	3.1	6	3	2	0	0	0	0	0	0	0	—	0	1	0	0	0.5	1.000

Bunny Hearn

HEARN, BUNN BL TL 5′11½″ 190 lbs.
B. May 21, 1891, Chapel Hill, N. C. D. Oct. 10, 1959, Wilson, N. C.

Year	Team	Lg	W	L	PCT	ERA	G	GS	CG	IP	H	BB	SO	ShO	Relief Pitching W	Relief Pitching L	Relief Pitching SV	Batting AB	Batting H	Batting HR	BA	PO	A	E	DP	TC/G	FA
1910	STL	N	1	3	.250	5.08	5	5	4	39	49	16	14	0	0	0	0	15	2	1	.133	2	7	0	1	1.8	1.000
1911			0	0	—	13.50	2	0	0	2.2	7	0	1	0	0	0	0	1	0	0	.000	0	0	0	0	0.0	.000
1913	NY	N	1	1	.500	2.77	2	2	1	13	13	7	8	0	0	0	0	5	2	0	.400	1	2	0	0	1.5	1.000
1915	PIT	F	6	11	.353	3.38	29	17	8	175.2	187	37	49	1	1	1	0	53	10	0	.189	7	50	0	1	2.0	1.000
1918	BOS	N	5	6	.455	2.49	17	12	9	126.1	119	29	30	1	0	0	0	45	8	0	.178	3	43	0	0	2.7	1.000
1920			0	3	.000	5.65	11	4	2	43	54	11	9	0	0	0	0	14	2	0	.143	2	15	3	0	1.8	.850
6 yrs.			13	24	.351	3.56	66	40	24	399.2	429	100	111	2	1	1	0	133	24	1	.180	15	117	3	2	2.0	.978

Bunny Hearn

HEARN, ELMER LAFAYETTE BL TL 5′ 8″ 160 lbs.
B. Jan. 13, 1904, Brooklyn, N. Y. D. Mar. 31, 1974, Venice, Fla.

Year	Team	Lg	W	L	PCT	ERA	G	GS	CG	IP	H	BB	SO	ShO	Relief Pitching W	Relief Pitching L	Relief Pitching SV	Batting AB	Batting H	Batting HR	BA	PO	A	E	DP	TC/G	FA
1926	BOS	N	4	9	.308	4.22	34	12	3	117.1	121	56	40	0	2	3	2	30	3	0	.100	2	38	0	1	1.2	1.000
1927			0	2	.000	4.26	8	0	0	12.2	16	9	5	0	0	2	0	5	2	0	.400	0	4	1	1	0.6	.800
1928			1	0	1.000	6.30	7	0	0	10	6	8	8	0	1	0	0	1	0	0	.000	0	1	0	0	0.1	1.000
1929			2	0	1.000	4.42	10	1	0	18.1	18	9	12	0	2	0	0	2	0	0	.000	1	5	0	2	0.6	1.000
4 yrs.			7	11	.389	4.38	59	13	3	158.1	161	82	65	0	5	5	2	38	5	0	.132	3	48	1	4	0.9	.981

Jim Hearn

HEARN, JAMES TOLBERT BR TR 6′ 3″ 205 lbs.
B. Apr. 11, 1921, Atlanta, Ga.

Year	Team	Lg	W	L	PCT	ERA	G	GS	CG	IP	H	BB	SO	ShO	Relief Pitching W	Relief Pitching L	Relief Pitching SV	Batting AB	Batting H	Batting HR	BA	PO	A	E	DP	TC/G	FA
1947	STL	N	12	7	.632	3.22	37	21	4	162	151	63	57	1	3	2	1	55	8	0	.145	6	25	1	2	0.9	.969
1948			8	6	.571	4.22	34	13	3	89.2	92	35	27	0	5	2	1	25	5	0	.200	1	8	0	0	0.3	1.000
1949			1	3	.250	5.14	17	4	0	42	48	23	18	0	1	1	0	10	1	0	.100	4	8	1	0	0.8	.923
1950	2 teams	STL N (6G 0–1)	NY N (16G 11–3)																								
"	total		11	4	.733	**2.49**	22	16	11	134	84	44	58	5	0	1	0	45	7	0	.156	9	23	1	2	1.5	.970
1951	NY	N	17	9	.654	3.62	34	34	11	211.1	204	82	66	0	0	0	0	74	12	1	.162	16	61	2	7	2.3	.975
1952			14	7	.667	3.78	37	34	11	223.2	208	97	89	1	0	0	1	77	14	3	.182	14	57	0	6	1.9	1.000
1953			9	12	.429	4.53	36	32	6	196.2	206	84	77	0	0	1	0	66	9	0	.136	9	44	3	2	1.6	.946
1954			8	8	.500	4.15	29	18	3	130	137	66	45	2	1	1	1	45	5	1	.111	8	29	2	3	1.3	.949
1955			14	16	.467	3.73	39	33	11	226.2	225	66	86	1	2	1	0	77	12	4	.156	19	48	5	6	1.8	.931
1956			5	11	.313	3.97	30	19	2	129.1	124	44	66	0	0	1	1	41	4	0	.098	7	22	3	2	1.1	.906
1957	PHI	N	5	1	.833	3.65	36	4	1	74	79	18	46	0	4	0	3	17	0	0	.000	9	16	3	1	0.8	.893
1958			5	3	.625	4.17	39	1	0	73.1	88	27	33	0	4	3	0	14	0	0	.000	3	10	1	2	0.4	.929
1959			0	2	.000	5.73	6	0	0	11	15	6	1	0	0	2	0	2	0	0	.000	1	4	0	0	0.8	1.000
13 yrs.			109	89	.551	3.81	396	229	63	1703.2	1661	655	669	10	20	15	8	548	77	9	.141	106	355	22	33	1.2	.954
WORLD SERIES																											
1951	NY	N	1	0	1.000	1.04	2	1	0	8.2	5	8	1	0	0	0	0	3	0	0	.000	0	2	0	1	1.0	1.000

Spencer Heath

HEATH, SPENCER PAUL BB TR 6′ 170 lbs.
B. Nov. 5, 1894, Chicago, Ill. D. Jan. 25, 1930, Chicago, Ill.

Year	Team	Lg	W	L	PCT	ERA	G	GS	CG	IP	H	BB	SO	ShO	Relief Pitching W	Relief Pitching L	Relief Pitching SV	Batting AB	Batting H	Batting HR	BA	PO	A	E	DP	TC/G	FA
1920	CHI	A	0	0	—	15.43	4	0	0	7	19	2	0	0	0	0	0	3	0	0	.000	0	3	3	0	1.5	.500

Jeff Heathcock

HEATHCOCK, RONALD JEFFREY BR TR 6′ 4″ 195 lbs.
B. Nov. 18, 1959, Covina, Calif.

Year	Team	Lg	W	L	PCT	ERA	G	GS	CG	IP	H	BB	SO	ShO	Relief Pitching W	Relief Pitching L	Relief Pitching SV	Batting AB	Batting H	Batting HR	BA	PO	A	E	DP	TC/G	FA
1983	HOU	N	2	1	.667	3.21	6	3	0	28	19	4	12	0	1	0	1	6	0	0	.000	3	4	0	1	1.2	1.000
1985			3	1	.750	3.36	14	7	1	56.1	50	13	25	0	1	1	1	16	1	0	.063	4	9	0	1	0.9	1.000
1987			4	2	.667	3.16	19	2	0	42.2	44	9	15	0	3	1	1	10	0	0	.000	3	7	1	0	0.6	.909
1988			0	5	.000	5.81	17	1	0	31	33	16	12	0	0	4	0	3	0	0	.000	3	7	1	0	0.6	.909
4 yrs.			9	9	.500	3.76	56	13	1	158	146	42	64	0	5	6	3	35	1	0	.029	13	27	2	2	0.8	.952

Neal Heaton

HEATON, NEAL BL TL 6′ 2″ 197 lbs.
B. Mar. 3, 1960, Jamaica, N. Y.

Year	Team	Lg	W	L	PCT	ERA	G	GS	CG	IP	H	BB	SO	ShO	Relief Pitching W	Relief Pitching L	Relief Pitching SV	Batting AB	Batting H	Batting HR	BA	PO	A	E	DP	TC/G	FA
1982	CLE	A	0	2	.000	5.23	8	4	0	31	32	16	14	0	0	0	0	0	0	0	—	2	3	0	0	0.6	1.000
1983			11	7	.611	4.16	39	16	4	149.1	157	44	75	3	4	2	7	0	0	0	—	7	14	0	0	0.5	1.000
1984			12	15	.444	5.21	38	34	4	198.2	231	75	75	1	0	1	0	0	0	0	—	9	19	2	0	0.8	.933
1985			9	17	.346	4.90	36	33	5	207.2	244	80	82	1	0	1	0	0	0	0	—	8	21	1	1	0.8	.967
1986	2 teams	CLE A (12G 3–6)	MIN A (21G 4–9)																								
"	total		7	15	.318	4.08	33	29	5	198.2	201	81	90	0	0	0	1	0	0	0		13	24	1	1	1.2	.974
1987	MON	N	13	10	.565	4.52	32	32	3	193.1	207	37	105	1	0	0	0	67	14	0	.209	5	28	3	1	1.1	.917
1988			3	10	.231	4.99	32	11	0	97.1	98	43	43	0	1	4	2	21	3	0	.143	6	14	1	2	0.7	.952
1989	PIT	N	6	7	.462	3.05	42	18	1	147.1	127	55	67	0	2	0	0	42	9	0	.214	6	28	1	1	0.8	.971
1990			12	9	.571	3.45	30	24	0	146	143	38	68	0	0	1	0	43	2	0	.047	5	22	2	1	1.0	.931
1991			3	3	.500	4.33	42	1	0	68.2	72	21	34	0	3	2	0	14	4	0	.286	1	8	1	0	0.2	.900

Neal Heaton *continued*

Year	Team		W	L	PCT	ERA	G	GS	CG	IP	H	BB	SO	ShO	Relief Pitching W	Relief Pitching L	Relief Pitching SV	Batting AB	Batting H	Batting HR	BA	PO	A	E	DP	TC/G	FA
1992	**2 teams**	**KC A** (31G 3–1)	**MIL A** (1G 0–0)																								
″	**total**		3	1	.750	4.07	32	0	0	42	43	23	31	0	3	1	0	0	0	0		5	2	1	0	0.3	.875
1993	**NY**	**A**	1	0	1.000	6.00	18	0	0	27	34	11	15	0	1	0	0	0	0	0	—	1	6	0	0	0.4	1.000
12 yrs.			80	96	.455	4.37	382	202	22	1507	1589	524	699	6	14	12	10	187	32	0	.171	68	189	13	7	0.7	.952

Dave Heaverlo

HEAVERLO, DAVID WALLACE BR TR 6′ 2″ 220 lbs.
B. Aug. 25, 1950, Ellensburg, Wash.

Year	Team		W	L	PCT	ERA	G	GS	CG	IP	H	BB	SO	ShO	Relief Pitching W	Relief Pitching L	Relief Pitching SV	Batting AB	Batting H	Batting HR	BA	PO	A	E	DP	TC/G	FA
1975	**SF**	**N**	3	1	.750	2.39	42	0	0	64	62	31	35	0	3	1	1	4	2	0	.500	7	10	1	1	0.4	.944
1976			4	4	.500	4.44	61	0	0	75	85	15	40	0	4	4	1	3	1	0	.333	7	15	2	1	0.4	.917
1977			5	1	.833	2.55	56	0	0	99	92	21	58	0	5	1	1	5	0	0	.000	10	20	1	2	0.6	.968
1978	**OAK**	**A**	3	6	.333	3.25	69	0	0	130	141	41	71	0	3	6	10	0	0	0	—	9	30	0	3	0.6	1.000
1979			4	11	.267	4.19	62	0	0	86	97	42	40	0	4	11	9	1	0	0	.000	9	13	2	1	0.4	.917
1980	**SEA**	**A**	6	3	.667	3.87	60	0	0	79	75	35	42	0	6	3	4	0	0	0	—	7	5	4	0	0.3	.750
1981	**OAK**	**A**	1	0	1.000	1.50	6	0	0	6	7	3	2	0	1	0	0	0	0	0	—	0	0	0	0	0.0	.000
7 yrs.			26	26	.500	3.41	356	0	0	539	559	188	288	0	26	26	26	13	3	0	.231	49	93	10	8	0.4	.934

Wally Hebert

HEBERT, WALLACE ANDREW (Preacher) BL TL 6′ 1″ 195 lbs.
B. Aug. 21, 1907, Lake Charles, La.

Year	Team		W	L	PCT	ERA	G	GS	CG	IP	H	BB	SO	ShO	Relief Pitching W	Relief Pitching L	Relief Pitching SV	Batting AB	Batting H	Batting HR	BA	PO	A	E	DP	TC/G	FA
1931	**STL**	**A**	6	7	.462	5.07	23	13	5	103	128	43	26	0	0	1	0	43	9	0	.209	7	11	0	0	0.8	1.000
1932			1	12	.077	6.48	35	15	2	108.1	145	45	29	0	0	1	1	34	12	0	.353	9	22	1	0	0.9	.969
1933			4	6	.400	5.30	33	10	3	88.1	114	35	19	0	2	1	0	23	9	0	.391	7	13	0	1	0.6	1.000
1943	**PIT**	**N**	10	11	.476	2.98	34	23	12	184	197	45	41	1	1	1	0	59	13	0	.220	13	43	4	5	1.8	.933
4 yrs.			21	36	.368	4.63	125	61	22	483.2	584	168	115	1	3	4	1	159	43	0	.270	36	89	5	6	1.0	.962

Guy Hecker

HECKER, GUY JACKSON (Blond Guy) BR TR 6′ 190 lbs.
B. Apr. 3, 1856, Youngsville, Pa. D. Dec. 3, 1938, Wooster, Ohio.
Manager 1890.

Year	Team		W	L	PCT	ERA	G	GS	CG	IP	H	BB	SO	ShO	Relief Pitching W	Relief Pitching L	Relief Pitching SV	Batting AB	Batting H	Batting HR	BA	PO	A	E	DP	TC/G	FA
1882	**LOU**	**AA**	6	6	.500	*1.30*	13	11	10	104	75	5	33	0	**1**	0	0	340	94	3	.276	699	68	31	43	9.9	.961
1883			28	25	.528	*3.33*	55	54	53	451	509	72	153	3	0	0	0	322	88	1	.273	144	100	24	7	3.0	.910
1884			**52**	20	.722	***1.80***	**76**	**73**	**72**	**670.2**	**526**	56	**385**	6	1	**1**	0	316	94	4	.297	55	145	12	3	2.6	.943
1885			30	23	.566	*2.17*	54	53	51	480	454	54	209	2	0	0	0	297	81	2	.273	174	106	15	16	4.0	.949
1886			26	23	.531	*2.87*	52	48	45	420.2	390	118	133	2	1	0	0	343	117	4	.341	243	10	23	12	3.0	.917
1887			18	12	.600	*4.16*	33	32	32	285.1	325	50	58	2	0	0	1	370	118	4	.319	429	82	29	27	5.9	.946
1888			8	17	.320	3.39	26	25	25	223.1	251	43	63	0	0	0	0	211	48	0	.227	305	57	25	12	6.6	.935
1889			5	13	.278	5.59	19	16	15	151.1	215	47	33	0	1	1	0	327	93	1	.284	616	55	23	45	8.2	.967
1890	**PIT**	**N**	2	9	.182	5.11	14	12	11	119.2	160	44	32	0	0	0	0	340	77	0	.226	627	53	28	26	7.9	.960
9 yrs.			175	148	.542	2.92	342	324	314	2906	2905	489	1099	15	4	2	1	*				3292	676	210	191	5.6	.950

Harry Hedgepath

HEDGEPATH, HARRY MALCOLM BL TL 6′ 1½″ 194 lbs.
B. Sept. 4, 1888, Fayetteville, N. C. D. July 30, 1966, Richmond, Va.

Year	Team		W	L	PCT	ERA	G	GS	CG	IP	H	BB	SO	ShO	Relief Pitching W	Relief Pitching L	Relief Pitching SV	Batting AB	Batting H	Batting HR	BA	PO	A	E	DP	TC/G	FA
1913	**WAS**	**A**	0	0	—	0.00	1	0	0	1	1	0	0	0	0	0	1	0	0	0	—	0	2	0	0	2.0	1.000

Mike Hedlund

HEDLUND, MICHAEL DAVID (Red) BR TR 6′ 1″ 182 lbs.
B. Aug. 11, 1946, Dallas, Tex. BB 1965, 1968

Year	Team		W	L	PCT	ERA	G	GS	CG	IP	H	BB	SO	ShO	Relief Pitching W	Relief Pitching L	Relief Pitching SV	Batting AB	Batting H	Batting HR	BA	PO	A	E	DP	TC/G	FA
1965	**CLE**	**A**	0	0	—	5.06	6	0	0	5.1	6	5	4	0	0	0	0	1	0	0	.000	0	0	0	0	0.0	.000
1968			0	0	—	10.80	3	0	0	1.2	6	2	0	0	0	0	0	0	0	0	—	0	1	0	0	0.3	1.000
1969	**KC**	**A**	3	6	.333	3.24	34	16	1	125	123	40	74	0	0	0	2	33	5	0	.152	9	24	1	3	1.0	.971
1970			2	3	.400	7.20	9	0	0	15	18	7	5	0	2	3	0	4	0	0	.000	0	1	0	0	0.1	1.000
1971			15	8	.652	2.71	32	30	7	206	168	72	76	1	0	0	0	68	6	0	.088	16	47	2	5	2.0	.969
1972			5	7	.417	4.78	29	16	1	113	119	41	52	0	1	0	0	32	6	0	.188	12	19	0	3	1.1	1.000
6 yrs.			25	24	.510	3.55	113	62	9	466	440	167	211	1	3	3	2	138	17	0	.123	37	92	3	11	1.2	.977

Danny Heep

HEEP, DANIEL WILLIAM BL TL 5′11″ 185 lbs.
B. July 3, 1957, San Antonio, Tex.

Year	Team		W	L	PCT	ERA	G	GS	CG	IP	H	BB	SO	ShO	Relief Pitching W	Relief Pitching L	Relief Pitching SV	Batting AB	Batting H	Batting HR	BA	PO	A	E	DP	TC/G	FA
1988	**LA**	**N**	0	0	—	9.00	1	0	0	2	2	0	0	0	0	0	0	149	36	0	.242	7	0	0	0	3.5	1.000
1990	**BOS**	**A**	0	0	—	9.00	1	0	0	1	4	0	0	0	0	0	0	69	12	0	.174	188	8	2	8	9.0	.990
2 yrs.			0	0		9.00	2	0	0	3	6	0	0	0	0	0	0	*				1558	82	22	78	2.9	.987

Bob Heffner

HEFFNER, ROBERT FREDERIC (Butch) BR TR 6′ 4″ 200 lbs.
B. Sept. 13, 1938, Allentown, Pa.

Year	Team		W	L	PCT	ERA	G	GS	CG	IP	H	BB	SO	ShO	Relief Pitching W	Relief Pitching L	Relief Pitching SV	Batting AB	Batting H	Batting HR	BA	PO	A	E	DP	TC/G	FA
1963	**BOS**	**A**	4	9	.308	4.26	20	19	3	124.2	131	36	77	1	0	0	0	43	5	0	.116	15	16	1	0	1.6	.969
1964			7	9	.438	4.08	55	10	1	158.2	152	44	112	1	6	4	6	44	7	1	.159	15	17	2	1	0.6	.941
1965			0	2	.000	7.16	27	1	0	49	59	18	42	0	0	2	0	6	0	0	.000	3	4	0	0	0.3	1.000
1966	**CLE**	**A**	0	1	.000	3.46	5	1	0	13	12	3	7	0	0	0	0	1	0	0	.000	0	0	0	0	0.0	.000
1968	**CAL**	**A**	0	0	—	2.25	7	0	0	8	6	6	3	0	0	0	0	0	0	0	—	0	1	0	0	0.1	1.000
5 yrs.			11	21	.344	4.51	114	31	4	353.1	360	107	241	2	6	6	6	94	12	1	.128	33	38	3	1	0.6	.959

Randy Heflin

HEFLIN, RANDOLPH RUTHERFORD BL TR 6′ 185 lbs.
B. Sept. 11, 1918, Fredericksburg, Va.

Year	Team		W	L	PCT	ERA	G	GS	CG	IP	H	BB	SO	ShO	Relief Pitching W	Relief Pitching L	Relief Pitching SV	Batting AB	Batting H	Batting HR	BA	PO	A	E	DP	TC/G	FA
1945	**BOS**	**A**	4	10	.286	4.06	20	14	6	102	102	61	39	2	0	1	0	35	3	0	.086	8	26	3	2	1.9	.919
1946			0	1	.000	2.45	5	1	0	14.2	16	12	6	0	0	1	0	3	2	0	.667	0	7	0	0	1.4	1.000
2 yrs.			4	11	.267	3.86	25	15	6	116.2	118	73	45	2	0	2	0	38	5	0	.132	8	33	3	2	1.8	.932

Jake Hehl

HEHL, HERMAN JACOB BR TR 5′11″ 180 lbs.
B. Dec. 8, 1899, Brooklyn, N. Y. D. July 4, 1961, Brooklyn, N. Y.

Year	Team		W	L	PCT	ERA	G	GS	CG	IP	H	BB	SO	ShO	Relief Pitching W	Relief Pitching L	Relief Pitching SV	Batting AB	Batting H	Batting HR	BA	PO	A	E	DP	TC/G	FA
1918	**BKN**	**N**	0	0	—	0.00	1	0	0	1	0	0	0	0	0	0	0	0	0	0	—	0	1	0	0	1.0	1.000

Emmett Heidrick

HEIDRICK, R. EMMETT (Snags) BL TR 6′ 185 lbs.
B. July 29, 1876, Queenstown, Pa. D. Jan. 20, 1916, Clarion, Pa.

Year	Team		W	L	PCT	ERA	G	GS	CG	IP	H	BB	SO	ShO	Relief Pitching W	Relief Pitching L	Relief Pitching SV	Batting AB	Batting H	Batting HR	BA	PO	A	E	DP	TC/G	FA
1902	**STL**	**A**	0	0	—	0.00	1	0	0	1	0	0	0	0	0	0	0	*				29	5	6	1	2.1	.850

Fred Heimach

HEIMACH, FREDERICK AMOS (Lefty) BL TL 6′ 175 lbs.
B. Jan. 27, 1901, Camden, N. J. D. June 1, 1973, Fort Myers, Fla.

Year	Team	Lg	W	L	PCT	ERA	G	GS	CG	IP	H	BB	SO	ShO	Relief W	Relief L	Relief SV	Batting AB	Batting H	Batting HR	BA	PO	A	E	DP	TC/G	FA
1920	PHI	A	0	1	.000	14.40	1	1	0	5	13	1	0	0	0	0	0	1	0	0	.000	1	5	0	0	6.0	1.000
1921			1	0	1.000	0.00	1	1	1	9	7	1	1	1	0	0	0	4	1	0	.250	1	5	0	0	6.0	1.000
1922			7	11	.389	5.03	37	19	7	171.2	220	63	47	0	3	2	1	60	15	0	.250	7	46	3	4	1.5	.946
1923			6	12	.333	4.32	40	19	10	208.1	238	69	63	0	1	1	0	118	30	1	.254	69	56	6	3	2.8	.954
1924			14	12	.538	4.73	40	26	10	198	243	60	60	0	3	0	0	90	29	0	.322	11	57	2	1	1.8	.971
1925			0	1	.000	3.98	10	0	0	20.1	24	9	6	0	0	1	0	6	1	0	.167	1	6	0	1	0.7	1.000
1926	2 teams	PHI A (13G 1–0)	BOS A (20G 2–9)																								
″	total		3	9	.250	4.98	33	14	6	133.2	147	47	25	0	1	1	0	54	14	0	.259	8	58	4	3	2.1	.943
1928	NY	A	2	3	.400	3.31	13	9	5	68	66	16	25	0	0	0	0	30	5	0	.167	0	16	0	2	1.2	1.000
1929			11	6	.647	4.01	35	10	3	134.2	141	29	26	3	7	2	4	49	9	1	.184	6	37	0	1	1.2	1.000
1930	BKN	N	0	2	.000	4.91	9	0	0	7.1	14	3	1	0	0	2	1	4	1	0	.250	0	3	0	1	0.3	1.000
1931			9	7	.563	3.46	31	10	7	135.1	145	23	43	1	4	2	1	61	12	0	.197	8	44	0	3	1.7	1.000
1932			9	4	.692	3.97	36	15	7	167.2	203	28	30	0	3	2	0	55	9	1	.164	10	41	0	1	1.4	1.000
1933			0	1	.000	10.01	10	3	0	29.2	49	11	7	0	0	1	0	10	2	0	.200	0	6	0	1	0.6	1.000
13 yrs.			62	69	.473	4.46	296	127	56	1288.2	1510	360	334	5	22	14	7	*				122	380	15	21	1.7	.971

Gorman Heimueller

HEIMUELLER, GORMAN JOHN BL TL 6′ 4″ 195 lbs.
B. Sept. 24, 1955, Los Angeles, Calif.

Year	Team	Lg	W	L	PCT	ERA	G	GS	CG	IP	H	BB	SO	ShO	Relief W	Relief L	Relief SV	Batting AB	Batting H	Batting HR	BA	PO	A	E	DP	TC/G	FA
1983	OAK	A	3	5	.375	4.41	16	14	2	83.2	93	29	31	1	0	0	0	0	0	0	—	7	23	0	1	1.9	1.000
1984			0	1	.000	6.14	6	0	0	14.2	21	7	3	0	0	1	0	0	0	0	—	1	3	0	1	0.7	1.000
2 yrs.			3	6	.333	4.67	22	14	2	98.1	114	36	34	1	0	1	0	0	0	0		8	26	0	2	1.5	1.000

Don Heinkel

HEINKEL, DONALD ELLIOTT BL TR 6′ 185 lbs.
B. Oct. 20, 1959, Racine, Wis.

Year	Team	Lg	W	L	PCT	ERA	G	GS	CG	IP	H	BB	SO	ShO	Relief W	Relief L	Relief SV	Batting AB	Batting H	Batting HR	BA	PO	A	E	DP	TC/G	FA
1988	DET	A	0	0	—	3.96	21	0	0	36.1	30	12	30	0	0	0	1	0	0	0	—	3	3	0	1	0.3	1.000
1989	STL	N	1	1	.500	5.81	7	5	0	26.1	40	7	16	0	0	0	0	6	0	0	.000	3	3	0	1	0.9	1.000
2 yrs.			1	1	.500	4.74	28	5	0	62.2	70	19	46	0	0	0	1	6	0	0	.000	6	6	0	2	0.4	1.000

Ken Heintzelman

HEINTZELMAN, KENNETH ALPHONSE BR TL 5′11½″ 185 lbs.
Father of Tom Heintzelman.
B. Oct. 14, 1915, Peruque, Mo.

Year	Team	Lg	W	L	PCT	ERA	G	GS	CG	IP	H	BB	SO	ShO	Relief W	Relief L	Relief SV	Batting AB	Batting H	Batting HR	BA	PO	A	E	DP	TC/G	FA
1937	PIT	N	1	0	1.000	2.00	1	1	1	9	6	3	4	0	0	0	0	4	0	0	.000	0	0	1	0	1.0	.000
1938			0	0	—	9.00	1	0	0	2	1	3	1	0	0	0	0	0	0	0	—	0	1	0	0	1.0	1.000
1939			1	1	.500	5.05	17	2	1	35.2	35	18	18	1	0	0	0	9	2	0	.222	2	5	0	0	0.4	1.000
1940			8	8	.500	4.47	39	16	5	165	193	65	71	2	3	2	3	54	9	0	.167	4	45	1	4	1.3	.980
1941			11	11	.500	3.44	35	24	13	196	206	83	81	2	1	3	0	63	8	0	.127	8	44	2	4	1.5	.963
1942			8	11	.421	4.57	27	18	5	130	143	63	39	3	3	1	0	35	3	0	.086	1	23	0	1	0.9	1.000
1946			8	12	.400	3.77	32	24	6	157.2	165	86	57	2	1	0	1	44	6	0	.136	7	39	0	3	1.4	1.000
1947	2 teams	PIT N (2G 0–0)	PHI N (24G 7–10)																								
″	total		7	10	.412	4.50	26	20	8	140	153	52	57	0	1	0	1	43	5	0	.116	2	14	2	1	0.7	.889
1948	PHI	N	6	11	.353	4.29	27	16	5	130	117	45	57	2	1	0	2	37	5	0	.135	2	22	0	1	0.9	1.000
1949			17	10	.630	3.02	33	32	15	250	239	93	65	**5**	0	1	0	83	13	0	.157	4	38	1	4	1.3	.977
1950			3	9	.250	4.09	23	17	4	125.1	122	54	39	1	1	0	0	38	2	0	.053	1	16	0	1	0.7	1.000
1951			6	12	.333	4.18	35	12	3	118.1	119	53	55	1	3	4	2	28	3	0	.107	4	17	0	3	0.6	1.000
1952			1	3	.250	3.16	23	1	0	42.2	41	12	20	0	1	2	1	2	0	0	.000	2	3	0	1	0.2	1.000
13 yrs.			77	98	.440	3.93	319	183	66	1501.2	1540	630	564	19	15	13	10	440	56	0	.127	37	267	7	23	1.0	.977
WORLD SERIES																											
1950	PHI	N	0	0	—	1.17	1	1	0	7.2	4	6	3	0	0	0	0	2	0	0	.000	0	2	0	0	2.0	1.000

Clarence Heise

HEISE, CLARENCE EDWARD (Lefty) BL TL 5′10″ 172 lbs.
B. Aug. 7, 1907, Topeka, Kans.

Year	Team	Lg	W	L	PCT	ERA	G	GS	CG	IP	H	BB	SO	ShO	Relief W	Relief L	Relief SV	Batting AB	Batting H	Batting HR	BA	PO	A	E	DP	TC/G	FA
1934	STL	N	0	0	—	4.50	1	0	0	2	3	0	1	0	0	0	0	0	0	0	—	0	0	0	0	0.0	.000

Jim Heise

HEISE, JAMES EDWARD BR TR 6′ 1″ 185 lbs.
B. Oct. 2, 1932, Scottsdale, Pa.

Year	Team	Lg	W	L	PCT	ERA	G	GS	CG	IP	H	BB	SO	ShO	Relief W	Relief L	Relief SV	Batting AB	Batting H	Batting HR	BA	PO	A	E	DP	TC/G	FA
1957	WAS	A	0	3	.000	8.05	8	2	0	19	25	16	8	0	0	1	0	4	0	0	.000	1	3	1	1	0.6	.800

Roy Heiser

HEISER, LEROY BARTON BR TR 6′ 4″ 190 lbs.
B. June 22, 1942, Baltimore, Md.

Year	Team	Lg	W	L	PCT	ERA	G	GS	CG	IP	H	BB	SO	ShO	Relief W	Relief L	Relief SV	Batting AB	Batting H	Batting HR	BA	PO	A	E	DP	TC/G	FA
1961	WAS	A	0	0	—	6.35	3	0	0	5.2	6	9	1	0	0	0	0	2	0	0	.000	0	0	1	0	0.3	.000

Crese Heisman

HEISMAN, CHRISTIAN ERNEST BR TL 6′ 2″ 175 lbs.
B. Apr. 16, 1880, Cincinnati, Ohio D. Nov. 19, 1951, Cincinnati, Ohio.

Year	Team	Lg	W	L	PCT	ERA	G	GS	CG	IP	H	BB	SO	ShO	Relief W	Relief L	Relief SV	Batting AB	Batting H	Batting HR	BA	PO	A	E	DP	TC/G	FA
1901	CIN	N	0	2	.000	5.93	3	2	1	13.2	18	6	6	0	0	0	0	5	2	0	.400	1	1	0	0	0.7	1.000
1902	2 teams	CIN N (5G 2–1)	BAL A (3G 0–3)																								
″	total		2	4	.333	4.41	8	6	4	49	53	22	17	0	0	0	0	21	4	0	.190	3	11	0	0	1.8	1.000
2 yrs.			2	6	.250	4.74	11	8	5	62.2	71	28	23	0	0	0	0	26	6	0	.231	4	12	0	0	1.5	1.000

Henry Heitmann

HEITMANN, HARRY ANTON BR TR 6′ 175 lbs.
B. Oct. 6, 1896, Albany, N. Y. D. Dec. 15, 1958, Brooklyn, N. Y.

Year	Team	Lg	W	L	PCT	ERA	G	GS	CG	IP	H	BB	SO	ShO	Relief W	Relief L	Relief SV	Batting AB	Batting H	Batting HR	BA	PO	A	E	DP	TC/G	FA
1918	BKN	N	0	1	.000	108.00	1	1	0	0.1	4	0	0	0	0	0	0	0	0	0	—	0	0	0	0	0.0	.000

Mel Held

HELD, MELVIN NICHOLAS (Country) BR TR 6′ 1″ 178 lbs.
B. Apr. 12, 1929, Edon, Ohio.

Year	Team	Lg	W	L	PCT	ERA	G	GS	CG	IP	H	BB	SO	ShO	Relief W	Relief L	Relief SV	Batting AB	Batting H	Batting HR	BA	PO	A	E	DP	TC/G	FA
1956	BAL	A	0	0	—	5.14	4	0	0	7	7	3	4	0	0	0	0	0	0	0	—	0	3	0	1	0.8	1.000

Rick Helling

HELLING, RICKY ALLEN BR TR 6′ 3″ 215 lbs.
B. Dec. 15, 1970, Devils Lake, N. D.

Year	Team	Lg	W	L	PCT	ERA	G	GS	CG	IP	H	BB	SO	ShO	Relief W	Relief L	Relief SV	Batting AB	Batting H	Batting HR	BA	PO	A	E	DP	TC/G	FA
1994	TEX	A	3	2	.600	5.88	9	9	1	52	62	18	25	1	0	0	0	0	0	0	—	2	3	0	0	0.6	1.000
1995			0	2	.000	6.57	3	3	0	12.1	17	8	5	0	0	0	0	0	0	0	—	0	1	0	0	0.3	1.000
2 yrs.			3	4	.429	6.02	12	12	1	64.1	79	26	30	1	0	0	0	0	0	0		2	4	0	0	0.5	1.000

Horace Helmbold

HELMBOLD, HORACE WILLING
B. Aug. 27, 1867, Philadelphia, Pa. Deceased.

Year	Team	Lg	W	L	PCT	ERA	G	GS	CG	IP	H	BB	SO	ShO	Relief Pitching W	Relief Pitching L	Relief Pitching SV	Batting AB	Batting H	Batting HR	BA	PO	A	E	DP	TC/G	FA
1890	PHI	AA	0	1	.000	*14.14*	1	1	1	7	17	6	3	0	0	0	0	3	0	0	.000	1	2	1	0	4.0	.750

Russ Heman

HEMAN, RUSSELL FREDERICK BR TR 6′ 4″ 200 lbs.
B. Feb. 10, 1933, Olive, Calif.

Year	Team	Lg	W	L	PCT	ERA	G	GS	CG	IP	H	BB	SO	ShO	Relief Pitching W	Relief Pitching L	Relief Pitching SV	Batting AB	Batting H	Batting HR	BA	PO	A	E	DP	TC/G	FA
1961	2 teams CLE A (6G 0–0) LA A (6G 0–0)																										
″	total		0	0		2.70	12	0	0	20	12	10	6	0	0	0	1	2	0	0	.000	1	4	0	0	0.4	1.000

George Hemming

HEMMING, GEORGE EARL (Old Wax Figger) BR TR 5′11″ 170 lbs.
B. Dec. 15, 1868, Carrollton, Ohio D. June 3, 1930, Springfield, Mass.

Year	Team	Lg	W	L	PCT	ERA	G	GS	CG	IP	H	BB	SO	ShO	Relief Pitching W	Relief Pitching L	Relief Pitching SV	Batting AB	Batting H	Batting HR	BA	PO	A	E	DP	TC/G	FA
1890	2 teams CLE P (3G 0–1) BKN P (19G 8–4)																										
″	total		8	5	.615	4.25	22	12	12	144	142	78	35	0	1	0	**3**	68	11	0	.162	4	43	5	1	2.3	.904
1891	BKN	N	8	15	.348	4.96	27	22	19	199.2	231	84	83	1	0	1	1	82	13	0	.159	9	44	6	1	2.2	.898
1892	2 teams CIN N (1G 0–1) LOU N (4G 2–2)																										
″	total		2	3	.400	5.05	5	4	4	41	46	19	12	0	0	1	0	16	2	0	.125	3	10	1	1	2.8	.929
1893	LOU	N	18	17	.514	5.18	41	32	32	332	373	176	79	1	2	0	1	158	32	0	.203	25	80	7	2	2.5	.938
1894	2 teams LOU N (35G 13–19) BAL N (6G 4–0)																										
″	total		17	19	.472	4.27	41	38	36	339.2	406	159	70	1	0	0	1	152	39	2	.257	27	55	5	1	2.1	.943
1895	BAL	N	20	13	.606	4.05	34	31	26	262.1	288	96	43	1	0	2	0	117	33	1	.282	7	46	4	2	1.7	.930
1896			15	6	.714	4.19	25	21	20	202	233	54	33	3	1	0	0	97	25	0	.258	16	37	4	2	2.0	.930
1897	LOU	N	3	4	.429	5.10	9	8	7	67	80	25	7	0	0	0	0	28	5	0	.179	9	16	2	0	2.7	.926
8 yrs.			91	82	.526	4.55	204	168	156	1587.2	1799	691	362	7	4	4	6	718	160	3	.223	100	331	34	10	2.2	.927

Bernie Henderson

HENDERSON, BERNARD (Barnyard) BL TR 5′ 9″ 175 lbs.
B. Apr. 12, 1899, Douglasville, Tex. D. June 4, 1966, Linden, Tex.

Year	Team	Lg	W	L	PCT	ERA	G	GS	CG	IP	H	BB	SO	ShO	Relief Pitching W	Relief Pitching L	Relief Pitching SV	Batting AB	Batting H	Batting HR	BA	PO	A	E	DP	TC/G	FA
1921	CLE	A	0	1	.000	9.00	2	1	0	3	5	0	1	0	0	0	0	1	0	0	.000	0	0	0	0	0.0	.000

Bill Henderson

HENDERSON, WILLIAM MAXWELL BR TR 6′ 190 lbs.
B. Nov. 4, 1901, Pensacola, Fla. D. Oct. 6, 1966, Pensacola, Fla.

Year	Team	Lg	W	L	PCT	ERA	G	GS	CG	IP	H	BB	SO	ShO	Relief Pitching W	Relief Pitching L	Relief Pitching SV	Batting AB	Batting H	Batting HR	BA	PO	A	E	DP	TC/G	FA
1930	NY	A	0	0	—	4.50	3	0	0	8	7	4	2	0	0	0	0	2	1	0	.500	0	2	0	0	0.7	1.000

Ed Henderson

HENDERSON, EDWARD J. BL TL 5′ 9″ 168 lbs.
Born Eugene J. Ball.
B. Dec. 25, 1884, Newark, N. J. D. Jan. 15, 1964, New York, N. Y.

Year	Team	Lg	W	L	PCT	ERA	G	GS	CG	IP	H	BB	SO	ShO	Relief Pitching W	Relief Pitching L	Relief Pitching SV	Batting AB	Batting H	Batting HR	BA	PO	A	E	DP	TC/G	FA
1914	2 teams PIT F (6G 0–1) IND F (2G 1–0)																										
″	total		1	1	.500	4.15	8	2	2	26	22	12	5	0	0	0	0	7	0	0	.000	2	4	0	0	0.8	1.000

Hardie Henderson

HENDERSON, JAMES HARDING BR TR
B. Oct. 31, 1862, Philadelphia, Pa. D. Feb. 6, 1903, Philadelphia, Pa.

Year	Team	Lg	W	L	PCT	ERA	G	GS	CG	IP	H	BB	SO	ShO	Relief Pitching W	Relief Pitching L	Relief Pitching SV	Batting AB	Batting H	Batting HR	BA	PO	A	E	DP	TC/G	FA
1883	2 teams PHI N (1G 0–1) BAL AA (45G 10–32)																										
″	total		10	33	.233	4.39	46	43	39	367.1	409	89	147	0	0	**1**	0	199	33	1	.166	33	63	26	3	2.0	.787
1884	BAL	AA	27	23	.540	*2.62*	52	52	50	439.1	382	**116**	346	4	0	0	0	203	46	0	.227	28	78	22	3	2.3	.828
1885			25	**35**	.417	*3.19*	61	61	59	539.1	**539**	**117**	263	0	0	0	0	229	51	1	.223	28	81	14	4	2.0	.886
1886	2 teams BAL AA (19G 3–15) BKN AA (14G 10–4)																										
″	total		13	19	.406	3.90	33	33	33	295.1	300	117	137	0	0	0	0	118	25	0	.212	22	55	5	3	2.5	.939
1887	BKN	AA	5	8	.385	*3.95*	13	12	12	111.2	127	63	28	0	**1**	0	0	41	5	0	.122	5	32	1	0	2.9	.974
1888	PIT	N	1	3	.250	5.35	5	5	4	35.1	43	20	9	0	0	0	0	18	5	0	.278	1	8	2	1	1.8	.818
6 yrs.			81	121	.401	3.50	210	206	197	1788.1	1800	522	930	4	1	1	0	808	165	2	.204	117	317	70	14	2.2	.861

Joe Henderson

HENDERSON, JOSEPH LEE BL TR 6′ 2″ 195 lbs.
B. July 4, 1946, Lake Cormorant, Miss.

Year	Team	Lg	W	L	PCT	ERA	G	GS	CG	IP	H	BB	SO	ShO	Relief Pitching W	Relief Pitching L	Relief Pitching SV	Batting AB	Batting H	Batting HR	BA	PO	A	E	DP	TC/G	FA
1974	CHI	A	1	0	1.000	8.40	5	3	0	15	21	11	12	0	1	0	0	1	0	0	.000	0	3	1	0	0.8	.750
1976	CIN	N	2	0	1.000	0.00	4	0	0	11	9	8	7	0	2	0	0	0	0	0	—	1	2	0	0	0.8	1.000
1977			0	2	.000	12.00	7	0	0	9	17	6	8	0	0	2	0	1	0	0	.000	0	0	0	0	0.0	.000
3 yrs.			3	2	.600	6.69	16	3	0	35	47	25	27	0	3	2	0	2	0	0	.000	1	5	1	0	0.4	.857

Rod Henderson

HENDERSON, RODNEY WOOD BR TR 6′ 4″ 195 lbs.
B. Mar. 11, 1971, Greensburg, Ky.

Year	Team	Lg	W	L	PCT	ERA	G	GS	CG	IP	H	BB	SO	ShO	Relief Pitching W	Relief Pitching L	Relief Pitching SV	Batting AB	Batting H	Batting HR	BA	PO	A	E	DP	TC/G	FA
1994	MON	N	0	1	.000	9.45	3	2	0	6.2	9	7	3	0	0	0	0	1	0	0	.000	1	2	0	0	1.0	1.000

Bob Hendley

HENDLEY, CHARLES ROBERT BR TL 6′ 2″ 190 lbs.
B. Apr. 30, 1939, Macon, Ga.

Year	Team	Lg	W	L	PCT	ERA	G	GS	CG	IP	H	BB	SO	ShO	Relief Pitching W	Relief Pitching L	Relief Pitching SV	Batting AB	Batting H	Batting HR	BA	PO	A	E	DP	TC/G	FA
1961	MIL	N	5	7	.417	3.90	19	13	3	97	96	39	44	0	1	0	0	31	1	0	.032	6	24	1	0	1.6	.968
1962			11	13	.458	3.60	35	29	7	200	188	59	112	2	0	1	1	59	7	1	.119	7	41	5	1	1.5	.906
1963			9	9	.500	3.93	41	24	7	169.1	153	64	105	3	0	2	3	47	5	0	.106	3	39	0	0	1.0	1.000
1964	SF	N	10	11	.476	3.64	30	29	4	163.1	161	59	104	1	0	0	0	47	5	0	.106	6	21	2	3	1.0	.931
1965	2 teams SF N (8G 0–0) CHI N (18G 4–4)																										
″	total		4	4	.500	5.96	26	12	2	77	86	38	46	0	1	1	0	17	0	0	.000	4	19	2	0	1.0	.920
1966	CHI	N	4	5	.444	3.91	43	6	0	89.2	98	39	65	0	4	3	7	18	3	0	.167	3	18	1	1	0.5	.955
1967	2 teams CHI N (7G 2–0) NY N (15G 3–3)																										
″	total		5	3	.625	3.90	22	13	2	83	82	31	46	0	2	0	1	24	2	0	.083	1	5	0	0	0.3	1.000
7 yrs.			48	52	.480	3.97	216	126	25	879.1	864	329	522	6	8	7	12	243	23	1	.095	30	167	11	5	1.0	.947

Ed Hendricks

HENDRICKS, EDWARD (Big Ed) BL TL 6′ 3″ 200 lbs.
B. June 20, 1885, Zeeland, Mich. D. Nov. 28, 1930, Jackson, Mich.

Year	Team	Lg	W	L	PCT	ERA	G	GS	CG	IP	H	BB	SO	ShO	Relief Pitching W	Relief Pitching L	Relief Pitching SV	Batting AB	Batting H	Batting HR	BA	PO	A	E	DP	TC/G	FA
1910	NY	N	0	1	.000	3.75	4	1	1	12	12	4	2	0	0	0	1	4	0	0	.000	1	1	0	0	0.5	1.000

Ellie Hendricks

HENDRICKS, ELROD JEROME BL TR 6′ 1″ 175 lbs.
B. Dec. 22, 1940, Charlotte Amalie, Virgin Islands.

Year	Team	Lg	W	L	PCT	ERA	G	GS	CG	IP	H	BB	SO	ShO	Relief Pitching W	Relief Pitching L	Relief Pitching SV	Batting AB	Batting H	Batting HR	BA	PO	A	E	DP	TC/G	FA
1978	BAL	A	0	0	—	0.00	1	0	0	2.1	1	1	0	0	0	0	0	*				303	21	3	3	6.2	.991

Don Hendrickson

HENDRICKSON, DONALD WILLIAM
B. July 14, 1915, Kewanna, Ind. D. Jan. 19, 1977, Norfolk, Va.
BR TR 6′ 2″ 204 lbs.

Year	Team		W	L	PCT	ERA	G	GS	CG	IP	H	BB	SO	ShO	Relief Pitching W	Relief Pitching L	Relief Pitching SV	Batting AB	Batting H	Batting HR	BA	PO	A	E	DP	TC/G	FA
1945	**BOS**	**N**	4	8	.333	4.91	37	2	1	73.1	74	39	14	0	3	8	5	18	3	0	.167	1	14	2	1	0.5	.882
1946			0	1	.000	4.50	2	0	0	2	4	2	2	0	0	1	0	1	0	0	.000	0	0	0	0	0.0	.000
2 yrs.			4	9	.308	4.90	39	2	1	75.1	78	41	16	0	3	9	5	19	3	0	.158	1	14	2	1	0.4	.882

Claude Hendrix

HENDRIX, CLAUDE RAYMOND
B. Apr. 13, 1889, Olathe, Kans. D. Mar. 22, 1944, Allentown, Pa.
BR TR 6′ 195 lbs.

Year	Team		W	L	PCT	ERA	G	GS	CG	IP	H	BB	SO	ShO	Relief Pitching W	Relief Pitching L	Relief Pitching SV	Batting AB	Batting H	Batting HR	BA	PO	A	E	DP	TC/G	FA
1911	**PIT**	**N**	4	6	.400	2.73	22	12	6	118.2	85	53	57	1	0	1	1	41	4	0	.098	12	45	1	2	2.6	.983
1912			24	9	**.727**	2.59	39	32	25	288.2	256	105	176	4	3	1	1	121	39	1	.322	7	91	3	2	2.6	.970
1913			14	15	.483	2.84	42	25	17	241	216	89	138	2	4	2	3	99	27	1	.273	6	67	4	6	1.8	.948
1914	**CHI**	**F**	**29**	11	.725	1.69	**49**	37	**34**	362	262	77	189	6	3	2	5	130	30	2	.231	10	137	5	5	3.1	.967
1915			16	15	.516	3.00	40	31	26	285	256	84	107	5	2	0	4	113	30	4	.265	11	69	3	2	2.1	.964
1916	**CHI**	**N**	8	16	.333	2.68	36	24	15	218	193	67	117	3	1	1	2	80	16	1	.200	10	65	4	2	2.2	.949
1917			10	12	.455	2.60	40	21	13	215	202	72	81	1	3	2	1	86	22	0	.256	6	52	4	1	1.5	.935
1918			19	7	**.731**	2.78	32	27	21	233	229	54	86	3	1	0	0	91	24	3	.264	6	75	2	1	2.6	.976
1919			10	14	.417	2.62	33	25	15	206.1	208	42	69	2	1	1	0	78	15	1	.192	5	67	1	0	2.2	.986
1920			9	12	.429	3.58	27	23	12	203.2	216	54	72	0	1	0	0	83	15	0	.181	4	56	5	1	2.4	.923
10 yrs.			143	117	.550	2.65	360	257	184	2371.1	2123	697	1092	27	19	10	17	*				77	724	32	22	2.3	.962
WORLD SERIES																											
1918	**CHI**	**N**	0	0	—	0.00	1	0	0	1	0	0	0	0	0	0	0	*				0	0	0	0	0.0	.000

Lafayette Henion

HENION, LAFAYETTE MARION
B. June 7, 1899, Eureka, Calif. D. July 22, 1955, San Luis Obispo, Calif.
BR TR 5′11″ 154 lbs.

Year	Team		W	L	PCT	ERA	G	GS	CG	IP	H	BB	SO	ShO	Relief Pitching W	Relief Pitching L	Relief Pitching SV	Batting AB	Batting H	Batting HR	BA	PO	A	E	DP	TC/G	FA
1919	**BKN**	**N**	0	0	—	6.00	1	0	0	3	2	2	2	0	0	0	0	1	0	0	.000	1	0	0	0	1.0	1.000

Tom Henke

HENKE, THOMAS ANTHONY (The Terminator)
B. Dec. 21, 1957, Kansas City, Mo.
BR TR 6′ 5″ 215 lbs.

Year	Team		W	L	PCT	ERA	G	GS	CG	IP	H	BB	SO	ShO	Relief Pitching W	Relief Pitching L	Relief Pitching SV	Batting AB	Batting H	Batting HR	BA	PO	A	E	DP	TC/G	FA
1982	**TEX**	**A**	1	0	1.000	1.15	8	0	0	15.2	14	8	9	0	1	0	0	0	0	0	—	2	2	0	0	0.5	1.000
1983			1	0	1.000	3.38	8	0	0	16	16	4	17	0	1	0	1	0	0	0	—	0	3	1	0	0.5	.750
1984			1	1	.500	6.35	25	0	0	28.1	36	20	25	0	1	1	2	0	0	0	—	1	2	0	0	0.1	1.000
1985	**TOR**	**A**	3	3	.500	2.02	28	0	0	40	29	8	42	0	3	3	13	0	0	0	—	3	3	0	0	0.2	1.000
1986			9	5	.643	3.35	63	0	0	91.1	63	32	118	0	9	5	27	0	0	0	—	2	2	0	1	0.1	1.000
1987			0	6	.000	2.49	72	0	0	94	62	25	128	0	0	6	**34**	0	0	0	—	9	12	0	1	0.3	1.000
1988			4	4	.500	2.91	52	0	0	68	60	24	66	0	4	4	25	0	0	0	—	1	9	0	1	0.2	1.000
1989			8	3	.727	1.92	64	0	0	89	66	25	116	0	8	3	20	0	0	0	—	3	10	1	0	0.2	.929
1990			2	4	.333	2.17	61	0	0	74.2	58	19	75	0	2	4	32	0	0	0	—	6	5	0	0	0.2	1.000
1991			0	2	.000	2.32	49	0	0	50.1	33	11	53	0	0	2	32	0	0	0	—	2	1	0	0	0.1	1.000
1992			3	2	.600	2.26	57	0	0	55.2	40	22	46	0	3	2	34	0	0	0	—	2	2	0	0	0.1	1.000
1993	**TEX**	**A**	5	5	.500	2.91	66	0	0	74.1	55	27	79	0	5	5	40	0	0	0	—	6	10	0	1	0.2	1.000
1994			3	6	.333	3.79	37	0	0	38	33	12	39	0	3	**6**	15	0	0	0	—	2	2	0	0	0.1	1.000
1995	**STL**	**N**	1	1	.500	1.82	52	0	0	54.1	42	18	48	0	1	1	36	1	0	0	.000	4	4	0	1	0.2	1.000
14 yrs.			41	42	.494	2.67	642	0	0	789.2	607	255	861	0	41	42	311 **5th**	1	0	0	.000	43	67	2	5	0.2	.982
LEAGUE CHAMPIONSHIP SERIES																											
1985	**TOR**	**A**	2	0	1.000	4.26	3	0	0	6.1	5	4	4	0	2	0	0	0	0	0	—	1	0	0	0	0.3	1.000
1989			0	0	—	0.00	3	0	0	2.2	0	0	3	0	0	0	0	0	0	0	—	0	1	0	0	0.3	1.000
1991			0	0	—	0.00	2	0	0	2.2	0	1	5	0	0	0	0	0	0	0	—	0	2	0	0	1.0	1.000
1992			0	0	—	0.00	4	0	0	4.2	3	2	2	0	0	0	3	0	0	0	—	0	0	0	0	0.0	.000
4 yrs.			2	0	1.000	1.65	12 **8th**	0	0	16.1	8	7	14	0	2	0	3 **6th**	0	0	0		1	3	0	0	0.3	1.000
WORLD SERIES																											
1992	**TOR**	**A**	0	0	—	2.70	3	0	0	3.1	2	2	1	0	0	0	2	0	0	0	—	0	2	0	0	0.7	1.000

Weldon Henley

HENLEY, WELDON
B. Oct. 20, 1880, Jasper, Ga. D. Nov. 17, 1960, Palatka, Fla.
BR TR 6′ 175 lbs.

Year	Team		W	L	PCT	ERA	G	GS	CG	IP	H	BB	SO	ShO	Relief Pitching W	Relief Pitching L	Relief Pitching SV	Batting AB	Batting H	Batting HR	BA	PO	A	E	DP	TC/G	FA
1903	**PHI**	**A**	12	10	.545	3.91	29	21	13	186.1	186	67	86	1	**2**	0	0	68	9	0	.132	8	52	3	2	2.2	.952
1904			15	17	.469	2.53	36	34	31	295.2	245	76	130	5	0	0	0	108	24	0	.222	16	115	7	3	3.8	.949
1905			4	11	.267	2.60	25	19	12	183.2	155	67	82	2	0	0	0	65	11	0	.169	10	77	6	1	3.7	.935
1907	**BKN**	**N**	1	5	.167	3.05	7	7	5	56	54	21	11	0	0	0	0	20	4	0	.200	7	24	2	0	4.1	.939
4 yrs.			32	43	.427	2.94	97	81	61	721.2	640	231	309	8	2	0	0	261	48	0	.184	41	268	18	6	3.3	.945

Mike Henneman

HENNEMAN, MICHAEL ALAN
B. Dec. 11, 1961, St. Charles, Mo.
BR TR 6′ 4″ 205 lbs.

Year	Team		W	L	PCT	ERA	G	GS	CG	IP	H	BB	SO	ShO	Relief Pitching W	Relief Pitching L	Relief Pitching SV	Batting AB	Batting H	Batting HR	BA	PO	A	E	DP	TC/G	FA
1987	**DET**	**A**	11	3	.786	2.98	55	0	0	96.2	86	30	75	0	11	3	7	1	0	0	.000	8	11	0	2	0.3	1.000
1988			9	6	.600	1.87	65	0	0	91.1	72	24	58	0	**9**	6	22	0	0	0	—	4	8	1	0	0.2	.923
1989			11	4	.733	3.70	60	0	0	90	84	51	69	0	**11**	4	8	0	0	0	—	5	12	0	2	0.3	1.000
1990			8	6	.571	3.05	69	0	0	94.1	90	33	50	0	8	6	22	0	0	0	—	7	16	3	2	0.4	.885
1991			10	2	.833	2.88	60	0	0	84.1	81	34	61	0	**10**	2	21	0	0	0	—	6	10	2	1	0.3	.889
1992			2	6	.250	3.96	60	0	0	77.1	75	20	58	0	2	6	24	0	0	0	—	9	9	1	1	0.3	.947
1993			5	3	.625	2.64	63	0	0	71.2	69	32	58	0	5	3	24	0	0	0	—	6	5	1	0	0.2	.917
1994			1	3	.250	5.19	30	0	0	34.2	43	17	27	0	1	3	8	0	0	0	—	6	4	0	0	0.3	1.000
1995	**2 teams**	**DET A** (29G 0–1)	**HOU N** (21G 0–1)																								
″	**total**		0	2	.000	2.15	50	0	0	50.1	45	13	43	0	0	2	26	0	0	0	—	3	2	0	0	0.1	1.000
9 yrs.			57	35	.620	3.05	512	0	0	690.2	645	254	499	0	57	35	162	1	0	0	.000	54	77	8	8	0.3	.942
LEAGUE CHAMPIONSHIP SERIES																											
1987	**DET**	**A**	1	0	1.000	10.80	3	0	0	5	6	6	3	0	1	0	0	0	0	0	—	0	2	0	0	0.7	1.000

George Hennessey

HENNESSEY, GEORGE (Three Star)
B. Oct. 28, 1907, Slatington, Pa. D. Jan. 15, 1988, Princeton, N. J.
BR TR 5′10″ 168 lbs.

Year	Team		W	L	PCT	ERA	G	GS	CG	IP	H	BB	SO	ShO	Relief Pitching W	Relief Pitching L	Relief Pitching SV	Batting AB	Batting H	Batting HR	BA	PO	A	E	DP	TC/G	FA
1937	**STL**	**A**	0	1	.000	10.29	5	0	0	7	15	6	4	0	0	1	0	0	0	0	—	0	2	0	0	0.4	1.000
1942	**PHI**	**N**	1	1	.500	2.65	5	1	0	17	11	10	2	0	1	0	0	5	0	0	.000	1	2	0	0	0.6	1.000
1945	**CHI**	**N**	0	0	—	7.36	2	0	0	3.2	7	1	2	0	0	0	0	0	0	0	—	1	1	0	0	1.0	1.000
3 yrs.			1	2	.333	5.20	12	1	0	27.2	33	17	8	0	1	1	0	5	0	0	.000	2	5	0	0	0.6	1.000

Phil Hennigan

HENNIGAN, PHILLIP WINSTON
B. Apr. 10, 1946, Jasper, Tex.
BR TR 5′11½″ 185 lbs.

Year	Team		W	L	PCT	ERA	G	GS	CG	IP	H	BB	SO	ShO	Relief W	Relief L	Relief SV	AB	H	HR	BA	PO	A	E	DP	TC/G	FA
1969	CLE	A	2	1	.667	3.31	9	0	0	16.1	14	4	10	0	2	1	0	2	0	0	.000	0	0	0	0	0.0	.000
1970			6	3	.667	4.00	42	1	0	72	69	44	43	0	6	2	3	7	1	0	.143	12	11	0	1	0.5	1.000
1971			4	3	.571	4.94	57	0	0	82	80	51	69	0	4	3	14	6	0	0	.000	5	8	0	1	0.2	1.000
1972			5	3	.625	2.69	38	1	0	67	54	18	44	0	5	2	6	12	1	0	.083	1	5	0	0	0.2	1.000
1973	NY	N	0	4	.000	6.23	30	0	0	43.1	50	16	22	0	0	4	3	3	1	0	.333	4	4	1	0	0.3	.889
5 yrs.			17	14	.548	4.26	176	2	0	280.2	267	133	188	0	17	12	26	30	3	0	.100	22	28	1	2	0.3	.980

Pete Henning

HENNING, ERNEST HERMAN
B. Dec. 28, 1887, Crown Point, Ind. D. Nov. 4, 1939, Dyer, Ind.
BR TR 5′11″ 185 lbs.

Year	Team		W	L	PCT	ERA	G	GS	CG	IP	H	BB	SO	ShO	Relief W	Relief L	Relief SV	AB	H	HR	BA	PO	A	E	DP	TC/G	FA
1914	KC	F	6	12	.333	4.83	28	14	7	138	153	58	45	0	1	**5**	1	44	8	0	.182	6	44	5	1	2.0	.909
1915			8	16	.333	3.17	40	20	15	207	181	76	73	1	2	3	2	68	14	0	.206	10	80	1	3	2.3	.989
2 yrs.			14	28	.333	3.83	68	34	22	345	334	134	118	1	3	8	3	112	22	0	.196	16	124	6	4	2.1	.959

Rick Henninger

HENNINGER, RICHARD LEE
B. Jan. 11, 1948, Hastings, Neb.
BR TR 6′6″ 225 lbs.

Year	Team		W	L	PCT	ERA	G	GS	CG	IP	H	BB	SO	ShO	Relief W	Relief L	Relief SV	AB	H	HR	BA	PO	A	E	DP	TC/G	FA
1973	TEX	A	1	0	1.000	2.74	6	2	0	23	23	11	6	0	1	0	0	0	0	0	—	1	1	0	0	0.3	1.000

Randy Hennis

HENNIS, RANDALL PHILIP
B. Dec. 16, 1965, Clearlake, Calif.
BR TR 6′6″ 220 lbs.

Year	Team		W	L	PCT	ERA	G	GS	CG	IP	H	BB	SO	ShO	Relief W	Relief L	Relief SV	AB	H	HR	BA	PO	A	E	DP	TC/G	FA
1990	HOU	N	0	0	—	0.00	3	1	0	9.2	1	3	4	0	0	0	0	2	0	0	.000	2	0	0	0	0.7	1.000

Bill Henry

HENRY, WILLIAM FRANCIS
B. Feb. 15, 1942, Long Beach, Calif.
BL TL 6′3″ 195 lbs.

Year	Team		W	L	PCT	ERA	G	GS	CG	IP	H	BB	SO	ShO	Relief W	Relief L	Relief SV	AB	H	HR	BA	PO	A	E	DP	TC/G	FA
1966	NY	A	0	0	—	0.00	2	0	0	3	0	2	3	0	0	0	0	0	0	0	—	0	2	0	0	1.0	1.000

Bill Henry

HENRY, WILLIAM RODMAN
B. Oct. 15, 1927, Alice, Tex.
BL TL 6′2″ 180 lbs.

Year	Team		W	L	PCT	ERA	G	GS	CG	IP	H	BB	SO	ShO	Relief W	Relief L	Relief SV	AB	H	HR	BA	PO	A	E	DP	TC/G	FA
1952	BOS	A	5	4	.556	3.87	13	10	5	76.2	75	36	23	0	0	0	0	31	8	0	.258	5	7	0	1	0.9	1.000
1953			5	5	.500	3.26	21	12	4	85.2	86	33	56	1	1	0	1	32	6	0	.188	4	11	1	0	0.8	.938
1954			3	7	.300	4.52	24	13	3	95.2	104	49	38	1	0	1	0	34	4	0	.118	4	13	0	0	0.7	1.000
1955			2	4	.333	3.32	17	7	0	59.2	56	21	23	0	1	1	0	19	2	0	.105	4	11	0	1	0.9	1.000
1958	CHI	N	5	4	.556	2.88	44	0	0	81.1	63	17	58	0	5	4	6	17	4	0	.235	2	8	0	1	0.2	1.000
1959			9	8	.529	2.68	**65**	0	0	134.1	111	26	115	0	9	8	12	31	6	0	.194	2	18	1	2	0.3	.952
1960	CIN	N	1	5	.167	3.19	51	0	0	67.2	62	20	58	0	1	5	17	8	0	0	.000	5	13	1	2	0.4	.947
1961			2	1	.667	2.19	47	0	0	53.1	50	15	53	0	2	1	16	5	0	0	.000	4	7	0	0	0.2	1.000
1962			4	2	.667	4.58	40	0	0	37.1	40	20	35	0	4	2	11	3	1	0	.333	2	2	0	0	0.1	1.000
1963			1	3	.250	4.15	47	0	0	52	55	11	45	0	1	3	14	6	1	0	.167	2	9	2	1	0.3	.846
1964			2	2	.500	0.87	37	0	0	52	31	12	28	0	2	2	6	6	3	0	.500	6	7	0	0	0.4	1.000
1965	2 teams	CIN N (3G 2–0) SF N (35G 2–2)																									
″	total		4	2	.667	3.26	38	0	0	47	43	9	40	0	4	2	4	5	1	0	.200	4	4	0	0	0.2	1.000
1966	SF	N	1	1	.500	2.49	35	0	0	21.2	15	10	15	0	1	1	1	2	0	0	.000	1	3	0	0	0.1	1.000
1967			2	0	1.000	2.05	28	1	0	22	16	9	23	0	2	0	2	1	0	0	.000	1	1	0	1	0.1	1.000
1968	2 teams	SF N (7G 0–2) PIT N (10G 0–0)																									
″	total		0	2	.000	7.48	17	1	0	21.2	33	6	9	0	0	1	0	3	0	0	.000	2	1	0	0	0.2	1.000
1969	HOU	N	0	0	—	0.00	3	0	0	5	2	2	2	0	0	0	0	0	0	0	—	0	0	0	0	0.0	.000
16 yrs.			46	50	.479	3.26	527	44	12	913	842	296	621	2	33	31	90	203	36	0	.177	48	115	5	9	0.3	.970
WORLD SERIES																											
1961	CIN	N	0	0	—	19.29	2	0	0	2.1	4	2	3	0	0	0	0	0	0	0	—	0	1	0	0	0.5	1.000

Butch Henry

HENRY, FLOYD BLUFORD
B. Oct. 7, 1968, El Paso, Tex.
BL TL 6′1″ 195 lbs.

Year	Team		W	L	PCT	ERA	G	GS	CG	IP	H	BB	SO	ShO	Relief W	Relief L	Relief SV	AB	H	HR	BA	PO	A	E	DP	TC/G	FA
1992	HOU	N	6	9	.400	4.02	28	28	2	165.2	185	41	96	1	0	0	0	54	8	1	.148	13	30	3	2	1.6	.935
1993	2 teams	CLR N (20G 2–8) MON N (10G 1–1)																									
″	total		3	9	.250	6.12	30	16	1	103	135	28	47	0	0	1	0	24	2	0	.083	5	12	1	1	0.6	.944
1994	MON	N	8	3	.727	2.43	24	15	0	107.1	97	20	70	0	0	0	1	31	9	0	.290	8	13	0	3	0.9	1.000
1995			7	9	.438	2.84	21	21	1	126.2	133	28	60	1	0	0	0	42	2	0	.048	11	25	0	3	1.7	1.000
4 yrs.			24	30	.444	3.81	103	80	4	502.2	550	117	273	2	0	1	1	151	21	1	.139	37	80	4	9	1.2	.967

Doug Henry

HENRY, RICHARD DOUGLAS
B. Dec. 10, 1963, Sacramento, Calif.
BR TR 6′4″ 185 lbs.

Year	Team		W	L	PCT	ERA	G	GS	CG	IP	H	BB	SO	ShO	Relief W	Relief L	Relief SV	AB	H	HR	BA	PO	A	E	DP	TC/G	FA
1991	MIL	A	2	1	.667	1.00	32	0	0	36	16	14	28	0	2	1	15	0	0	0	—	4	1	0	0	0.2	1.000
1992			1	4	.200	4.02	68	0	0	65	64	24	52	0	1	4	29	0	0	0	—	10	4	0	2	0.2	1.000
1993			4	4	.500	5.56	54	0	0	55	67	25	38	0	4	4	17	0	0	0	—	5	7	0	0	0.2	1.000
1994			2	3	.400	4.60	25	0	0	31.1	32	23	20	0	2	3	0	1	0	0	.000	2	3	0	0	0.2	1.000
1995	NY	N	3	6	.333	2.96	51	0	0	67	48	25	62	0	3	6	4	1	1	0	1.000	4	9	1	0	0.3	.929
5 yrs.			12	18	.400	3.72	230	0	0	254.1	227	111	200	0	12	18	65	2	1	0	.500	25	24	1	2	0.2	.980

Dutch Henry

HENRY, FRANK JOHN
B. May 12, 1902, Cleveland, Ohio D. Aug. 23, 1968, Cleveland, Ohio.
BL TL 6′1″ 173 lbs.

Year	Team		W	L	PCT	ERA	G	GS	CG	IP	H	BB	SO	ShO	Relief W	Relief L	Relief SV	AB	H	HR	BA	PO	A	E	DP	TC/G	FA
1921	STL	A	0	0	—	4.50	1	0	0	2	2	0	1	0	0	0	0	1	1	0	1.000	1	0	0	0	1.0	1.000
1922			0	0	—	5.40	4	0	0	5	7	5	3	0	0	0	0	0	0	0	—	0	1	0	0	0.3	1.000
1923	BKN	N	4	6	.400	3.91	17	9	5	94.1	105	28	28	2	1	1	0	35	8	0	.229	2	21	1	2	1.4	.958
1924			1	2	.333	5.67	16	4	0	46	69	15	11	0	1	1	0	20	5	0	.250	3	12	0	0	0.9	1.000
1927	NY	N	11	6	.647	4.23	45	15	7	163.2	184	31	40	1	**6**	2	4	55	13	0	.236	5	30	0	0	0.8	1.000
1928			3	6	.333	3.80	17	8	4	64	82	25	23	0	0	1	1	19	3	0	.158	4	17	1	5	1.3	.955
1929	2 teams	NY N (27G 5–6) CHI A (2G 1–0)																									
″	total		6	6	.500	4.10	29	10	5	116.1	149	38	29	0	1	3	1	35	8	0	.229	8	17	1	2	0.9	.962
1930	CHI	A	2	17	.105	4.88	35	16	4	155	211	48	35	0	2	2	0	51	12	0	.235	11	42	1	3	1.5	.981
8 yrs.			27	43	.386	4.39	164	62	25	646.1	809	190	170	3	11	10	6	216	50	0	.231	34	140	4	12	1.1	.978

Dwayne Henry

HENRY, DWAYNE ALLEN
B. Feb. 16, 1962, Elkton, Md.
BR TR 6′ 3″ 210 lbs.

Year	Team		W	L	PCT	ERA	G	GS	CG	IP	H	BB	SO	ShO	Relief Pitching W	Relief Pitching L	Relief Pitching SV	Batting AB	Batting H	Batting HR	BA	PO	A	E	DP	TC/G	FA
1984	TEX	A	0	1	.000	8.31	3	0	0	4.1	5	7	2	0	0	1	0	0	0	0	—	0	0	0	0	0.0	.000
1985			2	2	.500	2.57	16	0	0	21	16	7	20	0	2	2	3	0	0	0	—	1	2	1	1	0.3	.750
1986			1	0	1.000	4.66	19	0	0	19.1	14	22	17	0	1	0	0	0	0	0	—	0	4	0	0	0.2	1.000
1987			0	0	—	9.00	5	0	0	10	12	9	7	0	0	0	0	0	0	0	—	2	1	0	0	0.6	1.000
1988			0	1	.000	8.71	11	0	0	10.1	15	9	10	0	0	1	1	0	0	0	—	1	0	0	0	0.1	1.000
1989	ATL	N	0	2	.000	4.26	12	0	0	12.2	12	5	16	0	0	2	1	0	0	0	—	1	0	1	0	0.2	.500
1990			2	2	.500	5.63	34	0	0	38.1	41	25	34	0	2	2	0	0	0	0	—	4	1	0	0	0.1	1.000
1991	HOU	N	3	2	.600	3.19	52	0	0	67.2	51	39	51	0	3	2	2	1	0	0	.000	4	5	0	1	0.2	1.000
1992	CIN	N	3	3	.500	3.33	60	0	0	83.2	59	44	72	0	3	3	0	4	1	0	.250	5	13	2	0	0.3	.900
1993	2 teams	CIN N	(3G 0–1)		SEA A	(31G 2–1)																					
"	total		2	2	.500	6.44	34	1	0	58.2	62	39	37	0	2	2	2	1	0	0	.000	2	1	0	0	0.1	1.000
1995	DET	A	1	0	1.000	6.23	10	0	0	8.2	11	10	9	0	1	0	5	0	0	0	—	1	0	0	0	0.1	1.000
11 yrs.			14	15	.483	4.65	256	1	0	334.2	298	216	275	0	14	15	14	6	1	0	.167	21	27	4	2	0.2	.923

Earl Henry

HENRY, EARL CLIFFORD (Hook)
B. June 10, 1917, Roseville, Ohio.
BL TL 5′11″ 172 lbs.

Year	Team		W	L	PCT	ERA	G	GS	CG	IP	H	BB	SO	ShO	Relief Pitching W	Relief Pitching L	Relief Pitching SV	Batting AB	Batting H	Batting HR	BA	PO	A	E	DP	TC/G	FA
1944	CLE	A	1	1	.500	4.58	2	2	1	17.2	18	3	5	0	0	0	0	5	0	0	.000	1	4	0	0	2.5	1.000
1945			0	3	.000	5.40	15	1	0	21.2	20	20	10	0	0	2	0	4	2	0	.500	3	6	0	0	0.6	1.000
2 yrs.			1	4	.200	5.03	17	3	1	39.1	38	23	15	0	0	2	0	9	2	0	.222	4	10	0	0	0.8	1.000

Jim Henry

HENRY, JAMES FRANCIS
B. June 26, 1910, Danville, Va. D. Aug. 15, 1976, Memphis, Tenn.
BR TR 6′ 2″ 175 lbs.

Year	Team		W	L	PCT	ERA	G	GS	CG	IP	H	BB	SO	ShO	Relief Pitching W	Relief Pitching L	Relief Pitching SV	Batting AB	Batting H	Batting HR	BA	PO	A	E	DP	TC/G	FA
1936	BOS	A	5	1	.833	4.60	21	8	2	76.1	75	40	36	0	2	0	0	26	3	0	.115	3	13	0	0	0.8	1.000
1937			1	0	1.000	5.17	3	2	1	15.2	15	11	8	0	0	0	0	5	0	0	.000	0	2	0	1	0.7	1.000
1939	PHI	N	0	1	.000	5.09	9	1	0	23	24	8	7	0	0	1	1	5	0	0	.000	0	3	1	0	0.4	.750
3 yrs.			6	2	.750	4.77	33	11	3	115	114	59	51	0	2	1	1	36	3	0	.083	3	18	1	1	0.7	.955

John Henry

HENRY, JOHN MICHAEL
B. Sept. 2, 1863, Springfield, Mass. D. June 11, 1939, Hartford, Conn.
TL

Year	Team		W	L	PCT	ERA	G	GS	CG	IP	H	BB	SO	ShO	Relief Pitching W	Relief Pitching L	Relief Pitching SV	Batting AB	Batting H	Batting HR	BA	PO	A	E	DP	TC/G	FA
1884	CLE	N	1	4	.200	*3.64*	5	5	5	42	46	26	23	1	0	0	0	26	4	0	.154	7	12	1	0	2.2	.950
1885	BAL	AA	2	7	.222	*4.31*	9	9	9	71	71	13	31	0	0	0	0	34	9	0	.265	10	18	2	1	3.0	.933
1886	WAS	N	1	3	.250	*4.23*	4	4	4	27.2	35	15	19	0	0	0	0	14	5	0	.357	2	3	1	0	1.5	.833
3 yrs.			4	14	.222	4.09	18	18	18	140.2	152	54	73	1	0	0	0	*				75	37	13	2	2.1	.896

Roy Henshaw

HENSHAW, ROY KNIKLEBINE
B. July 29, 1911, Chicago, Ill. D. June 8, 1993, La Grange, Ill.
BR TL 5′ 8″ 155 lbs.

Year	Team		W	L	PCT	ERA	G	GS	CG	IP	H	BB	SO	ShO	Relief Pitching W	Relief Pitching L	Relief Pitching SV	Batting AB	Batting H	Batting HR	BA	PO	A	E	DP	TC/G	FA
1933	CHI	N	2	1	.667	4.19	21	0	0	38.2	32	20	16	0	2	1	0	10	2	0	.200	1	5	1	0	0.3	.857
1935			13	5	.722	3.28	31	18	7	142.2	135	68	53	3	4	0	1	51	13	0	.255	6	15	4	2	0.8	.840
1936			6	5	.545	3.97	39	14	6	129.1	152	56	69	2	1	3	1	44	6	0	.136	4	16	3	1	0.6	.870
1937	BKN	N	5	12	.294	5.07	42	16	5	156.1	176	69	98	0	1	3	2	48	8	0	.167	4	32	3	2	0.9	.923
1938	STL	N	5	11	.313	4.02	27	15	4	130	132	48	34	0	2	1	0	41	9	0	.220	3	23	1	0	1.0	.963
1942	DET	A	2	4	.333	4.09	23	2	0	61.2	63	27	24	0	2	3	1	12	1	0	.083	4	10	2	0	0.7	.875
1943			0	2	.000	3.79	26	3	0	71.1	75	33	33	0	0	1	2	18	2	0	.111	9	13	1	0	0.9	.957
1944			0	0	—	8.76	7	1	0	12.1	17	6	10	0	0	0	0	5	0	0	.000	3	2	0	0	0.7	1.000
8 yrs.			33	40	.452	4.16	216	69	22	742.1	782	327	337	5	12	12	7	229	41	0	.179	34	116	15	5	0.8	.909
WORLD SERIES																											
1935	CHI	N	0	0	—	7.36	1	0	0	3.2	2	5	2	0	0	0	0	1	0	0	.000	0	1	0	0	1.0	1.000

Phil Hensiek

HENSIEK, PHILIP FRANK (Sid)
B. Oct. 13, 1901, St. Louis, Mo. D. Feb. 21, 1972, St. Louis, Mo.
BR TR 6′ 160 lbs.

Year	Team		W	L	PCT	ERA	G	GS	CG	IP	H	BB	SO	ShO	Relief Pitching W	Relief Pitching L	Relief Pitching SV	Batting AB	Batting H	Batting HR	BA	PO	A	E	DP	TC/G	FA
1935	WAS	A	0	3	.000	9.69	6	1	0	13	21	9	6	0	0	2	1	3	2	0	.667	0	3	2	0	0.8	.600

Chuck Hensley

HENSLEY, CHARLES FLOYD
B. Mar. 11, 1959, Tulare, Calif.
BL TL 6′ 3″ 190 lbs.

Year	Team		W	L	PCT	ERA	G	GS	CG	IP	H	BB	SO	ShO	Relief Pitching W	Relief Pitching L	Relief Pitching SV	Batting AB	Batting H	Batting HR	BA	PO	A	E	DP	TC/G	FA
1986	SF	N	0	0	—	2.45	11	0	0	7.1	5	2	6	0	0	0	1	0	0	0	—	0	1	0	0	0.1	1.000

Pat Hentgen

HENTGEN, PATRICK GEORGE
B. Nov. 13, 1968, Detroit, Mich.
BR TR 6′ 2″ 210 lbs.

Year	Team		W	L	PCT	ERA	G	GS	CG	IP	H	BB	SO	ShO	Relief Pitching W	Relief Pitching L	Relief Pitching SV	Batting AB	Batting H	Batting HR	BA	PO	A	E	DP	TC/G	FA
1991	TOR	A	0	0	—	2.45	3	1	0	7.1	5	3	3	0	0	0	0	0	0	0	—	0	2	0	1	0.7	1.000
1992			5	2	.714	5.36	28	2	0	50.1	49	32	39	0	5	1	0	0	0	0	—	0	4	0	1	0.1	1.000
1993			19	9	.679	3.87	34	32	3	216.1	215	74	122	0	0	1	0	0	0	0	—	12	22	1	1	1.0	.971
1994			13	8	.619	3.40	24	24	6	174.2	158	59	147	3	0	0	0	0	0	0	—	12	21	0	2	1.4	1.000
1995			10	14	.417	5.11	30	30	2	200.2	236	90	135	0	0	0	0	0	0	0	—	12	18	2	2	1.1	.938
5 yrs.			47	33	.587	4.23	119	89	11	649.1	663	258	446	3	5	2	0	0	0	0		36	67	3	7	0.9	.972
LEAGUE CHAMPIONSHIP SERIES																											
1993	TOR	A	0	1	.000	18.00	1	1	0	3	9	2	3	0	0	0	0	0	0	0	—	1	0	0	0	1.0	1.000
WORLD SERIES																											
1993	TOR	A	1	0	1.000	1.50	1	1	0	6	5	3	6	0	0	0	0	3	0	0	.000	0	0	0	0	0.0	.000

Bill Hepler

HEPLER, WILLIAM LEWIS
B. Sept. 25, 1945, Covington, Va.
BL TL 6′ 160 lbs.

Year	Team		W	L	PCT	ERA	G	GS	CG	IP	H	BB	SO	ShO	Relief Pitching W	Relief Pitching L	Relief Pitching SV	Batting AB	Batting H	Batting HR	BA	PO	A	E	DP	TC/G	FA
1966	NY	N	3	3	.500	3.52	37	3	0	69	71	51	25	0	3	1	0	14	3	0	.214	3	11	2	0	0.4	.875

Ron Herbel

HERBEL, RONALD SAMUEL
B. Jan. 16, 1938, Denver, Colo.
BR TR 6′ 1″ 195 lbs.

Year	Team		W	L	PCT	ERA	G	GS	CG	IP	H	BB	SO	ShO	Relief Pitching W	Relief Pitching L	Relief Pitching SV	Batting AB	Batting H	Batting HR	BA	PO	A	E	DP	TC/G	FA
1963	SF	N	0	0	—	6.75	2	0	0	1.1	1	1	1	0	0	0	0	0	0	0	—	0	0	0	0	0.0	.000
1964			9	9	.500	3.07	40	22	7	161	162	61	98	2	0	1	1	47	0	0	.000	12	39	2	1	1.3	.962
1965			12	9	.571	3.85	47	21	1	170.2	172	47	106	0	4	2	1	49	1	0	.020	14	39	3	1	1.2	.946
1966			4	5	.444	4.16	32	18	0	129.2	149	39	55	0	0	1	1	38	1	0	.026	4	22	3	2	0.9	.897
1967			4	5	.444	3.08	42	11	1	125.2	125	35	52	1	2	1	1	28	3	0	.107	11	37	0	7	1.1	1.000
1968			0	0	—	3.35	28	2	0	43	55	15	18	0	0	0	0	3	0	0	.000	3	11	0	0	0.5	1.000
1969			4	1	.800	4.03	39	4	2	87	92	23	34	0	2	1	1	17	0	0	.000	8	16	1	1	0.6	.960

Year	Team	W	L	PCT	ERA	G	GS	CG	IP	H	BB	SO	ShO	Relief Pitching W	Relief Pitching L	Relief Pitching SV	Batting AB	Batting H	Batting HR	BA	PO	A	E	DP	TC/G	FA

Ron Herbel *continued*

Year	Team	W	L	PCT	ERA	G	GS	CG	IP	H	BB	SO	ShO	W	L	SV	AB	H	HR	BA	PO	A	E	DP	TC/G	FA
1970	**2 teams** SD N (64G 7–5) NY N (12G 2–2)																									
"	**total**	9	7	.563	4.57	**76**	1	0	124	128	41	61	0	**9**	6	10	13	0	0	.000	8	17	2	0	0.4	.926
1971	**ATL N**	0	1	.000	5.19	25	0	0	52	61	23	22	0	0	1	1	11	1	0	.091	3	7	0	3	0.4	1.000
9 yrs.		42	37	.532	3.82	331	79	11	894.1	945	285	447	3	17	13	16	206	6	0	.029	63	188	11	15	0.8	.958

Ernie Herbert

HERBERT, ERNIE ALBERT (Tex) BR TR 5′10″ 165 lbs.
B. Jan. 30, 1887, Hale, Mo. D. Jan. 13, 1968, Dallas, Tex.

Year	Team	W	L	PCT	ERA	G	GS	CG	IP	H	BB	SO	ShO	W	L	SV	AB	H	HR	BA	PO	A	E	DP	TC/G	FA
1913	**CIN N**	0	0	—	2.08	6	0	0	17.1	12	5	5	0	0	0	0	4	1	0	.250	0	1	0	0	0.2	1.000
1914	**STL F**	1	1	.500	3.75	18	2	0	50.1	56	27	24	0	0	1	1	13	7	0	.538	1	3	0	1	0.2	1.000
1915		1	0	1.000	3.38	11	1	1	48	48	18	23	0	0	0	0	18	5	0	.278	0	12	0	0	1.1	1.000
3 yrs.		2	1	.667	3.35	35	3	1	115.2	116	50	52	0	0	1	1	35	13	0	.371	1	16	0	1	0.5	1.000

Fred Herbert

HERBERT, FREDERICK BR TR 6′ 185 lbs.
Born Herbert Frederick Kemman.
B. Mar. 4, 1887, LaGrange, Ill. D. May 29, 1963, Tice, Fla.

Year	Team	W	L	PCT	ERA	G	GS	CG	IP	H	BB	SO	ShO	W	L	SV	AB	H	HR	BA	PO	A	E	DP	TC/G	FA
1915	**NY N**	1	1	.500	1.06	2	2	1	17	12	4	6	0	0	0	0	6	1	0	.167	0	5	0	0	2.5	1.000

Ray Herbert

HERBERT, RAYMOND ERNEST BR TR 5′11″ 185 lbs.
B. Dec. 15, 1929, Detroit, Mich.

Year	Team	W	L	PCT	ERA	G	GS	CG	IP	H	BB	SO	ShO	W	L	SV	AB	H	HR	BA	PO	A	E	DP	TC/G	FA
1950	**DET A**	1	2	.333	3.63	8	3	1	22.1	20	12	5	0	1	0	1	7	2	0	.286	1	8	0	1	1.1	1.000
1951		4	0	1.000	1.42	5	0	0	12.2	8	9	9	0	4	0	0	4	0	0	.000	0	1	1	0	0.4	.500
1953		4	6	.400	5.24	43	3	0	87.2	109	46	37	0	4	4	6	19	3	0	.158	9	28	2	2	0.9	.949
1954		3	6	.333	5.87	42	4	0	84.1	114	50	44	0	3	3	0	17	3	1	.176	7	24	1	2	0.8	.969
1955	**KC A**	1	8	.111	6.26	23	11	2	87.2	99	40	30	0	0	1	0	21	4	0	.190	8	24	0	0	1.4	1.000
1958		8	8	.500	3.50	42	16	5	175	161	55	108	0	1	3	3	52	10	0	.192	9	37	3	8	1.2	.939
1959		11	11	.500	4.85	37	26	10	183.2	196	62	99	2	0	1	1	57	12	1	.211	13	23	1	4	1.0	.973
1960		14	15	.483	3.28	37	33	14	252.2	256	72	122	0	0	1	1	76	13	0	.171	8	55	2	6	1.8	.969
1961	**2 teams** KC A (13G 3–6) CHI A (21G 9–6)																									
"	**total**	12	12	.500	4.55	34	32	5	221.1	245	66	84	0	1	0	0	81	15	2	.185	20	39	2	4	1.8	.967
1962	**CHI A**	20	9	**.690**	3.27	35	35	12	236.2	228	74	115	2	0	0	0	82	16	2	.195	21	50	0	8	2.0	1.000
1963		13	10	.565	3.24	33	33	14	224.2	230	35	105	**7**	0	0	0	63	14	1	.222	18	48	1	1	2.0	.985
1964		6	7	.462	3.47	20	19	1	111.2	117	17	40	1	0	0	0	36	5	0	.139	3	18	0	1	1.0	1.000
1965	**PHI N**	5	8	.385	3.86	25	19	4	130.2	162	19	51	1	0	0	1	41	11	0	.268	7	26	0	4	1.3	1.000
1966		2	5	.286	4.29	23	2	0	50.1	55	14	15	0	2	4	2	13	1	0	.077	2	8	0	1	0.4	1.000
14 yrs.		104	107	.493	4.01	407	236	68	1881.1	2000	571	864	13	16	17	15	569	109	7	.192	126	389	13	42	1.3	.975

Gil Heredia

HEREDIA, GILBERT BR TR 6′ 1″ 190 lbs.
B. Oct. 26, 1965, Nogales, Ariz.

Year	Team	W	L	PCT	ERA	G	GS	CG	IP	H	BB	SO	ShO	W	L	SV	AB	H	HR	BA	PO	A	E	DP	TC/G	FA
1991	**SF N**	0	2	.000	3.82	7	4	0	33	27	7	13	0	0	0	0	7	3	0	.429	2	2	0	0	0.6	1.000
1992	**2 teams** SF N (13G 2–3) MON N (7G 0–0)																									
"	**total**	2	3	.400	4.23	20	5	0	44.2	44	20	22	0	2	0	0	9	1	0	.111	0	5	0	0	0.3	1.000
1993	**MON N**	4	2	.667	3.92	20	9	1	57.1	66	14	40	0	0	0	2	13	2	0	.154	4	11	0	1	0.8	1.000
1994		6	3	.667	3.46	39	3	0	75.1	85	13	62	0	4	3	0	16	5	0	.313	5	12	1	0	0.5	.944
1995		5	6	.455	4.31	40	18	0	119	137	21	74	0	1	0	1	33	6	0	.182	9	21	0	0	0.8	1.000
5 yrs.		17	16	.515	3.99	126	39	1	329.1	359	75	211	0	7	3	3	78	17	0	.218	20	51	1	1	0.6	.986

Ubaldo Heredia

HEREDIA, UBALDO JOSE BR TR 6′ 2″ 180 lbs.
Born Ubaldo Jose Heredia (Martinez).
B. May 4, 1956, Ciudad Bolivar, Venezuela.

Year	Team	W	L	PCT	ERA	G	GS	CG	IP	H	BB	SO	ShO	W	L	SV	AB	H	HR	BA	PO	A	E	DP	TC/G	FA
1987	**MON N**	0	1	.000	5.40	2	2	0	10	10	3	6	0	0	0	0	2	0	0	.000	0	2	0	1	1.0	1.000

Wilson Heredia

HEREDIA, WILSON BR TR 6′ 175 lbs.
B. Mar. 30, 1972, La Romana, Dominican Republic.

Year	Team	W	L	PCT	ERA	G	GS	CG	IP	H	BB	SO	ShO	W	L	SV	AB	H	HR	BA	PO	A	E	DP	TC/G	FA
1995	**TEX A**	0	1	.000	3.75	6	0	0	12	9	15	6	0	0	1	0	0	0	0	—	0	1	0	0	0.2	1.000

Art Herman

HERMAN, ARTHUR
B. May 11, 1871, Louisville, Ky. D. Sept. 20, 1955, Los Angeles, Calif.

Year	Team	W	L	PCT	ERA	G	GS	CG	IP	H	BB	SO	ShO	W	L	SV	AB	H	HR	BA	PO	A	E	DP	TC/G	FA
1896	**LOU N**	4	6	.400	5.63	14	12	9	94.1	122	36	13	0	0	0	0	36	5	0	.139	1	20	4	1	1.8	.840
1897		0	1	.000	4.00	3	2	1	18	23	5	4	0	0	0	0	6	2	0	.333	0	6	0	0	2.0	1.000
2 yrs.		4	7	.364	5.37	17	14	10	112.1	145	41	17	0	0	0	0	42	7	0	.167	1	26	4	1	1.8	.871

Dustin Hermanson

HERMANSON, DUSTIN MICHAEL BR TR 6′ 3″ 195 lbs.
B. Dec. 21, 1972, Springfield, Ohio.

Year	Team	W	L	PCT	ERA	G	GS	CG	IP	H	BB	SO	ShO	W	L	SV	AB	H	HR	BA	PO	A	E	DP	TC/G	FA
1995	**SD N**	3	1	.750	6.82	26	0	0	31.2	35	22	19	0	3	1	0	0	0	0	—	4	4	0	2	0.3	1.000

Jesus Hernaiz

HERNAIZ, JESUS RAFAEL BR TR 6′ 2″ 175 lbs.
Born Jesus Rafael Hernaiz (Rodriguez).
B. Jan. 8, 1948, Santurce, Puerto Rico.

Year	Team	W	L	PCT	ERA	G	GS	CG	IP	H	BB	SO	ShO	W	L	SV	AB	H	HR	BA	PO	A	E	DP	TC/G	FA
1974	**PHI N**	2	3	.400	5.93	27	0	0	41	53	25	16	0	2	3	1	2	0	0	.000	4	6	3	0	0.5	.769

Evelio Hernandez

HERNANDEZ, GREGORIO EVELIO BR TR 6′ 1″ 180 lbs.
Born Gregorio Evelio Hernandez (Lopez).
B. Dec. 24, 1930, Guanabacoa, Cuba.

Year	Team	W	L	PCT	ERA	G	GS	CG	IP	H	BB	SO	ShO	W	L	SV	AB	H	HR	BA	PO	A	E	DP	TC/G	FA
1956	**WAS A**	1	1	.500	4.76	4	4	1	22.2	24	8	9	0	0	0	0	11	2	0	.182	1	3	0	0	1.0	1.000
1957		0	0	—	4.25	14	2	0	36	38	20	15	0	0	0	0	6	0	0	.000	2	3	1	0	0.4	.833
2 yrs.		1	1	.500	4.45	18	6	1	58.2	62	28	24	0	0	0	0	17	2	0	.118	3	6	1	0	0.6	.900

Guillermo Hernandez

HERNANDEZ, GUILLERMO (Willie) BL TL 6′ 3″ 180 lbs.
Born Guillermo Hernandez (Villanueva).
B. Nov. 14, 1954, Aguada, Puerto Rico.

Year	Team	W	L	PCT	ERA	G	GS	CG	IP	H	BB	SO	ShO	W	L	SV	AB	H	HR	BA	PO	A	E	DP	TC/G	FA
1977	**CHI N**	8	7	.533	3.03	67	1	0	110	94	28	78	0	8	6	4	16	1	0	.063	8	27	0	2	0.5	1.000
1978		8	2	.800	3.75	54	0	0	60	57	35	38	0	8	2	3	1	0	0	.000	2	12	0	0	0.3	1.000
1979		4	4	.500	5.01	51	2	0	79	85	39	53	0	4	3	0	8	2	0	.250	4	11	1	0	0.3	.938

Guillermo Hernandez *continued*

Year	Team	W	L	PCT	ERA	G	GS	CG	IP	H	BB	SO	ShO	Relief Pitching W	Relief Pitching L	Relief Pitching SV	Batting AB	Batting H	Batting HR	BA	PO	A	E	DP	TC/G	FA
1980		1	9	.100	4.42	53	7	0	108	115	45	75	0	1	3	0	19	4	0	.211	12	20	0	2	0.6	1.000
1981		0	0	—	3.86	12	0	0	14	14	8	13	0	0	0	2	0	0	0	—	0	3	0	0	0.3	1.000
1982		4	6	.400	3.00	75	0	0	75	74	24	54	0	4	6	10	3	0	0	.000	5	22	1	1	0.4	.964
1983	2 teams CHI N (11G 1–0) PHI N (63G 8–4)																									
"	total	9	4	.692	3.28	74	1	0	115.1	109	32	93	0	9	4	8	15	6	0	.400	2	17	0	3	0.3	1.000
1984	DET A	9	3	.750	1.92	**80**	0	0	140.1	96	36	112	0	9	3	32	0	0	0	—	5	14	0	1	0.2	1.000
1985		8	10	.444	2.70	74	0	0	106.2	82	14	76	0	8	**10**	31	1	0	0	.000	7	7	1	0	0.2	.933
1986		8	7	.533	3.55	64	0	0	88.2	87	21	77	0	8	7	24	0	0	0	—	6	13	0	0	0.3	1.000
1987		3	4	.429	3.67	45	0	0	49	53	20	30	0	3	4	8	0	0	0	—	2	4	1	1	0.2	.857
1988		6	5	.545	3.06	63	0	0	67.2	50	31	59	0	6	5	10	0	0	0	—	3	15	0	1	0.3	1.000
1989		2	2	.500	5.74	32	0	0	31.1	36	16	30	0	2	2	15	0	0	0	—	2	4	0	1	0.2	1.000
13 yrs.		70	63	.526	3.38	744	11	0	1045	952	349	788	0	70	55	147	63	13	0	.206	58	169	4	12	0.3	.983
LEAGUE CHAMPIONSHIP SERIES																										
1984	DET A	0	0	—	2.25	3	0	0	4	3	1	3	0	0	0	1	0	0	0	—	0	0	0	0	0.0	.000
1987		0	0	—	0.00	1	0	0	0.1	2	0	0	0	0	0	0	0	0	0	—	0	0	0	0	0.0	.000
2 yrs.		0	0		2.08	4	0	0	4.1	5	1	3	0	0	0	1	0	0	0		0	0	0	0	0.0	
WORLD SERIES																										
1983	PHI N	0	0	—	0.00	3	0	0	4	0	1	4	0	0	0	0	0	0	0	—	1	0	0	0	0.3	1.000
1984	DET A	0	0	—	1.69	3	0	0	5.1	4	0	0	0	0	0	2	0	0	0	—	0	1	0	0	0.3	1.000
2 yrs.		0	0		0.96	6	0	0	9.1	4	1	4	0	0	0	2	0	0	0		1	1	0	0	0.3	1.000

Jeremy Hernandez

HERNANDEZ, JEREMY STUART BR TR 6′ 5″ 195 lbs.
B. July 6, 1966, Burbank, Calif.

Year	Team	W	L	PCT	ERA	G	GS	CG	IP	H	BB	SO	ShO	Relief Pitching W	Relief Pitching L	Relief Pitching SV	Batting AB	Batting H	Batting HR	BA	PO	A	E	DP	TC/G	FA
1991	SD N	0	0	—	0.00	9	0	0	14.1	8	5	9	0	0	0	2	2	0	0	.000	0	3	0	1	0.3	1.000
1992		1	4	.200	4.17	26	0	0	36.2	39	11	25	0	1	4	1	2	0	0	.000	2	6	0	2	0.3	1.000
1993	2 teams SD N (21G 0–2) CLE A (49G 6–5)																									
"	total	6	7	.462	3.63	70	0	0	111.2	116	34	70	0	6	7	8	1	0	0	.000	3	17	1	1	0.3	.952
1994	FLA N	3	3	.500	2.70	21	0	0	23.1	16	14	13	0	3	3	9	1	0	0	.000	0	2	0	0	0.1	1.000
1995		0	0	—	11.57	7	0	0	7	12	3	5	0	0	0	0	1	0	0	.000	0	0	0	0	0.0	.000
5 yrs.		10	14	.417	3.64	133	0	0	193	191	67	122	0	10	14	20	7	0	0	.000	5	28	1	4	0.3	.971

Manny Hernandez

HERNANDEZ, MANUEL ANTONIO BR TR 6′ 150 lbs.
Born Manuel Antonio Hernandez (Montas).
B. May 7, 1961, La Romana, Dominican Republic.

Year	Team	W	L	PCT	ERA	G	GS	CG	IP	H	BB	SO	ShO	Relief Pitching W	Relief Pitching L	Relief Pitching SV	Batting AB	Batting H	Batting HR	BA	PO	A	E	DP	TC/G	FA
1986	HOU N	2	3	.400	3.90	9	4	0	27.2	33	12	9	0	1	0	0	6	0	0	.000	1	5	0	0	0.7	1.000
1987		0	4	.000	5.40	6	3	0	21.2	25	5	12	0	0	2	0	5	0	0	.000	2	4	1	0	1.2	.857
1989	NY N	0	0	—	0.00	1	0	0	1	0	0	1	0	0	0	0	0	0	0	—	0	0	0	0	0.0	.000
3 yrs.		2	7	.222	4.47	16	7	0	50.1	58	17	22	0	1	2	0	11	0	0	.000	3	9	1	0	0.8	.923

Ramon Hernandez

HERNANDEZ, RAMON BB TL 5′11″ 165 lbs.
Born Ramon Hernandez (Gonzalez).
B. Aug. 31, 1940, Carolina, Puerto Rico.

Year	Team	W	L	PCT	ERA	G	GS	CG	IP	H	BB	SO	ShO	Relief Pitching W	Relief Pitching L	Relief Pitching SV	Batting AB	Batting H	Batting HR	BA	PO	A	E	DP	TC/G	FA
1967	ATL N	0	2	.000	4.18	46	0	0	51.2	60	14	28	0	0	2	5	4	0	0	.000	2	12	0	1	0.3	1.000
1968	CHI N	0	0	—	9.00	8	0	0	9	14	0	3	0	0	0	0	0	0	0	—	0	3	1	0	0.5	.750
1971	PIT N	0	1	.000	0.75	10	0	0	12	5	2	7	0	0	1	4	2	1	0	.500	2	2	0	0	0.4	1.000
1972		5	0	1.000	1.67	53	0	0	70	50	22	47	0	5	0	14	12	2	0	.167	3	11	0	0	0.3	1.000
1973		4	5	.444	2.41	59	0	0	89.2	71	25	64	0	4	5	11	8	1	0	.125	3	16	1	2	0.3	.950
1974		5	2	.714	2.74	58	0	0	69	68	18	33	0	5	2	2	4	1	0	.250	2	9	1	1	0.2	.917
1975		7	2	.778	2.95	46	0	0	64	62	28	43	0	7	2	5	6	0	0	.000	1	13	0	0	0.3	1.000
1976	2 teams PIT N (37G 2–2) CHI N (2G 0–0)																									
"	total	2	2	.500	3.43	39	0	0	44.2	44	16	18	0	2	2	3	3	0	0	.000	0	7	2	1	0.2	.778
1977	2 teams CHI N (6G 0–0) BOS A (12G 0–1)																									
"	total	0	1	.000	6.53	18	0	0	20.2	25	10	12	0	0	1	2	1	0	0	.000	0	5	0	0	0.3	1.000
9 yrs.		23	15	.605	3.03	337	0	0	430.2	399	135	255	0	23	15	46	40	5	0	.125	13	78	5	5	0.3	.948
LEAGUE CHAMPIONSHIP SERIES																										
1972	PIT N	0	0	—	2.70	3	0	0	3.1	1	0	3	0	0	0	1	0	0	0	—	0	2	0	0	0.7	1.000
1974		0	0	—	0.00	2	0	0	4.1	3	1	2	0	0	0	0	1	0	0	.000	0	1	0	0	0.5	1.000
1975		0	1	.000	27.00	1	0	0	0.2	3	0	0	0	0	1	0	0	0	0	—	0	0	0	0	0.0	.000
3 yrs.		0	1	.000	3.24	6	0	0	8.1	7	1	5	0	0	1	1	1	0	0	.000	0	3	0	0	0.5	1.000

Roberto Hernandez

HERNANDEZ, ROBERTO MANUEL BR TR 6′ 4″ 220 lbs.
Born Roberto Manuel Hernandez (Rodriguez).
B. Nov. 11, 1964, Santurce, Puerto Rico.

Year	Team	W	L	PCT	ERA	G	GS	CG	IP	H	BB	SO	ShO	Relief Pitching W	Relief Pitching L	Relief Pitching SV	Batting AB	Batting H	Batting HR	BA	PO	A	E	DP	TC/G	FA
1991	CHI A	1	0	1.000	7.80	9	3	0	15	18	7	6	0	0	0	0	0	0	0	—	0	2	0	0	0.2	1.000
1992		7	3	.700	1.65	43	0	0	71	45	20	68	0	7	3	12	0	0	0	—	7	4	1	1	0.3	.917
1993		3	4	.429	2.29	70	0	0	78.2	66	20	71	0	3	4	38	0	0	0	—	2	11	1	1	0.2	.929
1994		4	4	.500	4.91	45	0	0	47.2	44	19	50	0	4	4	14	0	0	0	—	0	2	1	0	0.1	.667
1995		3	7	.300	3.92	60	0	0	59.2	63	28	84	0	3	7	32	0	0	0	—	2	5	1	0	0.1	.875
5 yrs.		18	18	.500	3.24	227	3	0	272	236	94	279	0	17	18	96	0	0	0		11	24	4	2	0.2	.897
LEAGUE CHAMPIONSHIP SERIES																										
1993	CHI A	0	0	—	0.00	4	0	0	4	4	0	1	0	0	0	1	0	0	0	—	0	0	0	0	0.0	.000

Rudy Hernandez

HERNANDEZ, RUDOLPH ALBERT BR TR 6′ 3″ 185 lbs.
Born Rudolph Albert Hernandez (Fuentes).
B. Dec. 10, 1931, Santiago, Dominican Republic.

Year	Team	W	L	PCT	ERA	G	GS	CG	IP	H	BB	SO	ShO	Relief Pitching W	Relief Pitching L	Relief Pitching SV	Batting AB	Batting H	Batting HR	BA	PO	A	E	DP	TC/G	FA
1960	WAS A	4	1	.800	4.41	21	0	0	34.2	34	21	22	0	4	1	0	6	1	0	.167	1	4	1	1	0.3	.833
1961		0	1	.000	3.00	7	0	0	9	8	3	4	0	0	1	0	0	0	0	—	1	3	0	0	0.6	1.000
2 yrs.		4	2	.667	4.12	28	0	0	43.2	42	24	26	0	4	2	0	6	1	0	.167	2	7	1	1	0.4	.900

Xavier Hernandez

HERNANDEZ, FRANCIS XAVIER BL TR 6′ 2″ 185 lbs.
B. Aug. 16, 1965, Port Arthur, Tex.

Year	Team	Lg	W	L	PCT	ERA	G	GS	CG	IP	H	BB	SO	ShO	Relief W	Relief L	Relief SV	AB	H	HR	BA	PO	A	E	DP	TC/G	FA
1989	TOR	A	1	0	1.000	4.76	7	0	0	22.2	25	8	7	0	1	0	0	0	0	0	—	1	2	1	0	0.6	.750
1990	HOU	N	2	1	.667	4.62	34	1	0	62.1	60	24	24	0	2	0	0	3	1	0	.333	3	5	0	0	0.2	1.000
1991			2	7	.222	4.71	32	6	0	63	66	32	55	0	2	2	3	10	0	0	.000	6	9	0	0	0.5	1.000
1992			9	1	.900	2.11	77	0	0	111	81	42	96	0	9	1	7	9	0	0	.000	9	7	1	0	0.2	.941
1993			4	5	.444	2.61	72	0	0	96.2	75	28	101	0	4	5	9	5	0	0	.000	1	8	0	0	0.1	1.000
1994	NY	A	4	4	.500	5.85	31	0	0	40	48	21	37	0	4	4	6	0	0	0	—	2	8	0	3	0.3	1.000
1995	CIN	N	7	2	.778	4.60	59	0	0	90	95	31	84	0	7	2	3	8	0	0	.000	10	7	0	0	0.3	1.000
7 yrs.			29	20	.592	3.76	312	7	0	485.2	450	186	404	0	29	14	28	35	1	0	.029	32	46	2	3	0.3	.975
LEAGUE CHAMPIONSHIP SERIES																											
1995	CIN	N	0	0	—	27.00	1	0	0	0.2	3	0	0	0	0	0	0	0	0	0	—	0	0	0	0	0.0	.000

Walt Herrell

HERRELL, WALTER WILLIAM
B. Feb. 19, 1889, Rockville, Md. D. Jan. 23, 1949, Front Royal, Va.

Year	Team	Lg	W	L	PCT	ERA	G	GS	CG	IP	H	BB	SO	ShO	Relief W	Relief L	Relief SV	AB	H	HR	BA	PO	A	E	DP	TC/G	FA
1911	WAS	A	0	0	—	18.00	1	0	0	2	5	2	0	0	0	0	0	1	0	0	.000	1	0	0	0	1.0	1.000

Tito Herrera

HERRERA, PROCOPIO (Bobby) BR TR 6′ 184 lbs.
Born Procopio Herrera (Rodriguez).
B. July 26, 1926, Nuevo Laredo, Mexico.

Year	Team	Lg	W	L	PCT	ERA	G	GS	CG	IP	H	BB	SO	ShO	Relief W	Relief L	Relief SV	AB	H	HR	BA	PO	A	E	DP	TC/G	FA
1951	STL	A	0	0	—	27.00	3	0	0	2.1	6	4	1	0	0	0	0	0	0	0	—	0	0	0	0	0.0	.000

Troy Herriage

HERRIAGE, WILLIAM TROY (Dutch) BR TR 6′ 1″ 170 lbs.
B. Dec. 20, 1930, Tipton, Okla.

Year	Team	Lg	W	L	PCT	ERA	G	GS	CG	IP	H	BB	SO	ShO	Relief W	Relief L	Relief SV	AB	H	HR	BA	PO	A	E	DP	TC/G	FA
1956	KC	A	1	13	.071	6.64	31	16	1	103	135	64	59	0	0	1	0	25	3	0	.120	0	11	3	0	0.5	.786

Tom Herrin

HERRIN, THOMAS EDWARD BR TR 6′ 3″ 190 lbs.
B. Sept. 12, 1929, Shreveport, La.

Year	Team	Lg	W	L	PCT	ERA	G	GS	CG	IP	H	BB	SO	ShO	Relief W	Relief L	Relief SV	AB	H	HR	BA	PO	A	E	DP	TC/G	FA
1954	BOS	A	1	2	.333	7.31	14	1	0	28.1	34	22	8	0	1	1	0	8	1	0	.125	4	9	0	2	0.9	1.000

Art Herring

HERRING, ARTHUR L. (Sandy) BR TR 5′ 7″ 168 lbs.
B. Mar. 10, 1907, Altus, Okla.

Year	Team	Lg	W	L	PCT	ERA	G	GS	CG	IP	H	BB	SO	ShO	Relief W	Relief L	Relief SV	AB	H	HR	BA	PO	A	E	DP	TC/G	FA
1929	DET	A	2	1	.667	4.78	4	4	2	32	38	19	15	0	0	0	0	14	3	0	.214	2	7	0	0	2.3	1.000
1930			3	3	.500	5.33	23	6	1	77.2	97	36	16	0	1	0	0	23	3	0	.130	4	14	0	1	0.8	1.000
1931			7	13	.350	4.31	35	16	9	165	186	67	64	0	1	4	1	55	11	0	.200	9	39	2	6	1.4	.960
1932			1	2	.333	5.24	12	0	0	22.1	25	15	12	0	1	2	2	4	0	0	.000	0	6	0	1	0.5	1.000
1933			1	2	.333	3.84	24	3	1	61	61	20	20	0	0	2	0	13	1	0	.077	0	11	0	2	0.5	1.000
1934	BKN	N	2	4	.333	6.20	14	4	2	49.1	63	29	15	0	1	3	0	14	2	0	.143	3	9	1	0	0.9	.923
1939	CHI	A	0	0	—	5.65	7	0	0	14.1	13	5	8	0	0	0	0	4	0	0	.000	0	3	0	0	0.4	1.000
1944	BKN	N	3	4	.429	3.42	12	6	3	55.1	59	17	19	1	1	0	1	15	3	0	.200	3	11	0	1	1.2	1.000
1945			7	4	.636	3.48	22	15	7	124	103	43	34	2	1	0	2	42	4	0	.095	7	27	0	4	1.5	1.000
1946			7	2	.778	3.35	35	2	0	86	91	29	34	0	5	2	5	22	4	0	.182	5	25	2	2	0.9	.938
1947	PIT	N	1	3	.250	8.44	11	0	0	10.2	18	4	6	0	1	3	2	2	0	0	.000	0	1	0	0	0.1	1.000
11 yrs.			34	38	.472	4.32	199	56	25	697.2	754	284	243	3	12	16	13	208	31	0	.149	33	153	5	17	1.0	.974

Bill Herring

HERRING, WILLIAM FRANCIS (Smoke) BR TR 6′ 3″ 185 lbs.
B. Oct. 31, 1893, New York, N. Y. D. Sept. 10, 1962, Honesdale, Pa.

Year	Team	Lg	W	L	PCT	ERA	G	GS	CG	IP	H	BB	SO	ShO	Relief W	Relief L	Relief SV	AB	H	HR	BA	PO	A	E	DP	TC/G	FA
1915	BKN	F	0	0	—	15.00	3	0	0	3	5	2	3	0	0	0	0	0	0	0	—	0	0	0	0	0.0	.000

Herb Herring

HERRING, HERBERT LEE BR TR 5′11″ 178 lbs.
B. July 22, 1891, Danville, Ark. D. Apr. 22, 1964, Tucson, Ariz.

Year	Team	Lg	W	L	PCT	ERA	G	GS	CG	IP	H	BB	SO	ShO	Relief W	Relief L	Relief SV	AB	H	HR	BA	PO	A	E	DP	TC/G	FA
1912	WAS	A	0	0	—	0.00	1	0	0	1	1	1	0	0	0	0	0	0	0	0	—	0	0	0	0	0.0	.000

Lefty Herring

HERRING, SILAS CLARKE BL TL 5′11″ 160 lbs.
B. Mar. 4, 1880, Philadelphia, Pa. D. Feb. 11, 1965, Massapequa, N. Y.

Year	Team	Lg	W	L	PCT	ERA	G	GS	CG	IP	H	BB	SO	ShO	Relief W	Relief L	Relief SV	AB	H	HR	BA	PO	A	E	DP	TC/G	FA
1899	WAS	N	0	0	—	0.00	2	0	0	2	0	2	0	0	0	0	0	*				0	1	0	0	0.5	1.000

LeRoy Herrmann

HERRMANN, LeROY GEORGE BR TR 5′10″ 185 lbs.
B. Feb. 27, 1906, Steward, Ill. D. July 3, 1972, Livermore, Calif.

Year	Team	Lg	W	L	PCT	ERA	G	GS	CG	IP	H	BB	SO	ShO	Relief W	Relief L	Relief SV	AB	H	HR	BA	PO	A	E	DP	TC/G	FA
1932	CHI	N	2	1	.667	6.39	7	0	0	12.2	18	9	5	0	2	1	0	2	1	0	.500	2	1	0	1	0.4	1.000
1933			0	1	.000	5.57	9	1	0	21	26	8	4	0	0	0	1	6	1	0	.167	1	1	1	0	0.3	.667
1935	CIN	N	3	5	.375	3.58	29	8	2	108	124	31	30	0	1	0	0	30	8	0	.267	4	23	1	1	1.0	.964
3 yrs.			5	7	.417	4.13	45	9	2	141.2	168	48	39	0	3	1	1	38	10	0	.263	7	25	2	2	0.8	.941

Marty Herrmann

HERRMANN, MARTIN JOHN (Lefty) BL TL 5′10″ 150 lbs.
B. Jan. 10, 1893, Oldenburg, Ind. D. Sept. 11, 1956, Cincinnati, Ohio.

Year	Team	Lg	W	L	PCT	ERA	G	GS	CG	IP	H	BB	SO	ShO	Relief W	Relief L	Relief SV	AB	H	HR	BA	PO	A	E	DP	TC/G	FA
1918	BKN	N	0	0	—	0.00	1	0	0	1	0	1	0	0	0	0	0	0	0	0	—	0	0	0	0	0.0	.000

Frank Hershey

HERSHEY, FRANK TR 175 lbs.
B. Dec. 13, 1877, Gorham, N. Y. D. Dec. 15, 1949, Canandaigua, N. Y.

Year	Team	Lg	W	L	PCT	ERA	G	GS	CG	IP	H	BB	SO	ShO	Relief W	Relief L	Relief SV	AB	H	HR	BA	PO	A	E	DP	TC/G	FA
1905	BOS	N	0	1	.000	6.75	1	1	0	4	5	2	1	0	0	0	0	1	0	0	.000	0	0	0	0	0.0	.000

Orel Hershiser

HERSHISER, OREL LEONARD QUINTON IV (Bulldog) BR TR 6′ 3″ 190 lbs.
B. Sept. 16, 1958, Buffalo, N. Y.

Year	Team	Lg	W	L	PCT	ERA	G	GS	CG	IP	H	BB	SO	ShO	Relief W	Relief L	Relief SV	AB	H	HR	BA	PO	A	E	DP	TC/G	FA
1983	LA	N	0	0	—	3.38	8	0	0	8	7	6	5	0	0	0	1	0	0	0	—	0	2	0	1	0.3	1.000
1984			11	8	.579	2.66	45	20	8	189.2	160	50	150	**4**	2	2	2	50	10	0	.200	17	28	5	2	1.1	.900
1985			19	3	**.864**	2.03	36	34	9	239.2	179	68	157	5	1	0	0	76	15	0	.197	20	45	7	4	2.0	.903
1986			14	14	.500	3.85	35	35	8	231.1	213	86	153	1	0	0	0	71	17	0	.239	22	36	3	6	1.7	.951
1987			16	16	.500	3.06	37	35	10	**264.2**	247	74	190	1	0	1	1	90	19	0	.211	37	34	5	6	2.1	.934
1988			**23**	8	.742	2.26	35	34	**15**	**267**	208	73	178	**8**	0	0	1	85	11	0	.129	32	60	6	6	2.8	.939
1989			15	**15**	.500	2.31	35	33	8	**256.2**	226	77	178	4	0	0	0	77	14	0	.182	24	51	4	2	2.3	.949
1990			1	1	.500	4.26	4	4	0	25.1	26	4	16	0	0	0	0	7	0	0	.000	1	3	0	0	1.0	1.000
1991			7	2	.778	3.46	21	21	0	112	112	32	73	0	0	0	0	31	8	0	.258	12	18	1	1	1.5	.968
1992			10	**15**	.400	3.67	33	33	1	210.2	209	69	130	0	0	0	0	68	15	0	.221	28	41	3	2	2.2	.958

Orel Hershiser *continued*

Year	Team	Lg	W	L	PCT	ERA	G	GS	CG	IP	H	BB	SO	ShO	Relief Pitching W	Relief Pitching L	Relief Pitching SV	Batting AB	Batting H	HR	BA	PO	A	E	DP	TC/G	FA
1993			12	14	.462	3.59	33	33	5	215.2	201	72	141	1	0	0	0	73	26	0	.356	20	43	3	1	1.9	.955
1994			6	6	.500	3.79	21	21	1	135.1	146	42	72	0	0	0	0	44	9	0	.205	22	24	2	3	2.3	.958
1995	CLE	A	16	6	.727	3.87	26	26	1	167.1	151	51	111	1	0	0	0	0	0	0	—	16	31	2	1	1.9	.959
13 yrs.			150	108	.581	3.06	369	329	66	2323.1	2085	704	1554	25	3	3	5	672	144	0	.214	251	416	41	35	1.9	.942
DIVISIONAL PLAYOFF SERIES																											
1995	CLE	A	1	0	1.000	0.00	1	1	0	7.1	3	2	7	0	0	0	0	0	0	0	—	0	0	0	0	0.0	.000
LEAGUE CHAMPIONSHIP SERIES																											
1985	LA	N	1	0	1.000	3.52	2	2	1	15.1	17	6	5	0	0	0	0	7	2	0	.286	2	2	0	1	2.0	1.000
1988			1	0	1.000	1.09	4	3	1	24.2	18	7	15	1	0	0	1	9	0	0	.000	3	3	0	0	1.5	1.000
1995	CLE	A	2	0	1.000	1.29	2	2	0	14	9	3	15	0	0	0	0	0	0	0	—	0	4	0	0	2.0	1.000
3 yrs.			4	0	1.000	1.83	8	7	2	54	44	16	35	1	0	0	1	16	2	0	.125	5	9	0	1	1.8	1.000
			3rd		**1st**	**3rd**		**4th**	**4th**	**4th**		**10th**	**8th**	**1st**													
WORLD SERIES																											
1988	LA	N	2	0	1.000	1.00	2	2	2	18	7	6	17	1	0	0	0	3	3	0	1.000	1	1	0	0	1.0	1.000
1995	CLE	A	1	1	.500	2.57	2	2	0	14	8	4	13	0	0	0	0	2	0	0	.000	1	7	1	1	4.5	.889
2 yrs.			3	1	.750	1.69	4	4	2	32	15	10	30	1	0	0	0	5	3	0	.600	2	8	1	1	2.8	.909

Joe Hesketh

HESKETH, JOSEPH THOMAS
B. Feb. 15, 1959, Lackawanna, N. Y.
BL TL 6′ 2″ 165 lbs.

Year	Team	Lg	W	L	PCT	ERA	G	GS	CG	IP	H	BB	SO	ShO	Relief Pitching W	Relief Pitching L	Relief Pitching SV	Batting AB	Batting H	HR	BA	PO	A	E	DP	TC/G	FA
1984	MON	N	2	2	.500	1.80	11	5	1	45	38	15	32	1	0	1	1	10	1	0	.100	2	6	1	1	0.8	.889
1985			10	5	.667	2.49	25	25	2	155.1	125	45	113	1	0	0	0	44	4	0	.091	3	22	0	0	1.0	1.000
1986			6	5	.545	5.01	15	15	0	82.2	92	31	67	0	0	0	0	23	0	0	.000	2	8	1	0	0.7	.909
1987			0	0	—	3.14	18	0	0	28.2	23	15	31	0	0	0	1	4	0	0	.000	1	1	1	0	0.2	.667
1988			4	3	.571	2.85	60	0	0	72.2	63	35	64	0	4	3	9	2	0	0	.000	6	14	0	2	0.3	1.000
1989			6	4	.600	5.77	43	0	0	48.1	54	26	44	0	6	4	3	2	1	0	.500	3	9	1	3	0.3	.923
1990	3 teams	MON N	(2G 1–0)		ATL N	(31G 0–2)	BOS A		(12G 0–4)																		
″	total		1	6	.143	4.53	45	2	0	59.2	69	25	50	0	1	4	5	1	0	0	.000	4	6	2	0	0.3	.833
1991	BOS	A	12	4	.750	3.29	39	17	0	153.1	142	53	104	0	2	0	0	0	0	0	—	13	19	1	1	0.8	.970
1992			8	9	.471	4.36	30	25	1	148.2	162	58	104	0	1	0	1	0	0	0	—	6	22	4	1	1.1	.875
1993			3	4	.429	5.06	28	5	0	53.1	62	29	34	0	2	1	1	0	0	0	—	2	7	1	1	0.4	.900
1994			8	5	.615	4.26	25	20	0	114	117	46	83	0	0	0	0	0	0	0	—	5	9	4	0	0.7	.778
11 yrs.			60	47	.561	3.78	339	114	4	961.2	947	378	726	2	16	13	21	86	6	0	.070	47	123	16	9	0.5	.914

Otto Hess

HESS, OTTO C.
B. Oct. 10, 1878, Berne, Switzerland D. Feb. 25, 1926, Tucson, Ariz.
BL TL 6′ 1″ 170 lbs.

Year	Team	Lg	W	L	PCT	ERA	G	GS	CG	IP	H	BB	SO	ShO	Relief Pitching W	Relief Pitching L	Relief Pitching SV	Batting AB	Batting H	HR	BA	PO	A	E	DP	TC/G	FA
1902	CLE	A	2	4	.333	5.98	7	4	4	43.2	67	23	13	0	0	**2**	0	14	1	0	.071	4	16	3	0	3.3	.870
1904			8	7	.533	1.67	21	16	15	151.1	134	31	64	4	1	0	0	100	12	0	.120	25	49	5	0	2.4	.937
1905			10	15	.400	3.16	26	25	22	213.2	179	72	109	4	0	1	0	175	44	2	.251	74	67	9	2	2.8	.940
1906			20	17	.541	1.83	43	36	33	334	274	85	167	7	1	0	**3**	154	31	0	.201	29	87	6	4	2.5	.951
1907			6	6	.500	2.89	17	14	7	93.1	84	37	36	0	0	0	1	30	4	0	.133	6	26	2	0	1.8	.941
1908			0	0	—	5.14	4	0	0	7	11	1	2	0	0	0	0	14	0	0	.000	4	3	0	0	0.9	1.000
1912	BOS	N	12	17	.414	3.76	33	31	21	254	270	90	80	0	0	2	0	94	23	0	.245	11	47	3	3	1.8	.951
1913			7	17	.292	3.83	29	27	19	218.1	231	70	80	2	0	0	0	83	26	2	.313	11	58	4	2	2.5	.945
1914			5	6	.455	3.03	14	11	7	89	89	33	24	1	1	0	1	47	11	1	.234	22	33	2	3	3.0	.965
1915			0	1	.000	3.86	4	1	1	14	16	6	5	0	0	0	0	5	2	0	.400	1	4	1	0	1.2	.833
10 yrs.			70	90	.438	2.98	198	165	129	1418.1	1355	448	580	18	3	5	5	*				187	390	35	14	2.4	.943

George Hesselbacher

HESSELBACHER, GEORGE EDWARD
B. Jan. 18, 1895, Philadelphia, Pa. D. Feb. 18, 1980, Rydal, Pa.
BR TR 6′ 2″ 175 lbs.

Year	Team	Lg	W	L	PCT	ERA	G	GS	CG	IP	H	BB	SO	ShO	Relief Pitching W	Relief Pitching L	Relief Pitching SV	Batting AB	Batting H	HR	BA	PO	A	E	DP	TC/G	FA
1916	PHI	A	0	4	.000	7.27	6	4	2	26	37	22	6	0	0	0	0	8	1	0	.125	0	14	0	0	2.3	1.000

Larry Hesterfer

HESTERFER, LAWRENCE
B. June 9, 1878, Newark, N. J. D. Sept. 22, 1943, Cedar Grove, N. Y.
BR TL 5′ 8″ 145 lbs.

Year	Team	Lg	W	L	PCT	ERA	G	GS	CG	IP	H	BB	SO	ShO	Relief Pitching W	Relief Pitching L	Relief Pitching SV	Batting AB	Batting H	HR	BA	PO	A	E	DP	TC/G	FA
1901	NY	N	0	1	.000	7.50	1	1	1	6	15	3	2	0	0	0	0	2	0	0	.000	0	1	0	0	1.0	1.000

Johnny Hetki

HETKI, JOHN EDWARD
B. May 12, 1922, Leavenworth, Kans.
BR TR 6′ 1″ 202 lbs.

Year	Team	Lg	W	L	PCT	ERA	G	GS	CG	IP	H	BB	SO	ShO	Relief Pitching W	Relief Pitching L	Relief Pitching SV	Batting AB	Batting H	HR	BA	PO	A	E	DP	TC/G	FA
1945	CIN	N	1	2	.333	3.58	5	2	2	32.2	28	11	9	0	0	1	0	11	1	0	.091	2	9	0	0	2.2	1.000
1946			6	6	.500	2.99	32	11	4	126.1	121	31	41	0	2	1	1	33	11	0	.333	6	24	1	0	1.0	.968
1947			3	4	.429	5.81	37	5	2	96	110	48	33	0	2	0	0	27	6	0	.222	3	19	0	0	0.6	1.000
1948			0	1	.000	9.45	3	0	0	6.2	8	3	3	0	0	1	0	1	0	0	.000	0	0	0	0	0.0	.000
1950			1	2	.333	5.09	22	1	0	53	53	27	21	0	1	1	0	9	2	0	.222	1	8	0	1	0.4	1.000
1952	STL	A	0	1	.000	3.86	3	1	0	9.1	15	2	4	0	0	0	0	1	0	0	.000	1	2	0	0	1.0	1.000
1953	PIT	N	3	6	.333	3.95	54	2	0	118.1	120	33	37	0	3	5	3	24	5	0	.208	9	20	0	1	0.5	1.000
1954			4	4	.500	4.99	58	1	0	83	102	30	27	0	4	3	9	9	2	0	.222	3	11	0	0	0.2	1.000
8 yrs.			18	26	.409	4.39	214	23	8	525.1	557	185	175	0	12	12	13	115	27	0	.235	25	93	1	2	0.6	.992

Eric Hetzel

HETZEL, ERIC PAUL
B. Sept. 25, 1963, Crowley, La.
BR TR 6′ 3″ 175 lbs.

Year	Team	Lg	W	L	PCT	ERA	G	GS	CG	IP	H	BB	SO	ShO	Relief Pitching W	Relief Pitching L	Relief Pitching SV	Batting AB	Batting H	HR	BA	PO	A	E	DP	TC/G	FA
1989	BOS	A	2	3	.400	6.26	12	11	0	50.1	61	28	33	0	0	1	0	0	0	0	—	3	1	0	1	0.3	1.000
1990			1	4	.200	5.91	9	8	0	35	39	21	20	0	0	0	0	0	0	0	—	2	3	0	0	0.6	1.000
2 yrs.			3	7	.300	6.12	21	19	0	85.1	100	49	53	0	0	1	0	0	0	0		5	4	0	1	0.4	1.000

Ed Heusser

HEUSSER, EDWARD BURLTON (The Wild Elk of the Wasatch)
B. May 7, 1909, Salt Lake County, Utah D. Mar. 1, 1956, Aurora, Colo.
BB TR 6′½″ 187 lbs.
BR 1935–1938

Year	Team	Lg	W	L	PCT	ERA	G	GS	CG	IP	H	BB	SO	ShO	Relief Pitching W	Relief Pitching L	Relief Pitching SV	Batting AB	Batting H	HR	BA	PO	A	E	DP	TC/G	FA
1935	STL	N	5	5	.500	2.92	33	11	2	123.1	125	27	39	0	2	1	2	34	4	0	.118	7	20	1	3	0.8	.964
1936			7	3	.700	5.43	42	3	0	104.1	130	38	26	0	6	2	3	26	7	1	.269	2	24	4	2	0.7	.867
1938	PHI	N	0	0	—	27.00	1	0	0	1	2	1	0	0	0	0	0	0	0	0	—	0	0	0	0	0.0	.000
1940	PHI	A	6	13	.316	4.99	41	6	2	110	144	42	39	0	4	9	5	30	5	1	.167	9	21	1	1	0.8	.968
1943	CIN	N	4	3	.571	3.46	26	10	2	91	97	23	28	1	2	0	0	27	5	0	.185	6	14	0	1	0.8	1.000
1944			13	11	.542	**2.38**	30	23	17	192.2	165	42	42	4	2	1	2	69	15	0	.217	11	33	1	1	1.5	.978
1945			11	16	.407	3.71	31	30	18	223	248	60	56	4	0	0	1	77	19	1	.247	9	45	1	2	1.8	.982

Ed Heusser *continued*

Year	Team	Lg	W	L	PCT	ERA	G	GS	CG	IP	H	BB	SO	ShO	Relief Pitching W	Relief Pitching L	Relief Pitching SV	Batting AB	Batting H	Batting HR	BA	PO	A	E	DP	TC/G	FA
1946			7	14	.333	3.22	29	21	9	167.2	167	39	47	1	0	1	2	53	11	0	.208	7	26	3	3	1.2	.917
1948	PHI	N	3	2	.600	4.99	33	0	0	74	89	28	22	0	3	2	3	19	3	0	.158	5	15	1	0	0.6	.952
9 yrs.			56	67	.455	3.69	266	104	50	1087	1167	300	299	10	19	16	18	335	69	3	.206	56	198	12	13	1.0	.955

Joe Heving

HEVING, JOSEPH WILLIAM BR TR 6′ 1″ 185 lbs.
Brother of Johnnie Heving.
B. Sept. 2, 1900, Covington, Ky. D. Apr. 11, 1970, Covington, Ky.

Year	Team	Lg	W	L	PCT	ERA	G	GS	CG	IP	H	BB	SO	ShO	Relief Pitching W	Relief Pitching L	Relief Pitching SV	Batting AB	Batting H	Batting HR	BA	PO	A	E	DP	TC/G	FA
1930	NY	N	7	5	.583	5.22	41	2	0	89.2	109	27	37	0	**7**	**5**	6	22	5	0	.227	11	33	2	2	1.1	.957
1931			1	6	.143	4.89	22	0	0	42.1	48	11	26	0	1	**6**	3	8	1	0	.125	2	12	0	0	0.6	1.000
1933	CHI	A	7	5	.583	2.67	40	6	3	118	113	27	47	1	5	1	6	38	8	0	.211	3	28	1	1	0.8	.969
1934			1	7	.125	7.26	33	2	0	88	133	48	40	0	1	5	4	27	5	0	.185	10	18	2	2	0.9	.933
1937	CLE	A	8	4	.667	4.83	40	0	0	72.2	92	30	35	0	8	4	5	19	5	0	.263	3	18	0	1	0.5	1.000
1938	2 teams	CLE A (3G 1–1) BOS A (16G 8–1)																									
″	total		9	2	.818	4.09	19	11	7	88	104	27	34	1	1	1	2	31	4	0	.129	8	22	1	4	1.6	.968
1939	BOS	A	11	3	.786	3.70	46	5	1	107	124	34	43	0	**11**	2	7	32	6	0	.188	8	17	3	2	0.6	.893
1940			12	7	.632	4.01	39	7	4	119	129	42	55	0	**8**	4	3	40	8	0	.200	8	22	4	3	0.9	.882
1941	CLE	A	5	2	.714	2.29	27	3	2	70.2	63	31	18	1	3	2	5	15	0	0	.000	8	22	0	0	1.1	1.000
1942			5	3	.625	4.86	27	2	0	46.1	52	25	13	0	5	2	3	7	0	0	.000	3	10	2	1	0.6	.867
1943			1	1	.500	2.75	30	1	0	72	58	34	34	0	1	1	9	14	1	0	.071	8	20	0	0	0.9	1.000
1944			8	3	.727	1.96	**63**	1	0	119.1	106	41	46	0	8	2	10	22	4	0	.182	5	29	4	0	0.6	.895
1945	BOS	N	1	0	1.000	3.38	3	0	0	5.1	5	3	1	0	1	0	0	1	0	0	.000	0	4	0	0	1.3	1.000
13 yrs.			76	48	.613	3.90	430	40	17	1038.1	1136	380	429	3	60	35	63	276	47	0	.170	77	255	19	16	0.8	.946

Jake Hewitt

HEWITT, CHARLES JACOB BL TL 5′ 7″ 150 lbs.
B. June 6, 1870, Madisonville, W. Va. D. May 18, 1959, Morgantown, W. Va.

Year	Team	Lg	W	L	PCT	ERA	G	GS	CG	IP	H	BB	SO	ShO	Relief Pitching W	Relief Pitching L	Relief Pitching SV	Batting AB	Batting H	Batting HR	BA	PO	A	E	DP	TC/G	FA
1895	PIT	N	1	0	1.000	4.15	4	2	1	13	13	2	4	0	0	0	2	6	1	0	.167	0	2	1	0	0.8	.667

Greg Heydeman

HEYDEMAN, GREGORY GEORGE BR TR 6′ 180 lbs.
B. Jan. 2, 1952, Carmel, Calif.

Year	Team	Lg	W	L	PCT	ERA	G	GS	CG	IP	H	BB	SO	ShO	Relief Pitching W	Relief Pitching L	Relief Pitching SV	Batting AB	Batting H	Batting HR	BA	PO	A	E	DP	TC/G	FA
1973	LA	N	0	0	—	4.50	1	0	0	2	2	1	1	0	0	0	0	0	0	0	—	0	0	0	0	0.0	.000

John Heyner

HEYNER, JOHN
B. Hyde Park, Ill. Deceased.

Year	Team	Lg	W	L	PCT	ERA	G	GS	CG	IP	H	BB	SO	ShO	Relief Pitching W	Relief Pitching L	Relief Pitching SV	Batting AB	Batting H	Batting HR	BA	PO	A	E	DP	TC/G	FA
1890	PIT	N	0	0	—	*13.50*	1	0	0	4	7	5	1	0	0	0	0	2	0	0	.000	0	1	0	0	1.0	1.000

Greg Hibbard

HIBBARD, JAMES GREGORY BL TL 6′ 180 lbs.
B. Sept. 13, 1964, New Orleans, La.

Year	Team	Lg	W	L	PCT	ERA	G	GS	CG	IP	H	BB	SO	ShO	Relief Pitching W	Relief Pitching L	Relief Pitching SV	Batting AB	Batting H	Batting HR	BA	PO	A	E	DP	TC/G	FA
1989	CHI	A	6	7	.462	3.21	23	23	2	137.1	142	41	55	0	0	0	0	0	0	0	—	5	27	0	4	1.4	1.000
1990			14	9	.609	3.16	33	33	3	211	202	55	92	1	0	0	0	0	0	0	—	7	29	0	2	1.1	1.000
1991			11	11	.500	4.31	32	29	5	194	196	57	71	0	1	0	0	0	0	0	—	9	28	2	2	1.2	.949
1992			10	7	.588	4.40	31	28	0	176	187	57	69	0	0	0	1	0	0	0	—	6	36	3	4	1.5	.933
1993	CHI	N	15	11	.577	3.96	31	31	1	191	209	47	82	0	0	0	0	65	6	0	.092	6	26	0	2	1.0	1.000
1994	SEA	A	1	5	.167	6.69	15	14	0	80.2	115	31	39	0	0	0	0	0	0	0	—	3	15	1	1	1.3	.947
6 yrs.			57	50	.533	4.05	165	158	11	990	1051	288	408	1	1	0	1	65	6	0	.092	36	161	6	15	1.2	.970

John Hibbard

HIBBARD, JOHN DENISON TL
B. Dec. 2, 1864, Chicago, Ill. D. Nov. 17, 1937, Hollywood, Calif.

Year	Team	Lg	W	L	PCT	ERA	G	GS	CG	IP	H	BB	SO	ShO	Relief Pitching W	Relief Pitching L	Relief Pitching SV	Batting AB	Batting H	Batting HR	BA	PO	A	E	DP	TC/G	FA
1884	CHI	N	1	1	.500	2.65	2	2	2	17	18	9	4	1	0	0	0	7	0	0	.000	1	3	0	0	2.0	1.000

Bryan Hickerson

HICKERSON, BRYAN DAVID BL TL 6′ 2″ 195 lbs.
B. Oct. 13, 1963, Bemidji, Minn.

Year	Team	Lg	W	L	PCT	ERA	G	GS	CG	IP	H	BB	SO	ShO	Relief Pitching W	Relief Pitching L	Relief Pitching SV	Batting AB	Batting H	Batting HR	BA	PO	A	E	DP	TC/G	FA
1991	SF	N	2	2	.500	3.60	17	6	0	50	53	17	43	0	0	0	0	12	0	0	.000	0	1	0	0	0.1	1.000
1992			5	3	.625	3.09	61	1	0	87.1	74	21	68	0	5	3	0	4	0	0	.000	1	5	0	0	0.1	1.000
1993			7	5	.583	4.26	47	15	0	120.1	137	39	69	0	0	2	0	28	4	0	.143	4	12	1	0	0.4	.941
1994			4	8	.333	5.40	28	14	0	98.1	118	38	59	0	1	1	1	27	5	0	.185	1	9	0	1	0.4	1.000
1995	2 teams	CHI N (38G 2–3) CLR N (18G 1–0)																									
″	total		3	3	.500	8.57	56	0	0	48.1	69	28	40	0	3	3	1	3	2	0	.667	3	3	0	1	0.1	1.000
5 yrs.			21	21	.500	4.72	209	36	0	404.1	451	143	279	0	9	9	2	74	11	0	.149	9	30	1	2	0.2	.975

Jim Hickey

HICKEY, JAMES ROBERT (Sid) BR TR 6′ 1″ 204 lbs.
B. Oct. 22, 1920, North Abington, Mass.

Year	Team	Lg	W	L	PCT	ERA	G	GS	CG	IP	H	BB	SO	ShO	Relief Pitching W	Relief Pitching L	Relief Pitching SV	Batting AB	Batting H	Batting HR	BA	PO	A	E	DP	TC/G	FA
1942	BOS	N	0	1	.000	20.25	1	1	0	1.1	4	2	0	0	0	0	0	1	0	0	.000	0	0	0	0	0.0	.000
1944			0	0	—	4.82	8	0	0	9.1	15	5	3	0	0	0	0	1	0	0	.000	0	3	0	0	0.4	1.000
2 yrs.			0	1	.000	6.75	9	1	0	10.2	19	7	3	0	0	0	0	2	0	0	.000	0	3	0	0	0.3	1.000

John Hickey

HICKEY, JOHN WILLIAM BR TL 5′10″ 170 lbs.
B. Nov. 3, 1881, Minneapolis, Minn. D. Dec. 28, 1941, Seattle, Wash.

Year	Team	Lg	W	L	PCT	ERA	G	GS	CG	IP	H	BB	SO	ShO	Relief Pitching W	Relief Pitching L	Relief Pitching SV	Batting AB	Batting H	Batting HR	BA	PO	A	E	DP	TC/G	FA
1904	CLE	A	0	1	.000	7.30	2	2	1	12.1	14	11	5	0	0	0	0	5	0	0	.000	0	5	0	0	2.5	1.000

Kevin Hickey

HICKEY, KEVIN JOHN BL TL 6′ 1″ 170 lbs.
B. Feb. 25, 1956, Chicago, Ill.

Year	Team	Lg	W	L	PCT	ERA	G	GS	CG	IP	H	BB	SO	ShO	Relief Pitching W	Relief Pitching L	Relief Pitching SV	Batting AB	Batting H	Batting HR	BA	PO	A	E	DP	TC/G	FA
1981	CHI	A	0	2	.000	3.68	41	0	0	44	38	18	17	0	0	2	3	0	0	0	—	3	11	0	0	0.3	1.000
1982			4	4	.500	3.00	60	0	0	78	73	30	38	0	4	4	6	0	0	0	—	5	20	1	4	0.4	.962
1983			1	2	.333	5.23	23	0	0	20.2	23	11	8	0	1	2	5	0	0	0	—	1	3	0	0	0.2	1.000
1989	BAL	A	2	3	.400	2.92	51	0	0	49.1	38	23	28	0	2	3	2	0	0	0	—	2	6	0	0	0.2	1.000
1990			1	3	.250	5.13	37	0	0	26.1	26	13	17	0	1	3	1	0	0	0	—	1	4	0	0	0.1	1.000
1991			1	0	1.000	9.00	19	0	0	14	15	6	10	0	1	0	0	0	0	0	—	1	1	0	0	0.1	1.000
6 yrs.			9	14	.391	3.91	231	0	0	232.1	213	101	118	0	9	14	17	0	0	0		13	45	1	4	0.3	.983

Ernie Hickman

HICKMAN, ERNEST P.
B. 1856, East St. Louis, Ill. D. Nov. 19, 1891, East St. Louis, Ill.

Year	Team	Lg	W	L	PCT	ERA	G	GS	CG	IP	H	BB	SO	ShO	Relief Pitching W	Relief Pitching L	Relief Pitching SV	Batting AB	Batting H	Batting HR	BA	PO	A	E	DP	TC/G	FA
1884	KC	U	4	13	.235	*4.52*	17	17	15	137.1	172	36	68	0	0	0	0	72	12	0	.167	12	32	15	1	2.8	.746

Jess Hickman

HICKMAN, JESSE OWENS BR TR 6′ 2″ 186 lbs.
B. Feb. 18, 1939, Lecompte, La.

Year	Team	Lg	W	L	PCT	ERA	G	GS	CG	IP	H	BB	SO	ShO	Relief Pitching W	Relief Pitching L	Relief Pitching SV	Batting AB	Batting H	HR	BA	PO	A	E	DP	TC/G	FA
1965	KC	A	0	1	.000	5.87	12	0	0	15.1	9	8	16	0	0	1	0	0	0	0	—	2	1	0	0	0.3	1.000
1966			0	0	—	0.00	1	0	0	1	0	1	0	0	0	0	0	0	0	0	—	0	0	0	0	0.0	.000
2 yrs.			0	1	.000	5.51	13	0	0	16.1	9	9	16	0	0	1	0	0	0	0		2	1	0	0	0.2	1.000

Jim Hickman

HICKMAN, JAMES LUCIUS BR TR 6′ 3″ 192 lbs.
B. May 10, 1937, Henning, Tenn.

Year	Team	Lg	W	L	PCT	ERA	G	GS	CG	IP	H	BB	SO	ShO	Relief Pitching W	Relief Pitching L	Relief Pitching SV	Batting AB	Batting H	HR	BA	PO	A	E	DP	TC/G	FA
1967	LA	N	0	0	—	4.50	1	0	0	2	2	0	0	0	0	0	0	*				265	7	8	0	2.3	.971

Piano Legs Hickman

HICKMAN, CHARLES TAYLOR BR TR 5′11½″ 215 lbs.
B. Mar. 4, 1876, Taylortown, Pa. D. Apr. 19, 1934, Morgantown, W. Va.

Year	Team	Lg	W	L	PCT	ERA	G	GS	CG	IP	H	BB	SO	ShO	Relief Pitching W	Relief Pitching L	Relief Pitching SV	Batting AB	Batting H	HR	BA	PO	A	E	DP	TC/G	FA
1897	BOS	N	0	0	—	5.87	2	0	0	7.2	10	5	0	0	0	0	1	3	2	1	.667	1	1	0	1	1.0	1.000
1898			1	2	.333	2.18	6	3	3	33	22	13	9	1	0	0	2	58	15	0	.259	79	5	4	8	4.6	.955
1899			6	0	1.000	4.48	11	9	5	66.1	52	40	14	2	0	0	1	63	25	0	.397	27	12	6	3	2.4	.867
1901	NY	N	3	5	.375	4.57	9	9	6	65	76	26	11	0	0	0	0	401	113	4	.282	194	277	87	19	4.4	.844
1902	CLE	A	0	1	.000	7.88	1	1	1	8	11	5	1	0	0	0	0	534	194	11	.363	1140	55	45	63	9.6	.964
1907	WAS	A	0	0	—	3.60	1	0	0	5	4	5	2	0	0	0	0	216	61	1	.282	1323	88	45	69	11.0	.969
6 yrs.			10	8	.556	4.28	30	22	15	185	175	94	37	3	0	0	4	*				5035	1174	357	272	6.4	.946

Kirby Higbe

HIGBE, WALTER KIRBY BR TR 5′11″ 190 lbs.
B. Apr. 8, 1915, Columbia, S. C. D. May 6, 1985, Columbia, S. C.

Year	Team	Lg	W	L	PCT	ERA	G	GS	CG	IP	H	BB	SO	ShO	Relief Pitching W	Relief Pitching L	Relief Pitching SV	Batting AB	Batting H	HR	BA	PO	A	E	DP	TC/G	FA
1937	CHI	N	1	0	1.000	5.40	1	0	0	5	4	1	2	0	1	0	0	3	0	0	.000	0	0	0	0	0.0	.000
1938			0	0	—	5.40	2	2	0	10	10	6	4	0	0	0	0	3	0	0	.000	1	4	0	1	2.5	1.000
1939	**2 teams**	**CHI N** (9G 2–1)	**PHI N** (34G 10–14)																								
″	**total**		12	15	.444	4.67	43	28	14	210	220	**123**	95	1	1	1	2	73	13	0	.178	9	19	0	0	0.7	1.000
1940	PHI	N	14	19	.424	3.72	41	36	20	283	242	**121**	**137**	1	1	0	1	103	17	0	.165	15	47	3	4	1.6	.954
1941	BKN	N	**22**	9	.710	3.14	**48**	**39**	19	298	244	**132**	121	2	1	2	3	112	21	0	.188	13	39	1	2	1.1	.981
1942			16	11	.593	3.25	38	32	13	221.2	180	106	115	2	1	2	0	77	8	0	.104	12	36	2	5	1.3	.960
1943			13	10	.565	3.70	35	27	8	185	189	95	108	1	1	2	0	65	9	1	.138	9	27	0	2	1.0	1.000
1946			17	8	.680	3.03	42	29	11	210.2	178	107	134	3	2	2	1	77	10	0	.130	13	40	3	2	1.3	.946
1947	**2 teams**	**BKN N** (4G 2–0)	**PIT N** (46G 11–17)																								
″	**total**		13	17	.433	3.81	50	33	10	240.2	222	**122**	109	1	2	1	5	77	11	1	.143	10	26	1	0	0.7	.973
1948	PIT	N	8	7	.533	3.36	56	8	3	158	140	83	86	0	6	4	10	48	10	1	.208	5	22	1	0	0.5	.964
1949	**2 teams**	**PIT N** (7G 0–2)	**NY N** (37G 2–0)																								
″	**total**		2	2	.500	5.08	44	3	0	95.2	97	53	43	0	2	1	2	18	1	0	.056	2	14	0	1	0.4	1.000
1950	NY	N	0	3	.000	4.93	18	1	0	34.2	37	30	17	0	0	2	0	4	1	0	.250	3	11	0	0	0.8	1.000
12 yrs.			118	101	.539	3.69	418	238	98	1952.1	1763	979	971	11	18	17	24	660	101	3	.153	92	285	11	17	0.9	.972
WORLD SERIES																											
1941	BKN	N	0	0	—	7.36	1	1	0	3.2	6	2	1	0	0	0	0	1	1	0	1.000	0	1	0	0	1.0	1.000

Irv Higginbotham

HIGGINBOTHAM, IRVING CLINTON BR TR 6′ 1″ 196 lbs.
B. Apr. 26, 1882, Homer, Neb. D. June 12, 1959, Seattle, Wash.

Year	Team	Lg	W	L	PCT	ERA	G	GS	CG	IP	H	BB	SO	ShO	Relief Pitching W	Relief Pitching L	Relief Pitching SV	Batting AB	Batting H	HR	BA	PO	A	E	DP	TC/G	FA
1906	STL	N	1	4	.200	3.23	7	6	4	47.1	50	11	14	0	0	0	0	18	4	0	.222	1	18	2	0	3.0	.905
1908			3	8	.273	3.20	19	11	7	107	113	33	38	1	0	1	0	38	5	0	.132	2	27	1	0	1.6	.967
1909	**2 teams**	**STL N** (3G 1–0)	**CHI N** (19G 5–2)																								
″	**total**		6	2	.750	2.12	22	7	5	89.1	69	22	34	0	3	1	0	29	6	0	.207	4	17	3	0	1.1	.875
3 yrs.			10	14	.417	2.81	48	24	16	243.2	232	66	86	1	3	2	0	85	15	0	.176	7	62	6	0	1.6	.920

Dennis Higgins

HIGGINS, DENNIS DEAN BR TR 6′ 3″ 180 lbs.
B. Aug. 4, 1939, Jefferson City, Mo.

Year	Team	Lg	W	L	PCT	ERA	G	GS	CG	IP	H	BB	SO	ShO	Relief Pitching W	Relief Pitching L	Relief Pitching SV	Batting AB	Batting H	HR	BA	PO	A	E	DP	TC/G	FA
1966	CHI	A	1	0	1.000	2.52	42	1	0	93	66	33	86	0	0	0	5	17	3	0	.176	4	15	0	2	0.5	1.000
1967			1	2	.333	5.84	9	0	0	12.1	13	10	8	0	1	2	0	1	0	0	.000	2	2	0	0	0.4	1.000
1968	WAS	A	4	4	.500	3.25	59	0	0	99.2	81	46	66	0	4	4	13	15	2	0	.133	2	11	0	0	0.2	1.000
1969			10	9	.526	3.48	55	0	0	85.1	79	56	71	0	10	9	16	11	1	0	.091	4	7	0	0	0.2	1.000
1970	CLE	A	4	6	.400	4.00	58	0	0	90	82	54	82	0	4	6	11	12	3	0	.250	7	14	1	0	0.4	.955
1971	STL	N	1	0	1.000	3.86	3	0	0	7	6	2	6	0	1	0	0	1	0	0	.000	1	1	0	0	0.7	1.000
1972			1	2	.333	3.97	15	1	0	22.2	19	22	20	0	1	1	1	1	0	0	.000	2	1	0	0	0.2	1.000
7 yrs.			22	23	.489	3.42	241	2	0	410	346	223	339	0	21	22	46	58	9	0	.155	22	51	1	2	0.3	.986

Thomas Higgins

HIGGINS, THOMAS EDWARD (Eddie, Irish) BR TR 6′½″ 174 lbs.
B. Mar. 18, 1888, Nevada, Ill. D. Feb. 14, 1959, Elgin, Ill.

Year	Team	Lg	W	L	PCT	ERA	G	GS	CG	IP	H	BB	SO	ShO	Relief Pitching W	Relief Pitching L	Relief Pitching SV	Batting AB	Batting H	HR	BA	PO	A	E	DP	TC/G	FA
1909	STL	N	3	3	.500	4.50	16	5	5	66	68	17	15	0	1	0	0	21	4	0	.190	4	20	0	0	1.5	1.000
1910			0	1	.000	4.35	2	0	0	10.1	15	7	1	0	0	1	0	5	2	0	.400	1	6	0	0	2.3	1.000
2 yrs.			3	4	.429	4.48	18	5	5	76.1	83	24	16	0	1	1	0	26	6	0	.231	5	26	0	0	1.6	1.000

Ed High

HIGH, EDWARD THOMAS (Lefty) TL
B. Dec. 26, 1876, Baltimore, Md. D. Feb. 20, 1926, Baltimore, Md.

Year	Team	Lg	W	L	PCT	ERA	G	GS	CG	IP	H	BB	SO	ShO	Relief Pitching W	Relief Pitching L	Relief Pitching SV	Batting AB	Batting H	HR	BA	PO	A	E	DP	TC/G	FA
1901	DET	A	1	0	1.000	3.50	4	1	1	18	21	6	4	0	0	0	0	7	0	0	.000	2	3	0	1	1.3	1.000

Ted Higuera

HIGUERA, TEODORO BB TL 5′10″ 180 lbs.
Born Teodoro Valenzuela Higuera (Valenzuela).
B. Nov. 9, 1958, Los Mochis, Mexico.

Year	Team	Lg	W	L	PCT	ERA	G	GS	CG	IP	H	BB	SO	ShO	Relief Pitching W	Relief Pitching L	Relief Pitching SV	Batting AB	Batting H	HR	BA	PO	A	E	DP	TC/G	FA
1985	MIL	A	15	8	.652	3.90	32	30	7	212.1	186	63	127	2	0	0	0	0	0	0	—	8	18	1	2	0.8	.963
1986			20	11	.645	2.79	34	34	15	248.1	226	74	207	4	0	0	0	0	0	0	—	9	26	0	1	1.0	1.000
1987			18	10	.643	3.85	35	35	14	261.2	236	87	240	3	0	0	0	0	0	0	—	9	23	2	3	1.0	.941
1988			16	9	.640	2.45	31	31	8	227.1	168	59	192	1	0	0	0	0	0	0	—	12	33	0	1	1.5	1.000
1989			9	6	.600	3.46	22	22	2	135.1	125	48	91	1	0	0	0	0	0	0	—	5	10	1	0	0.7	.938
1990			11	10	.524	3.76	27	27	4	170	167	50	129	1	0	0	0	0	0	0	—	7	18	2	2	1.0	.926
1991			3	2	.600	4.46	7	6	0	36.1	37	10	33	0	0	0	0	0	0	0	—	1	5	1	0	1.0	.857
1993			1	3	.250	7.20	8	8	0	30	43	16	27	0	0	0	0	0	0	0	—	3	0	0	0	0.4	1.000
1994			1	5	.167	7.06	17	12	0	58.2	74	36	35	0	0	0	0	0	0	0	—	1	10	0	3	0.6	1.000
9 yrs.			94	64	.595	3.61	213	205	50	1380	1262	443	1081	12	0	0	0	0	0	0		55	143	7	12	1.0	.966

Whitey Hilcher

HILCHER, WALTER FRANK BR TR 6′ 174 lbs.
B. Feb. 28, 1909, Chicago, Ill. D. Nov. 21, 1962, Minneapolis, Minn.

Year	Team	W	L	PCT	ERA	G	GS	CG	IP	H	BB	SO	ShO	Relief W	Relief L	Relief SV	Batting AB	Batting H	Batting HR	BA	PO	A	E	DP	TC/G	FA
1931	CIN N	0	1	.000	3.00	2	1	0	12	16	4	5	0	0	0	0	4	0	0	.000	0	1	0	0	0.5	1.000
1932		0	3	.000	7.71	11	2	0	18.2	24	10	4	0	0	1	0	3	1	0	.333	3	3	0	0	0.5	1.000
1935		2	0	1.000	2.79	4	2	1	19.1	19	5	9	1	1	0	0	6	1	0	.167	1	8	0	0	2.3	1.000
1936		1	2	.333	6.17	14	1	0	35	44	14	10	0	1	2	0	8	0	0	.000	1	5	1	1	0.5	.857
4 yrs.		3	6	.333	5.29	31	6	1	85	103	33	28	1	2	3	0	21	2	0	.095	5	17	1	1	0.7	.957

Oral Hildebrand

HILDEBRAND, ORAL CLYDE BR TR 6′ 3″ 175 lbs.
B. Apr. 7, 1907, Indianapolis, Ind. D. Sept. 8, 1977, Southport, Ind.

Year	Team	W	L	PCT	ERA	G	GS	CG	IP	H	BB	SO	ShO	Relief W	Relief L	Relief SV	Batting AB	Batting H	Batting HR	BA	PO	A	E	DP	TC/G	FA
1931	CLE A	2	1	.667	4.39	5	2	2	26.2	25	13	6	0	1	0	0	11	2	0	.182	1	4	0	0	1.0	1.000
1932		8	6	.571	3.69	27	15	7	129.1	124	62	49	0	2	0	0	48	7	0	.146	9	13	1	2	0.9	.957
1933		16	11	.593	3.76	36	31	15	220.1	205	88	90	**6**	1	1	0	84	16	0	.190	11	43	2	4	1.6	.964
1934		11	9	.550	4.50	33	28	10	198	225	99	72	1	0	0	1	76	13	0	.171	5	44	0	1	1.5	1.000
1935		9	8	.529	3.94	34	20	8	171.1	171	63	49	0	3	0	5	55	9	0	.164	6	35	2	1	1.3	.953
1936		10	11	.476	4.90	36	21	9	174.2	197	83	65	0	4	1	4	63	12	0	.190	4	26	0	1	0.8	1.000
1937	STL A	8	17	.320	5.14	30	27	12	201.1	228	87	75	1	1	1	1	70	14	0	.200	5	36	2	1	1.4	.953
1938		8	10	.444	5.69	23	23	10	163	194	73	66	0	0	0	0	59	15	0	.254	5	14	1	0	0.9	.950
1939	NY A	10	4	.714	3.06	21	15	7	126.2	102	41	50	1	0	0	2	44	8	0	.182	5	18	1	1	1.1	.958
1940		1	1	.500	1.86	13	0	0	19.1	19	14	5	0	1	1	0	3	0	0	.000	1	3	1	0	0.4	.800
10 yrs.		83	78	.516	4.35	258	182	80	1430.2	1490	623	527	9	13	4	13	513	96	0	.187	52	236	10	11	1.2	.966
WORLD SERIES																										
1939	NY A	0	0	—	0.00	1	1	0	4	2	0	3	0	0	0	0	1	0	0	.000	0	0	0	0	0.0	.000

Tom Hilgendorf

HILGENDORF, THOMAS EUGENE BB TL 6′ 1½″ 187 lbs.
B. Mar. 10, 1942, Clinton, Iowa.

Year	Team	W	L	PCT	ERA	G	GS	CG	IP	H	BB	SO	ShO	Relief W	Relief L	Relief SV	Batting AB	Batting H	Batting HR	BA	PO	A	E	DP	TC/G	FA
1969	STL N	0	0	—	1.50	6	0	0	6	3	2	2	0	0	0	2	1	1	0	1.000	0	1	0	0	0.2	1.000
1970		0	4	.000	3.86	23	0	0	21	22	13	13	0	0	4	3	1	0	0	.000	0	5	0	0	0.2	1.000
1972	CLE A	3	1	.750	2.68	19	5	1	47	51	21	25	0	1	0	0	13	1	0	.077	2	10	1	0	0.7	.923
1973		5	3	.625	3.14	48	1	1	94.2	87	36	58	0	5	2	6	0	0	0	—	4	20	1	1	0.5	.960
1974		4	3	.571	4.88	35	0	0	48	58	17	23	0	4	3	3	0	0	0	—	3	8	0	0	0.3	1.000
1975	PHI N	7	3	.700	2.13	53	0	0	97	82	38	52	0	7	3	0	12	3	0	.250	5	18	0	1	0.4	1.000
6 yrs.		19	14	.576	3.04	184	6	2	313.2	303	127	173	0	17	12	14	27	5	0	.185	14	62	2	2	0.4	.974

Carmen Hill

HILL, CARMEN PROCTOR (Bunker, Specs) BR TR 6′ 1″ 180 lbs.
B. Oct. 1, 1895, Royalton, Minn. D. Jan. 1, 1990, Indianapolis, Ind.

Year	Team	W	L	PCT	ERA	G	GS	CG	IP	H	BB	SO	ShO	Relief W	Relief L	Relief SV	Batting AB	Batting H	Batting HR	BA	PO	A	E	DP	TC/G	FA
1915	PIT N	2	1	.667	1.15	8	3	2	47	42	13	24	1	0	0	0	13	2	0	.154	3	14	0	1	2.1	1.000
1916		0	0	—	8.53	2	0	0	6.1	11	5	5	0	0	0	0	0	0	0	—	0	0	0	0	0.0	.000
1918		2	3	.400	1.24	6	4	3	43.2	24	17	15	0	1	0	0	12	2	0	.167	1	13	0	0	2.3	1.000
1919		0	0	—	9.00	4	0	0	5	12	1	1	0	0	0	0	0	0	0	—	0	2	0	1	0.5	1.000
1922	NY N	2	1	.667	4.76	8	4	0	28.1	33	5	6	0	1	0	0	11	2	0	.182	1	11	0	0	1.5	1.000
1926	PIT N	3	3	.500	3.40	6	6	4	39.2	42	9	8	1	0	0	0	17	3	0	.176	2	16	0	1	3.0	1.000
1927		22	11	.667	3.24	43	31	22	277.2	260	80	95	2	4	0	3	104	22	0	.212	11	64	4	0	1.8	.949
1928		16	10	.615	3.53	36	31	16	237	229	81	73	1	1	1	2	86	20	0	.233	7	44	5	2	1.6	.911
1929	2 teams PIT N (27G 2–3) STL N (3G 0–0)																									
″	total	2	3	.400	4.41	30	4	0	87.2	104	43	29	0	2	1	3	31	1	0	.032	3	22	3	1	0.9	.893
1930	STL N	0	1	.000	7.36	4	2	0	14.2	12	13	8	0	0	0	0	3	1	0	.333	1	2	0	0	0.8	1.000
10 yrs.		49	33	.598	3.44	147	85	47	787	769	267	264	5	9	2	8	277	53	0	.191	29	188	12	6	1.6	.948
WORLD SERIES																										
1927	PIT N	0	0	—	4.50	1	1	0	6	9	1	6	0	0	0	0	1	0	0	.000	0	0	0	0	0.0	.000

Dave Hill

HILL, DAVID BURNHAM BR TL 6′ 2″ 170 lbs.
B. Nov. 11, 1937, New Orleans, La.

Year	Team	W	L	PCT	ERA	G	GS	CG	IP	H	BB	SO	ShO	Relief W	Relief L	Relief SV	Batting AB	Batting H	Batting HR	BA	PO	A	E	DP	TC/G	FA
1957	KC A	0	0	—	27.00	2	0	0	2.1	6	3	1	0	0	0	0	0	0	0	—	0	0	0	0	0.0	.000

Donnie Hill

HILL, DONALD EARL BB TR 5′10″ 165 lbs.
B. Nov. 12, 1960, Pomona, Calif.

Year	Team	W	L	PCT	ERA	G	GS	CG	IP	H	BB	SO	ShO	Relief W	Relief L	Relief SV	Batting AB	Batting H	Batting HR	BA	PO	A	E	DP	TC/G	FA
1990	CAL A	0	0	—	0.00	1	0	0	1	0	1	1	0	0	0	0	*				87	136	9	24	4.4	.961

Garry Hill

HILL, GARRY ALTON BR TR 6′ 2″ 195 lbs.
B. Nov. 3, 1946, Rutherfordton, N. C.

Year	Team	W	L	PCT	ERA	G	GS	CG	IP	H	BB	SO	ShO	Relief W	Relief L	Relief SV	Batting AB	Batting H	Batting HR	BA	PO	A	E	DP	TC/G	FA
1969	ATL N	0	1	.000	18.00	1	1	0	2	6	1	2	0	0	0	0	0	0	0	—	0	1	0	0	1.0	1.000

Herbert Hill

HILL, HERBERT LEE BR TR 5′11″ 175 lbs.
B. Aug. 19, 1892, Hutchins, Tex. D. Sept. 2, 1970, Farmer's Branch, Tex.

Year	Team	W	L	PCT	ERA	G	GS	CG	IP	H	BB	SO	ShO	Relief W	Relief L	Relief SV	Batting AB	Batting H	Batting HR	BA	PO	A	E	DP	TC/G	FA
1915	CLE A	0	0	—	0.00	1	0	0	2	1	2	0	0	0	0	0	0	0	0	—	0	0	0	0	0.0	.000

Ken Hill

HILL, KENNETH WADE (Thrill) BR TR 6′ 4″ 200 lbs.
B. Dec. 14, 1965, Lynn, Mass.

Year	Team	W	L	PCT	ERA	G	GS	CG	IP	H	BB	SO	ShO	Relief W	Relief L	Relief SV	Batting AB	Batting H	Batting HR	BA	PO	A	E	DP	TC/G	FA
1988	STL N	0	1	.000	5.14	4	1	0	14	16	6	6	0	0	0	0	3	0	0	.000	0	3	0	0	0.8	1.000
1989		7	**15**	.318	3.80	33	33	2	196.2	186	**99**	112	1	0	0	0	59	9	0	.153	12	31	1	1	1.3	.977
1990		5	6	.455	5.49	17	14	1	78.2	79	33	58	0	0	0	0	19	4	0	.211	7	10	1	1	1.1	.944
1991		11	10	.524	3.57	30	30	0	181.1	147	67	121	0	0	0	0	50	5	0	.100	15	26	2	1	1.4	.953
1992	MON N	16	9	.640	2.68	33	33	3	218	187	75	150	3	0	0	0	62	11	1	.177	21	36	4	3	1.8	.934
1993		9	7	.563	3.23	28	28	2	183.2	163	74	90	0	0	0	0	52	6	0	.115	24	38	1	2	2.3	.984
1994		**16**	5	.762	3.32	23	23	2	154.2	145	44	85	1	0	0	0	48	7	0	.146	15	33	2	2	2.2	.960
1995	2 teams STL N (18G 6–7) CLE A (12G 4–1)																									
″	total	10	8	.556	4.62	30	29	1	185	202	77	98	0	0	0	0	31	6	0	.194	23	35	1	2	2.0	.983
8 yrs.		74	61	.548	3.67	198	191	11	1212	1125	475	720	5	0	0	0	324	48	1	.148	117	212	12	12	1.7	.965
DIVISIONAL PLAYOFF SERIES																										
1995	CLE A	1	0	1.000	0.00	1	0	0	1.1	1	0	2	0	1	0	0	0	0	0	—	0	2	0	0	2.0	1.000
LEAGUE CHAMPIONSHIP SERIES																										
1995	CLE A	1	0	1.000	0.00	1	1	0	7	5	3	6	0	0	0	0	0	0	0	—	1	1	0	0	2.0	1.000

Ken Hill *continued*

Year	Team	Lg	W	L	PCT	ERA	G	GS	CG	IP	H	BB	SO	ShO	Relief Pitching W	Relief Pitching L	Relief Pitching SV	Batting AB	Batting H	Batting HR	BA	PO	A	E	DP	TC/G	FA
WORLD SERIES																											
1995	CLE	A	0	1	.000	4.26	2	1	0	6.1	7	4	1	0	0	0	0	0	0	0	—	1	2	0	0	1.5	1.000

Milt Hill

HILL, MILTON GILES BR TR 6′ 180 lbs.
B. Aug. 22, 1965, Atlanta, Ga.

Year	Team	Lg	W	L	PCT	ERA	G	GS	CG	IP	H	BB	SO	ShO	Relief Pitching W	Relief Pitching L	Relief Pitching SV	Batting AB	Batting H	Batting HR	BA	PO	A	E	DP	TC/G	FA
1991	CIN	N	1	1	.500	3.78	22	0	0	33.1	36	8	20	0	1	1	0	1	0	0	.000	2	2	0	0	0.2	1.000
1992			0	0	—	3.15	14	0	0	20	15	5	10	0	0	0	1	0	0	0	—	3	2	0	0	0.4	1.000
1993			3	0	1.000	5.65	19	0	0	28.2	34	9	23	0	3	0	0	2	0	0	.000	4	0	1	0	0.3	.800
1994	2 teams	ATL N	(10G 0–0)	SEA A	(13G 1–0)																						
″	total		1	0	1.000	6.94	23	0	0	35	48	17	26	0	1	0	0	0	0	0		2	3	0	0	0.2	1.000
4 yrs.			5	1	.833	5.08	78	0	0	117	133	39	79	0	5	1	1	3	0	0	.000	11	7	1	0	0.2	.947

Red Hill

HILL, CLIFFORD JOSEPH BB TL
B. Jan. 20, 1893, Marshall, Tex. D. Aug. 11, 1938, El Paso, Tex.

Year	Team	Lg	W	L	PCT	ERA	G	GS	CG	IP	H	BB	SO	ShO	Relief Pitching W	Relief Pitching L	Relief Pitching SV	Batting AB	Batting H	Batting HR	BA	PO	A	E	DP	TC/G	FA
1917	PHI	A	0	0	—	6.75	1	0	0	2.2	5	1	0	0	0	0	0	0	0	0	—	0	2	0	0	2.0	1.000

Still Bill Hill

HILL, WILLIAM CICERO BL TL 6′ 1″ 201 lbs.
Brother of Hugh Hill.
B. Aug. 2, 1874, Chattanooga, Tenn. D. Jan. 28, 1938, Cincinnati, Ohio.

Year	Team	Lg	W	L	PCT	ERA	G	GS	CG	IP	H	BB	SO	ShO	Relief Pitching W	Relief Pitching L	Relief Pitching SV	Batting AB	Batting H	Batting HR	BA	PO	A	E	DP	TC/G	FA
1896	LOU	N	9	28	.243	4.31	43	39	32	319.2	353	155	104	0	0	1	2	116	24	0	.207	13	95	13	5	2.8	.893
1897			7	17	.292	3.62	27	26	20	199	209	69	55	1	0	0	0	74	7	0	.095	14	53	12	1	2.9	.848
1898	CIN	N	13	14	.481	3.98	33	32	26	262	261	119	75	2	0	0	0	98	13	0	.133	6	67	1	7	2.2	.986
1899	3 teams	CLE N	(11G 3–6)	BAL N	(8G 3–4)	BKN N	(2G 1–0)																				
″	total		7	10	.412	4.93	21	18	14	144.1	171	63	46	0	0	0	1	60	14	0	.233	4	40	8	2	2.5	.846
4 yrs.			36	69	.343	4.16	124	115	92	925	994	406	280	3	0	1	3	348	58	0	.167	37	255	34	15	2.6	.896

Homer Hillebrand

HILLEBRAND, HOMER HILLER HENRY BR TL 5′ 8″ 165 lbs.
B. Oct. 10, 1879, Freeport, Ill. D. Jan. 20, 1974, Elsinore, Calif.

Year	Team	Lg	W	L	PCT	ERA	G	GS	CG	IP	H	BB	SO	ShO	Relief Pitching W	Relief Pitching L	Relief Pitching SV	Batting AB	Batting H	Batting HR	BA	PO	A	E	DP	TC/G	FA
1905	PIT	N	4	2	.667	2.82	10	6	4	60.2	43	19	37	0	1	0	0	110	26	0	.236	190	20	7	8	6.0	.968
1906			3	2	.600	2.21	7	5	4	53	42	21	32	1	1	0	0	21	5	0	.238	4	19	0	2	3.3	1.000
1908			0	0	—	0.00	1	0	0	1	1	0	1	0	0	0	0	0	0	0	—	0	0	0	0	0.0	.000
3 yrs.			7	4	.636	2.51	18	11	8	114.2	86	40	70	1	2	0	0	*				194	39	7	10	5.5	.971

Shawn Hillegas

HILLEGAS, SHAWN PATRICK BR TR 6′ 3″ 205 lbs.
B. Aug. 21, 1964, Dos Palos, Calif.

Year	Team	Lg	W	L	PCT	ERA	G	GS	CG	IP	H	BB	SO	ShO	Relief Pitching W	Relief Pitching L	Relief Pitching SV	Batting AB	Batting H	Batting HR	BA	PO	A	E	DP	TC/G	FA
1987	LA	N	4	3	.571	3.57	12	10	0	58	52	31	51	0	0	0	0	14	0	0	.000	4	2	1	0	0.6	.857
1988	2 teams	LA N	(11G 3–4)	CHI A	(6G 3–2)																						
″	total		6	6	.500	3.72	17	16	0	96.2	84	35	56	0	0	0	0	15	2	0	.133	10	8	1	0	1.1	.947
1989	CHI	A	7	11	.389	4.74	50	13	0	119.2	132	51	76	0	5	4	3	0	0	0	—	5	13	3	1	0.4	.857
1990			0	0	—	0.79	7	0	0	11.1	4	5	5	0	0	0	0	0	0	0	—	2	2	0	0	0.6	1.000
1991	CLE	A	3	4	.429	4.34	51	3	0	83	67	46	66	0	3	4	7	0	0	0	—	7	8	0	1	0.3	1.000
1992	2 teams	NY A	(21G 1–8)	OAK A	(5G 0–0)																						
″	total		1	8	.111	5.23	26	9	1	86	104	37	49	1	0	3	0	0	0	0		7	5	3	0	0.6	.800
1993	OAK	A	3	6	.333	6.97	18	11	0	60.2	78	33	29	0	1	1	0	0	0	0	—	1	7	1	0	0.5	.889
7 yrs.			24	38	.387	4.61	181	62	1	515.1	521	238	332	1	9	12	10	29	2	0	.069	36	45	9	2	0.5	.900

Frank Hiller

HILLER, FRANK WALTER (Dutch) BR TR 6′ 200 lbs.
B. July 13, 1920, Newark, N. J. D. Jan. 8, 1987, West/chester, Pa.

Year	Team	Lg	W	L	PCT	ERA	G	GS	CG	IP	H	BB	SO	ShO	Relief Pitching W	Relief Pitching L	Relief Pitching SV	Batting AB	Batting H	Batting HR	BA	PO	A	E	DP	TC/G	FA
1946	NY	A	0	2	.000	4.76	3	1	0	11.1	13	6	4	0	0	1	0	4	1	0	.250	0	2	0	0	0.7	1.000
1948			5	2	.714	4.04	22	5	1	62.1	59	30	25	0	3	1	0	16	6	0	.375	3	11	0	0	0.6	1.000
1949			0	2	.000	5.87	4	0	0	7.2	9	7	3	0	0	2	1	2	1	0	.500	0	1	0	0	0.3	1.000
1950	CHI	N	12	5	.706	3.53	38	17	9	153	153	32	55	2	2	1	1	44	5	0	.114	14	29	1	0	1.2	.977
1951			6	12	.333	4.84	24	21	6	141.1	147	31	50	2	0	0	1	48	6	0	.125	13	30	1	2	1.8	.977
1952	CIN	N	5	8	.385	4.63	28	15	6	124.1	129	37	50	1	0	3	1	30	5	0	.167	9	25	1	0	1.3	.971
1953	NY	N	2	1	.667	6.15	19	1	0	33.2	43	15	10	0	2	0	0	4	2	0	.500	5	10	2	0	0.9	.882
7 yrs.			30	32	.484	4.42	138	60	22	533.2	553	158	197	5	7	8	4	148	26	0	.176	44	108	5	2	1.1	.968

John Hiller

HILLER, JOHN FREDERICK BR TL 6′ 1″ 185 lbs.
B. Apr. 8, 1943, Toronto, Ont., Canada.

Year	Team	Lg	W	L	PCT	ERA	G	GS	CG	IP	H	BB	SO	ShO	Relief Pitching W	Relief Pitching L	Relief Pitching SV	Batting AB	Batting H	Batting HR	BA	PO	A	E	DP	TC/G	FA
1965	DET	A	0	0	—	0.00	5	0	0	6	5	1	4	0	0	0	1	0	0	0	—	0	0	0	0	0.0	.000
1966			0	0	—	9.00	1	0	0	2	2	2	1	0	0	0	0	0	0	0	—	0	0	0	0	0.0	.000
1967			4	3	.571	2.63	23	6	2	65	57	9	49	2	1	1	3	15	2	0	.133	4	9	1	0	0.6	.929
1968			9	6	.600	2.39	39	12	4	128	92	51	78	1	4	3	2	37	3	0	.081	12	15	0	1	0.7	1.000
1969			4	4	.500	3.99	40	8	1	99.1	97	44	74	1	3	1	4	21	6	0	.286	2	11	1	0	0.3	.929
1970			6	6	.500	3.03	47	5	1	104	82	46	89	1	5	3	3	23	0	0	.000	3	10	0	0	0.3	1.000
1972			1	2	.333	2.05	24	3	1	44	39	13	26	0	0	0	3	4	0	0	.000	1	9	0	2	0.4	1.000
1973			10	5	.667	1.44	**65**	0	0	125	89	39	124	0	10	5	**38**	0	0	0	—	8	16	1	1	0.4	.960
1974			17	14	.548	2.64	59	0	0	150	127	62	134	0	**17**	**14**	13	0	0	0	—	2	11	1	0	0.2	.929
1975			2	3	.400	2.17	36	0	0	70.2	52	36	87	0	2	3	14	0	0	0	—	1	8	0	0	0.3	1.000
1976			12	8	.600	2.38	56	1	1	121	93	67	117	1	11	8	13	1	0	0	.000	2	13	1	0	0.3	.938
1977			8	14	.364	3.56	45	8	3	124	120	61	115	0	5	9	7	0	0	0	—	4	11	2	1	0.4	.882
1978			9	4	.692	2.34	51	0	0	92.1	64	35	74	0	9	4	15	0	0	0	—	1	9	0	0	0.2	1.000
1979			4	7	.364	5.24	43	0	0	79	83	55	46	0	4	7	9	0	0	0	—	4	10	0	0	0.3	1.000
1980			1	0	1.000	4.35	11	0	0	31	38	14	18	0	1	0	0	0	0	0	—	1	4	1	0	0.5	.833
15 yrs.			87	76	.534	2.83	545	43	13	1241.1	1040	535	1036	6	72	58	125	101	11	0	.109	45	136	8	5	0.3	.958
LEAGUE CHAMPIONSHIP SERIES																											
1972	DET	A	1	0	1.000	0.00	3	0	0	3.1	1	1	1	0	1	0	0	0	0	0	—	0	0	0	0	0.0	.000
WORLD SERIES																											
1968	DET	A	0	0	—	13.50	2	0	0	2	6	3	1	0	0	0	0	0	0	0	—	1	0	0	0	0.5	1.000

Dave Hillman

HILLMAN, DARIUS DUTTON BR TR 5′11″ 168 lbs.
B. Sept. 14, 1927, Dungannon, Va.

Year	Team	Lg	W	L	PCT	ERA	G	GS	CG	IP	H	BB	SO	ShO	Relief W	Relief L	Relief SV	AB	H	HR	BA	PO	A	E	DP	TC/G	FA
1955	CHI	N	0	0	—	5.31	25	3	0	57.2	63	25	23	0	0	0	0	10	1	0	.100	4	10	1	1	0.6	.933
1956			0	2	.000	2.19	2	2	0	12.1	11	5	6	0	0	0	0	4	0	0	.000	0	4	0	0	2.0	1.000
1957			6	11	.353	4.35	32	14	1	103.1	115	37	53	0	3	3	1	24	0	0	.000	11	12	1	3	0.8	.958
1958			4	8	.333	3.15	31	16	3	125.2	132	31	65	0	0	1	1	41	6	0	.146	7	20	1	0	0.9	.964
1959			8	11	.421	3.53	39	24	4	191	178	43	88	1	3	1	0	60	9	0	.150	28	31	2	0	1.6	.967
1960	BOS	A	0	3	.000	5.65	16	3	0	36.2	41	12	14	0	0	1	0	6	0	0	.000	1	9	0	0	0.6	1.000
1961			3	2	.600	2.77	28	1	0	78	70	23	39	0	3	2	0	17	0	0	.000	1	15	0	0	0.6	1.000
1962	2 teams	CIN N (2G 0–0)	NY N (13G 0–0)																								
″	total		0	0		6.98	15	1	0	19.1	29	9	8	0	0	0	1	1	0	0	.000	2	3	0	0	0.3	1.000
8 yrs.			21	37	.362	3.87	188	64	8	624	639	185	296	1	9	8	3	163	16	0	.098	54	104	5	4	0.9	.969

Eric Hillman

HILLMAN, JOHN ERIC BL TL 6′10″ 235 lbs.
B. Apr. 27, 1966, Gary, Ind.

Year	Team	Lg	W	L	PCT	ERA	G	GS	CG	IP	H	BB	SO	ShO	Relief W	Relief L	Relief SV	AB	H	HR	BA	PO	A	E	DP	TC/G	FA
1992	NY	N	2	2	.500	5.33	11	8	0	52.1	67	10	16	0	0	0	0	13	1	0	.077	1	7	0	0	0.7	1.000
1993			2	9	.182	3.97	27	22	3	145	173	24	60	1	0	1	0	44	7	0	.159	11	21	4	1	1.3	.889
1994			0	3	.000	7.79	11	6	0	34.2	45	11	20	0	0	0	0	8	0	0	.000	2	4	0	0	0.5	1.000
3 yrs.			4	14	.222	4.85	49	36	3	232	285	45	96	1	0	1	0	65	8	0	.123	14	32	4	1	1.0	.920

Charlie Hilsey

HILSEY, CHARLES T. 5′ 7″ 180 lbs.
B. Mar. 23, 1864, Philadelphia, Pa. D. Oct. 31, 1918, Philadelphia, Pa.

Year	Team	Lg	W	L	PCT	ERA	G	GS	CG	IP	H	BB	SO	ShO	Relief W	Relief L	Relief SV	AB	H	HR	BA	PO	A	E	DP	TC/G	FA
1883	PHI	N	0	3	.000	*5.54*	3	3	3	26	36	4	8	0	0	0	0	10	1	0	.100	1	4	2	0	2.3	.714
1884	PHI	AA	2	1	.667	*4.67*	3	3	3	27	29	5	10	0	0	0	0	24	5	0	.208	1	9	4	0	2.3	.714
2 yrs.			2	4	.333	5.09	6	6	6	53	65	9	18	0	0	0	0	34	6	0	.176	2	13	6	0	2.3	.714

Howard Hilton

HILTON, HOWARD JAMES BR TR 6′ 3″ 230 lbs.
B. Jan. 3, 1964, Oxnard, Calif.

Year	Team	Lg	W	L	PCT	ERA	G	GS	CG	IP	H	BB	SO	ShO	Relief W	Relief L	Relief SV	AB	H	HR	BA	PO	A	E	DP	TC/G	FA
1990	STL	N	0	0	—	0.00	2	0	0	3	2	3	2	0	0	0	0	0	0	0	—	0	0	0	0	0.0	.000

Sam Hinds

HINDS, SAMUEL RUSSELL BR TR 6′ 6″ 215 lbs.
B. July 11, 1953, Frederick, Md.

Year	Team	Lg	W	L	PCT	ERA	G	GS	CG	IP	H	BB	SO	ShO	Relief W	Relief L	Relief SV	AB	H	HR	BA	PO	A	E	DP	TC/G	FA
1977	MIL	A	0	3	.000	4.75	29	1	0	72	72	40	46	0	0	2	2	0	0	0	—	5	8	0	0	0.4	1.000

Paul Hines

HINES, PAUL A. BR TR 5′ 9½″ 173 lbs.
B. Mar. 1, 1852, Washington, D. C. D. July 10, 1935, Hyattsville, Md.

Year	Team	Lg	W	L	PCT	ERA	G	GS	CG	IP	H	BB	SO	ShO	Relief W	Relief L	Relief SV	AB	H	HR	BA	PO	A	E	DP	TC/G	FA
1884	PRO	N	0	0	—	*0.00*	1	0	0	1	3	0	0	0	0	0	0	*				159	8	14	4	2.8	.923

Dutch Hinrichs

HINRICHS, WILLIAM LOUIS BR TR 6′ 3″ 195 lbs.
B. Apr. 27, 1889, Orange, Calif. D. Aug. 18, 1972, Kingsburg, Calif.

Year	Team	Lg	W	L	PCT	ERA	G	GS	CG	IP	H	BB	SO	ShO	Relief W	Relief L	Relief SV	AB	H	HR	BA	PO	A	E	DP	TC/G	FA
1910	WAS	A	0	1	.000	2.57	3	0	0	7	10	3	5	0	0	1	1	4	0	0	.000	0	0	0	0	0.0	.000

Paul Hinrichs

HINRICHS, PAUL EDWIN (Herky) BR TR 6′ 180 lbs.
B. Aug. 31, 1925, Marengo, Iowa.

Year	Team	Lg	W	L	PCT	ERA	G	GS	CG	IP	H	BB	SO	ShO	Relief W	Relief L	Relief SV	AB	H	HR	BA	PO	A	E	DP	TC/G	FA
1951	BOS	A	0	0	—	21.60	4	0	0	3.1	7	4	1	0	0	0	0	0	0	0	—	0	1	0	0	0.3	1.000

Jerry Hinsley

HINSLEY, JERRY DEAN BR TR 5′11″ 165 lbs.
B. Apr. 9, 1944, Hugo, Okla.

Year	Team	Lg	W	L	PCT	ERA	G	GS	CG	IP	H	BB	SO	ShO	Relief W	Relief L	Relief SV	AB	H	HR	BA	PO	A	E	DP	TC/G	FA
1964	NY	N	0	2	.000	8.22	9	2	0	15.1	21	7	11	0	0	1	0	1	0	0	.000	0	1	1	0	0.2	.500
1967			0	0	—	3.60	2	0	0	5	6	4	3	0	0	0	0	0	0	0	—	1	0	0	1	0.5	1.000
2 yrs.			0	2	.000	7.08	11	2	0	20.1	27	11	14	0	0	1	0	1	0	0	.000	1	1	1	1	0.3	.667

Rich Hinton

HINTON, RICHARD MICHAEL BL TL 6′ 2″ 185 lbs.
B. May 22, 1947, Tucson, Ariz.

Year	Team	Lg	W	L	PCT	ERA	G	GS	CG	IP	H	BB	SO	ShO	Relief W	Relief L	Relief SV	AB	H	HR	BA	PO	A	E	DP	TC/G	FA
1971	CHI	A	2	4	.333	4.50	18	2	0	24	27	6	15	0	2	2	0	1	0	0	.000	0	7	0	1	0.4	1.000
1972	2 teams	NY A (7G 1–0)	TEX A (5G 0–1)																								
″	total		1	1	.500	3.86	12	3	0	28	27	18	17	0	0	1	0	5	1	0	.200	2	3	0	0	0.4	1.000
1975	CHI	A	1	0	1.000	4.82	15	0	0	37.1	41	15	30	0	1	0	0	0	0	0	—	1	9	0	1	0.7	1.000
1976	CIN	N	1	2	.333	7.50	12	1	0	18	30	11	8	0	1	2	0	1	0	0	.000	0	2	1	0	0.3	.667
1978	CHI	A	2	6	.250	4.02	29	4	2	80.2	78	28	48	0	1	3	1	0	0	0	—	3	8	1	0	0.4	.917
1979	2 teams	CHI A (16G 1–2)	SEA A (14G 0–2)																								
″	total		1	4	.200	5.81	30	3	0	62	80	13	34	0	1	1	2	0	0	0		6	10	1	1	0.6	.941
6 yrs.			8	17	.320	4.86	116	13	2	250	283	91	152	0	6	9	3	7	1	0	.143	12	39	3	3	0.5	.944

Herb Hippauf

HIPPAUF, HERBERT AUGUST BR TL 6′ 180 lbs.
B. May 9, 1939, New York, N. Y. D. July 17, 1995, Santa Clara, Calif.

Year	Team	Lg	W	L	PCT	ERA	G	GS	CG	IP	H	BB	SO	ShO	Relief W	Relief L	Relief SV	AB	H	HR	BA	PO	A	E	DP	TC/G	FA
1966	ATL	N	0	1	.000	13.50	3	0	0	2.2	6	1	1	0	0	1	0	0	0	0	—	0	0	1	0	0.3	.000

Harley Hisner

HISNER, HARLEY PARNELL BR TR 6′ 1″ 185 lbs.
B. Nov. 6, 1926, Naples, Ind.

Year	Team	Lg	W	L	PCT	ERA	G	GS	CG	IP	H	BB	SO	ShO	Relief W	Relief L	Relief SV	AB	H	HR	BA	PO	A	E	DP	TC/G	FA
1951	BOS	A	0	1	.000	4.50	1	1	0	6	7	4	3	0	0	0	0	2	1	0	.500	0	1	0	1	1.0	1.000

Sterling Hitchcock

HITCHCOCK, STERLING ALEX BL TL 6′ 1″ 200 lbs.
B. Apr. 29, 1971, Fayetteville, N. C.

Year	Team	Lg	W	L	PCT	ERA	G	GS	CG	IP	H	BB	SO	ShO	Relief W	Relief L	Relief SV	AB	H	HR	BA	PO	A	E	DP	TC/G	FA
1992	NY	A	0	2	.000	8.31	3	3	0	13	23	6	6	0	0	0	0	0	0	0	—	0	2	0	0	0.7	1.000
1993			1	2	.333	4.65	6	6	0	31	32	14	26	0	0	0	0	0	0	0	—	1	3	0	1	0.7	1.000
1994			4	1	.800	4.20	23	5	1	49.1	48	29	37	0	1	1	2	0	0	0	—	1	7	2	0	0.4	.800
1995			11	10	.524	4.70	27	27	4	168.1	155	68	121	1	0	0	0	0	0	0	—	4	12	0	1	0.6	1.000
4 yrs.			16	15	.516	4.78	59	41	5	261.2	258	117	190	1	1	1	2	0	0	0		6	24	2	2	0.5	.938
DIVISIONAL PLAYOFF SERIES																											
1995	NY	A	0	0	—	5.40	2	0	0	1.2	2	2	1	0	0	0	0	0	0	0	—	0	1	0	0	0.5	1.000

Bruce Hitt

HITT, BRUCE SMITH BR TR 6′ 1″ 190 lbs.
B. Mar. 14, 1897, Comanche, Tex. D. Nov. 10, 1973, Portland, Ore.

Year	Team	Lg	W	L	PCT	ERA	G	GS	CG	IP	H	BB	SO	ShO	Relief W	Relief L	Relief SV	AB	H	HR	BA	PO	A	E	DP	TC/G	FA
1917	STL	N	0	0	—	9.00	2	0	0	4	7	1	1	0	0	0	0	1	0	0	.000	0	2	0	0	1.0	1.000

Roy Hitt

HITT, ROY WESLEY (Rhino) BL TL 5′10″ 200 lbs.
B. June 22, 1887, Carleton, Neb. D. Feb. 8, 1956, Pomona, Calif.

Year	Team		W	L	PCT	ERA	G	GS	CG	IP	H	BB	SO	ShO	Relief W	Relief L	Relief SV	AB	H	HR	BA	PO	A	E	DP	TC/G	FA
1907	CIN	N	6	10	.375	3.40	21	18	14	153.1	143	56	63	2	0	0	0	56	10	0	.179	3	37	1	0	2.0	.976

Lloyd Hittle

HITTLE, LLOYD ELDON (Red) BR TL 5′10½″ 164 lbs.
B. Feb. 21, 1924, Lodi, Calif.

Year	Team		W	L	PCT	ERA	G	GS	CG	IP	H	BB	SO	ShO	Relief W	Relief L	Relief SV	AB	H	HR	BA	PO	A	E	DP	TC/G	FA
1949	WAS	A	5	7	.417	4.21	36	9	3	109	123	57	32	2	3	2	0	28	4	0	.143	5	17	1	0	0.6	.957
1950			2	4	.333	4.98	11	4	1	43.1	60	17	9	0	1	3	0	13	1	0	.077	3	14	1	1	1.6	.944
2 yrs.			7	11	.389	4.43	47	13	4	152.1	183	74	41	2	4	5	0	41	5	0	.122	8	31	2	1	0.9	.951

Myril Hoag

HOAG, MYRIL OLIVER BR TR 5′11″ 180 lbs.
B. Mar. 9, 1908, Davis, Calif. D. July 28, 1971, High Springs, Fla.

Year	Team		W	L	PCT	ERA	G	GS	CG	IP	H	BB	SO	ShO	Relief W	Relief L	Relief SV	AB	H	HR	BA	PO	A	E	DP	TC/G	FA
1939	STL	A	0	0	—	0.00	1	0	0	1	0	0	0	0	0	0	0	482	142	10	.295	12	2	0	0	0.6	1.000
1945	CLE	A	0	0	—	0.00	2	0	0	3	3	1	0	0	0	0	0	128	27	0	.211	26	3	1	0	0.8	.967
2 yrs.			0	0		0.00	3	0	0	4	3	1	0	0	0	0	0	*				1677	80	63	20	2.1	.965

Ed Hobaugh

HOBAUGH, EDWARD RUSSELL BR TR 6′ 176 lbs.
B. June 27, 1934, Kittanning, Pa.

Year	Team		W	L	PCT	ERA	G	GS	CG	IP	H	BB	SO	ShO	Relief W	Relief L	Relief SV	AB	H	HR	BA	PO	A	E	DP	TC/G	FA
1961	WAS	A	7	9	.438	4.42	26	18	3	126.1	142	64	67	0	0	2	0	41	4	0	.098	7	22	2	3	1.2	.935
1962			2	1	.667	3.76	26	2	0	69.1	66	25	37	0	2	0	1	12	2	0	.167	1	8	0	2	0.3	1.000
1963			0	0	—	6.19	9	1	0	16	20	6	11	0	0	0	0	2	1	1	.500	1	3	0	0	0.4	1.000
3 yrs.			9	10	.474	4.34	61	21	3	211.2	228	95	115	0	2	2	1	55	7	1	.127	9	33	2	5	0.7	.955

Glen Hobbie

HOBBIE, GLEN FREDERICK BR TR 6′2″ 195 lbs.
B. Apr. 24, 1936, Witt, Ill.

Year	Team		W	L	PCT	ERA	G	GS	CG	IP	H	BB	SO	ShO	Relief W	Relief L	Relief SV	AB	H	HR	BA	PO	A	E	DP	TC/G	FA
1957	CHI	N	0	0	—	10.38	2	0	0	4.1	6	5	3	0	0	0	0	2	0	0	.000	1	0	0	0	0.5	1.000
1958			10	6	.625	3.74	55	16	2	168.1	163	93	91	1	6	1	2	48	7	0	.146	12	44	5	5	1.1	.918
1959			16	13	.552	3.69	46	33	10	234	204	106	138	3	0	1	0	79	9	0	.114	18	40	4	2	1.3	.935
1960			16	**20**	.444	3.97	46	36	16	258.2	253	101	134	4	2	3	1	86	13	1	.151	19	67	5	4	2.0	.945
1961			7	13	.350	4.26	36	29	7	198.2	207	54	103	2	1	0	2	66	11	2	.167	16	53	4	1	2.0	.945
1962			5	14	.263	5.22	42	23	5	162	198	62	87	0	0	2	0	49	6	0	.122	8	31	0	1	0.9	1.000
1963			7	10	.412	3.92	36	24	4	165.1	172	49	94	1	1	0	0	50	4	0	.080	6	29	4	1	1.1	.897
1964	2 teams	CHI N (8G 0–3) STL N (13G 1–2)																									
″	total		1	5	.167	5.65	21	9	1	71.2	80	25	32	0	0	0	1	18	2	1	.111	6	18	0	0	1.1	1.000
8 yrs.			62	81	.434	4.20	284	170	45	1263	1283	495	682	11	10	7	6	398	52	4	.131	86	282	22	14	1.4	.944

Jack Hobbs

HOBBS, JOHN DOUGLAS BR TL 6′3″ 190 lbs.
B. Nov. 11, 1955, Philadelphia, Pa.

Year	Team		W	L	PCT	ERA	G	GS	CG	IP	H	BB	SO	ShO	Relief W	Relief L	Relief SV	AB	H	HR	BA	PO	A	E	DP	TC/G	FA
1981	MIN	A	0	0	—	3.00	4	0	0	6	5	6	1	0	0	0	0	0	0	0	—	1	0	0	0	0.3	1.000

Harry Hoch

HOCH, HARRY KELLER BR TR 5′10½″ 165 lbs.
B. Jan. 9, 1887, Woodside, Del. D. Oct. 26, 1981, Lewes, Del.

Year	Team		W	L	PCT	ERA	G	GS	CG	IP	H	BB	SO	ShO	Relief W	Relief L	Relief SV	AB	H	HR	BA	PO	A	E	DP	TC/G	FA
1908	PHI	N	2	1	.667	2.77	3	3	2	26	20	13	4	0	0	0	0	5	1	0	.200	2	9	0	1	3.7	1.000
1914	STL	A	0	2	.000	3.00	15	2	1	54	55	27	13	0	0	0	0	18	1	0	.056	4	23	0	1	1.8	1.000
1915			0	4	.000	7.20	12	3	1	40	52	26	9	0	0	1	0	10	2	0	.200	2	11	2	1	1.3	.867
3 yrs.			2	7	.222	4.35	30	8	4	120	127	66	26	0	0	1	0	33	4	0	.121	8	43	2	3	1.8	.962

Chuck Hockenbery

HOCKENBERY, CHARLES MARION BB TR 6′1″ 195 lbs.
B. Dec. 15, 1950, La Crosse, Wis.

Year	Team		W	L	PCT	ERA	G	GS	CG	IP	H	BB	SO	ShO	Relief W	Relief L	Relief SV	AB	H	HR	BA	PO	A	E	DP	TC/G	FA
1975	CAL	A	0	5	.000	5.27	16	4	0	41	48	19	15	0	0	1	1	0	0	0	—	1	6	0	1	0.4	1.000

George Hockette

HOCKETTE, GEORGE EDWARD (Lefty) BL TL 6′ 174 lbs.
B. Apr. 7, 1908, Perth, Miss. D. Jan. 20, 1974, Plantation, Fla.

Year	Team		W	L	PCT	ERA	G	GS	CG	IP	H	BB	SO	ShO	Relief W	Relief L	Relief SV	AB	H	HR	BA	PO	A	E	DP	TC/G	FA
1934	BOS	A	2	1	.667	1.65	3	3	3	27.1	22	6	14	2	0	0	0	11	3	0	.273	2	3	1	0	2.0	.833
1935			2	3	.400	5.16	23	4	0	61	83	12	11	0	2	1	0	14	2	0	.143	5	27	2	1	1.5	.941
2 yrs.			4	4	.500	4.08	26	7	3	88.1	105	18	25	2	2	1	0	25	5	0	.200	7	30	3	1	1.5	.925

Ed Hodge

HODGE, ED OLIVER BL TL 6′2″ 185 lbs.
B. Apr. 19, 1958, Bellflower, Calif.

Year	Team		W	L	PCT	ERA	G	GS	CG	IP	H	BB	SO	ShO	Relief W	Relief L	Relief SV	AB	H	HR	BA	PO	A	E	DP	TC/G	FA
1984	MIN	A	4	3	.571	4.77	25	15	0	100	116	29	59	0	0	0	0	0	0	0	—	2	6	0	0	0.3	1.000

Shovel Hodge

HODGE, CLARENCE CLEMENT BL TR 6′4″ 190 lbs.
B. July 6, 1893, Mount Andrew, Ala. D. Dec. 31, 1967, Ft. Walton Beach, Fla.

Year	Team		W	L	PCT	ERA	G	GS	CG	IP	H	BB	SO	ShO	Relief W	Relief L	Relief SV	AB	H	HR	BA	PO	A	E	DP	TC/G	FA
1920	CHI	A	1	1	.500	2.29	4	2	1	19.2	15	12	5	0	0	0	0	6	0	0	.000	0	3	0	0	0.8	1.000
1921			6	8	.429	6.56	36	11	6	142.2	191	54	25	0	4	1	2	52	17	0	.327	10	52	2	1	1.8	.969
1922			7	6	.538	4.14	35	8	2	139	154	65	37	0	5	2	1	58	12	0	.207	0	46	3	3	1.4	.939
3 yrs.			14	15	.483	5.17	75	21	9	301.1	360	131	67	0	9	3	3	116	29	0	.250	10	101	5	4	1.5	.957

Eli Hodkey

HODKEY, ALOYSIUS JOSEPH BL TL 6′4″ 185 lbs.
B. Nov. 3, 1917, Lorain, Ohio.

Year	Team		W	L	PCT	ERA	G	GS	CG	IP	H	BB	SO	ShO	Relief W	Relief L	Relief SV	AB	H	HR	BA	PO	A	E	DP	TC/G	FA
1946	PHI	N	0	1	.000	12.46	2	1	0	4.1	9	5	0	0	0	1	0	2	0	0	.000	0	0	0	0	0.0	.000

Charlie Hodnett

HODNETT, CHARLES
B. 1861, St. Louis, Mo. Deceased.

Year	Team		W	L	PCT	ERA	G	GS	CG	IP	H	BB	SO	ShO	Relief W	Relief L	Relief SV	AB	H	HR	BA	PO	A	E	DP	TC/G	FA
1883	STL	AA	2	2	.500	*1.41*	4	4	3	32	28	7	6	0	0	0	0	11	2	0	.182	0	6	0	0	1.2	1.000
1884	STL	U	12	2	.857	*2.01*	14	14	12	121	121	16	41	1	0	0	0	58	12	0	.207	5	22	6	1	1.6	.818
2 yrs.			14	4	.778	1.88	18	18	15	153	149	23	47	1	0	0	0	69	14	0	.203	5	28	6	1	1.6	.846

George Hodson

HODSON, GEORGE S.
B. June 1870, Pa. Deceased.

Year	Team		W	L	PCT	ERA	G	GS	CG	IP	H	BB	SO	ShO	Relief W	Relief L	Relief SV	AB	H	HR	BA	PO	A	E	DP	TC/G	FA
1894	BOS	N	4	4	.500	5.84	12	11	8	74	103	35	12	0	0	0	0	30	3	0	.100	1	10	4	1	1.3	.733
1895	PHI	N	1	2	.333	9.53	4	2	1	17	27	9	6	0	1	0	0	5	0	0	.000	1	1	0	0	0.5	1.000
2 yrs.			5	6	.455	6.53	16	13	9	91	130	44	18	0	1	0	0	35	3	0	.086	2	11	4	1	1.1	.765

Billy Hoeft

HOEFT, WILLIAM FREDERICK BL TL 6′ 3″ 180 lbs.
B. May 17, 1932, Oshkosh, Wis.

Year	Team	W	L	PCT	ERA	G	GS	CG	IP	H	BB	SO	ShO	Relief Pitching W	Relief Pitching L	Relief Pitching SV	Batting AB	Batting H	Batting HR	BA	PO	A	E	DP	TC/G	FA
1952	DET A	2	7	.222	4.32	34	10	1	125	123	63	67	0	0	2	4	40	6	0	.150	6	25	2	4	0.9	.939
1953		9	14	.391	4.83	29	27	9	197.2	223	58	90	0	0	0	2	64	11	0	.172	14	24	2	0	1.4	.950
1954		7	15	.318	4.58	34	25	10	175	180	59	114	4	1	1	1	52	10	0	.192	6	18	1	2	0.7	.960
1955		16	7	.696	2.99	32	29	17	220	187	75	133	**7**	0	1	0	82	17	0	.207	7	21	0	2	0.9	1.000
1956		20	14	.588	4.06	38	34	18	248	276	104	172	4	2	0	0	80	20	0	.250	5	28	1	1	0.9	.971
1957		9	11	.450	3.48	34	28	10	207	188	69	111	1	0	0	1	67	10	3	.149	8	28	2	2	1.1	.947
1958		10	9	.526	4.15	36	21	6	143	148	49	94	0	1	2	3	44	12	0	.273	6	15	3	2	0.7	.875
1959	3 teams DET A (2G 1–1) BOS A (5G 0–3) BAL A (16G 1–1)																									
″	total	2	5	.286	5.59	23	8	0	67.2	78	31	40	0	0	0	0	18	4	0	.222	4	12	1	1	0.7	.941
1960	BAL A	2	1	.667	4.34	19	0	0	18.2	18	14	14	0	2	1	0	1	0	0	.000	3	3	0	1	0.3	1.000
1961		7	4	.636	2.02	35	12	3	138	106	55	100	1	2	1	3	39	7	0	.179	9	25	0	2	1.0	1.000
1962		4	8	.333	4.59	57	4	0	113.2	103	43	73	0	4	6	7	19	3	0	.158	10	17	2	2	0.5	.931
1963	SF N	2	0	1.000	4.44	23	0	0	24.1	26	10	8	0	2	0	4	1	1	0	1.000	1	4	2	0	0.3	.714
1964	MIL N	4	0	1.000	3.80	42	0	0	73.1	76	18	47	0	4	0	4	9	2	0	.222	4	14	0	0	0.4	1.000
1965	CHI N	2	2	.500	2.81	29	2	1	51.1	41	20	44	0	1	1	1	11	3	0	.273	0	7	1	0	0.3	.875
1966	2 teams CHI N (36G 1–2) SF N (4G 0–2)																									
″	total	1	4	.200	4.84	40	0	0	44.2	47	17	33	0	1	4	3	4	1	0	.250	5	8	0	0	0.3	1.000
15 yrs.		97	101	.490	3.94	505	200	75	1847.1	1820	685	1140	17	20	19	33	531	107	3	.202	88	249	17	19	0.7	.952

Art Hoelskoetter

HOELSKOETTER, ARTHUR H. BR TR 6′ 2″
B. Sept. 30, 1882, St. Louis, Mo. D. Aug. 3, 1954, St. Louis, Mo.

Year	Team	W	L	PCT	ERA	G	GS	CG	IP	H	BB	SO	ShO	Relief Pitching W	Relief Pitching L	Relief Pitching SV	Batting AB	Batting H	Batting HR	BA	PO	A	E	DP	TC/G	FA
1905	STL N	0	1	.000	1.50	1	1	1	6	6	5	4	0	0	0	0	83	20	0	.241	40	46	4	4	3.8	.956
1906		2	4	.333	4.63	12	3	2	58.1	53	34	20	0	1	0	0	317	71	0	.224	109	173	19	10	3.2	.937
1907		0	0	—	5.73	2	0	0	11	9	10	8	0	0	0	0	396	98	2	.247	450	267	42	40	6.3	.945
3 yrs.		2	5	.286	4.54	15	4	3	75.1	68	49	32	0	1	0	0	*				786	551	81	61	5.0	.943

Joe Hoerner

HOERNER, JOSEPH WALTER BR TL 6′ 1″ 200 lbs.
B. Nov. 12, 1936, Dubuque, Iowa.

Year	Team	W	L	PCT	ERA	G	GS	CG	IP	H	BB	SO	ShO	Relief Pitching W	Relief Pitching L	Relief Pitching SV	Batting AB	Batting H	Batting HR	BA	PO	A	E	DP	TC/G	FA
1963	HOU N	0	0	—	0.00	1	0	0	3	2	0	2	0	0	0	0	1	0	0	.000	0	1	0	0	1.0	1.000
1964		0	0	—	4.91	7	0	0	11	13	6	4	0	0	0	0	1	0	0	.000	1	3	1	0	0.7	.800
1966	STL N	5	1	.833	1.54	57	0	0	76	57	21	63	0	5	1	13	8	1	1	.125	5	9	2	0	0.3	.875
1967		4	4	.500	2.59	57	0	0	66	52	20	50	0	4	4	15	11	2	0	.182	3	10	0	0	0.2	1.000
1968		8	2	.800	1.47	47	0	0	49	34	12	42	0	8	2	17	6	0	0	.000	2	6	1	0	0.2	.889
1969		2	3	.400	2.89	45	0	0	53	44	9	35	0	2	3	15	5	0	0	.000	3	9	0	1	0.3	1.000
1970	PHI N	9	5	.643	2.64	44	0	0	58	53	20	39	0	**9**	5	9	10	2	0	.200	2	1	1	0	0.1	.750
1971		4	5	.444	1.97	49	0	0	73	57	21	57	0	4	5	9	10	1	0	.100	2	10	2	0	0.3	.857
1972	2 teams PHI N (15G 0–2) ATL N (25G 1–3)																									
″	total	1	5	.167	4.40	40	0	0	45	55	13	31	0	1	5	5	5	0	0	.000	1	3	1	0	0.1	.800
1973	2 teams ATL N (20G 2–2) KC A (22G 2–0)																									
″	total	4	2	.667	5.63	42	0	0	32	45	17	25	0	4	2	6	0	0	0		0	1	0	0	0.0	1.000
1974	KC A	2	3	.400	3.86	30	0	0	35	32	12	24	0	2	3	2	0	0	0	—	0	1	0	0	0.0	1.000
1975	PHI N	0	0	—	2.57	25	0	0	21	25	8	20	0	0	0	0	2	0	0	.000	0	0	0	0	0.0	.000
1976	TEX A	0	4	.000	5.14	41	0	0	35	41	19	15	0	0	4	8	0	0	0	—	0	3	0	0	0.1	1.000
1977	CIN N	0	0	—	12.00	8	0	0	6	9	3	5	0	0	0	0	0	0	0	—	0	0	0	0	0.0	.000
14 yrs.		39	34	.534	2.99	493	0	0	563	519	181	412	0	39	34	99	59	6	1	.102	19	57	8	1	0.2	.905
WORLD SERIES																										
1967	STL N	0	0	—	40.50	2	0	0	0.2	4	1	0	0	0	0	0	0	0	0	—	0	0	0	0	0.0	.000
1968		0	1	.000	3.86	3	0	0	4.2	5	5	3	0	0	1	1	2	1	0	.500	0	0	0	0	0.0	.000
2 yrs.		0	1	.000	8.44	5	0	0	5.1	9	6	3	0	0	1	1	2	1	0	.500	0	0	0	0	0.0	

Frank Hoerst

HOERST, FRANK JOSEPH (Lefty) BL TL 6′ 3″ 192 lbs.
B. Aug. 11, 1917, Philadelphia, Pa.

Year	Team	W	L	PCT	ERA	G	GS	CG	IP	H	BB	SO	ShO	Relief Pitching W	Relief Pitching L	Relief Pitching SV	Batting AB	Batting H	Batting HR	BA	PO	A	E	DP	TC/G	FA
1940	PHI N	1	0	1.000	5.25	6	0	0	12	12	8	3	0	1	0	0	2	0	0	.000	1	6	0	1	1.2	1.000
1941		3	10	.231	5.20	37	11	1	105.2	111	50	33	0	1	1	0	22	4	0	.182	3	31	4	2	1.0	.895
1942		4	16	.200	5.20	33	22	5	150.2	162	78	52	0	0	0	1	46	7	0	.152	11	40	2	2	1.6	.962
1946		1	6	.143	4.61	18	7	2	68.1	77	36	17	0	0	1	0	17	1	0	.059	5	9	0	0	0.8	1.000
1947		1	1	.500	7.94	4	1	0	11.1	19	3	0	0	1	0	0	4	2	0	.500	2	2	0	0	1.0	1.000
5 yrs.		10	33	.233	5.17	98	41	8	348	381	175	105	0	3	2	1	91	14	0	.154	22	88	6	5	1.2	.948

Red Hoff

HOFF, CHESTER CORNELIUS BL TL 5′ 9″ 162 lbs.
B. May 8, 1891, Ossining, N. Y.

Year	Team	W	L	PCT	ERA	G	GS	CG	IP	H	BB	SO	ShO	Relief Pitching W	Relief Pitching L	Relief Pitching SV	Batting AB	Batting H	Batting HR	BA	PO	A	E	DP	TC/G	FA
1911	NY A	0	1	.000	2.18	5	1	0	20.2	21	7	10	0	0	0	0	11	3	0	.273	2	11	1	0	2.8	.929
1912		0	1	.000	6.89	5	1	0	15.2	20	6	14	0	0	0	0	5	1	0	.200	0	4	1	0	1.0	.800
1913		0	0	—	0.00	2	0	0	3	0	1	2	0	0	0	0	1	0	0	.000	0	0	0	0	0.0	.000
1915	STL A	2	2	.500	1.24	11	3	2	43.2	26	24	23	0	1	0	0	17	3	0	.176	2	17	3	0	2.0	.864
4 yrs.		2	4	.333	2.49	23	5	2	83	67	38	49	0	1	0	0	34	7	0	.206	4	32	5	0	1.8	.878

Bill Hoffer

HOFFER, WILLIAM LEOPOLD (Wizard) BR TR 5′ 9″ 155 lbs.
B. Nov. 8, 1870, Cedar Rapids, Iowa D. July 21, 1959, Cedar Rapids, Iowa.

Year	Team	W	L	PCT	ERA	G	GS	CG	IP	H	BB	SO	ShO	Relief Pitching W	Relief Pitching L	Relief Pitching SV	Batting AB	Batting H	Batting HR	BA	PO	A	E	DP	TC/G	FA
1895	BAL N	31	6	**.838**	3.21	41	38	32	314	296	124	80	**4**	2	1	0	126	27	0	.214	15	55	2	2	1.8	.972
1896		25	7	**.781**	3.38	35	35	32	309	317	95	93	3	0	0	0	125	38	0	.304	15	83	9	6	3.1	.916
1897		22	11	.667	4.30	38	33	29	303.1	350	104	62	1	1	2	0	139	33	1	.237	29	64	4	4	2.3	.959
1898	2 teams BAL N (4G 0–4) PIT N (4G 3–0)																									
″	total	3	4	.429	4.68	8	7	7	65.1	88	31	16	0	0	0	0	35	6	0	.171	7	13	1	0	1.8	.952
1899	PIT N	8	10	.444	3.63	23	19	15	163.2	169	64	44	2	1	1	0	91	18	0	.198	30	40	8	2	2.6	.897
1901	CLE A	3	8	.273	4.55	16	10	10	99	113	35	19	0	0	1	**3**	44	6	0	.136	8	31	3	1	2.5	.929
6 yrs.		92	46	.667	3.75	161	142	125	1254.1	1333	453	314	10	4	5	3	560	128	1	.229	104	286	27	15	2.4	.935

Bill Hoffman

HOFFMAN, WILLIAM JOSEPH BL TL 5′ 9″ 170 lbs.
B. Mar. 3, 1918, Philadelphia, Pa.

Year	Team	W	L	PCT	ERA	G	GS	CG	IP	H	BB	SO	ShO	Relief Pitching W	Relief Pitching L	Relief Pitching SV	Batting AB	Batting H	Batting HR	BA	PO	A	E	DP	TC/G	FA
1939	PHI N	0	0	—	13.50	3	0	0	6	8	7	1	0	0	0	0	1	0	0	.000	0	0	0	0	0.0	.000

Danny Hoffman

HOFFMAN, DANIEL JOHN BL TL 5′ 9″ 175 lbs.
B. Mar. 12, 1880, Canton, Conn. D. Mar. 14, 1922, Manchester, Conn.

Year	Team	Lg	W	L	PCT	ERA	G	GS	CG	IP	H	BB	SO	ShO	Relief W	Relief L	Relief SV	AB	H	HR	BA	PO	A	E	DP	TC/G	FA
1903	PHI	A	0	0	—	2.70	1	0	0	3.1	2	2	0	0	0	0	0	*				111	4	6	0	1.9	.950

Frank Hoffman

HOFFMAN, FRANK J. (The Texas Wonder) TR
B. Houston, Tex. Deceased.

Year	Team	Lg	W	L	PCT	ERA	G	GS	CG	IP	H	BB	SO	ShO	Relief W	Relief L	Relief SV	AB	H	HR	BA	PO	A	E	DP	TC/G	FA
1888	KC	AA	3	9	.250	2.77	12	12	12	104	102	42	38	0	0	0	0	39	6	0	.154	7	24	6	1	3.1	.838

Guy Hoffman

HOFFMAN, GUY ALAN BL TL 5′ 9″ 175 lbs.
B. July 9, 1956, Ottawa, Ill.

Year	Team	Lg	W	L	PCT	ERA	G	GS	CG	IP	H	BB	SO	ShO	Relief W	Relief L	Relief SV	AB	H	HR	BA	PO	A	E	DP	TC/G	FA
1979	CHI	A	0	5	.000	5.40	24	0	0	30	30	23	18	0	0	5	2	0	0	0	—	1	5	0	1	0.3	1.000
1980			1	0	1.000	2.61	23	1	0	38	38	17	24	0	1	0	1	0	0	0	—	1	1	0	0	0.1	1.000
1983			1	0	1.000	7.50	11	0	0	6	14	2	2	0	1	0	0	0	0	0	—	1	0	0	0	0.1	1.000
1986	CHI	N	6	2	.750	3.86	32	8	1	84	92	29	47	0	4	0	0	15	1	0	.067	1	9	1	0	0.3	.909
1987	CIN	N	9	10	.474	4.37	36	22	0	158.2	160	49	87	0	3	0	0	45	5	0	.111	3	21	0	0	0.7	1.000
1988	TEX	A	0	0	—	5.24	11	0	0	22.1	22	8	9	0	0	0	0	0	0	0	—	1	4	0	0	0.5	1.000
6 yrs.			17	17	.500	4.25	137	31	1	339	356	128	187	0	9	5	3	60	6	0	.100	8	40	1	1	0.4	.980

Trevor Hoffman

HOFFMAN, TREVOR WILLIAM BR TR 6′ 1″ 200 lbs.
Brother of Glenn Hoffman.
B. Oct. 13, 1967, Bellflower, Calif.

Year	Team	Lg	W	L	PCT	ERA	G	GS	CG	IP	H	BB	SO	ShO	Relief W	Relief L	Relief SV	AB	H	HR	BA	PO	A	E	DP	TC/G	FA
1993	2 teams	FLA N	(28G 2–2)		SD N	(39G 2–4)																					
″	total		4	6	.400	3.90	67	0	0	90	80	39	79	0	4	6	5	7	1	0	.143	6	11	0	0	0.3	1.000
1994	SD	N	4	4	.500	2.57	47	0	0	56	39	20	68	0	4	4	20	3	0	0	.000	4	5	0	1	0.2	1.000
1995			7	4	.636	3.88	55	0	0	53.1	48	14	52	0	7	4	31	2	1	0	.500	5	1	0	0	0.1	1.000
3 yrs.			15	14	.517	3.52	169	0	0	199.1	167	73	199	0	15	14	56	12	2	0	.167	15	17	0	1	0.2	1.000

John Hofford

HOFFORD, JOHN WILLIAM
B. May 25, 1863, Philadelphia, Pa. D. Dec. 16, 1915, Philadelphia, Pa.

Year	Team	Lg	W	L	PCT	ERA	G	GS	CG	IP	H	BB	SO	ShO	Relief W	Relief L	Relief SV	AB	H	HR	BA	PO	A	E	DP	TC/G	FA
1885	PIT	AA	0	3	.000	*3.60*	3	3	3	25	28	9	21	0	0	0	0	8	1	0	.125	1	5	0	0	2.0	1.000
1886			3	6	.333	*4.33*	9	9	9	81	88	40	25	0	0	0	0	34	10	0	.294	5	17	2	0	2.7	.917
2 yrs.			3	9	.250	4.16	12	12	12	106	116	49	46	0	0	0	0	42	11	0	.262	6	22	2	0	2.5	.933

Eddie Hogan

HOGAN, ROBERT EDWARD BR 5′ 7″ 153 lbs.
B. Apr. 1860, St. Louis, Mo. Deceased.

Year	Team	Lg	W	L	PCT	ERA	G	GS	CG	IP	H	BB	SO	ShO	Relief W	Relief L	Relief SV	AB	H	HR	BA	PO	A	E	DP	TC/G	FA
1882	STL	AA	0	1	.000	1.13	1	1	1	8	10	0	4	0	0	0	0	*				0	1	2	0	3.0	.333

George Hogan

HOGAN, GEORGE A. BR TR 6′ 160 lbs.
Brother of Happy Hogan.
B. Sept. 25, 1885, Marion, Ohio D. Feb. 22, 1922, Bartlesville, Okla.

Year	Team	Lg	W	L	PCT	ERA	G	GS	CG	IP	H	BB	SO	ShO	Relief W	Relief L	Relief SV	AB	H	HR	BA	PO	A	E	DP	TC/G	FA
1914	KC	F	0	1	.000	4.15	4	1	0	13	12	7	7	0	0	0	0	4	0	0	.000	0	5	1	1	1.5	.833

Bill Hogg

HOGG, WILLIAM JOHNSTON (Buffalo Bill) BR TR 6′ 200 lbs.
B. Sept. 11, 1881, Port Huron, Mich. D. Dec. 8, 1909, New Orleans, La.

Year	Team	Lg	W	L	PCT	ERA	G	GS	CG	IP	H	BB	SO	ShO	Relief W	Relief L	Relief SV	AB	H	HR	BA	PO	A	E	DP	TC/G	FA
1905	NY	A	9	13	.409	3.20	39	22	9	205	178	101	125	3	4	**3**	1	67	4	0	.060	5	35	2	3	1.1	.952
1906			14	13	.519	2.93	28	25	15	206	171	72	107	3	3	0	0	72	9	0	.125	5	35	1	4	1.5	.976
1907			10	8	.556	3.08	25	21	13	166.2	173	83	64	0	0	0	0	64	11	1	.172	7	47	2	0	2.2	.964
1908			4	16	.200	3.01	24	21	7	152.1	155	63	72	0	0	0	0	43	4	0	.093	5	37	1	0	1.8	.977
4 yrs.			37	50	.425	3.06	116	89	44	730	677	319	368	6	7	3	1	246	28	1	.114	22	154	6	7	1.6	.967

Brad Hogg

HOGG, CARTER BRADLEY BR TR 6′ 185 lbs.
B. Mar. 26, 1888, Buena Vista, Ga. D. Apr. 2, 1935, Buena Vista, Ga.

Year	Team	Lg	W	L	PCT	ERA	G	GS	CG	IP	H	BB	SO	ShO	Relief W	Relief L	Relief SV	AB	H	HR	BA	PO	A	E	DP	TC/G	FA
1911	BOS	N	0	3	.000	6.66	8	3	2	25.2	33	14	8	0	0	1	0	9	4	0	.444	2	8	1	0	1.4	.909
1912			1	1	.500	6.97	10	1	0	31	37	16	12	0	1	1	0	11	1	0	.091	0	6	0	0	0.6	1.000
1915	CHI	N	1	0	1.000	2.08	2	2	1	13	12	6	0	1	0	0	0	3	0	0	.000	0	6	0	0	3.0	1.000
1918	PHI	N	13	13	.500	2.53	29	25	17	228	201	61	81	3	1	0	1	79	18	0	.228	8	73	1	7	2.8	.988
1919			5	12	.294	4.43	22	19	13	150.1	163	55	48	0	0	1	0	60	17	0	.283	3	34	0	0	1.7	1.000
5 yrs.			20	29	.408	3.70	71	50	33	448	446	152	149	4	2	3	1	162	40	0	.247	13	127	2	7	2.0	.986

Chief Hogsett

HOGSETT, ELON CHESTER BL TL 6′ 190 lbs.
B. Nov. 2, 1903, Brownell, Kans.

Year	Team	Lg	W	L	PCT	ERA	G	GS	CG	IP	H	BB	SO	ShO	Relief W	Relief L	Relief SV	AB	H	HR	BA	PO	A	E	DP	TC/G	FA
1929	DET	A	1	2	.333	2.83	4	4	2	28.2	34	9	9	1	0	0	0	10	2	0	.200	1	8	0	1	2.3	1.000
1930			9	8	.529	5.42	33	17	4	146	174	63	54	0	2	1	1	58	17	1	.293	10	37	5	1	1.6	.904
1931			3	9	.250	5.93	22	12	5	112.1	150	33	47	0	0	2	2	47	11	0	.234	8	23	1	0	1.5	.969
1932			11	9	.550	3.54	47	15	7	178	201	66	56	0	**6**	3	7	57	14	2	.246	8	46	3	4	1.2	.947
1933			6	10	.375	4.50	45	2	0	116	137	56	39	0	6	**9**	9	38	8	0	.211	4	31	1	2	0.8	.972
1934			3	2	.600	4.29	26	0	0	50.1	61	19	23	0	3	2	3	13	3	0	.231	4	11	0	0	0.6	1.000
1935			6	6	.500	3.54	40	0	0	96.2	109	49	39	0	**6**	**6**	5	23	6	2	.261	5	31	2	2	0.9	.947
1936	2 teams	DET A	(3G 0–1)		STL A	(39G 13–15)																					
″	total		13	16	.448	5.58	42	29	10	219.1	286	91	68	0	1	2	1	70	10	0	.143	2	51	6	2	1.4	.898
1937	STL	A	6	19	.240	6.29	37	26	8	177.1	245	75	68	1	1	0	2	62	13	1	.210	8	28	3	2	1.1	.923
1938	WAS	A	5	6	.455	6.03	31	9	1	91	107	36	33	0	3	2	3	23	7	0	.304	7	18	2	2	0.9	.926
1944	DET	A	0	0	—	0.00	3	0	0	6.1	7	4	5	0	0	0	0	2	0	0	.000	0	1	1	0	0.7	.500
11 yrs.			63	87	.420	5.02	330	114	37	1222	1511	501	441	2	28	27	33	403	91	6	.226	57	285	24	16	1.1	.934
WORLD SERIES																											
1934	DET	A	0	0	—	1.23	3	0	0	7.1	6	3	3	0	0	0	0	3	0	0	.000	0	2	0	0	0.7	1.000
1935			0	0	—	0.00	1	0	0	1	0	1	0	0	0	0	0	0	0	0	—	1	0	0	0	1.0	1.000
2 yrs.			0	0		1.08	4	0	0	8.1	6	4	3	0	0	0	0	3	0	0	.000	1	2	0	0	0.8	1.000

Bobby Hogue

HOGUE, ROBERT CLINTON BR TR 5′10″ 195 lbs.
B. Apr. 5, 1921, Miami, Fla. D. Dec. 22, 1987, Miami, Fla.

Year	Team	Lg	W	L	PCT	ERA	G	GS	CG	IP	H	BB	SO	ShO	Relief W	Relief L	Relief SV	AB	H	HR	BA	PO	A	E	DP	TC/G	FA
1948	BOS	N	8	2	.800	3.23	40	1	0	86.1	88	19	43	0	8	2	2	21	2	0	.095	4	11	0	1	0.4	1.000
1949			2	2	.500	3.13	33	0	0	72	78	25	23	0	2	2	3	21	6	0	.286	3	21	0	1	0.7	1.000
1950			3	5	.375	5.03	36	1	0	62.2	69	31	15	0	3	5	7	13	3	0	.231	1	14	0	4	0.4	1.000

Bobby Hogue *continued*

Year	Team	Lg	W	L	PCT	ERA	G	GS	CG	IP	H	BB	SO	ShO	Relief Pitching W	Relief Pitching L	Relief Pitching SV	Batting AB	Batting H	Batting HR	BA	PO	A	E	DP	TC/G	FA
1951	3 teams BOS N (3G 0–0) STL A (18G 1–1) NY A (7G 1–0)																										
″	total		2	1	.667	4.29	28	0	0	42	39	29	13	0	2	1	1	5	3	0	.600	3	10	0	2	0.5	1.000
1952	2 teams NY A (27G 3–5) STL A (8G 0–1)																										
″	total		3	6	.333	4.66	35	1	0	63.2	62	38	14	0	3	5	4	13	3	0	.231	0	10	3	0	0.4	.769
5 yrs.			18	16	.529	3.97	172	3	0	326.2	336	142	108	0	18	15	17	73	17	0	.233	11	66	3	8	0.5	.962
WORLD SERIES																											
1951	NY	A	0	0	—	0.00	2	0	0	2.2	1	0	0	0	0	0	0	0	0	0	—	0	1	0	0	0.5	1.000

Cal Hogue

HOGUE, CALVIN GREY BR TR 6′ 185 lbs.
B. Oct. 24, 1927, Dayton, Ohio.

Year	Team	Lg	W	L	PCT	ERA	G	GS	CG	IP	H	BB	SO	ShO	Relief Pitching W	Relief Pitching L	Relief Pitching SV	Batting AB	Batting H	Batting HR	BA	PO	A	E	DP	TC/G	FA
1952	PIT	N	1	8	.111	4.84	19	12	3	83.2	79	68	34	0	0	0	0	24	6	0	.250	4	9	2	1	0.8	.867
1953			1	1	.500	5.21	3	2	2	19	19	16	10	0	0	0	0	5	0	0	.000	1	3	0	1	1.3	1.000
1954			0	1	.000	4.91	3	2	0	11	11	12	7	0	0	0	0	3	0	0	.000	0	2	0	0	0.7	1.000
3 yrs.			2	10	.167	4.91	25	16	5	113.2	109	96	51	0	0	0	0	32	6	0	.188	5	14	2	2	0.8	.905

Wally Holborow

HOLBOROW, WALTER ALBERT BR TR 5′11″ 187 lbs.
B. Nov. 30, 1913, New York, N. Y. D. July 14, 1986, Ft. Lauderdale, Fla.

Year	Team	Lg	W	L	PCT	ERA	G	GS	CG	IP	H	BB	SO	ShO	Relief Pitching W	Relief Pitching L	Relief Pitching SV	Batting AB	Batting H	Batting HR	BA	PO	A	E	DP	TC/G	FA
1944	WAS	A	0	0	—	0.00	1	0	0	3	0	2	1	0	0	0	0	0	0	0	—	1	0	0	0	1.0	1.000
1945			1	1	.500	2.30	15	1	1	31.1	20	16	14	1	0	1	0	2	0	0	.000	1	3	1	0	0.3	.800
1948	PHI	A	1	2	.333	5.71	5	1	1	17.1	32	7	3	0	1	1	0	4	2	0	.500	2	6	1	1	1.8	.889
3 yrs.			2	3	.400	3.31	21	2	2	51.2	52	25	18	1	1	2	0	6	2	0	.333	4	9	2	1	0.7	.867

Ken Holcombe

HOLCOMBE, KENNETH EDWARD BR TR 5′11½″ 169 lbs.
B. Aug. 23, 1918, Burnsville, N. C.

Year	Team	Lg	W	L	PCT	ERA	G	GS	CG	IP	H	BB	SO	ShO	Relief Pitching W	Relief Pitching L	Relief Pitching SV	Batting AB	Batting H	Batting HR	BA	PO	A	E	DP	TC/G	FA
1945	NY	A	3	3	.500	1.79	23	2	0	55.1	43	27	20	0	3	2	0	15	2	0	.133	2	10	1	1	0.6	.923
1948	CIN	N	0	0	—	7.71	2	0	0	2.1	3	0	2	0	0	0	0	0	0	0	—	0	0	0	0	0.0	.000
1950	CHI	A	3	10	.231	4.59	24	15	5	96	122	45	37	0	0	1	1	32	5	0	.156	6	16	2	1	1.0	.917
1951			11	12	.478	3.78	28	23	12	159.1	142	68	39	2	1	0	0	44	11	0	.250	8	42	3	5	1.9	.943
1952	2 teams CHI A (7G 0–5) STL A (12G 0–2)																										
″	total		0	7	.000	5.30	19	8	1	56	58	27	19	0	0	1	0	13	1	0	.077	2	15	2	0	1.0	.895
1953	BOS	A	1	0	1.000	6.00	3	0	0	6	9	3	1	0	1	0	1	2	0	0	.000	1	1	0	0	0.7	1.000
6 yrs.			18	32	.360	3.98	99	48	18	375	377	170	118	2	5	4	2	106	19	0	.179	19	84	8	7	1.1	.928

Fred Holdsworth

HOLDSWORTH, FREDERICK WILLIAM BR TR 6′ 1″ 190 lbs.
B. May 29, 1952, Detroit, Mich.

Year	Team	Lg	W	L	PCT	ERA	G	GS	CG	IP	H	BB	SO	ShO	Relief Pitching W	Relief Pitching L	Relief Pitching SV	Batting AB	Batting H	Batting HR	BA	PO	A	E	DP	TC/G	FA
1972	DET	A	0	1	.000	12.86	2	2	0	7	13	2	5	0	0	0	0	3	1	0	.333	1	0	0	0	0.5	1.000
1973			0	1	.000	6.60	5	2	0	15	13	6	9	0	0	0	0	0	0	0	—	2	0	1	0	0.6	.667
1974			0	3	.000	4.25	8	5	0	36	40	14	16	0	0	0	0	0	0	0	—	0	2	2	0	0.5	.500
1976	BAL	A	4	1	.800	2.02	16	0	0	40	24	13	24	0	4	1	2	0	0	0	—	4	3	0	0	0.4	1.000
1977	2 teams BAL A (12G 0–1) MON N (14G 3–3)																										
″	total		3	4	.429	4.02	26	6	0	56	52	34	25	0	0	1	0	10	0	0	.000	5	6	0	2	0.4	1.000
1978	MON	N	0	0	—	7.00	6	0	0	9	16	8	3	0	0	0	0	0	0	0	—	0	2	1	0	0.5	.667
1980	MIL	A	0	0	—	4.50	9	0	0	20	24	9	12	0	0	0	0	0	0	0	—	0	5	0	0	0.6	1.000
7 yrs.			7	10	.412	4.38	72	15	0	183	182	86	94	0	4	2	2	13	1	0	.077	12	18	4	2	0.5	.882

Walter Holke

HOLKE, WALTER HENRY (Union Man) BB TL 6′ 1½″ 185 lbs.
B. Dec. 25, 1892, St. Louis, Mo. D. Oct. 12, 1954, St. Louis, Mo.

Year	Team	Lg	W	L	PCT	ERA	G	GS	CG	IP	H	BB	SO	ShO	Relief Pitching W	Relief Pitching L	Relief Pitching SV	Batting AB	Batting H	Batting HR	BA	PO	A	E	DP	TC/G	FA
1923	PHI	N	0	0	—	0.00	1	0	0	0.1	1	0	0	0	0	0	0	*				17	2	1	1	10.0	.950

Al Holland

HOLLAND, ALFRED WILLIS BR TL 5′11″ 207 lbs.
B. Aug. 16, 1952, Roanoke, Va.

Year	Team	Lg	W	L	PCT	ERA	G	GS	CG	IP	H	BB	SO	ShO	Relief Pitching W	Relief Pitching L	Relief Pitching SV	Batting AB	Batting H	Batting HR	BA	PO	A	E	DP	TC/G	FA
1977	PIT	N	0	0	—	9.00	2	0	0	2	4	0	1	0	0	0	0	0	0	0	—	1	0	0	0	0.5	1.000
1979	SF	N	0	0	—	0.00	3	0	0	7	3	5	7	0	0	0	0	0	0	0	—	0	0	0	0	0.0	.000
1980			5	3	.625	1.76	54	0	0	82	71	34	65	0	5	3	7	5	1	0	.200	3	15	3	1	0.4	.857
1981			7	5	.583	2.41	47	3	0	101	87	44	78	0	6	5	7	16	1	0	.063	7	11	4	0	0.5	.818
1982			7	3	.700	3.33	58	7	0	129.2	115	40	97	0	5	0	5	34	2	0	.059	2	22	2	1	0.4	.923
1983	PHI	N	8	4	.667	2.26	68	0	0	91.2	63	30	100	0	8	4	25	7	0	0	.000	0	5	0	0	0.1	1.000
1984			5	10	.333	3.39	68	0	0	98.1	82	30	61	0	5	**10**	29	5	0	0	.000	1	8	0	0	0.1	1.000
1985	3 teams PHI N (3G 0–1) PIT N (38G 1–3) CAL A (15G 0–1)																										
″	total		1	5	.167	2.90	56	0	0	87	70	31	62	0	1	5	5	5	2	0	.400	4	9	0	1	0.2	1.000
1986	NY	A	1	0	1.000	5.09	25	1	0	40.2	44	9	37	0	1	0	0	0	0	0	—	0	2	2	0	0.2	.500
1987			0	0	—	14.21	3	0	0	6.1	9	9	5	0	0	0	0	0	0	0	—	0	1	0	0	0.3	1.000
10 yrs.			34	30	.531	2.98	384	11	0	645.2	548	232	513	0	31	27	78	72	6	0	.083	18	73	11	3	0.3	.892
LEAGUE CHAMPIONSHIP SERIES																											
1983	PHI	N	0	0	—	0.00	2	0	0	3	1	0	3	0	0	0	1	0	0	0	—	0	0	0	0	0.0	.000
WORLD SERIES																											
1983	PHI	N	0	0	—	0.00	2	0	0	3.2	1	0	5	0	0	0	1	0	0	0	—	0	0	0	0	0.0	.000

Bill Holland

HOLLAND, WILLIAM DAVID BL TL 6′ 1″ 190 lbs.
B. June 4, 1915, Varina, N. C.

Year	Team	Lg	W	L	PCT	ERA	G	GS	CG	IP	H	BB	SO	ShO	Relief Pitching W	Relief Pitching L	Relief Pitching SV	Batting AB	Batting H	Batting HR	BA	PO	A	E	DP	TC/G	FA
1939	WAS	A	0	1	.000	11.25	3	0	0	4	6	5	2	0	0	1	0	0	0	0	—	0	1	0	1	0.3	1.000

Mul Holland

HOLLAND, HOWARD ARTHUR BR TR 6′ 4″ 185 lbs.
B. Jan. 6, 1903, Franklin, Va. D. Feb. 16, 1969, Winchester, Va.

Year	Team	Lg	W	L	PCT	ERA	G	GS	CG	IP	H	BB	SO	ShO	Relief Pitching W	Relief Pitching L	Relief Pitching SV	Batting AB	Batting H	Batting HR	BA	PO	A	E	DP	TC/G	FA
1926	CIN	N	0	0	—	1.35	3	0	0	6.2	3	5	0	0	0	0	0	2	1	0	.500	1	5	0	0	2.0	1.000
1927	NY	N	1	0	1.000	0.00	2	0	0	2	0	3	0	0	1	0	0	0	0	0	—	0	0	0	0	0.0	.000
1929	STL	N	0	1	.000	9.42	8	0	0	14.1	13	7	5	0	0	1	0	4	1	0	.250	0	2	0	1	0.3	1.000
3 yrs.			1	1	.500	6.26	13	0	0	23	16	15	5	0	1	1	0	6	2	0	.333	1	7	0	1	0.6	1.000

Ed Holley

HOLLEY, EDWARD EDGAR BR TR 6′ 1½″ 195 lbs.
B. July 23, 1899, Benton, Ky. D. Oct. 26, 1986, Paducah, Ky.

Year	Team		W	L	PCT	ERA	G	GS	CG	IP	H	BB	SO	ShO	Relief Pitching W	Relief Pitching L	Relief Pitching SV	Batting AB	Batting H	Batting HR	BA	PO	A	E	DP	TC/G	FA
1928	CHI	N	0	0	—	3.77	13	1	0	31	31	16	10	0	0	0	0	5	0	0	.000	0	5	0	0	0.4	1.000
1932	PHI	N	11	14	.440	3.95	34	30	16	228	247	55	87	2	0	0	0	91	12	0	.132	11	39	5	3	1.6	.909
1933			13	15	.464	3.53	30	28	12	206.2	219	62	56	3	0	1	0	74	12	0	.162	8	32	0	2	1.3	1.000
1934	2 teams	PHI N (15G 1–8)	PIT N (5G 0–3)																								
″	total		1	11	.083	8.12	20	17	2	82	105	37	16	0	0	0	0	26	7	0	.269	0	13	2	2	0.8	.867
4 yrs.			25	40	.385	4.40	97	76	30	547.2	602	170	169	5	0	1	0	196	31	0	.158	19	89	7	7	1.2	.939

Bug Holliday

HOLLIDAY, JAMES WEAR BR TR 5′11″ 151 lbs.
B. Feb. 8, 1867, St. Louis, Mo. D. Feb. 15, 1910, Cincinnati, Ohio.

Year	Team		W	L	PCT	ERA	G	GS	CG	IP	H	BB	SO	ShO	Relief Pitching W	Relief Pitching L	Relief Pitching SV	Batting AB	Batting H	Batting HR	BA	PO	A	E	DP	TC/G	FA
1892	CIN	N	0	0	—	11.25	1	0	0	4	13	1	0	0	0	0	0	602	176	13	.292	234	29	22	6	2.1	.923
1896			0	0	—	0.00	1	0	0	1	4	2	0	0	0	0	0	84	27	0	.321	253	20	15	5	2.2	.948
2 yrs.			0	0		9.00	2	0	0	5	17	3	0	0	0	0	0	*				1773	151	135	36	2.3	.934

Carl Holling

HOLLING, CARL BR TR 6′ 1″ 172 lbs.
B. July 9, 1896, Dana, Calif. D. July 18, 1962, Sonoma, Calif.

Year	Team		W	L	PCT	ERA	G	GS	CG	IP	H	BB	SO	ShO	Relief Pitching W	Relief Pitching L	Relief Pitching SV	Batting AB	Batting H	Batting HR	BA	PO	A	E	DP	TC/G	FA
1921	DET	A	3	7	.300	4.30	35	11	4	136	162	58	38	0	1	3	4	48	13	0	.271	13	39	1	3	1.5	.981
1922			1	1	.500	15.43	5	1	0	9.1	21	5	2	0	1	0	0	2	0	0	.000	0	3	0	0	0.6	1.000
2 yrs.			4	8	.333	5.02	40	12	4	145.1	183	63	40	0	2	3	4	50	13	0	.260	13	42	1	3	1.4	.982

Al Hollingsworth

HOLLINGSWORTH, ALBERT WAYNE (Boots) BL TL 6′ 174 lbs.
B. Feb. 25, 1908, St. Louis, Mo.

Year	Team		W	L	PCT	ERA	G	GS	CG	IP	H	BB	SO	ShO	Relief Pitching W	Relief Pitching L	Relief Pitching SV	Batting AB	Batting H	Batting HR	BA	PO	A	E	DP	TC/G	FA
1935	CIN	N	6	13	.316	3.89	38	22	8	173.1	165	76	89	0	1	1	0	54	8	0	.148	9	39	4	0	1.4	.923
1936			9	10	.474	4.16	29	25	9	184	204	66	76	0	1	1	0	73	23	1	.315	10	28	2	2	1.4	.950
1937			9	15	.375	3.91	43	24	11	202.1	229	73	74	1	2	3	5	76	19	0	.250	4	51	4	2	1.4	.932
1938	2 teams	CIN N (9G 2–2)	PHI N (24G 5–16)																								
″	total		7	18	.280	4.36	33	25	12	208.1	220	89	93	1	2	1	0	79	18	0	.228	10	28	0	3	1.2	1.000
1939	2 teams	PHI N (15G 1–9)	BKN N (8G 1–2)																								
″	total		2	11	.154	5.67	23	15	4	87.1	111	38	35	0	1	1	0	28	3	0	.107	3	20	0	1	1.0	1.000
1940	WAS	A	1	0	1.000	5.50	3	2	0	18	18	11	7	0	0	0	0	6	1	0	.167	1	7	0	1	2.7	1.000
1942	STL	A	10	6	.625	2.96	33	18	7	161	173	52	60	1	1	2	4	56	10	0	.179	6	36	1	2	1.3	.977
1943			6	13	.316	4.21	35	20	9	154	169	51	63	1	1	2	3	50	7	0	.140	7	27	2	3	1.0	.944
1944			5	7	.417	4.47	26	10	3	92.2	108	37	22	2	2	1	1	28	2	0	.071	3	14	0	0	0.7	1.000
1945			12	9	.571	2.70	26	22	15	173.1	164	68	64	1	1	1	1	61	12	1	.197	14	38	0	2	2.0	1.000
1946	2 teams	STL A (5G 0–0)	CHI A (21G 3–2)																								
″	total		3	2	.600	4.91	26	2	0	66	86	26	25	0	3	1	1	14	0	0	.000	0	9	0	0	0.3	1.000
11 yrs.			70	104	.402	3.99	315	185	78	1520.1	1647	587	608	7	15	14	15	525	103	2	.196	67	297	13	16	1.2	.966
WORLD SERIES																											
1944	STL	A	0	0	—	2.25	1	0	0	4	5	2	1	0	0	0	0	1	0	0	.000	0	1	0	0	1.0	1.000

Bonnie Hollingsworth

HOLLINGSWORTH, JOHN BURNETTE BR TR 5′10½″ 170 lbs.
B. Dec. 26, 1895, Jacksboro, Tenn. D. Jan. 4, 1990, Knoxville, Tenn.

Year	Team		W	L	PCT	ERA	G	GS	CG	IP	H	BB	SO	ShO	Relief Pitching W	Relief Pitching L	Relief Pitching SV	Batting AB	Batting H	Batting HR	BA	PO	A	E	DP	TC/G	FA
1922	PIT	N	0	0	—	7.90	9	0	0	13.2	17	8	7	0	0	0	0	0	0	0	—	1	1	0	0	0.2	1.000
1923	WAS	A	3	7	.300	4.09	17	8	1	72.2	72	50	26	0	0	2	0	22	2	0	.091	3	14	1	0	1.1	.944
1924	BKN	N	1	0	1.000	6.75	3	1	1	8	7	9	6	0	0	0	0	3	0	0	.000	0	3	0	0	1.0	1.000
1928	BOS	N	0	2	.000	5.24	7	2	0	22.1	30	13	10	0	0	1	0	6	1	0	.167	0	7	0	0	1.0	1.000
4 yrs.			4	9	.308	4.94	36	11	2	116.2	126	80	49	0	0	3	0	31	3	0	.097	4	25	1	0	0.8	.967

Jessie Hollins

HOLLINS, JESSIE EDWARD BR TR 6′ 3″ 190 lbs.
B. Jan. 27, 1970, Conroe, Tex.

Year	Team		W	L	PCT	ERA	G	GS	CG	IP	H	BB	SO	ShO	Relief Pitching W	Relief Pitching L	Relief Pitching SV	Batting AB	Batting H	Batting HR	BA	PO	A	E	DP	TC/G	FA
1992	CHI	N	0	0	—	13.50	4	0	0	4.2	8	5	0	0	0	0	0	0	0	0	—	1	0	0	0	0.3	1.000

John Hollison

HOLLISON, JOHN HENRY (Swede) BR TL 5′ 8″ 162 lbs.
B. May 3, 1870, Chicago, Ill. D. Aug. 19, 1969, Chicago, Ill.

Year	Team		W	L	PCT	ERA	G	GS	CG	IP	H	BB	SO	ShO	Relief Pitching W	Relief Pitching L	Relief Pitching SV	Batting AB	Batting H	Batting HR	BA	PO	A	E	DP	TC/G	FA
1892	CHI	N	0	0	—	2.25	1	0	0	4	1	0	2	0	0	0	0	3	0	0	.000	0	1	0	0	1.0	1.000

Bobo Holloman

HOLLOMAN, ALVA LEE BR TR 6′ 2″ 207 lbs.
B. Mar. 7, 1925, Thomaston, Ga. D. May 1, 1987, Athens, Ga.

Year	Team		W	L	PCT	ERA	G	GS	CG	IP	H	BB	SO	ShO	Relief Pitching W	Relief Pitching L	Relief Pitching SV	Batting AB	Batting H	Batting HR	BA	PO	A	E	DP	TC/G	FA
1953	STL	A	3	7	.300	5.23	22	10	1	65.1	69	50	25	1	0	2	0	19	2	0	.105	8	9	3	1	0.9	.850

Jim Holloway

HOLLOWAY, JAMES MADISON BR TR 6′ 1″ 165 lbs.
B. Sept. 22, 1908, Plaquemine, La.

Year	Team		W	L	PCT	ERA	G	GS	CG	IP	H	BB	SO	ShO	Relief Pitching W	Relief Pitching L	Relief Pitching SV	Batting AB	Batting H	Batting HR	BA	PO	A	E	DP	TC/G	FA
1929	PHI	N	0	0	—	13.50	3	0	0	4.2	10	5	1	0	0	0	0	1	1	0	1.000	1	0	0	0	0.3	1.000

Ken Holloway

HOLLOWAY, KENNETH EUGENE BR TR 6′ 185 lbs.
Born Kenneth Eugene Hollaway.
B. Aug. 8, 1897, Thomas County, Ga. D. Sept. 25, 1968, Thomasville, Ga.

Year	Team		W	L	PCT	ERA	G	GS	CG	IP	H	BB	SO	ShO	Relief Pitching W	Relief Pitching L	Relief Pitching SV	Batting AB	Batting H	Batting HR	BA	PO	A	E	DP	TC/G	FA
1922	DET	A	0	0	—	0.00	1	0	0	1	1	0	1	0	0	0	0	0	0	0	—	0	0	0	0	0.0	.000
1923			11	10	.524	4.45	42	24	7	194	232	75	55	1	3	1	1	65	8	0	.123	15	54	2	2	1.7	.972
1924			14	6	.700	4.07	49	13	5	181.1	209	61	46	0	**9**	2	3	58	11	0	.190	13	53	4	2	1.4	.943
1925			13	4	.765	4.62	38	14	6	157.2	170	67	29	0	4	0	2	48	11	0	.229	7	32	1	1	1.1	.975
1926			4	6	.400	5.12	36	12	3	139	192	42	43	0	0	2	2	46	11	0	.239	3	37	0	1	1.1	1.000
1927			11	12	.478	4.07	36	23	11	183.1	210	61	36	1	1	2	6	62	8	0	.129	9	55	3	1	1.9	.955
1928			4	8	.333	4.34	30	11	5	120.1	137	32	32	0	1	1	2	33	4	0	.121	7	34	3	2	1.5	.932
1929	CLE	A	6	5	.545	3.03	25	11	6	119	118	37	32	2	1	0	0	41	7	0	.171	4	18	2	3	1.0	.917
1930	2 teams	CLE A (12G 1–1)	NY A (16G 0–0)																								
″	total		1	1	.500	6.72	28	2	0	64.1	101	22	19	0	0	0	2	25	3	0	.120	3	18	2	0	0.8	.913
9 yrs.			64	52	.552	4.40	285	110	43	1160	1370	397	293	4	19	8	18	378	63	0	.167	61	301	17	12	1.3	.955

Jeff Holly

HOLLY, JEFFREY OWEN BL TL 6' 5" 210 lbs.
B. Mar. 1, 1953, San Pedro, Calif.

Year	Team	W	L	PCT	ERA	G	GS	CG	IP	H	BB	SO	ShO	Relief Pitching W	Relief Pitching L	Relief Pitching SV	Batting AB	Batting H	Batting HR	BA	PO	A	E	DP	TC/G	FA
1977	MIN A	2	3	.400	6.94	18	5	0	48	57	12	32	0	1	0	0	0	0	0	—	4	4	1	0	0.5	.889
1978		1	1	.500	3.57	15	1	0	35.1	28	18	12	0	1	0	0	0	0	0	—	0	8	0	0	0.5	1.000
1979		0	0	—	7.50	6	0	0	6	10	3	5	0	0	0	0	0	0	0	—	0	1	0	0	0.2	1.000
3 yrs.		3	4	.429	5.64	39	6	0	89.1	95	33	49	0	2	0	0	0	0	0		4	13	1	0	0.5	.944

Brad Holman

HOLMAN, BRADLEY THOMAS BR TR 6' 5" 205 lbs.
Brother of Brian Holman.
B. Feb. 9, 1968, Kansas City, Mo.

Year	Team	W	L	PCT	ERA	G	GS	CG	IP	H	BB	SO	ShO	Relief Pitching W	Relief Pitching L	Relief Pitching SV	Batting AB	Batting H	Batting HR	BA	PO	A	E	DP	TC/G	FA
1993	SEA A	1	3	.250	3.72	19	0	0	36.1	27	16	17	0	1	3	3	0	0	0	—	1	3	0	0	0.2	1.000

Brian Holman

HOLMAN, BRIAN SCOTT BR TR 6' 4" 185 lbs.
Brother of Brad Holman.
B. Jan. 25, 1965, Denver, Colo.

Year	Team	W	L	PCT	ERA	G	GS	CG	IP	H	BB	SO	ShO	Relief Pitching W	Relief Pitching L	Relief Pitching SV	Batting AB	Batting H	Batting HR	BA	PO	A	E	DP	TC/G	FA
1988	MON N	4	8	.333	3.23	18	16	1	100.1	101	34	58	1	0	0	0	28	3	0	.107	4	11	1	0	0.9	.938
1989	2 teams MON N	(10G 1–2)		SEA A	(23G 8–10)																					
"	total	9	12	.429	3.67	33	25	6	191.1	194	77	105	2	0	1	0	8	1	0	.125	11	31	2	3	1.3	.955
1990	SEA A	11	11	.500	4.03	28	28	3	189.2	188	66	121	0	0	0	0	1	0	0	.000	16	17	1	0	1.2	.971
1991		13	14	.481	3.69	30	30	5	195.1	199	77	108	3	0	0	0	0	0	0	—	17	33	2	2	1.7	.962
4 yrs.		37	45	.451	3.71	109	99	15	676.2	682	254	392	6	0	1	0	37	4	0	.108	48	92	6	5	1.3	.959

Scott Holman

HOLMAN, RANDY SCOTT BR TR 6' 1" 190 lbs.
B. Sept. 18, 1958, Santa Paula, Calif.

Year	Team	W	L	PCT	ERA	G	GS	CG	IP	H	BB	SO	ShO	Relief Pitching W	Relief Pitching L	Relief Pitching SV	Batting AB	Batting H	Batting HR	BA	PO	A	E	DP	TC/G	FA
1980	NY N	0	0	—	1.29	4	0	0	7	6	1	3	0	0	0	0	0	0	0	—	0	0	1	0	0.3	.000
1982		2	1	.667	2.36	4	4	1	26.2	23	7	11	0	0	0	0	9	2	0	.222	1	8	0	0	2.3	1.000
1983		1	7	.125	3.74	35	10	0	101	90	52	44	0	0	1	0	23	5	0	.217	16	22	2	1	1.1	.950
3 yrs.		3	8	.273	3.34	43	14	1	134.2	119	60	58	0	0	1	0	32	7	0	.219	17	30	3	1	1.2	.940

Shawn Holman

HOLMAN, SHAWN LEROY BR TR 6' 2" 185 lbs.
B. Nov. 10, 1964, Sewickley, Pa.

Year	Team	W	L	PCT	ERA	G	GS	CG	IP	H	BB	SO	ShO	Relief Pitching W	Relief Pitching L	Relief Pitching SV	Batting AB	Batting H	Batting HR	BA	PO	A	E	DP	TC/G	FA
1989	DET A	0	0	—	1.80	5	0	0	10	8	11	9	0	0	0	0	0	0	0	—	0	1	0	0	0.2	1.000

Darren Holmes

HOLMES, DARREN LEE BR TR 6' 199 lbs.
B. Apr. 25, 1966, Asheville, N. C.

Year	Team	W	L	PCT	ERA	G	GS	CG	IP	H	BB	SO	ShO	Relief Pitching W	Relief Pitching L	Relief Pitching SV	Batting AB	Batting H	Batting HR	BA	PO	A	E	DP	TC/G	FA
1990	LA N	0	1	.000	5.19	14	0	0	17.1	15	11	19	0	0	1	0	0	0	0	—	1	1	0	0	0.1	1.000
1991	MIL A	1	4	.200	4.72	40	0	0	76.1	90	27	59	0	1	4	3	0	0	0	—	4	14	1	0	0.5	.947
1992		4	4	.500	2.55	41	0	0	42.1	35	11	31	0	4	4	6	0	0	0	—	5	4	1	1	0.2	.900
1993	CLR N	3	3	.500	4.05	62	0	0	66.2	56	20	60	0	3	3	25	0	0	0	—	7	6	1	1	0.2	.929
1994		0	3	.000	6.35	29	0	0	28.1	35	24	33	0	0	3	3	1	0	0	.000	2	3	1	0	0.2	.833
1995		6	1	.857	3.24	68	0	0	66.2	59	28	61	0	6	1	14	1	0	0	.000	6	13	1	0	0.3	.950
6 yrs.		14	16	.467	4.11	254	0	0	297.2	290	121	263	0	14	16	51	2	0	0	.000	25	41	5	2	0.3	.930
DIVISIONAL PLAYOFF SERIES																										
1995	CLR N	1	0	1.000	0.00	3	0	0	1.2	6	0	2	0	1	0	0	0	0	0	—	0	0	0	0	0.0	.000

Ducky Holmes

HOLMES, JAMES WILLIAM BL TR 5' 6" 170 lbs.
B. Jan. 28, 1869, Des Moines, Iowa D. Aug. 6, 1932, Truro, Iowa.

Year	Team	W	L	PCT	ERA	G	GS	CG	IP	H	BB	SO	ShO	Relief Pitching W	Relief Pitching L	Relief Pitching SV	Batting AB	Batting H	Batting HR	BA	PO	A	E	DP	TC/G	FA
1895	LOU N	1	0	1.000	5.79	2	1	1	14	16	4	0	0	0	0	0	161	60	3	.373	49	32	21	2	2.4	.794
1896		0	1	.000	7.50	2	1	0	12	26	8	3	0	0	0	0	141	38	0	.270	44	14	19	3	2.1	.753
2 yrs.		1	1	.500	6.58	4	2	1	26	42	12	3	0	0	0	0	*				1638	195	167	35	2.2	.916

Ed Holmes

HOLMES, ELWOOD MARTER (Chick) TR
B. Mar. 22, 1896, Beverly, N. J. D. Apr. 15, 1954, Camden, N. J.

Year	Team	W	L	PCT	ERA	G	GS	CG	IP	H	BB	SO	ShO	Relief Pitching W	Relief Pitching L	Relief Pitching SV	Batting AB	Batting H	Batting HR	BA	PO	A	E	DP	TC/G	FA
1918	PHI A	0	0	—	13.50	2	0	0	2	4	1	0	0	0	0	0	0	0	0	—	0	0	0	0	0.0	.000

Jim Holmes

HOLMES, JAMES SCOTT
B. Aug. 2, 1882, Lawrenceburg, Ky. D. Mar. 10, 1960, Jacksonville, Fla.

Year	Team	W	L	PCT	ERA	G	GS	CG	IP	H	BB	SO	ShO	Relief Pitching W	Relief Pitching L	Relief Pitching SV	Batting AB	Batting H	Batting HR	BA	PO	A	E	DP	TC/G	FA
1906	PHI A	0	1	.000	4.00	3	1	0	9	10	8	1	0	0	0	0	5	3	0	.600	1	3	0	0	1.3	1.000
1908	BKN N	1	4	.200	3.38	13	1	1	40	37	20	10	0	1	**3**	0	13	1	0	.077	0	4	2	0	0.5	.667
2 yrs.		1	5	.167	3.49	16	2	1	49	47	28	11	0	1	3	0	18	4	0	.222	1	7	2	0	0.6	.800

Herm Holshouser

HOLSHOUSER, HERMAN ALEXANDER BR TR 6' 170 lbs.
B. Jan. 20, 1907, Rockwell, N. C. D. July 26, 1994, Concord, N. C.

Year	Team	W	L	PCT	ERA	G	GS	CG	IP	H	BB	SO	ShO	Relief Pitching W	Relief Pitching L	Relief Pitching SV	Batting AB	Batting H	Batting HR	BA	PO	A	E	DP	TC/G	FA
1930	STL A	0	1	.000	7.80	25	1	0	62.1	103	28	37	0	0	1	1	16	2	0	.125	1	11	1	0	0.5	.923

Vern Holtgrave

HOLTGRAVE, LAVERN GEORGE (Woody) BR TR 6' 1" 183 lbs.
B. Oct. 18, 1942, Aviston, Ill.

Year	Team	W	L	PCT	ERA	G	GS	CG	IP	H	BB	SO	ShO	Relief Pitching W	Relief Pitching L	Relief Pitching SV	Batting AB	Batting H	Batting HR	BA	PO	A	E	DP	TC/G	FA
1965	DET A	0	0	—	6.00	1	0	0	3	4	2	2	0	0	0	0	0	0	0	—	0	0	0	0	0.0	.000

Brian Holton

HOLTON, BRIAN JOHN BR TR 6' 3" 190 lbs.
B. Nov. 29, 1959, McKeesport, Pa.

Year	Team	W	L	PCT	ERA	G	GS	CG	IP	H	BB	SO	ShO	Relief Pitching W	Relief Pitching L	Relief Pitching SV	Batting AB	Batting H	Batting HR	BA	PO	A	E	DP	TC/G	FA
1985	LA N	1	1	.500	9.00	3	0	0	4	9	1	1	0	1	1	0	0	0	0	—	0	1	0	0	0.3	1.000
1986		2	3	.400	4.44	12	3	0	24.1	28	6	24	0	2	1	0	5	0	0	.000	3	3	0	0	0.5	1.000
1987		3	2	.600	3.89	53	1	0	83.1	87	32	58	0	3	2	2	5	1	0	.200	8	14	0	2	0.4	1.000
1988		7	3	.700	1.70	45	0	0	84.2	69	26	49	0	7	3	1	10	0	0	.000	8	11	0	0	0.4	1.000
1989	BAL A	5	7	.417	4.02	39	12	0	116.1	140	39	51	0	2	4	0	0	0	0	—	22	9	1	1	0.8	.969
1990		2	3	.400	4.50	33	0	0	58	68	21	27	0	2	3	0	0	0	0	—	6	10	1	0	0.5	.941
6 yrs.		20	19	.513	3.62	185	16	0	370.2	401	125	210	0	17	14	3	20	1	0	.050	47	48	2	3	0.5	.979
LEAGUE CHAMPIONSHIP SERIES																										
1988	LA N	0	0	—	2.25	3	0	0	4	2	1	2	0	0	0	1	1	1	0	1.000	0	1	0	0	0.3	1.000
WORLD SERIES																										
1988	LA N	0	0	—	0.00	1	0	0	2	0	1	0	0	0	0	0	0	0	0	—	0	1	0	0	1.0	1.000

Ken Holtzman

HOLTZMAN, KENNETH DALE
B. Nov. 3, 1945, St. Louis, Mo.

BR TL 6′ 2″ 175 lbs.

Year	Team	W	L	PCT	ERA	G	GS	CG	IP	H	BB	SO	ShO	Relief Pitching W	Relief Pitching L	Relief Pitching SV	Batting AB	Batting H	Batting HR	BA	PO	A	E	DP	TC/G	FA
1965	CHI N	0	0	—	2.25	3	0	0	4	2	3	3	0	0	0	0	0	0	0	—	0	1	0	0	0.3	1.000
1966		11	16	.407	3.79	34	33	9	220.2	194	68	171	0	0	0	0	73	9	0	.123	12	24	4	2	1.2	.900
1967		9	0	1.000	2.53	12	12	3	92.2	76	44	62	0	0	0	0	35	7	0	.200	4	17	0	0	1.8	1.000
1968		11	14	.440	3.35	34	32	6	215	201	76	151	3	0	0	1	80	10	0	.125	2	42	1	3	1.3	.978
1969		17	13	.567	3.59	39	39	12	261	248	93	176	6	0	0	0	100	15	1	.150	6	40	3	2	1.3	.939
1970		17	11	.607	3.38	39	38	15	288	271	94	202	1	0	0	0	105	21	0	.200	11	44	2	1	1.5	.965
1971		9	15	.375	4.48	30	29	9	195	213	64	143	3	0	0	0	69	9	1	.130	6	28	3	2	1.2	.919
1972	OAK A	19	11	.633	2.51	39	37	16	265	232	52	134	4	1	0	0	90	16	0	.178	7	47	1	4	1.4	.982
1973		21	13	.618	2.97	40	40	16	297.1	275	66	157	4	0	0	0	0	0	0	—	15	42	5	2	1.5	.919
1974		19	17	.528	3.07	39	38	9	255	273	51	117	3	0	1	0	0	0	0	—	5	43	1	2	1.3	.980
1975		18	14	.563	3.14	39	38	13	266.1	217	108	122	2	1	0	0	2	0	0	.000	11	58	1	3	1.8	.986
1976	2 teams BAL A (13G 5–4) NY A (21G 9–7)																									
″	total	14	11	.560	3.65	34	34	16	246.2	265	70	66	3	0	0	0	0	0	0		19	42	3	2	1.9	.953
1977	NY A	2	3	.400	5.75	18	11	0	72	105	24	14	0	0	0	0	0	0	0	—	8	21	1	1	1.7	.967
1978	2 teams NY A (5G 1–0) CHI N (23G 0–3)																									
″	total	1	3	.250	5.60	28	9	0	70.2	82	44	39	0	0	0	2	10	2	0	.200	3	11	0	1	0.5	1.000
1979	CHI N	6	9	.400	4.58	23	20	3	118	133	53	44	2	0	0	0	43	10	0	.233	8	11	1	0	0.9	.950
15 yrs.		174	150	.537	3.49	451	410	127	2867.1	2787	910	1601	31	2	1	3	607	99	2	.163	117	471	26	25	1.4	.958

LEAGUE CHAMPIONSHIP SERIES

Year	Team	W	L	PCT	ERA	G	GS	CG	IP	H	BB	SO	ShO	Relief Pitching W	Relief Pitching L	Relief Pitching SV	Batting AB	Batting H	Batting HR	BA	PO	A	E	DP	TC/G	FA
1972	OAK A	0	1	.000	4.50	1	1	0	4	4	2	2	0	0	0	0	1	0	0	.000	0	1	0	0	1.0	1.000
1973		1	0	1.000	0.82	1	1	1	11	3	1	7	0	0	0	0	0	0	0	—	1	2	0	1	3.0	1.000
1974		1	0	1.000	0.00	1	1	1	9	5	2	3	1	0	0	0	0	0	0	—	0	1	0	0	1.0	1.000
1975		0	2	.000	4.09	2	2	0	11	12	1	7	0	0	0	0	0	0	0	—	1	1	0	0	1.0	1.000
4 yrs.		2	3	.400	2.06	5	5	2	35	24	6	19	1	0	0	0	1	0	0	.000	2	5	0	1	1.4	1.000
			5th					4th					1st													

WORLD SERIES

Year	Team	W	L	PCT	ERA	G	GS	CG	IP	H	BB	SO	ShO	Relief Pitching W	Relief Pitching L	Relief Pitching SV	Batting AB	Batting H	Batting HR	BA	PO	A	E	DP	TC/G	FA
1972	OAK A	1	0	1.000	2.13	3	2	0	12.2	11	3	4	0	0	0	0	5	0	0	.000	0	3	1	1	1.3	.750
1973		2	1	.667	4.22	3	3	0	10.2	13	5	6	0	0	0	0	3	2	0	.667	1	3	0	1	1.3	1.000
1974		1	0	1.000	1.50	2	2	0	12	13	4	10	0	0	0	0	4	2	1	.500	0	3	0	0	1.5	1.000
3 yrs.		4	1	.800	2.55	8	7	0	35.1	37	12	20	0	0	0	0	12	4	1	.333	1	9	1	2	1.4	.909

Mark Holzemer

HOLZEMER, MARK HAROLD
B. Aug. 20, 1969, Littleton, Colo.

BL TL 6′ 165 lbs.

Year	Team	W	L	PCT	ERA	G	GS	CG	IP	H	BB	SO	ShO	Relief Pitching W	Relief Pitching L	Relief Pitching SV	Batting AB	Batting H	Batting HR	BA	PO	A	E	DP	TC/G	FA
1993	CAL A	0	3	.000	8.87	5	4	0	23.1	34	13	10	0	0	0	0	0	0	0	—	0	5	0	0	1.0	1.000
1995		0	1	.000	5.40	12	0	0	8.1	11	7	5	0	0	1	0	0	0	0	—	1	3	0	0	0.3	1.000
2 yrs.		0	4	.000	7.96	17	4	0	31.2	45	20	15	0	0	1	0	0	0	0		1	8	0	0	0.5	1.000

Rick Honeycutt

HONEYCUTT, FREDERICK WAYNE
B. June 29, 1952, Chattanooga, Tenn.

BL TL 6′ 1″ 185 lbs.

Year	Team	W	L	PCT	ERA	G	GS	CG	IP	H	BB	SO	ShO	Relief Pitching W	Relief Pitching L	Relief Pitching SV	Batting AB	Batting H	Batting HR	BA	PO	A	E	DP	TC/G	FA
1977	SEA A	0	1	.000	4.34	10	3	0	29	26	11	17	0	0	0	0	0	0	0	—	0	2	0	0	0.2	1.000
1978		5	11	.313	4.89	26	24	4	134.1	150	49	50	1	0	0	0	0	0	0	—	9	28	2	1	1.5	.949
1979		11	12	.478	4.04	33	28	8	194	201	67	83	1	1	3	0	0	0	0	—	6	28	5	2	1.2	.872
1980		10	17	.370	3.95	30	30	9	203	221	60	79	1	0	0	0	0	0	0	—	9	32	2	1	1.4	.953
1981	TEX A	11	6	.647	3.30	20	20	8	128	120	17	40	2	0	0	0	0	0	0	—	3	30	3	1	1.8	.917
1982		5	17	.227	5.27	30	26	4	164	201	54	64	1	0	0	0	0	0	0	—	3	35	2	0	1.3	.950
1983	2 teams TEX A (25G 14–8) LA N (9G 2–3)																									
″	total	16	11	.593	**3.03**	34	32	6	213.2	214	50	74	2	0	0	0	12	1	0	.083	13	55	1	5	2.0	.986
1984	LA N	10	9	.526	2.84	29	28	6	183.2	180	51	75	2	0	0	0	56	8	0	.143	10	42	3	2	1.9	.945
1985		8	12	.400	3.42	31	25	1	142	141	49	67	0	0	1	1	38	5	0	.132	9	37	2	1	1.5	.958
1986		11	9	.550	3.32	32	28	0	171	164	45	100	0	1	0	0	43	3	0	.070	9	35	1	2	1.4	.978
1987	2 teams LA N (27G 2–12) OAK A (7G 1–4)																									
″	total	3	16	.158	4.72	34	24	1	139.1	158	54	102	1	0	1	0	30	7	0	.233	5	20	2	0	0.8	.926
1988	OAK A	3	2	.600	3.50	55	0	0	79.2	74	25	47	0	3	2	7	0	0	0	—	3	18	2	3	0.4	.913
1989		2	2	.500	2.35	64	0	0	76.2	56	26	52	0	2	2	12	0	0	0	—	4	16	1	1	0.3	.952
1990		2	2	.500	2.70	63	0	0	63.1	46	22	38	0	2	2	7	2	0	0	.000	0	15	1	0	0.3	.938
1991		2	4	.333	3.58	43	0	0	37.2	37	20	26	0	2	4	0	0	0	0	—	4	4	0	1	0.2	1.000
1992		1	4	.200	3.69	54	0	0	39	41	10	32	0	1	4	3	0	0	0	—	3	2	1	0	0.1	.833
1993		1	4	.200	2.81	52	0	0	41.2	30	20	21	0	1	4	1	0	0	0	—	2	5	1	1	0.2	.875
1994	TEX A	1	2	.333	7.20	42	0	0	25	37	9	18	0	1	2	1	0	0	0	—	2	7	1	0	0.2	.900
1995	2 teams OAK A (49G 5–1) NY A (3G 0–0)																									
″	total	5	1	.833	2.96	52	0	0	45.2	39	10	21	0	5	1	2	0	0	0	—	3	5	1	0	0.2	.889
19 yrs.		107	142	.430	3.73	734	268	47	2110.2	2136	649	1006	11	19	26	34	181	24	0	.133	97	416	31	21	0.7	.943

LEAGUE CHAMPIONSHIP SERIES

Year	Team	W	L	PCT	ERA	G	GS	CG	IP	H	BB	SO	ShO	Relief Pitching W	Relief Pitching L	Relief Pitching SV	Batting AB	Batting H	Batting HR	BA	PO	A	E	DP	TC/G	FA
1983	LA N	0	0	—	21.60	2	0	0	1.2	4	0	2	0	0	0	0	0	0	0	—	1	0	0	0	0.5	1.000
1985		0	0	—	13.50	2	0	0	1.1	4	2	1	0	0	0	0	0	0	0	—	0	1	0	0	0.5	1.000
1988	OAK A	1	0	1.000	0.00	3	0	0	2	0	2	0	0	1	0	0	0	0	0	—	0	0	0	0	0.0	.000
1989		0	0	—	32.40	3	0	0	1.2	6	5	1	0	0	0	0	0	0	0	—	0	0	0	0	0.0	.000
1990		0	0	—	0.00	3	0	0	1.2	0	0	0	0	0	0	1	0	0	0	—	0	1	0	0	0.3	1.000
1992		0	0	—	0.00	2	0	0	2	0	0	1	0	0	0	0	0	0	0	—	0	0	0	0	0.0	.000
6 yrs.		1	0	1.000	10.45	15	0	0	10.1	14	9	5	0	1	0	1	0	0	0		1	2	0	0	0.2	1.000
						1st																				

WORLD SERIES

Year	Team	W	L	PCT	ERA	G	GS	CG	IP	H	BB	SO	ShO	Relief Pitching W	Relief Pitching L	Relief Pitching SV	Batting AB	Batting H	Batting HR	BA	PO	A	E	DP	TC/G	FA
1988	OAK A	1	0	1.000	0.00	3	0	0	3.1	0	0	5	0	1	0	0	0	0	0	—	0	0	0	0	0.0	.000
1989		0	0	—	6.75	3	0	0	2.2	4	0	2	0	0	0	0	0	0	0	—	0	0	0	0	0.0	.000
1990		0	0	—	0.00	1	0	0	1.2	2	1	0	0	0	0	0	0	0	0	—	0	0	0	0	0.0	—
3 yrs.		1	0	1.000	2.35	7	0	0	7.2	6	1	7	0	1	0	0	0	0	0		0	0	0	0	0.0	

Don Hood

HOOD, DONALD HARRIS
B. Oct. 16, 1949, Florence, S. C.

BL TL 6′ 2″ 180 lbs.

Year	Team	W	L	PCT	ERA	G	GS	CG	IP	H	BB	SO	ShO	Relief Pitching W	Relief Pitching L	Relief Pitching SV	Batting AB	Batting H	Batting HR	BA	PO	A	E	DP	TC/G	FA
1973	BAL A	3	2	.600	3.94	8	4	1	32	31	6	18	1	2	0	1	0	0	0	—	1	3	2	1	0.8	.667
1974		1	1	.500	3.47	20	2	0	57	47	20	26	0	1	0	1	0	0	0	—	1	9	1	0	0.6	.909
1975	CLE A	6	10	.375	4.39	29	19	2	135.1	136	57	51	0	1	1	0	0	0	0	—	7	15	3	0	0.8	.880
1976		3	5	.375	4.85	33	6	0	78	89	41	32	0	2	1	1	0	0	0	—	10	12	2	0	0.7	.917
1977		2	1	.667	3.00	41	5	1	105	87	49	62	0	1	0	0	0	0	0	—	4	10	2	1	0.4	.875

Don Hood *continued*

Year	Team		W	L	PCT	ERA	G	GS	CG	IP	H	BB	SO	ShO	Relief Pitching W	Relief Pitching L	Relief Pitching SV	Batting AB	Batting H	HR	BA	PO	A	E	DP	TC/G	FA
1978			5	6	.455	4.47	36	19	1	155	166	77	73	0	0	1	0	0	0	0	—	6	26	1	2	0.9	.970
1979	**2 teams**	**CLE A**	(13G 1–0)		**NY A**	(27G 3–1)																					
"	**total**		4	1	.800	3.24	40	6	0	89	75	44	29	0	2	1	2	0	0	0		5	18	0	2	0.6	1.000
1980	**STL**	**N**	4	6	.400	3.40	33	8	1	82	90	34	35	0	1	4	0	20	4	0	.200	7	15	1	1	0.7	.957
1982	**KC**	**A**	4	0	1.000	3.51	30	3	0	66.2	71	22	31	0	1	0	1	0	0	0	—	6	11	1	0	0.6	.944
1983			2	3	.400	2.27	27	0	0	47.2	48	14	17	0	2	3	0	0	0	0	—	3	14	3	3	0.7	.850
10 yrs.			34	35	.493	3.79	297	72	6	847.2	840	364	374	1	13	11	6	20	4	0	.200	50	133	16	10	0.7	.920

Wally Hood

HOOD, WALLACE JAMES JR. BR TR 6′ 1″ 190 lbs.
Son of Wally Hood.
B. Sept. 24, 1925, Los Angeles, Calif.

Year	Team		W	L	PCT	ERA	G	GS	CG	IP	H	BB	SO	ShO	Relief W	Relief L	Relief SV	AB	H	HR	BA	PO	A	E	DP	TC/G	FA
1949	**NY**	**A**	0	0	—	0.00	2	0	0	2.1	0	1	2	0	0	0	0	0	0	0	—	0	0	0	0	0.0	.000

Chris Hook

HOOK, CHRISTOPHER WAYNE BR TR 6′ 5″ 230 lbs.
B. Aug. 4, 1968, San Diego, Calif.

Year	Team		W	L	PCT	ERA	G	GS	CG	IP	H	BB	SO	ShO	Relief W	Relief L	Relief SV	AB	H	HR	BA	PO	A	E	DP	TC/G	FA
1995	**SF**	**N**	5	1	.833	5.50	45	0	0	52.1	55	29	40	0	5	1	0	3	0	0	.000	5	4	0	1	0.2	1.000

Jay Hook

HOOK, JAMES WESLEY BL TR 6′ 2″ 182 lbs.
B. Nov. 18, 1936, Waukegan, Ill.

Year	Team		W	L	PCT	ERA	G	GS	CG	IP	H	BB	SO	ShO	Relief W	Relief L	Relief SV	AB	H	HR	BA	PO	A	E	DP	TC/G	FA
1957	**CIN**	**N**	0	1	.000	4.50	3	2	0	10	6	8	6	0	0	0	0	3	0	0	.000	2	1	0	0	1.0	1.000
1958			0	1	.000	12.00	1	1	0	3	3	2	5	0	0	0	0	1	0	0	.000	0	0	0	0	0.0	.000
1959			5	5	.500	5.13	17	15	4	79	79	39	37	0	0	0	0	24	3	0	.125	7	8	1	2	0.9	.938
1960			11	18	.379	4.50	36	33	10	222	222	73	103	2	0	0	0	72	6	0	.083	19	30	1	5	1.4	.980
1961			1	3	.250	7.76	22	5	0	62.2	83	22	36	0	1	0	0	15	2	0	.133	10	4	0	0	0.6	1.000
1962	**NY**	**N**	8	19	.296	4.84	37	34	13	213.2	230	71	113	0	1	0	0	69	14	0	.203	22	31	3	2	1.5	.946
1963			4	14	.222	5.48	41	20	3	152.2	168	53	89	0	1	0	1	38	9	0	.237	11	20	3	1	0.8	.912
1964			0	1	.000	9.31	3	2	0	9.2	17	7	5	0	0	0	0	3	0	0	.000	1	3	0	0	1.3	1.000
8 yrs.			29	62	.319	5.23	160	112	30	752.2	808	275	394	2	3	0	1	225	34	0	.151	72	97	8	10	1.1	.955

Cy Hooker

HOOKER, WILLIAM EDWARD TR 5′ 6″
Born William Edward Hoch.
B. Aug. 28, 1880, Richmond, Va. D. July 2, 1929, Richmond, Va.

Year	Team		W	L	PCT	ERA	G	GS	CG	IP	H	BB	SO	ShO	Relief W	Relief L	Relief SV	AB	H	HR	BA	PO	A	E	DP	TC/G	FA
1902	**CIN**	**N**	0	1	.000	4.50	1	1	1	8	11	0	0	0	0	0	0	3	0	0	.000	0	1	1	0	2.0	.500
1903			0	0	—	0.00	1	0	0	2.1	2	2	0	0	0	0	0	1	0	0	.000	0	0	0	0	0.0	.000
2 yrs.			0	1	.000	3.48	2	1	1	10.1	13	2	0	0	0	0	0	4	0	0	.000	0	1	1	0	1.0	.500

Bob Hooper

HOOPER, ROBERT NELSON BR TR 5′11″ 195 lbs.
B. May 30, 1922, Leamington, Ont., Canada
D. Mar. 17, 1980, New Brunswick, N. J.

Year	Team		W	L	PCT	ERA	G	GS	CG	IP	H	BB	SO	ShO	Relief W	Relief L	Relief SV	AB	H	HR	BA	PO	A	E	DP	TC/G	FA
1950	**PHI**	**A**	15	10	.600	5.02	45	20	3	170.1	181	91	58	0	3	6	5	56	7	1	.125	19	37	2	10	1.3	.966
1951			12	10	.545	4.38	38	23	9	189	192	61	64	0	1	1	5	72	15	1	.208	18	37	3	3	1.5	.948
1952			8	15	.348	5.18	43	14	4	144.1	158	68	40	0	6	4	6	41	8	2	.195	22	32	1	5	1.3	.982
1953	**CLE**	**A**	5	4	.556	4.02	43	0	0	69.1	50	38	16	0	5	4	7	12	1	0	.083	3	16	0	2	0.4	1.000
1954			0	0	—	4.93	17	0	0	34.2	39	16	12	0	0	0	2	5	0	0	.000	2	6	0	0	0.5	1.000
1955	**CIN**	**N**	0	2	.000	7.62	8	0	0	13	20	6	6	0	0	2	0	1	0	0	.000	0	4	0	0	0.5	1.000
6 yrs.			40	41	.494	4.80	194	57	16	620.2	640	280	196	0	15	17	25	187	31	4	.166	64	132	6	20	1.0	.970

Harry Hooper

HOOPER, HARRY BARTHOLOMEW BL TR 5′10″ 168 lbs.
B. Aug. 24, 1887, Bell Station, Calif. D. Dec. 18, 1974, Santa Cruz, Calif.
Hall of Fame 1971.

Year	Team		W	L	PCT	ERA	G	GS	CG	IP	H	BB	SO	ShO	Relief W	Relief L	Relief SV	AB	H	HR	BA	PO	A	E	DP	TC/G	FA
1913	**BOS**	**A**	0	0	—	0.00	1	0	0	1	0	1	0	0	0	0	0	*				124	14	7	3	2.0	.952

Leon Hooten

HOOTEN, MICHAEL LEON BR TR 5′11″ 180 lbs.
B. Apr. 4, 1948, Downey, Calif.

Year	Team		W	L	PCT	ERA	G	GS	CG	IP	H	BB	SO	ShO	Relief W	Relief L	Relief SV	AB	H	HR	BA	PO	A	E	DP	TC/G	FA
1974	**OAK**	**A**	0	0	—	3.12	6	0	0	8.2	6	4	1	0	0	0	0	0	0	0	—	0	2	0	0	0.3	1.000

Burt Hooton

HOOTON, BURT CARLTON (Happy) BR TR 6′ 1″ 210 lbs.
B. Feb. 7, 1950, Greenville, Tex.

Year	Team		W	L	PCT	ERA	G	GS	CG	IP	H	BB	SO	ShO	Relief W	Relief L	Relief SV	AB	H	HR	BA	PO	A	E	DP	TC/G	FA
1971	**CHI**	**N**	2	0	1.000	2.14	3	3	2	21	8	10	22	1	0	0	0	7	0	0	.000	3	0	1	0	1.3	.750
1972			11	14	.440	2.80	33	31	9	218.1	201	81	132	3	1	0	0	72	9	1	.125	13	35	1	2	1.5	.980
1973			14	17	.452	3.67	42	34	9	240	248	73	134	2	1	2	0	70	9	0	.129	21	32	4	0	1.4	.930
1974			7	11	.389	4.81	48	21	3	176	214	51	94	1	2	2	1	50	3	0	.060	15	39	1	1	1.1	.982
1975	**2 teams**	**CHI N**	(3G 0–2)		**LA N**	(31G 18–7)																					
"	**total**		18	9	.667	3.07	34	33	12	234.2	190	68	153	4	0	1	0	73	9	1	.123	13	29	1	0	1.3	.977
1976	**LA**	**N**	11	15	.423	3.26	33	33	8	226.2	203	60	116	4	0	0	0	62	6	0	.097	6	31	0	0	1.1	1.000
1977			12	7	.632	2.62	32	31	6	223	184	60	153	2	0	0	1	67	11	0	.164	11	31	0	4	1.3	1.000
1978			19	10	.655	2.71	32	32	10	236	196	61	104	3	0	0	0	67	10	0	.149	12	33	1	4	1.4	.978
1979			11	10	.524	2.97	29	29	12	212	191	63	129	1	0	0	0	75	11	0	.147	12	26	0	3	1.3	1.000
1980			14	8	.636	3.65	34	33	4	207	194	64	118	2	0	0	1	64	4	1	.063	23	26	4	2	1.6	.925
1981			11	6	.647	2.28	23	23	5	142	124	33	74	4	0	0	0	42	8	0	.190	4	18	0	2	1.0	1.000
1982			4	7	.364	4.03	21	21	2	120.2	130	33	51	2	0	0	0	35	3	1	.086	9	21	0	1	1.4	1.000
1983			9	8	.529	4.22	33	27	2	160	156	59	87	0	0	0	0	50	8	0	.160	8	24	2	1	1.0	.941
1984			3	6	.333	3.44	54	6	0	110	109	43	62	0	3	4	4	14	1	0	.071	6	15	0	1	0.4	1.000
1985	**TEX**	**A**	5	8	.385	5.23	29	20	2	124	149	40	62	0	0	0	0	0	0	0	—	9	13	1	0	0.8	.957
15 yrs.			151	136	.526	3.38	480	377	86	2651.1	2497	799	1491	29	7	9	7	748	92	4	.123	165	373	16	21	1.2	.971
DIVISIONAL PLAYOFF SERIES																											
1981	**LA**	**N**	1	0	1.000	1.29	1	1	0	7	3	3	2	0	0	0	0	3	0	0	.000	0	0	0	0	0.0	.000
LEAGUE CHAMPIONSHIP SERIES																											
1977	**LA**	**N**	0	0	—	16.20	1	1	0	1.2	2	4	1	0	0	0	0	1	1	0	1.000	0	1	0	0	1.0	1.000
1978			0	0	—	7.71	1	1	0	4.2	10	0	5	0	0	0	0	2	0	0	.000	1	0	0	0	1.0	1.000
1981			2	0	1.000	0.00	2	2	0	14.2	11	6	7	0	0	0	0	5	0	0	.000	0	1	0	0	0.5	1.000
3 yrs.			2	0	1.000	3.00	4	4	0	21	23	10	13	0	0	0	0	8	1	0	.125	1	2	0	0	0.8	1.000

Burt Hooton *continued*

Year	Team		W	L	PCT	ERA	G	GS	CG	IP	H	BB	SO	ShO	Relief W	Relief L	Relief SV	AB	H	HR	BA	PO	A	E	DP	TC/G	FA
WORLD SERIES																											
1977	LA	N	1	1	.500	3.75	2	2	1	12	8	2	9	0	0	0	0	5	0	0	.000	0	0	0	0	0.0	.000
1978			1	1	.500	6.48	2	2	0	8.1	13	3	6	0	0	0	0	0	0	0	—	1	0	0	0	0.5	1.000
1981			1	1	.500	1.59	2	2	0	11.1	8	9	3	0	0	0	0	4	0	0	.000	1	0	0	0	0.5	1.000
3 yrs.			3	3	.500	3.69	6	6	1	31.2	29	14	18	0	0	0	0	9	0	0	.000	2	0	0	0	0.3	1.000

Dick Hoover

HOOVER, RICHARD LLOYD BL TL 6′ 170 lbs.
B. Dec. 11, 1925, Columbus, Ohio D. Apr. 12, 1981, Lake Placid, Fla.

Year	Team		W	L	PCT	ERA	G	GS	CG	IP	H	BB	SO	ShO	Relief W	Relief L	Relief SV	AB	H	HR	BA	PO	A	E	DP	TC/G	FA
1952	BOS	N	0	0	—	7.71	2	0	0	4.2	8	3	0	0	0	0	0	0	0	0	—	1	0	0	0	0.5	1.000

John Hoover

HOOVER, JOHN NICKLAUS BR TR 6′ 2″ 190 lbs.
B. Dec. 22, 1962, Fresno, Calif.

Year	Team		W	L	PCT	ERA	G	GS	CG	IP	H	BB	SO	ShO	Relief W	Relief L	Relief SV	AB	H	HR	BA	PO	A	E	DP	TC/G	FA
1990	TEX	A	0	0	—	11.57	2	0	0	4.2	8	3	0	0	0	0	0	0	0	0	—	0	0	0	0	0.0	.000

John Hope

HOPE, JOHN ALAN BR TR 6′ 3″ 195 lbs.
B. Dec. 21, 1970, Ft. Lauderdale, Fla.

Year	Team		W	L	PCT	ERA	G	GS	CG	IP	H	BB	SO	ShO	Relief W	Relief L	Relief SV	AB	H	HR	BA	PO	A	E	DP	TC/G	FA
1993	PIT	N	0	2	.000	4.03	7	7	0	38	47	8	8	0	0	0	0	13	1	0	.077	1	10	1	0	1.7	.917
1994			0	0	—	5.79	9	0	0	14	18	4	6	0	0	0	0	3	1	0	.333	1	3	0	0	0.4	1.000
1995			0	0	—	30.86	3	0	0	2.1	8	4	2	0	0	0	0	0	0	0	—	0	0	0	0	0.0	.000
3 yrs.			0	2	.000	5.63	19	7	0	54.1	73	16	16	0	0	0	0	16	2	0	.125	2	13	1	0	0.8	.938

Sam Hope

HOPE, SAMUEL BR TR 5′10″
B. Dec. 4, 1878, Brooklyn, N. Y. D. June 30, 1946, Greenport, N. Y.

Year	Team		W	L	PCT	ERA	G	GS	CG	IP	H	BB	SO	ShO	Relief W	Relief L	Relief SV	AB	H	HR	BA	PO	A	E	DP	TC/G	FA
1907	PHI	A	0	0	—	0.00	1	0	0	0.1	3	0	0	0	0	0	0	0	0	0	—	0	1	0	0	1.0	1.000

Paul Hopkins

HOPKINS, PAUL HENRY BR TR 6′ 175 lbs.
B. Sept. 25, 1904, Chester, Pa.

Year	Team		W	L	PCT	ERA	G	GS	CG	IP	H	BB	SO	ShO	Relief W	Relief L	Relief SV	AB	H	HR	BA	PO	A	E	DP	TC/G	FA
1927	WAS	A	1	0	1.000	5.00	2	1	0	9	13	4	5	0	0	0	0	3	2	0	.667	0	4	0	0	2.0	1.000
1929	2 teams	WAS A (7G 0–1) STL A (2G 0–0)																									
″	total		0	1	.000	1.96	9	0	0	18.1	15	11	6	0	0	1	0	3	0	0	.000	1	2	0	0	0.3	1.000
2 yrs.			1	1	.500	2.96	11	1	0	27.1	28	15	11	0	0	1	0	6	2	0	.333	1	6	0	0	0.6	1.000

Bill Hopper

HOPPER, WILLIAM BOOTH (Bird Dog) BR TR 6′ 175 lbs.
B. Aug. 26, 1890, Jackson, Tenn. D. Jan. 14, 1965, Allen Park, Mich.

Year	Team		W	L	PCT	ERA	G	GS	CG	IP	H	BB	SO	ShO	Relief W	Relief L	Relief SV	AB	H	HR	BA	PO	A	E	DP	TC/G	FA
1913	STL	N	0	3	.000	3.75	3	3	2	24	20	8	3	0	0	0	0	8	3	0	.375	1	6	1	0	2.7	.875
1914			0	0	—	3.60	3	0	0	5	6	5	1	0	0	0	0	0	0	0	—	0	2	0	0	0.7	1.000
1915	WAS	A	0	1	.000	4.60	13	0	0	31.1	39	16	8	0	0	1	1	5	1	0	.200	3	13	2	1	1.4	.889
3 yrs.			0	4	.000	4.18	19	3	2	60.1	65	29	12	0	0	1	1	13	4	0	.308	4	21	3	1	1.5	.893

Jim Hopper

HOPPER, JAMES McDANIEL BR TR 6′ 1″ 175 lbs.
B. Sept. 1, 1919, Charlotte, N. C. D. Jan. 23, 1982, Charlotte, N. C.

Year	Team		W	L	PCT	ERA	G	GS	CG	IP	H	BB	SO	ShO	Relief W	Relief L	Relief SV	AB	H	HR	BA	PO	A	E	DP	TC/G	FA
1946	PIT	N	0	1	.000	10.38	2	1	0	4.1	6	3	1	0	0	0	0	0	0	0	—	0	1	0	0	0.5	1.000

Lefty Hopper

HOPPER, CLARENCE F. TL
B. May 27, 1874, Jersey City, N. J. Deceased.

Year	Team		W	L	PCT	ERA	G	GS	CG	IP	H	BB	SO	ShO	Relief W	Relief L	Relief SV	AB	H	HR	BA	PO	A	E	DP	TC/G	FA
1898	BKN	N	0	2	.000	4.91	2	2	2	11	14	5	5	0	0	0	0	4	0	0	.000	0	4	1	0	2.5	.800

John Horan

HORAN, PATRICK J. 5′10½″ 160 lbs.
B. 1863, Ireland Deceased.

Year	Team		W	L	PCT	ERA	G	GS	CG	IP	H	BB	SO	ShO	Relief W	Relief L	Relief SV	AB	H	HR	BA	PO	A	E	DP	TC/G	FA
1884	CHI	U	3	6	.333	3.40	13	10	9	98	94	24	55	0	0	0	0	68	6	0	.088	14	21	12	3	2.0	.745

Joe Horlen

HORLEN, JOEL EDWARD BR TR 6′ 170 lbs.
B. Aug. 14, 1937, San Antonio, Tex.

Year	Team		W	L	PCT	ERA	G	GS	CG	IP	H	BB	SO	ShO	Relief W	Relief L	Relief SV	AB	H	HR	BA	PO	A	E	DP	TC/G	FA
1961	CHI	A	1	3	.250	6.62	5	4	0	17.2	25	13	11	0	1	0	0	7	0	0	.000	3	3	0	1	1.2	1.000
1962			7	6	.538	4.89	20	19	5	108.2	108	43	63	1	0	0	0	38	2	0	.053	10	28	1	0	2.0	.974
1963			11	7	.611	3.27	33	21	3	124	122	55	61	0	0	2	0	40	9	0	.225	4	30	0	0	1.0	1.000
1964			13	9	.591	1.88	32	28	9	210.2	142	55	138	2	1	0	0	69	11	0	.159	14	46	0	3	1.9	1.000
1965			13	13	.500	2.88	34	34	7	219	203	39	125	4	0	0	0	68	9	0	.132	10	41	3	0	1.6	.944
1966			10	13	.435	2.43	37	29	4	211	185	53	124	2	1	0	1	60	4	0	.067	25	57	3	5	2.3	.965
1967			19	7	**.731**	**2.06**	35	35	13	258	188	58	103	**6**	0	0	0	83	14	0	.169	29	53	0	4	2.3	1.000
1968			12	14	.462	2.37	35	35	4	223.2	197	70	102	1	0	0	0	67	7	0	.104	14	47	3	3	1.8	.953
1969			13	16	.448	3.78	36	35	7	235.2	237	77	121	2	0	0	0	77	14	0	.182	13	32	3	0	1.3	.938
1970			6	16	.273	4.87	28	26	4	172	198	41	77	0	0	0	0	52	6	0	.115	22	42	1	1	2.3	.985
1971			8	9	.471	4.27	34	18	3	137	150	30	82	0	1	2	2	40	4	0	.100	10	27	2	0	1.1	.949
1972	OAK	A	3	4	.429	3.00	32	6	0	84	74	20	58	0	2	0	1	17	3	0	.176	5	15	0	0	0.6	1.000
12 yrs.			116	117	.498	3.11	361	290	59	2001.1	1829	554	1065	18	6	4	4	618	83	0	.134	159	421	16	17	1.7	.973
LEAGUE CHAMPIONSHIP SERIES																											
1972	OAK	A	0	1	.000	∞	1	0	0		0	1	0	0	0	1	0	0	0	0	—	0	0	0	0	0.0	.000
WORLD SERIES																											
1972	OAK	A	0	0	—	6.75	1	0	0	1.1	2	2	1	0	0	0	0	0	0	0	—	1	0	0	0	1.0	1.000

Trader Horne

HORNE, BERLYN DALE (Sonny) BB TR 5′ 9″ 155 lbs.
B. Apr. 12, 1899, Bachman, Ohio D. Feb. 3, 1983, Franklin, Ohio.

Year	Team		W	L	PCT	ERA	G	GS	CG	IP	H	BB	SO	ShO	Relief W	Relief L	Relief SV	AB	H	HR	BA	PO	A	E	DP	TC/G	FA
1929	CHI	N	1	1	.500	5.09	11	1	0	23	24	21	6	0	1	1	0	5	2	0	.400	2	6	0	0	0.7	1.000

Jack Horner

HORNER, WILLIAM FRANK BR
B. Sept. 21, 1863, Baltimore, Md. D. July 14, 1910, New Orleans, La.

Year	Team		W	L	PCT	ERA	G	GS	CG	IP	H	BB	SO	ShO	Relief W	Relief L	Relief SV	AB	H	HR	BA	PO	A	E	DP	TC/G	FA
1894	BAL	N	0	1	.000	9.00	2	1	1	11	15	7	2	0	0	0	1	6	1	0	.167	0	3	1	0	2.0	.750

Joe Hornung

HORNUNG, MICHAEL JOSEPH (Ubbo Ubbo) BR TR 5′ 8½″ 164 lbs.
B. June 12, 1857, Carthage, N. Y. D. Oct. 30, 1931, New York, N. Y.

Year	Team		W	L	PCT	ERA	G	GS	CG	IP	H	BB	SO	ShO	Relief W	Relief L	Relief SV	AB	H	HR	BA	PO	A	E	DP	TC/G	FA
1880	BUF	N	0	0	—	6.00	1	0	0	3	2	1	0	0	0	0	0	*				135	12	26	2	2.2	.850

Hanson Horsey

HORSEY, HANSON BR TR 5′11″ 165 lbs.
B. Nov. 26, 1889, Galena, Md. D. Dec. 1, 1949, Millington, Md.

Year	Team	W	L	PCT	ERA	G	GS	CG	IP	H	BB	SO	ShO	Relief Pitching W	Relief Pitching L	Relief Pitching SV	Batting AB	Batting H	Batting HR	BA	PO	A	E	DP	TC/G	FA
1912	CIN N	0	0	—	22.50	1	0	0	4	14	3	0	0	0	0	0	2	0	0	.000	0	0	0	0	0.0	.000

Vince Horsman

HORSMAN, VINCENT STANLEY JOSEPH BR TL 6′ 2″ 175 lbs.
B. Mar. 9, 1967, Halifax, Nova Scotia, Canada.

Year	Team	W	L	PCT	ERA	G	GS	CG	IP	H	BB	SO	ShO	Relief Pitching W	Relief Pitching L	Relief Pitching SV	Batting AB	Batting H	Batting HR	BA	PO	A	E	DP	TC/G	FA
1991	TOR A	0	0	—	0.00	4	0	0	4	2	3	2	0	0	0	0	0	0	0	—	0	0	0	0	0.0	.000
1992	OAK A	2	1	.667	2.49	58	0	0	43.1	39	21	18	0	2	1	1	0	0	0	—	1	5	0	0	0.1	1.000
1993		2	0	1.000	5.40	40	0	0	25	25	15	17	0	2	0	0	0	0	0	—	0	2	0	0	0.1	1.000
1994		0	1	.000	4.91	33	0	0	29.1	29	11	20	0	0	1	0	0	0	0	—	2	6	0	0	0.2	1.000
1995	MIN A	0	0	—	7.00	6	0	0	9	12	4	4	0	0	0	0	0	0	0	—	1	3	0	0	0.7	1.000
5 yrs.		4	2	.667	4.07	141	0	0	110.2	107	54	61	0	4	2	1	0	0	0		4	16	0	0	0.1	1.000

Oscar Horstmann

HORSTMANN, OSCAR THEODORE BR TR 5′11″ 165 lbs.
B. June 2, 1891, Alma, Mo. D. May 11, 1977, Salina, Kans.

Year	Team	W	L	PCT	ERA	G	GS	CG	IP	H	BB	SO	ShO	Relief Pitching W	Relief Pitching L	Relief Pitching SV	Batting AB	Batting H	Batting HR	BA	PO	A	E	DP	TC/G	FA
1917	STL N	9	4	.692	3.45	35	11	4	138.1	111	54	50	1	4	0	1	46	9	0	.196	3	40	2	2	1.3	.956
1918		0	2	.000	5.48	9	2	0	23	29	14	6	0	0	1	0	4	0	0	.000	1	12	0	0	1.4	1.000
1919		0	1	.000	3.00	6	2	0	15	14	12	5	0	0	0	0	2	1	0	.500	1	5	0	0	1.0	1.000
3 yrs.		9	7	.563	3.67	50	15	4	176.1	154	80	61	1	4	1	1	52	10	0	.192	5	57	2	2	1.3	.969

Elmer Horton

HORTON, ELMER E. (Herky Jerky)
B. Sept. 4, 1869, Hamilton, Ohio D. Aug. 12, 1920, Vienna, Ohio.

Year	Team	W	L	PCT	ERA	G	GS	CG	IP	H	BB	SO	ShO	Relief Pitching W	Relief Pitching L	Relief Pitching SV	Batting AB	Batting H	Batting HR	BA	PO	A	E	DP	TC/G	FA
1896	PIT N	0	2	.000	9.60	2	2	2	15	22	9	3	0	0	0	0	7	0	0	.000	4	0	2	0	3.0	.667
1898	BKN N	0	1	.000	10.00	1	1	1	9	16	6	0	0	0	0	0	4	1	0	.250	0	2	0	0	2.0	1.000
2 yrs.		0	3	.000	9.75	3	3	3	24	38	15	3	0	0	0	0	11	1	0	.091	4	2	2	0	2.7	.750

Ricky Horton

HORTON, RICKY NEAL BL TL 6′ 2″ 197 lbs.
B. July 30, 1959, Poughkeepsie, N. Y.

Year	Team	W	L	PCT	ERA	G	GS	CG	IP	H	BB	SO	ShO	Relief Pitching W	Relief Pitching L	Relief Pitching SV	Batting AB	Batting H	Batting HR	BA	PO	A	E	DP	TC/G	FA
1984	STL N	9	4	.692	3.44	37	18	1	125.2	140	39	76	1	1	0	1	31	2	0	.065	5	35	3	3	1.2	.930
1985		3	2	.600	2.91	49	3	0	89.2	84	34	59	0	2	2	1	16	1	0	.063	9	21	2	0	0.7	.938
1986		4	3	.571	2.24	42	9	1	100.1	77	26	49	0	1	0	3	18	1	0	.056	4	24	0	3	0.7	1.000
1987		8	3	.727	3.82	67	6	0	125	127	42	55	0	6	2	7	29	5	0	.172	12	31	2	2	0.7	.956
1988	2 teams CHI A (52G 6–10) LA N (12G 1–1)																									
″	total	7	11	.389	4.87	64	9	1	118.1	131	38	36	0	4	5	2	0	0	0		5	27	2	4	0.5	.941
1989	2 teams LA N (23G 0–0) STL N (11G 0–3)																									
″	total	0	3	.000	4.85	34	8	0	72.1	85	21	26	0	0	0	0	12	3	0	.250	2	13	0	2	0.4	1.000
1990	STL N	1	1	.500	4.93	32	0	0	42	52	22	18	0	1	1	1	4	0	0	.000	2	14	0	2	0.5	1.000
7 yrs.		32	27	.542	3.76	325	53	3	673.1	696	222	319	1	15	10	15	110	12	0	.109	39	165	9	16	0.7	.958
LEAGUE CHAMPIONSHIP SERIES																										
1985	STL N	0	0	—	9.00	3	0	0	3	4	2	1	0	0	0	0	0	0	0	—	1	2	0	0	1.0	1.000
1987		0	0	—	0.00	1	0	0	3	2	0	2	0	0	0	0	0	0	0	—	0	0	0	0	0.0	.000
1988	LA N	0	0	—	0.00	4	0	0	4.1	4	2	3	0	0	0	0	0	0	0	—	0	1	0	1	0.3	1.000
3 yrs.		0	0		2.61	8	0	0	10.1	10	4	6	0	0	0	0	0	0	0		1	3	0	1	0.5	1.000
WORLD SERIES																										
1985	STL N	0	0	—	6.75	3	0	0	4	4	5	5	0	0	0	0	1	0	0	.000	2	0	0	0	0.7	1.000
1987		0	0	—	6.00	2	0	0	3	5	0	1	0	0	0	0	0	0	0	—	0	1	0	0	0.5	1.000
2 yrs.		0	0		6.43	5	0	0	7	9	5	6	0	0	0	0	1	0	0	.000	2	1	0	0	0.6	1.000

Dave Hoskins

HOSKINS, DAVID TAYLOR BL TR 6′ 1″ 180 lbs.
B. Aug. 3, 1925, Greenwood, Miss. D. Apr. 2, 1970, Flint, Mich.

Year	Team	W	L	PCT	ERA	G	GS	CG	IP	H	BB	SO	ShO	Relief Pitching W	Relief Pitching L	Relief Pitching SV	Batting AB	Batting H	Batting HR	BA	PO	A	E	DP	TC/G	FA
1953	CLE A	9	3	.750	3.99	26	7	3	112.2	102	38	55	0	6	1	1	58	15	1	.259	7	18	0	1	1.0	1.000
1954		0	1	.000	3.04	14	1	0	26.2	29	10	9	0	0	1	0	8	0	0	.000	2	4	0	0	0.4	1.000
2 yrs.		9	4	.692	3.81	40	8	3	139.1	131	48	64	0	6	2	1	66	15	1	.227	9	22	0	1	0.8	1.000

Gene Host

HOST, EUGENE EARL (Slick, Twinkles) BB TL 5′11″ 190 lbs.
B. Jan. 1, 1933, Leeper, Pa.

Year	Team	W	L	PCT	ERA	G	GS	CG	IP	H	BB	SO	ShO	Relief Pitching W	Relief Pitching L	Relief Pitching SV	Batting AB	Batting H	Batting HR	BA	PO	A	E	DP	TC/G	FA
1956	DET A	0	0	—	7.71	1	1	0	4.2	9	2	5	0	0	0	0	2	0	0	.000	0	0	0	0	0.0	.000
1957	KC A	0	2	.000	7.23	11	2	0	23.2	29	14	9	0	0	1	0	5	0	0	.000	0	6	0	0	0.5	1.000
2 yrs.		0	2	.000	7.31	12	3	0	28.1	38	16	14	0	0	1	0	7	0	0	.000	0	6	0	0	0.5	1.000

Byron Houck

HOUCK, BYRON SIMON (Duke) BR TR 6′ 175 lbs.
B. Aug. 28, 1891, Prosper, Minn. D. June 17, 1969, Santa Cruz, Calif.

Year	Team	W	L	PCT	ERA	G	GS	CG	IP	H	BB	SO	ShO	Relief Pitching W	Relief Pitching L	Relief Pitching SV	Batting AB	Batting H	Batting HR	BA	PO	A	E	DP	TC/G	FA
1912	PHI A	8	8	.500	2.94	30	17	12	180.2	148	74	75	0	0	2	0	62	4	0	.065	7	50	4	2	2.0	.934
1913		14	6	.700	4.14	41	19	4	176	147	122	71	1	**8**	2	0	60	5	0	.083	12	42	1	1	1.3	.982
1914	2 teams PHI A (3G 0–0) BKN F (17G 2–6)																									
″	total	2	6	.250	3.15	20	12	3	103	109	49	49	0	0	0	0	33	8	1	.242	1	18	4	0	1.1	.826
1918	STL A	2	4	.333	2.39	27	2	0	71.2	58	29	29	0	1	3	2	20	3	0	.150	5	18	4	1	1.0	.852
4 yrs.		26	24	.520	3.30	118	50	19	531.1	462	274	224	1	9	7	2	175	20	1	.114	25	128	13	4	1.4	.922

Charlie Hough

HOUGH, CHARLES OLIVER BR TR 6′ 2″ 190 lbs.
B. Jan. 5, 1948, Honolulu, Hawaii.

Year	Team	W	L	PCT	ERA	G	GS	CG	IP	H	BB	SO	ShO	Relief Pitching W	Relief Pitching L	Relief Pitching SV	Batting AB	Batting H	Batting HR	BA	PO	A	E	DP	TC/G	FA
1970	LA N	0	0	—	5.29	8	0	0	17	18	11	8	0	0	0	2	3	1	0	.333	1	3	0	0	0.5	1.000
1971		0	0	—	4.50	4	0	0	4	3	3	4	0	0	0	0	0	0	0	—	0	1	0	0	0.3	1.000
1972		0	0	—	3.38	2	0	0	2.2	2	2	4	0	0	0	0	0	0	0	—	0	1	0	0	0.5	1.000
1973		4	2	.667	2.76	37	0	0	71.2	52	45	70	0	4	2	5	14	3	0	.214	4	11	1	1	0.4	.938
1974		9	4	.692	3.75	49	0	0	96	65	40	63	0	9	4	1	12	0	0	.000	3	14	1	1	0.4	.944
1975		3	7	.300	2.95	38	0	0	61	43	34	34	0	3	7	4	6	2	0	.333	4	7	2	0	0.3	.846
1976		12	8	.600	2.21	77	0	0	142.2	102	77	81	0	**12**	8	18	21	6	0	.286	3	22	1	0	0.3	.962
1977		6	12	.333	3.33	70	1	0	127	98	70	105	0	5	**12**	22	22	4	1	.182	6	15	1	1	0.3	.955
1978		5	5	.500	3.29	55	0	0	93	69	48	66	0	5	5	7	12	4	0	.333	5	11	0	2	0.3	1.000
1979		7	5	.583	4.77	42	14	0	151	152	66	76	0	1	2	0	38	6	0	.158	5	26	1	0	0.8	.969
1980	2 teams LA N (19G 1–3) TEX A (16G 2–2)																									
″	total	3	5	.375	4.55	35	3	2	93	91	58	72	1	2	3	1	2	1	0	.500	2	10	1	0	0.4	.923
1981	TEX A	4	1	.800	2.96	21	5	2	82	61	31	69	0	0	0	1	0	0	0	—	2	8	0	1	0.5	1.000
1982		16	13	.552	3.95	34	34	12	228	217	72	128	2	0	0	0	0	0	0	—	14	35	1	4	1.5	.980
1983		15	13	.536	3.18	34	33	11	252	219	95	152	3	1	0	0	0	0	0	—	25	46	2	4	2.1	.973
1984		16	14	.533	3.76	36	**36**	**17**	266	**260**	94	165	1	0	0	0	0	0	0	—	12	51	1	2	1.8	.984

Charlie Hough *continued*

Year	Team	Lg	W	L	PCT	ERA	G	GS	CG	IP	H	BB	SO	ShO	Relief Pitching W	Relief Pitching L	Relief Pitching SV	Batting AB	Batting H	Batting HR	BA	PO	A	E	DP	TC/G	FA
1985			14	16	.467	3.31	34	34	14	250.1	198	83	141	1	0	0	0	0	0	0	—	18	35	2	5	1.6	.964
1986			17	10	.630	3.79	33	33	7	230.1	188	89	146	2	0	0	0	0	0	0	—	20	32	1	2	1.6	.981
1987			18	13	.581	3.79	40	**40**	13	**285.1**	238	124	223	0	0	0	0	0	0	0	—	30	46	1	3	1.9	.987
1988			15	16	.484	3.32	34	34	10	252	202	**126**	174	0	0	0	0	0	0	0	—	27	43	1	4	2.1	.986
1989			10	13	.435	4.35	30	30	5	182	168	95	94	1	0	0	0	0	0	0	—	13	18	1	3	1.1	.969
1990			12	12	.500	4.07	32	32	5	218.2	190	119	114	0	0	0	0	0	0	0	—	11	31	2	2	1.4	.955
1991	CHI	A	9	10	.474	4.02	31	29	4	199.1	167	94	107	1	0	0	0	0	0	0	—	12	31	1	1	1.4	.977
1992			7	12	.368	3.93	27	27	4	176.1	160	66	76	0	0	0	0	0	0	0	—	7	20	0	1	1.0	1.000
1993	FLA	N	9	16	.360	4.27	34	34	0	204.1	202	71	126	0	0	0	0	63	2	0	.032	6	41	1	1	1.4	.979
1994			5	9	.357	5.15	21	21	1	113.2	118	52	65	1	0	0	0	33	4	0	.121	5	20	0	0	1.2	1.000
25 yrs.			216	216	.500	3.75	858	440	107	3799.1	3283	1665 **8th**	2363	13	42	43	61	226	33	1	.146	235	578	22	38	1.0	.974
LEAGUE CHAMPIONSHIP SERIES																											
1974	LA	N	0	0	—	7.71	1	0	0	2.1	4	0	2	0	0	0	0	0	0	0	—	0	0	1	0	1.0	.000
1977			0	0	—	4.50	1	0	0	2	2	0	3	0	0	0	0	0	0	0	—	0	1	0	0	1.0	1.000
1978			0	0	—	4.50	1	0	0	2	1	0	1	0	0	0	0	0	0	0	—	1	1	0	0	2.0	1.000
3 yrs.			0	0		5.68	3	0	0	6.1	7	0	6	0	0	0	0	0	0	0		1	2	1	0	1.3	.750
WORLD SERIES																											
1974	LA	N	0	0	—	0.00	1	0	0	2	0	1	4	0	0	0	0	0	0	0	—	0	0	0	0	0.0	.000
1977			0	0	—	1.80	2	0	0	5	3	0	5	0	0	0	0	0	0	0	—	0	0	0	0	0.0	.000
1978			0	0	—	8.44	2	0	0	5.1	10	2	5	0	0	0	0	0	0	0	—	1	0	0	0	0.5	1.000
3 yrs.			0	0		4.38	5	0	0	12.1	13	3	14	0	0	0	0	0	0	0		1	0	0	0	0.2	1.000

Fred House

HOUSE, WILLARD EDWIN BR TR 6′ 3″ 190 lbs.
B. Oct. 3, 1890, Cabool, Mo. D. Nov. 16, 1923, Kansas City, Mo.

Year	Team	Lg	W	L	PCT	ERA	G	GS	CG	IP	H	BB	SO	ShO	Relief Pitching W	Relief Pitching L	Relief Pitching SV	Batting AB	Batting H	Batting HR	BA	PO	A	E	DP	TC/G	FA
1913	DET	A	1	2	.333	5.20	19	2	0	53.2	64	17	16	0	1	1	0	10	0	0	.000	0	27	2	0	1.5	.931

Pat House

HOUSE, PATRICK LORY BL TL 6′ 3″ 185 lbs.
B. Sept. 1, 1940, Boise, Ida.

Year	Team	Lg	W	L	PCT	ERA	G	GS	CG	IP	H	BB	SO	ShO	Relief Pitching W	Relief Pitching L	Relief Pitching SV	Batting AB	Batting H	Batting HR	BA	PO	A	E	DP	TC/G	FA
1967	HOU	N	1	0	1.000	4.50	6	0	0	4	3	0	2	0	1	0	1	0	0	0	—	1	2	0	0	0.5	1.000
1968			1	1	.500	7.71	18	0	0	16.1	21	6	6	0	1	1	0	0	0	0	—	1	2	0	0	0.2	1.000
2 yrs.			2	1	.667	7.08	24	0	0	20.1	24	6	8	0	2	1	1	0	0	0		2	4	0	0	0.3	1.000

Tom House

HOUSE, THOMAS ROSS BL TL 5′11″ 190 lbs.
B. Apr. 29, 1947, Seattle, Wash.

Year	Team	Lg	W	L	PCT	ERA	G	GS	CG	IP	H	BB	SO	ShO	Relief Pitching W	Relief Pitching L	Relief Pitching SV	Batting AB	Batting H	Batting HR	BA	PO	A	E	DP	TC/G	FA
1971	ATL	N	1	0	1.000	3.00	11	1	0	21	20	3	11	0	0	0	0	5	2	0	.400	0	4	0	0	0.4	1.000
1972			0	0	—	3.00	8	0	0	9	7	6	7	0	0	0	2	1	0	0	.000	0	2	0	0	0.3	1.000
1973			4	2	.667	4.70	52	0	0	67	58	31	42	0	4	2	4	10	2	0	.200	1	10	0	0	0.2	1.000
1974			6	2	.750	1.92	56	0	0	103	74	27	64	0	6	2	11	10	4	0	.400	6	23	3	0	0.6	.906
1975			7	7	.500	3.19	58	0	0	79	79	36	36	0	7	7	11	9	1	0	.111	7	16	4	0	0.5	.852
1976	BOS	A	1	3	.250	4.30	36	0	0	44	39	19	27	0	1	3	4	0	0	0	—	3	11	1	0	0.4	.933
1977	2 teams		BOS A (8G 1–0)		SEA A (26G 4–5)																						
″	total		5	5	.500	4.64	34	11	1	97	109	25	45	0	1	1	1	0	0	0		1	11	1	1	0.4	.923
1978	SEA	A	5	4	.556	4.66	34	9	3	116	130	35	29	0	2	0	0	0	0	0	—	3	19	0	0	0.6	1.000
8 yrs.			29	23	.558	3.79	289	21	4	536	516	182	261	0	21	15	33	35	9	0	.257	21	96	9	1	0.4	.929

Charlie Householder

HOUSEHOLDER, CHARLES F. BR TR 5′ 7″ 150 lbs.
B. 1856, Harrisburg, Pa. Deceased.

Year	Team	Lg	W	L	PCT	ERA	G	GS	CG	IP	H	BB	SO	ShO	Relief Pitching W	Relief Pitching L	Relief Pitching SV	Batting AB	Batting H	Batting HR	BA	PO	A	E	DP	TC/G	FA
1884	CHI	U	0	0	—	3.00	2	0	0	3	4	0	3	0	0	0	0	*				99	66	37	7	2.3	.817

Frank Houseman

HOUSEMAN, FRANK
B. Baltimore, Md. Deceased.

Year	Team	Lg	W	L	PCT	ERA	G	GS	CG	IP	H	BB	SO	ShO	Relief Pitching W	Relief Pitching L	Relief Pitching SV	Batting AB	Batting H	Batting HR	BA	PO	A	E	DP	TC/G	FA
1886	BAL	AA	0	1	.000	3.38	1	1	1	8	6	1	5	0	0	0	0	4	1	0	.250	2	1	0	0	3.0	1.000

Joe Houser

HOUSER, JOSEPH WILLIAM BL TL 5′ 9½″ 160 lbs.
B. July 3, 1891, Steubenville, Ohio D. Jan. 3, 1953, Orlando, Fla.

Year	Team	Lg	W	L	PCT	ERA	G	GS	CG	IP	H	BB	SO	ShO	Relief Pitching W	Relief Pitching L	Relief Pitching SV	Batting AB	Batting H	Batting HR	BA	PO	A	E	DP	TC/G	FA
1914	BUF	F	0	1	.000	5.48	7	2	0	23	21	20	6	0	0	0	0	7	1	0	.143	1	11	0	0	1.5	1.000

Art Houtteman

HOUTTEMAN, ARTHUR JOSEPH BR TR 6′ 2″ 188 lbs.
B. Aug. 7, 1927, Detroit, Mich.

Year	Team	Lg	W	L	PCT	ERA	G	GS	CG	IP	H	BB	SO	ShO	Relief Pitching W	Relief Pitching L	Relief Pitching SV	Batting AB	Batting H	Batting HR	BA	PO	A	E	DP	TC/G	FA
1945	DET	A	0	2	.000	5.33	13	0	0	25.1	27	11	9	0	0	2	0	5	0	0	.000	2	8	0	1	0.8	1.000
1946			0	1	.000	9.00	1	1	0	8	15	0	2	0	0	0	0	2	1	0	.500	0	1	0	0	1.0	1.000
1947			7	2	.778	3.42	23	9	7	110.2	106	36	58	2	1	0	0	40	12	0	.300	4	17	2	2	1.0	.913
1948			2	16	.111	4.66	43	20	4	164.1	186	52	74	0	1	2	10	56	11	0	.196	9	47	4	5	1.4	.933
1949			15	10	.600	3.71	34	25	13	203.2	227	59	85	2	3	2	0	78	19	0	.244	14	59	2	7	2.2	.973
1950			19	12	.613	3.54	41	34	21	274.2	257	99	88	**4**	2	0	4	93	14	0	.151	15	63	4	2	2.0	.951
1952			8	**20**	.286	4.36	35	28	10	221	218	65	109	2	1	2	1	69	7	0	.101	16	40	1	3	1.6	.982
1953	2 teams	DET A	(16G 2–6)		CLE A (22G 7–7)																						
″	total		9	13	.409	4.61	38	22	9	177.2	200	54	68	2	2	2	4	53	8	1	.151	11	28	1	1	1.1	.975
1954	CLE	A	15	7	.682	3.35	32	25	11	188	198	59	68	1	1	2	0	65	18	1	.277	17	38	2	3	1.8	.965
1955			10	6	.625	3.98	35	12	3	124.1	126	44	53	1	6	1	0	38	6	0	.158	14	27	1	4	1.2	.976
1956			2	2	.500	6.56	22	4	0	46.2	60	31	19	0	1	0	1	12	2	0	.167	3	9	0	0	0.5	1.000
1957	2 teams	CLE A	(3G 0–0)		BAL A (5G 0–0)																						
″	total		0	0		13.50	8	1	0	10.2	26	6	6	0	0	0	0	2	1	0	.500	0	2	0	0	0.3	1.000
12 yrs.			87	91	.489	4.14	325	181	78	1555	1646	516	639	14	18	13	20	513	99	2	.193	105	339	17	28	1.4	.963
WORLD SERIES																											
1954	CLE	A	0	0	—	4.50	1	0	0	2	2	1	1	0	0	0	0	0	0	0	—	0	0	0	0	0.0	.000

Hick Hovlik

HOVLIK, EDWARD CHARLES BR TR 6′ 180 lbs.
Brother of Joe Hovlik.
B. Aug. 20, 1891, Cleveland, Ohio D. Mar. 19, 1955, Painesville, Ohio.

Year	Team		W	L	PCT	ERA	G	GS	CG	IP	H	BB	SO	ShO	Relief Pitching W	Relief Pitching L	Relief Pitching SV	Batting AB	Batting H	Batting HR	BA	PO	A	E	DP	TC/G	FA
1918	WAS	A	2	1	.667	1.29	8	2	1	28	25	10	10	0	1	0	0	8	1	0	.125	2	5	0	0	0.9	1.000
1919			0	0	—	12.71	3	0	0	5.2	12	9	3	0	0	0	1	2	0	0	.000	0	3	0	0	1.0	1.000
2 yrs.			2	1	.667	3.21	11	2	1	33.2	37	19	13	0	1	0	1	10	1	0	.100	2	8	0	0	0.9	1.000

Joe Hovlik

HOVLIK, JOSEPH BR TR 5′10½″ 194 lbs.
Brother of Hick Hovlik.
B. Aug. 16, 1884, Austria-Hungary D. Nov. 3, 1951, Oxford Junction, Iowa.

Year	Team		W	L	PCT	ERA	G	GS	CG	IP	H	BB	SO	ShO	Relief Pitching W	Relief Pitching L	Relief Pitching SV	Batting AB	Batting H	Batting HR	BA	PO	A	E	DP	TC/G	FA
1909	WAS	A	0	0	—	4.50	3	0	0	6	13	3	1	0	0	0	0	2	0	0	.000	0	3	0	0	1.0	1.000
1910			0	0	—	16.20	1	0	0	1.2	6	0	0	0	0	0	0	0	0	0	—	0	1	1	0	2.0	.500
1911	CHI	A	2	0	1.000	3.06	12	3	1	47	47	20	24	1	1	0	0	13	1	0	.077	2	18	0	0	1.7	1.000
3 yrs.			2	0	1.000	3.62	16	3	1	54.2	66	23	25	1	1	0	0	15	1	0	.067	2	22	1	0	1.6	.960

Bruce Howard

HOWARD, BRUCE ERNEST BB TR 6′ 2″ 180 lbs.
Father of Dave Howard.
B. Mar. 23, 1943, Salisbury, Md.

Year	Team		W	L	PCT	ERA	G	GS	CG	IP	H	BB	SO	ShO	Relief Pitching W	Relief Pitching L	Relief Pitching SV	Batting AB	Batting H	Batting HR	BA	PO	A	E	DP	TC/G	FA
1963	CHI	A	2	1	.667	2.65	7	0	0	17	12	14	9	0	2	1	1	4	1	0	.250	1	1	0	0	0.3	1.000
1964			2	1	.667	0.81	3	3	1	22.1	10	8	17	1	0	0	0	8	0	0	.000	1	3	0	0	1.3	1.000
1965			9	8	.529	3.47	30	22	1	148	123	72	120	1	2	1	0	41	6	0	.146	5	22	1	0	0.9	.964
1966			9	5	.643	2.30	27	21	4	149	110	44	85	2	1	0	0	43	3	0	.070	10	27	3	1	1.5	.925
1967			3	10	.231	3.43	30	17	1	112.2	102	52	76	0	1	1	0	28	5	0	.179	7	23	0	3	1.0	1.000
1968	2 teams BAL A (10G 0–2) WAS A (13G 1–4)																										
″	total		1	6	.143	4.74	23	12	0	79.2	92	49	42	0	0	0	0	23	2	1	.087	2	18	0	2	0.9	1.000
6 yrs.			26	31	.456	3.18	120	75	7	528.2	449	239	349	4	6	3	1	147	17	1	.116	26	94	4	6	1.0	.968

Chris Howard

HOWARD, CHRISTIAN BR TL 6′ 185 lbs.
B. Nov. 18, 1965, Lynn, Mass.

Year	Team		W	L	PCT	ERA	G	GS	CG	IP	H	BB	SO	ShO	Relief Pitching W	Relief Pitching L	Relief Pitching SV	Batting AB	Batting H	Batting HR	BA	PO	A	E	DP	TC/G	FA
1993	CHI	A	1	0	1.000	0.00	3	0	0	2.1	2	3	1	0	1	0	0	0	0	0	—	0	0	0	0	0.0	.000
1994	BOS	A	1	0	1.000	3.63	37	0	0	39.2	35	12	22	0	1	0	1	0	0	0	—	2	4	0	0	0.2	1.000
1995	TEX	A	0	0	—	0.00	4	0	0	4	3	1	2	0	0	0	0	0	0	0	—	0	0	0	0	0.0	.000
3 yrs.			2	0	1.000	3.13	44	0	0	46	40	16	25	0	2	0	1	0	0	0		2	4	0	0	0.1	1.000

Dave Howard

HOWARD, DAVID WAYNE BB TR 6′ 165 lbs.
Son of Bruce Howard.
B. Feb. 26, 1967, Sarasota, Fla.

Year	Team		W	L	PCT	ERA	G	GS	CG	IP	H	BB	SO	ShO	Relief Pitching W	Relief Pitching L	Relief Pitching SV	Batting AB	Batting H	Batting HR	BA	PO	A	E	DP	TC/G	FA
1994	KC	A	0	0	—	4.50	1	0	0	2	2	5	0	0	0	0	0	*				129	248	12	40	4.2	.969

Del Howard

HOWARD, GEORGE ELMER BL TR 6′ 180 lbs.
Brother of Ivon Howard.
B. Dec. 24, 1877, Kenney, Ill. D. Dec. 24, 1956, Seattle, Wash.

Year	Team		W	L	PCT	ERA	G	GS	CG	IP	H	BB	SO	ShO	Relief Pitching W	Relief Pitching L	Relief Pitching SV	Batting AB	Batting H	Batting HR	BA	PO	A	E	DP	TC/G	FA
1905	PIT	N	0	0	—	0.00	1	0	0	6	4	1	0	0	0	0	0	*				947	53	23	58	8.6	.978

Earl Howard

HOWARD, EARL NYCUM BR TR 6′ 1″ 160 lbs.
B. June 25, 1896, Everett, Pa. D. Apr. 4, 1937, Everett, Pa.

Year	Team		W	L	PCT	ERA	G	GS	CG	IP	H	BB	SO	ShO	Relief Pitching W	Relief Pitching L	Relief Pitching SV	Batting AB	Batting H	Batting HR	BA	PO	A	E	DP	TC/G	FA
1918	STL	N	0	0	—	0.00	1	0	0	2	0	2	0	0	0	0	0	0	0	0	—	1	2	0	1	3.0	1.000

Fred Howard

HOWARD, FRED IRVING III BR TR 6′ 3″ 190 lbs.
B. Sept. 2, 1956, Portland, Me.

Year	Team		W	L	PCT	ERA	G	GS	CG	IP	H	BB	SO	ShO	Relief Pitching W	Relief Pitching L	Relief Pitching SV	Batting AB	Batting H	Batting HR	BA	PO	A	E	DP	TC/G	FA
1979	CHI	A	1	5	.167	3.57	28	6	0	68	73	32	36	0	0	1	0	0	0	0	—	7	4	0	0	0.4	1.000

Lee Howard

HOWARD, LEE VINCENT BL TL 6′ 2″ 175 lbs.
B. Nov. 11, 1923, Staten Island, N. Y.

Year	Team		W	L	PCT	ERA	G	GS	CG	IP	H	BB	SO	ShO	Relief Pitching W	Relief Pitching L	Relief Pitching SV	Batting AB	Batting H	Batting HR	BA	PO	A	E	DP	TC/G	FA
1946	PIT	N	0	1	.000	2.02	3	2	1	13.1	14	9	6	0	0	0	0	5	0	0	.000	0	2	1	1	1.0	.667
1947			0	0	—	3.38	2	0	0	2.2	4	0	2	0	0	0	0	0	0	0	—	0	0	0	0	0.0	.000
2 yrs.			0	1	.000	2.25	5	2	1	16	18	9	8	0	0	0	0	5	0	0	.000	0	2	1	1	0.6	.667

Cal Howe

HOWE, CALVIN EARL BL TL 6′ 3″ 205 lbs.
B. Nov. 27, 1924, Rock Falls, Ill.

Year	Team		W	L	PCT	ERA	G	GS	CG	IP	H	BB	SO	ShO	Relief Pitching W	Relief Pitching L	Relief Pitching SV	Batting AB	Batting H	Batting HR	BA	PO	A	E	DP	TC/G	FA
1952	CHI	N	0	0	—	0.00	1	0	0	2	0	1	2	0	0	0	0	0	0	0	—	0	0	0	0	0.0	.000

Les Howe

HOWE, LESTER CURTIS (Lucky) BR TR 5′11½″ 170 lbs.
B. Aug. 24, 1895, Brooklyn, N. Y. D. July 16, 1976, Woodmere, N. Y.

Year	Team		W	L	PCT	ERA	G	GS	CG	IP	H	BB	SO	ShO	Relief Pitching W	Relief Pitching L	Relief Pitching SV	Batting AB	Batting H	Batting HR	BA	PO	A	E	DP	TC/G	FA
1923	BOS	A	1	0	1.000	2.40	12	2	0	30	23	7	7	0	1	0	0	6	0	0	.000	2	10	2	0	1.2	.857
1924			1	0	1.000	7.36	4	0	0	7.1	11	2	3	0	1	0	0	2	1	0	.500	0	2	0	0	0.5	1.000
2 yrs.			2	0	1.000	3.38	16	2	0	37.1	34	9	10	0	2	0	0	8	1	0	.125	2	12	2	0	1.0	.875

Steve Howe

HOWE, STEVEN ROY BL TL 6′ 1″ 180 lbs.
B. Mar. 10, 1958, Pontiac, Mich.

Year	Team		W	L	PCT	ERA	G	GS	CG	IP	H	BB	SO	ShO	Relief Pitching W	Relief Pitching L	Relief Pitching SV	Batting AB	Batting H	Batting HR	BA	PO	A	E	DP	TC/G	FA
1980	LA	N	7	9	.438	2.65	59	0	0	85	83	22	39	0	7	9	17	11	1	0	.091	3	20	1	0	0.4	.958
1981			5	3	.625	2.50	41	0	0	54	51	18	32	0	5	3	8	1	0	0	.000	1	5	0	0	0.1	1.000
1982			7	5	.583	2.08	66	0	0	99.1	87	17	49	0	7	5	13	7	0	0	.000	2	17	1	0	0.3	.950
1983			4	7	.364	1.44	46	0	0	68.2	55	12	52	0	4	7	18	8	1	0	.125	4	15	0	0	0.4	1.000
1985	2 teams LA N (19G 1–1) MIN A (13G 2–3)																										
″	total		3	4	.429	5.49	32	0	0	41	58	12	21	0	3	4	3	0	0	0		3	7	1	0	0.3	.909
1987	TEX	A	3	3	.500	4.31	24	0	0	31.1	33	8	19	0	3	3	1	0	0	0	—	4	4	0	0	0.3	1.000
1991	NY	A	3	1	.750	1.68	37	0	0	48.1	39	7	34	0	3	1	3	0	0	0	—	5	6	3	1	0.4	.786
1992			3	0	1.000	2.45	20	0	0	22	9	3	12	0	3	0	6	0	0	0	—	2	7	1	0	0.5	.900
1993			3	5	.375	4.97	51	0	0	50.2	58	10	19	0	3	5	4	0	0	0	—	2	13	1	0	0.3	.938
1994			3	0	1.000	1.80	40	0	0	40	28	7	18	0	3	0	15	0	0	0	—	2	4	0	0	0.2	1.000
1995			6	3	.667	4.96	56	0	0	49	66	17	28	0	6	3	2	0	0	0	—	3	11	0	1	0.3	1.000
11 yrs.			47	40	.540	2.93	472	0	0	589.1	567	133	323	0	47	40	90	27	2	0	.074	31	109	8	2	0.3	.946

Steve Howe *continued*

Year	Team	Lg	W	L	PCT	ERA	G	GS	CG	IP	H	BB	SO	ShO	Relief Pitching W	Relief Pitching L	Relief Pitching SV	Batting AB	Batting H	Batting HR	BA	PO	A	E	DP	TC/G	FA
DIVISIONAL PLAYOFF SERIES																											
1981	LA	N	0	0	—	0.00	2	0	0	2	1	0	2	0	0	0	0	0	0	0	—	0	0	0	0	0.0	.000
1995	NY	A	0	0	—	18.00	2	0	0	1	4	0	0	0	0	0	0	0	0	0	—	0	0	0	0	0.0	—
2 yrs.			0	0		6.00	4	0	0	3	5	0	2	0	0	0	0	0	0	0		0	0	0	0	0.0	
LEAGUE CHAMPIONSHIP SERIES																											
1981	LA	N	0	0	—	0.00	2	0	0	2	1	0	2	0	0	0	0	0	0	0	—	0	0	0	0	0.0	.000
WORLD SERIES																											
1981	LA	N	1	0	1.000	3.86	3	0	0	7	7	1	4	0	1	0	1	2	0	0	.000	0	1	1	0	0.7	.500

Dixie Howell

HOWELL, MILLARD — BL TR 6′ 2″ 210 lbs.
B. Jan. 7, 1920, Bowman, Ky. D. Mar. 18, 1960, Hollywood, Fla.

Year	Team	Lg	W	L	PCT	ERA	G	GS	CG	IP	H	BB	SO	ShO	Relief Pitching W	Relief Pitching L	Relief Pitching SV	Batting AB	Batting H	Batting HR	BA	PO	A	E	DP	TC/G	FA
1940	CLE	A	0	0	—	1.80	3	0	0	5	2	4	2	0	0	0	0	0	0	0	—	0	1	0	0	0.3	1.000
1949	CIN	N	0	1	.000	8.10	5	1	0	13.1	21	8	7	0	0	0	0	9	1	0	.111	0	3	0	0	0.6	1.000
1955	CHI	A	8	3	.727	2.93	35	0	0	73.2	70	25	25	0	**8**	3	9	21	8	0	.381	4	21	3	0	0.8	.893
1956			5	6	.455	4.62	34	1	0	64.1	79	36	28	0	4	6	4	17	4	2	.235	2	12	2	2	0.5	.875
1957			6	5	.545	3.29	37	0	0	68.1	64	30	37	0	6	5	6	27	5	3	.185	4	14	0	1	0.5	1.000
1958			0	0	—	0.00	1	0	0	1.2	0	0	0	0	0	0	0	0	0	0	—	0	1	0	0	1.0	1.000
6 yrs.			19	15	.559	3.78	115	2	0	226.1	236	103	99	0	18	14	19	74	18	5	.243	10	52	5	3	0.6	.925

Harry Howell

HOWELL, HENRY HARRY (Handsome Harry) — BR TR 5′ 9″
B. Nov. 14, 1876, New Jersey D. May 22, 1956, Spokane, Wash.

Year	Team	Lg	W	L	PCT	ERA	G	GS	CG	IP	H	BB	SO	ShO	Relief Pitching W	Relief Pitching L	Relief Pitching SV	Batting AB	Batting H	Batting HR	BA	PO	A	E	DP	TC/G	FA
1898	BKN	N	2	0	1.000	5.00	2	2	2	18	15	11	2	0	0	0	0	8	2	0	.250	1	5	0	1	3.0	1.000
1899	BAL	N	13	8	.619	3.91	28	25	21	209.1	248	69	58	0	1	0	1	82	12	0	.146	10	53	4	1	2.4	.940
1900	BKN	N	6	5	.545	3.75	21	10	7	110.1	131	36	26	2	1	1	0	42	12	1	.286	6	31	2	1	1.9	.949
1901	BAL	A	14	21	.400	3.67	37	34	32	294.2	333	79	93	1	1	1	0	188	41	2	.218	59	93	16	6	3.1	.905
1902			9	15	.375	4.12	26	23	19	199	243	48	33	1	1	0	0	347	93	2	.268	152	208	26	10	4.0	.933
1903	NY	A	9	6	.600	3.53	25	15	13	155.2	140	44	62	0	1	0	0	106	23	1	.217	38	81	7	3	3.2	.944
1904	STL	A	13	21	.382	2.19	34	33	32	299.2	254	60	122	2	0	1	0	113	25	1	.221	26	143	5	1	5.1	.971
1905			15	22	.405	1.98	38	37	35	323	252	101	198	4	0	0	0	135	26	1	.193	26	179	8	3	5.2	.962
1906			15	14	.517	2.11	35	33	30	276.2	233	61	140	6	0	1	1	104	13	0	.125	31	111	10	2	4.3	.934
1907			16	15	.516	1.93	42	35	26	316.1	258	88	118	2	0	0	3	114	27	2	.237	42	125	3	4	3.9	.982
1908			18	18	.500	1.89	41	32	27	324.1	279	70	117	2	5	1	1	120	22	1	.183	21	101	5	3	3.1	.961
1909			1	1	.500	3.13	10	3	0	37.1	42	8	16	0	1	1	0	34	6	0	.176	15	25	4	2	2.4	.909
1910			0	0	—	10.80	1	0	0	3.1	7	2	1	0	0	0	0	2	0	0	.000	0	1	0	0	1.0	1.000
13 yrs.			131	146	.473	2.74	340	282	244	2567.2	2435	677	986	20	11	6	6	*				427	1156	90	37	3.7	.946

Jay Howell

HOWELL, JAY CANFIELD — BR TR 6′ 3″ 200 lbs.
B. Nov. 26, 1955, Miami, Fla.

Year	Team	Lg	W	L	PCT	ERA	G	GS	CG	IP	H	BB	SO	ShO	Relief Pitching W	Relief Pitching L	Relief Pitching SV	Batting AB	Batting H	Batting HR	BA	PO	A	E	DP	TC/G	FA
1980	CIN	N	0	0	—	15.00	5	0	0	3	8	0	1	0	0	0	0	0	0	0	—	0	0	0	0	0.0	.000
1981	CHI	N	2	0	1.000	4.91	10	2	0	22	23	10	10	0	0	0	0	2	0	0	.000	2	9	0	1	1.1	1.000
1982	NY	A	2	3	.400	7.71	6	6	0	28	42	13	21	0	0	0	0	0	0	0	—	2	2	0	0	0.7	1.000
1983			1	5	.167	5.38	19	12	2	82	89	35	61	0	0	0	0	0	0	0	—	7	10	1	0	0.9	.944
1984			9	4	.692	2.69	61	1	0	103.2	86	34	109	0	8	4	7	0	0	0	—	11	16	1	3	0.5	.964
1985	OAK	A	9	8	.529	2.85	63	0	0	98	98	31	68	0	9	8	29	0	0	0	—	1	15	0	1	0.3	1.000
1986			3	6	.333	3.38	38	0	0	53.1	53	23	42	0	3	6	16	0	0	0	—	2	6	0	0	0.2	1.000
1987			3	4	.429	5.89	36	0	0	44.1	48	21	35	0	3	4	16	0	0	0	—	3	4	1	0	0.2	.875
1988	LA	N	5	3	.625	2.08	50	0	0	65	44	21	70	0	5	3	21	2	0	0	.000	7	6	1	0	0.3	.929
1989			5	3	.625	1.58	56	0	0	79.2	60	22	55	0	5	3	28	3	0	0	.000	5	10	1	2	0.3	.938
1990			5	5	.500	2.18	45	0	0	66	59	20	59	0	5	5	16	2	0	0	.000	3	8	0	0	0.2	1.000
1991			6	5	.545	3.18	44	0	0	51	39	11	40	0	6	5	16	0	0	0	—	5	6	1	1	0.3	.917
1992			1	3	.250	1.54	41	0	0	46.2	41	18	36	0	1	3	4	0	0	0	—	6	7	0	0	0.3	1.000
1993	ATL	N	3	3	.500	2.31	54	0	0	58.1	48	16	37	0	3	3	0	0	0	0	—	4	7	0	0	0.2	1.000
1994	TEX	A	4	1	.800	5.44	40	0	0	43	44	16	22	0	4	1	2	0	0	0	—	5	6	2	1	0.3	.846
15 yrs.			58	53	.523	3.34	568	21	2	844	782	291	666	0	52	45	155	9	0	0	.000	63	112	8	9	0.3	.956
LEAGUE CHAMPIONSHIP SERIES																											
1988	LA	N	0	1	.000	27.00	2	0	0	0.2	1	2	1	0	0	1	0	0	0	0	—	0	0	0	0	0.0	.000
WORLD SERIES																											
1988	LA	N	0	1	.000	3.38	2	0	0	2.2	3	1	2	0	0	1	1	0	0	0	—	0	0	0	0	0.0	.000

Ken Howell

HOWELL, KENNETH — BR TR 6′ 3″ 195 lbs.
B. Nov. 28, 1960, Detroit, Mich.

Year	Team	Lg	W	L	PCT	ERA	G	GS	CG	IP	H	BB	SO	ShO	Relief Pitching W	Relief Pitching L	Relief Pitching SV	Batting AB	Batting H	Batting HR	BA	PO	A	E	DP	TC/G	FA
1984	LA	N	5	5	.500	3.33	32	1	0	51.1	51	9	54	0	5	5	6	5	0	0	.000	6	6	0	0	0.4	1.000
1985			4	7	.364	3.77	56	0	0	86	66	35	85	0	4	7	12	4	0	0	.000	7	11	1	0	0.3	.947
1986			6	12	.333	3.87	62	0	0	97.2	86	63	104	0	6	**12**	12	5	0	0	.000	5	7	1	0	0.2	.923
1987			3	4	.429	4.91	40	2	0	55	54	29	60	0	2	3	1	4	1	0	.250	5	5	0	0	0.3	1.000
1988			0	1	.000	6.39	4	1	0	12.2	16	4	12	0	0	0	0	1	0	0	.000	0	1	0	0	0.3	1.000
1989	PHI	N	12	12	.500	3.44	33	32	1	204	155	86	164	1	0	0	0	65	6	0	.092	13	19	0	2	1.0	1.000
1990			8	7	.533	4.64	18	18	2	106.2	106	49	70	0	0	0	0	30	2	0	.067	6	11	2	0	1.1	.895
7 yrs.			38	48	.442	3.95	245	54	3	613.1	534	275	549	1	17	27	31	114	9	0	.079	42	60	4	2	0.4	.962
LEAGUE CHAMPIONSHIP SERIES																											
1985	LA	N	0	0	—	0.00	1	0	0	2	0	0	2	0	0	0	0	0	0	0	—	0	1	0	0	1.0	1.000

Roland Howell

HOWELL, ROLAND BOATNER (Billiken) — BR TR 6′ 4″ 210 lbs.
B. Jan. 3, 1892, Napoleonville, La. D. Mar. 31, 1973, Baton Rouge, La.

Year	Team	Lg	W	L	PCT	ERA	G	GS	CG	IP	H	BB	SO	ShO	Relief Pitching W	Relief Pitching L	Relief Pitching SV	Batting AB	Batting H	Batting HR	BA	PO	A	E	DP	TC/G	FA
1912	STL	N	0	0	—	27.00	3	0	0	1.2	5	5	0	0	0	0	0	0	0	0	—	0	0	0	0	0.0	.000

Peter Hoy

HOY, PETER ALEXANDER — BL TR 6′ 7″ 220 lbs.
B. June 29, 1966, Brockville, Ont., Canada.

Year	Team	Lg	W	L	PCT	ERA	G	GS	CG	IP	H	BB	SO	ShO	Relief Pitching W	Relief Pitching L	Relief Pitching SV	Batting AB	Batting H	Batting HR	BA	PO	A	E	DP	TC/G	FA
1992	BOS	A	0	0	—	7.36	5	0	0	3.2	8	2	2	0	0	0	0	0	0	0	—	0	1	0	1	0.2	1.000

Tex Hoyle

HOYLE, ROLAND EDISON BR TR 6′ 4″ 170 lbs.
B. July 17, 1921, Carbondale, Pa. D. July 4, 1994, Carbondale, Pa.

Year	Team	Lg	W	L	PCT	ERA	G	GS	CG	IP	H	BB	SO	ShO	Relief Pitching W	Relief Pitching L	Relief Pitching SV	Batting AB	Batting H	Batting HR	BA	PO	A	E	DP	TC/G	FA
1952	PHI	A	0	0	—	27.00	3	0	0	2.1	9	1	1	0	0	0	0	0	0	0	—	0	1	0	0	0.3	1.000

LaMarr Hoyt

HOYT, DEWEY LaMARR BR TR 6′ 3″ 195 lbs.
B. Jan. 1, 1955, Columbia, S. C.

Year	Team	Lg	W	L	PCT	ERA	G	GS	CG	IP	H	BB	SO	ShO	Relief Pitching W	Relief Pitching L	Relief Pitching SV	Batting AB	Batting H	Batting HR	BA	PO	A	E	DP	TC/G	FA
1979	CHI	A	0	0	—	0.00	2	0	0	3	2	0	0	0	0	0	0	0	0	0	—	0	0	0	0	0.0	.000
1980			9	3	.750	4.58	24	13	3	112	123	41	55	1	2	0	0	0	0	0	—	1	12	1	0	0.6	.929
1981			9	3	.750	3.56	43	1	0	91	80	28	60	0	9	3	10	0	0	0	—	6	8	0	1	0.3	1.000
1982			**19**	15	.559	3.53	39	32	14	239.2	248	48	124	2	4	0	0	0	0	0	—	16	26	0	3	1.1	1.000
1983			**24**	10	.706	3.66	36	36	11	260.2	236	31	148	1	0	0	0	0	0	0	—	21	56	2	4	2.2	.975
1984			13	**18**	.419	4.47	34	34	11	235.2	244	43	126	1	0	0	0	0	0	0	—	12	37	3	2	1.5	.942
1985	SD	N	16	8	.667	3.47	31	31	8	210.1	210	20	83	3	0	0	0	64	4	0	.063	12	40	1	4	1.7	.981
1986			8	11	.421	5.15	35	25	1	159	170	68	85	0	1	1	0	46	6	0	.130	8	17	2	1	0.8	.926
8 yrs.			98	68	.590	3.99	244	172	48	1311.1	1313	279	681	8	16	4	10	110	10	0	.091	76	196	9	15	1.2	.968
LEAGUE CHAMPIONSHIP SERIES																											
1983	CHI	A	1	0	1.000	1.00	1	1	1	9	5	0	4	0	0	0	0	0	0	0	—	2	1	0	0	3.0	1.000

Waite Hoyt

HOYT, WAITE CHARLES (Schoolboy) BR TR 6′ 180 lbs.
B. Sept. 9, 1899, Brooklyn, N. Y. D. Aug. 25, 1984, Cincinnati, Ohio.
Hall of Fame 1969.

Year	Team	Lg	W	L	PCT	ERA	G	GS	CG	IP	H	BB	SO	ShO	Relief Pitching W	Relief Pitching L	Relief Pitching SV	Batting AB	Batting H	Batting HR	BA	PO	A	E	DP	TC/G	FA
1918	NY	N	0	0	—	0.00	1	0	0	1	0	0	2	0	0	0	0	1	0	0	.000	0	0	0	0	0.0	.000
1919	BOS	A	4	6	.400	3.25	13	11	6	105.1	99	22	28	1	0	0	0	38	5	0	.132	6	33	2	1	3.2	.951
1920			6	6	.500	4.38	22	11	6	121.1	123	47	45	2	0	2	1	43	5	0	.116	3	35	0	1	1.7	1.000
1921	NY	A	19	13	.594	3.09	43	32	21	282.1	301	81	102	1	3	2	3	99	22	0	.222	15	65	5	5	2.0	.941
1922			19	12	.613	3.43	37	31	17	265	271	76	95	3	3	1	0	92	20	0	.217	9	58	2	1	1.9	.971
1923			17	9	.654	3.02	37	28	19	238.2	227	66	60	1	3	0	1	84	16	0	.190	17	58	3	1	2.1	.962
1924			18	13	.581	3.79	46	32	14	247	295	76	71	2	3	2	4	75	10	0	.133	12	57	3	2	1.6	.958
1925			11	14	.440	4.00	46	30	17	243	283	78	86	1	0	1	6	79	24	0	.304	7	73	2	3	1.8	.976
1926			16	12	.571	3.85	40	27	12	217.2	224	62	79	1	4	1	4	76	16	0	.211	12	38	3	3	1.3	.943
1927			**22**	7	**.759**	2.63	36	32	23	256.1	242	54	86	3	0	1	1	99	22	0	.222	12	60	1	1	2.0	.986
1928			23	7	.767	3.36	42	31	19	273	279	60	67	3	2	1	**8**	109	28	0	.257	12	56	1	6	1.6	.986
1929			10	9	.526	4.24	30	25	12	201.2	219	69	57	0	0	0	1	76	17	0	.224	8	37	2	1	1.6	.957
1930	2 teams		NY A (8G 2–2)			DET A (26G 9–8)																					
″	total		11	10	.524	4.71	34	27	10	183.1	240	56	35	1	1	0	4	62	10	0	.161	6	24	1	1	0.9	.968
1931	2 teams		DET A (16G 3–8)			PHI A (16G 10–5)																					
″	total		13	13	.500	4.97	32	26	14	203	254	69	40	2	0	2	0	73	17	0	.233	9	44	2	4	1.7	.964
1932	2 teams		BKN N (8G 1–3)			NY N (18G 5–7)																					
″	total		6	10	.375	4.35	26	16	3	124	141	37	36	0	2	1	1	37	3	0	.081	7	36	0	1	1.7	1.000
1933	PIT	N	5	7	.417	2.92	36	8	4	117	118	19	44	1	2	2	4	32	5	0	.156	5	30	1	3	1.0	.972
1934			15	6	.714	2.93	48	15	6	190.2	184	43	105	3	**7**	1	5	56	10	0	.179	3	37	2	0	0.9	.952
1935			7	11	.389	3.40	39	11	5	164	187	27	63	0	**5**	3	6	54	14	0	.259	5	34	2	3	1.1	.951
1936			7	5	.583	2.70	22	9	6	116.2	115	20	37	0	2	2	1	39	6	0	.154	2	30	2	1	1.5	.941
1937	2 teams		PIT N (11G 1–2)			BKN N (27G 7–7)																					
″	total		8	9	.471	3.41	38	19	10	195.1	211	36	65	1	2	2	2	60	5	0	.083	10	33	2	2	1.2	.956
1938	BKN	N	0	3	.000	4.96	6	1	0	16.1	24	5	3	0	0	2	0	3	0	0	.000	0	2	0	0	0.3	1.000
21 yrs.			237	182	.566	3.59	674	422	224	3762.2	4037	1003	1206	26	39	26	52	1287	255	0	.198	160	840	36	40	1.5	.965
WORLD SERIES																											
1921	NY	A	2	1	.667	0.00	3	3	3	27	18	11	18	1	0	0	0	9	2	0	.222	0	6	0	0	2.0	1.000
1922			0	1	.000	1.13	2	1	0	8	11	2	4	0	0	0	0	2	1	0	.500	1	2	0	0	1.5	1.000
1923			0	0	—	15.43	1	1	0	2.1	4	1	0	0	0	0	0	1	0	0	.000	0	0	0	0	0.0	.000
1926			1	1	.500	1.20	2	2	1	15	19	1	10	0	0	0	0	6	0	0	.000	0	0	0	0	0.0	.000
1927			1	0	1.000	4.91	1	1	0	7.1	8	1	2	0	0	0	0	3	0	0	.000	0	0	0	0	0.0	.000
1928			2	0	1.000	1.50	2	2	2	18	14	6	14	0	0	0	0	7	1	0	.143	0	3	1	0	2.0	.750
1931	PHI	A	0	1	.000	4.50	1	1	0	6	7	0	1	0	0	0	0	2	0	0	.000	0	0	0	0	0.0	.000
7 yrs.			6	4	.600	1.83	12	11	6	83.2	81	22	49	1	0	0	0	30	4	0	.133	1	11	1	0	1.1	.923
			5th				7th	2nd	6th	5th			8th														

Al Hrabosky

HRABOSKY, ALAN THOMAS (The Mad Hungarian) BR TL 5′11″ 185 lbs.
B. July 21, 1949, Oakland, Calif.

Year	Team	Lg	W	L	PCT	ERA	G	GS	CG	IP	H	BB	SO	ShO	Relief Pitching W	Relief Pitching L	Relief Pitching SV	Batting AB	Batting H	Batting HR	BA	PO	A	E	DP	TC/G	FA
1970	STL	N	2	1	.667	4.74	16	1	0	19	22	7	12	0	2	1	0	3	0	0	.000	1	0	0	0	0.1	1.000
1971			0	0	—	0.00	1	0	0	2	2	0	2	0	0	0	0	0	0	0	—	0	0	0	0	0.0	.000
1972			1	0	1.000	0.00	5	0	0	7	2	3	9	0	1	0	0	1	0	0	.000	0	0	0	0	0.0	.000
1973			2	4	.333	2.09	44	0	0	56	45	21	57	0	2	4	5	4	0	0	.000	2	5	2	1	0.2	.778
1974			8	1	.889	2.97	65	0	0	88	71	38	82	0	8	1	9	13	4	0	.308	3	7	3	0	0.2	.769
1975			13	3	.813	1.67	65	0	0	97	72	33	82	0	13	3	**22**	15	3	0	.200	0	6	0	0	0.1	1.000
1976			8	6	.571	3.30	68	0	0	95.1	89	39	73	0	8	6	13	7	0	0	.000	1	13	1	1	0.2	.933
1977			6	5	.545	4.40	65	0	0	86	82	41	68	0	6	5	10	8	0	0	.000	3	8	0	1	0.2	1.000
1978	KC	A	8	7	.533	2.88	58	0	0	75	52	35	60	0	8	7	20	0	0	0	—	3	9	0	1	0.2	1.000
1979			9	4	.692	3.74	58	0	0	65	67	41	39	0	9	4	11	0	0	0	—	2	4	2	0	0.1	.750
1980	ATL	N	4	2	.667	3.60	45	0	0	60	50	31	31	0	4	2	3	1	0	0	.000	3	2	0	0	0.1	1.000
1981			1	1	.500	1.06	24	0	0	34	24	9	13	0	1	1	1	1	0	0	.000	1	1	0	0	0.1	1.000
1982			2	1	.667	5.54	31	0	0	37.1	41	17	20	0	2	1	3	3	1	0	.333	1	3	0	0	0.1	1.000
13 yrs.			64	35	.646	3.11	545	1	0	721.2	619	315	548	0	64	35	97	56	8	0	.143	20	58	8	4	0.2	.907
LEAGUE CHAMPIONSHIP SERIES																											
1978	KC	A	0	0	—	3.00	3	0	0	3	3	0	2	0	0	0	0	0	0	0	—	0	0	0	0	0.0	.000

Bill Hubbell

HUBBELL, WILBERT WILLIAM BR TR 6′ 1½″ 195 lbs.
B. June 17, 1897, San Francisco, Calif. D. Aug. 3, 1980, Lakewood, Colo.

Year	Team	Lg	W	L	PCT	ERA	G	GS	CG	IP	H	BB	SO	ShO	Relief Pitching W	Relief Pitching L	Relief Pitching SV	Batting AB	Batting H	Batting HR	BA	PO	A	E	DP	TC/G	FA
1919	NY	N	1	1	.500	1.96	2	2	2	18.1	19	2	3	0	0	0	0	8	1	0	.125	1	4	0	0	2.5	1.000
1920	2 teams		NY N (14G 0–1)			PHI N (24G 9–9)																					
″	total		9	10	.474	3.55	38	18	9	180	202	57	34	1	1	2	4	58	8	0	.138	7	46	2	4	1.4	.964

Bill Hubbell *continued*

Year	Team	W	L	PCT	ERA	G	GS	CG	IP	H	BB	SO	ShO	Relief Pitching W	Relief Pitching L	Relief Pitching SV	Batting AB	Batting H	Batting HR	BA	PO	A	E	DP	TC/G	FA
1921	PHI N	9	16	.360	4.33	36	30	15	220.1	269	38	43	1	0	0	2	75	12	1	.160	9	57	6	1	2.0	.917
1922		7	15	.318	5.00	35	26	11	189	257	41	33	1	0	0	1	70	12	0	.171	8	45	1	2	1.5	.981
1923		1	6	.143	8.35	22	5	1	55	102	17	8	0	1	3	0	17	4	0	.235	2	15	0	0	0.8	1.000
1924		10	9	.526	4.83	36	22	9	179	233	45	30	2	2	2	2	59	13	0	.220	11	43	1	6	1.5	.982
1925	2 teams PHI N (2G 0–0) BKN N (33G 3–6)																									
"	total	3	6	.333	5.14	35	5	3	89.1	125	25	16	0	2	2	1	21	3	0	.143	5	29	2	1	1.0	.944
7 yrs.		40	63	.388	4.68	204	108	50	931	1207	225	167	5	6	9	10	308	53	1	.172	43	239	12	14	1.4	.959

Carl Hubbell

HUBBELL, CARL OWEN (King Carl, The Meal Ticket)
B. June 22, 1903, Carthage, Mo. D. Nov. 21, 1988, Scottsdale, Ariz.
Hall of Fame 1947.

BR TL 6′ 170 lbs.
BB 1928–1929, 1931–1932

Year	Team	W	L	PCT	ERA	G	GS	CG	IP	H	BB	SO	ShO	Relief Pitching W	Relief Pitching L	Relief Pitching SV	Batting AB	Batting H	Batting HR	BA	PO	A	E	DP	TC/G	FA
1928	NY N	10	6	.625	2.83	20	14	8	124	117	21	37	1	2	1	1	47	5	0	.106	6	40	5	2	2.5	.902
1929		18	11	.621	3.69	39	35	19	268	273	67	106	1	0	0	1	93	12	0	.129	16	76	1	7	2.4	.989
1930		17	12	.586	3.87	37	32	17	241.2	263	58	117	3	1	0	2	86	13	0	.151	12	39	3	3	1.5	.944
1931		14	12	.538	2.66	36	30	21	247	213	66	156	4	0	0	3	83	20	0	.241	9	38	4	0	1.4	.922
1932		18	11	.621	2.50	40	32	22	284	260	40	137	0	0	2	2	108	26	1	.241	18	83	4	5	2.6	.962
1933		**23**	12	.657	**1.66**	45	33	22	**308.2**	256	47	156	**10**	3	1	5	109	20	1	.183	23	94	2	5	2.6	.983
1934		21	12	.636	**2.30**	49	34	23	313	286	37	118	5	1	0	**8**	117	23	0	.197	17	82	2	4	2.1	.980
1935		23	12	.657	3.27	42	35	24	302.2	314	49	150	1	3	1	0	109	26	1	.239	5	85	1	5	2.2	.989
1936		**26**	6	**.813**	**2.31**	42	34	25	304	265	57	123	3	2	0	3	110	25	0	.227	14	65	2	7	1.9	.975
1937		**22**	8	**.733**	3.20	39	32	18	261.2	261	55	**159**	4	3	0	4	97	21	0	.216	11	47	2	3	1.5	.967
1938		13	10	.565	3.07	24	22	13	179	171	33	104	1	0	1	1	58	9	0	.155	6	27	0	4	1.4	1.000
1939		11	9	.550	2.75	29	18	10	154	150	24	62	0	2	0	2	53	8	1	.151	2	36	0	0	1.3	1.000
1940		11	12	.478	3.65	31	28	11	214.1	220	59	86	2	2	0	0	81	15	0	.185	4	52	2	3	1.9	.966
1941		11	9	.550	3.57	26	22	11	164	169	53	75	1	1	1	1	57	8	0	.140	3	20	1	4	0.9	.958
1942		11	8	.579	3.95	24	20	11	157.1	158	34	61	0	0	1	0	60	11	0	.183	6	32	4	0	1.8	.905
1943		4	4	.500	4.91	12	11	3	66	87	24	31	0	0	0	0	20	4	0	.200	3	8	0	2	0.9	1.000
16 yrs.		253	154	.622	2.98	535	432	258	3589.1	3463	724	1678	36	20	8	33	1288	246	4	.191	155	824	33	54	1.9	.967
WORLD SERIES																										
1933	NY N	2	0	1.000	0.00	2	2	2	20	13	6	15	0	0	0	0	7	2	0	.286	1	4	1	0	3.0	.833
1936		1	1	.500	2.25	2	2	1	16	15	2	10	0	0	0	0	6	2	0	.333	2	2	1	0	2.5	.800
1937		1	1	.500	3.77	2	2	1	14.1	12	4	7	0	0	0	0	6	0	0	.000	0	3	0	1	1.5	1.000
3 yrs.		4	2	.667	1.79	6	6	4	50.1	40	12	32	0	0	0	0	19	4	0	.211	3	9	2	1	2.3	.857

Earl Huckleberry

HUCKLEBERRY, EARL EUGENE
B. May 23, 1910, Konawa, Okla.

BR TR 5′11″ 165 lbs.

Year	Team	W	L	PCT	ERA	G	GS	CG	IP	H	BB	SO	ShO	Relief Pitching W	Relief Pitching L	Relief Pitching SV	Batting AB	Batting H	Batting HR	BA	PO	A	E	DP	TC/G	FA
1935	PHI A	1	0	1.000	9.45	1	1	0	6.2	8	4	2	0	0	0	0	3	0	0	.000	1	1	1	0	3.0	.667

John Hudek

HUDEK, JOHN RAYMOND
B. Aug. 8, 1966, Tampa, Fla.

BB TR 6′ 1″ 200 lbs.

Year	Team	W	L	PCT	ERA	G	GS	CG	IP	H	BB	SO	ShO	Relief Pitching W	Relief Pitching L	Relief Pitching SV	Batting AB	Batting H	Batting HR	BA	PO	A	E	DP	TC/G	FA
1994	HOU N	0	2	.000	2.97	42	0	0	39.1	24	18	39	0	0	2	16	0	0	0	—	4	3	0	0	0.2	1.000
1995		2	2	.500	5.40	19	0	0	20	19	5	29	0	2	2	7	1	1	0	1.000	1	5	0	0	0.3	1.000
2 yrs.		2	4	.333	3.79	61	0	0	59.1	43	23	68	0	2	4	23	1	1	0	1.000	5	8	0	0	0.2	1.000

Willis Hudlin

HUDLIN, GEORGE WILLIS (Ace)
B. May 23, 1906, Wagoner, Okla.

BR TR 6′ 190 lbs.

Year	Team	W	L	PCT	ERA	G	GS	CG	IP	H	BB	SO	ShO	Relief Pitching W	Relief Pitching L	Relief Pitching SV	Batting AB	Batting H	Batting HR	BA	PO	A	E	DP	TC/G	FA
1926	CLE A	1	3	.250	2.78	8	2	1	32.1	25	13	6	0	1	1	0	8	1	0	.125	6	15	0	0	2.6	1.000
1927		18	12	.600	4.01	43	30	18	264.2	**291**	83	65	1	4	0	0	96	24	1	.250	12	80	1	4	2.2	.989
1928		14	14	.500	4.04	42	26	10	220.1	231	90	62	0	6	0	7	72	14	0	.194	16	60	7	3	2.0	.916
1929		17	15	.531	3.34	40	33	22	280.1	299	73	60	2	3	1	1	97	19	0	.196	24	88	5	8	2.9	.957
1930		13	16	.448	4.57	37	33	13	216.2	255	76	60	1	1	2	1	73	16	0	.219	8	67	5	6	2.2	.938
1931		15	14	.517	4.60	44	34	15	254.1	313	88	83	1	1	1	4	100	20	0	.200	14	65	4	10	1.9	.952
1932		12	8	.600	4.71	33	21	12	181.2	204	59	65	0	1	1	2	64	13	0	.203	3	47	2	1	1.6	.962
1933		5	13	.278	3.97	34	17	6	147.1	161	61	44	0	0	2	1	41	6	1	.146	8	48	1	2	1.7	.982
1934		15	10	.600	4.75	36	26	15	195	210	65	58	1	1	3	4	68	14	1	.206	10	62	1	8	2.0	.986
1935		15	11	.577	3.69	36	29	14	231.2	252	61	45	3	0	1	5	86	24	1	.279	11	48	1	2	1.7	.983
1936		1	5	.167	9.00	27	7	1	64	112	31	20	0	1	0	0	18	2	0	.111	2	15	1	1	0.7	.944
1937		12	11	.522	4.10	35	23	10	175.2	213	40	31	2	4	0	2	59	10	0	.169	4	51	4	4	1.7	.932
1938		8	8	.500	4.89	29	15	8	127	158	45	27	0	2	4	1	43	5	0	.116	7	29	3	3	1.3	.923
1939		9	10	.474	4.91	27	20	7	143	175	42	28	0	1	2	3	48	9	1	.188	21	42	1	2	2.4	.984
1940	4 teams CLE A (4G 2–1) WAS A (8G 1–2) STL A (6G 0–1) NY N (1G 0–1)																									
"	total	3	5	.375	6.98	19	12	3	77.1	109	16	22	0	0	0	0	21	3	0	.143	4	17	2	0	1.2	.913
1944	STL A	0	1	.000	4.50	1	0	0	2	3	0	1	0	0	1	0	0	0	0	—	0	0	0	0	0.0	.000
16 yrs.		158	156	.503	4.41	491	328	155	2613.1	3011	843	677	11	26	19	31	894	180	5	.201	150	734	38	54	1.9	.959

Charles Hudson

HUDSON, CHARLES
B. Aug. 18, 1949, Ada, Okla.

BL TL 6′ 3″ 185 lbs.

Year	Team	W	L	PCT	ERA	G	GS	CG	IP	H	BB	SO	ShO	Relief Pitching W	Relief Pitching L	Relief Pitching SV	Batting AB	Batting H	Batting HR	BA	PO	A	E	DP	TC/G	FA
1972	STL N	1	0	1.000	5.11	12	0	0	12.1	10	7	4	0	1	0	0	0	0	0	—	1	3	0	0	0.3	1.000
1973	TEX A	4	2	.667	4.65	25	4	1	62	59	31	34	1	2	1	1	0	0	0	—	3	10	1	0	0.6	.929
1975	CAL A	0	1	.000	9.53	3	1	0	5.2	7	4	0	0	0	0	0	0	0	0	—	0	2	1	0	1.0	.667
3 yrs.		5	3	.625	5.06	40	5	1	80	76	42	38	1	3	1	1	0	0	0	—	4	15	2	0	0.5	.905

Charles Hudson

HUDSON, CHARLES LYNN
B. Mar. 16, 1959, Ennis, Tex.

BB TR 6′ 3″ 185 lbs.
BR 1983

Year	Team	W	L	PCT	ERA	G	GS	CG	IP	H	BB	SO	ShO	Relief Pitching W	Relief Pitching L	Relief Pitching SV	Batting AB	Batting H	Batting HR	BA	PO	A	E	DP	TC/G	FA
1983	PHI N	8	8	.500	3.35	26	26	3	169.1	158	53	101	0	0	0	0	54	5	0	.093	14	19	1	3	1.3	.971
1984		9	11	.450	4.04	30	30	1	173.2	181	52	94	1	0	0	0	56	5	0	.089	4	20	2	1	0.9	.923
1985		8	13	.381	3.78	38	26	3	193	188	74	122	0	0	2	0	57	8	0	.140	14	18	0	1	0.8	1.000
1986		7	10	.412	4.94	33	23	0	144	165	58	82	0	1	0	0	43	2	0	.047	12	20	1	0	1.0	.970
1987	NY A	11	7	.611	3.61	35	16	6	154.2	137	57	100	2	5	2	0	0	0	0	—	9	14	0	1	0.7	1.000

Charles Hudson *continued*

Year	Team	W	L	PCT	ERA	G	GS	CG	IP	H	BB	SO	ShO	Relief Pitching W	Relief Pitching L	Relief Pitching SV	Batting AB	Batting H	Batting HR	BA	PO	A	E	DP	TC/G	FA
1988		6	6	.500	4.49	28	12	1	106.1	93	36	58	0	2	2	2	0	0	0	—	9	10	0	3	0.7	1.000
1989	DET A	1	5	.167	6.34	18	7	0	66.2	75	31	23	0	0	2	0	0	0	0	—	7	5	1	1	0.7	.923
7 yrs.		50	60	.455	4.14	208	140	14	1007.2	997	361	580	3	8	8	2	210	20	0	.095	69	106	5	10	0.9	.972
LEAGUE CHAMPIONSHIP SERIES																										
1983	PHI N	1	0	1.000	2.00	1	1	1	9	4	2	9	0	0	0	0	4	0	0	.000	0	0	0	0	0.0	.000
WORLD SERIES																										
1983	PHI N	0	2	.000	8.64	2	2	0	8.1	9	1	6	0	0	0	0	2	0	0	.000	0	0	0	0	0.0	.000

Hal Hudson

HUDSON, HAL CAMPBELL (Lefty) BL TL 5′10″ 175 lbs.
B. May 4, 1927, Grosse Pointe, Mich.

Year	Team	W	L	PCT	ERA	G	GS	CG	IP	H	BB	SO	ShO	Relief Pitching W	Relief Pitching L	Relief Pitching SV	Batting AB	Batting H	Batting HR	BA	PO	A	E	DP	TC/G	FA
1952	2 teams STL A (3G 0–0) CHI A (2G 0–0)																									
″	total	0	0		8.38	5	0	0	9.2	16	7	4	0	0	0	0	1	0	0	.000	0	0	0	0	0.0	
1953	CHI A	0	0	—	0.00	1	0	0	0.2	0	0	0	0	0	0	0	0	0	0	—	0	0	0	0	0.0	.000
2 yrs.		0	0		7.84	6	0	0	10.1	16	7	4	0	0	0	0	1	0	0	.000	0	0	0	0	0.0	

Jesse Hudson

HUDSON, JESSE JAMES BL TL 6′ 2″ 165 lbs.
B. July 22, 1948, Mansfield, La.

Year	Team	W	L	PCT	ERA	G	GS	CG	IP	H	BB	SO	ShO	Relief Pitching W	Relief Pitching L	Relief Pitching SV	Batting AB	Batting H	Batting HR	BA	PO	A	E	DP	TC/G	FA
1969	NY N	0	0	—	4.50	1	0	0	2	2	2	3	0	0	0	0	0	0	0	—	0	1	0	0	1.0	1.000

Joe Hudson

HUDSON, JOSEPH PAUL BR TR 6′ 1″ 173 lbs.
B. Sept. 29, 1970, Philadelphia, Pa.

Year	Team	W	L	PCT	ERA	G	GS	CG	IP	H	BB	SO	ShO	Relief Pitching W	Relief Pitching L	Relief Pitching SV	Batting AB	Batting H	Batting HR	BA	PO	A	E	DP	TC/G	FA
1995	BOS A	0	1	.000	4.11	39	0	0	46	53	23	29	0	0	1	1	0	0	0	—	1	6	0	1	0.2	1.000
DIVISIONAL PLAYOFF SERIES																										
1995	BOS A	0	0	—	0.00	1	0	0	1	2	1	0	0	0	0	0	0	0	0	—	0	0	0	0	0.0	.000

Nat Hudson

HUDSON, NATHANIEL P. BR TR
B. Jan. 12, 1869, Chicago, Ill. D. Mar. 14, 1928, Chicago, Ill.

Year	Team	W	L	PCT	ERA	G	GS	CG	IP	H	BB	SO	ShO	Relief Pitching W	Relief Pitching L	Relief Pitching SV	Batting AB	Batting H	Batting HR	BA	PO	A	E	DP	TC/G	FA
1886	STL AA	16	10	.615	*3.03*	29	27	25	234.1	224	62	100	0	1	0	**1**	150	35	0	.233	53	38	6	2	2.2	.938
1887		4	4	.500	*4.97*	9	9	7	67	91	20	15	0	0	0	0	48	12	0	.250	9	7	3	0	1.3	.842
1888		25	10	**.714**	2.54	39	37	36	333	283	59	130	5	**1**	0	0	196	50	2	.255	89	55	9	4	2.6	.941
1889		3	2	.600	4.20	9	5	4	60	71	15	13	0	1	0	0	52	13	1	.250	20	12	3	0	1.9	.914
4 yrs.		48	26	.649	3.08	86	78	72	694.1	669	156	258	5	3	0	1	*				171	112	21	6	2.2	.931

Rex Hudson

HUDSON, REX HAUGHTON BB TR 5′11″ 165 lbs.
B. Aug. 11, 1953, Tulsa, Okla.

Year	Team	W	L	PCT	ERA	G	GS	CG	IP	H	BB	SO	ShO	Relief Pitching W	Relief Pitching L	Relief Pitching SV	Batting AB	Batting H	Batting HR	BA	PO	A	E	DP	TC/G	FA
1974	LA N	0	0	—	22.50	1	0	0	2	6	0	0	0	0	0	0	0	0	0	—	0	0	0	0	0.0	.000

Sid Hudson

HUDSON, SIDNEY CHARLES BR TR 6′ 4″ 180 lbs.
B. Jan. 3, 1915, Coalfield, Tenn.

Year	Team	W	L	PCT	ERA	G	GS	CG	IP	H	BB	SO	ShO	Relief Pitching W	Relief Pitching L	Relief Pitching SV	Batting AB	Batting H	Batting HR	BA	PO	A	E	DP	TC/G	FA
1940	WAS A	17	16	.515	4.57	38	31	19	252	272	81	96	3	0	2	1	93	22	0	.237	14	50	4	1	1.8	.941
1941		13	14	.481	3.46	33	33	17	249.2	242	97	108	3	0	0	0	86	16	0	.186	11	57	7	4	2.3	.907
1942		10	17	.370	4.36	35	31	19	239.1	266	70	72	1	1	1	2	89	19	0	.213	14	67	6	3	2.5	.931
1946		8	11	.421	3.60	31	15	6	142.1	160	37	35	1	5	1	1	43	12	0	.279	9	36	0	1	1.5	1.000
1947		6	9	.400	5.60	20	17	5	106	113	58	37	1	1	0	0	39	12	0	.308	7	20	0	1	1.4	1.000
1948		4	16	.200	5.88	39	29	4	182	217	107	53	0	0	0	1	59	14	0	.237	15	44	3	5	1.6	.952
1949		8	**17**	.320	4.22	40	27	11	209	234	91	54	2	1	1	1	67	16	0	.239	18	53	1	5	1.8	.986
1950		14	14	.500	4.09	30	30	17	237.2	261	98	75	0	0	0	0	93	20	0	.215	11	55	3	7	2.3	.957
1951		5	12	.294	5.13	23	19	8	138.2	168	52	43	0	0	0	0	44	12	0	.273	10	35	1	4	2.0	.978
1952	2 teams WAS A (7G 3–4) BOS A (21G 7–9)																									
″	total	10	13	.435	3.34	28	25	13	197	204	65	74	0	0	0	0	70	12	0	.171	23	57	3	7	3.0	.964
1953	BOS A	6	9	.400	3.52	30	17	4	156	164	49	60	0	2	1	2	50	7	0	.140	13	26	1	2	1.3	.975
1954		3	4	.429	4.42	33	5	0	71.1	83	30	27	0	3	1	5	13	2	0	.154	6	14	2	1	0.7	.909
12 yrs.		104	152	.406	4.28	380	279	123	2181	2384	835	734	11	13	7	13	746	164	0	.220	151	514	31	41	1.8	.955

Al Huenke

HUENKE, ALBERT A. BR TR 6′ 175 lbs.
B. June 26, 1891, New Bremen, Ohio D. Sept. 20, 1974, St. Marys, Ohio.

Year	Team	W	L	PCT	ERA	G	GS	CG	IP	H	BB	SO	ShO	Relief Pitching W	Relief Pitching L	Relief Pitching SV	Batting AB	Batting H	Batting HR	BA	PO	A	E	DP	TC/G	FA
1914	NY N	0	0	—	4.50	1	0	0	2	2	0	2	0	0	0	0	1	0	0	.000	0	0	0	0	0.0	.000

Phil Huffman

HUFFMAN, PHILLIP LEE BR TR 6′ 2″ 180 lbs.
B. June 20, 1958, Freeport, Tex.

Year	Team	W	L	PCT	ERA	G	GS	CG	IP	H	BB	SO	ShO	Relief Pitching W	Relief Pitching L	Relief Pitching SV	Batting AB	Batting H	Batting HR	BA	PO	A	E	DP	TC/G	FA
1979	TOR A	6	**18**	.250	5.77	31	31	2	173	220	68	56	1	0	0	0	0	0	0	—	7	30	0	0	1.2	1.000
1985	BAL A	0	0	—	15.43	2	1	0	4.2	7	5	2	0	0	0	0	0	0	0	—	2	0	0	0	1.0	1.000
2 yrs.		6	18	.250	6.03	33	32	2	177.2	227	73	58	1	0	0	0	0	0	0		9	30	0	0	1.2	1.000

Bill Hughes

HUGHES, WILLIAM NESBERT BR TR 5′10½″ 155 lbs.
B. Nov. 18, 1896, Philadelphia, Pa. D. Feb. 25, 1963, Birmingham, Ala.

Year	Team	W	L	PCT	ERA	G	GS	CG	IP	H	BB	SO	ShO	Relief Pitching W	Relief Pitching L	Relief Pitching SV	Batting AB	Batting H	Batting HR	BA	PO	A	E	DP	TC/G	FA
1921	PIT N	0	0	—	4.50	1	0	0	2	3	1	2	0	0	0	0	0	0	0	—	0	1	0	0	1.0	1.000

Bill Hughes

HUGHES, WILLIAM R. BL TL
B. Nov. 25, 1866, Bladinsville, Ill. D. Aug. 25, 1943, Santa Ana, Calif.

Year	Team	W	L	PCT	ERA	G	GS	CG	IP	H	BB	SO	ShO	Relief Pitching W	Relief Pitching L	Relief Pitching SV	Batting AB	Batting H	Batting HR	BA	PO	A	E	DP	TC/G	FA
1885	PHI AA	0	2	.000	*4.86*	2	2	2	16.2	18	10	4	0	0	0	0	*				92	3	7	2	6.8	.931

Dick Hughes

HUGHES, RICHARD HENRY BR TR 6′ 3″ 195 lbs.
B. Feb. 13, 1938, Stephens, Ark.

Year	Team	W	L	PCT	ERA	G	GS	CG	IP	H	BB	SO	ShO	Relief Pitching W	Relief Pitching L	Relief Pitching SV	Batting AB	Batting H	Batting HR	BA	PO	A	E	DP	TC/G	FA
1966	STL N	2	1	.667	1.71	6	2	1	21	12	7	20	1	1	1	1	5	2	0	.400	1	4	0	0	0.8	1.000
1967		16	6	**.727**	2.67	37	27	12	222.1	164	48	161	3	1	0	3	78	10	0	.128	10	28	1	1	1.1	.974
1968		2	2	.500	3.53	25	5	0	63.2	45	21	49	0	1	1	4	15	0	0	.000	7	10	0	3	0.7	1.000
3 yrs.		20	9	.690	2.79	68	34	13	307	221	76	230	4	3	2	8	98	12	0	.122	18	42	1	4	0.9	.984
WORLD SERIES																										
1967	STL N	0	1	.000	5.00	2	2	0	9	9	3	7	0	0	0	0	3	0	0	.000	1	0	0	0	0.5	1.000
1968		0	0	—	0.00	1	0	0	0.1	2	0	0	0	0	0	0	0	0	0	—	0	0	0	0	0.0	.000
2 yrs.		0	1	.000	4.82	3	2	0	9.1	11	3	7	0	0	0	0	3	0	0	.000	1	0	0	0	0.3	1.000

Ed Hughes

HUGHES, EDWARD J. BR TR 6′ 1″ 180 lbs.
Brother of Long Tom Hughes.
B. Oct. 5, 1880, Chicago, Ill. D. Oct. 11, 1927, McHenry, Ill.

Year	Team	W	L	PCT	ERA	G	GS	CG	IP	H	BB	SO	ShO	Relief W	Relief L	Relief SV	AB	H	HR	BA	PO	A	E	DP	TC/G	FA
1905	BOS A	3	2	.600	4.59	6	4	2	33.1	38	9	8	0	0	1	0	14	3	0	.214	5	2	2	0	9.0	.778
1906		0	0	—	5.40	2	0	0	10	15	3	3	0	0	0	0	3	0	0	.000	0	3	1	0	2.0	.750
2 yrs.		3	2	.600	4.78	8	4	2	43.1	53	12	11	0	0	1	0	21	4	0	.190	5	10	8	0	2.6	.652

Jim Hughes

HUGHES, JAMES JAY BR TR 185 lbs.
Brother of Mickey Hughes.
B. Jan. 22, 1874, Sacramento, Calif. D. June 2, 1924, Sacramento, Calif.

Year	Team	W	L	PCT	ERA	G	GS	CG	IP	H	BB	SO	ShO	Relief W	Relief L	Relief SV	AB	H	HR	BA	PO	A	E	DP	TC/G	FA
1898	BAL N	23	12	.657	3.20	38	35	31	300.2	268	100	81	5	2	1	0	164	37	2	.226	49	80	12	2	2.7	.915
1899	BKN N	**28**	6	**.824**	2.68	35	35	30	291.2	250	119	99	3	0	0	0	107	27	0	.252	19	74	7	4	2.9	.930
1901		17	12	.586	3.27	31	29	24	250.2	265	102	96	0	1	0	0	91	16	0	.176	18	66	6	5	2.9	.933
1902		15	11	.577	2.87	31	29	27	254	228	55	94	0	0	0	0	94	20	1	.213	21	71	4	5	3.0	.958
4 yrs.		83	41	.669	3.00	135	128	112	1097	1011	376	370	8	3	1	0	456	100	3	.219	107	291	29	16	2.8	.932

Jim Hughes

HUGHES, JAMES MICHAEL BR TR 6′ 3″ 190 lbs.
B. Aug. 11, 1951, Los Angeles, Calif.

Year	Team	W	L	PCT	ERA	G	GS	CG	IP	H	BB	SO	ShO	Relief W	Relief L	Relief SV	AB	H	HR	BA	PO	A	E	DP	TC/G	FA
1974	MIN A	0	2	.000	5.40	2	2	1	10	8	4	8	0	0	0	0	0	0	0	—	1	1	0	0	1.0	1.000
1975		16	14	.533	3.82	37	34	12	249.2	241	127	130	2	1	0	0	0	0	0	—	18	41	6	1	1.8	.908
1976		9	14	.391	4.98	37	26	3	177	190	73	87	0	2	1	0	0	0	0	—	13	21	5	2	1.1	.872
1977		0	0	—	2.25	2	0	0	4	4	1	1	0	0	0	0	0	0	0	—	0	0	0	0	0.0	.000
4 yrs.		25	30	.455	4.31	78	62	16	440.2	443	205	226	2	3	1	0	0	0	0		32	63	11	3	1.4	.896

Jim Hughes

HUGHES, JAMES ROBERT BR TR 6′ 1½″ 200 lbs.
B. Mar. 21, 1923, Chicago, Ill.

Year	Team	W	L	PCT	ERA	G	GS	CG	IP	H	BB	SO	ShO	Relief W	Relief L	Relief SV	AB	H	HR	BA	PO	A	E	DP	TC/G	FA
1952	BKN N	2	1	.667	1.45	6	0	0	18.2	16	11	8	0	2	1	0	4	0	0	.000	0	1	0	0	0.2	1.000
1953		4	3	.571	3.47	48	0	0	85.2	80	41	49	0	4	3	9	14	4	0	.286	8	9	0	0	0.4	1.000
1954		8	4	.667	3.22	**60**	0	0	86.2	76	44	58	0	8	4	**24**	16	3	0	.188	4	10	2	1	0.3	.875
1955		0	2	.000	4.22	24	0	0	42.2	41	19	20	0	0	2	6	10	0	0	.000	2	8	1	1	0.5	.909
1956	2 teams BKN N (5G 0–0) CHI N (25G 1–3)																									
″	total	1	3	.250	5.18	30	1	0	57.1	53	34	28	0	1	2	0	9	2	0	.222	2	5	0	2	0.2	1.000
1957	CHI A	0	0	—	10.80	4	0	0	5	12	3	2	0	0	0	0	0	0	0	—	0	1	0	0	0.3	1.000
6 yrs.		15	13	.536	3.83	172	1	0	296	278	152	165	0	15	12	39	53	9	0	.170	16	34	3	4	0.3	.943
WORLD SERIES																										
1953	BKN N	0	0	—	2.25	1	0	0	4	3	1	3	0	0	0	0	1	0	0	.000	0	0	1	0	1.0	.000

Long Tom Hughes

HUGHES, THOMAS JAMES BR TR 6′ 1″ 175 lbs.
Brother of Ed Hughes.
B. Nov. 29, 1878, Chicago, Ill. D. Feb. 8, 1956, Chicago, Ill.

Year	Team	W	L	PCT	ERA	G	GS	CG	IP	H	BB	SO	ShO	Relief W	Relief L	Relief SV	AB	H	HR	BA	PO	A	E	DP	TC/G	FA
1900	CHI N	1	1	.500	5.14	3	3	3	21	31	7	12	0	0	0	0	6	0	0	.000	0	6	0	0	2.0	1.000
1901		11	21	.344	3.24	37	35	32	308.1	309	115	225	1	1	0	0	118	14	0	.119	12	58	6	4	2.0	.921
1902	2 teams BAL A (13G 7–5) BOS A (9G 3–3)																									
″	total	10	8	.556	3.71	22	21	16	157.2	171	56	60	1	0	0	0	73	17	0	.233	13	45	4	1	2.5	.935
1903	BOS A	20	7	.741	2.57	33	31	25	244.2	232	60	112	5	0	1	0	93	26	1	.280	7	52	3	3	1.9	.952
1904	2 teams NY A (19G 7–11) WAS A (16G 2–13)																									
″	total	9	24	.273	3.59	35	32	26	260.2	274	82	123	2	0	**2**	1	111	26	1	.234	21	69	7	1	2.4	.928
1905	WAS A	17	20	.459	2.35	39	35	26	291.1	239	79	149	5	3	1	1	104	22	1	.212	9	69	5	0	2.1	.940
1906		7	17	.292	3.62	30	24	18	204	230	81	90	1	1	1	0	66	14	1	.212	6	43	5	1	1.8	.907
1907		7	14	.333	3.11	34	23	18	211	206	47	102	2	0	0	**4**	80	19	1	.237	6	61	1	0	2.0	.985
1908		18	15	.545	2.21	43	31	24	276.1	224	77	165	3	3	1	4	87	17	0	.195	8	87	11	4	2.5	.896
1909		4	7	.364	2.69	22	13	7	120.1	113	33	77	2	0	1	1	36	3	0	.083	2	36	6	0	2.0	.864
1911		11	17	.393	3.47	34	27	17	223	251	77	86	2	2	1	0	81	15	1	.185	8	51	5	3	1.9	.922
1912		13	10	.565	2.94	31	26	11	196	201	78	108	1	3	1	0	67	13	0	.194	6	57	7	1	2.3	.900
1913		4	12	.250	4.30	36	13	4	129.2	129	61	59	0	2	3	6	36	4	0	.111	9	41	5	1	1.5	.909
13 yrs.		132	173	.433	3.09	399	314	227	2644	2610	853	1368	25	15	12	17	958	190	6	.198	107	675	65	19	2.1	.923
WORLD SERIES																										
1903	BOS A	0	1	.000	9.00	1	1	0	2	4	2	0	0	0	0	0	0	0	0	—	0	0	0	0	0.0	.000

Mickey Hughes

HUGHES, MICHAEL F. TR 5′ 6″ 165 lbs.
Brother of Jim Hughes.
B. Oct. 25, 1866, New York, N. Y. D. Apr. 10, 1931, Jersey City, N. J.

Year	Team	W	L	PCT	ERA	G	GS	CG	IP	H	BB	SO	ShO	Relief W	Relief L	Relief SV	AB	H	HR	BA	PO	A	E	DP	TC/G	FA
1888	BKN AA	25	13	.658	2.13	40	40	40	363	281	98	159	2	0	0	0	139	19	0	.137	13	83	15	3	2.8	.865
1889		9	8	.529	4.35	20	17	13	153	172	86	54	0	0	1	0	68	12	0	.176	3	33	0	1	1.7	1.000
1890	2 teams BKN N (9G 4–4) PHI AA (6G 1–3)																									
″	total	5	7	.417	5.27	15	13	10	107.2	141	51	37	0	0	**1**	0	42	3	0	.071	2	20	7	2	1.8	.759
3 yrs.		39	28	.582	3.22	75	70	63	623.2	594	235	250	2	0	2	0	249	34	0	.137	18	136	22	6	2.3	.875

Tom Hughes

HUGHES, THOMAS EDWARD BL TR 6′ 2″ 180 lbs.
B. Sept. 13, 1934, Ancon, Canal Zone.

Year	Team	W	L	PCT	ERA	G	GS	CG	IP	H	BB	SO	ShO	Relief W	Relief L	Relief SV	AB	H	HR	BA	PO	A	E	DP	TC/G	FA
1959	STL N	0	2	.000	15.75	2	2	0	4	9	2	2	0	0	0	0	1	0	0	.000	0	0	0	0	0.0	.000

Tom Hughes

HUGHES, THOMAS L. BR TR 6′ 2″ 175 lbs.
B. Jan. 28, 1884, Coal Creek, Colo. D. Nov. 1, 1961, Los Angeles, Calif.

Year	Team	W	L	PCT	ERA	G	GS	CG	IP	H	BB	SO	ShO	Relief W	Relief L	Relief SV	AB	H	HR	BA	PO	A	E	DP	TC/G	FA
1906	NY A	1	0	1.000	4.20	3	1	1	15	11	1	5	0	0	0	0	5	1	0	.200	0	1	0	0	0.3	1.000
1907		2	0	1.000	2.67	4	3	2	27	16	11	10	0	0	0	0	7	1	0	.143	1	4	0	0	1.3	1.000
1909		7	8	.467	2.65	24	15	9	118.2	109	37	69	2	1	0	1	39	5	1	.128	8	29	1	0	1.6	.974
1910		7	9	.438	3.50	23	15	11	151.2	153	37	64	0	1	1	1	55	9	0	.164	4	57	4	1	2.8	.938
1914	BOS N	2	0	1.000	2.65	2	2	1	17	14	4	11	0	0	0	0	7	0	0	.000	2	6	0	0	4.0	1.000
1915		16	14	.533	2.12	**50**	25	17	280.1	208	58	171	4	**6**	0	**5**	90	9	1	.100	6	59	3	2	1.4	.956
1916		16	3	**.842**	2.35	40	13	7	161	121	51	97	1	**9**	2	5	52	10	0	.192	8	31	0	0	1.0	1.000
1917		5	3	.625	1.95	11	8	6	74	54	30	40	2	0	0	0	24	0	0	.000	4	17	1	1	2.0	.955
1918		0	2	.000	3.44	3	3	1	18.1	17	6	9	0	0	0	0	6	2	1	.333	0	7	0	0	2.3	1.000
9 yrs.		56	39	.589	2.56	160	85	55	863	703	235	476	9	17	3	12	285	37	3	.130	33	211	9	4	1.6	.964

Tommy Hughes

HUGHES, THOMAS OWEN BR TR 6′ 1″ 190 lbs.
B. Oct. 7, 1919, Wilkes-Barre, Pa. D. Nov. 28, 1990, Wilkes-Barre, Pa.

Year	Team		W	L	PCT	ERA	G	GS	CG	IP	H	BB	SO	ShO	Relief Pitching W	Relief Pitching L	Relief Pitching SV	Batting AB	Batting H	Batting HR	BA	PO	A	E	DP	TC/G	FA
1941	**PHI**	**N**	9	14	.391	4.45	34	24	5	170	187	82	59	2	3	2	0	55	11	0	.200	11	36	2	1	1.4	.959
1942			12	18	.400	3.06	40	31	19	253	224	99	77	0	1	0	1	80	8	0	.100	9	69	2	3	2.0	.975
1946			6	9	.400	4.38	29	13	3	111	123	44	34	2	2	0	1	31	3	0	.097	5	17	1	2	0.8	.957
1947			4	11	.267	3.47	29	15	4	127	121	59	44	1	1	1	1	40	2	0	.050	4	25	0	2	1.0	1.000
1948	**CIN**	**N**	0	4	.000	9.00	12	4	0	27	43	24	7	0	0	0	0	7	1	0	.143	2	4	0	0	0.5	1.000
5 yrs.			31	56	.356	3.92	144	87	31	688	698	308	221	5	7	3	3	213	25	0	.117	31	151	5	8	1.3	.973

Vern Hughes

HUGHES, VERNON ALEXANDER (Lefty) BL TL 5′10″ 155 lbs.
B. Apr. 15, 1893, Etna, Pa. D. Sept. 26, 1961, Sewickley, Pa.

Year	Team		W	L	PCT	ERA	G	GS	CG	IP	H	BB	SO	ShO	Relief Pitching W	Relief Pitching L	Relief Pitching SV	Batting AB	Batting H	Batting HR	BA	PO	A	E	DP	TC/G	FA
1914	**BAL**	**F**	0	0	—	3.18	3	0	0	5.2	5	3	0	0	0	0	0	1	0	0	.000	0	2	1	0	1.0	.667

Jim Hughey

HUGHEY, JAMES ULYSSES (Cold Water Jim) TR 6′
B. Mar. 8, 1869, Wakashma, Mich. D. Mar. 29, 1945, Coldwater, Mich.

Year	Team		W	L	PCT	ERA	G	GS	CG	IP	H	BB	SO	ShO	Relief Pitching W	Relief Pitching L	Relief Pitching SV	Batting AB	Batting H	Batting HR	BA	PO	A	E	DP	TC/G	FA
1891	**MIL**	**AA**	1	0	1.000	3.00	2	1	1	15	18	3	9	0	0	0	0	7	1	0	.143	0	5	0	0	2.5	1.000
1893	**CHI**	**N**	0	1	.000	11.00	2	2	1	9	14	3	4	0	0	0	0	2	0	0	.000	0	3	1	0	2.0	.750
1896	**PIT**	**N**	6	8	.429	4.99	25	14	11	155	171	67	48	0	2	0	0	65	14	0	.215	5	23	3	1	1.2	.903
1897			6	10	.375	5.06	25	17	13	149.1	193	45	38	0	1	1	1	63	8	0	.127	4	26	3	0	1.3	.909
1898	**STL**	**N**	7	24	.226	3.93	35	33	31	283.2	325	71	74	0	0	0	0	97	11	1	.113	8	67	11	2	2.5	.872
1899	**CLE**	**N**	4	**30**	.118	5.41	36	34	32	283	403	88	54	0	0	2	0	111	18	0	.162	9	48	12	3	1.9	.826
1900	**STL**	**N**	5	7	.417	5.19	20	12	11	112.2	147	40	23	0	0	0	0	41	7	0	.171	1	24	5	0	1.5	.833
7 yrs.			29	80	.266	4.87	145	113	100	1007.2	1271	317	250	0	3	3	1	386	59	1	.153	27	196	35	6	1.8	.864

Tex Hughson

HUGHSON, CECIL CARLTON BR TR 6′ 3″ 198 lbs.
B. Feb. 9, 1916, Buda, Tex. D. Aug. 6, 1993, Austin, Tex.

Year	Team		W	L	PCT	ERA	G	GS	CG	IP	H	BB	SO	ShO	Relief Pitching W	Relief Pitching L	Relief Pitching SV	Batting AB	Batting H	Batting HR	BA	PO	A	E	DP	TC/G	FA
1941	**BOS**	**A**	5	3	.625	4.13	12	8	4	61	70	13	22	0	1	0	0	17	1	0	.059	3	11	0	1	1.2	1.000
1942			**22**	6	.786	2.59	38	30	**22**	**281**	258	75	**113**	4	0	0	4	102	18	0	.176	16	59	1	7	2.0	.987
1943			12	15	.444	2.64	35	32	**20**	266	242	73	114	4	0	1	2	86	9	0	.105	10	61	2	3	2.1	.973
1944			18	5	**.783**	2.26	28	23	19	203.1	172	41	112	2	0	0	5	66	10	0	.152	9	35	2	0	1.6	.957
1946			20	11	.645	2.75	39	35	21	278	252	51	172	6	0	0	3	91	12	0	.132	18	34	1	0	1.4	.981
1947			12	11	.522	3.33	29	26	13	189.1	173	71	119	3	1	0	0	61	2	0	.033	10	25	1	3	1.2	.972
1948			3	1	.750	5.12	15	0	0	19.1	21	7	6	0	3	1	0	2	0	0	.000	1	1	1	0	0.2	.667
1949			4	2	.667	5.33	29	2	0	77.2	82	41	35	0	4	1	3	22	1	0	.045	3	5	0	2	0.3	1.000
8 yrs.			96	54	.640	2.94	225	156	99	1375.2	1270	372	693	19	9	3	17	447	53	0	.119	70	231	8	16	1.4	.974
WORLD SERIES																											
1946	**BOS**	**A**	0	1	.000	3.14	3	2	0	14.1	14	3	8	0	0	0	0	3	1	0	.333	0	1	1	0	0.7	.500

Rick Huisman

HUISMAN, RICHARD ALLEN BR TR 6′ 3″ 200 lbs.
B. May 17, 1969, Oak Park, Ill.

Year	Team		W	L	PCT	ERA	G	GS	CG	IP	H	BB	SO	ShO	Relief Pitching W	Relief Pitching L	Relief Pitching SV	Batting AB	Batting H	Batting HR	BA	PO	A	E	DP	TC/G	FA
1995	**KC**	**A**	0	0	—	7.45	7	0	0	9.2	14	1	12	0	0	0	0	0	0	0	—	0	1	0	0	0.1	1.000

Mark Huismann

HUISMANN, MARK LAWRENCE BR TR 6′ 3″ 195 lbs.
B. May 11, 1958, Lincoln, Neb.

Year	Team		W	L	PCT	ERA	G	GS	CG	IP	H	BB	SO	ShO	Relief Pitching W	Relief Pitching L	Relief Pitching SV	Batting AB	Batting H	Batting HR	BA	PO	A	E	DP	TC/G	FA
1983	**KC**	**A**	2	1	.667	5.58	13	0	0	30.2	29	17	20	0	2	1	0	0	0	0	—	1	2	0	0	0.2	1.000
1984			3	3	.500	4.20	38	0	0	75	84	21	54	0	3	3	3	0	0	0	—	7	10	3	0	0.5	.850
1985			1	0	1.000	1.93	9	0	0	18.2	14	3	9	0	1	0	0	0	0	0	—	1	3	0	0	0.4	1.000
1986	**2 teams**	**KC A** (10G 0–1)	**SEA A** (36G 3–3)																								
″	**total**		3	4	.429	3.79	46	1	0	97.1	98	25	72	0	3	3	5	0	0	0		12	12	3	1	0.6	.889
1987	**2 teams**	**SEA A** (6G 0–0)	**CLE A** (20G 2–3)																								
″	**total**		2	3	.400	5.04	26	0	0	50	48	12	38	0	2	3	2	0	0	0		4	8	3	0	0.6	.800
1988	**DET**	**A**	1	0	1.000	5.06	5	0	0	5.1	6	2	6	0	1	0	0	0	0	0	—	0	2	0	1	0.4	1.000
1989	**BAL**	**A**	0	0	—	6.35	8	0	0	11.1	13	0	13	0	0	0	1	0	0	0	—	3	3	0	0	0.8	1.000
1990	**PIT**	**N**	1	0	1.000	9.00	2	0	0	3	6	1	2	0	1	0	0	0	0	0	—	0	0	0	0	0.0	.000
1991			0	0	—	7.20	5	0	0	5	7	2	5	0	0	0	0	0	0	0	—	1	1	0	0	0.4	1.000
9 yrs.			13	11	.542	4.40	152	1	0	296.1	305	83	219	0	13	10	11	0	0	0		29	41	9	2	0.5	.886
LEAGUE CHAMPIONSHIP SERIES																											
1984	**KC**	**A**	0	0	—	10.13	1	0	0	2.2	6	1	2	0	0	0	0	0	0	0	—	0	0	0	0	0.0	.000

Harry Hulihan

HULIHAN, HARRY JOSEPH BR TL 5′11″ 170 lbs.
B. Apr. 18, 1899, Rutland, Vt. D. Sept. 11, 1980, Rutland, Vt.

Year	Team		W	L	PCT	ERA	G	GS	CG	IP	H	BB	SO	ShO	Relief Pitching W	Relief Pitching L	Relief Pitching SV	Batting AB	Batting H	Batting HR	BA	PO	A	E	DP	TC/G	FA
1922	**BOS**	**N**	2	3	.400	3.15	7	6	2	40	40	26	16	0	0	0	0	13	2	0	.154	0	6	1	0	1.0	.857

Jim Hulvey

HULVEY, JAMES HENSEL BB TR 6′ 180 lbs.
B. July 18, 1897, Mount Sidney, Va. D. Apr. 9, 1982, Mount Sidney, Va.

Year	Team		W	L	PCT	ERA	G	GS	CG	IP	H	BB	SO	ShO	Relief Pitching W	Relief Pitching L	Relief Pitching SV	Batting AB	Batting H	Batting HR	BA	PO	A	E	DP	TC/G	FA
1923	**PHI**	**A**	0	1	.000	7.71	1	1	0	7	10	2	2	0	0	0	0	2	1	0	.500	0	2	0	0	2.0	1.000

Tom Hume

HUME, THOMAS HUBERT BR TR 6′ 1″ 185 lbs.
B. Mar. 29, 1953, Cincinnati, Ohio.

Year	Team		W	L	PCT	ERA	G	GS	CG	IP	H	BB	SO	ShO	Relief Pitching W	Relief Pitching L	Relief Pitching SV	Batting AB	Batting H	Batting HR	BA	PO	A	E	DP	TC/G	FA
1977	**CIN**	**N**	3	3	.500	7.12	14	5	0	43	54	17	22	0	1	1	0	10	2	1	.200	1	6	0	0	0.5	1.000
1978			8	11	.421	4.14	42	23	3	174	198	50	90	0	2	0	1	45	3	0	.067	8	30	1	1	0.9	.974
1979			10	9	.526	2.76	57	12	2	163	162	33	80	0	5	5	17	46	8	0	.174	6	27	2	1	0.6	.943
1980			9	10	.474	2.56	78	0	0	137	121	38	68	0	9	10	25	16	3	0	.188	9	32	0	3	0.5	1.000
1981			9	4	.692	3.44	51	0	0	68	63	31	27	0	**9**	4	13	4	0	0	.000	2	12	0	0	0.3	1.000
1982			2	6	.250	3.11	46	0	0	63.2	57	21	22	0	2	6	17	5	0	0	.000	3	9	1	0	0.3	.923
1983			3	5	.375	4.77	48	0	0	66	66	41	34	0	3	5	9	5	0	0	.000	3	14	1	3	0.4	.944
1984			4	13	.235	5.64	54	8	0	113.1	142	41	59	0	3	8	3	22	3	0	.136	14	17	0	1	0.6	1.000
1985			3	5	.375	3.26	56	0	0	80	65	35	50	0	3	5	3	5	0	0	.000	4	12	1	1	0.3	.941
1986	**PHI**	**N**	4	1	.800	2.77	48	1	0	94.1	89	34	51	0	3	1	4	11	0	0	.000	8	19	1	1	0.6	.964
1987	**2 teams**	**PHI N** (38G 1–4)	**CIN N** (11G 1–0)																								
″	**total**		2	4	.333	5.36	49	6	0	84	89	43	33	0	1	1	0	15	3	0	.200	2	17	0	0	0.4	1.000
11 yrs.			57	71	.445	3.85	543	55	5	1086.1	1106	384	536	0	41	46	92	184	22	1	.120	60	195	7	11	0.5	.973
LEAGUE CHAMPIONSHIP SERIES																											
1979	**CIN**	**N**	0	1	.000	6.75	3	0	0	4	6	0	2	0	0	1	0	1	0	0	.000	0	2	0	0	0.7	1.000

Bill Humphrey

HUMPHREY, BYRON WILLIAM — BR TR 6′ 180 lbs.
B. June 17, 1911, Vienna, Mo. D. Feb. 13, 1992, Springfield, Mo.

Year	Team	Lg	W	L	PCT	ERA	G	GS	CG	IP	H	BB	SO	ShO	Relief Pitching W	Relief Pitching L	Relief Pitching SV	Batting AB	Batting H	Batting HR	BA	PO	A	E	DP	TC/G	FA
1938	BOS	A	0	0	—	9.00	2	0	0	2	5	1	0	0	0	0	0	0	0	0	—	0	0	0	0	0.0	.000

Bob Humphreys

HUMPHREYS, ROBERT WILLIAM — BR TR 5′11″ 165 lbs.
B. Aug. 18, 1935, Covington, Va.

Year	Team	Lg	W	L	PCT	ERA	G	GS	CG	IP	H	BB	SO	ShO	Relief Pitching W	Relief Pitching L	Relief Pitching SV	Batting AB	Batting H	Batting HR	BA	PO	A	E	DP	TC/G	FA
1962	DET	A	0	1	.000	7.20	4	0	0	5	8	2	3	0	0	1	1	0	0	0	—	1	1	0	0	0.5	1.000
1963	STL	N	0	1	.000	5.06	9	0	0	10.2	11	7	8	0	0	1	0	0	0	0	—	0	2	0	0	0.2	1.000
1964			2	0	1.000	2.53	28	0	0	42.2	32	15	36	0	2	0	2	4	1	0	.250	3	5	0	1	0.3	1.000
1965	CHI	N	2	0	1.000	3.15	41	0	0	65.2	59	27	38	0	2	0	0	3	0	0	.000	2	8	0	0	0.2	1.000
1966	WAS	A	7	3	.700	2.82	58	1	0	111.2	91	28	88	0	6	3	3	12	2	0	.167	8	13	0	2	0.4	1.000
1967			6	2	.750	4.17	48	2	0	105.2	93	41	54	0	5	1	4	15	2	0	.133	7	11	2	2	0.4	.900
1968			5	7	.417	3.69	56	0	0	92.2	78	30	56	0	5	7	2	5	2	0	.400	8	16	0	2	0.4	1.000
1969			3	3	.500	3.05	47	0	0	79.2	69	38	43	0	3	3	5	13	1	0	.077	1	16	1	0	0.4	.944
1970	2 teams	WAS A (5G 0–0) MIL A (23G 2–4)																									
″	total		2	4	.333	2.92	28	1	0	52.1	41	31	38	0	2	4	3	9	0	0	.000	5	6	0	1	0.4	1.000
9 yrs.			27	21	.563	3.36	319	4	0	566	482	219	364	0	25	20	20	61	8	0	.131	35	78	3	8	0.4	.974
WORLD SERIES																											
1964	STL	N	0	0	—	0.00	1	0	0	1	0	0	1	0	0	0	0	0	0	0	—	0	0	0	0	0.0	.000

Bert Humphries

HUMPHRIES, ALBERT — BR TR 5′11½″ 182 lbs.
B. Sept. 26, 1880, California, Pa. D. Sept. 21, 1945, Orlando, Fla.

Year	Team	Lg	W	L	PCT	ERA	G	GS	CG	IP	H	BB	SO	ShO	Relief Pitching W	Relief Pitching L	Relief Pitching SV	Batting AB	Batting H	Batting HR	BA	PO	A	E	DP	TC/G	FA
1910	PHI	N	0	0	—	4.66	5	0	0	9.2	13	3	3	0	0	0	1	2	0	0	.000	0	4	0	1	0.8	1.000
1911	2 teams	PHI N (11G 3–1) CIN N (14G 4–3)																									
″	total		7	4	.636	3.06	25	12	5	106	118	28	29	0	0	1	1	31	6	0	.194	4	29	1	1	1.4	.971
1912	CIN	N	9	11	.450	3.23	30	15	9	158.2	162	36	58	1	4	3	2	51	7	0	.137	6	33	3	1	1.4	.929
1913	CHI	N	16	4	**.800**	2.69	28	20	13	181	169	24	61	2	2	1	0	62	12	0	.194	8	37	4	1	1.8	.918
1914			10	11	.476	2.68	34	22	8	171	162	37	62	2	2	2	0	55	13	0	.236	10	55	2	1	2.0	.970
1915			8	13	.381	2.31	31	22	10	171.2	183	23	45	4	1	1	2	46	8	0	.174	4	38	4	4	1.5	.913
6 yrs.			50	43	.538	2.79	153	91	45	798	807	151	258	9	9	8	6	247	46	0	.186	32	196	14	9	1.6	.942

John Humphries

HUMPHRIES, JOHN WILLIAM — BR TR 6′1″ 185 lbs.
B. June 23, 1915, Clifton Forge, Va. D. June 24, 1965, New Orleans, La.

Year	Team	Lg	W	L	PCT	ERA	G	GS	CG	IP	H	BB	SO	ShO	Relief Pitching W	Relief Pitching L	Relief Pitching SV	Batting AB	Batting H	Batting HR	BA	PO	A	E	DP	TC/G	FA
1938	CLE	A	9	8	.529	5.23	**45**	6	1	103.1	105	63	56	0	**8**	3	6	29	3	0	.103	3	15	2	1	0.4	.900
1939			2	4	.333	8.26	15	1	0	28.1	30	32	12	0	2	3	2	7	0	0	.000	1	4	1	0	0.4	.833
1940			0	2	.000	8.29	19	1	1	33.2	35	29	17	0	0	1	1	6	0	0	.000	0	4	1	0	0.3	.800
1941	CHI	A	4	2	.667	1.84	14	6	4	73.1	63	22	25	4	0	0	1	23	2	0	.087	4	7	0	1	0.8	1.000
1942			12	12	.500	2.68	28	28	17	228.1	227	59	71	2	0	0	0	80	18	0	.225	11	41	2	1	1.9	.963
1943			11	11	.500	3.30	28	27	8	188.1	198	54	51	2	0	0	0	69	20	0	.290	6	36	3	1	1.6	.933
1944			8	10	.444	3.67	30	20	8	169	170	57	42	0	2	1	1	53	10	0	.189	3	22	2	0	0.9	.926
1945			6	14	.300	4.24	22	21	10	153	172	48	33	1	0	0	1	54	8	0	.148	3	19	6	0	1.3	.786
1946	PHI	N	0	0	—	4.01	10	1	0	24.2	24	9	10	0	0	0	0	8	2	0	.250	0	0	0	0	0.0	.000
9 yrs.			52	63	.452	3.78	211	111	49	1002	1024	373	317	9	12	8	12	329	63	0	.191	31	148	17	4	0.9	.913

Ben Hunt

HUNT, BENJAMIN FRANKLIN (Highpockets) — BL TL 6′5″ 190 lbs.
B. Nov. 10, 1888, Eufaula, Okla. D. Sept. 27, 1927, Greybull, Wyo.

Year	Team	Lg	W	L	PCT	ERA	G	GS	CG	IP	H	BB	SO	ShO	Relief Pitching W	Relief Pitching L	Relief Pitching SV	Batting AB	Batting H	Batting HR	BA	PO	A	E	DP	TC/G	FA
1910	BOS	A	2	3	.400	4.05	7	7	3	46.2	45	20	19	0	0	0	0	18	1	0	.056	1	14	2	0	2.4	.882
1913	STL	N	0	1	.000	3.38	2	1	0	8	6	9	6	0	0	0	0	2	0	0	.000	1	4	0	0	2.5	1.000
2 yrs.			2	4	.333	3.95	9	8	3	54.2	51	29	25	0	0	0	0	20	1	0	.050	2	18	2	0	2.4	.909

Ken Hunt

HUNT, KENNETH RAYMOND — BR TR 6′4″ 200 lbs.
B. Dec. 14, 1938, Ogden, Utah.

Year	Team	Lg	W	L	PCT	ERA	G	GS	CG	IP	H	BB	SO	ShO	Relief Pitching W	Relief Pitching L	Relief Pitching SV	Batting AB	Batting H	Batting HR	BA	PO	A	E	DP	TC/G	FA
1961	CIN	N	9	10	.474	3.96	29	22	4	136.1	130	66	75	0	0	0	0	39	7	0	.179	10	19	5	2	1.2	.853
WORLD SERIES																											
1961	CIN	N	0	0	—	0.00	1	0	0	1	0	1	1	0	0	0	0	0	0	0	—	0	1	0	0	1.0	1.000

Catfish Hunter

HUNTER, JAMES AUGUSTUS — BR TR 6′ 190 lbs.
B. Apr. 8, 1946, Hertford, N. C.
Hall of Fame 1987.

Year	Team	Lg	W	L	PCT	ERA	G	GS	CG	IP	H	BB	SO	ShO	Relief Pitching W	Relief Pitching L	Relief Pitching SV	Batting AB	Batting H	Batting HR	BA	PO	A	E	DP	TC/G	FA
1965	KC	A	8	8	.500	4.26	32	20	3	133	124	46	82	2	1	0	0	40	6	0	.150	4	16	2	1	0.7	.909
1966			9	11	.450	4.02	30	25	4	176.2	158	64	103	0	0	0	0	59	9	0	.153	10	14	3	1	0.9	.889
1967			13	17	.433	2.81	35	35	13	259.2	209	84	196	5	0	0	0	92	18	2	.196	15	16	1	1	0.9	.969
1968	OAK	A	13	13	.500	3.35	36	34	11	234	210	69	172	2	0	0	1	82	19	1	.232	16	20	4	0	1.1	.900
1969			12	15	.444	3.35	38	35	10	247	210	85	150	3	0	0	0	85	19	1	.224	17	32	0	4	1.3	1.000
1970			18	14	.563	3.81	40	**40**	9	262	253	74	178	1	0	0	0	90	18	1	.200	17	24	1	3	1.0	.976
1971			21	11	.656	2.96	37	37	16	274	225	80	181	4	0	0	0	103	36	1	.350	15	26	0	1	1.1	1.000
1972			21	7	**.750**	2.04	38	37	16	295	200	70	191	5	1	0	0	105	23	0	.219	23	30	2	1	1.4	.964
1973			21	5	**.808**	3.34	36	36	11	256.1	222	69	124	3	0	0	0	1	1	0	1.000	11	24	1	0	1.0	.972
1974			**25**	12	.676	**2.49**	41	41	23	318	268	46	143	6	0	0	0	0	0	0	—	25	27	3	1	1.3	.945
1975	NY	A	**23**	14	.622	2.58	39	39	**30**	**328**	248	83	177	7	0	0	0	0	0	0	—	23	26	3	0	1.3	.942
1976			17	15	.531	3.53	36	36	21	298.2	268	68	173	2	0	0	0	1	0	0	.000	24	30	2	2	1.6	.964
1977			9	9	.500	4.72	22	22	8	143	137	47	52	1	0	0	0	0	0	0	—	4	11	0	1	0.7	1.000
1978			12	6	.667	3.58	21	20	5	118	98	35	56	1	0	0	0	0	0	0	—	11	13	0	0	1.1	1.000
1979			2	9	.182	5.31	19	19	1	105	128	34	34	0	0	0	0	0	0	0	—	10	10	1	0	1.1	.952
15 yrs.			224	166	.574	3.26	500	476	181	3448.1	2958	954	2012	42	2	0	1	658	149	6	.226	225	319	23	16	1.1	.959
LEAGUE CHAMPIONSHIP SERIES																											
1971	OAK	A	0	1	.000	5.63	1	1	1	8	7	2	6	0	0	0	0	3	0	0	.000	0	0	0	0	0.0	.000
1972			0	0	—	1.17	2	2	0	15.1	10	5	9	0	0	0	0	6	1	0	.167	0	0	0	0	0.0	.000
1973			2	0	1.000	1.65	2	2	1	16.1	12	5	6	1	0	0	0	0	0	0	—	1	0	0	0	0.5	1.000
1974			1	1	.500	4.63	2	2	0	11.2	11	2	6	0	0	0	0	0	0	0	—	3	2	0	0	2.5	1.000
1976	NY	A	1	1	.500	4.50	2	2	1	12	10	1	5	0	0	0	0	0	0	0	—	0	3	0	0	1.5	1.000
1978			0	0	—	4.50	1	1	0	6	7	3	5	0	0	0	0	0	0	0	—	0	1	0	0	1.0	1.000
6 yrs.			4	3	.571	3.25	10	10	3	69.1	57	18	37	1	0	0	0	9	1	0	.111	4	6	0	0	1.0	1.000
			3rd	**5th**				**1st**	**2nd**	**2nd**		**7th**	**6th**	**1st**													

Catfish Hunter *continued*

Year	Team	W	L	PCT	ERA	G	GS	CG	IP	H	BB	SO	ShO	Relief Pitching W	Relief Pitching L	Relief Pitching SV	Batting AB	Batting H	Batting HR	BA	PO	A	E	DP	TC/G	FA
WORLD SERIES																										
1972	OAK A	2	0	1.000	2.81	3	2	0	16	12	6	11	0	0	0	0	5	1	0	.200	0	3	1	0	1.3	.750
1973		1	0	1.000	2.02	2	2	0	13.1	11	4	6	0	0	0	0	5	0	0	.000	1	2	1	0	2.0	.750
1974		1	0	1.000	1.17	2	1	0	7.2	5	2	5	0	0	0	1	2	0	0	.000	1	1	0	0	1.0	1.000
1976	NY A	0	1	.000	3.12	1	1	1	8.2	10	4	5	0	0	0	0	0	0	0	—	0	1	0	0	1.0	1.000
1977		0	1	.000	10.38	2	1	0	4.1	6	0	1	0	0	0	0	0	0	0	—	1	0	0	0	0.5	1.000
1978		1	1	.500	4.15	2	2	0	13	13	1	5	0	0	0	0	0	0	0	—	2	0	0	0	1.0	1.000
6 yrs.		5	3	.625	3.29	12	9	1	63	57	17	33	0	0	0	1	12	1	0	.083	5	7	2	0	1.2	.857
		8th				**7th**	**6th**		**10th**																	

George Hunter

HUNTER, GEORGE HENRY BB TL 5′ 8½″ 165 lbs.
Brother of Bill Hunter.
B. July 8, 1887, Buffalo, N. Y. D. Jan. 11, 1968, Harrisburg, Pa.

Year	Team	W	L	PCT	ERA	G	GS	CG	IP	H	BB	SO	ShO	Relief Pitching W	Relief Pitching L	Relief Pitching SV	Batting AB	Batting H	Batting HR	BA	PO	A	E	DP	TC/G	FA
1909	BKN N	4	10	.286	2.46	16	13	10	113.1	104	38	43	0	1	2	0	*				31	32	7	3	1.8	.900

Jim Hunter

HUNTER, JAMES MacGREGOR BR TR 6′ 3″ 205 lbs.
B. June 22, 1964, Jersey City, N. J.

Year	Team	W	L	PCT	ERA	G	GS	CG	IP	H	BB	SO	ShO	Relief Pitching W	Relief Pitching L	Relief Pitching SV	Batting AB	Batting H	Batting HR	BA	PO	A	E	DP	TC/G	FA
1991	MIL A	0	5	.000	7.26	8	6	0	31	45	17	14	0	0	1	0	0	0	0	—	3	7	0	1	1.3	1.000

Lem Hunter

HUNTER, ROBERT LEMUEL
B. Jan. 16, 1863, Warren, Ohio D. Nov. 9, 1956, West Lafayette, Ohio.

Year	Team	W	L	PCT	ERA	G	GS	CG	IP	H	BB	SO	ShO	Relief Pitching W	Relief Pitching L	Relief Pitching SV	Batting AB	Batting H	Batting HR	BA	PO	A	E	DP	TC/G	FA
1883	CLE N	0	0	—	1.42	1	0	0	6.1	10	2	4	0	0	0	0	*				0	1	0	0	0.5	1.000

Willard Hunter

HUNTER, WILLARD MITCHELL BR TL 6′ 2″ 180 lbs.
B. Mar. 8, 1934, Newark, N. J.

Year	Team	W	L	PCT	ERA	G	GS	CG	IP	H	BB	SO	ShO	Relief Pitching W	Relief Pitching L	Relief Pitching SV	Batting AB	Batting H	Batting HR	BA	PO	A	E	DP	TC/G	FA
1962	2 teams LA N (1G 0–0) NY N (27G 1–6)																									
″	total	1	6	.143	6.65	28	6	1	65	73	38	41	0	1	0	0	13	3	0	.231	5	7	1	0	0.5	.923
1964	NY N	3	3	.500	4.41	41	0	0	49	54	9	22	0	3	3	5	1	1	0	1.000	2	8	0	1	0.2	1.000
2 yrs.		4	9	.308	5.68	69	6	1	114	127	47	63	0	4	3	5	14	4	0	.286	7	15	1	1	0.3	.957

Walter Huntzinger

HUNTZINGER, WALTER HENRY (Shakes) BR TR 6′ 150 lbs.
B. Feb. 6, 1899, Pottsville, Pa. D. Aug. 11, 1981, Upper Darby, Pa.

Year	Team	W	L	PCT	ERA	G	GS	CG	IP	H	BB	SO	ShO	Relief Pitching W	Relief Pitching L	Relief Pitching SV	Batting AB	Batting H	Batting HR	BA	PO	A	E	DP	TC/G	FA
1923	NY N	0	1	.000	7.88	2	1	0	8	9	1	2	0	0	1	0	2	0	0	.000	0	1	0	0	0.5	1.000
1924		1	1	.500	4.45	12	2	0	32.1	41	9	6	0	0	0	1	8	4	0	.500	0	7	1	0	0.7	.875
1925		5	1	.833	3.50	26	1	0	64.1	68	17	19	0	5	1	0	11	1	0	.091	1	11	0	1	0.5	1.000
1926	2 teams STL N (9G 0–4) CHI N (11G 1–1)																									
″	total	1	5	.167	2.73	20	4	2	62.2	61	22	13	0	1	2	2	15	1	0	.067	2	20	1	1	1.1	.957
4 yrs.		7	8	.467	3.60	60	8	2	167.1	179	49	40	0	6	4	3	36	6	0	.167	3	39	2	2	0.7	.955

Tom Hurd

HURD, THOMAS CARR (Whitey) BR TR 5′ 9″ 155 lbs.
B. May 27, 1924, Danville, Va. D. Sept. 5, 1982, Waterloo, Iowa.

Year	Team	W	L	PCT	ERA	G	GS	CG	IP	H	BB	SO	ShO	Relief Pitching W	Relief Pitching L	Relief Pitching SV	Batting AB	Batting H	Batting HR	BA	PO	A	E	DP	TC/G	FA
1954	BOS A	2	0	1.000	3.03	16	0	0	29.2	21	12	14	0	2	0	1	3	1	0	.333	3	6	0	0	0.6	1.000
1955		8	6	.571	3.01	43	0	0	80.2	72	38	48	0	**8**	6	5	14	1	0	.071	4	12	0	1	0.4	1.000
1956		3	4	.429	5.33	40	0	0	76	84	47	34	0	3	4	5	12	6	0	.500	3	9	0	0	0.3	1.000
3 yrs.		13	10	.565	3.96	99	0	0	186.1	177	97	96	0	13	10	11	29	8	0	.276	10	27	0	1	0.4	1.000

Bruce Hurst

HURST, BRUCE VEE BL TL 6′ 4″ 200 lbs.
B. Mar. 24, 1958, St. George, Utah.

Year	Team	W	L	PCT	ERA	G	GS	CG	IP	H	BB	SO	ShO	Relief Pitching W	Relief Pitching L	Relief Pitching SV	Batting AB	Batting H	Batting HR	BA	PO	A	E	DP	TC/G	FA
1980	BOS A	2	2	.500	9.00	12	7	0	31	39	16	16	0	0	0	0	0	0	0	—	1	4	0	0	0.4	1.000
1981		2	0	1.000	4.30	5	5	0	23	23	12	11	0	0	0	0	0	0	0	—	0	2	0	0	0.4	1.000
1982		3	7	.300	5.77	28	19	0	117	161	40	53	0	0	1	0	0	0	0	—	6	22	1	1	1.0	.966
1983		12	12	.500	4.09	33	32	6	211.1	241	62	115	2	0	0	0	0	0	0	—	12	34	2	2	1.5	.958
1984		12	12	.500	3.92	33	33	9	218	232	88	136	2	0	0	0	0	0	0	—	10	30	0	1	1.2	1.000
1985		11	13	.458	4.51	35	31	6	229.1	243	70	189	1	0	2	0	0	0	0	—	11	32	3	0	1.3	.935
1986		13	8	.619	2.99	25	25	11	174.1	169	50	167	4	0	0	0	0	0	0	—	7	18	2	2	1.1	.926
1987		15	13	.536	4.41	33	33	15	238.2	239	76	190	3	0	0	0	0	0	0	—	12	34	3	2	1.5	.939
1988		18	6	.750	3.66	33	32	7	216.2	222	65	166	1	0	0	0	0	0	0	—	7	31	0	0	1.2	1.000
1989	SD N	15	11	.577	2.69	33	33	**10**	244.2	214	66	179	2	0	0	0	70	5	0	.071	8	42	0	2	1.5	1.000
1990		11	9	.550	3.14	33	33	9	223.2	188	63	162	**4**	0	0	0	67	6	0	.090	7	34	1	3	1.3	.976
1991		15	8	.652	3.29	31	31	4	221.2	201	59	141	0	0	0	0	67	9	0	.134	7	33	2	2	1.4	.952
1992		14	9	.609	3.85	32	32	6	217.1	223	51	131	4	0	0	0	69	11	0	.159	10	32	1	0	1.3	.977
1993	2 teams SD N (2G 0–1) CLR N (3G 0–1)																									
″	total	0	2	.000	7.62	5	5	0	13	15	6	9	0	0	0	0	1	0	0	.000	0	4	0	0	0.8	1.000
1994	TEX A	2	1	.667	7.11	8	8	0	38	53	16	24	0	0	0	0	0	0	0	—	0	3	0	0	0.4	1.000
15 yrs.		145	113	.562	3.92	379	359	83	2417.2	2463	740	1689	23	0	3	0	274	31	0	.113	98	355	15	15	1.2	.968
LEAGUE CHAMPIONSHIP SERIES																										
1986	BOS A	1	0	1.000	2.40	2	2	1	15	18	1	8	0	0	0	0	0	0	0	—	1	2	0	0	1.5	1.000
1988		0	2	.000	2.77	2	2	1	13	10	5	12	0	0	0	0	0	0	0	—	0	4	0	0	2.0	1.000
2 yrs.		1	2	.333	2.57	4	4	2	28	28	6	20	0	0	0	0	0	0	0		1	6	0	0	1.8	1.000
								4th																		
WORLD SERIES																										
1986	BOS A	2	0	1.000	1.96	3	3	1	23	18	6	17	0	0	0	0	3	0	0	.000	1	3	0	0	1.3	1.000

James Hurst

HURST, JAMES LAVON BL TL 6′ 160 lbs.
B. June 1, 1967, Plantation, Fla.

Year	Team	W	L	PCT	ERA	G	GS	CG	IP	H	BB	SO	ShO	Relief Pitching W	Relief Pitching L	Relief Pitching SV	Batting AB	Batting H	Batting HR	BA	PO	A	E	DP	TC/G	FA
1994	TEX A	0	0	—	10.13	8	0	0	10.2	17	8	5	0	0	0	0	0	0	0	—	0	2	0	0	0.3	1.000

Jonathan Hurst

HURST, JONATHAN BR TR 6′ 3″ 175 lbs.
B. Oct. 20, 1966, New York, N. Y.

Year	Team	W	L	PCT	ERA	G	GS	CG	IP	H	BB	SO	ShO	Relief Pitching W	Relief Pitching L	Relief Pitching SV	Batting AB	Batting H	Batting HR	BA	PO	A	E	DP	TC/G	FA
1992	MON N	1	1	.500	5.51	3	3	0	16.1	18	7	4	0	0	0	0	4	0	0	.000	2	2	0	0	1.3	1.000
1994	NY N	0	1	.000	12.60	7	0	0	10	15	5	6	0	0	1	0	0	0	0	—	1	1	0	0	0.3	1.000
2 yrs.		1	2	.333	8.20	10	3	0	26.1	33	12	10	0	0	1	0	4	0	0	.000	3	3	0	0	0.6	1.000

Edwin Hurtado

HURTADO, EDWIN AMILGAR BR TR 6′ 3″ 215 lbs.
B. Feb. 1, 1970, Barquisimeto, Venezuela.

Year	Team		W	L	PCT	ERA	G	GS	CG	IP	H	BB	SO	ShO	Relief Pitching W	Relief Pitching L	Relief Pitching SV	Batting AB	Batting H	Batting HR	BA	PO	A	E	DP	TC/G	FA
1995	TOR	A	5	2	.714	5.45	14	10	1	77.2	81	40	33	0	1	0	0	0	0	0	—	6	8	0	3	1.0	1.000

Bill Husted

HUSTED, WILLIAM J.
B. Oct. 11, 1866, Gloucester, N. J. D. May 17, 1941, Gloucester, N. J.

Year	Team		W	L	PCT	ERA	G	GS	CG	IP	H	BB	SO	ShO	Relief Pitching W	Relief Pitching L	Relief Pitching SV	Batting AB	Batting H	Batting HR	BA	PO	A	E	DP	TC/G	FA
1890	PHI	P	5	10	.333	4.88	18	17	12	129	148	67	33	0	0	0	0	56	6	0	.107	3	24	5	1	1.8	.844

Bert Husting

HUSTING, BERTHOLD JUNEAU (Pete) BR TR
B. Mar. 6, 1878, Fond du Lac, Wis. D. Sept. 3, 1948, Milwaukee, Wis.

Year	Team		W	L	PCT	ERA	G	GS	CG	IP	H	BB	SO	ShO	Relief Pitching W	Relief Pitching L	Relief Pitching SV	Batting AB	Batting H	Batting HR	BA	PO	A	E	DP	TC/G	FA
1900	PIT	N	0	0	—	5.63	2	0	0	8	10	5	7	0	0	0	0	3	0	0	.000	1	4	0	0	2.5	1.000
1901	MIL	A	10	15	.400	4.27	34	26	19	217.1	234	95	67	0	1	1	1	94	19	1	.202	22	82	9	4	3.1	.920
1902	2 teams	BOS A	(1G 0–1)		PHI A	(32G 14–5)																					
″	total		14	6	.700	3.99	33	28	18	212	255	99	48	1	1	0	0	86	14	0	.163	20	74	12	3	3.2	.887
3 yrs.			24	21	.533	4.16	69	54	37	437.1	499	199	122	1	2	1	1	183	33	1	.180	43	160	21	7	3.2	.906

Johnny Hutchings

HUTCHINGS, JOHN RICHARD JOSEPH BB TR 6′ 2″ 250 lbs.
B. Apr. 14, 1916, Chicago, Ill. D. Apr. 27, 1963, Indianapolis, Ind.

Year	Team		W	L	PCT	ERA	G	GS	CG	IP	H	BB	SO	ShO	Relief Pitching W	Relief Pitching L	Relief Pitching SV	Batting AB	Batting H	Batting HR	BA	PO	A	E	DP	TC/G	FA
1940	CIN	N	2	1	.667	3.50	19	4	0	54	53	18	18	0	2	0	0	13	2	0	.154	1	6	0	0	0.4	1.000
1941	2 teams	CIN N	(8G 0–0)		BOS N	(36G 1–6)																					
″	total		1	6	.143	4.13	44	7	1	106.2	122	26	41	1	0	2	2	27	4	0	.148	2	23	1	5	0.6	.962
1942	BOS	N	1	0	1.000	4.39	20	3	0	65.2	66	34	27	0	0	0	0	20	1	0	.050	3	10	1	1	0.7	.929
1944			1	4	.200	3.97	14	7	1	56.2	55	26	26	0	0	1	1	15	1	0	.067	1	8	0	1	0.6	1.000
1945			7	6	.538	3.75	57	12	3	185	173	75	99	2	3	3	3	54	13	0	.241	7	36	3	1	0.8	.935
1946			0	1	.000	9.00	1	1	0	3	5	1	1	0	0	0	0	1	0	0	.000	0	0	0	0	0.0	.000
6 yrs.			12	18	.400	3.96	155	34	5	471	474	180	212	3	5	6	6	130	21	0	.162	14	83	5	8	0.7	.951
WORLD SERIES																											
1940	CIN	N	0	0	—	9.00	1	0	0	1	2	1	0	0	0	0	0	0	0	0	—	0	1	0	0	1.0	1.000

Bill Hutchinson

HUTCHINSON, WILLIAM FORREST (Wild Bill) BR TR 5′ 9″ 175 lbs.
B. Dec. 17, 1859, New Haven, Conn. D. Mar. 19, 1926, Kansas City, Mo.

Year	Team		W	L	PCT	ERA	G	GS	CG	IP	H	BB	SO	ShO	Relief Pitching W	Relief Pitching L	Relief Pitching SV	Batting AB	Batting H	Batting HR	BA	PO	A	E	DP	TC/G	FA
1884	KC	U	1	1	.500	2.65	2	2	2	17	14	1	5	0	0	0	0	8	2	0	.250	1	12	0	0	6.5	1.000
1889	CHI	N	16	17	.485	3.54	37	36	33	318	306	117	136	3	0	0	0	133	21	1	.158	18	86	13	3	3.1	.889
1890			**42**	25	.627	2.70	**71**	**66**	**65**	**603**	505	199	289	5	1	**1**	**2**	261	53	2	.203	44	128	14	5	2.6	.925
1891			**44**	19	.698	2.81	**66**	**58**	**56**	**561**	**508**	178	261	4	**7**	0	1	243	45	2	.185	22	103	13	0	2.1	.906
1892			**37**	36	.507	2.74	**75**	**70**	**67**	**627**	**572**	187	**316**	5	1	2	0	263	57	1	.217	25	156	14	4	2.5	.928
1893			16	24	.400	4.75	44	40	38	348.1	420	156	80	2	0	1	0	162	41	0	.253	15	62	9	3	1.9	.895
1894			14	16	.467	6.06	36	34	28	277.2	373	140	59	0	1	0	0	136	42	6	.309	11	45	5	1	1.5	.918
1895			13	21	.382	4.73	38	35	30	291	371	129	85	2	0	0	0	126	25	0	.198	9	65	8	1	2.2	.902
1897	STL	N	1	4	.200	6.08	6	5	2	40	55	22	5	0	0	0	0	18	5	0	.278	0	7	1	0	1.3	.875
9 yrs.			184	163	.530	3.58	375	346	321	3083	3124	1129	1236	21	10	4	3	1350	291	12	.216	145	664	77	17	2.3	.913

Fred Hutchinson

HUTCHINSON, FREDERICK CHARLES BL TR 6′ 2″ 190 lbs.
B. Aug. 12, 1919, Seattle, Wash. D. Nov. 12, 1964, Bradenton, Fla.
Manager 1952–54, 1956–64.

Year	Team		W	L	PCT	ERA	G	GS	CG	IP	H	BB	SO	ShO	Relief Pitching W	Relief Pitching L	Relief Pitching SV	Batting AB	Batting H	Batting HR	BA	PO	A	E	DP	TC/G	FA
1939	DET	A	3	6	.333	5.21	13	12	3	84.2	95	51	22	0	0	0	0	34	13	0	.382	6	13	0	1	1.5	1.000
1940			3	7	.300	5.68	17	10	1	76	85	26	32	0	1	2	0	30	8	0	.267	2	16	2	1	1.2	.900
1946			14	11	.560	3.09	28	26	16	207	184	66	138	3	0	0	2	89	28	0	.315	11	47	1	3	2.1	.983
1947			18	10	.643	3.03	33	25	18	219.2	211	61	113	3	2	1	2	106	32	2	.302	15	40	1	1	1.7	.982
1948			13	11	.542	4.32	33	28	15	221	223	48	92	0	0	0	0	112	23	1	.205	19	45	0	5	1.9	1.000
1949			15	7	.682	2.96	33	21	9	188.2	167	52	54	4	3	2	1	73	18	0	.247	18	39	1	5	1.8	.983
1950			17	8	.680	3.96	39	26	10	231.2	269	48	71	1	4	1	0	95	31	0	.326	17	50	4	6	1.8	.944
1951			10	10	.500	3.68	31	20	9	188.1	204	27	53	2	4	1	2	85	16	0	.188	17	45	4	1	2.1	.939
1952			2	1	.667	3.38	12	1	0	37.1	40	9	12	0	2	0	0	18	1	0	.056	1	15	0	1	1.3	1.000
1953			0	0	—	2.79	3	0	0	9.2	9	0	4	0	0	0	0	6	1	1	.167	6	0	0	0	1.5	1.000
10 yrs.			95	71	.572	3.73	242	169	81	1464	1487	388	591	13	16	7	7	*				112	310	13	24	1.8	.970
WORLD SERIES																											
1940	DET	A	0	0	—	9.00	1	0	0	1	1	1	1	0	0	0	0	*				0	0	0	0	0.0	.000

Ira Hutchinson

HUTCHINSON, IRA KENDALL BR TR 5′10½″ 180 lbs.
B. Aug. 31, 1910, Chicago, Ill. D. Aug. 21, 1973, Chicago, Ill.

Year	Team		W	L	PCT	ERA	G	GS	CG	IP	H	BB	SO	ShO	Relief Pitching W	Relief Pitching L	Relief Pitching SV	Batting AB	Batting H	Batting HR	BA	PO	A	E	DP	TC/G	FA
1933	CHI	A	0	0	—	13.50	1	1	0	4	7	3	2	0	0	0	0	2	1	0	.500	0	0	0	0	0.0	.000
1937	BOS	N	4	6	.400	3.73	31	8	1	91.2	99	35	29	0	4	0	0	26	3	0	.115	5	24	1	1	1.0	.967
1938			9	8	.529	2.74	36	12	4	151	150	61	38	1	5	3	4	52	9	0	.173	14	33	1	4	1.3	.979
1939	BKN	N	5	2	.714	4.34	41	1	0	105.2	103	51	46	0	5	2	1	27	1	0	.037	3	28	0	2	0.8	1.000
1940	STL	N	4	2	.667	3.13	20	2	1	63.1	68	19	19	0	2	2	1	18	4	0	.222	2	14	1	1	0.9	.941
1941			1	5	.167	3.86	29	0	0	46.2	32	19	19	0	1	**5**	5	8	2	0	.250	2	10	2	3	0.5	.857
1944	BOS	N	9	7	.563	4.21	40	8	1	119.2	136	53	22	1	6	4	1	29	4	0	.138	3	29	0	4	0.8	1.000
1945			2	3	.400	5.02	11	0	0	28.2	33	8	4	0	2	3	1	9	0	0	.000	0	9	0	1	0.8	1.000
8 yrs.			34	33	.507	3.76	209	32	7	610.2	628	249	179	2	25	19	13	171	24	0	.140	29	147	5	16	0.9	.972

Herb Hutson

HUTSON, GEORGE HERBERT BR TR 6′ 2″ 205 lbs.
B. July 17, 1949, Savannah, Ga.

Year	Team		W	L	PCT	ERA	G	GS	CG	IP	H	BB	SO	ShO	Relief Pitching W	Relief Pitching L	Relief Pitching SV	Batting AB	Batting H	Batting HR	BA	PO	A	E	DP	TC/G	FA
1974	CHI	N	0	2	.000	3.41	20	2	0	29	24	15	22	0	0	0	0	2	0	0	.000	1	2	0	0	0.2	1.000

Mark Hutton

HUTTON, MARK STEVEN BR TR 6′ 6″ 240 lbs.
B. Feb. 6, 1970, South Adelaide, Australia.

Year	Team		W	L	PCT	ERA	G	GS	CG	IP	H	BB	SO	ShO	Relief Pitching W	Relief Pitching L	Relief Pitching SV	Batting AB	Batting H	Batting HR	BA	PO	A	E	DP	TC/G	FA
1993	NY	A	1	1	.500	5.73	7	4	0	22	24	17	12	0	0	0	0	0	0	0	—	1	2	1	0	0.6	.750
1994			0	0	—	4.91	2	0	0	3.2	4	0	1	0	0	0	0	0	0	0	—	0	0	0	0	0.0	.000
2 yrs.			1	1	.500	5.61	9	4	0	25.2	28	17	13	0	0	0	0	0	0	0		1	2	1	0	0.4	.750

Tom Hutton

HUTTON, THOMAS GEORGE BL TL 5′11″ 180 lbs.
B. Apr. 20, 1946, Los Angeles, Calif.

Year	Team		W	L	PCT	ERA	G	GS	CG	IP	H	BB	SO	ShO	Relief Pitching W	Relief Pitching L	Relief Pitching SV	Batting AB	Batting H	Batting HR	BA	PO	A	E	DP	TC/G	FA
1980	MON	N	0	0	—	27.00	1	0	0	1	3	1	1	0	0	0	0	*				2	0	0	0	0.7	1.000

Year	Team	Lg	W	L	PCT	ERA	G	GS	CG	IP	H	BB	SO	ShO	Relief Pitching W	Relief Pitching L	Relief Pitching SV	Batting AB	Batting H	Batting HR	BA	PO	A	E	DP	TC/G	FA

Dick Hyde

HYDE, RICHARD ELDE BR TR 5′11″ 170 lbs.
B. Aug. 3, 1928, Hindsboro, Ill.

Year	Team	Lg	W	L	PCT	ERA	G	GS	CG	IP	H	BB	SO	ShO	Relief W	Relief L	Relief SV	AB	H	HR	BA	PO	A	E	DP	TC/G	FA
1955	WAS	A	0	0	—	4.50	3	0	0	2	2	1	1	0	0	0	0	0	0	0	—	0	0	0	0	0.0	.000
1957			4	3	.571	4.12	52	2	0	109.1	104	56	46	0	4	3	1	18	3	0	.167	5	23	0	3	0.5	1.000
1958			10	3	.769	1.75	53	0	0	103	82	35	49	0	**10**	3	18	18	0	0	.000	7	25	1	1	0.6	.970
1959			2	5	.286	4.97	37	0	0	54.1	56	27	29	0	2	5	4	6	0	0	.000	3	20	3	0	0.7	.885
1960			0	1	.000	4.15	9	0	0	8.2	11	5	4	0	0	1	0	0	0	0	—	0	1	0	0	0.1	1.000
1961	BAL	A	1	2	.333	5.57	15	0	0	21	18	13	15	0	1	2	0	1	1	0	1.000	1	10	1	1	0.8	.917
6 yrs.			17	14	.548	3.56	169	2	0	298.1	273	137	144	0	17	14	23	43	4	0	.093	16	79	5	5	0.6	.950

Jim Hyndman

HYNDMAN, JAMES WILLIAM
B. July 1865, Kingston, Pa. Deceased.

Year	Team	Lg	W	L	PCT	ERA	G	GS	CG	IP	H	BB	SO	ShO	Relief W	Relief L	Relief SV	AB	H	HR	BA	PO	A	E	DP	TC/G	FA
1886	PHI	AA	0	1	.000	*27.00*	1	1	0	2	5	5	1	0	0	0	0	*				3	1	1	0	2.5	.800

Pat Hynes

HYNES, PATRICK J. TL
B. Mar. 12, 1884, St. Louis, Mo. D. Mar. 12, 1907, St. Louis, Mo.

Year	Team	Lg	W	L	PCT	ERA	G	GS	CG	IP	H	BB	SO	ShO	Relief W	Relief L	Relief SV	AB	H	HR	BA	PO	A	E	DP	TC/G	FA
1903	STL	N	0	1	.000	4.00	1	1	1	9	10	6	1	0	0	0	0	3	0	0	.000	1	0	1	0	2.0	.500
1904	STL	A	1	0	1.000	6.23	5	2	1	26	35	7	6	0	0	0	0	254	60	0	.236	73	5	8	0	1.3	.907
2 yrs.			1	1	.500	5.66	6	3	2	35	45	13	7	0	0	0	0	*				74	5	9	0	1.3	.898

Ham Iburg

IBURG, HERMAN EDWARD BR TR 5′11½″ 165 lbs.
B. Oct. 29, 1877, San Francisco, Calif. D. Feb. 11, 1945, San Francisco, Calif.

Year	Team	Lg	W	L	PCT	ERA	G	GS	CG	IP	H	BB	SO	ShO	Relief W	Relief L	Relief SV	AB	H	HR	BA	PO	A	E	DP	TC/G	FA
1902	PHI	N	11	18	.379	3.89	30	29	20	236	286	62	106	1	0	0	0	87	12	0	.138	8	59	4	1	2.4	.944

Gary Ignasiak

IGNASIAK, GARY RAYMOND BR TL 5′11″ 185 lbs.
Brother of Mike Ignasiak.
B. Sept. 1, 1949, Mt. Clemens, Mich.

Year	Team	Lg	W	L	PCT	ERA	G	GS	CG	IP	H	BB	SO	ShO	Relief W	Relief L	Relief SV	AB	H	HR	BA	PO	A	E	DP	TC/G	FA
1973	DET	A	0	0	—	3.60	3	0	0	5	5	3	4	0	0	0	0	0	0	0	—	0	1	0	0	0.3	1.000

Mike Ignasiak

IGNASIAK, MICHAEL JAMES BR TR 5′11″ 175 lbs.
Brother of Gary Ignasiak.
B. Mar. 12, 1967, Anchorville, Mich.

Year	Team	Lg	W	L	PCT	ERA	G	GS	CG	IP	H	BB	SO	ShO	Relief W	Relief L	Relief SV	AB	H	HR	BA	PO	A	E	DP	TC/G	FA
1991	MIL	A	2	1	.667	5.68	4	1	0	12.2	7	8	10	0	2	1	0	0	0	0	—	1	0	0	0	0.3	1.000
1993			1	1	.500	3.65	27	0	0	37	32	21	28	0	1	1	0	0	0	0	—	0	3	0	0	0.1	1.000
1994			3	1	.750	4.53	23	5	0	47.2	51	13	24	0	2	0	0	0	0	0	—	2	4	0	1	0.3	1.000
1995			4	1	.800	5.90	25	0	0	39.2	51	23	26	0	4	1	0	0	0	0	—	3	2	0	1	0.2	1.000
4 yrs.			10	4	.714	4.80	79	6	0	137	141	65	88	0	9	3	0	0	0	0		6	9	0	2	0.2	1.000

Blaise Ilsley

ILSLEY, BLAISE FRANCIS BL TL 6′1″ 195 lbs.
B. Apr. 9, 1964, Alpena, Mich.

Year	Team	Lg	W	L	PCT	ERA	G	GS	CG	IP	H	BB	SO	ShO	Relief W	Relief L	Relief SV	AB	H	HR	BA	PO	A	E	DP	TC/G	FA
1994	CHI	N	0	0	—	7.80	10	0	0	15	25	9	9	0	0	0	0	1	0	0	.000	4	1	0	0	0.5	1.000

Doc Imlay

IMLAY, HARRY MILLER BR TR 5′11″ 168 lbs.
B. Jan. 12, 1889, Allentown, N. J. D. Oct. 7, 1948, Bordentown, N. J.

Year	Team	Lg	W	L	PCT	ERA	G	GS	CG	IP	H	BB	SO	ShO	Relief W	Relief L	Relief SV	AB	H	HR	BA	PO	A	E	DP	TC/G	FA
1913	PHI	N	0	0	—	7.24	9	0	0	13.2	19	7	7	0	0	0	0	3	0	0	.000	1	5	0	0	0.7	1.000

Bob Ingersoll

INGERSOLL, ROBERT RANDOLPH BR TR 5′11½″ 175 lbs.
B. Jan. 8, 1883, Rapid City, S. D. D. Jan. 13, 1927, Minneapolis, Minn.

Year	Team	Lg	W	L	PCT	ERA	G	GS	CG	IP	H	BB	SO	ShO	Relief W	Relief L	Relief SV	AB	H	HR	BA	PO	A	E	DP	TC/G	FA
1914	CIN	N	0	0	—	3.00	4	0	0	6	5	5	2	0	0	0	0	1	1	0	1.000	0	1	0	0	0.3	1.000

Bert Inks

INKS, ALBERT JOHN BL TL 6′3″ 175 lbs.
B. Jan. 27, 1871, Ligonier, Ind. D. Oct. 3, 1941, Ligonier, Ind.

Year	Team	Lg	W	L	PCT	ERA	G	GS	CG	IP	H	BB	SO	ShO	Relief W	Relief L	Relief SV	AB	H	HR	BA	PO	A	E	DP	TC/G	FA
1891	BKN	N	3	10	.231	4.02	13	13	11	96.1	99	43	47	1	0	0	0	35	10	0	.286	2	18	2	0	1.7	.909
1892	2 teams	BKN N (9G 4–2) WAS N (3G 1–2)																									
″	total		5	4	.556	4.22	12	11	7	79	77	43	36	1	0	0	0	35	13	0	.371	3	18	4	0	2.1	.840
1894	2 teams	BAL N (22G 9–4) LOU N (8G 2–6)																									
″	total		11	10	.524	5.84	30	22	18	192.2	268	88	38	0	1	0	1	84	30	0	.357	11	33	8	0	1.7	.846
1895	LOU	N	7	20	.259	6.40	28	27	21	205.1	294	78	42	0	0	0	0	84	21	0	.250	5	53	6	0	2.3	.906
1896	2 teams	PHI N (3G 0–1) CIN N (3G 1–1)																									
″	total		1	2	.333	5.64	6	4	2	30.1	42	14	4	0	0	0	0	12	1	0	.083	2	2	1	0	0.8	.800
5 yrs.			27	46	.370	5.52	89	77	59	603.2	780	266	167	2	1	0	1	250	75	0	.300	23	124	21	0	1.9	.875

Jeff Innis

INNIS, JEFFREY DAVID BR TR 6′1″ 170 lbs.
B. July 5, 1962, Decatur, Ill.

Year	Team	Lg	W	L	PCT	ERA	G	GS	CG	IP	H	BB	SO	ShO	Relief W	Relief L	Relief SV	AB	H	HR	BA	PO	A	E	DP	TC/G	FA
1987	NY	N	0	1	.000	3.16	17	1	0	25.2	29	4	28	0	0	1	0	3	0	0	.000	3	2	0	0	0.3	1.000
1988			1	1	.500	1.89	12	0	0	19	19	2	14	0	1	1	0	0	0	0	—	0	0	0	0	0.0	.000
1989			0	1	.000	3.18	29	0	0	39.2	38	8	16	0	0	1	0	2	0	0	.000	7	8	1	0	0.6	.938
1990			1	3	.250	2.39	18	0	0	26.1	19	10	12	0	1	3	1	0	0	0	—	4	3	0	0	0.4	1.000
1991			0	2	.000	2.66	69	0	0	84.2	66	23	47	0	0	2	0	2	0	0	.000	13	26	1	1	0.6	.975
1992			6	9	.400	2.86	76	0	0	88	85	36	39	0	6	9	1	2	0	0	.000	13	21	0	1	0.4	1.000
1993			2	3	.400	4.11	67	0	0	76.2	81	38	36	0	2	3	3	0	0	0	—	7	13	0	1	0.3	1.000
7 yrs.			10	20	.333	3.05	288	1	0	360	337	121	192	0	10	20	5	9	0	0	.000	47	73	2	3	0.4	.984

Dane Iorg

IORG, DANE CHARLES BL TR 6′ 180 lbs.
Brother of Garth Iorg.
B. May 11, 1950, Eureka, Calif.

Year	Team	Lg	W	L	PCT	ERA	G	GS	CG	IP	H	BB	SO	ShO	Relief W	Relief L	Relief SV	AB	H	HR	BA	PO	A	E	DP	TC/G	FA
1986	SD	N	0	0	—	6.00	2	0	0	3	5	1	2	0	0	0	0	*				71	4	2	6	4.8	.974

Hooks Iott

IOTT, CLARENCE EUGENE BB TL 6′2″ 200 lbs.
B. Dec. 3, 1919, Mountain Grove, Mo. D. Aug. 17, 1980, St. Petersburg, Fla.

Year	Team	Lg	W	L	PCT	ERA	G	GS	CG	IP	H	BB	SO	ShO	Relief W	Relief L	Relief SV	AB	H	HR	BA	PO	A	E	DP	TC/G	FA
1941	STL	A	0	0	—	9.00	2	0	0	2	2	1	1	0	0	0	0	0	0	0	—	0	1	0	0	0.5	1.000
1947	2 teams	STL A (4G 0–1) NY N (20G 3–8)																									
″	total		3	9	.250	7.00	24	9	2	79.2	82	66	52	1	1	5	0	23	3	0	.130	2	13	0	1	0.6	1.000
2 yrs.			3	9	.250	7.05	26	9	2	81.2	84	67	53	1	1	5	0	23	3	0	.130	2	14	0	1	0.6	1.000

Daryl Irvine

IRVINE, DARYL KEITH BR TR 6′ 3″ 195 lbs.
B. Nov. 15, 1964, Harrisonburg, Va.

Year	Team	W	L	PCT	ERA	G	GS	CG	IP	H	BB	SO	ShO	Relief Pitching W	L	SV	Batting AB	H	HR	BA	PO	A	E	DP	TC/G	FA
1990	BOS A	1	1	.500	4.67	11	0	0	17.1	15	10	9	0	1	1	0	0	0	0	—	1	3	0	0	0.4	1.000
1991		0	0	—	6.00	9	0	0	18	25	9	8	0	0	0	0	0	0	0	—	3	3	1	0	0.8	.857
1992		3	4	.429	6.11	21	0	0	28	31	14	10	0	3	4	0	0	0	0	—	2	5	0	0	0.3	1.000
3 yrs.		4	5	.444	5.68	41	0	0	63.1	71	33	27	0	4	5	0	0	0	0		6	11	1	0	0.4	.944

Arthur Irwin

IRWIN, ARTHUR ALBERT BL TR 5′ 8½″ 158 lbs.
Brother of John Irwin.
B. Feb. 14, 1858, Toronto, Ont., Canada D. July 16, 1921, Atlantic Ocean.
Manager 1889, 1891–92, 1894–96, 1898–99.

Year	Team	W	L	PCT	ERA	G	GS	CG	IP	H	BB	SO	ShO	Relief Pitching W	L	SV	Batting AB	H	HR	BA	PO	A	E	DP	TC/G	FA
1884	PRO N	0	0	—	*3.00*	1	0	0	3	5	1	0	0	0	0	0	404	97	2	.240	98	345	53	27	5.8	.893
1889	WAS N	0	0	—	0.00	1	0	0	1	1	0	0	0	0	0	0	386	89	0	.231	50	155	36	11	4.8	.851
2 yrs.		0	0		2.25	2	0	0	4	6	1	0	0	0	0	0	*				1402	3268	647	303	5.2	.878

Bill Irwin

IRWIN, WILLIAM FRANKLIN (Phil) BR TR 6′ 195 lbs.
B. Sept. 16, 1859, Neville, Ohio D. Aug. 7, 1933, Ft. Thomas, Ky.

Year	Team	W	L	PCT	ERA	G	GS	CG	IP	H	BB	SO	ShO	Relief Pitching W	L	SV	Batting AB	H	HR	BA	PO	A	E	DP	TC/G	FA
1886	CIN AA	0	2	.000	*5.82*	2	2	2	17	18	8	6	0	0	0	0	6	0	0	.000	1	5	0	0	3.0	1.000

Frank Isbell

ISBELL, WILLIAM FRANK (Bald Eagle) BL TR 5′11″ 190 lbs.
B. Aug. 21, 1875, Delevan, N. Y. D. July 15, 1941, Wichita, Kans.

Year	Team	W	L	PCT	ERA	G	GS	CG	IP	H	BB	SO	ShO	Relief Pitching W	L	SV	Batting AB	H	HR	BA	PO	A	E	DP	TC/G	FA
1898	CHI N	4	7	.364	3.56	13	9	7	81	86	42	16	0	1	1	0	159	37	0	.233	54	43	19	5	2.4	.836
1901	CHI A	0	0	—	9.00	1	0	0	1	2	0	0	0	0	0	0	556	143	3	.257	1389	107	32	79	10.8	.979
1902		0	0	—	9.00	1	1	0	1	3	1	1	0	0	0	0	515	130	4	.252	1405	105	22	100	11.0	.986
1906		0	0	—	0.00	1	0	0	2	1	0	2	0	0	0	0	549	153	0	.279	1225	136	35	58	10.0	.975
1907		0	0	—	0.00	1	0	0	0.1	0	0	0	0	0	0	1	486	118	0	.243	285	386	30	42	5.6	.957
5 yrs.		4	7	.364	3.59	17	10	7	85.1	92	43	19	0	1	1	1	*				7643	1605	242	448	8.4	.974

Jason Isringhausen

ISRINGHAUSEN, JASON DERIK BR TR 6′ 3″ 195 lbs.
B. Sept. 7, 1972, Brighton, Ill.

Year	Team	W	L	PCT	ERA	G	GS	CG	IP	H	BB	SO	ShO	Relief Pitching W	L	SV	Batting AB	H	HR	BA	PO	A	E	DP	TC/G	FA
1995	NY N	9	2	.818	2.81	14	14	1	93	88	31	55	0	0	0	0	27	4	0	.148	8	11	2	1	1.5	.905

Pete Jablonowski

Playing record listed under Pete Appleton.

Al Jackson

JACKSON, ALVIN NEIL BL TL 5′10″ 169 lbs.
B. Dec. 25, 1935, Waco, Tex.

Year	Team	W	L	PCT	ERA	G	GS	CG	IP	H	BB	SO	ShO	Relief Pitching W	L	SV	Batting AB	H	HR	BA	PO	A	E	DP	TC/G	FA
1959	PIT N	0	0	—	6.50	8	3	0	18	30	8	13	0	0	0	0	5	1	0	.200	2	2	0	0	0.5	1.000
1961		1	0	1.000	3.42	3	2	1	23.2	20	4	15	0	0	0	0	8	0	0	.000	2	7	0	1	3.0	1.000
1962	NY N	8	20	.286	4.40	36	33	12	231.1	244	78	118	4	0	0	0	73	5	0	.068	21	59	2	1	2.3	.976
1963		13	17	.433	3.96	37	34	11	227	237	84	142	0	0	0	1	79	16	0	.203	15	46	3	5	1.7	.953
1964		11	16	.407	4.26	40	31	11	213.1	229	60	112	3	2	0	1	72	11	1	.153	23	36	4	2	1.6	.937
1965		8	20	.286	4.34	37	31	7	205.1	217	61	120	3	0	0	1	60	7	0	.117	10	48	3	2	1.6	.951
1966	STL N	13	15	.464	2.51	36	30	11	232.2	222	45	90	3	1	1	0	74	13	0	.176	16	63	5	4	2.3	.940
1967		9	4	.692	3.95	38	11	1	107	117	29	43	1	4	1	1	31	8	0	.258	10	29	1	2	1.1	.975
1968	NY N	3	7	.300	3.69	25	9	0	92.2	88	17	59	0	1	1	3	28	7	0	.250	7	17	0	1	1.0	1.000
1969	2 teams NY N (9G 0–0) CIN N (33G 1–0)																									
″	total	1	0	1.000	6.81	42	0	0	38.1	45	21	26	0	1	0	3	5	1	0	.200	7	4	2	0	0.3	.846
10 yrs.		67	99	.404	3.98	302	184	54	1389.1	1449	407	738	14	9	3	10	435	69	1	.159	113	311	20	18	1.5	.955

Charlie Jackson

JACKSON, CHARLES BERNARD TR
B. Aug. 4, 1876, Versailles, Ohio D. Nov. 23, 1957, Scottsbluff, Neb.

Year	Team	W	L	PCT	ERA	G	GS	CG	IP	H	BB	SO	ShO	Relief Pitching W	L	SV	Batting AB	H	HR	BA	PO	A	E	DP	TC/G	FA
1905	DET A	0	2	.000	5.73	2	2	1	11	14	7	3	0	0	0	0	4	1	0	.250	1	2	1	0	2.0	.750

Danny Jackson

JACKSON, DANNY LYNN BR TL 6′ 205 lbs.
B. Jan. 5, 1962, San Antonio, Tex.

Year	Team	W	L	PCT	ERA	G	GS	CG	IP	H	BB	SO	ShO	Relief Pitching W	L	SV	Batting AB	H	HR	BA	PO	A	E	DP	TC/G	FA
1983	KC A	1	1	.500	5.21	4	3	0	19	26	6	9	0	1	0	0	0	0	0	—	2	3	0	0	1.3	1.000
1984		2	6	.250	4.26	15	11	1	76	84	35	40	0	1	0	0	0	0	0	—	6	7	1	2	0.9	.929
1985		14	12	.538	3.42	32	32	4	208	209	76	114	3	0	0	0	0	0	0	—	8	27	3	2	1.2	.921
1986		11	12	.478	3.20	32	27	4	185.2	177	79	115	1	0	0	1	0	0	0	—	14	21	2	1	1.2	.946
1987		9	18	.333	4.02	36	34	11	224	219	109	152	2	0	0	0	0	0	0	—	13	23	2	2	1.1	.947
1988	CIN N	**23**	8	.742	2.73	35	35	**15**	260.2	206	71	161	6	0	0	0	90	13	0	.144	10	52	3	2	1.9	.954
1989		6	11	.353	5.60	20	20	1	115.2	122	57	70	0	0	0	0	36	8	0	.222	5	15	0	0	1.0	1.000
1990		6	6	.500	3.61	22	21	0	117.1	119	40	76	0	0	0	0	37	2	0	.054	4	13	1	0	0.8	.944
1991	CHI N	1	5	.167	6.75	17	14	0	70.2	89	48	31	0	0	0	0	23	2	0	.087	4	7	1	0	0.7	.917
1992	2 teams CHI N (19G 4–9) PIT N (15G 4–4)																									
″	total	8	13	.381	3.84	34	34	0	201.1	211	77	97	0	0	0	0	60	5	0	.083	9	33	8	2	1.5	.840
1993	PHI N	12	11	.522	3.77	32	32	2	210.1	214	80	120	1	0	0	0	65	5	0	.077	7	26	4	3	1.2	.892
1994		14	6	.700	3.26	25	25	4	179.1	183	46	129	1	0	0	0	57	9	0	.158	12	30	0	3	1.7	1.000
1995	STL N	2	12	.143	5.90	19	19	2	100.2	120	48	52	1	0	0	0	31	5	0	.161	7	12	3	1	1.2	.864
13 yrs.		109	121	.474	3.88	323	307	44	1968.2	1979	772	1166	15	2	0	1	399	49	0	.123	101	269	28	18	1.2	.930
LEAGUE CHAMPIONSHIP SERIES																										
1985	KC A	1	0	1.000	0.00	2	1	1	10	10	1	7	1	0	0	0	0	0	0	—	0	0	0	0	0.0	.000
1990	CIN N	1	0	1.000	2.38	2	2	0	11.1	8	7	8	0	0	0	0	3	0	0	.000	0	2	0	0	1.0	1.000
1992	PIT N	0	1	.000	21.60	1	1	0	1.2	4	2	0	0	0	0	0	0	0	0	—	0	0	0	0	0.0	.000
1993	PHI N	1	0	1.000	1.17	1	1	0	7.2	9	2	6	0	0	0	0	4	1	0	.250	0	0	0	0	0.0	.000
4 yrs.		3	1	.750	2.35	6	5	1	30.2	31	12	21	1 **1st**	0	0	0	7	1	0	.143	0	2	0	0	0.3	1.000
WORLD SERIES																										
1985	KC A	1	1	.500	1.69	2	2	1	16	9	5	12	0	0	0	0	6	0	0	.000	0	4	1	0	2.5	.800
1990	CIN N	0	0	—	10.13	1	1	0	2.2	6	2	0	0	0	0	0	1	0	0	.000	0	1	1	0	2.0	.500
1993	PHI N	0	1	.000	7.20	1	1	0	5	6	1	1	0	0	0	0	1	0	0	.000	0	0	0	0	0.0	.000
3 yrs.		1	2	.333	3.80	4	4	1	23.2	21	8	13	0	0	0	0	8	0	0	.000	0	5	2	0	1.8	.714

Darrell Jackson

JACKSON, DARRELL PRESTON B. Apr. 3, 1956, Los Angeles, Calif. BB TL 5′10″ 150 lbs.

Year	Team	Lg	W	L	PCT	ERA	G	GS	CG	IP	H	BB	SO	ShO	Relief Pitching W	Relief Pitching L	Relief Pitching SV	Batting AB	Batting H	Batting HR	BA	PO	A	E	DP	TC/G	FA
1978	MIN	A	4	6	.400	4.48	19	15	1	92.1	89	48	54	1	0	0	0	0	0	0	—	1	13	3	1	0.9	.824
1979			4	4	.500	4.30	24	8	1	69	89	26	43	0	1	0	0	0	0	0	—	3	13	1	2	0.7	.941
1980			9	9	.500	3.87	32	25	1	172	161	69	90	0	0	0	1	0	0	0	—	9	23	2	4	1.1	.941
1981			3	3	.500	4.36	14	5	0	33	35	19	26	0	1	1	0	0	0	0	—	0	2	0	0	0.1	1.000
1982			0	5	.000	6.25	13	7	0	44.2	51	24	16	0	0	1	0	0	0	0	—	1	7	3	1	0.8	.727
5 yrs.			20	27	.426	4.38	102	60	3	411	425	186	229	1	2	2	1	0	0	0		14	58	9	8	0.8	.889

Darrin Jackson

JACKSON, DARRIN JAY B. Aug. 22, 1963, Los Angeles, Calif. BR TR 6′ 185 lbs.

Year	Team	Lg	W	L	PCT	ERA	G	GS	CG	IP	H	BB	SO	ShO	Relief Pitching W	Relief Pitching L	Relief Pitching SV	Batting AB	Batting H	Batting HR	BA	PO	A	E	DP	TC/G	FA
1991	SD	N	0	0	—	9.00	1	0	0	2	3	2	0	0	0	0	0	*				7	0	0	0	1.8	1.000

Grant Jackson

JACKSON, GRANT DWIGHT (Buck) B. Sept. 28, 1942, Fostoria, Ohio. BB TL 6′ 180 lbs. BL 1971–1979

Year	Team	Lg	W	L	PCT	ERA	G	GS	CG	IP	H	BB	SO	ShO	Relief Pitching W	Relief Pitching L	Relief Pitching SV	Batting AB	Batting H	Batting HR	BA	PO	A	E	DP	TC/G	FA
1965	PHI	N	1	1	.500	7.24	6	2	0	13.2	17	5	15	0	1	1	0	4	0	0	.000	2	2	1	0	0.8	.800
1966			0	0	—	5.40	2	0	0	1.2	2	3	0	0	0	0	0	0	0	0	—	0	1	0	0	0.5	1.000
1967			2	3	.400	3.84	43	4	0	84.1	86	43	83	0	2	1	1	15	2	0	.133	1	5	1	0	0.2	.857
1968			1	6	.143	2.95	33	6	1	61	59	20	49	0	0	3	1	10	3	0	.300	3	9	1	2	0.4	.923
1969			14	18	.438	3.34	38	35	13	253	237	92	180	4	0	0	1	86	12	1	.140	8	36	5	2	1.3	.898
1970			5	15	.250	5.28	32	23	1	150	170	61	104	0	2	0	0	44	4	0	.091	13	21	1	0	1.1	.971
1971	BAL	A	4	3	.571	3.12	29	9	0	78	72	20	51	0	0	0	0	22	2	1	.091	3	11	1	1	0.5	.933
1972			1	1	.500	2.63	32	0	0	41	33	9	34	0	1	1	8	4	0	0	.000	1	6	0	1	0.2	1.000
1973			8	0	1.000	1.91	45	0	0	80	54	24	47	0	8	0	9	0	0	0	—	2	12	1	3	0.3	.933
1974			6	4	.600	2.55	49	0	0	67	48	22	56	0	6	4	12	0	0	0	—	2	3	1	0	0.1	.833
1975			4	3	.571	3.35	41	0	0	48.1	42	21	39	0	4	3	7	0	0	0	—	2	6	1	1	0.2	.889
1976	2 teams BAL A (13G 1–1) NY A (21G 6–0)																										
″	total		7	1	.875	2.54	34	2	1	78	57	25	39	1	5	1	4	0	0	0		1	6	0	0	0.2	1.000
1977	PIT	N	5	3	.625	3.86	49	2	0	91	81	39	41	0	5	2	4	18	6	0	.333	2	12	0	1	0.3	1.000
1978			7	5	.583	3.27	60	0	0	77	89	32	45	0	7	5	5	12	3	0	.250	2	14	1	0	0.3	.941
1979			8	5	.615	2.96	72	0	0	82	67	35	39	0	8	5	14	9	0	0	.000	2	9	0	0	0.2	1.000
1980			8	4	.667	2.92	61	0	0	71	71	20	31	0	8	4	9	10	0	0	.000	6	9	0	1	0.2	1.000
1981	2 teams PIT N (35G 1–2) MON N (10G 1–0)																										
″	total		2	2	.500	3.77	45	0	0	43	44	19	21	0	2	2	4	2	0	0	.000	4	3	1	0	0.2	.875
1982	2 teams KC A (20G 3–1) PIT N (1G 0–0)																										
″	total		3	1	.750	5.31	21	0	0	39	43	21	15	0	3	1	0	0	0	0		1	5	1	0	0.3	.857
18 yrs.			86	75	.534	3.46	692	83	16	1359	1272	511	889	5	62	33	79	236	32	2	.136	55	170	16	12	0.3	.934
LEAGUE CHAMPIONSHIP SERIES																											
1973	BAL	A	1	0	1.000	0.00	2	0	0	3	0	1	0	0	1	0	0	0	0	0	—	0	0	0	0	0.0	.000
1974			0	0	—	0.00	1	0	0	0.1	1	0	1	0	0	0	0	0	0	0	—	0	0	0	0	0.0	.000
1976	NY	A	0	0	—	8.10	2	0	0	3.1	4	1	3	0	0	0	0	0	0	0	—	0	1	0	0	0.5	1.000
1979	PIT	N	1	0	1.000	0.00	2	0	0	2	1	1	2	0	1	0	0	1	0	0	.000	0	0	0	0	0.0	.000
4 yrs.			2	0	1.000	3.12	7	0	0	8.2	6	3	6	0	2	0	0	1	0	0	.000	0	1	0	0	0.1	1.000
WORLD SERIES																											
1971	BAL	A	0	0	—	0.00	1	0	0	0.2	0	1	0	0	0	0	0	0	0	0	—	0	0	0	0	0.0	.000
1976	NY	A	0	0	—	4.91	1	0	0	3.2	4	0	3	0	0	0	0	0	0	0	—	0	3	0	0	3.0	1.000
1979	PIT	N	1	0	1.000	0.00	4	0	0	4.2	1	2	2	0	1	0	0	1	0	0	.000	0	0	0	0	0.0	.000
3 yrs.			1	0	1.000	2.00	6	0	0	9	5	3	5	0	1	0	0	1	0	0	.000	0	3	0	0	0.5	1.000

John Jackson

JACKSON, JOHN LEWIS B. July 15, 1909, Wynnefield, Pa. D. Oct. 24, 1956, Somers Point, N. J. BR TR 6′ 2″ 180 lbs.

Year	Team	Lg	W	L	PCT	ERA	G	GS	CG	IP	H	BB	SO	ShO	Relief Pitching W	Relief Pitching L	Relief Pitching SV	Batting AB	Batting H	Batting HR	BA	PO	A	E	DP	TC/G	FA
1933	PHI	N	2	2	.500	6.00	10	7	1	54	74	35	11	0	0	0	0	21	3	0	.143	1	2	1	0	0.4	.750

Larry Jackson

JACKSON, LAWRENCE CURTIS B. June 2, 1931, Nampa, Ida. D. Aug. 28, 1990, Boise, Ida. BR TR 6′ 1½″ 175 lbs.

Year	Team	Lg	W	L	PCT	ERA	G	GS	CG	IP	H	BB	SO	ShO	Relief Pitching W	Relief Pitching L	Relief Pitching SV	Batting AB	Batting H	Batting HR	BA	PO	A	E	DP	TC/G	FA
1955	STL	N	9	14	.391	4.31	37	25	4	177.1	189	72	88	1	4	2	2	57	3	0	.053	16	30	7	2	1.4	.868
1956			2	2	.500	4.11	51	1	0	85.1	75	45	50	0	2	1	9	11	1	0	.091	4	26	3	0	0.6	.909
1957			15	9	.625	3.47	41	22	6	210.1	196	57	96	2	7	2	1	72	13	0	.181	18	53	0	3	1.7	1.000
1958			13	13	.500	3.68	49	23	11	198	211	51	124	1	2	5	8	60	9	0	.150	12	22	3	0	0.8	.919
1959			14	13	.519	3.30	40	37	12	256	271	64	145	3	0	1	0	80	9	0	.113	18	37	2	5	1.4	.965
1960			18	13	.581	3.48	43	**38**	14	**282**	**277**	70	171	3	0	2	0	95	20	0	.211	20	38	4	5	1.4	.935
1961			14	11	.560	3.75	33	28	12	211	203	56	113	3	0	1	0	74	13	0	.176	17	42	1	5	1.8	.983
1962			16	11	.593	3.75	36	35	11	252.1	267	64	112	2	0	0	0	89	15	0	.169	19	50	3	3	2.0	.958
1963	CHI	N	14	18	.438	2.55	37	37	13	275	256	54	153	4	0	0	0	87	17	0	.195	21	58	4	4	2.2	.952
1964			**24**	11	.686	3.14	40	38	19	297.2	265	58	148	3	0	1	0	114	20	0	.175	24	85	0	6	2.7	1.000
1965			14	21	.400	3.85	39	39	12	257.1	268	57	131	4	0	0	0	86	11	1	.128	18	58	0	4	1.9	1.000
1966	2 teams CHI N (3G 0–2) PHI N (35G 15–13)																										
″	total		15	15	.500	3.32	38	35	12	255	257	62	112	5	1	0	0	92	13	1	.141	23	50	6	2	2.1	.924
1967	PHI	N	13	15	.464	3.10	40	37	11	261.2	242	54	139	4	1	0	0	87	14	0	.161	21	64	5	6	2.3	.944
1968			13	17	.433	2.77	34	34	12	243.2	229	60	127	2	0	0	0	85	12	0	.141	26	43	0	1	2.0	1.000
14 yrs.			194	183	.515	3.40	558	429	149	3262.2	3206	824	1709	37	17	15	20	1089	170	2	.156	257	656	38	46	1.7	.960

Mike Jackson

JACKSON, MICHAEL RAY B. Dec. 22, 1964, Houston, Tex. BR TR 6′ 1″ 185 lbs.

Year	Team	Lg	W	L	PCT	ERA	G	GS	CG	IP	H	BB	SO	ShO	Relief Pitching W	Relief Pitching L	Relief Pitching SV	Batting AB	Batting H	Batting HR	BA	PO	A	E	DP	TC/G	FA
1986	PHI	N	0	0	—	3.38	9	0	0	13.1	12	4	3	0	0	0	0	0	0	0	—	2	0	0	0	0.2	1.000
1987			3	10	.231	4.20	55	7	0	109.1	88	56	93	0	2	6	1	17	2	0	.118	5	12	1	0	0.3	.944
1988	SEA	A	6	5	.545	2.63	62	0	0	99.1	74	43	76	0	6	5	4	0	0	0	—	4	11	0	0	0.2	1.000
1989			4	6	.400	3.17	65	0	0	99.1	81	54	94	0	4	6	7	0	0	0	—	3	11	2	0	0.2	.875
1990			5	7	.417	4.54	63	0	0	77.1	64	44	69	0	5	7	3	0	0	0	—	5	12	0	3	0.3	1.000
1991			7	7	.500	3.25	72	0	0	88.2	64	34	74	0	7	**7**	14	0	0	0	—	2	8	1	1	0.2	.909
1992	SF	N	6	6	.500	3.73	67	0	0	82	76	33	80	0	6	6	2	2	0	0	.000	6	9	1	0	0.2	.938
1993			6	6	.500	3.03	**81**	0	0	77.1	58	24	70	0	6	6	1	3	2	0	.667	3	13	1	0	0.2	.941

Mike Jackson *continued*

Year	Team	W	L	PCT	ERA	G	GS	CG	IP	H	BB	SO	ShO	Relief Pitching W	Relief Pitching L	Relief Pitching SV	Batting AB	Batting H	Batting HR	BA	PO	A	E	DP	TC/G	FA
1994		3	2	.600	1.49	36	0	0	42.1	23	11	51	0	3	2	4	1	0	0	.000	0	7	0	1	0.2	1.000
1995	CIN N	6	1	.857	2.39	40	0	0	49	38	19	41	0	6	1	2	4	1	0	.250	2	3	0	0	0.1	1.000
10 yrs.		46	50	.479	3.30	550	7	0	738	578	322	651	0	45	46	38	27	5	0	.185	32	86	6	5	0.2	.952
DIVISIONAL PLAYOFF SERIES																										
1995	CIN N	0	0	—	0.00	3	0	0	3.2	4	0	1	0	0	0	0	1	1	0	1.000	1	1	0	0	0.7	1.000
LEAGUE CHAMPIONSHIP SERIES																										
1995	CIN N	0	1	.000	23.14	3	0	0	2.1	5	4	1	0	0	1	0	0	0	0	—	0	1	0	0	0.3	1.000

Mike Jackson

JACKSON, MICHAEL WARREN
B. Mar. 27, 1946, Paterson, N. J.
BL TL 6′ 3″ 190 lbs.

Year	Team	W	L	PCT	ERA	G	GS	CG	IP	H	BB	SO	ShO	Relief Pitching W	Relief Pitching L	Relief Pitching SV	Batting AB	Batting H	Batting HR	BA	PO	A	E	DP	TC/G	FA
1970	PHI N	1	1	.500	1.50	5	0	0	6	6	4	4	0	1	1	0	1	1	0	1.000	0	1	0	0	0.2	1.000
1971	STL N	0	0	—	0.00	1	0	0	1	1	1	0	0	0	0	0	1	0	0	.000	0	0	0	0	0.0	.000
1972	KC A	1	2	.333	6.30	7	3	0	20	24	14	15	0	0	1	0	5	0	0	.000	1	7	1	1	1.3	.889
1973	2 teams KC A (9G 0–0) CLE A (1G 0–0)																									
″	total	0	0		6.65	10	0	0	23	26	20	14	0	0	0	0	0	0	0		1	3	0	0	0.4	1.000
4 yrs.		2	3	.400	5.76	23	3	0	50	57	39	33	0	1	2	0	7	1	0	.143	2	11	1	1	0.6	.929

Roy Lee Jackson

JACKSON, ROY LEE
B. May 1, 1954, Opelika, Ala.
BR TR 6′ 2″ 190 lbs.

Year	Team	W	L	PCT	ERA	G	GS	CG	IP	H	BB	SO	ShO	Relief Pitching W	Relief Pitching L	Relief Pitching SV	Batting AB	Batting H	Batting HR	BA	PO	A	E	DP	TC/G	FA
1977	NY N	0	2	.000	6.00	4	4	0	24	25	15	13	0	0	0	0	6	0	0	.000	1	1	1	0	0.8	.667
1978		0	0	—	9.00	4	2	0	13	21	6	6	0	0	0	0	3	2	0	.667	1	4	1	6	1.5	.833
1979		1	0	1.000	2.25	8	0	0	16	11	5	10	0	1	0	0	1	1	0	1.000	2	1	0	1	0.4	1.000
1980		1	7	.125	4.18	24	8	1	71	78	20	58	0	0	1	1	16	3	0	.188	1	7	0	1	0.3	1.000
1981	TOR A	1	2	.333	2.61	39	0	0	62	65	25	27	0	1	2	7	0	0	0	—	5	10	1	0	0.4	.938
1982		8	8	.500	3.06	48	2	0	97	77	31	71	0	8	7	6	0	0	0	—	6	12	0	0	0.4	1.000
1983		8	3	.727	4.50	49	0	0	92	92	41	48	0	8	3	7	0	0	0	—	6	14	0	1	0.4	1.000
1984		7	8	.467	3.56	54	0	0	86	73	31	58	0	7	8	10	0	0	0	—	5	11	0	0	0.3	1.000
1985	SD N	2	3	.400	2.70	22	2	0	40	32	13	28	0	1	2	2	5	0	0	.000	5	5	1	0	0.5	.909
1986	MIN A	0	1	.000	3.86	28	0	0	58.1	57	16	32	0	0	1	1	0	0	0	—	3	6	0	0	0.3	1.000
10 yrs.		28	34	.452	3.77	280	18	1	559.1	531	203	351	0	26	24	34	31	6	0	.194	35	71	4	9	0.4	.964

Art Jacobs

JACOBS, ARTHUR EDWARD
B. Aug. 28, 1902, Luckey, Ohio D. June 8, 1967, Inglewood, Calif.
BL TL 5′10″ 170 lbs.

Year	Team	W	L	PCT	ERA	G	GS	CG	IP	H	BB	SO	ShO	Relief Pitching W	Relief Pitching L	Relief Pitching SV	Batting AB	Batting H	Batting HR	BA	PO	A	E	DP	TC/G	FA
1939	CIN N	0	0	—	9.00	1	0	0	1	2	1	0	0	0	0	1	0	0	0	—	0	0	0	0	0.0	.000

Bucky Jacobs

JACOBS, NEWTON SMITH
B. Mar. 21, 1913, Altavista, Va. D. July 15, 1990, Richmond, Va.
BR TR 5′11″ 155 lbs.

Year	Team	W	L	PCT	ERA	G	GS	CG	IP	H	BB	SO	ShO	Relief Pitching W	Relief Pitching L	Relief Pitching SV	Batting AB	Batting H	Batting HR	BA	PO	A	E	DP	TC/G	FA
1937	WAS A	1	1	.500	4.84	11	1	0	22.1	26	11	8	0	1	0	0	5	0	0	.000	1	5	0	0	0.5	1.000
1939		0	0	—	0.00	2	0	0	3	1	0	1	0	0	0	0	0	0	0	—	0	0	0	0	0.0	.000
1940		0	1	.000	6.00	9	0	0	15	16	9	6	0	0	1	0	1	0	0	.000	1	9	0	1	1.1	1.000
3 yrs.		1	2	.333	4.91	22	1	0	40.1	43	20	15	0	1	1	0	6	0	0	.000	2	14	0	1	0.7	1.000

Elmer Jacobs

JACOBS, WILLIAM ELMER
B. Aug. 10, 1892, Salem, Mo. D. Feb. 10, 1958, Salem, Mo.
BR TR 6′ 165 lbs.

Year	Team	W	L	PCT	ERA	G	GS	CG	IP	H	BB	SO	ShO	Relief Pitching W	Relief Pitching L	Relief Pitching SV	Batting AB	Batting H	Batting HR	BA	PO	A	E	DP	TC/G	FA
1914	PHI N	1	3	.250	4.80	14	7	1	50.2	65	20	17	0	0	0	0	14	0	0	.000	1	16	1	0	1.3	.944
1916	PIT N	6	10	.375	2.94	34	17	8	153	151	38	46	0	2	1	0	40	3	0	.075	3	37	2	0	1.2	.952
1917		6	19	.240	2.81	38	25	10	227.1	214	76	58	1	1	3	2	67	12	0	.179	8	75	2	3	2.2	.976
1918	2 teams PIT N (8G 0–1) PHI N (18G 9–5)																									
″	total	9	6	.600	2.95	26	18	12	146.1	122	56	35	4	0	1	1	45	8	0	.178	12	36	0	1	1.8	1.000
1919	2 teams PHI N (17G 6–10) STL N (17G 3–6)																									
″	total	9	16	.360	3.32	34	23	17	214	231	69	68	1	2	1	1	68	16	0	.235	6	68	3	1	2.3	.961
1920	STL N	4	8	.333	5.21	23	9	1	77.2	91	33	21	0	2	2	1	26	5	0	.192	3	28	2	1	1.4	.939
1924	CHI N	11	12	.478	3.74	38	22	13	190.1	181	72	50	1	2	2	1	54	6	0	.111	9	54	2	0	1.7	.969
1925		2	3	.400	5.17	18	4	1	55.2	63	22	19	1	1	2	1	13	3	0	.231	1	14	0	1	0.8	1.000
1927	CHI A	2	4	.333	4.60	25	8	2	74.1	105	37	22	1	0	0	0	20	3	0	.150	3	27	2	1	1.3	.938
9 yrs.		50	81	.382	3.55	250	133	65	1189.1	1223	423	336	9	10	12	7	347	56	0	.161	46	355	14	8	1.7	.966

Tony Jacobs

JACOBS, ANTHONY ROBERT
B. Aug. 5, 1925, Dixmoor, Ill. D. Dec. 21, 1980, Nashville, Tenn.
BB TR 5′ 9″ 150 lbs.

Year	Team	W	L	PCT	ERA	G	GS	CG	IP	H	BB	SO	ShO	Relief Pitching W	Relief Pitching L	Relief Pitching SV	Batting AB	Batting H	Batting HR	BA	PO	A	E	DP	TC/G	FA
1948	CHI N	0	0	—	4.50	1	0	0	2	3	0	2	0	0	0	0	0	0	0	—	0	1	0	0	1.0	1.000
1955	STL N	0	0	—	18.00	1	0	0	2	6	1	1	0	0	0	0	1	0	0	.000	0	2	0	0	2.0	1.000
2 yrs.		0	0		11.25	2	0	0	4	9	1	3	0	0	0	0	1	0	0	.000	0	3	0	0	1.5	1.000

Beany Jacobson

JACOBSON, ALBERT L.
B. June 5, 1881, Port Washington, Wis. D. Jan. 31, 1933, Decatur, Ill.
BL TL 6′ 170 lbs.

Year	Team	W	L	PCT	ERA	G	GS	CG	IP	H	BB	SO	ShO	Relief Pitching W	Relief Pitching L	Relief Pitching SV	Batting AB	Batting H	Batting HR	BA	PO	A	E	DP	TC/G	FA
1904	WAS A	6	23	.207	3.55	33	30	23	253.2	276	57	75	1	0	1	0	88	8	0	.091	13	95	6	0	3.5	.947
1905		7	8	.467	3.30	22	17	12	144.1	139	35	50	0	0	0	0	44	7	0	.159	8	37	5	1	2.3	.900
1906	STL A	9	9	.500	2.50	24	15	12	155	146	27	53	0	2	1	0	58	5	0	.086	13	47	3	1	2.6	.952
1907	2 teams STL A (7G 1–6) BOS A (2G 0–0)																									
″	total	1	6	.143	3.19	9	8	6	59.1	57	29	17	0	0	0	0	18	4	0	.222	4	18	2	0	2.7	.917
4 yrs.		23	46	.333	3.19	88	70	53	612.1	618	148	195	1	2	2	0	208	24	0	.115	38	197	16	2	2.9	.936

Larry Jacobus

JACOBUS, STUART LOUIS
B. Dec. 12, 1893, Cincinnati, Ohio D. Aug. 19, 1965, North College Hill, Ohio.
BB TR 6′ 2″ 186 lbs.

Year	Team	W	L	PCT	ERA	G	GS	CG	IP	H	BB	SO	ShO	Relief Pitching W	Relief Pitching L	Relief Pitching SV	Batting AB	Batting H	Batting HR	BA	PO	A	E	DP	TC/G	FA
1918	CIN N	0	1	.000	5.71	5	0	0	17.1	25	1	8	0	0	1	0	5	0	0	.000	0	4	0	0	0.8	1.000

Jason Jacome

JACOME, JASON JAMES
B. Nov. 24, 1970, Tulsa, Okla.
BL TL 6′ 1″ 155 lbs.

Year	Team	W	L	PCT	ERA	G	GS	CG	IP	H	BB	SO	ShO	Relief Pitching W	Relief Pitching L	Relief Pitching SV	Batting AB	Batting H	Batting HR	BA	PO	A	E	DP	TC/G	FA
1994	NY N	4	3	.571	2.67	8	8	1	54	54	17	30	1	0	0	0	16	1	0	.063	4	9	0	2	1.6	1.000
1995	2 teams NY N (5G 0–4) KC A (15G 4–6)																									
″	total	4	10	.286	6.34	20	19	1	105	134	36	50	0	0	0	0	7	0	0	.000	6	24	2	2	1.6	.938
2 yrs.		8	13	.381	5.09	28	27	2	159	188	53	80	1	0	0	0	23	1	0	.043	10	33	2	4	1.6	.956

Pat Jacquez

JACQUEZ, PATRICK THOMAS BR TR 6′ 200 lbs.
B. Apr. 23, 1947, Stockton, Calif.

Year	Team	Lg	W	L	PCT	ERA	G	GS	CG	IP	H	BB	SO	ShO	Relief W	Relief L	SV	AB	H	HR	BA	PO	A	E	DP	TC/G	FA
1971	CHI	A	0	0	—	4.50	2	0	0	2	4	2	1	0	0	0	0	1	0	0	.000	0	1	0	0	0.5	1.000

Paul Jaeckel

JAECKEL, PAUL HENRY (Jake) BR TR 5′10″ 170 lbs.
B. Apr. 1, 1942, East Los Angeles, Calif.

Year	Team	Lg	W	L	PCT	ERA	G	GS	CG	IP	H	BB	SO	ShO	Relief W	Relief L	SV	AB	H	HR	BA	PO	A	E	DP	TC/G	FA
1964	CHI	N	1	0	1.000	0.00	4	0	0	8	4	3	2	0	1	0	1	1	0	0	.000	1	1	0	0	0.5	1.000

Charlie Jaeger

JAEGER, CHARLES THOMAS BR TR 6′ 1″ 195 lbs.
B. Apr. 17, 1875, Ottawa, Ill. D. Sept. 27, 1942, Ottawa, Ill.

Year	Team	Lg	W	L	PCT	ERA	G	GS	CG	IP	H	BB	SO	ShO	Relief W	Relief L	SV	AB	H	HR	BA	PO	A	E	DP	TC/G	FA
1904	DET	A	3	3	.500	2.57	8	6	5	49	49	15	13	0	0	0	0	17	1	0	.059	2	15	2	0	2.4	.895

Joe Jaeger

JAEGER, JOSEPH PETER (Zip) BR TR 6′ 3″ 180 lbs.
B. Mar. 3, 1895, St. Cloud, Minn. D. Dec. 13, 1963, Hampton, Iowa.

Year	Team	Lg	W	L	PCT	ERA	G	GS	CG	IP	H	BB	SO	ShO	Relief W	Relief L	SV	AB	H	HR	BA	PO	A	E	DP	TC/G	FA
1920	CHI	N	0	0	—	12.00	2	0	0	3	6	4	0	0	0	0	0	1	0	0	.000	0	1	0	0	0.5	1.000

Sig Jakucki

JAKUCKI, SIGMUND (Jack) BR TR 6′ 2½″ 198 lbs.
B. Aug. 20, 1909, Camden, N. J. D. May 29, 1979, Galveston, Tex.

Year	Team	Lg	W	L	PCT	ERA	G	GS	CG	IP	H	BB	SO	ShO	Relief W	Relief L	SV	AB	H	HR	BA	PO	A	E	DP	TC/G	FA
1936	STL	A	0	3	.000	8.71	7	2	0	20.2	32	12	9	0	0	1	0	6	0	0	.000	1	4	1	1	0.9	.833
1944			13	9	.591	3.55	35	24	12	198	211	54	67	4	1	2	3	73	11	1	.151	7	44	0	2	1.5	1.000
1945			12	10	.545	3.51	30	24	15	192.1	188	65	55	1	2	0	2	70	13	2	.186	7	42	1	0	1.7	.980
3 yrs.			25	22	.532	3.79	72	50	27	411	431	131	131	5	3	3	5	149	24	3	.161	15	90	2	3	1.5	.981
WORLD SERIES																											
1944	STL	A	0	1	.000	9.00	1	1	0	3	5	0	4	0	0	0	0	0	0	0	—	0	1	0	0	1.0	1.000

Charlie Jamerson

JAMERSON, CHARLES DEWEY (Lefty) BL TL 6′ 1″ 195 lbs.
B. Jan. 26, 1900, Enfield, Ill. D. Aug. 4, 1980, Mockville, N. C.

Year	Team	Lg	W	L	PCT	ERA	G	GS	CG	IP	H	BB	SO	ShO	Relief W	Relief L	SV	AB	H	HR	BA	PO	A	E	DP	TC/G	FA
1924	BOS	A	0	0	—	18.00	1	0	0	1	1	3	0	0	0	0	0	0	0	0	—	0	0	0	0	0.0	.000

Bill James

JAMES, WILLIAM HENRY (Big Bill) BB TR 6′ 4″ 195 lbs.
B. Jan. 20, 1887, Detroit, Mich. D. May 24, 1942, Venice, Calif.

Year	Team	Lg	W	L	PCT	ERA	G	GS	CG	IP	H	BB	SO	ShO	Relief W	Relief L	SV	AB	H	HR	BA	PO	A	E	DP	TC/G	FA
1911	CLE	A	2	4	.333	4.88	8	6	4	51.2	58	32	21	0	0	0	0	17	1	0	.059	4	11	1	0	2.0	.938
1912			0	0	—	4.61	3	0	0	13.2	15	9	5	0	0	0	0	3	0	0	.000	1	2	3	0	2.0	.500
1914	STL	A	15	14	.517	2.85	44	35	20	284	269	109	109	3	0	0	2	89	10	0	.112	11	106	3	5	2.7	.975
1915	2 teams	STL A	(34G 7–10)	DET A	(11G 7–3)																						
″	total		14	13	.519	3.26	45	32	11	237.1	212	125	82	1	2	0	1	63	14	0	.222	14	84	8	3	2.4	.925
1916	DET	A	8	12	.400	3.68	30	20	8	151.2	141	79	61	0	2	0	1	44	3	0	.068	4	46	6	1	1.9	.893
1917			13	10	.565	2.09	34	23	10	198	163	96	62	2	2	1	1	57	12	0	.211	4	61	5	1	2.1	.929
1918			6	11	.353	3.76	19	18	8	122	127	68	42	1	1	0	0	46	5	0	.109	5	43	1	3	2.6	.980
1919	3 teams	DET A	(2G 1–0)	BOS A	(13G 3–5)	CHI A	(5G 3–2)																				
″	total		7	7	.500	3.71	20	13	7	121.1	129	58	26	2	0	2	0	39	6	0	.154	7	32	4	2	2.2	.907
8 yrs.			65	71	.478	3.20	203	147	68	1179.2	1114	576	408	9	7	3	5	358	51	0	.142	50	385	31	15	2.3	.933
WORLD SERIES																											
1919	CHI	A	0	0	—	5.79	1	0	0	4.2	8	3	2	0	0	0	0	2	0	0	.000	0	0	0	0	0.0	.000

Bill James

JAMES, WILLIAM LAWRENCE (Seattle Bill) BR TR 6′ 3″ 196 lbs.
B. Mar. 12, 1892, Iowa Hill, Calif. D. Mar. 10, 1971, Oroville, Calif.

Year	Team	Lg	W	L	PCT	ERA	G	GS	CG	IP	H	BB	SO	ShO	Relief W	Relief L	SV	AB	H	HR	BA	PO	A	E	DP	TC/G	FA
1913	BOS	N	6	10	.375	2.79	24	14	10	135.2	134	57	73	1	1	1	0	47	12	0	.255	7	35	7	2	2.0	.857
1914			26	7	**.788**	1.90	46	37	30	332.1	261	118	156	4	1	1	2	129	33	0	.256	4	85	10	7	2.2	.899
1915			5	4	.556	3.03	13	10	4	68.1	68	22	23	0	0	1	0	21	1	0	.048	2	25	0	0	2.1	1.000
1919			0	0	—	3.38	1	0	0	5.1	6	2	1	0	0	0	0	2	0	0	.000	0	3	0	0	3.0	1.000
4 yrs.			37	21	.638	2.28	84	61	44	541.2	469	199	253	5	2	3	2	199	46	0	.231	13	148	17	9	2.1	.904
WORLD SERIES																											
1914	BOS	N	2	0	1.000	0.00	2	1	1	11	2	6	9	1	1	0	0	4	0	0	.000	0	5	0	0	2.5	1.000

Bob James

JAMES, ROBERT HARVEY BR TR 6′ 4″ 215 lbs.
B. Aug. 15, 1958, Glendale, Calif.

Year	Team	Lg	W	L	PCT	ERA	G	GS	CG	IP	H	BB	SO	ShO	Relief W	Relief L	SV	AB	H	HR	BA	PO	A	E	DP	TC/G	FA
1978	MON	N	0	1	.000	9.00	4	1	0	4	4	4	3	0	0	0	0	0	0	0	—	0	1	0	0	0.3	1.000
1979			0	0	—	13.50	2	0	0	2	2	3	1	0	0	0	0	0	0	0	—	0	0	0	0	0.0	.000
1982	2 teams	MON N	(7G 0–0)	DET A	(12G 0–2)																						
″	total		0	2	.000	5.34	19	1	0	28.2	32	16	31	0	0	2	0	0	0	0		1	4	3	0	0.4	.625
1983	2 teams	DET A	(4G 0–0)	MON N	(27G 1–0)																						
″	total		1	0	1.000	3.50	31	0	0	54	42	26	60	0	1	0	7	7	2	0	.286	4	12	2	1	0.6	.889
1984	MON	N	6	6	.500	3.66	62	0	0	96	92	45	91	0	6	6	10	14	2	0	.143	5	7	4	0	0.3	.750
1985	CHI	A	8	7	.533	2.13	69	0	0	110	90	23	88	0	8	7	32	0	0	0	—	12	8	1	0	0.3	.952
1986			5	4	.556	5.25	49	0	0	58.1	61	23	32	0	5	4	14	0	0	0	—	3	6	0	0	0.2	1.000
1987			4	6	.400	4.67	43	0	0	54	54	17	34	0	4	6	10	0	0	0	—	3	9	3	1	0.3	.800
8 yrs.			24	26	.480	3.80	279	2	0	407	377	157	340	0	24	25	73	21	4	0	.190	28	47	13	2	0.3	.852

Jeff James

JAMES, JEFFREY LYNN (Jesse) BR TR 6′ 3″ 195 lbs.
B. Sept. 29, 1941, Indianapolis, Ind.

Year	Team	Lg	W	L	PCT	ERA	G	GS	CG	IP	H	BB	SO	ShO	Relief W	Relief L	SV	AB	H	HR	BA	PO	A	E	DP	TC/G	FA
1968	PHI	N	4	4	.500	4.28	29	13	1	115.2	112	46	83	1	0	0	0	33	4	0	.121	10	18	3	2	1.1	.903
1969			2	2	.500	5.34	6	5	1	32	36	14	21	0	0	0	0	11	2	0	.182	2	3	0	0	0.8	1.000
2 yrs.			6	6	.500	4.51	35	18	2	147.2	148	60	104	1	0	0	0	44	6	0	.136	12	21	3	2	1.0	.917

Johnny James

JAMES, JOHN PHILLIP BL TR 5′10″ 160 lbs.
B. July 23, 1933, Bonner's Ferry, Ida.

Year	Team	Lg	W	L	PCT	ERA	G	GS	CG	IP	H	BB	SO	ShO	Relief W	Relief L	SV	AB	H	HR	BA	PO	A	E	DP	TC/G	FA
1958	NY	A	0	0	—	0.00	1	0	0	3	2	4	1	0	0	0	0	1	0	0	.000	1	0	0	0	1.0	1.000
1960			5	1	.833	4.36	28	0	0	43.1	38	26	29	0	5	1	2	3	0	0	.000	2	9	0	0	0.4	1.000
1961	2 teams	NY A	(1G 0–0)	LA A	(36G 0–2)																						
″	total		0	2	.000	5.20	37	3	0	72.2	67	54	43	0	0	1	0	13	0	0	.000	1	12	0	1	0.4	1.000
3 yrs.			5	3	.625	4.76	66	3	0	119	107	84	73	0	5	2	2	17	0	0	.000	4	21	0	1	0.4	1.000

Lefty James

JAMES, WILLIAM A. BR TL 5′11½″ 175 lbs.
B. July 1, 1889, Glen Roy, Ohio D. May 3, 1933, Glen Roy, Ohio.

Year	Team	Lg	W	L	PCT	ERA	G	GS	CG	IP	H	BB	SO	ShO	Relief W	Relief L	Relief SV	Batting AB	Batting H	HR	BA	PO	A	E	DP	TC/G	FA
1912	CLE	A	0	1	.000	7.50	3	1	0	6	8	4	2	0	0	0	1	3	0	0	.000	0	2	1	0	1.0	.667
1913			2	2	.500	3.00	11	4	4	39	42	9	18	0	0	1	0	13	3	0	.231	0	8	3	0	1.0	.727
1914			0	3	.000	3.20	17	6	1	50.2	44	32	16	0	0	1	0	12	0	0	.000	3	21	0	0	1.4	1.000
3 yrs.			2	6	.250	3.39	31	11	5	95.2	94	45	36	0	0	2	1	28	3	0	.107	3	31	4	0	1.2	.895

Mike James

JAMES, MICHAEL ELMO BR TR 6′ 4″ 216 lbs.
B. Aug. 15, 1967, Fort Walton Beach, Fla.

Year	Team	Lg	W	L	PCT	ERA	G	GS	CG	IP	H	BB	SO	ShO	Relief W	Relief L	Relief SV	Batting AB	Batting H	HR	BA	PO	A	E	DP	TC/G	FA
1995	CAL	A	3	0	1.000	3.88	46	0	0	55.2	49	26	36	0	3	0	1	0	0	0	—	2	8	0	0	0.2	1.000

Rick James

JAMES, RICHARD LEE BR TR 6′ 2½″ 205 lbs.
B. Oct. 11, 1947, Sheffield, Ala.

Year	Team	Lg	W	L	PCT	ERA	G	GS	CG	IP	H	BB	SO	ShO	Relief W	Relief L	Relief SV	Batting AB	Batting H	HR	BA	PO	A	E	DP	TC/G	FA
1967	CHI	N	0	1	.000	13.50	3	1	0	4.2	9	2	2	0	0	0	0	1	0	0	.000	0	0	0	0	0.0	.000

Charlie Jamieson

JAMIESON, CHARLES DEVINE BL TL 5′ 8½″ 165 lbs.
B. Feb. 7, 1893, Paterson, N. J. D. Oct. 27, 1969, Paterson, N. J.

Year	Team	Lg	W	L	PCT	ERA	G	GS	CG	IP	H	BB	SO	ShO	Relief W	Relief L	Relief SV	Batting AB	Batting H	HR	BA	PO	A	E	DP	TC/G	FA
1916	WAS	A	0	0	—	4.50	1	0	0	4	2	3	2	0	0	0	0	145	36	0	.248	36	5	0	0	2.4	1.000
1917			0	0	—	38.57	1	0	0	2.1	10	2	1	0	0	0	0	382	98	0	.257	135	12	11	4	1.7	.930
1918	PHI	A	2	1	.667	4.30	5	2	1	23	24	13	2	0	1	0	0	416	84	0	.202	184	21	10	4	2.0	.953
1919	CLE	A	0	0	—	5.54	4	1	0	13	12	8	0	0	0	0	0	17	6	0	.353	5	2	1	0	1.1	.875
1922			0	0	—	3.18	2	0	0	5.2	7	4	2	0	0	0	0	567	183	3	.323	194	15	8	0	2.1	.963
5 yrs.			2	1	.667	6.19	13	3	1	48	55	30	7	0	1	0	0	*				3467	208	130	40	2.3	.966

Gerry Janeski

JANESKI, GERALD JOSEPH BR TR 6′ 4″ 205 lbs.
B. Apr. 18, 1946, Pasadena, Calif.

Year	Team	Lg	W	L	PCT	ERA	G	GS	CG	IP	H	BB	SO	ShO	Relief W	Relief L	Relief SV	Batting AB	Batting H	HR	BA	PO	A	E	DP	TC/G	FA
1970	CHI	A	10	17	.370	4.76	35	35	4	206	247	63	79	1	0	0	0	66	5	0	.076	15	37	5	6	1.6	.912
1971	WAS	A	1	5	.167	4.94	23	10	0	62	72	34	19	0	1	0	1	14	3	0	.214	7	12	0	2	0.8	1.000
1972	TEX	A	0	1	.000	2.77	4	1	0	13	11	7	7	0	0	0	0	2	0	0	.000	1	3	0	0	1.0	1.000
3 yrs.			11	23	.324	4.71	62	46	4	281	330	104	105	1	1	0	1	82	8	0	.098	23	52	5	8	1.3	.938

Larry Jansen

JANSEN, LAWRENCE JOSEPH BR TR 6′ 2″ 190 lbs.
B. July 16, 1920, Verboort, Ore.

Year	Team	Lg	W	L	PCT	ERA	G	GS	CG	IP	H	BB	SO	ShO	Relief W	Relief L	Relief SV	Batting AB	Batting H	HR	BA	PO	A	E	DP	TC/G	FA
1947	NY	N	21	5	**.808**	3.16	42	30	20	248	241	57	104	1	1	1	1	86	16	0	.186	19	42	4	3	1.5	.938
1948			18	12	.600	3.61	42	36	15	277	283	54	126	4	1	0	2	95	13	0	.137	20	56	1	7	1.8	.987
1949			15	16	.484	3.85	37	35	17	259.2	271	62	113	3	0	1	0	97	16	0	.165	14	57	1	1	1.9	.986
1950			19	13	.594	3.01	40	35	21	275	238	55	161	**5**	0	0	3	96	16	1	.167	30	45	1	7	1.9	.987
1951			**23**	11	.676	3.04	39	34	18	278.1	254	56	145	3	4	1	0	96	9	0	.094	29	54	1	3	2.2	.988
1952			11	11	.500	4.09	34	27	8	167.1	183	47	74	1	1	0	2	45	8	0	.178	9	38	3	5	1.5	.940
1953			11	16	.407	4.14	36	26	6	184.2	185	55	88	0	2	1	1	60	8	0	.133	11	27	0	2	1.1	1.000
1954			2	2	.500	5.98	13	7	0	40.2	57	15	15	0	1	1	0	14	4	0	.286	3	12	0	3	1.2	1.000
1956	CIN	N	2	3	.400	5.19	8	7	2	34.2	39	9	16	0	0	0	1	11	0	0	.000	3	4	0	0	0.9	1.000
9 yrs.			122	89	.578	3.58	291	237	107	1765.1	1751	410	842	17	10	5	10	600	90	1	.150	138	335	11	31	1.7	.977
WORLD SERIES																											
1951	NY	N	0	2	.000	6.30	3	2	0	10	8	4	6	0	0	0	0	2	0	0	.000	1	2	0	0	1.0	1.000

Kevin Jarvis

JARVIS, KEVIN THOMAS BL TR 6′ 2″ 200 lbs.
B. Aug. 1, 1969, Lexington, Ky.

Year	Team	Lg	W	L	PCT	ERA	G	GS	CG	IP	H	BB	SO	ShO	Relief W	Relief L	Relief SV	Batting AB	Batting H	HR	BA	PO	A	E	DP	TC/G	FA
1994	CIN	N	1	1	.500	7.13	6	3	0	17.2	22	5	10	0	0	1	0	4	1	0	.250	2	3	1	0	1.0	.833
1995			3	4	.429	5.70	19	11	1	79	91	32	33	1	0	0	0	21	3	0	.143	8	12	2	1	1.2	.909
2 yrs.			4	5	.444	5.96	25	14	1	96.2	113	37	43	1	0	1	0	25	4	0	.160	10	15	3	1	1.1	.893

Pat Jarvis

JARVIS, ROBERT PATRICK BR TR 5′10½″ 180 lbs.
B. Mar. 18, 1941, Carlyle, Ill.

Year	Team	Lg	W	L	PCT	ERA	G	GS	CG	IP	H	BB	SO	ShO	Relief W	Relief L	Relief SV	Batting AB	Batting H	HR	BA	PO	A	E	DP	TC/G	FA
1966	ATL	N	6	2	.750	2.31	10	9	3	62.1	46	12	41	1	0	0	0	22	0	0	.000	1	7	0	0	0.8	1.000
1967			15	10	.600	3.66	32	30	7	194	195	62	118	1	2	0	0	71	6	0	.085	11	24	4	1	1.2	.897
1968			16	12	.571	2.60	34	34	14	256	202	50	157	1	0	0	0	85	12	0	.141	18	29	2	2	1.4	.959
1969			13	11	.542	4.44	37	33	4	217	204	73	123	1	0	0	0	71	8	0	.113	19	31	0	1	1.4	1.000
1970			16	16	.500	3.61	36	34	11	254	240	72	173	1	0	1	0	82	15	0	.183	29	38	1	0	1.9	.985
1971			6	14	.300	4.11	35	23	3	162	162	51	68	3	2	1	1	47	5	0	.106	16	27	1	1	1.3	.977
1972			11	7	.611	4.09	37	6	0	99	94	44	56	0	8	5	2	24	3	0	.125	5	19	1	1	0.7	.960
1973	MON	N	2	1	.667	3.20	28	0	0	39.1	37	16	19	0	2	1	0	3	0	0	.000	4	5	2	0	0.4	.818
8 yrs.			85	73	.538	3.58	249	169	42	1283.2	1180	380	755	8	14	8	3	405	49	0	.121	103	180	11	6	1.2	.963
LEAGUE CHAMPIONSHIP SERIES																											
1969	ATL	N	0	1	.000	12.46	1	1	0	4.1	10	0	6	0	0	0	0	2	0	0	.000	1	2	0	1	3.0	1.000

Ray Jarvis

JARVIS, RAYMOND ARNOLD BR TR 6′ 2″ 198 lbs.
B. May 10, 1946, Providence, R. I.

Year	Team	Lg	W	L	PCT	ERA	G	GS	CG	IP	H	BB	SO	ShO	Relief W	Relief L	Relief SV	Batting AB	Batting H	HR	BA	PO	A	E	DP	TC/G	FA
1969	BOS	A	5	6	.455	4.75	29	12	2	100.1	105	43	36	0	2	0	1	29	2	0	.069	9	19	3	1	1.1	.903
1970			0	1	.000	3.94	15	0	0	16	17	14	8	0	0	1	0	0	0	0	—	1	3	1	0	0.3	.800
2 yrs.			5	7	.417	4.64	44	12	2	116.1	122	57	44	0	2	1	1	29	2	0	.069	10	22	4	1	0.8	.889

Hi Jasper

JASPER, HENRY W. BR TR 5′11″ 180 lbs.
B. Nov. 15, 1880, St. Louis, Mo. D. May 22, 1937, St. Louis, Mo.

Year	Team	Lg	W	L	PCT	ERA	G	GS	CG	IP	H	BB	SO	ShO	Relief W	Relief L	Relief SV	Batting AB	Batting H	HR	BA	PO	A	E	DP	TC/G	FA
1914	CHI	A	1	0	1.000	3.34	16	0	0	32.1	22	20	19	0	1	0	0	5	0	0	.000	2	13	0	1	0.9	1.000
1915			0	1	.000	4.60	3	2	1	15.2	8	9	15	0	0	0	0	7	2	0	.286	0	11	1	0	4.0	.917
1916	STL	N	5	6	.455	3.28	21	9	2	107	97	42	37	0	3	1	1	33	7	1	.212	3	35	0	2	1.8	1.000
1919	CLE	A	4	5	.444	3.59	12	10	5	82.2	83	28	25	0	1	0	0	29	3	0	.103	2	30	4	0	3.0	.889
4 yrs.			10	12	.455	3.48	52	21	8	237.2	210	99	96	0	5	1	1	74	12	1	.162	7	89	5	3	1.9	.950

Larry Jaster

JASTER, LARRY EDWARD BL TL 6′ 3″ 190 lbs.
B. Jan. 13, 1944, Midland, Mich.

Year	Team	Lg	W	L	PCT	ERA	G	GS	CG	IP	H	BB	SO	ShO	Relief W	Relief L	Relief SV	Batting AB	Batting H	HR	BA	PO	A	E	DP	TC/G	FA
1965	STL	N	3	0	1.000	1.61	4	3	3	28	21	7	10	0	0	0	0	10	2	0	.200	0	3	0	0	0.8	1.000
1966			11	5	.688	3.26	26	21	6	151.2	124	45	92	**5**	1	0	0	45	8	1	.178	6	20	0	3	1.0	1.000
1967			9	7	.563	3.01	34	23	2	152.1	141	44	87	1	1	0	3	50	5	0	.100	1	18	2	3	0.6	.905
1968			9	13	.409	3.51	31	21	3	153.2	153	38	70	1	2	1	0	43	6	1	.140	5	20	0	1	0.8	1.000
1969	MON	N	1	6	.143	5.49	24	11	1	77	95	28	39	0	0	0	0	19	8	0	.421	7	6	6	0	0.8	.684

Larry Jaster *continued*

Year	Team	Lg	W	L	PCT	ERA	G	GS	CG	IP	H	BB	SO	ShO	Relief Pitching W	Relief Pitching L	Relief Pitching SV	Batting AB	Batting H	Batting HR	BA	PO	A	E	DP	TC/G	FA
1970	**ATL**	**N**	1	1	.500	6.95	14	0	0	22	33	8	9	0	1	1	0	3	0	0	.000	0	8	0	0	0.6	1.000
1972			1	1	.500	5.25	5	1	0	12	12	8	6	0	1	0	0	1	0	0	.000	1	1	0	0	0.4	1.000
7 yrs.			35	33	.515	3.65	138	80	15	596.2	579	178	313	7	6	2	3	171	29	2	.170	20	76	8	7	0.8	.923
WORLD SERIES																											
1967	**STL**	**N**	0	0	—	0.00	1	0	0	0.1	2	0	0	0	0	0	0	0	0	0	—	0	0	0	0	0.0	.000
1968			0	0	—	∞	1	0	0		2	1	0	0	0	0	0	0	0	0	—	0	0	0	0	0.0	.000
2 yrs.			0	0		81.00	2	0	0	0.1	4	1	0	0	0	0	0	0	0	0		0	0	0	0	0.0	

Al Javery

JAVERY, ALVA WILLIAM (Bear Tracks)
B. June 5, 1918, Worcester, Mass. D. Sept. 13, 1977, Woodstock, Conn.
BR TR 6′ 3″ 183 lbs.

Year	Team	Lg	W	L	PCT	ERA	G	GS	CG	IP	H	BB	SO	ShO	Relief Pitching W	Relief Pitching L	Relief Pitching SV	Batting AB	Batting H	Batting HR	BA	PO	A	E	DP	TC/G	FA
1940	**BOS**	**N**	2	4	.333	5.51	29	4	1	83.1	99	36	42	0	2	3	1	23	2	0	.087	1	10	2	0	0.4	.846
1941			10	11	.476	4.31	34	23	9	160.2	181	65	54	1	2	0	1	58	6	0	.103	3	42	1	0	1.4	.978
1942			12	16	.429	3.03	42	**37**	19	261	251	78	85	5	0	1	0	86	9	0	.105	14	63	1	7	1.9	.987
1943			17	16	.515	3.21	41	35	19	**303**	**288**	99	134	5	2	3	0	104	17	0	.163	18	69	6	4	2.3	.935
1944			10	19	.345	3.54	40	33	11	254	248	118	137	3	2	0	3	79	12	0	.152	7	37	3	4	1.2	.936
1945			2	7	.222	6.28	17	14	2	77.1	92	51	18	1	0	1	0	29	6	0	.207	0	21	0	0	1.2	1.000
1946			0	1	.000	13.50	2	1	0	3.1	5	5	0	0	0	0	0	1	0	0	.000	0	0	1	0	0.5	.000
7 yrs.			53	74	.417	3.80	205	147	61	1142.2	1164	452	470	15	8	8	5	380	52	0	.137	43	242	14	15	1.5	.953

Joey Jay

JAY, JOSEPH RICHARD
B. Aug. 15, 1935, Middletown, Conn.
BB TR 6′ 4″ 228 lbs.
BR 1953

Year	Team	Lg	W	L	PCT	ERA	G	GS	CG	IP	H	BB	SO	ShO	Relief Pitching W	Relief Pitching L	Relief Pitching SV	Batting AB	Batting H	Batting HR	BA	PO	A	E	DP	TC/G	FA
1953	**MIL**	**N**	1	0	1.000	0.00	3	1	1	10	6	5	4	1	0	0	0	3	0	0	.000	0	0	0	0	0.0	.000
1954			1	0	1.000	6.50	15	1	0	18	21	16	13	0	1	0	0	0	0	0	—	0	3	0	0	0.2	1.000
1955			0	0	—	4.74	12	1	0	19	23	13	3	0	0	0	0	3	2	0	.667	0	1	0	1	0.1	1.000
1957			0	0	—	0.00	1	0	0	0.2	0	0	0	0	0	0	1	0	0	0	—	0	1	0	0	1.0	1.000
1958			7	5	.583	2.14	18	12	6	96.2	60	43	74	3	0	0	0	32	3	0	.094	9	13	1	0	1.3	.957
1959			6	11	.353	4.09	34	19	4	136.1	130	64	88	1	1	2	0	35	3	0	.086	13	28	2	3	1.3	.953
1960			9	8	.529	3.24	32	11	3	133.1	128	59	90	0	3	5	1	45	7	0	.156	13	18	1	1	1.0	.969
1961	**CIN**	**N**	**21**	10	.677	3.53	34	34	14	247.1	217	92	157	**4**	0	0	0	89	8	0	.090	23	32	2	2	1.7	.965
1962			21	14	.600	3.76	39	37	16	273	269	100	155	4	1	0	0	90	15	2	.167	14	39	1	3	1.4	.981
1963			7	18	.280	4.29	30	22	4	170	172	73	116	1	2	3	1	50	8	0	.160	14	24	3	3	1.4	.927
1964			11	11	.500	3.39	34	23	10	183	167	36	134	0	2	0	2	53	3	0	.057	6	24	1	1	0.9	.968
1965			9	8	.529	4.22	37	24	4	155.2	150	63	102	1	2	1	1	49	2	0	.041	9	26	1	1	1.0	.972
1966	**2 teams CIN N (12G 6–2) ATL N (9G 0–4)**																										
″	**total**		6	6	.500	5.05	21	18	1	103.1	117	43	63	1	0	0	1	34	4	0	.118	4	12	2	0	0.9	.889
13 yrs.			99	91	.521	3.77	310	203	63	1546.1	1460	607	999	16	12	11	7	483	55	2	.114	105	221	14	15	1.1	.959
WORLD SERIES																											
1961	**CIN**	**N**	1	1	.500	5.59	2	2	1	9.2	8	6	6	0	0	0	0	4	0	0	.000	1	0	0	0	0.5	1.000

Domingo Jean

JEAN, DOMINGO
Born Domingo Jean (Luisa).
B. Jan. 9, 1969, San Pedro de Macoris, Dominican Republic.
BR TR 6′ 2″ 175 lbs.

Year	Team	Lg	W	L	PCT	ERA	G	GS	CG	IP	H	BB	SO	ShO	Relief Pitching W	Relief Pitching L	Relief Pitching SV	Batting AB	Batting H	Batting HR	BA	PO	A	E	DP	TC/G	FA
1993	**NY**	**A**	1	1	.500	4.46	10	6	0	40.1	37	19	20	0	0	0	0	0	0	0	—	1	6	0	0	0.7	1.000

Tex Jeanes

JEANES, ERNEST LEE
B. Dec. 19, 1900, Maypearl, Tex. D. Apr. 5, 1973, Longview, Tex.
BR TR 6′ 176 lbs.

Year	Team	Lg	W	L	PCT	ERA	G	GS	CG	IP	H	BB	SO	ShO	Relief Pitching W	Relief Pitching L	Relief Pitching SV	Batting AB	Batting H	Batting HR	BA	PO	A	E	DP	TC/G	FA
1922	**CLE**	**A**	0	0	—	0.00	1	0	0		0	1	0	0	0	0	0	1	0	0	.000	1	1	0	0	0.5	1.000
1927	**NY**	**N**	0	0	—	9.00	1	0	0	1	2	2	0	0	0	0	0	20	6	0	.300	0	0	0	0	0.0	
2 yrs.			0	0		9.00	2	0	0	1	2	3	0	0	0	0	0	*				46	2	0	0	1.2	1.000

George Jeffcoat

JEFFCOAT, GEORGE EDWARD
Brother of Hal Jeffcoat.
B. Dec. 24, 1913, New Brookland, S. C. D. Oct. 13, 1978, Leesville, S. C.
BR TR 5′11½″ 175 lbs.

Year	Team	Lg	W	L	PCT	ERA	G	GS	CG	IP	H	BB	SO	ShO	Relief Pitching W	Relief Pitching L	Relief Pitching SV	Batting AB	Batting H	Batting HR	BA	PO	A	E	DP	TC/G	FA
1936	**BKN**	**N**	5	6	.455	4.52	40	5	3	95.2	84	63	46	0	4	3	3	23	3	0	.130	3	17	0	0	0.5	1.000
1937			1	3	.250	5.13	21	3	1	54.1	58	27	29	1	1	2	0	12	0	0	.000	0	10	0	0	0.5	1.000
1939			0	0	—	0.00	1	0	0	2	2	0	1	0	0	0	0	0	0	0	—	0	0	0	0	0.0	.000
1943	**BOS**	**N**	1	2	.333	3.06	8	1	0	17.2	15	10	10	0	0	2	0	4	2	0	.500	0	5	0	0	0.6	1.000
4 yrs.			7	11	.389	4.51	70	9	4	169.2	159	100	86	1	5	7	3	39	5	0	.128	3	32	0	0	0.5	1.000

Hal Jeffcoat

JEFFCOAT, HAROLD BENTLEY
Brother of George Jeffcoat.
B. Sept. 6, 1924, West Columbia, S. C.
BR TR 5′10½″ 185 lbs.

Year	Team	Lg	W	L	PCT	ERA	G	GS	CG	IP	H	BB	SO	ShO	Relief Pitching W	Relief Pitching L	Relief Pitching SV	Batting AB	Batting H	Batting HR	BA	PO	A	E	DP	TC/G	FA
1954	**CHI**	**N**	5	6	.455	5.19	43	3	1	104	110	58	35	0	4	4	7	31	8	1	.258	307	12	8	3	2.7	.976
1955			8	6	.571	2.95	50	1	0	100.2	107	53	32	0	8	6	6	23	4	1	.174	4	24	3	1	0.6	.903
1956	**CIN**	**N**	8	2	.800	3.84	38	16	2	171	189	55	55	0	2	0	2	54	8	0	.148	21	42	2	4	1.7	.969
1957			12	13	.480	4.52	37	31	10	207	236	46	63	1	0	1	0	69	14	4	.203	16	30	2	5	1.3	.958
1958			6	8	.429	3.72	49	0	0	75	76	26	35	0	6	8	9	9	5	0	.556	9	19	0	2	0.6	1.000
1959	**2 teams CIN N (17G 0–1) STL N (11G 0–1)**																										
″	**total**		0	2	.000	5.95	28	0	0	39.1	54	19	19	0	0	2	1	4	1	0	.250	5	5	0	1	0.4	1.000
6 yrs.			39	37	.513	4.22	245	51	13	697	772	257	239	1	20	21	25	*				1267	203	40	28	1.9	.974

Mike Jeffcoat

JEFFCOAT, JAMES MICHAEL
B. Aug. 3, 1959, Pine Bluff, Ark.
BL TL 6′ 2″ 185 lbs.

Year	Team	Lg	W	L	PCT	ERA	G	GS	CG	IP	H	BB	SO	ShO	Relief Pitching W	Relief Pitching L	Relief Pitching SV	Batting AB	Batting H	Batting HR	BA	PO	A	E	DP	TC/G	FA
1983	**CLE**	**A**	1	3	.250	3.31	11	2	0	32.2	32	13	9	0	1	1	0	0	0	0	—	2	4	0	0	0.5	1.000
1984			5	2	.714	2.99	63	1	0	75.1	82	24	41	0	4	2	1	0	0	0	—	2	13	0	3	0.2	1.000
1985	**2 teams CLE A (9G 0–0) SF N (19G 0–2)**																										
″	**total**		0	2	.000	4.55	28	1	0	31.2	35	12	14	0	0	2	0	1	0	0	.000	2	12	1	0	0.5	.933
1987	**TEX**	**A**	0	1	.000	12.86	2	2	0	7	11	4	1	0	0	0	0	0	0	0	—	0	0	0	0	0.0	.000
1988			0	2	.000	11.70	5	2	0	10	19	5	5	0	0	0	0	0	0	0	—	0	2	0	0	0.4	1.000
1989			9	6	.600	3.58	22	22	2	130.2	139	33	64	2	0	0	0	0	0	0	—	13	18	1	1	1.5	.969
1990			5	6	.455	4.47	44	12	1	110.2	122	28	58	0	2	1	5	0	0	0	—	4	10	1	3	0.3	.933
1991			5	3	.625	4.63	70	0	0	79.2	104	25	43	0	5	3	1	1	1	0	1.000	2	13	0	0	0.2	1.000

Mike Jeffcoat *continued*

Year	Team	W	L	PCT	ERA	G	GS	CG	IP	H	BB	SO	ShO	Relief Pitching W	Relief Pitching L	Relief Pitching SV	Batting AB	Batting H	Batting HR	BA	PO	A	E	DP	TC/G	FA
1992		0	1	.000	7.32	6	3	0	19.2	28	5	6	0	0	0	0	0	0	0	—	1	3	0	1	0.7	1.000
1994	**FLA N**	0	0	—	10.13	4	0	0	2.2	4	0	1	0	0	0	0	0	0	0	—	0	0	0	0	0.0	.000
10 yrs.		25	26	.490	4.37	255	45	3	500	576	149	242	2	12	9	7	2	1	0	.500	26	75	3	8	0.4	.971

Jesse Jefferson

JEFFERSON, JESSE HARRISON BR TR 6′ 3″ 188 lbs.
B. Mar. 3, 1949, Midlothian, Va.

Year	Team	W	L	PCT	ERA	G	GS	CG	IP	H	BB	SO	ShO	Relief Pitching W	Relief Pitching L	Relief Pitching SV	Batting AB	Batting H	Batting HR	BA	PO	A	E	DP	TC/G	FA
1973	**BAL A**	6	5	.545	4.10	18	15	3	101	104	46	52	0	1	0	0	0	0	0	—	5	20	0	0	1.4	1.000
1974		1	0	1.000	4.42	20	2	0	57	55	38	31	0	0	0	0	0	0	0	—	3	9	1	1	0.6	.923
1975	**2 teams BAL A** (4G 0–2) **CHI A** (22G 5–9)																									
″	**total**	5	11	.313	4.92	26	21	1	115.1	105	102	71	0	0	2	0	0	0	0		5	21	4	2	1.2	.867
1976	**CHI A**	2	5	.286	8.56	19	9	0	62	86	42	30	0	0	1	0	0	0	0	—	3	14	0	2	0.9	1.000
1977	**TOR A**	9	17	.346	4.31	33	33	8	217	224	83	114	0	0	0	0	0	0	0	—	12	38	8	2	1.8	.862
1978		7	16	.304	4.38	31	30	9	211.2	214	86	97	2	0	0	0	0	0	0	—	15	31	3	3	1.6	.939
1979		2	10	.167	5.51	34	10	2	116	150	45	43	0	0	3	1	0	0	0	—	10	22	4	1	1.1	.889
1980	**2 teams TOR A** (29G 4–13) **PIT N** (1G 1–0)																									
″	**total**	5	13	.278	5.23	30	19	2	129	133	54	57	2	1	1	0	1	0	0	.000	6	25	2	1	1.1	.939
1981	**CAL A**	2	4	.333	3.62	26	5	0	77	80	24	27	0	1	0	0	0	0	0	—	11	6	3	2	0.8	.850
9 yrs.		39	81	.325	4.81	237	144	25	1086	1151	520	522	4	3	7	1	1	0	0	.000	70	186	25	14	1.2	.911

Ferguson Jenkins

JENKINS, FERGUSON ARTHUR BR TR 6′ 5″ 205 lbs.
B. Dec. 13, 1943, Chatham, Ont., Canada.
Hall of Fame 1991.

Year	Team	W	L	PCT	ERA	G	GS	CG	IP	H	BB	SO	ShO	Relief Pitching W	Relief Pitching L	Relief Pitching SV	Batting AB	Batting H	Batting HR	BA	PO	A	E	DP	TC/G	FA
1965	**PHI N**	2	1	.667	2.19	7	0	0	12.1	7	2	10	0	2	1	1	1	0	0	.000	0	1	0	0	0.1	1.000
1966	**2 teams PHI N** (1G 0–0) **CHI N** (60G 6–8)																									
″	**total**	6	8	.429	3.32	61	12	2	184.1	150	52	150	1	2	5	5	51	7	1	.137	11	19	3	0	0.5	.909
1967	**CHI N**	20	13	.606	2.80	38	38	**20**	289.1	230	83	236	3	0	0	0	93	14	0	.151	20	49	2	4	1.9	.972
1968		20	15	.571	2.63	40	**40**	20	308	255	65	260	3	0	0	0	100	16	1	.160	14	41	0	5	1.4	1.000
1969		21	15	.583	3.21	43	**42**	23	311	284	71	**273**	7	0	0	1	108	15	1	.139	14	47	4	3	1.5	.938
1970		22	16	.579	3.39	40	39	**24**	313	265	60	274	3	0	0	0	113	14	3	.124	14	39	4	1	1.4	.930
1971		**24**	13	.649	2.77	39	**39**	**30**	**325**	**304**	37	263	3	0	0	0	115	28	6	.243	31	48	7	1	2.2	.919
1972		20	12	.625	3.21	36	36	23	289	253	62	184	5	0	0	0	109	20	1	.183	28	50	2	2	2.2	.975
1973		14	16	.467	3.89	38	38	7	271	267	57	170	2	0	0	0	84	10	0	.119	21	53	4	6	2.1	.949
1974	**TEX A**	**25**	12	.676	2.83	41	41	**29**	328	286	45	225	6	0	0	0	2	1	0	.500	24	41	4	3	1.7	.942
1975		17	18	.486	3.93	37	37	22	270	261	56	157	4	0	0	0	0	0	0	—	27	39	5	1	1.9	.930
1976	**BOS A**	12	11	.522	3.27	30	29	12	209	201	43	142	2	1	0	0	0	0	0	—	13	23	0	3	1.2	1.000
1977		10	10	.500	3.68	28	28	11	193	190	36	105	1	0	0	0	0	0	0	—	24	30	4	1	2.1	.931
1978	**TEX A**	18	8	.692	3.04	34	30	16	249	228	41	157	4	0	1	0	0	0	0	—	29	37	1	4	2.0	.985
1979		16	14	.533	4.07	37	37	10	259	252	81	164	3	0	0	0	0	0	0	—	25	50	3	5	2.1	.962
1980		12	12	.500	3.77	29	29	12	198	190	52	129	0	0	0	0	0	0	0	—	24	23	2	3	1.7	.959
1981		5	8	.385	4.50	19	16	1	106	122	40	63	0	0	1	0	0	0	0	—	10	22	0	3	1.7	1.000
1982	**CHI N**	14	15	.483	3.15	34	34	4	217.1	221	68	134	1	0	0	0	67	10	0	.149	18	30	4	0	1.5	.923
1983		6	9	.400	4.30	33	29	1	167.1	176	46	96	1	0	0	0	53	13	0	.245	16	18	0	0	1.0	1.000
19 yrs.		284	226	.557	3.34	664	594	267	4499.2	4142	997	3192	49	5	8	7	896	148	13	.165	363	660	49	45	1.6	.954
												9th														

Jack Jenkins

JENKINS, WARREN WASHINGTON BR TR 6′ 2″ 195 lbs.
B. Dec. 22, 1942, Covington, Va.

Year	Team	W	L	PCT	ERA	G	GS	CG	IP	H	BB	SO	ShO	Relief Pitching W	Relief Pitching L	Relief Pitching SV	Batting AB	Batting H	Batting HR	BA	PO	A	E	DP	TC/G	FA
1962	**WAS A**	0	1	.000	4.05	3	1	1	13.1	12	7	10	0	0	0	0	4	0	0	.000	0	1	0	1	0.3	1.000
1963		0	2	.000	5.84	4	2	0	12.1	16	12	5	0	0	0	0	3	1	0	.333	1	3	1	0	1.3	.800
1969	**LA N**	0	0	—	0.00	1	0	0	1	0	0	1	0	0	0	0	0	0	0	—	1	0	0	0	1.0	1.000
3 yrs.		0	3	.000	4.72	8	3	1	26.2	28	19	16	0	0	0	0	7	1	0	.143	2	4	1	1	0.9	.857

Bill Jensen

JENSEN, WILLIAM CHRISTIAN BL TR 5′11½″ 170 lbs.
B. Nov. 23, 1888, New Haven, Conn. D. Mar. 27, 1917, Philadelphia, Pa.

Year	Team	W	L	PCT	ERA	G	GS	CG	IP	H	BB	SO	ShO	Relief Pitching W	Relief Pitching L	Relief Pitching SV	Batting AB	Batting H	Batting HR	BA	PO	A	E	DP	TC/G	FA
1912	**DET A**	1	2	.333	5.40	4	3	1	25	30	14	4	0	0	0	0	11	0	0	.000	1	9	1	0	2.8	.909
1914	**PHI A**	0	1	.000	2.00	1	1	1	9	7	2	1	0	0	0	0	2	0	0	.000	0	3	0	0	3.0	1.000
2 yrs.		1	3	.250	4.50	5	4	2	34	37	16	5	0	0	0	0	13	0	0	.000	1	12	1	0	2.8	.929

Virgil Jester

JESTER, VIRGIL MILTON BR TR 5′11″ 188 lbs.
B. July 23, 1927, Denver, Colo.

Year	Team	W	L	PCT	ERA	G	GS	CG	IP	H	BB	SO	ShO	Relief Pitching W	Relief Pitching L	Relief Pitching SV	Batting AB	Batting H	Batting HR	BA	PO	A	E	DP	TC/G	FA
1952	**BOS N**	3	5	.375	3.33	19	8	4	73	80	23	25	1	0	1	0	19	4	0	.211	6	8	1	1	0.8	.933
1953	**MIL N**	0	0	—	22.50	2	0	0	2	4	4	0	0	0	0	0	0	0	0	—	0	1	0	0	0.5	1.000
2 yrs.		3	5	.375	3.84	21	8	4	75	84	27	25	1	0	1	0	19	4	0	.211	6	9	1	1	0.8	.938

German Jimenez

JIMENEZ, GERMAN BL TL 5′10″ 200 lbs.
Born German Jimenez (Camarena).
B. Dec. 5, 1962, Santiago, Mexico.

Year	Team	W	L	PCT	ERA	G	GS	CG	IP	H	BB	SO	ShO	Relief Pitching W	Relief Pitching L	Relief Pitching SV	Batting AB	Batting H	Batting HR	BA	PO	A	E	DP	TC/G	FA
1988	**ATL N**	1	6	.143	5.01	15	9	0	55.2	65	12	26	0	0	1	0	17	1	0	.059	0	6	0	0	0.4	1.000

Juan Jimenez

JIMENEZ, JUAN ANTONIO BR TR 6′ 1″ 165 lbs.
Born Juan Antonio Jimenez (Martes).
B. Mar. 8, 1949, La Torre, Dominican Republic.

Year	Team	W	L	PCT	ERA	G	GS	CG	IP	H	BB	SO	ShO	Relief Pitching W	Relief Pitching L	Relief Pitching SV	Batting AB	Batting H	Batting HR	BA	PO	A	E	DP	TC/G	FA
1974	**PIT N**	0	0	—	6.75	4	0	0	4	6	2	2	0	0	0	0	0	0	0	—	0	0	0	0	0.0	.000

Miguel Jimenez

JIMENEZ, MIGUEL ANTHONY BR TR 6′ 2″ 205 lbs.
B. Aug. 19, 1969, New York, N. Y.

Year	Team	W	L	PCT	ERA	G	GS	CG	IP	H	BB	SO	ShO	Relief Pitching W	Relief Pitching L	Relief Pitching SV	Batting AB	Batting H	Batting HR	BA	PO	A	E	DP	TC/G	FA
1993	**OAK A**	1	0	1.000	4.00	5	4	0	27	27	16	13	0	0	0	0	0	0	0	—	0	0	0	0	0.0	.000
1994		1	4	.200	7.41	8	7	0	34	38	32	22	0	0	0	0	0	0	0	—	2	6	1	1	1.1	.889
2 yrs.		2	4	.333	5.90	13	11	0	61	65	48	35	0	0	0	0	0	0	0		2	6	1	1	0.7	.889

Tommy John

JOHN, THOMAS EDWARD (T. J.) BR TL 6′ 3″ 180 lbs.
B. May 22, 1943, Terre Haute, Ind.

Year	Team	W	L	PCT	ERA	G	GS	CG	IP	H	BB	SO	ShO	Relief Pitching W	Relief Pitching L	Relief Pitching SV	Batting AB	Batting H	Batting HR	BA	PO	A	E	DP	TC/G	FA
1963	CLE A	0	2	.000	2.21	6	3	0	20.1	23	6	9	0	0	0	0	6	0	0	.000	1	3	0	0	0.7	1.000
1964		2	9	.182	3.91	25	14	2	94.1	97	35	65	1	0	0	0	24	5	0	.208	5	16	0	2	0.8	1.000
1965	CHI A	14	7	.667	3.09	39	27	6	183.2	162	58	126	1	1	1	3	59	10	1	.169	4	51	5	3	1.5	.917
1966		14	11	.560	2.62	34	33	10	223	195	57	138	**5**	0	0	0	69	10	2	.145	8	47	5	0	1.8	.917
1967		10	13	.435	2.47	31	29	9	178.1	143	47	110	**6**	0	1	0	51	8	0	.157	17	55	2	4	2.4	.973
1968		10	5	.667	1.98	25	25	5	177.1	135	49	117	1	0	0	0	62	12	1	.194	10	54	1	6	2.6	.985
1969		9	11	.450	3.25	33	33	6	232.1	230	90	128	2	0	0	0	79	9	0	.114	16	66	0	4	2.5	1.000
1970		12	17	.414	3.28	37	37	10	269	253	101	138	3	0	0	0	84	17	0	.202	15	65	8	3	2.4	.909
1971		13	16	.448	3.62	38	35	10	229	244	58	131	3	0	0	0	69	10	0	.145	9	34	3	2	1.2	.935
1972	LA N	11	5	.688	2.89	29	29	4	186.2	172	40	117	1	0	0	0	63	10	0	.159	11	45	0	3	1.9	1.000
1973		16	7	**.696**	3.10	36	31	4	218	202	50	116	2	0	0	0	74	15	0	.203	15	64	1	6	2.2	.988
1974		13	3	.813	2.59	22	22	5	153	133	42	78	3	0	0	0	51	6	0	.118	3	36	1	3	1.8	.975
1976		10	10	.500	3.09	31	31	6	207	207	61	91	2	0	0	0	64	7	0	.109	3	33	1	2	1.2	.973
1977		20	7	.741	2.78	31	31	11	220	225	50	123	3	0	0	0	79	14	1	.177	6	47	1	5	1.7	.981
1978		17	10	.630	3.30	33	30	7	213	230	53	124	0	1	0	1	66	8	0	.121	8	45	3	1	1.7	.946
1979	NY A	21	9	.700	2.97	37	36	17	276	268	65	111	3	1	0	0	0	0	0	—	15	51	3	5	1.9	.957
1980		22	9	.710	3.43	36	36	16	265	270	56	78	**6**	0	0	0	0	0	0	—	16	46	1	4	1.8	.984
1981		9	8	.529	2.64	20	20	7	140	135	39	50	0	0	0	0	0	0	0	—	11	27	0	2	1.9	1.000
1982	**2 teams** **NY A** (30G 10–10) **CAL A** (7G 4–2)																									
″	total	14	12	.538	3.69	37	33	10	221.2	239	39	68	2	0	0	0	0	0	0		10	48	2	1	1.6	.967
1983	CAL A	11	13	.458	4.33	34	34	9	234.2	**287**	49	65	0	0	0	0	0	0	0	—	16	39	0	4	1.6	1.000
1984		7	13	.350	4.52	32	29	4	181.1	223	56	47	1	0	0	0	0	0	0	—	15	27	0	2	1.3	1.000
1985	**2 teams** **CAL A** (12G 2–4) **OAK A** (11G 2–6)																									
″	total	4	10	.286	5.53	23	17	0	86.1	117	28	25	0	1	1	0	0	0	0		8	22	0	2	1.3	1.000
1986	NY A	5	3	.625	2.93	13	10	1	70.2	73	15	28	0	0	0	0	0	0	0	—	4	15	3	2	1.7	.864
1987		13	6	.684	4.03	33	33	3	187.2	212	47	63	1	0	0	0	0	0	0	—	4	31	5	1	1.2	.875
1988		9	8	.529	4.49	35	32	0	176.1	221	46	81	0	0	0	0	0	0	0	—	4	40	4	2	1.4	.917
1989		2	7	.222	5.80	10	10	0	63.2	87	22	18	0	0	0	0	0	0	0	—	3	21	0	0	2.4	1.000
26 yrs.		288	231	.555	3.34	760	700	162	4708.1	4783	1259	2245	46	4	3	4	900	141	5	.157	237	1028	49	69	1.7	.963
DIVISIONAL PLAYOFF SERIES																										
1981	NY A	0	1	.000	6.43	1	1	0	7	8	2	0	0	0	0	0	0	0	0	—	0	0	0	0	0.0	.000
LEAGUE CHAMPIONSHIP SERIES																										
1977	LA N	1	0	1.000	0.66	2	2	1	13.2	11	5	11	0	0	0	0	5	1	0	.200	0	1	0	0	0.5	1.000
1978		1	0	1.000	0.00	1	1	1	9	4	2	4	1	0	0	0	3	0	0	.000	0	0	0	0	0.0	.000
1980	NY A	0	0	—	2.70	1	1	0	6.2	8	1	3	0	0	0	0	0	0	0	—	0	1	0	0	1.0	1.000
1981		1	0	1.000	1.50	1	1	0	6	6	1	3	0	0	0	0	0	0	0	—	0	0	0	0	0.0	.000
1982	CAL A	1	1	.500	5.11	2	2	1	12.1	11	6	6	0	0	0	0	0	0	0	—	3	1	0	0	2.0	1.000
5 yrs.		4	1	.800	2.08	7	7	3	47.2	40	15	27	1	0	0	0	8	1	0	.125	3	3	0	0	0.9	1.000
		3rd		**7th**			**4th**	**2nd**	**8th**				**1st**													
WORLD SERIES																										
1977	LA N	0	1	.000	6.00	1	1	0	6	9	3	7	0	0	0	0	2	0	0	.000	0	0	0	0	0.0	.000
1978		1	0	1.000	3.07	2	2	0	14.2	14	4	6	0	0	0	0	0	0	0	—	0	4	0	0	2.0	1.000
1981	NY A	1	0	1.000	0.69	3	2	0	13	11	0	8	0	0	0	0	2	0	0	.000	0	3	0	0	1.0	1.000
3 yrs.		2	1	.667	2.67	6	5	0	33.2	34	7	21	0	0	0	0	4	0	0	.000	0	7	0	0	1.2	1.000

Augie Johns

JOHNS, AUGUSTUS FRANCIS (Lefty) BL TL 5′ 8½″ 170 lbs.
B. Sept. 10, 1899, St. Louis, Mo. D. Sept. 12, 1975, San Antonio, Tex.

Year	Team	W	L	PCT	ERA	G	GS	CG	IP	H	BB	SO	ShO	Relief Pitching W	Relief Pitching L	Relief Pitching SV	Batting AB	Batting H	Batting HR	BA	PO	A	E	DP	TC/G	FA
1926	DET A	6	4	.600	5.35	35	14	3	112.2	117	69	40	1	2	0	1	28	4	0	.143	4	16	0	0	0.6	1.000
1927		0	0	—	9.00	1	0	0	1	1	1	1	0	0	0	0	0	0	0	—	0	1	0	0	1.0	1.000
2 yrs.		6	4	.600	5.38	36	14	3	113.2	118	70	41	1	2	0	1	28	4	0	.143	4	17	0	0	0.6	1.000

Doug Johns

JOHNS, DOUGLAS ALAN BR TL 6′ 2″ 185 lbs.
B. Dec. 19, 1967, South Bend, Ind.

Year	Team	W	L	PCT	ERA	G	GS	CG	IP	H	BB	SO	ShO	Relief Pitching W	Relief Pitching L	Relief Pitching SV	Batting AB	Batting H	Batting HR	BA	PO	A	E	DP	TC/G	FA
1995	OAK A	5	3	.625	4.61	11	9	1	54.2	44	26	25	1	0	0	0	0	0	0	—	6	10	1	0	1.5	.941

Ollie Johns

JOHNS, OLIVER TRACY BL TL
B. Aug. 21, 1879, Trenton, Ohio D. June 17, 1961, Hamilton, Ohio.

Year	Team	W	L	PCT	ERA	G	GS	CG	IP	H	BB	SO	ShO	Relief Pitching W	Relief Pitching L	Relief Pitching SV	Batting AB	Batting H	Batting HR	BA	PO	A	E	DP	TC/G	FA
1905	CIN N	1	0	1.000	3.50	4	1	1	18	31	4	8	0	0	0	1	5	1	0	.200	2	4	1	0	1.8	.857

Abe Johnson

JOHNSON, ABRAHAM
B. Chicago, Ill. Deceased.

Year	Team	W	L	PCT	ERA	G	GS	CG	IP	H	BB	SO	ShO	Relief Pitching W	Relief Pitching L	Relief Pitching SV	Batting AB	Batting H	Batting HR	BA	PO	A	E	DP	TC/G	FA
1893	CHI N	0	0	—	36.00	1	0	0	1	2	2	0	0	0	0	1	0	0	0	—	0	0	0	0	0.0	.000

Adam Johnson

JOHNSON, ADAM RANKIN JR. BR TR 6′ 3″ 177 lbs.
Son of Adam Johnson.
B. Mar. 1, 1917, Hayden, Ariz.

Year	Team	W	L	PCT	ERA	G	GS	CG	IP	H	BB	SO	ShO	Relief Pitching W	Relief Pitching L	Relief Pitching SV	Batting AB	Batting H	Batting HR	BA	PO	A	E	DP	TC/G	FA
1941	PHI A	1	0	1.000	3.60	7	0	0	10	14	3	0	0	1	0	0	1	0	0	.000	1	3	0	0	0.6	1.000

Adam Johnson

JOHNSON, ADAM RANKIN SR. (Tex) BR TR 6′ 1½″ 185 lbs.
Father of Adam Johnson.
B. Feb. 4, 1888, Burnet, Tex. D. July 2, 1972, Williamsport, Pa.

Year	Team	W	L	PCT	ERA	G	GS	CG	IP	H	BB	SO	ShO	Relief Pitching W	Relief Pitching L	Relief Pitching SV	Batting AB	Batting H	Batting HR	BA	PO	A	E	DP	TC/G	FA
1914	**2 teams** **BOS A** (16G 4–9) **CHI F** (16G 9–5)																									
″	total	13	14	.481	**2.26**	32	27	16	219.1	180	63	84	4	1	1	0	67	8	0	.119	6	51	2	4	1.8	.966
1915	**2 teams** **CHI F** (11G 2–4) **BAL F** (23G 7–11)																									
″	total	9	15	.375	3.64	34	25	15	207.2	201	81	81	2	1	2	2	73	9	0	.123	2	40	0	2	1.2	1.000
1918	STL N	1	1	.500	2.74	6	1	0	23	20	7	4	0	1	0	0	4	1	0	.250	0	13	2	0	2.5	.867
3 yrs.		23	30	.434	2.92	72	53	31	450	401	151	169	6	3	3	2	144	18	0	.125	8	104	4	6	1.6	.966

Art Johnson

JOHNSON, ARTHUR GILBERT BB TL 6′ 1″ 167 lbs.
B. Feb. 15, 1897, Warren, Pa. D. June 7, 1982, Sarasota, Fla.

Year	Team	W	L	PCT	ERA	G	GS	CG	IP	H	BB	SO	ShO	Relief Pitching W	Relief Pitching L	Relief Pitching SV	Batting AB	Batting H	Batting HR	BA	PO	A	E	DP	TC/G	FA
1927	NY N	0	0	—	0.00	1	0	0	3	1	1	0	0	0	0	0	0	0	0	—	0	1	1	0	2.0	.500

Art Johnson

JOHNSON, ARTHUR HENRY (Lefty) BL TL 6′ 2″ 185 lbs.
B. July 16, 1916, Winchester, Mass.

Year	Team	Lg	W	L	PCT	ERA	G	GS	CG	IP	H	BB	SO	ShO	Relief W	Relief L	Relief SV	Bat AB	Bat H	HR	BA	PO	A	E	DP	TC/G	FA
1940	BOS	N	0	1	.000	10.50	2	1	0	6	10	3	1	0	0	0	0	1	0	0	.000	0	3	0	0	1.5	1.000
1941			7	15	.318	3.53	43	18	6	183.1	189	71	70	0	1	4	1	55	8	0	.145	7	40	4	4	1.2	.922
1942			0	0	—	1.42	4	0	0	6.1	4	5	0	0	0	0	0	1	0	0	.000	0	1	0	0	0.3	1.000
3 yrs.			7	16	.304	3.68	49	19	6	195.2	203	79	71	0	1	4	1	57	8	0	.140	7	44	4	4	1.1	.927

Bart Johnson

JOHNSON, CLAIR BARTH BR TR 6′ 5″ 190 lbs.
B. Jan. 3, 1950, Torrance, Calif.

Year	Team	Lg	W	L	PCT	ERA	G	GS	CG	IP	H	BB	SO	ShO	Relief W	Relief L	Relief SV	Bat AB	Bat H	HR	BA	PO	A	E	DP	TC/G	FA
1969	CHI	A	1	3	.250	3.22	4	3	0	22.1	22	6	18	0	0	1	0	6	1	0	.167	2	2	1	0	1.3	.800
1970			4	7	.364	4.80	18	15	2	90	92	46	71	1	0	0	0	29	8	0	.276	4	11	0	2	0.8	1.000
1971			12	10	.545	2.93	53	16	4	178	148	111	153	0	4	4	14	57	11	0	.193	12	19	3	0	0.6	.912
1972			0	3	.000	9.22	9	0	0	13.2	18	13	9	0	0	3	1	1	0	0	.000	0	3	0	0	0.3	1.000
1973			3	3	.500	4.13	22	9	0	80.2	76	40	56	0	1	0	0	0	0	0	—	4	10	0	0	0.6	1.000
1974			10	4	.714	2.73	18	18	8	122	105	32	76	2	0	0	0	0	0	0	—	6	7	0	0	0.7	1.000
1976			9	16	.360	4.73	32	32	8	211	231	62	91	3	0	0	0	0	0	0	—	22	30	1	0	1.7	.981
1977			4	5	.444	4.01	29	4	0	92	114	38	46	0	3	2	2	0	0	0	—	8	12	1	1	0.7	.952
8 yrs.			43	51	.457	3.93	185	97	22	809.2	806	348	520	6	8	10	17	93	20	0	.215	58	94	6	3	0.9	.962

Ben Johnson

JOHNSON, BENJAMIN FRANKLIN BR TR 6′ 2″ 190 lbs.
B. May 15, 1931, Greenwood, S. C.

Year	Team	Lg	W	L	PCT	ERA	G	GS	CG	IP	H	BB	SO	ShO	Relief W	Relief L	Relief SV	Bat AB	Bat H	HR	BA	PO	A	E	DP	TC/G	FA
1959	CHI	N	0	0	—	2.16	4	2	0	16.2	17	4	6	0	0	0	0	4	0	0	.000	2	1	0	0	0.8	1.000
1960			2	1	.667	4.91	17	0	0	29.1	39	11	9	0	2	1	1	2	0	0	.000	2	8	0	1	0.6	1.000
2 yrs.			2	1	.667	3.91	21	2	0	46	56	15	15	0	2	1	1	6	0	0	.000	4	9	0	1	0.6	1.000

Bill Johnson

JOHNSON, WILLIAM CHARLES BR TR 6′ 5″ 205 lbs.
B. Oct. 6, 1960, Wilmington, Del.

Year	Team	Lg	W	L	PCT	ERA	G	GS	CG	IP	H	BB	SO	ShO	Relief W	Relief L	Relief SV	Bat AB	Bat H	HR	BA	PO	A	E	DP	TC/G	FA
1983	CHI	N	1	0	1.000	4.38	10	0	0	12.1	17	3	4	0	1	0	0	0	0	0	—	1	4	0	0	0.5	1.000
1984			0	0	—	1.69	4	0	0	5.1	4	1	3	0	0	0	0	0	0	0	—	0	3	0	0	0.8	1.000
2 yrs.			1	0	1.000	3.57	14	0	0	17.2	21	4	7	0	1	0	0	0	0	0		1	7	0	0	0.6	1.000

Bob Johnson

JOHNSON, ROBERT DALE BL TR 6′ 4″ 220 lbs.
B. Apr. 25, 1943, Aurora, Ind.

Year	Team	Lg	W	L	PCT	ERA	G	GS	CG	IP	H	BB	SO	ShO	Relief W	Relief L	Relief SV	Bat AB	Bat H	HR	BA	PO	A	E	DP	TC/G	FA
1969	NY	N	0	0	—	0.00	2	0	0	1.2	1	1	1	0	0	0	1	0	0	0	—	0	0	0	0	0.0	.000
1970	KC	A	8	13	.381	3.07	40	26	10	214	178	82	206	1	0	1	4	57	6	0	.105	13	20	0	0	0.8	1.000
1971	PIT	N	9	10	.474	3.45	31	27	7	175	170	55	101	1	0	0	0	48	3	0	.063	14	20	3	2	1.2	.919
1972			4	4	.500	2.96	31	11	1	115.2	98	46	79	0	2	2	3	35	5	0	.143	6	7	1	1	0.5	.929
1973			4	2	.667	3.62	50	2	0	92	98	34	68	0	4	1	4	14	0	0	.000	2	4	1	1	0.1	.857
1974	CLE	A	3	4	.429	4.38	14	10	0	72	75	37	36	0	0	0	0	0	0	0	—	2	11	0	0	0.9	1.000
1977	ATL	N	0	1	.000	7.36	15	0	0	22	24	14	16	0	0	1	0	3	1	0	.333	0	1	0	0	0.1	1.000
7 yrs.			28	34	.452	3.48	183	76	18	692.1	644	269	507	2	6	5	12	157	15	0	.096	37	63	5	4	0.6	.952
LEAGUE CHAMPIONSHIP SERIES																											
1971	PIT	N	1	0	1.000	0.00	1	1	0	8	5	3	7	0	0	0	0	2	0	0	.000	0	0	0	0	0.0	.000
1972			0	0	—	3.00	2	0	0	6	4	2	7	0	0	0	0	1	0	0	.000	0	0	0	0	0.0	.000
2 yrs.			1	0	1.000	1.29	3	1	0	14	9	5	14	0	0	0	0	3	0	0	.000	0	0	0	0	0.0	
WORLD SERIES																											
1971	PIT	N	0	1	.000	9.00	2	1	0	5	5	3	3	0	0	0	0	3	0	0	.000	2	0	0	0	1.0	1.000

Chet Johnson

JOHNSON, CHESTER LILLIS BL TL 6′ 175 lbs.
Brother of Earl Johnson.
B. Aug. 1, 1917, Redmond, Wash. D. Apr. 10, 1983, Seattle, Wash.

Year	Team	Lg	W	L	PCT	ERA	G	GS	CG	IP	H	BB	SO	ShO	Relief W	Relief L	Relief SV	Bat AB	Bat H	HR	BA	PO	A	E	DP	TC/G	FA
1946	STL	A	0	0	—	5.00	5	3	0	18	20	13	8	0	0	0	0	6	0	0	.000	0	0	0	0	0.0	.000

Chief Johnson

JOHNSON, GEORGE HOWARD BR TR 5′11½″ 190 lbs.
B. Mar. 30, 1886, Winnebago, Neb. D. June 11, 1922, Des Moines, Iowa.

Year	Team	Lg	W	L	PCT	ERA	G	GS	CG	IP	H	BB	SO	ShO	Relief W	Relief L	Relief SV	Bat AB	Bat H	HR	BA	PO	A	E	DP	TC/G	FA
1913	CIN	N	14	16	.467	3.01	44	31	13	269	251	86	107	3	2	2	0	88	10	1	.114	1	75	6	2	1.9	.927
1914	2 teams	CIN N (1G 0–0) KC F (20G 9–10)																									
″	total		9	10	.474	3.26	21	20	12	138	163	35	79	2	0	0	0	49	6	1	.122	1	27	4	1	1.5	.875
1915	KC	F	18	17	.514	2.75	46	34	19	281.1	253	71	118	4	4	0	1	87	11	1	.126	13	94	12	4	2.6	.899
3 yrs.			41	43	.488	2.95	111	85	44	688.1	667	192	304	9	6	2	1	224	27	3	.121	15	196	22	7	2.1	.906

Connie Johnson

JOHNSON, CLIFFORD BR TR 6′ 4″ 200 lbs.
B. Dec. 27, 1922, Stone Mountain, Ga.

Year	Team	Lg	W	L	PCT	ERA	G	GS	CG	IP	H	BB	SO	ShO	Relief W	Relief L	Relief SV	Bat AB	Bat H	HR	BA	PO	A	E	DP	TC/G	FA
1953	CHI	A	4	4	.500	3.56	14	10	2	60.2	55	38	44	1	0	0	0	20	1	0	.050	1	6	0	0	0.5	1.000
1955			7	4	.636	3.45	17	16	5	99	95	52	72	2	0	0	0	33	5	0	.152	3	9	0	0	0.7	1.000
1956	2 teams	CHI A (5G 0–1) BAL A (26G 9–10)																									
″	total		9	11	.450	3.44	31	27	9	196	176	69	136	2	0	0	0	61	15	0	.246	9	16	1	0	0.8	.962
1957	BAL	A	14	11	.560	3.20	35	30	14	242	212	66	177	3	0	1	0	89	12	0	.135	10	22	1	0	0.9	.970
1958			6	9	.400	3.88	26	17	4	118.1	116	32	68	0	1	1	1	34	7	0	.206	3	13	0	0	0.6	1.000
5 yrs.			40	39	.506	3.44	123	100	34	716	654	257	497	8	1	2	1	237	40	0	.169	26	66	2	0	0.8	.979

Dane Johnson

JOHNSON, DANE EDWARD BR TR 6′ 5″ 205 lbs.
B. Feb. 10, 1963, Coral Gables, Fla.

Year	Team	Lg	W	L	PCT	ERA	G	GS	CG	IP	H	BB	SO	ShO	Relief W	Relief L	Relief SV	Bat AB	Bat H	HR	BA	PO	A	E	DP	TC/G	FA
1994	CHI	A	2	1	.667	6.57	15	0	0	12.1	16	11	7	0	2	1	0	0	0	0	—	0	1	0	0	0.1	1.000

Dave Johnson

JOHNSON, DAVID CHARLES BR TR 6′ 1″ 183 lbs.
B. Oct. 4, 1948, Abilene, Tex.

Year	Team	Lg	W	L	PCT	ERA	G	GS	CG	IP	H	BB	SO	ShO	Relief W	Relief L	Relief SV	Bat AB	Bat H	HR	BA	PO	A	E	DP	TC/G	FA
1974	BAL	A	2	2	.500	3.00	11	0	0	15	17	5	6	0	2	2	2	0	0	0	—	1	1	0	0	0.2	1.000
1975			0	1	.000	4.15	6	0	0	8.2	8	7	4	0	0	1	0	0	0	0	—	1	1	0	0	0.3	1.000
1977	MIN	A	2	5	.286	4.56	30	6	0	73	86	23	33	0	1	3	0	0	0	0	—	5	11	0	2	0.5	1.000
1978			0	2	.000	7.50	6	1	0	12	15	9	7	0	0	1	0	0	0	0	—	2	1	0	0	0.5	1.000
4 yrs.			4	10	.286	4.64	53	7	0	108.2	126	44	50	0	3	7	2	0	0	0		9	14	0	2	0.4	1.000

Dave Johnson

JOHNSON, DAVID WAYNE BR TR 5′10″ 180 lbs.
B. Oct. 24, 1959, Baltimore, Md.

Year	Team	Lg	W	L	PCT	ERA	G	GS	CG	IP	H	BB	SO	ShO	Relief Pitching W	Relief Pitching L	Relief Pitching SV	Batting AB	Batting H	Batting HR	BA	PO	A	E	DP	TC/G	FA
1987	PIT	N	0	0	—	9.95	5	0	0	6.1	13	2	4	0	0	0	0	0	0	0	—	1	1	0	1	0.4	1.000
1989	BAL	A	4	7	.364	4.23	14	14	4	89.1	90	28	26	0	0	0	0	0	0	0	—	6	5	0	0	0.8	1.000
1990			13	9	.591	4.10	30	29	3	180	196	43	68	0	0	0	0	0	0	0	—	13	10	2	1	0.8	.920
1991			4	8	.333	7.07	22	14	0	84	127	24	38	0	2	0	0	0	0	0	—	7	7	0	1	0.6	1.000
1993	DET	A	1	1	.500	12.96	6	0	0	8.1	13	5	7	0	1	1	0	0	0	0	—	1	0	1	0	0.3	.500
5 yrs.			22	25	.468	5.11	77	57	7	368	439	102	143	0	3	1	0	0	0	0		28	23	3	3	0.7	.944

Don Johnson

JOHNSON, DONALD ROY BR TR 6′ 3″ 200 lbs.
B. Nov. 12, 1926, Portland, Ore.

Year	Team	Lg	W	L	PCT	ERA	G	GS	CG	IP	H	BB	SO	ShO	Relief Pitching W	Relief Pitching L	Relief Pitching SV	Batting AB	Batting H	Batting HR	BA	PO	A	E	DP	TC/G	FA
1947	NY	A	4	3	.571	3.64	15	8	2	54.1	57	23	16	0	1	1	0	13	0	0	.000	2	7	2	2	0.7	.818
1950	2 teams	NY A (8G 1–0) STL A (25G 5–6)																									
″	total		6	6	.500	6.71	33	12	4	114	161	67	40	0	2	0	1	32	2	0	.063	2	19	3	0	0.7	.875
1951	2 teams	STL A (6G 0–1) WAS A (21G 7–11)																									
″	total		7	12	.368	4.76	27	23	8	158.2	165	76	60	1	0	0	0	50	5	0	.100	3	27	0	5	1.1	1.000
1952	WAS	A	0	5	.000	4.43	29	6	0	69	80	33	37	0	0	2	2	13	1	0	.077	6	9	0	0	0.5	1.000
1954	CHI	A	8	7	.533	3.13	46	16	3	144	129	43	68	3	2	3	7	35	1	0	.029	8	24	1	1	0.7	.970
1955	BAL	A	2	4	.333	5.82	31	5	0	68	89	35	27	0	2	1	1	10	0	0	.000	0	14	1	2	0.5	.933
1958	SF	N	0	1	.000	6.26	17	0	0	23	31	8	14	0	0	1	1	2	0	0	.000	1	3	0	0	0.2	1.000
7 yrs.			27	38	.415	4.78	198	70	17	631	712	285	262	4	7	8	12	155	9	0	.058	22	103	7	10	0.7	.947

Earl Johnson

JOHNSON, EARL DOUGLAS (Lefty) BL TL 6′ 3″ 190 lbs.
Brother of Chet Johnson.
B. Apr. 2, 1919, Redmond, Wash. D. Dec. 3, 1994, Seattle, Wash.

Year	Team	Lg	W	L	PCT	ERA	G	GS	CG	IP	H	BB	SO	ShO	Relief Pitching W	Relief Pitching L	Relief Pitching SV	Batting AB	Batting H	Batting HR	BA	PO	A	E	DP	TC/G	FA
1940	BOS	A	6	2	.750	4.09	17	10	2	70.1	69	39	26	0	2	1	0	27	2	0	.074	2	19	0	1	1.2	1.000
1941			4	5	.444	4.52	17	12	4	93.2	90	51	46	0	1	0	0	34	10	0	.294	3	27	0	3	1.8	1.000
1946			5	4	.556	3.71	29	5	1	80	78	39	40	1	5	3	3	22	5	0	.227	5	12	1	1	0.6	.944
1947			12	11	.522	2.97	45	17	6	142.1	129	62	65	3	4	3	8	44	12	0	.273	4	31	2	5	0.8	.946
1948			10	4	.714	4.53	35	3	1	91.1	98	42	45	0	**9**	2	5	31	3	0	.097	6	25	0	2	0.9	1.000
1949			3	6	.333	7.48	19	3	0	49.1	65	29	20	0	3	4	0	11	0	0	.000	3	5	1	0	0.5	.889
1950			0	0	—	7.24	11	0	0	13.2	18	8	6	0	0	0	0	2	0	0	.000	0	6	0	0	0.5	1.000
1951	DET	A	0	0	—	6.35	6	0	0	5.2	9	2	2	0	0	0	1	0	0	0	—	1	1	0	1	0.3	1.000
8 yrs.			40	32	.556	4.30	179	50	14	546.1	556	272	250	4	24	13	17	171	32	0	.187	24	126	4	13	0.9	.974
WORLD SERIES																											
1946	BOS	A	1	0	1.000	2.70	3	0	0	3.1	1	2	1	0	1	0	0	1	0	0	.000	0	2	0	0	0.7	1.000

Ellis Johnson

JOHNSON, ELLIS WALTER BR TR 6′½″ 180 lbs.
B. Dec. 8, 1892, Minneapolis, Minn. D. Jan. 14, 1965, Minneapolis, Minn.

Year	Team	Lg	W	L	PCT	ERA	G	GS	CG	IP	H	BB	SO	ShO	Relief Pitching W	Relief Pitching L	Relief Pitching SV	Batting AB	Batting H	Batting HR	BA	PO	A	E	DP	TC/G	FA
1912	CHI	A	0	0	—	3.29	4	0	0	13.2	11	10	8	0	0	0	0	3	0	0	.000	1	2	0	0	0.8	1.000
1915			0	0	—	9.00	1	0	0	2	3	0	3	0	0	0	0	0	0	0	—	0	0	0	0	0.0	.000
1917	PHI	A	0	2	.000	7.24	4	2	0	13.2	15	5	8	0	0	0	0	1	0	0	.000	0	5	0	0	1.3	1.000
3 yrs.			0	2	.000	5.52	9	2	0	29.1	29	15	19	0	0	0	0	4	0	0	.000	1	7	0	0	0.9	1.000

Ernie Johnson

JOHNSON, ERNEST THORWALD BR TR 6′ 3½″ 190 lbs.
B. June 16, 1924, Brattleboro, Vt.

Year	Team	Lg	W	L	PCT	ERA	G	GS	CG	IP	H	BB	SO	ShO	Relief Pitching W	Relief Pitching L	Relief Pitching SV	Batting AB	Batting H	Batting HR	BA	PO	A	E	DP	TC/G	FA
1950	BOS	N	2	0	1.000	6.97	16	1	0	20.2	37	13	15	0	2	0	0	2	1	0	.500	1	10	0	0	0.7	1.000
1952			6	3	.667	4.11	29	10	2	92	100	31	45	1	2	0	1	22	2	0	.091	9	21	1	3	1.1	.968
1953	MIL	N	4	3	.571	2.67	36	1	0	81	79	22	36	0	4	2	0	14	1	0	.071	4	15	2	1	0.6	.905
1954			5	2	.714	2.81	40	4	1	99.1	77	34	68	0	4	1	2	13	3	0	.231	4	22	0	2	0.6	1.000
1955			5	7	.417	3.42	40	2	0	92	81	55	43	0	5	5	4	20	2	0	.100	7	14	3	0	0.6	.875
1956			4	3	.571	3.71	36	0	0	51	54	21	26	0	4	3	6	4	1	0	.250	4	10	1	0	0.4	.933
1957			7	3	.700	3.88	30	0	0	65	67	26	44	0	7	3	4	17	6	1	.353	6	13	0	0	0.6	1.000
1958			3	1	.750	8.10	15	0	0	23.1	35	10	13	0	3	1	1	2	0	0	.000	2	4	1	0	0.5	.857
1959	BAL	A	4	1	.800	4.11	31	1	0	50.1	57	19	29	0	4	1	1	6	2	0	.333	1	10	1	0	0.4	.917
9 yrs.			40	23	.635	3.77	273	19	3	574.2	587	231	319	1	35	16	19	100	18	1	.180	38	119	9	6	0.6	.946
WORLD SERIES																											
1957	MIL	N	0	1	.000	1.29	3	0	0	7	2	1	8	0	0	1	0	1	0	0	.000	1	4	0	0	1.7	1.000

Fred Johnson

JOHNSON, FREDERICK EDWARD (Cactus) BR TR 6′ 185 lbs.
B. Mar. 10, 1894, Tolar, Tex. D. June 14, 1973, Kerrville, Tex.

Year	Team	Lg	W	L	PCT	ERA	G	GS	CG	IP	H	BB	SO	ShO	Relief Pitching W	Relief Pitching L	Relief Pitching SV	Batting AB	Batting H	Batting HR	BA	PO	A	E	DP	TC/G	FA
1922	NY	N	0	2	.000	4.00	2	2	1	18	20	1	8	0	0	0	0	4	0	0	.000	1	3	0	0	2.0	1.000
1923			2	0	1.000	4.24	3	2	1	17	11	7	5	0	1	0	0	6	0	0	.000	0	9	0	1	3.0	1.000
1938	STL	A	3	7	.300	5.61	17	6	3	69	91	27	24	0	0	**5**	3	25	6	0	.240	0	7	3	1	0.6	.700
1939			0	1	.000	6.43	5	2	1	14	23	9	2	0	0	0	0	4	0	0	.000	0	7	0	0	1.4	1.000
4 yrs.			5	10	.333	5.26	27	12	6	118	145	44	39	0	1	5	3	39	6	0	.154	1	26	3	2	1.1	.900

Hank Johnson

JOHNSON, HENRY WARD BR TR 5′11½″ 175 lbs.
BB 1933
B. May 21, 1906, Bradenton, Fla. D. Aug. 20, 1982, Bradenton, Fla.

Year	Team	Lg	W	L	PCT	ERA	G	GS	CG	IP	H	BB	SO	ShO	Relief Pitching W	Relief Pitching L	Relief Pitching SV	Batting AB	Batting H	Batting HR	BA	PO	A	E	DP	TC/G	FA
1925	NY	A	1	3	.250	6.85	24	4	2	67	88	37	25	1	0	1	0	17	1	0	.059	0	21	1	1	0.9	.955
1926			0	0	—	18.00	1	0	0	1	2	2	0	0	0	0	1	0	0	0	—	0	1	0	0	1.0	1.000
1928			14	9	.609	4.30	31	22	10	199	188	**104**	110	1	2	0	0	79	19	1	.241	9	42	2	2	1.7	.962
1929			3	3	.500	5.06	12	8	2	42.2	37	39	24	0	0	0	0	14	1	0	.071	1	5	1	0	0.6	.857
1930			14	11	.560	4.67	44	15	7	175.1	177	104	115	1	**9**	5	2	64	17	1	.266	5	40	2	3	1.1	.957
1931			13	8	.619	4.72	40	23	8	196.1	176	102	106	0	3	1	4	77	15	0	.195	4	24	0	0	0.7	1.000
1932			2	2	.500	4.88	5	4	2	31.1	34	15	27	0	0	0	0	13	3	0	.231	1	5	0	0	1.2	1.000
1933	BOS	A	8	6	.571	4.06	25	21	7	155.1	156	74	65	0	0	0	1	52	12	0	.231	3	25	0	2	1.1	1.000
1934			6	8	.429	5.36	31	14	7	124.1	162	53	66	1	0	2	1	43	10	0	.233	3	18	0	1	0.7	1.000
1935			2	1	.667	5.52	13	2	0	31	41	14	14	0	2	0	1	8	0	0	.000	2	1	0	0	0.2	1.000
1936	PHI	A	0	2	.000	7.71	3	3	0	11.2	16	10	6	0	0	0	0	4	1	0	.250	1	1	1	0	1.0	.667
1939	CIN	N	0	3	.000	2.01	20	0	0	31.1	30	13	10	0	0	3	1	5	2	0	.400	0	2	0	0	0.1	1.000
12 yrs.			63	56	.529	4.75	249	116	45	1066.1	1107	567	568	4	16	12	11	376	81	2	.215	29	185	7	9	0.9	.968

Jeff Johnson

JOHNSON, WILLIAM JEFFREY
B. Aug. 4, 1966, Durham, N. C.
BB TL 6' 3" 200 lbs.

Year	Team	Lg	W	L	PCT	ERA	G	GS	CG	IP	H	BB	SO	ShO	Relief W	Relief L	Relief SV	Batting AB	Batting H	Batting HR	BA	PO	A	E	DP	TC/G	FA
1991	NY	A	6	11	.353	5.95	23	23	0	127	156	33	62	0	0	0	0	0	0	0	—	4	24	3	3	1.3	.903
1992			2	3	.400	6.66	13	8	0	52.2	71	23	14	0	0	0	0	0	0	0	—	1	8	0	0	0.7	1.000
1993			0	2	.000	30.38	2	2	0	2.2	12	2	0	0	0	0	0	0	0	0	—	1	0	1	0	1.0	.500
3 yrs.			8	16	.333	6.52	38	33	0	182.1	239	58	76	0	0	0	0	0	0	0		6	32	4	3	1.1	.905

Jerry Johnson

JOHNSON, JERRY MICHAEL
B. Dec. 3, 1943, Miami, Fla.
BR TR 6' 3" 200 lbs.

Year	Team	Lg	W	L	PCT	ERA	G	GS	CG	IP	H	BB	SO	ShO	Relief W	Relief L	Relief SV	Batting AB	Batting H	Batting HR	BA	PO	A	E	DP	TC/G	FA
1968	PHI	N	4	4	.500	3.24	16	11	2	80.2	82	29	40	0	0	0	0	25	2	0	.080	4	17	0	3	1.3	1.000
1969			6	13	.316	4.29	33	21	4	147	151	57	82	2	0	0	1	43	9	0	.209	6	22	1	1	0.9	.966
1970	2 teams	STL N (7G 2–0)	SF N (33G 3–4)																								
"	total		5	4	.556	4.11	40	1	0	76.2	73	41	49	0	5	3	4	16	1	0	.063	3	9	1	0	0.3	.923
1971	SF	N	12	9	.571	2.97	67	0	0	109	93	48	85	0	**12**	**9**	18	13	2	0	.154	6	15	1	0	0.3	.955
1972			8	6	.571	4.44	48	0	0	73	73	40	57	0	8	6	8	9	0	0	.000	5	12	2	0	0.4	.895
1973	CLE	A	5	6	.455	6.18	39	1	0	59.2	70	39	45	0	5	6	5	0	0	0	—	3	11	1	0	0.4	.933
1974	HOU	N	2	1	.667	4.80	34	0	0	45	47	24	32	0	2	1	0	1	0	0	.000	3	6	2	2	0.3	.818
1975	SD	N	3	1	.750	5.17	21	4	0	54	60	31	18	0	2	0	0	12	1	0	.083	6	5	1	0	0.6	.917
1976			1	3	.250	5.31	24	1	0	39	39	26	27	0	1	2	0	3	0	0	.000	4	3	1	0	0.3	.875
1977	TOR	A	2	4	.333	4.60	43	0	0	86	91	54	54	0	2	4	5	0	0	0	—	4	11	1	2	0.4	.938
10 yrs.			48	51	.485	4.31	365	39	6	770	779	389	489	2	37	31	41	122	15	0	.123	44	111	11	8	0.5	.934
LEAGUE CHAMPIONSHIP SERIES																											
1971	SF	N	0	0	—	13.50	1	0	0	1.1	1	1	2	0	0	0	0	0	0	0	—	0	0	0	0	0.0	.000

Jim Johnson

JOHNSON, JAMES BRIAN
B. Nov. 3, 1945, Muskegon, Mich.
BL TL 5'11" 175 lbs.

Year	Team	Lg	W	L	PCT	ERA	G	GS	CG	IP	H	BB	SO	ShO	Relief W	Relief L	Relief SV	Batting AB	Batting H	Batting HR	BA	PO	A	E	DP	TC/G	FA
1970	SF	N	1	0	1.000	7.71	3	0	0	7	8	5	2	0	1	0	0	2	0	0	.000	0	2	0	0	0.7	1.000

Jing Johnson

JOHNSON, RUSSELL CONWELL
B. Oct. 9, 1894, Parker Ford, Pa. D. Dec. 6, 1950, Pottstown, Pa.
BR TR 5' 9" 172 lbs.

Year	Team	Lg	W	L	PCT	ERA	G	GS	CG	IP	H	BB	SO	ShO	Relief W	Relief L	Relief SV	Batting AB	Batting H	Batting HR	BA	PO	A	E	DP	TC/G	FA
1916	PHI	A	2	8	.200	3.74	12	12	8	84.1	90	39	25	0	0	0	0	27	2	1	.074	6	34	1	3	3.4	.976
1917			9	12	.429	2.78	34	23	13	191	184	56	55	0	0	0	0	59	12	0	.203	14	64	3	0	2.4	.963
1919			9	15	.375	3.61	34	25	12	202	222	62	67	0	2	1	0	72	14	1	.194	12	76	4	2	2.7	.957
1927			4	2	.667	3.48	17	3	2	51.2	42	16	16	0	2	1	0	12	2	0	.167	1	18	1	2	1.2	.950
1928			0	0	—	5.06	3	0	0	10.2	13	5	3	0	0	0	0	4	2	0	.500	1	3	0	1	1.3	1.000
5 yrs.			24	37	.393	3.35	100	63	35	539.2	551	178	166	0	4	2	0	174	32	2	.184	34	195	9	8	2.4	.962

Joe Johnson

JOHNSON, JOSEPH RICHARD
B. Oct. 30, 1961, Brookline, Mass.
BR TR 6' 2" 195 lbs.

Year	Team	Lg	W	L	PCT	ERA	G	GS	CG	IP	H	BB	SO	ShO	Relief W	Relief L	Relief SV	Batting AB	Batting H	Batting HR	BA	PO	A	E	DP	TC/G	FA
1985	ATL	N	4	4	.500	4.10	15	14	1	85.2	95	24	34	0	0	0	0	23	1	0	.043	4	7	1	0	0.8	.917
1986	2 teams	ATL N (17G 6–7)	TOR A (16G 7–2)																								
"	total		13	9	.591	4.42	33	30	2	175	195	57	88	0	0	1	0	26	3	0	.115	11	29	2	2	1.3	.952
1987	TOR	A	3	5	.375	5.13	14	14	0	66.2	77	18	27	0	0	0	0	0	0	0	—	7	8	0	0	1.1	1.000
3 yrs.			20	18	.526	4.48	62	58	3	327.1	367	99	149	0	0	1	0	49	4	0	.082	22	44	3	2	1.1	.957

John Henry Johnson

JOHNSON, JOHN HENRY
B. Aug. 21, 1956, Houston, Tex.
BL TL 6' 2" 190 lbs.

Year	Team	Lg	W	L	PCT	ERA	G	GS	CG	IP	H	BB	SO	ShO	Relief W	Relief L	Relief SV	Batting AB	Batting H	Batting HR	BA	PO	A	E	DP	TC/G	FA
1978	OAK	A	11	10	.524	3.39	33	30	7	186	164	82	91	2	0	0	0	0	0	0	—	8	16	4	0	0.8	.857
1979	2 teams	OAK A (14G 2–8)	TEX A (17G 2–6)																								
"	total		4	14	.222	4.63	31	25	2	167	168	72	96	0	1	0	0	0	0	0		5	18	0	3	0.7	1.000
1980	TEX	A	2	2	.500	2.31	33	0	0	39	27	15	44	0	2	2	4	0	0	0	—	0	5	0	0	0.2	1.000
1981			3	1	.750	2.63	24	0	0	24	19	6	8	0	3	1	2	0	0	0	—	1	7	0	1	0.3	1.000
1983	BOS	A	3	2	.600	3.71	34	1	0	53.1	58	20	51	0	3	1	1	0	0	0	—	2	5	1	0	0.2	.875
1984			1	2	.333	3.53	30	3	0	63.2	64	27	57	0	1	1	1	0	0	0	—	0	8	0	0	0.3	1.000
1986	MIL	A	2	1	.667	2.66	19	0	0	44	43	10	42	0	2	1	1	0	0	0	—	2	3	1	0	0.3	.833
1987			0	1	.000	9.57	10	2	0	26.1	42	18	18	0	0	0	0	0	0	0	—	0	5	0	1	0.5	1.000
8 yrs.			26	33	.441	3.89	214	61	9	603.1	585	250	407	2	12	6	9	0	0	0		18	67	6	5	0.4	.934

Johnny Johnson

JOHNSON, JOHN CLIFFORD (Swede)
B. Sept. 29, 1914, Belmore, Ohio D. June 26, 1991, Iron Mountain, Mich.
BL TL 6' 182 lbs.

Year	Team	Lg	W	L	PCT	ERA	G	GS	CG	IP	H	BB	SO	ShO	Relief W	Relief L	Relief SV	Batting AB	Batting H	Batting HR	BA	PO	A	E	DP	TC/G	FA
1944	NY	A	0	2	.000	4.05	22	1	0	26.2	25	24	11	0	0	1	3	6	3	0	.500	2	1	1	0	0.2	.750
1945	CHI	A	3	0	1.000	4.26	29	0	0	69.2	85	35	38	0	3	0	4	14	4	0	.286	1	10	1	1	0.4	.917
2 yrs.			3	2	.600	4.20	51	1	0	96.1	110	59	49	0	3	1	7	20	7	0	.350	3	11	2	1	0.3	.875

Ken Johnson

JOHNSON, KENNETH TRAVIS
B. June 16, 1933, West Palm Beach, Fla.
BR TR 6' 4" 210 lbs.

Year	Team	Lg	W	L	PCT	ERA	G	GS	CG	IP	H	BB	SO	ShO	Relief W	Relief L	Relief SV	Batting AB	Batting H	Batting HR	BA	PO	A	E	DP	TC/G	FA
1958	KC	A	0	0	—	27.00	2	0	0	2.1	6	3	1	0	0	0	0	0	0	0	—	1	1	0	0	1.0	1.000
1959			1	1	.500	4.09	2	2	0	11	11	5	8	0	0	0	0	3	0	0	.000	0	3	0	0	1.5	1.000
1960			5	10	.333	4.26	42	6	2	120.1	120	45	83	0	3	6	3	30	5	0	.167	6	27	0	0	0.8	1.000
1961	2 teams	KC A (6G 0–4)	CIN N (15G 6–2)																								
"	total		6	6	.500	4.00	21	12	3	92.1	82	29	46	1	0	3	1	26	6	0	.231	10	23	0	1	1.6	1.000
1962	HOU	N	7	16	.304	3.84	33	31	5	197	195	46	178	1	0	0	0	52	4	0	.077	9	37	4	1	1.5	.920
1963			11	17	.393	2.65	37	32	6	224	204	50	148	1	1	1	1	74	5	0	.068	8	51	1	4	1.6	.983
1964			11	16	.407	3.63	35	35	7	218	209	44	117	1	0	0	0	76	6	1	.079	9	50	6	4	1.9	.908
1965	2 teams	HOU N (8G 3–2)	MIL N (29G 13–8)																								
"	total		16	10	.615	3.42	37	34	9	231.1	217	48	151	1	0	0	2	79	9	0	.114	16	30	2	1	1.3	.958
1966	ATL	N	14	8	.636	3.30	32	31	11	215.2	213	46	105	2	0	0	0	70	10	1	.143	14	35	1	4	1.6	.980
1967			13	9	.591	2.74	29	29	6	210.1	191	38	85	0	0	0	0	71	9	0	.127	9	33	1	0	1.5	.977
1968			5	8	.385	3.47	31	16	1	135	145	25	57	0	1	2	0	40	7	0	.175	7	18	1	3	0.8	.962
1969	3 teams	ATL N (9G 0–1)	NY A (12G 1–2)	CHI N (9G 1–2)																							
"	total		2	5	.286	3.89	30	3	0	74	68	33	59	0	2	3	2	13	0	0	.000	3	13	0	1	0.5	1.000
1970	MON	N	0	0	—	7.50	3	0	0	6	9	1	4	0	0	0	0	0	0	0	—	1	1	0	0	0.7	1.000
13 yrs.			91	106	.462	3.46	334	231	50	1737.1	1670	413	1042	7	7	15	9	534	61	2	.114	93	322	16	19	1.3	.963

Ken Johnson *continued*

Year	Team	W	L	PCT	ERA	G	GS	CG	IP	H	BB	SO	ShO	Relief Pitching W	Relief Pitching L	Relief Pitching SV	Batting AB	Batting H	HR	BA	PO	A	E	DP	TC/G	FA
WORLD SERIES																										
1961	**CIN N**	0	0	—	0.00	1	0	0	0.2	0	0	0	0	0	0	0	0	0	0	—	0	0	0	0	0.0	.000

Ken Johnson

JOHNSON, KENNETH WANDERSEE (Hooks)
B. Jan. 14, 1923, Topeka, Kans.
BL TL 6′ 1″ 185 lbs.

Year	Team	W	L	PCT	ERA	G	GS	CG	IP	H	BB	SO	ShO	Relief Pitching W	Relief Pitching L	Relief Pitching SV	Batting AB	Batting H	HR	BA	PO	A	E	DP	TC/G	FA
1947	**STL N**	1	0	1.000	0.00	2	1	1	10	2	5	8	0	0	0	0	4	2	0	.500	0	2	0	0	1.0	1.000
1948		2	4	.333	4.76	13	4	0	45.1	43	30	20	0	2	1	0	20	6	0	.300	0	8	1	0	0.7	.889
1949		0	1	.000	6.42	14	2	0	33.2	29	35	18	0	0	0	0	8	2	0	.250	1	13	2	1	1.1	.875
1950	**2 teams STL N** (2G 0–0) **PHI N** (14G 4–1)																									
″	**total**	4	1	.800	3.88	16	9	3	62.2	62	46	33	1	1	0	0	19	3	0	.158	1	14	0	0	0.9	1.000
1951	**PHI N**	5	8	.385	4.57	20	18	4	106.1	103	68	58	3	0	0	0	35	5	0	.143	4	15	0	4	0.9	1.000
1952	**DET A**	0	0	—	6.35	9	1	0	11.1	12	11	10	0	0	0	0	3	1	0	.333	1	2	0	0	0.3	1.000
6 yrs.		12	14	.462	4.58	74	35	8	269.1	251	195	147	4	3	1	0	89	19	0	.213	7	54	3	5	0.9	.953

Lloyd Johnson

JOHNSON, LLOYD WILLIAM (Eppa)
B. Dec. 24, 1910, Santa Rosa, Calif. D. Oct. 8, 1980, Stockton, Calif.
BL TL 6′ 4″ 204 lbs.

Year	Team	W	L	PCT	ERA	G	GS	CG	IP	H	BB	SO	ShO	Relief Pitching W	Relief Pitching L	Relief Pitching SV	Batting AB	Batting H	HR	BA	PO	A	E	DP	TC/G	FA
1934	**PIT N**	0	0	—	0.00	1	0	0	1	1	0	0	0	0	0	0	0	0	0	—	0	0	0	0	0.0	.000

Louis Johnson

JOHNSON, JOHN LOUIS
Born John Louis Mercer.
B. Nov. 18, 1869, Pekin, Ill. D. Jan. 28, 1941, Kansas City, Mo.
TL 5′10″ 165 lbs.

Year	Team	W	L	PCT	ERA	G	GS	CG	IP	H	BB	SO	ShO	Relief Pitching W	Relief Pitching L	Relief Pitching SV	Batting AB	Batting H	HR	BA	PO	A	E	DP	TC/G	FA
1894	**PHI N**	1	1	.500	6.06	4	3	2	32.2	44	15	10	0	0	0	0	16	3	0	.188	0	8	2	0	2.5	.800

Mike Johnson

JOHNSON, MICHAEL NORTON
B. Mar. 2, 1951, Slayton, Minn.
BR TR 6′ 1″ 185 lbs.

Year	Team	W	L	PCT	ERA	G	GS	CG	IP	H	BB	SO	ShO	Relief Pitching W	Relief Pitching L	Relief Pitching SV	Batting AB	Batting H	HR	BA	PO	A	E	DP	TC/G	FA
1974	**SD N**	0	2	.000	4.71	18	0	0	21	29	15	15	0	0	2	0	0	0	0	—	0	2	0	1	0.1	1.000

Randy Johnson

JOHNSON, RANDALL DAVID
B. Sept. 10, 1963, Walnut Creek, Calif.
BR TL 6′10″ 225 lbs.

Year	Team	W	L	PCT	ERA	G	GS	CG	IP	H	BB	SO	ShO	Relief Pitching W	Relief Pitching L	Relief Pitching SV	Batting AB	Batting H	HR	BA	PO	A	E	DP	TC/G	FA
1988	**MON N**	3	0	1.000	2.42	4	4	1	26	23	7	25	0	0	0	0	9	1	0	.111	0	0	1	0	0.3	.000
1989	**2 teams MON N** (7G 0–4) **SEA A** (22G 7–9)																									
″	**total**	7	13	.350	4.82	29	28	2	160.2	147	96	130	0	0	0	0	7	1	0	.143	8	26	7	1	1.4	.829
1990	**SEA A**	14	11	.560	3.65	33	33	5	219.2	174	**120**	194	2	0	0	0	0	0	0	—	6	24	5	2	1.1	.857
1991		13	10	.565	3.98	33	33	2	201.1	151	**152**	228	1	0	0	0	0	0	0	—	0	23	5	3	0.8	.821
1992		12	14	.462	3.77	31	31	6	210.1	154	**144**	**241**	2	0	0	0	0	0	0	—	5	20	3	0	0.9	.893
1993		19	8	.704	3.24	35	34	10	255.1	185	99	**308**	3	0	0	1	0	0	0	—	10	29	0	2	1.1	1.000
1994		13	6	.684	3.19	23	23	**9**	172	132	72	**204**	**4**	0	0	0	0	0	0	—	12	27	0	0	1.7	1.000
1995		18	2	.900	2.48	30	30	6	214.1	159	65	294	3	0	0	0	0	0	0	—	7	24	1	0	1.1	.969
8 yrs.		99	64	.607	3.52	218	216	41	1459.2	1125	755	1624	15	0	0	1	16	2	0	.125	48	173	22	8	1.1	.909
DIVISIONAL PLAYOFF SERIES																										
1995	**SEA A**	2	0	1.000	2.70	2	1	0	10	5	6	16	0	1	0	0	0	0	0	—	0	0	0	0	0.0	.000
LEAGUE CHAMPIONSHIP SERIES																										
1995	**SEA A**	0	1	.000	2.35	2	2	0	15.1	12	2	13	0	0	0	0	0	0	0	—	1	1	0	0	1.0	1.000

Roy Johnson

JOHNSON, ROY J. (Hardrock)
B. Oct. 1, 1895, Madill, Okla. D. Jan. 10, 1986, Scottsdale, Ariz.
Manager 1944.
BR TR 6′ 185 lbs.

Year	Team	W	L	PCT	ERA	G	GS	CG	IP	H	BB	SO	ShO	Relief Pitching W	Relief Pitching L	Relief Pitching SV	Batting AB	Batting H	HR	BA	PO	A	E	DP	TC/G	FA
1918	**PHI A**	1	5	.167	3.42	10	8	3	50	47	27	14	0	0	1	0	15	1	0	.067	2	13	1	1	1.6	.938

Si Johnson

JOHNSON, SILAS KENNETH
B. Oct. 5, 1906, Danway, Ill. D. May 12, 1994, Sheridan, Ill.
BR TR 5′11½″ 185 lbs.

Year	Team	W	L	PCT	ERA	G	GS	CG	IP	H	BB	SO	ShO	Relief Pitching W	Relief Pitching L	Relief Pitching SV	Batting AB	Batting H	HR	BA	PO	A	E	DP	TC/G	FA
1928	**CIN N**	0	0	—	4.35	3	0	0	10.1	9	5	1	0	0	0	0	4	1	0	.250	0	4	0	0	1.3	1.000
1929		0	0	—	4.50	1	0	0	2	2	1	0	0	0	0	0	0	0	0	—	0	0	0	0	0.0	.000
1930		3	1	.750	4.94	35	3	0	78.1	86	31	47	0	2	1	0	17	4	0	.235	4	12	1	1	0.5	.941
1931		11	**19**	.367	3.77	42	33	14	262.1	273	74	95	0	0	2	0	87	13	0	.149	2	34	0	0	0.9	1.000
1932		13	15	.464	3.27	42	27	14	245	246	57	94	2	1	0	2	80	10	0	.125	7	55	7	1	1.6	.899
1933		7	18	.280	3.49	34	28	14	211.1	212	54	51	4	0	0	1	72	3	0	.042	3	44	3	3	1.5	.940
1934		7	**22**	.241	5.22	46	31	9	215.2	264	84	89	0	0	2	3	72	10	0	.139	6	32	0	1	0.8	1.000
1935		5	11	.313	6.23	30	20	4	130	155	59	40	1	0	0	0	41	1	0	.024	3	24	0	2	0.9	1.000
1936	**2 teams CIN N** (2G 0–0) **STL N** (12G 5–3)																									
″	**total**	5	3	.625	4.93	14	9	3	65.2	89	11	23	1	1	1	0	21	4	0	.190	1	8	0	1	0.6	1.000
1937	**STL N**	12	12	.500	3.32	38	21	12	192.1	222	43	64	1	3	3	1	65	9	0	.138	5	36	1	2	1.1	.976
1938		0	3	.000	7.47	6	3	0	15.2	27	6	4	0	0	0	0	1	0	0	.000	0	4	0	0	0.7	1.000
1940	**PHI N**	5	14	.263	4.88	37	14	5	138.1	145	42	58	0	1	**6**	1	43	6	0	.140	5	16	0	1	0.6	1.000
1941		5	12	.294	4.52	39	21	6	163.1	207	54	80	1	0	3	2	47	7	0	.149	4	27	0	1	0.8	1.000
1942		8	19	.296	3.69	39	26	10	195.1	198	72	78	1	1	1	0	58	6	0	.103	3	30	0	2	0.8	1.000
1943		8	3	.727	3.27	21	14	9	113	110	25	46	1	0	0	2	33	6	0	.182	4	21	1	1	1.2	.962
1946	**2 teams PHI N** (1G 0–0) **BOS N** (28G 6–5)																									
″	**total**	6	5	.545	2.77	29	12	5	130	141	35	43	1	0	0	1	38	6	0	.158	6	21	1	0	1.0	.964
1947	**BOS N**	6	8	.429	4.23	36	10	3	112.2	124	34	27	0	2	2	2	30	1	0	.033	3	36	0	3	1.1	1.000
17 yrs.		101	165	.380	4.09	492	272	108	2281.1	2510	687	840	13	11	21	15	709	87	0	.123	56	404	14	19	1.0	.970

Syl Johnson

JOHNSON, SYLVESTER
B. Dec. 31, 1900, Portland, Ore. D. Feb. 20, 1985, Portland, Ore.
BR TR 5′11½″ 180 lbs.

Year	Team	W	L	PCT	ERA	G	GS	CG	IP	H	BB	SO	ShO	Relief Pitching W	Relief Pitching L	Relief Pitching SV	Batting AB	Batting H	HR	BA	PO	A	E	DP	TC/G	FA
1922	**DET A**	7	3	.700	3.71	29	8	3	97	99	30	29	0	3	1	1	36	8	0	.222	3	17	2	0	0.8	.909
1923		12	7	.632	3.98	37	18	7	176.1	181	47	93	1	5	2	0	62	10	1	.161	5	17	1	0	0.6	.957
1924		5	4	.556	4.93	29	9	2	104	117	42	55	0	2	2	3	34	7	0	.206	2	17	0	0	0.7	1.000
1925		0	2	.000	3.46	6	0	0	13	11	10	5	0	0	2	0	3	0	0	.000	2	4	0	0	1.0	1.000
1926	**STL N**	0	3	.000	4.22	19	6	1	49	54	15	10	0	0	0	1	12	0	0	.000	0	10	0	1	0.5	1.000
1927		0	0	—	6.00	2	0	0	3	3	0	2	0	0	0	0	0	0	0	—	1	0	0	0	0.5	1.000
1928		8	4	.667	3.90	34	6	2	120	117	33	66	0	4	2	3	38	6	0	.158	3	20	1	2	0.7	.958

Syl Johnson *continued*

Year	Team	W	L	PCT	ERA	G	GS	CG	IP	H	BB	SO	ShO	Relief Pitching W	Relief Pitching L	Relief Pitching SV	Batting AB	Batting H	Batting HR	BA	PO	A	E	DP	TC/G	FA
1929		13	7	.650	3.60	42	19	12	182.1	186	56	80	3	3	2	3	60	7	1	.117	5	19	1	0	0.6	.960
1930		12	10	.545	4.65	32	24	9	187.2	215	38	92	2	2	1	2	70	15	0	.214	4	21	1	1	0.8	.962
1931		11	9	.550	3.00	32	24	12	186	186	29	82	2	1	0	2	60	14	0	.233	3	24	3	2	0.9	.900
1932		5	14	.263	4.92	32	22	7	164.2	199	35	70	1	1	1	2	51	10	0	.196	3	30	0	1	1.0	1.000
1933		3	3	.500	4.29	35	1	0	84	89	16	28	0	2	3	3	21	5	0	.238	1	12	0	0	0.4	1.000
1934	**2 teams** **CIN N** (2G 0–0) **PHI N** (42G 5–9)																									
"	**total**	5	9	.357	3.46	44	10	4	140.1	131	24	54	3	2	5	3	43	9	1	.209	5	10	1	1	0.4	.938
1935	**PHI N**	10	8	.556	3.56	37	18	8	174.2	182	31	89	1	3	1	6	58	14	1	.241	6	20	2	1	0.8	.929
1936		5	7	.417	4.30	39	8	1	111	129	29	48	0	1	4	7	36	9	0	.250	4	13	0	0	0.4	1.000
1937		4	10	.286	5.02	32	15	4	138	155	22	46	0	1	2	3	48	7	0	.146	8	25	1	2	1.1	.971
1938		2	7	.222	4.23	22	6	2	83	87	11	21	0	1	3	0	29	1	0	.034	2	9	0	0	0.5	1.000
1939		8	8	.500	3.81	22	14	6	111	112	15	37	0	2	0	2	33	5	0	.152	3	17	0	1	0.9	1.000
1940		2	2	.500	4.20	17	2	2	40.2	37	5	13	0	0	2	2	8	0	0	.000	3	6	0	1	0.5	1.000
19 yrs.		112	117	.489	4.06	542	210	82	2165.2	2290	488	920	13	33	33	43	702	127	4	.181	63	291	13	13	0.7	.965
WORLD SERIES																										
1928	**STL N**	0	0	—	4.50	2	0	0	2	4	1	1	0	0	0	0	0	0	0	—	0	0	0	0	0.0	.000
1930		0	0	—	7.20	2	0	0	5	4	3	4	0	0	0	0	0	0	0	—	0	0	0	0	0.0	.000
1931		0	1	.000	3.00	3	1	0	9	10	1	6	0	0	0	0	2	0	0	.000	0	1	0	0	0.3	1.000
3 yrs.		0	1	.000	4.50	7	1	0	16	18	5	11	0	0	0	0	2	0	0	.000	0	1	0	0	0.1	1.000

Tom Johnson

JOHNSON, THOMAS RAYMOND
B. Apr. 2, 1951, St. Paul, Minn.
BR TR 6′ 1″ 185 lbs.

Year	Team	W	L	PCT	ERA	G	GS	CG	IP	H	BB	SO	ShO	Relief Pitching W	Relief Pitching L	Relief Pitching SV	Batting AB	Batting H	Batting HR	BA	PO	A	E	DP	TC/G	FA
1974	**MIN A**	2	0	1.000	0.00	4	0	0	7	4	0	4	0	2	0	1	0	0	0	—	0	1	1	0	0.5	.500
1975		1	2	.333	4.19	18	0	0	38.2	40	21	17	0	1	2	3	0	0	0	—	5	5	1	0	0.6	.909
1976		3	1	.750	2.61	18	1	0	48.1	44	8	37	0	3	0	0	0	0	0	—	1	7	0	0	0.4	1.000
1977		16	7	.696	3.12	71	0	0	147	152	47	87	0	**16**	7	15	0	0	0	—	9	26	1	0	0.5	.972
1978		1	4	.200	5.51	18	0	0	32.2	42	17	21	0	1	4	3	0	0	0	—	0	6	0	0	0.3	1.000
5 yrs.		23	14	.622	3.39	129	1	0	273.2	282	93	166	0	23	13	22	0	0	0		15	45	3	0	0.5	.952

Vic Johnson

JOHNSON, VICTOR OSCAR
B. Aug. 3, 1920, Eau Claire, Wis.
BR TL 6′ 160 lbs.

Year	Team	W	L	PCT	ERA	G	GS	CG	IP	H	BB	SO	ShO	Relief Pitching W	Relief Pitching L	Relief Pitching SV	Batting AB	Batting H	Batting HR	BA	PO	A	E	DP	TC/G	FA
1944	**BOS A**	0	3	.000	6.26	7	5	0	27.1	42	15	7	0	0	0	0	10	0	0	.000	1	9	1	1	1.6	.909
1945		6	4	.600	4.01	26	9	4	85.1	90	46	21	1	3	0	2	30	5	0	.167	4	23	2	2	1.1	.931
1946	**CLE A**	0	1	.000	9.22	9	1	0	13.2	20	8	3	0	0	0	0	2	0	0	.000	1	5	1	1	0.8	.857
3 yrs.		6	8	.429	5.06	42	15	4	126.1	152	69	31	1	3	0	2	42	5	0	.119	6	37	4	4	1.1	.915

Walter Johnson

JOHNSON, WALTER PERRY (Barney, The Big Train)
B. Nov. 6, 1887, Humboldt, Kans. D. Dec. 10, 1946, Washington, D. C.
Manager 1929–35.
Hall of Fame 1936.
BR TR 6′ 1″ 200 lbs.

Year	Team	W	L	PCT	ERA	G	GS	CG	IP	H	BB	SO	ShO	Relief Pitching W	Relief Pitching L	Relief Pitching SV	Batting AB	Batting H	Batting HR	BA	PO	A	E	DP	TC/G	FA
1907	**WAS A**	5	9	.357	1.87	14	12	11	110.2	98	17	70	2	0	2	0	36	4	0	.111	5	20	3	1	2.0	.893
1908		14	14	.500	1.64	36	29	23	257.1	194	53	160	6	0	1	1	79	13	0	.165	4	56	4	3	1.8	.938
1909		13	25	.342	2.21	40	36	27	297	247	84	164	4	1	2	1	101	13	1	.129	15	73	7	2	2.4	.926
1910		25	17	.595	1.35	**45**	**42**	**38**	**373**	**269**	76	**313**	8	1	1	1	137	24	2	.175	23	90	6	3	2.6	.950
1911		25	13	.658	1.89	40	37	**36**	323.1	292	70	207	**6**	1	1	1	128	30	1	.234	14	95	4	8	2.8	.965
1912		33	12	.733	**1.39**	50	37	34	369	259	76	**303**	7	5	2	2	144	38	2	.264	15	93	4	4	2.2	.964
1913		**36**	7	**.837**	**1.09**	47	36	**29**	**346**	230	38	**243**	**11**	7	0	2	134	35	2	.261	22	82	0	7	2.2	1.000
1914		**28**	18	.609	1.72	**51**	**40**	**33**	**371.2**	**287**	74	**225**	**9**	4	3	1	136	30	3	.221	30	102	5	6	2.6	.964
1915		**27**	13	.675	1.55	47	**39**	**35**	**336.2**	258	56	**203**	**7**	2	0	4	147	34	2	.231	23	95	6	7	2.4	.952
1916		**25**	20	.556	1.89	48	38	**36**	**371**	**290**	82	**228**	3	4	3	1	142	33	1	.232	17	72	6	2	2.0	.937
1917		23	16	.590	2.30	47	34	30	328	259	67	**188**	8	5	1	3	130	33	0	.254	16	82	0	2	2.1	1.000
1918		**23**	13	.639	**1.27**	39	29	29	325	241	70	**162**	**8**	3	4	3	150	40	1	.267	22	71	2	4	2.2	.979
1919		20	14	.588	**1.49**	39	29	27	290.1	235	51	**147**	**7**	2	**4**	2	125	24	1	.192	23	69	1	5	2.2	.989
1920		8	10	.444	3.13	21	15	12	143.2	135	27	78	4	1	2	3	69	18	1	.261	7	28	3	0	1.7	.921
1921		17	14	.548	3.51	35	32	25	264	265	92	**143**	1	1	1	1	111	30	0	.270	4	51	1	1	1.6	.982
1922		15	16	.484	2.99	41	31	23	280	283	99	105	4	1	1	4	108	22	1	.204	11	66	0	2	1.9	1.000
1923		17	12	.586	3.48	42	35	18	261.1	263	69	**130**	3	1	2	4	93	18	0	.194	13	51	2	7	1.5	.970
1924		**23**	7	**.767**	**2.72**	38	**38**	20	277.2	233	77	**158**	**6**	0	0	0	113	32	1	.283	9	53	0	2	1.6	1.000
1925		20	7	.741	3.07	30	29	16	229	211	78	108	3	1	0	0	97	42	2	.433	5	37	0	2	1.4	1.000
1926		15	16	.484	3.61	33	33	22	261.2	259	73	125	2	0	0	0	103	20	1	.194	11	38	1	1	1.5	.980
1927		5	6	.455	5.10	18	15	7	107.2	113	26	48	1	0	0	0	46	16	2	.348	5	25	0	3	1.7	1.000
21 yrs.		417	279	.599	2.17	801	666	531	5924	4921	1355	3508	110	40	30	34	*				294	1349	55	72	2.1	.968
		2nd	**4th**		**7th**			**5th**	**3rd**			**7th**	**1st**													
WORLD SERIES																										
1924	**WAS A**	1	2	.333	2.63	3	2	2	24	30	11	20	0	1	0	0	9	1	0	.111	1	4	1	2	2.0	.833
1925		2	1	.667	2.08	3	3	3	26	26	4	15	1	0	0	0	11	1	0	.091	0	4	0	0	1.3	1.000
2 yrs.		3	3	.500	2.34	6	5	5	50	56	15	35	1	1	0	0	*				1	8	1	2	1.7	.900

Youngy Johnson

JOHNSON, JOHN GODFRED
B. July 22, 1877, San Francisco, Calif. D. Aug. 28, 1936, Berkeley, Calif.
TR

Year	Team	W	L	PCT	ERA	G	GS	CG	IP	H	BB	SO	ShO	Relief Pitching W	Relief Pitching L	Relief Pitching SV	Batting AB	Batting H	Batting HR	BA	PO	A	E	DP	TC/G	FA
1897	**PHI N**	1	2	.333	4.66	5	2	1	29	39	12	7	0	1	0	0	13	1	0	.077	2	4	0	1	1.2	1.000
1899	**NY N**	0	0	—	0.00	1	0	0	2	0	2	1	0	0	0	0	1	0	0	.000	0	1	1	0	2.0	.500
2 yrs.		1	2	.333	4.35	6	2	1	31	39	14	8	0	1	0	0	14	1	0	.071	2	5	1	1	1.3	.875

Joel Johnston

JOHNSTON, JOEL RAYMOND
B. Mar. 8, 1967, West Chester, Pa.
BR TR 6′ 5″ 218 lbs.

Year	Team	W	L	PCT	ERA	G	GS	CG	IP	H	BB	SO	ShO	Relief Pitching W	Relief Pitching L	Relief Pitching SV	Batting AB	Batting H	Batting HR	BA	PO	A	E	DP	TC/G	FA
1991	**KC A**	1	0	1.000	0.40	13	0	0	22.1	9	9	21	0	1	0	0	0	0	0	—	1	2	0	0	0.2	1.000
1992		0	0	—	13.50	5	0	0	2.2	3	2	0	0	0	0	0	0	0	0	—	0	0	0	0	0.0	.000
1993	**PIT N**	2	4	.333	3.38	33	0	0	53.1	38	19	31	0	2	4	2	6	2	0	.333	4	5	0	0	0.3	1.000
1994		0	0	—	29.70	4	0	0	3.1	14	4	5	0	0	0	0	0	0	0	—	0	1	2	0	0.8	.333
1995	**BOS A**	0	1	.000	11.25	4	0	0	4	2	3	4	0	0	1	0	0	0	0	—	0	0	0	0	0.0	.000
5 yrs.		3	5	.375	4.31	59	0	0	85.2	66	37	61	0	3	5	2	6	2	0	.333	5	8	2	0	0.3	.867

John Johnstone

JOHNSTONE, JOHN WILLIAM
B. Nov. 25, 1968, Liverpool, N. Y.
BR TR 6′ 3″ 195 lbs.

Year	Team	W	L	PCT	ERA	G	GS	CG	IP	H	BB	SO	ShO	Relief W	Relief L	Relief SV	Batting AB	Batting H	HR	BA	PO	A	E	DP	TC/G	FA
1993	FLA N	0	2	.000	5.91	7	0	0	10.2	16	7	5	0	0	2	0	0	0	0	—	1	1	0	0	0.3	1.000
1994		1	2	.333	5.91	17	0	0	21.1	23	16	23	0	1	2	0	0	0	0	—	0	3	0	0	0.2	1.000
1995		0	0	—	3.86	4	0	0	4.2	7	2	3	0	0	0	0	0	0	0	—	1	0	0	0	0.3	1.000
3 yrs.		1	4	.200	5.65	28	0	0	36.2	46	25	31	0	1	4	0	0	0	0		2	4	0	0	0.2	1.000

Roy Joiner

JOINER, ROY MERRILL (Pop)
B. Oct. 30, 1906, Red Bluff, Calif. D. Dec. 26, 1989, Red Bluff, Calif.
BL TL 6′ 170 lbs.

Year	Team	W	L	PCT	ERA	G	GS	CG	IP	H	BB	SO	ShO	Relief W	Relief L	Relief SV	Batting AB	Batting H	HR	BA	PO	A	E	DP	TC/G	FA
1934	CHI N	0	1	.000	8.21	20	2	0	34	61	8	9	0	0	0	0	10	2	0	.200	1	7	1	0	0.4	.889
1935		0	0	—	5.40	2	0	0	3.1	6	2	0	0	0	0	0	1	0	0	.000	0	3	0	0	1.5	1.000
1940	NY N	3	2	.600	3.40	30	2	0	53	66	17	25	0	2	1	1	11	3	0	.273	4	11	2	0	0.6	.882
3 yrs.		3	3	.500	5.28	52	4	0	90.1	133	27	34	0	2	1	1	22	5	0	.227	5	21	3	0	0.6	.897

Dave Jolly

JOLLY, DAVID (Gabby)
B. Oct. 14, 1924, Stony Point, N. C. D. May 27, 1963, Durham, N. C.
BR TR 6′ 170 lbs.

Year	Team	W	L	PCT	ERA	G	GS	CG	IP	H	BB	SO	ShO	Relief W	Relief L	Relief SV	Batting AB	Batting H	HR	BA	PO	A	E	DP	TC/G	FA
1953	MIL N	0	1	.000	3.52	24	0	0	38.1	34	27	23	0	0	1	0	2	1	0	.500	2	6	0	0	0.3	1.000
1954		11	6	.647	2.43	47	1	0	111.1	87	64	62	0	11	6	10	31	9	1	.290	4	21	1	3	0.6	.962
1955		2	3	.400	5.71	36	0	0	58.1	58	51	23	0	2	3	1	6	1	0	.167	2	15	2	2	0.5	.895
1956		2	3	.400	3.74	29	0	0	45.2	39	35	20	0	2	3	7	4	0	0	.000	0	5	1	1	0.2	.833
1957		1	1	.500	5.02	23	0	0	37.2	37	21	27	0	1	1	1	5	3	0	.600	1	7	0	0	0.3	1.000
5 yrs.		16	14	.533	3.77	159	1	0	291.1	255	198	155	0	16	14	19	48	14	1	.292	9	54	4	6	0.4	.940

Al Jones

JONES, ALFORNIA
B. Feb. 10, 1959, Charleston, Miss.
BR TR 6′ 4″ 210 lbs.

Year	Team	W	L	PCT	ERA	G	GS	CG	IP	H	BB	SO	ShO	Relief W	Relief L	Relief SV	Batting AB	Batting H	HR	BA	PO	A	E	DP	TC/G	FA
1983	CHI A	0	0	—	3.86	2	0	0	2.1	3	2	2	0	0	0	0	0	0	0	—	0	0	0	0	0.0	.000
1984		1	1	.500	4.43	20	0	0	20.1	23	11	15	0	1	1	5	0	0	0	—	0	3	0	0	0.2	1.000
1985		1	0	1.000	1.50	5	0	0	6	3	3	2	0	1	0	0	0	0	0	—	1	1	0	0	0.4	1.000
3 yrs.		2	1	.667	3.77	27	0	0	28.2	29	16	19	0	2	1	5	0	0	0		1	4	0	0	0.2	1.000

Alex Jones

JONES, ALEXANDER H.
B. Dec. 25, 1869, Bradford, Pa. D. Apr. 4, 1941, Woodville, Pa.
BL TL 5′ 6″ 135 lbs.

Year	Team	W	L	PCT	ERA	G	GS	CG	IP	H	BB	SO	ShO	Relief W	Relief L	Relief SV	Batting AB	Batting H	HR	BA	PO	A	E	DP	TC/G	FA
1889	PIT N	1	0	1.000	3.00	1	1	1	9	7	1	10	0	0	0	0	5	1	0	.200	0	3	0	1	3.0	1.000
1892	2 teams LOU N (18G 5–11) WAS N (4G 0–3)																									
″	total	5	14	.263	3.42	22	20	16	173.2	163	70	51	1	0	1	0	66	11	0	.167	12	43	7	3	2.8	.887
1894	PHI N	1	0	1.000	2.00	1	1	1	9	10	0	2	0	0	0	0	4	1	0	.250	0	2	0	0	2.0	1.000
1903	DET A	0	1	.000	12.46	2	2	0	8.2	19	6	2	0	0	0	0	4	0	0	.000	1	2	0	0	1.5	1.000
4 yrs.		7	15	.318	3.73	26	24	18	200.1	199	77	65	1	0	1	0	79	13	0	.165	13	50	7	4	2.7	.900

Art Jones

JONES, ARTHUR LENNOX
B. Feb. 7, 1906, Kershaw, S. C. D. Nov. 25, 1980, Columbia, S. C.
BR TR 6′ 165 lbs.

Year	Team	W	L	PCT	ERA	G	GS	CG	IP	H	BB	SO	ShO	Relief W	Relief L	Relief SV	Batting AB	Batting H	HR	BA	PO	A	E	DP	TC/G	FA
1932	BKN N	0	0	—	18.00	1	0	0	1	2	1	0	0	0	0	0	0	0	0	—	0	1	0	0	1.0	1.000

Baldy Jones

JONES, HENRY
Deceased.
TR

Year	Team	W	L	PCT	ERA	G	GS	CG	IP	H	BB	SO	ShO	Relief W	Relief L	Relief SV	Batting AB	Batting H	HR	BA	PO	A	E	DP	TC/G	FA
1890	PIT N	2	1	.667	3.48	5	4	2	31	35	14	13	0	0	0	0	9	2	0	.222	0	3	0	1	0.6	1.000

Barry Jones

JONES, BARRY LOUIS
B. Feb. 15, 1963, Centerville, Ind.
BR TR 6′ 4″ 225 lbs.

Year	Team	W	L	PCT	ERA	G	GS	CG	IP	H	BB	SO	ShO	Relief W	Relief L	Relief SV	Batting AB	Batting H	HR	BA	PO	A	E	DP	TC/G	FA
1986	PIT N	3	4	.429	2.89	26	0	0	37.1	29	21	29	0	3	4	3	5	1	0	.200	3	7	1	2	0.4	.909
1987		2	4	.333	5.61	32	0	0	43.1	55	23	28	0	2	4	1	3	0	0	.000	3	7	1	1	0.3	.909
1988	2 teams PIT N (42G 1–1) CHI A (17G 2–2)																									
″	total	3	3	.500	2.84	59	0	0	82.1	72	38	48	0	3	3	3	5	0	0	.000	7	12	2	3	0.4	.905
1989	CHI A	3	2	.600	2.37	22	0	0	30.1	22	8	17	0	3	2	1	0	0	0	—	1	9	2	1	0.5	.833
1990		11	4	.733	2.31	65	0	0	74	62	33	45	0	**11**	4	1	0	0	0	—	4	19	0	1	0.4	1.000
1991	MON N	4	9	.308	3.35	**77**	0	0	88.2	76	33	46	0	4	**9**	13	1	0	0	.000	5	19	3	1	0.4	.889
1992	2 teams PHI N (44G 5–6) NY N (17G 2–0)																									
″	total	7	6	.538	5.68	61	0	0	69.2	85	35	30	0	7	6	1	2	0	0	.000	4	13	0	2	0.3	1.000
1993	CHI A	0	1	.000	8.59	6	0	0	7.1	14	3	7	0	0	1	0	0	0	0	—	1	0	0	0	0.2	1.000
8 yrs.		33	33	.500	3.66	348	0	0	433	415	194	250	0	33	33	23	16	1	0	.063	28	86	9	11	0.4	.927

Bobby Jones

JONES, ROBERT JOSEPH
B. Feb. 10, 1970, Fresno, Calif.
BR TR 6′ 4″ 210 lbs.

Year	Team	W	L	PCT	ERA	G	GS	CG	IP	H	BB	SO	ShO	Relief W	Relief L	Relief SV	Batting AB	Batting H	HR	BA	PO	A	E	DP	TC/G	FA
1993	NY N	2	4	.333	3.65	9	9	0	61.2	61	22	35	0	0	0	0	20	1	0	.050	5	8	0	0	1.4	1.000
1994		12	7	.632	3.15	24	24	1	160	157	56	80	1	0	0	0	46	5	0	.109	11	33	0	3	1.8	1.000
1995		10	10	.500	4.19	30	30	3	195.2	209	53	127	1	0	0	0	56	9	0	.161	11	30	6	1	1.6	.872
3 yrs.		24	21	.533	3.71	63	63	4	417.1	427	131	242	2	0	0	0	122	15	0	.123	27	71	6	4	1.7	.942

Broadway Jones

JONES, JESSE FRANK
B. Nov. 15, 1898, Millsboro, Del. D. Sept. 7, 1977, Lewes, Del.
BR TR 5′ 9″ 154 lbs.

Year	Team	W	L	PCT	ERA	G	GS	CG	IP	H	BB	SO	ShO	Relief W	Relief L	Relief SV	Batting AB	Batting H	HR	BA	PO	A	E	DP	TC/G	FA
1923	PHI N	0	0	—	9.00	3	0	0	8	5	7	1	0	0	0	0	2	1	0	.500	0	1	0	0	0.3	1.000

Bumpus Jones

JONES, CHARLES LEANDER
B. Jan. 1, 1870, Cedarville, Ohio D. June 25, 1938, Xenia, Ohio.
BR TR

Year	Team	W	L	PCT	ERA	G	GS	CG	IP	H	BB	SO	ShO	Relief W	Relief L	Relief SV	Batting AB	Batting H	HR	BA	PO	A	E	DP	TC/G	FA
1892	CIN N	1	0	1.000	0.00	1	1	1	9	0	4	3	0	0	0	0	2	0	0	.000	0	0	1	0	1.0	.000
1893	2 teams CIN N (6G 1–3) NY N (1G 0–1)																									
″	total	1	4	.200	10.19	7	6	2	32.2	42	33	7	0	1	0	0	16	4	0	.250	1	6	1	1	1.1	.875
2 yrs.		2	4	.333	7.99	8	7	3	41.2	42	37	10	0	1	0	0	18	4	0	.222	1	6	2	1	1.1	.778

Calvin Jones

JONES, CALVIN DOUGLAS
B. Sept. 26, 1963, Compton, Calif.
BR TR 6′ 3″ 185 lbs.

Year	Team	W	L	PCT	ERA	G	GS	CG	IP	H	BB	SO	ShO	Relief W	Relief L	Relief SV	Batting AB	Batting H	HR	BA	PO	A	E	DP	TC/G	FA
1991	SEA A	2	2	.500	2.53	27	0	0	46.1	33	29	42	0	2	2	2	0	0	0	—	1	8	0	1	0.3	1.000
1992		3	5	.375	5.69	38	1	0	61.2	50	47	49	0	3	4	0	0	0	0	—	3	7	3	1	0.3	.769
2 yrs.		5	7	.417	4.33	65	1	0	108	83	76	91	0	5	6	2	0	0	0		4	15	3	2	0.3	.864

Charley Jones

JONES, CHARLES WESLEY (Long Charley)
Born Benjamin Wesley Rippay.
B. Apr. 3, 1850, Alamance County, N. C. Deceased.
BR TR 5′11½″ 202 lbs.

Year	Team		W	L	PCT	ERA	G	GS	CG	IP	H	BB	SO	ShO	Relief W	Relief L	Relief SV	Batting AB	Batting H	HR	BA	PO	A	E	DP	TC/G	FA
1887	NY	AA	0	0	—	*3.00*	2	0	0	3	2	4	0	0	0	0	0	*				151	11	27	2	3.0	.857

Cowboy Jones

JONES, ALBERT EDWARD (Bronco)
B. Aug. 23, 1874, Golden, Colo. D. Feb. 9, 1958, Inglewood, Calif.
BL TL 5′11″ 160 lbs.

Year	Team		W	L	PCT	ERA	G	GS	CG	IP	H	BB	SO	ShO	Relief W	Relief L	Relief SV	Batting AB	Batting H	HR	BA	PO	A	E	DP	TC/G	FA
1898	CLE	N	4	4	.500	3.00	9	9	7	72	76	29	26	0	0	0	0	28	2	0	.071	2	10	5	0	1.9	.706
1899	STL	N	6	5	.545	3.59	12	12	9	85.1	111	22	28	0	0	0	0	29	5	0	.172	2	30	3	0	2.9	.914
1900			13	19	.406	3.54	39	36	29	292.2	334	82	68	3	0	2	0	117	21	0	.179	10	100	10	1	3.1	.917
1901			2	6	.250	4.48	10	9	7	76.1	97	22	25	0	0	0	0	27	4	0	.148	7	25	0	1	3.2	1.000
4 yrs.			25	34	.424	3.61	70	66	52	526.1	618	155	147	3	0	2	0	201	32	0	.159	21	165	18	2	2.9	.912

Dale Jones

JONES, DALE ELDON (Nubs)
B. Dec. 17, 1918, Marquette, Neb. D. Nov. 8, 1980, Orlando, Fla.
BR TR 6′ 1″ 172 lbs.

Year	Team		W	L	PCT	ERA	G	GS	CG	IP	H	BB	SO	ShO	Relief W	Relief L	Relief SV	Batting AB	Batting H	HR	BA	PO	A	E	DP	TC/G	FA
1941	PHI	N	0	1	.000	7.56	2	1	0	8.1	13	6	2	0	0	0	0	3	1	0	.333	0	0	1	0	0.5	.000

Deacon Jones

JONES, CARROLL ELMER
B. Dec. 20, 1892, Arcadia, Kans. D. Dec. 28, 1952, Pittsburg, Kans.
BR TR 6′ 1″ 174 lbs.

Year	Team		W	L	PCT	ERA	G	GS	CG	IP	H	BB	SO	ShO	Relief W	Relief L	Relief SV	Batting AB	Batting H	HR	BA	PO	A	E	DP	TC/G	FA
1916	DET	A	0	0	—	2.57	1	0	0	7	7	5	2	0	0	0	0	2	0	0	.000	1	1	0	0	2.0	1.000
1917			4	4	.500	2.92	24	6	2	77	69	26	28	0	2	2	0	15	0	0	.000	1	30	1	0	1.3	.969
1918			3	1	.750	3.09	21	4	1	67	60	38	15	0	2	0	0	27	5	0	.185	3	25	1	2	1.3	.966
3 yrs.			7	5	.583	2.98	46	10	3	151	136	69	45	0	4	2	0	44	5	0	.114	5	56	2	2	1.3	.968

Dick Jones

JONES, DECATUR POINDEXTER
B. May 22, 1902, Meadville, Miss. D. Aug. 2, 1994, Burlingame, Calif.
BL TR 6′ 184 lbs.

Year	Team		W	L	PCT	ERA	G	GS	CG	IP	H	BB	SO	ShO	Relief W	Relief L	Relief SV	Batting AB	Batting H	HR	BA	PO	A	E	DP	TC/G	FA
1926	WAS	A	2	1	.667	4.29	4	3	1	21	20	11	3	0	0	0	0	10	2	0	.200	0	6	0	0	1.5	1.000
1927			0	0	—	21.60	2	0	0	3.1	8	5	1	0	0	0	0	0	0	0	—	1	0	0	0	0.5	1.000
2 yrs.			2	1	.667	6.66	6	3	1	24.1	28	16	4	0	0	0	0	10	2	0	.200	1	6	0	0	1.2	1.000

Doug Jones

JONES, DOUGLAS REID
B. June 24, 1957, Covina, Calif.
BR TR 6′ 3″ 195 lbs.

Year	Team		W	L	PCT	ERA	G	GS	CG	IP	H	BB	SO	ShO	Relief W	Relief L	Relief SV	Batting AB	Batting H	HR	BA	PO	A	E	DP	TC/G	FA
1982	MIL	A	0	0	—	10.13	4	0	0	2.2	5	1	1	0	0	0	0	0	0	0	—	1	0	0	0	0.3	1.000
1986	CLE	A	1	0	1.000	2.50	11	0	0	18	18	6	12	0	1	0	1	0	0	0	—	1	4	0	1	0.5	1.000
1987			6	5	.545	3.15	49	0	0	91.1	101	24	87	0	6	5	8	0	0	0	—	8	13	5	3	0.5	.808
1988			3	4	.429	2.27	51	0	0	83.1	69	16	72	0	3	4	37	0	0	0	—	7	11	2	0	0.4	.900
1989			7	10	.412	2.34	59	0	0	80.2	76	13	65	0	7	**10**	32	0	0	0	—	3	14	0	1	0.3	1.000
1990			5	5	.500	2.56	66	0	0	84.1	66	22	55	0	5	5	43	0	0	0	—	0	9	2	0	0.2	.818
1991			4	8	.333	5.54	36	4	0	63.1	87	17	48	0	1	**7**	7	0	0	0	—	7	10	0	1	0.5	1.000
1992	HOU	N	11	8	.579	1.85	80	0	0	111.2	96	17	93	0	**11**	8	36	4	0	0	.000	5	12	2	0	0.2	.895
1993			4	10	.286	4.54	71	0	0	85.1	102	21	66	0	4	10	26	0	0	0	—	2	12	1	0	0.2	.933
1994	PHI	N	2	4	.333	2.17	47	0	0	54	55	6	38	0	2	4	27	1	1	0	1.000	2	10	2	0	0.3	.857
1995	BAL	A	0	4	.000	5.01	52	0	0	46.2	55	16	42	0	0	4	22	0	0	0	—	4	6	1	3	0.2	.909
11 yrs.			43	58	.426	3.12	526	4	0	721.1	730	159	579	0	40	57	239	5	1	0	.200	40	101	15	9	0.3	.904

Earl Jones

JONES, EARL LESLIE (Lefty)
B. June 11, 1919, Fresno, Calif. D. Jan. 24, 1989, Fresno, Calif.
BL TL 5′10½″ 190 lbs.

Year	Team		W	L	PCT	ERA	G	GS	CG	IP	H	BB	SO	ShO	Relief W	Relief L	Relief SV	Batting AB	Batting H	HR	BA	PO	A	E	DP	TC/G	FA
1945	STL	A	0	0	—	2.54	10	0	0	28.1	18	18	13	0	0	0	1	10	2	1	.200	0	3	0	1	0.3	1.000

Elijah Jones

JONES, ELIJAH ALBERT
B. Jan. 27, 1882, Oxford, Mich. D. Apr. 29, 1943, Pontiac, Mich.
BR TR 5′11½″

Year	Team		W	L	PCT	ERA	G	GS	CG	IP	H	BB	SO	ShO	Relief W	Relief L	Relief SV	Batting AB	Batting H	HR	BA	PO	A	E	DP	TC/G	FA
1907	DET	A	0	1	.000	5.06	4	1	1	16	23	4	9	0	0	0	1	4	0	0	.000	0	4	2	0	1.5	.667
1909			1	1	.500	2.70	2	2	0	10	10	0	2	0	0	0	0	4	1	0	.250	1	1	0	0	1.0	1.000
2 yrs.			1	2	.333	4.15	6	3	1	26	33	4	11	0	0	0	1	8	1	0	.125	1	5	2	0	1.3	.750

Gary Jones

JONES, GARETH HOWELL
Brother of Steve Jones.
B. June 12, 1945, Huntington Park, Calif.
BL TL 6′ 191 lbs.

Year	Team		W	L	PCT	ERA	G	GS	CG	IP	H	BB	SO	ShO	Relief W	Relief L	Relief SV	Batting AB	Batting H	HR	BA	PO	A	E	DP	TC/G	FA
1970	NY	A	0	0	—	0.00	2	0	0	2	3	1	2	0	0	0	0	0	0	0	—	0	0	0	0	0.0	.000
1971			0	0	—	9.00	12	0	0	14	19	7	10	0	0	0	0	1	0	0	.000	1	1	1	0	0.3	.667
2 yrs.			0	0		7.88	14	0	0	16	22	8	12	0	0	0	0	1	0	0	.000	1	1	1	0	0.2	.667

Gordon Jones

JONES, GORDON BASSETT
B. Apr. 2, 1930, Portland, Ore. D. Apr. 25, 1994, Lodi, Calif.
BR TR 6′ 185 lbs.

Year	Team		W	L	PCT	ERA	G	GS	CG	IP	H	BB	SO	ShO	Relief W	Relief L	Relief SV	Batting AB	Batting H	HR	BA	PO	A	E	DP	TC/G	FA
1954	STL	N	4	4	.500	2.00	11	10	4	81	78	19	48	2	0	0	0	24	3	0	.125	7	11	1	0	1.7	.947
1955			1	4	.200	5.84	15	9	0	57	66	28	46	0	0	1	0	14	1	0	.071	1	4	0	1	0.3	1.000
1956			0	2	.000	5.56	5	1	0	11.1	14	5	6	0	0	1	0	2	0	0	.000	0	2	0	0	0.4	1.000
1957	NY	N	0	1	.000	6.17	10	0	0	11.2	16	3	5	0	0	1	0	2	1	0	.500	0	0	0	0	0.0	.000
1958	SF	N	3	1	.750	2.37	11	1	0	30.1	33	5	8	0	2	1	1	7	0	0	.000	2	9	1	1	1.1	.917
1959			3	2	.600	4.33	31	0	0	43.2	45	19	29	0	3	2	2	4	0	0	.000	1	6	0	1	0.2	1.000
1960	BAL	A	1	1	.500	4.42	29	0	0	55	59	13	30	0	1	1	2	5	2	0	.400	5	8	0	1	0.4	1.000
1961			0	0	—	5.40	3	0	0	5	5	0	4	0	0	0	1	0	0	0	—	1	0	0	0	0.3	1.000
1962	KC	A	3	2	.600	6.34	21	0	0	32.2	31	14	28	0	3	2	6	5	0	0	.000	1	3	0	0	0.2	1.000
1964	HOU	N	0	1	.000	4.14	34	0	0	50	58	14	28	0	0	1	0	4	1	0	.250	4	7	0	0	0.3	1.000
1965			0	0	—	0.00	1	0	0	1	0	0	0	0	0	0	0	0	0	0	—	0	0	0	0	0.0	.000
11 yrs.			15	18	.455	4.16	171	21	4	378.2	405	120	232	2	9	10	12	67	8	0	.119	22	50	2	4	0.4	.973

Jeff Jones

JONES, JEFFREY ALLEN
B. July 29, 1956, Detroit, Mich.
BR TR 6′ 3″ 210 lbs.

Year	Team		W	L	PCT	ERA	G	GS	CG	IP	H	BB	SO	ShO	Relief W	Relief L	Relief SV	Batting AB	Batting H	HR	BA	PO	A	E	DP	TC/G	FA
1980	OAK	A	1	3	.250	2.86	35	0	0	44	32	26	34	0	1	3	5	0	0	0	—	5	10	0	0	0.4	1.000
1981			4	1	.800	3.39	33	0	0	61	51	40	43	0	4	1	3	0	0	0	—	2	6	0	0	0.2	1.000
1982			3	1	.750	5.11	18	2	0	37	44	26	18	0	2	1	0	0	0	0	—	3	3	0	0	0.3	1.000
1983			1	1	.500	5.76	13	1	0	29.2	43	8	14	0	1	1	0	0	0	0	—	1	4	0	0	0.4	1.000
1984			0	3	.000	3.55	13	0	0	33	31	12	19	0	0	3	0	0	0	0	—	2	3	0	2	0.4	1.000
5 yrs.			9	9	.500	3.96	112	3	0	204.2	201	112	128	0	8	9	8	0	0	0		13	26	0	2	0.3	1.000

Jeff Jones *continued*

Year	Team	W	L	PCT	ERA	G	GS	CG	IP	H	BB	SO	ShO	Relief Pitching W	L	SV	Batting AB	H	HR	BA	PO	A	E	DP	TC/G	FA
LEAGUE CHAMPIONSHIP SERIES																										
1981	OAK A	0	0	—	4.50	1	0	0	2	2	1	0	0	0	0	0	0	0	0	—	1	0	0	0	1.0	1.000

Jim Jones

JONES, JAMES TILFORD (Sheriff) BR TR 5′10″ 162 lbs.
B. Dec. 25, 1876, London, Ky. D. May 6, 1953, London, Ky.

Year	Team	W	L	PCT	ERA	G	GS	CG	IP	H	BB	SO	ShO	Relief Pitching W	L	SV	Batting AB	H	HR	BA	PO	A	E	DP	TC/G	FA
1897	LOU N	0	0	—	18.90	1	0	0	6.2	19	5	0	0	0	0	0	4	1	0	.250	0	0	0	0	0.0	.000
1901	NY N	0	1	.000	10.80	1	1	1	5	6	2	3	0	0	0	0	91	19	0	.209	33	6	5	1	2.1	.886
2 yrs.		0	1	.000	15.43	2	1	1	11.2	25	7	3	0	0	0	0	*				155	15	20	3	2.1	.895

Jimmy Jones

JONES, JAMES CONDIA BR TR 6′ 2″ 175 lbs.
B. Apr. 20, 1964, Dallas, Tex.

Year	Team	W	L	PCT	ERA	G	GS	CG	IP	H	BB	SO	ShO	Relief Pitching W	L	SV	Batting AB	H	HR	BA	PO	A	E	DP	TC/G	FA
1986	SD N	2	0	1.000	2.50	3	3	1	18	10	3	15	1	0	0	0	6	1	0	.167	1	2	0	0	1.0	1.000
1987		9	7	.563	4.14	30	22	2	145.2	154	54	51	1	2	0	0	49	8	1	.163	15	28	0	1	1.4	1.000
1988		9	14	.391	4.12	29	29	3	179	192	44	82	0	0	0	0	55	9	1	.164	17	32	0	3	1.7	1.000
1989	NY A	2	1	.667	5.25	11	6	0	48	56	16	25	0	0	0	0	0	0	0	—	2	14	0	1	1.5	1.000
1990		1	2	.333	6.30	17	7	0	50	72	23	25	0	0	0	0	0	0	0	—	1	5	1	1	0.4	.857
1991	HOU N	6	8	.429	4.39	26	22	1	135.1	143	51	88	1	1	1	0	38	7	0	.184	8	26	2	2	1.4	.944
1992		10	6	.625	4.07	25	23	0	139.1	135	39	69	0	2	0	0	36	6	0	.167	9	17	0	1	1.0	1.000
1993	MON N	4	1	.800	6.35	12	6	0	39.2	47	9	21	0	1	0	0	9	1	0	.111	4	4	0	1	0.7	1.000
8 yrs.		43	39	.524	4.46	153	118	7	755	809	239	376	3	6	1	0	193	32	2	.166	57	128	3	10	1.2	.984

Johnny Jones

JONES, JOHN PAUL BR TR 6′ 1″ 151 lbs.
B. Aug. 25, 1892, Arcadia, La. D. June 5, 1980, Ruston, La.

Year	Team	W	L	PCT	ERA	G	GS	CG	IP	H	BB	SO	ShO	Relief Pitching W	L	SV	Batting AB	H	HR	BA	PO	A	E	DP	TC/G	FA
1919	NY N	0	0	—	5.40	2	0	0	6.2	9	3	3	0	0	0	1	3	0	0	.000	0	3	1	0	2.0	.750
1920	BOS N	1	0	1.000	6.52	3	1	0	9.2	16	5	6	0	0	0	0	4	1	0	.250	2	3	0	0	1.7	1.000
2 yrs.		1	0	1.000	6.06	5	1	0	16.1	25	8	9	0	0	0	1	7	1	0	.143	2	6	1	0	1.8	.889

Jumping Jack Jones

JONES, DANIEL ALBION TR
B. Oct. 23, 1860, Litchfield, Conn. D. Oct. 19, 1936, Wallingford, Conn.

Year	Team	W	L	PCT	ERA	G	GS	CG	IP	H	BB	SO	ShO	Relief Pitching W	L	SV	Batting AB	H	HR	BA	PO	A	E	DP	TC/G	FA
1883	2 teams DET N (12G 6–5) PHI AA (7G 5–2)																									
″	total	11	7	.611	3.14	19	19	16	157.2	161	25	61	0	0	0	0	67	14	0	.209	2	25	5	0	1.5	.844

Ken Jones

JONES, KENNETH FREDERICK (Broadway) BR TR 6′ 3″ 193 lbs.
B. Apr. 13, 1903, Dover, N. J. D. May 15, 1991, Hartford, Conn.

Year	Team	W	L	PCT	ERA	G	GS	CG	IP	H	BB	SO	ShO	Relief Pitching W	L	SV	Batting AB	H	HR	BA	PO	A	E	DP	TC/G	FA
1924	DET A	0	0	—	0.00	1	0	0	2	1	1	0	0	0	0	0	0	0	0	—	0	0	0	0	0.0	.000
1930	BOS N	0	1	.000	5.95	8	1	0	19.2	28	4	4	0	0	0	0	5	1	0	.200	0	6	2	0	1.0	.750
2 yrs.		0	1	.000	5.40	9	1	0	21.2	29	5	4	0	0	0	0	5	1	0	.200	0	6	2	0	0.9	.750

Mickey Jones

JONES, MICHAEL BL TL 5′11½″ 168 lbs.
B. July 6, 1865, Hamilton, Ont., Canada D. Mar. 24, 1894, Hamilton, Ont., Canada.

Year	Team	W	L	PCT	ERA	G	GS	CG	IP	H	BB	SO	ShO	Relief Pitching W	L	SV	Batting AB	H	HR	BA	PO	A	E	DP	TC/G	FA
1890	LOU AA	2	0	1.000	3.27	3	3	2	22	21	9	6	0	0	0	0	9	4	0	.444	2	4	2	0	2.7	.750

Mike Jones

JONES, MICHAEL CARL BL TL 6′ 6″ 215 lbs.
B. July 30, 1959, Rochester, N. Y.

Year	Team	W	L	PCT	ERA	G	GS	CG	IP	H	BB	SO	ShO	Relief Pitching W	L	SV	Batting AB	H	HR	BA	PO	A	E	DP	TC/G	FA
1980	KC A	0	1	.000	10.80	3	1	0	5	6	5	2	0	0	0	0	0	0	0	—	0	0	0	0	0.0	.000
1981		6	3	.667	3.20	12	11	0	76	74	28	29	0	0	0	0	0	0	0	—	3	14	0	0	1.4	1.000
1984		2	3	.400	4.89	23	12	0	81	86	36	43	0	0	0	0	0	0	0	—	2	7	0	0	0.4	1.000
1985		3	3	.500	4.78	33	1	0	64	62	39	32	0	3	2	0	0	0	0	—	6	8	0	0	0.4	1.000
4 yrs.		11	10	.524	4.42	71	25	0	226	228	108	106	0	3	2	0	0	0	0		11	29	0	0	0.6	1.000
DIVISIONAL PLAYOFF SERIES																										
1981	KC A	0	1	.000	2.25	1	1	0	8	9	0	2	0	0	0	0	0	0	0	—	0	0	0	0	0.0	.000
LEAGUE CHAMPIONSHIP SERIES																										
1984	KC A	0	0	—	6.75	1	0	0	1.1	1	0	0	0	0	0	0	0	0	0	—	0	0	0	0	0.0	.000

Odell Jones

JONES, ODELL BR TR 6′ 3″ 175 lbs.
B. Jan. 13, 1953, Tulare, Calif.

Year	Team	W	L	PCT	ERA	G	GS	CG	IP	H	BB	SO	ShO	Relief Pitching W	L	SV	Batting AB	H	HR	BA	PO	A	E	DP	TC/G	FA
1975	PIT N	0	0	—	0.00	2	0	0	3	1	0	2	0	0	0	0	0	0	0	—	0	1	0	0	0.5	1.000
1977		3	7	.300	5.08	34	15	1	108	118	31	66	0	1	1	0	28	4	0	.143	2	8	0	0	0.3	1.000
1978		2	0	1.000	2.00	3	1	0	9	7	4	10	0	1	0	0	1	0	0	.000	0	1	0	0	0.3	1.000
1979	SEA A	3	11	.214	6.05	25	19	3	119	151	58	72	0	0	2	0	0	0	0	—	8	9	4	0	0.8	.810
1981	PIT N	4	5	.444	3.33	13	8	0	54	51	23	30	0	1	1	0	10	2	0	.200	3	10	0	0	1.0	1.000
1983	TEX A	3	6	.333	3.09	42	0	0	67	56	22	50	0	3	6	10	0	0	0	—	3	5	0	0	0.2	1.000
1984		2	4	.333	3.64	33	0	0	59.1	62	23	28	0	2	4	2	0	0	0	—	5	10	0	1	0.5	1.000
1986	BAL A	2	2	.500	3.83	21	0	0	49.1	58	23	32	0	2	2	0	0	0	0	—	2	5	0	0	0.3	1.000
1988	MIL A	5	0	1.000	4.35	28	2	0	80.2	75	29	48	0	4	0	1	0	0	0	—	3	8	1	0	0.4	.917
9 yrs.		24	35	.407	4.42	201	45	4	549.1	579	213	338	0	14	16	13	39	6	0	.154	26	57	5	1	0.4	.943

Oscar Jones

JONES, OSCAR WINFIELD (Flip Flap) BR TR 5′ 7″ 163 lbs.
B. Jan. 21, 1879, London Grove, Pa. D. Oct. 8, 1946, Perkasie, Pa.

Year	Team	W	L	PCT	ERA	G	GS	CG	IP	H	BB	SO	ShO	Relief Pitching W	L	SV	Batting AB	H	HR	BA	PO	A	E	DP	TC/G	FA
1903	BKN N	20	16	.556	2.94	38	36	31	324.1	320	77	95	4	0	1	0	125	32	0	.256	13	75	9	2	2.6	.907
1904		17	**25**	.405	2.75	46	41	38	377	**387**	92	96	0	1	0	0	137	24	0	.175	16	78	10	2	2.3	.904
1905		8	15	.348	4.66	29	20	14	174	197	56	66	0	2	1	1	65	13	0	.200	3	32	4	0	1.3	.897
3 yrs.		45	56	.446	3.20	113	97	83	875.1	904	225	257	4	3	2	1	327	69	0	.211	32	185	23	4	2.1	.904

Percy Jones

JONES, PERCY LEE BR TL 5′11½″ 175 lbs.
B. Oct. 28, 1899, Harwood, Tex. D. Mar. 18, 1979, Dallas, Tex.

Year	Team	W	L	PCT	ERA	G	GS	CG	IP	H	BB	SO	ShO	Relief Pitching W	L	SV	Batting AB	H	HR	BA	PO	A	E	DP	TC/G	FA
1920	CHI N	0	0	—	11.57	4	0	0	7	15	3	0	0	0	0	0	2	0	0	.000	0	2	0	0	0.5	1.000
1921		3	5	.375	4.56	32	3	1	98.2	116	39	46	0	2	3	0	27	6	0	.222	6	14	0	0	0.6	1.000
1922		8	9	.471	4.72	44	24	7	164	197	69	46	2	2	0	1	47	4	0	.085	3	42	4	1	1.1	.918
1925		6	6	.500	4.65	28	13	6	124	123	71	60	1	2	1	0	39	6	0	.154	4	38	3	1	1.6	.933
1926		12	7	.632	3.09	30	20	10	160.1	151	90	80	2	4	0	2	50	13	0	.260	2	34	5	0	1.4	.878

Percy Jones *continued*

Year	Team	W	L	PCT	ERA	G	GS	CG	IP	H	BB	SO	ShO	Relief Pitching W	Relief Pitching L	Relief Pitching SV	Batting AB	Batting H	Batting HR	BA	PO	A	E	DP	TC/G	FA
1927		7	8	.467	4.07	30	11	5	112.2	123	72	37	1	3	1	0	40	14	0	.350	3	33	2	2	1.3	.947
1928		10	6	.625	4.03	39	18	9	154	164	56	41	1	3	0	3	56	11	0	.196	3	36	2	2	1.1	.951
1929	**BOS N**	7	15	.318	4.64	35	22	11	188.1	219	84	69	1	2	1	0	61	9	0	.148	14	42	1	2	1.6	.982
1930	**PIT N**	0	1	.000	6.63	9	2	0	19	26	11	3	0	0	0	0	2	0	0	.000	0	2	0	0	0.2	1.000
9 yrs.		53	57	.482	4.33	251	113	49	1028	1134	495	382	8	18	6	6	324	63	0	.194	35	243	17	8	1.2	.942

Randy Jones

JONES, RANDALL LEO
B. Jan. 12, 1950, Fullerton, Calif.
BR TL 6′ 178 lbs.

Year	Team	W	L	PCT	ERA	G	GS	CG	IP	H	BB	SO	ShO	Relief Pitching W	Relief Pitching L	Relief Pitching SV	Batting AB	Batting H	Batting HR	BA	PO	A	E	DP	TC/G	FA
1973	**SD N**	7	6	.538	3.16	20	19	6	139.2	129	37	77	1	0	0	0	48	8	0	.167	3	24	1	0	1.4	.964
1974		8	**22**	.267	4.46	40	34	4	208	217	78	124	1	0	1	2	65	10	0	.154	7	44	2	3	1.3	.962
1975		20	12	.625	**2.24**	37	36	18	285	242	56	103	6	1	0	0	83	11	0	.133	14	70	4	5	2.4	.955
1976		**22**	14	.611	2.74	40	**40**	**25**	**315.1**	**274**	50	93	5	0	0	0	103	6	0	.058	31	81	0	12	2.8	1.000
1977		6	12	.333	4.59	27	25	1	147	173	36	44	0	0	0	0	43	5	0	.116	8	47	2	0	2.1	.965
1978		13	14	.481	2.88	37	36	7	253	263	64	71	2	0	1	0	82	15	0	.183	15	51	4	5	1.9	.943
1979		11	12	.478	3.63	39	39	6	263	257	64	112	0	0	0	0	86	15	0	.174	15	60	3	2	2.0	.962
1980		5	13	.278	3.92	24	24	4	154	165	29	53	3	0	0	0	45	3	0	.067	12	38	1	0	2.1	.980
1981	**NY N**	1	8	.111	4.88	13	12	0	59	65	38	14	0	0	0	0	17	2	0	.118	2	19	0	0	1.6	1.000
1982		7	10	.412	4.60	28	20	2	107.2	130	51	44	1	0	0	0	27	4	0	.148	7	31	1	3	1.4	.974
10 yrs.		100	123	.448	3.42	305	285	73	1931.2	1915	503	735	19	1	2	2	599	79	0	.132	114	465	18	30	2.0	.970

Rick Jones

JONES, THOMAS FREDERICK
B. Apr. 16, 1955, Jacksonville, Fla.
BL TL 6′ 5″ 190 lbs.

Year	Team	W	L	PCT	ERA	G	GS	CG	IP	H	BB	SO	ShO	Relief Pitching W	Relief Pitching L	Relief Pitching SV	Batting AB	Batting H	Batting HR	BA	PO	A	E	DP	TC/G	FA
1976	**BOS A**	5	3	.625	3.38	24	14	1	104	133	26	45	0	1	0	0	0	0	0	—	8	13	0	2	0.9	1.000
1977	**SEA A**	1	4	.200	5.14	10	10	0	42	47	37	16	0	0	0	0	0	0	0	—	1	7	0	1	0.8	1.000
1978		0	2	.000	5.84	3	2	0	12.1	17	7	11	0	0	0	0	0	0	0	—	1	1	0	0	0.7	1.000
3 yrs.		6	9	.400	4.04	37	26	1	158.1	197	70	72	0	1	0	0	0	0	0		10	21	0	3	0.8	1.000

Sad Sam Jones

JONES, SAMUEL POND
B. July 26, 1892, Woodsfield, Ohio D. July 6, 1966, Barnesville, Ohio.
BR TR 6′ 170 lbs.

Year	Team	W	L	PCT	ERA	G	GS	CG	IP	H	BB	SO	ShO	Relief Pitching W	Relief Pitching L	Relief Pitching SV	Batting AB	Batting H	Batting HR	BA	PO	A	E	DP	TC/G	FA
1914	**CLE A**	0	0	—	2.70	1	0	0	3.1	2	2	0	0	0	0	0	2	1	0	.500	0	1	0	0	1.0	1.000
1915		4	9	.308	3.65	48	9	2	145.2	131	63	42	0	2	3	4	32	5	0	.156	6	46	4	2	1.2	.929
1916	**BOS A**	0	1	.000	3.67	12	0	0	27	25	10	7	0	0	1	1	6	2	0	.333	4	8	0	0	0.9	1.000
1917		0	1	.000	4.41	9	1	0	16.1	15	6	5	0	0	0	1	4	0	0	.000	3	5	0	2	0.9	1.000
1918		16	5	**.762**	2.25	24	21	16	184	151	70	44	5	0	0	0	57	10	0	.175	11	41	2	5	2.3	.963
1919		12	20	.375	3.75	35	31	21	245	258	95	67	5	0	3	1	81	11	0	.136	12	81	5	2	2.8	.949
1920		13	16	.448	3.94	37	33	20	274	302	79	86	3	0	2	0	92	20	0	.217	8	68	5	2	2.2	.938
1921		23	16	.590	3.22	40	38	25	298.2	318	78	98	**5**	1	0	1	100	24	2	.240	14	59	4	2	1.9	.948
1922	**NY A**	13	13	.500	3.67	45	28	21	260	270	76	81	0	1	0	**8**	87	23	1	.264	11	60	3	5	1.6	.959
1923		21	8	.724	3.63	39	27	18	243	239	69	68	3	2	2	4	85	19	0	.224	7	68	1	5	1.9	.987
1924		9	6	.600	3.63	36	21	8	178.2	187	76	53	3	2	1	3	51	9	1	.176	6	40	4	1	1.4	.920
1925		15	**21**	.417	4.63	43	31	14	246.2	267	104	92	1	4	3	2	80	13	0	.163	17	56	3	4	1.7	.961
1926		9	8	.529	4.98	39	23	6	161	186	80	69	1	2	1	5	49	10	0	.204	4	33	2	1	1.0	.949
1927	**STL A**	8	14	.364	4.32	30	26	11	189.2	211	102	72	0	0	0	0	55	6	0	.109	12	35	2	0	1.6	.959
1928	**WAS A**	17	7	.708	2.84	30	27	19	224.2	209	78	63	4	0	0	0	79	20	2	.253	16	49	0	5	2.2	1.000
1929		9	9	.500	3.92	24	24	8	153.2	156	49	36	1	0	0	0	51	8	0	.157	10	26	3	1	1.6	.923
1930		15	7	.682	4.07	25	25	14	183.1	195	61	60	1	0	0	0	61	9	0	.148	11	32	4	2	1.9	.915
1931		9	10	.474	4.32	25	24	8	148	185	47	58	1	0	0	1	48	15	0	.313	6	28	2	2	1.4	.944
1932	**CHI A**	10	15	.400	4.22	30	28	10	200.1	217	75	64	0	2	0	0	57	11	0	.193	17	50	3	2	2.3	.957
1933		10	12	.455	3.36	27	25	11	176.2	181	65	60	2	0	1	0	58	9	0	.155	6	34	3	3	1.6	.930
1934		8	12	.400	5.11	27	26	11	183.1	217	60	60	1	0	0	0	60	12	0	.200	11	27	2	1	1.5	.950
1935		8	7	.533	4.05	21	19	7	140	162	51	38	0	0	0	0	48	8	0	.167	5	29	0	1	1.6	1.000
22 yrs.		229	217	.513	3.84	647	487	250	3883	4084	1396	1223	36	16	17	31	1243	245	6	.197	197	876	52	48	1.7	.954
WORLD SERIES																										
1918	**BOS A**	0	1	.000	3.00	1	1	1	9	7	5	5	0	0	0	0	1	0	0	.000	0	4	0	0	4.0	1.000
1922	**NY A**	0	0	—	0.00	2	0	0	2	1	1	0	0	0	0	0	0	0	0	—	0	1	0	0	0.5	1.000
1923		0	1	.000	0.90	2	1	0	10	5	2	3	0	0	0	1	2	0	0	.000	0	3	0	1	1.5	1.000
1926		0	0	—	9.00	1	0	0	1	2	2	1	0	0	0	0	0	0	0	—	0	0	0	0	0.0	.000
4 yrs.		0	2	.000	2.05	6	2	1	22	15	10	9	0	0	0	1	3	0	0	.000	0	8	0	1	1.3	1.000

Sam Jones

JONES, SAMUEL (Sad Sam, Toothpick Sam)
B. Dec. 14, 1925, Stewartsville, Ohio D. Nov. 5, 1971, Morgantown, W. Va.
BR TR 6′ 4″ 192 lbs.

Year	Team	W	L	PCT	ERA	G	GS	CG	IP	H	BB	SO	ShO	Relief Pitching W	Relief Pitching L	Relief Pitching SV	Batting AB	Batting H	Batting HR	BA	PO	A	E	DP	TC/G	FA
1951	**CLE A**	0	1	.000	2.08	2	1	0	8.2	4	5	4	0	0	0	0	2	0	0	.000	1	1	0	0	1.0	1.000
1952		2	3	.400	7.25	14	4	0	36	38	37	28	0	1	0	1	10	1	0	.100	0	4	0	0	0.3	1.000
1955	**CHI N**	14	**20**	.412	4.10	36	34	12	241.2	175	**185**	**198**	4	1	1	0	77	14	0	.182	14	36	5	1	1.5	.909
1956		9	14	.391	3.91	33	28	8	188.2	155	**115**	**176**	2	1	0	0	57	10	0	.175	7	21	4	3	1.0	.875
1957	**STL N**	12	9	.571	3.60	28	27	10	182.2	164	71	154	2	1	0	0	63	10	0	.159	13	27	1	1	1.5	.976
1958		14	13	.519	2.88	35	35	14	250	204	**107**	**225**	2	0	0	0	90	9	0	.100	14	31	1	3	1.3	.978
1959	**SF N**	**21**	15	.583	**2.83**	50	35	16	270.2	232	**109**	209	**4**	4	1	4	85	11	0	.129	10	34	3	2	0.9	.936
1960		18	14	.563	3.19	39	35	13	234	200	91	190	3	2	1	0	80	16	0	.200	6	34	5	1	1.2	.889
1961		8	8	.500	4.49	37	17	2	128.1	134	57	105	0	2	1	1	36	5	0	.139	7	11	1	1	0.5	.947
1962	**DET A**	2	4	.333	3.65	30	6	1	81.1	77	35	73	0	1	1	1	21	2	1	.095	11	8	1	0	0.7	.950
1963	**STL N**	2	0	1.000	9.00	11	0	0	11	15	5	8	0	2	0	2	1	0	0	.000	1	1	0	0	0.2	1.000
1964	**BAL A**	0	0	—	2.61	7	0	0	10.1	5	5	6	0	0	0	0	0	0	0	—	0	1	0	1	0.1	1.000
12 yrs.		102	101	.502	3.59	322	222	76	1643.1	1403	822	1376	17	15	5	9	522	78	1	.149	84	209	21	13	1.0	.933

Sheldon Jones

JONES, SHELDON LESLIE (Available)
B. Feb. 2, 1922, Tecumseh, Neb. D. Apr. 18, 1991, Greenville, N. C.
BR TR 6′ 180 lbs.

Year	Team	W	L	PCT	ERA	G	GS	CG	IP	H	BB	SO	ShO	Relief Pitching W	Relief Pitching L	Relief Pitching SV	Batting AB	Batting H	Batting HR	BA	PO	A	E	DP	TC/G	FA
1946	**NY N**	1	2	.333	3.21	6	4	1	28	21	17	24	0	0	0	0	8	2	0	.250	1	4	0	0	0.8	1.000
1947		2	2	.500	3.88	15	6	0	55.2	51	29	24	0	2	0	0	16	2	0	.125	4	5	1	0	0.7	.900
1948		16	8	.667	3.35	55	21	8	201.1	204	90	82	2	5	4	5	64	13	0	.203	10	38	2	1	0.9	.960
1949		15	12	.556	3.34	42	27	11	207.1	198	88	79	1	5	0	0	66	8	0	.121	11	35	1	2	1.1	.979
1950		13	16	.448	4.61	40	28	11	199	188	90	97	2	2	3	2	57	6	0	.105	8	25	0	0	0.8	1.000

Sheldon Jones *continued*

Year	Team	Lg	W	L	PCT	ERA	G	GS	CG	IP	H	BB	SO	ShO	Relief W	Relief L	Relief SV	AB	H	HR	BA	PO	A	E	DP	TC/G	FA
1951			6	11	.353	4.26	41	12	2	120.1	119	52	58	0	4	4	4	31	3	0	.097	5	23	2	2	0.7	.933
1952	BOS	N	1	4	.200	4.76	39	1	0	70	81	31	40	0	1	3	1	8	1	0	.125	4	13	1	1	0.5	.944
1953	CHI	N	0	2	.000	5.40	22	2	0	38.1	47	16	9	0	0	1	0	7	0	0	.000	4	6	1	2	0.5	.909
8 yrs.			54	57	.486	3.96	260	101	33	920	909	413	413	5	19	15	12	257	35	0	.136	47	149	8	8	0.8	.961
WORLD SERIES																											
1951	NY	N	0	0	—	2.08	2	0	0	4.1	5	1	2	0	0	0	1	0	0	0	—	0	1	0	0	0.5	1.000

Sherman Jones

JONES, SHERMAN JARVIS (Roadblock)
B. Feb. 10, 1935, Winton, N. C.
BL TR 6′ 4″ 205 lbs.

Year	Team	Lg	W	L	PCT	ERA	G	GS	CG	IP	H	BB	SO	ShO	Relief W	Relief L	Relief SV	AB	H	HR	BA	PO	A	E	DP	TC/G	FA
1960	SF	N	1	1	.500	3.09	16	0	0	32	37	11	10	0	1	1	1	7	2	0	.286	0	4	1	0	0.3	.800
1961	CIN	N	1	1	.500	4.42	24	2	0	55	51	27	32	0	0	1	2	11	2	0	.182	5	8	0	0	0.5	1.000
1962	NY	N	0	4	.000	7.71	8	3	0	23.1	31	8	11	0	0	1	0	7	3	0	.429	3	5	0	0	1.0	1.000
3 yrs.			2	6	.250	4.73	48	5	0	110.1	119	46	53	0	1	3	3	25	7	0	.280	8	17	1	0	0.5	.962
WORLD SERIES																											
1961	CIN	N	0	0	—	0.00	1	0	0	0.2	0	0	0	0	0	0	0	0	0	0	—	0	0	0	0	0.0	.000

Stacy Jones

JONES, JOSEPH STACY
B. May 26, 1967, Gadsden, Ala.
BR TR 6′ 6″ 225 lbs.

Year	Team	Lg	W	L	PCT	ERA	G	GS	CG	IP	H	BB	SO	ShO	Relief W	Relief L	Relief SV	AB	H	HR	BA	PO	A	E	DP	TC/G	FA
1991	BAL	A	0	0	—	4.09	4	1	0	11	11	5	10	0	0	0	0	0	0	0	—	2	1	0	0	0.8	1.000

Steve Jones

JONES, STEVEN HOWELL
Brother of Gary Jones.
B. Apr. 22, 1941, Huntington Park, Calif.
BL TL 5′10″ 175 lbs.

Year	Team	Lg	W	L	PCT	ERA	G	GS	CG	IP	H	BB	SO	ShO	Relief W	Relief L	Relief SV	AB	H	HR	BA	PO	A	E	DP	TC/G	FA
1967	CHI	A	2	2	.500	4.21	11	3	0	25.2	21	12	17	0	1	0	0	4	1	0	.250	0	4	1	0	0.5	.800
1968	WAS	A	1	2	.333	5.91	7	0	0	10.2	8	7	11	0	1	2	0	1	0	0	.000	0	0	1	0	0.1	.000
1969	KC	A	2	3	.400	4.23	20	4	0	44.2	45	24	31	0	0	1	0	8	1	0	.125	7	6	1	0	0.7	.929
3 yrs.			5	7	.417	4.44	38	7	0	81	74	43	59	0	2	3	0	13	2	0	.154	7	10	3	0	0.5	.850

Tim Jones

JONES, TIMOTHY BRYON
B. Jan. 24, 1954, Sacramento, Calif.
BB TR 6′ 5″ 220 lbs.

Year	Team	Lg	W	L	PCT	ERA	G	GS	CG	IP	H	BB	SO	ShO	Relief W	Relief L	Relief SV	AB	H	HR	BA	PO	A	E	DP	TC/G	FA
1977	PIT	N	1	0	1.000	0.00	3	1	0	10	4	3	5	0	0	0	0	2	0	0	.000	1	0	0	0	0.3	1.000

Tim Jones

JONES, WILLIAM TIMOTHY
B. Dec. 1, 1962, Sumter, S. C.
BL TR 5′10″ 172 lbs.

Year	Team	Lg	W	L	PCT	ERA	G	GS	CG	IP	H	BB	SO	ShO	Relief W	Relief L	Relief SV	AB	H	HR	BA	PO	A	E	DP	TC/G	FA
1990	STL	N	0	0	—	6.75	1	0	0	1.1	1	2	0	0	0	0	0	*				26	40	1	7	3.7	.985

Todd Jones

JONES, TODD BARTON GIVIN
B. Apr. 24, 1968, Marietta, Ga.
BL TR 6′ 3″ 200 lbs.

Year	Team	Lg	W	L	PCT	ERA	G	GS	CG	IP	H	BB	SO	ShO	Relief W	Relief L	Relief SV	AB	H	HR	BA	PO	A	E	DP	TC/G	FA
1993	HOU	N	1	2	.333	3.13	27	0	0	37.1	28	15	25	0	1	2	2	0	0	0	—	4	2	0	0	0.2	1.000
1994			5	2	.714	2.72	48	0	0	72.2	52	26	63	0	5	2	5	5	2	0	.400	4	3	0	0	0.1	1.000
1995			6	5	.545	3.07	68	0	0	99.2	89	52	96	0	6	5	15	5	1	0	.200	3	11	1	1	0.2	.933
3 yrs.			12	9	.571	2.96	143	0	0	209.2	169	93	184	0	12	9	22	10	3	0	.300	11	16	1	1	0.2	.964

Claude Jonnard

JONNARD, CLAUDE ALFRED
Brother of Bubber Jonnard.
B. Nov. 23, 1897, Nashville, Tenn. D. Aug. 27, 1959, Nashville, Tenn.
BR TR 6′ 1″ 165 lbs.

Year	Team	Lg	W	L	PCT	ERA	G	GS	CG	IP	H	BB	SO	ShO	Relief W	Relief L	Relief SV	AB	H	HR	BA	PO	A	E	DP	TC/G	FA
1921	NY	N	0	0	—	0.00	1	0	0	4	4	0	7	0	0	0	1	1	0	0	.000	0	0	0	0	0.0	.000
1922			6	1	.857	3.84	33	0	0	96	96	28	44	0	6	1	**5**	24	1	0	.042	0	15	1	1	0.5	.938
1923			4	3	.571	3.28	**45**	1	1	96	105	35	45	0	3	3	**5**	26	1	0	.038	3	17	1	0	0.5	.952
1924			4	5	.444	2.41	34	3	1	89.2	80	24	40	0	4	3	5	22	1	0	.045	2	20	0	0	0.6	1.000
1926	STL	A	0	2	.000	6.00	12	3	0	36	46	24	13	0	0	0	1	7	0	0	.000	0	17	2	0	1.6	.895
1929	CHI	N	0	1	.000	7.48	12	2	0	27.2	41	11	11	0	0	0	0	10	2	0	.200	0	8	2	0	0.8	.800
6 yrs.			14	12	.538	3.79	137	9	2	349.1	372	122	160	0	13	7	17	90	5	0	.056	5	77	6	1	0.6	.932
WORLD SERIES																											
1923	NY	N	0	0	—	0.00	2	0	0	2	1	1	1	0	0	0	0	0	0	0	—	0	1	0	0	0.5	1.000
1924			0	0	—	0.00	1	0	0		0	1	0	0	0	0	0	0	0	0	—	0	0	0	0	0.0	.000
2 yrs.			0	0		0.00	3	0	0	2	1	2	1	0	0	0	0	0	0	0		0	1	0	0	0.3	1.000

Charlie Jordan

JORDAN, CHARLES T.
B. Oct. 4, 1871, Baltimore, Md. D. June 1, 1928, Hazleton, Pa.

Year	Team	Lg	W	L	PCT	ERA	G	GS	CG	IP	H	BB	SO	ShO	Relief W	Relief L	Relief SV	AB	H	HR	BA	PO	A	E	DP	TC/G	FA
1896	PHI	N	0	0	—	7.71	2	0	0	4.2	9	2	3	0	0	0	0	2	1	0	.500	0	1	0	0	0.5	1.000

Harry Jordan

JORDAN, HARRY J.
B. Feb. 14, 1873, Titusville, Pa. D. Mar. 1, 1920, Pittsburgh, Pa.

Year	Team	Lg	W	L	PCT	ERA	G	GS	CG	IP	H	BB	SO	ShO	Relief W	Relief L	Relief SV	AB	H	HR	BA	PO	A	E	DP	TC/G	FA
1894	PIT	N	1	0	1.000	4.00	1	1	1	9	10	2	1	0	0	0	0	3	0	0	.000	2	0	0	0	2.0	1.000
1895			0	2	.000	4.24	2	2	2	17	24	6	4	0	0	0	0	7	2	0	.286	1	2	1	0	2.0	.750
2 yrs.			1	2	.333	4.15	3	3	3	26	34	8	5	0	0	0	0	10	2	0	.200	3	2	1	0	2.0	.833

Milt Jordan

JORDAN, MILTON MIGNOT
B. May 24, 1927, Mineral Springs, Pa. D. May 13, 1993, Ithaca, N. Y.
BR TR 6′ 2½″ 207 lbs.

Year	Team	Lg	W	L	PCT	ERA	G	GS	CG	IP	H	BB	SO	ShO	Relief W	Relief L	Relief SV	AB	H	HR	BA	PO	A	E	DP	TC/G	FA
1953	DET	A	0	1	.000	5.82	8	1	0	17	26	5	4	0	0	0	0	2	1	0	.500	0	6	2	0	1.0	.750

Niles Jordan

JORDAN, NILES CHAPMAN
B. Dec. 1, 1925, Lyman, Wash.
BL TL 5′11″ 180 lbs.

Year	Team	Lg	W	L	PCT	ERA	G	GS	CG	IP	H	BB	SO	ShO	Relief W	Relief L	Relief SV	AB	H	HR	BA	PO	A	E	DP	TC/G	FA
1951	PHI	N	2	3	.400	3.19	5	5	2	36.2	35	8	11	1	0	0	0	13	1	0	.077	3	4	0	0	1.4	1.000
1952	CIN	N	0	1	.000	9.95	3	1	0	6.1	14	3	2	0	0	0	0	1	0	0	.000	0	1	0	1	0.3	1.000
2 yrs.			2	4	.333	4.19	8	6	2	43	49	11	13	1	0	0	0	14	1	0	.071	3	5	0	1	1.0	1.000

Ricardo Jordan

JORDAN, RICARDO
B. June 27, 1970, Boynton Beach, Fla.
BL TL 6′ 175 lbs.

Year	Team	Lg	W	L	PCT	ERA	G	GS	CG	IP	H	BB	SO	ShO	Relief W	Relief L	Relief SV	AB	H	HR	BA	PO	A	E	DP	TC/G	FA
1995	TOR	A	1	0	1.000	6.60	15	0	0	15	18	13	10	0	1	0	1	0	0	0	—	1	2	0	0	0.2	1.000

Rip Jordan

JORDAN, RAYMOND WILLIS (Lanky)
B. Sept. 28, 1889, Portland, Me. D. June 5, 1960, Meriden, Conn.
BL TR 6′ 172 lbs.

Year	Team	Lg	W	L	PCT	ERA	G	GS	CG	IP	H	BB	SO	ShO	Relief W	Relief L	Relief SV	AB	H	HR	BA	PO	A	E	DP	TC/G	FA
1912	CHI	A	0	0	—	6.10	3	0	0	10.1	13	0	0	0	0	0	0	4	0	0	.000	0	2	0	0	0.7	1.000
1919	WAS	A	0	0	—	11.25	1	1	0	4	6	2	2	0	0	0	0	1	0	0	.000	0	0	0	0	0.0	.000
2 yrs.			0	0		7.53	4	1	0	14.1	19	2	2	0	0	0	0	5	0	0	.000	0	2	0	0	0.5	1.000

Orville Jorgens

JORGENS, ORVILLE EDWARD
Brother of Arndt Jorgens.
B. June 4, 1908, Rockford, Ill. D. Jan. 11, 1992, Colorado Springs, Colo.
BR TR 6′ 1″ 180 lbs.

Year	Team	Lg	W	L	PCT	ERA	G	GS	CG	IP	H	BB	SO	ShO	Relief W	Relief L	Relief SV	AB	H	HR	BA	PO	A	E	DP	TC/G	FA
1935	PHI	N	10	15	.400	4.83	**53**	24	6	188.1	216	96	57	0	4	3	2	62	6	0	.097	9	55	2	0	1.2	.970
1936			8	8	.500	4.79	39	21	4	167.1	196	69	58	0	0	1	0	60	12	0	.200	5	39	0	3	1.1	1.000
1937			3	4	.429	4.41	52	9	1	140.2	159	68	34	0	2	0	3	35	5	0	.143	8	40	3	2	1.0	.941
3 yrs.			21	27	.438	4.70	144	54	11	496.1	571	233	149	0	6	4	5	157	23	0	.146	22	134	5	5	1.1	.969

Addie Joss

JOSS, ADRIAN
B. Apr. 12, 1880, Woodland, Wis. D. Apr. 14, 1911, Toledo, Ohio.
Hall of Fame 1978.
BR TR 6′ 3″ 185 lbs.

Year	Team	Lg	W	L	PCT	ERA	G	GS	CG	IP	H	BB	SO	ShO	Relief W	Relief L	Relief SV	AB	H	HR	BA	PO	A	E	DP	TC/G	FA
1902	CLE	A	17	13	.567	2.77	32	29	28	269.1	225	75	106	**5**	1	0	0	103	12	0	.117	17	107	6	4	3.9	.954
1903			18	13	.581	2.15	32	31	31	292.2	239	43	126	3	0	0	0	117	22	0	.188	15	112	7	4	4.1	.948
1904			14	10	.583	**1.59**	25	24	20	192.1	160	30	83	6	0	1	0	76	10	0	.132	32	61	3	3	3.4	.969
1905			20	12	.625	2.01	33	32	31	286	246	46	132	3	0	1	0	94	13	0	.138	25	106	4	1	3.9	.970
1906			21	9	.700	1.72	34	31	28	282	220	43	106	9	0	1	1	100	21	0	.210	33	94	4	2	3.6	.969
1907			**27**	11	.711	1.83	42	38	34	338.2	279	54	127	6	2	0	2	114	13	0	.114	21	143	3	6	4.0	.982
1908			24	11	.686	**1.16**	42	35	29	325	232	30	130	9	2	0	2	97	15	0	.155	23	109	5	3	3.3	.964
1909			14	13	.519	1.71	33	28	24	242.2	198	31	67	4	0	1	0	80	8	1	.100	12	78	2	0	2.8	.978
1910			5	5	.500	2.26	13	12	9	107.1	96	18	49	1	0	0	0	36	4	0	.111	7	42	2	1	3.9	.961
9 yrs.			160	97	.623	1.88 **2nd**	286	260	234	2336	1895	370	926	46	5	4	5	817	118	1	.144	185	852	36	24	3.6	.966

Bob Joyce

JOYCE, ROBERT EMMETT
B. Jan. 14, 1915, Stockton, Calif. D. Dec. 10, 1981, San Francisco, Calif.
BR TR 6′ 1″ 180 lbs.

Year	Team	Lg	W	L	PCT	ERA	G	GS	CG	IP	H	BB	SO	ShO	Relief W	Relief L	Relief SV	AB	H	HR	BA	PO	A	E	DP	TC/G	FA
1939	PHI	A	3	5	.375	6.69	30	6	1	107.2	156	37	25	0	3	1	0	35	3	0	.086	3	24	0	1	0.9	1.000
1946	NY	N	3	4	.429	5.34	14	7	2	60.2	79	20	24	0	0	0	0	19	3	1	.158	4	14	0	0	1.3	1.000
2 yrs.			6	9	.400	6.20	44	13	3	168.1	235	57	49	0	3	1	0	54	6	1	.111	7	38	0	1	1.0	1.000

Dick Joyce

JOYCE, RICHARD EDWARD
B. Nov. 18, 1943, Portland, Me.
BL TL 6′ 5″ 225 lbs.

Year	Team	Lg	W	L	PCT	ERA	G	GS	CG	IP	H	BB	SO	ShO	Relief W	Relief L	Relief SV	AB	H	HR	BA	PO	A	E	DP	TC/G	FA
1965	KC	A	0	1	.000	2.77	5	3	0	13	12	4	7	0	0	0	0	4	0	0	.000	0	2	0	0	0.4	1.000

Mike Joyce

Playing record listed under Mike O'Neill.

Mike Joyce

JOYCE, MICHAEL LEWIS
B. Feb. 12, 1941, Detroit, Mich.
BR TR 6′ 2″ 193 lbs.

Year	Team	Lg	W	L	PCT	ERA	G	GS	CG	IP	H	BB	SO	ShO	Relief W	Relief L	Relief SV	AB	H	HR	BA	PO	A	E	DP	TC/G	FA
1962	CHI	A	2	1	.667	3.32	25	1	0	43.1	40	14	9	0	2	1	2	7	3	0	.429	2	9	0	1	0.4	1.000
1963			0	0	—	8.44	6	0	0	10.2	13	8	7	0	0	0	0	0	0	0	—	0	1	0	0	0.2	1.000
2 yrs.			2	1	.667	4.33	31	1	0	54	53	22	16	0	2	1	2	7	3	0	.429	2	10	0	1	0.4	1.000

Oscar Judd

JUDD, THOMAS WILLIAM OSCAR (Ossie)
B. Feb. 14, 1908, London, Ont., Canada D. Dec. 27, 1995, Ingersoll, Ont., Canada.
BL TL 6′½″ 180 lbs.

Year	Team	Lg	W	L	PCT	ERA	G	GS	CG	IP	H	BB	SO	ShO	Relief W	Relief L	Relief SV	AB	H	HR	BA	PO	A	E	DP	TC/G	FA
1941	BOS	A	0	0	—	8.76	7	0	0	12.1	15	10	5	0	0	0	1	4	2	0	.500	0	4	1	0	0.7	.800
1942			8	10	.444	3.89	31	19	11	150.1	135	90	70	0	0	2	2	67	18	2	.269	6	29	1	1	1.2	.972
1943			11	6	.647	2.90	23	20	8	155.1	131	69	53	1	0	1	0	54	14	0	.259	9	41	3	4	2.3	.943
1944			1	1	.500	3.60	9	6	1	30	30	15	9	0	0	0	0	11	2	0	.182	1	4	0	0	0.6	1.000
1945	2 teams	BOS A (2G 0–1)	PHI N (23G 5–4)																								
″	total		5	5	.500	4.13	25	10	3	89.1	90	43	41	1	0	0	2	32	9	0	.281	4	23	0	0	1.1	1.000
1946	PHI	N	11	12	.478	3.53	30	24	12	173.1	169	90	65	1	0	1	2	79	25	1	.316	10	50	0	0	2.0	1.000
1947			4	15	.211	4.60	32	19	8	146.2	155	69	54	1	0	2	0	64	12	0	.188	7	33	1	3	1.3	.976
1948			0	2	.000	6.91	4	1	0	14.1	19	11	7	0	0	2	0	6	1	0	.167	1	2	1	0	1.0	.750
8 yrs.			40	51	.440	3.90	161	99	43	771.2	744	397	304	4	0	8	7	*				38	186	7	8	1.4	.970

Ralph Judd

JUDD, RALPH WESLEY
B. Dec. 7, 1901, Perrysburg, Ohio D. May 6, 1957, Lapeer, Mich.
BL TR 5′10″ 170 lbs.

Year	Team	Lg	W	L	PCT	ERA	G	GS	CG	IP	H	BB	SO	ShO	Relief W	Relief L	Relief SV	AB	H	HR	BA	PO	A	E	DP	TC/G	FA
1927	WAS	A	0	0	—	6.75	1	0	0	4	8	2	2	0	0	0	1	1	0	0	.000	0	0	0	0	0.0	.000
1929	NY	N	3	0	1.000	2.66	18	0	0	50.2	49	11	21	0	3	0	0	14	0	0	.000	2	12	0	1	0.8	1.000
1930			0	0	—	5.87	2	0	0	7.2	13	3	0	0	0	0	0	3	0	0	.000	0	2	1	0	1.5	.667
3 yrs.			3	0	1.000	3.32	21	0	0	62.1	70	16	23	0	3	0	1	18	0	0	.000	2	14	1	1	0.8	.941

Jeff Juden

JUDEN, JEFFREY DANIEL
B. Jan. 19, 1971, Salem, Mass.
BR TR 6′ 7″ 245 lbs.

Year	Team	Lg	W	L	PCT	ERA	G	GS	CG	IP	H	BB	SO	ShO	Relief W	Relief L	Relief SV	AB	H	HR	BA	PO	A	E	DP	TC/G	FA
1991	HOU	N	0	2	.000	6.00	4	3	0	18	19	7	11	0	0	0	0	5	0	0	.000	0	2	3	0	1.3	.400
1993			0	1	.000	5.40	2	0	0	5	4	4	7	0	0	1	0	0	0	0	—	0	0	0	0	0.0	.000
1994	PHI	N	1	4	.200	6.18	6	5	0	27.2	29	12	22	0	0	0	0	9	1	0	.111	1	3	1	0	0.8	.800
1995			2	4	.333	4.02	13	10	1	62.2	53	31	47	0	0	0	0	18	1	1	.056	3	8	0	0	0.8	1.000
4 yrs.			3	11	.214	4.92	25	18	1	113.1	105	54	87	0	0	1	0	32	2	1	.063	4	13	4	0	0.8	.810

Howie Judson

JUDSON, HOWARD KOLLS
B. Feb. 16, 1926, Hebron, Ill.
BR TR 6′ 1″ 195 lbs.

Year	Team	Lg	W	L	PCT	ERA	G	GS	CG	IP	H	BB	SO	ShO	Relief W	Relief L	Relief SV	AB	H	HR	BA	PO	A	E	DP	TC/G	FA
1948	CHI	A	4	5	.444	4.78	40	5	1	107.1	102	56	38	0	4	2	8	29	3	0	.103	2	22	1	2	0.6	.960
1949			1	14	.067	4.58	26	12	3	108	114	70	36	0	0	4	1	31	2	0	.065	2	24	2	0	1.1	.929
1950			2	3	.400	3.94	46	3	1	112	105	63	34	0	2	2	0	20	2	0	.100	6	14	4	1	0.5	.833
1951			5	6	.455	3.77	27	14	3	121.2	124	55	43	0	0	1	1	33	4	0	.121	2	25	1	2	1.0	.964
1952			0	1	.000	4.24	21	0	0	34	30	22	15	0	0	1	1	4	0	0	.000	1	6	1	0	0.4	.875

Howie Judson *continued*

Year	Team	Lg	W	L	PCT	ERA	G	GS	CG	IP	H	BB	SO	ShO	Relief W	Relief L	Relief SV	AB	H	HR	BA	PO	A	E	DP	TC/G	FA
1953	**CIN**	**N**	0	1	.000	5.59	10	6	0	38.2	58	11	11	0	0	0	0	9	1	0	.111	0	8	0	1	0.8	1.000
1954			5	7	.417	3.95	37	8	0	93.1	86	42	27	0	1	3	3	24	2	0	.083	4	10	1	1	0.4	.933
7 yrs.			17	37	.315	4.29	207	48	8	615	619	319	204	0	7	13	14	150	14	0	.093	17	109	10	7	0.7	.926

Ken Jungels

JUNGELS, KENNETH PETER (Curly)
B. June 23, 1916, Aurora, Ill. D. Sept. 9, 1975, West Bend, Wis.
BR TR 6′ 1″ 180 lbs.

Year	Team	Lg	W	L	PCT	ERA	G	GS	CG	IP	H	BB	SO	ShO	Relief W	Relief L	Relief SV	AB	H	HR	BA	PO	A	E	DP	TC/G	FA
1937	**CLE**	**A**	0	0	—	0.00	2	0	0	3	3	1	0	0	0	0	0	0	0	0	—	1	0	0	0	0.5	1.000
1938			1	0	1.000	8.80	9	0	0	15.1	21	18	7	0	1	0	0	5	0	0	.000	1	2	0	0	0.3	1.000
1940			0	0	—	2.70	2	0	0	3.1	3	1	1	0	0	0	0	1	0	0	.000	0	1	0	0	0.5	1.000
1941			0	0	—	7.24	6	0	0	13.2	17	8	6	0	0	0	0	2	0	0	.000	0	1	0	0	0.2	1.000
1942	**PIT**	**N**	0	0	—	6.59	6	0	0	13.2	12	4	7	0	0	0	0	2	1	0	.500	1	3	0	0	0.7	1.000
5 yrs.			1	0	1.000	6.80	25	0	0	49	56	32	21	0	1	0	0	10	1	0	.100	3	7	0	0	0.4	1.000

Mike Jurewicz

JUREWICZ, MICHAEL ALLEN
B. Sept. 20, 1945, Buffalo, N. Y.
BB TL 6′ 3″ 205 lbs.

Year	Team	Lg	W	L	PCT	ERA	G	GS	CG	IP	H	BB	SO	ShO	Relief W	Relief L	Relief SV	AB	H	HR	BA	PO	A	E	DP	TC/G	FA
1965	**NY**	**A**	0	0	—	7.71	2	0	0	2.1	5	1	2	0	0	0	0	0	0	0	—	0	0	0	0	0.0	.000

Al Jurisich

JURISICH, ALVIN JOSEPH
B. Aug. 25, 1921, New Orleans, La. D. Nov. 3, 1981, New Orleans, La.
BR TR 6′ 2″ 193 lbs.

Year	Team	Lg	W	L	PCT	ERA	G	GS	CG	IP	H	BB	SO	ShO	Relief W	Relief L	Relief SV	AB	H	HR	BA	PO	A	E	DP	TC/G	FA
1944	**STL**	**N**	7	9	.438	3.39	30	14	5	130	102	65	53	2	2	0	1	45	8	0	.178	5	18	1	2	0.8	.958
1945			3	3	.500	5.15	27	6	1	71.2	61	41	42	0	1	1	0	23	2	0	.087	3	8	0	0	0.4	1.000
1946	**PHI**	**N**	4	3	.571	3.69	13	10	2	68.1	71	31	34	1	0	0	1	23	3	0	.130	5	5	1	1	0.8	.909
1947			1	7	.125	4.94	34	12	5	118.1	110	52	48	0	1	2	3	31	1	0	.032	1	16	0	1	0.5	1.000
4 yrs.			15	22	.405	4.24	104	42	13	388.1	344	189	177	3	4	3	5	122	14	0	.115	14	47	2	4	0.6	.968
WORLD SERIES																											
1944	**STL**	**N**	0	0	—	27.00	1	0	0	0.2	2	1	0	0	0	0	0	0	0	0	—	0	0	0	0	0.0	.000

Walt Justis

JUSTIS, WALTER NEWTON (Smoke)
B. Aug. 17, 1883, Moore's Hill, Ind. D. Oct. 4, 1941, Lawrenceburg, Ind.
BR TR 5′11½″ 195 lbs.

Year	Team	Lg	W	L	PCT	ERA	G	GS	CG	IP	H	BB	SO	ShO	Relief W	Relief L	Relief SV	AB	H	HR	BA	PO	A	E	DP	TC/G	FA
1905	**DET**	**A**	0	0	—	8.10	2	0	0	3.1	4	6	0	0	0	0	0	0	0	0	—	0	0	0	0	0.0	.000

Earl Juul

JUUL, EARL HEROLD
Brother of Herb Juul.
B. May 21, 1893, Chicago, Ill. D. Jan. 4, 1942, Chicago, Ill.
BR TR 5′ 9½″ 150 lbs.

Year	Team	Lg	W	L	PCT	ERA	G	GS	CG	IP	H	BB	SO	ShO	Relief W	Relief L	Relief SV	AB	H	HR	BA	PO	A	E	DP	TC/G	FA
1914	**BKN**	**F**	0	3	.000	6.21	9	3	0	29	26	31	16	0	0	0	0	9	2	0	.222	0	7	1	0	0.9	.875

Herb Juul

JUUL, HERBERT VICTOR
Brother of Earl Juul.
B. Feb. 2, 1886, Chicago, Ill. D. Nov. 14, 1928, Chicago, Ill.
BL TL 5′11″ 150 lbs.

Year	Team	Lg	W	L	PCT	ERA	G	GS	CG	IP	H	BB	SO	ShO	Relief W	Relief L	Relief SV	AB	H	HR	BA	PO	A	E	DP	TC/G	FA
1911	**CIN**	**N**	0	0	—	4.50	1	0	0	4	3	4	2	0	0	0	0	2	0	0	.000	0	0	0	0	0.0	.000

Jim Kaat

KAAT, JAMES LEE (Kitty)
B. Nov. 7, 1938, Zeeland, Mich.
BL TL 6′ 4½″ 205 lbs.

Year	Team	Lg	W	L	PCT	ERA	G	GS	CG	IP	H	BB	SO	ShO	Relief W	Relief L	Relief SV	AB	H	HR	BA	PO	A	E	DP	TC/G	FA
1959	**WAS**	**A**	0	2	.000	12.60	3	2	0	5	7	4	2	0	0	0	0	1	0	0	.000	0	1	0	0	0.3	1.000
1960			1	5	.167	5.58	13	9	0	50	48	31	25	0	0	0	0	14	2	0	.143	0	11	0	1	0.8	1.000
1961	**MIN**	**A**	9	17	.346	3.90	36	29	8	200.2	188	82	122	1	0	1	0	63	15	0	.238	19	41	2	8	1.7	.968
1962			18	14	.563	3.14	39	35	16	269	243	75	173	**5**	1	0	1	100	18	1	.180	16	72	3	6	2.3	.967
1963			10	10	.500	4.19	31	27	7	178.1	195	38	105	1	0	1	1	61	8	1	.131	19	43	1	5	2.0	.984
1964			17	11	.607	3.22	36	34	13	243	231	60	171	0	0	1	1	83	14	3	.169	16	48	5	6	1.9	.928
1965			18	11	.621	2.83	45	**42**	7	264.1	**267**	63	154	2	0	0	2	93	23	1	.247	15	64	6	3	1.9	.929
1966			**25**	13	.658	2.75	41	**41**	**19**	**304.2**	**271**	55	205	3	0	0	0	118	23	2	.195	19	46	3	5	1.7	.956
1967			16	13	.552	3.04	42	38	13	263.1	**269**	42	211	2	0	0	0	99	17	1	.172	13	46	3	0	1.5	.952
1968			14	12	.538	2.94	30	29	9	208	192	40	130	2	0	0	0	77	12	0	.156	10	31	1	0	1.4	.976
1969			14	13	.519	3.49	40	32	10	242.1	252	75	139	0	3	1	1	87	18	2	.207	9	29	8	4	1.1	.826
1970			14	10	.583	3.56	45	34	4	230	244	58	120	1	1	0	0	76	15	1	.197	15	43	4	5	1.4	.935
1971			13	14	.481	3.32	39	38	15	260	275	47	137	4	0	0	0	93	15	0	.161	13	41	1	4	1.4	.982
1972			10	2	.833	2.07	15	15	5	113	94	20	64	0	0	0	0	45	13	2	.289	5	19	2	0	1.7	.923
1973	**2 teams**	**MIN A** (29G 11–12) **CHI A** (7G 4–1)																									
″	**total**		15	13	.536	4.37	36	35	10	224.1	250	43	109	3	1	0	0	0	0	0		10	26	1	2	1.0	.973
1974	**CHI**	**A**	21	13	.618	2.92	42	39	15	277	263	63	142	3	1	0	0	1	0	0	.000	14	33	2	3	1.2	.959
1975			20	14	.588	3.11	43	41	12	303.2	**321**	77	142	1	0	0	0	0	0	0	—	15	39	1	2	1.3	.982
1976	**PHI**	**N**	12	14	.462	3.48	38	35	7	227.2	241	32	83	1	0	1	0	79	14	1	.177	18	19	2	3	1.0	.949
1977			6	11	.353	5.40	35	27	2	160	211	40	55	0	0	1	0	53	10	0	.189	7	19	3	1	0.8	.897
1978			8	5	.615	4.11	26	24	2	140	150	32	48	1	0	0	0	48	7	0	.146	5	15	0	4	0.8	1.000
1979	**2 teams**	**PHI N** (3G 1–0) **NY A** (40G 2–3)																									
″	**total**		3	3	.500	3.95	43	2	0	66	73	19	25	0	3	3	2	1	0	0	.000	5	6	1	0	0.3	.917
1980	**2 teams**	**NY A** (4G 0–1) **STL N** (49G 8–7)																									
″	**total**		8	8	.500	3.93	53	14	6	135	148	37	37	1	3	3	4	35	5	1	.143	5	19	2	2	0.5	.923
1981	**STL**	**N**	6	6	.500	3.40	41	1	0	53	60	17	8	0	6	5	4	8	3	0	.375	4	13	2	1	0.5	.895
1982			5	3	.625	4.08	62	2	0	75	79	23	35	0	5	3	2	12	0	0	.000	8	14	2	0	0.4	.917
1983			0	0	—	3.89	24	0	0	34.2	48	10	19	0	0	0	0	4	0	0	.000	2	6	1	0	0.4	.889
25 yrs.			283	237	.544	3.45	898	625	180	4528	4620	1083	2461	31	24	20	18	1251	232	16	.185	262	744	56	65	1.2	.947
LEAGUE CHAMPIONSHIP SERIES																											
1970	**MIN**	**A**	0	1	.000	9.00	1	1	0	2	6	2	1	0	0	0	0	1	0	0	.000	0	0	0	0	0.0	.000
1976	**PHI**	**N**	0	0	—	3.00	1	1	0	6	2	2	1	0	0	0	0	2	1	0	.500	0	1	0	0	1.0	1.000
2 yrs.			0	1	.000	4.50	2	2	0	8	8	4	2	0	0	0	0	3	1	0	.333	0	1	0	0	0.5	1.000
WORLD SERIES																											
1965	**MIN**	**A**	1	2	.333	3.77	3	3	1	14.1	18	2	6	0	0	0	0	6	1	0	.167	5	2	0	0	2.3	1.000
1982	**STL**	**N**	0	0	—	3.86	4	0	0	2.1	4	2	2	0	0	0	0	0	0	0	—	0	0	0	0	0.0	.000
2 yrs.			1	2	.333	3.78	7	3	1	16.2	22	4	8	0	0	0	0	6	1	0	.167	5	2	0	0	1.0	1.000

George Kahler

KAHLER, GEORGE RUNNELLS (Krum)
B. Sept. 6, 1889, Athens, Ohio D. Feb. 7, 1924, Battle Creek, Mich.
BR TR 6′ 183 lbs.

Year	Team	W	L	PCT	ERA	G	GS	CG	IP	H	BB	SO	ShO	Relief Pitching W	Relief Pitching L	Relief Pitching SV	Batting AB	Batting H	Batting HR	BA	PO	A	E	DP	TC/G	FA
1910	CLE A	6	4	.600	1.60	12	12	8	95.1	80	46	38	2	0	0	0	35	5	0	.143	4	29	3	1	3.0	.917
1911		9	8	.529	3.27	30	17	10	154.1	153	66	97	0	1	0	1	54	9	0	.167	9	35	2	0	1.5	.957
1912		12	19	.387	3.69	41	32	17	246.1	263	**121**	104	3	0	0	1	80	9	0	.113	12	54	2	4	1.7	.971
1913		5	11	.313	3.14	24	15	5	117.2	118	32	43	0	0	2	0	33	2	0	.061	5	21	2	0	1.2	.929
1914		0	1	.000	3.86	2	1	1	14	17	7	3	0	0	0	0	5	0	0	.000	0	3	0	0	1.5	1.000
5 yrs.		32	43	.427	3.17	109	77	41	627.2	631	272	285	5	1	2	2	207	25	0	.121	30	142	9	5	1.7	.950

Don Kainer

KAINER, DONALD WAYNE
B. Sept. 3, 1955, Houston, Tex.
BR TR 6′ 3″ 205 lbs.

Year	Team	W	L	PCT	ERA	G	GS	CG	IP	H	BB	SO	ShO	Relief Pitching W	Relief Pitching L	Relief Pitching SV	Batting AB	Batting H	Batting HR	BA	PO	A	E	DP	TC/G	FA
1980	TEX A	0	0	—	1.80	4	3	0	20	22	9	10	0	0	0	0	0	0	0	—	1	9	0	1	2.5	1.000

Bob Kaiser

KAISER, ROBERT THOMAS
B. Apr. 29, 1950, Cincinnati, Ohio.
BB TL 5′10″ 175 lbs.

Year	Team	W	L	PCT	ERA	G	GS	CG	IP	H	BB	SO	ShO	Relief Pitching W	Relief Pitching L	Relief Pitching SV	Batting AB	Batting H	Batting HR	BA	PO	A	E	DP	TC/G	FA
1971	CLE A	0	0	—	4.50	5	0	0	6	8	3	4	0	0	0	0	0	0	0	—	0	1	0	0	0.2	1.000

Don Kaiser

KAISER, CLYDE DONALD (Tiger)
B. Feb. 3, 1935, Byng, Okla.
BR TR 6′ 5″ 195 lbs.

Year	Team	W	L	PCT	ERA	G	GS	CG	IP	H	BB	SO	ShO	Relief Pitching W	Relief Pitching L	Relief Pitching SV	Batting AB	Batting H	Batting HR	BA	PO	A	E	DP	TC/G	FA
1955	CHI N	0	0	—	5.40	11	0	0	18.1	20	5	11	0	0	0	0	2	0	0	.000	0	2	1	0	0.3	.667
1956		4	9	.308	3.59	27	22	5	150.1	144	52	74	1	0	0	0	47	2	0	.043	7	26	3	1	1.3	.917
1957		2	6	.250	5.00	20	13	1	72	91	28	23	0	0	0	0	19	2	0	.105	5	20	1	4	1.3	.962
3 yrs.		6	15	.286	4.15	58	35	6	240.2	255	85	108	1	0	0	0	68	4	0	.059	12	48	5	5	1.1	.923

Jeff Kaiser

KAISER, JEFFREY PATRICK
B. July 24, 1960, Wyandotte, Mich.
BR TL 6′ 3″ 195 lbs.

Year	Team	W	L	PCT	ERA	G	GS	CG	IP	H	BB	SO	ShO	Relief Pitching W	Relief Pitching L	Relief Pitching SV	Batting AB	Batting H	Batting HR	BA	PO	A	E	DP	TC/G	FA
1985	OAK A	0	0	—	14.58	15	0	0	16.2	25	20	10	0	0	0	0	0	0	0	—	4	3	0	1	0.5	1.000
1987	CLE A	0	0	—	16.20	2	0	0	3.1	4	3	2	0	0	0	0	0	0	0	—	1	0	0	0	0.5	1.000
1988		0	0	—	0.00	3	0	0	2.2	2	1	0	0	0	0	0	0	0	0	—	0	2	0	0	0.7	1.000
1989		0	1	.000	7.36	6	0	0	3.2	5	5	4	0	0	1	0	0	0	0	—	0	0	0	0	0.0	.000
1990		0	0	—	3.55	5	0	0	12.2	16	7	9	0	0	0	0	0	0	0	—	3	1	0	0	0.8	1.000
1991	DET A	0	1	.000	9.00	10	0	0	5	6	5	4	0	0	1	2	0	0	0	—	0	1	0	0	0.1	1.000
1993	2 teams CIN N (3G 0–0) NY N (6G 0–0)																									
″	total	0	0		7.88	9	0	0	8	10	5	9	0	0	0	0	0	0	0		0	1	0	0	0.1	1.000
7 yrs.		0	2	.000	9.17	50	0	0	52	68	46	38	0	0	2	2	0	0	0		8	8	0	1	0.3	1.000

George Kaiserling

KAISERLING, GEORGE
B. May 12, 1893, Steubenville, Ohio D. Mar. 2, 1918, Steubenville, Ohio.
BR TR 6′ 175 lbs.

Year	Team	W	L	PCT	ERA	G	GS	CG	IP	H	BB	SO	ShO	Relief Pitching W	Relief Pitching L	Relief Pitching SV	Batting AB	Batting H	Batting HR	BA	PO	A	E	DP	TC/G	FA
1914	IND F	17	10	.630	3.11	37	33	20	275.1	288	72	75	1	1	1	0	98	11	0	.112	10	70	2	3	2.2	.976
1915	NWK F	13	14	.481	2.24	41	29	16	261.1	246	73	75	5	1	0	2	79	12	0	.152	6	81	5	2	2.2	.946
2 yrs.		30	24	.556	2.68	78	62	36	536.2	534	145	150	6	2	1	2	177	23	0	.130	16	151	7	5	2.2	.960

Bill Kalfass

KALFASS, WILLIAM PHILIP (Lefty)
B. Mar. 3, 1916, New York, N. Y. D. Sept. 8, 1968, Brooklyn, N. Y.
BR TL 6′ 3½″ 190 lbs.

Year	Team	W	L	PCT	ERA	G	GS	CG	IP	H	BB	SO	ShO	Relief Pitching W	Relief Pitching L	Relief Pitching SV	Batting AB	Batting H	Batting HR	BA	PO	A	E	DP	TC/G	FA
1937	PHI A	1	0	1.000	3.00	3	1	1	12	10	10	9	0	0	0	0	4	0	0	.000	0	1	0	0	0.3	1.000

Rudy Kallio

KALLIO, RUDOLPH
B. Dec. 14, 1892, Portland, Ore. D. Apr. 6, 1979, Newport, Ore.
BR TR 5′10″ 160 lbs.

Year	Team	W	L	PCT	ERA	G	GS	CG	IP	H	BB	SO	ShO	Relief Pitching W	Relief Pitching L	Relief Pitching SV	Batting AB	Batting H	Batting HR	BA	PO	A	E	DP	TC/G	FA
1918	DET A	8	14	.364	3.62	30	22	10	181.1	178	76	70	2	1	2	0	56	9	0	.161	10	47	5	0	2.0	.919
1919		0	0	—	5.64	12	1	0	22.1	28	8	3	0	0	0	1	4	0	0	.000	1	4	0	1	0.4	1.000
1925	BOS A	1	4	.200	7.71	7	4	0	18.2	28	9	2	0	0	1	0	6	2	0	.333	1	4	0	0	0.7	1.000
3 yrs.		9	18	.333	4.17	49	27	10	222.1	234	93	75	2	1	3	1	66	11	0	.167	12	55	5	1	1.4	.931

Scott Kamieniecki

KAMIENIECKI, SCOTT ANDREW
B. Apr. 19, 1964, Mt. Clemens, Mich.
BR TR 6′ 195 lbs.

Year	Team	W	L	PCT	ERA	G	GS	CG	IP	H	BB	SO	ShO	Relief Pitching W	Relief Pitching L	Relief Pitching SV	Batting AB	Batting H	Batting HR	BA	PO	A	E	DP	TC/G	FA
1991	NY A	4	4	.500	3.90	9	9	0	55.1	54	22	34	0	0	0	0	0	0	0	—	5	9	0	0	1.6	1.000
1992		6	14	.300	4.36	28	28	4	188	193	74	88	0	0	0	0	0	0	0	—	15	19	0	3	1.2	1.000
1993		10	7	.588	4.08	30	20	2	154.1	163	59	72	0	0	1	1	0	0	0	—	17	23	0	0	1.3	1.000
1994		8	6	.571	3.76	22	16	1	117.1	115	59	71	0	1	0	0	0	0	0	—	8	17	1	1	1.2	.962
1995		7	6	.538	4.01	17	16	1	89.2	83	49	43	0	0	0	0	0	0	0	—	3	10	0	2	0.8	1.000
5 yrs.		35	37	.486	4.08	106	89	8	604.2	608	263	308	0	1	1	1	0	0	0		48	78	1	6	1.2	.992
DIVISIONAL PLAYOFF SERIES																										
1995	NY A	0	0	—	7.20	1	1	0	5	9	4	4	0	0	0	0	0	0	0	—	0	0	0	0	0.0	.000

Bob Kammeyer

KAMMEYER, ROBERT LYNN
B. Dec. 2, 1950, Kansas City, Mo.
BR TR 6′ 4″ 210 lbs.

Year	Team	W	L	PCT	ERA	G	GS	CG	IP	H	BB	SO	ShO	Relief Pitching W	Relief Pitching L	Relief Pitching SV	Batting AB	Batting H	Batting HR	BA	PO	A	E	DP	TC/G	FA
1978	NY A	0	0	—	5.82	7	0	0	21.2	24	6	11	0	0	0	0	0	0	0	—	0	7	0	0	1.0	1.000
1979		0	0	—	∞	1	0	0		7	0	0	0	0	0	0	0	0	0	—	0	0	0	0	0.0	.000
2 yrs.		0	0		9.14	8	0	0	21.2	31	6	11	0	0	0	0	0	0	0		0	7	0	0	0.9	1.000

Ike Kamp

KAMP, ALPHONSE FRANCIS
B. Sept. 5, 1900, Roxbury, Mass. D. Feb. 25, 1955, Boston, Mass.
BB TL 6′ 170 lbs.

Year	Team	W	L	PCT	ERA	G	GS	CG	IP	H	BB	SO	ShO	Relief Pitching W	Relief Pitching L	Relief Pitching SV	Batting AB	Batting H	Batting HR	BA	PO	A	E	DP	TC/G	FA
1924	BOS N	0	1	.000	5.14	1	1	0	7	9	5	4	0	0	0	0	1	0	0	.000	0	3	0	0	3.0	1.000
1925		2	4	.333	5.09	24	4	1	58.1	68	35	20	0	1	2	0	12	2	0	.167	4	14	1	1	0.8	.947
2 yrs.		2	5	.286	5.10	25	5	1	65.1	77	40	24	0	1	2	0	13	2	0	.154	4	17	1	1	0.9	.955

Harry Kane

KANE, HARRY (Klondike)
Born Harry Cohen.
B. July 27, 1883, Hamburg, Ark. D. Sept. 15, 1932, Portland, Ore.
BL TL

Year	Team	W	L	PCT	ERA	G	GS	CG	IP	H	BB	SO	ShO	Relief Pitching W	Relief Pitching L	Relief Pitching SV	Batting AB	Batting H	Batting HR	BA	PO	A	E	DP	TC/G	FA
1902	STL A	0	1	.000	5.48	4	1	1	23	34	16	7	0	0	0	0	9	1	0	.111	1	6	0	0	1.8	1.000
1903	DET A	0	2	.000	8.50	3	3	2	18	26	8	10	0	0	0	0	7	1	0	.143	0	3	1	0	1.3	.750
1905	PHI N	1	1	.500	1.59	2	2	2	17	12	8	12	1	0	0	0	6	1	0	.167	1	2	0	0	1.5	1.000
1906		1	3	.250	3.86	6	3	2	28	28	18	14	0	1	1	0	8	0	0	.000	2	9	0	0	1.8	1.000
4 yrs.		2	7	.222	4.81	15	9	7	86	100	50	43	1	1	1	0	30	3	0	.100	4	20	1	0	1.7	.960

Erv Kantlehner

KANTLEHNER, ERVING LESLIE BL TL 6′ 190 lbs.
B. July 31, 1892, San Jose, Calif. D. Feb. 3, 1990, Santa Barbara, Calif.

Year	Team	W	L	PCT	ERA	G	GS	CG	IP	H	BB	SO	ShO	Relief Pitching W	Relief Pitching L	Relief Pitching SV	Batting AB	Batting H	Batting HR	BA	PO	A	E	DP	TC/G	FA
1914	PIT N	3	2	.600	3.09	21	5	3	67	51	39	26	2	0	1	0	15	1	0	.067	3	17	2	1	1.0	.909
1915		5	12	.294	2.26	29	18	10	163	135	58	64	1	1	2	2	52	15	0	.288	3	49	1	1	1.8	.981
1916	2 teams PIT N (34G 5–15) PHI N (3G 0–0)																									
″	total	5	15	.250	3.30	37	21	7	169	158	60	51	2	2	3	2	46	8	0	.174	8	53	3	2	1.7	.953
3 yrs.		13	29	.310	2.84	87	44	20	399	344	157	141	5	3	6	4	113	24	0	.212	14	119	6	4	1.6	.957

Matt Karchner

KARCHNER, MATTHEW DEAN BR TR 6′ 4″ 245 lbs.
B. June 28, 1967, Berwick, Pa.

Year	Team	W	L	PCT	ERA	G	GS	CG	IP	H	BB	SO	ShO	Relief Pitching W	Relief Pitching L	Relief Pitching SV	Batting AB	Batting H	Batting HR	BA	PO	A	E	DP	TC/G	FA
1995	CHI A	4	2	.667	1.69	31	0	0	32	33	12	24	0	4	2	0	0	0	0	—	6	3	0	2	0.3	1.000

Paul Kardow

KARDOW, PAUL OTTO (Tex) BR TR 6′ 6″ 210 lbs.
B. Sept. 19, 1915, Humble, Tex. D. Apr. 27, 1968, San Antonio, Tex.

Year	Team	W	L	PCT	ERA	G	GS	CG	IP	H	BB	SO	ShO	Relief Pitching W	Relief Pitching L	Relief Pitching SV	Batting AB	Batting H	Batting HR	BA	PO	A	E	DP	TC/G	FA
1936	CLE A	0	0	—	4.50	2	0	0	2	1	2	0	0	0	0	0	0	0	0	—	0	0	0	0	0.0	.000

Ed Karger

KARGER, EDWIN (Loose) BR TL 5′11″ 185 lbs.
B. May 6, 1883, San Angelo, Tex. D. Sept. 9, 1957, Delta, Colo.

Year	Team	W	L	PCT	ERA	G	GS	CG	IP	H	BB	SO	ShO	Relief Pitching W	Relief Pitching L	Relief Pitching SV	Batting AB	Batting H	Batting HR	BA	PO	A	E	DP	TC/G	FA
1906	2 teams PIT N (6G 2–3) STL N (25G 5–16)																									
″	total	7	19	.269	2.62	31	22	17	219.2	214	52	81	0	1	**4**	1	84	18	1	.214	21	81	5	2	3.5	.953
1907	STL N	15	19	.441	2.03	38	32	28	310	251	64	132	6	1	2	1	111	19	2	.171	29	96	6	4	3.4	.954
1908		4	9	.308	3.06	22	15	9	141.1	148	50	34	1	0	0	0	54	13	0	.241	10	33	2	5	2.0	.956
1909	2 teams CIN N (9G 1–3) BOS A (12G 5–2)																									
″	total	6	5	.545	3.61	21	11	4	102.1	97	52	25	0	2	2	0	35	6	0	.171	5	33	6	0	2.1	.864
1910	BOS A	11	7	.611	3.19	27	25	16	183.1	162	53	81	1	0	0	1	68	20	2	.294	7	47	2	2	2.1	.964
1911		5	8	.385	3.37	25	18	6	131	134	42	57	1	0	0	0	47	11	1	.234	6	35	3	2	1.8	.932
6 yrs.		48	67	.417	2.79	164	123	80	1087.2	1006	313	410	9	4	8	3	399	87	6	.218	78	325	24	15	2.6	.944

Andy Karl

KARL, ANTON ANDREW BR TR 6′ 1½″ 175 lbs.
B. Apr. 8, 1914, Mount Vernon, N. Y. D. Apr. 8, 1989, La Jolla, Calif.

Year	Team	W	L	PCT	ERA	G	GS	CG	IP	H	BB	SO	ShO	Relief Pitching W	Relief Pitching L	Relief Pitching SV	Batting AB	Batting H	Batting HR	BA	PO	A	E	DP	TC/G	FA
1943	2 teams BOS A (11G 1–1) PHI N (9G 1–2)																									
″	total	2	3	.400	5.30	20	2	0	52.2	75	24	10	0	2	1	1	15	4	0	.267	6	19	1	0	1.3	.962
1944	PHI N	3	2	.600	2.33	38	0	0	89	76	21	26	0	3	2	2	15	3	0	.200	4	22	0	0	0.7	1.000
1945		9	8	.529	2.99	**67**	2	1	180.2	175	50	51	0	9	6	**15**	49	7	0	.143	10	38	2	3	0.7	.960
1946		3	7	.300	4.96	39	0	0	65.1	84	22	15	0	3	**7**	5	10	1	0	.100	3	17	0	0	0.5	1.000
1947	BOS N	2	3	.400	3.86	27	0	0	35	41	13	5	0	2	3	3	6	1	0	.167	5	13	0	2	0.7	1.000
5 yrs.		19	23	.452	3.51	191	4	1	422.2	451	130	107	0	19	19	26	95	16	0	.168	28	109	3	5	0.7	.979

Scott Karl

KARL, RANDALL SCOTT BL TL 6′ 2″ 195 lbs.
B. Aug. 9, 1971, Fontana, Calif.

Year	Team	W	L	PCT	ERA	G	GS	CG	IP	H	BB	SO	ShO	Relief Pitching W	Relief Pitching L	Relief Pitching SV	Batting AB	Batting H	Batting HR	BA	PO	A	E	DP	TC/G	FA
1995	MIL A	6	7	.462	4.14	25	18	1	124	141	50	59	0	0	0	0	0	0	0	—	5	21	3	3	1.2	.897

Bill Karns

KARNS, WILLIAM ARTHUR BL TL
B. Dec. 28, 1875, Richmond, Iowa D. Nov. 15, 1941, Seattle, Wash.

Year	Team	W	L	PCT	ERA	G	GS	CG	IP	H	BB	SO	ShO	Relief Pitching W	Relief Pitching L	Relief Pitching SV	Batting AB	Batting H	Batting HR	BA	PO	A	E	DP	TC/G	FA
1901	BAL A	1	0	1.000	6.35	3	1	1	17	30	9	5	0	0	0	0	7	1	0	.143	1	3	0	0	1.3	1.000

Ryan Karp

KARP, RYAN JASON BL TL 6′ 4″ 217 lbs.
B. Apr. 5, 1970, Los Angeles, Calif.

Year	Team	W	L	PCT	ERA	G	GS	CG	IP	H	BB	SO	ShO	Relief Pitching W	Relief Pitching L	Relief Pitching SV	Batting AB	Batting H	Batting HR	BA	PO	A	E	DP	TC/G	FA
1995	PHI N	0	0	—	4.50	1	0	0	2	1	3	2	0	0	0	0	0	0	0	—	0	0	0	0	0.0	.000

Herb Karpel

KARPEL, HERBERT (Lefty) BL TL 5′ 9½″ 180 lbs.
B. Dec. 27, 1917, Brooklyn, N. Y.

Year	Team	W	L	PCT	ERA	G	GS	CG	IP	H	BB	SO	ShO	Relief Pitching W	Relief Pitching L	Relief Pitching SV	Batting AB	Batting H	Batting HR	BA	PO	A	E	DP	TC/G	FA
1946	NY A	0	0	—	10.80	2	0	0	1.2	4	0	0	0	0	0	0	0	0	0	—	0	0	0	0	0.0	.000

Benn Karr

KARR, BENJAMIN JOYCE (Baldy) BL TR 6′ 175 lbs.
B. Nov. 28, 1893, Mt. Pleasant, Miss. D. Dec. 8, 1968, Memphis, Tenn.

Year	Team	W	L	PCT	ERA	G	GS	CG	IP	H	BB	SO	ShO	Relief Pitching W	Relief Pitching L	Relief Pitching SV	Batting AB	Batting H	Batting HR	BA	PO	A	E	DP	TC/G	FA
1920	BOS A	3	8	.273	4.81	26	2	0	91.2	109	24	21	0	3	**6**	1	75	21	1	.280	5	18	2	0	1.0	.920
1921		8	7	.533	3.67	26	7	5	117.2	123	38	37	0	**5**	3	0	62	16	0	.258	2	30	2	0	1.3	.941
1922		5	12	.294	4.47	41	13	7	183.1	212	45	41	0	0	5	1	98	21	0	.214	9	44	5	3	1.4	.914
1925	CLE A	11	12	.478	4.78	32	24	12	197.2	248	80	41	1	5	1	0	92	24	1	.261	14	57	4	5	2.3	.947
1926		5	6	.455	5.00	30	7	4	113.1	137	41	23	0	2	4	1	45	10	0	.222	6	35	2	0	1.4	.953
1927		3	3	.500	5.05	22	5	1	76.2	92	32	17	0	1	0	2	20	4	0	.200	4	29	2	0	1.6	.943
6 yrs.		35	48	.422	4.60	177	58	29	780.1	921	260	180	1	16	19	5	*				40	213	17	8	1.5	.937

Steve Karsay

KARSAY, STEFAN ANDREW BR TR 6′ 3″ 210 lbs.
B. Mar. 24, 1972, Flushing, N. Y.

Year	Team	W	L	PCT	ERA	G	GS	CG	IP	H	BB	SO	ShO	Relief Pitching W	Relief Pitching L	Relief Pitching SV	Batting AB	Batting H	Batting HR	BA	PO	A	E	DP	TC/G	FA
1993	OAK A	3	3	.500	4.04	8	8	0	49	49	16	33	0	0	0	0	0	0	0	—	2	3	0	0	0.6	1.000
1994		1	1	.500	2.57	4	4	1	28	26	8	15	0	0	0	0	0	0	0	—	3	4	0	0	1.8	1.000
2 yrs.		4	4	.500	3.51	12	12	1	77	75	24	48	0	0	0	0	0	0	0		5	7	0	0	1.0	1.000

John Katoll

KATOLL, JOHN (Katy) BR TR 5′11″ 195 lbs.
B. June 24, 1872, Germany D. June 18, 1955, Hartland, Ill.

Year	Team	W	L	PCT	ERA	G	GS	CG	IP	H	BB	SO	ShO	Relief Pitching W	Relief Pitching L	Relief Pitching SV	Batting AB	Batting H	Batting HR	BA	PO	A	E	DP	TC/G	FA
1898	CHI N	0	1	.000	0.82	2	1	1	11	8	1	3	0	0	0	0	4	0	0	.000	0	2	0	0	1.0	1.000
1899		1	1	.500	6.00	2	2	2	18	17	4	1	0	0	0	0	7	0	0	.000	0	6	2	0	4.0	.750
1901	CHI A	11	10	.524	2.81	27	25	19	208	231	53	59	0	0	0	0	80	10	1	.125	11	71	8	1	3.3	.911
1902	2 teams CHI A (1G 0–0) BAL A (15G 5–10)																									
″	total	5	10	.333	3.99	16	13	13	124	176	32	27	0	2	0	0	58	10	0	.172	12	55	6	0	3.8	.918
4 yrs.		17	22	.436	3.32	47	41	35	361	432	90	90	0	2	0	0	149	20	1	.134	23	134	16	1	3.5	.908

Bob Katz

KATZ, ROBERT CLYDE BR TR 5′11½″ 190 lbs.
B. Jan. 30, 1911, Lancaster, Pa. D. Dec. 14, 1962, St. Joseph, Mich.

Year	Team	W	L	PCT	ERA	G	GS	CG	IP	H	BB	SO	ShO	Relief Pitching W	Relief Pitching L	Relief Pitching SV	Batting AB	Batting H	Batting HR	BA	PO	A	E	DP	TC/G	FA
1944	CIN N	0	1	.000	3.93	6	2	0	18.1	17	7	4	0	0	0	0	4	0	0	.000	1	6	0	1	1.2	1.000

Curt Kaufman

KAUFMAN, CURT GERRARD BR TR 6′ 2″ 175 lbs.
B. July 19, 1957, Omaha, Neb.

Year	Team		W	L	PCT	ERA	G	GS	CG	IP	H	BB	SO	ShO	Relief Pitching W	L	SV	Batting AB	H	HR	BA	PO	A	E	DP	TC/G	FA
1982	NY	A	1	0	1.000	5.19	7	0	0	8.2	9	6	1	0	1	0	0	0	0	0	—	1	0	0	0	0.1	1.000
1983			0	0	—	3.12	4	0	0	8.2	10	4	8	0	0	0	0	0	0	0	—	0	1	0	0	0.3	1.000
1984	CAL	A	2	3	.400	4.57	29	1	0	69	68	20	41	0	2	3	1	0	0	0	—	1	12	0	2	0.4	1.000
3 yrs.			3	3	.500	4.48	40	1	0	86.1	87	30	50	0	3	3	1	0	0	0		2	13	0	2	0.4	1.000

Tony Kaufmann

KAUFMANN, ANTHONY CHARLES BR TR 5′11″ 165 lbs.
B. Dec. 16, 1900, Chicago, Ill. D. June 4, 1982, Elgin, Ill.

Year	Team		W	L	PCT	ERA	G	GS	CG	IP	H	BB	SO	ShO	Relief Pitching W	L	SV	Batting AB	H	HR	BA	PO	A	E	DP	TC/G	FA
1921	CHI	N	1	0	1.000	4.15	2	1	1	13	12	3	6	0	0	0	1	5	2	0	.400	0	1	0	0	0.5	1.000
1922			7	13	.350	4.06	37	14	4	153	161	57	45	1	2	**6**	3	45	9	1	.200	14	28	3	0	1.2	.933
1923			14	10	.583	3.10	33	24	18	206.1	209	67	72	2	1	0	3	74	16	2	.216	9	41	2	3	1.6	.962
1924			16	11	.593	4.02	34	26	16	208.1	218	66	79	3	1	2	0	76	24	1	.316	14	38	1	3	1.6	.981
1925			13	13	.500	4.50	31	23	14	196	221	77	49	2	2	3	2	78	15	2	.192	9	43	1	6	1.7	.981
1926			9	7	.563	3.02	26	21	14	169.2	169	44	52	1	0	0	2	60	15	1	.250	4	34	0	2	1.5	1.000
1927	3 teams	CHI N	(9G 3–3)		PHI N	(5G 0–3)	STL N	(1G 0–0)																			
″	total		3	6	.333	7.84	15	11	4	72.1	116	28	25	0	0	0	0	23	6	2	.261	4	21	0	1	1.6	1.000
1928	STL	N	0	0	—	9.64	4	1	0	4.2	8	4	2	0	0	0	0	0	0	0	—	0	1	0	0	0.3	1.000
1930			0	1	.000	7.84	2	1	0	10.1	15	4	2	0	0	0	0	3	1	0	.333	27	0	1	0	1.8	.964
1931			1	1	.500	6.06	15	1	0	49	65	17	13	0	1	1	1	18	2	0	.111	2	11	1	0	0.9	.929
1935			0	0	—	2.45	3	0	0	3.2	4	1	0	0	0	0	0	0	0	0	—	0	1	0	0	0.3	1.000
11 yrs.			64	62	.508	4.18	202	123	71	1086.1	1198	368	345	9	7	12	12	414	91	9	.220	83	220	9	15	1.4	.971

Steve Kealey

KEALEY, STEVEN WILLIAM BR TR 6′ 185 lbs.
B. May 13, 1947, Torrance, Calif.

Year	Team		W	L	PCT	ERA	G	GS	CG	IP	H	BB	SO	ShO	Relief Pitching W	L	SV	Batting AB	H	HR	BA	PO	A	E	DP	TC/G	FA
1968	CAL	A	0	1	.000	2.70	6	0	0	10	10	5	4	0	0	1	0	0	0	0	—	0	0	1	0	0.2	.000
1969			2	0	1.000	3.93	15	3	1	36.2	48	13	17	1	1	0	0	9	0	0	.000	1	2	0	0	0.2	1.000
1970			1	0	1.000	4.09	17	0	0	22	19	6	14	0	1	0	1	4	1	0	.250	0	1	1	0	0.1	.500
1971	CHI	A	2	2	.500	3.86	54	1	0	77	69	26	50	0	2	2	6	10	2	1	.200	5	11	2	0	0.3	.889
1972			3	2	.600	3.30	40	0	0	57.1	50	12	37	0	3	2	4	3	0	0	.000	3	6	2	0	0.3	.818
1973			0	0	—	15.09	7	0	0	11.1	23	7	4	0	0	0	0	0	0	0	—	1	0	0	0	0.1	1.000
6 yrs.			8	5	.615	4.28	139	4	1	214.1	219	69	126	1	7	5	11	26	3	1	.115	10	20	6	0	0.3	.833

Ed Keas

KEAS, EDWARD JAMES
B. Feb. 2, 1863, Dubuque, Iowa D. Jan. 12, 1940, Dubuque, Iowa.

Year	Team		W	L	PCT	ERA	G	GS	CG	IP	H	BB	SO	ShO	Relief Pitching W	L	SV	Batting AB	H	HR	BA	PO	A	E	DP	TC/G	FA
1888	CLE	AA	3	3	.500	2.29	6	6	6	51	53	12	18	0	0	0	0	23	2	0	.087	5	13	1	1	3.2	.947

Ed Keating

KEATING, ROBERT EDWARD BL TL 6′ 4″ 190 lbs.
B. Sept. 22, 1862, Springfield, Mass. D. Jan. 19, 1922, Springfield, Mass.

Year	Team		W	L	PCT	ERA	G	GS	CG	IP	H	BB	SO	ShO	Relief Pitching W	L	SV	Batting AB	H	HR	BA	PO	A	E	DP	TC/G	FA
1887	BAL	AA	0	1	.000	11.00	1	1	1	9	16	6	0	0	0	0	0	4	1	0	.250	0	4	0	0	4.0	1.000

Ray Keating

KEATING, RAYMOND HERBERT BR TR 5′11″ 185 lbs.
B. July 21, 1891, Bridgeport, Conn. D. Nov. 28, 1963, Sacramento, Calif.

Year	Team		W	L	PCT	ERA	G	GS	CG	IP	H	BB	SO	ShO	Relief Pitching W	L	SV	Batting AB	H	HR	BA	PO	A	E	DP	TC/G	FA
1912	NY	A	0	3	.000	5.80	6	5	3	35.2	36	18	21	0	0	0	0	16	6	0	.375	0	11	1	0	2.0	.917
1913			6	12	.333	3.21	28	21	9	151.1	146	51	83	2	0	0	0	43	3	0	.070	3	39	9	0	1.8	.824
1914			7	11	.389	2.96	34	25	14	210	198	67	109	0	1	0	1	71	12	0	.169	9	68	3	2	2.4	.963
1915			3	6	.333	3.63	11	10	8	79.1	66	45	37	1	1	0	0	26	4	0	.154	0	28	2	0	2.7	.933
1916			5	6	.455	3.07	14	11	6	91	91	37	35	0	0	0	0	29	7	0	.241	7	35	5	3	3.4	.894
1918			2	2	.500	3.91	15	6	1	48.1	39	30	16	0	1	0	0	16	3	0	.188	3	13	0	1	1.1	1.000
1919	BOS	N	7	11	.389	2.98	22	14	9	136	129	45	48	1	2	2	0	46	7	1	.152	7	44	1	4	2.4	.981
7 yrs.			30	51	.370	3.29	130	92	50	751.2	705	293	349	4	5	2	1	247	42	1	.170	29	238	21	10	2.2	.927

Cactus Keck

KECK, FRANK JOSEPH BR TR 5′11″ 170 lbs.
B. Jan. 13, 1899, St. Louis, Mo. D. Feb. 6, 1981, St. Louis, Mo.

Year	Team		W	L	PCT	ERA	G	GS	CG	IP	H	BB	SO	ShO	Relief Pitching W	L	SV	Batting AB	H	HR	BA	PO	A	E	DP	TC/G	FA
1922	CIN	N	7	6	.538	3.37	27	15	5	131	138	29	27	1	2	0	1	44	7	0	.159	2	17	4	2	0.9	.826
1923			3	6	.333	3.72	35	6	1	87	84	32	16	0	3	1	2	17	1	0	.059	5	25	3	1	0.9	.909
2 yrs.			10	12	.455	3.51	62	21	6	218	222	61	43	1	5	1	3	61	8	0	.131	7	42	7	3	0.9	.875

Bob Keefe

KEEFE, ROBERT FRANCIS BR TR 5′11″ 155 lbs.
B. June 16, 1882, Folsom, Calif. D. Dec. 7, 1964, Sacramento, Calif.

Year	Team		W	L	PCT	ERA	G	GS	CG	IP	H	BB	SO	ShO	Relief Pitching W	L	SV	Batting AB	H	HR	BA	PO	A	E	DP	TC/G	FA
1907	NY	A	3	5	.375	2.50	19	3	0	57.2	60	20	20	0	3	2	3	19	1	0	.053	1	20	2	0	1.2	.913
1911	CIN	N	12	13	.480	2.69	39	26	15	234.1	196	76	105	0	1	1	3	70	6	0	.086	13	36	8	1	1.5	.860
1912			1	3	.250	5.24	17	6	0	68.2	78	33	29	0	0	1	2	18	3	0	.167	3	18	4	1	1.5	.840
3 yrs.			16	21	.432	3.14	75	35	15	360.2	334	129	154	0	4	4	8	107	10	0	.093	17	74	14	2	1.4	.867

Dave Keefe

KEEFE, DAVID EDWIN BL TR 5′ 9″ 165 lbs.
B. Jan. 9, 1897, Williston, Vt. D. Feb. 4, 1978, Kansas City, Mo.

Year	Team		W	L	PCT	ERA	G	GS	CG	IP	H	BB	SO	ShO	Relief Pitching W	L	SV	Batting AB	H	HR	BA	PO	A	E	DP	TC/G	FA
1917	PHI	A	1	0	1.000	1.80	3	0	0	5	5	4	1	0	1	0	0	1	0	0	.000	0	2	0	0	0.7	1.000
1919			0	1	.000	4.00	1	1	1	9	8	3	5	0	0	0	0	3	0	0	.000	0	3	0	0	3.0	1.000
1920			6	7	.462	2.97	31	13	7	130.1	129	30	41	1	3	0	0	40	10	0	.250	4	39	3	2	1.5	.935
1921			2	9	.182	4.68	44	12	4	173	214	64	68	0	1	2	1	57	10	0	.175	5	37	7	2	1.1	.857
1922	CLE	A	0	0	—	6.19	18	1	0	36.1	47	12	11	0	0	0	0	6	2	0	.333	2	8	1	1	0.6	.909
5 yrs.			9	17	.346	4.15	97	27	12	353.2	403	113	126	1	5	2	1	107	22	0	.206	11	89	11	5	1.1	.901

George Keefe

KEEFE, GEORGE WASHINGTON BL TL 5′ 9″ 168 lbs.
B. Jan. 7, 1867, Washington, D. C. D. Aug. 24, 1935, Washington, D. C.

Year	Team		W	L	PCT	ERA	G	GS	CG	IP	H	BB	SO	ShO	Relief Pitching W	L	SV	Batting AB	H	HR	BA	PO	A	E	DP	TC/G	FA
1886	WAS	N	0	3	.000	5.17	4	4	4	31.1	28	15	5	0	0	0	0	14	0	0	.000	2	2	0	0	1.0	1.000
1887			0	1	.000	9.00	1	1	1	8	16	4	0	0	0	0	0	3	0	0	.000	0	0	1	0	1.0	.000
1888			6	7	.462	2.84	13	13	13	114	87	43	52	1	0	0	0	42	9	0	.214	2	28	2	0	2.5	.938
1889			8	18	.308	5.13	30	28	24	230	266	143	90	0	1	0	0	98	16	0	.163	6	33	3	0	1.4	.929
1890	BUF	P	6	16	.273	6.52	25	22	22	196	280	138	55	0	0	0	0	79	16	0	.203	2	49	10	1	2.4	.836
1891	WAS	AA	0	3	.000	2.68	5	4	4	37	44	17	11	0	0	0	1	14	2	0	.143	1	12	2	0	3.0	.867
6 yrs.			20	48	.294	5.05	78	72	68	616.1	721	360	213	1	1	0	1	250	43	0	.172	13	124	18	1	2.0	.884

John Keefe

KEEFE, JOHN THOMAS TL
B. July 16, 1867, Fitchburg, Mass. D. Aug. 10, 1937, Fitchburg, Mass.

Year	Team	Lg	W	L	PCT	ERA	G	GS	CG	IP	H	BB	SO	ShO	Relief W	Relief L	Relief SV	Batting AB	Batting H	HR	BA	PO	A	E	DP	TC/G	FA
1890	SYR	AA	17	**24**	.415	*4.32*	43	41	36	352.1	355	148	120	2	1	0	0	157	30	0	.191	14	71	4	2	2.1	.955

Tim Keefe

KEEFE, TIMOTHY JOHN (Sir Timothy) BR TR 5′10½″ 185 lbs.
B. Jan. 1, 1857, Cambridge, Mass. D. Apr. 23, 1933, Cambridge, Mass.
Hall of Fame 1964.

Year	Team	Lg	W	L	PCT	ERA	G	GS	CG	IP	H	BB	SO	ShO	Relief W	Relief L	Relief SV	Batting AB	Batting H	HR	BA	PO	A	E	DP	TC/G	FA
1880	TRO	N	6	6	.500	0.86	12	12	12	105	71	17	43	0	0	0	0	43	10	0	.233	7	22	0	0	2.4	1.000
1881			18	27	.400	*3.25*	45	45	45	402	442	81	103	4	0	0	0	152	35	0	.230	23	79	17	5	2.6	.857
1882			17	26	.395	*2.50*	43	42	41	375	368	81	116	1	**1**	0	0	189	43	1	.228	52	102	14	6	3.1	.917
1883	NY	AA	41	27	.603	*2.41*	**68**	**68**	**68**	**619**	486	98	**361**	5	0	0	0	259	57	0	.220	38	152	61	3	3.6	.757
1884			37	17	.685	*2.29*	58	58	57	491.2	388	75	323	4	0	0	0	213	50	3	.235	26	97	32	3	2.5	.794
1885	NY	N	32	13	.711	***1.58***	46	46	45	398	297	103	230	7	0	0	0	166	27	0	.163	30	80	13	0	2.6	.894
1886			**42**	20	.677	*2.53*	**64**	**64**	**62**	**540**	478	100	291	2	0	0	0	205	35	1	.171	29	107	15	3	2.3	.901
1887			35	19	.648	3.10	56	56	54	478.2	447	108	186	2	0	0	0	191	42	2	.220	18	102	15	1	2.3	.889
1888			**35**	12	**.745**	**1.74**	51	51	51	434.1	316	91	**333**	**8**	0	0	0	181	23	2	.127	30	79	11	1	2.3	.908
1889			28	13	.683	3.31	47	45	38	364	310	151	209	3	0	0	1	149	23	0	.154	10	78	8	3	2.0	.917
1890	NY	P	17	11	.607	3.38	30	30	23	229	228	85	88	1	0	0	0	92	10	2	.109	15	61	4	2	2.7	.950
1891	2 teams	NY N (8G 2–5)	PHI N (11G 3–6)																								
″	total		5	11	.313	4.45	19	17	13	133.1	155	55	64	0	0	0	1	50	7	0	.140	6	28	2	1	1.9	.944
1892	PHI	N	19	16	.543	2.36	39	38	31	313.1	264	100	127	2	1	0	0	117	10	1	.085	8	68	13	2	2.3	.854
1893			10	7	.588	4.40	22	22	17	178	202	79	53	0	0	0	0	79	18	0	.228	5	32	6	1	2.0	.860
14 yrs.			342	225	.603	2.62	600	594	557	5061.1	4452	1224	2527	39	2	0	2	*				297	1087	211	31	2.6	.868
			8th						**3rd**																		

Bob Keegan

KEEGAN, ROBERT CHARLES (Smiley) BR TR 6′ 2½″ 207 lbs.
B. Aug. 4, 1920, Rochester, N. Y.

Year	Team	Lg	W	L	PCT	ERA	G	GS	CG	IP	H	BB	SO	ShO	Relief W	Relief L	Relief SV	Batting AB	Batting H	HR	BA	PO	A	E	DP	TC/G	FA
1953	CHI	A	7	5	.583	2.74	22	11	4	98.2	80	33	32	2	2	0	1	28	9	0	.321	7	20	0	2	1.2	1.000
1954			16	9	.640	3.09	31	27	14	209.2	211	82	61	2	0	0	2	75	9	0	.120	5	36	1	3	1.4	.976
1955			2	5	.286	5.83	18	11	1	58.2	83	28	29	0	0	1	0	18	6	0	.333	2	11	1	0	0.8	.929
1956			5	7	.417	3.93	20	16	4	105.1	119	35	32	0	1	0	0	32	4	0	.125	6	18	1	0	1.3	.960
1957			10	8	.556	3.53	30	20	6	142.2	131	37	36	2	2	2	2	39	4	0	.103	5	23	0	1	0.9	1.000
1958			0	2	.000	6.07	14	2	0	29.2	44	18	8	0	0	2	0	4	0	0	.000	0	9	0	0	0.6	1.000
6 yrs.			40	36	.526	3.66	135	87	29	644.2	668	233	198	6	5	5	5	196	32	0	.163	25	117	3	6	1.1	.979

Ed Keegan

KEEGAN, EDWARD CHARLES BR TR 6′ 3″ 165 lbs.
B. July 8, 1939, Camden, N. J.

Year	Team	Lg	W	L	PCT	ERA	G	GS	CG	IP	H	BB	SO	ShO	Relief W	Relief L	Relief SV	Batting AB	Batting H	HR	BA	PO	A	E	DP	TC/G	FA
1959	PHI	N	0	3	.000	18.00	3	3	0	9	19	13	3	0	0	0	0	3	0	0	.000	0	1	0	0	0.3	1.000
1961	KC	A	0	0	—	4.50	6	0	0	6	6	5	3	0	0	0	1	0	0	0	—	1	0	0	0	0.2	1.000
1962	PHI	N	0	0	—	2.25	4	0	0	8	6	5	5	0	0	0	0	0	0	0	—	0	0	0	0	0.0	.000
3 yrs.			0	3	.000	9.00	13	3	0	23	31	23	11	0	0	0	1	3	0	0	.000	1	1	0	0	0.2	1.000

Burt Keeley

KEELEY, BURTON ELWOOD (Speed) BR TR 5′ 9″ 170 lbs.
B. Nov. 2, 1879, Wilmington, Ill. D. May 3, 1952, Ely, Minn.

Year	Team	Lg	W	L	PCT	ERA	G	GS	CG	IP	H	BB	SO	ShO	Relief W	Relief L	Relief SV	Batting AB	Batting H	HR	BA	PO	A	E	DP	TC/G	FA
1908	WAS	A	6	11	.353	2.97	28	17	12	169.2	173	48	68	1	0	**3**	1	49	5	0	.102	6	64	10	2	2.9	.875
1909			0	0	—	11.57	2	0	0	7	12	1	0	0	0	0	0	2	1	0	.500	0	7	0	0	3.5	1.000
2 yrs.			6	11	.353	3.31	30	17	12	176.2	185	49	68	1	0	3	1	51	6	0	.118	6	71	10	2	2.9	.885

Vic Keen

KEEN, HOWARD VICTOR BR TR 5′ 9″ 165 lbs.
B. Mar. 16, 1899, Bel Air, Md. D. Dec. 10, 1976, Salisbury, Md.

Year	Team	Lg	W	L	PCT	ERA	G	GS	CG	IP	H	BB	SO	ShO	Relief W	Relief L	Relief SV	Batting AB	Batting H	HR	BA	PO	A	E	DP	TC/G	FA
1918	PHI	A	0	1	.000	3.38	1	1	0	8	9	1	1	0	0	0	0	1	0	0	.000	0	0	0	0	0.0	.000
1921	CHI	N	0	3	.000	4.68	5	4	1	25	29	9	9	0	0	0	0	5	0	0	.000	0	7	1	1	1.6	.875
1922			1	2	.333	3.89	7	2	2	34.2	36	10	11	0	0	1	1	12	4	0	.333	0	8	1	0	1.3	.889
1923			12	8	.600	3.00	35	17	10	177	169	57	46	0	3	2	1	53	8	0	.151	5	35	3	2	1.2	.930
1924			15	14	.517	3.80	40	28	15	234.2	242	80	75	0	2	1	3	77	12	0	.156	6	42	1	1	1.2	.980
1925			2	6	.250	6.26	30	8	1	83.1	125	41	19	0	2	1	1	25	6	0	.240	1	26	1	2	0.9	.964
1926	STL	N	10	9	.526	4.56	26	21	12	152	179	42	29	1	0	1	0	53	3	0	.057	7	29	0	4	1.4	1.000
1927			2	1	.667	4.81	21	0	0	33.2	39	8	12	0	2	1	0	4	1	0	.250	1	8	0	0	0.4	1.000
8 yrs.			42	44	.488	4.11	165	81	41	748.1	828	248	202	1	9	7	6	230	34	0	.148	20	155	7	10	1.1	.962
WORLD SERIES																											
1926	STL	N	0	0	—	0.00	1	0	0	1	0	0	0	0	0	0	0	0	0	0	—	0	1	0	0	1.0	1.000

Jim Keenan

KEENAN, JAMES WILLIAM BR TR 5′10″ 186 lbs.
B. Feb. 10, 1858, New Haven, Conn. D. Sept. 21, 1926, Cincinnati, Ohio.

Year	Team	Lg	W	L	PCT	ERA	G	GS	CG	IP	H	BB	SO	ShO	Relief W	Relief L	Relief SV	Batting AB	Batting H	HR	BA	PO	A	E	DP	TC/G	FA
1884	IND	AA	0	0	—	3.00	1	0	0	3	2	0	0	0	0	0	0	249	73	3	.293	11	7	1	0	9.5	.947
1885	CIN	AA	0	0	—	*1.13*	1	0	0	8	7	1	0	0	0	0	0	132	35	1	.265	191	38	19	2	6.5	.923
1886			0	1	.000	*3.38*	2	0	0	8	8	3	2	0	0	**1**	0	148	40	3	.270	220	54	24	6	6.2	.919
3 yrs.			0	1	.000	2.37	4	0	0	19	17	4	2	0	0	1	0	*				3151	605	228	98	7.4	.943

Jim Keenan

KEENAN, JAMES WILLIAM (Sparkplug) BL TL 5′ 7″ 155 lbs.
B. May 25, 1899, Avon, N. Y. D. June 5, 1980, Seminole, Fla.

Year	Team	Lg	W	L	PCT	ERA	G	GS	CG	IP	H	BB	SO	ShO	Relief W	Relief L	Relief SV	Batting AB	Batting H	HR	BA	PO	A	E	DP	TC/G	FA
1920	PHI	N	0	0	—	3.00	1	0	0	3	3	1	2	0	0	0	0	1	0	0	.000	0	1	0	0	1.0	1.000
1921			1	2	.333	6.68	15	2	0	32.1	48	15	7	0	1	0	0	9	0	0	.000	0	6	0	0	0.4	1.000
2 yrs.			1	2	.333	6.37	16	2	0	35.1	51	16	9	0	1	0	0	10	0	0	.000	0	7	0	0	0.4	1.000

Kid Keenan

KEENAN, HARRY LEON TR 95 lbs.
B. 1875, Louisville, Ky. D. June 11, 1903, Covington, Ky.

Year	Team	Lg	W	L	PCT	ERA	G	GS	CG	IP	H	BB	SO	ShO	Relief W	Relief L	Relief SV	Batting AB	Batting H	HR	BA	PO	A	E	DP	TC/G	FA
1891	CIN	AA	0	1	.000	0.00	1	1	1	8	6	4	5	0	0	0	0	4	2	0	.500	0	1	0	0	1.0	1.000

Harry Keener

KEENER, JOSHUA HARRY (Beans) TR
B. Sept. 1869, Easton, Pa. D. Mar. 25, 1912, Easton, Pa.

Year	Team	Lg	W	L	PCT	ERA	G	GS	CG	IP	H	BB	SO	ShO	Relief W	Relief L	Relief SV	Batting AB	Batting H	HR	BA	PO	A	E	DP	TC/G	FA
1896	PHI	N	3	11	.214	5.88	16	13	11	113.1	144	39	28	0	0	1	0	51	16	0	.314	5	27	3	1	2.2	.914

Jeff Keener

KEENER, JEFFREY BRUCE
B. Jan. 14, 1959, Pana, Ill.
BL TR 6′ 180 lbs.

Year	Team	Lg	W	L	PCT	ERA	G	GS	CG	IP	H	BB	SO	ShO	Relief W	Relief L	Relief SV	Batting AB	Batting H	Batting HR	BA	PO	A	E	DP	TC/G	FA
1982	STL	N	1	1	.500	1.61	19	0	0	22.1	19	19	25	0	1	1	0	0	0	0	—	4	2	0	0	0.3	1.000
1983			0	0	—	8.31	4	0	0	4.1	6	1	4	0	0	0	0	0	0	0	—	0	1	0	0	0.3	1.000
2 yrs.			1	1	.500	2.70	23	0	0	26.2	25	20	29	0	1	1	0	0	0	0		4	3	0	0	0.3	1.000

Joe Keener

KEENER, JOSEPH DONALD
B. Apr. 21, 1953, San Pedro, Calif.
BR TR 6′ 4″ 200 lbs.

Year	Team	Lg	W	L	PCT	ERA	G	GS	CG	IP	H	BB	SO	ShO	Relief W	Relief L	Relief SV	Batting AB	Batting H	Batting HR	BA	PO	A	E	DP	TC/G	FA
1976	MON	N	0	1	.000	10.38	2	2	0	4.1	7	8	1	0	0	0	0	1	0	0	.000	0	1	0	0	0.5	1.000

Buster Keeton

KEETON, RICKEY
B. Mar. 18, 1957, Cincinnati, Ohio.
BR TR 6′ 2″ 190 lbs.

Year	Team	Lg	W	L	PCT	ERA	G	GS	CG	IP	H	BB	SO	ShO	Relief W	Relief L	Relief SV	Batting AB	Batting H	Batting HR	BA	PO	A	E	DP	TC/G	FA
1980	MIL	A	2	2	.500	4.82	5	5	0	28	35	9	8	0	0	0	0	0	0	0	—	4	3	0	1	1.4	1.000
1981			1	0	1.000	5.14	17	0	0	35	47	11	9	0	1	0	0	0	0	0	—	2	6	0	2	0.5	1.000
2 yrs.			3	2	.600	5.00	22	5	0	63	82	20	17	0	1	0	0	0	0	0		6	9	0	3	0.7	1.000

Frank Keffer

KEFFER, FRANK
B. Harrisburg, Pa. Deceased.

Year	Team	Lg	W	L	PCT	ERA	G	GS	CG	IP	H	BB	SO	ShO	Relief W	Relief L	Relief SV	Batting AB	Batting H	Batting HR	BA	PO	A	E	DP	TC/G	FA
1890	SYR	AA	1	1	.500	*5.63*	2	1	1	16	15	9	4	0	1	0	0	7	1	0	.143	1	5	1	0	3.5	.857

Chet Kehn

KEHN, CHESTER LAWRENCE
B. Oct. 30, 1921, San Diego, Calif. D. Apr. 5, 1984, San Diego, Calif.
BR TR 5′11″ 168 lbs.

Year	Team	Lg	W	L	PCT	ERA	G	GS	CG	IP	H	BB	SO	ShO	Relief W	Relief L	Relief SV	Batting AB	Batting H	Batting HR	BA	PO	A	E	DP	TC/G	FA
1942	BKN	N	0	0	—	7.04	3	1	0	7.2	8	4	3	0	0	0	0	2	2	0	1.000	2	2	0	0	1.3	1.000

Katsy Keifer

KEIFER, SHERMAN CARL (Kat)
B. Sept. 3, 1891, California, Pa. D. Feb. 19, 1927, Outwood, Ky.
BB TL

Year	Team	Lg	W	L	PCT	ERA	G	GS	CG	IP	H	BB	SO	ShO	Relief W	Relief L	Relief SV	Batting AB	Batting H	Batting HR	BA	PO	A	E	DP	TC/G	FA
1914	IND	F	1	0	1.000	2.00	1	1	1	9	6	2	2	0	0	0	0	3	1	0	.333	1	4	1	0	6.0	.833

Mike Kekich

KEKICH, MICHAEL DENNIS
B. Apr. 2, 1945, San Diego, Calif.
BR TL 6′ 1″ 196 lbs.

Year	Team	Lg	W	L	PCT	ERA	G	GS	CG	IP	H	BB	SO	ShO	Relief W	Relief L	Relief SV	Batting AB	Batting H	Batting HR	BA	PO	A	E	DP	TC/G	FA
1965	LA	N	0	1	.000	9.58	5	1	0	10.1	10	13	9	0	0	0	0	2	0	0	.000	0	0	0	0	0.0	.000
1968			2	10	.167	3.91	25	20	1	115	116	46	84	1	0	0	0	37	3	0	.081	1	17	1	0	0.8	.947
1969	NY	A	4	6	.400	4.54	28	13	1	105	91	49	66	0	1	0	1	27	3	0	.111	5	10	1	0	0.6	.938
1970			6	3	.667	4.82	26	14	1	99	103	55	63	0	0	0	0	32	3	0	.094	5	10	2	0	0.7	.882
1971			10	9	.526	4.08	37	24	3	170	167	82	93	0	2	0	0	52	8	0	.154	5	37	0	1	1.1	1.000
1972			10	13	.435	3.70	29	28	2	175.1	172	76	78	0	0	0	0	59	8	0	.136	4	26	0	3	1.0	1.000
1973	2 teams	NY A (5G 1–1) CLE A (16G 1–4)																									
″	total		2	5	.286	7.52	21	10	0	64.2	93	49	30	0	0	0	0	0	0	0		1	4	1	1	0.3	.833
1975	TEX	A	0	0	—	3.73	23	0	0	31.1	33	21	19	0	0	0	2	0	0	0	—	0	9	0	0	0.4	1.000
1977	SEA	A	5	4	.556	5.60	41	2	0	90	90	51	55	0	5	2	3	0	0	0	—	1	14	0	0	0.4	1.000
9 yrs.			39	51	.433	4.59	235	112	8	860.2	875	442	497	1	8	2	6	209	25	0	.120	22	127	5	5	0.7	.968

George Kelb

KELB, GEORGE FRANCIS (Lefty, Pugger)
B. July 17, 1870, Toledo, Ohio D. Oct. 20, 1936, Toledo, Ohio.
BL TL

Year	Team	Lg	W	L	PCT	ERA	G	GS	CG	IP	H	BB	SO	ShO	Relief W	Relief L	Relief SV	Batting AB	Batting H	Batting HR	BA	PO	A	E	DP	TC/G	FA
1898	CLE	N	0	1	.000	4.41	3	1	1	16.1	23	1	8	0	0	0	0	5	1	0	.200	1	3	0	0	1.3	1.000

Hal Kelleher

KELLEHER, HAROLD JOSEPH
B. June 24, 1914, Philadelphia, Pa. D. Aug. 27, 1989, Cape May Court House, N. J.
BR TR 6′ 165 lbs.

Year	Team	Lg	W	L	PCT	ERA	G	GS	CG	IP	H	BB	SO	ShO	Relief W	Relief L	Relief SV	Batting AB	Batting H	Batting HR	BA	PO	A	E	DP	TC/G	FA
1935	PHI	N	2	0	1.000	1.80	3	3	2	25	26	12	12	1	0	0	0	8	3	0	.375	2	6	1	0	3.0	.889
1936			0	5	.000	5.32	14	4	1	44	60	29	13	0	0	2	0	12	2	0	.167	1	11	1	0	0.9	.923
1937			2	4	.333	6.63	27	2	1	58.1	72	31	20	0	2	2	0	17	3	0	.176	3	12	2	1	0.6	.882
1938			0	0	—	18.41	6	0	0	7.1	16	9	4	0	0	0	0	2	1	0	.500	1	2	0	1	0.5	1.000
4 yrs.			4	9	.308	5.95	50	9	4	134.2	174	81	49	1	2	4	0	39	9	0	.231	7	31	4	2	0.8	.905

Ron Keller

KELLER, RONALD LEE
B. June 3, 1943, Indianapolis, Ind.
BR TR 6′ 2″ 200 lbs.

Year	Team	Lg	W	L	PCT	ERA	G	GS	CG	IP	H	BB	SO	ShO	Relief W	Relief L	Relief SV	Batting AB	Batting H	Batting HR	BA	PO	A	E	DP	TC/G	FA
1966	MIN	A	0	0	—	5.06	2	0	0	5.1	7	1	1	0	0	0	0	1	0	0	.000	0	1	0	0	0.5	1.000
1968			0	1	.000	2.81	7	1	0	16	18	4	11	0	0	0	0	1	0	0	.000	2	2	0	0	0.6	1.000
2 yrs.			0	1	.000	3.38	9	1	0	21.1	25	5	12	0	0	0	0	2	0	0	.000	2	3	0	0	0.6	1.000

Al Kellett

KELLETT, ALFRED HENRY
B. Oct. 30, 1901, Red Bank, N. J. D. July 14, 1960, New York, N. Y.
BR TR 6′ 3″ 200 lbs.

Year	Team	Lg	W	L	PCT	ERA	G	GS	CG	IP	H	BB	SO	ShO	Relief W	Relief L	Relief SV	Batting AB	Batting H	Batting HR	BA	PO	A	E	DP	TC/G	FA
1923	PHI	A	0	1	.000	6.30	5	0	0	10	11	8	1	0	0	1	0	3	1	0	.333	1	6	0	0	1.4	1.000
1924	BOS	A	0	0	—	∞	1	0	0		0	2	0	0	0	0	0	0	0	0	—	0	0	0	0	0.0	.000
2 yrs.			0	1	.000	8.10	6	0	0	10	11	10	1	0	0	1	0	3	1	0	.333	1	6	0	0	1.2	1.000

Dick Kelley

KELLEY, RICHARD ANTHONY
B. Jan. 8, 1940, Brighton, Mass. D. Dec. 12, 1991, Northridge, Calif.
BR TL 5′11½″ 174 lbs.

Year	Team	Lg	W	L	PCT	ERA	G	GS	CG	IP	H	BB	SO	ShO	Relief W	Relief L	Relief SV	Batting AB	Batting H	Batting HR	BA	PO	A	E	DP	TC/G	FA
1964	MIL	N	0	0	—	18.00	2	0	0	2	2	3	2	0	0	0	0	0	0	0	—	0	0	0	0	0.0	.000
1965			1	1	.500	3.00	21	4	0	45	37	20	31	0	1	0	0	8	0	0	.000	1	8	1	0	0.5	.900
1966	ATL	N	7	5	.583	3.22	20	13	2	81	75	21	50	2	0	1	0	28	1	0	.036	0	8	2	1	0.5	.800
1967			2	9	.182	3.77	39	9	1	98	88	42	75	1	1	4	2	16	4	0	.250	5	20	0	1	0.6	1.000
1968			2	4	.333	2.75	31	11	1	98.1	86	45	73	1	0	0	1	23	1	0	.043	7	20	1	3	0.9	.964
1969	SD	N	4	8	.333	3.57	27	23	1	136	113	61	96	1	0	0	0	47	5	0	.106	9	27	0	1	1.3	1.000
1971			2	3	.400	3.45	48	1	0	60	52	23	42	0	1	3	2	3	1	0	.333	5	8	0	1	0.3	1.000
7 yrs.			18	30	.375	3.39	188	61	5	520.1	453	215	369	5	3	8	5	125	12	0	.096	27	91	4	7	0.6	.967

Harry Kelley

KELLEY, HARRY LEROY
B. Feb. 13, 1906, Parkin, Ark. D. Mar. 23, 1958, Parkin, Ark.
BR TR 5′ 9½″ 170 lbs.

Year	Team	Lg	W	L	PCT	ERA	G	GS	CG	IP	H	BB	SO	ShO	Relief W	Relief L	Relief SV	Batting AB	Batting H	Batting HR	BA	PO	A	E	DP	TC/G	FA
1925	WAS	A	1	1	.500	9.00	6	1	0	16	30	12	7	0	1	0	0	4	0	0	.000	1	6	0	0	1.2	1.000
1926			0	0	—	8.10	7	1	0	10	17	8	6	0	0	0	0	1	0	0	.000	1	1	0	1	0.3	1.000
1936	PHI	A	15	12	.556	3.86	35	27	20	235.1	250	75	82	1	2	2	3	91	18	0	.198	5	36	3	3	1.3	.932

Harry Kelley *continued*

Year	Team	W	L	PCT	ERA	G	GS	CG	IP	H	BB	SO	ShO	Relief W	Relief L	SV	AB	H	HR	BA	PO	A	E	DP	TC/G	FA
1937		13	**21**	.382	5.36	41	29	14	205	267	79	68	0	4	3	0	71	16	0	.225	10	32	0	2	1.0	1.000
1938	**2 teams** **PHI A** (4G 0–2) **WAS A** (38G 9–8)																									
"	**total**	9	10	.474	5.12	42	17	7	156.1	179	56	47	2	2	1	1	50	12	0	.240	11	30	4	2	1.1	.911
1939	**WAS A**	4	3	.571	4.70	15	3	2	53.2	69	14	20	0	2	2	1	15	4	0	.267	1	9	1	0	0.7	.909
6 yrs.		42	47	.472	4.86	146	78	43	676.1	812	244	230	3	11	8	5	232	50	0	.216	29	114	8	8	1.0	.947

Tom Kelley

KELLEY, THOMAS HENRY BR TR 6′ 185 lbs.
B. Jan. 5, 1944, Manchester, Conn.

Year	Team	W	L	PCT	ERA	G	GS	CG	IP	H	BB	SO	ShO	Relief W	Relief L	SV	AB	H	HR	BA	PO	A	E	DP	TC/G	FA
1964	**CLE A**	0	0	—	5.59	6	0	0	9.2	9	9	7	0	0	0	0	0	0	0	—	1	2	1	0	0.7	.750
1965		2	1	.667	2.40	4	4	1	30	19	13	31	0	0	0	0	9	2	0	.222	1	3	0	1	1.0	1.000
1966		4	8	.333	4.34	31	7	1	95.1	97	42	64	0	3	4	0	28	4	0	.143	8	8	1	0	0.5	.941
1967		0	0	—	0.00	1	0	0	1	0	2	0	0	0	0	0	0	0	0	—	1	1	0	1	2.0	1.000
1971	**ATL N**	9	5	.643	2.96	28	20	5	143	140	69	68	0	0	0	0	43	2	0	.047	11	18	0	2	1.0	1.000
1972		5	7	.417	4.58	27	14	2	116	122	65	59	1	0	0	0	34	3	0	.088	4	6	1	0	0.4	.909
1973		0	1	.000	2.77	7	0	0	13	13	7	5	0	0	1	0	2	0	0	.000	0	1	0	0	0.1	1.000
7 yrs.		20	22	.476	3.75	104	45	9	408	400	207	234	1	3	5	0	116	11	0	.095	26	39	3	4	0.7	.956

Alex Kellner

KELLNER, ALEXANDER RAYMOND BR TL 6′ 200 lbs.
Brother of Walt Kellner.
B. Aug. 26, 1924, Tucson, Ariz.

Year	Team	W	L	PCT	ERA	G	GS	CG	IP	H	BB	SO	ShO	Relief W	Relief L	SV	AB	H	HR	BA	PO	A	E	DP	TC/G	FA
1948	**PHI A**	0	0	—	7.83	13	1	0	23	21	16	14	0	0	0	0	5	0	0	.000	0	2	0	0	0.2	1.000
1949		20	12	.625	3.75	38	27	19	245	243	129	94	0	4	2	1	92	20	0	.217	9	46	3	4	1.5	.948
1950		8	**20**	.286	5.47	36	29	15	225.1	253	112	85	0	0	1	2	80	16	0	.200	13	27	3	2	1.2	.930
1951		11	**14**	.440	4.46	33	29	11	209.2	218	93	94	1	0	1	2	79	18	0	.228	15	31	2	3	1.5	.958
1952		12	14	.462	4.36	34	33	14	231.1	223	86	105	2	0	0	0	82	17	1	.207	17	28	0	4	1.3	1.000
1953		11	12	.478	3.93	25	25	14	201.2	210	51	81	2	0	0	0	69	15	0	.217	5	28	2	2	1.4	.943
1954		6	17	.261	5.39	27	27	8	173.2	204	88	69	1	0	0	0	55	10	0	.182	6	32	0	2	1.4	1.000
1955	**KC A**	11	8	.579	4.20	30	24	6	162.2	164	60	75	3	0	1	0	56	12	0	.214	4	30	3	2	1.2	.919
1956		7	4	.636	4.32	20	17	5	91.2	103	33	44	0	1	0	0	30	6	0	.200	1	17	1	2	0.9	.947
1957		6	5	.545	4.27	28	21	3	132.2	141	41	72	0	0	0	0	47	11	3	.234	5	24	2	4	1.1	.935
1958	**2 teams** **KC A** (7G 0–2) **CIN N** (18G 7–3)																									
"	**total**	7	5	.583	3.35	25	13	4	115.2	114	28	64	0	3	0	0	39	11	0	.282	5	11	0	2	0.6	1.000
1959	**STL N**	2	1	.667	3.16	12	4	0	37	31	10	19	0	1	0	0	9	2	0	.222	3	4	1	0	0.7	.875
12 yrs.		101	112	.474	4.41	321	250	99	1849.1	1925	747	816	9	9	5	5	643	138	4	.215	83	280	17	27	1.2	.955

Walt Kellner

KELLNER, WALTER JOSEPH BR TR 6′ 200 lbs.
Brother of Alex Kellner.
B. Apr. 26, 1929, Tucson, Ariz.

Year	Team	W	L	PCT	ERA	G	GS	CG	IP	H	BB	SO	ShO	Relief W	Relief L	SV	AB	H	HR	BA	PO	A	E	DP	TC/G	FA
1952	**PHI A**	0	0	—	6.75	1	0	0	4	4	3	2	0	0	0	1	1	0	0	.000	0	0	0	0	0.0	.000
1953		0	0	—	6.00	2	0	0	3	1	4	4	0	0	0	0	0	0	0	—	0	1	0	1	0.5	1.000
2 yrs.		0	0		6.43	3	0	0	7	5	7	6	0	0	0	1	1	0	0	.000	0	1	0	1	0.3	1.000

Al Kellogg

KELLOGG, ALBERT CLEMENT TL 6′ 3″ 208 lbs.
B. Sept. 9, 1886, Providence, R. I. D. July 21, 1953, Portland, Ore.

Year	Team	W	L	PCT	ERA	G	GS	CG	IP	H	BB	SO	ShO	Relief W	Relief L	SV	AB	H	HR	BA	PO	A	E	DP	TC/G	FA
1908	**PHI A**	0	2	.000	5.82	3	3	2	17	20	9	8	0	0	0	0	8	1	0	.125	0	8	2	0	3.3	.800

Win Kellum

KELLUM, WINFORD ANSLEY BB TL 5′10″ 190 lbs.
B. Apr. 11, 1876, Waterford, Ont., Canada D. Aug. 10, 1951, Big Rapids, Mich.

Year	Team	W	L	PCT	ERA	G	GS	CG	IP	H	BB	SO	ShO	Relief W	Relief L	SV	AB	H	HR	BA	PO	A	E	DP	TC/G	FA
1901	**BOS A**	2	3	.400	6.38	6	6	5	48	61	7	8	0	0	0	0	18	3	0	.167	2	18	0	0	3.3	1.000
1904	**CIN N**	15	10	.600	2.60	31	24	22	224.2	206	46	70	1	**2**	1	2	82	13	0	.159	21	64	2	1	2.4	.977
1905	**STL N**	3	3	.500	2.92	11	7	5	74	70	10	19	1	0	1	0	25	5	0	.200	2	28	1	0	2.8	.968
3 yrs.		20	16	.556	3.19	48	37	32	346.2	337	63	97	2	2	2	2	125	21	0	.168	25	110	3	1	2.6	.978

Bob Kelly

KELLY, ROBERT EDWARD BR TR 6′ 180 lbs.
B. Oct. 4, 1927, Cleveland, Ohio.

Year	Team	W	L	PCT	ERA	G	GS	CG	IP	H	BB	SO	ShO	Relief W	Relief L	SV	AB	H	HR	BA	PO	A	E	DP	TC/G	FA
1951	**CHI N**	7	4	.636	4.66	35	11	4	123.2	130	55	48	0	2	0	0	31	5	0	.161	13	20	2	1	1.0	.943
1952		4	9	.308	3.59	31	15	3	125.1	114	46	50	2	0	3	0	37	8	0	.216	8	27	2	1	1.2	.946
1953	**2 teams** **CHI N** (14G 0–1) **CIN N** (28G 1–2)																									
"	**total**	1	3	.250	5.40	42	5	0	83.1	98	35	35	0	0	2	2	18	2	0	.111	3	18	1	2	0.5	.955
1958	**2 teams** **CIN N** (2G 0–0) **CLE A** (13G 0–2)																									
"	**total**	0	2	.000	5.16	15	4	0	29.2	32	16	13	0	0	1	0	4	1	0	.250	0	6	0	1	0.4	1.000
4 yrs.		12	18	.400	4.50	123	35	7	362	374	152	146	2	2	6	2	90	16	0	.178	24	71	5	5	0.8	.950

Bryan Kelly

KELLY, BRYAN KEITH BR TR 6′ 2″ 195 lbs.
B. Feb. 24, 1959, Silver Spring, Md.

Year	Team	W	L	PCT	ERA	G	GS	CG	IP	H	BB	SO	ShO	Relief W	Relief L	SV	AB	H	HR	BA	PO	A	E	DP	TC/G	FA
1986	**DET A**	1	2	.333	4.50	6	4	0	20	21	10	18	0	0	1	0	0	0	0	—	2	4	1	0	1.2	.857
1987		0	1	.000	5.06	5	0	0	10.2	12	7	10	0	0	1	0	0	0	0	—	0	0	0	0	0.0	.000
2 yrs.		1	3	.250	4.70	11	4	0	30.2	33	17	28	0	0	2	0	0	0	0		2	4	1	0	0.6	.857

Ed Kelly

KELLY, EDWARD LEO BR TR 5′11½″ 173 lbs.
B. Dec. 10, 1888, Pawtucket, R. I. D. Nov. 4, 1928, Red Lodge, Mont.

Year	Team	W	L	PCT	ERA	G	GS	CG	IP	H	BB	SO	ShO	Relief W	Relief L	SV	AB	H	HR	BA	PO	A	E	DP	TC/G	FA
1914	**BOS A**	0	0	—	0.00	3	0	0	2.1	1	1	4	0	0	0	0	1	0	0	.000	0	1	0	0	0.3	1.000

George Kelly

KELLY, GEORGE LANGE (Highpockets) BR TR 6′ 4″ 190 lbs.
Brother of Ren Kelly.
B. Sept. 10, 1895, San Francisco, Calif. D. Oct. 13, 1984, Burlingame, Calif.
Hall of Fame 1973.

Year	Team	W	L	PCT	ERA	G	GS	CG	IP	H	BB	SO	ShO	Relief W	Relief L	SV	AB	H	HR	BA	PO	A	E	DP	TC/G	FA
1917	**NY N**	1	0	1.000	0.00	1	0	0	5	4	1	2	0	1	0	0	*				62	4	2	1	5.2	.971

Herb Kelly

KELLY, HERBERT BARRETT
B. June 4, 1892, Mobile, Ala. D. May 18, 1973, Torrance, Calif.
BL TL 5′ 9″ 160 lbs.

Year	Team		W	L	PCT	ERA	G	GS	CG	IP	H	BB	SO	ShO	Relief W	Relief L	Relief SV	Batting AB	Batting H	HR	BA	PO	A	E	DP	TC/G	FA
1914	PIT	N	0	2	.000	2.45	5	2	2	25.2	24	7	6	0	0	0	0	9	2	0	.222	2	6	0	0	1.6	1.000
1915			1	1	.500	4.09	5	1	0	11	10	4	6	0	1	0	0	2	1	0	.500	1	8	1	1	2.0	.900
2 yrs.			1	3	.250	2.95	10	3	2	36.2	34	11	12	0	1	0	0	11	3	0	.273	3	14	1	1	1.8	.944

King Kelly

KELLY, MICHAEL JOSEPH
B. Dec. 31, 1857, Troy, N. Y. D. Nov. 8, 1894, Boston, Mass.
Manager 1887, 1890–91.
Hall of Fame 1945.
BR TR 5′10″ 170 lbs.

Year	Team		W	L	PCT	ERA	G	GS	CG	IP	H	BB	SO	ShO	Relief W	Relief L	Relief SV	Batting AB	Batting H	HR	BA	PO	A	E	DP	TC/G	FA
1880	CHI	N	0	0	—	0.00	1	0	0	3	3	1	1	0	0	0	0	344	100	1	.291	150	65	43	5	3.9	.833
1883			0	0	—	0.00	1	0	0	1	1	0	0	0	0	0	0	428	109	3	.255	164	139	58	4	4.3	.839
1884			0	1	.000	*8.44*	2	0	0	5.1	12	2	1	0	0	0	0	452	160	13	.354	201	141	86	10	3.7	.799
1887	BOS	N	1	0	1.000	3.46	3	0	0	13	17	14	0	0	0	**1**	0	484	156	8	.322	259	112	58	5	3.7	.865
1890	BOS	P	1	0	1.000	4.50	1	0	0	2	1	2	2	0	1	0	0	340	111	4	.326	387	141	59	11	4.3	.899
1891	CIN	AA	0	1	.000	5.28	3	0	0	15.1	21	7	0	0	0	1	0	350	100	2	.286	351	159	59	19	4.6	.896
1892	BOS	N	0	0	—	1.50	1	0	0	6	8	4	0	0	0	0	0	281	53	2	.189	340	101	47	13	6.2	.904
7 yrs.			2	2	.500	4.14	12	0	0	45.2	63	30	4	0	2	2	0	*				3587	1751	854	145	3.8	.862

Mike Kelly

KELLY, MICHAEL J.
B. Nov. 9, 1902, St. Louis, Mo.
BR TR 6′ 1″ 178 lbs.

Year	Team		W	L	PCT	ERA	G	GS	CG	IP	H	BB	SO	ShO	Relief W	Relief L	Relief SV	Batting AB	Batting H	HR	BA	PO	A	E	DP	TC/G	FA
1926	PHI	N	0	0	—	9.45	4	0	0	6.2	9	4	2	0	0	0	0	3	0	0	.000	0	0	0	0	0.0	.000

Ren Kelly

KELLY, REYNOLDS JOSEPH
Brother of George Kelly.
B. Nov. 18, 1899, San Francisco, Calif. D. Aug. 24, 1963, Millbrae, Calif.
BR TR 6′ 183 lbs.

Year	Team		W	L	PCT	ERA	G	GS	CG	IP	H	BB	SO	ShO	Relief W	Relief L	Relief SV	Batting AB	Batting H	HR	BA	PO	A	E	DP	TC/G	FA
1923	PHI	A	0	0	—	2.57	1	0	0	7	7	4	1	0	0	0	0	3	0	0	.000	0	0	0	0	0.0	.000

Bill Kelso

KELSO, WILLIAM EUGENE
B. Feb. 19, 1940, Kansas City, Mo.
BR TR 6′ 4″ 215 lbs.

Year	Team		W	L	PCT	ERA	G	GS	CG	IP	H	BB	SO	ShO	Relief W	Relief L	Relief SV	Batting AB	Batting H	HR	BA	PO	A	E	DP	TC/G	FA
1964	LA	A	2	0	1.000	2.28	10	1	1	23.2	19	9	21	1	1	0	0	6	0	0	.000	0	5	0	0	0.5	1.000
1966	CAL	A	1	1	.500	2.38	5	0	0	11.1	11	6	11	0	1	1	0	1	0	0	.000	1	1	0	0	0.4	1.000
1967			5	3	.625	2.97	69	1	0	112	85	63	91	0	5	2	11	19	2	0	.105	5	20	2	1	0.4	.926
1968	CIN	N	4	1	.800	3.98	35	0	0	54.1	56	15	39	0	4	1	1	8	0	0	.000	1	6	0	0	0.2	1.000
4 yrs.			12	5	.706	3.13	119	2	1	201.1	171	93	162	1	11	4	12	34	2	0	.059	7	32	2	1	0.3	.951

Russ Kemmerer

KEMMERER, RUSSELL PAUL (Dutch, Rusty)
B. Nov. 1, 1931, Pittsburgh, Pa.
BR TR 6′ 2″ 198 lbs.

Year	Team		W	L	PCT	ERA	G	GS	CG	IP	H	BB	SO	ShO	Relief W	Relief L	Relief SV	Batting AB	Batting H	HR	BA	PO	A	E	DP	TC/G	FA
1954	BOS	A	5	3	.625	3.82	19	9	2	75.1	71	41	37	1	2	0	0	21	3	0	.143	4	14	2	2	1.1	.900
1955			1	1	.500	7.27	7	2	0	17.1	18	15	13	0	1	0	0	3	0	0	.000	0	2	0	0	0.3	1.000
1957	2 teams	BOS A (1G 0–0)	WAS A (39G 7–11)																								
″	total		7	11	.389	4.95	40	26	6	176.1	219	73	82	0	1	0	0	46	3	2	.065	4	20	3	2	0.7	.889
1958	WAS	A	6	15	.286	4.61	40	30	6	224.1	234	74	111	0	0	0	0	69	11	0	.159	13	37	2	2	1.3	.962
1959			8	17	.320	4.50	37	28	8	206	221	71	89	0	0	0	0	60	8	0	.133	18	36	3	1	1.5	.947
1960	2 teams	WAS A (3G 0–2)	CHI A (36G 6–3)																								
″	total		6	5	.545	3.59	39	10	2	138	129	55	86	1	4	2	2	33	0	0	.000	12	22	1	1	0.9	.971
1961	CHI	A	3	3	.500	4.38	47	2	0	96.2	102	26	35	0	3	3	2	15	3	0	.200	8	21	2	2	0.7	.935
1962	2 teams	CHI A (20G 2–1)	HOU N (36G 5–3)																								
″	total		7	4	.636	4.03	56	2	0	96	102	26	40	0	7	2	3	11	4	0	.364	8	21	2	1	0.6	.935
1963	HOU	N	0	0	—	5.65	17	0	0	36.2	48	8	12	0	0	0	1	7	2	0	.286	5	8	0	1	0.8	1.000
9 yrs.			43	59	.422	4.46	302	109	24	1066.2	1144	389	505	2	18	7	8	265	34	2	.128	72	181	15	12	0.9	.944

Dutch Kemner

KEMNER, HERMAN JOHN
B. Mar. 4, 1899, Quincy, Ill. D. Jan. 16, 1988, Quincy, Ill.
BR TR 5′10½″ 175 lbs.

Year	Team		W	L	PCT	ERA	G	GS	CG	IP	H	BB	SO	ShO	Relief W	Relief L	Relief SV	Batting AB	Batting H	HR	BA	PO	A	E	DP	TC/G	FA
1929	CIN	N	0	0	—	7.63	9	0	0	15.1	19	8	10	0	0	0	1	4	1	0	.250	0	4	1	0	0.6	.800

Ed Kenna

KENNA, EDWARD BENNINGHAUS (The Pitching Poet)
B. Oct. 17, 1877, Charleston, W. Va. D. Mar. 22, 1912, Grant, Fla.
TR 6′ 180 lbs.

Year	Team		W	L	PCT	ERA	G	GS	CG	IP	H	BB	SO	ShO	Relief W	Relief L	Relief SV	Batting AB	Batting H	HR	BA	PO	A	E	DP	TC/G	FA
1902	PHI	A	1	1	.500	5.29	2	1	1	17	19	11	5	0	1	0	0	8	1	0	.125	1	7	1	0	4.5	.889

Bill Kennedy

KENNEDY, WILLIAM AULTON (Lefty)
B. Mar. 14, 1921, Carnesville, Ga. D. Apr. 9, 1983, Seattle, Wash.
BL TL 6′ 2″ 195 lbs.

Year	Team		W	L	PCT	ERA	G	GS	CG	IP	H	BB	SO	ShO	Relief W	Relief L	Relief SV	Batting AB	Batting H	HR	BA	PO	A	E	DP	TC/G	FA
1948	2 teams	CLE A (6G 1–0)	STL A (26G 7–8)																								
″	total		8	8	.500	5.21	32	23	3	143.1	148	117	89	0	0	0	0	47	13	0	.277	3	21	0	0	0.8	1.000
1949	STL	A	4	11	.267	4.69	48	16	2	153.2	172	73	69	0	2	1	1	40	6	0	.150	4	23	3	0	0.6	.900
1950			0	0	—	0.00	1	0	0	2	1	2	1	0	0	0	0	0	0	0	—	0	0	1	0	1.0	.000
1951			1	5	.167	5.63	19	5	1	56	76	37	29	0	0	2	0	16	2	0	.125	3	14	1	2	0.9	.944
1952	CHI	A	2	2	.500	2.80	**47**	1	0	70.2	54	38	46	0	2	1	5	13	3	0	.231	5	8	1	1	0.3	.929
1953	BOS	A	0	0	—	3.70	16	0	0	24.1	24	17	14	0	0	0	2	2	1	0	.500	2	3	2	0	0.4	.714
1956	CIN	N	0	0	—	18.00	1	0	0	2	6	0	0	0	0	0	0	0	0	0	—	0	0	0	0	0.0	.000
1957			0	2	.000	6.39	8	0	0	12.2	16	5	8	0	0	2	3	2	0	0	.000	0	3	0	1	0.4	1.000
8 yrs.			15	28	.349	4.71	172	45	6	464.2	497	289	256	0	4	6	11	120	25	0	.208	17	72	8	4	0.6	.918

Bill Kennedy

KENNEDY, WILLIAM GORMAN
B. Dec. 22, 1918, Alexandria, Va. D. Aug. 20, 1995, Alexandria, Va.
BL TL 6′ 1″ 175 lbs.

Year	Team		W	L	PCT	ERA	G	GS	CG	IP	H	BB	SO	ShO	Relief W	Relief L	Relief SV	Batting AB	Batting H	HR	BA	PO	A	E	DP	TC/G	FA
1942	WAS	A	0	1	.000	8.00	8	2	1	18	21	10	4	0	0	0	2	4	0	0	.000	1	6	0	1	0.9	1.000
1946			1	2	.333	6.00	21	2	0	39	40	29	18	0	1	1	3	8	1	0	.125	2	7	2	0	0.5	.818
1947			0	0	—	8.10	2	0	0	6.2	10	5	1	0	0	0	0	2	0	0	.000	0	2	0	0	1.0	1.000
3 yrs.			1	3	.250	6.79	31	4	1	63.2	71	44	23	0	1	1	5	14	1	0	.071	3	15	2	1	0.6	.900

Brickyard Kennedy

KENNEDY, WILLIAM P.
B. Oct. 7, 1867, Bellaire, Ohio D. Sept. 23, 1915, Bellaire, Ohio.
BR TR 5′11″ 160 lbs.

Year	Team		W	L	PCT	ERA	G	GS	CG	IP	H	BB	SO	ShO	Relief W	Relief L	Relief SV	Batting AB	Batting H	HR	BA	PO	A	E	DP	TC/G	FA
1892	BKN	N	13	8	.619	3.86	26	21	18	191	189	95	108	0	1	0	1	85	14	0	.165	17	32	2	1	1.9	.961
1893			25	20	.556	3.72	46	44	40	382.2	376	168	107	2	0	1	1	157	39	0	.248	12	109	10	6	2.8	.924
1894			24	20	.545	4.92	48	41	34	360.2	445	149	107	0	4	0	2	161	49	0	.304	7	82	8	4	2.0	.918
1895			19	12	.613	5.12	39	33	26	279.2	335	93	39	2	3	0	1	127	39	0	.307	5	66	5	1	1.9	.934
1896			17	20	.459	4.42	42	38	28	305.2	334	130	76	1	0	0	1	122	23	0	.189	10	87	5	2	2.4	.951

Brickyard Kennedy *continued*

Year	Team	W	L	PCT	ERA	G	GS	CG	IP	H	BB	SO	ShO	Relief Pitching W	Relief Pitching L	Relief Pitching SV	Batting AB	Batting H	Batting HR	BA	PO	A	E	DP	TC/G	FA
1897		18	20	.474	3.91	44	40	36	343.1	370	149	81	2	1	1	1	147	40	1	.272	14	87	4	4	2.4	.962
1898		16	22	.421	3.37	40	39	38	339.1	360	123	73	0	0	0	0	135	34	0	.252	15	108	6	5	3.2	.953
1899		22	9	.710	2.79	40	33	27	277.1	297	86	55	2	1	0	2	109	27	0	.248	14	67	8	2	2.2	.910
1900		20	13	.606	3.91	42	35	26	292	316	111	75	2	2	0	0	123	37	0	.301	20	73	5	3	2.3	.949
1901		3	5	.375	3.06	14	8	6	85.1	80	24	28	0	0	0	0	36	6	0	.167	3	20	1	1	1.7	.958
1902	NY N	1	4	.200	3.96	6	6	4	38.2	44	16	9	1	0	0	0	15	4	0	.267	4	7	2	0	2.2	.846
1903	PIT N	9	6	.600	3.45	18	15	10	125.1	130	57	39	1	0	1	0	58	21	0	.362	2	29	1	0	1.8	.969
12 yrs.		187	159	.540	3.96	405	353	293	3021	3276	1201	797	13	12	3	9	1275	333	1	.261	123	767	57	29	2.3	.940
WORLD SERIES 1903	PIT N	0	1	.000	5.14	1	1	0	7	11	3	3	0	0	0	0	2	1	0	.500	0	1	0	0	1.0	1.000

Monte Kennedy

KENNEDY, MONTIA CALVIN (Lefty)
B. May 11, 1922, Amelia, Va.
BR TL 6′ 2″ 185 lbs.

Year	Team	W	L	PCT	ERA	G	GS	CG	IP	H	BB	SO	ShO	Relief Pitching W	Relief Pitching L	Relief Pitching SV	Batting AB	Batting H	Batting HR	BA	PO	A	E	DP	TC/G	FA
1946	NY N	9	10	.474	3.42	38	27	10	186.2	153	**116**	71	1	0	0	1	64	15	0	.234	10	35	2	2	1.2	.957
1947		9	12	.429	4.85	34	24	9	148.1	158	88	60	0	1	1	0	48	8	0	.167	7	26	1	1	1.0	.971
1948		3	9	.250	4.01	25	16	7	114.1	118	57	63	1	0	0	0	31	4	0	.129	3	17	1	0	0.8	.952
1949		12	14	.462	3.43	38	32	14	223.1	208	100	95	4	0	0	1	83	12	1	.145	2	30	2	4	0.9	.941
1950		5	4	.556	4.72	36	17	5	114.1	120	53	41	0	2	0	2	36	2	0	.056	5	20	1	2	0.7	.962
1951		1	2	.333	2.25	29	5	1	68	68	31	22	0	0	1	0	15	3	0	.200	4	13	2	0	0.7	.895
1952		3	4	.429	3.02	31	6	2	83.1	73	31	48	1	2	1	0	22	2	0	.091	6	15	1	4	0.7	.955
1953		0	0	—	7.15	18	0	0	22.2	30	19	11	0	0	0	0	2	0	0	.000	2	4	0	2	0.3	1.000
8 yrs.		42	55	.433	3.84	249	127	48	961	928	495	411	7	5	3	4	301	46	1	.153	39	160	10	15	0.8	.952
WORLD SERIES 1951	NY N	0	0	—	6.00	2	0	0	3	3	1	4	0	0	0	0	0	0	0	—	0	1	0	0	0.5	1.000

Ted Kennedy

KENNEDY, THEODORE A.
B. Feb. 1865, Henry, Ill. D. Oct. 31, 1907, St. Louis, Mo.
BL

Year	Team	W	L	PCT	ERA	G	GS	CG	IP	H	BB	SO	ShO	Relief Pitching W	Relief Pitching L	Relief Pitching SV	Batting AB	Batting H	Batting HR	BA	PO	A	E	DP	TC/G	FA
1885	CHI N	7	2	.778	*3.43*	9	9	8	78.2	91	28	36	0	0	0	0	36	3	0	.083	3	18	2	0	2.3	.913
1886	2 teams PHI AA (20G 5–15) LOU AA (4G 0–4)																									
″	total	5	19	.208	4.66	24	23	23	204.2	249	81	82	0	0	**1**	0	81	4	0	.049	8	37	6	1	2.1	.882
2 yrs.		12	21	.364	4.32	33	32	31	283.1	340	109	118	0	0	1	0	117	7	0	.060	11	55	8	1	2.2	.892

Vern Kennedy

KENNEDY, LLOYD VERNON
B. Mar. 20, 1907, Kansas City, Mo. D. Jan. 18, 1993, Mendon, Mo.
BL TR 6′ 175 lbs.

Year	Team	W	L	PCT	ERA	G	GS	CG	IP	H	BB	SO	ShO	Relief Pitching W	Relief Pitching L	Relief Pitching SV	Batting AB	Batting H	Batting HR	BA	PO	A	E	DP	TC/G	FA
1934	CHI A	0	2	.000	3.72	3	3	1	19.1	21	9	7	0	0	0	0	7	2	0	.286	1	6	0	0	2.3	1.000
1935		11	11	.500	3.91	31	25	16	211.2	211	95	65	2	0	1	1	73	18	0	.247	8	54	2	3	2.1	.969
1936		21	9	.700	4.63	35	34	20	274.1	282	**147**	99	1	1	0	0	113	32	0	.283	13	50	2	5	1.9	.969
1937		14	13	.519	5.09	32	30	15	221	238	124	114	1	0	1	0	87	20	2	.230	9	40	3	1	1.6	.942
1938	DET A	12	9	.571	5.06	33	26	11	190.1	215	113	53	0	1	0	2	79	23	0	.291	6	46	3	4	1.7	.945
1939	2 teams DET A (4G 0–3) STL A (33G 9–17)																									
″	total	9	**20**	.310	5.80	37	31	13	212.2	254	124	64	1	0	1	0	74	12	0	.162	8	37	1	2	1.2	.978
1940	STL A	12	17	.414	5.59	34	32	18	222.1	263	122	70	0	1	0	0	84	25	2	.298	13	50	0	4	1.9	1.000
1941	2 teams STL A (6G 2–4) WAS A (17G 1–7)																									
″	total	3	11	.214	5.17	23	13	4	111.1	121	66	28	0	1	1	0	36	9	0	.250	5	24	2	1	1.3	.935
1942	CLE A	4	8	.333	4.08	28	12	4	108	99	50	37	0	0	2	1	30	6	0	.200	4	24	3	3	1.1	.903
1943		10	7	.588	2.45	28	17	8	146.2	130	59	63	1	3	1	0	52	12	0	.231	8	36	1	2	1.6	.978
1944	2 teams CLE A (12G 2–5) PHI N (12G 1–5)																									
″	total	3	10	.231	4.64	24	17	5	114.1	126	57	40	0	1	0	0	44	8	0	.182	8	25	3	1	1.5	.917
1945	2 teams PHI N (12G 0–3) CIN N (24G 5–12)																									
″	total	5	15	.250	4.28	36	23	11	193.2	213	83	51	1	0	2	1	64	14	0	.219	16	47	2	2	1.8	.969
12 yrs.		104	132	.441	4.67	344	263	126	2025.2	2173	1049	691	7	8	9	5	743	181	4	.244	99	439	22	28	1.6	.961

Art Kenney

KENNEY, ARTHUR JOSEPH
B. Apr. 29, 1916, Milford, Mass.
BL TL 6′ 175 lbs.

Year	Team	W	L	PCT	ERA	G	GS	CG	IP	H	BB	SO	ShO	Relief Pitching W	Relief Pitching L	Relief Pitching SV	Batting AB	Batting H	Batting HR	BA	PO	A	E	DP	TC/G	FA
1938	BOS N	0	0	—	15.43	2	0	0	2.1	3	8	2	0	0	0	0	0	0	0	—	0	1	0	0	0.5	1.000

Ed Kent

KENT, EDWARD C.
B. 1859, New York, N. Y. Deceased.
BR TR 5′ 6½″ 152 lbs.

Year	Team	W	L	PCT	ERA	G	GS	CG	IP	H	BB	SO	ShO	Relief Pitching W	Relief Pitching L	Relief Pitching SV	Batting AB	Batting H	Batting HR	BA	PO	A	E	DP	TC/G	FA
1884	TOL AA	0	1	.000	*6.00*	1	1	1	9	14	3	4	0	0	0	0	4	0	0	.000	1	4	1	0	6.0	.833

Maury Kent

KENT, MAURICE ALLEN
B. Sept. 17, 1885, Marshalltown, Iowa D. Apr. 19, 1966, Iowa City, Iowa.
BR TR 6′ 168 lbs.

Year	Team	W	L	PCT	ERA	G	GS	CG	IP	H	BB	SO	ShO	Relief Pitching W	Relief Pitching L	Relief Pitching SV	Batting AB	Batting H	Batting HR	BA	PO	A	E	DP	TC/G	FA
1912	BKN N	5	5	.500	4.84	20	9	2	93	107	46	24	1	1	1	0	35	8	0	.229	2	29	2	1	1.6	.939
1913		0	0	—	2.45	3	0	0	7.1	5	3	1	0	0	0	0	3	0	0	.000	0	1	0	0	0.3	1.000
2 yrs.		5	5	.500	4.66	23	9	2	100.1	112	49	25	1	1	1	0	38	8	0	.211	2	30	2	1	1.5	.941

Matt Keough

KEOUGH, MATTHEW LON
Son of Marty Keough.
B. July 3, 1955, Pomona, Calif.
BR TR 6′ 3″ 190 lbs.

Year	Team	W	L	PCT	ERA	G	GS	CG	IP	H	BB	SO	ShO	Relief Pitching W	Relief Pitching L	Relief Pitching SV	Batting AB	Batting H	Batting HR	BA	PO	A	E	DP	TC/G	FA
1977	OAK A	1	3	.250	4.81	7	6	0	43	39	22	23	0	0	0	0	0	0	0	—	3	4	1	0	1.1	.875
1978		8	15	.348	3.24	32	32	6	197.1	178	85	108	0	0	0	0	0	0	0	—	21	31	2	2	1.7	.963
1979		2	17	.105	5.03	30	28	7	177	220	78	95	1	0	0	0	0	0	0	—	23	28	3	5	1.8	.944
1980		16	13	.552	2.92	34	32	20	250	218	94	121	2	0	0	0	0	0	0	—	23	28	3	2	1.6	.944
1981		10	6	.625	3.41	19	19	10	140	125	45	60	2	0	0	0	0	0	0	—	10	13	2	2	1.3	.920
1982		11	**18**	.379	5.72	34	34	10	209.1	233	101	75	2	0	0	0	0	0	0	—	9	20	3	2	0.9	.906
1983	2 teams OAK A (14G 2–3) NY A (12G 3–4)																									
″	total	5	7	.417	5.33	26	16	0	99.2	109	51	54	0	2	0	0	0	0	0		6	9	1	0	0.6	.938
1985	STL N	0	1	.000	4.50	4	1	0	10	10	4	10	0	0	0	0	2	0	0	.000	0	2	0	0	0.5	1.000
1986	2 teams CHI N (19G 2–2) HOU N (10G 3–2)																									
″	total	5	4	.556	3.94	29	7	0	64	58	30	44	0	3	1	0	16	6	0	.375	3	6	1	2	0.3	.900
9 yrs.		58	84	.408	4.17	215	175	53	1190.1	1190	510	590	7	5	1	0	18	6	0	.333	98	141	16	15	1.2	.937

Matt Keough *continued*

Year	Team	Lg	W	L	PCT	ERA	G	GS	CG	IP	H	BB	SO	ShO	Relief Pitching W	Relief Pitching L	Relief Pitching SV	Batting AB	Batting H	Batting HR	BA	PO	A	E	DP	TC/G	FA
LEAGUE CHAMPIONSHIP SERIES																											
1981	**OAK**	**A**	0	1	.000	1.08	1	1	0	8.1	7	6	2	0	0	0	0	0	0	0	—	0	1	0	0	1.0	1.000

Kurt Kepshire

KEPSHIRE, KURT DAVID BL TR 6′ 1″ 180 lbs.
B. July 3, 1959, Bridgeport, Conn.

Year	Team	Lg	W	L	PCT	ERA	G	GS	CG	IP	H	BB	SO	ShO	Relief Pitching W	Relief Pitching L	Relief Pitching SV	Batting AB	Batting H	Batting HR	BA	PO	A	E	DP	TC/G	FA
1984	**STL**	**N**	6	5	.545	3.30	17	16	2	109	100	44	71	2	0	0	0	36	2	0	.056	4	10	3	0	1.0	.824
1985			10	9	.526	4.75	32	29	0	153.1	155	71	67	0	0	0	0	51	6	0	.118	5	19	1	1	0.8	.960
1986			0	1	.000	4.50	2	1	0	8	8	4	6	0	0	0	0	1	0	0	.000	1	2	0	0	1.5	1.000
3 yrs.			16	15	.516	4.16	51	46	2	270.1	263	119	144	2	0	0	0	88	8	0	.091	10	31	4	1	0.9	.911

Charlie Kerfeld

KERFELD, CHARLES PATRICK BR TR 6′ 6″ 225 lbs.
B. Sept. 28, 1963, Knob Noster, Mo.

Year	Team	Lg	W	L	PCT	ERA	G	GS	CG	IP	H	BB	SO	ShO	Relief Pitching W	Relief Pitching L	Relief Pitching SV	Batting AB	Batting H	Batting HR	BA	PO	A	E	DP	TC/G	FA
1985	**HOU**	**N**	4	2	.667	4.06	11	6	0	44.1	44	25	30	0	2	0	0	14	0	0	.000	5	2	1	1	0.7	.875
1986			11	2	.846	2.59	61	0	0	93.2	71	42	77	0	11	2	7	9	1	0	.111	7	9	0	1	0.3	1.000
1987			0	2	.000	6.67	21	0	0	29.2	34	21	17	0	0	2	0	3	0	0	.000	5	3	1	0	0.4	.889
1990	**2 teams**	**HOU N** (5G 0–2)	**ATL N** (25G 3–1)																								
″	**total**		3	3	.500	6.62	30	0	0	34	40	29	31	0	3	3	2	0	0	0		2	2	3	0	0.2	.571
4 yrs.			18	9	.667	4.20	123	6	0	201.2	189	117	155	0	16	7	9	26	1	0	.038	19	16	5	2	0.3	.875
LEAGUE CHAMPIONSHIP SERIES																											
1986	**HOU**	**N**	0	1	.000	2.25	3	0	0	4	2	1	4	0	0	1	0	0	0	0	—	0	0	1	0	0.3	.000

Gus Keriazakos

KERIAZAKOS, CONSTANTINE NICHOLAS BR TR 6′ 3″ 187 lbs.
B. July 28, 1931, West Orange, N. J.

Year	Team	Lg	W	L	PCT	ERA	G	GS	CG	IP	H	BB	SO	ShO	Relief Pitching W	Relief Pitching L	Relief Pitching SV	Batting AB	Batting H	Batting HR	BA	PO	A	E	DP	TC/G	FA
1950	**CHI**	**A**	0	1	.000	19.29	1	1	0	2.1	7	5	1	0	0	0	0	1	1	0	1.000	0	0	0	0	0.0	.000
1954	**WAS**	**A**	2	3	.400	3.77	22	3	2	59.2	59	30	33	0	1	1	0	15	1	0	.067	7	7	0	1	0.6	1.000
1955	**KC**	**A**	0	1	.000	12.34	5	1	0	11.2	15	7	8	0	0	1	0	3	0	0	.000	0	1	0	0	0.2	1.000
3 yrs.			2	5	.286	5.62	28	5	2	73.2	81	42	42	0	1	2	0	19	2	0	.105	7	8	0	1	0.5	1.000

Bill Kerksieck

KERKSIECK, WAYMAN WILLIAM BR TR 6′ 1″ 183 lbs.
B. Dec. 6, 1913, Ulm, Ark. D. Mar. 11, 1970, Stuttgart, Ark.

Year	Team	Lg	W	L	PCT	ERA	G	GS	CG	IP	H	BB	SO	ShO	Relief Pitching W	Relief Pitching L	Relief Pitching SV	Batting AB	Batting H	Batting HR	BA	PO	A	E	DP	TC/G	FA
1939	**PHI**	**N**	0	2	.000	7.18	23	2	1	62.2	81	32	13	0	0	0	0	12	1	0	.083	1	11	0	1	0.5	1.000

Jim Kern

KERN, JAMES LESTER BR TR 6′ 5″ 185 lbs.
B. Mar. 15, 1949, Gladwin, Mich.

Year	Team	Lg	W	L	PCT	ERA	G	GS	CG	IP	H	BB	SO	ShO	Relief Pitching W	Relief Pitching L	Relief Pitching SV	Batting AB	Batting H	Batting HR	BA	PO	A	E	DP	TC/G	FA
1974	**CLE**	**A**	0	1	.000	4.70	4	3	1	15.1	16	14	11	0	0	0	0	0	0	0	—	0	1	0	0	0.3	1.000
1975			1	2	.333	3.77	13	7	0	71.2	60	45	55	0	0	0	0	0	0	0	—	4	11	2	0	1.3	.882
1976			10	7	.588	2.36	50	2	0	118	91	50	111	0	9	6	15	0	0	0	—	7	14	3	2	0.5	.875
1977			8	10	.444	3.42	60	0	0	92	85	47	91	0	8	**10**	18	0	0	0	—	5	13	3	2	0.3	.857
1978			10	10	.500	3.08	58	0	0	99.1	77	58	95	0	10	10	13	1	0	0	.000	4	16	0	0	0.3	1.000
1979	**TEX**	**A**	13	5	.722	1.57	71	0	0	143	99	62	136	0	13	5	29	0	0	0	—	9	16	7	1	0.5	.781
1980			3	11	.214	4.86	38	1	0	63	65	45	40	0	3	**11**	2	0	0	0	—	0	12	0	1	0.3	1.000
1981			1	2	.333	2.70	23	0	0	30	21	22	20	0	1	2	6	0	0	0	—	3	3	1	0	0.3	.857
1982	**2 teams**	**CIN N** (50G 3–5)	**CHI A** (13G 2–1)																								
″	**total**		5	6	.455	3.46	63	1	0	104	81	60	66	0	4	6	5	7	0	0	.000	6	18	0	0	0.4	1.000
1983	**CHI**	**A**	0	0	—	0.00	1	0	0	0.2	1	0	0	0	0	0	0	0	0	0	—	0	0	0	0	0.0	.000
1984	**2 teams**	**PHI N** (8G 0–1)	**MIL A** (6G 1–0)																								
″	**total**		1	1	.500	7.50	14	0	0	18	26	13	12	0	1	1	0	1	0	0	.000	1	2	0	0	0.2	1.000
1985	**MIL**	**A**	0	1	.000	6.55	5	0	0	11	14	5	3	0	0	1	0	0	0	0	—	2	3	0	1	1.0	1.000
1986	**CLE**	**A**	1	1	.500	7.90	16	0	0	27.1	34	23	11	0	1	1	0	0	0	0	—	2	6	0	0	0.5	1.000
13 yrs.			53	57	.482	3.32	416	14	1	793.1	670	444	651	0	50	53	88	9	0	0	.000	43	115	16	7	0.4	.908

Dickie Kerr

KERR, RICHARD HENRY BL TL 5′ 7″ 155 lbs.
B. July 3, 1893, St. Louis, Mo. D. May 4, 1963, Houston, Tex.

Year	Team	Lg	W	L	PCT	ERA	G	GS	CG	IP	H	BB	SO	ShO	Relief Pitching W	Relief Pitching L	Relief Pitching SV	Batting AB	Batting H	Batting HR	BA	PO	A	E	DP	TC/G	FA
1919	**CHI**	**A**	13	7	.650	2.88	39	17	10	212.1	208	64	79	1	**7**	1	0	68	17	0	.250	7	66	4	0	2.0	.948
1920			21	9	.700	3.37	45	27	20	253.2	266	72	72	3	3	1	**5**	90	14	0	.156	8	81	1	2	2.0	.989
1921			19	17	.528	4.72	44	37	25	308.2	**357**	96	80	3	3	0	1	105	25	0	.238	10	81	7	4	2.2	.929
1925			0	1	.000	5.15	12	2	0	36.2	45	18	4	0	0	0	0	12	4	0	.333	1	11	1	3	1.1	.923
4 yrs.			53	34	.609	3.84	140	83	55	811.1	876	250	235	7	13	2	6	275	60	0	.218	26	239	13	9	2.0	.953
WORLD SERIES																											
1919	**CHI**	**A**	2	0	1.000	1.42	2	2	2	19	14	3	6	1	0	0	0	6	1	0	.167	1	4	0	0	2.5	1.000

Joe Kerrigan

KERRIGAN, JOSEPH THOMAS BR TR 6′ 5″ 205 lbs.
B. Nov. 30, 1954, Philadelphia, Pa.

Year	Team	Lg	W	L	PCT	ERA	G	GS	CG	IP	H	BB	SO	ShO	Relief Pitching W	Relief Pitching L	Relief Pitching SV	Batting AB	Batting H	Batting HR	BA	PO	A	E	DP	TC/G	FA
1976	**MON**	**N**	2	6	.250	3.81	38	0	0	56.2	63	23	22	0	2	6	1	2	0	0	.000	7	9	1	2	0.4	.941
1977			3	5	.375	3.24	66	0	0	89	80	33	43	0	3	5	11	8	0	0	.000	6	16	2	3	0.4	.917
1978	**BAL**	**A**	3	1	.750	4.77	26	2	0	71.2	75	36	41	0	2	1	3	0	0	0	—	1	19	1	3	0.8	.952
1980			0	0	—	4.50	1	0	0	2	3	0	1	0	0	0	0	0	0	0	—	0	2	0	0	2.0	1.000
4 yrs.			8	12	.400	3.90	131	2	0	219.1	221	92	107	0	7	12	15	10	0	0	.000	14	46	4	8	0.5	.938

Rick Kester

KESTER, RICHARD LEE BR TR 6′ 190 lbs.
B. July 7, 1946, Iola, Kans.

Year	Team	Lg	W	L	PCT	ERA	G	GS	CG	IP	H	BB	SO	ShO	Relief Pitching W	Relief Pitching L	Relief Pitching SV	Batting AB	Batting H	Batting HR	BA	PO	A	E	DP	TC/G	FA
1968	**ATL**	**N**	0	0	—	5.68	5	0	0	6.1	8	3	9	0	0	0	0	0	0	0	—	0	0	0	0	0.0	.000
1969			0	0	—	13.50	1	0	0	2	5	0	2	0	0	0	0	0	0	0	—	0	0	0	0	0.0	.000
1970			0	0	—	5.63	15	0	0	32	36	19	20	0	0	0	0	9	0	0	.000	0	3	2	0	0.3	.600
3 yrs.			0	0		6.02	21	0	0	40.1	49	22	31	0	0	0	0	9	0	0	.000	0	3	2	0	0.2	.600

Gus Ketchum

KETCHUM, AUGUSTUS FRANKLIN BR TR 5′ 9½″ 170 lbs.
B. Mar. 21, 1897, Royce City, Tex. D. Sept. 6, 1980, Oklahoma City, Okla.

Year	Team	Lg	W	L	PCT	ERA	G	GS	CG	IP	H	BB	SO	ShO	Relief Pitching W	Relief Pitching L	Relief Pitching SV	Batting AB	Batting H	Batting HR	BA	PO	A	E	DP	TC/G	FA
1922	**PHI**	**A**	0	1	.000	5.63	6	0	0	16	19	8	4	0	0	1	0	4	0	0	.000	0	1	0	0	0.2	1.000

Hank Keupper

KEUPPER, HENRY J. BL TL 6′ 1″ 185 lbs.
B. June 24, 1887, Staunton, Ill. D. Aug. 14, 1960, Marion, Ill.

Year	Team	Lg	W	L	PCT	ERA	G	GS	CG	IP	H	BB	SO	ShO	Relief Pitching W	Relief Pitching L	Relief Pitching SV	Batting AB	Batting H	Batting HR	BA	PO	A	E	DP	TC/G	FA
1914	**STL**	**F**	8	20	.286	4.27	42	25	12	213	256	49	70	1	3	1	0	68	17	0	.250	10	74	4	1	2.1	.955

Jimmy Key

KEY, JAMES EDWARD BR TL 6′ 1″ 180 lbs.
B. Apr. 22, 1961, Huntsville, Ala.

Year	Team	Lg	W	L	PCT	ERA	G	GS	CG	IP	H	BB	SO	ShO	Relief Pitching W	Relief Pitching L	Relief Pitching SV	Batting AB	Batting H	Batting HR	BA	PO	A	E	DP	TC/G	FA
1984	TOR	A	4	5	.444	4.65	63	0	0	62	70	32	44	0	4	5	10	0	0	0	—	9	11	1	0	0.3	.952
1985			14	6	.700	3.00	35	32	3	212.2	188	50	85	0	1	0	0	0	0	0	—	15	52	3	3	1.9	.957
1986			14	11	.560	3.57	36	35	4	232	222	74	141	2	0	0	0	0	0	0	—	18	42	0	4	1.7	1.000
1987			17	8	.680	**2.76**	36	36	8	261	210	66	161	1	0	0	0	0	0	0	—	17	44	3	5	1.8	.953
1988			12	5	.706	3.29	21	21	2	131.1	127	30	65	2	0	0	0	0	0	0	—	5	19	0	1	1.1	1.000
1989			13	14	.481	3.88	33	33	5	216	226	27	118	1	0	0	0	0	0	0	—	11	44	2	2	1.7	.965
1990			13	7	.650	4.25	27	27	0	154.2	169	22	88	0	0	0	0	0	0	0	—	8	22	1	3	1.1	.968
1991			16	12	.571	3.05	33	33	2	209.1	207	44	125	2	0	0	0	0	0	0	—	22	37	2	3	1.8	.967
1992			13	13	.500	3.53	33	33	4	216.2	205	59	117	2	0	0	0	0	0	0	—	18	27	1	2	1.4	.978
1993	NY	A	18	6	**.750**	3.00	34	34	4	236.2	219	43	173	2	0	0	0	0	0	0	—	14	33	4	1	1.5	.922
1994			**17**	4	.810	3.27	25	**25**	1	168	177	52	97	0	0	0	0	0	0	0	—	6	40	2	3	1.9	.958
1995			1	2	.333	5.64	5	5	0	30.1	40	6	14	0	0	0	0	0	0	0	—	4	3	0	2	1.4	1.000
12 yrs.			152	93	.620	3.40	381	314	33	2130.2	2060	505	1228	12	5	5	10	0	0	0		147	374	19	29	1.4	.965
LEAGUE CHAMPIONSHIP SERIES																											
1985	TOR	A	0	1	.000	5.19	2	2	0	8.2	15	2	5	0	0	0	0	0	0	0	—	0	3	0	0	1.5	1.000
1989			1	0	1.000	4.50	1	1	0	6	7	2	2	0	0	0	0	0	0	0	—	0	0	0	0	0.0	.000
1991			0	0	—	3.00	1	1	0	6	5	1	1	0	0	0	0	0	0	0	—	0	3	0	1	3.0	1.000
1992			0	0	—	0.00	1	0	0	3	2	2	1	0	0	0	0	0	0	0	—	0	0	0	0	0.0	.000
4 yrs.			1	1	.500	3.80	5	4	0	23.2	29	7	9	0	0	0	0	0	0	0		0	6	0	1	1.2	1.000
WORLD SERIES																											
1992	TOR	A	2	0	1.000	1.00	2	1	0	9	6	0	6	0	1	0	0	1	0	0	.000	2	4	0	0	3.0	1.000

Brian Keyser

KEYSER, BRIAN LEE BR TR 6′ 1″ 180 lbs.
B. Oct. 31, 1966, Castro Valley, Calif.

Year	Team	Lg	W	L	PCT	ERA	G	GS	CG	IP	H	BB	SO	ShO	Relief W	Relief L	Relief SV	AB	H	HR	BA	PO	A	E	DP	TC/G	FA
1995	CHI	A	5	6	.455	4.97	23	10	0	92.1	114	27	48	0	3	1	0	0	0	0	—	9	17	1	1	1.2	.963

Dana Kiecker

KIECKER, DANA ERVIN BR TR 6′ 3″ 180 lbs.
B. Feb. 25, 1961, Sleepy Eye, Minn.

Year	Team	Lg	W	L	PCT	ERA	G	GS	CG	IP	H	BB	SO	ShO	Relief W	Relief L	Relief SV	AB	H	HR	BA	PO	A	E	DP	TC/G	FA
1990	BOS	A	8	9	.471	3.97	32	25	0	152	145	54	93	0	0	0	0	0	0	0	—	18	27	2	1	1.5	.957
1991			2	3	.400	7.36	18	5	0	40.1	56	23	21	0	0	2	0	0	0	0	—	4	11	1	1	0.9	.938
2 yrs.			10	12	.455	4.68	50	30	0	192.1	201	77	114	0	0	2	0	0	0	0		22	38	3	2	1.3	.952
LEAGUE CHAMPIONSHIP SERIES																											
1990	BOS	A	0	0	—	1.59	1	1	0	5.2	6	1	2	0	0	0	0	0	0	0	—	0	0	0	0	0.0	.000

Joe Kiefer

KIEFER, JOSEPH WILLIAM (Harlem Joe, Smoke) BR TR 5′11″ 190 lbs.
B. July 19, 1899, West Leyden, N. Y. D. July 5, 1975, Utica, N. Y.

Year	Team	Lg	W	L	PCT	ERA	G	GS	CG	IP	H	BB	SO	ShO	Relief W	Relief L	Relief SV	AB	H	HR	BA	PO	A	E	DP	TC/G	FA
1920	CHI	A	0	1	.000	15.43	2	1	0	4.2	7	5	1	0	0	0	0	2	0	0	.000	0	0	0	0	0.0	.000
1925	BOS	A	0	2	.000	6.00	2	2	0	15	20	9	4	0	0	0	0	4	0	0	.000	1	7	1	0	4.5	.889
1926			0	2	.000	4.80	11	1	0	30	29	16	4	0	0	1	0	7	1	0	.143	0	10	1	1	1.0	.909
3 yrs.			0	5	.000	6.16	15	4	0	49.2	56	30	9	0	0	1	0	13	1	0	.077	1	17	2	1	1.3	.900

Mark Kiefer

KIEFER, MARK ANDREW BR TR 6′ 4″ 175 lbs.
Brother of Steve Kiefer.
B. Nov. 13, 1968, Orange, Calif.

Year	Team	Lg	W	L	PCT	ERA	G	GS	CG	IP	H	BB	SO	ShO	Relief W	Relief L	Relief SV	AB	H	HR	BA	PO	A	E	DP	TC/G	FA
1993	MIL	A	0	0	—	0.00	6	0	0	9.1	3	5	7	0	0	0	1	0	0	0	—	1	1	0	0	0.3	1.000
1994			1	0	1.000	8.44	7	0	0	10.2	15	8	8	0	1	0	0	0	0	0	—	0	1	0	0	0.1	1.000
1995			4	1	.800	3.44	24	0	0	49.2	37	27	41	0	4	1	0	0	0	0	—	0	3	0	1	0.1	1.000
3 yrs.			5	1	.833	3.75	37	0	0	69.2	55	40	56	0	5	1	1	0	0	0		1	5	0	1	0.2	1.000

John Kiely

KIELY, JOHN FRANCIS BR TR 6′ 3″ 210 lbs.
B. Oct. 4, 1964, Boston, Mass.

Year	Team	Lg	W	L	PCT	ERA	G	GS	CG	IP	H	BB	SO	ShO	Relief W	Relief L	Relief SV	AB	H	HR	BA	PO	A	E	DP	TC/G	FA
1991	DET	A	0	1	.000	14.85	7	0	0	6.2	13	9	1	0	0	1	0	0	0	0	—	0	0	0	0	0.0	.000
1992			4	2	.667	2.13	39	0	0	55	44	28	18	0	4	2	0	0	0	0	—	8	15	0	3	0.6	1.000
1993			0	2	.000	7.71	8	0	0	11.2	13	13	5	0	0	2	0	0	0	0	—	0	5	0	1	0.6	1.000
3 yrs.			4	5	.444	4.17	54	0	0	73.1	70	50	24	0	4	5	0	0	0	0		8	20	0	4	0.5	1.000

Leo Kiely

KIELY, LEO PATRICK BL TL 6′ 2″ 180 lbs.
B. Nov. 30, 1929, Hoboken, N. J. D. Jan. 18, 1984, Montclair, N. J.

Year	Team	Lg	W	L	PCT	ERA	G	GS	CG	IP	H	BB	SO	ShO	Relief W	Relief L	Relief SV	AB	H	HR	BA	PO	A	E	DP	TC/G	FA
1951	BOS	A	7	7	.500	3.34	17	16	4	113.1	106	39	46	0	0	1	0	35	5	0	.143	4	29	2	0	2.1	.943
1954			5	8	.385	3.50	28	19	4	131	153	58	59	1	0	0	0	50	9	1	.180	7	20	5	1	1.1	.844
1955			3	3	.500	2.80	33	4	0	90	91	37	36	0	3	2	6	26	5	0	.192	6	19	0	4	0.8	1.000
1956			2	2	.500	5.17	23	0	0	31.1	47	14	9	0	2	2	3	6	1	0	.167	3	5	0	0	0.3	1.000
1958			5	2	.714	3.00	47	0	0	81	77	18	26	0	5	2	12	13	0	0	.000	4	19	1	1	0.5	.958
1959			3	3	.500	4.20	41	0	0	55.2	67	18	30	0	3	3	7	8	0	0	.000	7	12	0	1	0.5	1.000
1960	KC	A	1	2	.333	1.74	20	0	0	20.2	21	5	6	0	1	2	1	1	0	0	.000	2	9	0	1	0.6	1.000
7 yrs.			26	27	.491	3.37	209	39	8	523	562	189	212	1	14	12	29	139	20	1	.144	33	113	8	8	0.7	.948

Darryl Kile

KILE, DARRYL ANDREW BR TR 6′ 5″ 185 lbs.
B. Dec. 2, 1968, Garden Grove, Calif.

Year	Team	Lg	W	L	PCT	ERA	G	GS	CG	IP	H	BB	SO	ShO	Relief W	Relief L	Relief SV	AB	H	HR	BA	PO	A	E	DP	TC/G	FA
1991	HOU	N	7	11	.389	3.69	37	22	0	153.2	144	84	100	0	0	2	0	38	0	0	.000	7	17	3	1	0.7	.889
1992			5	10	.333	3.95	22	22	2	125.1	124	63	90	0	0	0	0	32	5	0	.156	2	12	5	0	0.9	.737
1993			15	8	.652	3.51	32	26	4	171.2	152	69	141	2	1	0	0	53	5	1	.094	9	15	3	0	0.8	.889
1994			9	6	.600	4.57	24	24	0	147.2	153	**82**	105	0	0	0	0	47	7	0	.149	9	19	1	0	1.2	.966
1995			4	12	.250	4.96	25	21	0	127	114	73	113	0	0	0	0	36	4	0	.111	11	25	3	2	1.6	.923
5 yrs.			40	47	.460	4.09	140	115	6	725.1	687	371	549	2	1	2	0	206	21	1	.102	38	88	15	3	1.0	.894

John Kiley

KILEY, JOHN FREDERICK BL TL 5′ 7″ 147 lbs.
B. July 1, 1859, South Dedham, Mass. D. Dec. 18, 1940, Norwood, Mass.

Year	Team	Lg	W	L	PCT	ERA	G	GS	CG	IP	H	BB	SO	ShO	Relief W	Relief L	Relief SV	AB	H	HR	BA	PO	A	E	DP	TC/G	FA
1891	BOS	N	0	1	.000	6.75	1	1	1	8	13	5	1	0	0	0	0	*				15	1	12	0	2.0	.571

Paul Kilgus

KILGUS, PAUL NELSON BL TL 6′ 1″ 175 lbs.
B. Feb. 2, 1962, Bowling Green, Ky.

Year	Team		W	L	PCT	ERA	G	GS	CG	IP	H	BB	SO	ShO	Relief Pitching W	Relief Pitching L	Relief Pitching SV	Batting AB	Batting H	HR	BA	PO	A	E	DP	TC/G	FA
1987	TEX	A	2	7	.222	4.13	25	12	0	89.1	95	31	42	0	0	2	0	0	0	0	—	7	9	4	2	0.8	.800
1988			12	15	.444	4.16	32	32	5	203.1	190	71	88	3	0	0	0	0	0	0	—	11	34	2	4	1.5	.957
1989	CHI	N	6	10	.375	4.39	35	23	0	145.2	164	49	61	0	0	0	2	41	3	0	.073	10	25	2	0	1.1	.946
1990	TOR	A	0	0	—	6.06	11	0	0	16.1	19	7	7	0	0	0	0	0	0	0	—	1	3	0	0	0.4	1.000
1991	BAL	A	0	2	.000	5.08	38	0	0	62	60	24	32	0	0	2	1	0	0	0	—	14	13	2	2	0.8	.931
1993	STL	N	1	0	1.000	0.63	22	1	0	28.2	18	8	21	0	1	0	1	5	1	0	.200	4	3	0	0	0.3	1.000
6 yrs.			21	34	.382	4.19	163	68	5	545.1	546	190	251	3	1	4	4	46	4	0	.087	47	87	10	8	0.9	.931
LEAGUE CHAMPIONSHIP SERIES																											
1989	CHI	N	0	0	—	0.00	1	0	0	3	4	1	1	0	0	0	0	0	0	0	—	0	0	0	0	0.0	.000

Mike Kilkenny

KILKENNY, MICHAEL DAVID BR TL 6′ 3½″ 175 lbs.
B. Apr. 11, 1945, Bradford, Ont., Canada.

Year	Team		W	L	PCT	ERA	G	GS	CG	IP	H	BB	SO	ShO	Relief Pitching W	Relief Pitching L	Relief Pitching SV	Batting AB	Batting H	HR	BA	PO	A	E	DP	TC/G	FA
1969	DET	A	8	6	.571	3.37	39	15	6	128.1	99	63	97	4	1	1	2	37	2	0	.054	5	19	1	0	0.6	.960
1970			7	6	.538	5.16	36	21	3	129	141	70	105	0	1	0	0	39	3	0	.077	6	20	1	1	0.8	.963
1971			4	5	.444	5.02	30	11	2	86	83	44	47	0	0	0	1	24	2	0	.083	4	14	2	0	0.7	.900
1972	4 teams	DET A (1G 0–0) OAK A (1G 0–0) CLE A (22G 4–1) SD N (5G 0–0)																									
″	total		4	1	.800	3.78	29	7	1	64.1	59	42	49	0	2	0	1	14	1	0	.071	4	11	0	2	0.5	1.000
1973	CLE	A	0	0	—	22.50	5	0	0	2	5	5	3	0	0	0	0	0	0	0	—	0	1	0	0	0.2	1.000
5 yrs.			23	18	.561	4.44	139	54	12	409.2	387	224	301	4	4	1	4	114	8	0	.070	19	65	4	3	0.6	.955

Evans Killeen

KILLEEN, EVANS HENRY BR TR 6′ 190 lbs.
B. Feb. 27, 1936, Brooklyn, N. Y.

Year	Team		W	L	PCT	ERA	G	GS	CG	IP	H	BB	SO	ShO	Relief Pitching W	Relief Pitching L	Relief Pitching SV	Batting AB	Batting H	HR	BA	PO	A	E	DP	TC/G	FA
1959	KC	A	0	0	—	4.76	4	0	0	5.2	4	4	1	0	0	0	0	0	0	0	—	0	0	0	0	0.0	.000

Henry Killeen

KILLEEN, HENRY 5′ 9″ 150 lbs.
B. 1871, Troy, N. Y. Deceased.

Year	Team		W	L	PCT	ERA	G	GS	CG	IP	H	BB	SO	ShO	Relief Pitching W	Relief Pitching L	Relief Pitching SV	Batting AB	Batting H	HR	BA	PO	A	E	DP	TC/G	FA
1891	CLE	N	0	1	.000	6.23	1	1	1	8.2	11	8	3	0	0	0	0	3	0	0	.000	0	3	0	0	3.0	1.000

Frank Killen

KILLEN, FRANK BISSELL (Lefty) BL TL 6′ 1″ 200 lbs.
B. Nov. 30, 1870, Pittsburgh, Pa. D. Dec. 3, 1939, Pittsburgh, Pa.

Year	Team		W	L	PCT	ERA	G	GS	CG	IP	H	BB	SO	ShO	Relief Pitching W	Relief Pitching L	Relief Pitching SV	Batting AB	Batting H	HR	BA	PO	A	E	DP	TC/G	FA
1891	MIL	AA	7	4	.636	1.68	11	11	11	96.1	73	51	38	2	0	0	0	35	8	0	.229	3	22	3	1	2.5	.893
1892	WAS	N	29	26	.527	3.31	60	52	46	459.2	448	182	147	2	1	**3**	0	186	37	4	.199	21	121	22	2	2.6	.866
1893	PIT	N	**36**	14	.720	3.63	55	48	38	416	401	140	99	2	**5**	1	0	171	47	4	.275	16	103	14	2	2.4	.895
1894			14	11	.560	4.50	28	28	20	204	261	86	62	1	0	0	0	80	21	0	.263	6	44	5	2	2.0	.909
1895			5	5	.500	5.49	13	11	6	95	113	57	25	0	1	1	0	38	13	0	.342	1	26	0	1	2.1	1.000
1896			**30**	18	.625	3.41	**52**	**50**	**44**	**432.1**	476	119	134	**5**	1	0	0	173	40	2	.231	15	115	10	1	2.7	.929
1897			17	23	.425	4.46	42	41	**38**	337.1	417	76	99	1	0	1	0	129	32	1	.248	17	73	13	2	2.5	.874
1898	2 teams	PIT N (23G 10–11) WAS N (17G 6–9)																									
″	total		16	20	.444	3.68	40	39	32	306	350	70	91	0	0	0	0	120	32	0	.267	15	69	8	3	2.1	.913
1899	2 teams	WAS N (2G 0–2) BOS N (12G 7–5)																									
″	total		7	7	.500	4.45	14	14	12	111.1	126	30	26	0	0	0	0	46	8	0	.174	6	24	5	0	2.5	.857
1900	CHI	N	3	3	.500	4.67	6	6	6	54	65	11	4	0	0	0	0	20	3	0	.150	0	15	2	0	2.8	.882
10 yrs.			164	131	.556	3.78	321	300	253	2512	2730	822	725	13	8	6	0	998	241	11	.241	100	612	82	14	2.4	.897

Ed Killian

KILLIAN, EDWIN HENRY (Twilight Ed) BL TL 5′11″ 170 lbs.
B. Nov. 12, 1876, Racine, Wis. D. July 18, 1928, Detroit, Mich.

Year	Team		W	L	PCT	ERA	G	GS	CG	IP	H	BB	SO	ShO	Relief Pitching W	Relief Pitching L	Relief Pitching SV	Batting AB	Batting H	HR	BA	PO	A	E	DP	TC/G	FA
1903	CLE	A	3	4	.429	2.48	9	8	7	61.2	61	13	18	3	0	0	0	28	5	0	.179	2	20	2	0	2.7	.917
1904	DET	A	14	20	.412	2.44	40	34	32	331.2	293	93	124	4	0	**2**	1	126	18	0	.143	20	85	8	3	2.8	.929
1905			23	14	.622	2.27	39	37	33	313.1	263	102	110	**8**	2	0	0	118	32	0	.271	14	79	7	3	2.6	.930
1906			10	6	.625	3.43	21	16	14	149.2	165	54	47	0	1	0	2	53	9	0	.170	2	38	2	2	2.0	.952
1907			25	13	.658	1.78	42	34	29	314	286	91	96	3	**5**	0	1	122	39	0	.320	17	97	4	1	2.7	.966
1908			12	9	.571	2.99	27	23	15	180.2	170	53	47	0	0	0	1	73	10	0	.137	15	71	3	0	3.3	.966
1909			11	9	.550	1.71	25	19	14	173.1	150	49	54	3	1	0	1	62	10	0	.161	11	49	1	1	2.4	.984
1910			4	3	.571	3.04	11	9	5	74	75	27	20	1	0	1	0	27	4	0	.148	7	19	0	0	2.4	1.000
8 yrs.			102	78	.567	2.38	214	180	149	1598.1	1463	482	516	22	9	3	6	609	127	0	.209	88	458	27	10	2.7	.953
WORLD SERIES																											
1907	DET	A	0	0	—	2.25	1	0	0	4	3	1	1	0	0	0	0	2	1	0	.500	0	0	0	0	0.0	.000
1908			0	0	—	7.71	1	1	0	2.1	5	3	1	0	0	0	0	0	0	0	—	0	1	0	0	1.0	1.000
2 yrs.			0	0		4.26	2	1	0	6.1	8	4	2	0	0	0	0	2	1	0	.500	0	1	0	0	0.5	1.000

Jack Killilay

KILLILAY, JOHN WILLIAM BR TR 5′11″ 165 lbs.
B. May 24, 1887, Leavenworth, Kans. D. Oct. 21, 1968, Tulsa, Okla.

Year	Team		W	L	PCT	ERA	G	GS	CG	IP	H	BB	SO	ShO	Relief Pitching W	Relief Pitching L	Relief Pitching SV	Batting AB	Batting H	HR	BA	PO	A	E	DP	TC/G	FA
1911	BOS	A	4	2	.667	3.54	14	7	1	61	65	36	28	0	2	0	0	24	1	0	.042	1	17	0	0	1.3	1.000

Matt Kilroy

KILROY, MATTHEW ALOYSIUS (Matches) BL TL 5′ 9″ 175 lbs.
Brother of Mike Kilroy.
B. June 21, 1866, Philadelphia, Pa. D. Mar. 2, 1940, Philadelphia, Pa.

Year	Team		W	L	PCT	ERA	G	GS	CG	IP	H	BB	SO	ShO	Relief Pitching W	Relief Pitching L	Relief Pitching SV	Batting AB	Batting H	HR	BA	PO	A	E	DP	TC/G	FA
1886	BAL	AA	29	**34**	.460	*3.37*	**68**	**68**	**66**	583	476	182	**513**	5	0	0	0	218	38	0	.174	32	116	28	1	2.5	.841
1887			**46**	19	.708	*3.07*	**69**	**69**	**66**	**589.1**	**585**	157	217	**6**	0	0	0	239	59	0	.247	39	167	22	2	3.1	.904
1888			17	21	.447	4.04	40	40	35	321	347	79	135	2	0	0	0	145	26	0	.179	21	61	6	2	1.9	.932
1889			29	25	.537	2.85	59	56	**55**	480.2	476	142	217	5	0	0	0	208	57	1	.274	30	142	18	4	2.8	.905
1890	BOS	P	9	15	.375	4.26	30	27	18	217.2	268	87	48	0	1	1	1	93	20	0	.215	28	60	10	2	2.9	.898
1891	CIN	AA	1	4	.200	2.98	7	6	4	45.1	51	19	6	0	0	0	0	20	3	0	.150	3	14	2	0	2.4	.895
1892	WAS	N	1	1	.500	2.39	4	3	2	26.1	20	15	1	0	0	0	0	10	2	0	.200	3	14	2	0	4.8	.895
1893	LOU	N	3	2	.600	9.00	5	5	5	35	57	23	4	1	0	0	0	16	7	0	.438	1	12	1	0	2.8	.929
1894			0	5	.000	3.89	8	7	3	37	46	20	11	0	0	0	0	17	2	0	.118	6	13	4	0	2.9	.826
1898	CHI	N	6	7	.462	4.31	13	11	10	100.1	119	30	18	0	1	1	0	96	22	0	.229	21	31	4	2	2.2	.929
10 yrs.			141	133	.515	3.47	303	292	264	2435.2	2445	754	1170	19	2	2	1	*				184	630	97	13	2.7	.894

Mike Kilroy

KILROY, MICHAEL JOSEPH BR TR
Brother of Matt Kilroy.
B. Nov. 4, 1872, Philadelphia, Pa. D. Oct. 2, 1960, Philadelphia, Pa.

Year	Team	Lg	W	L	PCT	ERA	G	GS	CG	IP	H	BB	SO	ShO	Relief W	Relief L	Relief SV	Batting AB	Batting H	Batting HR	BA	PO	A	E	DP	TC/G	FA
1888	**BAL**	**AA**	0	1	.000	8.00	1	1	1	9	12	5	1	0	0	0	0	4	0	0	.000	1	1	0	0	2.0	1.000
1891	**PHI**	**N**	0	2	.000	9.90	3	1	0	10	15	4	3	0	0	1	0	5	2	0	.400	1	1	0	0	0.7	1.000
2 yrs.			0	3	.000	9.00	4	2	1	19	27	9	4	0	0	1	0	9	2	0	.222	2	2	0	0	1.0	1.000

Newt Kimball

KIMBALL, NEWELL W. BR TR 6′ 2½″ 190 lbs.
B. Mar. 27, 1915, Logan, Utah.

Year	Team	Lg	W	L	PCT	ERA	G	GS	CG	IP	H	BB	SO	ShO	Relief W	Relief L	Relief SV	Batting AB	Batting H	Batting HR	BA	PO	A	E	DP	TC/G	FA
1937	**CHI**	**N**	0	0	—	10.80	2	0	0	5	12	1	0	0	0	0	0	1	0	0	.000	0	2	0	0	1.0	1.000
1938			0	0	—	9.00	1	0	0	1	3	0	1	0	0	0	0	0	0	0	—	0	0	0	0	0.0	.000
1940	**2 teams**	**BKN N**	(21G 3–1)		**STL N**	(2G 1–0)																					
″	**total**		4	1	.800	3.02	23	1	1	47.2	40	21	27	0	3	1	1	11	2	0	.182	4	5	0	0	0.4	1.000
1941	**BKN**	**N**	3	1	.750	3.63	15	5	1	52	43	29	17	0	1	0	1	14	3	0	.214	4	10	0	0	0.9	1.000
1942			2	0	1.000	3.68	14	1	0	29.1	27	19	8	0	1	0	0	5	1	0	.200	0	0	0	0	0.0	.000
1943	**2 teams**	**BKN N**	(5G 1–1)		**PHI N**	(34G 1–6)																					
″	**total**		2	7	.222	3.84	39	6	2	100.2	94	47	35	0	1	4	3	19	3	0	.158	5	10	4	2	0.5	.789
6 yrs.			11	9	.550	3.78	94	13	4	235.2	219	117	88	0	6	5	5	50	9	0	.180	13	27	4	2	0.5	.909

Sam Kimber

KIMBER, SAMUEL JACKSON BR TR 5′10½″ 168 lbs.
B. Oct. 29, 1852, Philadelphia, Pa. D. Nov. 7, 1925, Philadelphia, Pa.

Year	Team	Lg	W	L	PCT	ERA	G	GS	CG	IP	H	BB	SO	ShO	Relief W	Relief L	Relief SV	Batting AB	Batting H	Batting HR	BA	PO	A	E	DP	TC/G	FA
1884	**BKN**	**AA**	17	20	.459	*3.91*	40	40	40	352.1	363	69	119	3	0	0	0	138	20	0	.145	32	67	30	0	3.2	.767
1885	**PRO**	**N**	0	1	.000	11.25	1	1	1	8	15	5	4	0	0	0	0	3	0	0	.000	0	4	1	0	5.0	.800
2 yrs.			17	21	.447	4.07	41	41	41	360.1	378	74	123	3	0	0	0	141	20	0	.142	32	71	31	0	3.3	.769

Harry Kimberlin

KIMBERLIN, HARRY LYDLE (Murphy) BR TR 6′ 3″ 175 lbs.
B. Mar. 13, 1909, Sullivan, Mo. BB 1938

Year	Team	Lg	W	L	PCT	ERA	G	GS	CG	IP	H	BB	SO	ShO	Relief W	Relief L	Relief SV	Batting AB	Batting H	Batting HR	BA	PO	A	E	DP	TC/G	FA
1936	**STL**	**A**	0	0	—	5.40	13	0	0	20	24	16	4	0	0	0	0	1	0	0	.000	0	2	0	0	0.2	1.000
1937			0	2	.000	2.35	3	2	1	15.1	16	9	5	0	0	0	0	5	1	0	.200	0	3	1	0	1.3	.750
1938			0	0	—	3.38	1	1	1	8	8	3	1	0	0	0	0	1	0	0	.000	0	0	0	0	0.0	.000
1939			1	2	.333	5.49	17	3	0	41	59	19	11	0	1	0	0	9	3	0	.333	2	8	1	0	0.6	.909
4 yrs.			1	4	.200	4.70	34	6	2	84.1	107	47	21	0	1	0	0	16	4	0	.250	2	13	2	0	0.5	.882

Hal Kime

KIME, HAROLD LEE (Lefty) BL TL 5′ 9″ 160 lbs.
B. Mar. 15, 1899, West Salem, Ohio D. May 16, 1939, Columbus, Ohio.

Year	Team	Lg	W	L	PCT	ERA	G	GS	CG	IP	H	BB	SO	ShO	Relief W	Relief L	Relief SV	Batting AB	Batting H	Batting HR	BA	PO	A	E	DP	TC/G	FA
1920	**STL**	**N**	0	0	—	2.57	4	0	0	7	9	2	1	0	0	0	0	1	0	0	.000	0	3	0	0	0.8	1.000

Chad Kimsey

KIMSEY, CLYDE ELIAS BL TR 6′ 3½″ 200 lbs.
B. Aug. 6, 1906, Copperhill, Tenn. D. Dec. 3, 1942, Pryor, Okla.

Year	Team	Lg	W	L	PCT	ERA	G	GS	CG	IP	H	BB	SO	ShO	Relief W	Relief L	Relief SV	Batting AB	Batting H	Batting HR	BA	PO	A	E	DP	TC/G	FA
1929	**STL**	**A**	3	6	.333	5.04	24	3	1	64.1	88	19	13	0	1	**5**	1	30	8	2	.267	7	25	1	2	1.4	.970
1930			6	10	.375	6.35	42	4	1	113.1	139	45	32	0	6	**7**	1	70	24	2	.343	2	32	2	0	0.9	.944
1931			4	6	.400	4.39	42	1	0	94.1	121	27	27	0	4	**5**	7	37	10	2	.270	6	31	3	1	1.0	.925
1932	**2 teams**	**STL A**	(33G 4–2)		**CHI A**	(7G 1–1)																					
″	**total**		5	3	.625	3.83	40	0	0	89.1	93	38	19	0	5	3	5	20	6	0	.300	4	30	2	2	0.9	.944
1933	**CHI**	**A**	4	1	.800	5.53	28	2	0	96	124	36	19	0	4	0	0	33	5	0	.152	2	28	0	2	1.1	1.000
1936	**DET**	**A**	2	3	.400	4.85	22	0	0	52	58	29	11	0	2	3	3	16	5	0	.313	3	18	1	0	1.0	.955
6 yrs.			24	29	.453	5.07	198	10	2	509.1	623	194	121	0	22	23	17	*				24	164	9	7	1.0	.954

Ellis Kinder

KINDER, ELLIS RAYMOND (Old Folks) BR TR 6′ 215 lbs.
B. July 26, 1914, Atkins, Ark. D. Oct. 16, 1968, Jackson, Tenn.

Year	Team	Lg	W	L	PCT	ERA	G	GS	CG	IP	H	BB	SO	ShO	Relief W	Relief L	Relief SV	Batting AB	Batting H	Batting HR	BA	PO	A	E	DP	TC/G	FA
1946	**STL**	**A**	3	3	.500	3.32	33	7	1	86.2	78	36	59	0	0	0	1	19	1	0	.053	2	10	0	2	0.4	1.000
1947			8	15	.348	4.49	34	26	10	194.1	201	82	110	2	0	0	1	62	8	0	.129	5	18	2	2	0.7	.920
1948	**BOS**	**A**	10	7	.588	3.74	28	22	10	178	183	63	53	1	1	2	0	62	6	0	.097	5	20	1	2	0.9	.962
1949			23	6	**.793**	3.36	43	30	19	252	251	99	138	**6**	2	1	4	92	12	0	.130	7	28	1	1	0.8	.972
1950			14	12	.538	4.26	48	23	11	207	212	78	95	1	3	4	9	71	13	1	.183	7	30	3	0	0.8	.925
1951			11	2	.846	2.55	**63**	2	1	127	108	46	84	0	**10**	1	**14**	34	4	0	.118	5	13	0	1	0.3	1.000
1952			5	6	.455	2.58	23	10	4	97.2	85	28	50	0	1	2	4	32	0	0	.000	4	16	0	2	0.9	1.000
1953			10	6	.625	1.85	**69**	0	0	107	84	38	39	0	**10**	6	**27**	29	11	0	.379	10	18	0	0	0.4	1.000
1954			8	8	.500	3.62	48	2	0	107	106	36	67	0	7	**8**	15	27	5	0	.185	2	11	2	0	0.3	.867
1955			5	5	.500	2.84	43	0	0	66.2	57	15	31	0	5	5	18	12	3	0	.250	2	7	0	1	0.2	1.000
1956	**2 teams**	**STL N**	(22G 2–0)		**CHI A**	(29G 3–1)																					
″	**total**		5	1	.833	3.09	51	0	0	55.1	56	17	23	0	5	1	9	4	0	0	.000	3	3	0	0	0.1	1.000
1957	**CHI**	**A**	0	0	—	0.00	1	0	0	1	0	1	0	0	0	0	0	0	0	0	—	0	0	0	0	0.0	.000
12 yrs.			102	71	.590	3.43	484	122	56	1479.2	1421	539	749	10	44	30	102	444	63	1	.142	52	174	9	11	0.5	.962

Clyde King

KING, CLYDE EDWARD BB TR 6′ 1″ 175 lbs.
B. May 23, 1925, Goldsboro, N. C.
Manager 1969–70, 1974–75, 1982.

Year	Team	Lg	W	L	PCT	ERA	G	GS	CG	IP	H	BB	SO	ShO	Relief W	Relief L	Relief SV	Batting AB	Batting H	Batting HR	BA	PO	A	E	DP	TC/G	FA
1944	**BKN**	**N**	2	1	.667	3.09	14	3	1	43.2	42	12	14	0	0	0	0	10	2	0	.200	0	3	0	0	0.2	1.000
1945			5	5	.500	4.09	42	2	0	112.1	131	48	29	0	5	4	3	32	4	0	.125	5	27	2	2	0.8	.941
1947			6	5	.545	2.77	29	9	2	87.2	85	29	31	0	2	2	0	26	3	0	.115	5	11	1	1	0.6	.941
1948			0	1	.000	8.03	9	0	0	12.1	14	6	5	0	0	1	0	2	0	0	.000	0	4	0	0	0.4	1.000
1951			14	7	.667	4.15	48	3	1	121.1	118	50	33	0	**13**	6	6	29	4	0	.138	12	21	0	4	0.7	1.000
1952			2	0	1.000	5.06	23	0	0	42.2	56	12	17	0	2	0	0	5	0	0	.000	6	11	1	1	0.8	.944
1953	**CIN**	**N**	3	6	.333	5.21	35	4	0	76	78	32	21	0	2	4	2	10	0	0	.000	6	11	0	3	0.5	1.000
7 yrs.			32	25	.561	4.14	200	21	4	496	524	189	150	0	24	17	11	114	13	0	.114	34	88	4	11	0.6	.968

Eric King

KING, ERIC STEVEN BR TR 6′ 2″ 180 lbs.
B. Apr. 10, 1964, Oxnard, Calif.

Year	Team	Lg	W	L	PCT	ERA	G	GS	CG	IP	H	BB	SO	ShO	Relief W	Relief L	Relief SV	Batting AB	Batting H	Batting HR	BA	PO	A	E	DP	TC/G	FA
1986	**DET**	**A**	11	4	.733	3.51	33	16	3	138.1	108	63	79	1	3	0	3	0	0	0	—	19	15	1	0	1.1	.971
1987			6	9	.400	4.89	55	4	0	116	111	60	89	0	6	7	9	0	0	0	—	15	22	1	3	0.7	.974
1988			4	1	.800	3.41	23	5	0	68.2	60	34	45	0	1	0	3	0	0	0	—	3	8	2	0	0.6	.846
1989	**CHI**	**A**	9	10	.474	3.39	25	25	1	159.1	144	64	72	1	0	0	0	0	0	0	—	15	20	3	2	1.5	.921
1990			12	4	.750	3.28	25	25	2	151	135	40	70	2	0	0	0	0	0	0	—	8	15	0	1	0.9	1.000

Eric King *continued*

Year	Team	Lg	W	L	PCT	ERA	G	GS	CG	IP	H	BB	SO	ShO	Relief W	Relief L	Relief SV	Batting AB	Batting H	Batting HR	BA	PO	A	E	DP	TC/G	FA
1991	CLE	A	6	11	.353	4.60	25	24	2	150.2	166	44	59	1	0	0	0	0	0	0	—	9	14	2	2	1.0	.920
1992	DET	A	4	6	.400	5.22	17	14	0	79.1	90	28	45	0	0	0	1	0	0	0	—	6	5	1	0	0.7	.917
7 yrs.			52	45	.536	3.97	203	113	8	863.1	814	333	459	5	10	7	16	0	0	0		75	99	10	8	0.9	.946
LEAGUE CHAMPIONSHIP SERIES																											
1987	DET	A	0	0	—	1.69	2	0	0	5.1	3	2	4	0	0	0	0	0	0	0	—	1	1	0	0	1.0	1.000

Kevin King

KING, KEVIN RAY BL TL 6′ 4″ 170 lbs.
B. Feb. 11, 1969, Atwater, Calif.

Year	Team	Lg	W	L	PCT	ERA	G	GS	CG	IP	H	BB	SO	ShO	Relief W	Relief L	Relief SV	Batting AB	Batting H	Batting HR	BA	PO	A	E	DP	TC/G	FA
1993	SEA	A	0	1	.000	6.17	13	0	0	11.2	9	4	8	0	0	1	0	0	0	0	—	0	1	1	0	0.2	.500
1994			0	2	.000	7.04	19	0	0	15.1	21	17	6	0	0	2	0	0	0	0	—	1	3	0	0	0.2	1.000
1995			0	0	—	12.27	2	0	0	3.2	7	1	3	0	0	0	0	0	0	0	—	0	0	1	0	0.5	.000
3 yrs.			0	3	.000	7.34	34	0	0	30.2	37	22	17	0	0	3	0	0	0	0		1	4	2	0	0.2	.714

Nellie King

KING, NELSON JOSEPH BR TR 6′ 6″ 185 lbs.
B. Mar. 15, 1928, Shenandoah, Pa.

Year	Team	Lg	W	L	PCT	ERA	G	GS	CG	IP	H	BB	SO	ShO	Relief W	Relief L	Relief SV	Batting AB	Batting H	Batting HR	BA	PO	A	E	DP	TC/G	FA
1954	PIT	N	0	0	—	5.14	4	0	0	7	10	1	3	0	0	0	0	0	0	0	—	0	3	0	1	0.8	1.000
1955			1	3	.250	2.98	17	4	0	54.1	60	14	21	0	0	1	0	12	0	0	.000	7	6	0	1	0.8	1.000
1956			4	1	.800	3.15	38	0	0	60	54	19	25	0	4	1	5	6	0	0	.000	6	5	0	0	0.3	1.000
1957			2	1	.667	4.50	36	0	0	52	69	16	23	0	2	1	1	5	0	0	.000	6	6	0	0	0.3	1.000
4 yrs.			7	5	.583	3.58	95	4	0	173.1	193	50	72	0	6	3	6	23	0	0	.000	19	20	0	2	0.4	1.000

Silver King

KING, CHARLES FREDERICK BR TR 6′ 170 lbs.
Born Charles Frederick Koenig.
B. Jan. 11, 1868, St. Louis, Mo. D. May 21, 1938, St. Louis, Mo.

Year	Team	Lg	W	L	PCT	ERA	G	GS	CG	IP	H	BB	SO	ShO	Relief W	Relief L	Relief SV	Batting AB	Batting H	Batting HR	BA	PO	A	E	DP	TC/G	FA
1886	KC	N	1	3	.250	*4.85*	5	5	5	39	43	9	23	0	0	0	0	22	1	0	.045	0	13	3	0	2.3	.813
1887	STL	AA	32	12	.727	*3.78*	46	44	43	390	401	109	128	2	**1**	0	1	222	46	0	.207	35	70	16	1	1.9	.868
1888			**45**	21	.682	**1.64**	**66**	**65**	**64**	**585.2**	437	76	258	**6**	**1**	0	0	207	43	1	.208	33	119	12	4	2.4	.927
1889			33	17	.660	3.14	56	53	47	458	462	125	188	2	0	1	1	189	43	0	.228	19	91	5	2	1.9	.957
1890	CHI	P	30	22	.577	**2.69**	56	56	48	461	420	163	185	**4**	0	0	0	185	31	1	.168	22	139	6	5	2.9	.964
1891	PIT	N	14	**29**	.326	3.11	48	44	40	384.1	382	144	160	3	0	0	1	148	25	0	.169	19	67	10	5	2.0	.896
1892	NY	N	23	24	.489	3.24	52	47	46	419.1	397	174	177	1	1	0	0	167	35	2	.210	22	81	11	4	2.2	.904
1893	2 teams	NY N	(7G 3–4)	CIN N	(17G 5–6)																						
″	total		8	10	.444	6.08	24	21	12	154	188	82	43	1	0	0	1	54	9	0	.167	8	32	3	1	1.8	.930
1896	WAS	N	10	7	.588	4.09	22	16	12	145.1	179	43	35	0	**3**	1	1	58	16	0	.276	6	19	1	0	1.2	.962
1897			6	9	.400	4.79	23	19	12	154	196	45	32	0	0	1	1	57	11	0	.193	2	40	2	1	1.9	.955
10 yrs.			202	154	.567	3.18	398	370	329	3190.2	3105	970	1229	19	6	3	6	*				166	671	69	23	2.1	.924

Brian Kingman

KINGMAN, BRIAN PAUL BR TR 6′ 2″ 200 lbs.
B. July 27, 1954, Los Angeles, Calif.

Year	Team	Lg	W	L	PCT	ERA	G	GS	CG	IP	H	BB	SO	ShO	Relief W	Relief L	Relief SV	Batting AB	Batting H	Batting HR	BA	PO	A	E	DP	TC/G	FA
1979	OAK	A	8	7	.533	4.30	18	17	5	113	113	33	58	1	1	0	0	0	0	0	—	8	8	2	0	1.0	.889
1980			8	**20**	.286	3.84	32	30	10	211	209	82	116	1	0	1	0	0	0	0	—	7	22	3	2	1.0	.906
1981			3	6	.333	3.96	18	15	3	100	112	32	52	1	0	0	0	0	0	0	—	4	9	2	0	0.8	.867
1982			4	12	.250	4.48	23	20	3	122.2	131	57	46	0	1	0	1	0	0	0	—	3	9	1	0	0.6	.923
1983	SF	N	0	0	—	7.71	3	0	0	4.2	10	1	1	0	0	0	0	0	0	0	—	0	0	0	0	0.0	.000
5 yrs.			23	45	.338	4.13	94	82	21	551.1	575	205	273	3	2	1	1	0	0	0		22	48	8	2	0.8	.897
LEAGUE CHAMPIONSHIP SERIES																											
1981	OAK	A	0	0	—	81.00	1	0	0	0.1	3	0	0	0	0	0	0	0	0	0	—	0	0	0	0	0.0	.000

Dave Kingman

KINGMAN, DAVID ARTHUR (Kong) BR TR 6′ 6″ 210 lbs.
B. Dec. 21, 1948, Pendleton, Ore.

Year	Team	Lg	W	L	PCT	ERA	G	GS	CG	IP	H	BB	SO	ShO	Relief W	Relief L	Relief SV	Batting AB	Batting H	Batting HR	BA	PO	A	E	DP	TC/G	FA
1973	SF	N	0	0	—	9.00	2	0	0	4	3	6	4	0	0	0	0	*				168	9	4	9	5.3	.978

Dennis Kinney

KINNEY, DENNIS PAUL BL TL 6′ 1″ 175 lbs.
B. Feb. 26, 1952, Toledo, Ohio.

Year	Team	Lg	W	L	PCT	ERA	G	GS	CG	IP	H	BB	SO	ShO	Relief W	Relief L	Relief SV	Batting AB	Batting H	Batting HR	BA	PO	A	E	DP	TC/G	FA
1978	2 teams	CLE A	(18G 0–2)	SD N	(7G 0–1)																						
″	total		0	3	.000	4.73	25	0	0	45.2	43	18	21	0	0	3	5	1	0	0	.000	4	4	1	1	0.4	.889
1979	SD	N	0	0	—	3.50	13	0	0	18	17	8	11	0	0	0	0	1	0	0	.000	0	2	1	0	0.2	.667
1980			4	6	.400	4.23	50	0	0	83	79	37	40	0	4	6	1	12	1	0	.083	2	13	0	0	0.3	1.000
1981	DET	A	0	0	—	9.00	6	0	0	4	5	4	3	0	0	0	0	0	0	0	—	1	0	0	0	0.2	1.000
1982	OAK	A	0	0	—	8.31	3	0	0	4.1	9	4	0	0	0	0	0	0	0	0	—	0	1	0	0	0.3	1.000
5 yrs.			4	9	.308	4.53	97	0	0	155	153	71	75	0	4	9	6	14	1	0	.071	7	20	2	1	0.3	.931

Walt Kinney

KINNEY, WALTER WILLIAM BL TL 6′ 2″ 186 lbs.
B. Sept. 9, 1893, Denison, Tex. D. July 1, 1971, Escondido, Calif.

Year	Team	Lg	W	L	PCT	ERA	G	GS	CG	IP	H	BB	SO	ShO	Relief W	Relief L	Relief SV	Batting AB	Batting H	Batting HR	BA	PO	A	E	DP	TC/G	FA
1918	BOS	A	0	0	—	1.80	5	0	0	15	5	8	4	0	0	0	0	5	0	0	.000	2	3	0	0	0.8	1.000
1919	PHI	A	9	15	.375	3.64	43	21	13	202.2	199	91	97	0	3	2	2	88	25	1	.284	14	63	6	3	1.9	.928
1920			2	4	.333	3.10	10	8	5	61	59	28	19	1	0	0	0	26	9	0	.346	4	15	1	0	2.0	.950
1923			0	1	.000	7.50	5	1	0	12	11	9	9	0	0	1	0	6	1	1	.167	1	1	0	0	0.4	1.000
4 yrs.			11	20	.355	3.59	63	30	18	290.2	274	136	129	1	3	3	2	125	35	2	.280	21	82	7	3	1.7	.936

Mike Kinnunen

KINNUNEN, MICHAEL JOHN BL TL 6′ 1″ 185 lbs.
B. Apr. 1, 1958, Seattle, Wash.

Year	Team	Lg	W	L	PCT	ERA	G	GS	CG	IP	H	BB	SO	ShO	Relief W	Relief L	Relief SV	Batting AB	Batting H	Batting HR	BA	PO	A	E	DP	TC/G	FA
1980	MIN	A	0	0	—	5.04	21	0	0	25	29	9	8	0	0	0	0	0	0	0	—	6	3	0	0	0.4	1.000
1986	BAL	A	0	0	—	6.43	9	0	0	7	8	5	1	0	0	0	0	0	0	0	—	1	2	0	0	0.3	1.000
1987			0	0	—	4.95	18	0	0	20	27	16	14	0	0	0	0	0	0	0	—	0	2	0	0	0.1	1.000
3 yrs.			0	0		5.19	48	0	0	52	64	30	23	0	0	0	0	0	0	0		7	7	0	0	0.3	1.000

Ed Kinsella

KINSELLA, EDWARD WILLIAM (Rube) BR TR 6′ 1½″ 175 lbs.
B. Jan. 15, 1882, Lexington, Ill. D. Jan. 17, 1976, Bloomington, Ill.

Year	Team	Lg	W	L	PCT	ERA	G	GS	CG	IP	H	BB	SO	ShO	Relief W	Relief L	Relief SV	Batting AB	Batting H	Batting HR	BA	PO	A	E	DP	TC/G	FA
1905	PIT	N	0	1	.000	2.65	3	2	2	17	19	3	11	0	0	0	0	3	0	0	.000	0	1	1	0	0.7	.500
1910	STL	A	1	3	.250	3.78	10	5	2	50	62	16	10	0	0	0	0	12	3	0	.250	0	22	2	2	2.4	.917
2 yrs.			1	4	.200	3.49	13	7	4	67	81	19	21	0	0	0	0	15	3	0	.200	0	23	3	2	2.0	.885

Matt Kinzer

KINZER, MATTHEW ROY
B. June 17, 1963, Indianapolis, Ind.
BR TR 6' 2" 210 lbs.

Year	Team	W	L	PCT	ERA	G	GS	CG	IP	H	BB	SO	ShO	Relief W	Relief L	Relief SV	AB	H	HR	BA	PO	A	E	DP	TC/G	FA
1989	STL N	0	2	.000	12.82	8	1	0	13.1	25	4	8	0	0	1	0	1	0	0	.000	0	0	0	0	0.0	.000
1990	DET A	0	0	—	16.20	1	0	0	1.2	3	3	1	0	0	0	0	0	0	0	—	0	0	0	0	0.0	.000
2 yrs.		0	2	.000	13.20	9	1	0	15	28	7	9	0	0	1	0	1	0	0	.000	0	0	0	0	0.0	

Harry Kinzy

KINZY, HENRY HERSHEL (Slim)
B. July 19, 1910, Hallsville, Tex.
BR TR 6' 4" 185 lbs.

Year	Team	W	L	PCT	ERA	G	GS	CG	IP	H	BB	SO	ShO	Relief W	Relief L	Relief SV	AB	H	HR	BA	PO	A	E	DP	TC/G	FA
1934	CHI A	0	1	.000	4.98	13	2	1	34.1	38	31	12	0	0	0	0	10	3	0	.300	1	6	1	0	0.6	.875

Fred Kipp

KIPP, FRED LEO
B. Oct. 1, 1931, Piqua, Kans.
BL TL 6' 4" 200 lbs.

Year	Team	W	L	PCT	ERA	G	GS	CG	IP	H	BB	SO	ShO	Relief W	Relief L	Relief SV	AB	H	HR	BA	PO	A	E	DP	TC/G	FA
1957	BKN N	0	0	—	9.00	1	0	0	4	6	0	3	0	0	0	0	1	0	0	.000	0	1	0	0	1.0	1.000
1958	LA N	6	6	.500	5.01	40	9	0	102.1	107	45	58	0	2	3	0	36	9	0	.250	7	18	0	0	0.6	1.000
1959		0	0	—	0.00	2	0	0	2.2	2	3	1	0	0	0	0	0	0	0	—	0	2	0	0	1.0	1.000
1960	NY A	0	1	.000	6.23	4	0	0	4.1	4	0	2	0	0	1	0	0	0	0	—	0	1	0	0	0.3	1.000
4 yrs.		6	7	.462	5.08	47	9	0	113.1	119	48	64	0	2	4	0	37	9	0	.243	7	22	0	0	0.6	1.000

Bob Kipper

KIPPER, ROBERT WAYNE
B. July 8, 1964, Aurora, Ill.
BR TL 6' 2" 190 lbs.

Year	Team	W	L	PCT	ERA	G	GS	CG	IP	H	BB	SO	ShO	Relief W	Relief L	Relief SV	AB	H	HR	BA	PO	A	E	DP	TC/G	FA
1985	2 teams CAL A (2G 0–1) PIT N (5G 1–2)																									
"	total	1	3	.250	7.07	7	5	0	28	28	10	13	0	0	0	0	8	2	0	.250	1	5	1	0	1.0	.857
1986	PIT N	6	8	.429	4.03	20	19	0	114	123	34	81	0	0	0	0	33	1	0	.030	1	15	1	2	0.9	.941
1987		5	9	.357	5.94	24	20	1	110.2	117	52	83	1	0	0	0	33	8	0	.242	3	16	0	1	0.8	1.000
1988		2	6	.250	3.74	50	0	0	65	54	26	39	0	2	6	0	4	0	0	.000	4	16	0	1	0.4	1.000
1989		3	4	.429	2.93	52	0	0	83	55	33	58	0	3	4	4	9	1	0	.111	3	10	2	1	0.3	.867
1990		5	2	.714	3.02	41	1	0	62.2	44	26	35	0	5	1	3	7	1	0	.143	5	8	0	0	0.3	1.000
1991		2	2	.500	4.65	52	0	0	60	66	22	38	0	2	2	4	1	0	0	.000	1	6	2	0	0.2	.778
1992	MIN A	3	3	.500	4.42	25	0	0	38.2	40	14	22	0	3	3	0	0	0	0	—	0	6	0	1	0.2	1.000
8 yrs.		27	37	.422	4.34	271	45	1	562	527	217	369	1	15	16	11	95	13	0	.137	18	82	6	6	0.4	.943
LEAGUE CHAMPIONSHIP SERIES																										
1991	PIT N	0	0	—	4.50	1	0	0	2	2	0	1	0	0	0	0	0	0	0	—	0	1	0	0	1.0	1.000

Thornton Kipper

KIPPER, THORNTON JOHN
B. Sept. 27, 1928, Bagley, Wis.
BR TR 6' 3" 190 lbs.

Year	Team	W	L	PCT	ERA	G	GS	CG	IP	H	BB	SO	ShO	Relief W	Relief L	Relief SV	AB	H	HR	BA	PO	A	E	DP	TC/G	FA
1953	PHI N	3	3	.500	4.73	20	3	0	45.2	59	12	15	0	3	0	0	11	1	0	.091	6	5	0	1	0.6	1.000
1954		0	0	—	7.90	11	0	0	13.2	22	12	5	0	0	0	1	2	0	0	.000	0	4	0	0	0.4	1.000
1955		0	1	.000	4.99	24	0	0	39.2	47	22	15	0	0	1	0	3	1	0	.333	1	5	0	0	0.3	1.000
3 yrs.		3	4	.429	5.27	55	3	0	99	128	46	35	0	3	1	1	16	2	0	.125	7	14	0	1	0.4	1.000

Clay Kirby

KIRBY, CLAYTON LAWS
B. June 25, 1948, Washington, D. C. D. Oct. 11, 1991, Arlington, Va.
BR TR 6' 3" 175 lbs.

Year	Team	W	L	PCT	ERA	G	GS	CG	IP	H	BB	SO	ShO	Relief W	Relief L	Relief SV	AB	H	HR	BA	PO	A	E	DP	TC/G	FA
1969	SD N	7	**20**	.259	3.79	35	35	2	216	204	100	113	0	0	0	0	66	4	0	.061	17	23	4	4	1.3	.909
1970		10	16	.385	4.52	36	34	6	215	198	120	154	1	0	0	0	74	11	0	.149	6	23	2	1	0.9	.935
1971		15	13	.536	2.83	38	36	13	267	213	103	231	2	0	0	0	86	8	0	.093	17	33	2	1	1.4	.962
1972		12	14	.462	3.13	34	34	9	238.2	197	116	175	2	0	0	0	74	5	0	.068	11	29	5	3	1.3	.889
1973		8	18	.308	4.79	34	31	4	191.2	214	66	129	2	0	0	0	54	5	0	.093	9	19	3	1	0.9	.903
1974	CIN N	12	9	.571	3.27	36	35	7	231	210	91	160	1	0	0	0	74	7	0	.095	11	27	10	1	1.3	.792
1975		10	6	.625	4.70	26	19	1	111	113	54	48	0	3	1	0	32	6	0	.188	7	9	3	0	0.7	.842
1976	MON N	1	8	.111	5.72	22	15	0	78.2	81	63	51	0	0	0	0	18	1	0	.056	1	9	0	1	0.5	1.000
8 yrs.		75	104	.419	3.83	261	239	42	1549	1430	713	1061	8	3	1	0	478	47	0	.098	79	172	29	12	1.1	.896

John Kirby

KIRBY, JOHN F. (Chickenhearted)
B. Jan. 13, 1865, St. Louis, Mo. D. Oct. 6, 1931, St. Louis, Mo.
TR 5' 8" 172 lbs.

Year	Team	W	L	PCT	ERA	G	GS	CG	IP	H	BB	SO	ShO	Relief W	Relief L	Relief SV	AB	H	HR	BA	PO	A	E	DP	TC/G	FA
1884	KC U	0	1	.000	*4.09*	2	2	1	11	13	2	1	0	0	0	0	7	1	0	.143	2	6	3	0	3.7	.727
1885	STL N	5	8	.385	3.55	14	14	14	129.1	118	44	46	0	0	0	0	50	3	0	.060	5	22	7	1	2.4	.794
1886		11	25	.306	*3.30*	41	41	38	325	329	134	129	1	0	0	0	136	15	0	.110	16	61	9	2	2.0	.895
1887	2 teams IND N (8G 1–6) CLE AA (5G 0–5)																									
"	total	1	11	.083	7.25	13	13	10	103	132	71	13	0	0	0	0	47	7	0	.149	3	18	2	0	1.4	.913
1888	KC AA	1	4	.200	4.19	5	5	5	43	48	7	11	0	0	0	0	16	1	0	.063	1	11	3	0	3.0	.800
5 yrs.		18	49	.269	4.09	75	75	68	611.1	640	258	200	1	0	0	0	256	27	0	.105	27	118	24	3	2.1	.858

LaRue Kirby

KIRBY, LaRUE
B. Dec. 30, 1889, Eureka, Mich. D. June 10, 1961, Lansing, Mich.
BB TR 6' 185 lbs.

Year	Team	W	L	PCT	ERA	G	GS	CG	IP	H	BB	SO	ShO	Relief W	Relief L	Relief SV	AB	H	HR	BA	PO	A	E	DP	TC/G	FA
1912	NY N	1	0	1.000	5.73	3	1	1	11	13	6	2	0	0	0	1	5	1	0	.200	2	3	0	0	1.7	1.000
1915	STL F	0	0	—	5.14	1	0	0	7	7	2	7	0	0	0	0	178	38	0	.213	100	7	3	2	2.2	.973
2 yrs.		1	0	1.000	5.50	4	1	1	18	20	8	9	0	0	0	1	*				190	18	7	4	2.0	.967

Mike Kircher

KIRCHER, MICHAEL ANDREW
Born Wolfgang Andrew Kerscher.
B. Sept. 30, 1897, Rochester, N. Y. D. June 26, 1972, Rochester, N. Y.
BB TR 6' 180 lbs.

Year	Team	W	L	PCT	ERA	G	GS	CG	IP	H	BB	SO	ShO	Relief W	Relief L	Relief SV	AB	H	HR	BA	PO	A	E	DP	TC/G	FA
1919	PHI A	0	0	—	7.88	2	0	0	8	15	3	2	0	0	0	0	3	0	0	.000	0	0	0	0	0.0	.000
1920	STL N	2	1	.667	5.40	9	3	1	36.2	50	5	5	0	1	0	0	11	3	0	.273	3	4	1	0	0.9	.875
1921		0	1	.000	8.10	3	0	0	3.1	4	1	2	0	0	1	0	0	0	0	—	0	0	0	0	0.0	—
3 yrs.		2	2	.500	6.00	14	3	1	48	69	9	9	0	1	1	0	14	3	0	.214	3	4	1	0	0.7	.875

Bill Kirk

KIRK, WILLIAM PARTLEMORE
B. July 19, 1935, Coatesville, Pa.
BL TL 6' 165 lbs.

Year	Team	W	L	PCT	ERA	G	GS	CG	IP	H	BB	SO	ShO	Relief W	Relief L	Relief SV	AB	H	HR	BA	PO	A	E	DP	TC/G	FA
1961	KC A	0	0	—	12.00	1	1	0	3	6	1	3	0	0	0	0	0	0	0	—	0	0	0	0	0.0	.000

Don Kirkwood

KIRKWOOD, DONALD PAUL
B. Sept. 24, 1949, Pontiac, Mich.
BR TR 6' 3" 175 lbs.

Year	Team	W	L	PCT	ERA	G	GS	CG	IP	H	BB	SO	ShO	Relief W	Relief L	Relief SV	AB	H	HR	BA	PO	A	E	DP	TC/G	FA
1974	CAL A	0	0	—	9.00	3	0	0	7	12	6	4	0	0	0	0	0	0	0	—	0	0	0	0	0.0	.000
1975		6	5	.545	3.11	44	2	0	84	85	28	49	0	6	4	7	0	0	0	—	3	12	3	1	0.4	.833
1976		6	12	.333	4.61	28	26	4	158	167	57	78	0	0	1	0	0	0	0	—	18	26	5	3	1.8	.898

Don Kirkwood *continued*

Year	Team		W	L	PCT	ERA	G	GS	CG	IP	H	BB	SO	ShO	Relief Pitching W	Relief Pitching L	Relief Pitching SV	Batting AB	Batting H	Batting HR	BA	PO	A	E	DP	TC/G	FA
1977	2 teams	CAL A (13G 1–0)			CHI A (16G 1–1)																						
"	total		2	1	.667	5.15	29	0	0	57.2	69	19	34	0	2	1	1	0	0	0		5	14	1	1	0.7	.950
1978	TOR	A	4	5	.444	4.24	16	9	3	68	76	25	29	0	1	1	0	0	0	0	—	4	12	0	0	1.0	1.000
5 yrs.			18	23	.439	4.37	120	37	7	374.2	409	135	194	0	9	7	8	0	0	0		30	64	9	5	0.9	.913

Harry Kirsch

KIRSCH, HARRY LOUIS (Casey)
B. Oct. 17, 1887, Pittsburgh, Pa. D. Dec. 25, 1925, Overbrook, Pa.
BR TR 5′11″ 170 lbs.

Year	Team		W	L	PCT	ERA	G	GS	CG	IP	H	BB	SO	ShO	Relief W	Relief L	SV	AB	H	HR	BA	PO	A	E	DP	TC/G	FA
1910	CLE	A	0	0	—	6.00	2	0	0	3	5	1	5	0	0	0	0	0	0	0	—	0	0	0	0	0.0	.000

Garland Kiser

KISER, GARLAND ROUTHARD
B. July 8, 1968, Charlotte, N. C.
BL TL 6′ 3″ 190 lbs.

Year	Team		W	L	PCT	ERA	G	GS	CG	IP	H	BB	SO	ShO	Relief W	Relief L	SV	AB	H	HR	BA	PO	A	E	DP	TC/G	FA
1991	CLE	A	0	0	—	9.64	7	0	0	4.2	7	4	3	0	0	0	0	0	0	0	—	0	0	0	0	0.0	.000

Rube Kisinger

KISINGER, CHARLES SAMUEL
B. Dec. 13, 1876, Adrian, Mich. D. July 14, 1941, Huron, Ohio.
BR TR 6′ 190 lbs.

Year	Team		W	L	PCT	ERA	G	GS	CG	IP	H	BB	SO	ShO	Relief W	Relief L	SV	AB	H	HR	BA	PO	A	E	DP	TC/G	FA
1902	DET	A	2	3	.400	3.12	5	5	5	43.1	48	14	7	0	0	0	0	19	3	0	.158	1	13	2	0	3.2	.875
1903			7	9	.438	2.96	16	14	13	118.2	118	27	33	2	**2**	0	0	47	6	0	.128	1	43	1	0	2.8	.978
2 yrs.			9	12	.429	3.00	21	19	18	162	166	41	40	2	2	0	0	66	9	0	.136	2	56	3	0	2.9	.951

Bruce Kison

KISON, BRUCE EUGENE
B. Feb. 18, 1950, Pasco, Wash.
BR TR 6′ 4″ 178 lbs.

Year	Team		W	L	PCT	ERA	G	GS	CG	IP	H	BB	SO	ShO	Relief W	Relief L	SV	AB	H	HR	BA	PO	A	E	DP	TC/G	FA
1971	PIT	N	6	5	.545	3.41	18	13	2	95	93	36	60	0	1	1	0	31	2	0	.065	8	18	1	5	1.5	.963
1972			9	7	.563	3.26	32	18	6	152	123	69	102	1	0	0	3	53	10	0	.189	9	15	1	2	0.8	.960
1973			3	0	1.000	3.09	7	7	0	43.2	36	24	26	0	0	0	0	12	1	0	.083	2	7	0	0	1.3	1.000
1974			9	8	.529	3.49	40	16	1	129	123	57	71	0	4	4	2	37	4	0	.108	10	25	2	2	0.9	.946
1975			12	11	.522	3.23	33	29	6	192	160	92	89	0	1	0	0	59	7	0	.119	11	39	1	5	1.5	.980
1976			14	9	.609	3.08	31	29	6	193	180	52	98	1	0	0	1	59	12	0	.203	16	31	2	2	1.6	.959
1977			9	10	.474	4.90	33	32	3	193	209	55	122	1	0	0	0	69	18	1	.261	11	33	2	0	1.4	.957
1978			6	6	.500	3.19	28	11	0	96	81	39	62	0	2	2	0	29	4	1	.138	11	14	0	1	0.9	1.000
1979			13	7	.650	3.19	33	25	3	172	157	45	105	1	2	1	0	55	8	1	.145	10	30	1	2	1.2	.976
1980	CAL	A	3	6	.333	4.93	13	13	2	73	73	32	28	1	0	0	0	0	0	0	—	2	11	3	0	1.2	.813
1981			1	1	.500	3.48	11	4	0	44	40	14	19	0	0	0	0	0	0	0	—	3	9	0	1	1.1	1.000
1982			10	5	.667	3.17	33	16	3	142	120	44	86	1	1	2	1	0	0	0	—	19	24	1	2	1.3	.977
1983			11	5	.688	4.05	26	17	4	126.2	128	43	83	1	3	0	2	0	0	0	—	5	22	0	2	1.0	1.000
1984			4	5	.444	5.37	20	7	0	65.1	72	28	66	0	2	1	2	0	0	0	—	7	3	2	1	0.6	.833
1985	BOS	A	5	3	.625	4.11	22	9	0	92	98	32	56	0	2	1	1	0	0	0	—	16	16	0	2	1.5	1.000
15 yrs.			115	88	.567	3.66	380	246	36	1808.2	1693	662	1073	7	18	12	12	404	66	3	.163	140	297	16	27	1.2	.965
LEAGUE CHAMPIONSHIP SERIES																											
1971	PIT	N	1	0	1.000	0.00	1	0	0	4.2	2	2	3	0	1	0	0	2	0	0	.000	0	1	0	0	1.0	1.000
1972			1	0	1.000	0.00	2	0	0	2.1	1	0	3	0	1	0	0	0	0	0	—	0	0	0	0	0.0	.000
1974			1	0	1.000	0.00	1	1	0	6.2	2	6	5	0	0	0	0	3	0	0	.000	1	1	0	0	2.0	1.000
1975			0	0	—	4.50	1	0	0	2	2	1	1	0	0	0	0	0	0	0	—	0	0	0	0	0.0	.000
1982	CAL	A	1	0	1.000	1.93	2	2	1	14	8	3	12	0	0	0	0	0	0	0	—	0	0	0	0	0.0	.000
5 yrs.			4	0	1.000	1.21	7	3	1	29.2	15	12	24	0	2	0	0	5	0	0	.000	1	2	0	0	0.4	1.000
			3rd		1st	1st																					
WORLD SERIES																											
1971	PIT	N	1	0	1.000	0.00	2	0	0	6.1	1	2	3	0	1	0	0	2	0	0	.000	0	1	0	0	0.5	1.000
1979			0	1	.000	108.00	1	1	0	0.1	3	2	0	0	0	0	0	0	0	0	—	0	1	0	0	1.0	1.000
2 yrs.			1	1	.500	5.40	3	1	0	6.2	4	4	3	0	1	0	0	2	0	0	.000	0	2	0	0	0.7	1.000

Bill Kissinger

KISSINGER, WILLIAM FRANCIS (Shang)
B. Aug. 15, 1871, Dayton, Ky. D. Apr. 20, 1929, Cincinnati, Ohio.
BR TR 185 lbs.

Year	Team		W	L	PCT	ERA	G	GS	CG	IP	H	BB	SO	ShO	Relief W	Relief L	SV	AB	H	HR	BA	PO	A	E	DP	TC/G	FA
1895	2 teams	BAL N (2G 1–0)			STL N (24G 4–12)																						
"	total		5	12	.294	6.51	26	16	10	152	240	53	34	0	2	2	0	102	25	0	.245	14	47	7	1	1.9	.897
1896	STL	N	2	9	.182	6.49	20	12	11	136	209	55	22	0	0	0	1	73	22	0	.301	10	45	8	2	2.6	.873
1897			0	4	.000	11.49	7	4	2	31.1	51	15	5	0	0	0	0	39	13	0	.333	14	8	4	0	1.9	.846
3 yrs.			7	25	.219	6.99	53	32	23	319.1	500	123	61	0	2	2	1	214	60	0	.280	38	100	19	3	2.2	.879

Frank Kitson

KITSON, FRANK R.
B. Sept. 11, 1869, Hopkins, Mich. D. Apr. 14, 1930, Allegan, Mich.
BL TR 5′11″ 165 lbs.

Year	Team		W	L	PCT	ERA	G	GS	CG	IP	H	BB	SO	ShO	Relief W	Relief L	SV	AB	H	HR	BA	PO	A	E	DP	TC/G	FA
1898	BAL	N	8	5	.615	3.24	17	13	13	119.1	123	35	32	1	0	0	0	86	27	0	.314	16	33	6	0	2.0	.891
1899			22	16	.579	2.76	40	37	34	329.2	329	66	75	2	0	1	0	134	27	0	.201	12	69	2	1	2.1	.976
1900	BKN	N	15	13	.536	4.19	40	30	21	253.1	283	56	55	2	2	0	**4**	109	32	0	.294	13	39	5	0	1.4	.912
1901			19	11	.633	2.98	38	32	26	280.2	312	67	127	5	1	**2**	2	133	35	1	.263	19	56	4	2	1.9	.949
1902			19	12	.613	2.84	31	31	28	259.2	251	48	107	3	0	1	0	113	30	1	.265	7	69	3	1	2.5	.962
1903	DET	A	15	16	.484	2.58	31	28	28	257.2	277	38	102	2	**2**	1	0	116	21	0	.181	15	69	3	0	2.4	.966
1904			8	13	.381	3.07	26	24	19	199.2	211	38	69	0	0	0	1	72	15	1	.208	6	68	4	2	3.0	.949
1905			12	14	.462	3.47	33	27	21	225.2	230	57	78	3	2	0	1	87	16	0	.184	5	65	7	0	2.3	.909
1906	WAS	A	6	14	.300	3.65	30	21	15	197	196	57	59	1	1	**2**	0	90	22	1	.244	5	62	3	1	2.3	.957
1907	2 teams	WAS A (5G 0–3)			NY A (12G 4–0)																						
"	total		4	3	.571	3.39	17	7	5	93	116	26	25	0	1	0	0	31	7	0	.226	4	21	3	0	1.8	.893
10 yrs.			128	117	.522	3.17	303	250	210	2215.2	2328	488	729	19	9	7	8	*				102	551	40	7	2.2	.942

Mal Kittridge

KITTRIDGE, MALACHI JEDDIDAH
B. Oct. 12, 1869, Clinton, Mass. D. June 23, 1928, Gary, Ind.
Manager 1904.
BR TR 5′ 7″ 170 lbs.

Year	Team		W	L	PCT	ERA	G	GS	CG	IP	H	BB	SO	ShO	Relief W	Relief L	SV	AB	H	HR	BA	PO	A	E	DP	TC/G	FA
1896	CHI	N	0	0	—	5.40	1	0	0	1.2	2	1	0	0	0	0	0	*				458	113	34	9	6.3	.944

Hugo Klaerner

KLAERNER, HUGO EMIL (Dutch)
B. Oct. 15, 1908, Fredericksburg, Tex. D. Jan. 3, 1982, Fredericksburg, Tex.
BR TR 5′11″ 190 lbs.

Year	Team		W	L	PCT	ERA	G	GS	CG	IP	H	BB	SO	ShO	Relief W	Relief L	SV	AB	H	HR	BA	PO	A	E	DP	TC/G	FA
1934	CHI	A	0	2	.000	10.90	3	3	1	17.1	24	16	9	0	0	0	0	6	2	0	.333	0	8	0	0	2.7	1.000

Fred Klages

KLAGES, FREDERICK ALBERT ANTHONY BR TR 6′ 2″ 185 lbs.
B. Oct. 31, 1943, Ambridge, Pa.

Year	Team	W	L	PCT	ERA	G	GS	CG	IP	H	BB	SO	ShO	Relief Pitching W	L	SV	Batting AB	H	HR	BA	PO	A	E	DP	TC/G	FA
1966	CHI A	1	0	1.000	1.72	3	3	0	15.2	9	7	6	0	0	0	0	6	3	0	.500	3	2	0	0	1.7	1.000
1967		4	4	.500	3.83	11	9	0	44.2	43	16	17	0	1	0	0	12	0	0	.000	2	4	0	0	0.5	1.000
2 yrs.		5	4	.556	3.28	14	12	0	60.1	52	23	23	0	1	0	0	18	3	0	.167	5	6	0	0	0.8	1.000

Al Klawitter

KLAWITTER, ALBERT C. BR TR 5′11½″ 187 lbs.
B. Apr. 12, 1888, Wilkes-Barre, Pa. D. May 2, 1950, Milwaukee, Wis.

Year	Team	W	L	PCT	ERA	G	GS	CG	IP	H	BB	SO	ShO	Relief Pitching W	L	SV	Batting AB	H	HR	BA	PO	A	E	DP	TC/G	FA
1909	NY N	1	1	.500	2.00	6	3	2	27	24	13	6	0	0	0	1	9	3	0	.333	3	12	0	0	2.5	1.000
1910		0	0	—	9.00	1	0	0	1	2	2	0	0	0	0	0	0	0	0	—	0	0	1	0	1.0	.000
1913	DET A	1	2	.333	5.91	8	3	1	32	39	15	10	0	0	1	0	11	0	0	.000	0	12	1	0	1.6	.923
3 yrs.		2	3	.400	4.20	15	6	3	60	65	30	16	0	0	1	1	20	3	0	.150	3	24	2	0	1.9	.931

Tom Klawitter

KLAWITTER, THOMAS CARL BR TL 6′ 2″ 190 lbs.
B. June 24, 1958, LaCrosse, Wis.

Year	Team	W	L	PCT	ERA	G	GS	CG	IP	H	BB	SO	ShO	Relief Pitching W	L	SV	Batting AB	H	HR	BA	PO	A	E	DP	TC/G	FA
1985	MIN A	0	0	—	6.75	7	2	0	9.1	7	13	5	0	0	0	0	0	0	0	—	0	2	0	0	0.3	1.000

Hal Kleine

KLEINE, HAROLD JOHN BL TL 6′ 2″ 193 lbs.
B. June 8, 1923, St. Louis, Mo. D. Dec. 10, 1957, St. Louis, Mo.

Year	Team	W	L	PCT	ERA	G	GS	CG	IP	H	BB	SO	ShO	Relief Pitching W	L	SV	Batting AB	H	HR	BA	PO	A	E	DP	TC/G	FA
1944	CLE A	1	2	.333	5.75	11	6	1	40.2	38	36	13	0	0	0	0	14	2	0	.143	1	6	1	0	0.7	.875
1945		0	0	—	3.86	3	0	0	7	8	7	5	0	0	0	0	3	1	0	.333	0	1	0	0	0.3	1.000
2 yrs.		1	2	.333	5.48	14	6	1	47.2	46	43	18	0	0	0	0	17	3	0	.176	1	7	1	0	0.6	.889

Ted Kleinhans

KLEINHANS, THEODORE OTTO BR TL 6′ 170 lbs.
B. Apr. 8, 1899, Deer Park, Wis. D. July 24, 1985, Redington Beach, Fla.

Year	Team	W	L	PCT	ERA	G	GS	CG	IP	H	BB	SO	ShO	Relief Pitching W	L	SV	Batting AB	H	HR	BA	PO	A	E	DP	TC/G	FA
1934	2 teams PHI N (5G 0–0) CIN N (24G 2–6)																									
″	total	2	6	.250	5.99	29	9	0	85.2	118	41	25	0	1	1	0	24	3	0	.125	5	27	2	1	1.2	.941
1936	NY A	1	1	.500	5.83	19	0	0	29.1	36	23	10	0	1	1	1	6	1	0	.167	1	5	0	0	0.3	1.000
1937	CIN N	1	2	.333	2.30	7	3	1	27.1	29	12	13	0	0	0	0	8	2	0	.250	2	2	0	0	0.6	1.000
1938		0	0	—	9.00	1	0	0	1	2	0	0	0	0	0	0	0	0	0	—	0	0	0	0	0.0	.000
4 yrs.		4	9	.308	5.27	56	12	1	143.1	185	76	48	0	2	2	1	38	6	0	.158	8	34	2	1	0.8	.955

Nub Kleinke

KLEINKE, NORBERT GEORGE BR TR 6′ 1″ 170 lbs.
B. May 19, 1911, Fond du Lac, Wis. D. Mar. 16, 1950, Pacific Ocean.

Year	Team	W	L	PCT	ERA	G	GS	CG	IP	H	BB	SO	ShO	Relief Pitching W	L	SV	Batting AB	H	HR	BA	PO	A	E	DP	TC/G	FA
1935	STL N	0	0	—	4.97	4	2	0	12.2	19	3	5	0	0	0	0	2	0	0	.000	1	2	0	0	0.8	1.000
1937		1	1	.500	4.79	5	2	1	20.2	25	7	9	0	0	1	0	8	0	0	.000	1	6	0	0	1.4	1.000
2 yrs.		1	1	.500	4.86	9	4	1	33.1	44	10	14	0	0	1	0	10	0	0	.000	2	8	0	0	1.1	1.000

Ed Klepfer

KLEPFER, EDWARD LLOYD (Big Ed) BR TR 6′ 185 lbs.
B. Mar. 17, 1888, Summerville, Pa. D. Aug. 9, 1950, Tulsa, Okla.

Year	Team	W	L	PCT	ERA	G	GS	CG	IP	H	BB	SO	ShO	Relief Pitching W	L	SV	Batting AB	H	HR	BA	PO	A	E	DP	TC/G	FA
1911	NY A	0	0	—	6.75	2	0	0	4	5	2	4	0	0	0	0	1	0	0	.000	0	2	0	0	1.0	1.000
1913		0	1	.000	7.66	8	1	0	24.2	38	12	10	0	0	0	0	6	1	0	.167	0	8	1	1	1.1	.889
1915	2 teams CHI A (3G 1–0) CLE A (8G 1–6)																									
″	total	2	6	.250	2.26	11	9	3	55.2	58	16	16	0	0	0	0	15	2	0	.133	0	20	2	1	2.0	.909
1916	CLE A	6	6	.500	2.52	31	13	4	143	136	46	62	1	0	2	2	40	1	0	.025	12	36	1	1	1.6	.980
1917		14	4	.778	2.37	41	27	9	213	208	55	66	0	2	1	1	62	2	0	.032	6	60	8	3	1.8	.892
1919		0	0	—	7.36	5	0	0	7.1	12	6	7	0	0	0	0	1	0	0	.000	0	2	0	0	0.4	1.000
6 yrs.		22	17	.564	2.81	98	50	16	447.2	457	137	165	1	2	3	3	125	6	0	.048	18	128	12	6	1.6	.924

Eddie Klieman

KLIEMAN, EDWARD FREDERICK (Babe) BR TR 6′ 1″ 190 lbs.
B. Mar. 21, 1918, Norwood, Ohio D. Nov. 15, 1979, Homosassa, Fla.

Year	Team	W	L	PCT	ERA	G	GS	CG	IP	H	BB	SO	ShO	Relief Pitching W	L	SV	Batting AB	H	HR	BA	PO	A	E	DP	TC/G	FA
1943	CLE A	0	1	.000	1.00	1	1	1	9	8	5	2	0	0	0	0	3	0	0	.000	0	2	0	0	2.0	1.000
1944		11	13	.458	3.38	47	19	5	178.1	185	70	44	1	5	3	5	57	6	0	.105	15	35	1	2	1.1	.980
1945		5	8	.385	3.85	38	12	4	126.1	123	49	33	1	1	2	4	40	8	1	.200	12	37	2	3	1.3	.961
1946		0	0	—	6.60	9	0	0	15	18	10	2	0	0	0	0	1	0	0	.000	0	0	0	0	0.0	.000
1947		5	4	.556	3.03	**58**	0	0	92	78	39	21	0	5	4	**17**	19	2	0	.105	12	20	1	3	0.6	.970
1948		3	2	.600	2.60	44	0	0	79.2	62	46	18	0	3	2	4	14	2	0	.143	4	21	0	1	0.6	1.000
1949	2 teams WAS A (2G 0–0) CHI A (18G 2–0)																									
″	total	2	0	1.000	4.25	20	0	0	36	41	18	10	0	2	0	3	9	3	0	.333	3	9	0	1	0.6	1.000
1950	PHI A	0	0	—	9.53	5	0	0	5.2	10	2	0	0	0	0	0	1	0	0	.000	0	0	1	0	0.2	.000
8 yrs.		26	28	.481	3.49	222	32	10	542	525	239	130	2	16	11	33	144	21	1	.146	46	124	5	10	0.8	.971
WORLD SERIES																										
1948	CLE A	0	0	—	∞	1	0	0		1	2	0	0	0	0	0	0	0	0	—	0	0	0	0	0.0	.000

Ron Klimkowski

KLIMKOWSKI, RONALD BERNARD BR TR 6′ 2″ 190 lbs.
B. Mar. 1, 1944, Jersey City, N. J.

Year	Team	W	L	PCT	ERA	G	GS	CG	IP	H	BB	SO	ShO	Relief Pitching W	L	SV	Batting AB	H	HR	BA	PO	A	E	DP	TC/G	FA
1969	NY A	0	0	—	0.64	3	1	0	14	6	5	3	0	0	0	0	3	0	0	.000	3	0	0	0	1.0	1.000
1970		6	7	.462	2.66	45	3	1	98	80	33	40	1	5	5	1	19	1	0	.053	5	18	1	0	0.5	.958
1971	OAK A	2	2	.500	3.40	26	0	0	45	37	23	25	0	2	2	2	5	2	0	.400	9	8	1	1	0.7	.944
1972	NY A	0	3	.000	4.06	16	2	0	31	32	15	11	0	0	1	1	6	0	0	.000	0	6	1	1	0.4	.857
4 yrs.		8	12	.400	2.92	90	6	1	188	155	76	79	1	7	8	4	33	3	0	.091	17	32	3	2	0.6	.942

Bob Kline

KLINE, ROBERT GEORGE (Junior) BR TR 6′ 3″ 200 lbs.
B. Dec. 9, 1909, Enterprise, Ohio D. Mar. 16, 1987, Westerville, Ohio.

Year	Team	W	L	PCT	ERA	G	GS	CG	IP	H	BB	SO	ShO	Relief Pitching W	L	SV	Batting AB	H	HR	BA	PO	A	E	DP	TC/G	FA
1930	BOS A	0	0	—	0.00	1	0	0	1	1	0	0	0	0	0	0	0	0	0	—	0	0	0	0	0.0	.000
1931		5	5	.500	4.41	28	10	3	98	110	35	25	0	2	0	0	27	9	0	.333	2	30	2	1	1.2	.941
1932		11	13	.458	5.28	47	19	4	172	203	76	31	1	5	2	2	54	7	0	.130	16	44	1	6	1.3	.984
1933		7	8	.467	4.54	46	8	1	127	127	67	16	0	4	4	4	34	6	0	.176	3	46	1	2	1.1	.980
1934	2 teams PHI A (20G 6–2) WAS A (6G 1–0)																									
″	total	7	2	.778	7.21	26	0	0	43.2	60	17	15	0	**7**	2	1	9	3	0	.333	2	16	0	1	0.7	1.000
5 yrs.		30	28	.517	5.05	148	37	8	441.2	501	195	87	1	18	8	7	124	25	0	.202	23	136	4	10	1.1	.975

Bobby Kline

KLINE, JOHN ROBERT BR TR 6′ 179 lbs.
B. Jan. 27, 1929, St. Petersburg, Fla.

Year	Team	W	L	PCT	ERA	G	GS	CG	IP	H	BB	SO	ShO	Relief Pitching W	L	SV	Batting AB	H	HR	BA	PO	A	E	DP	TC/G	FA
1955	WAS A	0	0	—	27.00	1	0	0	1	4	1	0	0	0	0	0	*				107	164	16	38	3.7	.944

Ron Kline

KLINE, RONALD LEE BR TR 6′ 3″ 205 lbs.
B. Mar. 9, 1932, Callery, Pa.

Year	Team	Lg	W	L	PCT	ERA	G	GS	CG	IP	H	BB	SO	ShO	Relief W	Relief L	Relief SV	AB	H	HR	BA	PO	A	E	DP	TC/G	FA
1952	PIT	N	0	7	.000	5.49	27	11	0	78.2	74	66	27	0	0	1	0	19	0	0	.000	3	8	0	2	0.4	1.000
1955			6	13	.316	4.15	36	19	2	136.2	161	53	48	1	2	0	2	38	5	0	.132	20	30	2	2	1.4	.962
1956			14	**18**	.438	3.38	44	39	9	264	263	81	125	2	0	0	2	79	10	0	.127	17	42	4	3	1.4	.937
1957			9	16	.360	4.04	40	31	11	205	214	61	88	2	0	1	0	66	4	0	.061	18	27	1	2	1.1	.978
1958			13	**16**	.448	3.53	32	32	11	237.1	220	92	109	2	0	0	0	74	2	0	.027	20	40	3	4	2.0	.952
1959			11	13	.458	4.26	33	29	7	186	186	70	91	0	1	0	0	59	8	0	.136	15	27	2	1	1.3	.955
1960	STL	N	4	9	.308	6.04	34	17	1	117.2	133	43	54	0	1	2	1	35	5	0	.143	8	23	0	1	0.9	1.000
1961	2 teams	LA A (26G 3–6) DET A (10G 5–3)																									
″	total		8	9	.471	4.14	36	20	3	161	172	61	97	1	1	3	1	49	6	0	.122	10	28	3	2	1.1	.927
1962	DET	A	3	6	.333	4.31	36	4	0	77.1	88	28	47	0	3	3	2	16	2	0	.125	13	11	2	2	0.7	.923
1963	WAS	A	3	8	.273	2.79	62	1	0	93.2	85	30	49	0	3	**8**	17	11	1	0	.091	3	14	1	2	0.3	.944
1964			10	7	.588	2.32	61	0	0	81.1	81	21	40	0	10	7	14	6	1	0	.167	2	13	1	1	0.3	.938
1965			7	6	.538	2.63	74	0	0	99.1	106	32	52	0	7	6	**29**	7	0	0	.000	3	13	0	1	0.2	1.000
1966			6	4	.600	2.39	63	0	0	90.1	79	17	46	0	6	4	23	6	1	0	.167	6	7	1	0	0.2	.929
1967	MIN	A	7	1	.875	3.77	54	0	0	71.2	71	15	36	0	7	1	5	5	0	0	.000	2	11	0	0	0.2	1.000
1968	PIT	N	12	5	.706	1.68	56	0	0	112.2	94	31	48	0	**12**	5	7	16	0	0	.000	4	15	0	0	0.3	1.000
1969	3 teams	PIT N (20G 1–3) SF N (7G 0–2) BOS A (16G 0–1)																									
″	total		1	6	.143	5.19	43	0	0	59	77	28	29	0	1	6	4	5	0	0	.000	3	10	0	1	0.3	1.000
1970	ATL	N	0	0	—	7.50	5	0	0	6	9	2	3	0	0	0	1	0	0	0	—	0	0	0	0	0.0	.000
17 yrs.			114	144	.442	3.75	736	203	44	2077.2	2113	731	989	8	54	47	108	491	45	0	.092	147	319	20	24	0.7	.959

Steve Kline

KLINE, STEVEN JACK BR TR 6′ 3″ 205 lbs.
B. Oct. 6, 1947, Wenatchee, Wash.

Year	Team	Lg	W	L	PCT	ERA	G	GS	CG	IP	H	BB	SO	ShO	Relief W	Relief L	Relief SV	AB	H	HR	BA	PO	A	E	DP	TC/G	FA
1970	NY	A	6	6	.500	3.42	16	15	5	100	99	24	49	0	0	0	0	28	5	0	.179	14	14	0	2	1.8	1.000
1971			12	13	.480	2.96	31	30	15	222	206	37	81	1	0	0	0	66	9	0	.136	24	49	1	1	2.4	.986
1972			16	9	.640	2.40	32	32	11	236	210	44	58	4	0	0	0	76	7	0	.092	20	50	7	3	2.4	.909
1973			4	7	.364	4.01	14	13	2	74	76	31	19	1	0	0	0	0	0	0	—	1	12	0	0	0.9	1.000
1974	2 teams	NY A (4G 2–2) CLE A (16G 3–8)																									
″	total		5	10	.333	4.64	20	15	1	97	96	36	23	0	0	0	0	0	0	0		5	17	0	4	1.1	1.000
1977	ATL	N	0	0	—	6.75	16	0	0	20	21	12	10	0	0	0	1	0	0	0	—	0	2	1	0	0.2	.667
6 yrs.			43	45	.489	3.27	129	105	34	749	708	184	240	6	0	0	1	170	21	0	.124	64	144	9	10	1.7	.959

Bill Kling

KLING, WILLIAM BL TR 6′ 190 lbs.
Brother of Johnny Kling.
B. Jan. 14, 1867, Kansas City, Mo. D. Aug. 26, 1934, Kansas City, Mo.

Year	Team	Lg	W	L	PCT	ERA	G	GS	CG	IP	H	BB	SO	ShO	Relief W	Relief L	Relief SV	AB	H	HR	BA	PO	A	E	DP	TC/G	FA
1891	PHI	N	4	2	.667	4.32	12	7	4	75	90	32	26	0	0	0	0	31	6	0	.194	1	13	1	0	1.2	.933
1892	BAL	N	0	2	.000	11.45	2	2	0	11	17	7	7	0	0	0	0	4	1	0	.250	0	2	0	0	1.0	1.000
1895	LOU	N	0	0	—	0.00	1	0	0	1	0	1	0	0	0	0	0	1	0	0	.000	0	0	0	0	0.0	.000
3 yrs.			4	4	.500	5.17	15	9	4	87	107	40	33	0	0	0	0	36	7	0	.194	1	15	1	0	1.1	.941

Scott Klingenbeck

KLINGENBECK, SCOTT EDWARD BR TR 6′ 2″ 205 lbs.
B. Feb. 3, 1971, Cincinnati, Ohio.

Year	Team	Lg	W	L	PCT	ERA	G	GS	CG	IP	H	BB	SO	ShO	Relief W	Relief L	Relief SV	AB	H	HR	BA	PO	A	E	DP	TC/G	FA
1994	BAL	A	1	0	1.000	3.86	1	1	0	7	6	4	5	0	0	0	0	0	0	0	—	1	0	0	0	1.0	1.000
1995	2 teams	BAL A (6G 2–2) MIN A (18G 0–2)																									
″	total		2	4	.333	7.12	24	9	0	79.2	101	42	42	0	0	0	0	0	0	0	—	8	10	1	0	0.8	.947
2 yrs.			3	4	.429	6.85	25	10	0	86.2	107	46	47	0	0	0	0	0	0	0	—	9	10	1	0	0.8	.950

Bob Klinger

KLINGER, ROBERT HAROLD BR TR 6′ 180 lbs.
B. June 4, 1908, Allenton, Mo. D. Aug. 19, 1977, Villa Ridge, Mo.

Year	Team	Lg	W	L	PCT	ERA	G	GS	CG	IP	H	BB	SO	ShO	Relief W	Relief L	Relief SV	AB	H	HR	BA	PO	A	E	DP	TC/G	FA
1938	PIT	N	12	5	.706	2.99	28	21	10	159.1	152	42	58	1	2	0	1	60	10	0	.167	4	34	0	2	1.4	1.000
1939			14	**17**	.452	4.36	37	33	10	225	251	81	64	2	1	1	0	84	17	0	.202	7	62	3	5	1.9	.958
1940			8	13	.381	5.39	39	22	3	142	196	53	48	0	2	0	3	42	6	0	.143	6	33	0	1	1.0	1.000
1941			9	4	.692	3.93	35	9	3	116.2	127	30	36	0	7	0	4	32	8	0	.250	4	25	1	3	0.9	.967
1942			8	11	.421	3.24	37	19	8	152.2	151	45	58	1	1	2	1	40	8	0	.200	14	35	1	0	1.4	.980
1943			11	8	.579	2.72	33	25	14	195	185	58	65	3	0	2	0	65	16	0	.246	14	37	0	2	1.5	1.000
1946	BOS	A	3	2	.600	2.37	28	1	0	57	49	25	16	0	3	2	**9**	16	5	0	.313	1	11	1	0	0.5	.923
1947			1	1	.500	3.86	28	0	0	42	42	24	12	0	1	1	5	9	1	0	.111	4	4	0	0	0.3	1.000
8 yrs.			66	61	.520	3.68	265	130	48	1089.2	1153	358	357	7	17	8	23	348	71	0	.204	54	241	6	13	1.1	.980
WORLD SERIES																											
1946	BOS	A	0	1	.000	13.50	1	0	0	0.2	2	1	0	0	0	1	0	0	0	0	—	1	0	0	0	1.0	1.000

Joe Klink

KLINK, JOSEPH CHARLES BL TL 5′11″ 170 lbs.
B. Feb. 3, 1962, Johnstown, Pa.

Year	Team	Lg	W	L	PCT	ERA	G	GS	CG	IP	H	BB	SO	ShO	Relief W	Relief L	Relief SV	AB	H	HR	BA	PO	A	E	DP	TC/G	FA
1987	MIN	A	0	1	.000	6.65	12	0	0	23	37	11	17	0	0	1	0	0	0	0	—	0	2	0	0	0.2	1.000
1990	OAK	A	0	0	—	2.04	40	0	0	39.2	34	18	19	0	0	0	1	0	0	0	—	1	1	0	0	0.1	1.000
1991			10	3	.769	4.35	62	0	0	62	60	21	34	0	**10**	3	2	0	0	0	—	4	8	0	1	0.2	1.000
1993	FLA	N	0	2	.000	5.02	59	0	0	37.2	37	24	22	0	0	2	0	2	0	0	.000	3	2	0	0	0.1	1.000
4 yrs.			10	6	.625	4.27	173	0	0	162.1	168	74	92	0	10	6	3	2	0	0	.000	8	13	0	2	0.1	1.000
WORLD SERIES																											
1990	OAK	A	0	0	—	0.00	1	0	0		0	1	0	0	0	0	0	0	0	0	—	0	0	0	0	0.0	.000

Johnny Klippstein

KLIPPSTEIN, JOHN CALVIN BR TR 6′ 1″ 173 lbs.
B. Oct. 17, 1927, Washington, D. C.

Year	Team	Lg	W	L	PCT	ERA	G	GS	CG	IP	H	BB	SO	ShO	Relief W	Relief L	Relief SV	AB	H	HR	BA	PO	A	E	DP	TC/G	FA
1950	CHI	N	2	9	.182	5.25	33	11	3	104.2	112	64	51	0	1	1	1	33	11	1	.333	7	15	3	3	0.8	.880
1951			6	6	.500	4.29	35	11	1	123.2	125	53	56	1	4	0	2	37	4	1	.108	4	23	0	3	0.8	1.000
1952			9	14	.391	4.44	41	25	7	202.2	208	89	110	2	4	0	3	63	11	1	.175	6	43	0	4	1.2	1.000
1953			10	11	.476	4.83	48	20	5	167.2	169	107	113	0	2	4	6	58	9	1	.155	5	21	2	1	0.6	.929
1954			4	11	.267	5.29	36	21	4	148	155	96	69	0	0	2	1	45	6	0	.133	15	27	0	3	1.2	1.000
1955	CIN	N	9	10	.474	3.39	39	14	3	138	120	60	68	2	4	2	0	31	2	0	.065	9	23	3	0	0.9	.914
1956			12	11	.522	4.09	37	29	11	211	219	82	86	0	2	0	1	71	7	0	.099	10	42	1	3	1.4	.981
1957			8	11	.421	5.05	46	18	3	146	146	68	99	1	3	2	3	41	3	0	.073	10	17	0	0	0.6	1.000

Johnny Klippstein *continued*

Year	Team	W	L	PCT	ERA	G	GS	CG	IP	H	BB	SO	ShO	Relief W	Relief L	Relief SV	AB	H	HR	BA	PO	A	E	DP	TC/G	FA
1958	2 teams CIN N (12G 3–2) LA N (45G 3–5)																									
″	total	6	7	.462	4.10	57	4	0	123	118	58	95	0	5	6	10	28	2	0	.071	8	11	0	1	0.3	1.000
1959	LA N	4	0	1.000	5.91	28	0	0	45.2	48	33	30	0	4	0	2	7	1	0	.143	2	7	2	0	0.4	.818
1960	CLE A	5	5	.500	2.91	49	0	0	74.1	53	35	46	0	5	5	**14**	14	2	0	.143	13	9	1	0	0.5	.957
1961	WAS A	2	2	.500	6.78	42	1	0	71.2	83	43	41	0	2	1	0	7	1	0	.143	3	14	0	2	0.4	1.000
1962	CIN N	7	6	.538	4.47	40	7	0	108.2	113	64	67	0	6	3	4	24	3	1	.125	3	22	0	1	0.6	1.000
1963	PHI N	5	6	.455	1.93	49	1	0	112	80	46	86	0	5	5	8	26	1	0	.038	5	15	0	0	0.4	1.000
1964	2 teams PHI N (11G 2–1) MIN A (33G 0–4)																									
″	total	2	5	.286	2.65	44	0	0	68	66	28	52	0	2	5	3	6	0	0	.000	2	19	1	2	0.5	.955
1965	MIN A	9	3	.750	2.24	56	0	0	76.1	59	31	59	0	9	3	5	8	0	0	.000	0	11	2	0	0.2	.846
1966		1	1	.500	3.40	26	0	0	39.2	35	20	26	0	1	1	3	3	0	0	.000	4	4	0	0	0.3	1.000
1967	DET A	0	0	—	5.40	5	0	0	6.2	6	1	4	0	0	0	0	0	0	0	—	0	1	0	0	0.2	1.000
18 yrs.		101	118	.461	4.24	711	162	37	1967.2	1915	978	1158	6	59	40	66	502	63	5	.125	106	324	15	23	0.6	.966
WORLD SERIES																										
1959	LA N	0	0	—	0.00	1	0	0	2	1	0	2	0	0	0	0	0	0	0	—	0	1	0	0	1.0	1.000
1965	MIN A	0	0	—	0.00	2	0	0	2.2	2	2	3	0	0	0	0	0	0	0	—	0	0	0	0	0.0	.000
2 yrs.		0	0		0.00	3	0	0	4.2	3	2	5	0	0	0	0	0	0	0		0	1	0	0	0.3	1.000

Fred Klobedanz

KLOBEDANZ, FREDERICK AUGUSTUS (Kloby) BL TL 5′11″ 190 lbs.
B. June 13, 1871, Waterbury, Conn. D. Apr. 12, 1940, Waterbury, Conn.

Year	Team	W	L	PCT	ERA	G	GS	CG	IP	H	BB	SO	ShO	Relief W	Relief L	Relief SV	AB	H	HR	BA	PO	A	E	DP	TC/G	FA
1896	BOS N	6	4	.600	3.01	10	9	9	80.2	69	31	26	0	1	0	0	41	13	2	.317	3	15	2	1	2.0	.900
1897		26	7	**.788**	4.60	38	37	30	309.1	344	125	92	2	0	0	0	148	48	1	.324	10	47	2	4	1.5	.966
1898		19	10	.655	3.89	35	33	25	270.2	281	99	51	0	0	0	0	127	27	3	.213	50	67	8	4	2.9	.936
1899		1	4	.200	4.86	5	5	4	33.1	39	9	8	0	0	0	0	11	2	1	.182	0	11	0	0	2.2	1.000
1902		1	0	1.000	1.13	1	1	1	8	9	2	4	0	0	0	0	2	1	0	.500	1	0	0	0	1.0	1.000
5 yrs.		53	25	.679	4.12	89	85	69	702	742	266	181	2	1	0	0	329	91	7	.277	64	140	12	9	2.2	.944

Stan Klopp

KLOPP, STANLEY HAROLD (Betz) BR TR 6′ 1½″ 180 lbs.
B. Dec. 22, 1910, Womelsdorf, Pa. D. Mar. 11, 1980, Robesonia, Pa.

Year	Team	W	L	PCT	ERA	G	GS	CG	IP	H	BB	SO	ShO	Relief W	Relief L	Relief SV	AB	H	HR	BA	PO	A	E	DP	TC/G	FA
1944	BOS N	1	2	.333	4.27	24	0	0	46.1	47	33	17	0	1	2	0	7	2	0	.286	1	6	1	0	0.3	.875

Brent Knackert

KNACKERT, BRENT BRADLEY BR TR 6′ 3″ 185 lbs.
B. Aug. 1, 1969, Los Angeles, Calif.

Year	Team	W	L	PCT	ERA	G	GS	CG	IP	H	BB	SO	ShO	Relief W	Relief L	Relief SV	AB	H	HR	BA	PO	A	E	DP	TC/G	FA
1990	SEA A	1	1	.500	6.51	24	2	0	37.1	50	21	28	0	1	1	0	0	0	0	—	4	4	2	0	0.4	.800

Chris Knapp

KNAPP, ROBERT CHRISTIAN BR TR 6′ 5″ 195 lbs.
B. Sept. 16, 1953, Cherry Point, N. C.

Year	Team	W	L	PCT	ERA	G	GS	CG	IP	H	BB	SO	ShO	Relief W	Relief L	Relief SV	AB	H	HR	BA	PO	A	E	DP	TC/G	FA
1975	CHI A	0	0	—	4.50	2	0	0	2	2	4	3	0	0	0	0	0	0	0	—	0	0	0	0	0.0	.000
1976		3	1	.750	4.85	11	6	1	52	54	32	41	0	1	0	0	0	0	0	—	2	5	1	1	0.7	.875
1977		12	7	.632	4.81	27	26	4	146	166	61	103	0	0	0	0	0	0	0	—	8	19	2	1	1.1	.931
1978	CAL A	14	8	.636	4.21	30	29	6	188.1	178	67	126	0	0	0	0	0	0	0	—	4	20	4	1	0.9	.857
1979		5	5	.500	5.51	20	18	3	98	109	35	36	0	0	0	0	0	0	0	—	8	14	1	1	1.1	.957
1980		2	11	.154	6.15	32	20	1	117	133	51	46	0	1	1	1	0	0	0	—	2	14	1	0	0.5	.941
6 yrs.		36	32	.529	5.00	122	99	15	603.1	642	250	355	0	2	1	1	0	0	0		24	72	9	4	0.9	.914
LEAGUE CHAMPIONSHIP SERIES																										
1979	CAL A	0	1	.000	7.71	1	1	0	2.1	5	1	0	0	0	0	0	0	0	0	—	0	0	0	0	0.0	.000

Frank Knauss

KNAUSS, FRANK H. BL TL 158 lbs.
B. 1868, Cleveland, Ohio Deceased.

Year	Team	W	L	PCT	ERA	G	GS	CG	IP	H	BB	SO	ShO	Relief W	Relief L	Relief SV	AB	H	HR	BA	PO	A	E	DP	TC/G	FA
1890	COL AA	17	12	.586	*2.81*	37	34	28	275.2	206	106	148	3	0	0	2	106	24	1	.226	9	48	5	1	1.7	.919
1891	CLE N	0	3	.000	7.20	3	3	1	15	23	8	6	0	0	0	0	6	1	0	.167	1	3	0	0	1.3	1.000
1892	CIN N	0	0	—	3.38	1	0	0	8	13	5	2	0	0	0	0	3	1	0	.333	1	2	1	1	4.0	.750
1894	CLE N	0	1	.000	5.73	2	2	1	11	7	14	2	0	0	0	0	4	0	0	.000	0	5	0	0	2.5	1.000
1895	NY N	0	0	—	17.18	1	1	0	3.2	9	2	1	0	0	0	0	1	0	0	.000	0	1	2	0	3.0	.333
5 yrs.		17	16	.515	3.30	44	40	30	313.1	258	135	159	3	0	0	2	120	26	1	.217	11	59	8	2	1.8	.897

Rudy Kneisch

KNEISCH, RUDOLPH FRANK BR TL 5′10½″ 175 lbs.
B. Apr. 10, 1899, Baltimore, Md. D. Apr. 6, 1965, Baltimore, Md.

Year	Team	W	L	PCT	ERA	G	GS	CG	IP	H	BB	SO	ShO	Relief W	Relief L	Relief SV	AB	H	HR	BA	PO	A	E	DP	TC/G	FA
1926	DET A	0	1	.000	2.65	2	2	1	17	18	6	4	0	0	0	0	5	0	0	.000	2	5	0	1	3.5	1.000

Phil Knell

KNELL, PHILIP H. BR TL 5′ 7½″ 154 lbs.
B. Mar. 2, 1865, Mill Valley, Calif. D. June 5, 1944, Santa Monica, Calif.

Year	Team	W	L	PCT	ERA	G	GS	CG	IP	H	BB	SO	ShO	Relief W	Relief L	Relief SV	AB	H	HR	BA	PO	A	E	DP	TC/G	FA
1888	PIT N	1	2	.333	3.76	3	3	3	26.1	20	18	15	0	0	0	0	11	1	0	.091	2	5	2	0	3.0	.778
1890	PHI P	22	11	.667	3.83	35	31	30	286.2	287	166	99	2	2	1	0	132	29	0	.220	24	67	10	4	2.7	.901
1891	COL AA	28	27	.509	2.92	58	52	47	462	363	226	228	**5**	1	**2**	0	215	34	0	.158	48	120	13	1	2.7	.928
1892	2 teams WAS N (22G 9–13) PHI N (11G 5–5)																									
″	total	14	18	.438	3.78	33	30	24	250	243	111	117	1	2	0	0	102	11	0	.108	21	40	9	1	2.1	.871
1894	2 teams PIT N (1G 0–0) LOU N (32G 7–21)																									
″	total	7	21	.250	5.49	33	28	25	254	341	110	67	0	0	0	0	116	31	1	.267	16	38	13	2	2.0	.806
1895	2 teams LOU N (10G 0–6) CLE N (20G 7–5)																									
″	total	7	11	.389	5.76	30	19	12	173.1	224	74	49	0	2	1	0	81	17	0	.210	15	41	7	2	2.1	.889
6 yrs.		79	90	.467	4.05	192	163	141	1452.1	1478	705	575	8	7	4	0	657	123	1	.187	126	311	54	10	2.4	.890

Bob Knepper

KNEPPER, ROBERT WESLEY BL TL 6′ 3″ 195 lbs.
B. May 25, 1954, Akron, Ohio.

Year	Team	W	L	PCT	ERA	G	GS	CG	IP	H	BB	SO	ShO	Relief W	Relief L	Relief SV	AB	H	HR	BA	PO	A	E	DP	TC/G	FA
1976	SF N	1	2	.333	3.24	4	4	0	25	26	7	11	0	0	0	0	9	1	0	.111	1	4	0	1	1.3	1.000
1977		11	9	.550	3.36	27	27	6	166	151	72	100	2	0	0	0	55	10	0	.182	10	21	1	1	1.2	.969
1978		17	11	.607	2.63	36	35	16	260	218	85	147	**6**	0	0	0	79	5	0	.063	4	33	0	3	1.0	1.000
1979		9	12	.429	4.65	34	34	6	207	241	77	123	2	0	0	0	66	12	1	.182	8	26	5	1	1.1	.872
1980		9	16	.360	4.10	35	33	8	215	242	61	103	1	0	0	0	66	10	0	.152	7	45	3	3	1.6	.945
1981	HOU N	9	5	.643	2.18	22	22	6	157	128	38	75	5	0	0	0	47	7	1	.149	6	26	3	1	1.6	.914
1982		5	15	.250	4.45	33	29	4	180	193	60	108	0	0	0	1	52	3	0	.058	8	32	1	3	1.2	.976

Bob Knepper *continued*

Year	Team	W	L	PCT	ERA	G	GS	CG	IP	H	BB	SO	ShO	Relief Pitching W	L	SV	Batting AB	H	HR	BA	PO	A	E	DP	TC/G	FA
1983		6	13	.316	3.19	35	29	4	203	202	71	125	3	1	1	0	66	12	1	.182	2	40	3	4	1.3	.933
1984		15	10	.600	3.20	35	34	11	233.2	223	55	140	3	0	0	0	76	13	1	.171	7	32	2	2	1.2	.951
1985		15	13	.536	3.55	37	37	4	241	253	54	131	0	0	0	0	78	11	1	.141	5	30	3	1	1.0	.921
1986		17	12	.586	3.14	40	38	8	258	232	62	143	**5**	1	0	0	91	9	0	.099	23	47	3	6	1.8	.959
1987		8	**17**	.320	5.27	33	31	1	177.2	226	54	76	0	0	0	0	51	5	0	.098	7	39	2	2	1.5	.958
1988		14	5	.737	3.14	27	27	3	175	156	67	103	2	0	0	0	48	6	0	.125	6	39	2	3	1.7	.957
1989	**2 teams HOU N** (22G 4–10) **SF N** (13G 3–2)																									
"	**total**	7	12	.368	5.13	35	26	1	165	190	75	64	1	1	0	0	43	8	1	.186	8	29	2	1	1.1	.949
1990	**SF N**	3	3	.500	5.68	12	7	0	44.1	56	19	24	0	0	1	0	13	3	0	.231	1	8	0	0	0.8	1.000
15 yrs.		146	155	.485	3.68	445	413	78	2707.2	2737	857	1473	30	3	2	1	840	115	6	.137	103	451	30	32	1.3	.949
DIVISIONAL PLAYOFF SERIES																										
1981	**HOU N**	0	1	.000	5.40	1	1	0	5	6	2	4	0	0	0	0	1	0	0	.000	0	0	0	0	0.0	.000
LEAGUE CHAMPIONSHIP SERIES																										
1986	**HOU N**	0	0	—	3.52	2	2	0	15.1	13	1	9	0	0	0	0	5	0	0	.000	0	0	0	0	0.0	.000

Charlie Knepper

KNEPPER, CHARLES
B. Feb. 18, 1871, Anderson, Ind. D. Feb. 6, 1946, Muncie, Ind.
BR TR 6′ 4″ 190 lbs.

Year	Team	W	L	PCT	ERA	G	GS	CG	IP	H	BB	SO	ShO	Relief W	L	SV	AB	H	HR	BA	PO	A	E	DP	TC/G	FA
1899	**CLE N**	4	22	.154	5.78	27	26	26	219.2	307	77	43	0	0	0	0	89	12	0	.135	8	49	6	2	2.3	.905

Lou Knerr

KNERR, WALLACE LUTHER
B. Aug. 21, 1921, Denver, Pa. D. Mar. 27, 1980, Reading, Pa.
BR TR 6′ 1″ 210 lbs.

Year	Team	W	L	PCT	ERA	G	GS	CG	IP	H	BB	SO	ShO	Relief W	L	SV	AB	H	HR	BA	PO	A	E	DP	TC/G	FA
1945	**PHI A**	5	11	.313	4.22	27	17	5	130	142	74	41	0	1	0	0	47	9	0	.191	10	24	1	3	1.3	.971
1946		3	**16**	.158	5.40	30	22	6	148.1	171	67	58	0	0	1	0	50	9	0	.180	4	26	0	0	1.0	1.000
1947	**WAS A**	0	0	—	11.00	6	0	0	9	17	8	5	0	0	0	0	1	1	0	1.000	0	3	1	0	0.7	.750
3 yrs.		8	27	.229	5.04	63	39	11	287.1	330	149	104	0	1	1	0	98	19	0	.194	14	53	2	3	1.1	.971

Elmer Knetzer

KNETZER, ELMER ELLSWORTH (Baron)
B. July 22, 1885, Carrick, Pa. D. Oct. 3, 1975, Pittsburgh, Pa.
BR TR 5′10″ 180 lbs.

Year	Team	W	L	PCT	ERA	G	GS	CG	IP	H	BB	SO	ShO	Relief W	L	SV	AB	H	HR	BA	PO	A	E	DP	TC/G	FA
1909	**BKN N**	1	3	.250	3.03	5	4	3	35.2	33	22	7	0	0	0	0	12	0	0	.000	2	14	1	0	3.4	.941
1910		7	5	.583	3.19	20	15	10	132.2	122	60	56	3	0	0	0	38	2	0	.053	3	32	4	0	2.0	.897
1911		11	12	.478	3.49	35	20	11	204	202	93	66	3	2	3	0	62	6	0	.097	7	51	3	2	1.7	.951
1912		7	9	.438	4.55	33	16	4	140.1	135	70	61	1	2	1	0	37	5	0	.135	4	34	2	0	1.2	.950
1914	**PIT F**	19	11	.633	2.88	37	30	20	272	257	88	146	3	4	0	1	91	9	0	.099	6	88	6	2	2.7	.940
1915		18	15	.545	2.58	41	33	22	279	256	89	120	3	1	1	3	91	12	0	.132	12	80	3	2	2.3	.968
1916	**2 teams BOS N** (2G 0–2) **CIN N** (36G 5–12)																									
"	**total**	5	14	.263	3.01	38	16	12	176.1	172	47	72	0	0	**5**	1	52	8	0	.154	5	63	2	1	1.8	.971
1917	**CIN N**	0	0	—	2.96	11	0	0	27.1	29	12	7	0	0	0	1	3	0	0	.000	2	9	1	0	1.1	.917
8 yrs.		68	69	.496	3.15	220	134	82	1267.1	1206	481	535	13	9	10	6	386	42	0	.109	41	371	22	7	2.0	.949

Jack Knight

KNIGHT, ELMA RUSSELL
B. Jan. 12, 1895, Pittsboro, Miss. D. July 30, 1976, San Antonio, Tex.
BL TR 6′ 175 lbs.

Year	Team	W	L	PCT	ERA	G	GS	CG	IP	H	BB	SO	ShO	Relief W	L	SV	AB	H	HR	BA	PO	A	E	DP	TC/G	FA
1922	**STL N**	0	0	—	9.00	1	1	0	4	9	3	1	0	0	0	0	2	1	0	.500	0	1	0	0	1.0	1.000
1925	**PHI N**	7	6	.538	6.84	33	11	4	105.1	161	36	19	0	3	2	3	44	9	0	.205	4	20	1	0	0.8	.960
1926		3	12	.200	6.62	35	15	5	142.2	206	48	29	0	1	1	2	56	12	2	.214	13	56	3	5	2.0	.958
1927	**BOS N**	0	0	—	15.00	3	0	0	3	6	2	0	0	0	0	0	0	0	0	—	1	3	0	1	1.3	1.000
4 yrs.		10	18	.357	6.85	72	27	9	255	382	89	49	0	4	3	5	102	22	2	.216	18	80	4	6	1.4	.961

Joe Knight

KNIGHT, JOSEPH WILLIAM (Quiet Joe)
B. Sept. 28, 1859, Port Stanley, Ont., Canada
D. Oct. 16, 1938, Lynhurst, Ont., Canada.
BL TL 5′11″ 185 lbs.

Year	Team	W	L	PCT	ERA	G	GS	CG	IP	H	BB	SO	ShO	Relief W	L	SV	AB	H	HR	BA	PO	A	E	DP	TC/G	FA
1884	**PHI N**	2	4	.333	*5.47*	6	6	6	51	66	21	8	0	0	0	0	*				3	12	4	0	3.2	.789

Lon Knight

KNIGHT, ALONZO P.
B. June 16, 1853, Philadelphia, Pa. D. Apr. 23, 1932, Philadelphia, Pa.
Manager 1883–84.
BR TR 5′11½″ 165 lbs.

Year	Team	W	L	PCT	ERA	G	GS	CG	IP	H	BB	SO	ShO	Relief W	L	SV	AB	H	HR	BA	PO	A	E	DP	TC/G	FA
1876	**PHI N**	10	22	.313	2.62	34	32	27	282	383	34	12	0	0	0	0	240	60	0	.250	156	48	40	10	3.9	.836
1884	**PHI AA**	0	1	.000	9.00	2	1	1	14	24	4	2	0	0	0	0	484	131	1	.271	47	22	11	1	1.6	.863
1885	**2 teams PHI AA** (1G 0–0) **PRO N** (1G 0–0)																									
"	**total**	0	0		4.00	2	0	0	9	8	6	2	0	0	0	0	200	38	0	.190	88	17	7	5	2.0	.938
3 yrs.		10	23	.303	2.95	38	33	28	305	415	44	16	0	0	0	0	*				833	212	147	35	2.2	.877

Hub Knolls

KNOLLS, OSCAR EDWARD
B. Dec. 18, 1883, Valparaiso, Ind. D. July 1, 1946, Chicago, Ill.
TR 6′ 2″ 190 lbs.

Year	Team	W	L	PCT	ERA	G	GS	CG	IP	H	BB	SO	ShO	Relief W	L	SV	AB	H	HR	BA	PO	A	E	DP	TC/G	FA
1906	**BKN N**	0	0	—	4.05	2	0	0	6.2	13	2	3	0	0	0	0	1	1	0	1.000	0	0	1	0	0.5	.000

Jack Knott

KNOTT, JOHN HENRY
B. Mar. 2, 1907, Dallas, Tex. D. Oct. 13, 1981, Brownwood, Tex.
BR TR 6′ 2½″ 200 lbs.

Year	Team	W	L	PCT	ERA	G	GS	CG	IP	H	BB	SO	ShO	Relief W	L	SV	AB	H	HR	BA	PO	A	E	DP	TC/G	FA
1933	**STL A**	1	8	.111	5.01	20	9	0	82.2	88	33	19	0	0	2	0	23	7	0	.304	2	15	1	0	0.9	.944
1934		10	3	.769	4.96	45	10	2	138	149	67	56	0	**7**	0	4	30	4	0	.133	5	31	2	0	0.8	.947
1935		11	8	.579	4.60	48	19	7	187.2	219	78	45	2	5	4	**7**	61	7	0	.115	7	44	2	1	1.1	.962
1936		9	17	.346	7.29	47	23	9	192.2	272	93	60	0	3	3	6	57	4	0	.070	3	33	2	1	0.8	.947
1937		8	18	.308	4.89	38	22	8	191.1	220	91	74	0	2	5	2	57	8	0	.140	2	26	1	1	0.8	.966
1938	**2 teams STL A** (7G 1–2) **CHI A** (20G 5–10)																									
"	**total**	6	12	.333	4.19	27	22	9	161	170	69	43	0	0	1	0	50	6	0	.120	4	35	3	5	1.6	.929
1939	**CHI A**	11	6	.647	4.15	25	23	8	149.2	157	41	56	0	0	0	0	53	8	0	.151	4	23	2	2	1.2	.931
1940		11	9	.550	4.56	25	23	4	158	166	52	44	2	0	0	0	57	5	0	.088	4	29	3	2	1.4	.917
1941	**PHI A**	13	11	.542	4.40	27	26	11	194.1	212	81	54	0	0	0	0	65	5	0	.077	7	26	1	2	1.3	.971
1942		2	10	.167	5.57	20	14	4	95.1	127	36	31	0	1	0	0	29	4	0	.138	7	24	1	3	1.6	.969
1946		0	1	.000	5.68	3	1	0	6.1	7	1	2	0	0	1	0	0	0	0	—	0	0	0	0	0.0	.000
11 yrs.		82	103	.443	4.97	325	192	62	1557	1787	642	484	4	18	16	19	482	58	0	.120	45	286	18	17	1.1	.948

Ed Knouff

KNOUFF, EDWARD (Fred) BR TR 210 lbs.
B. June 1868, Philadelphia, Pa. D. Sept. 14, 1900, Philadelphia, Pa.

Year	Team	Lg	W	L	PCT	ERA	G	GS	CG	IP	H	BB	SO	ShO	Relief Pitching W	Relief Pitching L	Relief Pitching SV	Batting AB	Batting H	Batting HR	BA	PO	A	E	DP	TC/G	FA
1885	PHI	AA	7	6	.538	3.65	14	13	12	106	103	44	43	0	0	0	0	48	9	0	.188	4	22	4	2	2.0	.867
1886	BAL	AA	0	1	.000	2.00	1	1	1	9	2	5	8	0	0	0	0	3	0	0	.000	0	5	0	0	5.0	1.000
1887	2 teams	BAL AA	(9G 2–6)		STL AA	(6G 4–2)																					
″	total		6	8	.429	6.21	15	15	12	113	119	77	45	1	0	0	0	87	19	0	.218	20	28	7	2	2.0	.873
1888	2 teams	STL AA	(9G 5–4)		CLE AA	(2G 0–1)																					
″	total		5	5	.500	2.50	11	11	10	90	74	40	27	0	0	0	0	37	4	0	.108	6	18	3	0	2.3	.889
1889	PHI	AA	2	0	1.000	3.96	3	3	2	25	37	9	5	0	0	0	0	12	3	0	.250	1	2	0	0	1.0	1.000
5 yrs.			20	20	.500	4.17	44	43	37	343	335	175	128	1	0	0	0	187	35	0	.187	31	75	14	4	2.1	.883

Darold Knowles

KNOWLES, DAROLD DUANE BL TL 6′ 180 lbs.
B. Dec. 9, 1941, Brunswick, Mo.

Year	Team	Lg	W	L	PCT	ERA	G	GS	CG	IP	H	BB	SO	ShO	Relief Pitching W	Relief Pitching L	Relief Pitching SV	Batting AB	Batting H	Batting HR	BA	PO	A	E	DP	TC/G	FA
1965	BAL	A	0	1	.000	9.20	5	1	0	14.2	14	10	12	0	0	0	0	4	0	0	.000	3	3	0	0	1.2	1.000
1966	PHI	N	6	5	.545	3.05	69	0	0	100.1	98	46	88	0	6	5	13	16	4	0	.250	3	28	5	1	0.5	.861
1967	WAS	A	6	8	.429	2.70	61	1	0	113.1	91	52	85	0	6	7	14	16	1	0	.063	6	28	5	4	0.6	.872
1968			1	1	.500	2.18	32	0	0	41.1	38	12	37	0	1	1	4	4	1	0	.250	1	8	1	0	0.3	.900
1969			9	2	.818	2.24	53	0	0	84.1	73	31	59	0	9	2	13	13	1	0	.077	6	12	0	0	0.3	1.000
1970			2	14	.125	2.04	71	0	0	119	100	58	71	0	2	**14**	27	20	1	0	.050	8	25	2	2	0.5	.943
1971	2 teams	WAS A	(12G 2–2)		OAK A	(43G 5–2)																					
″	total		7	4	.636	3.57	55	0	0	68	57	22	56	0	7	4	9	10	1	0	.100	1	17	1	0	0.3	.947
1972	OAK	A	5	1	.833	1.36	54	0	0	66	49	37	36	0	5	1	11	12	3	0	.250	2	26	1	0	0.5	.966
1973			6	8	.429	3.09	52	5	1	99	87	49	46	1	4	7	9	0	0	0	—	3	27	5	0	0.7	.857
1974			3	3	.500	4.25	45	1	0	53	61	35	18	0	2	3	3	0	0	0	—	2	12	0	2	0.3	1.000
1975	CHI	N	6	9	.400	5.83	58	0	0	88	107	36	63	0	6	9	15	15	1	0	.067	6	26	0	1	0.6	1.000
1976			5	7	.417	2.88	58	0	0	72	61	22	39	0	5	7	9	7	1	0	.143	3	23	2	2	0.5	.929
1977	TEX	A	5	2	.714	3.24	42	0	0	50	50	23	14	0	5	2	4	0	0	0	—	3	14	2	3	0.5	.895
1978	MON	N	3	3	.500	2.38	60	0	0	72	63	30	34	0	3	3	6	6	1	0	.167	2	20	1	2	0.4	.957
1979	STL	N	2	5	.286	4.04	48	0	0	49	54	17	22	0	2	5	6	2	0	0	.000	2	7	4	0	0.3	.692
1980			0	1	.000	9.00	2	0	0	2	3	0	1	0	0	1	0	0	0	0	—	0	0	0	0	0.0	.000
16 yrs.			66	74	.471	3.12	765	8	1	1092	1006	480	681	1	63	71	143	125	15	0	.120	51	276	29	17	0.5	.919
LEAGUE CHAMPIONSHIP SERIES																											
1971	OAK	A	0	0	—	0.00	1	0	0	0.1	1	0	0	0	0	0	0	0	0	0	—	0	0	0	0	0.0	.000
WORLD SERIES																											
1973	OAK	A	0	0	—	0.00	7	0	0	6.1	4	5	5	0	0	0	2	0	0	0	—	0	1	1	1	0.3	.500

Tom Knowlson

KNOWLSON, THOMAS HERBERT (Doc) BB TR 5′11″ 178 lbs.
B. Apr. 23, 1895, Ridgway, Pa. D. Apr. 11, 1943, Miami Shores, Fla.

Year	Team	Lg	W	L	PCT	ERA	G	GS	CG	IP	H	BB	SO	ShO	Relief Pitching W	Relief Pitching L	Relief Pitching SV	Batting AB	Batting H	Batting HR	BA	PO	A	E	DP	TC/G	FA
1915	PHI	A	4	6	.400	3.49	18	9	8	100.2	99	60	24	0	1	0	0	36	3	0	.083	2	32	5	2	2.2	.872

Bill Knowlton

KNOWLTON, WILLIAM YOUNG BR TR
B. Aug. 18, 1892, Philadelphia, Pa. D. Feb. 25, 1944, Philadelphia, Pa.

Year	Team	Lg	W	L	PCT	ERA	G	GS	CG	IP	H	BB	SO	ShO	Relief Pitching W	Relief Pitching L	Relief Pitching SV	Batting AB	Batting H	Batting HR	BA	PO	A	E	DP	TC/G	FA
1920	PHI	A	0	1	.000	4.76	1	1	0	5.2	9	3	5	0	0	0	0	2	0	0	.000	0	3	1	0	4.0	.750

Kurt Knudsen

KNUDSEN, KURT DAVID BR TR 6′ 2″ 185 lbs.
B. Feb. 20, 1967, Arlington Heights, Ill.

Year	Team	Lg	W	L	PCT	ERA	G	GS	CG	IP	H	BB	SO	ShO	Relief Pitching W	Relief Pitching L	Relief Pitching SV	Batting AB	Batting H	Batting HR	BA	PO	A	E	DP	TC/G	FA
1992	DET	A	2	3	.400	4.58	48	1	0	70.2	70	41	51	0	2	2	5	0	0	0	—	6	7	0	2	0.3	1.000
1993			3	2	.600	4.78	30	0	0	37.2	41	16	29	0	3	2	2	0	0	0	—	4	3	0	0	0.2	1.000
1994			1	0	1.000	13.50	4	0	0	5.1	7	11	1	0	1	0	0	0	0	0	—	0	0	0	0	0.0	.000
3 yrs.			6	5	.545	5.07	82	1	0	113.2	118	68	81	0	6	4	7	0	0	0		10	10	0	2	0.2	1.000

Mark Knudson

KNUDSON, MARK RICHARD BR TR 6′ 5″ 215 lbs.
B. Oct. 28, 1960, Denver, Colo.

Year	Team	Lg	W	L	PCT	ERA	G	GS	CG	IP	H	BB	SO	ShO	Relief Pitching W	Relief Pitching L	Relief Pitching SV	Batting AB	Batting H	Batting HR	BA	PO	A	E	DP	TC/G	FA
1985	HOU	N	0	2	.000	9.00	2	2	0	11	21	3	4	0	0	0	0	2	0	0	.000	1	1	0	0	1.0	1.000
1986	2 teams	HOU N	(9G 1–5)		MIL A	(4G 0–1)																					
″	total		1	6	.143	5.22	13	8	0	60.1	70	20	29	0	0	0	0	10	0	0	.000	4	5	0	0	0.7	1.000
1987	MIL	A	4	4	.500	5.37	15	8	1	62	88	14	26	0	2	1	0	0	0	0	—	5	4	1	0	0.7	.900
1988			0	0	—	1.13	5	0	0	16	17	2	7	0	0	0	0	0	0	0	—	0	3	0	0	0.6	1.000
1989			8	5	.615	3.35	40	7	1	123.2	110	29	47	0	2	4	0	0	0	0	—	12	10	0	2	0.6	1.000
1990			10	9	.526	4.12	30	27	4	168.1	187	40	56	2	1	0	0	0	0	0	—	13	16	2	2	1.0	.935
1991			1	3	.250	7.97	12	7	0	35	54	15	23	0	0	0	0	0	0	0	—	4	3	0	0	0.6	1.000
1993	CLR	N	0	0	—	22.24	4	0	0	5.2	16	5	3	0	0	0	0	1	0	0	.000	0	1	1	0	0.5	.500
8 yrs.			24	29	.453	4.72	121	59	6	482	563	128	195	2	5	5	0	13	0	0	.000	39	43	4	4	0.7	.953

Kevin Kobel

KOBEL, KEVIN RICHARD BR TL 6′ 180 lbs.
B. Oct. 2, 1953, Buffalo, N. Y.

Year	Team	Lg	W	L	PCT	ERA	G	GS	CG	IP	H	BB	SO	ShO	Relief Pitching W	Relief Pitching L	Relief Pitching SV	Batting AB	Batting H	Batting HR	BA	PO	A	E	DP	TC/G	FA
1973	MIL	A	0	1	.000	8.64	2	1	0	8.1	9	8	4	0	0	0	0	0	0	0	—	0	1	0	0	0.5	1.000
1974			6	14	.300	3.99	34	24	3	169	166	54	74	2	0	1	0	0	0	0	—	8	29	0	3	1.1	1.000
1976			0	1	.000	11.25	3	0	0	4	6	3	1	0	0	1	0	0	0	0	—	0	1	0	0	0.3	1.000
1978	NY	N	5	6	.455	2.92	32	11	1	108	95	30	51	0	1	2	0	25	4	0	.160	4	16	2	1	0.7	.909
1979			6	8	.429	3.50	30	27	1	162	169	46	67	1	0	0	0	46	9	0	.196	13	26	3	2	1.4	.929
1980			1	4	.200	7.13	14	1	0	24	36	11	8	0	1	4	0	2	0	0	.000	0	4	0	0	0.3	1.000
6 yrs.			18	34	.346	3.88	115	64	5	475.1	481	152	205	3	2	8	0	73	13	0	.178	25	77	5	6	0.9	.953

Alan Koch

KOCH, ALAN GOODMAN BR TR 6′ 4″ 195 lbs.
B. Mar. 25, 1938, Decatur, Ala.

Year	Team	Lg	W	L	PCT	ERA	G	GS	CG	IP	H	BB	SO	ShO	Relief Pitching W	Relief Pitching L	Relief Pitching SV	Batting AB	Batting H	Batting HR	BA	PO	A	E	DP	TC/G	FA
1963	DET	A	1	1	.500	10.80	7	1	0	10	21	9	5	0	1	1	0	3	2	0	.667	0	2	0	0	0.3	1.000
1964	2 teams	DET A	(3G 0–0)		WAS A	(32G 3–10)																					
″	total		3	10	.231	4.96	35	14	1	118	116	46	68	0	0	3	0	32	8	0	.250	2	12	2	0	0.5	.875
2 yrs.			4	11	.267	5.41	42	15	1	128	137	55	73	0	1	4	0	35	10	0	.286	2	14	2	0	0.4	.889

Dick Koecher

KOECHER, RICHARD FINLAY (Highpockets) BL TL 6′ 5″ 196 lbs.
B. Mar. 30, 1926, Philadelphia, Pa.

Year	Team		W	L	PCT	ERA	G	GS	CG	IP	H	BB	SO	ShO	Relief Pitching W	L	SV	Batting AB	H	HR	BA	PO	A	E	DP	TC/G	FA
1946	PHI	N	0	1	.000	10.13	1	1	0	2.2	7	1	2	0	0	0	0	1	0	0	.000	0	0	0	0	0.0	.000
1947			0	2	.000	4.76	3	2	1	17	20	10	4	0	0	0	0	4	0	0	.000	0	5	0	0	1.7	1.000
1948			0	1	.000	3.00	3	0	0	6	4	3	2	0	0	1	0	0	0	0	—	0	1	0	0	0.3	1.000
3 yrs.			0	4	.000	4.91	7	3	1	25.2	31	14	8	0	0	1	0	5	0	0	.000	0	6	0	0	0.9	1.000

Mark Koenig

KOENIG, MARK ANTHONY BB TR 6′ 180 lbs.
B. July 19, 1904, San Francisco, Calif. D. Apr. 22, 1993, Willows, Calif.

Year	Team		W	L	PCT	ERA	G	GS	CG	IP	H	BB	SO	ShO	Relief Pitching W	L	SV	Batting AB	H	HR	BA	PO	A	E	DP	TC/G	FA
1930	DET	A	0	1	.000	10.00	2	1	0	9	11	8	6	0	0	0	0	341	81	1	.238	53	81	8	16	5.1	.944
1931			0	0	—	6.43	3	0	0	7	7	11	3	0	0	0	0	364	92	1	.253	191	238	28	41	4.9	.939
2 yrs.			0	1	.000	8.44	5	1	0	16	18	19	9	0	0	0	0	*				1987	2929	350	514	4.9	.934

Will Koenigsmark

KOENIGSMARK, WILLIAM THOMAS BR TR 6′ 4″ 180 lbs.
B. Feb. 27, 1896, Waterloo, Ill. D. July 1, 1972, Waterloo, Ill.

Year	Team		W	L	PCT	ERA	G	GS	CG	IP	H	BB	SO	ShO	Relief Pitching W	L	SV	Batting AB	H	HR	BA	PO	A	E	DP	TC/G	FA
1919	STL	N	0	0	—	∞	1	0	0		2	1	0	0	0	0	0	0	0	0	—	0	0	0	0	0.0	.000

Elmer Koestner

KOESTNER, ELMER JOSEPH (Bob) BR TR 6′ 1½″ 175 lbs.
B. Nov. 30, 1885, Piper City, Ill. D. Oct. 27, 1959, Fairbury, Ill.

Year	Team		W	L	PCT	ERA	G	GS	CG	IP	H	BB	SO	ShO	Relief Pitching W	L	SV	Batting AB	H	HR	BA	PO	A	E	DP	TC/G	FA
1910	CLE	A	5	10	.333	3.04	27	13	8	145	145	63	44	1	2	**4**	2	48	15	0	.313	9	41	4	3	2.0	.926
1914	2 teams	CHI N (4G 0–0) CIN N (5G 0–0)																									
″	total		0	0		4.01	9	1	0	24.2	24	13	12	0	0	0	0	6	2	0	.333	1	6	1	1	0.9	.875
2 yrs.			5	10	.333	3.18	36	14	8	169.2	169	76	56	1	2	4	2	54	17	0	.315	10	47	5	4	1.7	.919

Joe Kohlman

KOHLMAN, JOSEPH JAMES (Blackie) BR TR 6′ 160 lbs.
B. Jan. 28, 1913, Philadelphia, Pa. D. Mar. 16, 1974, Philadelphia, Pa.

Year	Team		W	L	PCT	ERA	G	GS	CG	IP	H	BB	SO	ShO	Relief Pitching W	L	SV	Batting AB	H	HR	BA	PO	A	E	DP	TC/G	FA
1937	WAS	A	1	0	1.000	4.15	2	2	1	13	15	3	3	0	0	0	0	5	1	0	.200	0	1	0	0	0.5	1.000
1938			0	0	—	6.28	7	0	0	14.1	12	11	5	0	0	0	0	3	0	0	.000	2	3	0	1	0.7	1.000
2 yrs.			1	0	1.000	5.27	9	2	1	27.1	27	14	8	0	0	0	0	8	1	0	.125	2	4	0	1	0.7	1.000

Eddie Kolb

KOLB, EDWARD WILLIAM BR TR
B. July 20, 1880, Cincinnati, Ohio Deceased.

Year	Team		W	L	PCT	ERA	G	GS	CG	IP	H	BB	SO	ShO	Relief Pitching W	L	SV	Batting AB	H	HR	BA	PO	A	E	DP	TC/G	FA
1899	CLE	N	0	1	.000	10.13	1	1	1	8	18	5	1	0	0	0	0	4	1	0	.250	0	0	1	0	1.0	.000

Ray Kolp

KOLP, RAYMOND CARL (Jockey) BR TR 5′10½″ 187 lbs.
B. Oct. 1, 1894, New Berlin, Ohio D. July 29, 1967, New Orleans, La.

Year	Team		W	L	PCT	ERA	G	GS	CG	IP	H	BB	SO	ShO	Relief Pitching W	L	SV	Batting AB	H	HR	BA	PO	A	E	DP	TC/G	FA
1921	STL	A	8	7	.533	4.97	37	18	5	166.2	208	51	43	1	1	2	0	55	7	0	.127	12	45	0	3	1.5	1.000
1922			14	4	.778	3.93	32	18	9	169.2	199	36	54	1	2	1	0	57	17	0	.298	13	18	1	0	1.0	.969
1923			5	12	.294	3.89	34	17	11	171.1	178	54	44	1	0	2	1	54	6	0	.111	10	37	5	2	1.5	.904
1924			5	7	.417	5.68	25	12	5	96.2	131	25	29	1	2	0	0	30	6	0	.200	7	18	0	1	1.0	1.000
1927	CIN	N	3	3	.500	3.06	24	5	2	82.1	86	29	28	1	1	2	3	30	6	0	.200	4	17	0	3	0.9	1.000
1928			13	10	.565	3.19	44	24	12	209	219	55	61	1	3	1	3	70	15	1	.214	11	50	1	4	1.4	.984
1929			8	10	.444	4.03	30	16	4	145.1	151	39	27	1	2	1	0	49	8	0	.163	7	38	2	1	1.6	.957
1930			7	12	.368	4.22	37	19	5	168.1	180	34	40	2	1	2	3	49	12	1	.245	8	30	1	0	1.1	.974
1931			4	9	.308	4.96	30	10	2	107	144	39	24	0	2	1	1	32	4	0	.125	3	17	0	2	0.7	1.000
1932			6	10	.375	3.89	32	19	7	159.2	176	27	42	2	0	0	1	49	9	0	.184	6	23	0	3	0.9	1.000
1933			6	9	.400	3.53	30	14	4	150.1	168	23	28	0	3	2	3	45	7	0	.156	5	39	2	0	1.5	.957
1934			0	2	.000	4.52	28	2	0	61.2	78	12	19	0	0	0	3	12	1	0	.083	0	21	0	3	0.8	1.000
12 yrs.			79	95	.454	4.08	383	174	66	1688	1918	424	439	11	17	14	18	532	98	2	.184	86	353	12	22	1.2	.973

Hal Kolstad

KOLSTAD, HAROLD EVERETTE BR TR 5′ 9″ 190 lbs.
B. June 1, 1935, Rice Lake, Wis.

Year	Team		W	L	PCT	ERA	G	GS	CG	IP	H	BB	SO	ShO	Relief Pitching W	L	SV	Batting AB	H	HR	BA	PO	A	E	DP	TC/G	FA
1962	BOS	A	0	2	.000	5.43	27	2	0	61.1	65	35	36	0	0	2	2	18	1	0	.056	6	10	1	1	0.6	.941
1963			0	2	.000	13.09	7	0	0	11	16	6	6	0	0	2	0	1	0	0	.000	1	1	0	0	0.3	1.000
2 yrs.			0	4	.000	6.59	34	2	0	72.1	81	41	42	0	0	4	2	19	1	0	.053	7	11	1	1	0.6	.947

Ed Konetchy

KONETCHY, EDWARD JOSEPH (Big Ed) BR TR 6′ 2½″ 195 lbs.
B. Sept. 3, 1885, LaCrosse, Wis. D. May 27, 1947, Fort Worth, Tex.

Year	Team		W	L	PCT	ERA	G	GS	CG	IP	H	BB	SO	ShO	Relief Pitching W	L	SV	Batting AB	H	HR	BA	PO	A	E	DP	TC/G	FA
1910	STL	N	0	0	—	4.50	1	0	0	4	4	1	0	0	0	0	0	520	157	3	.302	922	71	25	46	11.3	.975
1913			1	0	1.000	0.00	1	0	0	4.2	1	4	3	0	1	0	0	502	137	7	.273	1610	122	24	61	11.4	.986
1918	BOS	N	0	1	.000	6.75	1	1	1	8	14	2	3	0	0	0	0	437	103	2	.236	1584	97	26	71	11.2	.985
3 yrs.			1	1	.500	4.32	3	1	1	16.2	19	7	6	0	1	0	0	*				21378	1297	224	1087	11.0	.990

Doug Konieczny

KONIECZNY, DOUGLAS JAMES BR TR 6′ 4″ 220 lbs.
B. Sept. 27, 1951, Detroit, Mich.

Year	Team		W	L	PCT	ERA	G	GS	CG	IP	H	BB	SO	ShO	Relief Pitching W	L	SV	Batting AB	H	HR	BA	PO	A	E	DP	TC/G	FA
1973	HOU	N	0	1	.000	5.54	2	2	0	13	12	4	6	0	0	0	0	4	0	0	.000	1	1	0	0	1.0	1.000
1974			0	3	.000	7.88	6	3	0	16	18	12	8	0	0	0	0	4	0	0	.000	1	2	0	0	0.5	1.000
1975			6	13	.316	4.47	32	29	4	171	184	87	89	1	0	0	0	50	8	0	.160	7	21	4	1	1.0	.875
1977			1	1	.500	6.00	4	4	0	21	26	8	7	0	0	0	0	7	1	0	.143	5	3	0	0	2.0	1.000
4 yrs.			7	18	.280	4.93	44	38	4	221	240	111	110	1	0	0	0	65	9	0	.138	14	27	4	1	1.0	.911

Alex Konikowski

KONIKOWSKI, ALEXANDER JAMES (Whitey) BR TR 6′ 1″ 187 lbs.
B. June 8, 1928, Throop, Pa.

Year	Team		W	L	PCT	ERA	G	GS	CG	IP	H	BB	SO	ShO	Relief Pitching W	L	SV	Batting AB	H	HR	BA	PO	A	E	DP	TC/G	FA
1948	NY	N	2	3	.400	7.56	22	1	0	33.1	46	17	9	0	2	2	1	2	0	0	.000	3	8	0	1	0.5	1.000
1951			0	0	—	0.00	3	0	0	4	2	0	5	0	0	0	0	0	0	0	—	1	0	0	0	0.3	1.000
1954			0	0	—	7.50	10	0	0	12	10	12	6	0	0	0	0	1	0	0	.000	0	1	0	0	0.1	1.000
3 yrs.			2	3	.400	6.93	35	1	0	49.1	58	29	20	0	2	2	1	3	0	0	.000	4	9	0	1	0.4	1.000
WORLD SERIES																											
1951	NY	N	0	0	—	0.00	1	0	0	1	1	0	0	0	0	0	0	0	0	0	—	0	0	0	0	0.0	.000

Jim Konstanty

KONSTANTY, CASIMIR JAMES BR TR 6′ 1½″ 202 lbs.
B. Mar. 2, 1917, Strykersville, N. Y. D. June 11, 1976, Oneonta, N. Y.

Year	Team		W	L	PCT	ERA	G	GS	CG	IP	H	BB	SO	ShO	Relief Pitching W	L	SV	Batting AB	H	HR	BA	PO	A	E	DP	TC/G	FA
1944	CIN	N	6	4	.600	2.80	20	12	5	112.2	113	33	19	1	2	1	0	34	10	0	.294	10	25	0	1	1.8	1.000
1946	BOS	N	0	1	.000	5.28	10	1	0	15.1	17	7	9	0	0	0	0	2	0	0	.000	2	5	0	1	0.7	1.000
1948	PHI	N	1	0	1.000	0.93	6	0	0	9.2	7	2	7	0	1	0	2	3	0	0	.000	0	1	0	0	0.2	1.000

Jim Konstanty *continued*

Year	Team	W	L	PCT	ERA	G	GS	CG	IP	H	BB	SO	ShO	Relief Pitching W	Relief Pitching L	Relief Pitching SV	Batting AB	Batting H	Batting HR	BA	PO	A	E	DP	TC/G	FA
1949		9	5	.643	3.25	53	0	0	97	98	29	43	0	9	5	7	17	3	0	.176	3	25	2	0	0.6	.933
1950		16	7	.696	2.66	**74**	0	0	152	108	50	56	0	**16**	**7**	**22**	37	4	0	.108	12	22	2	3	0.5	.944
1951		4	11	.267	4.05	58	1	0	115.2	127	31	27	0	4	**10**	9	19	3	0	.158	8	29	1	1	0.7	.974
1952		5	3	.625	3.94	42	2	2	80	87	21	16	1	4	2	6	14	1	0	.071	6	16	3	1	0.6	.880
1953		14	10	.583	4.43	48	19	7	170.2	198	42	45	0	4	3	5	50	11	0	.220	6	33	0	5	0.8	1.000
1954	2 teams PHI N (33G 2–3) NY A (9G 1–1)																									
"	total	3	4	.429	3.01	42	1	0	68.2	73	18	14	0	3	4	5	16	0	0	.000	5	13	0	0	0.4	1.000
1955	NY A	7	2	.778	2.32	45	0	0	73.2	68	24	19	0	7	2	11	8	1	0	.125	8	11	2	1	0.5	.905
1956	2 teams NY A (8G 0–0) STL N (27G 1–1)																									
"	total	1	1	.500	4.65	35	0	0	50.1	61	12	13	0	1	1	7	2	0	0	.000	1	5	0	1	0.2	1.000
11 yrs.		66	48	.579	3.46	433	36	14	945.2	957	269	268	2	51	35	74	202	33	0	.163	61	185	10	14	0.6	.961
WORLD SERIES																										
1950	PHI N	0	1	.000	2.40	3	1	0	15	9	4	3	0	0	0	0	4	1	0	.250	1	1	0	0	0.7	1.000

Dennis Konuszewski

KONUSZEWSKI, DENNIS JOHN
B. Feb. 4, 1971, Bridgeport, Mich.
BR TR 6′ 3″ 210 lbs.

Year	Team	W	L	PCT	ERA	G	GS	CG	IP	H	BB	SO	ShO	Relief Pitching W	Relief Pitching L	Relief Pitching SV	Batting AB	Batting H	Batting HR	BA	PO	A	E	DP	TC/G	FA
1995	PIT N	0	0	—	54.00	1	0	0	0.1	3	1	0	0	0	0	0	0	0	0	—	0	0	0	0	0.0	.000

Ernie Koob

KOOB, ERNEST GERALD
B. Sept. 11, 1892, Keeler, Mich. D. Nov. 12, 1941, Lemay, Mo.
BL TL 5′10″ 160 lbs.

Year	Team	W	L	PCT	ERA	G	GS	CG	IP	H	BB	SO	ShO	Relief Pitching W	Relief Pitching L	Relief Pitching SV	Batting AB	Batting H	Batting HR	BA	PO	A	E	DP	TC/G	FA
1915	STL A	4	5	.444	2.36	28	13	6	133.2	119	50	37	0	0	0	1	37	5	0	.135	3	32	0	3	1.3	1.000
1916		11	8	.579	2.54	33	20	10	166.2	153	56	26	2	2	1	2	41	0	0	.000	4	36	0	1	1.2	1.000
1917		6	14	.300	3.91	39	18	3	133.2	139	57	47	1	1	2	1	35	4	0	.114	4	44	7	3	1.4	.873
1919		2	3	.400	4.64	25	4	0	66	77	23	11	0	2	1	0	15	0	0	.000	2	21	1	2	1.0	.958
4 yrs.		23	30	.434	3.13	125	55	19	500	488	186	121	3	5	4	4	128	9	0	.070	13	133	8	9	1.2	.948

Cal Koonce

KOONCE, CALVIN LEE
B. Nov. 18, 1940, Fayetteville, N. C. D. Oct. 28, 1993, Winston-Salem, N. C.
BR TR 6′ 1″ 185 lbs.

Year	Team	W	L	PCT	ERA	G	GS	CG	IP	H	BB	SO	ShO	Relief Pitching W	Relief Pitching L	Relief Pitching SV	Batting AB	Batting H	Batting HR	BA	PO	A	E	DP	TC/G	FA
1962	CHI N	10	10	.500	3.97	35	30	3	190.2	200	86	84	1	0	0	0	64	6	0	.094	17	29	3	1	1.4	.939
1963		2	6	.250	4.58	21	13	0	72.2	75	32	44	0	0	0	0	19	2	0	.105	2	18	0	1	1.0	1.000
1964		3	0	1.000	2.03	6	2	0	31	30	7	17	0	1	0	0	10	0	0	.000	0	14	0	2	2.3	1.000
1965		7	9	.438	3.69	38	23	3	173	181	52	88	1	0	0	0	49	5	0	.102	8	31	0	3	1.0	1.000
1966		5	5	.500	3.81	45	5	0	108.2	113	35	65	0	4	4	2	23	3	0	.130	6	25	1	1	0.7	.969
1967	2 teams CHI N (34G 2–2) NY N (11G 3–3)																									
"	total	5	5	.500	3.75	45	6	2	96	97	28	52	1	2	2	2	20	2	0	.100	13	21	0	3	0.8	1.000
1968	NY N	6	4	.600	2.42	55	2	0	96.2	80	32	50	0	5	4	11	14	0	0	.000	13	11	0	0	0.4	1.000
1969		6	3	.667	4.99	40	0	0	83	85	42	48	0	6	3	7	17	4	0	.235	7	18	0	2	0.6	1.000
1970	2 teams NY N (13G 0–2) BOS A (23G 3–4)																									
"	total	3	6	.333	3.49	36	8	1	98	89	43	47	0	0	2	2	22	2	0	.091	10	24	1	2	1.0	.971
1971	BOS A	0	1	.000	5.57	13	1	0	21	22	11	9	0	0	0	0	1	0	0	.000	5	4	0	1	0.7	1.000
10 yrs.		47	49	.490	3.78	334	90	9	970.2	972	368	504	3	18	15	24	239	24	0	.100	81	195	5	16	0.8	.982

Jerry Koosman

KOOSMAN, JEROME MARTIN (Kooz)
B. Dec. 23, 1942, Appleton, Minn.
BR TL 6′ 2″ 205 lbs.

Year	Team	W	L	PCT	ERA	G	GS	CG	IP	H	BB	SO	ShO	Relief Pitching W	Relief Pitching L	Relief Pitching SV	Batting AB	Batting H	Batting HR	BA	PO	A	E	DP	TC/G	FA
1967	NY N	0	2	.000	6.04	9	3	0	22.1	22	19	11	0	0	0	0	2	0	0	.000	0	5	0	1	0.6	1.000
1968		19	12	.613	2.08	35	34	17	263.2	221	69	178	7	0	0	0	91	7	1	.077	5	42	0	2	1.3	1.000
1969		17	9	.654	2.28	32	32	16	241	187	68	180	6	0	0	0	84	4	0	.048	4	37	1	3	1.3	.976
1970		12	7	.632	3.14	30	29	5	212	189	71	118	1	1	0	0	70	6	0	.086	7	20	0	1	0.9	1.000
1971		6	11	.353	3.04	26	24	4	166	160	51	96	0	0	0	0	50	8	0	.160	6	23	1	2	1.2	.967
1972		11	12	.478	4.14	34	24	4	163	155	52	147	1	2	0	1	47	4	0	.085	4	23	1	1	0.8	.964
1973		14	15	.483	2.84	35	35	12	263	234	76	156	3	0	0	0	78	8	0	.103	5	41	2	1	1.4	.958
1974		15	11	.577	3.36	35	35	13	265	258	85	188	0	0	0	0	86	16	0	.186	8	41	4	2	1.5	.925
1975		14	13	.519	3.41	36	34	11	240	234	98	173	4	0	0	2	78	14	0	.179	10	32	3	3	1.3	.933
1976		21	10	.677	2.70	34	32	17	247	205	66	200	3	0	0	0	79	17	0	.215	5	39	3	1	1.4	.936
1977		8	**20**	.286	3.49	32	32	6	227	195	81	192	1	0	0	0	72	8	1	.111	4	25	4	0	1.0	.879
1978		3	15	.167	3.75	38	32	3	235	221	84	160	0	0	0	2	70	6	0	.086	4	48	6	4	1.5	.897
1979	MIN A	20	13	.606	3.38	37	36	10	264	268	83	157	2	0	0	0	0	0	0	—	10	50	5	6	1.8	.923
1980		16	13	.552	4.04	38	34	8	243	252	69	149	0	1	1	2	0	0	0	—	7	41	3	2	1.3	.941
1981	2 teams MIN A (19G 3–9) CHI A (8G 1–4)																									
"	total	4	**13**	.235	4.02	27	16	3	121	125	41	76	1	0	2	5	0	0	0		7	17	1	0	0.9	.960
1982	CHI A	11	7	.611	3.84	42	19	3	173.1	194	38	88	1	2	3	3	0	0	0	—	12	24	1	3	0.9	.973
1983		11	7	.611	4.77	37	24	2	169.2	176	53	90	1	1	0	2	0	0	0	—	5	26	2	2	0.9	.939
1984	PHI N	14	15	.483	3.25	36	34	3	224	232	60	137	1	0	0	0	74	8	0	.108	9	34	4	1	1.3	.915
1985		6	4	.600	4.62	19	18	3	99.1	107	34	60	1	0	0	0	34	3	0	.088	4	14	1	1	1.0	.947
19 yrs.		222	209	.515	3.36	612	527	140	3839.1	3635	1198	2556	33	7	6	17	915	109	2	.119	116	582	42	36	1.2	.943
LEAGUE CHAMPIONSHIP SERIES																										
1969	NY N	0	0	—	11.57	1	1	0	4.2	7	4	5	0	0	0	0	2	0	0	.000	0	1	0	0	1.0	1.000
1973		1	0	1.000	2.00	1	1	1	9	8	0	9	0	0	0	0	4	2	0	.500	0	0	0	0	0.0	.000
1983	CHI A	0	0	—	54.00	1	0	0	0.1	1	2	0	0	0	0	0	0	0	0	—	0	0	0	0	0.0	.000
3 yrs.		1	0	1.000	6.43	3	2	1	14	16	6	14	0	0	0	0	6	2	0	.333	0	1	0	0	0.3	1.000
WORLD SERIES																										
1969	NY N	2	0	1.000	2.04	2	2	1	17.2	7	4	9	0	0	0	0	7	1	0	.143	0	2	0	0	1.0	1.000
1973		1	0	1.000	3.12	2	2	0	8.2	9	7	8	0	0	0	0	4	0	0	.000	0	1	1	0	1.0	.500
2 yrs.		3	0	1.000 **1st**	2.39	4	4	1	26.1	16	11	17	0	0	0	0	11	1	0	.091	0	3	1	0	1.0	.750

Howie Koplitz

KOPLITZ, HOWARD DEAN
B. May 4, 1938, Oshkosh, Wis.
BR TR 5′10½″ 190 lbs.

Year	Team	W	L	PCT	ERA	G	GS	CG	IP	H	BB	SO	ShO	Relief Pitching W	Relief Pitching L	Relief Pitching SV	Batting AB	Batting H	Batting HR	BA	PO	A	E	DP	TC/G	FA
1961	DET A	2	0	1.000	2.25	4	1	1	12	16	8	9	0	1	0	0	4	0	0	.000	0	1	0	0	0.3	1.000
1962		3	0	1.000	5.26	10	6	1	37.2	54	10	10	0	0	0	0	13	3	0	.231	3	7	0	1	1.0	1.000
1964	WAS A	0	0	—	4.76	6	1	0	17	20	13	9	0	0	0	0	4	0	0	.000	1	3	0	0	0.7	1.000

Howie Koplitz *continued*

Year	Team	Lg	W	L	PCT	ERA	G	GS	CG	IP	H	BB	SO	ShO	Relief Pitching W	Relief Pitching L	Relief Pitching SV	Batting AB	Batting H	Batting HR	BA	PO	A	E	DP	TC/G	FA
1965			4	7	.364	4.05	33	11	0	106.2	97	48	59	0	2	2	1	30	3	0	.100	8	23	0	2	0.9	1.000
1966			0	0	—	0.00	1	0	0	2	0	1	0	0	0	0	0	0	0	0	—	0	1	0	0	1.0	1.000
5 yrs.			9	7	.563	4.21	54	19	2	175.1	187	80	87	0	3	2	1	51	6	0	.118	12	35	0	3	0.9	1.000

George Korince

KORINCE, GEORGE EUGENE (Moose)
B. Jan. 10, 1946, Ottawa, Ont., Canada.

BR TR 6′ 3″ 210 lbs.

Year	Team	Lg	W	L	PCT	ERA	G	GS	CG	IP	H	BB	SO	ShO	Relief Pitching W	Relief Pitching L	Relief Pitching SV	Batting AB	Batting H	Batting HR	BA	PO	A	E	DP	TC/G	FA
1966	DET	A	0	0	—	0.00	2	0	0	3	1	3	2	0	0	0	0	0	0	0	—	0	0	0	0	0.0	.000
1967			1	0	1.000	5.14	9	0	0	14	10	11	11	0	1	0	0	1	0	0	.000	1	2	0	0	0.3	1.000
2 yrs.			1	0	1.000	4.24	11	0	0	17	11	14	13	0	1	0	0	1	0	0	.000	1	2	0	0	0.3	1.000

Jim Korwan

KORWAN, JAMES
B. Mar. 4, 1874, Brooklyn, N. Y. D. Jan. 24, 1899, Brooklyn, N. Y.

BR TR 6′ 1″ 181 lbs.

Year	Team	Lg	W	L	PCT	ERA	G	GS	CG	IP	H	BB	SO	ShO	Relief Pitching W	Relief Pitching L	Relief Pitching SV	Batting AB	Batting H	Batting HR	BA	PO	A	E	DP	TC/G	FA
1894	BKN	N	0	0	—	14.40	1	0	0	5	9	5	2	0	0	0	0	2	0	0	.000	0	1	0	0	1.0	1.000
1897	CHI	N	1	2	.333	5.82	5	4	3	34	47	28	12	0	0	0	0	12	0	0	.000	5	14	1	0	4.0	.950
2 yrs.			1	2	.333	6.92	6	4	3	39	56	33	14	0	0	0	0	14	0	0	.000	5	15	1	0	3.5	.952

Bill Koski

KOSKI, WILLIAM JOHN (T-Bone)
B. Feb. 6, 1932, Madera, Calif.

BR TR 6′ 4″ 185 lbs.

Year	Team	Lg	W	L	PCT	ERA	G	GS	CG	IP	H	BB	SO	ShO	Relief Pitching W	Relief Pitching L	Relief Pitching SV	Batting AB	Batting H	Batting HR	BA	PO	A	E	DP	TC/G	FA
1951	PIT	N	0	1	.000	6.67	13	1	0	27	26	28	6	0	0	0	0	4	0	0	.000	0	2	0	0	0.2	1.000

Dave Koslo

KOSLO, GEORGE BERNARD
Born George Bernard Koslowski.
B. Mar. 31, 1920, Menasha, Wis. D. Dec. 1, 1975, Menasha, Wis.

BL TL 5′11″ 180 lbs.

Year	Team	Lg	W	L	PCT	ERA	G	GS	CG	IP	H	BB	SO	ShO	Relief Pitching W	Relief Pitching L	Relief Pitching SV	Batting AB	Batting H	Batting HR	BA	PO	A	E	DP	TC/G	FA
1941	NY	N	1	2	.333	1.90	4	3	2	23.2	17	10	12	0	0	0	0	9	1	0	.111	0	3	1	0	1.0	.750
1942			3	6	.333	5.08	19	11	3	78	79	32	42	1	0	0	0	25	3	0	.120	1	13	1	0	0.8	.933
1946			14	**19**	.424	3.63	40	**35**	17	265.1	**251**	101	121	3	0	1	1	88	11	0	.125	10	61	3	1	1.9	.959
1947			15	10	.600	4.39	39	31	10	217.1	223	82	86	3	2	1	0	78	10	0	.128	13	36	2	2	1.3	.961
1948			8	10	.444	3.87	35	18	5	149	168	62	58	3	2	2	3	44	5	0	.114	8	24	0	1	0.9	1.000
1949			11	14	.440	**2.50**	38	23	15	212	193	43	64	0	1	1	4	69	10	2	.145	7	39	0	4	1.2	1.000
1950			13	15	.464	3.91	40	22	7	186.2	190	68	56	2	5	3	3	65	8	1	.123	5	37	2	3	1.1	.955
1951			10	9	.526	3.31	39	16	5	149.2	153	45	54	2	5	0	3	50	5	0	.100	7	38	0	2	1.2	1.000
1952			10	7	.588	3.19	41	17	8	166.1	154	47	67	2	2	1	5	54	2	0	.037	16	33	4	7	1.3	.925
1953			6	12	.333	4.76	37	12	2	111.2	135	36	36	0	3	4	2	30	1	0	.033	7	22	1	3	0.8	.967
1954	2 teams	BAL A (3G 0–1)	MIL N (12G 1–1)																								
″	total		1	2	.333	3.13	15	1	0	31.2	33	12	10	0	1	1	1	4	0	0	.000	1	1	0	0	0.1	1.000
1955	MIL	N	0	1	.000	∞	1	0	0		1	0	0	0	0	1	0	0	0	0	—	0	0	0	0	0.0	.000
12 yrs.			92	107	.462	3.68	348	189	74	1591.1	1597	538	606	16	21	15	22	516	56	3	.109	75	307	14	23	1.1	.965
WORLD SERIES																											
1951	NY	N	1	1	.500	3.00	2	2	1	15	12	7	6	0	0	0	0	5	0	0	.000	2	2	0	0	2.0	1.000

Joe Kostal

KOSTAL, JOSEPH WILLIAM (Cudgy)
B. Mar. 17, 1876, Chicago, Ill. D. Oct. 10, 1933, Guelph, Ont., Canada.

BR TR 5′ 6″ 130 lbs.

Year	Team	Lg	W	L	PCT	ERA	G	GS	CG	IP	H	BB	SO	ShO	Relief Pitching W	Relief Pitching L	Relief Pitching SV	Batting AB	Batting H	Batting HR	BA	PO	A	E	DP	TC/G	FA
1896	LOU	N	0	0	—	0.00	2	0	0	2	4	0	0	0	0	0	0	0	0	0	—	0	0	1	0	0.5	.000

Sandy Koufax

KOUFAX, SANFORD
Born Sanford Braun.
B. Dec. 30, 1935, Brooklyn, N. Y.
Hall of Fame 1972.

BR TL 6′ 2″ 210 lbs.

Year	Team	Lg	W	L	PCT	ERA	G	GS	CG	IP	H	BB	SO	ShO	Relief Pitching W	Relief Pitching L	Relief Pitching SV	Batting AB	Batting H	Batting HR	BA	PO	A	E	DP	TC/G	FA
1955	BKN	N	2	2	.500	3.02	12	5	2	41.2	33	28	30	2	0	1	0	12	0	0	.000	1	6	1	0	0.7	.875
1956			2	4	.333	4.91	16	10	0	58.2	66	29	30	0	0	0	0	17	2	0	.118	4	3	0	0	0.4	1.000
1957			5	4	.556	3.88	34	13	2	104.1	83	51	122	0	1	0	0	26	0	0	.000	3	4	1	0	0.2	.875
1958	LA	N	11	11	.500	4.48	40	26	5	158.2	132	105	131	0	3	1	1	49	6	0	.122	6	21	1	3	0.7	.964
1959			8	6	.571	4.05	35	23	6	153.1	136	92	173	1	0	0	2	54	6	0	.111	4	16	1	1	0.6	.952
1960			8	13	.381	3.91	37	26	7	175	133	100	197	2	1	0	1	57	7	0	.123	6	18	0	1	0.6	1.000
1961			18	13	.581	3.52	42	35	15	255.2	212	96	**269**	2	1	0	1	77	5	0	.065	7	26	2	2	0.8	.943
1962			14	7	.667	**2.54**	28	26	11	184.1	134	57	216	2	0	0	1	69	6	1	.087	3	16	2	0	0.8	.905
1963			**25**	5	.833	**1.88**	40	40	20	311	214	58	**306**	**11**	0	0	0	110	7	1	.064	4	34	3	1	1.0	.927
1964			19	5	**.792**	**1.74**	29	28	15	223	154	53	223	**7**	0	0	1	74	7	0	.095	9	18	2	1	1.0	.931
1965			**26**	8	**.765**	**2.04**	43	41	**27**	**335.2**	216	71	**382**	8	0	0	2	113	20	0	.177	10	36	0	2	1.1	1.000
1966			**27**	9	.750	**1.73**	41	**41**	**27**	**323**	241	77	**317**	**5**	0	0	0	118	9	0	.076	7	30	1	2	0.9	.974
12 yrs.			165	87	.655 **10th**	2.76	397	314	137	2324.1	1754	817	2396	40	6	2	9	776	75	2	.097	64	228	14	13	0.8	.954
WORLD SERIES																											
1959	LA	N	0	1	.000	1.00	2	1	0	9	5	1	7	0	0	0	0	2	0	0	.000	0	0	0	0	0.0	.000
1963			2	0	1.000	1.50	2	2	2	18	12	3	23	0	0	0	0	6	0	0	.000	1	3	0	0	2.0	1.000
1965			2	1	.667	0.38	3	3	2	24	13	5	29	2	0	0	0	9	1	0	.111	1	4	0	0	1.7	1.000
1966			0	1	.000	1.50	1	1	0	6	6	2	2	0	0	0	0	2	0	0	.000	0	1	0	0	1.0	1.000
4 yrs.			4	3	.571	0.95 **5th**	8	7	4	57	36	11	61 **4th**	2 **4th**	0	0	0	19	1	0	.053	2	8	0	0	1.3	1.000

Joe Koukalik

KOUKALIK, JOSEPH
B. Mar. 3, 1880, Chicago, Ill. D. Dec. 27, 1945, Chicago, Ill.

BR TR 5′ 8″ 160 lbs.

Year	Team	Lg	W	L	PCT	ERA	G	GS	CG	IP	H	BB	SO	ShO	Relief Pitching W	Relief Pitching L	Relief Pitching SV	Batting AB	Batting H	Batting HR	BA	PO	A	E	DP	TC/G	FA
1904	BKN	N	0	1	.000	1.13	1	1	1	8	10	4	1	0	0	0	0	3	0	0	.000	0	1	1	0	2.0	.500

Lou Koupal

KOUPAL, LOUIS LADDIE
B. Dec. 19, 1898, Tabor, S. D. D. Dec. 8, 1961, San Gabriel, Calif.

BR TR 5′11″ 175 lbs.

Year	Team	Lg	W	L	PCT	ERA	G	GS	CG	IP	H	BB	SO	ShO	Relief Pitching W	Relief Pitching L	Relief Pitching SV	Batting AB	Batting H	Batting HR	BA	PO	A	E	DP	TC/G	FA
1925	PIT	N	0	0	—	9.00	6	0	0	9	14	7	0	0	0	0	0	1	0	0	.000	0	3	0	0	0.5	1.000
1926			0	2	.000	3.20	6	2	1	19.2	22	8	7	0	0	0	0	4	1	0	.250	1	4	0	0	0.8	1.000
1928	BKN	N	1	0	1.000	2.41	17	1	1	37.1	43	15	10	0	0	0	1	9	1	0	.111	1	14	0	1	0.9	1.000

Lou Koupal *continued*

Year	Team	W	L	PCT	ERA	G	GS	CG	IP	H	BB	SO	ShO	Relief W	Relief L	Relief SV	AB	H	HR	BA	PO	A	E	DP	TC/G	FA
1929	2 teams BKN N (18G 0–1) PHI N (15G 5–5)																									
"	total	5	6	.455	4.96	33	15	3	127	155	54	35	0	0	0	6	46	5	0	.109	4	23	3	1	0.9	.900
1930	PHI N	0	4	.000	8.59	13	4	1	36.2	52	17	11	0	0	1	0	12	1	0	.083	0	4	0	0	0.3	1.000
1937	STL A	4	9	.308	6.56	26	13	6	105.2	150	55	24	0	0	0	0	32	3	0	.094	3	19	0	1	0.8	1.000
6 yrs.		10	21	.323	5.58	101	35	12	335.1	436	156	87	0	0	1	7	104	11	0	.106	9	67	3	3	0.8	.962

Fabian Kowalik

KOWALIK, FABIAN LORENZ BR TR 5′11″ 185 lbs.
B. Apr. 22, 1908, Falls City, Tex. D. Aug. 14, 1954, Karnes City, Tex. BB 1932, 1935

Year	Team	W	L	PCT	ERA	G	GS	CG	IP	H	BB	SO	ShO	Relief W	Relief L	Relief SV	AB	H	HR	BA	PO	A	E	DP	TC/G	FA
1932	CHI A	0	1	.000	6.97	2	1	0	10.1	16	4	2	0	0	0	0	13	5	0	.385	2	2	1	0	1.3	.800
1935	CHI N	2	2	.500	4.42	20	2	1	55	60	19	20	0	2	0	1	15	3	0	.200	3	15	3	1	1.0	.857
1936	3 teams CHI N (6G 0–2) PHI N (22G 1–5) BOS N (1G 0–1)																									
"	total	1	8	.111	5.82	29	9	3	102	142	40	20	0	0	2	1	67	15	0	.224	7	17	4	10	0.8	.857
3 yrs.		3	11	.214	5.43	51	12	4	167.1	218	63	42	0	2	2	2	95	23	0	.242	12	34	8	11	0.9	.852
WORLD SERIES																										
1935	CHI N	0	0	—	2.08	1	0	0	4.1	3	1	1	0	0	0	0	2	1	0	.500	0	2	1	0	3.0	.667

Joe Kraemer

KRAEMER, JOSEPH WAYNE BL TL 6′2″ 185 lbs.
B. Sept. 10, 1964, Olympia, Wash.

Year	Team	W	L	PCT	ERA	G	GS	CG	IP	H	BB	SO	ShO	Relief W	Relief L	Relief SV	AB	H	HR	BA	PO	A	E	DP	TC/G	FA
1989	CHI N	0	1	.000	4.91	1	1	0	3.2	7	2	5	0	0	0	0	1	0	0	.000	0	0	0	0	0.0	.000
1990		0	0	—	7.20	18	0	0	25	31	14	16	0	0	0	0	0	0	0	—	2	4	1	1	0.4	.857
2 yrs.		0	1	.000	6.91	19	1	0	28.2	38	16	21	0	0	0	0	1	0	0	.000	2	4	1	1	0.4	.857

Joe Krakauskas

KRAKAUSKAS, JOSEPH VICTOR LAWRENCE BL TL 6′1″ 203 lbs.
B. Mar. 28, 1915, Montreal, Que., Canada
D. July 8, 1960, Hamilton, Ont., Canada.

Year	Team	W	L	PCT	ERA	G	GS	CG	IP	H	BB	SO	ShO	Relief W	Relief L	Relief SV	AB	H	HR	BA	PO	A	E	DP	TC/G	FA
1937	WAS A	4	1	.800	2.70	5	4	3	40	33	22	18	0	1	0	0	16	2	0	.125	1	4	3	0	1.6	.625
1938		7	5	.583	3.12	29	10	5	121.1	99	88	104	1	2	1	0	33	6	0	.182	3	16	1	0	0.7	.950
1939		11	17	.393	4.60	39	29	12	217.1	230	114	110	0	0	3	1	77	16	0	.208	6	26	3	2	0.9	.914
1940		1	6	.143	6.44	32	10	2	109	137	73	68	0	0	2	2	32	8	0	.250	2	24	2	3	0.9	.929
1941	CLE A	1	2	.333	4.10	12	5	0	41.2	39	29	25	0	0	1	0	13	1	0	.077	2	11	0	0	1.1	1.000
1942		0	0	—	3.86	3	0	0	7	7	4	2	0	0	0	0	2	0	0	.000	0	4	0	0	1.3	1.000
1946		2	5	.286	5.51	29	5	0	47.1	60	25	20	0	2	2	1	10	0	0	.000	2	12	1	0	0.5	.933
7 yrs.		26	36	.419	4.53	149	63	22	583.2	605	355	347	1	5	9	4	183	33	0	.180	16	97	10	5	0.8	.919

Jack Kralick

KRALICK, JOHN FRANCIS BL TL 6′2″ 180 lbs.
B. June 1, 1935, Youngstown, Ohio.

Year	Team	W	L	PCT	ERA	G	GS	CG	IP	H	BB	SO	ShO	Relief W	Relief L	Relief SV	AB	H	HR	BA	PO	A	E	DP	TC/G	FA
1959	WAS A	0	0	—	6.57	6	0	0	12.1	13	6	7	0	0	0	0	2	0	0	.000	2	6	0	2	1.3	1.000
1960		8	6	.571	3.04	35	18	7	151	139	45	71	2	2	0	1	41	5	0	.122	7	22	0	2	0.8	1.000
1961	MIN A	13	11	.542	3.61	33	33	11	242	257	64	137	2	0	0	0	86	13	1	.151	12	47	1	4	1.8	.983
1962		12	11	.522	3.86	39	37	7	242.2	239	61	139	1	0	0	0	89	18	2	.202	21	40	1	5	1.6	.984
1963	2 teams MIN A (5G 1–4) CLE A (28G 13–9)																									
"	total	14	13	.519	3.03	33	32	11	223	215	49	129	4	0	0	0	66	12	1	.182	18	30	1	2	1.5	.980
1964	CLE A	12	7	.632	3.21	30	29	8	190.2	196	51	119	3	0	0	0	64	10	0	.156	8	32	1	2	1.4	.976
1965		5	11	.313	4.92	30	16	1	86	106	21	34	0	2	2	0	21	3	0	.143	3	15	3	0	0.7	.857
1966		3	4	.429	3.82	27	4	0	68.1	69	20	31	0	3	1	0	13	1	0	.077	6	16	1	0	0.9	.957
1967		0	2	.000	9.00	2	0	0	2	4	1	1	0	0	2	0	0	0	0	—	0	3	0	1	1.5	1.000
9 yrs.		67	65	.508	3.56	235	169	45	1218	1238	318	668	12	7	5	1	382	62	4	.162	77	211	8	18	1.3	.973

Steve Kraly

KRALY, STEVE CHARLES (Lefty) BL TL 5′10″ 152 lbs.
B. Apr. 18, 1929, Whiting, Ind.

Year	Team	W	L	PCT	ERA	G	GS	CG	IP	H	BB	SO	ShO	Relief W	Relief L	Relief SV	AB	H	HR	BA	PO	A	E	DP	TC/G	FA
1953	NY A	0	2	.000	3.24	5	3	0	25	19	16	8	0	0	0	1	7	0	0	.000	2	6	0	0	1.6	1.000

Jack Kramer

KRAMER, JOHN HENRY BR TR 6′2″ 190 lbs.
B. Jan. 5, 1918, New Orleans, La. D. May 18, 1995, Metairie, La.

Year	Team	W	L	PCT	ERA	G	GS	CG	IP	H	BB	SO	ShO	Relief W	Relief L	Relief SV	AB	H	HR	BA	PO	A	E	DP	TC/G	FA
1939	STL A	9	16	.360	5.83	40	31	10	211.2	269	127	68	2	0	2	0	66	9	1	.136	7	34	2	0	1.1	.953
1940		3	7	.300	6.26	16	9	1	64.2	86	26	12	0	1	2	0	20	1	0	.050	2	15	1	1	1.1	.944
1941		4	3	.571	5.16	29	3	0	59.1	69	40	20	0	4	1	2	8	0	0	.000	2	14	3	1	0.7	.842
1943		0	0	—	8.00	3	0	0	9	11	8	4	0	0	0	0	2	1	0	.500	1	1	0	0	0.7	1.000
1944		17	13	.567	2.49	33	31	18	257	233	75	124	1	1	0	0	85	14	2	.165	10	62	3	5	2.3	.960
1945		10	15	.400	3.36	29	25	15	193	190	73	99	3	1	0	2	61	9	0	.148	10	39	1	4	1.7	.980
1946		13	11	.542	3.19	31	28	13	194.2	190	68	69	3	0	0	0	59	8	0	.136	12	32	1	2	1.5	.978
1947		11	16	.407	4.97	33	28	9	199.1	206	89	77	1	1	1	1	62	7	0	.113	7	38	2	3	1.4	.957
1948	BOS A	18	5	**.783**	4.35	29	29	14	205	233	64	72	2	0	0	0	73	11	1	.151	5	26	1	1	1.1	.969
1949		6	8	.429	5.16	21	18	7	111.2	126	49	24	2	1	1	1	35	9	0	.257	3	19	0	2	1.0	1.000
1950	NY N	3	6	.333	3.53	35	9	1	86.2	91	39	27	0	2	1	1	20	2	1	.100	10	14	0	2	0.7	1.000
1951	2 teams NY N (4G 0–0) NY A (19G 1–3)																									
"	total	1	3	.250	5.76	23	4	0	45.1	57	24	17	0	1	3	0	10	1	0	.100	4	4	3	0	0.5	.727
12 yrs.		95	103	.480	4.24	322	215	88	1637.1	1761	682	613	14	12	11	7	501	72	5	.144	73	298	17	21	1.2	.956
WORLD SERIES																										
1944	STL A	1	0	1.000	0.00	2	1	1	11	9	4	12	0	0	0	0	4	0	0	.000	0	3	0	0	1.5	1.000

Randy Kramer

KRAMER, RANDALL JOHN BR TR 6′2″ 170 lbs.
B. Sept. 20, 1960, Palo Alto, Calif.

Year	Team	W	L	PCT	ERA	G	GS	CG	IP	H	BB	SO	ShO	Relief W	Relief L	Relief SV	AB	H	HR	BA	PO	A	E	DP	TC/G	FA
1988	PIT N	1	2	.333	5.40	5	1	0	10	12	1	7	0	1	1	0	2	0	0	.000	1	0	0	0	0.2	1.000
1989		5	9	.357	3.96	35	15	1	111.1	90	61	52	1	1	1	2	33	5	0	.152	10	10	0	0	0.6	1.000
1990	2 teams PIT N (12G 0–1) CHI N (10G 0–2)																									
"	total	0	3	.000	4.50	22	4	0	46	47	21	27	0	0	1	0	6	0	0	.000	9	5	0	1	0.6	1.000
1992	SEA A	0	1	.000	7.71	4	4	0	16.1	30	7	6	0	0	0	0	0	0	0	—	1	0	0	0	0.3	1.000
4 yrs.		6	15	.286	4.51	66	24	1	183.2	179	90	92	1	2	3	2	41	5	0	.122	21	15	0	1	0.5	1.000

Tom Kramer

KRAMER, THOMAS JOSEPH
B. Jan. 9, 1968, Canicinnati, Ohio.
BB TR 6′ 185 lbs.

Year	Team	Lg	W	L	PCT	ERA	G	GS	CG	IP	H	BB	SO	ShO	Relief W	Relief L	Relief SV	Batting AB	Batting H	HR	BA	PO	A	E	DP	TC/G	FA
1991	CLE	A	0	0	—	17.36	4	0	0	4.2	10	6	4	0	0	0	0	0	0	0	—	1	0	0	0	0.3	1.000
1993			7	3	.700	4.02	39	16	1	121	126	59	71	0	2	1	0	0	0	0	—	9	13	1	0	0.6	.957
2 yrs.			7	3	.700	4.51	43	16	1	125.2	136	65	75	0	2	1	0	0	0	0		10	13	1	0	0.6	.958

Gene Krapp

KRAPP, EUGENE HAMLET (Rubber)
B. May 12, 1887, Rochester, N. Y. D. Apr. 13, 1923, Detroit, Mich.
BR TR 5′ 7″ 168 lbs.

Year	Team	Lg	W	L	PCT	ERA	G	GS	CG	IP	H	BB	SO	ShO	Relief W	Relief L	Relief SV	Batting AB	Batting H	HR	BA	PO	A	E	DP	TC/G	FA
1911	CLE	A	13	9	.591	3.44	34	26	14	214.2	182	**136**	130	1	2	0	1	74	17	0	.230	16	78	7	0	3.0	.931
1912			2	5	.286	4.60	9	7	4	58.2	57	42	22	0	0	0	0	22	7	0	.318	3	28	0	1	3.4	1.000
1914	BUF	F	14	14	.500	2.49	36	29	18	252.2	198	115	106	1	1	1	0	77	11	0	.143	16	98	7	7	3.4	.942
1915			9	19	.321	3.51	38	30	14	231	188	123	93	1	1	0	0	70	9	0	.129	13	100	3	6	3.1	.974
4 yrs.			38	47	.447	3.23	117	92	50	757	625	416	351	3	4	1	1	243	44	0	.181	48	304	17	14	3.2	.954

Tex Kraus

KRAUS, JOHN WILLIAM (Texas Jack)
B. Apr. 26, 1918, San Antonio, Tex. D. Jan. 2, 1976, San Antonio, Tex.
BR TL 6′ 4″ 190 lbs.

Year	Team	Lg	W	L	PCT	ERA	G	GS	CG	IP	H	BB	SO	ShO	Relief W	Relief L	Relief SV	Batting AB	Batting H	HR	BA	PO	A	E	DP	TC/G	FA
1943	PHI	N	9	15	.375	3.16	34	25	10	199.2	197	78	48	1	0	1	2	60	4	0	.067	5	49	1	3	1.6	.982
1945			4	9	.308	5.40	19	13	0	81.2	96	40	28	0	1	0	0	25	3	0	.120	3	17	1	1	1.1	.952
1946	NY	N	2	1	.667	6.12	17	1	0	25	25	15	7	0	2	1	0	3	0	0	.000	1	9	1	0	0.6	.909
3 yrs.			15	25	.375	4.00	70	39	10	306.1	318	133	83	1	3	2	2	88	7	0	.080	9	75	3	4	1.2	.966

Harry Krause

KRAUSE, HARRY WILLIAM (Hal)
B. July 12, 1887, San Francisco, Calif. D. Oct. 23, 1940, San Francisco, Calif.
BB TL 5′10″ 165 lbs.

Year	Team	Lg	W	L	PCT	ERA	G	GS	CG	IP	H	BB	SO	ShO	Relief W	Relief L	Relief SV	Batting AB	Batting H	HR	BA	PO	A	E	DP	TC/G	FA
1908	PHI	A	1	1	.500	2.57	4	2	2	21	20	4	10	0	0	0	0	7	0	0	.000	3	1	2	0	1.5	.667
1909			18	8	.692	**1.39**	32	21	16	213	151	49	139	7	**4**	2	0	77	12	0	.156	7	48	4	3	1.8	.932
1910			6	6	.500	2.88	16	11	9	112.1	99	42	60	2	0	1	0	38	8	0	.211	7	24	4	1	2.2	.886
1911			11	8	.579	3.04	27	19	12	169	155	47	85	1	2	1	2	59	15	0	.254	5	31	2	0	1.4	.947
1912	2 teams	PHI A (4G 0–2)	CLE A (2G 0–1)																								
″	total		0	3	.000	12.60	6	4	0	10	21	4	4	0	0	0	0	4	1	0	.250	0	2	0	0	0.3	1.000
5 yrs.			36	26	.581	2.50	85	57	39	525.1	446	146	298	10	6	4	2	185	36	0	.195	22	106	12	4	1.6	.914

Lew Krausse

KRAUSSE, LEWIS BERNARD, JR.
Son of Lew Krausse.
B. Apr. 25, 1943, Media, Pa.
BR TR 6′ 175 lbs.

Year	Team	Lg	W	L	PCT	ERA	G	GS	CG	IP	H	BB	SO	ShO	Relief W	Relief L	Relief SV	Batting AB	Batting H	HR	BA	PO	A	E	DP	TC/G	FA
1961	KC	A	2	5	.286	4.85	12	8	2	55.2	49	46	32	1	0	0	0	17	2	0	.118	1	4	1	0	0.5	.833
1964			0	2	.000	7.36	5	4	0	14.2	22	9	9	0	0	0	0	2	0	0	.000	1	2	1	0	0.8	.750
1965			2	4	.333	5.04	7	5	0	25	29	8	22	0	0	1	0	7	0	0	.000	2	0	0	0	0.3	1.000
1966			14	9	.609	2.99	36	22	4	177.2	144	63	87	1	1	3	3	52	8	0	.154	11	15	1	1	0.8	.963
1967			7	17	.292	4.28	48	19	0	160	140	67	96	0	3	3	6	41	6	1	.146	5	26	2	2	0.7	.939
1968	OAK	A	10	11	.476	3.11	36	25	2	185	147	62	105	0	2	1	4	56	9	0	.161	11	20	0	2	0.9	1.000
1969			7	7	.500	4.44	43	16	4	140	134	48	85	2	1	3	7	48	8	4	.167	5	17	1	4	0.5	.957
1970	MIL	A	13	18	.419	4.75	37	35	8	216	235	67	130	1	0	0	0	65	9	0	.138	21	27	1	0	1.3	.980
1971			8	12	.400	2.95	43	22	1	180	164	62	92	0	1	2	0	44	1	0	.023	17	22	2	0	1.0	.951
1972	BOS	A	1	3	.250	6.34	24	7	0	61	74	28	35	0	0	0	1	16	2	0	.125	5	11	0	0	0.7	1.000
1973	STL	N	0	0	—	0.00	1	0	0	2	2	1	1	0	0	0	0	0	0	0	—	0	1	0	0	1.0	1.000
1974	ATL	N	4	3	.571	4.16	29	4	0	67	65	32	27	0	3	2	0	6	2	1	.333	5	8	0	0	0.4	1.000
12 yrs.			68	91	.428	4.00	321	167	21	1284	1205	493	721	5	11	15	21	354	47	6	.133	84	153	9	9	0.8	.963

Lew Krausse

KRAUSSE, LEWIS BERNARD, SR.
Father of Lew Krausse.
B. June 8, 1912, Media, Pa. D. Sept. 6, 1988, Sarasota, Fla.
BR TR 6′½″ 167 lbs.

Year	Team	Lg	W	L	PCT	ERA	G	GS	CG	IP	H	BB	SO	ShO	Relief W	Relief L	Relief SV	Batting AB	Batting H	HR	BA	PO	A	E	DP	TC/G	FA
1931	PHI	A	1	0	1.000	3.97	3	1	1	11.1	6	6	1	0	0	0	0	2	0	0	.000	1	3	0	1	1.3	1.000
1932			4	1	.800	4.58	20	3	2	57	64	24	16	1	2	1	0	15	2	0	.133	3	17	1	1	1.0	.952
2 yrs.			5	1	.833	4.48	23	4	3	68.1	70	30	17	1	2	1	0	17	2	0	.118	4	20	1	2	1.1	.960

Ken Kravec

KRAVEC, KENNETH PETER
B. July 29, 1951, Cleveland, Ohio.
BL TL 6′ 2″ 185 lbs.

Year	Team	Lg	W	L	PCT	ERA	G	GS	CG	IP	H	BB	SO	ShO	Relief W	Relief L	Relief SV	Batting AB	Batting H	HR	BA	PO	A	E	DP	TC/G	FA
1975	CHI	A	0	1	.000	6.23	2	1	0	4.1	1	8	1	0	0	0	0	0	0	0	—	0	4	0	0	2.0	1.000
1976			1	5	.167	4.86	9	8	1	50	49	32	38	0	0	0	0	0	0	0	—	0	7	1	0	0.9	.875
1977			11	8	.579	4.10	26	25	6	167	161	57	125	1	0	0	0	0	0	0	—	6	26	1	2	1.3	.970
1978			11	16	.407	4.08	30	30	7	203	188	95	154	2	0	0	0	0	0	0	—	7	25	3	1	1.2	.914
1979			15	13	.536	3.74	36	35	10	250	208	111	132	3	0	0	1	0	0	0	—	8	35	1	1	1.2	.977
1980			3	6	.333	6.91	20	15	0	82	100	44	37	0	0	0	0	0	0	0	—	7	13	0	0	1.0	1.000
1981	CHI	N	1	6	.143	5.08	24	12	0	78	80	39	50	0	0	1	0	15	0	0	.000	3	16	1	0	0.8	.950
1982			1	1	.500	6.12	13	2	0	25	27	18	20	0	1	1	0	3	0	0	.000	1	3	0	0	0.3	1.000
8 yrs.			43	56	.434	4.46	160	128	24	859.1	814	404	557	6	1	2	1	18	0	0	.000	32	129	7	4	1.0	.958

Ray Krawczyk

KRAWCZYK, RAYMOND ALLEN
B. Oct. 9, 1959, Sewickley, Pa.
BR TR 6′ 2″ 190 lbs.

Year	Team	Lg	W	L	PCT	ERA	G	GS	CG	IP	H	BB	SO	ShO	Relief W	Relief L	Relief SV	Batting AB	Batting H	HR	BA	PO	A	E	DP	TC/G	FA
1984	PIT	N	0	0	—	3.38	4	0	0	5.1	7	4	3	0	0	0	0	0	0	0	—	0	0	0	0	0.0	.000
1985			0	2	.000	14.04	8	0	0	8.1	20	6	9	0	0	2	0	0	0	0	—	0	2	1	1	0.4	.667
1986			0	1	.000	7.30	12	0	0	12.1	17	10	7	0	0	1	0	0	0	0	—	2	0	1	0	0.3	.667
1988	CAL	A	0	1	.000	4.81	14	1	0	24.1	29	8	17	0	0	0	1	0	0	0	—	2	6	0	0	0.6	1.000
1989	MIL	A	0	0	—	13.50	1	0	0	2	4	1	6	0	0	0	0	0	0	0	—	0	0	0	0	0.0	.000
5 yrs.			0	4	.000	7.05	39	1	0	52.1	77	29	42	0	0	3	1	0	0	0		4	8	2	1	0.4	.857

Ray Kremer

KREMER, REMY PETER (Wiz)
B. Mar. 23, 1893, Oakland, Calif. D. Feb. 8, 1965, Pinole, Calif.
BR TR 6′ 1″ 190 lbs.

Year	Team	Lg	W	L	PCT	ERA	G	GS	CG	IP	H	BB	SO	ShO	Relief W	Relief L	Relief SV	Batting AB	Batting H	HR	BA	PO	A	E	DP	TC/G	FA
1924	PIT	N	18	10	.643	3.19	**41**	30	17	259.1	262	51	64	**4**	3	1	1	86	13	0	.151	3	59	2	2	1.6	.969
1925			17	8	.680	3.69	40	27	14	214.2	232	47	62	0	3	2	2	71	14	0	.197	1	39	0	1	1.0	1.000
1926			**20**	6	**.769**	**2.61**	37	26	18	231.1	221	51	74	3	2	0	5	83	21	1	.253	4	46	1	0	1.4	.980
1927			19	8	.704	**2.47**	35	28	18	226	205	53	63	3	2	2	2	83	14	2	.169	7	37	1	0	1.3	.978
1928			15	13	.536	4.64	34	31	17	219	253	68	61	1	0	0	0	78	14	0	.179	7	33	2	0	1.2	.952
1929			18	10	.643	4.26	34	27	14	221.2	226	60	66	0	3	0	0	86	11	1	.128	4	39	0	0	1.3	1.000
1930			**20**	12	.625	5.02	39	**38**	18	**276**	**366**	63	58	1	0	1	0	102	16	1	.157	7	38	2	7	1.2	.957

Ray Kremer *continued*

Year	Team	W	L	PCT	ERA	G	GS	CG	IP	H	BB	SO	ShO	Relief Pitching W	L	SV	Batting AB	H	HR	BA	PO	A	E	DP	TC/G	FA
1931		11	15	.423	3.33	30	30	15	230	246	65	58	1	0	0	0	75	17	0	.227	1	27	1	1	1.0	.966
1932		4	3	.571	4.29	11	10	3	56.2	61	16	6	1	0	0	0	19	2	0	.105	1	7	1	0	0.8	.889
1933		1	0	1.000	10.35	7	0	0	20	36	9	4	0	1	0	0	4	0	0	.000	2	6	0	2	1.1	1.000
10 yrs.		143	85	.627	3.76	308	247	134	1954.2	2108	483	516	14	14	6	10	687	122	5	.178	37	331	10	13	1.2	.974
WORLD SERIES																										
1925	PIT N	2	1	.667	3.00	3	2	2	21	17	4	9	0	1	0	0	7	1	0	.143	2	5	1	0	2.7	.875
1927		0	1	.000	3.60	1	1	0	5	5	3	1	0	0	0	0	2	1	0	.500	0	0	0	0	0.0	.000
2 yrs.		2	2	.500	3.12	4	3	2	26	22	7	10	0	1	0	0	9	2	0	.222	2	5	1	0	2.0	.875

Jim Kremmel

KREMMEL, JAMES LOUIS BL TL 6′ 175 lbs.
B. Feb. 28, 1948, Belleville, Ill.

Year	Team	W	L	PCT	ERA	G	GS	CG	IP	H	BB	SO	ShO	Relief Pitching W	L	SV	Batting AB	H	HR	BA	PO	A	E	DP	TC/G	FA
1973	TEX A	0	2	.000	9.00	4	2	0	9	15	6	6	0	0	0	0	0	0	0	—	0	1	0	0	0.3	1.000
1974	CHI N	0	2	.000	5.23	23	2	0	31	37	18	22	0	0	1	0	3	0	0	.000	1	4	1	1	0.3	.833
2 yrs.		0	4	.000	6.07	27	4	0	40	52	24	28	0	0	1	0	3	0	0	.000	1	5	1	1	0.3	.857

Red Kress

KRESS, RALPH BR TR 5′11½″ 165 lbs.
B. Jan. 2, 1907, Columbia, Calif. D. Nov. 29, 1962, Los Angeles, Calif.

Year	Team	W	L	PCT	ERA	G	GS	CG	IP	H	BB	SO	ShO	Relief Pitching W	L	SV	Batting AB	H	HR	BA	PO	A	E	DP	TC/G	FA
1935	WAS A	0	0	—	12.71	3	0	0	5.2	8	5	5	0	0	0	0	252	75	2	.298	12	25	1	4	5.4	.974
1946	NY N	0	0	—	12.27	1	0	0	3.2	5	1	1	0	0	0	0	1	0	0	.000	318	400	55	99	5.2	.929
2 yrs.		0	0		12.54	4	0	0	9.1	13	6	6	0	0	0	0	*				3977	2944	343	743	5.4	.953

Lou Kretlow

KRETLOW, LOUIS HENRY BR TR 6′2″ 185 lbs.
B. June 27, 1921, Apache, Okla.

Year	Team	W	L	PCT	ERA	G	GS	CG	IP	H	BB	SO	ShO	Relief Pitching W	L	SV	Batting AB	H	HR	BA	PO	A	E	DP	TC/G	FA
1946	DET A	1	0	1.000	3.00	1	1	1	9	7	2	4	0	0	0	0	4	2	0	.500	0	1	0	0	1.0	1.000
1948		2	1	.667	4.63	5	2	1	23.1	21	11	9	0	1	0	0	8	4	0	.500	0	5	0	0	1.0	1.000
1949		3	2	.600	6.16	25	10	1	76	85	69	40	0	2	1	0	26	0	0	.000	2	23	2	1	1.1	.926
1950	2 teams STL A (9G 0–2) CHI A (11G 0–0)																									
″	total	0	2	.000	7.07	20	3	0	35.2	42	45	24	0	0	1	0	7	0	0	.000	0	3	0	0	0.2	1.000
1951	CHI A	6	9	.400	4.20	26	18	7	137	129	74	89	1	0	1	0	48	4	0	.083	5	22	3	2	1.2	.900
1952		4	4	.500	2.96	19	11	4	79	52	56	63	2	0	0	1	20	1	0	.050	1	9	0	2	0.5	1.000
1953	2 teams CHI A (9G 0–0) STL A (22G 1–5)																									
″	total	1	5	.167	4.78	31	14	0	101.2	105	82	52	0	0	0	0	29	5	0	.172	6	13	4	1	0.7	.826
1954	BAL A	6	11	.353	4.37	32	20	5	166.2	169	82	82	0	0	1	0	51	8	0	.157	4	30	0	2	1.1	1.000
1955		0	4	.000	8.22	15	5	0	38.1	50	27	26	0	0	0	0	11	1	0	.091	1	11	0	0	0.8	1.000
1956	KC A	4	9	.308	5.31	25	20	3	118.2	121	74	61	0	0	0	0	33	2	0	.061	5	16	2	1	0.9	.913
10 yrs.		27	47	.365	4.87	199	104	22	785.1	781	522	450	3	3	4	1	237	27	0	.114	24	133	11	9	0.8	.935

Rick Kreuger

KREUGER, RICHARD ALLEN BR TL 6′2″ 185 lbs.
B. Nov. 3, 1948, Grand Rapids, Mich.

Year	Team	W	L	PCT	ERA	G	GS	CG	IP	H	BB	SO	ShO	Relief Pitching W	L	SV	Batting AB	H	HR	BA	PO	A	E	DP	TC/G	FA
1975	BOS A	0	0	—	4.50	2	0	0	4	3	1	1	0	0	0	0	0	0	0	—	1	2	0	0	1.5	1.000
1976		2	1	.667	4.06	8	4	1	31	31	16	12	0	0	0	0	0	0	0	—	1	8	0	1	1.1	1.000
1977		0	1	.000	∞	1	0	0		2	0	0	0	0	1	0	0	0	0	—	0	0	0	0	0.0	.000
1978	CLE A	0	0	—	3.86	6	0	0	9.1	6	3	7	0	0	0	0	0	0	0	—	1	1	0	0	0.3	1.000
4 yrs.		2	2	.500	4.47	17	4	1	44.1	42	20	20	0	0	1	0	0	0	0		3	11	0	1	0.8	1.000

Frank Kreutzer

KREUTZER, FRANKLIN JAMES BR TL 6′1″ 175 lbs.
B. Feb. 7, 1939, Buffalo, N. Y.

Year	Team	W	L	PCT	ERA	G	GS	CG	IP	H	BB	SO	ShO	Relief Pitching W	L	SV	Batting AB	H	HR	BA	PO	A	E	DP	TC/G	FA
1962	CHI A	0	0	—	0.00	1	0	0	1.1	0	1	1	0	0	0	0	0	0	0	—	0	0	0	0	0.0	.000
1963		1	0	1.000	1.80	1	1	0	5	3	1	0	0	0	0	0	2	0	0	.000	0	1	0	0	1.0	1.000
1964	2 teams CHI A (17G 3–1) WAS A (13G 2–6)																									
″	total	5	7	.417	4.10	30	11	0	85.2	85	41	59	0	2	2	1	19	1	0	.053	8	16	1	0	0.8	.960
1965	WAS A	2	6	.250	4.32	33	14	2	85.1	73	54	65	1	0	1	0	22	1	1	.045	4	6	3	0	0.4	.769
1966		0	5	.000	6.03	9	6	0	31.1	30	10	24	0	0	0	0	8	2	0	.250	4	4	0	0	0.9	1.000
1969		0	0	—	4.50	4	0	0	2	3	2	2	0	0	0	0	0	0	0	—	0	1	0	0	0.3	1.000
6 yrs.		8	18	.308	4.40	78	32	2	210.2	194	109	151	1	2	3	1	51	4	1	.078	16	28	4	0	0.6	.917

Krieger

KRIEGER
Deceased.

Year	Team	W	L	PCT	ERA	G	GS	CG	IP	H	BB	SO	ShO	Relief Pitching W	L	SV	Batting AB	H	HR	BA	PO	A	E	DP	TC/G	FA
1884	KC U	0	1	.000	0.00	1	1	0	7	9	5	3	0	0	0	0	*				1	1	0	0	1.0	1.000

Kurt Krieger

KRIEGER, KURT FERDINAND (Dutch) BR TR 6′3″ 212 lbs.
B. Sept. 16, 1926, Traisen, Austria D. Aug. 16, 1970, St. Louis, Mo.

Year	Team	W	L	PCT	ERA	G	GS	CG	IP	H	BB	SO	ShO	Relief Pitching W	L	SV	Batting AB	H	HR	BA	PO	A	E	DP	TC/G	FA
1949	STL N	0	0	—	0.00	1	0	0	1	0	1	0	0	0	0	0	0	0	0	—	0	0	0	0	0.0	.000
1951		0	0	—	15.75	2	0	0	4	6	5	3	0	0	0	0	0	0	0	—	0	1	0	0	0.5	1.000
2 yrs.		0	0		12.60	3	0	0	5	6	6	3	0	0	0	0	0	0	0		0	1	0	0	0.3	1.000

Howie Krist

KRIST, HOWARD WILBUR (Spud) BL TR 6′1″ 175 lbs.
B. Feb. 28, 1916, West Henrietta, N. Y. D. Apr. 23, 1989, Buffalo, N. Y.

Year	Team	W	L	PCT	ERA	G	GS	CG	IP	H	BB	SO	ShO	Relief Pitching W	L	SV	Batting AB	H	HR	BA	PO	A	E	DP	TC/G	FA
1937	STL N	3	1	.750	4.23	6	4	1	27.2	34	10	6	0	1	0	0	9	0	0	.000	2	3	0	0	0.8	1.000
1938		0	0	—	0.00	2	0	0	1.1	1	0	1	0	0	0	0	0	0	0	—	0	0	0	0	0.0	.000
1941		10	0	1.000	4.03	37	8	2	114	107	35	36	0	6	0	2	38	9	0	.237	4	19	0	0	0.6	1.000
1942		13	3	.813	2.51	34	8	3	118.1	103	43	47	0	**8**	2	1	42	6	0	.143	2	16	1	1	0.6	.947
1943		11	5	.688	2.90	34	17	9	164.1	141	62	57	3	2	1	3	60	10	0	.167	1	13	3	1	0.5	.824
1946		0	2	.000	6.75	15	0	0	18.2	22	8	3	0	0	2	0	0	0	0	—	0	4	0	1	0.3	1.000
6 yrs.		37	11	.771	3.32	128	37	15	444.1	408	158	150	3	17	5	6	149	25	0	.168	9	55	4	3	0.5	.941
WORLD SERIES																										
1943	STL N	0	0	—	0.00	1	0	0		1	0	0	0	0	0	0	0	0	0	—	0	0	0	0	0.0	.000

Rick Krivda

KRIVDA, RICK MICHAEL BR TL 6′1″ 180 lbs.
B. Jan. 19, 1970, McKeesport, Pa.

Year	Team	W	L	PCT	ERA	G	GS	CG	IP	H	BB	SO	ShO	Relief Pitching W	L	SV	Batting AB	H	HR	BA	PO	A	E	DP	TC/G	FA
1995	BAL A	2	7	.222	4.54	13	13	1	75.1	76	25	53	0	0	0	0	0	0	0	—	0	7	1	0	0.6	.875

Gus Krock

KROCK, AUGUST H.
B. May 9, 1866, Milwaukee, Wis. D. Mar. 22, 1905, Pasadena, Calif.
TL 6′ 196 lbs.

Year	Team		W	L	PCT	ERA	G	GS	CG	IP	H	BB	SO	ShO	Relief Pitching W	Relief Pitching L	Relief Pitching SV	Batting AB	Batting H	Batting HR	BA	PO	A	E	DP	TC/G	FA
1888	CHI	N	25	14	.641	2.44	39	39	39	339.2	295	45	161	4	0	0	0	134	22	1	.164	4	61	12	1	2.0	.844
1889	3 teams	CHI N (7G 3–3) IND N (4G 2–2) WAS N (6G 2–4)																									
″	total		7	9	.438	5.57	17	17	14	140.2	199	50	43	0	0	0	0	61	11	0	.180	4	25	6	0	2.1	.829
1890	BUF	P	0	3	.000	6.12	4	3	3	25	43	15	5	0	0	0	0	12	1	0	.083	0	9	0	0	2.3	1.000
3 yrs.			32	26	.552	3.49	60	59	56	505.1	537	110	209	4	0	0	0	207	34	1	.164	8	95	18	1	2.0	.851

Rube Kroh

KROH, FLOYD MYRON
B. Aug. 25, 1886, Friendship, N. Y. D. Mar. 17, 1944, New Orleans, La.
BL TL 6′ 2″ 186 lbs.

Year	Team		W	L	PCT	ERA	G	GS	CG	IP	H	BB	SO	ShO	Relief Pitching W	Relief Pitching L	Relief Pitching SV	Batting AB	Batting H	Batting HR	BA	PO	A	E	DP	TC/G	FA
1906	BOS	A	1	0	1.000	0.00	1	1	1	9	2	4	5	1	0	0	0	3	0	0	.000	0	4	0	0	4.0	1.000
1907			1	4	.200	2.62	7	5	1	34.1	33	8	8	0	0	0	0	11	3	0	.273	1	12	2	0	2.1	.867
1908	CHI	N	0	0	—	1.50	2	1	0	12	9	4	11	0	0	0	0	4	0	0	.000	0	4	0	0	2.0	1.000
1909			9	4	.692	1.65	17	13	10	120.1	97	30	51	2	0	0	0	40	6	0	.150	6	37	1	2	2.6	.977
1910			3	1	.750	4.46	6	4	1	34.1	33	15	16	0	2	0	0	12	3	0	.250	0	12	0	0	2.0	1.000
1912	BOS	N	0	0	—	5.68	3	1	0	6.1	8	6	1	0	0	0	0	2	1	0	.500	0	4	0	0	1.3	1.000
6 yrs.			14	9	.609	2.29	36	25	13	216.1	182	67	92	3	2	0	0	72	13	0	.181	7	73	3	2	2.3	.964

Gary Kroll

KROLL, GARY MELVIN
B. July 8, 1941, Culver City, Calif.
BR TR 6′ 6″ 220 lbs.

Year	Team		W	L	PCT	ERA	G	GS	CG	IP	H	BB	SO	ShO	Relief Pitching W	Relief Pitching L	Relief Pitching SV	Batting AB	Batting H	Batting HR	BA	PO	A	E	DP	TC/G	FA
1964	2 teams	PHI N (2G 0–0) NY N (8G 0–1)																									
″	total		0	1	.000	4.01	10	2	0	24.2	22	17	26	0	0	0	0	3	1	0	.333	1	8	1	0	1.0	.900
1965	NY	N	6	6	.500	4.45	32	11	1	87	83	41	62	0	4	1	1	26	3	0	.115	4	14	2	3	0.6	.900
1966	HOU	N	0	0	—	3.80	10	0	0	23.2	26	11	22	0	0	0	0	3	0	0	.000	1	4	0	0	0.5	1.000
1969	CLE	A	0	0	—	4.13	19	0	0	24	16	22	28	0	0	0	0	0	0	0	—	0	3	0	0	0.2	1.000
4 yrs.			6	7	.462	4.24	71	13	1	159.1	147	91	138	0	4	1	1	32	4	0	.125	6	29	3	3	0.5	.921

Marc Kroon

KROON, MARC JASON
B. Apr. 2, 1973, Bronx, N. Y.
BB TR 6′ 2″ 195 lbs.

Year	Team		W	L	PCT	ERA	G	GS	CG	IP	H	BB	SO	ShO	Relief Pitching W	Relief Pitching L	Relief Pitching SV	Batting AB	Batting H	Batting HR	BA	PO	A	E	DP	TC/G	FA
1995	SD	N	0	1	.000	10.80	2	0	0	1.2	1	2	2	0	0	1	0	0	0	0	—	0	0	0	0	0.0	.000

Bill Krueger

KRUEGER, WILLIAM CULP
B. Apr. 24, 1958, Waukegan, Ill.
BL TL 6′ 5″ 205 lbs.

Year	Team		W	L	PCT	ERA	G	GS	CG	IP	H	BB	SO	ShO	Relief Pitching W	Relief Pitching L	Relief Pitching SV	Batting AB	Batting H	Batting HR	BA	PO	A	E	DP	TC/G	FA
1983	OAK	A	7	6	.538	3.61	17	16	2	109.2	104	53	58	0	1	0	0	0	0	0	—	3	7	1	0	0.6	.909
1984			10	10	.500	4.75	26	24	1	142	156	85	61	0	0	0	0	0	0	0	—	6	12	0	1	0.7	1.000
1985			9	10	.474	4.52	32	23	2	151.1	165	69	56	0	1	0	0	0	0	0	—	3	23	2	0	0.9	.929
1986			1	2	.333	6.03	11	3	0	34.1	40	13	10	0	0	1	1	0	0	0	—	2	8	1	1	1.0	.909
1987	2 teams	OAK A (9G 0–3) LA N (2G 0–0)																									
″	total		0	3	.000	6.75	11	0	0	8	12	9	4	0	0	3	0	0	0	0		0	0	0	0	0.0	
1988	LA	N	0	0	—	11.57	1	1	0	2.1	4	2	1	0	0	0	0	0	0	0		0	2	0	0	2.0	1.000
1989	MIL	A	3	2	.600	3.84	34	5	0	93.2	96	33	72	0	1	0	3	0	0	0	—	5	11	0	0	0.5	1.000
1990			6	8	.429	3.98	30	17	0	129	137	54	64	0	2	3	0	0	0	0	—	2	17	0	2	0.6	1.000
1991	SEA	A	11	8	.579	3.60	35	25	1	175	194	60	91	0	1	1	0	0	0	0	—	5	30	0	2	1.0	1.000
1992	2 teams	MIN A (27G 10–6) MON N (9G 0–2)																									
″	total		10	8	.556	4.53	36	29	2	178.2	189	53	99	2	0	1	0	3	0	0	.000	4	11	0	0	0.4	1.000
1993	DET	A	6	4	.600	3.40	32	7	0	82	90	30	60	0	3	2	0	0	0	0	—	2	10	0	1	0.4	1.000
1994	2 teams	DET A (16G 0–2) SD N (8G 3–2)																									
″	total		3	4	.429	6.38	24	9	1	60.2	68	24	47	0	0	1	0	12	6	0	.500	1	11	0	1	0.5	1.000
1995	2 teams	SD N (6G 0–0) SEA A (6G 2–1)																									
″	total		2	1	.667	6.18	12	5	0	27.2	50	8	16	0	1	0	0	0	0	0	—	0	2	0	1	0.2	1.000
13 yrs.			68	66	.507	4.35	301	164	9	1194.1	1305	493	639	2	10	12	4	15	6	0	.400	33	144	4	9	0.6	.978

Abe Kruger

KRUGER, ABRAHAM
B. Feb. 14, 1885, Morris Run, Pa. D. July 4, 1962, Elmira, N. Y.
BR TR 6′ 2″ 190 lbs.

Year	Team		W	L	PCT	ERA	G	GS	CG	IP	H	BB	SO	ShO	Relief Pitching W	Relief Pitching L	Relief Pitching SV	Batting AB	Batting H	Batting HR	BA	PO	A	E	DP	TC/G	FA
1908	BKN	N	0	1	.000	4.26	2	1	0	6.1	5	3	2	0	0	0	0	2	0	0	.000	0	6	0	0	3.0	1.000

Mike Krukow

KRUKOW, MICHAEL EDWARD
B. Jan. 21, 1952, Long Beach, Calif.
BR TR 6′ 5″ 205 lbs.

Year	Team		W	L	PCT	ERA	G	GS	CG	IP	H	BB	SO	ShO	Relief Pitching W	Relief Pitching L	Relief Pitching SV	Batting AB	Batting H	Batting HR	BA	PO	A	E	DP	TC/G	FA
1976	CHI	N	0	0	—	9.00	2	0	0	4	6	2	1	0	0	0	0	1	0	0	.000	0	0	0	0	0.0	.000
1977			8	14	.364	4.40	34	33	1	172	195	61	106	1	0	0	0	55	11	0	.200	15	26	3	3	1.3	.932
1978			9	3	.750	3.91	27	20	3	138	125	53	81	1	0	0	0	45	11	0	.244	9	19	0	1	1.0	1.000
1979			9	9	.500	4.20	28	28	0	165	172	81	119	1	0	0	0	51	16	1	.314	11	12	0	3	0.8	1.000
1980			10	15	.400	4.39	34	34	3	205	200	80	130	0	0	0	0	65	16	1	.246	10	19	5	3	1.0	.853
1981			9	9	.500	3.69	25	**25**	2	144	146	55	101	1	0	0	0	50	9	0	.180	13	21	2	2	1.4	.944
1982	PHI	N	13	11	.542	3.12	33	33	7	208	211	82	138	2	0	0	0	72	13	0	.181	19	35	1	1	1.7	.982
1983	SF	N	11	11	.500	3.95	31	31	2	184.1	189	76	136	1	0	0	0	63	16	1	.254	13	18	5	1	1.2	.861
1984			11	12	.478	4.56	35	33	3	199.1	**234**	78	141	1	0	0	1	72	10	0	.139	12	20	1	3	0.9	.970
1985			8	11	.421	3.38	28	28	6	194.2	176	49	150	1	0	0	0	55	12	1	.218	6	27	1	3	1.2	.971
1986			20	9	.690	3.05	34	34	10	245	204	55	178	2	0	0	0	82	12	0	.146	17	33	4	1	1.6	.926
1987			5	6	.455	4.80	30	28	3	163	182	46	104	0	0	0	0	54	9	0	.167	9	30	1	5	1.3	.975
1988			7	4	.636	3.54	20	20	1	124.2	111	31	75	0	0	0	0	41	3	1	.073	8	18	0	0	1.3	1.000
1989			4	3	.571	3.98	8	8	0	43	37	18	18	0	0	0	0	16	1	0	.063	4	6	0	1	1.3	1.000
14 yrs.			124	117	.515	3.90	369	355	41	2190	2188	767	1478	10	0	0	1	722	139	5	.193	146	284	23	27	1.2	.949
LEAGUE CHAMPIONSHIP SERIES																											
1987	SF	N	1	0	1.000	2.00	1	1	1	9	9	1	3	0	0	0	0	2	0	0	.000	2	2	0	1	4.0	1.000

Al Krumm

KRUMM, ALBERT
B. Jan. 1865, Pa. Deceased.
TR

Year	Team		W	L	PCT	ERA	G	GS	CG	IP	H	BB	SO	ShO	Relief Pitching W	Relief Pitching L	Relief Pitching SV	Batting AB	Batting H	Batting HR	BA	PO	A	E	DP	TC/G	FA
1889	PIT	N	0	1	.000	10.00	1	1	1	9	8	10	4	0	0	0	0	4	0	0	.000	0	0	0	0	0.0	.000

Johnny Kucab

KUCAB, JOHN ALBERT BR TR 6′ 2″ 185 lbs.
B. Dec. 17, 1919, Olyphant, Pa. D. May 26, 1977, Youngstown, Ohio.

Year	Team	W	L	PCT	ERA	G	GS	CG	IP	H	BB	SO	ShO	Relief Pitching W	L	SV	Batting AB	H	HR	BA	PO	A	E	DP	TC/G	FA
1950	PHI A	1	1	.500	3.46	4	2	2	26	29	8	8	0	0	0	0	9	1	0	.111	0	3	0	0	0.8	1.000
1951		4	3	.571	4.22	30	1	0	74.2	76	23	23	0	4	2	4	16	0	0	.000	3	6	1	1	0.3	.900
1952		0	1	.000	5.26	25	0	0	51.1	64	20	17	0	0	1	2	10	2	0	.200	3	9	2	1	0.6	.857
3 yrs.		5	5	.500	4.44	59	3	2	152	169	51	48	0	4	3	6	35	3	0	.086	6	18	3	2	0.5	.889

Jack Kucek

KUCEK, JOHN ANDREW CHARLES BR TR 6′ 2″ 200 lbs.
B. June 8, 1953, Warren, Ohio.

Year	Team	W	L	PCT	ERA	G	GS	CG	IP	H	BB	SO	ShO	Relief Pitching W	L	SV	Batting AB	H	HR	BA	PO	A	E	DP	TC/G	FA
1974	CHI A	1	4	.200	5.21	9	7	0	38	48	21	25	0	0	0	0	0	0	0	—	4	8	0	0	1.3	1.000
1975		0	0	—	4.91	2	0	0	3.2	9	4	2	0	0	0	0	0	0	0	—	0	0	0	0	0.0	.000
1976		0	0	—	9.00	2	0	0	5	9	4	2	0	0	0	0	0	0	0	—	0	0	0	0	0.0	.000
1977		0	1	.000	3.60	8	3	0	35	35	10	25	0	0	0	0	0	0	0	—	7	8	1	0	2.0	.938
1978		2	3	.400	3.29	10	5	3	52	42	27	30	0	0	0	1	0	0	0	—	4	5	0	0	0.9	1.000
1979	2 teams CHI A (1G 0–0) PHI N (4G 1–0)																				0	0	0	0	0.0	
″	total	1	0	1.000	7.20	5	0	0	5	6	4	2	0	1	0	0	0	0	0		0	0	0	0	0.0	
1980	TOR A	3	8	.273	6.75	23	12	0	68	83	41	35	0	1	2	1	0	0	0	—	1	10	4	1	0.7	.733
7 yrs.		7	16	.304	5.10	59	27	3	206.2	232	111	121	0	2	2	2	0	0	0		16	31	5	1	0.9	.904

Johnny Kucks

KUCKS, JOHN CHARLES BR TR 6′ 3″ 170 lbs.
B. July 27, 1933, Hoboken, N. J.

Year	Team	W	L	PCT	ERA	G	GS	CG	IP	H	BB	SO	ShO	Relief Pitching W	L	SV	Batting AB	H	HR	BA	PO	A	E	DP	TC/G	FA
1955	NY A	8	7	.533	3.41	29	13	3	126.2	122	44	49	1	2	3	0	40	2	0	.050	3	24	3	0	1.0	.900
1956		18	9	.667	3.85	34	31	12	224.1	223	72	67	3	2	0	0	77	11	0	.143	13	40	5	5	1.7	.914
1957		8	10	.444	3.56	37	23	4	179.1	169	59	78	1	1	1	2	55	6	0	.109	9	47	1	5	1.5	.982
1958		8	8	.500	3.93	34	15	4	126	132	39	46	1	2	5	4	40	5	0	.125	6	25	1	2	0.9	.969
1959	2 teams NY A (9G 0–1) KC A (33G 8–11)																									
″	total	8	12	.400	4.34	42	24	6	168	184	51	60	1	0	1	1	49	4	0	.082	11	36	1	4	1.1	.979
1960	KC A	4	10	.286	6.00	31	17	1	114	140	43	38	0	2	0	0	30	4	0	.133	3	22	3	1	0.9	.893
6 yrs.		54	56	.491	4.10	207	123	30	938.1	970	308	338	7	9	10	7	291	32	0	.110	45	194	14	17	1.2	.945
WORLD SERIES																										
1955	NY A	0	0	—	6.00	2	0	0	3	4	1	1	0	0	0	0	0	0	0	—	0	1	0	0	0.5	1.000
1956		1	0	1.000	0.82	3	1	1	11	6	3	2	1	0	0	0	3	0	0	.000	1	2	0	1	1.0	1.000
1957		0	0	—	0.00	1	0	0	0.2	1	1	1	0	0	0	0	0	0	0	—	0	0	0	0	0.0	.000
1958		0	0	—	2.08	2	0	0	4.1	4	1	0	0	0	0	0	1	1	0	1.000	0	0	0	0	0.0	.000
4 yrs.		1	0	1.000	1.89	8	1	1	19	15	6	4	1	0	0	0	4	1	0	.250	1	3	0	1	0.5	1.000

Bert Kuczynski

KUCZYNSKI, BERNARD CARL BR TR 6′ 195 lbs.
B. Jan. 8, 1920, Philadelphia, Pa.

Year	Team	W	L	PCT	ERA	G	GS	CG	IP	H	BB	SO	ShO	Relief Pitching W	L	SV	Batting AB	H	HR	BA	PO	A	E	DP	TC/G	FA
1943	PHI A	0	1	.000	4.01	6	1	0	24.2	36	9	8	0	0	0	0	6	0	0	.000	0	5	0	0	0.8	1.000

Fred Kuhaulua

KUHAULUA, FRED MAHELE BL TL 5′11″ 175 lbs.
B. Feb. 23, 1953, Honolulu, Hawaii.

Year	Team	W	L	PCT	ERA	G	GS	CG	IP	H	BB	SO	ShO	Relief Pitching W	L	SV	Batting AB	H	HR	BA	PO	A	E	DP	TC/G	FA
1977	CAL A	0	0	—	15.63	3	1	0	6.1	15	7	3	0	0	0	0	0	0	0	—	0	1	0	0	0.3	1.000
1981	SD N	1	0	1.000	2.48	5	4	0	29	28	9	16	0	0	0	0	9	1	0	.111	0	1	0	0	0.2	1.000
2 yrs.		1	0	1.000	4.84	8	5	0	35.1	43	16	19	0	0	0	0	9	1	0	.111	0	2	0	0	0.3	1.000

Bub Kuhn

KUHN, BERNARD DANIEL BL TR 6′ 4″ 182 lbs.
B. Oct. 12, 1899, Vicksburg, Mich. D. Nov. 20, 1956, Detroit, Mich.

Year	Team	W	L	PCT	ERA	G	GS	CG	IP	H	BB	SO	ShO	Relief Pitching W	L	SV	Batting AB	H	HR	BA	PO	A	E	DP	TC/G	FA
1924	CLE A	0	1	.000	27.00	1	0	0	1	4	0	0	0	0	1	0	0	0	0	—	0	1	0	0	1.0	1.000

John Kull

KULL, JOHN A. BL TL 6′ 2″ 190 lbs.
B. June 24, 1882, Shenandoah, Pa. D. Mar. 30, 1936, Schuylkill, Pa.

Year	Team	W	L	PCT	ERA	G	GS	CG	IP	H	BB	SO	ShO	Relief Pitching W	L	SV	Batting AB	H	HR	BA	PO	A	E	DP	TC/G	FA
1909	PHI A	1	0	1.000	3.00	1	0	0	3	3	5	4	0	1	0	0	1	1	0	1.000	0	1	0	0	1.0	1.000

John Kume

KUME, JOHN MICHAEL BR TR 6′ 1″ 200 lbs.
B. May 19, 1926, Premier, W. Va.

Year	Team	W	L	PCT	ERA	G	GS	CG	IP	H	BB	SO	ShO	Relief Pitching W	L	SV	Batting AB	H	HR	BA	PO	A	E	DP	TC/G	FA
1955	KC A	0	2	.000	7.99	6	4	0	23.2	35	15	7	0	0	0	0	8	1	0	.125	1	4	0	0	0.8	1.000

Bill Kunkel

KUNKEL, WILLIAM GUSTAVE JAMES BR TR 6′ 1″ 187 lbs.
Father of Jeff Kunkel.
B. July 7, 1936, Hoboken, N. J. D. May 4, 1985, Red Bank, N. J.

Year	Team	W	L	PCT	ERA	G	GS	CG	IP	H	BB	SO	ShO	Relief Pitching W	L	SV	Batting AB	H	HR	BA	PO	A	E	DP	TC/G	FA
1961	KC A	3	4	.429	5.18	58	2	0	88.2	103	32	46	0	3	2	4	8	1	0	.125	10	13	3	2	0.4	.885
1962		0	0	—	3.52	9	0	0	7.2	8	4	6	0	0	0	0	0	0	0	—	0	1	0	0	0.1	1.000
1963	NY A	3	2	.600	2.72	22	0	0	46.1	42	13	31	0	3	2	0	6	2	0	.333	2	4	0	0	0.3	1.000
3 yrs.		6	6	.500	4.29	89	2	0	142.2	153	49	83	0	6	4	4	14	3	0	.214	12	18	3	2	0.4	.909

Jeff Kunkel

KUNKEL, JEFFREY WILLIAM BR TR 6′ 2″ 175 lbs.
Son of Bill Kunkel.
B. Mar. 25, 1962, West Palm Beach, Fla.

Year	Team	W	L	PCT	ERA	G	GS	CG	IP	H	BB	SO	ShO	Relief Pitching W	L	SV	Batting AB	H	HR	BA	PO	A	E	DP	TC/G	FA
1988	TEX A	0	0	—	0.00	1	0	0	1	0	0	1	0	0	0	0	154	35	2	.227	81	120	17	22	4.4	.922
1989		0	0	—	21.60	1	0	0	1.2	4	3	0	0	0	0	0	293	79	8	.270	143	168	22	27	3.1	.934
2 yrs.		0	0		13.50	2	0	0	2.2	4	3	1	0	0	0	0	*				446	631	65	117	3.1	.943

Earl Kunz

KUNZ, EARL DEWEY (Pinch) BR TR 5′10″ 170 lbs.
B. Dec. 25, 1899, Sacramento, Calif. D. Apr. 14, 1963, Sacramento, Calif.

Year	Team	W	L	PCT	ERA	G	GS	CG	IP	H	BB	SO	ShO	Relief Pitching W	L	SV	Batting AB	H	HR	BA	PO	A	E	DP	TC/G	FA
1923	PIT N	1	2	.333	5.52	21	2	1	45.2	48	24	12	0	1	1	1	12	1	0	.083	1	8	4	0	0.6	.692

Ryan Kurosaki

KUROSAKI, RYAN YOSHITOMO BR TR 5′10″ 160 lbs.
B. July 3, 1952, Honolulu, Hawaii.

Year	Team	W	L	PCT	ERA	G	GS	CG	IP	H	BB	SO	ShO	Relief Pitching W	L	SV	Batting AB	H	HR	BA	PO	A	E	DP	TC/G	FA
1975	STL N	0	0	—	7.62	7	0	0	13	15	7	6	0	0	0	0	1	0	0	.000	0	1	0	0	0.1	1.000

Hal Kurtz

KURTZ, HAROLD JAMES (Bud) BR TR 6′ 3″ 205 lbs.
B. Aug. 20, 1943, Washington, D. C.

Year	Team	W	L	PCT	ERA	G	GS	CG	IP	H	BB	SO	ShO	Relief Pitching W	L	SV	Batting AB	H	HR	BA	PO	A	E	DP	TC/G	FA
1968	CLE A	1	0	1.000	5.21	28	0	0	38	37	15	16	0	1	0	1	4	0	0	.000	0	5	1	1	0.2	.833

Ed Kusel

KUSEL, EDWARD D.
B. Feb. 15, 1886, Cleveland, Ohio D. Oct. 20, 1948, Cleveland, Ohio.
TR 6′ 165 lbs.

Year	Team	W	L	PCT	ERA	G	GS	CG	IP	H	BB	SO	ShO	Relief W	Relief L	Relief SV	AB	H	HR	BA	PO	A	E	DP	TC/G	FA
1909	STL A	0	3	.000	7.13	3	3	3	24	43	1	2	0	0	0	0	10	3	0	.300	2	5	0	0	2.3	1.000

Emil Kush

KUSH, EMIL BENEDICT (Moe)
B. Nov. 4, 1916, Chicago, Ill. D. Nov. 26, 1969, River Grove, Ill.
BR TR 5′11″ 185 lbs.

Year	Team	W	L	PCT	ERA	G	GS	CG	IP	H	BB	SO	ShO	Relief W	Relief L	Relief SV	AB	H	HR	BA	PO	A	E	DP	TC/G	FA
1941	CHI N	0	0	—	2.25	2	0	0	4	2	0	2	0	0	0	0	1	0	0	.000	0	0	0	0	0.0	.000
1942		0	0	—	0.00	1	0	0	2	1	1	1	0	0	0	0	1	0	0	.000	0	2	0	0	2.0	1.000
1946		9	2	.818	3.05	40	6	1	129.2	120	43	50	1	8	0	2	38	8	0	.211	9	37	2	2	1.2	.958
1947		8	3	.727	3.36	47	1	1	91	80	53	44	0	7	3	5	20	5	0	.250	5	21	1	1	0.6	.963
1948		1	4	.200	4.38	34	1	0	72	70	37	31	0	1	3	3	13	2	0	.154	6	15	1	0	0.6	.955
1949		3	3	.500	3.78	26	0	0	47.2	51	24	22	0	3	3	2	9	3	0	.333	6	10	0	2	0.6	1.000
6 yrs.		21	12	.636	3.48	150	8	2	346.1	324	158	150	1	19	9	12	82	18	0	.220	26	85	4	5	0.8	.965

Craig Kusick

KUSICK, CRAIG ROBERT
B. Sept. 30, 1948, Milwaukee, Wis.
BR TR 6′ 3″ 210 lbs.

Year	Team	W	L	PCT	ERA	G	GS	CG	IP	H	BB	SO	ShO	Relief W	Relief L	Relief SV	AB	H	HR	BA	PO	A	E	DP	TC/G	FA
1979	TOR A	0	0	—	4.50	1	0	0	4	3	0	0	0	0	0	0	*				89	5	1	7	6.3	.989

Marty Kutyna

KUTYNA, MARION JOHN
B. Nov. 14, 1932, Philadelphia, Pa.
BR TR 6′ 190 lbs.

Year	Team	W	L	PCT	ERA	G	GS	CG	IP	H	BB	SO	ShO	Relief W	Relief L	Relief SV	AB	H	HR	BA	PO	A	E	DP	TC/G	FA
1959	KC A	0	0	—	0.00	4	0	0	7.1	7	1	1	0	0	0	1	0	0	0	—	1	3	0	0	1.0	1.000
1960		3	2	.600	3.94	51	0	0	61.2	64	32	20	0	3	2	4	5	1	0	.200	3	12	1	1	0.3	.938
1961	WAS A	6	8	.429	3.97	50	6	0	143	147	48	64	0	5	4	3	34	7	0	.206	13	36	1	4	1.0	.980
1962		5	6	.455	4.04	54	0	0	78	83	27	25	0	5	6	0	8	1	0	.125	6	18	1	0	0.5	.960
4 yrs.		14	16	.467	3.88	159	6	0	290	301	108	110	0	13	12	8	47	9	0	.191	23	69	3	5	0.6	.968

Jerry Kutzler

KUTZLER, JERRY SCOTT
B. Mar. 25, 1965, Waukegan, Ill.
BL TR 6′ 1″ 175 lbs.

Year	Team	W	L	PCT	ERA	G	GS	CG	IP	H	BB	SO	ShO	Relief W	Relief L	Relief SV	AB	H	HR	BA	PO	A	E	DP	TC/G	FA
1990	CHI A	2	1	.667	6.03	7	7	0	31.1	38	14	21	0	0	0	0	0	0	0	—	2	2	0	0	0.6	1.000

Bob Kuzava

KUZAVA, ROBERT LeROY (Sarge)
B. May 28, 1923, Wyandotte, Mich.
BB TL 6′ 2″ 202 lbs.

Year	Team	W	L	PCT	ERA	G	GS	CG	IP	H	BB	SO	ShO	Relief W	Relief L	Relief SV	AB	H	HR	BA	PO	A	E	DP	TC/G	FA
1946	CLE A	1	0	1.000	3.00	2	2	0	12	9	11	4	0	0	0	0	5	1	0	.200	0	4	1	0	2.5	.800
1947		1	1	.500	4.15	4	4	1	21.2	22	9	9	1	0	0	0	9	1	0	.111	0	8	0	0	2.0	1.000
1949	CHI A	10	6	.625	4.02	29	18	9	156.2	139	91	83	1	2	0	0	56	2	0	.036	8	17	3	1	1.0	.893
1950	2 teams CHI A (10G 1–3) WAS A (22G 8–7)																									
″	total	9	10	.474	4.33	32	29	9	199.1	199	102	105	1	0	0	0	62	6	1	.097	8	30	3	5	1.3	.927
1951	2 teams WAS A (8G 3–3) NY A (23G 8–4)																									
″	total	11	7	.611	3.61	31	16	7	134.2	133	55	72	1	5	1	5	39	6	0	.154	9	17	2	0	0.9	.929
1952	NY A	8	8	.500	3.45	28	12	6	133	115	63	67	1	3	2	3	43	4	0	.093	4	16	0	2	0.7	1.000
1953		6	5	.545	3.31	33	6	2	92.1	92	34	48	2	4	1	4	21	1	0	.048	1	8	0	0	0.3	1.000
1954	2 teams NY A (20G 1–3) BAL A (4G 1–3)																									
″	total	2	6	.250	4.97	24	7	0	63.1	76	29	37	0	1	1	1	13	0	0	.000	0	5	0	1	0.2	1.000
1955	2 teams BAL A (6G 0–1) PHI N (17G 1–0)																									
″	total	1	1	.500	6.25	23	5	0	44.2	57	16	18	0	0	0	0	8	1	0	.125	3	6	0	0	0.4	1.000
1957	2 teams PIT N (4G 0–0) STL N (3G 0–0)																									
″	total	0	0		6.23	7	0	0	4.1	7	5	3	0	0	0	0	0	0	0		0	1	0	0	0.1	1.000
10 yrs.		49	44	.527	4.05	213	99	34	862	849	415	446	7	15	5	13	256	22	1	.086	33	112	9	9	0.7	.942
WORLD SERIES																										
1951	NY A	0	0	—	0.00	1	0	0	1	0	0	0	0	0	0	1	0	0	0	—	0	0	0	0	0.0	.000
1952		0	0	—	0.00	1	0	0	2.2	0	0	2	0	0	0	1	1	0	0	.000	0	0	0	0	0.0	.000
1953		0	0	—	13.50	1	0	0	0.2	2	0	1	0	0	0	0	1	0	0	.000	0	0	0	0	0.0	.000
3 yrs.		0	0		2.08	3	0	0	4.1	2	0	3	0	0	0	2	2	0	0	.000	0	0	0	0	0.0	

Clem Labine

LABINE, CLEMENT WALTER
B. Aug. 6, 1926, Lincoln, R. I.
BR TR 6′ 180 lbs.

Year	Team	W	L	PCT	ERA	G	GS	CG	IP	H	BB	SO	ShO	Relief W	Relief L	Relief SV	AB	H	HR	BA	PO	A	E	DP	TC/G	FA
1950	BKN N	0	0	—	4.50	1	0	0	2	2	1	0	0	0	0	0	0	0	0	—	0	0	0	0	0.0	.000
1951		5	1	.833	2.20	14	6	5	65.1	52	20	39	2	0	0	0	21	3	0	.143	6	6	1	1	0.9	.923
1952		8	4	.667	5.14	25	9	0	77	76	47	43	0	6	1	0	22	1	0	.045	8	17	1	1	1.0	.962
1953		11	6	.647	2.77	37	7	0	110.1	92	30	44	0	**10**	4	7	28	2	0	.071	8	19	0	2	0.7	1.000
1954		7	6	.538	4.15	47	2	0	108.1	101	56	43	0	6	5	5	30	1	0	.033	7	24	3	1	0.7	.912
1955		13	5	.722	3.24	**60**	8	1	144.1	121	55	67	0	**10**	2	11	31	3	3	.097	21	30	1	2	0.9	.981
1956		10	6	.625	3.35	62	3	1	115.2	111	39	75	0	9	6	**19**	23	2	0	.087	13	18	2	1	0.5	.939
1957		5	7	.417	3.44	58	0	0	104.2	104	27	67	0	5	**7**	**17**	20	2	0	.100	6	28	1	2	0.6	.971
1958	LA N	6	6	.500	4.15	52	2	0	104	112	33	43	0	5	5	14	18	1	0	.056	3	21	2	2	0.5	.923
1959		5	10	.333	3.93	56	0	0	84.2	91	25	37	0	5	**10**	9	16	0	0	.000	9	18	0	2	0.5	1.000
1960	3 teams LA N (13G 0–1) DET A (14G 0–3) PIT N (15G 3–0)																									
″	total	3	4	.429	3.64	42	0	0	66.2	74	31	42	0	3	4	6	8	1	0	.125	4	12	2	1	0.4	.889
1961	PIT N	4	1	.800	3.69	56	1	0	92.2	102	31	49	0	4	1	8	10	1	0	.100	12	12	1	0	0.4	.960
1962	NY N	0	0	—	11.25	3	0	0	4	5	1	2	0	0	0	0	0	0	0	—	0	2	0	0	0.7	1.000
13 yrs.		77	56	.579	3.63	513	38	7	1079.2	1043	396	551	2	63	45	96	227	17	3	.075	97	207	14	15	0.6	.956
WORLD SERIES																										
1953	BKN N	0	2	.000	3.60	3	0	0	5	10	1	3	0	0	2	1	2	0	0	.000	0	2	0	1	0.7	1.000
1955		1	0	1.000	2.89	4	0	0	9.1	6	2	2	0	1	0	1	4	0	0	.000	0	3	0	0	0.8	1.000
1956		1	0	1.000	0.00	2	1	1	12	8	3	7	1	0	0	0	4	1	0	.250	0	3	0	0	1.5	1.000
1959	LA N	0	0	—	0.00	1	0	0	1	0	0	1	0	0	0	0	0	0	0	—	0	0	0	0	0.0	.000
1960	PIT N	0	0	—	13.50	3	0	0	4	13	1	2	0	0	0	0	0	0	0	—	0	2	0	0	0.7	1.000
5 yrs.		2	2	.500	3.16	13 **6th**	1	1	31.1	37	7	15	1	1	2	2	10	1	0	.100	0	10	0	1	0.8	1.000

Bob Lacey

LACEY, ROBERT JOSEPH
B. Aug. 25, 1953, Fredericksburg, Va.
BR TL 6′ 5″ 210 lbs.

Year	Team	W	L	PCT	ERA	G	GS	CG	IP	H	BB	SO	ShO	Relief W	Relief L	Relief SV	AB	H	HR	BA	PO	A	E	DP	TC/G	FA
1977	OAK A	6	8	.429	3.02	64	0	0	122	100	43	69	0	6	8	7	0	0	0	—	3	38	3	1	0.7	.932
1978		8	9	.471	3.01	**74**	0	0	119.2	126	35	60	0	8	9	5	0	0	0	—	8	27	3	1	0.5	.921
1979		1	5	.167	5.81	42	0	0	48	66	24	33	0	1	5	4	0	0	0	—	3	7	0	0	0.2	1.000

Bob Lacey *continued*

Year	Team	W	L	PCT	ERA	G	GS	CG	IP	H	BB	SO	ShO	Relief Pitching W	Relief Pitching L	Relief Pitching SV	Batting AB	Batting H	Batting HR	BA	PO	A	E	DP	TC/G	FA
1980		3	2	.600	2.92	47	1	1	80	68	21	45	1	2	2	6	0	0	0	—	3	12	0	0	0.3	1.000
1981	2 teams CLE A (14G 0–0) TEX A (1G 0–0)																									
"	total	0	0		7.77	15	0	0	22	37	3	11	0	0	0	0	0	0	0		1	3	0	0	0.3	1.000
1983	CAL A	1	2	.333	5.19	8	0	0	8.2	12	0	7	0	1	2	0	0	0	0	—	0	1	0	0	0.1	1.000
1984	SF N	1	3	.250	3.88	34	1	0	51	55	13	26	0	1	2	0	6	2	0	.333	1	10	0	0	0.3	1.000
7 yrs.		20	29	.408	3.67	284	2	1	451.1	464	139	251	1	19	28	22	6	2	0	.333	19	98	6	2	0.4	.951

Marcel Lachemann

LACHEMANN, MARCEL ERNEST BR TR 6′ 1″ 185 lbs.
Brother of Rene Lachemann.
B. June 13, 1941, Los Angeles, Calif.
Manager 1994–95.

Year	Team	W	L	PCT	ERA	G	GS	CG	IP	H	BB	SO	ShO	Relief Pitching W	Relief Pitching L	Relief Pitching SV	Batting AB	Batting H	Batting HR	BA	PO	A	E	DP	TC/G	FA
1969	OAK A	4	1	.800	3.95	28	0	0	43.1	43	19	16	0	4	1	2	2	0	0	.000	2	10	1	1	0.5	.923
1970		3	3	.500	2.79	41	0	0	58	58	18	39	0	3	3	3	8	0	0	.000	1	15	1	1	0.4	.941
1971		0	0	—	54.00	1	0	0	0.1	2	1	0	0	0	0	0	0	0	0	—	0	1	0	0	1.0	1.000
3 yrs.		7	4	.636	3.45	70	0	0	101.2	103	38	55	0	7	4	5	10	0	0	.000	3	26	2	2	0.4	.935

Al Lachowicz

LACHOWICZ, ALLEN ROBERT BR TR 6′ 3″ 185 lbs.
B. Sept. 6, 1960, Pittsburgh, Pa.

Year	Team	W	L	PCT	ERA	G	GS	CG	IP	H	BB	SO	ShO	Relief Pitching W	Relief Pitching L	Relief Pitching SV	Batting AB	Batting H	Batting HR	BA	PO	A	E	DP	TC/G	FA
1983	TEX A	0	1	.000	2.25	2	1	0	8	9	2	8	0	0	0	0	0	0	0	—	1	1	0	0	1.0	1.000

Lackey

LACKEY
B. Columbus, Ohio Deceased.

Year	Team	W	L	PCT	ERA	G	GS	CG	IP	H	BB	SO	ShO	Relief Pitching W	Relief Pitching L	Relief Pitching SV	Batting AB	Batting H	Batting HR	BA	PO	A	E	DP	TC/G	FA
1890	PHI AA	0	0	—	9.00	1	0	0	2	1	3	1	0	0	0	0	1	0	0	.000	0	0	0	0	0.0	.000

George LaClaire

LaCLAIRE, GEORGE LEWIS BR TR 5′ 9″ 170 lbs.
B. Oct. 18, 1886, Milton, Vt. D. Oct. 10, 1918, Farnham, Que., Canada.

Year	Team	W	L	PCT	ERA	G	GS	CG	IP	H	BB	SO	ShO	Relief Pitching W	Relief Pitching L	Relief Pitching SV	Batting AB	Batting H	Batting HR	BA	PO	A	E	DP	TC/G	FA
1914	PIT F	5	2	.714	4.01	22	7	5	103.1	99	25	49	1	2	0	0	34	5	0	.147	6	28	0	2	1.5	1.000
1915	3 teams PIT F (14G 1–0) BUF F (1G 0–0) BAL F (18G 2–8)																									
"	total	3	8	.273	2.85	33	12	7	132.2	123	36	42	1	1	2	1	37	4	0	.108	0	46	0	2	1.4	1.000
2 yrs.		8	10	.444	3.36	55	19	12	236	222	61	91	2	3	2	1	71	9	0	.127	6	74	0	4	1.5	1.000

Frank LaCorte

LaCORTE, FRANK JOSEPH BR TR 6′ 1″ 180 lbs.
B. Oct. 13, 1951, San Jose, Calif.

Year	Team	W	L	PCT	ERA	G	GS	CG	IP	H	BB	SO	ShO	Relief Pitching W	Relief Pitching L	Relief Pitching SV	Batting AB	Batting H	Batting HR	BA	PO	A	E	DP	TC/G	FA
1975	ATL N	0	3	.000	5.14	3	2	0	14	13	6	10	0	0	1	0	5	0	0	.000	0	2	0	1	0.7	1.000
1976		3	12	.200	4.71	19	17	1	105	97	53	79	0	0	1	0	33	3	0	.091	5	14	3	0	1.2	.864
1977		1	8	.111	11.68	14	7	0	37	67	29	28	0	0	2	0	10	2	0	.200	2	6	0	0	0.6	1.000
1978		0	1	.000	3.60	2	2	0	15	9	4	7	0	0	0	0	4	0	0	.000	0	1	0	0	0.5	1.000
1979	2 teams ATL N (6G 0–0) HOU N (12G 1–2)																									
"	total	1	2	.333	5.60	18	3	0	35.1	30	15	30	0	0	0	0	4	0	0	.000	0	1	1	0	0.1	.500
1980	HOU N	8	5	.615	2.82	55	0	0	83	61	43	66	0	8	5	11	6	1	0	.167	1	3	1	0	0.1	.800
1981		4	2	.667	3.64	37	0	0	42	41	21	40	0	4	2	5	3	1	0	.333	2	4	0	0	0.2	1.000
1982		1	5	.167	4.48	55	0	0	76.1	71	46	51	0	1	5	7	7	0	0	.000	2	4	2	0	0.1	.750
1983		4	4	.500	5.06	37	0	0	53.1	35	28	48	0	4	4	3	5	1	0	.200	1	6	0	0	0.2	1.000
1984	CAL A	1	2	.333	7.06	13	1	0	29.1	33	13	13	0	0	2	0	0	0	0	—	0	4	1	0	0.4	.800
10 yrs.		23	44	.343	5.01	253	32	1	490.1	457	258	372	0	17	22	26	77	8	0	.104	13	45	8	1	0.3	.879
DIVISIONAL PLAYOFF SERIES																										
1981	HOU N	0	0	—	0.00	2	0	0	3.2	2	1	5	0	0	0	0	0	0	0	—	0	0	0	0	0.0	.000
LEAGUE CHAMPIONSHIP SERIES																										
1980	HOU N	1	1	.500	3.00	2	0	0	3	7	2	2	0	1	1	0	1	0	0	.000	0	0	0	0	0.0	.000

Mike LaCoss

LaCOSS, MICHAEL JAMES BR TR 6′ 5″ 185 lbs.
Born Michael James Marks.
B. May 30, 1956, Glendale, Calif.

Year	Team	W	L	PCT	ERA	G	GS	CG	IP	H	BB	SO	ShO	Relief Pitching W	Relief Pitching L	Relief Pitching SV	Batting AB	Batting H	Batting HR	BA	PO	A	E	DP	TC/G	FA
1978	CIN N	4	8	.333	4.50	16	15	2	96	104	46	31	1	0	0	0	30	2	0	.067	8	13	0	0	1.3	1.000
1979		14	8	.636	3.50	35	32	6	206	202	79	73	1	0	0	0	70	9	0	.129	15	34	2	4	1.5	.961
1980		10	12	.455	4.63	34	29	4	169	207	68	59	2	2	0	0	55	5	0	.091	9	34	3	4	1.4	.935
1981		4	7	.364	6.12	20	13	1	78	102	30	22	1	2	0	1	19	0	0	.000	6	14	1	0	1.0	.952
1982	HOU N	6	6	.500	2.90	41	8	0	115	107	54	51	0	3	3	0	24	6	0	.250	7	16	3	3	0.6	.885
1983		5	7	.417	4.43	38	17	2	138	142	56	53	0	0	1	1	35	3	0	.086	6	27	0	1	0.9	1.000
1984		7	5	.583	4.02	39	18	2	132	132	55	86	1	1	0	3	31	4	0	.129	9	20	2	2	0.8	.935
1985	KC A	1	1	.500	5.09	21	0	0	40.2	49	29	26	0	1	1	1	0	0	0	—	1	8	0	1	0.4	1.000
1986	SF N	10	13	.435	3.57	37	31	4	204.1	179	70	86	1	0	0	0	61	14	2	.230	19	34	1	2	1.5	.981
1987		13	10	.565	3.68	39	26	2	171	184	63	79	1	1	0	0	50	3	0	.060	15	43	2	4	1.5	.967
1988		7	7	.500	3.62	19	19	1	114.1	99	47	70	1	0	0	0	33	8	0	.242	10	32	0	1	2.2	1.000
1989		10	10	.500	3.17	45	18	1	150.1	143	65	78	0	3	5	6	41	3	0	.073	12	20	4	1	0.8	.889
1990		6	4	.600	3.94	13	12	1	77.2	75	39	39	0	0	0	0	23	1	0	.043	5	8	1	1	1.1	.929
1991		1	5	.167	7.23	18	5	0	47.1	61	24	30	0	0	3	0	9	2	0	.222	4	5	1	0	0.6	.900
14 yrs.		98	103	.488	4.02	415	243	26	1739.2	1786	725	783	9	13	13	12	481	60	2	.125	126	308	20	24	1.1	.956
LEAGUE CHAMPIONSHIP SERIES																										
1979	CIN N	0	1	.000	10.80	1	1	0	1.2	1	4	0	0	0	0	0	0	0	0	—	0	1	0	0	1.0	1.000
1987	SF N	0	0	—	0.00	2	0	0	3.1	1	3	2	0	0	0	0	0	0	0	—	0	2	0	0	1.0	1.000
1989		0	0	—	9.00	1	1	0	3	7	0	2	0	0	0	0	1	0	0	.000	0	0	1	0	1.0	.000
3 yrs.		0	1	.000	5.63	4	2	0	8	9	7	4	0	0	0	0	1	0	0	.000	0	3	1	0	1.0	.750
WORLD SERIES																										
1989	SF N	0	0	—	6.23	2	0	0	4.1	4	3	2	0	0	0	0	1	0	0	.000	1	0	0	0	0.5	1.000

Pete Ladd

LADD, PETER LINWOOD (Bigfoot) BR TR 6′ 3″ 228 lbs.
B. July 17, 1956, Portland, Me.

Year	Team	W	L	PCT	ERA	G	GS	CG	IP	H	BB	SO	ShO	Relief Pitching W	Relief Pitching L	Relief Pitching SV	Batting AB	Batting H	Batting HR	BA	PO	A	E	DP	TC/G	FA
1979	HOU N	1	1	.500	3.00	10	0	0	12	8	8	6	0	1	1	0	1	0	0	.000	3	2	0	0	0.5	1.000
1982	MIL A	1	3	.250	4.00	16	0	0	18	16	6	12	0	1	3	3	0	0	0	—	1	0	0	0	0.1	1.000
1983		3	4	.429	2.55	44	0	0	49.1	30	16	41	0	3	4	25	0	0	0	—	1	5	0	0	0.1	1.000

Pete Ladd *continued*

Year	Team	W	L	PCT	ERA	G	GS	CG	IP	H	BB	SO	ShO	Relief Pitching W	Relief Pitching L	Relief Pitching SV	Batting AB	Batting H	Batting HR	BA	PO	A	E	DP	TC/G	FA
1984		4	9	.308	5.24	54	1	0	91	94	38	75	0	4	8	3	0	0	0	—	5	4	1	0	0.2	.900
1985		0	0	—	4.53	29	0	0	45.2	58	10	22	0	0	0	2	0	0	0	—	3	5	1	0	0.3	.889
1986	SEA A	8	6	.571	3.82	52	0	0	70.2	69	18	53	0	8	6	6	0	0	0	—	2	5	1	0	0.2	.875
6 yrs.		17	23	.425	4.14	205	1	0	286.2	275	96	209	0	17	22	39	1	0	0	.000	15	21	3	0	0.2	.923
LEAGUE CHAMPIONSHIP SERIES																										
1982	MIL A	0	0	—	0.00	3	0	0	3.1	0	0	5	0	0	0	2	0	0	0	—	0	1	0	0	0.3	1.000
WORLD SERIES																										
1982	MIL A	0	0	—	0.00	1	0	0	0.2	1	2	0	0	0	0	0	0	0	0	—	0	0	0	0	0.0	.000

Doyle Lade

LADE, DOYLE MARION (Porky) BR TR 5′10″ 183 lbs.
B. Feb. 17, 1921, Fairbury, Neb. BB 1946–1947

Year	Team	W	L	PCT	ERA	G	GS	CG	IP	H	BB	SO	ShO	Relief W	Relief L	SV	AB	H	HR	BA	PO	A	E	DP	TC/G	FA
1946	CHI N	0	2	.000	4.11	3	2	0	15.1	15	3	8	0	0	1	0	5	1	0	.200	0	4	0	0	1.3	1.000
1947		11	10	.524	3.94	34	25	7	187.1	202	79	62	1	0	0	0	60	13	0	.217	10	46	1	2	1.7	.982
1948		5	6	.455	4.02	19	12	6	87.1	99	31	29	0	0	0	0	32	5	0	.156	11	19	0	1	1.6	1.000
1949		4	5	.444	5.00	36	13	5	129.2	141	58	43	1	0	0	1	32	7	0	.219	10	23	1	0	0.9	.971
1950		5	6	.455	4.74	34	12	2	117.2	126	50	36	0	2	1	2	35	10	0	.286	10	36	0	2	1.4	1.000
5 yrs.		25	29	.463	4.39	126	64	20	537.1	583	221	178	2	2	2	3	164	36	0	.220	41	128	2	5	1.4	.988

Steve Ladew

LADEW, STEPHEN
B. St. Louis, Mo. Deceased.

Year	Team	W	L	PCT	ERA	G	GS	CG	IP	H	BB	SO	ShO	Relief W	Relief L	SV	AB	H	HR	BA	PO	A	E	DP	TC/G	FA
1889	KC AA	0	0	—	4.50	1	0	0	2	1	3	0	0	0	0	0	*				1	1	0	0	1.0	1.000

Flip Lafferty

LAFFERTY, FRANK BERNARD TR
B. May 4, 1854, Scranton, Pa. D. Feb. 8, 1910, Wilmington, Del.

Year	Team	W	L	PCT	ERA	G	GS	CG	IP	H	BB	SO	ShO	Relief W	Relief L	SV	AB	H	HR	BA	PO	A	E	DP	TC/G	FA
1876	PHI N	0	1	.000	0.00	1	1	1	9	5	0	0	0	0	0	0	*				1	2	1	1	4.0	.750

Ed Lafitte

LAFITTE, EDWARD FRANCIS (Doc) BR TR 6′2″ 188 lbs.
B. Apr. 7, 1886, New Orleans, La. D. Apr. 12, 1971, Jenkintown, Pa.

Year	Team	W	L	PCT	ERA	G	GS	CG	IP	H	BB	SO	ShO	Relief W	Relief L	SV	AB	H	HR	BA	PO	A	E	DP	TC/G	FA
1909	DET A	0	1	.000	3.86	3	1	1	14	22	2	11	0	0	0	1	4	1	0	.250	1	4	0	0	1.7	1.000
1911		11	8	.579	3.92	29	20	15	172.1	205	52	63	0	0	1	1	70	11	1	.157	12	41	4	0	1.8	.930
1912		0	0	—	16.20	1	0	0	1.2	2	2	0	0	0	0	0	0	0	0	—	1	1	0	0	2.0	1.000
1914	BKN F	16	16	.500	2.63	42	33	23	290.2	260	**127**	137	0	1	2	2	101	26	1	.257	11	101	4	3	2.8	.966
1915	2 teams BKN F	(17G 6–9)		BUF F	(14G 2–2)																					
″	total	8	11	.421	3.80	31	21	8	168	179	79	51	0	0	1	1	70	16	0	.229	8	44	2	0	1.6	.963
5 yrs.		35	36	.493	3.34	106	75	47	646.2	668	262	262	0	1	4	5	245	54	2	.220	33	191	10	3	2.1	.957

Ed Lagger

LAGGER, EDWIN JOSEPH BR TR 6′3″ 200 lbs.
B. July 14, 1912, Joliet, Ill. D. Nov. 10, 1981, Joliet, Ill.

Year	Team	W	L	PCT	ERA	G	GS	CG	IP	H	BB	SO	ShO	Relief W	Relief L	SV	AB	H	HR	BA	PO	A	E	DP	TC/G	FA
1934	PHI A	0	0	—	11.00	8	0	0	18	27	14	2	0	0	0	0	6	0	0	.000	2	9	1	1	1.5	.917

Lerrin LaGrow

LaGROW, LERRIN HARRIS BR TR 6′5″ 220 lbs.
B. July 8, 1948, Phoenix, Ariz.

Year	Team	W	L	PCT	ERA	G	GS	CG	IP	H	BB	SO	ShO	Relief W	Relief L	SV	AB	H	HR	BA	PO	A	E	DP	TC/G	FA
1970	DET A	0	1	.000	7.50	10	0	0	12	16	6	7	0	0	1	0	1	0	0	.000	1	1	0	0	0.2	1.000
1972		0	1	.000	1.33	16	0	0	27	22	6	9	0	0	1	2	0	0	0	—	2	4	0	0	0.4	1.000
1973		1	5	.167	4.33	21	3	0	54	54	23	33	0	0	3	3	0	0	0	—	5	11	2	0	0.9	.889
1974		8	19	.296	4.67	37	34	11	216	245	80	85	0	0	0	0	0	0	0	—	12	48	4	1	1.7	.938
1975		7	14	.333	4.38	32	26	7	164.1	183	66	75	2	0	0	0	0	0	0	—	6	17	4	3	0.8	.852
1976	STL N	0	1	.000	1.48	8	2	1	24.1	21	7	10	0	0	0	0	5	0	0	.000	1	4	0	0	0.6	1.000
1977	CHI A	7	3	.700	2.45	66	0	0	99	81	35	63	0	7	3	25	0	0	0	—	5	17	1	2	0.3	.957
1978		6	5	.545	4.40	52	0	0	88	85	38	41	0	6	5	16	0	0	0	—	4	20	1	3	0.5	.960
1979	2 teams CHI A	(11G 0–3)		LA N	(31G 5–1)																					
″	total	5	4	.556	5.24	42	2	0	55	65	34	31	0	5	2	5	3	1	0	.333	0	8	1	0	0.2	.889
1980	PHI N	0	2	.000	4.15	25	0	0	39	42	17	21	0	0	2	3	4	1	0	.250	1	6	0	0	0.3	1.000
10 yrs.		34	55	.382	4.11	309	67	19	778.2	814	312	375	2	18	17	54	13	2	0	.154	37	136	13	9	0.6	.930
LEAGUE CHAMPIONSHIP SERIES																										
1972	DET A	0	0	—	0.00	1	0	0	1	0	0	1	0	0	0	0	0	0	0	—	0	0	0	0	0.0	.000

Jeff Lahti

LAHTI, JEFFREY ALLEN BR TR 6′ 180 lbs.
B. Oct. 8, 1956, Oregon City, Ore.

Year	Team	W	L	PCT	ERA	G	GS	CG	IP	H	BB	SO	ShO	Relief W	Relief L	SV	AB	H	HR	BA	PO	A	E	DP	TC/G	FA
1982	STL N	5	4	.556	3.81	33	1	0	56.2	53	21	22	0	5	3	0	13	1	0	.077	9	15	1	1	0.8	.960
1983		3	3	.500	3.16	53	0	0	74	64	29	26	0	3	3	0	10	0	0	.000	6	14	0	3	0.4	1.000
1984		4	2	.667	3.72	63	0	0	84.2	69	34	45	0	4	2	1	6	1	0	.167	4	15	1	1	0.3	.950
1985		5	2	.714	1.84	52	0	0	68.1	63	26	41	0	5	2	19	9	0	0	.000	5	9	1	1	0.3	.933
1986		0	0	—	0.00	4	0	0	2.1	3	1	3	0	0	0	0	0	0	0	—	0	0	0	0	0.0	.000
5 yrs.		17	11	.607	3.12	205	1	0	286	252	111	137	0	17	10	20	38	2	0	.053	24	53	3	6	0.4	.962
LEAGUE CHAMPIONSHIP SERIES																										
1985	STL N	1	0	1.000	0.00	2	0	0	2	2	0	1	0	1	0	0	0	0	0	—	0	0	0	0	0.0	.000
WORLD SERIES																										
1982	STL N	0	0	—	10.80	2	0	0	1.2	4	1	1	0	0	0	0	0	0	0	—	0	1	0	0	0.5	1.000
1985		0	0	—	12.27	3	0	0	3.2	10	0	2	0	0	0	1	0	0	0	—	0	0	0	0	0.0	.000
2 yrs.		0	0	—	11.81	5	0	0	5.1	14	1	3	0	0	0	1	0	0	0	—	0	1	0	0	0.2	1.000

Eddie Lake

LAKE, EDWARD ERVING BR TR 5′7″ 159 lbs.
B. Mar. 18, 1916, Antioch, Calif. D. June 7, 1995, Castro Valley, Calif.

Year	Team	W	L	PCT	ERA	G	GS	CG	IP	H	BB	SO	ShO	Relief W	Relief L	SV	AB	H	HR	BA	PO	A	E	DP	TC/G	FA
1944	BOS A	0	0	—	4.19	6	0	0	19.1	20	11	7	0	0	0	0	*				3	3	1	1	3.5	.857

Joe Lake

LAKE, JOSEPH HENRY BR TR 6′ 185 lbs.
B. Jan. 6, 1881, Brooklyn, N. Y. D. June 30, 1950, Brooklyn, N. Y.

Year	Team	W	L	PCT	ERA	G	GS	CG	IP	H	BB	SO	ShO	Relief W	Relief L	SV	AB	H	HR	BA	PO	A	E	DP	TC/G	FA
1908	NY A	9	**22**	.290	3.17	38	27	19	269.1	252	77	118	2	2	2	0	112	21	1	.188	9	64	10	1	2.2	.880
1909		14	11	.560	1.88	31	26	17	215.1	180	59	117	3	2	0	1	81	14	0	.173	3	94	10	2	3.5	.907
1910	STL A	11	17	.393	2.20	35	29	24	261.1	243	77	141	1	1	1	2	81	21	0	.259	5	88	9	2	2.9	.912

Joe Lake *continued*

Year	Team	W	L	PCT	ERA	G	GS	CG	IP	H	BB	SO	ShO	Relief Pitching W	Relief Pitching L	Relief Pitching SV	Batting AB	Batting H	Batting HR	BA	PO	A	E	DP	TC/G	FA
1911		10	15	.400	3.30	30	25	14	215.1	245	40	69	2	1	1	0	80	21	0	.263	15	88	7	0	3.7	.936
1912	2 teams STL A (11G 1–7) DET A (26G 9–11)																									
″	total	10	18	.357	3.44	37	20	15	219.2	260	55	114	0	5	**4**	1	81	12	1	.148	4	73	5	1	2.2	.939
1913	DET A	8	7	.533	3.28	28	12	6	137	149	24	35	0	4	1	1	45	12	1	.267	6	59	4	1	2.5	.942
6 yrs.		62	90	.408	2.85	199	139	95	1318	1329	332	594	8	15	9	5	480	101	3	.210	42	466	45	7	2.8	.919

Al Lakeman

LAKEMAN, ALBERT WESLEY (Moose) BR TR 6′ 2″ 195 lbs.
B. Dec. 31, 1918, Cincinnati, Ohio D. May 25, 1976, Spartanburg, S. C.

Year	Team	W	L	PCT	ERA	G	GS	CG	IP	H	BB	SO	ShO	Relief Pitching W	Relief Pitching L	Relief Pitching SV	Batting AB	Batting H	Batting HR	BA	PO	A	E	DP	TC/G	FA
1948	PHI N	0	0	—	13.50	1	0	0	0.2	1	0	0	0	0	0	0	*				57	7	2	2	3.9	.970

Jack Lamabe

LAMABE, JOHN ALEXANDER BR TR 6′ 1″ 198 lbs.
B. Oct. 3, 1936, Farmingdale, N. Y.

Year	Team	W	L	PCT	ERA	G	GS	CG	IP	H	BB	SO	ShO	Relief Pitching W	Relief Pitching L	Relief Pitching SV	Batting AB	Batting H	Batting HR	BA	PO	A	E	DP	TC/G	FA
1962	PIT N	3	1	.750	2.88	46	0	0	78	70	40	56	0	3	1	2	9	0	0	.000	3	17	0	1	0.4	1.000
1963	BOS A	7	4	.636	3.15	65	2	0	151.1	139	46	93	0	7	3	6	32	3	1	.094	11	26	1	0	0.6	.974
1964		9	13	.409	5.89	39	25	3	177.1	235	57	109	0	1	2	1	52	6	0	.115	12	26	3	1	1.1	.927
1965	2 teams BOS A (14G 0–3) HOU N (3G 0–2)																									
″	total	0	5	.000	6.87	17	2	0	38	51	17	23	0	0	3	0	8	1	0	.125	2	7	0	1	0.5	1.000
1966	CHI A	7	9	.438	3.93	34	17	3	121.1	116	35	67	2	2	0	0	35	2	0	.057	13	16	0	0	0.9	1.000
1967	3 teams CHI A (3G 1–0) NY N (16G 0–3) STL N (23G 3–4)																									
″	total	4	7	.364	3.20	42	3	1	84.1	74	19	56	1	3	5	5	15	2	0	.133	5	13	1	0	0.5	.947
1968	CHI N	3	2	.600	4.30	42	0	0	60.2	68	24	30	0	3	2	1	5	1	0	.200	3	8	0	1	0.3	1.000
7 yrs.		33	41	.446	4.24	285	49	7	711	753	238	434	3	19	16	15	156	15	1	.096	49	113	5	4	0.6	.970
WORLD SERIES																										
1967	STL N	0	1	.000	6.75	3	0	0	2.2	5	0	4	0	0	1	0	0	0	0	—	0	1	0	1	0.3	1.000

Al LaMacchia

LaMACCHIA, ALFRED ANTHONY BR TR 5′10½″ 190 lbs.
B. July 22, 1921, St. Louis, Mo.

Year	Team	W	L	PCT	ERA	G	GS	CG	IP	H	BB	SO	ShO	Relief Pitching W	Relief Pitching L	Relief Pitching SV	Batting AB	Batting H	Batting HR	BA	PO	A	E	DP	TC/G	FA
1943	STL A	0	1	.000	11.25	1	1	0	4	9	2	2	0	0	0	0	2	0	0	.000	0	0	0	0	0.0	.000
1945		2	0	1.000	2.00	5	0	0	9	6	3	2	0	2	0	0	1	0	0	.000	0	2	0	0	0.4	1.000
1946	2 teams STL A (8G 0–0) WAS A (2G 0–1)																									
″	total	0	1	.000	7.64	10	0	0	17.2	23	9	3	0	0	1	0	3	0	0	.000	1	1	0	0	0.2	1.000
3 yrs.		2	2	.500	6.46	16	1	0	30.2	38	14	7	0	2	1	0	6	0	0	.000	1	3	0	0	0.3	1.000

Frank LaManna

LaMANNA, FRANK (Hank) BR TR 6′ 2½″ 195 lbs.
B. Aug. 22, 1919, Watertown, Pa. D. Sept. 1, 1980, Syracuse, N. Y.

Year	Team	W	L	PCT	ERA	G	GS	CG	IP	H	BB	SO	ShO	Relief Pitching W	Relief Pitching L	Relief Pitching SV	Batting AB	Batting H	Batting HR	BA	PO	A	E	DP	TC/G	FA
1940	BOS N	1	0	1.000	4.72	5	1	1	13.1	13	8	3	0	0	0	0	5	1	0	.200	2	2	1	1	1.0	.800
1941		5	4	.556	5.33	35	4	0	72.2	77	56	23	0	4	2	1	32	9	0	.281	9	20	1	1	0.8	.967
1942		0	1	.000	5.40	5	0	0	6.2	5	3	2	0	0	1	0	2	0	0	.000	0	1	0	0	0.2	1.000
3 yrs.		6	5	.545	5.24	45	5	1	92.2	95	67	28	0	4	3	1	39	10	0	.256	11	23	2	2	0.7	.944

Frank Lamanske

LAMANSKE, FRANK JAMES (Lefty) BL TL 5′11″ 170 lbs.
B. Sept. 30, 1906, Oglesby, Ill. D. Aug. 4, 1971, Olney, Ill.

Year	Team	W	L	PCT	ERA	G	GS	CG	IP	H	BB	SO	ShO	Relief Pitching W	Relief Pitching L	Relief Pitching SV	Batting AB	Batting H	Batting HR	BA	PO	A	E	DP	TC/G	FA
1935	BKN N	0	0	—	7.36	2	0	0	3.2	5	1	1	0	0	0	0	1	0	0	.000	1	1	0	0	1.0	1.000

Wayne LaMaster

LaMASTER, NOBLE WAYNE BL TL 5′ 8″ 170 lbs.
B. Feb. 13, 1907, Speed, Ind. D. Aug. 4, 1989, New Albany, Ind.

Year	Team	W	L	PCT	ERA	G	GS	CG	IP	H	BB	SO	ShO	Relief Pitching W	Relief Pitching L	Relief Pitching SV	Batting AB	Batting H	Batting HR	BA	PO	A	E	DP	TC/G	FA
1937	PHI N	15	**19**	.441	5.31	50	30	10	220.1	255	82	135	1	3	4	4	79	15	0	.190	10	23	4	1	0.7	.892
1938	2 teams PHI N (18G 4–7) BKN N (3G 0–1)																									
″	total	4	8	.333	7.32	21	12	1	75	97	34	38	1	0	2	0	28	10	0	.357	7	15	0	1	1.0	1.000
2 yrs.		19	27	.413	5.82	71	42	11	295.1	352	116	173	2	3	6	4	107	25	0	.234	17	38	4	2	0.8	.932

John Lamb

LAMB, JOHN ANDREW BR TR 6′ 3″ 180 lbs.
B. July 20, 1946, Sharon, Conn.

Year	Team	W	L	PCT	ERA	G	GS	CG	IP	H	BB	SO	ShO	Relief Pitching W	Relief Pitching L	Relief Pitching SV	Batting AB	Batting H	Batting HR	BA	PO	A	E	DP	TC/G	FA
1970	PIT N	0	1	.000	2.81	23	0	0	32	23	13	24	0	0	1	3	3	0	0	.000	0	2	0	0	0.1	1.000
1971		0	0	—	0.00	2	0	0	4	3	1	1	0	0	0	0	1	0	0	.000	0	1	0	0	0.5	1.000
1973		0	1	.000	6.07	22	0	0	29.2	37	10	11	0	0	1	2	3	0	0	.000	3	5	0	0	0.4	1.000
3 yrs.		0	2	.000	4.11	47	0	0	65.2	63	24	36	0	0	2	5	7	0	0	.000	3	8	0	0	0.2	1.000

Ray Lamb

LAMB, RAYMOND RICHARD BR TR 6′ 1″ 170 lbs.
B. Dec. 28, 1944, Glendale, Calif.

Year	Team	W	L	PCT	ERA	G	GS	CG	IP	H	BB	SO	ShO	Relief Pitching W	Relief Pitching L	Relief Pitching SV	Batting AB	Batting H	Batting HR	BA	PO	A	E	DP	TC/G	FA
1969	LA N	0	1	.000	1.80	10	0	0	15	12	7	11	0	0	1	1	1	0	0	.000	2	3	0	0	0.5	1.000
1970		6	1	.857	3.79	35	0	0	57	59	27	32	0	6	1	0	4	0	0	.000	3	3	0	1	0.2	1.000
1971	CLE A	6	12	.333	3.36	43	21	3	158	147	69	91	1	0	2	1	43	4	0	.093	6	19	2	0	0.6	.926
1972		5	6	.455	3.08	34	9	0	108	101	29	64	0	4	1	0	21	0	0	.000	2	13	1	0	0.5	.938
1973		3	3	.500	4.60	32	1	0	86	98	42	60	0	3	2	2	0	0	0	—	5	10	1	1	0.5	.938
5 yrs.		20	23	.465	3.54	154	31	3	424	417	174	258	1	13	7	4	69	4	0	.058	18	48	4	2	0.5	.943

Clay Lambert

LAMBERT, CLAYTON PATRICK BR TR 6′ 2″ 185 lbs.
B. Mar. 26, 1917, Summit, Ill. D. Apr. 3, 1981, Ogden, Utah.

Year	Team	W	L	PCT	ERA	G	GS	CG	IP	H	BB	SO	ShO	Relief Pitching W	Relief Pitching L	Relief Pitching SV	Batting AB	Batting H	Batting HR	BA	PO	A	E	DP	TC/G	FA
1946	CIN N	2	2	.500	4.27	23	4	2	52.2	48	20	20	0	1	1	1	13	2	0	.154	1	6	0	0	0.3	1.000
1947		0	0	—	15.88	3	0	0	5.2	12	6	1	0	0	0	0	1	0	0	.000	0	2	0	0	0.7	1.000
2 yrs.		2	2	.500	5.40	26	4	2	58.1	60	26	21	0	1	1	1	14	2	0	.143	1	8	0	0	0.3	1.000

Gene Lambert

LAMBERT, EUGENE MARION BR TR 5′11″ 175 lbs.
B. Apr. 26, 1921, Crenshaw, Miss.

Year	Team	W	L	PCT	ERA	G	GS	CG	IP	H	BB	SO	ShO	Relief Pitching W	Relief Pitching L	Relief Pitching SV	Batting AB	Batting H	Batting HR	BA	PO	A	E	DP	TC/G	FA
1941	PHI N	0	1	.000	2.00	2	1	0	9	11	2	3	0	0	0	0	2	0	0	.000	0	1	0	0	0.5	1.000
1942		0	0	—	9.00	1	0	0	1	3	0	1	0	0	0	0	0	0	0	—	0	1	0	0	1.0	1.000
2 yrs.		0	1	.000	2.70	3	1	0	10	14	2	4	0	0	0	0	2	0	0	.000	0	2	0	0	0.7	1.000

Otis Lambeth

LAMBETH, OTIS SAMUEL
B. May 13, 1890, Berlin, Kans. D. June 5, 1976, Moran, Kans.
BR TR 6′ 175 lbs.

Year	Team	Lg	W	L	PCT	ERA	G	GS	CG	IP	H	BB	SO	ShO	Relief Pitching W	Relief Pitching L	Relief Pitching SV	Batting AB	Batting H	HR	BA	PO	A	E	DP	TC/G	FA
1916	CLE	A	4	3	.571	2.92	15	9	3	74	69	38	28	0	1	0	1	27	3	0	.111	2	14	3	1	1.3	.842
1917			7	6	.538	3.14	26	10	2	97.1	97	30	27	0	3	3	2	32	6	0	.188	6	23	3	1	1.2	.906
1918			0	0	—	6.43	2	0	0	7	10	6	3	0	0	0	0	1	1	0	1.000	0	2	0	0	1.0	1.000
3 yrs.			11	9	.550	3.18	43	19	5	178.1	176	74	58	0	4	3	3	60	10	0	.167	8	39	6	2	1.2	.887

Fred Lamline

LAMLINE, FREDERICK ARTHUR (Dutch)
Born Frederick Arthur Lamlein.
B. Aug. 14, 1887, Port Huron, Mich. D. Sept. 20, 1970, Port Huron, Mich.
BR TR 5′11″ 171 lbs.

Year	Team	Lg	W	L	PCT	ERA	G	GS	CG	IP	H	BB	SO	ShO	Relief Pitching W	Relief Pitching L	Relief Pitching SV	Batting AB	Batting H	HR	BA	PO	A	E	DP	TC/G	FA
1912	CHI	A	0	0	—	31.50	1	0	0	2	7	2	1	0	0	0	0	0	0	0	—	0	1	0	0	1.0	1.000
1915	STL	N	0	0	—	2.84	4	0	0	19	21	3	11	0	0	0	0	8	1	0	.125	0	5	0	0	1.3	1.000
2 yrs.			0	0		5.57	5	0	0	21	28	5	12	0	0	0	0	8	1	0	.125	0	6	0	0	1.2	1.000

Dennis Lamp

LAMP, DENNIS PATRICK
B. Sept. 23, 1952, Los Angeles, Calif.
BR TR 6′ 4″ 200 lbs.

Year	Team	Lg	W	L	PCT	ERA	G	GS	CG	IP	H	BB	SO	ShO	Relief Pitching W	Relief Pitching L	Relief Pitching SV	Batting AB	Batting H	HR	BA	PO	A	E	DP	TC/G	FA
1977	CHI	N	0	2	.000	6.30	11	3	0	30	43	8	12	0	0	1	0	8	3	0	.375	1	8	1	0	0.9	.900
1978			7	15	.318	3.29	37	36	6	224	221	56	73	3	0	0	0	73	15	0	.205	18	51	1	1	1.9	.986
1979			11	10	.524	3.51	38	32	6	200	223	46	86	1	0	0	0	58	9	0	.155	17	45	3	3	1.7	.954
1980			10	14	.417	5.19	41	37	2	203	259	82	83	1	1	2	0	61	6	0	.098	8	47	2	3	1.4	.965
1981	CHI	A	7	6	.538	2.41	27	10	3	127	103	43	71	0	3	1	0	0	0	0	—	5	23	1	4	1.1	.966
1982			11	8	.579	3.99	44	27	3	189.2	206	59	78	2	1	1	5	0	0	0	—	9	39	5	1	1.2	.906
1983			7	7	.500	3.71	49	5	1	116.1	123	29	44	0	4	5	15	0	0	0	—	9	16	0	2	0.5	1.000
1984	TOR	A	8	8	.500	4.55	56	4	0	85	97	38	45	0	5	7	9	0	0	0	—	9	15	2	3	0.5	.923
1985			11	0	1.000	3.32	53	1	0	105.2	96	27	68	0	11	0	2	0	0	0	—	11	21	0	3	0.6	1.000
1986			2	6	.250	5.05	40	2	0	73	93	23	30	0	2	4	2	0	0	0	—	5	11	1	2	0.4	.941
1987	OAK	A	1	3	.250	5.08	36	5	0	56.2	76	22	36	0	0	0	0	0	0	0	—	1	9	0	0	0.3	1.000
1988	BOS	A	7	6	.538	3.48	46	0	0	82.2	92	19	49	0	7	6	0	0	0	0	—	5	18	1	0	0.5	.958
1989			4	2	.667	2.32	42	0	0	112.1	96	27	61	0	4	2	2	0	0	0	—	12	20	0	3	0.8	1.000
1990			3	5	.375	4.68	47	1	0	105.2	114	30	49	0	3	5	0	0	0	0	—	12	14	0	0	0.6	1.000
1991			6	3	.667	4.70	51	0	0	92	100	31	57	0	6	3	0	0	0	0	—	2	12	1	2	0.3	.933
1992	PIT	N	1	1	.500	5.14	21	0	0	28	33	9	15	0	1	1	0	1	0	0	.000	4	4	0	0	0.4	1.000
16 yrs.			96	96	.500	3.93	639	163	21	1831	1975	549	857	7	48	38	35	201	33	0	.164	128	353	18	27	0.8	.964
LEAGUE CHAMPIONSHIP SERIES																											
1983	CHI	A	0	0	—	0.00	3	0	0	2	0	2	1	0	0	0	0	0	0	0	—	0	0	0	0	0.0	.000
1985	TOR	A	0	0	—	0.00	3	0	0	9.1	2	1	10	0	0	0	0	0	0	0	—	0	0	0	0	0.0	.000
1990	BOS	A	0	0	—	108.00	1	0	0	0.1	2	2	0	0	0	0	0	0	0	0	—	0	0	0	0	0.0	.000
3 yrs.			0	0		3.09	7	0	0	11.2	4	5	11	0	0	0	0	0	0	0		0	0	0	0	0.0	

Henry Lampe

LAMPE, HENRY JOSEPH
B. Sept. 19, 1872, Boston, Mass. D. Sept. 16, 1936, Dorchester, Mass.
BR TL 5′11½″ 175 lbs.

Year	Team	Lg	W	L	PCT	ERA	G	GS	CG	IP	H	BB	SO	ShO	Relief Pitching W	Relief Pitching L	Relief Pitching SV	Batting AB	Batting H	HR	BA	PO	A	E	DP	TC/G	FA
1894	BOS	N	0	1	.000	11.81	2	1	0	5.1	17	7	1	0	0	0	0	2	0	0	.000	1	2	1	0	2.0	.750
1895	PHI	N	0	2	.000	7.57	7	3	2	44	68	33	18	0	0	0	0	16	2	0	.125	1	11	4	0	2.3	.750
2 yrs.			0	3	.000	8.03	9	4	2	49.1	85	40	19	0	0	0	0	18	2	0	.111	2	13	5	0	2.2	.750

Dick Lanahan

LANAHAN, RICHARD ANTHONY
B. Sept. 27, 1911, Washington, D. C. D. Mar. 12, 1975, Rochester, Minn.
BL TL 6′ 186 lbs.

Year	Team	Lg	W	L	PCT	ERA	G	GS	CG	IP	H	BB	SO	ShO	Relief Pitching W	Relief Pitching L	Relief Pitching SV	Batting AB	Batting H	HR	BA	PO	A	E	DP	TC/G	FA
1935	WAS	A	0	3	.000	5.66	3	3	0	20.2	27	17	10	0	0	0	0	6	1	0	.167	0	4	0	0	1.3	1.000
1937			0	1	.000	12.71	6	2	0	11.1	16	13	2	0	0	0	0	1	0	0	.000	1	4	0	0	0.8	1.000
1940	PIT	N	6	8	.429	4.25	40	8	4	108	121	42	45	0	2	**6**	2	34	4	0	.118	3	22	1	3	0.6	.962
1941			0	1	.000	5.25	7	0	0	12	13	3	5	0	0	1	0	1	0	0	.000	0	2	0	0	0.3	1.000
4 yrs.			6	13	.316	5.15	56	13	4	152	177	75	62	0	2	7	2	42	5	0	.119	4	32	1	3	0.7	.973

Les Lancaster

LANCASTER, LESTER WAYNE
B. Apr. 21, 1962, Dallas, Tex.
BR TR 6′ 2″ 200 lbs.

Year	Team	Lg	W	L	PCT	ERA	G	GS	CG	IP	H	BB	SO	ShO	Relief Pitching W	Relief Pitching L	Relief Pitching SV	Batting AB	Batting H	HR	BA	PO	A	E	DP	TC/G	FA
1987	CHI	N	8	3	.727	4.90	27	18	0	132.1	138	51	78	0	1	0	0	49	4	0	.082	12	14	0	0	1.0	1.000
1988			4	6	.400	3.78	44	3	1	85.2	89	34	36	0	3	6	5	20	1	0	.050	6	17	0	0	0.5	1.000
1989			4	2	.667	1.36	42	0	0	72.2	60	15	56	0	4	2	8	11	2	0	.182	8	5	0	1	0.3	1.000
1990			9	5	.643	4.62	55	6	1	109	121	40	65	1	6	4	6	20	1	0	.050	9	19	0	1	0.5	1.000
1991			9	7	.563	3.52	64	11	1	156	150	49	102	0	4	4	3	28	5	0	.179	13	14	0	1	0.4	1.000
1992	DET	A	3	4	.429	6.33	41	1	0	86.2	101	51	35	0	3	3	0	0	0	0	—	3	9	1	4	0.3	.923
1993	STL	N	4	1	.800	2.93	50	0	0	61.1	56	21	36	0	4	1	0	4	0	0	.000	3	6	0	0	0.2	1.000
7 yrs.			41	28	.594	4.05	323	39	3	703.2	715	261	408	1	25	20	22	132	13	0	.098	54	84	1	7	0.4	.993
LEAGUE CHAMPIONSHIP SERIES																											
1989	CHI	N	1	1	.500	6.00	3	0	0	6	6	1	3	0	1	1	0	1	0	0	.000	0	1	0	0	0.3	1.000

Gary Lance

LANCE, GARY DEAN
B. Sept. 21, 1948, Greenville, S. C.
BB TR 6′ 3″ 195 lbs.

Year	Team	Lg	W	L	PCT	ERA	G	GS	CG	IP	H	BB	SO	ShO	Relief Pitching W	Relief Pitching L	Relief Pitching SV	Batting AB	Batting H	HR	BA	PO	A	E	DP	TC/G	FA
1977	KC	A	0	1	.000	4.50	1	0	0	2	2	2	0	0	0	1	0	0	0	0	—	0	0	0	0	0.0	.000

Bill Landis

LANDIS, WILLIAM HENRY
B. Oct. 8, 1942, Hanford, Calif.
BL TL 6′ 2″ 178 lbs.

Year	Team	Lg	W	L	PCT	ERA	G	GS	CG	IP	H	BB	SO	ShO	Relief Pitching W	Relief Pitching L	Relief Pitching SV	Batting AB	Batting H	HR	BA	PO	A	E	DP	TC/G	FA
1963	KC	A	0	0	—	0.00	1	0	0	1.2	0	1	3	0	0	0	0	0	0	0	—	0	0	0	0	0.0	.000
1967	BOS	A	1	0	1.000	5.26	18	1	0	25.2	24	11	23	0	1	0	0	2	0	0	.000	0	1	0	0	0.1	1.000
1968			3	3	.500	3.15	38	1	0	60	48	30	59	0	3	2	3	6	0	0	.000	2	3	0	0	0.1	1.000
1969			5	5	.500	5.25	45	5	0	82.1	82	49	50	0	4	3	1	11	0	0	.000	2	16	2	0	0.4	.900
4 yrs.			9	8	.529	4.46	102	7	0	169.2	154	91	135	0	8	5	4	19	0	0	.000	4	20	2	0	0.3	.923

Doc Landis

LANDIS, SAMUEL H.
B. Aug. 16, 1854, Philadelphia, Pa. Deceased.
BR 5′11″ 172 lbs.

Year	Team	Lg	W	L	PCT	ERA	G	GS	CG	IP	H	BB	SO	ShO	Relief Pitching W	Relief Pitching L	Relief Pitching SV	Batting AB	Batting H	HR	BA	PO	A	E	DP	TC/G	FA
1882	2 teams	PHI AA (2G 1–1) BAL AA (42G 11–27)																									
″	total		12	**28**	.300	3.32	44	41	37	358	**425**	47	75	0	0	0	0	187	31	0	.166	41	107	18	3	2.8	.892

Year	Team	Lg	W	L	PCT	ERA	G	GS	CG	IP	H	BB	SO	ShO	Relief Pitching W	Relief Pitching L	Relief Pitching SV	Batting AB	Batting H	Batting HR	BA	PO	A	E	DP	TC/G	FA

Larry Landreth

LANDRETH, LARRY ROBERT BR TR 6′ 1″ 175 lbs.
B. Mar. 11, 1955, Stratford, Ont., Canada.

Year	Team	Lg	W	L	PCT	ERA	G	GS	CG	IP	H	BB	SO	ShO	W	L	SV	AB	H	HR	BA	PO	A	E	DP	TC/G	FA
1976	MON	N	1	2	.333	4.09	3	3	0	11	13	10	7	0	0	0	0	3	0	0	.000	0	1	0	0	0.3	1.000
1977			0	2	.000	10.00	4	1	0	9	16	8	5	0	0	1	0	2	0	0	.000	0	0	0	0	0.0	.000
2 yrs.			1	4	.200	6.75	7	4	0	20	29	18	12	0	0	1	0	5	0	0	.000	0	1	0	0	0.1	1.000

Bill Landrum

LANDRUM, THOMAS WILLIAM BR TR 6′ 2″ 185 lbs.
Son of Joe Landrum.
B. Aug. 17, 1957, Columbia, S. C.

Year	Team	Lg	W	L	PCT	ERA	G	GS	CG	IP	H	BB	SO	ShO	W	L	SV	AB	H	HR	BA	PO	A	E	DP	TC/G	FA
1986	CIN	N	0	0	—	6.75	10	0	0	13.1	23	4	14	0	0	0	0	2	0	0	.000	0	1	0	0	0.1	1.000
1987			3	2	.600	4.71	44	2	0	65	68	34	42	0	3	1	2	5	1	0	.200	3	12	0	4	0.3	1.000
1988	CHI	N	1	0	1.000	5.84	7	0	0	12.1	19	3	6	0	1	0	0	2	0	0	.000	2	0	0	0	0.3	1.000
1989	PIT	N	2	3	.400	1.67	56	0	0	81	60	28	51	0	2	3	26	3	0	0	.000	8	10	0	0	0.3	1.000
1990			7	3	.700	2.13	54	0	0	71.2	69	21	39	0	7	3	13	9	1	0	.111	11	6	0	0	0.3	1.000
1991			4	4	.500	3.18	61	0	0	76.1	76	19	45	0	4	4	17	4	0	0	.000	4	8	0	0	0.2	1.000
1992	MON	N	1	1	.500	7.20	18	0	0	20	27	9	7	0	1	1	0	0	0	0	—	2	2	0	0	0.2	1.000
1993	CIN	N	0	2	.000	3.74	18	0	0	21.2	18	6	14	0	0	2	0	0	0	0	—	1	6	0	0	0.4	1.000
8 yrs.			18	15	.545	3.39	268	2	0	361.1	360	124	218	0	18	14	58	25	2	0	.080	31	45	0	4	0.3	1.000
LEAGUE CHAMPIONSHIP SERIES																											
1990	PIT	N	0	0	—	0.00	2	0	0	2	0	0	1	0	0	0	0	0	0	0	—	0	0	0	0	0.0	.000
1991			0	0	—	9.00	1	0	0	1	2	2	2	0	0	0	0	0	0	0	—	0	0	0	0	0.0	.000
2 yrs.			0	0		3.00	3	0	0	3	2	2	3	0	0	0	0	0	0	0		0	0	0	0	0.0	

Joe Landrum

LANDRUM, JOSEPH BUTLER BR TR 5′11″ 180 lbs.
Father of Bill Landrum.
B. Dec. 13, 1928, Columbia, S. C.

Year	Team	Lg	W	L	PCT	ERA	G	GS	CG	IP	H	BB	SO	ShO	W	L	SV	AB	H	HR	BA	PO	A	E	DP	TC/G	FA
1950	BKN	N	0	0	—	8.10	7	0	0	6.2	12	1	5	0	0	0	1	0	0	0	—	1	3	0	0	0.6	1.000
1952			1	3	.250	5.21	9	5	2	38	46	10	17	0	0	0	0	8	1	0	.125	4	5	1	0	1.1	.900
2 yrs.			1	3	.250	5.64	16	5	2	44.2	58	11	22	0	0	0	1	8	1	0	.125	5	8	1	0	0.9	.929

Jerry Lane

LANE, JERALD HAL BR TR 6′½″ 205 lbs.
B. Feb. 7, 1926, Ashland, N. Y. D. July 24, 1988, Chattanooga, Tenn.

Year	Team	Lg	W	L	PCT	ERA	G	GS	CG	IP	H	BB	SO	ShO	W	L	SV	AB	H	HR	BA	PO	A	E	DP	TC/G	FA
1953	WAS	A	1	4	.200	4.92	20	2	0	56.2	64	16	26	0	1	2	0	9	1	0	.111	1	8	0	0	0.4	1.000
1954	CIN	N	1	0	1.000	1.69	3	0	0	10.2	9	3	2	0	1	0	0	4	0	0	.000	0	0	0	0	0.0	.000
1955			0	2	.000	4.91	8	0	0	11	11	6	5	0	0	2	1	0	0	0	—	1	3	0	0	0.5	1.000
3 yrs.			2	6	.250	4.48	31	2	0	78.1	84	25	33	0	2	4	1	13	1	0	.077	2	11	0	0	0.4	1.000

Sam Lanford

LANFORD, LEWIS GROVER BL TR 5′ 9″ 155 lbs.
B. Jan. 8, 1886, Woodruff, S. C. D. Sept. 14, 1970, Woodruff, S. C.

Year	Team	Lg	W	L	PCT	ERA	G	GS	CG	IP	H	BB	SO	ShO	W	L	SV	AB	H	HR	BA	PO	A	E	DP	TC/G	FA
1907	WAS	A	0	1	.000	5.14	2	1	0	7	10	5	2	0	0	0	0	3	1	0	.333	0	2	1	0	1.5	.667

Walt Lanfranconi

LANFRANCONI, WALTER OSWALD BR TR 5′ 7½″ 155 lbs.
B. Nov. 9, 1916, Barre, Vt. D. Aug. 18, 1986, Barre, Vt.

Year	Team	Lg	W	L	PCT	ERA	G	GS	CG	IP	H	BB	SO	ShO	W	L	SV	AB	H	HR	BA	PO	A	E	DP	TC/G	FA
1941	CHI	N	0	1	.000	3.00	2	1	0	6	7	2	1	0	0	0	0	1	0	0	.000	0	1	0	0	0.5	1.000
1947	BOS	N	4	4	.500	2.95	36	4	1	64	65	27	18	0	3	1	1	10	0	0	.000	1	20	0	0	0.6	1.000
2 yrs.			4	5	.444	2.96	38	5	1	70	72	29	19	0	3	1	1	11	0	0	.000	1	21	0	0	0.6	1.000

Chip Lang

LANG, ROBERT DAVID BR TR 6′ 4″ 210 lbs.
B. Aug. 21, 1952, Pittsburgh, Pa.

Year	Team	Lg	W	L	PCT	ERA	G	GS	CG	IP	H	BB	SO	ShO	W	L	SV	AB	H	HR	BA	PO	A	E	DP	TC/G	FA
1975	MON	N	0	0	—	9.00	1	1	0	2	2	3	2	0	0	0	0	0	0	0	—	0	0	0	0	0.0	.000
1976			1	3	.250	4.19	29	2	0	62.1	56	34	30	0	1	1	0	6	1	0	.167	6	10	1	1	0.6	.941
2 yrs.			1	3	.250	4.34	30	3	0	64.1	58	37	32	0	1	1	0	6	1	0	.167	6	10	1	1	0.6	.941

Marty Lang

LANG, MARTIN JOHN (Lefty) BR TL 5′11″ 160 lbs.
B. Sept. 27, 1905, Hooper, Neb. D. Jan. 13, 1968, Lakewood, Colo.

Year	Team	Lg	W	L	PCT	ERA	G	GS	CG	IP	H	BB	SO	ShO	W	L	SV	AB	H	HR	BA	PO	A	E	DP	TC/G	FA
1930	PIT	N	0	0	—	54.00	2	0	0	1.2	9	3	2	0	0	0	0	0	0	0	—	0	0	0	0	0.0	.000

Dick Lange

LANGE, RICHARD OTTO BR TR 5′10″ 185 lbs.
B. Sept. 1, 1948, Harbor Beach, Mich.

Year	Team	Lg	W	L	PCT	ERA	G	GS	CG	IP	H	BB	SO	ShO	W	L	SV	AB	H	HR	BA	PO	A	E	DP	TC/G	FA
1972	CAL	A	0	0	—	4.50	2	1	0	8	7	2	8	0	0	0	0	3	0	0	.000	0	2	0	0	1.0	1.000
1973			2	1	.667	4.44	17	4	1	52.2	61	21	27	0	1	0	0	0	0	0	—	3	7	0	2	0.6	1.000
1974			3	8	.273	3.79	21	18	1	114	111	47	57	0	0	0	0	0	0	0	—	5	11	1	1	0.8	.941
1975			4	6	.400	5.21	30	8	1	102	119	53	45	0	2	2	1	0	0	0	—	6	13	0	2	0.6	1.000
4 yrs.			9	15	.375	4.46	70	31	3	276.2	298	123	137	0	3	2	1	3	0	0	.000	14	33	1	5	0.7	.979

Erv Lange

LANGE, ERWIN HENRY BR TR 5′10″ 170 lbs.
B. Aug. 12, 1887, Forest Park, Ill. D. Apr. 24, 1971, Maywood, Ill.

Year	Team	Lg	W	L	PCT	ERA	G	GS	CG	IP	H	BB	SO	ShO	W	L	SV	AB	H	HR	BA	PO	A	E	DP	TC/G	FA
1914	CHI	F	12	10	.545	2.23	36	22	10	190	162	55	87	2	3	1	2	51	9	0	.176	4	43	5	3	1.4	.904

Frank Lange

LANGE, FRANK HERMAN (Seagan) BR TR 5′11″ 180 lbs.
B. Oct. 28, 1883, Columbus, Wis. D. Dec. 26, 1945, Madison, Wis.

Year	Team	Lg	W	L	PCT	ERA	G	GS	CG	IP	H	BB	SO	ShO	W	L	SV	AB	H	HR	BA	PO	A	E	DP	TC/G	FA
1910	CHI	A	9	4	.692	1.65	23	15	6	130.2	93	54	98	1	1	0	0	51	13	0	.255	5	29	5	1	1.7	.872
1911			8	8	.500	3.23	29	22	8	161.2	151	77	104	1	0	1	0	76	22	0	.289	7	41	9	2	2.0	.842
1912			10	10	.500	3.27	31	21	11	165.1	165	68	96	2	3	1	3	65	14	0	.215	6	42	5	1	1.7	.906
1913			1	3	.250	4.87	12	3	0	40.2	46	20	20	0	0	1	0	18	3	0	.167	1	17	0	3	1.5	1.000
4 yrs.			28	25	.528	2.96	95	61	25	498.1	455	219	318	4	4	3	3	*				19	129	19	7	1.8	.886

Rick Langford

LANGFORD, JAMES RICK BR TR 6′ 180 lbs.
B. Mar. 20, 1952, Farmville, Va.

Year	Team	Lg	W	L	PCT	ERA	G	GS	CG	IP	H	BB	SO	ShO	W	L	SV	AB	H	HR	BA	PO	A	E	DP	TC/G	FA
1976	PIT	N	0	1	.000	6.26	12	1	0	23	27	14	17	0	0	1	0	5	1	0	.200	2	4	0	1	0.5	1.000
1977	OAK	A	8	**19**	.296	4.02	37	31	6	208	223	73	141	1	1	0	0	0	0	0	—	23	29	0	3	1.4	1.000
1978			7	13	.350	3.43	37	24	4	175.2	169	56	92	2	1	1	0	0	0	0	—	27	23	0	2	1.4	1.000
1979			12	16	.429	4.27	34	29	14	219	233	57	101	1	1	0	0	0	0	0	—	26	36	0	3	1.8	1.000
1980			19	12	.613	3.26	35	33	**28**	**290**	276	64	102	2	1	0	0	0	0	0	—	28	45	1	1	2.1	.986

Rick Langford *continued*

Year	Team	W	L	PCT	ERA	G	GS	CG	IP	H	BB	SO	ShO	Relief Pitching W	L	SV	Batting AB	H	HR	BA	PO	A	E	DP	TC/G	FA
1981		12	10	.545	3.00	24	24	**18**	195	190	58	84	2	0	0	0	0	0	0	—	17	23	3	3	1.7	.930
1982		11	16	.407	4.21	32	31	15	237.1	265	49	79	2	0	0	0	1	0	0	.000	16	39	2	3	1.7	.965
1983		0	4	.000	12.15	7	7	0	20	43	10	2	0	0	0	0	0	0	0	—	1	2	0	0	0.4	1.000
1984		0	0	—	8.31	3	1	0	8.2	15	2	2	0	0	0	0	0	0	0	—	0	0	0	0	0.0	.000
1985		3	5	.375	3.51	23	3	0	59	60	15	21	0	3	3	0	0	0	0	—	2	9	0	1	0.5	1.000
1986		1	10	.091	7.36	16	11	0	55	69	18	30	0	0	2	0	0	0	0	—	5	1	0	0	0.4	1.000
11 yrs.		73	106	.408	4.01	260	195	85	1490.2	1570	416	671	10	7	7	0	6	1	0	.167	147	211	6	17	1.4	.984
DIVISIONAL PLAYOFF SERIES																										
1981	OAK A	1	0	1.000	1.23	1	1	0	7.1	10	0	3	0	0	0	0	0	0	0	—	0	0	0	0	0.0	.000

Mark Langston

LANGSTON, MARK EDWARD
B. Aug. 20, 1960, San Diego, Calif.

BR TL 6′ 2″ 175 lbs.

Year	Team	W	L	PCT	ERA	G	GS	CG	IP	H	BB	SO	ShO	Relief Pitching W	L	SV	Batting AB	H	HR	BA	PO	A	E	DP	TC/G	FA
1984	SEA A	17	10	.630	3.40	35	33	5	225	188	**118**	**204**	2	1	0	0	0	0	0	—	15	30	2	2	1.3	.957
1985		7	14	.333	5.47	24	24	2	126.2	122	91	72	0	0	0	0	0	0	0	—	9	26	2	4	1.5	.946
1986		12	14	.462	4.85	37	36	9	239.1	234	123	**245**	0	0	0	0	0	0	0	—	7	27	6	3	1.1	.850
1987		19	13	.594	3.84	35	35	14	272	242	114	**262**	3	0	0	0	0	0	0	—	8	41	2	3	1.5	.961
1988		15	11	.577	3.34	35	35	9	261.1	222	110	235	3	0	0	0	0	0	0	—	11	45	4	6	1.7	.933
1989	2 teams SEA A (10G 4–5) MON N (24G 12–9)																									
″	total	16	14	.533	2.74	34	34	8	250	198	112	235	5	0	0	0	64	11	0	.172	15	28	2	2	1.3	.956
1990	CAL A	10	17	.370	4.40	33	33	5	223	215	104	195	1	0	0	0	0	0	0	—	7	42	3	0	1.6	.942
1991		19	8	.704	3.00	34	34	7	246.1	190	96	183	0	0	0	0	0	0	0	—	15	34	3	2	1.5	.942
1992		13	14	.481	3.66	32	32	9	229	206	74	174	2	0	0	0	2	0	0	.000	7	41	3	1	1.5	.941
1993		16	11	.593	3.20	35	35	7	256.1	220	85	196	0	0	0	0	0	0	0	—	10	47	2	4	1.7	.966
1994		7	8	.467	4.68	18	18	2	119.1	121	54	109	1	0	0	0	0	0	0	—	3	27	2	1	1.8	.938
1995		15	7	.682	4.63	31	31	2	200.1	212	64	142	1	0	0	0	0	0	0	—	2	43	3	2	1.5	.938
12 yrs.		166	141	.541	3.81	383	380	79	2648.2	2370	1145	2252	18	1	0	0	66	11	0	.167	109	431	34	30	1.5	.941

Max Lanier

LANIER, HUBERT MAX
Father of Hal Lanier.
B. Aug. 18, 1915, Denton, N. C.

BR TL 5′11″ 180 lbs.

Year	Team	W	L	PCT	ERA	G	GS	CG	IP	H	BB	SO	ShO	Relief Pitching W	L	SV	Batting AB	H	HR	BA	PO	A	E	DP	TC/G	FA
1938	STL N	0	3	.000	4.20	18	3	1	45	57	28	14	0	0	2	0	10	1	0	.100	3	9	2	1	0.8	.857
1939		2	1	.667	2.39	7	6	2	37.2	29	13	14	0	0	0	0	14	4	0	.286	1	6	0	0	1.0	1.000
1940		9	6	.600	3.34	35	11	4	105	113	38	49	2	5	3	3	30	6	0	.200	5	26	3	1	1.0	.912
1941		10	8	.556	2.82	35	18	8	153	126	59	93	2	2	3	3	52	10	0	.192	10	37	0	2	1.3	1.000
1942		13	8	.619	2.98	34	20	8	160	137	60	93	2	5	0	2	47	12	0	.255	5	38	2	1	1.3	.956
1943		15	7	.682	1.90	32	25	14	213.1	195	75	123	2	2	0	3	73	12	0	.164	8	43	1	2	1.6	.981
1944		17	12	.586	2.65	33	30	16	224.1	192	71	141	5	3	0	0	77	14	0	.182	8	39	3	3	1.5	.940
1945		2	2	.500	1.73	4	3	3	26	22	8	16	0	0	1	0	11	2	0	.182	0	4	0	0	1.0	1.000
1946		6	0	1.000	1.93	6	6	6	56	45	19	36	2	0	0	0	25	5	0	.200	1	10	0	1	1.8	1.000
1949		5	4	.556	3.82	15	15	4	92	92	35	37	1	0	0	0	27	2	0	.074	2	12	0	2	0.9	1.000
1950		11	9	.550	3.13	27	27	10	181.1	173	68	89	2	0	0	0	68	11	0	.162	12	31	1	2	1.6	.977
1951		11	9	.550	3.26	31	23	9	160	149	50	59	2	1	0	1	53	8	0	.151	9	28	2	5	1.3	.949
1952	NY N	7	12	.368	3.94	37	16	6	137	124	65	47	1	2	3	5	41	11	0	.268	13	37	3	4	1.4	.943
1953	2 teams NY N (3G 0–0) STL A (10G 0–1)																									
″	total	0	1	.000	7.16	13	1	0	27.2	36	22	10	0	0	0	0	7	1	0	.143	1	4	0	1	0.4	1.000
14 yrs.		108	82	.568	3.01	327	204	91	1618.1	1490	611	821	21	20	12	17	535	99	0	.185	78	324	17	25	1.3	.959
WORLD SERIES																										
1942	STL N	1	0	1.000	0.00	2	0	0	4	3	1	1	0	1	0	0	1	1	0	1.000	0	1	2	0	1.5	.333
1943		0	1	.000	1.76	3	2	0	15.1	13	3	13	0	0	0	0	4	1	0	.250	0	3	1	0	1.3	.750
1944		1	0	1.000	2.19	2	2	0	12.1	8	8	11	0	0	0	0	4	2	0	.500	1	1	0	1	1.0	1.000
3 yrs.		2	1	.667	1.71	7	4	0	31.2	24	12	25	0	1	0	0	9	4	0	.444	1	5	3	1	1.3	.667

Johnny Lanning

LANNING, JOHN YOUNG (Tobacco Chewin' Johnny)
Brother of Tom Lanning.
B. Sept. 6, 1910, Asheville, N. C. D. Nov. 8, 1989, Asheville, N. C.

BR TR 6′ 1″ 185 lbs.

Year	Team	W	L	PCT	ERA	G	GS	CG	IP	H	BB	SO	ShO	Relief Pitching W	L	SV	Batting AB	H	HR	BA	PO	A	E	DP	TC/G	FA
1936	BOS N	7	11	.389	3.65	28	20	3	153	154	55	33	1	1	0	0	52	7	1	.135	8	28	3	1	1.4	.923
1937		5	7	.417	3.93	32	11	4	116.2	107	40	37	1	2	0	2	33	4	0	.121	7	23	0	3	0.9	1.000
1938		8	7	.533	3.72	32	18	4	138	146	52	39	1	3	1	0	48	9	0	.188	7	24	3	3	1.1	.912
1939		5	6	.455	3.42	37	6	3	129	120	53	45	0	3	2	4	42	6	0	.143	12	25	3	0	1.1	.925
1940	PIT N	8	4	.667	4.05	38	7	2	115.2	119	39	42	0	5	2	2	35	7	0	.200	8	22	3	2	0.9	.909
1941		11	11	.500	3.13	34	23	9	175.2	175	47	41	0	2	1	1	56	6	0	.107	12	41	0	2	1.6	1.000
1942		6	8	.429	3.32	34	8	2	119.1	125	26	31	1	4	2	1	29	4	0	.138	13	20	1	4	1.0	.971
1943		4	1	.800	2.33	12	2	0	27	23	9	11	0	4	0	2	6	1	0	.167	1	3	2	0	0.5	.667
1945		0	0	—	36.00	1	0	0	2	8	0	0	0	0	0	0	0	0	0	—	0	1	0	0	1.0	1.000
1946		4	5	.444	3.07	27	9	3	91	97	31	16	0	2	2	1	21	3	0	.143	5	22	0	1	1.0	1.000
1947	BOS N	0	0	—	9.82	3	0	0	3.2	4	6	0	0	0	0	0	0	0	0	—	0	3	0	0	1.0	1.000
11 yrs.		58	60	.492	3.58	278	104	30	1071	1078	358	295	4	26	10	13	322	47	1	.146	73	212	15	16	1.1	.950

Les Lanning

LANNING, LESTER ALFRED (Red)
B. May 13, 1895, Harvard, Ill. D. June 13, 1962, Bristol, Conn.

BL TL 5′ 9″ 165 lbs.

Year	Team	W	L	PCT	ERA	G	GS	CG	IP	H	BB	SO	ShO	Relief Pitching W	L	SV	Batting AB	H	HR	BA	PO	A	E	DP	TC/G	FA
1916	PHI A	0	3	.000	8.14	6	3	1	24.1	38	17	9	0	0	0	0	*				10	8	1	0	1.3	.947

Tom Lanning

LANNING, THOMAS NEWTON
Brother of Johnny Lanning.
B. Apr. 22, 1907, Biltmore, N. C. D. Nov. 4, 1967, Marietta, Ga.

BL TL 6′ 1″ 165 lbs.

Year	Team	W	L	PCT	ERA	G	GS	CG	IP	H	BB	SO	ShO	Relief Pitching W	L	SV	Batting AB	H	HR	BA	PO	A	E	DP	TC/G	FA
1938	PHI N	0	1	.000	6.43	3	1	0	7	9	2	2	0	0	0	0	1	1	0	1.000	1	0	0	0	0.3	1.000

Gene Lansing

LANSING, EUGENE HEWITT (Jigger)
B. Jan. 11, 1898, Albany, N. Y. D. Jan. 18, 1945, Rensselaer, N. Y.

BR TR 6′ 1″ 185 lbs.

Year	Team	W	L	PCT	ERA	G	GS	CG	IP	H	BB	SO	ShO	Relief Pitching W	L	SV	Batting AB	H	HR	BA	PO	A	E	DP	TC/G	FA
1922	BOS N	0	1	.000	5.98	15	1	0	40.2	46	22	14	0	0	1	0	11	0	0	.000	1	8	1	0	0.7	.900

Paul LaPalme

LaPALME, PAUL EDMORE (Lefty) BL TL 5'10" 175 lbs.
B. Dec. 14, 1923, Springfield, Mass.

Year	Team	W	L	PCT	ERA	G	GS	CG	IP	H	BB	SO	ShO	Relief Pitching W	Relief Pitching L	Relief Pitching SV	Batting AB	Batting H	Batting HR	BA	PO	A	E	DP	TC/G	FA
1951	PIT N	1	5	.167	6.29	22	8	1	54.1	79	31	24	1	0	2	0	10	1	0	.100	4	6	0	0	0.5	1.000
1952		1	2	.333	3.92	31	2	0	59.2	56	37	25	0	1	2	0	10	1	0	.100	1	15	1	1	0.5	.941
1953		8	16	.333	4.59	35	24	7	176.1	191	64	86	1	1	1	2	59	5	0	.085	5	23	4	1	0.9	.875
1954		4	10	.286	5.52	33	15	2	120.2	147	54	57	0	1	1	0	35	5	0	.143	7	19	0	1	0.8	1.000
1955	STL N	4	3	.571	2.75	56	0	0	91.2	76	34	39	0	4	3	3	19	4	0	.211	7	19	1	1	0.5	.963
1956	3 teams STL N (1G 0–0) CIN N (11G 2–4) CHI A (29G 3–1)																									
"	total	5	5	.500	3.93	41	2	0	73.1	61	33	27	0	4	4	2	10	2	0	.200	1	16	0	2	0.4	1.000
1957	CHI A	1	4	.200	3.35	35	0	0	40.1	35	19	19	0	1	4	7	4	2	0	.500	4	10	1	2	0.4	.933
7 yrs.		24	45	.348	4.42	253	51	10	616.1	645	272	277	2	12	17	14	147	20	0	.136	29	108	7	8	0.6	.951

Andy Lapihuska

LAPIHUSKA, ANDREW (Apples) BL TR 5'10½" 175 lbs.
B. Nov. 1, 1922, Delmont, N. J.

Year	Team	W	L	PCT	ERA	G	GS	CG	IP	H	BB	SO	ShO	Relief Pitching W	Relief Pitching L	Relief Pitching SV	Batting AB	Batting H	Batting HR	BA	PO	A	E	DP	TC/G	FA
1942	PHI N	0	2	.000	5.23	3	2	0	20.2	17	13	8	0	0	0	0	7	2	0	.286	1	5	0	0	2.0	1.000
1943		0	0	—	23.14	1	0	0	2.1	5	3	0	0	0	0	0	2	0	0	.000	0	0	0	0	0.0	.000
2 yrs.		0	2	.000	7.04	4	2	0	23	22	16	8	0	0	0	0	9	2	0	.222	1	5	0	0	1.5	1.000

Dave LaPoint

LaPOINT, DAVID JEFFREY BL TL 6'3" 205 lbs.
B. July 29, 1959, Glens Falls, N. Y.

Year	Team	W	L	PCT	ERA	G	GS	CG	IP	H	BB	SO	ShO	Relief Pitching W	Relief Pitching L	Relief Pitching SV	Batting AB	Batting H	Batting HR	BA	PO	A	E	DP	TC/G	FA
1980	MIL A	1	0	1.000	6.00	5	3	0	15	17	13	5	0	1	0	1	0	0	0	—	0	0	0	0	0.0	.000
1981	STL N	1	0	1.000	4.09	3	2	0	11	12	2	4	0	0	0	0	5	0	0	.000	1	2	0	0	1.0	1.000
1982		9	3	.750	3.42	42	21	0	152.2	170	52	81	0	1	0	0	38	2	0	.053	2	13	1	0	0.4	.938
1983		12	9	.571	3.95	37	29	1	191.1	191	84	113	0	2	1	0	59	9	0	.153	11	24	0	1	0.9	1.000
1984		12	10	.545	3.96	33	33	2	193	205	77	130	1	0	0	0	59	4	0	.068	2	23	1	4	0.8	.962
1985	SF N	7	17	.292	3.57	31	31	2	206.2	215	74	122	1	0	0	0	60	10	0	.167	8	23	1	1	1.0	.969
1986	2 teams DET A (16G 3–6) SD N (24G 1–4)																									
"	total	4	10	.286	5.02	40	12	0	129	152	56	77	0	0	3	0	8	0	0	.000	5	16	1	2	0.6	.955
1987	2 teams STL N (6G 1–1) CHI A (14G 6–3)																									
"	total	7	4	.636	3.56	20	14	2	98.2	95	36	51	1	1	1	0	4	0	0	.000	2	26	1	0	1.5	.966
1988	2 teams CHI A (25G 10–11) PIT N (8G 4–2)																									
"	total	14	13	.519	3.25	33	33	2	213.1	205	57	98	1	0	0	0	16	1	0	.063	7	24	1	1	1.0	.969
1989	NY A	6	9	.400	5.62	20	20	0	113.2	146	45	51	0	0	0	0	0	0	0	—	2	10	0	1	0.6	1.000
1990		7	10	.412	4.11	28	27	2	157.2	180	57	67	0	0	0	0	0	0	0	—	6	23	2	3	1.1	.935
1991	PHI N	0	1	.000	16.20	2	2	0	5	10	6	3	0	0	0	0	2	0	0	.000	0	2	1	0	1.5	.667
12 yrs.		80	86	.482	4.02	294	227	11	1487	1598	559	802	4	5	5	1	251	26	0	.104	46	186	9	13	0.8	.963
WORLD SERIES																										
1982	STL N	0	0	—	3.24	2	1	0	8.1	10	2	3	0	0	0	0	0	0	0	—	0	2	1	0	1.5	.667

Pat Larkin

LARKIN, PATRICK CLIBORN BL TL 6' 180 lbs.
B. June 14, 1960, Arcadia, Calif.

Year	Team	W	L	PCT	ERA	G	GS	CG	IP	H	BB	SO	ShO	Relief Pitching W	Relief Pitching L	Relief Pitching SV	Batting AB	Batting H	Batting HR	BA	PO	A	E	DP	TC/G	FA
1983	SF N	0	0	—	4.35	5	0	0	10.1	13	3	6	0	0	0	0	1	0	0	.000	0	2	1	0	0.6	.667

Steve Larkin

LARKIN, STEPHEN PATRICK BR TR 6'1" 195 lbs.
B. Dec. 9, 1910, Cincinnati, Ohio D. May 2, 1969, Norristown, Pa.

Year	Team	W	L	PCT	ERA	G	GS	CG	IP	H	BB	SO	ShO	Relief Pitching W	Relief Pitching L	Relief Pitching SV	Batting AB	Batting H	Batting HR	BA	PO	A	E	DP	TC/G	FA
1934	DET A	0	0	—	1.50	2	1	0	6	8	5	8	0	0	0	0	3	1	0	.333	1	2	1	0	2.0	.750

Terry Larkin

LARKIN, FRANK S. BR TR
B. 1856, Brooklyn, N. Y. D. Sept. 16, 1894, Brooklyn, N. Y.

Year	Team	W	L	PCT	ERA	G	GS	CG	IP	H	BB	SO	ShO	Relief Pitching W	Relief Pitching L	Relief Pitching SV	Batting AB	Batting H	Batting HR	BA	PO	A	E	DP	TC/G	FA
1876	NY N	0	1	.000	3.00	1	1	1	9	9	0	0	0	0	0	0	4	0	0	.000	0	2	2	0	4.0	.500
1877	HAR N	29	**25**	.537	2.14	56	56	55	501	510	**53**	96	4	0	0	0	228	52	1	.228	31	99	20	1	2.5	.867
1878	CHI N	29	26	.527	2.24	56	56	56	506	511	31	163	1	0	0	0	226	65	0	.288	20	95	21	0	2.3	.846
1879		31	23	.574	2.44	58	58	57	513.1	514	30	142	4	0	0	0	228	50	0	.219	10	80	9	1	1.6	.909
1880	TRO N	0	5	.000	8.76	5	5	3	38	83	10	5	0	0	0	0	20	3	0	.150	5	11	1	2	2.1	.941
5 yrs.		89	80	.527	2.43	176	176	172	1567.1	1627	124	406	9	0	0	0	*				189	432	93	20	2.9	.870

Dave LaRoche

LaROCHE, DAVID EUGENE BL TL 6'2" 200 lbs.
B. May 14, 1948, Colorado Springs, Colo.

Year	Team	W	L	PCT	ERA	G	GS	CG	IP	H	BB	SO	ShO	Relief Pitching W	Relief Pitching L	Relief Pitching SV	Batting AB	Batting H	Batting HR	BA	PO	A	E	DP	TC/G	FA
1970	CAL A	4	1	.800	3.42	38	0	0	50	41	21	44	0	4	1	4	8	2	0	.250	5	7	0	1	0.3	1.000
1971		5	1	.833	2.50	56	0	0	72	55	27	63	0	5	1	9	11	1	0	.091	0	8	1	0	0.2	.889
1972	MIN A	5	7	.417	2.84	62	0	0	95	72	39	79	0	5	7	10	11	1	0	.091	2	15	0	0	0.3	1.000
1973	CHI N	4	1	.800	5.83	45	0	0	54	55	29	34	0	4	1	4	4	2	0	.500	5	13	3	1	0.5	.857
1974		5	6	.455	4.79	49	4	0	92	103	47	49	0	4	5	5	27	9	0	.333	3	14	0	0	0.3	1.000
1975	CLE A	5	3	.625	2.19	61	0	0	82.1	61	57	94	0	5	3	17	0	0	0	—	7	13	0	0	0.3	1.000
1976		1	4	.200	2.25	61	0	0	96	57	49	104	0	1	4	21	0	0	0	—	3	9	3	0	0.2	.800
1977	2 teams CLE A (13G 2–2) CAL A (46G 6–5)																									
"	total	8	7	.533	3.51	59	0	0	100	79	44	79	0	8	7	17	0	0	0	—	6	10	0	3	0.3	1.000
1978	CAL A	10	9	.526	2.81	59	0	0	96	73	48	70	0	10	9	25	0	0	0	—	2	14	0	0	0.3	1.000
1979		7	11	.389	5.55	53	1	0	86	107	32	59	0	6	11	10	0	0	0	—	4	17	0	0	0.4	1.000
1980		3	5	.375	4.08	52	9	1	128	122	39	89	0	2	0	4	0	0	0	—	5	16	1	0	0.4	.955
1981	NY A	4	1	.800	2.49	26	1	0	47	38	16	24	0	4	1	0	0	0	0	—	5	4	0	0	0.3	1.000
1982		4	2	.667	3.42	25	0	0	50	54	11	31	0	4	2	0	0	0	0	—	1	3	0	0	0.2	1.000
1983		0	0	—	18.00	1	0	0	1	2	0	0	0	0	0	0	0	0	0	—	0	1	0	0	1.0	1.000
14 yrs.		65	58	.528	3.53	647	15	1	1049.1	919	459	819	0	62	52	126	61	15	0	.246	48	144	8	5	0.3	.960
LEAGUE CHAMPIONSHIP SERIES																										
1979	CAL A	0	0	—	6.75	1	0	0	1.1	2	1	1	0	0	0	0	0	0	0	—	0	0	0	0	0.0	.000
WORLD SERIES																										
1981	NY A	0	0	—	0.00	1	0	0	1	0	0	2	0	0	0	0	0	0	0	—	0	0	0	0	0.0	.000

John LaRose

LaROSE, HENRY JOHN BL TL 6'1" 185 lbs.
B. Oct. 25, 1951, Pawtucket, R. I.

Year	Team	W	L	PCT	ERA	G	GS	CG	IP	H	BB	SO	ShO	Relief Pitching W	Relief Pitching L	Relief Pitching SV	Batting AB	Batting H	Batting HR	BA	PO	A	E	DP	TC/G	FA
1978	BOS A	0	0	—	22.50	1	0	0	2	3	3	0	0	0	0	0	0	0	0	—	0	1	0	0	1.0	1.000

Don Larsen

LARSEN, DON JAMES
B. Aug. 7, 1929, Michigan City, Ind.
BR TR 6′ 4″ 215 lbs.

Year	Team	W	L	PCT	ERA	G	GS	CG	IP	H	BB	SO	ShO	Relief Pitching W	Relief Pitching L	Relief Pitching SV	Batting AB	Batting H	Batting HR	BA	PO	A	E	DP	TC/G	FA
1953	STL A	7	12	.368	4.16	38	22	7	192.2	201	64	96	2	1	2	2	81	23	3	.284	8	29	2	1	1.0	.949
1954	BAL A	3	**21**	.125	4.37	29	28	12	201.2	213	89	80	1	0	1	0	88	22	1	.250	14	34	1	3	1.7	.980
1955	NY A	9	2	.818	3.06	19	13	5	97	81	51	44	1	1	1	2	41	6	2	.146	5	13	1	3	1.0	.947
1956		11	5	.688	3.26	38	20	6	179.2	133	96	107	1	2	1	1	79	19	2	.241	13	23	3	3	1.0	.923
1957		10	4	.714	3.74	27	20	4	139.2	113	87	81	1	2	0	0	56	14	0	.250	10	20	2	2	1.2	.938
1958		9	6	.600	3.07	19	19	5	114.1	100	52	55	3	0	0	0	49	15	4	.306	5	14	2	2	1.1	.905
1959		6	7	.462	4.33	25	18	3	124.2	122	76	69	1	0	0	0	47	12	0	.255	5	22	2	1	1.2	.931
1960	KC A	1	10	.091	5.38	22	15	0	83.2	97	42	43	0	0	1	0	29	6	0	.207	4	8	1	1	0.6	.923
1961	2 teams KC A (8G 1–0) CHI A (25G 7–2)																									
″	total	8	2	.800	4.13	33	4	0	89.1	85	40	66	0	6	1	2	45	14	2	.311	8	17	0	0	0.7	1.000
1962	SF N	5	4	.556	4.38	49	0	0	86.1	83	47	58	0	5	4	11	25	5	0	.200	4	15	0	3	0.4	1.000
1963		7	7	.500	3.05	46	0	0	62	46	30	44	0	7	7	3	11	2	0	.182	4	12	1	0	0.4	.941
1964	2 teams SF N (6G 0–1) HOU N (30G 4–8)																									
″	total	4	9	.308	2.45	36	10	2	113.2	102	26	64	1	1	4	1	32	3	0	.094	9	19	1	1	0.8	.966
1965	2 teams HOU N (1G 0–0) BAL A (27G 1–2)																									
″	total	1	2	.333	2.88	28	2	0	59.1	61	23	41	0	1	1	1	13	3	0	.231	6	16	1	1	0.8	.957
1967	CHI N	0	0	—	9.00	3	0	0	4	5	2	1	0	0	0	0	0	0	0	—	0	2	0	1	0.7	1.000
14 yrs.		81	91	.471	3.78	412	171	44	1548	1442	725	849	11	26	23	23	*				95	244	17	22	0.9	.952
WORLD SERIES																										
1955	NY A	0	1	.000	11.25	1	1	0	4	5	2	2	0	0	0	0	2	0	0	.000	0	1	0	0	1.0	1.000
1956		1	0	1.000	0.00	2	2	1	10.2	1	4	7	1	0	0	0	3	1	0	.333	0	1	0	0	0.5	1.000
1957		1	1	.500	3.72	2	1	0	9.2	8	5	6	0	1	0	0	2	0	0	.000	0	1	0	0	0.5	1.000
1958		1	0	1.000	0.96	2	2	0	9.1	9	6	9	0	0	0	0	2	0	0	.000	1	0	0	0	0.5	1.000
1962	SF N	1	0	1.000	3.86	3	0	0	2.1	1	2	0	0	1	0	0	0	0	0	—	1	0	0	0	0.3	1.000
5 yrs.		4	2	.667	2.75	10	6	1	36	24	19	24	1	2	0	0	*				2	3	0	0	0.5	1.000

Dan Larson

LARSON, DANIEL JAMES
B. July 4, 1954, Los Angeles, Calif.
BR TR 6′ 175 lbs.

Year	Team	W	L	PCT	ERA	G	GS	CG	IP	H	BB	SO	ShO	Relief Pitching W	Relief Pitching L	Relief Pitching SV	Batting AB	Batting H	Batting HR	BA	PO	A	E	DP	TC/G	FA
1976	HOU N	5	8	.385	3.03	13	13	5	92	81	28	42	0	0	0	0	31	9	0	.290	7	13	0	2	1.5	1.000
1977		1	7	.125	5.79	32	10	1	98	108	45	44	0	1	3	1	28	6	0	.214	11	14	2	0	0.8	.926
1978	PHI N	0	0	—	9.00	1	0	0	1	1	1	2	0	0	0	0	0	0	0	—	0	0	0	0	0.0	.000
1979		1	1	.500	4.26	3	3	0	19	17	9	9	0	0	0	0	5	0	0	.000	1	4	0	1	1.7	1.000
1980		0	5	.000	3.13	12	7	0	46	46	24	17	0	0	0	0	13	2	0	.154	4	4	0	0	0.7	1.000
1981		3	0	1.000	4.18	5	4	1	28	27	15	15	0	0	0	0	9	1	0	.111	6	2	0	0	1.6	1.000
1982	CHI N	0	4	.000	5.67	12	6	0	39.2	51	18	22	0	0	0	0	11	3	0	.273	10	7	0	2	1.4	1.000
7 yrs.		10	25	.286	4.39	78	43	7	323.2	331	140	151	0	1	3	1	97	21	0	.216	39	44	2	5	1.1	.976

Al Lary

LARY, ALFRED ALLEN
Brother of Frank Lary.
B. Sept. 26, 1929, Northport, Ala.
BR TR 6′ 3″ 185 lbs.

Year	Team	W	L	PCT	ERA	G	GS	CG	IP	H	BB	SO	ShO	Relief Pitching W	Relief Pitching L	Relief Pitching SV	Batting AB	Batting H	Batting HR	BA	PO	A	E	DP	TC/G	FA
1954	CHI N	0	0	—	3.00	1	1	0	6	3	7	4	0	0	0	0	2	1	0	.500	1	1	0	0	2.0	1.000
1962		0	1	.000	7.15	15	3	0	34	42	15	18	0	0	0	0	6	1	0	.167	1	5	1	0	0.5	.857
2 yrs.		0	1	.000	6.53	16	4	0	40	45	22	22	0	0	0	0	8	2	0	.250	2	6	1	0	0.6	.889

Frank Lary

LARY, FRANK STRONG (Mule, The Yankee Killer)
Brother of Al Lary.
B. Apr. 10, 1930, Northport, Ala.
BR TR 5′11″ 175 lbs.

Year	Team	W	L	PCT	ERA	G	GS	CG	IP	H	BB	SO	ShO	Relief Pitching W	Relief Pitching L	Relief Pitching SV	Batting AB	Batting H	Batting HR	BA	PO	A	E	DP	TC/G	FA
1954	DET A	0	0	—	2.45	3	0	0	3.2	4	3	5	0	0	0	0	0	0	0	—	0	0	0	0	0.0	.000
1955		14	15	.483	3.10	36	31	16	235	232	89	98	2	1	1	1	82	16	0	.195	14	46	3	4	1.8	.952
1956		**21**	13	.618	3.15	41	**38**	20	**294**	**289**	116	165	3	0	0	1	103	19	1	.184	15	45	3	3	1.5	.952
1957		11	16	.407	3.98	40	35	12	237.2	250	72	107	2	0	1	3	73	9	0	.123	14	43	1	4	1.5	.983
1958		16	15	.516	2.90	39	34	**19**	**260.1**	249	68	131	3	0	2	1	88	15	1	.170	20	39	1	1	1.5	.983
1959		17	10	.630	3.55	32	32	11	223	225	46	137	3	0	0	0	80	10	1	.125	15	34	3	1	1.6	.942
1960		15	15	.500	3.51	38	**36**	**15**	**274.1**	**262**	62	149	2	0	0	1	93	17	2	.183	14	37	4	2	1.4	.927
1961		23	9	.719	3.24	36	36	**22**	275.1	252	66	146	4	0	0	0	108	25	1	.231	32	55	1	5	2.4	.989
1962		2	6	.250	5.74	17	14	2	80	98	21	41	1	0	1	0	24	4	0	.167	7	8	3	0	1.1	.833
1963		4	9	.308	3.27	16	14	6	107.1	90	26	46	0	0	0	0	35	8	0	.229	26	14	0	1	2.5	1.000
1964	3 teams DET A (6G 0–2) NY N (13G 2–3) MIL N (5G 1–0)																									
″	total	3	5	.375	5.03	24	14	3	87.2	101	24	37	1	0	0	1	27	2	0	.074	11	13	1	1	1.0	.960
1965	2 teams NY N (14G 1–3) CHI A (14G 1–0)																									
″	total	2	3	.400	3.32	28	8	0	84	71	23	37	0	0	0	3	21	5	0	.238	6	17	1	1	0.9	.958
12 yrs.		128	116	.525	3.49	350	292	126	2162.1	2123	616	1099	21	1	5	11	734	130	6	.177	174	351	21	23	1.6	.962

Fred Lasher

LASHER, FREDERICK WALTER
B. Aug. 19, 1941, Poughkeepsie, N. Y.
BR TR 6′ 3″ 190 lbs.

Year	Team	W	L	PCT	ERA	G	GS	CG	IP	H	BB	SO	ShO	Relief Pitching W	Relief Pitching L	Relief Pitching SV	Batting AB	Batting H	Batting HR	BA	PO	A	E	DP	TC/G	FA
1963	MIN A	0	0	—	4.76	11	0	0	11.1	12	11	10	0	0	0	0	1	0	0	.000	1	4	1	0	0.5	.833
1967	DET A	2	1	.667	3.90	17	0	0	30	25	11	28	0	2	1	9	9	1	0	.111	1	4	0	0	0.3	1.000
1968		5	1	.833	3.33	34	0	0	48.2	37	22	32	0	5	1	5	9	1	0	.111	3	10	1	1	0.4	.929
1969		2	1	.667	3.07	32	0	0	44	34	22	26	0	2	1	0	4	0	0	.000	2	8	0	0	0.3	1.000
1970	2 teams DET A (12G 1–3) CLE A (43G 1–7)																									
″	total	2	10	.167	4.18	55	1	0	66.2	67	42	52	0	2	9	8	9	0	0	.000	1	8	4	0	0.2	.692
1971	CAL A	0	0	—	36.00	2	0	0	1	4	2	0	0	0	0	0	0	0	0	—	0	0	0	0	0.0	.000
6 yrs.		11	13	.458	3.88	151	1	0	201.2	179	110	148	0	11	12	22	32	2	0	.063	8	34	6	1	0.3	.875
WORLD SERIES																										
1968	DET A	0	0	—	0.00	1	0	0	2	1	0	1	0	0	0	0	0	0	0	—	0	1	0	0	1.0	1.000

Bill Laskey

LASKEY, WILLIAM ALAN
B. Dec. 20, 1957, Toledo, Ohio.
BR TR 6′ 5″ 190 lbs.

Year	Team	W	L	PCT	ERA	G	GS	CG	IP	H	BB	SO	ShO	Relief Pitching W	Relief Pitching L	Relief Pitching SV	Batting AB	Batting H	Batting HR	BA	PO	A	E	DP	TC/G	FA
1982	SF N	13	12	.520	3.14	32	31	7	189.1	186	43	88	1	0	0	0	62	8	0	.129	17	30	2	2	1.5	.959
1983		13	10	.565	4.19	25	25	1	148.1	151	45	81	0	0	0	0	47	5	0	.106	11	16	1	0	1.1	.964
1984		9	14	.391	4.33	35	34	2	207.2	222	50	71	0	1	0	0	63	4	0	.063	12	23	0	0	1.0	1.000

Bill Laskey *continued*

Year	Team	Lg	W	L	PCT	ERA	G	GS	CG	IP	H	BB	SO	ShO	Relief W	Relief L	Relief SV	AB	H	HR	BA	PO	A	E	DP	TC/G	FA
1985	2 teams	SF N (19G 5–11) MON N (11G 0–5)																									
″	total		5	16	.238	4.91	30	26	0	148.1	165	53	60	0	0	0	0	37	5	0	.135	12	26	2	1	1.3	.950
1986	SF	N	1	1	.500	4.28	20	0	0	27.1	28	13	8	0	1	1	1	1	0	0	.000	3	6	1	1	0.5	.900
1988	CLE	A	1	0	1.000	5.18	17	0	0	24.1	32	6	17	0	1	0	1	0	0	0	—	0	4	0	0	0.2	1.000
6 yrs.			42	53	.442	4.14	159	116	10	745.1	784	210	325	1	3	1	2	210	22	0	.105	55	105	6	4	1.0	.964

Bill Lasley

LASLEY, WILLARD ALMOND BB TR 6′ 175 lbs.
B. July 13, 1902, Marietta, Ohio D. Aug. 21, 1990, Seattle, Wash.

Year	Team	Lg	W	L	PCT	ERA	G	GS	CG	IP	H	BB	SO	ShO	Relief W	Relief L	Relief SV	AB	H	HR	BA	PO	A	E	DP	TC/G	FA
1924	STL	A	0	0	—	6.75	2	0	0	4	7	2	0	0	0	0	0	1	0	0	.000	0	0	0	0	0.0	.000

Tom Lasorda

LASORDA, THOMAS CHARLES BL TL 5′10″ 175 lbs.
B. Sept. 22, 1927, Norristown, Pa.
Manager 1976–95.

Year	Team	Lg	W	L	PCT	ERA	G	GS	CG	IP	H	BB	SO	ShO	Relief W	Relief L	Relief SV	AB	H	HR	BA	PO	A	E	DP	TC/G	FA
1954	BKN	N	0	0	—	5.00	4	0	0	9	8	5	5	0	0	0	0	1	0	0	.000	0	1	0	0	0.3	1.000
1955			0	0	—	13.50	4	1	0	4	5	6	4	0	0	0	0	0	0	0	—	0	0	0	0	0.0	.000
1956	KC	A	0	4	.000	6.15	18	5	0	45.1	40	45	28	0	0	0	1	13	1	0	.077	3	9	1	0	0.7	.923
3 yrs.			0	4	.000	6.48	26	6	0	58.1	53	56	37	0	0	0	1	14	1	0	.071	3	10	1	0	0.5	.929

Bill Latham

LATHAM, WILLIAM CAROL, JR. BL TL 6′ 2″ 190 lbs.
B. Aug. 29, 1960, Birmingham, Ala.

Year	Team	Lg	W	L	PCT	ERA	G	GS	CG	IP	H	BB	SO	ShO	Relief W	Relief L	Relief SV	AB	H	HR	BA	PO	A	E	DP	TC/G	FA
1985	NY	N	1	3	.250	3.97	7	3	0	22.2	21	7	10	0	0	1	0	3	1	0	.333	0	7	0	0	1.0	1.000
1986	MIN	A	0	1	.000	7.31	7	2	0	16	24	6	8	0	0	0	0	0	0	0	—	0	1	1	0	0.3	.500
2 yrs.			1	4	.200	5.35	14	5	0	38.2	45	13	18	0	0	1	0	3	1	0	.333	0	8	1	0	0.6	.889

Bill Lathrop

LATHROP, WILLIAM GEORGE BR TR 6′ 2½″ 184 lbs.
B. Aug. 12, 1891, Hanover, Wis. D. Nov. 20, 1958, Janesville, Wis.

Year	Team	Lg	W	L	PCT	ERA	G	GS	CG	IP	H	BB	SO	ShO	Relief W	Relief L	Relief SV	AB	H	HR	BA	PO	A	E	DP	TC/G	FA
1913	CHI	A	0	1	.000	4.24	6	0	0	17	16	12	9	0	0	1	0	4	0	0	.000	0	6	0	0	1.0	1.000
1914			1	2	.333	2.64	19	1	0	47.2	41	19	7	0	1	1	0	12	0	0	.000	0	19	0	0	1.0	1.000
2 yrs.			1	3	.250	3.06	25	1	0	64.2	57	31	16	0	1	2	0	16	0	0	.000	0	25	0	0	1.0	1.000

Barry Latman

LATMAN, ARNOLD BARRY BR TR 6′ 3″ 210 lbs.
B. May 21, 1936, Los Angeles, Calif.

Year	Team	Lg	W	L	PCT	ERA	G	GS	CG	IP	H	BB	SO	ShO	Relief W	Relief L	Relief SV	AB	H	HR	BA	PO	A	E	DP	TC/G	FA
1957	CHI	A	1	2	.333	8.03	7	2	0	12.1	12	13	9	0	1	1	1	1	0	0	.000	1	2	0	1	0.4	1.000
1958			3	0	1.000	0.76	13	3	1	47.2	27	17	28	1	1	0	0	12	1	0	.083	2	5	1	0	0.6	.875
1959			8	5	.615	3.75	37	21	5	156	138	72	97	2	0	0	0	47	6	0	.128	5	13	1	1	0.5	.947
1960	CLE	A	7	7	.500	4.03	31	20	4	147.1	146	72	94	0	1	1	0	41	9	0	.220	10	18	1	0	0.9	.966
1961			13	5	.722	4.02	45	18	4	176.2	163	54	108	2	6	0	5	55	4	0	.073	10	13	2	2	0.6	.920
1962			8	13	.381	4.17	45	21	7	179.1	179	72	117	1	2	2	5	53	10	1	.189	17	22	7	3	1.0	.848
1963			7	12	.368	4.94	38	21	4	149.1	146	52	133	2	1	1	2	44	8	1	.182	18	31	3	1	1.4	.942
1964	LA	A	6	10	.375	3.85	40	18	2	138	128	52	81	1	3	2	2	40	5	0	.125	9	17	3	2	0.7	.897
1965	CAL	A	1	1	.500	2.84	18	0	0	31.2	30	16	18	0	1	1	0	2	0	0	.000	0	2	1	0	0.2	.667
1966	HOU	N	2	7	.222	2.71	31	9	1	103	88	35	74	1	1	2	1	26	4	0	.154	5	16	1	0	0.7	.955
1967			3	6	.333	4.52	39	1	0	77.2	73	34	70	0	3	6	0	11	1	0	.091	2	13	0	0	0.4	1.000
11 yrs.			59	68	.465	3.91	344	134	28	1219	1130	489	829	10	20	16	16	332	48	2	.145	79	152	20	10	0.7	.920

Bill Lattimore

LATTIMORE, WILLIAM HERSHEL (Slothful Bill) BL TL 5′ 9″ 165 lbs.
B. May 5, 1884, Roxton, Tex. D. Oct. 30, 1919, Colorado Springs, Colo.

Year	Team	Lg	W	L	PCT	ERA	G	GS	CG	IP	H	BB	SO	ShO	Relief W	Relief L	Relief SV	AB	H	HR	BA	PO	A	E	DP	TC/G	FA
1908	CLE	A	1	2	.333	4.50	4	4	1	24	24	7	5	1	0	0	0	9	4	0	.444	0	5	0	0	1.3	1.000

Chuck Lauer

LAUER, JOHN CHARLES TR
B. 1865, Pittsburgh, Pa. Deceased.

Year	Team	Lg	W	L	PCT	ERA	G	GS	CG	IP	H	BB	SO	ShO	Relief W	Relief L	Relief SV	AB	H	HR	BA	PO	A	E	DP	TC/G	FA
1884	PIT	AA	0	2	.000	*7.58*	3	3	2	19	23	9	8	0	0	0	0	*				16	3	3	0	1.6	.864

George Lauzerique

LAUZERIQUE, GEORGE ALBERT BR TR 6′ 1″ 180 lbs.
B. July 22, 1947, Havana, Cuba.

Year	Team	Lg	W	L	PCT	ERA	G	GS	CG	IP	H	BB	SO	ShO	Relief W	Relief L	Relief SV	AB	H	HR	BA	PO	A	E	DP	TC/G	FA
1967	KC	A	0	2	.000	2.25	3	2	0	16	11	6	10	0	0	0	0	3	0	0	.000	0	3	0	0	1.0	1.000
1968	OAK	A	0	0	—	0.00	1	0	0	1	0	1	0	0	0	0	0	0	0	0	—	0	1	0	0	1.0	1.000
1969			3	4	.429	4.70	19	8	1	61.1	58	27	39	0	0	2	0	20	2	0	.100	2	14	0	1	0.8	1.000
1970	MIL	A	1	2	.333	6.94	11	4	1	35	41	14	24	0	0	0	0	10	2	1	.200	3	3	0	0	0.5	1.000
4 yrs.			4	8	.333	5.00	34	14	2	113.1	110	48	73	0	0	2	0	33	4	1	.121	5	21	0	1	0.8	1.000

Gary Lavelle

LAVELLE, GARY ROBERT BB TL 6′ 2″ 190 lbs.
B. Jan. 3, 1949, Scranton, Pa. BL 1981
BR 1982–1983

Year	Team	Lg	W	L	PCT	ERA	G	GS	CG	IP	H	BB	SO	ShO	Relief W	Relief L	Relief SV	AB	H	HR	BA	PO	A	E	DP	TC/G	FA
1974	SF	N	0	3	.000	2.12	10	0	0	17	14	10	12	0	0	3	0	2	0	0	.000	0	2	1	0	0.3	.667
1975			6	3	.667	2.96	65	0	0	82	80	48	51	0	6	3	8	9	1	0	.111	6	11	1	2	0.3	.944
1976			10	6	.625	2.69	65	0	0	110.1	102	52	71	0	10	6	12	13	1	0	.077	5	11	4	0	0.3	.800
1977			7	7	.500	2.06	73	0	0	118	106	37	93	0	7	7	20	14	0	0	.000	5	20	1	2	0.4	.962
1978			13	10	.565	3.31	67	0	0	98	96	44	63	0	**13**	10	14	15	1	0	.067	2	19	2	1	0.3	.913
1979			7	9	.438	2.51	70	0	0	97	86	42	80	0	7	9	20	4	1	0	.250	4	13	1	0	0.3	.944
1980			6	8	.429	3.42	62	0	0	100	106	36	66	0	6	8	9	11	0	0	.000	3	16	0	0	0.3	1.000
1981			2	6	.250	3.82	34	3	0	66	58	23	45	0	2	4	4	11	3	0	.273	3	16	1	3	0.6	.950
1982			10	7	.588	2.67	68	0	0	104.2	97	29	76	0	10	7	8	13	2	0	.154	8	26	2	0	0.5	.944
1983			7	4	.636	2.59	56	0	0	87	73	19	68	0	7	4	20	14	0	0	.000	5	20	1	2	0.5	.962
1984			5	4	.556	2.76	77	0	0	101	92	42	71	0	5	4	12	5	0	0	.000	1	13	0	0	0.2	1.000
1985	TOR	A	5	7	.417	3.10	69	0	0	72.2	54	36	50	0	5	7	8	0	0	0	—	2	9	0	1	0.2	1.000
1987	2 teams	TOR A (23G 2–3) OAK A (6G 0–0)																									
″	total		2	3	.400	5.91	29	0	0	32	40	22	23	0	2	3	1	0	0	0		4	5	0	0	0.3	1.000
13 yrs.			80	77	.510	2.93	745	3	0	1085.2	1004	440	769	0	80	75	136	111	9	0	.081	48	181	14	11	0.3	.942
LEAGUE CHAMPIONSHIP SERIES																											
1985	TOR	A	0	0	—	0.00	1	0	0		0	1	0	0	0	0	0	0	0	0	—	0	0	0	0	0.0	.000

Jimmy Lavender

LAVENDER, JAMES SANFORD
Born James Sanford Lamlein.
B. Mar. 25, 1884, Barnesville, Ga. D. Jan. 12, 1960, Cartersville, Ga.
BR TR 5′11″ 165 lbs.

Year	Team		W	L	PCT	ERA	G	GS	CG	IP	H	BB	SO	ShO	Relief Pitching W	Relief Pitching L	Relief Pitching SV	Batting AB	Batting H	HR	BA	PO	A	E	DP	TC/G	FA
1912	CHI	N	16	13	.552	3.04	42	31	15	251.2	240	89	109	3	1	1	3	87	13	0	.149	8	64	4	5	1.8	.947
1913			10	14	.417	3.66	40	20	10	204	206	98	91	0	3	2	2	68	8	0	.118	2	46	2	0	1.3	.960
1914			11	11	.500	3.07	37	28	11	214.1	191	87	87	2	1	2	0	63	11	0	.175	5	71	2	0	2.1	.974
1915			10	16	.385	2.58	41	24	13	220	178	67	117	1	2	4	3	67	9	0	.134	14	67	1	3	2.0	.988
1916			10	14	.417	2.82	36	25	9	188	163	62	91	4	1	1	2	53	8	0	.151	3	47	2	0	1.4	.962
1917	PHI	N	5	8	.385	3.55	28	14	7	129.1	119	44	52	0	1	0	1	36	5	0	.139	3	30	3	0	1.3	.917
6 yrs.			62	76	.449	3.09	224	142	65	1207.1	1097	447	547	10	9	10	11	374	54	0	.144	35	325	14	8	1.7	.963

Ron Law

LAW, RONALD DAVID
B. Mar. 14, 1946, Hamilton, Ont., Canada.
BR TR 6′ 2″ 165 lbs.

Year	Team		W	L	PCT	ERA	G	GS	CG	IP	H	BB	SO	ShO	Relief Pitching W	Relief Pitching L	Relief Pitching SV	Batting AB	Batting H	HR	BA	PO	A	E	DP	TC/G	FA
1969	CLE	A	3	4	.429	4.99	35	1	0	52.1	68	34	29	0	3	4	1	7	1	0	.143	4	9	1	1	0.4	.929

Vance Law

LAW, VANCE AARON
Son of Vern Law.
B. Oct. 1, 1956, Boise, Ida.
BR TR 6′ 2″ 185 lbs.

Year	Team		W	L	PCT	ERA	G	GS	CG	IP	H	BB	SO	ShO	Relief Pitching W	Relief Pitching L	Relief Pitching SV	Batting AB	Batting H	HR	BA	PO	A	E	DP	TC/G	FA
1986	MON	N	0	0	—	2.25	3	0	0	4	3	2	0	0	0	0	0	360	81	5	.225	31	54	3	8	4.4	.966
1987			0	0	—	5.40	3	0	0	3.1	5	0	2	0	0	0	0	436	119	12	.273	258	308	11	54	3.9	.981
1991	OAK	A	0	0	—	0.00	1	0	0	0.2	1	1	0	0	0	0	0	134	28	0	.209	112	272	19	22	2.7	.953
3 yrs.			0	0		3.38	7	0	0	8	9	3	2	0	0	0	0	*				1628	2497	123	383	3.3	.971

Vern Law

LAW, VERNON SANDERS (Deacon)
Father of Vance Law.
B. Mar. 12, 1930, Meridian, Ida.
BR TR 6′ 2″ 195 lbs.

Year	Team		W	L	PCT	ERA	G	GS	CG	IP	H	BB	SO	ShO	Relief Pitching W	Relief Pitching L	Relief Pitching SV	Batting AB	Batting H	HR	BA	PO	A	E	DP	TC/G	FA
1950	PIT	N	7	9	.438	4.92	27	17	5	128	137	49	57	1	1	0	0	41	3	0	.073	5	15	2	1	0.8	.909
1951			6	9	.400	4.50	28	14	2	114	109	51	41	1	3	3	2	32	11	1	.344	10	15	2	2	1.0	.926
1954			9	13	.409	5.51	39	18	7	161.2	201	56	57	0	4	0	3	52	12	1	.231	12	23	1	2	0.9	.972
1955			10	10	.500	3.81	43	24	8	200.2	221	61	82	1	1	1	1	63	16	1	.254	14	35	4	3	1.2	.925
1956			8	16	.333	4.32	39	32	6	195.2	218	49	60	0	1	3	2	57	10	1	.175	12	31	0	3	1.1	1.000
1957			10	8	.556	2.87	31	25	9	172.2	172	32	55	3	2	0	1	63	12	0	.190	13	23	2	2	1.2	.947
1958			14	12	.538	3.96	35	29	6	202.1	235	39	56	1	2	0	3	62	12	2	.194	16	31	0	3	1.3	1.000
1959			18	9	.667	2.98	34	33	20	266	245	53	110	2	0	0	1	96	16	1	.167	20	47	1	5	2.0	.985
1960			20	9	.690	3.08	35	35	**18**	271.2	266	40	120	3	0	0	0	94	17	1	.181	28	50	2	6	2.3	.975
1961			3	4	.429	4.70	11	10	1	59.1	72	18	20	0	0	0	0	19	5	0	.263	7	13	0	1	1.8	1.000
1962			10	7	.588	3.94	23	20	7	139.1	156	27	78	2	0	0	0	45	14	0	.311	7	27	2	3	1.6	.944
1963			4	5	.444	4.93	18	12	1	76.2	91	13	31	1	0	1	0	23	5	0	.217	5	20	0	1	1.4	1.000
1964			12	13	.480	3.61	35	29	7	192	203	32	93	5	0	1	0	61	19	1	.311	16	36	1	3	1.5	.981
1965			17	9	.654	2.15	29	28	13	217.1	182	35	101	4	1	0	0	82	20	1	.244	29	36	1	2	2.3	.985
1966			12	8	.600	4.05	31	28	8	177.2	203	24	88	4	2	0	0	66	16	1	.242	11	36	0	4	1.5	1.000
1967			2	6	.250	4.18	25	10	1	97	122	18	43	0	0	2	0	27	3	0	.111	8	15	1	0	1.0	.958
16 yrs.			162	147	.524	3.77	483	364	119	2672	2833	597	1092	28	17	11	13	883	191	11	.216	213	453	19	41	1.4	.972
WORLD SERIES																											
1960	PIT	N	2	0	1.000	3.44	3	3	0	18.1	22	3	8	0	0	0	0	6	2	0	.333	0	6	0	0	2.0	1.000

Bob Lawrence

LAWRENCE, ROBERT ANDREW (Larry)
B. Dec. 14, 1899, Brooklyn, N. Y. D. Nov. 6, 1983, Jamaica, N. Y.
BR TR 5′11″ 180 lbs.

Year	Team		W	L	PCT	ERA	G	GS	CG	IP	H	BB	SO	ShO	Relief Pitching W	Relief Pitching L	Relief Pitching SV	Batting AB	Batting H	HR	BA	PO	A	E	DP	TC/G	FA
1924	CHI	A	0	0	—	9.00	1	0	0	1	1	1	1	0	0	0	0	0	0	0	—	0	0	0	0	0.0	.000

Brooks Lawrence

LAWRENCE, BROOKS ULYSSES (Bull)
B. Jan. 30, 1925, Springfield, Ohio.
BR TR 6′ 205 lbs.

Year	Team		W	L	PCT	ERA	G	GS	CG	IP	H	BB	SO	ShO	Relief Pitching W	Relief Pitching L	Relief Pitching SV	Batting AB	Batting H	HR	BA	PO	A	E	DP	TC/G	FA
1954	STL	N	15	6	.714	3.74	35	18	8	158.2	141	72	72	0	6	4	1	53	10	0	.189	13	26	1	4	1.1	.975
1955			3	8	.273	6.56	46	10	2	96	102	58	52	1	1	3	1	21	2	0	.095	11	16	1	2	0.6	.964
1956	CIN	N	19	10	.655	3.99	49	30	11	218.2	210	71	96	1	6	1	0	70	11	0	.157	13	53	2	5	1.4	.971
1957			16	13	.552	3.52	49	32	12	250.1	234	76	121	1	1	2	4	82	14	0	.171	34	32	4	3	1.4	.943
1958			8	13	.381	4.13	46	23	6	181	194	55	74	2	2	5	5	53	6	0	.113	6	33	2	2	0.9	.951
1959			7	12	.368	4.77	43	14	3	128.1	144	45	64	0	4	5	10	40	6	0	.150	7	22	3	1	0.7	.906
1960			1	0	1.000	10.57	7	0	0	7.2	9	8	2	0	1	0	1	0	0	0	—	0	3	0	0	0.4	1.000
7 yrs.			69	62	.527	4.25	275	127	42	1040.2	1034	385	481	5	21	20	22	319	49	0	.154	84	185	13	17	1.0	.954

Al Lawson

LAWSON, ALFRED WILLIAM
B. Mar. 24, 1869, London, England D. Nov. 29, 1954, San Antonio, Tex.
BR TR 5′11″ 165 lbs.

Year	Team		W	L	PCT	ERA	G	GS	CG	IP	H	BB	SO	ShO	Relief Pitching W	Relief Pitching L	Relief Pitching SV	Batting AB	Batting H	HR	BA	PO	A	E	DP	TC/G	FA
1890	2 teams	BOS N (1G 0–1) PIT N (2G 0–2)																									
"	total		0	3	.000	6.63	3	3	2	19	27	14	3	0	0	0	0	6	0	0	.000	0	5	3	0	2.7	.625

Bob Lawson

LAWSON, ROBERT BAKER
B. Aug. 23, 1876, Brookneal, Va. D. Oct. 28, 1952, Durham, N. C.
BR TR 5′10″ 170 lbs.

Year	Team		W	L	PCT	ERA	G	GS	CG	IP	H	BB	SO	ShO	Relief Pitching W	Relief Pitching L	Relief Pitching SV	Batting AB	Batting H	HR	BA	PO	A	E	DP	TC/G	FA
1901	BOS	N	2	2	.500	3.33	6	4	4	46	45	28	12	0	0	0	0	27	4	1	.148	6	18	4	0	2.8	.857
1902	BAL	A	0	2	.000	4.85	3	2	1	13	21	3	5	0	0	0	0	6	1	0	.167	0	7	0	0	2.3	1.000
2 yrs.			2	4	.333	3.66	9	6	5	59	66	31	17	0	0	0	0	33	5	1	.152	6	25	4	0	2.7	.886

Roxie Lawson

LAWSON, ALFRED VOYLE
B. Apr. 13, 1906, Donnellson, Iowa D. Apr. 9, 1977, Stockport, Iowa.
BR TR 6′ 170 lbs.

Year	Team		W	L	PCT	ERA	G	GS	CG	IP	H	BB	SO	ShO	Relief Pitching W	Relief Pitching L	Relief Pitching SV	Batting AB	Batting H	HR	BA	PO	A	E	DP	TC/G	FA
1930	CLE	A	1	2	.333	6.15	7	4	2	33.2	46	23	10	0	0	0	0	11	1	0	.091	2	6	0	0	1.1	1.000
1931			0	2	.000	7.60	17	3	0	55.2	72	36	20	0	0	0	0	14	2	0	.143	5	7	1	1	0.8	.923
1933	DET	A	0	1	.000	7.31	4	2	0	16	17	17	6	0	0	0	0	5	0	0	.000	0	5	0	0	1.3	1.000
1935			3	1	.750	1.58	7	4	4	40	34	24	16	2	0	0	2	13	4	0	.308	2	2	1	0	0.7	.800
1936			8	6	.571	5.48	41	8	3	128	139	71	34	0	5	**5**	3	45	10	0	.222	7	28	1	1	0.9	.972
1937			18	7	.720	5.26	37	29	15	217.1	236	115	68	0	3	1	1	81	21	0	.259	16	33	2	2	1.4	.961
1938			8	9	.471	5.46	27	16	5	127	154	82	39	0	3	0	1	45	2	0	.044	9	26	2	0	1.4	.946

Roxie Lawson *continued*

Year	Team	W	L	PCT	ERA	G	GS	CG	IP	H	BB	SO	ShO	Relief Pitching W	Relief L	Relief SV	Batting AB	Batting H	HR	BA	PO	A	E	DP	TC/G	FA
1939	2 teams DET A (2G 1–1) STL A (36G 3–7)																									
″	total	4	8	.333	5.28	38	15	5	162	188	90	47	0	2	0	0	47	8	0	.170	8	26	1	1	0.9	.971
1940	STL A	5	3	.625	5.13	30	2	0	72	77	54	18	0	5	1	4	22	1	0	.045	3	12	0	2	0.5	1.000
9 yrs.		47	39	.547	5.37	208	83	34	851.2	963	512	258	2	18	7	11	283	49	0	.173	52	145	8	7	1.0	.961

Steve Lawson

LAWSON, STEVEN GEORGE BR TL 6′ 1″ 175 lbs.
B. Dec. 28, 1950, Oakland, Calif.

Year	Team	W	L	PCT	ERA	G	GS	CG	IP	H	BB	SO	ShO	Relief Pitching W	Relief L	Relief SV	Batting AB	Batting H	HR	BA	PO	A	E	DP	TC/G	FA
1972	TEX A	0	0	—	2.81	13	0	0	16	13	10	13	0	0	0	1	1	1	0	1.000	0	2	0	0	0.2	1.000

Bill Laxton

LAXTON, WILLIAM HENRY BL TL 6′ 1″ 190 lbs.
B. Jan. 5, 1948, Camden, N. J.

Year	Team	W	L	PCT	ERA	G	GS	CG	IP	H	BB	SO	ShO	Relief Pitching W	Relief L	Relief SV	Batting AB	Batting H	HR	BA	PO	A	E	DP	TC/G	FA
1970	PHI N	0	0	—	13.50	2	0	0	2	2	2	2	0	0	0	0	0	0	0	—	0	0	0	0	0.0	.000
1971	SD N	0	2	.000	6.75	18	0	0	28	32	26	23	0	0	2	0	0	0	0	—	1	4	0	0	0.3	1.000
1974		0	1	.000	4.00	30	1	0	45	37	38	40	0	0	1	0	5	1	0	.200	2	4	0	0	0.2	1.000
1976	DET A	0	5	.000	4.09	26	3	0	94.2	77	51	74	0	0	2	2	0	0	0	—	4	5	2	0	0.4	.818
1977	2 teams SEA A (43G 3–2) CLE A (2G 0–0)																									
″	total	3	2	.600	4.96	45	0	0	74.1	64	41	50	0	3	2	3	0	0	0		3	6	0	0	0.2	1.000
5 yrs.		3	10	.231	4.72	121	4	0	244	212	158	189	0	3	7	5	5	1	0	.200	10	19	2	0	0.3	.935

Tim Layana

LAYANA, TIMOTHY JOSEPH BR TR 6′ 2″ 195 lbs.
B. Mar. 2, 1964, Inglewood, Calif.

Year	Team	W	L	PCT	ERA	G	GS	CG	IP	H	BB	SO	ShO	Relief Pitching W	Relief L	Relief SV	Batting AB	Batting H	HR	BA	PO	A	E	DP	TC/G	FA
1990	CIN N	5	3	.625	3.49	55	0	0	80	71	44	53	0	5	3	2	5	0	0	.000	10	9	0	1	0.3	1.000
1991		0	2	.000	6.97	22	0	0	20.2	23	11	14	0	0	2	0	1	0	0	.000	3	4	1	1	0.4	.875
1993	SF N	0	0	—	22.50	1	0	0	2	7	1	1	0	0	0	0	0	0	0	—	0	1	0	0	1.0	1.000
3 yrs.		5	5	.500	4.56	78	0	0	102.2	101	56	68	0	5	5	2	6	0	0	.000	13	14	1	2	0.4	.964

Danny Lazar

LAZAR, JOHN DANIEL BL TL 6′ 1″ 190 lbs.
B. Nov. 14, 1943, East Chicago, Ind.

Year	Team	W	L	PCT	ERA	G	GS	CG	IP	H	BB	SO	ShO	Relief Pitching W	Relief L	Relief SV	Batting AB	Batting H	HR	BA	PO	A	E	DP	TC/G	FA
1968	CHI A	0	1	.000	4.05	8	1	0	13.1	14	4	11	0	0	0	0	2	0	0	.000	1	2	0	0	0.4	1.000
1969		0	0	—	6.53	9	3	0	20.2	21	11	9	0	0	0	0	4	0	0	.000	2	2	0	0	0.4	1.000
2 yrs.		0	1	.000	5.56	17	4	0	34	35	15	20	0	0	0	0	6	0	0	.000	3	4	0	0	0.4	1.000

Jack Lazorko

LAZORKO, JACK THOMAS BR TR 5′11″ 198 lbs.
B. Mar. 30, 1956, Hoboken, N. J.

Year	Team	W	L	PCT	ERA	G	GS	CG	IP	H	BB	SO	ShO	Relief Pitching W	Relief L	Relief SV	Batting AB	Batting H	HR	BA	PO	A	E	DP	TC/G	FA
1984	MIL A	0	1	.000	4.31	15	1	0	39.2	37	22	24	0	0	1	1	0	0	0	—	3	5	0	0	0.5	1.000
1985	SEA A	0	0	—	3.54	15	0	0	20.1	23	8	7	0	0	0	1	0	0	0	—	4	4	0	1	0.5	1.000
1986	DET A	0	0	—	4.05	3	0	0	6.2	8	4	3	0	0	0	0	0	0	0	—	1	1	0	0	0.7	1.000
1987	CAL A	5	6	.455	4.59	26	11	2	117.2	108	44	55	0	2	1	0	0	0	0	—	8	25	0	1	1.3	1.000
1988		0	1	.000	3.35	10	3	0	37.2	37	16	19	0	0	0	0	0	0	0	—	2	7	0	0	0.9	1.000
5 yrs.		5	8	.385	4.22	69	15	2	222	213	94	108	0	2	2	2	0	0	0		18	42	0	2	0.9	1.000

Charlie Lea

LEA, CHARLES WILLIAM BR TR 6′ 4″ 194 lbs.
B. Dec. 25, 1956, Orleans, France.

Year	Team	W	L	PCT	ERA	G	GS	CG	IP	H	BB	SO	ShO	Relief Pitching W	Relief L	Relief SV	Batting AB	Batting H	HR	BA	PO	A	E	DP	TC/G	FA
1980	MON N	7	5	.583	3.72	21	19	0	104	103	55	56	0	0	0	0	37	3	0	.081	4	10	0	0	0.7	1.000
1981		5	4	.556	4.64	16	11	2	64	63	26	31	2	0	0	0	15	2	0	.133	5	8	0	2	0.8	1.000
1982		12	10	.545	3.24	27	27	4	177.2	145	56	115	2	0	0	0	65	8	0	.123	6	22	1	1	1.1	.966
1983		16	11	.593	3.12	33	33	8	222	195	84	137	4	0	0	0	70	8	0	.114	19	27	2	0	1.5	.958
1984		15	10	.600	2.89	30	30	8	224.1	198	68	123	0	0	0	0	72	8	0	.111	19	33	1	1	1.8	.981
1987		0	1	.000	36.00	1	1	0	1	4	2	1	0	0	0	0	0	0	0	—	0	0	0	0	0.0	.000
1988	MIN A	7	7	.500	4.85	24	23	0	130	156	50	72	0	0	0	0	0	0	0	—	12	12	0	1	1.0	1.000
7 yrs.		62	48	.564	3.54	152	144	22	923	864	341	535	8	0	0	0	259	29	0	.112	65	112	4	5	1.2	.978

Rick Leach

LEACH, RICHARD MAX BL TL 6′ 1″ 180 lbs.
B. May 4, 1957, Ann Arbor, Mich.

Year	Team	W	L	PCT	ERA	G	GS	CG	IP	H	BB	SO	ShO	Relief Pitching W	Relief L	Relief SV	Batting AB	Batting H	HR	BA	PO	A	E	DP	TC/G	FA
1984	TOR A	0	0	—	27.00	1	0	0	1	2	2	0	0	0	0	0	*				149	14	0	15	3.3	1.000

Terry Leach

LEACH, TERRY HESTER BR TR 6′ 215 lbs.
B. Mar. 13, 1954, Selma, Ala.

Year	Team	W	L	PCT	ERA	G	GS	CG	IP	H	BB	SO	ShO	Relief Pitching W	Relief L	Relief SV	Batting AB	Batting H	HR	BA	PO	A	E	DP	TC/G	FA
1981	NY N	1	1	.500	2.57	21	1	0	35	26	12	16	0	1	0	0	1	0	0	.000	4	7	0	0	0.5	1.000
1982		2	1	.667	4.17	21	1	1	45.1	46	18	30	1	1	1	3	8	1	0	.125	0	8	1	0	0.4	.889
1985		3	4	.429	2.91	22	4	1	55.2	48	14	30	1	0	3	1	12	2	0	.167	5	14	0	0	0.9	1.000
1986		0	0	—	2.70	6	0	0	6.2	6	3	4	0	0	0	0	0	0	0	—	0	2	0	0	0.3	1.000
1987		11	1	.917	3.22	44	12	1	131.1	132	29	61	1	4	0	0	33	2	0	.061	18	21	2	3	0.9	.951
1988		7	2	.778	2.54	52	0	0	92	95	24	51	0	7	2	3	14	2	0	.143	10	22	0	0	0.6	1.000
1989	2 teams NY N (10G 0–0) KC A (30G 5–6)																									
″	total	5	6	.455	4.17	40	3	0	95	97	40	36	0	4	4	0	4	0	0	.000	7	25	4	0	0.9	.889
1990	MIN A	2	5	.286	3.20	55	0	0	81.2	84	21	46	0	2	5	2	0	0	0	—	12	11	1	0	0.4	.958
1991		1	2	.333	3.61	50	0	0	67.1	82	14	32	0	1	2	0	0	0	0	—	8	13	0	2	0.4	1.000
1992	CHI A	6	5	.545	1.95	51	0	0	73.2	57	20	22	0	6	5	0	0	0	0	—	9	13	1	1	0.5	.957
1993		0	0	—	2.81	14	0	0	16	15	2	3	0	0	0	1	0	0	0	—	1	0	0	0	0.1	1.000
11 yrs.		38	27	.585	3.15	376	21	3	699.2	688	197	331	3	26	22	10	72	7	0	.097	74	136	9	6	0.6	.959
LEAGUE CHAMPIONSHIP SERIES																										
1988	NY N	0	0	—	0.00	3	0	0	5	4	1	4	0	0	0	0	0	0	0	—	1	0	0	0	0.3	1.000
WORLD SERIES																										
1991	MIN A	0	0	—	3.86	2	0	0	2.1	2	0	2	0	0	0	0	0	0	0	—	0	0	0	0	0.0	.000

Luis Leal

LEAL, LUIS ENRIQUE BR TR 6′ 3″ 205 lbs.
Born Luis Enrique Leal (Alvarado).
B. Mar. 21, 1957, Barquisimento, Venezuela.

Year	Team	W	L	PCT	ERA	G	GS	CG	IP	H	BB	SO	ShO	Relief Pitching W	Relief L	Relief SV	Batting AB	Batting H	HR	BA	PO	A	E	DP	TC/G	FA
1980	TOR A	3	4	.429	4.50	13	10	1	60	72	31	26	0	0	0	0	0	0	0	—	3	7	1	0	0.8	.909
1981		7	**13**	.350	3.67	29	19	3	130	127	44	71	0	1	3	1	0	0	0	—	4	19	0	0	0.8	1.000
1982		12	15	.444	3.93	38	38	10	249.2	250	79	111	0	0	0	0	0	0	0	—	17	31	0	2	1.3	1.000

Luis Leal *continued*

Year	Team	W	L	PCT	ERA	G	GS	CG	IP	H	BB	SO	ShO	Relief Pitching W	Relief Pitching L	Relief Pitching SV	Batting AB	Batting H	Batting HR	BA	PO	A	E	DP	TC/G	FA
1983		13	12	.520	4.31	35	35	7	217.1	216	65	116	1	0	0	0	0	0	0	—	20	23	1	2	1.3	.977
1984		13	8	.619	3.89	35	35	6	222.1	221	77	134	2	0	0	0	0	0	0	—	12	30	0	3	1.2	1.000
1985		3	6	.333	5.75	15	14	0	67.1	82	24	33	0	0	1	0	0	0	0	—	5	10	1	1	1.1	.938
6 yrs.		51	58	.468	4.14	165	151	27	946.2	968	320	491	3	1	4	1	0	0	0		61	120	3	8	1.1	.984

King Lear

LEAR, CHARLES BERNARD BR TR 6′ 175 lbs.
B. Jan. 23, 1891, Greencastle, Pa. D. Oct. 31, 1976, Greencastle, Pa.

Year	Team	W	L	PCT	ERA	G	GS	CG	IP	H	BB	SO	ShO	Relief Pitching W	Relief Pitching L	Relief Pitching SV	Batting AB	Batting H	Batting HR	BA	PO	A	E	DP	TC/G	FA
1914	CIN N	1	2	.333	3.07	17	4	3	55.2	55	19	20	1	0	0	1	16	3	0	.188	1	14	1	0	0.9	.938
1915		6	10	.375	3.01	40	15	9	167.2	169	45	46	0	1	3	0	47	8	0	.170	4	29	3	2	0.9	.917
2 yrs.		7	12	.368	3.02	57	19	12	223.1	224	64	66	1	1	3	1	63	11	0	.175	5	43	4	2	0.9	.923

Frank Leary

LEARY, FRANCIS PATRICK TR
B. Feb. 26, 1881, Wayland, Mass. D. Oct. 4, 1907, Natick, Mass.

Year	Team	W	L	PCT	ERA	G	GS	CG	IP	H	BB	SO	ShO	Relief Pitching W	Relief Pitching L	Relief Pitching SV	Batting AB	Batting H	Batting HR	BA	PO	A	E	DP	TC/G	FA
1907	CIN N	0	1	.000	1.13	2	1	0	8	7	6	4	0	0	1	0	2	0	0	.000	0	4	0	0	2.0	1.000

Jack Leary

LEARY, JOHN J. TL 5′11″ 186 lbs.
B. 1858, New Haven, Conn. Deceased.

Year	Team	W	L	PCT	ERA	G	GS	CG	IP	H	BB	SO	ShO	Relief Pitching W	Relief Pitching L	Relief Pitching SV	Batting AB	Batting H	Batting HR	BA	PO	A	E	DP	TC/G	FA
1880	BOS N	0	1	.000	15.00	1	1	0	3	8	0	1	0	0	0	0	3	0	0	.000	0	2	0	0	1.0	1.000
1881	DET N	0	2	.000	4.15	2	2	1	13	13	2	2	0	0	0	0	11	3	0	.273	5	2	2	0	2.3	.778
1882	2 teams PIT AA (3G 1–0) BAL AA (3G 2–1)																									
″	total	3	1	.750	3.43	6	5	4	44.2	57	11	7	0	0	0	0	275	79	2	.287	78	81	49	2	3.0	.764
1884	2 teams ALT U (3G 0–3) CHI U (2G 0–2)																									
″	total	0	5	.000	5.29	5	4	3	34	45	7	13	0	0	1	0	73	10	0	.137	72	112	44	14	5.3	.807
4 yrs.		3	9	.250	4.56	14	12	8	94.2	123	20	23	0	0	1	0	*				191	217	115	16	3.7	.780

Tim Leary

LEARY, TIMOTHY JAMES BR TR 6′ 3″ 205 lbs.
B. Mar. 21, 1958, Santa Monica, Calif.

Year	Team	W	L	PCT	ERA	G	GS	CG	IP	H	BB	SO	ShO	Relief Pitching W	Relief Pitching L	Relief Pitching SV	Batting AB	Batting H	Batting HR	BA	PO	A	E	DP	TC/G	FA
1981	NY N	0	0	—	0.00	1	1	0	2	0	1	3	0	0	0	0	1	0	0	.000	0	0	0	0	0.0	.000
1983		1	1	.500	3.38	2	2	1	10.2	15	4	9	0	0	0	0	3	1	0	.333	1	3	0	0	2.0	1.000
1984		3	3	.500	4.02	20	7	0	53.2	61	18	29	0	3	0	0	10	3	1	.300	3	4	1	0	0.4	.875
1985	MIL A	1	4	.200	4.05	5	5	0	33.1	40	8	29	0	0	0	0	0	0	0	—	1	7	0	0	1.6	1.000
1986		12	12	.500	4.21	33	30	3	188.1	216	53	110	2	0	0	0	0	0	0	—	22	26	1	1	1.5	.980
1987	LA N	3	11	.214	4.76	39	12	0	107.2	121	36	61	0	1	4	1	23	7	0	.304	9	18	0	2	0.7	1.000
1988		17	11	.607	2.91	35	34	9	228.2	201	56	180	6	0	0	0	67	18	0	.269	24	34	1	4	1.7	.983
1989	2 teams LA N (19G 6–7) CIN N (14G 2–7)																									
″	total	8	14	.364	3.52	33	31	2	207	205	68	123	0	1	1	0	59	7	0	.119	20	31	2	2	1.6	.962
1990	NY A	9	**19**	.321	4.11	31	31	6	208	202	78	138	1	0	0	0	0	0	0	—	14	36	4	4	1.7	.926
1991		4	10	.286	6.49	28	18	1	120.2	150	57	83	0	0	2	0	0	0	0	—	9	12	1	3	0.8	.955
1992	2 teams NY A (18G 5–6) SEA A (8G 3–4)																									
″	total	8	10	.444	5.36	26	23	3	141	131	87	46	0	0	0	0	0	0	0		10	18	0	3	1.1	1.000
1993	SEA A	11	9	.550	5.05	33	27	0	169.1	202	58	68	0	0	1	0	0	0	0	—	14	28	0	3	1.3	1.000
1994	TEX A	1	1	.500	8.14	6	3	0	21	26	11	9	0	0	0	0	0	0	0	—	3	4	0	0	1.2	1.000
13 yrs.		78	105	.426	4.36	292	224	25	1491.1	1570	535	888	9	5	8	1	163	36	1	.221	130	221	10	22	1.2	.972
LEAGUE CHAMPIONSHIP SERIES																										
1988	LA N	0	1	.000	6.23	2	1	0	4.1	8	3	3	0	0	0	0	1	0	0	.000	0	1	0	0	0.5	1.000
WORLD SERIES																										
1988	LA N	0	0	—	1.35	2	0	0	6.2	6	2	4	0	0	0	0	0	0	0	—	1	3	0	1	2.0	1.000

Razor Ledbetter

LEDBETTER, RALPH OVERTON BR TR 6′ 3″ 190 lbs.
B. Dec. 8, 1894, Rutherford College, N. C. D. Feb. 1, 1969, West Palm Beach, Fla.

Year	Team	W	L	PCT	ERA	G	GS	CG	IP	H	BB	SO	ShO	Relief Pitching W	Relief Pitching L	Relief Pitching SV	Batting AB	Batting H	Batting HR	BA	PO	A	E	DP	TC/G	FA
1915	DET A	0	0	—	0.00	1	0	0	1	1	0	0	0	0	0	0	0	0	0	—	0	1	0	0	1.0	1.000

Bill Lee

LEE, WILLIAM CRUTCHER (Big Bill) BR TR 6′ 3″ 195 lbs.
B. Oct. 21, 1909, Plaquemine, La. D. June 15, 1977, Plaquemine, La.

Year	Team	W	L	PCT	ERA	G	GS	CG	IP	H	BB	SO	ShO	Relief Pitching W	Relief Pitching L	Relief Pitching SV	Batting AB	Batting H	Batting HR	BA	PO	A	E	DP	TC/G	FA
1934	CHI N	13	14	.481	3.40	35	29	16	214.1	218	74	104	4	0	0	1	76	10	0	.132	15	48	4	2	1.9	.940
1935		20	6	**.769**	2.96	39	32	18	252	241	84	100	3	2	0	1	102	24	0	.235	12	52	7	4	1.8	.901
1936		18	11	.621	3.31	43	33	20	258.2	238	93	102	**4**	1	2	1	87	12	1	.138	12	61	7	5	1.9	.912
1937		14	15	.483	3.54	42	**34**	17	272.1	289	73	108	2	0	1	3	87	15	1	.172	20	70	5	5	2.3	.947
1938		**22**	9	**.710**	**2.66**	44	**37**	19	291	281	74	121	**9**	1	1	2	101	20	0	.198	18	61	5	3	1.9	.940
1939		19	15	.559	3.44	37	**36**	20	282.1	295	85	105	1	0	1	0	103	13	1	.126	15	80	5	3	2.7	.950
1940		9	17	.346	5.03	37	30	9	211.1	246	70	70	1	1	1	0	76	10	0	.132	10	42	6	3	1.6	.897
1941		8	14	.364	3.76	28	22	12	167.1	179	43	62	0	0	1	1	59	11	2	.186	10	39	6	3	2.0	.891
1942		13	13	.500	3.85	32	30	18	219.2	221	67	75	1	0	0	0	69	11	0	.159	10	55	2	2	2.1	.970
1943	2 teams CHI N (13G 3–7) PHI N (13G 1–5)																									
″	total	4	12	.250	4.01	26	19	6	139	153	48	35	0	0	0	3	43	8	0	.186	9	21	3	1	1.3	.909
1944	PHI N	10	11	.476	3.15	31	28	11	208.1	199	57	50	3	0	0	1	72	14	0	.194	17	47	4	2	2.2	.941
1945	2 teams PHI N (13G 3–6) BOS N (16G 6–3)																									
″	total	9	9	.500	3.58	29	26	8	183.2	219	66	25	1	0	0	0	55	8	0	.145	5	46	1	1	1.8	.981
1946	BOS N	10	9	.526	4.18	25	21	8	140	148	45	32	0	1	0	0	47	8	0	.170	6	35	1	0	1.7	.976
1947	CHI N	0	2	.000	4.50	14	2	0	24	26	14	9	0	0	0	0	3	1	0	.333	4	5	2	0	0.8	.818
14 yrs.		169	157	.518	3.54	462	379	182	2864	2953	893	998	29	6	7	13	980	165	5	.168	163	662	58	34	1.9	.934
WORLD SERIES																										
1935	CHI N	0	0	—	3.48	2	1	0	10.1	11	5	5	0	0	0	1	1	0	0	.000	1	1	0	0	1.0	1.000
1938		0	2	.000	2.45	2	2	0	11	15	1	8	0	0	0	0	3	0	0	.000	1	0	0	0	0.5	1.000
2 yrs.		0	2	.000	2.95	4	3	0	21.1	26	6	13	0	0	0	1	4	0	0	.000	2	1	0	0	0.8	1.000

Bill Lee

LEE, WILLIAM FRANCIS (Spaceman) BL TL 6′ 3″ 205 lbs.
B. Dec. 28, 1946, Burbank, Calif.

Year	Team	W	L	PCT	ERA	G	GS	CG	IP	H	BB	SO	ShO	Relief Pitching W	Relief Pitching L	Relief Pitching SV	Batting AB	Batting H	Batting HR	BA	PO	A	E	DP	TC/G	FA
1969	BOS A	1	3	.250	4.50	20	1	0	52	56	28	45	0	1	2	0	10	0	0	.000	2	6	1	0	0.4	.889
1970		2	2	.500	4.62	11	5	0	37	48	14	19	0	0	0	1	11	0	0	.000	1	10	0	1	1.0	1.000
1971		9	2	.818	2.74	47	3	0	102	102	46	74	0	8	2	2	23	5	0	.217	2	19	1	0	0.5	.955
1972		7	4	.636	3.20	47	0	0	84.1	75	32	43	0	7	4	5	16	3	1	.188	6	24	0	2	0.6	1.000
1973		17	11	.607	2.74	38	33	18	285.1	275	76	120	1	1	0	1	0	0	0	—	10	57	6	2	1.9	.918

Bill Lee *continued*

Year	Team	W	L	PCT	ERA	G	GS	CG	IP	H	BB	SO	ShO	Relief Pitching W	Relief Pitching L	Relief Pitching SV	Batting AB	Batting H	Batting HR	BA	PO	A	E	DP	TC/G	FA
1974		17	15	.531	3.51	38	37	16	282	**320**	67	95	1	0	0	0	0	0	0	—	9	69	8	3	2.3	.907
1975		17	9	.654	3.95	41	34	17	260	274	69	78	4	0	0	0	0	0	0	—	9	54	5	4	1.7	.926
1976		5	7	.417	5.63	24	14	1	96	124	28	29	0	1	0	3	0	0	0	—	2	22	2	1	1.0	.923
1977		9	5	.643	4.42	27	16	4	128.1	155	29	31	0	0	1	1	0	0	0	—	3	32	1	4	1.3	.972
1978		10	10	.500	3.46	28	24	8	177	198	59	44	1	0	0	0	0	0	0	—	9	32	3	2	1.6	.932
1979	MON N	16	10	.615	3.04	33	33	6	222	230	46	59	3	0	0	0	74	16	0	.216	11	41	1	2	1.6	.981
1980		4	6	.400	4.96	24	18	2	118	156	22	34	0	1	1	0	41	9	0	.220	7	19	0	2	1.1	1.000
1981		5	6	.455	2.93	31	7	0	89	90	14	34	0	3	3	6	22	8	1	.364	12	27	0	1	1.3	1.000
1982		0	0	—	4.38	7	0	0	12.1	19	1	8	0	0	0	0	0	0	0	—	0	3	0	0	0.4	1.000
14 yrs.		119	90	.569	3.62	416	225	72	1945.1	2122	531	713	10	22	13	19	197	41	2	.208	83	415	28	24	1.3	.947
DIVISIONAL PLAYOFF SERIES																										
1981	MON N	0	0	—	0.00	1	0	0	0.2	2	0	1	0	0	0	0	0	0	0	—	0	0	0	0	0.0	.000
LEAGUE CHAMPIONSHIP SERIES																										
1981	MON N	0	0	—	0.00	1	0	0	0.1	1	0	0	0	0	0	0	0	0	0	—	0	0	0	0	0.0	.000
WORLD SERIES																										
1975	BOS A	0	0	—	3.14	2	2	0	14.1	12	3	7	0	0	0	0	6	1	0	.167	0	1	0	0	0.5	1.000

Bob Lee

LEE, ROBERT DEAN (Horse, Moose) BR TR 6′ 3″ 225 lbs.
B. Nov. 26, 1937, Ottumwa, Iowa.

Year	Team	W	L	PCT	ERA	G	GS	CG	IP	H	BB	SO	ShO	Relief Pitching W	Relief Pitching L	Relief Pitching SV	Batting AB	Batting H	Batting HR	BA	PO	A	E	DP	TC/G	FA
1964	LA A	6	5	.545	1.51	64	5	0	137	87	58	111	0	5	4	19	22	0	0	.000	9	10	2	1	0.3	.905
1965	CAL A	9	7	.563	1.92	69	0	0	131.1	95	42	89	0	9	7	23	21	3	1	.143	3	18	0	0	0.3	1.000
1966		5	4	.556	2.74	61	0	0	101.2	90	31	46	0	5	4	16	11	0	0	.000	4	16	1	1	0.3	.952
1967	2 teams LA N (4G 0–0) CIN N (27G 3–3)																									
″	total	3	3	.500	4.55	31	1	0	57.1	57	28	35	0	2	3	2	8	3	0	.375	3	6	1	1	0.3	.900
1968	CIN N	2	4	.333	5.15	44	1	0	64.2	73	37	34	0	2	4	3	5	1	0	.200	4	5	0	0	0.2	1.000
5 yrs.		25	23	.521	2.71	269	7	0	492	402	196	315	0	23	22	63	67	7	1	.104	23	55	4	3	0.3	.951

Don Lee

LEE, DONALD EDWARD BR TR 6′ 4″ 205 lbs.
Son of Thornton Lee.
B. Feb. 26, 1934, Globe, Ariz.

Year	Team	W	L	PCT	ERA	G	GS	CG	IP	H	BB	SO	ShO	Relief Pitching W	Relief Pitching L	Relief Pitching SV	Batting AB	Batting H	Batting HR	BA	PO	A	E	DP	TC/G	FA
1957	DET A	1	3	.250	4.66	11	6	0	38.2	48	18	19	0	0	1	0	12	2	0	.167	1	6	0	0	0.6	1.000
1958		0	0	—	9.00	1	0	0	2	1	1	0	0	0	0	0	0	0	0	—	0	0	0	0	0.0	.000
1960	WAS A	8	7	.533	3.44	44	20	1	165	160	64	88	0	3	2	3	43	5	1	.116	6	31	0	3	0.8	1.000
1961	MIN A	3	6	.333	3.52	37	10	4	115	93	35	65	0	1	0	3	30	2	0	.067	8	29	2	1	1.1	.949
1962	2 teams MIN A (9G 3–3) LA A (27G 8–8)																									
″	total	11	11	.500	3.46	36	31	5	205.1	204	63	102	2	0	1	2	68	13	0	.191	13	28	1	1	1.2	.976
1963	LA A	8	11	.421	3.68	40	22	3	154	148	51	89	2	2	0	1	45	7	0	.156	8	21	1	4	0.8	.967
1964		5	4	.556	2.72	33	8	0	89.1	99	25	73	0	3	1	2	23	6	0	.261	1	12	0	0	0.4	1.000
1965	2 teams CAL A (10G 0–1) HOU N (7G 0–0)																									
″	total	0	1	.000	5.32	17	0	0	22	29	8	15	0	0	1	0	4	1	0	.250	3	4	1	0	0.5	.875
1966	2 teams HOU N (9G 2–0) CHI N (16G 2–1)																									
″	total	4	1	.800	4.86	25	0	0	37	45	16	16	0	4	1	0	1	1	0	1.000	3	9	1	2	0.5	.923
9 yrs.		40	44	.476	3.61	244	97	13	828.1	827	281	467	4	13	7	11	226	37	1	.164	43	140	6	11	0.8	.968

Mark Lee

LEE, MARK LINDEN BR TR 6′ 4″ 225 lbs.
B. June 14, 1953, Inglewood, Calif.

Year	Team	W	L	PCT	ERA	G	GS	CG	IP	H	BB	SO	ShO	Relief Pitching W	Relief Pitching L	Relief Pitching SV	Batting AB	Batting H	Batting HR	BA	PO	A	E	DP	TC/G	FA
1978	SD N	5	1	.833	3.28	56	0	0	85	74	36	31	0	5	1	2	5	0	0	.000	5	22	1	0	0.5	.964
1979		2	4	.333	4.29	46	1	0	65	88	25	25	0	2	3	5	6	2	0	.333	3	14	1	1	0.4	.944
1980	PIT N	0	1	.000	4.50	4	0	0	6	5	3	2	0	0	1	0	0	0	0	—	2	2	0	0	1.0	1.000
1981		0	2	.000	2.70	12	0	0	20	17	5	5	0	0	2	2	2	1	0	.500	6	7	1	0	1.2	.929
4 yrs.		7	8	.467	3.63	118	1	0	176	184	69	63	0	7	7	9	13	3	0	.231	16	45	3	1	0.5	.953

Mark Lee

LEE, MARK OWEN BL TL 6′ 3″ 198 lbs.
B. July 20, 1964, Williston, N. D.

Year	Team	W	L	PCT	ERA	G	GS	CG	IP	H	BB	SO	ShO	Relief Pitching W	Relief Pitching L	Relief Pitching SV	Batting AB	Batting H	Batting HR	BA	PO	A	E	DP	TC/G	FA
1988	KC A	0	0	—	3.60	4	0	0	5	6	1	0	0	0	0	0	0	0	0	—	0	1	0	1	0.3	1.000
1990	MIL A	1	0	1.000	2.11	11	0	0	21.1	20	4	14	0	1	0	0	0	0	0	—	1	1	0	0	0.2	1.000
1991		2	5	.286	3.86	62	0	0	67.2	72	31	43	0	2	5	1	0	0	0	—	0	13	0	2	0.2	1.000
1995	BAL A	2	0	1.000	4.86	39	0	0	33.1	31	18	27	0	2	0	1	0	0	0	—	2	1	1	0	0.1	.750
4 yrs.		5	5	.500	3.82	116	0	0	127.1	129	54	84	0	5	5	2	0	0	0		3	16	1	3	0.2	.950

Mike Lee

LEE, MICHAEL RANDALL BL TL 6′ 5″ 220 lbs.
B. May 19, 1941, Bell, Calif.

Year	Team	W	L	PCT	ERA	G	GS	CG	IP	H	BB	SO	ShO	Relief Pitching W	Relief Pitching L	Relief Pitching SV	Batting AB	Batting H	Batting HR	BA	PO	A	E	DP	TC/G	FA
1960	CLE A	0	0	—	2.00	7	0	0	9	6	11	6	0	0	0	0	0	0	0	—	0	0	0	0	0.0	.000
1963	LA A	1	1	.500	3.81	6	4	0	26	30	14	11	0	0	0	0	7	0	0	.000	1	10	0	0	1.8	1.000
2 yrs.		1	1	.500	3.34	13	4	0	35	36	25	17	0	0	0	0	7	0	0	.000	1	10	0	0	0.8	1.000

Roy Lee

LEE, ROY EDWIN BL TL 5′11½″ 175 lbs.
B. Sept. 28, 1917, Elmira, N. Y. D. Nov. 11, 1985, St. Louis, Mo.

Year	Team	W	L	PCT	ERA	G	GS	CG	IP	H	BB	SO	ShO	Relief Pitching W	Relief Pitching L	Relief Pitching SV	Batting AB	Batting H	Batting HR	BA	PO	A	E	DP	TC/G	FA
1945	NY N	0	2	.000	11.57	3	1	0	7	8	3	0	0	0	1	0	1	0	0	.000	0	0	0	0	0.0	.000

Thornton Lee

LEE, THORNTON STARR (Lefty) BL TL 6′ 3″ 205 lbs.
Father of Don Lee.
B. Sept. 13, 1906, Sonoma, Calif.

Year	Team	W	L	PCT	ERA	G	GS	CG	IP	H	BB	SO	ShO	Relief Pitching W	Relief Pitching L	Relief Pitching SV	Batting AB	Batting H	Batting HR	BA	PO	A	E	DP	TC/G	FA
1933	CLE A	1	1	.500	4.15	3	2	2	17.1	13	11	7	0	0	0	0	8	3	0	.375	0	3	0	0	1.0	1.000
1934		1	1	.500	5.04	24	6	0	85.2	105	44	41	0	0	0	0	21	2	0	.095	4	18	2	1	1.0	.917
1935		7	10	.412	4.04	32	20	8	180.2	179	71	81	1	2	1	1	61	12	0	.197	11	41	3	3	1.7	.945
1936		3	5	.375	4.89	43	8	2	127	138	67	49	0	1	2	3	41	5	0	.122	3	35	2	0	0.9	.950
1937	CHI A	12	10	.545	3.52	30	25	13	204.2	209	60	80	2	0	0	0	71	15	0	.211	9	34	3	0	1.5	.935
1938		13	12	.520	3.49	33	30	18	245.1	252	94	77	1	0	1	1	97	25	4	.258	1	46	5	2	1.6	.904
1939		15	11	.577	4.21	33	29	15	235	260	70	81	2	0	1	3	91	15	0	.165	6	45	2	0	1.6	.962
1940		12	13	.480	3.47	28	27	24	228	223	56	87	1	0	0	0	84	23	0	.274	5	31	4	2	1.4	.900
1941		22	11	.667	**2.37**	35	34	**30**	300.1	258	92	130	3	0	0	1	114	29	0	.254	10	52	5	2	1.9	.925
1942		2	6	.250	3.32	11	8	6	76	82	31	25	1	0	0	0	30	6	0	.200	1	7	1	2	0.8	.889

Thornton Lee *continued*

Year	Team		W	L	PCT	ERA	G	GS	CG	IP	H	BB	SO	ShO	Relief W	Relief L	Relief SV	AB	H	HR	BA	PO	A	E	DP	TC/G	FA
1943			5	9	.357	4.18	19	19	7	127	129	50	35	1	0	0	0	42	3	0	.071	3	17	3	1	1.2	.870
1944			3	9	.250	3.02	15	14	6	113.1	105	25	39	0	0	0	0	42	4	0	.095	3	32	2	2	2.5	.946
1945			15	12	.556	2.44	29	28	19	228.1	208	76	108	1	1	0	0	78	14	0	.179	6	38	2	4	1.6	.957
1946			2	4	.333	3.53	7	7	2	43.1	39	23	23	0	0	0	0	15	4	0	.267	0	7	2	1	1.3	.778
1947			3	7	.300	4.47	21	11	2	86.2	86	56	57	1	0	3	1	29	6	0	.207	4	15	2	1	1.0	.905
1948	NY	N	1	3	.250	4.41	11	4	1	32.2	41	12	17	0	0	1	0	11	1	0	.091	1	7	0	0	0.7	1.000
16 yrs.			117	124	.485	3.56	374	272	155	2331.1	2327	838	937	14	4	9	10	835	167	4	.200	67	428	38	21	1.4	.929

Tom Lee

LEE, THOMAS FRANK
B. June 8, 1862, Milwaukee, Wis. D. Mar. 4, 1886, Milwaukee, Wis.

Year	Team		W	L	PCT	ERA	G	GS	CG	IP	H	BB	SO	ShO	Relief W	Relief L	Relief SV	AB	H	HR	BA	PO	A	E	DP	TC/G	FA
1884	2 teams	CHI N (5G 1–4)	BAL U (15G 5–8)																								
"	total		6	12	.333	3.50	20	19	17	167.1	176	44	95	0	0	0	0	106	26	0	.245	31	52	15	5	3.2	.847

Watty Lee

LEE, WYATT ARNOLD (Indian)
B. Aug. 12, 1879, Lynch Station, Va. D. Mar. 6, 1936, Washington, D. C.
BL TL 5′10½″ 171 lbs.

Year	Team		W	L	PCT	ERA	G	GS	CG	IP	H	BB	SO	ShO	Relief W	Relief L	Relief SV	AB	H	HR	BA	PO	A	E	DP	TC/G	FA
1901	WAS	A	16	16	.500	4.40	36	33	25	262	328	45	63	2	1	1	0	129	33	0	.256	16	82	7	3	2.4	.933
1902			5	7	.417	5.05	13	10	10	98	118	20	24	0	1	1	0	391	100	4	.256	176	46	19	1	2.2	.921
1903			8	12	.400	3.08	22	20	15	166.2	169	40	70	2	1	0	0	231	48	0	.208	113	64	9	5	2.7	.952
1904	PIT	N	1	2	.333	8.74	5	3	1	22.2	34	9	5	0	0	1	0	12	4	0	.333	1	7	1	0	1.8	.889
4 yrs.			30	37	.448	4.29	76	66	51	549.1	649	114	162	4	3	3	0	*									
																						306	199	36	9	2.4	.933

Sam Leever

LEEVER, SAMUEL (The Goshen Schoolmaster)
B. Dec. 23, 1871, Goshen, Ohio D. May 19, 1953, Goshen, Ohio.
BR TR 5′10½″ 175 lbs.

Year	Team		W	L	PCT	ERA	G	GS	CG	IP	H	BB	SO	ShO	Relief W	Relief L	Relief SV	AB	H	HR	BA	PO	A	E	DP	TC/G	FA
1898	PIT	N	1	0	1.000	2.45	5	3	2	33	26	5	15	0	0	0	0	12	3	0	.250	3	5	0	0	1.6	1.000
1899			21	23	.477	3.18	**51**	39	35	**379**	353	122	121	4	2	**5**	**3**	146	33	0	.226	10	100	6	2	2.3	.948
1900			15	13	.536	2.71	30	29	25	232.2	236	48	84	3	0	0	0	88	18	1	.205	8	52	4	0	2.1	.938
1901			14	5	.737	2.86	21	20	18	176	182	39	82	2	1	0	0	71	13	0	.183	3	54	2	0	2.8	.966
1902			16	7	.696	2.39	28	26	23	222	203	31	86	4	0	0	2	90	16	0	.178	4	42	2	0	1.7	.958
1903			25	7	**.781**	**2.06**	36	34	30	284.1	255	60	90	**7**	0	0	1	115	19	0	.165	12	76	4	1	2.6	.957
1904			18	11	.621	2.17	34	32	26	253.1	224	54	63	1	1	0	0	99	26	1	.263	11	67	1	2	2.3	.987
1905			19	6	.760	2.70	33	29	20	230	199	54	81	3	1	0	0	88	9	0	.102	7	70	8	1	2.6	.906
1906			22	7	.759	2.32	36	31	25	260.1	232	48	76	6	1	1	0	95	20	0	.211	11	52	3	1	1.8	.955
1907			14	9	.609	1.66	31	24	17	216.2	182	46	65	5	2	1	0	73	11	0	.151	4	39	2	1	1.5	.956
1908			15	7	.682	2.10	38	20	14	192.2	179	41	28	4	2	2	2	61	9	0	.148	8	44	2	0	1.4	.963
1909			8	1	.889	2.83	19	4	2	70	74	14	23	0	6	1	2	24	4	0	.167	0	23	0	0	1.2	1.000
1910			6	5	.545	2.76	26	8	4	111	104	25	33	0	3	2	2	31	2	0	.065	3	35	0	3	1.5	1.000
13 yrs.			194	101	.658 8th	2.47	388	299	241	2661	2449	587	847	39	19	12	12	993	183	2	.184	84	659	34	11	2.0	.956
WORLD SERIES																											
1903	PIT	N	0	2	.000	6.30	2	2	1	10	13	3	2	0	0	0	0	4	0	0	.000	0	2	0	0	1.0	1.000

Bill Lefebvre

LEFEBVRE, WILFRID HENRY (Lefty)
B. Nov. 11, 1915, Natick, R. I.
BL TL 5′11½″ 180 lbs.

Year	Team		W	L	PCT	ERA	G	GS	CG	IP	H	BB	SO	ShO	Relief W	Relief L	Relief SV	AB	H	HR	BA	PO	A	E	DP	TC/G	FA
1938	BOS	A	0	0	—	13.50	1	0	0	4	8	0	0	0	0	0	0	1	1	1	1.000	0	0	0	0	0.0	.000
1939			1	1	.500	5.81	5	3	0	26.1	35	14	8	0	0	0	0	10	3	0	.300	1	2	0	0	0.6	1.000
1943	WAS	A	2	0	1.000	4.45	6	3	1	32.1	33	16	10	0	1	0	0	14	4	0	.286	1	6	0	1	1.2	1.000
1944			2	4	.333	4.52	24	4	2	69.2	86	21	18	0	1	1	3	62	16	0	.258	17	14	1	3	1.2	.969
4 yrs.			5	5	.500	5.03	36	10	3	132.1	162	51	36	0	2	1	3	*									
																						19	22	1	4	1.1	.976

Craig Lefferts

LEFFERTS, CRAIG LINDSAY
B. Sept. 29, 1957, Munich, West Germany.
BL TL 6′ 1″ 180 lbs.

Year	Team		W	L	PCT	ERA	G	GS	CG	IP	H	BB	SO	ShO	Relief W	Relief L	Relief SV	AB	H	HR	BA	PO	A	E	DP	TC/G	FA
1983	CHI	N	3	4	.429	3.13	56	5	0	89	80	29	60	0	2	3	1	18	2	0	.111	8	13	1	0	0.4	.955
1984	SD	N	3	4	.429	2.13	62	0	0	105.2	88	24	56	0	3	4	10	17	5	0	.294	5	10	1	2	0.3	.938
1985			7	6	.538	3.35	60	0	0	83.1	75	30	48	0	7	6	2	4	1	0	.250	4	11	0	1	0.3	1.000
1986			9	8	.529	3.09	**83**	0	0	107.2	98	44	72	0	9	8	4	8	1	1	.125	3	24	0	3	0.3	1.000
1987	2 teams	SD N (33G 2–2)	SF N (44G 3–3)																								
"	total		5	5	.500	3.83	77	0	0	98.2	92	33	57	0	5	5	6	7	2	0	.286	5	11	2	1	0.2	.889
1988	SF	N	3	8	.273	2.92	64	0	0	92.1	74	23	58	0	3	8	11	9	0	0	.000	2	11	0	0	0.2	1.000
1989			2	4	.333	2.69	70	0	0	107	93	22	71	0	2	4	20	7	0	0	.000	5	9	0	2	0.2	1.000
1990	SD	N	7	5	.583	2.52	56	0	0	78.2	68	22	60	0	7	5	23	4	1	0	.250	6	10	0	2	0.3	1.000
1991			1	6	.143	3.91	54	0	0	69	74	14	48	0	1	6	23	6	0	0	.000	3	12	0	1	0.3	1.000
1992	2 teams	SD N (27G 13–9)	BAL A (5G 1–3)																								
"	total		14	12	.538	3.76	32	32	1	196.1	214	41	104	0	0	0	0	52	4	0	.077	8	28	2	0	1.2	.947
1993	TEX	A	3	9	.250	6.05	52	8	0	83.1	102	28	58	0	2	4	0	0	0	0	—	6	12	1	0	0.4	.947
1994	CAL	A	1	1	.500	4.67	30	0	0	34.2	50	12	27	0	1	1	1	0	0	0	—	1	3	1	0	0.2	.800
12 yrs.			58	72	.446	3.43	696	45	1	1145.2	1108	322	719	0	42	54	101	132	16	1	.121	56	154	8	12	0.3	.963
LEAGUE CHAMPIONSHIP SERIES																											
1984	SD	N	2	0	1.000	0.00	3	0	0	4	1	1	1	0	2	0	0	0	0	0	—	0	0	0	0	0.0	.000
1987	SF	N	0	0	—	0.00	3	0	0	2	3	1	0	0	0	0	0	0	0	0	—	0	2	0	1	0.7	1.000
1989			0	0	—	9.00	2	0	0	1	1	2	1	0	0	0	0	0	0	0	—	0	0	0	0	0.0	.000
3 yrs.			2	0	1.000	1.29	8	0	0	7	5	4	2	0	2	0	0	0	0	0		0	2	0	1	0.3	1.000
WORLD SERIES																											
1984	SD	N	0	0	—	0.00	3	0	0	6	2	1	7	0	0	0	1	0	0	0	—	0	0	0	0	0.0	.000
1989	SF	N	0	0	—	3.38	3	0	0	2.2	2	2	1	0	0	0	0	0	0	0	—	0	1	1	0	0.7	.500
2 yrs.			0	0		1.04	6	0	0	8.2	4	3	8	0	0	0	1	0	0	0		0	1	1	0	0.3	.500

Phil Leftwich

LEFTWICH, PHILLIP DALE
B. May 19, 1969, Lynchburg, Va.
BR TR 6′ 5″ 205 lbs.

Year	Team		W	L	PCT	ERA	G	GS	CG	IP	H	BB	SO	ShO	Relief W	Relief L	Relief SV	AB	H	HR	BA	PO	A	E	DP	TC/G	FA
1993	CAL	A	4	6	.400	3.79	12	12	1	80.2	81	27	31	0	0	0	0	0	0	0	—	5	11	1	2	1.4	.941
1994			5	10	.333	5.68	20	20	1	114	127	42	67	0	0	0	0	0	0	0	—	9	15	3	0	1.4	.889
2 yrs.			9	16	.360	4.90	32	32	2	194.2	208	69	98	0	0	0	0	0	0	0		14	26	4	2	1.4	.909

Regis Leheny

LEHENY, REGIS FRANCIS BL TL 6′½″ 180 lbs.
B. Jan. 5, 1908, Pittsburgh, Pa. D. Nov. 2, 1976, Pittsburgh, Pa.

Year	Team		W	L	PCT	ERA	G	GS	CG	IP	H	BB	SO	ShO	Relief Pitching W	L	SV	Batting AB	H	HR	BA	PO	A	E	DP	TC/G	FA
1932	BOS	A	0	0	—	16.88	2	0	0	2.2	5	3	1	0	0	0	0	1	0	0	.000	0	2	0	0	1.0	1.000

Jim Lehew

LEHEW, JAMES ANTHONY BR TR 6′ 185 lbs.
B. Aug. 19, 1937, Baltimore, Md.

Year	Team		W	L	PCT	ERA	G	GS	CG	IP	H	BB	SO	ShO	Relief Pitching W	L	SV	Batting AB	H	HR	BA	PO	A	E	DP	TC/G	FA
1961	BAL	A	0	0	—	0.00	2	0	0	2	1	0	0	0	0	0	0	0	0	0	—	0	1	0	0	0.5	1.000
1962			0	0	—	1.86	6	0	0	9.2	10	3	2	0	0	0	0	1	0	0	.000	0	4	0	0	0.7	1.000
2 yrs.			0	0		1.54	8	0	0	11.2	11	3	2	0	0	0	0	1	0	0	.000	0	5	0	0	0.6	1.000

Ken Lehman

LEHMAN, KENNETH KARL BL TL 6′ 170 lbs.
B. June 10, 1928, Seattle, Wash.

Year	Team		W	L	PCT	ERA	G	GS	CG	IP	H	BB	SO	ShO	Relief Pitching W	L	SV	Batting AB	H	HR	BA	PO	A	E	DP	TC/G	FA
1952	BKN	N	1	2	.333	5.28	4	3	0	15.1	19	6	7	0	1	0	0	4	0	0	.000	0	4	0	0	1.0	1.000
1956			2	3	.400	5.66	25	4	0	49.1	65	23	29	0	2	1	0	10	3	0	.300	4	11	1	0	0.6	.938
1957	2 teams	BKN N (3G 0–0)	BAL A (30G 8–3)																								
″	total		8	3	.727	2.52	33	3	1	75	64	23	35	0	7	1	6	22	5	0	.227	8	9	3	3	0.6	.850
1958	BAL	A	2	1	.667	3.48	31	1	1	62	64	18	36	0	2	1	0	14	1	0	.071	3	11	0	0	0.5	1.000
1961	PHI	N	1	1	.500	4.26	41	2	0	63.1	61	25	27	0	1	0	1	6	0	0	.000	6	16	0	1	0.5	1.000
5 yrs.			14	10	.583	3.91	134	13	2	265	273	95	134	0	13	3	7	56	9	0	.161	21	51	4	4	0.6	.947
WORLD SERIES																											
1952	BKN	N	0	0	—	0.00	1	0	0	2	2	1	0	0	0	0	0	0	0	0	—	0	1	0	0	1.0	1.000

Norm Lehr

LEHR, NORMAN CARL MICHAEL (King) BR TR 6′ 168 lbs.
B. May 28, 1901, Rochester, N. Y. D. July 17, 1968, Livonia, N. Y.

Year	Team		W	L	PCT	ERA	G	GS	CG	IP	H	BB	SO	ShO	Relief Pitching W	L	SV	Batting AB	H	HR	BA	PO	A	E	DP	TC/G	FA
1926	CLE	A	0	0	—	3.07	4	0	0	14.2	11	4	4	0	0	0	0	4	0	0	.000	1	7	1	0	2.3	.889

Hank Leiber

LEIBER, HENRY EDWARD BR TR 6′ 1½″ 205 lbs.
B. Jan. 17, 1911, Phoenix, Ariz. D. Nov. 8, 1993, Tucson, Ariz.

Year	Team		W	L	PCT	ERA	G	GS	CG	IP	H	BB	SO	ShO	Relief Pitching W	L	SV	Batting AB	H	HR	BA	PO	A	E	DP	TC/G	FA
1942	NY	N	0	1	.000	6.00	1	1	1	9	9	5	5	0	0	0	0	*				3	1	0	0	4.0	1.000

Charlie Leibrandt

LEIBRANDT, CHARLES LOUIS, JR. BR TL 6′ 3″ 195 lbs.
B. Oct. 4, 1956, Chicago, Ill.

Year	Team		W	L	PCT	ERA	G	GS	CG	IP	H	BB	SO	ShO	Relief Pitching W	L	SV	Batting AB	H	HR	BA	PO	A	E	DP	TC/G	FA
1979	CIN	N	0	0	—	0.00	3	0	0	4	2	2	1	0	0	0	0	0	0	0	—	1	0	0	1	0.3	1.000
1980			10	9	.526	4.24	36	27	5	174	200	54	62	2	0	0	0	56	11	0	.196	10	35	3	3	1.3	.938
1981			1	1	.500	3.60	7	4	1	30	28	15	9	1	0	0	0	8	0	0	.000	0	7	0	0	1.0	1.000
1982			5	7	.417	5.10	36	11	0	107.2	130	48	34	0	2	1	2	25	2	0	.080	5	18	1	0	0.7	.958
1984	KC	A	11	7	.611	3.63	23	23	0	143.2	158	38	53	0	0	0	0	0	0	0	—	9	15	3	1	1.2	.889
1985			17	9	.654	2.69	33	33	8	237.2	223	68	108	3	0	0	0	0	0	0	—	19	53	1	2	2.2	.986
1986			14	11	.560	4.09	35	34	8	231.1	238	63	108	1	0	0	0	0	0	0	—	14	43	1	3	1.7	.983
1987			16	11	.593	3.41	35	35	8	240.1	235	74	151	3	0	0	0	0	0	0	—	15	55	4	4	2.1	.946
1988			13	12	.520	3.19	35	35	7	243	244	62	125	2	0	0	0	0	0	0	—	19	43	3	2	1.9	.954
1989			5	11	.313	5.14	33	27	3	161	196	54	73	1	0	0	0	0	0	0	—	6	26	2	0	1.0	.941
1990	ATL	N	9	11	.450	3.16	24	24	5	162.1	164	35	76	2	0	0	0	50	9	0	.180	10	28	0	2	1.6	1.000
1991			15	13	.536	3.49	36	36	1	229.2	212	56	128	1	0	0	0	70	3	0	.043	14	53	2	1	1.9	.971
1992			15	7	.682	3.36	32	31	5	193	191	42	104	2	0	0	0	58	7	0	.121	20	44	3	1	2.1	.955
1993	TEX	A	9	10	.474	4.55	26	26	1	150.1	169	45	89	0	0	0	0	0	0	0	—	9	45	2	5	2.2	.964
14 yrs.			140	119	.541	3.71	394	346	52	2308	2390	656	1121	18	2	1	2	267	32	0	.120	151	465	25	25	1.6	.961
LEAGUE CHAMPIONSHIP SERIES																											
1979	CIN	N	0	0	—	0.00	1	0	0	0.1	0	0	0	0	0	0	0	0	0	0	—	0	0	0	0	0.0	.000
1984	KC	A	0	1	.000	1.13	1	1	1	8	3	4	6	0	0	0	0	0	0	0	—	1	2	0	0	3.0	1.000
1985			1	2	.333	5.28	3	2	0	15.1	17	4	6	0	1	0	0	0	0	0	—	3	7	0	0	3.3	1.000
1991	ATL	N	0	0	—	1.35	1	1	0	6.2	8	3	6	0	0	0	0	1	0	0	.000	0	1	0	0	1.0	1.000
1992			0	0	—	1.93	2	0	0	4.2	4	3	3	0	0	0	0	1	0	0	.000	0	1	0	0	0.5	1.000
5 yrs.			1	3 5th	.250	3.09	8	4	1	35	32	14	21	0	1	0	0	2	0	0	.000	4	11	0	0	1.9	1.000
WORLD SERIES																											
1985	KC	A	0	1	.000	2.76	2	2	0	16.1	10	4	10	0	0	0	0	4	0	0	.000	1	2	0	0	1.5	1.000
1991	ATL	N	0	2	.000	11.25	2	1	0	4	8	1	3	0	0	1	0	0	0	0	—	0	1	0	0	0.5	1.000
1992			0	1	.000	9.00	1	0	0	2	3	0	0	0	0	1	0	0	0	0	—	1	0	0	0	1.0	1.000
3 yrs.			0	4	.000	4.84	5	3	0	22.1	21	5	13	0	0	2	0	4	0	0	.000	2	3	0	0	1.0	1.000

Lefty Leifield

LEIFIELD, ALBERT PETER BL TL 6′ 1″ 165 lbs.
B. Sept. 5, 1883, Trenton, Ill. D. Oct. 10, 1970, Alexandria, Va.

Year	Team		W	L	PCT	ERA	G	GS	CG	IP	H	BB	SO	ShO	Relief Pitching W	L	SV	Batting AB	H	HR	BA	PO	A	E	DP	TC/G	FA
1905	PIT	N	5	2	.714	2.89	8	7	6	56	52	14	10	1	0	0	0	20	7	0	.350	5	19	0	0	3.0	1.000
1906			18	13	.581	1.87	37	31	24	255.2	214	68	111	8	3	0	1	88	11	0	.125	12	78	3	3	2.5	.968
1907			20	16	.556	2.33	40	33	24	286	270	100	112	6	3	2	0	102	15	0	.147	18	94	6	3	3.0	.949
1908			15	14	.517	2.10	34	26	18	218.2	168	86	87	5	2	1	2	75	17	0	.227	6	62	5	4	2.1	.932
1909			19	8	.704	2.37	32	26	13	201.2	172	54	43	3	3	1	0	73	14	0	.192	6	53	3	1	1.9	.952
1910			15	12	.556	2.64	40	30	13	218.1	197	67	64	3	5	0	1	60	11	0	.183	13	75	2	2	2.3	.978
1911			16	16	.500	2.63	42	37	26	318	301	82	111	2	0	0	1	102	24	0	.235	12	82	7	6	2.3	.931
1912	2 teams	PIT N (6G 1–2)	CHI N (13G 7–2)																								
″	total		8	4	.667	2.86	19	10	5	94.1	97	31	31	1	3	1	0	33	4	0	.121	10	31	1	2	2.2	.976
1913	CHI	N	0	1	.000	5.48	6	1	0	21.1	28	5	4	0	0	1	0	7	0	0	.000	0	10	0	0	1.7	1.000
1918	STL	A	2	6	.250	2.55	15	6	3	67	61	19	22	1	1	1	0	19	1	0	.053	2	23	0	1	1.7	1.000
1919			6	4	.600	2.93	19	9	6	92	96	25	18	2	1	1	0	30	3	0	.100	1	30	0	1	1.6	1.000
1920			0	0	—	7.00	4	0	0	9	17	3	3	0	0	0	0	2	0	0	.000	0	1	0	0	0.3	1.000
12 yrs.			124	96	.564	2.47	296	216	138	1838	1673	554	616	32	21	8	5	611	107	0	.175	85	558	27	23	2.3	.960
WORLD SERIES																											
1909	PIT	N	0	1	.000	11.25	1	1	0	4	7	1	0	0	0	0	0	1	0	0	.000	0	5	0	0	5.0	1.000

Dave Leiper

LEIPER, DAVID PAUL BL TL 6′ 1″ 160 lbs.
B. June 18, 1962, Whittier, Calif.

Year	Team		W	L	PCT	ERA	G	GS	CG	IP	H	BB	SO	ShO	Relief Pitching W	L	SV	Batting AB	H	HR	BA	PO	A	E	DP	TC/G	FA
1984	OAK	A	1	0	1.000	9.00	8	0	0	7	12	5	3	0	1	0	0	0	0	0	—	1	2	0	0	0.4	1.000
1986			2	2	.500	4.83	33	0	0	31.2	28	18	15	0	2	2	1	0	0	0	—	0	6	0	0	0.2	1.000

Dave Leiper *continued*

Year	Team	W	L	PCT	ERA	G	GS	CG	IP	H	BB	SO	ShO	Relief W	Relief L	SV	AB	H	HR	BA	PO	A	E	DP	TC/G	FA
1987	2 teams OAK A (45G 2–1) SD N (12G 1–0)																									
"	total	3	1	.750	3.95	57	0	0	68.1	65	23	43	0	3	1	2	0	0	0		5	14	2	1	0.4	.905
1988	SD N	3	0	1.000	2.17	35	0	0	54	45	14	33	0	3	0	1	2	1	0	.500	3	9	0	1	0.3	1.000
1989		0	1	.000	5.02	22	0	0	28.2	40	20	7	0	0	1	0	1	0	0	.000	4	7	1	0	0.5	.917
1994	OAK A	0	0	—	1.93	26	0	0	18.2	13	6	14	0	0	0	1	0	0	0	—	0	1	0	1	0.0	1.000
1995	2 teams OAK A (24G 1–1) MON N (26G 0–2)																									
"	total	1	3	.250	3.22	50	0	0	44.2	39	19	22	0	1	3	2	1	0	0	.000	1	8	0	0	0.2	1.000
7 yrs.		10	7	.588	3.66	231	0	0	253	242	105	137	0	10	7	7	4	1	0	.250	14	47	3	3	0.3	.953

Jack Leiper

LEIPER, JOHN HENRY THOMAS
B. Dec. 23, 1867, Chester, Pa. D. Aug. 23, 1960, West Goshen, Pa.
BL TL 5′11″

Year	Team	W	L	PCT	ERA	G	GS	CG	IP	H	BB	SO	ShO	Relief W	Relief L	SV	AB	H	HR	BA	PO	A	E	DP	TC/G	FA
1891	COL AA	2	2	.500	5.40	6	5	4	45	41	39	19	0	0	0	0	21	3	0	.143	4	8	3	1	2.1	.800

John Leister

LEISTER, JOHN WILLIAM
B. Jan. 3, 1961, San Antonio, Tex.
BR TR 6′ 2″ 200 lbs.

Year	Team	W	L	PCT	ERA	G	GS	CG	IP	H	BB	SO	ShO	Relief W	Relief L	SV	AB	H	HR	BA	PO	A	E	DP	TC/G	FA
1987	BOS A	0	2	.000	9.20	8	6	0	30.1	49	12	16	0	0	0	0	0	0	0	—	2	2	0	0	0.5	1.000
1990		0	0	—	4.76	2	1	0	5.2	7	4	3	0	0	0	0	0	0	0	—	0	0	0	0	0.0	.000
2 yrs.		0	2	.000	8.50	10	7	0	36	56	16	19	0	0	0	0	0	0	0		2	2	0	0	0.4	1.000

Al Leiter

LEITER, ALOIS TERRY
Brother of Mark Leiter.
B. Oct. 23, 1965, Toms River, N. J.
BL TL 6′ 2″ 200 lbs.

Year	Team	W	L	PCT	ERA	G	GS	CG	IP	H	BB	SO	ShO	Relief W	Relief L	SV	AB	H	HR	BA	PO	A	E	DP	TC/G	FA
1987	NY A	2	2	.500	6.35	4	4	0	22.2	24	15	28	0	0	0	0	0	0	0	—	0	2	0	0	0.5	1.000
1988		4	4	.500	3.92	14	14	0	57.1	49	33	60	0	0	0	0	0	0	0	—	0	11	1	0	0.9	.917
1989	2 teams NY A (4G 1–2) TOR A (1G 0–0)																									
"	total	1	2	.333	5.67	5	5	0	33.1	32	23	26	0	0	0	0	0	0	0		1	2	0	0	0.6	1.000
1990	TOR A	0	0	—	0.00	4	0	0	6.1	1	2	5	0	0	0	0	0	0	0	—	1	1	0	0	0.5	1.000
1991		0	0	—	27.00	3	0	0	1.2	3	5	1	0	0	0	0	0	0	0	—	0	1	0	0	0.3	1.000
1992		0	0	—	9.00	1	0	0	1	1	2	0	0	0	0	0	0	0	0	—	0	0	0	0	0.0	.000
1993		9	6	.600	4.11	34	12	1	105	93	56	66	1	3	1	2	0	0	0	—	4	12	1	0	0.5	.941
1994		6	7	.462	5.08	20	20	1	111.2	125	65	100	0	0	0	0	0	0	0	—	3	13	0	1	0.8	1.000
1995		11	11	.500	3.64	28	28	2	183	162	108	153	1	0	0	0	0	0	0	—	7	15	0	2	0.8	1.000
9 yrs.		33	32	.508	4.36	113	83	4	522	490	309	439	2	3	1	2	0	0	0		16	57	2	3	0.7	.973
LEAGUE CHAMPIONSHIP SERIES																										
1993	TOR A	0	0	—	3.38	2	0	0	2.2	4	2	2	0	0	0	0	0	0	0	—	0	0	0	0	0.0	.000
WORLD SERIES																										
1993	TOR A	1	0	1.000	7.71	3	0	0	7	12	2	5	0	1	0	0	1	1	0	1.000	0	0	0	0	0.0	.000

Mark Leiter

LEITER, MARK EDWARD
Brother of Al Leiter.
B. Apr. 13, 1963, Joliet, Ill.
BR TR 6′ 3″ 200 lbs.

Year	Team	W	L	PCT	ERA	G	GS	CG	IP	H	BB	SO	ShO	Relief W	Relief L	SV	AB	H	HR	BA	PO	A	E	DP	TC/G	FA
1990	NY A	1	1	.500	6.84	8	3	0	26.1	33	9	21	0	0	1	0	0	0	0	—	0	8	0	1	1.0	1.000
1991	DET A	9	7	.563	4.21	38	15	1	134.2	125	50	103	0	2	1	1	0	0	0	—	3	17	1	1	0.6	.952
1992		8	5	.615	4.18	35	14	1	112	116	43	75	0	3	2	0	0	0	0	—	8	15	1	0	0.7	.958
1993		6	6	.500	4.72	27	13	1	106.2	111	44	70	0	1	2	0	0	0	0	—	5	11	2	1	0.7	.889
1994	CAL A	4	7	.364	4.72	40	7	0	95.1	99	35	71	0	2	4	2	0	0	0	—	5	16	1	0	0.6	.955
1995	SF N	10	12	.455	3.82	30	29	7	195.2	185	55	129	1	0	1	0	61	6	0	.098	7	19	4	4	1.0	.867
6 yrs.		38	38	.500	4.35	178	81	10	670.2	669	236	469	1	8	11	3	61	6	0	.098	28	86	9	7	0.7	.927

Bill Leith

LEITH, WILLIAM (Shady Bill)
B. May 31, 1873, Mattewan, N. Y. D. July 16, 1940, Beacon, N. Y.
TL

Year	Team	W	L	PCT	ERA	G	GS	CG	IP	H	BB	SO	ShO	Relief W	Relief L	SV	AB	H	HR	BA	PO	A	E	DP	TC/G	FA
1899	WAS N	0	0	—	18.00	1	0	0	2	4	2	1	0	0	0	0	1	0	0	.000	0	0	1	0	1.0	.000

Doc Leitner

LEITNER, GEORGE ALOYSIUS
B. Sept. 14, 1865, Piermont, N. Y. D. May 18, 1937, New York, N. Y.
BR TR 5′11½″ 185 lbs.

Year	Team	W	L	PCT	ERA	G	GS	CG	IP	H	BB	SO	ShO	Relief W	Relief L	SV	AB	H	HR	BA	PO	A	E	DP	TC/G	FA
1887	IND N	2	6	.250	5.68	8	8	8	65	69	41	27	0	0	0	0	27	4	0	.148	0	5	3	0	1.0	.625

Dummy Leitner

LEITNER, GEORGE MICHAEL
B. June 19, 1871, Parkton, Md. D. Feb. 20, 1960, Baltimore, Md.
BL TR 5′ 7″ 120 lbs.

Year	Team	W	L	PCT	ERA	G	GS	CG	IP	H	BB	SO	ShO	Relief W	Relief L	SV	AB	H	HR	BA	PO	A	E	DP	TC/G	FA
1901	2 teams PHI A (1G 0–0) NY N (2G 0–2)																									
"	total	0	2	.000	4.05	3	2	2	20	28	5	4	0	0	0	0	8	1	0	.125	0	3	0	0	1.0	1.000
1902	2 teams CLE A (1G 0–0) CHI A (1G 0–0)																									
"	total	0	0		7.50	2	1	0	12	20	3	0	0	0	0	0	7	1	0	.143	1	5	0	2	3.0	1.000
2 yrs.		0	2	.000	5.34	5	3	2	32	48	8	4	0	0	0	0	15	2	0	.133	1	8	0	2	1.8	1.000

Bill Lelivelt

LELIVELT, WILLIAM JOHN
Brother of Jack Lelivelt.
B. Oct. 21, 1884, Chicago, Ill. D. Feb. 14, 1968, Chicago, Ill.
BR TR 6′ 195 lbs.

Year	Team	W	L	PCT	ERA	G	GS	CG	IP	H	BB	SO	ShO	Relief W	Relief L	SV	AB	H	HR	BA	PO	A	E	DP	TC/G	FA
1909	DET A	0	1	.000	4.50	4	2	1	20	27	2	4	0	0	0	1	6	2	0	.333	1	7	0	0	2.0	1.000
1910		0	1	.000	1.00	1	1	1	9	6	3	2	0	0	0	0	2	1	0	.500	0	3	0	1	3.0	1.000
2 yrs.		0	2	.000	3.41	5	3	2	29	33	5	6	0	0	0	1	8	3	0	.375	1	10	0	1	2.2	1.000

Dave Lemanczyk

LEMANCZYK, DAVID LAWRENCE
B. Aug. 17, 1950, Syracuse, N. Y.
BR TR 6′ 4″ 235 lbs.

Year	Team	W	L	PCT	ERA	G	GS	CG	IP	H	BB	SO	ShO	Relief W	Relief L	SV	AB	H	HR	BA	PO	A	E	DP	TC/G	FA
1973	DET A	0	0	—	13.50	1	0	0	2	4	0	0	0	0	0	0	0	0	0	—	0	0	0	0	0.0	.000
1974		2	1	.667	3.99	22	3	0	79	79	44	52	0	1	0	0	0	0	0	—	6	12	0	1	0.8	1.000
1975		2	7	.222	4.46	26	6	4	109	120	46	67	0	2	1	0	0	0	0	—	9	14	1	1	0.9	.958
1976		4	6	.400	5.11	20	10	1	81	86	34	51	0	2	0	0	0	0	0	—	8	14	2	0	1.2	.917
1977	TOR A	13	16	.448	4.25	34	34	11	252	278	87	105	0	0	0	0	0	0	0	—	25	37	4	4	1.9	.939

Dave Lemanczyk *continued*

Year	Team	W	L	PCT	ERA	G	GS	CG	IP	H	BB	SO	ShO	Relief Pitching W	Relief Pitching L	Relief Pitching SV	Batting AB	Batting H	Batting HR	BA	PO	A	E	DP	TC/G	FA
1978		4	14	.222	6.26	29	20	3	136.2	170	65	62	0	0	0	0	0	0	0	—	2	22	2	1	0.9	.923
1979		8	10	.444	3.71	22	20	11	143	137	45	63	3	0	0	0	0	0	0	—	12	20	2	2	1.5	.941
1980	**2 teams** **TOR A** (10G 2–5) **CAL A** (21G 2–4)																									
"	**total**	4	9	.308	4.75	31	10	0	110	138	42	29	0	1	3	0	0	0	0		5	15	0	1	0.6	1.000
8 yrs.		37	63	.370	4.62	185	103	30	912.2	1012	363	429	3	6	4	0	0	0	0		67	134	11	10	1.1	.948

Denny Lemaster

LEMASTER, DENVER CLAYTON BR TL 6′ 1″ 182 lbs.
B. Feb. 25, 1939, Corona, Calif.

Year	Team	W	L	PCT	ERA	G	GS	CG	IP	H	BB	SO	ShO	Relief Pitching W	Relief Pitching L	Relief Pitching SV	Batting AB	Batting H	Batting HR	BA	PO	A	E	DP	TC/G	FA
1962	**MIL N**	3	4	.429	3.01	17	12	4	86.2	75	32	69	1	0	0	0	33	4	0	.121	3	7	3	0	0.8	.769
1963		11	14	.440	3.04	46	31	10	237	199	85	190	1	1	0	1	74	14	2	.189	12	26	2	1	0.9	.950
1964		17	11	.607	4.15	39	35	9	221	216	75	185	3	1	0	1	67	9	0	.134	11	35	0	3	1.2	1.000
1965		7	13	.350	4.43	32	23	4	146.1	140	58	111	1	0	1	0	45	4	0	.089	10	23	3	1	1.1	.917
1966	**ATL N**	11	8	.579	3.74	27	27	10	171	170	41	139	3	0	0	0	59	7	0	.119	7	18	0	0	0.9	1.000
1967		9	9	.500	3.34	31	31	8	215.1	184	72	148	2	0	0	0	67	7	0	.104	7	35	0	0	1.4	1.000
1968	**HOU N**	10	15	.400	2.81	33	32	7	224	231	72	146	2	0	0	0	65	2	0	.031	7	27	4	1	1.2	.895
1969		13	17	.433	3.16	38	37	11	245	232	72	173	1	0	0	1	88	15	1	.170	12	33	0	1	1.2	1.000
1970		7	12	.368	4.56	39	21	3	162	169	65	103	0	1	1	3	45	8	1	.178	8	17	1	1	0.7	.962
1971		0	2	.000	3.45	42	0	0	60	59	22	28	0	0	2	2	6	1	0	.167	1	10	0	1	0.3	1.000
1972	**MON N**	2	0	1.000	7.78	13	0	0	19.2	28	6	13	0	2	0	0	3	1	0	.333	0	1	0	0	0.1	1.000
11 yrs.		90	105	.462	3.58	357	249	66	1788	1703	600	1305	14	5	4	8	552	72	4	.130	78	232	13	9	0.9	.960

Dick LeMay

LeMAY, RICHARD PAUL BL TL 6′ 3″ 190 lbs.
B. Aug. 28, 1938, Cincinnati, Ohio.

Year	Team	W	L	PCT	ERA	G	GS	CG	IP	H	BB	SO	ShO	Relief Pitching W	Relief Pitching L	Relief Pitching SV	Batting AB	Batting H	Batting HR	BA	PO	A	E	DP	TC/G	FA
1961	**SF N**	3	6	.333	3.56	27	5	1	83.1	65	36	54	0	2	6	3	26	2	0	.077	3	15	2	1	0.7	.900
1962		0	1	.000	7.71	9	0	0	9.1	9	9	5	0	0	1	1	0	0	0	—	0	2	0	0	0.2	1.000
1963	**CHI N**	0	1	.000	5.28	9	1	0	15.1	26	4	10	0	0	1	0	2	0	0	.000	0	3	1	0	0.4	.750
3 yrs.		3	8	.273	4.17	45	6	1	108	100	49	69	0	2	8	4	28	2	0	.071	3	20	3	1	0.6	.885

Bob Lemon

LEMON, ROBERT GRANVILLE BL TR 6′ 180 lbs.
B. Sept. 22, 1920, San Bernardino, Calif.
Manager 1970–72, 1977–79, 1981–82.
Hall of Fame 1976.

Year	Team	W	L	PCT	ERA	G	GS	CG	IP	H	BB	SO	ShO	Relief Pitching W	Relief Pitching L	Relief Pitching SV	Batting AB	Batting H	Batting HR	BA	PO	A	E	DP	TC/G	FA
1946	**CLE A**	4	5	.444	2.49	32	5	1	94	77	68	39	0	3	2	1	89	16	1	.180	1	1	0	0	2.0	1.000
1947		11	5	.688	3.44	37	15	6	167.1	150	97	65	1	1	2	3	56	18	2	.321	13	46	1	4	1.5	.983
1948		20	14	.588	2.82	43	37	**20**	**293.2**	231	129	147	**10**	1	1	2	119	34	5	.286	23	86	4	8	2.6	.965
1949		22	10	.688	2.99	37	33	22	279.2	211	137	138	2	2	1	1	108	29	7	.269	34	71	4	5	2.9	.963
1950		**23**	11	.676	3.84	44	**37**	**22**	**288**	**281**	146	**170**	3	1	0	3	136	37	6	.272	22	66	4	6	2.1	.957
1951		17	**14**	.548	3.52	42	**34**	17	263.1	**244**	124	132	1	0	0	2	102	21	3	.206	21	60	2	5	2.0	.976
1952		22	11	.667	2.50	42	**36**	**28**	**309.2**	236	105	131	5	0	1	4	124	28	2	.226	32	79	2	7	2.7	.982
1953		21	15	.583	3.36	41	36	23	**286.2**	**283**	110	98	5	1	1	1	112	26	2	.232	31	74	3	15	2.6	.972
1954		**23**	7	.767	2.72	36	33	**21**	258.1	228	92	110	2	1	0	0	98	21	2	.214	22	57	3	8	2.3	.963
1955		**18**	10	.643	3.88	35	31	5	211.1	218	74	100	0	1	0	2	78	19	1	.244	16	43	1	3	1.7	.983
1956		20	14	.588	3.03	39	35	**21**	255.1	230	89	94	2	0	0	3	93	18	5	.194	24	61	6	6	2.3	.934
1957		6	11	.353	4.60	21	17	2	117.1	129	64	45	0	1	2	0	46	3	1	.065	12	31	0	5	2.0	1.000
1958		0	1	.000	5.33	11	1	0	25.1	41	16	8	0	0	0	0	13	3	0	.231	1	7	0	1	0.7	1.000
13 yrs.		207	128	.618	3.23	460	350	188	2850	2559	1251	1277	31	12	10	22	*				298	713	33	80	2.2	.968
WORLD SERIES																										
1948	**CLE A**	2	0	1.000	1.65	2	2	1	16.1	16	7	6	0	0	0	0	7	0	0	.000	3	9	0	1	6.0	1.000
1954		0	2	.000	6.75	2	2	1	13.1	16	8	11	0	0	0	0	6	0	0	.000	2	2	0	0	2.0	1.000
2 yrs.		2	2	.500	3.94	4	4	2	29.2	32	15	17	0	0	0	0	*				5	11	0	1	4.0	1.000

Dave Lemonds

LEMONDS, DAVID LEE BL TL 6′ 1½″ 180 lbs.
B. July 5, 1948, Charlotte, N. C.

Year	Team	W	L	PCT	ERA	G	GS	CG	IP	H	BB	SO	ShO	Relief Pitching W	Relief Pitching L	Relief Pitching SV	Batting AB	Batting H	Batting HR	BA	PO	A	E	DP	TC/G	FA
1969	**CHI N**	0	1	.000	3.60	2	1	0	5	5	5	0	0	0	0	0	1	0	0	.000	0	1	0	0	0.5	1.000
1972	**CHI A**	4	7	.364	2.95	31	18	0	94.2	87	38	69	0	1	1	0	25	3	0	.120	7	11	0	2	0.6	1.000
2 yrs.		4	8	.333	2.98	33	19	0	99.2	92	43	69	0	1	1	0	26	3	0	.115	7	12	0	2	0.6	1.000

Mark Lemongello

LEMONGELLO, MARK BR TR 6′ 1″ 180 lbs.
B. July 21, 1955, Jersey City, N. J.

Year	Team	W	L	PCT	ERA	G	GS	CG	IP	H	BB	SO	ShO	Relief Pitching W	Relief Pitching L	Relief Pitching SV	Batting AB	Batting H	Batting HR	BA	PO	A	E	DP	TC/G	FA
1976	**HOU N**	3	1	.750	2.79	4	4	1	29	26	7	9	0	0	0	0	8	0	0	.000	1	9	0	0	2.5	1.000
1977		9	14	.391	3.47	34	30	5	215	237	52	83	0	0	1	0	69	6	0	.087	23	30	5	1	1.7	.914
1978		9	14	.391	3.94	33	30	9	210	204	66	77	1	0	0	1	64	11	0	.172	15	34	2	1	1.5	.961
1979	**TOR A**	1	9	.100	6.29	18	10	2	83	97	34	40	0	1	2	0	0	0	0	—	8	15	2	0	1.4	.920
4 yrs.		22	38	.367	4.06	89	74	17	537	564	159	209	1	1	3	1	141	17	0	.121	47	88	9	2	1.6	.938

Ed Lennon

LENNON, EDWARD FRANCIS BR TR 5′11″ 170 lbs.
B. Aug. 17, 1897, Philadelphia, Pa. D. Sept. 13, 1947, Philadelphia, Pa.

Year	Team	W	L	PCT	ERA	G	GS	CG	IP	H	BB	SO	ShO	Relief Pitching W	Relief Pitching L	Relief Pitching SV	Batting AB	Batting H	Batting HR	BA	PO	A	E	DP	TC/G	FA
1928	**PHI N**	0	0	—	8.76	5	0	0	12.1	19	10	6	0	0	0	0	4	0	0	.000	0	1	1	0	0.4	.500

Danilo Leon

LEON, DANILO ENRIQUE BR TR 6′ 1″ 170 lbs.
Born Danilo Enrique Leon (Lineco).
B. Apr. 3, 1967, La Concepcion, Venezuela.

Year	Team	W	L	PCT	ERA	G	GS	CG	IP	H	BB	SO	ShO	Relief Pitching W	Relief Pitching L	Relief Pitching SV	Batting AB	Batting H	Batting HR	BA	PO	A	E	DP	TC/G	FA
1992	**TEX A**	1	1	.500	5.89	15	0	0	18.1	18	10	15	0	1	1	0	0	0	0	—	3	1	0	0	0.3	1.000

Max Leon

LEON, MAXIMINO BR TR 5′10″ 145 lbs.
Born Maximino Leon (Molino).
B. Feb. 4, 1950, Pozo Hondo, Mexico.

Year	Team	W	L	PCT	ERA	G	GS	CG	IP	H	BB	SO	ShO	Relief Pitching W	Relief Pitching L	Relief Pitching SV	Batting AB	Batting H	Batting HR	BA	PO	A	E	DP	TC/G	FA
1973	**ATL N**	2	2	.500	5.33	12	1	1	27	30	9	18	0	1	2	0	7	2	0	.286	1	2	0	0	0.3	1.000
1974		4	7	.364	2.64	34	2	1	75	68	14	38	1	3	6	3	15	2	0	.133	4	15	1	2	0.6	.950
1975		2	1	.667	4.13	50	1	0	85	90	33	53	0	1	1	6	9	3	0	.333	3	19	3	0	0.5	.880

Max Leon *continued*

Year	Team		W	L	PCT	ERA	G	GS	CG	IP	H	BB	SO	ShO	Relief Pitching W	Relief Pitching L	Relief Pitching SV	Batting AB	Batting H	Batting HR	BA	PO	A	E	DP	TC/G	FA
1976			2	4	.333	2.75	30	0	0	36	32	15	16	0	2	4	3	2	0	0	.000	1	3	0	0	0.1	1.000
1977			4	4	.500	3.95	31	9	0	82	89	25	44	0	2	2	1	19	6	0	.316	9	12	1	0	0.7	.955
1978			0	0	—	6.00	5	0	0	6	6	4	1	0	0	0	0	0	0	0	—	0	1	0	0	0.2	1.000
6 yrs.			14	18	.438	3.70	162	13	2	311	315	100	170	1	9	15	13	52	13	0	.250	18	52	5	2	0.5	.933

Sid Leon

LEON, ISIDORO (Izzy)
Born Isidoro Leon (Becerra).
B. Jan. 4, 1911, Cruces, Cuba.

BR TR 5′10″ 160 lbs.

Year	Team		W	L	PCT	ERA	G	GS	CG	IP	H	BB	SO	ShO	Relief Pitching W	Relief Pitching L	Relief Pitching SV	Batting AB	Batting H	Batting HR	BA	PO	A	E	DP	TC/G	FA
1945	**PHI**	**N**	0	4	.000	5.35	14	4	0	38.2	49	19	11	0	0	0	0	9	1	0	.111	2	8	1	0	0.8	.909

Dennis Leonard

LEONARD, DENNIS PATRICK
B. May 8, 1951, Brooklyn, N. Y.

BR TR 6′ 1″ 190 lbs.

Year	Team		W	L	PCT	ERA	G	GS	CG	IP	H	BB	SO	ShO	Relief Pitching W	Relief Pitching L	Relief Pitching SV	Batting AB	Batting H	Batting HR	BA	PO	A	E	DP	TC/G	FA
1974	**KC**	**A**	0	4	.000	5.32	5	4	0	22	28	12	8	0	0	0	0	0	0	0	—	3	7	0	1	2.0	1.000
1975			15	7	.682	3.77	32	30	8	212.1	212	90	146	0	1	0	0	0	0	0	—	14	28	2	4	1.4	.955
1976			17	10	.630	3.51	35	34	16	259	247	70	150	2	0	0	0	0	0	0	—	11	23	6	2	1.1	.850
1977			**20**	12	.625	3.04	38	37	21	293	246	79	244	5	0	0	1	0	0	0	—	21	29	4	2	1.4	.926
1978			21	17	.553	3.33	40	**40**	20	294.2	**283**	78	183	4	0	0	0	0	0	0	—	16	43	1	2	1.5	.983
1979			14	12	.538	4.08	32	32	12	236	226	56	126	**5**	0	0	0	0	0	0	—	19	32	1	2	1.6	.981
1980			20	11	.645	3.79	38	**38**	9	280	271	80	155	3	0	0	0	0	0	0	—	9	41	1	4	1.3	.980
1981			13	11	.542	2.99	26	**26**	9	**202**	**202**	41	107	2	0	0	0	0	0	0	—	13	31	0	3	1.7	1.000
1982			10	6	.625	5.10	21	21	2	130.2	145	46	58	0	0	0	0	0	0	0	—	16	18	3	2	1.8	.919
1983			6	3	.667	3.71	10	10	1	63	69	19	31	0	0	0	0	0	0	0	—	2	11	2	2	1.5	.867
1985			0	0	—	0.00	2	0	0	2	1	0	1	0	0	0	0	0	0	0	—	0	0	0	0	0.0	.000
1986			8	13	.381	4.44	33	30	5	192.2	207	51	114	2	0	0	0	0	0	0	—	11	29	4	4	1.3	.909
12 yrs.			144	106	.576	3.69	312	302	103	2187.1	2137	622	1323	23	1	0	1	0	0	0		135	292	24	28	1.4	.947
DIVISIONAL PLAYOFF SERIES																											
1981	**KC**	**A**	0	1	.000	1.13	1	1	0	8	7	1	3	0	0	0	0	0	0	0	—	0	0	0	0	0.0	.000
LEAGUE CHAMPIONSHIP SERIES																											
1976	**KC**	**A**	0	0	—	19.29	2	2	0	2.1	9	2	0	0	0	0	0	0	0	0	—	0	0	0	0	0.0	.000
1977			1	1	.500	3.00	2	1	1	9	5	2	4	0	0	1	0	0	0	0	—	0	0	0	0	0.0	.000
1978			0	2	.000	3.75	2	2	1	12	13	2	11	0	0	0	0	0	0	0	—	1	0	0	0	0.5	1.000
1980			1	0	1.000	2.25	1	1	0	8	7	1	8	0	0	0	0	0	0	0	—	0	0	0	0	0.0	.000
4 yrs.			2	3 **5th**	.400	4.31	7	6 **9th**	2 **4th**	31.1	34	7	23	0	0	1	0	0	0	0		1	0	0	0	0.1	1.000
WORLD SERIES																											
1980	**KC**	**A**	1	1	.500	6.75	2	2	0	10.2	15	2	5	0	0	0	0	0	0	0	—	0	0	1	0	0.5	.000

Dutch Leonard

LEONARD, EMIL JOHN
B. Mar. 25, 1909, Auburn, Ill. D. Apr. 17, 1983, Springfield, Ill.

BR TR 6′ 175 lbs.

Year	Team		W	L	PCT	ERA	G	GS	CG	IP	H	BB	SO	ShO	Relief Pitching W	Relief Pitching L	Relief Pitching SV	Batting AB	Batting H	Batting HR	BA	PO	A	E	DP	TC/G	FA
1933	**BKN**	**N**	2	3	.400	2.92	10	3	2	40	42	10	6	0	1	1	0	11	0	0	.000	4	10	2	0	1.6	.875
1934			14	11	.560	3.28	44	20	11	183.2	210	34	58	2	5	3	5	67	12	0	.179	11	42	0	4	1.2	1.000
1935			2	9	.182	3.92	43	11	4	137.2	152	29	41	0	0	4	**8**	39	1	0	.026	2	26	1	0	0.7	.966
1936			0	0	—	3.66	16	0	0	32	34	5	8	0	0	0	1	5	2	0	.400	1	12	0	0	0.8	1.000
1938	**WAS**	**A**	12	15	.444	3.43	33	31	15	223.1	221	53	68	3	1	0	0	82	19	0	.232	9	46	4	3	1.8	.932
1939			20	8	.714	3.54	34	34	21	269.1	**273**	59	88	2	0	0	0	95	21	0	.221	10	56	2	3	2.0	.971
1940			14	**19**	.424	3.49	35	35	23	289	**328**	78	124	2	0	0	0	101	16	0	.158	15	72	4	7	2.6	.956
1941			18	13	.581	3.45	34	33	19	256	271	54	91	4	0	0	0	88	9	0	.102	20	37	3	7	1.8	.950
1942			2	2	.500	4.11	6	5	1	35	28	5	15	1	0	0	0	10	1	0	.100	1	7	0	0	1.3	1.000
1943			11	13	.458	3.28	31	30	15	219.2	218	46	51	2	0	0	1	67	7	0	.104	10	55	2	5	2.2	.970
1944			14	14	.500	3.06	32	31	17	229.1	222	37	62	3	0	1	0	79	18	0	.228	7	53	3	2	2.0	.952
1945			17	7	.708	2.13	31	29	12	216	208	35	96	4	1	0	1	78	18	0	.231	8	44	2	0	1.7	.963
1946			10	10	.500	3.56	26	23	7	161.2	182	36	62	2	0	0	0	53	9	0	.170	4	47	3	2	2.1	.944
1947	**PHI**	**N**	17	12	.586	2.68	32	29	19	235	224	57	103	3	1	1	0	80	14	0	.175	18	51	0	2	2.2	1.000
1948			11	**18**	.379	2.51	34	30	16	225.2	226	54	92	1	1	1	0	83	12	0	.145	15	57	2	2	2.2	.973
1949	**CHI**	**N**	7	16	.304	4.15	33	28	10	180	198	43	83	1	0	0	0	59	12	0	.203	13	36	3	1	1.6	.942
1950			5	1	.833	3.77	35	1	0	74	70	27	28	0	4	1	6	16	1	0	.063	5	15	0	1	0.6	1.000
1951			10	6	.625	2.64	41	1	0	81.2	69	28	30	0	10	5	3	21	0	0	.000	6	21	0	2	0.7	1.000
1952			2	2	.500	2.16	45	0	0	66.2	56	24	37	0	2	2	11	10	2	0	.200	6	22	1	0	0.6	.966
1953			2	3	.400	4.60	45	0	0	62.2	72	24	27	0	2	3	8	10	3	0	.300	9	10	0	0	0.4	1.000
20 yrs.			190	182	.511	3.25	640	374	192	3218.1	3304	738	1170	30	28	22	44	1054	177	0	.168	174	719	32	41	1.4	.965

Dutch Leonard

LEONARD, HUBERT BENJAMIN
B. Apr. 16, 1892, Birmingham, Ohio D. July 11, 1952, Fresno, Calif.

BL TL 5′10½″ 185 lbs.

Year	Team		W	L	PCT	ERA	G	GS	CG	IP	H	BB	SO	ShO	Relief Pitching W	Relief Pitching L	Relief Pitching SV	Batting AB	Batting H	Batting HR	BA	PO	A	E	DP	TC/G	FA
1913	**BOS**	**A**	14	16	.467	2.39	42	27	14	259.1	245	94	144	3	3	3	1	83	15	0	.181	6	62	8	0	1.8	.895
1914			19	5	.792	**1.01**[1]	36	25	17	222.2	141	60	174	7	4	0	3	69	10	0	.145	6	41	2	1	1.4	.959
1915			15	7	.682	2.36	32	21	10	183.1	130	67	116	2	4	2	0	53	14	0	.264	3	30	2	0	1.1	.943
1916			18	12	.600	2.36	48	34	17	274	244	66	144	6	2	0	6	85	17	0	.200	7	49	3	1	1.2	.949
1917			16	17	.485	2.17	37	36	26	294.1	257	72	144	4	0	0	1	104	9	0	.087	5	60	1	2	1.8	.985
1918			8	6	.571	2.72	16	16	12	125.2	119	53	47	3	0	0	0	43	8	0	.186	4	25	2	2	1.9	.935
1919	**DET**	**A**	14	13	.519	2.77	29	28	18	217.1	212	65	102	4	0	1	0	71	11	0	.155	7	40	3	1	1.7	.940
1920			10	17	.370	4.33	28	27	10	191.1	192	63	76	3	0	1	0	57	12	0	.211	7	41	2	0	1.8	.960
1921			11	13	.458	3.75	36	32	16	245	273	63	120	1	0	2	1	82	14	0	.171	4	50	3	1	1.6	.947
1924			3	2	.600	4.56	9	7	3	51.1	69	17	26	0	0	0	1	19	4	0	.211	0	11	1	0	1.3	.917
1925			11	4	.733	4.51	18	18	9	125.2	143	43	65	0	0	0	0	50	10	0	.200	5	17	1	0	1.3	.957
11 yrs.			139	112	.554	2.77	331	271	152	2190	2025	663	1158	33	13	9	13	716	124	0	.173	54	426	28	8	1.5	.945
WORLD SERIES																											
1915	**BOS**	**A**	1	0	1.000	1.00	1	1	1	9	3	0	6	0	0	0	0	3	0	0	.000	0	2	0	0	2.0	1.000
1916			1	0	1.000	1.00	1	1	1	9	5	4	3	0	0	0	0	3	0	0	.000	0	1	0	0	1.0	1.000
2 yrs.			2	0	1.000	1.00	2	2	2	18	8	4	9	0	0	0	0	6	0	0	.000	0	3	0	0	1.5	1.000

Elmer Leonard

LEONARD, ELMER ELLSWORTH (Tiny) BR TR 6′ 3½″ 210 lbs.
B. Nov. 12, 1888, Napa, Calif. D. May 27, 1981, Napa, Calif.

Year	Team	W	L	PCT	ERA	G	GS	CG	IP	H	BB	SO	ShO	Relief W	Relief L	Relief SV	AB	H	HR	BA	PO	A	E	DP	TC/G	FA
1911	PHI A	2	2	.500	2.84	5	1	1	19	26	10	10	0	1	2	0	7	2	0	.286	0	3	0	0	0.6	1.000

Dave Leonhard

LEONHARD, DAVID PAUL BR TR 5′11″ 165 lbs.
B. Jan. 22, 1941, Arlington, Va.

Year	Team	W	L	PCT	ERA	G	GS	CG	IP	H	BB	SO	ShO	Relief W	Relief L	Relief SV	AB	H	HR	BA	PO	A	E	DP	TC/G	FA
1967	BAL A	0	0	—	3.14	3	2	0	14.1	11	6	9	0	0	0	1	5	0	0	.000	3	3	0	0	2.0	1.000
1968		7	7	.500	3.13	28	18	5	126.1	95	57	61	2	1	0	1	31	4	0	.129	10	26	2	1	1.4	.947
1969		7	4	.636	2.49	37	3	1	94	78	38	37	1	6	2	1	21	2	0	.095	9	11	0	1	0.5	1.000
1970		0	0	—	5.14	23	0	0	28	32	18	14	0	0	0	1	1	0	0	.000	0	9	0	1	0.4	1.000
1971		2	3	.400	2.83	12	6	1	54	51	19	18	1	1	0	1	18	5	0	.278	3	13	0	0	1.3	1.000
1972		0	0	—	4.50	14	0	0	20	20	12	7	0	0	0	0	1	1	0	1.000	2	3	0	0	0.4	1.000
6 yrs.		16	14	.533	3.15	117	29	7	336.2	287	150	146	4	8	2	5	77	12	0	.156	27	65	2	3	0.8	.979
WORLD SERIES																										
1969	BAL A	0	0	—	4.50	1	0	0	2	1	1	1	0	0	0	0	0	0	0	—	0	1	0	0	1.0	1.000
1971		0	0	—	0.00	1	0	0	1	0	1	0	0	0	0	0	0	0	0	—	0	0	0	0	0.0	.000
2 yrs.		0	0		3.00	2	0	0	3	1	2	1	0	0	0	0	0	0	0		0	1	0	0	0.5	1.000

Rudy Leopold

LEOPOLD, RUDOLPH MATAS BL TL 6′ 160 lbs.
B. July 27, 1905, Grand Cane, La. D. Sept. 3, 1965, Baton Rouge, La.

Year	Team	W	L	PCT	ERA	G	GS	CG	IP	H	BB	SO	ShO	Relief W	Relief L	Relief SV	AB	H	HR	BA	PO	A	E	DP	TC/G	FA
1928	CHI A	0	0	—	3.86	2	0	0	2.1	3	0	0	0	0	0	0	1	0	0	.000	0	0	1	0	0.5	.000

Randy Lerch

LERCH, RANDY LOUIS BL TL 6′ 5″ 195 lbs.
B. Oct. 9, 1954, Sacramento, Calif.

Year	Team	W	L	PCT	ERA	G	GS	CG	IP	H	BB	SO	ShO	Relief W	Relief L	Relief SV	AB	H	HR	BA	PO	A	E	DP	TC/G	FA
1975	PHI N	0	0	—	6.43	3	0	0	7	6	1	8	0	0	0	0	0	0	0	—	0	0	0	0	0.0	.000
1976		0	0	—	3.00	1	0	0	3	3	0	0	0	0	0	1	1	1	0	1.000	0	0	0	0	0.0	.000
1977		10	6	.625	5.06	32	28	3	169	207	75	81	0	1	0	0	54	9	0	.167	16	33	2	4	1.6	.961
1978		11	8	.579	3.96	33	28	5	184	183	70	96	0	0	0	0	60	15	3	.250	9	32	2	3	1.3	.953
1979		10	13	.435	3.74	37	35	6	214	228	60	92	1	0	0	0	72	11	1	.153	13	38	1	5	1.4	.981
1980		4	14	.222	5.16	30	22	2	150	178	55	57	0	1	0	0	45	12	0	.267	8	29	1	1	1.3	.974
1981	MIL A	7	9	.438	4.30	23	18	1	111	134	43	53	0	2	1	0	0	0	0	—	4	21	1	1	1.1	.962
1982	2 teams MIL A (21G 8–7) MON N (6G 2–0)																									
″	total	10	7	.588	4.69	27	24	1	132.1	149	59	37	1	0	0	0	8	2	0	.250	5	17	2	0	0.9	.917
1983	2 teams MON N (19G 1–3) SF N (7G 1–0)																									
″	total	2	3	.400	6.02	26	5	0	49.1	54	26	30	0	1	1	0	9	2	0	.222	3	6	0	1	0.3	1.000
1984	SF N	5	3	.625	4.23	37	4	0	72.1	80	36	48	0	5	2	2	15	2	0	.133	5	12	0	1	0.5	1.000
1986	PHI N	1	1	.500	7.88	4	0	0	8	10	7	5	0	1	1	0	3	1	0	.333	0	1	0	0	0.3	1.000
11 yrs.		60	64	.484	4.52	253	164	18	1100	1232	432	507	2	11	5	3	267	55	4	.206	63	189	9	16	1.0	.966
DIVISIONAL PLAYOFF SERIES																										
1981	MIL A	0	0	—	1.50	1	1	0	6	3	4	3	0	0	0	0	0	0	0	—	0	0	0	0	0.0	.000
LEAGUE CHAMPIONSHIP SERIES																										
1978	PHI N	0	0	—	5.06	1	1	0	5.1	7	0	0	0	0	0	0	2	0	0	.000	0	1	0	0	1.0	1.000

Louis LeRoy

LeROY, LOUIS PAUL BR TR 5′10″ 180 lbs.
B. Feb. 18, 1879, Omro, Wis. D. Oct. 10, 1944, Shawano, Wis.

Year	Team	W	L	PCT	ERA	G	GS	CG	IP	H	BB	SO	ShO	Relief W	Relief L	Relief SV	AB	H	HR	BA	PO	A	E	DP	TC/G	FA
1905	NY A	1	1	.500	3.75	3	3	2	24	26	1	8	0	0	0	0	8	1	0	.125	2	5	0	0	2.3	1.000
1906		2	0	1.000	2.22	11	2	1	44.2	33	12	28	0	1	0	1	14	2	0	.143	2	17	0	0	1.7	1.000
1910	BOS A	0	0	—	11.25	1	0	0	4	7	2	3	0	0	0	0	1	0	0	.000	0	1	0	0	1.0	1.000
3 yrs.		3	1	.750	3.22	15	5	3	72.2	66	15	39	0	1	0	1	23	3	0	.130	4	23	0	0	1.8	1.000

Barry Lersch

LERSCH, BARRY LEE BB TR 6′ 175 lbs.
B. Sept. 7, 1944, Denver, Colo. BL 1973–1974

Year	Team	W	L	PCT	ERA	G	GS	CG	IP	H	BB	SO	ShO	Relief W	Relief L	Relief SV	AB	H	HR	BA	PO	A	E	DP	TC/G	FA
1969	PHI N	0	3	.000	7.00	10	0	0	18	20	10	13	0	0	3	2	3	0	0	.000	2	6	0	0	0.8	1.000
1970		6	3	.667	3.26	42	11	3	138	119	47	92	0	2	0	3	31	2	0	.065	6	18	2	3	0.6	.923
1971		5	14	.263	3.79	38	30	3	214	203	50	113	0	0	0	0	59	10	0	.169	14	30	2	2	1.2	.957
1972		4	6	.400	3.04	36	8	3	100.2	86	33	48	1	0	2	0	23	0	0	.000	7	15	2	0	0.7	.917
1973		3	6	.333	4.39	42	4	0	98.1	105	27	51	0	3	4	1	17	3	0	.176	5	13	1	2	0.5	.947
1974	STL N	0	0	—	54.00	1	0	0	1	3	5	0	0	0	0	0	0	0	0	—	0	0	0	0	0.0	.000
6 yrs.		18	32	.360	3.82	169	53	9	570	536	172	317	1	5	9	6	133	15	0	.113	34	82	7	7	0.7	.943

Don Leshnock

LESHNOCK, DONALD LEE BR TL 6′ 3″ 195 lbs.
B. Nov. 25, 1946, Youngstown, Ohio.

Year	Team	W	L	PCT	ERA	G	GS	CG	IP	H	BB	SO	ShO	Relief W	Relief L	Relief SV	AB	H	HR	BA	PO	A	E	DP	TC/G	FA
1972	DET A	0	0	—	0.00	1	0	0	1	2	0	2	0	0	0	0	0	0	0	—	0	0	0	0	0.0	.000

Curtis Leskanic

LESKANIC, CURTIS JOHN BR TR 6′ 180 lbs.
B. Apr. 2, 1968, Homestead, Pa.

Year	Team	W	L	PCT	ERA	G	GS	CG	IP	H	BB	SO	ShO	Relief W	Relief L	Relief SV	AB	H	HR	BA	PO	A	E	DP	TC/G	FA
1993	CLR N	1	5	.167	5.37	18	8	0	57	59	27	30	0	0	1	0	13	2	0	.154	5	5	1	2	0.6	.909
1994		1	1	.500	5.64	8	3	0	22.1	27	10	17	0	0	0	0	6	1	0	.167	1	2	0	0	0.4	1.000
1995		6	3	.667	3.40	**76**	0	0	98	83	33	107	0	6	3	10	7	1	0	.143	9	17	0	1	0.3	1.000
3 yrs.		8	9	.471	4.31	102	11	0	177.1	169	70	154	0	6	4	10	26	4	0	.154	15	24	1	3	0.4	.975
DIVISIONAL PLAYOFF SERIES																										
1995	CLR N	0	1	.000	6.00	3	0	0	3	3	0	4	0	0	1	0	0	0	0	—	0	0	0	0	0.0	.000

Brad Lesley

LESLEY, BRADLEY JAY (The Animal) BR TR 6′ 6″ 220 lbs.
B. Sept. 11, 1958, Turlock, Calif.

Year	Team	W	L	PCT	ERA	G	GS	CG	IP	H	BB	SO	ShO	Relief W	Relief L	Relief SV	AB	H	HR	BA	PO	A	E	DP	TC/G	FA
1982	CIN N	0	2	.000	2.58	28	0	0	38.1	27	13	29	0	0	2	4	1	0	0	.000	2	5	0	0	0.3	1.000
1983		0	0	—	2.16	5	0	0	8.1	9	0	5	0	0	0	0	0	0	0	—	0	1	0	0	0.2	1.000
1984		0	1	.000	5.12	16	0	0	19.1	17	14	7	0	0	1	2	2	1	0	.500	1	4	1	0	0.4	.833
1985	MIL A	1	0	1.000	9.95	5	0	0	6.1	8	2	5	0	1	0	0	0	0	0	—	0	1	0	0	0.2	1.000
4 yrs.		1	3	.250	3.86	54	0	0	72.1	61	29	46	0	1	3	6	3	1	0	.333	3	11	1	0	0.3	.933

Walt Leverenz

LEVERENZ, WALTER FRED (Tiny)
B. July 21, 1887, Chicago, Ill. D. Mar. 19, 1973, Atascadero, Calif.
BL TL 5′10″ 175 lbs.

Year	Team	Lg	W	L	PCT	ERA	G	GS	CG	IP	H	BB	SO	ShO	Relief W	Relief L	Relief SV	Batting AB	Batting H	Batting HR	BA	PO	A	E	DP	TC/G	FA
1913	STL	A	6	17	.261	2.58	30	27	13	202.2	159	89	87	2	0	0	1	68	12	0	.176	11	52	5	2	2.3	.926
1914			1	12	.077	3.80	27	16	5	111.1	107	63	41	0	0	2	0	33	6	0	.182	6	28	6	0	1.4	.850
1915			0	2	.000	8.00	5	1	0	9	11	8	3	0	0	1	1	1	0	0	.000	0	3	0	0	0.6	1.000
3 yrs.			7	31	.184	3.15	62	44	18	323	277	160	131	2	0	3	2	102	18	0	.176	17	83	11	2	1.8	.901

Dixie Leverett

LEVERETT, GORHAM VANCE
B. Mar. 29, 1894, Georgetown, Tex. D. Feb. 20, 1957, Beaverton, Ore.
BR TR 5′11″ 190 lbs.

Year	Team	Lg	W	L	PCT	ERA	G	GS	CG	IP	H	BB	SO	ShO	Relief W	Relief L	Relief SV	Batting AB	Batting H	Batting HR	BA	PO	A	E	DP	TC/G	FA
1922	CHI	A	13	10	.565	3.32	33	27	16	224.2	224	79	60	4	0	0	2	83	21	0	.253	12	51	2	2	2.0	.969
1923			10	13	.435	4.06	38	24	9	192.2	212	64	64	0	1	3	3	60	16	0	.267	6	49	3	2	1.5	.948
1924			2	3	.400	5.82	21	11	4	99	123	41	29	0	0	0	0	32	6	0	.188	4	25	2	1	1.5	.935
1926			1	1	.500	6.00	6	3	1	24	31	7	12	0	0	0	0	7	1	0	.143	1	7	1	1	1.5	.889
1929	BOS	N	3	7	.300	6.36	24	12	3	97.2	135	30	28	0	0	1	1	32	6	0	.188	5	20	1	0	1.1	.962
5 yrs.			29	34	.460	4.50	122	77	33	638	725	221	193	4	1	4	6	214	50	0	.234	28	152	9	6	1.5	.952

Hod Leverette

LEVERETTE, HORACE WILBUR
B. Feb. 4, 1889, Shreveport, La. D. Apr. 10, 1958, St. Petersburg, Fla.
BR TR 6′ 180 lbs.

Year	Team	Lg	W	L	PCT	ERA	G	GS	CG	IP	H	BB	SO	ShO	Relief W	Relief L	Relief SV	Batting AB	Batting H	Batting HR	BA	PO	A	E	DP	TC/G	FA
1920	STL	A	0	2	.000	5.23	3	2	0	10.1	9	12	0	0	0	0	0	3	0	0	.000	0	7	0	0	2.3	1.000

Dutch Levsen

LEVSEN, EMIL HENRY
B. Apr. 29, 1898, Wyoming, Iowa D. Mar. 12, 1972, St. Louis Park, Minn.
BR TR 6′ 180 lbs.

Year	Team	Lg	W	L	PCT	ERA	G	GS	CG	IP	H	BB	SO	ShO	Relief W	Relief L	Relief SV	Batting AB	Batting H	Batting HR	BA	PO	A	E	DP	TC/G	FA
1923	CLE	A	0	0	—	0.00	3	0	0	4.1	4	0	1	0	0	0	0	1	0	0	.000	0	6	0	0	2.0	1.000
1924			1	1	.500	4.41	4	1	1	16.1	22	4	3	0	0	1	0	5	0	0	.000	2	4	0	0	1.5	1.000
1925			1	2	.333	5.55	4	3	2	24.1	30	16	9	0	0	0	0	8	2	0	.250	1	2	1	0	1.0	.750
1926			16	13	.552	3.41	33	31	18	237.1	235	85	53	2	0	2	0	83	17	0	.205	12	55	2	7	2.1	.971
1927			3	7	.300	5.49	25	13	2	80.1	96	37	15	1	0	1	0	25	5	0	.200	2	27	2	3	1.2	.935
1928			0	3	.000	5.44	11	3	0	41.1	39	31	7	0	0	1	0	13	0	0	.000	0	12	3	0	1.4	.800
6 yrs.			21	26	.447	4.17	80	51	23	404	426	173	88	3	0	5	0	135	24	0	.178	17	106	8	10	1.6	.939

Dennis Lewallyn

LEWALLYN, DENNIS DALE
B. Aug. 11, 1953, Pensacola, Fla.
BR TR 6′ 4″ 195 lbs.

Year	Team	Lg	W	L	PCT	ERA	G	GS	CG	IP	H	BB	SO	ShO	Relief W	Relief L	Relief SV	Batting AB	Batting H	Batting HR	BA	PO	A	E	DP	TC/G	FA
1975	LA	N	0	0	—	0.00	2	0	0	3	1	0	0	0	0	0	0	0	0	0	—	1	0	0	0	0.5	1.000
1976			1	1	.500	2.16	4	2	0	16.2	12	6	4	0	0	0	0	5	0	0	.000	0	5	0	0	1.3	1.000
1977			3	1	.750	4.24	5	1	0	17	22	4	8	0	2	1	1	6	0	0	.000	2	1	0	0	0.6	1.000
1978			0	0	—	0.00	1	0	0	2	2	0	0	0	0	0	0	0	0	0	—	0	0	0	0	0.0	.000
1979			0	1	.000	5.25	7	0	0	12	19	5	1	0	0	1	0	2	1	0	.500	1	4	0	0	0.7	1.000
1980	TEX	A	0	0	—	7.50	4	0	0	6	7	4	1	0	0	0	0	0	0	0	—	0	2	0	0	0.5	1.000
1981	CLE	A	0	0	—	5.54	7	0	0	13	16	2	11	0	0	0	0	0	0	0	—	0	1	0	0	0.1	1.000
1982			0	1	.000	6.97	4	0	0	10.1	13	1	3	0	0	1	0	0	0	0	—	2	0	0	0	0.5	1.000
8 yrs.			4	4	.500	4.50	34	3	0	80	92	22	28	0	2	3	1	13	1	0	.077	6	13	0	0	0.6	1.000

Dan Lewandowski

LEWANDOWSKI, DANIEL WILLIAM
B. Jan. 6, 1928, Buffalo, N. Y.
BR TR 6′ 180 lbs.

Year	Team	Lg	W	L	PCT	ERA	G	GS	CG	IP	H	BB	SO	ShO	Relief W	Relief L	Relief SV	Batting AB	Batting H	Batting HR	BA	PO	A	E	DP	TC/G	FA
1951	STL	N	0	1	.000	9.00	2	0	0	1	3	1	1	0	0	1	0	0	0	0	—	0	0	0	0	0.0	.000

Lewis

LEWIS
B. Brooklyn, N. Y. Deceased.

Year	Team	Lg	W	L	PCT	ERA	G	GS	CG	IP	H	BB	SO	ShO	Relief W	Relief L	Relief SV	Batting AB	Batting H	Batting HR	BA	PO	A	E	DP	TC/G	FA
1890	BUF	P	0	1	.000	60.00	1	1	0	3	13	7	1	0	0	0	0	*				2	3	0	0	2.5	1.000

Burt Lewis

LEWIS, WILLIAM BURTON
B. Oct. 3, 1895, Tonawanda, N. Y. D. Mar. 24, 1950, Tonawanda, N. Y.
BR TR 6′ 2″ 176 lbs.

Year	Team	Lg	W	L	PCT	ERA	G	GS	CG	IP	H	BB	SO	ShO	Relief W	Relief L	Relief SV	Batting AB	Batting H	Batting HR	BA	PO	A	E	DP	TC/G	FA
1924	PHI	N	0	0	—	6.00	12	0	0	18	23	7	3	0	0	0	0	5	0	0	.000	2	4	0	1	0.5	1.000

Duffy Lewis

LEWIS, GEORGE EDWARD
B. Apr. 18, 1888, San Francisco, Calif. D. June 17, 1979, Salem, N. H.
BR TR 5′10½″ 165 lbs.

Year	Team	Lg	W	L	PCT	ERA	G	GS	CG	IP	H	BB	SO	ShO	Relief W	Relief L	Relief SV	Batting AB	Batting H	Batting HR	BA	PO	A	E	DP	TC/G	FA
1913	BOS	A	0	0	—	0.00	1	0	0	1	0	0	1	0	0	0	0	*				261	28	17	9	2.1	.944

Jim Lewis

LEWIS, JAMES MARTIN
B. Oct. 12, 1955, Miami, Fla.
BR TR 6′ 3″ 190 lbs.

Year	Team	Lg	W	L	PCT	ERA	G	GS	CG	IP	H	BB	SO	ShO	Relief W	Relief L	Relief SV	Batting AB	Batting H	Batting HR	BA	PO	A	E	DP	TC/G	FA
1979	SEA	A	0	0	—	18.00	2	0	0	2	10	1	0	0	0	0	0	0	0	0	—	0	0	1	0	0.5	.000
1982	NY	A	0	0	—	54.00	1	0	0	0.2	3	3	0	0	0	0	0	0	0	0	—	0	0	0	0	0.0	.000
1983	MIN	A	0	0	—	6.50	6	0	0	18	24	7	8	0	0	0	0	0	0	0	—	1	3	0	0	0.7	1.000
1985	SEA	A	0	1	.000	7.71	2	1	0	4.2	8	1	1	0	0	0	0	0	0	0	—	0	0	0	0	0.0	.000
4 yrs.			0	1	.000	8.88	11	1	0	25.1	45	12	9	0	0	0	0	0	0	0		1	3	1	0	0.5	.800

Jim Lewis

LEWIS, JAMES STEVEN
B. July 20, 1964, Jackson, Mich.
BR TR 6′ 2″ 200 lbs.

Year	Team	Lg	W	L	PCT	ERA	G	GS	CG	IP	H	BB	SO	ShO	Relief W	Relief L	Relief SV	Batting AB	Batting H	Batting HR	BA	PO	A	E	DP	TC/G	FA
1991	SD	N	0	0	—	4.15	12	0	0	13	14	11	10	0	0	0	0	2	0	0	.000	0	5	1	0	0.5	.833

Richie Lewis

LEWIS, RICHIE TODD
B. Jan. 25, 1966, Muncie, Ind.
BR TR 5′10″ 175 lbs.

Year	Team	Lg	W	L	PCT	ERA	G	GS	CG	IP	H	BB	SO	ShO	Relief W	Relief L	Relief SV	Batting AB	Batting H	Batting HR	BA	PO	A	E	DP	TC/G	FA
1992	BAL	A	1	1	.500	10.80	2	2	0	6.2	13	7	4	0	0	0	0	0	0	0	—	1	1	0	0	1.0	1.000
1993	FLA	N	6	3	.667	3.26	57	0	0	77.1	68	43	65	0	6	3	0	2	1	0	.500	3	13	1	1	0.3	.941
1994			1	4	.200	5.67	45	0	0	54	62	38	45	0	1	4	0	5	0	0	.000	6	5	2	1	0.3	.846
1995			0	1	.000	3.75	21	1	0	36	30	15	32	0	0	1	0	1	0	0	.000	8	2	2	0	0.6	.833
4 yrs.			8	9	.471	4.40	125	3	0	174	173	103	146	0	7	8	0	8	1	0	.125	18	21	5	2	0.4	.886

Scott Lewis

LEWIS, SCOTT ALLEN
B. Dec. 5, 1965, Grant's Pass, Ore.
BR TR 6′ 3″ 190 lbs.

Year	Team	Lg	W	L	PCT	ERA	G	GS	CG	IP	H	BB	SO	ShO	Relief W	Relief L	Relief SV	Batting AB	Batting H	Batting HR	BA	PO	A	E	DP	TC/G	FA
1990	CAL	A	1	1	.500	2.20	2	2	1	16.1	10	2	9	0	0	0	0	0	0	0	—	0	1	0	0	0.5	1.000
1991			3	5	.375	6.27	16	11	0	60.1	81	21	37	0	1	0	0	0	0	0	—	4	8	1	0	0.8	.923
1992			4	0	1.000	3.99	21	2	0	38.1	36	14	18	0	3	0	0	0	0	0	—	3	8	0	2	0.5	1.000
1993			1	2	.333	4.22	15	4	0	32	37	12	10	0	0	1	0	0	0	0	—	5	1	2	0	0.5	.750
1994			0	1	.000	6.10	20	0	0	31	46	10	10	0	0	1	0	0	0	0	—	0	5	0	0	0.3	1.000
5 yrs.			9	9	.500	5.01	74	19	1	178	210	59	84	0	4	2	0	0	0	0		12	23	3	2	0.5	.921

Ted Lewis

LEWIS, EDWARD MORGAN (Parson) BR TR 5′10½″ 158 lbs.
B. Dec. 25, 1872, Machynlleth, Wales D. May 24, 1936, Durham, N. H.

Year	Team	Lg	W	L	PCT	ERA	G	GS	CG	IP	H	BB	SO	ShO	Relief Pitching W	Relief Pitching L	Relief Pitching SV	Batting AB	Batting H	Batting HR	BA	PO	A	E	DP	TC/G	FA
1896	BOS	N	1	4	.200	3.24	6	5	4	41.2	37	27	12	0	0	0	0	18	2	0	.111	6	10	0	1	2.7	1.000
1897			21	12	.636	3.85	38	34	30	290	316	125	65	2	1	1	1	113	28	0	.248	6	46	3	1	1.4	.945
1898			26	8	**.765**	2.90	41	33	29	313.1	267	109	72	1	3	0	2	131	37	0	.282	15	72	4	4	2.2	.956
1899			17	11	.607	3.49	29	25	23	234.2	245	73	60	2	**3**	1	0	96	25	0	.260	17	35	6	0	2.0	.897
1900			13	12	.520	4.13	30	22	19	209	215	86	66	1	**4**	0	0	73	10	0	.137	8	36	5	1	1.6	.898
1901	BOS	A	16	17	.485	3.53	39	34	31	316.1	299	91	103	1	0	2	1	121	21	0	.174	7	84	7	1	2.5	.929
6 yrs.			94	64	.595	3.53	183	153	136	1405	1379	511	378	7	11	4	4	552	123	0	.223	59	283	25	8	2.0	.932

Terry Ley

LEY, TERRENCE RICHARD BL TL 6′ 190 lbs.
B. Feb. 21, 1947, Portland, Ore.

Year	Team	Lg	W	L	PCT	ERA	G	GS	CG	IP	H	BB	SO	ShO	Relief Pitching W	Relief Pitching L	Relief Pitching SV	Batting AB	Batting H	Batting HR	BA	PO	A	E	DP	TC/G	FA
1971	NY	A	0	0	—	5.00	6	0	0	9	9	9	7	0	0	0	0	0	0	0	—	1	3	1	0	0.8	.800

Al Libke

LIBKE, ALBERT WALTER (Big Al) BL TR 6′ 4″ 215 lbs.
B. Sept. 12, 1918, Tacoma, Wash.

Year	Team	Lg	W	L	PCT	ERA	G	GS	CG	IP	H	BB	SO	ShO	Relief Pitching W	Relief Pitching L	Relief Pitching SV	Batting AB	Batting H	Batting HR	BA	PO	A	E	DP	TC/G	FA
1945	CIN	N	0	0	—	0.00	4	0	0	4.1	3	3	2	0	0	0	0	449	127	4	.283	236	15	9	7	2.3	.965
1946			0	0	—	3.60	1	1	0	5	4	3	2	0	0	0	0	431	109	5	.253	191	14	6	4	1.8	.972
2 yrs.			0	0		1.93	5	1	0	9.1	7	6	4	0	0	0	0	*				427	29	15	11	2.0	.968

Don Liddle

LIDDLE, DONALD EUGENE BL TL 5′10″ 165 lbs.
B. May 25, 1925, Mt. Carmel, Ill.

Year	Team	Lg	W	L	PCT	ERA	G	GS	CG	IP	H	BB	SO	ShO	Relief Pitching W	Relief Pitching L	Relief Pitching SV	Batting AB	Batting H	Batting HR	BA	PO	A	E	DP	TC/G	FA
1953	MIL	N	7	6	.538	3.08	31	15	4	128.2	119	55	63	0	3	1	2	34	3	0	.088	5	20	2	2	0.9	.926
1954	NY	N	9	4	.692	3.06	28	19	4	126.2	100	55	44	3	1	1	0	37	7	0	.189	6	19	1	1	0.9	.962
1955			10	4	.714	4.23	33	13	4	106.1	97	61	56	0	4	1	1	27	5	0	.185	5	15	1	0	0.6	.952
1956	2 teams	NY N (11G 1–2) STL N (14G 1–2)																									
″	total		2	4	.333	5.59	25	7	1	66	81	32	35	0	1	0	1	14	2	0	.143	7	10	1	1	0.7	.944
4 yrs.			28	18	.609	3.75	117	54	13	427.2	397	203	198	3	9	3	4	112	17	0	.152	23	64	5	4	0.8	.946
WORLD SERIES																											
1954	NY	N	1	0	1.000	1.29	2	1	0	7	5	1	2	0	0	0	0	3	0	0	.000	0	1	1	0	1.0	.500

Dutch Lieber

LIEBER, CHARLES EDWIN BR TR 6′½″ 180 lbs.
B. Feb. 1, 1910, Alameda, Calif. D. Dec. 31, 1961, Sawtelle, Calif.

Year	Team	Lg	W	L	PCT	ERA	G	GS	CG	IP	H	BB	SO	ShO	Relief Pitching W	Relief Pitching L	Relief Pitching SV	Batting AB	Batting H	Batting HR	BA	PO	A	E	DP	TC/G	FA
1935	PHI	A	1	1	.500	3.09	18	1	0	46.2	45	19	14	0	1	1	2	14	2	0	.143	3	10	1	1	0.8	.929
1936			0	1	.000	7.71	3	0	0	11.2	17	6	1	0	0	1	0	3	0	0	.000	0	5	0	0	1.7	1.000
2 yrs.			1	2	.333	4.01	21	1	0	58.1	62	25	15	0	1	2	2	17	2	0	.118	3	15	1	1	0.9	.947

Jon Lieber

LIEBER, JONATHAN RAY BL TR 6′ 3″ 220 lbs.
B. Apr. 2, 1970, Council Bluffs, Iowa.

Year	Team	Lg	W	L	PCT	ERA	G	GS	CG	IP	H	BB	SO	ShO	Relief Pitching W	Relief Pitching L	Relief Pitching SV	Batting AB	Batting H	Batting HR	BA	PO	A	E	DP	TC/G	FA
1994	PIT	N	6	7	.462	3.73	17	17	1	108.2	116	25	71	0	0	0	0	39	4	0	.103	10	8	2	1	1.2	.900
1995			4	7	.364	6.32	21	12	0	72.2	103	14	45	0	1	0	0	21	1	0	.048	2	16	1	0	0.9	.947
2 yrs.			10	14	.417	4.76	38	29	1	181.1	219	39	116	0	1	0	0	60	5	0	.083	12	24	3	1	1.0	.923

Glenn Liebhardt

LIEBHARDT, GLENN IGNATIUS (Sandy) BR TR 5′10½″ 170 lbs.
Son of Glenn Liebhardt.
B. July 31, 1910, Cleveland, Ohio D. Mar. 14, 1992, Winston-Salem, N. C.

Year	Team	Lg	W	L	PCT	ERA	G	GS	CG	IP	H	BB	SO	ShO	Relief Pitching W	Relief Pitching L	Relief Pitching SV	Batting AB	Batting H	Batting HR	BA	PO	A	E	DP	TC/G	FA
1930	PHI	A	0	1	.000	11.00	5	0	0	9	14	8	2	0	0	1	0	2	0	0	.000	0	1	1	0	0.4	.500
1936	STL	A	0	0	—	8.78	24	0	0	55.1	98	27	20	0	0	0	0	11	0	0	.000	0	4	1	0	0.2	.800
1938			0	0	—	6.00	2	0	0	3	4	0	1	0	0	0	0	0	0	0	—	0	1	0	0	0.5	1.000
3 yrs.			0	1	.000	8.96	31	0	0	67.1	116	35	23	0	0	1	0	13	0	0	.000	0	6	2	0	0.3	.750

Glenn Liebhardt

LIEBHARDT, GLENN JOHN BR TR 5′10″ 175 lbs.
Father of Glenn Liebhardt.
B. Mar. 10, 1883, Milton, Ind. D. July 13, 1956, Cleveland, Ohio.

Year	Team	Lg	W	L	PCT	ERA	G	GS	CG	IP	H	BB	SO	ShO	Relief Pitching W	Relief Pitching L	Relief Pitching SV	Batting AB	Batting H	Batting HR	BA	PO	A	E	DP	TC/G	FA
1906	CLE	A	2	0	1.000	1.50	2	2	2	18	13	1	9	0	0	0	0	8	0	0	.000	0	7	0	0	3.5	1.000
1907			18	14	.563	2.05	38	34	27	280.1	254	85	110	4	0	0	1	87	14	0	.161	9	92	4	3	2.8	.962
1908			15	16	.484	2.20	39	26	19	262	222	81	146	3	3	2	0	80	14	0	.175	14	78	4	4	2.5	.958
1909			1	5	.167	2.92	12	4	1	52.1	54	16	15	0	1	1	1	15	0	0	.000	5	7	1	0	1.1	.923
4 yrs.			36	35	.507	2.17	91	66	49	612.2	543	183	280	7	4	3	2	190	28	0	.147	28	184	9	7	2.4	.959

Gene Lillard

LILLARD, ROBERT EUGENE BR TR 5′10½″ 178 lbs.
Brother of Bill Lillard.
B. Nov. 12, 1913, Santa Barbara, Calif. D. Apr. 12, 1991, Goleta, Calif.

Year	Team	Lg	W	L	PCT	ERA	G	GS	CG	IP	H	BB	SO	ShO	Relief Pitching W	Relief Pitching L	Relief Pitching SV	Batting AB	Batting H	Batting HR	BA	PO	A	E	DP	TC/G	FA
1939	CHI	N	3	5	.375	6.55	20	7	2	55	68	36	31	0	1	1	0	10	1	0	.100	11	13	2	2	3.7	.923
1940	STL	N	0	1	.000	13.50	2	1	0	4.2	8	4	2	0	0	1	0	0	0	0	—	0	1	0	0	0.5	1.000
2 yrs.			3	6	.333	7.09	22	8	2	59.2	76	40	33	0	1	2	0	*				13	25	2	2	1.4	.950

Jim Lillie

LILLIE, JAMES J. (Grasshopper)
Born James J. Lilly.
B. July 27, 1861, New Haven, Conn. D. Nov. 9, 1890, Kansas City, Mo.

Year	Team	Lg	W	L	PCT	ERA	G	GS	CG	IP	H	BB	SO	ShO	Relief Pitching W	Relief Pitching L	Relief Pitching SV	Batting AB	Batting H	Batting HR	BA	PO	A	E	DP	TC/G	FA
1883	BUF	N	0	1	.000	*3.00*	3	0	0	12	16	2	4	0	0	1	0	201	47	1	.234	84	13	22	3	2.2	.815
1884			0	1	.000	6.23	2	1	0	13	22	5	4	0	0	0	0	471	105	3	.223	190	46	40	7	2.4	.855
1886	KC	N	0	0	—	*4.50*	1	0	0	6	8	1	0	0	0	0	0	416	73	0	.175	196	31	35	5	2.3	.866
3 yrs.			0	2	.000	4.65	6	1	0	31	46	8	8	0	0	1	0	*				669	122	127	18	2.3	.862

Derek Lilliquist

LILLIQUIST, DEREK JANSEN BL TL 6′ 200 lbs.
B. Feb. 20, 1966, Winter Park, Fla.

Year	Team	Lg	W	L	PCT	ERA	G	GS	CG	IP	H	BB	SO	ShO	Relief Pitching W	Relief Pitching L	Relief Pitching SV	Batting AB	Batting H	Batting HR	BA	PO	A	E	DP	TC/G	FA
1989	ATL	N	8	10	.444	3.97	32	30	0	165.2	202	34	79	0	0	0	0	63	12	0	.190	9	20	2	1	1.0	.935
1990	2 teams	ATL N (12G 2–8) SD N (16G 3–3)																									
″	total		5	11	.313	5.31	28	18	1	122	136	42	63	1	0	1	0	43	11	2	.256	4	7	0	0	0.4	1.000
1991	SD	N	0	2	.000	8.79	6	2	0	14.1	25	4	7	0	0	0	0	2	0	0	.000	1	4	0	0	0.8	1.000
1992	CLE	A	5	3	.625	1.75	71	0	0	61.2	39	18	47	0	5	3	6	0	0	0	—	3	9	0	0	0.2	1.000
1993			4	4	.500	2.25	56	2	0	64	64	19	40	0	4	4	10	0	0	0	—	1	9	1	0	0.2	.909

Derek Lilliquist *continued*

Year	Team	W	L	PCT	ERA	G	GS	CG	IP	H	BB	SO	ShO	Relief Pitching W	Relief Pitching L	Relief Pitching SV	Batting AB	Batting H	Batting HR	BA	PO	A	E	DP	TC/G	FA
1994		1	3	.250	4.91	36	0	0	29.1	34	8	15	0	1	3	1	0	0	0	—	0	2	0	0	0.1	1.000
1995	**BOS A**	2	1	.667	6.26	28	0	0	23	27	9	9	0	2	1	0	0	0	0	—	2	2	0	0	0.1	1.000
7 yrs.		25	34	.424	4.11	257	52	1	480	527	134	260	1	12	12	17	108	23	2	.213	20	53	3	1	0.3	.961

Jose Lima

LIMA, JOSE DESIDERIO RODRIGUEZ BR TR 6′ 2″ 170 lbs.
B. Sept. 20, 1972, Santiago, Dominican Republic.

Year	Team	W	L	PCT	ERA	G	GS	CG	IP	H	BB	SO	ShO	Relief Pitching W	Relief Pitching L	Relief Pitching SV	Batting AB	Batting H	Batting HR	BA	PO	A	E	DP	TC/G	FA
1994	**DET A**	0	1	.000	13.50	3	1	0	6.2	11	3	7	0	0	0	0	0	0	0	—	1	0	0	0	0.3	1.000
1995		3	9	.250	6.11	15	15	0	73.2	85	18	37	0	0	0	0	0	0	0	—	5	2	0	0	0.5	1.000
2 yrs.		3	10	.231	6.72	18	16	0	80.1	96	21	44	0	0	0	0	0	0	0		6	2	0	0	0.4	1.000

Ezra Lincoln

LINCOLN, EZRA PERRY BL TL 5′11″ 160 lbs.
B. Nov. 17, 1868, Raynham, Mass. D. May 7, 1951, Taunton, Mass.

Year	Team	W	L	PCT	ERA	G	GS	CG	IP	H	BB	SO	ShO	Relief Pitching W	Relief Pitching L	Relief Pitching SV	Batting AB	Batting H	Batting HR	BA	PO	A	E	DP	TC/G	FA
1890	**2 teams** **CLE N** (15G 3–11) **SYR AA** (3G 0–3)																									
″	**total**	3	14	.176	5.28	18	18	15	138	190	57	28	0	0	0	0	59	8	0	.136	6	29	2	0	2.1	.946

Vive Lindaman

LINDAMAN, VIVAN ALEXANDER BR TR 6′ 1″ 200 lbs.
B. Oct. 28, 1877, Charles City, Iowa D. Feb. 13, 1927, Charles City, Iowa.

Year	Team	W	L	PCT	ERA	G	GS	CG	IP	H	BB	SO	ShO	Relief Pitching W	Relief Pitching L	Relief Pitching SV	Batting AB	Batting H	Batting HR	BA	PO	A	E	DP	TC/G	FA
1906	**BOS N**	12	23	.343	2.43	39	37	32	307.1	303	90	115	2	0	0	0	106	14	0	.132	13	85	14	2	2.9	.875
1907		11	15	.423	3.63	34	28	24	260	252	108	90	2	0	1	1	90	11	0	.122	12	62	4	1	2.3	.949
1908		12	16	.429	2.36	43	30	21	270.2	246	70	68	2	0	1	1	85	15	0	.176	9	68	2	0	1.8	.975
1909		1	6	.143	4.64	15	6	6	66	75	28	13	1	0	1	0	22	6	0	.273	2	16	2	0	1.3	.900
4 yrs.		36	60	.375	2.92	131	101	83	904	876	296	286	7	0	3	2	303	46	0	.152	36	231	22	3	2.2	.924

Paul Lindblad

LINDBLAD, PAUL AARON BL TL 6′ 1″ 185 lbs.
B. Aug. 9, 1941, Chanute, Kans.

Year	Team	W	L	PCT	ERA	G	GS	CG	IP	H	BB	SO	ShO	Relief Pitching W	Relief Pitching L	Relief Pitching SV	Batting AB	Batting H	Batting HR	BA	PO	A	E	DP	TC/G	FA
1965	**KC A**	0	1	.000	11.05	4	0	0	7.1	12	0	12	0	0	1	0	1	0	0	.000	1	3	1	0	1.3	.800
1966		5	10	.333	4.17	38	14	0	121	138	37	69	0	2	3	1	34	5	0	.147	6	22	1	1	0.8	.966
1967		5	8	.385	3.58	46	10	1	115.2	106	35	83	1	3	3	6	34	7	1	.206	4	17	0	1	0.5	1.000
1968	**OAK A**	4	3	.571	2.40	47	1	0	56.1	51	14	42	0	4	2	2	8	3	0	.375	4	9	0	1	0.3	1.000
1969		9	6	.600	4.14	60	0	0	78.1	72	33	64	0	9	6	9	12	4	0	.333	2	11	0	0	0.2	1.000
1970		8	2	.800	2.71	62	0	0	63	52	28	42	0	8	2	3	6	0	0	.000	1	10	0	0	0.2	1.000
1971	**2 teams** **OAK A** (8G 1–0) **WAS A** (43G 6–4)																									
″	**total**	7	4	.636	2.80	51	0	0	99.2	76	31	54	0	7	4	8	22	4	0	.182	4	21	0	1	0.5	1.000
1972	**TEX A**	5	8	.385	2.61	**66**	0	0	100	95	29	51	0	5	8	9	15	3	0	.200	0	15	0	1	0.2	1.000
1973	**OAK A**	1	5	.167	3.69	36	3	0	78	89	28	33	0	1	2	2	0	0	0	—	5	9	0	0	0.4	1.000
1974		4	4	.500	2.05	45	2	0	101	85	30	46	0	3	3	6	0	0	0	—	1	19	1	1	0.5	.952
1975		9	1	.900	2.72	68	0	0	122.1	105	43	58	0	9	1	7	1	0	0	.000	10	23	2	3	0.5	.943
1976		6	5	.545	3.05	65	0	0	115	111	24	37	0	6	5	5	0	0	0	—	9	21	1	1	0.5	.968
1977	**TEX A**	4	5	.444	4.18	42	1	0	99	103	29	46	0	4	4	4	0	0	0	—	7	16	0	0	0.5	1.000
1978	**2 teams** **TEX A** (18G 1–1) **NY A** (7G 0–0)																									
″	**total**	1	1	.500	3.88	25	1	0	58	62	23	34	0	1	1	2	0	0	0		2	9	0	1	0.4	1.000
14 yrs.		68	63	.519	3.28	655	32	1	1214.2	1157	384	671	1	62	45	64	133	26	1	.195	56	205	6	11	0.4	.978
LEAGUE CHAMPIONSHIP SERIES																										
1975	**OAK A**	0	0	—	0.00	2	0	0	4.2	5	1	0	0	0	0	0	0	0	0	—	1	4	0	0	2.5	1.000
WORLD SERIES																										
1973	**OAK A**	1	0	1.000	0.00	3	0	0	3.1	4	1	1	0	1	0	0	1	0	0	.000	0	0	0	0	0.0	.000
1978	**NY A**	0	0	—	11.57	1	0	0	2.1	4	0	1	0	0	0	0	0	0	0	—	0	0	0	0	0.0	.000
2 yrs.		1	0	1.000	4.76	4	0	0	5.2	8	1	2	0	1	0	0	1	0	0	.000	0	0	0	0	0.0	

Lymie Linde

LINDE, LYMAN GILBERT BR TR 5′11″ 185 lbs.
B. Sept. 20, 1920, Beaver Dam, Wis.

Year	Team	W	L	PCT	ERA	G	GS	CG	IP	H	BB	SO	ShO	Relief Pitching W	Relief Pitching L	Relief Pitching SV	Batting AB	Batting H	Batting HR	BA	PO	A	E	DP	TC/G	FA
1947	**CLE A**	0	0	—	27.00	1	0	0	0.2	3	1	0	0	0	0	0	0	0	0	—	0	0	0	0	0.0	.000
1948		0	0	—	5.40	3	0	0	10	9	4	0	0	0	0	0	2	0	0	.000	0	1	1	0	0.7	.500
2 yrs.		0	0		6.75	4	0	0	10.2	12	5	0	0	0	0	0	2	0	0	.000	0	1	1	0	0.5	.500

Johnny Lindell

LINDELL, JOHN HARLAN BR TR 6′ 4½″ 217 lbs.
B. Aug. 30, 1916, Greeley, Colo. D. Aug. 27, 1985, Newport Beach, Calif.

Year	Team	W	L	PCT	ERA	G	GS	CG	IP	H	BB	SO	ShO	Relief Pitching W	Relief Pitching L	Relief Pitching SV	Batting AB	Batting H	Batting HR	BA	PO	A	E	DP	TC/G	FA
1942	**NY A**	2	1	.667	3.76	23	2	0	52.2	52	22	28	0	2	0	1	24	6	0	.250	5	7	1	2	0.6	.923
1953	**2 teams** **PIT N** (27G 5–16) **PHI N** (5G 1–1)																									
″	**total**	6	17	.261	4.66	32	26	15	199	195	**139**	118	1	1	0	0	109	33	4	.303	269	11	10	1	2.4	.966
2 yrs.		8	18	.308	4.47	55	28	15	251.2	247	161	146	1	3	0	1	*				1801	104	42	30	2.6	.978

Ernie Lindemann

LINDEMANN, ERNEST BR TR
B. June 10, 1883, New York, N. Y. D. Dec. 27, 1951, Brooklyn, N. Y.

Year	Team	W	L	PCT	ERA	G	GS	CG	IP	H	BB	SO	ShO	Relief Pitching W	Relief Pitching L	Relief Pitching SV	Batting AB	Batting H	Batting HR	BA	PO	A	E	DP	TC/G	FA
1907	**BOS N**	0	0	—	5.68	1	1	0	6.1	6	4	3	0	0	0	0	2	1	0	.500	0	3	0	0	3.0	1.000

Carl Lindquist

LINDQUIST, CARL EMIL (Lindy) BR TR 6′ 2″ 185 lbs.
B. May 9, 1919, Morris Run, Pa.

Year	Team	W	L	PCT	ERA	G	GS	CG	IP	H	BB	SO	ShO	Relief Pitching W	Relief Pitching L	Relief Pitching SV	Batting AB	Batting H	Batting HR	BA	PO	A	E	DP	TC/G	FA
1943	**BOS N**	0	2	.000	6.23	2	2	0	13	17	4	1	0	0	0	0	4	0	0	.000	1	4	0	0	2.5	1.000
1944		0	0	—	3.12	5	0	0	8.2	8	2	4	0	0	0	0	1	0	0	.000	1	0	0	0	0.2	1.000
2 yrs.		0	2	.000	4.98	7	2	0	21.2	25	6	5	0	0	0	0	5	0	0	.000	2	4	0	0	0.9	1.000

Jim Lindsey

LINDSEY, JAMES KENDRICK BR TR 6′ 1″ 175 lbs.
B. Jan. 24, 1898, Greensburg, La. D. Oct. 25, 1963, Jackson, La.

Year	Team	W	L	PCT	ERA	G	GS	CG	IP	H	BB	SO	ShO	Relief Pitching W	Relief Pitching L	Relief Pitching SV	Batting AB	Batting H	Batting HR	BA	PO	A	E	DP	TC/G	FA
1922	**CLE A**	4	5	.444	6.02	29	5	0	83.2	105	24	29	0	4	2	1	24	4	0	.167	1	17	1	1	0.7	.947
1924		0	0	—	21.00	3	0	0	3	8	3	0	0	0	0	0	0	0	0	—	0	1	0	0	0.3	1.000
1929	**STL N**	1	1	.500	5.51	2	2	1	16.1	20	2	8	0	0	0	0	5	1	0	.200	0	3	0	0	1.5	1.000
1930		7	5	.583	4.43	39	6	3	105.2	131	46	50	0	4	2	5	28	8	0	.286	1	9	1	0	0.3	.909
1931		6	4	.600	2.77	35	2	1	74.2	77	45	32	1	5	4	7	9	1	0	.111	0	15	1	1	0.5	.938
1932		3	3	.500	4.94	33	5	0	89.1	96	38	31	0	3	2	3	21	3	0	.143	0	16	1	1	0.5	.941
1933		0	0	—	4.50	1	0	0	2	2	1	1	0	0	0	0	0	0	0	—	0	0	0	0	0.0	.000

Jim Lindsey *continued*

Year	Team	Lg	W	L	PCT	ERA	G	GS	CG	IP	H	BB	SO	ShO	Relief W	Relief L	Relief SV	AB	H	HR	BA	PO	A	E	DP	TC/G	FA
1934	2 teams	CIN N (4G 0–0) STL N (11G 0–1)																									
"	total		0	1	.000	6.00	15	0	0	18	25	5	9	0	0	1	1	1	0	0	.000	0	3	0	0	0.2	1.000
1937	BKN	N	0	1	.000	3.52	20	0	0	38.1	43	12	15	0	0	1	2	6	1	0	.167	0	7	1	0	0.4	.875
9 yrs.			21	20	.512	4.70	177	20	5	431	507	176	175	1	16	12	19	94	18	0	.191	2	71	5	3	0.4	.936
WORLD SERIES																											
1930	STL	N	0	0	—	1.93	2	0	0	4.2	1	1	2	0	0	0	0	1	1	0	1.000	0	1	0	0	0.5	1.000
1931			0	0	—	5.40	2	0	0	3.1	4	3	2	0	0	0	0	0	0	0	—	0	0	0	0	0.0	.000
2 yrs.			0	0		3.38	4	0	0	8	5	4	4	0	0	0	0	1	1	0	1.000	0	1	0	0	0.3	1.000

Axel Lindstrom

LINDSTROM, AXEL OLAF BR TR 5′10″ 180 lbs.
B. Aug. 26, 1895, Gustavberg, Sweden D. June 24, 1940, Asheville, N. C.

Year	Team	Lg	W	L	PCT	ERA	G	GS	CG	IP	H	BB	SO	ShO	Relief W	Relief L	Relief SV	AB	H	HR	BA	PO	A	E	DP	TC/G	FA
1916	PHI	A	0	0	—	4.50	1	0	0	4	2	0	1	0	0	0	1	2	1	0	.500	0	1	0	0	1.0	1.000

Dick Lines

LINES, RICHARD GEORGE BR TL 6′ 1″ 175 lbs.
B. Aug. 17, 1938, Montreal, Que., Canada.

Year	Team	Lg	W	L	PCT	ERA	G	GS	CG	IP	H	BB	SO	ShO	Relief W	Relief L	Relief SV	AB	H	HR	BA	PO	A	E	DP	TC/G	FA
1966	WAS	A	5	2	.714	2.28	53	0	0	83	63	24	49	0	5	2	2	10	0	0	.000	4	23	1	3	0.5	.964
1967			2	5	.286	3.36	54	0	0	85.2	83	24	54	0	2	5	4	9	1	0	.111	5	16	3	2	0.4	.875
2 yrs.			7	7	.500	2.83	107	0	0	168.2	146	48	103	0	7	7	6	19	1	0	.053	9	39	4	5	0.5	.923

Fred Link

LINK, FREDERICK THEODORE (Laddie) BL TL 6′ 170 lbs.
B. Mar. 11, 1886, Columbus, Ohio D. May 22, 1939, Houston, Tex.

Year	Team	Lg	W	L	PCT	ERA	G	GS	CG	IP	H	BB	SO	ShO	Relief W	Relief L	Relief SV	AB	H	HR	BA	PO	A	E	DP	TC/G	FA
1910	2 teams	CLE A (22G 5–6) STL A (3G 0–1)																									
"	total		5	7	.417	3.42	25	16	6	139.2	139	62	57	1	1	0	1	49	8	0	.163	4	42	4	0	2.0	.920

Ed Linke

LINKE, EDWARD KARL BR TR 5′11″ 180 lbs.
B. Nov. 9, 1911, Chicago, Ill. D. June 21, 1988, Chicago, Ill.

Year	Team	Lg	W	L	PCT	ERA	G	GS	CG	IP	H	BB	SO	ShO	Relief W	Relief L	Relief SV	AB	H	HR	BA	PO	A	E	DP	TC/G	FA
1933	WAS	A	1	0	1.000	5.06	3	2	0	16	15	11	6	0	0	0	0	6	1	0	.167	2	3	1	0	2.0	.833
1934			2	2	.500	4.15	7	4	2	34.2	38	9	9	0	0	0	0	11	2	0	.182	3	7	0	0	1.4	1.000
1935			11	7	.611	5.01	40	22	10	178	211	80	51	1	2	1	3	68	20	1	.294	4	30	2	3	0.9	.944
1936			1	5	.167	7.10	13	6	1	52	73	14	11	0	1	1	0	15	6	1	.400	1	17	1	1	1.5	.947
1937			6	1	.857	5.60	36	7	0	128.2	158	59	61	0	3	1	3	46	10	0	.217	1	23	1	1	0.7	.960
1938	STL	A	1	7	.125	7.94	21	2	0	39.2	60	33	18	0	1	**5**	0	10	2	0	.200	1	11	1	1	0.6	.923
6 yrs.			22	22	.500	5.61	120	43	13	449	555	206	156	1	7	8	6	156	41	2	.263	12	91	6	6	0.9	.945

Royce Lint

LINT, ROYCE JAMES BL TL 6′ 1″ 165 lbs.
B. Jan. 1, 1921, Birmingham, Ala.

Year	Team	Lg	W	L	PCT	ERA	G	GS	CG	IP	H	BB	SO	ShO	Relief W	Relief L	Relief SV	AB	H	HR	BA	PO	A	E	DP	TC/G	FA
1954	STL	N	2	3	.400	4.86	30	4	1	70.1	75	30	36	1	1	3	0	10	1	0	.100	8	14	3	0	0.8	.880

Doug Linton

LINTON, DOUGLAS WARREN BR TR 6′ 1″ 185 lbs.
B. Feb. 9, 1965, Santa Ana, Calif.

Year	Team	Lg	W	L	PCT	ERA	G	GS	CG	IP	H	BB	SO	ShO	Relief W	Relief L	Relief SV	AB	H	HR	BA	PO	A	E	DP	TC/G	FA
1992	TOR	A	1	3	.250	8.63	8	3	0	24	31	17	16	0	0	1	0	0	0	0	—	0	2	0	1	0.3	1.000
1993	2 teams	TOR A (4G 0–1) CAL A (19G 2–0)																									
"	total		2	1	.667	7.36	23	1	0	36.2	46	23	23	0	2	0	0	0	0	0		2	3	0	0	0.2	1.000
1994	NY	N	6	2	.750	4.47	32	3	0	50.1	74	20	29	0	5	1	0	7	0	0	.000	1	6	1	0	0.3	.875
1995	KC	A	0	1	.000	7.25	7	2	0	22.1	22	10	13	0	0	0	0	0	0	0	—	0	5	0	0	0.7	1.000
4 yrs.			9	7	.563	6.48	70	9	0	133.1	173	70	81	0	7	2	0	7	0	0	.000	3	16	1	1	0.3	.950

Frank Linzy

LINZY, FRANK ALFRED BR TR 6′ 1″ 190 lbs.
B. Sept. 15, 1940, Fort Gibson, Okla.

Year	Team	Lg	W	L	PCT	ERA	G	GS	CG	IP	H	BB	SO	ShO	Relief W	Relief L	Relief SV	AB	H	HR	BA	PO	A	E	DP	TC/G	FA
1963	SF	N	0	0	—	4.86	8	1	0	16.2	22	10	14	0	0	0	0	3	0	0	.000	2	4	0	0	0.8	1.000
1965			9	3	.750	1.43	57	0	0	81.2	76	23	35	0	9	3	21	18	4	1	.222	8	39	0	2	0.8	1.000
1966			7	11	.389	2.96	51	0	0	100.1	107	34	57	0	7	**11**	16	20	3	0	.150	6	21	3	1	0.6	.900
1967			7	7	.500	1.51	57	0	0	95.2	67	34	38	0	7	7	17	15	0	0	.000	8	32	0	2	0.7	1.000
1968			9	8	.529	2.08	57	0	0	95.1	76	27	36	0	9	**8**	12	11	0	0	.000	7	33	0	4	0.7	1.000
1969			14	9	.609	3.65	58	0	0	116	129	38	62	0	**14**	9	11	30	8	0	.267	6	37	3	2	0.8	.935
1970	2 teams	SF N (20G 2–1) STL N (47G 3–5)																									
"	total		5	6	.455	4.66	67	0	0	87	99	34	35	0	5	6	3	11	0	0	.000	3	20	0	1	0.3	1.000
1971	STL	N	4	3	.571	2.14	50	0	0	59	49	27	24	0	4	3	6	4	2	0	.500	6	13	0	0	0.4	1.000
1972	MIL	A	2	2	.500	3.04	47	0	0	77	70	27	24	0	2	2	12	9	1	0	.111	2	18	1	3	0.4	.952
1973			2	6	.250	3.57	42	1	0	63	68	21	21	0	2	6	13	0	0	0	—	3	12	2	1	0.4	.882
1974	PHI	N	3	2	.600	3.24	22	0	0	25	27	7	12	0	3	2	0	0	0	0	—	0	7	0	1	0.3	1.000
11 yrs.			62	57	.521	2.85	516	2	0	816.2	790	282	358	0	62	57	111	121	18	1	.149	51	236	9	17	0.6	.970

Angelo LiPetri

LiPETRI, MICHAEL ANGELO BR TR 6′ 1½″ 180 lbs.
B. July 6, 1930, Brooklyn, N. Y.

Year	Team	Lg	W	L	PCT	ERA	G	GS	CG	IP	H	BB	SO	ShO	Relief W	Relief L	Relief SV	AB	H	HR	BA	PO	A	E	DP	TC/G	FA
1956	PHI	N	0	0	—	3.27	6	0	0	11	7	3	8	0	0	0	0	1	0	0	.000	1	2	0	0	0.5	1.000
1958			0	0	—	11.25	4	0	0	4	6	0	1	0	0	0	0	0	0	0	—	1	1	0	0	0.5	1.000
2 yrs.			0	0		5.40	10	0	0	15	13	3	9	0	0	0	0	1	0	0	.000	2	3	0	0	0.5	1.000

Tom Lipp

LIPP, THOMAS CHARLES 5′11½″ 170 lbs.
B. June 4, 1870, Baltimore, Md. D. May 30, 1932, Baltimore, Md.

Year	Team	Lg	W	L	PCT	ERA	G	GS	CG	IP	H	BB	SO	ShO	Relief W	Relief L	Relief SV	AB	H	HR	BA	PO	A	E	DP	TC/G	FA
1897	PHI	N	0	1	.000	15.00	1	1	0	3	8	2	1	0	0	0	0	1	1	0	1.000	0	0	0	0	0.0	.000

Nig Lipscomb

LIPSCOMB, GERARD BR TR 6′ 175 lbs.
B. Feb. 24, 1911, Rutherfordton, N. C. D. Feb. 27, 1978, Huntersville, N. C.

Year	Team	Lg	W	L	PCT	ERA	G	GS	CG	IP	H	BB	SO	ShO	Relief W	Relief L	Relief SV	AB	H	HR	BA	PO	A	E	DP	TC/G	FA
1937	STL	A	0	0	—	6.52	3	0	0	9.2	13	5	1	0	0	0	0	*				73	82	6	28	5.2	.963

Felipe Lira

LIRA, ANTONIO FELIPE BR TR 6′ 170 lbs.
B. Apr. 26, 1972, Santa Teresa, Venezuela

Year	Team	Lg	W	L	PCT	ERA	G	GS	CG	IP	H	BB	SO	ShO	Relief W	Relief L	Relief SV	AB	H	HR	BA	PO	A	E	DP	TC/G	FA
1995	DET	A	9	13	.409	4.31	37	22	0	146.1	151	56	89	0	2	3	1	0	0	0	—	13	15	0	1	0.8	1.000

Hod Lisenbee

LISENBEE, HORACE MILTON BR TR 5′11″ 170 lbs.
B. Sept. 23, 1898, Clarksville, Tenn. D. Nov. 14, 1987, Clarksville, Tenn.

Year	Team	W	L	PCT	ERA	G	GS	CG	IP	H	BB	SO	ShO	Relief Pitching W	Relief Pitching L	Relief Pitching SV	Batting AB	Batting H	Batting HR	BA	PO	A	E	DP	TC/G	FA
1927	WAS A	18	9	.667	3.57	39	34	17	242	221	78	105	4	2	1	0	83	11	0	.133	11	45	4	2	1.5	.933
1928		2	6	.250	6.08	16	9	3	77	102	32	13	0	1	0	0	23	4	0	.174	2	15	1	0	1.1	.944
1929	BOS A	0	0	—	5.19	5	0	0	8.2	10	4	2	0	0	0	0	2	0	0	.000	0	3	0	0	0.6	1.000
1930		10	17	.370	4.40	37	31	15	237.1	254	86	47	0	1	0	0	75	20	0	.267	3	37	4	1	1.2	.909
1931		5	12	.294	5.19	41	17	6	164.2	190	49	42	0	2	1	0	53	12	0	.226	7	30	5	0	1.0	.881
1932		0	4	.000	5.65	19	6	3	73.1	87	25	13	0	0	0	0	21	1	0	.048	2	12	1	0	0.8	.933
1936	PHI A	1	7	.125	6.20	19	7	4	85.2	115	24	17	0	0	1	0	25	3	0	.120	2	15	2	0	1.0	.895
1945	CIN N	1	3	.250	5.49	31	3	0	80.1	97	16	14	0	1	2	1	19	0	0	.000	2	11	0	0	0.4	1.000
8 yrs.		37	58	.389	4.81	207	107	48	969	1076	314	253	4	7	5	1	301	51	0	.169	29	168	17	3	1.0	.921

Ad Liska

LISKA, ADOLPH JAMES BR TR 5′11½″ 160 lbs.
B. July 10, 1906, Dwight, Neb.

Year	Team	W	L	PCT	ERA	G	GS	CG	IP	H	BB	SO	ShO	Relief Pitching W	Relief Pitching L	Relief Pitching SV	Batting AB	Batting H	Batting HR	BA	PO	A	E	DP	TC/G	FA
1929	WAS A	3	9	.250	4.77	24	10	4	94.1	87	42	33	0	0	3	0	29	5	0	.172	7	34	0	0	1.7	1.000
1930		9	7	.563	3.29	32	16	7	150.2	140	71	40	1	0	1	1	52	5	0	.096	14	56	0	4	2.2	1.000
1931		0	1	.000	6.75	2	1	0	4	9	1	2	0	0	0	0	1	0	0	.000	0	2	0	0	1.0	1.000
1932	PHI N	2	0	1.000	1.69	8	0	0	26.2	22	10	6	0	2	0	1	7	0	0	.000	2	12	1	0	1.9	.933
1933		3	1	.750	4.52	45	1	0	75.2	96	26	23	0	3	1	1	14	1	0	.071	4	33	1	3	0.8	.974
5 yrs.		17	18	.486	3.87	111	28	11	351.1	354	150	104	1	5	5	3	103	11	0	.107	27	137	2	7	1.5	.988

Mark Littell

LITTELL, MARK ALAN BL TR 6′ 3″ 210 lbs.
B. Jan. 17, 1953, Cape Girardeau, Mo.

Year	Team	W	L	PCT	ERA	G	GS	CG	IP	H	BB	SO	ShO	Relief Pitching W	Relief Pitching L	Relief Pitching SV	Batting AB	Batting H	Batting HR	BA	PO	A	E	DP	TC/G	FA
1973	KC A	1	3	.250	5.68	8	7	1	38	44	23	16	0	0	0	0	0	0	0	—	2	5	0	0	0.9	1.000
1975		1	2	.333	3.70	7	3	1	24.1	19	15	19	0	1	0	0	0	0	0	—	4	6	1	0	1.6	.909
1976		8	4	.667	2.08	60	1	0	104	68	60	92	0	8	3	16	1	0	0	.000	3	9	0	1	0.2	1.000
1977		8	4	.667	3.60	48	5	0	105	73	55	106	0	6	4	12	1	0	0	.000	7	7	1	1	0.3	.933
1978	STL N	4	8	.333	2.80	72	2	0	106	80	59	130	0	4	7	11	7	0	0	.000	4	10	1	0	0.2	.933
1979		9	4	.692	2.20	63	0	0	82	60	39	67	0	9	4	13	14	0	0	.000	6	7	1	1	0.2	.929
1980		0	2	.000	9.00	14	0	0	11	14	7	7	0	0	2	2	1	0	0	.000	0	1	0	0	0.1	1.000
1981		1	3	.250	4.39	28	1	0	41	36	31	22	0	1	2	2	8	2	0	.250	5	4	2	0	0.4	.818
1982		0	1	.000	5.23	16	0	0	20.2	22	15	7	0	0	1	0	2	0	0	.000	0	2	1	0	0.2	.667
9 yrs.		32	31	.508	3.32	316	19	2	532	416	304	466	0	29	23	56	34	2	0	.059	31	51	7	3	0.3	.921
LEAGUE CHAMPIONSHIP SERIES																										
1976	KC A	0	1	.000	1.93	3	0	0	4.2	4	1	3	0	0	1	0	0	0	0	—	0	1	0	0	0.3	1.000
1977		0	0	—	3.00	2	0	0	3	5	3	1	0	0	0	0	0	0	0	—	0	0	0	0	0.0	.000
2 yrs.		0	1	.000	2.35	5	0	0	7.2	9	4	4	0	0	1	0	0	0	0	—	0	1	0	0	0.2	1.000

Jeff Little

LITTLE, DONALD JEFFREY BR TL 6′ 6″ 220 lbs.
B. Dec. 25, 1954, Fremont, Ohio.

Year	Team	W	L	PCT	ERA	G	GS	CG	IP	H	BB	SO	ShO	Relief Pitching W	Relief Pitching L	Relief Pitching SV	Batting AB	Batting H	Batting HR	BA	PO	A	E	DP	TC/G	FA
1980	STL N	1	1	.500	3.79	7	2	0	19	18	9	17	0	0	0	0	6	1	0	.167	0	1	0	0	0.1	1.000
1982	MIN A	2	0	1.000	4.21	33	0	0	36.1	33	27	26	0	2	0	0	0	0	0	—	0	3	0	0	0.1	1.000
2 yrs.		3	1	.750	4.07	40	2	0	55.1	51	36	43	0	2	0	0	6	1	0	.167	0	4	0	0	0.1	1.000

Dick Littlefield

LITTLEFIELD, RICHARD BERNARD BL TL 6′ 180 lbs.
B. Mar. 18, 1926, Detroit, Mich.

Year	Team	W	L	PCT	ERA	G	GS	CG	IP	H	BB	SO	ShO	Relief Pitching W	Relief Pitching L	Relief Pitching SV	Batting AB	Batting H	Batting HR	BA	PO	A	E	DP	TC/G	FA
1950	BOS A	2	2	.500	9.26	15	2	0	23.1	27	24	13	0	2	0	1	4	0	0	.000	1	6	0	1	0.5	1.000
1951	CHI A	1	1	.500	8.38	4	2	0	9.2	9	17	7	0	1	0	0	1	0	0	.000	1	1	0	1	0.5	1.000
1952	2 teams DET A (28G 0–3) STL A (7G 2–3)																									
″	total	2	6	.250	3.54	35	6	3	94	81	42	66	0	1	3	1	23	2	0	.087	4	4	0	1	0.2	1.000
1953	STL A	7	12	.368	5.08	36	22	2	152.1	153	84	104	0	2	1	0	42	8	0	.190	9	19	0	0	0.8	1.000
1954	2 teams BAL A (3G 0–0) PIT N (23G 10–11)																									
″	total	10	11	.476	3.86	26	21	7	161	148	91	97	1	1	0	0	50	8	0	.160	5	14	3	0	0.8	.864
1955	PIT N	5	12	.294	5.12	35	17	4	130	148	68	70	1	1	3	0	34	6	0	.176	7	12	3	1	0.6	.864
1956	3 teams PIT N (6G 0–0) STL N (3G 0–2) NY N (31G 4–4)																									
″	total	4	6	.400	4.37	40	11	0	119.1	101	49	80	0	1	2	2	28	2	0	.071	10	14	1	1	0.6	.960
1957	CHI N	2	3	.400	5.35	48	2	0	65.2	76	37	51	0	2	1	4	11	2	0	.182	2	7	4	0	0.3	.692
1958	MIL N	0	1	.000	4.26	4	0	0	6.1	7	1	7	0	0	1	1	0	0	0	—	0	0	0	0	0.0	.000
9 yrs.		33	54	.379	4.71	243	83	16	761.2	750	413	495	2	11	11	9	193	28	0	.145	39	77	11	5	0.5	.913

John Littlefield

LITTLEFIELD, JOHN ANDREW BR TR 6′ 2″ 200 lbs.
B. Jan. 5, 1954, Covina, Calif.

Year	Team	W	L	PCT	ERA	G	GS	CG	IP	H	BB	SO	ShO	Relief Pitching W	Relief Pitching L	Relief Pitching SV	Batting AB	Batting H	Batting HR	BA	PO	A	E	DP	TC/G	FA
1980	STL N	5	5	.500	3.14	52	0	0	66	71	20	22	0	5	5	9	11	0	0	.000	2	12	1	3	0.3	.933
1981	SD N	2	3	.400	3.66	42	0	0	64	53	28	21	0	2	3	2	1	0	0	.000	6	9	1	1	0.4	.938
2 yrs.		7	8	.467	3.39	94	0	0	130	124	48	43	0	7	8	11	12	0	0	.000	8	21	2	4	0.3	.935

Carlisle Littlejohn

LITTLEJOHN, CHARLES CARLISLE BR TR 5′10″ 175 lbs.
B. Oct. 6, 1901, Irene, Tex. D. Oct. 27, 1977, Kansas City, Mo.

Year	Team	W	L	PCT	ERA	G	GS	CG	IP	H	BB	SO	ShO	Relief Pitching W	Relief Pitching L	Relief Pitching SV	Batting AB	Batting H	Batting HR	BA	PO	A	E	DP	TC/G	FA
1927	STL N	3	1	.750	4.50	14	2	1	42	47	14	16	0	2	0	0	12	5	0	.417	1	5	1	0	0.5	.857
1928		2	1	.667	3.66	12	2	1	32	36	14	6	0	1	1	0	11	0	0	.000	0	8	1	0	0.8	.889
2 yrs.		5	2	.714	4.14	26	4	2	74	83	28	22	0	3	1	0	23	5	0	.217	1	13	2	0	0.6	.875

Greg Litton

LITTON, JON GREGORY BR TR 6′ 175 lbs.
B. July 13, 1964, New Orleans, La.

Year	Team	W	L	PCT	ERA	G	GS	CG	IP	H	BB	SO	ShO	Relief Pitching W	Relief Pitching L	Relief Pitching SV	Batting AB	Batting H	Batting HR	BA	PO	A	E	DP	TC/G	FA
1991	SF N	0	0	—	9.00	1	0	0	1	1	3	0	0	0	0	0	*				44	66	3	5	1.7	.973

Bud Lively

LIVELY, EVERETT ADRIAN (Red) BR TR 6′½″ 200 lbs.
Son of Jack Lively.
B. Feb. 14, 1925, Birmingham, Ala.

Year	Team	W	L	PCT	ERA	G	GS	CG	IP	H	BB	SO	ShO	Relief Pitching W	Relief Pitching L	Relief Pitching SV	Batting AB	Batting H	Batting HR	BA	PO	A	E	DP	TC/G	FA
1947	CIN N	4	7	.364	4.68	38	17	3	123	126	63	52	1	0	1	0	32	6	0	.188	8	21	2	0	0.8	.935
1948		0	0	—	2.38	10	0	0	22.2	13	11	12	0	0	0	0	2	0	0	.000	1	1	0	1	0.2	1.000
1949		4	6	.400	3.92	31	10	3	103.1	91	53	30	1	0	1	1	26	4	0	.154	4	15	1	1	0.6	.950
3 yrs.		8	13	.381	4.16	79	27	6	249	230	127	94	2	0	2	1	60	10	0	.167	13	37	3	2	0.7	.943

Mickey Lolich *continued*

Year	Team		W	L	PCT	ERA	G	GS	CG	IP	H	BB	SO	ShO	Relief Pitching W	Relief Pitching L	Relief Pitching SV	Batting AB	Batting H	Batting HR	BA	PO	A	E	DP	TC/G	FA
1976	NY	N	8	13	.381	3.22	31	30	5	193	184	52	120	2	0	0	0	54	7	0	.130	9	27	6	1	1.4	.857
1978	SD	N	2	1	.667	1.54	20	2	0	35	30	11	13	0	1	0	1	3	0	0	.000	1	6	0	0	0.3	1.000
1979			0	2	.000	4.78	27	5	0	49	59	22	20	0	0	0	0	6	0	0	.000	0	9	0	0	0.3	1.000
16 yrs.			217	191	.532	3.44	586	496	195	3639	3366	1099	2832	41	8	4	11	821	90	0	.110	100	448	38	16	1.0	.935
LEAGUE CHAMPIONSHIP SERIES																											
1972	DET	A	0	1	.000	1.42	2	2	0	19	14	5	10	0	0	0	0	7	0	0	.000	1	3	0	0	2.0	1.000
WORLD SERIES																											
1968	DET	A	3	0	1.000 1st	1.67	3	3	3	27	20	6	21	0	0	0	0	12	3	1	.250	1	4	0	0	1.7	1.000

Tim Lollar

LOLLAR, WILLIAM TIMOTHY — BL TL 6′ 3″ 200 lbs.
B. Mar. 17, 1956, Poplar Bluff, Mo.

Year	Team		W	L	PCT	ERA	G	GS	CG	IP	H	BB	SO	ShO	Relief Pitching W	Relief Pitching L	Relief Pitching SV	Batting AB	Batting H	Batting HR	BA	PO	A	E	DP	TC/G	FA
1980	NY	A	1	0	1.000	3.38	14	1	0	32	33	20	13	0	0	0	2	0	0	0	—	1	7	1	1	0.6	.889
1981	SD	N	2	8	.200	6.08	24	11	0	77	87	51	38	0	1	2	1	18	3	1	.167	4	22	1	1	1.1	.963
1982			16	9	.640	3.13	34	34	4	232.2	192	87	150	2	0	0	0	85	21	3	.247	7	38	0	4	1.3	1.000
1983			7	12	.368	4.61	30	30	1	175.2	170	85	135	0	0	0	0	58	14	1	.241	4	19	0	1	0.8	1.000
1984			11	13	.458	3.91	31	31	3	195.2	168	105	131	2	0	0	0	68	15	3	.221	1	22	0	1	0.7	1.000
1985	2 teams	CHI A (18G 3–5)			BOS A	(16G 5–5)																					
″	total		8	10	.444	4.62	34	23	1	150	140	98	105	0	1	0	1	1	0	0	.000	8	13	0	0	0.6	1.000
1986	BOS	A	2	0	1.000	6.91	32	1	0	43	51	34	28	0	1	0	0	1	1	0	1.000	4	7	0	1	0.3	1.000
7 yrs.			47	52	.475	4.27	199	131	9	906	841	480	600	4	3	2	4	231	54	8	.234	29	128	2	9	0.8	.987
LEAGUE CHAMPIONSHIP SERIES																											
1984	SD	N	0	0	—	6.23	1	1	0	4.1	3	4	3	0	0	0	0	1	0	0	.000	0	0	0	0	0.0	.000
WORLD SERIES																											
1984	SD	N	0	1	.000	21.60	1	1	0	1.2	4	4	0	0	0	0	0	0	0	0	—	0	0	0	0	0.0	.000

Vic Lombardi

LOMBARDI, VICTOR ALVIN — BL TL 5′ 7″ 158 lbs.
B. Sept. 20, 1922, Reedley, Calif.

Year	Team		W	L	PCT	ERA	G	GS	CG	IP	H	BB	SO	ShO	Relief Pitching W	Relief Pitching L	Relief Pitching SV	Batting AB	Batting H	Batting HR	BA	PO	A	E	DP	TC/G	FA
1945	BKN	N	10	11	.476	3.31	38	24	9	203.2	195	86	64	0	3	1	4	71	13	0	.183	8	38	3	5	1.3	.939
1946			13	10	.565	2.89	41	25	13	193	170	84	60	2	1	2	3	61	14	0	.230	4	44	3	1	1.2	.941
1947			12	11	.522	2.99	33	20	7	174.2	156	65	72	3	3	1	3	66	16	0	.242	8	35	0	2	1.3	1.000
1948	PIT	N	10	9	.526	3.70	38	17	9	163	156	67	54	0	3	1	4	48	10	0	.208	3	37	0	0	1.1	1.000
1949			5	5	.500	4.57	34	12	4	134	149	68	64	0	1	2	1	49	17	0	.347	9	28	0	1	1.1	1.000
1950			0	5	.000	6.60	39	2	0	76.1	93	48	26	0	0	3	1	16	4	0	.250	4	15	0	3	0.5	1.000
6 yrs.			50	51	.495	3.68	223	100	42	944.2	919	418	340	5	11	10	16	311	74	0	.238	36	197	6	12	1.1	.975
WORLD SERIES																											
1947	BKN	N	0	1	.000	12.15	2	2	0	6.2	14	1	5	0	0	0	0	3	0	0	.000	0	0	0	0	0.0	.000

Lou Lombardo

LOMBARDO, LOUIS — BL TL 6′ 2″ 210 lbs.
B. Nov. 18, 1928, Carlstadt, N. J.

Year	Team		W	L	PCT	ERA	G	GS	CG	IP	H	BB	SO	ShO	Relief Pitching W	Relief Pitching L	Relief Pitching SV	Batting AB	Batting H	Batting HR	BA	PO	A	E	DP	TC/G	FA
1948	NY	N	0	0	—	6.75	2	0	0	5.1	5	5	0	0	0	0	0	2	0	0	.000	0	2	0	0	1.0	1.000

Kevin Lomon

LOMON, KEVIN DALE — BR TR 6′ 1″ 195 lbs.
B. Nov. 20, 1971, Fort Smith, Ark.

Year	Team		W	L	PCT	ERA	G	GS	CG	IP	H	BB	SO	ShO	Relief Pitching W	Relief Pitching L	Relief Pitching SV	Batting AB	Batting H	Batting HR	BA	PO	A	E	DP	TC/G	FA
1995	NY	N	0	1	.000	6.75	6	0	0	9.1	17	5	6	0	0	1	0	0	0	0	—	1	0	1	0	0.3	.500

Jim Lonborg

LONBORG, JAMES REYNOLD — BR TR 6′ 5″ 200 lbs.
B. Apr. 16, 1942, Santa Maria, Calif.

Year	Team		W	L	PCT	ERA	G	GS	CG	IP	H	BB	SO	ShO	Relief Pitching W	Relief Pitching L	Relief Pitching SV	Batting AB	Batting H	Batting HR	BA	PO	A	E	DP	TC/G	FA
1965	BOS	A	9	17	.346	4.47	32	31	7	185.1	193	65	113	1	0	0	0	59	8	0	.136	12	24	5	0	1.3	.878
1966			10	10	.500	3.86	45	23	3	181.2	173	55	131	1	1	1	2	54	5	0	.093	18	21	2	2	0.9	.951
1967			**22**	9	.710	3.16	39	**39**	15	273.1	228	83	**246**	2	0	0	0	99	14	0	.141	19	24	1	2	1.1	.977
1968			6	10	.375	4.29	23	17	4	113.1	89	59	73	1	0	2	0	39	11	1	.282	8	6	0	0	0.6	1.000
1969			7	11	.389	4.51	29	23	4	143.2	148	65	100	0	1	0	0	41	4	0	.098	13	18	2	1	1.1	.939
1970			4	1	.800	3.18	9	4	0	34	33	9	21	0	2	0	0	9	4	1	.444	2	5	0	1	0.8	1.000
1971			10	7	.588	4.13	27	26	5	168	167	67	100	1	1	0	0	53	9	0	.170	15	28	1	3	1.6	.977
1972	MIL	A	14	12	.538	2.83	33	30	11	223	197	76	143	2	0	0	1	69	10	0	.145	9	25	3	2	1.1	.919
1973	PHI	N	13	16	.448	4.88	38	30	6	199.1	218	80	106	0	2	1	0	59	8	0	.136	10	26	5	2	1.1	.878
1974			17	13	.567	3.21	39	39	16	283	280	70	121	3	0	0	0	94	9	1	.096	16	26	2	1	1.1	.955
1975			8	6	.571	4.13	27	26	6	159	161	45	72	2	0	0	1	44	1	0	.023	24	18	1	0	1.6	.977
1976			18	10	.643	3.08	33	32	8	222	210	50	118	1	0	0	1	67	11	0	.164	21	16	0	0	1.1	1.000
1977			11	4	.733	4.10	25	25	4	158	157	50	76	1	0	0	0	48	5	0	.104	10	17	0	3	1.1	1.000
1978			8	10	.444	5.21	22	22	1	114	132	45	48	0	0	0	0	34	6	0	.176	11	14	0	1	1.1	1.000
1979			0	1	.000	11.57	4	1	0	7	14	4	7	0	0	0	0	1	0	0	.000	1	0	0	0	0.3	1.000
15 yrs.			157	137	.534	3.86	425	368	90	2464.2	2400	823	1475	15	7	4	4	770	105	3	.136	189	268	22	18	1.1	.954
LEAGUE CHAMPIONSHIP SERIES																											
1976	PHI	N	0	1	.000	1.69	1	1	0	5.1	2	2	2	0	0	0	0	1	0	0	.000	0	2	0	0	2.0	1.000
1977			0	1	.000	11.25	1	1	0	4	5	1	1	0	0	0	0	1	0	0	.000	0	2	0	0	2.0	1.000
2 yrs.			0	2	.000	5.79	2	2	0	9.1	7	3	3	0	0	0	0	2	0	0	.000	0	4	0	0	2.0	1.000
WORLD SERIES																											
1967	BOS	A	2	1	.667	2.63	3	3	2	24	14	2	11	1	0	0	0	9	0	0	.000	1	2	0	0	1.0	1.000

Bill Long

LONG, WILLIAM DOUGLAS — BR TR 6′ 185 lbs.
B. Feb. 29, 1960, Cincinnati, Ohio.

Year	Team		W	L	PCT	ERA	G	GS	CG	IP	H	BB	SO	ShO	Relief Pitching W	Relief Pitching L	Relief Pitching SV	Batting AB	Batting H	Batting HR	BA	PO	A	E	DP	TC/G	FA
1985	CHI	A	0	1	.000	10.29	4	3	0	14	25	5	13	0	0	0	0	0	0	0	—	2	3	0	0	1.3	1.000
1987			8	8	.500	4.37	29	23	5	169	179	28	72	2	1	1	1	0	0	0	—	14	25	3	2	1.4	.929
1988			8	11	.421	4.03	47	18	3	174	187	43	77	0	2	2	2	0	0	0	—	7	25	0	0	0.7	1.000

Bill Long *continued*

Year	Team	W	L	PCT	ERA	G	GS	CG	IP	H	BB	SO	ShO	Relief Pitching W	Relief Pitching L	Relief Pitching SV	Batting AB	Batting H	Batting HR	BA	PO	A	E	DP	TC/G	FA
1989		5	5	.500	3.92	30	8	0	98.2	101	37	51	0	2	0	1	0	0	0	—	9	15	0	0	0.8	1.000
1990	2 teams CHI A (4G 0–1) CHI N (42G 6–1)																									
"	total	6	2	.750	4.55	46	0	0	61.1	72	23	34	0	6	2	5	5	0	0	.000	6	11	1	0	0.4	.944
1991	MON N	0	0	—	10.80	3	0	0	1.2	4	4	0	0	0	0	0	0	0	0	—	0	0	0	0	0.0	.000
6 yrs.		27	27	.500	4.37	159	52	8	518.2	568	140	247	2	11	5	9	5	0	0	.000	38	79	4	2	0.8	.967

Bob Long

LONG, ROBERT EARL BR TR 6′ 3″ 178 lbs.
B. Nov. 11, 1954, Jasper, Tenn.

Year	Team	W	L	PCT	ERA	G	GS	CG	IP	H	BB	SO	ShO	Relief Pitching W	Relief Pitching L	Relief Pitching SV	Batting AB	Batting H	Batting HR	BA	PO	A	E	DP	TC/G	FA
1981	PIT N	1	2	.333	5.85	5	3	0	20	23	10	8	0	0	0	0	4	0	0	.000	1	1	0	0	0.4	1.000
1985	SEA A	0	0	—	3.76	28	0	0	38.1	30	17	29	0	0	0	0	0	0	0	—	3	3	0	0	0.2	1.000
2 yrs.		1	2	.333	4.47	33	3	0	58.1	53	27	37	0	0	0	0	4	0	0	.000	4	4	0	0	0.2	1.000

Lep Long

LONG, LESTER BR TR 5′10″ 153 lbs.
B. July 12, 1888, Summit, N. J. D. Oct. 21, 1958, Birmingham, Ala.

Year	Team	W	L	PCT	ERA	G	GS	CG	IP	H	BB	SO	ShO	Relief Pitching W	Relief Pitching L	Relief Pitching SV	Batting AB	Batting H	Batting HR	BA	PO	A	E	DP	TC/G	FA
1911	PHI A	0	0	—	4.50	4	0	0	8	15	5	4	0	0	0	0	3	0	0	.000	1	2	0	0	0.8	1.000

Red Long

LONG, NELSON BR TR 6′ 1″ 190 lbs.
B. Sept. 28, 1876, Burlington, Ont., Canada
D. Aug. 11, 1929, Hamilton, Ont., Canada.

Year	Team	W	L	PCT	ERA	G	GS	CG	IP	H	BB	SO	ShO	Relief Pitching W	Relief Pitching L	Relief Pitching SV	Batting AB	Batting H	Batting HR	BA	PO	A	E	DP	TC/G	FA
1902	BOS N	0	0	—	1.13	1	1	1	8	4	3	5	0	0	0	0	*				8	6	0	0	4.7	1.000

Tom Long

LONG, THOMAS FRANCIS BL TL 5′ 9″ 154 lbs.
B. Apr. 22, 1898, Memphis, Tenn. D. Sept. 16, 1973, Louisville, Ky.

Year	Team	W	L	PCT	ERA	G	GS	CG	IP	H	BB	SO	ShO	Relief Pitching W	Relief Pitching L	Relief Pitching SV	Batting AB	Batting H	Batting HR	BA	PO	A	E	DP	TC/G	FA
1924	BKN N	0	0	—	9.00	1	0	0	2	2	2	0	0	0	0	0	0	0	0	—	0	0	0	0	0.0	.000

Brian Looney

LOONEY, BRIAN JAMES BL TL 5′10″ 180 lbs.
B. Sept. 26, 1969, New Haven, Conn.

Year	Team	W	L	PCT	ERA	G	GS	CG	IP	H	BB	SO	ShO	Relief Pitching W	Relief Pitching L	Relief Pitching SV	Batting AB	Batting H	Batting HR	BA	PO	A	E	DP	TC/G	FA
1993	MON N	0	0	—	3.00	3	1	0	6	8	2	7	0	0	0	0	1	0	0	.000	0	1	0	0	0.3	1.000
1994		0	0	—	22.50	1	0	0	2	4	0	2	0	0	0	0	0	0	0	—	0	0	0	0	0.0	.000
1995	BOS A	0	1	.000	17.36	3	1	0	4.2	12	4	2	0	0	0	0	0	0	0	—	0	1	0	0	0.3	1.000
3 yrs.		0	1	.000	11.37	7	2	0	12.2	24	6	11	0	0	0	0	1	0	0	.000	0	2	0	0	0.3	1.000

Pete Loos

LOOS, IVAN TR
B. Mar. 23, 1878, Philadelphia, Pa. D. Feb. 23, 1956, Darby, Pa.

Year	Team	W	L	PCT	ERA	G	GS	CG	IP	H	BB	SO	ShO	Relief Pitching W	Relief Pitching L	Relief Pitching SV	Batting AB	Batting H	Batting HR	BA	PO	A	E	DP	TC/G	FA
1901	PHI A	0	1	.000	27.00	1	1	0	1	2	4	0	0	0	0	0	0	0	0	—	0	1	0	0	1.0	1.000

Ed Lopat

LOPAT, EDMUND WALTER (Steady Eddie) BL TL 5′10″ 185 lbs.
Born Edmund Walter Lopatynski.
B. June 21, 1918, New York, N. Y. D. June 15, 1992, Darien, Conn.
Manager 1963–64.

Year	Team	W	L	PCT	ERA	G	GS	CG	IP	H	BB	SO	ShO	Relief Pitching W	Relief Pitching L	Relief Pitching SV	Batting AB	Batting H	Batting HR	BA	PO	A	E	DP	TC/G	FA
1944	CHI A	11	10	.524	3.26	27	25	13	210	217	59	75	1	0	0	0	81	25	0	.309	9	44	0	4	2.0	1.000
1945		10	13	.435	4.11	26	24	17	199.1	226	56	74	1	0	0	1	82	24	1	.293	15	32	2	0	1.9	.959
1946		13	13	.500	2.73	29	29	20	231	216	48	89	2	0	0	0	87	22	0	.253	8	48	0	4	1.9	1.000
1947		16	13	.552	2.81	31	31	22	252.2	241	73	109	3	0	0	0	96	19	0	.198	12	36	2	0	1.6	.960
1948	NY A	17	11	.607	3.65	33	31	13	226.2	246	66	83	3	1	0	0	81	14	0	.173	6	50	3	3	1.8	.949
1949		15	10	.600	3.26	31	30	14	215.1	222	69	70	4	0	0	1	76	20	1	.263	7	42	2	5	1.6	.961
1950		18	8	.692	3.47	35	32	15	236.1	244	65	72	3	1	0	1	82	19	0	.232	10	47	2	4	1.7	.966
1951		21	9	.700	2.91	31	31	20	234.2	209	71	93	5	0	0	0	84	15	3	.179	9	50	3	4	2.0	.952
1952		10	5	.667	2.53	20	19	10	149.1	127	53	56	2	0	0	0	52	9	0	.173	6	30	1	2	1.9	.973
1953		16	4	**.800**	**2.42**	25	24	9	178.1	169	32	50	3	0	0	0	63	12	0	.190	8	38	2	1	1.9	.958
1954		12	4	.750	3.55	26	23	7	170	189	33	54	0	0	0	0	57	1	0	.018	3	28	1	1	1.2	.969
1955	2 teams NY A (16G 4–8) BAL A (10G 3–4)																									
"	total	7	12	.368	3.91	26	19	4	135.2	158	25	34	1	0	3	0	46	7	0	.152	7	23	1	2	1.2	.968
12 yrs.		166	112	.597	3.21	340	318	164	2439.1	2464	650	859	28	2	3	3	887	187	5	.211	100	468	19	30	1.7	.968
WORLD SERIES																										
1949	NY A	1	0	1.000	6.35	1	1	0	5.2	9	1	4	0	0	0	0	3	1	0	.333	0	1	0	0	1.0	1.000
1950		0	0	—	2.25	1	1	0	8	9	0	5	0	0	0	0	2	1	0	.500	1	4	0	0	5.0	1.000
1951		2	0	1.000	0.50	2	2	2	18	10	3	4	0	0	0	0	8	1	0	.125	2	4	0	1	3.0	1.000
1952		0	1	.000	4.76	2	2	0	11.1	14	4	3	0	0	0	0	3	1	0	.333	0	1	0	0	0.5	1.000
1953		1	0	1.000	2.00	1	1	1	9	9	4	3	0	0	0	0	3	0	0	.000	0	2	0	0	2.0	1.000
5 yrs.		4	1	.800	2.60	7	7	3	52	51	12	19	0	0	0	0	19	4	0	.211	3	12	0	1	2.1	1.000

Art Lopatka

LOPATKA, ARTHUR JOSEPH BB TL 5′10″ 170 lbs.
B. May 28, 1919, Chicago, Ill.

Year	Team	W	L	PCT	ERA	G	GS	CG	IP	H	BB	SO	ShO	Relief Pitching W	Relief Pitching L	Relief Pitching SV	Batting AB	Batting H	Batting HR	BA	PO	A	E	DP	TC/G	FA
1945	STL N	1	0	1.000	1.54	4	1	1	11.2	7	3	5	0	0	0	0	4	1	0	.250	1	0	0	0	0.3	1.000
1946	PHI N	0	1	.000	16.88	4	1	0	5.1	13	4	4	0	0	0	0	0	0	0	—	0	1	0	0	0.3	1.000
2 yrs.		1	1	.500	6.35	8	2	1	17	20	7	9	0	0	0	0	4	1	0	.250	1	1	0	0	0.3	1.000

Albie Lopez

LOPEZ, ALBERT ANTHONY BR TR 6′ 1″ 205 lbs.
B. Aug. 18, 1971, Mesa, Ariz.

Year	Team	W	L	PCT	ERA	G	GS	CG	IP	H	BB	SO	ShO	Relief Pitching W	Relief Pitching L	Relief Pitching SV	Batting AB	Batting H	Batting HR	BA	PO	A	E	DP	TC/G	FA
1993	CLE A	3	1	.750	5.98	9	9	0	49.2	49	32	25	0	0	0	0	0	0	0	—	5	6	2	0	1.4	.846
1994		1	2	.333	4.24	4	4	1	17	20	6	18	1	0	0	0	0	0	0	—	2	0	1	0	0.8	.667
1995		0	0	—	3.13	6	2	0	23	17	7	22	0	0	0	0	0	0	0	—	1	2	0	0	0.5	1.000
3 yrs.		4	3	.571	4.92	19	15	1	89.2	86	45	65	1	0	0	0	0	0	0		8	8	3	0	1.0	.842

Aurelio Lopez

LOPEZ, AURELIO ALEJANDRO BR TR 6′ 225 lbs.
Born Aurelio Alejandro Lopez (Rios).
B. Sept. 21, 1948, Tecamachalco, Mexico D. Sept. 22, 1992, Matehuala, Mexico.

Year	Team	W	L	PCT	ERA	G	GS	CG	IP	H	BB	SO	ShO	Relief Pitching W	Relief Pitching L	Relief Pitching SV	Batting AB	Batting H	Batting HR	BA	PO	A	E	DP	TC/G	FA
1974	KC A	0	0	—	5.63	8	1	0	16	21	10	5	0	0	0	0	0	0	0	—	0	4	2	0	0.8	.667
1978	STL N	4	2	.667	4.29	25	4	0	65	52	32	46	0	2	1	0	14	3	0	.214	0	5	1	0	0.2	.833
1979	DET A	10	5	.667	2.41	61	0	0	127	95	51	106	0	10	5	21	0	0	0	—	9	15	1	1	0.4	.960
1980		13	6	.684	3.77	67	1	0	124	125	45	97	0	**13**	5	21	0	0	0	—	5	11	1	1	0.3	.941
1981		5	2	.714	3.62	29	3	0	82	70	31	53	0	3	2	3	0	0	0	—	5	10	0	1	0.5	1.000

Aurelio Lopez *continued*

Year	Team		W	L	PCT	ERA	G	GS	CG	IP	H	BB	SO	ShO	Relief Pitching W	Relief Pitching L	Relief Pitching SV	Batting AB	Batting H	Batting HR	BA	PO	A	E	DP	TC/G	FA
1982			3	1	.750	5.27	19	0	0	41	41	19	26	0	3	1	3	0	0	0	—	3	5	0	0	0.4	1.000
1983			9	8	.529	2.81	57	0	0	115.1	87	49	90	0	9	8	18	0	0	0	—	2	13	1	0	0.3	.938
1984			10	1	.909	2.94	71	0	0	137.2	109	52	94	0	**10**	1	14	0	0	0	—	6	11	2	2	0.3	.895
1985			3	7	.300	4.80	51	0	0	86.1	82	41	53	0	3	7	5	0	0	0	—	5	10	1	1	0.3	.938
1986	**HOU**	**N**	3	3	.500	3.46	45	0	0	78	64	25	44	0	3	3	7	9	0	0	.000	2	6	2	0	0.2	.800
1987			2	1	.667	4.50	26	0	0	38	39	12	21	0	2	1	1	1	0	0	.000	0	7	1	0	0.3	.875
11 yrs.			62	36	.633	3.56	459	9	0	910.1	785	367	635	0	58	34	93	24	3	0	.125	37	97	12	6	0.3	.918
LEAGUE CHAMPIONSHIP SERIES																											
1984	**DET**	**A**	1	0	1.000	0.00	1	0	0	3	4	1	2	0	1	0	0	0	0	0	—	0	0	0	0	0.0	.000
1986	**HOU**	**N**	0	1	.000	8.10	2	0	0	3.1	7	4	3	0	0	1	0	0	0	0	—	0	0	0	0	0.0	.000
2 yrs.			1	1	.500	4.26	3	0	0	6.1	11	5	5	0	1	1	0	0	0	0		0	0	0	0	0.0	
WORLD SERIES																											
1984	**DET**	**A**	1	0	1.000	0.00	2	0	0	3	1	1	4	0	1	0	0	0	0	0	—	0	0	0	0	0.0	.000

Marcelino Lopez

LOPEZ, MARCELINO PONS BR TL 6′ 3″ 195 lbs.
B. Sept. 23, 1943, Havana, Cuba.

Year	Team		W	L	PCT	ERA	G	GS	CG	IP	H	BB	SO	ShO	Relief Pitching W	Relief Pitching L	Relief Pitching SV	Batting AB	Batting H	Batting HR	BA	PO	A	E	DP	TC/G	FA
1963	**PHI**	**N**	1	0	1.000	6.00	4	2	0	6	8	7	2	0	0	0	0	2	0	0	.000	1	2	0	0	0.8	1.000
1965	**CAL**	**A**	14	13	.519	2.93	35	32	8	215.1	185	82	122	1	0	0	1	69	14	1	.203	12	57	2	4	2.0	.972
1966			7	14	.333	3.93	37	32	6	199	188	68	132	2	0	0	1	58	11	0	.190	17	40	2	1	1.6	.966
1967	**2 teams**	**CAL A** (4G 0–2) **BAL A** (4G 1–0)																									
″	**total**		1	2	.333	4.72	8	7	0	26.2	26	19	21	0	0	0	0	7	1	0	.143	0	1	2	0	0.4	.333
1969	**BAL**	**A**	5	3	.625	4.41	27	4	0	69.1	65	34	57	0	4	2	0	14	3	0	.214	2	4	1	1	0.3	.857
1970			1	1	.500	2.07	25	3	0	61	47	37	49	0	0	1	0	13	1	0	.077	2	6	4	1	0.5	.667
1971	**MIL**	**A**	2	7	.222	4.63	31	11	0	68	64	60	42	0	1	3	0	17	1	0	.059	5	13	1	2	0.6	.947
1972	**CLE**	**A**	0	0	—	5.63	4	2	0	8	8	10	1	0	0	0	0	1	0	0	.000	0	1	0	0	0.3	1.000
8 yrs.			31	40	.437	3.62	171	93	14	653.1	591	317	426	3	5	6	2	181	31	1	.171	39	124	12	9	1.0	.931
LEAGUE CHAMPIONSHIP SERIES																											
1969	**BAL**	**A**	0	0	—	0.00	1	0	0	0.1	1	2	0	0	0	0	0	0	0	0	—	0	0	0	0	0.0	.000
WORLD SERIES																											
1970	**BAL**	**A**	0	0	—	0.00	1	0	0	0.1	0	0	0	0	0	0	0	0	0	0	—	0	0	0	0	0.0	.000

Ramon Lopez

LOPEZ, JOSE RAMON BR TR 6′ 175 lbs.
Born Jose Ramon Lopez (Hevia).
B. May 26, 1933, Las Villas, Cuba D. Sept. 4, 1982, Miami, Fla.

Year	Team		W	L	PCT	ERA	G	GS	CG	IP	H	BB	SO	ShO	Relief Pitching W	Relief Pitching L	Relief Pitching SV	Batting AB	Batting H	Batting HR	BA	PO	A	E	DP	TC/G	FA
1966	**CAL**	**A**	0	1	.000	5.14	4	1	0	7	4	4	2	0	0	0	0	0	0	0	—	2	0	1	0	0.8	.667

Bris Lord

LORD, BRISCOE ROBOTHAM (The Human Eyeball) BR TR 5′ 9″ 185 lbs.
B. Sept. 21, 1883, Upland, Pa. D. Nov. 13, 1964, Annapolis, Md.

Year	Team		W	L	PCT	ERA	G	GS	CG	IP	H	BB	SO	ShO	Relief Pitching W	Relief Pitching L	Relief Pitching SV	Batting AB	Batting H	Batting HR	BA	PO	A	E	DP	TC/G	FA
1907	**PHI**	**A**	0	0	—	9.00	1	0	0	1	3	0	0	0	0	0	0	*				94	9	4	3	1.8	.963

Lefty Lorenzen

LORENZEN, ADOLPH ANDREAS BL TL 5′10″ 164 lbs.
B. Jan. 12, 1893, Davenport, Iowa D. Mar. 5, 1963, Davenport, Iowa.

Year	Team		W	L	PCT	ERA	G	GS	CG	IP	H	BB	SO	ShO	Relief Pitching W	Relief Pitching L	Relief Pitching SV	Batting AB	Batting H	Batting HR	BA	PO	A	E	DP	TC/G	FA
1913	**DET**	**A**	0	0	—	18.00	1	0	0	2	4	3	0	0	0	0	0	2	1	0	.500	0	3	0	1	3.0	1.000

Andrew Lorraine

LORRAINE, ANDREW JASON BL TL 6′ 3″ 195 lbs.
B. Aug. 11, 1972, Los Angeles, Calif.

Year	Team		W	L	PCT	ERA	G	GS	CG	IP	H	BB	SO	ShO	Relief Pitching W	Relief Pitching L	Relief Pitching SV	Batting AB	Batting H	Batting HR	BA	PO	A	E	DP	TC/G	FA
1994	**CAL**	**A**	0	2	.000	10.61	4	3	0	18.2	30	11	10	0	0	0	0	0	0	0	—	2	3	0	0	1.3	1.000
1995	**CHI**	**A**	0	0	—	3.38	5	0	0	8	3	2	5	0	0	0	0	0	0	0	—	1	0	0	0	0.2	1.000
2 yrs.			0	2	.000	8.44	9	3	0	26.2	33	13	15	0	0	0	0	0	0	0		3	3	0	0	0.7	1.000

Joe Lotz

LOTZ, JOSEPH PETER (Smokey) BR TR 5′ 8½″ 175 lbs.
B. Jan. 2, 1891, Remsen, Iowa D. Jan. 1, 1971, Castro Valley, Calif.

Year	Team		W	L	PCT	ERA	G	GS	CG	IP	H	BB	SO	ShO	Relief Pitching W	Relief Pitching L	Relief Pitching SV	Batting AB	Batting H	Batting HR	BA	PO	A	E	DP	TC/G	FA
1916	**STL**	**N**	0	3	.000	4.28	12	3	1	40	31	17	18	0	0	0	0	12	4	0	.333	1	8	0	0	0.8	1.000

Art Loudell

LOUDELL, ARTHUR BR TR 5′11″ 173 lbs.
Born Arthur Laudel.
B. Apr. 10, 1882, Latham, Mo. D. Feb. 19, 1961, Kansas City, Mo.

Year	Team		W	L	PCT	ERA	G	GS	CG	IP	H	BB	SO	ShO	Relief Pitching W	Relief Pitching L	Relief Pitching SV	Batting AB	Batting H	Batting HR	BA	PO	A	E	DP	TC/G	FA
1910	**DET**	**A**	1	1	.500	3.38	5	2	1	21.1	23	14	12	0	0	0	0	7	1	0	.143	0	3	0	0	0.6	1.000

Larry Loughlin

LOUGHLIN, LARRY JOHN BL TL 6′ 1″ 190 lbs.
B. Aug. 16, 1941, Tacoma, Wash.

Year	Team		W	L	PCT	ERA	G	GS	CG	IP	H	BB	SO	ShO	Relief Pitching W	Relief Pitching L	Relief Pitching SV	Batting AB	Batting H	Batting HR	BA	PO	A	E	DP	TC/G	FA
1967	**PHI**	**N**	0	0	—	15.19	3	0	0	5.1	9	4	5	0	0	0	0	1	1	0	1.000	0	0	1	0	0.3	.000

Don Loun

LOUN, DONALD NELSON BR TL 6′ 2″ 185 lbs.
B. Nov. 9, 1940, Frederick, Md.

Year	Team		W	L	PCT	ERA	G	GS	CG	IP	H	BB	SO	ShO	Relief Pitching W	Relief Pitching L	Relief Pitching SV	Batting AB	Batting H	Batting HR	BA	PO	A	E	DP	TC/G	FA
1964	**WAS**	**A**	1	1	.500	2.08	2	2	1	13	13	3	3	1	0	0	0	4	0	0	.000	2	4	0	0	3.0	1.000

Slim Love

LOVE, EDWARD HAUGHTON BL TL 6′ 7″ 195 lbs.
B. Aug. 1, 1890, Love, Miss. D. Nov. 30, 1942, Memphis, Tenn.

Year	Team		W	L	PCT	ERA	G	GS	CG	IP	H	BB	SO	ShO	Relief Pitching W	Relief Pitching L	Relief Pitching SV	Batting AB	Batting H	Batting HR	BA	PO	A	E	DP	TC/G	FA
1913	**WAS**	**A**	1	0	1.000	1.62	5	1	0	16.2	14	6	5	0	0	0	1	5	1	0	.200	0	1	2	0	0.6	.333
1916	**NY**	**A**	2	0	1.000	4.91	20	1	0	47.2	46	23	21	0	1	0	0	14	0	0	.000	0	14	1	0	0.8	.933
1917			6	5	.545	2.35	33	9	2	130.1	115	57	82	0	4	0	1	36	6	0	.167	3	27	3	1	1.0	.909
1918			13	12	.520	3.07	38	29	13	228.2	207	**116**	95	1	1	1	1	74	17	0	.230	7	39	4	5	1.3	.920
1919	**DET**	**A**	6	4	.600	3.01	22	8	4	89.2	92	40	46	0	3	1	1	27	6	0	.222	1	15	2	3	0.8	.889
1920			0	0	—	8.31	1	0	0	4.1	6	4	2	0	0	0	0	0	0	0	—	0	1	0	0	1.0	1.000
6 yrs.			28	21	.571	3.04	119	48	19	517.1	480	246	251	1	9	2	4	156	30	0	.192	11	97	12	9	1.0	.900

Vance Lovelace

LOVELACE, VANCE ODELL
B. Aug. 9, 1963, Tampa, Fla.

BL TL 6′ 5″ 205 lbs.

Year	Team	Lg	W	L	PCT	ERA	G	GS	CG	IP	H	BB	SO	ShO	Relief Pitching W	L	SV	Batting AB	H	HR	BA	PO	A	E	DP	TC/G	FA
1988	CAL	A	0	0	—	13.50	3	0	0	1.1	2	3	0	0	0	0	0	0	0	0	—	0	0	0	0	0.0	.000
1989			0	0	—	0.00	1	0	0	1	0	1	1	0	0	0	0	0	0	0	—	0	0	0	0	0.0	.000
1990	SEA	A	0	0	—	3.86	5	0	0	2.1	3	6	1	0	0	0	0	0	0	0	—	0	0	0	0	0.0	.000
3 yrs.			0	0		5.79	9	0	0	4.2	5	10	2	0	0	0	0	0	0	0		0	0	0	0	0.0	

Lynn Lovenguth

LOVENGUTH, LYNN RICHARD
B. Nov. 29, 1922, Camden, N. J.

BL TR 5′10½″ 170 lbs.

Year	Team	Lg	W	L	PCT	ERA	G	GS	CG	IP	H	BB	SO	ShO	Relief Pitching W	L	SV	Batting AB	H	HR	BA	PO	A	E	DP	TC/G	FA
1955	PHI	N	0	1	.000	4.50	14	0	0	18	17	10	14	0	0	1	0	2	0	0	.000	0	1	0	1	0.1	1.000
1957	STL	N	0	1	.000	2.00	2	1	0	9	6	6	6	0	0	0	0	2	0	0	.000	0	0	0	0	0.0	.000
2 yrs.			0	2	.000	3.67	16	1	0	27	23	16	20	0	0	1	0	4	0	0	.000	0	1	0	1	0.1	1.000

John Lovett

LOVETT, JOHN
B. May 6, 1878, Monday, Ohio D. Dec. 5, 1937, Murray City, Ohio.

Year	Team	Lg	W	L	PCT	ERA	G	GS	CG	IP	H	BB	SO	ShO	Relief Pitching W	L	SV	Batting AB	H	HR	BA	PO	A	E	DP	TC/G	FA
1903	STL	N	0	1	.000	5.40	3	1	0	5	6	5	3	0	0	0	0	3	1	0	.333	0	1	0	0	0.3	1.000

Tom Lovett

LOVETT, THOMAS JOSEPH
B. Dec. 7, 1863, Providence, R. I. D. Mar. 19, 1928, Providence, R. I.

BR 5′ 8″ 165 lbs.

Year	Team	Lg	W	L	PCT	ERA	G	GS	CG	IP	H	BB	SO	ShO	Relief Pitching W	L	SV	Batting AB	H	HR	BA	PO	A	E	DP	TC/G	FA
1885	PHI	AA	7	8	.467	*3.70*	16	16	15	138.2	130	38	56	1	0	0	0	58	13	0	.224	10	20	13	0	2.5	.698
1889	BKN	AA	17	10	.630	4.32	29	28	23	229	234	65	92	1	0	0	0	100	19	2	.190	8	49	3	2	2.1	.950
1890	BKN	N	30	11	**.732**	2.78	44	41	39	372	327	141	124	4	1	0	0	164	33	1	.201	11	79	10	3	2.2	.900
1891			23	19	.548	3.69	44	43	39	365.2	361	129	129	3	0	0	0	153	25	0	.163	23	59	6	2	2.0	.932
1893			3	5	.375	6.56	14	8	6	96	134	35	15	0	1	0	1	50	9	0	.180	12	17	4	2	1.7	.879
1894	BOS	N	8	6	.571	5.97	15	13	10	104	155	36	23	0	1	1	0	49	7	1	.143	6	14	1	1	1.4	.952
6 yrs.			88	59	.599	3.94	162	149	132	1305.1	1341	444	439	9	3	1	1	574	106	4	.185	70	238	37	10	2.0	.893

Pete Lovrich

LOVRICH, PETER
B. Oct. 16, 1942, Blue Island, Ill.

BR TR 6′ 4″ 200 lbs.

Year	Team	Lg	W	L	PCT	ERA	G	GS	CG	IP	H	BB	SO	ShO	Relief Pitching W	L	SV	Batting AB	H	HR	BA	PO	A	E	DP	TC/G	FA
1963	KC	A	1	1	.500	7.84	20	1	0	20.2	25	10	16	0	1	0	0	0	0	0	—	0	1	0	0	0.1	1.000

Grover Lowdermilk

LOWDERMILK, GROVER CLEVELAND (Slim)
Brother of Lou Lowdermilk.
B. Jan. 15, 1885, Sandborn, Ind. D. Mar. 31, 1968, Odin, Ill.

BR TR 6′ 4″ 190 lbs.

Year	Team	Lg	W	L	PCT	ERA	G	GS	CG	IP	H	BB	SO	ShO	Relief Pitching W	L	SV	Batting AB	H	HR	BA	PO	A	E	DP	TC/G	FA
1909	STL	N	0	2	.000	6.21	7	3	1	29	28	30	14	0	0	0	0	10	1	0	.100	0	8	1	0	1.3	.889
1911			0	1	.000	7.29	11	2	1	33.1	37	33	15	0	0	0	0	9	1	0	.111	0	11	0	0	1.0	1.000
1912	CHI	N	0	1	.000	9.69	2	1	1	13	17	14	8	0	0	0	0	4	0	0	.000	0	4	3	0	3.5	.571
1915	2 teams	STL A (38G 9–17) DET A (7G 4–1)																									
″	total		13	18	.419	3.24	45	34	14	250.1	200	157	148	1	3	2	0	80	10	0	.125	6	73	9	3	2.0	.898
1916	2 teams	DET A (1G 0–0) CLE A (10G 1–5)																									
″	total		1	5	.167	3.14	11	9	2	51.2	52	48	28	0	0	0	0	18	3	0	.167	2	15	2	1	1.7	.895
1917	STL	A	2	1	.667	1.42	3	2	2	19	16	4	9	1	0	1	0	7	0	0	.000	1	5	0	0	2.0	1.000
1918			2	6	.250	3.15	13	11	4	80	74	38	25	0	0	0	0	28	7	0	.250	5	33	1	1	3.0	.974
1919	2 teams	STL A (7G 0–0) CHI A (20G 5–5)																									
″	total		5	5	.500	2.57	27	11	5	108.2	101	47	49	0	0	2	0	35	3	0	.086	3	35	4	4	1.6	.905
1920	CHI	A	0	0	—	6.75	3	0	0	5.1	9	5	0	0	0	0	0	0	0	0	—	1	4	1	0	2.0	.833
9 yrs.			23	39	.371	3.58	122	73	30	590.1	534	376	296	2	3	5	0	191	25	0	.131	18	188	21	9	1.9	.907
WORLD SERIES																											
1919	CHI	A	0	0	—	9.00	1	0	0	1	2	1	0	0	0	0	0	0	0	0	—	0	1	0	0	1.0	1.000

Lou Lowdermilk

LOWDERMILK, LOUIS BAILEY
Brother of Grover Lowdermilk.
B. Feb. 23, 1887, Sandborn, Ind. D. Dec. 27, 1975, Centralia, Ill.

BR TL 6′ 1″ 180 lbs.

Year	Team	Lg	W	L	PCT	ERA	G	GS	CG	IP	H	BB	SO	ShO	Relief Pitching W	L	SV	Batting AB	H	HR	BA	PO	A	E	DP	TC/G	FA
1911	STL	N	3	4	.429	3.46	16	3	3	65	72	29	20	1	2	2	0	18	2	0	.111	0	11	1	0	0.8	.917
1912			1	1	.500	3.00	4	1	1	15	14	9	2	0	0	1	1	4	1	0	.250	0	5	0	0	1.3	1.000
2 yrs.			4	5	.444	3.38	20	4	4	80	86	38	22	1	2	3	1	22	3	0	.136	0	16	1	0	0.9	.941

Bobby Lowe

LOWE, ROBERT LINCOLN (Link)
B. July 10, 1868, Pittsburgh, Pa. D. Dec. 8, 1951, Detroit, Mich.
Manager 1904.

BR TR 5′10″ 150 lbs.

Year	Team	Lg	W	L	PCT	ERA	G	GS	CG	IP	H	BB	SO	ShO	Relief Pitching W	L	SV	Batting AB	H	HR	BA	PO	A	E	DP	TC/G	FA
1891	BOS	N	0	0	—	9.00	1	0	0	1	3	1	0	0	0	0	0	*				103	82	11	2	3.8	.944

George Lowe

LOWE, GEORGE WESLEY
B. Apr. 25, 1895, Ridgefield Park, N. J. D. Sept. 3, 1981, Somers Point, N. J.

BR TR 6′ 2″ 180 lbs.

Year	Team	Lg	W	L	PCT	ERA	G	GS	CG	IP	H	BB	SO	ShO	Relief Pitching W	L	SV	Batting AB	H	HR	BA	PO	A	E	DP	TC/G	FA
1920	CIN	N	0	0	—	0.00	1	0	0	2	1	1	0	0	0	0	0	0	0	0	—	0	0	0	0	0.0	.000

Turk Lown

LOWN, OMAR JOSEPH
B. May 30, 1924, Brooklyn, N. Y.

BR TR 6′ 180 lbs.

Year	Team	Lg	W	L	PCT	ERA	G	GS	CG	IP	H	BB	SO	ShO	Relief Pitching W	L	SV	Batting AB	H	HR	BA	PO	A	E	DP	TC/G	FA
1951	CHI	N	4	9	.308	5.46	31	18	3	127	125	90	39	1	1	2	0	39	8	0	.205	9	23	0	1	1.0	1.000
1952			4	11	.267	4.37	33	19	5	156.2	154	93	73	0	1	2	0	50	7	0	.140	12	33	1	2	1.4	.978
1953			8	7	.533	5.16	49	12	2	148.1	166	84	76	0	7	3	3	48	6	0	.125	12	33	0	4	0.9	1.000
1954			0	2	.000	6.14	15	0	0	22	23	15	16	0	0	2	0	0	0	0	—	2	6	1	0	0.6	.889
1956			9	8	.529	3.58	61	0	0	110.2	95	78	74	0	9	8	13	23	5	1	.217	9	13	1	1	0.4	.957
1957			5	7	.417	3.77	**67**	0	0	93	74	51	51	0	5	**7**	12	10	2	0	.200	5	22	1	4	0.4	.964
1958	3 teams	CHI N (4G 0–0) CIN N (11G 0–2) CHI A (27G 3–3)																									
″	total		3	5	.375	4.31	42	0	0	56.1	63	43	53	0	3	5	8	10	3	0	.300	6	5	1	1	0.3	.917
1959	CHI	A	9	2	.818	2.89	60	0	0	93.1	73	42	63	0	**9**	2	**15**	12	3	0	.250	2	21	1	0	0.4	.958
1960			2	3	.400	3.88	45	0	0	67.1	60	34	39	0	2	3	5	5	1	0	.200	4	13	2	1	0.4	.895
1961			7	5	.583	2.76	59	0	0	101	87	35	50	0	7	5	11	14	0	0	.000	6	15	2	1	0.4	.913
1962			4	2	.667	3.04	42	0	0	56.1	58	25	40	0	4	2	6	3	0	0	.000	7	14	1	1	0.5	.955
11 yrs.			55	61	.474	4.12	504	49	10	1032	978	590	574	1	48	41	73	214	35	1	.164	74	198	11	16	0.6	.961
WORLD SERIES																											
1959	CHI	A	0	0	—	0.00	3	0	0	3.1	2	1	3	0	0	0	0	0	0	0	—	0	0	0	0	0.0	.000

Sam Lowry

LOWRY, SAMUEL JOSEPH (Mose) BR TR 5′11″ 160 lbs.
B. Mar. 25, 1920, Philadelphia, Pa. D. Dec. 1, 1992, Philadelphia, Pa.

Year	Team	W	L	PCT	ERA	G	GS	CG	IP	H	BB	SO	ShO	Relief Pitching W	Relief Pitching L	Relief Pitching SV	Batting AB	Batting H	Batting HR	BA	PO	A	E	DP	TC/G	FA
1942	PHI A	0	0	—	6.00	1	0	0	3	3	1	0	0	0	0	0	1	0	0	.000	0	0	0	0	0.0	.000
1943		0	0	—	5.00	5	0	0	18	18	9	3	0	0	0	0	6	1	0	.167	1	5	0	0	1.2	1.000
2 yrs.		0	0		5.14	6	0	0	21	21	10	3	0	0	0	0	7	1	0	.143	1	5	0	0	1.0	1.000

Mike Loynd

LOYND, MICHAEL WALLACE BR TR 6′ 4″ 210 lbs.
B. Mar. 26, 1964, St. Louis, Mo.

Year	Team	W	L	PCT	ERA	G	GS	CG	IP	H	BB	SO	ShO	Relief Pitching W	Relief Pitching L	Relief Pitching SV	Batting AB	Batting H	Batting HR	BA	PO	A	E	DP	TC/G	FA
1986	TEX A	2	2	.500	5.36	9	8	0	42	49	19	33	0	0	0	1	0	0	0	—	5	5	1	0	1.2	.909
1987		1	5	.167	6.10	26	8	0	69.1	82	38	48	0	1	0	1	0	0	0	—	5	6	3	0	0.5	.786
2 yrs.		3	7	.300	5.82	35	16	0	111.1	131	57	81	0	1	0	2	0	0	0		10	11	4	0	0.7	.840

Pat Luby

LUBY, JOHN PERKINS TR 6′ 185 lbs.
B. June 1869, Charleston, S. C. D. Apr. 24, 1899, Charleston, S. C.

Year	Team	W	L	PCT	ERA	G	GS	CG	IP	H	BB	SO	ShO	Relief Pitching W	Relief Pitching L	Relief Pitching SV	Batting AB	Batting H	Batting HR	BA	PO	A	E	DP	TC/G	FA
1890	CHI N	20	9	.690	3.19	34	31	26	267.2	226	95	85	0	0	0	1	116	31	3	.267	31	44	3	0	2.2	.962
1891		8	11	.421	4.76	30	24	18	206	221	94	52	0	1	0	1	98	24	2	.245	14	42	3	2	1.8	.949
1892		10	16	.385	3.13	31	27	24	247.1	247	106	64	1	2	0	1	163	31	2	.190	28	62	9	3	2.1	.909
1895	LOU N	1	5	.167	6.81	11	6	5	71.1	115	19	12	0	0	0	0	53	15	0	.283	54	25	5	5	4.7	.940
4 yrs.		39	41	.488	3.91	106	88	73	792.1	809	314	213	1	3	0	3	*				127	173	20	10	2.4	.938

Gary Lucas

LUCAS, GARY PAUL BL TL 6′ 5″ 200 lbs.
B. Nov. 8, 1954, Riverside, Calif.

Year	Team	W	L	PCT	ERA	G	GS	CG	IP	H	BB	SO	ShO	Relief Pitching W	Relief Pitching L	Relief Pitching SV	Batting AB	Batting H	Batting HR	BA	PO	A	E	DP	TC/G	FA
1980	SD N	5	8	.385	3.24	46	18	0	150	138	43	85	0	1	1	3	35	6	0	.171	9	23	0	4	0.7	1.000
1981		7	7	.500	2.00	**57**	0	0	90	78	36	53	0	7	7	13	10	1	0	.100	5	15	0	0	0.4	1.000
1982		1	10	.091	3.24	65	0	0	97.1	89	29	64	0	1	**10**	16	14	0	0	.000	6	19	0	0	0.4	1.000
1983		5	8	.385	2.87	62	0	0	91	85	34	60	0	5	8	17	12	0	0	.000	5	10	3	1	0.3	.833
1984	MON N	0	3	.000	2.72	55	0	0	53	54	20	42	0	0	3	8	4	0	0	.000	2	15	0	1	0.3	1.000
1985		6	2	.750	3.19	49	0	0	67.2	63	24	31	0	6	2	2	5	0	0	.000	2	11	0	1	0.3	1.000
1986	CAL A	4	1	.800	3.15	27	0	0	45.2	45	6	31	0	4	1	2	0	0	0	—	6	9	0	0	0.6	1.000
1987		1	5	.167	3.63	48	0	0	74.1	66	35	44	0	1	5	3	0	0	0	—	3	17	2	1	0.5	.909
8 yrs.		29	44	.397	3.01	409	18	0	669	618	227	410	0	25	37	64	80	7	0	.087	38	119	5	8	0.4	.969
LEAGUE CHAMPIONSHIP SERIES																										
1986	CAL A	0	0	—	11.57	4	0	0	2.1	3	1	2	0	0	0	0	0	0	0	—	0	0	0	0	0.0	.000

Ray Lucas

LUCAS, RAY WESLEY (Luke) BR TR 6′ 2″ 175 lbs.
B. Oct. 2, 1908, Springfield, Ohio D. Oct. 9, 1969, Harrison, Mich.

Year	Team	W	L	PCT	ERA	G	GS	CG	IP	H	BB	SO	ShO	Relief Pitching W	Relief Pitching L	Relief Pitching SV	Batting AB	Batting H	Batting HR	BA	PO	A	E	DP	TC/G	FA
1929	NY N	0	0	—	0.00	3	0	0	8	3	3	1	0	0	0	1	2	1	0	.500	0	3	0	1	1.0	1.000
1930		0	0	—	6.97	6	0	0	10.1	9	10	1	0	0	0	0	1	0	0	.000	0	6	0	0	1.0	1.000
1931		0	0	—	4.50	1	0	0	2	1	1	0	0	0	0	0	0	0	0	—	0	0	0	0	0.0	.000
1933	BKN N	0	0	—	7.20	2	0	0	5	6	4	0	0	0	0	0	0	0	0	—	1	1	0	0	1.0	1.000
1934		1	1	.500	6.75	10	2	0	30.2	39	14	3	0	1	0	0	6	2	0	.333	2	12	1	1	1.5	.933
5 yrs.		1	1	.500	5.79	22	2	0	56	58	32	5	0	1	0	1	9	3	0	.333	3	22	1	2	1.2	.962

Red Lucas

LUCAS, CHARLES FREDERICK (The Nashville Narcissus) BL TR 5′ 9½″ 170 lbs.
B. Apr. 28, 1902, Columbia, Tenn. D. July 9, 1986, Nashville, Tenn.

Year	Team	W	L	PCT	ERA	G	GS	CG	IP	H	BB	SO	ShO	Relief Pitching W	Relief Pitching L	Relief Pitching SV	Batting AB	Batting H	Batting HR	BA	PO	A	E	DP	TC/G	FA
1923	NY N	0	0	—	0.00	3	0	0	5.1	9	4	3	0	0	0	1	2	0	0	.000	1	3	0	0	1.3	1.000
1924	BOS N	1	4	.200	5.16	27	4	1	83.2	112	18	30	0	1	1	0	33	11	0	.333	5	23	0	1	1.0	1.000
1926	CIN N	8	5	.615	3.68	39	11	7	154	161	30	34	1	3	1	2	76	23	0	.303	9	21	1	3	5.2	.968
1927		18	11	.621	3.38	37	23	19	239.2	231	39	51	4	4	3	2	150	47	0	.313	14	63	4	4	1.8	.951
1928		13	9	.591	3.39	27	19	13	167.1	164	42	35	**4**	3	2	1	73	23	0	.315	8	37	0	3	1.7	1.000
1929		19	12	.613	3.60	32	32	**28**	270	267	58	72	2	0	0	0	140	41	0	.293	12	63	4	3	2.5	.949
1930		14	16	.467	5.38	33	28	18	210.2	270	44	53	1	0	2	1	113	38	2	.336	8	30	0	0	1.2	1.000
1931		14	13	.519	3.59	29	29	**24**	238	261	39	56	0	0	0	0	153	43	0	.281	8	54	1	3	2.2	.984
1932		13	17	.433	2.94	31	31	**28**	269.1	261	35	63	0	0	0	0	150	43	0	.287	17	55	2	4	2.4	.973
1933		10	16	.385	3.40	29	29	21	219.2	248	18	40	3	0	0	0	122	35	1	.287	3	52	0	5	1.9	1.000
1934	PIT N	10	9	.526	4.38	29	21	12	172.2	198	40	44	1	0	1	0	105	23	0	.219	7	24	2	2	1.1	.939
1935		8	6	.571	3.44	20	19	8	125.2	136	23	29	2	0	0	0	66	21	0	.318	7	23	1	1	1.5	.968
1936		15	4	.789	3.18	27	22	12	175.2	178	26	53	0	3	0	0	108	26	0	.241	8	33	1	4	1.6	.976
1937		8	10	.444	4.27	20	20	9	126.1	150	23	20	1	0	0	0	82	22	0	.268	9	19	0	1	1.4	1.000
1938		6	3	.667	3.54	13	13	4	84	90	16	19	0	0	0	0	46	5	0	.109	3	14	0	1	1.3	1.000
15 yrs.		157	135	.538	3.72	396	301	204	2542	2736	455	602	19	14	10	7	*				125	550	16	36	1.7	.977

Joe Lucey

LUCEY, JOSEPH EARL (Scootch) BR TR 6′ 168 lbs.
B. Mar. 27, 1897, Holyoke, Mass. D. July 30, 1980, Holyoke, Mass.

Year	Team	W	L	PCT	ERA	G	GS	CG	IP	H	BB	SO	ShO	Relief Pitching W	Relief Pitching L	Relief Pitching SV	Batting AB	Batting H	Batting HR	BA	PO	A	E	DP	TC/G	FA
1925	BOS A	0	1	.000	9.00	7	2	0	11	18	14	2	0	0	0	0	15	2	0	.133	0	0	0	0	0.0	

Con Lucid

LUCID, CORNELIUS CECIL 5′ 7″ 170 lbs.
B. Feb. 24, 1874, Dublin, Ireland D. June 25, 1931, Houston, Tex.

Year	Team	W	L	PCT	ERA	G	GS	CG	IP	H	BB	SO	ShO	Relief Pitching W	Relief Pitching L	Relief Pitching SV	Batting AB	Batting H	Batting HR	BA	PO	A	E	DP	TC/G	FA
1893	LOU N	0	1	.000	15.00	2	1	0	6	10	10	0	0	0	0	0	3	1	0	.333	0	1	1	0	1.0	.500
1894	BKN N	5	3	.625	6.56	10	9	7	71.1	87	44	15	0	0	0	0	33	7	0	.212	3	3	2	0	0.8	.750
1895	2 teams BKN N (21G 10–7) PHI N (10G 6–3)																									
″	total	16	10	.615	5.66	31	29	19	206.2	244	107	43	3	1	0	0	82	23	0	.280	8	36	4	1	1.5	.917
1896	PHI N	1	4	.200	8.36	5	5	5	42	75	17	3	0	0	0	0	16	2	0	.125	3	4	1	1	1.6	.875
1897	STL N	1	5	.167	3.67	6	6	5	49	66	26	4	0	0	0	0	17	3	0	.176	2	16	4	1	3.7	.818
5 yrs.		23	23	.500	6.02	54	50	36	375	482	204	65	3	1	0	0	151	36	0	.238	16	60	12	3	1.6	.864

Lou Lucier

LUCIER, LOUIS JOSEPH BR TR 5′ 8″ 160 lbs.
B. Mar. 23, 1918, Northbridge, Mass.

Year	Team	W	L	PCT	ERA	G	GS	CG	IP	H	BB	SO	ShO	Relief Pitching W	Relief Pitching L	Relief Pitching SV	Batting AB	Batting H	Batting HR	BA	PO	A	E	DP	TC/G	FA
1943	BOS A	3	4	.429	3.89	16	9	3	74	94	33	23	0	0	0	0	20	4	0	.200	7	29	1	4	2.3	.973
1944	2 teams BOS A (3G 0–0) PHI N (1G 0–0)																									
″	total	0	0		7.36	4	0	0	7.1	10	9	3	0	0	0	0	1	0	0	.000	0	0	0	0	0.0	
1945	PHI N	0	1	.000	2.21	13	0	0	20.1	14	5	5	0	0	1	1	4	1	0	.250	1	8	0	1	0.7	1.000
3 yrs.		3	5	.375	3.81	33	9	3	101.2	118	47	31	0	0	1	1	25	5	0	.200	8	37	1	5	1.4	.978

Year	Team		W	L	PCT	ERA	G	GS	CG	IP	H	BB	SO	ShO	Relief Pitching W	Relief Pitching L	Relief Pitching SV	Batting AB	Batting H	Batting HR	BA	PO	A	E	DP	TC/G	FA

Willie Ludolph

LUDOLPH, WILLIAM FRANCIS (Wee Willie) BR TR 6′ 1½″ 170 lbs.
B. Jan. 21, 1900, San Francisco, Calif. D. Apr. 8, 1952, Oakland, Calif.

Year	Team		W	L	PCT	ERA	G	GS	CG	IP	H	BB	SO	ShO	W	L	SV	AB	H	HR	BA	PO	A	E	DP	TC/G	FA
1924	DET	A	0	0	—	4.76	3	0	0	5.2	5	2	1	0	0	0	0	1	0	0	.000	1	2	0	0	1.0	1.000

Steve Luebber

LUEBBER, STEPHEN LEE BR TR 6′ 3″ 185 lbs.
B. July 9, 1949, Clinton, Mo.

Year	Team		W	L	PCT	ERA	G	GS	CG	IP	H	BB	SO	ShO	W	L	SV	AB	H	HR	BA	PO	A	E	DP	TC/G	FA
1971	MIN	A	2	5	.286	5.03	18	12	0	68	73	37	35	0	1	0	1	19	1	0	.053	2	12	0	1	0.8	1.000
1972			0	0	—	0.00	2	0	0	2	3	2	1	0	0	0	0	0	0	0	—	0	1	0	0	0.5	1.000
1976			4	5	.444	4.00	38	12	2	119.1	109	62	45	1	0	1	2	0	0	0	—	5	17	6	1	0.7	.786
1979	TOR	A	0	0	—	∞	1	0	0		2	1	0	0	0	0	0	0	0	0	—	0	0	0	0	0.0	.000
1981	BAL	A	0	0	—	7.41	7	0	0	17	26	4	12	0	0	0	0	0	0	0	—	3	3	0	0	0.9	1.000
5 yrs.			6	10	.375	4.62	66	24	2	206.1	213	106	93	1	1	1	3	19	1	0	.053	10	33	6	2	0.7	.878

Larry Luebbers

LUEBBERS, LARRY CHRISTOPHER BR TR 6′ 6″ 190 lbs.
B. Oct. 11, 1969, Cincinnati, Ohio.

Year	Team		W	L	PCT	ERA	G	GS	CG	IP	H	BB	SO	ShO	W	L	SV	AB	H	HR	BA	PO	A	E	DP	TC/G	FA
1993	CIN	N	2	5	.286	4.54	14	14	0	77.1	74	38	38	0	0	0	0	24	6	0	.250	4	8	2	1	1.0	.857

Dick Luebke

LUEBKE, RICHARD RAYMOND BR TL 6′ 4″ 200 lbs.
B. Apr. 8, 1935, Chicago, Ill. D. Dec. 4, 1974, San Diego, Calif.

Year	Team		W	L	PCT	ERA	G	GS	CG	IP	H	BB	SO	ShO	W	L	SV	AB	H	HR	BA	PO	A	E	DP	TC/G	FA
1962	BAL	A	0	1	.000	2.70	10	0	0	13.1	12	6	7	0	0	1	0	0	0	0	—	1	0	0	0	0.1	1.000

Rick Luecken

LUECKEN, RICHARD FRED BR TR 6′ 6″ 210 lbs.
B. Nov. 15, 1960, McAllen, Tex.

Year	Team		W	L	PCT	ERA	G	GS	CG	IP	H	BB	SO	ShO	W	L	SV	AB	H	HR	BA	PO	A	E	DP	TC/G	FA
1989	KC	A	2	1	.667	3.42	19	0	0	23.2	23	13	16	0	2	1	1	0	0	0	—	2	2	0	0	0.2	1.000
1990	2 teams	ATL N	(36G 1–4)	TOR A	(1G 0–0)																						
"	total		1	4	.200	5.83	37	0	0	54	75	31	35	0	1	4	1	3	1	0	.333	5	6	0	0	0.3	1.000
2 yrs.			3	5	.375	5.10	56	0	0	77.2	98	44	51	0	3	5	2	3	1	0	.333	7	8	0	0	0.3	1.000

Urbano Lugo

LUGO, RAFAEL URBANO BR TR 6′ 185 lbs.
Born Rafael Urbano Lugo (Colina).
B. Aug. 12, 1962, Punto Fijo, Venezuela.

Year	Team		W	L	PCT	ERA	G	GS	CG	IP	H	BB	SO	ShO	W	L	SV	AB	H	HR	BA	PO	A	E	DP	TC/G	FA
1985	CAL	A	3	4	.429	3.69	20	10	1	83	86	29	42	0	0	0	0	0	0	0	—	4	13	2	2	0.9	.895
1986			1	1	.500	3.80	6	3	0	21.1	21	6	9	0	0	0	0	0	0	0	—	2	2	0	0	0.7	1.000
1987			0	2	.000	9.32	7	5	0	28	42	18	24	0	0	0	0	0	0	0	—	2	2	0	0	0.6	1.000
1988			0	0	—	9.00	1	0	0	2	2	1	1	0	0	0	0	0	0	0	—	0	0	0	0	0.0	.000
1989	MON	N	0	0	—	6.75	3	0	0	4	4	0	3	0	0	0	0	0	0	0	—	1	0	0	0	0.3	1.000
1990	DET	A	2	0	1.000	7.03	13	1	0	24.1	30	13	12	0	2	0	0	0	0	0	—	0	7	0	0	0.5	1.000
6 yrs.			6	7	.462	5.31	50	19	1	162.2	185	67	91	0	2	0	0	0	0	0		9	24	2	2	0.7	.943

Bill Luhrsen

LUHRSEN, WILLIAM FERDINAND (Wild Bill) BR TR 5′ 9″ 165 lbs.
B. Apr. 14, 1884, Buckley, Ill. D. Aug. 15, 1973, Little Rock, Ark.

Year	Team		W	L	PCT	ERA	G	GS	CG	IP	H	BB	SO	ShO	W	L	SV	AB	H	HR	BA	PO	A	E	DP	TC/G	FA
1913	PIT	N	3	1	.750	2.48	5	3	2	29	25	16	11	0	1	0	0	10	0	0	.000	1	12	0	1	2.6	1.000

Al Lukens

LUKENS, ALBERT P. 5′ 9″ 168 lbs.
B. 1872, Vineland, N. J. Deceased.

Year	Team		W	L	PCT	ERA	G	GS	CG	IP	H	BB	SO	ShO	W	L	SV	AB	H	HR	BA	PO	A	E	DP	TC/G	FA
1894	PHI	N	0	1	.000	10.20	3	2	1	15	26	10	0	0	0	0	0	8	0	0	.000	0	1	0	0	0.3	1.000

Ralph Lumenti

LUMENTI, RAPHAEL ANTHONY (Commuter) BL TL 6′ 3″ 185 lbs.
B. Dec. 21, 1936, Milford, Mass.

Year	Team		W	L	PCT	ERA	G	GS	CG	IP	H	BB	SO	ShO	W	L	SV	AB	H	HR	BA	PO	A	E	DP	TC/G	FA
1957	WAS	A	0	1	.000	6.75	3	2	0	9.1	9	5	8	0	0	0	0	2	0	0	.000	0	1	0	1	0.3	1.000
1958			1	2	.333	8.57	8	4	0	21	21	36	20	0	0	0	0	8	2	0	.250	0	4	0	0	0.5	1.000
1959			0	0	—	0.00	2	0	0	3	2	1	2	0	0	0	0	0	0	0	—	0	0	0	0	0.0	.000
3 yrs.			1	3	.250	7.29	13	6	0	33.1	32	42	30	0	0	0	0	10	2	0	.200	0	5	0	1	0.4	1.000

Memo Luna

LUNA, GUILLERMO ROMERO BL TL 6′ 168 lbs.
B. June 25, 1930, Tacubaya, Mexico.

Year	Team		W	L	PCT	ERA	G	GS	CG	IP	H	BB	SO	ShO	W	L	SV	AB	H	HR	BA	PO	A	E	DP	TC/G	FA
1954	STL	N	0	1	.000	27.00	1	1	0	0.2	2	2	0	0	0	0	0	0	0	0	—	0	0	0	0	0.0	.000

Jack Lundbom

LUNDBOM, JOHN FREDERICK BR TR 6′ 2″ 187 lbs.
B. Mar. 10, 1877, Manistee, Mich. D. Oct. 31, 1949, Manistee, Mich.

Year	Team		W	L	PCT	ERA	G	GS	CG	IP	H	BB	SO	ShO	W	L	SV	AB	H	HR	BA	PO	A	E	DP	TC/G	FA
1902	CLE	A	1	1	.500	6.62	8	3	1	34	48	16	7	0	1	0	0	15	4	0	.267	0	8	0	1	1.0	1.000

Carl Lundgren

LUNDGREN, CARL LEONARD BR TR 5′11″ 175 lbs.
B. Feb. 16, 1880, Marengo, Ill. D. Aug. 21, 1934, Marengo, Ill.

Year	Team		W	L	PCT	ERA	G	GS	CG	IP	H	BB	SO	ShO	W	L	SV	AB	H	HR	BA	PO	A	E	DP	TC/G	FA
1902	CHI	N	9	9	.500	1.97	18	18	17	160	158	45	68	1	0	0	0	66	7	0	.106	9	33	8	3	2.5	.840
1903			10	9	.526	2.94	27	20	16	193	191	60	67	0	1	0	**3**	61	7	0	.115	8	40	1	0	1.8	.980
1904			17	10	.630	2.60	31	27	25	242	203	77	106	2	1	0	1	90	20	0	.222	21	56	4	2	2.6	.951
1905			13	5	.722	2.24	23	19	16	169	132	53	69	3	0	0	0	61	11	0	.180	11	51	3	1	2.8	.954
1906			17	6	.739	2.21	27	24	21	207.2	160	89	103	5	0	0	2	67	12	0	.179	13	55	1	2	2.5	.986
1907			18	7	.720	1.17	28	25	21	207	130	92	84	7	3	0	0	66	7	0	.106	6	56	1	1	2.3	.984
1908			6	9	.400	4.22	23	15	9	138.2	149	56	38	1	1	0	0	47	7	0	.149	6	24	1	1	1.3	.968
1909			0	1	.000	4.15	2	1	0	4.1	6	4	0	0	0	0	0	2	1	0	.500	0	0	0	0	0.0	.000
8 yrs.			90	56	.616	2.42	179	149	125	1321.2	1129	476	535	19	6	0	6	460	72	0	.157	74	315	19	10	2.2	.953

Del Lundgren

LUNDGREN, EBIN DELMAR BR TR 5′ 8″ 160 lbs.
B. Sept. 21, 1899, Lindsborg, Kans. D. Oct. 19, 1984, Lindsborg, Kans.

Year	Team		W	L	PCT	ERA	G	GS	CG	IP	H	BB	SO	ShO	W	L	SV	AB	H	HR	BA	PO	A	E	DP	TC/G	FA
1924	PIT	N	0	1	.000	6.48	8	1	0	16.2	25	3	4	0	0	0	0	3	0	0	.000	0	6	0	0	0.8	1.000
1926	BOS	A	0	2	.000	8.07	17	1	0	29	35	24	10	0	0	1	0	4	0	0	.000	1	9	1	0	0.6	.909
1927			5	12	.294	6.27	30	17	5	136.1	160	87	39	2	0	2	0	44	7	0	.159	6	22	0	1	0.9	1.000
3 yrs.			5	15	.250	6.58	55	19	5	182	220	114	53	2	0	3	0	51	7	0	.137	7	37	1	1	0.8	.978

Dolf Luque

LUQUE, ADOLFO DOMINGO de GUZMAN (The Pride Of Havana) BR TR 5′ 7″ 160 lbs.
B. Aug. 4, 1890, Havana, Cuba D. July 3, 1957, Havana, Cuba.

Year	Team		W	L	PCT	ERA	G	GS	CG	IP	H	BB	SO	ShO	W	L	SV	AB	H	HR	BA	PO	A	E	DP	TC/G	FA
1914	BOS	N	0	1	.000	4.15	2	1	1	8.2	5	4	1	0	0	0	0	2	0	0	.000	1	0	0	0	0.5	1.000
1915			0	0	—	3.60	2	1	0	5	6	4	3	0	0	0	0	2	0	0	.000	0	2	0	0	1.0	1.000

Dolf Luque *continued*

Year	Team		W	L	PCT	ERA	G	GS	CG	IP	H	BB	SO	ShO	Relief Pitching W	L	SV	Batting AB	H	HR	BA	PO	A	E	DP	TC/G	FA
1918	CIN	N	6	3	.667	3.80	12	10	9	83	84	32	26	1	0	0	0	28	9	0	.321	2	23	1	1	2.2	.962
1919			9	3	.750	2.63	30	9	6	106	89	36	40	2	3	0	3	32	4	0	.125	6	35	0	0	1.3	1.000
1920			13	9	.591	2.51	37	23	10	207.2	168	60	72	1	1	1	1	64	17	0	.266	11	47	4	2	1.7	.935
1921			17	19	.472	3.38	41	36	25	304	318	64	102	**3**	0	1	3	111	30	0	.270	21	76	5	3	2.5	.951
1922			13	**23**	.361	3.31	39	33	18	261	266	72	79	0	3	2	0	86	18	0	.209	13	61	3	0	2.0	.961
1923			**27**	8	**.771**	**1.93**	41	37	28	322	279	88	151	**6**	1	0	2	104	21	1	.202	17	71	2	4	2.2	.978
1924			10	15	.400	3.16	31	28	13	219.1	229	53	86	2	0	1	0	73	13	1	.178	11	57	6	1	2.3	.919
1925			16	18	.471	**2.63**	36	36	22	291	263	78	140	**4**	0	0	0	102	26	2	.255	15	84	7	3	2.9	.934
1926			13	16	.448	3.43	34	30	16	233.2	231	77	83	1	1	1	0	78	27	0	.346	12	65	3	2	2.4	.963
1927			13	12	.520	3.20	29	27	17	230.2	225	56	76	2	1	0	0	83	18	0	.217	18	64	5	4	3.0	.943
1928			11	10	.524	3.57	33	29	11	234.1	254	84	72	1	0	1	1	67	8	0	.119	15	42	3	3	1.8	.950
1929			5	16	.238	4.50	32	22	8	176	213	56	43	1	0	1	0	54	15	1	.278	9	40	0	2	1.5	1.000
1930	BKN	N	14	8	.636	4.30	31	24	16	199	221	58	62	2	1	0	2	75	18	0	.240	8	45	1	0	1.7	.981
1931			7	6	.538	4.56	19	15	5	102.2	122	27	25	0	2	0	0	30	4	0	.133	3	19	0	1	1.2	1.000
1932	NY	N	6	7	.462	4.01	38	5	1	110	128	32	32	0	6	3	5	25	1	0	.040	19	23	1	2	1.1	.977
1933			8	2	.800	2.69	35	0	0	80.1	75	19	23	0	**8**	2	4	19	5	0	.263	3	19	0	0	0.6	1.000
1934			4	3	.571	3.83	26	0	0	42.1	54	17	12	0	4	3	7	7	2	0	.286	4	14	2	1	0.8	.900
1935			1	0	1.000	0.00	2	0	0	3.2	1	1	2	0	1	0	0	1	1	0	1.000	0	0	0	0	0.0	.000
20 yrs.			193	179	.519	3.24	550	366	206	3220.1	3231	918	1130	26	32	16	28	1043	237	5	.227	188	787	43	29	1.8	.958
WORLD SERIES																											
1919	CIN	N	0	0	—	0.00	2	0	0	5	1	0	6	0	0	0	0	1	0	0	.000	1	0	0	0	0.5	1.000
1933	NY	N	1	0	1.000	0.00	1	0	0	4.1	2	2	5	0	1	0	0	1	1	0	1.000	1	0	0	0	1.0	1.000
2 yrs.			1	0	1.000	0.00	3	0	0	9.1	3	2	11	0	1	0	0	2	1	0	.500	2	0	0	0	0.7	1.000

Johnny Lush

LUSH, JOHN CHARLES BL TL 5′ 9½″ 165 lbs.
B. Oct. 8, 1885, Williamsport, Pa. D. Nov. 18, 1946, Beverly Hills, Calif.

Year	Team		W	L	PCT	ERA	G	GS	CG	IP	H	BB	SO	ShO	Relief Pitching W	L	SV	Batting AB	H	HR	BA	PO	A	E	DP	TC/G	FA
1904	PHI	N	0	6	.000	3.59	7	6	3	42.2	52	27	27	0	0	0	0	369	102	2	.276	583	44	35	28	6.5	.947
1905			2	0	1.000	1.59	2	2	1	17	12	8	8	0	0	0	0	16	5	0	.313	6	6	4	0	3.2	.750
1906			18	15	.545	2.37	37	35	24	281	254	119	151	5	0	0	0	212	56	0	.264	75	95	13	3	3.0	.929
1907	**2 teams**	**PHI N** (8G 3–5)		**STL N** (20G 7–10)																							
″	**total**		10	15	.400	2.64	28	27	20	201.1	180	63	91	6	0	0	0	122	31	0	.254	19	54	7	4	2.1	.913
1908	STL	N	11	18	.379	2.12	38	32	23	250.2	221	57	93	3	1	0	1	89	15	0	.169	15	73	7	0	2.5	.926
1909			11	18	.379	3.13	34	28	21	221.1	215	69	66	2	0	1	0	92	22	0	.239	9	64	4	0	2.1	.948
1910			14	13	.519	3.20	36	24	13	225.1	235	70	54	1	4	3	1	93	21	0	.226	8	56	5	2	1.9	.928
7 yrs.			66	85	.437	2.68	182	154	105	1239.1	1169	413	490	17	5	4	2	*				715	392	75	37	3.7	.937

Jim Lyle

LYLE, JAMES CHARLES BR TR 6′ 1″ 180 lbs.
B. July 24, 1900, Lake, Miss. D. Oct. 10, 1977, Williamsport, Pa.

Year	Team		W	L	PCT	ERA	G	GS	CG	IP	H	BB	SO	ShO	Relief Pitching W	L	SV	Batting AB	H	HR	BA	PO	A	E	DP	TC/G	FA
1925	WAS	A	0	0	—	6.00	1	0	0	3	5	1	3	0	0	0	0	1	0	0	.000	0	0	0	0	0.0	.000

Sparky Lyle

LYLE, ALBERT WALTER BL TL 6′ 1″ 182 lbs.
B. July 22, 1944, Du Bois, Pa.

Year	Team		W	L	PCT	ERA	G	GS	CG	IP	H	BB	SO	ShO	Relief Pitching W	L	SV	Batting AB	H	HR	BA	PO	A	E	DP	TC/G	FA
1967	BOS	A	1	2	.333	2.28	27	0	0	43.1	33	14	42	0	1	2	5	8	2	0	.250	2	5	0	0	0.3	1.000
1968			6	1	.857	2.74	49	0	0	65.2	67	14	52	0	6	1	11	8	1	0	.125	5	6	3	0	0.3	.786
1969			8	3	.727	2.54	71	0	0	102.2	91	48	93	0	8	3	17	17	2	0	.118	3	19	3	3	0.4	.880
1970			1	7	.125	3.90	63	0	0	67	62	34	51	0	1	7	20	13	0	0	.000	1	7	0	0	0.1	1.000
1971			6	4	.600	2.77	50	0	0	52	41	23	37	0	6	4	16	3	3	0	1.000	2	10	0	1	0.2	1.000
1972	NY	A	9	5	.643	1.91	59	0	0	108.1	84	29	75	0	9	5	**35**	21	4	0	.190	4	11	0	0	0.3	1.000
1973			5	9	.357	2.51	51	0	0	82.1	66	18	63	0	5	**9**	27	0	0	0	—	2	13	2	2	0.3	.882
1974			9	3	.750	1.66	66	0	0	114	93	43	89	0	9	3	15	1	0	0	.000	3	11	1	2	0.2	.933
1975			5	7	.417	3.12	49	0	0	89.1	94	36	65	0	5	7	6	0	0	0	—	2	16	4	1	0.4	.818
1976			7	8	.467	2.26	64	0	0	103.2	82	42	61	0	7	8	**23**	0	0	0	—	3	11	2	1	0.3	.875
1977			13	5	.722	2.17	**72**	0	0	137	131	33	68	0	13	5	26	0	0	0	—	2	22	2	0	0.4	.923
1978			9	3	.750	3.47	59	0	0	111.2	116	33	33	0	9	3	9	0	0	0	—	9	18	1	3	0.5	.964
1979	TEX	A	5	8	.385	3.13	67	0	0	95	78	28	48	0	5	8	13	0	0	0	—	2	11	2	0	0.2	.867
1980	**2 teams**	**TEX A** (49G 3–2)		**PHI N** (10G 0–0)																							
″	**total**		3	2	.600	4.26	59	0	0	95	108	34	49	0	3	2	10	0	0	0		4	10	0	0	0.2	1.000
1981	PHI	N	9	6	.600	4.44	48	0	0	75	85	33	29	0	**9**	6	2	5	2	0	.400	6	17	0	0	0.5	1.000
1982	**2 teams**	**PHI N** (34G 3–3)		**CHI A** (11G 0–0)																							
″	**total**		3	3	.500	4.62	45	0	0	48.2	61	19	18	0	3	3	3	2	1	0	.500	4	11	1	1	0.4	.938
16 yrs.			99	76	.566	2.88	899 **10th**	0	0	1390.2	1292	481	873	0	99 **5th**	76	238	78	15	0	.192	54	198	21	14	0.3	.923
DIVISIONAL PLAYOFF SERIES																											
1981	PHI	N	0	0	—	0.00	3	0	0	2.1	4	2	1	0	0	0	0	0	0	0	—	0	0	0	0	0.0	.000
LEAGUE CHAMPIONSHIP SERIES																											
1976	NY	A	0	0	—	0.00	1	0	0	1	0	1	0	0	0	0	1	0	0	0	—	0	0	0	0	0.0	.000
1977			2	0	1.000	0.96	4	0	0	9.1	7	0	3	0	2	0	0	0	0	0	—	0	0	0	0	0.0	.000
1978			0	0	—	13.50	1	0	0	1.1	3	0	0	0	0	0	0	0	0	0	—	1	1	0	0	2.0	1.000
3 yrs.			2	0	1.000	2.31	6	0	0	11.2	10	1	3	0	2	0	1	0	0	0		1	1	0	0	0.3	1.000
WORLD SERIES																											
1976	NY	A	0	0	—	0.00	2	0	0	2.2	1	0	3	0	0	0	0	0	0	0	—	0	0	0	0	0.0	.000
1977			1	0	1.000	1.93	2	0	0	4.2	2	0	2	0	1	0	0	2	0	0	.000	0	0	0	0	0.0	.000
2 yrs.			1	0	1.000	1.23	4	0	0	7.1	3	0	5	0	1	0	0	2	0	0	.000	0	0	0	0	0.0	

Adrian Lynch

LYNCH, ADRIAN RYAN BB TR 6′ 1½″ 185 lbs.
B. Feb. 9, 1897, Laurens, Iowa D. Mar. 16, 1934, Davenport, Iowa.

Year	Team		W	L	PCT	ERA	G	GS	CG	IP	H	BB	SO	ShO	Relief Pitching W	L	SV	Batting AB	H	HR	BA	PO	A	E	DP	TC/G	FA
1920	STL	A	2	0	1.000	5.24	5	3	1	22.1	23	17	8	0	0	0	0	9	2	0	.222	0	4	1	0	1.0	.800

Ed Lynch

LYNCH, EDWARD FRANCIS BR TR 6′ 5″ 210 lbs.
B. Feb. 25, 1956, Brooklyn, N. Y.

Year	Team	W	L	PCT	ERA	G	GS	CG	IP	H	BB	SO	ShO	Relief W	Relief L	Relief SV	AB	H	HR	BA	PO	A	E	DP	TC/G	FA
1980	NY N	1	1	.500	5.21	5	4	0	19	24	5	9	0	0	0	0	6	2	0	.333	1	3	0	1	0.8	1.000
1981		4	5	.444	2.92	17	13	0	80	79	21	27	0	0	1	0	21	3	0	.143	7	9	1	0	1.0	.941
1982		4	8	.333	3.55	43	12	0	139.1	145	40	51	0	1	3	2	33	0	0	.000	6	18	0	0	0.6	1.000
1983		10	10	.500	4.28	30	27	1	174.2	208	41	44	0	1	0	0	52	8	0	.154	10	24	0	0	1.1	1.000
1984		9	8	.529	4.50	40	13	0	124	169	24	62	0	5	0	2	27	6	0	.222	9	13	1	0	0.6	.957
1985		10	8	.556	3.44	31	29	6	191	188	27	65	1	0	0	0	52	4	0	.077	15	14	2	2	1.0	.935
1986	2 teams NY N (1G 0–0) CHI N (23G 7–5)																									
″	total	7	5	.583	3.73	24	13	1	101.1	107	23	58	1	3	1	0	30	1	0	.033	7	12	0	2	0.8	1.000
1987	CHI N	2	9	.182	5.38	58	8	0	110.1	130	48	80	0	0	5	4	16	3	0	.188	9	17	0	2	0.4	1.000
8 yrs.		47	54	.465	4.00	248	119	8	939.2	1050	229	396	2	10	10	8	237	27	0	.114	64	110	4	7	0.7	.978

Jack Lynch

LYNCH, JOHN H. BR TR 5′ 8″ 185 lbs.
B. Feb. 5, 1857, New York, N. Y. D. Apr. 19, 1923, Bronx, N. Y.

Year	Team	W	L	PCT	ERA	G	GS	CG	IP	H	BB	SO	ShO	Relief W	Relief L	Relief SV	AB	H	HR	BA	PO	A	E	DP	TC/G	FA
1881	BUF N	10	9	.526	*3.59*	20	19	17	165.2	203	29	32	0	0	0	0	78	13	0	.167	15	39	5	0	2.3	.915
1883	NY AA	13	15	.464	*4.09*	29	29	29	255	263	25	119	1	0	0	0	107	20	0	.187	18	46	20	0	2.9	.762
1884		37	15	.712	*2.64*	54	53	53	487	410	42	286	5	0	**1**	0	195	30	0	.154	24	80	37	3	2.6	.738
1885		23	21	.523	*3.61*	44	43	43	379	410	42	177	1	**1**	0	0	153	30	0	.196	11	34	4	0	1.1	.918
1886		20	30	.400	*3.95*	51	50	50	432.2	485	116	193	1	0	0	0	169	27	0	.160	9	65	11	0	1.7	.871
1887		7	14	.333	*5.10*	21	21	21	187	245	36	45	0	0	0	0	83	14	0	.169	27	59	8	1	4.1	.915
1890	BKN AA	0	1	.000	12.00	1	1	1	9	22	5	1	0	0	0	0	4	3	0	.750	2	5	0	0	7.0	1.000
7 yrs.		110	105	.512	3.69	220	216	214	1915.1	2038	295	853	8	1	1	0	789	137	0	.174	106	328	85	4	2.3	.836

Mike Lynch

LYNCH, MICHAEL JOSEPH BR TR 6′ 2″ 170 lbs.
B. June 28, 1880, Holyoke, Mass. D. Apr. 2, 1927, Garrison, N. Y.

Year	Team	W	L	PCT	ERA	G	GS	CG	IP	H	BB	SO	ShO	Relief W	Relief L	Relief SV	AB	H	HR	BA	PO	A	E	DP	TC/G	FA
1904	PIT N	15	11	.577	2.71	27	24	24	222.2	200	91	95	1	1	1	0	87	20	0	.230	11	49	6	1	2.4	.909
1905		17	8	.680	3.80	33	22	13	206	191	107	106	0	**5**	1	2	81	11	0	.136	16	53	3	2	2.2	.958
1906		6	5	.545	2.42	18	12	7	119	101	31	48	0	2	0	0	39	8	0	.205	4	31	1	1	2.0	.972
1907	2 teams PIT N (7G 2–2) NY N (12G 3–6)																									
″	total	5	8	.385	3.00	19	14	9	108	105	52	43	0	0	0	0	39	11	0	.282	7	35	0	3	2.2	1.000
4 yrs.		43	32	.573	3.05	97	72	53	655.2	597	281	292	1	8	2	2	246	50	0	.203	38	168	10	7	2.2	.954

Thomas Lynch

LYNCH, THOMAS S. BL 5′11″ 175 lbs.
B. 1863, Peru, Ill. D. May 13, 1923, Peru, Ill.

Year	Team	W	L	PCT	ERA	G	GS	CG	IP	H	BB	SO	ShO	Relief W	Relief L	Relief SV	AB	H	HR	BA	PO	A	E	DP	TC/G	FA
1884	CHI N	0	0	—	*2.57*	1	1	0	7	7	3	2	0	0	0	0	*				8	1	0	0	4.5	1.000

Red Lynn

LYNN, JAPHET MONROE BR TR 6′ 162 lbs.
B. Dec. 27, 1913, Kenney, Tex. D. Oct. 27, 1977, Bellville, Tex.

Year	Team	W	L	PCT	ERA	G	GS	CG	IP	H	BB	SO	ShO	Relief W	Relief L	Relief SV	AB	H	HR	BA	PO	A	E	DP	TC/G	FA
1939	2 teams DET A (4G 0–1) NY N (26G 1–0)																									
″	total	1	1	.500	3.88	30	0	0	58	55	24	25	0	1	1	1	8	0	0	.000	2	6	2	0	0.3	.800
1940	NY N	4	3	.571	3.83	33	0	0	42.1	40	24	25	0	4	3	3	4	0	0	.000	1	3	0	0	0.1	1.000
1944	CHI N	5	4	.556	4.06	22	7	4	84.1	80	37	35	1	0	2	1	29	6	0	.207	7	20	0	2	1.2	1.000
3 yrs.		10	8	.556	3.95	85	7	4	184.2	175	85	85	1	5	6	5	41	6	0	.146	10	29	2	2	0.5	.951

Al Lyons

LYONS, ALBERT HAROLD BR TR 6′ 2″ 195 lbs.
B. July 18, 1918, St. Joseph, Mo. D. Dec. 20, 1965, Inglewood, Calif.

Year	Team	W	L	PCT	ERA	G	GS	CG	IP	H	BB	SO	ShO	Relief W	Relief L	Relief SV	AB	H	HR	BA	PO	A	E	DP	TC/G	FA
1944	NY A	0	0	—	4.54	11	0	0	39.2	43	24	14	0	0	0	0	26	9	0	.346	1	4	0	0	0.5	1.000
1946		0	1	.000	5.40	2	1	0	8.1	11	6	4	0	0	0	0	4	0	0	.000	1	2	0	0	1.5	1.000
1947	2 teams NY A (6G 1–0) PIT N (13G 1–2)																									
″	total	2	2	.500	7.78	19	0	0	39.1	54	21	23	0	2	2	0	16	6	0	.375	4	11	1	2	0.8	.938
1948	BOS N	1	0	1.000	7.82	7	0	0	12.2	17	8	5	0	1	0	0	12	2	0	.167	7	8	0	0	1.4	1.000
4 yrs.		3	3	.500	6.30	39	1	0	100	125	59	46	0	3	2	0	58	17	1	.293	13	25	1	2	0.9	.974

George Lyons

LYONS, GEORGE TONY (Smooth) BR TR 5′11″ 180 lbs.
B. Jan. 25, 1891, Bible Grove, Ill. D. Aug. 12, 1981, Nevada, Mo.

Year	Team	W	L	PCT	ERA	G	GS	CG	IP	H	BB	SO	ShO	Relief W	Relief L	Relief SV	AB	H	HR	BA	PO	A	E	DP	TC/G	FA
1920	STL N	2	1	.667	3.09	7	2	1	23.1	21	9	5	0	1	0	0	7	1	0	.143	1	9	0	1	1.4	1.000
1924	STL A	3	2	.600	4.93	25	6	2	76.2	95	44	25	0	1	0	0	20	5	0	.250	5	24	0	0	1.2	1.000
2 yrs.		5	3	.625	4.50	32	8	3	100	116	53	30	0	2	0	0	27	6	0	.222	6	33	0	1	1.2	1.000

Harry Lyons

LYONS, HARRY P. BR TR 5′10½″ 157 lbs.
B. Mar. 25, 1866, Chester, Pa. D. June 30, 1912, Mauricetown, N. J.

Year	Team	W	L	PCT	ERA	G	GS	CG	IP	H	BB	SO	ShO	Relief W	Relief L	Relief SV	AB	H	HR	BA	PO	A	E	DP	TC/G	FA
1890	ROC AA	0	0	—	*12.27*	1	0	0	3.2	8	1	2	0	0	0	0	*				4	5	1	1	3.3	.900

Hersh Lyons

LYONS, HERSCHEL ENGLEBERT BR TR 5′11″ 195 lbs.
B. July 23, 1915, Fresno, Calif.

Year	Team	W	L	PCT	ERA	G	GS	CG	IP	H	BB	SO	ShO	Relief W	Relief L	Relief SV	AB	H	HR	BA	PO	A	E	DP	TC/G	FA
1941	STL N	0	0	—	0.00	1	0	0	1.1	1	3	1	0	0	0	0	0	0	0	—	0	0	0	0	0.0	.000

Steve Lyons

LYONS, STEPHEN JOHN (Psycho) BL TR 6′ 3″ 190 lbs.
B. June 3, 1960, Tacoma, Wash.

Year	Team	W	L	PCT	ERA	G	GS	CG	IP	H	BB	SO	ShO	Relief W	Relief L	Relief SV	AB	H	HR	BA	PO	A	E	DP	TC/G	FA
1990	CHI A	0	0	—	4.50	1	0	0	2	2	4	1	0	0	0	0	146	28	1	.192	253	6	7	0	2.2	.974
1991	BOS A	0	0	—	0.00	1	0	0	1	2	0	1	0	0	0	0	212	51	4	.241	118	43	3	6	2.1	.982
2 yrs.		0	0		3.00	2	0	0	3	4	4	2	0	0	0	0	*				1477	727	67	170	2.8	.970

Ted Lyons

LYONS, THEODORE AMAR BB TR 5′11″ 200 lbs.
B. Dec. 28, 1900, Lake Charles, La. D. July 25, 1986, Sulphur, La.
Manager 1946–48.
Hall of Fame 1955.

Year	Team	W	L	PCT	ERA	G	GS	CG	IP	H	BB	SO	ShO	Relief W	Relief L	Relief SV	AB	H	HR	BA	PO	A	E	DP	TC/G	FA
1923	CHI A	2	1	.667	6.35	9	1	0	22.2	30	15	6	0	2	0	0	5	1	0	.200	3	7	0	1	1.1	1.000
1924		12	11	.522	4.87	41	22	12	216.1	279	72	52	0	1	1	3	77	17	0	.221	3	45	5	2	1.3	.906
1925		**21**	11	.656	3.26	43	32	19	262.2	274	83	45	**5**	2	2	3	97	18	0	.186	8	80	4	3	2.1	.957
1926		18	16	.529	3.01	39	31	24	283.2	268	106	51	3	1	3	2	104	22	0	.212	16	91	5	3	2.9	.955
1927		**22**	14	.611	2.84	39	34	**30**	**307.2**	**291**	67	71	2	0	2	2	110	28	1	.255	13	79	2	3	2.4	.979
1928		15	14	.517	3.98	39	27	21	240	276	68	60	0	3	1	6	91	23	0	.253	20	60	7	6	2.2	.920
1929		14	20	.412	4.10	37	31	21	259.1	276	76	57	1	1	3	2	91	20	0	.220	21	66	5	4	2.4	.946

Year	Team	Lg	W	L	PCT	ERA	G	GS	CG	IP	H	BB	SO	ShO	Relief W	Relief L	Relief SV	Batting AB	Batting H	HR	BA	PO	A	E	DP	TC/G	FA

Ted Lyons *continued*

Year	Team	Lg	W	L	PCT	ERA	G	GS	CG	IP	H	BB	SO	ShO	Relief W	Relief L	Relief SV	Batting AB	Batting H	HR	BA	PO	A	E	DP	TC/G	FA
1930			22	15	.595	3.78	42	36	**29**	**297.2**	**331**	57	69	1	2	1	1	122	38	1	.311	14	77	6	5	2.3	.938
1931			4	6	.400	4.01	22	12	7	101	117	33	16	0	1	1	0	33	5	0	.152	4	18	1	3	1.0	.957
1932			10	15	.400	3.28	33	26	19	230.2	243	71	58	1	0	1	2	73	19	1	.260	11	42	2	1	1.7	.964
1933			10	**21**	.323	4.38	36	27	14	228	260	74	74	2	4	3	1	91	26	1	.286	10	49	1	3	1.7	.983
1934			11	13	.458	4.87	30	24	21	205.1	249	66	53	0	0	1	1	97	20	1	.206	12	50	4	4	2.2	.939
1935			15	8	.652	3.02	23	22	19	190.2	194	56	54	3	0	1	0	82	18	0	.220	9	31	0	2	1.7	1.000
1936			10	13	.435	5.14	26	24	15	182	227	45	48	1	0	1	0	70	11	0	.157	12	38	0	2	1.9	1.000
1937			12	7	.632	4.15	22	22	11	169.1	182	45	45	0	0	0	0	57	12	0	.211	6	33	0	3	1.8	1.000
1938			9	11	.450	3.70	23	23	17	194.2	238	52	54	1	0	0	0	72	14	0	.194	9	46	1	1	2.4	.982
1939			14	6	.700	2.76	21	21	16	172.2	162	26	65	0	0	0	0	61	18	0	.295	9	22	3	3	1.6	.912
1940			12	8	.600	3.24	22	22	17	186.1	188	37	72	**4**	0	0	0	75	18	0	.240	12	24	3	1	1.8	.923
1941			12	10	.545	3.70	22	22	19	187.1	199	37	63	2	0	0	0	74	20	0	.270	17	36	1	3	2.5	.981
1942			14	6	.700	**2.10**	20	20	20	180.1	167	26	50	1	0	0	0	67	16	0	.239	8	41	1	4	2.5	.980
1946			1	4	.200	2.32	5	5	5	42.2	38	9	10	0	0	0	0	14	0	0	.000	2	10	0	0	2.4	1.000
21 yrs.			260	230	.531	3.67	594	484	356	4161	4489	1121	1073	27	17	21	23	*				219	945	51	57	2.0	.958

Toby Lyons

LYONS, THOMAS A.
B. Mar. 27, 1869, Cambridge, Mass. D. Aug. 27, 1920, Boston, Mass.

Year	Team	Lg	W	L	PCT	ERA	G	GS	CG	IP	H	BB	SO	ShO	Relief W	Relief L	Relief SV	Batting AB	Batting H	HR	BA	PO	A	E	DP	TC/G	FA
1890	SYR	AA	0	2	.000	*10.48*	3	3	2	22.1	40	21	6	0	0	0	0	12	4	0	.333	1	6	0	0	2.3	1.000

Rick Lysander

LYSANDER, RICHARD EUGENE BR TR 6′ 2″ 195 lbs.
B. Feb. 21, 1953, Huntington Park, Calif.

Year	Team	Lg	W	L	PCT	ERA	G	GS	CG	IP	H	BB	SO	ShO	Relief W	Relief L	Relief SV	Batting AB	Batting H	HR	BA	PO	A	E	DP	TC/G	FA
1980	OAK	A	0	0	—	7.71	5	0	0	14	24	4	5	0	0	0	0	0	0	0	—	2	3	0	0	1.0	1.000
1983	MIN	A	5	12	.294	3.38	61	4	1	125	132	43	58	1	4	9	3	0	0	0	—	19	14	1	2	0.6	.971
1984			4	3	.571	3.65	36	0	0	56.2	62	27	22	0	4	3	5	0	0	0	—	8	6	1	1	0.4	.933
1985			0	2	.000	6.05	35	1	0	61	72	22	26	0	0	1	3	0	0	0	—	7	5	0	0	0.3	1.000
4 yrs.			9	17	.346	4.31	137	5	1	256.2	290	96	111	1	8	13	11	0	0	0		36	28	2	3	0.5	.970

Bill Lyston

LYSTON, WILLIAM EDWARD TR
B. 1863, Baltimore, Md. D. Aug. 4, 1944, Baltimore, Md.

Year	Team	Lg	W	L	PCT	ERA	G	GS	CG	IP	H	BB	SO	ShO	Relief W	Relief L	Relief SV	Batting AB	Batting H	HR	BA	PO	A	E	DP	TC/G	FA
1891	COL	AA	0	1	.000	10.50	1	1	1	6	10	6	1	0	0	0	0	2	0	0	.000	1	0	0	0	1.0	1.000
1894	CLE	N	0	1	.000	9.82	1	1	0	3.2	5	4	0	0	0	0	0	2	0	0	.000	0	0	0	0	0.0	.000
2 yrs.			0	2	.000	10.24	2	2	1	9.2	15	10	1	0	0	0	0	4	0	0	.000	1	0	0	0	0.5	1.000

Duke Maas

MAAS, DUANE FREDERICK BR TR 5′10″ 170 lbs.
B. Jan. 31, 1929, Utica, Mich. D. Dec. 7, 1976, Mt. Clemens, Mich.

Year	Team	Lg	W	L	PCT	ERA	G	GS	CG	IP	H	BB	SO	ShO	Relief W	Relief L	Relief SV	Batting AB	Batting H	HR	BA	PO	A	E	DP	TC/G	FA
1955	DET	A	5	6	.455	4.88	18	16	5	86.2	91	50	42	2	0	0	0	30	5	0	.167	2	17	0	0	1.1	1.000
1956			0	7	.000	6.54	26	7	0	63.1	81	32	34	0	0	1	0	16	3	0	.188	5	8	2	0	0.6	.867
1957			10	14	.417	3.28	45	26	8	219.1	210	65	116	2	1	2	6	71	6	1	.085	8	41	1	2	1.1	.980
1958	2 teams	KC A (10G 4–5) NY A (22G 7–3)																									
″	total		11	8	.579	3.85	32	20	5	156.2	142	49	69	2	2	2	1	51	6	0	.118	12	19	1	0	1.0	.969
1959	NY	A	14	8	.636	4.43	38	21	3	138	149	53	67	1	5	0	4	40	5	0	.125	5	28	1	2	0.9	.971
1960			5	1	.833	4.09	35	1	0	70.1	70	35	28	0	5	0	4	6	0	0	.000	8	13	2	3	0.7	.913
1961			0	0	—	54.00	1	0	0	0.1	2	0	0	0	0	0	0	0	0	0	—	0	0	0	0	0.0	.000
7 yrs.			45	44	.506	4.19	195	91	21	734.2	745	284	356	7	13	5	15	214	25	1	.117	40	126	7	7	0.9	.960

WORLD SERIES

Year	Team	Lg	W	L	PCT	ERA	G	GS	CG	IP	H	BB	SO	ShO	Relief W	Relief L	Relief SV	Batting AB	Batting H	HR	BA	PO	A	E	DP	TC/G	FA
1958	NY	A	0	0	—	81.00	1	0	0	0.1	2	1	0	0	0	0	0	0	0	0	—	0	0	0	0	0.0	.000
1960			0	0	—	4.50	1	0	0	2	2	0	1	0	0	0	0	0	0	0	—	0	0	0	0	0.0	.000
2 yrs.			0	0		15.43	2	0	0	2.1	4	1	1	0	0	0	0	0	0	0		0	0	0	0	0.0	

Bob Mabe

MABE, ROBERT LEE BR TR 5′11″ 165 lbs.
B. Oct. 8, 1929, Danville, Va.

Year	Team	Lg	W	L	PCT	ERA	G	GS	CG	IP	H	BB	SO	ShO	Relief W	Relief L	Relief SV	Batting AB	Batting H	HR	BA	PO	A	E	DP	TC/G	FA
1958	STL	N	3	9	.250	4.51	31	13	4	111.2	113	41	74	0	1	1	0	24	1	0	.042	11	17	1	1	0.9	.966
1959	CIN	N	4	2	.667	5.46	18	1	0	29.2	29	19	8	0	4	2	3	7	0	0	.000	1	3	0	2	0.2	1.000
1960	BAL	A	0	0	—	27.00	2	0	0	0.2	4	1	0	0	0	0	0	0	0	0	—	0	0	0	0	0.0	.000
3 yrs.			7	11	.389	4.82	51	14	4	142	146	61	82	0	5	3	3	31	1	0	.032	12	20	1	3	0.6	.970

Mac MacArthur

MacARTHUR, MALCOLM M. TR 5′ 9½″ 164 lbs.
B. Jan. 19, 1862, Glasgow, Scotland D. Oct. 18, 1932, Detroit, Mich.

Year	Team	Lg	W	L	PCT	ERA	G	GS	CG	IP	H	BB	SO	ShO	Relief W	Relief L	Relief SV	Batting AB	Batting H	HR	BA	PO	A	E	DP	TC/G	FA
1884	IND	AA	1	5	.167	*5.02*	6	6	6	52	57	21	19	0	0	0	0	21	2	0	.095	1	12	5	1	3.0	.722

Frank MacCormick

MacCORMICK, FRANK LOUIS BR TR 6′ 4″ 210 lbs.
B. Sept. 21, 1954, Jersey City, N. J.

Year	Team	Lg	W	L	PCT	ERA	G	GS	CG	IP	H	BB	SO	ShO	Relief W	Relief L	Relief SV	Batting AB	Batting H	HR	BA	PO	A	E	DP	TC/G	FA
1976	DET	A	0	5	.000	5.73	9	8	0	33	35	34	14	0	0	0	0	3	0	0	.000	4	3	0	0	0.8	1.000
1977	SEA	A	0	0	—	3.86	3	3	0	7	4	12	4	0	0	0	0	0	0	0	—	0	1	0	0	0.3	1.000
2 yrs.			0	5	.000	5.40	12	11	0	40	39	46	18	0	0	0	0	3	0	0	.000	4	4	0	0	0.7	1.000

Bill MacDonald

MacDONALD, WILLIAM PAUL BR TR 5′10″ 170 lbs.
B. Mar. 28, 1929, Alameda, Calif. D. May 4, 1991, Shasta Lake, Calif.

Year	Team	Lg	W	L	PCT	ERA	G	GS	CG	IP	H	BB	SO	ShO	Relief W	Relief L	Relief SV	Batting AB	Batting H	HR	BA	PO	A	E	DP	TC/G	FA
1950	PIT	N	8	10	.444	4.29	32	20	6	153	138	88	60	2	1	1	1	49	6	0	.122	5	15	1	1	0.7	.952
1953			0	1	.000	12.27	4	1	0	7.1	12	8	4	0	0	0	0	0	0	0	—	0	1	0	0	0.3	1.000
2 yrs.			8	11	.421	4.66	36	21	6	160.1	150	96	64	2	1	1	1	49	6	0	.122	5	16	1	1	0.6	.955

Bob MacDonald

MacDONALD, ROBERT JOSEPH BL TL 6′ 3″ 200 lbs.
B. Apr. 27, 1965, East Orange, N. J.

Year	Team	Lg	W	L	PCT	ERA	G	GS	CG	IP	H	BB	SO	ShO	Relief W	Relief L	Relief SV	Batting AB	Batting H	HR	BA	PO	A	E	DP	TC/G	FA
1990	TOR	A	0	0	—	0.00	4	0	0	2.1	0	2	0	0	0	0	0	0	0	0	—	0	0	0	0	0.0	.000
1991			3	3	.500	2.85	45	0	0	53.2	51	25	24	0	3	3	0	0	0	0	—	4	5	0	0	0.2	1.000
1992			1	0	1.000	4.37	27	0	0	47.1	50	16	26	0	1	0	0	0	0	0	—	2	2	0	0	0.1	1.000
1993	DET	A	3	3	.500	5.35	68	0	0	65.2	67	33	39	0	3	3	3	0	0	0	—	3	13	1	0	0.3	.941
1995	NY	A	1	1	.500	4.86	33	0	0	46.1	50	22	41	0	1	1	0	0	0	0	—	2	4	0	0	0.2	1.000
5 yrs.			8	7	.533	4.35	177	0	0	215.1	218	98	130	0	8	7	3	0	0	0		11	24	1	0	0.2	.972

Bob MacDonald *continued*

LEAGUE CHAMPIONSHIP SERIES

Year	Team	W	L	PCT	ERA	G	GS	CG	IP	H	BB	SO	ShO	Relief Pitching W	Relief Pitching L	Relief Pitching SV	Batting AB	Batting H	Batting HR	BA	PO	A	E	DP	TC/G	FA
1991	TOR A	0	0	—	9.00	1	0	0	1	1	1	0	0	0	0	0	0	0	0	—	0	0	0	0	0.0	.000

Harry Mace

MACE, HARRY F. 5′11″ 185 lbs.
B. 1870, Washington, D. C. Deceased.

Year	Team	W	L	PCT	ERA	G	GS	CG	IP	H	BB	SO	ShO	Relief Pitching W	Relief Pitching L	Relief Pitching SV	Batting AB	Batting H	Batting HR	BA	PO	A	E	DP	TC/G	FA
1891	WAS AA	0	1	.000	7.31	3	1	1	16	18	8	3	0	0	0	0	6	0	0	.000	0	4	1	0	1.7	.800

Danny MacFayden

MacFAYDEN, DANIEL KNOWLES (Deacon Danny) BR TR 5′11″ 170 lbs.
B. June 10, 1905, North Truro, Mass. D. Aug. 26, 1972, Brunswick, Me.

Year	Team	W	L	PCT	ERA	G	GS	CG	IP	H	BB	SO	ShO	Relief Pitching W	Relief Pitching L	Relief Pitching SV	Batting AB	Batting H	Batting HR	BA	PO	A	E	DP	TC/G	FA
1926	BOS A	0	1	.000	4.85	3	1	1	13	10	7	1	0	0	0	0	3	1	0	.333	1	6	0	2	2.3	1.000
1927		5	8	.385	4.27	34	16	6	160.1	176	59	42	1	2	1	2	46	13	1	.283	3	35	3	0	1.2	.927
1928		9	15	.375	4.75	33	28	9	195	215	78	61	0	0	0	0	63	9	0	.143	8	42	0	1	1.5	1.000
1929		10	18	.357	3.62	32	26	14	221	225	81	61	**4**	0	2	0	74	13	0	.176	6	60	3	2	2.2	.957
1930		11	14	.440	4.21	36	33	18	269.1	293	93	76	1	1	0	2	92	13	0	.141	17	60	3	4	2.2	.963
1931		16	12	.571	4.02	35	32	17	230.2	263	79	74	2	1	0	0	81	10	0	.123	12	56	1	5	2.0	.986
1932	2 teams BOS A (12G 1–10) NY A (17G 7–5)																									
″	total	8	15	.348	4.39	29	26	14	199	228	70	62	0	0	0	1	74	8	0	.108	11	35	7	4	1.8	.868
1933	NY A	3	2	.600	5.88	25	6	2	90.1	120	37	28	0	0	1	0	34	1	0	.029	4	19	2	2	1.0	.920
1934		4	3	.571	4.50	22	11	4	96	110	31	41	0	0	0	0	39	4	0	.103	3	15	1	1	0.9	.947
1935	2 teams CIN N (7G 1–2) BOS N (28G 5–13)																									
″	total	6	15	.286	5.04	35	24	8	187.2	239	47	59	1	0	2	0	62	9	0	.145	8	55	4	2	1.9	.940
1936	BOS N	17	13	.567	2.87	37	31	21	266.2	268	66	86	2	2	1	0	83	8	0	.096	9	75	4	5	2.4	.955
1937		14	14	.500	2.93	32	32	16	246	250	60	70	2	0	0	0	83	13	0	.157	13	62	4	3	2.5	.949
1938		14	9	.609	2.95	29	29	19	219.2	211	64	58	5	0	0	0	77	9	0	.117	11	41	1	2	1.8	.981
1939		8	14	.364	3.90	33	28	8	191.2	221	59	46	0	0	0	2	67	12	0	.179	9	47	3	0	1.8	.949
1940	PIT N	5	4	.556	3.55	35	8	0	91.1	112	27	24	0	4	2	2	28	5	0	.179	2	22	1	2	0.7	.960
1941	WAS A	0	1	.000	10.29	5	0	0	7	12	5	3	0	0	1	0	0	0	0	—	0	3	0	1	0.6	1.000
1943	BOS N	2	1	.667	5.91	10	1	0	21.1	31	9	5	0	2	1	0	4	1	0	.250	1	4	0	0	0.5	1.000
17 yrs.		132	159	.454	3.96	465	332	157	2706	2984	872	797	18	12	11	9	910	129	1	.142	118	637	37	36	1.7	.953

Julio Machado

MACHADO, JULIO SEGUNDO (Iguana Man) BR TR 5′ 9″ 165 lbs.
Born Julio Segundo Machado (Rondon).
B. Dec. 1, 1965, Zulia, Venezuela.

Year	Team	W	L	PCT	ERA	G	GS	CG	IP	H	BB	SO	ShO	Relief Pitching W	Relief Pitching L	Relief Pitching SV	Batting AB	Batting H	Batting HR	BA	PO	A	E	DP	TC/G	FA
1989	NY N	0	1	.000	3.27	10	0	0	11	9	3	14	0	0	1	0	0	0	0	—	2	0	0	0	0.2	1.000
1990	2 teams NY N (27G 4–1) MIL A (10G 0–0)																									
″	total	4	1	.800	2.47	37	0	0	47.1	41	25	39	0	4	1	3	0	0	0		2	4	0	0	0.2	1.000
1991	MIL A	3	3	.500	3.45	54	0	0	88.2	65	55	98	0	3	3	3	0	0	0	—	4	7	1	1	0.2	.917
3 yrs.		7	5	.583	3.12	101	0	0	147	115	83	151	0	7	5	6	0	0	0		8	11	1	1	0.2	.950

Chuck Machemehl

MACHEMEHL, CHARLES WALTER BR TR 6′ 4″ 200 lbs.
B. Apr. 20, 1947, Brenham, Tex.

Year	Team	W	L	PCT	ERA	G	GS	CG	IP	H	BB	SO	ShO	Relief Pitching W	Relief Pitching L	Relief Pitching SV	Batting AB	Batting H	Batting HR	BA	PO	A	E	DP	TC/G	FA
1971	CLE A	0	2	.000	6.50	14	0	0	18	16	15	9	0	0	2	3	2	1	0	.500	1	3	0	0	0.3	1.000

Bill Mack

MACK, WILLIAM FRANCIS BL TL 6′ 1″ 155 lbs.
B. Feb. 12, 1885, Elmira, N. Y. D. Sept. 30, 1971, Elmira, N. Y.

Year	Team	W	L	PCT	ERA	G	GS	CG	IP	H	BB	SO	ShO	Relief Pitching W	Relief Pitching L	Relief Pitching SV	Batting AB	Batting H	Batting HR	BA	PO	A	E	DP	TC/G	FA
1908	CHI N	0	0	—	2.84	2	0	0	6.1	5	1	2	0	0	0	0	3	2	0	.667	0	2	1	0	1.5	.667

Frank Mack

MACK, FRANK GEORGE (Stubby) BR TR 6′ 1½″ 180 lbs.
B. Feb. 2, 1900, Oklahoma City, Okla. D. July 2, 1971, Clearwater, Fla.

Year	Team	W	L	PCT	ERA	G	GS	CG	IP	H	BB	SO	ShO	Relief Pitching W	Relief Pitching L	Relief Pitching SV	Batting AB	Batting H	Batting HR	BA	PO	A	E	DP	TC/G	FA
1922	CHI A	2	2	.500	3.67	8	4	1	34.1	36	16	11	1	0	0	0	12	3	0	.250	2	5	0	0	0.9	1.000
1923		0	1	.000	4.24	11	0	0	23.1	23	11	6	0	0	1	0	6	0	0	.000	0	7	0	1	0.6	1.000
1925		0	0	—	9.45	8	0	0	13.1	24	13	6	0	0	0	0	3	1	0	.333	0	2	0	0	0.3	1.000
3 yrs.		2	3	.400	4.94	27	4	1	71	83	40	23	1	0	1	0	21	4	0	.190	2	14	0	1	0.6	1.000

Tony Mack

MACK, TONY LYNN BR TR 5′10″ 175 lbs.
B. Apr. 30, 1961, Lexington, Ky.

Year	Team	W	L	PCT	ERA	G	GS	CG	IP	H	BB	SO	ShO	Relief Pitching W	Relief Pitching L	Relief Pitching SV	Batting AB	Batting H	Batting HR	BA	PO	A	E	DP	TC/G	FA
1985	CAL A	0	1	.000	15.43	1	1	0	2.1	8	0	0	0	0	0	0	0	0	0	—	0	0	0	0	0.0	.000

Ken MacKenzie

MacKENZIE, KENNETH PURVIS BR TL 6′ 185 lbs.
B. Mar. 10, 1934, Gore Bay, Ont., Canada.

Year	Team	W	L	PCT	ERA	G	GS	CG	IP	H	BB	SO	ShO	Relief Pitching W	Relief Pitching L	Relief Pitching SV	Batting AB	Batting H	Batting HR	BA	PO	A	E	DP	TC/G	FA
1960	MIL N	0	1	.000	6.48	9	0	0	8.1	9	3	9	0	0	1	0	1	0	0	.000	1	0	0	0	0.1	1.000
1961		0	1	.000	5.14	5	0	0	7	8	2	5	0	0	1	0	2	0	0	.000	0	3	0	0	0.6	1.000
1962	NY N	5	4	.556	4.95	42	1	0	80	87	34	51	0	5	3	1	12	1	0	.083	3	16	2	3	0.5	.905
1963	2 teams NY N (34G 3–1) STL N (8G 0–0)																									
″	total	3	1	.750	4.88	42	0	0	66.1	72	15	48	0	3	1	3	10	0	0	.000	3	6	2	0	0.3	.818
1964	SF N	0	0	—	5.00	10	0	0	9	9	3	3	0	0	0	1	0	0	0	—	1	3	0	0	0.4	1.000
1965	HOU N	0	3	.000	3.86	21	0	0	37.1	46	6	26	0	0	3	0	11	3	0	.273	0	6	0	1	0.3	1.000
6 yrs.		8	10	.444	4.80	129	1	0	208	231	63	142	0	8	9	5	36	4	0	.111	8	34	4	4	0.4	.913

Johnny Mackinson

MACKINSON, JOHN JOSEPH BR TR 5′10½″ 160 lbs.
B. Oct. 29, 1923, Orange, N. J. D. Oct. 17, 1989, Reseda, Calif.

Year	Team	W	L	PCT	ERA	G	GS	CG	IP	H	BB	SO	ShO	Relief Pitching W	Relief Pitching L	Relief Pitching SV	Batting AB	Batting H	Batting HR	BA	PO	A	E	DP	TC/G	FA
1953	PHI A	0	0	—	0.00	1	0	0	1.1	1	2	0	0	0	0	0	0	0	0	—	0	0	0	0	0.0	.000
1955	STL N	0	1	.000	7.84	8	1	0	20.2	24	10	8	0	0	1	0	4	0	0	.000	0	4	0	0	0.5	1.000
2 yrs.		0	1	.000	7.36	9	1	0	22	25	12	8	0	0	1	0	4	0	0	.000	0	4	0	0	0.4	1.000

Bill MacLeod

MacLEOD, WILLIAM DANIEL BL TL 6′ 2″ 190 lbs.
B. May 13, 1942, Gloucester, Mass.

Year	Team	W	L	PCT	ERA	G	GS	CG	IP	H	BB	SO	ShO	Relief Pitching W	Relief Pitching L	Relief Pitching SV	Batting AB	Batting H	Batting HR	BA	PO	A	E	DP	TC/G	FA
1962	BOS A	0	1	.000	5.40	2	0	0	1.2	4	1	2	0	0	1	0	0	0	0	—	0	0	0	0	0.0	.000

Max Macon

MACON, MAX CULLEN BL TL 6′ 3″ 175 lbs.
B. Oct. 14, 1915, Pensacola, Fla. D. Aug. 5, 1989, Jupiter, Fla.

Year	Team	Lg	W	L	PCT	ERA	G	GS	CG	IP	H	BB	SO	ShO	Relief W	Relief L	Relief SV	Batting AB	Batting H	HR	BA	PO	A	E	DP	TC/G	FA
1938	STL	N	4	11	.267	4.11	38	12	5	129.1	133	61	39	1	2	2	2	36	11	0	.306	3	32	2	2	0.9	.946
1940	BKN	N	1	0	1.000	22.50	2	0	0	2	5	0	1	0	1	0	0	1	1	0	1.000	0	0	0	0	0.0	.000
1942			5	3	.625	1.93	14	8	4	84	67	33	27	1	2	0	1	43	12	0	.279	9	15	1	0	1.8	.960
1943			7	5	.583	5.96	25	9	0	77	89	32	21	0	3	2	0	55	9	0	.164	14	19	1	4	1.2	.971
1944	BOS	N	0	0	—	21.00	1	0	0	3	10	1	1	0	0	0	0	366	100	3	.273	671	51	17	62	7.8	.977
1947			0	0	—	0.00	1	0	0	2	1	1	1	0	0	0	0	1	0	0	.000	0	1	0	0	1.0	1.000
6 yrs.			17	19	.472	4.24	81	29	9	297.1	305	128	90	2	8	4	3	*				697	118	21	68	4.7	.975

Harry MacPherson

MacPHERSON, HARRY WILLIAM BR TR 5′10″ 150 lbs.
B. July 10, 1926, North Andover, Mass.

Year	Team	Lg	W	L	PCT	ERA	G	GS	CG	IP	H	BB	SO	ShO	Relief W	Relief L	Relief SV	Batting AB	Batting H	HR	BA	PO	A	E	DP	TC/G	FA
1944	BOS	N	0	0	—	0.00	1	0	0	1	0	1	1	0	0	0	0	0	0	0	—	0	0	0	0	0.0	.000

Jimmy Macullar

MACULLAR, JAMES F. (Little Mac) BR TL 5′ 6″ 155 lbs.
B. Jan. 16, 1855, Boston, Mass. D. Apr. 8, 1924, Baltimore, Md.
Manager 1879.

Year	Team	Lg	W	L	PCT	ERA	G	GS	CG	IP	H	BB	SO	ShO	Relief W	Relief L	Relief SV	Batting AB	Batting H	HR	BA	PO	A	E	DP	TC/G	FA
1886	BAL	AA	0	0	—	9.00	1	0	0	2	4	0	1	0	0	0	0	*				139	120	42	9	4.4	.860

Keith MacWhorter

MacWHORTER, KEITH BR TR 6′ 4″ 190 lbs.
B. Dec. 30, 1955, Worcester, Mass.

Year	Team	Lg	W	L	PCT	ERA	G	GS	CG	IP	H	BB	SO	ShO	Relief W	Relief L	Relief SV	Batting AB	Batting H	HR	BA	PO	A	E	DP	TC/G	FA
1980	BOS	A	0	3	.000	5.57	14	2	0	42	46	18	21	0	0	1	0	0	0	0	—	5	7	1	1	0.9	.923

Kid Madden

MADDEN, MICHAEL JOSEPH TL 5′ 7½″ 130 lbs.
B. Oct. 22, 1867, Portland, Me. D. Mar. 16, 1896, Portland, Me.

Year	Team	Lg	W	L	PCT	ERA	G	GS	CG	IP	H	BB	SO	ShO	Relief W	Relief L	Relief SV	Batting AB	Batting H	HR	BA	PO	A	E	DP	TC/G	FA
1887	BOS	N	21	14	.600	3.79	37	37	36	321	317	122	81	3	0	0	0	132	32	1	.242	5	59	13	1	2.0	.831
1888			7	11	.389	2.95	20	18	17	165	142	24	53	1	0	0	0	67	11	0	.164	4	41	4	0	2.5	.918
1889			10	10	.500	4.40	22	19	18	178	194	71	64	1	1	0	1	86	25	0	.291	9	35	4	2	2.0	.917
1890	BOS	P	3	2	.600	4.79	10	7	5	62	85	25	24	1	1	0	1	38	7	0	.184	9	20	4	2	2.5	.879
1891	2 teams	BOS AA (1G 0–1)	BAL AA (32G 13–12)																								
″	total		13	13	.500	4.19	33	28	21	232	249	94	62	1	1	0	1	110	31	1	.282	14	80	16	5	2.8	.855
5 yrs.			54	50	.519	3.92	122	109	97	958	987	336	284	7	3	0	3	433	106	2	.245	41	235	41	10	2.3	.871

Len Madden

MADDEN, LEONARD JOSEPH (Lefty) BL TL 6′ 2″ 165 lbs.
B. July 2, 1890, Toledo, Ohio D. Sept. 9, 1949, Toledo, Ohio.

Year	Team	Lg	W	L	PCT	ERA	G	GS	CG	IP	H	BB	SO	ShO	Relief W	Relief L	Relief SV	Batting AB	Batting H	HR	BA	PO	A	E	DP	TC/G	FA
1912	CHI	N	0	1	.000	2.92	6	2	0	12.1	16	9	5	0	0	0	0	4	1	0	.250	0	3	2	0	0.8	.600

Mike Madden

MADDEN, MICHAEL ANTHONY BL TL 6′ 1″ 185 lbs.
B. Jan. 13, 1957, Denver, Colo.

Year	Team	Lg	W	L	PCT	ERA	G	GS	CG	IP	H	BB	SO	ShO	Relief W	Relief L	Relief SV	Batting AB	Batting H	HR	BA	PO	A	E	DP	TC/G	FA
1983	HOU	N	9	5	.643	3.14	28	13	0	94.2	76	45	44	0	3	0	0	22	1	0	.045	7	15	1	4	0.8	.957
1984			2	3	.400	5.53	17	7	0	40.2	46	35	29	0	1	0	0	6	2	0	.333	0	2	0	0	0.1	1.000
1985			0	0	—	4.26	13	0	0	19	29	11	16	0	0	0	0	0	0	0	—	2	1	0	0	0.2	1.000
1986			1	2	.333	4.08	13	6	0	39.2	47	22	30	0	1	0	0	9	0	0	.000	1	5	0	0	0.5	1.000
4 yrs.			12	10	.545	3.94	71	26	0	194	198	113	119	0	5	0	0	37	3	0	.081	10	23	1	4	0.5	.971

Morris Madden

MADDEN, MORRIS DeWAYNE BL TL 6′ 155 lbs.
B. Aug. 31, 1960, Laurens, S. C.

Year	Team	Lg	W	L	PCT	ERA	G	GS	CG	IP	H	BB	SO	ShO	Relief W	Relief L	Relief SV	Batting AB	Batting H	HR	BA	PO	A	E	DP	TC/G	FA
1987	DET	A	0	0	—	16.20	2	0	0	1.2	4	3	0	0	0	0	0	0	0	0	—	0	0	0	0	0.0	.000
1988	PIT	N	0	0	—	0.00	5	0	0	5.2	5	7	3	0	0	0	0	0	0	0	—	0	2	0	0	0.4	1.000
1989			2	2	.500	7.07	9	3	0	14	17	13	6	0	1	0	0	1	0	0	.000	1	0	2	0	0.3	.333
3 yrs.			2	2	.500	5.91	16	3	0	21.1	26	23	9	0	1	0	0	1	0	0	.000	1	2	2	0	0.3	.600

Nick Maddox

MADDOX, NICHOLAS BL TR 6′ 175 lbs.
B. Nov. 9, 1886, Govans, Md. D. Nov. 27, 1954, Pittsburgh, Pa.

Year	Team	Lg	W	L	PCT	ERA	G	GS	CG	IP	H	BB	SO	ShO	Relief W	Relief L	Relief SV	Batting AB	Batting H	HR	BA	PO	A	E	DP	TC/G	FA
1907	PIT	N	5	1	.833	0.83	6	6	6	54	32	13	38	1	0	0	0	20	5	0	.250	2	12	1	0	2.5	.933
1908			23	8	.742	2.28	36	32	22	260.2	209	90	70	4	2	0	1	94	25	0	.266	8	77	3	3	2.4	.966
1909			13	8	.619	2.21	31	27	17	203.1	173	39	56	4	1	0	0	67	15	0	.224	6	54	2	3	2.0	.968
1910			2	3	.400	3.40	20	7	2	87.1	73	28	29	0	1	1	0	28	6	0	.214	1	24	1	2	1.3	.962
4 yrs.			43	20	.683	2.29	93	72	47	605.1	487	170	193	9	4	1	1	209	51	0	.244	17	167	7	8	2.1	.963
WORLD SERIES																											
1909	PIT	N	1	0	1.000	1.00	1	1	1	9	10	2	4	0	0	0	0	4	0	0	.000	0	1	0	0	1.0	1.000

Greg Maddux

MADDUX, GREGORY ALAN BR TR 6′ 170 lbs.
Brother of Mike Maddux.
B. Apr. 14, 1966, San Angelo, Tex.

Year	Team	Lg	W	L	PCT	ERA	G	GS	CG	IP	H	BB	SO	ShO	Relief W	Relief L	Relief SV	Batting AB	Batting H	HR	BA	PO	A	E	DP	TC/G	FA
1986	CHI	N	2	4	.333	5.52	6	5	1	31	44	11	20	0	0	1	0	12	4	0	.333	1	6	1	0	1.3	.875
1987			6	14	.300	5.61	30	27	1	155.2	181	74	101	1	0	0	0	42	5	0	.119	16	50	4	7	2.3	.943
1988			18	8	.692	3.18	34	34	9	249	230	81	140	3	0	0	0	96	19	0	.198	28	45	3	3	2.2	.961
1989			19	12	.613	2.95	35	35	7	238.1	222	82	135	1	0	0	0	81	17	0	.210	35	41	3	4	2.3	.962
1990			15	15	.500	3.46	35	**35**	8	237	**242**	71	144	2	0	0	0	83	12	0	.145	39	55	0	6	2.7	1.000
1991			15	11	.577	3.35	37	**37**	7	**263**	232	66	198	2	0	0	0	88	18	1	.205	39	50	2	5	2.5	.978
1992			**20**	11	.645	2.18	35	**35**	9	**268**	201	70	199	4	0	0	0	88	15	1	.170	30	64	3	1	2.8	.969
1993	ATL	N	20	10	.667	**2.36**	36	**36**	**8**	**267**	228	52	197	1	0	0	0	91	15	0	.165	39	59	7	5	2.9	.933
1994			**16**	6	.727	**1.56**	25	25	**10**	**202**	150	31	156	**3**	0	0	0	63	14	0	.222	20	37	4	4	2.4	.934
1995			**19**	2	**.905**	**1.63**	28	28	**10**	**209.2**	147	23	181	**3**	0	0	0	72	11	0	.153	18	53	0	4	2.5	1.000
10 yrs.			150	93	.617	2.88	301	297	70	2120.2	1877	561	1471	20	0	1	0	716	130	2	.182	265	460	27	39	2.5	.964
DIVISIONAL PLAYOFF SERIES																											
1995	ATL	N	1	0	1.000	4.50	2	2	0	14	19	2	7	0	0	0	0	6	1	0	.167	1	4	0	1	2.5	1.000
LEAGUE CHAMPIONSHIP SERIES																											
1989	CHI	N	0	1	.000	13.50	2	2	0	7.1	13	4	5	0	0	0	0	3	0	0	.000	0	0	1	0	0.5	.000
1993	ATL	N	1	1	.500	4.97	2	2	0	12.2	11	7	11	0	0	0	0	4	1	0	.250	3	5	1	0	4.5	.889
1995			1	0	1.000	1.13	1	1	0	8	7	2	4	0	0	0	0	3	0	0	.000	1	1	0	0	2.0	1.000
3 yrs.			2	2	.500	6.11	5	5	0	28	31	13	20	0	0	0	0	10	1	0	.100	4	6	2	0	2.4	.833
WORLD SERIES																											
1995	ATL	N	1	1	.500	2.25	2	2	1	16	9	3	8	0	0	0	0	3	0	0	.000	2	4	0	0	3.0	1.000

Mike Maddux

MADDUX, MICHAEL AUSLEY
Brother of Greg Maddux.
B. Aug. 27, 1961, Dayton, Ohio.
BL TR 6′ 2″ 180 lbs.

Year	Team	W	L	PCT	ERA	G	GS	CG	IP	H	BB	SO	ShO	Relief Pitching W	Relief Pitching L	Relief Pitching SV	Batting AB	Batting H	Batting HR	BA	PO	A	E	DP	TC/G	FA
1986	PHI N	3	7	.300	5.42	16	16	0	78	88	34	44	0	0	0	0	22	1	0	.045	5	10	2	0	1.1	.882
1987		2	0	1.000	2.65	7	2	0	17	17	5	15	0	1	0	0	3	0	0	.000	1	1	1	0	0.4	.667
1988		4	3	.571	3.76	25	11	0	88.2	91	34	59	0	2	0	0	23	3	0	.130	8	18	4	1	1.2	.867
1989		1	3	.250	5.15	16	4	2	43.2	52	14	26	1	0	1	1	10	0	0	.000	7	12	0	1	1.2	1.000
1990	LA N	0	1	.000	6.53	11	2	0	20.2	24	4	11	0	0	0	0	2	0	0	.000	0	2	0	0	0.2	1.000
1991	SD N	7	2	.778	2.46	64	1	0	98.2	78	27	57	0	6	2	5	13	1	0	.077	9	18	1	1	0.4	.964
1992		2	2	.500	2.37	50	1	0	79.2	71	24	60	0	2	1	5	9	1	0	.111	9	18	1	1	0.6	.964
1993	NY N	3	8	.273	3.60	58	0	0	75	67	27	57	0	3	8	5	3	0	0	.000	6	16	1	1	0.4	.957
1994		2	1	.667	5.11	27	0	0	44	45	13	32	0	2	1	2	3	0	0	.000	2	11	1	2	0.5	.929
1995	2 teams PIT N (8G 1–0) BOS A (36G 4–1)																									
″	total	5	1	.833	4.10	44	4	0	98.2	100	18	69	0	3	1	1	0	0	0	—	9	12	1	2	0.5	.955
10 yrs.		29	28	.509	3.87	318	41	2	644	633	200	430	1	19	14	19	88	6	0	.068	56	118	12	9	0.6	.935
DIVISIONAL PLAYOFF SERIES																										
1995	BOS A	0	0	—	0.00	2	0	0	3	2	1	1	0	0	0	0	0	0	0	—	1	2	0	0	1.5	1.000

Tony Madigan

MADIGAN, WILLIAM J.
B. 1868, Washington, D. C. D. Dec. 4, 1954, Washington, D. C.
TR 5′ 5½″ 126 lbs.

Year	Team	W	L	PCT	ERA	G	GS	CG	IP	H	BB	SO	ShO	Relief Pitching W	Relief Pitching L	Relief Pitching SV	Batting AB	Batting H	Batting HR	BA	PO	A	E	DP	TC/G	FA
1886	WAS N	1	13	.071	*5.06*	14	13	13	115.2	159	44	29	0	0	0	0	48	4	0	.083	3	28	3	1	2.3	.912

Dave Madison

MADISON, DAVID PLEDGER
B. Feb. 1, 1921, Brooksville, Miss. D. Dec. 8, 1985, Macon, Miss.
BR TR 6′ 3″ 190 lbs.

Year	Team	W	L	PCT	ERA	G	GS	CG	IP	H	BB	SO	ShO	Relief Pitching W	Relief Pitching L	Relief Pitching SV	Batting AB	Batting H	Batting HR	BA	PO	A	E	DP	TC/G	FA
1950	NY A	0	0	—	6.00	1	0	0	3	3	1	1	0	0	0	0	0	0	0	—	0	0	0	0	0.0	.000
1952	2 teams STL A (31G 4–2) DET A (10G 1–1)																									
″	total	5	3	.625	4.94	41	5	0	93	94	58	42	0	3	2	0	19	2	0	.105	2	17	1	2	0.5	.950
1953	DET A	3	4	.429	6.82	32	1	0	62	76	44	27	0	3	3	0	11	1	0	.091	2	13	2	0	0.5	.882
3 yrs.		8	7	.533	5.70	74	6	0	158	173	103	70	0	6	5	0	30	3	0	.100	4	30	3	2	0.5	.919

Alex Madrid

MADRID, ALEXANDER
B. Apr. 18, 1963, Springerville, Ariz.
BR TR 6′ 3″ 200 lbs.

Year	Team	W	L	PCT	ERA	G	GS	CG	IP	H	BB	SO	ShO	Relief Pitching W	Relief Pitching L	Relief Pitching SV	Batting AB	Batting H	Batting HR	BA	PO	A	E	DP	TC/G	FA
1987	MIL A	0	0	—	15.19	3	0	0	5.1	11	1	1	0	0	0	0	0	0	0	—	0	0	0	0	0.0	.000
1988	PHI N	1	1	.500	2.76	5	2	1	16.1	15	6	2	0	0	0	0	3	0	0	.000	0	2	0	0	0.4	1.000
1989		1	2	.333	5.47	6	3	0	24.2	32	14	13	0	0	0	0	6	0	0	.000	0	2	0	0	0.3	1.000
3 yrs.		2	3	.400	5.63	14	5	1	46.1	58	21	16	0	0	0	0	9	0	0	.000	0	4	0	0	0.3	1.000

Hector Maestri

MAESTRI, HECTOR ANIBAL
Born Hector Anibal Maestri (Garcia).
B. Apr. 19, 1935, Havana, Cuba.
BR TR 5′10″ 170 lbs.

Year	Team	W	L	PCT	ERA	G	GS	CG	IP	H	BB	SO	ShO	Relief Pitching W	Relief Pitching L	Relief Pitching SV	Batting AB	Batting H	Batting HR	BA	PO	A	E	DP	TC/G	FA
1960	WAS A	0	0	—	0.00	1	0	0	2	1	1	1	0	0	0	0	0	0	0	—	0	0	0	0	0.0	.000
1961		0	1	.000	1.50	1	1	0	6	6	2	2	0	0	0	0	1	0	0	.000	0	1	0	0	1.0	1.000
2 yrs.		0	1	.000	1.13	2	1	0	8	7	3	3	0	0	0	0	1	0	0	.000	0	1	0	0	0.5	1.000

Bill Magee

MAGEE, WILLIAM J.
B. 1875 Deceased.
BR TR 5′10″ 154 lbs.

Year	Team	W	L	PCT	ERA	G	GS	CG	IP	H	BB	SO	ShO	Relief Pitching W	Relief Pitching L	Relief Pitching SV	Batting AB	Batting H	Batting HR	BA	PO	A	E	DP	TC/G	FA
1897	LOU N	4	12	.250	5.39	22	16	13	155.1	186	99	44	1	0	1	0	62	13	0	.210	4	42	7	1	2.4	.868
1898		16	15	.516	3.93	38	33	29	295.1	294	129	55	3	0	1	0	111	14	0	.126	11	65	6	3	2.2	.927
1899	3 teams LOU N (12G 3–7) PHI N (9G 3–5) WAS N (8G 1–4)																									
″	total	7	16	.304	6.15	29	26	17	183	227	88	28	1	0	1	0	73	13	0	.178	8	51	7	0	2.3	.894
1901	2 teams STL N (1G 0–0) NY N (6G 0–4)																									
″	total	0	4	.000	5.72	7	6	4	50.1	64	15	17	0	0	0	0	18	4	0	.222	4	10	0	0	2.0	1.000
1902	2 teams NY N (2G 0–0) PHI N (8G 2–4)																									
″	total	2	4	.333	3.68	10	8	6	58.2	66	19	17	0	0	0	0	20	4	0	.200	0	16	4	1	2.0	.800
5 yrs.		29	51	.363	4.88	106	89	69	742.2	837	350	161	5	0	3	0	284	48	0	.169	27	184	24	5	2.2	.898

Sal Maglie

MAGLIE, SALVATORE ANTHONY (The Barber)
B. Apr. 26, 1917, Niagara Falls, N. Y. D. Dec. 28, 1992, Niagara Falls, N. Y.
BR TR 6′ 2″ 180 lbs.

Year	Team	W	L	PCT	ERA	G	GS	CG	IP	H	BB	SO	ShO	Relief Pitching W	Relief Pitching L	Relief Pitching SV	Batting AB	Batting H	Batting HR	BA	PO	A	E	DP	TC/G	FA
1945	NY N	5	4	.556	2.35	13	10	7	84.1	72	22	32	3	0	1	0	30	5	0	.167	1	17	0	1	1.4	1.000
1950		18	4	**.818**	2.71	47	16	12	206	169	86	96	**5**	5	2	1	66	8	0	.121	12	51	1	3	1.4	.984
1951		**23**	6	.793	2.93	42	37	22	298	254	86	146	3	1	0	4	112	17	1	.152	23	53	0	7	1.8	1.000
1952		18	8	.692	2.92	35	31	12	216	199	75	112	5	1	1	1	69	5	0	.072	18	41	3	3	1.8	.952
1953		8	9	.471	4.15	27	24	9	145.1	158	47	80	3	0	0	0	48	13	0	.271	8	15	1	1	0.9	.958
1954		14	6	.700	3.26	34	32	9	218.1	222	70	117	1	0	0	2	63	8	0	.127	4	41	2	3	1.4	.957
1955	2 teams NY N (23G 9–5) CLE A (10G 0–2)																									
″	total	9	7	.563	3.77	33	23	6	155.1	168	55	82	0	1	0	2	45	5	0	.111	6	14	1	2	0.6	.952
1956	2 teams CLE A (2G 0–0) BKN N (28G 13–5)																									
″	total	13	5	.722	2.89	30	26	9	196	160	54	110	3	0	0	0	70	9	0	.129	9	20	0	5	1.0	1.000
1957	2 teams BKN N (19G 6–6) NY A (6G 2–0)																									
″	total	8	6	.571	2.69	25	20	5	127.1	116	33	59	2	0	0	4	37	3	0	.081	10	17	1	1	1.1	.964
1958	2 teams NY A (7G 1–1) STL N (10G 2–6)																									
″	total	3	7	.300	4.72	17	13	2	76.1	73	34	28	0	0	0	0	23	3	1	.130	5	11	1	0	1.0	.941
10 yrs.		119	62	.657 **9th**	3.15	303	232	93	1723	1591	562	862	25	8	4	14	563	76	2	.135	96	280	10	26	1.3	.974
WORLD SERIES																										
1951	NY N	0	1	.000	7.20	1	1	0	5	8	2	3	0	0	0	0	1	0	0	.000	0	0	0	0	0.0	.000
1954		0	0	—	2.57	1	1	0	7	7	2	2	0	0	0	0	3	0	0	.000	0	2	0	0	2.0	1.000
1956	BKN N	1	1	.500	2.65	2	2	2	17	14	6	15	0	0	0	0	5	0	0	.000	0	1	0	0	0.5	1.000
3 yrs.		1	2	.333	3.41	4	4	2	29	29	10	20	0	0	0	0	9	0	0	.000	0	3	0	0	0.8	1.000

Mike Magnante

MAGNANTE, MICHAEL ANTHONY
B. June 17, 1965, Glendale, Calif.
BL TL 6′ 1″ 180 lbs.

Year	Team	W	L	PCT	ERA	G	GS	CG	IP	H	BB	SO	ShO	Relief Pitching W	Relief Pitching L	Relief Pitching SV	Batting AB	Batting H	Batting HR	BA	PO	A	E	DP	TC/G	FA
1991	KC A	0	1	.000	2.45	38	0	0	55	55	23	42	0	0	1	0	0	0	0	—	3	6	1	1	0.3	.900
1992		4	9	.308	4.94	44	12	0	89.1	115	35	31	0	1	4	0	0	0	0	—	9	20	0	3	0.7	1.000
1993		1	2	.333	4.08	7	6	0	35.1	37	11	16	0	0	0	0	0	0	0	—	4	6	0	1	1.4	1.000

Mike Magnante *continued*

Year	Team	W	L	PCT	ERA	G	GS	CG	IP	H	BB	SO	ShO	Relief Pitching W	Relief Pitching L	Relief Pitching SV	Batting AB	Batting H	Batting HR	BA	PO	A	E	DP	TC/G	FA
1994		2	3	.400	4.60	36	1	0	47	55	16	21	0	2	2	0	0	0	0	—	4	7	1	1	0.3	.917
1995		1	1	.500	4.23	28	0	0	44.2	45	16	28	0	1	1	0	0	0	0	—	8	9	2	2	0.7	.895
5 yrs.		8	16	.333	4.15	153	19	0	271.1	307	101	138	0	4	8	0	0	0	0		28	48	4	8	0.5	.950

Jim Magnuson

MAGNUSON, JAMES ROBERT BR TL 6′ 2″ 190 lbs.
B. Aug. 18, 1946, Marinette, Wis. D. May 30, 1991, Green Bay, Wis.

Year	Team	W	L	PCT	ERA	G	GS	CG	IP	H	BB	SO	ShO	Relief Pitching W	Relief Pitching L	Relief Pitching SV	Batting AB	Batting H	Batting HR	BA	PO	A	E	DP	TC/G	FA
1970	CHI A	1	5	.167	4.80	13	6	0	45	45	16	20	0	0	0	0	11	0	0	.000	3	6	0	0	0.7	1.000
1971		2	1	.667	4.50	15	4	0	30	30	16	11	0	0	0	0	4	0	0	.000	2	4	0	1	0.4	1.000
1973	NY A	0	1	.000	4.28	8	0	0	27.1	38	9	9	0	0	1	0	0	0	0	—	3	5	1	2	1.1	.889
3 yrs.		3	7	.300	4.57	36	10	0	102.1	113	41	40	0	0	1	0	15	0	0	.000	8	15	1	3	0.7	.958

Joe Magrane

MAGRANE, JOSEPH DAVID BR TL 6′ 6″ 225 lbs.
B. July 2, 1964, Des Moines, Iowa.

Year	Team	W	L	PCT	ERA	G	GS	CG	IP	H	BB	SO	ShO	Relief Pitching W	Relief Pitching L	Relief Pitching SV	Batting AB	Batting H	Batting HR	BA	PO	A	E	DP	TC/G	FA
1987	STL N	9	7	.563	3.54	27	26	4	170.1	157	60	101	2	0	0	0	52	7	1	.135	10	26	3	3	1.4	.923
1988		5	9	.357	**2.18**	24	24	4	165.1	133	51	100	3	0	0	0	48	8	1	.167	16	37	5	0	2.4	.914
1989		18	9	.667	2.91	34	33	9	234.2	219	72	127	3	0	0	0	80	11	1	.138	11	31	2	1	1.3	.955
1990		10	17	.370	3.59	31	31	3	203.1	204	59	100	2	0	0	0	55	7	0	.127	8	38	1	1	1.5	.979
1992		1	2	.333	4.02	5	5	0	31.1	34	15	20	0	0	0	0	10	2	1	.200	1	5	0	0	1.2	1.000
1993	2 teams STL N (22G 8–10) CAL A (8G 3–2)																									
″	total	11	12	.478	4.66	30	28	0	164	175	58	62	0	0	1	0	35	4	0	.114	12	36	2	3	1.7	.960
1994	CAL A	2	6	.250	7.30	20	11	1	74	89	51	33	0	0	1	0	0	0	0	—	2	10	0	1	0.6	1.000
7 yrs.		56	62	.475	3.65	171	158	21	1043	1011	366	543	10	0	2	0	280	39	4	.139	60	183	13	9	1.5	.949
LEAGUE CHAMPIONSHIP SERIES																										
1987	STL N	0	0	—	9.00	1	1	0	4	4	2	3	0	0	0	0	1	0	0	.000	0	1	0	0	1.0	1.000
WORLD SERIES																										
1987	STL N	0	1	.000	8.59	2	2	0	7.1	9	5	5	0	0	0	0	0	0	0	—	1	1	0	0	1.0	1.000

Pete Magrini

MAGRINI, PETER ALEXANDER BR TR 6′ 195 lbs.
B. June 8, 1942, San Francisco, Calif.

Year	Team	W	L	PCT	ERA	G	GS	CG	IP	H	BB	SO	ShO	Relief Pitching W	Relief Pitching L	Relief Pitching SV	Batting AB	Batting H	Batting HR	BA	PO	A	E	DP	TC/G	FA
1966	BOS A	0	1	.000	9.82	3	1	0	7.1	8	8	3	0	0	0	0	3	0	0	.000	0	1	1	0	0.7	.500

Art Mahaffey

MAHAFFEY, ARTHUR BR TR 6′ 1″ 185 lbs.
B. June 4, 1938, Cincinnati, Ohio.

Year	Team	W	L	PCT	ERA	G	GS	CG	IP	H	BB	SO	ShO	Relief Pitching W	Relief Pitching L	Relief Pitching SV	Batting AB	Batting H	Batting HR	BA	PO	A	E	DP	TC/G	FA
1960	PHI N	7	3	.700	2.31	14	12	5	93.1	78	34	56	1	0	0	0	30	3	0	.100	6	13	0	0	1.4	1.000
1961		11	**19**	.367	4.10	36	32	12	219.1	205	70	158	3	0	1	0	63	8	0	.127	14	28	3	2	1.3	.933
1962		19	14	.576	3.94	41	39	20	274	253	81	177	2	0	1	0	92	13	2	.141	14	24	0	1	0.9	1.000
1963		7	10	.412	3.99	26	22	6	149	143	48	97	1	1	0	0	50	10	0	.200	11	22	1	0	1.3	.971
1964		12	9	.571	4.52	34	29	2	157.1	161	82	80	2	1	0	0	50	6	1	.120	6	19	0	2	0.7	1.000
1965		2	5	.286	6.21	22	9	1	71	82	32	52	0	0	0	0	21	2	0	.095	4	6	1	0	0.5	.909
1966	STL N	1	4	.200	6.43	12	5	0	35	37	21	19	0	0	0	1	7	0	0	.000	1	4	0	0	0.4	1.000
7 yrs.		59	64	.480	4.17	185	148	46	999	959	368	639	9	2	2	1	313	42	3	.134	56	116	5	5	1.0	.972

Lou Mahaffey

MAHAFFEY, LOUIS WOOD BR TR 5′ 9″ 170 lbs.
B. Jan. 3, 1874, Madison, Wis. D. Oct. 26, 1949, Torrance, Calif.

Year	Team	W	L	PCT	ERA	G	GS	CG	IP	H	BB	SO	ShO	Relief Pitching W	Relief Pitching L	Relief Pitching SV	Batting AB	Batting H	Batting HR	BA	PO	A	E	DP	TC/G	FA
1898	LOU N	0	1	.000	3.00	1	1	1	9	10	5	1	0	0	0	0	4	0	0	.000	0	1	0	0	1.0	1.000

Roy Mahaffey

MAHAFFEY, LEE ROY (Popeye) BR TR 6′ 180 lbs.
B. Feb. 9, 1903, Belton, S. C. D. July 23, 1969, Anderson, S. C.

Year	Team	W	L	PCT	ERA	G	GS	CG	IP	H	BB	SO	ShO	Relief Pitching W	Relief Pitching L	Relief Pitching SV	Batting AB	Batting H	Batting HR	BA	PO	A	E	DP	TC/G	FA
1926	PIT N	0	0	—	0.00	4	0	0	4.2	5	1	3	0	0	0	0	2	0	0	.000	0	0	1	0	0.3	.000
1927		1	0	1.000	7.71	2	1	0	9.1	9	9	4	0	0	0	0	5	2	0	.400	0	1	0	0	0.5	1.000
1930	PHI A	9	5	.643	5.01	33	16	6	152.2	186	53	38	0	0	0	0	59	7	1	.119	5	25	2	4	1.0	.938
1931		15	4	.789	4.21	30	20	8	162.1	161	82	59	0	3	0	2	63	12	2	.190	4	19	1	0	0.8	.958
1932		13	13	.500	5.09	37	28	13	222.2	245	96	106	0	2	3	0	87	15	1	.172	11	35	3	3	1.3	.939
1933		13	10	.565	5.17	33	23	9	179.1	198	74	66	0	2	2	0	65	14	0	.215	7	29	1	1	1.1	.973
1934		6	7	.462	5.37	37	14	3	129	142	55	37	0	2	0	2	48	13	0	.271	5	19	2	0	0.7	.923
1935		8	4	.667	3.90	27	17	5	136	153	42	39	0	2	0	0	51	9	0	.176	2	21	1	3	0.9	.958
1936	STL A	2	6	.250	8.10	21	9	1	60	82	40	13	0	1	0	1	16	1	0	.063	0	3	1	0	0.2	.750
9 yrs.		67	49	.578	5.01	224	128	45	1056	1181	452	365	0	12	5	5	396	73	4	.184	34	152	12	11	0.9	.939
WORLD SERIES																										
1931	PHI A	0	0	—	9.00	1	0	0	1	1	1	0	0	0	0	0	0	0	0	—	0	1	0	0	1.0	1.000

Art Mahan

MAHAN, ARTHUR LEO BL TL 5′11″ 178 lbs.
B. June 8, 1913, Somerville, Mass.

Year	Team	W	L	PCT	ERA	G	GS	CG	IP	H	BB	SO	ShO	Relief Pitching W	Relief Pitching L	Relief Pitching SV	Batting AB	Batting H	Batting HR	BA	PO	A	E	DP	TC/G	FA
1940	PHI N	0	0	—	0.00	1	0	0	1	1	0	0	0	0	0	0	*				1380	102	12	120	10.2	.992

Mickey Mahler

MAHLER, MICHAEL JAMES BB TL 6′ 3″ 189 lbs.
Brother of Rick Mahler.
B. July 30, 1952, Montgomery, Ala.

Year	Team	W	L	PCT	ERA	G	GS	CG	IP	H	BB	SO	ShO	Relief Pitching W	Relief Pitching L	Relief Pitching SV	Batting AB	Batting H	Batting HR	BA	PO	A	E	DP	TC/G	FA
1977	ATL N	1	2	.333	6.26	5	5	0	23	31	9	14	0	0	0	0	6	3	0	.500	0	3	1	1	0.8	.750
1978		4	11	.267	4.67	34	21	1	135	130	66	92	0	0	0	0	41	4	0	.098	4	15	0	1	0.6	1.000
1979		5	11	.313	5.85	26	18	1	100	123	47	71	0	2	0	0	27	3	0	.111	4	13	1	1	0.7	.944
1980	PIT N	0	0	—	63.00	2	0	0	1	4	3	1	0	0	0	0	0	0	0	—	0	0	0	0	0.0	.000
1981	CAL A	0	0	—	0.00	6	0	0	6	1	2	5	0	0	0	0	0	0	0	—	0	1	0	0	0.2	1.000
1982		2	0	1.000	1.13	6	0	0	8	9	6	5	0	2	0	0	0	0	0	—	0	1	0	0	0.2	1.000
1985	2 teams MON N (9G 1–4) DET A (3G 1–2)																									
″	total	2	6	.250	3.00	12	9	1	69	59	28	46	1	1	0	1	16	3	0	.188	2	6	2	2	0.8	.800
1986	2 teams TEX A (29G 0–2) TOR A (2G 0–0)																									
″	total	0	2	.000	4.08	31	5	0	64	72	29	28	0	0	0	3	0	0	0		3	9	0	2	0.4	1.000
8 yrs.		14	32	.304	4.68	122	58	3	406	429	190	262	1	5	0	4	90	13	0	.144	13	48	4	7	0.5	.938

Rick Mahler

MAHLER, RICHARD KEITH BR TR 6′ 1″ 195 lbs.
Brother of Mickey Mahler.
B. Aug. 5, 1953, Austin, Tex.

Year	Team	Lg	W	L	PCT	ERA	G	GS	CG	IP	H	BB	SO	ShO	Relief Pitching W	Relief Pitching L	Relief Pitching SV	Batting AB	Batting H	Batting HR	BA	PO	A	E	DP	TC/G	FA
1979	ATL	N	0	0	—	6.14	15	0	0	22	28	11	12	0	0	0	0	2	1	0	.500	1	3	1	0	0.3	.800
1980			0	0	—	2.25	2	0	0	4	2	0	1	0	0	0	0	0	0	0	—	0	1	0	0	0.5	1.000
1981			8	6	.571	2.81	34	14	1	112	109	43	54	0	2	0	2	27	4	0	.148	14	19	2	0	1.0	.943
1982			9	10	.474	4.21	39	33	5	205.1	213	62	105	2	0	0	0	58	11	1	.190	19	36	1	5	1.4	.982
1983			0	0	—	5.02	10	0	0	14.1	16	9	7	0	0	0	0	2	0	0	.000	1	1	1	1	0.3	.667
1984			13	10	.565	3.12	38	29	9	222	209	62	106	1	0	0	0	71	21	0	.296	20	42	2	5	1.7	.969
1985			17	15	.531	3.48	39	**39**	6	266.2	**272**	79	107	1	0	0	0	90	14	0	.156	21	45	4	9	1.8	.943
1986			14	**18**	.438	4.88	39	**39**	7	237.2	**283**	95	137	1	0	0	0	83	16	0	.193	23	41	3	2	1.7	.955
1987			8	13	.381	4.98	39	28	3	197	212	85	95	1	2	1	0	65	11	0	.169	13	42	1	2	1.4	.982
1988			9	16	.360	3.69	39	34	5	249	**279**	42	131	0	2	0	0	72	9	0	.125	22	43	3	4	1.7	.956
1989	CIN	N	9	13	.409	3.83	40	31	5	220.2	**242**	51	102	2	0	0	0	62	11	0	.177	8	35	1	2	1.1	.977
1990			7	6	.538	4.28	35	16	2	134.2	134	39	68	1	1	1	4	35	4	0	.114	11	17	1	1	0.8	.966
1991	2 teams	MON N	(10G 1–3)		ATL N	(13G 1–1)																					
″	total		2	4	.333	4.50	23	8	0	66	70	28	27	0	0	1	0	14	2	0	.143	7	13	1	0	0.9	.952
13 yrs.			96	111	.464	3.99	392	271	43	1951.1	2069	606	952	9	7	3	6	581	104	1	.179	160	338	21	31	1.3	.960
LEAGUE CHAMPIONSHIP SERIES																											
1982	ATL	N	0	0	—	0.00	1	0	0	1.2	3	2	0	0	0	0	0	0	0	0	—	0	1	0	0	1.0	1.000
1990	CIN	N	0	0	—	0.00	1	0	0	1.2	2	0	0	0	0	0	0	0	0	0	—	0	0	0	0	0.0	.000
2 yrs.			0	0		0.00	2	0	0	3.1	5	2	0	0	0	0	0	0	0	0		0	1	0	0	0.5	1.000

Pat Mahomes

MAHOMES, PATRICK LAVON BR TR 6′ 1″ 175 lbs.
B. Aug. 9, 1970, Bryan, Tex.

Year	Team	Lg	W	L	PCT	ERA	G	GS	CG	IP	H	BB	SO	ShO	Relief Pitching W	Relief Pitching L	Relief Pitching SV	Batting AB	Batting H	Batting HR	BA	PO	A	E	DP	TC/G	FA
1992	MIN	A	3	4	.429	5.04	14	13	0	69.2	73	37	44	0	0	0	0	0	0	0	—	5	4	0	0	0.6	1.000
1993			1	5	.167	7.71	12	5	0	37.1	47	16	23	0	1	0	0	0	0	0	—	4	4	0	1	0.7	1.000
1994			9	5	.643	4.72	21	21	0	120	121	62	53	0	0	0	0	0	0	0	—	11	12	1	2	1.1	.958
1995			4	10	.286	6.37	47	7	0	94.2	100	47	67	0	4	6	3	0	0	0	—	11	9	0	3	0.4	1.000
4 yrs.			17	24	.415	5.62	94	46	0	321.2	341	162	187	0	5	6	3	0	0	0		31	29	1	6	0.6	.984

Al Mahon

MAHON, ALFRED GWINN (Lefty) BL TL 5′11″ 160 lbs.
B. Sept. 23, 1909, Albion, Neb. D. Dec. 26, 1977, New Haven, Conn.

Year	Team	Lg	W	L	PCT	ERA	G	GS	CG	IP	H	BB	SO	ShO	Relief Pitching W	Relief Pitching L	Relief Pitching SV	Batting AB	Batting H	Batting HR	BA	PO	A	E	DP	TC/G	FA
1930	PHI	A	0	0	—	22.85	3	0	0	4.1	11	7	0	0	0	0	0	1	0	0	.000	0	2	0	0	0.7	1.000

Bob Mahoney

MAHONEY, ROBERT PAUL BR TR 6′ 1″ 185 lbs.
B. June 20, 1928, LeRoy, Minn.

Year	Team	Lg	W	L	PCT	ERA	G	GS	CG	IP	H	BB	SO	ShO	Relief Pitching W	Relief Pitching L	Relief Pitching SV	Batting AB	Batting H	Batting HR	BA	PO	A	E	DP	TC/G	FA
1951	2 teams	CHI A	(3G 0–0)		STL A	(30G 2–5)																					
″	total		2	5	.286	4.52	33	4	0	87.2	91	46	33	0	2	2	0	18	4	0	.222	4	12	1	2	0.5	.941
1952	STL	A	0	0	—	18.00	3	0	0	3	8	4	1	0	0	0	0	0	0	0	—	0	0	0	0	0.0	.000
2 yrs.			2	5	.286	4.96	36	4	0	90.2	99	50	34	0	2	2	0	18	4	0	.222	4	12	1	2	0.5	.941

Chris Mahoney

MAHONEY, CHRISTOPHER JOHN BR TR 5′ 9″ 160 lbs.
B. June 11, 1885, Milton, Mass. D. July 15, 1954, Visalia, Calif.

Year	Team	Lg	W	L	PCT	ERA	G	GS	CG	IP	H	BB	SO	ShO	Relief Pitching W	Relief Pitching L	Relief Pitching SV	Batting AB	Batting H	Batting HR	BA	PO	A	E	DP	TC/G	FA
1910	BOS	A	0	1	.000	3.27	2	1	0	11	16	5	6	0	0	0	1	7	1	0	.143	1	6	0	1	2.3	1.000

Mike Mahoney

MAHONEY, GEORGE W. BR 6′ 4″ 220 lbs.
B. Dec. 5, 1873, Boston, Mass. D. Jan. 3, 1940, Boston, Mass.

Year	Team	Lg	W	L	PCT	ERA	G	GS	CG	IP	H	BB	SO	ShO	Relief Pitching W	Relief Pitching L	Relief Pitching SV	Batting AB	Batting H	Batting HR	BA	PO	A	E	DP	TC/G	FA
1897	BOS	N	0	0	—	18.00	1	0	0	1	3	1	1	0	0	0	0	*				1	1	0	0	1.0	1.000

Duster Mails

MAILS, JOHN WALTER (The Great) BL TL 6′ 195 lbs.
B. Oct. 1, 1894, San Quentin, Calif. D. July 5, 1974, San Francisco, Calif.

Year	Team	Lg	W	L	PCT	ERA	G	GS	CG	IP	H	BB	SO	ShO	Relief Pitching W	Relief Pitching L	Relief Pitching SV	Batting AB	Batting H	Batting HR	BA	PO	A	E	DP	TC/G	FA
1915	BKN	N	0	1	.000	3.60	2	0	0	5	6	5	3	0	0	1	0	1	0	0	.000	0	2	0	0	1.0	1.000
1916			0	1	.000	3.63	11	0	0	17.1	15	9	13	0	0	1	0	4	1	0	.250	0	2	0	0	0.2	1.000
1920	CLE	A	7	0	1.000	1.85	9	8	6	63.1	54	18	25	2	0	0	0	20	4	0	.200	3	10	0	0	1.4	1.000
1921			14	8	.636	3.94	34	24	10	194.1	210	89	87	2	2	1	2	64	6	0	.094	7	33	2	0	1.2	.952
1922			4	7	.364	5.28	26	13	4	104	122	40	54	1	1	1	0	31	5	0	.161	6	24	0	1	1.2	1.000
1925	STL	N	7	7	.500	4.60	21	16	9	131	145	58	49	0	0	1	0	45	6	0	.133	4	24	3	1	1.5	.903
1926			0	1	.000	0.00	1	0	0	1	2	1	1	0	0	1	0	0	0	0	—	0	1	1	0	2.0	.500
7 yrs.			32	25	.561	4.10	104	61	29	516	554	220	232	5	3	6	2	165	22	0	.133	20	96	6	2	1.2	.951
WORLD SERIES																											
1920	CLE	A	1	0	1.000	0.00	2	1	1	15.2	6	6	6	1	0	0	0	5	0	0	.000	1	4	0	1	2.5	1.000

Alex Main

MAIN, MILES GRANT BL TR 6′ 5″ 195 lbs.
B. May 13, 1884, Montrose, Mich. D. Dec. 29, 1965, Royal Oak, Mich.

Year	Team	Lg	W	L	PCT	ERA	G	GS	CG	IP	H	BB	SO	ShO	Relief Pitching W	Relief Pitching L	Relief Pitching SV	Batting AB	Batting H	Batting HR	BA	PO	A	E	DP	TC/G	FA
1914	DET	A	6	6	.500	2.67	32	12	5	138.1	131	59	55	1	1	1	3	40	4	0	.100	6	60	4	5	2.2	.943
1915	KC	F	13	14	.481	2.54	35	28	18	230	181	75	91	2	1	0	3	76	15	0	.197	8	86	5	3	2.8	.949
1918	PHI	N	2	2	.500	4.63	8	4	1	35	30	16	14	1	0	0	0	11	1	0	.091	1	10	0	1	1.4	1.000
3 yrs.			21	22	.488	2.77	75	44	24	403.1	342	150	160	4	2	1	6	127	20	0	.157	15	156	9	9	2.4	.950

Woody Main

MAIN, FORREST HARRY BR TR 6′ 3½″ 195 lbs.
B. Feb. 12, 1922, Delano, Calif. D. June 27, 1992, Whittier, Calif.

Year	Team	Lg	W	L	PCT	ERA	G	GS	CG	IP	H	BB	SO	ShO	Relief Pitching W	Relief Pitching L	Relief Pitching SV	Batting AB	Batting H	Batting HR	BA	PO	A	E	DP	TC/G	FA
1948	PIT	N	1	1	.500	8.33	17	0	0	27	35	19	12	0	1	1	0	2	0	0	.000	2	6	0	0	0.5	1.000
1950			1	0	1.000	4.87	12	0	0	20.1	21	11	12	0	1	0	1	5	2	0	.400	1	4	0	0	0.4	1.000
1952			2	12	.143	4.46	48	11	2	153.1	149	52	79	0	0	7	2	37	2	0	.054	8	15	4	0	0.6	.852
1953			0	0	—	11.25	2	0	0	4	5	2	4	0	0	0	0	0	0	0	—	0	0	0	0	0.0	.000
4 yrs.			4	13	.235	5.14	79	11	2	204.2	210	84	107	0	2	8	3	44	4	0	.091	11	25	4	0	0.5	.900

Jim Mains

MAINS, JAMES ROYAL BR TR 6′ 2″ 190 lbs.
B. June 12, 1922, Bridgton, Me. D. Mar. 17, 1969, Bridgton, Me.

Year	Team	Lg	W	L	PCT	ERA	G	GS	CG	IP	H	BB	SO	ShO	Relief Pitching W	Relief Pitching L	Relief Pitching SV	Batting AB	Batting H	Batting HR	BA	PO	A	E	DP	TC/G	FA
1943	PHI	A	0	1	.000	5.63	1	1	1	8	9	3	4	0	0	0	0	2	0	0	.000	0	1	0	0	1.0	1.000

Willard Mains

MAINS, WILLARD EBEN (Grasshopper) TR 6′ 2″ 190 lbs.
B. July 7, 1868, North Windham, Me. D. May 23, 1923, Bridgton, Me.

Year	Team	Lg	W	L	PCT	ERA	G	GS	CG	IP	H	BB	SO	ShO	Relief W	Relief L	Relief SV	Batting AB	Batting H	HR	BA	PO	A	E	DP	TC/G	FA
1888	CHI	N	1	1	.500	4.91	2	2	1	11	8	6	5	0	0	0	0	7	1	0	.143	0	2	1	0	1.0	.667
1891	2 teams	CIN AA (30G 12–12) MIL AA (2G 0–2)																									
"	total		12	14	.462	3.07	32	25	20	214	210	117	78	0	1	**2**	0	95	25	1	.263	4	70	7	1	2.5	.914
1896	BOS	N	3	2	.600	5.48	8	5	3	42.2	43	31	13	0	0	0	1	22	6	0	.273	2	9	0	0	1.4	1.000
3 yrs.			16	17	.485	3.53	42	32	24	267.2	261	154	96	0	1	2	1	124	32	1	.258	6	81	8	1	2.2	.916

Frank Makosky

MAKOSKY, FRANK (Dins) BR TR 6′ 1″ 185 lbs.
B. Jan. 20, 1910, Boonton, N. J. D. Jan. 10, 1987, Stroudsburg, Pa.

Year	Team	Lg	W	L	PCT	ERA	G	GS	CG	IP	H	BB	SO	ShO	Relief W	Relief L	Relief SV	Batting AB	Batting H	HR	BA	PO	A	E	DP	TC/G	FA
1937	NY	A	5	2	.714	4.97	26	1	1	58	64	24	27	0	5	1	3	16	5	0	.313	3	21	0	0	0.9	1.000

Tom Makowski

MAKOWSKI, THOMAS ANTHONY BR TL 5′11″ 185 lbs.
B. Dec. 22, 1950, Buffalo, N. Y.

Year	Team	Lg	W	L	PCT	ERA	G	GS	CG	IP	H	BB	SO	ShO	Relief W	Relief L	Relief SV	Batting AB	Batting H	HR	BA	PO	A	E	DP	TC/G	FA
1975	DET	A	0	0	—	4.82	3	0	0	9.1	10	9	3	0	0	0	0	0	0	0	—	0	4	1	0	1.7	.800

Bill Malarkey

MALARKEY, WILLIAM JOHN BR TR 5′10″ 185 lbs.
B. Nov. 26, 1878, Port Byron, Ill. D. Dec. 12, 1956, Phoenix, Ariz.

Year	Team	Lg	W	L	PCT	ERA	G	GS	CG	IP	H	BB	SO	ShO	Relief W	Relief L	Relief SV	Batting AB	Batting H	HR	BA	PO	A	E	DP	TC/G	FA
1908	NY	N	0	2	.000	2.57	15	0	0	35	31	10	12	0	0	2	1	6	0	0	.000	1	9	1	0	0.7	.909

John Malarkey

MALARKEY, JOHN S. TR 5′11″ 155 lbs.
B. May 4, 1872, Springfield, Ohio D. Oct. 29, 1949, Cincinnati, Ohio.

Year	Team	Lg	W	L	PCT	ERA	G	GS	CG	IP	H	BB	SO	ShO	Relief W	Relief L	Relief SV	Batting AB	Batting H	HR	BA	PO	A	E	DP	TC/G	FA
1894	WAS	N	2	1	.667	4.15	3	3	3	26	42	5	3	0	0	0	0	14	1	0	.071	1	1	1	0	0.8	.667
1895			0	8	.000	5.99	22	8	5	100.2	135	60	32	0	0	1	2	37	5	0	.135	3	15	1	0	0.9	.947
1896			0	1	.000	1.29	1	1	0	7	9	3	0	0	0	0	0	2	1	0	.500	2	1	0	0	3.0	1.000
1899	CHI	N	0	1	.000	13.00	1	1	1	9	19	5	7	0	0	0	0	5	1	0	.200	0	4	0	0	4.0	1.000
1902	BOS	N	8	10	.444	2.59	21	19	17	170.1	158	58	39	1	1	0	1	62	13	1	.210	8	59	8	1	3.4	.893
1903			11	16	.407	3.09	32	27	25	253	266	96	98	2	0	**2**	0	87	14	0	.161	16	75	11	5	3.2	.892
6 yrs.			21	37	.362	3.64	80	59	51	566	629	227	179	3	1	3	3	207	35	1	.169	30	155	21	6	2.5	.898

Carlos Maldonado

MALDONADO, CARLOS CESAR BB TR 6′ 2″ 175 lbs.
Born Carlos Cesar Maldonado (Delgado).
B. Oct. 18, 1966, Chepo, Panama.

Year	Team	Lg	W	L	PCT	ERA	G	GS	CG	IP	H	BB	SO	ShO	Relief W	Relief L	Relief SV	Batting AB	Batting H	HR	BA	PO	A	E	DP	TC/G	FA
1990	KC	A	0	0	—	9.00	4	0	0	6	9	4	9	0	0	0	0	0	0	0	—	0	0	0	0	0.0	.000
1991			0	0	—	8.22	5	0	0	7.2	11	9	1	0	0	0	0	0	0	0	—	0	0	1	0	0.2	.000
1993	MIL	A	2	2	.500	4.58	29	0	0	37.1	40	17	18	0	2	2	1	0	0	0	—	3	5	1	1	0.3	.889
3 yrs.			2	2	.500	5.65	38	0	0	51	60	30	28	0	2	2	1	0	0	0		3	5	2	1	0.3	.800

Cy Malis

MALIS, CYRUS SOL BR TR 5′11″ 175 lbs.
B. Feb. 26, 1907, Philadelphia, Pa. D. Jan. 12, 1971, North Hollywood, Calif.

Year	Team	Lg	W	L	PCT	ERA	G	GS	CG	IP	H	BB	SO	ShO	Relief W	Relief L	Relief SV	Batting AB	Batting H	HR	BA	PO	A	E	DP	TC/G	FA
1934	PHI	N	0	0	—	4.91	1	0	0	3.2	4	2	1	0	0	0	0	0	0	0	—	1	0	0	0	1.0	1.000

Mal Mallette

MALLETTE, MALCOLM FRANCIS BL TL 6′ 2″ 200 lbs.
B. Jan. 30, 1922, Syracuse, N. Y.

Year	Team	Lg	W	L	PCT	ERA	G	GS	CG	IP	H	BB	SO	ShO	Relief W	Relief L	Relief SV	Batting AB	Batting H	HR	BA	PO	A	E	DP	TC/G	FA
1950	BKN	N	0	0	—	0.00	2	0	0	1.1	2	1	2	0	0	0	0	0	0	0	—	0	0	0	0	0.0	.000

Rob Mallicoat

MALLICOAT, ROBBIN DALE BL TL 6′ 3″ 180 lbs.
B. Nov. 16, 1964, St. Helens, Ore.

Year	Team	Lg	W	L	PCT	ERA	G	GS	CG	IP	H	BB	SO	ShO	Relief W	Relief L	Relief SV	Batting AB	Batting H	HR	BA	PO	A	E	DP	TC/G	FA
1987	HOU	N	0	0	—	6.75	4	1	0	6.2	8	6	4	0	0	0	0	0	0	0	—	1	1	0	0	0.5	1.000
1991			0	2	.000	3.86	24	0	0	23.1	22	13	18	0	0	2	1	1	0	0	.000	1	0	1	0	0.1	.500
1992			0	0	—	7.23	23	0	0	23.2	26	19	20	0	0	0	0	1	0	0	.000	0	3	0	0	0.1	1.000
3 yrs.			0	2	.000	5.70	51	1	0	53.2	56	38	42	0	0	2	1	2	0	0	.000	2	4	1	0	0.1	.857

Alex Malloy

MALLOY, ARCHIBALD ALEXANDER (Lick) BR TR 6′ 2″ 180 lbs.
B. Oct. 31, 1886, Laurinburg, N. C. D. Mar. 1, 1961, Ferris, Tex.

Year	Team	Lg	W	L	PCT	ERA	G	GS	CG	IP	H	BB	SO	ShO	Relief W	Relief L	Relief SV	Batting AB	Batting H	HR	BA	PO	A	E	DP	TC/G	FA
1910	STL	A	0	6	.000	2.56	7	6	4	52.2	47	17	27	0	0	0	0	16	1	0	.063	2	17	2	1	3.0	.905

Bob Malloy

MALLOY, ROBERT PAUL BR TR 5′11″ 185 lbs.
B. May 28, 1918, Canonsburg, Pa.

Year	Team	Lg	W	L	PCT	ERA	G	GS	CG	IP	H	BB	SO	ShO	Relief W	Relief L	Relief SV	Batting AB	Batting H	HR	BA	PO	A	E	DP	TC/G	FA
1943	CIN	N	0	0	—	6.30	6	0	0	10	14	8	4	0	0	0	0	3	2	0	.667	0	1	0	0	0.2	1.000
1944			1	1	.500	3.09	9	0	0	23.1	22	11	4	0	1	1	0	7	0	0	.000	1	6	0	1	0.8	1.000
1946			2	5	.286	2.75	27	3	1	72	71	26	24	0	1	4	2	18	5	0	.278	0	13	4	1	0.6	.765
1947			0	0	—	18.00	1	0	0	1	3	0	1	0	0	0	0	0	0	0	—	0	0	0	0	0.0	.000
1949	STL	A	1	1	.500	2.79	5	0	0	9.2	6	7	2	0	1	1	0	3	0	0	.000	2	1	0	0	0.6	1.000
5 yrs.			4	7	.364	3.26	48	3	1	116	116	52	35	0	3	6	2	31	7	0	.226	3	21	4	2	0.6	.857

Bob Malloy

MALLOY, ROBERT WILLIAM BR TR 6′ 5″ 200 lbs.
B. Nov. 24, 1964, Garland, Tex.

Year	Team	Lg	W	L	PCT	ERA	G	GS	CG	IP	H	BB	SO	ShO	Relief W	Relief L	Relief SV	Batting AB	Batting H	HR	BA	PO	A	E	DP	TC/G	FA
1987	TEX	A	0	0	—	6.55	2	2	0	11	13	3	8	0	0	0	0	0	0	0	—	0	1	0	0	0.5	1.000
1990	MON	N	0	0	—	0.00	1	0	0	2	1	1	1	0	0	0	0	0	0	0	—	0	0	0	0	0.0	.000
2 yrs.			0	0		5.54	3	2	0	13	14	4	9	0	0	0	0	0	0	0		0	1	0	0	0.3	1.000

Herm Malloy

MALLOY, HERMAN BR TR 6′
B. June 1, 1885, Massillon, Ohio D. May 9, 1942, Nimishillen, Ohio.

Year	Team	Lg	W	L	PCT	ERA	G	GS	CG	IP	H	BB	SO	ShO	Relief W	Relief L	Relief SV	Batting AB	Batting H	HR	BA	PO	A	E	DP	TC/G	FA
1907	DET	A	0	1	.000	5.63	1	1	1	8	13	5	6	0	0	0	0	4	0	0	.000	0	2	0	0	2.0	1.000
1908			0	2	.000	3.71	3	2	2	17	20	4	8	0	0	0	0	9	3	0	.333	2	10	1	0	4.3	.923
2 yrs.			0	3	.000	4.32	4	3	3	25	33	9	14	0	0	0	0	13	3	0	.231	2	12	1	0	3.8	.933

Chuck Malone

MALONE, CHARLES RAY BR TR 6′ 7″ 250 lbs.
B. June 8, 1965, Harrisburg, Ark.

Year	Team	Lg	W	L	PCT	ERA	G	GS	CG	IP	H	BB	SO	ShO	Relief W	Relief L	Relief SV	Batting AB	Batting H	HR	BA	PO	A	E	DP	TC/G	FA
1990	PHI	N	1	0	1.000	3.68	7	0	0	7.1	3	11	7	0	1	0	0	0	0	0	—	0	0	0	0	0.0	.000

Pat Malone

MALONE, PERCE LEIGH BL TR 6′ 200 lbs.
BB 1935–1937
B. Sept. 25, 1902, Altoona, Pa. D. May 13, 1943, Altoona, Pa.

Year	Team	Lg	W	L	PCT	ERA	G	GS	CG	IP	H	BB	SO	ShO	Relief W	Relief L	Relief SV	Batting AB	Batting H	HR	BA	PO	A	E	DP	TC/G	FA
1928	CHI	N	18	13	.581	2.84	42	25	16	250.2	218	99	155	2	2	4	2	95	18	1	.189	5	54	3	2	1.5	.952
1929			**22**	10	.688	3.57	40	30	19	267	283	102	**166**	**5**	4	1	2	105	22	2	.210	10	35	1	5	1.1	.978

Pat Malone *continued*

Year	Team		W	L	PCT	ERA	G	GS	CG	IP	H	BB	SO	ShO	Relief Pitching W	L	SV	Batting AB	H	HR	BA	PO	A	E	DP	TC/G	FA
1930			**20**	9	.690	3.94	45	35	**22**	271.2	290	96	142	2	1	1	4	105	26	4	.248	16	40	1	1	1.3	.982
1931			16	9	.640	3.90	36	30	12	228.1	229	88	112	2	3	0	0	79	17	1	.215	6	46	2	2	1.5	.963
1932			15	17	.469	3.38	37	33	17	237	222	78	120	2	1	1	0	78	14	1	.179	8	33	2	1	1.2	.953
1933			10	14	.417	3.91	31	26	13	186.1	186	59	72	2	2	0	0	63	10	0	.159	11	35	2	1	1.5	.958
1934			14	7	.667	3.53	34	21	8	191	200	55	111	1	2	0	0	64	11	0	.172	4	32	0	1	1.1	1.000
1935	NY	A	3	5	.375	5.43	29	2	0	56.1	53	33	25	0	3	4	3	15	0	0	.000	1	10	2	1	0.4	.846
1936			12	4	.750	3.81	35	9	5	134.2	144	60	72	0	**8**	2	**9**	51	10	0	.196	1	17	1	0	0.5	.947
1937			4	4	.500	5.48	28	9	3	92	109	35	49	0	1	3	6	33	1	0	.030	1	9	0	0	0.4	1.000
10 yrs.			134	92	.593	3.74	357	220	115	1915	1934	705	1024	16	27	16	26	688	129	9	.188	63	311	14	14	1.1	.964
WORLD SERIES																											
1929	CHI	N	0	2	.000	4.15	3	2	1	13	12	7	11	0	0	0	0	4	1	0	.250	0	1	0	0	0.3	1.000
1932			0	0	—	0.00	1	0	0	2.2	1	4	4	0	0	0	0	0	0	0	—	0	0	0	0	0.0	.000
1936	NY	A	0	1	.000	1.80	2	0	0	5	2	1	2	0	0	1	1	1	1	0	1.000	0	2	0	0	1.0	1.000
3 yrs.			0	3	.000	3.05	6	2	1	20.2	15	12	17	0	0	1	1	5	2	0	.400	0	3	0	0	0.5	1.000

Charlie Maloney

MALONEY, CHARLES MICHAEL
B. May 22, 1886, Cambridge, Mass. D. Jan. 17, 1967, Arlington, Mass.
BR TR 5′ 8″ 155 lbs.

Year	Team		W	L	PCT	ERA	G	GS	CG	IP	H	BB	SO	ShO	Relief Pitching W	L	SV	Batting AB	H	HR	BA	PO	A	E	DP	TC/G	FA
1908	BOS	N	0	0	—	4.50	1	0	0	2	3	1	0	0	0	0	0	0	0	0	—	0	1	0	0	1.0	1.000

Jim Maloney

MALONEY, JAMES WILLIAM
B. June 2, 1940, Fresno, Calif.
BL TR 6′ 2″ 190 lbs.

Year	Team		W	L	PCT	ERA	G	GS	CG	IP	H	BB	SO	ShO	Relief Pitching W	L	SV	Batting AB	H	HR	BA	PO	A	E	DP	TC/G	FA
1960	CIN	N	2	6	.250	4.66	11	10	2	63.2	61	37	48	1	0	0	0	18	2	0	.111	3	9	0	1	1.1	1.000
1961			6	7	.462	4.37	27	11	1	94.2	86	59	57	0	1	3	2	29	11	1	.379	6	13	1	0	0.7	.950
1962			9	7	.563	3.51	22	17	3	115.1	90	66	105	0	2	0	1	43	8	0	.186	7	10	2	1	0.9	.895
1963			23	7	.767	2.77	33	33	13	250.1	183	88	265	6	0	0	0	89	15	0	.169	8	30	3	1	1.2	.927
1964			15	10	.600	2.71	31	31	11	216	175	83	214	2	0	0	0	73	11	1	.151	10	23	2	1	1.1	.943
1965			20	9	.690	2.54	33	33	14	255.1	189	110	244	5	0	0	0	89	20	0	.225	18	33	1	0	1.6	.981
1966			16	8	.667	2.80	32	32	10	224.2	174	90	216	**5**	0	0	0	81	18	0	.222	12	29	2	3	1.3	.953
1967			15	11	.577	3.25	30	29	6	196.1	181	72	153	3	0	1	0	69	11	0	.159	7	29	1	0	1.2	.973
1968			16	10	.615	3.61	33	32	8	207	183	80	181	5	1	0	0	74	18	2	.243	16	21	2	1	1.2	.949
1969			12	5	.706	2.77	30	27	6	179	135	86	102	3	0	0	0	55	11	3	.200	13	25	1	2	1.3	.974
1970			0	1	.000	11.12	7	3	0	17	26	15	7	0	0	0	1	3	0	0	.000	0	5	0	0	0.7	1.000
1971	CAL	A	0	3	.000	5.10	13	4	0	30	35	24	13	0	0	0	0	5	1	0	.200	1	5	0	0	0.5	1.000
12 yrs.			134	84	.615	3.19	302	262	74	1849.1	1518	810	1605	30	4	4	4	628	126	7	.201	101	232	15	10	1.1	.957
WORLD SERIES																											
1961	CIN	N	0	0	—	27.00	1	0	0	0.2	4	1	1	0	0	0	0	0	0	0	—	0	0	0	0	0.0	.000

Paul Maloy

MALOY, PAUL AUGUSTUS (Biff)
B. June 4, 1892, Bascom, Ohio D. Mar. 18, 1976, Sandusky, Ohio.
BR TR 5′11″ 185 lbs.

Year	Team		W	L	PCT	ERA	G	GS	CG	IP	H	BB	SO	ShO	Relief Pitching W	L	SV	Batting AB	H	HR	BA	PO	A	E	DP	TC/G	FA
1913	BOS	A	0	0	—	9.00	2	0	0	2	2	1	0	0	0	0	0	0	0	0	—	0	0	1	0	0.5	.000

Gordon Maltzberger

MALTZBERGER, GORDON RALPH (Maltzy)
B. Sept. 4, 1912, Utopia, Tex. D. Dec. 11, 1974, Rialto, Calif.
BR TR 6′ 170 lbs.

Year	Team		W	L	PCT	ERA	G	GS	CG	IP	H	BB	SO	ShO	Relief Pitching W	L	SV	Batting AB	H	HR	BA	PO	A	E	DP	TC/G	FA
1943	CHI	A	7	4	.636	2.46	37	0	0	98.2	86	24	48	0	7	4	**14**	25	3	0	.120	5	20	0	2	0.7	1.000
1944			10	5	.667	2.96	46	0	0	91.1	81	19	49	0	**10**	5	**12**	22	3	0	.136	1	16	2	0	0.4	.895
1946			2	0	1.000	1.59	19	0	0	39.2	30	6	17	0	2	0	2	6	0	0	.000	1	4	0	1	0.3	1.000
1947			1	4	.200	3.39	33	0	0	63.2	61	25	22	0	1	4	5	7	1	0	.143	4	14	0	1	0.5	1.000
4 yrs.			20	13	.606	2.70	135	0	0	293.1	258	74	136	0	20	13	33	60	7	0	.117	11	54	2	4	0.5	.970

Al Mamaux

MAMAUX, ALBERT LEON
B. May 30, 1894, Pittsburgh, Pa. D. Jan. 2, 1963, Santa Monica, Calif.
BR TR 6′½″ 168 lbs.

Year	Team		W	L	PCT	ERA	G	GS	CG	IP	H	BB	SO	ShO	Relief Pitching W	L	SV	Batting AB	H	HR	BA	PO	A	E	DP	TC/G	FA
1913	PIT	N	0	0	—	3.00	1	0	0	3	2	2	2	0	0	0	0	1	0	0	.000	0	1	0	0	1.0	1.000
1914			5	2	.714	1.71	13	6	4	63	41	24	30	2	1	1	0	20	5	0	.250	4	23	2	0	2.2	.931
1915			21	8	.724	2.04	38	31	17	251.2	182	96	152	8	3	0	0	92	15	0	.163	5	48	2	2	1.4	.964
1916			21	15	.583	2.53	45	37	26	310	264	**136**	163	1	1	0	2	110	21	0	.191	7	82	1	1	2.0	.989
1917			2	11	.154	5.25	16	13	5	85.2	92	50	22	0	0	1	0	31	7	0	.226	3	20	1	0	1.5	.958
1918	BKN	N	0	1	.000	6.75	2	1	0	8	14	2	2	0	0	0	0	2	0	0	.000	0	6	0	0	3.0	1.000
1919			10	12	.455	2.66	30	22	16	199.1	174	66	80	2	1	0	0	63	11	0	.175	4	56	3	0	2.1	.952
1920			12	8	.600	2.69	41	17	9	190.2	172	63	101	2	5	1	4	60	10	0	.167	6	46	3	1	1.3	.945
1921			3	3	.500	3.14	12	1	0	43	36	13	21	0	3	2	1	11	2	0	.182	1	14	1	0	1.3	.938
1922			1	4	.200	3.70	37	7	1	87.2	97	33	35	0	0	2	3	17	4	1	.235	2	22	0	0	0.6	1.000
1923			0	2	.000	8.31	5	1	0	13	20	6	5	0	0	1	0	2	1	0	.500	0	3	0	1	0.6	1.000
1924	NY	A	1	1	.500	5.68	14	2	0	38	44	20	12	0	0	1	0	13	1	0	.077	1	6	2	0	0.6	.778
12 yrs.			76	67	.531	2.90	254	138	78	1293	1138	511	625	15	14	9	10	422	77	1	.182	33	327	15	5	1.5	.960
WORLD SERIES																											
1920	BKN	N	0	0	—	4.50	3	0	0	4	2	0	5	0	0	0	0	1	0	0	.000	0	1	0	0	0.3	1.000

Hal Manders

MANDERS, HAROLD CARL
B. June 14, 1917, Waukee, Iowa.
BR TR 6′ 187 lbs.

Year	Team		W	L	PCT	ERA	G	GS	CG	IP	H	BB	SO	ShO	Relief Pitching W	L	SV	Batting AB	H	HR	BA	PO	A	E	DP	TC/G	FA
1941	DET	A	1	0	1.000	2.35	8	0	0	15.1	13	8	7	0	1	0	0	4	0	0	.000	0	2	0	0	0.3	1.000
1942			2	0	1.000	4.09	18	0	0	33	39	15	14	0	2	0	0	4	1	0	.250	1	7	0	0	0.4	1.000
1946	2 teams	DET A (2G 0–0) CHI N (2G 0–1)																									
″	total		0	1	.000	9.75	4	1	0	12	19	5	7	0	0	0	0	4	1	0	.250	0	0	0	0	0.0	
3 yrs.			3	1	.750	4.77	30	1	0	60.1	71	28	28	0	3	0	0	12	2	0	.167	1	9	0	0	0.3	1.000

Leo Mangum

MANGUM, LEO ALLAN (Blackie)
B. May 24, 1896, Durham, N. C. D. July 9, 1974, Lima, Ohio.
BR TR 6′ 1″ 187 lbs.

Year	Team		W	L	PCT	ERA	G	GS	CG	IP	H	BB	SO	ShO	Relief Pitching W	L	SV	Batting AB	H	HR	BA	PO	A	E	DP	TC/G	FA
1924	CHI	A	1	4	.200	7.09	13	7	1	47	69	25	12	0	1	0	0	14	1	0	.071	3	11	2	1	1.2	.875
1925			1	0	1.000	7.80	7	0	0	15	25	6	6	0	1	0	0	4	2	0	.500	0	2	0	1	0.3	1.000
1928	NY	N	0	0	—	15.00	1	1	0	3	6	5	1	0	0	0	0	1	1	0	1.000	0	3	0	1	3.0	1.000
1932	BOS	N	0	0	—	5.23	7	0	0	10.1	17	0	3	0	0	0	0	2	0	0	.000	2	6	0	0	1.1	1.000
1933			4	3	.571	3.32	25	5	2	84	93	11	28	1	2	1	0	22	2	0	.091	2	27	0	1	1.2	1.000

Leo Mangum *continued*

Year	Team	W	L	PCT	ERA	G	GS	CG	IP	H	BB	SO	ShO	Relief Pitching W	Relief Pitching L	Relief Pitching SV	Batting AB	Batting H	Batting HR	BA	PO	A	E	DP	TC/G	FA
1934		5	3	.625	5.72	29	3	1	94.1	127	23	28	0	4	2	1	32	9	0	.281	2	27	1	2	1.0	.967
1935		0	0	—	3.86	3	0	0	4.2	6	2	0	0	0	0	0	0	0	0	—	0	1	0	0	0.3	1.000
7 yrs.		11	10	.524	5.37	85	16	4	258.1	343	72	78	1	8	3	1	75	15	0	.200	9	77	3	6	1.0	.966

Ernie Manning

MANNING, ERNEST DEVON (Ed) BL TR 6′ 175 lbs.
B. Oct. 9, 1890, Florala, Ala. D. Apr. 28, 1973, Pensacola, Fla.

Year	Team	W	L	PCT	ERA	G	GS	CG	IP	H	BB	SO	ShO	Relief Pitching W	Relief Pitching L	Relief Pitching SV	Batting AB	Batting H	Batting HR	BA	PO	A	E	DP	TC/G	FA
1914	STL A	0	0	—	3.60	4	0	0	10	11	3	3	0	0	0	0	4	0	0	.000	3	4	0	0	1.4	1.000

Jack Manning

MANNING, JOHN E. BR TR 5′ 8½″ 158 lbs.
B. Dec. 20, 1853, Braintree, Mass. D. Aug. 15, 1929, Boston, Mass.
Manager 1877.

Year	Team	W	L	PCT	ERA	G	GS	CG	IP	H	BB	SO	ShO	Relief Pitching W	Relief Pitching L	Relief Pitching SV	Batting AB	Batting H	Batting HR	BA	PO	A	E	DP	TC/G	FA
1876	BOS N	18	5	.783	2.14	34	20	13	197.1	213	32	24	0	**4**	0	**5**	288	76	2	.264	85	37	26	3	1.6	.824
1877	CIN N	0	4	.000	6.95	10	4	2	44	83	7	6	0	0	0	1	252	80	0	.317	233	84	51	8	5.5	.861
1878	BOS N	1	0	1.000	14.29	3	1	1	11.1	24	5	2	0	0	0	0	248	63	0	.254	61	12	23	1	1.5	.760
3 yrs.		19	9	.679	3.53	47	25	16	252.2	320	44	32	0	4	0	6	*				1037	246	224	31	2.1	.851

Jim Manning

MANNING, JAMES BENJAMIN BR TR 6′ 1″ 185 lbs.
B. July 21, 1943, L'Anse, Mich.

Year	Team	W	L	PCT	ERA	G	GS	CG	IP	H	BB	SO	ShO	Relief Pitching W	Relief Pitching L	Relief Pitching SV	Batting AB	Batting H	Batting HR	BA	PO	A	E	DP	TC/G	FA
1962	MIN A	0	0	—	5.14	5	1	0	7	14	1	3	0	0	0	0	1	0	0	.000	3	1	0	0	0.8	1.000

Rube Manning

MANNING, WALTER S. BR TR 6′ 180 lbs.
B. Apr. 29, 1883, Chambersburg, Pa. D. Apr. 23, 1930, Williamsport, Pa.

Year	Team	W	L	PCT	ERA	G	GS	CG	IP	H	BB	SO	ShO	Relief Pitching W	Relief Pitching L	Relief Pitching SV	Batting AB	Batting H	Batting HR	BA	PO	A	E	DP	TC/G	FA
1907	NY A	0	1	.000	3.00	1	1	1	9	8	3	3	0	0	0	0	3	0	0	.000	0	2	0	0	2.0	1.000
1908		13	16	.448	2.94	41	26	19	245	228	86	113	2	4	1	1	91	17	0	.187	5	70	2	0	1.8	.974
1909		7	11	.389	3.17	26	21	11	173	167	48	71	2	1	1	1	60	11	0	.183	5	51	1	0	2.2	.982
1910		2	4	.333	3.70	16	9	4	75.1	80	25	25	0	0	0	0	26	5	0	.192	1	22	0	2	1.4	1.000
4 yrs.		22	32	.407	3.14	84	57	35	502.1	483	162	212	4	5	2	2	180	33	0	.183	11	145	3	2	1.9	.981

Ramon Manon

MANON, RAMON BR TR 6′ 150 lbs.
Born Ramon Manon (Reyes).
B. Jan. 20, 1968, Santo Domingo, Dominican Republic.

Year	Team	W	L	PCT	ERA	G	GS	CG	IP	H	BB	SO	ShO	Relief Pitching W	Relief Pitching L	Relief Pitching SV	Batting AB	Batting H	Batting HR	BA	PO	A	E	DP	TC/G	FA
1990	TEX A	0	0	—	13.50	1	0	0	2	3	3	0	0	0	0	0	0	0	0	—	2	0	0	0	2.0	1.000

Tom Mansell

MANSELL, THOMAS E. BL TR 5′ 8″ 160 lbs.
Brother of Mike Mansell. Brother of John Mansell.
B. Jan. 1, 1855, Auburn, N. Y. D. Oct. 6, 1934, Auburn, N. Y.

Year	Team	W	L	PCT	ERA	G	GS	CG	IP	H	BB	SO	ShO	Relief Pitching W	Relief Pitching L	Relief Pitching SV	Batting AB	Batting H	Batting HR	BA	PO	A	E	DP	TC/G	FA
1883	DET N	0	0	—	16.20	1	0	0	6.2	21	5	3	0	0	0	0	*				65	3	23	1	2.2	.747

Lou Manske

MANSKE, LOUIS HUGO BL TL 6′
B. July 4, 1884, Milwaukee, Wis. D. Apr. 27, 1963, Milwaukee, Wis.

Year	Team	W	L	PCT	ERA	G	GS	CG	IP	H	BB	SO	ShO	Relief Pitching W	Relief Pitching L	Relief Pitching SV	Batting AB	Batting H	Batting HR	BA	PO	A	E	DP	TC/G	FA
1906	PIT N	1	0	1.000	5.63	2	1	0	8	12	5	6	0	0	0	0	4	0	0	.000	0	0	0	0	0.0	.000

Matt Mantei

MANTEI, MATTHEW BRUCE BR TR 6′ 1″ 181 lbs.
B. July 7, 1973, Tampa, Fla.

Year	Team	W	L	PCT	ERA	G	GS	CG	IP	H	BB	SO	ShO	Relief Pitching W	Relief Pitching L	Relief Pitching SV	Batting AB	Batting H	Batting HR	BA	PO	A	E	DP	TC/G	FA
1995	FLA N	0	1	.000	4.72	12	0	0	13.1	12	13	15	0	0	1	0	0	0	0	—	1	2	0	2	0.3	1.000

Barry Manuel

MANUEL, BARRY PAUL BR TR 5′11″ 175 lbs.
B. Aug. 12, 1965, Mamou, La.

Year	Team	W	L	PCT	ERA	G	GS	CG	IP	H	BB	SO	ShO	Relief Pitching W	Relief Pitching L	Relief Pitching SV	Batting AB	Batting H	Batting HR	BA	PO	A	E	DP	TC/G	FA
1991	TEX A	1	0	1.000	1.13	8	0	0	16	7	6	5	0	1	0	0	0	0	0	—	0	6	0	0	0.8	1.000
1992		1	0	1.000	4.76	3	0	0	5.2	6	1	9	0	1	0	0	0	0	0	—	0	0	0	0	0.0	.000
2 yrs.		2	0	1.000	2.08	11	0	0	21.2	13	7	14	0	2	0	0	0	0	0		0	6	0	0	0.5	1.000

Moxie Manuel

MANUEL, MARK GARFIELD BR TB 5′11″ 170 lbs.
B. Oct. 16, 1881, Metropolis, Ill. D. Apr. 26, 1924, Memphis, Tenn.

Year	Team	W	L	PCT	ERA	G	GS	CG	IP	H	BB	SO	ShO	Relief Pitching W	Relief Pitching L	Relief Pitching SV	Batting AB	Batting H	Batting HR	BA	PO	A	E	DP	TC/G	FA
1905	WAS A	0	0	—	5.40	3	1	1	10	9	3	3	0	0	0	0	4	1	0	.250	1	5	2	0	2.7	.750
1908	CHI A	3	4	.429	3.28	18	6	3	60.1	52	25	25	0	2	1	1	16	1	0	.063	3	22	3	1	1.6	.893
2 yrs.		3	4	.429	3.58	21	7	4	70.1	61	28	28	0	2	1	1	20	2	0	.100	4	27	5	1	1.7	.861

Dick Manville

MANVILLE, RICHARD WESLEY BR TR 6′ 4″ 192 lbs.
B. Dec. 25, 1926, Des Moines, Iowa.

Year	Team	W	L	PCT	ERA	G	GS	CG	IP	H	BB	SO	ShO	Relief Pitching W	Relief Pitching L	Relief Pitching SV	Batting AB	Batting H	Batting HR	BA	PO	A	E	DP	TC/G	FA
1950	BOS N	0	0	—	0.00	1	0	0	2	0	3	2	0	0	0	0	0	0	0	—	0	0	0	0	0.0	.000
1952	CHI N	0	0	—	7.94	11	0	0	17	25	12	6	0	0	0	0	2	1	0	.500	2	4	0	0	0.5	1.000
2 yrs.		0	0		7.11	12	0	0	19	25	15	8	0	0	0	0	2	1	0	.500	2	4	0	0	0.5	1.000

Josias Manzanillo

MANZANILLO, JOSIAS BR TR 6′ 190 lbs.
Born Josias Manzanillo (Adams).
Brother of Ravelo Manzanillo.
B. Oct. 16, 1967, San Pedro de Macoris, Dominican Republic.

Year	Team	W	L	PCT	ERA	G	GS	CG	IP	H	BB	SO	ShO	Relief Pitching W	Relief Pitching L	Relief Pitching SV	Batting AB	Batting H	Batting HR	BA	PO	A	E	DP	TC/G	FA
1991	BOS A	0	0	—	18.00	1	0	0	1	2	3	1	0	0	0	0	0	0	0	—	0	0	0	0	0.0	.000
1993	2 teams MIL A (10G 1–1) NY N (6G 0–0)																									
"	total	1	1	.500	6.83	16	1	0	29	30	19	21	0	1	0	1	1	0	0	.000	2	5	0	1	0.4	1.000
1994	NY N	3	2	.600	2.66	37	0	0	47.1	34	13	48	0	3	2	2	4	0	0	.000	7	3	1	0	0.3	.909
1995	2 teams NY N (12G 1–2) NY A (11G 0–0)																									
"	total	1	2	.333	4.86	23	0	0	33.1	37	15	25	0	1	2	0	0	0	0	—	2	3	0	1	0.2	1.000
4 yrs.		5	5	.500	4.55	77	1	0	110.2	103	50	95	0	5	4	3	5	0	0	.000	11	11	1	2	0.3	.957

Ravelo Manzanillo

MANZANILLO, RAVELO BL TL 6′ 210 lbs.
Born Ravelo Manzanillo (Adams).
Brother of Josias Manzanillo.
B. Oct. 17, 1963, San Pedro de Macoris, Dominican Republic.

Year	Team	W	L	PCT	ERA	G	GS	CG	IP	H	BB	SO	ShO	Relief Pitching W	Relief Pitching L	Relief Pitching SV	Batting AB	Batting H	Batting HR	BA	PO	A	E	DP	TC/G	FA
1988	CHI A	0	1	.000	5.79	2	2	0	9.1	7	12	10	0	0	0	0	0	0	0	—	0	1	0	0	0.5	1.000
1994	PIT N	4	2	.667	4.14	46	0	0	50	45	42	39	0	4	2	1	3	2	0	.667	2	8	1	0	0.2	.909
1995		0	0	—	4.91	5	0	0	3.2	3	2	1	0	0	0	0	1	0	0	.000	0	1	0	0	0.2	1.000
3 yrs.		4	3	.571	4.43	53	2	0	63	55	56	50	0	4	2	1	4	2	0	.500	2	10	1	0	0.2	.923

Rolla Mapel

MAPEL, ROLLA HAMILTON (Lefty) — BL TL 5′11½″ 165 lbs.
B. Mar. 9, 1890, Lee's Summit, Mo. D. Apr. 6, 1966, San Diego, Calif.

Year	Team	Lg	W	L	PCT	ERA	G	GS	CG	IP	H	BB	SO	ShO	Relief Pitching W	Relief Pitching L	Relief Pitching SV	Batting AB	Batting H	Batting HR	BA	PO	A	E	DP	TC/G	FA
1919	**STL**	**A**	0	3	.000	4.50	4	3	2	20	17	17	2	0	0	0	0	6	1	0	.167	0	11	0	0	2.8	1.000

Paul Marak

MARAK, PAUL PATRICK — BR TR 6′ 2″ 175 lbs.
B. Aug. 2, 1965, Lakenheath, England.

Year	Team	Lg	W	L	PCT	ERA	G	GS	CG	IP	H	BB	SO	ShO	Relief Pitching W	Relief Pitching L	Relief Pitching SV	Batting AB	Batting H	Batting HR	BA	PO	A	E	DP	TC/G	FA
1990	**ATL**	**N**	1	2	.333	3.69	7	7	1	39	39	19	15	1	0	0	0	11	1	0	.091	6	9	0	1	2.1	1.000

Georges Maranda

MARANDA, GEORGES HENRI — BR TR 6′ 2″ 195 lbs.
B. Jan. 15, 1932, Levis, Que., Canada.

Year	Team	Lg	W	L	PCT	ERA	G	GS	CG	IP	H	BB	SO	ShO	Relief Pitching W	Relief Pitching L	Relief Pitching SV	Batting AB	Batting H	Batting HR	BA	PO	A	E	DP	TC/G	FA
1960	**SF**	**N**	1	4	.200	4.62	17	4	0	50.2	50	30	28	0	0	1	0	12	2	0	.167	5	17	1	1	1.4	.957
1962	**MIN**	**A**	1	3	.250	4.46	32	4	0	72.2	69	35	36	0	0	2	0	16	4	0	.250	3	16	1	2	0.6	.950
2 yrs.			2	7	.222	4.52	49	8	0	123.1	119	65	64	0	0	3	0	28	6	0	.214	8	33	2	3	0.9	.953

Firpo Marberry

MARBERRY, FREDERICK — BR TR 6′ 1″ 190 lbs.
B. Nov. 30, 1898, Streetman, Tex. D. June 30, 1976, Mexia, Tex.

Year	Team	Lg	W	L	PCT	ERA	G	GS	CG	IP	H	BB	SO	ShO	Relief Pitching W	Relief Pitching L	Relief Pitching SV	Batting AB	Batting H	Batting HR	BA	PO	A	E	DP	TC/G	FA
1923	**WAS**	**A**	4	0	1.000	2.82	11	4	2	44.2	42	17	18	0	0	0	0	14	2	0	.143	1	10	1	0	1.1	.917
1924			11	12	.478	3.09	**50**	14	6	195.1	190	70	68	0	6	**5**	**15**	59	8	0	.136	8	39	2	3	1.0	.959
1925			8	6	.571	3.47	**55**	0	0	93.1	84	45	53	0	8	**6**	**15**	19	5	0	.263	6	26	0	1	0.6	1.000
1926			12	7	.632	3.00	**64**	5	3	138	120	66	43	0	9	**5**	**22**	34	6	0	.176	5	31	2	2	0.6	.947
1927			10	7	.588	4.64	56	10	2	155.1	177	68	74	0	8	2	9	41	5	0	.122	9	25	0	4	0.6	1.000
1928			13	13	.500	3.85	**48**	11	7	161.1	160	42	76	1	7	**9**	3	46	5	0	.109	8	27	1	2	0.8	.972
1929			19	12	.613	3.06	**49**	26	16	250.1	233	69	121	0	3	4	**11**	82	19	0	.232	15	35	0	1	1.0	1.000
1930			15	5	.750	4.09	33	22	9	185	190	53	56	2	0	3	1	73	24	0	.329	7	33	1	2	1.2	.976
1931			16	4	.800	3.45	45	25	11	219	211	63	88	2	3	1	7	82	19	1	.232	3	36	1	4	0.9	.975
1932			8	4	.667	4.01	**54**	15	8	197.2	202	72	66	1	1	1	**13**	66	11	0	.167	9	45	1	5	1.0	.982
1933	**DET**	**A**	16	11	.593	3.29	37	32	15	238.1	232	61	84	1	2	0	2	90	11	0	.122	11	37	4	3	1.4	.923
1934			15	5	.750	4.57	38	19	6	155.2	174	48	64	1	6	0	3	55	12	0	.218	10	20	2	2	0.8	.938
1935			0	1	.000	4.26	5	2	1	19	22	9	7	0	0	0	0	5	1	0	.200	0	3	0	0	0.6	1.000
1936	**2 teams**	**NY N**	(1G 0–0)	**WAS A**	(5G 0–2)																						
″	**total**		0	2	.000	3.77	6	1	0	14.1	12	3	4	0	0	1	0	3	0	0	.000	0	3	2	0	0.8	.600
14 yrs.			147	89	.623	3.63	551	186	86	2067.1	2049	686	822	8	53	37	101	669	128	1	.191	92	370	17	29	0.9	.965
WORLD SERIES																											
1924	**WAS**	**A**	0	1	.000	1.13	4	1	0	8	9	4	10	0	0	0	2	2	0	0	.000	1	1	0	1	0.5	1.000
1925			0	0	—	0.00	2	0	0	2.1	3	0	2	0	0	0	1	0	0	0	—	0	0	0	0	0.0	.000
1934	**DET**	**A**	0	0	—	21.60	2	0	0	1.2	5	1	0	0	0	0	0	0	0	0	—	0	1	0	0	0.5	1.000
3 yrs.			0	1	.000	3.75	8	1	0	12	17	5	12	0	0	0	3	2	0	0	.000	1	2	0	1	0.4	1.000
																	4th										

Walt Marbet

MARBET, WALTER WILLIAM — BR TR 6′ 1″ 175 lbs.
B. Sept. 13, 1890, Plymouth County, Iowa D. Sept. 24, 1956, Hohenwald, Tenn.

Year	Team	Lg	W	L	PCT	ERA	G	GS	CG	IP	H	BB	SO	ShO	Relief Pitching W	Relief Pitching L	Relief Pitching SV	Batting AB	Batting H	Batting HR	BA	PO	A	E	DP	TC/G	FA
1913	**STL**	**N**	0	1	.000	16.20	3	1	0	3.1	9	4	1	0	0	0	0	0	0	0	—	0	0	0	0	0.0	.000

Phil Marchildon

MARCHILDON, PHILIP JOSEPH — BR TR 5′10½″ 170 lbs.
B. Oct. 25, 1913, Penetanguishene, Ont., Canada.

Year	Team	Lg	W	L	PCT	ERA	G	GS	CG	IP	H	BB	SO	ShO	Relief Pitching W	Relief Pitching L	Relief Pitching SV	Batting AB	Batting H	Batting HR	BA	PO	A	E	DP	TC/G	FA
1940	**PHI**	**A**	0	2	.000	7.20	2	2	1	10	12	8	4	0	0	0	0	2	0	0	.000	0	3	0	0	1.5	1.000
1941			10	15	.400	3.57	30	27	14	204.1	188	118	74	1	1	1	0	66	11	0	.167	11	22	1	1	1.1	.971
1942			17	14	.548	4.20	38	31	18	244	215	**140**	110	1	2	0	1	84	20	0	.238	13	35	2	3	1.3	.960
1945			0	1	.000	4.00	3	2	0	9	5	11	2	0	0	1	0	2	1	0	.500	1	2	0	0	1.0	1.000
1946			13	**16**	.448	3.49	36	29	16	226.2	197	114	95	1	2	0	1	75	5	0	.067	9	33	4	0	1.3	.913
1947			19	9	.679	3.22	35	35	21	276.2	228	**141**	128	2	0	0	0	98	15	1	.153	7	34	3	2	1.3	.932
1948			9	15	.375	4.53	33	30	12	226.1	214	131	66	1	0	1	0	72	5	0	.069	10	36	4	5	1.5	.920
1949			0	3	.000	11.81	7	6	0	16	24	19	2	0	0	0	0	6	1	0	.167	1	3	1	0	0.7	.800
1950	**BOS**	**A**	0	0	—	6.75	1	0	0	1.1	1	2	0	0	0	0	0	0	0	0	—	0	0	0	0	0.0	.000
9 yrs.			68	75	.476	3.93	185	162	82	1214.1	1084	684	481	6	5	3	2	405	58	1	.143	52	168	15	11	1.3	.936

Johnny Marcum

MARCUM, JOHN ALFRED (Footsie) — BL TR 5′11″ 197 lbs.
B. Sept. 9, 1909, Campbellsburg, Ky. D. Sept. 10, 1984, Louisville, Ky.

Year	Team	Lg	W	L	PCT	ERA	G	GS	CG	IP	H	BB	SO	ShO	Relief Pitching W	Relief Pitching L	Relief Pitching SV	Batting AB	Batting H	Batting HR	BA	PO	A	E	DP	TC/G	FA
1933	**PHI**	**A**	3	2	.600	1.95	5	5	4	37	28	20	14	2	0	0	0	12	2	0	.167	5	6	0	0	2.2	1.000
1934			14	11	.560	4.50	37	31	17	232	257	88	92	2	1	2	0	112	30	1	.268	14	42	3	2	1.6	.949
1935			17	12	.586	4.08	39	27	19	242.2	256	83	99	2	2	0	3	119	37	2	.311	11	32	5	1	1.2	.896
1936	**BOS**	**A**	8	13	.381	4.81	31	23	9	174	194	52	57	1	1	2	1	88	18	2	.205	7	31	2	3	1.3	.950
1937			13	11	.542	4.85	37	23	9	183.2	230	47	59	1	5	1	3	86	23	0	.267	13	38	1	1	1.4	.981
1938			5	6	.455	4.09	15	11	7	92.1	113	25	25	0	1	0	0	37	5	0	.135	3	15	0	0	1.2	1.000
1939	**2 teams**	**STL A**	(12G 2–5)	**CHI A**	(19G 3–3)																						
″	**total**		5	8	.385	6.60	31	12	4	137.2	191	29	46	0	0	3	0	79	26	0	.329	8	17	1	2	0.8	.962
7 yrs.			65	63	.508	4.66	195	132	69	1099.1	1269	344	392	8	10	8	7	*				61	181	12	9	1.3	.953

Leo Marentette

MARENTETTE, LEO JOHN — BR TR 6′ 2″ 200 lbs.
B. Feb. 18, 1941, Detroit, Mich.

Year	Team	Lg	W	L	PCT	ERA	G	GS	CG	IP	H	BB	SO	ShO	Relief Pitching W	Relief Pitching L	Relief Pitching SV	Batting AB	Batting H	Batting HR	BA	PO	A	E	DP	TC/G	FA
1965	**DET**	**A**	0	0	—	0.00	2	0	0	3	1	1	3	0	0	0	0	0	0	0	—	0	1	0	0	0.5	1.000
1969	**MON**	**N**	0	0	—	6.75	3	0	0	5.1	9	1	4	0	0	0	0	1	0	0	.000	2	0	0	0	0.7	1.000
2 yrs.			0	0		4.32	5	0	0	8.1	10	2	7	0	0	0	0	1	0	0	.000	2	1	0	0	0.6	1.000

Joe Margoneri

MARGONERI, JOSEPH EMANUEL — BL TL 6′ 185 lbs.
B. Jan. 13, 1930, Somerset, Pa.

Year	Team	Lg	W	L	PCT	ERA	G	GS	CG	IP	H	BB	SO	ShO	Relief Pitching W	Relief Pitching L	Relief Pitching SV	Batting AB	Batting H	Batting HR	BA	PO	A	E	DP	TC/G	FA
1956	**NY**	**N**	6	6	.500	3.93	23	13	2	91.2	88	49	49	0	1	1	0	29	3	1	.103	3	15	1	0	0.8	.947
1957			1	1	.500	5.24	13	2	1	34.1	44	21	18	0	0	1	0	8	0	0	.000	1	5	0	1	0.5	1.000
2 yrs.			7	7	.500	4.29	36	15	3	126	132	70	67	0	1	2	0	37	3	1	.081	4	20	1	1	0.7	.960

Juan Marichal

MARICHAL, JUAN ANTONIO (Manito, The Dominican Dandy) BR TR 6′ 185 lbs.
Born Juan Antonio Marichal (Sanchez).
B. Oct. 20, 1937, Laguna Verde, Dominican Republic.
Hall of Fame 1983.

Year	Team	W	L	PCT	ERA	G	GS	CG	IP	H	BB	SO	ShO	Relief Pitching W	Relief Pitching L	Relief Pitching SV	Batting AB	Batting H	Batting HR	BA	PO	A	E	DP	TC/G	FA
1960	SF N	6	2	.750	2.66	11	11	6	81.1	59	28	58	1	0	0	0	31	4	0	.129	5	13	0	1	1.6	1.000
1961		13	10	.565	3.89	29	27	9	185	183	48	124	3	1	1	0	59	7	0	.119	10	27	3	1	1.4	.925
1962		18	11	.621	3.36	37	36	18	262.2	233	90	153	3	0	0	1	89	21	0	.236	15	43	4	0	1.7	.935
1963		**25**	8	.758	2.41	41	40	18	**321.1**	259	61	248	5	1	0	0	112	20	1	.179	18	39	2	1	1.4	.966
1964		21	8	.724	2.48	33	33	**22**	269	241	52	206	4	0	0	0	97	14	0	.144	29	42	3	2	2.2	.959
1965		22	13	.629	2.13	39	37	24	295.1	224	46	240	**10**	1	0	1	98	17	0	.173	23	43	3	3	1.8	.957
1966		25	6	**.806**	2.23	37	36	25	307.1	228	36	222	4	1	0	0	112	28	1	.250	23	47	4	2	2.0	.946
1967		14	10	.583	2.76	26	26	18	202.1	195	42	166	2	0	0	0	79	14	0	.177	15	22	2	1	1.5	.949
1968		**26**	9	.743	2.43	38	38	**30**	**325.2**	**295**	46	218	5	0	0	0	123	20	0	.163	33	64	6	3	2.7	.942
1969		21	11	.656	**2.10**	37	36	27	300	244	54	205	**8**	0	0	0	109	15	0	.138	21	64	2	3	2.4	.977
1970		12	10	.545	4.11	34	33	14	243	269	48	123	1	0	0	0	85	5	0	.059	25	43	1	1	2.0	.986
1971		18	11	.621	2.94	37	37	18	279	244	56	159	4	0	0	0	105	14	2	.133	28	52	7	3	2.4	.920
1972		6	16	.273	3.71	25	24	6	165	176	46	72	0	0	1	0	51	10	0	.196	17	24	6	1	1.9	.872
1973		11	15	.423	3.79	34	32	9	209	231	37	87	2	0	0	0	69	13	0	.188	25	44	4	5	2.1	.945
1974	BOS A	5	1	.833	4.87	11	9	0	57.1	61	14	21	0	1	0	0	0	0	0	—	4	8	0	0	1.1	1.000
1975	LA N	0	1	.000	13.50	2	2	0	6	11	5	1	0	0	0	0	2	0	0	.000	0	2	0	0	1.0	1.000
16 yrs.		243	142	.631	2.89	471	457	244	3509.1	3153	709	2303	52	5	2	2	1221	202	4	.165	291	577	47	27	1.9	.949
LEAGUE CHAMPIONSHIP SERIES																										
1971	SF N	0	1	.000	2.25	1	1	1	8	4	0	6	0	0	0	0	3	0	0	.000	2	4	0	0	6.0	1.000
WORLD SERIES																										
1962	SF N	0	0	—	0.00	1	1	0	4	2	2	4	0	0	0	0	2	0	0	.000	1	0	0	1	1.0	1.000

Dan Marion

MARION, DONALD G. BR TR 6′ 1″ 187 lbs.
B. July 31, 1890, Cleveland, Ohio D. Jan. 18, 1933, Milwaukee, Wis.

Year	Team	W	L	PCT	ERA	G	GS	CG	IP	H	BB	SO	ShO	Relief W	Relief L	Relief SV	AB	H	HR	BA	PO	A	E	DP	TC/G	FA
1914	BKN F	3	2	.600	3.93	17	9	4	89.1	97	38	41	0	0	0	0	36	7	0	.194	3	21	2	0	1.5	.923
1915		10	9	.526	3.20	35	25	15	208.1	193	64	46	2	0	1	0	74	13	0	.176	8	66	6	2	2.3	.925
2 yrs.		13	11	.542	3.42	52	34	19	297.2	290	102	87	2	0	1	0	110	20	0	.182	11	87	8	2	2.0	.925

Duke Markell

MARKELL, HARRY DUQUESNE BR TR 6′ 1½″ 209 lbs.
Born Harry Duquesne Makowsky.
B. Aug. 17, 1923, Paris, France D. June 14, 1984, Fort Lauderdale, Fla.

Year	Team	W	L	PCT	ERA	G	GS	CG	IP	H	BB	SO	ShO	Relief W	Relief L	Relief SV	AB	H	HR	BA	PO	A	E	DP	TC/G	FA
1951	STL A	1	1	.500	6.33	5	2	1	21.1	25	20	10	0	0	0	0	6	1	0	.167	1	1	0	0	0.4	1.000

Cliff Markle

MARKLE, CLIFFORD MONROE BR TR 5′ 8½″ 160 lbs.
B. May 3, 1894, Dravosburg, Pa. D. May 24, 1974, Temple City, Calif.

Year	Team	W	L	PCT	ERA	G	GS	CG	IP	H	BB	SO	ShO	Relief W	Relief L	Relief SV	AB	H	HR	BA	PO	A	E	DP	TC/G	FA
1915	NY A	2	0	1.000	0.39	3	2	2	23	15	6	12	0	0	0	0	4	0	0	.000	1	4	1	0	2.0	.833
1916		4	3	.571	4.53	11	7	3	45.2	41	31	14	1	0	1	0	13	0	0	.000	1	12	0	0	1.2	1.000
1921	CIN N	2	6	.250	3.76	10	6	5	67	75	20	23	0	1	1	0	24	3	0	.125	6	11	2	1	1.9	.895
1922		4	5	.444	3.81	25	3	2	75.2	75	33	34	1	3	3	0	20	3	0	.150	4	15	0	0	0.8	1.000
1924	NY A	0	3	.000	8.87	7	3	0	23.1	29	20	7	0	0	0	0	8	0	0	.000	1	3	1	0	0.7	.800
5 yrs.		12	17	.414	4.10	56	21	12	234.2	235	110	90	2	4	5	0	69	6	0	.087	13	45	4	1	1.1	.935

Dick Marlowe

MARLOWE, RICHARD BURTON BR TR 6′ 2″ 165 lbs.
B. June 27, 1929, Hickory, N. C. D. Dec. 30, 1968, Toledo, Ohio.

Year	Team	W	L	PCT	ERA	G	GS	CG	IP	H	BB	SO	ShO	Relief W	Relief L	Relief SV	AB	H	HR	BA	PO	A	E	DP	TC/G	FA
1951	DET A	0	1	.000	32.40	2	1	0	1.2	5	2	1	0	0	0	0	0	0	0	—	0	0	0	0	0.0	.000
1952		0	2	.000	7.36	4	1	0	11	21	3	3	0	0	1	0	2	0	0	.000	1	0	0	0	0.3	1.000
1953		6	7	.462	5.26	42	11	2	119.2	152	42	52	0	3	1	0	32	7	0	.219	7	17	1	0	0.6	.960
1954		5	4	.556	4.18	38	2	0	84	76	40	39	0	5	2	2	18	3	0	.167	5	11	1	0	0.4	.941
1955		1	0	1.000	1.80	4	1	1	15	12	4	9	0	0	0	1	4	0	0	.000	0	1	0	0	0.3	1.000
1956	2 teams DET A (7G 1–1) CHI A (1G 0–0)																									
"	total	1	1	.500	6.00	8	1	0	12	14	10	4	0	1	0	0	1	0	0	.000	2	1	0	0	0.4	1.000
6 yrs.		13	15	.464	4.99	98	17	3	243.1	280	101	108	0	9	4	3	57	10	0	.175	15	30	2	0	0.5	.957

Lou Marone

MARONE, LOUIS STEPHEN BR TL 5′11″ 185 lbs.
B. Dec. 3, 1945, San Diego, Calif.

Year	Team	W	L	PCT	ERA	G	GS	CG	IP	H	BB	SO	ShO	Relief W	Relief L	Relief SV	AB	H	HR	BA	PO	A	E	DP	TC/G	FA
1969	PIT N	1	1	.500	2.57	29	0	0	35	24	13	25	0	1	1	0	0	0	0	—	1	4	1	0	0.2	.833
1970		0	0	—	4.50	1	0	0	2	2	0	0	0	0	0	0	0	0	0	—	0	0	0	0	0.0	.000
2 yrs.		1	1	.500	2.68	30	0	0	37	26	13	25	0	1	1	0	0	0	0		1	4	1	0	0.2	.833

Rube Marquard

MARQUARD, RICHARD WILLIAM BB TL 6′ 3″ 180 lbs.
B. Oct. 9, 1889, Cleveland, Ohio D. June 1, 1980, Baltimore, Md.
Hall of Fame 1971.

Year	Team	W	L	PCT	ERA	G	GS	CG	IP	H	BB	SO	ShO	Relief W	Relief L	Relief SV	AB	H	HR	BA	PO	A	E	DP	TC/G	FA
1908	NY N	0	1	.000	3.60	1	1	0	5	6	2	2	0	0	0	0	1	0	0	.000	0	1	0	0	1.0	1.000
1909		5	13	.278	2.60	29	21	8	173	155	73	109	0	2	0	0	54	8	0	.148	3	45	4	1	1.8	.923
1910		4	4	.500	4.46	13	8	2	70.2	65	40	52	0	0	1	0	27	3	0	.111	0	17	2	1	1.5	.895
1911		24	7	**.774**	2.50	45	33	22	277.2	221	106	**237**	5	2	1	2	104	17	1	.163	6	46	4	1	1.2	.929
1912		**26**	11	.703	2.57	43	38	22	294.2	286	80	175	1	2	1	0	96	21	0	.219	2	58	1	0	1.4	.984
1913		23	10	.697	2.50	42	33	20	288	248	49	151	4	5	0	2	105	23	0	.219	4	46	2	2	1.2	.962
1914		12	22	.353	3.06	39	33	15	268	261	47	92	4	1	0	2	84	15	0	.179	5	77	3	0	2.2	.965
1915	2 teams NY N (27G 9–8) BKN N (6G 2–2)																									
"	total	11	10	.524	4.04	33	23	10	193.2	207	38	92	2	4	1	2	63	7	0	.111	6	51	6	2	1.9	.905
1916	BKN N	13	6	.684	1.58	36	21	15	205	169	38	107	2	3	0	5	63	9	0	.143	4	35	2	1	1.1	.951
1917		19	12	.613	2.55	37	29	14	232.2	200	60	117	2	5	1	0	75	15	0	.200	5	47	3	1	1.5	.945
1918		9	**18**	.333	2.64	34	29	19	239	231	59	89	4	0	0	0	76	13	0	.171	5	58	3	1	1.9	.955
1919		3	3	.500	2.29	8	7	3	59	54	10	29	0	0	0	0	23	6	0	.261	1	11	0	0	1.5	1.000
1920		10	7	.588	3.23	28	26	10	189.2	181	35	89	1	0	0	0	59	10	0	.169	7	30	1	2	1.4	.974
1921	CIN N	17	14	.548	3.39	39	35	18	265.2	291	50	88	2	0	1	0	95	19	0	.200	7	51	1	6	1.5	.983
1922	BOS N	11	15	.423	5.09	39	25	7	198	255	66	57	0	3	1	1	63	14	0	.222	4	51	4	4	1.5	.932

Rube Marquard *continued*

Year	Team	Lg	W	L	PCT	ERA	G	GS	CG	IP	H	BB	SO	ShO	Relief Pitching W	Relief Pitching L	Relief Pitching SV	Batting AB	Batting H	Batting HR	BA	PO	A	E	DP	TC/G	FA
1923			11	14	.440	3.73	38	29	11	239	265	65	78	3	0	2	0	86	12	0	.140	0	58	2	5	1.6	.967
1924			1	2	.333	3.00	6	6	1	36	33	13	10	0	0	0	0	11	3	0	.273	0	9	0	0	1.5	1.000
1925			2	8	.200	5.75	26	8	0	72	105	27	19	0	0	4	0	22	3	0	.136	4	6	1	0	0.4	.909
18 yrs.			201	177	.532	3.08	536	405	197	3306.2	3233	858	1593	30	27	13	14	1107	198	1	.179	63	697	39	27	1.5	.951
WORLD SERIES																											
1911	**NY**	**N**	0	1	.000	1.54	3	2	2	11.2	9	1	8	0	0	0	0	2	0	0	.000	0	2	0	0	0.7	1.000
1912			2	0	1.000	0.50	2	2	2	18	14	2	9	0	0	0	0	4	0	0	.000	0	4	1	0	2.5	.800
1913			0	1	.000	7.00	2	1	0	9	10	3	3	0	0	0	0	1	0	0	.000	0	8	0	0	4.0	1.000
1916	**BKN**	**N**	0	2	.000	4.91	2	2	0	11	12	6	9	0	0	0	0	3	0	0	.000	0	2	0	0	1.0	1.000
1920			0	1	.000	2.00	2	1	0	9	7	3	6	0	0	0	0	1	0	0	.000	0	1	0	0	0.5	1.000
5 yrs.			2	5	.286	2.76	11	8	4	58.2	52	15	35	0	0	0	0	11	0	0	.000	0	17	1	0	1.6	.944
				2nd			**10th**	**10th**																			

Isidro Marquez

MARQUEZ, ISIDRO
Born Isidro Marquez (Espinoza).
B. May 14, 1965, Navajoa, Mexico.
BR TR 6′ 3″ 190 lbs.

Year	Team	Lg	W	L	PCT	ERA	G	GS	CG	IP	H	BB	SO	ShO	Relief Pitching W	Relief Pitching L	Relief Pitching SV	Batting AB	Batting H	Batting HR	BA	PO	A	E	DP	TC/G	FA
1995	**CHI**	**A**	0	1	.000	6.75	7	0	0	6.2	9	2	8	0	0	1	0	0	0	0	—	1	0	0	0	0.1	1.000

Jim Marquis

MARQUIS, JAMES MILBURN
B. Nov. 18, 1900, Yoakum, Tex. D. Aug. 5, 1992, Jackson, Calif.
BR TR 5′11″ 174 lbs.

Year	Team	Lg	W	L	PCT	ERA	G	GS	CG	IP	H	BB	SO	ShO	Relief Pitching W	Relief Pitching L	Relief Pitching SV	Batting AB	Batting H	Batting HR	BA	PO	A	E	DP	TC/G	FA
1925	**NY**	**A**	0	0	—	9.82	2	0	0	7.1	12	6	0	0	0	0	0	2	0	0	.000	0	4	1	0	2.5	.800

Connie Marrero

MARRERO, CONRADO EUGENIO
Born Conrado Eugenio Marrero (Ramos).
B. Apr. 25, 1911, Las Villas, Cuba.
BR TR 5′ 7″ 158 lbs.

Year	Team	Lg	W	L	PCT	ERA	G	GS	CG	IP	H	BB	SO	ShO	Relief Pitching W	Relief Pitching L	Relief Pitching SV	Batting AB	Batting H	Batting HR	BA	PO	A	E	DP	TC/G	FA
1950	**WAS**	**A**	6	10	.375	4.50	27	19	8	152	159	55	63	1	1	0	1	49	6	0	.122	4	14	0	0	0.7	1.000
1951			11	9	.550	3.90	25	25	16	187	198	71	66	2	0	0	0	61	10	0	.164	5	29	3	1	1.5	.919
1952			11	8	.579	2.88	22	22	16	184.1	175	53	77	2	0	0	0	63	5	0	.079	7	18	1	2	1.2	.962
1953			8	7	.533	3.03	22	20	10	145.2	130	48	65	2	0	0	2	48	6	0	.125	5	19	2	1	1.2	.923
1954			3	6	.333	4.75	22	8	1	66.1	74	22	26	0	2	2	0	15	0	0	.000	1	9	0	1	0.5	1.000
5 yrs.			39	40	.494	3.67	118	94	51	735.1	736	249	297	7	3	2	3	236	27	0	.114	22	89	6	5	1.0	.949

Buck Marrow

MARROW, CHARLES KENNON
B. Aug. 29, 1909, Tarboro, N. C. D. Nov. 21, 1982, Newport News, Va.
BR TR 6′ 4″ 200 lbs.

Year	Team	Lg	W	L	PCT	ERA	G	GS	CG	IP	H	BB	SO	ShO	Relief Pitching W	Relief Pitching L	Relief Pitching SV	Batting AB	Batting H	Batting HR	BA	PO	A	E	DP	TC/G	FA
1932	**DET**	**A**	2	5	.286	4.81	18	7	2	63.2	70	29	31	0	1	0	1	19	3	0	.158	6	14	1	0	1.2	.952
1937	**BKN**	**N**	1	2	.333	6.61	6	3	1	16.1	19	9	2	0	0	0	0	5	0	0	.000	1	4	0	0	0.8	1.000
1938			0	1	.000	4.58	15	0	0	19.2	23	11	6	0	0	1	0	1	0	0	.000	2	4	0	1	0.4	1.000
3 yrs.			3	8	.273	5.06	39	10	3	99.2	112	49	39	0	1	1	1	25	3	0	.120	9	22	1	1	0.8	.969

Ed Mars

MARS, EDWARD M.
B. Dec. 4, 1866, Chicago, Ill. D. Dec. 9, 1941, Chicago, Ill.
5′ 9″ 166 lbs.

Year	Team	Lg	W	L	PCT	ERA	G	GS	CG	IP	H	BB	SO	ShO	Relief Pitching W	Relief Pitching L	Relief Pitching SV	Batting AB	Batting H	Batting HR	BA	PO	A	E	DP	TC/G	FA
1890	**SYR**	**AA**	9	5	.643	*4.67*	16	14	14	121.1	132	49	59	0	0	0	0	51	14	0	.275	3	28	2	1	2.1	.939

Cuddles Marshall

MARSHALL, CLARENCE WESTLY
B. Apr. 28, 1925, Bellingham, Wash.
BR TR 6′ 3″ 200 lbs.

Year	Team	Lg	W	L	PCT	ERA	G	GS	CG	IP	H	BB	SO	ShO	Relief Pitching W	Relief Pitching L	Relief Pitching SV	Batting AB	Batting H	Batting HR	BA	PO	A	E	DP	TC/G	FA
1946	**NY**	**A**	3	4	.429	5.33	23	11	1	81	96	56	32	0	2	0	0	28	4	0	.143	2	18	0	2	0.9	1.000
1948			0	0	—	0.00	1	0	0	1	0	3	0	0	0	0	0	0	0	0	—	0	0	0	0	0.0	.000
1949			3	0	1.000	5.11	21	2	0	49.1	48	48	13	0	3	0	3	9	1	0	.111	0	14	1	1	0.7	.933
1950	**STL**	**A**	1	3	.250	7.88	28	2	0	53.2	72	51	24	0	1	2	1	12	4	0	.333	0	5	2	0	0.3	.714
4 yrs.			7	7	.500	5.98	73	15	1	185	216	158	69	0	6	2	4	49	9	0	.184	2	37	3	3	0.6	.929

Mike Marshall

MARSHALL, MICHAEL GRANT
B. Jan. 15, 1943, Adrian, Mich.
BR TR 5′10″ 180 lbs.

Year	Team	Lg	W	L	PCT	ERA	G	GS	CG	IP	H	BB	SO	ShO	Relief Pitching W	Relief Pitching L	Relief Pitching SV	Batting AB	Batting H	Batting HR	BA	PO	A	E	DP	TC/G	FA
1967	**DET**	**A**	1	3	.250	1.98	37	0	0	59	51	20	41	0	1	3	10	9	2	0	.222	11	8	0	0	0.5	1.000
1969	**SEA**	**A**	3	10	.231	5.13	20	14	3	87.2	99	35	47	1	0	1	0	27	7	1	.259	14	22	2	2	1.9	.947
1970	**2 teams**	**HOU N**	(4G 0–1)	**MON N**	(24G 3–7)																						
″	**total**		3	8	.273	3.86	28	5	0	70	64	33	43	0	3	4	3	11	1	0	.091	4	20	0	2	0.9	1.000
1971	**MON**	**N**	5	8	.385	4.30	66	0	0	111	100	50	85	0	5	8	23	16	3	0	.188	6	30	2	2	0.6	.947
1972			14	8	.636	1.78	**65**	0	0	116	82	47	95	0	**14**	8	18	22	3	0	.136	5	17	1	0	0.4	.957
1973			14	11	.560	2.66	**92**	0	0	179	163	75	124	0	**14**	**11**	**31**	33	8	0	.242	14	37	1	2	0.6	.981
1974	**LA**	**N**	15	12	.556	2.42	**106**[1]	0	0	208	191	56	143	0	**15**	**12**	**21**	34	8	0	.235	9	33	2	4	0.4	.955
1975			9	14	.391	3.30	57	0	0	109	98	39	64	0	9	**14**	13	15	1	0	.067	6	23	3	6	0.6	.906
1976	**2 teams**	**LA N**	(30G 4–3)	**ATL N**	(24G 2–1)																						
″	**total**		6	4	.600	3.99	54	0	0	99.1	99	39	56	0	6	4	14	11	1	0	.091	7	24	0	1	0.6	1.000
1977	**2 teams**	**ATL N**	(4G 1–0)	**TEX A**	(12G 2–2)																						
″	**total**		3	2	.600	4.71	16	4	0	42	54	15	24	0	1	2	1	1	1	0	1.000	2	7	1	1	0.6	.900
1978	**MIN**	**A**	10	12	.455	2.36	54	0	0	99	80	37	56	0	10	**12**	21	0	0	0	—	9	19	1	1	0.5	.966
1979			10	15	.400	2.64	**90**	1	0	143	132	48	81	0	10	**14**	**32**	0	0	0	—	11	31	1	4	0.5	.977
1980			1	3	.250	6.19	18	0	0	32	42	12	13	0	1	3	1	0	0	0	—	4	7	0	0	0.6	1.000
1981	**NY**	**N**	3	2	.600	2.61	20	0	0	31	26	8	8	0	3	2	0	0	0	0	—	3	5	1	0	0.4	.889
14 yrs.			97	112	.464	3.14	723	24	3	1386	1281	514	880	1	92	98	188	179	35	1	.196	105	283	15	25	0.6	.963
															9th												
LEAGUE CHAMPIONSHIP SERIES																											
1974	**LA**	**N**	0	0	—	0.00	2	0	0	3	0	0	1	0	0	0	0	0	0	0	—	0	0	0	0	0.0	.000
WORLD SERIES																											
1974	**LA**	**N**	0	1	.000	1.00	5	0	0	9	6	1	10	0	0	1	1	0	0	0	—	0	4	0	0	0.8	1.000

Rube Marshall

MARSHALL, ROY DeVERNE (Cy)
B. July 19, 1890, Salineville, Ohio D. June 11, 1980, Dover, Ohio.
BR TR 5′11″ 170 lbs.

Year	Team	Lg	W	L	PCT	ERA	G	GS	CG	IP	H	BB	SO	ShO	Relief Pitching W	Relief Pitching L	Relief Pitching SV	Batting AB	Batting H	Batting HR	BA	PO	A	E	DP	TC/G	FA
1912	**PHI**	**N**	0	1	.000	21.00	2	1	0	3	12	1	2	0	0	0	0	0	0	0	—	0	1	0	0	0.5	1.000
1913			0	1	.000	4.57	14	3	0	45.1	54	22	18	0	0	0	1	11	1	0	.091	0	13	0	0	0.9	1.000

Rube Marshall *continued*

Year	Team	W	L	PCT	ERA	G	GS	CG	IP	H	BB	SO	ShO	Relief Pitching W	Relief Pitching L	Relief Pitching SV	Batting AB	Batting H	Batting HR	BA	PO	A	E	DP	TC/G	FA
1914		6	7	.462	3.75	27	19	7	134.1	144	50	49	0	1	0	1	43	6	0	.140	7	38	3	1	1.8	.938
1915	BUF F	3	1	.750	3.94	21	4	2	59.1	62	33	21	0	0	0	0	17	5	0	.294	0	15	1	0	0.8	.938
4 yrs.		9	10	.474	4.17	64	27	9	242	272	106	90	0	1	0	2	71	12	0	.169	7	67	4	1	1.2	.949

Barney Martin

MARTIN, BARNES ROBERTSON BR TR 5′11″ 170 lbs.
Father of Jerry Martin.
B. Mar. 3, 1923, Columbia, S. C.

Year	Team	W	L	PCT	ERA	G	GS	CG	IP	H	BB	SO	ShO	Relief Pitching W	Relief Pitching L	Relief Pitching SV	Batting AB	Batting H	Batting HR	BA	PO	A	E	DP	TC/G	FA
1953	CIN N	0	0	—	9.00	1	0	0	2	3	1	1	0	0	0	0	0	0	0	—	0	0	0	0	0.0	.000

Doc Martin

MARTIN, HAROLD WINTHROP BR TR 5′11″ 165 lbs.
B. Sept. 23, 1887, Roxbury, Mass. D. Apr. 14, 1935, Milton, Mass.

Year	Team	W	L	PCT	ERA	G	GS	CG	IP	H	BB	SO	ShO	Relief Pitching W	Relief Pitching L	Relief Pitching SV	Batting AB	Batting H	Batting HR	BA	PO	A	E	DP	TC/G	FA
1908	PHI A	0	1	.000	13.50	1	1	0	2	2	3	2	0	0	0	0	1	0	0	.000	0	0	0	0	0.0	.000
1911		1	1	.500	4.50	11	3	1	38	40	17	21	0	0	1	0	14	3	0	.214	1	12	2	0	1.4	.867
1912		0	0	—	10.38	2	0	0	4.1	5	5	4	0	0	0	0	3	0	0	.000	0	3	0	0	1.5	1.000
3 yrs.		1	2	.333	5.48	14	4	1	44.1	47	25	27	0	0	1	0	18	3	0	.167	1	15	2	0	1.3	.889

Freddie Martin

MARTIN, FRED TURNER BR TR 6′1″ 185 lbs.
B. June 27, 1915, Williams, Okla. D. June 11, 1979, Chicago, Ill.

Year	Team	W	L	PCT	ERA	G	GS	CG	IP	H	BB	SO	ShO	Relief Pitching W	Relief Pitching L	Relief Pitching SV	Batting AB	Batting H	Batting HR	BA	PO	A	E	DP	TC/G	FA
1946	STL N	2	1	.667	4.08	6	3	2	28.2	29	8	19	0	0	1	0	11	3	0	.273	2	7	1	1	1.7	.900
1949		6	0	1.000	2.44	21	5	3	70	65	20	30	0	2	0	0	20	6	0	.300	4	13	1	0	0.9	.944
1950		4	2	.667	5.12	30	2	0	63.1	87	30	19	0	4	0	0	15	4	0	.267	8	13	1	0	0.7	.955
3 yrs.		12	3	.800	3.78	57	10	5	162	181	58	68	0	6	1	0	46	13	0	.283	14	33	3	1	0.9	.940

John Martin

MARTIN, JOHN ROBERT BB TL 6′ 190 lbs.
B. Apr. 11, 1956, Wyandotte, Mich.

Year	Team	W	L	PCT	ERA	G	GS	CG	IP	H	BB	SO	ShO	Relief Pitching W	Relief Pitching L	Relief Pitching SV	Batting AB	Batting H	Batting HR	BA	PO	A	E	DP	TC/G	FA
1980	STL N	2	3	.400	4.29	9	5	1	42	39	9	23	0	0	1	0	11	3	0	.273	0	5	0	0	0.6	1.000
1981		8	5	.615	3.41	17	15	4	103	85	26	36	0	0	0	0	33	7	0	.212	3	20	0	0	1.4	1.000
1982		4	5	.444	4.23	24	7	0	66	56	30	21	0	1	2	0	11	1	0	.091	2	8	1	0	0.5	.909
1983	2 teams STL N (26G 3–1) DET A (15G 0–0)																									
″	total	3	1	.750	4.18	41	5	0	79.2	75	30	40	0	2	0	1	18	4	0	.222	3	16	1	0	0.5	.950
4 yrs.		17	14	.548	3.93	91	32	5	290.2	255	95	120	0	3	3	1	73	15	0	.205	8	49	2	0	0.6	.966

Morrie Martin

MARTIN, MORRIS WEBSTER BL TL 6′ 173 lbs.
B. Sept. 3, 1922, Dixon, Mo.

Year	Team	W	L	PCT	ERA	G	GS	CG	IP	H	BB	SO	ShO	Relief Pitching W	Relief Pitching L	Relief Pitching SV	Batting AB	Batting H	Batting HR	BA	PO	A	E	DP	TC/G	FA
1949	BKN N	1	3	.250	7.04	10	4	0	30.2	39	15	15	0	1	0	0	10	2	0	.200	0	7	1	0	0.8	.875
1951	PHI A	11	4	.733	3.78	35	13	3	138	139	63	35	1	5	0	0	50	11	0	.220	6	33	2	5	1.2	.951
1952		0	2	.000	6.39	5	5	0	25.1	32	15	13	0	0	0	0	9	1	0	.111	0	3	0	0	0.6	1.000
1953		10	12	.455	4.43	58	11	2	156.1	158	59	64	0	8	5	7	42	4	0	.095	2	26	0	4	0.5	1.000
1954	2 teams PHI A (13G 2–4) CHI A (35G 5–4)																									
″	total	7	8	.467	3.52	48	8	3	122.2	109	43	55	0	4	5	5	32	6	0	.188	4	19	1	1	0.5	.958
1955	CHI A	2	3	.400	3.63	37	0	0	52	50	22	22	0	2	3	2	10	3	0	.300	2	15	0	0	0.5	1.000
1956	2 teams CHI A (10G 1–0) BAL A (9G 1–1)																									
″	total	2	1	.667	6.17	19	0	0	23.1	31	9	12	0	2	1	0	5	1	0	.200	1	4	1	1	0.3	.833
1957	STL N	0	0	—	2.53	4	1	0	10.2	5	4	7	0	0	0	0	2	0	0	.000	1	3	0	0	1.0	1.000
1958	2 teams STL N (17G 3–1) CLE A (14G 2–0)																									
″	total	5	1	.833	3.74	31	0	0	43.1	39	20	21	0	5	1	1	5	0	0	.000	2	5	0	2	0.2	1.000
1959	CHI N	0	0	—	19.29	3	0	0	2.1	5	1	1	0	0	0	0	0	0	0	—	0	1	0	0	0.3	1.000
10 yrs.		38	34	.528	4.29	250	42	8	604.2	607	251	245	1	27	15	15	165	28	0	.170	18	116	5	13	0.6	.964

Pat Martin

MARTIN, PATRICK FRANCIS BL TL 5′11½″ 170 lbs.
B. Apr. 13, 1894, Brooklyn, N. Y. D. Feb. 4, 1949, Brooklyn, N. Y.

Year	Team	W	L	PCT	ERA	G	GS	CG	IP	H	BB	SO	ShO	Relief Pitching W	Relief Pitching L	Relief Pitching SV	Batting AB	Batting H	Batting HR	BA	PO	A	E	DP	TC/G	FA
1919	PHI A	0	2	.000	4.09	2	2	1	11	11	8	6	0	0	0	0	3	0	0	.000	0	2	1	0	1.5	.667
1920		1	4	.200	6.12	8	5	2	32.1	48	25	14	0	0	0	0	10	4	0	.400	0	6	3	0	1.1	.667
2 yrs.		1	6	.143	5.61	10	7	3	43.1	59	33	20	0	0	0	0	13	4	0	.308	0	8	4	0	1.2	.667

Paul Martin

MARTIN, PAUL CHARLES BR TR 6′6″ 235 lbs.
B. Mar. 10, 1932, Brownstone, Pa.

Year	Team	W	L	PCT	ERA	G	GS	CG	IP	H	BB	SO	ShO	Relief Pitching W	Relief Pitching L	Relief Pitching SV	Batting AB	Batting H	Batting HR	BA	PO	A	E	DP	TC/G	FA
1955	PIT N	0	1	.000	13.50	7	1	0	7.1	13	17	3	0	0	0	0	0	0	0	—	0	1	0	0	0.1	1.000

Pepper Martin

MARTIN, JOHN LEONARD ROOSEVELT (The Wild Hoss Of The Osage) BR TR 5′8″ 170 lbs.
B. Feb. 29, 1904, Temple, Okla. D. Mar. 5, 1965, McAlester, Okla.

Year	Team	W	L	PCT	ERA	G	GS	CG	IP	H	BB	SO	ShO	Relief Pitching W	Relief Pitching L	Relief Pitching SV	Batting AB	Batting H	Batting HR	BA	PO	A	E	DP	TC/G	FA
1934	STL N	0	0	—	4.50	1	0	0	2	1	0	0	0	0	0	0	454	131	5	.289	2	0	0	0	0.5	1.000
1936		0	0	—	0.00	1	0	0	2	1	2	0	0	0	0	0	572	177	11	.309	282	10	10	2	2.7	.967
2 yrs.		0	0		2.25	2	0	0	4	2	2	0	0	0	0	0	*				1692	775	124	58	2.5	.952

Ray Martin

MARTIN, RAYMOND JOSEPH BR TR 6′2″ 177 lbs.
B. Mar. 13, 1925, Norwood, Mass.

Year	Team	W	L	PCT	ERA	G	GS	CG	IP	H	BB	SO	ShO	Relief Pitching W	Relief Pitching L	Relief Pitching SV	Batting AB	Batting H	Batting HR	BA	PO	A	E	DP	TC/G	FA
1943	BOS N	0	0	—	8.10	2	0	0	3.1	3	1	1	0	0	0	0	1	0	0	.000	0	2	0	0	1.0	1.000
1947		1	0	1.000	1.00	1	1	1	9	7	4	2	0	0	0	0	3	0	0	.000	3	2	0	0	5.0	1.000
1948		0	0	—	0.00	2	0	0	2.1	0	1	0	0	0	0	0	0	0	0	—	0	0	0	0	0.0	.000
3 yrs.		1	0	1.000	2.45	5	1	1	14.2	10	6	3	0	0	0	0	4	0	0	.000	3	4	0	0	1.4	1.000

Renie Martin

MARTIN, DONALD RENIE BR TR 6′4″ 190 lbs.
B. Aug. 30, 1955, Dover, Del.

Year	Team	W	L	PCT	ERA	G	GS	CG	IP	H	BB	SO	ShO	Relief Pitching W	Relief Pitching L	Relief Pitching SV	Batting AB	Batting H	Batting HR	BA	PO	A	E	DP	TC/G	FA
1979	KC A	0	3	.000	5.14	25	0	0	35	32	14	25	0	0	3	5	0	0	0	—	5	8	1	0	0.6	.929
1980		10	10	.500	4.40	32	20	2	137	133	70	68	0	2	0	2	0	0	0	—	10	18	4	5	1.0	.875
1981		4	5	.444	2.76	29	0	0	62	55	29	25	0	4	5	4	0	0	0	—	3	15	2	2	0.7	.900
1982	SF N	7	10	.412	4.66	29	25	1	141	148	64	63	0	0	0	0	49	13	0	.265	8	28	5	2	1.4	.878
1983		2	4	.333	4.20	37	6	0	94.1	95	51	43	0	2	1	1	26	9	0	.346	15	16	0	0	0.8	1.000
1984	2 teams SF N (12G 1–1) PHI N (9G 0–2)																									
″	total	1	3	.250	4.15	21	0	0	39	46	28	13	0	1	3	0	8	3	0	.375	3	14	0	1	0.8	1.000
6 yrs.		24	35	.407	4.27	173	51	3	508.1	509	256	237	0	9	12	12	83	25	0	.301	44	99	12	10	0.9	.923

Renie Martin *continued*

Year	Team	Lg	W	L	PCT	ERA	G	GS	CG	IP	H	BB	SO	ShO	Relief Pitching W	Relief Pitching L	Relief Pitching SV	Batting AB	Batting H	Batting HR	BA	PO	A	E	DP	TC/G	FA
DIVISIONAL PLAYOFF SERIES																											
1981	KC	A	0	0	—	0.00	2	0	0	5.1	1	2	2	0	0	0	0	0	0	0	—	0	0	0	0	0.0	.000
WORLD SERIES																											
1980	KC	A	0	0	—	2.79	3	0	0	9.2	11	3	2	0	0	0	0	0	0	0	—	0	0	0	0	0.0	.000

Speed Martin

MARTIN, ELWOOD GOOD
B. Sept. 15, 1893, Wawawai, Wash. D. June 14, 1983, Lemon Grove, Calif.
BR TR 6′ 165 lbs.

Year	Team	Lg	W	L	PCT	ERA	G	GS	CG	IP	H	BB	SO	ShO	Relief Pitching W	Relief Pitching L	Relief Pitching SV	Batting AB	Batting H	Batting HR	BA	PO	A	E	DP	TC/G	FA
1917	STL	A	0	2	.000	5.74	9	2	0	15.2	20	5	5	0	0	0	0	2	0	0	.000	3	11	1	0	1.7	.933
1918	CHI	N	6	2	.750	1.84	9	5	4	53.2	47	14	16	1	3	0	0	16	3	0	.188	4	18	1	1	2.6	.957
1919			8	8	.500	2.47	35	14	7	163.2	158	52	54	2	2	1	2	44	8	0	.182	9	53	3	3	1.9	.954
1920			4	15	.211	4.83	35	13	6	136	165	50	44	0	1	5	2	44	7	1	.159	6	44	4	1	1.5	.926
1921			11	15	.423	4.35	37	28	13	217.1	245	68	86	1	2	1	1	73	17	0	.233	9	65	1	1	2.0	.987
1922			1	0	1.000	7.50	1	1	0	6	10	2	2	0	0	0	0	1	0	0	.000	0	0	0	0	0.0	.000
6 yrs.			30	42	.417	3.78	126	63	30	592.1	645	191	207	4	8	7	5	180	35	1	.194	31	191	10	6	1.8	.957

Joe Martina

MARTINA, JOHN JOSEPH (Oyster Joe)
B. July 8, 1889, New Orleans, La. D. Mar. 22, 1962, New Orleans, La.
BR TR 6′ 183 lbs.

Year	Team	Lg	W	L	PCT	ERA	G	GS	CG	IP	H	BB	SO	ShO	Relief Pitching W	Relief Pitching L	Relief Pitching SV	Batting AB	Batting H	Batting HR	BA	PO	A	E	DP	TC/G	FA
1924	WAS	A	6	8	.429	4.67	24	14	8	125.1	129	56	57	0	2	2	0	43	14	0	.326	3	20	1	2	1.0	.958
WORLD SERIES																											
1924	WAS	A	0	0	—	0.00	1	0	0	1	0	0	1	0	0	0	0	0	0	0	—	0	0	0	0	0.0	.000

Buck Martinez

MARTINEZ, JOHN ALBERT
B. Nov. 7, 1948, Redding, Calif.
BR TR 5′10″ 190 lbs.

Year	Team	Lg	W	L	PCT	ERA	G	GS	CG	IP	H	BB	SO	ShO	Relief Pitching W	Relief Pitching L	Relief Pitching SV	Batting AB	Batting H	Batting HR	BA	PO	A	E	DP	TC/G	FA
1979	MIL	A	0	0	—	9.00	1	0	0	1	1	1	0	0	0	0	0	*				292	26	9	8	5.8	.972

Dave Martinez

MARTINEZ, DAVID
B. Sept. 26, 1964, New York, N. Y.
BL TL 5′10″ 150 lbs.

Year	Team	Lg	W	L	PCT	ERA	G	GS	CG	IP	H	BB	SO	ShO	Relief Pitching W	Relief Pitching L	Relief Pitching SV	Batting AB	Batting H	Batting HR	BA	PO	A	E	DP	TC/G	FA
1990	MON	N	0	0	—	54.00	1	0	0	0.1	2	2	0	0	0	0	0	391	109	11	.279	77	2	1	1	1.7	.988
1995	CHI	A	0	0	—	0.00	1	0	0	1	0	2	0	0	0	0	0	303	93	5	.307	283	10	6	1	2.2	.980
2 yrs.			0	0		13.50	2	0	0	1.1	2	4	0	0	0	0	0	*				2470	106	40	85	2.5	.985

Dennis Martinez

MARTINEZ, JOSE DENNIS (El Presidente)
Born Jose Dennis Martinez (Emilia).
B. May 14, 1955, Granada, Nicaragua.
BR TR 6′ 1″ 175 lbs.

Year	Team	Lg	W	L	PCT	ERA	G	GS	CG	IP	H	BB	SO	ShO	Relief Pitching W	Relief Pitching L	Relief Pitching SV	Batting AB	Batting H	Batting HR	BA	PO	A	E	DP	TC/G	FA
1976	BAL	A	1	2	.333	2.57	4	2	1	28	23	8	18	0	1	0	0	0	0	0	—	3	4	0	0	1.8	1.000
1977			14	7	.667	4.10	42	13	5	167	157	64	107	0	8	4	4	0	0	0	—	9	26	1	2	0.9	.972
1978			16	11	.593	3.52	40	38	15	276.1	257	93	142	2	0	0	0	0	0	0	—	27	51	1	6	2.0	.987
1979			15	16	.484	3.67	40	**39**	**18**	**292**	279	78	132	3	0	0	0	0	0	0	—	26	59	5	3	2.3	.944
1980			6	4	.600	3.96	25	12	2	100	103	44	42	0	0	1	1	0	0	0	—	5	16	0	1	0.8	1.000
1981			**14**	5	.737	3.32	25	24	9	179	173	62	88	2	0	0	0	0	0	0	—	20	44	2	4	2.6	.970
1982			16	12	.571	4.21	40	39	10	252	262	87	111	2	0	0	0	0	0	0	—	13	38	1	2	1.3	.981
1983			7	16	.304	5.53	32	25	4	153	209	45	71	0	1	0	0	0	0	0	—	16	42	1	0	1.8	.983
1984			6	9	.400	5.02	34	20	2	141.2	145	37	77	0	1	2	0	0	0	0	—	17	19	2	4	1.1	.947
1985			13	11	.542	5.15	33	31	3	180	203	63	68	1	1	0	0	0	0	0	—	17	26	1	0	1.3	.977
1986	2 teams	BAL A	(4G 0–0)		MON N	(19G 3–6)																					
″	total		3	6	.333	4.73	23	15	1	104.2	114	30	65	1	0	0	0	30	3	0	.100	4	25	1	0	1.3	.967
1987	MON	N	11	4	.733	3.30	22	22	2	144.2	133	40	84	1	0	0	0	46	3	0	.065	10	23	1	3	1.5	.971
1988			15	13	.536	2.72	34	34	9	235.1	215	55	120	2	0	0	0	78	15	0	.192	19	39	6	3	1.9	.906
1989			16	7	.696	3.18	34	33	5	232	227	49	142	2	0	1	0	72	9	0	.125	11	50	2	6	1.9	.968
1990			10	11	.476	2.95	32	32	7	226	191	49	156	2	0	0	0	68	7	0	.103	16	35	1	2	1.6	.981
1991			14	11	.560	**2.39**	31	31	**9**	222	187	62	123	**5**	0	0	0	72	11	0	.153	21	48	4	5	2.4	.945
1992			16	11	.593	2.47	32	32	6	226.1	172	60	147	0	0	0	0	74	14	0	.189	20	45	4	3	2.2	.942
1993			15	9	.625	3.85	35	34	2	224.2	211	64	138	0	0	0	1	69	11	0	.159	17	46	1	1	1.8	.984
1994	CLE	A	11	6	.647	3.52	24	24	7	176.2	166	44	92	3	0	0	0	0	0	0	—	11	33	0	2	1.8	1.000
1995			12	5	.706	3.08	28	28	3	187	174	46	99	2	0	0	0	0	0	0	—	15	46	4	3	2.3	.938
20 yrs.			231	176	.568	3.60	610	528	120	3748.1	3601	1080	2022	28	12	8	6	509	73	0	.143	297	715	38	50	1.7	.964
DIVISIONAL PLAYOFF SERIES																											
1995	CLE	A	0	0	—	3.00	1	1	0	6	5	0	2	0	0	0	0	0	0	0	—	0	1	0	0	1.0	1.000
LEAGUE CHAMPIONSHIP SERIES																											
1979	BAL	A	0	0	—	3.24	1	1	0	8.1	8	0	4	0	0	0	0	0	0	0	—	2	0	0	0	2.0	1.000
1995	CLE	A	1	1	.500	2.02	2	2	0	13.1	10	3	7	0	0	0	0	0	0	0	—	1	1	0	0	1.0	1.000
2 yrs.			1	1	.500	2.49	3	3	0	21.2	18	3	11	0	0	0	0	0	0	0		3	1	0	0	1.3	1.000
WORLD SERIES																											
1979	BAL	A	0	0	—	18.00	2	1	0	2	6	0	0	0	0	0	0	0	0	0	—	0	1	0	1	0.5	1.000
1995	CLE	A	0	1	.000	3.48	2	2	0	10.1	12	8	5	0	0	0	0	3	0	0	.000	0	3	1	0	2.0	.750
2 yrs.			0	1	.000	5.84	4	3	0	12.1	18	8	5	0	0	0	0	3	0	0	.000	0	4	1	1	1.3	.800

Fred Martinez

MARTINEZ, ALFREDO
B. Mar. 15, 1957, Los Angeles, Calif.
BR TR 6′ 3″ 185 lbs.

Year	Team	Lg	W	L	PCT	ERA	G	GS	CG	IP	H	BB	SO	ShO	Relief Pitching W	Relief Pitching L	Relief Pitching SV	Batting AB	Batting H	Batting HR	BA	PO	A	E	DP	TC/G	FA
1980	CAL	A	7	9	.438	4.53	30	23	4	149	150	59	57	1	0	0	0	0	0	0	—	3	17	2	0	0.7	.909
1981			0	0	—	3.00	2	0	0	6	5	3	4	0	0	0	0	0	0	0	—	0	2	0	0	1.0	1.000
2 yrs.			7	9	.438	4.47	32	23	4	155	155	62	61	1	0	0	0	0	0	0		3	19	2	0	0.8	.917

Jose Martinez

MARTINEZ, JOSE MIGUEL
Born Jose Martinez (Martinez).
B. Apr. 1, 1971, Guayabin, Dominican Republic.
BR TR 6′ 2″ 180 lbs.

Year	Team	Lg	W	L	PCT	ERA	G	GS	CG	IP	H	BB	SO	ShO	Relief Pitching W	Relief Pitching L	Relief Pitching SV	Batting AB	Batting H	Batting HR	BA	PO	A	E	DP	TC/G	FA
1994	SD	N	0	2	.000	6.75	4	1	0	12	18	5	7	0	0	1	0	2	0	0	.000	0	2	0	0	0.5	1.000

Marty Martinez

MARTINEZ, ORLANDO
Born Orlando Martinez Oliva.
B. Aug. 23, 1941, Havana, Cuba.
Manager 1986.

BB TR 6′ 170 lbs.
BR 1962

Year	Team	W	L	PCT	ERA	G	GS	CG	IP	H	BB	SO	ShO	Relief Pitching W	Relief Pitching L	Relief Pitching SV	Batting AB	Batting H	HR	BA	PO	A	E	DP	TC/G	FA
1969	HOU N	0	0	—	9.00	1	0	0	1	1	0	0	0	0	0	0	*				6	18	2	2	2.2	.923

Pedro Martinez

MARTINEZ, PEDRO
Born Pedro Martinez (Aquino).
B. Nov. 29, 1968, Villa Mella, Dominican Republic.

BL TL 6′ 2″ 155 lbs.

Year	Team	W	L	PCT	ERA	G	GS	CG	IP	H	BB	SO	ShO	Relief Pitching W	Relief Pitching L	Relief Pitching SV	Batting AB	Batting H	HR	BA	PO	A	E	DP	TC/G	FA
1993	SD N	3	1	.750	2.43	32	0	0	37	23	13	32	0	3	1	0	4	0	0	.000	2	4	1	0	0.2	.857
1994		3	2	.600	2.90	48	1	0	68.1	52	49	52	0	3	2	3	5	0	0	.000	5	17	4	1	0.5	.846
1995	HOU N	0	0	—	7.40	25	0	0	20.2	29	16	17	0	0	0	0	0	0	0	—	3	2	0	0	0.2	1.000
3 yrs.		6	3	.667	3.50	105	1	0	126	104	78	101	0	6	3	3	9	0	0	.000	10	23	5	1	0.4	.868

Pedro Martinez

MARTINEZ, PEDRO
Born Pedro Jaime (Martinez).
Brother of Ramon Martinez.
B. July 25, 1971, Manoguayabo, Dominican Republic.

BR TR 5′11″ 150 lbs.

Year	Team	W	L	PCT	ERA	G	GS	CG	IP	H	BB	SO	ShO	Relief Pitching W	Relief Pitching L	Relief Pitching SV	Batting AB	Batting H	HR	BA	PO	A	E	DP	TC/G	FA
1992	LA N	0	1	.000	2.25	2	1	0	8	6	1	8	0	0	0	0	2	0	0	.000	0	0	0	0	0.0	.000
1993		10	5	.667	2.61	65	2	0	107	76	57	119	0	**10**	3	2	4	0	0	.000	4	4	0	1	0.1	1.000
1994	MON N	11	5	.688	3.42	24	23	1	144.2	115	45	142	1	0	0	1	44	4	0	.091	9	15	4	0	1.2	.857
1995		14	10	.583	3.51	30	30	2	194.2	158	66	174	2	0	0	0	63	7	0	.111	13	23	2	0	1.3	.947
4 yrs.		35	21	.625	3.25	121	56	3	454.1	355	169	443	3	10	3	3	113	11	0	.097	26	42	6	1	0.6	.919

Ramon Martinez

MARTINEZ, RAMON
Born Ramon Jaime (Martinez).
Brother of Pedro Martinez.
B. Mar. 22, 1968, Santo Domingo, Dominican Republic.

BR TR 6′ 4″ 165 lbs.

Year	Team	W	L	PCT	ERA	G	GS	CG	IP	H	BB	SO	ShO	Relief Pitching W	Relief Pitching L	Relief Pitching SV	Batting AB	Batting H	HR	BA	PO	A	E	DP	TC/G	FA
1988	LA N	1	3	.250	3.79	9	6	0	35.2	27	22	23	0	0	0	0	7	0	0	.000	1	5	0	0	0.7	1.000
1989		6	4	.600	3.19	15	15	2	98.2	79	41	89	2	0	0	0	37	6	0	.162	11	14	0	1	1.7	1.000
1990		20	6	.769	2.92	33	33	**12**	234.1	191	67	223	3	0	0	0	80	10	0	.125	16	27	1	0	1.3	.977
1991		17	13	.567	3.27	33	33	6	220.1	190	69	150	4	0	0	0	77	9	1	.117	22	21	2	0	1.4	.956
1992		8	11	.421	4.00	25	25	1	150.2	141	69	101	1	0	0	0	50	6	0	.120	10	18	2	1	1.2	.933
1993		10	12	.455	3.44	32	32	4	211.2	202	**104**	127	3	0	0	0	70	9	0	.129	28	31	0	4	1.8	1.000
1994		12	7	.632	3.97	24	24	4	170	160	56	119	**3**	0	0	0	66	18	0	.273	21	17	3	0	1.7	.927
1995		17	7	.708	3.66	30	30	4	206.1	176	**81**	138	2	0	0	0	64	11	0	.172	16	27	3	2	1.5	.935
8 yrs.		91	63	.591	3.48	201	198	33	1327.2	1166	509	970	18	0	0	0	451	69	1	.153	125	160	11	8	1.5	.963
DIVISIONAL PLAYOFF SERIES																										
1995	LA N	0	1	.000	14.54	1	1	0	4.1	10	2	3	0	0	0	0	1	0	0	.000	0	1	0	0	1.0	1.000

Rogelio Martinez

MARTINEZ, ROGELIO (Limonar)
Born Rogelio Martinez (Ulloa).
B. Nov. 5, 1918, Cidra, Cuba.

BR TR 6′ 180 lbs.

Year	Team	W	L	PCT	ERA	G	GS	CG	IP	H	BB	SO	ShO	Relief Pitching W	Relief Pitching L	Relief Pitching SV	Batting AB	Batting H	HR	BA	PO	A	E	DP	TC/G	FA
1950	WAS A	0	1	.000	27.00	2	1	0	1.1	4	2	0	0	0	0	0	0	0	0	—	0	0	0	0	0.0	.000

Silvio Martinez

MARTINEZ, SILVIO RAMON
Born Silvio Ramon Martinez (Cabrera).
B. Aug. 19, 1955, Santiago, Dominican Republic.

BR TR 5′10″ 170 lbs.

Year	Team	W	L	PCT	ERA	G	GS	CG	IP	H	BB	SO	ShO	Relief Pitching W	Relief Pitching L	Relief Pitching SV	Batting AB	Batting H	HR	BA	PO	A	E	DP	TC/G	FA
1977	CHI A	0	1	.000	5.57	10	0	0	21	28	12	10	0	0	1	1	0	0	0	—	2	4	1	1	0.7	.857
1978	STL N	9	8	.529	3.65	22	22	5	138	114	71	45	2	0	0	0	47	8	0	.170	9	18	3	0	1.4	.900
1979		15	8	.652	3.26	32	29	7	207	204	67	102	2	0	0	0	62	8	0	.129	17	15	4	3	1.1	.889
1980		5	10	.333	4.80	25	20	2	120	127	48	39	0	1	0	0	35	3	0	.086	4	12	2	2	0.7	.889
1981		2	5	.286	3.99	18	16	0	97	95	39	34	0	0	0	0	35	7	0	.200	6	13	1	0	1.1	.950
5 yrs.		31	32	.492	3.87	107	87	14	583	568	237	230	4	1	1	1	179	26	0	.145	38	62	11	6	1.0	.901

Tippy Martinez

MARTINEZ, FELIX ANTHONY
B. May 31, 1950, La Junta, Colo.

BL TL 5′10″ 180 lbs.

Year	Team	W	L	PCT	ERA	G	GS	CG	IP	H	BB	SO	ShO	Relief Pitching W	Relief Pitching L	Relief Pitching SV	Batting AB	Batting H	HR	BA	PO	A	E	DP	TC/G	FA
1974	NY A	0	0	—	4.15	10	0	0	13	14	9	10	0	0	0	0	0	0	0	—	1	1	0	0	0.2	1.000
1975		1	2	.333	2.68	23	2	0	37	27	32	20	0	1	0	8	0	0	0	—	2	2	1	0	0.2	.800
1976	2 teams NY A (11G 2–0) BAL A (28G 3–1)																									
″	total	5	1	.833	2.33	39	0	0	69.2	50	42	45	0	5	1	10	0	0	0		11	15	0	1	0.7	1.000
1977	BAL A	5	1	.833	2.70	41	0	0	50	47	27	29	0	5	1	9	0	0	0	—	2	12	0	3	0.3	1.000
1978		3	3	.500	4.83	42	0	0	69	77	40	57	0	3	3	5	0	0	0	—	8	13	0	1	0.5	1.000
1979		10	3	.769	2.88	39	0	0	78	59	31	61	0	10	3	3	0	0	0	—	4	13	1	2	0.5	.944
1980		4	4	.500	3.00	53	0	0	81	69	34	68	0	4	4	10	0	0	0	—	5	16	0	3	0.4	1.000
1981		3	3	.500	2.90	37	0	0	59	48	32	50	0	3	3	11	0	0	0	—	3	13	3	0	0.5	.842
1982		8	8	.500	3.41	76	0	0	95	81	37	78	0	8	8	16	0	0	0	—	6	10	0	1	0.2	1.000
1983		9	3	.750	2.35	65	0	0	103.1	76	37	81	0	9	3	21	0	0	0	—	5	23	0	1	0.4	1.000
1984		4	9	.308	3.91	55	0	0	89.2	88	51	71	0	4	9	17	0	0	0	—	2	14	2	0	0.3	.889
1985		3	3	.500	5.40	49	0	0	70	70	37	47	0	3	3	4	0	0	0	—	9	10	1	1	0.4	.950
1986		0	2	.000	5.63	14	0	0	16	18	12	11	0	0	2	1	0	0	0	—	0	3	1	0	0.3	.750
1988	MIN A	0	0	—	18.00	3	0	0	4	8	4	3	0	0	0	0	0	0	0	—	0	0	0	0	0.0	.000
14 yrs.		55	42	.567	3.45	546	2	0	834.2	732	425	631	0	55	40	115	0	0	0		58	145	9	13	0.4	.958
LEAGUE CHAMPIONSHIP SERIES																										
1983	BAL A	1	0	1.000	0.00	2	0	0	6	5	3	5	0	1	0	0	0	0	0	—	0	2	0	0	1.0	1.000
WORLD SERIES																										
1979	BAL A	0	0	—	6.75	3	0	0	1.1	3	0	1	0	0	0	0	0	0	0	—	0	0	0	0	0.0	.000
1983		0	0	—	3.00	3	0	0	3	3	0	0	0	0	0	2	0	0	0	—	0	0	0	0	0.0	.000
2 yrs.		0	0		4.15	6	0	0	4.1	6	0	1	0	0	0	2	0	0	0		0	0	0	0	0.0	

Wedo Martini

MARTINI, GUIDO JOE (Southern)
B. July 1, 1913, Birmingham, Ala. D. Oct. 28, 1970, Philadelphia, Pa.

BR TR 5′10″ 165 lbs.

Year	Team	W	L	PCT	ERA	G	GS	CG	IP	H	BB	SO	ShO	Relief Pitching W	Relief Pitching L	Relief Pitching SV	Batting AB	Batting H	HR	BA	PO	A	E	DP	TC/G	FA
1935	PHI A	0	2	.000	17.05	3	2	0	6.1	8	11	1	0	0	0	0	2	0	0	.000	0	4	0	0	1.3	1.000

Joe Marty

MARTY, JOSEPH ANTON BR TR 6′ 182 lbs.
B. Sept. 1, 1913, Sacramento, Calif. D. Oct. 4, 1984, Sacramento, Calif.

Year	Team		W	L	PCT	ERA	G	GS	CG	IP	H	BB	SO	ShO	Relief W	Relief L	Relief SV	Batting AB	Batting H	HR	BA	PO	A	E	DP	TC/G	FA
1939	PHI	N	0	0	—	4.50	1	0	0	4	2	3	1	0	0	0	0	*				196	4	5	0	2.4	.976

Randy Martz

MARTZ, RANDY CARL BL TR 6′ 4″ 210 lbs.
B. May 28, 1956, Harrisburg, Pa.

Year	Team		W	L	PCT	ERA	G	GS	CG	IP	H	BB	SO	ShO	Relief W	Relief L	Relief SV	Batting AB	Batting H	HR	BA	PO	A	E	DP	TC/G	FA
1980	CHI	N	1	2	.333	2.10	6	6	0	30	28	11	5	0	0	0	0	9	1	0	.111	7	6	0	0	2.2	1.000
1981			5	7	.417	3.67	33	14	1	108	103	49	32	0	2	0	6	28	6	0	.214	7	18	0	2	0.8	1.000
1982			11	10	.524	4.21	28	24	1	147.2	157	36	40	0	1	1	1	42	6	0	.143	15	27	1	1	1.5	.977
1983	CHI	A	0	0	—	3.60	1	1	0	5	4	4	1	0	0	0	0	0	0	0	—	1	0	0	0	1.0	1.000
4 yrs.			17	19	.472	3.78	68	45	2	290.2	292	100	78	0	3	1	7	79	13	0	.165	30	51	1	3	1.2	.988

Del Mason

MASON, ADELBERT WILLIAM BR TR 6′ 160 lbs.
B. Oct. 29, 1883, Newfane, N. Y. D. Dec. 31, 1962, Winter Park, Fla.

Year	Team		W	L	PCT	ERA	G	GS	CG	IP	H	BB	SO	ShO	Relief W	Relief L	Relief SV	Batting AB	Batting H	HR	BA	PO	A	E	DP	TC/G	FA
1904	WAS	A	0	3	.000	6.00	5	3	2	33	45	13	16	0	0	1	0	15	0	0	.000	3	6	0	0	1.8	1.000
1906	CIN	N	0	1	.000	4.50	2	1	1	12	10	6	4	0	0	0	0	5	0	0	.000	1	2	0	0	1.5	1.000
1907			5	12	.294	3.14	25	17	13	146	144	55	45	1	2	1	0	44	8	0	.182	6	44	1	4	2.0	.980
3 yrs.			5	16	.238	3.72	32	21	16	191	199	74	65	1	2	2	0	64	8	0	.125	10	52	1	4	2.0	.984

Ernie Mason

MASON, ERNEST
B. New Orleans, La. D. July 30, 1904, Covington, La.

Year	Team		W	L	PCT	ERA	G	GS	CG	IP	H	BB	SO	ShO	Relief W	Relief L	Relief SV	Batting AB	Batting H	HR	BA	PO	A	E	DP	TC/G	FA
1894	STL	N	0	2	.000	7.15	4	2	2	22.2	34	10	3	0	0	1	0	12	3	0	.250	2	2	1	0	1.0	.800

Hank Mason

MASON, HENRY BR TR 6′ 185 lbs.
B. June 19, 1931, Marshall, Mo.

Year	Team		W	L	PCT	ERA	G	GS	CG	IP	H	BB	SO	ShO	Relief W	Relief L	Relief SV	Batting AB	Batting H	HR	BA	PO	A	E	DP	TC/G	FA
1958	PHI	N	0	0	—	10.80	1	0	0	5	7	2	3	0	0	0	0	2	0	0	.000	0	0	0	0	0.0	.000
1960			0	0	—	9.53	3	0	0	5.2	9	5	3	0	0	0	0	1	0	0	.000	0	1	0	0	0.3	1.000
2 yrs.			0	0		10.13	4	0	0	10.2	16	7	6	0	0	0	0	3	0	0	.000	0	1	0	0	0.3	1.000

Mike Mason

MASON, MICHAEL PAUL BL TL 6′ 2″ 205 lbs.
B. Nov. 21, 1958, Faribault, Minn.

Year	Team		W	L	PCT	ERA	G	GS	CG	IP	H	BB	SO	ShO	Relief W	Relief L	Relief SV	Batting AB	Batting H	HR	BA	PO	A	E	DP	TC/G	FA
1982	TEX	A	1	2	.333	5.09	4	4	0	23	21	9	8	0	0	0	0	0	0	0	—	1	5	0	0	1.5	1.000
1983			0	2	.000	5.91	5	0	0	10.2	10	6	9	0	0	2	0	0	0	0	—	1	2	0	0	0.6	1.000
1984			9	13	.409	3.61	36	24	4	184.1	159	51	113	0	3	0	0	0	0	0	—	4	22	0	0	0.7	1.000
1985			8	15	.348	4.83	38	30	1	179	212	73	92	1	0	0	0	0	0	0	—	4	30	4	0	1.0	.895
1986			7	3	.700	4.33	27	22	2	135	135	56	85	1	0	0	0	0	0	0	—	9	19	0	1	1.0	1.000
1987	2 teams	TEX A (8G 0–2)	CHI N (17G 4–1)																								
″	total		4	3	.571	5.64	25	10	0	67	80	45	49	0	2	0	0	9	2	0	.222	2	10	1	2	0.5	.923
1988	MIN	A	0	1	.000	10.80	5	0	0	6.2	8	9	7	0	0	1	0	0	0	0	—	0	0	0	0	0.0	.000
7 yrs.			29	39	.426	4.53	140	90	7	605.2	625	249	363	2	5	3	0	9	2	0	.222	21	88	5	3	0.8	.956

Roger Mason

MASON, ROGER LeROY BR TR 6′ 6″ 215 lbs.
B. Sept. 18, 1958, Bellaire, Mich.

Year	Team		W	L	PCT	ERA	G	GS	CG	IP	H	BB	SO	ShO	Relief W	Relief L	Relief SV	Batting AB	Batting H	HR	BA	PO	A	E	DP	TC/G	FA
1984	DET	A	1	1	.500	4.50	5	2	0	22	23	10	15	0	0	0	1	0	0	0	—	5	1	0	0	1.5	1.000
1985	SF	N	1	3	.250	2.12	5	5	1	29.2	28	11	26	1	0	0	0	11	1	0	.091	4	2	0	0	1.2	1.000
1986			3	4	.429	4.80	11	11	1	60	56	30	43	0	0	0	0	21	1	0	.048	6	4	1	0	1.0	.909
1987			1	1	.500	4.50	5	5	0	26	30	10	18	0	0	0	0	8	1	0	.125	3	3	0	2	1.2	1.000
1989	HOU	N	0	0	—	20.25	2	0	0	1.1	2	2	3	0	0	0	0	0	0	0	—	1	0	0	0	0.5	1.000
1991	PIT	N	3	2	.600	3.03	24	0	0	29.2	21	6	21	0	3	2	3	0	0	0	—	1	5	0	1	0.3	1.000
1992			5	7	.417	4.09	65	0	0	88	80	33	56	0	5	7	8	10	0	0	.000	6	7	1	0	0.2	.929
1993	2 teams	SD N (34G 0–7)	PHI N (34G 5–5)																								
″	total		5	12	.294	4.06	68	0	0	99.2	90	34	71	0	5	**12**	0	6	1	0	.167	2	8	0	0	0.1	1.000
1994	2 teams	PHI N (6G 1–1)	NY N (41G 2–4)																								
″	total		3	5	.375	3.75	47	0	0	60	55	25	33	0	3	5	1	0	0	0		3	3	0	0	0.1	1.000
9 yrs.			22	35	.386	4.02	232	23	2	416.1	385	161	286	1	16	26	13	56	4	0	.071	31	33	2	3	0.3	.970
LEAGUE CHAMPIONSHIP SERIES																											
1991	PIT	N	0	0	—	0.00	3	0	0	4.1	3	1	2	0	0	0	1	1	0	0	.000	0	0	0	0	0.0	.000
1992			0	0	—	0.00	2	0	0	3.1	0	2	1	0	0	0	0	0	0	0	—	2	0	0	0	1.0	1.000
1993	PHI	N	0	0	—	0.00	2	0	0	3	1	0	2	0	0	0	0	0	0	0	—	0	0	0	0	0.0	.000
3 yrs.			0	0		0.00	7	0	0	10.2	4	3	5	0	0	0	1	1	0	0	.000	2	0	0	0	0.3	1.000
WORLD SERIES																											
1993	PHI	N	0	0	—	1.17	4	0	0	7.2	4	1	7	0	0	0	0	1	0	0	.000	0	0	0	0	0.0	.000

Walt Masters

MASTERS, WALTER THOMAS BR TR 5′10½″ 180 lbs.
B. Mar. 28, 1907, Pen Argyl, Pa. D. July 10, 1992, Ottawa, Ont., Canada.

Year	Team		W	L	PCT	ERA	G	GS	CG	IP	H	BB	SO	ShO	Relief W	Relief L	Relief SV	Batting AB	Batting H	HR	BA	PO	A	E	DP	TC/G	FA
1931	WAS	A	0	0	—	2.00	3	0	0	9	7	4	1	0	0	0	1	2	0	0	.000	0	4	0	1	1.3	1.000
1937	PHI	N	0	0	—	36.00	1	0	0	1	5	1	0	0	0	0	0	0	0	0	—	0	0	0	0	0.0	.000
1939	PHI	A	0	0	—	6.55	4	0	0	11	15	8	2	0	0	0	0	2	0	0	.000	0	3	1	0	1.0	.750
3 yrs.			0	0		6.00	8	0	0	21	27	13	3	0	0	0	1	4	0	0	.000	0	7	1	1	1.0	.875

Paul Masterson

MASTERSON, PAUL NICKALIS (Lefty) BL TL 5′11″ 165 lbs.
B. Oct. 16, 1915, Chicago, Ill.

Year	Team		W	L	PCT	ERA	G	GS	CG	IP	H	BB	SO	ShO	Relief W	Relief L	Relief SV	Batting AB	Batting H	HR	BA	PO	A	E	DP	TC/G	FA
1940	PHI	N	0	0	—	7.20	2	0	0	5	5	2	3	0	0	0	0	1	0	0	.000	0	1	0	0	0.5	1.000
1941			1	0	1.000	4.76	2	1	1	11.1	11	6	8	0	0	0	0	4	0	0	.000	0	2	0	0	1.0	1.000
1942			0	0	—	6.48	4	0	0	8.1	10	5	3	0	0	0	0	0	0	0	—	0	2	0	0	0.5	1.000
3 yrs.			1	0	1.000	5.84	8	1	1	24.2	26	13	14	0	0	0	0	5	0	0	.000	0	5	0	0	0.6	1.000

Walt Masterson

MASTERSON, WALTER EDWARD BR TR 6′ 2″ 189 lbs.
B. June 22, 1920, Philadelphia, Pa.

Year	Team		W	L	PCT	ERA	G	GS	CG	IP	H	BB	SO	ShO	Relief W	Relief L	Relief SV	Batting AB	Batting H	HR	BA	PO	A	E	DP	TC/G	FA
1939	WAS	A	2	2	.500	5.55	24	5	1	58.1	66	48	12	0	1	0	0	13	2	0	.154	2	9	2	0	0.5	.846
1940			3	13	.188	4.90	31	19	3	130.1	128	88	68	0	1	1	2	38	7	0	.184	5	16	1	0	0.7	.955
1941			4	3	.571	5.97	34	6	1	78.1	101	53	40	0	2	0	3	19	2	0	.105	4	17	1	2	0.6	.955
1942			5	9	.357	3.34	25	15	8	142.2	138	54	63	4	0	2	2	45	7	0	.156	8	22	7	0	1.5	.811
1945			1	2	.333	1.08	4	2	1	25	21	10	14	1	0	2	0	9	1	0	.111	2	4	0	0	1.5	1.000

Walt Masterson *continued*

Year	Team		W	L	PCT	ERA	G	GS	CG	IP	H	BB	SO	ShO	Relief Pitching W	Relief Pitching L	Relief Pitching SV	Batting AB	Batting H	HR	BA	PO	A	E	DP	TC/G	FA
1946			5	6	.455	6.01	29	9	2	91.1	105	67	61	0	4	2	1	25	2	0	.080	5	15	1	0	0.7	.952
1947			12	16	.429	3.13	35	31	14	253	215	97	135	4	0	0	1	83	11	0	.133	14	51	6	4	2.0	.915
1948			8	15	.348	3.83	33	27	9	188	171	122	72	2	0	0	2	57	11	0	.193	10	24	3	1	1.1	.919
1949	**2 teams**	**WAS A**	(10G 3–2)		**BOS A**	(18G 3–4)																					
″	**total**		6	6	.500	3.75	28	12	4	108	100	56	36	0	2	2	4	35	3	0	.086	4	21	1	1	0.9	.962
1950	**BOS**	**A**	8	6	.571	5.64	33	15	6	129.1	145	82	60	0	1	2	1	44	6	0	.136	8	26	2	6	1.1	.944
1951			3	0	1.000	3.34	30	1	0	59.1	53	32	39	0	3	0	2	11	2	0	.182	1	12	1	0	0.5	.929
1952	**2 teams**	**BOS A**	(5G 1–1)		**WAS A**	(24G 9–8)																					
″	**total**		10	9	.526	4.13	29	22	11	170	171	83	92	0	1	0	2	52	6	0	.115	16	31	1	3	1.7	.979
1953	**WAS**	**A**	10	12	.455	3.63	29	20	10	166.1	145	62	95	4	1	2	0	51	7	0	.137	10	27	4	1	1.4	.902
1956	**DET**	**A**	1	1	.500	4.17	35	0	0	49.2	54	32	28	0	1	1	0	4	1	0	.250	3	6	2	1	0.3	.818
14 yrs.			78	100	.438	4.15	399	184	70	1649.2	1613	886	815	15	17	14	20	486	68	0	.140	92	281	32	19	1.0	.921

Len Matarazzo

MATARAZZO, LEONARD BR TR 6′ 4″ 195 lbs.
B. Sept. 12, 1928, New Castle, Pa.

Year	Team		W	L	PCT	ERA	G	GS	CG	IP	H	BB	SO	ShO	Relief Pitching W	Relief Pitching L	Relief Pitching SV	Batting AB	Batting H	HR	BA	PO	A	E	DP	TC/G	FA
1952	**PHI**	**A**	0	0	—	0.00	1	0	0	1	1	1	0	0	0	0	0	0	0	0	—	0	0	0	0	0.0	.000

Bobby Mathews

MATHEWS, ROBERT T. BR TR 5′ 5½″ 140 lbs.
B. Nov. 21, 1851, Baltimore, Md. D. Apr. 17, 1898, Baltimore, Md.

Year	Team		W	L	PCT	ERA	G	GS	CG	IP	H	BB	SO	ShO	Relief Pitching W	Relief Pitching L	Relief Pitching SV	Batting AB	Batting H	HR	BA	PO	A	E	DP	TC/G	FA
1876	**NY**	**N**	21	34	.382	2.86	56	56	55	516	**693**	24	37	2	0	0	0	218	40	0	.183	41	78	28	0	2.6	.810
1877	**CIN**	**N**	3	12	.200	4.04	15	15	13	129.1	208	17	9	0	0	0	0	59	10	0	.169	8	19	7	0	2.0	.794
1879	**PRO**	**N**	12	8	.600	2.29	27	25	15	189	194	26	90	0	0	0	**1**	173	35	1	.202	24	46	13	1	1.6	.843
1881	**2 teams**	**PRO N**	(14G 4–8)		**BOS N**	(5G 1–0)																					
″	**total**		5	8	.385	3.02	19	15	11	125.1	143	32	33	1	0	0	**2**	128	23	0	.180	30	21	11	2	1.5	.823
1882	**BOS**	**N**	19	15	.559	*2.87*	34	32	31	285	278	22	153	0	**1**	**1**	0	169	38	0	.225	11	34	12	1	1.2	.789
1883	**PHI**	**AA**	30	13	.698	*2.46*	44	44	41	381	396	31	203	1	0	0	0	167	31	0	.186	15	68	12	2	2.0	.874
1884			30	18	.625	*3.32*	49	49	48	430.2	401	49	286	3	0	0	0	184	34	0	.185	8	78	25	1	2.2	.775
1885			30	17	.638	*2.43*	48	48	46	422.1	394	57	286	2	0	0	0	179	30	0	.168	8	67	10	1	1.7	.882
1886			13	9	.591	*3.96*	24	24	22	197.2	226	53	93	0	0	0	0	88	21	0	.239	5	46	9	3	2.4	.850
1887			3	4	.429	*6.67*	7	7	7	58	75	25	9	0	0	0	0	25	5	0	.200	2	14	2	1	2.6	.889
10 yrs.			166	138	.546	3.00	323	315	289	2734.1	3008	336	1199	9	1	1	3	*				152	471	129	12	1.9	.828

Greg Mathews

MATHEWS, GREGORY INMAN BR TL 6′ 2″ 180 lbs.
B. May 17, 1962, Harbor City, Calif. BB 1986

Year	Team		W	L	PCT	ERA	G	GS	CG	IP	H	BB	SO	ShO	Relief Pitching W	Relief Pitching L	Relief Pitching SV	Batting AB	Batting H	HR	BA	PO	A	E	DP	TC/G	FA
1986	**STL**	**N**	11	8	.579	3.65	23	22	1	145.1	139	44	67	0	0	0	0	43	2	0	.047	3	17	0	1	0.9	1.000
1987			11	11	.500	3.73	32	32	2	197.2	184	71	108	1	0	0	0	68	13	0	.191	3	31	4	2	1.2	.895
1988			4	6	.400	4.24	13	13	1	68	61	33	31	0	0	0	0	23	4	0	.174	3	13	2	0	1.4	.889
1990			0	5	.000	5.33	11	10	0	50.2	53	30	18	0	0	1	0	14	3	0	.214	2	15	1	1	1.6	.944
1992	**PHI**	**N**	2	3	.400	5.16	14	7	0	52.1	54	24	27	0	1	0	0	14	0	0	.000	1	6	0	0	0.5	1.000
5 yrs.			28	33	.459	4.08	93	84	4	514	491	202	251	1	1	1	0	162	22	0	.136	12	82	7	4	1.1	.931
LEAGUE CHAMPIONSHIP SERIES																											
1987	**STL**	**N**	1	0	1.000	3.48	2	2	0	10.1	6	3	10	0	0	0	0	2	2	0	1.000	0	0	0	0	0.0	.000
WORLD SERIES																											
1987	**STL**	**N**	0	0	—	2.45	1	1	0	3.2	2	2	3	0	0	0	0	1	0	0	.000	0	1	0	0	1.0	1.000

T. J. Mathews

MATHEWS, TIMOTHY JAY BR TR 6′ 2″ 200 lbs.
Son of Nelson Mathews.
B. Jan. 9, 1970, Belleville, Ill.

Year	Team		W	L	PCT	ERA	G	GS	CG	IP	H	BB	SO	ShO	Relief Pitching W	Relief Pitching L	Relief Pitching SV	Batting AB	Batting H	HR	BA	PO	A	E	DP	TC/G	FA
1995	**STL**	**N**	1	1	.500	1.52	23	0	0	29.2	21	11	28	0	1	1	2	2	0	0	.000	4	5	1	1	0.4	.900

Terry Mathews

MATHEWS, TERRY ALAN BL TR 6′ 2″ 200 lbs.
B. Oct. 5, 1964, Alexandria, Va.

Year	Team		W	L	PCT	ERA	G	GS	CG	IP	H	BB	SO	ShO	Relief Pitching W	Relief Pitching L	Relief Pitching SV	Batting AB	Batting H	HR	BA	PO	A	E	DP	TC/G	FA
1991	**TEX**	**A**	4	0	1.000	3.61	34	2	0	57.1	54	18	51	0	4	0	1	0	0	0	—	8	5	0	0	0.4	1.000
1992			2	4	.333	5.95	40	0	0	42.1	48	31	26	0	2	4	0	0	0	0	—	5	4	0	1	0.2	1.000
1994	**FLA**	**N**	2	1	.667	3.35	24	2	0	43	45	9	21	0	1	0	0	6	3	0	.500	5	6	0	1	0.5	1.000
1995			4	4	.500	3.38	57	0	0	82.2	70	27	72	0	4	4	3	13	6	0	.462	6	9	0	0	0.3	1.000
4 yrs.			12	9	.571	3.91	155	4	0	225.1	217	85	170	0	11	8	4	19	9	0	.474	24	24	0	2	0.3	1.000

Christy Mathewson

MATHEWSON, CHRISTOPHER (Big Six, Matty) BR TR 6′ 1½″ 195 lbs.
Brother of Henry Mathewson.
B. Aug. 12, 1880, Factoryville, Pa. D. Oct. 7, 1925, Saranac Lake, N. Y.
Manager 1916–18.
Hall of Fame 1936.

Year	Team		W	L	PCT	ERA	G	GS	CG	IP	H	BB	SO	ShO	Relief Pitching W	Relief Pitching L	Relief Pitching SV	Batting AB	Batting H	HR	BA	PO	A	E	DP	TC/G	FA
1900	**NY**	**N**	0	3	.000	5.08	6	1	1	33.2	37	20	15	0	0	2	0	11	2	0	.182	1	9	0	0	2.0	1.000
1901			20	17	.541	2.41	40	38	36	336	288	97	221	5	0	1	0	130	28	0	.215	21	108	1	1	3.3	.992
1902			14	17	.452	2.11	34	32	29	276.2	241	73	159	**8**	1	0	0	127	26	2	.205	49	82	10	8	3.4	.929
1903			30	13	.698	2.26	45	42	37	366.1	321	100	**267**	3	1	0	2	124	28	1	.226	18	93	3	0	2.5	.974
1904			33	12	.733	2.03	48	**46**	33	367.2	306	78	**212**	4	**2**	0	0	133	30	0	.226	32	116	6	0	3.2	.961
1905			**31**	8	**.795**	**1.27**	43	37	33	339	252	64	**206**	**8**	2	1	3	127	30	2	.236	15	116	4	4	3.1	.970
1906			22	12	.647	2.97	38	35	22	266.2	262	77	128	6	1	0	1	91	24	0	.264	15	90	1	1	2.8	.991
1907			**24**	13	.649	1.99	41	36	31	316	250	53	**178**	**8**	1	0	2	107	20	0	.187	16	87	6	0	2.7	.945
1908			**37**	11	.771	**1.43**	**56**	**44**	**34**	**390.2**	**285**	42	**259**	**12**	3	1	**5**	129	20	0	.155	27	141	2	1	3.0	.988
1909			25	6	**.806**	**1.14**	37	33	26	275.1	192	36	149	8	2	0	2	95	25	1	.263	19	96	4	3	3.2	.966
1910			**27**	9	.750	1.90	38	35	**27**	318	292	60	184	2	2	1	0	107	25	1	.234	12	114	4	6	3.4	.969
1911			26	13	.667	**1.99**	45	37	29	307	**303**	38	141	5	2	0	3	112	22	0	.196	31	107	2	2	3.1	.986
1912			23	12	.657	2.12	43	34	27	**310**	311	34	134	0	2	2	5	110	29	0	.264	15	74	4	4	2.2	.957
1913			25	11	.694	**2.06**	40	35	25	306	**291**	21	93	4	3	0	2	103	19	0	.184	13	100	3	3	2.9	.974
1914			24	13	.649	3.00	41	35	29	312	314	23	80	5	3	0	2	105	23	0	.219	15	91	5	7	2.7	.955

Christy Mathewson *continued*

Year	Team	W	L	PCT	ERA	G	GS	CG	IP	H	BB	SO	ShO	Relief W	Relief L	Relief SV	Batting AB	Batting H	Batting HR	BA	PO	A	E	DP	TC/G	FA
1915		8	14	.364	3.58	27	24	11	186	199	20	57	1	0	0	0	51	8	0	.157	8	54	1	3	2.3	.984
1916	**2 teams** **NY N** (12G 3–4) **CIN N** (1G 1–0)																									
"	**total**	4	4	.500	3.01	13	7	5	74.2	74	8	19	1	1	2	2	22	3	0	.136	6	28	0	1	2.6	1.000
17 yrs.		373 **3rd**	188	.665 **7th**	2.13 **5th**	635	551	435	4781.2	4218	844	2502	80 3rd	26	10	29	1684	362	7	.215	313	1506	56	44	2.9	.970
WORLD SERIES																										
1905	**NY N**	3	0	1.000	0.00	3	3	3	27	14	1	18	3	0	0	0	8	2	0	.250	2	8	1	0	3.7	.909
1911		1	2	.333	2.00	3	3	2	27	25	2	13	0	0	0	0	7	2	0	.286	2	9	1	0	4.0	.917
1912		0	2	.000	1.57	3	3	3	28.2	23	5	10	0	0	0	0	12	2	0	.167	1	12	0	0	4.3	1.000
1913		1	1	.500	0.95	2	2	2	19	14	2	7	1	0	0	0	5	3	0	.600	1	5	0	0	3.0	1.000
4 yrs.		5 **8th**	5 **2nd**	.500	1.15 **8th**	11 **10th**	11 **2nd**	10 **1st**	101.2 **2nd**	76	10	48 **9th**	4 **1st**	0	0	0	32	9	0	.281	6	34	2	0	3.8	.952

Henry Mathewson

MATHEWSON, HENRY BR TR 6′ 3″ 175 lbs.
Brother of Christy Mathewson.
B. Dec. 24, 1886, Factoryville, Pa. D. July 1, 1917, Factoryville, Pa.

Year	Team	W	L	PCT	ERA	G	GS	CG	IP	H	BB	SO	ShO	Relief W	Relief L	Relief SV	Batting AB	Batting H	Batting HR	BA	PO	A	E	DP	TC/G	FA
1906	**NY N**	0	1	.000	5.40	2	1	1	10	7	14	2	0	0	0	1	2	0	0	.000	0	4	0	2	2.0	1.000
1907		0	0	—	0.00	1	0	0	1	1	0	0	0	0	0	1	0	0	0	—	0	0	0	0	0.0	.000
2 yrs.		0	1	.000	4.91	3	1	1	11	8	14	2	0	0	0	2	2	0	0	.000	0	4	0	2	1.3	1.000

Carl Mathias

MATHIAS, CARL LYNWOOD (Stubby) BB TL 5′11″ 195 lbs.
B. June 13, 1936, Bechtelsville, Pa.

Year	Team	W	L	PCT	ERA	G	GS	CG	IP	H	BB	SO	ShO	Relief W	Relief L	Relief SV	Batting AB	Batting H	Batting HR	BA	PO	A	E	DP	TC/G	FA
1960	**CLE A**	0	1	.000	3.52	7	0	0	15.1	14	8	13	0	0	1	0	1	0	0	.000	1	3	0	0	0.6	1.000
1961	**WAS A**	0	1	.000	11.20	4	3	0	13.2	22	4	7	0	0	0	0	5	1	0	.200	1	2	0	0	0.8	1.000
2 yrs.		0	2	.000	7.14	11	3	0	29	36	12	20	0	0	1	0	6	1	0	.167	2	5	0	0	0.6	1.000

Ron Mathis

MATHIS, RONALD VANCE BR TR 6′ 180 lbs.
B. Sept. 25, 1958, Kansas City, Mo.

Year	Team	W	L	PCT	ERA	G	GS	CG	IP	H	BB	SO	ShO	Relief W	Relief L	Relief SV	Batting AB	Batting H	Batting HR	BA	PO	A	E	DP	TC/G	FA
1985	**HOU N**	3	5	.375	6.04	23	8	0	70	83	27	34	0	0	2	1	14	1	0	.071	5	10	1	0	0.7	.938
1987		0	1	.000	5.25	8	0	0	12	10	11	8	0	0	1	0	2	0	0	.000	2	2	1	0	0.6	.800
2 yrs.		3	6	.333	5.93	31	8	0	82	93	38	42	0	0	3	1	16	1	0	.063	7	12	2	0	0.7	.905

Jon Matlack

MATLACK, JONATHAN TRUMPBOUR BL TL 6′ 3″ 205 lbs.
B. Jan. 19, 1950, West Chester, Pa.

Year	Team	W	L	PCT	ERA	G	GS	CG	IP	H	BB	SO	ShO	Relief W	Relief L	Relief SV	Batting AB	Batting H	Batting HR	BA	PO	A	E	DP	TC/G	FA
1971	**NY N**	0	3	.000	4.14	7	6	0	37	31	15	24	0	0	0	0	11	3	0	.273	1	2	0	0	0.4	1.000
1972		15	10	.600	2.32	34	32	8	244	215	71	169	4	1	0	0	78	10	0	.128	8	33	1	1	1.2	.976
1973		14	16	.467	3.20	34	34	14	242	210	99	205	3	0	0	0	65	9	0	.138	4	40	1	3	1.3	.978
1974		13	15	.464	2.41	34	34	14	265	221	76	195	**7**	0	0	0	79	8	0	.101	5	40	0	1	1.3	1.000
1975		16	12	.571	3.38	33	32	8	229	224	58	154	3	0	0	0	70	7	0	.100	3	28	3	1	1.0	.912
1976		17	10	.630	2.95	35	35	16	262	236	57	153	**6**	0	0	0	88	17	0	.193	10	35	1	0	1.3	.978
1977		7	15	.318	4.21	26	26	5	169	175	43	123	3	0	0	0	50	3	0	.060	4	27	1	1	1.2	.969
1978	**TEX A**	15	13	.536	2.27	35	33	18	270	252	51	157	2	0	0	1	0	0	0	—	17	42	5	2	1.8	.922
1979		5	4	.556	4.13	13	13	2	85	98	15	35	0	0	0	0	0	0	0	—	3	16	2	1	1.6	.905
1980		10	10	.500	3.68	35	34	8	235	265	48	142	1	0	0	1	0	0	0	—	5	25	4	0	1.0	.882
1981		4	7	.364	4.15	17	16	1	104	101	41	43	1	0	0	0	0	0	0	—	2	20	2	0	1.4	.917
1982		7	7	.500	3.53	33	14	1	147.2	158	37	78	0	2	2	1	0	0	0	—	4	24	0	1	0.8	1.000
1983		2	4	.333	4.66	25	9	2	73.1	90	27	38	0	0	1	0	0	0	0	—	2	14	1	3	0.7	.941
13 yrs.		125	126	.498	3.18	361	318	97	2363	2276	638	1516	30	3	3	3	441	57	0	.129	68	346	21	14	1.2	.952
LEAGUE CHAMPIONSHIP SERIES																										
1973	**NY N**	1	0	1.000	0.00	1	1	1	9	2	3	9	1 **1st**	0	0	0	2	0	0	.000	0	1	0	0	1.0	1.000
WORLD SERIES																										
1973	**NY N**	1	2	.333	2.16	3	3	0	16.2	10	5	11	0	0	0	0	4	1	0	.250	0	1	0	0	0.3	1.000

Al Mattern

MATTERN, ALONZO ALBERT BL TR 5′10″ 165 lbs.
B. June 16, 1883, West Rush, N. Y. D. Nov. 6, 1958, West Rush, N. Y.

Year	Team	W	L	PCT	ERA	G	GS	CG	IP	H	BB	SO	ShO	Relief W	Relief L	Relief SV	Batting AB	Batting H	Batting HR	BA	PO	A	E	DP	TC/G	FA
1908	**BOS N**	1	3	.250	2.08	5	3	1	30.1	30	6	8	1	0	1	0	8	1	0	.125	1	8	0	0	1.8	1.000
1909		16	20	.444	2.85	47	32	24	316.1	**322**	**108**	98	2	3	4	3	101	17	0	.168	21	100	10	2	2.8	.924
1910		16	19	.457	2.98	**51**	37	17	305	288	121	94	6	4	2	1	98	16	0	.163	12	90	3	1	2.1	.971
1911		4	15	.211	4.97	33	21	11	186.1	228	63	51	0	0	2	0	63	11	0	.175	6	61	2	0	2.1	.971
1912		0	1	.000	7.11	2	1	0	6.1	10	1	3	0	0	0	0	2	0	0	.000	0	2	0	0	1.0	1.000
5 yrs.		37	58	.389	3.37	138	94	53	844.1	878	299	254	9	7	9	4	272	45	0	.165	40	261	15	3	2.3	.953

C. V. Matterson

MATTERSON, C. V.
B. Ohio Deceased.

Year	Team	W	L	PCT	ERA	G	GS	CG	IP	H	BB	SO	ShO	Relief W	Relief L	Relief SV	Batting AB	Batting H	Batting HR	BA	PO	A	E	DP	TC/G	FA
1884	**STL U**	1	0	1.000	*9.00*	1	1	0	6	9	3	3	0	0	0	0	*				0	0	0	0	0.0	

Henry Matteson

MATTESON, HENRY EDSON BR TR 5′10½″ 160 lbs.
B. Sept. 7, 1884, Guy's Mills, Pa. D. Sept. 1, 1943, Westfield, N. Y.

Year	Team	W	L	PCT	ERA	G	GS	CG	IP	H	BB	SO	ShO	Relief W	Relief L	Relief SV	Batting AB	Batting H	Batting HR	BA	PO	A	E	DP	TC/G	FA
1914	**PHI N**	3	2	.600	3.10	15	3	2	58	58	23	28	0	2	1	0	22	4	0	.182	1	7	0	0	0.5	1.000
1918	**WAS A**	5	3	.625	1.73	14	6	2	67.2	57	15	17	0	3	1	0	19	2	0	.105	2	15	1	1	1.3	.944
2 yrs.		8	5	.615	2.36	29	9	4	125.2	115	38	45	0	5	2	0	41	6	0	.146	3	22	1	1	0.9	.962

Bill Matthews

MATTHEWS, WILLIAM CALVIN TR
B. Jan. 12, 1878, Mahanoy City, Pa. D. Jan. 23, 1946, Mahanoy City, Pa.

Year	Team	W	L	PCT	ERA	G	GS	CG	IP	H	BB	SO	ShO	Relief W	Relief L	Relief SV	Batting AB	Batting H	Batting HR	BA	PO	A	E	DP	TC/G	FA
1909	**BOS A**	0	0	—	3.24	5	1	0	16.2	16	10	6	0	0	0	0	8	0	0	.000	1	3	0	0	0.8	1.000

Joe Matthews

MATTHEWS, JOHN JOSEPH (Lefty) BB TL 6′ 170 lbs.
B. Sept. 29, 1898, Baltimore, Md. D. Feb. 8, 1968, Hagerstown, Md.

Year	Team	W	L	PCT	ERA	G	GS	CG	IP	H	BB	SO	ShO	Relief W	Relief L	Relief SV	Batting AB	Batting H	Batting HR	BA	PO	A	E	DP	TC/G	FA
1922	**BOS N**	0	1	.000	3.60	3	1	0	10	5	6	0	0	0	0	0	2	0	0	.000	0	1	0	0	0.3	1.000

Dale Matthewson

MATTHEWSON, DALE WESLEY BR TR 5′11½″ 145 lbs.
B. May 15, 1923, Catasauqua, Pa. D. Feb. 20, 1984, Blairsville, Ga.

Year	Team	W	L	PCT	ERA	G	GS	CG	IP	H	BB	SO	ShO	Relief Pitching W	Relief Pitching L	Relief Pitching SV	Batting AB	Batting H	HR	BA	PO	A	E	DP	TC/G	FA
1943	PHI N	0	3	.000	4.85	11	1	0	26	26	8	8	0	0	2	0	2	0	0	.000	1	4	0	1	0.5	1.000
1944		0	0	—	3.94	17	0	0	32	27	16	8	0	0	0	0	3	1	0	.333	3	5	1	0	0.5	.889
2 yrs.		0	3	.000	4.34	28	1	0	58	53	24	16	0	0	2	0	5	1	0	.200	4	9	1	1	0.5	.929

Mike Mattimore

MATTIMORE, MICHAEL JOSEPH BL TL 5′ 8½″ 160 lbs.
B. 1859, Renovo, Pa. D. Apr. 28, 1931, Butte, Mont.

Year	Team	W	L	PCT	ERA	G	GS	CG	IP	H	BB	SO	ShO	Relief Pitching W	Relief Pitching L	Relief Pitching SV	Batting AB	Batting H	HR	BA	PO	A	E	DP	TC/G	FA
1887	NY N	3	3	.500	2.35	7	7	6	57.1	47	28	12	1	0	0	0	32	8	0	.250	8	5	1	0	1.6	.929
1888	PHI AA	15	10	.600	3.38	26	24	24	221	221	65	80	4	0	**1**	0	142	38	0	.268	32	71	10	6	2.7	.912
1889	2 teams PHI AA (5G 2–1) KC AA (1G 0–0)																									
″	total	2	1	.667	5.56	6	1	1	34	46	15	7	0	2	0	1	148	29	1	.196	98	12	15	2	2.8	.880
1890	BKN AA	6	13	.316	4.44	19	19	19	178.1	201	76	33	0	0	0	0	129	17	0	.132	20	38	12	0	2.1	.829
4 yrs.		26	27	.491	3.80	58	51	50	490.2	515	184	132	5	2	1	1	*				158	126	38	8	2.5	.882

Earl Mattingly

MATTINGLY, LAURENCE EARL BR TR 5′10½″ 164 lbs.
B. Nov. 4, 1904, New Port, Md. D. Sept. 8, 1993, Brookeville, Md.

Year	Team	W	L	PCT	ERA	G	GS	CG	IP	H	BB	SO	ShO	Relief Pitching W	Relief Pitching L	Relief Pitching SV	Batting AB	Batting H	HR	BA	PO	A	E	DP	TC/G	FA
1931	BKN N	0	1	.000	2.51	8	0	0	14.1	15	10	6	0	0	1	0	3	0	0	.000	0	5	0	1	0.6	1.000

Rick Matula

MATULA, RICHARD CARLTON BR TR 6′ 190 lbs.
B. Nov. 22, 1953, Wharton, Tex.

Year	Team	W	L	PCT	ERA	G	GS	CG	IP	H	BB	SO	ShO	Relief Pitching W	Relief Pitching L	Relief Pitching SV	Batting AB	Batting H	HR	BA	PO	A	E	DP	TC/G	FA
1979	ATL N	8	10	.444	4.16	28	28	1	171	193	64	67	0	0	0	0	53	5	0	.094	15	23	0	6	1.4	1.000
1980		11	13	.458	4.58	33	30	3	177	195	60	62	1	0	0	0	57	6	0	.105	20	28	1	5	1.5	.980
1981		0	0	—	6.43	5	0	0	7	8	2	0	0	0	0	0	1	0	0	.000	1	1	0	0	0.4	1.000
3 yrs.		19	23	.452	4.41	66	58	4	355	396	126	129	1	0	0	0	111	11	0	.099	36	52	1	11	1.3	.989

Harry Matuzak

MATUZAK, HENRY GEORGE (Matty) BR TR 5′11½″ 185 lbs.
B. Jan. 27, 1910, Omer, Mich. D. Nov. 16, 1978, Fairhope, Ala.

Year	Team	W	L	PCT	ERA	G	GS	CG	IP	H	BB	SO	ShO	Relief Pitching W	Relief Pitching L	Relief Pitching SV	Batting AB	Batting H	HR	BA	PO	A	E	DP	TC/G	FA
1934	PHI A	0	3	.000	4.88	11	0	0	24	28	10	9	0	0	3	0	6	1	0	.167	0	7	1	0	0.7	.875
1936		0	1	.000	7.20	6	1	0	15	21	4	8	0	0	1	0	3	0	0	.000	0	3	1	0	0.7	.750
2 yrs.		0	4	.000	5.77	17	1	0	39	49	14	17	0	0	4	0	9	1	0	.111	0	10	2	0	0.7	.833

Hal Mauck

MAUCK, ALFRED MARIS BR TR 5′11″ 185 lbs.
B. Mar. 6, 1869, Princeton, Ind. D. Apr. 27, 1921, Princeton, Ind.

Year	Team	W	L	PCT	ERA	G	GS	CG	IP	H	BB	SO	ShO	Relief Pitching W	Relief Pitching L	Relief Pitching SV	Batting AB	Batting H	HR	BA	PO	A	E	DP	TC/G	FA
1893	CHI N	8	10	.444	4.41	23	18	12	143	168	60	23	1	2	1	0	61	9	0	.148	2	32	4	0	1.7	.895

Al Maul

MAUL, ALBERT JOSEPH (Smiling Al) BR TR 6′ 175 lbs.
B. Oct. 9, 1865, Philadelphia, Pa. D. May 3, 1958, Philadelphia, Pa.

Year	Team	W	L	PCT	ERA	G	GS	CG	IP	H	BB	SO	ShO	Relief Pitching W	Relief Pitching L	Relief Pitching SV	Batting AB	Batting H	HR	BA	PO	A	E	DP	TC/G	FA
1884	PHI U	0	1	.000	*4.50*	1	1	1	8	10	1	7	0	0	0	0	4	0	0	.000	0	1	0	0	1.0	1.000
1887	PHI N	4	2	.667	5.54	7	5	4	50.1	72	15	18	0	**2**	0	0	56	17	1	.304	30	10	5	2	2.6	.889
1888	PIT N	0	2	.000	6.35	3	1	1	17	26	5	12	0	0	1	0	259	54	0	.208	450	20	16	22	6.5	.967
1889		1	4	.200	9.86	6	4	4	42	64	28	11	0	0	1	0	257	71	4	.276	125	32	10	5	2.4	.940
1890	PIT P	16	12	.571	3.79	30	28	26	246.2	258	104	81	2	0	1	0	162	42	0	.259	51	84	16	5	3.3	.894
1891	PIT N	1	2	.333	2.31	8	3	3	39	44	16	13	0	0	0	1	149	28	0	.188	61	13	9	3	1.7	.892
1893	WAS N	12	21	.364	5.30	37	33	29	297	355	144	72	1	1	0	0	134	34	0	.254	28	70	12	1	2.5	.891
1894		11	15	.423	5.98	28	26	21	201.2	272	73	34	0	0	0	0	124	30	2	.242	30	51	9	1	2.3	.900
1895		10	5	.667	**2.45**	16	16	14	135.2	136	37	34	0	0	0	0	72	18	0	.250	18	32	4	3	2.7	.926
1896		5	2	.714	3.63	8	8	7	62	75	20	18	0	0	0	0	28	8	0	.286	2	10	1	1	1.6	.923
1897	2 teams WAS N (1G 0–1) BAL N (2G 0–0)																									
″	total	0	1	.000	7.45	3	3	0	9.2	13	9	2	0	0	0	0	4	1	0	.250	0	2	0	0	0.7	1.000
1898	BAL N	20	7	.741	2.10	28	28	26	239.2	207	49	31	1	0	0	0	93	19	0	.204	9	38	2	0	1.7	.959
1899	BKN N	2	0	1.000	4.50	4	4	2	26	35	6	2	0	0	0	0	11	3	0	.273	0	9	1	0	2.5	.900
1900	PHI N	2	3	.400	6.16	5	4	3	38	53	3	6	0	1	0	0	15	3	0	.200	0	11	1	0	2.4	.917
1901	NY N	0	2	.000	11.37	3	3	2	19	39	8	5	0	0	0	0	8	3	0	.375	1	7	0	0	2.7	1.000
15 yrs.		84	79	.515	4.43	187	167	143	1431.2	1659	518	346	4	4	3	1	*				805	390	86	43	3.1	.933

Ernie Maun

MAUN, ERNEST GERALD BR TR 6′ 165 lbs.
B. Feb. 3, 1901, Clearwater, Kans. D. Jan. 1, 1987, Corpus Christi, Tex.

Year	Team	W	L	PCT	ERA	G	GS	CG	IP	H	BB	SO	ShO	Relief Pitching W	Relief Pitching L	Relief Pitching SV	Batting AB	Batting H	HR	BA	PO	A	E	DP	TC/G	FA
1924	NY N	1	1	.500	5.91	22	0	0	35	46	10	5	0	1	1	1	3	2	0	.667	1	6	0	0	0.3	1.000
1926	PHI N	1	4	.200	6.45	14	5	0	37.2	57	18	9	0	1	1	0	12	3	0	.250	1	9	0	0	0.7	1.000
2 yrs.		2	5	.286	6.19	36	5	0	72.2	103	28	14	0	2	2	1	15	5	0	.333	2	15	0	0	0.5	1.000

Dick Mauney

MAUNEY, RICHARD BR TR 5′11½″ 164 lbs.
B. Jan. 26, 1920, Concord, N. C. D. Feb. 6, 1970, Albemarle, N. C.

Year	Team	W	L	PCT	ERA	G	GS	CG	IP	H	BB	SO	ShO	Relief Pitching W	Relief Pitching L	Relief Pitching SV	Batting AB	Batting H	HR	BA	PO	A	E	DP	TC/G	FA
1945	PHI N	6	10	.375	3.08	20	16	6	122.2	127	27	35	2	0	2	1	41	6	0	.146	8	29	2	0	2.0	.949
1946		6	4	.600	2.70	24	7	3	90	98	18	31	1	3	2	2	24	4	0	.167	8	17	0	0	1.0	1.000
1947		0	0	—	3.86	9	1	0	16.1	15	7	6	0	0	0	1	2	0	0	.000	1	7	1	0	1.0	.889
3 yrs.		12	14	.462	2.99	53	24	9	229	240	52	72	3	3	4	4	67	10	0	.149	17	53	3	0	1.4	.959

Harry Maupin

MAUPIN, HARRY CARR TR 5′ 7″ 150 lbs.
B. July 11, 1872, Wellsville, Mo. D. Aug. 25, 1952, Parsons, Kans.

Year	Team	W	L	PCT	ERA	G	GS	CG	IP	H	BB	SO	ShO	Relief Pitching W	Relief Pitching L	Relief Pitching SV	Batting AB	Batting H	HR	BA	PO	A	E	DP	TC/G	FA
1898	STL N	0	2	.000	5.50	2	2	2	18	22	3	3	0	0	0	0	7	3	0	.429	0	1	0	0	0.5	1.000
1899	CLE N	0	3	.000	12.60	5	3	2	25	55	7	3	0	0	0	0	10	0	0	.000	0	2	1	0	0.6	.667
2 yrs.		0	5	.000	9.63	7	5	4	43	77	10	6	0	0	0	0	17	3	0	.176	0	3	1	0	0.6	.750

Ralph Mauriello

MAURIELLO, RALPH (Tami) BR TR 6′ 3″ 195 lbs.
B. Aug. 25, 1934, Brooklyn, N. Y.

Year	Team	W	L	PCT	ERA	G	GS	CG	IP	H	BB	SO	ShO	Relief Pitching W	Relief Pitching L	Relief Pitching SV	Batting AB	Batting H	HR	BA	PO	A	E	DP	TC/G	FA
1958	LA N	1	1	.500	4.63	3	2	0	11.2	10	8	11	0	0	0	0	4	0	0	.000	0	1	0	0	0.3	1.000

Tim Mauser

MAUSER, TIMOTHY EDWARD BR TR 6′ 185 lbs.
B. Oct. 4, 1966, Fort Worth, Tex.

Year	Team	W	L	PCT	ERA	G	GS	CG	IP	H	BB	SO	ShO	Relief Pitching W	Relief Pitching L	Relief Pitching SV	Batting AB	Batting H	HR	BA	PO	A	E	DP	TC/G	FA
1991	PHI N	0	0	—	7.59	3	0	0	10.2	18	3	6	0	0	0	0	3	0	0	.000	0	1	0	0	0.3	1.000
1993	2 teams PHI N (8G 0–0) SD N (28G 0–1)																									
″	total	0	1	.000	4.00	36	0	0	54	51	24	46	0	0	1	0	6	0	0	.000	6	11	1	2	0.5	.944

Tim Mauser *continued*

Year	Team		W	L	PCT	ERA	G	GS	CG	IP	H	BB	SO	ShO	Relief W	Relief L	Relief SV	Batting AB	Batting H	Batting HR	BA	PO	A	E	DP	TC/G	FA
1994	SD	N	2	4	.333	3.49	35	0	0	49	50	19	32	0	2	4	2	4	1	0	.250	2	5	0	2	0.2	1.000
1995			0	1	.000	9.53	5	0	0	5.2	4	9	9	0	0	1	0	1	0	0	.000	0	0	0	0	0.0	.000
4 yrs.			2	6	.250	4.37	79	0	0	119.1	123	55	93	0	2	6	2	14	1	0	.071	8	17	1	4	0.3	.962

Brian Maxcy

MAXCY, DAVID BRIAN
B. May 4, 1971, Amory, Miss.
BR TR 6′ 1″ 170 lbs.

Year	Team		W	L	PCT	ERA	G	GS	CG	IP	H	BB	SO	ShO	Relief W	Relief L	Relief SV	Batting AB	Batting H	Batting HR	BA	PO	A	E	DP	TC/G	FA
1995	DET	A	4	5	.444	6.88	41	0	0	52.1	61	31	20	0	4	5	0	0	0	0	—	6	14	2	1	0.5	.909

Larry Maxie

MAXIE, LARRY HANS
B. Oct. 10, 1940, Upland, Calif.
BR TR 6′ 4″ 220 lbs.

Year	Team		W	L	PCT	ERA	G	GS	CG	IP	H	BB	SO	ShO	Relief W	Relief L	Relief SV	Batting AB	Batting H	Batting HR	BA	PO	A	E	DP	TC/G	FA
1969	ATL	N	0	0	—	3.00	2	0	0	3	1	1	1	0	0	0	0	0	0	0	—	0	2	0	0	1.0	1.000

Bert Maxwell

MAXWELL, JAMES ALBERT
B. Oct. 17, 1886, Texarkana, Ark. D. Dec. 10, 1961, Brady, Tex.
BB TR 6′ 180 lbs.

Year	Team		W	L	PCT	ERA	G	GS	CG	IP	H	BB	SO	ShO	Relief W	Relief L	Relief SV	Batting AB	Batting H	Batting HR	BA	PO	A	E	DP	TC/G	FA
1906	PIT	N	0	1	.000	5.63	1	1	0	8	8	2	1	0	0	0	0	3	0	0	.000	0	3	0	1	3.0	1.000
1908	PHI	A	0	0	—	11.08	4	0	0	13	23	9	7	0	0	0	0	5	0	0	.000	1	3	0	0	1.0	1.000
1911	NY	N	1	2	.333	2.90	4	3	3	31	37	7	8	0	0	0	0	9	1	0	.111	3	11	1	1	3.8	.933
1914	BKN	F	3	4	.429	3.28	12	8	6	71.1	76	24	19	1	0	0	1	23	2	0	.087	5	23	1	2	2.4	.966
4 yrs.			4	7	.364	4.16	21	12	9	123.1	144	42	35	1	0	0	1	40	3	0	.075	9	40	2	4	2.4	.961

Buckshot May

MAY, WILLIAM HERBERT
B. Dec. 13, 1899, Bakersfield, Calif. D. Mar. 15, 1984, Bakersfield, Calif.
BR TR 6′ 2″ 169 lbs.

Year	Team		W	L	PCT	ERA	G	GS	CG	IP	H	BB	SO	ShO	Relief W	Relief L	Relief SV	Batting AB	Batting H	Batting HR	BA	PO	A	E	DP	TC/G	FA
1924	PIT	N	0	0	—	0.00	1	0	0	1	2	0	1	0	0	0	0	0	0	0	—	0	0	0	0	0.0	.000

Darrell May

MAY, DARRELL KEVIN
B. June 13, 1972, San Bernardino, Calif.
BL TL 6′ 2″ 170 lbs.

Year	Team		W	L	PCT	ERA	G	GS	CG	IP	H	BB	SO	ShO	Relief W	Relief L	Relief SV	Batting AB	Batting H	Batting HR	BA	PO	A	E	DP	TC/G	FA
1995	ATL	N	0	0	—	11.25	2	0	0	4	10	0	1	0	0	0	0	0	0	0	—	0	1	0	0	0.5	1.000

Jakie May

MAY, FRANK SPRUIELL
B. Nov. 25, 1895, Youngville, N. C. D. June 3, 1970, Wendell, N. C.
BR TL 5′ 8″ 178 lbs.

Year	Team		W	L	PCT	ERA	G	GS	CG	IP	H	BB	SO	ShO	Relief W	Relief L	Relief SV	Batting AB	Batting H	Batting HR	BA	PO	A	E	DP	TC/G	FA
1917	STL	N	0	0	—	3.38	15	1	0	29.1	29	11	18	0	0	0	0	4	0	0	.000	3	14	0	1	1.1	1.000
1918			5	6	.455	3.83	29	15	6	152.2	149	69	61	0	2	0	0	45	3	1	.067	6	33	2	0	1.4	.951
1919			3	12	.200	3.22	28	19	8	125.2	99	**87**	58	1	0	1	0	37	6	0	.162	1	30	1	0	1.1	.969
1920			1	4	.200	3.06	16	5	3	70.2	65	37	33	0	0	1	0	22	5	0	.227	0	10	0	0	0.6	1.000
1921			1	3	.250	4.71	5	5	1	21	29	12	5	0	0	0	0	6	2	0	.333	0	3	1	0	0.8	.750
1924	CIN	N	3	3	.500	3.00	38	3	2	99	104	29	59	0	2	2	**6**	27	3	1	.111	2	21	0	0	0.6	1.000
1925			8	9	.471	3.87	36	12	7	137.1	146	45	74	1	2	4	2	43	8	0	.186	5	30	0	2	1.0	1.000
1926			13	9	.591	3.22	45	15	9	167.2	175	44	103	1	5	**4**	3	48	7	0	.146	6	30	1	5	0.8	.973
1927			15	12	.556	3.51	44	28	17	235.2	242	70	121	2	2	0	1	76	14	0	.184	6	51	0	2	1.3	1.000
1928			3	5	.375	4.42	21	11	1	79.1	99	35	39	1	2	2	1	27	8	0	.296	4	12	0	1	0.8	1.000
1929			10	14	.417	4.61	41	24	10	199	219	75	92	0	4	1	3	64	13	0	.203	6	40	1	2	1.1	.979
1930			3	11	.214	5.77	26	18	5	112.1	147	41	44	1	0	1	0	39	5	0	.128	6	23	1	1	1.2	.967
1931	CHI	N	5	5	.500	3.87	31	4	1	79	81	43	38	0	3	4	2	22	5	0	.227	4	14	0	3	0.6	1.000
1932			2	2	.500	4.36	35	0	0	53.2	61	19	20	0	2	2	1	8	1	0	.125	4	10	2	0	0.5	.875
14 yrs.			72	95	.431	3.88	410	160	70	1562.1	1645	617	765	7	24	22	19	468	80	2	.171	53	321	9	17	0.9	.977
WORLD SERIES																											
1932	CHI	N	0	1	.000	11.57	2	0	0	4.2	9	3	4	0	0	1	0	2	0	0	.000	1	0	0	0	0.5	1.000

Rudy May

MAY, RUDOLPH
B. July 18, 1944, Coffeyville, Kans.
BL TL 6′ 2″ 205 lbs.

Year	Team		W	L	PCT	ERA	G	GS	CG	IP	H	BB	SO	ShO	Relief W	Relief L	Relief SV	Batting AB	Batting H	Batting HR	BA	PO	A	E	DP	TC/G	FA
1965	CAL	A	4	9	.308	3.92	30	19	2	124	111	78	76	1	0	0	0	30	6	0	.200	4	15	0	0	0.6	1.000
1969			10	13	.435	3.44	43	25	4	180.1	142	66	133	0	3	2	2	49	4	0	.082	6	26	6	3	0.9	.842
1970			7	13	.350	4.00	38	34	2	209	190	81	164	2	1	1	0	69	6	0	.087	5	33	3	1	1.1	.927
1971			11	12	.478	3.03	32	31	7	208	160	87	156	2	0	1	0	68	10	0	.147	7	31	4	3	1.3	.905
1972			12	11	.522	2.94	35	30	10	205	162	82	169	3	1	0	1	62	7	0	.113	2	24	5	2	0.9	.839
1973			7	17	.292	4.38	34	28	10	185	177	80	134	4	0	2	0	0	0	0	—	2	39	1	0	1.2	.976
1974	2 teams	CAL A (18G 0–1)	NY A (17G 8–4)																								
″	total		8	5	.615	3.19	35	18	8	141	104	58	102	2	1	0	2	0	0	0		4	19	0	0	0.7	1.000
1975	NY	A	14	12	.538	3.06	32	31	13	212	179	99	145	1	0	0	0	0	0	0	—	9	25	2	0	1.1	.944
1976	2 teams	NY A (11G 4–3)	BAL A (24G 11–7)																								
″	total		15	10	.600	3.72	35	32	7	220.1	205	70	109	2	0	0	0	0	0	0		13	31	5	3	1.4	.898
1977	BAL	A	18	14	.563	3.61	37	37	11	252	243	78	105	4	0	0	0	0	0	0	—	6	33	4	1	1.2	.907
1978	MON	N	8	10	.444	3.88	27	23	4	144	141	42	87	1	0	1	0	42	6	0	.143	5	15	3	2	0.9	.870
1979			10	3	.769	2.30	33	7	2	94	88	31	67	1	6	1	0	21	3	0	.143	6	15	0	0	0.6	1.000
1980	NY	A	15	5	.750	**2.47**	41	17	3	175	144	39	133	1	4	2	3	0	0	0	—	5	26	2	2	0.8	.939
1981			6	11	.353	4.14	27	22	4	148	137	41	79	0	0	1	1	0	0	0	—	11	28	1	0	1.5	.975
1982			6	6	.500	2.89	41	6	0	106	109	14	85	0	4	3	3	0	0	0	—	2	19	1	1	0.5	.955
1983			1	5	.167	6.87	15	0	0	18.1	22	12	16	0	1	5	0	0	0	0	—	0	3	0	0	0.2	1.000
16 yrs.			152	156	.494	3.46	535	360	87	2622	2314	958	1760	24	21	19	12	341	42	0	.123	87	382	37	18	0.9	.927
DIVISIONAL PLAYOFF SERIES																											
1981	NY	A	0	0	—	0.00	1	0	0	2	1	0	1	0	0	0	0	0	0	0	—	0	0	1	0	1.0	.000
LEAGUE CHAMPIONSHIP SERIES																											
1980	NY	A	0	1	.000	3.38	1	1	1	8	6	3	4	0	0	0	0	0	0	0	—	2	2	0	0	4.0	1.000
1981			0	0	—	8.10	1	1	0	3.1	6	0	5	0	0	0	0	0	0	0	—	0	0	0	0	0.0	.000
2 yrs.			0	1	.000	4.76	2	2	1	11.1	12	3	9	0	0	0	0	0	0	0		2	2	0	0	2.0	1.000
WORLD SERIES																											
1981	NY	A	0	0	—	2.84	3	0	0	6.1	5	1	5	0	0	0	0	1	0	0	.000	0	1	0	0	0.3	1.000

Scott May

MAY, SCOTT FRANCIS BR TR 6′ 1″ 185 lbs.
B. Nov. 11, 1961, West Bend, Wis.

Year	Team		W	L	PCT	ERA	G	GS	CG	IP	H	BB	SO	ShO	Relief Pitching W	Relief Pitching L	Relief Pitching SV	Batting AB	Batting H	Batting HR	BA	PO	A	E	DP	TC/G	FA
1988	TEX	A	0	0	—	8.59	3	1	0	7.1	8	4	4	0	0	0	0	0	0	0	—	1	0	0	1	0.3	1.000
1991	CHI	N	0	0	—	18.00	2	0	0	2	6	1	1	0	0	0	0	0	0	0	—	0	0	0	0	0.0	.000
2 yrs.			0	0		10.61	5	1	0	9.1	14	5	5	0	0	0	0	0	0	0		1	0	0	1	0.2	1.000

Ed Mayer

MAYER, EDWIN DAVID BL TL 6′ 2″ 185 lbs.
B. Nov. 30, 1931, San Francisco, Calif.

Year	Team		W	L	PCT	ERA	G	GS	CG	IP	H	BB	SO	ShO	Relief Pitching W	Relief Pitching L	Relief Pitching SV	Batting AB	Batting H	Batting HR	BA	PO	A	E	DP	TC/G	FA
1957	CHI	N	0	0	—	5.87	3	1	0	7.2	8	2	3	0	0	0	0	2	1	0	.500	1	3	0	0	1.3	1.000
1958			2	2	.500	3.80	19	0	0	23.2	15	16	14	0	2	2	1	5	1	0	.200	1	3	1	0	0.3	.800
2 yrs.			2	2	.500	4.31	22	1	0	31.1	23	18	17	0	2	2	1	7	2	0	.286	2	6	1	0	0.4	.889

Erskine Mayer

MAYER, ERSKINE JOHN BR TR 6′ 168 lbs.
Born James Erskine.
Brother of Sam Mayer.
B. Jan. 16, 1889, Atlanta, Ga. D. Mar. 10, 1957, Los Angeles, Calif.

Year	Team		W	L	PCT	ERA	G	GS	CG	IP	H	BB	SO	ShO	Relief Pitching W	Relief Pitching L	Relief Pitching SV	Batting AB	Batting H	Batting HR	BA	PO	A	E	DP	TC/G	FA
1912	PHI	N	0	1	.000	6.33	7	1	0	21.1	27	7	5	0	0	0	0	3	0	0	.000	1	6	1	2	1.1	.875
1913			9	9	.500	3.11	39	20	7	170.2	172	46	51	2	3	1	1	50	6	0	.120	3	48	1	2	1.3	.981
1914			21	19	.525	2.58	48	39	24	321	308	91	116	4	3	1	2	108	21	1	.194	14	105	5	1	2.6	.960
1915			21	15	.583	2.36	43	33	20	274.2	240	59	114	2	4	1	2	88	21	1	.239	14	74	2	3	2.1	.978
1916			7	7	.500	3.15	28	16	7	140	148	33	62	2	1	0	0	38	5	0	.132	9	50	3	3	2.2	.952
1917			11	6	.647	2.76	28	18	11	160	160	33	64	1	1	1	0	51	10	0	.196	5	43	3	4	1.8	.941
1918	2 teams	PHI N (13G 7–4)	PIT N (15G 9–3)																								
″	total		16	7	.696	2.65	28	27	18	227.1	230	53	41	1	0	0	0	79	15	0	.190	10	58	0	2	2.4	1.000
1919	2 teams	PIT N (18G 5–3)	CHI A (6G 1–3)																								
″	total		6	6	.500	5.30	24	12	6	112	130	23	29	0	2	1	1	36	6	0	.167	2	27	1	0	1.3	.967
8 yrs.			91	70	.565	2.96	245	166	93	1427	1415	345	482	12	14	5	6	453	84	2	.185	58	411	16	17	2.0	.967
WORLD SERIES																											
1915	PHI	N	0	1	.000	2.38	2	2	1	11.1	16	2	7	0	0	0	0	4	0	0	.000	2	3	0	0	2.5	1.000
1919	CHI	A	0	0	—	0.00	1	0	0	1	0	1	0	0	0	0	0	0	0	0	—	0	0	0	0	0.0	.000
2 yrs.			0	1	.000	2.19	3	2	1	12.1	16	3	7	0	0	0	0	4	0	0	.000	2	3	0	0	1.7	1.000

Sam Mayer

MAYER, SAMUEL FRANKEL BR TL 5′10″ 164 lbs.
Born Samuel Frankel Erskine.
Brother of Erskine Mayer.
B. Feb. 28, 1893, Atlanta, Ga. D. July 1, 1962, Atlanta, Ga.

Year	Team		W	L	PCT	ERA	G	GS	CG	IP	H	BB	SO	ShO	Relief Pitching W	Relief Pitching L	Relief Pitching SV	Batting AB	Batting H	Batting HR	BA	PO	A	E	DP	TC/G	FA
1915	WAS	A	0	0	—	0.00	1	0	0		0	2	0	0	0	0	0	*				14	1	0	1	1.3	1.000

Al Mays

MAYS, ALBERT C. BR
B. May 17, 1865, Canal Dover, Ohio D. May 17, 1905, Parkersburg, W. Va.

Year	Team		W	L	PCT	ERA	G	GS	CG	IP	H	BB	SO	ShO	Relief Pitching W	Relief Pitching L	Relief Pitching SV	Batting AB	Batting H	Batting HR	BA	PO	A	E	DP	TC/G	FA
1885	LOU	AA	6	11	.353	*2.76*	17	17	17	150	129	43	61	0	0	0	0	61	13	0	.213	5	23	0	0	1.6	1.000
1886	NY	AA	11	28	.282	*3.39*	41	40	39	350	330	140	163	1	0	0	0	135	16	1	.119	9	71	11	3	2.2	.879
1887			17	**34**	.333	*4.73*	52	52	50	441.1	551	136	124	0	0	0	0	221	45	2	.204	36	146	28	4	3.3	.867
1888	BKN	AA	9	9	.500	2.80	18	18	17	160.2	150	32	67	1	0	0	0	63	5	0	.079	7	45	6	2	3.1	.897
1889	COL	AA	10	7	.588	4.82	21	19	13	140	167	56	52	1	0	0	0	54	7	0	.130	6	36	4	1	2.0	.913
1890			0	1	.000	*8.00*	1	1	1	9	14	8	2	0	0	0	0	3	0	0	.000	0	0	1	0	1.0	.000
6 yrs.			53	90	.371	3.91	150	147	137	1251	1341	415	469	3	0	0	0	537	86	3	.160	63	321	50	10	2.6	.885

Carl Mays

MAYS, CARL WILLIAM (Sub) BL TR 5′11½″ 195 lbs.
B. Nov. 12, 1891, Liberty, Ky. D. Apr. 4, 1971, El Cajon, Calif.

Year	Team		W	L	PCT	ERA	G	GS	CG	IP	H	BB	SO	ShO	Relief Pitching W	Relief Pitching L	Relief Pitching SV	Batting AB	Batting H	Batting HR	BA	PO	A	E	DP	TC/G	FA
1915	BOS	A	6	5	.545	2.60	38	6	2	131.2	119	21	65	0	**5**	3	**7**	38	9	0	.237	9	44	2	0	1.4	.964
1916			18	13	.581	2.39	44	24	14	245	208	74	76	2	6	3	3	77	18	0	.234	13	117	6	5	3.1	.956
1917			22	9	.710	1.74	35	33	27	289	230	74	91	2	1	0	0	107	27	0	.252	22	118	1	5	4.0	.993
1918			21	13	.618	2.21	35	33	**30**	293.1	230	81	114	**8**	0	1	0	104	30	0	.288	16	122	8	3	4.2	.945
1919	2 teams	BOS A (21G 5–11)	NY A (13G 9–3)																								
″	total		14	14	.500	2.11	34	29	26	265	227	77	107	3	0	0	2	98	22	0	.224	19	86	5	6	3.2	.955
1920	NY	A	26	11	.703	3.06	45	37	26	312	310	84	92	**6**	4	0	2	109	26	0	.239	19	106	1	5	2.8	.992
1921			**27**	9	**.750**	3.05	**49**	38	30	**336.2**	332	76	70	1	1	0	**7**	143	49	2	.343	8	104	2	4	2.3	.982
1922			12	14	.462	3.60	34	29	21	240	257	50	41	1	0	1	2	92	23	0	.250	8	94	5	4	3.1	.953
1923			5	2	.714	6.20	23	7	2	81.1	119	32	16	0	2	0	0	27	4	1	.148	8	32	1	2	1.8	.976
1924	CIN	N	20	9	.690	3.15	37	27	15	226	238	36	63	2	4	1	0	83	24	1	.289	13	94	5	5	3.0	.955
1925			3	5	.375	3.31	12	5	3	51.2	60	13	10	0	1	2	2	16	4	0	.250	3	15	2	3	1.7	.900
1926			19	12	.613	3.14	39	33	**24**	281	286	53	58	3	0	1	1	98	22	0	.224	16	117	4	10	3.5	.971
1927			3	7	.300	3.51	14	9	6	82	89	10	17	0	1	0	0	32	13	1	.406	5	38	0	1	3.1	1.000
1928			4	1	.800	3.88	14	7	4	62.2	67	22	10	1	0	0	1	27	8	0	.296	3	17	1	0	1.5	.952
1929	NY	N	7	2	.778	4.32	37	8	1	123	140	31	32	0	6	1	4	34	12	0	.353	12	34	1	3	1.3	.979
15 yrs.			207	126	.622	2.92	490	325	231	3020.1	2912	734	862	29	31	13	31	1085	291	5	.268	174	1138	44	56	2.8	.968
WORLD SERIES																											
1916	BOS	A	0	1	.000	5.06	2	1	0	5.1	8	3	2	0	0	0	1	1	0	0	.000	0	4	0	0	2.0	1.000
1918			2	0	1.000	1.00	2	2	2	18	10	3	5	0	0	0	0	5	1	0	.200	0	8	0	0	4.0	1.000
1921	NY	A	1	2	.333	1.73	3	3	3	26	20	0	9	1	0	0	0	9	1	0	.111	0	8	0	0	2.7	1.000
1922			0	1	.000	4.50	1	1	0	8	9	2	1	0	0	0	0	2	0	0	.000	0	4	0	0	4.0	1.000
4 yrs.			3	4	.429	2.20	8	7	5	57.1	47	8	17	1	0	0	1	17	2	0	.118	0	24	0	0	3.0	1.000

Matt Maysey

MAYSEY, MATTHEW SAMUEL BR TR 6′ 4″ 225 lbs.
B. Jan. 8, 1967, Hamilton, Ont., Canada.

Year	Team		W	L	PCT	ERA	G	GS	CG	IP	H	BB	SO	ShO	Relief Pitching W	Relief Pitching L	Relief Pitching SV	Batting AB	Batting H	Batting HR	BA	PO	A	E	DP	TC/G	FA
1992	MON	N	0	0	—	3.86	2	0	0	2.1	4	0	1	0	0	0	0	0	0	0	—	0	0	0	0	0.0	.000
1993	MIL	A	1	2	.333	5.73	23	0	0	22	28	13	10	0	1	2	1	1	1	0	1.000	1	2	2	0	0.2	.600
2 yrs.			1	2	.333	5.55	25	0	0	24.1	32	13	11	0	1	2	1	1	1	0	1.000	1	2	2	0	0.2	.600

Jack McAdams

McADAMS, GEORGE D. BR TR 6′ 1½″ 170 lbs.
B. Dec. 17, 1886, Benton, Ark. D. May 21, 1937, San Francisco, Calif.

Year	Team		W	L	PCT	ERA	G	GS	CG	IP	H	BB	SO	ShO	Relief Pitching W	Relief Pitching L	Relief Pitching SV	Batting AB	Batting H	Batting HR	BA	PO	A	E	DP	TC/G	FA
1911	STL	N	0	0	—	3.72	6	0	0	9.2	7	5	4	0	0	0	0	1	0	0	.000	2	2	0	0	0.7	1.000

Bill McAfee

McAFEE, WILLIAM FORT
B. Sept. 7, 1907, Smithville, Ga. D. July 8, 1958, Culpeper, Va.
BR TR 6′ 2″ 186 lbs.

Year	Team	Lg	W	L	PCT	ERA	G	GS	CG	IP	H	BB	SO	ShO	Relief W	Relief L	Relief SV	AB	H	HR	BA	PO	A	E	DP	TC/G	FA
1930	CHI	N	0	0	—	0.00	2	0	0	1	3	2	0	0	0	0	0	0	0	0	—	0	0	0	0	0.0	.000
1931	BOS	N	0	1	.000	6.37	18	1	0	29.2	39	10	9	0	0	0	0	3	0	0	.000	0	8	0	2	0.4	1.000
1932	WAS	A	6	1	.857	3.92	8	5	2	41.1	47	22	10	0	3	0	0	18	2	0	.111	2	14	0	0	2.0	1.000
1933			3	2	.600	6.62	27	1	0	53	64	21	14	0	3	2	5	15	4	1	.267	1	12	1	2	0.5	.929
1934	STL	A	1	0	1.000	5.84	28	0	0	61.2	84	26	11	0	1	0	0	16	3	0	.188	3	10	2	0	0.5	.867
5 yrs.			10	4	.714	5.69	83	7	2	186.2	237	81	44	0	7	2	5	52	9	1	.173	6	44	3	4	0.6	.943

Jimmy McAleer

McALEER, JAMES ROBERT
B. July 10, 1864, Youngstown, Ohio D. Apr. 29, 1931, Youngstown, Ohio.
Manager 1901–11.
BR TR 6′ 175 lbs.

Year	Team	Lg	W	L	PCT	ERA	G	GS	CG	IP	H	BB	SO	ShO	Relief W	Relief L	Relief SV	AB	H	HR	BA	PO	A	E	DP	TC/G	FA
1901	CLE	A	0	0	—	0.00	1	0	0	0.1	2	3	0	0	0	0	0	*				247	29	13	9	2.6	.955

John McAleese

McALEESE, JOHN JAMES
B. Aug. 22, 1878, Sharon, Pa. D. Nov. 14, 1950, New York, N. Y.
BR TR 5′ 8″

Year	Team	Lg	W	L	PCT	ERA	G	GS	CG	IP	H	BB	SO	ShO	Relief W	Relief L	Relief SV	AB	H	HR	BA	PO	A	E	DP	TC/G	FA
1901	CHI	A	0	0	—	9.00	1	0	0	3	7	1	1	0	0	0	0	*				0	1	0	0	1.0	1.000

Jack McAllister

Playing record listed under Andy Coakley.

Sport McAllister

McALLISTER, LEWIS WILLIAM
B. July 23, 1874, Austin, Miss. D. July 17, 1962, Wyandotte, Mich.
BB TR 5′11″ 180 lbs.

Year	Team	Lg	W	L	PCT	ERA	G	GS	CG	IP	H	BB	SO	ShO	Relief W	Relief L	Relief SV	AB	H	HR	BA	PO	A	E	DP	TC/G	FA
1896	CLE	N	0	0	—	6.75	1	0	0	4	9	2	0	0	0	0	0	27	6	0	.222	6	2	1	0	1.3	.889
1897			1	2	.333	4.50	4	3	3	28	29	9	10	0	0	0	0	137	30	0	.219	74	21	9	1	2.5	.913
1898			3	4	.429	4.55	9	7	6	65.1	73	23	9	0	0	0	0	57	13	0	.228	15	17	2	0	2.0	.941
1899			0	1	.000	9.56	3	1	1	16	29	10	2	0	0	0	0	418	99	1	.237	218	59	28	11	2.6	.908
4 yrs.			4	7	.364	5.32	17	11	10	113.1	140	44	21	0	0	0	0	*				1176	409	130	65	4.2	.924

Ernie McAnally

McANALLY, ERNEST LEE
B. Aug. 15, 1946, Pittsburg, Tex.
BR TR 6′ 1″ 190 lbs.

Year	Team	Lg	W	L	PCT	ERA	G	GS	CG	IP	H	BB	SO	ShO	Relief W	Relief L	Relief SV	AB	H	HR	BA	PO	A	E	DP	TC/G	FA
1971	MON	N	11	12	.478	3.89	31	25	8	178	150	87	98	2	0	0	0	60	7	1	.117	12	28	6	2	1.5	.870
1972			6	15	.286	3.81	29	27	4	170	165	71	102	2	0	0	0	53	6	0	.113	9	40	4	1	1.8	.925
1973			7	9	.438	4.04	27	24	4	147	158	54	72	0	0	0	0	49	9	0	.184	4	25	7	4	1.3	.806
1974			6	13	.316	4.47	25	21	5	129	126	56	79	2	0	1	0	42	5	0	.119	5	24	1	1	1.2	.967
4 yrs.			30	49	.380	4.02	112	97	21	624	599	268	351	6	0	1	0	204	27	1	.132	30	117	18	8	1.5	.891

Jamie McAndrew

McANDREW, JAMES BRIAN
Son of Jim McAndrew.
B. Sept. 2, 1967, Williamsport, Pa.
BR TR 6′ 2″ 190 lbs.

Year	Team	Lg	W	L	PCT	ERA	G	GS	CG	IP	H	BB	SO	ShO	Relief W	Relief L	Relief SV	AB	H	HR	BA	PO	A	E	DP	TC/G	FA
1995	MIL	A	2	3	.400	4.71	10	4	0	36.1	37	12	19	0	0	1	0	0	0	0	—	3	3	1	0	0.7	.857

Jim McAndrew

McANDREW, JAMES CLEMENT
Father of Jamie McAndrew.
B. Jan. 11, 1944, Lost Nation, Iowa.
BR TR 6′ 2″ 185 lbs.

Year	Team	Lg	W	L	PCT	ERA	G	GS	CG	IP	H	BB	SO	ShO	Relief W	Relief L	Relief SV	AB	H	HR	BA	PO	A	E	DP	TC/G	FA
1968	NY	N	4	7	.364	2.28	12	12	2	79	66	17	46	1	0	0	0	22	1	0	.045	8	8	0	2	1.3	1.000
1969			6	7	.462	3.47	27	21	4	135	112	44	90	2	0	0	0	37	5	0	.135	10	14	0	1	0.9	1.000
1970			10	14	.417	3.57	32	27	9	184	166	38	111	3	0	1	2	54	8	0	.148	13	17	0	1	0.9	1.000
1971			2	5	.286	4.40	24	10	0	90	78	32	42	0	0	1	0	23	1	0	.043	10	17	4	1	1.3	.871
1972			11	8	.579	2.80	28	23	4	160.2	133	38	81	0	1	0	1	43	2	0	.047	16	16	1	0	1.2	.970
1973			3	8	.273	5.38	23	12	0	80.1	109	31	38	0	0	1	1	15	2	0	.133	3	9	2	0	0.6	.857
1974	SD	N	1	4	.200	5.57	15	5	1	42	48	13	16	0	0	1	0	7	1	0	.143	0	5	0	0	0.3	1.000
7 yrs.			37	53	.411	3.65	161	110	20	771	712	213	424	6	1	4	4	201	20	0	.100	60	86	7	5	1.0	.954

Dixie McArthur

McARTHUR, OLAND ALEXANDER
B. Feb. 1, 1892, Vernon, Ala. D. May 31, 1986, West Point, Miss.
BR TR 6′ 1″ 185 lbs.

Year	Team	Lg	W	L	PCT	ERA	G	GS	CG	IP	H	BB	SO	ShO	Relief W	Relief L	Relief SV	AB	H	HR	BA	PO	A	E	DP	TC/G	FA
1914	PIT	N	0	0	—	0.00	1	0	0	1	1	0	1	0	0	0	0	0	0	0	—	0	0	0	0	0.0	.000

Tom McAvoy

McAVOY, THOMAS JOHN
B. Aug. 12, 1936, Brooklyn, N. Y.
BL TL 6′ 3″ 200 lbs.

Year	Team	Lg	W	L	PCT	ERA	G	GS	CG	IP	H	BB	SO	ShO	Relief W	Relief L	Relief SV	AB	H	HR	BA	PO	A	E	DP	TC/G	FA
1959	WAS	A	0	0	—	0.00	1	0	0	2.2	1	2	0	0	0	0	0	1	0	0	.000	0	1	0	0	1.0	1.000

Wickey McAvoy

McAVOY, JAMES EUGENE
B. Oct. 20, 1894, Rochester, N. Y. D. July 6, 1973, Rochester, N. Y.
BR TR 5′11″ 172 lbs.

Year	Team	Lg	W	L	PCT	ERA	G	GS	CG	IP	H	BB	SO	ShO	Relief W	Relief L	Relief SV	AB	H	HR	BA	PO	A	E	DP	TC/G	FA
1918	PHI	A	0	0	—	0.00	1	0	0	0.2	0	0	0	0	0	0	0	*				14	7	0	0	5.3	1.000

Al McBean

McBEAN, ALVIN O'NEAL
B. May 15, 1938, Charlotte Amalie, Virgin Islands.
BR TR 5′11½″ 165 lbs.

Year	Team	Lg	W	L	PCT	ERA	G	GS	CG	IP	H	BB	SO	ShO	Relief W	Relief L	Relief SV	AB	H	HR	BA	PO	A	E	DP	TC/G	FA
1961	PIT	N	3	2	.600	3.75	27	2	0	74.1	72	42	49	0	3	1	0	15	4	1	.267	4	23	1	1	1.0	.964
1962			15	10	.600	3.70	33	29	6	189.2	212	65	119	2	0	0	0	67	14	0	.209	17	31	5	4	1.6	.906
1963			13	3	.813	2.57	55	7	2	122.1	100	39	74	1	11	2	11	31	6	1	.194	11	29	6	2	0.8	.870
1964			8	3	.727	1.91	58	0	0	89.2	76	17	41	0	**8**	3	22	12	1	0	.083	3	38	4	5	0.8	.911
1965			6	6	.500	2.29	62	1	0	114	111	42	54	0	5	6	18	27	6	0	.222	6	27	1	1	0.5	.971
1966			4	3	.571	3.22	47	0	0	86.2	95	24	54	0	4	3	3	10	1	0	.100	7	17	1	0	0.5	.960
1967			7	4	.636	2.54	51	8	5	131	118	43	54	0	3	2	4	29	6	0	.207	9	26	2	1	0.7	.946
1968			9	12	.429	3.58	36	28	9	198.1	204	63	100	2	0	1	0	67	13	1	.194	16	54	3	3	2.0	.959
1969	2 teams	SD N (1G 0–1)	LA N (31G 2–6)																								
″	total		2	7	.222	4.07	32	1	0	55.1	56	23	27	0	2	6	4	5	1	0	.200	0	5	1	0	0.2	.833
1970	2 teams	LA N (1G 0–0)	PIT N (7G 0–0)																								
″	total		0	0		7.36	8	0	0	11	14	7	3	0	0	0	1	1	0	0	.000	0	2	0	1	0.3	1.000
10 yrs.			67	50	.573	3.13	409	76	22	1072.1	1058	365	575	5	36	24	63	264	52	3	.197	73	252	24	18	0.9	.931

Pryor McBee

McBEE, PRYOR EDWARD (Lefty)
B. June 20, 1901, Blanco, Okla. D. Apr. 19, 1963, Roseville, Calif.
BR TL 6′ 1″ 190 lbs.

Year	Team		W	L	PCT	ERA	G	GS	CG	IP	H	BB	SO	ShO	Relief Pitching W	Relief Pitching L	Relief Pitching SV	Batting AB	Batting H	Batting HR	BA	PO	A	E	DP	TC/G	FA
1926	CHI	A	0	0	—	6.75	1	0	0	1.1	1	3	1	0	0	0	0	0	0	0	—	0	0	0	0	0.0	.000

Dick McBride

McBRIDE, JAMES DICKSON
B. 1845, Philadelphia, Pa. D. Oct. 10, 1916, Philadelphia, Pa.
TR 5′ 9″ 150 lbs.

Year	Team		W	L	PCT	ERA	G	GS	CG	IP	H	BB	SO	ShO	Relief Pitching W	Relief Pitching L	Relief Pitching SV	Batting AB	Batting H	Batting HR	BA	PO	A	E	DP	TC/G	FA
1876	BOS	N	0	4	.000	2.73	4	4	3	33	53	5	2	0	0	0	0	16	3	0	.188	0	5	1	0	1.2	.833

Ken McBride

McBRIDE, KENNETH FAYE
B. Aug. 12, 1935, Huntsville, Ala.
BR TR 6′ 1″ 190 lbs.

Year	Team		W	L	PCT	ERA	G	GS	CG	IP	H	BB	SO	ShO	Relief Pitching W	Relief Pitching L	Relief Pitching SV	Batting AB	Batting H	Batting HR	BA	PO	A	E	DP	TC/G	FA
1959	CHI	A	0	1	.000	3.18	11	2	0	22.2	20	17	12	0	0	0	1	6	1	0	.167	0	9	1	0	0.9	.900
1960			0	1	.000	3.86	5	0	0	4.2	6	3	4	0	0	1	0	0	0	0	—	1	0	0	0	0.2	1.000
1961	LA	A	12	15	.444	3.65	38	36	11	241.2	229	102	180	1	0	1	1	83	7	0	.084	19	53	2	5	1.9	.973
1962			11	5	.688	3.50	24	23	6	149.1	136	70	83	4	0	0	0	55	9	1	.164	20	41	2	7	2.6	.968
1963			13	12	.520	3.26	36	36	11	251	198	82	147	2	0	0	0	87	15	0	.172	22	52	3	3	2.1	.961
1964			4	13	.235	5.26	29	21	0	116.1	104	75	66	0	1	0	1	28	6	0	.214	13	29	1	4	1.5	.977
1965	CAL	A	0	3	.000	6.14	8	4	0	22	24	14	11	0	0	0	0	5	0	0	.000	3	1	0	0	0.5	1.000
7 yrs.			40	50	.444	3.79	151	122	28	807.2	717	363	503	7	1	2	3	264	38	1	.144	78	185	9	19	1.8	.967

Pete McBride

McBRIDE, PETER WILLIAM
B. July 9, 1875, Adams, Mass. D. July 3, 1944, North Adams, Mass.
BR TR 5′10″ 170 lbs.

Year	Team		W	L	PCT	ERA	G	GS	CG	IP	H	BB	SO	ShO	Relief Pitching W	Relief Pitching L	Relief Pitching SV	Batting AB	Batting H	Batting HR	BA	PO	A	E	DP	TC/G	FA
1898	CLE	N	0	1	.000	6.43	1	1	1	7	9	4	6	0	0	0	0	2	2	0	1.000	0	1	0	0	1.0	1.000
1899	STL	N	2	4	.333	4.08	11	6	4	64	65	40	26	0	0	0	0	27	5	1	.185	3	13	6	0	1.8	.727
2 yrs.			2	5	.286	4.31	12	7	5	71	74	44	32	0	0	0	0	29	7	1	.241	3	14	6	0	1.8	.739

Dick McCabe

McCABE, RICHARD JAMES
B. Feb. 21, 1896, Mamaroneck, N. Y. D. Apr. 11, 1950, Buffalo, N. Y.
BR TR 5′10½″ 159 lbs.

Year	Team		W	L	PCT	ERA	G	GS	CG	IP	H	BB	SO	ShO	Relief Pitching W	Relief Pitching L	Relief Pitching SV	Batting AB	Batting H	Batting HR	BA	PO	A	E	DP	TC/G	FA
1918	BOS	A	0	1	.000	2.79	3	1	0	9.2	13	2	3	0	0	0	0	2	0	0	.000	1	3	0	0	1.3	1.000
1922	CHI	A	1	0	1.000	5.40	3	0	0	3.1	4	0	1	0	1	0	0	0	0	0	—	0	0	0	0	0.0	.000
2 yrs.			1	1	.500	3.46	6	1	0	13	17	2	4	0	1	0	0	2	0	0	.000	1	3	0	0	0.7	1.000

Ralph McCabe

McCABE, RALPH HERBERT
B. Oct. 21, 1918, Napanee, Ont., Canada D. May 3, 1974, Windsor, Ont., Canada.
BR TR 6′ 4″ 195 lbs.

Year	Team		W	L	PCT	ERA	G	GS	CG	IP	H	BB	SO	ShO	Relief Pitching W	Relief Pitching L	Relief Pitching SV	Batting AB	Batting H	Batting HR	BA	PO	A	E	DP	TC/G	FA
1946	CLE	A	0	1	.000	11.25	1	1	0	4	5	2	3	0	0	0	0	1	0	0	.000	1	0	0	0	1.0	1.000

Tim McCabe

McCABE, TIMOTHY J.
B. Oct. 19, 1894, Ironton, Mo. D. Apr. 12, 1977, Ironton, Mo.
BR TR 6′ 190 lbs.

Year	Team		W	L	PCT	ERA	G	GS	CG	IP	H	BB	SO	ShO	Relief Pitching W	Relief Pitching L	Relief Pitching SV	Batting AB	Batting H	Batting HR	BA	PO	A	E	DP	TC/G	FA
1915	STL	A	3	1	.750	2.38	7	4	4	41.2	25	9	17	1	0	0	0	15	1	0	.067	0	10	1	0	1.6	.909
1916			2	0	1.000	3.16	13	0	0	25.2	29	7	7	0	2	0	0	4	0	0	.000	1	14	0	0	1.2	1.000
1917			0	0	—	23.14	1	0	0	2.1	4	4	2	0	0	0	0	0	0	0	—	0	1	0	0	1.0	1.000
1918			0	0	—	13.50	1	0	0	1.1	2	1	0	0	0	0	0	0	0	0	—	0	0	0	0	0.0	.000
4 yrs.			5	1	.833	3.55	22	4	4	71	60	21	26	1	2	0	0	19	1	0	.053	1	25	1	0	1.2	.963

Harry McCaffrey

McCAFFREY, HARRY CHARLES
B. Nov. 25, 1858, St. Louis, Mo. D. Apr. 19, 1928, St. Louis, Mo.
BR TR 5′10½″ 185 lbs.

Year	Team		W	L	PCT	ERA	G	GS	CG	IP	H	BB	SO	ShO	Relief Pitching W	Relief Pitching L	Relief Pitching SV	Batting AB	Batting H	Batting HR	BA	PO	A	E	DP	TC/G	FA
1885	CIN	AA	1	0	1.000	*6.00*	1	1	1	9	13	2	2	0	0	0	0	*				74	50	17	5	3.5	.879

Bill McCahan

McCAHAN, WILLIAM GLENN
B. June 7, 1921, Philadelphia, Pa. D. July 3, 1986, Fort Worth, Tex.
BR TR 5′11″ 200 lbs.

Year	Team		W	L	PCT	ERA	G	GS	CG	IP	H	BB	SO	ShO	Relief Pitching W	Relief Pitching L	Relief Pitching SV	Batting AB	Batting H	Batting HR	BA	PO	A	E	DP	TC/G	FA
1946	PHI	A	1	1	.500	1.00	4	2	2	18	16	9	6	1	0	0	0	5	2	0	.400	1	3	0	0	1.0	1.000
1947			10	5	.667	3.32	29	19	10	165.1	160	62	47	1	1	0	0	55	9	0	.164	7	33	1	4	1.4	.976
1948			4	7	.364	5.71	17	15	5	86.2	98	65	20	0	0	0	0	31	8	0	.258	6	10	1	0	1.0	.941
1949			1	1	.500	2.61	7	4	0	20.2	23	9	3	0	0	0	0	5	1	0	.200	0	3	0	0	0.4	1.000
4 yrs.			16	14	.533	3.84	57	40	17	290.2	297	145	76	2	1	0	0	96	20	0	.208	14	49	2	4	1.1	.969

Dutch McCall

McCALL, ROBERT LEONARD
B. Dec. 27, 1920, Columbia, Tenn. D. Jan. 7, 1996, Little Rock, Ark.
BL TL 6′ 1½″ 185 lbs.

Year	Team		W	L	PCT	ERA	G	GS	CG	IP	H	BB	SO	ShO	Relief Pitching W	Relief Pitching L	Relief Pitching SV	Batting AB	Batting H	Batting HR	BA	PO	A	E	DP	TC/G	FA
1948	CHI	N	4	13	.235	4.82	30	20	5	151.1	158	85	89	0	0	3	0	53	9	0	.170	5	31	3	5	1.3	.923

Larry McCall

McCALL, LARRY STEPHEN
B. Sept. 8, 1952, Asheville, N. C.
BL TR 6′ 2″ 195 lbs.

Year	Team		W	L	PCT	ERA	G	GS	CG	IP	H	BB	SO	ShO	Relief Pitching W	Relief Pitching L	Relief Pitching SV	Batting AB	Batting H	Batting HR	BA	PO	A	E	DP	TC/G	FA
1977	NY	A	0	1	.000	7.50	2	0	0	6	12	1	0	0	0	1	0	0	0	0	—	1	0	1	0	1.0	.500
1978			1	1	.500	5.63	5	1	0	16	20	6	7	0	1	0	0	0	0	0	—	0	4	0	1	0.8	1.000
1979	TEX	A	1	0	1.000	2.25	2	1	0	8	7	3	3	0	0	0	0	0	0	0	—	0	1	0	1	0.5	1.000
3 yrs.			2	2	.500	5.10	9	2	0	30	39	10	10	0	1	1	0	0	0	0		1	5	1	2	0.8	.857

Windy McCall

McCALL, JOHN WILLIAM
B. July 18, 1925, San Francisco, Calif.
BL TL 6′ 180 lbs.

Year	Team		W	L	PCT	ERA	G	GS	CG	IP	H	BB	SO	ShO	Relief Pitching W	Relief Pitching L	Relief Pitching SV	Batting AB	Batting H	Batting HR	BA	PO	A	E	DP	TC/G	FA
1948	BOS	A	0	1	.000	20.25	1	1	0	1.1	6	1	0	0	0	0	0	0	0	0	—	0	1	0	0	1.0	1.000
1949			0	0	—	11.57	5	0	0	9.1	13	10	8	0	0	0	0	3	2	0	.667	0	0	0	0	0.0	.000
1950	PIT	N	0	0	—	9.45	2	0	0	6.2	12	4	5	0	0	0	0	2	0	0	.000	1	1	0	0	1.0	1.000
1954	NY	N	2	5	.286	3.25	33	4	0	61	50	29	38	0	2	3	2	11	0	0	.000	3	5	3	0	0.3	.727
1955			6	5	.545	3.69	42	6	4	95	86	37	50	0	3	3	3	17	2	0	.118	6	16	0	4	0.5	1.000
1956			3	4	.429	3.61	46	4	0	77.1	74	20	41	0	3	1	7	15	3	0	.200	4	6	1	0	0.2	.909
1957			0	0	—	15.00	5	0	0	3	8	2	2	0	0	0	0	0	0	0	—	0	0	0	0	0.0	.000
7 yrs.			11	15	.423	4.22	134	15	4	253.2	249	103	144	0	8	7	12	48	7	0	.146	14	29	4	4	0.4	.915

Randy McCament

McCAMENT, LARRY RANDALL
B. July 29, 1962, Albuquerque, N. M.
BR TR 6′ 3″ 195 lbs.

Year	Team		W	L	PCT	ERA	G	GS	CG	IP	H	BB	SO	ShO	Relief Pitching W	Relief Pitching L	Relief Pitching SV	Batting AB	Batting H	Batting HR	BA	PO	A	E	DP	TC/G	FA
1989	SF	N	1	1	.500	3.93	25	0	0	36.2	32	23	12	0	1	1	0	3	1	0	.333	3	8	1	1	0.5	.917
1990			0	0	—	3.00	3	0	0	6	8	5	5	0	0	0	0	1	0	0	.000	1	0	0	0	0.3	1.000
2 yrs.			1	1	.500	3.80	28	0	0	42.2	40	28	17	0	1	1	0	4	1	0	.250	4	8	1	1	0.5	.923

Gene McCann

McCANN, HENRY EUGENE
B. June 13, 1876, Baltimore, Md. D. Apr. 26, 1943, New York, N. Y.
TR 5′10″

Year	Team	W	L	PCT	ERA	G	GS	CG	IP	H	BB	SO	ShO	Relief Pitching W	L	SV	Batting AB	H	HR	BA	PO	A	E	DP	TC/G	FA
1901	BKN N	2	3	.400	3.44	6	5	3	34	34	16	9	0	0	0	0	10	0	0	.000	2	11	2	0	2.5	.867
1902		1	2	.333	2.40	3	3	3	30	32	12	9	0	0	0	0	12	1	0	.083	4	10	1	0	5.0	.933
2 yrs.		3	5	.375	2.95	9	8	6	64	66	28	18	0	0	0	0	22	1	0	.045	6	21	3	0	3.3	.900

Arch McCarthy

McCARTHY, ARCHIBALD JOSEPH
B. Jan. 21, 1881, Ypsilanti, Mich. Deceased.
TR 6′ 160 lbs.

Year	Team	W	L	PCT	ERA	G	GS	CG	IP	H	BB	SO	ShO	Relief Pitching W	L	SV	Batting AB	H	HR	BA	PO	A	E	DP	TC/G	FA
1902	DET A	2	7	.222	6.13	10	8	8	72	90	31	10	0	1	0	0	28	2	0	.071	2	13	3	1	1.8	.833

Bill McCarthy

McCARTHY, WILLIAM THOMAS
B. Apr. 11, 1882, Ashland, Mass. D. May 29, 1939, Boston, Mass.
BR TR 5′11″ 180 lbs.

Year	Team	W	L	PCT	ERA	G	GS	CG	IP	H	BB	SO	ShO	Relief Pitching W	L	SV	Batting AB	H	HR	BA	PO	A	E	DP	TC/G	FA
1906	BOS N	0	0	—	9.00	1	0	0	2	2	3	0	0	0	0	0	1	0	0	.000	0	0	0	0	0.0	.000

Johnny McCarthy

McCARTHY, JOHN JOSEPH
B. Jan. 7, 1910, Chicago, Ill. D. Sept. 13, 1973, Mundelein, Ill.
BL TL 6′ 1½″ 185 lbs.

Year	Team	W	L	PCT	ERA	G	GS	CG	IP	H	BB	SO	ShO	Relief Pitching W	L	SV	Batting AB	H	HR	BA	PO	A	E	DP	TC/G	FA
1939	NY N	0	0	—	7.20	1	0	0	5	8	2	0	0	0	0	0	*				89	9	4	13	7.8	.961

Tom McCarthy

McCARTHY, THOMAS MICHAEL
B. June 18, 1961, Lundstahl, West Germany.
BR TR 6′ 180 lbs.

Year	Team	W	L	PCT	ERA	G	GS	CG	IP	H	BB	SO	ShO	Relief Pitching W	L	SV	Batting AB	H	HR	BA	PO	A	E	DP	TC/G	FA
1985	BOS A	0	0	—	10.80	3	0	0	5	7	4	2	0	0	0	0	0	0	0	—	1	0	0	0	0.3	1.000
1988	CHI A	2	0	1.000	1.38	6	0	0	13	9	2	5	0	2	0	1	0	0	0	—	1	3	0	0	0.7	1.000
1989		1	2	.333	3.51	31	0	0	66.2	72	20	27	0	1	2	0	0	0	0	—	4	13	0	2	0.5	1.000
3 yrs.		3	2	.600	3.61	40	0	0	84.2	88	26	34	0	3	2	1	0	0	0		6	16	0	2	0.6	1.000

Tom McCarthy

McCARTHY, THOMAS PATRICK
B. May 22, 1884, Fort Wayne, Ind. D. Mar. 28, 1933, Mishawaka, Ind.
TR 5′ 7″ 170 lbs.

Year	Team	W	L	PCT	ERA	G	GS	CG	IP	H	BB	SO	ShO	Relief Pitching W	L	SV	Batting AB	H	HR	BA	PO	A	E	DP	TC/G	FA
1908	3 teams CIN N (1G 0–1) PIT N (2G 0–0) BOS N (14G 6–3)																									
″	total	6	4	.600	1.82	17	13	7	103.2	86	37	31	2	0	0	0	41	6	0	.146	4	36	1	0	2.4	.976
1909	BOS N	0	5	.000	3.50	8	7	3	46.1	47	28	11	0	0	0	0	16	2	0	.125	3	14	1	0	2.3	.944
2 yrs.		6	9	.400	2.34	25	20	10	150	133	65	42	2	0	0	0	57	8	0	.140	7	50	2	0	2.4	.966

Tommy McCarthy

McCARTHY, THOMAS FRANCIS MICHAEL
B. July 24, 1863, Boston, Mass. D. Aug. 5, 1922, Boston, Mass.
Manager 1890.
Hall of Fame 1946.
BR TR 5′7″ 170 lbs.

Year	Team	W	L	PCT	ERA	G	GS	CG	IP	H	BB	SO	ShO	Relief Pitching W	L	SV	Batting AB	H	HR	BA	PO	A	E	DP	TC/G	FA
1884	BOS U	0	7	.000	*4.82*	7	6	5	56	73	14	18	0	0	1	0	209	45	0	.215	45	30	18	2	1.7	.806
1886	PHI N	0	0	—	0.00	1	0	0	1	0	1	1	0	0	0	0	27	5	0	.185	69	8	12	0	2.2	.865
1888	STL AA	0	0	—	4.15	2	0	0	4.1	3	2	1	0	0	0	0	511	140	1	.274	8	1	2	0	1.2	.818
1889		0	0	—	7.20	1	0	0	5	4	6	1	0	0	0	0	604	176	2	.291	230	39	33	11	2.1	.891
1891		0	0	—	9.00	1	0	0	1	2	0	0	0	0	0	0	570	176	8	.309	205	95	43	11	2.5	.875
1894	BOS N	0	0	—	4.50	1	0	0	2	1	3	0	0	0	0	0	539	188	13	.349	225	92	47	14	2.6	.871
6 yrs.		0	7	.000	4.93	13	6	5	69.1	83	26	21	0	0	1	0	*				2190	486	342	83	2.3	.887

John McCarty

McCARTY, JOHN A.
B. St. Louis, Mo. Deceased.
TR

Year	Team	W	L	PCT	ERA	G	GS	CG	IP	H	BB	SO	ShO	Relief Pitching W	L	SV	Batting AB	H	HR	BA	PO	A	E	DP	TC/G	FA
1889	KC AA	8	6	.571	3.91	15	14	13	119.2	147	61	36	0	0	0	0	79	18	0	.228	20	33	14	0	3.2	.791

Kirk McCaskill

McCASKILL, KIRK EDWARD
B. Apr. 9, 1961, Kapuskasing, Ont., Canada.
BR TR 6′ 1″ 185 lbs.

Year	Team	W	L	PCT	ERA	G	GS	CG	IP	H	BB	SO	ShO	Relief Pitching W	L	SV	Batting AB	H	HR	BA	PO	A	E	DP	TC/G	FA
1985	CAL A	12	12	.500	4.70	30	29	6	189.2	189	64	102	1	0	0	0	0	0	0	—	11	27	3	1	1.4	.927
1986		17	10	.630	3.36	34	33	10	246.1	207	92	202	2	0	0	0	0	0	0	—	24	26	1	0	1.5	.980
1987		4	6	.400	5.67	14	13	1	74.2	84	34	56	1	0	0	0	0	0	0	—	8	12	1	1	1.5	.952
1988		8	6	.571	4.31	23	23	4	146.1	155	61	98	2	0	0	0	0	0	0	—	12	18	3	2	1.4	.909
1989		15	10	.600	2.93	32	32	6	212	202	59	107	4	0	0	0	0	0	0	—	16	42	3	5	1.9	.951
1990		12	11	.522	3.25	29	29	2	174.1	161	72	78	1	0	0	0	0	0	0	—	19	29	3	2	1.8	.941
1991		10	**19**	.345	4.26	30	30	1	177.2	193	66	71	0	0	0	0	0	0	0	—	17	25	1	4	1.4	.977
1992	CHI A	12	13	.480	4.18	34	34	0	209	193	95	109	0	0	0	0	0	0	0	—	24	31	2	0	1.7	.965
1993		4	8	.333	5.23	30	14	0	113.2	144	36	65	0	0	1	2	0	0	0	—	7	23	2	4	1.1	.938
1994		1	4	.200	3.42	40	0	0	52.2	51	22	37	0	1	4	3	0	0	0	—	4	8	0	0	0.3	1.000
1995		6	4	.600	4.89	55	1	0	81	97	33	50	0	6	4	2	0	0	0	—	5	13	2	0	0.4	.900
11 yrs.		101	103	.495	4.03	351	238	30	1677.1	1676	634	975	11	7	9	7	0	0	0		147	254	21	19	1.2	.950
LEAGUE CHAMPIONSHIP SERIES																										
1986	CAL A	0	2	.000	7.71	2	2	0	9.1	16	5	7	0	0	0	0	0	0	0	—	0	0	0	0	0.0	.000
1993	CHI A	0	0	—	0.00	3	0	0	3.2	3	1	3	0	0	0	0	0	0	0	—	0	2	0	0	0.7	1.000
2 yrs.		0	2	.000	5.54	5	2	0	13	19	6	10	0	0	0	0	0	0	0		0	2	0	0	0.4	1.000

Steve McCatty

McCATTY, STEVEN EARL
B. Mar. 20, 1954, Detroit, Mich.
BR TR 6′ 3″ 195 lbs.

Year	Team	W	L	PCT	ERA	G	GS	CG	IP	H	BB	SO	ShO	Relief Pitching W	L	SV	Batting AB	H	HR	BA	PO	A	E	DP	TC/G	FA
1977	OAK A	0	0	—	5.14	4	2	0	14	16	7	9	0	0	0	0	0	0	0	—	0	0	0	0	0.0	.000
1978		0	0	—	4.50	9	0	0	20	26	9	10	0	0	0	0	0	0	0	—	2	1	1	0	0.4	.750
1979		11	12	.478	4.21	31	23	8	186	207	80	87	0	2	1	0	0	0	0	—	12	20	3	3	1.1	.914
1980		14	14	.500	3.85	33	31	11	222	202	99	114	1	0	1	0	0	0	0	—	13	26	1	2	1.2	.975
1981		**14**	7	.667	**2.32**	22	22	16	186	140	61	91	**4**	0	0	0	0	0	0	—	11	26	1	2	1.7	.974
1982		6	3	.667	3.99	21	20	2	128.2	124	70	66	0	0	0	0	0	0	0	—	12	13	0	0	1.2	1.000
1983		6	9	.400	3.99	38	24	3	167	156	82	65	2	0	0	5	0	0	0	—	7	16	1	1	0.6	.958
1984		8	14	.364	4.76	33	30	4	179.2	206	71	63	0	1	1	0	0	0	0	—	15	16	2	1	1.0	.939
1985		4	4	.500	5.57	30	9	1	85.2	95	41	36	0	1	1	0	0	0	0	—	4	13	1	4	0.6	.944
9 yrs.		63	63	.500	3.99	221	161	45	1189	1172	520	541	7	4	4	5	0	0	0		76	131	10	13	1.0	.954
DIVISIONAL PLAYOFF SERIES																										
1981	OAK A	1	0	1.000	1.00	1	1	1	9	6	4	3	0	0	0	0	0	0	0	—	0	0	0	0	0.0	.000
LEAGUE CHAMPIONSHIP SERIES																										
1981	OAK A	0	1	.000	13.50	1	1	0	3.1	6	2	2	0	0	0	0	0	0	0	—	1	1	0	0	2.0	1.000

Al McCauley

McCAULEY, ALLEN A. BL TL 6′ 180 lbs.
B. Mar. 4, 1863, Indianapolis, Ind. D. Aug. 24, 1917, Indianapolis, Ind.

Year	Team	Lg	W	L	PCT	ERA	G	GS	CG	IP	H	BB	SO	ShO	Relief Pitching W	Relief Pitching L	Relief Pitching SV	Batting AB	Batting H	Batting HR	BA	PO	A	E	DP	TC/G	FA
1884	IND	AA	2	7	.222	5.09	10	9	9	76	87	25	34	0	0	0	0	*				40	23	4	4	3.7	.940

Joe McClain

McCLAIN, JOSEPH FRED BR TR 6′ 183 lbs.
B. May 5, 1933, Johnson City, Tenn.

Year	Team	Lg	W	L	PCT	ERA	G	GS	CG	IP	H	BB	SO	ShO	Relief Pitching W	Relief Pitching L	Relief Pitching SV	Batting AB	Batting H	Batting HR	BA	PO	A	E	DP	TC/G	FA
1961	WAS	A	8	18	.308	3.86	33	29	7	212	221	48	76	2	0	0	1	68	14	0	.206	15	24	1	0	1.2	.975
1962			0	4	.000	9.38	10	4	0	24	33	11	6	0	0	0	0	7	1	0	.143	1	5	0	1	0.6	1.000
2 yrs.			8	22	.267	4.42	43	33	7	236	254	59	82	2	0	0	1	75	15	0	.200	16	29	1	1	1.1	.978

Paul McClellan

McCLELLAN, PAUL WILLIAM BR TR 6′ 2″ 180 lbs.
B. Feb. 3, 1966, San Mateo, Calif.

Year	Team	Lg	W	L	PCT	ERA	G	GS	CG	IP	H	BB	SO	ShO	Relief Pitching W	Relief Pitching L	Relief Pitching SV	Batting AB	Batting H	Batting HR	BA	PO	A	E	DP	TC/G	FA
1990	SF	N	0	1	.000	11.74	4	1	0	7.2	14	6	2	0	0	0	0	2	1	0	.500	1	2	0	1	0.8	1.000
1991			3	6	.333	4.56	13	12	1	71	68	25	44	0	0	0	0	21	3	0	.143	4	6	0	1	0.8	1.000
2 yrs.			3	7	.300	5.26	17	13	1	78.2	82	31	46	0	0	0	0	23	4	0	.174	5	8	0	2	0.8	1.000

Jim McCloskey

McCLOSKEY, JAMES ELLWOOD BL TL 5′ 9½″ 180 lbs.
B. May 26, 1910, Danville, Pa. D. Aug. 18, 1971, Jersey City, N. J.

Year	Team	Lg	W	L	PCT	ERA	G	GS	CG	IP	H	BB	SO	ShO	Relief Pitching W	Relief Pitching L	Relief Pitching SV	Batting AB	Batting H	Batting HR	BA	PO	A	E	DP	TC/G	FA
1936	BOS	N	0	0	—	11.25	4	1	0	8	14	3	2	0	0	0	0	1	0	0	.000	0	3	0	0	0.8	1.000

John McCloskey

McCLOSKEY, JAMES JOHN
B. Aug. 20, 1882, Wyoming, Pa. D. Mar. 1, 1919, Lewisburg, Pa.

Year	Team	Lg	W	L	PCT	ERA	G	GS	CG	IP	H	BB	SO	ShO	Relief Pitching W	Relief Pitching L	Relief Pitching SV	Batting AB	Batting H	Batting HR	BA	PO	A	E	DP	TC/G	FA
1906	PHI	N	3	2	.600	2.85	9	4	3	41	46	9	6	0	1	0	0	15	3	0	.200	0	10	0	0	1.1	1.000
1907			0	0	—	7.00	3	0	0	9	15	6	3	0	0	0	0	4	0	0	.000	0	3	1	0	1.3	.750
2 yrs.			3	2	.600	3.60	12	4	3	50	61	15	9	0	1	0	0	19	3	0	.158	0	13	1	0	1.2	.929

Bob McClure

McCLURE, ROBERT CRAIG BR TL 5′11″ 170 lbs.
B. Apr. 29, 1952, Oakland, Calif.

Year	Team	Lg	W	L	PCT	ERA	G	GS	CG	IP	H	BB	SO	ShO	Relief Pitching W	Relief Pitching L	Relief Pitching SV	Batting AB	Batting H	Batting HR	BA	PO	A	E	DP	TC/G	FA
1975	KC	A	1	0	1.000	0.00	12	0	0	15.1	4	14	15	0	1	0	1	0	0	0	—	0	0	0	0	0.0	.000
1976			0	0	—	9.00	8	0	0	4	3	8	3	0	0	0	0	0	0	0	—	0	0	0	0	0.0	.000
1977	MIL	A	2	1	.667	2.54	68	0	0	71	64	34	57	0	2	1	6	0	0	0	—	2	19	2	2	0.3	.913
1978			2	6	.250	3.74	44	0	0	65	53	30	47	0	2	6	9	0	0	0	—	1	8	1	0	0.2	.900
1979			5	2	.714	3.88	36	0	0	51	53	24	37	0	5	2	5	0	0	0	—	1	7	3	1	0.3	.727
1980			5	8	.385	3.07	52	5	2	91	83	37	47	1	1	7	10	0	0	0	—	3	9	0	0	0.2	1.000
1981			0	0	—	3.38	4	0	0	8	7	4	6	0	0	0	0	0	0	0	—	1	0	0	0	0.3	1.000
1982			12	7	.632	4.22	34	26	5	172.2	160	74	99	0	2	0	0	0	0	0	—	4	23	3	3	0.9	.900
1983			9	9	.500	4.50	24	23	4	142	152	68	68	0	0	0	0	0	0	0	—	4	19	1	1	1.0	.958
1984			4	8	.333	4.38	39	18	1	139.2	154	52	68	0	0	2	1	0	0	0	—	4	21	2	2	0.7	.926
1985			4	1	.800	4.31	38	1	0	85.2	91	30	57	0	4	1	3	0	0	0	—	3	11	0	2	0.4	1.000
1986	2 teams MIL A (13G 2–1) MON N (52G 2–5)																										
″	total		4	6	.400	3.19	65	0	0	79	71	33	53	0	4	6	6	4	1	0	.250	2	12	1	1	0.2	.933
1987	MON	N	6	1	.857	3.44	52	0	0	52.1	47	20	33	0	6	1	5	2	0	0	.000	3	8	0	0	0.2	1.000
1988	2 teams MON N (19G 1–3) NY N (14G 1–0)																										
″	total		2	3	.400	5.40	33	0	0	30	35	8	19	0	2	3	3	2	0	0	.000	0	5	0	0	0.2	1.000
1989	CAL	A	6	1	.857	1.55	48	0	0	52.1	39	15	36	0	6	1	3	0	0	0	—	2	4	0	0	0.1	1.000
1990			2	0	1.000	6.43	11	0	0	7	7	3	6	0	2	0	0	0	0	0	—	0	1	0	0	0.1	1.000
1991	2 teams CAL A (13G 0–0) STL N (32G 1–1)																										
″	total		1	1	.500	4.96	45	0	0	32.2	37	13	20	0	1	1	0	1	1	0	1.000	1	5	0	0	0.1	1.000
1992	STL	N	2	2	.500	3.17	71	0	0	54	52	25	24	0	2	2	0	0	0	0	—	2	8	0	1	0.1	1.000
1993	FLA	N	1	1	.500	7.11	14	0	0	6.1	13	5	6	0	1	1	0	0	0	0	—	0	1	0	0	0.1	1.000
19 yrs.			68	57	.544	3.81	698	73	12	1159	1125	497	701	1	41	34	52	9	2	0	.222	33	161	13	13	0.3	.937
DIVISIONAL PLAYOFF SERIES																											
1981	MIL	A	0	0	—	0.00	3	0	0	3.1	4	0	2	0	0	0	0	0	0	0	—	0	0	0	0	0.0	.000
LEAGUE CHAMPIONSHIP SERIES																											
1982	MIL	A	1	0	1.000	0.00	1	0	0	1.2	2	0	0	0	1	0	0	0	0	0	—	0	0	0	0	0.0	.000
WORLD SERIES																											
1982	MIL	A	0	2	.000	4.15	5	0	0	4.1	5	3	5	0	0	2	2	0	0	0	—	0	0	0	0	0.0	.000

Harry McCluskey

McCLUSKEY, HARRY ROBERT (Lefty) BL TL 5′11½″ 173 lbs.
B. May 29, 1892, Clay Center, Ohio D. June 7, 1962, Toledo, Ohio.

Year	Team	Lg	W	L	PCT	ERA	G	GS	CG	IP	H	BB	SO	ShO	Relief Pitching W	Relief Pitching L	Relief Pitching SV	Batting AB	Batting H	Batting HR	BA	PO	A	E	DP	TC/G	FA
1915	CIN	N	0	0	—	5.40	3	0	0	5	4	0	2	0	0	0	0	2	0	0	.000	0	0	0	0	0.0	.000

Alex McColl

McCOLL, ALEXANDER BOYD (Red) BB TR 6′ 1″ 178 lbs.
B. Mar. 29, 1894, Eagleville, Ohio D. Feb. 6, 1991, Kingsville, Ohio.

Year	Team	Lg	W	L	PCT	ERA	G	GS	CG	IP	H	BB	SO	ShO	Relief Pitching W	Relief Pitching L	Relief Pitching SV	Batting AB	Batting H	Batting HR	BA	PO	A	E	DP	TC/G	FA
1933	WAS	A	1	0	1.000	2.65	4	1	1	17	13	7	5	0	0	0	0	6	2	0	.333	0	4	1	0	1.3	.800
1934			3	4	.429	3.86	42	2	1	112	129	36	29	0	2	3	1	31	3	0	.097	6	32	2	3	1.0	.950
2 yrs.			4	4	.500	3.70	46	3	2	129	142	43	34	0	2	3	1	37	5	0	.135	6	36	3	3	1.0	.933
WORLD SERIES																											
1933	WAS	A	0	0	—	0.00	1	0	0	2	0	0	0	0	0	0	0	0	0	0	—	0	1	0	0	1.0	1.000

Ralph McConnaughey

McCONNAUGHEY, RALPH JAMES BR TR 5′ 8½″ 166 lbs.
B. Aug. 5, 1889, Vandergrift, Pa. D. June 4, 1966, Detroit, Mich.

Year	Team	Lg	W	L	PCT	ERA	G	GS	CG	IP	H	BB	SO	ShO	Relief Pitching W	Relief Pitching L	Relief Pitching SV	Batting AB	Batting H	Batting HR	BA	PO	A	E	DP	TC/G	FA
1914	IND	F	0	2	.000	4.85	7	2	1	26	23	16	7	0	0	0	0	8	1	0	.125	0	7	0	1	1.0	1.000

George McConnell

McCONNELL, GEORGE NEELY BR TR 6′ 3″ 190 lbs.
B. Sept. 16, 1877, Shelbyville, Tenn. D. May 10, 1964, Chattanooga, Tenn.

Year	Team	Lg	W	L	PCT	ERA	G	GS	CG	IP	H	BB	SO	ShO	Relief Pitching W	Relief Pitching L	Relief Pitching SV	Batting AB	Batting H	Batting HR	BA	PO	A	E	DP	TC/G	FA
1909	NY	A	0	1	.000	2.25	2	1	0	4	3	3	4	0	0	1	0	43	9	0	.209	124	14	5	7	11.0	.965
1912			8	12	.400	2.75	23	20	19	176.2	172	52	91	0	0	1	0	91	27	0	.297	24	75	8	3	4.3	.925
1913			4	15	.211	3.20	35	20	8	180	162	60	72	0	0	1	3	67	12	0	.179	11	74	3	2	2.4	.966
1914	CHI	N	0	1	.000	1.29	1	1	0	7	3	3	3	0	0	0	0	2	0	0	.000	0	3	0	0	3.0	1.000
1915	CHI	F	**25**	10	**.714**	2.20	44	35	23	303	262	89	151	4	3	1	1	125	31	1	.248	8	105	3	4	2.6	.974
1916	CHI	N	4	12	.250	2.57	28	21	8	171.1	137	35	82	1	0	2	0	57	9	0	.158	9	50	3	3	2.2	.952
6 yrs.			41	51	.446	2.60	133	98	58	842	739	242	403	5	3	5	4	*				176	321	22	19	3.5	.958

Billy McCool

McCOOL, WILLIAM JOHN
B. July 14, 1944, Batesville, Ind.
BR TL 6′ 2″ 195 lbs.

Year	Team	Lg	W	L	PCT	ERA	G	GS	CG	IP	H	BB	SO	ShO	Relief W	Relief L	Relief SV	AB	H	HR	BA	PO	A	E	DP	TC/G	FA
1964	CIN	N	6	5	.545	2.42	40	3	0	89.1	66	29	87	0	5	3	7	17	0	0	.000	1	8	0	0	0.2	1.000
1965			9	10	.474	4.27	62	2	0	105.1	93	47	120	0	9	**8**	21	27	1	0	.037	2	15	0	0	0.3	1.000
1966			8	8	.500	2.48	57	0	0	105.1	76	41	104	0	8	8	18	18	3	0	.167	3	25	0	3	0.5	1.000
1967			3	7	.300	3.42	31	11	0	97.1	92	56	83	0	0	3	2	26	2	0	.077	1	14	2	0	0.5	.882
1968			3	4	.429	4.97	30	4	0	50.2	59	41	30	0	2	3	2	8	1	0	.125	3	6	2	0	0.4	.818
1969	SD	N	3	5	.375	4.27	54	0	0	59	59	42	35	0	3	5	7	1	0	0	.000	0	10	1	0	0.2	.909
1970	STL	N	0	3	.000	6.14	18	0	0	22	20	16	12	0	0	3	1	4	0	0	.000	0	5	0	0	0.3	1.000
7 yrs.			32	42	.432	3.59	292	20	0	529	465	272	471	0	27	33	58	101	7	0	.069	10	83	5	3	0.3	.949

Harry McCormick

McCORMICK, PATRICK HENRY
B. Oct. 25, 1855, Syracuse, N. Y. D. Aug. 8, 1889, Syracuse, N. Y.
BR TR 5′ 9″ 155 lbs.

Year	Team	Lg	W	L	PCT	ERA	G	GS	CG	IP	H	BB	SO	ShO	Relief W	Relief L	Relief SV	AB	H	HR	BA	PO	A	E	DP	TC/G	FA
1879	SYR	N	18	33	.353	2.99	54	54	49	457.1	517	31	96	5	0	0	0	230	51	1	.222	19	68	14	0	1.7	.861
1881	WOR	N	1	8	.111	3.56	9	9	9	78.1	89	15	7	1	0	0	0	45	6	0	.133	8	10	2	0	1.7	.900
1882	CIN	AA	14	11	.560	*1.52*	25	25	24	219.2	177	42	33	3	0	0	0	93	12	0	.129	13	76	5	0	3.5	.947
1883			8	6	.571	*2.87*	15	15	14	128.2	139	27	21	1	0	0	0	55	17	0	.309	6	32	4	0	2.8	.905
4 yrs.			41	58	.414	2.66	103	103	96	884	922	115	157	10	0	0	0	423	86	1	.203	46	186	25	0	2.2	.903

Jerry McCormick

McCORMICK, JOHN
B. Philadelphia, Pa. D. Sept. 19, 1905, Philadelphia, Pa.

Year	Team	Lg	W	L	PCT	ERA	G	GS	CG	IP	H	BB	SO	ShO	Relief W	Relief L	Relief SV	AB	H	HR	BA	PO	A	E	DP	TC/G	FA
1884	PHI	U	0	0	—	*9.00*	1	0	0	2	5	0	3	0	0	0	0	*				138	196	84	10	4.5	.799

Jim McCormick

McCORMICK, JAMES
B. Nov. 3, 1856, Glasgow, Scotland D. Mar. 10, 1918, Paterson, N. J.
Manager 1879–80, 1882.
BR TR 5′10½″ 215 lbs.

Year	Team	Lg	W	L	PCT	ERA	G	GS	CG	IP	H	BB	SO	ShO	Relief W	Relief L	Relief SV	AB	H	HR	BA	PO	A	E	DP	TC/G	FA
1878	IND	N	5	8	.385	1.69	14	14	12	117	128	15	36	1	0	0	0	56	8	0	.143	9	33	3	3	2.6	.933
1879	CLE	N	20	**40**	.333	2.42	62	60	59	546.1	582	**74**	197	3	1	0	0	282	62	0	.220	97	120	15	4	2.9	.935
1880			**45**	28	.616	1.85	**74**	**74**	**72**	**657.2**	**585**	75	260	7	0	0	0	289	71	0	.246	38	135	26	4	2.5	.869
1881			26	30	.464	2.45	59	58	**57**	526	484	84	178	2	0	0	0	309	79	0	.256	55	92	18	4	2.3	.891
1882			**36**	29	.554	*2.37*	**68**	**67**	**65**	**595.2**	**550**	**103**	200	4	**1**	0	0	262	57	2	.218	45	100	15	1	2.2	.906
1883			28	12	**.700**	***1.84***	43	41	36	342	316	65	145	1	1	0	1	157	37	0	.236	28	101	17	4	3.3	.884
1884	2 teams CLE N (42G 19–22) CIN U (24G 21–3)																										
"	total		40	25	.615	**2.37**	66	66	63	569	508	89	343	10	0	0	0	300	77	0	.257	54	119	9	6	2.3	.951
1885	2 teams PRO N (4G 1–3) CHI N (24G 20–4)																										
"	total		21	7	.750	2.43	28	28	28	252	221	60	96	3	0	0	0	117	26	0	.222	23	75	5	3	3.6	.951
1886	CHI	N	31	11	.738	*2.82*	42	42	38	347.2	341	100	172	2	0	0	0	174	41	2	.236	22	75	6	3	2.2	.942
1887	PIT	N	13	23	.361	4.30	36	36	36	322.1	377	84	77	0	0	0	0	136	33	0	.243	13	88	8	1	3.0	.927
10 yrs.			265	213	.554	2.43	492	486	466 **10th**	4275.2	4092	749	1704	33	3	0	1	*				384	938	122	33	2.6	.916

Mike McCormick

McCORMICK, MICHAEL FRANCIS
B. Sept. 29, 1938, Pasadena, Calif.
BL TL 6′ 2″ 195 lbs.

Year	Team	Lg	W	L	PCT	ERA	G	GS	CG	IP	H	BB	SO	ShO	Relief W	Relief L	Relief SV	AB	H	HR	BA	PO	A	E	DP	TC/G	FA
1956	NY	N	0	1	.000	9.45	3	2	0	6.2	7	10	4	0	0	0	0	1	0	0	.000	0	1	0	0	0.3	1.000
1957			3	1	.750	4.10	24	5	1	74.2	79	32	50	0	2	0	0	22	6	0	.273	3	9	1	2	0.5	.923
1958	SF	N	11	8	.579	4.59	42	28	8	178.1	192	60	82	2	2	0	1	54	12	0	.222	11	37	2	5	1.2	.960
1959			12	16	.429	3.99	47	31	7	225.2	213	86	151	3	2	2	4	66	7	0	.106	12	42	3	1	1.2	.947
1960			15	12	.556	**2.70**	40	34	15	253	228	65	154	4	0	2	3	88	16	0	.182	12	55	2	7	1.7	.971
1961			13	16	.448	3.20	40	35	13	250	235	75	163	3	0	2	0	80	15	0	.188	12	37	0	1	1.2	1.000
1962			5	5	.500	5.38	28	15	1	98.2	112	45	42	0	0	0	0	28	3	1	.107	1	18	1	1	0.7	.950
1963	BAL	A	6	8	.429	4.30	25	21	2	136	132	66	75	0	0	0	0	46	8	1	.174	9	21	2	0	1.3	.938
1964			0	2	.000	5.19	4	2	0	17.1	21	8	13	0	0	0	0	6	1	0	.167	1	2	0	0	0.8	1.000
1965	WAS	A	8	8	.500	3.36	44	21	3	158	158	36	88	1	1	2	1	41	3	0	.073	8	22	0	1	0.7	1.000
1966			11	14	.440	3.46	41	32	8	216	193	51	101	3	1	0	0	66	14	2	.212	5	34	0	1	1.0	1.000
1967	SF	N	**22**	10	.688	2.85	40	35	14	262.1	220	81	150	5	2	1	0	84	10	1	.119	10	36	0	0	1.1	1.000
1968			12	14	.462	3.58	38	28	9	198.1	196	49	121	2	3	1	1	58	6	1	.103	9	23	1	0	0.9	.970
1969			11	9	.550	3.34	32	28	9	197	175	77	76	0	0	0	0	66	9	1	.136	3	33	0	3	1.1	1.000
1970	2 teams SF N (23G 3–4) NY A (9G 2–0)																										
"	total		5	4	.556	6.18	32	15	1	99	106	49	49	0	1	0	2	30	5	0	.167	5	16	0	2	0.7	1.000
1971	KC	A	0	0	—	9.00	4	1	0	10	14	5	2	0	0	0	0	2	0	0	.000	1	8	0	0	2.3	1.000
16 yrs.			134	128	.511	3.73	484	333	91	2381	2281	795	1321	23	14	10	12	738	115	7	.156	102	394	12	24	1.0	.976

Bill McCorry

McCORRY, WILLIAM CHARLES
B. July 9, 1887, Saranac Lake, N. Y. D. Mar. 22, 1973, Augusta, Ga.
BL TR 5′ 9″ 157 lbs.

Year	Team	Lg	W	L	PCT	ERA	G	GS	CG	IP	H	BB	SO	ShO	Relief W	Relief L	Relief SV	AB	H	HR	BA	PO	A	E	DP	TC/G	FA
1909	STL	A	0	2	.000	9.00	2	2	2	15	29	6	10	0	0	0	0	5	0	0	.000	0	1	0	0	0.5	1.000

Les McCrabb

McCRABB, LESTER WILLIAM (Buster)
B. Nov. 4, 1914, Wakefield, Pa.
BR TR 5′11″ 175 lbs.

Year	Team	Lg	W	L	PCT	ERA	G	GS	CG	IP	H	BB	SO	ShO	Relief W	Relief L	Relief SV	AB	H	HR	BA	PO	A	E	DP	TC/G	FA
1939	PHI	A	1	2	.333	4.04	5	4	2	35.2	42	10	11	0	0	0	0	13	0	0	.000	1	6	0	0	1.4	1.000
1940			0	0	—	6.94	4	0	0	11.2	19	2	4	0	0	0	0	4	1	0	.250	0	4	0	0	1.0	1.000
1941			9	13	.409	5.49	26	23	11	157.1	188	49	40	1	1	0	2	56	8	0	.143	9	24	4	1	1.4	.892
1942			0	0	—	31.50	1	0	0	4	14	2	0	0	0	0	0	1	0	0	.000	0	2	0	0	2.0	1.000
1950			0	0	—	27.00	2	0	0	1.1	7	0	2	0	0	0	0	0	0	0	—	0	0	0	0	0.0	.000
5 yrs.			10	15	.400	5.96	38	27	13	210	270	63	57	1	1	0	2	74	9	0	.122	10	36	4	1	1.3	.920

Ed McCreery

McCREERY, ESLEY PORTERFIELD
B. Dec. 24, 1889, Cripple Creek, Colo. D. Oct. 19, 1960, Sacramento, Calif.
BR TR 6′ 1″ 195 lbs.

Year	Team	Lg	W	L	PCT	ERA	G	GS	CG	IP	H	BB	SO	ShO	Relief W	Relief L	Relief SV	AB	H	HR	BA	PO	A	E	DP	TC/G	FA
1914	DET	A	1	0	1.000	11.25	3	1	0	4	6	3	4	0	0	0	0	1	0	0	.000	0	1	0	0	0.3	1.000

Tom McCreery

McCREERY, THOMAS LIVINGSTON BB TR 5′11″ 180 lbs.
B. Oct. 19, 1874, Beaver, Pa. D. July 3, 1941, Beaver, Pa.

Year	Team	W	L	PCT	ERA	G	GS	CG	IP	H	BB	SO	ShO	Relief W	Relief L	Relief SV	Batting AB	Batting H	Batting HR	BA	PO	A	E	DP	TC/G	FA
1895	LOU N	3	1	.750	5.36	8	4	3	48.2	51	38	14	1	0	0	1	108	35	0	.324	31	23	10	4	2.0	.844
1896		0	1	.000	36.00	1	1	0	1	4	5	0	0	0	0	0	441	155	7	.351	180	22	18	5	1.9	.918
1900	PIT N	0	0	—	12.00	1	0	0	3	3	1	0	0	0	0	0	132	29	1	.220	186	32	33	4	1.8	.869
3 yrs.		3	2	.600	6.32	10	5	3	52.2	58	44	14	1	0	0	1	*				2196	233	171	84	3.3	.934

Lance McCullers

McCULLERS, LANCE GRAYE BB TR 6′1″ 185 lbs.
B. Mar. 8, 1964, Tampa, Fla.

Year	Team	W	L	PCT	ERA	G	GS	CG	IP	H	BB	SO	ShO	Relief W	Relief L	Relief SV	Batting AB	Batting H	Batting HR	BA	PO	A	E	DP	TC/G	FA
1985	SD N	0	2	.000	2.31	21	0	0	35	23	16	27	0	0	2	5	4	0	0	.000	2	6	2	0	0.5	.800
1986		10	10	.500	2.78	70	7	0	136	103	58	92	0	9	6	5	22	2	0	.091	6	16	2	1	0.3	.917
1987		8	10	.444	3.72	78	0	0	123.1	115	59	126	0	8	**10**	16	14	1	0	.071	9	17	2	1	0.4	.929
1988		3	6	.333	2.49	60	0	0	97.2	70	55	81	0	3	6	10	8	2	0	.250	6	14	2	1	0.4	.909
1989	NY A	4	3	.571	4.57	52	1	0	84.2	83	37	82	0	4	2	3	0	0	0	—	5	10	2	0	0.3	.882
1990	2 teams NY A (11G 1–0) DET A (9G 1–0)																									
″	total	2	0	1.000	3.02	20	1	0	44.2	32	19	31	0	2	0	0	0	0	0		4	2	0	0	0.3	1.000
1992	TEX A	1	0	1.000	5.40	5	0	0	5	1	8	3	0	1	0	0	0	0	0	—	1	2	0	1	0.6	1.000
7 yrs.		28	31	.475	3.25	306	9	0	526.1	427	252	442	0	27	26	39	48	5	0	.104	33	67	10	4	0.4	.909

Charlie McCullough

McCULLOUGH, CHARLES F.
B. 1867, Dublin, Ireland Deceased.

Year	Team	W	L	PCT	ERA	G	GS	CG	IP	H	BB	SO	ShO	Relief W	Relief L	Relief SV	Batting AB	Batting H	Batting HR	BA	PO	A	E	DP	TC/G	FA
1890	2 teams BKN AA (26G 4–21) SYR AA (3G 1–2)																									
″	total	5	23	.179	4.88	29	28	27	241.2	276	116	69	0	0	0	0	95	3	0	.032	4	42	6	0	1.8	.885

Paul McCullough

McCULLOUGH, PAUL WILLARD BR TR 5′9½″ 190 lbs.
B. July 28, 1898, New Castle, Pa. D. Nov. 7, 1970, New Castle, Pa.

Year	Team	W	L	PCT	ERA	G	GS	CG	IP	H	BB	SO	ShO	Relief W	Relief L	Relief SV	Batting AB	Batting H	Batting HR	BA	PO	A	E	DP	TC/G	FA
1929	WAS A	0	0	—	8.59	3	0	0	7.1	7	2	3	0	0	0	0	1	0	0	.000	0	0	0	0	0.0	.000

Phil McCullough

McCULLOUGH, PINSON LAMAR BR TR 6′4″ 204 lbs.
B. July 22, 1917, Stockbridge, Ga.

Year	Team	W	L	PCT	ERA	G	GS	CG	IP	H	BB	SO	ShO	Relief W	Relief L	Relief SV	Batting AB	Batting H	Batting HR	BA	PO	A	E	DP	TC/G	FA
1942	WAS A	0	0	—	6.00	1	0	0	3	5	2	2	0	0	0	0	1	0	0	.000	0	1	0	0	1.0	1.000

Jeff McCurry

McCURRY, JEFFREY DEE BR TR 6′7″ 210 lbs.
B. Jan. 21, 1970, Tokyo, Japan.

Year	Team	W	L	PCT	ERA	G	GS	CG	IP	H	BB	SO	ShO	Relief W	Relief L	Relief SV	Batting AB	Batting H	Batting HR	BA	PO	A	E	DP	TC/G	FA
1995	PIT N	1	4	.200	5.02	55	0	0	61	82	30	27	0	1	4	1	3	0	0	.000	1	12	0	0	0.2	1.000

Lindy McDaniel

McDANIEL, LYNDALL DALE BR TR 6′3″ 195 lbs.
Brother of Von McDaniel.
B. Dec. 13, 1935, Hollis, Okla.

Year	Team	W	L	PCT	ERA	G	GS	CG	IP	H	BB	SO	ShO	Relief W	Relief L	Relief SV	Batting AB	Batting H	Batting HR	BA	PO	A	E	DP	TC/G	FA
1955	STL N	0	0	—	4.74	4	2	0	19	22	7	7	0	0	0	0	5	1	0	.200	3	3	0	0	1.5	1.000
1956		7	6	.538	3.40	39	7	1	116.1	121	42	59	0	5	2	0	32	7	0	.219	9	24	3	0	0.9	.917
1957		15	9	.625	3.49	30	26	10	191	196	53	75	1	3	0	0	74	19	1	.257	12	33	1	3	1.5	.978
1958		5	7	.417	5.80	26	17	2	108.2	139	31	47	1	0	2	0	30	2	0	.067	4	26	1	3	1.2	.968
1959		14	12	.538	3.82	62	7	1	132	144	41	86	0	13	8	**15**	29	1	0	.034	7	31	3	3	0.7	.927
1960		12	4	.750	2.09	65	2	1	116.1	85	24	105	0	12	2	**26**	26	6	0	.231	5	21	0	2	0.4	1.000
1961		10	6	.625	4.87	55	0	0	94.1	117	31	65	0	10	6	9	17	4	0	.235	5	22	0	1	0.5	1.000
1962		3	10	.231	4.12	55	2	0	107	96	29	79	0	2	**9**	14	21	2	0	.095	10	25	1	2	0.7	.972
1963	CHI N	13	7	.650	2.86	57	0	0	88	82	27	75	0	13	7	**22**	22	2	1	.091	3	16	1	0	0.4	.950
1964		1	7	.125	3.88	63	0	0	95	104	23	71	0	1	7	15	16	2	0	.125	3	18	1	1	0.3	.955
1965		5	6	.455	2.59	71	0	0	128.2	115	47	92	0	5	6	2	8	0	0	.000	5	30	0	1	0.5	1.000
1966	SF N	10	5	.667	2.66	64	0	0	121.2	103	35	93	0	10	5	6	22	2	0	.091	8	24	0	0	0.5	1.000
1967		2	6	.250	3.72	41	3	0	72.2	69	24	48	0	2	4	3	11	1	0	.091	5	19	0	1	0.6	1.000
1968	2 teams SF N (12G 0–0) NY A (24G 4–1)																									
″	total	4	1	.800	3.31	36	0	0	70.2	60	17	52	0	4	1	10	15	0	0	.000	10	20	1	0	0.9	.968
1969	NY A	5	6	.455	3.55	51	0	0	83.2	84	23	60	0	5	6	5	8	0	0	.000	3	21	2	0	0.5	.923
1970		9	5	.643	2.01	62	0	0	112	88	23	81	0	9	5	29	24	4	0	.167	7	19	3	2	0.5	.897
1971		5	10	.333	5.01	44	0	0	70	82	24	39	0	5	10	4	9	1	0	.111	2	14	0	0	0.4	1.000
1972		3	1	.750	2.25	37	0	0	68	54	25	47	0	3	1	0	7	2	1	.286	5	14	1	2	0.5	.950
1973		12	6	.667	2.86	47	3	1	160.1	148	49	93	0	**12**	4	10	2	0	0	.000	9	35	1	7	1.0	.978
1974	KC A	1	4	.200	3.45	38	5	2	107	109	24	47	0	0	2	1	0	0	0	—	8	21	1	0	0.8	.967
1975		5	1	.833	4.15	40	0	0	78	81	24	40	0	5	1	1	0	0	0	—	4	11	2	0	0.4	.882
21 yrs.		141	119	.542	3.45	987 **4th**	74	18	2140.1	2099	623	1361	2	119 **2nd**	88	172	378	56	3	.148	127	447	22	28	0.6	.963

Von McDaniel

McDANIEL, MAX VON BR TR 6′2½″ 180 lbs.
Brother of Lindy McDaniel.
B. Apr. 18, 1939, Hollis, Okla. D. Aug. 20, 1995, Lawton, Okla.

Year	Team	W	L	PCT	ERA	G	GS	CG	IP	H	BB	SO	ShO	Relief W	Relief L	Relief SV	Batting AB	Batting H	Batting HR	BA	PO	A	E	DP	TC/G	FA
1957	STL N	7	5	.583	3.22	17	13	4	86.2	71	31	45	2	1	0	0	26	0	0	.000	3	9	0	3	0.7	1.000
1958		0	0	—	13.50	2	1	0	2	5	5	0	0	0	0	0	0	0	0	—	0	0	0	0	0.0	.000
2 yrs.		7	5	.583	3.45	19	14	4	88.2	76	36	45	2	1	0	0	26	0	0	.000	3	9	0	3	0.6	1.000

Mickey McDermott

McDERMOTT, MAURICE JOSEPH BL TL 6′2″ 170 lbs.
B. Aug. 29, 1928, Poughkeepsie, N. Y.

Year	Team	W	L	PCT	ERA	G	GS	CG	IP	H	BB	SO	ShO	Relief W	Relief L	Relief SV	Batting AB	Batting H	Batting HR	BA	PO	A	E	DP	TC/G	FA
1948	BOS A	0	0	—	6.17	7	0	0	23.1	16	35	17	0	0	0	0	8	3	0	.375	1	8	0	0	1.3	1.000
1949		5	4	.556	4.05	12	12	6	80	63	52	50	2	0	0	0	33	7	0	.212	2	14	1	0	1.4	.941
1950		7	3	.700	5.19	38	15	4	130	119	124	96	0	3	0	5	44	16	0	.364	5	25	2	1	0.8	.938
1951		8	8	.500	3.35	34	19	9	172	141	92	127	1	0	1	3	66	18	1	.273	4	34	2	5	1.2	.950
1952		10	9	.526	3.72	30	21	7	162	139	92	117	2	2	3	0	62	14	1	.226	10	24	2	1	1.2	.944
1953		18	10	.643	3.01	32	30	8	206.1	169	109	92	4	0	0	0	93	28	1	.301	5	40	2	3	1.5	.957
1954	WAS A	7	15	.318	3.44	30	26	11	196.1	172	110	95	1	0	0	1	95	19	0	.200	3	39	2	2	1.5	.955
1955		10	10	.500	3.75	31	20	8	156	140	102	78	1	2	1	1	95	25	1	.263	3	30	2	1	1.1	.943
1956	NY A	2	6	.250	4.24	23	9	1	87	85	47	38	0	0	0	0	52	11	1	.212	2	13	0	2	0.7	1.000
1957	KC A	1	4	.200	5.48	29	4	0	69	68	50	29	0	1	2	0	49	12	4	.245	12	17	2	0	1.0	.935

Mickey McDermott *continued*

Year	Team	W	L	PCT	ERA	G	GS	CG	IP	H	BB	SO	ShO	Relief Pitching W	Relief Pitching L	Relief Pitching SV	Batting AB	Batting H	Batting HR	BA	PO	A	E	DP	TC/G	FA
1958	DET A	0	0	—	9.00	2	0	0	2	6	2	0	0	0	0	0	3	1	0	.333	0	0	0	0	0.0	.000
1961	2 teams STL N (19G 1–0) KC A (4G 0–0)																									
"	total	1	0	1.000	5.51	23	0	0	32.2	43	25	18	0	1	0	4	19	2	0	.105	2	3	1	0	0.3	.833
12 yrs.		69	69	.500	3.91	291	156	54	1316.2	1161	840	757	11	9	7	14	*				49	247	16	15	1.1	.949
WORLD SERIES																										
1956	NY A	0	0	—	3.00	1	0	0	3	2	3	3	0	0	0	0	*				0	0	0	0	0.0	.000

Mike McDermott

McDERMOTT, MICHAEL H.
B. May 6, 1864, Fall River, Mass. D. May 7, 1947, Fall River, Mass.
TR 5′10″ 152 lbs.

Year	Team	W	L	PCT	ERA	G	GS	CG	IP	H	BB	SO	ShO	Relief Pitching W	Relief Pitching L	Relief Pitching SV	Batting AB	Batting H	Batting HR	BA	PO	A	E	DP	TC/G	FA
1889	LOU AA	1	8	.111	4.16	9	9	9	84.1	108	34	22	0	0	0	0	33	6	0	.182	1	17	1	1	2.1	.947

Mike McDermott

McDERMOTT, MICHAEL JOSEPH
B. Sept. 7, 1862, St. Louis, Mo. D. June 30, 1943, St. Louis, Mo.
TR 5′ 8″ 145 lbs.

Year	Team	W	L	PCT	ERA	G	GS	CG	IP	H	BB	SO	ShO	Relief Pitching W	Relief Pitching L	Relief Pitching SV	Batting AB	Batting H	Batting HR	BA	PO	A	E	DP	TC/G	FA
1895	LOU N	4	19	.174	5.99	33	26	18	207.1	258	103	42	0	0	0	0	82	13	0	.159	6	57	14	2	2.3	.818
1896		2	7	.222	7.34	12	10	4	65	87	44	12	1	0	0	0	27	8	0	.296	5	20	4	0	2.4	.862
1897	2 teams CLE N (9G 4–5) STL N (4G 1–2)																									
"	total	5	7	.417	5.72	13	11	5	83.1	98	44	15	0	2	0	0	34	10	0	.294	4	28	1	1	2.5	.970
3 yrs.		11	33	.250	6.17	58	47	27	355.2	443	191	69	1	2	0	0	143	31	0	.217	15	105	19	3	2.4	.863

Danny McDevitt

McDEVITT, DANIEL EUGENE
B. Nov. 18, 1932, New York, N. Y.
BL TL 5′10″ 175 lbs.

Year	Team	W	L	PCT	ERA	G	GS	CG	IP	H	BB	SO	ShO	Relief Pitching W	Relief Pitching L	Relief Pitching SV	Batting AB	Batting H	Batting HR	BA	PO	A	E	DP	TC/G	FA
1957	BKN N	7	4	.636	3.25	22	17	5	119	105	72	90	2	0	0	0	39	6	0	.154	11	26	4	1	1.9	.902
1958	LA N	2	6	.250	7.45	13	10	2	48.1	71	31	26	0	0	0	0	15	2	0	.133	0	8	3	0	0.8	.727
1959		10	8	.556	3.97	39	22	6	145	149	51	106	2	1	0	4	46	5	0	.109	11	22	4	2	0.9	.892
1960		0	4	.000	4.25	24	7	0	53	51	42	30	0	0	2	0	10	2	0	.200	2	9	0	0	0.5	1.000
1961	2 teams NY A (8G 1–2) MIN A (16G 1–0)																									
"	total	2	2	.500	4.08	24	3	0	39.2	38	27	23	0	2	0	1	4	0	0	.000	1	10	1	0	0.5	.917
1962	KC A	0	3	.000	5.82	33	1	0	51	47	41	28	0	0	2	2	9	2	0	.222	4	12	1	1	0.5	.941
6 yrs.		21	27	.438	4.40	155	60	13	456	461	264	303	4	3	4	7	123	17	0	.138	29	87	13	4	0.8	.899

Ben McDonald

McDONALD, LARRY BENARD
B. Nov. 24, 1967, Baton Rouge, La.
BR TR 6′ 7″ 212 lbs.

Year	Team	W	L	PCT	ERA	G	GS	CG	IP	H	BB	SO	ShO	Relief Pitching W	Relief Pitching L	Relief Pitching SV	Batting AB	Batting H	Batting HR	BA	PO	A	E	DP	TC/G	FA
1989	BAL A	1	0	1.000	8.59	6	0	0	7.1	8	4	3	0	1	0	0	0	0	0	—	0	2	0	0	0.3	1.000
1990		8	5	.615	2.43	21	15	3	118.2	88	35	65	2	0	0	0	0	0	0	—	15	14	1	1	1.4	.967
1991		6	8	.429	4.84	21	21	1	126.1	126	43	85	0	0	0	0	0	0	0	—	12	8	0	1	1.0	1.000
1992		13	13	.500	4.24	35	35	4	227	213	74	158	2	0	0	0	0	0	0	—	22	29	0	2	1.5	1.000
1993		13	14	.481	3.39	34	34	7	220.1	185	86	171	1	0	0	0	0	0	0	—	15	42	2	2	1.7	.966
1994		14	7	.667	4.06	24	24	5	157.1	151	54	94	1	0	0	0	0	0	0	—	7	25	0	1	1.3	1.000
1995		3	6	.333	4.16	14	13	1	80	67	38	62	0	0	0	0	0	0	0	—	5	13	1	0	1.4	.947
7 yrs.		58	53	.523	3.89	155	142	21	937	838	334	638	6	1	0	0	0	0	0		76	133	4	7	1.4	.981

Hank McDonald

McDONALD, HENRY MONROE
B. Jan. 16, 1911, Santa Monica, Calif. D. Oct. 17, 1982, Hemet, Calif.
BR TR 6′ 3½″ 200 lbs.

Year	Team	W	L	PCT	ERA	G	GS	CG	IP	H	BB	SO	ShO	Relief Pitching W	Relief Pitching L	Relief Pitching SV	Batting AB	Batting H	Batting HR	BA	PO	A	E	DP	TC/G	FA
1931	PHI A	2	4	.333	3.71	19	10	1	70.1	62	41	23	1	1	1	0	21	2	0	.095	5	9	1	0	0.8	.933
1933	2 teams PHI A (4G 1–1) STL A (25G 0–4)																									
"	total	1	5	.167	8.02	29	6	0	70.2	97	38	23	0	1	1	0	18	2	0	.111	6	14	1	1	0.7	.952
2 yrs.		3	9	.250	5.87	48	16	1	141	159	79	46	1	2	2	0	39	4	0	.103	11	23	2	1	0.8	.944

Jim McDonald

McDONALD, JIMMIE LeROY (Hot Rod)
B. May 17, 1927, Grant's Pass, Ore.
BR TR 5′10½″ 185 lbs.
BB 1950–1951

Year	Team	W	L	PCT	ERA	G	GS	CG	IP	H	BB	SO	ShO	Relief Pitching W	Relief Pitching L	Relief Pitching SV	Batting AB	Batting H	Batting HR	BA	PO	A	E	DP	TC/G	FA
1950	BOS A	1	0	1.000	3.79	9	0	0	19	23	10	5	0	1	0	0	3	1	0	.333	3	7	0	0	1.1	1.000
1951	STL A	4	7	.364	4.07	16	11	5	84	84	46	28	0	0	0	1	29	6	0	.207	9	16	2	1	1.7	.926
1952	NY A	3	4	.429	3.50	26	5	1	69.1	71	40	20	0	2	3	0	19	6	0	.316	7	24	0	1	1.2	1.000
1953		9	7	.563	3.82	27	18	6	129.2	128	39	43	2	1	1	0	41	4	0	.098	7	30	1	6	1.4	.974
1954		4	1	.800	3.17	16	10	3	71	54	45	20	1	0	0	0	19	4	0	.211	7	14	0	2	1.3	1.000
1955	BAL A	3	5	.375	7.14	21	8	0	51.2	76	30	20	0	1	0	0	11	2	0	.182	2	15	1	2	0.9	.944
1956	CHI A	0	2	.000	8.68	8	3	0	18.2	29	7	10	0	0	0	0	5	0	0	.000	1	3	1	0	0.6	.800
1957		0	1	.000	2.01	10	0	0	22.1	18	10	12	0	0	1	0	1	0	0	.000	3	3	1	0	0.7	.857
1958		0	0	—	19.29	3	0	0	2.1	6	4	0	0	0	0	0	0	0	0	—	0	1	0	1	0.3	1.000
9 yrs.		24	27	.471	4.27	136	55	15	468	489	231	158	3	5	5	1	128	23	0	.180	39	113	6	13	1.2	.962
WORLD SERIES																										
1953	NY A	1	0	1.000	5.87	1	1	0	7.2	12	0	3	0	0	0	0	2	1	0	.500	3	0	0	0	3.0	1.000

John McDonald

McDONALD, JOHN JOSEPH
Born John Joseph McDonnell.
B. Jan. 27, 1883, Throop, Pa. D. Apr. 9, 1950, Roselle, N. J.
TR 6′ 1″ 170 lbs.

Year	Team	W	L	PCT	ERA	G	GS	CG	IP	H	BB	SO	ShO	Relief Pitching W	Relief Pitching L	Relief Pitching SV	Batting AB	Batting H	Batting HR	BA	PO	A	E	DP	TC/G	FA
1907	WAS A	0	0	—	9.00	1	0	0	6	12	2	3	0	0	0	0	3	1	0	.333	0	2	1	0	3.0	.667

John McDougal

McDOUGAL, JOHN H.
B. Sept. 19, 1871, Aledo, Ill. D. Apr. 28, 1936, Galesburg, Ill.
TR 170 lbs.

Year	Team	W	L	PCT	ERA	G	GS	CG	IP	H	BB	SO	ShO	Relief Pitching W	Relief Pitching L	Relief Pitching SV	Batting AB	Batting H	Batting HR	BA	PO	A	E	DP	TC/G	FA
1895	STL N	4	10	.286	8.32	18	14	10	114.2	187	46	23	0	0	1	0	41	6	0	.146	6	21	4	0	1.7	.871
1896		0	1	.000	8.10	3	1	0	10	13	4	0	0	0	0	0	3	0	0	.000	1	6	1	0	2.7	.875
2 yrs.		4	11	.267	8.30	21	15	10	124.2	200	50	23	0	0	1	0	44	6	0	.136	7	27	5	0	1.9	.872

Sandy McDougal

McDOUGAL, JOHN AUCHANBOLT
B. May 21, 1874, Buffalo, N. Y. D. Oct. 2, 1910, Buffalo, N. Y.
BR TR 5′10″ 155 lbs.

Year	Team	W	L	PCT	ERA	G	GS	CG	IP	H	BB	SO	ShO	Relief Pitching W	Relief Pitching L	Relief Pitching SV	Batting AB	Batting H	Batting HR	BA	PO	A	E	DP	TC/G	FA
1895	BKN N	0	0	—	12.00	1	0	0	3	3	5	2	0	0	0	1	1	0	0	.000	0	0	0	0	0.0	.000
1905	STL N	1	4	.200	3.43	5	5	5	44.2	50	12	10	0	0	0	0	15	2	0	.133	0	27	0	0	5.4	1.000
2 yrs.		1	4	.200	3.97	6	5	5	47.2	53	17	12	0	0	0	1	16	2	0	.125	0	27	0	0	4.5	1.000

Jack McDowell

McDOWELL, JACK BURNS (Black Jack) BR TR 6′ 5″ 180 lbs.
B. Jan. 16, 1966, Van Nuys, Calif.

Year	Team	W	L	PCT	ERA	G	GS	CG	IP	H	BB	SO	ShO	Relief W	Relief L	SV	AB	H	HR	BA	PO	A	E	DP	TC/G	FA
1987	CHI A	3	0	1.000	1.93	4	4	0	28	16	6	15	0	0	0	0	0	0	0	—	1	6	0	0	1.8	1.000
1988		5	10	.333	3.97	26	26	1	158.2	147	68	84	0	0	0	0	0	0	0	—	12	16	5	1	1.3	.848
1990		14	9	.609	3.82	33	33	4	205	189	77	165	0	0	0	0	0	0	0	—	17	20	1	3	1.2	.974
1991		17	10	.630	3.41	35	**35**	**15**	253.2	212	82	191	3	0	0	0	0	0	0	—	19	32	0	1	1.5	1.000
1992		20	10	.667	3.18	34	34	**13**	260.2	247	75	178	1	0	0	0	0	0	0	—	16	27	2	3	1.3	.956
1993		**22**	10	.688	3.37	34	34	10	256.2	261	69	158	**4**	0	0	0	0	0	0	—	23	43	3	2	2.0	.957
1994		10	9	.526	3.73	25	**25**	6	181	186	42	127	2	0	0	0	0	0	0	—	8	24	0	0	1.3	1.000
1995	NY A	15	10	.600	3.93	30	30	8	217.2	211	78	157	2	0	0	0	0	0	0	—	18	23	1	1	1.4	.976
8 yrs.		106	68	.609	3.56	221	221	57	1561.1	1469	497	1075	12	0	0	0	0	0	0		114	191	12	11	1.4	.962
DIVISIONAL PLAYOFF SERIES																										
1995	NY A	0	2	.000	9.00	2	1	0	7	8	4	6	0	0	1	0	0	0	0	—	0	0	0	0	0.0	.000
LEAGUE CHAMPIONSHIP SERIES																										
1993	CHI A	0	2	.000	10.00	2	2	0	9	18	5	5	0	0	0	0	0	0	0	—	0	1	1	0	1.0	.500

Roger McDowell

McDOWELL, ROGER ALAN BR TR 6′ 1″ 175 lbs.
B. Dec. 21, 1960, Cincinnati, Ohio

Year	Team	W	L	PCT	ERA	G	GS	CG	IP	H	BB	SO	ShO	Relief W	Relief L	SV	AB	H	HR	BA	PO	A	E	DP	TC/G	FA
1985	NY N	6	5	.545	2.83	62	2	0	127.1	108	37	70	0	6	4	17	19	3	0	.158	17	27	4	2	0.8	.917
1986		14	9	.609	3.02	75	0	0	128	107	42	65	0	**14**	9	22	18	5	0	.278	17	30	0	0	0.6	1.000
1987		7	5	.583	4.16	56	0	0	88.2	95	28	32	0	7	5	25	13	3	0	.231	10	17	0	1	0.5	1.000
1988		5	5	.500	2.63	62	0	0	89	80	31	46	0	5	5	16	9	3	0	.333	11	19	1	2	0.5	.968
1989	2 teams NY N (25G 1–5) PHI N (44G 3–3)																									
″	total	4	8	.333	1.96	69	0	0	92	79	38	47	0	4	8	23	3	1	0	.333	17	25	3	3	0.7	.933
1990	PHI N	6	8	.429	3.86	72	0	0	86.1	92	35	39	0	6	8	22	2	0	0	.000	1	23	5	2	0.4	.828
1991	2 teams PHI N (38G 3–6) LA N (33G 6–3)																									
″	total	9	9	.500	2.93	71	0	0	101.1	100	48	50	0	9	**9**	10	2	0	0	.000	8	25	3	3	0.5	.917
1992	LA N	6	10	.375	4.09	65	0	0	83.2	103	42	50	0	6	**10**	14	3	0	0	.000	8	21	3	2	0.5	.906
1993		5	3	.625	2.25	54	0	0	68	76	30	27	0	5	3	2	2	1	0	.500	11	24	3	3	0.7	.921
1994		0	3	.000	5.23	32	0	0	41.1	50	22	29	0	0	3	0	1	0	0	.000	2	7	0	0	0.3	1.000
1995	TEX A	7	4	.636	4.02	64	0	0	85	86	34	49	0	7	4	4	0	0	0	—	8	20	1	3	0.5	.966
11 yrs.		69	69	.500	3.24	682	2	0	990.2	976	387	504	0	69	68	155	72	16	0	.222	110	238	23	21	0.5	.938
LEAGUE CHAMPIONSHIP SERIES																										
1986	NY N	0	0	—	0.00	2	0	0	7	1	0	3	0	0	0	0	1	0	0	.000	3	1	0	0	2.0	1.000
1988		0	1	.000	4.50	4	0	0	6	6	2	5	0	0	1	0	0	0	0	—	0	3	1	0	1.0	.750
2 yrs.		0	1	.000	2.08	6	0	0	13	7	2	8	0	0	1	0	1	0	0	.000	3	4	1	0	1.3	.875
WORLD SERIES																										
1986	NY N	1	0	1.000	4.91	5	0	0	7.1	10	6	2	0	1	0	0	0	0	0	—	1	4	0	0	1.0	1.000

Sam McDowell

McDOWELL, SAMUEL EDWARD (Sudden Sam) BL TL 6′ 5″ 190 lbs.
B. Sept. 21, 1942, Pittsburgh, Pa.

Year	Team	W	L	PCT	ERA	G	GS	CG	IP	H	BB	SO	ShO	Relief W	Relief L	SV	AB	H	HR	BA	PO	A	E	DP	TC/G	FA
1961	CLE A	0	0	—	0.00	1	1	0	6.1	3	5	5	0	0	0	0	2	0	0	.000	0	2	0	0	2.0	1.000
1962		3	7	.300	6.06	25	13	0	87.2	81	70	70	0	2	0	1	26	4	0	.154	4	14	2	0	0.8	.900
1963		3	5	.375	4.85	14	12	3	65	63	44	63	1	0	0	0	19	4	0	.211	4	7	0	0	0.8	1.000
1964		11	6	.647	2.70	31	24	6	173.1	148	100	177	2	2	0	1	56	8	0	.143	7	20	2	1	0.9	.931
1965		17	11	.607	**2.18**	42	35	14	273	178	**132**	**325**	3	1	0	4	95	12	0	.126	6	46	4	0	1.3	.929
1966		9	8	.529	2.87	35	28	8	194.1	130	102	**225**	**5**	0	0	3	60	12	0	.200	11	30	2	2	1.2	.953
1967		13	15	.464	3.85	37	37	10	236.1	201	**123**	236	1	0	0	0	82	15	1	.183	9	31	5	2	1.2	.889
1968		15	14	.517	1.81	38	37	11	269	181	**110**	**283**	3	0	0	0	85	13	0	.153	10	30	4	7	1.2	.909
1969		18	14	.563	2.94	39	38	18	285	222	102	**279**	4	0	0	1	92	16	0	.174	5	39	4	5	1.2	.917
1970		20	12	.625	2.92	39	39	19	**305**	236	**131**	**304**	1	0	0	0	105	13	1	.124	4	35	4	1	1.0	.907
1971		13	17	.433	3.39	35	31	8	215	160	**153**	192	2	2	0	1	73	13	0	.178	3	26	4	2	0.9	.879
1972	SF N	10	8	.556	4.34	28	25	4	164	155	86	122	0	0	0	0	59	7	0	.119	8	21	1	0	1.1	.967
1973	2 teams SF N (18G 1–2) NY A (16G 5–8)																									
″	total	6	10	.375	4.11	34	18	2	135.2	118	93	110	1	0	1	3	12	2	0	.167	7	20	0	1	0.8	1.000
1974	NY A	1	6	.143	4.69	13	7	0	48	42	41	33	0	0	1	0	0	0	0	—	1	2	1	0	0.3	.750
1975	PIT N	2	1	.667	2.83	14	1	0	35	30	20	29	0	1	1	0	8	0	0	.000	1	5	0	2	0.4	1.000
15 yrs.		141	134	.513	3.17	425	346	103	2492.2	1948	1312	2453	23	8	3	14	774	119	2	.154	80	328	33	23	1.0	.925

Chuck McElroy

McELROY, CHARLES DWAYNE BL TL 6′ 160 lbs.
B. Oct. 1, 1967, Port Arthur, Tex.

Year	Team	W	L	PCT	ERA	G	GS	CG	IP	H	BB	SO	ShO	Relief W	Relief L	SV	AB	H	HR	BA	PO	A	E	DP	TC/G	FA
1989	PHI N	0	0	—	1.74	11	0	0	10.1	12	4	8	0	0	0	0	0	0	0	—	1	0	0	0	0.1	1.000
1990		0	1	.000	7.71	16	0	0	14	24	10	16	0	0	1	0	0	0	0	—	1	0	1	0	0.1	.500
1991	CHI N	6	2	.750	1.95	71	0	0	101.1	73	57	92	0	6	2	3	10	3	0	.300	8	14	0	1	0.3	1.000
1992		4	7	.364	3.55	72	0	0	83.2	73	51	83	0	4	7	6	6	4	0	.667	3	8	1	2	0.2	.917
1993		2	2	.500	4.56	49	0	0	47.1	51	25	31	0	2	2	0	6	0	0	.000	3	5	0	1	0.2	1.000
1994	CIN N	1	2	.333	2.34	52	0	0	57.2	52	15	38	0	1	2	5	6	1	0	.167	1	5	0	0	0.1	1.000
1995		3	4	.429	6.02	44	0	0	40.1	46	15	27	0	3	4	0	3	0	0	.000	2	4	0	1	0.1	1.000
7 yrs.		16	18	.471	3.43	315	0	0	354.2	331	177	295	0	16	18	14	31	8	0	.258	19	36	2	5	0.2	.965

Jim McElroy

McELROY, JAMES D. 5′10″ 170 lbs.
B. 1863, San Francisco, Calif. D. Feb. 24, 1889, Albuquerque, N. M.

Year	Team	W	L	PCT	ERA	G	GS	CG	IP	H	BB	SO	ShO	Relief W	Relief L	SV	AB	H	HR	BA	PO	A	E	DP	TC/G	FA
1884	2 teams PHI N (13G 1–12) WIL U (1G 0–1)																									
″	total	1	13	.071	5.12	14	14	13	116	125	54	48	0	0	0	0	50	7	0	.140	13	25	10	1	2.8	.792

Will McEnaney

McENANEY, WILLIAM HENRY BL TL 6′ 180 lbs.
B. Feb. 14, 1952, Springfield, Ohio.

Year	Team	W	L	PCT	ERA	G	GS	CG	IP	H	BB	SO	ShO	Relief W	Relief L	SV	AB	H	HR	BA	PO	A	E	DP	TC/G	FA
1974	CIN N	2	1	.667	4.33	24	0	0	27	24	9	13	0	2	1	2	0	0	0	—	0	1	0	0	0.0	1.000
1975		5	2	.714	2.47	70	0	0	91	92	23	48	0	5	2	15	14	0	0	.000	6	8	0	0	0.2	1.000
1976		2	6	.250	4.88	55	0	0	72	97	23	28	0	2	6	7	6	1	0	.167	4	13	3	1	0.4	.850

Will McEnaney *continued*

Year	Team		W	L	PCT	ERA	G	GS	CG	IP	H	BB	SO	ShO	Relief Pitching W	Relief Pitching L	Relief Pitching SV	Batting AB	Batting H	Batting HR	BA	PO	A	E	DP	TC/G	FA
1977	MON	N	3	5	.375	3.93	69	0	0	87	92	22	38	0	3	5	3	8	0	0	.000	5	12	0	1	0.2	1.000
1978	PIT	N	0	0	—	10.00	6	0	0	9	15	2	6	0	0	0	0	0	0	0	—	1	1	0	0	0.3	1.000
1979	STL	N	0	3	.000	2.95	45	0	0	64	60	16	15	0	0	3	2	3	0	0	.000	2	19	0	2	0.5	1.000
6 yrs.			12	17	.414	3.75	269	0	0	350	380	95	148	0	12	17	29	31	1	0	.032	18	54	3	4	0.3	.960
LEAGUE CHAMPIONSHIP SERIES																											
1975	CIN	N	0	0	—	6.75	1	0	0	1.1	1	0	1	0	0	0	0	0	0	0	—	0	0	0	0	0.0	.000
WORLD SERIES																											
1975	CIN	N	0	0	—	2.70	5	0	0	6.2	3	2	5	0	0	0	1	1	1	0	1.000	0	0	0	0	0.0	.000
1976			0	0	—	0.00	2	0	0	4.2	2	1	2	0	0	0	2	0	0	0	—	1	0	0	0	0.5	1.000
2 yrs.			0	0		1.59	7	0	0	11.1	5	3	7	0	0	0	3 4th	1	1	0	1.000	1	0	0	0	0.1	1.000

Lou McEvoy

McEVOY, LOUIS ANTHONY
B. May 30, 1902, Williamsburg, Kans. D. Dec. 17, 1953, Webster Groves, Mo.
BR TR 6′ 2½″ 203 lbs.

Year	Team		W	L	PCT	ERA	G	GS	CG	IP	H	BB	SO	ShO	Relief Pitching W	Relief Pitching L	Relief Pitching SV	Batting AB	Batting H	Batting HR	BA	PO	A	E	DP	TC/G	FA
1930	NY	A	1	3	.250	6.71	28	1	0	52.1	64	29	14	0	1	2	3	16	2	0	.125	2	8	3	0	0.5	.769
1931			0	0	—	12.41	6	0	0	12.1	19	12	3	0	0	0	1	4	0	0	.000	1	4	0	0	0.8	1.000
2 yrs.			1	3	.250	7.79	34	1	0	64.2	83	41	17	0	1	2	4	20	2	0	.100	3	12	3	0	0.5	.833

Barney McFadden

McFADDEN, BERNARD JOSEPH
B. Feb. 22, 1874, Eckley, Pa. D. Apr. 28, 1924, Mauch Chunk, Pa.
BR TR 6′ 1″ 195 lbs.

Year	Team		W	L	PCT	ERA	G	GS	CG	IP	H	BB	SO	ShO	Relief Pitching W	Relief Pitching L	Relief Pitching SV	Batting AB	Batting H	Batting HR	BA	PO	A	E	DP	TC/G	FA
1901	CIN	N	3	3	.500	6.07	8	5	4	46	54	40	11	0	1	1	0	20	3	0	.150	4	15	3	3	2.8	.864
1902	PHI	N	0	1	.000	8.00	1	1	1	9	14	7	3	0	0	0	0	3	0	0	.000	0	2	0	1	2.0	1.000
2 yrs.			3	4	.429	6.38	9	6	5	55	68	47	14	0	1	1	0	23	3	0	.130	4	17	3	4	2.7	.875

Dan McFarlan

McFARLAN, ANDERSON DANIEL
Brother of Alex McFarlan.
B. Nov. 26, 1874, Gainesville, Tex. D. Sept. 24, 1924, Louisville, Ky.

Year	Team		W	L	PCT	ERA	G	GS	CG	IP	H	BB	SO	ShO	Relief Pitching W	Relief Pitching L	Relief Pitching SV	Batting AB	Batting H	Batting HR	BA	PO	A	E	DP	TC/G	FA
1895	LOU	N	0	7	.000	6.65	7	7	6	46	80	15	10	0	0	0	0	21	5	0	.238	3	13	0	0	2.3	1.000
1899	2 teams	BKN N (1G 0–0)	WAS N (32G 8–18)																								
″	total		8	18	.308	4.67	33	28	22	217.2	274	67	41	1	0	0	0	88	16	0	.182	9	51	8	4	2.1	.882
2 yrs.			8	25	.242	5.02	40	35	28	263.2	354	82	51	1	0	0	0	109	21	0	.193	12	64	8	4	2.1	.905

Chappie McFarland

McFARLAND, CHARLES A.
Brother of Monte McFarland.
B. Mar. 13, 1875, White Hall, Ill. D. Dec. 14, 1924, Houston, Tex.
TR 6′ 1″

Year	Team		W	L	PCT	ERA	G	GS	CG	IP	H	BB	SO	ShO	Relief Pitching W	Relief Pitching L	Relief Pitching SV	Batting AB	Batting H	Batting HR	BA	PO	A	E	DP	TC/G	FA
1902	STL	N	0	1	.000	5.73	2	1	1	11	11	3	3	0	0	0	0	4	0	0	.000	0	5	0	0	2.5	1.000
1903			9	18	.333	3.07	28	26	25	229	253	48	76	1	0	**2**	0	74	8	0	.108	5	75	6	5	3.1	.930
1904			14	17	.452	3.21	32	31	28	269.1	266	56	111	1	0	0	0	99	13	0	.131	13	106	6	3	3.9	.952
1905			8	18	.308	3.82	31	28	22	250	281	65	85	3	0	0	1	85	14	0	.165	12	75	4	1	2.9	.956
1906	3 teams	STL N (6G 2–1)	PIT N (6G 1–3)	BKN N (1G 0–1)																							
″	total		3	5	.375	2.87	13	10	5	81.2	82	20	32	1	0	0	1	31	7	0	.226	5	25	1	1	2.4	.968
5 yrs.			34	59	.366	3.35	106	96	81	841	893	192	307	6	0	2	2	293	42	0	.143	35	286	17	10	3.2	.950

Chris McFarland

McFARLAND, CHRISTOPHER
B. Aug. 17, 1861, Fall River, Mass. D. May 24, 1918, New Bedford, Mass.
5′ 9″ 170 lbs.

Year	Team		W	L	PCT	ERA	G	GS	CG	IP	H	BB	SO	ShO	Relief Pitching W	Relief Pitching L	Relief Pitching SV	Batting AB	Batting H	Batting HR	BA	PO	A	E	DP	TC/G	FA
1884	BAL	U	0	1	.000	*15.00*	1	1	0	3	9	1	3	0	0	0	0	*				4	0	3	0	1.8	.571

Monte McFarland

McFARLAND, LAMONT AMOS
Brother of Chappie McFarland.
B. Nov. 7, 1872, White Hall, Ill. D. Nov. 15, 1913, Peoria, Ill.

Year	Team		W	L	PCT	ERA	G	GS	CG	IP	H	BB	SO	ShO	Relief Pitching W	Relief Pitching L	Relief Pitching SV	Batting AB	Batting H	Batting HR	BA	PO	A	E	DP	TC/G	FA
1895	CHI	N	2	0	1.000	5.14	2	2	2	14	21	5	5	0	0	0	0	7	1	0	.143	0	4	0	0	2.0	1.000
1896			0	4	.000	7.20	4	3	2	25	32	21	3	0	0	1	0	12	0	0	.000	2	8	0	0	2.5	1.000
2 yrs.			2	4	.333	6.46	6	5	4	39	53	26	8	0	0	1	0	19	1	0	.053	2	12	0	0	2.3	1.000

Jack McFetridge

McFETRIDGE, JOHN REED
B. Aug. 25, 1869, Philadelphia, Pa. D. Jan. 10, 1917, Philadelphia, Pa.
6′ 175 lbs.

Year	Team		W	L	PCT	ERA	G	GS	CG	IP	H	BB	SO	ShO	Relief Pitching W	Relief Pitching L	Relief Pitching SV	Batting AB	Batting H	Batting HR	BA	PO	A	E	DP	TC/G	FA
1890	PHI	N	1	0	1.000	1.00	1	1	1	9	5	2	4	0	0	0	0	4	3	0	.750	0	1	0	0	1.0	1.000
1903			1	11	.083	4.91	14	13	11	102.2	120	49	31	0	0	0	0	34	6	0	.176	2	24	3	0	2.1	.897
2 yrs.			2	11	.154	4.59	15	14	12	111.2	125	51	35	0	0	0	0	38	9	0	.237	2	25	3	0	2.0	.900

Andy McGaffigan

McGAFFIGAN, ANDREW JOSEPH
B. Oct. 25, 1956, West Palm Beach, Fla.
BR TR 6′ 3″ 185 lbs.

Year	Team		W	L	PCT	ERA	G	GS	CG	IP	H	BB	SO	ShO	Relief Pitching W	Relief Pitching L	Relief Pitching SV	Batting AB	Batting H	Batting HR	BA	PO	A	E	DP	TC/G	FA
1981	NY	A	0	0	—	2.57	2	0	0	7	5	3	2	0	0	0	0	0	0	0	—	0	0	0	0	0.0	.000
1982	SF	N	1	0	1.000	0.00	4	0	0	8	5	1	4	0	1	0	0	1	0	0	.000	0	0	0	0	0.0	.000
1983			3	9	.250	4.29	43	16	0	134.1	131	39	93	0	1	0	2	30	2	0	.067	8	4	2	0	0.3	.857
1984	2 teams	MON N (21G 3–4)	CIN N (9G 0–2)																								
″	total		3	6	.333	3.52	30	6	0	69	60	23	57	0	1	3	1	10	0	0	.000	3	6	1	1	0.3	.900
1985	CIN	N	3	3	.500	3.72	15	15	2	94.1	88	30	83	0	0	0	0	29	1	0	.034	8	12	1	2	1.4	.952
1986	MON	N	10	5	.667	2.65	48	14	1	142.2	114	55	104	1	5	1	2	33	2	0	.061	6	17	5	1	0.6	.821
1987			5	2	.714	2.39	69	0	0	120.1	105	42	100	0	5	2	12	17	0	0	.000	5	17	4	2	0.4	.846
1988			6	0	1.000	2.76	63	0	0	91.1	81	37	71	0	6	0	4	5	0	0	.000	7	8	1	0	0.3	.938
1989			3	5	.375	4.68	57	0	0	75	85	30	40	0	3	5	2	1	1	0	1.000	3	8	2	0	0.2	.846
1990	2 teams	SF N (4G 0–0)	KC A (24G 4–3)																								
″	total		4	3	.571	3.89	28	11	0	83.1	85	32	53	0	1	0	1	0	0	0		5	6	1	0	0.4	.917
1991	KC	A	0	0	—	4.50	4	0	0	8	14	2	3	0	0	0	0	0	0	0	—	0	0	0	0	0.0	.000
11 yrs.			38	33	.535	3.38	363	62	3	833.1	773	294	610	1	23	11	24	126	6	0	.048	45	78	17	6	0.4	.879

Jack McGeachy

McGEACHY, JOHN CHARLES BR TR 5′ 8″ 165 lbs.
B. May 13, 1864, Clinton, Mass. D. Apr. 5, 1930, Cambridge, Mass.

Year	Team	Lg	W	L	PCT	ERA	G	GS	CG	IP	H	BB	SO	ShO	Relief W	Relief L	Relief SV	Batting AB	Batting H	HR	BA	PO	A	E	DP	TC/G	FA
1887	IND	N	0	1	.000	11.37	1	0	0	6.1	13	4	3	0	0	1	0	405	109	1	.269	102	28	22	5	2.3	.855
1888			0	0	—	7.20	1	0	0	5	5	3	0	0	0	0	0	452	99	0	.219	194	28	16	5	2.0	.933
1889			0	0	—	11.57	3	0	0	4.2	7	6	3	0	0	0	0	532	142	2	.267	189	36	20	8	1.8	.918
3 yrs.			0	1	.000	10.13	5	0	0	16	25	13	6	0	0	1	0	*				1061	147	128	22	2.2	.904

Bill McGee

McGEE, WILLIAM HENRY (Fiddler Bill) BR TR 6′ 1″ 215 lbs.
B. Nov. 16, 1909, Batchtown, Ill. D. Feb. 11, 1987, St. Louis, Mo.

Year	Team	Lg	W	L	PCT	ERA	G	GS	CG	IP	H	BB	SO	ShO	Relief W	Relief L	Relief SV	Batting AB	Batting H	HR	BA	PO	A	E	DP	TC/G	FA
1935	STL	N	1	0	1.000	1.00	1	1	1	9	3	1	2	0	0	0	0	3	1	0	.333	0	0	0	0	0.0	.000
1936			1	1	.500	8.04	7	2	0	15.2	23	4	8	0	0	0	0	4	1	0	.250	0	5	0	0	0.7	1.000
1937			1	0	1.000	2.63	4	1	1	13.2	13	4	9	0	0	0	0	5	1	0	.200	0	4	0	0	1.0	1.000
1938			7	12	.368	3.21	47	25	10	216	216	78	104	1	1	2	5	67	14	0	.209	11	39	3	2	1.1	.943
1939			12	5	.706	3.81	43	17	5	156	155	59	56	4	4	3	0	55	8	0	.145	3	33	0	3	0.8	1.000
1940			16	10	.615	3.80	38	31	11	217.2	222	96	78	3	1	2	0	73	13	0	.178	8	33	2	1	1.1	.953
1941	2 teams	STL N (4G 0–1)	NY N (22G 2–9)																								
″	total		2	10	.167	4.92	26	17	1	120.2	134	67	43	0	0	1	0	35	5	0	.143	3	17	0	0	0.8	1.000
1942	NY	N	6	3	.667	2.93	31	8	2	104.1	95	46	40	1	4	0	1	29	3	0	.103	6	16	1	1	0.7	.957
8 yrs.			46	41	.529	3.74	197	102	31	853	861	355	340	9	10	8	6	271	46	0	.170	31	147	6	7	0.9	.967

Connie McGeehan

McGEEHAN, CORNELIUS BERNARD
Brother of Dan McGeehan.
B. Aug. 25, 1882, Drifton, Pa. D. July 4, 1907, Hazleton, Pa.

Year	Team	Lg	W	L	PCT	ERA	G	GS	CG	IP	H	BB	SO	ShO	Relief W	Relief L	Relief SV	Batting AB	Batting H	HR	BA	PO	A	E	DP	TC/G	FA
1903	PHI	A	1	0	1.000	4.50	3	0	0	10	9	1	4	0	1	0	0	6	0	0	.000	2	4	0	0	1.5	1.000

Kevin McGehee

McGEHEE, GEORGE KEVIN BR TR 6′ 190 lbs.
B. Jan. 18, 1969, Alexandria, La.

Year	Team	Lg	W	L	PCT	ERA	G	GS	CG	IP	H	BB	SO	ShO	Relief W	Relief L	Relief SV	Batting AB	Batting H	HR	BA	PO	A	E	DP	TC/G	FA
1993	BAL	A	0	0	—	5.94	5	0	0	16.2	18	7	7	0	0	0	0	0	0	0	—	2	2	0	0	0.8	1.000

Pat McGehee

McGEHEE, PATRICK HENRY BL TR 6′ 2½″ 180 lbs.
B. July 2, 1888, Meadville, Miss. D. Dec. 30, 1946, Paducah, Ky.

Year	Team	Lg	W	L	PCT	ERA	G	GS	CG	IP	H	BB	SO	ShO	Relief W	Relief L	Relief SV	Batting AB	Batting H	HR	BA	PO	A	E	DP	TC/G	FA
1912	DET	A	0	0	—	0.00	1	1	0		1	1	0	0	0	0	0	0	0	0	—	0	0	0	0	0.0	.000

Randy McGilberry

McGILBERRY, RANDALL KENT BB TR 6′ 1″ 195 lbs.
B. Oct. 29, 1953, Mobile, Ala.

Year	Team	Lg	W	L	PCT	ERA	G	GS	CG	IP	H	BB	SO	ShO	Relief W	Relief L	Relief SV	Batting AB	Batting H	HR	BA	PO	A	E	DP	TC/G	FA
1977	KC	A	0	1	.000	5.14	3	0	0	7	7	1	1	0	0	1	0	0	0	0	—	1	2	0	0	1.0	1.000
1978			0	1	.000	4.56	18	0	0	25.2	27	18	12	0	0	1	0	0	0	0	—	2	6	3	0	0.6	.727
2 yrs.			0	2	.000	4.68	21	0	0	32.2	34	19	13	0	0	2	0	0	0	0		3	8	3	0	0.7	.786

Bill McGill

McGILL, WILLIAM JOHN (Parson) BR TR 6′ 2″
B. June 29, 1880, Galva, Kans. D. Aug. 7, 1959, Alva, Okla.

Year	Team	Lg	W	L	PCT	ERA	G	GS	CG	IP	H	BB	SO	ShO	Relief W	Relief L	Relief SV	Batting AB	Batting H	HR	BA	PO	A	E	DP	TC/G	FA
1907	STL	A	1	0	1.000	3.44	2	2	1	18.1	22	2	8	0	0	0	0	9	0	0	.000	2	5	1	0	4.0	.875

Willie McGill

McGILL, WILLIAM VANESS (Kid) TL 5′ 6½″ 170 lbs.
B. Nov. 10, 1873, Atlanta, Ga. D. Aug. 29, 1944, Indianapolis, Ind.

Year	Team	Lg	W	L	PCT	ERA	G	GS	CG	IP	H	BB	SO	ShO	Relief W	Relief L	Relief SV	Batting AB	Batting H	HR	BA	PO	A	E	DP	TC/G	FA
1890	CLE	P	11	9	.550	4.12	24	20	19	183.2	222	96	82	0	1	0	0	68	10	0	.147	5	52	4	1	2.4	.934
1891	2 teams	CIN AA (8G 2–5)	STL AA (33G 18–9)																								
″	total		20	14	.588	3.42	41	37	26	297.2	276	163	166	1	1	1	1	103	15	0	.146	8	46	8	0	1.5	.871
1892	CIN	N	1	1	.500	5.29	3	3	1	17	18	5	7	0	0	0	0	7	2	0	.286	0	4	0	0	1.3	1.000
1893	CHI	N	17	18	.486	4.61	39	34	26	302.2	311	181	91	1	1	2	0	124	29	0	.234	7	42	6	3	1.4	.891
1894			7	19	.269	5.84	27	23	22	208	272	117	58	0	2	1	0	82	20	0	.244	4	30	4	0	1.4	.895
1895	PHI	N	10	8	.556	5.55	20	20	13	146	177	81	70	0	0	0	0	63	14	0	.222	3	32	4	1	2.0	.897
1896			5	4	.556	5.31	12	11	7	79.2	87	53	29	0	0	0	0	29	6	0	.207	0	22	4	0	2.2	.846
7 yrs.			71	73	.493	4.62	166	148	114	1234.2	1363	696	503	2	5	4	1	476	96	0	.202	27	228	30	5	1.7	.895

John McGillen

McGILLEN, JOHN JOSEPH BL TL 6′ 1″ 175 lbs.
B. Aug. 6, 1917, Eddystone, Pa. D. Aug. 11, 1987, Upland, Pa.

Year	Team	Lg	W	L	PCT	ERA	G	GS	CG	IP	H	BB	SO	ShO	Relief W	Relief L	Relief SV	Batting AB	Batting H	HR	BA	PO	A	E	DP	TC/G	FA
1944	PHI	A	0	0	—	18.00	2	0	0	1	1	2	0	0	0	0	0	0	0	0	—	0	0	0	0	0.0	.000

Jim McGinley

McGINLEY, JAMES WILLIAM BR TR 5′ 9½″ 165 lbs.
B. Oct. 2, 1878, Groveland, Mass. D. Sept. 20, 1961, Haverhill, Mass.

Year	Team	Lg	W	L	PCT	ERA	G	GS	CG	IP	H	BB	SO	ShO	Relief W	Relief L	Relief SV	Batting AB	Batting H	HR	BA	PO	A	E	DP	TC/G	FA
1904	STL	N	2	1	.667	2.00	3	3	3	27	28	6	6	0	0	0	0	11	1	0	.091	0	1	0	1	0.3	1.000
1905			0	1	.000	15.00	1	1	0	3	5	2	0	0	0	0	0	1	1	0	1.000	0	0	0	0	0.0	.000
2 yrs.			2	2	.500	3.30	4	4	3	30	33	8	6	0	0	0	0	12	2	0	.167	0	1	0	1	0.3	1.000

Dan McGinn

McGINN, DANIEL MICHAEL BL TL 6′ 185 lbs.
B. Nov. 29, 1943, Omaha, Neb.

Year	Team	Lg	W	L	PCT	ERA	G	GS	CG	IP	H	BB	SO	ShO	Relief W	Relief L	Relief SV	Batting AB	Batting H	HR	BA	PO	A	E	DP	TC/G	FA
1968	CIN	N	0	1	.000	5.25	14	0	0	12	13	11	16	0	0	1	0	2	0	0	.000	0	3	1	0	0.3	.750
1969	MON	N	7	10	.412	3.94	74	1	0	132.1	123	65	112	0	7	**10**	6	29	5	1	.172	3	30	6	0	0.5	.846
1970			7	10	.412	5.43	52	19	3	131	154	78	83	2	2	1	0	35	4	0	.114	6	29	3	1	0.7	.921
1971			1	4	.200	5.96	28	6	1	71	74	42	40	0	0	1	0	17	4	0	.235	4	15	1	3	0.7	.950
1972	CHI	N	0	5	.000	5.86	42	2	0	63	78	29	42	0	0	3	4	8	2	0	.250	2	6	1	0	0.2	.889
5 yrs.			15	30	.333	5.10	210	28	4	409.1	442	225	293	2	9	16	10	91	15	1	.165	15	83	12	4	0.5	.891

Gus McGinnis

McGINNIS, ALBERT TL 5′11″ 168 lbs.
B. 1871, Painesville, Ohio Deceased.

Year	Team	Lg	W	L	PCT	ERA	G	GS	CG	IP	H	BB	SO	ShO	Relief W	Relief L	Relief SV	Batting AB	Batting H	HR	BA	PO	A	E	DP	TC/G	FA
1893	2 teams	CHI N (13G 2–5)	PHI N (5G 1–3)																								
″	total		3	8	.273	4.99	18	9	7	104.2	124	48	25	1	1	1	0	40	9	0	.225	4	27	1	1	1.7	.969

Jumbo McGinnis

McGINNIS, GEORGE WASHINGTON 5′10″ 197 lbs.
B. Feb. 22, 1864, Alton, Ill. D. May 18, 1934, St. Louis, Mo.

Year	Team	Lg	W	L	PCT	ERA	G	GS	CG	IP	H	BB	SO	ShO	Relief W	Relief L	Relief SV	Batting AB	Batting H	HR	BA	PO	A	E	DP	TC/G	FA
1882	STL	AA	25	17	.595	*2.47*	44	44	42	379.1	376	52	134	3	0	0	0	203	44	0	.217	19	104	14	2	2.6	.898
1883			28	16	.636	*2.33*	45	45	41	382.2	325	69	128	**6**	0	0	0	180	36	0	.200	15	86	22	3	2.5	.821
1884			24	16	.600	*2.84*	40	40	39	354.1	331	35	141	5	0	0	0	146	34	0	.233	8	71	12	1	2.3	.868

Jumbo McGinnis *continued*

Year	Team	W	L	PCT	ERA	G	GS	CG	IP	H	BB	SO	ShO	Relief Pitching W	Relief Pitching L	Relief Pitching SV	Batting AB	Batting H	Batting HR	BA	PO	A	E	DP	TC/G	FA
1885		6	6	.500	*3.38*	13	13	12	112	98	19	41	3	0	0	0	50	11	0	.220	1	15	6	1	1.6	.727
1886	2 teams STL AA (10G 5–5) BAL AA (26G 11–13)																									
"	total	16	18	.471	3.58	36	35	34	297	342	75	100	1	0	0	0	122	23	1	.189	12	54	11	1	2.0	.857
1887	CIN AA	3	5	.375	*5.45*	8	8	8	69.1	85	43	18	0	0	0	0	31	6	0	.194	1	14	1	0	2.0	.938
6 yrs.		102	78	.567	2.92	186	185	176	1594.2	1557	293	562	18	0	0	0	732	154	1	.210	56	344	66	8	2.3	.858

Joe McGinnity

McGINNITY, JOSEPH JEROME (Iron Man)
Born Joseph Jerome McGinty.
B. Mar. 19, 1871, Rock Island, Ill. D. Nov. 14, 1929, Brooklyn, N. Y.
Hall of Fame 1946.
BR TR 5′11″ 206 lbs.

Year	Team	W	L	PCT	ERA	G	GS	CG	IP	H	BB	SO	ShO	Relief Pitching W	Relief Pitching L	Relief Pitching SV	Batting AB	Batting H	Batting HR	BA	PO	A	E	DP	TC/G	FA
1899	BAL N	**28**	17	.622	2.68	48	41	38	366.1	358	93	74	4	**3**	2	2	145	28	0	.193	21	96	10	0	2.5	.921
1900	BKN N	**29**	9	.763	2.90	44	37	32	**347**	350	**113**	93	1	3	0	0	145	28	0	.193	18	75	12	4	2.3	.886
1901	BAL A	26	20	.565	3.56	**48**	**43**	**39**	**382**	**412**	96	75	1	2	1	1	148	31	0	.209	17	104	9	2	2.7	.931
1902	2 teams BAL A (25G 13–10) NY N (19G 8–8)																									
"	total	21	18	.538	2.84	44	39	35	351.2	341	78	106	1	0	1	0	153	33	0	.216	30	91	12	4	2.6	.910
1903	NY N	**31**	20	.608	2.43	**55**	**48**	**44**	**434**	391	109	171	3	**2**	**2**	2	165	34	0	.206	31	94	16	3	2.6	.887
1904		**35**	8	**.814**	**1.61**	**51**	44	38	**408**	307	86	144	**9**	**2**	0	**5**	142	25	0	.176	28	127	13	1	3.3	.923
1905		21	15	.583	2.87	**46**	38	26	320	289	71	125	2	0	1	3	120	28	0	.233	23	94	7	3	2.7	.944
1906		**27**	12	.692	2.25	**45**	37	32	339.2	316	71	105	3	2	1	2	115	15	0	.130	22	105	13	4	3.1	.907
1907		18	18	.500	3.16	**47**	34	23	310.1	320	58	120	3	3	**4**	**4**	103	18	0	.175	18	94	4	0	2.5	.966
1908		11	7	.611	2.27	37	20	7	186	192	37	55	5	**4**	1	4	61	11	0	.180	10	50	5	4	1.8	.923
10 yrs.		247	144	.632	2.65	465	381	314	3445	3276	812	1068	32	21	13	23	1297	251	0	.194	218	930	101	25	2.6	.919
WORLD SERIES																										
1905	NY N	1	1	.500	0.00	2	2	1	17	10	3	6	1	0	0	0	5	0	0	.000	0	6	0	0	3.0	1.000

Lynn McGlothen

McGLOTHEN, LYNN EVERETT
B. Mar. 27, 1950, Monroe, La. D. Aug. 14, 1984, Dubach, La.
BL TR 6′ 2″ 185 lbs.

Year	Team	W	L	PCT	ERA	G	GS	CG	IP	H	BB	SO	ShO	Relief Pitching W	Relief Pitching L	Relief Pitching SV	Batting AB	Batting H	Batting HR	BA	PO	A	E	DP	TC/G	FA
1972	BOS A	8	7	.533	3.41	22	22	4	145.1	135	59	112	1	0	0	0	53	10	0	.189	17	31	0	2	2.2	1.000
1973		1	2	.333	8.22	6	3	0	23	39	8	16	0	0	1	0	0	0	0	—	3	2	0	0	0.8	1.000
1974	STL N	16	12	.571	2.70	31	31	8	237	212	89	142	3	0	0	0	83	15	0	.181	19	37	1	3	1.8	.982
1975		15	13	.536	3.92	35	34	9	239	231	97	146	2	0	0	0	80	7	0	.087	10	25	2	3	1.1	.946
1976		13	15	.464	3.91	33	32	10	205	209	68	106	4	0	0	0	71	15	0	.211	20	18	0	3	1.2	1.000
1977	SF N	2	9	.182	5.63	21	15	2	80	94	52	42	0	0	1	0	19	2	0	.105	3	4	1	0	0.4	.875
1978	2 teams SF N (5G 0–0) CHI N (49G 5–3)																									
"	total	5	3	.625	3.30	54	2	0	92.2	92	43	69	0	5	2	0	16	3	0	.188	1	7	1	1	0.2	.889
1979	CHI N	13	14	.481	4.12	42	29	6	212	236	55	147	1	3	1	2	71	16	0	.225	15	15	0	0	0.7	1.000
1980		12	14	.462	4.80	39	27	2	182	211	64	119	2	0	1	0	51	10	0	.196	3	21	2	0	0.7	.923
1981	2 teams CHI N (20G 1–4) CHI A (11G 0–0)																									
"	total	1	4	.200	4.56	31	6	0	77	85	35	38	0	1	1	0	12	1	0	.083	6	13	0	0	0.6	1.000
1982	NY A	0	0	—	10.80	4	0	0	5	9	2	2	0	0	0	0	0	0	0	—	1	1	0	0	0.5	1.000
11 yrs.		86	93	.480	3.98	318	201	41	1498	1553	572	939	13	9	7	2	456	79	0	.173	98	174	7	12	0.9	.975

Pat McGlothin

McGLOTHIN, EZRA MAC
B. Oct. 20, 1920, Coalfield, Tenn.
BL TR 6′ 3½″ 180 lbs.

Year	Team	W	L	PCT	ERA	G	GS	CG	IP	H	BB	SO	ShO	Relief Pitching W	Relief Pitching L	Relief Pitching SV	Batting AB	Batting H	Batting HR	BA	PO	A	E	DP	TC/G	FA
1949	BKN N	1	1	.500	4.60	7	0	0	15.2	13	5	11	0	1	1	0	3	0	0	.000	3	5	1	0	1.3	.889
1950		0	0	—	13.50	1	0	0	2	5	1	2	0	0	0	0	0	0	0	—	0	0	0	0	0.0	.000
2 yrs.		1	1	.500	5.60	8	0	0	17.2	18	6	13	0	1	1	0	3	0	0	.000	3	5	1	0	1.1	.889

Jim McGlothlin

McGLOTHLIN, JAMES MILTON (Red)
B. Oct. 6, 1943, Los Angeles, Calif. D. Dec. 23, 1975, Union, Ky.
BR TR 6′ 1″ 185 lbs.

Year	Team	W	L	PCT	ERA	G	GS	CG	IP	H	BB	SO	ShO	Relief Pitching W	Relief Pitching L	Relief Pitching SV	Batting AB	Batting H	Batting HR	BA	PO	A	E	DP	TC/G	FA
1965	CAL A	0	3	.000	3.50	3	3	1	18	18	7	9	0	0	0	0	6	0	0	.000	1	1	0	1	0.7	1.000
1966		3	1	.750	4.52	19	11	0	67.2	79	19	41	0	0	0	0	17	1	0	.059	10	7	1	0	0.9	.944
1967		12	8	.600	2.96	32	29	9	197.1	163	56	137	**6**	1	0	0	57	8	0	.140	15	33	4	4	1.6	.923
1968		10	15	.400	3.54	40	32	8	208.1	187	60	135	0	0	0	3	63	7	0	.111	19	35	1	4	1.4	.982
1969		8	16	.333	3.18	37	35	4	201	188	58	96	1	0	0	0	58	7	0	.121	14	38	2	0	1.5	.963
1970	CIN N	14	10	.583	3.58	35	34	5	211	192	86	97	3	0	0	0	66	8	1	.121	16	55	0	6	2.0	1.000
1971		8	12	.400	3.21	30	26	6	171	151	47	93	0	0	0	0	51	7	1	.137	11	33	4	3	1.6	.917
1972		9	8	.529	3.91	31	21	3	145	165	49	69	1	1	3	0	46	8	1	.174	10	22	4	2	1.2	.889
1973	2 teams CIN N (24G 3–3) CHI A (5G 0–1)																									
"	total	3	4	.429	6.06	29	10	0	81.2	104	36	32	0	0	0	0	16	2	0	.125	3	19	0	1	0.8	1.000
9 yrs.		67	77	.465	3.61	256	201	36	1301	1247	418	709	11	2	3	3	380	48	3	.126	99	243	16	21	1.4	.955
LEAGUE CHAMPIONSHIP SERIES																										
1972	CIN N	0	0	—	0.00	1	0	0	1	0	0	0	0	0	0	0	0	0	0	—	0	0	0	0	0.0	.000
WORLD SERIES																										
1970	CIN N	0	0	—	8.31	1	1	0	4.1	6	2	2	0	0	0	0	2	0	0	.000	0	0	0	0	0.0	.000
1972		0	0	—	12.00	1	1	0	3	2	2	3	0	0	0	0	1	0	0	.000	0	1	0	0	1.0	1.000
2 yrs.		0	0		9.82	2	2	0	7.1	8	4	5	0	0	0	0	3	0	0	.000	0	1	0	0	0.5	1.000

Stoney McGlynn

McGLYNN, ULYSSES SIMPSON GRANT
B. May 26, 1872, Lancaster, Pa. D. Aug. 26, 1941, Manitowoc, Wis.
BR TR 5′11″ 185 lbs.

Year	Team	W	L	PCT	ERA	G	GS	CG	IP	H	BB	SO	ShO	Relief Pitching W	Relief Pitching L	Relief Pitching SV	Batting AB	Batting H	Batting HR	BA	PO	A	E	DP	TC/G	FA
1906	STL N	2	2	.500	2.44	6	6	6	48	43	15	25	0	0	0	0	17	1	0	.059	1	23	1	1	4.2	.960
1907		14	**25**	.359	2.91	45	**39**	**33**	**352.1**	**329**	**112**	109	3	1	1	1	125	25	0	.200	22	94	12	4	2.8	.906
1908		1	6	.143	3.45	16	6	4	75.2	76	17	23	0	1	0	1	26	2	0	.077	1	29	4	1	2.1	.882
3 yrs.		17	33	.340	2.95	67	51	43	476	448	144	157	3	2	1	2	168	28	0	.167	24	146	17	6	2.8	.909

Mickey McGowan

McGOWAN, TULLIS EARL
B. Nov. 26, 1921, Dothan, Ala.
BL TL 6′ 2″ 200 lbs.

Year	Team	W	L	PCT	ERA	G	GS	CG	IP	H	BB	SO	ShO	Relief Pitching W	Relief Pitching L	Relief Pitching SV	Batting AB	Batting H	Batting HR	BA	PO	A	E	DP	TC/G	FA
1948	NY N	0	0	—	7.36	3	0	0	3.2	3	4	2	0	0	0	0	1	0	0	.000	0	1	0	0	0.3	1.000

Howard McGraner

McGRANER, HOWARD (Muck)
B. Sept. 11, 1889, Hamley Run, Ohio D. Oct. 22, 1952, Zaleski, Ohio.
BL TL 5′ 7″ 155 lbs.

Year	Team	W	L	PCT	ERA	G	GS	CG	IP	H	BB	SO	ShO	Relief Pitching W	Relief Pitching L	Relief Pitching SV	Batting AB	Batting H	Batting HR	BA	PO	A	E	DP	TC/G	FA
1912	CIN N	1	0	1.000	7.11	4	0	0	19	22	7	5	0	1	0	0	8	2	0	.250	0	8	0	0	2.0	1.000

Bob McGraw

McGRAW, ROBERT EMMETT
B. Apr. 10, 1895, La Veta, Colo. D. June 2, 1978, Seal Beach, Calif.
BR TR 6′ 2″ 160 lbs.

Year	Team	W	L	PCT	ERA	G	GS	CG	IP	H	BB	SO	ShO	Relief Pitching W	Relief Pitching L	Relief Pitching SV	Batting AB	Batting H	Batting HR	BA	PO	A	E	DP	TC/G	FA
1917	NY A	0	1	.000	0.82	2	2	1	11	9	3	3	0	0	0	0	3	0	0	.000	0	2	0	0	1.0	1.000
1918		0	1	.000	∞	1	1	0		0	4	0	0	0	0	0	0	0	0	—	0	0	0	0	0.0	.000
1919	2 teams NY A (6G 1–0) BOS A (10G 0–2)																									
″	total	1	2	.333	5.44	16	1	0	43	44	27	9	0	1	1	0	13	1	0	.077	0	9	0	0	0.6	1.000
1920	NY A	0	0	—	4.67	15	0	0	27	24	20	11	0	0	0	0	7	0	0	.000	2	3	0	0	0.3	1.000
1925	BKN N	0	2	.000	3.20	2	2	2	19.2	14	13	3	0	0	0	0	6	1	0	.167	0	2	0	0	1.0	1.000
1926		9	13	.409	4.59	33	21	10	174.1	197	67	49	0	1	2	1	55	8	0	.145	7	37	2	0	1.4	.957
1927	2 teams BKN N (1G 0–1) STL N (18G 4–5)																									
″	total	4	6	.400	5.23	19	13	4	98	126	32	39	1	0	1	0	34	6	1	.176	5	25	1	0	1.6	.968
1928	PHI N	7	8	.467	4.64	39	3	0	132	150	56	28	0	5	**8**	1	36	4	0	.111	2	29	2	1	0.8	.939
1929		5	5	.500	5.73	41	4	0	86.1	113	43	22	0	4	4	4	20	4	0	.200	5	24	2	4	0.8	.935
9 yrs.		26	38	.406	4.89	168	47	17	591.1	677	265	164	1	11	16	6	174	24	1	.138	21	131	7	5	0.9	.956

John McGraw

McGRAW, JOHN
Born Roy Elmer Hoar.
B. Dec. 8, 1890, Intercourse, Pa. D. Apr. 27, 1967, Torrance, Calif.
BR TR 5′ 9″ 160 lbs.

Year	Team	W	L	PCT	ERA	G	GS	CG	IP	H	BB	SO	ShO	Relief Pitching W	Relief Pitching L	Relief Pitching SV	Batting AB	Batting H	Batting HR	BA	PO	A	E	DP	TC/G	FA
1914	BKN F	0	0	—	0.00	1	0	0	2	0	0	2	0	0	0	0	0	0	0	—	0	0	0	0	0.0	.000

Tug McGraw

McGRAW, FRANK EDWIN
B. Aug. 30, 1944, Martinez, Calif.
BR TL 6′ 170 lbs.

Year	Team	W	L	PCT	ERA	G	GS	CG	IP	H	BB	SO	ShO	Relief Pitching W	Relief Pitching L	Relief Pitching SV	Batting AB	Batting H	Batting HR	BA	PO	A	E	DP	TC/G	FA
1965	NY N	2	7	.222	3.32	37	9	2	97.2	88	48	57	0	0	1	1	23	3	0	.130	5	14	3	2	0.6	.864
1966		2	9	.182	5.34	15	12	1	62.1	72	25	34	0	0	0	0	17	4	0	.235	3	9	0	0	0.8	1.000
1967		0	3	.000	7.79	4	4	0	17.1	13	13	18	0	0	0	0	4	1	0	.250	1	4	0	0	1.3	1.000
1969		9	3	.750	2.24	42	4	1	100.1	89	47	92	0	8	2	12	24	4	0	.167	6	19	4	2	0.7	.862
1970		4	6	.400	3.26	57	0	0	91	77	49	81	0	4	6	10	13	4	0	.308	9	17	3	0	0.5	.897
1971		11	4	.733	1.70	51	1	0	111	73	41	109	0	11	4	8	18	4	1	.222	2	12	1	2	0.3	.933
1972		8	6	.571	1.70	54	0	0	106	71	40	92	0	8	6	27	20	2	0	.100	6	13	0	0	0.4	1.000
1973		5	6	.455	3.87	60	2	0	118.2	106	55	81	0	5	6	25	24	4	0	.167	8	19	1	1	0.5	.964
1974		6	11	.353	4.15	41	4	1	89	96	32	54	1	4	9	3	14	1	0	.071	2	13	3	0	0.4	.833
1975	PHI N	9	6	.600	2.97	56	0	0	103	84	36	55	0	9	6	14	13	2	0	.154	4	15	1	2	0.4	.950
1976		7	6	.538	2.50	58	0	0	97.1	81	42	76	0	7	6	11	7	1	0	.143	4	12	4	0	0.3	.800
1977		7	3	.700	2.62	45	0	0	79	62	24	58	0	7	3	9	10	4	0	.400	2	13	0	2	0.3	1.000
1978		8	7	.533	3.20	55	1	0	90	82	23	63	0	8	6	9	4	0	0	.000	4	13	1	2	0.3	.944
1979		4	3	.571	5.14	65	1	0	84	83	29	57	0	4	3	16	6	1	0	.167	6	4	0	0	0.2	1.000
1980		5	4	.556	1.47	57	0	0	92	62	23	75	0	5	4	20	8	2	0	.250	3	15	0	1	0.3	1.000
1981		2	4	.333	2.66	34	0	0	44	35	14	26	0	2	4	10	1	0	0	.000	3	4	0	0	0.2	1.000
1982		3	3	.500	4.31	34	0	0	39.2	50	12	25	0	3	3	5	2	0	0	.000	4	7	0	1	0.3	1.000
1983		2	1	.667	3.56	34	1	0	55.2	58	19	30	0	2	0	0	3	1	0	.333	1	10	1	1	0.4	.917
1984		2	0	1.000	3.79	25	0	0	38	36	10	26	0	2	0	0	3	1	0	.333	2	6	1	0	0.4	.889
19 yrs.		96	92	.511	3.13	824	39	5	1516	1318	582	1109	1	89	69	180	214	39	1	.182	75	219	23	16	0.4	.927
DIVISIONAL PLAYOFF SERIES																										
1981	PHI N	1	0	1.000	0.00	2	0	0	4	2	0	2	0	1	0	0	0	0	0	—	0	0	0	0	0.0	.000
LEAGUE CHAMPIONSHIP SERIES																										
1969	NY N	0	0	—	0.00	1	0	0	3	1	1	1	0	0	0	1	0	0	0	—	0	0	0	0	0.0	.000
1973		0	0	—	0.00	2	0	0	5	4	3	3	0	0	0	1	1	0	0	.000	2	0	1	0	1.5	.667
1976	PHI N	0	0	—	11.57	2	0	0	2.1	4	1	5	0	0	0	0	0	0	0	—	0	1	0	0	0.5	1.000
1977		0	0	—	0.00	2	0	0	3	1	2	3	0	0	0	1	0	0	0	—	0	0	0	0	0.0	.000
1978		0	1	.000	1.59	3	0	0	5.2	3	5	5	0	0	0	0	0	0	0	—	0	0	0	0	0.0	.000
1980		0	1	.000	4.50	5	0	0	8	8	4	5	0	0	1	2	1	0	0	.000	0	0	0	0	0.0	.000
6 yrs.		0	2	.000	2.67	15	0	0	27	21	16	22	0	0	2	5	2	0	0	.000	2	1	1	0	0.3	.750
						1st					**10th**					**2nd**										
WORLD SERIES																										
1973	NY N	1	0	1.000	2.63	5	0	0	13.2	8	9	14	0	1	0	1	3	1	0	.333	0	3	0	0	0.6	1.000
1980	PHI N	1	1	.500	1.17	4	0	0	7.2	7	8	10	0	1	1	2	0	0	0	—	0	1	0	0	0.3	1.000
2 yrs.		2	1	.667	2.11	9	0	0	21.1	15	17	24	0	2	1	3	3	1	0	.333	0	4	0	0	0.4	1.000
																4th										

Scott McGregor

McGREGOR, SCOTT HOUSTON
B. Jan. 18, 1954, Inglewood, Calif.
BB TL 6′ 1″ 190 lbs.

Year	Team	W	L	PCT	ERA	G	GS	CG	IP	H	BB	SO	ShO	Relief Pitching W	Relief Pitching L	Relief Pitching SV	Batting AB	Batting H	Batting HR	BA	PO	A	E	DP	TC/G	FA
1976	BAL A	0	1	.000	3.60	3	2	0	15	17	5	6	0	0	0	0	0	0	0	—	2	3	0	0	1.7	1.000
1977		3	5	.375	4.42	29	5	1	114	119	30	55	0	1	4	4	0	0	0	—	3	15	1	1	0.7	.947
1978		15	13	.536	3.32	35	32	13	233	217	47	94	4	1	0	1	0	0	0	—	11	38	2	5	1.5	.961
1979		13	6	.684	3.34	27	23	7	175	165	23	81	2	0	0	0	0	0	0	—	10	21	0	0	1.1	1.000
1980		20	8	.714	3.32	36	36	12	252	254	58	119	4	0	0	0	0	0	0	—	8	28	0	0	1.0	1.000
1981		13	5	.722	3.26	24	22	8	160	167	40	82	3	0	0	0	0	0	0	—	8	29	0	2	1.5	1.000
1982		14	12	.538	4.61	37	37	7	226.1	238	52	84	1	0	0	0	0	0	0	—	11	30	0	1	1.1	1.000
1983		18	7	.720	3.18	36	36	12	260	271	45	86	2	0	0	0	0	0	0	—	19	35	2	2	1.6	.964
1984		15	12	.556	3.94	30	30	10	196.1	216	54	67	3	0	0	0	0	0	0	—	14	35	1	2	1.7	.980
1985		14	14	.500	4.81	35	34	8	204	226	65	86	1	0	0	0	0	0	0	—	13	26	1	2	1.1	.975
1986		11	15	.423	4.52	34	33	4	203	216	57	95	2	0	0	0	0	0	0	—	12	27	1	2	1.2	.975
1987		2	7	.222	6.64	26	15	1	85.1	112	35	39	1	0	0	0	0	0	0	—	7	25	1	1	1.3	.970
1988		0	3	.000	8.83	4	4	0	17.1	27	7	10	0	0	0	0	0	0	0	—	1	5	0	0	1.5	1.000
13 yrs.		138	108	.561	3.99	356	309	83	2141.1	2245	518	904	23	2	4	5	0	0	0		119	317	9	18	1.3	.980
LEAGUE CHAMPIONSHIP SERIES																										
1979	BAL A	1	0	1.000	0.00	1	1	1	9	6	1	4	1	0	0	0	0	0	0	—	0	0	0	0	0.0	.000
1983		0	1	.000	1.35	1	1	0	6.2	6	3	2	0	0	0	0	0	0	0	—	1	1	0	0	2.0	1.000
2 yrs.		1	1	.500	0.57	2	2	1	15.2	12	4	6	1	0	0	0	0	0	0		1	1	0	0	1.0	1.000
													1st													

Scott McGregor *continued*

Year	Team	Lg	W	L	PCT	ERA	G	GS	CG	IP	H	BB	SO	ShO	Relief Pitching W	Relief Pitching L	Relief Pitching SV	Batting AB	Batting H	HR	BA	PO	A	E	DP	TC/G	FA
WORLD SERIES																											
1979	BAL	A	1	1	.500	3.18	2	2	1	17	16	2	8	0	0	0	0	4	0	0	.000	1	2	0	0	1.5	1.000
1983			1	1	.500	1.06	2	2	1	17	9	2	12	1	0	0	0	5	0	0	.000	0	0	0	0	0.0	.000
2 yrs.			2	2	.500	2.12	4	4	2	34	25	4	20	1	0	0	0	9	0	0	.000	1	2	0	0	0.8	1.000

Slim McGrew

McGREW, WALTER HOWARD BR TR 6′ 7½″ 235 lbs.
B. Aug. 5, 1899, Yoakum, Tex. D. Aug. 21, 1967, Houston, Tex.

Year	Team	Lg	W	L	PCT	ERA	G	GS	CG	IP	H	BB	SO	ShO	Relief Pitching W	Relief Pitching L	Relief Pitching SV	Batting AB	Batting H	HR	BA	PO	A	E	DP	TC/G	FA
1922	WAS	A	0	0	—	10.80	1	0	0	1.2	4	2	1	0	0	0	0	1	0	0	.000	0	2	0	0	2.0	1.000
1923			0	0	—	12.60	3	0	0	5	11	3	1	0	0	0	0	1	0	0	.000	0	3	1	0	1.3	.750
1924			0	1	.000	5.01	6	2	0	23.1	25	12	8	0	0	0	0	8	0	0	.000	0	3	0	0	0.5	1.000
3 yrs.			0	1	.000	6.60	10	2	0	30	40	17	10	0	0	0	0	10	0	0	.000	0	8	1	0	0.9	.889

McGuire

McGUIRE TL
Deceased.

Year	Team	Lg	W	L	PCT	ERA	G	GS	CG	IP	H	BB	SO	ShO	Relief Pitching W	Relief Pitching L	Relief Pitching SV	Batting AB	Batting H	HR	BA	PO	A	E	DP	TC/G	FA
1894	CIN	N	0	0	—	10.50	1	0	0	6	15	5	1	0	0	0	0	4	1	0	.250	0	2	0	0	2.0	1.000

Deacon McGuire

McGUIRE, JAMES THOMAS BR TR 6′ 1″ 185 lbs.
B. Nov. 18, 1863, Youngstown, Ohio D. Oct. 31, 1936, Duck Lake, Mich.
Manager 1898, 1907–11.

Year	Team	Lg	W	L	PCT	ERA	G	GS	CG	IP	H	BB	SO	ShO	Relief Pitching W	Relief Pitching L	Relief Pitching SV	Batting AB	Batting H	HR	BA	PO	A	E	DP	TC/G	FA
1890	ROC	AA	0	0	—	*6.75*	1	0	0	4	10	1	1	0	0	0	0	*				231	61	32	1	6.8	.901

Tom McGuire

McGUIRE, THOMAS PATRICK (Elmer) BR TR 6′ 175 lbs.
B. Feb. 1, 1892, Chicago, Ill. D. Dec. 7, 1959, Phoenix, Ariz.

Year	Team	Lg	W	L	PCT	ERA	G	GS	CG	IP	H	BB	SO	ShO	Relief Pitching W	Relief Pitching L	Relief Pitching SV	Batting AB	Batting H	HR	BA	PO	A	E	DP	TC/G	FA
1914	CHI	F	5	7	.417	3.70	24	12	7	131.1	143	57	37	0	0	3	0	70	19	1	.271	4	52	4	2	1.9	.933
1919	CHI	A	0	0	—	9.00	1	0	0	3	5	3	0	0	0	0	0	1	0	0	.000	0	3	0	0	3.0	1.000
2 yrs.			5	7	.417	3.82	25	12	7	134.1	148	60	37	0	0	3	0	71	19	1	.268	4	55	4	2	1.9	.937

Bill McGunnigle

McGUNNIGLE, WILLIAM HENRY (Gunner) BR TR 5′ 9″ 155 lbs.
B. Jan. 1, 1855, Boston, Mass. D. Mar. 9, 1899, Brockton, Mass.
Manager 1888–91, 1896.

Year	Team	Lg	W	L	PCT	ERA	G	GS	CG	IP	H	BB	SO	ShO	Relief Pitching W	Relief Pitching L	Relief Pitching SV	Batting AB	Batting H	HR	BA	PO	A	E	DP	TC/G	FA
1879	BUF	N	9	5	.643	2.63	14	13	13	120	113	16	62	2	0	**1**	0	171	30	0	.175	64	35	9	2	2.3	.917
1880			2	3	.400	3.41	5	5	4	37	43	8	3	1	0	0	0	26	4	0	.154	6	4	2	0	1.3	.833
2 yrs.			11	8	.579	2.81	19	18	17	157	156	24	65	3	0	1	0	*				70	39	11	2	2.1	.908

Marty McHale

McHALE, MARTIN JOSEPH BR TR 5′11½″ 174 lbs.
B. Oct. 30, 1888, Stoneham, Mass. D. May 7, 1979, Hempstead, N. Y.

Year	Team	Lg	W	L	PCT	ERA	G	GS	CG	IP	H	BB	SO	ShO	Relief Pitching W	Relief Pitching L	Relief Pitching SV	Batting AB	Batting H	HR	BA	PO	A	E	DP	TC/G	FA
1910	BOS	A	0	2	.000	4.61	2	2	1	13.2	15	6	14	0	0	0	0	6	0	0	.000	0	3	0	0	1.5	1.000
1911			0	0	—	9.64	4	1	0	9.1	19	3	3	0	0	0	0	3	0	0	.000	0	4	0	0	1.0	1.000
1913	NY	A	2	4	.333	2.96	7	6	4	48.2	49	10	11	1	0	0	0	15	0	0	.000	0	11	1	2	1.7	.917
1914			7	16	.304	2.97	31	23	12	191	195	33	75	0	1	0	1	60	12	0	.200	3	45	9	2	1.8	.842
1915			3	7	.300	4.25	13	11	6	78.1	86	19	25	0	0	0	0	21	3	0	.143	7	22	1	0	2.3	.967
1916	2 teams	BOS A (2G 0–1) CLE A (5G 0–0)																									
″	total		0	1	.000	4.67	7	1	0	17.1	17	10	3	0	0	0	0	2	0	0	.000	1	5	0	0	0.9	1.000
6 yrs.			12	30	.286	3.57	64	44	23	358.1	381	81	131	1	1	0	1	107	15	0	.140	11	90	11	4	1.8	.902

Vance McIlree

McILREE, VANCE ELMER BR TR 6′ 160 lbs.
B. Oct. 14, 1897, Riverside, Iowa D. May 6, 1959, Kansas City, Mo.

Year	Team	Lg	W	L	PCT	ERA	G	GS	CG	IP	H	BB	SO	ShO	Relief Pitching W	Relief Pitching L	Relief Pitching SV	Batting AB	Batting H	HR	BA	PO	A	E	DP	TC/G	FA
1921	WAS	A	0	0	—	9.00	1	0	0	1	1	0	0	0	0	0	0	0	0	0	—	0	0	0	0	0.0	.000

Irish McIlveen

McILVEEN, HENRY COOKE BL TL 5′11½″ 180 lbs.
B. July 27, 1880, Belfast, Ireland D. Oct. 18, 1960, Lorain, Ohio.

Year	Team	Lg	W	L	PCT	ERA	G	GS	CG	IP	H	BB	SO	ShO	Relief Pitching W	Relief Pitching L	Relief Pitching SV	Batting AB	Batting H	HR	BA	PO	A	E	DP	TC/G	FA
1906	PIT	N	0	1	.000	7.71	2	1	0	7	10	2	3	0	0	0	0	*				1	2	0	0	1.5	1.000

Stover McIlwain

McILWAIN, STOVER WILLIAM (Smokey) BR TR 6′ 2″ 195 lbs.
B. Sept. 22, 1939, Savannah, Ga. D. Jan. 15, 1966, Buffalo, N. Y.

Year	Team	Lg	W	L	PCT	ERA	G	GS	CG	IP	H	BB	SO	ShO	Relief Pitching W	Relief Pitching L	Relief Pitching SV	Batting AB	Batting H	HR	BA	PO	A	E	DP	TC/G	FA
1957	CHI	A	0	0	—	0.00	1	0	0	1	2	1	0	0	0	0	0	0	0	0	—	0	0	0	0	0.0	.000
1958			0	0	—	2.25	1	1	0	4	4	0	4	0	0	0	0	1	0	0	.000	1	0	0	0	1.0	1.000
2 yrs.			0	0		1.80	2	1	0	5	6	1	4	0	0	0	0	1	0	0	.000	1	0	0	0	0.5	1.000

Harry McIntire

McINTIRE, JOHN REID (Rocks) BR TR 5′11″ 180 lbs.
B. Jan. 11, 1879, Dayton, Ohio D. Jan. 9, 1949, Daytona Beach, Fla.

Year	Team	Lg	W	L	PCT	ERA	G	GS	CG	IP	H	BB	SO	ShO	Relief Pitching W	Relief Pitching L	Relief Pitching SV	Batting AB	Batting H	HR	BA	PO	A	E	DP	TC/G	FA
1905	BKN	N	8	25	.242	3.70	40	35	29	309	**340**	101	135	1	0	1	1	138	34	1	.246	13	73	11	2	2.2	.887
1906			13	21	.382	2.97	39	31	25	276	254	89	121	4	2	2	3	103	18	0	.175	10	78	3	4	2.2	.967
1907			7	15	.318	2.39	28	22	19	199.2	178	79	49	3	1	0	0	69	15	0	.217	7	56	6	2	2.5	.913
1908			11	20	.355	2.69	40	35	26	288	259	90	108	4	0	1	2	100	20	0	.200	6	76	4	5	2.2	.953
1909			7	17	.292	3.63	32	26	20	228	200	91	84	2	0	1	0	76	13	0	.171	6	62	4	3	2.3	.944
1910	CHI	N	13	9	.591	3.07	28	19	10	176	152	50	65	2	4	1	0	66	17	1	.258	4	48	3	0	2.0	.945
1911			11	7	.611	4.11	25	17	9	149	147	33	56	1	2	0	0	53	14	0	.264	1	42	0	0	1.7	1.000
1912			1	2	.333	3.80	4	3	2	23.2	22	6	8	0	0	1	0	10	3	0	.300	1	6	1	0	2.0	.875
1913	CIN	N	0	1	.000	27.00	1	0	0	1	3	0	0	0	0	1	0	0	0	0	—	0	0	0	0	0.0	.000
9 yrs.			71	117	.378	3.22	237	188	140	1650.1	1555	539	626	17	9	8	6	*				48	441	32	16	2.1	.939
WORLD SERIES																											
1910	CHI	N	0	1	.000	6.75	2	0	0	5.1	4	3	3	0	0	1	0	*				0	2	1	0	1.5	.667

Joe McIntosh

McINTOSH, JOSEPH ANTHONY BB TR 6′ 2″ 185 lbs.
B. Aug. 4, 1951, Billings, Mont.

Year	Team	Lg	W	L	PCT	ERA	G	GS	CG	IP	H	BB	SO	ShO	Relief Pitching W	Relief Pitching L	Relief Pitching SV	Batting AB	Batting H	HR	BA	PO	A	E	DP	TC/G	FA
1974	SD	N	0	4	.000	3.65	10	5	0	37	36	17	22	0	0	0	0	10	0	0	.000	1	4	0	1	0.5	1.000
1975			8	15	.348	3.69	37	28	4	183	195	60	71	1	1	3	0	48	9	0	.188	12	26	0	1	1.0	1.000
2 yrs.			8	19	.296	3.68	47	33	4	220	231	77	93	1	1	3	0	58	9	0	.155	13	30	0	2	0.9	1.000

Frank McIntyre

McINTYRE, FRANK W.
B. July 12, 1859, Walled Lake, Mich. D. July 8, 1887, Detroit, Mich.

Year	Team	W	L	PCT	ERA	G	GS	CG	IP	H	BB	SO	ShO	Relief Pitching W	Relief Pitching L	Relief Pitching SV	Batting AB	Batting H	HR	BA	PO	A	E	DP	TC/G	FA
1883	2 teams DET N (1G 1–0) COL AA (2G 1–1)																									
"	total	2	1	.667	3.60	3	3	3	30	31	8	6	0	0	0	0	11	0	0	.000	0	4	0	0	1.3	1.000

Doc McJames

McJAMES, JAMES McCUTCHEN TR
Born James McCutchen James.
B. Aug. 27, 1873, Williamsburg, S. C. D. Sept. 23, 1901, Charleston, S. C.

Year	Team	W	L	PCT	ERA	G	GS	CG	IP	H	BB	SO	ShO	Relief Pitching W	Relief Pitching L	Relief Pitching SV	Batting AB	Batting H	HR	BA	PO	A	E	DP	TC/G	FA
1895	WAS N	1	1	.500	1.59	2	2	2	17	17	16	9	0	0	0	0	7	1	0	.143	0	4	0	0	2.0	1.000
1896		12	20	.375	4.27	37	33	29	280.1	310	135	103	0	0	0	1	111	18	0	.162	9	66	9	2	2.3	.893
1897		15	23	.395	3.61	44	39	33	323.2	361	137	**156**	**3**	2	1	2	124	21	0	.169	7	72	7	1	2.0	.919
1898	BAL N	27	15	.643	2.36	45	42	40	374	327	113	178	2	1	1	0	149	27	0	.181	12	70	7	1	2.0	.921
1899	BKN N	19	15	.559	3.50	37	34	27	275.1	295	122	105	1	1	0	1	112	19	0	.170	6	78	7	3	2.5	.923
1901		5	6	.455	4.75	13	12	6	91	104	40	42	0	0	1	0	34	1	0	.029	2	17	5	0	1.8	.792
6 yrs.		79	80	.497	3.43	178	162	137	1361.1	1414	563	593	6	4	3	4	537	87	0	.162	36	307	35	7	2.1	.907

Archie McKain

McKAIN, ARCHIE RICHARD (Happy) BB TL 5′10″ 175 lbs.
B. May 12, 1911, Delphos, Kans. D. May 21, 1985, Salina, Kans. BL 1941, 1943

Year	Team	W	L	PCT	ERA	G	GS	CG	IP	H	BB	SO	ShO	Relief Pitching W	Relief Pitching L	Relief Pitching SV	Batting AB	Batting H	HR	BA	PO	A	E	DP	TC/G	FA
1937	BOS A	8	8	.500	4.66	36	18	3	137	152	64	66	0	2	0	2	49	13	0	.265	4	27	3	0	0.9	.912
1938		5	4	.556	4.52	37	5	1	99.2	119	44	27	0	3	3	6	31	2	0	.065	10	26	2	1	1.0	.947
1939	DET A	5	6	.455	3.68	32	11	4	129.2	120	54	49	1	4	2	4	41	9	2	.220	1	15	2	0	0.6	.889
1940		5	0	1.000	2.82	27	0	0	51	48	25	24	0	5	0	3	7	1	0	.143	2	16	0	0	0.7	1.000
1941	2 teams DET A (15G 2–1) STL A (8G 0–1)																									
"	total	2	2	.500	5.60	23	0	0	53	74	15	16	0	2	2	1	13	0	0	.000	2	24	0	2	1.1	1.000
1943	STL A	1	1	.500	3.94	10	0	0	16	16	6	6	0	1	1	0	1	0	0	.000	1	4	1	0	0.6	.833
6 yrs.		26	21	.553	4.26	165	34	8	486.1	529	208	188	1	17	8	16	142	25	2	.176	20	112	8	3	0.8	.943
WORLD SERIES																										
1940	DET A	0	0	—	3.00	1	0	0	3	4	0	0	0	0	0	0	0	0	0	—	0	1	0	0	1.0	1.000

Hal McKain

McKAIN, HAROLD LEROY BL TR 5′11″ 185 lbs.
B. July 10, 1906, Logan, Iowa D. Jan. 24, 1970, Sacramento, Calif.

Year	Team	W	L	PCT	ERA	G	GS	CG	IP	H	BB	SO	ShO	Relief Pitching W	Relief Pitching L	Relief Pitching SV	Batting AB	Batting H	HR	BA	PO	A	E	DP	TC/G	FA
1927	CLE A	0	1	.000	4.09	2	1	0	11	18	4	5	0	0	0	0	4	0	0	.000	0	5	0	0	2.5	1.000
1929	CHI A	6	9	.400	3.65	34	10	4	158	158	85	33	1	3	4	1	44	10	0	.227	4	54	3	4	1.8	.951
1930		6	4	.600	5.56	32	5	0	89	108	42	52	0	6	1	5	31	13	0	.419	2	23	2	0	0.8	.926
1931		6	9	.400	5.71	27	8	3	112	134	57	39	0	6	3	0	42	5	0	.119	5	31	2	0	1.4	.947
1932		0	0	—	11.12	8	0	0	11.1	17	5	7	0	0	0	0	1	0	0	.000	1	4	1	0	0.8	.833
5 yrs.		18	23	.439	4.93	103	24	7	381.1	435	193	136	1	15	8	6	122	28	0	.230	12	117	8	4	1.3	.942

Reeve McKay

McKAY, REEVE STEWART TR 6′ 1½″ 168 lbs.
B. Nov. 16, 1881, Morgan, Tex. D. Jan. 18, 1946, Dallas, Tex.

Year	Team	W	L	PCT	ERA	G	GS	CG	IP	H	BB	SO	ShO	Relief Pitching W	Relief Pitching L	Relief Pitching SV	Batting AB	Batting H	HR	BA	PO	A	E	DP	TC/G	FA
1915	STL A	0	0	—	9.00	1	0	0	1	1	0	0	0	0	0	0	0	0	0	—	0	1	0	0	1.0	1.000

Jim McKee

McKEE, JAMES MARION BR TR 6′ 7″ 215 lbs.
B. Feb. 1, 1947, Columbus, Ohio.

Year	Team	W	L	PCT	ERA	G	GS	CG	IP	H	BB	SO	ShO	Relief Pitching W	Relief Pitching L	Relief Pitching SV	Batting AB	Batting H	HR	BA	PO	A	E	DP	TC/G	FA
1972	PIT N	1	0	1.000	0.00	2	0	0	5	2	1	4	0	1	0	0	0	0	0	—	0	0	0	0	0.0	.000
1973		0	1	.000	5.67	15	1	0	27	31	17	13	0	0	0	0	4	0	0	.000	0	4	2	0	0.4	.667
2 yrs.		1	1	.500	4.78	17	1	0	32	33	18	17	0	1	0	0	4	0	0	.000	0	4	2	0	0.4	.667

Rogers McKee

McKEE, ROGERS HORNSBY BL TL 6′ 1″ 160 lbs.
B. Sept. 16, 1926, Shelby, N. C.

Year	Team	W	L	PCT	ERA	G	GS	CG	IP	H	BB	SO	ShO	Relief Pitching W	Relief Pitching L	Relief Pitching SV	Batting AB	Batting H	HR	BA	PO	A	E	DP	TC/G	FA
1943	PHI N	1	0	1.000	6.08	4	1	1	13.1	12	10	1	0	0	0	0	5	1	0	.200	0	4	0	0	1.0	1.000
1944		0	0	—	4.50	1	0	0	2	2	1	0	0	0	0	0	0	0	0	—	1	0	0	0	1.0	1.000
2 yrs.		1	0	1.000	5.87	5	1	1	15.1	14	11	1	0	0	0	0	5	1	0	.200	1	4	0	0	1.0	1.000

Tim McKeithan

McKEITHAN, EMMETT JAMES BR TR 6′ 2″ 182 lbs.
B. Nov. 2, 1906, Lawndale, N. C. D. Aug. 20, 1969, Forest City, N. C.

Year	Team	W	L	PCT	ERA	G	GS	CG	IP	H	BB	SO	ShO	Relief Pitching W	Relief Pitching L	Relief Pitching SV	Batting AB	Batting H	HR	BA	PO	A	E	DP	TC/G	FA
1932	PHI A	0	1	.000	7.11	4	2	0	12.2	18	5	0	0	0	0	0	3	0	0	.000	0	4	0	0	1.0	1.000
1933		1	0	1.000	4.00	3	1	0	9	10	4	3	0	1	0	0	3	1	0	.333	1	2	0	0	1.0	1.000
1934		0	0	—	15.75	3	0	0	4	7	5	0	0	0	0	0	1	0	0	.000	0	0	0	0	0.0	.000
3 yrs.		1	1	.500	7.36	10	3	0	25.2	35	14	3	0	1	0	0	7	1	0	.143	1	6	0	0	0.7	1.000

Russ McKelvy

McKELVY, RUSSELL ERRETT BR TR
B. Sept. 8, 1854, Swissvale, Pa. D. Oct. 19, 1915, Omaha, Neb.

Year	Team	W	L	PCT	ERA	G	GS	CG	IP	H	BB	SO	ShO	Relief Pitching W	Relief Pitching L	Relief Pitching SV	Batting AB	Batting H	HR	BA	PO	A	E	DP	TC/G	FA
1878	IND N	0	2	.000	2.16	4	1	1	25	38	3	3	0	0	**1**	0	*				121	27	28	2	2.7	.841

Kit McKenna

McKENNA, JAMES WILLIAM
B. Feb. 10, 1873, Lynchburg, Va. D. Mar. 31, 1941, Lynchburg, Va.

Year	Team	W	L	PCT	ERA	G	GS	CG	IP	H	BB	SO	ShO	Relief Pitching W	Relief Pitching L	Relief Pitching SV	Batting AB	Batting H	HR	BA	PO	A	E	DP	TC/G	FA
1898	BKN N	2	6	.250	5.63	14	9	7	100.2	118	57	27	0	1	0	0	40	9	0	.225	1	34	1	0	2.6	.972
1899	BAL N	2	3	.400	4.60	8	4	4	45	66	19	7	0	1	0	1	17	1	0	.059	2	10	0	0	1.3	1.000
2 yrs.		4	9	.308	5.31	22	13	11	145.2	184	76	34	0	2	0	1	57	10	0	.175	3	44	1	0	2.1	.979

Limb McKenry

McKENRY, FRANK GORDON (Big Pete) BR TR 6′ 205 lbs.
B. Aug. 13, 1888, Piney Flats, Tenn. D. Nov. 1, 1956, Fresno, Calif.

Year	Team	W	L	PCT	ERA	G	GS	CG	IP	H	BB	SO	ShO	Relief Pitching W	Relief Pitching L	Relief Pitching SV	Batting AB	Batting H	HR	BA	PO	A	E	DP	TC/G	FA
1915	CIN N	5	5	.500	2.94	21	11	5	110.1	94	39	37	0	1	0	0	33	5	0	.152	3	36	2	3	2.0	.951
1916		1	1	.500	4.30	6	1	0	14.2	14	8	2	0	1	1	0	5	2	0	.400	0	4	0	0	0.7	1.000
2 yrs.		6	6	.500	3.10	27	12	5	125	108	47	39	0	2	1	0	38	7	0	.184	3	40	2	3	1.7	.956

Joel McKeon

McKEON, JOEL JACOB BL TL 6′ 185 lbs.
B. Feb. 25, 1963, Covington, Ky.

Year	Team	W	L	PCT	ERA	G	GS	CG	IP	H	BB	SO	ShO	Relief Pitching W	Relief Pitching L	Relief Pitching SV	Batting AB	Batting H	HR	BA	PO	A	E	DP	TC/G	FA
1986	CHI A	3	1	.750	2.45	30	0	0	33	18	17	18	0	3	1	1	0	0	0	—	2	2	0	0	0.1	1.000
1987		1	2	.333	9.43	13	0	0	21	27	15	14	0	1	2	0	0	0	0	—	4	0	0	0	0.3	1.000
2 yrs.		4	3	.571	5.17	43	0	0	54	45	32	32	0	4	3	1	0	0	0		6	2	0	0	0.2	1.000

Larry McKeon

McKEON, LAWRENCE G.
B. Mar. 25, 1866, New York, N. Y. D. July 18, 1915, Indianapolis, Ind.
5′10″ 168 lbs.

Year	Team	W	L	PCT	ERA	G	GS	CG	IP	H	BB	SO	ShO	Relief W	Relief L	Relief SV	Batting AB	Batting H	HR	BA	PO	A	E	DP	TC/G	FA
1884	IND AA	18	**41**	.305	*3.50*	61	60	59	512	488	94	308	2	0	0	0	247	53	0	.215	80	131	23	3	3.3	.902
1885	CIN AA	20	13	.606	*2.86*	33	33	32	290	273	50	117	2	0	0	0	121	20	0	.165	18	41	1	0	1.8	.983
1886	2 teams CIN AA	(19G 8–8)		KC N	(3G 0–2)																					
″	total	8	10	.444	5.75	22	22	19	177	218	62	49	0	0	0	0	84	19	0	.226	25	37	2	4	2.6	.969
3 yrs.		46	64	.418	3.71	116	115	110	979	979	206	474	4	0	0	0	452	92	0	.204	123	209	26	7	2.8	.927

Denny McLain

McLAIN, DENNIS DALE
B. Mar. 29, 1944, Chicago, Ill.
BR TR 6′ 1″ 185 lbs.

Year	Team	W	L	PCT	ERA	G	GS	CG	IP	H	BB	SO	ShO	Relief W	Relief L	Relief SV	Batting AB	Batting H	HR	BA	PO	A	E	DP	TC/G	FA
1963	DET A	2	1	.667	4.29	3	3	2	21	20	16	22	0	0	0	0	5	1	1	.200	0	6	2	2	2.7	.750
1964		4	5	.444	4.05	19	16	3	100	84	37	70	0	0	1	0	37	5	0	.135	4	6	1	0	0.6	.909
1965		16	6	.727	2.61	33	29	13	220.1	174	62	192	4	1	0	1	74	4	0	.054	17	30	1	1	1.5	.979
1966		20	14	.588	3.92	38	38	14	264.1	205	104	192	4	0	0	0	93	17	0	.183	14	34	0	2	1.3	1.000
1967		17	16	.515	3.79	37	37	10	235	209	73	161	3	0	0	0	85	10	0	.118	21	22	5	4	1.3	.896
1968		**31**	6	**.838**	1.96	41	**41**	**28**	**336**	241	63	280	6	0	0	0	111	18	0	.162	36	40	1	3	1.9	.987
1969		**24**	9	.727	2.80	42	**41**	23	**325**	**288**	67	181	**9**	0	0	0	106	17	0	.160	26	24	2	1	1.2	.962
1970		3	5	.375	4.65	14	14	1	91	100	28	52	0	0	0	0	31	2	0	.065	7	14	0	1	1.5	1.000
1971	WAS A	10	**22**	.313	4.27	33	32	9	217	233	72	103	3	1	0	0	58	6	0	.103	27	26	0	1	1.6	1.000
1972	2 teams OAK A	(5G 1–2)		ATL N	(15G 3–5)																					
″	total	4	7	.364	6.39	20	13	2	76	92	26	29	0	1	1	1	16	2	0	.125	2	10	1	0	0.6	.923
10 yrs.		131	91	.590	3.39	280	264	105	1885.2	1646	548	1282	29	3	2	2	616	82	1	.133	154	212	13	15	1.4	.966
WORLD SERIES																										
1968	DET A	1	2	.333	3.24	3	3	1	16.2	18	4	13	0	0	0	0	6	0	0	.000	0	3	1	0	1.3	.750

Barney McLaughlin

McLAUGHLIN, BERNARD
Brother of Frank McLaughlin.
B. 1857, Ireland D. Feb. 13, 1921, Lowell, Mass.
BR TR 5′ 8″ 163 lbs.

Year	Team	W	L	PCT	ERA	G	GS	CG	IP	H	BB	SO	ShO	Relief W	Relief L	Relief SV	Batting AB	Batting H	HR	BA	PO	A	E	DP	TC/G	FA
1884	KC U	1	3	.250	*5.36*	7	4	4	48.2	62	15	14	0	1	0	0	*				58	49	24	8	2.9	.817

Bo McLaughlin

McLAUGHLIN, MICHAEL DUANE
B. Oct. 23, 1953, Oakland, Calif.
BR TR 6′ 5″ 210 lbs.

Year	Team	W	L	PCT	ERA	G	GS	CG	IP	H	BB	SO	ShO	Relief W	Relief L	Relief SV	Batting AB	Batting H	HR	BA	PO	A	E	DP	TC/G	FA
1976	HOU N	4	5	.444	2.85	17	11	4	79	71	17	32	2	0	0	1	19	0	0	.000	10	10	0	2	1.2	1.000
1977		4	7	.364	4.24	46	6	0	85	81	34	59	0	3	4	5	9	0	0	.000	7	15	2	1	0.5	.917
1978		0	1	.000	5.09	12	1	0	23	30	16	10	0	0	0	2	3	0	0	.000	1	3	0	0	0.3	1.000
1979	2 teams HOU N	(12G 1–2)		ATL N	(37G 1–1)																					
″	total	2	3	.400	5.05	49	1	0	66	85	20	57	0	1	3	0	6	0	0	.000	3	4	1	0	0.2	.875
1981	OAK A	0	0	—	11.25	11	0	0	12	17	9	3	0	0	0	1	0	0	0	—	2	1	0	0	0.3	1.000
1982		0	4	.000	4.84	21	2	1	48.1	51	27	27	0	0	2	0	0	0	0	—	0	0	0	0	0.0	.000
6 yrs.		10	20	.333	4.48	156	21	5	313.1	335	123	188	2	4	9	9	37	0	0	.000	23	33	3	3	0.4	.949

Byron McLaughlin

McLAUGHLIN, BYRON SCOTT
B. Sept. 29, 1955, Van Nuys, Calif.
BR TR 6′ 1″ 175 lbs.

Year	Team	W	L	PCT	ERA	G	GS	CG	IP	H	BB	SO	ShO	Relief W	Relief L	Relief SV	Batting AB	Batting H	HR	BA	PO	A	E	DP	TC/G	FA
1977	SEA A	0	0	—	36.00	1	0	0	1	5	0	1	0	0	0	0	0	0	0	—	0	0	0	0	0.0	.000
1978		4	8	.333	4.37	20	17	4	107	97	39	87	0	0	0	0	0	0	0	—	3	8	2	0	0.6	.846
1979		7	7	.500	4.21	47	7	1	124	114	60	74	0	6	2	14	0	0	0	—	6	11	1	0	0.4	.944
1980		3	6	.333	6.82	45	4	0	91	124	50	41	0	2	4	2	0	0	0	—	1	8	1	1	0.2	.900
1983	CAL A	2	4	.333	5.17	16	7	0	55.2	63	22	45	0	0	1	0	0	0	0	—	2	8	0	2	0.5	1.000
5 yrs.		16	25	.390	5.11	129	35	5	378.2	403	171	248	0	8	7	16	0	0	0		12	43	4	3	0.4	.932

Frank McLaughlin

McLAUGHLIN, FRANCIS EDWARD
Brother of Barney McLaughlin.
B. June 19, 1856, Lowell, Mass. D. Apr. 5, 1917, Lowell, Mass.
BR TR 5′ 9″ 160 lbs.

Year	Team	W	L	PCT	ERA	G	GS	CG	IP	H	BB	SO	ShO	Relief W	Relief L	Relief SV	Batting AB	Batting H	HR	BA	PO	A	E	DP	TC/G	FA
1883	PIT AA	0	0	—	*13.00*	2	0	0	9	14	3	1	0	0	0	0	114	25	1	.219	17	40	20	2	5.1	.740
1884	KC U	0	0	—	*5.40*	2	1	0	10	15	2	3	0	0	0	0	257	60	3	.233	114	133	62	15	4.5	.799
2 yrs.		0	0		9.00	4	1	0	19	29	5	4	0	0	0	0	*				155	258	107	21	4.5	.794

Jim McLaughlin

McLAUGHLIN, JAMES THOMAS
B. Nov. 18, 1860, Cleveland, Ohio D. Nov. 16, 1895, Cleveland, Ohio.
BL TL 157 lbs.

Year	Team	W	L	PCT	ERA	G	GS	CG	IP	H	BB	SO	ShO	Relief W	Relief L	Relief SV	Batting AB	Batting H	HR	BA	PO	A	E	DP	TC/G	FA
1884	BAL AA	1	2	.333	*3.68*	3	2	2	22	27	11	8	0	0	**1**	0	*				3	7	1	0	1.8	.909

Joey McLaughlin

McLAUGHLIN, JOEY RICHARD
B. July 11, 1956, Tulsa, Okla.
BR TR 6′ 2″ 205 lbs.

Year	Team	W	L	PCT	ERA	G	GS	CG	IP	H	BB	SO	ShO	Relief W	Relief L	Relief SV	Batting AB	Batting H	HR	BA	PO	A	E	DP	TC/G	FA
1977	ATL N	0	0	—	15.00	3	2	0	6	10	3	0	0	0	0	0	1	0	0	.000	0	3	0	0	1.0	1.000
1979		5	3	.625	2.48	37	0	0	69	54	34	40	0	5	3	5	11	2	0	.182	4	8	2	0	0.4	.857
1980	TOR A	6	9	.400	4.50	55	10	0	136	159	53	70	0	4	5	4	0	0	0	—	12	15	0	2	0.5	1.000
1981		1	5	.167	2.85	40	0	0	60	55	21	38	0	1	5	10	0	0	0	—	7	6	0	0	0.3	1.000
1982		8	6	.571	3.21	44	0	0	70	54	30	49	0	8	6	8	0	0	0	—	6	10	0	3	0.4	1.000
1983		7	4	.636	4.45	50	0	0	64.2	63	37	47	0	7	4	9	0	0	0	—	6	6	0	1	0.2	1.000
1984	2 teams TOR A	(6G 0–0)		TEX A	(15G 2–1)																					
″	total	2	1	.667	3.95	21	0	0	43.1	45	20	24	0	2	1	0	0	0	0		3	5	1	2	0.4	.889
7 yrs.		29	28	.509	3.85	250	12	0	449	440	198	268	0	27	24	36	12	2	0	.167	38	53	3	8	0.4	.968

Jud McLaughlin

McLAUGHLIN, JUSTIN THEODORE
B. Mar. 24, 1912, Brighton, Mass. D. Sept. 27, 1964, Cambridge, Mass.
BL TL 5′11″ 155 lbs.

Year	Team	W	L	PCT	ERA	G	GS	CG	IP	H	BB	SO	ShO	Relief W	Relief L	Relief SV	Batting AB	Batting H	HR	BA	PO	A	E	DP	TC/G	FA
1931	BOS A	0	0	—	12.00	9	0	0	12	23	8	3	0	0	0	0	0	0	0	—	1	4	1	1	0.7	.833
1932		0	0	—	15.00	1	0	0	3	5	4	0	0	0	0	0	1	0	0	.000	0	1	0	0	1.0	1.000
1933		0	0	—	6.23	6	0	0	8.2	14	5	1	0	0	0	0	0	0	0	—	0	1	0	0	0.2	1.000
3 yrs.		0	0		10.27	16	0	0	23.2	42	17	4	0	0	0	0	1	0	0	.000	1	6	1	1	0.5	.875

Pat McLaughlin

McLAUGHLIN, PATRICK ELMER BR TR 6′ 2″ 175 lbs.
B. Aug. 17, 1910, Taylor, Tex.

Year	Team		W	L	PCT	ERA	G	GS	CG	IP	H	BB	SO	ShO	Relief Pitching W	Relief Pitching L	Relief Pitching SV	Batting AB	Batting H	Batting HR	BA	PO	A	E	DP	TC/G	FA
1937	DET	A	0	2	.000	6.34	10	3	0	32.2	39	16	8	0	0	0	0	10	1	0	.100	1	3	0	0	0.4	1.000
1940	PHI	A	0	0	—	16.20	1	0	0	1.2	4	1	0	0	0	0	0	0	0	0	—	0	1	0	0	1.0	1.000
1945	DET	A	0	0	—	9.00	1	0	0	1	2	0	0	0	0	0	0	0	0	0	—	0	0	1	0	1.0	.000
3 yrs.			0	2	.000	6.88	12	3	0	35.1	45	17	8	0	0	0	0	10	1	0	.100	1	4	1	0	0.5	.833

Warren McLaughlin

McLAUGHLIN, WARREN A. TL
B. Jan. 22, 1876, N. Plainfield, N. J. D. Oct. 22, 1923, Plainfield, N. J.

Year	Team		W	L	PCT	ERA	G	GS	CG	IP	H	BB	SO	ShO	Relief Pitching W	Relief Pitching L	Relief Pitching SV	Batting AB	Batting H	Batting HR	BA	PO	A	E	DP	TC/G	FA
1900	PHI	N	0	0	—	4.50	1	0	0	6	4	6	1	0	0	0	0	2	1	0	.500	0	2	1	0	3.0	.667
1902	PIT	N	3	0	1.000	2.77	3	3	3	26	27	9	13	0	0	0	0	11	4	0	.364	1	1	0	0	0.7	1.000
1903	PHI	N	0	2	.000	7.04	3	2	2	23	38	11	3	0	0	1	0	10	2	0	.200	0	4	0	0	1.3	1.000
3 yrs.			3	2	.600	4.75	7	5	5	55	69	26	17	0	0	1	0	23	7	0	.304	1	7	1	0	1.3	.889

Mac McLean

McLEAN, ALBERT ELDON BR TR 6′ 175 lbs.
B. Sept. 20, 1912, Chicago, Ill. D. Sept. 29, 1990, Ashboro, N. C.

Year	Team		W	L	PCT	ERA	G	GS	CG	IP	H	BB	SO	ShO	Relief Pitching W	Relief Pitching L	Relief Pitching SV	Batting AB	Batting H	Batting HR	BA	PO	A	E	DP	TC/G	FA
1935	WAS	A	0	0	—	7.27	4	0	0	8.2	12	5	3	0	0	0	0	2	0	0	.000	0	0	0	0	0.0	.000

Wayne McLeland

McLELAND, WAYNE GAFFNEY (Nubbin) BR TR 6′ 180 lbs.
B. Aug. 29, 1924, Milton, Iowa

Year	Team		W	L	PCT	ERA	G	GS	CG	IP	H	BB	SO	ShO	Relief Pitching W	Relief Pitching L	Relief Pitching SV	Batting AB	Batting H	Batting HR	BA	PO	A	E	DP	TC/G	FA
1951	DET	A	0	1	.000	8.18	6	1	0	11	20	4	0	0	0	0	0	1	0	0	.000	2	3	1	0	1.0	.833
1952			0	0	—	10.13	4	0	0	2.2	4	6	0	0	0	0	0	0	0	0	—	0	0	0	0	0.0	.000
2 yrs.			0	1	.000	8.56	10	1	0	13.2	24	10	0	0	0	0	0	1	0	0	.000	2	3	1	0	0.6	.833

Cal McLish

McLISH, CALVIN COOLIDGE JULIUS CAESAR TUSKAHOMA (Buster) BB TR 6′ 179 lbs.
B. Dec. 1, 1925, Anadarko, Okla.

Year	Team		W	L	PCT	ERA	G	GS	CG	IP	H	BB	SO	ShO	Relief Pitching W	Relief Pitching L	Relief Pitching SV	Batting AB	Batting H	Batting HR	BA	PO	A	E	DP	TC/G	FA
1944	BKN	N	3	10	.231	7.82	23	13	3	84	110	48	24	0	0	2	0	32	7	0	.219	3	9	0	0	0.5	1.000
1946			0	0	—	∞	1	0	0		1	0	0	0	0	0	0	0	0	0	—	0	0	0	0	0.0	.000
1947	PIT	N	0	0	—	18.00	1	0	0	1	2	0	0	0	0	0	0	0	0	0	—	1	1	0	0	2.0	1.000
1948			0	0	—	9.00	2	1	0	5	8	2	1	0	0	0	0	1	0	0	.000	0	2	0	0	1.0	1.000
1949	CHI	N	1	1	.500	5.87	8	2	0	23	31	12	6	0	0	0	0	9	3	1	.333	3	6	1	1	1.3	.900
1951			4	10	.286	4.45	30	17	5	145.2	159	52	46	1	0	1	0	42	5	0	.119	14	22	1	6	1.2	.973
1956	CLE	A	2	4	.333	4.96	37	2	0	61.2	67	32	27	0	1	3	1	9	1	0	.111	5	14	0	0	0.5	1.000
1957			9	7	.563	2.74	42	7	2	144.1	117	67	88	0	7	5	1	43	8	2	.186	6	27	1	2	0.8	.971
1958			16	8	.667	2.99	39	30	13	225.2	214	70	97	0	0	0	1	64	6	0	.094	15	38	1	4	1.4	.981
1959			19	8	.704	3.63	35	32	13	235.1	**253**	72	113	0	0	0	1	74	14	0	.189	25	49	2	4	2.2	.974
1960	CIN	N	4	14	.222	4.16	37	21	2	151.1	170	48	56	1	0	3	0	41	2	0	.049	13	33	1	0	1.3	.979
1961	CHI	A	10	13	.435	4.38	31	27	4	162.1	178	47	80	0	0	0	1	54	9	0	.167	16	32	0	1	1.5	1.000
1962	PHI	N	11	5	.688	4.25	32	24	5	154.2	184	45	71	1	1	0	1	51	4	0	.078	17	20	0	2	1.2	1.000
1963			13	11	.542	3.26	32	32	10	209.2	184	56	98	2	0	0	0	69	14	0	.203	13	47	4	7	2.0	.938
1964			0	1	.000	3.38	2	1	0	5.1	6	1	6	0	0	0	0	1	0	0	.000	0	2	0	0	1.0	1.000
15 yrs.			92	92	.500	4.01	352	209	57	1609	1684	552	713	5	9	14	6	490	73	3	.149	131	302	11	27	1.3	.975

Sam McMackin

McMACKIN, SAMUEL TL
B. 1872, Cleveland, Ohio D. Feb. 11, 1903, Columbus, Ohio.

Year	Team		W	L	PCT	ERA	G	GS	CG	IP	H	BB	SO	ShO	Relief Pitching W	Relief Pitching L	Relief Pitching SV	Batting AB	Batting H	Batting HR	BA	PO	A	E	DP	TC/G	FA
1902	2 teams	CHI A (1G 0–0) DET A (1G 0–1)																									
″	total		0	1	.000	2.38	2	1	1	11.1	10	4	4	0	0	0	0	5	2	0	.400	1	6	0	0	3.5	1.000

Jack McMahan

McMAHAN, JACK WALLY BR TL 6′ 175 lbs.
B. July 22, 1932, Hot Springs, Ark.

Year	Team		W	L	PCT	ERA	G	GS	CG	IP	H	BB	SO	ShO	Relief Pitching W	Relief Pitching L	Relief Pitching SV	Batting AB	Batting H	Batting HR	BA	PO	A	E	DP	TC/G	FA
1956	2 teams	PIT N (11G 0–0) KC A (23G 0–5)																									
″	total		0	5	.000	5.04	34	9	0	75	87	40	22	0	0	0	0	15	0	0	.000	3	14	0	1	0.5	1.000

Doc McMahon

McMAHON, HENRY JOHN
B. Dec. 19, 1886, Woburn, Mass. D. Dec. 11, 1929, Woburn, Mass.

Year	Team		W	L	PCT	ERA	G	GS	CG	IP	H	BB	SO	ShO	Relief Pitching W	Relief Pitching L	Relief Pitching SV	Batting AB	Batting H	Batting HR	BA	PO	A	E	DP	TC/G	FA
1908	BOS	A	1	0	1.000	3.00	1	1	1	9	14	0	3	0	0	0	0	5	2	0	.400	1	2	1	0	4.0	.750

Don McMahon

McMAHON, DONALD JOHN BR TR 6′ 2″ 215 lbs.
B. Jan. 4, 1930, Brooklyn, N. Y. D. July 22, 1987, Los Angeles, Calif.

Year	Team		W	L	PCT	ERA	G	GS	CG	IP	H	BB	SO	ShO	Relief Pitching W	Relief Pitching L	Relief Pitching SV	Batting AB	Batting H	Batting HR	BA	PO	A	E	DP	TC/G	FA
1957	MIL	N	2	3	.400	1.54	32	0	0	46.2	33	29	46	0	2	3	9	8	2	0	.250	1	5	1	1	0.2	.857
1958			7	2	.778	3.68	38	0	0	58.2	50	29	37	0	7	2	8	9	1	0	.111	5	7	1	0	0.3	.923
1959			5	3	.625	2.57	60	0	0	80.2	81	37	55	0	5	3	**15**	9	2	0	.222	4	10	2	0	0.3	.875
1960			3	6	.333	5.94	48	0	0	63.2	66	32	50	0	3	6	10	11	0	0	.000	1	13	1	0	0.3	.933
1961			6	4	.600	2.84	53	0	0	92	84	51	55	0	6	4	8	16	3	0	.188	7	23	3	1	0.6	.909
1962	2 teams	MIL N (2G 0–1) HOU N (51G 5–5)																									
″	total		5	6	.455	1.69	53	0	0	79.2	56	33	72	0	5	6	8	12	1	0	.083	4	11	0	0	0.3	1.000
1963	HOU	N	1	5	.167	4.05	49	2	0	80	83	26	51	0	1	3	5	12	1	0	.083	5	12	1	2	0.4	.944
1964	CLE	A	6	4	.600	2.41	70	0	0	101	67	52	92	0	6	4	16	14	2	0	.143	5	10	0	0	0.2	1.000
1965			3	3	.500	3.28	58	0	0	85	79	37	60	0	3	3	11	9	2	0	.222	10	15	0	3	0.4	1.000
1966	2 teams	CLE A (12G 1–1) BOS A (49G 8–7)																									
″	total		9	8	.529	2.69	61	0	0	90.1	73	44	62	0	9	8	10	13	1	0	.077	7	10	0	1	0.3	1.000
1967	2 teams	BOS A (11G 1–2) CHI A (52G 5–0)																									
″	total		6	2	.750	1.98	63	0	0	109.1	68	40	84	0	6	2	5	13	2	0	.154	7	16	1	1	0.4	.958
1968	2 teams	CHI A (25G 2–1) DET A (20G 3–1)																									
″	total		5	2	.714	1.98	45	0	0	81.2	53	30	65	0	5	2	1	7	1	0	.143	3	8	0	0	0.2	1.000
1969	2 teams	DET A (34G 3–5) SF N (13G 3–1)																									
″	total		6	6	.500	3.54	47	0	0	61	38	27	59	0	6	6	13	9	1	0	.111	0	11	0	1	0.2	1.000
1970	SF	N	9	5	.643	2.97	61	0	0	94	70	45	74	0	**9**	5	19	14	2	0	.143	8	9	0	0	0.3	1.000
1971			10	6	.625	4.06	61	0	0	82	73	37	71	0	10	6	4	7	0	0	.000	8	14	0	1	0.4	1.000
1972			3	3	.500	3.71	44	0	0	63	46	21	45	0	3	3	5	4	1	0	.250	4	7	0	1	0.3	1.000
1973			4	0	1.000	1.50	22	0	0	30	21	7	20	0	4	0	6	1	1	0	1.000	3	5	0	0	0.4	1.000
1974			0	0	—	3.00	9	0	0	12	13	2	5	0	0	0	0	0	0	0	—	1	1	0	0	0.2	1.000
18 yrs.			90	68	.570	2.96	874	2	0	1310.2	1054	579	1003	0	90 **10th**	66	153	168	23	0	.137	83	187	10	12	0.3	.964

Don McMahon *continued*

Year	Team	Lg	W	L	PCT	ERA	G	GS	CG	IP	H	BB	SO	ShO	Relief W	Relief L	Relief SV	AB	H	HR	BA	PO	A	E	DP	TC/G	FA
LEAGUE CHAMPIONSHIP SERIES																											
1971	SF	N	0	0	—	0.00	2	0	0	3	0	0	3	0	0	0	0	0	0	0	—	1	1	0	0	1.0	1.000
WORLD SERIES																											
1957	MIL	N	0	0	—	0.00	3	0	0	5	3	3	5	0	0	0	0	0	0	0	—	0	2	0	0	0.7	1.000
1958			0	0	—	5.40	3	0	0	3.1	3	3	5	0	0	0	0	0	0	0	—	1	0	0	0	0.3	1.000
1968	DET	A	0	0	—	13.50	2	0	0	2	4	0	1	0	0	0	0	0	0	0	—	1	0	0	0	0.5	1.000
3 yrs.			0	0		4.35	8	0	0	10.1	10	6	11	0	0	0	0	0	0	0		2	2	0	0	0.5	1.000

Sadie McMahon

McMAHON, JOHN JOSEPH
B. Sept. 19, 1867, Wilmington, Del. D. Feb. 20, 1954, Delaware City, Del.
BR TR 5′ 9″ 165 lbs.

Year	Team	Lg	W	L	PCT	ERA	G	GS	CG	IP	H	BB	SO	ShO	Relief W	Relief L	Relief SV	AB	H	HR	BA	PO	A	E	DP	TC/G	FA
1889	PHI	AA	14	12	.538	3.53	30	27	29	242	230	102	117	2	0	1	0	104	16	0	.154	7	62	6	6	2.5	.920
1890	2 teams	PHI AA (48G 29–18) BAL AA (12G 7–3)																									
″	total		**36**	21	.632	3.29	**60**	**57**	**55**	**509**	**498**	166	**291**	1	0	1	1	214	44	2	.206	42	140	12	8	3.2	.938
1891	BAL	AA	**35**	24	.593	2.81	61	**58**	**53**	**503**	493	149	219	**5**	2	0	1	210	43	1	.205	14	141	11	4	2.6	.934
1892	BAL	N	19	25	.432	3.24	48	46	44	397	430	145	118	2	0	0	1	177	25	0	.141	15	95	13	2	2.5	.894
1893			23	18	.561	4.37	43	40	35	346.1	378	156	79	0	0	1	1	148	36	0	.243	16	75	18	2	2.5	.835
1894			25	8	.758	4.21	35	33	26	275.2	317	111	60	0	0	1	0	126	36	0	.286	17	62	5	2	2.4	.940
1895			10	4	.714	2.94	15	15	15	122.1	110	32	37	**4**	0	0	0	51	16	0	.314	3	23	2	0	1.9	.929
1896			11	9	.550	3.48	22	22	19	175.2	195	55	33	0	0	0	0	73	9	0	.123	3	48	5	1	2.5	.911
1897	BKN	N	0	6	.000	5.86	9	7	5	63	75	29	13	0	0	1	0	25	5	0	.200	3	16	1	0	2.2	.950
9 yrs.			173	127	.577	3.51	323	305	281	2634	2726	945	967	14	2	5	4	1128	230	3	.204	120	662	73	25	2.6	.915

John McMakin

McMAKIN, JOHN WEAVER (Spartanburg John)
B. Mar. 6, 1878, Spartanburg, S. C. D. Sept. 25, 1956, Lyman, S. C.
BR TL 5′11″ 165 lbs.

Year	Team	Lg	W	L	PCT	ERA	G	GS	CG	IP	H	BB	SO	ShO	Relief W	Relief L	Relief SV	AB	H	HR	BA	PO	A	E	DP	TC/G	FA
1902	BKN	N	2	2	.500	3.09	4	4	4	32	34	11	6	0	0	0	0	11	2	0	.182	0	9	0	0	2.3	1.000

Joe McManus

McMANUS, JOAB LOGAN
B. Sept. 7, 1887, Palmyra, Ill. D. Dec. 23, 1955, Beckley, W. Va.
BR TR 6′ 1″ 185 lbs.

Year	Team	Lg	W	L	PCT	ERA	G	GS	CG	IP	H	BB	SO	ShO	Relief W	Relief L	Relief SV	AB	H	HR	BA	PO	A	E	DP	TC/G	FA
1913	CIN	N	0	0	—	18.00	1	0	0	2	3	4	1	0	0	0	0	0	0	0	—	0	1	0	0	1.0	1.000

Pat McManus

McMANUS, PATRICK
B. Ireland D. Oct. 6, 1917, Brooklyn, N. Y.

Year	Team	Lg	W	L	PCT	ERA	G	GS	CG	IP	H	BB	SO	ShO	Relief W	Relief L	Relief SV	AB	H	HR	BA	PO	A	E	DP	TC/G	FA
1879	TRO	N	0	2	.000	3.00	2	2	2	21	24	1	6	0	0	0	0	8	1	0	.125	2	5	0	0	3.5	1.000

Greg McMichael

McMICHAEL, GREGORY WINSTON
B. Dec. 1, 1966, Knoxville, Tenn.
BR TR 6′ 3″ 215 lbs.

Year	Team	Lg	W	L	PCT	ERA	G	GS	CG	IP	H	BB	SO	ShO	Relief W	Relief L	Relief SV	AB	H	HR	BA	PO	A	E	DP	TC/G	FA
1993	ATL	N	2	3	.400	2.06	74	0	0	91.2	68	29	89	0	2	3	19	4	0	0	.000	7	18	1	2	0.4	.962
1994			4	6	.400	3.84	51	0	0	58.2	66	19	47	0	4	**6**	21	1	0	0	.000	2	6	2	0	0.2	.800
1995			7	2	.778	2.79	67	0	0	80.2	64	32	74	0	7	2	2	6	0	0	.000	4	6	1	0	0.2	.909
3 yrs.			13	11	.542	2.77	192	0	0	231	198	80	210	0	13	11	42	11	0	0	.000	13	30	4	2	0.2	.915
DIVISIONAL PLAYOFF SERIES																											
1995	ATL	N	0	0	—	6.75	2	0	0	1.1	1	2	1	0	0	0	0	0	0	0	—	0	0	0	0	0.0	.000
LEAGUE CHAMPIONSHIP SERIES																											
1993	ATL	N	0	1	.000	6.75	4	0	0	4	7	2	1	0	0	1	0	0	0	0	—	0	1	0	0	0.3	1.000
1995			1	0	1.000	0.00	3	0	0	2.2	0	1	2	0	1	0	1	0	0	0	—	0	0	0	0	0.0	.000
2 yrs.			1	1	.500	4.05	7	0	0	6.2	7	3	3	0	1	1	1	0	0	0		0	1	0	0	0.1	1.000
WORLD SERIES																											
1995	ATL	N	0	0	—	2.70	3	0	0	3.1	3	2	2	0	0	0	0	0	0	0	—	0	1	0	0	0.3	1.000

George McMullen

McMULLEN, GEORGE
B. Calif. Deceased.

Year	Team	Lg	W	L	PCT	ERA	G	GS	CG	IP	H	BB	SO	ShO	Relief W	Relief L	Relief SV	AB	H	HR	BA	PO	A	E	DP	TC/G	FA
1887	NY	AA	2	1	.667	7.71	3	3	2	21	25	19	2	0	0	0	0	12	1	0	.083	2	6	5	0	3.3	.615

Craig McMurtry

McMURTRY, JOE CRAIG
B. Nov. 5, 1959, Temple, Tex.
BR TR 6′ 5″ 195 lbs.

Year	Team	Lg	W	L	PCT	ERA	G	GS	CG	IP	H	BB	SO	ShO	Relief W	Relief L	Relief SV	AB	H	HR	BA	PO	A	E	DP	TC/G	FA
1983	ATL	N	15	9	.625	3.08	36	35	6	224.2	204	88	105	3	0	0	0	70	6	0	.086	15	51	3	3	1.9	.957
1984			9	17	.346	4.32	37	30	0	183.1	184	102	99	0	0	2	0	52	6	0	.115	10	48	1	2	1.6	.983
1985			0	3	.000	6.60	17	6	0	45	56	27	28	0	0	0	1	14	1	0	.071	2	12	2	0	0.9	.875
1986			1	6	.143	4.74	37	5	0	79.2	82	43	50	0	1	3	0	16	2	0	.125	6	11	0	1	0.5	1.000
1988	TEX	A	3	3	.500	2.25	32	0	0	60	37	24	35	0	3	3	3	0	0	0	—	8	10	2	3	0.6	.900
1989			0	0	—	7.43	19	0	0	23	29	13	14	0	0	0	0	0	0	0	—	1	5	1	0	0.4	.857
1990			0	3	.000	4.32	23	3	0	41.2	43	30	14	0	0	1	0	0	0	0	—	1	8	0	3	0.4	1.000
1995	HOU	N	0	1	.000	7.84	11	0	0	10.1	15	9	4	0	0	1	0	1	0	0	.000	1	3	0	0	0.4	1.000
8 yrs.			28	42	.400	4.08	212	79	6	667.2	650	336	349	3	4	10	4	153	15	0	.098	44	148	9	12	0.9	.955

Edgar McNabb

McNABB, EDGAR J.
B. Oct. 24, 1865, Coshocton, Ohio D. Feb. 28, 1894, Pittsburgh, Pa.
BR TR 5′11½″ 170 lbs.

Year	Team	Lg	W	L	PCT	ERA	G	GS	CG	IP	H	BB	SO	ShO	Relief W	Relief L	Relief SV	AB	H	HR	BA	PO	A	E	DP	TC/G	FA
1893	BAL	N	8	7	.533	4.12	21	14	12	142	167	53	18	0	1	1	0	67	13	0	.194	11	31	5	1	2.2	.894

Dave McNally

McNALLY, DAVID ARTHUR
B. Oct. 31, 1942, Billings, Mont.
BR TL 5′11″ 185 lbs.

Year	Team	Lg	W	L	PCT	ERA	G	GS	CG	IP	H	BB	SO	ShO	Relief W	Relief L	Relief SV	AB	H	HR	BA	PO	A	E	DP	TC/G	FA
1962	BAL	A	1	0	1.000	0.00	1	1	1	9	2	3	4	1	0	0	0	3	0	0	.000	0	2	0	0	2.0	1.000
1963			7	8	.467	4.58	29	20	2	125.2	133	55	78	0	0	0	1	38	2	0	.053	6	16	0	0	0.8	1.000
1964			9	11	.450	3.67	30	23	5	159.1	157	51	88	3	1	0	0	51	7	0	.137	5	26	1	6	1.1	.969
1965			11	6	.647	2.85	35	29	6	198.2	163	73	116	2	0	0	0	65	6	0	.092	6	38	2	3	1.3	.957
1966			13	6	.684	3.17	34	33	5	213	212	64	158	1	0	0	0	77	15	0	.195	7	36	0	2	1.3	1.000
1967			7	7	.500	4.54	24	22	3	119	134	39	70	1	0	0	0	38	6	0	.158	3	11	1	2	0.6	.933
1968			22	10	.688	1.95	35	35	18	273	175	55	202	5	0	0	0	86	11	3	.128	6	28	1	1	1.0	.971
1969			20	7	.741	3.22	41	40	11	268.2	232	84	166	4	0	0	0	94	8	1	.085	6	28	1	2	0.9	.971
1970			**24**	9	.727	3.22	40	**40**	16	296	**277**	78	185	1	0	0	0	105	14	1	.133	10	37	1	4	1.2	.979
1971			21	5	**.808**	2.89	30	30	11	224	188	58	91	1	0	0	0	74	12	2	.162	10	39	1	1	1.7	.980

Dave McNally *continued*

Year	Team	W	L	PCT	ERA	G	GS	CG	IP	H	BB	SO	ShO	Relief Pitching W	Relief Pitching L	Relief Pitching SV	Batting AB	Batting H	Batting HR	BA	PO	A	E	DP	TC/G	FA
1972		13	17	.433	2.95	36	36	12	241	220	68	120	6	0	0	0	79	12	2	.152	9	43	3	5	1.5	.945
1973		17	17	.500	3.21	38	38	17	266	247	81	87	4	0	0	0	0	0	0	—	13	51	2	4	1.7	.970
1974		16	10	.615	3.58	39	37	13	259	260	81	111	4	0	0	1	0	0	0	—	13	50	5	7	1.7	.926
1975	MON N	3	6	.333	5.26	12	12	0	77	88	36	36	0	0	0	0	21	4	0	.190	3	12	3	0	1.5	.833
14 yrs.		184	119	.607	3.24	424	396	120	2729.1	2488	826	1512	33	1	0	2	731	97	9	.133	97	417	21	37	1.3	.961
LEAGUE CHAMPIONSHIP SERIES																										
1969	BAL A	1	0	1.000	0.00	1	1	1	11	3	5	11	1	0	0	0	4	0	0	.000	0	0	0	0	0.0	.000
1970		1	0	1.000	3.00	1	1	1	9	6	5	5	0	0	0	0	5	2	0	.400	0	0	0	0	0.0	.000
1971		1	0	1.000	3.86	1	1	0	7	7	1	5	0	0	0	0	2	0	0	.000	0	2	0	0	2.0	1.000
1973		0	1	.000	5.87	1	1	0	7.2	7	2	7	0	0	0	0	0	0	0	—	0	0	0	0	0.0	.000
1974		0	1	.000	1.59	1	1	0	5.2	6	2	2	0	0	0	0	0	0	0	—	0	0	0	0	0.0	.000
5 yrs.		3	2	.600	2.68	5	5	2	40.1	29	15	30	1	0	0	0	11	2	0	.182	0	2	0	0	0.4	1.000
								4th				**10th**	**1st**													
WORLD SERIES																										
1966	BAL A	1	0	1.000	1.59	2	2	1	11.1	6	7	5	1	0	0	0	3	0	0	.000	0	0	0	0	0.0	.000
1969		0	1	.000	2.81	2	2	1	16	11	5	13	0	0	0	0	5	1	1	.200	1	1	0	0	1.0	1.000
1970		1	0	1.000	3.00	1	1	1	9	9	2	5	0	0	0	0	4	1	1	.250	0	1	0	0	1.0	1.000
1971		2	1	.667	1.98	4	2	1	13.2	10	5	12	0	0	0	0	4	0	0	.000	0	2	0	0	0.5	1.000
4 yrs.		4	2	.667	2.34	9	7	4	50	36	19	35	1	0	0	0	16	2	2	.125	1	4	0	0	0.6	1.000

Tim McNamara

McNAMARA, TIMOTHY AUGUSTINE BR TR 5′11″ 170 lbs.
B. Nov. 20, 1898, Millville, Mass. D. Nov. 5, 1994, North Smithfield, R. I.

Year	Team	W	L	PCT	ERA	G	GS	CG	IP	H	BB	SO	ShO	Relief Pitching W	Relief Pitching L	Relief Pitching SV	Batting AB	Batting H	Batting HR	BA	PO	A	E	DP	TC/G	FA
1922	BOS N	3	4	.429	2.42	24	5	4	70.2	55	26	16	2	0	3	0	17	2	0	.118	3	14	0	0	0.7	1.000
1923		3	13	.188	4.91	32	16	3	139.1	185	29	32	0	1	1	0	39	7	0	.179	7	23	2	2	1.0	.938
1924		8	12	.400	5.18	35	21	6	179	242	31	35	2	2	0	0	43	6	0	.140	12	45	0	2	1.6	1.000
1925		0	0	—	81.00	1	0	0	0.2	6	2	1	0	0	0	0	0	0	0	—	0	0	0	0	0.0	.000
1926	NY N	0	0	—	9.00	6	0	0	6	7	4	4	0	0	0	0	0	0	0	—	0	2	0	0	0.3	1.000
5 yrs.		14	29	.326	4.78	98	42	13	395.2	495	92	88	4	3	4	0	99	15	0	.152	22	84	2	4	1.1	.981

Gordon McNaughton

McNAUGHTON, GORDON JOSEPH (Big Train) BR TR 6′ 1″ 190 lbs.
B. July 31, 1910, Chicago, Ill. D. Aug. 6, 1942, Chicago, Ill.

Year	Team	W	L	PCT	ERA	G	GS	CG	IP	H	BB	SO	ShO	Relief Pitching W	Relief Pitching L	Relief Pitching SV	Batting AB	Batting H	Batting HR	BA	PO	A	E	DP	TC/G	FA
1932	BOS A	0	1	.000	6.43	6	2	0	21	21	22	6	0	0	0	0	8	2	0	.250	2	6	0	1	1.3	1.000

Harry McNeal

McNEAL, JOHN HARLEY (The Cleveland Kid) BR TR 6′ 3″ 175 lbs.
B. Aug. 11, 1877, Iberia, Ohio D. Jan. 11, 1945, Cleveland, Ohio.

Year	Team	W	L	PCT	ERA	G	GS	CG	IP	H	BB	SO	ShO	Relief Pitching W	Relief Pitching L	Relief Pitching SV	Batting AB	Batting H	Batting HR	BA	PO	A	E	DP	TC/G	FA
1901	CLE A	5	5	.500	4.43	12	10	9	85.1	120	30	15	0	0	0	0	37	6	0	.162	2	15	2	0	1.6	.895

Ed McNichol

McNICHOL, EDWIN BRIGGS BR TR 5′ 5″ 170 lbs.
B. Jan. 10, 1879, Martins Ferry, Ohio D. Nov. 1, 1952, Salineville, Ohio.

Year	Team	W	L	PCT	ERA	G	GS	CG	IP	H	BB	SO	ShO	Relief Pitching W	Relief Pitching L	Relief Pitching SV	Batting AB	Batting H	Batting HR	BA	PO	A	E	DP	TC/G	FA
1904	BOS N	2	12	.143	4.28	17	15	12	122	120	74	39	1	0	0	0	43	4	0	.093	1	28	1	1	1.8	.967

Frank McPartlin

McPARTLIN, FRANK TR 6′ 180 lbs.
B. Feb. 16, 1872, Hoosick Falls, N. Y. D. Nov. 13, 1943, New York, N. Y.

Year	Team	W	L	PCT	ERA	G	GS	CG	IP	H	BB	SO	ShO	Relief Pitching W	Relief Pitching L	Relief Pitching SV	Batting AB	Batting H	Batting HR	BA	PO	A	E	DP	TC/G	FA
1899	NY N	0	0	—	4.50	1	0	0	4	4	3	2	0	0	0	0	1	0	0	.000	0	2	1	0	3.0	.667

John McPherson

McPHERSON, JOHN JACOB
B. Mar. 9, 1869, Easton, Pa. D. Sept. 30, 1941, Easton, Pa.

Year	Team	W	L	PCT	ERA	G	GS	CG	IP	H	BB	SO	ShO	Relief Pitching W	Relief Pitching L	Relief Pitching SV	Batting AB	Batting H	Batting HR	BA	PO	A	E	DP	TC/G	FA
1901	PHI A	0	1	.000	11.25	1	1	0	4	7	4	0	0	0	0	0	1	0	0	.000	0	3	1	1	4.0	.750
1904	PHI N	1	10	.091	3.66	15	12	11	128	130	46	32	1	0	0	0	47	3	0	.064	7	38	2	0	3.1	.957
2 yrs.		1	11	.083	3.89	16	13	11	132	137	50	32	1	0	0	0	48	3	0	.063	7	41	3	1	3.2	.941

Herb McQuaid

McQUAID, HERBERT GEORGE BR TR 6′ 2″ 185 lbs.
B. Mar. 29, 1899, San Francisco, Calif. D. Apr. 4, 1966, Richmond, Calif.

Year	Team	W	L	PCT	ERA	G	GS	CG	IP	H	BB	SO	ShO	Relief Pitching W	Relief Pitching L	Relief Pitching SV	Batting AB	Batting H	Batting HR	BA	PO	A	E	DP	TC/G	FA
1923	CIN N	1	0	1.000	2.36	12	1	0	34.1	31	10	9	0	0	0	0	7	0	0	.000	1	12	0	1	1.1	1.000
1926	NY A	1	0	1.000	6.10	17	1	0	38.1	48	13	6	0	1	0	0	7	0	0	.000	2	12	0	0	0.8	1.000
2 yrs.		2	0	1.000	4.33	29	2	0	72.2	79	23	15	0	1	0	0	14	0	0	.000	3	24	0	1	0.9	1.000

Mike McQueen

McQUEEN, MICHAEL ROBERT BL TL 6′ 188 lbs.
B. Aug. 30, 1950, Oklahoma City, Okla.

Year	Team	W	L	PCT	ERA	G	GS	CG	IP	H	BB	SO	ShO	Relief Pitching W	Relief Pitching L	Relief Pitching SV	Batting AB	Batting H	Batting HR	BA	PO	A	E	DP	TC/G	FA
1969	ATL N	0	0	—	3.00	1	1	0	3	2	3	3	0	0	0	0	0	0	0	—	0	0	0	0	0.0	.000
1970		1	5	.167	5.59	22	8	1	66	67	31	54	0	0	0	1	20	6	0	.300	0	7	1	0	0.4	.875
1971		4	1	.800	3.54	17	3	0	56	47	23	38	0	2	0	1	19	4	0	.211	1	4	0	1	0.3	1.000
1972		0	5	.000	4.62	23	7	1	78	79	44	40	0	0	0	1	23	2	0	.087	0	8	1	1	0.4	.889
1974	CIN N	0	0	—	5.40	10	0	0	15	17	11	5	0	0	0	0	1	1	0	1.000	1	0	0	0	0.1	1.000
5 yrs.		5	11	.313	4.67	73	19	2	218	212	112	140	0	2	0	3	63	13	0	.206	2	19	2	2	0.3	.913

George McQuillan

McQUILLAN, GEORGE WATT BR TR 5′11½″ 175 lbs.
B. May 1, 1885, Brooklyn, N. Y. D. Mar. 30, 1940, Columbus, Ohio.

Year	Team	W	L	PCT	ERA	G	GS	CG	IP	H	BB	SO	ShO	Relief Pitching W	Relief Pitching L	Relief Pitching SV	Batting AB	Batting H	Batting HR	BA	PO	A	E	DP	TC/G	FA
1907	PHI N	4	0	1.000	0.66	6	5	5	41	21	11	28	3	0	0	0	11	4	0	.364	1	2	0	0	0.5	1.000
1908		23	17	.575	1.53	48	42	32	359.2	263	91	114	7	0	0	2	119	18	0	.151	14	95	6	1	2.4	.948
1909		13	16	.448	2.14	41	28	16	247.2	202	54	96	4	2	2	2	76	9	0	.118	8	56	0	2	1.6	1.000
1910		9	6	.600	**1.60**	24	17	13	152.1	109	50	71	3	0	1	1	47	7	0	.149	3	39	1	3	1.8	.977
1911	CIN N	2	6	.250	4.68	19	5	2	77	92	31	28	0	1	2	0	22	2	0	.091	3	16	2	1	1.1	.905
1913	PIT N	8	6	.571	3.43	25	16	7	141.2	144	35	59	0	2	0	1	39	4	0	.103	6	32	0	0	1.5	1.000
1914		13	17	.433	2.98	45	28	15	259.1	248	60	96	0	1	2	4	73	5	0	.068	11	68	2	3	1.8	.975
1915	2 teams PIT N (30G 8–10) PHI N (9G 4–3)																									
″	total	12	13	.480	2.62	39	28	14	212.2	220	50	69	0	1	0	1	67	5	0	.075	5	58	4	0	1.7	.940
1916	PHI N	1	7	.125	2.76	21	3	1	62	58	15	22	0	1	4	2	11	1	0	.091	0	17	2	0	0.9	.895
1918	CLE A	0	1	.000	2.35	5	1	0	23	25	4	7	0	0	0	1	4	0	0	.000	2	7	0	0	1.8	1.000
10 yrs.		85	89	.489	2.38	273	173	105	1576.1	1382	401	590	17	8	11	14	469	55	0	.117	53	390	17	10	1.7	.963

Hugh McQuillan

McQUILLAN, HUGH A. (Handsome Hugh)
B. Sept. 15, 1897, New York, N. Y. D. Aug. 26, 1947, New York, N. Y.
BR TR 6′ 170 lbs.

Year	Team	W	L	PCT	ERA	G	GS	CG	IP	H	BB	SO	ShO	Relief Pitching W	Relief Pitching L	Relief Pitching SV	Batting AB	Batting H	Batting HR	BA	PO	A	E	DP	TC/G	FA
1918	**BOS N**	1	0	1.000	3.00	1	1	1	9	7	5	1	0	0	0	0	4	1	0	.250	0	3	0	1	3.0	1.000
1919		2	3	.400	3.45	16	7	2	60	66	14	13	0	0	0	1	18	4	0	.222	8	14	4	1	1.4	.846
1920		11	15	.423	3.55	38	26	17	225.2	230	70	53	1	1	1	5	74	19	1	.257	5	76	5	4	2.3	.942
1921		13	17	.433	4.00	45	31	13	250	284	90	94	2	2	1	5	88	18	1	.205	10	68	9	2	1.9	.897
1922	**2 teams** **BOS N** (28G 5–10) **NY N** (15G 6–5)																									
″	**total**	11	15	.423	4.06	43	30	8	230.1	265	90	57	0	3	2	1	79	14	0	.177	5	55	9	4	1.6	.870
1923	**NY N**	15	14	.517	3.41	38	32	15	229.2	224	66	75	5	2	0	0	82	14	0	.171	8	48	2	3	1.5	.966
1924		14	8	.636	2.69	27	23	14	184	179	43	49	1	0	0	3	67	14	0	.209	2	39	4	1	1.7	.911
1925		2	3	.400	6.04	14	11	2	70	95	23	23	0	0	0	1	21	3	0	.143	2	20	0	2	1.6	1.000
1926		11	10	.524	3.72	33	22	12	167	171	42	47	1	0	2	0	53	7	0	.132	10	46	2	5	1.8	.966
1927	**2 teams** **NY N** (11G 5–4) **BOS N** (13G 3–5)																									
″	**total**	8	9	.471	5.11	24	20	7	135.2	182	46	34	0	1	2	0	41	9	0	.220	4	35	4	1	1.8	.907
10 yrs.		88	94	.484	3.83	279	203	91	1561.1	1703	489	446	10	9	8	16	527	103	2	.195	54	404	39	24	1.8	.922
WORLD SERIES																										
1922	**NY N**	1	0	1.000	3.00	1	1	1	9	8	2	4	0	0	0	0	4	1	0	.250	0	0	0	0	0.0	.000
1923		0	1	.000	5.00	2	1	0	9	11	4	3	0	0	0	0	3	0	0	.000	0	1	0	0	0.5	1.000
1924		0	0	—	2.57	3	1	0	7	2	6	2	0	0	0	1	1	1	0	1.000	0	2	0	1	0.7	1.000
3 yrs.		1	1	.500	3.60	6	3	1	25	21	12	9	0	0	0	1	8	2	0	.250	0	3	0	1	0.5	1.000

Norm McRae

McRAE, NORMAN
B. Sept. 26, 1947, Elizabeth, N. J.
BR TR 6′ 1″ 195 lbs.

Year	Team	W	L	PCT	ERA	G	GS	CG	IP	H	BB	SO	ShO	Relief Pitching W	Relief Pitching L	Relief Pitching SV	Batting AB	Batting H	Batting HR	BA	PO	A	E	DP	TC/G	FA
1969	**DET A**	0	0	—	6.00	3	0	0	3	2	1	3	0	0	0	0	0	0	0	—	0	0	0	0	0.0	.000
1970		0	0	—	2.90	19	0	0	31	26	25	16	0	0	0	0	1	0	0	.000	3	7	2	1	0.6	.833
2 yrs.		0	0		3.18	22	0	0	34	28	26	19	0	0	0	0	1	0	0	.000	3	7	2	1	0.5	.833

Trick McSorley

McSORLEY, JOHN BERNARD
B. Dec. 16, 1852, St. Louis, Mo. D. Feb. 9, 1936, St. Louis, Mo.
BR TR 5′ 4″ 142 lbs.

Year	Team	W	L	PCT	ERA	G	GS	CG	IP	H	BB	SO	ShO	Relief Pitching W	Relief Pitching L	Relief Pitching SV	Batting AB	Batting H	Batting HR	BA	PO	A	E	DP	TC/G	FA
1884	**TOL AA**	0	0	—	*4.50*	1	0	0	2	5	0	1	0	0	0	0	*				154	10	7	13	7.4	.959

Bill McTigue

McTIGUE, WILLIAM PATRICK
B. Jan. 3, 1891, Nashville, Tenn. D. May 8, 1920, Nashville, Tenn.
BL TL 6′ 1½″ 175 lbs.

Year	Team	W	L	PCT	ERA	G	GS	CG	IP	H	BB	SO	ShO	Relief Pitching W	Relief Pitching L	Relief Pitching SV	Batting AB	Batting H	Batting HR	BA	PO	A	E	DP	TC/G	FA
1911	**BOS N**	0	5	.000	7.05	14	8	0	37	37	49	23	0	0	1	0	12	1	0	.083	1	6	1	0	0.6	.875
1912		2	0	1.000	5.45	10	1	1	34.2	39	18	17	0	1	0	0	13	1	0	.077	1	10	0	2	1.1	1.000
1916	**DET A**	0	0	—	5.06	3	0	0	5.1	5	5	1	0	0	0	0	1	0	0	.000	1	3	0	0	1.3	1.000
3 yrs.		2	5	.286	6.19	27	9	1	77	81	72	41	0	1	1	0	26	2	0	.077	3	19	1	2	0.9	.957

Cal McVey

McVEY, CALVIN ALEXANDER
B. Aug. 30, 1850, Montrose, Iowa D. Aug. 20, 1926, San Francisco, Calif.
Manager 1878–79.
BR TR 5′ 9″ 170 lbs.

Year	Team	W	L	PCT	ERA	G	GS	CG	IP	H	BB	SO	ShO	Relief Pitching W	Relief Pitching L	Relief Pitching SV	Batting AB	Batting H	Batting HR	BA	PO	A	E	DP	TC/G	FA
1876	**CHI N**	5	1	.833	1.52	11	6	5	59.1	57	2	9	0	0	0	2	308	107	1	.347	511	24	27	21	7.6	.952
1877		4	8	.333	4.50	17	10	6	92	129	11	20	0	1	**1**	**2**	266	98	0	.368	179	75	42	4	3.9	.858
1879	**CIN N**	0	2	.000	8.36	3	1	1	14	34	2	7	0	0	**1**	0	354	105	0	.297	83	107	42	6	3.6	.819
3 yrs.		9	11	.450	3.76	31	17	12	165.1	220	15	36	0	1	2	4	*				1525	214	155	64	6.4	.918

Doug McWeeny

McWEENY, DOUGLAS LAWRENCE (Buzz)
B. Aug. 17, 1896, Chicago, Ill. D. Jan. 1, 1953, Melrose Park, Ill.
BR TR 6′ 2″ 190 lbs.

Year	Team	W	L	PCT	ERA	G	GS	CG	IP	H	BB	SO	ShO	Relief Pitching W	Relief Pitching L	Relief Pitching SV	Batting AB	Batting H	Batting HR	BA	PO	A	E	DP	TC/G	FA
1921	**CHI A**	3	6	.333	6.08	27	9	4	97.2	127	45	46	0	1	0	2	31	1	0	.032	3	21	1	0	0.9	.960
1922		0	1	.000	5.91	4	1	0	10.2	13	7	5	0	0	0	0	1	0	0	.000	0	1	0	0	0.3	1.000
1924		1	3	.250	4.57	13	5	2	43.1	47	17	18	0	1	0	0	9	0	0	.000	3	22	0	0	1.9	1.000
1926	**BKN N**	11	13	.458	3.04	42	25	10	216.1	213	84	96	1	2	0	1	64	7	0	.109	12	44	5	1	1.5	.918
1927		4	8	.333	3.56	34	22	6	164.1	167	70	73	0	0	1	1	47	2	0	.043	10	38	5	0	1.6	.906
1928		14	14	.500	3.17	42	32	12	244	218	**114**	79	**4**	0	2	1	81	14	0	.173	7	72	3	3	2.0	.963
1929		4	10	.286	6.10	36	24	4	146	167	93	59	0	0	2	1	48	5	0	.104	7	23	2	1	0.9	.938
1930	**CIN N**	0	2	.000	7.36	8	2	0	25.2	28	20	10	0	0	1	0	7	1	0	.143	1	5	0	0	0.8	1.000
8 yrs.		37	57	.394	4.17	206	120	38	948	980	450	386	5	4	6	6	288	30	0	.104	43	226	16	5	1.4	.944

Larry McWilliams

McWILLIAMS, LARRY DEAN
B. Feb. 10, 1954, Wichita, Kans.
BL TL 6′ 5″ 180 lbs.

Year	Team	W	L	PCT	ERA	G	GS	CG	IP	H	BB	SO	ShO	Relief Pitching W	Relief Pitching L	Relief Pitching SV	Batting AB	Batting H	Batting HR	BA	PO	A	E	DP	TC/G	FA
1978	**ATL N**	9	3	.750	2.82	15	15	3	99	84	35	42	1	0	0	0	32	2	0	.063	10	19	0	1	1.9	1.000
1979		3	2	.600	5.59	13	13	1	66	69	22	32	0	0	0	0	24	5	0	.208	2	17	1	2	1.5	.950
1980		9	14	.391	4.94	30	30	4	164	188	39	77	1	0	0	0	51	8	0	.157	11	24	3	1	1.3	.921
1981		2	1	.667	3.08	6	5	2	38	31	8	23	1	0	0	0	10	1	0	.100	4	9	0	2	2.2	1.000
1982	**2 teams** **ATL N** (27G 2–3) **PIT N** (19G 6–5)																									
″	**total**	8	8	.500	3.84	46	20	2	159.1	158	44	118	2	2	2	1	38	7	0	.184	9	40	0	2	1.1	1.000
1983	**PIT N**	15	8	.652	3.25	35	35	8	238	205	87	199	4	0	0	0	79	9	0	.114	10	40	5	5	1.6	.909
1984		12	11	.522	2.93	34	32	7	227.1	226	78	149	2	0	0	1	74	9	0	.122	15	32	0	4	1.4	1.000
1985		7	9	.438	4.70	30	19	2	126.1	139	62	52	0	1	1	0	40	5	0	.125	4	21	0	0	0.8	1.000
1986		3	11	.214	5.15	49	15	0	122.1	129	49	80	0	2	3	0	29	4	0	.138	7	17	0	2	0.5	1.000
1987	**ATL N**	0	1	.000	5.75	9	2	0	20.1	25	7	13	0	0	0	0	5	1	0	.200	1	3	0	1	0.4	1.000
1988	**STL N**	6	9	.400	3.90	42	17	2	136	130	45	70	1	1	3	1	37	6	0	.162	5	24	2	0	0.7	.935
1989	**2 teams** **PHI N** (40G 2–11) **KC A** (8G 2–2)																									
″	**total**	4	13	.235	4.11	48	21	3	153.1	154	57	78	1	0	1	0	27	3	0	.111	7	26	2	2	0.7	.943
1990	**KC A**	0	0	—	9.72	13	0	0	8.1	10	9	7	0	0	0	0	0	0	0	—	0	3	0	0	0.2	1.000
13 yrs.		78	90	.464	3.99	370	224	34	1558.1	1548	542	940	13	6	10	3	446	60	0	.135	85	275	13	22	1.0	.965

Rusty Meacham

MEACHAM, RUSSELL LOREN
B. Jan. 27, 1968, Stuart, Fla.
BR TR 6′ 3″ 155 lbs.

Year	Team	W	L	PCT	ERA	G	GS	CG	IP	H	BB	SO	ShO	Relief Pitching W	Relief Pitching L	Relief Pitching SV	Batting AB	Batting H	Batting HR	BA	PO	A	E	DP	TC/G	FA
1991	**DET A**	2	1	.667	5.20	10	4	0	27.2	35	11	14	0	0	0	0	0	0	0	—	4	4	0	0	0.8	1.000
1992	**KC A**	10	4	.714	2.74	64	0	0	101.2	88	21	64	0	**10**	4	2	0	0	0	—	13	18	1	1	0.5	.969
1993		2	2	.500	5.57	15	0	0	21	31	5	13	0	2	2	0	0	0	0	—	2	4	0	1	0.4	1.000
1994		3	3	.500	3.73	36	0	0	50.2	51	12	36	0	3	3	4	0	0	0	—	1	9	0	1	0.3	1.000
1995		4	3	.571	4.98	49	0	0	59.2	72	19	30	0	4	3	2	0	0	0	—	5	9	1	2	0.3	.933
5 yrs.		21	13	.618	3.94	174	4	0	260.2	277	68	157	0	19	12	8	0	0	0		25	44	2	5	0.4	.972

Johnny Meador

MEADOR, JOHN DAVIS
B. Dec. 4, 1892, Madison, N. C. D. Apr. 11, 1970, Winston-Salem, N. C.
BR TR 5′10½″ 165 lbs.

Year	Team	W	L	PCT	ERA	G	GS	CG	IP	H	BB	SO	ShO	Relief W	Relief L	Relief SV	AB	H	HR	BA	PO	A	E	DP	TC/G	FA
1920	PIT N	0	2	.000	4.21	12	2	0	36.1	48	7	5	0	0	0	0	6	1	0	.167	2	13	0	0	1.3	1.000

Lee Meadows

MEADOWS, HENRY LEE (Specs)
B. July 12, 1894, Oxford, N. C. D. Jan. 29, 1963, Daytona Beach, Fla.
BL TR 6′ 190 lbs.
BB 1920–1921, 1926, 1929

Year	Team	W	L	PCT	ERA	G	GS	CG	IP	H	BB	SO	ShO	Relief W	Relief L	Relief SV	AB	H	HR	BA	PO	A	E	DP	TC/G	FA
1915	STL N	13	11	.542	2.99	39	26	14	244	232	88	104	1	3	0	0	83	8	0	.096	3	53	3	2	1.5	.949
1916		12	**23**	.343	2.58	**51**	36	11	289	261	119	120	1	5	3	2	95	15	0	.158	6	83	6	2	1.9	.937
1917		15	9	.625	3.09	43	37	18	265.1	253	90	100	4	3	0	2	89	9	0	.101	4	66	4	0	1.7	.946
1918		8	14	.364	3.59	30	23	12	165.1	176	56	49	0	1	2	1	55	7	0	.127	6	41	4	4	1.7	.922
1919	2 teams STL N (22G 4–10) PHI N (18G 8–10)																									
″	total	12	**20**	.375	2.69	40	29	18	241.1	228	79	116	4	2	2	0	80	9	0	.112	7	81	8	0	2.4	.917
1920	PHI N	16	14	.533	2.84	35	33	19	247	249	90	95	3	1	0	0	82	14	0	.171	10	70	7	1	2.5	.920
1921		11	16	.407	4.31	28	27	15	194.1	226	62	52	2	1	0	0	62	13	3	.210	9	69	6	6	3.0	.929
1922		12	18	.400	4.03	33	33	19	237	264	71	62	2	0	0	0	86	27	0	.314	8	71	1	2	2.4	.988
1923	2 teams PHI N (8G 1–3) PIT N (31G 16–10)																									
″	total	17	13	.567	3.83	39	30	17	246.2	290	59	76	1	1	1	1	98	26	1	.265	8	64	1	7	1.9	.986
1924	PIT N	13	12	.520	3.26	36	30	15	229.1	240	51	61	3	1	1	0	82	16	0	.195	3	55	4	0	1.7	.935
1925		19	10	.655	3.67	35	31	20	255.1	272	67	87	1	1	2	1	97	17	1	.175	6	62	0	4	1.9	1.000
1926		**20**	9	.690	3.97	36	31	15	226.2	254	52	54	1	3	0	0	88	20	0	.227	9	69	3	6	2.3	.963
1927		19	10	.655	3.40	40	**38**	**25**	299.1	**315**	66	84	2	0	0	0	115	18	0	.157	5	64	5	5	1.9	.932
1928		1	1	.500	8.10	4	2	1	10	18	5	3	0	0	0	0	4	2	0	.500	0	2	0	0	0.5	1.000
1929		0	0	—	13.50	1	0	0	0.2	2	1	0	0	0	0	0	1	0	0	.000	0	0	0	0	0.0	.000
15 yrs.		188	180	.511	3.38	490	406	219	3151.1	3280	956	1063	25	22	11	7	1117	201	5	.180	84	850	52	39	2.0	.947
WORLD SERIES																										
1925	PIT N	0	1	.000	3.38	1	1	0	8	6	0	4	0	0	0	0	1	0	0	.000	0	2	0	0	2.0	1.000
1927		0	1	.000	9.95	1	1	0	6.1	7	1	6	0	0	0	0	2	0	0	.000	0	1	0	0	1.0	1.000
2 yrs.		0	2	.000	6.28	2	2	0	14.1	13	1	10	0	0	0	0	3	0	0	.000	0	3	0	0	1.5	1.000

Rufe Meadows

MEADOWS, RUFUS RIVERS
B. Aug. 25, 1907, Chase City, Va. D. May 10, 1970, Wichita, Kans.
BL TL 5′11″ 175 lbs.

Year	Team	W	L	PCT	ERA	G	GS	CG	IP	H	BB	SO	ShO	Relief W	Relief L	Relief SV	AB	H	HR	BA	PO	A	E	DP	TC/G	FA
1926	CIN N	0	0	—	0.00	1	0	0	0.1	0	0	0	0	0	0	0	1	0	0	.000	0	0	0	0	0.0	.000

Dave Meads

MEADS, DAVID DONALD
B. Jan. 7, 1964, Montclair, N. J.
BL TL 6′½″ 175 lbs.

Year	Team	W	L	PCT	ERA	G	GS	CG	IP	H	BB	SO	ShO	Relief W	Relief L	Relief SV	AB	H	HR	BA	PO	A	E	DP	TC/G	FA
1987	HOU N	5	3	.625	5.55	45	0	0	48.2	60	16	32	0	5	3	0	3	1	0	.333	1	4	0	1	0.1	1.000
1988		3	1	.750	3.18	22	2	0	39.2	37	14	27	0	2	0	0	4	1	0	.250	3	6	1	0	0.5	.900
2 yrs.		8	4	.667	4.48	67	2	0	88.1	97	30	59	0	7	3	0	7	2	0	.286	4	10	1	1	0.2	.933

George Meakim

MEAKIM, GEORGE CLINTON
B. July 11, 1865, Brooklyn, N. Y. D. Feb. 17, 1923, Queens, N. Y.
BR TR 5′ 7½″ 154 lbs.

Year	Team	W	L	PCT	ERA	G	GS	CG	IP	H	BB	SO	ShO	Relief W	Relief L	Relief SV	AB	H	HR	BA	PO	A	E	DP	TC/G	FA
1890	LOU AA	12	7	.632	*2.91*	28	21	16	192	173	63	123	3	1	0	1	72	11	0	.153	16	29	8	2	1.8	.849
1891	PHI AA	1	4	.200	6.94	6	6	4	35	51	22	13	0	0	0	0	15	3	0	.200	6	18	4	1	4.7	.857
1892	2 teams CHI N (1G 0–1) CIN N (3G 1–1)																									
″	total	1	2	.333	9.53	4	4	2	22.2	37	11	4	0	0	0	0	10	2	0	.200	3	3	1	0	1.8	.857
1895	LOU N	1	0	1.000	2.57	1	1	1	7	7	4	2	0	0	0	0	3	1	0	.333	1	1	0	0	2.0	1.000
4 yrs.		15	13	.536	4.03	39	32	23	256.2	268	100	142	3	1	0	1	100	17	0	.170	26	51	13	3	2.3	.856

Jim Mecir

MECIR, JAMES JASON
B. May 16, 1970, Bayside, N. Y.
BB TR 6′ 1″ 195 lbs.

Year	Team	W	L	PCT	ERA	G	GS	CG	IP	H	BB	SO	ShO	Relief W	Relief L	Relief SV	AB	H	HR	BA	PO	A	E	DP	TC/G	FA
1995	SEA A	0	0	—	0.00	2	0	0	4.2	5	2	3	0	0	0	0	0	0	0	—	0	0	0	0	0.0	.000

Doc Medich

MEDICH, GEORGE FRANCIS
B. Dec. 9, 1948, Aliquippa, Pa.
BR TR 6′ 5″ 225 lbs.

Year	Team	W	L	PCT	ERA	G	GS	CG	IP	H	BB	SO	ShO	Relief W	Relief L	Relief SV	AB	H	HR	BA	PO	A	E	DP	TC/G	FA
1972	NY A	0	0	—	∞	1	1	0		2	2	0	0	0	0	0	0	0	0	—	0	0	0	0	0.0	.000
1973		14	9	.609	2.95	34	32	11	235	217	74	145	3	0	0	0	0	0	0	—	14	25	5	0	1.3	.886
1974		19	15	.559	3.60	38	38	17	280	275	91	154	4	0	0	0	0	0	0	—	18	35	3	3	1.5	.946
1975		16	16	.500	3.50	38	37	15	272.1	271	72	132	2	0	0	0	0	0	0	—	18	27	2	1	1.2	.957
1976	PIT N	8	11	.421	3.51	29	26	3	179.1	193	48	86	0	0	0	0	52	5	0	.096	6	36	2	2	1.5	.955
1977	3 teams OAK A (26G 10–6) SEA A (3G 2–0) NY N (1G 0–1)																									
″	total	12	7	.632	4.53	30	29	2	177	187	54	80	0	1	0	0	2	0	0	.000	12	18	2	0	1.1	.938
1978	TEX A	9	8	.529	3.74	28	22	6	171	166	52	71	2	0	0	2	0	0	0	—	11	31	1	2	1.5	.977
1979		10	7	.588	4.17	29	19	4	149	156	49	58	1	0	2	0	0	0	0	—	6	33	2	0	1.4	.951
1980		14	11	.560	3.93	34	32	6	204	230	56	91	0	0	0	0	0	0	0	—	9	27	3	3	1.1	.923
1981		10	6	.625	3.08	20	20	4	143	136	33	65	**4**	0	0	0	0	0	0	—	15	26	1	1	2.1	.976
1982	2 teams TEX A (21G 7–11) MIL A (10G 5–4)																									
″	total	12	15	.444	5.04	31	31	3	185.2	203	93	73	0	0	0	0	0	0	0		8	27	0	0	1.1	1.000
11 yrs.		124	105	.541	3.78	312	287	71	1996.1	2036	624	955	16	1	2	2	54	5	0	.093	117	285	21	12	1.4	.950
WORLD SERIES																										
1982	MIL A	0	0	—	18.00	1	0	0	2	5	1	0	0	0	0	0	0	0	0	—	0	0	0	0	0.0	.000

Irv Medlinger

MEDLINGER, IRVING JOHN
B. June 18, 1927, Chicago, Ill. D. Sept. 3, 1975, Wheeling, Ill.
BL TL 5′11″ 185 lbs.

Year	Team	W	L	PCT	ERA	G	GS	CG	IP	H	BB	SO	ShO	Relief W	Relief L	Relief SV	AB	H	HR	BA	PO	A	E	DP	TC/G	FA
1949	STL A	0	0	—	27.00	3	0	0	4	11	3	4	0	0	0	0	0	0	0	—	0	0	0	0	0.0	.000
1951		0	0	—	8.38	6	0	0	9.2	10	12	5	0	0	0	0	0	0	0	—	0	1	0	0	0.2	1.000
2 yrs.		0	0		13.83	9	0	0	13.2	21	15	9	0	0	0	0	0	0	0		0	1	0	0	0.1	1.000

Scott Medvin

MEDVIN, SCOTT HOWARD
B. Sept. 16, 1961, North Olmsted, Ohio.
BR TR 6′ 1″ 195 lbs.

Year	Team	W	L	PCT	ERA	G	GS	CG	IP	H	BB	SO	ShO	Relief W	Relief L	Relief SV	AB	H	HR	BA	PO	A	E	DP	TC/G	FA
1988	PIT N	3	0	1.000	4.88	17	0	0	27.2	23	9	16	0	3	0	0	3	0	0	.000	0	6	0	0	0.4	1.000
1989		0	1	.000	5.68	6	0	0	6.1	6	5	4	0	0	1	0	0	0	0	—	1	2	0	0	0.5	1.000
1990	SEA A	0	1	.000	6.23	5	0	0	4.1	7	2	1	0	0	1	0	0	0	0	—	1	2	1	0	0.8	.750
3 yrs.		3	2	.600	5.17	28	0	0	38.1	36	16	21	0	3	2	0	3	0	0	.000	2	10	1	0	0.5	.923

Pete Meegan

MEEGAN, PETER J. (Steady Pete)
B. Nov. 13, 1863, San Francisco, Calif. D. Mar. 15, 1905, San Francisco, Calif.

Year	Team	Lg	W	L	PCT	ERA	G	GS	CG	IP	H	BB	SO	ShO	Relief W	Relief L	Relief SV	AB	H	HR	BA	PO	A	E	DP	TC/G	FA
1884	RIC	AA	5	9	.357	*4.37*	17	17	17	140	140	27	71	1	0	0	0	59	8	0	.136	10	34	10	0	3.0	.815
1885	PIT	AA	7	8	.467	*3.39*	18	16	14	146	146	38	58	1	**1**	0	0	67	13	0	.194	13	36	8	1	2.6	.860
2 yrs.			12	17	.414	3.87	35	33	31	286	286	65	129	2	1	0	0	126	21	0	.167	23	70	18	1	2.8	.838

Bill Meehan

MEEHAN, WILLIAM THOMAS BR TR 5′ 9″ 155 lbs.
B. Sept. 4, 1889, Osceola Mills, Pa. D. Oct. 8, 1982, Douglas, Wyo.

Year	Team	Lg	W	L	PCT	ERA	G	GS	CG	IP	H	BB	SO	ShO	Relief W	Relief L	Relief SV	AB	H	HR	BA	PO	A	E	DP	TC/G	FA
1915	PHI	A	0	1	.000	11.25	1	1	0	4	7	3	4	0	0	0	0	1	1	0	1.000	1	2	0	0	3.0	1.000

Roy Meeker

MEEKER, CHARLES ROY (Lefty) BL TL 5′ 9″ 175 lbs.
B. Sept. 15, 1900, Lead Mine, Mo. D. Mar. 25, 1929, Orlando, Fla.

Year	Team	Lg	W	L	PCT	ERA	G	GS	CG	IP	H	BB	SO	ShO	Relief W	Relief L	Relief SV	AB	H	HR	BA	PO	A	E	DP	TC/G	FA
1923	PHI	A	3	0	1.000	3.60	5	2	2	25	24	13	12	0	1	0	0	9	1	0	.111	0	5	0	0	1.0	1.000
1924			5	12	.294	4.68	30	14	5	146	166	81	37	1	1	2	0	48	11	0	.229	7	28	1	2	1.2	.972
1926	CIN	N	0	2	.000	6.43	7	1	1	21	24	9	5	0	0	1	0	6	0	0	.000	0	6	0	0	0.9	1.000
3 yrs.			8	14	.364	4.73	42	17	8	192	214	103	54	1	2	3	0	63	12	0	.190	7	39	1	2	1.1	.979

Jouett Meekin

MEEKIN, GEORGE JOUETT BR TR 6′ 1″ 180 lbs.
B. Feb. 21, 1867, New Albany, Ind. D. Dec. 14, 1944, New Albany, Ind.

Year	Team	Lg	W	L	PCT	ERA	G	GS	CG	IP	H	BB	SO	ShO	Relief W	Relief L	Relief SV	AB	H	HR	BA	PO	A	E	DP	TC/G	FA
1891	LOU	AA	9	16	.360	4.44	28	25	24	221	223	106	141	2	0	0	0	94	21	1	.223	15	38	3	3	1.8	.946
1892	2 teams	LOU N (19G 7–10) WAS N (14G 3–10)																									
″	total		10	20	.333	3.79	33	32	30	268.1	280	126	125	1	0	0	0	109	11	2	.101	15	56	7	1	2.3	.910
1893	WAS	N	10	15	.400	4.96	31	28	24	245	289	140	91	1	0	0	0	113	29	3	.257	14	53	7	3	2.2	.905
1894	NY	N	33	9	**.786**	3.70	52	48	40	409	404	171	133	1	1	1	2	170	48	5	.282	15	60	4	3	1.5	.949
1895			16	11	.593	5.30	29	29	24	225.2	296	73	76	1	0	0	0	96	28	1	.292	10	44	5	1	2.0	.915
1896			26	14	.650	3.82	42	41	34	334.1	378	127	110	0	0	1	0	144	43	2	.299	17	62	8	3	2.1	.908
1897			20	11	.645	3.76	37	34	30	303.2	328	99	83	2	0	1	0	137	41	0	.299	14	56	11	2	2.2	.864
1898			16	18	.471	3.77	38	37	34	320	329	108	82	1	0	0	0	129	27	0	.209	18	51	9	0	2.1	.885
1899	2 teams	NY N (18G 5–11) BOS N (13G 7–6)																									
″	total		12	17	.414	3.72	31	31	28	256.1	280	93	53	0	0	0	0	99	19	1	.192	7	37	5	1	1.6	.898
1900	PIT	N	0	2	.000	6.92	2	2	1	13	20	8	3	0	0	0	0	4	0	0	.000	0	0	2	0	1.0	.000
10 yrs.			152	133	.533	4.08	323	307	269	2596.1	2827	1051	897	9	1	3	2	1095	267	15	.244	125	457	61	17	1.9	.905

Phil Meeler

MEELER, CHARLES PHILIP, JR. BR TR 6′ 5″ 215 lbs.
B. July 23, 1948, South Boston, Va.

Year	Team	Lg	W	L	PCT	ERA	G	GS	CG	IP	H	BB	SO	ShO	Relief W	Relief L	Relief SV	AB	H	HR	BA	PO	A	E	DP	TC/G	FA
1972	DET	A	0	1	.000	4.50	7	0	0	8	10	7	5	0	0	1	0	2	0	0	.000	1	1	0	0	0.3	1.000

Russ Meers

MEERS, RUSSELL HARLAN (Babe) BL TL 5′10″ 170 lbs.
B. Nov. 28, 1918, Tilton, Ill. D. Nov. 16, 1994, Lancaster, Pa.

Year	Team	Lg	W	L	PCT	ERA	G	GS	CG	IP	H	BB	SO	ShO	Relief W	Relief L	Relief SV	AB	H	HR	BA	PO	A	E	DP	TC/G	FA
1941	CHI	N	0	1	.000	1.13	1	1	0	8	5	0	5	0	0	0	0	2	0	0	.000	1	0	0	0	1.0	1.000
1946			1	2	.333	3.18	7	2	0	11.1	10	10	2	0	1	0	0	1	1	0	1.000	0	3	0	0	0.4	1.000
1947			2	0	1.000	4.48	35	1	0	64.1	61	38	28	0	2	0	0	14	2	0	.143	3	12	2	0	0.5	.882
3 yrs.			3	3	.500	3.98	43	4	0	83.2	76	48	35	0	3	0	0	17	3	0	.176	4	15	2	0	0.5	.905

Heinie Meine

MEINE, HENRY WILLIAM (The Count of Luxemburg) BR TR 5′11″ 180 lbs.
B. May 1, 1896, St. Louis, Mo. D. Mar. 18, 1968, St. Louis, Mo.

Year	Team	Lg	W	L	PCT	ERA	G	GS	CG	IP	H	BB	SO	ShO	Relief W	Relief L	Relief SV	AB	H	HR	BA	PO	A	E	DP	TC/G	FA
1922	STL	A	0	0	—	4.50	1	0	0	4	5	2	0	0	0	0	0	1	0	0	.000	1	2	0	0	3.0	1.000
1929	PIT	N	7	6	.538	4.50	22	13	7	108	120	34	19	1	1	1	1	39	4	0	.103	2	19	1	1	1.0	.955
1930			6	8	.429	6.14	20	16	4	117.1	168	44	18	0	0	0	1	41	5	0	.122	6	35	0	5	2.0	1.000
1931			**19**	13	.594	2.98	36	**35**	22	**284**	278	87	58	3	0	1	0	96	14	0	.146	15	59	4	7	2.2	.949
1932			12	9	.571	3.86	28	25	13	172.1	193	45	32	1	0	0	1	61	10	0	.164	7	35	4	3	1.6	.913
1933			15	8	.652	3.65	32	29	12	207.1	227	50	50	2	2	0	0	75	13	0	.173	11	31	1	1	1.3	.977
1934			7	6	.538	4.32	26	14	2	106.1	134	25	22	0	3	0	0	28	3	0	.107	3	19	1	0	0.9	.957
7 yrs.			66	50	.569	3.95	165	132	60	999.1	1125	287	199	7	6	2	3	341	49	0	.144	45	200	11	17	1.6	.957

Frank Meinke

MEINKE, FRANK LOUIS BR 5′10½″ 172 lbs.
Father of Bob Meinke.
B. Oct. 18, 1863, Chicago, Ill. D. Nov. 8, 1931, Chicago, Ill.

Year	Team	Lg	W	L	PCT	ERA	G	GS	CG	IP	H	BB	SO	ShO	Relief W	Relief L	Relief SV	AB	H	HR	BA	PO	A	E	DP	TC/G	FA
1884	DET	N	8	23	.258	*3.18*	35	31	31	289	341	63	124	1	0	**1**	0	341	56	6	.164	80	214	44	20	3.5	.870
1885			0	1	.000	3.60	1	1	0	5	13	4	0	0	0	0	0	3	0	0	.000	1	2	0	0	1.5	1.000
2 yrs.			8	24	.250	3.18	36	32	31	294	354	67	124	1	0	1	0	*				81	216	44	20	3.5	.871

Sam Mejias

MEJIAS, SAMUEL ELIAS BR TR 6′ 170 lbs.
B. May 9, 1952, Santiago, Dominican Republic.

Year	Team	Lg	W	L	PCT	ERA	G	GS	CG	IP	H	BB	SO	ShO	Relief W	Relief L	Relief SV	AB	H	HR	BA	PO	A	E	DP	TC/G	FA
1978	MON	N	0	0	—	0.00	1	0	0	1	0	0	0	0	0	0	0	*				19	1	0	0	1.2	1.000

Jose Melendez

MELENDEZ, JOSE LUIS BR TR 6′ 2″ 175 lbs.
Born Jose Luis Melendéz (Garcia).
B. Sept. 2, 1965, Naguabo, Puerto Rico.

Year	Team	Lg	W	L	PCT	ERA	G	GS	CG	IP	H	BB	SO	ShO	Relief W	Relief L	Relief SV	AB	H	HR	BA	PO	A	E	DP	TC/G	FA
1990	SEA	A	0	0	—	11.81	3	0	0	5.1	8	3	7	0	0	0	0	0	0	0	—	0	0	0	0	0.0	.000
1991	SD	N	8	5	.615	3.27	31	9	0	93.2	77	24	60	0	3	2	3	20	2	0	.100	4	11	2	0	0.5	.882
1992			6	7	.462	2.92	56	3	0	89.1	82	20	82	0	6	4	0	5	0	0	.000	2	8	1	1	0.2	.909
1993	BOS	A	2	1	.667	2.25	9	0	0	16	10	5	14	0	2	1	0	0	0	0	—	1	3	0	0	0.4	1.000
1994			0	1	.000	6.06	10	0	0	16.1	20	8	9	0	0	1	0	0	0	0	—	0	3	0	0	0.3	1.000
5 yrs.			16	14	.533	3.47	109	12	0	220.2	197	60	172	0	11	8	3	25	2	0	.080	7	25	3	1	0.3	.914

Steve Melter

MELTER, STEPHEN BLAZIUS BR TR 6′ 2″ 180 lbs.
B. Jan. 2, 1886, Cherokee, Iowa D. Jan. 28, 1962, Mishawaka, Ind.

Year	Team	Lg	W	L	PCT	ERA	G	GS	CG	IP	H	BB	SO	ShO	Relief W	Relief L	Relief SV	AB	H	HR	BA	PO	A	E	DP	TC/G	FA
1909	STL	N	0	1	.000	3.50	23	1	0	64.1	79	20	24	0	0	1	1	15	2	0	.133	5	21	0	2	1.1	1.000

Cliff Melton

MELTON, CLIFFORD GEORGE (Mountain Music) BL TL 6′ 5½″ 203 lbs.
B. Jan. 3, 1912, Brevard, N. C. D. July 28, 1986, Baltimore, Md.

Year	Team	Lg	W	L	PCT	ERA	G	GS	CG	IP	H	BB	SO	ShO	Relief W	Relief L	Relief SV	AB	H	HR	BA	PO	A	E	DP	TC/G	FA
1937	NY	N	20	9	.690	2.61	46	27	14	248	216	55	142	2	4	1	**7**	82	10	0	.122	10	68	1	3	1.7	.987
1938			14	14	.500	3.89	36	31	10	243	266	61	101	1	1	0	0	80	14	0	.175	5	64	4	1	2.0	.945
1939			12	15	.444	3.56	41	23	9	207.1	214	65	95	2	3	2	5	66	12	0	.182	6	49	4	0	1.4	.932
1940			10	11	.476	4.91	37	21	4	166.2	185	68	91	1	3	2	2	54	12	0	.222	6	38	0	4	1.2	1.000
1941			8	11	.421	3.01	42	22	9	194.1	181	61	100	3	1	1	1	61	7	0	.115	4	58	2	1	1.5	.969

Cliff Melton *continued*

Year	Team	W	L	PCT	ERA	G	GS	CG	IP	H	BB	SO	ShO	Relief Pitching W	L	SV	Batting AB	H	HR	BA	PO	A	E	DP	TC/G	FA
1942		11	5	.688	2.63	23	17	12	143.2	122	33	61	2	0	0	1	47	11	0	.234	7	44	1	1	2.3	.981
1943		9	13	.409	3.19	34	28	6	186.1	184	69	55	2	0	1	0	54	8	0	.148	6	57	3	4	1.9	.955
1944		2	2	.500	4.06	13	10	1	64.1	78	19	15	0	0	0	0	25	3	0	.120	1	19	1	1	1.6	.952
8 yrs.		86	80	.518	3.42	272	179	65	1453.2	1446	431	660	13	12	7	16	469	77	0	.164	45	397	16	15	1.7	.965
WORLD SERIES																										
1937	NY N	0	2	.000	4.91	3	2	0	11	12	6	7	0	0	0	0	2	0	0	.000	0	0	1	0	0.3	.000

Rube Melton

MELTON, REUBEN FRANKLIN BR TR 6' 5" 205 lbs.
B. Feb. 27, 1917, Cramerton, N. C. D. Sept. 11, 1971, Greer, S. C.

Year	Team	W	L	PCT	ERA	G	GS	CG	IP	H	BB	SO	ShO	Relief Pitching W	L	SV	Batting AB	H	HR	BA	PO	A	E	DP	TC/G	FA
1941	PHI N	1	5	.167	4.73	25	5	2	83.2	81	47	57	0	1	2	0	19	2	0	.105	0	11	2	0	0.5	.846
1942		9	20	.310	3.70	42	29	10	209.1	180	**114**	107	1	1	1	4	65	8	1	.123	8	33	1	2	1.0	.976
1943	BKN N	5	8	.385	3.92	30	17	4	119.1	102	79	63	2	1	1	0	38	4	0	.105	1	20	3	1	0.8	.875
1944		9	13	.409	3.46	37	23	6	187.1	178	96	91	1	2	0	0	57	7	0	.123	8	34	2	2	1.2	.955
1946		6	3	.667	1.99	24	12	3	99.2	72	52	44	2	1	1	1	28	3	0	.107	1	20	1	0	0.9	.955
1947		0	1	.000	13.50	4	1	0	4.2	7	7	1	0	0	0	0	1	1	0	1.000	0	0	0	0	0.0	.000
6 yrs.		30	50	.375	3.62	162	87	25	704	620	395	363	6	6	5	5	208	25	1	.120	18	118	9	5	0.9	.938

Mario Mendoza

MENDOZA, MARIO BR TR 5'11" 170 lbs.
Born Mario Mendoza (Aizpuru).
B. Dec. 26, 1950, Chihuahua, Mexico.

Year	Team	W	L	PCT	ERA	G	GS	CG	IP	H	BB	SO	ShO	Relief Pitching W	L	SV	Batting AB	H	HR	BA	PO	A	E	DP	TC/G	FA
1977	PIT N	0	0	—	13.50	1	0	0	2	3	2	0	0	0	0	0	*				77	187	10	21	3.1	.964

Mike Mendoza

MENDOZA, MICHAEL JOSEPH BR TR 6' 5" 215 lbs.
B. Nov. 26, 1955, Inglewood, Calif.

Year	Team	W	L	PCT	ERA	G	GS	CG	IP	H	BB	SO	ShO	Relief Pitching W	L	SV	Batting AB	H	HR	BA	PO	A	E	DP	TC/G	FA
1979	HOU N	0	0	—	0.00	1	0	0	1	0	0	0	0	0	0	0	*				0	0	0	0	0.0	.000

Jock Menefee

MENEFEE, JOHN BR TR 6' 165 lbs.
B. Jan. 15, 1868, Rowlesburg, West Virginia D. Mar. 11, 1953, Belle Vernon, Pa.

Year	Team	W	L	PCT	ERA	G	GS	CG	IP	H	BB	SO	ShO	Relief Pitching W	L	SV	Batting AB	H	HR	BA	PO	A	E	DP	TC/G	FA
1892	PIT N	0	0	—	11.25	1	0	0	4	10	2	0	0	0	0	0	3	0	0	.000	1	2	0	0	1.5	1.000
1893	LOU N	8	7	.533	4.24	15	15	14	129.1	150	40	30	1	0	0	0	73	20	0	.274	19	38	5	2	2.8	.919
1894	2 teams LOU N (28G 8–17) PIT N (13G 5–8)																									
"	total	13	25	.342	4.68	41	37	33	323.1	417	89	76	1	0	1	0	126	25	0	.198	30	79	8	0	2.8	.932
1895	PIT N	0	1	.000	16.20	2	1	0	1.2	2	7	0	0	0	0	0	0	0	0	—	1	1	1	0	1.5	.667
1898	NY N	0	1	.000	4.82	1	1	1	9.1	11	2	3	0	0	0	0	5	0	0	.000	0	3	1	0	4.0	.750
1900	CHI N	9	4	.692	3.85	16	13	11	117	140	35	30	0	1	0	0	46	5	0	.109	3	21	3	1	1.7	.889
1901		8	13	.381	3.80	21	20	19	182.1	201	34	55	0	0	1	0	152	39	0	.257	67	48	12	2	2.6	.906
1902		12	10	.545	2.42	22	21	20	197.1	202	26	60	5	1	0	0	216	50	0	.231	230	57	13	7	4.5	.957
1903		8	8	.500	3.00	20	17	13	147	157	38	39	1	1	1	0	64	13	0	.203	31	56	8	0	4.3	.916
9 yrs.		58	69	.457	3.81	139	125	111	1111.1	1290	273	293	8	3	3	0	*				382	305	51	12	3.3	.931

Tony Menendez

MENENDEZ, ANTONIO GUSTAVO BR TR 6' 2" 190 lbs.
Born Antonio Gustavo Menendez (Remon).
B. Feb. 20, 1965, Havana, Cuba.

Year	Team	W	L	PCT	ERA	G	GS	CG	IP	H	BB	SO	ShO	Relief Pitching W	L	SV	Batting AB	H	HR	BA	PO	A	E	DP	TC/G	FA
1992	CIN N	1	0	1.000	1.93	3	0	0	4.2	1	0	5	0	1	0	0	0	0	0	—	0	0	0	0	0.0	.000
1993	PIT N	2	0	1.000	3.00	14	0	0	21	20	4	13	0	2	0	0	1	0	0	.000	1	2	1	0	0.3	.750
1994	SF N	0	1	.000	21.60	6	0	0	3.1	8	2	2	0	0	1	0	0	0	0	—	0	0	0	0	0.0	.000
3 yrs.		3	1	.750	4.97	23	0	0	29	29	6	20	0	3	1	0	1	0	0	.000	1	2	1	0	0.2	.750

Paul Menhart

MENHART, PAUL GERARD BR TR 6' 2" 190 lbs.
B. Mar. 25, 1969, St. Louis, Mo.

Year	Team	W	L	PCT	ERA	G	GS	CG	IP	H	BB	SO	ShO	Relief Pitching W	L	SV	Batting AB	H	HR	BA	PO	A	E	DP	TC/G	FA
1995	TOR A	1	4	.200	4.92	21	9	1	78.2	72	47	50	0	1	1	0	0	0	0	—	2	11	1	1	0.7	.929

Mike Meola

MEOLA, EMILE MICHAEL BR TR 5'11" 175 lbs.
B. Oct. 19, 1905, New York, N. Y. D. Sept. 1, 1976, Fair Lawn, N. J.

Year	Team	W	L	PCT	ERA	G	GS	CG	IP	H	BB	SO	ShO	Relief Pitching W	L	SV	Batting AB	H	HR	BA	PO	A	E	DP	TC/G	FA
1933	BOS A	0	0	—	23.14	3	0	0	2.1	5	2	1	0	0	0	0	0	0	0	—	0	0	0	0	0.0	.000
1936	2 teams STL A (9G 0–1) BOS A (6G 0–2)																									
"	total	0	3	.000	7.30	15	3	1	40.2	58	23	14	0	0	1	1	9	2	0	.222	1	11	0	0	0.8	1.000
2 yrs.		0	3	.000	8.16	18	3	1	43	63	25	15	0	0	1	1	9	2	0	.222	1	11	0	0	0.7	1.000

Jose Mercedes

MERCEDES, JOSE MIGUEL BR TR 6' 1" 180 lbs.
Born Jose Miguel Mercedes (Santana).
B. Mar. 5, 1971, El Seibo, Dominican Republic.

Year	Team	W	L	PCT	ERA	G	GS	CG	IP	H	BB	SO	ShO	Relief Pitching W	L	SV	Batting AB	H	HR	BA	PO	A	E	DP	TC/G	FA
1994	MIL A	2	0	1.000	2.32	19	0	0	31	22	16	11	0	2	0	0	0	0	0	—	1	3	1	0	0.3	.800
1995		0	1	.000	9.82	5	0	0	7.1	12	8	6	0	0	1	0	0	0	0	—	0	0	0	0	0.0	.000
2 yrs.		2	1	.667	3.76	24	0	0	38.1	34	24	17	0	2	1	0	0	0	0		1	3	1	0	0.2	.800

Jack Mercer

MERCER, HARRY VERNON
B. Mar. 10, 1889, Zanesville, Ohio D. June 25, 1945, Dayton, Ohio.

Year	Team	W	L	PCT	ERA	G	GS	CG	IP	H	BB	SO	ShO	Relief Pitching W	L	SV	Batting AB	H	HR	BA	PO	A	E	DP	TC/G	FA
1910	PIT N	0	0	—	0.00	1	0	0	1	0	2	1	0	0	0	0	0	0	0	—	0	0	0	0	0.0	.000

Mark Mercer

MERCER, MARK KENNETH BL TL 6' 5" 220 lbs.
B. May 22, 1954, Fort Bragg, N. C.

Year	Team	W	L	PCT	ERA	G	GS	CG	IP	H	BB	SO	ShO	Relief Pitching W	L	SV	Batting AB	H	HR	BA	PO	A	E	DP	TC/G	FA
1981	TEX A	0	1	.000	4.50	7	0	0	8	7	7	8	0	0	1	2	0	0	0	—	0	2	0	0	0.3	1.000

Win Mercer

MERCER, GEORGE BARCLAY BR TR 5' 7" 140 lbs.
B. June 20, 1874, Chester, W. Va. D. Jan. 12, 1903, San Francisco, Calif.

Year	Team	W	L	PCT	ERA	G	GS	CG	IP	H	BB	SO	ShO	Relief Pitching W	L	SV	Batting AB	H	HR	BA	PO	A	E	DP	TC/G	FA
1894	WAS N	17	23	.425	3.76	49	38	30	333	431	125	69	0	2	1	3	162	46	2	.284	20	69	6	1	1.8	.937
1895		13	23	.361	4.46	43	38	32	311	430	96	84	0	0	1	2	196	50	1	.255	44	76	25	3	2.5	.828
1896		25	18	.581	4.13	46	45	38	366.1	456	117	94	2	1	0	0	156	38	1	.244	37	89	21	3	3.1	.857
1897		20	20	.500	3.25	45	**42**	34	332	395	102	88	**3**	0	1	2	135	43	0	.319	0	0	0	0	0.0	.000
1898		12	18	.400	4.81	33	30	24	233.2	309	71	52	0	0	1	0	249	80	2	.321	91	116	29	8	2.9	.877

Win Mercer *continued*

Year	Team	Lg	W	L	PCT	ERA	G	GS	CG	IP	H	BB	SO	ShO	Relief Pitching W	Relief Pitching L	Relief Pitching SV	Batting AB	Batting H	Batting HR	BA	PO	A	E	DP	TC/G	FA
1899			7	14	.333	4.60	23	21	21	186	234	53	28	0	0	0	0	375	112	1	.299	109	156	40	8	3.0	.869
1900	NY	N	13	17	.433	3.86	33	29	26	242.2	303	58	39	1	0	1	0	248	73	0	.294	75	149	32	11	3.4	.875
1901	WAS	A	9	13	.409	4.56	24	22	19	179.2	217	50	31	1	0	0	1	140	42	0	.300	92	57	15	10	3.3	.909
1902	DET	A	15	18	.455	3.04	35	33	28	281.2	282	80	40	4	0	0	1	100	18	0	.180	13	103	8	2	3.5	.935
9 yrs.			131	164	.444	3.98	331	298	252	2466	3057	752	525	11	3	5	9	*				481	815	176	46	2.7	.880

Kent Mercker

MERCKER, KENT FRANKLIN
B. Feb. 1, 1968, Dublin, Ohio.
BL TL 6′ 1″ 175 lbs.

Year	Team	Lg	W	L	PCT	ERA	G	GS	CG	IP	H	BB	SO	ShO	Relief Pitching W	Relief Pitching L	Relief Pitching SV	Batting AB	Batting H	Batting HR	BA	PO	A	E	DP	TC/G	FA
1989	ATL	N	0	0	—	12.46	2	1	0	4.1	8	6	4	0	0	0	0	1	0	0	.000	0	0	0	0	0.0	.000
1990			4	7	.364	3.17	36	0	0	48.1	43	24	39	0	4	7	7	3	0	0	.000	2	1	1	0	0.1	.750
1991			5	3	.625	2.58	50	4	0	73.1	56	35	62	0	4	3	6	10	1	0	.100	2	7	1	1	0.2	.900
1992			3	2	.600	3.42	53	0	0	68.1	51	35	49	0	3	2	6	5	0	0	.000	1	2	0	0	0.1	1.000
1993			3	1	.750	2.86	43	6	0	66	52	36	59	0	2	0	0	13	0	0	.000	1	4	1	0	0.1	.833
1994			9	4	.692	3.45	20	17	2	112.1	90	45	111	1	0	0	0	37	2	0	.054	4	15	0	1	0.9	1.000
1995			7	8	.467	4.15	29	26	0	143	140	61	102	0	0	0	0	48	5	0	.104	5	23	1	2	1.0	.966
7 yrs.			31	25	.554	3.49	233	54	2	515.2	440	242	426	1	13	12	19	117	8	0	.068	15	52	4	4	0.3	.944
DIVISIONAL PLAYOFF SERIES																											
1995	ATL	N	0	0	—	0.00	1	0	0	0.1	0	0	0	0	0	0	0	0	0	0	—	0	0	0	0	0.0	.000
LEAGUE CHAMPIONSHIP SERIES																											
1991	ATL	N	0	1	.000	13.50	1	0	0	0.2	0	2	0	0	0	1	0	0	0	0	—	0	0	0	0	0.0	.000
1992			0	0	—	0.00	2	0	0	3	1	1	1	0	0	0	0	0	0	0	—	0	0	0	0	0.0	.000
1993			0	0	—	1.80	5	0	0	5	3	2	4	0	0	0	0	0	0	0	—	0	0	0	0	0.0	.000
3 yrs.			0	1	.000	2.08	8	0	0	8.2	4	5	5	0	0	1	0	0	0	0		0	0	0	0	0.0	
WORLD SERIES																											
1991	ATL	N	0	0	—	0.00	2	0	0	1	0	0	1	0	0	0	0	0	0	0	—	0	0	0	0	0.0	.000
1995			0	0	—	4.50	1	0	0	2	1	2	2	0	0	0	0	0	0	0	—	0	0	0	0	0.0	.000
2 yrs.			0	0		3.00	3	0	0	3	1	2	3	0	0	0	0	0	0	0		0	0	0	0	0.0	

Spike Merena

MERENA, JOHN JOSEPH
B. Nov. 18, 1909, Paterson, N. J. D. Mar. 9, 1977, Bridgeport, Conn.
BL TL 6′ 185 lbs.

Year	Team	Lg	W	L	PCT	ERA	G	GS	CG	IP	H	BB	SO	ShO	Relief Pitching W	Relief Pitching L	Relief Pitching SV	Batting AB	Batting H	Batting HR	BA	PO	A	E	DP	TC/G	FA
1934	BOS	A	1	2	.333	2.92	4	3	2	24.2	20	16	7	1	0	0	0	7	1	0	.143	0	2	0	0	0.5	1.000

Ron Meridith

MERIDITH, RONALD KNOX
B. Nov. 26, 1956, San Pedro, Calif.
BL TL 6′ 175 lbs.

Year	Team	Lg	W	L	PCT	ERA	G	GS	CG	IP	H	BB	SO	ShO	Relief Pitching W	Relief Pitching L	Relief Pitching SV	Batting AB	Batting H	Batting HR	BA	PO	A	E	DP	TC/G	FA
1984	CHI	N	0	0	—	3.38	3	0	0	5.1	6	2	4	0	0	0	0	0	0	0	—	1	0	0	0	0.3	1.000
1985			3	2	.600	4.47	32	0	0	46.1	53	24	23	0	3	2	1	4	1	0	.250	0	9	0	1	0.3	1.000
1986	TEX	A	1	0	1.000	3.00	5	0	0	3	2	1	2	0	1	0	0	0	0	0	—	0	2	0	0	0.4	1.000
1987			1	0	1.000	6.10	11	0	0	20.2	25	12	17	0	1	0	0	0	0	0	—	0	5	0	1	0.5	1.000
4 yrs.			5	2	.714	4.78	51	0	0	75.1	86	39	46	0	5	2	1	4	1	0	.250	1	16	0	2	0.3	1.000

Brett Merriman

MERRIMAN, BRETT ALAN
B. July 15, 1966, Jacksonville, Ill.
BR TR 6′ 2″ 210 lbs.

Year	Team	Lg	W	L	PCT	ERA	G	GS	CG	IP	H	BB	SO	ShO	Relief Pitching W	Relief Pitching L	Relief Pitching SV	Batting AB	Batting H	Batting HR	BA	PO	A	E	DP	TC/G	FA
1993	MIN	A	1	1	.500	9.67	19	0	0	27	36	23	14	0	1	1	0	0	0	0	—	1	4	0	0	0.3	1.000
1994			0	1	.000	6.35	15	0	0	17	18	14	10	0	0	1	0	0	0	0	—	0	1	0	0	0.1	1.000
2 yrs.			1	2	.333	8.39	34	0	0	44	54	37	24	0	1	2	0	0	0	0		1	5	0	0	0.2	1.000

George Merritt

MERRITT, GEORGE WASHINGTON
B. Apr. 14, 1880, Paterson, N. J. D. Feb. 21, 1938, Memphis, Tenn.
TR 6′ 160 lbs.

Year	Team	Lg	W	L	PCT	ERA	G	GS	CG	IP	H	BB	SO	ShO	Relief Pitching W	Relief Pitching L	Relief Pitching SV	Batting AB	Batting H	Batting HR	BA	PO	A	E	DP	TC/G	FA
1901	PIT	N	3	0	1.000	4.88	3	3	3	24	28	5	5	0	0	0	0	11	3	0	.273	1	5	0	0	2.0	1.000
1903			0	0	—	2.25	1	0	0	4	4	1	2	0	0	0	0	27	4	0	.148	4	1	0	0	2.5	1.000
2 yrs.			3	0	1.000	4.50	4	3	3	28	32	6	7	0	0	0	0	*				14	6	1	0	1.6	.952

Jim Merritt

MERRITT, JAMES JOSEPH
B. Dec. 9, 1943, Altadena, Calif.
BL TL 6′ 3″ 175 lbs.

Year	Team	Lg	W	L	PCT	ERA	G	GS	CG	IP	H	BB	SO	ShO	Relief Pitching W	Relief Pitching L	Relief Pitching SV	Batting AB	Batting H	Batting HR	BA	PO	A	E	DP	TC/G	FA
1965	MIN	A	5	4	.556	3.17	16	9	1	76.2	68	20	61	0	1	1	2	22	3	0	.136	2	13	1	1	1.0	.938
1966			7	14	.333	3.38	31	18	5	144	112	33	124	1	0	3	3	39	4	0	.103	7	20	0	0	0.9	1.000
1967			13	7	.650	2.53	37	28	11	227.2	196	30	161	4	1	0	0	74	10	0	.135	4	32	3	1	1.1	.923
1968			12	16	.429	3.25	38	34	11	238.1	207	52	181	1	1	0	1	71	10	0	.141	7	38	0	2	1.2	1.000
1969	CIN	N	17	9	.654	4.37	42	36	8	251	269	61	144	1	0	0	0	77	11	1	.143	7	33	1	1	1.0	.976
1970			20	12	.625	4.08	35	35	12	234	248	53	136	1	0	0	0	83	14	3	.169	5	30	2	1	1.1	.946
1971			1	11	.083	4.37	28	11	0	107	115	31	38	0	1	2	0	29	4	0	.138	5	10	1	1	0.6	.938
1972			1	0	1.000	4.50	4	1	0	8	13	2	4	0	1	0	0	2	0	0	.000	0	1	0	0	0.3	1.000
1973	TEX	A	5	13	.278	4.05	35	19	8	160	191	34	65	1	0	2	1	0	0	0	—	7	22	2	1	0.9	.935
1974			0	0	—	4.09	26	1	0	33	46	6	18	0	0	0	0	0	0	0	—	1	4	3	0	0.3	.625
1975			0	0	—	0.00	5	0	0	3.2	3	0	0	0	0	0	0	0	0	0	—	0	0	0	0	0.0	.000
11 yrs.			81	86	.485	3.65	297	192	56	1483.1	1468	322	932	9	5	8	7	397	56	4	.141	45	203	13	8	0.9	.950
LEAGUE CHAMPIONSHIP SERIES																											
1970	CIN	N	1	0	1.000	1.69	1	1	0	5.1	3	0	2	0	0	0	0	2	0	0	.000	0	2	0	0	2.0	1.000
WORLD SERIES																											
1965	MIN	A	0	0	—	2.70	2	0	0	3.1	2	0	1	0	0	0	0	0	0	0	—	0	2	0	0	1.0	1.000
1970	CIN	N	0	1	.000	21.60	1	1	0	1.2	3	1	0	0	0	0	0	1	0	0	.000	0	0	0	0	0.0	.000
2 yrs.			0	1	.000	9.00	3	1	0	5	5	1	1	0	0	0	0	1	0	0	.000	0	2	0	0	0.7	1.000

Lloyd Merritt

MERRITT, LLOYD WESLEY
B. Apr. 8, 1933, St. Louis, Mo.
BR TR 6′ 189 lbs.

Year	Team	Lg	W	L	PCT	ERA	G	GS	CG	IP	H	BB	SO	ShO	Relief Pitching W	Relief Pitching L	Relief Pitching SV	Batting AB	Batting H	Batting HR	BA	PO	A	E	DP	TC/G	FA
1957	STL	N	1	2	.333	3.31	44	0	0	65.1	60	28	35	0	1	2	7	7	0	0	.000	3	13	2	0	0.4	.889

Sam Mertes

MERTES, SAMUEL BLAIR (Sandow)
B. Aug. 6, 1872, San Francisco, Calif. D. Mar. 11, 1945, San Francisco, Calif.
BR TR 5′10″ 185 lbs.

Year	Team	Lg	W	L	PCT	ERA	G	GS	CG	IP	H	BB	SO	ShO	Relief Pitching W	Relief Pitching L	Relief Pitching SV	Batting AB	Batting H	Batting HR	BA	PO	A	E	DP	TC/G	FA
1902	CHI	A	1	0	1.000	1.17	1	0	0	7.2	6	0	0	0	1	0	0	*				86	5	9	1	2.7	.910

Jim Mertz

MERTZ, JAMES VERLIN
B. Aug. 10, 1916, Lima, Ohio
BR TR 5′10½″ 170 lbs.

Year	Team	W	L	PCT	ERA	G	GS	CG	IP	H	BB	SO	ShO	Relief Pitching W	Relief Pitching L	Relief Pitching SV	Batting AB	Batting H	Batting HR	BA	PO	A	E	DP	TC/G	FA
1943	WAS A	5	7	.417	4.63	33	10	2	116.2	109	58	53	0	2	1	3	38	7	0	.184	3	26	3	2	1.0	.906

Jose Mesa

MESA, JOSE RAMON
Born Jose Ramon Nova (Mesa).
B. May 22, 1966, Pueblo Viejo, Dominican Republic.
BR TR 6′ 3″ 170 lbs.

Year	Team	W	L	PCT	ERA	G	GS	CG	IP	H	BB	SO	ShO	Relief Pitching W	Relief Pitching L	Relief Pitching SV	Batting AB	Batting H	Batting HR	BA	PO	A	E	DP	TC/G	FA
1987	BAL A	1	3	.250	6.03	6	5	0	31.1	38	15	17	0	0	0	0	0	0	0	—	1	1	0	0	0.3	1.000
1990		3	2	.600	3.86	7	7	0	46.2	37	27	24	0	0	0	0	0	0	0	—	3	5	1	1	1.3	.889
1991		6	11	.353	5.97	23	23	2	123.2	151	62	64	1	0	0	0	0	0	0	—	17	17	0	0	1.5	1.000
1992	2 teams BAL A (13G 3–8) CLE A (15G 4–4)																									
″	total	7	12	.368	4.59	28	27	1	160.2	169	70	62	1	0	0	0	0	0	0		12	21	2	0	1.3	.943
1993	CLE A	10	12	.455	4.92	34	33	3	208.2	232	62	118	0	0	0	0	0	0	0	—	15	29	3	0	1.4	.936
1994		7	5	.583	3.82	51	0	0	73	71	26	63	0	7	5	2	0	0	0	—	3	11	2	0	0.3	.875
1995		3	0	1.000	1.13	62	0	0	64	49	17	58	0	3	0	**46**	0	0	0	—	6	10	1	0	0.3	.941
7 yrs.		37	45	.451	4.55	211	95	6	708	747	279	406	2	10	5	48	0	0	0		57	94	9	1	0.8	.944
DIVISIONAL PLAYOFF SERIES																										
1995	CLE A	0	0	—	0.00	2	0	0	2	0	2	0	0	0	0	0	0	0	0	—	0	0	0	0	0.0	.000
LEAGUE CHAMPIONSHIP SERIES																										
1995	CLE A	0	0	—	2.25	4	0	0	4	3	1	1	0	0	0	1	0	0	0	—	1	2	0	1	0.8	1.000
WORLD SERIES																										
1995	CLE A	1	0	1.000	4.50	2	0	0	4	5	1	4	0	1	0	1	0	0	0	—	0	0	0	0	0.0	.000

Bud Messenger

MESSENGER, ANDREW WARREN
B. Feb. 1, 1898, Grand Blanc, Mich. D. Nov. 4, 1971, Lansing, Mich.
BR TR 6′ 175 lbs.

Year	Team	W	L	PCT	ERA	G	GS	CG	IP	H	BB	SO	ShO	Relief Pitching W	Relief Pitching L	Relief Pitching SV	Batting AB	Batting H	Batting HR	BA	PO	A	E	DP	TC/G	FA
1924	CLE A	2	0	1.000	4.32	5	2	1	25	28	14	4	0	1	0	0	8	1	0	.125	0	6	0	0	1.2	1.000

Andy Messersmith

MESSERSMITH, JOHN ALEXANDER
B. Aug. 6, 1945, Toms River, N. J.
BR TR 6′ 1″ 200 lbs.

Year	Team	W	L	PCT	ERA	G	GS	CG	IP	H	BB	SO	ShO	Relief Pitching W	Relief Pitching L	Relief Pitching SV	Batting AB	Batting H	Batting HR	BA	PO	A	E	DP	TC/G	FA
1968	CAL A	4	2	.667	2.21	28	5	2	81.1	44	35	74	1	2	0	4	20	2	0	.100	6	12	1	0	0.7	.947
1969		16	11	.593	2.52	40	33	10	250	169	100	211	2	0	0	2	77	12	0	.156	17	29	5	2	1.3	.902
1970		11	10	.524	3.00	37	26	6	195	144	78	162	1	3	0	5	70	11	1	.157	12	23	4	3	1.1	.897
1971		20	13	.606	2.99	38	38	14	277	224	121	179	4	0	0	0	93	16	2	.172	18	49	5	2	1.9	.931
1972		8	11	.421	2.81	25	21	10	170	125	68	142	3	0	0	2	53	10	0	.189	9	24	0	0	1.3	1.000
1973	LA N	14	10	.583	2.70	33	33	10	249.2	196	77	177	3	0	0	0	89	15	0	.169	19	35	5	0	1.8	.915
1974		**20**	6	**.769**	2.59	39	39	13	292	227	94	221	3	0	0	0	96	23	1	.240	18	44	9	3	1.8	.873
1975		19	14	.576	2.29	42	**40**	**19**	**322**	244	96	213	**7**	0	0	1	108	17	0	.157	11	43	5	1	1.4	.915
1976	ATL N	11	11	.500	3.04	29	28	12	207	166	74	135	3	0	0	1	67	12	0	.179	14	33	5	2	1.8	.904
1977		5	4	.556	4.41	16	16	1	102	101	39	69	0	0	0	0	34	4	1	.118	5	15	2	1	1.4	.909
1978	NY A	0	3	.000	5.64	6	5	0	22.1	24	15	16	0	0	0	0	0	0	0	—	2	2	0	4	0.7	1.000
1979	LA N	2	4	.333	4.94	11	11	1	62	55	34	26	0	0	0	0	22	2	0	.091	5	9	0	1	1.3	1.000
12 yrs.		130	99	.568	2.86	344	295	98	2230.1	1719	831	1625	27	5	0	15	729	124	5	.170	136	318	41	19	1.4	.917
LEAGUE CHAMPIONSHIP SERIES																										
1974	LA N	1	0	1.000	2.57	1	1	1	7	8	3	0	0	0	0	0	3	0	0	.000	1	2	0	0	3.0	1.000
WORLD SERIES																										
1974	LA N	0	2	.000	4.50	2	2	0	14	11	7	12	0	0	0	0	4	2	0	.500	1	4	1	0	3.0	.833

Tom Metcalf

METCALF, THOMAS JOHN
B. July 16, 1940, Amherst, Wis.
BR TR 6′ 2½″ 174 lbs.

Year	Team	W	L	PCT	ERA	G	GS	CG	IP	H	BB	SO	ShO	Relief Pitching W	Relief Pitching L	Relief Pitching SV	Batting AB	Batting H	Batting HR	BA	PO	A	E	DP	TC/G	FA
1963	NY A	1	0	1.000	2.77	8	0	0	13	12	3	3	0	1	0	0	0	0	0	—	0	2	0	0	0.3	1.000

Dewey Metivier

METIVIER, GEORGE DEWEY
B. May 6, 1898, Cambridge, Mass. D. Mar. 2, 1947, Cambridge, Mass.
BL TR 5′11″ 175 lbs.
BL 1922

Year	Team	W	L	PCT	ERA	G	GS	CG	IP	H	BB	SO	ShO	Relief Pitching W	Relief Pitching L	Relief Pitching SV	Batting AB	Batting H	Batting HR	BA	PO	A	E	DP	TC/G	FA
1922	CLE A	2	0	1.000	4.50	2	2	2	18	18	3	1	0	0	0	0	6	1	0	.167	1	2	0	0	1.5	1.000
1923		4	2	.667	6.50	26	5	1	73.1	111	38	9	0	3	1	1	20	3	0	.150	2	22	1	2	1.0	.960
1924		1	5	.167	5.31	26	6	1	76.1	110	34	14	0	1	1	3	24	3	0	.125	5	14	0	1	0.7	1.000
3 yrs.		7	7	.500	5.74	54	13	4	167.2	239	75	24	0	4	2	4	50	7	0	.140	8	38	1	3	0.9	.979

Butch Metzger

METZGER, CLARENCE EDWARD
B. May 23, 1952, Lafayette, Ind.
BR TR 6′ 1″ 185 lbs.

Year	Team	W	L	PCT	ERA	G	GS	CG	IP	H	BB	SO	ShO	Relief Pitching W	Relief Pitching L	Relief Pitching SV	Batting AB	Batting H	Batting HR	BA	PO	A	E	DP	TC/G	FA
1974	SF N	1	0	1.000	3.46	10	0	0	13	11	12	5	0	1	0	0	0	0	0	—	1	1	0	0	0.2	1.000
1975	SD N	1	0	1.000	7.20	4	0	0	5	6	4	6	0	1	0	0	0	0	0	—	0	1	0	0	0.3	1.000
1976		11	4	.733	2.92	77	0	0	123.1	119	52	89	0	11	4	16	8	0	0	.000	5	17	1	0	0.3	.957
1977	2 teams SD N (17G 0–0) STL N (58G 4–2)																									
″	total	4	2	.667	3.59	75	1	0	115.1	105	50	54	0	4	2	7	7	0	0	.000	5	12	0	1	0.2	1.000
1978	NY N	1	3	.250	6.57	25	0	0	37	48	22	21	0	1	3	0	0	0	0	—	1	4	0	0	0.2	1.000
5 yrs.		18	9	.667	3.74	191	1	0	293.2	289	140	175	0	18	9	23	15	0	0	.000	12	35	1	1	0.3	.979

Bob Meyer

MEYER, ROBERT BERNARD
B. Aug. 4, 1939, Toledo, Ohio.
BR TL 6′ 2″ 185 lbs.

Year	Team	W	L	PCT	ERA	G	GS	CG	IP	H	BB	SO	ShO	Relief Pitching W	Relief Pitching L	Relief Pitching SV	Batting AB	Batting H	Batting HR	BA	PO	A	E	DP	TC/G	FA
1964	3 teams NY A (7G 0–3) LA A (6G 1–1) KC A (9G 1–4)																									
″	total	2	8	.200	4.37	22	13	2	78.1	78	58	55	0	0	2	0	21	0	0	.000	4	10	1	1	0.7	.933
1969	SEA A	0	3	.000	3.31	6	5	1	32.2	30	10	17	0	0	0	0	11	1	0	.091	0	3	3	0	1.0	.500
1970	MIL A	0	1	.000	6.50	10	0	0	18	24	12	20	0	0	0	0	3	1	0	.333	0	3	0	0	0.3	1.000
3 yrs.		2	12	.143	4.40	38	18	3	129	132	80	92	0	0	2	0	35	2	0	.057	4	16	4	1	0.6	.833

Brian Meyer

MEYER, BRIAN SCOTT
B. Jan. 29, 1963, Camden, N. J.
BR TR 6′ 1″ 190 lbs.

Year	Team	W	L	PCT	ERA	G	GS	CG	IP	H	BB	SO	ShO	Relief Pitching W	Relief Pitching L	Relief Pitching SV	Batting AB	Batting H	Batting HR	BA	PO	A	E	DP	TC/G	FA
1988	HOU N	0	0	—	1.46	8	0	0	12.1	9	4	10	0	0	0	0	0	0	0	—	0	5	0	0	0.6	1.000
1989		0	1	.000	4.50	12	0	0	18	16	13	13	0	0	1	1	0	0	0	—	2	2	0	0	0.3	1.000
1990		0	4	.000	2.21	14	0	0	20.1	16	6	6	0	0	4	1	1	0	0	.000	2	7	0	0	0.6	1.000
3 yrs.		0	5	.000	2.84	34	0	0	50.2	41	23	29	0	0	5	2	1	0	0	.000	4	14	0	0	0.5	1.000

Jack Meyer

MEYER, JOHN ROBERT
B. Mar. 23, 1932, Philadelphia, Pa. D. Mar. 9, 1967, Philadelphia, Pa.
BR TR 6′ 1″ 175 lbs.

Year	Team		W	L	PCT	ERA	G	GS	CG	IP	H	BB	SO	ShO	Relief Pitching W	Relief Pitching L	Relief Pitching SV	Batting AB	Batting H	Batting HR	BA	PO	A	E	DP	TC/G	FA
1955	PHI	N	6	11	.353	3.43	50	5	0	110.1	75	66	97	0	5	**7**	**16**	20	2	0	.100	6	13	1	0	0.4	.950
1956			7	11	.389	4.41	41	7	2	96	86	51	66	0	6	6	2	20	4	1	.200	4	17	1	2	0.5	.955
1957			0	2	.000	5.73	19	2	0	37.2	44	28	34	0	0	2	0	6	1	0	.167	5	6	0	0	0.6	1.000
1958			3	6	.333	3.59	37	5	1	90.1	77	33	87	0	3	2	2	18	5	0	.278	4	7	1	1	0.3	.917
1959			5	3	.625	3.36	47	1	1	93.2	76	53	71	0	5	2	1	14	1	0	.071	4	14	1	2	0.4	.947
1960			3	1	.750	4.32	7	4	0	25	25	11	18	0	1	0	0	8	1	0	.125	1	4	0	0	0.7	1.000
1961			0	0	—	9.00	1	0	0	2	2	2	2	0	0	0	0	0	0	0	—	0	0	0	0	0.0	.000
7 yrs.			24	34	.414	3.92	202	24	4	455	385	244	375	0	20	19	21	86	14	1	.163	24	61	4	5	0.4	.955

Russ Meyer

MEYER, RUSSELL CHARLES (The Mad Monk)
B. Oct. 25, 1923, Peru, Ill.
BB TR 6′ 1″ 175 lbs.

Year	Team		W	L	PCT	ERA	G	GS	CG	IP	H	BB	SO	ShO	Relief Pitching W	Relief Pitching L	Relief Pitching SV	Batting AB	Batting H	Batting HR	BA	PO	A	E	DP	TC/G	FA
1946	CHI	N	0	0	—	3.18	4	1	0	17	21	10	10	0	0	0	1	5	1	0	.200	0	4	0	0	1.0	1.000
1947			3	2	.600	3.40	23	2	1	45	43	14	22	0	3	1	0	12	3	0	.250	1	6	0	0	0.3	1.000
1948			10	10	.500	3.66	29	26	8	164.2	157	77	89	3	0	2	0	56	6	0	.107	12	26	1	0	1.3	.974
1949	PHI	N	17	8	.680	3.08	37	28	14	213	199	70	78	2	2	1	1	70	10	0	.143	14	28	1	3	1.2	.977
1950			9	11	.450	5.30	32	25	3	159.2	193	67	74	0	0	1	1	50	7	0	.140	8	31	0	4	1.2	1.000
1951			8	9	.471	3.48	28	24	7	168	172	55	65	2	0	1	0	48	5	0	.104	5	21	1	1	1.0	.963
1952			13	14	.481	3.14	37	32	14	232.1	235	65	92	1	0	1	1	79	7	1	.089	8	37	4	6	1.3	.918
1953	BKN	N	15	5	.750	4.56	34	32	10	191.1	201	63	106	2	0	1	0	75	11	0	.147	8	33	3	1	1.3	.932
1954			11	6	.647	3.99	36	28	6	180.1	193	49	70	2	0	0	0	47	2	0	.043	5	27	3	0	1.0	.914
1955			6	2	.750	5.42	18	11	2	73	86	31	26	1	1	1	0	27	1	0	.037	1	21	0	1	1.2	1.000
1956	2 teams	CHI N	(20G 1–6)		CIN N	(1G 0–0)																					
″	total		1	6	.143	6.21	21	9	0	58	72	26	29	0	0	1	0	12	1	0	.083	4	18	0	2	1.0	1.000
1957	BOS	A	0	0	—	5.40	2	1	0	5	10	3	1	0	0	0	0	1	1	0	1.000	0	4	0	0	2.0	1.000
1959	KC	A	1	0	1.000	4.50	18	0	0	24	24	11	10	0	1	0	1	2	0	0	.000	2	2	0	0	0.2	1.000
13 yrs.			94	73	.563	3.99	319	219	65	1531.1	1606	541	672	13	7	10	5	484	55	1	.114	68	258	13	18	1.1	.962
WORLD SERIES																											
1950	PHI	N	0	1	.000	5.40	2	0	0	1.2	4	0	1	0	0	1	0	0	0	0	—	0	1	0	0	0.5	1.000
1953	BKN	N	0	0	—	6.23	1	0	0	4.1	8	4	5	0	0	0	0	1	0	0	.000	0	1	0	0	1.0	1.000
1955			0	0	—	0.00	1	0	0	5.2	4	2	4	0	0	0	0	2	0	0	.000	0	1	0	0	1.0	1.000
3 yrs.			0	1	.000	3.09	4	0	0	11.2	16	6	10	0	0	1	0	3	0	0	.000	0	3	0	0	0.8	1.000

Levi Meyerle

MEYERLE, LEVI SAMUEL (Long Levi)
B. July 1845, Philadelphia, Pa. D. Nov. 4, 1921, Philadelphia, Pa.
BR TR 6′ 1″ 177 lbs.

Year	Team		W	L	PCT	ERA	G	GS	CG	IP	H	BB	SO	ShO	Relief Pitching W	Relief Pitching L	Relief Pitching SV	Batting AB	Batting H	Batting HR	BA	PO	A	E	DP	TC/G	FA
1876	PHI	N	0	2	.000	5.00	2	2	2	18	28	1	0	0	0	0	0	*				98	110	52	5	4.6	.800

Dan Miceli

MICELI, DANIEL
B. Sept. 9, 1970, Newark, N. J.
BR TR 6′ 1″ 185 lbs.

Year	Team		W	L	PCT	ERA	G	GS	CG	IP	H	BB	SO	ShO	Relief Pitching W	Relief Pitching L	Relief Pitching SV	Batting AB	Batting H	Batting HR	BA	PO	A	E	DP	TC/G	FA
1993	PIT	N	0	0	—	5.06	9	0	0	5.1	6	3	4	0	0	0	0	0	0	0	—	0	0	0	0	0.0	.000
1994			2	1	.667	5.93	28	0	0	27.1	28	11	27	0	2	1	2	3	0	0	.000	1	5	0	0	0.2	1.000
1995			4	4	.500	4.66	58	0	0	58	61	28	56	0	4	4	21	1	0	0	.000	2	5	0	0	0.1	1.000
3 yrs.			6	5	.545	5.06	95	0	0	90.2	95	42	87	0	6	5	23	4	0	0	.000	3	10	0	0	0.1	1.000

Gene Michael

MICHAEL, EUGENE RICHARD (Stick)
B. June 2, 1938, Kent, Ohio.
Manager 1981–82, 1986–87.
BB TR 6′ 2″ 183 lbs.

Year	Team		W	L	PCT	ERA	G	GS	CG	IP	H	BB	SO	ShO	Relief Pitching W	Relief Pitching L	Relief Pitching SV	Batting AB	Batting H	Batting HR	BA	PO	A	E	DP	TC/G	FA
1968	NY	A	0	0	—	0.00	1	0	0	3	5	0	3	0	0	0	0	*				10	20	3	7	3.0	.909

John Michaels

MICHAELS, JOHN JOSEPH
B. July 10, 1907, Bridgeport, Conn.
BL TL 5′10½″ 154 lbs.

Year	Team		W	L	PCT	ERA	G	GS	CG	IP	H	BB	SO	ShO	Relief Pitching W	Relief Pitching L	Relief Pitching SV	Batting AB	Batting H	Batting HR	BA	PO	A	E	DP	TC/G	FA
1932	BOS	A	1	6	.143	5.13	28	8	2	80.2	101	27	16	0	0	0	0	21	3	0	.143	5	24	3	1	1.1	.906

John Michaelson

MICHAELSON, JOHN AUGUST (Mike)
B. Aug. 12, 1893, Taivalkosi, Finland D. Apr. 16, 1968, Woodruff, Wis.
BR TR 5′ 9″ 165 lbs.

Year	Team		W	L	PCT	ERA	G	GS	CG	IP	H	BB	SO	ShO	Relief Pitching W	Relief Pitching L	Relief Pitching SV	Batting AB	Batting H	Batting HR	BA	PO	A	E	DP	TC/G	FA
1921	CHI	A	0	0	—	10.13	2	0	0	2.2	4	1	1	0	0	0	0	0	0	0	—	0	0	0	0	0.0	.000

Glenn Mickens

MICKENS, GLENN ROGER
B. July 26, 1930, Wilmar, Calif.
BR TR 6′ 175 lbs.

Year	Team		W	L	PCT	ERA	G	GS	CG	IP	H	BB	SO	ShO	Relief Pitching W	Relief Pitching L	Relief Pitching SV	Batting AB	Batting H	Batting HR	BA	PO	A	E	DP	TC/G	FA
1953	BKN	N	0	1	.000	11.37	4	2	0	6.1	11	4	5	0	0	0	0	2	0	0	.000	0	2	1	0	0.8	.667

Jim Middleton

MIDDLETON, JAMES BLAINE (Rifle Jim)
B. May 28, 1889, Argos, Ind. D. Jan. 12, 1974, Argos, Ind.
BR TR 5′11½″ 165 lbs.

Year	Team		W	L	PCT	ERA	G	GS	CG	IP	H	BB	SO	ShO	Relief Pitching W	Relief Pitching L	Relief Pitching SV	Batting AB	Batting H	Batting HR	BA	PO	A	E	DP	TC/G	FA
1917	NY	N	1	1	.500	2.75	13	0	0	36	35	8	9	0	1	1	1	8	0	0	.000	2	13	0	0	1.2	1.000
1921	DET	A	6	11	.353	5.03	38	10	2	121.2	149	44	31	0	4	**8**	**7**	34	5	0	.147	9	38	2	0	1.3	.959
2 yrs.			7	12	.368	4.51	51	10	2	157.2	184	52	40	0	5	9	8	42	5	0	.119	11	51	2	0	1.3	.969

John Middleton

MIDDLETON, JOHN WAYNE (Lefty)
B. Apr. 11, 1900, Mt. Calm, Tex. D. Nov. 3, 1986, Amarillo, Tex.
BL TL 6′ 1″ 185 lbs.

Year	Team		W	L	PCT	ERA	G	GS	CG	IP	H	BB	SO	ShO	Relief Pitching W	Relief Pitching L	Relief Pitching SV	Batting AB	Batting H	Batting HR	BA	PO	A	E	DP	TC/G	FA
1922	CLE	A	0	1	.000	7.36	2	1	0	7.1	8	6	2	0	0	0	0	3	1	0	.333	0	2	0	0	1.0	1.000

Dick Midkiff

MIDKIFF, RICHARD JAMES
B. Sept. 28, 1914, Gonzales, Tex. D. Oct. 30, 1956, Temple, Tex.
BR TR 6′ 2″ 195 lbs.

Year	Team		W	L	PCT	ERA	G	GS	CG	IP	H	BB	SO	ShO	Relief Pitching W	Relief Pitching L	Relief Pitching SV	Batting AB	Batting H	Batting HR	BA	PO	A	E	DP	TC/G	FA
1938	BOS	A	1	1	.500	5.09	13	2	0	35.1	43	21	10	0	1	0	0	10	2	0	.200	2	7	0	0	0.7	1.000

Gary Mielke

MIELKE, GARY ROGER
B. Jan. 28, 1963, St. James, Minn.
BR TR 6′ 3″ 185 lbs.

Year	Team		W	L	PCT	ERA	G	GS	CG	IP	H	BB	SO	ShO	Relief Pitching W	Relief Pitching L	Relief Pitching SV	Batting AB	Batting H	Batting HR	BA	PO	A	E	DP	TC/G	FA
1987	TEX	A	0	0	—	6.00	3	0	0	3	3	1	3	0	0	0	0	0	0	0	—	0	0	0	0	0.0	.000
1989			1	0	1.000	3.26	43	0	0	49.2	52	25	26	0	1	0	1	0	0	0	—	3	6	1	0	0.2	.900
1990			0	3	.000	3.73	33	0	0	41	42	15	13	0	0	3	0	0	0	0	—	2	7	0	0	0.3	1.000
3 yrs.			1	3	.250	3.56	79	0	0	93.2	97	41	42	0	1	3	1	0	0	0		5	13	1	0	0.2	.947

Pete Mikkelsen

MIKKELSEN, PETER JAMES
B. Oct. 25, 1939, Staten Island, N. Y.
BR TR 6′ 2″ 210 lbs.

Year	Team	W	L	PCT	ERA	G	GS	CG	IP	H	BB	SO	ShO	Relief W	Relief L	Relief SV	Batting AB	Batting H	Batting HR	BA	PO	A	E	DP	TC/G	FA
1964	NY A	7	4	.636	3.56	50	0	0	86	79	41	63	0	7	4	12	16	1	0	.063	9	17	0	1	0.5	1.000
1965		4	9	.308	3.28	41	3	0	82.1	78	36	69	0	4	6	1	10	1	0	.100	5	20	4	1	0.7	.862
1966	PIT N	9	8	.529	3.07	71	0	0	126	106	51	76	0	9	8	14	20	3	0	.150	7	20	1	0	0.4	.964
1967	2 teams PIT N (32G 1–2) CHI N (7G 0–0)																									
"	total	1	2	.333	4.55	39	0	0	63.1	59	24	30	0	1	2	2	4	0	0	.000	3	6	2	0	0.3	.818
1968	2 teams CHI N (3G 0–0) STL N (5G 0–0)																									
"	total	0	0		2.61	8	0	0	20.2	17	8	13	0	0	0	0	4	1	0	.250	0	3	2	0	0.6	.600
1969	LA N	7	5	.583	2.78	48	0	0	81	57	30	51	0	7	5	4	6	1	0	.167	7	17	2	0	0.5	.923
1970		4	2	.667	2.76	33	0	0	62	48	20	47	0	4	2	6	6	2	0	.333	5	10	0	0	0.5	1.000
1971		8	5	.615	3.65	41	0	0	74	67	17	46	0	8	5	5	10	2	0	.200	9	13	2	0	0.6	.917
1972		5	5	.500	4.06	33	0	0	57.2	65	23	41	0	5	5	5	7	0	0	.000	1	9	1	0	0.3	.909
9 yrs.		45	40	.529	3.38	364	3	0	653	576	250	436	0	45	37	49	83	11	0	.133	46	115	14	2	0.5	.920
WORLD SERIES																										
1964	NY A	0	1	.000	5.79	4	0	0	4.2	4	2	4	0	0	1	0	0	0	0	—	0	2	0	0	0.5	1.000

John Miklos

MIKLOS, JOHN JOSEPH (Hank)
B. Nov. 27, 1910, Chicago, Ill.
BL TL 5′11″ 185 lbs.

Year	Team	W	L	PCT	ERA	G	GS	CG	IP	H	BB	SO	ShO	Relief W	Relief L	Relief SV	Batting AB	Batting H	Batting HR	BA	PO	A	E	DP	TC/G	FA
1944	CHI N	0	0	—	7.71	2	0	0	7	9	3	0	0	0	0	0	2	0	0	.000	0	4	0	0	2.0	1.000

Bob Milacki

MILACKI, ROBERT
B. July 28, 1964, Trenton, N. J.
BR TR 6′ 4″ 220 lbs.

Year	Team	W	L	PCT	ERA	G	GS	CG	IP	H	BB	SO	ShO	Relief W	Relief L	Relief SV	Batting AB	Batting H	Batting HR	BA	PO	A	E	DP	TC/G	FA
1988	BAL A	2	0	1.000	0.72	3	3	1	25	9	9	18	1	0	0	0	0	0	0	—	4	3	0	1	2.3	1.000
1989		14	12	.538	3.74	37	**36**	3	243	233	88	113	2	0	0	0	0	0	0	—	27	28	2	5	1.5	.965
1990		5	8	.385	4.46	27	24	1	135.1	143	61	60	1	0	0	0	0	0	0	—	21	16	1	2	1.4	.974
1991		10	9	.526	4.01	31	26	3	184	175	53	108	1	1	0	0	0	0	0	—	23	24	2	4	1.6	.959
1992		6	8	.429	5.84	23	20	0	115.2	140	44	51	0	0	0	1	0	0	0	—	14	10	0	0	1.0	1.000
1993	CLE A	1	1	.500	3.38	5	2	0	16	19	11	7	0	1	0	0	0	0	0	—	0	3	0	0	0.6	1.000
1994	KC A	0	5	.000	6.14	10	10	0	55.2	68	20	17	0	0	0	0	0	0	0	—	8	13	1	0	2.2	.955
7 yrs.		38	43	.469	4.31	136	121	8	774.2	787	286	374	5	2	0	1	0	0	0		97	97	6	12	1.5	.970

Carl Miles

MILES, CARL THOMAS
B. Mar. 22, 1918, Trenton, Mo.
BB TL 5′11″ 178 lbs.

Year	Team	W	L	PCT	ERA	G	GS	CG	IP	H	BB	SO	ShO	Relief W	Relief L	Relief SV	Batting AB	Batting H	Batting HR	BA	PO	A	E	DP	TC/G	FA
1940	PHI A	0	0	—	13.50	2	0	0	8	9	8	6	0	0	0	0	4	3	0	.750	0	1	0	0	0.5	1.000

Jim Miles

MILES, JAMES CHARLIE
B. Aug. 8, 1943, Grenada, Miss.
BR TR 6′ 2″ 210 lbs.

Year	Team	W	L	PCT	ERA	G	GS	CG	IP	H	BB	SO	ShO	Relief W	Relief L	Relief SV	Batting AB	Batting H	Batting HR	BA	PO	A	E	DP	TC/G	FA
1968	WAS A	0	0	—	12.46	3	0	0	4.1	8	2	5	0	0	0	0	0	0	0	—	0	0	0	0	0.0	.000
1969		0	1	.000	6.20	10	1	0	20.1	19	15	15	0	0	0	0	3	1	0	.333	2	5	0	1	0.7	1.000
2 yrs.		0	1	.000	7.30	13	1	0	24.2	27	17	20	0	0	0	0	3	1	0	.333	2	5	0	1	0.5	1.000

Sam Militello

MILITELLO, SAM SALVATORE
B. Nov. 26, 1969, Tampa, Fla.
BR TR 6′ 3″ 200 lbs.

Year	Team	W	L	PCT	ERA	G	GS	CG	IP	H	BB	SO	ShO	Relief W	Relief L	Relief SV	Batting AB	Batting H	Batting HR	BA	PO	A	E	DP	TC/G	FA
1992	NY A	3	3	.500	3.45	9	9	0	60	43	32	42	0	0	0	0	0	0	0	—	2	4	2	0	0.9	.750
1993		1	1	.500	6.75	3	2	0	9.1	10	7	5	0	0	0	0	0	0	0	—	2	1	0	0	1.0	1.000
2 yrs.		4	4	.500	3.89	12	11	0	69.1	53	39	47	0	0	0	0	0	0	0		4	5	2	0	0.9	.818

Johnny Miljus

MILJUS, JOHN KENNETH (Big Serb)
B. June 30, 1895, Pittsburgh, Pa. D. Feb. 11, 1976, Fort Harrison, Mont.
BR TR 6′ 1″ 178 lbs.

Year	Team	W	L	PCT	ERA	G	GS	CG	IP	H	BB	SO	ShO	Relief W	Relief L	Relief SV	Batting AB	Batting H	Batting HR	BA	PO	A	E	DP	TC/G	FA
1915	PIT F	0	0	—	0.00	1	0	0	1	1	0	0	0	0	0	0	0	0	0	—	0	1	0	0	1.0	1.000
1917	BKN N	0	1	.000	0.60	4	1	1	15	14	8	9	0	0	0	0	5	0	0	.000	0	4	2	0	1.5	.667
1920		1	0	1.000	3.09	9	0	0	23.1	24	4	9	0	1	0	0	6	2	0	.333	0	9	0	1	1.0	1.000
1921		6	3	.667	4.23	28	9	3	93.2	115	27	37	0	2	0	1	30	5	0	.167	4	33	1	1	1.4	.974
1927	PIT N	8	3	.727	1.90	19	6	3	75.2	62	17	24	2	4	1	0	28	5	0	.179	4	23	0	2	1.4	1.000
1928	2 teams PIT N (21G 5–7) CLE A (11G 1–4)																									
"	total	6	11	.353	4.19	32	14	4	120.1	136	53	45	0	3	2	2	41	11	0	.268	5	25	1	1	1.0	.968
1929	CLE A	8	8	.500	5.19	34	15	4	128.1	174	64	42	0	4	1	2	43	11	0	.256	9	28	3	1	1.2	.925
7 yrs.		29	26	.527	3.92	127	45	15	457.1	526	173	166	2	14	4	5	153	34	0	.222	22	123	7	6	1.2	.954
WORLD SERIES																										
1927	PIT N	0	1	.000	1.35	2	0	0	6.2	4	4	6	0	0	1	0	2	0	0	.000	1	2	0	0	1.5	1.000

Bill Miller

MILLER, WILLIAM FRANCIS (Wild Bill)
B. Apr. 12, 1910, Hannibal, Mo. D. Feb. 26, 1982, Hannibal, Mo.
BR TR 6′ 180 lbs.

Year	Team	W	L	PCT	ERA	G	GS	CG	IP	H	BB	SO	ShO	Relief W	Relief L	Relief SV	Batting AB	Batting H	Batting HR	BA	PO	A	E	DP	TC/G	FA
1937	STL A	0	1	.000	13.50	1	1	0	4	7	4	1	0	0	0	0	1	0	0	.000	0	1	0	0	1.0	1.000

Bill Miller

MILLER, WILLIAM PAUL (Hooks)
B. July 26, 1927, Minersville, Pa.
BL TL 6′ 175 lbs.

Year	Team	W	L	PCT	ERA	G	GS	CG	IP	H	BB	SO	ShO	Relief W	Relief L	Relief SV	Batting AB	Batting H	Batting HR	BA	PO	A	E	DP	TC/G	FA
1952	NY A	4	6	.400	3.48	21	13	5	88	78	49	45	2	0	1	0	28	6	0	.214	2	15	1	0	0.9	.944
1953		2	1	.667	4.76	13	3	0	34	46	19	17	0	1	0	1	10	2	0	.200	1	10	0	0	0.8	1.000
1954		0	1	.000	6.35	2	1	0	5.2	9	1	6	0	0	0	0	1	0	0	.000	0	0	0	0	0.0	.000
1955	BAL A	0	1	.000	13.50	5	1	0	4	3	10	4	0	0	0	0	1	1	0	1.000	0	1	0	0	0.2	1.000
4 yrs.		6	9	.400	4.24	41	18	5	131.2	136	79	72	2	1	1	1	40	9	0	.225	3	26	1	0	0.7	.967

Bob Miller

MILLER, ROBERT GERALD
B. July 15, 1935, Berwyn, Ill.
BR TL 6′ 1″ 185 lbs.

Year	Team	W	L	PCT	ERA	G	GS	CG	IP	H	BB	SO	ShO	Relief W	Relief L	Relief SV	Batting AB	Batting H	Batting HR	BA	PO	A	E	DP	TC/G	FA
1953	DET A	1	2	.333	5.94	13	1	0	36.1	46	21	9	0	1	1	0	8	1	0	.125	5	7	0	0	0.9	1.000
1954		1	1	.500	2.45	32	1	0	69.2	62	26	27	0	1	1	1	15	2	0	.133	4	9	1	0	0.4	.929
1955		2	1	.667	2.49	7	3	1	25.1	26	12	11	0	0	0	0	9	2	0	.222	1	3	0	0	0.6	1.000
1956		0	2	.000	5.68	11	3	0	31.2	37	22	16	0	0	0	0	7	1	0	.143	2	3	2	1	0.6	.714
1962	2 teams CIN N (6G 0–0) NY N (17G 2–2)																									
"	total	2	2	.500	10.17	23	0	0	25.2	38	11	12	0	2	2	0	2	0	0	.000	2	4	0	1	0.3	1.000
5 yrs.		6	8	.429	4.72	86	8	1	188.2	206	92	75	0	4	4	1	41	6	0	.146	14	26	3	2	0.5	.930

Bob Miller

MILLER, ROBERT JOHN BR TR 6′ 3″ 190 lbs.
B. June 16, 1926, Detroit, Mich.

Year	Team	W	L	PCT	ERA	G	GS	CG	IP	H	BB	SO	ShO	Relief Pitching W	Relief Pitching L	Relief Pitching SV	Batting AB	Batting H	Batting HR	BA	PO	A	E	DP	TC/G	FA
1949	**PHI N**	0	0	—	0.00	3	0	0	2.2	2	2	0	0	0	0	0	0	0	0	—	0	1	0	0	0.3	1.000
1950		11	6	.647	3.57	35	21	7	174	190	57	44	2	0	0	1	61	11	0	.180	15	40	0	2	1.6	1.000
1951		2	1	.667	6.82	17	3	0	34.1	47	18	10	0	1	1	0	7	3	0	.429	1	3	0	0	0.2	1.000
1952		0	1	.000	6.00	3	1	0	9	13	1	2	0	0	0	0	1	0	0	.000	1	3	0	0	1.3	1.000
1953		8	9	.471	4.00	35	20	8	157.1	169	42	63	3	2	1	2	55	10	0	.182	8	24	0	3	0.9	1.000
1954		7	9	.438	4.56	30	16	5	150	176	39	42	0	4	1	0	50	8	1	.160	13	31	2	4	1.5	.957
1955		8	4	.667	2.41	40	0	0	89.2	80	28	28	0	8	4	1	18	5	0	.278	3	17	0	1	0.5	1.000
1956		3	6	.333	3.24	49	6	3	122.1	115	34	53	1	1	4	5	22	2	0	.091	9	19	0	1	0.6	1.000
1957		2	5	.286	2.69	32	1	0	60.1	61	17	12	0	2	5	6	8	2	1	.250	4	7	0	2	0.3	1.000
1958		1	1	.500	11.69	17	0	0	22.1	36	9	9	0	1	1	0	1	0	0	.000	1	3	0	0	0.2	1.000
10 yrs.		42	42	.500	3.96	261	68	23	822	889	247	263	6	19	17	15	223	41	2	.184	55	148	2	13	0.8	.990
WORLD SERIES																										
1950	**PHI N**	0	1	.000	27.00	1	1	0	0.1	2	0	0	0	0	0	0	0	0	0	—	0	0	0	0	0.0	.000

Bob Miller

MILLER, ROBERT LANE BR TR 6′ 1″ 180 lbs.
Born Robert Lane Gemeinweiser.
B. Feb. 18, 1939, St. Louis, Mo. D. Aug. 6, 1993, Rancho Bernardo, Calif.

Year	Team	W	L	PCT	ERA	G	GS	CG	IP	H	BB	SO	ShO	Relief Pitching W	Relief Pitching L	Relief Pitching SV	Batting AB	Batting H	Batting HR	BA	PO	A	E	DP	TC/G	FA
1957	**STL N**	0	0	—	7.00	5	0	0	9	13	5	7	0	0	0	0	0	0	0	—	1	2	0	0	0.6	1.000
1959		4	3	.571	3.31	11	10	3	70.2	66	21	43	0	0	0	0	24	5	0	.208	6	16	0	1	2.0	1.000
1960		4	3	.571	3.42	15	7	0	52.2	53	17	33	0	1	0	0	14	2	0	.143	3	11	0	0	0.9	1.000
1961		1	3	.250	4.24	34	5	0	74.1	82	46	39	0	1	1	3	14	5	0	.357	2	18	3	3	0.7	.870
1962	**NY N**	1	12	.077	4.89	33	21	1	143.2	146	62	91	0	0	1	1	41	5	0	.122	14	32	2	3	1.5	.958
1963	**LA N**	10	8	.556	2.89	42	23	2	187	171	65	125	0	4	2	1	57	4	0	.070	15	54	2	5	1.7	.972
1964		7	7	.500	2.62	**74**	2	0	137.2	115	63	94	0	6	7	9	19	3	0	.158	8	36	1	2	0.6	.978
1965		6	7	.462	2.97	61	1	0	103	82	26	77	0	6	6	9	16	0	0	.000	2	29	4	0	0.6	.886
1966		4	2	.667	2.77	46	0	0	84.1	70	29	58	0	4	2	5	13	1	0	.077	3	10	5	1	0.4	.722
1967		2	9	.182	4.31	52	4	0	85.2	88	27	32	0	2	6	0	8	1	0	.125	6	21	3	1	0.6	.900
1968	**MIN A**	0	3	.000	2.74	45	0	0	72.1	65	24	41	0	0	3	2	7	1	0	.143	3	15	0	2	0.4	1.000
1969		5	5	.500	3.02	48	11	1	119.1	118	32	57	0	0	4	3	31	0	0	.000	7	25	0	2	0.7	1.000
1970	**3 teams** **CLE A** (15G 2–2) **CHI N** (7G 0–0) **CHI A** (15G 4–6)																									
″	**total**	6	8	.429	4.79	37	15	0	107	129	54	55	0	2	0	3	28	5	0	.179	7	22	0	2	0.8	1.000
1971	**3 teams** **CHI N** (2G 0–0) **SD N** (38G 7–3) **PIT N** (16G 1–2)																									
″	**total**	8	5	.615	1.64	56	0	0	98.2	83	40	51	0	8	5	10	12	0	0	.000	16	17	1	3	0.6	.971
1972	**PIT N**	5	2	.714	2.65	36	0	0	54.1	54	24	18	0	5	2	3	4	0	0	.000	2	8	1	1	0.3	.909
1973	**3 teams** **DET A** (22G 4–2) **SD N** (18G 0–0) **NY N** (1G 0–0)																									
″	**total**	4	2	.667	3.67	41	0	0	73.2	63	34	39	0	4	2	1	2	0	0	.000	4	7	0	1	0.3	1.000
1974	**NY N**	2	2	.500	3.58	58	0	0	78	89	39	35	0	2	2	2	9	1	0	.111	7	12	0	0	0.3	1.000
17 yrs.		69	81	.460	3.37	694	99	7	1551.1	1487	608	895	0	45	43	52	299	33	0	.110	106	335	22	27	0.7	.952
LEAGUE CHAMPIONSHIP SERIES																										
1969	**MIN A**	0	1	.000	5.40	1	1	0	1.2	5	0	0	0	0	0	0	0	0	0	—	0	0	0	0	0.0	.000
1971	**PIT N**	0	0	—	6.00	1	0	0	3	3	3	3	0	0	0	0	1	0	0	.000	1	0	0	0	1.0	1.000
1972		0	0	—	0.00	1	0	0	1	0	0	1	0	0	0	0	0	0	0	—	0	0	0	0	0.0	.000
3 yrs.		0	1	.000	4.76	3	1	0	5.2	8	3	4	0	0	0	0	1	0	0	.000	1	0	0	0	0.3	1.000
WORLD SERIES																										
1965	**LA N**	0	0	—	0.00	2	0	0	1.1	0	0	0	0	0	0	0	0	0	0	—	0	0	0	0	0.0	.000
1966		0	0	—	0.00	1	0	0	3	2	2	1	0	0	0	0	0	0	0	—	0	1	0	0	1.0	1.000
1971	**PIT N**	0	1	.000	3.86	3	0	0	4.2	7	1	2	0	0	0	0	0	0	0	—	1	1	0	0	0.7	1.000
3 yrs.		0	1	.000	2.00	6	0	0	9	9	3	3	0	0	0	0	0	0	0		1	2	0	0	0.5	1.000

Bob Miller

MILLER, ROBERT W.
B. 1862 Deceased.

Year	Team	W	L	PCT	ERA	G	GS	CG	IP	H	BB	SO	ShO	Relief Pitching W	Relief Pitching L	Relief Pitching SV	Batting AB	Batting H	Batting HR	BA	PO	A	E	DP	TC/G	FA
1890	**ROC AA**	3	7	.300	*4.29*	13	12	11	92.1	89	26	20	0	0	0	1	40	6	0	.150	2	22	2	0	1.6	.923
1891	**WAS AA**	2	5	.286	4.29	7	7	3	42	53	24	13	0	0	0	0	18	2	0	.111	3	13	2	0	2.6	.889
2 yrs.		5	12	.294	4.29	20	19	14	134.1	142	50	33	0	0	0	1	58	8	0	.138	5	35	4	0	1.9	.909

Burt Miller

MILLER, HERBERT A.
B. Oct. 28, 1875, Riley, Mich. Deceased.

Year	Team	W	L	PCT	ERA	G	GS	CG	IP	H	BB	SO	ShO	Relief Pitching W	Relief Pitching L	Relief Pitching SV	Batting AB	Batting H	Batting HR	BA	PO	A	E	DP	TC/G	FA
1897	**LOU N**	0	1	.000	7.94	4	1	1	17	32	3	3	0	0	0	0	6	1	0	.167	1	4	0	0	1.3	1.000

Cyclone Miller

MILLER, JOSEPH H. TL 5′ 9½″ 165 lbs.
B. Sept. 24, 1859, Springfield, Mass. D. Oct. 13, 1916, New London, Conn.

Year	Team	W	L	PCT	ERA	G	GS	CG	IP	H	BB	SO	ShO	Relief Pitching W	Relief Pitching L	Relief Pitching SV	Batting AB	Batting H	Batting HR	BA	PO	A	E	DP	TC/G	FA
1884	**3 teams** **CHI U** (1G 1–0) **PRO N** (6G 2–2) **PHI N** (1G 0–1)																									
″	**total**	3	3	.500	3.25	8	7	4	52.2	57	17	26	0	0	**1**	0	31	2	0	.065	2	14	0	0	1.3	1.000
1886	**PHI AA**	10	8	.556	*2.97*	19	19	19	169.2	158	59	99	1	0	0	0	66	9	0	.136	5	39	2	1	2.2	.957
2 yrs.		13	11	.542	3.04	27	26	23	222.1	215	76	125	1	0	1	0	97	11	0	.113	7	53	2	1	1.9	.968

Dyar Miller

MILLER, DYAR K. BR TR 6′ 1″ 195 lbs.
B. May 29, 1946, Batesville, Ind.

Year	Team	W	L	PCT	ERA	G	GS	CG	IP	H	BB	SO	ShO	Relief Pitching W	Relief Pitching L	Relief Pitching SV	Batting AB	Batting H	Batting HR	BA	PO	A	E	DP	TC/G	FA
1975	**BAL A**	6	3	.667	2.72	30	0	0	46.1	32	16	33	0	6	3	8	0	0	0	—	1	8	1	0	0.3	.900
1976		2	4	.333	2.93	49	0	0	89	79	36	37	0	2	4	7	0	0	0	—	1	10	2	1	0.3	.846
1977	**2 teams** **BAL A** (12G 2–2) **CAL A** (41G 4–4)																									
″	**total**	6	6	.500	3.53	53	0	0	114.2	106	40	58	0	6	6	5	0	0	0		9	11	0	1	0.4	1.000
1978	**CAL A**	6	2	.750	2.66	41	0	0	84.2	85	41	34	0	6	2	1	0	0	0	—	6	4	1	0	0.3	.909
1979	**2 teams** **CAL A** (14G 1–0) **TOR A** (10G 0–0)																									
″	**total**	1	0	1.000	5.58	24	1	0	50	71	18	23	0	1	0	0	0	0	0		4	3	0	0	0.3	1.000
1980	**NY N**	1	2	.333	1.93	31	0	0	42	37	11	28	0	1	2	1	1	0	0	.000	0	4	2	1	0.2	.667
1981		1	0	1.000	3.32	23	0	0	38	49	15	22	0	1	0	0	3	1	0	.333	2	2	1	1	0.2	.800
7 yrs.		23	17	.575	3.23	251	1	0	464.2	459	177	235	0	23	17	22	4	1	0	.250	23	42	7	4	0.3	.903

Elmer Miller

MILLER, ELMER JOSEPH BL TL 5′11″ 189 lbs.
B. Apr. 17, 1904, Detroit, Mich. D. Jan. 8, 1987, Corona, Calif.

Year	Team	W	L	PCT	ERA	G	GS	CG	IP	H	BB	SO	ShO	Relief Pitching W	Relief Pitching L	Relief Pitching SV	Batting AB	Batting H	Batting HR	BA	PO	A	E	DP	TC/G	FA
1929	**PHI N**	0	1	.000	11.12	8	2	0	11.1	12	21	5	0	0	0	0	*				11	5	1	0	1.4	.941

Frank Miller

MILLER, FRANK LEE (Bullet) BR TR 6′ 188 lbs.
B. Mar. 13, 1886, Allegan, Mich. D. Feb. 19, 1974, Allegan, Mich.

Year	Team	W	L	PCT	ERA	G	GS	CG	IP	H	BB	SO	ShO	Relief Pitching W	Relief Pitching L	Relief Pitching SV	Batting AB	Batting H	Batting HR	BA	PO	A	E	DP	TC/G	FA
1913	CHI A	0	1	.000	27.00	1	1	0	1.2	4	3	2	0	0	0	0	0	0	0	—	0	1	0	0	1.0	1.000
1916	PIT N	7	10	.412	2.29	30	20	10	173	135	49	88	2	0	2	1	51	7	0	.137	3	44	3	0	1.7	.940
1917		10	19	.345	3.13	38	28	14	224	216	60	92	5	1	2	1	76	9	0	.118	4	69	1	0	1.9	.986
1918		11	8	.579	2.38	23	23	14	170.1	152	37	47	2	0	0	0	57	6	0	.105	2	53	3	1	2.5	.948
1919		13	12	.520	3.03	32	26	16	201.2	170	34	59	3	0	0	0	66	7	0	.106	10	63	2	2	2.3	.973
1922	BOS N	11	13	.458	3.51	31	23	14	200	213	60	65	2	2	1	1	68	8	0	.118	4	51	3	0	1.9	.948
1923		0	3	.000	4.58	8	6	0	39.1	54	11	6	0	0	0	1	7	1	0	.143	1	5	0	0	0.8	1.000
7 yrs.		52	66	.441	3.01	163	127	68	1010	944	254	359	14	3	5	4	325	38	0	.117	24	286	12	3	2.0	.963

Fred Miller

MILLER, FREDERICK HOLMAN (Speedy) BL TL 6′ 2″ 190 lbs.
B. June 28, 1886, Fairfield, Ind. D. May 2, 1953, Brookville, Ind.

Year	Team	W	L	PCT	ERA	G	GS	CG	IP	H	BB	SO	ShO	Relief Pitching W	Relief Pitching L	Relief Pitching SV	Batting AB	Batting H	Batting HR	BA	PO	A	E	DP	TC/G	FA
1910	BKN N	1	1	.500	4.71	6	2	0	21	25	13	2	0	0	0	0	8	2	0	.250	0	9	0	0	1.5	1.000

Jake Miller

MILLER, WALTER BL TL 6′ 2″ 170 lbs.
Brother of Russ Miller.
B. Feb. 28, 1898, Wagram, Ohio D. Aug. 20, 1975, Venice, Fla.

Year	Team	W	L	PCT	ERA	G	GS	CG	IP	H	BB	SO	ShO	Relief Pitching W	Relief Pitching L	Relief Pitching SV	Batting AB	Batting H	Batting HR	BA	PO	A	E	DP	TC/G	FA
1924	CLE A	0	1	.000	3.00	2	2	1	12	13	5	4	0	0	0	0	5	0	0	.000	1	3	1	1	2.5	.800
1925		10	13	.435	3.31	32	22	13	190.1	207	62	51	0	2	2	2	71	13	0	.183	22	43	3	1	2.1	.956
1926		7	4	.636	3.27	18	11	5	82.2	99	18	24	3	2	0	1	24	2	0	.083	8	16	0	0	1.3	1.000
1927		10	8	.556	3.21	34	23	11	185.1	189	48	53	0	0	1	0	58	8	0	.138	9	48	3	2	1.8	.950
1928		8	9	.471	4.44	25	23	8	158	203	43	37	0	0	0	0	52	7	0	.135	11	39	1	2	2.0	.980
1929		14	12	.538	3.58	29	29	14	206	227	60	58	2	0	0	0	75	15	0	.200	15	47	5	3	2.3	.925
1930		4	5	.444	7.13	24	9	1	88.1	147	38	31	0	2	0	0	33	10	0	.303	10	26	5	1	1.7	.878
1931		2	1	.667	4.35	10	5	1	41.1	45	19	17	1	1	0	0	13	1	0	.077	5	11	1	0	1.7	.941
1933	CHI A	5	6	.455	5.62	26	14	4	105.2	130	47	30	2	0	1	0	37	7	0	.189	2	31	3	1	1.4	.917
9 yrs.		60	59	.504	4.09	200	138	58	1069.2	1260	340	305	8	7	4	3	368	63	0	.171	83	264	22	11	1.8	.940

John Miller

MILLER, JOHN ERNEST BR TR 6′ 2″ 210 lbs.
B. May 30, 1941, Baltimore, Md.

Year	Team	W	L	PCT	ERA	G	GS	CG	IP	H	BB	SO	ShO	Relief Pitching W	Relief Pitching L	Relief Pitching SV	Batting AB	Batting H	Batting HR	BA	PO	A	E	DP	TC/G	FA
1962	BAL A	1	1	.500	0.90	2	1	0	10	2	5	4	0	1	0	0	3	0	0	.000	0	3	0	0	1.5	1.000
1963		1	1	.500	3.18	3	2	0	17	12	14	16	0	0	0	0	6	0	0	.000	2	1	0	0	1.0	1.000
1965		6	4	.600	3.18	16	16	1	93.1	75	58	71	0	0	0	0	30	3	0	.100	4	17	2	1	1.4	.913
1966		4	8	.333	4.74	23	16	0	100.2	92	58	81	0	2	1	0	34	4	0	.118	8	16	0	2	1.0	1.000
1967		0	0	—	7.50	2	0	0	6	7	3	6	0	0	0	0	0	0	0	—	0	1	0	0	0.5	1.000
5 yrs.		12	14	.462	3.89	46	35	1	227	188	138	178	0	3	1	0	73	7	0	.096	14	38	2	3	1.2	.963

Ken Miller

MILLER, KENNETH ALBERT (Whitey) BR TR 6′ 1″ 195 lbs.
B. May 2, 1915, St. Louis, Mo. D. Apr. 3, 1991, St. Louis, Mo.

Year	Team	W	L	PCT	ERA	G	GS	CG	IP	H	BB	SO	ShO	Relief Pitching W	Relief Pitching L	Relief Pitching SV	Batting AB	Batting H	Batting HR	BA	PO	A	E	DP	TC/G	FA
1944	NY N	0	1	.000	0.00	4	0	0	5	1	4	2	0	0	1	0	1	0	0	.000	1	1	1	0	0.8	.667

Kurt Miller

MILLER, KURT EVERETT BR TR 6′ 5″ 205 lbs.
B. Aug. 24, 1972, Tucson, Ariz.

Year	Team	W	L	PCT	ERA	G	GS	CG	IP	H	BB	SO	ShO	Relief Pitching W	Relief Pitching L	Relief Pitching SV	Batting AB	Batting H	Batting HR	BA	PO	A	E	DP	TC/G	FA
1994	FLA N	1	3	.250	8.10	4	4	0	20	26	7	11	0	0	0	0	6	1	0	.167	3	4	0	2	1.8	1.000

Larry Miller

MILLER, LARRY DON BL TL 6′ 195 lbs.
B. June 19, 1937, Topeka, Kans.

Year	Team	W	L	PCT	ERA	G	GS	CG	IP	H	BB	SO	ShO	Relief Pitching W	Relief Pitching L	Relief Pitching SV	Batting AB	Batting H	Batting HR	BA	PO	A	E	DP	TC/G	FA
1964	LA N	4	8	.333	4.18	16	14	1	79.2	87	28	50	0	1	0	0	26	7	0	.269	3	12	0	0	0.9	1.000
1965	NY N	1	4	.200	5.02	28	5	0	57.1	66	25	36	0	1	0	0	11	2	0	.182	4	9	3	0	0.6	.813
1966		0	2	.000	7.56	4	1	0	8.1	9	4	7	0	0	1	0	2	1	0	.500	0	0	0	0	0.0	.000
3 yrs.		5	14	.263	4.71	48	20	1	145.1	162	57	93	0	2	1	0	39	10	0	.256	7	21	3	0	0.6	.903

Ox Miller

MILLER, JOHN ANTHONY BR TR 6′ 1″ 190 lbs.
B. May 4, 1915, Gause, Tex.

Year	Team	W	L	PCT	ERA	G	GS	CG	IP	H	BB	SO	ShO	Relief Pitching W	Relief Pitching L	Relief Pitching SV	Batting AB	Batting H	Batting HR	BA	PO	A	E	DP	TC/G	FA
1943	2 teams WAS A (3G 0–0) STL A (2G 0–0)																									
″	total	0	0		11.25	5	0	0	12	17	8	4	0	0	0	0	2	0	0	.000	2	7	0	0	1.8	1.000
1945	STL A	2	1	.667	1.59	4	3	3	28.1	23	5	4	0	0	0	0	11	2	0	.182	0	2	1	0	0.8	.667
1946		1	3	.250	6.88	11	3	0	35.1	52	15	12	0	1	2	1	7	2	0	.286	7	7	0	1	1.3	1.000
1947	CHI N	1	2	.333	10.13	4	4	1	16	31	5	7	0	0	0	0	7	3	1	.429	1	1	0	0	0.5	1.000
4 yrs.		4	6	.400	6.38	24	10	4	91.2	123	33	27	0	1	2	1	27	7	1	.259	10	17	1	1	1.2	.964

Paul Miller

MILLER, PAUL ROBERT BR TR 6′ 5″ 215 lbs.
B. Apr. 27, 1965, Burlington, Wis.

Year	Team	W	L	PCT	ERA	G	GS	CG	IP	H	BB	SO	ShO	Relief Pitching W	Relief Pitching L	Relief Pitching SV	Batting AB	Batting H	Batting HR	BA	PO	A	E	DP	TC/G	FA
1991	PIT N	0	0	—	5.40	1	1	0	5	4	3	2	0	0	0	0	3	0	0	.000	0	0	0	0	0.0	.000
1992		1	0	1.000	2.38	6	0	0	11.1	11	1	5	0	1	0	0	3	0	0	.000	0	1	0	0	0.2	1.000
1993		0	0	—	5.40	3	2	0	10	15	2	2	0	0	0	0	2	0	0	.000	0	1	1	0	0.7	.500
3 yrs.		1	0	1.000	4.10	10	3	0	26.1	30	6	9	0	1	0	0	8	0	0	.000	0	2	1	0	0.3	.667

Ralph Miller

MILLER, RALPH DARWIN BR TR 5′11″ 170 lbs.
B. Mar. 15, 1873, Cincinnati, Ohio D. May 8, 1973, Cincinnati, Ohio.

Year	Team	W	L	PCT	ERA	G	GS	CG	IP	H	BB	SO	ShO	Relief Pitching W	Relief Pitching L	Relief Pitching SV	Batting AB	Batting H	Batting HR	BA	PO	A	E	DP	TC/G	FA
1898	BKN N	4	14	.222	5.34	23	21	16	151.2	161	86	43	0	1	0	0	62	12	0	.194	9	49	6	0	2.7	.906
1899	BAL N	1	3	.250	4.76	6	4	3	34	42	13	3	0	1	0	1	11	2	0	.182	0	7	2	0	1.5	.778
2 yrs.		5	17	.227	5.24	29	25	19	185.2	203	99	46	0	2	0	1	73	14	0	.192	9	56	8	0	2.4	.890

Ralph Miller

MILLER, RALPH HENRY (Lefty) BR TL 6′ 1½″ 190 lbs.
Brother of Bing Miller.
B. Jan. 14, 1899, Vinton, Iowa D. Feb. 18, 1967, White Bear Lake, Minn.

Year	Team	W	L	PCT	ERA	G	GS	CG	IP	H	BB	SO	ShO	Relief Pitching W	Relief Pitching L	Relief Pitching SV	Batting AB	Batting H	Batting HR	BA	PO	A	E	DP	TC/G	FA
1921	WAS A	0	0	—	0.00	1	0	0	1	0	0	0	0	0	0	0	0	0	0	—	0	0	0	0	0.0	.000

Randy Miller

MILLER, RANDALL SCOTT BR TR 6′ 1″ 180 lbs.
B. Mar. 18, 1953, Oxnard, Calif.

Year	Team	W	L	PCT	ERA	G	GS	CG	IP	H	BB	SO	ShO	Relief Pitching W	Relief Pitching L	Relief Pitching SV	Batting AB	Batting H	Batting HR	BA	PO	A	E	DP	TC/G	FA
1977	BAL A	0	0	—	27.00	1	0	0	1	4	0	0	0	0	0	0	0	0	0	—	0	0	0	0	0.0	.000
1978	MON N	0	1	.000	10.29	5	0	0	7	11	3	6	0	0	1	0	1	0	0	.000	0	2	1	0	0.6	.667
2 yrs.		0	1	.000	12.38	6	0	0	8	15	3	6	0	0	1	0	1	0	0	.000	0	2	1	0	0.5	.667

Red Miller

MILLER, LEO ALPHONSO
B. Feb. 11, 1897, Philadelphia, Pa. D. Oct. 20, 1973, Orlando, Fla.
BR TR 5'11" 195 lbs.

Year	Team	W	L	PCT	ERA	G	GS	CG	IP	H	BB	SO	ShO	Relief Pitching W	Relief Pitching L	Relief Pitching SV	Batting AB	Batting H	Batting HR	BA	PO	A	E	DP	TC/G	FA
1923	PHI N	0	0	—	32.40	1	0	0	1.2	6	1	0	0	0	0	0	1	0	0	.000	0	0	0	0	0.0	.000

Roger Miller

MILLER, ROGER WESLEY
B. Aug. 1, 1954, Connellsville, Pa. D. Apr. 26, 1993, Mill Run, Pa.
BR TR 6' 3" 200 lbs.

Year	Team	W	L	PCT	ERA	G	GS	CG	IP	H	BB	SO	ShO	Relief Pitching W	Relief Pitching L	Relief Pitching SV	Batting AB	Batting H	Batting HR	BA	PO	A	E	DP	TC/G	FA
1974	MIL A	0	0	—	13.50	2	0	0	2	3	0	2	0	0	0	0	0	0	0	—	0	0	0	0	0.0	.000

Ronnie Miller

MILLER, ROLAND ARTHUR
B. Aug. 28, 1918, Mason City, Iowa
BB TR 5'11" 167 lbs.

Year	Team	W	L	PCT	ERA	G	GS	CG	IP	H	BB	SO	ShO	Relief Pitching W	Relief Pitching L	Relief Pitching SV	Batting AB	Batting H	Batting HR	BA	PO	A	E	DP	TC/G	FA
1941	WAS A	0	0	—	4.50	1	0	0	2	2	1	0	0	0	0	0	0	0	0	—	0	0	0	0	0.0	.000

Roscoe Miller

MILLER, ROSCOE CLYDE (Roxy, Rubberlegs)
B. Dec. 2, 1876, Greenville, Ind. D. Apr. 18, 1913, Corydon, Ind.
BR TR 6' 2" 190 lbs.

Year	Team	W	L	PCT	ERA	G	GS	CG	IP	H	BB	SO	ShO	Relief Pitching W	Relief Pitching L	Relief Pitching SV	Batting AB	Batting H	Batting HR	BA	PO	A	E	DP	TC/G	FA
1901	DET A	23	13	.639	2.95	38	36	35	332	339	98	79	3	1	0	1	130	27	0	.208	19	112	5	4	3.6	.963
1902	2 teams DET A (20G 6–12) NY N (10G 1–8)																									
"	total	7	20	.259	3.98	30	27	22	221.1	235	68	54	1	0	0	1	81	12	0	.148	21	53	4	4	2.6	.949
1903	NY N	2	5	.286	4.13	15	8	6	85	101	24	30	0	0	0	**3**	31	5	0	.161	8	17	2	1	1.8	.926
1904	PIT N	7	8	.467	3.35	19	17	11	134.1	133	39	35	2	0	0	0	46	2	0	.043	2	34	2	0	2.0	.947
4 yrs.		39	46	.459	3.45	102	88	74	772.2	808	229	198	6	1	0	5	288	46	0	.160	50	216	13	9	2.7	.953

Russ Miller

MILLER, RUSSELL LEWIS
Brother of Jake Miller.
B. Mar. 25, 1900, Etna, Ohio D. Apr. 30, 1962, Bucyrus, Ohio.
BR TR 5'11" 165 lbs.

Year	Team	W	L	PCT	ERA	G	GS	CG	IP	H	BB	SO	ShO	Relief Pitching W	Relief Pitching L	Relief Pitching SV	Batting AB	Batting H	Batting HR	BA	PO	A	E	DP	TC/G	FA
1927	PHI N	1	1	.500	5.28	2	2	1	15.1	21	3	4	0	0	0	0	3	1	0	.333	0	3	0	0	1.5	1.000
1928		0	12	.000	5.42	33	12	1	108	137	34	19	0	0	3	1	27	4	0	.148	6	27	1	0	1.0	.971
2 yrs.		1	13	.071	5.40	35	14	2	123.1	158	37	23	0	0	3	1	30	5	0	.167	6	30	1	0	1.1	.973

Stu Miller

MILLER, STUART LEONARD
B. Dec. 26, 1927, Northampton, Mass.
BR TR 5'11½" 165 lbs.

Year	Team	W	L	PCT	ERA	G	GS	CG	IP	H	BB	SO	ShO	Relief Pitching W	Relief Pitching L	Relief Pitching SV	Batting AB	Batting H	Batting HR	BA	PO	A	E	DP	TC/G	FA
1952	STL N	6	3	.667	2.05	12	11	6	88	63	26	64	2	1	0	0	25	3	0	.120	12	24	1	2	3.1	.973
1953		7	8	.467	5.56	40	18	8	137.2	161	47	79	2	0	1	4	43	8	0	.186	22	38	3	4	1.6	.952
1954		2	3	.400	5.79	19	4	0	46.2	55	29	22	0	1	2	2	13	4	0	.308	8	16	1	3	1.3	.960
1956	2 teams STL N (3G 0–1) PHI N (24G 5–8)																									
"	total	5	9	.357	4.50	27	15	2	114	121	56	60	0	2	1	1	26	4	0	.154	9	19	0	1	1.0	1.000
1957	NY N	7	9	.438	3.63	38	13	0	124	110	45	60	0	6	3	1	35	2	0	.057	12	24	1	6	1.0	.973
1958	SF N	6	9	.400	**2.47**	41	20	4	182	160	49	119	1	0	2	0	50	6	0	.120	9	34	1	4	1.1	.977
1959		8	7	.533	2.84	59	9	2	167.2	164	57	95	0	7	4	8	45	2	0	.044	15	40	2	1	1.0	.965
1960		7	6	.538	3.90	47	3	2	101.2	100	31	65	0	5	5	2	25	5	0	.200	5	25	2	2	0.7	.938
1961		14	5	.737	2.66	63	0	0	122	95	37	89	0	**14**	5	**17**	20	4	0	.200	10	29	0	4	0.6	1.000
1962		5	8	.385	4.12	59	0	0	107	107	42	78	0	5	8	19	16	2	0	.125	6	17	0	1	0.4	1.000
1963	BAL A	5	8	.385	2.24	**71**	0	0	112.1	93	53	114	0	5	**8**	**27**	16	5	0	.313	7	22	1	1	0.4	.967
1964		7	7	.500	3.06	66	0	0	97	77	34	87	0	7	7	23	9	1	0	.111	8	15	2	2	0.4	.920
1965		14	7	.667	1.89	67	0	0	119.1	87	32	104	0	14	7	24	16	1	0	.063	18	16	0	2	0.5	1.000
1966		9	4	.692	2.25	51	0	0	92	65	22	67	0	9	4	18	19	2	0	.105	5	11	0	1	0.3	1.000
1967		3	10	.231	2.55	42	0	0	81.1	63	36	60	0	3	**10**	8	11	0	0	.000	6	10	0	1	0.4	1.000
1968	ATL N	0	0	—	54.00	2	0	0	0.2	1	4	1	0	0	0	0	0	0	0	—	0	1	0	0	0.5	1.000
16 yrs.		105	103	.505	3.24	704	93	24	1693.1	1522	600	1164	5	79	67	154	369	49	0	.133	152	341	14	35	0.7	.972
WORLD SERIES																										
1962	SF N	0	0	—	0.00	2	0	0	1.1	1	2	0	0	0	0	0	0	0	0	—	0	1	0	0	0.5	1.000

Walt Miller

MILLER, WALTER W.
B. Oct. 19, 1884, Spiceland, Ind. D. Mar. 1, 1956, Marion, Ind.
BR TR 5'11½" 180 lbs.

Year	Team	W	L	PCT	ERA	G	GS	CG	IP	H	BB	SO	ShO	Relief Pitching W	Relief Pitching L	Relief Pitching SV	Batting AB	Batting H	Batting HR	BA	PO	A	E	DP	TC/G	FA
1911	BKN N	0	1	.000	6.55	3	2	0	11	16	6	0	0	0	0	0	4	0	0	.000	0	2	0	1	0.7	1.000

Billy Milligan

MILLIGAN, WILLIAM JOSEPH
B. Aug. 19, 1878, Buffalo, N. Y. D. Oct. 14, 1928, Buffalo, N. Y.
BR TL 5' 7"

Year	Team	W	L	PCT	ERA	G	GS	CG	IP	H	BB	SO	ShO	Relief Pitching W	Relief Pitching L	Relief Pitching SV	Batting AB	Batting H	Batting HR	BA	PO	A	E	DP	TC/G	FA
1901	PHI A	0	3	.000	4.36	6	3	2	33	43	14	5	0	0	1	0	15	5	1	.333	1	8	0	0	1.3	1.000
1904	NY N	0	1	.000	5.40	5	1	1	25	36	4	6	0	0	0	2	9	1	0	.111	1	7	1	0	1.8	.889
2 yrs.		0	4	.000	4.81	11	4	3	58	79	18	11	0	0	1	2	24	6	1	.250	2	15	1	0	1.5	.944

Jocko Milligan

MILLIGAN, JOHN
B. Aug. 8, 1861, Philadelphia, Pa. D. Aug. 29, 1923, Philadelphia, Pa.
BR TR 6' 195 lbs.

Year	Team	W	L	PCT	ERA	G	GS	CG	IP	H	BB	SO	ShO	Relief Pitching W	Relief Pitching L	Relief Pitching SV	Batting AB	Batting H	Batting HR	BA	PO	A	E	DP	TC/G	FA
1890	PHI P	0	0	—	0.00	1	0	0		0	0	0	0	0	0	0	*				477	101	37	5	9.3	.940

John Milligan

MILLIGAN, JOHN ALEXANDER
B. Jan. 22, 1904, Schuylerville, N. Y. D. May 15, 1972, Fort Pierce, Fla.
BR TL 5'10" 172 lbs.

Year	Team	W	L	PCT	ERA	G	GS	CG	IP	H	BB	SO	ShO	Relief Pitching W	Relief Pitching L	Relief Pitching SV	Batting AB	Batting H	Batting HR	BA	PO	A	E	DP	TC/G	FA
1928	PHI N	2	5	.286	4.37	13	7	3	68	69	32	22	0	0	1	0	20	1	0	.050	4	20	2	0	2.0	.923
1929		0	1	.000	16.76	8	3	0	9.2	29	10	2	0	0	1	0	3	1	0	.333	0	4	0	0	0.5	1.000
1930		1	2	.333	3.18	9	2	1	28.1	26	21	7	0	0	1	0	9	1	0	.111	3	11	0	1	1.6	1.000
1931		0	0	—	3.38	3	0	0	8	11	4	6	0	0	0	0	2	0	0	.000	0	0	0	0	0.0	.000
1934	WAS A	0	0	—	10.13	2	0	0	2.2	6	0	1	0	0	0	0	0	0	0	—	0	1	0	0	0.5	1.000
5 yrs.		3	8	.273	5.17	35	12	4	116.2	141	67	38	0	0	3	0	34	3	0	.088	7	36	2	1	1.3	.956

Bob Milliken

MILLIKEN, ROBERT FOGLE (Bobo)
B. Aug. 25, 1926, Majorsville, W. Va.
BR TR 6' 195 lbs.

Year	Team	W	L	PCT	ERA	G	GS	CG	IP	H	BB	SO	ShO	Relief Pitching W	Relief Pitching L	Relief Pitching SV	Batting AB	Batting H	Batting HR	BA	PO	A	E	DP	TC/G	FA
1953	BKN N	8	4	.667	3.37	37	10	3	117.2	94	42	65	0	5	2	2	34	4	0	.118	3	11	0	1	0.4	1.000
1954		5	2	.714	4.02	24	3	0	62.2	58	18	25	0	5	0	2	17	3	0	.176	3	5	0	1	0.3	1.000
2 yrs.		13	6	.684	3.59	61	13	3	180.1	152	60	90	0	10	2	4	51	7	0	.137	6	16	0	2	0.4	1.000
WORLD SERIES																										
1953	BKN N	0	0	—	0.00	1	0	0	2	2	1	0	0	0	0	0	0	0	0	—	0	0	0	0	0.0	.000

Alan Mills

MILLS, ALAN BERNARD
B. Oct. 18, 1966, Lakeland, Fla.
BR TR 6′ 1″ 190 lbs.

Year	Team	W	L	PCT	ERA	G	GS	CG	IP	H	BB	SO	ShO	Relief Pitching W	Relief Pitching L	Relief Pitching SV	Batting AB	Batting H	Batting HR	BA	PO	A	E	DP	TC/G	FA
1990	NY A	1	5	.167	4.10	36	0	0	41.2	48	33	24	0	1	5	0	0	0	0	—	3	10	2	0	0.4	.867
1991		1	1	.500	4.41	6	2	0	16.1	16	8	11	0	1	0	0	0	0	0	—	0	5	0	0	0.8	1.000
1992	BAL A	10	4	.714	2.61	35	3	0	103.1	78	54	60	0	9	3	2	0	0	0	—	9	17	0	2	0.7	1.000
1993		5	4	.556	3.23	45	0	0	100.1	80	51	68	0	5	4	4	0	0	0	—	7	11	3	2	0.5	.857
1994		3	3	.500	5.16	47	0	0	45.1	43	24	44	0	3	3	2	0	0	0	—	3	2	0	0	0.1	1.000
1995		3	0	1.000	7.43	21	0	0	23	30	18	16	0	3	0	0	0	0	0	—	0	1	0	0	0.0	1.000
6 yrs.		23	17	.575	3.76	190	5	0	330	295	188	223	0	22	15	8	0	0	0		22	46	5	4	0.4	.932

Art Mills

MILLS, ARTHUR GRANT
Son of Willie Mills.
B. Mar. 2, 1903, Utica, N. Y. D. July 23, 1975, Utica, N. Y.
BR TR 5′10″ 155 lbs.

Year	Team	W	L	PCT	ERA	G	GS	CG	IP	H	BB	SO	ShO	Relief Pitching W	Relief Pitching L	Relief Pitching SV	Batting AB	Batting H	Batting HR	BA	PO	A	E	DP	TC/G	FA
1927	BOS N	0	1	.000	3.82	15	1	0	37.2	41	18	7	0	0	1	0	7	0	0	.000	6	12	0	0	1.2	1.000
1928		0	0	—	12.91	4	0	0	7.2	17	8	0	0	0	0	0	1	0	0	.000	1	1	0	0	0.5	1.000
2 yrs.		0	1	.000	5.36	19	1	0	45.1	58	26	7	0	0	1	0	8	0	0	.000	7	13	0	0	1.1	1.000

Dick Mills

MILLS, RICHARD ALAN
B. Jan. 29, 1945, Boston, Mass.
BR TR 6′ 3″ 195 lbs.

Year	Team	W	L	PCT	ERA	G	GS	CG	IP	H	BB	SO	ShO	Relief Pitching W	Relief Pitching L	Relief Pitching SV	Batting AB	Batting H	Batting HR	BA	PO	A	E	DP	TC/G	FA
1970	BOS A	0	0	—	2.25	2	0	0	4	6	3	3	0	0	0	0	0	0	0	—	0	1	1	0	1.0	.500

Lefty Mills

MILLS, HOWARD ROBINSON
B. May 12, 1910, Dedham, Mass. D. Sept. 23, 1982, Riverside, Calif.
BL TL 6′ 1″ 187 lbs.

Year	Team	W	L	PCT	ERA	G	GS	CG	IP	H	BB	SO	ShO	Relief Pitching W	Relief Pitching L	Relief Pitching SV	Batting AB	Batting H	Batting HR	BA	PO	A	E	DP	TC/G	FA
1934	STL A	0	0	—	4.15	4	0	0	8.2	10	11	2	0	0	0	0	3	1	0	.333	0	1	0	0	0.3	1.000
1937		1	1	.500	6.39	2	2	1	12.2	16	10	10	0	0	0	0	5	0	0	.000	0	3	1	0	2.0	.750
1938		10	12	.455	5.31	30	27	15	210.1	216	116	134	1	0	0	0	66	6	0	.091	4	28	5	1	1.2	.865
1939		4	11	.267	6.55	34	14	4	144.1	147	113	103	0	2	2	2	47	11	1	.234	2	20	3	0	0.7	.880
1940		0	6	.000	7.78	26	5	1	59	64	52	18	0	0	1	0	13	2	0	.154	3	13	1	1	0.7	.941
5 yrs.		15	30	.333	6.06	96	48	21	435	453	302	267	1	2	3	2	134	20	1	.149	9	65	10	2	0.9	.881

Willie Mills

MILLS, WILLIAM GRANT (Wee Willie)
Father of Art Mills.
B. Aug. 15, 1877, Schenevus, N. Y. D. July 5, 1914, Norwood, N. Y.
BR TR 5′ 7″ 150 lbs.

Year	Team	W	L	PCT	ERA	G	GS	CG	IP	H	BB	SO	ShO	Relief Pitching W	Relief Pitching L	Relief Pitching SV	Batting AB	Batting H	Batting HR	BA	PO	A	E	DP	TC/G	FA
1901	NY N	0	2	.000	8.44	2	2	2	16	21	4	3	0	0	0	0	6	1	0	.167	1	2	0	0	1.5	1.000

Al Milnar

MILNAR, ALBERT JOSEPH (Happy)
Born Albert Joseph Mlinar.
B. Dec. 26, 1913, Cleveland, Ohio.
BL TL 6′ 2″ 195 lbs.

Year	Team	W	L	PCT	ERA	G	GS	CG	IP	H	BB	SO	ShO	Relief Pitching W	Relief Pitching L	Relief Pitching SV	Batting AB	Batting H	Batting HR	BA	PO	A	E	DP	TC/G	FA
1936	CLE A	1	2	.333	7.36	4	3	1	22	26	18	9	0	0	0	0	10	3	0	.300	0	5	1	1	1.5	.833
1938		3	1	.750	5.00	23	5	2	68.1	90	26	29	0	2	0	1	26	4	1	.154	2	12	0	2	0.6	1.000
1939		14	12	.538	3.79	37	26	12	209	212	99	76	2	2	1	3	79	20	0	.253	8	37	0	1	1.2	1.000
1940		18	10	.643	3.27	37	33	15	242.1	242	99	99	**4**	0	0	3	94	17	0	.181	2	26	4	2	0.9	.875
1941		12	19	.387	4.36	35	30	9	229.1	236	116	82	1	0	3	0	82	14	2	.171	10	29	1	3	1.1	.975
1942		6	8	.429	4.13	28	19	8	157	146	85	35	2	1	0	0	70	12	1	.171	5	38	1	3	1.6	.977
1943	2 teams CLE A (16G 1–3) STL A (3G 1–2)																									
″	total	2	5	.286	7.38	19	8	1	53.2	74	44	19	0	1	1	0	25	6	0	.240	4	13	0	0	0.9	1.000
1946	2 teams STL A (4G 1–1) PHI N (1G 0–0)																									
″	total	1	1	.500	4.91	5	3	1	14.2	17	8	1	1	0	0	0	4	3	0	.750	0	3	0	0	0.6	1.000
8 yrs.		57	58	.496	4.22	188	127	49	996.1	1043	495	350	10	6	5	7	390	79	4	.203	31	163	7	12	1.1	.965

George Milstead

MILSTEAD, GEORGE EARL (Cowboy)
B. Sept. 26, 1903, Cleburne, Tex. D. Aug. 9, 1977, Cleburne, Tex.
BL TL 5′10″ 144 lbs.

Year	Team	W	L	PCT	ERA	G	GS	CG	IP	H	BB	SO	ShO	Relief Pitching W	Relief Pitching L	Relief Pitching SV	Batting AB	Batting H	Batting HR	BA	PO	A	E	DP	TC/G	FA
1924	CHI N	1	1	.500	6.07	13	2	1	29.2	41	13	6	0	0	0	0	6	1	0	.167	1	9	0	0	0.8	1.000
1925		1	1	.500	3.00	5	3	1	21	26	8	7	0	0	0	0	7	0	0	.000	0	5	0	2	1.0	1.000
1926		1	5	.167	3.58	18	4	0	55.1	63	24	14	0	1	2	2	19	1	0	.053	5	24	1	2	1.7	.967
3 yrs.		3	7	.300	4.16	36	9	2	106	130	45	27	0	1	2	2	32	2	0	.063	6	38	1	4	1.3	.978

Larry Milton

MILTON, SAMUEL LAWRENCE
B. May 4, 1879, Owensboro, Ky. D. May 16, 1942, Tulsa, Okla.
TR

Year	Team	W	L	PCT	ERA	G	GS	CG	IP	H	BB	SO	ShO	Relief Pitching W	Relief Pitching L	Relief Pitching SV	Batting AB	Batting H	Batting HR	BA	PO	A	E	DP	TC/G	FA
1903	STL N	0	0	—	2.25	1	0	0	4	3	1	0	0	0	0	0	2	1	0	.500	0	3	0	0	3.0	1.000

Michael Mimbs

MIMBS, MICHAEL RANDALL
B. Feb. 13, 1969, Macon, Ga.
BL TL 6′ 2″ 182 lbs.

Year	Team	W	L	PCT	ERA	G	GS	CG	IP	H	BB	SO	ShO	Relief Pitching W	Relief Pitching L	Relief Pitching SV	Batting AB	Batting H	Batting HR	BA	PO	A	E	DP	TC/G	FA
1995	PHI N	9	7	.563	4.15	35	19	2	136.2	127	75	93	1	2	0	1	35	5	0	.143	6	22	1	4	0.8	.966

Cotton Minahan

MINAHAN, EDMUND JOSEPH
B. Dec. 10, 1882, Springfield, Ohio D. May 20, 1958, East Orange, N. J.
BR TR 6′ 190 lbs.

Year	Team	W	L	PCT	ERA	G	GS	CG	IP	H	BB	SO	ShO	Relief Pitching W	Relief Pitching L	Relief Pitching SV	Batting AB	Batting H	Batting HR	BA	PO	A	E	DP	TC/G	FA
1907	CIN N	0	2	.000	1.29	2	2	1	14	12	13	4	0	0	0	0	5	0	0	.000	0	2	1	0	1.5	.667

Rudy Minarcin

MINARCIN, RUDY ANTHONY (Buster)
B. Mar. 25, 1930, North Vandergrift, Pa.
BR TR 6′ 195 lbs.

Year	Team	W	L	PCT	ERA	G	GS	CG	IP	H	BB	SO	ShO	Relief Pitching W	Relief Pitching L	Relief Pitching SV	Batting AB	Batting H	Batting HR	BA	PO	A	E	DP	TC/G	FA
1955	CIN N	5	9	.357	4.90	41	12	3	115.2	116	51	45	1	2	1	1	28	5	0	.179	8	28	1	2	0.9	.973
1956	BOS A	1	0	1.000	2.79	3	1	0	9.2	9	8	5	0	1	0	0	2	1	0	.500	0	3	0	0	1.0	1.000
1957		0	0	—	4.43	26	0	0	44.2	44	30	20	0	0	0	2	2	0	0	.000	2	7	0	1	0.3	1.000
3 yrs.		6	9	.400	4.66	70	13	3	170	169	89	70	1	3	1	3	32	6	0	.188	10	38	1	3	0.7	.980

Nate Minchey

MINCHEY, NATHAN DEREK
B. Aug. 31, 1969, Austin, Tex.
BR TR 6′ 8″ 225 lbs.

Year	Team	W	L	PCT	ERA	G	GS	CG	IP	H	BB	SO	ShO	Relief Pitching W	Relief Pitching L	Relief Pitching SV	Batting AB	Batting H	Batting HR	BA	PO	A	E	DP	TC/G	FA
1993	BOS A	1	2	.333	3.55	5	5	1	33	35	8	18	0	0	0	0	0	0	0	—	1	3	1	0	1.0	.800
1994		2	3	.400	8.61	6	5	0	23	44	14	15	0	0	0	0	0	0	0	—	0	4	0	0	0.7	1.000
2 yrs.		3	5	.375	5.63	11	10	1	56	79	22	33	0	0	0	0	0	0	0		1	7	1	0	0.8	.889

Ray Miner

MINER, RAYMOND THEODORE (Lefty)
B. Apr. 4, 1897, Glens Falls, N. Y. D. Sept. 15, 1963, Glen Ridge, N. Y.
BR TL 5′11″ 160 lbs.

Year	Team	W	L	PCT	ERA	G	GS	CG	IP	H	BB	SO	ShO	Relief Pitching W	Relief Pitching L	Relief Pitching SV	Batting AB	Batting H	Batting HR	BA	PO	A	E	DP	TC/G	FA
1921	PHI A	0	0	—	36.00	1	0	0	1	2	3	0	0	0	0	0	0	0	0	—	0	0	0	0	0.0	.000

Craig Minetto

MINETTO, CRAIG STEPHEN
B. Apr. 25, 1954, Stockton, Calif.
BL TL 6′ 185 lbs.

Year	Team	W	L	PCT	ERA	G	GS	CG	IP	H	BB	SO	ShO	Relief Pitching W	Relief Pitching L	Relief Pitching SV	Batting AB	Batting H	Batting HR	BA	PO	A	E	DP	TC/G	FA
1978	OAK A	0	0	—	3.75	4	1	0	12	13	7	3	0	0	0	0	0	0	0	—	2	1	0	0	0.8	1.000
1979		1	5	.167	5.57	36	13	0	118	131	58	64	0	0	0	0	0	0	0	—	4	10	0	0	0.4	1.000
1980		0	2	.000	7.88	7	1	0	8	11	3	5	0	0	1	1	0	0	0	—	0	0	0	0	0.0	.000
1981		0	0	—	2.57	8	0	0	7	7	4	4	0	0	0	0	0	0	0	—	0	0	0	0	0.0	.000
4 yrs.		1	7	.125	5.40	55	15	0	145	162	72	76	0	0	1	1	0	0	0		6	11	0	0	0.3	1.000

Steve Mingori

MINGORI, STEPHEN BERNARD
B. Feb. 29, 1944, Kansas City, Mo.
BL TL 5′10″ 165 lbs.

Year	Team	W	L	PCT	ERA	G	GS	CG	IP	H	BB	SO	ShO	Relief Pitching W	Relief Pitching L	Relief Pitching SV	Batting AB	Batting H	Batting HR	BA	PO	A	E	DP	TC/G	FA
1970	CLE A	1	0	1.000	2.70	21	0	0	20	17	12	16	0	1	0	1	1	0	0	.000	3	3	1	0	0.3	.857
1971		1	2	.333	1.42	54	0	0	57	31	24	45	0	1	2	4	2	1	0	.500	2	12	0	1	0.3	1.000
1972		0	6	.000	3.95	41	0	0	57	67	36	47	0	0	6	10	8	1	0	.125	4	11	1	0	0.4	.938
1973	2 teams CLE A (5G 0–0) KC A (19G 3–3)																									
″	total	3	3	.500	3.57	24	1	0	68	69	33	50	0	3	2	1	0	0	0		5	10	0	3	0.6	1.000
1974	KC A	2	3	.400	2.82	36	0	0	67	53	23	43	0	2	3	2	0	0	0	—	6	16	0	3	0.6	1.000
1975		0	3	.000	2.52	36	0	0	50	42	20	25	0	0	3	2	1	0	0	.000	3	9	2	2	0.4	.857
1976		5	5	.500	2.33	55	0	0	85	73	25	38	0	5	5	10	0	0	0	—	9	24	0	1	0.6	1.000
1977		2	4	.333	3.09	43	0	0	64	59	19	19	0	2	4	4	0	0	0	—	3	14	1	1	0.4	.944
1978		1	4	.200	2.74	45	0	0	69	64	16	28	0	1	4	7	0	0	0	—	3	13	1	0	0.4	.941
1979		3	3	.500	5.74	30	1	0	47	69	17	18	0	3	2	1	0	0	0	—	6	4	2	0	0.4	.833
10 yrs.		18	33	.353	3.04	385	2	0	584	544	225	329	0	18	31	42	12	2	0	.167	44	116	8	11	0.4	.952
LEAGUE CHAMPIONSHIP SERIES																										
1976	KC A	0	0	—	2.70	3	0	0	3.1	4	0	1	0	0	0	1	0	0	0	—	0	0	0	0	0.0	.000
1977		0	0	—	0.00	3	0	0	1.1	0	0	1	0	0	0	0	0	0	0	—	0	0	0	0	0.0	.000
1978		0	0	—	7.36	1	0	0	3.2	5	3	0	0	0	0	0	0	0	0	—	0	0	0	0	0.0	.000
3 yrs.		0	0		4.32	7	0	0	8.1	9	3	2	0	0	0	1	0	0	0		0	0	0	0	0.0	

Paul Minner

MINNER, PAUL EDISON (Lefty)
B. July 30, 1923, New Wilmington, Pa.
BL TL 6′ 5″ 200 lbs.

Year	Team	W	L	PCT	ERA	G	GS	CG	IP	H	BB	SO	ShO	Relief Pitching W	Relief Pitching L	Relief Pitching SV	Batting AB	Batting H	Batting HR	BA	PO	A	E	DP	TC/G	FA
1946	BKN N	0	1	.000	6.75	3	0	0	4	6	3	3	0	0	1	0	0	0	0	—	0	0	1	0	0.3	.000
1948		4	3	.571	2.44	28	2	0	62.2	61	26	23	0	3	3	1	21	4	0	.190	2	14	1	2	0.6	.941
1949		3	1	.750	3.80	27	1	0	47.1	49	18	17	0	3	1	2	14	3	0	.214	2	11	1	0	0.5	.929
1950	CHI N	8	13	.381	4.11	39	24	9	190.1	217	72	99	1	0	0	4	65	14	1	.215	12	45	2	4	1.5	.966
1951		6	**17**	.261	3.79	33	28	14	201.2	219	64	68	3	0	0	1	71	18	1	.254	10	53	1	6	1.9	.984
1952		14	9	.609	3.74	28	27	12	180.2	180	54	61	2	0	0	0	64	15	1	.234	15	40	1	3	2.0	.982
1953		12	15	.444	4.21	31	27	9	201	227	40	64	2	2	0	1	68	15	1	.221	11	56	3	2	2.3	.957
1954		11	11	.500	3.96	32	29	12	218	236	50	79	0	0	1	1	76	13	2	.171	15	42	1	6	1.8	.983
1955		9	9	.500	3.48	22	22	7	157.2	173	47	53	1	0	0	0	56	13	0	.232	4	39	1	3	2.0	.977
1956		2	5	.286	6.89	10	9	1	47	60	19	14	0	0	0	0	12	3	0	.250	4	10	1	0	1.5	.933
10 yrs.		69	84	.451	3.94	253	169	64	1310.1	1428	393	481	9	8	6	10	447	98	6	.219	75	310	13	26	1.6	.967
WORLD SERIES																										
1949	BKN N	0	0	—	0.00	1	0	0	1	1	0	0	0	0	0	0	0	0	0	—	0	1	0	0	1.0	1.000

Don Minnick

MINNICK, DONALD ATHEY
B. Apr. 14, 1931, Lynchburg, Va.
BR TR 6′ 3″ 195 lbs.

Year	Team	W	L	PCT	ERA	G	GS	CG	IP	H	BB	SO	ShO	Relief Pitching W	Relief Pitching L	Relief Pitching SV	Batting AB	Batting H	Batting HR	BA	PO	A	E	DP	TC/G	FA
1957	WAS A	0	1	.000	4.82	2	1	0	9.1	14	2	7	0	0	0	0	2	0	0	.000	0	1	0	0	0.5	1.000

Blas Minor

MINOR, BLAS
B. Mar. 20, 1966, Merced, Calif.
BR TR 6′ 3″ 195 lbs.

Year	Team	W	L	PCT	ERA	G	GS	CG	IP	H	BB	SO	ShO	Relief Pitching W	Relief Pitching L	Relief Pitching SV	Batting AB	Batting H	Batting HR	BA	PO	A	E	DP	TC/G	FA
1992	PIT N	0	0	—	4.50	1	0	0	2	3	0	0	0	0	0	0	0	0	0	—	0	1	1	1	2.0	.500
1993		8	6	.571	4.10	65	0	0	94.1	94	26	84	0	8	6	2	10	2	0	.200	8	15	0	0	0.4	1.000
1994		0	1	.000	8.05	17	0	0	19	27	9	17	0	0	1	1	0	0	0	—	1	2	0	0	0.2	1.000
1995	NY N	4	2	.667	3.66	35	0	0	46.2	44	13	43	0	4	2	1	2	0	0	.000	3	7	0	0	0.3	1.000
4 yrs.		12	9	.571	4.44	118	0	0	162	168	48	144	0	12	9	4	12	2	0	.167	12	25	1	1	0.3	.974

Jim Minshall

MINSHALL, JAMES EDWARD
B. July 4, 1947, Covington, Ky.
BR TR 6′ 6″ 215 lbs.

Year	Team	W	L	PCT	ERA	G	GS	CG	IP	H	BB	SO	ShO	Relief Pitching W	Relief Pitching L	Relief Pitching SV	Batting AB	Batting H	Batting HR	BA	PO	A	E	DP	TC/G	FA
1974	PIT N	0	1	.000	0.00	5	0	0	4	1	2	3	0	0	1	0	0	0	0	—	0	0	0	0	0.0	.000
1975		0	0	—	0.00	1	0	0	1	0	2	2	0	0	0	0	0	0	0	—	0	0	0	0	0.0	.000
2 yrs.		0	1	.000	0.00	6	0	0	5	1	4	5	0	0	1	0	0	0	0		0	0	0	0	0.0	

Greg Minton

MINTON, GREGORY BRIAN (Moon Man)
B. July 29, 1951, Lubbock, Tex.
BB TR 6′ 2″ 180 lbs.

Year	Team	W	L	PCT	ERA	G	GS	CG	IP	H	BB	SO	ShO	Relief Pitching W	Relief Pitching L	Relief Pitching SV	Batting AB	Batting H	Batting HR	BA	PO	A	E	DP	TC/G	FA
1975	SF N	1	1	.500	6.88	4	2	0	17	19	11	6	0	0	0	0	6	0	0	.000	2	4	0	1	1.5	1.000
1976		0	3	.000	4.91	10	2	0	25.2	32	12	7	0	0	2	0	5	1	0	.200	3	4	2	0	0.9	.778
1977		1	1	.500	4.50	2	2	0	14	14	4	5	0	0	0	0	3	1	0	.333	2	4	0	0	3.0	1.000
1978		0	1	.000	7.88	11	0	0	16	22	8	6	0	0	1	0	1	0	0	.000	2	2	0	1	0.4	1.000
1979		4	3	.571	1.80	46	0	0	80	59	27	33	0	4	3	4	4	0	0	.000	3	23	1	2	0.6	.963
1980		4	6	.400	2.47	68	0	0	91	81	34	42	0	4	6	19	8	1	0	.125	8	21	1	2	0.4	.967
1981		4	5	.444	2.89	55	0	0	84	84	36	29	0	4	5	21	12	0	0	.000	11	25	0	1	0.7	1.000
1982		10	4	.714	1.83	78	0	0	123	108	42	58	0	10	4	30	17	3	0	.176	11	22	3	2	0.5	.917
1983		7	11	.389	3.54	73	0	0	106.2	117	47	38	0	7	**11**	22	11	6	1	.545	5	18	1	0	0.3	.958
1984		4	9	.308	3.76	74	1	0	124.1	130	57	48	0	3	9	19	21	1	0	.048	8	31	2	1	0.6	.951
1985		5	4	.556	3.54	68	0	0	96.2	98	54	37	0	5	4	4	8	0	0	.000	7	27	1	1	0.5	.971
1986		4	4	.500	3.93	48	0	0	68.2	63	34	34	0	4	4	5	5	2	0	.400	7	19	2	1	0.6	.929
1987	2 teams SF N (15G 1–0) CAL A (41G 5–4)																									
″	total	6	4	.600	3.17	56	0	0	99.1	101	39	44	0	6	4	11	2	0	0	.000	7	23	0	2	0.5	1.000
1988	CAL A	4	5	.444	2.85	44	0	0	79	67	34	46	0	4	5	7	0	0	0	—	11	15	0	3	0.6	1.000
1989		4	3	.571	2.20	62	0	0	90	76	37	42	0	4	3	8	0	0	0	—	8	20	0	0	0.5	1.000
1990		1	1	.500	2.35	11	0	0	15.1	11	7	4	0	1	1	0	0	0	0	—	0	3	0	0	0.3	1.000
16 yrs.		59	65	.476	3.10	710	7	0	1130.2	1082	483	479	0	56	62	150	103	15	1	.146	95	261	13	17	0.5	.965

Steve Mintz

MINTZ, STEPHEN WAYNE
B. Nov. 24, 1968, Wilmington, N. C.

BL TR 5′11″ 190 lbs.

Year	Team	W	L	PCT	ERA	G	GS	CG	IP	H	BB	SO	ShO	Relief Pitching W	Relief Pitching L	Relief Pitching SV	Batting AB	Batting H	Batting HR	BA	PO	A	E	DP	TC/G	FA
1995	SF N	1	2	.333	7.45	14	0	0	19.1	26	12	7	0	1	2	0	3	0	0	.000	1	2	0	0	0.2	1.000

Gino Minutelli

MINUTELLI, GINO MICHAEL
B. May 23, 1964, Wilmington, Del.

BL TL 6′ 180 lbs.

Year	Team	W	L	PCT	ERA	G	GS	CG	IP	H	BB	SO	ShO	Relief Pitching W	Relief Pitching L	Relief Pitching SV	Batting AB	Batting H	Batting HR	BA	PO	A	E	DP	TC/G	FA
1990	CIN N	0	0	—	9.00	2	0	0	1	0	2	0	0	0	0	0	0	0	0	—	0	0	0	0	0.0	.000
1991		0	2	.000	6.04	16	3	0	25.1	30	18	21	0	0	1	0	3	0	0	.000	1	5	0	0	0.4	1.000
1993	SF N	0	1	.000	3.77	9	0	0	14.1	7	15	10	0	0	1	0	4	0	0	.000	0	1	0	0	0.1	1.000
3 yrs.		0	3	.000	5.31	27	3	0	40.2	37	35	31	0	0	2	0	7	0	0	.000	1	6	0	0	0.3	1.000

Paul Mirabella

MIRABELLA, PAUL THOMAS
B. Mar. 20, 1954, Belleville, N. J.

BL TL 6′ 1″ 190 lbs.

Year	Team	W	L	PCT	ERA	G	GS	CG	IP	H	BB	SO	ShO	Relief Pitching W	Relief Pitching L	Relief Pitching SV	Batting AB	Batting H	Batting HR	BA	PO	A	E	DP	TC/G	FA
1978	TEX A	3	2	.600	5.79	10	4	0	28	30	17	23	0	1	1	1	0	0	0	—	0	3	0	0	0.3	1.000
1979	NY A	0	4	.000	9.00	10	1	0	14	16	10	4	0	0	3	0	0	0	0	—	0	2	0	0	0.2	1.000
1980	TOR A	5	12	.294	4.33	33	22	3	131	151	66	53	1	0	0	0	0	0	0	—	9	20	1	1	0.9	.967
1981		0	0	—	7.20	8	1	0	15	20	7	9	0	0	0	0	0	0	0	—	1	0	0	0	0.1	1.000
1982	TEX A	1	1	.500	4.80	40	0	0	50.2	46	22	29	0	1	1	3	0	0	0	—	2	6	1	2	0.2	.889
1983	BAL A	0	0	—	5.59	3	2	0	9.2	9	7	4	0	0	0	0	0	0	0	—	0	1	1	0	0.7	.500
1984	SEA A	2	5	.286	4.37	52	1	0	68	74	32	41	0	2	4	3	0	0	0	—	4	11	0	1	0.3	1.000
1985		0	0	—	1.32	10	0	0	13.2	9	4	8	0	0	0	0	0	0	0	—	0	1	0	0	0.1	1.000
1986		0	0	—	8.53	8	0	0	6.1	13	3	6	0	0	0	0	0	0	0	—	0	1	0	0	0.1	1.000
1987	MIL A	2	1	.667	4.91	29	0	0	29.1	30	16	14	0	2	1	2	0	0	0	—	7	5	1	1	0.4	.923
1988		2	2	.500	1.65	38	0	0	60	44	21	33	0	2	2	4	0	0	0	—	6	10	0	1	0.4	1.000
1989		0	0	—	7.63	13	0	0	15.1	18	7	6	0	0	0	0	0	0	0	—	0	6	2	0	0.6	.750
1990		4	2	.667	3.97	44	2	0	59	66	27	28	0	4	1	0	0	0	0	—	4	7	1	1	0.3	.917
13 yrs.		19	29	.396	4.45	298	33	3	500	526	239	258	1	12	13	13	0	0	0		33	73	7	7	0.4	.938

Angel Miranda

MIRANDA, ANGEL LUIS
Born Angel Luis Miranda (Andujar).
B. Nov. 9, 1969, Arecibo, Puerto Rico.

BL TL 6′ 1″ 160 lbs.

Year	Team	W	L	PCT	ERA	G	GS	CG	IP	H	BB	SO	ShO	Relief Pitching W	Relief Pitching L	Relief Pitching SV	Batting AB	Batting H	Batting HR	BA	PO	A	E	DP	TC/G	FA
1993	MIL A	4	5	.444	3.30	22	17	2	120	100	52	88	0	0	0	0	0	0	0	—	4	13	2	1	0.9	.895
1994		2	5	.286	5.28	8	8	1	46	39	27	24	0	0	0	0	0	0	0	—	1	3	0	0	0.5	1.000
1995		4	5	.444	5.23	30	10	0	74	83	49	45	0	2	2	1	0	0	0	—	5	9	0	1	0.5	1.000
3 yrs.		10	15	.400	4.28	60	35	3	240	222	128	157	0	2	2	1	0	0	0		10	25	2	2	0.6	.946

Bobby Mitchell

MITCHELL, ROBERT McKASHA
B. Feb. 6, 1856, Cincinnati, Ohio D. May 1, 1933, Springfield, Ohio.

BL TL 5′ 5″ 135 lbs.

Year	Team	W	L	PCT	ERA	G	GS	CG	IP	H	BB	SO	ShO	Relief Pitching W	Relief Pitching L	Relief Pitching SV	Batting AB	Batting H	Batting HR	BA	PO	A	E	DP	TC/G	FA
1877	CIN N	6	5	.545	3.51	12	12	11	100	123	11	41	1	0	0	0	49	10	0	.204	10	14	2	0	1.9	.923
1878		7	2	.778	2.14	9	9	9	80	69	18	51	1	0	0	0	49	12	0	.245	4	21	4	1	2.4	.862
1879	CLE N	7	15	.318	3.28	23	22	20	194.2	236	42	90	0	0	**1**	0	109	16	0	.147	23	24	20	0	2.1	.701
1882	STL AA	0	1	.000	*7.71*	1	1	0	7	12	2	2	0	0	0	0	4	0	0	.000	0	2	1	0	1.5	.667
4 yrs.		20	23	.465	3.18	45	44	40	381.2	440	73	184	2	0	1	0	211	38	0	.180	37	61	27	1	2.1	.784

Charlie Mitchell

MITCHELL, CHARLES ROSS
Brother of John Mitchell.
B. June 24, 1962, Dickson, Tenn.

BR TR 6′ 3″ 170 lbs.

Year	Team	W	L	PCT	ERA	G	GS	CG	IP	H	BB	SO	ShO	Relief Pitching W	Relief Pitching L	Relief Pitching SV	Batting AB	Batting H	Batting HR	BA	PO	A	E	DP	TC/G	FA
1984	BOS A	0	0	—	2.76	10	0	0	16.1	14	6	7	0	0	0	0	0	0	0	—	1	3	1	0	0.5	.800
1985		0	0	—	16.20	2	0	0	1.2	5	0	2	0	0	0	0	0	0	0	—	1	1	0	0	1.0	1.000
2 yrs.		0	0		4.00	12	0	0	18	19	6	9	0	0	0	0	0	0	0		2	4	1	0	0.6	.857

Clarence Mitchell

MITCHELL, CLARENCE ELMER
B. Feb. 22, 1891, Franklin, Neb. D. Nov. 6, 1963, Grand Island, Neb.

BL TL 5′11½″ 190 lbs.

Year	Team	W	L	PCT	ERA	G	GS	CG	IP	H	BB	SO	ShO	Relief Pitching W	Relief Pitching L	Relief Pitching SV	Batting AB	Batting H	Batting HR	BA	PO	A	E	DP	TC/G	FA
1911	DET A	1	0	1.000	8.16	5	1	0	14.1	20	7	4	0	1	0	0	4	2	0	.500	0	2	0	0	0.4	1.000
1916	CIN N	11	10	.524	3.14	29	24	17	194.2	211	45	52	1	0	1	0	117	28	0	.239	70	56	3	9	3.4	.977
1917		9	15	.375	3.22	32	20	10	159.1	166	34	37	2	2	3	1	90	25	0	.278	73	49	4	5	2.9	.968
1918	BKN N	0	1	.000	108.00	1	1	0	0.1	4	0	0	0	0	0	0	24	6	0	.250	6	0	1	0	0.8	.857
1919		7	5	.583	3.06	23	11	9	108.2	123	23	43	0	1	0	0	49	18	1	.367	4	36	1	1	1.8	.976
1920		5	2	.714	3.09	19	7	3	78.2	85	23	18	1	0	1	1	107	25	0	.234	98	36	2	8	4.0	.985
1921		11	9	.550	2.89	37	18	13	190	206	46	39	**3**	2	2	2	91	24	0	.264	30	64	4	7	2.4	.959
1922		0	3	.000	14.21	5	3	0	12.2	28	7	1	0	0	0	0	155	45	3	.290	366	34	3	32	8.6	.993
1923	PHI N	9	10	.474	4.72	29	19	8	139.1	170	46	42	1	1	1	0	78	21	1	.269	4	18	3	2	0.9	.880
1924		6	13	.316	5.62	30	26	9	165	223	58	36	1	0	1	1	102	26	0	.255	10	51	0	3	2.0	1.000
1925		10	17	.370	5.28	32	26	12	199.1	245	51	46	1	0	1	1	92	18	0	.196	20	62	0	9	2.4	1.000
1926		9	14	.391	4.58	28	25	12	178.2	232	55	52	0	1	0	1	78	19	0	.244	18	62	1	3	2.5	.988
1927		6	3	.667	4.09	13	12	8	94.2	99	28	17	1	0	0	0	42	10	1	.238	1	25	1	1	2.1	.963
1928	2 teams PHI N (3G 0–0) STL N (19G 8–9)																									
″	total	8	9	.471	3.53	22	18	9	155.2	162	40	31	1	1	0	0	60	8	0	.133	6	51	1	3	2.6	.983
1929	STL N	8	11	.421	4.27	25	22	16	173	221	60	39	0	0	0	0	66	18	0	.273	1	37	1	1	1.6	.974
1930	2 teams STL N (1G 1–0) NY N (24G 10–3)																									
″	total	11	3	.786	4.02	25	17	5	132	156	38	41	0	1	2	0	49	13	0	.265	10	35	0	1	1.8	1.000
1931	NY N	13	11	.542	4.07	27	25	13	190.1	221	52	39	0	0	0	0	73	16	1	.219	13	33	6	2	1.9	.885
1932		1	3	.250	4.15	8	3	1	30.1	41	11	7	0	0	1	2	10	2	0	.200	2	3	1	0	0.8	.833
18 yrs.		125	139	.473	4.12	390	278	145	2217	2613	624	544	12	10	13	9	*				732	654	32	87	2.9	.977
WORLD SERIES																										
1920	BKN N	0	0	—	0.00	1	0	0	4.2	3	3	1	0	0	0	0	3	1	0	.333	1	0	0	0	1.0	1.000
1928	STL N	0	0	—	1.59	1	0	0	5.2	2	2	2	0	0	0	0	2	0	0	.000	0	1	1	0	2.0	.500
2 yrs.		0	0		0.87	2	0	0	10.1	5	5	3	0	0	0	0	*				1	1	1	0	1.5	.667

Craig Mitchell

MITCHELL, CRAIG SETON
B. Apr. 14, 1954, Santa Rosa, Calif.

BR TR 6′ 3″ 180 lbs.

Year	Team	W	L	PCT	ERA	G	GS	CG	IP	H	BB	SO	ShO	Relief Pitching W	Relief Pitching L	Relief Pitching SV	Batting AB	Batting H	Batting HR	BA	PO	A	E	DP	TC/G	FA
1975	OAK A	0	1	.000	12.27	1	1	0	3.2	6	2	2	0	0	0	0	0	0	0	—	1	1	0	1	2.0	1.000
1976		0	0	—	3.00	1	0	0	3	3	0	0	0	0	0	0	0	0	0	—	0	1	1	0	2.0	.500
1977		0	1	.000	7.50	3	1	0	6	9	2	1	0	0	0	0	0	0	0	—	1	1	1	0	1.0	.667
3 yrs.		0	2	.000	7.82	5	2	0	12.2	18	4	3	0	0	0	0	0	0	0		2	3	2	1	1.4	.714

Fred Mitchell

MITCHELL, FREDERICK FRANCIS
Born Frederick Francis Yapp.
B. June 5, 1878, Cambridge, Mass. D. Oct. 13, 1970, Newton, Mass.
Manager 1917–23.
BR TR 5′ 9½″ 185 lbs.

Year	Team	W	L	PCT	ERA	G	GS	CG	IP	H	BB	SO	ShO	Relief W	Relief L	Relief SV	AB	H	HR	BA	PO	A	E	DP	TC/G	FA
1901	BOS A	6	6	.500	3.81	17	13	10	108.2	115	51	34	0	1	0	0	44	7	0	.159	2	34	6	2	2.1	.857
1902	2 teams BOS A (1G 0–1) PHI A (18G 5–7)																									
″	total	5	8	.385	3.87	19	14	9	111.2	128	64	24	0	1	1	1	49	9	0	.184	6	45	4	4	2.8	.927
1903	PHI N	11	15	.423	4.48	28	28	24	227	250	102	69	1	0	0	0	95	19	0	.200	10	50	10	3	2.5	.857
1904	2 teams PHI N (13G 4–7) BKN N (8G 2–5)																									
″	total	6	12	.333	3.56	21	21	19	174.2	206	48	45	1	0	0	0	106	24	0	.226	85	83	11	5	5.4	.939
1905	BKN N	3	7	.300	4.78	12	10	9	96	107	38	44	0	0	0	0	79	15	0	.190	71	44	13	2	5.1	.898
5 yrs.		31	48	.392	4.10	97	86	71	718	806	303	216	2	2	1	1	*				436	325	55	18	4.2	.933

John Mitchell

MITCHELL, JOHN KYLE
Brother of Charlie Mitchell.
B. Aug. 11, 1965, Dickson, Tenn.
BR TR 6′ 2″ 165 lbs.

Year	Team	W	L	PCT	ERA	G	GS	CG	IP	H	BB	SO	ShO	Relief W	Relief L	Relief SV	AB	H	HR	BA	PO	A	E	DP	TC/G	FA
1986	NY N	0	1	.000	3.60	4	1	0	10	10	4	2	0	0	0	0	2	0	0	.000	3	1	0	0	1.0	1.000
1987		3	6	.333	4.11	20	19	1	111.2	124	36	57	0	0	0	0	35	4	0	.114	16	21	6	3	2.2	.860
1988		0	0	—	0.00	1	0	0	1	2	1	1	0	0	0	0	1	0	0	.000	0	0	0	0	0.0	.000
1989		0	1	.000	6.00	2	0	0	3	3	4	4	0	0	1	0	0	0	0	—	0	0	0	0	0.0	.000
1990	BAL A	6	6	.500	4.64	24	17	0	114.1	133	48	43	0	0	0	0	0	0	0	—	7	19	2	3	1.2	.929
5 yrs.		9	14	.391	4.35	51	37	1	240	272	93	107	0	0	1	0	38	4	0	.105	26	41	8	6	1.5	.893

Monroe Mitchell

MITCHELL, MONROE BARR
B. Sept. 11, 1901, Starkville, Miss. D. Sept. 4, 1976, Valdosta, Ga.
BR TR 6′ 1½″ 170 lbs.

Year	Team	W	L	PCT	ERA	G	GS	CG	IP	H	BB	SO	ShO	Relief W	Relief L	Relief SV	AB	H	HR	BA	PO	A	E	DP	TC/G	FA
1923	WAS A	2	4	.333	6.48	10	6	3	41.2	57	22	8	1	0	0	2	12	3	0	.250	3	8	1	0	1.2	.917

Paul Mitchell

MITCHELL, PAUL MICHAEL
B. Aug. 19, 1949, Worcester, Mass.
BR TR 6′ 1″ 195 lbs.

Year	Team	W	L	PCT	ERA	G	GS	CG	IP	H	BB	SO	ShO	Relief W	Relief L	Relief SV	AB	H	HR	BA	PO	A	E	DP	TC/G	FA
1975	BAL A	3	0	1.000	3.63	11	4	1	57	41	19	31	0	2	0	0	0	0	0	—	2	5	0	0	0.6	1.000
1976	OAK A	9	7	.563	4.25	26	26	4	142	169	30	67	1	0	0	0	0	0	0	—	7	17	0	0	0.9	1.000
1977	2 teams OAK A (5G 0–3) SEA A (9G 3–3)																									
″	total	3	6	.333	6.41	14	12	0	53.1	71	23	25	0	0	0	0	0	0	0		5	11	0	0	1.1	1.000
1978	SEA A	8	14	.364	4.18	29	29	4	168	173	79	75	2	0	0	0	0	0	0	—	7	20	0	2	0.9	1.000
1979	2 teams SEA A (10G 1–4) MIL A (18G 3–3)																									
″	total	4	7	.364	5.30	28	14	1	112	127	25	50	0	0	0	0	0	0	0		5	13	0	1	0.6	1.000
1980	MIL A	5	5	.500	3.54	17	11	1	89	92	15	29	1	0	0	1	0	0	0	—	6	16	0	0	1.3	1.000
6 yrs.		32	39	.451	4.45	125	96	11	621.1	673	191	277	4	2	0	1	0	0	0		32	82	0	3	0.9	1.000

Roy Mitchell

MITCHELL, ALBERT ROY
B. Apr. 19, 1885, Belton, Tex. D. Sept. 8, 1959, Temple, Tex.
BR TR 5′ 9½″ 170 lbs.

Year	Team	W	L	PCT	ERA	G	GS	CG	IP	H	BB	SO	ShO	Relief W	Relief L	Relief SV	AB	H	HR	BA	PO	A	E	DP	TC/G	FA
1910	STL A	4	2	.667	2.60	6	6	6	52	43	12	23	0	0	0	0	19	4	0	.211	0	20	0	1	3.3	1.000
1911		4	8	.333	3.84	28	12	8	133.2	134	45	40	1	1	1	0	49	11	0	.224	5	39	5	0	1.8	.898
1912		3	4	.429	4.65	13	8	5	62	81	17	22	0	1	0	0	19	6	0	.316	3	11	0	1	1.1	1.000
1913		13	16	.448	3.01	33	27	21	245.1	265	47	59	4	2	1	1	88	13	0	.148	17	69	6	2	2.8	.935
1914		4	5	.444	4.35	28	9	4	103.1	134	38	38	0	2	0	**4**	34	7	0	.206	5	32	3	0	1.4	.925
1918	2 teams CHI A (2G 0–1) CIN N (5G 4–0)																									
″	total	4	1	.800	2.42	7	5	3	48.1	45	9	12	2	1	0	0	16	3	0	.188	2	14	2	0	2.6	.889
1919	CIN N	0	1	.000	2.32	7	1	0	31	32	9	10	0	0	0	0	10	0	0	.000	1	15	1	0	2.4	.941
7 yrs.		32	37	.464	3.42	122	68	47	675.2	734	177	204	7	7	2	5	235	44	0	.187	33	200	17	4	2.0	.932

Willie Mitchell

MITCHELL, WILLIAM
B. Dec. 1, 1889, Pleasant Grove, Miss. D. Nov. 23, 1973, Sardis, Miss.
BR TL 6′ 176 lbs.

Year	Team	W	L	PCT	ERA	G	GS	CG	IP	H	BB	SO	ShO	Relief W	Relief L	Relief SV	AB	H	HR	BA	PO	A	E	DP	TC/G	FA
1909	CLE A	1	2	.333	1.57	3	3	3	23	18	10	8	0	0	0	0	7	2	0	.286	2	7	1	1	3.3	.900
1910		12	8	.600	2.60	35	18	11	183.2	155	55	102	1	2	2	0	63	10	0	.159	9	46	4	1	1.7	.932
1911		7	14	.333	3.76	30	22	9	177.1	190	60	78	0	1	2	0	64	7	0	.109	9	47	6	0	2.1	.903
1912		5	8	.385	2.80	29	15	8	163.2	149	56	94	0	1	0	1	53	6	0	.113	8	30	6	0	1.5	.864
1913		14	8	.636	1.74	34	22	14	217	153	88	141	4	4	1	0	70	10	0	.143	10	44	4	3	1.7	.931
1914		12	17	.414	3.19	39	32	16	257	228	124	179	3	0	1	1	81	7	0	.086	4	46	6	1	1.4	.893
1915		11	14	.440	2.82	36	30	12	236	210	84	149	1	1	1	1	79	10	0	.127	3	48	8	1	1.6	.864
1916	2 teams CLE A (12G 2–5) DET A (23G 7–5)																									
″	total	9	10	.474	3.78	35	23	8	171.1	174	67	84	2	1	1	1	47	9	0	.191	5	30	4	1	1.1	.897
1917	DET A	12	8	.600	2.19	30	22	12	185.1	172	46	80	5	0	0	0	59	7	0	.119	11	40	4	2	1.8	.927
1918		0	1	.000	9.00	1	1	0	4	3	5	2	0	0	0	0	2	0	0	.000	1	2	0	0	3.0	1.000
1919		1	2	.333	5.27	3	2	0	13.2	12	10	4	0	0	1	0	5	1	0	.200	1	4	0	0	1.7	1.000
11 yrs.		84	92	.477	2.86	275	190	93	1632	1464	605	921	16	10	9	4	530	69	0	.130	63	344	43	10	1.6	.904

Vinegar Bend Mizell

MIZELL, WILMER DAVID
B. Aug. 13, 1930, Leakesville, Miss.
BR TL 6′ 3½″ 205 lbs.

Year	Team	W	L	PCT	ERA	G	GS	CG	IP	H	BB	SO	ShO	Relief W	Relief L	Relief SV	AB	H	HR	BA	PO	A	E	DP	TC/G	FA
1952	STL N	10	8	.556	3.65	30	30	7	190	171	**103**	146	2	0	0	0	68	3	0	.044	7	25	4	1	1.2	.889
1953		13	11	.542	3.49	33	33	10	224.1	193	114	173	1	0	0	0	83	7	1	.084	13	35	7	2	1.7	.873
1956		14	14	.500	3.62	33	33	11	208.2	172	92	153	3	0	0	0	75	8	0	.107	19	30	2	2	1.5	.961
1957		8	10	.444	3.74	33	21	7	149.1	136	51	87	2	1	1	0	45	4	0	.089	8	29	0	3	1.1	1.000
1958		10	14	.417	3.42	30	29	8	189.2	178	91	80	2	0	0	0	61	7	0	.115	6	31	3	3	1.3	.925
1959		13	10	.565	4.20	31	30	8	201.1	196	89	108	1	1	0	0	75	14	0	.187	9	23	3	1	1.1	.914
1960	2 teams STL N (9G 1–3) PIT N (23G 13–5)																									
″	total	14	8	.636	3.50	32	32	8	211	205	74	113	3	0	0	0	69	9	0	.130	9	28	0	1	1.2	1.000
1961	PIT N	7	10	.412	5.04	25	17	2	100	120	31	37	1	1	0	0	23	3	0	.130	6	7	2	1	0.6	.867
1962	2 teams PIT N (4G 1–1) NY N (17G 0–2)																									
″	total	1	3	.250	6.63	21	5	0	54.1	63	35	21	0	0	2	0	14	2	0	.143	2	9	0	0	0.5	1.000
9 yrs.		90	88	.506	3.85	268	230	61	1528.2	1434	680	918	15	3	3	0	513	57	1	.111	79	217	21	14	1.2	.934
WORLD SERIES																										
1960	PIT N	0	1	.000	15.43	2	1	0	2.1	4	2	1	0	0	0	0	0	0	0	—	0	0	0	0	0.0	.000

Dave Mlicki

MLICKI, DAVID JOHN
B. June 8, 1968, Cleveland, Ohio.
BR TR 6′ 4″ 185 lbs.

Year	Team		W	L	PCT	ERA	G	GS	CG	IP	H	BB	SO	ShO	Relief Pitching W	L	SV	Batting AB	H	HR	BA	PO	A	E	DP	TC/G	FA
1992	CLE	A	0	2	.000	4.98	4	4	0	21.2	23	16	16	0	0	0	0	0	0	0	—	6	3	0	1	2.3	1.000
1993			0	0	—	3.38	3	3	0	13.1	11	6	7	0	0	0	0	0	0	0	—	1	1	0	0	0.7	1.000
1995	NY	N	9	7	.563	4.26	29	25	0	160.2	160	54	123	0	1	0	0	39	2	0	.051	10	15	1	3	0.9	.962
3 yrs.			9	9	.500	4.28	36	32	0	195.2	194	76	146	0	1	0	0	39	2	0	.051	17	19	1	4	1.0	.973

Kevin Mmahat

MMAHAT, KEVIN PAUL
B. Nov. 9, 1964, Memphis, Tenn.
BL TL 6′ 5″ 220 lbs.

Year	Team		W	L	PCT	ERA	G	GS	CG	IP	H	BB	SO	ShO	Relief Pitching W	L	SV	Batting AB	H	HR	BA	PO	A	E	DP	TC/G	FA
1989	NY	A	0	2	.000	12.91	4	2	0	7.2	13	8	3	0	0	0	0	0	0	0	—	0	1	1	0	0.5	.500

Mike Modak

MODAK, MICHAEL
B. May 18, 1922, Campbell, Ohio.
BR TR 5′10½″ 195 lbs.

Year	Team		W	L	PCT	ERA	G	GS	CG	IP	H	BB	SO	ShO	Relief Pitching W	L	SV	Batting AB	H	HR	BA	PO	A	E	DP	TC/G	FA
1945	CIN	N	1	2	.333	5.74	20	3	1	42.1	52	23	7	1	0	1	1	10	1	0	.100	0	5	1	0	0.3	.833

Dennis Moeller

MOELLER, DENNIS MICHAEL
B. Sept. 15, 1967, Tarzana, Calif.
BR TL 6′ 2″ 195 lbs.

Year	Team		W	L	PCT	ERA	G	GS	CG	IP	H	BB	SO	ShO	Relief Pitching W	L	SV	Batting AB	H	HR	BA	PO	A	E	DP	TC/G	FA
1992	KC	A	0	3	.000	7.00	5	4	0	18	24	11	6	0	0	0	0	0	0	0	—	0	5	0	0	1.0	1.000
1993	PIT	N	1	0	1.000	9.92	10	0	0	16.1	26	7	13	0	1	0	0	0	0	0	—	2	2	0	0	0.4	1.000
2 yrs.			1	3	.250	8.39	15	4	0	34.1	50	18	19	0	1	0	0	0	0	0		2	7	0	0	0.6	1.000

Joe Moeller

MOELLER, JOSEPH DOUGLAS
B. Feb. 15, 1943, Blue Island, Ill.
BR TR 6′ 5″ 192 lbs.

Year	Team		W	L	PCT	ERA	G	GS	CG	IP	H	BB	SO	ShO	Relief Pitching W	L	SV	Batting AB	H	HR	BA	PO	A	E	DP	TC/G	FA
1962	LA	N	6	5	.545	5.25	19	15	1	85.2	87	58	46	0	0	1	1	33	7	0	.212	6	18	0	2	1.3	1.000
1964			7	13	.350	4.21	27	24	1	145.1	153	31	97	0	0	0	0	45	3	0	.067	9	24	1	1	1.3	.971
1966			2	4	.333	2.52	29	8	0	78.2	73	14	31	0	1	1	0	12	2	0	.167	5	21	1	1	0.9	.963
1967			0	0	—	9.00	6	0	0	5	9	3	2	0	0	0	0	0	0	0	—	0	1	0	0	0.2	1.000
1968			1	1	.500	5.06	3	3	0	16	17	2	11	0	0	0	0	7	0	0	.000	0	3	0	0	1.0	1.000
1969			1	0	1.000	3.35	23	4	0	51	54	13	25	0	0	0	1	10	2	0	.200	6	13	0	1	0.8	1.000
1970			7	9	.438	3.93	31	19	2	135	131	43	63	1	1	0	4	39	6	0	.154	6	15	2	1	0.7	.913
1971			2	4	.333	3.82	28	1	0	66	72	12	32	0	2	3	1	9	0	0	.000	3	14	1	1	0.6	.944
8 yrs.			26	36	.419	4.02	166	74	4	582.2	596	176	307	1	4	5	7	155	20	0	.129	35	109	5	7	0.9	.966
WORLD SERIES																											
1966	LA	N	0	0	—	4.50	1	0	0	2	1	1	0	0	0	0	0	0	0	0	—	0	0	0	0	0.0	.000

Ron Moeller

MOELLER, RONALD RALPH (The Kid)
B. Oct. 13, 1938, Cincinnati, Ohio.
BL TL 6′ 180 lbs.

Year	Team		W	L	PCT	ERA	G	GS	CG	IP	H	BB	SO	ShO	Relief Pitching W	L	SV	Batting AB	H	HR	BA	PO	A	E	DP	TC/G	FA
1956	BAL	A	0	1	.000	4.15	4	1	0	8.2	10	3	2	0	0	0	0	1	0	0	.000	0	1	0	0	0.3	1.000
1958			0	0	—	4.15	4	0	0	4.1	6	3	3	0	0	0	0	0	0	0	—	0	2	0	0	0.5	1.000
1961	LA	A	4	8	.333	5.83	33	18	1	112.2	122	83	87	1	0	1	0	29	6	0	.207	5	21	3	2	0.9	.897
1963	2 teams	LA A (3G 0–0) WAS A (8G 2–0)																									
″	total		2	0	1.000	6.33	11	3	0	27	36	11	12	0	0	0	0	9	2	0	.222	0	3	0	0	0.3	1.000
4 yrs.			6	9	.400	5.78	52	22	1	152.2	174	100	104	1	0	1	0	39	8	0	.205	5	27	3	2	0.7	.914

Sam Moffett

MOFFETT, SAMUEL R.
Brother of Joe Moffett.
B. Mar. 14, 1857, Wheeling, W. Va. D. May 5, 1907, Butte, Mont.
BR TR 6′ 175 lbs.

Year	Team		W	L	PCT	ERA	G	GS	CG	IP	H	BB	SO	ShO	Relief Pitching W	L	SV	Batting AB	H	HR	BA	PO	A	E	DP	TC/G	FA
1884	CLE	N	3	19	.136	*3.87*	24	22	21	197.2	236	58	84	0	0	0	0	256	47	0	.184	102	68	23	4	2.8	.881
1887	IND	N	1	5	.167	3.78	6	6	6	50	47	23	3	0	0	0	0	41	5	0	.122	8	7	3	0	1.6	.833
1888			2	5	.286	4.66	7	7	6	56	62	17	7	1	0	0	0	35	4	0	.114	4	5	3	1	1.2	.750
3 yrs.			6	29	.171	4.00	37	35	33	303.2	345	98	94	1	0	0	0	*				114	80	29	5	2.5	.870

Randy Moffitt

MOFFITT, RANDALL JAMES
B. Oct. 13, 1948, Long Beach, Calif.
BR TR 6′ 3″ 190 lbs.

Year	Team		W	L	PCT	ERA	G	GS	CG	IP	H	BB	SO	ShO	Relief Pitching W	L	SV	Batting AB	H	HR	BA	PO	A	E	DP	TC/G	FA
1972	SF	N	1	5	.167	3.68	40	0	0	71	72	30	37	0	1	5	4	8	0	0	.000	4	12	1	0	0.4	.941
1973			4	4	.500	2.43	60	0	0	100	86	31	65	0	4	4	14	17	1	0	.059	6	10	3	2	0.3	.842
1974			5	7	.417	4.50	61	1	0	102	99	29	49	0	5	7	15	16	5	0	.313	12	16	0	1	0.5	1.000
1975			4	5	.444	3.89	55	0	0	74	73	32	39	0	4	5	11	14	3	0	.214	4	10	3	1	0.3	.824
1976			6	6	.500	2.27	58	0	0	103	92	35	50	0	6	6	14	14	2	0	.143	11	13	3	0	0.5	.889
1977			4	9	.308	3.58	64	0	0	88	91	39	68	0	4	9	11	3	0	0	.000	8	15	1	1	0.4	.958
1978			8	4	.667	3.29	70	0	0	82	79	33	52	0	8	4	12	7	1	0	.143	3	7	1	0	0.2	.909
1979			2	5	.286	7.71	28	0	0	35	53	14	16	0	2	5	2	4	0	0	.000	1	5	0	0	0.2	1.000
1980			1	1	.500	4.76	13	0	0	17	18	4	10	0	1	1	0	1	0	0	.000	0	3	0	1	0.2	1.000
1981			0	0	—	8.18	10	0	0	11	15	2	11	0	0	0	0	0	0	0	—	0	0	1	0	0.1	.000
1982	HOU	N	2	4	.333	3.02	30	0	0	41.2	36	13	20	0	2	4	3	2	0	0	.000	3	2	0	0	0.2	1.000
1983	TOR	A	6	2	.750	3.77	45	0	0	57.1	52	24	38	0	6	2	10	0	0	0	—	1	8	0	1	0.2	1.000
12 yrs.			43	52	.453	3.65	534	1	0	782	766	286	455	0	43	52	96	86	12	0	.140	53	101	13	7	0.3	.922

Herb Moford

MOFORD, HERBERT
B. Aug. 6, 1928, Brooksville, Ky.
BR TR 6′ 1″ 175 lbs.

Year	Team		W	L	PCT	ERA	G	GS	CG	IP	H	BB	SO	ShO	Relief Pitching W	L	SV	Batting AB	H	HR	BA	PO	A	E	DP	TC/G	FA
1955	STL	N	1	1	.500	7.88	14	1	0	24	29	15	8	0	1	0	2	2	0	0	.000	1	9	0	0	0.7	1.000
1958	DET	A	4	9	.308	3.61	25	11	6	109.2	83	42	58	0	0	2	1	37	1	0	.027	5	24	0	2	1.2	1.000
1959	BOS	A	0	2	.000	11.42	4	2	0	8.2	10	6	7	0	0	0	0	1	0	0	.000	0	2	0	0	0.5	1.000
1962	NY	N	0	1	.000	7.20	7	0	0	15	21	1	5	0	0	1	0	4	1	0	.250	2	1	0	0	0.4	1.000
4 yrs.			5	13	.278	5.03	50	14	6	157.1	143	64	78	0	1	3	3	44	2	0	.045	8	36	0	2	0.9	1.000

George Mogridge

MOGRIDGE, GEORGE ANTHONY
B. Feb. 18, 1889, Rochester, N. Y. D. Mar. 4, 1962, Rochester, N. Y.
BL TL 6′ 2″ 165 lbs.

Year	Team		W	L	PCT	ERA	G	GS	CG	IP	H	BB	SO	ShO	Relief Pitching W	L	SV	Batting AB	H	HR	BA	PO	A	E	DP	TC/G	FA
1911	CHI	A	0	2	.000	4.97	4	1	0	12.2	12	1	5	0	0	1	0	5	2	0	.400	3	2	0	0	1.3	1.000
1912			3	4	.429	4.04	17	7	2	64.2	69	15	31	0	1	1	3	16	2	0	.125	4	16	2	0	1.3	.909
1915	NY	A	2	3	.400	1.76	6	6	3	41	33	11	11	1	0	0	0	12	1	0	.083	1	11	1	0	2.2	.923
1916			6	12	.333	2.31	30	21	10	194.2	174	45	66	2	1	0	0	66	14	0	.212	15	61	4	2	2.7	.950
1917			9	11	.450	2.98	29	25	15	196.1	185	39	46	1	1	0	0	69	11	0	.159	16	61	0	1	2.7	1.000
1918			16	13	.552	2.27	**45**	19	13	230.1	232	43	62	1	4	**7**	**7**	79	15	0	.190	13	76	1	5	2.0	.989
1919			10	7	.588	2.50	35	18	13	187	159	46	58	3	1	1	0	48	6	0	.125	10	51	2	2	1.8	.968

George Mogridge *continued*

Year	Team	W	L	PCT	ERA	G	GS	CG	IP	H	BB	SO	ShO	Relief Pitching			Batting			BA	PO	A	E	DP	TC/G	FA
														W	L	SV	AB	H	HR							
1920		5	9	.357	4.31	26	15	7	125.1	146	36	35	0	0	1	1	42	7	0	.167	3	37	1	1	1.6	.976
1921	WAS A	18	14	.563	3.00	38	36	21	288	301	66	101	4	1	0	0	98	15	0	.153	18	78	2	3	2.6	.980
1922		18	13	.581	3.58	34	32	18	251.2	300	72	61	3	0	2	0	86	21	1	.244	12	59	6	5	2.3	.922
1923		13	13	.500	3.11	33	28	17	211	228	56	62	3	0	1	1	75	17	0	.227	11	60	5	6	2.3	.934
1924		16	11	.593	3.76	30	30	13	213	217	61	48	2	0	0	0	74	13	0	.176	7	53	2	4	2.1	.968
1925	2 teams WAS A (10G 4–3) STL A (2G 1–1)																									
″	total	5	4	.556	3.95	12	10	4	68.1	73	23	21	0	0	1	0	23	2	0	.087	3	18	3	1	2.0	.875
1926	BOS N	6	10	.375	4.50	39	10	2	142	173	36	46	0	5	3	3	46	8	0	.174	12	43	3	5	1.5	.948
1927		6	4	.600	3.70	20	1	0	48.2	48	15	26	0	**6**	3	5	15	3	0	.200	1	13	0	0	0.7	1.000
15 yrs.		133	130	.506	3.20	398	259	138	2274.2	2350	565	679	20	20	21	20	754	137	1	.182	129	639	32	35	2.0	.960
WORLD SERIES																										
1924	WAS A	1	0	1.000	2.25	2	1	0	12	7	6	5	0	0	0	0	5	0	0	.000	0	0	0	0	0.0	.000

George Mohart

MOHART, GEORGE BENJAMIN BR TR 5′ 9″ 165 lbs.
B. Mar. 6, 1892, Buffalo, N. Y. D. Oct. 2, 1970, Silver Creek, N. Y.

Year	Team	W	L	PCT	ERA	G	GS	CG	IP	H	BB	SO	ShO	Relief Pitching			Batting			BA	PO	A	E	DP	TC/G	FA
														W	L	SV	AB	H	HR							
1920	BKN N	0	1	.000	1.77	13	1	0	35.2	33	7	13	0	0	1	0	8	1	0	.125	3	13	0	0	1.2	1.000
1921		0	0	—	3.86	2	0	0	7	8	1	1	0	0	0	0	2	1	0	.500	0	1	0	0	0.5	1.000
2 yrs.		0	1	.000	2.11	15	1	0	42.2	41	8	14	0	0	1	0	10	2	0	.200	3	14	0	0	1.1	1.000

Mike Mohler

MOHLER, MICHAEL ROSS BR TL 6′ 2″ 195 lbs.
B. July 26, 1968, Dayton, Ohio.

Year	Team	W	L	PCT	ERA	G	GS	CG	IP	H	BB	SO	ShO	Relief Pitching			Batting			BA	PO	A	E	DP	TC/G	FA
														W	L	SV	AB	H	HR							
1993	OAK A	1	6	.143	5.60	42	9	0	64.1	57	44	42	0	1	1	0	0	0	0	—	2	9	1	2	0.3	.917
1994		0	1	.000	7.71	1	1	0	2.1	2	2	4	0	0	0	0	0	0	0	—	0	0	0	0	0.0	.000
1995		1	1	.500	3.04	28	0	0	23.2	16	18	15	0	1	1	1	0	0	0	—	2	2	0	0	0.1	1.000
3 yrs.		2	8	.200	4.98	71	10	0	90.1	75	64	61	0	2	2	1	0	0	0		4	11	1	2	0.2	.938

Dale Mohorcic

MOHORCIC, DALE ROBERT BR TR 6′ 3″ 220 lbs.
B. Jan. 25, 1956, Cleveland, Ohio.

Year	Team	W	L	PCT	ERA	G	GS	CG	IP	H	BB	SO	ShO	Relief Pitching			Batting			BA	PO	A	E	DP	TC/G	FA
														W	L	SV	AB	H	HR							
1986	TEX A	2	4	.333	2.51	58	0	0	79	86	15	29	0	2	4	7	0	0	0	—	5	12	0	3	0.3	1.000
1987		7	6	.538	2.99	74	0	0	99.1	88	19	48	0	7	6	16	0	0	0	—	9	23	2	3	0.5	.941
1988	2 teams TEX A (43G 2–6) NY A (13G 2–2)																									
″	total	4	8	.333	4.22	56	0	0	74.2	83	29	44	0	4	**8**	6	0	0	0		7	9	1	0	0.3	.941
1989	NY A	2	1	.667	4.99	32	0	0	57.2	65	18	24	0	2	1	2	0	0	0	—	5	10	0	2	0.5	1.000
1990	MON N	1	2	.333	3.23	34	0	0	53	56	18	29	0	1	2	2	8	1	0	.125	2	9	0	2	0.3	1.000
5 yrs.		16	21	.432	3.49	254	0	0	363.2	378	99	174	0	16	21	33	8	1	0	.125	28	63	3	10	0.4	.968

Bill Moisan

MOISAN, WILLIAM JOSEPH BL TR 6′ 1″ 170 lbs.
B. July 30, 1925, Bradford, Mass.

Year	Team	W	L	PCT	ERA	G	GS	CG	IP	H	BB	SO	ShO	Relief Pitching			Batting			BA	PO	A	E	DP	TC/G	FA
														W	L	SV	AB	H	HR							
1953	CHI N	0	0	—	5.40	3	0	0	5	5	2	1	0	0	0	0	0	0	0	—	0	1	0	0	0.3	1.000

Carlton Molesworth

MOLESWORTH, CARLTON BL TL 5′ 6″ 200 lbs.
B. Feb. 15, 1876, Frederick, Md. D. July 25, 1961, Frederick, Md.

Year	Team	W	L	PCT	ERA	G	GS	CG	IP	H	BB	SO	ShO	Relief Pitching			Batting			BA	PO	A	E	DP	TC/G	FA
														W	L	SV	AB	H	HR							
1895	WAS N	0	2	.000	14.63	4	3	1	16	33	15	7	0	0	0	0	7	1	0	.143	0	2	0	0	0.5	1.000

Rich Moloney

MOLONEY, RICHARD HENRY BR TR 6′ 3″ 185 lbs.
B. June 7, 1950, Brookline, Mass.

Year	Team	W	L	PCT	ERA	G	GS	CG	IP	H	BB	SO	ShO	Relief Pitching			Batting			BA	PO	A	E	DP	TC/G	FA
														W	L	SV	AB	H	HR							
1970	CHI A	0	0	—	0.00	1	0	0	1	2	0	1	0	0	0	0	0	0	0	—	0	0	0	0	0.0	.000

Vince Molyneaux

MOLYNEAUX, VINCENT LEO BR TR 6′ 180 lbs.
B. Aug. 17, 1888, Lewiston, N. Y. D. May 4, 1950, Stamford, Conn.

Year	Team	W	L	PCT	ERA	G	GS	CG	IP	H	BB	SO	ShO	Relief Pitching			Batting			BA	PO	A	E	DP	TC/G	FA
														W	L	SV	AB	H	HR							
1917	STL A	0	0	—	4.91	7	0	0	22	18	20	4	0	0	0	0	4	0	0	.000	0	9	0	0	1.3	1.000
1918	BOS A	1	0	1.000	3.38	6	0	0	10.2	3	8	1	0	1	0	0	2	0	0	.000	1	3	0	1	0.7	1.000
2 yrs.		1	0	1.000	4.41	13	0	0	32.2	21	28	5	0	1	0	0	6	0	0	.000	1	12	0	1	1.0	1.000

Rinty Monahan

MONAHAN, EDWARD FRANCIS BR TR 6′ 1″ 195 lbs.
B. Apr. 28, 1928, Brooklyn, N. Y.

Year	Team	W	L	PCT	ERA	G	GS	CG	IP	H	BB	SO	ShO	Relief Pitching			Batting			BA	PO	A	E	DP	TC/G	FA
														W	L	SV	AB	H	HR							
1953	PHI A	0	0	—	4.22	4	0	0	10.2	11	7	2	0	0	0	0	2	0	0	.000	0	1	0	0	0.3	1.000

Bill Monbouquette

MONBOUQUETTE, WILLIAM CHARLES BR TR 5′11″ 190 lbs.
B. Aug. 11, 1936, Medford, Mass.

Year	Team	W	L	PCT	ERA	G	GS	CG	IP	H	BB	SO	ShO	Relief Pitching			Batting			BA	PO	A	E	DP	TC/G	FA
														W	L	SV	AB	H	HR							
1958	BOS A	3	4	.429	3.31	10	8	3	54.1	52	20	30	0	0	0	0	17	3	0	.176	1	7	1	1	0.9	.889
1959		7	7	.500	4.15	34	17	4	151.2	165	33	87	0	2	1	0	46	3	0	.065	11	22	0	3	1.0	1.000
1960		14	11	.560	3.64	35	30	12	215	217	68	134	3	2	0	0	65	6	0	.092	18	28	0	3	1.3	1.000
1961		14	14	.500	3.39	32	32	12	236.1	233	100	161	1	0	0	0	69	9	0	.130	16	28	1	2	1.4	.978
1962		15	13	.536	3.33	35	35	11	235.1	227	65	153	4	0	0	0	73	7	0	.096	7	21	1	0	0.8	.966
1963		20	10	.667	3.81	37	36	13	266.2	**258**	42	174	1	0	1	0	88	10	0	.114	31	37	0	3	1.8	1.000
1964		13	14	.481	4.04	36	35	7	234	**258**	40	120	5	0	0	1	72	6	0	.083	15	38	0	2	1.5	1.000
1965		10	**18**	.357	3.70	35	35	10	228.2	239	40	110	2	0	0	0	68	4	0	.059	21	38	2	2	1.7	.967
1966	DET A	7	8	.467	4.73	30	14	2	102.2	120	22	61	1	3	0	0	26	4	0	.154	11	10	1	1	0.7	.955
1967	2 teams DET A (2G 0–0) NY A (33G 6–5)																									
″	total	6	5	.545	2.33	35	10	2	135.1	123	17	55	1	2	1	1	32	5	0	.156	11	19	1	1	0.9	.968
1968	2 teams NY A (17G 5–7) SF N (7G 0–1)																									
″	total	5	8	.385	4.35	24	11	2	101.1	103	15	37	0	1	4	1	26	3	0	.115	13	18	0	1	1.3	1.000
11 yrs.		114	112	.504	3.68	343	263	78	1961.1	1995	462	1122	18	10	7	3	582	60	0	.103	155	266	7	19	1.2	.984

Sid Monge

MONGE, ISIDRO PEDROZA BB TL 6′ 2″ 185 lbs.
B. Apr. 11, 1951, Agua Prieta, Mexico.

Year	Team	W	L	PCT	ERA	G	GS	CG	IP	H	BB	SO	ShO	Relief Pitching			Batting			BA	PO	A	E	DP	TC/G	FA
														W	L	SV	AB	H	HR							
1975	CAL A	0	2	.000	4.18	4	2	2	23.2	22	10	17	0	0	0	0	0	0	0	—	1	2	0	0	0.8	1.000
1976		6	7	.462	3.36	32	13	2	118	108	49	53	0	2	2	0	0	0	0	—	6	15	2	1	0.7	.913
1977	2 teams CAL A (4G 0–1) CLE A (33G 1–2)																									
″	total	1	3	.250	5.44	37	0	0	51.1	61	33	29	0	1	3	4	0	0	0		1	7	2	1	0.3	.800
1978	CLE A	4	3	.571	2.76	48	2	0	84.2	71	51	54	0	4	2	6	0	0	0	—	4	11	2	1	0.4	.882
1979		12	10	.545	2.40	76	0	0	131	96	64	108	0	12	10	19	0	0	0	—	6	17	3	2	0.3	.885

Sid Monge *continued*

Year	Team	W	L	PCT	ERA	G	GS	CG	IP	H	BB	SO	ShO	Relief W	Relief L	Relief SV	Batting AB	Batting H	HR	BA	PO	A	E	DP	TC/G	FA
1980		3	5	.375	3.54	67	0	0	94	80	40	61	0	3	5	14	0	0	0	—	4	6	0	0	0.1	1.000
1981		3	5	.375	4.34	31	0	0	58	58	21	41	0	3	5	4	0	0	0	—	5	4	0	0	0.3	1.000
1982	PHI N	7	1	.875	3.75	47	0	0	72	70	22	43	0	7	1	2	9	1	0	.111	5	14	1	0	0.4	.950
1983	2 teams PHI N (14G 3–0) SD N (47G 7–3)																									
"	total	10	3	.769	3.70	61	0	0	80.1	85	37	39	0	10	3	7	11	1	0	.091	4	10	0	0	0.2	1.000
1984	2 teams SD N (13G 2–1) DET A (19G 1–0)																									
"	total	3	1	.750	4.41	32	0	0	51	57	29	26	0	3	1	0	1	0	0	.000	1	3	1	0	0.2	.800
10 yrs.		49	40	.551	3.53	435	17	4	764	708	356	471	0	45	32	56	21	2	0	.095	37	89	11	5	0.3	.920

Ed Monroe

MONROE, EDWARD OLIVER (Peck) BR TR 6′ 5″ 187 lbs.
B. Feb. 22, 1895, Louisville, Ky. D. Apr. 29, 1969, Louisville, Ky.

Year	Team	W	L	PCT	ERA	G	GS	CG	IP	H	BB	SO	ShO	Relief W	Relief L	Relief SV	Batting AB	Batting H	HR	BA	PO	A	E	DP	TC/G	FA
1917	NY A	1	0	1.000	3.45	9	1	1	28.2	35	6	12	0	0	0	1	12	2	0	.167	0	9	2	1	1.2	.818
1918		0	0	—	4.50	1	0	0	2	1	2	1	0	0	0	0	0	0	0	—	0	1	1	1	2.0	.500
2 yrs.		1	0	1.000	3.52	10	1	1	30.2	36	8	13	0	0	0	1	12	2	0	.167	0	10	3	2	1.3	.769

Larry Monroe

MONROE, LAWRENCE JAMES BR TR 6′ 4″ 200 lbs.
B. June 20, 1956, Detroit, Mich.

Year	Team	W	L	PCT	ERA	G	GS	CG	IP	H	BB	SO	ShO	Relief W	Relief L	Relief SV	Batting AB	Batting H	HR	BA	PO	A	E	DP	TC/G	FA
1976	CHI A	0	1	.000	4.09	8	2	0	22	23	13	9	0	0	0	0	0	0	0	—	5	1	0	0	0.8	1.000

Zack Monroe

MONROE, ZACHARY CHARLES BR TR 6′ 198 lbs.
B. July 8, 1931, Peoria, Ill.

Year	Team	W	L	PCT	ERA	G	GS	CG	IP	H	BB	SO	ShO	Relief W	Relief L	Relief SV	Batting AB	Batting H	HR	BA	PO	A	E	DP	TC/G	FA
1958	NY A	4	2	.667	3.26	21	6	1	58	57	27	18	0	1	1	1	17	2	0	.118	7	10	1	2	0.9	.944
1959		0	0	—	5.40	3	0	0	3.1	3	2	1	0	0	0	0	0	0	0	—	0	1	0	0	0.3	1.000
2 yrs.		4	2	.667	3.38	24	6	1	61.1	60	29	19	0	1	1	1	17	2	0	.118	7	11	1	2	0.8	.947
WORLD SERIES																										
1958	NY A	0	0	—	27.00	1	0	0	1	3	1	1	0	0	0	0	0	0	0	—	0	0	0	0	0.0	.000

John Montague

MONTAGUE, JOHN EVANS BR TR 6′ 2″ 213 lbs.
B. Sept. 12, 1947, Newport News, Va.

Year	Team	W	L	PCT	ERA	G	GS	CG	IP	H	BB	SO	ShO	Relief W	Relief L	Relief SV	Batting AB	Batting H	HR	BA	PO	A	E	DP	TC/G	FA
1973	MON N	0	0	—	3.52	4	0	0	7.2	8	2	7	0	0	0	0	1	0	0	.000	0	0	0	0	0.0	.000
1974		3	4	.429	3.14	46	1	0	83	73	38	43	0	3	3	3	10	1	0	.100	6	5	3	1	0.3	.786
1975	2 teams MON N (12G 0–1) PHI N (3G 0–0)																									
"	total	0	1	.000	6.35	15	0	0	22.2	31	10	10	0	0	1	2	1	0	0	.000	0	5	1	1	0.4	.833
1977	SEA A	8	12	.400	4.30	47	15	2	182	193	75	98	0	4	4	4	0	0	0	—	11	33	0	1	0.9	1.000
1978		1	3	.250	6.18	19	0	0	43.2	52	24	14	0	1	3	2	0	0	0	—	2	5	1	0	0.4	.875
1979	2 teams SEA A (41G 6–4) CAL A (14G 2–0)																									
"	total	8	4	.667	5.51	55	1	0	134	141	56	66	0	8	3	7	0	0	0	—	6	21	2	0	0.5	.931
1980	CAL A	4	2	.667	5.11	37	0	0	74	97	21	22	0	4	2	3	0	0	0		4	13	0	1	0.5	1.000
7 yrs.		24	26	.480	4.76	223	17	2	547	595	226	260	0	20	16	21	12	1	0	.083	29	82	7	4	0.5	.941
LEAGUE CHAMPIONSHIP SERIES																										
1979	CAL A	0	1	.000	9.00	2	0	0	4	4	2	2	0	0	1	0	0	0	0	—	1	2	0	0	1.5	1.000

Rafael Montalvo

MONTALVO, RAFAEL EDGARDO BR TR 6′ 185 lbs.
Born Rafael Edgardo Montalvo (Torres).
B. Mar. 31, 1964, Rio Piedras, Puerto Rico.

Year	Team	W	L	PCT	ERA	G	GS	CG	IP	H	BB	SO	ShO	Relief W	Relief L	Relief SV	Batting AB	Batting H	HR	BA	PO	A	E	DP	TC/G	FA
1986	HOU N	0	0	—	9.00	1	0	0	1	1	2	0	0	0	0	0	0	0	0	—	1	1	0	0	2.0	1.000

Aurelio Monteagudo

MONTEAGUDO, AURELIO FAUSTINO BR TR 5′11″ 180 lbs.
Born Aurelio Faustino Monteagudo (Cintra).
Son of Rene Monteagudo.
B. Nov. 19, 1943, Caibarien, Cuba D. Nov. 10, 1990, Saltillo, Mexico.

Year	Team	W	L	PCT	ERA	G	GS	CG	IP	H	BB	SO	ShO	Relief W	Relief L	Relief SV	Batting AB	Batting H	HR	BA	PO	A	E	DP	TC/G	FA
1963	KC A	0	0	—	2.57	4	0	0	7	4	3	3	0	0	0	0	0	0	0	—	0	3	0	0	0.8	1.000
1964		0	4	.000	8.90	11	6	0	31.1	40	10	14	0	0	0	0	7	2	0	.286	3	3	1	1	0.6	.857
1965		0	0	—	3.86	4	0	0	7	5	4	5	0	0	0	0	0	0	0	—	0	0	0	0	0.0	.000
1966	2 teams KC A (6G 0–0) HOU N (10G 0–0)																									
"	total	0	0		3.86	16	0	0	28	26	18	10	0	0	0	1	1	0	0	.000	0	4	0	2	0.3	1.000
1967	CHI A	0	1	.000	20.25	1	1	0	1.1	4	2	0	0	0	0	0	0	0	0	—	0	0	0	0	0.0	.000
1970	KC A	1	1	.500	3.00	21	0	0	27	20	9	18	0	1	1	0	2	0	0	.000	1	2	1	0	0.2	.750
1973	CAL A	2	1	.667	4.20	15	0	0	30	23	16	8	0	2	1	3	0	0	0	—	6	3	0	1	0.6	1.000
7 yrs.		3	7	.300	5.06	72	7	0	131.2	122	62	58	0	3	2	4	10	2	0	.200	10	15	2	4	0.4	.926

Rene Monteagudo

MONTEAGUDO, RENE BL TL 5′ 7″ 165 lbs.
Born Rene Monteagudo (Miranda).
Father of Aurelio Monteagudo.
B. Mar. 12, 1916, Havana, Cuba D. Sept. 14, 1973, Hialeah, Fla.

Year	Team	W	L	PCT	ERA	G	GS	CG	IP	H	BB	SO	ShO	Relief W	Relief L	Relief SV	Batting AB	Batting H	HR	BA	PO	A	E	DP	TC/G	FA
1938	WAS A	1	1	.500	5.73	5	3	2	22	26	15	13	0	0	0	0	6	3	0	.500	0	1	0	0	0.2	1.000
1940		2	6	.250	6.08	27	8	3	100.2	128	52	64	0	0	1	2	33	6	0	.182	5	11	1	1	0.6	.941
1945	PHI N	0	0	—	7.49	14	0	0	45.2	67	28	16	0	0	0	0	193	58	0	.301	12	1	1	0	1.6	.929
3 yrs.		3	7	.300	6.42	46	11	5	168.1	221	95	93	0	0	1	2	*				79	25	10	4	1.3	.912

John Montefusco

MONTEFUSCO, JOHN JOSEPH (The Count) BR TR 6′ 1″ 180 lbs.
B. May 25, 1950, Long Branch, N. J.

Year	Team	W	L	PCT	ERA	G	GS	CG	IP	H	BB	SO	ShO	Relief W	Relief L	Relief SV	Batting AB	Batting H	HR	BA	PO	A	E	DP	TC/G	FA
1974	SF N	3	2	.600	4.85	7	5	1	39	41	19	34	1	1	0	0	14	4	2	.286	0	4	0	0	0.6	1.000
1975		15	9	.625	2.88	35	34	10	244	210	86	215	4	0	0	0	80	7	1	.087	11	25	1	0	1.1	.973
1976		16	14	.533	2.84	37	36	11	253.1	224	74	172	**6**	0	0	0	78	8	0	.103	12	21	3	0	1.0	.917
1977		7	12	.368	3.50	26	25	4	157	170	46	110	0	0	0	0	49	6	1	.122	10	12	1	0	0.9	.957
1978		11	9	.550	3.80	36	36	3	239	233	68	177	0	0	0	0	70	4	0	.057	8	28	2	2	1.1	.947
1979		3	8	.273	3.94	22	22	0	137	145	51	76	0	0	0	0	42	7	0	.167	9	20	1	2	1.4	.967
1980		4	8	.333	4.38	22	17	1	113	120	39	85	0	1	0	0	30	1	0	.033	6	9	0	1	0.7	1.000
1981	ATL N	2	3	.400	3.51	26	9	0	77	75	27	34	0	0	0	1	15	1	0	.067	6	12	1	1	0.7	.947
1982	SD N	10	11	.476	4.00	32	32	1	184.1	177	41	83	0	0	0	0	58	5	0	.086	11	29	3	0	1.3	.930
1983	2 teams SD N (31G 9–4) NY A (6G 5–0)																									
"	total	14	4	.778	3.31	37	16	1	133.1	133	42	67	0	6	1	4	19	1	0	.053	5	16	3	0	0.6	.875

John Montefusco *continued*

Year	Team	Lg	W	L	PCT	ERA	G	GS	CG	IP	H	BB	SO	ShO	Relief W	Relief L	Relief SV	Batting AB	Batting H	Batting HR	BA	PO	A	E	DP	TC/G	FA
1984	NY	A	5	3	.625	3.58	11	11	0	55.1	55	13	23	0	0	0	0	0	0	0	—	1	7	1	1	0.8	.889
1985			0	0	—	10.29	3	1	0	7	12	2	2	0	0	0	0	0	0	0	—	1	1	0	0	0.7	1.000
1986			0	0	—	2.19	4	0	0	12.1	9	5	3	0	0	0	0	0	0	0	—	2	3	0	1	1.3	1.000
13 yrs.			90	83	.520	3.54	298	244	32	1651.2	1604	513	1081	11	8	1	5	455	44	4	.097	82	187	16	8	1.0	.944

Manny Montejo

MONTEJO, MANUEL (Pete)
Born Manuel Montejo (Bofill).
B. Oct. 16, 1935, Caibarien, Cuba.
BR TR 5′11″ 150 lbs.

Year	Team	Lg	W	L	PCT	ERA	G	GS	CG	IP	H	BB	SO	ShO	Relief W	Relief L	Relief SV	Batting AB	Batting H	Batting HR	BA	PO	A	E	DP	TC/G	FA
1961	DET	A	0	0	—	3.86	12	0	0	16.1	13	6	15	0	0	0	0	0	0	0	—	0	0	0	0	0.0	.000

Rich Monteleone

MONTELEONE, RICHARD
B. Mar. 22, 1963, Tampa, Fla.
BR TR 6′ 2″ 205 lbs.

Year	Team	Lg	W	L	PCT	ERA	G	GS	CG	IP	H	BB	SO	ShO	Relief W	Relief L	Relief SV	Batting AB	Batting H	Batting HR	BA	PO	A	E	DP	TC/G	FA
1987	SEA	A	0	0	—	6.43	3	0	0	7	10	4	2	0	0	0	0	0	0	0	—	0	3	0	0	1.0	1.000
1988	CAL	A	0	0	—	0.00	3	0	0	4.1	4	1	3	0	0	0	0	0	0	0	—	0	1	0	0	0.3	1.000
1989			2	2	.500	3.18	24	0	0	39.2	39	13	27	0	2	2	0	0	0	0	—	1	9	1	1	0.5	.909
1990	NY	A	0	1	.000	6.14	5	0	0	7.1	8	2	8	0	0	1	0	0	0	0	—	1	1	0	0	0.4	1.000
1991			3	1	.750	3.64	26	0	0	47	42	19	34	0	3	1	0	0	0	0	—	1	10	1	1	0.5	.917
1992			7	3	.700	3.30	47	0	0	92.2	82	27	62	0	7	3	0	0	0	0	—	6	7	0	1	0.3	1.000
1993			7	4	.636	4.94	42	0	0	85.2	85	35	50	0	7	4	0	0	0	0	—	9	11	1	0	0.5	.952
1994	SF	N	4	3	.571	3.18	39	0	0	45.1	43	13	16	0	4	3	0	3	0	0	.000	2	3	0	0	0.1	1.000
1995	CAL	A	1	0	1.000	2.00	9	0	0	9	8	3	5	0	1	0	0	0	0	0	—	0	1	0	0	0.1	1.000
9 yrs.			24	14	.632	3.78	198	0	0	338	321	117	207	0	24	14	0	3	0	0	.000	20	46	3	3	0.3	.957

Jeff Montgomery

MONTGOMERY, JEFFREY THOMAS
B. Jan. 7, 1962, Wellston, Ohio.
BR TR 5′11″ 170 lbs.

Year	Team	Lg	W	L	PCT	ERA	G	GS	CG	IP	H	BB	SO	ShO	Relief W	Relief L	Relief SV	Batting AB	Batting H	Batting HR	BA	PO	A	E	DP	TC/G	FA
1987	CIN	N	2	2	.500	6.52	14	1	0	19.1	25	9	13	0	2	1	0	2	0	0	.000	1	3	0	0	0.3	1.000
1988	KC	A	7	2	.778	3.45	45	0	0	62.2	54	30	47	0	7	2	1	0	0	0	—	3	10	1	0	0.3	.929
1989			7	3	.700	1.37	63	0	0	92	66	25	94	0	7	3	18	0	0	0	—	11	6	2	1	0.3	.895
1990			6	5	.545	2.39	73	0	0	94.1	81	34	94	0	6	5	24	0	0	0	—	3	13	0	0	0.2	1.000
1991			4	4	.500	2.90	67	0	0	90	83	28	77	0	4	4	33	0	0	0	—	10	8	0	0	0.3	1.000
1992			1	6	.143	2.18	65	0	0	82.2	61	27	69	0	1	6	39	0	0	0	—	12	13	1	2	0.4	.962
1993			7	5	.583	2.27	69	0	0	87.1	65	23	66	0	7	5	**45**	0	0	0	—	6	13	0	0	0.3	1.000
1994			2	3	.400	4.03	42	0	0	44.2	48	15	50	0	2	3	27	0	0	0	—	2	2	1	0	0.1	.800
1995			2	3	.400	3.43	54	0	0	65.2	60	25	49	0	2	3	31	0	0	0	—	13	4	1	1	0.3	.944
9 yrs.			38	33	.535	2.72	492	1	0	638.2	543	216	559	0	38	32	218	2	0	0	.000	61	72	6	4	0.3	.957

Monty Montgomery

MONTGOMERY, MONTY BRYSON
B. Sept. 1, 1946, Albemarle, N. C.
BR TR 6′ 3″ 200 lbs.

Year	Team	Lg	W	L	PCT	ERA	G	GS	CG	IP	H	BB	SO	ShO	Relief W	Relief L	Relief SV	Batting AB	Batting H	Batting HR	BA	PO	A	E	DP	TC/G	FA
1971	KC	A	3	0	1.000	2.14	3	2	0	21	16	3	12	0	1	0	0	7	0	0	.000	2	3	0	0	1.7	1.000
1972			3	3	.500	3.05	9	8	1	56	55	17	24	1	0	0	0	17	3	0	.176	3	7	0	2	1.1	1.000
2 yrs.			6	3	.667	2.81	12	10	1	77	71	20	36	1	1	0	0	24	3	0	.125	5	10	0	2	1.3	1.000

Ray Monzant

MONZANT, RAMON SEGUNDO
Born Ramon Segundo Monzant (Espina).
B. Jan. 4, 1933, Maracaibo, Venezuela.
BR TR 6′ 160 lbs.

Year	Team	Lg	W	L	PCT	ERA	G	GS	CG	IP	H	BB	SO	ShO	Relief W	Relief L	Relief SV	Batting AB	Batting H	Batting HR	BA	PO	A	E	DP	TC/G	FA
1954	NY	N	0	0	—	4.70	6	1	0	7.2	8	11	5	0	0	0	0	2	0	0	.000	0	0	1	0	0.2	.000
1955			4	8	.333	3.99	28	12	3	94.2	98	43	54	0	2	1	0	24	3	0	.125	7	10	2	0	0.7	.895
1956			1	0	1.000	4.15	4	1	1	13	8	7	11	0	0	0	0	4	0	0	.000	0	2	0	0	0.5	1.000
1957			3	2	.600	3.99	24	2	0	49.2	55	16	37	0	3	0	0	10	3	0	.300	1	2	0	0	0.1	1.000
1958	SF	N	8	11	.421	4.72	43	16	4	150.2	160	57	93	1	3	5	1	49	8	0	.163	16	26	2	4	1.0	.955
1960			0	0	—	9.00	1	0	0	1	1	0	1	0	0	0	0	0	0	0	—	0	1	0	0	1.0	1.000
6 yrs.			16	21	.432	4.38	106	32	8	316.2	330	134	201	1	8	6	1	89	14	0	.157	24	41	5	4	0.7	.929

Leo Moon

MOON, LEO (Lefty)
B. June 22, 1899, Belmont, N. C. D. Aug. 25, 1970, New Orleans, La.
BR TL 5′11″ 165 lbs.

Year	Team	Lg	W	L	PCT	ERA	G	GS	CG	IP	H	BB	SO	ShO	Relief W	Relief L	Relief SV	Batting AB	Batting H	Batting HR	BA	PO	A	E	DP	TC/G	FA
1932	CLE	A	0	0	—	11.12	1	0	0	5.2	11	7	1	0	0	0	0	2	1	0	.500	0	2	0	0	2.0	1.000

Jim Mooney

MOONEY, JIM IRVING
B. Sept. 4, 1906, Mooresburg, Tenn. D. Apr. 27, 1979, Johnson City, Tenn.
BR TL 5′11″ 168 lbs.

Year	Team	Lg	W	L	PCT	ERA	G	GS	CG	IP	H	BB	SO	ShO	Relief W	Relief L	Relief SV	Batting AB	Batting H	Batting HR	BA	PO	A	E	DP	TC/G	FA
1931	NY	N	7	1	.875	2.01	10	8	6	71.2	71	16	38	2	1	0	0	25	4	0	.160	1	10	0	1	1.1	1.000
1932			6	10	.375	5.05	29	18	4	124.2	154	42	37	1	0	1	0	41	5	0	.122	2	21	2	2	0.9	.920
1933	STL	N	2	5	.286	3.72	21	8	2	77.1	87	26	14	0	0	1	1	20	1	0	.050	2	22	1	0	1.2	.960
1934			2	4	.333	5.47	32	7	1	82.1	114	49	27	0	2	0	1	19	1	0	.053	3	12	2	0	0.5	.882
4 yrs.			17	20	.459	4.25	92	41	13	356	426	133	116	3	3	2	2	105	11	0	.105	8	65	5	3	0.8	.936
WORLD SERIES																											
1934	STL	N	0	0	—	0.00	1	0	0	1	1	0	0	0	0	0	0	0	0	0	—	0	1	0	0	1.0	1.000

Bill Mooneyham

MOONEYHAM, WILLIAM CRAIG
B. Aug. 16, 1960, Livermore, Calif.
BR TR 6′ 175 lbs.

Year	Team	Lg	W	L	PCT	ERA	G	GS	CG	IP	H	BB	SO	ShO	Relief W	Relief L	Relief SV	Batting AB	Batting H	Batting HR	BA	PO	A	E	DP	TC/G	FA
1986	OAK	A	4	5	.444	4.52	45	6	0	99.2	103	67	75	0	4	3	2	0	0	0	—	5	17	2	1	0.5	.917

Balor Moore

MOORE, BALOR LILBON
B. Jan. 25, 1951, Smithville, Tex.
BL TL 6′ 2″ 178 lbs.

Year	Team	Lg	W	L	PCT	ERA	G	GS	CG	IP	H	BB	SO	ShO	Relief W	Relief L	Relief SV	Batting AB	Batting H	Batting HR	BA	PO	A	E	DP	TC/G	FA
1970	MON	N	0	2	.000	7.20	6	2	0	10	14	8	6	0	0	0	0	3	1	0	.333	1	2	1	1	0.7	.750
1972			9	9	.500	3.47	22	22	6	147.2	122	59	161	3	0	0	0	55	8	0	.145	4	21	3	0	1.3	.893
1973			7	16	.304	4.49	35	32	3	176.1	151	109	151	1	0	0	0	53	3	0	.057	11	19	4	2	1.0	.882
1974			0	2	.000	3.86	8	2	0	14	13	15	16	0	0	0	0	2	0	0	.000	0	1	1	0	0.3	.500
1977	CAL	A	0	2	.000	3.97	7	3	0	22.2	28	10	14	0	0	0	0	0	0	0	—	0	2	1	0	0.4	.667
1978	TOR	A	6	9	.400	4.86	37	18	2	144.1	165	54	75	0	2	0	0	0	0	0	—	4	29	3	2	1.0	.917
1979			5	7	.417	4.86	34	16	5	139	135	79	51	0	0	0	0	0	0	0	—	4	22	4	1	0.9	.867
1980			1	1	.500	5.26	31	3	0	65	76	31	22	0	1	0	1	0	0	0	—	2	10	2	1	0.5	.857
8 yrs.			28	48	.368	4.51	180	98	16	719	704	365	496	4	3	0	1	113	12	0	.106	26	106	19	7	0.8	.874

Barry Moore

MOORE, ROBERT BARRY — BL TL 6′ 1″ 190 lbs.
B. Apr. 3, 1943, Statesville, N. C.

Year	Team	W	L	PCT	ERA	G	GS	CG	IP	H	BB	SO	ShO	Relief Pitching W	Relief Pitching L	Relief Pitching SV	Batting AB	Batting H	Batting HR	BA	PO	A	E	DP	TC/G	FA
1965	WAS A	0	0	—	0.00	1	0	0	1	1	1	0	0	0	0	0	0	0	0	—	0	0	0	0	0.0	.000
1966		3	3	.500	3.75	12	11	1	62.1	55	39	28	0	0	0	0	19	2	0	.105	2	13	0	0	1.3	1.000
1967		7	11	.389	3.76	27	26	3	143.2	127	71	74	1	0	0	0	46	6	0	.130	6	31	2	2	1.4	.949
1968		4	6	.400	3.37	32	18	0	117.2	116	42	56	0	0	0	3	31	3	0	.097	9	24	1	1	1.1	.971
1969		9	8	.529	4.30	31	25	4	134	123	67	51	0	0	2	0	43	9	0	.209	3	14	1	2	0.6	.944
1970	2 teams CLE A (13G 3–5) CHI A (24G 0–4)																									
″	total	3	9	.250	5.30	37	19	0	141	155	80	69	0	0	0	0	40	7	0	.175	11	28	2	1	1.1	.951
6 yrs.		26	37	.413	4.16	140	99	8	599.2	577	300	278	1	0	2	3	179	27	0	.151	31	110	6	6	1.0	.959

Bill Moore

MOORE, WILLIAM CHRISTOPHER — BR TR 6′ 3″ 195 lbs.
B. Sept. 3, 1902, Corning, N. Y. D. Jan. 24, 1984, Corning, N. Y.

Year	Team	W	L	PCT	ERA	G	GS	CG	IP	H	BB	SO	ShO	Relief Pitching W	Relief Pitching L	Relief Pitching SV	Batting AB	Batting H	Batting HR	BA	PO	A	E	DP	TC/G	FA
1925	DET A	0	0	—	∞	1	0	0		0	3	0	0	0	0	0	0	0	0	—	0	0	0	0	0.0	.000

Bob Moore

MOORE, ROBERT DEVELL — BR TR 6′ 5″ 215 lbs.
B. Nov. 8, 1958, Sweetwater, La.

Year	Team	W	L	PCT	ERA	G	GS	CG	IP	H	BB	SO	ShO	Relief Pitching W	Relief Pitching L	Relief Pitching SV	Batting AB	Batting H	Batting HR	BA	PO	A	E	DP	TC/G	FA
1985	SF N	0	0	—	3.24	11	0	0	16.2	18	10	10	0	0	0	0	2	0	0	.000	0	1	1	0	0.2	.500

Brad Moore

MOORE, BRADLEY ALAN — BR TR 6′ 1″ 185 lbs.
B. June 21, 1964, Loveland, Colo.

Year	Team	W	L	PCT	ERA	G	GS	CG	IP	H	BB	SO	ShO	Relief Pitching W	Relief Pitching L	Relief Pitching SV	Batting AB	Batting H	Batting HR	BA	PO	A	E	DP	TC/G	FA
1988	PHI N	0	0	—	0.00	5	0	0	5.2	4	4	2	0	0	0	0	0	0	0	—	2	1	0	0	0.6	1.000
1990		0	0	—	3.38	3	0	0	2.2	4	2	1	0	0	0	0	0	0	0	—	0	1	0	0	0.3	1.000
2 yrs.		0	0		1.08	8	0	0	8.1	8	6	3	0	0	0	0	0	0	0		2	2	0	0	0.5	1.000

Carlos Moore

MOORE, CARLOS WHITMAN — BR TR 6′ 1½″ 180 lbs.
B. Aug. 13, 1906, Clinton, Tenn. D. July 2, 1958, New Orleans, La.

Year	Team	W	L	PCT	ERA	G	GS	CG	IP	H	BB	SO	ShO	Relief Pitching W	Relief Pitching L	Relief Pitching SV	Batting AB	Batting H	Batting HR	BA	PO	A	E	DP	TC/G	FA
1930	WAS A	0	0	—	2.31	4	0	0	11.2	9	4	2	0	0	0	0	4	0	0	.000	2	1	0	0	0.8	1.000

Cy Moore

MOORE, WILLIAM AUSTIN — BR TR 6′ 1″ 190 lbs.
B. Feb. 7, 1905, Elberton, Ga. D. Mar. 28, 1972, Augusta, Ga.

Year	Team	W	L	PCT	ERA	G	GS	CG	IP	H	BB	SO	ShO	Relief Pitching W	Relief Pitching L	Relief Pitching SV	Batting AB	Batting H	Batting HR	BA	PO	A	E	DP	TC/G	FA
1929	BKN N	3	3	.500	5.56	32	4	0	68	87	31	17	0	2	1	2	16	3	0	.188	2	11	0	1	0.4	1.000
1930		0	0	—	0.00	1	0	0		2	0	0	0	0	0	0	0	0	0	—	0	0	0	0	0.0	.000
1931		1	2	.333	3.79	23	1	1	61.2	62	13	35	0	1	1	0	13	2	0	.154	2	12	0	0	0.6	1.000
1932		0	3	.000	4.81	20	2	0	48.2	56	17	23	0	0	2	0	14	3	0	.214	5	11	1	0	0.9	.941
1933	PHI N	8	9	.471	3.74	36	18	9	161.1	177	42	53	3	2	0	1	48	3	0	.063	6	35	1	1	1.2	.976
1934		4	9	.308	6.47	35	15	3	126.2	163	65	55	0	2	0	0	42	6	0	.143	2	21	2	2	0.7	.920
6 yrs.		16	26	.381	4.86	147	40	13	466.1	547	168	183	3	7	4	3	133	17	0	.128	17	90	4	4	0.8	.964

Dee Moore

MOORE, D. C. — BR TR 6′ 200 lbs.
B. Apr. 6, 1914, Hedley, Tex.

Year	Team	W	L	PCT	ERA	G	GS	CG	IP	H	BB	SO	ShO	Relief Pitching W	Relief Pitching L	Relief Pitching SV	Batting AB	Batting H	Batting HR	BA	PO	A	E	DP	TC/G	FA
1936	CIN N	0	0	—	0.00	2	1	0	7	3	2	3	0	0	0	0	*				5	3	1	0	3.0	.889

Donnie Moore

MOORE, DONNIE RAY — BL TR 6′ 175 lbs.
B. Feb. 13, 1954, Lubbock, Tex. D. July 18, 1989, Anaheim, Calif.

Year	Team	W	L	PCT	ERA	G	GS	CG	IP	H	BB	SO	ShO	Relief Pitching W	Relief Pitching L	Relief Pitching SV	Batting AB	Batting H	Batting HR	BA	PO	A	E	DP	TC/G	FA
1975	CHI N	0	0	—	4.00	4	1	0	9	12	4	8	0	0	0	0	3	0	0	.000	2	0	0	0	0.5	1.000
1977		4	2	.667	4.04	27	1	0	49	51	18	34	0	4	2	0	10	3	0	.300	4	11	2	1	0.6	.882
1978		9	7	.563	4.11	71	1	0	103	117	31	50	0	9	7	4	15	4	0	.267	10	16	2	0	0.4	.929
1979		1	4	.200	5.18	39	1	0	73	95	25	43	0	1	3	1	13	2	0	.154	6	15	2	0	0.6	.913
1980	STL N	1	1	.500	6.14	11	0	0	22	25	5	10	0	1	1	0	4	3	0	.750	1	1	1	0	0.3	.667
1981	MIL A	0	0	—	6.75	3	0	0	4	4	4	2	0	0	0	0	0	0	0	—	1	1	0	0	0.7	1.000
1982	ATL N	3	1	.750	4.23	16	0	0	27.2	32	7	17	0	3	1	1	1	0	0	.000	7	3	0	1	0.6	1.000
1983		2	3	.400	3.67	43	0	0	68.2	72	10	41	0	2	3	6	8	4	0	.500	2	8	0	0	0.2	1.000
1984		4	5	.444	2.94	47	0	0	64.1	63	18	47	0	4	5	16	3	0	0	.000	3	10	1	1	0.3	.929
1985	CAL A	8	8	.500	1.92	65	0	0	103	91	21	72	0	8	8	31	0	0	0	—	4	12	2	1	0.3	.889
1986		4	5	.444	2.97	49	0	0	72.2	60	22	53	0	4	5	21	0	0	0	—	2	7	1	0	0.2	.900
1987		2	2	.500	2.70	14	0	0	26.2	28	13	17	0	2	2	5	0	0	0	—	0	2	0	0	0.1	1.000
1988		5	2	.714	4.91	27	0	0	33	48	8	22	0	5	2	4	0	0	0	—	3	4	0	0	0.3	1.000
13 yrs.		43	40	.518	3.66	416	4	0	656	698	186	416	0	43	39	89	57	16	0	.281	45	90	11	4	0.4	.925
LEAGUE CHAMPIONSHIP SERIES																										
1982	ATL N	0	0	—	0.00	2	0	0	2.2	2	0	1	0	0	0	0	0	0	0	—	1	0	0	0	0.5	1.000
1986	CAL A	0	1	.000	7.20	3	0	0	5	8	2	0	0	0	1	1	0	0	0	—	1	0	0	0	0.3	1.000
2 yrs.		0	1	.000	4.70	5	0	0	7.2	10	2	1	0	0	1	1	0	0	0		2	0	0	0	0.4	1.000

Earl Moore

MOORE, EARL ALONZO (Steam Engine In Boots) — BR TR 6′ 195 lbs.
B. July 29, 1879, Pickerington, Ohio D. Nov. 28, 1961, Columbus, Ohio.

Year	Team	W	L	PCT	ERA	G	GS	CG	IP	H	BB	SO	ShO	Relief Pitching W	Relief Pitching L	Relief Pitching SV	Batting AB	Batting H	Batting HR	BA	PO	A	E	DP	TC/G	FA
1901	CLE A	16	14	.533	2.90	31	30	28	251.1	234	107	99	4	0	0	0	99	16	0	.162	9	45	7	2	2.0	.885
1902		17	17	.500	2.95	36	34	29	293	304	**101**	84	4	1	0	1	113	24	0	.212	7	79	3	4	2.5	.966
1903		19	9	.679	**1.77**	29	27	27	238.2	189	56	142	3	0	1	1	84	8	0	.095	5	56	5	0	2.3	.924
1904		12	11	.522	2.25	26	24	22	227.2	186	61	139	1	0	1	0	86	12	0	.140	6	40	8	1	2.1	.852
1905		15	15	.500	2.64	31	30	28	269	232	92	131	3	0	0	0	94	10	0	.106	14	72	7	0	3.0	.925
1906		1	1	.500	3.94	5	4	2	29.2	27	18	8	0	0	0	0	10	0	0	.000	0	6	1	1	1.4	.857
1907	2 teams CLE A (3G 1–1) NY A (12G 2–6)																									
″	total	3	7	.300	4.10	15	11	4	83.1	90	38	35	0	0	0	1	29	6	0	.207	1	27	2	0	2.0	.933
1908	PHI N	2	1	.667	0.00	3	3	3	26	20	8	16	1	0	0	0	9	2	0	.222	0	4	0	0	1.3	1.000
1909		18	12	.600	2.10	38	34	24	299.2	238	**108**	173	4	2	1	0	96	9	0	.094	10	54	6	1	1.8	.914
1910		22	15	.595	2.58	46	35	19	283	228	121	**185**	6	3	3	0	87	20	0	.230	3	57	4	2	1.4	.938
1911		15	**19**	.441	2.63	42	36	21	308.1	265	164	174	5	0	2	1	101	11	0	.109	3	63	5	2	1.7	.930
1912		9	14	.391	3.31	31	24	10	182.1	186	77	79	1	2	0	0	56	6	0	.107	4	34	3	2	1.3	.927
1913	2 teams PHI N (12G 1–3) CHI N (7G 1–1)																									
″	total	2	4	.333	4.82	19	6	0	80.1	84	52	36	0	0	0	1	24	1	0	.042	2	29	2	1	1.7	.939
1914	BUF F	10	14	.417	4.30	36	27	14	194.2	184	99	96	2	0	1	2	56	9	0	.161	2	51	7	1	1.7	.883
14 yrs.		161	153	.513	2.78	388	325	231	2767	2467	1102	1397	34	8	9	7	944	134	0	.142	66	617	60	17	1.9	.919

Euel Moore

MOORE, EUEL WALTON (Chief) BR TR 6′ 2″ 185 lbs.
B. May 27, 1908, Reagan, Okla. D. Feb. 12, 1989, Tishomingo, Okla.

Year	Team	W	L	PCT	ERA	G	GS	CG	IP	H	BB	SO	ShO	Relief Pitching W	Relief Pitching L	Relief Pitching SV	Batting AB	Batting H	HR	BA	PO	A	E	DP	TC/G	FA
1934	PHI N	5	7	.417	4.05	20	16	3	122.1	145	41	38	0	0	1	1	46	5	0	.109	0	22	2	0	1.2	.917
1935	2 teams PHI N (15G 1–6) NY N (6G 1–0)																									
″	total	2	6	.250	7.45	21	8	1	48.1	72	24	18	0	1	0	1	17	6	0	.353	0	12	2	2	0.7	.857
1936	PHI N	2	3	.400	6.96	20	5	1	54.1	76	12	19	0	0	2	1	18	4	0	.222	1	7	4	1	0.6	.667
3 yrs.		9	16	.360	5.48	61	29	5	225	293	77	75	0	1	3	3	81	15	0	.185	1	41	8	3	0.8	.840

Gene Moore

MOORE, EUGENE SR. (Blue Goose) BL TL 6′ 2″ 185 lbs.
Father of Gene Moore.
B. Nov. 9, 1885, Lancaster, Tex. D. Aug. 31, 1938, Dallas, Tex.

Year	Team	W	L	PCT	ERA	G	GS	CG	IP	H	BB	SO	ShO	Relief Pitching W	Relief Pitching L	Relief Pitching SV	Batting AB	Batting H	HR	BA	PO	A	E	DP	TC/G	FA
1909	PIT N	0	0	—	18.00	1	0	0	2	4	3	2	0	0	0	0	1	0	0	.000	0	0	0	0	0.0	.000
1910		2	1	.667	3.12	4	1	0	17.1	19	7	9	0	2	1	0	6	0	0	.000	1	5	0	1	1.5	1.000
1912	CIN N	0	1	.000	4.91	5	2	0	14.2	17	11	6	0	0	0	1	4	0	0	.000	0	3	0	0	0.6	1.000
3 yrs.		2	2	.500	4.76	10	3	0	34	40	21	17	0	2	1	1	11	0	0	.000	1	8	0	1	0.9	1.000

George Moore

MOORE, GEORGE RAYMOND BB TR 5′10″ 165 lbs.
B. Nov. 25, 1872, Cambridge, Mass. D. Nov. 17, 1948, Barnstable, Mass.

Year	Team	W	L	PCT	ERA	G	GS	CG	IP	H	BB	SO	ShO	Relief Pitching W	Relief Pitching L	Relief Pitching SV	Batting AB	Batting H	HR	BA	PO	A	E	DP	TC/G	FA
1905	PIT N	0	0	—	0.00	1	0	0	3	2	0	1	0	0	0	0	1	0	0	.000	0	0	0	0	0.0	.000

Jim Moore

MOORE, JAMES STANFORD BR TR 6′ 165 lbs.
B. Dec. 14, 1903, Prescott, Ark. D. May 19, 1973, Seattle, Wash.

Year	Team	W	L	PCT	ERA	G	GS	CG	IP	H	BB	SO	ShO	Relief Pitching W	Relief Pitching L	Relief Pitching SV	Batting AB	Batting H	HR	BA	PO	A	E	DP	TC/G	FA
1928	CLE A	0	1	.000	2.00	1	1	1	9	5	5	1	0	0	0	0	3	0	0	.000	0	1	0	0	1.0	1.000
1929		0	0	—	9.53	2	0	0	5.2	6	4	0	0	0	0	0	2	0	0	.000	0	3	0	0	1.5	1.000
1930	CHI A	2	1	.667	3.60	9	5	2	40	42	12	11	0	0	0	1	13	3	0	.231	1	8	0	0	1.0	1.000
1931		0	2	.000	4.95	33	4	0	83.2	93	27	15	0	0	0	0	16	1	0	.063	2	25	3	1	0.9	.900
1932		0	0	—	0.00	1	0	0	1	1	1	2	0	0	0	0	1	0	0	.000	0	0	0	0	0.0	.000
5 yrs.		2	4	.333	4.52	46	10	3	139.1	147	49	29	0	0	0	1	35	4	0	.114	3	37	3	1	0.9	.930

Marcus Moore

MOORE, MARCUS BRAYMONT BB TR 6′ 5″ 195 lbs.
B. Nov. 2, 1970, Oakland, Calif.

Year	Team	W	L	PCT	ERA	G	GS	CG	IP	H	BB	SO	ShO	Relief Pitching W	Relief Pitching L	Relief Pitching SV	Batting AB	Batting H	HR	BA	PO	A	E	DP	TC/G	FA
1993	CLR N	3	1	.750	6.84	27	0	0	26.1	30	20	13	0	3	1	0	1	0	0	.000	0	1	2	0	0.1	.333
1994		1	1	.500	6.15	29	0	0	33.2	33	21	33	0	1	1	0	1	0	0	.000	2	3	0	0	0.2	1.000
2 yrs.		4	2	.667	6.45	56	0	0	60	63	41	46	0	4	2	0	2	0	0	.000	2	4	2	0	0.1	.750

Mike Moore

MOORE, MICHAEL WAYNE BR TR 6′ 4″ 205 lbs.
B. Nov. 26, 1959, Carnegie, Okla.

Year	Team	W	L	PCT	ERA	G	GS	CG	IP	H	BB	SO	ShO	Relief Pitching W	Relief Pitching L	Relief Pitching SV	Batting AB	Batting H	HR	BA	PO	A	E	DP	TC/G	FA
1982	SEA A	7	14	.333	5.36	28	27	1	144.1	159	79	73	1	0	0	0	0	0	0	—	13	27	5	2	1.6	.889
1983		6	8	.429	4.71	22	21	3	128	130	60	108	2	0	0	0	0	0	0	—	7	24	1	0	1.5	.969
1984		7	17	.292	4.97	34	33	6	212	236	85	158	0	0	0	0	0	0	0	—	18	41	7	0	1.9	.894
1985		17	10	.630	3.46	35	34	14	247	230	70	155	2	0	0	0	0	0	0	—	21	43	2	1	1.9	.970
1986		11	13	.458	4.30	38	**37**	11	266	**279**	94	146	1	0	0	1	0	0	0	—	23	33	4	1	1.6	.933
1987		9	**19**	.321	4.71	33	33	12	231	**268**	84	115	0	0	0	0	1	0	0	.000	22	34	2	4	1.8	.966
1988		9	15	.375	3.78	37	32	9	228.2	196	63	182	3	1	0	1	0	0	0	—	19	29	1	3	1.3	.980
1989	OAK A	19	11	.633	2.61	35	35	6	241.2	193	83	172	3	0	0	0	0	0	0	—	25	37	2	5	1.8	.969
1990		13	15	.464	4.65	33	33	3	199.1	204	84	73	0	0	0	0	0	0	0	—	22	31	1	1	1.6	.981
1991		17	8	.680	2.96	33	33	3	210	176	105	153	1	0	0	0	0	0	0	—	28	30	2	3	1.8	.967
1992		17	12	.586	4.12	36	**36**	2	223	229	103	117	0	0	0	0	0	0	0	—	17	22	3	5	1.2	.929
1993	DET A	13	9	.591	5.22	36	**36**	4	213.2	227	89	89	3	0	0	0	0	0	0	—	27	43	2	3	2.0	.972
1994		11	10	.524	5.42	25	**25**	4	154.1	152	**89**	62	0	0	0	0	0	0	0	—	21	30	0	2	2.0	1.000
1995		5	15	.250	7.53	25	25	1	132.2	179	68	64	0	0	0	0	0	0	0	—	14	20	1	3	1.4	.971
14 yrs.		161	176	.478	4.39	450	440	79	2831.2	2858	1156	1667	16	1	0	2	1	0	0	.000	277	444	33	33	1.7	.956
LEAGUE CHAMPIONSHIP SERIES																										
1989	OAK A	1	0	1.000	0.00	1	1	0	7	3	2	3	0	0	0	0	0	0	0	—	0	1	0	0	1.0	1.000
1990		1	0	1.000	1.50	1	1	0	6	4	1	5	0	0	0	0	0	0	0	—	0	0	0	0	0.0	.000
1992		0	2	.000	7.45	2	2	0	9.2	11	5	7	0	0	0	0	0	0	0	—	1	1	0	0	1.0	1.000
3 yrs.		2	2	.500	3.57	4	4	0	22.2	18	8	15	0	0	0	0	0	0	0		1	2	0	0	0.8	1.000
WORLD SERIES																										
1989	OAK A	2	0	1.000	2.08	2	2	0	13	9	3	10	0	0	0	0	3	1	0	.333	0	3	0	0	1.5	1.000
1990		0	1	.000	6.75	1	1	0	2.2	8	0	1	0	0	0	0	0	0	0	—	0	0	0	0	0.0	.000
2 yrs.		2	1	.667	2.87	3	3	0	15.2	17	3	11	0	0	0	0	3	1	0	.333	0	3	0	0	1.0	1.000

Ray Moore

MOORE, RAYMOND LEROY (Farmer) BR TR 6′ 195 lbs.
B. June 1, 1926, Meadows, Md. D. Mar. 2, 1995, Clinton, Md.

Year	Team	W	L	PCT	ERA	G	GS	CG	IP	H	BB	SO	ShO	Relief Pitching W	Relief Pitching L	Relief Pitching SV	Batting AB	Batting H	HR	BA	PO	A	E	DP	TC/G	FA
1952	BKN N	1	2	.333	4.76	14	2	0	28.1	29	26	11	0	1	0	0	3	0	0	.000	0	5	0	1	0.4	1.000
1953		0	1	.000	3.38	1	1	1	8	6	4	4	0	0	0	0	3	0	0	.000	1	0	1	0	2.0	.500
1955	BAL A	10	10	.500	3.92	46	14	3	151.2	128	80	80	1	3	**7**	6	44	6	0	.136	3	20	3	2	0.6	.885
1956		12	7	.632	4.18	32	27	9	185	161	99	105	1	1	1	0	70	19	2	.271	6	22	4	4	1.0	.875
1957		11	13	.458	3.72	34	32	7	227.1	196	**112**	117	1	0	1	0	84	18	3	.214	3	30	0	5	1.0	1.000
1958	CHI A	9	7	.563	3.82	32	20	4	136.2	107	70	73	2	2	3	2	44	9	1	.205	6	20	0	0	0.8	1.000
1959		3	6	.333	4.12	29	8	0	89.2	86	46	49	0	2	1	0	23	2	0	.087	3	14	1	0	0.6	.944
1960	2 teams CHI A (14G 1–1) WAS A (37G 3–2)																									
″	total	4	3	.571	3.54	51	0	0	86.1	68	38	32	0	4	3	13	16	1	0	.063	5	7	0	0	0.2	1.000
1961	MIN A	4	4	.500	3.67	46	0	0	56.1	49	38	45	0	4	4	14	4	0	0	.000	6	6	0	0	0.3	1.000
1962		8	3	.727	4.73	49	0	0	64.2	55	30	58	0	8	3	9	5	0	0	.000	6	3	0	2	0.2	1.000
1963		1	3	.250	6.98	31	1	0	38.2	50	17	38	0	1	2	2	3	1	0	.333	2	6	1	0	0.3	.889
11 yrs.		63	59	.516	4.06	365	105	24	1072.2	935	560	612	5	26	25	46	299	56	6	.187	41	133	10	14	0.5	.946
WORLD SERIES																										
1959	CHI A	0	0	—	9.00	1	0	0	1	1	0	1	0	0	0	0	0	0	0	—	0	0	0	0	0.0	.000

Roy Moore

MOORE, ROY DANIEL BB TL 6′ 185 lbs.
B. Dec. 26, 1898, Austin, Tex. D. Apr. 5, 1951, Seattle, Wash.

Year	Team	W	L	PCT	ERA	G	GS	CG	IP	H	BB	SO	ShO	Relief Pitching W	Relief Pitching L	Relief Pitching SV	Batting AB	Batting H	HR	BA	PO	A	E	DP	TC/G	FA
1920	PHI A	1	13	.071	4.68	24	16	7	132.2	161	64	45	0	0	0	0	50	10	1	.200	5	40	3	4	2.0	.938
1921		10	10	.500	4.51	29	26	12	191.2	206	122	64	0	0	0	0	74	19	3	.257	9	60	4	5	2.5	.945

Roy Moore *continued*

Year	Team	W	L	PCT	ERA	G	GS	CG	IP	H	BB	SO	ShO	Relief Pitching W	Relief Pitching L	Relief Pitching SV	Batting AB	Batting H	Batting HR	BA	PO	A	E	DP	TC/G	FA
1922	**2 teams** **PHI A** (15G 0–3) **DET A** (9G 0–0)																									
″	**total**	0	3	.000	7.17	24	6	0	70.1	94	42	38	0	0	1	2	26	8	0	.308	4	14	2	1	0.8	.900
1923	**DET A**	0	0	—	3.00	3	0	0	12	15	11	7	0	0	0	1	5	0	0	.000	0	6	0	0	1.5	1.000
4 yrs.		11	26	.297	4.98	80	48	19	406.2	476	239	154	0	0	1	3	155	37	4	.239	18	120	9	10	1.8	.939

Terry Moore

MOORE, TERRY BLUFORD BR TR 5′11″ 195 lbs.
B. May 27, 1912, Vernon, Ala. D. Mar. 29, 1995, Collinsville, Ill.
Manager 1954.

Year	Team	W	L	PCT	ERA	G	GS	CG	IP	H	BB	SO	ShO	Relief Pitching W	Relief Pitching L	Relief Pitching SV	Batting AB	Batting H	Batting HR	BA	PO	A	E	DP	TC/G	FA
1939	**STL N**	0	0	—	0.00	1	0	0	1	0	0	1	0	0	0	0	*				354	11	6	3	3.2	.984

Tommy Moore

MOORE, TOMMY JOE BR TR 5′11″ 175 lbs.
B. July 7, 1948, Lynwood, Calif.

Year	Team	W	L	PCT	ERA	G	GS	CG	IP	H	BB	SO	ShO	Relief Pitching W	Relief Pitching L	Relief Pitching SV	Batting AB	Batting H	Batting HR	BA	PO	A	E	DP	TC/G	FA
1972	**NY N**	0	0	—	2.92	3	1	0	12.1	12	1	5	0	0	0	0	3	1	0	.333	1	2	0	0	1.0	1.000
1973		0	1	.000	10.80	3	1	0	3.1	6	3	1	0	0	0	0	0	0	0	—	1	0	1	0	0.7	.500
1975	**2 teams** **STL N** (10G 0–0) **TEX A** (12G 0–2)																									
″	**total**	0	2	.000	6.07	22	0	0	40	46	24	21	0	0	2	0	2	1	0	.500	5	8	2	1	0.7	.867
1977	**SEA A**	2	1	.667	4.91	14	1	0	33	36	21	13	0	2	0	0	0	0	0	—	2	2	0	0	0.3	1.000
4 yrs.		2	4	.333	5.38	42	3	0	88.2	100	49	40	0	2	2	0	5	2	0	.400	9	12	3	1	0.6	.875

Whitey Moore

MOORE, LLOYD ALBERT BR TR 6′ 1″ 195 lbs.
B. June 10, 1912, Tuscarawas, Ohio D. Dec. 10, 1987, Uhrichsville, Ohio.

Year	Team	W	L	PCT	ERA	G	GS	CG	IP	H	BB	SO	ShO	Relief Pitching W	Relief Pitching L	Relief Pitching SV	Batting AB	Batting H	Batting HR	BA	PO	A	E	DP	TC/G	FA
1936	**CIN N**	1	0	1.000	5.40	1	0	0	5	3	3	4	0	1	0	0	2	0	0	.000	0	0	0	0	0.0	.000
1937		0	3	.000	4.89	13	6	0	38.2	32	39	27	0	0	0	0	8	0	0	.000	1	7	0	0	0.6	1.000
1938		6	4	.600	3.49	19	11	3	90.1	66	42	38	1	2	0	0	26	2	0	.077	2	15	1	1	0.9	.944
1939		13	12	.520	3.45	42	24	9	187.2	177	95	81	2	4	0	3	61	6	0	.098	9	32	1	0	1.0	.976
1940		8	8	.500	3.63	25	15	5	116.2	100	56	60	1	2	2	1	39	5	0	.128	3	9	1	0	0.5	.923
1941		2	1	.667	4.38	23	4	1	61.2	62	45	17	0	1	0	0	18	3	0	.167	2	10	2	2	0.6	.857
1942	**2 teams** **CIN N** (1G 0–0) **STL N** (9G 0–1)																									
″	**total**	0	1	.000	4.05	10	0	0	13.1	10	12	1	0	0	1	0	2	0	0	.000	1	0	0	0	0.1	1.000
7 yrs.		30	29	.508	3.75	133	60	18	513.1	450	292	228	4	10	3	4	156	16	0	.103	18	73	5	3	0.7	.948
WORLD SERIES																										
1939	**CIN N**	0	0	—	0.00	1	0	0	3	0	0	2	0	0	0	0	1	0	0	.000	0	2	0	0	2.0	1.000
1940		0	0	—	3.24	3	0	0	8.1	8	6	7	0	0	0	0	2	0	0	.000	0	1	0	0	0.3	1.000
2 yrs.		0	0		2.38	4	0	0	11.1	8	6	9	0	0	0	0	3	0	0	.000	0	3	0	0	0.8	1.000

Wilcy Moore

MOORE, WILLIAM WILCY (Cy) BR TR 6′ 195 lbs.
B. May 20, 1897, Bonita, Tex. D. Mar. 29, 1963, Hollis, Okla.

Year	Team	W	L	PCT	ERA	G	GS	CG	IP	H	BB	SO	ShO	Relief Pitching W	Relief Pitching L	Relief Pitching SV	Batting AB	Batting H	Batting HR	BA	PO	A	E	DP	TC/G	FA
1927	**NY A**	19	7	.731	**2.28**	50	12	6	213	185	59	75	1	**13**	3	**13**	75	6	1	.080	18	89	1	1	2.2	.991
1928		4	4	.500	4.18	35	2	0	60.1	71	31	18	0	3	3	2	14	2	0	.143	4	21	3	1	0.8	.893
1929		6	4	.600	4.06	41	0	0	62	64	19	21	0	6	4	8	15	1	0	.067	1	25	2	0	0.7	.929
1931	**BOS A**	11	13	.458	3.88	53	15	8	185.1	195	55	37	1	7	2	**10**	56	9	0	.161	2	70	1	2	1.4	.986
1932	**2 teams** **BOS A** (37G 4–10) **NY A** (10G 2–0)																									
″	**total**	6	10	.375	4.61	47	3	0	109.1	125	48	36	0	5	**8**	8	30	1	0	.033	6	34	1	3	0.9	.976
1933	**NY A**	5	6	.455	5.52	35	0	0	62	92	20	17	0	5	6	8	15	2	0	.133	3	15	3	1	0.6	.857
6 yrs.		51	44	.537	3.69	261	32	14	692	732	232	204	2	39	26	49	205	21	1	.102	34	254	11	8	1.1	.963
WORLD SERIES																										
1927	**NY A**	1	0	1.000	0.84	2	1	1	10.2	11	2	2	0	0	0	1	5	1	0	.200	0	5	1	0	3.0	.833
1932		1	0	1.000	0.00	1	0	0	5.1	2	0	1	0	1	0	0	3	1	0	.333	0	1	0	0	1.0	1.000
2 yrs.		2	0	1.000	0.56	3	1	1	16	13	2	3	0	1	0	1	8	2	0	.250	0	6	1	0	2.3	.857

Bob Moorhead

MOORHEAD, CHARLES ROBERT BR TR 6′ 1″ 208 lbs.
B. Jan. 23, 1938, Chambersburg, Pa. D. Dec. 3, 1986, Lemoyne, Pa.

Year	Team	W	L	PCT	ERA	G	GS	CG	IP	H	BB	SO	ShO	Relief Pitching W	Relief Pitching L	Relief Pitching SV	Batting AB	Batting H	Batting HR	BA	PO	A	E	DP	TC/G	FA
1962	**NY N**	0	2	.000	4.53	38	7	0	105.1	118	42	63	0	0	1	0	22	1	0	.045	7	28	4	4	1.0	.897
1965		0	1	.000	4.40	9	0	0	14.1	16	5	5	0	0	1	0	0	0	0	—	0	5	0	0	0.6	1.000
2 yrs.		0	3	.000	4.51	47	7	0	119.2	134	47	68	0	0	2	0	22	1	0	.045	7	33	4	4	0.9	.909

Bob Moose

MOOSE, ROBERT RALPH BR TR 6′ 200 lbs.
B. Oct. 9, 1947, Export, Pa. D. Oct. 9, 1976, Martins Ferry, Ohio.

Year	Team	W	L	PCT	ERA	G	GS	CG	IP	H	BB	SO	ShO	Relief Pitching W	Relief Pitching L	Relief Pitching SV	Batting AB	Batting H	Batting HR	BA	PO	A	E	DP	TC/G	FA
1967	**PIT N**	1	0	1.000	3.68	2	2	1	14.2	14	4	7	0	0	0	0	6	2	0	.333	3	1	0	0	2.0	1.000
1968		8	12	.400	2.74	38	22	3	170.2	136	41	126	3	0	4	3	54	5	0	.093	13	36	3	4	1.4	.942
1969		14	3	.824	2.91	44	19	6	170	149	62	165	1	0	0	4	53	4	0	.075	7	31	4	0	1.0	.905
1970		11	10	.524	3.98	28	27	9	190	186	64	119	2	0	0	0	66	12	0	.182	10	22	3	2	1.3	.914
1971		11	7	.611	4.11	30	18	3	140	169	35	68	1	4	1	1	39	4	0	.103	11	24	4	2	1.3	.897
1972		13	10	.565	2.91	31	30	6	226	213	47	144	3	0	0	1	71	12	0	.169	20	33	2	1	1.8	.964
1973		12	13	.480	3.53	33	29	6	201.1	219	70	111	3	1	1	0	67	9	0	.134	13	39	2	7	1.6	.963
1974		1	5	.167	7.50	7	6	0	36	59	7	15	0	0	0	0	11	2	0	.182	1	15	0	1	2.3	1.000
1975		2	2	.500	3.71	23	5	1	68	63	25	34	0	1	0	0	18	3	0	.167	6	16	1	2	1.0	.957
1976		3	9	.250	3.70	53	2	0	87.2	100	32	38	0	3	7	10	12	3	1	.250	3	14	2	0	0.4	.895
10 yrs.		76	71	.517	3.50	289	160	35	1304.1	1308	387	827	13	9	13	19	397	56	1	.141	87	231	21	19	1.2	.938
LEAGUE CHAMPIONSHIP SERIES																										
1970	**PIT N**	0	1	.000	3.52	1	1	0	7.2	4	2	4	0	0	0	0	4	0	0	.000	1	2	0	0	3.0	1.000
1971		0	0	—	0.00	1	0	0	2	0	0	0	0	0	0	0	0	0	0	—	0	0	0	0	0.0	.000
1972		0	1	.000	54.00	2	1	0	0.2	5	0	0	0	0	0	0	0	0	0	—	0	0	0	0	0.0	.000
3 yrs.		0	2	.000	6.10	4	2	0	10.1	9	2	4	0	0	0	0	4	0	0	.000	1	2	0	0	0.8	1.000
WORLD SERIES																										
1971	**PIT N**	0	0	—	6.52	3	1	0	9.2	12	2	7	0	0	0	0	2	0	0	.000	0	3	0	0	1.0	1.000

Jake Mooty

MOOTY, J. T. BR TR 5′10½″ 170 lbs.
B. Apr. 13, 1913, Bennett, Tex. D. Apr. 20, 1970, Fort Worth, Tex.

Year	Team	W	L	PCT	ERA	G	GS	CG	IP	H	BB	SO	ShO	Relief Pitching W	Relief Pitching L	Relief Pitching SV	Batting AB	Batting H	Batting HR	BA	PO	A	E	DP	TC/G	FA
1936	**CIN N**	0	0	—	3.95	8	0	0	13.2	10	4	11	0	0	0	1	1	0	0	.000	0	1	0	0	0.1	1.000
1937		0	3	.000	8.31	14	2	0	39	54	22	11	0	0	1	1	8	0	0	.000	4	8	2	0	1.0	.857
1940	**CHI N**	6	6	.500	2.92	20	12	6	114	101	49	42	0	2	0	1	38	10	0	.263	5	16	1	0	1.1	.955

Jake Mooty *continued*

Year	Team	Lg	W	L	PCT	ERA	G	GS	CG	IP	H	BB	SO	ShO	Relief Pitching W	Relief Pitching L	Relief Pitching SV	Batting AB	Batting H	Batting HR	BA	PO	A	E	DP	TC/G	FA
1941			8	9	.471	3.35	33	14	7	153.1	143	56	45	1	3	0	4	50	10	0	.200	3	36	0	6	1.2	1.000
1942			2	5	.286	4.70	19	10	1	84.1	89	44	28	0	0	1	1	28	6	0	.214	3	22	2	0	1.4	.926
1943			0	0	—	0.00	2	0	0	1	2	1	1	0	0	0	0	0	0	0	—	0	0	0	0	0.0	.000
1944	DET	A	0	0	—	4.45	15	0	0	28.1	35	18	7	0	0	0	0	7	1	0	.143	3	4	1	0	0.5	.875
7 yrs.			16	23	.410	4.03	111	38	14	433.2	434	194	145	1	5	2	8	132	27	0	.205	18	87	6	6	1.0	.946

Carl Moran

MORAN, CARL WILLIAM (Bugs) BR TR 6′4″ 210 lbs.
B. Sept. 26, 1950, Portsmouth, Va.

Year	Team	Lg	W	L	PCT	ERA	G	GS	CG	IP	H	BB	SO	ShO	Relief Pitching W	Relief Pitching L	Relief Pitching SV	Batting AB	Batting H	Batting HR	BA	PO	A	E	DP	TC/G	FA
1974	CHI	A	1	3	.250	4.70	15	5	0	46	57	23	17	0	0	1	0	0	0	0	—	2	3	0	1	0.3	1.000

Charley Moran

MORAN, CHARLES BARTHELL (Uncle Charlie) BR TR 5′8″ 180 lbs.
B. Feb. 22, 1878, Nashville, Tenn. D. June 14, 1949, Horse Cave, Ky.

Year	Team	Lg	W	L	PCT	ERA	G	GS	CG	IP	H	BB	SO	ShO	Relief Pitching W	Relief Pitching L	Relief Pitching SV	Batting AB	Batting H	Batting HR	BA	PO	A	E	DP	TC/G	FA
1903	STL	N	0	1	.000	5.25	3	2	2	24	30	19	7	0	0	0	0	*				2	4	0	0	1.5	1.000

Harry Moran

MORAN, HARRY EDWIN BL TL 6′1″ 165 lbs.
B. Apr. 2, 1889, Slater, W. Va. D. Nov. 28, 1962, Beckley, W. Va.

Year	Team	Lg	W	L	PCT	ERA	G	GS	CG	IP	H	BB	SO	ShO	Relief Pitching W	Relief Pitching L	Relief Pitching SV	Batting AB	Batting H	Batting HR	BA	PO	A	E	DP	TC/G	FA
1912	DET	A	0	1	.000	4.91	5	2	1	14.2	19	12	3	0	0	0	0	5	1	0	.200	1	4	0	0	1.0	1.000
1914	BUF	F	11	8	.579	4.27	34	16	7	154	159	53	73	2	3	1	1	51	10	0	.196	5	37	2	4	1.3	.955
1915	NWK	F	13	10	.565	2.54	34	23	13	205.2	193	66	87	2	2	0	0	61	11	0	.180	9	72	7	1	2.6	.920
3 yrs.			24	19	.558	3.34	73	41	21	374.1	371	131	163	4	5	1	1	117	22	0	.188	15	113	9	5	1.9	.934

Hiker Moran

MORAN, ALBERT THOMAS BR TR 6′4½″ 185 lbs.
B. Jan. 1, 1912, Rochester, N. Y.

Year	Team	Lg	W	L	PCT	ERA	G	GS	CG	IP	H	BB	SO	ShO	Relief Pitching W	Relief Pitching L	Relief Pitching SV	Batting AB	Batting H	Batting HR	BA	PO	A	E	DP	TC/G	FA
1938	BOS	N	0	0	—	0.00	1	0	0	3	1	1	0	0	0	0	0	0	0	0	—	0	0	0	0	0.0	.000
1939			1	1	.500	4.50	6	2	1	20	21	11	4	0	0	0	0	5	1	0	.200	1	3	1	0	0.8	.800
2 yrs.			1	1	.500	3.91	7	2	1	23	22	12	4	0	0	0	0	5	1	0	.200	1	3	1	0	0.7	.800

Sam Moran

MORAN, SAMUEL TL 160 lbs.
B. Sept. 16, 1870, Rochester, N. Y. D. Aug. 29, 1897, Rochester, N. Y.

Year	Team	Lg	W	L	PCT	ERA	G	GS	CG	IP	H	BB	SO	ShO	Relief Pitching W	Relief Pitching L	Relief Pitching SV	Batting AB	Batting H	Batting HR	BA	PO	A	E	DP	TC/G	FA
1895	PIT	N	2	4	.333	7.47	10	6	6	62.2	78	51	19	0	0	0	0	26	4	1	.154	1	15	1	1	1.7	.941

Forrest More

MORE, FORREST T. BR TR 6′ 180 lbs.
B. Sept. 30, 1883, Hayden, Ind. D. Aug. 17, 1968, Columbus, Ind.

Year	Team	Lg	W	L	PCT	ERA	G	GS	CG	IP	H	BB	SO	ShO	Relief Pitching W	Relief Pitching L	Relief Pitching SV	Batting AB	Batting H	Batting HR	BA	PO	A	E	DP	TC/G	FA
1909	2 teams	STL N (15G 1–5)	BOS N (10G 0–4)																								
″	total		1	9	.100	4.74	25	6	4	98.2	95	40	27	0	0	**5**	0	28	3	0	.107	2	34	2	2	1.5	.947

Dave Morehead

MOREHEAD, DAVID MICHAEL (Moe) BR TR 6′1″ 185 lbs.
B. Sept. 5, 1942, San Diego, Calif.

Year	Team	Lg	W	L	PCT	ERA	G	GS	CG	IP	H	BB	SO	ShO	Relief Pitching W	Relief Pitching L	Relief Pitching SV	Batting AB	Batting H	Batting HR	BA	PO	A	E	DP	TC/G	FA
1963	BOS	A	10	13	.435	3.81	29	29	6	174.2	137	99	136	1	0	0	0	57	6	0	.105	17	26	2	4	1.6	.956
1964			8	15	.348	4.97	32	30	3	166.2	156	112	139	1	0	0	0	54	5	0	.093	9	18	1	1	0.9	.964
1965			10	**18**	.357	4.06	34	33	5	192.2	157	113	163	2	0	0	0	61	8	0	.131	16	17	1	1	1.0	.971
1966			1	2	.333	5.46	12	5	0	28	31	7	20	0	0	0	0	6	3	0	.500	2	2	0	0	0.3	1.000
1967			5	4	.556	4.34	10	9	1	47.2	48	22	40	1	1	0	0	12	1	0	.083	2	4	0	1	0.6	1.000
1968			1	4	.200	2.45	11	9	3	55	52	20	28	1	0	0	0	16	2	0	.125	2	3	1	1	0.5	.833
1969	KC	A	2	3	.400	5.73	21	2	0	33	28	28	32	0	2	1	0	2	0	0	.000	1	3	0	0	0.2	1.000
1970			3	5	.375	3.61	28	17	1	122	121	62	69	0	0	1	1	36	6	0	.167	7	10	2	0	0.7	.895
8 yrs.			40	64	.385	4.15	177	134	19	819.2	730	463	627	6	3	2	1	244	31	0	.127	56	83	7	8	0.8	.952
WORLD SERIES																											
1967	BOS	A	0	0	—	0.00	2	0	0	3.1	0	4	3	0	0	0	0	0	0	0	—	0	0	0	0	0.0	.000

Seth Morehead

MOREHEAD, SETH MARVIN (Moe) BL TL 6′½″ 195 lbs.
B. Aug. 15, 1934, Houston, Tex.

Year	Team	Lg	W	L	PCT	ERA	G	GS	CG	IP	H	BB	SO	ShO	Relief Pitching W	Relief Pitching L	Relief Pitching SV	Batting AB	Batting H	Batting HR	BA	PO	A	E	DP	TC/G	FA
1957	PHI	N	1	1	.500	3.68	34	1	1	58.2	57	20	36	0	0	1	1	6	0	0	.000	3	7	1	0	0.3	.909
1958			1	6	.143	5.85	27	11	0	92.1	121	26	54	0	0	0	0	22	4	0	.182	3	10	5	1	0.7	.722
1959	2 teams	PHI N (3G 0–2)	CHI N (11G 0–1)																								
″	total		0	3	.000	6.59	14	5	0	28.2	40	11	17	0	0	0	0	5	1	0	.200	1	1	0	0	0.1	1.000
1960	CHI	N	2	9	.182	3.94	45	7	2	123.1	123	46	64	0	2	4	4	29	4	0	.138	8	19	0	1	0.6	1.000
1961	MIL	N	1	0	1.000	6.46	12	0	0	15.1	16	7	13	0	1	0	0	0	0	0	—	0	2	0	0	0.2	1.000
5 yrs.			5	19	.208	4.81	132	24	3	318.1	357	110	184	0	3	5	5	62	9	0	.145	15	39	6	2	0.5	.900

Ramon Morel

MOREL, RAMON RAFAEL BR TR 6′2″ 175 lbs.
B. Aug. 15, 1974, Villa Gonzalez, Dominican Republic.

Year	Team	Lg	W	L	PCT	ERA	G	GS	CG	IP	H	BB	SO	ShO	Relief Pitching W	Relief Pitching L	Relief Pitching SV	Batting AB	Batting H	Batting HR	BA	PO	A	E	DP	TC/G	FA
1995	PIT	N	0	1	.000	2.84	5	0	0	6.1	6	2	3	0	0	1	0	0	0	0	—	1	2	0	0	0.6	1.000

Lew Moren

MOREN, LEWIS HOWARD (Hicks) BR TR 5′11″ 150 lbs.
B. Aug. 4, 1883, Pittsburgh, Pa. D. Nov. 2, 1966, Pittsburgh, Pa.

Year	Team	Lg	W	L	PCT	ERA	G	GS	CG	IP	H	BB	SO	ShO	Relief Pitching W	Relief Pitching L	Relief Pitching SV	Batting AB	Batting H	Batting HR	BA	PO	A	E	DP	TC/G	FA
1903	PIT	N	0	1	.000	9.00	1	1	1	6	9	2	2	0	0	0	0	2	0	0	.000	1	1	0	0	2.0	1.000
1904			0	0	—	9.00	1	0	0	4	7	4	0	0	0	0	0	2	0	0	.000	0	3	0	0	3.0	1.000
1907	PHI	N	11	18	.379	2.54	37	31	21	255	202	101	98	3	0	1	1	74	6	0	.081	3	72	2	3	2.1	.974
1908			8	9	.471	2.92	28	16	9	154	146	49	72	4	1	1	0	49	12	0	.245	6	43	2	1	1.8	.961
1909			16	15	.516	2.66	39	31	19	253.2	223	91	108	2	3	3	1	90	10	0	.111	8	46	5	3	1.5	.915
1910			13	14	.481	3.55	34	26	12	205.1	207	82	74	1	3	2	1	74	11	0	.149	11	56	5	2	2.1	.931
6 yrs.			48	57	.457	2.95	140	105	62	878	794	329	354	10	7	7	3	291	39	0	.134	29	221	14	9	1.9	.947

Angel Moreno

MORENO, ANGEL BL TL 5′9″ 165 lbs.
Born Angel Moreno (Veneroso).
B. June 6, 1955, La Mendosa, Mexico.

Year	Team	Lg	W	L	PCT	ERA	G	GS	CG	IP	H	BB	SO	ShO	Relief Pitching W	Relief Pitching L	Relief Pitching SV	Batting AB	Batting H	Batting HR	BA	PO	A	E	DP	TC/G	FA
1981	CAL	A	1	3	.250	2.90	8	4	1	31	27	14	12	0	0	0	0	0	0	0	—	0	5	1	0	0.8	.833
1982			3	7	.300	4.74	13	8	2	49.1	55	23	22	0	1	1	1	0	0	0	—	2	8	2	0	0.9	.833
2 yrs.			4	10	.286	4.03	21	12	3	80.1	82	37	34	0	1	1	1	0	0	0		2	13	3	0	0.9	.833

Julio Moreno

MORENO, JULIO BR TR 5′ 8″ 165 lbs.
Born Julio Moreno (Gonzalez).
B. Jan. 28, 1921, Guines, Cuba D. Jan. 2, 1987, Miami, Fla.

Year	Team	W	L	PCT	ERA	G	GS	CG	IP	H	BB	SO	ShO	Relief W	Relief L	Relief SV	Batting AB	Batting H	Batting HR	BA	PO	A	E	DP	TC/G	FA
1950	WAS A	1	1	.500	4.64	4	3	1	21.1	22	12	7	0	0	0	0	8	1	0	.125	3	3	0	0	1.5	1.000
1951		5	11	.313	4.88	31	18	5	132.2	132	80	37	0	1	2	2	40	7	0	.175	10	24	0	1	1.1	1.000
1952		9	9	.500	3.97	26	22	7	147.1	154	52	62	0	0	1	0	49	6	0	.122	8	21	1	0	1.2	.967
1953		3	1	.750	2.80	12	2	1	35.1	41	13	13	0	2	1	0	9	0	0	.000	1	5	0	0	0.5	1.000
4 yrs.		18	22	.450	4.25	73	45	14	336.2	349	157	119	0	3	4	2	106	14	0	.132	22	53	1	1	1.0	.987

Roger Moret

MORET, ROGELIO BB TL 6′ 4″ 170 lbs.
Born Rogelio Moret Torres.
B. Sept. 16, 1949, Guayama, Puerto Rico.

Year	Team	W	L	PCT	ERA	G	GS	CG	IP	H	BB	SO	ShO	Relief W	Relief L	Relief SV	Batting AB	Batting H	Batting HR	BA	PO	A	E	DP	TC/G	FA
1970	BOS A	1	0	1.000	3.38	3	1	0	8	7	4	2	0	1	0	0	3	0	0	.000	0	1	0	0	0.3	1.000
1971		4	3	.571	2.92	13	7	4	71	50	40	47	1	0	1	0	23	2	0	.087	1	11	0	1	0.9	1.000
1972		0	0	—	3.60	3	0	0	5	5	6	4	0	0	0	0	1	0	0	.000	0	0	0	0	0.0	.000
1973		13	2	.867	3.17	30	15	5	156	138	67	90	2	1	0	3	0	0	0	—	5	22	1	3	0.9	.964
1974		9	10	.474	3.75	31	21	10	173	158	79	111	1	1	1	2	0	0	0	—	4	16	1	1	0.7	.952
1975		14	3	.824	3.60	36	16	4	145	132	76	80	1	4	0	1	0	0	0	—	2	18	0	1	0.6	1.000
1976	ATL N	3	5	.375	5.03	27	12	1	77	84	27	30	0	0	0	1	23	3	0	.130	0	13	0	1	0.5	1.000
1977	TEX A	3	3	.500	3.75	18	8	0	72	59	38	39	0	1	0	4	0	0	0	—	1	7	0	0	0.4	1.000
1978		0	1	.000	4.91	7	2	0	14.2	23	2	5	0	0	0	1	0	0	0	—	1	1	0	0	0.3	1.000
9 yrs.		47	27	.635	3.67	168	82	24	721.2	656	339	408	5	8	2	12	50	5	0	.100	14	89	2	7	0.6	.981
LEAGUE CHAMPIONSHIP SERIES																										
1975	BOS A	1	0	1.000	0.00	1	0	0	1	1	1	0	0	1	0	0	0	0	0	—	0	0	0	0	0.0	.000
WORLD SERIES																										
1975	BOS A	0	0	—	0.00	3	0	0	1.2	2	3	1	0	0	0	0	0	0	0	—	0	1	0	0	0.3	1.000

Dave Morey

MOREY, DAVID BEALE BL TR 6′ 185 lbs.
B. Feb. 25, 1889, Malden, Mass. D. Jan. 4, 1986, Oak Bluffs, Mass.

Year	Team	W	L	PCT	ERA	G	GS	CG	IP	H	BB	SO	ShO	Relief W	Relief L	Relief SV	Batting AB	Batting H	Batting HR	BA	PO	A	E	DP	TC/G	FA
1913	PHI A	0	0	—	4.50	2	0	0	4	2	2	1	0	0	0	0	1	0	0	.000	0	2	0	0	1.0	1.000

Bill Morgan

MORGAN, HENRY WILLIAM
B. Brooklyn, N. Y. Deceased.

Year	Team	W	L	PCT	ERA	G	GS	CG	IP	H	BB	SO	ShO	Relief W	Relief L	Relief SV	Batting AB	Batting H	Batting HR	BA	PO	A	E	DP	TC/G	FA
1884	RIC AA	2	3	.400	*4.15*	5	5	5	39	37	2	35	0	0	0	0	*				14	9	7	0	1.8	.767

Cy Morgan

MORGAN, CYRIL ARLON BR TR 6′ 170 lbs.
B. Dec. 11, 1896, Lakeville, Mass. D. Sept. 11, 1946, Lakeville, Mass.

Year	Team	W	L	PCT	ERA	G	GS	CG	IP	H	BB	SO	ShO	Relief W	Relief L	Relief SV	Batting AB	Batting H	Batting HR	BA	PO	A	E	DP	TC/G	FA
1921	BOS N	1	1	.500	6.53	17	0	0	30.1	37	17	8	0	1	1	1	5	0	0	.000	0	13	0	0	0.8	1.000
1922		0	0	—	27.00	2	0	0	1.1	8	2	0	0	0	0	0	0	0	0	—	0	0	0	0	0.0	.000
2 yrs.		1	1	.500	7.39	19	0	0	31.2	45	19	8	0	1	1	1	5	0	0	.000	0	13	0	0	0.7	1.000

Cy Morgan

MORGAN, HARRY RICHARD BR TR 6′ 175 lbs.
B. Nov. 10, 1878, Pomeroy, Ohio D. June 28, 1962, Wheeling, W. Va.

Year	Team	W	L	PCT	ERA	G	GS	CG	IP	H	BB	SO	ShO	Relief W	Relief L	Relief SV	Batting AB	Batting H	Batting HR	BA	PO	A	E	DP	TC/G	FA
1903	STL A	0	2	.000	4.15	2	1	1	13	12	6	6	0	0	1	0	4	1	0	.250	1	2	0	0	1.5	1.000
1904		0	2	.000	3.71	8	3	2	51	51	10	24	0	0	0	0	18	1	0	.056	3	22	1	0	3.3	.962
1905		2	5	.286	3.61	13	8	5	77.1	82	37	44	1	0	0	0	31	8	0	.258	5	34	8	1	3.6	.830
1907	2 teams STL A (10G 2–5) BOS A (16G 6–6)																									
″	total	8	11	.421	3.30	26	19	13	169.1	154	51	64	2	1	0	0	55	4	0	.073	6	59	4	3	2.7	.942
1908	BOS A	14	13	.519	2.46	30	26	17	205	166	90	99	2	1	1	1	63	8	0	.127	11	65	2	1	2.6	.974
1909	2 teams BOS A (12G 2–6) PHI A (28G 16–11)																									
″	total	18	17	.514	1.81	40	36	26	293.1	204	102	111	5	1	1	1	94	9	0	.096	6	100	4	1	2.8	.964
1910	PHI A	18	12	.600	1.55	36	34	23	290.2	214	**117**	134	3	0	1	0	99	14	0	.141	5	104	4	1	3.1	.965
1911		15	7	.682	2.70	38	30	15	249.2	217	113	136	2	1	1	1	94	15	0	.160	14	81	5	2	2.6	.950
1912		3	8	.273	3.75	16	14	5	93.2	75	51	47	0	1	0	0	30	1	0	.033	2	41	5	0	3.0	.896
1913	CIN N	0	1	.000	15.43	1	1	0	2.1	5	1	2	0	0	0	0	1	0	0	.000	0	2	0	0	2.0	1.000
10 yrs.		78	78	.500	2.51	210	172	107	1445.1	1180	578	667	15	5	5	3	489	61	0	.125	53	510	33	9	2.9	.945

Mike Morgan

MORGAN, MICHAEL THOMAS BR TR 6′ 3″ 195 lbs.
B. Oct. 8, 1959, Tulare, Calif.

Year	Team	W	L	PCT	ERA	G	GS	CG	IP	H	BB	SO	ShO	Relief W	Relief L	Relief SV	Batting AB	Batting H	Batting HR	BA	PO	A	E	DP	TC/G	FA
1978	OAK A	0	3	.000	7.30	3	3	1	12.1	19	8	0	0	0	0	0	0	0	0	—	1	4	0	1	1.7	1.000
1979		2	10	.167	5.96	13	13	2	77	102	50	17	0	0	0	0	0	0	0	—	9	15	1	0	1.9	.960
1982	NY A	7	11	.389	4.37	30	23	2	150.1	167	67	71	0	2	1	0	0	0	0	—	4	26	0	3	1.0	1.000
1983	TOR A	0	3	.000	5.16	16	4	0	45.1	48	21	22	0	0	1	0	0	0	0	—	2	10	1	0	0.8	.923
1985	SEA A	1	1	.500	12.00	2	2	0	6	11	5	2	0	0	0	0	0	0	0	—	0	1	0	0	0.5	1.000
1986		11	**17**	.393	4.53	37	33	9	216.1	243	86	116	1	0	0	1	0	0	0	—	14	27	2	5	1.2	.953
1987		12	17	.414	4.65	34	31	8	207	245	53	85	2	0	0	0	0	0	0	—	18	35	2	5	1.6	.964
1988	BAL A	1	6	.143	5.43	22	10	2	71.1	70	23	29	0	1	0	1	0	0	0	—	9	9	0	1	0.8	1.000
1989	LA N	8	11	.421	2.53	40	19	0	152.2	130	33	72	0	2	0	0	36	3	0	.083	20	41	2	2	1.6	.968
1990		11	15	.423	3.75	33	33	6	211	216	60	106	**4**	0	0	0	71	8	0	.113	25	39	1	3	2.0	.985
1991		14	10	.583	2.78	34	33	5	236.1	197	61	140	1	0	0	1	76	7	0	.092	25	41	2	3	2.0	.971
1992	CHI N	16	8	.667	2.55	34	34	6	240	203	79	123	1	0	0	0	74	8	0	.108	19	45	3	3	2.0	.955
1993		10	15	.400	4.03	32	32	1	207.2	206	74	111	1	0	0	0	66	4	0	.061	11	33	1	3	1.4	.978
1994		2	10	.167	6.69	15	15	1	80.2	111	35	57	0	0	0	0	24	3	0	.125	3	8	3	0	0.9	.786
1995	2 teams CHI N (4G 2–1) STL N (17G 5–6)																									
″	total	7	7	.500	3.56	21	21	1	131.1	133	34	61	0	0	0	0	38	2	0	.053	13	27	1	2	2.0	.976
15 yrs.		102	144	.415	3.98	366	306	44	2045.1	2101	689	1012	10	5	2	3	385	35	0	.091	173	361	19	31	1.5	.966

Tom Morgan

MORGAN, TOM STEPHEN (Plowboy) BR TR 6′ 1″ 180 lbs.
B. May 20, 1930, El Monte, Calif. D. Jan. 13, 1987, Anaheim, Calif.

Year	Team	W	L	PCT	ERA	G	GS	CG	IP	H	BB	SO	ShO	Relief W	Relief L	Relief SV	Batting AB	Batting H	Batting HR	BA	PO	A	E	DP	TC/G	FA
1951	NY A	9	3	.750	3.68	27	16	4	124.2	119	36	57	2	1	0	2	44	12	1	.273	12	27	4	2	1.6	.907
1952		5	4	.556	3.07	16	12	2	93.2	86	33	35	1	0	0	2	33	6	1	.182	6	29	0	3	2.2	1.000
1954		11	5	.688	3.34	32	17	7	143	149	40	34	4	3	1	1	49	7	1	.143	11	38	0	2	1.5	1.000
1955		7	3	.700	3.25	40	1	0	72	72	24	17	0	7	3	10	18	4	0	.222	6	24	1	2	0.8	.968
1956		6	7	.462	4.16	41	0	0	71.1	74	27	20	0	6	**7**	11	13	2	0	.154	2	18	2	5	0.5	.909

Tom Morgan *continued*

Year	Team	Lg	W	L	PCT	ERA	G	GS	CG	IP	H	BB	SO	ShO	Relief W	Relief L	Relief SV	AB	H	HR	BA	PO	A	E	DP	TC/G	FA
1957	KC	A	9	7	.563	4.64	46	13	5	143.2	160	61	32	0	6	2	7	33	3	0	.091	20	37	1	6	1.3	.983
1958	DET	A	2	5	.286	3.16	39	1	0	62.2	70	4	32	0	2	5	1	10	2	0	.200	2	9	1	1	0.3	.917
1959			1	4	.200	3.98	46	1	0	92.2	94	18	39	0	1	3	9	23	9	2	.391	4	15	0	2	0.4	1.000
1960	2 teams	DET A (22G 3–2)	WAS A (14G 1–3)																								
"	total		4	5	.444	4.25	36	0	0	53	69	15	23	0	4	5	1	5	0	0	.000	4	10	0	1	0.4	1.000
1961	LA	A	8	2	.800	2.36	59	0	0	91.2	74	17	39	0	8	2	10	12	1	0	.083	8	18	2	2	0.5	.929
1962			5	2	.714	2.91	48	0	0	58.2	53	19	29	0	5	2	9	6	0	0	.000	1	6	0	1	0.1	1.000
1963			0	0	—	5.51	13	0	0	16.1	20	6	7	0	0	0	1	1	0	0	.000	0	2	0	0	0.2	1.000
12 yrs.			67	47	.588	3.61	443	61	18	1023.1	1040	300	364	7	43	30	64	247	46	5	.186	76	233	11	27	0.7	.966
WORLD SERIES																											
1951	NY	A	0	0	—	0.00	1	0	0	2	2	1	3	0	0	0	0	0	0	0	—	0	1	0	0	1.0	1.000
1955			0	0	—	4.91	2	0	0	3.2	3	3	1	0	0	0	0	0	0	0	—	0	0	0	0	0.0	.000
1956			0	1	.000	9.00	2	0	0	4	6	4	3	0	0	1	0	1	1	0	1.000	0	0	0	0	0.0	.000
3 yrs.			0	1	.000	5.59	5	0	0	9.2	11	8	7	0	0	1	0	1	1	0	1.000	0	1	0	0	0.2	1.000

Gene Moriarity

MORIARITY, EUGENE JOHN BL TL 5′ 8″ 190 lbs.
B. Jan. 5, 1865, Holyoke, Mass. Deceased.

Year	Team	Lg	W	L	PCT	ERA	G	GS	CG	IP	H	BB	SO	ShO	Relief W	Relief L	Relief SV	AB	H	HR	BA	PO	A	E	DP	TC/G	FA
1884	IND	AA	0	2	.000	*5.27*	2	2	2	13.2	16	7	4	0	0	0	0	53	9	0	.170	16	7	6	0	2.1	.793
1885	DET	N	0	0	—	*9.00*	1	0	0	2	3	1	1	0	0	0	0	39	1	0	.026	23	12	9	0	3.7	.795
2 yrs.			0	2	.000	5.74	3	2	2	15.2	19	8	5	0	0	0	0	*				135	28	38	0	2.8	.811

John Morlan

MORLAN, JOHN GLEN BR TR 6′ 178 lbs.
B. Nov. 22, 1947, Columbus, Ohio.

Year	Team	Lg	W	L	PCT	ERA	G	GS	CG	IP	H	BB	SO	ShO	Relief W	Relief L	Relief SV	AB	H	HR	BA	PO	A	E	DP	TC/G	FA
1973	PIT	N	2	2	.500	3.95	10	7	1	41	42	23	23	0	0	0	0	11	2	0	.182	3	3	0	0	0.6	1.000
1974			0	3	.000	4.29	39	0	0	65	54	48	38	0	0	3	0	7	0	0	.000	4	6	1	0	0.3	.909
2 yrs.			2	5	.286	4.16	49	7	1	106	96	71	61	0	0	3	0	18	2	0	.111	7	9	1	0	0.3	.941

Dan Morogiello

MOROGIELLO, DANIEL JOSEPH BL TL 6′ 1″ 200 lbs.
B. Mar. 26, 1955, Brooklyn, N. Y.

Year	Team	Lg	W	L	PCT	ERA	G	GS	CG	IP	H	BB	SO	ShO	Relief W	Relief L	Relief SV	AB	H	HR	BA	PO	A	E	DP	TC/G	FA
1983	BAL	A	0	1	.000	2.39	22	0	0	37.2	39	10	15	0	0	1	1	0	0	0	—	0	3	1	0	0.2	.750

Jim Moroney

MORONEY, JAMES FRANCIS BL TL 6′ 1″ 175 lbs.
B. Dec. 4, 1885, Boston, Mass. D. Feb. 26, 1929, Philadelphia, Pa.

Year	Team	Lg	W	L	PCT	ERA	G	GS	CG	IP	H	BB	SO	ShO	Relief W	Relief L	Relief SV	AB	H	HR	BA	PO	A	E	DP	TC/G	FA
1906	BOS	N	0	3	.000	5.33	3	3	3	27	28	12	11	0	0	0	0	10	1	0	.100	0	9	1	0	3.3	.900
1910	PHI	N	1	2	.333	2.14	12	2	1	42	43	11	13	0	1	0	1	10	0	0	.000	1	11	2	0	1.2	.857
1912	CHI	N	1	1	.500	4.56	10	3	1	23.2	25	17	5	0	0	0	1	6	3	0	.500	0	7	2	0	0.9	.778
3 yrs.			2	6	.250	3.69	25	8	5	92.2	96	40	29	0	1	0	2	26	4	0	.154	1	27	5	0	1.3	.848

Bill Morrell

MORRELL, WILLARD BLACKMER BL TR 6′ 172 lbs.
B. Apr. 9, 1893, Hyde Park, Mass. D. Aug. 5, 1975, Birmingham, Ala. BR 1926

Year	Team	Lg	W	L	PCT	ERA	G	GS	CG	IP	H	BB	SO	ShO	Relief W	Relief L	Relief SV	AB	H	HR	BA	PO	A	E	DP	TC/G	FA
1926	WAS	A	3	3	.500	5.30	26	2	1	69.2	83	29	16	0	2	2	1	17	4	0	.235	3	15	1	0	0.7	.947
1930	NY	N	0	0	—	1.13	2	0	0	8	6	1	3	0	0	0	0	2	0	0	.000	2	1	0	0	1.5	1.000
1931			5	3	.625	4.36	20	7	2	66	83	27	16	0	1	1	1	18	2	0	.111	6	10	1	2	0.9	.941
3 yrs.			8	6	.571	4.64	48	9	3	143.2	172	57	35	0	3	3	2	37	6	0	.162	11	26	2	2	0.8	.949

John Morrill

MORRILL, JOHN FRANCIS (Honest John) BR TR 5′10½″ 155 lbs.
B. Feb. 19, 1855, Boston, Mass. D. Apr. 2, 1932, Boston, Mass.
Manager 1882–89.

Year	Team	Lg	W	L	PCT	ERA	G	GS	CG	IP	H	BB	SO	ShO	Relief W	Relief L	Relief SV	AB	H	HR	BA	PO	A	E	DP	TC/G	FA
1880	BOS	N	0	0	—	0.84	3	0	0	10.2	9	1	0	0	0	0	0	342	81	2	.237	238	160	78	21	7.0	.836
1881			0	1	.000	6.35	3	0	0	5.2	9	1	0	0	0	**1**	1	311	90	1	.289	764	61	26	33	10.3	.969
1882			0	0	—	0.00	1	0	0	2	3	0	2	0	0	0	0	349	101	2	.289	752	34	34	23	9.8	.959
1883			1	0	1.000	*2.77*	2	1	1	13	15	4	5	0	0	0	0	404	129	6	.319	819	44	31	34	8.9	.965
1884			0	1	.000	*7.43*	7	1	1	23	34	6	13	0	0	0	**2**	438	114	3	.260	1006	86	41	37	9.6	.964
1886			0	0	—	0.00	1	0	0	4	5	0	2	0	0	0	0	430	106	7	.247	1010	87	41	61	10.3	.964
1889	WAS	N	0	0	—	0.00	1	0	0	0.1	0	0	0	0	0	0	0	146	27	2	.185	535	245	61	44	7.1	.927
7 yrs.			1	2	.333	4.30	18	2	2	58.2	75	12	22	0	0	1	3	*				9838	1167	520	517	9.0	.955

Bugs Morris

Playing record listed under Bugs Bennett.

Danny Morris

MORRIS, DANNY WALKER BR TR 6′ 1″ 200 lbs.
B. June 11, 1946, Greenville, Ky.

Year	Team	Lg	W	L	PCT	ERA	G	GS	CG	IP	H	BB	SO	ShO	Relief W	Relief L	Relief SV	AB	H	HR	BA	PO	A	E	DP	TC/G	FA
1968	MIN	A	0	1	.000	1.69	3	2	0	10.2	11	4	6	0	0	0	0	3	0	0	.000	0	2	0	1	0.7	1.000
1969			0	1	.000	5.06	3	1	0	5.1	5	4	1	0	0	0	0	0	0	0	—	0	1	0	0	0.3	1.000
2 yrs.			0	2	.000	2.81	6	3	0	16	16	8	7	0	0	0	0	3	0	0	.000	0	3	0	1	0.5	1.000

E. Morris

MORRIS, E.
B. Trenton, N. J. Deceased.

Year	Team	Lg	W	L	PCT	ERA	G	GS	CG	IP	H	BB	SO	ShO	Relief W	Relief L	Relief SV	AB	H	HR	BA	PO	A	E	DP	TC/G	FA
1884	BAL	U	0	0	—	*9.00*	1	0	0	1	2	2	0	0	0	0	0	*				0	0	2	0	1.0	.000

Ed Morris

MORRIS, EDWARD (Cannonball) BR TL 5′ 7″ 165 lbs.
B. Sept. 29, 1862, Brooklyn, N. Y. D. Apr. 12, 1937, Pittsburgh, Pa.

Year	Team	Lg	W	L	PCT	ERA	G	GS	CG	IP	H	BB	SO	ShO	Relief W	Relief L	Relief SV	AB	H	HR	BA	PO	A	E	DP	TC/G	FA
1884	COL	AA	34	13	**.723**	*2.18*	52	52	47	429.2	335	51	302	3	0	0	0	199	37	0	.186	29	88	24	3	2.3	.830
1885	PIT	AA	39	24	.619	*2.35*	**63**	**63**	**63**	**581**	459	101	**298**	**7**	0	0	0	237	44	0	.186	26	93	20	4	2.2	.856
1886			**41**	20	.672	*2.45*	64	63	63	555.1	455	118	326	**12**	0	0	**1**	227	38	1	.167	21	90	10	2	1.9	.917
1887	PIT	N	14	22	.389	4.31	38	38	37	317.2	375	71	91	1	0	0	0	126	25	0	.198	5	52	5	1	1.6	.919
1888			29	24	.547	2.31	**55**	**55**	**54**	480	**470**	74	135	5	0	0	0	189	19	0	.101	20	106	8	3	2.4	.940
1889			6	13	.316	4.13	21	21	18	170	196	48	40	0	0	0	0	72	7	0	.097	5	27	1	0	1.6	.970
1890	PIT	P	8	7	.533	4.86	18	15	15	144.1	178	35	25	1	0	0	0	63	9	0	.143	3	28	4	1	1.9	.886
7 yrs.			171	123	.582	2.82	311	307	297	2678	2468	498	1217	29	0	0	1	1113	179	1	.161	109	484	72	14	2.1	.892

Ed Morris

MORRIS, WALTER EDWARD BR TR 6′ 2″ 185 lbs.
B. Dec. 7, 1899, Foshee, Ala. D. Mar. 3, 1932, Century, Fla.

Year	Team	W	L	PCT	ERA	G	GS	CG	IP	H	BB	SO	ShO	Relief W	Relief L	Relief SV	Batting AB	Batting H	Batting HR	BA	PO	A	E	DP	TC/G	FA
1922	CHI N	0	0	—	8.25	5	0	0	12	22	6	5	0	0	0	0	4	1	0	.250	0	3	2	0	1.0	.600
1928	BOS A	19	15	.559	3.53	47	29	20	257.2	255	80	104	0	3	2	5	91	14	0	.154	4	48	0	4	1.1	1.000
1929		14	14	.500	4.45	33	26	17	208.1	227	95	73	2	2	1	1	69	16	1	.232	6	38	3	1	1.4	.936
1930		4	9	.308	4.13	18	9	3	65.1	67	38	28	0	2	2	0	19	6	0	.316	4	11	2	0	0.9	.882
1931		5	7	.417	4.75	37	14	3	130.2	131	74	46	0	1	1	0	38	6	0	.158	11	27	5	1	1.2	.884
5 yrs.		42	45	.483	4.19	140	78	43	674	702	293	256	2	8	6	6	221	43	1	.195	25	127	12	6	1.2	.927

Jack Morris

MORRIS, JOHN SCOTT BR TR 6′ 3″ 195 lbs.
B. May 16, 1955, St. Paul, Minn.

Year	Team	W	L	PCT	ERA	G	GS	CG	IP	H	BB	SO	ShO	Relief W	Relief L	Relief SV	Batting AB	Batting H	Batting HR	BA	PO	A	E	DP	TC/G	FA
1977	DET A	1	1	.500	3.72	7	6	1	46	38	23	28	0	0	0	0	0	0	0	—	2	8	0	0	1.4	1.000
1978		3	5	.375	4.33	28	7	0	106	107	49	48	0	3	4	0	0	0	0	—	5	15	2	3	0.8	.909
1979		17	7	.708	3.27	27	27	9	198	179	59	113	1	0	0	0	0	0	0	—	14	23	2	3	1.4	.949
1980		16	15	.516	4.18	36	36	11	250	252	87	112	2	0	0	0	0	0	0	—	31	43	2	2	2.1	.974
1981		**14**	7	.667	3.05	25	25	15	198	153	**78**	97	1	0	0	0	0	0	0	—	16	28	0	2	1.8	1.000
1982		17	16	.515	4.06	37	37	17	266.1	247	96	135	3	0	0	0	0	0	0	—	26	31	1	2	1.6	.983
1983		20	13	.606	3.34	37	37	20	**293.2**	257	83	**232**	1	0	0	0	0	0	0	—	29	26	2	2	1.5	.965
1984		19	11	.633	3.60	35	35	9	240.1	221	87	148	1	0	0	0	0	0	0	—	29	32	3	4	1.8	.953
1985		16	11	.593	3.33	35	35	13	257	212	110	191	4	0	0	0	0	0	0	—	25	25	4	2	1.5	.926
1986		21	8	.724	3.27	35	35	15	267	229	82	223	**6**	0	0	0	0	0	0	—	27	27	2	4	1.6	.964
1987		18	11	.621	3.38	34	34	13	266	227	93	208	0	0	0	0	1	0	0	.000	31	18	0	1	1.4	1.000
1988		15	13	.536	3.94	34	34	10	235	225	83	168	2	0	0	0	0	0	0	—	31	21	1	1	1.6	.981
1989		6	14	.300	4.86	24	24	10	170.1	189	59	115	0	0	0	0	0	0	0	—	17	22	1	3	1.7	.975
1990		15	18	.455	4.51	36	**36**	**11**	249.2	231	97	162	3	0	0	0	0	0	0	—	38	14	2	2	1.5	.963
1991	MIN A	18	12	.600	3.43	35	**35**	10	246.2	226	92	163	2	0	0	0	0	0	0	—	23	25	0	2	1.4	1.000
1992	TOR A	**21**	6	.778	4.04	34	34	6	240.2	222	80	132	1	0	0	0	0	0	0	—	20	26	1	2	1.4	.979
1993		7	12	.368	6.19	27	27	4	152.2	189	65	103	1	0	0	0	0	0	0	—	11	10	2	0	0.9	.913
1994	CLE A	10	6	.625	5.60	23	23	1	141.1	163	67	100	0	0	0	0	0	0	0	—	12	19	4	1	1.5	.886
18 yrs.		254	186	.577	3.90	549	527	175	3824.2	3567	1390	2478	28	3	4	0	1	0	0	.000	387	413	29	36	1.5	.965
LEAGUE CHAMPIONSHIP SERIES																										
1984	DET A	1	0	1.000	1.29	1	1	0	7	5	1	4	0	0	0	0	0	0	0	—	1	1	0	0	2.0	1.000
1987		0	1	.000	6.75	1	1	1	8	6	3	7	0	0	0	0	0	0	0	—	0	0	0	0	0.0	.000
1991	MIN A	2	0	1.000	4.05	2	2	0	13.1	17	1	7	0	0	0	0	0	0	0	—	3	2	0	0	2.5	1.000
1992	TOR A	0	1	.000	6.57	2	2	1	12.1	11	9	6	0	0	0	0	0	0	0	—	0	4	0	1	2.0	1.000
4 yrs.		3	2	.600	4.87	6	6 **9th**	2 **4th**	40.2	39	14	24	0	0	0	0	0	0	0		4	7	0	1	1.8	1.000
WORLD SERIES																										
1984	DET A	2	0	1.000	2.00	2	2	2	18	13	3	13	0	0	0	0	0	0	0	—	5	1	0	0	3.0	1.000
1991	MIN A	2	0	1.000	1.17	3	3	1	23	18	9	15	1	0	0	0	2	0	0	.000	3	3	0	0	2.0	1.000
1992	TOR A	0	2	.000	8.44	2	2	0	10.2	13	6	12	0	0	0	0	2	0	0	.000	0	1	0	0	0.5	1.000
3 yrs.		4	2	.667	2.96	7	7	3	51.2	44	18	40	1	0	0	0	4	0	0	.000	8	5	0	0	1.9	1.000

John Morris

MORRIS, JOHN WALLACE BR TL 6′ 2″ 195 lbs.
B. Aug. 23, 1941, Lewes, Del.

Year	Team	W	L	PCT	ERA	G	GS	CG	IP	H	BB	SO	ShO	Relief W	Relief L	Relief SV	Batting AB	Batting H	Batting HR	BA	PO	A	E	DP	TC/G	FA
1966	PHI N	1	1	.500	5.27	13	0	0	13.2	15	3	8	0	1	1	0	0	0	0	—	1	3	0	0	0.3	1.000
1968	BAL A	2	0	1.000	2.56	19	0	0	31.2	19	17	22	0	2	0	0	6	0	0	.000	1	5	0	0	0.3	1.000
1969	SEA A	0	0	—	6.39	6	0	0	12.2	16	8	8	0	0	0	0	1	1	0	1.000	2	6	0	1	1.3	1.000
1970	MIL A	4	3	.571	3.95	20	9	2	73	70	22	40	0	1	0	0	17	3	0	.176	2	15	0	3	0.9	1.000
1971		2	2	.500	3.71	43	1	0	68	69	27	42	0	2	2	1	5	1	0	.200	3	16	1	1	0.5	.950
1972	SF N	0	0	—	4.50	7	0	0	6	9	2	5	0	0	0	0	0	0	0	—	0	1	0	0	0.1	1.000
1973		1	0	1.000	9.00	7	0	0	6	12	3	3	0	1	0	0	1	0	0	.000	0	1	0	0	0.1	1.000
1974		1	1	.500	3.00	17	0	0	21	17	4	9	0	1	1	1	1	1	0	1.000	0	1	0	0	0.1	1.000
8 yrs.		11	7	.611	3.96	132	10	2	232	227	86	137	0	8	4	2	31	6	0	.194	9	48	1	5	0.4	.983

Bill Morrisette

MORRISETTE, WILLIAM LEE BR TR 6′ 176 lbs.
B. Jan. 17, 1893, Baltimore, Md. D. Mar. 25, 1966, Virginia Beach, Va.

Year	Team	W	L	PCT	ERA	G	GS	CG	IP	H	BB	SO	ShO	Relief W	Relief L	Relief SV	Batting AB	Batting H	Batting HR	BA	PO	A	E	DP	TC/G	FA
1915	PHI A	2	0	1.000	1.35	4	1	1	20	15	5	11	0	1	0	0	7	2	0	.286	1	6	1	0	2.0	.875
1916		0	0	—	6.75	1	0	0	4	6	5	2	0	0	0	0	1	0	0	.000	0	4	0	0	4.0	1.000
1920	DET A	1	1	.500	4.33	8	3	1	27	25	19	15	0	0	0	0	8	0	0	.000	0	5	0	0	0.6	1.000
3 yrs.		3	1	.750	3.35	13	4	2	51	46	29	28	0	1	0	0	16	2	0	.125	1	15	1	0	1.3	.941

Guy Morrison

MORRISON, WALTER GUY BR TR 5′11″ 185 lbs.
B. Aug. 29, 1895, Hinton, W. Va. D. Aug. 14, 1934, Grand Rapids, Mich.

Year	Team	W	L	PCT	ERA	G	GS	CG	IP	H	BB	SO	ShO	Relief W	Relief L	Relief SV	Batting AB	Batting H	Batting HR	BA	PO	A	E	DP	TC/G	FA
1927	BOS N	1	2	.333	4.46	11	3	1	34.1	40	15	6	0	1	0	0	8	1	1	.125	2	14	3	0	1.7	.842
1928		0	0	—	12.00	1	0	0	3	4	3	0	0	0	0	0	0	0	0	—	0	2	0	0	2.0	1.000
2 yrs.		1	2	.333	5.06	12	3	1	37.1	44	18	6	0	1	0	0	8	1	1	.125	2	16	3	0	1.8	.857

Hank Morrison

MORRISON, STEPHEN HENRY BR TR 5′10″ 180 lbs.
B. May 22, 1866, Olneyville, R. I. D. Sept. 30, 1927, Attleboro, Mass.

Year	Team	W	L	PCT	ERA	G	GS	CG	IP	H	BB	SO	ShO	Relief W	Relief L	Relief SV	Batting AB	Batting H	Batting HR	BA	PO	A	E	DP	TC/G	FA
1887	IND N	3	4	.429	7.58	7	7	5	57	79	27	13	0	0	0	0	26	3	0	.115	2	4	2	0	1.0	.750

Jim Morrison

MORRISON, JAMES FORREST BR TR 5′11″ 175 lbs.
B. Sept. 23, 1952, Pensacola, Fla.

Year	Team	W	L	PCT	ERA	G	GS	CG	IP	H	BB	SO	ShO	Relief W	Relief L	Relief SV	Batting AB	Batting H	Batting HR	BA	PO	A	E	DP	TC/G	FA
1988	ATL N	0	0	—	0.00	3	0	0	3.2	3	2	1	0	0	0	0	*				0	7	1	0	1.6	.875

Johnny Morrison

MORRISON, JOHN DEWEY (Jughandle Johnny) BR TR 5′11″ 188 lbs.
Brother of Phil Morrison.
B. Oct. 22, 1895, Pelleville, Ky. D. Mar. 20, 1966, Louisville, Ky.

Year	Team	W	L	PCT	ERA	G	GS	CG	IP	H	BB	SO	ShO	Relief W	Relief L	Relief SV	Batting AB	Batting H	Batting HR	BA	PO	A	E	DP	TC/G	FA
1920	PIT N	1	0	1.000	0.00	2	1	1	7	4	1	3	1	0	0	0	3	0	0	.000	0	2	0	0	1.0	1.000
1921		9	7	.563	2.88	21	17	11	144	131	33	52	**3**	0	0	0	42	5	0	.119	3	37	0	2	1.9	1.000
1922		17	11	.607	3.43	45	33	20	286.1	315	87	104	**5**	1	1	1	101	20	0	.198	3	69	2	0	1.6	.973
1923		25	13	.658	3.49	42	37	27	301.2	287	110	114	2	1	0	2	115	21	0	.183	5	70	2	1	1.8	.974
1924		11	16	.407	3.75	**41**	25	10	237.2	213	73	85	0	6	1	2	77	13	0	.169	3	50	3	2	1.4	.946

Johnny Morrison *continued*

Year	Team	Lg	W	L	PCT	ERA	G	GS	CG	IP	H	BB	SO	ShO	Relief Pitching W	Relief Pitching L	Relief Pitching SV	Batting AB	Batting H	Batting HR	BA	PO	A	E	DP	TC/G	FA
1925			17	14	.548	3.88	**44**	26	10	211	245	60	60	0	**6**	3	**4**	73	13	0	.178	1	43	2	2	1.0	.957
1926			6	8	.429	3.38	26	14	6	122.1	119	44	39	2	1	1	2	39	3	0	.077	2	20	0	3	0.8	1.000
1927			3	2	.600	4.19	21	2	1	53.2	63	21	21	0	2	2	3	13	2	0	.154	0	6	1	1	0.3	.857
1929	**BKN**	**N**	13	7	.650	4.48	39	10	4	136.2	150	61	57	0	**10**	2	**8**	43	7	0	.163	1	15	2	1	0.5	.889
1930			1	2	.333	5.45	16	0	0	34.2	47	16	11	0	1	2	1	5	0	0	.000	1	6	1	0	0.5	.875
10 yrs.			103	80	.563	3.65	297	165	90	1535	1574	506	546	13	28	12	23	511	84	0	.164	19	318	13	12	1.2	.963
WORLD SERIES																											
1925	**PIT**	**N**	0	0	—	2.89	3	0	0	9.1	11	1	7	0	0	0	0	2	1	0	.500	0	3	0	0	1.0	1.000

Mike Morrison

MORRISON, MICHAEL BR TR 5′ 8½″ 156 lbs.
B. Feb. 6, 1867, Erie, Pa. D. June 16, 1955, Erie, Pa.

Year	Team	Lg	W	L	PCT	ERA	G	GS	CG	IP	H	BB	SO	ShO	Relief Pitching W	Relief Pitching L	Relief Pitching SV	Batting AB	Batting H	Batting HR	BA	PO	A	E	DP	TC/G	FA
1887	**CLE**	**AA**	12	25	.324	*4.92*	40	40	35	316.2	385	**205**	158	0	0	0	0	141	27	0	.191	17	114	12	4	3.1	.916
1888			1	3	.250	5.40	4	4	4	35	40	19	14	0	0	0	0	17	4	0	.235	5	7	3	0	3.8	.800
1890	**2 teams**	**SYR AA**	(17G 6–9)		**BAL AA**	(4G 1–2)																					
″	**total**		7	11	.389	5.53	21	18	16	153	146	101	82	1	1	0	0	129	30	1	.233	43	41	8	4	2.4	.913
3 yrs.			20	39	.339	5.14	65	62	55	504.2	571	325	• 254	1	1	0	0	287	61	1	.213	65	162	23	8	2.8	.908

Phil Morrison

MORRISON, PHILIP MELVIN BB TR 6′ 2″ 190 lbs.
Brother of Johnny Morrison.
B. Oct. 18, 1894, Rockport, Ind. D. Jan. 18, 1955, Lexington, Ky.

Year	Team	Lg	W	L	PCT	ERA	G	GS	CG	IP	H	BB	SO	ShO	Relief Pitching W	Relief Pitching L	Relief Pitching SV	Batting AB	Batting H	Batting HR	BA	PO	A	E	DP	TC/G	FA
1921	**PIT**	**N**	0	0	—	0.00	1	0	0	0.2	1	0	1	0	0	0	0	0	0	0	—	0	0	0	0	0.0	.000

Deacon Morrissey

MORRISSEY, MICHAEL JOSEPH TR 5′ 4″ 140 lbs.
B. May 3, 1876, Baltimore, Md. D. Feb. 22, 1939, Baltimore, Md.

Year	Team	Lg	W	L	PCT	ERA	G	GS	CG	IP	H	BB	SO	ShO	Relief Pitching W	Relief Pitching L	Relief Pitching SV	Batting AB	Batting H	Batting HR	BA	PO	A	E	DP	TC/G	FA
1901	**BOS**	**A**	0	0	—	2.08	1	0	0	4.1	5	2	1	0	0	0	0	3	0	0	.000	0	2	0	0	2.0	1.000
1902	**CHI**	**N**	1	3	.250	2.25	5	5	5	40	40	8	13	0	0	0	0	22	2	0	.091	4	13	2	0	2.7	.895
2 yrs.			1	3	.250	2.23	6	5	5	44.1	45	10	14	0	0	0	0	25	2	0	.080	4	15	2	0	2.6	.905

Carl Morton

MORTON, CARL WENDLE BR TR 6′ 200 lbs.
B. Jan. 18, 1944, Kansas City, Mo. D. Apr. 12, 1983, Tulsa, Okla.

Year	Team	Lg	W	L	PCT	ERA	G	GS	CG	IP	H	BB	SO	ShO	Relief Pitching W	Relief Pitching L	Relief Pitching SV	Batting AB	Batting H	Batting HR	BA	PO	A	E	DP	TC/G	FA
1969	**MON**	**N**	0	3	.000	4.66	8	5	0	29	29	18	16	0	0	0	1	7	0	0	.000	3	7	0	0	1.3	1.000
1970			18	11	.621	3.60	43	37	10	285	281	**125**	154	4	0	0	0	93	15	2	.161	29	42	2	2	1.7	.973
1971			10	18	.357	4.79	36	35	9	214	252	83	84	0	0	0	1	77	14	2	.182	28	37	2	4	1.9	.970
1972			7	13	.350	3.92	27	27	3	172	170	53	51	1	0	0	0	52	7	0	.135	24	25	1	0	1.9	.980
1973	**ATL**	**N**	15	10	.600	3.41	38	37	10	256.1	254	70	112	4	0	0	0	94	17	3	.181	26	36	2	2	1.7	.969
1974			16	12	.571	3.14	38	38	7	275	**293**	89	113	1	0	0	0	89	10	0	.112	25	36	1	3	1.6	.984
1975			17	16	.515	3.50	39	39	11	278	**302**	82	78	2	0	0	0	94	15	0	.160	29	40	2	3	1.8	.972
1976			4	9	.308	4.18	26	24	1	140	172	45	42	1	0	0	0	45	8	0	.178	18	26	1	1	1.7	.978
8 yrs.			87	92	.486	3.73	255	242	51	1649.1	1753	565	650	13	0	0	2	551	86	7	.156	182	249	11	15	1.7	.975

Charlie Morton

MORTON, CHARLES HAZEN BR TR 150 lbs.
B. Oct. 12, 1854, Kingsville, Ohio D. Dec. 9, 1921, Massillon, Ohio.
Manager 1884–85, 1890.

Year	Team	Lg	W	L	PCT	ERA	G	GS	CG	IP	H	BB	SO	ShO	Relief Pitching W	Relief Pitching L	Relief Pitching SV	Batting AB	Batting H	Batting HR	BA	PO	A	E	DP	TC/G	FA
1884	**TOL**	**AA**	0	1	.000	*3.09*	3	1	1	23.1	18	5	7	0	0	0	0	*				42	25	18	1	2.2	.788

Guy Morton

MORTON, GUY, SR. (Alabama Blossom) BR TR 6′ 1″ 175 lbs.
Father of Guy Morton.
B. June 1, 1893, Vernon, Ala. D. Oct. 18, 1934, Sheffield, Ala.

Year	Team	Lg	W	L	PCT	ERA	G	GS	CG	IP	H	BB	SO	ShO	Relief Pitching W	Relief Pitching L	Relief Pitching SV	Batting AB	Batting H	Batting HR	BA	PO	A	E	DP	TC/G	FA
1914	**CLE**	**A**	1	13	.071	3.02	25	13	5	128	116	55	80	0	0	2	1	35	1	0	.029	2	30	5	1	1.5	.865
1915			16	15	.516	2.14	34	27	15	240	189	60	134	6	2	2	1	82	12	0	.146	3	69	4	2	2.2	.947
1916			12	8	.600	2.89	27	18	9	149.2	139	42	88	0	1	3	0	57	12	0	.211	7	38	6	1	1.9	.882
1917			10	10	.500	2.74	35	18	6	161	158	59	62	1	3	3	2	47	4	0	.085	5	42	6	0	1.5	.887
1918			14	8	.636	2.64	30	28	13	214.2	189	77	123	1	1	0	0	77	12	0	.156	6	52	7	2	2.2	.892
1919			9	9	.500	2.81	26	20	9	147.1	128	47	64	3	1	1	0	56	9	0	.161	1	40	6	0	1.8	.872
1920			8	6	.571	4.47	29	17	5	137	140	57	72	1	2	0	1	46	10	0	.217	2	25	6	0	1.1	.818
1921			8	3	.727	2.76	30	6	2	107.2	98	32	45	2	**5**	1	0	35	6	0	.171	1	20	2	1	0.8	.913
1922			14	9	.609	4.00	38	23	13	202.2	218	85	102	3	2	2	0	68	13	0	.191	6	64	3	3	1.9	.959
1923			6	6	.500	4.24	33	14	3	129.1	133	56	54	2	1	1	1	44	7	0	.159	2	32	3	0	1.1	.919
1924			0	1	.000	6.57	10	0	0	12.1	12	13	6	0	0	1	0	1	0	0	.000	0	3	2	0	0.5	.600
11 yrs.			98	88	.527	3.13	317	184	80	1629.2	1520	583	830	19	18	16	6	548	86	0	.157	35	415	50	10	1.6	.900

Kevin Morton

MORTON, KEVIN JOSEPH BR TL 6′ 2″ 185 lbs.
B. Aug. 3, 1968, Norwalk, Conn.

Year	Team	Lg	W	L	PCT	ERA	G	GS	CG	IP	H	BB	SO	ShO	Relief Pitching W	Relief Pitching L	Relief Pitching SV	Batting AB	Batting H	Batting HR	BA	PO	A	E	DP	TC/G	FA
1991	**BOS**	**A**	6	5	.545	4.59	16	15	1	86.1	93	40	45	0	0	0	0	0	0	0	—	4	16	0	2	1.3	1.000

Sparrow Morton

MORTON, WILLIAM P. TL
Deceased.

Year	Team	Lg	W	L	PCT	ERA	G	GS	CG	IP	H	BB	SO	ShO	Relief Pitching W	Relief Pitching L	Relief Pitching SV	Batting AB	Batting H	Batting HR	BA	PO	A	E	DP	TC/G	FA
1884	**PHI**	**N**	0	2	.000	*5.29*	2	2	2	17	16	11	5	0	0	0	0	8	3	0	.375	2	3	2	0	3.5	.714

Earl Moseley

MOSELEY, EARL VICTOR BR TR 5′ 9½″ 168 lbs.
B. Sept. 7, 1884, Middleburg, Ohio D. July 1, 1963, Alliance, Ohio.

Year	Team	Lg	W	L	PCT	ERA	G	GS	CG	IP	H	BB	SO	ShO	Relief Pitching W	Relief Pitching L	Relief Pitching SV	Batting AB	Batting H	Batting HR	BA	PO	A	E	DP	TC/G	FA
1913	**BOS**	**A**	8	5	.615	3.13	24	15	7	120.2	105	49	62	3	1	1	0	37	3	0	.081	8	37	2	1	2.0	.957
1914	**IND**	**F**	19	18	.514	3.47	43	38	29	316.2	303	123	205	4	1	2	1	109	12	0	.110	13	86	7	3	2.5	.934
1915	**NWK**	**F**	16	16	.500	**1.91**	38	32	22	268	222	99	142	5	1	2	0	88	13	0	.148	7	63	4	1	1.9	.946
1916	**CIN**	**N**	7	10	.412	3.89	31	15	7	150.1	145	69	60	0	2	2	1	46	4	0	.087	2	33	1	2	1.2	.972
4 yrs.			50	49	.505	3.01	136	100	65	855.2	775	340	469	12	5	7	2	280	32	0	.114	30	219	14	7	1.9	.947

Walter Moser

MOSER, WALTER FREDERICK BR TR 5′ 9″ 170 lbs.
B. Feb. 27, 1881, Concord, N. C. D. Dec. 10, 1946, Philadelphia, Pa.

Year	Team	W	L	PCT	ERA	G	GS	CG	IP	H	BB	SO	ShO	Relief W	Relief L	Relief SV	AB	H	HR	BA	PO	A	E	DP	TC/G	FA
1906	PHI N	0	4	.000	3.59	6	4	4	42.2	49	15	17	0	0	0	0	14	0	0	.000	3	8	2	1	2.2	.846
1911	2 teams BOS A (6G 0–1) STL A (2G 0–2)																									
"	total	0	3	.000	6.11	8	5	1	28	48	15	13	0	0	0	0	8	1	0	.125	1	9	2	0	1.5	.833
2 yrs.		0	7	.000	4.58	14	9	5	70.2	97	30	30	0	0	0	0	22	1	0	.045	4	17	4	1	1.8	.840

John Moses

MOSES, JOHN WILLIAM BB TL 5′10″ 165 lbs.
B. Aug. 9, 1957, Los Angeles, Calif.

Year	Team	W	L	PCT	ERA	G	GS	CG	IP	H	BB	SO	ShO	Relief W	Relief L	Relief SV	AB	H	HR	BA	PO	A	E	DP	TC/G	FA
1989	MIN A	0	0	—	0.00	1	0	0	1	0	1	0	0	0	0	0	242	68	1	.281	16	2	1	0	1.0	.947
1990		0	0	—	13.50	2	0	0	2	5	2	0	0	0	0	0	172	38	1	.221	108	2	0	0	1.1	1.000
2 yrs.		0	0		9.00	3	0	0	3	5	3	0	0	0	0	0	*				1115	36	14	8	1.7	.988

Paul Moskau

MOSKAU, PAUL RICHARD BR TR 6′ 2″ 200 lbs.
B. Dec. 20, 1953, St. Joseph, Mo.

Year	Team	W	L	PCT	ERA	G	GS	CG	IP	H	BB	SO	ShO	Relief W	Relief L	Relief SV	AB	H	HR	BA	PO	A	E	DP	TC/G	FA
1977	CIN N	6	6	.500	4.00	20	19	2	108	116	40	71	2	0	0	0	38	7	1	.184	6	19	0	1	1.3	1.000
1978		6	4	.600	3.97	26	25	2	145	139	57	88	1	0	0	1	49	10	1	.204	5	13	0	1	0.7	1.000
1979		5	4	.556	3.91	21	15	1	106	107	51	58	0	1	0	0	37	3	0	.081	3	19	2	3	1.1	.917
1980		9	7	.563	4.00	33	19	2	153	147	41	94	1	5	0	2	44	7	0	.159	11	22	3	4	1.1	.917
1981		2	1	.667	4.91	27	1	0	55	54	32	32	0	2	1	2	6	0	0	.000	4	12	1	0	0.6	.941
1982	PIT N	1	3	.250	4.37	13	5	0	35	43	8	15	0	0	1	0	11	1	0	.091	3	4	0	0	0.5	1.000
1983	CHI N	3	2	.600	6.75	8	8	0	32	44	14	16	0	0	0	0	11	2	0	.182	3	5	2	0	1.3	.800
7 yrs.		32	27	.542	4.22	148	92	7	634	650	243	374	4	8	2	5	196	30	2	.153	35	94	8	9	0.9	.942

Jim Mosolf

MOSOLF, JAMES FREDERICK BL TR 5′10″ 186 lbs.
B. Aug. 21, 1905, Puyallup, Wash. D. Dec. 28, 1979, Dallas, Ore.

Year	Team	W	L	PCT	ERA	G	GS	CG	IP	H	BB	SO	ShO	Relief W	Relief L	Relief SV	AB	H	HR	BA	PO	A	E	DP	TC/G	FA
1930	PIT N	0	0	—	27.00	1	0	0	0.1	1	0	1	0	0	0	0	*				7	0	0	0	2.3	1.000

Mal Moss

MOSS, CHARLES MALCOLM BR TL 6′ 175 lbs.
B. Apr. 18, 1905, Sullivan, Ind. D. Feb. 6, 1983, Savannah, Ga.

Year	Team	W	L	PCT	ERA	G	GS	CG	IP	H	BB	SO	ShO	Relief W	Relief L	Relief SV	AB	H	HR	BA	PO	A	E	DP	TC/G	FA
1930	CHI N	0	0	—	6.27	12	1	0	18.2	18	14	4	0	0	0	1	11	3	0	.273	3	4	0	0	0.6	1.000

Ray Moss

MOSS, RAYMOND EARL BR TR 6′ 1″ 185 lbs.
B. Dec. 5, 1901, Chattanooga, Tenn.

Year	Team	W	L	PCT	ERA	G	GS	CG	IP	H	BB	SO	ShO	Relief W	Relief L	Relief SV	AB	H	HR	BA	PO	A	E	DP	TC/G	FA
1926	BKN N	0	0	—	9.00	1	0	0	1	3	0	0	0	0	0	0	1	0	0	.000	0	0	0	0	0.0	.000
1927		1	0	1.000	3.24	1	1	0	8.1	11	1	1	0	0	0	0	3	1	0	.333	0	1	0	0	1.0	1.000
1928		0	3	.000	4.92	22	5	1	60.1	62	35	5	1	0	1	1	25	8	0	.320	3	15	2	1	0.9	.900
1929		11	6	.647	5.04	39	20	7	182	214	81	59	2	2	1	0	66	5	0	.076	5	32	1	0	1.0	.974
1930		9	6	.600	5.10	36	11	5	118.1	127	55	30	0	3	3	1	39	6	0	.154	4	16	1	2	0.6	.952
1931	2 teams BKN N (1G 0–0) BOS N (12G 1–3)																									
"	total	1	3	.250	4.50	13	5	0	46	57	17	14	0	1	0	0	15	2	0	.133	1	10	0	0	0.8	1.000
6 yrs.		22	18	.550	4.95	112	42	13	416	474	189	109	3	6	5	2	149	22	0	.148	13	74	4	3	0.8	.956

Don Mossi

MOSSI, DONALD LOUIS (The Sphinx) BL TL 6′ 1″ 195 lbs.
B. Jan. 11, 1929, St. Helena, Calif.

Year	Team	W	L	PCT	ERA	G	GS	CG	IP	H	BB	SO	ShO	Relief W	Relief L	Relief SV	AB	H	HR	BA	PO	A	E	DP	TC/G	FA
1954	CLE A	6	1	.857	1.94	40	5	2	93	56	39	55	0	4	0	7	19	3	0	.158	4	11	0	1	0.4	1.000
1955		4	3	.571	2.42	57	1	0	81.2	81	18	69	0	4	3	9	9	1	0	.111	7	19	0	2	0.5	1.000
1956		6	5	.545	3.59	48	3	0	87.2	79	33	59	0	6	3	11	20	3	0	.150	3	15	1	1	0.4	.947
1957		11	10	.524	4.13	36	22	6	159	166	57	97	1	1	1	2	55	12	0	.218	7	21	0	2	0.8	1.000
1958		7	8	.467	3.90	43	5	0	101.2	106	30	55	0	7	4	3	26	3	0	.115	8	17	0	1	0.6	1.000
1959	DET A	17	9	.654	3.36	34	30	15	228	210	49	125	3	0	1	0	77	13	1	.169	12	38	1	5	1.5	.980
1960		9	8	.529	3.47	23	22	9	158.1	158	32	69	2	1	0	0	43	5	0	.116	2	27	0	2	1.3	1.000
1961		15	7	.682	2.96	35	34	12	240.1	237	47	137	1	0	0	1	79	13	1	.165	7	40	1	8	1.4	.979
1962		11	13	.458	4.19	35	27	8	180.1	195	36	121	1	0	2	1	55	9	0	.164	9	19	0	3	0.8	1.000
1963		7	7	.500	3.74	24	16	3	122.2	110	17	68	0	2	0	2	39	8	0	.205	6	20	0	1	1.1	1.000
1964	CHI A	3	1	.750	2.92	34	0	0	40	37	7	36	0	3	1	7	6	1	0	.167	2	5	0	0	0.2	1.000
1965	KC A	5	8	.385	3.74	51	0	0	55.1	59	20	41	0	5	8	7	8	0	0	.000	2	7	0	2	0.2	1.000
12 yrs.		101	80	.558	3.43	460	165	55	1548	1494	385	932	8	33	23	50	436	71	2	.163	69	239	3	28	0.7	.990
WORLD SERIES																										
1954	CLE A	0	0	—	0.00	3	0	0	4	3	0	1	0	0	0	0	0	0	0	—	0	2	0	0	0.7	1.000

Earl Mossor

MOSSOR, EARL DALTON BL TR 6′ 1″ 175 lbs.
B. July 21, 1925, Forbus, Tenn. D. Dec. 29, 1988, Batavia, Ohio.

Year	Team	W	L	PCT	ERA	G	GS	CG	IP	H	BB	SO	ShO	Relief W	Relief L	Relief SV	AB	H	HR	BA	PO	A	E	DP	TC/G	FA
1951	BKN N	0	0	—	32.40	3	0	0	1.2	2	7	1	0	0	0	0	1	1	0	1.000	0	0	0	0	0.0	.000

Glen Moulder

MOULDER, GLEN HUBERT BR TR 6′ 180 lbs.
B. Sept. 28, 1917, Cleveland, Okla. D. Nov. 27, 1994, Decatur, Ga.

Year	Team	W	L	PCT	ERA	G	GS	CG	IP	H	BB	SO	ShO	Relief W	Relief L	Relief SV	AB	H	HR	BA	PO	A	E	DP	TC/G	FA
1946	BKN N	0	0	—	4.50	1	0	0	2	2	1	1	0	0	0	0	0	0	0	—	0	0	0	0	0.0	.000
1947	STL A	4	2	.667	3.82	32	2	0	73	78	43	23	0	3	1	2	17	4	0	.235	4	16	1	1	0.7	.952
1948	CHI A	3	6	.333	6.41	33	9	0	85.2	108	54	26	0	1	2	2	20	6	0	.300	3	17	3	0	0.7	.870
3 yrs.		7	8	.467	5.21	66	11	0	160.2	188	98	50	0	4	3	4	37	10	0	.270	7	33	4	1	0.7	.909

Frank Mountain

MOUNTAIN, FRANK HENRY BR TR 5′11″ 185 lbs.
B. May 17, 1860, Ft. Edward, N. Y. D. Nov. 19, 1939, Schenectady, N. Y.

Year	Team	W	L	PCT	ERA	G	GS	CG	IP	H	BB	SO	ShO	Relief W	Relief L	Relief SV	AB	H	HR	BA	PO	A	E	DP	TC/G	FA
1880	TRO N	1	1	.500	5.29	2	2	2	17	23	6	2	0	0	0	0	9	2	0	.222	0	4	0	0	2.0	1.000
1881	DET N	3	4	.429	5.25	7	7	7	60	80	18	13	0	0	0	0	25	4	0	.160	6	6	1	0	1.9	.923
1882	3 teams WOR N (5G 0–5) PHI AA (8G 2–5) WOR N (13G 2–11)																									
"	total	4	21	.160	3.76	26	26	24	213	257	46	44	0	0	0	0	122	32	2	.262	31	54	10	3	2.6	.895
1883	COL AA	26	**33**	.441	*3.60*	59	59	57	503	**546**	**123**	159	4	0	0	0	276	60	3	.217	55	106	26	3	2.6	.861
1884		23	17	.575	*2.45*	42	41	40	360.2	289	78	156	5	0	0	**1**	210	50	4	.238	30	90	10	0	2.2	.923
1885	PIT AA	1	4	.200	*4.30*	5	5	5	46	56	24	7	0	0	0	0	20	2	0	.100	1	10	2	0	2.6	.846
1886		0	2	.000	*7.88*	2	2	2	16	22	14	2	0	0	0	0	55	8	0	.145	160	9	9	6	9.9	.949
7 yrs.		58	82	.414	3.47	143	142	137	1215.2	1273	309	383	9	0	0	1	*				283	279	58	12	3.1	.906

Billy Mountjoy

MOUNTJOY, WILLIAM HENRY (Medicine Bill) BL TR 5′ 6″ 150 lbs.
B. Dec. 11, 1858, London, Ont., Canada. D. May 19, 1894, London, Ont., Canada.

Year	Team	Lg	W	L	PCT	ERA	G	GS	CG	IP	H	BB	SO	ShO	Relief Pitching W	Relief Pitching L	Relief Pitching SV	Batting AB	Batting H	Batting HR	BA	PO	A	E	DP	TC/G	FA
1883	CIN	AA	0	1	.000	2.25	1	1	1	8	9	2	3	0	0	0	0	3	0	0	.000	0	1	0	0	1.0	1.000
1884			19	12	.613	*2.93*	33	33	32	289	274	43	96	3	0	0	0	119	18	0	.151	15	65	6	3	2.5	.930
1885	2 teams	CIN AA (17G 10–7)	BAL AA (6G 2–4)																								
"	total		12	11	.522	3.75	23	23	23	206.2	221	65	65	2	0	0	0	78	11	0	.141	4	37	5	1	1.9	.891
3 yrs.			31	24	.564	3.25	57	57	56	503.2	504	110	164	5	0	0	0	200	29	0	.145	19	103	11	4	2.2	.917

Charlie Moyer

MOYER, CHARLES EDWARD
B. Aug. 15, 1885, Andover, Ohio D. Nov. 18, 1962, Jacksonville, Fla.

Year	Team	Lg	W	L	PCT	ERA	G	GS	CG	IP	H	BB	SO	ShO	Relief Pitching W	Relief Pitching L	Relief Pitching SV	Batting AB	Batting H	Batting HR	BA	PO	A	E	DP	TC/G	FA
1910	WAS	A	0	3	.000	3.24	6	3	2	25	22	13	3	0	0	0	0	8	1	0	.125	0	16	0	0	2.7	1.000

Jamie Moyer

MOYER, JAMIE BL TL 6′ 170 lbs.
B. Nov. 11, 1962, Sellersville, Pa.

Year	Team	Lg	W	L	PCT	ERA	G	GS	CG	IP	H	BB	SO	ShO	Relief Pitching W	Relief Pitching L	Relief Pitching SV	Batting AB	Batting H	Batting HR	BA	PO	A	E	DP	TC/G	FA
1986	CHI	N	7	4	.636	5.05	16	16	1	87.1	107	42	45	1	0	0	0	22	2	0	.091	2	22	0	0	1.5	1.000
1987			12	15	.444	5.10	35	33	1	201	210	97	147	0	1	0	0	61	14	0	.230	15	37	4	3	1.6	.929
1988			9	15	.375	3.48	34	30	3	202	212	55	121	1	1	0	0	60	5	0	.083	11	45	1	3	1.7	.982
1989	TEX	A	4	9	.308	4.86	15	15	1	76	84	33	44	0	0	0	0	0	0	0	—	5	14	0	2	1.3	1.000
1990			2	6	.250	4.66	33	10	1	102.1	115	39	58	0	1	1	0	0	0	0	—	6	14	0	2	0.6	1.000
1991	STL	N	0	5	.000	5.74	8	7	0	31.1	38	16	20	0	0	0	0	8	0	0	.000	0	5	0	0	0.6	1.000
1993	BAL	A	12	9	.571	3.43	25	25	3	152	154	38	90	1	0	0	0	0	0	0	—	14	25	1	1	1.6	.975
1994			5	7	.417	4.77	23	23	0	149	158	38	87	0	0	0	0	0	0	0	—	12	17	0	1	1.3	1.000
1995			8	6	.571	5.21	27	18	0	115.2	117	30	65	0	0	1	0	0	0	0	—	8	20	0	4	1.0	1.000
9 yrs.			59	76	.437	4.51	216	177	10	1116.2	1195	388	677	3	3	2	0	151	21	0	.139	73	199	6	16	1.3	.978

Ron Mrozinski

MROZINSKI, RONALD FRANK BR TL 5′11″ 160 lbs.
B. Sept. 16, 1930, White Haven, Pa.

Year	Team	Lg	W	L	PCT	ERA	G	GS	CG	IP	H	BB	SO	ShO	Relief Pitching W	Relief Pitching L	Relief Pitching SV	Batting AB	Batting H	Batting HR	BA	PO	A	E	DP	TC/G	FA
1954	PHI	N	1	1	.500	4.50	15	4	1	48	49	25	26	0	0	0	0	12	1	0	.083	3	3	0	1	0.4	1.000
1955			0	2	.000	6.55	22	1	0	34.1	38	19	18	0	0	1	1	4	0	0	.000	0	5	1	2	0.3	.833
2 yrs.			1	3	.250	5.36	37	5	1	82.1	87	44	44	0	0	1	1	16	1	0	.063	3	8	1	3	0.3	.917

Phil Mudrock

MUDROCK, PHILIP RAY BR TR 6′ 1″ 190 lbs.
B. June 12, 1937, Louisville, Colo.

Year	Team	Lg	W	L	PCT	ERA	G	GS	CG	IP	H	BB	SO	ShO	Relief Pitching W	Relief Pitching L	Relief Pitching SV	Batting AB	Batting H	Batting HR	BA	PO	A	E	DP	TC/G	FA
1963	CHI	N	0	0	—	9.00	1	0	0	1	2	0	0	0	0	0	0	0	0	0	—	0	0	0	0	0.0	.000

Gordy Mueller

MUELLER, JOSEPH GORDON BR TR 6′ 4″ 200 lbs.
B. Dec. 10, 1922, Baltimore, Md.

Year	Team	Lg	W	L	PCT	ERA	G	GS	CG	IP	H	BB	SO	ShO	Relief Pitching W	Relief Pitching L	Relief Pitching SV	Batting AB	Batting H	Batting HR	BA	PO	A	E	DP	TC/G	FA
1950	BOS	A	0	0	—	10.29	8	0	0	7	11	13	1	0	0	0	0	1	0	0	.000	2	1	0	0	0.4	1.000

Les Mueller

MUELLER, LESLIE CLYDE BR TR 6′ 3″ 190 lbs.
B. Mar. 4, 1919, Belleville, Ill.

Year	Team	Lg	W	L	PCT	ERA	G	GS	CG	IP	H	BB	SO	ShO	Relief Pitching W	Relief Pitching L	Relief Pitching SV	Batting AB	Batting H	Batting HR	BA	PO	A	E	DP	TC/G	FA
1941	DET	A	0	0	—	4.85	4	0	0	13	9	10	8	0	0	0	0	3	0	0	.000	0	3	0	0	0.8	1.000
1945			6	8	.429	3.68	26	18	6	134.2	117	58	42	2	0	0	1	44	8	1	.182	6	20	3	0	1.1	.897
2 yrs.			6	8	.429	3.78	30	18	6	147.2	126	68	50	2	0	0	1	47	8	1	.170	6	23	3	0	1.1	.906
WORLD SERIES																											
1945	DET	A	0	0	—	0.00	1	0	0	2	0	1	1	0	0	0	0	0	0	0	—	0	0	0	0	0.0	.000

Willie Mueller

MUELLER, WILLARD LAWRENCE BR TR 6′ 4″ 220 lbs.
B. Aug. 30, 1956, West Bend, Wis.

Year	Team	Lg	W	L	PCT	ERA	G	GS	CG	IP	H	BB	SO	ShO	Relief Pitching W	Relief Pitching L	Relief Pitching SV	Batting AB	Batting H	Batting HR	BA	PO	A	E	DP	TC/G	FA
1978	MIL	A	1	0	1.000	6.39	5	0	0	12.2	16	6	6	0	1	0	0	0	0	0	—	1	2	0	0	0.6	1.000
1981			0	0	—	4.50	1	0	0	2	4	0	1	0	0	0	0	0	0	0	—	1	0	0	0	1.0	1.000
2 yrs.			1	0	1.000	6.14	6	0	0	14.2	20	6	7	0	1	0	0	0	0	0		2	2	0	0	0.7	1.000

Billy Muffett

MUFFETT, BILLY ARNOLD (Muff) BR TR 6′ 1″ 198 lbs.
B. Sept. 21, 1930, Hammond, Ind.

Year	Team	Lg	W	L	PCT	ERA	G	GS	CG	IP	H	BB	SO	ShO	Relief Pitching W	Relief Pitching L	Relief Pitching SV	Batting AB	Batting H	Batting HR	BA	PO	A	E	DP	TC/G	FA
1957	STL	N	3	2	.600	2.25	23	0	0	44	35	13	21	0	3	2	8	7	0	0	.000	2	4	1	1	0.3	.857
1958			4	6	.400	4.93	35	6	1	84	107	42	41	0	3	3	5	20	4	0	.200	3	12	1	1	0.5	.938
1959	SF	N	0	0	—	5.40	5	0	0	6.2	11	3	3	0	0	0	0	0	0	0	—	0	1	0	0	0.2	1.000
1960	BOS	A	6	4	.600	3.24	23	14	4	125	116	36	75	1	1	1	0	41	11	0	.268	11	17	1	1	1.3	.966
1961			3	11	.214	5.67	38	11	2	112.2	130	36	47	0	2	3	2	23	5	1	.217	6	18	0	1	0.6	1.000
1962			0	0	—	9.00	1	1	0	4	8	2	1	0	0	0	0	1	0	0	.000	0	0	0	0	0.0	.000
6 yrs.			16	23	.410	4.33	125	32	7	376.1	407	132	188	1	9	9	15	92	20	1	.217	22	52	3	4	0.6	.961

Joe Muich

MUICH, IGNATIUS ANDREW BR TR 6′ 2″ 175 lbs.
B. Nov. 23, 1903, St. Louis, Mo. D. July 2, 1993, St. Louis, Mo.

Year	Team	Lg	W	L	PCT	ERA	G	GS	CG	IP	H	BB	SO	ShO	Relief Pitching W	Relief Pitching L	Relief Pitching SV	Batting AB	Batting H	Batting HR	BA	PO	A	E	DP	TC/G	FA
1924	BOS	N	0	0	—	11.00	3	0	0	9	19	5	1	0	0	0	0	3	0	0	.000	0	2	0	0	0.7	1.000

Joe Muir

MUIR, JOSEPH ALLEN BL TL 6′ 1″ 172 lbs.
B. Nov. 26, 1922, Oriole, Md. D. June 25, 1980, Baltimore, Md.

Year	Team	Lg	W	L	PCT	ERA	G	GS	CG	IP	H	BB	SO	ShO	Relief Pitching W	Relief Pitching L	Relief Pitching SV	Batting AB	Batting H	Batting HR	BA	PO	A	E	DP	TC/G	FA
1951	PIT	N	0	2	.000	2.76	9	1	0	16.1	11	7	5	0	0	2	0	1	0	0	.000	1	7	0	0	0.9	1.000
1952			2	3	.400	6.31	12	5	1	35.2	42	18	17	0	0	1	0	9	1	0	.111	4	5	1	1	0.8	.900
2 yrs.			2	5	.286	5.19	21	6	1	52	53	25	22	0	0	3	0	10	1	0	.100	5	12	1	1	0.9	.944

Hugh Mulcahy

MULCAHY, HUGH NOYES (Losing Pitcher) BR TR 6′ 2″ 190 lbs.
B. Sept. 9, 1913, Brighton, Mass.

Year	Team	Lg	W	L	PCT	ERA	G	GS	CG	IP	H	BB	SO	ShO	Relief Pitching W	Relief Pitching L	Relief Pitching SV	Batting AB	Batting H	Batting HR	BA	PO	A	E	DP	TC/G	FA
1935	PHI	N	1	5	.167	4.78	18	5	0	52.2	62	25	11	0	1	1	1	17	0	0	.000	4	18	3	0	1.3	.880
1936			1	1	.500	3.22	3	2	2	22.1	20	12	2	0	0	0	0	8	2	0	.250	2	6	1	0	3.0	.889
1937			8	18	.308	5.13	**56**	26	9	215.2	256	**97**	54	1	1	**5**	3	73	11	0	.151	13	64	3	3	1.4	.963
1938			10	**20**	.333	4.61	46	34	15	267.1	294	120	90	0	1	1	1	94	16	0	.170	13	54	0	**4**	1.5	1.000
1939			9	16	.360	4.99	38	32	14	225.2	246	93	59	1	0	2	4	76	12	0	.158	12	48	6	1	1.7	.909
1940			13	**22**	.371	3.60	36	36	21	280	**283**	91	82	3	0	0	0	94	19	0	.202	22	65	1	9	2.4	.989
1945			1	3	.250	3.81	5	4	1	28.1	33	9	2	0	0	0	0	7	0	0	.000	3	10	1	0	2.8	.929
1946			2	4	.333	4.45	16	5	1	62.2	69	33	12	0	0	2	0	16	3	0	.188	5	18	0	0	1.4	1.000
1947	PIT	N	0	0	—	4.05	2	1	0	6.2	8	7	2	0	0	0	0	3	1	0	.333	1	3	0	1	2.0	1.000
9 yrs.			45	89	.336	4.49	220	145	63	1161.1	1271	487	314	5	3	11	9	388	64	0	.165	75	286	15	18	1.7	.960

Terry Mulholland

MULHOLLAND, TERENCE JOHN
B. Mar. 9, 1963, Uniontown, Pa.
BR TL 6' 3" 200 lbs.

Year	Team	W	L	PCT	ERA	G	GS	CG	IP	H	BB	SO	ShO	Relief Pitching W	Relief Pitching L	Relief Pitching SV	Batting AB	Batting H	Batting HR	BA	PO	A	E	DP	TC/G	FA
1986	**SF N**	1	7	.125	4.94	15	10	0	54.2	51	35	27	0	0	0	0	19	1	0	.053	1	9	3	0	0.9	.769
1988		2	1	.667	3.72	9	6	2	46	50	7	18	1	0	0	0	14	0	0	.000	7	7	0	0	1.6	1.000
1989	**2 teams SF N** (5G 0–0) **PHI N** (20G 4–7)																									
"	**total**	4	7	.364	4.92	25	18	2	115.1	137	36	66	1	0	0	0	36	2	0	.056	2	25	4	1	1.2	.871
1990	**PHI N**	9	10	.474	3.34	33	26	6	180.2	172	42	75	1	0	0	0	62	6	0	.097	8	17	3	0	0.8	.893
1991		16	13	.552	3.61	34	34	8	232	231	49	142	3	0	0	0	80	7	0	.087	12	28	5	2	1.3	.889
1992		13	11	.542	3.81	32	32	**12**	229	227	46	125	2	0	0	0	83	8	0	.096	6	47	3	0	1.8	.946
1993		12	9	.571	3.25	29	28	7	191	177	40	116	2	0	0	0	62	4	0	.065	5	27	2	1	1.2	.941
1994	**NY A**	6	7	.462	6.49	24	19	2	120.2	150	37	72	0	0	0	0	0	0	0	—	4	15	1	0	0.8	.950
1995	**SF N**	5	13	.278	5.80	29	24	2	149	190	38	65	0	0	0	0	49	5	1	.102	5	23	3	2	1.1	.903
9 yrs.		68	78	.466	4.24	230	197	41	1318.1	1385	330	706	10	0	0	0	405	33	1	.081	50	198	24	6	1.2	.912
LEAGUE CHAMPIONSHIP SERIES																										
1993	**PHI N**	0	1	.000	7.20	1	1	0	5	9	1	2	0	0	0	0	2	0	0	.000	0	2	0	0	2.0	1.000
WORLD SERIES																										
1993	**PHI N**	1	0	1.000	6.75	2	2	0	10.2	14	3	5	0	0	0	0	0	0	0	—	1	1	0	0	1.0	1.000

Tony Mullane

MULLANE, ANTHONY JOHN (Count, The Apollo of the Box)
B. Jan. 30, 1859, Cork, Ireland D. Apr. 25, 1944, Chicago, Ill.
BB TB 5'10½" 165 lbs.
BL 1882

Year	Team	W	L	PCT	ERA	G	GS	CG	IP	H	BB	SO	ShO	Relief Pitching W	Relief Pitching L	Relief Pitching SV	Batting AB	Batting H	Batting HR	BA	PO	A	E	DP	TC/G	FA
1881	**DET N**	1	4	.200	4.91	5	5	5	44	55	17	7	0	0	0	0	19	5	0	.263	8	7	2	0	3.4	.882
1882	**LOU AA**	30	24	.556	*1.88*	**55**	**55**	51	460.1	418	**78**	**170**	5	0	0	0	303	78	0	.257	187	191	24	10	4.9	.940
1883	**STL AA**	35	15	**.700**	*2.19*	53	49	49	460.2	372	74	191	3	**1**	0	**1**	307	69	0	.225	66	108	27	6	2.3	.866
1884	**TOL AA**	36	26	.581	*2.52*	67	65	64	567	481	89	325	**7**	0	**1**	0	352	97	3	.276	139	161	41	10	3.4	.880
1886	**CIN AA**	33	27	.550	*3.70*	63	56	55	529.2	**501**	166	250	1	**4**	0	0	324	73	0	.225	114	117	27	10	2.6	.895
1887		31	17	.646	*3.24*	48	48	47	416.1	414	121	97	**6**	0	0	0	199	44	3	.221	40	73	7	6	2.1	.942
1888		26	16	.619	2.84	44	42	41	380.1	341	75	186	4	**1**	0	**1**	175	44	1	.251	62	85	14	2	3.0	.913
1889		11	9	.550	2.99	33	24	17	220	218	89	112	0	1	0	**5**	196	58	0	.296	78	80	22	10	2.7	.878
1890	**CIN N**	12	10	.545	2.24	25	21	21	209	175	96	91	0	1	0	1	286	79	0	.276	114	116	37	7	3.1	.861
1891		23	26	.469	3.23	51	47	42	426.1	390	187	124	1	2	2	0	209	31	0	.148	33	100	9	3	2.2	.937
1892		21	13	.618	2.59	37	34	30	295	222	127	109	3	2	0	1	118	20	0	.169	38	87	9	6	3.4	.933
1893	**2 teams CIN N** (15G 6–6) **BAL N** (34G 12–16)																									
"	**total**	18	22	.450	4.44	49	39	34	367	407	189	95	0	3	1	**2**	166	41	1	.247	27	90	8	3	2.4	.936
1894	**2 teams BAL N** (21G 6–9) **CLE N** (4G 1–2)																									
"	**total**	7	11	.389	6.59	25	19	12	155.2	201	100	46	0	0	1	**4**	66	22	0	.333	10	31	4	2	1.8	.911
13 yrs.		284	220	.563	3.05	555	504	468 **9th**	4531.1	4195	1408	1803	30	15	5	15	*				916	1246	231	75	2.9	.903

Dick Mulligan

MULLIGAN, RICHARD CHARLES
B. Mar. 18, 1918, Swoyersville, Pa. D. Dec. 15, 1992, Victoria, Tex.
BL TL 6' 167 lbs.

Year	Team	W	L	PCT	ERA	G	GS	CG	IP	H	BB	SO	ShO	Relief Pitching W	Relief Pitching L	Relief Pitching SV	Batting AB	Batting H	Batting HR	BA	PO	A	E	DP	TC/G	FA
1941	**WAS A**	0	1	.000	5.00	1	1	1	9	11	2	2	0	0	0	0	3	0	0	.000	0	2	0	0	2.0	1.000
1946	**2 teams PHI N** (19G 2–2) **BOS N** (4G 1–0)																									
"	**total**	3	2	.600	4.24	23	5	1	70	67	36	20	0	1	0	1	15	0	0	.000	4	13	0	0	0.7	1.000
1947	**BOS N**	0	0	—	9.00	1	0	0	2	4	1	1	0	0	0	0	0	0	0	—	0	0	0	0	0.0	.000
3 yrs.		3	3	.500	4.44	25	6	2	81	82	39	23	0	1	0	1	18	0	0	.000	4	15	0	0	0.8	1.000

Joe Mulligan

MULLIGAN, JOSEPH IGNATIUS (Big Joe)
B. July 31, 1913, Weymouth, Mass. D. June 5, 1986, West Roxbury, Mass.
BR TR 6' 4" 210 lbs.

Year	Team	W	L	PCT	ERA	G	GS	CG	IP	H	BB	SO	ShO	Relief Pitching W	Relief Pitching L	Relief Pitching SV	Batting AB	Batting H	Batting HR	BA	PO	A	E	DP	TC/G	FA
1934	**BOS A**	1	0	1.000	3.63	14	2	1	44.2	46	27	13	0	0	0	0	12	0	0	.000	2	10	0	1	0.9	1.000

George Mullin

MULLIN, GEORGE JOSEPH (Wabash George)
B. July 4, 1880, Toledo, Ohio D. Jan. 7, 1944, Wabash, Ind.
BR TR 5'11" 188 lbs.

Year	Team	W	L	PCT	ERA	G	GS	CG	IP	H	BB	SO	ShO	Relief Pitching W	Relief Pitching L	Relief Pitching SV	Batting AB	Batting H	Batting HR	BA	PO	A	E	DP	TC/G	FA
1902	**DET A**	13	16	.448	3.67	35	30	25	260	282	95	78	0	1	1	0	120	39	0	.325	30	79	9	3	3.0	.924
1903		19	15	.559	2.25	41	36	31	320.2	284	**106**	170	6	1	1	**2**	126	35	1	.278	38	108	10	1	3.7	.936
1904		17	23	.425	2.40	45	44	42	382.1	345	**131**	161	7	1	0	0	151	45	0	.298	28	163	13	5	4.3	.936
1905		21	21	.500	2.51	44	**41**	35	**347.2**	**303**	**138**	168	1	1	1	0	135	35	0	.259	20	134	6	7	3.6	.963
1906		21	18	.538	2.78	40	40	35	330	315	**108**	123	2	0	0	0	142	32	0	.225	21	113	6	2	3.5	.957
1907		20	20	.500	2.59	46	42	35	357.1	**346**	106	146	5	1	0	3	157	34	0	.217	15	133	6	1	3.3	.961
1908		17	13	.567	3.10	39	30	26	290.2	301	71	121	1	3	0	0	125	32	1	.256	21	102	5	2	3.3	.961
1909		**29**	8	**.784**	2.22	40	35	29	303.2	258	78	124	3	**4**	0	1	126	27	0	.214	12	99	3	2	2.7	.974
1910		21	12	.636	2.87	38	32	27	289	260	102	98	5	2	0	0	129	33	1	.256	22	97	8	1	3.2	.937
1911		18	10	.643	3.07	30	29	25	234.1	245	61	87	2	0	1	0	98	28	0	.286	9	55	4	2	2.3	.941
1912		12	17	.414	3.54	30	29	22	226	214	92	88	2	0	1	0	90	25	0	.278	8	70	6	1	2.8	.929
1913	**2 teams DET A** (7G 1–6) **WAS A** (12G 3–5)																									
"	**total**	4	11	.267	3.94	19	16	7	109.2	122	43	30	0	1	0	0	41	11	0	.268	2	41	2	1	2.4	.956
1914	**IND F**	14	10	.583	2.70	36	20	11	203	202	91	74	1	**8**	0	2	77	24	0	.312	9	45	5	1	1.6	.915
1915	**NWK F**	2	2	.500	5.85	5	4	3	32.1	41	16	14	0	0	0	0	10	1	0	.100	1	5	0	1	1.2	1.000
14 yrs.		228	196	.538	2.82	488	428	353	3686.2	3518	1238	1482	35	23	5	8	*				236	1244	83	30	3.1	.947
WORLD SERIES																										
1907	**DET A**	0	2	.000	2.12	2	2	2	17	16	6	7	0	0	0	0	6	0	0	.000	1	4	0	0	2.5	1.000
1908		1	0	1.000	1.00	1	1	1	9	7	1	8	0	0	0	0	3	1	0	.333	0	2	0	0	2.0	1.000
1909		2	1	.667	2.25	4	3	3	32	22	8	20	1	0	0	0	16	3	0	.188	0	12	0	0	3.0	1.000
3 yrs.		3	3	.500	2.02	7	6	6 **6th**	58	45	15	35	1	0	0	0	*				1	18	0	0	2.7	1.000

Dominic Mulrenan

MULRENAN, DOMINIC JOSEPH
B. Dec. 18, 1893, Woburn, Mass. D. July 27, 1964, Melrose, Mass.
BR TR 5'11" 170 lbs.

Year	Team	W	L	PCT	ERA	G	GS	CG	IP	H	BB	SO	ShO	Relief Pitching W	Relief Pitching L	Relief Pitching SV	Batting AB	Batting H	Batting HR	BA	PO	A	E	DP	TC/G	FA
1921	**CHI A**	2	8	.200	7.23	12	10	3	56	84	36	10	0	0	1	0	20	3	0	.150	4	17	2	0	1.9	.913

Frank Mulroney

MULRONEY, FRANCIS JOSEPH
B. Apr. 8, 1903, Mallard, Iowa D. Nov. 11, 1985, Aberdeen, Wash.
BR TR 6' 170 lbs.

Year	Team	W	L	PCT	ERA	G	GS	CG	IP	H	BB	SO	ShO	Relief Pitching W	Relief Pitching L	Relief Pitching SV	Batting AB	Batting H	Batting HR	BA	PO	A	E	DP	TC/G	FA
1930	**BOS A**	0	1	.000	3.00	2	0	0	3	3	0	2	0	0	1	0	0	0	0	—	0	1	0	0	0.5	1.000

Bob Muncrief

MUNCRIEF, ROBERT CLEVELAND
B. Jan. 28, 1916, Madill, Okla. D. Feb. 6, 1996, Duncanville, Tex.
BR TR 6′ 2″ 190 lbs.

Year	Team	Lg	W	L	PCT	ERA	G	GS	CG	IP	H	BB	SO	ShO	Relief Pitching W	Relief Pitching L	Relief Pitching SV	Batting AB	Batting H	Batting HR	BA	PO	A	E	DP	TC/G	FA
1937	STL	A	0	0	—	4.50	1	1	0	2	3	2	0	0	0	0	0	0	0	0	—	0	0	0	0	0.0	.000
1939			0	0	—	15.00	2	0	0	3	7	3	1	0	0	0	0	0	0	0	—	0	0	0	0	0.0	.000
1941			13	9	.591	3.65	36	24	12	214.1	221	53	67	2	1	0	1	76	18	0	.237	13	36	2	2	1.4	.961
1942			6	8	.429	3.89	24	18	7	134.1	149	31	39	1	0	0	0	45	5	0	.111	9	25	0	2	1.4	1.000
1943			13	12	.520	2.81	35	27	12	205	211	48	80	3	1	1	1	66	10	0	.152	10	28	1	2	1.1	.974
1944			13	8	.619	3.08	33	27	12	219.1	216	50	88	3	0	1	1	78	18	0	.231	16	35	1	1	1.6	.981
1945			13	4	.765	2.72	27	15	10	145.2	132	44	54	0	3	2	1	45	3	0	.067	9	22	2	1	1.2	.939
1946			3	12	.200	4.99	29	14	4	115.1	149	31	49	1	0	1	0	32	1	0	.031	7	13	2	1	0.8	.909
1947			8	14	.364	4.90	31	23	7	176.1	210	51	74	0	2	1	0	57	6	0	.105	6	29	0	2	1.1	1.000
1948	CLE	A	5	4	.556	3.98	21	9	1	72.1	76	31	24	1	2	0	0	18	2	0	.111	4	10	0	2	0.7	1.000
1949	2 teams	PIT N (13G 1–5)	CHI N (34G 5–6)																								
″	total		6	11	.353	5.12	47	7	2	110.2	124	44	47	0	4	7	5	21	5	0	.238	5	22	0	1	0.6	1.000
1951	NY	A	0	0	—	9.00	2	0	0	3	5	4	2	0	0	0	0	0	0	0	—	1	2	1	0	2.0	.750
12 yrs.			80	82	.494	3.80	288	165	67	1401.1	1503	392	525	11	13	13	9	438	68	0	.155	80	222	9	14	1.1	.971
WORLD SERIES																											
1944	STL	A	0	1	.000	1.35	2	0	0	6.2	5	4	4	0	0	1	0	1	0	0	.000	0	1	0	0	0.5	1.000
1948	CLE	A	0	0	—	0.00	1	0	0	2	1	0	0	0	0	0	0	0	0	0	—	1	0	0	0	1.0	1.000
2 yrs.			0	1	.000	1.04	3	0	0	8.2	6	4	4	0	0	1	0	1	0	0	.000	1	1	0	0	0.7	1.000

George Munger

MUNGER, GEORGE DAVID (Red)
B. Oct. 4, 1918, Houston, Tex.
BR TR 6′ 2″ 210 lbs.

Year	Team	Lg	W	L	PCT	ERA	G	GS	CG	IP	H	BB	SO	ShO	Relief Pitching W	Relief Pitching L	Relief Pitching SV	Batting AB	Batting H	Batting HR	BA	PO	A	E	DP	TC/G	FA
1943	STL	N	9	5	.643	3.95	32	9	5	93.1	101	42	45	0	4	2	2	28	6	0	.214	3	24	1	3	0.9	.964
1944			11	3	.786	1.34	21	12	7	121	92	41	55	2	2	1	2	44	5	0	.114	8	33	2	5	2.0	.953
1946			2	2	.500	3.33	10	7	2	48.2	47	12	28	0	0	0	1	16	4	0	.250	1	16	0	3	1.7	1.000
1947			16	5	.762	3.37	40	31	13	224.1	218	76	123	6	0	0	3	81	15	0	.185	5	55	2	1	1.5	.968
1948			10	11	.476	4.50	39	25	7	166	179	74	72	2	0	2	0	50	8	0	.160	8	37	0	5	1.2	1.000
1949			15	8	.652	3.87	35	28	12	188.1	179	87	82	2	0	2	2	66	17	1	.258	4	38	1	2	1.2	.977
1950			7	8	.467	3.90	32	20	5	154.2	158	70	61	1	1	1	0	51	7	0	.137	3	32	0	2	1.1	1.000
1951			4	6	.400	5.32	23	11	3	94.2	106	46	44	0	2	2	0	29	5	0	.172	7	25	1	2	1.4	.970
1952	2 teams	STL N (1G 0–1)	PIT N (5G 0–3)																								
″	total		0	4	.000	7.92	6	5	0	30.2	37	11	9	0	0	0	0	9	0	0	.000	1	12	0	3	2.2	1.000
1956	PIT	N	3	4	.429	4.04	35	13	0	107	126	41	45	0	1	1	2	28	3	0	.107	4	16	2	1	0.6	.909
10 yrs.			77	56	.579	3.83	273	161	54	1228.2	1243	500	564	13	10	11	12	402	70	1	.174	44	288	9	27	1.2	.974
WORLD SERIES																											
1946	STL	N	1	0	1.000	1.00	1	1	1	9	9	3	2	0	0	0	0	4	1	0	.250	1	0	0	0	1.0	1.000

Van Lingle Mungo

MUNGO, VAN LINGLE
B. June 8, 1911, Pageland, S. C. D. Feb. 12, 1985, Pageland, S. C.
BR TR 6′ 2″ 185 lbs.

Year	Team	Lg	W	L	PCT	ERA	G	GS	CG	IP	H	BB	SO	ShO	Relief Pitching W	Relief Pitching L	Relief Pitching SV	Batting AB	Batting H	Batting HR	BA	PO	A	E	DP	TC/G	FA
1931	BKN	N	3	1	.750	2.32	5	4	2	31	27	13	12	1	0	0	0	12	3	0	.250	1	4	0	0	1.0	1.000
1932			13	11	.542	4.43	39	33	11	223.1	224	**115**	107	1	0	1	2	79	16	0	.203	15	48	2	4	1.7	.969
1933			16	15	.516	2.72	41	28	18	248	223	84	110	3	2	2	0	84	15	0	.179	15	55	3	1	1.8	.959
1934			18	16	.529	3.37	45	**38**	22	**315.1**	**300**	**104**	184	3	1	1	3	121	30	0	.248	14	67	3	3	1.9	.964
1935			16	10	.615	3.65	37	26	18	214.1	205	90	143	**4**	1	2	2	90	26	0	.289	10	45	2	1	1.5	.965
1936			18	19	.486	3.35	45	**37**	22	311.2	275	**118**	**238**	2	1	2	3	123	22	0	.179	12	67	8	7	1.9	.908
1937			9	11	.450	2.91	25	21	14	161	136	56	122	0	0	0	3	64	16	0	.250	12	41	0	0	2.1	1.000
1938			4	11	.267	3.92	24	18	6	133.1	133	72	72	2	1	1	0	47	9	0	.191	4	31	0	2	1.5	1.000
1939			4	5	.444	3.26	14	10	1	77.1	70	33	34	0	1	0	0	29	10	0	.345	4	10	0	0	0.9	1.000
1940			1	0	1.000	2.45	7	0	0	22	24	10	9	0	1	0	1	7	0	0	.000	0	3	0	0	0.4	1.000
1941			0	0	—	4.50	2	0	0	2	1	2	0	0	0	0	0	0	0	0	—	0	1	0	0	0.5	1.000
1942	NY	N	1	2	.333	5.94	9	5	0	36.1	38	21	27	0	0	0	0	14	3	0	.214	2	6	0	2	0.9	1.000
1943			3	7	.300	3.91	45	13	2	154.1	140	79	83	2	0	0	2	44	7	0	.159	5	36	0	1	0.9	1.000
1945			14	7	.667	3.20	26	26	7	183	161	71	101	2	0	0	0	73	17	0	.233	6	34	5	1	1.7	.889
14 yrs.			120	115	.511	3.47	364	259	123	2113	1957	868	1242	20	8	9	16	787	174	0	.221	100	448	23	22	1.6	.960

Manny Muniz

MUNIZ, MANUEL
Born Manuel Muniz (Rodriguez).
B. Dec. 31, 1947, Caguas, Puerto Rico
BR TR 5′11″ 190 lbs.

Year	Team	Lg	W	L	PCT	ERA	G	GS	CG	IP	H	BB	SO	ShO	Relief Pitching W	Relief Pitching L	Relief Pitching SV	Batting AB	Batting H	Batting HR	BA	PO	A	E	DP	TC/G	FA
1971	PHI	N	0	1	.000	7.20	5	0	0	10	9	8	6	0	0	1	0	1	0	0	.000	0	1	0	0	0.2	1.000

Scott Munninghoff

MUNNINGHOFF, SCOTT ANDREW
B. Dec. 5, 1958, Cincinnati, Ohio
BR TR 6′ 175 lbs.

Year	Team	Lg	W	L	PCT	ERA	G	GS	CG	IP	H	BB	SO	ShO	Relief Pitching W	Relief Pitching L	Relief Pitching SV	Batting AB	Batting H	Batting HR	BA	PO	A	E	DP	TC/G	FA
1980	PHI	N	0	0	—	4.50	4	0	0	6	8	5	2	0	0	0	0	1	1	0	1.000	2	1	0	0	0.8	1.000

Les Munns

MUNNS, LESLIE ERNEST (Big Ed, Nemo)
B. Dec. 1, 1908, Fort Bragg, Calif.
BR TR 6′ 5″ 212 lbs.

Year	Team	Lg	W	L	PCT	ERA	G	GS	CG	IP	H	BB	SO	ShO	Relief Pitching W	Relief Pitching L	Relief Pitching SV	Batting AB	Batting H	Batting HR	BA	PO	A	E	DP	TC/G	FA
1934	BKN	N	3	7	.300	4.71	33	9	4	99.1	106	60	41	0	1	1	0	29	7	0	.241	7	29	1	0	1.1	.973
1935			1	3	.250	5.55	21	5	0	58.1	74	33	13	0	1	0	1	16	3	0	.188	7	4	3	0	0.7	.786
1936	STL	N	0	3	.000	3.00	7	1	0	24	23	12	4	0	0	3	1	9	1	0	.111	2	10	0	0	1.7	1.000
3 yrs.			4	13	.235	4.76	61	15	4	181.2	203	105	58	0	2	4	2	54	11	0	.204	16	43	4	0	1.0	.937

Bobby Munoz

MUNOZ, ROBERTO
Born Roberto Munoz (Sbert).
B. Mar. 3, 1968, Rio Piedras, Puerto Rico.
BR TR 6′ 7″ 237 lbs.

Year	Team	Lg	W	L	PCT	ERA	G	GS	CG	IP	H	BB	SO	ShO	Relief Pitching W	Relief Pitching L	Relief Pitching SV	Batting AB	Batting H	Batting HR	BA	PO	A	E	DP	TC/G	FA
1993	NY	A	3	3	.500	5.32	38	0	0	45.2	48	26	33	0	3	3	0	0	0	0	—	1	6	0	1	0.2	1.000
1994	PHI	N	7	5	.583	2.67	21	14	1	104.1	101	35	59	0	0	0	1	34	7	1	.206	8	18	1	1	1.3	.963
1995			0	2	.000	5.74	3	3	0	15.2	15	9	6	0	0	0	0	5	0	0	.000	0	3	1	0	1.3	.750
3 yrs.			10	10	.500	3.69	62	17	1	165.2	164	70	98	0	3	3	1	39	7	1	.179	9	27	2	2	0.6	.947

Mike Munoz

MUNOZ, MICHAEL ANTHONY
B. July 12, 1965, Baldwin Park, Calif.
BL TL 6′ 2″ 190 lbs.

Year	Team	Lg	W	L	PCT	ERA	G	GS	CG	IP	H	BB	SO	ShO	Relief Pitching W	Relief Pitching L	Relief Pitching SV	Batting AB	Batting H	Batting HR	BA	PO	A	E	DP	TC/G	FA
1989	LA	N	0	0	—	16.88	3	0	0	2.2	5	2	3	0	0	0	0	0	0	0	—	1	1	0	0	0.7	1.000
1990			0	1	.000	3.18	8	0	0	5.2	6	3	2	0	0	1	0	1	0	0	.000	0	0	0	0	0.0	.000
1991	DET	A	0	0	—	9.64	6	0	0	9.1	14	5	3	0	0	0	0	0	0	0	—	0	3	0	0	0.5	1.000

Mike Munoz *continued*

Year	Team	W	L	PCT	ERA	G	GS	CG	IP	H	BB	SO	ShO	Relief W	Relief L	Relief SV	AB	H	HR	BA	PO	A	E	DP	TC/G	FA
1992		1	2	.333	3.00	65	0	0	48	44	25	23	0	1	2	2	0	0	0	—	8	12	0	0	0.3	1.000
1993	2 teams DET A (8G 0–1) CLR N (21G 2–1)																									
″	total	2	2	.500	4.71	29	0	0	21	25	15	17	0	2	2	0	0	0	0		1	5	0	0	0.2	1.000
1994	CLR N	4	2	.667	3.74	57	0	0	45.2	37	31	32	0	4	2	1	0	0	0	—	6	12	1	2	0.3	.947
1995		2	4	.333	7.42	64	0	0	43.2	54	27	37	0	2	4	2	2	1	0	.500	5	7	0	0	0.2	1.000
7 yrs.		9	11	.450	5.06	232	0	0	176	185	108	117	0	9	11	5	3	1	0	.333	21	40	1	2	0.3	.984
DIVISIONAL PLAYOFF SERIES																										
1995	CLR N	0	1	.000	13.50	4	0	0	1.1	4	1	1	0	0	1	0	0	0	0	—	0	0	0	0	0.0	.000

BR TR 6′ 3″ 210 lbs.

MUNOZ, JUAN OSCAR
B. Sept. 25, 1969, Hialeah, Fla.

Oscar Munoz

Year	Team	W	L	PCT	ERA	G	GS	CG	IP	H	BB	SO	ShO	Relief W	Relief L	Relief SV	AB	H	HR	BA	PO	A	E	DP	TC/G	FA
1995	MIN A	2	1	.667	5.60	10	3	0	35.1	40	17	25	0	2	0	0	0	0	0	—	1	4	0	0	0.5	1.000

BR TR 6′ 2″ 188 lbs.

MURA, STEPHEN ANDREW
B. Feb. 12, 1955, New Orleans, La.

Steve Mura

Year	Team	W	L	PCT	ERA	G	GS	CG	IP	H	BB	SO	ShO	Relief W	Relief L	Relief SV	AB	H	HR	BA	PO	A	E	DP	TC/G	FA
1978	SD N	0	2	.000	11.25	5	2	0	8	15	5	5	0	0	0	0	1	0	0	.000	0	1	2	0	0.6	.333
1979		4	4	.500	3.08	38	5	0	73	57	37	59	0	3	2	2	10	0	0	.000	5	8	1	0	0.4	.929
1980		8	7	.533	3.67	37	23	3	169	149	86	109	1	0	0	2	51	7	0	.137	9	26	1	3	1.0	.972
1981		5	**14**	.263	4.27	23	22	2	139	156	50	70	0	0	1	0	44	6	0	.136	14	26	1	0	1.8	.976
1982	STL N	12	11	.522	4.05	35	30	7	184.1	196	80	84	1	0	0	0	53	3	0	.057	14	22	2	3	1.1	.947
1983	CHI A	0	0	—	4.38	6	0	0	12.1	13	6	4	0	0	0	0	0	0	0	—	0	1	1	0	0.3	.500
1985	OAK A	1	1	.500	4.13	23	1	0	48	41	25	29	0	1	1	1	0	0	0	—	2	6	1	0	0.4	.889
7 yrs.		30	39	.435	3.99	167	83	12	633.2	627	289	360	2	4	4	5	159	16	0	.101	44	90	9	6	0.9	.937

BL TL 6′ 180 lbs.

MURAKAMI, MASANORI
B. May 6, 1944, Otsuki, Japan.

Masanori Murakami

Year	Team	W	L	PCT	ERA	G	GS	CG	IP	H	BB	SO	ShO	Relief W	Relief L	Relief SV	AB	H	HR	BA	PO	A	E	DP	TC/G	FA
1964	SF N	1	0	1.000	1.80	9	0	0	15	8	1	15	0	1	0	1	3	0	0	.000	0	0	0	0	0.0	.000
1965		4	1	.800	3.75	45	1	0	74.1	57	22	85	0	4	1	8	13	2	0	.154	0	4	0	0	0.1	1.000
2 yrs.		5	1	.833	3.43	54	1	0	89.1	65	23	100	0	5	1	9	16	2	0	.125	0	4	0	0	0.1	1.000

BR TL 6′ 185 lbs.

MURCHISON, THOMAS MALCOLM
B. Oct. 8, 1896, Liberty, N. C. D. Oct. 20, 1962, Liberty, N. C.

Tim Murchison

Year	Team	W	L	PCT	ERA	G	GS	CG	IP	H	BB	SO	ShO	Relief W	Relief L	Relief SV	AB	H	HR	BA	PO	A	E	DP	TC/G	FA
1917	STL N	0	0	—	0.00	1	0	0	1	0	2	2	0	0	0	0	0	0	0	—	0	0	0	0	0.0	.000
1920	CLE A	0	0	—	0.00	2	0	0	5	3	4	0	0	0	0	0	1	0	0	.000	0	4	0	0	2.0	1.000
2 yrs.		0	0		0.00	3	0	0	6	3	6	2	0	0	0	0	1	0	0	.000	0	4	0	0	1.3	1.000

BR TR 6′ 3″ 195 lbs.

MURFF, JOHN ROBERT
B. Apr. 1, 1921, Burlington, Tex.

Red Murff

Year	Team	W	L	PCT	ERA	G	GS	CG	IP	H	BB	SO	ShO	Relief W	Relief L	Relief SV	AB	H	HR	BA	PO	A	E	DP	TC/G	FA
1956	MIL N	0	0	—	4.44	14	1	0	24.1	25	7	18	0	0	0	1	5	1	0	.200	4	4	1	0	0.6	.889
1957		2	2	.500	4.85	12	1	0	26	31	11	13	0	2	2	2	6	0	0	.000	1	7	0	0	0.7	1.000
2 yrs.		2	2	.500	4.65	26	2	0	50.1	56	18	31	0	2	2	3	11	1	0	.091	5	11	1	0	0.7	.941

MURPHY, ROBERT J.
B. Dec. 26, 1866, Dutchess County, N.Y. Deceased.

Bob Murphy

Year	Team	W	L	PCT	ERA	G	GS	CG	IP	H	BB	SO	ShO	Relief W	Relief L	Relief SV	AB	H	HR	BA	PO	A	E	DP	TC/G	FA
1890	NY N	1	0	1.000	5.50	3	2	1	18	23	10	8	0	0	0	0	9	1	0	.111	0	2	0	0	0.7	1.000

TR 5′ 9″ 130 lbs.

MURPHY, CORNELIUS B. (Razzle Dazzle)
B. Oct. 15, 1863, Worcester, Mass. D. Aug. 1, 1914, Worcester, Mass.

Con Murphy

Year	Team	W	L	PCT	ERA	G	GS	CG	IP	H	BB	SO	ShO	Relief W	Relief L	Relief SV	AB	H	HR	BA	PO	A	E	DP	TC/G	FA
1884	PHI N	0	3	.000	*6.58*	3	3	3	26	37	6	10	0	0	0	0	10	0	0	.000	0	8	0	0	2.7	1.000
1890	2 teams BKN P (20G 4–10) BKN AA (12G 3–9)																									
″	total	7	19	.269	5.19	32	26	21	234	289	128	55	0	0	**2**	2	119	24	1	.202	15	67	8	3	2.3	.911
2 yrs.		7	22	.241	5.33	35	29	24	260	326	134	65	0	0	2	2	129	24	1	.186	15	75	8	3	2.3	.918

BR TR 6′ 2″ 195 lbs.

MURPHY, DANIEL LEE
B. Sept. 18, 1964, Artesia, Calif.

Dan Murphy

Year	Team	W	L	PCT	ERA	G	GS	CG	IP	H	BB	SO	ShO	Relief W	Relief L	Relief SV	AB	H	HR	BA	PO	A	E	DP	TC/G	FA
1989	SD N	0	0	—	5.68	7	0	0	6.1	6	4	1	0	0	0	0	0	0	0	—	0	1	0	0	0.1	1.000

BL TR 5′11″ 185 lbs.

MURPHY, DANIEL FRANCIS
B. Aug. 23, 1942, Beverly, Mass.

Danny Murphy

Year	Team	W	L	PCT	ERA	G	GS	CG	IP	H	BB	SO	ShO	Relief W	Relief L	Relief SV	AB	H	HR	BA	PO	A	E	DP	TC/G	FA
1969	CHI A	2	1	.667	2.01	17	0	0	31.1	28	10	16	0	2	1	4	1	0	0	.000	40	1	1	1	2.0	.976
1970		2	3	.400	5.67	51	0	0	81	82	49	42	0	2	3	5	6	2	1	.333	4	10	1	1	0.3	.933
2 yrs.		4	4	.500	4.65	68	0	0	112.1	110	59	58	0	4	4	9	*				54	16	2	2	0.7	.972

TR 6′ 1″ 186 lbs.

MURPHY, EDWARD J.
B. Jan. 22, 1877, Auburn, N. Y. D. Jan. 29, 1935, Weedsport, N. Y.

Ed Murphy

Year	Team	W	L	PCT	ERA	G	GS	CG	IP	H	BB	SO	ShO	Relief W	Relief L	Relief SV	AB	H	HR	BA	PO	A	E	DP	TC/G	FA
1898	PHI N	1	2	.333	5.10	7	3	2	30	41	10	8	0	0	0	0	14	5	0	.357	3	12	2	2	2.4	.882
1901	STL N	10	9	.526	4.20	23	21	16	165	201	32	42	0	0	0	0	64	16	1	.250	7	52	1	1	2.6	.983
1902		9	7	.563	3.02	23	17	12	164	187	31	37	1	1	0	1	61	16	0	.262	8	52	3	1	2.7	.952
1903		4	8	.333	3.31	15	12	9	106	108	38	16	0	1	1	0	64	13	0	.203	71	34	4	4	4.5	.963
4 yrs.		24	26	.480	3.64	68	53	39	465	537	111	103	1	2	1	1	203	50	1	.246	89	150	10	8	3.2	.960

5′11″ 160 lbs.

MURPHY, JOSEPH AKIN
B. Sept. 7, 1866, St. Louis, Mo. D. Mar. 28, 1951, Coral Gables, Fla.

Joe Murphy

Year	Team	W	L	PCT	ERA	G	GS	CG	IP	H	BB	SO	ShO	Relief W	Relief L	Relief SV	AB	H	HR	BA	PO	A	E	DP	TC/G	FA
1886	3 teams CIN AA (5G 2–3) STL N (4G 0–4) STL AA (1G 1–0)																									
″	total	3	7	.300	6.07	10	10	9	86	100	40	25	0	0	0	0	35	3	0	.086	3	8	1	0	1.1	.917
1887	STL AA	1	0	1.000	*5.00*	1	1	1	9	13	4	5	0	0	0	0	6	1	0	.167	1	3	0	0	4.0	1.000
2 yrs.		4	7	.364	5.97	11	11	10	95	113	44	30	0	0	0	0	41	4	0	.098	4	11	1	0	1.3	.938

MURPHY, JOHN H.
B. Mar. 8, 1867, Philadelphia, Pa. Deceased.

John Murphy

Year	Team	W	L	PCT	ERA	G	GS	CG	IP	H	BB	SO	ShO	Relief W	Relief L	Relief SV	AB	H	HR	BA	PO	A	E	DP	TC/G	FA
1884	2 teams ALT U (14G 5–6) WIL U (7G 0–6)																									
″	total	5	12	.294	3.61	21	16	15	159.2	193	11	73	0	1	0	0	125	16	0	.128	27	54	19	4	2.5	.810

Johnny Murphy

MURPHY, JOHN JOSEPH (Fireman, Fordham Johnny, Grandma)
B. July 14, 1908, New York, N. Y. D. Jan. 14, 1970, New York, N. Y.
BR TR 6′ 2″ 190 lbs.

Year	Team	W	L	PCT	ERA	G	GS	CG	IP	H	BB	SO	ShO	Relief Pitching W	Relief Pitching L	Relief Pitching SV	Batting AB	Batting H	Batting HR	BA	PO	A	E	DP	TC/G	FA
1932	NY A	0	0	—	16.20	2	0	0	3.1	7	3	2	0	0	0	0	1	1	0	1.000	0	1	0	0	0.5	1.000
1934		14	10	.583	3.12	40	20	10	207.2	193	76	70	0	3	2	4	71	7	0	.099	19	41	3	6	1.6	.952
1935		10	5	.667	4.08	40	8	4	117	110	55	28	0	**6**	4	5	32	5	0	.156	6	21	2	0	0.7	.931
1936		9	3	.750	3.38	27	5	2	88	90	36	34	0	5	2	5	36	13	0	.361	9	19	3	4	1.1	.903
1937		13	4	.765	4.17	39	4	0	110	121	50	36	0	**12**	4	10	35	8	0	.229	9	39	3	1	1.3	.941
1938		8	2	.800	4.24	32	2	1	91.1	90	41	43	0	**8**	1	**11**	32	2	0	.063	7	21	1	0	0.9	.966
1939		3	6	.333	4.40	38	0	0	61.1	57	28	30	0	3	6	**19**	11	2	0	.182	3	12	1	1	0.4	.938
1940		8	4	.667	3.69	35	1	0	63.1	58	15	23	0	**8**	4	9	13	1	0	.077	2	15	0	0	0.5	1.000
1941		8	3	.727	1.98	35	0	0	77.1	68	40	29	0	**8**	3	**15**	18	1	0	.056	3	11	1	1	0.4	.933
1942		4	10	.286	3.41	31	0	0	58	66	23	24	0	4	**10**	**11**	13	2	0	.154	4	13	3	1	0.6	.850
1943		12	4	.750	2.51	37	0	0	68	44	30	31	0	**12**	4	8	19	1	0	.053	4	12	2	1	0.5	.889
1946		4	2	.667	3.40	27	0	0	45	40	19	19	0	4	2	7	6	0	0	.000	6	11	2	2	0.7	.895
1947	BOS A	0	0	—	2.80	32	0	0	54.2	41	28	9	0	0	0	3	11	3	0	.273	5	10	1	0	0.5	.938
13 yrs.		93	53	.637	3.50	415	40	17	1045	985	444	378	0	73	42	107	298	46	0	.154	77	226	22	17	0.8	.932
WORLD SERIES																										
1936	NY A	0	0	—	3.38	1	0	0	2.2	1	1	1	0	0	0	1	2	1	0	.500	0	0	0	0	0.0	.000
1937		0	0	—	0.00	1	0	0	0.1	0	0	0	0	0	0	1	0	0	0	—	0	0	0	0	0.0	.000
1938		0	0	—	0.00	1	0	0	2	2	1	1	0	0	0	1	0	0	0	—	0	0	0	0	0.0	.000
1939		1	0	1.000	2.70	1	0	0	3.1	5	0	2	0	1	0	0	2	0	0	.000	0	3	0	0	3.0	1.000
1941		1	0	1.000	0.00	2	0	0	6	2	1	3	0	1	0	0	2	0	0	.000	1	0	0	0	0.5	1.000
1943		0	0	—	0.00	2	0	0	2	1	1	1	0	0	0	1	0	0	0	—	0	1	0	0	0.5	1.000
6 yrs.		2	0	1.000	1.10	8	0	0	16.1	11	4	8	0	2	0	4 **2nd**	6	1	0	.167	1	4	0	0	0.6	1.000

Rob Murphy

MURPHY, ROBERT ALBERT, JR.
B. May 26, 1960, Miami, Fla.
BL TL 6′ 2″ 200 lbs.

Year	Team	W	L	PCT	ERA	G	GS	CG	IP	H	BB	SO	ShO	Relief Pitching W	Relief Pitching L	Relief Pitching SV	Batting AB	Batting H	Batting HR	BA	PO	A	E	DP	TC/G	FA
1985	CIN N	0	0	—	6.00	2	0	0	3	2	2	1	0	0	0	0	0	0	0	—	0	0	0	0	0.0	.000
1986		6	0	1.000	0.72	34	0	0	50.1	26	21	36	0	6	0	1	3	0	0	.000	1	9	0	0	0.3	1.000
1987		8	5	.615	3.04	87	0	0	100.2	91	32	99	0	8	5	3	5	1	0	.200	7	14	0	0	0.2	1.000
1988		0	6	.000	3.08	**76**	0	0	84.2	69	38	74	0	0	6	3	0	0	0	—	4	14	0	2	0.2	1.000
1989	BOS A	5	7	.417	2.74	74	0	0	105	97	41	107	0	5	7	9	0	0	0	—	7	15	0	1	0.3	1.000
1990		0	6	.000	6.32	68	0	0	57	85	32	54	0	0	6	7	0	0	0	—	4	7	1	2	0.2	.917
1991	SEA A	0	1	.000	3.00	57	0	0	48	47	19	34	0	0	1	4	0	0	0	—	2	8	2	0	0.2	.833
1992	HOU N	3	1	.750	4.04	59	0	0	55.2	56	21	42	0	3	1	0	1	0	0	.000	2	12	0	0	0.2	1.000
1993	STL N	5	7	.417	4.87	73	0	0	64.2	73	20	41	0	5	7	1	2	1	0	.500	3	8	1	1	0.2	.917
1994	2 teams STL N (50G 4–3) NY A (3G 0–0)																									
″	total	4	3	.571	4.29	53	0	0	42	38	13	25	0	4	3	2	0	0	0		0	7	0	1	0.1	1.000
1995	2 teams LA N (6G 0–1) FLA N (8G 1–1)																									
″	total	1	2	.333	10.95	14	0	0	12.1	14	8	7	0	1	2	0	1	1	0	1.000	0	3	0	0	0.2	1.000
11 yrs.		32	38	.457	3.64	597	0	0	623.1	598	247	520	0	32	38	30	12	3	0	.250	30	97	4	7	0.2	.969
LEAGUE CHAMPIONSHIP SERIES																										
1990	BOS A	0	0	—	13.50	1	0	0	0.2	2	1	0	0	0	0	0	0	0	0	—	0	0	0	0	0.0	.000

Tom Murphy

MURPHY, THOMAS ANDREW
B. Dec. 30, 1945, Cleveland, Ohio.
BR TR 6′ 3″ 185 lbs.

Year	Team	W	L	PCT	ERA	G	GS	CG	IP	H	BB	SO	ShO	Relief Pitching W	Relief Pitching L	Relief Pitching SV	Batting AB	Batting H	Batting HR	BA	PO	A	E	DP	TC/G	FA
1968	CAL A	5	6	.455	2.17	15	15	3	99.1	67	28	56	0	0	0	0	28	0	0	.000	5	11	3	0	1.3	.842
1969		10	16	.385	4.21	36	35	4	215.2	213	69	100	0	0	0	0	71	10	0	.141	14	38	5	6	1.6	.912
1970		16	13	.552	4.24	39	38	5	227	223	81	99	2	0	0	0	76	14	1	.184	22	29	5	3	1.4	.911
1971		6	17	.261	3.78	37	36	7	243	228	82	89	0	0	0	0	75	13	0	.173	19	49	4	2	1.9	.944
1972	2 teams CAL A (6G 0–0) KC A (18G 4–4)																									
″	total	4	4	.500	3.36	24	9	1	80.1	90	24	36	1	1	0	1	14	0	0	.000	3	20	1	1	1.0	.958
1973	STL N	3	7	.300	3.76	19	13	2	88.2	89	22	42	0	1	0	0	23	4	0	.174	8	16	1	0	1.3	.960
1974	MIL A	10	10	.500	1.90	70	0	0	123	97	51	47	0	10	10	20	2	1	0	.500	4	30	0	2	0.5	1.000
1975		1	9	.100	4.60	52	0	0	72.1	85	27	32	0	1	**9**	20	0	0	0	—	6	11	2	1	0.4	.895
1976	2 teams MIL A (15G 0–1) BOS A (37G 4–5)																									
″	total	4	6	.400	4.17	52	0	0	99.1	116	34	39	0	4	6	9	0	0	0		7	16	2	1	0.5	.920
1977	2 teams BOS A (16G 0–1) TOR A (19G 2–1)																									
″	total	2	2	.500	4.79	35	1	0	82.2	107	30	39	0	1	2	2	0	0	0		5	14	0	0	0.5	1.000
1978	TOR A	6	9	.400	3.93	50	0	0	94	87	37	36	0	6	9	7	0	0	0	—	4	24	0	1	0.6	1.000
1979		1	2	.333	5.50	10	0	0	18	23	8	6	0	1	2	0	0	0	0	—	3	5	0	1	0.8	1.000
12 yrs.		68	101	.402	3.78	439	147	22	1443.1	1425	493	621	3	25	38	59	289	42	1	.145	100	263	23	18	0.9	.940

Walter Murphy

MURPHY, WALTER JOSEPH
B. Sept. 27, 1907, New York, N. Y. D. Mar. 23, 1976, Houston, Tex.
BR TR 6′ 1½″ 180 lbs.

Year	Team	W	L	PCT	ERA	G	GS	CG	IP	H	BB	SO	ShO	Relief Pitching W	Relief Pitching L	Relief Pitching SV	Batting AB	Batting H	Batting HR	BA	PO	A	E	DP	TC/G	FA
1931	BOS A	0	0	—	9.00	2	0	0	2	4	1	0	0	0	0	0	0	0	0	—	0	0	0	0	0.0	.000

Amby Murray

MURRAY, JOSEPH AMBROSE
B. June 14, 1913, Fall River, Mass.
BL TL 5′ 7″ 150 lbs.

Year	Team	W	L	PCT	ERA	G	GS	CG	IP	H	BB	SO	ShO	Relief Pitching W	Relief Pitching L	Relief Pitching SV	Batting AB	Batting H	Batting HR	BA	PO	A	E	DP	TC/G	FA
1936	BOS N	0	0	—	4.09	4	1	0	11	15	3	2	0	0	0	0	4	1	0	.250	0	3	0	0	0.8	1.000

Dale Murray

MURRAY, DALE ALBERT
B. Feb. 2, 1950, Cuero, Tex.
BR TR 6′ 4″ 205 lbs.

Year	Team	W	L	PCT	ERA	G	GS	CG	IP	H	BB	SO	ShO	Relief Pitching W	Relief Pitching L	Relief Pitching SV	Batting AB	Batting H	Batting HR	BA	PO	A	E	DP	TC/G	FA
1974	MON N	1	1	.500	1.03	32	0	0	70	46	23	31	0	1	1	10	10	0	0	.000	3	13	2	0	0.6	.889
1975		15	8	.652	3.97	63	0	0	111	134	39	43	0	**15**	8	9	14	3	0	.214	9	30	3	1	0.7	.929
1976		4	9	.308	3.26	**81**	0	0	113.1	117	37	35	0	4	**9**	13	8	0	0	.000	8	38	1	3	0.6	.979
1977	CIN N	7	2	.778	4.94	61	1	0	102	125	46	42	0	7	2	4	12	2	0	.167	8	17	5	3	0.5	.833
1978	2 teams CIN N (15G 1–1) NY N (53G 8–5)																									
″	total	9	6	.600	3.78	68	0	0	119	119	53	62	0	9	6	7	10	0	0	.000	9	30	4	1	0.6	.907
1979	2 teams NY N (58G 4–8) MON N (9G 1–2)																									
″	total	5	10	.333	4.57	67	0	0	110.1	119	55	41	0	5	10	5	8	0	0	.000	5	19	1	3	0.4	.960
1980	MON N	0	1	.000	6.21	16	0	0	29	39	12	16	0	0	1	0	3	0	0	.000	4	1	1	0	0.4	.833
1981	TOR A	1	0	1.000	1.20	11	0	0	15	12	5	12	0	1	0	0	0	0	0	—	2	6	1	0	0.8	.889

Dale Murray *continued*

Year	Team	W	L	PCT	ERA	G	GS	CG	IP	H	BB	SO	ShO	Relief Pitching W	Relief Pitching L	Relief Pitching SV	Batting AB	Batting H	Batting HR	BA	PO	A	E	DP	TC/G	FA
1982		8	7	.533	3.16	56	0	0	111	115	32	60	0	8	7	11	0	0	0	—	5	32	2	2	0.7	.949
1983	NY A	2	4	.333	4.48	40	0	0	94.1	113	22	45	0	2	4	1	0	0	0	—	5	15	2	1	0.6	.909
1984		1	2	.333	4.94	19	0	0	23.2	30	5	13	0	1	2	0	0	0	0	—	0	4	1	0	0.3	.800
1985	2 teams NY A (3G 0–0) TEX A (1G 0–0)																									
"	total	0	0		15.00	4	0	0	3	7	0	0	0	0	0	0	0	0	0		0	1	0	0	0.3	1.000
12 yrs.		53	50	.515	3.85	518	1	0	901.2	976	329	400	0	53	50	60	65	5	0	.077	58	206	23	14	0.6	.920

George Murray

MURRAY, GEORGE KING (Smiler) BR TR 6′ 2″ 200 lbs.
B. Sept. 23, 1898, Charlotte, N. C. D. Oct. 18, 1955, Memphis, Tenn.

Year	Team	W	L	PCT	ERA	G	GS	CG	IP	H	BB	SO	ShO	Relief Pitching W	Relief Pitching L	Relief Pitching SV	Batting AB	Batting H	Batting HR	BA	PO	A	E	DP	TC/G	FA
1922	NY A	4	2	.667	3.97	22	3	0	56.2	53	26	14	0	4	1	0	18	5	1	.278	0	15	1	2	0.7	.938
1923	BOS A	7	11	.389	4.91	39	18	5	177.2	190	87	40	0	3	1	0	55	9	0	.164	5	41	3	1	1.3	.939
1924		2	9	.182	6.72	28	7	0	80.1	97	32	27	0	1	3	0	22	4	0	.182	2	20	2	0	0.9	.917
1926	WAS A	6	3	.667	5.64	12	12	5	81.1	89	37	28	0	0	0	0	36	5	0	.139	3	17	0	1	1.7	1.000
1927		1	1	.500	7.00	7	3	0	18	18	15	5	0	0	1	0	6	1	0	.167	0	0	0	0	0.0	.000
1933	CHI A	0	0	—	7.71	2	0	0	2.1	3	2	0	0	0	0	0	0	0	0	—	0	1	0	0	0.5	1.000
6 yrs.		20	26	.435	5.38	110	43	10	416.1	450	199	114	0	8	6	0	137	24	1	.175	10	94	6	4	1.0	.945

Jim Murray

MURRAY, JAMES FRANCIS (Big Jim) BB TL 6′ 2″ 200 lbs.
B. Dec. 31, 1900, Scranton, Pa. D. July 15, 1973, New York, N. Y.

Year	Team	W	L	PCT	ERA	G	GS	CG	IP	H	BB	SO	ShO	Relief Pitching W	Relief Pitching L	Relief Pitching SV	Batting AB	Batting H	Batting HR	BA	PO	A	E	DP	TC/G	FA
1922	BKN N	0	0	—	4.50	4	0	0	6	8	3	3	0	0	0	1	2	1	0	.500	1	0	0	0	0.3	1.000

Joe Murray

MURRAY, JOSEPH AMBROSE BL TL 6′ 165 lbs.
B. Nov. 11, 1920, Wilkes-Barre, Pa.

Year	Team	W	L	PCT	ERA	G	GS	CG	IP	H	BB	SO	ShO	Relief Pitching W	Relief Pitching L	Relief Pitching SV	Batting AB	Batting H	Batting HR	BA	PO	A	E	DP	TC/G	FA
1950	PHI A	0	3	.000	5.70	8	2	0	30	34	21	8	0	0	1	0	11	0	0	.000	3	7	0	0	1.3	1.000

Matt Murray

MURRAY, MATTHEW MICHAEL BL TR 6′ 6″ 240 lbs.
B. Sept. 26, 1970, Boston, Mass.

Year	Team	W	L	PCT	ERA	G	GS	CG	IP	H	BB	SO	ShO	Relief Pitching W	Relief Pitching L	Relief Pitching SV	Batting AB	Batting H	Batting HR	BA	PO	A	E	DP	TC/G	FA
1995	2 teams ATL N (4G 0–2) BOS A (2G 0–1)																									
"	total	0	3	.000	9.64	6	2	0	14	21	8	4	0	0	2	0	2	1	0	.500	1	5	0	1	1.0	1.000

Pat Murray

MURRAY, PATRICK JOSEPH BR TL 6′ 175 lbs.
B. July 18, 1897, Scottsville, N. Y. D. Nov. 5, 1983, Rochester, N. Y.

Year	Team	W	L	PCT	ERA	G	GS	CG	IP	H	BB	SO	ShO	Relief Pitching W	Relief Pitching L	Relief Pitching SV	Batting AB	Batting H	Batting HR	BA	PO	A	E	DP	TC/G	FA
1919	PHI N	0	2	.000	6.29	8	2	1	34.1	50	12	11	0	0	0	0	12	0	0	.000	1	9	1	0	1.4	.909

Dennis Musgraves

MUSGRAVES, DENNIS EUGENE BR TR 6′ 4″ 188 lbs.
B. Dec. 25, 1943, Indianapolis, Ind.

Year	Team	W	L	PCT	ERA	G	GS	CG	IP	H	BB	SO	ShO	Relief Pitching W	Relief Pitching L	Relief Pitching SV	Batting AB	Batting H	Batting HR	BA	PO	A	E	DP	TC/G	FA
1965	NY N	0	0	—	0.56	5	1	0	16	11	7	11	0	0	0	0	2	0	0	.000	1	2	0	0	0.6	1.000

Stan Musial

MUSIAL, STANLEY FRANK (Stan the Man) BL TL 6′ 175 lbs.
B. Nov. 21, 1920, Donora, Pa.
Hall of Fame 1969.

Year	Team	W	L	PCT	ERA	G	GS	CG	IP	H	BB	SO	ShO	Relief Pitching W	Relief Pitching L	Relief Pitching SV	Batting AB	Batting H	Batting HR	BA	PO	A	E	DP	TC/G	FA
1952	STL N	0	0	—	0.00	1	0	0		0	0	0	0	0	0	0	*				20	1	0	0	1.9	1.000

Jeff Musselman

MUSSELMAN, JEFFREY JOSEPH BL TL 6′ 180 lbs.
B. June 21, 1963, Doylestown, Pa.

Year	Team	W	L	PCT	ERA	G	GS	CG	IP	H	BB	SO	ShO	Relief Pitching W	Relief Pitching L	Relief Pitching SV	Batting AB	Batting H	Batting HR	BA	PO	A	E	DP	TC/G	FA
1986	TOR A	0	0	—	10.13	6	0	0	5.1	8	5	4	0	0	0	0	0	0	0	—	1	1	0	0	0.3	1.000
1987		12	5	.706	4.15	68	1	0	89	75	54	54	0	**12**	5	3	0	0	0	—	9	15	0	2	0.4	1.000
1988		8	5	.615	3.18	15	15	0	85	80	30	39	0	0	0	0	0	0	0	—	3	8	1	1	0.8	.917
1989	2 teams TOR A (5G 0–1) NY N (20G 3–2)																									
"	total	3	3	.500	5.30	25	3	0	37.1	46	23	14	0	3	2	0	0	0	0		6	12	2	0	0.8	.900
1990	NY N	0	2	.000	5.63	28	0	0	32	40	11	14	0	0	2	0	1	0	0	.000	5	5	0	0	0.4	1.000
5 yrs.		23	15	.605	4.31	142	19	0	248.2	249	123	125	0	15	9	3	1	0	0	.000	24	41	3	3	0.5	.956

Ron Musselman

MUSSELMAN, RALPH RONALD BR TR 6′ 2″ 185 lbs.
B. Nov. 11, 1954, Wilmington, N. C.

Year	Team	W	L	PCT	ERA	G	GS	CG	IP	H	BB	SO	ShO	Relief Pitching W	Relief Pitching L	Relief Pitching SV	Batting AB	Batting H	Batting HR	BA	PO	A	E	DP	TC/G	FA
1982	SEA A	1	0	1.000	3.45	12	0	0	15.2	18	6	9	0	1	0	0	0	0	0	—	1	4	1	0	0.5	.833
1984	TOR A	0	2	.000	2.11	11	0	0	21.1	18	10	9	0	0	2	1	0	0	0	—	0	3	0	0	0.3	1.000
1985		3	0	1.000	4.47	25	4	0	52.1	59	24	29	0	3	0	0	0	0	0	—	2	4	1	0	0.3	.857
3 yrs.		4	2	.667	3.73	48	4	0	89.1	95	40	47	0	4	2	1	0	0	0		3	11	2	0	0.3	.875

Paul Musser

MUSSER, PAUL BR TR 6′ 175 lbs.
B. June 24, 1889, Millheim, Pa. D. July 7, 1973, State College, Pa.

Year	Team	W	L	PCT	ERA	G	GS	CG	IP	H	BB	SO	ShO	Relief Pitching W	Relief Pitching L	Relief Pitching SV	Batting AB	Batting H	Batting HR	BA	PO	A	E	DP	TC/G	FA
1912	WAS A	1	0	1.000	2.61	7	2	0	20.2	16	16	10	0	0	0	1	7	0	0	.000	3	6	0	0	1.3	1.000
1919	BOS A	0	2	.000	4.12	5	4	1	19.2	26	8	14	0	0	0	0	8	0	0	.000	2	3	0	0	1.0	1.000
2 yrs.		1	2	.333	3.35	12	6	1	40.1	42	24	24	0	0	0	1	15	0	0	.000	5	9	0	0	1.2	1.000

Barney Mussill

MUSSILL, BERNARD JAMES BR TL 6′ 1″ 200 lbs.
B. Oct. 1, 1919, Bowerhill, Pa.

Year	Team	W	L	PCT	ERA	G	GS	CG	IP	H	BB	SO	ShO	Relief Pitching W	Relief Pitching L	Relief Pitching SV	Batting AB	Batting H	Batting HR	BA	PO	A	E	DP	TC/G	FA
1944	PHI N	0	1	.000	6.05	16	0	0	19.1	20	13	5	0	0	1	0	1	0	0	.000	0	4	0	0	0.3	1.000

Mike Mussina

MUSSINA, MICHAEL COLE BR TR 6′ 2″ 185 lbs.
B. Dec. 8, 1968, Williamsport, Pa.

Year	Team	W	L	PCT	ERA	G	GS	CG	IP	H	BB	SO	ShO	Relief Pitching W	Relief Pitching L	Relief Pitching SV	Batting AB	Batting H	Batting HR	BA	PO	A	E	DP	TC/G	FA
1991	BAL A	4	5	.444	2.87	12	12	2	87.2	77	21	52	0	0	0	0	0	0	0	—	4	11	0	1	1.3	1.000
1992		18	5	**.783**	2.54	32	32	8	241	212	48	130	4	0	0	0	0	0	0	—	13	31	1	0	1.4	.978
1993		14	6	.700	4.46	25	25	3	167.2	163	44	117	2	0	0	0	0	0	0	—	12	19	0	1	1.2	1.000
1994		16	5	.762	3.06	24	24	3	176.1	163	42	99	0	0	0	0	0	0	0	—	14	28	1	1	1.8	.977
1995		19	9	.679	3.29	32	32	7	221.2	187	50	158	4	0	0	0	0	0	0	—	13	26	2	3	1.3	.951
5 yrs.		71	30	.703	3.22	125	125	23	894.1	802	205	556	10	0	0	0	0	0	0		56	115	4	6	1.4	.977

Alex Mustaikis

MUSTAIKIS, ALEXANDER DOMINICK BR TR 6′ 3″ 180 lbs.
B. Mar. 26, 1909, Chelsea, Mass. D. Jan. 17, 1970, Scranton, Pa.

Year	Team	W	L	PCT	ERA	G	GS	CG	IP	H	BB	SO	ShO	Relief Pitching W	Relief Pitching L	Relief Pitching SV	Batting AB	Batting H	Batting HR	BA	PO	A	E	DP	TC/G	FA
1940	BOS A	0	1	.000	9.00	6	1	0	15	15	15	6	0	0	0	0	6	2	0	.333	2	7	1	1	1.7	.900

Jeff Mutis

MUTIS, JEFFREY THOMAS
B. Dec. 20, 1966, Allentown, Pa.
BL TL 6′ 2″ 185 lbs.

Year	Team		W	L	PCT	ERA	G	GS	CG	IP	H	BB	SO	ShO	Relief Pitching W	L	SV	Batting AB	H	HR	BA	PO	A	E	DP	TC/G	FA
1991	CLE	A	0	3	.000	11.68	3	3	0	12.1	23	7	6	0	0	0	0	0	0	0	—	1	1	0	0	0.7	1.000
1992			0	2	.000	9.53	3	2	0	11.1	24	6	8	0	0	0	0	0	0	0	—	0	2	0	0	0.7	1.000
1993			3	6	.333	5.78	17	13	1	81	93	33	29	1	0	0	0	0	0	0	—	3	17	0	1	1.2	1.000
1994	FLA	N	1	0	1.000	5.40	35	0	0	38.1	51	15	30	0	1	0	0	3	0	0	.000	2	6	1	1	0.3	.889
4 yrs.			4	11	.267	6.48	58	18	1	143	191	61	73	1	1	0	0	3	0	0	.000	6	26	1	2	0.6	.970

Elmer Myers

MYERS, ELMER GLENN
B. Mar. 2, 1894, York Springs, Pa. D. July 29, 1976, Collingwood, N. J.
BR TR 6′ 2″ 185 lbs.

Year	Team		W	L	PCT	ERA	G	GS	CG	IP	H	BB	SO	ShO	Relief Pitching W	L	SV	Batting AB	H	HR	BA	PO	A	E	DP	TC/G	FA
1915	PHI	A	1	0	1.000	0.00	1	1	1	9	2	5	12	1	0	0	0	3	0	0	.000	1	0	1	0	2.0	.500
1916			14	23	.378	3.66	44	35	31	315	280	**168**	182	2	1	1	1	126	27	0	.214	16	106	5	4	2.9	.961
1917			9	16	.360	4.42	38	23	13	201.2	221	79	88	2	1	2	3	73	18	0	.247	15	60	4	0	2.1	.949
1918			4	8	.333	4.63	18	15	5	95.1	101	42	17	1	0	0	1	35	5	0	.143	4	35	2	3	2.3	.951
1919	CLE	A	8	7	.533	3.74	23	15	6	134.2	134	43	38	1	2	0	1	46	11	0	.239	12	38	1	1	2.2	.980
1920	2 teams	CLE A (16G 2–4)	BOS A (12G 9–1)																								
″	total		11	5	.688	3.27	28	17	11	167.2	183	47	50	1	0	1	1	63	18	0	.286	10	39	4	0	1.9	.925
1921	BOS	A	8	12	.400	4.87	30	20	11	172	217	53	40	0	3	3	0	65	14	0	.215	7	45	1	4	1.8	.981
1922			0	1	.000	17.47	3	1	0	5.2	10	3	1	0	0	0	0	1	0	0	.000	0	2	0	0	0.7	1.000
8 yrs.			55	72	.433	4.06	185	127	78	1101	1148	440	428	8	7	7	7	412	93	0	.226	65	325	18	12	2.2	.956

Henry Myers

MYERS, HENRY C.
B. May 1858, Philadelphia, Pa. D. Apr. 18, 1895, Philadelphia, Pa.
Manager 1882.
BR TR 5′ 9″ 159 lbs.

Year	Team		W	L	PCT	ERA	G	GS	CG	IP	H	BB	SO	ShO	Relief Pitching W	L	SV	Batting AB	H	HR	BA	PO	A	E	DP	TC/G	FA
1882	BAL	AA	0	2	.000	*6.58*	6	2	1	26	30	4	7	0	0	0	0	*				1	2	0	0	3.0	1.000

Joe Myers

MYERS, JOSEPH WILLIAM
B. Mar. 18, 1882, Wilmington, Del. D. Feb. 11, 1956, Delaware City, Del.
BR TR 5′10½″ 205 lbs.

Year	Team		W	L	PCT	ERA	G	GS	CG	IP	H	BB	SO	ShO	Relief Pitching W	L	SV	Batting AB	H	HR	BA	PO	A	E	DP	TC/G	FA
1905	PHI	A	0	0	—	3.60	1	1	1	5	3	3	5	0	0	0	0	2	0	0	.000	0	1	0	0	1.0	1.000

Mike Myers

MYERS, MICHAEL STANLEY
B. June 26, 1969, Cook County, Ill.
BL TL 6′ 3″ 197 lbs.

Year	Team		W	L	PCT	ERA	G	GS	CG	IP	H	BB	SO	ShO	Relief Pitching W	L	SV	Batting AB	H	HR	BA	PO	A	E	DP	TC/G	FA
1995	2 teams	FLA N (2G 0–0)	DET A (11G 1–0)																								
″	total		1	0	1.000	7.56	13	0	0	8.1	11	7	4	0	1	0	0	0	0	0	—	1	1	0	0	0.2	1.000

Randy Myers

MYERS, RANDALL KIRK
B. Sept. 19, 1962, Vancouver, Wash.
BL TL 6′ 1″ 190 lbs.

Year	Team		W	L	PCT	ERA	G	GS	CG	IP	H	BB	SO	ShO	Relief Pitching W	L	SV	Batting AB	H	HR	BA	PO	A	E	DP	TC/G	FA
1985	NY	N	0	0	—	0.00	1	0	0	2	0	1	2	0	0	0	0	0	0	0	—	0	1	0	0	1.0	1.000
1986			0	0	—	4.22	10	0	0	10.2	11	9	13	0	0	0	0	0	0	0	—	0	2	0	0	0.2	1.000
1987			3	6	.333	3.96	54	0	0	75	61	30	92	0	3	6	6	7	2	0	.286	5	9	1	0	0.3	.933
1988			7	3	.700	1.72	55	0	0	68	45	17	69	0	7	3	26	4	1	0	.250	4	3	0	1	0.1	1.000
1989			7	4	.636	2.35	65	0	0	84.1	62	40	88	0	7	4	24	5	0	0	.000	3	11	0	0	0.2	1.000
1990	CIN	N	4	6	.400	2.08	66	0	0	86.2	59	38	98	0	4	6	31	4	1	0	.250	1	12	0	0	0.2	1.000
1991			6	13	.316	3.55	58	12	1	132	116	80	108	0	4	7	6	29	5	0	.172	6	12	2	0	0.3	.900
1992	SD	N	3	6	.333	4.29	66	0	0	79.2	84	34	66	0	3	6	38	7	1	0	.143	2	12	0	0	0.2	1.000
1993	CHI	N	2	4	.333	3.11	73	0	0	75.1	65	26	86	0	2	4	**53**	2	1	0	.500	1	7	0	0	0.1	1.000
1994			1	5	.167	3.79	38	0	0	40.1	40	16	32	0	1	5	21	1	0	0	.000	0	3	1	0	0.1	.750
1995			1	2	.333	3.88	57	0	0	55.2	49	28	59	0	1	2	**38**	0	0	0	—	2	9	0	0	0.2	1.000
11 yrs.			34	49	.410	3.17	543	12	1	709.2	592	319	713	0	32	43	243	59	11	0	.186	24	81	4	1	0.2	.963
LEAGUE CHAMPIONSHIP SERIES																											
1988	NY	N	2	0	1.000	0.00	3	0	0	4.2	1	2	0	0	2	0	0	0	0	0	—	0	1	0	0	0.3	1.000
1990	CIN	N	0	0	—	0.00	4	0	0	5.2	2	3	7	0	0	0	3	0	0	0	—	0	0	0	0	0.0	.000
2 yrs.			2	0	1.000	0.00	7	0	0	10.1	3	5	7	0	2	0	3 **6th**	0	0	0		0	1	0	0	0.1	1.000
WORLD SERIES																											
1990	CIN	N	0	0	—	0.00	3	0	0	3	2	0	3	0	0	0	1	0	0	0	—	0	0	0	0	0.0	.000

Bob Myrick

MYRICK, ROBERT HOWARD
B. Oct. 1, 1952, Hattiesburg, Miss.
BR TL 6′ 1″ 195 lbs.

Year	Team		W	L	PCT	ERA	G	GS	CG	IP	H	BB	SO	ShO	Relief Pitching W	L	SV	Batting AB	H	HR	BA	PO	A	E	DP	TC/G	FA
1976	NY	N	1	1	.500	3.21	21	1	0	28	34	13	11	0	1	0	0	3	0	0	.000	0	7	0	1	0.3	1.000
1977			2	2	.500	3.62	44	4	0	87	86	33	49	0	2	1	2	11	2	0	.182	3	15	0	0	0.4	1.000
1978			0	3	.000	3.24	17	0	0	25	18	13	13	0	0	3	0	2	0	0	.000	1	5	0	1	0.4	1.000
3 yrs.			3	6	.333	3.47	82	5	0	140	138	59	73	0	3	4	2	16	2	0	.125	4	27	0	2	0.4	1.000

Chris Nabholz

NABHOLZ, CHRISTOPHER WILLIAM
B. Jan. 5, 1967, Harrisburg, Pa.
BL TL 6′ 5″ 210 lbs.

Year	Team		W	L	PCT	ERA	G	GS	CG	IP	H	BB	SO	ShO	Relief Pitching W	L	SV	Batting AB	H	HR	BA	PO	A	E	DP	TC/G	FA
1990	MON	N	6	2	.750	2.83	11	11	1	70	43	32	53	1	0	0	0	21	0	0	.000	3	10	1	0	1.3	.929
1991			8	7	.533	3.63	24	24	1	153.2	134	57	99	0	0	0	0	52	6	0	.115	9	28	1	2	1.6	.974
1992			11	12	.478	3.32	32	32	1	195	176	74	130	1	0	0	0	65	8	0	.123	14	41	2	3	1.8	.965
1993			9	8	.529	4.09	26	21	1	116.2	100	63	74	0	0	0	0	39	5	0	.128	6	17	0	1	0.9	1.000
1994	2 teams	CLE A (6G 0–1)	BOS A (8G 3–4)																								
″	total		3	5	.375	7.64	14	12	0	53	67	38	28	0	0	0	0	0	0	0		1	9	0	2	0.7	1.000
1995	CHI	N	0	1	.000	5.40	34	0	0	23.1	22	14	21	0	0	1	0	1	0	0	.000	1	5	0	0	0.2	1.000
6 yrs.			37	35	.514	3.94	141	100	4	611.2	542	278	405	2	0	1	0	178	19	0	.107	34	110	4	8	1.0	.973

Jack Nabors

NABORS, HERMAN JOHN
B. Nov. 19, 1887, Montevallo, Ala. D. Nov. 20, 1923, Wilton, Ala.
BR TR 6′ 3″ 185 lbs.

Year	Team		W	L	PCT	ERA	G	GS	CG	IP	H	BB	SO	ShO	Relief Pitching W	L	SV	Batting AB	H	HR	BA	PO	A	E	DP	TC/G	FA
1915	PHI	A	0	5	.000	5.50	10	7	2	54	58	35	18	0	0	0	0	16	2	0	.125	2	18	5	0	2.5	.800
1916			1	20	.048	3.47	40	30	11	212.2	206	95	74	0	0	0	1	69	7	0	.101	4	58	13	0	1.9	.827
1917			0	0	—	3.00	2	0	0	3	2	1	2	0	0	0	0	0	0	0	—	0	2	0	0	1.0	1.000
3 yrs.			1	25	.038	3.87	52	37	13	269.2	266	131	94	0	0	0	1	85	9	0	.106	6	78	18	0	2.0	.824

Bill Nagel

NAGEL, WILLIAM TAYLOR
B. Aug. 19, 1915, Memphis, Tenn. D. Oct. 8, 1981, Freehold, N. J.
BR TR 6′ 1″ 190 lbs.

Year	Team		W	L	PCT	ERA	G	GS	CG	IP	H	BB	SO	ShO	Relief Pitching W	L	SV	Batting AB	H	HR	BA	PO	A	E	DP	TC/G	FA
1939	PHI	A	0	0	—	12.00	1	0	0	3	7	1	0	0	0	0	0	*				134	218	21	32	3.7	.944

Year	Team	Lg	W	L	PCT	ERA	G	GS	CG	IP	H	BB	SO	ShO	Relief Pitching W	Relief Pitching L	Relief Pitching SV	Batting AB	Batting H	Batting HR	BA	PO	A	E	DP	TC/G	FA

Judge Nagle

NAGLE, WALTER HAROLD (Lucky) BR TR 6′ 176 lbs.
B. Mar. 10, 1880, Santa Rosa, Calif. D. May 27, 1971, Santa Rosa, Calif.

1911 2 teams PIT N (8G 4–2) BOS A (5G 1–1)

Year	Team	Lg	W	L	PCT	ERA	G	GS	CG	IP	H	BB	SO	ShO	W	L	SV	AB	H	HR	BA	PO	A	E	DP	TC/G	FA
"	total		5	3	.625	3.48	13	4	1	54.1	60	12	23	0	4	0	1	17	2	0	.118	3	11	0	1	1.1	1.000

Charles Nagy

NAGY, CHARLES HARRISON BL TR 6′ 3″ 200 lbs.
B. May 5, 1967, Bridgeport, Conn.

Year	Team	Lg	W	L	PCT	ERA	G	GS	CG	IP	H	BB	SO	ShO	W	L	SV	AB	H	HR	BA	PO	A	E	DP	TC/G	FA
1990	CLE	A	2	4	.333	5.91	9	8	0	45.2	58	21	26	0	0	0	0	0	0	0	—	3	8	1	2	1.3	.917
1991			10	15	.400	4.13	33	33	6	211.1	228	66	109	1	0	0	0	0	0	0	—	17	20	2	4	1.2	.949
1992			17	10	.630	2.96	33	33	10	252	245	57	169	3	0	0	0	0	0	0	—	22	43	1	3	2.0	.985
1993			2	6	.250	6.29	9	9	1	48.2	66	13	30	0	0	0	0	0	0	0	—	8	14	1	2	2.6	.957
1994			10	8	.556	3.45	23	23	3	169.1	175	48	108	0	0	0	0	0	0	0	—	9	26	2	1	1.6	.946
1995			16	6	.727	4.55	29	29	2	178	194	61	139	1	0	0	0	0	0	0	—	19	34	1	4	1.9	.981
6 yrs.			57	49	.538	3.97	136	135	22	905	966	266	581	5	0	0	0	0	0	0		78	145	8	16	1.7	.965
DIVISIONAL PLAYOFF SERIES																											
1995	CLE	A	1	0	1.000	1.29	1	1	0	7	4	5	6	0	0	0	0	0	0	0	—	2	1	0	0	3.0	1.000
LEAGUE CHAMPIONSHIP SERIES																											
1995	CLE	A	0	0	—	1.13	1	1	0	8	5	0	6	0	0	0	0	0	0	0	—	0	1	0	0	1.0	1.000
WORLD SERIES																											
1995	CLE	A	0	0	—	6.43	1	1	0	7	8	1	4	0	0	0	0	0	0	0	—	1	1	0	0	2.0	1.000

Mike Nagy

NAGY, MICHAEL TIMOTHY BR TR 6′ 3″ 195 lbs.
B. Mar. 25, 1948, New York, N. Y.

Year	Team	Lg	W	L	PCT	ERA	G	GS	CG	IP	H	BB	SO	ShO	W	L	SV	AB	H	HR	BA	PO	A	E	DP	TC/G	FA
1969	BOS	A	12	2	.857	3.11	33	28	7	196.2	183	106	84	1	0	0	0	65	5	0	.077	17	29	3	6	1.5	.939
1970			6	5	.545	4.47	23	20	4	129	138	64	56	0	0	0	0	44	11	0	.250	12	15	1	1	1.2	.964
1971			1	3	.250	6.63	12	7	0	38	46	20	9	0	0	1	0	12	1	0	.083	3	5	0	1	0.7	1.000
1972			0	0	—	9.00	1	0	0	2	3	0	2	0	0	0	0	0	0	0	—	0	0	0	0	0.0	.000
1973	STL	N	0	2	.000	4.20	9	7	0	40.2	44	15	14	0	0	0	0	11	1	0	.091	1	5	0	1	0.7	1.000
1974	HOU	N	1	1	.500	8.53	9	0	0	12.2	17	5	5	0	1	1	0	1	0	0	.000	0	2	0	0	0.2	1.000
6 yrs.			20	13	.606	4.15	87	62	11	419	431	210	170	1	1	2	0	133	18	0	.135	33	56	4	9	1.1	.957

Steve Nagy

NAGY, STEPHEN BL TL 5′ 9″ 174 lbs.
B. May 28, 1919, Franklin, N. J.

Year	Team	Lg	W	L	PCT	ERA	G	GS	CG	IP	H	BB	SO	ShO	W	L	SV	AB	H	HR	BA	PO	A	E	DP	TC/G	FA
1947	PIT	N	1	3	.250	5.79	6	1	0	14	18	9	4	0	1	2	0	4	1	0	.250	2	2	0	0	0.7	1.000
1950	WAS	A	2	5	.286	6.58	9	9	2	53.1	69	29	17	0	0	0	0	22	5	1	.227	3	8	0	0	1.2	1.000
2 yrs.			3	8	.273	6.42	15	10	2	67.1	87	38	21	0	1	2	0	26	6	1	.231	5	10	0	0	1.0	1.000

Sam Nahem

NAHEM, SAMUEL RALPH (Subway) BR TR 6′ 1½″ 190 lbs.
B. Oct. 19, 1915, New York, N. Y.

Year	Team	Lg	W	L	PCT	ERA	G	GS	CG	IP	H	BB	SO	ShO	W	L	SV	AB	H	HR	BA	PO	A	E	DP	TC/G	FA
1938	BKN	N	1	0	1.000	3.00	1	1	1	9	6	4	2	0	0	0	0	5	2	0	.400	0	1	0	0	1.0	1.000
1941	STL	N	5	2	.714	2.98	26	8	2	81.2	76	38	31	0	1	1	1	23	4	0	.174	6	21	2	0	1.1	.931
1942	PHI	N	1	3	.250	4.94	35	2	0	74.2	72	40	38	0	1	2	0	20	2	0	.100	6	19	1	2	0.7	.962
1948			3	3	.500	7.02	28	1	0	59	68	45	30	0	3	2	0	13	2	0	.154	1	9	4	0	0.5	.714
4 yrs.			10	8	.556	4.69	90	12	3	224.1	222	127	101	0	5	5	1	61	10	0	.164	13	50	7	2	0.8	.900

Pete Naktenis

NAKTENIS, PETER ERNEST BL TL 6′ 1″ 185 lbs.
B. June 12, 1914, Aberdeen, Wash.

Year	Team	Lg	W	L	PCT	ERA	G	GS	CG	IP	H	BB	SO	ShO	W	L	SV	AB	H	HR	BA	PO	A	E	DP	TC/G	FA
1936	PHI	A	0	1	.000	12.54	7	1	0	18.2	24	27	18	0	0	0	0	5	1	0	.200	1	0	0	0	0.1	1.000
1939	CIN	N	0	0	—	2.25	3	0	0	4	2	0	1	0	0	0	0	0	0	0	—	0	2	0	0	0.7	1.000
2 yrs.			0	1	.000	10.72	10	1	0	22.2	26	27	19	0	0	0	0	5	1	0	.200	1	2	0	0	0.3	1.000

Buddy Napier

NAPIER, SKELTON LeROY BR TR 5′11″ 165 lbs.
B. Dec. 18, 1889, Byronville, Ga. D. Mar. 29, 1968, Hutchins, Tex.

Year	Team	Lg	W	L	PCT	ERA	G	GS	CG	IP	H	BB	SO	ShO	W	L	SV	AB	H	HR	BA	PO	A	E	DP	TC/G	FA
1912	STL	A	1	2	.333	4.97	7	2	0	25.1	33	5	10	0	1	0	0	7	0	0	.000	0	7	0	0	1.0	1.000
1918	CHI	N	0	0	—	5.40	1	0	0	6.2	10	4	2	0	0	0	0	3	1	0	.333	1	1	0	0	2.0	1.000
1920	CIN	N	4	2	.667	1.29	9	5	5	49	47	7	17	1	1	0	0	14	3	0	.214	4	12	0	1	1.8	1.000
1921			0	2	.000	5.56	22	6	1	56.2	72	13	14	0	0	0	1	14	2	0	.143	4	20	1	0	1.1	.960
4 yrs.			5	6	.455	3.92	39	13	6	137.2	162	29	43	1	2	0	1	38	6	0	.158	9	40	1	1	1.3	.980

Cholly Naranjo

NARANJO, LAZARO RAMON GONZALO BL TR 5′11½″ 165 lbs.
B. Nov. 25, 1934, Havana, Cuba.

Year	Team	Lg	W	L	PCT	ERA	G	GS	CG	IP	H	BB	SO	ShO	W	L	SV	AB	H	HR	BA	PO	A	E	DP	TC/G	FA
1956	PIT	N	1	2	.333	4.46	17	3	0	34.1	37	17	26	0	1	1	0	7	1	0	.143	8	9	0	0	1.0	1.000

Ray Narleski

NARLESKI, RAYMOND EDMOND BR TR 6′ 1″ 175 lbs.
Son of Bill Narleski.
B. Nov. 25, 1928, Camden, N. J.

Year	Team	Lg	W	L	PCT	ERA	G	GS	CG	IP	H	BB	SO	ShO	W	L	SV	AB	H	HR	BA	PO	A	E	DP	TC/G	FA
1954	CLE	A	3	3	.500	2.22	42	2	1	89	59	44	52	0	3	2	13	16	0	0	.000	5	10	2	2	0.4	.882
1955			9	1	.900	3.71	**60**	1	1	111.2	91	52	94	0	**8**	1	**19**	24	7	0	.292	1	11	2	0	0.2	.857
1956			3	2	.600	1.52	32	0	0	59.1	36	19	42	0	3	2	4	8	2	0	.250	2	5	0	1	0.2	1.000
1957			11	5	.688	3.09	46	15	7	154.1	136	70	93	1	5	0	16	43	4	1	.093	4	10	2	0	0.3	.875
1958			13	10	.565	4.07	44	24	7	183.1	179	91	102	0	2	1	1	54	11	0	.204	6	16	1	0	0.5	.957
1959	DET	A	4	12	.250	5.78	42	10	1	104.1	105	59	71	0	2	**7**	5	21	2	0	.095	4	8	2	0	0.3	.857
6 yrs.			43	33	.566	3.60	266	52	17	702	606	335	454	1	23	13	58	166	26	1	.157	22	60	9	3	0.3	.901
WORLD SERIES																											
1954	CLE	A	0	0	—	2.25	2	0	0	4	1	1	2	0	0	0	0	0	0	0	—	0	1	0	0	0.5	1.000

Buster Narum

NARUM, LESLIE FERDINAND BR TR 6′ 1″ 194 lbs.
B. Nov. 16, 1940, Philadelphia, Pa.

Year	Team	Lg	W	L	PCT	ERA	G	GS	CG	IP	H	BB	SO	ShO	W	L	SV	AB	H	HR	BA	PO	A	E	DP	TC/G	FA
1963	BAL	A	0	0	—	3.00	7	0	0	9	8	5	5	0	0	0	0	1	1	1	1.000	1	2	0	0	0.4	1.000
1964	WAS	A	9	15	.375	4.30	38	32	7	199	195	73	121	2	0	0	0	66	4	1	.061	9	16	1	2	0.7	.962
1965			4	12	.250	4.46	46	24	2	173.2	176	91	86	0	1	1	0	46	2	1	.043	17	39	3	2	1.3	.949
1966			0	0	—	21.60	3	0	0	3.1	11	4	0	0	0	0	0	0	0	0	—	0	0	0	0	0.0	.000
1967			1	0	1.000	3.09	2	2	0	11.2	8	4	8	0	0	0	0	5	0	0	.000	1	1	0	0	1.0	1.000
5 yrs.			14	27	.341	4.45	96	58	9	396.2	398	177	220	2	1	1	0	118	7	3	.059	28	58	4	4	0.9	.956

Billy Nash

NASH, WILLIAM MITCHELL
B. June 24, 1865, Richmond, Va. D. Nov. 15, 1929, East Orange, N. J.
Manager 1896.

BR TR 5′ 8½″ 167 lbs.

Year	Team	W	L	PCT	ERA	G	GS	CG	IP	H	BB	SO	ShO	Relief W	Relief L	Relief SV	Batting AB	Batting H	HR	BA	PO	A	E	DP	TC/G	FA
1889	BOS N	0	0	—	0.00	1	0	0	1	0	1	0	0	0	0	0	481	132	3	.274	77	87	34	8	4.4	.828
1890	BOS P	0	0	—	0.00	1	0	0	0.1	1	0	0	0	0	0	0	488	130	5	.266	198	307	78	37	4.5	.866
2 yrs.		0	0		0.00	2	0	0	1.1	1	1	0	0	0	0	0	*				2413	3344	666	291	4.1	.896

Jim Nash

NASH, JAMES EDWIN
B. Feb. 9, 1945, Hawthorne, Nev.

BR TR 6′ 5″ 215 lbs.

Year	Team	W	L	PCT	ERA	G	GS	CG	IP	H	BB	SO	ShO	Relief W	Relief L	Relief SV	Batting AB	Batting H	HR	BA	PO	A	E	DP	TC/G	FA
1966	KC A	12	1	.923	2.06	18	17	5	127	95	47	98	0	0	0	1	49	5	0	.102	6	5	0	0	0.6	1.000
1967		12	17	.414	3.76	37	34	8	222.1	200	87	186	2	0	0	0	70	7	0	.100	9	23	1	1	0.9	.970
1968	OAK A	13	13	.500	2.28	34	33	12	228.2	185	55	169	6	0	0	0	74	5	2	.068	9	20	1	2	0.9	.967
1969		8	8	.500	3.67	26	19	3	115.1	112	30	75	1	2	0	0	36	4	0	.111	9	14	3	0	1.0	.885
1970	ATL N	13	9	.591	4.08	34	33	6	212	211	90	153	2	0	1	0	80	7	2	.087	18	27	2	1	1.4	.957
1971		9	7	.563	4.94	32	19	2	133	166	50	65	0	0	1	2	47	7	0	.149	7	16	2	1	0.8	.920
1972	2 teams ATL N (11G 1–1) PHI N (9G 0–8)																									
″	total	1	9	.100	5.90	20	12	0	68.2	81	42	25	0	1	0	1	19	3	0	.158	2	10	1	2	0.6	.923
7 yrs.		68	64	.515	3.59	201	167	36	1107	1050	401	771	11	3	2	4	375	38	4	.101	60	115	10	7	0.9	.946

Phil Nastu

NASTU, PHILIP
B. Mar. 8, 1955, Bridgeport, Conn.

BL TL 6′ 2″ 180 lbs.

Year	Team	W	L	PCT	ERA	G	GS	CG	IP	H	BB	SO	ShO	Relief W	Relief L	Relief SV	Batting AB	Batting H	HR	BA	PO	A	E	DP	TC/G	FA
1978	SF N	0	1	.000	5.63	3	1	0	8	8	2	5	0	0	0	0	1	0	0	.000	1	0	0	0	0.3	1.000
1979		3	4	.429	4.32	25	14	1	100	105	41	47	0	0	0	0	24	1	0	.042	6	14	1	4	0.8	.952
1980		0	0	—	6.00	6	0	0	6	10	5	1	0	0	0	0	0	0	0	—	1	2	0	0	0.5	1.000
3 yrs.		3	5	.375	4.50	34	15	1	114	123	48	53	0	0	0	0	25	1	0	.040	8	16	1	4	0.7	.960

Jaime Navarro

NAVARRO, JAIME
Born Jaime Navarro (Cintron).
Son of Julio Navarro.
B. Mar. 27, 1967, Bayamon, Puerto Rico.

BR TR 6′ 4″ 210 lbs.

Year	Team	W	L	PCT	ERA	G	GS	CG	IP	H	BB	SO	ShO	Relief W	Relief L	Relief SV	Batting AB	Batting H	HR	BA	PO	A	E	DP	TC/G	FA
1989	MIL A	7	8	.467	3.12	19	17	1	109.2	119	32	56	0	1	0	0	0	0	0	—	6	16	2	0	1.3	.917
1990		8	7	.533	4.46	32	22	3	149.1	176	41	75	0	0	0	1	0	0	0	—	10	19	1	2	0.9	.967
1991		15	12	.556	3.92	34	34	10	234	237	73	114	2	0	0	0	0	0	0	—	16	28	3	3	1.4	.936
1992		17	11	.607	3.33	34	34	5	246	224	64	100	3	0	0	0	0	0	0	—	17	18	4	1	1.1	.897
1993		11	12	.478	5.33	35	34	5	214.1	254	73	114	1	0	0	0	0	0	0	—	14	21	2	2	1.1	.946
1994		4	9	.308	6.62	29	10	0	89.2	115	35	65	0	2	3	0	0	0	0	—	4	7	0	1	0.4	1.000
1995	CHI N	14	6	.700	3.28	29	29	1	200.1	194	56	128	1	0	0	0	65	12	0	.185	14	13	1	1	1.0	.964
7 yrs.		76	65	.539	4.13	212	180	25	1243.1	1319	374	652	7	3	3	1	65	12	0	.185	81	122	13	10	1.0	.940

Julio Navarro

NAVARRO, JULIO (Whiplash)
Born Julio Navarro (Ventura).
Father of Jaime Navarro.
B. Jan. 9, 1936, Vieques, Puerto Rico.

BR TR 6′ 175 lbs.

Year	Team	W	L	PCT	ERA	G	GS	CG	IP	H	BB	SO	ShO	Relief W	Relief L	Relief SV	Batting AB	Batting H	HR	BA	PO	A	E	DP	TC/G	FA
1962	LA A	1	1	.500	4.70	9	0	0	15.1	20	4	11	0	1	1	0	2	1	0	.500	0	2	0	0	0.2	1.000
1963		4	5	.444	2.89	57	0	0	90.1	75	32	53	0	4	5	12	15	3	0	.200	5	20	1	3	0.5	.962
1964	2 teams LA A (5G 0–0) DET A (26G 2–1)																									
″	total	2	1	.667	3.58	31	0	0	50.1	45	21	44	0	2	1	3	7	0	0	.000	2	7	0	1	0.3	1.000
1965	DET A	0	2	.000	4.20	15	1	0	30	25	12	22	0	0	2	1	4	0	0	.000	2	6	0	0	0.5	1.000
1966		0	0	—	∞	1	0	0		2	0	0	0	0	0	0	0	0	0	—	0	0	0	0	0.0	.000
1970	ATL N	0	0	—	4.15	17	0	0	26	24	1	21	0	0	0	1	6	1	0	.167	2	3	0	0	0.3	1.000
6 yrs.		7	9	.438	3.65	130	1	0	212	191	70	151	0	7	9	17	34	5	0	.147	11	38	1	4	0.4	.980

Earl Naylor

NAYLOR, EARL EUGENE
B. May 19, 1919, Kansas City, Mo. D. Jan. 16, 1990, Winter Haven, Fla.

BR TR 6′ 190 lbs.

Year	Team	W	L	PCT	ERA	G	GS	CG	IP	H	BB	SO	ShO	Relief W	Relief L	Relief SV	Batting AB	Batting H	HR	BA	PO	A	E	DP	TC/G	FA
1942	PHI N	0	5	.000	6.12	20	4	1	60.1	68	29	19	0	0	2	0	*				68	11	1	0	1.5	.988

Rollie Naylor

NAYLOR, ROLEINE CECIL
B. Feb. 4, 1892, Crum, Tex. D. June 18, 1966, Fort Worth, Tex.

BR TR 6′ 1½″ 180 lbs.

Year	Team	W	L	PCT	ERA	G	GS	CG	IP	H	BB	SO	ShO	Relief W	Relief L	Relief SV	Batting AB	Batting H	HR	BA	PO	A	E	DP	TC/G	FA
1917	PHI A	2	2	.500	1.64	5	5	3	33	30	11	11	0	0	0	0	11	1	0	.091	7	11	0	0	3.6	1.000
1919		5	18	.217	3.34	31	23	17	204.2	210	64	68	0	1	0	0	71	12	0	.169	14	50	5	5	2.2	.928
1920		10	23	.303	3.47	42	36	20	251.1	306	86	90	0	2	0	0	86	14	0	.163	13	70	2	4	2.0	.976
1921		3	13	.188	4.84	32	19	6	169.1	214	55	39	0	0	1	0	52	6	0	.115	6	38	2	1	1.4	.957
1922		10	15	.400	4.73	35	26	11	171.1	212	51	37	0	0	2	0	55	11	1	.200	10	46	0	3	1.6	1.000
1923		12	7	.632	3.46	26	20	9	143	149	59	27	2	1	0	0	45	11	0	.244	9	29	4	4	1.6	.905
1924		0	5	.000	6.34	10	7	1	38.1	53	20	10	0	0	1	0	8	3	0	.375	0	12	0	0	1.2	1.000
7 yrs.		42	83	.336	3.93	181	136	67	1011	1174	346	282	2	4	4	0	328	58	1	.177	59	256	13	17	1.8	.960

Mike Naymick

NAYMICK, MICHAEL JOHN
B. Sept. 6, 1917, Berlin, Pa.

BR TR 6′ 8″ 225 lbs.

Year	Team	W	L	PCT	ERA	G	GS	CG	IP	H	BB	SO	ShO	Relief W	Relief L	Relief SV	Batting AB	Batting H	HR	BA	PO	A	E	DP	TC/G	FA
1939	CLE A	0	1	.000	1.93	2	1	1	4.2	3	5	3	0	0	0	0	3	0	0	.000	0	0	0	0	0.0	.000
1940		1	2	.333	5.10	13	4	0	30	36	17	15	0	0	0	0	6	1	0	.167	2	9	0	0	0.8	1.000
1943		4	4	.500	2.30	29	4	0	62.2	32	47	41	0	4	1	2	16	3	0	.188	2	17	4	0	0.8	.826
1944	2 teams CLE A (7G 0–0) STL N (1G 0–0)																									
″	total	0	0		9.00	8	0	0	15	18	11	5	0	0	0	0	1	0	0	.000	2	3	1	1	0.8	.833
4 yrs.		5	7	.417	3.93	52	9	1	112.1	89	80	64	0	4	1	2	26	4	0	.154	6	29	5	1	0.8	.875

Denny Neagle

NEAGLE, DENNIS EDWARD
B. Sept. 13, 1968, Gambrills, Md.

BL TL 6′ 4″ 200 lbs.

Year	Team	W	L	PCT	ERA	G	GS	CG	IP	H	BB	SO	ShO	Relief W	Relief L	Relief SV	Batting AB	Batting H	HR	BA	PO	A	E	DP	TC/G	FA
1991	MIN A	0	1	.000	4.05	7	3	0	20	28	7	14	0	0	0	0	0	0	0	—	0	1	0	0	0.1	1.000
1992	PIT N	4	6	.400	4.48	55	6	0	86.1	81	43	77	0	3	3	2	11	0	0	.000	2	11	0	0	0.2	1.000
1993		3	5	.375	5.31	50	7	0	81.1	82	37	73	0	1	2	1	14	0	0	.000	1	5	0	0	0.1	1.000
1994		9	10	.474	5.12	24	24	2	137	135	49	122	0	0	0	0	42	8	1	.190	3	21	1	2	1.0	.960
1995		13	8	.619	3.43	31	**31**	5	**209.2**	**221**	45	150	1	0	0	0	74	9	1	.122	13	32	1	5	1.5	.978
5 yrs.		29	30	.492	4.35	167	71	7	534.1	547	181	436	1	4	5	3	141	17	2	.121	19	70	2	7	0.5	.978

Denny Neagle *continued*

Year	Team	W	L	PCT	ERA	G	GS	CG	IP	H	BB	SO	ShO	Relief Pitching W	Relief Pitching L	Relief Pitching SV	Batting AB	Batting H	Batting HR	BA	PO	A	E	DP	TC/G	FA
LEAGUE CHAMPIONSHIP SERIES																										
1992	PIT N	0	0	—	27.00	2	0	0	1.2	4	3	0	0	0	0	0	0	0	0	—	0	0	0	0	0.0	.000

Jack Neagle

NEAGLE, JOHN HENRY
B. Jan. 2, 1858, Syracuse, N. Y. D. Sept. 20, 1904, Syracuse, N. Y.
BR TR 5′ 6″ 155 lbs.

Year	Team	W	L	PCT	ERA	G	GS	CG	IP	H	BB	SO	ShO	Relief Pitching W	Relief Pitching L	Relief Pitching SV	Batting AB	Batting H	Batting HR	BA	PO	A	E	DP	TC/G	FA
1879	CIN N	0	1	.000	3.46	2	2	1	13	13	5	4	0	0	0	0	12	2	0	.167	1	2	2	0	1.3	.600
1883	3 teams PHI N (8G 1–7) BAL AA (6G 1–4) PIT AA (16G 3–12)																									
″	total	5	23	.179	5.94	30	28	22	221.1	292	66	63	0	0	1	0	209	41	0	.196	45	40	19	0	1.7	.817
1884	PIT AA	11	26	.297	*3.73*	38	38	37	326	354	70	85	2	0	0	0	148	22	0	.149	25	57	29	1	2.5	.739
3 yrs.		16	50	.242	4.59	70	68	60	560.1	659	141	152	2	0	1	0	*				71	99	50	1	2.0	.773

Joe Neale

NEALE, JOSEPH HUNT
B. May 7, 1866, Wadsworth, Ohio D. Dec. 30, 1913, Akron, Ohio.
BR TR 5′ 8″ 153 lbs.

Year	Team	W	L	PCT	ERA	G	GS	CG	IP	H	BB	SO	ShO	Relief Pitching W	Relief Pitching L	Relief Pitching SV	Batting AB	Batting H	Batting HR	BA	PO	A	E	DP	TC/G	FA
1886	LOU AA	0	1	.000	*7.71*	1	1	0	7	11	7	0	0	0	0	0	5	0	0	.000	1	5	0	0	2.0	1.000
1887		1	4	.200	*6.97*	5	4	4	41.1	60	15	11	0	**1**	0	0	19	1	0	.053	1	11	2	1	2.8	.857
1890	STL AA	5	3	.625	*3.39*	10	9	8	69	53	15	23	0	0	0	0	30	2	0	.067	4	6	0	0	0.9	1.000
1891		6	4	.600	4.24	15	11	9	110.1	109	36	24	1	0	0	**3**	51	6	1	.118	6	36	3	0	3.0	.933
4 yrs.		12	12	.500	4.59	31	25	21	227.2	233	73	58	1	1	0	3	105	9	1	.086	12	58	5	1	2.2	.933

Ron Necciai

NECCIAI, RONALD ANDREW
B. June 18, 1932, Gallatin, Pa.
BR TR 6′ 5″ 185 lbs.

Year	Team	W	L	PCT	ERA	G	GS	CG	IP	H	BB	SO	ShO	Relief Pitching W	Relief Pitching L	Relief Pitching SV	Batting AB	Batting H	Batting HR	BA	PO	A	E	DP	TC/G	FA
1952	PIT N	1	6	.143	7.08	12	9	0	54.2	63	32	31	0	0	0	0	17	1	0	.059	4	7	2	2	1.1	.846

Ron Negray

NEGRAY, RONALD ALVIN
B. Feb. 26, 1930, Akron, Ohio.
BR TR 6′ 1″ 185 lbs.

Year	Team	W	L	PCT	ERA	G	GS	CG	IP	H	BB	SO	ShO	Relief Pitching W	Relief Pitching L	Relief Pitching SV	Batting AB	Batting H	Batting HR	BA	PO	A	E	DP	TC/G	FA
1952	BKN N	0	0	—	3.46	4	1	0	13	15	5	5	0	0	0	0	2	0	0	.000	0	2	0	0	0.5	1.000
1955	PHI N	4	3	.571	3.52	19	10	2	71.2	71	21	30	0	1	0	0	24	0	0	.000	5	9	0	2	0.7	1.000
1956		2	3	.400	4.18	39	4	0	66.2	72	24	44	0	2	2	3	7	3	0	.429	4	11	1	1	0.4	.938
1958	LA N	0	0	—	7.15	4	0	0	11.1	12	7	2	0	0	0	0	2	0	0	.000	0	2	0	0	0.5	1.000
4 yrs.		6	6	.500	4.04	66	15	2	162.2	170	57	81	0	3	2	3	35	3	0	.086	9	24	1	3	0.5	.971

Jim Neher

NEHER, JAMES GILMORE
B. Feb. 5, 1889, Rochester, N. Y. D. Nov. 11, 1951, Buffalo, N. Y.
BR TR 5′11″ 185 lbs.

Year	Team	W	L	PCT	ERA	G	GS	CG	IP	H	BB	SO	ShO	Relief Pitching W	Relief Pitching L	Relief Pitching SV	Batting AB	Batting H	Batting HR	BA	PO	A	E	DP	TC/G	FA
1912	CLE A	0	0	—	0.00	1	0	0	1	0	0	0	0	0	0	0	0	0	0	—	0	0	0	0	0.0	.000

Art Nehf

NEHF, ARTHUR NEUKOM
B. July 31, 1892, Terre Haute, Ind. D. Dec. 18, 1960, Phoenix, Ariz.
BL TL 5′ 9½″ 176 lbs.

Year	Team	W	L	PCT	ERA	G	GS	CG	IP	H	BB	SO	ShO	Relief Pitching W	Relief Pitching L	Relief Pitching SV	Batting AB	Batting H	Batting HR	BA	PO	A	E	DP	TC/G	FA
1915	BOS N	5	4	.556	2.53	12	10	6	78.1	60	21	39	4	0	0	0	28	4	0	.143	7	17	2	3	2.2	.923
1916		7	5	.583	2.01	22	13	6	121	110	20	36	1	1	1	0	40	5	0	.125	7	29	2	2	1.7	.947
1917		17	8	.680	2.16	38	23	17	233.1	197	39	101	5	4	2	0	70	12	0	.171	9	63	1	3	1.9	.986
1918		15	15	.500	2.69	32	31	**28**	284.1	**274**	76	96	2	0	0	0	95	16	0	.168	15	97	3	2	3.4	.974
1919	2 teams BOS N (22G 8–9) NY N (13G 9–2)																									
″	total	17	11	.607	2.49	35	31	22	270.2	221	59	77	3	0	1	0	98	21	1	.214	14	77	2	2	2.6	.978
1920	NY N	21	12	.636	3.08	40	33	22	280.2	273	45	79	5	2	0	0	97	26	0	.268	18	83	2	11	2.6	.981
1921		20	10	.667	3.63	41	34	18	260.2	266	55	67	2	1	1	1	89	18	0	.202	17	77	2	3	2.3	.979
1922		19	13	.594	3.29	37	35	20	268.1	286	64	60	3	0	1	1	98	25	1	.255	14	64	3	3	2.2	.963
1923		13	10	.565	4.50	34	27	7	196	219	49	50	1	1	1	2	63	12	0	.190	14	47	1	5	1.8	.984
1924		14	4	.778	3.62	30	20	11	171.2	167	42	72	0	1	0	2	57	13	5	.228	6	50	1	2	1.8	.982
1925		11	9	.550	3.77	29	20	8	155	193	50	63	1	4	1	1	51	11	0	.216	8	42	0	5	1.7	1.000
1926	2 teams NY N (2G 0–0) CIN N (7G 0–1)																									
″	total	0	1	.000	4.34	9	0	0	18.2	27	6	4	0	0	1	0	6	1	0	.167	0	9	1	0	1.1	.900
1927	2 teams CIN N (21G 3–5) CHI N (8G 1–1)																									
″	total	4	6	.400	4.02	29	7	3	71.2	84	23	33	1	3	1	5	20	4	0	.200	3	19	0	0	0.8	1.000
1928	CHI N	13	7	.650	2.65	31	21	10	176.2	190	52	40	2	0	2	0	58	11	1	.190	3	48	2	3	1.7	.962
1929		8	5	.615	5.59	32	15	4	120.2	148	39	27	0	1	2	1	45	13	0	.289	9	27	0	3	1.1	1.000
15 yrs.		184	120	.605	3.20	451	320	182	2707.2	2715	640	844	30	18	14	13	915	192	8	.210	144	749	22	47	2.0	.976
WORLD SERIES																										
1921	NY N	1	2	.333	1.38	3	3	3	26	13	13	8	1	0	0	0	9	0	0	.000	1	4	1	0	2.0	.833
1922		1	0	1.000	2.25	2	2	1	16	11	3	6	0	0	0	0	3	0	0	.000	0	3	1	0	2.0	.750
1923		1	1	.500	2.76	2	2	1	16.1	10	6	7	1	0	0	0	6	1	0	.167	0	6	0	1	3.0	1.000
1924		1	1	.500	1.83	3	2	1	19.2	15	9	7	0	0	0	0	7	3	0	.429	0	6	0	0	2.0	1.000
1929	CHI N	0	0	—	18.00	2	0	0	1	1	1	0	0	0	0	0	0	0	0	—	0	0	0	0	0.0	.000
5 yrs.		4	4	.500	2.16	12	9	6	79	50	32	28	2	0	0	0	25	4	0	.160	1	19	2	1	1.8	.909
						7th	**6th**	**6th**	**7th**		**2nd**		**4th**													

Gary Neibauer

NEIBAUER, GARY WAYNE
B. Oct. 29, 1944, Billings, Mont.
BR TR 6′ 3″ 200 lbs.

Year	Team	W	L	PCT	ERA	G	GS	CG	IP	H	BB	SO	ShO	Relief Pitching W	Relief Pitching L	Relief Pitching SV	Batting AB	Batting H	Batting HR	BA	PO	A	E	DP	TC/G	FA
1969	ATL N	1	2	.333	3.88	29	0	0	58	42	31	42	0	1	2	0	10	0	0	.000	4	7	0	1	0.4	1.000
1970		0	3	.000	4.85	7	0	0	13	11	8	9	0	0	3	0	2	0	0	.000	0	1	0	0	0.1	1.000
1971		1	0	1.000	2.14	6	1	0	21	14	9	6	0	1	0	1	5	0	0	.000	2	3	0	1	0.8	1.000
1972	2 teams ATL N (8G 0–0) PHI N (9G 0–2)																									
″	total	0	2	.000	6.25	17	2	0	36	44	20	15	0	0	0	0	8	1	0	.125	0	4	0	0	0.2	1.000
1973	ATL N	2	1	.667	7.29	16	1	0	21	24	19	9	0	2	1	0	4	1	1	.250	2	0	0	0	0.1	1.000
5 yrs.		4	8	.333	4.77	75	4	0	149	135	87	81	0	4	6	1	29	2	1	.069	8	15	0	2	0.3	1.000
LEAGUE CHAMPIONSHIP SERIES																										
1969	ATL N	0	0	—	0.00	1	0	0	1	0	0	1	0	0	0	0	0	0	0	—	0	0	0	0	0.0	.000

Jim Neidlinger

NEIDLINGER, JAMES LLEWELLYN
B. Sept. 24, 1964, Vallejo, Calif.
BB TR 6′ 4″ 180 lbs.

Year	Team	W	L	PCT	ERA	G	GS	CG	IP	H	BB	SO	ShO	Relief Pitching W	Relief Pitching L	Relief Pitching SV	Batting AB	Batting H	Batting HR	BA	PO	A	E	DP	TC/G	FA
1990	LA N	5	3	.625	3.28	12	12	0	74	67	15	46	0	0	0	0	25	3	0	.120	8	5	0	0	1.1	1.000

Al Neiger

NEIGER, ALVIN EDWARD — BL TL 6′ 195 lbs.
B. Mar. 26, 1939, Wilmington, Del.

Year	Team	W	L	PCT	ERA	G	GS	CG	IP	H	BB	SO	ShO	Relief Pitching W	Relief Pitching L	Relief Pitching SV	Batting AB	Batting H	HR	BA	PO	A	E	DP	TC/G	FA
1960	PHI N	0	0	—	5.68	6	0	0	12.2	16	4	3	0	0	0	0	2	1	0	.500	1	2	0	0	0.5	1.000

Ernie Neitzke

NEITZKE, ERNEST FREDERICK — BR TR 5′10″ 180 lbs.
B. Nov. 13, 1894, Toledo, Ohio D. Apr. 27, 1977, Sylvania, Ohio.

Year	Team	W	L	PCT	ERA	G	GS	CG	IP	H	BB	SO	ShO	Relief Pitching W	Relief Pitching L	Relief Pitching SV	Batting AB	Batting H	HR	BA	PO	A	E	DP	TC/G	FA
1921	BOS A	0	0	—	6.14	2	0	0	7.1	8	4	1	0	0	0	0	*				13	4	2	0	1.9	.895

Bots Nekola

NEKOLA, FRANCIS JOSEPH — BL TL 5′11½″ 175 lbs.
B. Dec. 10, 1906, New York, N. Y. D. Mar. 11, 1987, Rockville Centre, N. Y.

Year	Team	W	L	PCT	ERA	G	GS	CG	IP	H	BB	SO	ShO	Relief Pitching W	Relief Pitching L	Relief Pitching SV	Batting AB	Batting H	HR	BA	PO	A	E	DP	TC/G	FA
1929	NY A	0	0	—	4.34	9	1	0	18.2	21	15	2	0	0	0	0	4	2	0	.500	1	8	0	1	1.0	1.000
1933	DET A	0	0	—	27.00	2	0	0	1.1	4	1	0	0	0	0	0	0	0	0	—	0	0	0	0	0.0	.000
2 yrs.		0	0		5.85	11	1	0	20	25	16	2	0	0	0	0	4	2	0	.500	1	8	0	1	0.8	1.000

Andy Nelson

NELSON, ANDREW A. — TL
B. St. Paul, Minn.

Year	Team	W	L	PCT	ERA	G	GS	CG	IP	H	BB	SO	ShO	Relief Pitching W	Relief Pitching L	Relief Pitching SV	Batting AB	Batting H	HR	BA	PO	A	E	DP	TC/G	FA
1908	CHI A	0	0	—	2.00	2	1	0	9	11	4	1	0	0	0	0	2	0	0	.000	1	0	0	0	0.5	1.000

Bill Nelson

NELSON, WILLIAM F. — TR
B. Sept. 28, 1863, Terre Haute, Ind. D. June 23, 1941, Terre Haute, Ind.

Year	Team	W	L	PCT	ERA	G	GS	CG	IP	H	BB	SO	ShO	Relief Pitching W	Relief Pitching L	Relief Pitching SV	Batting AB	Batting H	HR	BA	PO	A	E	DP	TC/G	FA
1884	PIT AA	1	2	.333	*4.50*	3	3	3	26	26	8	6	0	0	0	0	12	2	0	.167	4	5	5	0	4.7	.643

Emmett Nelson

NELSON, GEORGE EMMETT (Ramrod) — BR TR 6′3″ 180 lbs.
B. Feb. 26, 1905, Viborg, S. D. D. Aug. 25, 1967, Sioux Falls, S. D.

Year	Team	W	L	PCT	ERA	G	GS	CG	IP	H	BB	SO	ShO	Relief Pitching W	Relief Pitching L	Relief Pitching SV	Batting AB	Batting H	HR	BA	PO	A	E	DP	TC/G	FA
1935	CIN N	4	4	.500	4.33	19	7	3	60.1	70	23	14	1	1	1	1	15	2	0	.133	2	16	0	1	0.9	1.000
1936		1	0	1.000	3.18	6	1	0	17	24	4	3	0	1	0	0	6	1	0	.167	1	3	0	1	0.7	1.000
2 yrs.		5	4	.556	4.07	25	8	3	77.1	94	27	17	1	2	1	1	21	3	0	.143	3	19	0	2	0.9	1.000

Gene Nelson

NELSON, WAYLAND EUGENE — BR TR 6′ 172 lbs.
B. Dec. 3, 1960, Tampa, Fla.

Year	Team	W	L	PCT	ERA	G	GS	CG	IP	H	BB	SO	ShO	Relief Pitching W	Relief Pitching L	Relief Pitching SV	Batting AB	Batting H	HR	BA	PO	A	E	DP	TC/G	FA
1981	NY A	3	1	.750	4.85	8	7	0	39	40	23	16	0	0	0	0	0	0	0	—	3	6	1	0	1.3	.900
1982	SEA A	6	9	.400	4.62	22	19	2	122.2	133	60	71	1	0	1	0	0	0	0	—	10	20	1	2	1.4	.968
1983		0	3	.000	7.88	10	5	1	32	38	21	11	0	0	0	0	0	0	0	—	5	6	1	0	1.2	.917
1984	CHI A	3	5	.375	4.46	20	9	2	74.2	72	17	36	0	2	0	1	0	0	0	—	11	8	0	1	0.9	1.000
1985		10	10	.500	4.26	46	18	1	145.2	144	67	101	0	4	3	2	1	0	0	.000	10	19	1	0	0.7	.967
1986		6	6	.500	3.85	54	1	0	114.2	118	41	70	0	6	5	6	0	0	0	—	8	17	0	3	0.5	1.000
1987	OAK A	6	5	.545	3.93	54	6	0	123.2	120	35	94	0	5	2	3	0	0	0	—	8	13	2	0	0.4	.913
1988		9	6	.600	3.06	54	1	0	111.2	93	38	67	0	**9**	5	3	0	0	0	—	4	11	0	1	0.3	1.000
1989		3	5	.375	3.26	50	0	0	80	60	30	70	0	3	5	3	0	0	0	—	6	3	0	0	0.2	1.000
1990		3	3	.500	1.57	51	0	0	74.2	55	17	38	0	3	3	5	0	0	0	—	4	8	1	0	0.3	.923
1991		1	5	.167	6.84	44	0	0	48.2	60	23	23	0	1	5	0	0	0	0	—	4	4	0	0	0.2	1.000
1992		3	1	.750	6.45	28	2	0	51.2	68	22	23	0	2	1	0	0	0	0	—	3	4	0	0	0.3	1.000
1993	2 teams CAL A (46G 0–5) TEX A (6G 0–0)																									
″	total	0	5	.000	3.12	52	0	0	60.2	60	24	35	0	0	5	5	0	0	0		4	8	0	1	0.2	1.000
13 yrs.		53	64	.453	4.13	493	68	6	1079.2	1061	418	655	1	35	35	28	1	0	0	.000	80	127	7	8	0.4	.967
LEAGUE CHAMPIONSHIP SERIES																										
1988	OAK A	2	0	1.000	0.00	2	0	0	4.2	5	1	0	0	2	0	0	0	0	0	—	0	0	0	0	0.0	.000
1989		0	0	—	0.00	1	0	0	1.1	1	0	2	0	0	0	0	0	0	0	—	0	0	0	0	0.0	.000
1990		0	0	—	0.00	1	0	0	1.2	3	0	0	0	0	0	0	0	0	0	—	0	0	0	0	0.0	.000
3 yrs.		2	0	1.000	0.00	4	0	0	7.2	9	1	2	0	2	0	0	0	0	0		0	0	0	0	0.0	
WORLD SERIES																										
1988	OAK A	0	0	—	1.42	3	0	0	6.1	4	3	3	0	0	0	0	0	0	0	—	1	2	0	0	1.0	1.000
1989		0	0	—	54.00	2	0	0	1	4	2	1	0	0	0	0	0	0	0	—	0	0	0	0	0.0	.000
1990		0	0	—	0.00	2	0	0	5	3	2	0	0	0	0	0	0	0	0	—	0	0	0	0	0.0	.000
3 yrs.		0	0		5.11	7	0	0	12.1	11	7	4	0	0	0	0	0	0	0		1	2	0	0	0.4	1.000

Jeff Nelson

NELSON, JEFFREY ALLAN — BR TR 6′8″ 225 lbs.
B. Nov. 17, 1966, Baltimore, Md.

Year	Team	W	L	PCT	ERA	G	GS	CG	IP	H	BB	SO	ShO	Relief Pitching W	Relief Pitching L	Relief Pitching SV	Batting AB	Batting H	HR	BA	PO	A	E	DP	TC/G	FA
1992	SEA A	1	7	.125	3.44	66	0	0	81	71	44	46	0	1	7	6	0	0	0	—	3	12	2	2	0.3	.882
1993		5	3	.625	4.35	71	0	0	60	57	34	61	0	5	3	1	0	0	0	—	3	12	0	2	0.2	1.000
1994		0	0	—	2.76	28	0	0	42.1	35	20	44	0	0	0	0	0	0	0	—	1	5	2	1	0.3	.750
1995		7	3	.700	2.17	62	0	0	78.2	58	27	96	0	7	3	2	0	0	0	—	2	10	1	1	0.2	.923
4 yrs.		13	13	.500	3.16	227	0	0	262	221	125	247	0	13	13	9	0	0	0		9	39	5	6	0.2	.906
DIVISIONAL PLAYOFF SERIES																										
1995	SEA A	0	1	.000	3.18	3	0	0	5.2	7	3	7	0	0	1	0	0	0	0	—	0	1	0	0	0.3	1.000
LEAGUE CHAMPIONSHIP SERIES																										
1995	SEA A	0	0	—	0.00	3	0	0	3	3	5	3	0	0	0	0	0	0	0	—	0	3	0	1	1.0	1.000

Jim Nelson

NELSON, JAMES LORIN — BR TR 6′ 180 lbs.
B. July 4, 1947, Birmingham, Ala.

Year	Team	W	L	PCT	ERA	G	GS	CG	IP	H	BB	SO	ShO	Relief Pitching W	Relief Pitching L	Relief Pitching SV	Batting AB	Batting H	HR	BA	PO	A	E	DP	TC/G	FA
1970	PIT N	4	2	.667	3.44	15	10	1	68	64	38	42	1	0	0	0	20	4	0	.200	7	4	2	1	0.9	.846
1971		2	2	.500	2.31	17	2	0	35	27	26	11	0	2	1	0	6	3	0	.500	4	3	0	0	0.4	1.000
2 yrs.		6	4	.600	3.06	32	12	1	103	91	64	53	1	2	1	0	26	7	0	.269	11	7	2	1	0.6	.900

Luke Nelson

NELSON, LUTHER MARTIN — BR TR 6′ 180 lbs.
B. Dec. 4, 1893, Cable, Ill. D. Nov. 14, 1985, Moline, Ill.

Year	Team	W	L	PCT	ERA	G	GS	CG	IP	H	BB	SO	ShO	Relief Pitching W	Relief Pitching L	Relief Pitching SV	Batting AB	Batting H	HR	BA	PO	A	E	DP	TC/G	FA
1919	NY A	3	0	1.000	2.96	9	1	0	24.1	22	11	11	0	2	0	0	7	1	0	.143	1	5	0	0	0.7	1.000

Lynn Nelson

NELSON, LYNN BERNARD (Line Drive) — BL TR 5′10½″ 170 lbs.
B. Feb. 24, 1905, Sheldon, N. D. D. Feb. 15, 1955, Kansas City, Mo.

Year	Team	W	L	PCT	ERA	G	GS	CG	IP	H	BB	SO	ShO	Relief Pitching W	Relief Pitching L	Relief Pitching SV	Batting AB	Batting H	HR	BA	PO	A	E	DP	TC/G	FA
1930	CHI N	3	2	.600	5.09	37	3	0	81.1	97	28	29	0	2	2	0	18	4	0	.222	6	22	1	1	0.8	.966
1933		5	5	.500	3.21	24	3	3	75.2	65	30	20	0	4	3	1	21	5	0	.238	1	20	0	1	0.9	1.000
1934		0	1	.000	36.00	2	1	0	1	4	1	0	0	0	0	0	0	0	0	—	0	0	0	0	0.0	.000
1937	PHI A	4	9	.308	5.90	30	4	1	116	140	51	49	0	4	**7**	2	113	40	4	.354	19	15	0	0	0.9	1.000
1938		10	11	.476	5.65	32	23	13	191	215	79	75	0	0	2	2	112	31	0	.277	4	36	2	0	1.3	.952

Lynn Nelson *continued*

Year	Team	W	L	PCT	ERA	G	GS	CG	IP	H	BB	SO	ShO	Relief Pitching W	L	SV	Batting AB	H	HR	BA	PO	A	E	DP	TC/G	FA
1939		10	13	.435	4.78	35	24	12	197.2	233	64	75	2	2	0	1	80	15	0	.188	11	27	2	6	1.1	.950
1940	DET A	1	1	.500	10.93	6	2	0	14	23	9	7	0	1	0	0	23	8	1	.348	0	3	0	0	0.5	1.000
7 yrs.		33	42	.440	5.25	166	60	29	676.2	777	262	255	2	13	14	6	*				41	123	5	8	1.0	.970

Mel Nelson

NELSON, MELVIN FREDERICK BR TL 6′ 185 lbs.
B. May 30, 1936, San Diego, Calif.

Year	Team	W	L	PCT	ERA	G	GS	CG	IP	H	BB	SO	ShO	Relief Pitching W	L	SV	Batting AB	H	HR	BA	PO	A	E	DP	TC/G	FA
1960	STL N	0	1	.000	3.38	2	1	0	8	7	2	7	0	0	0	0	2	1	0	.500	0	1	0	0	0.5	1.000
1963	LA A	2	3	.400	5.30	36	3	0	52.2	55	32	41	0	2	0	1	11	1	0	.091	1	15	0	0	0.4	1.000
1965	MIN A	0	4	.000	4.12	28	3	0	54.2	57	23	31	0	0	3	3	9	1	0	.111	2	8	0	0	0.4	1.000
1967		0	0	—	54.00	1	0	0	0.1	3	0	0	0	0	0	0	0	0	0	—	0	0	0	0	0.0	.000
1968	STL N	2	1	.667	2.91	18	4	1	52.2	49	9	16	0	0	1	1	12	2	0	.167	3	9	0	0	0.7	1.000
1969		0	1	.000	12.60	8	0	0	5	13	3	3	0	0	1	0	0	0	0	—	1	0	0	0	0.1	1.000
6 yrs.		4	10	.286	4.41	93	11	1	173.1	184	69	98	0	2	5	5	34	5	0	.147	7	33	0	0	0.4	1.000
WORLD SERIES																										
1968	STL N	0	0	—	0.00	1	0	0	1	0	0	1	0	0	0	0	0	0	0	—	0	0	0	0	0.0	.000

Red Nelson

NELSON, ALBERT FRANCIS BR TR 5′11″ 190 lbs.
Born Albert W. Horazdovsky.
B. May 19, 1886, Cleveland, Ohio D. Oct. 26, 1956, St. Petersburg, Fla.

Year	Team	W	L	PCT	ERA	G	GS	CG	IP	H	BB	SO	ShO	Relief Pitching W	L	SV	Batting AB	H	HR	BA	PO	A	E	DP	TC/G	FA
1910	STL A	5	1	.833	2.55	7	6	6	60	57	14	30	1	0	0	0	23	6	1	.261	4	36	1	1	5.9	.976
1911		3	9	.250	5.22	16	13	6	81	103	44	24	0	1	0	0	27	3	0	.111	0	22	2	0	1.5	.917
1912	2 teams STL A (8G 0–2) PHI N (4G 2–0)																									
″	total	2	2	.500	5.30	12	5	1	37.1	46	19	11	0	0	0	1	13	2	0	.154	0	8	1	0	0.8	.889
1913	2 teams PHI N (2G 0–0) CIN N (2G 0–0)																									
″	total	0	0		8.10	4	0	0	10	15	8	3	0	0	0	0	3	1	0	.333	0	4	0	0	1.0	1.000
4 yrs.		10	12	.455	4.54	39	24	13	188.1	221	85	68	1	1	0	1	66	12	1	.182	4	70	4	1	2.0	.949

Roger Nelson

NELSON, ROGER EUGENE (Spider) BR TR 6′3″ 200 lbs.
B. June 7, 1944, Altadena, Calif.

Year	Team	W	L	PCT	ERA	G	GS	CG	IP	H	BB	SO	ShO	Relief Pitching W	L	SV	Batting AB	H	HR	BA	PO	A	E	DP	TC/G	FA
1967	CHI A	0	1	.000	1.29	5	0	0	7	4	0	4	0	0	1	0	0	0	0	—	1	2	0	1	0.6	1.000
1968	BAL A	4	3	.571	2.41	19	6	0	71	49	26	70	0	2	1	1	16	1	0	.063	3	8	0	0	0.6	1.000
1969	KC A	7	13	.350	3.31	29	29	8	193.1	170	65	82	1	0	0	0	58	8	0	.138	19	25	5	3	1.7	.898
1970		0	2	.000	10.00	4	2	0	9	18	0	3	0	0	0	0	0	0	0	—	0	3	0	0	0.8	1.000
1971		0	1	.000	5.29	13	1	0	34	35	5	29	0	0	1	0	6	2	0	.333	2	9	0	0	0.8	1.000
1972		11	6	.647	2.08	34	19	10	173.1	120	31	120	6	1	1	2	54	5	0	.093	8	33	1	1	1.2	.976
1973	CIN N	3	2	.600	3.46	14	8	1	54.2	49	24	17	0	0	0	0	18	2	0	.111	3	12	0	2	1.1	1.000
1974		4	4	.500	3.39	14	12	1	85	67	35	42	0	0	0	1	28	5	0	.179	6	10	2	1	1.3	.889
1976	KC A	0	0	—	2.00	3	0	0	9	4	4	4	0	0	0	0	0	0	0	—	1	1	0	0	0.7	1.000
9 yrs.		29	32	.475	3.06	135	77	20	636.1	516	190	371	7	3	4	4	180	23	0	.128	43	103	8	8	1.1	.948
LEAGUE CHAMPIONSHIP SERIES																										
1973	CIN N	0	0	—	0.00	1	0	0	2.1	0	1	0	0	0	0	0	1	0	0	.000	0	0	0	0	0.0	.000

Robb Nen

NEN, ROBERT ALLEN BR TR 6′4″ 200 lbs.
Son of Dick Nen.
B. Nov. 28, 1969, San Pedro, Calif.

Year	Team	W	L	PCT	ERA	G	GS	CG	IP	H	BB	SO	ShO	Relief Pitching W	L	SV	Batting AB	H	HR	BA	PO	A	E	DP	TC/G	FA
1993	2 teams TEX A (9G 1–1) FLA N (15G 1–0)																									
″	total	2	1	.667	6.75	24	4	0	56	63	46	39	0	0	0	0	4	0	0	.000	6	6	0	2	0.5	1.000
1994	FLA N	5	5	.500	2.95	44	0	0	58	46	17	60	0	5	5	15	3	0	0	.000	3	6	1	1	0.2	.900
1995		0	7	.000	3.29	62	0	0	65.2	62	23	68	0	0	7	23	0	0	0	—	3	9	0	1	0.2	1.000
3 yrs.		7	13	.350	4.26	130	4	0	179.2	171	86	167	0	5	12	38	7	0	0	.000	12	21	1	4	0.3	.971

Hal Neubauer

NEUBAUER, HAROLD CHARLES BR TR 6′½″ 185 lbs.
B. May 13, 1902, Hoboken, N. J. D. Sept. 9, 1949, Barrington, R. I.

Year	Team	W	L	PCT	ERA	G	GS	CG	IP	H	BB	SO	ShO	Relief Pitching W	L	SV	Batting AB	H	HR	BA	PO	A	E	DP	TC/G	FA
1925	BOS A	1	0	1.000	12.19	7	0	0	10.1	17	11	4	0	1	0	0	0	0	0	—	0	3	0	0	0.4	1.000

Tex Neuer

NEUER, JOHN S. TL
B. June 8, 1877, Fremont, Ohio D. Jan. 14, 1966, Northumberland, Pa.

Year	Team	W	L	PCT	ERA	G	GS	CG	IP	H	BB	SO	ShO	Relief Pitching W	L	SV	Batting AB	H	HR	BA	PO	A	E	DP	TC/G	FA
1907	NY A	4	2	.667	2.17	7	6	6	54	40	19	22	3	0	0	0	21	2	0	.095	4	11	1	0	2.3	.938

Dan Neumeier

NEUMEIER, DANIEL GEORGE BR TR 6′5″ 205 lbs.
B. Mar. 9, 1948, Shawano, Wis.

Year	Team	W	L	PCT	ERA	G	GS	CG	IP	H	BB	SO	ShO	Relief Pitching W	L	SV	Batting AB	H	HR	BA	PO	A	E	DP	TC/G	FA
1972	CHI A	0	0	—	7.36	3	0	0	3.2	2	3	0	0	0	0	0	1	0	0	.000	0	0	0	0	0.0	.000

Ernie Nevel

NEVEL, ERNIE WYRE BR TR 5′11″ 190 lbs.
B. Aug. 17, 1919, Charleston, Mo. D. July 10, 1988, Springfield, Mo.

Year	Team	W	L	PCT	ERA	G	GS	CG	IP	H	BB	SO	ShO	Relief Pitching W	L	SV	Batting AB	H	HR	BA	PO	A	E	DP	TC/G	FA
1950	NY A	0	1	.000	9.95	3	1	0	6.1	10	6	3	0	0	0	0	1	0	0	.000	0	2	0	0	0.7	1.000
1951		0	0	—	0.00	1	0	0	4	1	1	1	0	0	0	1	1	0	0	.000	0	0	0	0	0.0	.000
1953	CIN N	0	0	—	6.10	10	0	0	10.1	16	1	5	0	0	0	0	0	0	0	—	0	2	0	0	0.2	1.000
3 yrs.		0	1	.000	6.10	14	1	0	20.2	27	8	9	0	0	0	1	2	0	0	.000	0	4	0	0	0.3	1.000

Ernie Nevers

NEVERS, ERNEST ALONZO BR TR 6′ 205 lbs.
B. June 11, 1902, Willow River, Minn. D. May 3, 1976, San Rafael, Calif.

Year	Team	W	L	PCT	ERA	G	GS	CG	IP	H	BB	SO	ShO	Relief Pitching W	L	SV	Batting AB	H	HR	BA	PO	A	E	DP	TC/G	FA
1926	STL A	2	4	.333	4.46	11	7	4	74.2	82	24	16	0	0	0	0	27	5	0	.185	8	27	0	1	3.2	1.000
1927		3	8	.273	4.94	27	5	2	94.2	105	35	22	0	3	4	2	32	7	0	.219	5	31	4	0	1.5	.900
1928		1	0	1.000	3.00	6	0	0	9	9	2	1	0	1	0	0	1	0	0	.000	1	2	0	0	0.5	1.000
3 yrs.		6	12	.333	4.64	44	12	6	178.1	196	61	39	0	4	4	2	60	12	0	.200	14	60	4	1	1.8	.949

Don Newcombe

NEWCOMBE, DONALD (Newk) BL TR 6′4″ 220 lbs.
B. June 14, 1926, Madison, N. J.

Year	Team	W	L	PCT	ERA	G	GS	CG	IP	H	BB	SO	ShO	Relief Pitching W	L	SV	Batting AB	H	HR	BA	PO	A	E	DP	TC/G	FA
1949	BKN N	17	8	.680	3.17	38	31	19	244.1	223	73	149	**5**	0	0	1	96	22	0	.229	17	40	0	2	1.5	1.000
1950		19	11	.633	3.70	40	35	20	267.1	258	75	130	4	0	0	3	97	24	1	.247	19	43	2	3	1.6	.969
1951		20	9	.690	3.28	40	36	18	272	235	91	**164**	3	1	1	0	103	23	0	.223	24	45	3	3	1.8	.958
1954		9	8	.529	4.55	29	25	6	144.1	158	49	82	0	0	0	0	47	15	0	.319	11	16	2	2	1.0	.931
1955		20	5	**.800**	3.20	34	31	17	233.2	222	38	143	1	1	0	0	117	42	7	.359	15	24	4	5	1.3	.907

Don Newcombe *continued*

Year	Team	W	L	PCT	ERA	G	GS	CG	IP	H	BB	SO	ShO	Relief Pitching W	Relief Pitching L	Relief Pitching SV	Batting AB	Batting H	Batting HR	BA	PO	A	E	DP	TC/G	FA
1956		**27**	7	**.794**	3.06	38	36	18	268	219	46	139	5	2	0	0	111	26	2	.234	25	39	1	5	1.7	.985
1957		11	12	.478	3.49	28	28	12	198.2	199	33	90	4	0	0	0	74	17	1	.230	13	41	2	1	2.0	.964
1958	2 teams	LA N (11G 0–6)			CIN N (20G 7–7)																					
"	total	7	13	.350	4.67	31	26	8	167.2	212	36	69	0	0	1	1	72	26	1	.361	11	19	0	2	1.0	1.000
1959	CIN N	13	8	.619	3.16	30	29	17	222	216	27	100	2	0	0	1	105	32	3	.305	14	31	1	4	1.5	.978
1960	2 teams	CIN N (16G 4–6)			CLE A (20G 2–3)																					
"	total	6	9	.400	4.48	36	17	1	136.2	160	22	63	0	2	1	1	56	11	0	.196	10	15	3	0	0.8	.893
10 yrs.		149	90	.623	3.56	344	294	136	2154.2	2102	490	1129	24	6	3	7	*				159	313	18	27	1.4	.963
WORLD SERIES																										
1949	BKN N	0	2	.000	3.09	2	2	1	11.2	10	3	11	0	0	0	0	4	0	0	.000	1	1	0	0	1.0	1.000
1955		0	1	.000	9.53	1	1	0	5.2	8	2	4	0	0	0	0	3	0	0	.000	0	1	0	0	1.0	1.000
1956		0	1	.000	21.21	2	2	0	4.2	11	3	4	0	0	0	0	1	0	0	.000	0	2	0	0	1.0	1.000
3 yrs.		0	4	.000	8.59	5	5	1	22	29	8	19	0	0	0	0	*				1	4	0	0	1.0	1.000

Tom Newell

NEWELL, THOMAS DEAN
B. May 17, 1963, Monrovia, Calif.

BR TR 6′ 1″ 185 lbs.

Year	Team	W	L	PCT	ERA	G	GS	CG	IP	H	BB	SO	ShO	Relief Pitching W	Relief Pitching L	Relief Pitching SV	Batting AB	Batting H	Batting HR	BA	PO	A	E	DP	TC/G	FA
1987	PHI N	0	0	—	108.00	2	0	0	0.1	4	3	1	0	0	0	0	0	0	0	—	0	0	0	0	0.0	.000

Don Newhauser

NEWHAUSER, DONALD LOUIS
B. Nov. 7, 1947, Miami, Fla.

BR TR 6′ 4″ 200 lbs.

Year	Team	W	L	PCT	ERA	G	GS	CG	IP	H	BB	SO	ShO	Relief Pitching W	Relief Pitching L	Relief Pitching SV	Batting AB	Batting H	Batting HR	BA	PO	A	E	DP	TC/G	FA
1972	BOS A	4	2	.667	2.43	31	0	0	37	30	25	27	0	4	2	4	2	0	0	.000	0	6	0	0	0.2	1.000
1973		0	0	—	0.00	9	0	0	12	9	13	8	0	0	0	1	0	0	0	—	0	0	0	0	0.0	.000
1974		0	1	.000	9.00	2	0	0	4	5	4	2	0	0	1	0	0	0	0	—	1	1	0	0	1.0	1.000
3 yrs.		4	3	.571	2.38	42	0	0	53	44	42	37	0	4	3	5	2	0	0	.000	1	7	0	0	0.2	1.000

Hal Newhouser

NEWHOUSER, HAROLD (Prince Hal)
B. May 20, 1921, Detroit, Mich.
Hall of Fame 1992.

BL TL 6′ 2″ 180 lbs.

Year	Team	W	L	PCT	ERA	G	GS	CG	IP	H	BB	SO	ShO	Relief Pitching W	Relief Pitching L	Relief Pitching SV	Batting AB	Batting H	Batting HR	BA	PO	A	E	DP	TC/G	FA
1939	DET A	0	1	.000	5.40	1	1	1	5	3	4	4	0	0	0	0	1	0	0	.000	0	1	0	0	1.0	1.000
1940		9	9	.500	4.86	28	20	7	133.1	149	76	89	0	1	0	0	40	8	0	.200	5	31	1	0	1.3	.973
1941		9	11	.450	4.79	33	27	5	173	166	137	106	1	0	1	0	60	9	0	.150	4	37	0	4	1.2	1.000
1942		8	14	.364	2.45	38	23	11	183.2	137	114	103	1	0	2	5	52	8	0	.154	10	45	1	3	1.5	.982
1943		8	17	.320	3.04	37	25	10	195.2	163	**111**	144	1	1	1	1	65	12	0	.185	8	49	1	1	1.6	.983
1944		**29**	9	.763	2.22	47	34	25	312.1	264	102	**187**	6	4	2	2	120	29	0	.242	9	61	1	5	1.5	.986
1945		**25**	9	**.735**	**1.81**	40	**36**	**29**	**313.1**	239	110	**212**	**8**	1	0	2	109	28	0	.257	16	66	0	5	2.0	1.000
1946		**26**	9	.743	**1.94**	37	34	29	292.1	215	98	275	6	0	1	1	103	13	2	.126	15	47	3	4	1.8	.954
1947		17	**17**	.500	2.87	40	36	**24**	285	**268**	110	176	3	0	1	2	96	19	0	.198	23	52	4	3	2.0	.949
1948		**21**	12	.636	3.01	39	35	19	272.1	249	99	143	2	1	1	1	92	19	0	.207	11	52	1	5	1.6	.984
1949		18	11	.621	3.36	38	35	22	292	**277**	111	144	3	1	0	1	91	18	0	.198	7	69	3	3	2.1	.962
1950		15	13	.536	4.34	35	30	15	213.2	232	81	87	1	1	0	3	74	13	0	.176	10	37	2	1	1.4	.959
1951		6	6	.500	3.92	15	14	7	96.1	98	19	37	1	0	0	0	29	9	0	.310	3	22	2	4	1.8	.926
1952		9	9	.500	3.74	25	19	8	154	148	47	57	0	3	0	0	46	10	0	.217	10	31	3	2	1.8	.932
1953		0	1	.000	7.06	7	4	0	21.2	31	8	6	0	0	0	1	8	4	0	.500	1	4	0	0	0.7	1.000
1954	CLE A	7	2	.778	2.51	26	1	0	46.2	34	18	25	0	7	1	7	13	2	0	.154	3	7	0	0	0.4	1.000
1955		0	0	—	0.00	2	0	0	2.1	1	4	1	0	0	0	0	0	0	0	—	0	0	0	0	0.0	.000
17 yrs.		207	150	.580	3.06	488	374	212	2992.2	2674	1249	1796	33	20	10	26	999	201	2	.201	135	611	22	40	1.6	.971
WORLD SERIES																										
1945	DET A	2	1	.667	6.10	3	3	2	20.2	25	4	22	0	0	0	0	8	0	0	.000	2	6	1	0	3.0	.889
1954	CLE A	0	0	—	∞	1	0	0		1	1	0	0	0	0	0	0	0	0	—	0	0	0	0	0.0	.000
2 yrs.		2	1	.667	6.53	4	3	2	20.2	26	5	22	0	0	0	0	8	0	0	.000	2	6	1	0	2.3	.889

Floyd Newkirk

NEWKIRK, FLOYD ELMO (Three-Finger)
Brother of Joel Newkirk.
B. July 16, 1908, Norris City, Ill. D. Apr. 15, 1976, Clayton, Mo.

BR TR 5′11″ 178 lbs.

Year	Team	W	L	PCT	ERA	G	GS	CG	IP	H	BB	SO	ShO	Relief Pitching W	Relief Pitching L	Relief Pitching SV	Batting AB	Batting H	Batting HR	BA	PO	A	E	DP	TC/G	FA
1934	NY A	0	0	—	0.00	1	0	0	1	1	1	0	0	0	0	0	0	0	0	—	0	2	0	0	2.0	1.000

Joel Newkirk

NEWKIRK, JOEL IVAN (Sailor)
Brother of Floyd Newkirk.
B. June 1, 1896, Kyana, Ind. D. Jan. 22, 1966, El Dorado, Ill.

BR TR 6′ 180 lbs.

Year	Team	W	L	PCT	ERA	G	GS	CG	IP	H	BB	SO	ShO	Relief Pitching W	Relief Pitching L	Relief Pitching SV	Batting AB	Batting H	Batting HR	BA	PO	A	E	DP	TC/G	FA
1919	CHI N	0	0	—	13.50	1	0	0	2	2	3	1	0	0	0	0	1	0	0	.000	0	1	0	0	1.0	1.000
1920		0	1	.000	5.40	2	1	0	6.2	8	6	2	0	0	0	0	3	0	0	.000	0	0	1	0	0.5	.000
2 yrs.		0	1	.000	7.27	3	1	0	8.2	10	9	3	0	0	0	0	4	0	0	.000	0	1	1	0	0.7	.500

Maury Newlin

NEWLIN, MAURICE MILTON (Newley, Newt)
B. June 22, 1914, Bloomingdale, Ind. D. Aug. 14, 1978, Houston, Tex.

BR TR 6′ 176 lbs.

Year	Team	W	L	PCT	ERA	G	GS	CG	IP	H	BB	SO	ShO	Relief Pitching W	Relief Pitching L	Relief Pitching SV	Batting AB	Batting H	Batting HR	BA	PO	A	E	DP	TC/G	FA
1940	STL A	1	0	1.000	6.00	1	1	0	6	4	2	3	0	0	0	0	2	1	0	.500	0	0	0	0	0.0	.000
1941		0	2	.000	6.51	14	0	0	27.2	43	12	10	0	0	2	1	6	0	0	.000	0	9	1	0	0.7	.900
2 yrs.		1	2	.333	6.42	15	1	0	33.2	47	14	13	0	0	2	1	8	1	0	.125	0	9	1	0	0.7	.900

Fred Newman

NEWMAN, FREDERICK WILLIAM
B. Feb. 21, 1942, Boston, Mass. D. June 24, 1987, Framingham, Mass.

BR TR 6′ 3″ 180 lbs.

Year	Team	W	L	PCT	ERA	G	GS	CG	IP	H	BB	SO	ShO	Relief Pitching W	Relief Pitching L	Relief Pitching SV	Batting AB	Batting H	Batting HR	BA	PO	A	E	DP	TC/G	FA
1962	LA A	0	1	.000	9.95	4	1	0	6.1	11	3	4	0	0	0	0	1	0	0	.000	0	0	0	0	0.0	.000
1963		1	5	.167	5.32	12	8	0	44	56	15	16	0	0	0	0	16	4	0	.250	3	6	1	0	0.8	.900
1964		13	10	.565	2.75	32	28	7	190	177	39	83	2	0	0	0	61	11	1	.180	16	49	3	6	2.1	.956
1965	CAL A	14	16	.467	2.93	36	36	10	260.2	225	64	109	2	0	0	0	74	7	1	.095	25	83	3	4	3.1	.973
1966		4	7	.364	4.73	21	19	1	102.2	112	31	42	0	0	0	0	30	6	0	.200	8	21	1	1	1.4	.967
1967		1	0	1.000	1.42	3	1	0	6.1	8	2	0	0	1	0	0	1	0	0	.000	0	0	0	0	0.0	.000
6 yrs.		33	39	.458	3.41	108	93	18	610	589	154	254	4	1	0	0	183	28	2	.153	52	159	8	11	2.0	.963

Jeff Newman

NEWMAN, JEFFREY LYNN
B. Sept. 11, 1948, Ft. Worth, Tex.
Manager 1986.

BR TR 6′ 2″ 215 lbs.

Year	Team	W	L	PCT	ERA	G	GS	CG	IP	H	BB	SO	ShO	Relief Pitching W	L	SV	Batting AB	H	HR	BA	PO	A	E	DP	TC/G	FA
1977	OAK A	0	0	—	0.00	1	0	0	1	1	0	0	0	0	0	0	*				140	18	3	1	3.7	.981

Ray Newman

NEWMAN, RAYMOND FRANCIS
B. June 20, 1945, Evansville, Ind.

BL TL 6′ 5″ 205 lbs.

Year	Team	W	L	PCT	ERA	G	GS	CG	IP	H	BB	SO	ShO	Relief Pitching W	L	SV	Batting AB	H	HR	BA	PO	A	E	DP	TC/G	FA
1971	CHI N	1	2	.333	3.55	30	0	0	38	30	17	35	0	1	2	2	6	0	0	.000	1	6	0	0	0.2	1.000
1972	MIL A	0	0	—	0.00	4	0	0	7	4	2	1	0	0	0	1	1	1	0	1.000	0	2	0	0	0.5	1.000
1973		2	1	.667	2.95	11	0	0	18.1	19	5	10	0	2	1	1	0	0	0	—	0	6	0	0	0.5	1.000
3 yrs.		3	3	.500	2.98	45	0	0	63.1	53	24	46	0	3	3	4	7	1	0	.143	1	14	0	0	0.3	1.000

Bobo Newsom

NEWSOM, LOUIS NORMAN (Buck)
B. Aug. 11, 1907, Hartsville, S. C. D. Dec. 7, 1962, Orlando, Fla.

BR TR 6′ 3″ 200 lbs.

Year	Team	W	L	PCT	ERA	G	GS	CG	IP	H	BB	SO	ShO	Relief Pitching W	L	SV	Batting AB	H	HR	BA	PO	A	E	DP	TC/G	FA
1929	BKN N	0	3	.000	10.61	3	2	0	9.1	15	5	6	0	0	1	0	2	0	0	.000	0	2	0	1	0.7	1.000
1930		0	0	—	0.00	2	0	0	3	2	2	1	0	0	0	0	0	0	0	—	0	0	0	0	0.0	.000
1932	CHI N	0	0	—	0.00	1	0	0	1	1	0	0	0	0	0	0	0	0	0	—	0	1	0	0	1.0	1.000
1934	STL A	16	**20**	.444	4.01	47	32	15	262.1	259	**149**	135	2	3	4	5	93	17	0	.183	13	49	2	1	1.4	.969
1935	2 teams STL A (7G 0–6) WAS A (28G 11–12)																									
"	total	11	**18**	.379	4.52	35	29	18	241	276	97	87	2	0	2	3	84	23	0	.274	6	37	2	4	1.3	.956
1936	WAS A	17	15	.531	4.32	43	**38**	24	285.2	294	146	156	4	0	0	2	108	23	0	.213	11	50	1	5	1.4	.984
1937	2 teams WAS A (11G 3–4) BOS A (30G 13–10)																									
"	total	16	14	.533	4.74	41	**37**	17	275.1	271	**167**	166	1	1	1	0	100	22	1	.220	11	41	3	1	1.3	.945
1938	STL A	20	16	.556	5.08	44	**40**	**31**	**329.2**	**334**	192	226	0	0	0	1	124	31	0	.250	11	38	2	1	1.2	.961
1939	2 teams STL A (6G 3–1) DET A (35G 17–10)																									
"	total	20	11	.645	3.58	41	**37**	**24**	291.2	272	126	192	3	0	0	2	115	22	0	.191	12	39	3	1	1.3	.944
1940	DET A	21	5	.808	2.83	36	34	20	264	235	100	164	3	1	1	0	107	23	0	.215	3	32	3	3	1.1	.921
1941		12	**20**	.375	4.60	43	36	12	250.1	265	118	175	2	1	1	2	88	9	0	.102	5	36	2	2	1.0	.953
1942	2 teams WAS A (30G 11–17) BKN N (6G 2–2)																									
"	total	13	19	.406	4.73	36	34	17	245.2	264	106	**134**	3	1	0	0	86	12	0	.140	6	34	5	3	1.3	.889
1943	3 teams BKN N (22G 9–4) STL A (10G 1–6) WAS A (6G 3–3)																									
"	total	13	13	.500	4.22	38	27	8	217.1	220	113	123	1	4	1	1	74	18	0	.243	5	34	0	4	1.0	1.000
1944	PHI A	13	15	.464	2.82	37	33	18	265	243	82	142	2	0	0	1	88	10	0	.114	3	45	0	0	1.3	1.000
1945		8	**20**	.286	3.29	36	34	16	257.1	255	103	127	3	0	1	0	86	14	0	.163	12	28	2	1	1.2	.952
1946	2 teams PHI A (10G 3–5) WAS A (24G 11–8)																									
"	total	14	13	.519	2.93	34	31	17	236.2	224	90	114	3	0	0	1	81	12	0	.148	4	25	0	1	0.9	1.000
1947	2 teams WAS A (14G 4–6) NY A (17G 7–5)																									
"	total	11	11	.500	3.34	31	28	7	199.1	208	67	82	2	0	0	0	71	11	0	.155	5	18	2	1	0.8	.920
1948	NY N	0	4	.000	4.21	11	4	0	25.2	35	13	9	0	0	1	0	7	3	0	.429	1	4	1	0	0.5	.833
1952	2 teams WAS A (10G 1–1) PHI A (14G 3–3)																									
"	total	4	4	.500	3.88	24	5	1	60.1	54	32	27	0	3	2	3	17	2	0	.118	3	14	0	1	0.7	1.000
1953	PHI A	2	1	.667	4.89	17	2	1	38.2	44	24	16	0	1	0	0	6	1	0	.167	1	7	0	1	0.5	1.000
20 yrs.		211	222	.487	3.98	600	483	246	3759.1	3771	1732 **6th**	2082	31	15	15	21	1337	253	1	.189	112	534	28	31	1.1	.958
WORLD SERIES																										
1940	DET A	2	1	.667	1.38	3	3	3	26	18	4	17	1	0	0	0	10	1	0	.100	2	0	0	0	0.7	1.000
1947	NY A	0	1	.000	19.29	2	1	0	2.1	6	2	0	0	0	0	0	0	0	0	—	0	1	0	0	0.5	1.000
2 yrs.		2	2	.500	2.86	5	4	3	28.1	24	6	17	1	0	0	0	10	1	0	.100	2	1	0	0	0.6	1.000

Dick Newsome

NEWSOME, HEBER HAMPTON
B. Dec. 13, 1909, Ahoskie, N. C. D. Dec. 15, 1965, Ahoskie, N. C.

BR TR 6′ 185 lbs.

Year	Team	W	L	PCT	ERA	G	GS	CG	IP	H	BB	SO	ShO	Relief Pitching W	L	SV	Batting AB	H	HR	BA	PO	A	E	DP	TC/G	FA
1941	BOS A	19	10	.655	4.13	36	29	17	213.2	235	79	58	2	2	1	0	78	19	0	.244	19	53	2	5	2.1	.973
1942		8	10	.444	5.01	24	23	11	158	174	67	40	0	0	0	0	55	13	0	.236	11	36	4	4	2.1	.922
1943		8	13	.381	4.49	25	22	8	154.1	166	68	40	2	0	0	0	48	7	0	.146	8	25	1	2	1.4	.971
3 yrs.		35	33	.515	4.50	85	74	36	526	575	214	138	4	2	1	0	181	39	0	.215	38	114	7	11	1.9	.956

Doc Newton

NEWTON, EUSTACE JAMES
B. Oct. 26, 1877, Indianapolis, Ind. D. May 14, 1931, Memphis, Tenn.

BL TL 6′ 185 lbs.

Year	Team	W	L	PCT	ERA	G	GS	CG	IP	H	BB	SO	ShO	Relief Pitching W	L	SV	Batting AB	H	HR	BA	PO	A	E	DP	TC/G	FA
1900	CIN N	9	15	.375	4.14	35	27	22	234.2	255	100	88	1	2	1	0	86	17	0	.198	6	50	10	0	1.9	.848
1901	2 teams CIN N (20G 4–14) BKN N (13G 6–5)																									
"	total	10	19	.345	3.62	33	30	26	273.1	300	89	110	0	0	1	0	110	18	0	.164	14	78	18	3	3.3	.836
1902	BKN N	15	14	.517	2.42	31	28	26	264.1	208	87	107	5	**2**	0	0	109	19	0	.174	27	59	5	1	2.8	.945
1905	NY A	2	2	.500	2.11	11	7	2	59.2	61	24	15	0	0	0	0	22	3	0	.136	1	16	5	0	2.0	.773
1906		7	5	.583	3.17	21	15	6	125	118	33	52	2	1	0	0	41	9	0	.220	2	50	6	1	2.8	.897
1907		7	10	.412	3.18	19	15	10	133	132	31	70	0	2	0	0	37	4	0	.108	6	43	4	2	2.8	.925
1908		4	5	.444	2.95	23	13	6	88.1	78	41	49	1	0	1	1	25	4	0	.160	2	27	3	0	1.4	.906
1909		0	3	.000	2.82	4	4	1	22.1	27	11	11	0	0	0	0	6	1	0	.167	1	11	4	0	4.0	.750
8 yrs.		54	73	.425	3.22	177	139	99	1200.2	1179	416	502	9	7	3	1	436	75	0	.172	59	334	55	7	2.5	.877

Chet Nichols

NICHOLS, CHESTER RAYMOND, JR.
Son of Chet Nichols.
B. Feb. 22, 1931, Providence, R. I. D. Mar. 27, 1995, Lincoln, R. I.

BB TL 6′ 1½″ 165 lbs.

Year	Team	W	L	PCT	ERA	G	GS	CG	IP	H	BB	SO	ShO	Relief Pitching W	L	SV	Batting AB	H	HR	BA	PO	A	E	DP	TC/G	FA
1951	BOS N	11	8	.579	**2.88**	33	19	12	156	142	69	71	3	2	1	2	51	7	0	.137	6	36	0	2	1.3	1.000
1954	MIL N	9	11	.450	4.41	35	20	5	122.1	132	65	55	1	2	3	1	35	3	0	.086	3	27	0	3	0.9	1.000
1955		9	8	.529	4.00	34	21	6	144	139	67	44	0	1	1	1	52	8	0	.154	6	35	2	3	1.3	.953
1956		0	1	.000	6.75	2	0	0	4	9	3	2	0	0	1	0	1	0	0	.000	0	2	0	0	1.0	1.000
1960	BOS A	0	2	.000	4.26	6	1	0	12.2	12	4	11	0	0	1	0	3	0	0	.000	0	4	0	0	0.7	1.000
1961		3	2	.600	2.09	26	2	0	51.2	40	26	20	0	3	1	3	9	1	0	.111	3	23	0	1	1.0	1.000
1962		1	1	.500	3.00	29	1	0	57	61	22	33	0	0	1	3	9	0	0	.000	4	15	0	2	0.7	1.000
1963		1	3	.250	4.78	21	7	0	52.2	61	24	27	0	0	0	0	13	3	0	.231	2	8	1	1	0.5	.909
1964	CIN N	0	0	—	6.00	3	0	0	3	4	0	3	0	0	0	0	0	0	0	—	0	0	0	0	0.0	.000
9 yrs.		34	36	.486	3.64	189	71	23	603.1	600	280	266	4	8	9	10	173	22	0	.127	24	150	3	12	0.9	.983

Chet Nichols

NICHOLS, CHESTER RAYMOND, SR.
Father of Chet Nichols.
B. July 3, 1897, Woonsocket, R. I. D. July 11, 1982, Pawtucket, R. I.
BR TR 5′10″ 160 lbs.

Year	Team	Lg	W	L	PCT	ERA	G	GS	CG	IP	H	BB	SO	ShO	Relief Pitching W	Relief Pitching L	Relief Pitching SV	Batting AB	Batting H	Batting HR	BA	PO	A	E	DP	TC/G	FA
1926	PIT	N	0	0	—	8.22	3	0	0	7.2	13	5	2	0	0	0	0	3	1	0	.333	0	3	0	0	1.0	1.000
1927			0	3	.000	5.86	8	0	0	27.2	34	17	9	0	0	3	0	9	1	0	.111	0	6	0	0	0.8	1.000
1928	NY	N	0	0	—	23.63	3	0	0	2.2	11	3	1	0	0	0	0	0	0	0	—	0	1	0	0	0.3	1.000
1930	PHI	N	1	2	.333	6.79	16	5	1	59.2	76	16	15	0	0	0	0	20	6	0	.300	1	17	0	0	1.1	1.000
1931			0	1	.000	9.53	3	0	0	5.2	10	1	1	0	0	1	0	2	0	0	.000	1	1	0	0	0.7	1.000
1932			0	2	.000	6.98	11	0	0	19.1	23	14	5	0	0	2	1	4	0	0	.000	2	5	0	1	0.6	1.000
6 yrs.			1	8	.111	7.19	44	5	1	122.2	167	56	33	0	0	6	1	38	8	0	.211	4	33	0	1	0.8	1.000

Dolan Nichols

NICHOLS, DOLAN LEVON (Nick)
B. Feb. 28, 1930, Tishomingo, Miss. D. Nov. 20, 1989, Tupelo, Miss.
BR TR 6′ 195 lbs.

Year	Team	Lg	W	L	PCT	ERA	G	GS	CG	IP	H	BB	SO	ShO	Relief Pitching W	Relief Pitching L	Relief Pitching SV	Batting AB	Batting H	Batting HR	BA	PO	A	E	DP	TC/G	FA
1958	CHI	N	0	4	.000	5.01	24	0	0	41.1	46	16	9	0	0	4	1	5	0	0	.000	0	13	0	0	0.5	1.000

Kid Nichols

NICHOLS, CHARLES AUGUSTUS (Nick)
B. Sept. 14, 1869, Madison, Wis. D. Apr. 11, 1953, Kansas City, Mo.
Manager 1904–05.
Hall of Fame 1949.
BB TR 5′10½″ 175 lbs.

Year	Team	Lg	W	L	PCT	ERA	G	GS	CG	IP	H	BB	SO	ShO	Relief Pitching W	Relief Pitching L	Relief Pitching SV	Batting AB	Batting H	Batting HR	BA	PO	A	E	DP	TC/G	FA
1890	BOS	N	27	19	.587	2.21	48	47	47	427	374	112	222	**7**	0	0	0	174	43	0	.247	15	85	14	1	2.3	.877
1891			30	17	.638	2.39	52	48	45	425.2	413	103	240	5	0	1	**3**	183	36	0	.197	30	100	7	5	2.6	.949
1892			35	16	.686	2.83	53	51	50	454	404	121	187	5	1	0	0	197	39	2	.198	36	88	5	4	2.2	.961
1893			34	14	.708	3.52	52	44	44	425	426	118	94	1	4	1	1	177	39	2	.220	22	81	7	5	2.1	.936
1894			32	13	.711	4.75	50	46	40	407	488	121	113	**3**	1	1	0	170	50	0	.294	35	67	7	3	2.1	.936
1895			26	16	.619	3.41	47	42	42	379.2	417	86	140	1	0	0	**3**	157	37	0	.236	29	73	4	2	2.2	.962
1896			**30**	14	.682	2.81	49	43	37	375	387	101	102	3	2	1	1	147	28	1	.190	23	92	1	3	2.3	.991
1897			**31**	11	.738	2.64	**46**	40	37	**368**	362	72	136	2	2	0	**3**	147	39	3	.265	29	62	3	1	2.0	.968
1898			**31**	12	.721	2.13	**50**	42	40	388	316	85	138	5	2	0	**4**	158	38	2	.241	28	78	5	1	2.2	.955
1899			21	19	.525	2.94	42	37	37	349	326	82	108	4	1	2	1	136	26	1	.191	25	71	5	5	2.4	.950
1900			13	16	.448	3.07	29	27	25	231.1	215	72	53	**4**	0	2	0	90	18	1	.200	19	48	1	1	2.3	.985
1901			19	16	.543	3.22	38	34	33	321	306	90	143	4	2	1	0	163	46	4	.282	73	72	10	4	3.1	.935
1904	STL	N	21	13	.618	2.02	36	35	35	317	268	50	134	3	0	0	1	109	17	0	.156	13	84	5	1	2.8	.951
1905	2 teams	STL N (7G 1–5)	PHI N (17G 10–6)																								
″	total		11	11	.500	3.11	24	23	20	191	193	46	66	1	0	0	0	75	15	0	.200	5	32	5	1	1.7	.881
1906	PHI	N	0	1	.000	9.82	4	2	1	11	17	13	1	0	0	0	0	3	0	0	.000	0	1	0	0	0.3	1.000
15 yrs.			361 **6th**	208	.634	2.95	620	561	533 **4th**	5069.2	4912	1272	1877	48	15	9	17	*				382	1034	79	37	2.3	.947

Rod Nichols

NICHOLS, RODNEY LEA
B. Dec. 29, 1964, Burlington, Iowa.
BR TR 6′ 2″ 190 lbs.

Year	Team	Lg	W	L	PCT	ERA	G	GS	CG	IP	H	BB	SO	ShO	Relief Pitching W	Relief Pitching L	Relief Pitching SV	Batting AB	Batting H	Batting HR	BA	PO	A	E	DP	TC/G	FA
1988	CLE	A	1	7	.125	5.06	11	10	3	69.1	73	23	31	0	0	1	0	0	0	0	—	5	9	1	0	1.4	.933
1989			4	6	.400	4.40	15	11	0	71.2	81	24	42	0	0	2	0	0	0	0	—	4	8	0	2	0.8	1.000
1990			0	3	.000	7.88	4	2	0	16	24	6	3	0	0	1	0	0	0	0	—	0	4	0	0	1.0	1.000
1991			2	11	.154	3.54	31	16	3	137.1	145	30	76	1	0	1	1	0	0	0	—	10	14	1	1	0.8	.960
1992			4	3	.571	4.53	30	9	0	105.1	114	31	56	0	2	2	0	0	0	0	—	4	14	0	0	0.6	1.000
1993	LA	N	0	1	.000	5.68	4	0	0	6.1	9	2	3	0	0	1	0	0	0	0	—	1	2	0	1	0.8	1.000
1995	ATL	N	0	0	—	5.40	5	0	0	6.2	14	5	3	0	0	0	0	0	0	0	—	0	2	1	0	0.6	.667
7 yrs.			11	31	.262	4.43	100	48	6	412.2	460	121	214	1	2	8	1	0	0	0		24	53	3	4	0.8	.962

Tricky Nichols

NICHOLS, FREDERICK C.
B. July 26, 1850, Bridgeport, Conn. D. Aug. 22, 1897, Bridgeport, Conn.
BR TR 5′ 7½″ 150 lbs.

Year	Team	Lg	W	L	PCT	ERA	G	GS	CG	IP	H	BB	SO	ShO	Relief Pitching W	Relief Pitching L	Relief Pitching SV	Batting AB	Batting H	Batting HR	BA	PO	A	E	DP	TC/G	FA
1876	BOS	N	1	0	1.000	1.00	1	1	1	9	7	0	0	0	0	0	0	4	0	0	.000	0	2	0	0	2.0	1.000
1877	STL	N	18	23	.439	2.60	42	39	35	350	376	**53**	80	1	**2**	0	0	186	31	0	.167	32	62	8	1	1.8	.922
1878	PRO	N	4	7	.364	4.22	11	10	10	98	157	8	21	0	0	**1**	0	49	9	0	.184	6	27	1	2	3.1	.971
1880	WOR	N	0	2	.000	4.08	2	2	2	17.2	29	4	4	0	0	0	0	7	0	0	.000	0	3	3	0	3.0	.500
1882	BAL	AA	1	12	.077	*5.02*	16	13	12	118.1	155	17	21	0	0	0	0	95	15	0	.158	26	36	13	0	2.5	.827
5 yrs.			24	44	.353	3.37	72	65	60	593	724	82	126	1	2	1	0	*				64	130	25	3	2.1	.886

Frank Nicholson

NICHOLSON, FRANK COLLINS
B. Aug. 29, 1889, Berlin, Pa. D. Nov. 10, 1972, Jersey Shore, Pa.
BR TR 6′ 2″ 175 lbs.

Year	Team	Lg	W	L	PCT	ERA	G	GS	CG	IP	H	BB	SO	ShO	Relief Pitching W	Relief Pitching L	Relief Pitching SV	Batting AB	Batting H	Batting HR	BA	PO	A	E	DP	TC/G	FA
1912	PHI	N	0	0	—	6.75	2	0	0	4	8	2	1	0	0	0	0	0	0	0	—	0	1	0	0	0.5	1.000

Chris Nichting

NICHTING, CHRISTOPHER THOMAS
B. May 13, 1966, Cincinnati, Ohio.
BR TR 6′ 1″ 205 lbs.

Year	Team	Lg	W	L	PCT	ERA	G	GS	CG	IP	H	BB	SO	ShO	Relief Pitching W	Relief Pitching L	Relief Pitching SV	Batting AB	Batting H	Batting HR	BA	PO	A	E	DP	TC/G	FA
1995	TEX	A	0	0	—	7.03	13	0	0	24.1	36	13	6	0	0	0	0	0	0	0	—	5	7	0	0	0.9	1.000

George Nicol

NICOL, GEORGE EDWARD
B. Oct. 17, 1870, Barry, Ill. D. Aug. 10, 1924, Milwaukee, Wis.
TL 5′ 7″ 155 lbs.

Year	Team	Lg	W	L	PCT	ERA	G	GS	CG	IP	H	BB	SO	ShO	Relief Pitching W	Relief Pitching L	Relief Pitching SV	Batting AB	Batting H	Batting HR	BA	PO	A	E	DP	TC/G	FA
1890	STL	AA	2	1	.667	*4.76*	3	3	2	17	11	19	16	0	0	0	0	7	2	0	.286	2	0	0	0	0.7	1.000
1891	CHI	N	0	1	.000	4.91	3	2	0	11	14	10	12	0	0	1	0	6	2	0	.333	0	0	3	0	1.0	.000
1894	2 teams	PIT N (8G 3–4)	LOU N (1G 0–1)																								
″	total		3	5	.375	7.93	9	6	4	53.1	76	38	14	0	2	0	0	128	47	0	.367	32	9	10	1	1.5	.804
3 yrs.			5	7	.417	6.86	15	11	6	81.1	101	67	42	0	2	1	0	*				34	9	13	1	1.4	.768

Dave Nied

NIED, DAVID GLEN
B. Dec. 22, 1968, Dallas, Tex.
BR TR 6′ 2″ 175 lbs.

Year	Team	Lg	W	L	PCT	ERA	G	GS	CG	IP	H	BB	SO	ShO	Relief Pitching W	Relief Pitching L	Relief Pitching SV	Batting AB	Batting H	Batting HR	BA	PO	A	E	DP	TC/G	FA
1992	ATL	N	3	0	1.000	1.17	6	2	0	23	10	5	19	0	2	0	0	7	2	0	.286	0	2	0	0	0.3	1.000
1993	CLR	N	5	9	.357	5.17	16	16	1	87	99	42	46	0	0	0	0	23	4	0	.174	4	16	0	0	1.3	1.000
1994			9	7	.563	4.80	22	22	2	122	137	47	74	1	0	0	0	40	4	0	.100	4	12	0	2	0.7	1.000
1995			0	0	—	20.77	2	0	0	4.1	11	3	3	0	0	0	0	0	0	0	—	0	0	0	0	0.0	.000
4 yrs.			17	16	.515	4.87	46	40	3	236.1	257	97	142	1	2	0	0	70	10	0	.143	8	30	0	2	0.8	1.000

Tom Niedenfuer

NIEDENFUER, THOMAS EDWARD
B. Aug. 13, 1959, St. Louis Park, Minn.

BR TR 6' 5" 225 lbs.

Year	Team	W	L	PCT	ERA	G	GS	CG	IP	H	BB	SO	ShO	Relief W	Relief L	Relief SV	AB	H	HR	BA	PO	A	E	DP	TC/G	FA
1981	**LA N**	3	1	.750	3.81	17	0	0	26	25	6	12	0	3	1	2	0	0	0	—	4	2	0	0	0.4	1.000
1982		3	4	.429	2.71	55	0	0	69.2	71	25	60	0	3	4	9	3	0	0	.000	1	7	0	0	0.1	1.000
1983		8	3	.727	1.90	66	0	0	94.2	55	29	66	0	8	3	11	4	0	0	.000	8	8	1	0	0.3	.941
1984		2	5	.286	2.47	33	0	0	47.1	39	23	45	0	2	5	11	3	0	0	.000	1	5	1	0	0.2	.857
1985		7	9	.438	2.71	64	0	0	106.1	86	24	102	0	7	9	19	9	1	0	.111	8	7	0	0	0.2	1.000
1986		6	6	.500	3.71	60	0	0	80	86	29	55	0	6	6	11	4	2	0	.500	9	10	1	1	0.3	.950
1987	**2 teams** **LA N** (15G 1–0) **BAL A** (45G 3–5)																									
"	**total**	4	5	.444	4.46	60	0	0	68.2	68	31	47	0	4	5	14	0	0	0	—	7	6	1	2	0.2	.929
1988	**BAL A**	3	4	.429	3.51	52	0	0	59	59	19	40	0	3	4	18	0	0	0	—	3	5	1	1	0.2	.889
1989	**SEA A**	0	3	.000	6.69	25	0	0	36.1	46	15	15	0	0	3	0	0	0	0	—	6	5	2	0	0.5	.846
1990	**STL N**	0	6	.000	3.46	52	0	0	65	66	25	32	0	0	6	2	3	0	0	.000	3	7	2	0	0.2	.833
10 yrs.		36	46	.439	3.29	484	0	0	653	601	226	474	0	36	46	97	26	3	0	.115	50	62	9	4	0.3	.926
DIVISIONAL PLAYOFF SERIES																										
1981	**LA N**	0	0	—	0.00	1	0	0	0.1	1	1	1	0	0	0	0	0	0	0	—	0	0	0	0	0.0	.000
LEAGUE CHAMPIONSHIP SERIES																										
1981	**LA N**	0	0	—	0.00	1	0	0	0.1	2	0	0	0	0	0	0	0	0	0	—	0	1	0	0	1.0	1.000
1983		0	0	—	0.00	2	0	0	2	0	1	3	0	0	0	1	0	0	0	—	0	1	0	0	0.5	1.000
1985		0	2	.000	6.35	3	0	0	5.2	5	2	5	0	0	2	1	1	0	0	.000	2	0	0	0	0.7	1.000
3 yrs.		0	2	.000	4.50	6	0	0	8	7	3	8	0	0	2	2	1	0	0	.000	2	2	0	0	0.7	1.000
WORLD SERIES																										
1981	**LA N**	0	0	—	0.00	2	0	0	5	3	1	0	0	0	0	0	0	0	0	—	0	0	0	0	0.0	.000

Dick Niehaus

NIEHAUS, RICHARD J.
B. Oct. 24, 1892, Covington, Ky. D. Mar. 12, 1957, Atlanta, Ga.

BL TL 5'11" 165 lbs.

Year	Team	W	L	PCT	ERA	G	GS	CG	IP	H	BB	SO	ShO	Relief W	Relief L	Relief SV	AB	H	HR	BA	PO	A	E	DP	TC/G	FA
1913	**STL N**	0	2	.000	4.13	3	3	2	24	20	13	4	0	0	0	0	7	2	0	.286	0	9	1	0	3.3	.900
1914		1	0	1.000	3.12	8	1	1	17.1	18	8	6	0	0	0	0	4	1	0	.250	1	3	2	0	0.8	.667
1915		2	1	.667	3.97	15	2	0	45.1	48	22	21	0	1	0	0	14	1	0	.071	1	14	2	0	1.1	.882
1920	**CLE A**	1	2	.333	3.60	19	3	0	40	42	16	12	0	1	0	2	9	4	0	.444	0	5	0	0	0.3	1.000
4 yrs.		4	5	.444	3.77	45	9	3	126.2	128	59	43	0	2	0	2	34	8	0	.235	2	31	5	0	0.8	.868

Joe Niekro

NIEKRO, JOSEPH FRANKLIN
Brother of Phil Niekro.
B. Nov. 7, 1944, Martins Ferry, Ohio.

BR TR 6' 1" 185 lbs.

Year	Team	W	L	PCT	ERA	G	GS	CG	IP	H	BB	SO	ShO	Relief W	Relief L	Relief SV	AB	H	HR	BA	PO	A	E	DP	TC/G	FA
1967	**CHI N**	10	7	.588	3.34	36	22	7	169.2	171	32	77	2	1	1	0	46	9	0	.196	10	26	0	1	1.0	1.000
1968		14	10	.583	4.31	34	29	2	177.1	204	59	65	1	1	0	2	60	6	0	.100	9	33	0	2	1.2	1.000
1969	**2 teams** **CHI N** (4G 0–1) **SD N** (37G 8–17)																									
"	**total**	8	18	.308	3.70	41	34	8	221.1	237	51	62	3	0	0	0	56	7	0	.125	21	34	5	2	1.5	.917
1970	**DET A**	12	13	.480	4.06	38	34	6	213	221	72	101	2	1	0	0	66	13	0	.197	17	35	1	1	1.4	.981
1971		6	7	.462	4.50	31	15	0	122	136	49	43	0	2	0	1	30	4	0	.133	9	25	1	1	1.1	.971
1972		3	2	.600	3.83	18	7	1	47	62	8	24	0	0	1	1	12	3	0	.250	5	4	0	1	0.5	1.000
1973	**ATL N**	2	4	.333	4.13	20	0	0	24	23	11	12	0	2	4	3	3	1	0	.333	2	5	0	2	0.3	1.000
1974		3	2	.600	3.56	27	2	0	43	36	18	31	0	3	2	0	5	0	0	.000	4	8	0	1	0.4	1.000
1975	**HOU N**	6	4	.600	3.07	40	4	1	88	79	39	54	1	3	4	4	14	3	0	.214	7	13	0	0	0.5	1.000
1976		4	8	.333	3.36	36	13	0	118	107	56	77	0	0	2	0	27	5	1	.185	9	13	3	1	0.7	.880
1977		13	8	.619	3.03	44	14	9	181	155	64	101	2	4	4	5	50	7	0	.140	11	31	0	7	1.0	1.000
1978		14	14	.500	3.86	35	29	10	203	190	73	97	1	1	0	0	65	9	0	.138	18	21	0	3	1.1	1.000
1979		**21**	11	.656	3.00	38	38	11	264	221	107	119	**5**	0	0	0	83	10	0	.120	14	39	0	4	1.4	1.000
1980		20	12	.625	3.55	37	36	11	256	268	79	127	2	1	0	0	80	22	0	.275	17	37	2	2	1.5	.964
1981		9	9	.500	2.82	24	24	5	166	150	47	77	2	0	0	0	51	9	0	.176	11	23	0	1	1.4	1.000
1982		17	12	.586	2.47	35	35	16	270	224	64	130	5	0	0	0	89	8	0	.090	22	42	3	2	1.9	.955
1983		15	14	.517	3.48	38	**38**	9	263.2	238	101	152	1	0	0	0	85	8	0	.094	9	36	4	0	1.3	.918
1984		16	12	.571	3.04	38	**38**	6	248.1	223	89	127	1	0	0	0	83	11	0	.133	19	39	2	5	1.6	.967
1985	**2 teams** **HOU N** (32G 9–12) **NY A** (3G 2–1)																									
"	**total**	11	13	.458	3.83	35	35	4	225.1	211	107	121	1	0	0	0	68	17	0	.250	17	36	1	1	1.5	.981
1986	**NY A**	9	10	.474	4.87	25	25	0	125.2	139	63	59	0	0	0	0	0	0	0	—	9	13	1	2	0.9	.957
1987	**2 teams** **NY A** (8G 3–4) **MIN A** (19G 4–9)																									
"	**total**	7	13	.350	5.33	27	26	1	147	155	64	84	0	0	0	0	0	0	0		11	16	2	1	1.1	.931
1988	**MIN A**	1	1	.500	10.03	5	2	0	11.2	16	9	7	0	1	0	0	0	0	0	—	2	3	0	1	1.0	1.000
22 yrs.		221	204	.520	3.59	702	500	107	3585	3466	1262	1747	29	20	18	16	973	152	1	.156	253	532	25	41	1.2	.969
DIVISIONAL PLAYOFF SERIES																										
1981	**HOU N**	0	0	—	0.00	1	1	0	8	7	3	4	0	0	0	0	2	0	0	.000	0	0	0	0	0.0	.000
LEAGUE CHAMPIONSHIP SERIES																										
1980	**HOU N**	0	0	—	0.00	1	1	0	10	6	1	2	0	0	0	0	3	0	0	.000	1	0	0	0	1.0	1.000
WORLD SERIES																										
1987	**MIN A**	0	0	—	0.00	1	0	0	2	1	1	1	0	0	0	0	0	0	0	—	0	1	0	0	1.0	1.000

Phil Niekro

NIEKRO, PHILIP HENRY (Knucksie)
Brother of Joe Niekro.
B. Apr. 1, 1939, Blaine, Ohio.

BR TR 6' 1" 180 lbs.

Year	Team	W	L	PCT	ERA	G	GS	CG	IP	H	BB	SO	ShO	Relief W	Relief L	Relief SV	AB	H	HR	BA	PO	A	E	DP	TC/G	FA
1964	**MIL N**	0	0	—	4.80	10	0	0	15	15	7	8	0	0	0	0	0	0	0	—	0	2	0	1	0.2	1.000
1965		2	3	.400	2.89	41	1	0	74.2	73	26	49	0	1	3	6	10	1	0	.100	6	17	1	2	0.6	.958
1966	**ATL N**	4	3	.571	4.11	28	0	0	50.1	48	23	17	0	4	3	2	8	0	0	.000	2	18	0	1	0.7	1.000
1967		11	9	.550	**1.87**	46	20	10	207	164	55	129	1	1	2	9	57	7	0	.123	10	40	4	4	1.2	.926
1968		14	12	.538	2.59	37	34	15	256.2	228	45	140	5	0	1	2	77	8	2	.104	18	59	4	4	2.2	.951
1969		23	13	.639	2.57	40	35	21	284	235	57	193	4	0	0	1	95	20	0	.211	24	51	3	4	2.0	.962
1970		12	18	.400	4.27	34	32	10	230	222	68	168	3	1	0	0	79	12	1	.152	14	38	1	4	1.6	.981
1971		15	14	.517	2.98	42	36	18	269	248	70	173	4	1	0	2	92	14	0	.152	19	44	2	6	1.5	.969
1972		16	12	.571	3.06	38	36	17	282	254	53	164	1	0	1	0	93	18	1	.194	26	40	4	4	1.8	.943
1973		13	10	.565	3.31	42	30	9	245	214	89	131	1	2	1	4	82	10	1	.122	30	41	4	4	1.8	.947
1974		**20**	13	.606	2.38	41	39	**18**	**302**	249	88	195	6	0	0	1	104	20	0	.192	22	42	0	3	1.6	1.000
1975		15	15	.500	3.20	39	37	13	276	285	72	144	1	0	1	1	99	17	0	.172	21	41	0	2	1.6	1.000

Phil Niekro *continued*

Year	Team	W	L	PCT	ERA	G	GS	CG	IP	H	BB	SO	ShO	Relief Pitching W	Relief Pitching L	Relief Pitching SV	Batting AB	Batting H	HR	BA	PO	A	E	DP	TC/G	FA
1976		17	11	.607	3.29	38	37	10	271	249	101	173	2	0	0	0	94	18	1	.191	19	41	2	2	1.6	.968
1977		16	**20**	.444	4.04	44	**43**	**20**	**330**	**315**	**164**	**262**	2	1	0	0	109	19	0	.174	20	51	0	5	1.6	1.000
1978		19	**18**	.514	2.88	44	**42**	**22**	**334**	**295**	102	248	4	0	0	1	120	27	0	.225	17	65	2	4	1.9	.976
1979		**21**	**20**	.512	3.39	44	**44**	**23**	**342**	**311**	**113**	208	1	0	0	0	123	24	0	.195	31	56	1	3	2.0	.989
1980		15	**18**	.455	3.63	40	**38**	11	275	256	85	176	3	1	0	1	90	12	0	.133	18	40	1	6	1.5	.983
1981		7	7	.500	3.11	22	22	3	139	120	56	62	3	0	0	0	52	4	0	.077	10	22	0	2	1.5	1.000
1982		17	4	**.810**	3.61	35	35	4	234.1	225	73	144	2	0	0	0	87	17	1	.195	18	38	1	4	1.6	.982
1983		11	10	.524	3.97	34	33	2	201.2	212	105	128	0	0	0	0	65	12	0	.185	15	27	2	6	1.3	.955
1984	NY A	16	8	.667	3.09	32	31	5	215.2	219	76	136	1	0	0	0	0	0	0	—	13	36	1	4	1.6	.980
1985		16	12	.571	4.09	33	33	7	220	203	**120**	149	1	0	0	0	0	0	0	—	11	20	0	5	0.9	1.000
1986	CLE A	11	11	.500	4.32	34	32	5	210.1	241	95	81	0	2	0	0	0	0	0	—	9	32	4	2	1.3	.911
1987	3 teams CLE A (22G 7–11) TOR A (3G 0–2) ATL N (1G 0–0)																									
"	total	7	13	.350	6.30	26	26	2	138.2	163	66	64	0	0	0	0	1	0	0	.000	13	17	0	1	1.2	1.000
24 yrs.		318	274	.537	3.35	864	716	245	5403.1	5044	1809	3342	45	14	12	30	1537	260	7	.169	386	878	37	83	1.5	.972
			5th						**4th**		**3rd**	**8th**														
LEAGUE CHAMPIONSHIP SERIES																										
1969	ATL N	0	1	.000	4.50	1	1	0	8	9	4	4	0	0	0	0	3	0	0	.000	0	3	0	0	3.0	1.000
1982		0	0	—	3.00	1	1	0	6	6	4	5	0	0	0	0	0	0	0	—	1	1	0	0	2.0	1.000
2 yrs.		0	1	.000	3.86	2	2	0	14	15	8	9	0	0	0	0	3	0	0	.000	1	4	0	0	2.5	1.000

Jerry Nielsen

NIELSEN, GERALD ARTHUR BL TL 6′ 3″ 185 lbs.
B. Aug. 5, 1966, Sacramento, Calif.

Year	Team	W	L	PCT	ERA	G	GS	CG	IP	H	BB	SO	ShO	Relief Pitching W	Relief Pitching L	Relief Pitching SV	Batting AB	Batting H	HR	BA	PO	A	E	DP	TC/G	FA
1992	NY A	1	0	1.000	4.58	20	0	0	19.2	17	18	12	0	1	0	0	0	0	0	—	1	4	0	0	0.3	1.000
1993	CAL A	0	0	—	8.03	10	0	0	12.1	18	4	8	0	0	0	0	0	0	0	—	1	1	0	0	0.2	1.000
2 yrs.		1	0	1.000	5.91	30	0	0	32	35	22	20	0	1	0	0	0	0	0		2	5	0	0	0.2	1.000

Scott Nielsen

NIELSEN, JEFFREY SCOTT BR TR 6′ 1″ 190 lbs.
B. Dec. 18, 1958, Salt Lake City, Utah.

Year	Team	W	L	PCT	ERA	G	GS	CG	IP	H	BB	SO	ShO	Relief Pitching W	Relief Pitching L	Relief Pitching SV	Batting AB	Batting H	HR	BA	PO	A	E	DP	TC/G	FA
1986	NY A	4	4	.500	4.02	10	9	2	56	66	12	20	2	0	0	0	0	0	0	—	0	5	0	2	0.5	1.000
1987	CHI A	3	5	.375	6.24	19	7	1	66.1	83	25	23	1	1	0	2	0	0	0	—	4	9	2	0	0.8	.867
1988	NY A	1	2	.333	6.86	7	2	0	19.2	27	13	4	0	1	0	0	0	0	0	—	0	5	0	2	0.7	1.000
1989		1	0	1.000	13.50	2	0	0	0.2	2	1	0	0	1	0	0	0	0	0	—	0	0	0	0	0.0	.000
4 yrs.		9	11	.450	5.49	38	18	3	142.2	178	51	47	3	3	0	2	0	0	0		4	19	2	4	0.7	.920

Randy Niemann

NIEMANN, RANDAL HAROLD BL TL 6′ 4″ 200 lbs.
B. Nov. 15, 1955, Scotia, Calif.

Year	Team	W	L	PCT	ERA	G	GS	CG	IP	H	BB	SO	ShO	Relief Pitching W	Relief Pitching L	Relief Pitching SV	Batting AB	Batting H	HR	BA	PO	A	E	DP	TC/G	FA
1979	HOU N	3	2	.600	3.76	26	7	3	67	68	22	24	2	0	1	1	15	2	0	.133	1	7	0	0	0.3	1.000
1980		0	1	.000	5.45	22	1	0	33	40	12	18	0	0	1	1	6	2	0	.333	4	8	0	0	0.5	1.000
1982	PIT N	1	1	.500	5.09	20	0	0	35.1	34	17	26	0	1	1	1	2	2	0	1.000	4	7	0	0	0.6	1.000
1983		0	1	.000	9.22	8	1	0	13.2	20	7	8	0	0	0	0	1	0	0	.000	2	2	0	1	0.5	1.000
1984	CHI A	0	0	—	1.69	5	0	0	5.1	5	5	5	0	0	0	0	0	0	0	—	2	1	0	0	0.6	1.000
1985	NY N	0	0	—	0.00	4	0	0	4.2	5	0	2	0	0	0	0	0	0	0	—	0	2	0	0	0.5	1.000
1986		2	3	.400	3.79	31	1	0	35.2	44	12	18	0	1	3	0	6	2	0	.333	3	9	0	1	0.4	1.000
1987	MIN A	1	0	1.000	8.44	6	0	0	5.1	3	7	1	0	1	0	0	0	0	0	—	0	1	0	0	0.2	1.000
8 yrs.		7	8	.467	4.64	122	10	3	200	219	82	102	2	3	6	3	30	8	0	.267	16	37	0	2	0.4	1.000

Jack Niemes

NIEMES, JACOB LELAND BR TL 6′ 1″ 180 lbs.
B. Oct. 19, 1919, Cincinnati, Ohio D. Mar. 4, 1966, Hamilton, Ohio.

Year	Team	W	L	PCT	ERA	G	GS	CG	IP	H	BB	SO	ShO	Relief Pitching W	Relief Pitching L	Relief Pitching SV	Batting AB	Batting H	HR	BA	PO	A	E	DP	TC/G	FA
1943	CIN N	0	0	—	6.00	3	0	0	3	5	2	1	0	0	0	0	0	0	0	—	0	0	0	0	0.0	.000

Chuck Nieson

NIESON, CHARLES BASSETT BR TR 6′ 2″ 185 lbs.
B. Sept. 24, 1942, Hanford, Calif.

Year	Team	W	L	PCT	ERA	G	GS	CG	IP	H	BB	SO	ShO	Relief Pitching W	Relief Pitching L	Relief Pitching SV	Batting AB	Batting H	HR	BA	PO	A	E	DP	TC/G	FA
1964	MIN A	0	0	—	4.50	2	0	0	2	1	1	5	0	0	0	0	0	0	0	—	0	0	0	0	0.0	.000

Juan Nieves

NIEVES, JUAN MANUEL BL TL 6′ 3″ 175 lbs.
Born Juan Manuel Nieves (Cruz).
B. Jan. 5, 1965, Santurce, Puerto Rico.

Year	Team	W	L	PCT	ERA	G	GS	CG	IP	H	BB	SO	ShO	Relief Pitching W	Relief Pitching L	Relief Pitching SV	Batting AB	Batting H	HR	BA	PO	A	E	DP	TC/G	FA
1986	MIL A	11	12	.478	4.92	35	33	4	184.2	224	77	116	3	1	0	0	0	0	0	—	4	18	2	2	0.7	.917
1987		14	8	.636	4.88	34	33	3	195.2	199	100	163	1	0	0	0	0	0	0	—	6	23	5	2	1.0	.853
1988		7	5	.583	4.08	25	15	1	110.1	84	50	73	1	1	0	1	0	0	0	—	4	14	1	0	0.8	.947
3 yrs.		32	25	.561	4.71	94	81	8	490.2	507	227	352	5	2	0	1	0	0	0		14	55	8	4	0.8	.896

Johnny Niggeling

NIGGELING, JOHN ARNOLD BR TR 6′ 170 lbs.
B. July 10, 1903, Remsen, Iowa D. Sept. 16, 1963, Le Mars, Iowa.

Year	Team	W	L	PCT	ERA	G	GS	CG	IP	H	BB	SO	ShO	Relief Pitching W	Relief Pitching L	Relief Pitching SV	Batting AB	Batting H	HR	BA	PO	A	E	DP	TC/G	FA
1938	BOS N	1	0	1.000	9.00	2	0	0	2	4	1	1	0	1	0	0	0	0	0	—	0	0	0	0	0.0	.000
1939	CIN N	2	1	.667	5.80	10	5	2	40.1	51	13	20	1	0	0	0	13	2	0	.154	1	6	2	2	0.9	.778
1940	STL A	7	11	.389	4.45	28	20	10	153.2	148	69	82	0	0	0	0	51	9	0	.176	9	22	2	5	1.2	.939
1941		7	9	.438	3.80	24	20	13	168.1	168	63	68	1	0	1	0	60	10	0	.167	9	28	0	0	1.5	1.000
1942		15	11	.577	2.66	28	27	16	206.1	173	93	107	3	0	0	0	72	10	0	.139	3	36	0	0	1.4	1.000
1943	2 teams STL A (20G 6–8) WAS A (6G 4–2)																									
"	total	10	10	.500	2.59	26	26	12	201.1	149	74	97	3	0	0	0	67	8	0	.119	10	38	0	4	1.8	1.000
1944	WAS A	10	8	.556	2.32	24	24	14	206	164	88	121	3	0	0	0	69	9	0	.130	7	29	0	2	1.5	1.000
1945		7	12	.368	3.16	26	25	8	176.2	161	73	90	2	0	0	0	59	7	0	.119	6	25	2	2	1.3	.939
1946	2 teams WAS A (8G 3–2) BOS N (8G 2–5)																									
"	total	5	7	.417	3.56	16	14	6	96	93	42	34	0	0	1	0	29	4	0	.138	5	19	1	1	1.6	.960
9 yrs.		64	69	.481	3.22	184	161	81	1250.2	1111	516	620	13	1	2	0	420	59	0	.140	50	203	7	16	1.4	.973

Al Nipper

NIPPER, ALBERT SAMUEL BR TR 6′ 188 lbs.
B. Apr. 2, 1959, San Diego, Calif.

Year	Team	W	L	PCT	ERA	G	GS	CG	IP	H	BB	SO	ShO	Relief Pitching W	Relief Pitching L	Relief Pitching SV	Batting AB	Batting H	HR	BA	PO	A	E	DP	TC/G	FA
1983	BOS A	1	1	.500	2.25	3	2	1	16	17	7	5	0	0	0	0	0	0	0	—	1	2	0	0	1.0	1.000
1984		11	6	.647	3.89	29	24	6	182.2	183	52	84	0	0	0	0	0	0	0	—	28	31	1	0	2.1	.983
1985		9	12	.429	4.06	25	25	5	162	157	82	85	0	0	0	0	0	0	0	—	24	28	5	4	2.3	.912
1986		10	12	.455	5.38	26	26	3	159	186	47	79	0	0	0	0	0	0	0	—	28	28	1	4	2.2	.982
1987		11	12	.478	5.43	30	30	6	174	196	62	89	0	0	0	0	0	0	0	—	20	27	2	2	1.6	.959

Al Nipper *continued*

Year	Team		W	L	PCT	ERA	G	GS	CG	IP	H	BB	SO	ShO	Relief Pitching W	Relief L	Relief SV	Batting AB	Batting H	HR	BA	PO	A	E	DP	TC/G	FA
1988	**CHI**	**N**	2	4	.333	3.04	22	12	0	80	72	34	27	0	0	1	1	23	2	0	.087	4	7	1	1	0.5	.917
1990	**CLE**	**A**	2	3	.400	6.75	9	5	0	24	35	19	12	0	0	0	0	0	0	0	—	1	1	0	1	0.2	1.000
7 yrs.			46	50	.479	4.52	144	124	21	797.2	846	303	381	0	0	1	1	23	2	0	.087	106	124	10	12	1.7	.958
WORLD SERIES																											
1986	**BOS**	**A**	0	1	.000	7.11	2	1	0	6.1	10	2	2	0	0	0	0	0	0	0	—	1	2	0	0	1.5	1.000

Merlin Nippert

NIPPERT, MERLIN LEE BR TR 6′ 1″ 175 lbs.
B. Sept. 1, 1938, Mangum, Okla.

Year	Team		W	L	PCT	ERA	G	GS	CG	IP	H	BB	SO	ShO	Relief Pitching W	Relief L	Relief SV	Batting AB	Batting H	HR	BA	PO	A	E	DP	TC/G	FA
1962	**BOS**	**A**	0	0	—	4.50	4	0	0	6	4	4	3	0	0	0	0	0	0	0	—	0	1	1	0	0.5	.500

Ron Nischwitz

NISCHWITZ, RONALD LEE BB TL 6′ 3″ 205 lbs.
B. July 1, 1937, Dayton, Ohio.

Year	Team		W	L	PCT	ERA	G	GS	CG	IP	H	BB	SO	ShO	Relief Pitching W	Relief L	Relief SV	Batting AB	Batting H	HR	BA	PO	A	E	DP	TC/G	FA
1961	**DET**	**A**	0	1	.000	5.56	6	1	0	11.1	13	8	8	0	0	0	0	2	0	0	.000	1	1	1	0	0.5	.667
1962			4	5	.444	3.90	48	0	0	64.2	73	26	28	0	4	5	4	12	5	0	.417	2	13	1	2	0.3	.938
1963	**CLE**	**A**	0	2	.000	6.48	14	0	0	16.2	17	8	10	0	0	2	1	1	0	0	.000	2	3	1	1	0.4	.833
1965	**DET**	**A**	1	0	1.000	2.78	20	0	0	22.2	21	6	12	0	1	0	1	3	0	0	.000	2	3	0	0	0.3	1.000
4 yrs.			5	8	.385	4.21	88	1	0	115.1	124	48	58	0	5	7	6	18	5	0	.278	7	20	3	3	0.3	.900

Otho Nitcholas

NITCHOLAS, OTHO JAMES (Nick) BR TR 6′ 195 lbs.
B. Sept. 13, 1908, McKinney, Tex.

Year	Team		W	L	PCT	ERA	G	GS	CG	IP	H	BB	SO	ShO	Relief Pitching W	Relief L	Relief SV	Batting AB	Batting H	HR	BA	PO	A	E	DP	TC/G	FA
1945	**BKN**	**N**	1	0	1.000	5.30	7	0	0	18.2	19	1	4	0	1	0	0	4	1	0	.250	1	3	0	0	0.6	1.000

C. J. Nitkowski

NITKOWSKI, CHRISTOPHER JOHN BL TL 6′ 2″ 185 lbs.
B. Mar. 9, 1973, Suffern, N. Y.

Year	Team		W	L	PCT	ERA	G	GS	CG	IP	H	BB	SO	ShO	Relief Pitching W	Relief L	Relief SV	Batting AB	Batting H	HR	BA	PO	A	E	DP	TC/G	FA
1995	**2 teams**	**CIN N**	(9G 1–3)	**DET A**	(11G 1–4)																						
″	**total**		2	7	.222	6.66	20	18	0	71.2	94	35	31	0	0	0	0	10	2	0	.200	5	8	2	0	0.8	.867

Willard Nixon

NIXON, WILLARD LEE BL TR 6′ 2″ 195 lbs.
B. June 17, 1928, Taylorsville, Ga.

Year	Team		W	L	PCT	ERA	G	GS	CG	IP	H	BB	SO	ShO	Relief Pitching W	Relief L	Relief SV	Batting AB	Batting H	HR	BA	PO	A	E	DP	TC/G	FA
1950	**BOS**	**A**	8	6	.571	6.04	22	15	2	101.1	126	58	57	0	2	0	2	36	5	0	.139	7	14	1	3	1.0	.955
1951			7	4	.636	4.90	33	14	2	125	136	56	70	1	2	0	1	45	13	1	.289	2	23	1	1	0.8	.962
1952			5	4	.556	4.86	23	13	5	103.2	115	61	50	0	0	0	0	53	11	0	.208	7	18	0	4	1.1	1.000
1953			4	8	.333	3.93	23	15	5	116.2	114	59	57	1	0	1	0	42	8	0	.190	7	18	2	1	1.2	.926
1954			11	12	.478	4.06	31	30	8	199.2	182	87	102	2	0	0	0	68	18	1	.265	17	34	1	6	1.7	.981
1955			12	10	.545	4.07	31	31	7	208	207	85	95	3	0	0	0	69	18	0	.261	18	43	1	3	2.0	.984
1956			9	8	.529	4.21	23	22	9	145.1	142	57	74	1	0	0	0	54	11	0	.204	7	31	1	4	1.7	.974
1957			12	13	.480	3.68	29	29	11	191	207	56	96	1	0	0	0	75	22	0	.293	8	28	0	4	1.2	1.000
1958			1	7	.125	6.02	10	8	2	43.1	48	11	15	0	1	0	0	17	5	0	.294	1	8	0	1	0.9	1.000
9 yrs.			69	72	.489	4.39	225	177	51	1234	1277	530	616	9	5	1	3	459	111	2	.242	74	217	7	27	1.3	.977

Junior Noboa

NOBOA, MILCIADES ARTURO BR TR 5′10″ 155 lbs.
Born Milciades Arturo Noboa (Diaz).
B. Nov. 10, 1964, Azua, Dominican Republic.

Year	Team		W	L	PCT	ERA	G	GS	CG	IP	H	BB	SO	ShO	Relief Pitching W	Relief L	Relief SV	Batting AB	Batting H	HR	BA	PO	A	E	DP	TC/G	FA
1990	**MON**	**N**	0	0	—	0.00	1	0	0	0.2	0	1	0	0	0	0	0	*				7	13	0	4	1.0	1.000

Gary Nolan

NOLAN, GARY LYNN BR TR 6′ 2½″ 197 lbs.
B. May 27, 1948, Herlong, Calif.

Year	Team		W	L	PCT	ERA	G	GS	CG	IP	H	BB	SO	ShO	Relief Pitching W	Relief L	Relief SV	Batting AB	Batting H	HR	BA	PO	A	E	DP	TC/G	FA
1967	**CIN**	**N**	14	8	.636	2.58	33	32	8	226.2	193	62	206	5	1	0	0	67	7	0	.104	12	28	1	1	1.2	.976
1968			9	4	.692	2.40	23	22	4	150	105	49	111	2	0	0	0	46	6	1	.130	5	16	0	1	0.9	1.000
1969			8	8	.500	3.55	16	15	2	109	102	40	83	1	0	1	0	35	8	0	.229	4	10	0	1	0.9	1.000
1970			18	7	.720	3.26	37	37	4	251	226	96	181	2	0	0	0	82	13	0	.159	17	28	1	1	1.2	.978
1971			12	15	.444	3.16	35	35	9	245	208	59	146	0	0	0	0	75	11	0	.147	15	38	0	4	1.5	1.000
1972			15	5	**.750**	1.99	25	25	6	176	147	30	90	2	0	0	0	60	7	0	.117	14	19	0	2	1.3	1.000
1973			0	1	.000	3.48	2	2	0	10.1	6	7	3	0	0	0	0	2	0	0	.000	0	1	0	0	0.5	1.000
1975			15	9	.625	3.16	32	32	5	211	202	29	74	1	0	0	0	68	12	0	.176	12	22	0	1	1.1	1.000
1976			15	9	.625	3.46	34	34	7	239	232	27	113	1	0	0	0	79	8	0	.101	9	22	0	0	0.9	1.000
1977	**2 teams**	**CIN N**	(8G 4–1)	**CAL A**	(5G 0–3)																						
″	**total**		4	4	.500	6.16	13	13	0	57	84	14	32	0	0	0	0	15	1	0	.067	7	5	1	0	1.0	.923
10 yrs.			110	70	.611	3.08	250	247	45	1675	1505	413	1039	14	1	1	0	529	73	1	.138	95	189	3	11	1.1	.990
LEAGUE CHAMPIONSHIP SERIES																											
1970	**CIN**	**N**	1	0	1.000	0.00	1	1	1	9	8	4	6	0	0	0	0	3	1	0	.333	0	2	0	0	2.0	1.000
1972			0	0	—	1.50	1	1	0	6	4	1	4	0	0	0	0	2	0	0	.000	0	0	0	0	0.0	.000
1975			0	0	—	3.00	1	1	0	6	5	0	5	0	0	0	0	2	0	0	.000	0	0	0	0	0.0	.000
1976			0	0	—	1.59	1	1	0	5.2	6	2	1	0	0	0	0	0	0	0	—	1	0	0	0	1.0	1.000
4 yrs.			1	0	1.000	1.35	4	4	1	26.2	23	7	16	0	0	0	0	7	1	0	.143	1	2	0	0	0.8	1.000
					1st	**2nd**																					
WORLD SERIES																											
1970	**CIN**	**N**	0	1	.000	7.71	2	2	0	9.1	9	3	9	0	0	0	0	3	0	0	.000	0	1	0	0	0.5	1.000
1972			0	1	.000	3.38	2	2	0	10.2	7	2	3	0	0	0	0	3	0	0	.000	0	2	0	0	1.0	1.000
1975			0	0	—	6.00	2	2	0	6	6	1	2	0	0	0	0	1	0	0	.000	1	0	0	0	0.5	1.000
1976			1	0	1.000	2.70	1	1	0	6.2	8	1	1	0	0	0	0	0	0	0	—	0	1	0	0	1.0	1.000
4 yrs.			1	2	.333	4.96	7	7	0	32.2	30	7	15	0	0	0	0	7	0	0	.000	1	4	0	0	0.7	1.000

The Only Nolan

NOLAN, EDWARD SYLVESTER BL TR 5′ 8″ 171 lbs.
B. Nov. 7, 1857, Paterson, N. J. D. May 18, 1913, Paterson, N. J.

Year	Team		W	L	PCT	ERA	G	GS	CG	IP	H	BB	SO	ShO	Relief Pitching W	Relief L	Relief SV	Batting AB	Batting H	HR	BA	PO	A	E	DP	TC/G	FA
1878	**IND**	**N**	13	22	.371	2.57	38	38	37	347	357	**56**	125	1	0	0	0	152	37	0	.243	19	80	11	5	2.8	.900
1881	**CLE**	**N**	8	14	.364	3.05	22	21	20	180	183	38	54	0	0	**1**	0	168	41	0	.244	32	37	9	2	1.9	.885
1883	**PIT**	**AA**	0	7	.000	*4.25*	7	7	6	55	81	10	23	0	0	0	0	26	8	0	.308	2	11	5	0	2.3	.722
1884	**WIL**	**U**	1	4	.200	*2.92*	5	5	5	40	44	7	52	0	0	0	0	33	9	0	.273	5	11	1	0	1.9	.941
1885	**PHI**	**N**	1	5	.167	4.17	7	7	6	54	55	24	20	0	0	0	0	26	2	0	.077	1	11	3	0	1.9	.800
5 yrs.			23	52	.307	2.98	79	78	74	676	720	135	274	1	0	1	0	*				59	150	29	7	2.2	.878

Dick Nold

NOLD, RICHARD LOUIS BR TR 6′ 2″ 190 lbs.
B. May 4, 1943, San Francisco, Calif.

Year	Team	Lg	W	L	PCT	ERA	G	GS	CG	IP	H	BB	SO	ShO	Relief Pitching W	Relief Pitching L	Relief Pitching SV	Batting AB	Batting H	HR	BA	PO	A	E	DP	TC/G	FA
1967	WAS	A	0	2	.000	4.87	7	3	0	20.1	19	13	10	0	0	0	0	3	0	0	.000	1	2	0	0	0.4	1.000

Dickie Noles

NOLES, DICKIE RAY BR TR 6′ 2″ 160 lbs.
B. Nov. 19, 1956, Charlotte, N. C.

Year	Team	Lg	W	L	PCT	ERA	G	GS	CG	IP	H	BB	SO	ShO	Relief Pitching W	Relief Pitching L	Relief Pitching SV	Batting AB	Batting H	HR	BA	PO	A	E	DP	TC/G	FA
1979	PHI	N	3	4	.429	3.80	14	14	0	90	80	38	42	0	0	0	0	30	3	0	.100	4	17	1	1	1.6	.955
1980			1	4	.200	3.89	48	3	0	81	80	42	57	0	0	4	6	13	4	0	.308	8	10	2	0	0.4	.900
1981			2	2	.500	4.19	13	8	0	58	57	23	34	0	0	0	0	19	2	0	.105	1	5	2	0	0.6	.750
1982	CHI	N	10	13	.435	4.42	31	30	2	171	180	61	85	2	0	0	0	56	6	0	.107	14	26	2	0	1.4	.952
1983			5	10	.333	4.72	24	18	1	116.1	133	37	59	1	0	1	0	38	9	0	.237	11	14	1	0	1.1	.962
1984	2 teams CHI N (21G 2–2) TEX A (18G 2–3)																										
″	total		4	5	.444	5.15	39	7	0	108.1	120	46	53	0	4	3	0	10	0	0	.000	2	6	1	1	0.2	.889
1985	TEX	A	4	8	.333	5.06	28	13	0	110.1	129	33	59	0	1	1	1	0	0	0	—	13	16	3	2	1.1	.906
1986	CLE	A	3	2	.600	5.10	32	0	0	54.2	56	30	32	0	3	2	0	0	0	0	—	5	8	0	0	0.4	1.000
1987	2 teams CHI N (41G 4–2) DET A (4G 0–0)																										
″	total		4	2	.667	3.53	45	1	0	66.1	61	28	33	0	4	1	4	11	0	0	.000	6	15	0	0	0.5	1.000
1988	BAL	A	0	2	.000	24.30	2	2	0	3.1	11	0	1	0	0	0	0	0	0	0	—	0	0	0	0	0.0	.000
1990	PHI	N	0	1	.000	27.00	1	0	0	0.1	2	0	0	0	0	1	0	0	0	0	—	0	0	0	0	0.0	.000
11 yrs.			36	53	.404	4.56	277	96	3	859.2	909	338	455	3	12	13	11	177	24	0	.136	64	117	12	4	0.7	.938
DIVISIONAL PLAYOFF SERIES																											
1981	PHI	N	0	0	—	4.50	1	1	0	4	4	2	5	0	0	0	0	0	0	0	—	0	0	0	0	0.0	.000
LEAGUE CHAMPIONSHIP SERIES																											
1980	PHI	N	0	0	—	0.00	2	0	0	2.2	1	3	0	0	0	0	0	0	0	0	—	1	2	0	1	1.5	1.000
WORLD SERIES																											
1980	PHI	N	0	0	—	1.93	1	0	0	4.2	5	2	6	0	0	0	0	0	0	0	—	1	0	0	0	1.0	1.000

Eric Nolte

NOLTE, ERIC CARL BL TL 6′ 3″ 205 lbs.
B. Apr. 28, 1964, Canoga Park, Calif.

Year	Team	Lg	W	L	PCT	ERA	G	GS	CG	IP	H	BB	SO	ShO	Relief Pitching W	Relief Pitching L	Relief Pitching SV	Batting AB	Batting H	HR	BA	PO	A	E	DP	TC/G	FA
1987	SD	N	2	6	.250	3.21	12	12	1	67.1	57	36	44	0	0	0	0	21	2	0	.095	5	7	0	0	1.0	1.000
1988			0	0	—	6.00	2	0	0	3	3	2	1	0	0	0	0	0	0	0	—	0	0	0	0	0.0	.000
1989			0	0	—	11.00	3	1	0	9	15	7	8	0	0	0	0	2	0	0	.000	0	3	0	0	1.0	1.000
1991	2 teams SD N (6G 3–2) TEX A (3G 0–0)																										
″	total		3	2	.600	10.22	9	6	0	24.2	40	13	16	0	0	0	0	9	1	0	.111	0	3	0	0	0.3	1.000
4 yrs.			5	8	.385	5.63	26	19	1	104	115	58	69	0	0	0	0	32	3	0	.094	5	13	0	0	0.7	1.000

Hideo Nomo

NOMO, HIDEO (The Tornado) BR TR 6′ 2″ 210 lbs.
B. Aug. 31, 1968, Osaka, Japan

Year	Team	Lg	W	L	PCT	ERA	G	GS	CG	IP	H	BB	SO	ShO	Relief Pitching W	Relief Pitching L	Relief Pitching SV	Batting AB	Batting H	HR	BA	PO	A	E	DP	TC/G	FA
1995	LA	N	13	6	.684	2.54	28	28	4	191.1	124	78	**236**	**3**	0	0	0	66	6	0	.091	6	12	3	2	0.8	.857
DIVISIONAL PLAYOFF SERIES																											
1995	LA	N	0	1	.000	9.00	1	1	0	5	7	2	6	0	0	0	0	2	0	0	.000	0	0	0	0	0.0	.000

Jerry Nops

NOPS, JEREMIAH H. BL TL 5′ 8½″ 168 lbs.
B. June 23, 1875, Toledo, Ohio D. Mar. 26, 1937, Camden, N. J.

Year	Team	Lg	W	L	PCT	ERA	G	GS	CG	IP	H	BB	SO	ShO	Relief Pitching W	Relief Pitching L	Relief Pitching SV	Batting AB	Batting H	HR	BA	PO	A	E	DP	TC/G	FA
1896	2 teams PHI N (1G 1–0) BAL N (3G 2–1)																										
″	total		3	1	.750	5.90	4	4	4	29	40	3	9	0	0	0	0	13	1	0	.077	1	6	2	0	2.3	.778
1897	BAL	N	20	6	.769	2.81	30	25	23	220.2	235	52	69	1	1	1	0	92	18	0	.196	10	38	4	0	1.7	.923
1898			16	9	.640	3.56	33	29	23	235	241	78	91	2	1	0	0	91	20	0	.220	6	36	8	0	1.5	.840
1899			17	11	.607	4.03	33	33	26	259	296	71	60	2	0	0	0	105	29	0	.276	7	53	7	1	2.0	.896
1900	BKN	N	4	4	.500	3.84	9	8	6	68	79	18	22	1	0	0	0	25	4	0	.160	5	12	5	2	2.4	.773
1901	BAL	A	12	10	.545	4.08	27	23	17	176.2	192	59	43	1	0	0	1	59	13	0	.220	2	34	10	0	1.7	.783
6 yrs.			72	41	.637	3.70	136	122	99	988.1	1083	281	294	7	2	1	1	385	85	0	.221	31	179	36	3	1.8	.854

Wayne Nordhagen

NORDHAGEN, WAYNE OREN BR TR 6′ 2″ 205 lbs.
B. July 4, 1948, Thief River Falls, Minn.

Year	Team	Lg	W	L	PCT	ERA	G	GS	CG	IP	H	BB	SO	ShO	Relief Pitching W	Relief Pitching L	Relief Pitching SV	Batting AB	Batting H	HR	BA	PO	A	E	DP	TC/G	FA
1979	CHI	A	0	0	—	9.00	2	0	0	2	2	1	2	0	0	0	0	*				35	3	1	0	1.9	.974

John Noriega

NORIEGA, JOHN ALAN BR TR 6′ 4″ 185 lbs.
B. Dec. 20, 1943, Ogden, Utah.

Year	Team	Lg	W	L	PCT	ERA	G	GS	CG	IP	H	BB	SO	ShO	Relief Pitching W	Relief Pitching L	Relief Pitching SV	Batting AB	Batting H	HR	BA	PO	A	E	DP	TC/G	FA
1969	CIN	N	0	0	—	5.63	5	0	0	8	12	3	4	0	0	0	0	0	0	0	—	0	1	1	0	0.4	.500
1970			0	0	—	8.00	8	0	0	18	25	10	6	0	0	0	0	4	1	0	.250	1	7	0	0	1.0	1.000
2 yrs.			0	0		7.27	13	0	0	26	37	13	10	0	0	0	0	4	1	0	.250	1	8	1	0	0.8	.900

Fred Norman

NORMAN, FREDIE HUBERT BB TL 5′ 8″ 155 lbs.
B. Aug. 20, 1942, San Antonio, Tex. BL 1962–1964, 1966–1967, 1970

Year	Team	Lg	W	L	PCT	ERA	G	GS	CG	IP	H	BB	SO	ShO	Relief Pitching W	Relief Pitching L	Relief Pitching SV	Batting AB	Batting H	HR	BA	PO	A	E	DP	TC/G	FA
1962	KC	A	0	0	—	2.25	2	0	0	4	4	1	2	0	0	0	0	0	0	0	—	0	0	0	0	0.0	.000
1963			0	1	.000	11.37	2	2	0	6.1	9	7	6	0	0	0	0	1	0	0	.000	1	1	0	0	1.0	1.000
1964	CHI	N	0	4	.000	6.54	8	5	0	31.2	34	21	20	0	0	0	0	11	1	0	.091	2	4	0	1	0.8	1.000
1966			0	0	—	4.50	2	0	0	4	5	2	6	0	0	0	0	0	0	0	—	0	0	0	0	0.0	.000
1967			0	0	—	0.00	1	0	0	1	0	0	3	0	0	0	0	0	0	0	—	0	0	0	0	0.0	.000
1970	2 teams LA N (30G 2–0) STL N (1G 0–0)																										
″	total		2	0	1.000	5.14	31	0	0	63	66	33	47	0	2	0	1	7	1	0	.143	2	8	3	0	0.4	.769
1971	2 teams STL N (4G 0–0) SD N (20G 3–12)																										
″	total		3	12	.200	3.57	24	18	5	131	121	63	81	0	0	0	0	38	9	0	.237	3	18	3	0	1.0	.875
1972	SD	N	9	11	.450	3.44	42	28	10	211.2	195	88	167	6	1	0	2	64	8	0	.125	9	24	2	4	0.8	.943
1973	2 teams SD N (12G 1–7) CIN N (24G 12–6)																										
″	total		13	13	.500	3.60	36	35	8	240.1	208	101	161	3	0	0	0	80	6	0	.075	9	37	4	1	1.4	.920
1974	CIN	N	13	12	.520	3.15	35	26	8	186	170	68	141	2	0	3	0	61	8	0	.131	5	14	2	1	0.6	.905
1975			12	4	.750	3.73	34	26	2	188	163	84	119	0	1	0	0	60	7	0	.117	9	19	2	2	0.9	.933
1976			12	7	.632	3.10	33	24	8	180	153	70	126	3	1	0	0	50	7	0	.140	4	14	0	0	0.5	1.000
1977			14	13	.519	3.38	35	34	8	221	200	98	160	1	0	0	0	73	8	0	.110	9	31	4	2	1.3	.909

Fred Norman *continued*

Year	Team	W	L	PCT	ERA	G	GS	CG	IP	H	BB	SO	ShO	Relief Pitching W	Relief Pitching L	Relief Pitching SV	Batting AB	Batting H	Batting HR	BA	PO	A	E	DP	TC/G	FA
1978		11	9	.550	3.71	36	31	0	177	173	82	111	0	1	0	1	50	7	0	.140	6	25	2	0	0.9	.939
1979		11	13	.458	3.65	34	31	5	195	193	57	95	0	0	1	0	59	9	0	.153	4	26	3	1	1.0	.909
1980	MON N	4	4	.500	4.13	48	8	2	98	96	40	58	0	0	1	4	20	1	0	.050	1	11	1	0	0.3	.923
16 yrs.		104	103	.502	3.64	403	268	56	1938	1790	815	1303	15	6	5	8	574	72	0	.125	64	232	26	12	0.8	.919
LEAGUE CHAMPIONSHIP SERIES																										
1973	CIN N	0	0	—	1.80	1	1	0	5	1	3	3	0	0	0	0	1	0	0	.000	1	0	0	0	1.0	1.000
1975		1	0	1.000	1.50	1	1	0	6	4	5	4	0	0	0	0	1	0	0	.000	0	1	0	0	1.0	1.000
1979		0	0	—	18.00	1	0	0	2	4	1	1	0	0	0	0	1	0	0	.000	0	0	0	0	0.0	.000
3 yrs.		1	0	1.000	4.15	3	2	0	13	9	9	8	0	0	0	0	3	0	0	.000	1	1	0	0	0.7	1.000
WORLD SERIES																										
1975	CIN N	0	1	.000	9.00	2	1	0	4	8	3	2	0	0	0	0	1	0	0	.000	0	0	0	0	0.0	.000
1976		0	0	—	4.26	1	1	0	6.1	9	2	2	0	0	0	0	0	0	0	—	0	1	0	0	1.0	1.000
2 yrs.		0	1	.000	6.10	3	2	0	10.1	17	5	4	0	0	0	0	1	0	0	.000	0	1	0	0	0.3	1.000

Mike Norris

NORRIS, MICHAEL KELVIN
B. Mar. 19, 1955, San Francisco, Calif.
BR TR 6′ 2″ 175 lbs.

Year	Team	W	L	PCT	ERA	G	GS	CG	IP	H	BB	SO	ShO	Relief Pitching W	Relief Pitching L	Relief Pitching SV	Batting AB	Batting H	Batting HR	BA	PO	A	E	DP	TC/G	FA
1975	OAK A	1	0	1.000	0.00	4	3	1	16.2	6	8	5	1	0	0	0	0	0	0	—	1	4	1	0	1.5	.833
1976		4	5	.444	4.78	24	19	1	96	91	56	44	1	0	0	0	0	0	0	—	11	29	2	1	1.8	.952
1977		2	7	.222	4.79	16	12	1	77	77	31	35	1	0	0	0	1	0	0	.000	8	17	2	1	1.7	.926
1978		0	5	.000	5.51	14	5	1	49	46	35	36	0	0	0	0	0	0	0	—	5	5	2	0	0.9	.833
1979		5	8	.385	4.81	29	18	3	146	146	94	96	0	0	0	0	0	0	0	—	6	17	1	0	0.8	.958
1980		22	9	.710	2.54	33	33	24	284	215	83	180	1	0	0	0	0	0	0	—	25	52	3	3	2.4	.963
1981		12	9	.571	3.75	23	23	12	173	145	63	78	2	0	0	0	0	0	0	—	16	25	1	0	1.8	.976
1982		7	11	.389	4.76	28	28	7	166.1	154	84	83	1	0	0	0	0	0	0	—	22	21	2	1	1.6	.956
1983		4	5	.444	3.76	16	16	2	88.2	68	36	63	0	0	0	0	0	0	0	—	3	4	1	1	0.5	.875
1990		1	0	1.000	3.00	14	0	0	27	24	9	16	0	1	0	0	0	0	0	—	3	3	0	0	0.4	1.000
10 yrs.		58	59	.496	3.89	201	157	52	1123.2	972	499	636	7	1	0	0	1	0	0	.000	100	177	15	7	1.5	.949
DIVISIONAL PLAYOFF SERIES																										
1981	OAK A	1	0	1.000	0.00	1	1	1	9	4	3	2	1	0	0	0	0	0	0	—	0	0	1	0	1.0	.000
LEAGUE CHAMPIONSHIP SERIES																										
1981	OAK A	0	1	.000	3.68	1	1	0	7.1	6	2	4	0	0	0	0	0	0	0	—	1	2	0	0	3.0	1.000

Lou North

NORTH, LOUIS ALEXANDER
B. June 15, 1891, Elgin, Ill. D. May 16, 1974, Shelton, Conn.
BR TR 5′11″ 175 lbs.

Year	Team	W	L	PCT	ERA	G	GS	CG	IP	H	BB	SO	ShO	Relief Pitching W	Relief Pitching L	Relief Pitching SV	Batting AB	Batting H	Batting HR	BA	PO	A	E	DP	TC/G	FA
1913	DET A	0	1	.000	15.00	1	1	0	6	10	9	3	0	0	0	0	2	0	0	.000	0	1	1	0	2.0	.500
1917	STL N	0	0	—	3.97	5	0	0	11.1	14	4	4	0	0	0	0	3	0	0	.000	0	5	0	0	1.0	1.000
1920		3	2	.600	3.27	24	6	3	88	90	32	37	0	1	1	1	31	7	0	.226	2	18	1	0	0.9	.952
1921		4	4	.500	3.54	40	0	0	86.1	81	32	28	0	4	4	**7**	19	3	0	.158	4	11	2	1	0.4	.882
1922		10	3	.769	4.45	**53**	10	4	149.2	164	64	84	0	5	1	4	47	11	1	.234	9	49	1	3	1.1	.983
1923		3	4	.429	5.15	34	3	0	71.2	90	31	24	0	2	**4**	1	22	4	0	.182	3	18	0	2	0.6	1.000
1924	2 teams STL N (6G 0–0) BOS N (9G 1–2)																									
″	total	1	2	.333	5.76	15	5	1	50	60	28	19	0	0	0	0	13	2	0	.154	2	8	2	0	0.8	.833
7 yrs.		21	16	.568	4.43	172	25	8	463	509	200	199	0	12	10	13	137	27	1	.197	20	110	7	6	0.8	.949

Jake Northrop

NORTHROP, GEORGE HOWARD
B. Mar. 5, 1888, Monroeton, Pa. D. Nov. 16, 1945, Monroeton, Pa.
BL TR 5′11″ 170 lbs.

Year	Team	W	L	PCT	ERA	G	GS	CG	IP	H	BB	SO	ShO	Relief Pitching W	Relief Pitching L	Relief Pitching SV	Batting AB	Batting H	Batting HR	BA	PO	A	E	DP	TC/G	FA
1918	BOS N	5	1	.833	1.35	7	4	4	40	26	3	4	1	2	0	0	13	2	0	.154	0	14	0	0	2.0	1.000
1919		1	5	.167	4.58	11	3	2	37.1	43	10	9	0	0	3	0	8	4	0	.500	7	14	0	1	1.9	1.000
2 yrs.		6	6	.500	2.91	18	7	6	77.1	69	13	13	1	2	3	0	21	6	0	.286	7	28	0	1	1.9	1.000

Elisha Norton

NORTON, ELISHA STRONG
B. Aug. 17, 1873, Conneaut, Ohio D. Mar. 5, 1950, Aspinwall, Pa.
BR TR

Year	Team	W	L	PCT	ERA	G	GS	CG	IP	H	BB	SO	ShO	Relief Pitching W	Relief Pitching L	Relief Pitching SV	Batting AB	Batting H	Batting HR	BA	PO	A	E	DP	TC/G	FA
1896	WAS N	3	1	.750	3.07	8	5	2	44	49	14	13	0	1	0	0	19	4	0	.211	0	10	1	0	1.4	.909
1897		2	1	.667	6.88	4	2	1	17	31	11	3	0	1	0	0	18	5	0	.278	8	3	3	1	2.0	.786
2 yrs.		5	2	.714	4.13	12	7	3	61	80	25	16	0	2	0	0	37	9	0	.243	8	13	4	1	1.7	.840

Tom Norton

NORTON, THOMAS JOHN
B. Apr. 26, 1950, Elyria, Ohio.
BR TR 6′ 1″ 200 lbs.

Year	Team	W	L	PCT	ERA	G	GS	CG	IP	H	BB	SO	ShO	Relief Pitching W	Relief Pitching L	Relief Pitching SV	Batting AB	Batting H	Batting HR	BA	PO	A	E	DP	TC/G	FA
1972	MIN A	0	1	.000	2.81	21	0	0	32	31	14	22	0	0	1	0	0	0	0	—	4	9	0	0	0.6	1.000

Randy Nosek

NOSEK, RANDALL WILLIAM
B. Jan. 8, 1967, Omaha, Neb.
BR TR 6′ 4″ 215 lbs.

Year	Team	W	L	PCT	ERA	G	GS	CG	IP	H	BB	SO	ShO	Relief Pitching W	Relief Pitching L	Relief Pitching SV	Batting AB	Batting H	Batting HR	BA	PO	A	E	DP	TC/G	FA
1989	DET A	0	2	.000	13.50	2	2	0	5.1	7	10	4	0	0	0	0	0	0	0	—	0	0	0	0	0.0	.000
1990		1	1	.500	7.71	3	2	0	7	7	9	3	0	0	0	0	0	0	0	—	0	0	0	0	0.0	.000
2 yrs.		1	3	.250	10.22	5	4	0	12.1	14	19	7	0	0	0	0	0	0	0		0	0	0	0	0.0	

Don Nottebart

NOTTEBART, DONALD EDWARD
B. Jan. 23, 1936, West Newton, Mass.
BR TR 6′ 1″ 190 lbs.

Year	Team	W	L	PCT	ERA	G	GS	CG	IP	H	BB	SO	ShO	Relief Pitching W	Relief Pitching L	Relief Pitching SV	Batting AB	Batting H	Batting HR	BA	PO	A	E	DP	TC/G	FA
1960	MIL N	1	0	1.000	4.11	5	1	0	15.1	14	15	8	0	1	0	1	5	0	0	.000	2	6	0	0	1.6	1.000
1961		6	7	.462	4.06	38	11	2	126.1	117	48	66	0	3	2	3	38	7	0	.184	9	31	1	1	1.1	.976
1962		2	2	.500	3.23	39	0	0	64	64	20	36	0	2	2	2	6	2	0	.333	4	17	0	3	0.5	1.000
1963	HOU N	11	8	.579	3.17	31	27	9	193	170	39	118	2	0	0	0	66	11	0	.167	14	30	1	2	1.5	.978
1964		6	11	.353	3.90	28	24	2	157	165	37	90	0	1	0	0	47	3	0	.064	14	44	3	3	2.2	.951
1965		4	15	.211	4.67	29	25	3	158	166	55	77	0	0	1	0	48	5	0	.104	8	40	1	1	1.7	.980
1966	CIN N	5	4	.556	3.07	59	1	0	111.1	97	43	69	0	5	4	11	24	4	0	.167	9	20	0	1	0.5	1.000
1967		0	3	.000	1.93	47	0	0	79.1	75	19	48	0	0	3	4	3	0	0	.000	4	17	2	2	0.5	.913
1969	2 teams NY A (4G 0–0) CHI N (16G 1–1)																									
″	total	1	1	.500	6.38	20	0	0	24	34	7	13	0	1	1	0	1	0	0	.000	2	4	0	0	0.3	1.000
9 yrs.		36	51	.414	3.65	296	89	16	928.1	902	283	525	2	13	13	21	238	32	0	.134	66	209	8	13	1.0	.972

Chet Nourse

NOURSE, CHESTER LINWOOD
B. Aug. 7, 1887, Ipswich, Mass. D. Apr. 20, 1958, Clearwater, Fla.
BR TR 6′ 3″ 185 lbs.

Year	Team	Lg	W	L	PCT	ERA	G	GS	CG	IP	H	BB	SO	ShO	Relief Pitching W	L	SV	Batting AB	H	HR	BA	PO	A	E	DP	TC/G	FA
1909	BOS	A	0	0	—	7.20	3	0	0	5	5	5	3	0	0	0	0	2	0	0	.000	1	2	2	0	1.7	.600

Rafael Novoa

NOVOA, RAFAEL ANGEL
B. Oct. 26, 1967, New York, N. Y.
BL TL 6′ 180 lbs.

Year	Team	Lg	W	L	PCT	ERA	G	GS	CG	IP	H	BB	SO	ShO	Relief Pitching W	L	SV	Batting AB	H	HR	BA	PO	A	E	DP	TC/G	FA
1990	SF	N	0	1	.000	6.75	7	2	0	18.2	21	13	14	0	0	0	1	5	1	0	.200	0	0	0	0	0.0	.000
1993	MIL	A	0	3	.000	4.50	15	7	2	56	58	22	17	0	0	0	0	0	0	0	—	4	6	0	0	0.7	1.000
2 yrs.			0	4	.000	5.06	22	9	2	74.2	79	35	31	0	0	0	1	5	1	0	.200	4	6	0	0	0.5	1.000

Wynn Noyes

NOYES, WINFIELD CHARLES
B. June 16, 1889, Pleasanton, Neb. D. Apr. 8, 1969, Cashmere, Wash.
BR TR 6′ 180 lbs.

Year	Team	Lg	W	L	PCT	ERA	G	GS	CG	IP	H	BB	SO	ShO	Relief Pitching W	L	SV	Batting AB	H	HR	BA	PO	A	E	DP	TC/G	FA
1913	BOS	N	0	0	—	4.79	11	0	0	20.2	22	6	5	0	0	0	0	4	1	0	.250	2	5	0	0	0.6	1.000
1917	PHI	A	10	10	.500	2.95	27	22	11	171	156	77	64	1	1	1	1	52	6	0	.115	7	43	4	4	2.0	.926
1919	2 teams	PHI A (10G 1–5)	CHI A (1G 0–0)																								
″	total		1	5	.167	5.89	11	7	3	55	76	15	24	0	0	0	0	18	3	0	.167	2	16	1	0	1.7	.947
3 yrs.			11	15	.423	3.76	49	29	14	246.2	254	98	93	1	1	1	1	74	10	0	.135	11	64	5	4	1.6	.938

Edwin Nunez

NUNEZ, EDWIN
Born Edwin Nunez (Martinez).
B. May 27, 1963, Humacao, Puerto Rico.
BR TR 6′ 5″ 207 lbs.

Year	Team	Lg	W	L	PCT	ERA	G	GS	CG	IP	H	BB	SO	ShO	Relief Pitching W	L	SV	Batting AB	H	HR	BA	PO	A	E	DP	TC/G	FA
1982	SEA	A	1	2	.333	4.58	8	5	0	35.1	36	16	27	0	0	0	0	0	0	0	—	2	5	1	0	1.0	.875
1983			0	4	.000	4.38	14	5	0	37	40	22	35	0	0	0	0	0	0	0	—	0	6	0	1	0.4	1.000
1984			2	2	.500	3.18	37	0	0	68	55	21	57	0	2	2	7	0	0	0	—	4	6	1	0	0.3	.909
1985			7	3	.700	3.09	70	0	0	90.1	79	34	58	0	7	3	16	0	0	0	—	5	12	0	1	0.2	1.000
1986			1	2	.333	5.82	14	1	0	21.2	25	5	17	0	0	2	0	0	0	0	—	1	1	0	0	0.1	1.000
1987			3	4	.429	3.80	48	0	0	47.1	45	18	34	0	3	4	12	0	0	0	—	2	5	0	0	0.1	1.000
1988	2 teams	SEA A (14G 1–4)	NY N (10G 1–0)																								
″	total		2	4	.333	6.85	24	3	0	43.1	66	17	27	0	2	1	0	0	0	0		6	8	2	1	0.7	.875
1989	DET	A	3	4	.429	4.17	27	0	0	54	49	36	41	0	3	4	1	0	0	0	—	3	9	0	2	0.4	1.000
1990			3	1	.750	2.24	42	0	0	80.1	65	37	66	0	3	1	6	0	0	0	—	7	5	1	1	0.3	.923
1991	MIL	A	2	1	.667	6.04	23	0	0	25.1	28	13	24	0	2	1	8	0	0	0	—	0	3	1	0	0.2	.750
1992	2 teams	MIL A (10G 1–1)	TEX A (39G 0–2)																								
″	total		1	3	.250	4.85	49	0	0	59.1	63	22	49	0	1	3	3	0	0	0		3	4	1	0	0.2	.875
1993	OAK	A	3	6	.333	3.81	56	0	0	75.2	89	29	58	0	3	6	1	0	0	0	—	7	8	1	1	0.3	.938
1994			0	0	—	12.00	15	0	0	15	26	10	15	0	0	0	0	0	0	0	—	0	4	0	0	0.3	1.000
13 yrs.			28	36	.438	4.19	427	14	0	652.2	666	280	508	0	26	27	54	0	0	0		40	76	8	7	0.3	.935

Jose Nunez

NUNEZ, JOSE
Born Jose Nunez (Jimenez).
B. Jan. 13, 1964, Jarabocoa, Dominican Republic.
BR TR 6′ 3″ 175 lbs.

Year	Team	Lg	W	L	PCT	ERA	G	GS	CG	IP	H	BB	SO	ShO	Relief Pitching W	L	SV	Batting AB	H	HR	BA	PO	A	E	DP	TC/G	FA
1987	TOR	A	5	2	.714	5.01	37	9	0	97	91	58	99	0	3	1	0	0	0	0	—	5	7	0	1	0.3	1.000
1988			0	1	.000	3.07	13	2	0	29.1	28	17	18	0	0	1	0	0	0	0	—	1	4	0	0	0.4	1.000
1989			0	0	—	2.53	6	1	0	10.2	8	2	14	0	0	0	0	0	0	0	—	1	0	1	0	0.3	.500
1990	CHI	N	4	7	.364	6.53	21	10	0	60.2	61	34	40	0	1	2	0	11	0	0	.000	11	7	2	1	1.0	.900
4 yrs.			9	10	.474	5.05	77	22	0	197.2	188	111	171	0	4	4	0	11	0	0	.000	18	18	3	2	0.5	.923

Howie Nunn

NUNN, HOWARD RALPH
B. Oct. 18, 1935, Westfield, N. C.
BR TR 6′ 173 lbs.

Year	Team	Lg	W	L	PCT	ERA	G	GS	CG	IP	H	BB	SO	ShO	Relief Pitching W	L	SV	Batting AB	H	HR	BA	PO	A	E	DP	TC/G	FA
1959	STL	N	2	2	.500	7.59	16	0	0	21.1	23	15	20	0	2	2	0	1	0	0	.000	0	6	0	1	0.4	1.000
1961	CIN	N	2	1	.667	3.58	24	0	0	37.2	35	24	26	0	2	1	0	8	2	0	.250	1	6	0	1	0.3	1.000
1962			0	0	—	5.59	6	0	0	9.2	15	3	4	0	0	0	0	1	0	0	.000	2	2	0	0	0.7	1.000
3 yrs.			4	3	.571	5.11	46	0	0	68.2	73	42	50	0	4	3	0	10	2	0	.200	3	14	0	2	0.4	1.000

Joe Nuxhall

NUXHALL, JOSEPH HENRY
B. July 30, 1928, Hamilton, Ohio.
BL TL 6′ 3″ 195 lbs.

Year	Team	Lg	W	L	PCT	ERA	G	GS	CG	IP	H	BB	SO	ShO	Relief Pitching W	L	SV	Batting AB	H	HR	BA	PO	A	E	DP	TC/G	FA
1944	CIN	N	0	0	—	67.50	1	0	0	0.2	2	5	0	0	0	0	0	0	0	0	—	0	0	0	0	0.0	.000
1952			1	4	.200	3.22	37	5	2	92.1	83	42	52	0	1	2	1	23	2	0	.087	3	24	1	4	0.8	.964
1953			9	11	.450	4.32	30	17	5	141.2	136	69	52	1	2	2	2	49	16	3	.327	6	18	3	0	0.9	.889
1954			12	5	.706	3.89	35	14	5	166.2	188	59	85	1	5	1	0	52	9	3	.173	4	29	1	5	1.0	.971
1955			17	12	.586	3.47	50	33	14	257	240	78	98	**5**	2	0	3	86	17	3	.198	12	35	3	4	1.0	.940
1956			13	11	.542	3.72	44	32	10	200.2	196	87	120	2	2	0	3	59	11	2	.186	6	31	2	3	0.9	.949
1957			10	10	.500	4.75	39	28	6	174.1	192	53	99	2	1	0	1	59	14	0	.237	11	20	4	1	0.9	.886
1958			12	11	.522	3.79	36	26	5	175.2	169	63	111	0	4	0	0	62	13	0	.210	6	29	3	3	1.1	.921
1959			9	9	.500	4.24	28	21	6	131.2	155	35	75	1	2	0	1	44	11	0	.250	6	19	1	1	0.9	.962
1960			1	8	.111	4.42	38	6	0	112	130	27	72	0	0	3	0	26	2	0	.077	8	26	1	4	0.9	.971
1961	KC	A	5	8	.385	5.34	37	13	1	128	135	65	81	0	1	2	1	65	19	2	.292	10	13	3	1	0.7	.885
1962	2 teams	LA A (5G 0–0)	CIN N (12G 5–0)																								
″	total		5	0	1.000	3.03	17	9	1	71.1	66	30	59	0	1	0	1	26	7	1	.269	2	11	0	1	0.8	1.000
1963	CIN	N	15	8	.652	2.61	35	29	14	217.1	194	39	169	2	0	0	2	76	12	0	.158	5	33	5	2	1.2	.884
1964			9	8	.529	4.07	32	22	7	154.2	146	51	111	4	1	1	2	54	7	1	.130	5	20	2	1	0.8	.926
1965			11	4	.733	3.45	32	16	5	148.2	142	31	117	1	1	1	2	45	8	0	.178	5	13	0	0	0.6	1.000
1966			6	8	.429	4.50	35	16	2	130	136	42	71	1	2	1	0	40	4	0	.100	6	20	3	1	0.8	.897
16 yrs.			135	117	.536	3.90	526	287	83	2302.2	2310	776	1372	20	25	13	19	*				95	341	32	31	0.9	.932

Rich Nye

NYE, RICHARD RAYMOND
B. Aug. 4, 1944, Oakland, Calif.
BL TL 6′ 4″ 185 lbs.

Year	Team	Lg	W	L	PCT	ERA	G	GS	CG	IP	H	BB	SO	ShO	Relief Pitching W	L	SV	Batting AB	H	HR	BA	PO	A	E	DP	TC/G	FA
1966	CHI	N	0	2	.000	2.12	3	2	0	17	16	7	9	0	0	0	0	4	1	0	.250	0	1	0	0	0.3	1.000
1967			13	10	.565	3.20	35	30	7	205	179	52	119	0	0	1	0	75	16	0	.213	10	35	1	2	1.3	.978
1968			7	12	.368	3.80	27	20	6	132.2	145	34	74	1	1	0	1	44	8	0	.182	6	22	2	2	1.1	.933
1969			3	5	.375	5.09	34	5	1	69	72	21	39	0	0	0	3	16	1	0	.063	1	10	0	0	0.3	1.000
1970	2 teams	MON N (8G 3–2)	STL N (6G 0–0)																								
″	total		3	2	.600	4.14	14	6	2	54.1	60	26	26	0	0	0	0	19	4	0	.211	5	7	0	1	0.9	1.000
5 yrs.			26	31	.456	3.71	113	63	16	478	472	140	267	1	1	1	4	158	30	0	.190	22	75	3	5	0.9	.970

Jerry Nyman

NYMAN, GERALD SMITH
B. Nov. 23, 1942, Logan, Utah
BL TL 5'10" 165 lbs.

Year	Team	W	L	PCT	ERA	G	GS	CG	IP	H	BB	SO	ShO	Relief Pitching W	Relief Pitching L	Relief Pitching SV	Batting AB	Batting H	Batting HR	BA	PO	A	E	DP	TC/G	FA
1968	CHI A	2	1	.667	2.01	8	7	1	40.1	38	16	27	1	0	0	0	13	2	0	.154	2	6	2	1	1.3	.800
1969		4	4	.500	5.29	20	10	2	64.2	58	39	40	1	0	0	0	20	1	0	.050	0	9	0	0	0.4	1.000
1970	SD N	0	2	.000	16.20	2	2	0	5	8	2	2	0	0	0	0	0	0	0	—	0	0	0	0	0.0	.000
3 yrs.		6	7	.462	4.58	30	19	3	110	104	57	69	2	0	0	0	33	3	0	.091	2	15	2	1	0.6	.895

Prince Oana

OANA, HENRY KAUHANE
B. Jan. 22, 1908, Waipahu, Hawaii D. June 19, 1976, Austin, Tex.
BR TR 6'2" 193 lbs.

Year	Team	W	L	PCT	ERA	G	GS	CG	IP	H	BB	SO	ShO	Relief Pitching W	Relief Pitching L	Relief Pitching SV	Batting AB	Batting H	Batting HR	BA	PO	A	E	DP	TC/G	FA
1943	DET A	3	2	.600	4.50	10	0	0	34	34	19	15	0	3	2	0	26	10	1	.385	14	0	0	0	3.5	1.000
1945		0	0	—	1.59	3	1	0	11.1	3	7	3	0	0	0	1	5	1	0	.200	0	1	0	0	0.3	1.000
2 yrs.		3	2	.600	3.77	13	1	0	45.1	37	26	18	0	3	2	1	*				14	7	2	2	1.4	.913

Henry Oberbeck

OBERBECK, HENRY A.
B. May 17, 1858, St. Louis, Mo. D. Aug. 26, 1921, St. Louis, Mo.

Year	Team	W	L	PCT	ERA	G	GS	CG	IP	H	BB	SO	ShO	Relief Pitching W	Relief Pitching L	Relief Pitching SV	Batting AB	Batting H	Batting HR	BA	PO	A	E	DP	TC/G	FA
1884	2 teams BAL U (2G 0–0) KC U (6G 0–5)																									
"	total	0	5	.000	5.30	8	5	3	35.2	56	5	7	0	0	1	0	*				28	2	1	3	5.2	.968

Doc Oberlander

OBERLANDER, HARTMAN LOUIS
B. May 12, 1864, Waukegan, Ill. D. Nov. 14, 1922, Pryor, Okla.
TL

Year	Team	W	L	PCT	ERA	G	GS	CG	IP	H	BB	SO	ShO	Relief Pitching W	Relief Pitching L	Relief Pitching SV	Batting AB	Batting H	Batting HR	BA	PO	A	E	DP	TC/G	FA
1888	CLE AA	1	2	.333	5.26	3	3	3	25.2	27	18	23	0	0	0	0	14	3	0	.214	0	4	1	0	1.7	.800

Frank Oberlin

OBERLIN, FRANK RUFUS (Flossie)
B. Mar. 29, 1876, Elsie, Mich. D. Jan. 6, 1952, Ashley, Ind.
BR TR 6'1" 165 lbs.

Year	Team	W	L	PCT	ERA	G	GS	CG	IP	H	BB	SO	ShO	Relief Pitching W	Relief Pitching L	Relief Pitching SV	Batting AB	Batting H	Batting HR	BA	PO	A	E	DP	TC/G	FA
1906	BOS A	1	3	.250	3.18	4	4	4	34	38	13	13	0	0	0	0	13	2	0	.154	1	16	2	0	4.8	.895
1907	2 teams BOS A (12G 1–5) WAS A (11G 2–6)																									
"	total	3	11	.214	4.47	23	12	5	94.2	105	36	36	0	1	2	0	31	3	0	.097	1	26	5	0	1.3	.844
1909	WAS A	1	4	.200	3.73	9	4	1	41	41	16	13	0	1	0	0	14	2	0	.143	1	8	0	0	1.0	1.000
1910		0	6	.000	2.98	8	6	6	57.1	52	23	18	0	0	0	0	19	1	0	.053	3	17	5	0	3.1	.800
4 yrs.		5	24	.172	3.77	44	26	16	227	236	88	80	0	2	2	0	77	8	0	.104	6	67	12	0	1.9	.859

Billy O'Brien

O'BRIEN, WILLIAM SMITH
B. Mar. 14, 1860, Albany, N. Y. D. May 26, 1911, Kansas City, Mo.
BR 6' 185 lbs.

Year	Team	W	L	PCT	ERA	G	GS	CG	IP	H	BB	SO	ShO	Relief Pitching W	Relief Pitching L	Relief Pitching SV	Batting AB	Batting H	Batting HR	BA	PO	A	E	DP	TC/G	FA
1884	STP U	1	0	1.000	*1.80*	2	0	0	10	8	3	7	0	1	0	0	*				25	28	11	1	4.6	.828

Bob O'Brien

O'BRIEN, ROBERT ALLEN
B. Apr. 23, 1949, Pittsburgh, Pa.
BL TL 5'10" 170 lbs.

Year	Team	W	L	PCT	ERA	G	GS	CG	IP	H	BB	SO	ShO	Relief Pitching W	Relief Pitching L	Relief Pitching SV	Batting AB	Batting H	Batting HR	BA	PO	A	E	DP	TC/G	FA
1971	LA N	2	2	.500	3.00	14	4	1	42	42	13	15	1	1	1	0	9	1	0	.111	1	3	0	0	0.3	1.000

Buck O'Brien

O'BRIEN, THOMAS JOSEPH
B. May 9, 1882, Brockton, Mass. D. July 25, 1959, Boston, Mass.
BR TR 5'10" 188 lbs.

Year	Team	W	L	PCT	ERA	G	GS	CG	IP	H	BB	SO	ShO	Relief Pitching W	Relief Pitching L	Relief Pitching SV	Batting AB	Batting H	Batting HR	BA	PO	A	E	DP	TC/G	FA
1911	BOS A	5	1	.833	0.38	6	5	5	47.2	30	21	31	2	1	0	0	16	2	0	.125	3	14	0	1	2.8	1.000
1912		20	13	.606	2.58	37	34	25	275.2	237	90	115	2	2	0	0	94	13	0	.138	10	83	5	1	2.6	.949
1913	2 teams BOS A (15G 4–9) CHI A (6G 0–2)																									
"	total	4	11	.267	3.73	21	15	6	108.2	124	48	58	0	0	2	0	33	5	0	.152	2	33	0	0	1.7	1.000
3 yrs.		29	25	.537	2.63	64	54	36	432	391	159	204	4	3	2	0	143	20	0	.140	15	130	5	2	2.3	.967
WORLD SERIES																										
1912	BOS A	0	2	.000	7.00	2	2	0	9	12	3	4	0	0	0	0	2	0	0	.000	1	6	0	0	3.5	1.000

Dan O'Brien

O'BRIEN, DANIEL JOQUES
B. Apr. 22, 1954, St. Petersburg, Fla.
BR TR 6'4" 215 lbs.

Year	Team	W	L	PCT	ERA	G	GS	CG	IP	H	BB	SO	ShO	Relief Pitching W	Relief Pitching L	Relief Pitching SV	Batting AB	Batting H	Batting HR	BA	PO	A	E	DP	TC/G	FA
1978	STL N	0	2	.000	4.50	7	2	0	18	22	8	12	0	0	1	0	3	0	0	.000	0	2	0	0	0.3	1.000
1979		1	1	.500	8.18	6	0	0	11	21	3	5	0	1	1	0	2	0	0	.000	0	0	0	0	0.0	.000
2 yrs.		1	3	.250	5.90	13	2	0	29	43	11	17	0	1	2	0	5	0	0	.000	0	2	0	0	0.2	1.000

Darby O'Brien

O'BRIEN, JOHN F.
B. Apr. 15, 1867, Troy, N. Y. D. Mar. 11, 1892, West Troy, N. Y.
BR TR 5'10" 165 lbs.

Year	Team	W	L	PCT	ERA	G	GS	CG	IP	H	BB	SO	ShO	Relief Pitching W	Relief Pitching L	Relief Pitching SV	Batting AB	Batting H	Batting HR	BA	PO	A	E	DP	TC/G	FA
1888	CLE AA	11	19	.367	3.30	30	30	30	259	245	99	135	1	0	0	0	109	20	0	.183	16	63	9	2	2.8	.898
1889	CLE N	22	17	.564	4.15	41	41	39	346.2	345	167	122	1	0	0	0	140	35	0	.250	25	70	7	3	2.5	.931
1890	CLE P	8	16	.333	3.40	25	25	22	206.1	229	93	54	0	0	0	0	96	15	0	.156	9	46	2	2	2.2	.965
1891	BOS AA	18	13	.581	3.65	40	30	22	268.2	300	127	87	0	3	1	2	128	30	0	.234	11	50	4	4	1.6	.938
4 yrs.		59	65	.476	3.68	136	126	113	1080.2	1119	486	398	2	3	1	2	473	100	0	.211	61	229	22	11	2.2	.929

Darby O'Brien

O'BRIEN, WILLIAM D.
B. Sept. 1, 1863, Peoria, Ill. D. June 15, 1893, Peoria, Ill.
BR TR 6'1" 186 lbs.

Year	Team	W	L	PCT	ERA	G	GS	CG	IP	H	BB	SO	ShO	Relief Pitching W	Relief Pitching L	Relief Pitching SV	Batting AB	Batting H	Batting HR	BA	PO	A	E	DP	TC/G	FA
1887	NY AA	0	0	—	*7.36*	1	0	0	3.2	4	5	0	0	0	0	0	*				312	28	31	9	2.7	.916

Eddie O'Brien

O'BRIEN, EDWARD JOSEPH
Brother of Johnny O'Brien.
B. Dec. 11, 1930, South Amboy, N. J.
BR TR 5'9" 165 lbs.

Year	Team	W	L	PCT	ERA	G	GS	CG	IP	H	BB	SO	ShO	Relief Pitching W	Relief Pitching L	Relief Pitching SV	Batting AB	Batting H	Batting HR	BA	PO	A	E	DP	TC/G	FA
1956	PIT N	0	0	—	0.00	1	0	0	2	1	0	0	0	0	0	0	53	14	0	.264	122	207	23	39	4.3	.935
1957		1	0	1.000	2.19	3	1	1	12.1	11	3	10	0	0	0	0	4	0	0	.000	0	2	0	1	0.7	1.000
1958		0	0	—	13.50	1	0	0	2	4	1	1	0	0	0	0	0	0	0	—	0	0	0	0	0.0	.000
3 yrs.		1	0	1.000	3.31	5	1	1	16.1	16	4	11	0	0	0	0	*				304	282	29	55	3.3	.953

Johnny O'Brien

O'BRIEN, JOHN THOMAS
Brother of Eddie O'Brien.
B. Dec. 11, 1930, South Amboy, N. J.
BR TR 5'9" 170 lbs.

Year	Team	W	L	PCT	ERA	G	GS	CG	IP	H	BB	SO	ShO	Relief Pitching W	Relief Pitching L	Relief Pitching SV	Batting AB	Batting H	Batting HR	BA	PO	A	E	DP	TC/G	FA
1956	PIT N	1	0	1.000	2.84	8	0	0	19	8	9	9	0	1	0	0	104	18	0	.173	172	210	7	48	5.0	.982
1957		0	3	.000	6.08	16	1	0	40	46	24	19	0	0	2	0	35	11	0	.314	14	16	4	2	1.3	.882
1958	STL N	0	0	—	22.50	1	0	0	2	7	2	2	0	0	0	0	3	0	0	.000	3	1	0	0	0.6	1.000
3 yrs.		1	3	.250	5.61	25	1	0	61	61	35	30	0	1	2	0	*				511	629	35	144	4.1	.970

Tom O'Brien

O'BRIEN, THOMAS H.
B. June 22, 1860, Salem, Mass. D. Apr. 21, 1921, Worcester, Mass.
BR TR 6'1" 185 lbs.

Year	Team	W	L	PCT	ERA	G	GS	CG	IP	H	BB	SO	ShO	Relief Pitching W	Relief Pitching L	Relief Pitching SV	Batting AB	Batting H	Batting HR	BA	PO	A	E	DP	TC/G	FA
1887	NY AA	0	0	—	0.00	1	0	0	1	1	1	0	0	0	0	0	*				47	9	17	2	3.2	.767

Walter Ockey

OCKEY, WALTER ANDREW (Footie)
Born Walter Andrew Okypch.
B. Jan. 4, 1920, New York, N. Y. D. Dec. 4, 1971, Staten Island, N. Y.
BR TR 6' 175 lbs.

Year	Team	Lg	W	L	PCT	ERA	G	GS	CG	IP	H	BB	SO	ShO	Relief W	Relief L	Relief SV	AB	H	HR	BA	PO	A	E	DP	TC/G	FA
1944	NY	N	0	0	—	3.38	2	0	0	2.2	2	2	1	0	0	0	0	0	0	0	—	0	2	0	0	1.0	1.000

Pat O'Connell

O'CONNELL, PATRICK H.
B. June 10, 1861, Bangor, Me. D. Jan. 24, 1943, Lewiston, Me.
BL TR 5'10" 175 lbs.

Year	Team	Lg	W	L	PCT	ERA	G	GS	CG	IP	H	BB	SO	ShO	Relief W	Relief L	Relief SV	AB	H	HR	BA	PO	A	E	DP	TC/G	FA
1886	BAL	AA	0	0	—	6.00	1	0	0	3	4	2	1	0	0	0	0	*				65	4	17	0	2.0	.802

Andy O'Connor

O'CONNOR, ANDREW JAMES
B. Sept. 14, 1884, Roxbury, Mass. D. Sept. 26, 1980, Norwood, Mass.
BR TR 6' 160 lbs.

Year	Team	Lg	W	L	PCT	ERA	G	GS	CG	IP	H	BB	SO	ShO	Relief W	Relief L	Relief SV	AB	H	HR	BA	PO	A	E	DP	TC/G	FA
1908	NY	A	0	1	.000	10.13	1	1	1	8	15	7	5	0	0	0	0	3	0	0	.000	0	2	1	0	3.0	.667

Frank O'Connor

O'CONNOR, FRANK HENRY
B. Sept. 15, 1870, Keeseville, N. Y. D. Dec. 26, 1913, Brattleboro, Vt.
BL TL 6' 185 lbs.

Year	Team	Lg	W	L	PCT	ERA	G	GS	CG	IP	H	BB	SO	ShO	Relief W	Relief L	Relief SV	AB	H	HR	BA	PO	A	E	DP	TC/G	FA
1893	PHI	N	0	0	—	11.25	3	1	0	4	2	9	0	0	0	0	1	2	2	1	1.000	0	1	0	0	0.3	1.000

Jack O'Connor

O'CONNOR, JACK WILLIAM
B. June 2, 1958, Twenty-Nine Palms, Calif.
BL TL 6' 3" 215 lbs.

Year	Team	Lg	W	L	PCT	ERA	G	GS	CG	IP	H	BB	SO	ShO	Relief W	Relief L	Relief SV	AB	H	HR	BA	PO	A	E	DP	TC/G	FA
1981	MIN	A	3	2	.600	5.91	28	0	0	35	46	30	16	0	3	2	0	0	0	0	—	2	8	2	3	0.4	.833
1982			8	9	.471	4.29	23	19	6	126	122	57	56	1	0	0	0	0	0	0	—	3	6	0	0	0.4	1.000
1983			2	3	.400	5.86	27	8	0	83	107	36	56	0	1	0	0	0	0	0	—	2	6	0	0	0.3	1.000
1984			0	0	—	1.93	2	0	0	4.2	1	4	0	0	0	0	0	0	0	0	—	0	0	0	0	0.0	.000
1985	MON	N	0	2	.000	4.94	20	1	0	23.2	21	13	16	0	0	1	0	0	0	0	—	0	1	0	1	0.1	1.000
1987	BAL	A	1	1	.500	4.30	29	0	0	46	46	23	33	0	1	1	2	0	0	0	—	3	2	1	1	0.2	.833
6 yrs.			14	17	.452	4.89	129	28	6	318.1	343	163	177	1	5	4	2	0	0	0		10	23	3	5	0.3	.917

Hank O'Day

O'DAY, HENRY FRANCIS (Peep)
B. July 8, 1862, Chicago, Ill. D. July 2, 1935, Chicago, Ill.
Manager 1912, 1914.
TR 6' 180 lbs.

Year	Team	Lg	W	L	PCT	ERA	G	GS	CG	IP	H	BB	SO	ShO	Relief W	Relief L	Relief SV	AB	H	HR	BA	PO	A	E	DP	TC/G	FA
1884	TOL	AA	9	28	.243	*3.75*	41	40	35	326.2	335	66	163	2	0	0	**1**	242	51	0	.211	61	95	20	5	2.6	.886
1885	PIT	AA	5	7	.417	*3.67*	12	12	10	103	110	16	36	0	0	0	0	49	12	0	.245	8	19	4	2	2.1	.871
1886	WAS	N	2	2	.500	1.65	6	6	6	49	41	17	47	0	0	0	0	19	1	0	.053	4	14	2	1	3.3	.900
1887			8	20	.286	4.17	30	30	29	254.2	255	109	86	0	0	0	0	116	23	0	.198	15	59	6	4	2.1	.925
1888			16	**29**	.356	3.10	46	46	46	403	359	117	186	2	0	0	0	166	23	0	.139	19	67	8	1	2.0	.915
1889	2 teams	WAS N (13G 2–10) NY N (10G 9–1)																									
"	total		11	11	.500	4.31	23	23	19	186	200	92	51	0	0	0	0	75	11	0	.147	12	34	3	1	2.1	.939
1890	NY	P	22	13	.629	4.21	43	35	32	329	356	163	94	1	1	0	**3**	150	34	1	.227	11	71	7	0	2.1	.921
7 yrs.			73	110	.399	3.74	201	192	177	1651.1	1656	580	663	5	1	0	4	*				130	359	50	14	2.2	.907

Paul O'Dea

O'DEA, PAUL (Lefty)
B. July 3, 1920, Cleveland, Ohio D. Dec. 11, 1978, Cleveland, Ohio.
BL TL 6' 200 lbs.

Year	Team	Lg	W	L	PCT	ERA	G	GS	CG	IP	H	BB	SO	ShO	Relief W	Relief L	Relief SV	AB	H	HR	BA	PO	A	E	DP	TC/G	FA
1944	CLE	A	0	0	—	2.08	3	0	0	4.1	5	6	0	0	0	0	0	173	55	0	.318	93	3	5	3	2.1	.950
1945			0	0	—	13.50	1	0	0	2	4	2	0	0	0	0	0	221	52	1	.235	118	5	1	2	2.3	.992
2 yrs.			0	0		5.68	4	0	0	6.1	9	8	0	0	0	0	0	*				211	8	6	5	2.2	.973

Billy O'Dell

O'DELL, WILLIAM OLIVER (Digger)
B. Feb. 10, 1933, Whitmere, S. C.
BB TL 5'11" 170 lbs.

Year	Team	Lg	W	L	PCT	ERA	G	GS	CG	IP	H	BB	SO	ShO	Relief W	Relief L	Relief SV	AB	H	HR	BA	PO	A	E	DP	TC/G	FA
1954	BAL	A	1	1	.500	2.76	7	2	1	16.1	15	5	6	0	0	0	0	3	0	0	.000	0	5	0	0	0.7	1.000
1956			0	0	—	1.13	4	1	0	8	6	6	6	0	0	0	0	1	0	0	.000	0	0	0	0	0.0	.000
1957			4	10	.286	2.69	35	15	2	140.1	107	39	97	1	0	1	4	34	5	0	.147	5	14	2	1	0.6	.905
1958			14	11	.560	2.97	41	25	12	221.1	201	51	137	3	2	1	8	72	8	1	.111	12	32	0	2	1.1	1.000
1959			10	12	.455	2.93	38	24	6	199.1	163	67	88	2	2	4	1	60	5	1	.083	7	44	3	3	1.4	.944
1960	SF	N	8	13	.381	3.20	43	24	6	202.2	198	72	145	1	1	3	2	56	6	0	.107	9	29	1	0	0.9	.974
1961			7	5	.583	3.59	46	14	4	130.1	132	33	110	1	3	2	2	39	4	0	.103	8	17	0	1	0.5	1.000
1962			19	14	.576	3.53	43	39	20	280.2	**282**	66	195	2	1	0	0	90	12	0	.133	15	39	5	0	1.4	.915
1963			14	10	.583	3.16	36	33	10	222.1	218	70	116	3	0	1	1	78	16	0	.205	5	27	1	0	0.9	.970
1964			8	7	.533	5.40	36	8	1	85	82	35	54	0	**8**	3	2	22	0	0	.000	5	10	1	0	0.4	.938
1965	MIL	N	10	6	.625	2.18	62	1	0	111.1	87	30	78	0	**10**	5	18	23	4	0	.174	12	13	0	1	0.4	1.000
1966	2 teams	ATL N (24G 2–3) PIT N (37G 3–2)																									
"	total		5	5	.500	2.64	61	2	0	112.2	118	41	67	0	4	5	10	24	3	0	.125	7	10	0	2	0.3	1.000
1967	PIT	N	5	6	.455	5.82	27	11	1	86.2	88	41	34	0	1	1	0	26	3	0	.115	3	12	0	1	0.6	1.000
13 yrs.			105	100	.512	3.29	479	199	63	1817	1697	556	1133	13	32	26	48	528	66	2	.125	88	252	13	11	0.7	.963
WORLD SERIES																											
1962	SF	N	0	1	.000	4.38	3	1	0	12.1	12	3	9	0	0	0	1	3	1	0	.333	0	0	0	0	0.0	.000

Ted Odenwald

ODENWALD, THEODORE JOSEPH (Lefty)
B. Jan. 4, 1902, Hudson, Wis. D. Oct. 23, 1965, Shakopee, Minn.
BR TL 5'10" 147 lbs.

Year	Team	Lg	W	L	PCT	ERA	G	GS	CG	IP	H	BB	SO	ShO	Relief W	Relief L	Relief SV	AB	H	HR	BA	PO	A	E	DP	TC/G	FA
1921	CLE	A	1	0	1.000	1.56	10	0	0	17.1	16	6	4	0	1	0	0	3	0	0	.000	0	5	0	0	0.5	1.000
1922			0	0	—	40.50	1	0	0	1.1	6	2	2	0	0	0	0	0	0	0	—	1	0	0	0	1.0	1.000
2 yrs.			1	0	1.000	4.34	11	0	0	18.2	22	8	6	0	1	0	0	3	0	0	.000	1	5	0	0	0.5	1.000

Blue Moon Odom

ODOM, JOHNNY LEE
B. May 29, 1945, Macon, Ga.
BR TR 6' 178 lbs.

Year	Team	Lg	W	L	PCT	ERA	G	GS	CG	IP	H	BB	SO	ShO	Relief W	Relief L	Relief SV	AB	H	HR	BA	PO	A	E	DP	TC/G	FA
1964	KC	A	1	2	.333	10.06	5	5	1	17	29	11	10	1	0	0	0	5	0	0	.000	2	2	1	1	1.0	.800
1965			0	0	—	9.00	1	0	0	1	2	2	0	0	0	0	0	0	0	0	—	0	1	0	0	1.0	1.000
1966			5	5	.500	2.49	14	14	4	90.1	70	53	47	2	0	0	0	31	3	0	.097	12	20	1	2	2.4	.970
1967			3	8	.273	5.04	29	17	0	103.2	94	68	67	0	0	0	0	28	8	0	.286	9	17	3	2	1.0	.897
1968	OAK	A	16	10	.615	2.45	32	31	9	231.1	179	98	143	4	0	0	0	78	17	1	.218	10	43	2	1	1.7	.964
1969			15	6	.714	2.92	32	32	10	231.1	179	112	150	3	0	0	0	79	21	5	.266	27	32	4	4	2.0	.937
1970			9	8	.529	3.81	29	29	4	156	128	100	88	1	0	0	0	54	13	3	.241	22	30	4	2	1.9	.929
1971			10	12	.455	4.28	25	25	3	141	147	71	69	1	0	0	0	50	8	1	.160	15	19	6	3	1.6	.850
1972			15	6	.714	2.50	31	30	4	194.1	164	87	86	2	0	0	0	66	8	2	.121	15	33	7	2	1.8	.873
1973			5	12	.294	4.49	30	24	3	150.1	153	67	83	0	1	0	0	1	0	0	.000	8	20	4	3	1.1	.875

Year	Team	W	L	PCT	ERA	G	GS	CG	IP	H	BB	SO	ShO	Relief Pitching W	Relief Pitching L	Relief Pitching SV	Batting AB	Batting H	Batting HR	BA	PO	A	E	DP	TC/G	FA

Blue Moon Odom *continued*

Year	Team	W	L	PCT	ERA	G	GS	CG	IP	H	BB	SO	ShO	Relief W	Relief L	Relief SV	AB	H	HR	BA	PO	A	E	DP	TC/G	FA
1974		1	5	.167	3.83	34	5	1	87	85	52	52	0	1	0	1	0	0	0	—	7	16	5	1	0.8	.821
1975	3 teams OAK A (7G 0–2) CLE A (3G 1–0) ATL N (15G 1–7)																									
"	total	2	9	.182	7.22	25	13	1	77.1	101	47	44	1	0	1	0	13	1	0	.077	13	8	2	0	0.9	.913
1976	CHI A	2	2	.500	5.79	8	4	0	28	31	20	18	0	0	0	0	0	0	0	—	1	2	2	0	0.6	.600
13 yrs.		84	85	.497	3.70	295	229	40	1508.2	1362	788	857	15	2	1	1	405	79	12	.195	141	243	41	21	1.4	.904
LEAGUE CHAMPIONSHIP SERIES																										
1972	OAK A	2	0	1.000	0.00	2	2	1	14	5	2	5	1	0	0	0	4	1	0	.250	2	1	0	0	1.5	1.000
1973		0	0	—	1.80	1	0	0	5	6	2	4	0	0	0	0	0	0	0	—	0	1	0	0	1.0	1.000
1974		0	0	—	0.00	1	0	0	3.1	1	0	1	0	0	0	0	0	0	0	—	0	0	0	0	0.0	.000
3 yrs.		2	0	1.000	0.40	4	2	1	22.1	12	4	10	1 1st	0	0	0	4	1	0	.250	2	2	0	0	1.0	1.000
WORLD SERIES																										
1972	OAK A	0	1	.000	1.59	2	2	0	11.1	5	6	13	0	0	0	0	4	0	0	.000	1	3	0	0	2.0	1.000
1973		0	0	—	3.86	2	0	0	4.2	5	2	2	0	0	0	0	1	0	0	.000	0	1	0	0	0.5	1.000
1974		1	0	1.000	0.00	2	0	0	1.1	0	1	2	0	1	0	0	0	0	0	—	0	0	0	0	0.0	.000
3 yrs.		1	1	.500	2.08	6	2	0	17.1	10	9	17	0	1	0	0	5	0	0	.000	1	4	0	0	0.8	1.000

Dave Odom

ODOM, DAVID EVERETT (Porky) BR TR 6′ 1″ 220 lbs.
B. June 5, 1918, Dinuba, Calif. D. Nov. 19, 1987, Myrtle Beach, S. C.

Year	Team	W	L	PCT	ERA	G	GS	CG	IP	H	BB	SO	ShO	Relief W	Relief L	Relief SV	AB	H	HR	BA	PO	A	E	DP	TC/G	FA
1943	BOS N	0	3	.000	5.27	22	3	1	54.2	54	30	17	0	0	0	2	12	0	0	.000	3	5	1	0	0.4	.889

George O'Donnell

O'DONNELL, GEORGE DANA BR TR 6′ 3″ 175 lbs.
B. May 27, 1929, Winchester, Ill.

Year	Team	W	L	PCT	ERA	G	GS	CG	IP	H	BB	SO	ShO	Relief W	Relief L	Relief SV	AB	H	HR	BA	PO	A	E	DP	TC/G	FA
1954	PIT N	3	9	.250	4.53	21	10	3	87.1	105	21	8	0	1	1	1	23	2	1	.087	7	19	0	1	1.2	1.000

John O'Donoghue

O'DONOGHUE, JOHN EUGENE BR TL 6′ 4″ 203 lbs.
Father of John O'Donoghue.
B. Oct. 7, 1939, Kansas City, Mo.

Year	Team	W	L	PCT	ERA	G	GS	CG	IP	H	BB	SO	ShO	Relief W	Relief L	Relief SV	AB	H	HR	BA	PO	A	E	DP	TC/G	FA
1963	KC A	0	1	.000	1.50	1	1	0	6	6	2	1	0	0	0	0	2	0	0	.000	0	0	0	0	0.0	.000
1964		10	14	.417	4.92	39	32	2	173.2	202	65	79	1	1	0	0	55	13	1	.236	8	27	3	4	1.0	.921
1965		9	**18**	.333	3.95	34	30	4	177.2	183	66	82	1	0	2	0	55	12	1	.218	8	36	4	2	1.4	.917
1966	CLE A	6	8	.429	3.83	32	13	2	108	109	23	49	0	2	2	0	33	5	0	.152	5	24	0	0	0.9	1.000
1967		8	9	.471	3.24	33	17	5	130.2	120	33	81	2	1	0	2	40	4	1	.100	7	35	0	3	1.3	1.000
1968	BAL A	0	0	—	6.14	16	0	0	22	34	7	11	0	0	0	2	2	0	0	.000	0	5	0	0	0.3	1.000
1969	SEA A	2	2	.500	2.96	55	0	0	70	58	37	48	0	2	2	6	13	1	0	.077	3	9	1	2	0.2	.923
1970	2 teams MIL A (25G 2–0) MON N (9G 2–3)																									
"	total	4	3	.571	5.20	34	3	0	45	49	20	19	0	4	1	0	6	0	0	.000	2	11	1	2	0.4	.929
1971	MON N	0	0	—	4.76	13	0	0	17	19	7	7	0	0	0	0	0	0	0	—	2	2	0	0	0.3	1.000
9 yrs.		39	55	.415	4.08	257	96	13	750	780	260	377	4	10	7	10	206	35	3	.170	35	149	9	13	0.8	.953

John O'Donoghue

O'DONOGHUE, JOHN PRESTON BL TL 6′ 6″ 198 lbs.
Son of John O'Donoghue.
B. May 26, 1969, Wilmington, Del.

Year	Team	W	L	PCT	ERA	G	GS	CG	IP	H	BB	SO	ShO	Relief W	Relief L	Relief SV	AB	H	HR	BA	PO	A	E	DP	TC/G	FA
1993	BAL A	0	1	.000	4.58	11	1	0	19.2	22	10	16	0	0	0	0	0	0	0	—	1	1	1	0	0.3	.667

Lefty O'Doul

O'DOUL, FRANCIS JOSEPH BL TL 6′ 180 lbs.
B. Mar. 4, 1897, San Francisco, Calif. D. Dec. 7, 1969, San Francisco, Calif.

Year	Team	W	L	PCT	ERA	G	GS	CG	IP	H	BB	SO	ShO	Relief W	Relief L	Relief SV	AB	H	HR	BA	PO	A	E	DP	TC/G	FA
1919	NY A	0	0	—	3.60	3	0	0	5	7	4	2	0	0	0	0	16	4	0	.250	1	1	0	0	0.5	1.000
1920		0	0	—	4.91	2	0	0	3.2	4	2	2	0	0	0	0	12	2	0	.167	0	0	0	0	0.0	
1922		0	0	—	3.38	6	0	0	16	24	12	5	0	0	0	0	9	3	0	.333	1	4	0	1	0.8	1.000
1923	BOS A	1	1	.500	5.43	23	0	0	53	69	31	10	0	1	1	0	35	5	0	.143	2	21	1	0	1.0	.958
4 yrs.		1	1	.500	4.87	34	0	0	77.2	104	49	19	0	1	1	0	*				1594	61	61	7	2.1	.964

Bryan Oelkers

OELKERS, BRYAN ALOIS BL TL 6′ 2″ 190 lbs.
B. Mar. 11, 1961, Zaragoza, Spain.

Year	Team	W	L	PCT	ERA	G	GS	CG	IP	H	BB	SO	ShO	Relief W	Relief L	Relief SV	AB	H	HR	BA	PO	A	E	DP	TC/G	FA
1983	MIN A	0	5	.000	8.65	10	8	0	34.1	56	17	13	0	0	0	0	0	0	0	—	1	1	0	0	0.2	1.000
1986	CLE A	3	3	.500	4.70	35	4	0	69	70	40	33	0	3	2	1	0	0	0	—	5	4	0	0	0.3	1.000
2 yrs.		3	8	.273	6.01	45	12	0	103.1	126	57	46	0	3	2	1	0	0	0		6	5	0	0	0.2	1.000

Joe Oeschger

OESCHGER, JOSEPH CARL BR TR 6′ 190 lbs.
B. May 24, 1891, Chicago, Ill. D. July 29, 1986, Rohnert Park, Calif.

Year	Team	W	L	PCT	ERA	G	GS	CG	IP	H	BB	SO	ShO	Relief W	Relief L	Relief SV	AB	H	HR	BA	PO	A	E	DP	TC/G	FA
1914	PHI N	4	8	.333	3.77	32	10	5	124	129	54	47	0	3	0	1	40	3	0	.075	4	29	3	0	1.1	.917
1915		1	0	1.000	3.42	6	1	1	23.2	21	9	8	0	0	0	0	7	0	0	.000	1	6	0	0	1.2	1.000
1916		1	0	1.000	2.37	14	0	0	30.1	18	14	17	0	1	0	0	5	0	0	.000	1	10	0	2	0.8	1.000
1917		16	14	.533	2.75	42	30	18	262	241	72	123	5	3	0	0	88	10	0	.114	5	57	2	2	1.5	.969
1918		6	**18**	.250	3.03	30	23	13	184	159	83	60	2	0	3	**3**	60	5	0	.083	8	45	3	2	1.9	.946
1919	3 teams PHI N (5G 0–1) NY N (5G 0–1) BOS N (7G 4–2)																									
"	total	4	4	.500	3.94	17	12	6	102.2	127	39	24	1	0	1	0	38	2	0	.053	6	22	1	0	1.7	.966
1920	BOS N	15	13	.536	3.46	38	30	20	299	294	99	80	5	0	1	0	101	18	0	.178	10	70	5	3	2.2	.941
1921		20	14	.588	3.52	46	36	19	299	303	**97**	68	**3**	2	1	0	110	28	0	.255	11	93	5	2	2.4	.954
1922		6	21	.222	5.06	46	23	10	195.2	234	81	51	1	2	3	1	63	12	0	.190	6	51	1	3	1.3	.983
1923		5	15	.250	5.68	44	19	6	166.1	227	54	33	1	2	2	2	52	12	0	.231	7	38	0	3	1.0	1.000
1924	2 teams NY N (10G 2–0) PHI N (19G 2–7)																									
"	total	4	7	.364	4.01	29	10	0	94.1	123	30	18	0	2	2	0	27	8	0	.296	3	18	1	2	0.8	.955
1925	BKN N	1	2	.333	6.08	21	3	1	37	60	19	6	0	0	1	0	8	1	0	.125	2	8	1	0	0.5	.909
12 yrs.		83	116	.417	3.81	365	197	99	1818	1936	651	535	18	15	14	7	599	99	0	.165	64	447	22	19	1.5	.959

Curly Ogden

OGDEN, WARREN HARVEY BR TR 6′ 1½″ 180 lbs.
Brother of Jack Ogden.
B. Jan. 24, 1901, Ogden, Pa. D. Aug. 6, 1964, Chester, Pa.

Year	Team	W	L	PCT	ERA	G	GS	CG	IP	H	BB	SO	ShO	Relief W	Relief L	Relief SV	AB	H	HR	BA	PO	A	E	DP	TC/G	FA
1922	PHI A	1	4	.200	3.11	15	6	4	72.1	59	33	20	0	0	0	0	29	7	0	.241	5	16	2	0	1.5	.913
1923		1	2	.333	5.63	18	2	0	46.1	63	32	14	0	1	0	0	17	5	0	.294	3	13	1	0	0.9	.941
1924	2 teams PHI A (5G 0–3) WAS A (16G 9–5)																									
"	total	9	8	.529	2.83	21	17	9	120.2	97	58	27	3	0	2	0	50	13	0	.260	7	24	0	0	1.5	1.000

Curly Ogden *continued*

Year	Team	Lg	W	L	PCT	ERA	G	GS	CG	IP	H	BB	SO	ShO	Relief Pitching W	Relief Pitching L	Relief Pitching SV	Batting AB	Batting H	Batting HR	BA	PO	A	E	DP	TC/G	FA
1925	WAS	A	3	1	.750	4.50	17	4	2	42	45	18	6	1	1	0	0	12	3	0	.250	1	10	1	0	0.7	.917
1926			4	4	.500	4.30	22	9	4	96.1	114	45	21	0	1	1	0	27	5	0	.185	7	18	1	0	1.2	.962
5 yrs.			18	19	.486	3.79	93	38	19	377.2	378	186	88	4	3	3	0	135	33	0	.244	23	81	5	0	1.2	.954
WORLD SERIES																											
1924	WAS	A	0	0	—	0.00	1	1	0	0.1	0	1	1	0	0	0	0	0	0	0	—	0	0	0	0	0.0	.000

Jack Ogden

OGDEN, JOHN MAHLON
Brother of Curly Ogden.
B. Nov. 5, 1897, Ogden, Pa. D. Nov. 9, 1977, Philadelphia, Pa.
BR TR 6′ 190 lbs.

Year	Team	Lg	W	L	PCT	ERA	G	GS	CG	IP	H	BB	SO	ShO	Relief Pitching W	Relief Pitching L	Relief Pitching SV	Batting AB	Batting H	Batting HR	BA	PO	A	E	DP	TC/G	FA
1918	NY	N	0	0	—	3.12	5	0	0	8.2	8	3	1	0	0	0	0	1	0	0	.000	0	1	0	0	0.2	1.000
1928	STL	A	15	16	.484	4.15	38	31	18	242.2	257	80	67	1	2	1	2	85	17	0	.200	15	35	1	3	1.3	.980
1929			4	8	.333	4.93	34	14	7	131.1	154	44	32	0	0	2	0	45	11	0	.244	6	28	2	4	1.1	.944
1931	CIN	N	4	8	.333	2.93	22	9	3	89	79	32	24	1	1	3	1	27	4	0	.148	8	15	4	0	1.2	.852
1932			2	2	.500	5.21	24	3	1	57	72	22	20	0	1	1	0	12	2	0	.167	4	14	1	0	0.8	.947
5 yrs.			25	34	.424	4.24	123	57	29	528.2	570	181	144	2	4	7	3	170	34	0	.200	33	93	8	7	1.1	.940

Chad Ogea

OGEA, CHAD WAYNE
B. Nov. 9, 1970, Lake Charles, La.
BR TR 6′ 2″ 200 lbs.

Year	Team	Lg	W	L	PCT	ERA	G	GS	CG	IP	H	BB	SO	ShO	Relief Pitching W	Relief Pitching L	Relief Pitching SV	Batting AB	Batting H	Batting HR	BA	PO	A	E	DP	TC/G	FA
1994	CLE	A	0	1	.000	6.06	4	1	0	16.1	21	10	11	0	0	0	0	0	0	0	—	0	2	0	0	0.5	1.000
1995			8	3	.727	3.05	20	14	1	106.1	95	29	57	0	0	0	0	0	0	0	—	3	14	0	1	0.9	1.000
2 yrs.			8	4	.667	3.45	24	15	1	122.2	116	39	68	0	0	0	0	0	0	0		3	16	0	1	0.8	1.000
LEAGUE CHAMPIONSHIP SERIES																											
1995	CLE	A	0	0	—	0.00	1	0	0	0.2	1	0	2	0	0	0	0	0	0	0	—	0	0	0	0	0.0	.000

Joe Ogrodowski

OGRODOWSKI, JOSEPH ANTHONY
B. Nov. 20, 1906, Hoytville, Pa. D. June 24, 1959, Elmira, N. Y.
BR TR 5′11″ 165 lbs.

Year	Team	Lg	W	L	PCT	ERA	G	GS	CG	IP	H	BB	SO	ShO	Relief Pitching W	Relief Pitching L	Relief Pitching SV	Batting AB	Batting H	Batting HR	BA	PO	A	E	DP	TC/G	FA
1925	BOS	N	0	0	—	54.00	1	0	0	1	6	3	0	0	0	0	0	0	0	0	—	0	0	0	0	0.0	.000

Bill O'Hara

O'HARA, WILLIAM ALEXANDER
B. Aug. 14, 1883, Toronto, Ont., Canada D. June 15, 1931, Jersey City, N. J.
BL TR 5′10″

Year	Team	Lg	W	L	PCT	ERA	G	GS	CG	IP	H	BB	SO	ShO	Relief Pitching W	Relief Pitching L	Relief Pitching SV	Batting AB	Batting H	Batting HR	BA	PO	A	E	DP	TC/G	FA
1910	STL	N	0	0	—	0.00	1	0	0	1	0	0	0	0	0	0	0	*				202	19	5	4	2.0	.978

Joe Ohl

OHL, JOSEPH EARL
Born Joseph Earl von Ohl.
B. Jan. 10, 1888, Jobstown, N. J. D. Dec. 18, 1951, Camden, N. J.
BL TL

Year	Team	Lg	W	L	PCT	ERA	G	GS	CG	IP	H	BB	SO	ShO	Relief Pitching W	Relief Pitching L	Relief Pitching SV	Batting AB	Batting H	Batting HR	BA	PO	A	E	DP	TC/G	FA
1909	WAS	A	0	0	—	2.08	4	0	0	8.2	7	1	2	0	0	0	0	2	0	0	.000	5	0	0	0	1.3	1.000

Bob Ojeda

OJEDA, ROBERT MICHAEL (Bobby O.)
B. Dec. 17, 1957, Los Angeles, Calif.
BL TL 6′ 1″ 185 lbs.

Year	Team	Lg	W	L	PCT	ERA	G	GS	CG	IP	H	BB	SO	ShO	Relief Pitching W	Relief Pitching L	Relief Pitching SV	Batting AB	Batting H	Batting HR	BA	PO	A	E	DP	TC/G	FA
1980	BOS	A	1	1	.500	6.92	7	7	0	26	39	14	12	0	0	0	0	0	0	0	—	1	3	0	0	0.6	1.000
1981			6	2	.750	3.14	10	10	2	66	50	25	28	0	0	0	0	0	0	0	—	3	10	1	1	1.4	.929
1982			4	6	.400	5.63	22	14	0	78.1	95	29	52	0	1	0	0	0	0	0	—	2	7	1	0	0.5	.900
1983			12	7	.632	4.04	29	28	5	173.2	173	73	94	0	0	0	0	0	0	0	—	11	23	1	2	1.2	.971
1984			12	12	.500	3.99	33	32	8	216.2	211	96	137	**5**	0	0	0	0	0	0	—	10	32	2	3	1.3	.955
1985			9	11	.450	4.00	39	22	5	157.2	166	48	102	0	2	1	1	0	0	0	—	13	23	3	0	1.0	.923
1986	NY	N	18	5	**.783**	2.57	32	30	7	217.1	185	52	148	2	1	0	0	71	8	0	.113	9	37	1	3	1.5	.979
1987			3	5	.375	3.88	10	7	0	46.1	45	10	21	0	0	1	0	14	1	0	.071	5	6	0	2	1.1	1.000
1988			10	13	.435	2.88	29	29	5	190.1	158	33	133	5	0	0	0	61	10	0	.164	13	36	2	5	1.8	.961
1989			13	11	.542	3.47	31	31	5	192	179	78	95	2	0	0	0	66	7	0	.106	16	36	1	3	1.7	.981
1990			7	6	.538	3.66	38	12	0	118	123	40	62	0	3	1	0	30	4	0	.133	8	31	2	1	1.1	.951
1991	LA	N	12	9	.571	3.18	31	31	2	189.1	181	70	120	1	0	0	0	56	9	1	.161	14	32	0	1	1.5	1.000
1992			6	9	.400	3.63	29	29	2	166.1	169	81	94	1	0	0	0	49	5	0	.102	5	37	2	0	1.5	.955
1993	CLE	A	2	1	.667	4.40	9	7	0	43	48	21	27	0	0	0	0	0	0	0	—	3	9	0	1	1.3	1.000
1994	NY	A	0	0	—	24.00	2	2	0	3	11	6	3	0	0	0	0	0	0	0	—	0	1	0	0	0.5	1.000
15 yrs.			115	98	.540	3.65	351	291	41	1884	1833	676	1128	16	7	3	1	347	44	1	.127	113	323	16	22	1.3	.965
LEAGUE CHAMPIONSHIP SERIES																											
1986	NY	N	1	0	1.000	2.57	2	2	1	14	15	4	6	0	0	0	0	5	0	0	.000	2	4	0	0	3.0	1.000
WORLD SERIES																											
1986	NY	N	1	0	1.000	2.08	2	2	0	13	13	5	9	0	0	0	0	2	0	0	.000	0	2	0	0	1.0	1.000

Frank Okrie

OKRIE, FRANK ANTHONY (Lefty)
Father of Len Okrie.
B. Oct. 28, 1896, Detroit, Mich. D. Oct. 16, 1959, Detroit, Mich.
BL TL 5′11½″ 175 lbs.

Year	Team	Lg	W	L	PCT	ERA	G	GS	CG	IP	H	BB	SO	ShO	Relief Pitching W	Relief Pitching L	Relief Pitching SV	Batting AB	Batting H	Batting HR	BA	PO	A	E	DP	TC/G	FA
1920	DET	A	1	2	.333	5.27	21	1	1	41	44	18	9	0	1	1	0	5	1	0	.200	0	41	1	0	2.0	.976

Red Oldham

OLDHAM, JOHN CYRUS
B. July 15, 1893, Zion, Md. D. Jan. 28, 1961, Costa Mesa, Calif.
BB TL 6′ 176 lbs.
BL 1922, 1925–1926

Year	Team	Lg	W	L	PCT	ERA	G	GS	CG	IP	H	BB	SO	ShO	Relief Pitching W	Relief Pitching L	Relief Pitching SV	Batting AB	Batting H	Batting HR	BA	PO	A	E	DP	TC/G	FA
1914	DET	A	2	4	.333	3.38	9	7	3	45.1	42	8	23	0	0	0	0	15	4	0	.267	1	10	4	0	1.7	.733
1915			3	0	1.000	2.81	17	2	1	57.2	52	17	17	0	2	0	4	14	2	0	.143	0	18	3	0	1.2	.857
1920			8	13	.381	3.85	39	23	11	215.1	248	91	62	1	1	2	1	69	12	0	.174	6	78	4	1	2.3	.955
1921			11	14	.440	4.24	40	28	12	229.1	258	81	67	1	0	5	1	85	19	2	.224	6	66	4	2	1.9	.947
1922			10	13	.435	4.67	43	28	9	212	256	59	72	0	1	2	3	73	19	0	.260	7	57	3	1	1.6	.955
1925	PIT	N	3	2	.600	3.91	11	4	3	53	66	18	10	0	1	0	1	18	6	0	.333	1	15	1	1	1.5	.941
1926			2	2	.500	5.62	17	2	0	41.2	56	18	16	0	2	1	2	9	2	0	.222	3	9	1	1	0.8	.923
7 yrs.			39	48	.448	4.15	176	94	39	854.1	978	292	267	2	7	10	12	283	64	2	.226	24	253	20	6	1.7	.933
WORLD SERIES																											
1925	PIT	N	0	0	—	0.00	1	0	0	1	0	0	2	0	0	0	1	0	0	0	—	0	0	0	0	0.0	.000

Steve Olin

OLIN, STEVEN ROBERT
B. Oct. 4, 1965, Portland, Ore. D. Mar. 22, 1993, Little Lake Nellie, Fla.
BR TR 6′ 3″ 185 lbs.

Year	Team	Lg	W	L	PCT	ERA	G	GS	CG	IP	H	BB	SO	ShO	Relief Pitching W	Relief Pitching L	Relief Pitching SV	Batting AB	Batting H	Batting HR	BA	PO	A	E	DP	TC/G	FA
1989	CLE	A	1	4	.200	3.75	25	0	0	36	35	14	24	0	1	4	1	0	0	0	—	2	5	0	0	0.3	1.000
1990			4	4	.500	3.41	50	1	0	92.1	96	26	64	0	3	4	1	0	0	0	—	3	24	3	1	0.6	.900

Steve Olin *continued*

Year	Team	W	L	PCT	ERA	G	GS	CG	IP	H	BB	SO	ShO	Relief Pitching W	Relief Pitching L	Relief Pitching SV	Batting AB	Batting H	Batting HR	BA	PO	A	E	DP	TC/G	FA
1991		3	6	.333	3.36	48	0	0	56.1	61	23	38	0	3	6	17	0	0	0	—	3	8	0	2	0.2	1.000
1992		8	5	.615	2.34	72	0	0	88.1	80	27	47	0	8	5	29	0	0	0	—	4	17	0	1	0.3	1.000
4 yrs.		16	19	.457	3.10	195	1	0	273	272	90	173	0	15	19	48	0	0	0		12	54	3	4	0.4	.957

Omar Olivares

OLIVARES, OMAR BR TR 6′ 1″ 185 lbs.
Born Omar Olivares (Palqu).
Son of Ed Olivares.
B. July 6, 1967, Mayaguez, Puerto Rico.

Year	Team	W	L	PCT	ERA	G	GS	CG	IP	H	BB	SO	ShO	Relief Pitching W	Relief Pitching L	Relief Pitching SV	Batting AB	Batting H	Batting HR	BA	PO	A	E	DP	TC/G	FA
1990	STL N	1	1	.500	2.92	9	6	0	49.1	45	17	20	0	0	0	0	17	3	1	.176	7	8	0	0	1.7	1.000
1991		11	7	.611	3.71	28	24	0	167.1	148	61	91	0	0	0	1	53	12	0	.226	16	30	2	5	1.7	.958
1992		9	9	.500	3.84	32	30	1	197	189	63	124	0	0	0	0	68	16	1	.235	15	40	0	4	1.7	1.000
1993		5	3	.625	4.17	58	9	0	118.2	134	54	63	0	3	0	1	26	7	0	.269	9	36	4	3	0.8	.918
1994		3	4	.429	5.74	14	12	1	73.2	84	37	26	0	0	0	1	28	6	1	.214	7	14	1	1	1.6	.955
1995	2 teams CLR N (11G 1–3) PHI N (5G 0–1)																									
"	total	1	4	.200	6.91	16	6	0	41.2	55	23	22	0	0	2	0	9	2	1	.222	4	8	0	1	0.8	1.000
6 yrs.		30	28	.517	4.21	157	87	2	647.2	655	255	346	0	3	2	3	201	46	4	.229	58	136	7	14	1.3	.965

Darren Oliver

OLIVER, DARREN CHRISTOPHER BR TL 6′ 170 lbs.
Son of Bob Oliver.
B. Oct. 6, 1970, Kansas City, Mo.

Year	Team	W	L	PCT	ERA	G	GS	CG	IP	H	BB	SO	ShO	Relief Pitching W	Relief Pitching L	Relief Pitching SV	Batting AB	Batting H	Batting HR	BA	PO	A	E	DP	TC/G	FA
1993	TEX A	0	0	—	2.70	2	0	0	3.1	2	1	4	0	0	0	0	0	0	0	—	0	1	1	0	1.0	.500
1994		4	0	1.000	3.42	43	0	0	50	40	35	50	0	4	0	2	0	0	0	—	5	14	0	3	0.4	1.000
1995		4	2	.667	4.22	17	7	0	49	47	32	39	0	1	0	0	0	0	0	—	4	8	0	1	0.7	1.000
3 yrs.		8	2	.800	3.78	62	7	0	102.1	89	68	93	0	5	0	2	0	0	0		9	23	1	4	0.5	.970

Dick Oliver

Playing record listed under Dick Barrett.

Francisco Oliveras

OLIVERAS, FRANCISCO JAVIER BR TR 5′10″ 170 lbs.
Born Francisco Javier Oliveras (Noa).
B. Jan. 31, 1963, Santurce, Puerto Rico.

Year	Team	W	L	PCT	ERA	G	GS	CG	IP	H	BB	SO	ShO	Relief Pitching W	Relief Pitching L	Relief Pitching SV	Batting AB	Batting H	Batting HR	BA	PO	A	E	DP	TC/G	FA
1989	MIN A	3	4	.429	4.53	12	8	1	55.2	64	15	24	0	0	1	0	0	0	0	—	0	6	1	2	0.6	.857
1990	SF N	2	2	.500	2.77	33	2	0	55.1	47	21	41	0	2	1	2	5	0	0	.000	1	5	0	1	0.2	1.000
1991		6	6	.500	3.86	55	1	0	79.1	69	22	48	0	6	5	3	10	2	0	.200	3	12	1	0	0.3	.938
1992		0	3	.000	3.63	16	7	0	44.2	41	10	17	0	0	0	0	7	1	0	.143	0	9	1	0	0.6	.900
4 yrs.		11	15	.423	3.71	116	18	1	235	221	68	130	0	8	7	5	22	3	0	.136	4	32	3	3	0.3	.923

Chi Chi Olivo

OLIVO, FEDERICO EMILIO BR TR 6′ 2″ 215 lbs.
Born Federico Emilio Olivo (Maldonado).
Brother of Diomedes Olivo.
B. Mar. 18, 1928, Guayubin, Dominican Republic
D. Feb. 3, 1977, Guayubin, Dominican Republic.

Year	Team	W	L	PCT	ERA	G	GS	CG	IP	H	BB	SO	ShO	Relief Pitching W	Relief Pitching L	Relief Pitching SV	Batting AB	Batting H	Batting HR	BA	PO	A	E	DP	TC/G	FA
1961	MIL N	0	0	—	18.00	3	0	0	2	3	5	1	0	0	0	0	0	0	0	—	0	0	0	0	0.0	.000
1964		2	1	.667	3.75	38	0	0	60	55	21	45	0	2	1	5	4	1	0	.250	3	13	0	0	0.4	1.000
1965		0	1	.000	1.38	8	0	0	13	12	5	11	0	0	1	0	0	0	0	—	0	1	0	0	0.1	1.000
1966	ATL N	5	4	.556	4.23	47	0	0	66	59	19	41	0	5	4	7	9	1	0	.111	0	9	0	0	0.2	1.000
4 yrs.		7	6	.538	3.96	96	0	0	141	129	50	98	0	7	6	12	13	2	0	.154	3	23	0	0	0.3	1.000

Diomedes Olivo

OLIVO, DIOMEDES ANTONIO BL TL 6′ 1″ 195 lbs.
Born Diomedes Antonio Olivo (Maldonado).
Brother of Chi Chi Olivo.
B. Jan. 22, 1919, Guayubin, Dominican Republic
D. Feb. 15, 1977, Santo Domingo, Dominican Republic.

Year	Team	W	L	PCT	ERA	G	GS	CG	IP	H	BB	SO	ShO	Relief Pitching W	Relief Pitching L	Relief Pitching SV	Batting AB	Batting H	Batting HR	BA	PO	A	E	DP	TC/G	FA
1960	PIT N	0	0	—	2.79	4	0	0	9.2	8	5	10	0	0	0	0	1	0	0	.000	0	1	0	0	0.3	1.000
1962		5	1	.833	2.77	62	1	0	84.1	88	25	66	0	5	1	7	16	3	0	.188	6	10	1	0	0.3	.941
1963	STL N	0	5	.000	5.40	19	0	0	13.1	16	9	9	0	0	5	0	0	0	0	—	1	4	0	0	0.3	1.000
3 yrs.		5	6	.455	3.10	85	1	0	107.1	112	39	85	0	5	6	7	17	3	0	.176	7	15	1	0	0.3	.957

Jim Ollom

OLLOM, JAMES DONALD BR TL 6′ 4″ 210 lbs.
B. July 8, 1945, Snohomish, Wash.

Year	Team	W	L	PCT	ERA	G	GS	CG	IP	H	BB	SO	ShO	Relief Pitching W	Relief Pitching L	Relief Pitching SV	Batting AB	Batting H	Batting HR	BA	PO	A	E	DP	TC/G	FA
1966	MIN A	0	0	—	3.60	3	1	0	10	6	1	11	0	0	0	0	2	0	0	.000	0	1	0	0	0.3	1.000
1967		0	1	.000	5.40	21	2	0	35	33	11	17	0	0	0	0	5	1	0	.200	1	6	1	0	0.4	.875
2 yrs.		0	1	.000	5.00	24	3	0	45	39	12	28	0	0	0	0	7	1	0	.143	1	7	1	0	0.4	.889

Fred Olmstead

OLMSTEAD, FREDERIC WILLIAM BR TR 5′11″ 170 lbs.
B. July 3, 1881, Grand Rapids, Mich. D. Oct. 22, 1936, Muskogee, Okla.

Year	Team	W	L	PCT	ERA	G	GS	CG	IP	H	BB	SO	ShO	Relief Pitching W	Relief Pitching L	Relief Pitching SV	Batting AB	Batting H	Batting HR	BA	PO	A	E	DP	TC/G	FA
1908	CHI A	0	0	—	13.50	1	0	0	2	6	1	1	0	0	0	0	1	0	0	.000	0	0	0	0	0.0	.000
1909		3	2	.600	1.81	8	6	5	54.2	52	12	21	0	0	0	0	21	2	0	.095	1	17	0	0	2.3	1.000
1910		10	12	.455	1.95	32	20	14	184.1	174	50	68	4	2	1	0	65	10	0	.154	8	66	6	2	2.5	.925
1911		6	6	.500	4.21	25	11	7	117.2	146	30	45	1	3	0	2	37	7	0	.189	7	29	2	0	1.5	.947
4 yrs.		19	20	.487	2.74	66	37	26	358.2	378	93	135	5	5	1	2	124	19	0	.153	16	112	8	2	2.1	.941

Al Olmsted

OLMSTED, ALAN RAY BR TL 6′ 2″ 195 lbs.
B. Mar. 18, 1957, St. Louis, Mo.

Year	Team	W	L	PCT	ERA	G	GS	CG	IP	H	BB	SO	ShO	Relief Pitching W	Relief Pitching L	Relief Pitching SV	Batting AB	Batting H	Batting HR	BA	PO	A	E	DP	TC/G	FA
1980	STL N	1	1	.500	2.83	5	5	0	35	32	14	14	0	0	0	0	11	2	0	.182	2	9	0	0	2.2	1.000

Hank Olmsted

OLMSTED, HENRY THEODORE BR TR 5′ 8½″ 147 lbs.
B. Jan. 12, 1879, Sac Bay, Mich. D. Jan. 6, 1969, Bradenton, Fla.

Year	Team	W	L	PCT	ERA	G	GS	CG	IP	H	BB	SO	ShO	Relief Pitching W	Relief Pitching L	Relief Pitching SV	Batting AB	Batting H	Batting HR	BA	PO	A	E	DP	TC/G	FA
1905	BOS A	1	2	.333	3.24	3	3	3	25	18	12	6	0	0	0	0	8	1	0	.125	3	5	1	0	3.0	.889

Ole Olsen

OLSEN, ARTHUR BR TR 5′10″ 163 lbs.
B. Sept. 12, 1894, South Norwalk, Conn. D. Sept. 12, 1980, Norwalk, Conn.

Year	Team	W	L	PCT	ERA	G	GS	CG	IP	H	BB	SO	ShO	Relief Pitching W	Relief Pitching L	Relief Pitching SV	Batting AB	Batting H	Batting HR	BA	PO	A	E	DP	TC/G	FA
1922	DET A	7	6	.538	4.53	37	15	5	137	147	40	52	0	1	3	3	39	7	0	.179	8	36	1	2	1.2	.978
1923		1	1	.500	6.31	17	2	1	41.1	42	17	12	0	0	0	0	8	1	0	.125	1	6	2	0	0.5	.778
2 yrs.		8	7	.533	4.95	54	17	6	178.1	189	57	64	0	1	3	3	47	8	0	.170	9	42	3	2	1.0	.944

Vern Olsen

OLSEN, VERN JARL BR TL 6′½″ 175 lbs.
B. Mar. 16, 1918, Hillsboro, Ore. D. July 13, 1989, Maywood, Ill.

Year	Team	W	L	PCT	ERA	G	GS	CG	IP	H	BB	SO	ShO	Relief Pitching W	Relief Pitching L	Relief Pitching SV	Batting AB	Batting H	Batting HR	BA	PO	A	E	DP	TC/G	FA
1939	CHI N	1	0	1.000	0.00	4	0	0	7.2	2	7	3	0	1	0	0	1	0	0	.000	0	1	0	0	0.3	1.000
1940		13	9	.591	2.97	34	20	9	172.2	172	62	71	4	2	1	0	57	15	0	.263	9	53	0	1	1.8	1.000
1941		10	8	.556	3.15	37	23	10	185.2	202	59	73	2	0	0	1	63	15	1	.238	9	48	2	2	1.6	.966
1942		6	9	.400	4.49	32	17	4	140.1	161	55	46	1	0	2	1	48	9	0	.188	8	37	0	1	1.4	1.000
1946		0	0	—	2.79	5	0	0	9.2	10	9	8	0	0	0	0	0	0	0	—	0	2	0	0	0.4	1.000
5 yrs.		30	26	.536	3.40	112	60	23	516	547	192	201	7	3	3	2	169	39	1	.231	26	141	2	4	1.5	.988

Gregg Olson

OLSON, GREGGORY WILLIAM BR TR 6′4″ 210 lbs.
B. Oct. 11, 1966, Scribner, Neb.

Year	Team	W	L	PCT	ERA	G	GS	CG	IP	H	BB	SO	ShO	Relief Pitching W	Relief Pitching L	Relief Pitching SV	Batting AB	Batting H	Batting HR	BA	PO	A	E	DP	TC/G	FA
1988	BAL A	1	1	.500	3.27	10	0	0	11	10	10	9	0	1	1	0	0	0	0	—	1	2	0	0	0.3	1.000
1989		5	2	.714	1.69	64	0	0	85	57	46	90	0	5	2	27	0	0	0	—	5	12	1	0	0.3	.944
1990		6	5	.545	2.42	64	0	0	74.1	57	31	74	0	6	5	37	0	0	0	—	4	4	0	1	0.1	1.000
1991		4	6	.400	3.18	72	0	0	73.2	74	29	72	0	4	6	31	0	0	0	—	6	11	3	0	0.3	.850
1992		1	5	.167	2.05	60	0	0	61.1	46	24	58	0	1	5	36	0	0	0	—	5	9	0	2	0.2	1.000
1993		0	2	.000	1.60	50	0	0	45	37	18	44	0	0	2	29	1	0	0	.000	2	7	0	0	0.2	1.000
1994	ATL N	0	2	.000	9.20	16	0	0	14.2	19	13	10	0	0	2	1	1	0	0	.000	0	0	0	0	0.0	.000
1995	2 teams CLE A (3G 0–0) KC A (20G 3–3)																									
″	total	3	3	.500	4.09	23	0	0	33	28	19	21	0	3	3	3	0	0	0	—	1	5	0	1	0.3	1.000
8 yrs.		20	26	.435	2.67	359	0	0	398	328	190	378	0	20	26	164	2	0	0	.000	24	50	4	4	0.2	.949

Ted Olson

OLSON, THEODORE OTTO BR TR 6′2½″ 185 lbs.
B. Aug. 27, 1912, Quincy, Mass. D. Dec. 9, 1980, Weymouth, Mass.

Year	Team	W	L	PCT	ERA	G	GS	CG	IP	H	BB	SO	ShO	Relief Pitching W	Relief Pitching L	Relief Pitching SV	Batting AB	Batting H	Batting HR	BA	PO	A	E	DP	TC/G	FA
1936	BOS A	1	1	.500	7.36	5	3	1	18.1	24	8	5	0	0	0	0	7	1	0	.143	1	4	0	0	1.0	1.000
1937		0	0	—	7.24	11	0	0	32.1	42	15	11	0	0	0	0	10	3	0	.300	3	11	2	0	1.5	.875
1938		0	0	—	6.43	2	0	0	7	9	2	2	0	0	0	0	1	0	0	.000	0	1	0	0	0.5	1.000
3 yrs.		1	1	.500	7.18	18	3	1	57.2	75	25	18	0	0	0	0	18	4	0	.222	4	16	2	0	1.2	.909

Ed Olwine

OLWINE, EDWARD R. BR TL 6′2″ 165 lbs.
B. May 28, 1958, Greenville, Ohio.

Year	Team	W	L	PCT	ERA	G	GS	CG	IP	H	BB	SO	ShO	Relief Pitching W	Relief Pitching L	Relief Pitching SV	Batting AB	Batting H	Batting HR	BA	PO	A	E	DP	TC/G	FA
1986	ATL N	0	0	—	3.40	37	0	0	47.2	35	17	37	0	0	0	1	3	1	0	.333	3	5	0	0	0.2	1.000
1987		0	1	.000	5.01	27	0	0	23.1	25	8	12	0	0	1	1	0	0	0	—	0	3	1	0	0.1	.750
1988		0	0	—	6.75	16	0	0	18.2	22	4	5	0	0	0	1	0	0	0	—	1	1	0	0	0.1	1.000
3 yrs.		0	1	.000	4.52	80	0	0	89.2	82	29	54	0	0	1	3	3	1	0	.333	4	9	1	0	0.2	.929

Randy O'Neal

O'NEAL, RANDALL JEFFREY BR TR 6′2″ 195 lbs.
B. Aug. 30, 1960, Ashland, Ky.

Year	Team	W	L	PCT	ERA	G	GS	CG	IP	H	BB	SO	ShO	Relief Pitching W	Relief Pitching L	Relief Pitching SV	Batting AB	Batting H	Batting HR	BA	PO	A	E	DP	TC/G	FA
1984	DET A	2	1	.667	3.38	4	3	0	18.2	16	6	12	0	0	0	0	0	0	0	—	2	1	1	0	1.0	.750
1985		5	5	.500	3.24	28	12	1	94.1	82	36	52	0	0	0	1	0	0	0	—	9	17	2	1	1.0	.929
1986		3	7	.300	4.33	37	11	1	122.2	121	44	68	0	0	3	2	0	0	0	—	15	19	2	0	1.0	.944
1987	2 teams ATL N (16G 4–2) STL N (1G 0–0)																									
″	total	4	2	.667	5.32	17	11	0	66	81	26	37	0	0	0	0	20	3	0	.150	4	17	0	1	1.2	1.000
1988	STL N	2	3	.400	4.58	10	8	0	53	57	10	20	0	0	1	0	19	0	0	.000	3	14	0	1	1.7	1.000
1989	PHI N	0	1	.000	6.23	20	1	0	39	46	9	29	0	0	1	0	5	0	0	.000	2	9	1	0	0.6	.917
1990	SF N	1	0	1.000	3.83	26	0	0	47	58	18	30	0	1	0	0	6	1	0	.167	1	8	0	1	0.3	1.000
7 yrs.		17	19	.472	4.35	142	46	2	440.2	461	149	248	0	1	5	3	50	4	0	.080	36	85	6	4	0.9	.953

Skinny O'Neal

O'NEAL, ORAN HERBERT BR TR 5′11″ 160 lbs.
B. May 2, 1899, Gatewood, Mo. D. June 2, 1981, Springfield, Mo.

Year	Team	W	L	PCT	ERA	G	GS	CG	IP	H	BB	SO	ShO	Relief Pitching W	Relief Pitching L	Relief Pitching SV	Batting AB	Batting H	Batting HR	BA	PO	A	E	DP	TC/G	FA
1925	PHI N	0	0	—	9.30	11	1	0	20.1	35	12	6	0	0	0	0	6	1	0	.167	1	3	0	0	0.4	1.000
1927		0	0	—	9.00	2	0	0	5	9	2	2	0	0	0	0	1	0	0	.000	0	4	0	0	2.0	1.000
2 yrs.		0	0		9.24	13	1	0	25.1	44	14	8	0	0	0	0	7	1	0	.143	1	7	0	0	0.6	1.000

Ed O'Neill

O'NEILL, EDWARD J. TR 5′11″ 180 lbs.
B. Mar. 11, 1859, Fall River, Mass. D. Sept. 30, 1892, Fall River, Mass.

Year	Team	W	L	PCT	ERA	G	GS	CG	IP	H	BB	SO	ShO	Relief Pitching W	Relief Pitching L	Relief Pitching SV	Batting AB	Batting H	Batting HR	BA	PO	A	E	DP	TC/G	FA
1890	2 teams TOL AA (2G 0–1) PHI AA (6G 0–6)																									
″	total	0	7	.000	9.26	8	8	8	68	111	45	19	0	0	0	0	40	5	0	.125	9	19	5	0	2.8	.848

Emmett O'Neill

O'NEILL, ROBERT EMMETT (Pinky) BR TR 6′3″ 185 lbs.
B. Jan. 13, 1918, San Mateo, Calif. D. Oct. 11, 1993, Sparks, Nev.

Year	Team	W	L	PCT	ERA	G	GS	CG	IP	H	BB	SO	ShO	Relief Pitching W	Relief Pitching L	Relief Pitching SV	Batting AB	Batting H	Batting HR	BA	PO	A	E	DP	TC/G	FA
1943	BOS A	1	4	.200	4.53	11	5	1	57.2	56	46	20	0	1	0	0	16	3	0	.188	3	13	0	0	1.5	1.000
1944		6	11	.353	4.63	28	22	8	151.2	154	89	68	1	0	0	0	55	10	0	.182	3	19	1	0	0.8	.957
1945		8	11	.421	5.15	24	22	10	141.2	134	117	55	1	0	0	0	50	9	1	.180	5	31	3	3	1.6	.923
1946	2 teams CHI N (1G 0–0) CHI A (2G 0–0)																									
″	total	0	0		0.00	3	0	0	4.2	4	8	1	0	0	0	0	1	0	0	.000	0	1	1	1	0.7	.500
4 yrs.		15	26	.366	4.76	66	49	19	355.2	348	260	144	2	1	0	0	122	22	1	.180	11	64	5	4	1.2	.938

Harry O'Neill

O'NEILL, JOSEPH HENRY BR TR 6′ 180 lbs.
B. Feb. 20, 1897, Ridgetown, Ont., Canada
D. Sept. 5, 1969, Ridgetown, Ont., Canada.

Year	Team	W	L	PCT	ERA	G	GS	CG	IP	H	BB	SO	ShO	Relief Pitching W	Relief Pitching L	Relief Pitching SV	Batting AB	Batting H	Batting HR	BA	PO	A	E	DP	TC/G	FA
1922	PHI A	0	0	—	3.00	1	0	0	3	2	1	0	0	0	0	0	1	0	0	.000	0	2	0	0	2.0	1.000
1923		0	0	—	0.00	3	0	0	2	1	3	2	0	0	0	0	0	0	0	—	0	0	0	0	0.0	.000
2 yrs.		0	0		1.80	4	0	0	5	3	4	2	0	0	0	0	1	0	0	.000	0	2	0	0	0.5	1.000

Year	Team	Lg	W	L	PCT	ERA	G	GS	CG	IP	H	BB	SO	ShO	Relief Pitching W	Relief Pitching L	Relief Pitching SV	Batting AB	Batting H	Batting HR	BA	PO	A	E	DP	TC/G	FA

Mike O'Neill

O'NEILL, MICHAEL JOYCE BR TR 5′11″ 185 lbs.
Played as Mike Joyce in 1901.
Brother of Steve O'Neill. Brother of Jack O'Neill. Brother of Jim O'Neill.
B. Sept. 7, 1877, Galway, Ireland D. Aug. 12, 1959, Scranton, Pa.

Year	Team	Lg	W	L	PCT	ERA	G	GS	CG	IP	H	BB	SO	ShO	W	L	SV	AB	H	HR	BA	PO	A	E	DP	TC/G	FA
1901	STL	N	2	2	.500	1.32	5	4	4	41	29	10	16	1	0	0	0	15	6	0	.400	1	6	1	0	1.6	.875
1902			18	14	.563	2.93	36	32	29	288.1	297	66	105	2	**2**	0	0	135	43	2	.319	24	73	8	0	2.7	.924
1903			4	13	.235	4.77	19	17	12	115	184	43	39	0	0	0	0	110	25	0	.227	28	41	6	3	2.3	.920
1904			10	14	.417	2.09	25	24	23	220	229	50	68	1	0	0	0	91	21	0	.231	16	69	8	3	3.3	.914
4 yrs.			34	43	.442	2.87	85	77	68	664.1	739	169	228	4	2	0	0	*				87	190	26	6	2.7	.914

Paul O'Neill

O'NEILL, PAUL ANDREW BL TL 6′ 4″ 200 lbs.
B. Feb. 25, 1963, Columbus, Ohio.

Year	Team	Lg	W	L	PCT	ERA	G	GS	CG	IP	H	BB	SO	ShO	W	L	SV	AB	H	HR	BA	PO	A	E	DP	TC/G	FA
1987	CIN	N	0	0	—	13.50	1	0	0	2	2	4	2	0	0	0	0	*				3	1	0	0	2.0	1.000

Tip O'Neill

O'NEILL, JAMES EDWARD BR TR 6′ 1½″ 167 lbs.
B. May 25, 1858, Woodstock, Ont., Canada
D. Dec. 31, 1915, Montreal, Que., Canada.

Year	Team	Lg	W	L	PCT	ERA	G	GS	CG	IP	H	BB	SO	ShO	W	L	SV	AB	H	HR	BA	PO	A	E	DP	TC/G	FA
1883	NY	N	5	12	.294	*4.07*	19	19	15	148	182	64	55	0	0	0	0	76	15	0	.197	17	24	5	0	1.8	.891
1884	STL	AA	11	4	.733	*2.68*	17	14	14	141	125	51	36	0	1	0	0	297	82	3	.276	75	37	22	1	1.6	.836
2 yrs.			16	16	.500	3.39	36	33	29	289	307	115	91	0	1	0	0	*				1810	135	177	16	2.0	.917

Steve Ontiveros

ONTIVEROS, STEVEN BR TR 6′ 180 lbs.
B. Mar. 5, 1961, Tularosa, N. M.

Year	Team	Lg	W	L	PCT	ERA	G	GS	CG	IP	H	BB	SO	ShO	W	L	SV	AB	H	HR	BA	PO	A	E	DP	TC/G	FA
1985	OAK	A	1	3	.250	1.93	39	0	0	74.2	45	19	36	0	1	3	8	0	0	0	—	7	14	1	1	0.6	.955
1986			2	2	.500	4.71	46	0	0	72.2	72	25	54	0	2	2	10	0	0	0	—	2	10	0	1	0.3	1.000
1987			10	8	.556	4.00	35	22	2	150.2	141	50	97	1	1	2	1	0	0	0	—	14	29	1	0	1.3	.977
1988			3	4	.429	4.61	10	10	0	54.2	57	21	30	0	0	0	0	0	0	0	—	6	12	0	0	1.8	1.000
1989	PHI	N	2	1	.667	3.82	6	5	0	30.2	34	15	12	0	0	0	0	12	1	0	.083	4	9	0	2	2.2	1.000
1990			0	0	—	2.70	5	0	0	10	9	3	6	0	0	0	0	0	0	0	—	2	3	0	0	1.0	1.000
1993	SEA	A	0	2	.000	1.00	14	0	0	18	18	6	13	0	0	2	0	0	0	0	—	0	2	1	2	0.2	.667
1994	OAK	A	6	4	.600	**2.65**	27	13	2	115.1	93	26	56	0	1	2	0	0	0	0	—	15	22	0	2	1.4	1.000
1995			9	6	.600	4.37	22	22	2	129.2	144	38	77	1	0	0	0	0	0	0	—	17	26	0	4	2.0	1.000
9 yrs.			33	30	.524	3.62	204	72	6	656.1	613	203	381	2	5	11	19	12	1	0	.083	67	127	3	12	1.0	.985

Jose Oquendo

OQUENDO, JOSE MANUEL BB TR 5′10″ 160 lbs.
Born Jose Manuel Oquendo (Contreras). BR 1984
B. July 4, 1963, Rio Piedras, Puerto Rico.

Year	Team	Lg	W	L	PCT	ERA	G	GS	CG	IP	H	BB	SO	ShO	W	L	SV	AB	H	HR	BA	PO	A	E	DP	TC/G	FA
1987	STL	N	0	0	—	27.00	1	0	0	1	4	1	0	0	0	0	0	248	71	1	.286	182	326	21	65	4.6	.960
1988			0	1	.000	4.50	1	0	0	4	4	6	1	0	0	1	0	451	125	7	.277	268	315	11	61	3.6	.981
1991			0	0	—	27.00	1	0	0	1	2	2	1	0	0	0	0	366	88	1	.240	356	523	6	108	5.4	.993
3 yrs.			0	1	.000	12.00	3	0	0	6	10	9	2	0	0	1	0	*				1924	2734	82	543	4.1	.983

Mike Oquist

OQUIST, MICHAEL LEE BR TR 6′ 2″ 170 lbs.
B. May 30, 1968, La Junta, Colo.

Year	Team	Lg	W	L	PCT	ERA	G	GS	CG	IP	H	BB	SO	ShO	W	L	SV	AB	H	HR	BA	PO	A	E	DP	TC/G	FA
1993	BAL	A	0	0	—	3.86	5	0	0	11.2	12	4	8	0	0	0	0	0	0	0	—	1	0	0	0	0.2	1.000
1994			3	3	.500	6.17	15	9	0	58.1	75	30	39	0	2	0	0	0	0	0	—	6	7	0	0	0.9	1.000
1995			2	1	.667	4.17	27	0	0	54	51	41	27	0	2	1	0	0	0	0	—	1	8	0	0	0.3	1.000
3 yrs.			5	4	.556	5.08	47	9	0	124	138	75	74	0	4	1	0	0	0	0		8	15	0	0	0.5	1.000

Don O'Riley

O'RILEY, DONALD LEE BR TR 6′ 3″ 205 lbs.
B. Mar. 12, 1945, Topeka, Kans.

Year	Team	Lg	W	L	PCT	ERA	G	GS	CG	IP	H	BB	SO	ShO	W	L	SV	AB	H	HR	BA	PO	A	E	DP	TC/G	FA
1969	KC	A	1	1	.500	6.94	18	0	0	23.1	32	15	10	0	1	1	1	3	0	0	.000	3	1	0	0	0.2	1.000
1970			0	0	—	5.48	9	2	0	23	26	9	13	0	0	0	0	3	0	0	.000	2	1	0	0	0.3	1.000
2 yrs.			1	1	.500	6.22	27	2	0	46.1	58	24	23	0	1	1	1	6	0	0	.000	5	2	0	0	0.3	1.000

Jesse Orosco

OROSCO, JESSE RUSSELL BR TL 6′ 2″ 174 lbs.
B. Apr. 21, 1957, Santa Barbara, Calif.

Year	Team	Lg	W	L	PCT	ERA	G	GS	CG	IP	H	BB	SO	ShO	W	L	SV	AB	H	HR	BA	PO	A	E	DP	TC/G	FA
1979	NY	N	1	2	.333	4.89	18	2	0	35	33	22	22	0	1	2	0	6	0	0	.000	2	9	0	1	0.6	1.000
1981			0	1	.000	1.59	8	0	0	17	13	6	18	0	0	1	1	2	0	0	.000	1	2	0	0	0.4	1.000
1982			4	10	.286	2.72	54	2	0	109.1	92	40	89	0	4	8	4	14	2	0	.143	4	16	0	1	0.4	1.000
1983			13	7	.650	1.47	62	0	0	110	76	38	84	0	**13**	7	17	12	4	0	.333	5	19	0	0	0.4	1.000
1984			10	6	.625	2.59	60	0	0	87	58	34	85	0	10	6	31	4	1	0	.250	2	11	1	1	0.2	.929
1985			8	6	.571	2.73	54	0	0	79	66	34	68	0	8	6	17	7	3	0	.429	3	8	1	2	0.2	.917
1986			8	6	.571	2.33	58	0	0	81	64	35	62	0	8	6	21	3	0	0	.000	5	8	0	0	0.2	1.000
1987			3	9	.250	4.44	58	0	0	77	78	31	78	0	3	9	16	8	0	0	.000	4	9	0	1	0.2	1.000
1988	LA	N	3	2	.600	2.72	55	0	0	53	41	30	43	0	3	2	9	2	0	0	.000	1	10	0	1	0.2	1.000
1989	CLE	A	3	4	.429	2.08	69	0	0	78	54	26	79	0	3	4	3	0	0	0	—	6	13	0	1	0.3	1.000
1990			5	4	.556	3.90	55	0	0	64.2	58	38	55	0	5	4	2	0	0	0	—	1	14	1	1	0.3	.938
1991			2	0	1.000	3.74	47	0	0	45.2	52	15	36	0	2	0	0	0	0	0	—	3	3	0	0	0.1	1.000
1992	MIL	A	3	1	.750	3.23	59	0	0	39	33	13	40	0	3	1	1	0	0	0	—	2	3	0	0	0.1	1.000
1993			3	5	.375	3.18	57	0	0	56.2	47	17	67	0	3	5	8	1	0	0	.000	1	19	0	0	0.4	1.000
1994			3	1	.750	5.08	40	0	0	39	32	26	36	0	3	1	0	0	0	0	—	3	3	0	1	0.2	1.000
1995	BAL	A	2	4	.333	3.26	65	0	0	49.2	28	27	58	0	2	4	3	0	0	0	—	3	8	0	0	0.2	1.000
16 yrs.			71	68	.511	2.96	819	4	0	1021	825	432	920	0	71	66	133	59	10	0	.169	46	155	3	10	0.2	.985
LEAGUE CHAMPIONSHIP SERIES																											
1986	NY	N	3	0	1.000	3.38	4	0	0	8	5	2	10	0	3	0	0	0	0	0	—	1	1	0	0	0.5	1.000
1988	LA	N	0	0	—	7.71	4	0	0	2.1	4	3	0	0	0	0	0	0	0	0	—	1	0	0	0	0.3	1.000
2 yrs.			3	0	1.000	4.35	8	0	0	10.1	9	5	10	0	3	0	0	0	0	0		2	1	0	0	0.4	1.000
WORLD SERIES																											
1986	NY	N	0	0	—	0.00	4	0	0	5.2	2	0	6	0	0	0	2	1	1	0	1.000	0	0	0	0	0.0	.000

Jim O'Rourke

O'ROURKE, JAMES HENRY (Orator Jim)
Brother of John O'Rourke. Father of Queenie O'Rourke.
B. Sept. 1, 1850, Bridgeport, Conn. D. Jan. 8, 1919, Bridgeport, Conn.
Manager 1881–84, 1893.
Hall of Fame 1945.

BR TR 5′ 8″ 185 lbs.

Year	Team	W	L	PCT	ERA	G	GS	CG	IP	H	BB	SO	ShO	Relief W	Relief L	Relief SV	AB	H	HR	BA	PO	A	E	DP	TC/G	FA
1883	BUF N	0	0	—	*6.43*	2	0	0	7	10	1	1	0	0	0	1	436	143	1	.328	170	7	28	1	2.9	.863
1884		0	1	.000	*2.84*	4	0	0	12.2	7	1	3	0	0	**1**	1	467	162	5	.347	350	23	30	12	3.4	.926
2 yrs.		0	1	.000	4.12	6	0	0	19.2	17	2	4	0	0	1	2	*				4149	790	505	102	3.0	.907

Mike O'Rourke

O'ROURKE, MICHAEL J.
Deceased.

Year	Team	W	L	PCT	ERA	G	GS	CG	IP	H	BB	SO	ShO	Relief W	Relief L	Relief SV	AB	H	HR	BA	PO	A	E	DP	TC/G	FA
1890	BAL AA	1	2	.333	3.95	5	5	5	41	45	10	8	0	0	0	0	26	3	0	.115	3	12	0	0	1.9	1.000

Dave Orr

ORR, DAVID L.
B. Sept. 29, 1859, New York, N. Y. D. June 3, 1915, Brooklyn, N. Y.
Manager 1887.

BL TR 5′11″ 250 lbs.

Year	Team	W	L	PCT	ERA	G	GS	CG	IP	H	BB	SO	ShO	Relief W	Relief L	Relief SV	AB	H	HR	BA	PO	A	E	DP	TC/G	FA
1885	NY AA	0	0	—	*7.20*	3	0	0	10	11	5	1	0	0	0	0	*				148	1	9	4	11.3	.943

Joe Orrell

ORRELL, FORREST GORDON
B. Oct. 6, 1917, National City, Calif. D. Jan. 12, 1993, Chula Vista, Calif.

BR TR 6′ 4″ 210 lbs.

Year	Team	W	L	PCT	ERA	G	GS	CG	IP	H	BB	SO	ShO	Relief W	Relief L	Relief SV	AB	H	HR	BA	PO	A	E	DP	TC/G	FA
1943	DET A	0	0	—	3.72	10	0	0	19.1	18	11	2	0	0	0	1	4	1	0	.250	2	3	0	0	0.5	1.000
1944		2	1	.667	2.42	10	2	0	22.1	26	11	10	0	1	0	0	4	1	0	.250	1	8	0	0	0.9	1.000
1945		2	3	.400	3.00	12	5	1	48	46	24	14	0	0	1	0	15	2	0	.133	4	8	1	0	1.1	.923
3 yrs.		4	4	.500	3.01	32	7	1	89.2	90	46	26	0	1	1	1	23	4	0	.174	7	19	1	0	0.8	.963

Phil Ortega

ORTEGA, FILOMENO CORONADO (Kemo)
B. Oct. 7, 1939, Gilbert, Ariz.

BR TR 6′ 2″ 170 lbs.

Year	Team	W	L	PCT	ERA	G	GS	CG	IP	H	BB	SO	ShO	Relief W	Relief L	Relief SV	AB	H	HR	BA	PO	A	E	DP	TC/G	FA
1960	LA N	0	0	—	17.05	3	1	0	6.1	12	5	4	0	0	0	0	1	0	0	.000	0	1	0	0	0.3	1.000
1961		0	2	.000	5.54	4	2	1	13	10	2	15	0	0	0	0	4	1	0	.250	0	1	0	1	0.3	1.000
1962		0	2	.000	6.88	24	3	0	53.2	60	39	30	0	0	0	1	7	0	0	.000	2	7	1	0	0.4	.900
1963		0	0	—	18.00	1	0	0	1	2	0	1	0	0	0	0	0	0	0	—	0	0	0	0	0.0	.000
1964		7	9	.438	4.00	34	25	4	157.1	149	56	107	3	1	0	1	44	6	0	.136	6	18	2	1	0.8	.923
1965	WAS A	12	15	.444	5.11	35	29	4	179.2	176	97	88	2	2	0	0	53	11	0	.208	11	26	1	1	1.1	.974
1966		12	12	.500	3.92	33	31	5	197.1	158	53	121	1	1	0	0	54	3	0	.056	11	28	3	1	1.3	.929
1967		10	10	.500	3.03	34	34	5	219.2	189	57	122	2	0	0	0	66	4	0	.061	13	33	1	2	1.4	.979
1968		5	12	.294	4.98	31	16	1	115.2	115	62	57	1	1	3	0	24	4	0	.167	4	20	4	3	0.9	.857
1969	CAL A	0	0	—	10.13	5	0	0	8	13	7	4	0	0	0	0	0	0	0	—	1	1	0	0	0.4	1.000
10 yrs.		46	62	.426	4.43	204	141	20	951.2	884	378	549	9	5	3	2	253	29	0	.115	48	135	12	9	1.0	.938

Al Orth

ORTH, ALBERT LEWIS (The Curveless Wonder)
B. Sept. 5, 1872, Tipton, Ind. D. Oct. 8, 1948, Lynchburg, Va.

BL TR 6′ 200 lbs.

Year	Team	W	L	PCT	ERA	G	GS	CG	IP	H	BB	SO	ShO	Relief W	Relief L	Relief SV	AB	H	HR	BA	PO	A	E	DP	TC/G	FA
1895	PHI N	8	1	.889	3.89	11	10	9	88	103	22	25	0	0	0	1	45	16	1	.356	2	14	3	0	1.7	.842
1896		15	10	.600	4.41	25	23	19	196	244	46	23	0	2	0	0	82	21	1	.256	10	54	7	2	2.8	.901
1897		14	19	.424	4.62	36	34	29	282.1	349	82	64	2	0	1	0	152	50	1	.329	20	70	7	1	2.3	.928
1898		15	13	.536	3.02	32	28	25	250	290	53	52	1	0	1	0	123	36	1	.293	9	63	3	1	2.3	.960
1899		14	3	.824	**2.49**	21	15	13	144.2	149	19	35	3	**3**	0	1	62	13	1	.210	5	19	6	0	1.4	.800
1900		12	13	.480	3.78	33	30	24	262	302	60	68	2	1	1	1	129	40	1	.310	23	68	5	3	2.7	.948
1901		20	12	.625	2.27	35	33	30	281.2	250	32	92	**6**	1	1	0	128	36	1	.281	25	83	6	2	2.9	.947
1902	WAS A	19	18	.514	3.97	38	37	36	324	367	40	76	1	0	0	0	175	38	2	.217	46	97	12	3	2.9	.923
1903		10	22	.313	4.34	36	32	30	279.2	326	62	88	2	0	0	**2**	162	49	0	.302	55	98	15	3	3.4	.911
1904	2 teams WAS A (10G 3–4) NY A (20G 11–6)																									
"	total	14	10	.583	3.41	30	25	18	211.1	210	34	70	2	0	1	0	166	41	0	.247	53	74	10	1	2.7	.927
1905	NY A	18	16	.529	2.86	40	37	26	305.1	273	61	121	6	1	1	0	131	24	1	.183	31	98	10	1	3.3	.928
1906		**27**	17	.614	2.34	45	39	**36**	**338.2**	**317**	66	133	3	**5**	0	0	135	37	1	.274	13	103	8	1	2.7	.935
1907		14	**21**	.400	2.61	36	33	21	248.2	244	53	78	2	1	2	0	105	34	1	.324	9	95	9	1	3.1	.920
1908		2	13	.133	3.42	21	17	8	139.1	134	30	22	1	0	1	0	69	20	0	.290	6	42	1	2	2.3	.980
1909		0	0	—	12.00	1	1	0	3	6	1	1	0	0	0	0	34	9	0	.265	10	16	0	0	3.7	1.000
15 yrs.		202	188	.518	3.37	440	394	324	3354.2	3564	661	948	31	14	9	5	*				317	994	102	21	2.8	.928

Baby Ortiz

ORTIZ, OLIVERIO
Born Oliverio Ortiz (Nunez).
Brother of Roberto Ortiz.
B. Dec. 5, 1919, Camaguey, Cuba D. Mar. 27, 1984, Central Senado, Cuba.

BR TR 6′ 190 lbs.

Year	Team	W	L	PCT	ERA	G	GS	CG	IP	H	BB	SO	ShO	Relief W	Relief L	Relief SV	AB	H	HR	BA	PO	A	E	DP	TC/G	FA
1944	WAS A	0	2	.000	6.23	2	2	1	13	13	6	4	0	0	0	0	6	1	0	.167	0	0	0	0	0.0	.000

Ossie Orwoll

ORWOLL, OSWALD CHRISTIAN
B. Nov. 17, 1900, Portland, Ore. D. May 8, 1967, Decorah, Iowa.

BL TL 6′ 174 lbs.

Year	Team	W	L	PCT	ERA	G	GS	CG	IP	H	BB	SO	ShO	Relief W	Relief L	Relief SV	AB	H	HR	BA	PO	A	E	DP	TC/G	FA
1928	PHI A	6	5	.545	4.58	27	8	3	106	110	50	53	0	3	0	2	170	52	0	.306	328	41	7	32	6.2	.981
1929		0	2	.000	4.80	12	0	0	30	32	6	12	0	0	2	1	51	13	0	.255	18	6	0	1	1.1	1.000
2 yrs.		6	7	.462	4.63	39	8	3	136	142	56	65	0	3	2	3	*				346	47	7	33	4.9	.983

Bob Osborn

OSBORN, JOHN BODE
B. Apr. 17, 1903, San Diego, Tex. D. Apr. 19, 1960, Paris, Tex.

BR TR 6′ 1″ 175 lbs.

Year	Team	W	L	PCT	ERA	G	GS	CG	IP	H	BB	SO	ShO	Relief W	Relief L	Relief SV	AB	H	HR	BA	PO	A	E	DP	TC/G	FA
1925	CHI N	0	0	—	0.00	1	0	0	2	6	0	0	0	0	0	0	0	0	0	—	0	1	0	0	1.0	1.000
1926		6	5	.545	3.63	31	15	6	136.1	157	58	43	0	2	0	1	41	6	0	.146	9	39	1	4	1.6	.980
1927		5	5	.500	4.18	24	12	2	107.2	125	48	45	0	1	1	0	39	8	0	.205	8	19	3	1	1.3	.900
1929		0	0	—	3.00	3	1	0	9	8	2	1	0	0	0	0	4	1	0	.250	0	1	0	0	0.3	1.000
1930		10	6	.625	4.97	35	13	3	126.2	147	53	42	0	5	3	1	42	4	0	.095	10	34	1	2	1.3	.978
1931	PIT N	6	1	.857	5.01	27	2	0	64.2	85	20	9	0	**6**	1	0	18	3	0	.167	2	12	1	0	0.6	.933
6 yrs.		27	17	.614	4.32	121	43	11	446.1	528	181	140	0	14	5	2	144	22	0	.153	29	106	6	7	1.2	.957

Danny Osborn

OSBORN, DANNY LEON
B. June 19, 1946, Springfield, Mo.

BR TR 6′ 2″ 195 lbs.

Year	Team	W	L	PCT	ERA	G	GS	CG	IP	H	BB	SO	ShO	Relief W	Relief L	Relief SV	AB	H	HR	BA	PO	A	E	DP	TC/G	FA
1975	CHI A	3	0	1.000	4.50	24	0	0	58	57	37	38	0	3	0	0	0	0	0	—	3	5	1	0	0.4	.889

Donovan Osborne

OSBORNE, DONOVAN ALAN — BB TL 6′ 2″ 195 lbs.
B. June 21, 1969, Roseville, Calif.

Year	Team	Lg	W	L	PCT	ERA	G	GS	CG	IP	H	BB	SO	ShO	Relief Pitching W	Relief Pitching L	Relief Pitching SV	Batting AB	Batting H	Batting HR	BA	PO	A	E	DP	TC/G	FA
1992	STL	N	11	9	.550	3.77	34	29	0	179	193	38	104	0	1	1	0	58	7	0	.121	6	18	2	2	0.8	.923
1993			10	7	.588	3.76	26	26	1	155.2	153	47	83	0	0	0	0	49	10	0	.204	8	24	0	1	1.2	1.000
1995			4	6	.400	3.81	19	19	0	113.1	112	34	82	0	0	0	0	31	5	0	.161	3	16	0	0	1.0	1.000
3 yrs.			25	22	.532	3.78	79	74	1	448	458	119	269	0	1	1	0	138	22	0	.159	17	58	2	3	1.0	.974

Fred Osborne

OSBORNE, FREDERICK W. — TL
B. May 1865 Deceased.

Year	Team	Lg	W	L	PCT	ERA	G	GS	CG	IP	H	BB	SO	ShO	Relief Pitching W	Relief Pitching L	Relief Pitching SV	Batting AB	Batting H	Batting HR	BA	PO	A	E	DP	TC/G	FA
1890	PIT	N	0	5	.000	*8.38*	8	5	5	58	82	45	14	0	0	0	0	*				67	19	18	0	2.4	.827

Tiny Osborne

OSBORNE, EARNEST PRESTON — BL TR 6′ 4½″ 215 lbs.
Father of Bobo Osborne.
B. Apr. 9, 1893, Porterdale, Ga. D. Jan. 5, 1969, Atlanta, Ga.

Year	Team	Lg	W	L	PCT	ERA	G	GS	CG	IP	H	BB	SO	ShO	Relief Pitching W	Relief Pitching L	Relief Pitching SV	Batting AB	Batting H	Batting HR	BA	PO	A	E	DP	TC/G	FA
1922	CHI	N	9	5	.643	4.50	41	14	7	184	183	95	81	1	2	1	3	67	9	0	.134	3	26	0	1	0.7	1.000
1923			8	15	.348	4.56	37	25	8	179.2	174	89	69	1	1	3	1	60	12	0	.200	3	39	2	0	1.2	.955
1924	2 teams	CHI N (2G 0–0)	BKN N (21G 6–5)																								
″	total		6	5	.545	5.03	23	13	6	107.1	126	56	54	0	1	0	1	36	9	0	.250	2	21	3	0	1.1	.885
1925	BKN	N	8	15	.348	4.94	41	22	10	175	210	75	59	0	2	4	1	57	14	0	.246	3	34	1	1	0.9	.974
4 yrs.			31	40	.437	4.72	142	74	31	646	693	315	263	2	6	8	6	220	44	0	.200	11	120	6	2	1.0	.956

Wayne Osborne

OSBORNE, WAYNE HAROLD (Ossie) — BL TR 6′ 2½″ 172 lbs.
B. Oct. 11, 1912, Watsonville, Calif. D. Mar. 13, 1987, Vancouver, Wash.

Year	Team	Lg	W	L	PCT	ERA	G	GS	CG	IP	H	BB	SO	ShO	Relief Pitching W	Relief Pitching L	Relief Pitching SV	Batting AB	Batting H	Batting HR	BA	PO	A	E	DP	TC/G	FA
1935	PIT	N	0	0	—	6.75	2	0	0	1.1	1	0	1	0	0	0	0	0	0	0	—	0	1	0	0	0.5	1.000
1936	BOS	N	1	1	.500	5.85	5	3	0	20	31	9	8	0	0	0	0	8	2	0	.250	1	4	0	1	1.0	1.000
2 yrs.			1	1	.500	5.91	7	3	0	21.1	32	9	9	0	0	0	0	8	2	0	.250	1	5	0	1	0.9	1.000

Pat Osburn

OSBURN, LARRY PATRICK — BL TL 6′ 4″ 195 lbs.
B. May 4, 1949, Murray, Ky.

Year	Team	Lg	W	L	PCT	ERA	G	GS	CG	IP	H	BB	SO	ShO	Relief Pitching W	Relief Pitching L	Relief Pitching SV	Batting AB	Batting H	Batting HR	BA	PO	A	E	DP	TC/G	FA
1974	CIN	N	0	0	—	8.00	6	0	0	9	11	4	4	0	0	0	0	2	0	0	.000	1	3	0	0	0.7	1.000
1975	MIL	A	0	1	.000	6.17	6	1	0	11.2	19	9	1	0	0	0	0	0	0	0	—	2	3	0	0	0.8	1.000
2 yrs.			0	1	.000	6.97	12	1	0	20.2	30	13	5	0	0	0	0	2	0	0	.000	3	6	0	0	0.8	1.000

Charlie Osgood

OSGOOD, CHARLES BENJAMIN — BR TR 5′10″ 180 lbs.
B. Nov. 23, 1926, Somerville, Mass.

Year	Team	Lg	W	L	PCT	ERA	G	GS	CG	IP	H	BB	SO	ShO	Relief Pitching W	Relief Pitching L	Relief Pitching SV	Batting AB	Batting H	Batting HR	BA	PO	A	E	DP	TC/G	FA
1944	BKN	N	0	0	—	3.00	1	0	0	3	2	3	0	0	0	0	0	0	0	0	—	0	0	0	0	0.0	.000

Dan Osinski

OSINSKI, DANIEL — BR TR 6′ 1½″ 190 lbs.
B. Nov. 17, 1933, Chicago, Ill.

Year	Team	Lg	W	L	PCT	ERA	G	GS	CG	IP	H	BB	SO	ShO	Relief Pitching W	Relief Pitching L	Relief Pitching SV	Batting AB	Batting H	Batting HR	BA	PO	A	E	DP	TC/G	FA
1962	2 teams	KC A (4G 0–0)	LA A (33G 6–4)																								
″	total		6	4	.600	3.97	37	0	0	59	53	38	48	0	6	4	4	11	0	0	.000	3	10	1	0	0.4	.929
1963	LA	A	8	8	.500	3.28	47	16	4	159.1	145	80	100	1	4	2	0	45	5	0	.111	8	21	3	2	0.7	.906
1964			3	3	.500	3.48	47	4	1	93	87	39	88	1	2	2	2	18	1	0	.056	6	19	1	0	0.6	.962
1965	MIL	N	0	3	.000	2.82	61	0	0	83	81	40	54	0	0	3	6	6	1	0	.167	5	12	0	0	0.3	1.000
1966	BOS	A	4	3	.571	3.61	44	1	0	67.1	68	28	44	0	3	3	2	6	2	0	.333	4	8	0	0	0.3	1.000
1967			3	1	.750	2.54	34	0	0	63.2	61	14	38	0	3	1	2	9	3	0	.333	3	9	0	0	0.4	1.000
1969	CHI	A	5	5	.500	3.56	51	0	0	60.2	56	23	27	0	5	5	2	3	0	0	.000	1	21	0	1	0.4	1.000
1970	HOU	N	0	1	.000	9.00	3	0	0	4	5	2	1	0	0	1	0	0	0	0	—	0	0	0	0	0.0	.000
8 yrs.			29	28	.509	3.34	324	21	5	590	556	264	400	2	23	21	18	98	12	0	.122	30	100	5	3	0.4	.963
WORLD SERIES																											
1967	BOS	A	0	0	—	6.75	2	0	0	1.1	2	0	0	0	0	0	0	0	0	0	—	0	0	0	0	0.0	.000

Claude Osteen

OSTEEN, CLAUDE WILSON — BL TL 5′11″ 160 lbs.
B. Aug. 9, 1939, Caney Springs, Tenn.

Year	Team	Lg	W	L	PCT	ERA	G	GS	CG	IP	H	BB	SO	ShO	Relief Pitching W	Relief Pitching L	Relief Pitching SV	Batting AB	Batting H	Batting HR	BA	PO	A	E	DP	TC/G	FA
1957	CIN	N	0	0	—	2.25	3	0	0	4	4	3	3	0	0	0	0	1	0	0	.000	0	0	0	0	0.0	.000
1959			0	0	—	7.04	2	0	0	7.2	11	9	3	0	0	0	0	2	0	0	.000	0	1	0	0	0.5	1.000
1960			0	1	.000	5.03	20	3	0	48.1	53	30	15	0	0	0	0	12	1	0	.083	0	13	1	0	0.7	.929
1961	2 teams	CIN N (1G 0–0)	WAS A (3G 1–1)																								
″	total		1	1	.500	4.82	4	3	0	18.2	14	9	14	0	0	0	0	7	1	0	.143	0	3	0	1	0.6	1.000
1962	WAS	A	8	13	.381	3.65	28	22	7	150.1	140	47	59	2	0	0	1	48	10	0	.208	4	30	0	2	1.2	1.000
1963			9	14	.391	3.35	40	29	8	212.1	222	60	109	2	1	1	0	70	12	1	.171	11	30	3	2	1.1	.932
1964			15	13	.536	3.33	37	36	13	257	256	64	133	0	0	0	0	90	14	1	.156	9	51	0	5	1.6	1.000
1965	LA	N	15	15	.500	2.79	40	40	9	287	253	78	162	1	0	0	0	99	12	0	.121	11	82	3	6	2.4	.969
1966			17	14	.548	2.85	39	38	8	240.1	238	65	137	3	0	0	0	76	16	1	.211	10	49	4	0	1.6	.937
1967			17	17	.500	3.22	39	39	14	288.1	**298**	52	152	5	0	0	0	101	18	2	.178	11	53	2	2	1.7	.970
1968			12	**18**	.400	3.08	39	36	5	254	267	54	119	3	0	0	0	84	15	0	.179	11	50	1	2	1.6	.984
1969			20	15	.571	2.66	41	41	16	321	**293**	74	183	7	0	0	0	111	24	1	.216	19	69	3	0	2.2	.967
1970			16	14	.533	3.82	37	37	11	259	280	52	114	4	0	0	0	93	19	1	.204	10	40	1	5	1.4	.980
1971			14	11	.560	3.51	38	38	11	259	262	63	109	4	0	0	0	86	16	0	.186	22	66	1	4	2.3	.989
1972			20	11	.645	2.64	33	33	14	252	232	69	100	4	0	0	0	88	24	1	.273	9	40	1	2	1.5	.980
1973			16	11	.593	3.31	33	33	12	236.2	227	61	86	3	0	0	0	78	12	0	.154	9	53	2	3	1.9	.969
1974	2 teams	HOU N (23G 9–9)	STL N (8G 0–2)																								
″	total		9	11	.450	3.80	31	23	7	161	184	58	51	2	0	1	0	53	13	0	.245	11	28	2	2	1.3	.951
1975	CHI	A	7	16	.304	4.36	37	37	5	204.1	237	92	63	0	0	0	0	0	0	0	—	12	41	2	1	1.5	.964
18 yrs.			196	195	.501	3.30	541	488	140	3461	3471	940	1612	40	1	2	1	1099	207	8	.188	159	699	26	37	1.6	.971
WORLD SERIES																											
1965	LA	N	1	1	.500	0.64	2	2	1	14	9	5	4	1	0	0	0	3	1	0	.333	2	3	0	1	2.5	1.000
1966			0	1	.000	1.29	1	1	0	7	3	1	3	0	0	0	0	2	0	0	.000	1	0	0	0	1.0	1.000
2 yrs.			1	2	.333	0.86	3	3	1	21	12	6	7	1	0	0	0	5	1	0	.200	3	3	0	1	2.0	1.000

Darrell Osteen

OSTEEN, MILTON DARRELL — BR TR 6′ 1″ 170 lbs.
B. Feb. 14, 1943, Oklahoma City, Okla.

Year	Team	Lg	W	L	PCT	ERA	G	GS	CG	IP	H	BB	SO	ShO	Relief Pitching W	Relief Pitching L	Relief Pitching SV	Batting AB	Batting H	Batting HR	BA	PO	A	E	DP	TC/G	FA
1965	CIN	N	0	0	—	0.00	3	0	0	3	2	4	1	0	0	0	0	0	0	0	—	0	1	0	0	0.3	1.000
1966			0	2	.000	12.00	13	0	0	15	26	9	17	0	0	2	1	2	1	0	.500	0	1	0	0	0.1	1.000

Darrell Osteen *continued*

Year	Team	W	L	PCT	ERA	G	GS	CG	IP	H	BB	SO	ShO	Relief W	Relief L	Relief SV	Batting AB	Batting H	HR	BA	PO	A	E	DP	TC/G	FA
1967		0	2	.000	6.28	10	0	0	14.1	10	13	13	0	0	2	2	1	0	0	.000	1	3	0	0	0.4	1.000
1970	OAK A	1	0	1.000	6.00	3	1	0	6	9	3	3	0	0	0	0	2	0	0	.000	0	0	0	0	0.0	.000
4 yrs.		1	4	.200	7.98	29	1	0	38.1	47	29	34	0	0	4	3	5	1	0	.200	1	5	0	0	0.2	1.000

Fred Ostendorf

OSTENDORF, FREDERICK K.
B. Aug. 5, 1890, Baltimore, Md. D. Mar. 2, 1965, Kecoughtan, Va.
BL TL 6′½″ 169 lbs.

Year	Team	W	L	PCT	ERA	G	GS	CG	IP	H	BB	SO	ShO	Relief W	Relief L	Relief SV	Batting AB	Batting H	HR	BA	PO	A	E	DP	TC/G	FA
1914	IND F	0	0	—	22.50	1	0	0	2	5	2	0	0	0	0	0	1	0	0	.000	0	1	0	0	1.0	1.000

Bill Oster

OSTER, WILLIAM CHARLES
B. Jan. 2, 1933, New York, N. Y.
BL TL 6′ 3″ 198 lbs.

Year	Team	W	L	PCT	ERA	G	GS	CG	IP	H	BB	SO	ShO	Relief W	Relief L	Relief SV	Batting AB	Batting H	HR	BA	PO	A	E	DP	TC/G	FA
1954	PHI A	0	1	.000	6.32	8	1	0	15.2	19	12	5	0	0	0	0	3	1	0	.333	0	3	0	0	0.4	1.000

Fritz Ostermueller

OSTERMUELLER, FREDERICK RAYMOND
B. Sept. 15, 1907, Quincy, Ill. D. Dec. 17, 1957, Quincy, Ill.
BL TL 5′11″ 175 lbs.

Year	Team	W	L	PCT	ERA	G	GS	CG	IP	H	BB	SO	ShO	Relief W	Relief L	Relief SV	Batting AB	Batting H	HR	BA	PO	A	E	DP	TC/G	FA
1934	BOS A	10	13	.435	3.49	33	24	10	198.2	200	99	75	0	4	0	3	78	13	0	.167	8	52	2	2	1.9	.968
1935		7	8	.467	3.92	22	19	10	137.2	135	78	41	0	0	0	1	49	14	0	.286	9	27	5	1	1.9	.878
1936		10	16	.385	4.87	43	23	7	181	210	84	90	1	2	4	2	64	15	0	.234	10	42	1	1	1.2	.981
1937		3	7	.300	4.98	25	7	2	86.2	101	44	29	0	1	4	1	33	11	0	.333	9	17	3	0	1.2	.897
1938		13	5	.722	4.58	31	18	10	176.2	199	58	46	1	3	1	2	74	16	0	.216	15	30	4	3	1.6	.918
1939		11	7	.611	4.24	34	20	8	159.1	173	58	61	0	3	1	4	56	9	0	.161	12	22	2	2	1.1	.944
1940		5	9	.357	4.95	31	16	5	143.2	166	70	80	0	1	2	0	54	17	0	.315	2	21	1	0	0.8	.958
1941	STL A	0	3	.000	4.50	15	2	0	46	45	23	20	0	0	3	0	14	3	0	.214	3	10	1	0	0.9	.929
1942		3	1	.750	3.71	10	4	2	43.2	46	17	21	0	0	0	0	16	3	0	.188	2	6	0	0	0.8	1.000
1943	2 teams STL A (11G 0–2) BKN N (7G 1–1)																									
″	total	1	3	.250	4.18	18	4	0	56	57	25	19	0	1	2	0	18	2	0	.111	0	12	0	0	0.7	1.000
1944	2 teams BKN N (10G 2–1) PIT N (28G 11–7)																									
″	total	13	8	.619	2.81	38	28	17	246.1	247	77	97	1	0	0	2	93	22	0	.237	9	41	2	2	1.4	.962
1945	PIT N	5	4	.556	4.57	14	11	4	80.2	74	37	29	1	0	0	0	28	9	0	.321	8	14	1	0	1.6	.957
1946		13	10	.565	2.84	27	25	16	193.1	193	56	57	2	0	0	0	64	21	0	.328	9	33	1	0	1.6	.977
1947		12	10	.545	3.84	26	24	12	183	181	68	66	3	0	0	0	64	12	0	.188	9	25	0	4	1.3	1.000
1948		8	11	.421	4.42	23	22	10	134.1	143	41	43	2	0	0	0	44	8	0	.182	3	21	0	0	1.0	1.000
15 yrs.		114	115	.498	3.99	390	247	113	2067	2170	835	774	11	15	17	15	749	175	0	.234	108	373	23	15	1.3	.954

Joe Ostrowski

OSTROWSKI, JOSEPH PAUL (Professor)
B. Nov. 15, 1916, West Wyoming, Pa.
BL TL 6′ 180 lbs.

Year	Team	W	L	PCT	ERA	G	GS	CG	IP	H	BB	SO	ShO	Relief W	Relief L	Relief SV	Batting AB	Batting H	HR	BA	PO	A	E	DP	TC/G	FA
1948	STL A	4	6	.400	5.97	26	9	3	78.1	108	17	20	0	1	0	3	18	4	0	.222	5	23	0	0	1.1	1.000
1949		8	8	.500	4.79	40	13	4	141	185	27	34	0	2	2	2	37	7	0	.189	8	22	1	0	0.8	.968
1950	2 teams STL A (9G 2–4) NY A (21G 1–1)																									
″	total	3	5	.375	3.65	30	11	3	101	107	22	30	0	1	0	3	27	5	0	.185	4	16	1	1	0.7	.952
1951	NY A	6	4	.600	3.49	34	3	2	95.1	103	18	30	0	4	4	5	28	3	0	.107	5	14	0	2	0.6	1.000
1952		2	2	.500	5.63	20	1	0	40	56	14	17	0	2	2	2	8	0	0	.000	2	3	0	1	0.3	1.000
5 yrs.		23	25	.479	4.54	150	37	12	455.2	559	98	131	0	10	8	15	118	19	0	.161	24	78	2	4	0.7	.981
WORLD SERIES																										
1951	NY A	0	0	—	0.00	1	0	0	2	1	0	1	0	0	0	0	0	0	0	—	0	0	0	0	0.0	.000

Al Osuna

OSUNA, ALFONSO
B. Aug. 10, 1965, Inglewood, Calif.
BR TL 6′ 3″ 200 lbs.

Year	Team	W	L	PCT	ERA	G	GS	CG	IP	H	BB	SO	ShO	Relief W	Relief L	Relief SV	Batting AB	Batting H	HR	BA	PO	A	E	DP	TC/G	FA
1990	HOU N	2	0	1.000	4.76	12	0	0	11.1	10	6	6	0	2	0	0	0	0	0	—	1	1	0	0	0.2	1.000
1991		7	6	.538	3.42	71	0	0	81.2	59	46	68	0	7	6	12	2	0	0	.000	4	10	1	2	0.2	.933
1992		6	3	.667	4.23	66	0	0	61.2	52	38	37	0	6	3	0	0	0	0	—	2	11	0	0	0.2	1.000
1993		1	1	.500	3.20	44	0	0	25.1	17	13	21	0	1	1	2	0	0	0	—	0	2	1	0	0.1	.667
1994	LA N	2	0	1.000	6.23	15	0	0	8.2	13	4	7	0	2	0	0	0	0	0	—	0	0	0	0	0.0	.000
5 yrs.		18	10	.643	3.86	208	0	0	188.2	151	107	139	0	18	10	14	2	0	0	.000	7	24	2	2	0.2	.939

Antonio Osuna

OSUNA, ANTONIO PEDRO
B. Apr. 12, 1973, Sinaloa, Mexico.
BR TR 5′11″ 160 lbs.

Year	Team	W	L	PCT	ERA	G	GS	CG	IP	H	BB	SO	ShO	Relief W	Relief L	Relief SV	Batting AB	Batting H	HR	BA	PO	A	E	DP	TC/G	FA
1995	LA N	2	4	.333	4.43	39	0	0	44.2	39	20	46	0	2	4	0	2	0	0	.000	0	7	0	2	0.2	1.000
DIVISIONAL PLAYOFF SERIES																										
1995	LA N	0	1	.000	2.70	3	0	0	3.1	3	1	3	0	0	1	0	0	0	0	—	0	0	1	0	0.3	.000

Bill Otey

OTEY, WILLIAM TILFORD (Steamboat Bill)
B. Dec. 16, 1886, Dayton, Ohio D. Apr. 23, 1931, Dayton, Ohio.
BL TL 6′ 2½″ 181 lbs.

Year	Team	W	L	PCT	ERA	G	GS	CG	IP	H	BB	SO	ShO	Relief W	Relief L	Relief SV	Batting AB	Batting H	HR	BA	PO	A	E	DP	TC/G	FA
1907	PIT N	0	1	.000	4.41	3	2	1	16.1	23	4	5	0	0	0	0	4	1	0	.250	0	3	1	0	1.3	.750
1910	WAS A	0	1	.000	3.38	9	1	1	34.2	40	6	12	0	0	0	0	13	5	0	.385	3	5	1	0	1.0	.889
1911		1	3	.250	6.34	12	2	0	49.2	68	15	16	0	1	2	0	17	1	0	.059	3	19	4	0	2.2	.846
3 yrs.		1	5	.167	5.01	24	5	2	100.2	131	25	33	0	1	2	0	34	7	0	.206	6	27	6	0	1.6	.846

Harry Otis

OTIS, HARRY GEORGE (Cannonball)
B. Oct. 5, 1886, W. New York, N. J. D. Jan. 29, 1976, Trenton, N. J.
BR TL 6′ 180 lbs.

Year	Team	W	L	PCT	ERA	G	GS	CG	IP	H	BB	SO	ShO	Relief W	Relief L	Relief SV	Batting AB	Batting H	HR	BA	PO	A	E	DP	TC/G	FA
1909	CLE A	2	2	.500	1.37	5	3	0	26.1	26	18	6	0	1	0	0	9	1	0	.111	0	9	1	0	2.0	.900

Denny O'Toole

O'TOOLE, DENNIS JOSEPH
Brother of Jim O'Toole.
B. Mar. 13, 1949, Chicago, Ill.
BR TR 6′ 3″ 195 lbs.

Year	Team	W	L	PCT	ERA	G	GS	CG	IP	H	BB	SO	ShO	Relief W	Relief L	Relief SV	Batting AB	Batting H	HR	BA	PO	A	E	DP	TC/G	FA
1969	CHI A	0	0	—	6.75	2	0	0	4	5	2	4	0	0	0	0	0	0	0	—	0	0	0	0	0.0	.000
1970		0	0	—	3.00	3	0	0	3	5	2	3	0	0	0	0	0	0	0	—	0	0	0	0	0.0	.000
1971		0	0	—	0.00	1	0	0	2	0	1	2	0	0	0	0	0	0	0	—	0	0	0	0	0.0	.000
1972		0	0	—	5.40	3	0	0	5	10	2	5	0	0	0	0	0	0	0	—	0	1	0	0	0.3	1.000
1973		0	0	—	5.63	6	0	0	16	23	3	8	0	0	0	0	0	0	0	—	0	3	0	0	0.5	1.000
5 yrs.		0	0		5.10	15	0	0	30	43	10	22	0	0	0	0	0	0	0		0	4	0	0	0.3	1.000

Jim O'Toole

O'TOOLE, JAMES JEROME
Brother of Denny O'Toole.
B. Jan. 10, 1937, Chicago, Ill.
BB TL 6′ 190 lbs.

Year	Team		W	L	PCT	ERA	G	GS	CG	IP	H	BB	SO	ShO	Relief Pitching W	L	SV	Batting AB	H	HR	BA	PO	A	E	DP	TC/G	FA
1958	CIN	N	0	1	.000	1.29	1	1	0	7	4	5	4	0	0	0	0	2	0	0	.000	0	0	0	0	0.0	.000
1959			5	8	.385	5.15	28	19	3	129.1	144	73	68	1	0	0	0	37	5	0	.135	5	24	0	2	1.0	1.000
1960			12	12	.500	3.80	34	31	7	196.1	198	66	124	2	0	0	1	66	7	0	.106	8	23	5	1	1.1	.861
1961			19	9	.679	3.10	39	35	11	252.2	229	93	178	3	1	0	2	93	16	0	.172	16	42	2	2	1.5	.967
1962			16	13	.552	3.50	36	34	11	251.2	222	87	170	3	2	0	0	91	10	0	.110	10	33	1	1	1.2	.977
1963			17	14	.548	2.88	33	32	12	234.1	208	57	146	5	0	0	0	74	11	0	.149	14	29	5	1	1.5	.896
1964			17	7	.708	2.66	30	30	9	220	194	51	145	3	0	0	0	70	7	0	.100	12	29	2	1	1.4	.953
1965			3	10	.231	5.92	29	22	2	127.2	154	47	71	0	0	0	1	45	4	0	.089	5	17	2	1	0.8	.917
1966			5	7	.417	3.55	25	24	2	142	139	49	96	0	0	0	0	47	6	0	.128	5	20	1	0	1.0	.962
1967	CHI	A	4	3	.571	2.82	15	10	1	54.1	53	18	37	1	0	0	0	13	1	0	.077	5	6	2	1	0.9	.846
10 yrs.			98	84	.538	3.57	270	238	58	1615.1	1545	546	1039	18	3	0	4	538	67	0	.125	80	223	20	10	1.2	.938
WORLD SERIES																											
1961	CIN	N	0	2	.000	3.00	2	2	0	12	11	7	4	0	0	0	0	3	0	0	.000	1	0	0	0	0.5	1.000

Marty O'Toole

O'TOOLE, MARTIN JAMES
B. Nov. 27, 1888, William Penn, Pa. D. Feb. 18, 1949, Aberdeen, Wash.
BR TR 5′11″ 175 lbs.

Year	Team		W	L	PCT	ERA	G	GS	CG	IP	H	BB	SO	ShO	Relief Pitching W	L	SV	Batting AB	H	HR	BA	PO	A	E	DP	TC/G	FA
1908	CIN	N	1	0	1.000	2.40	3	2	1	15	15	7	5	0	0	0	0	5	1	0	.200	2	3	0	0	1.7	1.000
1911	PIT	N	3	2	.600	2.37	5	5	3	38	28	20	34	0	0	0	0	14	5	0	.357	4	9	1	0	2.8	.929
1912			15	17	.469	2.71	37	36	17	275.1	237	**159**	150	**6**	0	1	0	99	22	0	.222	3	75	3	1	2.2	.963
1913			6	8	.429	3.30	26	15	7	144.2	148	55	58	0	0	2	1	53	7	0	.132	5	36	2	2	1.7	.953
1914	2 teams	PIT N (19G 1–8)	NY N (10G 1–1)																								
″	total		2	9	.182	4.56	29	14	3	126.1	126	59	49	0	0	2	0	40	8	0	.200	1	28	0	0	1.0	1.000
5 yrs.			27	36	.429	3.21	100	72	31	599.1	554	300	296	6	0	5	1	211	43	0	.204	15	151	6	3	1.7	.965

Jim Otten

OTTEN, JAMES EDWARD
B. July 1, 1951, Lewiston, Mont.
BR TR 6′ 2″ 195 lbs.

Year	Team		W	L	PCT	ERA	G	GS	CG	IP	H	BB	SO	ShO	Relief Pitching W	L	SV	Batting AB	H	HR	BA	PO	A	E	DP	TC/G	FA
1974	CHI	A	0	1	.000	5.63	5	1	0	16	22	12	11	0	0	0	0	0	0	0	—	0	2	0	0	0.4	1.000
1975			0	0	—	6.75	2	0	0	5.1	4	7	3	0	0	0	0	0	0	0	—	0	1	0	0	0.5	1.000
1976			0	0	—	4.50	2	0	0	6	9	2	3	0	0	0	0	0	0	0	—	0	0	0	0	0.0	.000
1980	STL	N	0	5	.000	5.56	31	4	0	55	71	26	38	0	0	1	0	5	1	0	.200	0	11	0	2	0.4	1.000
1981			1	0	1.000	5.25	24	0	0	36	44	20	20	0	1	0	0	2	0	0	.000	0	3	1	0	0.2	.750
5 yrs.			1	6	.143	5.48	64	5	0	118.1	150	67	75	0	1	1	0	7	1	0	.143	0	17	1	2	0.3	.944

Dave Otto

OTTO, DAVID ALAN
B. Nov. 12, 1964, Chicago, Ill.
BL TL 6′ 7″ 210 lbs.

Year	Team		W	L	PCT	ERA	G	GS	CG	IP	H	BB	SO	ShO	Relief Pitching W	L	SV	Batting AB	H	HR	BA	PO	A	E	DP	TC/G	FA
1987	OAK	A	0	0	—	9.00	3	0	0	6	7	1	3	0	0	0	0	0	0	0	—	1	0	0	0	0.3	1.000
1988			0	0	—	1.80	3	2	0	10	9	6	7	0	0	0	0	0	0	0	—	1	1	0	0	0.7	1.000
1989			0	0	—	2.70	1	1	0	6.2	6	2	4	0	0	0	0	0	0	0	—	0	1	0	0	1.0	1.000
1990			0	0	—	7.71	2	0	0	2.1	3	3	2	0	0	0	0	0	0	0	—	0	2	0	1	1.0	1.000
1991	CLE	A	2	8	.200	4.23	18	14	1	100	108	27	47	0	0	0	0	0	0	0	—	1	16	1	0	1.0	.944
1992			5	9	.357	7.06	18	16	0	80.1	110	33	32	0	0	0	0	0	0	0	—	3	14	1	1	1.0	.944
1993	PIT	N	3	4	.429	5.03	28	8	0	68	85	28	30	0	1	1	0	18	4	0	.222	4	13	0	1	0.6	1.000
1994	CHI	N	0	1	.000	3.80	36	0	0	45	49	22	19	0	0	1	0	2	0	0	.000	1	5	1	1	0.2	.857
8 yrs.			10	22	.313	5.06	109	41	1	318.1	377	122	144	0	1	2	0	20	4	0	.200	11	52	3	4	0.6	.955

Orval Overall

OVERALL, ORVAL
B. Feb. 2, 1881, Farmersville, Calif. D. July 14, 1947, Fresno, Calif.
BB TR 6′ 2″ 214 lbs.

Year	Team		W	L	PCT	ERA	G	GS	CG	IP	H	BB	SO	ShO	Relief Pitching W	L	SV	Batting AB	H	HR	BA	PO	A	E	DP	TC/G	FA
1905	CIN	N	17	22	.436	2.86	42	39	32	318	290	147	173	2	1	1	0	117	17	0	.145	10	82	13	2	2.5	.876
1906	2 teams	CIN N (13G 3–5)	CHI N (18G 12–3)																								
″	total		15	8	.652	2.74	31	24	19	226.1	193	97	127	2	2	0	1	84	15	0	.179	8	56	5	2	2.2	.928
1907	CHI	N	23	8	.742	1.70	35	30	26	265.1	199	69	139	**8**	1	2	3	94	20	0	.213	14	76	3	2	2.7	.968
1908			15	11	.577	1.92	37	27	16	225	165	78	167	4	3	0	2	70	9	0	.129	13	51	5	1	1.9	.928
1909			20	11	.645	1.42	38	32	23	285	204	80	**205**	**9**	1	0	2	96	22	2	.229	12	69	3	3	2.2	.964
1910			12	6	.667	2.68	23	21	11	144.2	106	54	92	4	0	1	1	41	5	0	.122	5	43	0	0	1.9	1.000
1913			4	5	.444	3.31	11	9	6	68	73	26	30	1	0	0	0	24	6	0	.250	2	24	0	0	2.4	1.000
7 yrs.			106	71	.599	2.24 **8th**	217	182	133	1532.1	1230	551	933	30	8	4	9	526	94	2	.179	64	401	29	10	2.3	.941
WORLD SERIES																											
1906	CHI	N	0	0	—	1.50	2	0	0	12	10	3	8	0	0	0	0	4	1	0	.250	0	2	0	0	1.0	1.000
1907			1	0	1.000	1.00	2	2	1	18	14	4	11	0	0	0	0	5	1	0	.200	0	6	0	0	3.0	1.000
1908			2	0	1.000	0.98	3	2	2	18.1	7	7	15	1	0	0	0	6	2	0	.333	0	3	0	0	1.0	1.000
1910			0	1	.000	9.00	1	1	0	3	6	1	1	0	0	0	0	1	0	0	.000	0	0	0	0	0.0	.000
4 yrs.			3	1	.750	1.58	8	5	3	51.1	37	15	35	1	0	0	0	16	4	0	.250	0	11	0	0	1.4	1.000

Stubby Overmire

OVERMIRE, FRANK W.
B. May 16, 1919, Moline, Mich. D. Mar. 3, 1977, Lakeland, Fla.
BR TL 5′ 7″ 170 lbs.

Year	Team		W	L	PCT	ERA	G	GS	CG	IP	H	BB	SO	ShO	Relief Pitching W	L	SV	Batting AB	H	HR	BA	PO	A	E	DP	TC/G	FA
1943	DET	A	7	6	.538	3.18	29	18	8	147	135	38	48	3	0	0	1	42	7	0	.167	10	23	0	2	1.1	1.000
1944			11	11	.500	3.07	32	28	11	199.2	214	41	57	3	0	0	1	63	11	0	.175	12	46	1	3	1.8	.983
1945			9	9	.500	3.88	31	22	9	162.1	189	42	36	0	0	0	4	53	10	0	.189	11	33	2	2	1.5	.957
1946			5	7	.417	4.62	24	13	3	97.1	106	29	34	0	1	3	1	33	5	0	.152	5	25	2	0	1.3	.938
1947			11	5	.688	3.77	28	17	7	140.2	142	44	33	3	3	0	0	47	7	0	.149	10	21	1	2	1.1	.969
1948			3	4	.429	5.97	37	4	0	66.1	89	31	14	0	3	3	3	14	1	0	.071	6	16	0	1	0.6	1.000
1949			1	3	.250	9.87	14	1	0	17.1	29	9	3	0	1	2	0	3	1	0	.333	1	5	0	0	0.4	1.000
1950	STL	A	9	12	.429	4.19	31	19	8	161	200	45	39	2	1	2	0	48	8	0	.167	4	24	1	0	0.9	.966
1951	2 teams	STL A (8G 1–6)	NY A (15G 1–1)																								
″	total		2	7	.222	4.04	23	11	4	98	111	39	27	0	0	2	0	21	2	0	.095	9	14	3	0	1.1	.885
1952	STL	A	0	3	.000	3.73	17	4	0	41	44	7	10	0	0	0	0	11	2	0	.182	2	10	0	1	0.7	1.000
10 yrs.			58	67	.464	3.96	266	137	50	1130.2	1259	325	301	11	9	12	10	335	54	0	.161	70	217	10	11	1.1	.966
WORLD SERIES																											
1945	DET	A	0	1	.000	3.00	1	1	0	6	4	2	2	0	0	0	0	1	0	0	.000	0	1	0	0	1.0	1.000

Mike Overy

OVERY, HARRY MICHAEL BR TR 6′ 2″ 190 lbs.
B. Jan. 27, 1951, Clinton, Ill.

Year	Team	Lg	W	L	PCT	ERA	G	GS	CG	IP	H	BB	SO	ShO	Relief Pitching W	Relief Pitching L	Relief Pitching SV	Batting AB	Batting H	Batting HR	BA	PO	A	E	DP	TC/G	FA
1976	CAL	A	0	2	.000	6.43	5	0	0	7	6	3	8	0	0	2	0	0	0	0	—	0	2	1	0	0.6	.667

Ernie Ovitz

OVITZ, ERNEST GAYHART BR TR 5′ 8½″ 156 lbs.
B. Oct. 7, 1885, Mineral Point, Wis. D. Sept. 11, 1980, Green Bay, Wis.

Year	Team	Lg	W	L	PCT	ERA	G	GS	CG	IP	H	BB	SO	ShO	Relief Pitching W	Relief Pitching L	Relief Pitching SV	Batting AB	Batting H	Batting HR	BA	PO	A	E	DP	TC/G	FA
1911	CHI	N	0	0	—	4.50	1	0	0	2	3	3	0	0	0	0	0	0	0	0	—	0	0	0	0	0.0	.000

Bob Owchinko

OWCHINKO, ROBERT DENNIS BL TL 6′ 2″ 190 lbs.
B. Jan. 1, 1955, Detroit, Mich.

Year	Team	Lg	W	L	PCT	ERA	G	GS	CG	IP	H	BB	SO	ShO	Relief Pitching W	Relief Pitching L	Relief Pitching SV	Batting AB	Batting H	Batting HR	BA	PO	A	E	DP	TC/G	FA
1976	SD	N	0	2	.000	16.62	2	2	0	4.1	11	3	4	0	0	0	0	1	0	0	.000	0	1	0	0	0.5	1.000
1977			9	12	.429	4.45	30	28	3	170	191	67	101	2	1	0	0	49	4	0	.082	2	21	0	1	0.8	1.000
1978			10	13	.435	3.56	36	33	4	202	198	78	94	1	0	0	0	63	11	0	.175	6	30	0	3	1.0	1.000
1979			6	12	.333	3.74	42	20	2	149	144	55	66	0	2	5	0	33	4	0	.121	2	24	2	2	0.7	.929
1980	CLE	A	2	9	.182	5.29	29	14	1	114	138	47	66	1	1	0	0	0	0	0	—	3	18	1	0	0.8	.955
1981	OAK	A	4	3	.571	3.23	29	0	0	39	34	19	26	0	4	3	2	0	0	0	—	0	6	1	1	0.2	.857
1982			2	4	.333	5.21	54	0	0	102	111	52	67	0	2	4	3	0	0	0	—	7	7	0	1	0.3	1.000
1983	PIT	N	0	0	—	∞	1	0	0		2	0	0	0	0	0	0	0	0	0	—	0	0	0	0	0.0	.000
1984	CIN	N	3	5	.375	4.12	49	4	0	94	91	39	60	0	2	3	2	12	2	0	.167	4	11	0	0	0.3	1.000
1986	MON	N	1	0	1.000	3.60	3	3	0	15	17	3	6	0	0	0	0	5	1	0	.200	0	2	0	0	0.7	1.000
10 yrs.			37	60	.381	4.29	275	104	10	889.1	937	363	490	4	12	15	7	163	22	0	.135	24	120	4	8	0.5	.973
LEAGUE CHAMPIONSHIP SERIES																											
1981	OAK	A	0	0	—	5.40	1	0	0	1.2	3	0	0	0	0	0	0	0	0	0	—	0	1	0	0	1.0	1.000

Frank Owen

OWEN, FRANK MALCOLM (Yip) BB TR 5′11″ 160 lbs.
B. Dec. 23, 1879, Ypsilanti, Mich. D. Nov. 24, 1942, Dearborn, Mich.

Year	Team	Lg	W	L	PCT	ERA	G	GS	CG	IP	H	BB	SO	ShO	Relief Pitching W	Relief Pitching L	Relief Pitching SV	Batting AB	Batting H	Batting HR	BA	PO	A	E	DP	TC/G	FA
1901	DET	A	1	3	.250	4.34	8	5	3	56	70	30	17	0	0	0	0	20	1	0	.050	7	24	2	2	3.7	.939
1903	CHI	A	8	12	.400	3.50	26	20	15	167.1	167	44	66	1	1	**2**	1	57	7	0	.123	11	68	3	4	3.2	.963
1904			21	15	.583	1.94	37	36	34	315	243	61	103	4	0	0	1	107	23	2	.215	21	130	0	8	4.1	1.000
1905			21	13	.618	2.10	42	38	32	334	276	56	125	3	0	1	0	124	18	0	.145	20	120	3	1	3.4	.979
1906			22	13	.629	2.33	42	36	27	293	289	54	66	7	3	1	2	103	14	0	.136	22	110	3	1	3.2	.978
1907			2	3	.400	2.49	11	4	2	47	43	13	15	0	0	1	0	16	4	0	.250	5	16	0	0	1.9	1.000
1908			6	7	.462	3.41	25	14	5	140	142	37	48	1	2	0	0	50	9	0	.180	6	54	4	2	2.6	.938
1909			1	1	.500	4.50	3	2	1	16	19	3	3	0	0	0	0	6	1	0	.167	0	5	0	0	1.7	1.000
8 yrs.			82	67	.550	2.55	194	155	119	1368.1	1249	298	443	16	6	5	4	483	77	2	.159	92	527	15	18	3.3	.976
WORLD SERIES																											
1906	CHI	A	0	0	—	3.00	1	0	0	6	6	3	2	0	0	0	0	2	0	0	.000	1	4	0	0	5.0	1.000

Jim Owens

OWENS, JAMES PHILIP (Bear) BR TR 5′11″ 180 lbs.
B. Jan. 16, 1934, Gifford, Pa.

Year	Team	Lg	W	L	PCT	ERA	G	GS	CG	IP	H	BB	SO	ShO	Relief Pitching W	Relief Pitching L	Relief Pitching SV	Batting AB	Batting H	Batting HR	BA	PO	A	E	DP	TC/G	FA
1955	PHI	N	0	2	.000	8.31	3	2	0	8.2	13	7	6	0	0	0	0	1	0	0	.000	0	1	0	0	0.3	1.000
1956			0	4	.000	7.28	10	5	0	29.2	35	22	22	0	0	1	0	6	1	0	.167	2	5	0	2	0.7	1.000
1958			1	0	1.000	2.57	1	1	0	7	4	5	3	0	0	0	0	2	0	0	.000	0	1	0	0	1.0	1.000
1959			12	12	.500	3.21	31	30	11	221.1	203	73	135	1	0	0	1	75	9	0	.120	8	33	1	4	1.4	.976
1960			4	14	.222	5.04	31	22	6	150	182	64	83	0	0	1	0	44	3	0	.068	6	22	2	0	1.0	.933
1961			5	10	.333	4.47	20	17	3	106.2	119	32	38	0	0	1	0	27	2	0	.074	4	13	2	3	0.9	.895
1962			2	4	.333	6.33	23	12	1	69.2	90	33	21	0	0	0	0	14	2	0	.143	5	8	0	0	0.6	1.000
1963	CIN	N	0	2	.000	5.31	19	3	0	42.1	42	24	29	0	0	1	4	8	1	0	.125	4	9	1	0	0.7	.929
1964	HOU	N	8	7	.533	3.28	48	11	0	118	115	32	88	0	6	2	6	29	3	0	.103	2	17	2	0	0.4	.905
1965			6	5	.545	3.28	50	0	0	71.1	64	29	53	0	6	5	8	8	1	0	.125	2	11	0	0	0.3	1.000
1966			4	7	.364	4.68	40	0	0	50	53	17	32	0	4	7	2	4	0	0	.000	0	12	0	1	0.3	1.000
1967			0	1	.000	4.22	10	0	0	10.2	12	2	6	0	0	1	0	0	0	0	—	0	0	0	0	0.0	.000
12 yrs.			42	68	.382	4.31	286	103	21	885.1	932	340	516	1	16	19	21	218	22	0	.101	33	132	8	10	0.6	.954

Rick Ownbey

OWNBEY, RICHARD WAYNE BR TR 6′ 3″ 185 lbs.
B. Oct. 20, 1957, Corona, Calif.

Year	Team	Lg	W	L	PCT	ERA	G	GS	CG	IP	H	BB	SO	ShO	Relief Pitching W	Relief Pitching L	Relief Pitching SV	Batting AB	Batting H	Batting HR	BA	PO	A	E	DP	TC/G	FA
1982	NY	N	1	2	.333	3.75	8	8	2	50.1	44	43	28	0	0	0	0	15	3	0	.200	1	7	2	0	1.3	.800
1983			1	3	.250	4.67	10	4	0	34.2	31	21	19	0	1	0	0	9	1	0	.111	1	6	1	1	0.8	.875
1984	STL	N	0	3	.000	4.74	4	4	0	19	23	8	11	0	0	0	0	4	0	0	.000	1	1	0	0	0.5	1.000
1986			1	3	.250	3.80	17	3	0	42.2	47	19	25	0	0	2	0	7	0	0	.000	4	4	2	0	0.6	.800
4 yrs.			3	11	.214	4.11	39	19	2	146.2	145	91	83	0	1	2	0	35	4	0	.114	7	18	5	1	0.8	.833

Doc Ozmer

OZMER, HORACE ROBERT BR TR 5′10½″ 185 lbs.
B. May 25, 1901, Atlanta, Ga. D. Dec. 28, 1970, Atlanta, Ga.

Year	Team	Lg	W	L	PCT	ERA	G	GS	CG	IP	H	BB	SO	ShO	Relief Pitching W	Relief Pitching L	Relief Pitching SV	Batting AB	Batting H	Batting HR	BA	PO	A	E	DP	TC/G	FA
1923	PHI	A	0	0	—	4.50	1	0	0	2	1	1	1	0	0	0	0	0	0	0	—	1	1	0	0	2.0	1.000

John Pacella

PACELLA, JOHN LEWIS BR TR 6′ 3″ 195 lbs.
B. Sept. 15, 1956, Brooklyn, N. Y.

Year	Team	Lg	W	L	PCT	ERA	G	GS	CG	IP	H	BB	SO	ShO	Relief Pitching W	Relief Pitching L	Relief Pitching SV	Batting AB	Batting H	Batting HR	BA	PO	A	E	DP	TC/G	FA
1977	NY	N	0	0	—	0.00	3	0	0	4	2	2	1	0	0	0	0	0	0	0	—	0	0	1	0	0.3	.000
1979			0	2	.000	4.50	4	3	0	16	16	4	12	0	0	0	0	4	0	0	.000	2	1	0	0	0.8	1.000
1980			3	4	.429	5.14	32	15	0	84	89	59	68	0	0	0	0	20	2	0	.100	6	9	1	0	0.5	.938
1982	2 teams	NY A (3G 0–1)	MIN A (21G 1–2)																								
″	total		1	3	.250	7.30	24	2	0	61.2	74	46	22	0	1	1	2	0	0	0		3	2	0	0	0.2	1.000
1984	BAL	A	0	1	.000	6.75	6	1	0	14.2	15	9	8	0	0	1	0	0	0	0	—	0	1	1	0	0.3	.500
1986	DET	A	0	0	—	4.09	5	0	0	11	10	13	5	0	0	0	1	0	0	0	—	3	4	0	0	1.4	1.000
6 yrs.			4	10	.286	5.74	74	21	0	191.1	206	133	116	0	1	2	3	24	2	0	.083	14	17	3	0	0.5	.912

Pat Pacillo

PACILLO, PATRICK MICHAEL BR TR 6′ 2″ 205 lbs.
B. July 23, 1963, Jersey City, N. J.

Year	Team	Lg	W	L	PCT	ERA	G	GS	CG	IP	H	BB	SO	ShO	Relief Pitching W	Relief Pitching L	Relief Pitching SV	Batting AB	Batting H	Batting HR	BA	PO	A	E	DP	TC/G	FA
1987	CIN	N	3	3	.500	6.13	12	7	0	39.2	41	19	23	0	1	0	0	11	1	0	.091	2	5	0	0	0.6	1.000
1988			1	0	1.000	5.06	6	0	0	10.2	14	4	11	0	1	0	0	1	0	0	.000	0	1	1	0	0.3	.500
2 yrs.			4	3	.571	5.90	18	7	0	50.1	55	23	34	0	2	0	0	12	1	0	.083	2	6	1	0	0.5	.889

Gene Packard

PACKARD, EUGENE MILO BL TL 5′10″ 155 lbs.
B. July 13, 1887, Colorado Springs, Colo. D. May 19, 1959, Riverside, Calif.

Year	Team	W	L	PCT	ERA	G	GS	CG	IP	H	BB	SO	ShO	Relief W	Relief L	Relief SV	AB	Batting H	HR	BA	PO	A	E	DP	TC/G	FA
1912	CIN N	1	0	1.000	3.00	1	1	1	9	7	4	2	0	0	0	0	4	1	0	.250	1	2	0	0	3.0	1.000
1913		7	11	.389	2.97	39	21	9	190.2	208	64	73	2	1	2	0	61	11	0	.180	7	46	5	1	1.5	.914
1914	KC F	21	13	.618	2.89	42	34	24	302	282	88	154	4	3	0	4	116	28	1	.241	27	121	6	7	3.5	.961
1915		20	11	.645	2.68	42	31	21	281.2	250	74	108	5	2	2	2	95	22	1	.232	23	114	7	3	3.4	.951
1916	CHI N	10	6	.625	2.78	37	16	5	155.1	154	38	36	2	4	1	5	54	7	0	.130	17	64	3	2	2.1	.964
1917	2 teams CHI N (2G 0–0) STL N (34G 9–6)																									
″	total	9	6	.600	2.55	36	11	6	155	141	25	45	0	6	0	2	52	15	0	.288	5	43	0	2	1.3	1.000
1918	STL N	12	12	.500	3.50	30	23	10	182.1	184	33	46	1	3	1	2	69	12	0	.174	2	50	2	5	1.7	.963
1919	PHI N	6	8	.429	4.15	21	16	10	134.1	167	30	24	1	0	1	1	51	7	0	.137	9	36	0	3	2.1	1.000
8 yrs.		86	67	.562	3.01	248	153	86	1410.1	1393	356	488	15	19	7	16	502	103	2	.205	91	476	23	23	2.3	.961

Joe Pactwa

PACTWA, JOSEPH MARTIN BL TL 5′11″ 185 lbs.
B. June 2, 1948, Hammond, Ind.

Year	Team	W	L	PCT	ERA	G	GS	CG	IP	H	BB	SO	ShO	Relief W	Relief L	Relief SV	AB	Batting H	HR	BA	PO	A	E	DP	TC/G	FA
1975	CAL A	1	0	1.000	3.86	4	3	0	16.1	23	10	3	0	0	0	0	0	0	0	—	0	2	0	0	0.5	1.000

Dave Pagan

PAGAN, DAVID PERCY BR TR 6′ 2″ 175 lbs.
B. Sept. 15, 1949, Nipawin, Sask., Canada.

Year	Team	W	L	PCT	ERA	G	GS	CG	IP	H	BB	SO	ShO	Relief W	Relief L	Relief SV	AB	Batting H	HR	BA	PO	A	E	DP	TC/G	FA
1973	NY A	0	0	—	2.84	4	1	0	12.2	16	1	9	0	0	0	0	0	0	0	—	2	1	0	0	0.8	1.000
1974		1	3	.250	5.14	16	6	1	49	49	28	39	0	0	1	0	0	0	0	—	3	5	0	0	0.5	1.000
1975		0	0	—	4.06	13	0	0	31	30	13	18	0	0	0	1	0	0	0	—	5	1	1	0	0.5	.857
1976	2 teams NY A (7G 1–1) BAL A (20G 1–4)																									
″	total	2	5	.286	4.73	27	7	1	70.1	72	27	47	0	0	3	1	0	0	0		6	2	1	0	0.3	.889
1977	2 teams SEA A (24G 1–1) PIT N (1G 0–0)																									
″	total	1	1	.500	5.87	25	4	1	69	87	26	34	1	0	1	2	0	0	0		3	11	0	0	0.6	1.000
5 yrs.		4	9	.308	4.97	85	18	3	232	254	95	147	1	0	5	4	0	0	0		19	20	2	0	0.5	.951

Joe Page

PAGE, JOSEPH FRANCIS (Fireman, The Gay Reliever) BL TL 6′ 3″ 200 lbs.
B. Oct. 28, 1917, Cherry Valley, Pa. D. Apr. 21, 1980, Latrobe, Pa.

Year	Team	W	L	PCT	ERA	G	GS	CG	IP	H	BB	SO	ShO	Relief W	Relief L	Relief SV	AB	Batting H	HR	BA	PO	A	E	DP	TC/G	FA
1944	NY A	5	7	.417	4.56	19	16	4	102.2	100	52	63	0	0	0	0	32	5	0	.156	3	14	1	1	0.9	.944
1945		6	3	.667	2.82	20	9	4	102	95	46	50	0	2	0	0	36	9	0	.250	2	12	1	1	0.8	.933
1946		9	8	.529	3.57	31	17	6	136	126	72	77	1	2	4	3	43	7	1	.163	2	23	5	1	1.0	.833
1947		14	8	.636	2.48	56	2	0	141.1	105	72	116	0	**14**	**7**	**17**	46	10	1	.217	2	18	0	0	0.4	1.000
1948		7	8	.467	4.26	**55**	1	0	107.2	116	66	77	0	7	**8**	16	24	7	0	.292	3	14	0	0	0.3	1.000
1949		13	8	.619	2.59	**60**	0	0	135.1	103	75	99	0	**13**	**8**	**27**	40	7	0	.175	4	15	1	1	0.3	.950
1950		3	7	.300	5.04	37	0	0	55.1	66	31	33	0	3	7	13	8	2	0	.250	1	6	0	0	0.2	1.000
1954	PIT N	0	0	—	11.17	7	0	0	9.2	16	7	4	0	0	0	0	0	0	0	—	0	2	0	0	0.3	1.000
8 yrs.		57	49	.538	3.53	285	45	14	790	727	421	519	1	41	34	76	229	47	2	.205	17	104	8	4	0.5	.938
WORLD SERIES																										
1947	NY A	1	1	.500	4.15	4	0	0	13	12	2	7	0	1	1	1	4	0	0	.000	1	2	0	0	0.8	1.000
1949		1	0	1.000	2.00	3	0	0	9	6	3	8	0	1	0	1	4	0	0	.000	0	2	0	1	0.7	1.000
2 yrs.		2	1	.667	3.27	7	0	0	22	18	5	15	0	2	1	2	8	0	0	.000	1	4	0	1	0.7	1.000

Phil Page

PAGE, PHILIPPE RAUSAC BR TL 6′ 2″ 175 lbs.
B. Aug. 23, 1905, Springfield, Mass. D. July 27, 1958, Springfield, Mass.

Year	Team	W	L	PCT	ERA	G	GS	CG	IP	H	BB	SO	ShO	Relief W	Relief L	Relief SV	AB	Batting H	HR	BA	PO	A	E	DP	TC/G	FA
1928	DET A	2	0	1.000	2.45	3	2	2	22	21	10	3	0	0	0	0	9	2	0	.222	4	5	0	3	3.0	1.000
1929		0	2	.000	8.17	10	4	1	25.1	29	19	6	0	0	1	0	8	1	0	.125	2	2	1	0	0.5	.800
1930		0	1	.000	9.75	12	0	0	12	23	9	2	0	0	1	0	0	0	0	—	1	4	0	0	0.4	1.000
1934	BKN N	1	0	1.000	5.40	6	0	0	10	13	6	4	0	1	0	0	1	0	0	.000	2	5	1	0	1.3	.875
4 yrs.		3	3	.500	6.23	31	6	3	69.1	86	44	15	0	1	2	0	18	3	0	.167	9	16	2	3	0.9	.926

Sam Page

PAGE, SAMUEL WALTER BL TR 6′ 172 lbs.
B. Feb. 11, 1916, Woodruff, S. C.

Year	Team	W	L	PCT	ERA	G	GS	CG	IP	H	BB	SO	ShO	Relief W	Relief L	Relief SV	AB	Batting H	HR	BA	PO	A	E	DP	TC/G	FA
1939	PHI A	0	3	.000	6.95	4	3	1	22	34	15	11	0	0	1	0	7	3	0	.429	0	6	0	1	1.5	1.000

Vance Page

PAGE, VANCE LINWOOD BR TR 6′ 180 lbs.
B. Sept. 15, 1905, Elm City, N. C. D. July 14, 1951, Wilson, N. C.

Year	Team	W	L	PCT	ERA	G	GS	CG	IP	H	BB	SO	ShO	Relief W	Relief L	Relief SV	AB	Batting H	HR	BA	PO	A	E	DP	TC/G	FA
1938	CHI N	5	4	.556	3.84	13	9	3	68	90	13	18	0	0	0	1	26	4	0	.154	9	25	0	1	2.6	1.000
1939		7	7	.500	3.88	27	17	8	139.1	169	37	43	1	1	0	1	47	12	0	.255	4	33	0	1	1.4	1.000
1940		1	3	.250	4.42	30	1	0	59	65	26	22	0	1	3	2	13	4	0	.308	1	15	1	0	0.6	.941
1941		2	2	.500	4.28	25	3	1	48.1	48	30	17	0	2	2	1	7	2	0	.286	2	12	0	0	0.6	1.000
4 yrs.		15	16	.484	4.03	95	30	12	314.2	372	106	100	1	4	5	5	93	22	0	.237	16	85	1	2	1.1	.990
WORLD SERIES																										
1938	CHI N	0	0	—	13.50	1	0	0	1.1	2	0	0	0	0	0	0	0	0	0	—	0	1	0	0	1.0	1.000

Pat Paige

PAIGE, GEORGE LYNN BL TR 5′10″ 175 lbs.
Born George Lynn Page.
B. May 5, 1882, Paw Paw, Mich. D. June 8, 1939, Berlin, Wis.

Year	Team	W	L	PCT	ERA	G	GS	CG	IP	H	BB	SO	ShO	Relief W	Relief L	Relief SV	AB	Batting H	HR	BA	PO	A	E	DP	TC/G	FA
1911	CLE A	1	0	1.000	4.50	2	1	1	16	21	7	6	0	0	0	0	7	1	0	.143	2	7	0	0	4.5	1.000

Satchel Paige

PAIGE, LEROY ROBERT BR TR 6′ 3½″ 180 lbs.
B. July 7, 1906, Mobile, Ala. D. June 8, 1982, Kansas City, Mo.
Hall of Fame 1971.

Year	Team	W	L	PCT	ERA	G	GS	CG	IP	H	BB	SO	ShO	Relief W	Relief L	Relief SV	AB	Batting H	HR	BA	PO	A	E	DP	TC/G	FA
1948	CLE A	6	1	.857	2.48	21	7	3	72.2	61	25	45	2	2	1	1	23	2	0	.087	2	12	0	0	0.7	1.000
1949		4	7	.364	3.04	31	5	1	83	70	33	54	0	3	4	5	16	1	0	.063	5	10	0	0	0.5	1.000
1951	STL A	3	4	.429	4.79	23	3	0	62	67	29	48	0	3	2	5	16	2	0	.125	2	5	0	0	0.3	1.000
1952		12	10	.545	3.07	46	6	3	138	116	57	91	2	**8**	**8**	10	39	5	0	.128	5	23	0	2	0.6	1.000
1953		3	9	.250	3.53	57	4	0	117.1	114	39	51	0	2	**8**	11	29	2	0	.069	3	12	0	1	0.3	1.000
1965	KC A	0	0	—	0.00	1	1	0	3	1	0	1	0	0	0	0	1	0	0	.000	0	0	0	0	0.0	.000
6 yrs.		28	31	.475	3.29	179	26	7	476	429	183	290	4	18	23	32	124	12	0	.097	17	62	0	3	0.4	1.000
WORLD SERIES																										
1948	CLE A	0	0	—	0.00	1	0	0	0.2	0	0	0	0	0	0	0	0	0	0	—	0	0	0	0	0.0	.000

Phil Paine

PAINE, PHILLIPS STEERE (Flip) BR TR 6′ 2″ 180 lbs.
B. June 8, 1930, Chepachet, R. I. D. Feb. 19, 1978, Lebanon, Pa.

Year	Team		W	L	PCT	ERA	G	GS	CG	IP	H	BB	SO	ShO	Relief Pitching W	L	SV	Batting AB	H	HR	BA	PO	A	E	DP	TC/G	FA
1951	BOS	N	2	0	1.000	3.06	21	0	0	35.1	36	20	17	0	2	0	0	4	0	0	.000	2	5	0	0	0.3	1.000
1954	MIL	N	1	0	1.000	3.86	11	0	0	14	14	12	11	0	1	0	0	0	0	0	—	0	1	1	0	0.2	.500
1955			2	0	1.000	2.49	15	0	0	25.1	20	14	26	0	2	0	0	3	1	0	.333	1	6	2	0	0.6	.778
1956			0	0	—	∞	1	0	0		3	0	0	0	0	0	0	0	0	0	—	0	0	0	0	0.0	.000
1957			0	0	—	0.00	1	0	0	2	1	3	2	0	0	0	0	0	0	0	—	0	1	0	0	1.0	1.000
1958	STL	N	5	1	.833	3.56	46	0	0	73.1	70	31	45	0	5	1	1	7	2	0	.286	6	12	1	0	0.4	.947
6 yrs.			10	1	.909	3.36	95	0	0	150	144	80	101	0	10	1	1	14	3	0	.214	9	25	4	0	0.4	.895

Lance Painter

PAINTER, LANCE TELFORD BL TL 6′ 1″ 195 lbs.
B. July 21, 1967, Bedford, England.

Year	Team		W	L	PCT	ERA	G	GS	CG	IP	H	BB	SO	ShO	Relief Pitching W	L	SV	Batting AB	H	HR	BA	PO	A	E	DP	TC/G	FA
1993	CLR	N	2	2	.500	6.00	10	6	1	39	52	9	16	0	0	0	0	10	3	0	.300	1	9	0	0	1.0	1.000
1994			4	6	.400	6.11	15	14	0	73.2	91	26	41	0	0	0	0	21	3	0	.143	5	11	0	0	1.1	1.000
1995			3	0	1.000	4.37	33	1	0	45.1	55	10	36	0	2	0	1	9	1	0	.111	3	6	0	0	0.3	1.000
3 yrs.			9	8	.529	5.58	58	21	1	158	198	45	93	0	2	0	1	40	7	0	.175	9	26	0	0	0.6	1.000
DIVISIONAL PLAYOFF SERIES																											
1995	CLR	N	0	0	—	5.40	1	1	0	5	5	2	4	0	0	0	0	2	0	0	.000	0	0	0	0	0.0	.000

Vicente Palacios

PALACIOS, VICENTE BR TR 6′ 3″ 165 lbs.
Born Vicente Palacios (Diaz).
B. July 19, 1963, Veracruz, Mexico.

Year	Team		W	L	PCT	ERA	G	GS	CG	IP	H	BB	SO	ShO	Relief Pitching W	L	SV	Batting AB	H	HR	BA	PO	A	E	DP	TC/G	FA
1987	PIT	N	2	1	.667	4.30	6	4	0	29.1	27	9	13	0	0	0	0	9	1	0	.111	2	1	0	0	0.5	1.000
1988			1	2	.333	6.66	7	3	0	24.1	28	15	15	0	0	1	0	8	0	0	.000	3	5	0	0	1.1	1.000
1990			0	0	—	0.00	7	0	0	15	4	2	8	0	0	0	3	4	0	0	.000	2	0	0	0	0.3	1.000
1991			6	3	.667	3.75	36	7	1	81.2	69	38	64	1	4	1	3	14	1	0	.071	4	9	0	0	0.4	1.000
1992			3	2	.600	4.25	20	8	0	53	56	27	33	0	2	0	0	14	1	0	.071	5	7	1	1	0.6	.923
1994	STL	N	3	8	.273	4.44	31	17	1	117.2	104	43	95	1	1	1	1	33	0	0	.000	6	16	2	0	0.8	.917
1995			2	3	.400	5.80	20	5	0	40.1	48	19	34	0	1	1	0	6	1	0	.167	3	4	0	0	0.3	1.000
7 yrs.			17	19	.472	4.36	127	44	2	361.1	336	153	262	2	8	4	7	88	4	0	.045	25	42	3	1	0.6	.957

Mike Palagyi

PALAGYI, MICHAEL RAYMOND BR TR 6′ 2″ 185 lbs.
B. July 4, 1917, Conneaut, Ohio.

Year	Team		W	L	PCT	ERA	G	GS	CG	IP	H	BB	SO	ShO	Relief Pitching W	L	SV	Batting AB	H	HR	BA	PO	A	E	DP	TC/G	FA
1939	WAS	A	0	0	—	∞	1	0	0		0	3	0	0	0	0	0	0	0	0	—	0	0	0	0	0.0	.000

Erv Palica

PALICA, ERVIN MARTIN BR TR 6′ 1½″ 180 lbs.
Born Ervin Martin Pavliecivich.
B. Feb. 9, 1928, Lomita, Calif. D. May 29, 1982, Huntington Beach, Calif.

Year	Team		W	L	PCT	ERA	G	GS	CG	IP	H	BB	SO	ShO	Relief Pitching W	L	SV	Batting AB	H	HR	BA	PO	A	E	DP	TC/G	FA
1947	BKN	N	0	1	.000	3.00	3	0	0	3	2	2	1	0	0	1	0	0	0	0	—	0	0	0	0	0.0	.000
1948			6	6	.500	4.45	41	10	3	125.1	111	58	74	0	3	3	3	39	5	0	.128	5	16	0	1	0.5	1.000
1949			8	9	.471	3.62	49	1	0	97	93	49	44	0	8	8	6	19	3	0	.158	3	18	3	2	0.5	.875
1950			13	8	.619	3.58	43	19	10	201.1	176	98	131	2	2	2	1	68	15	1	.221	8	16	3	1	0.6	.889
1951			2	6	.250	4.75	19	8	0	53	55	20	15	0	2	1	0	13	2	0	.154	5	12	0	0	0.9	1.000
1953			0	0	—	12.00	4	0	0	6	10	8	3	0	0	0	0	1	1	0	1.000	0	2	0	0	0.5	1.000
1954			3	3	.500	5.32	25	3	0	67.2	77	31	25	0	3	2	0	16	4	0	.250	1	6	1	0	0.3	.875
1955	BAL	A	5	11	.313	4.14	33	25	5	169.2	165	83	68	1	0	0	2	55	13	0	.236	15	23	4	2	1.3	.905
1956			4	11	.267	4.49	29	14	2	116.1	117	50	62	0	2	3	0	32	5	0	.156	2	20	2	2	0.8	.917
9 yrs.			41	55	.427	4.22	246	80	20	839.1	806	399	423	3	20	20	12	243	48	1	.198	39	113	13	8	0.7	.921
WORLD SERIES																											
1949	BKN	N	0	0	—	0.00	1	0	0	2	1	1	1	0	0	0	0	0	0	0	—	0	1	0	0	1.0	1.000

Donn Pall

PALL, DONN STEVEN BR TR 6′ 2″ 185 lbs.
B. Jan. 11, 1962, Chicago, Ill.

Year	Team		W	L	PCT	ERA	G	GS	CG	IP	H	BB	SO	ShO	Relief Pitching W	L	SV	Batting AB	H	HR	BA	PO	A	E	DP	TC/G	FA
1988	CHI	A	0	2	.000	3.45	17	0	0	28.2	39	8	16	0	0	2	0	0	0	0	—	4	6	0	1	0.6	1.000
1989			4	5	.444	3.31	53	0	0	87	90	19	58	0	4	5	6	0	0	0	—	5	7	2	0	0.3	.857
1990			3	5	.375	3.32	56	0	0	76	63	24	39	0	3	5	2	0	0	0	—	1	11	0	2	0.2	1.000
1991			7	2	.778	2.41	51	0	0	71	59	20	40	0	7	2	0	0	0	0	—	4	8	1	0	0.3	.923
1992			5	2	.714	4.93	39	0	0	73	79	27	27	0	5	2	1	0	0	0	—	5	6	1	2	0.3	.917
1993	2 teams	CHI A (39G 2–3)	PHI N (8G 1–0)																								
″	total		3	3	.500	3.07	47	0	0	76.1	77	14	40	0	3	3	1	0	0	0		5	13	1	0	0.4	.947
1994	2 teams	NY A (26G 1–2)	CHI N (2G 0–0)																								
″	total		1	2	.333	3.69	28	0	0	39	51	10	23	0	1	2	0	0	0	0		4	4	0	0	0.3	1.000
7 yrs.			23	21	.523	3.43	291	0	0	451	458	122	243	0	23	21	10	0	0	0		28	55	5	5	0.3	.943

Mike Palm

PALM, RICHARD PAUL BR TR 6′ 3½″ 190 lbs.
B. Feb. 13, 1925, Boston, Mass.

Year	Team		W	L	PCT	ERA	G	GS	CG	IP	H	BB	SO	ShO	Relief Pitching W	L	SV	Batting AB	H	HR	BA	PO	A	E	DP	TC/G	FA
1948	BOS	A	0	0	—	6.00	3	0	0	3	6	5	1	0	0	0	0	3	0	0	.000	0	0	0	0	0.0	.000

Palmer

PALMER
B. St. Louis, Mo. Deceased.

Year	Team		W	L	PCT	ERA	G	GS	CG	IP	H	BB	SO	ShO	Relief Pitching W	L	SV	Batting AB	H	HR	BA	PO	A	E	DP	TC/G	FA
1885	STL	N	0	4	.000	*3.44*	4	4	4	34	46	20	9	0	0	0	0	11	1	0	.091	1	2	1	0	1.0	.750

David Palmer

PALMER, DAVID WILLIAM BR TR 6′ 1″ 195 lbs.
B. Aug. 19, 1957, Glens Falls, N. Y.

Year	Team		W	L	PCT	ERA	G	GS	CG	IP	H	BB	SO	ShO	Relief Pitching W	L	SV	Batting AB	H	HR	BA	PO	A	E	DP	TC/G	FA
1978	MON	N	0	1	.000	2.70	5	1	0	10	9	2	7	0	0	0	0	1	0	0	.000	0	5	1	0	1.2	.833
1979			10	2	.833	2.63	36	11	2	123	110	30	72	1	1	0	2	31	1	0	.032	7	17	1	0	0.7	.960
1980			8	6	.571	2.98	24	19	3	130	124	30	73	1	0	0	0	45	9	0	.200	9	26	2	0	1.5	.946
1982			6	4	.600	3.18	13	13	1	73.2	60	36	46	0	0	0	0	24	1	0	.042	7	10	1	1	1.4	.944
1984			7	3	.700	3.84	20	19	1	105.1	101	44	66	1	0	1	0	33	5	1	.152	20	13	1	1	1.7	.971
1985			7	10	.412	3.71	24	23	0	135.2	128	67	106	0	0	0	0	36	4	0	.111	17	21	1	5	1.6	.974
1986	ATL	N	11	10	.524	3.65	35	35	2	209.2	181	102	170	0	0	0	0	66	12	1	.182	18	33	0	3	1.5	1.000
1987			8	11	.421	4.90	28	28	0	152.1	169	64	111	0	0	0	0	48	6	1	.125	9	25	1	2	1.3	.971

David Palmer *continued*

Year	Team	W	L	PCT	ERA	G	GS	CG	IP	H	BB	SO	ShO	Relief Pitching W	Relief Pitching L	Relief Pitching SV	Batting AB	Batting H	Batting HR	BA	PO	A	E	DP	TC/G	FA
1988	**PHI N**	7	9	.438	4.47	22	22	1	129	129	48	85	1	0	0	0	39	10	2	.256	14	12	1	2	1.2	.963
1989	**DET A**	0	3	.000	7.79	5	5	0	17.1	25	11	12	0	0	0	0	0	0	0	—	2	1	1	0	0.8	.750
10 yrs.		64	59	.520	3.78	212	176	10	1086	1036	434	748	4	1	1	2	323	48	5	.149	103	163	10	14	1.3	.964

Jim Palmer

PALMER, JAMES ALVIN
B. Oct. 15, 1945, New York, N. Y.
Hall of Fame 1990.

BR TR 6′ 3″ 190 lbs.

Year	Team	W	L	PCT	ERA	G	GS	CG	IP	H	BB	SO	ShO	Relief Pitching W	Relief Pitching L	Relief Pitching SV	Batting AB	Batting H	Batting HR	BA	PO	A	E	DP	TC/G	FA
1965	**BAL A**	5	4	.556	3.72	27	6	0	92	75	56	75	0	4	2	1	26	5	1	.192	6	17	3	1	1.0	.885
1966		15	10	.600	3.46	30	30	6	208.1	176	91	147	0	0	0	0	73	7	1	.096	14	26	1	2	1.4	.976
1967		3	1	.750	2.94	9	9	2	49	34	20	23	1	0	0	0	13	1	0	.077	2	9	0	1	1.2	1.000
1969		16	4	**.800**	2.34	26	23	11	181	131	64	123	6	2	0	0	64	13	0	.203	7	11	1	1	0.7	.947
1970		20	10	.667	2.71	39	39	17	**305**	263	100	199	**5**	0	0	0	113	17	1	.150	21	42	2	4	1.7	.969
1971		20	9	.690	2.68	37	37	20	282	231	106	184	3	0	0	0	102	20	0	.196	27	41	5	3	2.0	.932
1972		21	10	.677	2.07	36	36	18	274.1	219	70	184	3	0	0	0	98	22	0	.224	14	37	3	4	1.5	.944
1973		22	9	.710	**2.40**	38	37	19	296	225	113	158	6	0	0	1	0	0	0	—	24	35	2	3	1.6	.967
1974		7	12	.368	3.27	26	26	5	179	176	69	84	2	0	0	0	0	0	0	—	15	33	1	2	1.9	.980
1975		**23**	11	.676	**2.09**	39	38	25	323	253	80	193	**10**	0	0	1	0	0	0	—	30	52	6	7	2.3	.932
1976		**22**	13	.629	2.51	40	**40**	23	**315**	255	84	159	6	0	0	0	0	0	0	—	27	49	1	2	1.9	.987
1977		**20**	11	.645	2.91	39	**39**	**22**	**319**	263	99	193	3	0	0	0	0	0	0	—	20	48	2	5	1.8	.971
1978		21	12	.636	2.46	38	38	19	**296**	246	97	138	6	0	0	0	0	0	0	—	27	43	2	5	1.9	.972
1979		10	6	.625	3.29	23	22	7	156	144	43	67	0	0	0	0	0	0	0	—	10	23	0	1	1.4	1.000
1980		16	10	.615	3.98	34	33	4	224	238	74	109	0	0	0	0	0	0	0	—	14	37	2	6	1.6	.962
1981		7	8	.467	3.76	22	22	5	127	117	46	35	0	0	0	0	0	0	0	—	12	26	0	2	1.7	1.000
1982		15	5	**.750**	3.13	36	32	8	227	195	63	103	2	0	1	1	0	0	0	—	16	37	2	3	1.5	.964
1983		5	4	.556	4.23	14	11	0	76.2	86	19	34	0	0	0	0	0	0	0	—	5	8	1	0	1.0	.929
1984		0	3	.000	9.17	5	3	0	17.2	22	17	4	0	0	1	0	0	0	0	—	1	3	0	1	0.8	1.000
19 yrs.		268	152	.638	2.86	558	521	211	3948	3349	1311	2212	53	6	4	4	489	85	3	.174	292	577	34	53	1.6	.962
LEAGUE CHAMPIONSHIP SERIES																										
1969	**BAL A**	1	0	1.000	2.00	1	1	1	9	10	2	4	0	0	0	0	5	0	0	.000	0	1	0	0	1.0	1.000
1970		1	0	1.000	1.00	1	1	1	9	7	3	12	0	0	0	0	4	1	0	.250	1	1	0	0	2.0	1.000
1971		1	0	1.000	3.00	1	1	1	9	7	3	8	0	0	0	0	5	1	0	.200	1	0	0	0	1.0	1.000
1973		1	0	1.000	1.84	3	2	1	14.2	11	8	15	1	0	0	0	0	0	0	—	1	1	0	1	0.7	1.000
1974		0	1	.000	1.00	1	1	1	9	4	1	4	0	0	0	0	0	0	0	—	0	2	0	0	2.0	1.000
1979		0	0	—	3.00	1	1	0	9	7	2	3	0	0	0	0	0	0	0	—	1	1	0	0	2.0	1.000
6 yrs.		4	1	.800	1.96	8	7	5	59.2	46	19	46	1	0	0	0	14	2	0	.143	4	6	0	1	1.1	1.000
		3rd		**7th**	**6th**		**4th**	**1st**	**3rd**		**4th**	**1st**	**1st**													
WORLD SERIES																										
1966	**BAL A**	1	0	1.000	0.00	1	1	1	9	4	3	6	1	0	0	0	4	0	0	.000	0	2	0	0	2.0	1.000
1969		0	1	.000	6.00	1	1	0	6	5	4	5	0	0	0	0	2	0	0	.000	1	0	1	0	2.0	.500
1970		1	0	1.000	4.60	2	2	0	15.2	11	9	9	0	0	0	0	7	1	0	.143	0	0	0	0	0.0	.000
1971		1	0	1.000	2.65	2	2	0	17	15	9	15	0	0	0	0	4	0	0	.000	2	1	0	0	1.5	1.000
1979		0	1	.000	3.60	2	2	0	15	18	5	8	0	0	0	0	4	0	0	.000	2	1	0	1	1.5	1.000
1983		1	0	1.000	0.00	1	0	0	2	2	1	1	0	1	0	0	0	0	0	—	0	0	0	0	0.0	.000
6 yrs.		4	2	.667	3.20	9	8	1	64.2	55	31	44	1	1	0	0	21	1	0	.048	5	4	1	1	1.1	.900
							10th		**9th**		**4th**															

Lowell Palmer

PALMER, LOWELL RAYMOND
B. Aug. 18, 1947, Sacramento, Calif.

BR TR 6′ 1″ 190 lbs.

Year	Team	W	L	PCT	ERA	G	GS	CG	IP	H	BB	SO	ShO	Relief Pitching W	Relief Pitching L	Relief Pitching SV	Batting AB	Batting H	Batting HR	BA	PO	A	E	DP	TC/G	FA
1969	**PHI N**	2	8	.200	5.20	26	9	1	90	91	47	68	1	1	2	0	22	3	1	.136	4	13	0	1	0.7	1.000
1970		1	2	.333	5.47	38	5	0	102	98	55	85	0	1	1	0	27	4	0	.148	7	10	0	1	0.4	1.000
1971		0	0	—	6.00	3	1	0	15	13	13	6	0	0	0	0	5	1	0	.200	2	1	0	0	1.0	1.000
1972	**2 teams** **CLE A** (1G 0–0) **STL N** (16G 0–3)																									
″	**total**	0	3	.000	3.89	17	2	0	37	32	28	28	0	0	1	0	5	0	0	.000	3	4	0	0	0.4	1.000
1974	**SD N**	2	5	.286	5.67	22	8	1	73	68	59	52	0	1	2	0	23	2	0	.087	1	9	1	1	0.5	.909
5 yrs.		5	18	.217	5.28	106	25	2	317	302	202	239	1	3	6	0	82	10	1	.122	17	37	1	3	0.5	.982

Emilio Palmero

PALMERO, EMILIO ANTONIO
B. June 13, 1895, Guanabocoa, Cuba D. July 15, 1970, Toledo, Ohio.

BL TL 5′11″ 157 lbs.
BB 1915–1916

Year	Team	W	L	PCT	ERA	G	GS	CG	IP	H	BB	SO	ShO	Relief Pitching W	Relief Pitching L	Relief Pitching SV	Batting AB	Batting H	Batting HR	BA	PO	A	E	DP	TC/G	FA
1915	**NY N**	0	2	.000	3.09	3	2	1	11.2	10	9	8	0	0	0	0	4	1	0	.250	0	5	0	0	1.7	1.000
1916		0	3	.000	8.04	4	2	0	15.2	17	8	8	0	0	2	0	3	0	0	.000	0	7	0	0	1.8	1.000
1921	**STL A**	4	7	.364	5.00	24	9	4	90	109	49	26	0	2	1	0	37	8	0	.216	2	31	2	2	1.4	.943
1926	**WAS A**	2	2	.500	4.76	7	3	0	17	22	15	6	0	1	0	0	3	1	0	.333	0	4	1	0	0.7	.800
1928	**BOS N**	0	1	.000	5.40	3	1	0	6.2	14	2	0	0	0	0	0	1	0	0	.000	0	1	0	0	0.3	1.000
5 yrs.		6	15	.286	5.17	41	17	5	141	172	83	48	0	3	3	0	48	10	0	.208	2	48	3	2	1.3	.943

Ed Palmquist

PALMQUIST, EDWIN LEE
B. June 10, 1933, Los Angeles, Calif.

BR TR 6′ 3″ 195 lbs.

Year	Team	W	L	PCT	ERA	G	GS	CG	IP	H	BB	SO	ShO	Relief Pitching W	Relief Pitching L	Relief Pitching SV	Batting AB	Batting H	Batting HR	BA	PO	A	E	DP	TC/G	FA
1960	**LA N**	0	1	.000	2.54	22	0	0	39	34	16	23	0	0	1	0	7	0	0	.000	1	7	0	1	0.4	1.000
1961	**2 teams** **LA N** (5G 0–1) **MIN A** (9G 1–1)																									
″	**total**	1	2	.333	8.49	14	2	0	29.2	43	20	18	0	1	1	1	3	0	0	.000	2	6	1	1	0.6	.889
2 yrs.		1	3	.250	5.11	36	2	0	68.2	77	36	41	0	1	2	1	10	0	0	.000	3	13	1	2	0.5	.941

Jim Panther

PANTHER, JAMES EDWARD
B. Mar. 1, 1945, Burlington, Iowa.

BR TR 6′ 1″ 190 lbs.

Year	Team	W	L	PCT	ERA	G	GS	CG	IP	H	BB	SO	ShO	Relief Pitching W	Relief Pitching L	Relief Pitching SV	Batting AB	Batting H	Batting HR	BA	PO	A	E	DP	TC/G	FA
1971	**OAK A**	0	1	.000	10.50	4	0	0	6	10	5	4	0	0	1	0	1	0	0	.000	1	1	0	0	0.5	1.000
1972	**TEX A**	5	9	.357	4.12	58	4	0	94	101	46	44	0	5	5	0	8	1	0	.125	5	17	1	0	0.4	.957
1973	**ATL N**	2	3	.400	7.55	23	0	0	31	45	9	8	0	2	3	0	0	0	0	—	2	1	1	0	0.2	.750
3 yrs.		7	13	.350	5.22	85	4	0	131	156	60	56	0	7	9	0	9	1	0	.111	8	19	2	0	0.3	.931

John Papa

PAPA, JOHN PAUL BR TR 5′11″ 190 lbs.
B. Dec. 5, 1940, Bridgeport, Conn.

Year	Team	Lg	W	L	PCT	ERA	G	GS	CG	IP	H	BB	SO	ShO	Relief W	Relief L	Relief SV	AB	H	HR	BA	PO	A	E	DP	TC/G	FA
1961	BAL	A	0	0	—	18.00	2	0	0	1	2	3	3	0	0	0	0	0	0	0	—	0	0	0	0	0.0	.000
1962			0	0	—	27.00	1	0	0	1	3	1	0	0	0	0	0	0	0	0	—	0	0	0	0	0.0	.000
2 yrs.			0	0		22.50	3	0	0	2	5	4	3	0	0	0	0	0	0	0		0	0	0	0	0.0	

Al Papai

PAPAI, ALFRED THOMAS BR TR 6′ 3″ 185 lbs.
B. May 7, 1917, Divernon, Ill. D. Sept. 7, 1995, Springfield, Ill.

Year	Team	Lg	W	L	PCT	ERA	G	GS	CG	IP	H	BB	SO	ShO	Relief W	Relief L	Relief SV	AB	H	HR	BA	PO	A	E	DP	TC/G	FA
1948	STL	N	0	1	.000	5.06	10	0	0	16	14	7	8	0	0	1	0	2	0	0	.000	1	4	0	0	0.5	1.000
1949	STL	A	4	11	.267	5.06	42	15	6	142.1	175	81	31	0	2	3	2	38	3	0	.079	13	39	2	4	1.3	.963
1950	2 teams	BOS A	(16G 4–2)	STL N	(13G 1–0)																						
″	total		5	2	.714	6.33	29	3	2	69.2	82	42	26	0	4	0	2	20	3	0	.150	2	11	0	2	0.4	1.000
1955	CHI	A	0	0	—	3.86	7	0	0	11.2	10	8	5	0	0	0	0	2	0	0	.000	2	7	1	0	1.4	.900
4 yrs.			9	14	.391	5.37	88	18	8	239.2	281	138	70	0	6	4	4	62	6	0	.097	18	61	3	6	0.9	.963

Larry Pape

PAPE, LAURENCE ALBERT BR TR 5′11″ 175 lbs.
B. July 21, 1883, Norwood, Ohio D. July 21, 1918, Swissvale, Pa.

Year	Team	Lg	W	L	PCT	ERA	G	GS	CG	IP	H	BB	SO	ShO	Relief W	Relief L	Relief SV	AB	H	HR	BA	PO	A	E	DP	TC/G	FA
1909	BOS	A	2	0	1.000	2.01	11	3	2	58.1	46	12	18	1	0	0	2	21	3	0	.143	3	6	1	0	0.9	.900
1911			10	8	.556	2.45	27	19	10	176.1	167	63	49	1	1	0	0	64	13	0	.203	8	76	7	0	3.4	.923
1912			1	1	.500	4.99	13	2	1	48.2	74	16	17	0	1	0	1	17	4	0	.235	1	17	1	0	1.5	.947
3 yrs.			13	9	.591	2.80	51	24	13	283.1	287	91	84	2	2	0	3	102	20	0	.196	12	99	9	0	2.4	.925

Frank Papish

PAPISH, FRANK RICHARD (Pap) BR TL 6′ 2″ 192 lbs.
B. Oct. 21, 1917, Pueblo, Colo. D. Aug. 30, 1965, Pueblo, Colo.

Year	Team	Lg	W	L	PCT	ERA	G	GS	CG	IP	H	BB	SO	ShO	Relief W	Relief L	Relief SV	AB	H	HR	BA	PO	A	E	DP	TC/G	FA
1945	CHI	A	4	4	.500	3.74	19	5	3	84.1	75	40	45	0	4	4	1	26	6	0	.231	2	24	1	0	1.4	.963
1946			7	5	.583	2.74	31	15	6	138	122	63	66	2	0	1	0	43	8	0	.186	11	23	3	2	1.2	.919
1947			12	12	.500	3.26	38	26	6	199	185	98	79	1	2	0	3	58	5	0	.086	11	27	2	2	1.1	.950
1948			2	8	.200	5.00	32	14	2	95.1	97	75	41	0	0	1	4	27	5	0	.185	2	14	1	2	0.5	.941
1949	CLE	A	1	0	1.000	3.19	25	3	1	62	54	39	23	0	1	0	1	8	1	0	.125	1	14	0	2	0.6	1.000
1950	PIT	N	0	0	—	27.00	4	1	0	2.1	8	4	1	0	0	0	0	0	0	0	—	1	0	0	0	0.3	1.000
6 yrs.			26	29	.473	3.58	149	64	18	581	541	319	255	3	7	6	9	162	25	0	.154	28	102	7	8	0.9	.949

John Pappalau

PAPPALAU, JOHN JOSEPH BR TR 6′ 175 lbs.
B. Apr. 3, 1875, Albany, N. Y. D. May 12, 1944, Albany, N. Y.

Year	Team	Lg	W	L	PCT	ERA	G	GS	CG	IP	H	BB	SO	ShO	Relief W	Relief L	Relief SV	AB	H	HR	BA	PO	A	E	DP	TC/G	FA
1897	CLE	N	0	1	.000	10.50	2	1	1	12	22	6	3	0	0	0	0	5	0	0	.000	1	3	0	0	2.0	1.000

Milt Pappas

PAPPAS, MILTON STEPHEN (Gimpy) BR TR 6′ 3″ 190 lbs.
Born Miltiades Stergios Papastegios.
B. May 11, 1939, Detroit, Mich.

Year	Team	Lg	W	L	PCT	ERA	G	GS	CG	IP	H	BB	SO	ShO	Relief W	Relief L	Relief SV	AB	H	HR	BA	PO	A	E	DP	TC/G	FA
1957	BAL	A	0	0	—	1.00	4	0	0	9	6	3	3	0	0	0	0	1	0	0	.000	0	2	0	0	0.5	1.000
1958			10	10	.500	4.06	31	21	3	135.1	135	48	72	0	1	1	0	42	6	1	.143	9	28	2	3	1.2	.949
1959			15	9	.625	3.27	33	27	15	209.1	175	75	120	4	1	0	3	79	11	0	.139	6	36	3	2	1.4	.933
1960			15	11	.577	3.37	30	27	11	205.2	184	83	126	3	2	1	0	70	3	1	.043	8	36	1	3	1.5	.978
1961			13	9	.591	3.04	26	23	11	177.2	134	78	89	4	1	0	1	66	9	3	.136	24	34	1	2	2.3	.983
1962			12	10	.545	4.03	35	32	9	205.1	200	75	130	1	0	0	0	69	6	4	.087	20	38	3	3	1.7	.951
1963			16	9	.640	3.03	34	32	11	216.2	186	69	120	4	0	0	0	71	9	2	.127	26	41	2	4	2.0	.971
1964			16	7	.696	2.97	37	36	13	251.2	225	48	157	7	0	0	0	93	12	0	.129	25	30	0	2	1.5	1.000
1965			13	9	.591	2.60	34	34	9	221.1	192	52	127	3	0	0	0	70	5	0	.071	15	21	3	4	1.1	.923
1966	CIN	N	12	11	.522	4.29	33	32	6	209.2	224	39	133	2	0	1	0	75	8	1	.107	16	32	1	2	1.5	.980
1967			16	13	.552	3.35	34	32	5	217.2	218	38	129	3	2	0	0	72	7	1	.097	13	36	0	3	1.4	1.000
1968	2 teams	CIN N	(15G 2–5)	ATL N	(22G 10–8)																						
″	total		12	13	.480	3.47	37	30	3	184	181	32	118	1	0	1	0	53	7	1	.132	4	29	1	0	0.9	.971
1969	ATL	N	6	10	.375	3.63	26	24	1	144	149	44	72	0	0	0	0	45	7	2	.156	17	20	2	1	1.5	.949
1970	2 teams	ATL N	(11G 2–2)	CHI N	(21G 10–8)																						
″	total		12	10	.545	3.34	32	23	7	180.1	179	43	105	2	1	0	0	60	12	2	.200	12	21	1	4	1.1	.971
1971	CHI	N	17	14	.548	3.52	35	35	14	261	279	62	99	**5**	0	0	0	91	14	0	.154	19	30	0	1	1.4	1.000
1972			17	7	.708	2.77	29	28	10	195	187	29	80	3	0	0	0	68	13	1	.191	20	27	0	2	1.6	1.000
1973			7	12	.368	4.28	30	29	1	162	192	40	48	1	0	0	0	48	3	1	.063	11	25	3	2	1.3	.923
17 yrs.			209	164	.560	3.40	520	465	129	3185.2	3046	858	1728	43	8	4	4	1073	132	20	.123	245	486	23	38	1.4	.969
LEAGUE CHAMPIONSHIP SERIES																											
1969	ATL	N	0	0	—	11.57	1	0	0	2.1	4	0	4	0	0	0	0	1	0	0	.000	0	0	0	0	0.0	.000

Chan Ho Park

PARK, CHAN HO BR TR 6′ 2″ 185 lbs.
B. June 3, 1973, Kongju, South Korea.

Year	Team	Lg	W	L	PCT	ERA	G	GS	CG	IP	H	BB	SO	ShO	Relief W	Relief L	Relief SV	AB	H	HR	BA	PO	A	E	DP	TC/G	FA
1994	LA	N	0	0	—	11.25	2	0	0	4	5	5	6	0	0	0	0	0	0	0	—	0	0	0	0	0.0	.000
1995			0	0	—	4.50	2	1	0	4	2	2	7	0	0	0	0	1	0	0	.000	0	0	0	0	0.0	.000
2 yrs.			0	0		7.88	4	1	0	8	7	7	13	0	0	0	0	1	0	0	.000	0	0	0	0	0.0	

Jim Park

PARK, JAMES BR TR 6′ 2″ 175 lbs.
B. Nov. 10, 1892, Richmond, Ky. D. Dec. 17, 1970, Lexington, Ky.

Year	Team	Lg	W	L	PCT	ERA	G	GS	CG	IP	H	BB	SO	ShO	Relief W	Relief L	Relief SV	AB	H	HR	BA	PO	A	E	DP	TC/G	FA
1915	STL	A	2	0	1.000	1.19	3	3	1	22.2	18	9	5	0	0	0	0	10	4	0	.400	1	4	0	0	1.7	1.000
1916			1	4	.200	2.62	26	6	1	79	69	25	26	0	1	0	0	20	2	0	.100	3	17	3	1	0.9	.870
1917			1	1	.500	6.64	13	0	0	20.1	27	12	9	0	1	1	0	2	0	0	.000	0	7	1	0	0.6	.875
3 yrs.			4	5	.444	3.02	42	9	2	122	114	46	40	0	2	1	0	32	6	0	.188	4	28	4	1	0.9	.889

Clay Parker

PARKER, JAMES CLAYTON BR TR 6′ 1″ 185 lbs.
B. Dec. 19, 1962, Columbia, La.

Year	Team	Lg	W	L	PCT	ERA	G	GS	CG	IP	H	BB	SO	ShO	Relief W	Relief L	Relief SV	AB	H	HR	BA	PO	A	E	DP	TC/G	FA
1987	SEA	A	0	0	—	10.57	3	1	0	7.2	15	4	8	0	0	0	0	0	0	0	—	0	1	0	0	0.3	1.000
1989	NY	A	4	5	.444	3.67	22	17	2	120	123	31	53	0	0	0	0	0	0	0	—	7	20	0	1	1.2	1.000
1990	2 teams	NY A	(5G 1–1)	DET A	(24G 2–2)																						
″	total		3	3	.500	3.58	29	3	0	73	64	32	40	0	2	1	0	0	0	0		5	10	0	1	0.5	1.000
1992	SEA	A	0	2	.000	7.56	8	6	0	33.1	47	11	20	0	0	0	0	0	0	0	—	1	4	1	0	0.8	.833
4 yrs.			7	10	.412	4.42	62	27	2	234	249	78	121	0	2	1	0	0	0	0		13	35	1	2	0.8	.980

Doc Parker

PARKER, HARLEY PARK BR TR 6' 2" 200 lbs.
Brother of Jay Parker.
B. June 14, 1872, Theresa, N. Y. D. Mar. 3, 1941, Chicago, Ill.

Year	Team	W	L	PCT	ERA	G	GS	CG	IP	H	BB	SO	ShO	Relief W	Relief L	Relief SV	AB	H	HR	BA	PO	A	E	DP	TC/G	FA
1893	CHI N	0	0	—	13.50	1	0	0	2	5	1	0	0	0	0	1	1	0	0	.000	0	0	0	0	0.0	.000
1895		4	2	.667	3.68	7	6	5	51.1	65	9	9	1	0	0	0	22	7	0	.318	3	12	1	1	2.3	.938
1896		1	5	.167	6.16	9	7	7	73	100	27	15	0	0	0	0	36	10	0	.278	5	22	3	1	3.0	.900
1901	CIN N	0	1	.000	15.75	1	1	1	8	26	2	0	0	0	0	0	3	0	0	.000	1	1	0	1	2.0	1.000
4 yrs.		5	8	.385	5.90	18	14	13	134.1	196	39	24	1	0	0	1	62	17	0	.274	9	35	4	3	2.5	.917

Harry Parker

PARKER, HARRY WILLIAM BR TR 6' 3" 190 lbs.
B. Sept. 14, 1947, Highland, Ill.

Year	Team	W	L	PCT	ERA	G	GS	CG	IP	H	BB	SO	ShO	Relief W	Relief L	Relief SV	AB	H	HR	BA	PO	A	E	DP	TC/G	FA
1970	STL N	1	1	.500	3.27	7	4	0	22	24	15	9	0	1	1	0	8	2	0	.250	4	4	0	0	1.1	1.000
1971		0	0	—	7.20	4	0	0	5	6	2	2	0	0	0	0	0	0	0	—	0	0	0	0	0.0	.000
1973	NY N	8	4	.667	3.35	38	9	0	96.2	79	36	63	0	4	2	5	23	4	0	.174	4	14	0	0	0.5	1.000
1974		4	12	.250	3.92	40	16	1	131	145	46	58	0	0	2	4	36	0	0	.000	5	15	1	1	0.5	.952
1975	2 teams NY N (18G 2–3) STL N (14G 0–1)																									
"	total	2	4	.333	5.06	32	1	0	53.1	58	29	35	0	2	3	3	3	0	0	.000	0	11	0	0	0.3	1.000
1976	CLE A	0	0	—	0.00	3	0	0	7	3	0	5	0	0	0	0	0	0	0	—	1	1	0	0	0.7	1.000
6 yrs.		15	21	.417	3.86	124	30	1	315	315	128	172	0	7	8	12	70	6	0	.086	14	45	1	1	0.5	.983
LEAGUE CHAMPIONSHIP SERIES																										
1973	NY N	0	1	.000	9.00	1	0	0	1	1	0	0	0	0	1	0	0	0	0	—	0	0	0	0	0.0	.000
WORLD SERIES																										
1973	NY N	0	1	.000	0.00	3	0	0	3.1	2	2	2	0	0	1	0	0	0	0	—	0	0	0	0	0.0	.000

Jay Parker

PARKER, JAY BR TR 5'11" 185 lbs.
Brother of Doc Parker.
B. July 8, 1874, Theresa, N. Y. D. June 8, 1935, Hartford, Mich.

Year	Team	W	L	PCT	ERA	G	GS	CG	IP	H	BB	SO	ShO	Relief W	Relief L	Relief SV	AB	H	HR	BA	PO	A	E	DP	TC/G	FA
1899	PIT N	0	0	—	∞	1	1	0		0	2	0	0	0	0	0	0	0	0	—	0	0	0	0	0.0	.000

Roy Parker

PARKER, ROY WILLIAM BR TR 6' 3" 200 lbs.
B. Feb. 29, 1896, Union, Mo. D. May 17, 1954, Tulsa, Okla.

Year	Team	W	L	PCT	ERA	G	GS	CG	IP	H	BB	SO	ShO	Relief W	Relief L	Relief SV	AB	H	HR	BA	PO	A	E	DP	TC/G	FA
1919	STL N	0	0	—	31.50	2	0	0	2	6	1	0	0	0	0	0	0	0	0	—	0	1	0	0	0.5	1.000

Slicker Parks

PARKS, VERNON HENRY BR TR 5'10" 158 lbs.
B. Nov. 10, 1895, Dallas, Mich. D. Feb. 21, 1978, Royal Oak, Mich.

Year	Team	W	L	PCT	ERA	G	GS	CG	IP	H	BB	SO	ShO	Relief W	Relief L	Relief SV	AB	H	HR	BA	PO	A	E	DP	TC/G	FA
1921	DET A	3	2	.600	5.68	10	1	0	25.1	33	16	10	0	3	2	0	9	1	0	.111	0	3	0	0	0.3	1.000

Roy Parmelee

PARMELEE, LeROY EARL (Bud) BR TR 6' 1" 190 lbs.
B. Apr. 25, 1907, Lambertville, Mich. D. Aug. 31, 1981, Monroe, Mich.

Year	Team	W	L	PCT	ERA	G	GS	CG	IP	H	BB	SO	ShO	Relief W	Relief L	Relief SV	AB	H	HR	BA	PO	A	E	DP	TC/G	FA
1929	NY N	1	0	1.000	9.00	2	1	0	7	13	3	1	0	0	0	0	2	1	0	.500	0	2	0	0	1.0	1.000
1930		0	1	.000	9.43	11	1	0	21	18	26	19	0	0	0	0	4	1	0	.250	1	4	1	0	0.5	.833
1931		2	2	.500	3.68	13	5	4	58.2	47	33	30	0	0	0	0	20	4	0	.200	5	11	0	1	1.2	1.000
1932		0	3	.000	3.91	8	3	0	25.1	25	14	23	0	0	0	0	5	2	0	.400	1	6	1	0	1.0	.875
1933		13	8	.619	3.17	32	32	14	218.1	191	77	132	3	0	0	0	81	19	1	.235	8	44	4	4	1.8	.929
1934		10	6	.625	3.42	22	20	7	152.2	134	60	83	3	0	0	0	55	11	2	.200	9	39	1	1	2.2	.980
1935		14	10	.583	4.22	34	31	13	226	214	**97**	79	1	1	0	0	86	18	0	.209	16	55	5	2	2.2	.934
1936	STL N	11	11	.500	4.56	37	28	9	221	226	107	79	0	0	1	2	76	15	0	.197	16	42	2	1	1.6	.967
1937	CHI N	7	8	.467	5.13	33	18	8	145.2	165	79	55	0	0	1	0	52	9	2	.173	13	33	2	2	1.5	.958
1939	PHI A	1	6	.143	6.45	14	5	0	44.2	42	35	13	0	1	2	1	15	2	0	.133	2	10	1	0	0.9	.923
10 yrs.		59	55	.518	4.27	206	144	55	1120.1	1075	531	514	6	2	4	3	396	82	5	.207	71	246	17	11	1.6	.949

Mel Parnell

PARNELL, MELVIN LLOYD (Dusty) BL TL 6' 180 lbs.
B. June 13, 1922, New Orleans, La.

Year	Team	W	L	PCT	ERA	G	GS	CG	IP	H	BB	SO	ShO	Relief W	Relief L	Relief SV	AB	H	HR	BA	PO	A	E	DP	TC/G	FA
1947	BOS A	2	3	.400	6.39	15	5	1	50.2	60	27	23	0	1	1	0	18	1	0	.056	0	7	1	0	0.5	.875
1948		15	8	.652	3.14	35	27	16	212	205	90	77	1	0	2	0	80	13	0	.163	9	48	1	3	1.7	.983
1949		**25**	7	.781	**2.77**	39	33	**27**	**295.1**	258	134	122	4	1	1	2	114	29	0	.254	8	53	0	5	1.6	1.000
1950		18	10	.643	3.61	40	31	21	249	244	106	93	2	0	1	3	98	19	0	.194	7	67	1	6	1.9	.987
1951		18	11	.621	3.26	36	29	11	221	229	77	77	3	2	0	2	81	25	0	.309	8	42	3	2	1.5	.943
1952		12	12	.500	3.62	33	29	15	214	207	89	107	3	0	0	2	84	8	1	.095	15	38	0	4	1.6	1.000
1953		21	8	.724	3.06	38	34	12	241	217	**116**	136	5	1	0	0	94	21	0	.223	10	27	2	4	1.0	.949
1954		3	7	.300	3.70	19	15	4	92.1	104	35	38	1	0	0	0	34	3	0	.088	3	17	1	1	1.1	.952
1955		2	3	.400	7.83	13	9	0	46	62	25	18	0	0	0	1	19	6	0	.316	2	9	1	0	0.9	.917
1956		7	6	.538	3.77	21	20	6	131.1	129	59	41	1	0	1	0	46	7	0	.152	7	19	2	2	1.3	.929
10 yrs.		123	75	.621	3.50	289	232	113	1752.2	1715	758	732	20	5	6	10	668	132	1	.198	69	327	12	27	1.4	.971

Rube Parnham

PARNHAM, JAMES ARTHUR BR TR 6' 3" 185 lbs.
B. Feb. 1, 1894, Heidelberg, Pa. D. Nov. 25, 1963, McKeesport, Pa.

Year	Team	W	L	PCT	ERA	G	GS	CG	IP	H	BB	SO	ShO	Relief W	Relief L	Relief SV	AB	H	HR	BA	PO	A	E	DP	TC/G	FA
1916	PHI A	2	1	.667	0.36	4	3	2	24.2	27	13	8	0	0	0	0	11	3	0	.273	1	12	0	0	3.3	1.000
1917		0	1	.000	4.09	2	2	0	11	12	9	4	0	0	0	0	3	0	0	.000	1	3	0	0	2.0	1.000
2 yrs.		2	2	.500	1.51	6	5	2	35.2	39	22	12	0	0	0	0	14	3	0	.214	2	15	0	0	2.8	1.000

Jose Parra

PARRA, JOSE MIGUEL BR TR 5'11" 160 lbs.
B. Nov. 28, 1972, Jacaqua Santiago, Dominican Republic.

Year	Team	W	L	PCT	ERA	G	GS	CG	IP	H	BB	SO	ShO	Relief W	Relief L	Relief SV	AB	H	HR	BA	PO	A	E	DP	TC/G	FA
1995	2 teams LA N (8G 0–0) MIN A (12G 1–5)																									
"	total	1	5	.167	7.13	20	12	0	72	93	28	36	0	0	0	0	0	0	0	—	4	9	2	1	0.8	.867

Jeff Parrett

PARRETT, JEFFREY DALE BR TR 6' 4" 185 lbs.
B. Aug. 26, 1961, Indianapolis, Ind.

Year	Team	W	L	PCT	ERA	G	GS	CG	IP	H	BB	SO	ShO	Relief W	Relief L	Relief SV	AB	H	HR	BA	PO	A	E	DP	TC/G	FA
1986	MON N	0	1	.000	4.87	12	0	0	20.1	19	13	21	0	0	1	0	2	1	0	.500	1	2	0	1	0.3	1.000
1987		7	6	.538	4.21	45	0	0	62	53	30	56	0	7	6	6	5	0	0	.000	3	9	2	1	0.3	.857
1988		12	4	.750	2.65	61	0	0	91.2	66	45	62	0	**12**	4	6	0	0	0	—	7	9	1	0	0.3	.941
1989	PHI N	12	6	.667	2.98	72	0	0	105.2	90	44	98	0	**12**	6	6	5	0	0	.000	2	9	0	0	0.2	1.000
1990	2 teams PHI N (47G 4–9) ATL N (20G 1–1)																									
"	total	5	10	.333	4.64	67	5	0	108.2	119	55	86	0	4	7	2	11	1	0	.091	1	18	4	1	0.3	.826

Jeff Parrett *continued*

Year	Team	Lg	W	L	PCT	ERA	G	GS	CG	IP	H	BB	SO	ShO	Relief W	Relief L	Relief SV	Batting AB	Batting H	HR	BA	PO	A	E	DP	TC/G	FA
1991	ATL	N	1	2	.333	6.33	18	0	0	21.1	31	12	14	0	1	2	1	0	0	0	—	3	5	1	1	0.5	.889
1992	OAK	A	9	1	.900	3.02	66	0	0	98.1	81	42	78	0	9	1	0	0	0	0	—	5	7	1	2	0.2	.923
1993	CLR	N	3	3	.500	5.38	40	6	0	73.2	78	45	66	0	1	2	1	11	1	0	.091	3	9	1	0	0.3	.923
1995	STL	N	4	7	.364	3.64	59	0	0	76.2	71	28	71	0	4	7	0	2	1	0	.500	7	6	2	0	0.3	.867
9 yrs.			53	40	.570	3.84	440	11	0	658.1	608	314	552	0	50	36	22	36	4	0	.111	32	74	12	6	0.3	.898
LEAGUE CHAMPIONSHIP SERIES																											
1992	OAK	A	0	0	—	11.57	3	0	0	2.1	6	0	1	0	0	0	0	0	0	0	—	0	1	0	0	0.3	1.000

Steve Parris

PARRIS, STEVEN MICHAEL
B. Dec. 17, 1967, Joliet, Ill.
BR TR 6′ 190 lbs.

Year	Team	Lg	W	L	PCT	ERA	G	GS	CG	IP	H	BB	SO	ShO	Relief W	Relief L	Relief SV	Batting AB	Batting H	HR	BA	PO	A	E	DP	TC/G	FA
1995	PIT	N	6	6	.500	5.38	15	15	1	82	89	33	61	1	0	0	0	28	7	0	.250	4	10	0	0	0.9	1.000

Mike Parrott

PARROTT, MICHAEL EVERETT
B. Dec. 6, 1954, Oxnard, Calif.
BR TR 6′ 4″ 210 lbs.

Year	Team	Lg	W	L	PCT	ERA	G	GS	CG	IP	H	BB	SO	ShO	Relief W	Relief L	Relief SV	Batting AB	Batting H	HR	BA	PO	A	E	DP	TC/G	FA
1977	BAL	A	0	0	—	2.25	3	0	0	4	4	2	2	0	0	0	0	0	0	0	—	1	0	0	0	0.3	1.000
1978	SEA	A	1	5	.167	5.14	27	10	0	82.1	108	32	41	0	0	1	1	0	0	0	—	7	11	1	1	0.7	.947
1979			14	12	.538	3.77	38	30	13	229	231	86	127	2	1	0	0	0	0	0	—	27	39	0	1	1.7	1.000
1980			1	16	.059	7.28	27	16	1	94	136	42	53	0	0	2	3	0	0	0	—	11	28	2	2	1.5	.951
1981			3	6	.333	5.08	24	12	0	85	102	28	43	0	0	0	1	0	0	0	—	6	15	0	0	0.9	1.000
5 yrs.			19	39	.328	4.88	119	68	14	494.1	581	190	266	2	1	3	5	0	0	0		52	93	3	4	1.2	.980

Tom Parrott

PARROTT, THOMAS WILLIAM (Tacky Tom)
Brother of Jiggs Parrott.
B. Apr. 10, 1868, Portland, Ore. D. Jan. 1, 1932, Dundee, Ore.
BR TR 5′10½″ 170 lbs.

Year	Team	Lg	W	L	PCT	ERA	G	GS	CG	IP	H	BB	SO	ShO	Relief W	Relief L	Relief SV	Batting AB	Batting H	HR	BA	PO	A	E	DP	TC/G	FA
1893	2 teams	CHI N (4G 0–3) CIN N (22G 10–7)																									
″	total		10	10	.500	4.48	26	20	13	181	209	87	40	1	3	0	0	95	20	1	.211	20	47	6	1	2.4	.918
1894	CIN	N	17	19	.472	5.60	41	36	31	308.2	402	126	61	1	0	1	1	229	74	4	.323	143	87	22	10	3.7	.913
1895			11	18	.379	5.47	41	31	23	263.1	382	76	57	0	3	1	**3**	201	69	3	.343	151	70	13	12	3.7	.944
1896	STL	N	1	1	.500	6.21	7	2	2	42	62	18	8	0	0	0	0	474	138	7	.291	334	27	18	7	3.1	.953
4 yrs.			39	48	.448	5.33	115	89	69	795	1055	307	166	2	6	2	4	*				648	231	59	30	3.3	.937

Jiggs Parson

PARSON, WILLIAM EDWIN
B. Dec. 28, 1885, Parker, S. D. D. May 19, 1967, Los Angeles, Calif.
BR TR 6′ 2″ 180 lbs.

Year	Team	Lg	W	L	PCT	ERA	G	GS	CG	IP	H	BB	SO	ShO	Relief W	Relief L	Relief SV	Batting AB	Batting H	HR	BA	PO	A	E	DP	TC/G	FA
1910	BOS	N	0	2	.000	3.82	10	4	0	35.1	35	26	7	0	0	1	0	12	1	0	.083	0	11	1	0	1.2	.917
1911			0	1	.000	6.48	7	0	0	25	36	15	7	0	0	1	0	10	2	0	.200	0	5	1	0	0.9	.833
2 yrs.			0	3	.000	4.92	17	4	0	60.1	71	41	14	0	0	2	0	22	3	0	.136	0	16	2	0	1.1	.889

Bill Parsons

PARSONS, WILLIAM RAYMOND
B. Aug. 17, 1948, Riverside, Calif.
BR TR 6′ 6″ 195 lbs.

Year	Team	Lg	W	L	PCT	ERA	G	GS	CG	IP	H	BB	SO	ShO	Relief W	Relief L	Relief SV	Batting AB	Batting H	HR	BA	PO	A	E	DP	TC/G	FA
1971	MIL	A	13	17	.433	3.20	36	35	12	245	219	93	139	4	0	0	0	72	12	1	.167	22	35	0	4	1.6	1.000
1972			13	13	.500	3.91	33	30	10	214	194	68	111	2	0	0	0	67	11	0	.164	8	22	0	1	0.9	1.000
1973			3	6	.333	6.79	20	17	0	59.2	59	67	30	0	0	0	0	0	0	0	—	2	9	1	0	0.6	.917
1974	OAK	A	0	0	—	0.00	4	0	0	2	1	3	2	0	0	0	0	0	0	0	—	0	0	0	0	0.0	.000
4 yrs.			29	36	.446	3.89	93	82	22	520.2	473	231	282	6	0	0	0	139	23	1	.165	32	66	1	5	1.1	.990

Charlie Parsons

PARSONS, CHARLES JAMES
B. July 18, 1863, Cherry Flats, Pa. D. Mar. 24, 1936, Mansfield, Pa.
BL TL 5′10″ 160 lbs.

Year	Team	Lg	W	L	PCT	ERA	G	GS	CG	IP	H	BB	SO	ShO	Relief W	Relief L	Relief SV	Batting AB	Batting H	HR	BA	PO	A	E	DP	TC/G	FA
1886	BOS	N	0	2	.000	3.94	2	2	2	16	20	4	5	0	0	0	0	8	3	0	.375	0	1	0	0	0.5	1.000
1887	NY	AA	1	1	.500	*4.50*	4	4	4	34	51	6	5	0	0	0	0	15	3	0	.200	1	8	2	0	2.8	.818
1890	CLE	N	0	1	.000	6.00	2	1	0	9	12	6	2	0	0	0	0	4	3	0	.750	0	2	3	0	2.5	.400
3 yrs.			1	4	.200	4.58	8	7	6	59	83	16	12	0	0	0	0	27	9	0	.333	1	11	5	0	2.1	.706

Tom Parsons

PARSONS, THOMAS ANTHONY (Long Tom)
B. Sept. 13, 1939, Lakeville, Conn.
BR TR 6′ 7″ 210 lbs.

Year	Team	Lg	W	L	PCT	ERA	G	GS	CG	IP	H	BB	SO	ShO	Relief W	Relief L	Relief SV	Batting AB	Batting H	HR	BA	PO	A	E	DP	TC/G	FA
1963	PIT	N	0	1	.000	8.31	1	1	0	4.1	7	2	2	0	0	0	0	2	0	0	.000	0	1	0	0	1.0	1.000
1964	NY	N	1	2	.333	4.19	4	2	1	19.1	20	6	10	0	1	0	0	7	0	0	.000	0	2	0	0	0.5	1.000
1965			1	10	.091	4.67	35	11	1	90.2	108	17	58	1	0	3	1	18	1	0	.056	4	22	0	1	0.7	1.000
3 yrs.			2	13	.133	4.72	40	14	2	114.1	135	25	70	1	1	3	1	27	1	0	.037	4	25	0	1	0.7	1.000

Stan Partenheimer

PARTENHEIMER, STANWOOD WENDELL (Party)
Son of Steve Partenheimer.
B. Oct. 21, 1922, Chicopee Falls, Mass. D. Jan. 28, 1989, Wilson, N. C.
BR TL 5′11″ 175 lbs.
BL 1944

Year	Team	Lg	W	L	PCT	ERA	G	GS	CG	IP	H	BB	SO	ShO	Relief W	Relief L	Relief SV	Batting AB	Batting H	HR	BA	PO	A	E	DP	TC/G	FA
1944	BOS	A	0	0	—	18.00	1	1	0	1	3	2	0	0	0	0	0	1	0	0	.000	0	0	0	0	0.0	.000
1945	STL	N	0	0	—	6.08	8	2	0	13.1	12	16	6	0	0	0	0	3	0	0	.000	0	4	0	0	0.5	1.000
2 yrs.			0	0		6.91	9	3	0	14.1	15	18	6	0	0	0	0	4	0	0	.000	0	4	0	0	0.4	1.000

Bill Paschall

PASCHALL, WILLIAM HERBERT
B. Apr. 22, 1954, Norfolk, Va.
BR TR 6′ 175 lbs.

Year	Team	Lg	W	L	PCT	ERA	G	GS	CG	IP	H	BB	SO	ShO	Relief W	Relief L	Relief SV	Batting AB	Batting H	HR	BA	PO	A	E	DP	TC/G	FA
1978	KC	A	0	1	.000	3.38	2	0	0	8	6	0	5	0	0	1	1	0	0	0	—	0	0	0	0	0.0	.000
1979			0	1	.000	6.43	7	0	0	14	18	5	3	0	0	1	0	0	0	0	—	0	2	0	0	0.3	1.000
1981			0	0	—	4.50	2	0	0	2	2	0	1	0	0	0	0	0	0	0	—	0	0	0	0	0.0	.000
3 yrs.			0	2	.000	5.25	11	0	0	24	26	5	9	0	0	2	1	0	0	0		0	2	0	0	0.2	1.000

Camilo Pascual

PASCUAL, CAMILO ALBERTO (Little Patato)
Born Camilo Alberto Pascual (Lus).
Brother of Carlos Pascual.
B. Jan. 20, 1934, Havana, Cuba.
BR TR 5′11″ 175 lbs.

Year	Team	Lg	W	L	PCT	ERA	G	GS	CG	IP	H	BB	SO	ShO	Relief W	Relief L	Relief SV	Batting AB	Batting H	HR	BA	PO	A	E	DP	TC/G	FA
1954	WAS	A	4	7	.364	4.22	48	4	1	119.1	126	61	60	0	4	4	3	30	4	0	.133	6	34	0	2	0.8	1.000
1955			2	12	.143	6.14	43	16	1	129	158	70	82	0	0	4	3	32	7	0	.219	8	31	2	1	1.0	.951
1956			6	18	.250	5.87	39	27	6	188.2	194	89	162	0	1	1	2	58	8	0	.138	8	31	2	2	1.1	.951
1957			8	17	.320	4.10	29	26	8	175.2	168	76	113	2	0	3	0	50	7	0	.140	7	37	1	1	1.6	.978
1958			8	12	.400	3.15	31	27	6	177.1	166	60	146	2	0	0	0	57	9	0	.158	12	27	3	2	1.4	.929
1959			17	10	.630	2.64	32	30	**17**	238.2	202	69	185	**6**	0	0	0	86	26	0	.302	18	55	0	4	2.3	1.000
1960			12	8	.600	3.03	26	22	8	151.2	139	53	143	3	0	1	2	51	9	1	.176	6	21	0	1	1.0	1.000

Camilo Pascual *continued*

Year	Team	W	L	PCT	ERA	G	GS	CG	IP	H	BB	SO	ShO	Relief W	Relief L	Relief SV	Batting AB	Batting H	HR	BA	PO	A	E	DP	TC/G	FA
1961	MIN A	15	16	.484	3.46	35	33	15	252.1	205	100	**221**	**8**	0	1	0	85	14	0	.165	14	40	1	0	1.6	.982
1962		20	11	.645	3.32	34	33	**18**	257.2	236	59	**206**	**5**	0	0	0	97	26	2	.268	28	32	1	4	1.8	.984
1963		21	9	.700	2.46	31	31	**18**	248.1	205	81	**202**	3	0	0	0	92	23	0	.250	20	29	2	2	1.6	.961
1964		15	12	.556	3.30	36	36	14	267.1	245	98	213	1	0	0	0	94	17	0	.181	19	38	4	2	1.7	.934
1965		9	3	.750	3.35	27	27	5	156	126	63	96	1	0	0	0	60	12	2	.200	14	32	1	1	1.7	.979
1966		8	6	.571	4.89	21	19	2	103	113	30	56	0	0	0	0	37	8	0	.216	11	25	0	1	1.7	1.000
1967	WAS A	12	10	.545	3.28	28	27	5	164.2	147	43	106	1	0	0	0	51	9	0	.176	10	25	1	1	1.3	.972
1968		13	12	.520	2.69	31	31	8	201	181	59	111	4	0	0	0	65	12	0	.185	19	35	0	0	1.7	1.000
1969	2 teams WAS A (14G 2–5) CIN N (5G 0–0)																									
"	total	2	5	.286	7.07	19	14	0	62.1	63	42	37	0	0	0	0	17	4	0	.235	5	7	0	0	0.6	1.000
1970	LA N	0	0	—	2.57	10	0	0	14	12	5	8	0	0	0	0	0	0	0	—	1	3	0	1	0.4	1.000
1971	CLE A	2	2	.500	3.13	9	1	0	23	17	11	20	0	2	1	0	5	3	0	.600	4	5	2	1	1.2	.818
18 yrs.		174	170	.506	3.63	529	404	132	2930	2703	1069	2167	36	7	15	10	967	198	5	.205	210	507	20	26	1.4	.973
WORLD SERIES																										
1965	MIN A	0	1	.000	5.40	1	1	0	5	8	1	0	0	0	0	0	1	0	0	.000	0	1	0	0	1.0	1.000

Carlos Pascual

PASCUAL, CARLOS ALBERTO (Patato) BR TR 5′ 6″ 165 lbs.
Born Carlos Alberto Pascual (Lus).
Brother of Camilo Pascual.
B. Mar. 13, 1931, Havana, Cuba.

Year	Team	W	L	PCT	ERA	G	GS	CG	IP	H	BB	SO	ShO	Relief W	Relief L	Relief SV	Batting AB	Batting H	HR	BA	PO	A	E	DP	TC/G	FA
1950	WAS A	1	1	.500	2.12	2	2	2	17	12	8	3	0	0	0	0	4	1	0	.250	0	1	1	0	1.0	.500

Larry Pashnick

PASHNICK, LARRY JOHN BR TR 6′ 3″ 205 lbs.
B. Apr. 25, 1956, Lincoln Park, Mich.

Year	Team	W	L	PCT	ERA	G	GS	CG	IP	H	BB	SO	ShO	Relief W	Relief L	Relief SV	Batting AB	Batting H	HR	BA	PO	A	E	DP	TC/G	FA
1982	DET A	4	4	.500	4.01	28	13	1	94.1	110	25	19	0	1	0	0	0	0	0	—	6	12	0	1	0.6	1.000
1983		1	3	.250	5.26	12	6	0	37.2	48	18	17	0	1	0	0	0	0	0	—	6	6	0	0	1.0	1.000
1984	MIN A	2	1	.667	3.52	13	1	0	38.1	38	11	10	0	2	0	0	0	0	0	—	3	6	0	0	0.7	1.000
3 yrs.		7	8	.467	4.17	53	20	1	170.1	196	54	46	0	4	0	0	0	0	0	—	15	24	0	1	0.7	1.000

Claude Passeau

PASSEAU, CLAUDE WILLIAM BR TR 6′ 3″ 198 lbs.
B. Apr. 9, 1909, Waynesboro, Miss.

Year	Team	W	L	PCT	ERA	G	GS	CG	IP	H	BB	SO	ShO	Relief W	Relief L	Relief SV	Batting AB	Batting H	HR	BA	PO	A	E	DP	TC/G	FA
1935	PIT N	0	1	.000	12.00	1	1	0	3	7	2	1	0	0	0	0	1	0	0	.000	0	2	0	1	2.0	1.000
1936	PHI N	11	15	.423	3.48	49	21	8	217.1	247	55	85	2	3	**7**	3	78	22	2	.282	7	49	2	4	1.2	.966
1937		14	18	.438	4.34	50	**34**	18	**292.1**	**348**	79	135	1	2	1	2	107	21	1	.196	14	60	1	3	1.5	.987
1938		11	18	.379	4.52	44	33	15	239	281	93	100	0	0	0	1	80	13	0	.163	14	60	4	4	1.8	.949
1939	2 teams PHI N (8G 2–4) CHI N (34G 13–9)																									
"	total	15	13	.536	3.28	42	35	17	274.1	269	73	**137**	2	1	2	3	97	16	1	.165	11	58	0	2	1.6	1.000
1940	CHI N	20	13	.606	2.50	46	31	20	280.2	259	59	124	4	4	1	5	98	20	1	.204	17	62	7	0	1.9	.919
1941		14	14	.500	3.35	34	30	20	231	262	52	80	3	1	1	0	86	19	3	.221	6	45	1	4	1.5	.981
1942		19	14	.576	2.68	35	34	24	278.1	**284**	74	89	3	0	0	0	105	19	2	.181	12	61	0	9	2.1	1.000
1943		15	12	.556	2.91	35	31	18	257	245	66	93	2	0	1	1	96	19	0	.198	13	55	0	5	1.9	1.000
1944		15	9	.625	2.89	34	27	18	227	234	50	89	2	0	0	3	80	13	0	.163	12	42	0	5	1.6	1.000
1945		17	9	.654	2.46	34	27	19	227	205	59	98	**5**	1	0	1	91	17	2	.187	17	52	0	3	2.0	1.000
1946		9	8	.529	3.13	21	21	10	129.1	118	42	47	2	0	0	0	49	10	3	.204	6	30	1	3	1.8	.973
1947		2	6	.250	6.25	19	6	1	63.1	97	24	26	1	1	1	2	14	0	0	.000	1	7	1	1	0.5	.889
13 yrs.		162	150	.519	3.32	444	331	188	2719.2	2856	728	1104	27	13	14	21	982	189	15	.192	130	583	17	44	1.6	.977
WORLD SERIES																										
1945	CHI N	1	0	1.000	2.70	3	2	1	16.2	7	8	3	1	0	0	0	7	0	0	.000	1	3	0	0	1.3	1.000

Frank Pastore

PASTORE, FRANK ENRICO BR TR 6′ 2″ 188 lbs.
B. Aug. 21, 1957, Alhambra, Calif.

Year	Team	W	L	PCT	ERA	G	GS	CG	IP	H	BB	SO	ShO	Relief W	Relief L	Relief SV	Batting AB	Batting H	HR	BA	PO	A	E	DP	TC/G	FA
1979	CIN N	6	7	.462	4.26	30	9	2	95	102	23	63	1	2	3	4	25	4	0	.160	5	13	0	2	0.6	1.000
1980		13	7	.650	3.26	27	27	9	185	161	42	110	2	0	0	0	64	10	0	.156	10	25	3	1	1.4	.921
1981		4	9	.308	4.02	22	22	2	132	125	35	81	1	0	0	0	44	5	0	.114	5	13	0	0	0.8	1.000
1982		8	13	.381	3.97	31	29	3	188.1	210	57	94	2	0	0	0	58	10	1	.172	6	24	1	2	1.0	.968
1983		9	12	.429	4.88	36	29	4	184.1	207	64	93	1	0	0	0	59	11	1	.186	15	19	0	3	0.9	1.000
1984		3	8	.273	6.50	24	16	1	98.1	110	40	53	0	1	0	0	28	2	0	.071	6	16	1	2	1.0	.957
1985		2	1	.667	3.83	17	6	1	54	60	16	29	0	1	0	0	14	2	0	.143	3	9	1	1	0.8	.923
1986	MIN A	3	1	.750	4.01	33	1	0	49.1	54	24	18	0	3	1	2	0	0	0	—	1	5	0	0	0.2	1.000
8 yrs.		48	58	.453	4.29	220	139	22	986.1	1029	301	541	7	7	4	6	292	44	2	.151	51	124	6	11	0.8	.967
LEAGUE CHAMPIONSHIP SERIES																										
1979	CIN N	0	0	—	2.57	1	1	0	7	7	3	1	0	0	0	0	0	0	0	—	0	0	0	0	0.0	.000

Jim Pastorius

PASTORIUS, JAMES W. BL TL 5′ 9″ 165 lbs.
B. July 12, 1881, Pittsburgh, Pa. D. May 10, 1941, Pittsburgh, Pa.

Year	Team	W	L	PCT	ERA	G	GS	CG	IP	H	BB	SO	ShO	Relief W	Relief L	Relief SV	Batting AB	Batting H	HR	BA	PO	A	E	DP	TC/G	FA
1906	BKN N	10	14	.417	3.61	29	24	16	211.2	225	69	58	3	1	2	0	71	10	0	.141	11	56	3	4	2.4	.957
1907		16	12	.571	2.35	28	26	20	222	218	77	70	4	2	0	0	73	15	0	.205	7	60	2	4	2.5	.971
1908		4	20	.167	2.44	28	25	16	213.2	171	74	54	2	0	1	0	62	8	0	.129	6	66	2	1	2.6	.973
1909		1	9	.100	5.76	12	9	5	79.2	91	58	23	1	0	1	0	25	2	0	.080	4	26	3	1	2.8	.909
4 yrs.		31	55	.360	3.12	97	84	57	727	705	278	205	10	3	4	0	231	35	0	.152	28	208	10	10	2.5	.959

Joe Pate

PATE, JOSEPH WILLIAM BL TL 5′10″ 184 lbs.
B. June 6, 1892, Alice, Tex. D. Dec. 26, 1948, Fort Worth, Tex.

Year	Team	W	L	PCT	ERA	G	GS	CG	IP	H	BB	SO	ShO	Relief W	Relief L	Relief SV	Batting AB	Batting H	HR	BA	PO	A	E	DP	TC/G	FA
1926	PHI A	9	0	1.000	2.71	47	2	0	113	109	51	24	0	9	0	6	27	4	0	.148	4	46	0	2	1.1	1.000
1927		0	3	.000	5.20	32	0	0	53.2	67	21	14	0	0	3	6	10	3	0	.300	1	16	2	0	0.6	.895
2 yrs.		9	3	.750	3.51	79	2	0	166.2	176	72	38	0	9	3	12	37	7	0	.189	5	62	2	2	0.9	.971

Casey Patten

PATTEN, CASE LYMAN (Pat) BB TL 6′ 175 lbs.
B. May 7, 1876, Westport, N. Y. D. May 31, 1935, Rochester, N. Y.

Year	Team	W	L	PCT	ERA	G	GS	CG	IP	H	BB	SO	ShO	Relief W	Relief L	Relief SV	Batting AB	Batting H	HR	BA	PO	A	E	DP	TC/G	FA
1901	WAS A	18	10	.643	3.93	32	30	26	254.1	285	74	109	4	0	1	0	96	13	1	.135	21	60	4	2	2.7	.953
1902		17	16	.515	4.05	36	34	33	299.2	331	89	92	1	0	0	1	125	12	0	.096	22	82	10	1	2.9	.912
1903		11	22	.333	3.60	36	34	32	300	313	80	133	0	0	0	1	106	14	0	.132	16	91	7	1	3.2	.939

Casey Patten *continued*

Year	Team	Lg	W	L	PCT	ERA	G	GS	CG	IP	H	BB	SO	ShO	Relief Pitching W	Relief Pitching L	Relief Pitching SV	Batting AB	Batting H	Batting HR	BA	PO	A	E	DP	TC/G	FA
1904			14	23	.378	3.07	45	39	37	357.2	**367**	79	150	2	0	**2**	**3**	126	16	0	.127	32	111	7	5	3.3	.953
1905			14	22	.389	3.14	42	37	29	309.2	300	86	113	2	1	**3**	0	106	16	0	.151	28	81	9	3	2.8	.924
1906			19	16	.543	2.17	38	32	28	282.2	253	79	96	7	1	**2**	0	94	11	1	.117	18	80	4	2	2.7	.961
1907			12	16	.429	3.56	36	29	20	237.1	272	63	58	1	0	1	0	87	11	0	.126	12	58	12	1	2.3	.854
1908	**2 teams**	**WAS A** (4G 0–2) **BOS A** (1G 0–1)																									
"	**total**		0	3	.000	5.14	5	4	1	21	33	7	6	0	0	0	0	6	1	0	.167	0	5	1	1	1.2	.833
8 yrs.			105	128	.451	3.36	270	239	206	2062.1	2154	557	757	17	2	9	5	746	94	2	.126	149	568	54	16	2.8	.930

Bob Patterson

PATTERSON, ROBERT CHANDLER BR TR 6′ 2″ 185 lbs.
B. May 16, 1959, Jacksonville, Fla.

Year	Team	Lg	W	L	PCT	ERA	G	GS	CG	IP	H	BB	SO	ShO	Relief W	Relief L	Relief SV	AB	H	HR	BA	PO	A	E	DP	TC/G	FA
1985	**SD**	**N**	0	0	—	24.75	3	0	0	4	13	3	1	0	0	0	0	0	0	0	—	0	0	0	0	0.0	.000
1986	**PIT**	**N**	2	3	.400	4.95	11	5	0	36.1	49	5	20	0	1	2	0	8	1	0	.125	1	9	0	1	0.9	1.000
1987			1	4	.200	6.70	15	7	0	43	49	22	27	0	0	0	0	12	1	0	.083	0	7	0	0	0.5	1.000
1989			4	3	.571	4.05	12	3	0	26.2	23	8	20	0	3	1	1	3	0	0	.000	1	2	0	0	0.3	1.000
1990			8	5	.615	2.95	55	5	0	94.2	88	21	70	0	6	3	5	19	1	0	.053	9	10	0	0	0.3	1.000
1991			4	3	.571	4.11	54	1	0	65.2	67	15	57	0	4	3	2	4	1	0	.250	4	9	0	1	0.2	1.000
1992			6	3	.667	2.92	60	0	0	64.2	59	23	43	0	6	3	9	6	2	0	.333	3	7	0	1	0.2	1.000
1993	**TEX**	**A**	2	4	.333	4.78	52	0	0	52.2	59	11	46	0	2	4	1	0	0	0	—	3	7	0	0	0.2	1.000
1994	**CAL**	**A**	2	3	.400	4.07	47	0	0	42	35	15	30	0	2	3	1	0	0	0	—	2	1	0	0	0.1	1.000
1995			5	2	.714	3.04	62	0	0	53.1	48	13	41	0	5	2	0	0	0	0	—	0	5	0	0	0.1	1.000
10 yrs.			34	30	.531	4.14	371	21	0	483	490	136	355	0	29	21	19	52	6	0	.115	23	57	0	3	0.2	1.000
LEAGUE CHAMPIONSHIP SERIES																											
1990	**PIT**	**N**	0	0	—	0.00	2	0	0	1	1	2	0	0	0	0	1	0	0	0	—	0	1	0	0	0.5	1.000
1991			0	0	—	0.00	1	0	0	2	1	0	3	0	0	0	0	0	0	0	—	0	0	0	0	0.0	.000
1992			0	0	—	5.40	2	0	0	1.2	3	1	1	0	0	0	0	0	0	0	—	0	0	0	0	0.0	.000
3 yrs.			0	0		1.93	5	0	0	4.2	5	3	4	0	0	0	1	0	0	0		0	1	0	0	0.2	1.000

Daryl Patterson

PATTERSON, DARYL ALAN BL TR 6′ 4″ 192 lbs.
B. Nov. 21, 1943, Coalinga, Calif.

Year	Team	Lg	W	L	PCT	ERA	G	GS	CG	IP	H	BB	SO	ShO	Relief W	Relief L	Relief SV	AB	H	HR	BA	PO	A	E	DP	TC/G	FA
1968	**DET**	**A**	2	3	.400	2.12	38	1	0	68	53	27	49	0	2	3	7	13	0	0	.000	4	9	1	0	0.4	.929
1969			0	2	.000	2.82	18	0	0	22.1	15	19	12	0	0	2	0	1	0	0	.000	1	0	0	0	0.1	1.000
1970			7	1	.875	4.85	43	0	0	78	81	39	55	0	7	1	2	11	0	0	.000	5	8	1	0	0.3	.929
1971	**3 teams**	**DET A** (12G 0–1) **OAK A** (4G 0–0) **STL N** (13G 0–1)																									
"	**total**		0	2	.000	4.93	29	2	0	42	39	25	18	0	0	2	1	6	0	0	.000	3	3	1	0	0.2	.857
1974	**PIT**	**N**	2	1	.667	7.29	14	0	0	21	35	9	8	0	2	1	1	4	0	0	.000	0	4	0	0	0.3	1.000
5 yrs.			11	9	.550	4.09	142	3	0	231.1	223	119	142	0	11	9	11	35	0	0	.000	13	24	3	0	0.3	.925
WORLD SERIES																											
1968	**DET**	**A**	0	0	—	0.00	2	0	0	3	1	1	0	0	0	0	0	0	0	0	—	0	1	0	0	0.5	1.000

Dave Patterson

PATTERSON, DAVID GLENN BR TR 6′ 170 lbs.
B. July 25, 1956, Springfield, Mo.

Year	Team	Lg	W	L	PCT	ERA	G	GS	CG	IP	H	BB	SO	ShO	Relief W	Relief L	Relief SV	AB	H	HR	BA	PO	A	E	DP	TC/G	FA
1979	**LA**	**N**	4	1	.800	5.26	36	0	0	53	62	22	34	0	4	1	6	7	1	0	.143	6	5	0	1	0.3	1.000

Gil Patterson

PATTERSON, GILBERT THOMAS BR TR 6′ 1″ 185 lbs.
B. Sept. 5, 1955, Philadelphia, Pa.

Year	Team	Lg	W	L	PCT	ERA	G	GS	CG	IP	H	BB	SO	ShO	Relief W	Relief L	Relief SV	AB	H	HR	BA	PO	A	E	DP	TC/G	FA
1977	**NY**	**A**	1	2	.333	5.45	10	6	0	33	38	20	29	0	0	0	1	0	0	0	—	5	6	1	0	1.2	.917

Jeff Patterson

PATTERSON, JEFFREY SIMMONS BR TR 6′ 2″ 200 lbs.
B. Oct. 1, 1968, Anaheim, Calif.

Year	Team	Lg	W	L	PCT	ERA	G	GS	CG	IP	H	BB	SO	ShO	Relief W	Relief L	Relief SV	AB	H	HR	BA	PO	A	E	DP	TC/G	FA
1995	**NY**	**A**	0	0	—	2.70	3	0	0	3.1	3	3	3	0	0	0	0	0	0	0	—	0	0	0	0	0.0	.000

Ken Patterson

PATTERSON, KENNETH BRIAN BL TL 6′ 4″ 210 lbs.
B. July 8, 1964, Costa Mesa, Calif.

Year	Team	Lg	W	L	PCT	ERA	G	GS	CG	IP	H	BB	SO	ShO	Relief W	Relief L	Relief SV	AB	H	HR	BA	PO	A	E	DP	TC/G	FA
1988	**CHI**	**A**	0	2	.000	4.79	9	2	0	20.2	25	7	8	0	0	1	1	0	0	0	—	1	2	0	0	0.3	1.000
1989			6	1	.857	4.52	50	1	0	65.2	64	28	43	0	6	1	0	0	0	0	—	3	4	0	1	0.1	1.000
1990			2	1	.667	3.39	43	0	0	66.1	58	34	40	0	2	1	2	0	0	0	—	2	12	1	0	0.3	.933
1991			3	0	1.000	2.83	43	0	0	63.2	48	35	32	0	3	0	1	0	0	0	—	1	6	3	1	0.2	.700
1992	**CHI**	**N**	2	3	.400	3.89	32	1	0	41.2	41	27	23	0	2	3	0	1	0	0	.000	4	6	1	0	0.3	.909
1993	**CAL**	**A**	1	1	.500	4.58	46	0	0	59	54	35	36	0	1	1	1	0	0	0	—	1	8	1	0	0.2	.900
1994			0	0	—	0.00	1	0	0	0.2	0	0	1	0	0	0	0	0	0	0	—	0	0	0	0	0.0	.000
7 yrs.			14	8	.636	3.88	224	4	0	317.2	290	166	183	0	14	7	5	1	0	0	.000	12	38	6	2	0.3	.893

Reggie Patterson

PATTERSON, REGINALD ALLEN BR TR 6′ 4″ 180 lbs.
B. Nov. 7, 1958, Birmingham, Ala.

Year	Team	Lg	W	L	PCT	ERA	G	GS	CG	IP	H	BB	SO	ShO	Relief W	Relief L	Relief SV	AB	H	HR	BA	PO	A	E	DP	TC/G	FA
1981	**CHI**	**A**	0	1	.000	14.14	6	1	0	7	14	6	2	0	0	0	0	0	0	0	—	0	3	0	0	0.5	1.000
1983	**CHI**	**N**	1	2	.333	4.82	5	2	0	18.2	17	6	10	0	0	1	0	6	0	0	.000	3	1	0	1	0.8	1.000
1984			0	1	.000	10.50	3	1	0	6	10	2	5	0	0	0	0	2	0	0	.000	1	1	0	0	0.7	1.000
1985			3	0	1.000	3.00	8	5	1	39	36	10	17	0	0	0	0	10	1	0	.100	4	4	0	0	1.0	1.000
4 yrs.			4	4	.500	5.22	22	9	1	70.2	77	24	34	0	0	1	0	18	1	0	.056	8	9	0	1	0.8	1.000

Roy Patterson

PATTERSON, ROY LEWIS (Pat) BR TR 6′ 185 lbs.
B. Dec. 17, 1876, Stoddard, Wis. D. Apr. 14, 1953, St. Croix Falls, Wis.

Year	Team	Lg	W	L	PCT	ERA	G	GS	CG	IP	H	BB	SO	ShO	Relief W	Relief L	Relief SV	AB	H	HR	BA	PO	A	E	DP	TC/G	FA
1901	**CHI**	**A**	20	16	.556	3.37	41	35	30	312.1	345	62	127	4	2	2	0	117	26	1	.222	9	88	6	2	2.5	.942
1902			19	14	.576	3.06	34	30	26	268	262	67	61	2	2	**2**	0	105	20	0	.190	17	83	6	4	3.1	.943
1903			15	15	.500	2.70	34	30	26	293	275	69	89	2	1	0	1	105	11	0	.105	23	98	6	2	3.7	.953
1904			9	9	.500	2.29	22	17	14	165	148	24	64	4	1	0	0	58	6	0	.103	7	49	2	2	2.6	.966
1905			4	6	.400	1.83	13	9	7	88.2	73	16	29	1	0	1	0	30	8	0	.267	5	32	1	2	2.9	.974
1906			10	7	.588	2.09	21	18	12	142	119	17	45	3	0	0	1	49	3	0	.061	9	46	2	0	2.7	.965
1907			4	6	.400	2.63	19	13	4	96	105	18	27	1	0	0	0	31	3	0	.097	5	36	0	0	2.2	1.000
7 yrs.			81	73	.526	2.75	184	152	119	1365	1327	273	442	17	6	5	2	495	77	1	.156	75	432	23	12	2.9	.957

Year	Team	W	L	PCT	ERA	G	GS	CG	IP	H	BB	SO	ShO	Relief Pitching W	Relief Pitching L	Relief Pitching SV	Batting AB	Batting H	HR	BA	PO	A	E	DP	TC/G	FA

Marty Pattin

PATTIN, MARTIN WILLIAM — BR TR 5′11″ 180 lbs.
B. Apr. 6, 1943, Charleston, Ill.

Year	Team	W	L	PCT	ERA	G	GS	CG	IP	H	BB	SO	ShO	Relief W	Relief L	SV	AB	H	HR	BA	PO	A	E	DP	TC/G	FA
1968	CAL A	4	4	.500	2.79	52	4	0	84	67	37	66	0	3	3	3	12	1	0	.083	6	5	0	0	0.2	1.000
1969	SEA A	7	12	.368	5.62	34	27	2	158.2	166	71	126	1	0	0	0	58	9	0	.155	5	18	2	2	0.7	.920
1970	MIL A	14	12	.538	3.40	37	29	11	233	204	71	161	0	1	1	0	70	9	0	.129	18	40	1	3	1.6	.983
1971		14	14	.500	3.12	36	36	9	265	225	73	169	5	0	0	0	83	7	0	.084	18	36	1	0	1.5	.982
1972	BOS A	17	13	.567	3.23	38	35	13	253.1	232	65	168	4	0	1	0	86	12	2	.140	19	38	1	2	1.5	.983
1973		15	15	.500	4.31	34	30	11	219.1	238	69	119	2	1	0	1	0	0	0	—	13	36	2	3	1.5	.961
1974	KC A	3	7	.300	4.00	25	11	2	117	121	28	50	0	2	3	0	0	0	0	—	5	14	1	1	0.8	.950
1975		10	10	.500	3.25	44	15	5	177	173	45	89	1	4	4	5	0	0	0	—	13	22	3	1	0.8	.921
1976		8	14	.364	2.49	44	15	4	141	114	38	65	1	1	8	5	0	0	0	—	9	20	1	1	0.7	.967
1977		10	3	.769	3.59	31	10	4	128	115	37	55	0	5	1	0	0	0	0	—	6	19	0	0	0.8	1.000
1978		3	3	.500	3.32	32	5	2	78.2	72	25	30	0	2	1	4	0	0	0	—	3	4	0	2	0.2	1.000
1979		5	2	.714	4.60	31	7	1	94	109	21	41	0	2	1	3	0	0	0	—	4	13	1	0	0.6	.944
1980		4	0	1.000	3.64	37	0	0	89	97	23	40	0	4	0	4	0	0	0	—	4	9	1	1	0.4	.929
13 yrs.		114	109	.511	3.62	475	224	64	2038	1933	603	1179	14	25	23	25	309	38	2	.123	123	274	14	16	0.9	.966
LEAGUE CHAMPIONSHIP SERIES																										
1976	KC A	0	0	—	27.00	2	0	0	0.1	0	1	0	0	0	0	0	0	0	0	—	0	0	0	0	0.0	.000
1977		0	0	—	1.50	1	0	0	6	6	0	0	0	0	0	0	0	0	0	—	1	2	0	1	3.0	1.000
1978		0	0	—	27.00	1	0	0	0.2	2	0	0	0	0	0	0	0	0	0	—	0	0	0	0	0.0	.000
3 yrs.		0	0		5.14	4	0	0	7	8	1	0	0	0	0	0	0	0	0		1	2	0	1	0.8	1.000
WORLD SERIES																										
1980	KC A	0	0	—	0.00	1	0	0	1	0	0	2	0	0	0	0	0	0	0	—	0	0	0	0	0.0	.000

Jimmy Pattison

PATTISON, JAMES WELLS — BL TL 6′ 185 lbs.
B. Dec. 18, 1908, Bronx, N. Y. D. Feb. 22, 1991, Melbourne, Fla.

Year	Team	W	L	PCT	ERA	G	GS	CG	IP	H	BB	SO	ShO	Relief W	Relief L	SV	AB	H	HR	BA	PO	A	E	DP	TC/G	FA
1929	BKN N	0	1	.000	4.63	6	0	0	11.2	9	4	5	0	0	1	0	2	1	0	.500	0	2	0	0	0.3	1.000

Harry Patton

PATTON, HARRY CLAUDE
B. June 29, 1884, Gillespie, Ill. D. June 9, 1930, St. Louis, Mo.

Year	Team	W	L	PCT	ERA	G	GS	CG	IP	H	BB	SO	ShO	Relief W	Relief L	SV	AB	H	HR	BA	PO	A	E	DP	TC/G	FA
1910	STL N	0	0	—	2.25	1	0	0	4	4	2	2	0	0	0	0	0	0	0	—	0	3	0	0	3.0	1.000

Mike Paul

PAUL, MICHAEL GEORGE — BL TL 6′ 175 lbs.
B. Apr. 18, 1945, Detroit, Mich.

Year	Team	W	L	PCT	ERA	G	GS	CG	IP	H	BB	SO	ShO	Relief W	Relief L	SV	AB	H	HR	BA	PO	A	E	DP	TC/G	FA
1968	CLE A	5	8	.385	3.93	36	7	0	91.2	72	35	87	0	2	5	3	24	4	0	.167	3	9	1	0	0.4	.923
1969		5	10	.333	3.61	47	12	0	117.1	104	54	98	0	4	3	2	27	0	0	.000	1	14	1	1	0.3	.938
1970		2	8	.200	4.81	30	15	1	88	91	45	70	0	0	1	0	26	4	0	.154	2	6	1	1	0.3	.889
1971		2	7	.222	5.95	17	12	1	62	78	14	33	0	0	0	0	19	1	0	.053	2	6	0	0	0.5	1.000
1972	TEX A	8	9	.471	2.17	49	20	2	162	149	52	108	1	1	1	1	48	8	0	.167	7	19	0	3	0.5	1.000
1973	2 teams TEX A (36G 5–4) CHI N (11G 0–1)																									
″	total	5	5	.500	4.71	47	11	1	105	121	45	55	0	1	1	2	4	0	0	.000	4	22	1	2	0.6	.963
1974	CHI N	0	1	.000	36.00	2	0	0	1	4	1	1	0	0	1	0	0	0	0	—	0	0	0	0	0.0	.000
7 yrs.		27	48	.360	3.92	228	77	5	627	619	246	452	1	8	12	8	148	17	0	.115	19	76	4	7	0.4	.960

Gene Paulette

PAULETTE, EUGENE EDWARD — BR TR 6′ 150 lbs.
B. May 26, 1891, Centralia, Ill. D. Feb. 8, 1966, Little Rock, Ark.

Year	Team	W	L	PCT	ERA	G	GS	CG	IP	H	BB	SO	ShO	Relief W	Relief L	SV	AB	H	HR	BA	PO	A	E	DP	TC/G	FA
1918	STL N	0	0	—	0.00	1	0	0	0.1	1	0	0	0	0	0	0	*				29	1	2	0	3.6	.938

Gil Paulsen

PAULSEN, GUILFORD PAUL HANS — BR TR 6′ 2½″ 190 lbs.
B. Nov. 14, 1902, Graettinger, Iowa D. Apr. 2, 1994, Harlan, Iowa.

Year	Team	W	L	PCT	ERA	G	GS	CG	IP	H	BB	SO	ShO	Relief W	Relief L	SV	AB	H	HR	BA	PO	A	E	DP	TC/G	FA
1925	STL N	0	0	—	0.00	1	0	0	2	1	0	1	0	0	0	0	0	0	0	—	0	1	0	0	1.0	1.000

Dave Pavlas

PAVLAS, DAVID LEE — BR TR 6′ 7″ 180 lbs.
B. Aug. 12, 1962, Frankfurt, Germany.

Year	Team	W	L	PCT	ERA	G	GS	CG	IP	H	BB	SO	ShO	Relief W	Relief L	SV	AB	H	HR	BA	PO	A	E	DP	TC/G	FA
1990	CHI N	2	0	1.000	2.11	13	0	0	21.1	23	6	12	0	2	0	0	1	0	0	.000	1	2	0	0	0.2	1.000
1991		0	0	—	18.00	1	0	0	1	3	0	0	0	0	0	0	0	0	0	—	0	0	0	0	0.0	.000
1995	NY A	0	0	—	3.18	4	0	0	5.2	8	0	3	0	0	0	0	0	0	0	—	0	0	0	0	0.0	.000
3 yrs.		2	0	1.000	2.89	18	0	0	28	34	6	15	0	2	0	0	1	0	0	.000	1	2	0	0	0.2	1.000

Roger Pavlik

PAVLIK, ROGER ALLEN — BR TR 6′ 3″ 220 lbs.
B. Oct. 4, 1967, Houston, Tex.

Year	Team	W	L	PCT	ERA	G	GS	CG	IP	H	BB	SO	ShO	Relief W	Relief L	SV	AB	H	HR	BA	PO	A	E	DP	TC/G	FA
1992	TEX A	4	4	.500	4.21	13	12	1	62	66	34	45	0	0	0	0	0	0	0	—	6	3	1	0	0.8	.900
1993		12	6	.667	3.41	26	26	2	166.1	151	80	131	0	0	0	0	0	0	0	—	10	27	3	2	1.5	.925
1994		2	5	.286	7.69	11	11	0	50.1	61	30	31	0	0	0	0	0	0	0	—	2	8	0	1	0.9	1.000
1995		10	10	.500	4.37	31	31	2	191.2	174	90	149	1	0	0	0	0	0	0	—	20	32	1	4	1.7	.981
4 yrs.		28	25	.528	4.36	81	80	5	470.1	452	234	356	1	0	0	0	0	0	0		38	70	5	7	1.4	.956

John Pawlowski

PAWLOWSKI, JOHN — BR TR 6′ 2″ 175 lbs.
B. Sept. 6, 1963, Johnson City, N. Y.

Year	Team	W	L	PCT	ERA	G	GS	CG	IP	H	BB	SO	ShO	Relief W	Relief L	SV	AB	H	HR	BA	PO	A	E	DP	TC/G	FA
1987	CHI A	0	0	—	4.91	2	0	0	3.2	7	3	2	0	0	0	0	0	0	0	—	0	0	0	0	0.0	.000
1988		1	0	1.000	8.36	6	0	0	14	20	3	10	0	1	0	0	0	0	0	—	1	2	0	0	0.5	1.000
2 yrs.		1	0	1.000	7.64	8	0	0	17.2	27	6	12	0	1	0	0	0	0	0		1	2	0	0	0.4	1.000

Mike Paxton

PAXTON, MICHAEL DeWAYNE — BR TR 5′11″ 190 lbs.
B. Sept. 3, 1953, Memphis, Tenn.

Year	Team	W	L	PCT	ERA	G	GS	CG	IP	H	BB	SO	ShO	Relief W	Relief L	SV	AB	H	HR	BA	PO	A	E	DP	TC/G	FA
1977	BOS A	10	5	.667	3.83	29	12	2	108	134	25	58	1	4	1	0	0	0	0	—	4	15	0	1	0.7	1.000
1978	CLE A	12	11	.522	3.86	33	27	5	191	179	63	96	2	1	1	1	0	0	0	—	17	20	1	2	1.2	.974
1979		8	8	.500	5.91	33	24	3	160	210	52	70	0	0	0	0	0	0	0	—	16	20	0	3	1.1	1.000
1980		0	0	—	12.38	4	0	0	8	13	6	6	0	0	0	0	0	0	0	—	2	0	0	0	0.5	1.000
4 yrs.		30	24	.556	4.70	99	63	10	467	536	146	230	3	5	2	1	0	0	0		39	55	1	6	1.0	.989

George Payne

PAYNE, GEORGE WASHINGTON — BR TR 5′11″ 172 lbs.
B. May 23, 1890, Mt. Vernon, Ky. D. Jan. 24, 1959, Bellflower, Calif.

Year	Team	W	L	PCT	ERA	G	GS	CG	IP	H	BB	SO	ShO	Relief W	Relief L	SV	AB	H	HR	BA	PO	A	E	DP	TC/G	FA
1920	CHI A	1	1	.500	5.46	12	0	0	29.2	39	9	9	0	1	1	0	8	1	0	.125	1	3	0	0	0.3	1.000

Harley Payne

PAYNE, HARLEY FENWICK (Lady) BB TL 6′ 160 lbs.
B. Jan. 9, 1868, Windsor, Ont., Canada. D. Dec. 29, 1935, Orwell, Ohio.

Year	Team		W	L	PCT	ERA	G	GS	CG	IP	H	BB	SO	ShO	Relief Pitching W	L	SV	Batting AB	H	HR	BA	PO	A	E	DP	TC/G	FA
1896	BKN	N	14	16	.467	3.39	34	28	24	241.2	284	58	52	2	2	2	0	98	21	0	.214	12	76	7	1	2.7	.926
1897			14	17	.452	4.63	40	38	30	280	350	71	86	1	0	0	0	110	26	0	.236	13	68	5	1	2.1	.942
1898			1	0	1.000	4.00	1	1	1	9	11	3	2	0	0	0	0	4	3	0	.750	0	4	0	0	4.0	1.000
1899	PIT	N	1	3	.250	3.76	5	5	2	26.1	33	4	8	0	0	0	0	10	1	0	.100	0	18	2	0	4.0	.900
4 yrs.			30	36	.455	4.04	80	72	57	557	678	136	148	3	2	2	0	222	51	0	.230	25	166	14	2	2.5	.932

Mike Payne

PAYNE, MICHAEL EARL BR TR 5′11″ 165 lbs.
B. Nov. 15, 1961, Woonsocket, R. I.

Year	Team		W	L	PCT	ERA	G	GS	CG	IP	H	BB	SO	ShO	Relief Pitching W	L	SV	Batting AB	H	HR	BA	PO	A	E	DP	TC/G	FA
1984	ATL	N	0	1	.000	6.35	3	1	0	5.2	7	3	3	0	0	0	0	1	0	0	.000	0	1	0	0	0.3	1.000

Mike Pazik

PAZIK, MICHAEL JOSEPH BL TL 6′2″ 195 lbs.
B. Jan. 26, 1950, Lynn, Mass.

Year	Team		W	L	PCT	ERA	G	GS	CG	IP	H	BB	SO	ShO	Relief Pitching W	L	SV	Batting AB	H	HR	BA	PO	A	E	DP	TC/G	FA
1975	MIN	A	0	4	.000	8.24	5	3	0	19.2	28	10	8	0	0	1	0	0	0	0	—	0	0	0	0	0.0	.000
1976			0	0	—	7.00	5	0	0	9	13	4	6	0	0	0	0	0	0	0	—	0	0	0	0	0.0	.000
1977			1	0	1.000	2.50	3	3	0	18	18	6	6	0	0	0	0	0	0	0	—	2	3	0	0	1.7	1.000
3 yrs.			1	4	.200	5.79	13	6	0	46.2	59	20	20	0	0	1	0	0	0	0		2	3	0	0	0.4	1.000

Frank Pearce

PEARCE, FRANKLIN JOHNSON
B. Mar. 30, 1860, Jefferson County, Ky. D. Nov. 13, 1926, Louisville, Ky.

Year	Team		W	L	PCT	ERA	G	GS	CG	IP	H	BB	SO	ShO	Relief Pitching W	L	SV	Batting AB	H	HR	BA	PO	A	E	DP	TC/G	FA
1876	LOU	N	0	0	—	4.50	1	0	0	4	5	1	1	0	0	0	0	2	0	0	.000	0	0	0	0	0.0	.000

Frank Pearce

PEARCE, FRANKLIN THOMAS BR TR 6′ 170 lbs.
B. Aug. 31, 1905, Middletown, Ky. D. Sept. 3, 1950, Van Buren, N. Y.

Year	Team		W	L	PCT	ERA	G	GS	CG	IP	H	BB	SO	ShO	Relief Pitching W	L	SV	Batting AB	H	HR	BA	PO	A	E	DP	TC/G	FA
1933	PHI	N	5	4	.556	3.62	20	7	3	82	78	29	18	1	2	2	0	26	5	0	.192	7	16	2	3	1.3	.920
1934			0	2	.000	7.20	7	1	0	20	25	5	4	0	0	1	0	3	2	0	.667	0	2	0	0	0.3	1.000
1935			0	0	—	8.31	5	0	0	13	22	6	7	0	0	0	0	4	2	0	.500	1	5	2	1	1.6	.750
3 yrs.			5	6	.455	4.77	32	8	3	115	125	40	29	1	2	3	0	33	9	0	.273	8	23	4	4	1.1	.886

George Pearce

PEARCE, GEORGE THOMAS BL TL 5′10½″ 175 lbs.
B. Jan. 10, 1888, Aurora, Ill. D. Oct. 11, 1935, Joliet, Ill.

Year	Team		W	L	PCT	ERA	G	GS	CG	IP	H	BB	SO	ShO	Relief Pitching W	L	SV	Batting AB	H	HR	BA	PO	A	E	DP	TC/G	FA
1912	CHI	N	0	0	—	5.52	3	2	0	14.2	15	12	9	0	0	0	0	6	1	0	.167	0	7	0	0	2.3	1.000
1913			13	5	.722	2.31	25	21	14	163.1	137	59	73	3	1	0	0	55	4	0	.073	6	41	3	0	2.0	.940
1914			8	12	.400	3.51	30	16	4	141	122	65	78	0	2	3	1	45	4	0	.089	1	45	3	1	1.6	.939
1915			13	9	.591	3.32	36	20	8	176	158	77	96	2	4	1	0	56	11	0	.196	1	49	6	0	1.6	.893
1916			0	0	—	2.08	4	1	0	4.1	6	1	0	0	0	0	0	0	0	0	—	0	1	0	0	0.3	1.000
1917	STL	N	1	1	.500	3.48	5	0	0	10.1	7	3	4	0	1	1	0	4	0	0	.000	1	4	1	1	1.2	.833
6 yrs.			35	27	.565	3.11	103	60	26	509.2	445	217	260	5	8	5	1	166	20	0	.120	9	147	13	2	1.6	.923

Jim Pearce

PEARCE, JAMES MADISON BR TR 6′6″ 180 lbs.
B. June 9, 1925, Zebulon, N. C.

Year	Team		W	L	PCT	ERA	G	GS	CG	IP	H	BB	SO	ShO	Relief Pitching W	L	SV	Batting AB	H	HR	BA	PO	A	E	DP	TC/G	FA
1949	WAS	A	0	1	.000	8.44	2	1	0	5.1	9	5	1	0	0	0	0	2	0	0	.000	0	5	1	0	3.0	.833
1950			2	1	.667	6.04	20	3	1	56.2	58	37	18	0	1	1	0	13	2	0	.154	2	9	0	0	0.6	1.000
1953			0	1	.000	7.71	4	1	0	9.1	15	6	0	0	0	0	0	1	0	0	.000	0	1	1	0	0.5	.500
1954	CIN	N	1	0	1.000	0.00	2	1	1	11	7	5	3	0	0	0	0	3	0	0	.000	1	2	0	0	1.5	1.000
1955			0	1	.000	10.80	2	1	0	3.1	8	0	0	0	0	0	0	0	0	0	—	1	0	0	0	0.5	1.000
5 yrs.			3	4	.429	5.78	30	7	2	85.2	97	53	22	0	1	1	0	19	2	0	.105	4	17	2	0	0.8	.913

Frank Pears

PEARS, FRANK H. TR 5′9″ 145 lbs.
B. Aug. 30, 1866, Kentucky D. Nov. 29, 1923, St. Louis, Mo.

Year	Team		W	L	PCT	ERA	G	GS	CG	IP	H	BB	SO	ShO	Relief Pitching W	L	SV	Batting AB	H	HR	BA	PO	A	E	DP	TC/G	FA
1889	KC	AA	0	2	.000	4.91	3	2	2	22	21	9	5	0	0	0	0	11	1	0	.091	1	3	0	0	1.0	1.000
1893	STL	N	0	0	—	13.50	1	0	0	4	9	2	0	0	0	0	0	2	0	0	.000	0	1	0	0	1.0	1.000
2 yrs.			0	2	.000	6.23	4	2	2	26	30	11	5	0	0	0	0	13	1	0	.077	1	4	0	0	1.0	1.000

Alex Pearson

PEARSON, ALEXANDER FRANKLIN BR TR 5′10½″ 160 lbs.
B. Mar. 9, 1877, Greensboro, Pa. D. Oct. 30, 1966, Rochester, Pa.

Year	Team		W	L	PCT	ERA	G	GS	CG	IP	H	BB	SO	ShO	Relief Pitching W	L	SV	Batting AB	H	HR	BA	PO	A	E	DP	TC/G	FA
1902	STL	N	2	6	.250	3.95	11	10	8	82	90	22	24	0	0	0	0	34	9	0	.265	1	22	2	0	2.3	.920
1903	CLE	A	1	2	.333	3.56	4	3	2	30.1	34	3	12	0	0	0	0	12	1	0	.083	1	10	1	0	3.0	.917
2 yrs.			3	8	.273	3.85	15	13	10	112.1	124	25	36	0	0	0	0	46	10	0	.217	2	32	3	0	2.5	.919

Ike Pearson

PEARSON, ISSAC OVERTON BR TR 6′1″ 180 lbs.
B. Mar. 1, 1917, Grenada, Miss. D. Mar. 17, 1985, Sarasota, Fla.

Year	Team		W	L	PCT	ERA	G	GS	CG	IP	H	BB	SO	ShO	Relief Pitching W	L	SV	Batting AB	H	HR	BA	PO	A	E	DP	TC/G	FA
1939	PHI	N	2	13	.133	5.76	26	13	4	125	144	56	29	0	0	2	0	37	2	0	.054	6	30	1	1	1.4	.973
1940			3	14	.176	5.45	29	20	5	145.1	160	57	43	1	0	1	1	44	9	0	.205	3	37	2	3	1.4	.952
1941			4	14	.222	3.57	46	10	0	136	139	70	38	0	4	4	6	40	5	0	.125	8	28	1	2	0.8	.973
1942			1	6	.143	4.54	35	7	0	85.1	87	50	21	0	1	1	0	23	1	0	.043	2	17	0	2	0.5	1.000
1946			1	0	1.000	3.77	5	2	1	14.1	19	8	6	1	0	0	0	5	1	1	.200	1	3	1	0	1.0	.800
1948	CHI	A	2	3	.400	4.92	23	2	0	53	62	27	12	0	1	2	1	10	2	0	.200	1	13	0	2	0.6	1.000
6 yrs.			13	50	.206	4.83	164	54	10	559	611	268	149	2	6	10	8	159	20	1	.126	21	128	5	10	0.9	.968

Monte Pearson

PEARSON, MONTGOMERY MARCELLUS BR TR 6′ 175 lbs.
B. Sept. 2, 1909, Oakland, Calif. D. Jan. 27, 1978, Fresno, Calif.

Year	Team		W	L	PCT	ERA	G	GS	CG	IP	H	BB	SO	ShO	Relief Pitching W	L	SV	Batting AB	H	HR	BA	PO	A	E	DP	TC/G	FA
1932	CLE	A	0	0	—	10.13	8	0	0	8	10	11	5	0	0	0	0	0	0	0	—	0	6	0	0	0.8	1.000
1933			10	5	.667	**2.33**	19	16	10	135.1	111	55	54	0	0	0	0	50	13	0	.260	1	26	2	2	1.5	.931
1934			18	13	.581	4.52	39	33	19	254.2	257	130	140	0	2	1	2	92	25	1	.272	15	48	2	5	1.7	.969
1935			8	13	.381	4.90	30	24	10	181.2	199	103	90	1	2	1	0	62	11	0	.177	8	42	2	5	1.7	.962
1936	NY	A	19	7	**.731**	3.71	33	31	15	223	191	135	118	1	1	0	1	91	23	1	.253	12	39	1	3	1.6	.981
1937			9	3	.750	3.17	22	20	7	144.2	145	64	71	1	0	0	1	51	11	0	.216	5	23	1	3	1.3	.966
1938			16	7	.696	3.97	28	27	17	202	198	113	98	1	0	0	0	76	13	0	.171	11	40	2	8	1.9	.962
1939			12	5	.706	4.49	22	20	8	146.1	151	70	76	0	0	1	0	53	17	0	.321	3	29	0	5	1.5	1.000
1940			7	5	.583	3.69	16	16	7	109.2	108	44	43	1	0	0	0	33	4	0	.121	6	29	0	2	2.2	1.000
1941	CIN	N	1	3	.250	5.18	7	4	1	24.1	22	15	8	0	0	0	0	5	0	0	.000	1	3	0	0	0.6	1.000
10 yrs.			100	61	.621	4.00	224	191	94	1429.2	1392	740	703	5	5	3	4	513	117	2	.228	62	285	10	33	1.6	.972

Monte Pearson *continued*

Year	Team	Lg	W	L	PCT	ERA	G	GS	CG	IP	H	BB	SO	ShO	Relief Pitching W	Relief Pitching L	Relief Pitching SV	Batting AB	Batting H	Batting HR	BA	PO	A	E	DP	TC/G	FA
WORLD SERIES																											
1936	**NY**	**A**	1	0	1.000	2.00	1	1	1	9	7	2	7	0	0	0	0	4	2	0	.500	1	2	0	0	3.0	1.000
1937			1	0	1.000	1.04	1	1	0	8.2	5	2	4	0	0	0	0	3	0	0	.000	0	2	0	0	2.0	1.000
1938			1	0	1.000	1.00	1	1	1	9	5	2	9	0	0	0	0	3	1	0	.333	2	0	0	0	2.0	1.000
1939			1	0	1.000	0.00	1	1	1	9	2	1	8	1	0	0	0	2	0	0	.000	0	5	0	0	5.0	1.000
4 yrs.			4	0	1.000	1.01	4	4	3	35.2	19	7	28	1	0	0	0	12	3	0	.250	3	9	0	0	3.0	1.000
					1st	***7th***																					

Marv Peasley

PEASLEY, MARVIN WARREN BL TL 6′ 1″ 175 lbs.
B. July 16, 1888, Jonesport, Me. D. Dec. 27, 1948, San Francisco, Calif.

Year	Team	Lg	W	L	PCT	ERA	G	GS	CG	IP	H	BB	SO	ShO	Relief Pitching W	Relief Pitching L	Relief Pitching SV	Batting AB	Batting H	Batting HR	BA	PO	A	E	DP	TC/G	FA
1910	**DET**	**A**	0	1	.000	8.10	2	1	0	10	13	11	4	0	0	0	0	3	0	0	.000	0	3	0	0	1.5	1.000

George Pechiney

PECHINEY, GEORGE ADOLPHE BR TR 5′ 9″ 184 lbs.
B. Sept. 20, 1861, Cincinnati, Ohio D. July 14, 1943, Cincinnati, Ohio.

Year	Team	Lg	W	L	PCT	ERA	G	GS	CG	IP	H	BB	SO	ShO	Relief Pitching W	Relief Pitching L	Relief Pitching SV	Batting AB	Batting H	Batting HR	BA	PO	A	E	DP	TC/G	FA
1885	**CIN**	**AA**	7	4	.636	*2.02*	11	11	11	98	95	30	49	1	0	0	0	40	6	0	.150	4	20	4	0	2.5	.857
1886			15	21	.417	*4.14*	40	40	35	330.1	355	133	110	2	0	0	0	144	30	1	.208	20	45	8	2	1.7	.890
1887	**CLE**	**AA**	1	9	.100	*7.12*	10	10	10	86	118	44	24	0	0	0	0	36	9	0	.250	0	23	5	1	2.8	.821
3 yrs.			23	34	.404	4.23	61	61	56	514.1	568	207	183	3	0	0	0	220	45	1	.205	24	88	17	3	2.0	.868

Bill Pecota

PECOTA, WILLIAM JOSEPH BR TR 6′ 2″ 195 lbs.
B. Feb. 16, 1960, Redwood City, Calif.

Year	Team	Lg	W	L	PCT	ERA	G	GS	CG	IP	H	BB	SO	ShO	Relief Pitching W	Relief Pitching L	Relief Pitching SV	Batting AB	Batting H	Batting HR	BA	PO	A	E	DP	TC/G	FA
1991	**KC**	**A**	0	0	—	4.50	1	0	0	2	4	0	0	0	0	0	0	398	114	6	.286	7	31	1	1	2.8	.974
1992	**NY**	**N**	0	0	—	9.00	1	0	0	1	1	0	0	0	0	0	0	269	61	2	.227	92	218	12	33	2.5	.963
2 yrs.			0	0		6.00	2	0	0	3	5	0	0	0	0	0	0	*				662	1083	38	178	2.6	.979

Steve Peek

PEEK, STEPHEN GEORGE BB TR 6′ 2″ 195 lbs.
B. July 30, 1914, Springfield, Mass. D. Sept. 20, 1991, Syracuse, N. Y.

Year	Team	Lg	W	L	PCT	ERA	G	GS	CG	IP	H	BB	SO	ShO	Relief Pitching W	Relief Pitching L	Relief Pitching SV	Batting AB	Batting H	Batting HR	BA	PO	A	E	DP	TC/G	FA
1941	**NY**	**A**	4	2	.667	5.06	17	8	2	80	85	39	18	0	0	0	0	28	1	0	.036	3	18	2	0	1.4	.913

Red Peery

PEERY, GEORGE ALLAN BL TL 5′11″ 160 lbs.
B. Aug. 15, 1906, Payson, Utah D. May 6, 1985, Salt Lake City, Utah.

Year	Team	Lg	W	L	PCT	ERA	G	GS	CG	IP	H	BB	SO	ShO	Relief Pitching W	Relief Pitching L	Relief Pitching SV	Batting AB	Batting H	Batting HR	BA	PO	A	E	DP	TC/G	FA
1927	**PIT**	**N**	0	0	—	0.00	1	0	0	1	0	1	0	0	0	0	0	0	0	0	—	0	1	0	0	1.0	1.000
1929	**BOS**	**N**	0	1	.000	5.11	9	1	0	44	53	9	3	0	0	0	0	14	3	0	.214	1	10	0	0	1.2	1.000
2 yrs.			0	1	.000	5.00	10	1	0	45	53	10	3	0	0	0	0	14	3	0	.214	1	11	0	0	1.2	1.000

Heinie Peitz

PEITZ, HENRY CLEMENT BR TR 5′11″ 165 lbs.
Brother of Joe Peitz.
B. Nov. 28, 1870, St. Louis, Mo. D. Oct. 23, 1943, Cincinnati, Ohio.

Year	Team	Lg	W	L	PCT	ERA	G	GS	CG	IP	H	BB	SO	ShO	Relief Pitching W	Relief Pitching L	Relief Pitching SV	Batting AB	Batting H	Batting HR	BA	PO	A	E	DP	TC/G	FA
1894	**STL**	**N**	0	0	—	9.00	1	0	0	3	7	2	0	0	0	0	0	338	89	3	.263	3	0	0	0	3.0	1.000
1897	**CIN**	**N**	0	1	.000	7.88	2	1	1	8	9	4	0	0	0	0	0	266	78	1	.293	388	116	33	16	5.4	.939
1899			0	0	—	5.40	1	0	0	5	6	1	3	0	0	0	0	290	79	1	.272	320	136	33	18	4.8	.933
3 yrs.			0	1	.000	7.31	4	1	1	16	22	7	3	0	0	0	0	*				4693	1484	260	207	5.3	.960

Barney Pelty

PELTY, BARNEY BR TR 5′ 9″ 175 lbs.
Born Barney Peltheimer.
B. Sept. 10, 1880, Farmington, Mo. D. May 24, 1939, Farmington, Mo.

Year	Team	Lg	W	L	PCT	ERA	G	GS	CG	IP	H	BB	SO	ShO	Relief Pitching W	Relief Pitching L	Relief Pitching SV	Batting AB	Batting H	Batting HR	BA	PO	A	E	DP	TC/G	FA
1903	**STL**	**A**	3	3	.500	2.40	7	6	5	48.2	49	15	20	0	0	0	1	20	3	0	.150	3	11	3	0	2.4	.824
1904			15	18	.455	2.84	39	35	31	301	270	77	126	2	2	0	0	118	15	0	.127	27	92	9	3	3.0	.930
1905			14	14	.500	2.75	31	28	26	258.2	222	68	114	1	1	0	0	98	15	0	.153	15	92	6	3	3.6	.947
1906			16	11	.593	1.59	34	30	25	260.2	189	59	92	4	1	0	2	95	16	0	.168	21	107	13	0	4.1	.908
1907			12	**21**	.364	2.57	36	31	29	273	234	64	85	5	0	**3**	1	95	16	0	.168	25	91	7	5	3.4	.943
1908			7	4	.636	1.99	20	13	7	122	104	32	36	1	1	1	0	42	5	0	.119	8	45	1	2	2.6	.981
1909			11	11	.500	2.30	27	23	17	199.1	158	53	88	5	0	2	0	91	15	0	.165	33	90	9	6	3.6	.932
1910			5	11	.313	3.48	27	19	12	165.1	157	70	48	3	1	1	0	56	5	0	.089	10	74	5	4	3.2	.944
1911			7	15	.318	2.83	28	22	18	207	197	69	59	1	0	2	0	65	9	0	.138	9	61	2	1	2.5	.972
1912	**2 teams**	**STL A** (6G 1–5) **WAS A** (11G 1–4)																									
″	**total**		2	9	.182	4.37	17	10	3	82.1	83	25	25	0	1	2	0	21	2	0	.095	3	21	1	2	1.5	.960
10 yrs.			92	117	.440	2.62	266	217	173	1918	1663	532	693	22	7	11	4	701	101	0	.144	154	684	56	26	3.2	.937

Alejandro Pena

PENA, ALEJANDRO BR TR 6′ 1″ 200 lbs.
Born Alejandro Pena (Vasquez).
B. June 25, 1959, Cambiaso, Dominican Republic.

Year	Team	Lg	W	L	PCT	ERA	G	GS	CG	IP	H	BB	SO	ShO	Relief Pitching W	Relief Pitching L	Relief Pitching SV	Batting AB	Batting H	Batting HR	BA	PO	A	E	DP	TC/G	FA
1981	**LA**	**N**	1	1	.500	2.88	14	0	0	25	18	11	14	0	1	1	2	6	0	0	.000	1	5	1	0	0.5	.857
1982			0	2	.000	4.79	29	0	0	35.2	37	21	20	0	0	2	0	0	0	0	—	3	11	2	1	0.6	.875
1983			12	9	.571	2.75	34	26	4	177	152	51	120	3	2	1	1	60	6	1	.100	13	32	4	4	1.4	.918
1984			12	6	.667	**2.48**	28	28	8	199.1	186	46	135	**4**	0	0	0	66	8	0	.121	17	21	4	1	1.5	.905
1985			0	1	.000	8.31	2	1	0	4.1	7	3	2	0	0	1	0	1	0	0	.000	0	1	1	0	1.0	.500
1986			1	2	.333	4.89	24	10	0	70	74	30	46	0	0	1	1	17	3	0	.176	1	8	0	0	0.4	1.000
1987			2	7	.222	3.50	37	7	0	87.1	82	37	76	0	2	2	11	13	1	0	.077	4	1	1	0	0.2	.833
1988			6	7	.462	1.91	60	0	0	94.1	75	27	83	0	6	7	12	6	0	0	.000	9	10	2	1	0.3	.905
1989			4	3	.571	2.13	53	0	0	76	62	18	75	0	4	3	5	1	1	0	1.000	1	5	1	0	0.1	.857
1990	**NY**	**N**	3	3	.500	3.20	52	0	0	76	71	22	76	0	3	3	5	6	1	0	.167	2	4	0	0	0.1	1.000
1991	**2 teams**	**NY N** (44G 6–1) **ATL N** (15G 2–0)																									
″	**total**		8	1	.889	2.40	59	0	0	82.1	74	22	62	0	8	1	15	1	0	0	.000	6	9	1	1	0.3	.938
1992	**ATL**	**N**	1	6	.143	4.07	41	0	0	42	40	13	34	0	1	6	15	2	0	0	.000	2	1	0	0	0.1	1.000
1994	**PIT**	**N**	3	2	.600	5.02	22	0	0	28.2	22	10	27	0	3	2	7	1	0	0	.000	1	1	1	0	0.1	.667
1995	**3 teams**	**BOS A** (17G 1–1) **FLA N** (13G 2–0) **ATL N** (14G 0–0)																									
″	**total**		3	1	.750	4.72	44	0	0	55.1	55	19	64	0	3	1	0	1	0	0	.000	2	3	0	0	0.1	1.000
14 yrs.			56	51	.523	3.10	499	72	12	1053.1	955	330	834	7	33	31	74	181	20	1	.110	62	112	18	8	0.4	.906
DIVISIONAL PLAYOFF SERIES																											
1995	**ATL**	**N**	2	0	1.000	0.00	3	0	0	3	3	1	2	0	2	0	0	0	0	0	—	0	0	0	0	0.0	.000

Alejandro Pena *continued*

LEAGUE CHAMPIONSHIP SERIES

Year	Team		W	L	PCT	ERA	G	GS	CG	IP	H	BB	SO	ShO	Relief Pitching W	Relief Pitching L	Relief Pitching SV	Batting AB	Batting H	Batting HR	BA	PO	A	E	DP	TC/G	FA
1981	LA	N	0	0	—	0.00	2	0	0	2.1	1	0	0	0	0	0	0	0	0	0	—	0	0	0	0	0.0	.000
1983			0	0	—	6.75	1	0	0	2.2	4	1	3	0	0	0	0	1	1	0	1.000	0	0	0	0	0.0	.000
1988			1	1	.500	4.15	3	0	0	4.1	1	5	1	0	1	1	1	0	0	0	—	0	0	0	0	0.0	.000
1991	ATL	N	0	0	—	0.00	4	0	0	4.1	1	0	4	0	0	0	3	0	0	0	—	1	2	0	0	0.8	1.000
1995			0	0	—	0.00	3	0	0	3	2	1	4	0	0	0	0	0	0	0	—	0	0	0	0	0.0	.000
5 yrs.			1	1	.500	2.16	13 5th	0	0	16.2	9	7	12	0	1	1	4 3rd	1	1	0	1.000	1	2	0	0	0.2	1.000

WORLD SERIES

Year	Team		W	L	PCT	ERA	G	GS	CG	IP	H	BB	SO	ShO	Relief Pitching W	Relief Pitching L	Relief Pitching SV	Batting AB	Batting H	Batting HR	BA	PO	A	E	DP	TC/G	FA
1988	LA	N	1	0	1.000	0.00	2	0	0	5	2	1	7	0	1	0	0	0	0	0	—	0	0	0	0	0.0	.000
1991	ATL	N	0	1	.000	3.38	3	0	0	5.1	6	3	7	0	0	1	0	0	0	0	—	0	0	0	0	0.0	.000
1995			0	1	.000	9.00	2	0	0	1	3	2	0	0	0	1	0	0	0	0	—	0	0	0	0	0.0	.000
3 yrs.			1	2	.333	2.38	7	0	0	11.1	11	6	14	0	1	2	0	0	0	0		0	0	0	0	0.0	

Hipolito Pena

PENA, HIPOLITO
Born Hipolito Pena (Concepcion).
B. Jan. 30, 1964, Fantino, Dominican Republic.
BL TL 6′ 3″ 168 lbs.

Year	Team		W	L	PCT	ERA	G	GS	CG	IP	H	BB	SO	ShO	Relief Pitching W	Relief Pitching L	Relief Pitching SV	Batting AB	Batting H	Batting HR	BA	PO	A	E	DP	TC/G	FA
1986	PIT	N	0	3	.000	8.64	10	1	0	8.1	7	3	6	0	0	2	1	0	0	0	—	0	1	0	0	0.1	1.000
1987			0	3	.000	4.56	16	1	0	25.2	16	26	16	0	0	2	1	6	1	0	.167	1	4	0	0	0.3	1.000
1988	NY	A	1	1	.500	3.14	16	0	0	14.1	10	9	10	0	1	1	0	0	0	0	—	1	2	0	1	0.2	1.000
3 yrs.			1	7	.125	4.84	42	2	0	48.1	33	38	32	0	1	5	2	6	1	0	.167	2	7	0	1	0.2	1.000

Jim Pena

PENA, JAMES PATRICK
B. Sept. 17, 1964, Los Angeles, Calif.
BL TL 6′ 1″ 185 lbs.

Year	Team		W	L	PCT	ERA	G	GS	CG	IP	H	BB	SO	ShO	Relief Pitching W	Relief Pitching L	Relief Pitching SV	Batting AB	Batting H	Batting HR	BA	PO	A	E	DP	TC/G	FA
1992	SF	N	1	1	.500	3.48	25	2	0	44	49	20	32	0	0	1	0	5	1	0	.200	1	11	3	1	0.6	.800

Jose Pena

PENA, JOSE
Born Jose Pena (Gutierrez).
B. Dec. 3, 1942, Ciudad Juarez, Mexico.
BR TR 6′ 2″ 190 lbs.

Year	Team		W	L	PCT	ERA	G	GS	CG	IP	H	BB	SO	ShO	Relief Pitching W	Relief Pitching L	Relief Pitching SV	Batting AB	Batting H	Batting HR	BA	PO	A	E	DP	TC/G	FA
1969	CIN	N	1	1	.500	18.00	6	0	0	5	10	5	3	0	1	1	0	0	0	0	—	0	1	0	0	0.2	1.000
1970	LA	N	4	3	.571	4.42	29	0	0	57	51	29	31	0	4	3	4	8	1	0	.125	1	14	0	0	0.5	1.000
1971			2	0	1.000	3.56	21	0	0	43	32	18	44	0	2	0	1	3	2	0	.667	0	4	0	0	0.2	1.000
1972			0	0	—	8.59	5	0	0	7.1	13	6	4	0	0	0	0	0	0	0	—	1	0	0	0	0.2	1.000
4 yrs.			7	4	.636	4.97	61	0	0	112.1	106	58	82	0	7	4	5	11	3	0	.273	2	19	0	0	0.3	1.000

Orlando Pena

PENA, ORLANDO GREGORIO
Born Orlando Gregorio Pena (Quevara).
B. Nov. 17, 1933, Victoria de las Tunas, Cuba.
BR TR 5′11″ 154 lbs.

Year	Team		W	L	PCT	ERA	G	GS	CG	IP	H	BB	SO	ShO	Relief Pitching W	Relief Pitching L	Relief Pitching SV	Batting AB	Batting H	Batting HR	BA	PO	A	E	DP	TC/G	FA
1958	CIN	N	1	0	1.000	0.60	9	0	0	15	10	4	11	0	1	0	3	0	0	0	—	1	1	0	0	0.2	1.000
1959			5	9	.357	4.76	46	8	1	136	150	39	76	0	2	4	5	34	3	0	.088	12	16	1	1	0.6	.966
1960			0	1	.000	2.89	4	0	0	9.1	8	3	9	0	0	1	0	1	0	0	.000	0	0	0	0	0.0	.000
1962	KC	A	6	4	.600	3.01	13	12	6	89.2	71	27	56	1	0	0	0	31	5	0	.161	5	9	1	0	1.2	.933
1963			12	**20**	.375	3.69	35	33	9	217	218	53	128	3	1	0	0	62	9	1	.145	11	26	0	0	1.1	1.000
1964			12	14	.462	4.43	40	32	5	219.1	231	73	184	0	0	0	0	75	12	1	.160	6	27	7	2	1.0	.825
1965	2 teams	KC A (12G 0–6)	DET A (30G 4–6)																								
″	total		4	12	.250	4.18	42	5	0	92.2	96	33	79	0	4	7	4	17	3	0	.176	4	10	2	0	0.4	.875
1966	DET	A	4	2	.667	3.08	54	0	0	108	105	35	79	0	4	2	7	18	2	0	.111	8	26	1	2	0.6	.971
1967	2 teams	DET A (2G 0–1)	CLE A (48G 0–3)																								
″	total		0	4	.000	3.59	50	1	0	90.1	72	22	74	0	0	3	8	8	0	0	.000	7	11	2	0	0.4	.900
1970	PIT	N	2	1	.667	4.74	23	0	0	38	38	7	25	0	2	1	2	6	0	0	.000	4	8	3	1	0.7	.800
1971	BAL	A	0	1	.000	3.00	5	0	0	15	16	5	4	0	0	1	0	3	0	0	.000	0	3	1	1	0.8	.750
1973	2 teams	BAL A (11G 1–1)	STL N (42G 4–4)																								
″	total		5	5	.500	2.94	53	2	0	107	96	22	61	0	5	5	7	7	1	0	.143	4	19	1	0	0.5	.958
1974	2 teams	STL N (42G 5–2)	CAL A (4G 0–0)																								
″	total		5	2	.714	2.21	46	0	0	53	51	21	28	0	5	2	4	2	1	0	.500	2	7	0	4	0.2	1.000
1975	CAL	A	0	2	.000	2.13	7	0	0	12.2	13	8	4	0	0	2	0	0	0	0	—	0	0	0	0	0.0	.000
14 yrs.			56	77	.421	3.70	427	93	21	1203	1175	352	818	4	24	28	40	264	36	2	.136	64	163	19	11	0.6	.923

Ramon Pena

PENA, RAMON ARTURO
Born Ramon Arturo Pena (Padilla).
Brother of Tony Pena.
B. May 5, 1962, Santiago, Dominican Republic.
BR TR 5′10″ 155 lbs.

Year	Team		W	L	PCT	ERA	G	GS	CG	IP	H	BB	SO	ShO	Relief Pitching W	Relief Pitching L	Relief Pitching SV	Batting AB	Batting H	Batting HR	BA	PO	A	E	DP	TC/G	FA
1989	DET	A	0	0	—	6.00	8	0	0	18	26	8	12	0	0	0	0	0	0	0	—	1	5	0	1	0.8	1.000

Russ Pence

PENCE, RUSSELL WILLIAM
B. Mar. 11, 1900, Marine, Ill. D. Aug. 11, 1971, Hot Springs, Ark.
BR TR 6′ 185 lbs.

Year	Team		W	L	PCT	ERA	G	GS	CG	IP	H	BB	SO	ShO	Relief Pitching W	Relief Pitching L	Relief Pitching SV	Batting AB	Batting H	Batting HR	BA	PO	A	E	DP	TC/G	FA
1921	CHI	A	0	0	—	8.44	4	0	0	5.1	6	7	2	0	0	0	0	1	0	0	.000	1	2	0	0	0.8	1.000

Ken Penner

PENNER, KENNETH WILLIAM
B. Apr. 24, 1896, Booneville, Ind. D. May 28, 1959, Sacramento, Calif.
BL TR 5′11½″ 170 lbs.

Year	Team		W	L	PCT	ERA	G	GS	CG	IP	H	BB	SO	ShO	Relief Pitching W	Relief Pitching L	Relief Pitching SV	Batting AB	Batting H	Batting HR	BA	PO	A	E	DP	TC/G	FA
1916	CLE	A	1	0	1.000	4.26	4	2	0	12.2	14	4	5	0	0	0	0	2	0	0	.000	0	7	1	1	2.0	.875
1929	CHI	N	0	1	.000	2.84	5	0	0	12.2	14	6	3	0	0	1	0	4	1	0	.250	0	3	0	0	0.6	1.000
2 yrs.			1	1	.500	3.55	9	2	0	25.1	28	10	8	0	0	1	0	6	1	0	.167	0	10	1	1	1.2	.909

Brad Pennington

PENNINGTON, BRAD LEE
B. Apr. 14, 1969, Salem, Ind.
BL TL 6′ 5″ 205 lbs.

Year	Team		W	L	PCT	ERA	G	GS	CG	IP	H	BB	SO	ShO	Relief Pitching W	Relief Pitching L	Relief Pitching SV	Batting AB	Batting H	Batting HR	BA	PO	A	E	DP	TC/G	FA
1993	BAL	A	3	2	.600	6.55	34	0	0	33	34	25	39	0	3	2	4	0	0	0	—	1	2	0	0	0.1	1.000
1994			0	1	.000	12.00	8	0	0	6	9	8	7	0	0	1	0	0	0	0	—	0	0	1	0	0.1	.000
1995	2 teams	BAL A (8G 0–1)	CIN N (6G 0–0)																								
″	total		0	1	.000	6.61	14	0	0	16.1	12	22	17	0	0	1	0	2	0	0	.000	1	0	1	0	0.1	.500
3 yrs.			3	4	.429	7.16	56	0	0	55.1	55	55	63	0	3	4	4	2	0	0	.000	2	2	2	0	0.1	.667

Kewpie Pennington

PENNINGTON, GEORGE LOUIS — BR TR 5′ 8½″ 168 lbs.
B. Sept. 24, 1896, New York, N. Y. D. May 3, 1953, Newark, N. J.

Year	Team	W	L	PCT	ERA	G	GS	CG	IP	H	BB	SO	ShO	Relief Pitching W	Relief Pitching L	Relief Pitching SV	Batting AB	Batting H	Batting HR	BA	PO	A	E	DP	TC/G	FA
1917	STL A	0	0	—	0.00	1	0	0	1	1	0	0	0	0	0	0	0	0	0	—	0	0	0	0	0.0	.000

Herb Pennock

PENNOCK, HERBERT JEFFERIS (The Knight of Kennett Square) — BB TL 6′ 160 lbs.
B. Feb. 10, 1894, Kennett Square, Pa. D. Jan. 30, 1948, New York, N. Y.
Hall of Fame 1948.

Year	Team	W	L	PCT	ERA	G	GS	CG	IP	H	BB	SO	ShO	Relief Pitching W	Relief Pitching L	Relief Pitching SV	Batting AB	Batting H	Batting HR	BA	PO	A	E	DP	TC/G	FA
1912	PHI A	1	2	.333	4.50	17	2	1	50	48	30	38	0	1	1	2	15	2	0	.133	2	15	1	0	1.1	.944
1913		2	1	.667	5.13	14	4	1	33.1	30	22	17	0	1	0	0	9	1	0	.111	0	9	0	0	0.6	1.000
1914		11	4	.733	2.79	28	14	8	151.2	136	65	90	3	2	2	3	56	12	0	.214	9	37	3	1	1.8	.939
1915	2 teams PHI A (11G 3–6) BOS A (5G 0–0)																									
″	total	3	6	.333	6.36	16	9	3	58	69	39	31	1	0	1	1	24	6	0	.250	2	15	2	1	1.2	.895
1916	BOS A	0	2	.000	3.04	9	2	0	26.2	23	8	12	0	0	0	1	8	1	0	.125	3	4	0	0	0.8	1.000
1917		5	5	.500	3.31	24	5	4	100.2	90	23	35	1	2	3	1	24	4	0	.167	1	30	2	2	1.4	.939
1919		16	8	.667	2.71	32	26	16	219	223	48	70	5	1	0	0	75	13	0	.173	13	45	2	5	1.9	.967
1920		16	13	.552	3.68	37	31	19	242.1	244	61	68	4	3	0	2	77	20	0	.260	6	53	1	0	1.6	.983
1921		12	14	.462	4.04	32	31	15	222.2	268	59	91	1	0	0	0	85	18	1	.212	11	59	2	3	2.3	.972
1922		10	17	.370	4.32	32	26	15	202	230	74	59	1	1	1	1	65	9	0	.138	8	56	1	1	2.0	.985
1923	NY A	19	6	**.760**	3.33	35	27	21	224.1	235	68	93	1	1	0	3	83	16	0	.193	4	66	1	4	2.0	.986
1924		21	9	.700	2.83	40	34	25	286.1	302	64	101	4	1	0	3	101	16	2	.158	10	61	0	5	1.8	1.000
1925		16	17	.485	2.96	47	31	21	**277**	267	71	88	2	1	2	2	99	20	0	.202	7	54	4	3	1.4	.938
1926		23	11	.676	3.62	40	33	19	266.1	294	43	78	1	2	1	2	85	18	0	.212	2	73	1	6	1.9	.987
1927		19	8	.704	3.00	34	26	18	209.2	225	48	51	1	2	0	2	69	15	0	.217	4	45	1	2	1.5	.980
1928		17	6	.739	2.56	28	24	19	211	215	40	53	**5**	0	0	3	74	15	0	.203	5	59	1	3	2.3	.985
1929		9	11	.450	4.90	27	23	8	158	205	28	49	1	0	1	2	51	9	0	.176	4	31	0	2	1.3	1.000
1930		11	7	.611	4.32	25	19	11	156.1	194	20	46	1	1	1	0	60	11	0	.183	3	36	1	1	1.6	.975
1931		11	6	.647	4.28	25	25	12	189.1	247	30	65	1	0	0	0	66	10	1	.152	1	37	1	4	1.6	.974
1932		9	5	.643	4.60	22	21	9	146.2	191	38	54	1	0	1	0	53	8	0	.151	4	29	1	1	1.5	.971
1933		7	4	.636	5.54	23	5	2	65	96	21	22	1	3	3	4	21	5	0	.238	2	12	1	1	0.7	.933
1934	BOS A	2	0	1.000	3.05	30	2	1	62	68	16	16	0	1	0	1	14	3	0	.214	0	8	0	0	0.3	1.000
22 yrs.		240	162	.597	3.61	617	420	248	3558.1	3900	916	1227	35	23	17	33	1214	232	4	.191	101	834	26	45	1.6	.973
WORLD SERIES																										
1914	PHI A	0	0	—	0.00	1	0	0	3	2	2	3	0	0	0	0	1	0	0	.000	0	1	0	0	1.0	1.000
1923	NY A	2	0	1.000	3.63	3	2	1	17.1	19	1	8	0	0	0	1	6	0	0	.000	0	2	0	0	0.7	1.000
1926		2	0	1.000	1.23	3	2	2	22	13	4	8	0	0	0	0	7	1	0	.143	0	6	0	0	2.0	1.000
1927		1	0	1.000	1.00	1	1	1	9	3	0	1	0	0	0	0	4	0	0	.000	1	1	0	0	2.0	1.000
1932		0	0	—	2.25	2	0	0	4	2	1	4	0	0	0	2	1	0	0	.000	0	1	0	0	0.5	1.000
5 yrs.		5	0	1.000	1.95	10	5	4	55.1	39	8	24	0	0	0	3	19	1	0	.053	1	11	0	0	1.2	1.000
		8th		**1st**												**4th**										

Paul Penson

PENSON, PAUL EUGENE — BR TR 6′ 1″ 185 lbs.
B. July 12, 1931, Kansas City, Kans.

Year	Team	W	L	PCT	ERA	G	GS	CG	IP	H	BB	SO	ShO	Relief Pitching W	Relief Pitching L	Relief Pitching SV	Batting AB	Batting H	Batting HR	BA	PO	A	E	DP	TC/G	FA
1954	PHI N	1	1	.500	4.50	5	3	0	16	14	14	3	0	0	0	0	7	0	0	.000	0	1	1	0	0.4	.500

Gene Pentz

PENTZ, EUGENE DAVID — BR TR 6′ 1″ 200 lbs.
B. June 21, 1953, Johnstown, Pa.

Year	Team	W	L	PCT	ERA	G	GS	CG	IP	H	BB	SO	ShO	Relief Pitching W	Relief Pitching L	Relief Pitching SV	Batting AB	Batting H	Batting HR	BA	PO	A	E	DP	TC/G	FA
1975	DET A	0	4	.000	3.20	13	0	0	25.1	27	20	21	0	0	4	0	0	0	0	—	2	2	2	0	0.5	.667
1976	HOU N	3	3	.500	2.95	40	0	0	64	62	31	36	0	3	3	5	5	1	0	.200	3	12	0	2	0.4	1.000
1977		5	2	.714	3.83	41	4	0	87	76	44	51	0	4	0	2	13	0	0	.000	5	13	0	0	0.4	1.000
1978		0	0	—	6.00	10	0	0	15	12	13	8	0	0	0	0	1	0	0	.000	3	6	0	0	0.9	1.000
4 yrs.		8	9	.471	3.62	104	4	0	191.1	177	108	116	0	7	7	7	19	1	0	.053	13	33	2	2	0.5	.958

Jimmy Peoples

PEOPLES, JAMES ELSWORTH — TR 5′ 8″ 200 lbs.
B. Oct. 8, 1863, Big Beaver, Mich. D. Aug. 29, 1920, Detroit, Mich.

Year	Team	W	L	PCT	ERA	G	GS	CG	IP	H	BB	SO	ShO	Relief Pitching W	Relief Pitching L	Relief Pitching SV	Batting AB	Batting H	Batting HR	BA	PO	A	E	DP	TC/G	FA
1885	CIN AA	0	2	.000	*12.00*	2	2	1	15	30	2	4	0	0	0	0	*				142	168	46	21	4.9	.871

Bob Pepper

PEPPER, ROBERT ERNEST — BR TR 6′ 2″ 178 lbs.
B. May 3, 1895, Rosston, Pa. D. Apr. 8, 1968, Fort Cliff, Pa.

Year	Team	W	L	PCT	ERA	G	GS	CG	IP	H	BB	SO	ShO	Relief Pitching W	Relief Pitching L	Relief Pitching SV	Batting AB	Batting H	Batting HR	BA	PO	A	E	DP	TC/G	FA
1915	PHI A	0	0	—	1.80	1	0	0	5	6	4	0	0	0	0	0	2	0	0	.000	1	1	0	0	2.0	1.000

Laurin Pepper

PEPPER, HUGH McLAURIN — BR TR 5′11″ 190 lbs.
B. Jan. 18, 1931, Vaughan, Miss.

Year	Team	W	L	PCT	ERA	G	GS	CG	IP	H	BB	SO	ShO	Relief Pitching W	Relief Pitching L	Relief Pitching SV	Batting AB	Batting H	Batting HR	BA	PO	A	E	DP	TC/G	FA
1954	PIT N	1	5	.167	7.99	14	8	0	50.2	63	43	17	0	0	0	0	17	4	0	.235	1	17	1	0	1.4	.947
1955		0	1	.000	10.35	14	1	0	20	30	25	7	0	0	0	0	2	0	0	.000	1	2	0	1	0.2	1.000
1956		1	1	.500	3.00	11	7	0	30	30	25	12	0	0	0	0	6	0	0	.000	2	2	0	0	0.4	1.000
1957		0	1	.000	8.00	5	1	0	9	11	5	4	0	0	1	0	0	0	0	—	1	0	0	0	0.2	1.000
4 yrs.		2	8	.200	7.06	44	17	0	109.2	134	98	40	0	0	1	0	25	4	0	.160	5	21	1	1	0.6	.963

Bill Peppers

PEPPERS, HARRISON — BL
B. Sept. 1866, Ky. D. Nov. 5, 1903, Webb City, Mo.

Year	Team	W	L	PCT	ERA	G	GS	CG	IP	H	BB	SO	ShO	Relief Pitching W	Relief Pitching L	Relief Pitching SV	Batting AB	Batting H	Batting HR	BA	PO	A	E	DP	TC/G	FA
1894	LOU N	0	1	.000	6.75	2	1	0	8	10	4	0	0	0	0	0	4	0	0	.000	0	1	0	0	0.5	1.000

Luis Peraza

PERAZA, LUIS — BR TR 5′11″ 185 lbs.
Born Luis Peraza (Rios).
B. June 17, 1942, Rio Piedras, Puerto Rico.

Year	Team	W	L	PCT	ERA	G	GS	CG	IP	H	BB	SO	ShO	Relief Pitching W	Relief Pitching L	Relief Pitching SV	Batting AB	Batting H	Batting HR	BA	PO	A	E	DP	TC/G	FA
1969	PHI N	0	0	—	6.00	8	0	0	9	12	2	7	0	0	0	0	1	0	0	.000	0	1	0	0	0.1	1.000

Oswald Peraza

PERAZA, OSWALD JOSE — BR TR 6′ 4″ 172 lbs.
B. Oct. 19, 1962, Puerto Cabello, Venezuela.

Year	Team	W	L	PCT	ERA	G	GS	CG	IP	H	BB	SO	ShO	Relief Pitching W	Relief Pitching L	Relief Pitching SV	Batting AB	Batting H	Batting HR	BA	PO	A	E	DP	TC/G	FA
1988	BAL A	5	7	.417	5.55	19	15	1	86	98	37	61	0	0	0	0	0	0	0	—	8	11	3	1	1.2	.864

Troy Percival

PERCIVAL, TROY EUGENE — BR TR 6′ 3″ 200 lbs.
B. Aug. 9, 1969, Fontana, Calif.

Year	Team	W	L	PCT	ERA	G	GS	CG	IP	H	BB	SO	ShO	Relief Pitching W	Relief Pitching L	Relief Pitching SV	Batting AB	Batting H	Batting HR	BA	PO	A	E	DP	TC/G	FA
1995	CAL A	3	2	.600	1.95	62	0	0	74	37	26	94	0	3	2	3	0	0	0	—	2	4	0	0	0.1	1.000

Hub Perdue

PERDUE, HERBERT RODNEY (The Gallatin Squash)
B. June 7, 1882, Bethpage, Tenn. D. Oct. 31, 1968, Gallatin, Tenn.
BR TR 5′10½″ 192 lbs.

Year	Team	W	L	PCT	ERA	G	GS	CG	IP	H	BB	SO	ShO	Relief Pitching W	Relief Pitching L	Relief Pitching SV	Batting AB	Batting H	Batting HR	BA	PO	A	E	DP	TC/G	FA
1911	BOS N	6	10	.375	4.98	24	19	9	137.1	180	41	40	0	0	0	1	48	10	0	.208	6	36	5	4	2.0	.894
1912		13	16	.448	3.80	37	30	20	249	295	54	101	1	0	2	3	87	12	0	.138	6	45	4	1	1.5	.927
1913		16	13	.552	3.26	38	32	16	212.1	201	39	91	3	2	0	1	67	7	0	.104	7	21	3	0	0.8	.903
1914	2 teams BOS N (9G 2–5) STL N (22G 8–8)																									
″	total	10	13	.435	3.57	31	28	14	204.1	220	46	56	0	0	0	1	62	9	0	.145	2	41	2	0	1.5	.956
1915	STL N	6	12	.333	4.21	31	13	5	115.1	141	19	29	1	3	**5**	1	36	4	0	.111	1	32	1	0	1.1	.971
5 yrs.		51	64	.443	3.85	161	122	64	918.1	1037	199	317	5	5	7	7	300	42	0	.140	22	175	15	5	1.3	.929

Carlos Perez

PEREZ, CARLOS
Born Carlos Gross (Perez).
Brother of Melido Perez. Brother of Pascual Perez.
B. Apr. 14, 1971, Nigua, Dominican Republic.
BL TL 6′ 3″ 195 lbs.

Year	Team	W	L	PCT	ERA	G	GS	CG	IP	H	BB	SO	ShO	Relief Pitching W	Relief Pitching L	Relief Pitching SV	Batting AB	Batting H	Batting HR	BA	PO	A	E	DP	TC/G	FA
1995	MON N	10	8	.556	3.69	28	23	2	141.1	142	28	106	1	0	0	0	45	6	1	.133	6	23	2	1	1.1	.935

George Perez

PEREZ, GEORGE THOMAS
B. Dec. 29, 1937, San Fernando, Calif.
BR TR 6′ 2½″ 200 lbs.

Year	Team	W	L	PCT	ERA	G	GS	CG	IP	H	BB	SO	ShO	Relief Pitching W	Relief Pitching L	Relief Pitching SV	Batting AB	Batting H	Batting HR	BA	PO	A	E	DP	TC/G	FA
1958	PIT N	0	1	.000	5.40	4	0	0	8.1	9	4	2	0	0	1	1	2	0	0	.000	0	0	0	0	0.0	.000

Melido Perez

PEREZ, MELIDO TURPEN
Born Melido Turpen Gross (Perez).
Brother of Carlos Perez. Brother of Pascual Perez.
B. Feb. 15, 1966, San Cristobal, Dominican Republic.
BR TR 6′ 4″ 180 lbs.

Year	Team	W	L	PCT	ERA	G	GS	CG	IP	H	BB	SO	ShO	Relief Pitching W	Relief Pitching L	Relief Pitching SV	Batting AB	Batting H	Batting HR	BA	PO	A	E	DP	TC/G	FA
1987	KC A	1	1	.500	7.84	3	3	0	10.1	18	5	5	0	0	0	0	0	0	0	—	0	0	1	0	0.3	.000
1988	CHI A	12	10	.545	3.79	32	32	3	197	186	72	138	1	0	0	0	0	0	0	—	8	18	1	1	0.8	.963
1989		11	14	.440	5.01	31	31	2	183.1	187	90	141	0	0	0	0	0	0	0	—	9	19	1	3	0.9	.966
1990		13	14	.481	4.61	35	35	3	197	177	86	161	3	0	0	0	0	0	0	—	4	20	1	0	0.7	.960
1991		8	7	.533	3.12	49	8	0	135.2	111	52	128	0	7	3	1	0	0	0	—	9	19	3	1	0.6	.903
1992	NY A	13	16	.448	2.87	33	33	10	247.2	212	93	218	1	0	0	0	0	0	0	—	15	28	10	0	1.6	.811
1993		6	14	.300	5.19	25	25	0	163	173	64	148	0	0	0	0	0	0	0	—	5	17	0	0	0.9	1.000
1994		9	4	.692	4.10	22	22	1	151.1	134	58	109	0	0	0	0	0	0	0	—	15	15	1	1	1.4	.968
1995		5	5	.500	5.58	13	12	1	69.1	70	31	44	0	0	0	0	0	0	0	—	4	4	1	0	0.7	.889
9 yrs.		78	85	.479	4.17	243	201	20	1354.2	1268	551	1092	5	7	3	1	0	0	0		69	140	19	6	0.9	.917

Mike Perez

PEREZ, MICHAEL IRVIN
Born Michael Irvin Perez (Ortega).
B. Oct. 19, 1964, Yauco, Puerto Rico.
BR TR 6′ 185 lbs.

Year	Team	W	L	PCT	ERA	G	GS	CG	IP	H	BB	SO	ShO	Relief Pitching W	Relief Pitching L	Relief Pitching SV	Batting AB	Batting H	Batting HR	BA	PO	A	E	DP	TC/G	FA
1990	STL N	1	0	1.000	3.95	13	0	0	13.2	12	3	5	0	1	0	1	1	0	0	.000	3	2	0	0	0.4	1.000
1991		0	2	.000	5.82	14	0	0	17	19	7	7	0	0	2	0	0	0	0	—	0	2	0	0	0.1	1.000
1992		9	3	.750	1.84	77	0	0	93	70	32	46	0	9	3	0	4	0	0	.000	9	15	0	2	0.3	1.000
1993		7	2	.778	2.48	65	0	0	72.2	65	20	58	0	7	2	7	1	0	0	.000	2	12	0	2	0.2	1.000
1994		2	3	.400	8.71	36	0	0	31	52	10	20	0	2	3	12	0	0	0	—	1	4	2	1	0.2	.714
1995	CHI N	2	6	.250	3.66	68	0	0	71.1	72	27	49	0	2	6	2	4	0	0	.000	5	8	1	1	0.2	.929
6 yrs.		21	16	.568	3.47	273	0	0	298.2	290	99	185	0	21	16	22	10	0	0	.000	20	43	3	6	0.2	.955

Pascual Perez

PEREZ, PASCUAL
Born Pascual Gross (Perez).
Brother of Carlos Perez. Brother of Melido Perez.
B. May 17, 1957, San Cristobal, Dominican Republic.
BR TR 6′ 2″ 162 lbs.

Year	Team	W	L	PCT	ERA	G	GS	CG	IP	H	BB	SO	ShO	Relief Pitching W	Relief Pitching L	Relief Pitching SV	Batting AB	Batting H	Batting HR	BA	PO	A	E	DP	TC/G	FA
1980	PIT N	0	1	.000	3.75	2	2	0	12	15	2	7	0	0	0	0	4	1	0	.250	1	1	0	0	1.0	1.000
1981		2	7	.222	3.98	17	13	2	86	92	34	46	0	0	1	0	22	3	0	.136	7	13	1	0	1.2	.952
1982	ATL N	4	4	.500	3.06	16	11	0	79.1	85	17	29	0	2	0	0	18	3	0	.167	9	11	1	2	1.3	.952
1983		15	8	.652	3.43	33	33	7	215.1	213	51	144	1	0	0	0	75	12	0	.160	24	33	4	2	1.8	.934
1984		14	8	.636	3.74	30	30	4	211.2	208	51	145	1	0	0	0	66	5	0	.076	19	40	1	1	2.0	.983
1985		1	13	.071	6.14	22	22	0	95.1	115	57	57	0	0	0	0	25	3	0	.120	7	9	1	0	0.8	.941
1987	MON N	7	0	1.000	2.30	10	10	2	70.1	52	16	58	0	0	0	0	24	1	0	.042	6	17	3	0	2.6	.885
1988		12	8	.600	2.44	27	27	4	188	133	44	131	2	0	0	0	54	2	0	.037	13	38	0	2	1.9	1.000
1989		9	13	.409	3.31	33	28	2	198.1	178	45	152	0	1	1	0	54	11	0	.204	17	26	2	1	1.4	.956
1990	NY A	1	2	.333	1.29	3	3	0	14	8	3	12	0	0	0	0	0	0	0	—	0	0	0	0	0.0	.000
1991		2	4	.333	3.18	14	14	0	73.2	68	24	41	0	0	0	0	0	0	0	—	2	10	2	1	1.0	.857
11 yrs.		67	68	.496	3.44	207	193	21	1244	1167	344	822	4	3	2	0	342	41	0	.120	105	198	15	9	1.5	.953
LEAGUE CHAMPIONSHIP SERIES																										
1982	ATL N	0	1	.000	5.19	2	1	0	8.2	10	2	4	0	0	0	0	3	0	0	.000	0	1	0	0	0.5	1.000

Yorkis Perez

PEREZ, YORKIS MIGUEL
Born Yorkis Miguel Perez (Vargas).
B. Sept. 30, 1967, Bajos de Haina, Dominican Republic.
BL TL 6′ 180 lbs.

Year	Team	W	L	PCT	ERA	G	GS	CG	IP	H	BB	SO	ShO	Relief Pitching W	Relief Pitching L	Relief Pitching SV	Batting AB	Batting H	Batting HR	BA	PO	A	E	DP	TC/G	FA
1991	CHI N	1	0	1.000	2.08	3	0	0	4.1	2	2	3	0	1	0	0	0	0	0	—	0	1	0	0	0.3	1.000
1994	FLA N	3	0	1.000	3.54	44	0	0	40.2	33	14	41	0	3	0	0	2	0	0	.000	5	1	0	0	0.1	1.000
1995		2	6	.250	5.21	69	0	0	46.2	35	28	47	0	2	6	1	2	0	0	.000	1	4	0	0	0.1	1.000
3 yrs.		6	6	.500	4.32	116	0	0	91.2	70	44	91	0	6	6	1	4	0	0	.000	6	6	0	0	0.1	1.000

Cecil Perkins

PERKINS, CECIL BOYCE
B. Dec. 1, 1940, Baltimore, Md.
BR TR 6′ 175 lbs.

Year	Team	W	L	PCT	ERA	G	GS	CG	IP	H	BB	SO	ShO	Relief Pitching W	Relief Pitching L	Relief Pitching SV	Batting AB	Batting H	Batting HR	BA	PO	A	E	DP	TC/G	FA
1967	NY A	0	1	.000	9.00	2	1	0	5	6	2	1	0	0	0	0	1	0	0	.000	1	1	0	0	1.0	1.000

Charlie Perkins

PERKINS, CHARLES SULLIVAN (Lefty)
B. Sept. 9, 1905, Ensley, Ala. D. May 25, 1988, Salem, Ore.
BR TL 6′ 1″ 175 lbs.

Year	Team	W	L	PCT	ERA	G	GS	CG	IP	H	BB	SO	ShO	Relief Pitching W	Relief Pitching L	Relief Pitching SV	Batting AB	Batting H	Batting HR	BA	PO	A	E	DP	TC/G	FA
1930	PHI A	0	0	—	6.46	8	1	0	23.2	25	15	15	0	0	0	0	8	1	0	.125	1	5	1	0	0.9	.857
1934	BKN N	0	3	.000	8.51	11	2	0	24.1	37	14	5	0	0	1	0	7	2	0	.286	1	3	2	0	0.5	.667
2 yrs.		0	3	.000	7.50	19	3	0	48	62	29	20	0	0	1	0	15	3	0	.200	2	8	3	0	0.7	.769

John Perkovich

PERKOVICH, JOHN JOSEPH
B. Mar. 10, 1924, Chicago, Ill.
BR TR 5′11″ 175 lbs.

Year	Team	W	L	PCT	ERA	G	GS	CG	IP	H	BB	SO	ShO	Relief W	Relief L	Relief SV	Batting AB	Batting H	Batting HR	BA	PO	A	E	DP	TC/G	FA
1950	CHI A	0	0	—	7.20	1	0	0	5	7	1	3	0	0	0	0	1	0	0	.000	0	0	0	0	0.0	.000

Harry Perkowski

PERKOWSKI, HARRY WALTER
B. Sept. 6, 1922, Dante, Va.
BL TL 6′2½″ 196 lbs.

Year	Team	W	L	PCT	ERA	G	GS	CG	IP	H	BB	SO	ShO	Relief W	Relief L	Relief SV	Batting AB	Batting H	Batting HR	BA	PO	A	E	DP	TC/G	FA
1947	CIN N	0	0	—	3.68	3	1	0	7.1	12	3	2	0	0	0	0	1	0	0	.000	0	1	0	0	0.3	1.000
1949		1	1	.500	4.56	5	3	2	23.2	21	14	3	0	0	0	0	9	3	0	.333	0	2	0	0	0.4	1.000
1950		0	0	—	5.24	22	0	0	34.1	36	23	19	0	0	0	0	22	7	0	.318	2	11	0	1	0.6	1.000
1951		3	6	.333	2.82	35	7	1	102	96	46	56	0	0	2	1	25	1	0	.040	1	22	0	2	0.7	1.000
1952		12	10	.545	3.80	33	24	11	194	197	89	86	1	0	2	0	75	12	0	.160	6	43	1	3	1.5	.980
1953		12	11	.522	4.52	33	25	7	193	204	62	70	2	2	0	2	69	14	0	.203	9	35	0	0	1.3	1.000
1954		2	8	.200	6.11	28	12	3	95.2	100	62	32	1	0	2	0	25	4	1	.160	5	12	1	2	0.6	.944
1955	CHI N	3	4	.429	5.29	25	4	0	47.2	53	25	28	0	3	1	2	13	2	0	.154	8	12	0	0	0.8	1.000
8 yrs.		33	40	.452	4.37	184	76	24	697.2	719	324	296	4	5	7	5	239	43	1	.180	31	138	2	8	0.9	.988

Jon Perlman

PERLMAN, JONATHAN SAMUEL
B. Dec. 13, 1956, Dallas, Tex.
BL TR 6′3″ 185 lbs.

Year	Team	W	L	PCT	ERA	G	GS	CG	IP	H	BB	SO	ShO	Relief W	Relief L	Relief SV	Batting AB	Batting H	Batting HR	BA	PO	A	E	DP	TC/G	FA
1985	CHI N	1	0	1.000	11.42	6	0	0	8.2	10	8	4	0	1	0	0	1	0	0	.000	0	2	0	0	0.3	1.000
1987	SF N	0	0	—	3.97	10	0	0	11.1	11	4	3	0	0	0	0	0	0	0	—	2	1	1	0	0.4	.750
1988	CLE A	0	2	.000	5.49	10	0	0	19.2	25	11	10	0	0	2	0	0	0	0	—	1	7	0	0	0.8	1.000
3 yrs.		1	2	.333	6.35	26	0	0	39.2	46	23	17	0	1	2	0	1	0	0	.000	3	10	1	0	0.5	.929

Len Perme

PERME, LEONARD JOHN
B. Nov. 25, 1917, Cleveland, Ohio
BL TL 6′ 170 lbs.

Year	Team	W	L	PCT	ERA	G	GS	CG	IP	H	BB	SO	ShO	Relief W	Relief L	Relief SV	Batting AB	Batting H	Batting HR	BA	PO	A	E	DP	TC/G	FA
1942	CHI A	0	1	.000	1.38	4	1	1	13	5	4	4	0	0	0	0	3	1	0	.333	0	2	0	1	0.5	1.000
1946		0	0	—	8.31	4	0	0	4.1	6	7	2	0	0	0	0	0	0	0	—	0	3	0	0	0.8	1.000
2 yrs.		0	1	.000	3.12	8	1	1	17.1	11	11	6	0	0	0	0	3	1	0	.333	0	5	0	1	0.6	1.000

Hub Pernoll

PERNOLL, HENRY HUBBARD
B. Mar. 14, 1888, Grant's Pass, Ore. D. Feb. 18, 1944, Grant's Pass, Ore.
BR TL 5′8″ 175 lbs.

Year	Team	W	L	PCT	ERA	G	GS	CG	IP	H	BB	SO	ShO	Relief W	Relief L	Relief SV	Batting AB	Batting H	Batting HR	BA	PO	A	E	DP	TC/G	FA
1910	DET A	4	3	.571	2.96	11	5	4	54.2	54	14	25	0	0	2	0	16	1	0	.063	4	31	1	1	3.3	.972
1912		0	0	—	6.00	3	0	0	9	9	4	3	0	0	0	0	3	0	0	.000	0	3	0	0	1.0	1.000
2 yrs.		4	3	.571	3.39	14	5	4	63.2	63	18	28	0	0	2	0	19	1	0	.053	4	34	1	1	2.8	.974

Ron Perranoski

PERRANOSKI, RONALD PETER
Born Ronald Peter Perzanowski.
B. Apr. 1, 1936, Paterson, N. J.
BL TL 6′ 180 lbs.

Year	Team	W	L	PCT	ERA	G	GS	CG	IP	H	BB	SO	ShO	Relief W	Relief L	Relief SV	Batting AB	Batting H	Batting HR	BA	PO	A	E	DP	TC/G	FA
1961	LA N	7	5	.583	2.65	53	1	0	91.2	82	41	56	0	7	5	6	12	1	0	.083	5	17	1	1	0.4	.957
1962		6	6	.500	2.85	**70**	0	0	107.1	103	36	68	0	6	6	20	14	1	0	.071	3	17	4	3	0.3	.833
1963		16	3	**.842**	1.67	**69**	0	0	129	112	43	75	0	**16**	3	21	24	3	0	.125	6	24	1	0	0.4	.968
1964		5	7	.417	3.09	72	0	0	125.1	128	46	79	0	5	7	14	19	2	0	.105	6	32	2	2	0.6	.950
1965		6	6	.500	2.24	59	0	0	104.2	85	40	53	0	6	6	17	19	3	0	.158	4	15	2	1	0.4	.905
1966		6	7	.462	3.18	55	0	0	82	82	31	50	0	6	7	7	8	2	0	.250	7	23	1	1	0.6	.968
1967		6	7	.462	2.45	**70**	0	0	110	97	45	75	0	6	7	16	10	1	0	.100	4	26	1	2	0.4	.968
1968	MIN A	8	7	.533	3.10	66	0	0	87	86	38	65	0	8	7	6	7	0	0	.000	4	13	1	0	0.3	.944
1969		9	10	.474	2.11	75	0	0	119.2	85	52	62	0	9	10	**31**	24	2	0	.083	4	23	1	2	0.4	.964
1970		7	8	.467	2.43	67	0	0	111	108	42	55	0	7	8	**34**	24	1	0	.042	0	15	1	0	0.2	.938
1971	2 teams MIN A (36G 1–4) DET A (11G 0–1)																									
″	total	1	5	.167	5.49	47	0	0	60.2	76	31	29	0	1	5	7	5	0	0	.000	1	10	3	0	0.3	.786
1972	2 teams DET A (17G 0–1) LA N (9G 2–0)																									
″	total	2	1	.667	5.30	26	0	0	35.2	42	16	15	0	2	1	0	1	0	0	.000	1	3	0	0	0.2	1.000
1973	CAL A	0	2	.000	4.09	8	0	0	11	11	7	5	0	0	2	0	0	0	0	—	0	3	0	0	0.4	1.000
13 yrs.		79	74	.516	2.79	737	1	0	1175	1097	468	687	0	79	74	179	167	16	0	.096	45	221	18	12	0.4	.937
LEAGUE CHAMPIONSHIP SERIES																										
1969	MIN A	0	1	.000	5.79	3	0	0	4.2	8	0	2	0	0	1	0	1	0	0	.000	0	0	0	0	0.0	.000
1970		0	0	—	19.29	2	0	0	2.1	5	1	3	0	0	0	0	0	0	0	—	0	1	0	1	0.5	1.000
2 yrs.		0	1	.000	10.29	5	0	0	7	13	1	5	0	0	1	0	1	0	0	.000	0	1	0	1	0.2	1.000
WORLD SERIES																										
1963	LA N	0	0	—	0.00	1	0	0	0.2	1	0	1	0	0	0	1	0	0	0	—	0	0	0	0	0.0	.000
1965		0	0	—	7.36	2	0	0	3.2	3	4	1	0	0	0	0	0	0	0	—	0	1	0	1	0.5	1.000
1966		0	0	—	5.40	2	0	0	3.1	4	1	2	0	0	0	0	0	0	0	—	0	2	1	0	1.5	.667
3 yrs.		0	0		5.87	5	0	0	7.2	8	5	4	0	0	0	1	0	0	0		0	3	1	1	0.8	.750

Bill Perrin

PERRIN, WILLIAM JOSEPH (Lefty)
B. June 23, 1910, New Orleans, La. D. June 30, 1974, New Orleans, La.
BR TL 5′11″ 172 lbs.

Year	Team	W	L	PCT	ERA	G	GS	CG	IP	H	BB	SO	ShO	Relief W	Relief L	Relief SV	Batting AB	Batting H	Batting HR	BA	PO	A	E	DP	TC/G	FA
1934	CLE A	0	1	.000	14.40	1	1	0	5	13	2	3	0	0	0	0	2	0	0	.000	0	2	0	0	2.0	1.000

George Perring

PERRING, GEORGE WILSON
B. Aug. 13, 1884, Sharon, Wis. D. Aug. 20, 1960, Beloit, Wis.
BR TR 6′ 190 lbs.

Year	Team	W	L	PCT	ERA	G	GS	CG	IP	H	BB	SO	ShO	Relief W	Relief L	Relief SV	Batting AB	Batting H	Batting HR	BA	PO	A	E	DP	TC/G	FA
1914	KC F	0	0	—	13.50	1	0	0	0.2	2	1	0	0	0	0	0	*				133	236	29	16	4.5	.927

Pol Perritt

PERRITT, WILLIAM DAYTON
B. Aug. 30, 1892, Arcadia, La. D. Oct. 15, 1947, Shreveport, La.
BR TR 6′2″ 168 lbs.

Year	Team	W	L	PCT	ERA	G	GS	CG	IP	H	BB	SO	ShO	Relief W	Relief L	Relief SV	Batting AB	Batting H	Batting HR	BA	PO	A	E	DP	TC/G	FA
1912	STL N	1	1	.500	3.19	6	3	1	31	25	10	13	0	0	0	0	9	2	0	.222	0	8	0	0	1.3	1.000
1913		6	14	.300	5.25	36	21	8	175	205	64	64	0	3	0	0	59	12	0	.203	10	46	3	1	1.6	.949
1914		16	13	.552	2.36	41	32	18	286	248	93	115	3	2	1	2	92	13	0	.141	8	67	9	1	2.0	.893
1915	NY N	12	18	.400	2.66	35	30	16	220	226	59	91	4	1	1	0	68	11	0	.162	7	40	8	0	1.6	.855
1916		18	11	.621	2.62	40	29	17	251	243	56	115	5	2	**5**	2	83	7	0	.084	12	55	4	2	1.8	.944
1917		17	7	.708	1.88	35	26	14	215	186	45	72	5	2	3	1	70	11	0	.157	11	63	2	4	2.2	.974
1918		18	13	.581	2.74	35	31	19	233	212	38	60	6	1	1	0	80	14	0	.175	12	54	3	1	2.0	.957
1919		1	1	.500	7.11	11	3	0	19	27	12	2	0	1	0	1	4	0	0	.000	0	8	0	0	0.7	1.000

Pol Perritt *continued*

Year	Team	W	L	PCT	ERA	G	GS	CG	IP	H	BB	SO	ShO	Relief W	Relief L	Relief SV	Batting AB	Batting H	HR	BA	PO	A	E	DP	TC/G	FA
1920		0	0	—	1.80	8	0	0	15	9	4	3	0	0	0	2	4	0	0	.000	1	5	0	0	0.8	1.000
1921	2 teams NY N (5G 2–0) DET A (4G 1–0)																									
"	total	3	0	1.000	4.38	9	3	0	24.2	35	9	8	0	2	0	0	8	2	0	.250	1	3	1	0	0.6	.800
10 yrs.		92	78	.541	2.89	256	178	93	1469.2	1416	390	543	23	14	11	8	477	72	0	.151	62	349	30	9	1.7	.932
WORLD SERIES																										
1917	NY N	0	0	—	2.16	3	0	0	8.1	9	3	3	0	0	0	0	2	2	0	1.000	0	1	0	0	0.3	1.000

Gaylord Perry

PERRY, GAYLORD JACKSON
Brother of Jim Perry.
B. Sept. 15, 1938, Williamston, N. C.
Hall of Fame 1991.

BR TR 6′ 4″ 205 lbs.

Year	Team	W	L	PCT	ERA	G	GS	CG	IP	H	BB	SO	ShO	Relief W	Relief L	Relief SV	Batting AB	Batting H	HR	BA	PO	A	E	DP	TC/G	FA
1962	SF N	3	1	.750	5.23	13	7	1	43	54	14	20	0	0	0	0	13	3	0	.231	3	5	1	1	0.7	.889
1963		1	6	.143	4.03	31	4	0	76	84	29	52	0	1	5	2	18	4	0	.222	4	12	0	0	0.5	1.000
1964		12	11	.522	2.75	44	19	5	206.1	179	43	155	2	6	5	5	56	3	0	.054	12	26	0	3	0.9	1.000
1965		8	12	.400	4.19	47	26	6	195.2	194	70	170	0	0	1	1	64	10	0	.156	18	40	1	4	1.3	.983
1966		21	8	.724	2.99	36	35	13	255.2	242	40	201	3	1	0	0	86	16	0	.186	16	40	1	2	1.6	.982
1967		15	17	.469	2.61	39	37	18	293	231	84	230	3	0	1	1	91	13	0	.143	20	64	3	2	2.2	.966
1968		16	15	.516	2.45	39	38	19	290.2	240	59	173	3	0	0	1	97	11	0	.113	31	62	2	3	2.4	.979
1969		19	14	.576	2.49	40	39	26	**325**	290	91	233	3	0	0	0	117	14	1	.120	18	67	0	2	2.1	1.000
1970		**23**	13	.639	3.20	41	**41**	23	**329**	**292**	84	214	**5**	0	0	0	120	14	1	.117	30	67	4	5	2.5	.960
1971		16	12	.571	2.76	37	37	14	280	255	67	158	2	0	0	0	98	10	1	.102	21	41	5	5	1.8	.925
1972	CLE A	**24**	16	.600	1.92	41	40	**29**	343	253	82	234	5	0	0	1	110	17	1	.155	18	61	2	7	2.0	.975
1973		19	19	.500	3.38	41	41	**29**	344	315	115	238	7	0	0	0	0	0	0	—	19	55	0	1	1.8	1.000
1974		21	13	.618	2.52	37	37	28	322	230	99	216	4	0	0	0	0	0	0	—	26	45	3	4	2.0	.959
1975	2 teams CLE A (15G 6–9) TEX A (22G 12–8)																									
"	total	18	17	.514	3.24	37	37	25	305.2	277	70	233	5	0	0	0	0	0	0		19	43	1	3	1.7	.984
1976	TEX A	15	14	.517	3.24	32	32	21	250	232	52	143	2	0	0	0	0	0	0	—	11	24	2	1	1.2	.946
1977		15	12	.556	3.37	34	34	13	238	239	56	177	4	0	0	0	0	0	0	—	14	28	1	2	1.3	.977
1978	SD N	**21**	6	**.778**	2.72	37	37	5	261	241	66	154	2	0	0	0	87	8	0	.092	13	40	2	6	1.5	.964
1979		12	11	.522	3.05	32	32	10	233	225	67	140	0	0	0	0	71	6	1	.085	11	41	2	2	1.7	.963
1980	2 teams TEX A (24G 6–9) NY A (10G 4–4)																									
"	total	10	13	.435	3.67	34	32	6	206	224	64	135	2	1	0	0	0	0	0		13	32	1	3	1.4	.978
1981	ATL N	8	9	.471	3.93	23	23	3	151	**182**	24	60	0	0	0	0	48	12	1	.250	11	19	3	0	1.4	.909
1982	SEA A	10	12	.455	4.40	32	32	6	216.2	245	54	116	0	0	0	0	0	0	0	—	11	35	3	1	1.5	.939
1983	2 teams SEA A (16G 3–10) KC A (14G 4–4)																									
"	total	7	14	.333	4.64	30	30	3	186.1	214	49	82	1	0	0	0	0	0	0		10	30	1	1	1.4	.976
22 yrs.		314	265	.542	3.10	777	690	303	5351	4938	1379	3534	53	9	12	11	1076	141	6	.131	349	877	38	58	1.6	.970
			6th						6th			6th														
LEAGUE CHAMPIONSHIP SERIES																										
1971	SF N	1	1	.500	6.14	2	2	1	14.2	19	3	11	0	0	0	0	4	1	0	.250	1	2	0	0	1.5	1.000

Jim Perry

PERRY, JAMES EVAN, JR.
Brother of Gaylord Perry.
B. Oct. 30, 1935, Williamston, N. C.

BB TR 6′ 4″ 190 lbs.

Year	Team	W	L	PCT	ERA	G	GS	CG	IP	H	BB	SO	ShO	Relief W	Relief L	Relief SV	Batting AB	Batting H	HR	BA	PO	A	E	DP	TC/G	FA
1959	CLE A	12	10	.545	2.65	44	13	8	153	122	55	79	2	5	4	4	50	15	0	.300	12	24	0	1	0.8	1.000
1960		**18**	10	**.643**	3.62	41	**36**	10	261.1	257	91	120	**4**	1	0	1	91	22	0	.242	23	40	2	4	1.6	.969
1961		10	17	.370	4.71	35	35	6	223.2	238	87	90	1	0	0	0	73	12	0	.164	17	37	5	5	1.7	.915
1962		12	12	.500	4.14	35	27	7	193.2	213	59	74	3	0	0	0	60	11	0	.183	12	39	1	3	1.5	.981
1963	2 teams CLE A (5G 0–0) MIN A (35G 9–9)																									
"	total	9	9	.500	3.83	40	25	5	178.2	179	59	72	1	0	1	1	53	11	0	.208	8	30	2	1	1.0	.950
1964	MIN A	6	3	.667	3.44	42	1	0	65.1	61	23	55	0	6	2	2	13	2	0	.154	3	9	0	0	0.3	1.000
1965		12	7	.632	2.63	36	19	4	167.2	142	47	88	2	5	0	0	53	9	0	.170	7	26	1	3	0.9	.971
1966		11	7	.611	2.54	33	25	8	184.1	149	53	122	1	0	0	0	59	13	1	.220	9	22	1	0	1.0	.969
1967		8	7	.533	3.03	37	11	3	130.2	123	50	94	2	3	4	0	42	8	1	.190	4	15	1	2	0.5	.950
1968		8	6	.571	2.27	32	18	3	139	113	26	69	2	1	0	1	42	6	2	.143	10	26	3	1	1.2	.923
1969		20	6	.769	2.82	46	36	12	261.2	244	66	153	3	3	0	0	93	16	0	.172	12	31	1	3	1.0	.977
1970		**24**	12	.667	3.03	40	**40**	13	279	258	57	168	4	0	0	0	97	24	1	.247	11	47	1	3	1.4	.983
1971		17	17	.500	4.23	40	39	8	270	263	102	126	0	0	0	1	92	17	0	.185	17	44	0	4	1.5	1.000
1972		13	16	.448	3.34	35	35	5	218	191	60	85	2	0	0	0	71	11	0	.155	21	28	6	3	1.6	.891
1973	DET A	14	13	.519	4.03	35	34	7	203	225	55	66	1	0	0	0	0	0	0	—	12	33	3	1	1.4	.938
1974	CLE A	17	12	.586	2.96	36	36	8	252	242	64	71	3	0	0	0	0	0	0	—	7	42	2	1	1.4	.961
1975	2 teams CLE A (8G 1–6) OAK A (15G 3–4)																									
"	total	4	10	.286	5.38	23	17	2	105.1	107	44	44	1	0	1	0	0	0	0		6	13	0	1	0.8	1.000
17 yrs.		215	174	.553	3.45	630	447	109	3286.1	3127	998	1576	32	24	12	10	889	177	5	.199	191	506	29	36	1.2	.960
LEAGUE CHAMPIONSHIP SERIES																										
1969	MIN A	0	0	—	3.38	1	1	0	8	6	3	3	0	0	0	0	3	0	0	.000	0	1	0	0	1.0	1.000
1970		0	1	.000	13.50	2	1	0	5.1	10	1	3	0	0	0	0	1	0	0	.000	1	0	0	0	0.5	1.000
2 yrs.		0	1	.000	7.43	3	2	0	13.1	16	4	6	0	0	0	0	4	0	0	.000	1	1	0	0	0.7	1.000
WORLD SERIES																										
1965	MIN A	0	0	—	4.50	2	0	0	4	5	2	4	0	0	0	0	0	0	0	—	0	1	0	0	0.5	1.000

Pat Perry

PERRY, WILLIAM PATRICK (Atlas)
B. Feb. 4, 1959, Taylorville, Ill.

BL TL 6′ 1″ 190 lbs.

Year	Team	W	L	PCT	ERA	G	GS	CG	IP	H	BB	SO	ShO	Relief W	Relief L	Relief SV	Batting AB	Batting H	HR	BA	PO	A	E	DP	TC/G	FA
1985	STL N	1	0	1.000	0.00	6	0	0	12.1	3	3	6	0	1	0	0	2	1	0	.500	0	1	0	0	0.2	1.000
1986		2	3	.400	3.80	46	0	0	68.2	59	34	29	0	2	3	2	8	0	0	.000	10	11	1	4	0.5	.955
1987	2 teams STL N (45G 4–2) CIN N (12G 1–0)																									
"	total	5	2	.714	3.56	57	0	0	81	60	25	39	0	5	2	2	7	1	0	.143	12	12	1	2	0.4	.960

Pat Perry *continued*

Year	Team		W	L	PCT	ERA	G	GS	CG	IP	H	BB	SO	ShO	Relief Pitching W	Relief Pitching L	Relief Pitching SV	Batting AB	Batting H	Batting HR	BA	PO	A	E	DP	TC/G	FA
1988	2 teams	CIN N	(12G 2–2)		CHI N	(35G 2–2)																					
″	total		4	4	.500	4.14	47	0	0	58.2	61	16	35	0	4	4	1	3	1	1	.333	4	7	0	0	0.2	1.000
1989	CHI	N	0	1	.000	1.77	19	0	0	35.2	23	16	20	0	0	1	1	6	1	0	.167	2	3	1	0	0.3	.833
1990	LA	N	0	0	—	8.10	7	0	0	6.2	9	5	2	0	0	0	0	1	0	0	.000	0	1	2	0	0.4	.333
6 yrs.			12	10	.545	3.46	182	0	0	263	215	99	131	0	12	10	6	27	4	1	.148	28	35	5	6	0.4	.926

Scott Perry

PERRY, HERBERT SCOTT BL TR 6′ 1″ 195 lbs.
B. Apr. 17, 1891, Denison, Tex. D. Oct. 27, 1959, Kansas City, Mo.

Year	Team		W	L	PCT	ERA	G	GS	CG	IP	H	BB	SO	ShO	Relief Pitching W	Relief Pitching L	Relief Pitching SV	Batting AB	Batting H	Batting HR	BA	PO	A	E	DP	TC/G	FA
1915	STL	A	0	0	—	13.50	1	1	0	2	5	1	0	0	0	0	0	0	0	0	—	0	0	0	0	0.0	.000
1916	CHI	N	2	1	.667	2.54	4	3	2	28.1	30	3	10	1	0	0	0	11	3	0	.273	2	9	0	0	2.8	1.000
1917	CIN	N	0	0	—	6.75	4	1	0	13.1	17	8	4	0	0	0	0	5	0	0	.000	1	3	2	0	1.5	.667
1918	PHI	A	20	**19**	.513	1.98	44	**36**	**30**	**332.1**	**295**	111	81	4	3	2	2	112	15	0	.134	16	96	4	6	2.6	.966
1919			4	17	.190	3.58	25	21	12	183.2	193	72	38	0	0	2	1	59	8	0	.136	14	76	4	2	3.8	.957
1920			11	**25**	.306	3.62	42	34	20	263.2	310	65	79	1	1	2	1	83	13	1	.157	10	70	5	1	2.0	.941
1921			3	6	.333	4.11	12	8	5	70	77	24	19	0	0	1	1	26	1	0	.038	5	24	1	1	2.5	.967
7 yrs.			40	68	.370	3.07	132	104	69	893.1	927	284	231	6	4	7	5	296	40	1	.135	48	278	16	10	2.6	.953

Parson Perryman

PERRYMAN, EMMETT KEY BR TR 6′ 4½″ 193 lbs.
B. Oct. 24, 1888, Everette Springs, Ga. D. Sept. 12, 1966, Starke, Fla.

Year	Team		W	L	PCT	ERA	G	GS	CG	IP	H	BB	SO	ShO	Relief Pitching W	Relief Pitching L	Relief Pitching SV	Batting AB	Batting H	Batting HR	BA	PO	A	E	DP	TC/G	FA
1915	STL	A	2	4	.333	3.93	24	3	0	50.1	52	16	19	0	2	1	0	6	0	0	.000	1	19	0	1	0.8	1.000

Robert Person

PERSON, ROBERT ALAN BR TR 6′ 180 lbs.
B. Oct. 6, 1969, Lowell, Mass.

Year	Team		W	L	PCT	ERA	G	GS	CG	IP	H	BB	SO	ShO	Relief Pitching W	Relief Pitching L	Relief Pitching SV	Batting AB	Batting H	Batting HR	BA	PO	A	E	DP	TC/G	FA
1995	NY	N	1	0	1.000	0.75	3	1	0	12	5	2	10	0	0	0	0	3	2	0	.667	0	0	0	0	0.0	.000

Bill Pertica

PERTICA, WILLIAM ANDREW BR TR 5′ 9″ 165 lbs.
B. Mar. 5, 1897, Santa Barbara, Calif. D. Dec. 28, 1967, Los Angeles, Calif.

Year	Team		W	L	PCT	ERA	G	GS	CG	IP	H	BB	SO	ShO	Relief Pitching W	Relief Pitching L	Relief Pitching SV	Batting AB	Batting H	Batting HR	BA	PO	A	E	DP	TC/G	FA
1918	BOS	A	0	0	—	3.00	1	0	0	3	3	0	1	0	0	0	0	1	0	0	.000	0	1	0	0	1.0	1.000
1921	STL	N	14	10	.583	3.37	38	31	15	208.1	212	70	67	2	0	1	2	70	10	0	.143	8	40	1	0	1.3	.980
1922			8	8	.500	5.91	34	15	2	117.1	153	65	30	0	4	2	0	33	6	0	.182	2	33	3	0	1.1	.921
1923			0	0	—	3.86	1	1	0	2.1	2	3	0	0	0	0	0	1	0	0	.000	1	1	0	0	2.0	1.000
4 yrs.			22	18	.550	4.27	74	47	17	331	370	138	98	2	4	3	2	105	16	0	.152	11	75	4	0	1.2	.956

Stan Perzanowski

PERZANOWSKI, STANLEY BB TR 6′ 2″ 170 lbs.
B. Aug. 25, 1950, East Chicago, Ind.

Year	Team		W	L	PCT	ERA	G	GS	CG	IP	H	BB	SO	ShO	Relief Pitching W	Relief Pitching L	Relief Pitching SV	Batting AB	Batting H	Batting HR	BA	PO	A	E	DP	TC/G	FA
1971	CHI	A	0	1	.000	12.00	5	0	0	6	14	3	5	0	0	1	1	2	0	0	.000	1	0	0	0	0.2	1.000
1974			0	0	—	22.50	2	1	0	2	8	2	2	0	0	0	0	0	0	0	—	0	1	0	0	0.5	1.000
1975	TEX	A	3	3	.500	3.00	12	8	1	66	59	25	26	0	0	0	0	0	0	0	—	6	17	2	0	2.1	.920
1976			0	0	—	9.75	5	0	0	12	20	4	6	0	0	0	0	0	0	0	—	2	2	0	0	0.8	1.000
1978	MIN	A	2	7	.222	5.24	13	7	1	56.2	59	26	31	0	0	3	1	0	0	0	—	3	11	1	1	1.2	.933
5 yrs.			5	11	.313	5.11	37	16	2	142.2	160	60	70	0	0	4	2	2	0	0	.000	12	31	3	1	1.2	.935

Jeff Peterek

PETEREK, JEFFREY ALLEN BR TR 6′ 2″ 195 lbs.
B. Sept. 22, 1963, Michigan City, Ind.

Year	Team		W	L	PCT	ERA	G	GS	CG	IP	H	BB	SO	ShO	Relief Pitching W	Relief Pitching L	Relief Pitching SV	Batting AB	Batting H	Batting HR	BA	PO	A	E	DP	TC/G	FA
1989	MIL	A	0	2	.000	4.02	7	4	0	31.1	31	14	16	0	0	0	0	0	0	0	—	3	4	0	0	1.0	1.000

Gary Peters

PETERS, GARY CHARLES BL TL 6′ 2″ 200 lbs.
B. Apr. 21, 1937, Grove City, Pa.

Year	Team		W	L	PCT	ERA	G	GS	CG	IP	H	BB	SO	ShO	Relief Pitching W	Relief Pitching L	Relief Pitching SV	Batting AB	Batting H	Batting HR	BA	PO	A	E	DP	TC/G	FA
1959	CHI	A	0	0	—	0.00	2	0	0	1	2	2	1	0	0	0	0	0	0	0	—	0	0	0	0	0.0	.000
1960			0	0	—	2.70	2	0	0	3.1	4	1	4	0	0	0	0	0	0	0	—	0	0	0	0	0.0	.000
1961			0	0	—	1.74	3	0	0	10.1	10	2	6	0	0	0	1	3	1	0	.333	3	6	0	1	3.0	1.000
1962			0	1	.000	5.68	5	0	0	6.1	8	1	4	0	0	1	0	0	0	0	—	0	2	0	0	0.4	1.000
1963			19	8	.704	**2.33**	41	30	13	243	192	68	189	4	0	2	1	81	21	3	.259	17	30	2	4	1.2	.959
1964			**20**	8	.714	2.50	37	36	11	273.2	217	104	205	3	0	0	0	120	25	4	.208	16	41	3	4	1.6	.950
1965			10	12	.455	3.62	33	30	1	176.1	181	63	95	0	0	0	0	72	13	1	.181	12	32	1	0	1.4	.978
1966			12	10	.545	**1.98**	30	27	11	204.2	156	45	129	4	0	1	0	81	19	1	.235	7	41	1	4	1.6	.980
1967			16	11	.593	2.28	38	36	11	260	187	91	215	3	0	0	0	99	21	2	.212	15	50	2	5	1.8	.970
1968			4	13	.235	3.76	31	25	6	162.2	146	60	110	1	0	0	1	72	15	2	.208	12	21	0	3	1.1	1.000
1969			10	15	.400	4.53	36	32	7	218.2	238	78	140	3	0	0	0	71	12	2	.169	6	25	1	1	0.9	.969
1970	BOS	A	16	11	.593	4.05	34	34	10	222	221	83	155	4	0	0	0	82	20	1	.244	7	27	3	3	1.1	.919
1971			14	11	.560	4.37	34	32	9	214	241	70	100	1	0	0	1	96	26	3	.271	13	27	2	2	1.2	.952
1972			3	3	.500	4.34	33	4	0	85	91	38	67	0	2	1	1	30	6	0	.200	3	10	0	0	0.4	1.000
14 yrs.			124	103	.546	3.25	359	286	79	2081	1894	706	1420	23	2	5	5	*				111	312	15	27	1.2	.966

Johnny Peters

PETERS, JOHN PAUL BR TR 180 lbs.
B. Apr. 8, 1850, Louisiana, Mo. D. Jan. 4, 1924, St. Louis, Mo.

Year	Team		W	L	PCT	ERA	G	GS	CG	IP	H	BB	SO	ShO	Relief Pitching W	Relief Pitching L	Relief Pitching SV	Batting AB	Batting H	Batting HR	BA	PO	A	E	DP	TC/G	FA
1876	CHI	N	0	0	—	0.00	1	0	0	1	1	1	0	0	0	0	1	*				95	193	21	16	4.6	.932

Ray Peters

PETERS, RAYMOND JAMES BR TR 6′ 5½″ 210 lbs.
B. Aug. 27, 1946, Buffalo, N. Y.

Year	Team		W	L	PCT	ERA	G	GS	CG	IP	H	BB	SO	ShO	Relief Pitching W	Relief Pitching L	Relief Pitching SV	Batting AB	Batting H	Batting HR	BA	PO	A	E	DP	TC/G	FA
1970	MIL	A	0	2	.000	31.50	2	2	0	2	7	5	1	0	0	0	0	0	0	0	—	0	1	0	0	0.5	1.000

Rube Peters

PETERS, OTTO CASPER BR TR 6′ 1″ 195 lbs.
B. Mar. 15, 1885, Grantfork, Ill. D. Feb. 7, 1965, Pequannock, N. J.

Year	Team		W	L	PCT	ERA	G	GS	CG	IP	H	BB	SO	ShO	Relief Pitching W	Relief Pitching L	Relief Pitching SV	Batting AB	Batting H	Batting HR	BA	PO	A	E	DP	TC/G	FA
1912	CHI	A	5	6	.455	4.14	28	11	4	108.2	134	33	39	0	1	1	0	31	6	0	.194	6	52	3	3	2.2	.951
1914	BKN	F	2	2	.500	3.82	11	3	1	37.2	52	16	13	0	1	0	0	11	1	0	.091	2	12	1	1	1.4	.933
2 yrs.			7	8	.467	4.06	39	14	5	146.1	186	49	52	0	2	1	0	42	7	0	.167	8	64	4	4	1.9	.947

Steve Peters

PETERS, STEVEN BRADLEY
B. Nov. 14, 1962, Oklahoma City, Okla.
BL TL 5′10″ 170 lbs.

Year	Team	W	L	PCT	ERA	G	GS	CG	IP	H	BB	SO	ShO	Relief Pitching W	Relief Pitching L	Relief Pitching SV	Batting AB	Batting H	Batting HR	BA	PO	A	E	DP	TC/G	FA
1987	STL N	0	0	—	1.80	12	0	0	15	17	6	11	0	0	0	1	2	0	0	.000	1	5	0	1	0.5	1.000
1988		3	3	.500	6.40	44	0	0	45	57	22	30	0	3	3	0	3	0	0	.000	3	4	1	0	0.2	.875
2 yrs.		3	3	.500	5.25	56	0	0	60	74	28	41	0	3	3	1	5	0	0	.000	4	9	1	1	0.3	.929

Adam Peterson

PETERSON, ADAM CHARLES
B. Dec. 11, 1965, Long Beach, Calif.
BR TR 6′ 3″ 190 lbs.

Year	Team	W	L	PCT	ERA	G	GS	CG	IP	H	BB	SO	ShO	Relief Pitching W	Relief Pitching L	Relief Pitching SV	Batting AB	Batting H	Batting HR	BA	PO	A	E	DP	TC/G	FA
1987	CHI A	0	0	—	13.50	1	1	0	4	8	3	1	0	0	0	0	0	0	0	—	1	0	0	0	1.0	1.000
1988		0	1	.000	13.50	2	2	0	6	6	6	5	0	0	0	0	0	0	0	—	0	0	1	0	0.5	.000
1989		0	1	.000	15.19	3	2	0	5.1	13	2	3	0	0	0	0	0	0	0	—	1	0	1	0	0.7	.500
1990		2	5	.286	4.55	20	11	2	85	90	26	29	0	0	1	0	0	0	0	—	4	7	1	0	0.6	.917
1991	SD N	3	4	.429	4.45	13	11	0	54.2	50	28	37	0	0	0	0	13	0	0	.000	4	5	0	1	0.7	1.000
5 yrs.		5	11	.313	5.46	39	27	2	155	167	65	75	0	0	1	0	13	0	0	.000	10	12	3	1	0.6	.880

Fritz Peterson

PETERSON, FRED INGLES
B. Feb. 8, 1942, Chicago, Ill.
BB TL 6′ 185 lbs.

Year	Team	W	L	PCT	ERA	G	GS	CG	IP	H	BB	SO	ShO	Relief Pitching W	Relief Pitching L	Relief Pitching SV	Batting AB	Batting H	Batting HR	BA	PO	A	E	DP	TC/G	FA
1966	NY A	12	11	.522	3.31	34	32	11	215	196	40	96	2	0	0	0	67	15	0	.224	16	36	4	1	1.6	.929
1967		8	14	.364	3.47	36	30	6	181.1	179	43	102	1	2	1	0	48	7	0	.146	13	35	2	4	1.4	.960
1968		12	11	.522	2.63	36	27	6	212.1	187	29	115	2	1	1	0	63	5	0	.079	6	56	2	6	1.8	.969
1969		17	16	.515	2.55	37	37	16	272	228	43	150	4	0	0	0	80	9	0	.113	15	53	3	5	1.9	.958
1970		20	11	.645	2.91	39	37	8	260	247	40	127	2	1	0	0	90	20	2	.222	12	52	3	7	1.7	.955
1971		15	13	.536	3.05	37	35	16	274	269	42	139	4	1	0	1	85	7	0	.082	14	54	1	7	1.9	.986
1972		17	15	.531	3.24	35	35	12	250	270	44	100	3	0	0	0	82	19	0	.232	13	44	1	6	1.7	.983
1973		8	15	.348	3.95	31	31	6	184.1	207	49	59	0	0	0	0	0	0	0	—	11	30	2	3	1.4	.953
1974	2 teams	NY A (3G 0–0)			CLE A (29G 9–14)																					
″	total	9	14	.391	4.36	32	30	3	161	200	39	57	0	0	0	0	0	0	0		8	31	2	2	1.3	.951
1975	CLE A	14	8	.636	3.94	25	25	6	146.1	154	40	47	2	0	0	0	0	0	0	—	8	26	1	3	1.4	.971
1976	2 teams	CLE A (9G 0–3)			TEX A (4G 1–0)																					
″	total	1	3	.250	5.08	13	11	0	62	80	17	23	0	0	0	0	0	0	0		0	12	0	0	0.9	1.000
11 yrs.		133	131	.504	3.30	355	330	90	2218.1	2217	426	1015	20	5	2	1	515	82	2	.159	116	429	21	44	1.6	.963

Jim Peterson

PETERSON, JAMES NIELS
B. Aug. 18, 1908, Philadelphia, Pa. D. Apr. 8, 1975, Palm Beach, Fla.
BR TR 6′½″ 200 lbs.

Year	Team	W	L	PCT	ERA	G	GS	CG	IP	H	BB	SO	ShO	Relief Pitching W	Relief Pitching L	Relief Pitching SV	Batting AB	Batting H	Batting HR	BA	PO	A	E	DP	TC/G	FA
1931	PHI A	0	1	.000	6.23	6	1	1	13	18	4	7	0	0	0	0	2	1	0	.500	0	2	0	0	0.3	1.000
1933		2	5	.286	4.96	32	5	0	90.2	114	36	18	0	2	3	0	27	4	0	.148	6	31	0	0	1.2	1.000
1937	BKN N	0	0	—	7.94	3	0	0	5.2	8	2	4	0	0	0	0	0	0	0	—	0	4	0	0	1.3	1.000
3 yrs.		2	6	.250	5.27	41	6	1	109.1	140	42	29	0	2	3	0	29	5	0	.172	6	37	0	0	1.0	1.000

Kent Peterson

PETERSON, KENT FRANKLIN
B. Dec. 21, 1925, Goshen, Utah D. Apr. 27, 1995, Highland, Utah.
BR TL 5′10″ 170 lbs.

Year	Team	W	L	PCT	ERA	G	GS	CG	IP	H	BB	SO	ShO	Relief Pitching W	Relief Pitching L	Relief Pitching SV	Batting AB	Batting H	Batting HR	BA	PO	A	E	DP	TC/G	FA
1944	CIN N	0	0	—	0.00	1	0	0	1	0	0	0	0	0	0	0	0	0	0	—	0	0	0	0	0.0	.000
1947		6	13	.316	4.25	37	17	3	152.1	156	62	78	1	2	2	2	44	3	0	.068	2	18	1	0	0.6	.952
1948		2	15	.118	4.60	43	17	2	137	146	59	64	0	0	3	1	36	5	0	.139	8	24	1	2	0.8	.970
1949		4	5	.444	6.24	30	7	2	66.1	66	46	28	0	1	2	0	18	1	0	.056	0	10	0	1	0.3	1.000
1950		0	3	.000	7.20	9	2	0	20	25	17	6	0	0	1	0	3	1	0	.333	0	1	0	0	0.1	1.000
1951		1	1	.500	6.52	9	0	0	9.2	13	8	5	0	1	1	0	1	0	0	.000	1	2	0	0	0.3	1.000
1952	PHI N	0	0	—	0.00	3	0	0	7	2	2	7	0	0	0	2	1	0	0	.000	0	0	0	0	0.0	.000
1953		0	1	.000	6.67	15	0	0	27	26	21	20	0	0	1	0	7	0	0	.000	1	3	0	0	0.3	1.000
8 yrs.		13	38	.255	4.95	147	43	7	420.1	434	215	208	1	4	10	5	110	10	0	.091	12	58	2	3	0.5	.972

Sid Peterson

PETERSON, SIDNEY HERBERT
B. Jan. 31, 1918, Havelock, N. D.
BR TR 6′ 3″ 200 lbs.

Year	Team	W	L	PCT	ERA	G	GS	CG	IP	H	BB	SO	ShO	Relief Pitching W	Relief Pitching L	Relief Pitching SV	Batting AB	Batting H	Batting HR	BA	PO	A	E	DP	TC/G	FA
1943	STL A	2	0	1.000	2.70	3	0	0	10	15	3	0	0	2	0	0	2	0	0	.000	0	2	0	0	0.7	1.000

Mark Petkovsek

PETKOVSEK, MARK JOSEPH
B. Nov. 18, 1965, Beaumont, Tex.
BR TR 6′ 185 lbs.

Year	Team	W	L	PCT	ERA	G	GS	CG	IP	H	BB	SO	ShO	Relief Pitching W	Relief Pitching L	Relief Pitching SV	Batting AB	Batting H	Batting HR	BA	PO	A	E	DP	TC/G	FA
1991	TEX A	0	1	.000	14.46	4	1	0	9.1	21	4	6	0	0	0	0	0	0	0	—	1	0	0	0	0.3	1.000
1993	PIT N	3	0	1.000	6.96	26	0	0	32.1	43	9	14	0	3	0	0	0	0	0	—	0	10	0	0	0.4	1.000
1995	STL N	6	6	.500	4.00	26	21	1	137.1	136	35	71	1	1	0	0	37	3	0	.081	8	17	0	1	1.0	1.000
3 yrs.		9	7	.563	5.08	56	22	1	179	200	48	91	1	4	0	0	37	3	0	.081	9	27	0	1	0.6	1.000

Dan Petry

PETRY, DANIEL JOSEPH
B. Nov. 13, 1958, Palo Alto, Calif.
BR TR 6′ 4″ 185 lbs.

Year	Team	W	L	PCT	ERA	G	GS	CG	IP	H	BB	SO	ShO	Relief Pitching W	Relief Pitching L	Relief Pitching SV	Batting AB	Batting H	Batting HR	BA	PO	A	E	DP	TC/G	FA
1979	DET A	6	5	.545	3.95	15	15	2	98	90	33	43	0	0	0	0	0	0	0	—	9	11	2	0	1.5	.909
1980		10	9	.526	3.93	27	25	4	165	156	83	88	3	1	0	0	0	0	0	—	12	32	3	3	1.7	.936
1981		10	9	.526	3.00	23	22	7	141	115	57	79	2	0	0	0	0	0	0	—	14	26	1	6	1.8	.976
1982		15	9	.625	3.22	35	35	8	246	220	100	132	1	0	0	0	0	0	0	—	28	48	0	4	2.2	1.000
1983		19	11	.633	3.92	38	**38**	9	266.1	256	99	122	2	0	0	0	0	0	0	—	30	43	2	10	2.0	.973
1984		18	8	.692	3.24	35	35	7	233.1	231	66	144	2	0	0	0	0	0	0	—	38	34	1	4	2.1	.986
1985		15	13	.536	3.36	34	34	8	238.2	190	81	109	0	0	0	0	0	0	0	—	36	26	0	3	1.8	1.000
1986		5	10	.333	4.66	20	20	2	116	122	53	56	0	0	0	0	0	0	0	—	16	18	0	1	1.7	1.000
1987		9	7	.563	5.61	30	21	0	134.2	148	76	93	0	2	0	0	0	0	0	—	16	21	2	0	1.3	.949
1988	CAL A	3	9	.250	4.38	22	22	4	139.2	139	59	64	1	0	0	0	0	0	0	—	20	25	0	2	2.0	1.000
1989		3	2	.600	5.47	19	4	0	51	53	23	21	0	2	0	0	0	0	0	—	5	7	0	0	0.6	1.000
1990	DET A	10	9	.526	4.45	32	23	1	149.2	148	77	73	0	2	0	0	0	0	0	—	19	23	0	2	1.3	1.000
1991	3 teams	DET A (17G 2–3)			ATL N (10G 0–0)				BOS A (13G 0–0)																	
″	total	2	3	.400	4.97	40	6	0	101.1	116	45	39	0	0	0	1	5	1	0	.200	12	22	1	3	0.9	.971
13 yrs.		125	104	.546	3.94	370	300	52	2080.2	1984	852	1063	11	7	0	1	5	1	0	.200	255	336	12	38	1.6	.980
LEAGUE CHAMPIONSHIP SERIES																										
1984	DET A	0	0	—	2.57	1	1	0	7	4	1	4	0	0	0	0	0	0	0	—	0	0	0	0	0.0	.000
1987		0	0	—	0.00	1	0	0	3.1	1	0	1	0	0	0	0	0	0	0	—	0	1	0	0	1.0	1.000
2 yrs.		0	0		1.74	2	1	0	10.1	5	1	5	0	0	0	0	0	0	0		0	1	0	0	0.5	1.000
WORLD SERIES																										
1984	DET A	0	1	.000	9.00	2	2	0	8	14	5	4	0	0	0	0	0	0	0	—	1	1	0	0	1.0	1.000

Jay Pettibone

PETTIBONE, HARRY JONATHAN BR TR 6′ 4″ 185 lbs.
B. June 21, 1957, Mt. Clemens, Mich.

Year	Team	W	L	PCT	ERA	G	GS	CG	IP	H	BB	SO	ShO	Relief W	Relief L	Relief SV	AB	H	HR	BA	PO	A	E	DP	TC/G	FA
1983	MIN A	0	4	.000	5.33	4	4	1	27	28	8	10	0	0	0	0	0	0	0	—	4	4	0	0	2.0	1.000

Bob Pettit

PETTIT, ROBERT HENRY BL TR 5′ 9″ 160 lbs.
B. July 19, 1861, Williamstown, Mass. D. Nov. 1, 1910, Derby, Conn.

Year	Team	W	L	PCT	ERA	G	GS	CG	IP	H	BB	SO	ShO	Relief W	Relief L	Relief SV	AB	H	HR	BA	PO	A	E	DP	TC/G	FA
1887	CHI N	0	0	—	0.00	1	0	0	1	3	2	0	0	0	0	**1**	*				35	8	6	0	1.4	.878

Leon Pettit

PETTIT, LEON ARTHUR (Lefty) BL TL 5′10½″ 165 lbs.
B. June 23, 1902, Waynesburg, Pa. D. Nov. 21, 1974, Columbia, Tenn.

Year	Team	W	L	PCT	ERA	G	GS	CG	IP	H	BB	SO	ShO	Relief W	Relief L	Relief SV	AB	H	HR	BA	PO	A	E	DP	TC/G	FA
1935	WAS A	8	5	.615	4.95	41	7	1	109	129	58	45	0	**6**	3	3	25	2	0	.080	9	19	3	0	0.8	.903
1937	PHI N	0	1	.000	11.25	3	1	0	4	6	4	0	0	0	0	0	0	0	0	—	2	0	0	0	0.7	1.000
2 yrs.		8	6	.571	5.18	44	8	1	113	135	62	45	0	6	3	3	25	2	0	.080	11	19	3	0	0.8	.909

Paul Pettit

PETTIT, GEORGE WILLIAM PAUL (Lefty) BL TL 6′ 2″ 195 lbs.
B. Nov. 29, 1931, Los Angeles, Calif.

Year	Team	W	L	PCT	ERA	G	GS	CG	IP	H	BB	SO	ShO	Relief W	Relief L	Relief SV	AB	H	HR	BA	PO	A	E	DP	TC/G	FA
1951	PIT N	0	0	—	3.38	2	0	0	2.2	2	1	0	0	0	0	0	1	0	0	.000	0	0	0	0	0.0	.000
1953		1	2	.333	7.71	10	5	0	28	33	20	14	0	0	0	0	8	2	0	.250	2	6	0	0	0.8	1.000
2 yrs.		1	2	.333	7.34	12	5	0	30.2	35	21	14	0	0	0	0	9	2	0	.222	2	6	0	0	0.7	1.000

Andy Pettitte

PETTITTE, ANDREW EUGENE BL TL 6′ 5″ 235 lbs.
B. June 15, 1972, Baton Rouge, La.

Year	Team	W	L	PCT	ERA	G	GS	CG	IP	H	BB	SO	ShO	Relief W	Relief L	Relief SV	AB	H	HR	BA	PO	A	E	DP	TC/G	FA
1995	NY A	12	9	.571	4.17	31	26	3	175	183	63	114	0	0	0	0	0	0	0	—	5	26	1	0	1.0	.969
DIVISIONAL PLAYOFF SERIES																										
1995	NY A	0	0	—	5.14	1	1	0	7	9	3	0	0	0	0	0	0	0	0	—	0	3	0	0	3.0	1.000

Charlie Petty

PETTY, CHARLES E. TR
B. June 28, 1866, Nashville, Tenn. Deceased.

Year	Team	W	L	PCT	ERA	G	GS	CG	IP	H	BB	SO	ShO	Relief W	Relief L	Relief SV	AB	H	HR	BA	PO	A	E	DP	TC/G	FA
1889	CIN AA	2	3	.400	5.52	5	5	5	44	44	20	10	0	0	0	0	20	6	0	.300	1	9	0	0	2.0	1.000
1893	NY N	5	2	.714	3.33	9	6	4	54	66	28	12	0	2	0	0	22	7	1	.318	2	11	2	0	1.7	.867
1894	2 teams WAS N (16G 3–8) CLE N (4G 0–2)																									
″	total	3	10	.231	6.23	20	15	10	130	198	46	18	0	0	0	0	53	9	0	.170	8	18	6	0	1.6	.813
3 yrs.		10	15	.400	5.41	34	26	19	228	308	94	40	0	2	0	0	95	22	1	.232	11	38	8	0	1.7	.860

Jesse Petty

PETTY, JESSE LEE (The Silver Fox) BR TL 6′ 195 lbs.
B. Nov. 23, 1894, Orr, Okla. D. Oct. 23, 1971, St. Paul, Minn.

Year	Team	W	L	PCT	ERA	G	GS	CG	IP	H	BB	SO	ShO	Relief W	Relief L	Relief SV	AB	H	HR	BA	PO	A	E	DP	TC/G	FA
1921	CLE A	0	0	—	2.00	4	0	0	9	10	0	0	0	0	0	0	2	0	0	.000	0	7	0	0	1.8	1.000
1925	BKN N	9	9	.500	4.88	28	21	7	153	188	47	39	0	3	0	0	50	7	0	.140	6	30	5	1	1.5	.878
1926		17	**17**	.500	2.84	38	33	23	275.2	246	79	101	1	2	1	1	97	17	0	.175	8	51	7	0	1.7	.894
1927		13	18	.419	2.98	42	33	19	271.2	263	53	101	2	2	1	1	91	9	0	.099	7	47	6	3	1.4	.900
1928		15	15	.500	4.04	40	31	15	234	264	56	74	2	1	2	1	81	9	0	.111	4	34	1	4	1.0	.974
1929	PIT N	11	10	.524	3.71	36	25	12	184.1	197	42	58	1	1	0	0	67	7	0	.104	1	36	1	0	1.1	.974
1930	2 teams PIT N (10G 1–6) CHI N (9G 1–3)																									
″	total	2	9	.182	5.69	19	10	0	80.2	118	19	34	0	1	1	1	25	4	0	.160	0	16	0	0	0.8	1.000
7 yrs.		67	78	.462	3.68	207	153	76	1208.1	1286	296	407	6	10	5	4	413	53	0	.128	26	221	20	8	1.3	.925

Pretzels Pezzullo

PEZZULLO, JOHN BL TL 5′11½″ 180 lbs.
B. Dec. 10, 1910, Bridgeport, Conn. D. May 16, 1990, Dallas, Tex.

Year	Team	W	L	PCT	ERA	G	GS	CG	IP	H	BB	SO	ShO	Relief W	Relief L	Relief SV	AB	H	HR	BA	PO	A	E	DP	TC/G	FA
1935	PHI N	3	5	.375	6.40	41	7	2	84.1	115	45	24	0	1	1	1	24	6	0	.250	2	9	1	0	0.3	.917
1936		0	0	—	4.50	1	0	0	2	1	6	0	0	0	0	0	0	0	0	—	0	0	0	0	0.0	.000
2 yrs.		3	5	.375	6.36	42	7	2	86.1	116	51	24	0	1	1	1	24	6	0	.250	2	9	1	0	0.3	.917

Bill Pfann

PFANN, WILLIAM F. 6′ 205 lbs.
B. June 1863, Brooklyn, N. Y. D. June 3, 1904, Hamilton, Ont., Canada.

Year	Team	W	L	PCT	ERA	G	GS	CG	IP	H	BB	SO	ShO	Relief W	Relief L	Relief SV	AB	H	HR	BA	PO	A	E	DP	TC/G	FA
1894	CIN N	0	1	.000	27.00	1	1	0	3	10	4	0	0	0	0	0	1	0	0	.000	0	2	0	0	2.0	1.000

Big Jeff Pfeffer

PFEFFER, FRANCIS XAVIER BR TR 6′ 1″ 185 lbs.
Brother of Jeff Pfeffer.
B. Mar. 31, 1882, Champaign, Ill. D. Dec. 19, 1954, Kankakee, Ill.

Year	Team	W	L	PCT	ERA	G	GS	CG	IP	H	BB	SO	ShO	Relief W	Relief L	Relief SV	AB	H	HR	BA	PO	A	E	DP	TC/G	FA
1905	CHI N	4	4	.500	2.50	15	11	9	101	84	36	56	0	0	0	0	40	8	0	.200	4	24	0	0	1.9	1.000
1906	BOS N	13	22	.371	2.95	35	35	33	302.1	270	114	158	4	0	0	0	158	31	1	.196	32	93	5	1	2.7	.962
1907		6	8	.429	3.00	19	16	12	144	129	61	65	1	0	0	0	60	15	0	.250	4	38	2	0	2.3	.955
1908		0	0	—	12.60	4	0	0	10	18	8	3	0	0	0	0	2	0	0	.000	0	1	0	0	0.3	1.000
1910	CHI N	1	0	1.000	3.27	13	1	1	41.1	43	16	11	0	0	0	0	17	3	0	.176	1	10	0	0	0.8	1.000
1911	BOS N	7	5	.583	4.73	26	6	4	97	116	57	24	1	4	2	2	46	9	1	.196	10	25	0	0	1.2	1.000
6 yrs.		31	39	.443	3.30	112	69	59	695.2	660	292	317	6	4	2	2	*				51	191	7	1	1.9	.972

Fred Pfeffer

PFEFFER, NATHANIEL FREDERICK (Dandelion, Fritz) BR TR 5′10½″ 184 lbs.
B. Mar. 17, 1860, Louisville, Ky. D. Apr. 10, 1932, Chicago, Ill.
Manager 1892.

Year	Team	W	L	PCT	ERA	G	GS	CG	IP	H	BB	SO	ShO	Relief W	Relief L	Relief SV	AB	H	HR	BA	PO	A	E	DP	TC/G	FA
1884	CHI N	0	0	—	*9.00*	1	0	0	1	3	1	0	0	0	0	0	467	135	25	.289	169	282	76	35	6.2	.856
1885		2	1	.667	*2.56*	5	2	2	31.2	26	8	13	0	**1**	0	**2**	469	113	6	.241	328	397	86	66	7.1	.894
1892	LOU N	0	0	—	1.80	1	0	0	5	4	5	0	0	0	0	0	470	121	2	.257	344	340	73	66	6.4	.904
1894		0	0	—	2.57	1	0	0	7	8	6	0	0	0	0	0	409	126	5	.308	394	402	72	68	6.9	.917
4 yrs.		2	1	.667	2.62	8	2	2	44.2	41	20	13	0	1	0	2	*				5054	5526	980	951	6.9	.915

Jeff Pfeffer

PFEFFER, EDWARD JOSEPH BR TR 6′ 3″ 210 lbs.
Brother of Big Jeff Pfeffer.
B. Mar. 4, 1888, Seymour, Ill. D. Aug. 15, 1972, Chicago, Ill.

Year	Team	W	L	PCT	ERA	G	GS	CG	IP	H	BB	SO	ShO	Relief W	Relief L	Relief SV	AB	H	HR	BA	PO	A	E	DP	TC/G	FA
1911	STL A	0	0	—	7.20	2	0	0	10	11	4	4	0	0	0	0	4	0	0	.000	0	2	0	0	1.0	1.000
1913	BKN N	0	1	.000	3.33	5	2	1	24.1	28	13	13	0	0	0	0	7	0	0	.000	2	6	0	1	1.6	1.000
1914		23	12	.657	1.97	43	34	27	315	264	91	135	3	0	2	4	116	23	0	.198	4	65	2	3	1.7	.972
1915		19	14	.576	2.10	40	34	26	291.2	243	76	84	6	1	2	3	106	27	0	.255	9	62	2	0	1.8	.973
1916		25	11	.694	1.92	41	36	30	328.2	274	63	128	6	1	0	1	122	34	0	.279	8	66	3	3	1.7	.961

Jeff Pfeffer *continued*

Year	Team	W	L	PCT	ERA	G	GS	CG	IP	H	BB	SO	ShO	Relief Pitching W	L	SV	Batting AB	H	HR	BA	PO	A	E	DP	TC/G	FA
1917		11	15	.423	2.23	30	30	24	266	225	66	115	3	0	0	0	100	13	0	.130	6	69	4	0	2.5	.949
1918		1	0	1.000	0.00	1	1	1	9	2	3	1	1	0	0	0	4	1	0	.250	1	4	0	0	5.0	1.000
1919		17	13	.567	2.66	30	30	26	267	270	49	92	4	0	0	0	97	20	0	.206	14	78	5	3	3.2	.948
1920		16	9	.640	3.01	30	28	20	215	225	45	80	2	1	0	0	74	18	0	.243	4	47	3	2	1.8	.944
1921	**2 teams** **BKN N**	(6G 1–5)		**STL N**	(18G 9–3)																					
″	**total**	10	8	.556	4.35	24	18	9	130.1	151	37	30	1	2	0	0	40	4	0	.100	4	29	1	1	1.4	.971
1922	**STL N**	19	12	.613	3.58	44	32	19	261.1	286	58	83	1	3	1	2	98	24	0	.245	4	65	1	3	1.6	.986
1923		8	9	.471	4.02	26	18	7	152.1	171	40	32	1	1	1	0	55	7	0	.127	3	31	1	2	1.3	.971
1924	**2 teams** **STL N**	(16G 4–5)		**PIT N**	(15G 5–3)																					
″	**total**	9	8	.529	4.35	31	16	4	136.2	170	47	39	0	4	3	0	51	9	0	.176	0	25	1	3	0.8	.962
13 yrs.		158	112	.585	2.77	347	279	194	2407.1	2320	592	836	28	13	9	10	874	180	0	.206	59	549	23	21	1.8	.964
WORLD SERIES																										
1916	**BKN N**	0	1	.000	2.53	3	1	0	10.2	7	4	5	0	0	0	1	4	1	0	.250	0	2	0	0	0.7	1.000
1920		0	0	—	3.00	1	0	0	3	4	2	1	0	0	0	0	1	0	0	.000	0	0	0	0	0.0	.000
2 yrs.		0	1	.000	2.63	4	1	0	13.2	11	6	6	0	0	0	1	5	1	0	.200	0	2	0	0	0.5	1.000

Jack Pfiester

PFIESTER, JOHN ALBERT (Jack the Giant Killer)
Born John Albert Hagenbush.
B. May 24, 1878, Cincinnati, Ohio D. Sept. 3, 1953, Loveland, Ohio.
BR TL 5′11″ 180 lbs.

Year	Team	W	L	PCT	ERA	G	GS	CG	IP	H	BB	SO	ShO	Relief Pitching W	L	SV	Batting AB	H	HR	BA	PO	A	E	DP	TC/G	FA
1903	**PIT N**	0	3	.000	6.16	3	3	2	19	26	10	15	0	0	0	0	6	0	0	.000	2	3	1	0	2.0	.833
1904		1	1	.500	7.20	3	2	1	20	28	9	6	0	0	0	0	7	2	0	.286	0	6	0	0	2.0	1.000
1906	**CHI N**	20	8	.714	1.56	31	29	20	241.2	173	63	153	4	1	0	0	84	4	0	.048	21	62	7	1	2.9	.922
1907		15	9	.625	**1.15**	30	22	13	195	143	48	90	3	2	1	0	64	6	0	.094	8	44	7	0	2.0	.881
1908		12	10	.545	2.00	33	29	18	252	204	70	117	3	0	1	0	79	8	0	.101	13	56	2	2	2.2	.972
1909		17	6	.739	2.43	29	25	13	196.2	179	49	73	5	1	0	0	65	11	0	.169	6	69	2	1	2.7	.974
1910		6	3	.667	1.79	14	13	5	100.1	82	26	34	2	0	0	0	33	3	0	.091	8	25	3	0	2.6	.917
1911		0	4	.000	4.01	6	5	3	33.2	34	18	15	0	0	0	0	11	2	0	.182	1	13	1	1	2.5	.933
8 yrs.		71	44	.617	2.04	149	128	75	1058.1	869	293	503	17	4	2	0	349	36	0	.103	59	278	23	5	2.4	.936
WORLD SERIES																										
1906	**CHI N**	0	2	.000	6.10	2	1	1	10.1	7	3	11	0	0	0	0	2	0	0	.000	0	2	1	0	1.5	.667
1907		1	0	1.000	1.00	1	1	1	9	9	1	3	0	0	0	0	2	0	0	.000	0	0	0	0	0.0	.000
1908		0	1	.000	7.88	1	1	0	8	10	3	1	0	0	0	0	2	0	0	.000	0	0	0	0	0.0	.000
1910		0	0	—	0.00	1	0	0	6.2	9	1	1	0	0	0	0	2	0	0	.000	0	1	0	0	1.0	1.000
4 yrs.		1	3	.250	3.97	5	3	2	34	35	8	16	0	0	0	0	8	0	0	.000	0	3	1	0	0.8	.750

Dan Pfister

PFISTER, DANIEL ALBIN
B. Dec. 20, 1936, Plainfield, N. J.
BR TR 6′ 187 lbs.

Year	Team	W	L	PCT	ERA	G	GS	CG	IP	H	BB	SO	ShO	Relief Pitching W	L	SV	Batting AB	H	HR	BA	PO	A	E	DP	TC/G	FA
1961	**KC A**	0	0	—	15.43	2	0	0	2.1	5	4	3	0	0	0	0	0	0	0	—	0	0	0	0	0.0	.000
1962		4	14	.222	4.54	41	25	2	196.1	175	106	123	0	0	1	1	65	12	0	.185	24	30	2	2	1.4	.964
1963		1	0	1.000	1.93	3	1	0	9.1	8	3	9	0	0	0	0	3	0	0	.000	0	3	0	0	1.0	1.000
1964		1	5	.167	6.53	19	3	0	41.1	50	29	21	0	1	3	0	6	0	0	.000	4	6	3	0	0.7	.769
4 yrs.		6	19	.240	4.87	65	29	2	249.1	238	142	156	0	1	4	1	74	12	0	.162	28	39	5	2	1.1	.931

Lee Pfund

PFUND, LeROY HERBERT
B. Oct. 18, 1918, Oak Park, Ill.
BR TR 6′ 1″ 185 lbs.

Year	Team	W	L	PCT	ERA	G	GS	CG	IP	H	BB	SO	ShO	Relief Pitching W	L	SV	Batting AB	H	HR	BA	PO	A	E	DP	TC/G	FA
1945	**BKN N**	3	2	.600	5.20	15	10	2	62.1	69	35	27	0	0	0	0	22	4	0	.182	4	14	2	1	1.3	.900

Bill Phebus

PHEBUS, RAYMOND WILLIAM
B. Aug. 2, 1909, Cherryvale, Kans. D. Oct. 11, 1989, Bartow, Fla.
BR TR 5′ 9″ 170 lbs.

Year	Team	W	L	PCT	ERA	G	GS	CG	IP	H	BB	SO	ShO	Relief Pitching W	L	SV	Batting AB	H	HR	BA	PO	A	E	DP	TC/G	FA
1936	**WAS A**	0	0	—	2.45	2	1	0	7.1	4	4	4	0	0	0	0	1	0	0	.000	0	0	0	0	0.0	.000
1937		3	2	.600	2.21	6	5	4	40.2	33	24	12	1	0	0	1	8	0	0	.000	1	4	1	0	1.0	.833
1938		0	0	—	11.37	5	0	0	6.1	9	7	2	0	0	0	1	1	0	0	.000	0	3	0	0	0.6	1.000
3 yrs.		3	2	.600	3.31	13	6	4	54.1	46	35	18	1	0	0	2	10	0	0	.000	1	7	1	0	0.7	.889

Ray Phelps

PHELPS, RAYMOND CLIFFORD
B. Dec. 11, 1903, Dunlap, Tenn. D. July 7, 1971, Fort Pierce, Fla.
BR TR 6′ 2″ 200 lbs.

Year	Team	W	L	PCT	ERA	G	GS	CG	IP	H	BB	SO	ShO	Relief Pitching W	L	SV	Batting AB	H	HR	BA	PO	A	E	DP	TC/G	FA
1930	**BKN N**	14	7	.667	4.11	36	24	11	179.2	198	52	64	2	2	1	0	68	10	1	.147	10	43	0	4	1.5	1.000
1931		7	9	.438	5.00	28	26	3	149.1	184	44	50	2	0	0	0	51	8	0	.157	4	31	1	6	1.3	.972
1932		4	5	.444	5.90	20	8	4	79.1	101	27	21	1	1	3	0	23	2	0	.087	3	20	4	1	1.4	.852
1935	**CHI A**	4	8	.333	4.82	27	17	4	125	126	55	38	0	0	1	1	41	5	0	.122	7	32	2	1	1.5	.951
1936		4	6	.400	6.03	15	4	2	68.2	91	42	17	0	3	3	0	26	6	0	.231	3	18	1	1	1.5	.955
5 yrs.		33	35	.485	4.93	126	79	24	602	700	220	190	5	6	8	1	209	31	1	.148	27	144	8	13	1.4	.955

Deacon Phillippe

PHILLIPPE, CHARLES LOUIS
B. May 23, 1872, Rural Retreat, Va. D. Mar. 30, 1952, Avalon, Pa.
BR TR 6′½″ 180 lbs.

Year	Team	W	L	PCT	ERA	G	GS	CG	IP	H	BB	SO	ShO	Relief Pitching W	L	SV	Batting AB	H	HR	BA	PO	A	E	DP	TC/G	FA
1899	**LOU N**	21	17	.553	3.17	42	38	33	321	331	64	68	2	**3**	0	1	128	26	0	.203	15	77	7	3	2.3	.929
1900	**PIT N**	20	13	.606	2.84	38	33	29	279	274	42	75	1	2	1	0	105	19	0	.181	9	57	3	1	1.8	.957
1901		22	12	.647	2.22	37	32	30	296	274	38	103	1	1	1	2	113	26	1	.230	15	89	6	2	3.0	.945
1902		20	9	.690	2.05	31	30	29	272	265	26	122	5	0	0	0	113	25	1	.221	5	59	3	1	2.2	.955
1903		24	7	.774	2.43	36	33	31	289.1	269	29	123	4	0	0	2	124	26	0	.210	14	65	4	1	2.2	.952
1904		10	10	.500	3.24	21	19	17	166.2	183	26	82	3	1	0	1	65	8	0	.123	8	41	1	3	2.4	.980
1905		22	13	.629	2.19	38	33	25	279	235	48	133	5	3	0	0	97	9	0	.093	4	74	5	2	2.2	.940
1906		15	10	.600	2.47	33	24	19	218.2	216	26	90	3	2	1	0	82	20	0	.244	5	61	3	2	2.1	.957
1907		13	11	.542	2.61	35	26	17	214	214	36	61	1	3	0	2	65	12	0	.185	8	53	1	1	1.8	.984
1908		0	0	—	11.25	5	0	0	12	20	3	1	0	0	0	0	4	1	0	.250	0	1	0	0	0.2	1.000
1909		8	3	.727	2.32	22	13	7	131.2	121	14	38	1	2	0	0	42	3	0	.071	6	26	0	1	1.5	1.000
1910		14	2	.875	2.29	31	8	5	121.2	111	9	30	1	**7**	1	4	41	9	1	.220	8	18	1	0	0.9	.963
1911		0	0	—	7.50	3	0	0	6	5	2	3	0	0	0	0	1	1	0	1.000	0	3	0	0	1.0	1.000
13 yrs.		189	107	.639	2.59	372	289	242	2607	2518	363	929	27	24	4	12	980	185	3	.189	97	624	34	17	2.0	.955

Deacon Phillippe *continued*

Year	Team	W	L	PCT	ERA	G	GS	CG	IP	H	BB	SO	ShO	Relief W	Relief L	SV	AB	H	HR	BA	PO	A	E	DP	TC/G	FA
WORLD SERIES																										
1903	PIT N	3	2	.600	3.27	5	5	5	44	38	3	20	0	0	0	0	18	4	0	.222	2	9	1	0	2.4	.917
1909		0	0	—	0.00	2	0	0	6	2	1	2	0	0	0	0	1	0	0	.000	1	2	2	0	2.5	.600
2 yrs.		3	2	.600	2.88	7	5	5	50	40	4	22	0	0	0	0	19	4	0	.211	3	11	3	0	2.4	.824

Bill Phillips

PHILLIPS, WILLIAM CORCORAN (Silver Bill, Whoa Bill) BR TR 5′11″ 180 lbs.
B. Nov. 9, 1868, Allenport, Pa. D. Oct. 25, 1941, Charleroi, Pa.
Manager 1914–15.

Year	Team	W	L	PCT	ERA	G	GS	CG	IP	H	BB	SO	ShO	Relief W	Relief L	SV	AB	H	HR	BA	PO	A	E	DP	TC/G	FA
1890	PIT N	1	9	.100	7.57	10	10	9	82	123	29	25	0	0	0	0	46	11	0	.239	2	17	1	0	1.4	.950
1895	CIN N	6	7	.462	6.03	18	9	6	109	126	44	15	0	3	2	2	48	15	0	.313	16	24	3	0	2.4	.930
1899		17	9	.654	3.32	33	27	18	227.2	234	71	43	1	2	1	1	92	12	0	.130	20	51	11	4	2.4	.866
1900		9	11	.450	4.28	29	24	17	208.1	229	67	51	3	1	0	0	79	13	0	.165	13	76	5	7	3.2	.947
1901		14	20	.412	4.64	37	36	29	281.1	364	67	109	1	0	0	0	109	22	0	.202	12	100	10	3	3.2	.918
1902		16	16	.500	2.48	34	33	30	272	266	55	85	0	0	0	0	114	39	0	.342	18	80	6	3	3.1	.942
1903		8	6	.571	3.35	16	13	11	118.1	134	30	46	1	0	0	0	57	10	0	.175	3	45	5	0	3.3	.906
7 yrs.		71	78	.477	4.08	177	152	120	1298.2	1476	363	374	6	6	3	3	545	122	0	.224	84	393	41	17	2.8	.921

Buz Phillips

PHILLIPS, ALBERT ABERNATHY BR TR 5′11½″ 185 lbs.
B. May 25, 1904, Newton, N. C. D. Nov. 6, 1964, Baltimore, Md.

Year	Team	W	L	PCT	ERA	G	GS	CG	IP	H	BB	SO	ShO	Relief W	Relief L	SV	AB	H	HR	BA	PO	A	E	DP	TC/G	FA
1930	PHI N	0	0	—	8.04	14	1	0	43.2	68	18	9	0	0	0	0	13	6	1	.462	2	5	0	0	0.5	1.000

Ed Phillips

PHILLIPS, NORMAN EDWIN BR TR 6′ 1″ 190 lbs.
B. Sept. 20, 1944, Ardmore, Okla.

Year	Team	W	L	PCT	ERA	G	GS	CG	IP	H	BB	SO	ShO	Relief W	Relief L	SV	AB	H	HR	BA	PO	A	E	DP	TC/G	FA
1970	BOS A	0	2	.000	5.25	18	0	0	24	29	10	23	0	0	2	0	3	0	0	.000	0	1	0	0	0.1	1.000

Jack Phillips

PHILLIPS, JACK DORN (Stretch) BR TR 6′ 4″ 193 lbs.
B. Sept. 6, 1921, Clarence, N. Y.

Year	Team	W	L	PCT	ERA	G	GS	CG	IP	H	BB	SO	ShO	Relief W	Relief L	SV	AB	H	HR	BA	PO	A	E	DP	TC/G	FA
1950	PIT N	0	0	—	7.20	1	0	0	5	7	1	2	0	0	0	0	*				71	1	1	8	7.3	.986

John Phillips

PHILLIPS, JOHN STEPHEN BR TR 6′ 1″ 185 lbs.
B. May 24, 1919, St. Louis, Mo. D. June 16, 1958, St. Louis, Mo.

Year	Team	W	L	PCT	ERA	G	GS	CG	IP	H	BB	SO	ShO	Relief W	Relief L	SV	AB	H	HR	BA	PO	A	E	DP	TC/G	FA
1945	NY N	0	0	—	10.38	1	0	0	4.1	5	4	0	0	0	0	0	*				1	0	0	0	1.0	1.000

Red Phillips

PHILLIPS, CLARENCE LEMUEL BR TR 6′ 3½″ 195 lbs.
B. Nov. 3, 1908, Pauls Valley, Okla. D. Feb. 1, 1988, Wichita, Kans.

Year	Team	W	L	PCT	ERA	G	GS	CG	IP	H	BB	SO	ShO	Relief W	Relief L	SV	AB	H	HR	BA	PO	A	E	DP	TC/G	FA
1934	DET A	2	0	1.000	6.17	7	1	1	23.1	31	16	3	0	1	0	1	12	3	0	.250	1	1	0	1	0.3	1.000
1936		2	4	.333	6.49	22	6	3	87.1	124	22	15	0	1	1	0	33	10	0	.303	3	15	1	2	0.9	.947
2 yrs.		4	4	.500	6.42	29	7	4	110.2	155	38	18	0	2	1	1	45	13	0	.289	4	16	1	3	0.7	.952

Taylor Phillips

PHILLIPS, WILLIAM TAYLOR (Tay) BL TL 5′11″ 185 lbs.
B. June 18, 1933, Atlanta, Ga.

Year	Team	W	L	PCT	ERA	G	GS	CG	IP	H	BB	SO	ShO	Relief W	Relief L	SV	AB	H	HR	BA	PO	A	E	DP	TC/G	FA
1956	MIL N	5	3	.625	2.26	23	6	3	87.2	69	33	36	0	2	1	2	21	0	0	.000	9	23	0	2	1.4	1.000
1957		3	2	.600	5.55	27	6	0	73	82	40	36	0	2	1	2	20	2	0	.100	4	14	0	2	0.7	1.000
1958	CHI N	7	10	.412	4.76	39	27	5	170.1	178	79	102	1	1	0	1	54	3	0	.056	7	35	5	3	1.2	.894
1959	2 teams CHI N (7G 0–2) PHI N (32G 1–4)																									
"	total	1	6	.143	5.54	39	5	1	79.2	94	42	40	0	0	3	1	15	1	0	.067	6	16	2	1	0.6	.917
1960	PHI N	0	1	.000	8.36	10	1	0	14	21	4	6	0	0	0	0	1	0	0	.000	1	2	0	0	0.3	1.000
1963	CHI A	0	0	—	10.29	9	0	0	14	16	13	13	0	0	0	0	2	0	0	.000	1	2	0	0	0.3	1.000
6 yrs.		16	22	.421	4.82	147	45	9	438.2	460	211	233	1	5	5	6	113	6	0	.053	28	92	7	8	0.9	.945

Tom Phillips

PHILLIPS, THOMAS GERARD BR TR 6′ 2″ 190 lbs.
B. Apr. 5, 1889, Philipsburg, Pa. D. Apr. 12, 1929, Philipsburg, Pa.

Year	Team	W	L	PCT	ERA	G	GS	CG	IP	H	BB	SO	ShO	Relief W	Relief L	SV	AB	H	HR	BA	PO	A	E	DP	TC/G	FA
1915	STL A	1	3	.250	2.96	5	4	1	27.1	28	12	5	0	0	0	0	9	1	0	.111	2	5	3	0	2.0	.700
1919	CLE A	3	2	.600	2.95	22	3	2	55	55	34	18	0	1	1	0	11	4	0	.364	1	11	1	0	0.6	.923
1921	WAS A	1	0	1.000	2.00	1	1	1	9	9	3	2	0	0	0	0	3	0	0	.000	0	1	1	0	2.0	.500
1922		3	7	.300	4.89	17	7	2	70	72	22	19	1	2	1	0	20	3	0	.150	2	14	0	1	0.9	1.000
4 yrs.		8	12	.400	3.74	45	15	6	161.1	164	71	44	1	3	2	0	43	8	0	.186	5	31	5	1	0.9	.878

Tom Phoebus

PHOEBUS, THOMAS HAROLD BR TR 5′ 8″ 185 lbs.
B. Apr. 7, 1942, Baltimore, Md.

Year	Team	W	L	PCT	ERA	G	GS	CG	IP	H	BB	SO	ShO	Relief W	Relief L	SV	AB	H	HR	BA	PO	A	E	DP	TC/G	FA
1966	BAL A	2	1	.667	1.23	3	3	2	22	16	6	17	2	0	0	0	6	1	0	.167	0	2	0	0	0.7	1.000
1967		14	9	.609	3.33	33	33	7	208	177	114	179	4	0	0	0	76	11	1	.145	12	22	1	0	1.1	.971
1968		15	15	.500	2.62	36	36	9	240.2	186	105	193	3	0	0	0	82	15	1	.183	20	29	1	2	1.4	.980
1969		14	7	.667	3.52	35	33	6	202	180	87	117	2	0	0	0	75	15	0	.200	18	22	0	1	1.1	1.000
1970		5	5	.500	3.07	27	21	3	135	106	62	72	0	0	0	0	43	7	0	.163	14	20	1	0	1.3	.971
1971	SD N	3	11	.214	4.47	29	21	2	133	144	64	80	0	0	0	0	36	6	0	.167	13	15	3	1	1.1	.903
1972	2 teams SD N (1G 0–1) CHI N (37G 3–3)																									
"	total	3	4	.429	4.04	38	2	0	89	79	51	67	0	3	2	6	17	2	0	.118	7	15	0	2	0.6	1.000
7 yrs.		56	52	.519	3.33	201	149	29	1029.2	888	489	725	11	3	2	6	335	57	2	.170	84	125	6	6	1.1	.972
WORLD SERIES																										
1970	BAL A	1	0	1.000	0.00	1	0	0	1.2	1	0	0	0	1	0	0	0	0	0	—	0	0	0	0	0.0	.000

Steve Phoenix

PHOENIX, STEVEN ROBERT BR TR 6′ 2″ 175 lbs.
B. Jan. 31, 1968, Phoenix, Ariz.

Year	Team	W	L	PCT	ERA	G	GS	CG	IP	H	BB	SO	ShO	Relief W	Relief L	SV	AB	H	HR	BA	PO	A	E	DP	TC/G	FA
1994	OAK A	0	0	—	6.23	2	0	0	4.1	4	2	3	0	0	0	0	0	0	0	—	0	0	0	0	0.0	.000
1995		0	0	—	32.40	1	0	0	1.2	3	3	3	0	0	0	0	0	0	0	—	0	0	0	0	0.0	.000
2 yrs.		0	0		13.50	3	0	0	6	7	5	6	0	0	0	0	0	0	0		0	0	0	0	0.0	

Bill Phyle

PHYLE, WILLIAM JOSEPH
B. June 25, 1875, Duluth, Minn. D. Aug. 6, 1953, Los Angeles, Calif.
TR

Year	Team		W	L	PCT	ERA	G	GS	CG	IP	H	BB	SO	ShO	Relief W	Relief L	Relief SV	AB	H	HR	BA	PO	A	E	DP	TC/G	FA
1898	CHI	N	2	1	.667	0.78	3	3	3	23	24	6	4	2	0	0	0	9	1	0	.111	0	4	1	0	1.7	.800
1899			1	8	.111	4.20	10	9	9	83.2	92	29	10	0	0	0	1	34	6	0	.176	6	23	2	1	3.1	.935
1901	NY	N	7	10	.412	4.27	24	19	16	168.2	208	54	62	0	0	0	1	66	12	0	.182	17	48	7	0	2.9	.903
3 yrs.			10	19	.345	3.96	37	31	28	275.1	324	89	76	2	0	0	2	182	32	0	.176	54	116	15	3	3.1	.919

Doug Piatt

PIATT, DOUGLAS WILLIAM
B. Sept. 26, 1965, Beaver, Pa.
BL TR 6′ 1″ 185 lbs.

Year	Team		W	L	PCT	ERA	G	GS	CG	IP	H	BB	SO	ShO	Relief W	Relief L	Relief SV	AB	H	HR	BA	PO	A	E	DP	TC/G	FA
1991	MON	N	0	0	—	2.60	21	0	0	34.2	29	17	29	0	0	0	0	1	0	0	.000	2	4	0	1	0.3	1.000

Wiley Piatt

PIATT, WILEY HAROLD (Iron Man)
B. July 13, 1874, Blue Creek, Ohio D. Sept. 20, 1946, Cincinnati, Ohio.
BL TL 5′10″ 175 lbs.

Year	Team		W	L	PCT	ERA	G	GS	CG	IP	H	BB	SO	ShO	Relief W	Relief L	Relief SV	AB	H	HR	BA	PO	A	E	DP	TC/G	FA
1898	PHI	N	24	14	.632	3.18	39	37	33	306	285	97	121	**6**	1	0	0	122	32	0	.262	9	66	15	2	2.3	.833
1899			23	15	.605	3.45	39	38	31	305	323	86	89	2	1	0	0	122	33	0	.270	3	53	4	1	1.5	.933
1900			9	10	.474	4.65	22	20	16	160.2	194	71	47	1	0	1	0	68	17	0	.250	2	30	8	0	1.8	.800
1901	2 teams	PHI A	(18G 5–12)			CHI A	(7G 4–2)																				
″	total		9	14	.391	4.13	25	22	19	191.2	218	74	64	1	1	1	1	75	15	0	.200	3	31	4	0	1.5	.895
1902	CHI	A	12	12	.500	3.51	32	30	22	246	263	66	96	2	0	0	0	85	17	0	.200	8	57	13	1	2.4	.833
1903	BOS	N	8	13	.381	3.18	25	23	18	181	198	61	100	0	0	1	0	71	16	0	.225	3	37	9	0	2.0	.816
6 yrs.			85	78	.521	3.60	182	170	139	1390.1	1481	455	517	12	3	3	1	543	130	0	.239	28	274	53	4	2.0	.851

Hipolito Pichardo

PICHARDO, HIPOLITO ANTONIO
Born Hipolito Antonio Pichardo (Balbina).
B. Aug. 22, 1969, Esperanza, Dominican Republic.
BR TR 6′ 1″ 160 lbs.

Year	Team		W	L	PCT	ERA	G	GS	CG	IP	H	BB	SO	ShO	Relief W	Relief L	Relief SV	AB	H	HR	BA	PO	A	E	DP	TC/G	FA
1992	KC	A	9	6	.600	3.95	31	24	1	143.2	148	49	59	1	0	1	0	0	0	0	—	19	16	2	2	1.2	.946
1993			7	8	.467	4.04	30	25	2	165	183	53	70	0	0	1	0	0	0	0	—	20	27	0	1	1.6	1.000
1994			5	3	.625	4.92	45	0	0	67.2	82	24	36	0	5	3	3	0	0	0	—	4	16	5	2	0.6	.800
1995			8	4	.667	4.36	44	0	0	64	66	30	43	0	8	4	1	2	0	0	.000	2	12	0	1	0.3	1.000
4 yrs.			29	21	.580	4.19	150	49	3	440.1	479	156	208	1	13	9	4	2	0	0	.000	45	71	7	6	0.8	.943

Ron Piche

PICHE, RONALD JACQUES
B. May 22, 1935, Verdun, Que., Canada.
BR TR 5′11″ 165 lbs.

Year	Team		W	L	PCT	ERA	G	GS	CG	IP	H	BB	SO	ShO	Relief W	Relief L	Relief SV	AB	H	HR	BA	PO	A	E	DP	TC/G	FA
1960	MIL	N	3	5	.375	3.56	37	0	0	48	48	23	38	0	3	5	9	7	0	0	.000	4	4	1	1	0.2	.889
1961			2	2	.500	3.47	12	1	1	23.1	20	16	16	0	1	2	1	5	0	0	.000	0	6	0	1	0.5	1.000
1962			3	2	.600	4.85	14	8	2	52	54	29	28	0	0	0	0	18	1	0	.056	7	9	0	1	1.1	1.000
1963			1	1	.500	3.40	37	1	0	53	53	25	40	0	1	1	0	7	0	0	.000	8	13	0	0	0.6	1.000
1965	CAL	A	0	3	.000	6.86	14	1	0	19.2	20	12	14	0	0	2	0	1	0	0	.000	2	3	0	0	0.4	1.000
1966	STL	N	1	3	.250	4.26	20	0	0	25.1	21	18	21	0	1	3	2	4	0	0	.000	1	2	0	0	0.2	1.000
6 yrs.			10	16	.385	4.19	134	11	3	221.1	216	123	157	0	6	13	12	42	1	0	.024	22	37	1	3	0.4	.983

Charlie Pickett

PICKETT, CHARLES ALBERT
B. Mar. 1, 1883, Delaware, Ohio D. May 20, 1969, Springfield, Ohio.
BR TR 6′ 1″ 175 lbs.

Year	Team		W	L	PCT	ERA	G	GS	CG	IP	H	BB	SO	ShO	Relief W	Relief L	Relief SV	AB	H	HR	BA	PO	A	E	DP	TC/G	FA
1910	STL	N	0	0	—	1.50	2	0	0	6	7	2	2	0	0	0	0	0	0	0	—	0	2	1	0	1.5	.667

Clarence Pickrel

PICKREL, CLARENCE DOUGLAS
B. Mar. 28, 1911, Gretna, Va. D. Nov. 4, 1983, Rocky Mount, Va.
BR TR 6′ 1″ 180 lbs.

Year	Team		W	L	PCT	ERA	G	GS	CG	IP	H	BB	SO	ShO	Relief W	Relief L	Relief SV	AB	H	HR	BA	PO	A	E	DP	TC/G	FA
1933	PHI	N	1	0	1.000	3.95	9	0	0	13.2	20	3	6	0	1	0	0	1	0	0	.000	0	0	0	0	0.0	.000
1934	BOS	N	0	0	—	5.06	10	1	0	16	24	7	9	0	0	0	0	2	0	0	.000	1	0	0	0	0.1	1.000
2 yrs.			1	0	1.000	4.55	19	1	0	29.2	44	10	15	0	1	0	0	3	0	0	.000	1	0	0	0	0.1	1.000

Jeff Pico

PICO, JEFFREY MARK
B. Feb. 12, 1966, Antioch, Calif.
BR TR 6′ 1″ 180 lbs.

Year	Team		W	L	PCT	ERA	G	GS	CG	IP	H	BB	SO	ShO	Relief W	Relief L	Relief SV	AB	H	HR	BA	PO	A	E	DP	TC/G	FA
1988	CHI	N	6	7	.462	4.15	29	13	3	112.2	108	37	57	2	2	1	1	34	5	0	.147	5	18	1	3	0.8	.958
1989			3	1	.750	3.77	53	5	0	90.2	99	31	38	0	2	0	2	10	1	0	.100	4	22	3	2	0.5	.897
1990			4	4	.500	4.79	31	8	0	92	120	37	37	0	0	1	2	22	6	0	.273	13	16	1	2	1.0	.967
3 yrs.			13	12	.520	4.24	113	26	3	295.1	327	105	132	2	4	2	5	66	12	0	.182	22	56	5	7	0.7	.940

Mario Picone

PICONE, MARIO PETER (Babe)
B. July 5, 1926, Brooklyn, N. Y.
BR TR 5′11″ 180 lbs.

Year	Team		W	L	PCT	ERA	G	GS	CG	IP	H	BB	SO	ShO	Relief W	Relief L	Relief SV	AB	H	HR	BA	PO	A	E	DP	TC/G	FA
1947	NY	N	0	0	—	7.71	2	1	0	7	10	2	1	0	0	0	0	2	1	0	.500	0	2	0	0	1.0	1.000
1952			0	1	.000	7.00	2	1	0	9	11	5	3	0	0	0	0	2	0	0	.000	0	3	0	1	1.5	1.000
1954	2 teams	NY N	(5G 0–0)			CIN N	(4G 0–1)																				
″	total		0	1	.000	5.63	9	1	0	24	22	18	7	0	0	0	0	2	0	0	.000	2	5	0	0	0.8	1.000
3 yrs.			0	2	.000	6.30	13	3	0	40	43	25	11	0	0	0	0	6	1	0	.167	2	10	0	1	0.9	1.000

Al Piechota

PIECHOTA, ALOYSIUS EDWARD
B. Jan. 19, 1914, Chicago, Ill.
BR TR 6′ 195 lbs.

Year	Team		W	L	PCT	ERA	G	GS	CG	IP	H	BB	SO	ShO	Relief W	Relief L	Relief SV	AB	H	HR	BA	PO	A	E	DP	TC/G	FA
1940	BOS	N	2	5	.286	5.75	21	8	2	61	68	41	18	0	1	1	0	20	4	0	.200	2	12	0	0	0.7	1.000
1941			0	0	—	0.00	1	0	0	1	0	1	0	0	0	0	0	0	0	0	—	0	0	0	0	0.0	.000
2 yrs.			2	5	.286	5.66	22	8	2	62	68	42	18	0	1	1	0	20	4	0	.200	2	12	0	0	0.6	1.000

Cy Pieh

PIEH, EDWIN JOHN
B. Sept. 29, 1886, Waunakee, Wis. D. Sept. 12, 1945, Jacksonville, Fla.
BR TR 6′ 2″ 190 lbs.

Year	Team		W	L	PCT	ERA	G	GS	CG	IP	H	BB	SO	ShO	Relief W	Relief L	Relief SV	AB	H	HR	BA	PO	A	E	DP	TC/G	FA
1913	NY	A	1	0	1.000	4.35	4	0	0	10.1	10	7	6	0	1	0	0	4	1	0	.250	0	8	0	1	2.0	1.000
1914			4	4	.500	5.05	18	4	1	62.1	68	29	24	0	3	2	0	17	2	0	.118	1	13	1	0	0.8	.933
1915			4	5	.444	2.87	21	8	3	94	78	39	46	2	2	0	0	30	2	0	.067	3	28	2	1	1.6	.939
3 yrs.			9	9	.500	3.78	43	12	4	166.2	156	75	76	2	6	2	0	51	5	0	.098	4	49	3	2	1.3	.946

Billy Pierce

PIERCE, WALTER WILLIAM
B. Apr. 2, 1927, Detroit, Mich.
BL TL 5′10″ 160 lbs.

Year	Team		W	L	PCT	ERA	G	GS	CG	IP	H	BB	SO	ShO	Relief W	Relief L	Relief SV	AB	H	HR	BA	PO	A	E	DP	TC/G	FA
1945	DET	A	0	0	—	1.80	5	0	0	10	6	10	10	0	0	0	0	2	0	0	.000	0	2	0	0	0.4	1.000
1948			3	0	1.000	6.34	22	5	0	55.1	47	51	36	0	1	0	0	17	5	0	.294	2	9	0	0	0.5	1.000
1949	CHI	A	7	15	.318	3.88	32	26	8	171.2	145	112	95	0	1	0	0	51	9	0	.176	12	33	4	2	1.5	.918
1950			12	16	.429	3.98	33	29	15	219.1	189	137	118	1	1	0	1	77	20	0	.260	4	30	1	1	1.1	.971
1951			15	**14**	.517	3.03	37	28	18	240.1	237	73	113	1	0	3	2	79	16	0	.203	11	38	2	4	1.4	.961

Billy Pierce *continued*

Year	Team	Lg	W	L	PCT	ERA	G	GS	CG	IP	H	BB	SO	ShO	Relief Pitching W	Relief Pitching L	Relief Pitching SV	Batting AB	Batting H	Batting HR	BA	PO	A	E	DP	TC/G	FA
1952			15	12	.556	2.57	33	32	14	255.1	214	79	144	4	0	0	1	91	17	0	.187	13	43	1	3	1.7	.982
1953			18	12	.600	2.72	40	33	19	271.1	216	102	**186**	7	3	0	3	87	11	0	.126	11	33	4	1	1.2	.917
1954			9	10	.474	3.48	36	26	12	188.2	179	86	148	4	0	0	3	57	11	0	.193	7	19	1	1	0.8	.963
1955			15	10	.600	**1.97**	33	26	16	205.2	162	64	157	6	2	0	1	70	12	0	.171	7	25	0	1	1.0	1.000
1956			20	9	.690	3.32	35	33	**21**	276.1	261	100	192	1	0	1	1	102	16	0	.157	4	33	3	2	1.1	.925
1957			**20**	12	.625	3.26	37	34	**16**	257	228	71	171	4	0	1	2	99	17	0	.172	8	45	2	2	1.5	.964
1958			17	11	.607	2.68	35	32	**19**	245	204	66	144	3	0	0	2	83	17	0	.205	11	26	1	3	1.1	.974
1959			14	15	.483	3.62	34	33	12	224	217	62	114	2	0	0	0	68	13	0	.191	11	40	2	4	1.6	.962
1960			14	7	.667	3.62	32	30	8	196.1	201	46	108	1	1	0	0	67	12	0	.179	7	29	2	2	1.2	.947
1961			10	9	.526	3.80	39	28	5	180	190	54	106	1	3	0	3	56	8	0	.143	7	31	3	1	1.1	.927
1962	SF	N	16	6	.727	3.49	30	23	7	162.1	147	35	76	2	0	0	1	56	12	0	.214	4	24	1	3	1.0	.966
1963			3	11	.214	4.27	38	13	3	99	106	20	52	1	0	5	8	31	4	0	.129	4	20	0	2	0.6	1.000
1964			3	0	1.000	2.20	34	1	0	49	40	10	29	0	2	0	4	9	3	0	.333	1	7	1	0	0.3	.889
18 yrs.			211	169	.555	3.27	585	432	193	3306.2	2989	1178	1999	38	14	10	32	1102	203	0	.184	124	487	28	32	1.1	.956
WORLD SERIES																											
1959	CHI	A	0	0	—	0.00	3	0	0	4	2	2	3	0	0	0	0	0	0	0	—	0	0	1	0	0.3	.000
1962	SF	N	1	1	.500	2.40	2	2	1	15	8	2	5	0	0	0	0	5	0	0	.000	1	0	0	0	0.5	1.000
2 yrs.			1	1	.500	1.89	5	2	1	19	10	4	8	0	0	0	0	5	0	0	.000	1	0	1	0	0.4	.500

BL TL 6′ 1″ 185 lbs.

PIERCE, EDWARD JOHN
B. Oct. 6, 1968, Arcadia, Calif.

Eddie Pierce

Year	Team	Lg	W	L	PCT	ERA	G	GS	CG	IP	H	BB	SO	ShO	Relief W	Relief L	Relief SV	AB	H	HR	BA	PO	A	E	DP	TC/G	FA
1992	KC	A	0	0	—	3.38	2	1	0	5.1	9	4	3	0	0	0	0	0	0	0	—	0	1	0	0	0.5	1.000

BR TR 6′ 1″ 187 lbs.

PIERCE, JEFFREY CHARLES
B. June 7, 1969, Poughkeepsie, N. Y.

Jeff Pierce

Year	Team	Lg	W	L	PCT	ERA	G	GS	CG	IP	H	BB	SO	ShO	Relief W	Relief L	Relief SV	AB	H	HR	BA	PO	A	E	DP	TC/G	FA
1995	BOS	A	0	3	.000	6.60	12	0	0	15	16	14	12	0	0	3	0	0	0	0	—	0	2	0	0	0.2	1.000

BL TL 5′ 7″ 156 lbs.

PIERCE, RAYMOND LESTER (Lefty)
B. June 6, 1897, Emporia, Kans. D. May 4, 1963, Denver, Colo.

Ray Pierce

Year	Team	Lg	W	L	PCT	ERA	G	GS	CG	IP	H	BB	SO	ShO	Relief W	Relief L	Relief SV	AB	H	HR	BA	PO	A	E	DP	TC/G	FA
1924	CHI	N	0	0	—	7.36	6	0	0	7.1	7	4	2	0	0	0	0	0	0	0	—	0	1	0	0	0.2	1.000
1925	PHI	N	5	4	.556	5.50	23	8	4	90	134	24	18	0	1	1	0	28	5	0	.179	4	22	0	2	1.1	1.000
1926			2	7	.222	5.63	37	7	1	84.2	128	35	18	0	2	2	0	24	3	0	.125	2	18	1	2	0.6	.952
3 yrs.			7	11	.389	5.64	66	15	5	182	269	63	38	0	3	3	0	52	8	0	.154	6	41	1	4	0.7	.979

BR TL 6′ 1″ 190 lbs.

PIERCE, TONY MICHAEL
B. Jan. 29, 1946, Brunswick, Ga.

Tony Pierce

Year	Team	Lg	W	L	PCT	ERA	G	GS	CG	IP	H	BB	SO	ShO	Relief W	Relief L	Relief SV	AB	H	HR	BA	PO	A	E	DP	TC/G	FA
1967	KC	A	3	4	.429	3.04	49	6	0	97.2	79	30	61	0	2	1	7	20	0	0	.000	9	9	0	0	0.4	1.000
1968	OAK	A	1	2	.333	3.86	17	3	0	32.2	39	10	16	0	0	0	1	6	0	0	.000	1	8	0	1	0.5	1.000
2 yrs.			4	6	.400	3.25	66	9	0	130.1	118	40	77	0	2	1	8	26	0	0	.000	10	17	0	1	0.4	1.000

BR TR 6′ 1½″ 170 lbs.

PIERCY, WILLIAM BENTON (Wild Bill)
B. May 2, 1896, El Monte, Calif. D. Aug. 28, 1951, Long Beach, Calif.

Bill Piercy

Year	Team	Lg	W	L	PCT	ERA	G	GS	CG	IP	H	BB	SO	ShO	Relief W	Relief L	Relief SV	AB	H	HR	BA	PO	A	E	DP	TC/G	FA
1917	NY	A	0	1	.000	3.00	1	1	1	9	9	2	4	0	0	0	0	2	0	0	.000	0	3	1	0	4.0	.750
1921			5	4	.556	2.98	14	10	5	81.2	82	28	35	1	1	1	0	28	6	0	.214	3	20	4	2	1.9	.852
1922	BOS	A	3	9	.250	4.67	29	12	7	121.1	140	62	24	1	0	1	0	34	5	0	.147	4	42	0	2	1.6	1.000
1923			8	17	.320	3.41	30	24	11	187.1	193	73	51	0	0	4	0	53	7	0	.132	10	65	4	3	2.6	.949
1924			5	7	.417	6.20	22	18	3	114.2	147	64	20	0	0	0	0	36	5	0	.139	4	35	4	0	2.0	.907
1926	CHI	N	6	5	.545	4.48	19	5	1	90.1	96	37	31	0	4	3	0	35	9	0	.257	5	23	3	1	1.6	.903
6 yrs.			27	43	.386	4.29	115	70	28	604.1	667	266	165	2	5	9	0	188	32	0	.170	26	188	16	8	2.0	.930
WORLD SERIES																											
1921	NY	A	0	0	—	0.00	1	0	0	1	2	0	2	0	0	0	0	0	0	0	—	0	0	0	0	0.0	.000

BR TR 5′ 7″ 153 lbs.

PIERETTI, MARINO PAUL (Chick)
B. Sept. 23, 1920, Lucca, Italy D. Jan. 30, 1981, San Francisco, Calif.

Marino Pieretti

Year	Team	Lg	W	L	PCT	ERA	G	GS	CG	IP	H	BB	SO	ShO	Relief W	Relief L	Relief SV	AB	H	HR	BA	PO	A	E	DP	TC/G	FA
1945	WAS	A	14	13	.519	3.32	44	27	14	233.1	235	91	66	3	1	1	2	81	18	0	.222	17	52	3	2	1.6	.958
1946			2	2	.500	5.95	30	2	1	62	70	40	20	0	1	1	0	14	3	0	.214	6	14	1	0	0.7	.952
1947			2	4	.333	4.21	23	10	2	83.1	97	47	32	1	0	1	0	26	6	0	.231	4	14	5	0	1.0	.783
1948	2 teams	WAS A (8G 0–2) CHI A (21G 8–10)																									
″	total		8	12	.400	5.47	29	19	4	131.2	135	59	34	0	1	1	1	41	7	0	.171	6	31	1	1	1.3	.974
1949	CHI	A	4	6	.400	5.51	39	9	0	116	131	54	25	0	2	1	4	38	9	0	.237	7	31	2	1	1.0	.950
1950	CLE	A	0	1	.000	4.18	29	1	0	47.1	45	30	11	0	0	1	1	7	2	0	.286	5	12	2	1	0.7	.895
6 yrs.			30	38	.441	4.53	194	68	21	673.2	713	321	188	4	5	6	8	207	45	0	.217	45	154	14	5	1.1	.934

BR TR 5′10½″ 195 lbs.

PIEROTTI, ALBERT FELIX
B. Oct. 24, 1895, Boston, Mass. D. Feb. 12, 1964, Everett, Mass.

Al Pierotti

Year	Team	Lg	W	L	PCT	ERA	G	GS	CG	IP	H	BB	SO	ShO	Relief W	Relief L	Relief SV	AB	H	HR	BA	PO	A	E	DP	TC/G	FA
1920	BOS	N	1	1	.500	2.88	6	2	2	25	23	9	12	0	0	0	0	8	2	0	.250	1	5	0	0	1.0	1.000
1921			0	1	.000	21.60	2	0	0	1.2	3	3	1	0	0	1	0	1	0	0	.000	0	1	1	0	1.0	.500
2 yrs.			1	2	.333	4.05	8	2	2	26.2	26	12	13	0	0	1	0	9	2	0	.222	1	6	1	0	1.0	.875

BR TR 6′ 1″ 155 lbs.

PIERRO, WILLIAM LEONARD (Wild Bill)
B. Apr. 15, 1926, Brooklyn, N. Y.

Bill Pierro

Year	Team	Lg	W	L	PCT	ERA	G	GS	CG	IP	H	BB	SO	ShO	Relief W	Relief L	Relief SV	AB	H	HR	BA	PO	A	E	DP	TC/G	FA
1950	PIT	N	0	2	.000	10.55	12	3	0	29	33	28	13	0	0	0	0	9	2	0	.222	0	3	0	0	0.3	1.000

BL TL 6′ 2″ 180 lbs.

PIERSON, WILLIAM MORRIS (Wild Bill)
B. June 14, 1899, Atlantic City, N. J. D. Feb. 20, 1959, Atlantic City, N. J.

Bill Pierson

Year	Team	Lg	W	L	PCT	ERA	G	GS	CG	IP	H	BB	SO	ShO	Relief W	Relief L	Relief SV	AB	H	HR	BA	PO	A	E	DP	TC/G	FA
1918	PHI	A	0	1	.000	3.32	8	1	0	21.2	20	20	6	0	0	0	0	4	1	0	.250	1	2	1	0	0.5	.750
1919			0	0	—	3.52	2	1	0	7.2	9	8	4	0	0	0	0	3	1	0	.333	0	4	0	0	2.0	1.000
1924			0	0	—	3.38	1	0	0	2.2	3	3	0	0	0	0	0	0	0	0	—	0	1	0	0	1.0	1.000
3 yrs.			0	1	.000	3.38	11	2	0	32	32	31	10	0	0	0	0	7	2	0	.286	1	7	1	0	0.8	.889

Dave Pierson

PIERSON, DAVID P.
Brother of Dick Pierson.
B. Aug. 20, 1855, Wilkes-Barre, Pa. D. Nov. 11, 1922, Trenton, N. J.
BR TR 5′ 7″ 142 lbs.

Year	Team	W	L	PCT	ERA	G	GS	CG	IP	H	BB	SO	ShO	Relief Pitching W	Relief Pitching L	Relief Pitching SV	Batting AB	Batting H	Batting HR	BA	PO	A	E	DP	TC/G	FA
1876	CIN N	0	1	.000	∞	1	1	0		2	0	0	0	0	0	0	*				159	58	59	6	4.2	.786

George Piktuzis

PIKTUZIS, GEORGE RICHARD
B. Jan. 3, 1932, Chicago, Ill.
BR TL 6′ 2″ 200 lbs.

Year	Team	W	L	PCT	ERA	G	GS	CG	IP	H	BB	SO	ShO	Relief Pitching W	Relief Pitching L	Relief Pitching SV	Batting AB	Batting H	Batting HR	BA	PO	A	E	DP	TC/G	FA
1956	CHI N	0	0	—	7.20	2	0	0	5	6	2	3	0	0	0	0	0	0	0	—	0	0	0	0	0.0	.000

Duane Pillette

PILLETTE, DUANE XAVIER (Dee)
Son of Herman Pillette.
B. July 24, 1922, Detroit, Mich.
BR TR 6′ 3″ 195 lbs.

Year	Team	W	L	PCT	ERA	G	GS	CG	IP	H	BB	SO	ShO	Relief Pitching W	Relief Pitching L	Relief Pitching SV	Batting AB	Batting H	Batting HR	BA	PO	A	E	DP	TC/G	FA
1949	NY A	2	4	.333	4.34	12	3	2	37.1	43	19	9	0	1	2	0	11	0	0	.000	4	9	0	2	1.1	1.000
1950	2 teams NY A (4G 0–0) STL A (24G 3–5)																									
″	total	3	5	.375	6.58	28	7	1	80.2	113	47	22	0	1	4	2	22	3	0	.136	3	14	4	2	0.8	.810
1951	STL A	6	**14**	.300	4.99	35	24	6	191	205	115	65	1	1	1	0	59	8	0	.136	19	25	1	1	1.3	.978
1952		10	13	.435	3.59	30	30	9	205.1	222	55	62	1	0	0	0	66	12	0	.182	14	25	0	4	1.3	1.000
1953		7	13	.350	4.48	31	25	5	166.2	181	62	58	1	0	1	0	53	7	1	.132	14	20	2	3	1.2	.944
1954	BAL A	10	14	.417	3.12	25	25	11	179	158	67	66	1	0	0	0	53	7	0	.132	12	43	2	4	2.3	.965
1955		0	3	.000	6.53	7	5	0	20.2	31	14	13	0	0	0	0	6	1	0	.167	0	5	1	0	0.9	.833
1956	PHI N	0	0	—	6.56	20	0	0	23.1	32	12	10	0	0	0	0	1	0	0	.000	1	3	0	0	0.2	1.000
8 yrs.		38	66	.365	4.40	188	119	34	904	985	391	305	4	3	8	2	271	38	1	.140	67	144	10	16	1.2	.955

Herman Pillette

PILLETTE, HERMAN POLYCARP (Old Folks)
Father of Duane Pillette.
B. Dec. 26, 1895, St. Paul, Ore. D. Apr. 30, 1960, Sacramento, Calif.
BR TR 6′ 2″ 190 lbs.

Year	Team	W	L	PCT	ERA	G	GS	CG	IP	H	BB	SO	ShO	Relief Pitching W	Relief Pitching L	Relief Pitching SV	Batting AB	Batting H	Batting HR	BA	PO	A	E	DP	TC/G	FA
1917	CIN N	0	0	—	18.00	1	0	0	1	4	0	0	0	0	0	0	0	0	0	—	0	0	0	0	0.0	.000
1922	DET A	19	12	.613	2.85	40	37	18	274.2	270	95	71	4	1	0	1	99	17	0	.172	11	82	4	5	2.4	.959
1923		14	**19**	.424	3.85	47	37	14	250.1	280	83	64	0	3	2	1	85	21	0	.247	17	86	11	2	2.4	.904
1924		1	1	.500	4.78	19	3	1	37.2	46	14	13	0	0	0	1	11	4	0	.364	2	11	1	0	0.7	.929
4 yrs.		34	32	.515	3.45	107	77	33	563.2	600	192	148	4	4	2	3	195	42	0	.215	30	179	16	7	2.1	.929

Squiz Pillion

PILLION, CECIL RANDOLPH
B. Apr. 13, 1894, Hartford, Conn. D. Sept. 30, 1962, Pittsburgh, Pa.
BL TL 6′ 178 lbs.

Year	Team	W	L	PCT	ERA	G	GS	CG	IP	H	BB	SO	ShO	Relief Pitching W	Relief Pitching L	Relief Pitching SV	Batting AB	Batting H	Batting HR	BA	PO	A	E	DP	TC/G	FA
1915	PHI A	0	0	—	6.75	2	0	0	5.1	10	2	0	0	0	0	0	1	0	0	.000	0	2	0	0	1.0	1.000

Horacio Pina

PINA, HORACIO
Born Horacio Pina (Garcia).
B. Mar. 12, 1945, Coahuila, Mexico.
BR TR 6′ 2″ 177 lbs.

Year	Team	W	L	PCT	ERA	G	GS	CG	IP	H	BB	SO	ShO	Relief Pitching W	Relief Pitching L	Relief Pitching SV	Batting AB	Batting H	Batting HR	BA	PO	A	E	DP	TC/G	FA
1968	CLE A	1	1	.500	1.72	12	3	0	31.1	24	15	24	0	0	0	2	6	0	0	.000	1	4	0	1	0.4	1.000
1969		4	2	.667	5.21	31	4	0	46.2	44	27	32	0	3	1	1	6	3	0	.500	3	8	0	1	0.4	1.000
1970	WAS A	5	3	.625	2.79	61	0	0	71	66	35	41	0	5	3	6	3	0	0	.000	5	15	1	0	0.3	.952
1971		1	1	.500	3.57	56	0	0	58	47	31	38	0	1	1	2	1	0	0	.000	3	14	0	2	0.3	1.000
1972	TEX A	2	7	.222	3.20	60	0	0	76	61	43	60	0	2	7	15	5	1	0	.200	5	22	2	4	0.5	.931
1973	OAK A	6	3	.667	2.76	47	0	0	88	58	34	41	0	6	3	8	0	0	0	—	6	26	0	4	0.7	1.000
1974	2 teams CHI N (34G 3–4) CAL A (11G 1–2)																									
″	total	4	6	.400	3.66	45	0	0	59	58	31	38	0	4	6	4	5	1	0	.200	4	15	1	0	0.4	.950
1978	PHI N	0	0	—	0.00	2	0	0	2	0	0	4	0	0	0	0	1	0	0	.000	1	0	0	0	0.5	1.000
8 yrs.		23	23	.500	3.25	314	7	0	432	358	216	278	0	21	21	38	27	5	0	.185	28	104	4	12	0.4	.971
LEAGUE CHAMPIONSHIP SERIES																										
1973	OAK A	0	0	—	0.00	1	0	0	2	3	1	1	0	0	0	0	0	0	0	—	0	0	0	0	0.0	.000
WORLD SERIES																										
1973	OAK A	0	0	—	0.00	2	0	0	3	6	2	0	0	0	0	0	0	0	0	—	0	0	0	0	0.0	.000

George Pinckney

PINCKNEY, GEORGE BURTON
B. Jan. 11, 1862, Orange Prairie, Ill. D. Nov. 10, 1926, Peoria, Ill.
BR TR 5′ 7″ 160 lbs.

Year	Team	W	L	PCT	ERA	G	GS	CG	IP	H	BB	SO	ShO	Relief Pitching W	Relief Pitching L	Relief Pitching SV	Batting AB	Batting H	Batting HR	BA	PO	A	E	DP	TC/G	FA
1886	BKN AA	0	0	—	*4.50*	1	0	0	2	2	0	0	0	0	0	0	*				73	110	32	11	6.0	.851

Ed Pinnance

PINNANCE, EDWARD D.
B. Oct. 22, 1879, Walpole Island, Ont., Canada
D. Dec. 12, 1944, Walpole Island, Ont., Canada.
BL TR 6′ 1″ 180 lbs.

Year	Team	W	L	PCT	ERA	G	GS	CG	IP	H	BB	SO	ShO	Relief Pitching W	Relief Pitching L	Relief Pitching SV	Batting AB	Batting H	Batting HR	BA	PO	A	E	DP	TC/G	FA
1903	PHI A	0	0	—	2.57	2	1	0	7	5	2	2	0	0	0	1	3	0	0	.000	1	1	0	0	1.0	1.000

Lerton Pinto

PINTO, WILLIAM LERTON
B. Apr. 8, 1899, Chillicothe, Ohio D. May 13, 1983, Oxnard, Calif.
BL TL 6′ 190 lbs.

Year	Team	W	L	PCT	ERA	G	GS	CG	IP	H	BB	SO	ShO	Relief Pitching W	Relief Pitching L	Relief Pitching SV	Batting AB	Batting H	Batting HR	BA	PO	A	E	DP	TC/G	FA
1922	PHI N	0	1	.000	5.11	9	0	0	24.2	31	14	4	0	0	1	0	9	1	0	.111	0	5	2	0	0.8	.714
1924		0	0	—	9.00	3	0	0	4	7	0	1	0	0	0	0	1	0	0	.000	0	1	0	0	0.3	1.000
2 yrs.		0	1	.000	5.65	12	0	0	28.2	38	14	5	0	0	1	0	10	1	0	.100	0	6	2	0	0.7	.750

Ed Pipgras

PIPGRAS, EDWARD JOHN
Brother of George Pipgras.
B. June 15, 1904, Schleswig, Iowa D. Apr. 13, 1964, Currie, Minn.
BR TR 6′ 2½″ 175 lbs.

Year	Team	W	L	PCT	ERA	G	GS	CG	IP	H	BB	SO	ShO	Relief Pitching W	Relief Pitching L	Relief Pitching SV	Batting AB	Batting H	Batting HR	BA	PO	A	E	DP	TC/G	FA
1932	BKN N	0	1	.000	5.40	5	1	0	10	16	6	5	0	0	1	0	2	0	0	.000	2	1	0	0	0.6	1.000

George Pipgras

PIPGRAS, GEORGE WILLIAM
Brother of Ed Pipgras.
B. Dec. 20, 1899, Ida Grove, Iowa D. Oct. 19, 1986, Gainesville, Fla.
BR TR 6′ 1½″ 185 lbs.

Year	Team	W	L	PCT	ERA	G	GS	CG	IP	H	BB	SO	ShO	Relief Pitching W	Relief Pitching L	Relief Pitching SV	Batting AB	Batting H	Batting HR	BA	PO	A	E	DP	TC/G	FA
1923	NY A	1	3	.250	5.94	8	2	2	33.1	34	25	12	0	0	2	0	9	0	0	.000	0	8	0	0	1.0	1.000
1924		0	1	.000	9.98	9	1	0	15.1	20	18	4	0	0	0	1	3	1	0	.333	1	9	0	0	1.1	1.000
1927		10	3	.769	4.11	29	21	9	166.1	148	77	81	1	0	0	0	67	16	1	.239	6	33	1	1	1.4	.975
1928		**24**	13	.649	3.38	46	**38**	22	**300.2**	**314**	103	139	4	0	1	3	115	18	0	.157	7	49	4	2	1.3	.933
1929		18	12	.600	4.23	39	33	13	225.1	229	95	125	3	2	1	0	84	12	0	.143	4	30	1	2	0.9	.971
1930		15	15	.500	4.11	44	30	15	221	230	70	111	**3**	1	2	4	80	12	1	.150	12	30	5	1	1.1	.894
1931		7	6	.538	3.79	36	14	6	137.2	134	58	59	0	3	2	3	41	1	0	.024	2	20	2	0	0.7	.917

George Pipgras *continued*

Year	Team	W	L	PCT	ERA	G	GS	CG	IP	H	BB	SO	ShO	Relief Pitching W	Relief Pitching L	Relief Pitching SV	Batting AB	Batting H	Batting HR	BA	PO	A	E	DP	TC/G	FA
1932		16	9	.640	4.19	32	27	14	219	235	87	111	2	1	2	0	82	18	0	.220	9	35	7	1	1.6	.863
1933	**2 teams** **NY A** (4G 2–2) **BOS A** (22G 9–8)																									
″	**total**	11	10	.524	3.90	26	21	12	161.1	172	57	70	2	1	2	1	57	10	0	.175	8	25	2	3	1.3	.943
1934	**BOS A**	0	0	—	8.10	2	1	0	3.1	4	3	0	0	0	0	0	1	0	0	.000	0	2	0	0	1.0	1.000
1935		0	1	.000	14.40	5	1	0	5	9	5	2	0	0	0	0	0	0	0	—	0	1	0	0	0.2	1.000
11 yrs.		102	73	.583	4.09	276	189	93	1488.1	1529	598	714	15	8	12	12	539	88	2	.163	49	242	22	10	1.1	.930
WORLD SERIES																										
1927	**NY A**	1	0	1.000	2.00	1	1	1	9	7	1	2	0	0	0	0	3	1	0	.333	1	2	0	0	3.0	1.000
1928		1	0	1.000	2.00	1	1	1	9	4	4	8	0	0	0	0	2	0	0	.000	0	1	0	0	1.0	1.000
1932		1	0	1.000	4.50	1	1	0	8	9	3	1	0	0	0	0	5	0	0	.000	0	0	0	0	0.0	.000
3 yrs.		3	0	1.000 **1st**	2.77	3	3	2	26	20	8	11	0	0	0	0	10	1	0	.100	1	3	0	0	1.3	1.000

Cotton Pippen

PIPPEN, HENRY HAROLD BR TR 6′ 2″ 180 lbs.
B. Apr. 2, 1911, Cisco, Tex. D. Feb. 15, 1981, Williams, Calif.

Year	Team	W	L	PCT	ERA	G	GS	CG	IP	H	BB	SO	ShO	Relief Pitching W	Relief Pitching L	Relief Pitching SV	Batting AB	Batting H	Batting HR	BA	PO	A	E	DP	TC/G	FA
1936	**STL N**	0	2	.000	7.71	6	3	0	21	37	8	8	0	0	0	0	6	1	0	.167	2	8	0	0	1.7	1.000
1939	**2 teams** **PHI A** (25G 4–11) **DET A** (3G 0–1)																									
″	**total**	4	12	.250	6.11	28	19	5	132.2	187	46	38	0	0	1	1	40	5	0	.125	10	26	3	4	1.4	.923
1940	**DET A**	1	2	.333	6.75	4	3	0	21.1	29	10	9	0	0	0	0	8	0	0	.000	2	4	0	0	1.5	1.000
3 yrs.		5	16	.238	6.38	38	25	5	175	253	64	55	0	0	1	1	54	6	0	.111	14	38	3	4	1.4	.945

Gerry Pirtle

PIRTLE, GERALD EUGENE BR TR 6′ 1″ 185 lbs.
B. Dec. 3, 1947, Tulsa, Okla.

Year	Team	W	L	PCT	ERA	G	GS	CG	IP	H	BB	SO	ShO	Relief Pitching W	Relief Pitching L	Relief Pitching SV	Batting AB	Batting H	Batting HR	BA	PO	A	E	DP	TC/G	FA
1978	**MON N**	0	2	.000	5.88	19	0	0	26	33	23	14	0	0	2	0	0	0	0	—	2	4	1	0	0.4	.857

Skip Pitlock

PITLOCK, LEE PATRICK THOMAS BL TL 6′ 2″ 180 lbs.
B. Nov. 6, 1947, Hillside, Ill.

Year	Team	W	L	PCT	ERA	G	GS	CG	IP	H	BB	SO	ShO	Relief Pitching W	Relief Pitching L	Relief Pitching SV	Batting AB	Batting H	Batting HR	BA	PO	A	E	DP	TC/G	FA
1970	**SF N**	5	5	.500	4.66	18	15	1	87	92	48	56	0	0	0	0	25	2	1	.080	3	15	0	0	1.0	1.000
1974	**CHI A**	3	3	.500	4.42	40	5	0	106	103	55	68	0	2	2	1	0	0	0	—	5	10	4	2	0.5	.789
1975		0	0	—	0.00	1	0	0		1	0	0	0	0	0	0	0	0	0	—	0	0	0	0	0.0	.000
3 yrs.		8	8	.500	4.52	59	20	1	193	196	103	124	0	2	2	1	25	2	1	.080	8	25	4	2	0.6	.892

Togie Pittinger

PITTINGER, CHARLES RENO BL TR 6′ 2″ 175 lbs.
B. Jan. 12, 1872, Greencastle, Pa. D. Jan. 14, 1909, Greencastle, Pa.

Year	Team	W	L	PCT	ERA	G	GS	CG	IP	H	BB	SO	ShO	Relief Pitching W	Relief Pitching L	Relief Pitching SV	Batting AB	Batting H	Batting HR	BA	PO	A	E	DP	TC/G	FA
1900	**BOS N**	2	9	.182	5.13	18	13	8	114	135	54	27	0	0	0	0	46	6	0	.130	9	23	5	2	2.1	.865
1901		13	16	.448	3.01	34	33	27	281.1	288	76	129	1	0	0	0	100	11	0	.110	8	86	4	4	2.9	.959
1902		27	16	.628	2.52	46	40	36	389.1	360	**128**	174	7	**2**	**3**	0	147	20	0	.136	20	83	6	2	2.4	.945
1903		19	**23**	.452	3.48	44	39	35	351.2	**396**	**143**	140	2	**2**	1	0	128	14	1	.109	14	84	15	1	2.6	.867
1904		15	21	.417	2.66	38	37	35	335.1	298	**144**	146	5	0	0	0	121	13	0	.107	22	114	12	2	3.9	.919
1905	**PHI N**	23	14	.622	3.10	**46**	37	29	337	311	104	136	4	3	2	2	122	19	0	.156	9	82	5	2	2.1	.948
1906		8	10	.444	3.40	20	16	9	129.2	128	50	43	2	1	1	0	44	4	0	.091	7	31	2	0	2.0	.950
1907		9	5	.643	3.00	16	12	8	102	101	35	37	1	2	0	0	36	5	0	.139	4	25	0	0	1.8	1.000
8 yrs.		116	114	.504	3.10	262	227	187	2040.1	2017	734	832	22	10	7	2	744	92	1	.124	93	528	49	13	2.6	.927

Jim Pittsley

PITTSLEY, JAMES MICHAEL BR TR 6′ 7″ 215 lbs.
B. Apr. 3, 1974, Du Bois, Iowa.

Year	Team	W	L	PCT	ERA	G	GS	CG	IP	H	BB	SO	ShO	Relief Pitching W	Relief Pitching L	Relief Pitching SV	Batting AB	Batting H	Batting HR	BA	PO	A	E	DP	TC/G	FA
1995	**KC A**	0	0	—	13.50	1	1	0	3.1	7	1	0	0	0	0	0	0	0	0	—	0	0	0	0	0.0	.000

Stan Pitula

PITULA, STANLEY BR TR 5′10″ 170 lbs.
B. Mar. 23, 1931, Hackensack, N. J. D. Aug. 15, 1965, Hackensack, N. J.

Year	Team	W	L	PCT	ERA	G	GS	CG	IP	H	BB	SO	ShO	Relief Pitching W	Relief Pitching L	Relief Pitching SV	Batting AB	Batting H	Batting HR	BA	PO	A	E	DP	TC/G	FA
1957	**CLE A**	2	2	.500	4.98	23	5	1	59.2	67	32	17	0	0	0	0	15	3	0	.200	2	9	0	1	0.5	1.000

Juan Pizarro

PIZARRO, JUAN ROMAN BL TL 5′11″ 170 lbs.
Born Juan Roman Pizarro (Cordova).
B. Feb. 7, 1937, Santurce, Puerto Rico.

Year	Team	W	L	PCT	ERA	G	GS	CG	IP	H	BB	SO	ShO	Relief Pitching W	Relief Pitching L	Relief Pitching SV	Batting AB	Batting H	Batting HR	BA	PO	A	E	DP	TC/G	FA
1957	**MIL N**	5	6	.455	4.62	24	10	3	99.1	99	51	68	0	3	1	0	36	9	1	.250	0	15	1	1	0.7	.938
1958		6	4	.600	2.70	16	10	7	96.2	75	47	84	1	1	1	1	32	8	0	.250	3	16	0	2	1.2	1.000
1959		6	2	.750	3.77	29	14	6	133.2	117	70	126	2	0	0	0	41	5	0	.122	7	18	0	0	0.9	1.000
1960		6	7	.462	4.55	21	17	3	114.2	105	72	88	0	1	1	0	40	11	0	.275	1	17	2	0	1.0	.900
1961	**CHI A**	14	7	.667	3.05	39	25	12	194.2	164	89	188	1	0	0	2	69	17	0	.246	8	22	3	1	0.8	.909
1962		12	14	.462	3.81	36	32	9	203.1	182	97	173	1	3	0	1	69	11	0	.159	10	23	1	1	0.9	.971
1963		16	8	.667	2.39	32	28	10	214.2	177	63	163	3	2	0	1	73	13	2	.178	6	22	0	1	0.9	1.000
1964		19	9	.679	2.56	33	33	11	239	193	55	162	4	0	0	0	90	19	3	.211	8	32	0	2	1.2	1.000
1965		6	3	.667	3.43	18	18	2	97	96	37	65	1	0	0	0	34	8	1	.235	3	17	1	2	1.2	.952
1966		8	6	.571	3.76	34	9	1	88.2	91	39	42	0	4	2	3	26	4	0	.154	5	18	0	1	0.7	1.000
1967	**PIT N**	8	10	.444	3.95	50	9	1	107	99	52	96	1	7	5	9	27	7	0	.259	1	13	1	0	0.3	.933
1968	**2 teams** **PIT N** (12G 1–1) **BOS A** (19G 6–8)																									
″	**total**	7	9	.438	3.56	31	12	6	118.2	111	54	90	0	2	3	2	33	5	0	.152	7	23	1	3	1.0	.968
1969	**3 teams** **BOS A** (6G 0–1) **CLE A** (48G 3–3) **OAK A** (3G 1–1)																									
″	**total**	4	5	.444	3.35	57	4	1	99.1	84	58	52	0	3	5	7	20	5	0	.250	6	18	1	0	0.4	.960
1970	**CHI N**	0	0	—	4.50	12	0	0	16	16	9	14	0	0	0	1	3	0	0	.000	0	4	0	0	0.3	1.000
1971		7	6	.538	3.48	16	14	6	101	78	40	67	3	0	0	0	34	6	1	.176	4	16	0	0	1.3	1.000
1972		4	5	.444	3.97	16	7	1	59	66	32	24	0	3	0	1	21	3	0	.143	2	15	0	1	1.1	1.000
1973	**2 teams** **CHI N** (2G 0–1) **HOU N** (15G 2–2)																									
″	**total**	2	3	.400	7.24	17	1	0	27.1	34	12	13	0	2	2	0	4	0	0	.000	2	7	1	0	0.6	.900
1974	**PIT N**	1	1	.500	1.88	7	2	0	24	20	11	7	0	0	0	0	6	2	0	.333	1	3	0	0	0.6	1.000
18 yrs.		131	105	.555	3.43	488	245	79	2034	1807	888	1522	17	31	20	28	658	133	8	.202	74	299	12	15	0.8	.969
LEAGUE CHAMPIONSHIP SERIES																										
1974	**PIT N**	0	0	—	0.00	1	0	0	0.2	0	1	0	0	0	0	0	0	0	0	—	0	0	0	0	0.0	.000

Juan Pizarro *continued*

WORLD SERIES

Year	Team	Lg	W	L	PCT	ERA	G	GS	CG	IP	H	BB	SO	ShO	Relief Pitching W	Relief Pitching L	Relief Pitching SV	Batting AB	Batting H	Batting HR	BA	PO	A	E	DP	TC/G	FA
1957	**MIL**	**N**	0	0	—	10.80	1	0	0	1.2	3	2	1	0	0	0	0	1	0	0	.000	0	0	0	0	0.0	.000
1958			0	0	—	5.40	1	0	0	1.2	2	1	3	0	0	0	0	0	0	0	—	0	1	0	0	1.0	1.000
2 yrs.			0	0		8.10	2	0	0	3.1	5	3	4	0	0	0	0	1	0	0	.000	0	1	0	0	0.5	1.000

Gordon Pladson

PLADSON, GORDON CECIL BR TR 6′ 4″ 210 lbs.
B. July 31, 1956, New Westminster, B. C., Canada.

Year	Team	Lg	W	L	PCT	ERA	G	GS	CG	IP	H	BB	SO	ShO	Relief Pitching W	Relief Pitching L	Relief Pitching SV	Batting AB	Batting H	Batting HR	BA	PO	A	E	DP	TC/G	FA
1979	**HOU**	**N**	0	0	—	4.50	4	0	0	4	9	2	2	0	0	0	0	0	0	0	—	0	0	0	0	0.0	.000
1980			0	4	.000	4.39	12	6	0	41	38	16	13	0	0	0	0	10	0	0	.000	3	9	2	0	1.2	.857
1981			0	0	—	9.00	2	0	0	4	9	3	3	0	0	0	0	0	0	0	—	0	0	0	0	0.0	.000
1982			0	0	—	54.00	2	0	0	1.1	10	2	0	0	0	0	0	0	0	0	—	0	0	0	0	0.0	.000
4 yrs.			0	4	.000	6.08	20	6	0	50.1	66	23	18	0	0	0	0	10	0	0	.000	3	9	2	0	0.7	.857

Emil Planeta

PLANETA, EMIL JOSEPH BR TR 6′ 190 lbs.
B. Jan. 13, 1909, Higganum, Conn. D. Feb. 2, 1963, Rocky Hill, Conn.

Year	Team	Lg	W	L	PCT	ERA	G	GS	CG	IP	H	BB	SO	ShO	Relief Pitching W	Relief Pitching L	Relief Pitching SV	Batting AB	Batting H	Batting HR	BA	PO	A	E	DP	TC/G	FA
1931	**NY**	**N**	0	0	—	10.13	2	0	0	5.1	7	4	0	0	0	0	0	1	0	0	.000	0	0	0	0	0.0	.000

Eddie Plank

PLANK, EDWARD ARTHUR BR TR 6′ 1″ 205 lbs.
B. Apr. 9, 1952, Chicago, Ill.

Year	Team	Lg	W	L	PCT	ERA	G	GS	CG	IP	H	BB	SO	ShO	Relief Pitching W	Relief Pitching L	Relief Pitching SV	Batting AB	Batting H	Batting HR	BA	PO	A	E	DP	TC/G	FA
1978	**SF**	**N**	0	0	—	3.86	5	0	0	7	6	2	1	0	0	0	0	0	0	0	—	0	0	0	0	0.0	.000
1979			0	0	—	6.75	4	0	0	4	9	2	1	0	0	0	0	0	0	0	—	1	0	1	0	0.5	.500
2 yrs.			0	0		4.91	9	0	0	11	15	4	2	0	0	0	0	0	0	0		1	0	1	0	0.2	.500

Eddie Plank

PLANK, EDWARD STEWART (Hank) BL TL 5′11½″ 175 lbs.
B. Aug. 31, 1875, Gettysburg, Pa. D. Feb. 24, 1926, Gettysburg, Pa.
Hall of Fame 1946.

Year	Team	Lg	W	L	PCT	ERA	G	GS	CG	IP	H	BB	SO	ShO	Relief Pitching W	Relief Pitching L	Relief Pitching SV	Batting AB	Batting H	Batting HR	BA	PO	A	E	DP	TC/G	FA
1901	**PHI**	**A**	17	13	.567	3.31	33	32	28	260.2	254	68	90	1	0	0	0	99	18	0	.182	6	63	5	2	2.2	.932
1902			20	15	.571	3.30	36	32	31	300	319	61	107	1	2	1	0	120	35	0	.292	18	74	5	2	2.7	.948
1903			23	16	.590	2.38	**43**	**40**	33	336	317	65	176	3	1	1	0	134	25	1	.187	23	85	4	1	2.6	.964
1904			26	17	.605	2.14	44	44	37	357.1	311	86	201	7	0	1	0	129	31	0	.240	22	103	3	4	3.0	.977
1905			24	12	.667	2.26	41	**41**	**36**	346.2	287	75	210	4	0	0	0	126	29	0	.230	24	82	6	0	2.7	.946
1906			19	6	**.760**	2.25	26	25	21	211.2	173	51	108	5	0	1	0	73	17	0	.233	16	46	2	2	2.5	.969
1907			24	16	.600	2.20	43	40	33	343.2	282	85	183	**8**	1	0	0	123	26	1	.211	33	88	2	4	2.9	.984
1908			14	16	.467	2.17	34	28	21	244.2	202	46	135	4	2	2	1	89	16	0	.180	17	45	2	1	1.9	.969
1909			19	10	.655	1.70	34	33	24	275.1	215	62	132	3	0	0	0	96	21	1	.219	11	82	1	3	2.8	.989
1910			16	10	.615	2.01	38	32	22	250.1	218	55	123	1	0	0	2	86	11	0	.128	9	64	1	1	1.9	.986
1911			23	8	.742	2.10	40	30	24	256.2	237	77	149	**6**	3	1	**4**	94	18	0	.191	7	71	2	2	2.0	.975
1912			26	6	.813	2.22	37	30	24	259.2	234	83	110	5	5	0	2	90	24	0	.267	6	68	0	1	2.0	1.000
1913			18	10	.643	2.60	41	29	18	242.2	211	57	151	7	4	0	4	75	8	0	.107	6	59	2	2	1.6	.970
1914			15	7	.682	2.87	34	22	12	185.1	178	42	110	4	4	1	3	60	9	0	.150	7	36	1	2	1.3	.977
1915	**STL**	**F**	21	11	.656	2.08	42	31	23	268.1	212	54	147	6	2	3	3	93	24	0	.258	13	58	1	4	1.7	.986
1916	**STL**	**A**	16	15	.516	2.33	37	26	17	235.2	203	67	88	3	3	3	3	81	15	0	.185	6	51	2	6	1.6	.966
1917			5	6	.455	1.79	20	13	8	131	105	38	26	1	0	1	1	38	4	0	.105	5	33	1	0	2.0	.974
17 yrs.			326	194	.627	2.34	623	528	412	4505.2	3958	1072	2246	69	27	15	23	1606	331	3	.206	229	1108	40	37	2.2	.971
			10th											**5th**													

WORLD SERIES

Year	Team	Lg	W	L	PCT	ERA	G	GS	CG	IP	H	BB	SO	ShO	Relief Pitching W	Relief Pitching L	Relief Pitching SV	Batting AB	Batting H	Batting HR	BA	PO	A	E	DP	TC/G	FA
1905	**PHI**	**A**	0	2	.000	1.59	2	2	2	17	14	4	11	0	0	0	0	6	1	0	.167	1	6	0	0	3.5	1.000
1911			1	1	.500	1.86	2	1	1	9.2	6	0	8	0	0	1	0	3	0	0	.000	0	2	0	0	1.0	1.000
1913			1	1	.500	0.95	2	2	2	19	9	3	7	0	0	0	0	7	1	0	.143	1	3	1	0	2.5	.800
1914			0	1	.000	1.00	1	1	1	9	7	4	6	0	0	0	0	2	0	0	.000	0	1	0	0	1.0	1.000
4 yrs.			2	5	.286	1.32	7	6	6	54.2	36	11	32	0	0	1	0	18	2	0	.111	2	12	1	0	2.1	.933
				2nd		**10th**			**6th**																		

Erik Plantenberg

PLANTENBERG, ERIK JOHN BR TL 6′ 1″ 190 lbs.
B. Oct. 30, 1968, Renton, Wash.

Year	Team	Lg	W	L	PCT	ERA	G	GS	CG	IP	H	BB	SO	ShO	Relief Pitching W	Relief Pitching L	Relief Pitching SV	Batting AB	Batting H	Batting HR	BA	PO	A	E	DP	TC/G	FA
1993	**SEA**	**A**	0	0	—	6.52	20	0	0	9.2	11	12	3	0	0	0	1	0	0	0	—	3	1	0	1	0.2	1.000
1994			0	0	—	0.00	6	0	0	7	4	7	1	0	0	0	0	0	0	0	—	0	3	1	0	0.7	.750
2 yrs.			0	0		3.78	26	0	0	16.2	15	19	4	0	0	0	1	0	0	0		3	4	1	1	0.3	.875

Bill Pleis

PLEIS, WILLIAM BL TL 5′10″ 170 lbs.
B. Aug. 5, 1937, St. Louis, Mo.

Year	Team	Lg	W	L	PCT	ERA	G	GS	CG	IP	H	BB	SO	ShO	Relief Pitching W	Relief Pitching L	Relief Pitching SV	Batting AB	Batting H	Batting HR	BA	PO	A	E	DP	TC/G	FA
1961	**MIN**	**A**	4	2	.667	4.95	37	0	0	56.1	59	34	32	0	4	2	2	9	1	0	.111	3	3	1	0	0.2	.857
1962			2	5	.286	4.40	21	4	0	45	46	14	31	0	2	2	3	14	4	0	.286	4	4	1	0	0.4	.889
1963			6	2	.750	4.37	36	4	1	68	67	16	37	0	4	1	0	16	2	0	.125	3	10	0	1	0.4	1.000
1964			4	1	.800	3.91	47	0	0	50.2	43	31	42	0	4	1	4	4	1	0	.250	6	6	0	1	0.3	1.000
1965			4	4	.500	2.98	41	2	0	51.1	49	27	33	0	4	2	4	7	0	0	.000	1	7	0	1	0.2	1.000
1966			1	2	.333	1.93	8	0	0	9.1	5	4	9	0	1	2	0	0	0	0	—	0	1	1	0	0.3	.500
6 yrs.			21	16	.568	4.07	190	10	1	280.2	269	126	184	0	19	10	13	50	8	0	.160	17	31	3	3	0.3	.941

WORLD SERIES

Year	Team	Lg	W	L	PCT	ERA	G	GS	CG	IP	H	BB	SO	ShO	Relief Pitching W	Relief Pitching L	Relief Pitching SV	Batting AB	Batting H	Batting HR	BA	PO	A	E	DP	TC/G	FA
1965	**MIN**	**A**	0	0	—	9.00	1	0	0	1	2	0	0	0	0	0	0	0	0	0	—	0	1	0	0	1.0	1.000

Dan Plesac

PLESAC, DANIEL THOMAS BL TL 6′ 5″ 205 lbs.
B. Feb. 4, 1962, Gary, Ind.

Year	Team	Lg	W	L	PCT	ERA	G	GS	CG	IP	H	BB	SO	ShO	Relief Pitching W	Relief Pitching L	Relief Pitching SV	Batting AB	Batting H	Batting HR	BA	PO	A	E	DP	TC/G	FA
1986	**MIL**	**A**	10	7	.588	2.97	51	0	0	91	81	29	75	0	10	7	14	0	0	0	—	1	11	0	0	0.2	1.000
1987			5	6	.455	2.61	57	0	0	79.1	63	23	89	0	5	6	23	0	0	0	—	0	12	2	1	0.2	.857
1988			1	2	.333	2.41	50	0	0	52.1	46	12	52	0	1	2	30	0	0	0	—	0	6	0	0	0.1	1.000
1989			3	4	.429	2.35	52	0	0	61.1	47	17	52	0	3	4	33	0	0	0	—	2	8	0	0	0.2	1.000
1990			3	7	.300	4.43	66	0	0	69	67	31	65	0	3	7	24	0	0	0	—	1	7	0	1	0.1	1.000
1991			2	7	.222	4.29	45	10	0	92.1	92	39	61	0	0	4	8	0	0	0	—	2	5	0	0	0.2	1.000
1992			5	4	.556	2.96	44	4	0	79	64	35	54	0	4	3	1	0	0	0	—	1	8	0	1	0.2	1.000
1993	**CHI**	**N**	2	1	.667	4.74	57	0	0	62.2	74	21	47	0	2	1	0	1	0	0	.000	0	9	1	2	0.2	.900

Dan Plesac *continued*

Year	Team	W	L	PCT	ERA	G	GS	CG	IP	H	BB	SO	ShO	Relief Pitching W	L	SV	Batting AB	H	HR	BA	PO	A	E	DP	TC/G	FA
1994		2	3	.400	4.61	54	0	0	54.2	61	13	53	0	2	3	1	4	0	0	.000	0	3	0	0	0.1	1.000
1995	PIT N	4	4	.500	3.58	58	0	0	60.1	53	27	57	0	4	4	3	4	1	0	.250	1	8	0	1	0.2	1.000
10 yrs.		37	45	.451	3.49	534	14	0	702	648	247	605	0	34	41	137	9	1	0	.111	8	77	3	6	0.2	.966

Norman Plitt

PLITT, NORMAN WILLIAM (Duke) BR TR 5′11″ 180 lbs.
B. Feb. 21, 1893, York, Pa. D. Feb. 1, 1954, New York, N. Y.

Year	Team	W	L	PCT	ERA	G	GS	CG	IP	H	BB	SO	ShO	Relief Pitching W	L	SV	Batting AB	H	HR	BA	PO	A	E	DP	TC/G	FA
1918	BKN N	0	0	—	4.50	1	0	0	2	3	1	0	0	0	0	0	1	1	0	1.000	0	0	0	0	0.0	.000
1927	2 teams BKN N (19G 2–6) NY N (3G 1–0)																									
″	total	3	6	.333	4.78	22	8	1	69.2	82	37	9	0	2	1	0	19	4	0	.211	4	19	2	1	1.1	.920
2 yrs.		3	6	.333	4.77	23	8	1	71.2	85	38	9	0	2	1	0	20	5	0	.250	4	19	2	1	1.1	.920

Tim Plodinec

PLODINEC, TIMOTHY ALFRED BR TR 6′ 4″ 190 lbs.
B. Jan. 27, 1947, Aliquippa, Pa.

Year	Team	W	L	PCT	ERA	G	GS	CG	IP	H	BB	SO	ShO	Relief Pitching W	L	SV	Batting AB	H	HR	BA	PO	A	E	DP	TC/G	FA
1972	STL N	0	0	—	27.00	1	0	0	0.1	3	0	0	0	0	0	0	0	0	0	—	0	0	0	0	0.0	.000

Eric Plunk

PLUNK, ERIC VAUGHN BR TR 6′ 5″ 210 lbs.
B. Sept. 3, 1963, Wilmington, Calif.

Year	Team	W	L	PCT	ERA	G	GS	CG	IP	H	BB	SO	ShO	Relief Pitching W	L	SV	Batting AB	H	HR	BA	PO	A	E	DP	TC/G	FA
1986	OAK A	4	7	.364	5.31	26	15	0	120.1	91	102	98	0	0	1	0	0	0	0	—	3	6	1	0	0.4	.900
1987		4	6	.400	4.74	32	11	0	95	91	62	90	0	3	2	2	0	0	0	—	1	9	0	0	0.3	1.000
1988		7	2	.778	3.00	49	0	0	78	62	39	79	0	7	2	5	0	0	0	—	2	5	1	0	0.2	.875
1989	2 teams OAK A (23G 1–1) NY A (27G 7–5)																									
″	total	8	6	.571	3.28	50	7	0	104.1	82	64	85	0	4	3	1	0	0	0		2	7	1	0	0.2	.900
1990	NY A	6	3	.667	2.72	47	0	0	72.2	58	43	67	0	6	3	0	0	0	0	—	3	18	2	2	0.5	.913
1991		2	5	.286	4.76	43	8	0	111.2	128	62	103	0	2	2	0	0	0	0	—	4	7	2	0	0.3	.846
1992	CLE A	9	6	.600	3.64	58	0	0	71.2	61	38	50	0	9	6	4	0	0	0	—	7	7	1	0	0.3	.933
1993		4	5	.444	2.79	70	0	0	71	61	30	77	0	4	5	15	0	0	0	—	5	2	1	0	0.1	.875
1994		7	2	.778	2.54	41	0	0	71	61	37	73	0	7	2	3	0	0	0	—	8	3	0	0	0.3	1.000
1995		6	2	.750	2.67	56	0	0	64	48	27	71	0	6	2	2	0	0	0	—	2	7	0	1	0.2	1.000
10 yrs.		57	44	.564	3.73	472	41	0	859.2	743	504	793	0	48	28	32	0	0	0		37	71	9	3	0.2	.923
DIVISIONAL PLAYOFF SERIES																										
1995	CLE A	0	0	—	0.00	1	0	0	1.1	1	1	1	0	0	0	0	0	0	0	—	0	1	0	0	1.0	1.000
LEAGUE CHAMPIONSHIP SERIES																										
1988	OAK A	0	0	—	0.00	1	0	0	0.1	1	0	1	0	0	0	0	0	0	0	—	0	0	0	0	0.0	.000
1995	CLE A	0	0	—	9.00	3	0	0	2	1	3	2	0	0	0	0	0	0	0	—	0	0	0	0	0.0	.000
2 yrs.		0	0		7.71	4	0	0	2.1	2	3	3	0	0	0	0	0	0	0		0	0	0	0	0.0	
WORLD SERIES																										
1988	OAK A	0	0	—	0.00	2	0	0	1.2	0	0	3	0	0	0	0	0	0	0	—	0	0	0	0	0.0	.000

Jeff Plympton

PLYMPTON, JEFFREY HUNTER BR TR 6′ 2″ 205 lbs.
B. Nov. 24, 1965, Framingham, Mass.

Year	Team	W	L	PCT	ERA	G	GS	CG	IP	H	BB	SO	ShO	Relief Pitching W	L	SV	Batting AB	H	HR	BA	PO	A	E	DP	TC/G	FA
1991	BOS A	0	0	—	0.00	4	0	0	5.1	5	4	2	0	0	0	0	0	0	0	—	0	0	0	0	0.0	.000

Ray Poat

POAT, RAYMOND WILLIS BR TR 6′ 2″ 200 lbs.
B. Dec. 19, 1917, Chicago, Ill. D. Apr. 29, 1990, Oak Lawn, Ill.

Year	Team	W	L	PCT	ERA	G	GS	CG	IP	H	BB	SO	ShO	Relief Pitching W	L	SV	Batting AB	H	HR	BA	PO	A	E	DP	TC/G	FA
1942	CLE A	1	3	.250	5.40	4	4	1	18.1	24	9	8	1	0	0	0	5	0	0	.000	1	3	0	1	1.0	1.000
1943		2	5	.286	4.40	17	4	1	45	44	20	31	0	0	4	0	13	2	0	.154	1	8	0	0	0.5	1.000
1944		4	8	.333	5.13	36	6	1	80.2	82	37	40	0	3	4	1	17	0	0	.000	6	11	1	3	0.5	.944
1947	NY N	4	3	.571	2.55	7	7	5	60	53	13	25	0	0	0	0	21	4	1	.190	5	8	0	1	1.9	1.000
1948		11	10	.524	4.34	39	24	7	157.2	162	67	57	3	2	3	0	56	7	0	.125	2	20	1	5	0.6	.957
1949	2 teams NY N (2G 0–0) PIT N (11G 0–1)																									
″	total	0	1	.000	7.04	13	2	0	38.1	60	16	17	0	0	0	0	10	1	0	.100	1	6	1	0	0.6	.875
6 yrs.		22	30	.423	4.55	116	47	15	400	425	162	178	4	5	11	1	122	14	1	.115	16	56	3	10	0.6	.960

Bud Podbielan

PODBIELAN, CLARENCE ANTHONY BR TR 6′ 1½″ 170 lbs.
B. Mar. 6, 1924, Curlew, Wash. D. Oct. 26, 1982, Syracuse, N. Y.

Year	Team	W	L	PCT	ERA	G	GS	CG	IP	H	BB	SO	ShO	Relief Pitching W	L	SV	Batting AB	H	HR	BA	PO	A	E	DP	TC/G	FA
1949	BKN N	0	1	.000	3.65	7	1	0	12.1	9	9	5	0	0	1	0	3	0	0	.000	0	5	0	0	0.7	1.000
1950		5	4	.556	5.33	20	10	2	72.2	93	29	28	0	1	2	1	28	3	0	.107	4	17	0	0	1.0	1.000
1951		2	2	.500	3.50	27	5	1	79.2	67	36	26	0	2	1	0	23	7	0	.304	6	16	0	0	0.8	1.000
1952	2 teams BKN N (3G 0–0) CIN N (24G 4–5)																									
″	total	4	5	.444	3.15	27	7	4	88.2	82	29	23	1	1	1	1	25	4	0	.160	7	11	2	2	0.7	.900
1953	CIN N	6	16	.273	4.73	36	24	8	186.1	214	67	74	1	1	1	1	56	7	0	.125	11	29	1	5	1.1	.976
1954		7	10	.412	5.36	27	24	4	131	157	58	42	0	0	0	0	42	6	0	.143	12	13	0	1	0.9	1.000
1955		1	2	.333	3.21	17	2	0	42	36	11	26	0	1	0	0	5	2	0	.400	0	9	0	0	0.5	1.000
1957		0	1	.000	6.19	5	3	1	16	18	4	13	0	0	0	0	5	0	0	.000	0	0	0	0	0.0	.000
1959	CLE A	0	1	.000	5.84	6	0	0	12.1	17	2	5	0	0	1	0	1	0	0	.000	1	3	0	0	0.7	1.000
9 yrs.		25	42	.373	4.49	172	76	20	641	693	245	242	2	6	7	3	188	29	0	.154	41	103	3	8	0.9	.980

Johnny Podgajny

PODGAJNY, JOHN SIGMUND (Specs) BR TR 6′ 2″ 173 lbs.
B. June 10, 1920, Chester, Pa. D. Mar. 2, 1971, Chester, Pa.

Year	Team	W	L	PCT	ERA	G	GS	CG	IP	H	BB	SO	ShO	Relief Pitching W	L	SV	Batting AB	H	HR	BA	PO	A	E	DP	TC/G	FA
1940	PHI N	1	3	.250	2.83	4	4	3	35	33	1	12	0	0	0	0	12	2	0	.167	2	9	1	0	3.0	.917
1941		9	12	.429	4.62	34	24	8	181.1	191	70	53	0	1	0	0	62	8	0	.129	10	40	2	4	1.5	.962
1942		6	14	.300	3.91	43	23	6	186.2	191	63	40	0	0	1	0	60	11	0	.183	6	39	3	2	1.1	.938
1943	2 teams PHI N (13G 4–4) PIT N (15G 0–4)																									
″	total	4	8	.333	4.39	28	10	3	98.1	114	29	20	0	1	2	0	27	6	0	.222	7	35	5	0	1.7	.894
1946	CLE A	0	0	—	5.00	6	0	0	9	13	2	4	0	0	0	0	0	0	0	—	2	1	0	0	0.5	1.000
5 yrs.		20	37	.351	4.20	115	61	20	510.1	542	165	129	0	2	3	0	161	27	0	.168	27	124	11	6	1.4	.932

Johnny Podres

PODRES, JOHN JOSEPH BL TL 5′11″ 170 lbs.
B. Sept. 30, 1932, Witherbee, N. Y.

Year	Team	W	L	PCT	ERA	G	GS	CG	IP	H	BB	SO	ShO	Relief Pitching W	L	SV	Batting AB	H	HR	BA	PO	A	E	DP	TC/G	FA
1953	BKN N	9	4	.692	4.23	33	18	3	115	126	64	82	1	4	0	0	36	11	0	.306	6	17	1	0	0.7	.958
1954		11	7	.611	4.27	29	21	6	151.2	147	53	79	2	1	0	0	60	17	0	.283	11	15	1	0	0.9	.963
1955		9	10	.474	3.95	27	24	5	159.1	160	57	114	2	0	0	0	60	11	0	.183	7	21	1	2	1.1	.966
1957		12	9	.571	**2.66**	31	27	10	196	168	44	109	**6**	1	0	3	72	15	0	.208	9	32	1	3	1.4	.976
1958	LA N	13	15	.464	3.72	39	31	10	210.1	208	78	143	2	0	1	1	71	9	0	.127	7	25	2	3	0.9	.941

Johnny Podres *continued*

Year	Team	W	L	PCT	ERA	G	GS	CG	IP	H	BB	SO	ShO	Relief Pitching W	L	SV	Batting AB	H	HR	BA	PO	A	E	DP	TC/G	FA
1959		14	9	.609	4.11	34	29	6	195	192	74	145	2	1	0	0	65	16	0	.246	6	37	2	5	1.3	.956
1960		14	12	.538	3.08	34	33	8	227.2	217	71	159	1	1	0	0	66	9	0	.136	8	30	1	4	1.1	.974
1961		18	5	**.783**	3.74	32	29	6	182.2	192	51	124	1	2	0	0	69	16	0	.232	6	26	1	2	1.0	.970
1962		15	13	.536	3.81	40	40	8	255	270	71	178	0	0	0	0	88	14	1	.159	4	31	6	1	1.0	.854
1963		14	12	.538	3.54	37	34	10	198.1	196	64	134	5	0	0	1	64	9	1	.141	2	33	0	1	0.9	1.000
1964		0	2	.000	16.88	2	2	0	2.2	5	3	0	0	0	0	0	0	0	0	—	0	0	0	0	0.0	.000
1965		7	6	.538	3.43	27	22	2	134	126	39	63	1	0	2	1	45	8	0	.178	3	15	1	1	0.7	.947
1966	2 teams LA N (1G 0–0) DET A (36G 4–5)																									
"	total	4	5	.444	3.38	37	13	2	109.1	108	35	54	1	2	1	4	30	7	0	.233	7	15	1	1	0.6	.957
1967	DET A	3	1	.750	3.84	21	8	0	63.1	58	11	34	0	1	0	1	20	2	0	.100	3	7	0	1	0.5	1.000
1969	SD N	5	6	.455	4.29	17	9	1	65	66	28	17	0	2	1	0	16	1	0	.063	1	9	0	0	0.6	1.000
15 yrs.		148	116	.561	3.67	440	340	77	2265.1	2239	743	1435	24	15	5	11	762	145	2	.190	80	313	18	24	0.9	.956
WORLD SERIES																										
1953	BKN N	0	1	.000	3.38	1	1	0	2.2	1	2	0	0	0	0	0	1	1	0	1.000	0	1	0	0	1.0	1.000
1955		2	0	1.000	1.00	2	2	2	18	15	4	10	1	0	0	0	7	1	0	.143	0	2	0	0	1.0	1.000
1959	LA N	1	0	1.000	4.82	2	2	0	9.1	7	6	4	0	0	0	0	4	2	0	.500	0	1	0	1	0.5	1.000
1963		1	0	1.000	1.08	1	1	0	8.1	6	1	4	0	0	0	0	4	1	0	.250	0	2	1	0	3.0	.667
4 yrs.		4	1	.800	2.11	6	6	2	38.1	29	13	18	1	0	0	0	16	5	0	.313	0	6	1	1	1.2	.857

Joe Poetz

POETZ, JOSEPH FRANK
B. June 22, 1900, St. Louis, Mo. D. Feb. 7, 1942, St. Louis, Mo.
BR TR 5′10½″ 185 lbs.

Year	Team	W	L	PCT	ERA	G	GS	CG	IP	H	BB	SO	ShO	Relief Pitching W	L	SV	Batting AB	H	HR	BA	PO	A	E	DP	TC/G	FA
1926	NY N	0	1	.000	3.38	2	1	0	8	5	8	0	0	0	0	0	1	0	0	.000	1	2	0	0	1.5	1.000

Boots Poffenberger

POFFENBERGER, CLETUS ELWOOD
B. July 1, 1915, Williamsport, Md.
BR TR 5′10″ 178 lbs.

Year	Team	W	L	PCT	ERA	G	GS	CG	IP	H	BB	SO	ShO	Relief Pitching W	L	SV	Batting AB	H	HR	BA	PO	A	E	DP	TC/G	FA
1937	DET A	10	5	.667	4.65	29	16	5	137.1	147	79	35	0	3	1	3	51	11	0	.216	8	32	1	3	1.4	.976
1938		6	7	.462	4.82	25	15	8	125	147	66	28	0	0	2	1	44	8	0	.182	5	17	1	1	0.9	.957
1939	BKN N	0	0	—	5.40	3	1	0	5	7	4	2	0	0	0	0	1	0	0	.000	0	2	0	0	0.7	1.000
3 yrs.		16	12	.571	4.75	57	32	13	267.1	301	149	65	0	3	3	4	96	19	0	.198	13	51	2	4	1.2	.970

Tom Poholsky

POHOLSKY, THOMAS GEORGE
B. Aug. 26, 1929, Detroit, Mich.
BR TR 6′ 3″ 205 lbs.

Year	Team	W	L	PCT	ERA	G	GS	CG	IP	H	BB	SO	ShO	Relief Pitching W	L	SV	Batting AB	H	HR	BA	PO	A	E	DP	TC/G	FA
1950	STL N	0	0	—	3.68	5	1	0	14.2	16	3	2	0	0	0	0	2	0	0	.000	0	2	0	0	0.4	1.000
1951		7	13	.350	4.43	38	26	10	195	204	68	70	1	1	2	1	67	14	0	.209	10	43	3	2	1.5	.946
1954		5	7	.417	3.06	25	13	4	106	101	20	55	0	0	2	0	27	4	0	.148	8	18	0	2	1.0	1.000
1955		9	11	.450	3.81	30	24	8	151	143	35	66	2	0	0	0	44	8	0	.182	14	20	0	0	1.1	1.000
1956		9	14	.391	3.59	33	29	7	203	210	44	95	2	0	0	0	69	11	0	.159	12	35	0	3	1.4	1.000
1957	CHI N	1	7	.125	4.93	28	11	1	84	117	22	28	0	0	0	0	19	2	0	.105	8	16	1	1	0.9	.960
6 yrs.		31	52	.373	3.93	159	104	30	753.2	791	192	316	5	1	4	1	228	39	0	.171	52	134	4	8	1.2	.979

Jennings Poindexter

POINDEXTER, CHESTER JENNINGS (Jinx)
B. Sept. 30, 1910, Pauls Valley, Okla. D. Mar. 3, 1983, Norman, Okla.
BL TL 5′10″ 165 lbs.

Year	Team	W	L	PCT	ERA	G	GS	CG	IP	H	BB	SO	ShO	Relief Pitching W	L	SV	Batting AB	H	HR	BA	PO	A	E	DP	TC/G	FA
1936	BOS A	0	2	.000	6.75	3	3	0	10.2	13	16	2	0	0	0	0	4	0	0	.000	0	2	0	0	0.7	1.000
1939	PHI N	0	0	—	4.15	11	1	0	30.1	29	15	12	0	0	0	0	10	2	0	.200	1	5	0	0	0.5	1.000
2 yrs.		0	2	.000	4.83	14	4	0	41	42	31	14	0	0	0	0	14	2	0	.143	1	7	0	0	0.6	1.000

Lou Polchow

POLCHOW, LOUIS WILLIAM
B. Mar. 14, 1881, Mankato, Minn. D. Aug. 15, 1912, Good Thunder, Minn.
5′ 9″

Year	Team	W	L	PCT	ERA	G	GS	CG	IP	H	BB	SO	ShO	Relief Pitching W	L	SV	Batting AB	H	HR	BA	PO	A	E	DP	TC/G	FA
1902	CLE A	0	1	.000	5.63	1	1	1	8	9	4	2	0	0	0	0	4	0	0	.000	0	2	0	0	2.0	1.000

Dick Pole

POLE, RICHARD HENRY
B. Oct. 13, 1950, Trout Creek, Mich.
BR TR 6′ 3″ 200 lbs.

Year	Team	W	L	PCT	ERA	G	GS	CG	IP	H	BB	SO	ShO	Relief Pitching W	L	SV	Batting AB	H	HR	BA	PO	A	E	DP	TC/G	FA
1973	BOS A	3	2	.600	5.56	12	7	0	55	70	18	24	0	0	0	0	0	0	0	—	3	7	0	0	0.8	1.000
1974		1	1	.500	4.20	15	2	0	45	55	13	32	0	1	0	1	0	0	0	—	5	8	1	0	0.9	.929
1975		4	6	.400	4.42	18	11	2	89.2	102	32	42	1	1	0	0	0	0	0	—	4	15	1	1	1.1	.950
1976		6	5	.545	4.31	31	15	1	121	131	48	49	0	1	1	0	1	0	0	.000	6	13	1	0	0.6	.950
1977	SEA A	7	12	.368	5.16	25	24	3	122	127	57	51	0	0	0	0	0	0	0	—	2	9	1	0	0.5	.917
1978		4	11	.267	6.48	21	18	2	98.2	122	41	41	0	0	1	0	0	0	0	—	10	9	0	0	0.9	1.000
6 yrs.		25	37	.403	5.05	122	77	8	531.1	607	209	239	1	3	2	1	1	0	0	.000	30	61	4	1	0.8	.958
WORLD SERIES																										
1975	BOS A	0	0	—	∞	1	0	0		0	2	0	0	0	0	0	0	0	0	—	0	0	0	0	0.0	.000

Ken Polivka

POLIVKA, KENNETH LYLE (Soup)
B. Jan. 21, 1921, Chicago, Ill. D. July 23, 1988, Aurora, Ill.
BL TL 5′10½″ 183 lbs.

Year	Team	W	L	PCT	ERA	G	GS	CG	IP	H	BB	SO	ShO	Relief Pitching W	L	SV	Batting AB	H	HR	BA	PO	A	E	DP	TC/G	FA
1947	CIN N	0	0	—	3.00	2	0	0	3	3	3	1	0	0	0	0	0	0	0	—	0	0	0	0	0.0	.000

Howie Pollet

POLLET, HOWARD JOSEPH
B. June 26, 1921, New Orleans, La. D. Aug. 8, 1974, Houston, Tex.
BL TL 6′ 1½″ 175 lbs.

Year	Team	W	L	PCT	ERA	G	GS	CG	IP	H	BB	SO	ShO	Relief Pitching W	L	SV	Batting AB	H	HR	BA	PO	A	E	DP	TC/G	FA
1941	STL N	5	2	.714	1.93	9	8	6	70	55	27	37	2	0	0	0	28	5	0	.179	0	18	0	0	2.0	1.000
1942		7	5	.583	2.88	27	13	5	109.1	102	39	42	2	1	1	0	31	7	0	.226	4	16	2	1	0.8	.909
1943		8	4	.667	**1.75**	16	14	12	118.1	83	32	61	5	0	0	0	43	7	0	.163	1	17	0	0	1.1	1.000
1946		**21**	10	.677	**2.10**	40	32	22	**266**	228	86	107	4	0	0	5	87	14	0	.161	8	59	4	9	1.8	.944
1947		9	11	.450	4.34	37	24	9	176.1	195	87	73	0	1	0	2	65	15	0	.231	5	33	0	5	1.0	1.000
1948		13	8	.619	4.54	36	26	11	186.1	216	67	80	0	2	0	0	68	8	0	.118	5	44	2	2	1.4	.961
1949		20	9	.690	2.77	39	28	17	230.2	228	59	108	**5**	3	1	1	82	16	0	.195	9	33	2	2	1.1	.955
1950		14	13	.519	3.29	37	30	14	232.1	228	68	117	2	1	1	2	84	12	0	.143	13	40	4	5	1.5	.930
1951	2 teams STL N (6G 0–3) PIT N (21G 6–10)																									
"	total	6	13	.316	4.98	27	23	4	141	159	59	57	1	0	2	1	37	5	0	.135	5	26	0	2	1.1	1.000
1952	PIT N	7	16	.304	4.12	31	30	9	214	217	71	90	1	0	0	0	68	13	0	.191	7	48	3	2	1.9	.948
1953	2 teams PIT N (5G 1–1) CHI N (25G 5–6)																									
"	total	6	7	.462	4.79	30	18	2	124	147	50	53	0	0	1	1	34	5	0	.147	8	15	3	2	0.9	.885
1954	CHI N	8	10	.444	3.58	20	20	4	128.1	131	54	58	2	0	0	0	47	13	0	.277	6	22	0	1	1.4	1.000

Howie Pollet *continued*

Year	Team	W	L	PCT	ERA	G	GS	CG	IP	H	BB	SO	ShO	Relief W	Relief L	Relief SV	Batting AB	Batting H	HR	BA	PO	A	E	DP	TC/G	FA
1955		4	3	.571	5.61	24	7	1	61	62	27	27	1	3	0	5	15	6	0	.400	7	15	0	1	0.9	1.000
1956	2 teams CHI A (11G 3–1) PIT N (19G 0–4)																									
"	total	3	5	.375	3.62	30	4	0	49.2	45	19	24	0	3	4	3	9	3	0	.333	4	10	0	0	0.5	1.000
14 yrs.		131	116	.530	3.51	403	277	116	2107.1	2096	745	934	25	14	10	20	698	129	0	.185	82	396	20	32	1.2	.960
WORLD SERIES																										
1942	STL N	0	0	—	0.00	1	0	0	0.1	0	0	0	0	0	0	0	0	0	0	—	0	0	0	0	0.0	.000
1946		0	1	.000	3.48	2	2	1	10.1	12	4	3	0	0	0	0	4	0	0	.000	0	0	0	0	0.0	.000
2 yrs.		0	1	.000	3.38	3	2	1	10.2	12	4	3	0	0	0	0	4	0	0	.000	0	0	0	0	0.0	

Lou Polli

POLLI, LOUIS AMERICO (Crip) BR TR 5′10½″ 165 lbs.
B. July 9, 1901, Barre, Vt.

Year	Team	W	L	PCT	ERA	G	GS	CG	IP	H	BB	SO	ShO	Relief W	Relief L	Relief SV	Batting AB	Batting H	HR	BA	PO	A	E	DP	TC/G	FA
1932	STL A	0	0	—	5.40	5	0	0	6.2	13	3	5	0	0	0	0	2	1	0	.500	0	0	1	0	0.2	.000
1944	NY N	0	2	.000	4.54	19	0	0	35.2	42	20	6	0	0	2	3	6	0	0	.000	0	7	0	0	0.4	1.000
2 yrs.		0	2	.000	4.68	24	0	0	42.1	55	23	11	0	0	2	3	8	1	0	.125	0	7	1	0	0.3	.875

John Poloni

POLONI, JOHN PAUL BL TL 6′ 5″ 210 lbs.
B. Feb. 28, 1954, Dearborn, Mich.

Year	Team	W	L	PCT	ERA	G	GS	CG	IP	H	BB	SO	ShO	Relief W	Relief L	Relief SV	Batting AB	Batting H	HR	BA	PO	A	E	DP	TC/G	FA
1977	TEX A	1	0	1.000	6.43	2	1	0	7	8	1	5	0	0	0	0	0	0	0	—	0	0	0	0	0.0	.000

John Pomorski

POMORSKI, JOHN LEON BR TR 6′ 178 lbs.
B. Dec. 30, 1905, Brooklyn, N. Y. D. Dec. 6, 1977, Brampton, Ont., Canada.

Year	Team	W	L	PCT	ERA	G	GS	CG	IP	H	BB	SO	ShO	Relief W	Relief L	Relief SV	Batting AB	Batting H	HR	BA	PO	A	E	DP	TC/G	FA
1934	CHI A	0	0	—	5.40	3	0	0	1.2	1	2	0	0	0	0	0	0	0	0	—	1	0	0	0	0.3	1.000

Arlie Pond

POND, ERASMUS ARLINGTON BR TR 5′10″ 160 lbs.
B. Jan. 19, 1872, Rutland, Vt. D. Sept. 19, 1930, Cebu, Philippines.

Year	Team	W	L	PCT	ERA	G	GS	CG	IP	H	BB	SO	ShO	Relief W	Relief L	Relief SV	Batting AB	Batting H	HR	BA	PO	A	E	DP	TC/G	FA
1895	BAL N	0	1	.000	5.93	6	1	1	13.2	10	12	13	0	0	0	2	6	2	0	.333	0	3	0	1	0.4	1.000
1896		16	8	.667	3.49	28	26	21	214.1	232	57	80	2	1	0	0	81	19	0	.235	3	46	5	0	1.9	.907
1897		18	9	.667	3.52	32	28	23	248	267	72	59	0	1	0	0	90	22	0	.244	16	52	6	2	2.2	.919
1898		1	1	.500	0.45	3	2	1	20	8	9	4	1	0	0	0	7	2	0	.286	0	2	0	0	0.7	1.000
4 yrs.		35	19	.648	3.45	69	57	46	496	517	150	156	3	2	0	2	184	45	0	.245	19	103	11	3	1.9	.917

Elmer Ponder

PONDER, CHARLES ELMER BR TR 6′ 178 lbs.
B. June 26, 1893, Reed, Okla. D. Apr. 20, 1974, Albuquerque, N. M.

Year	Team	W	L	PCT	ERA	G	GS	CG	IP	H	BB	SO	ShO	Relief W	Relief L	Relief SV	Batting AB	Batting H	HR	BA	PO	A	E	DP	TC/G	FA
1917	PIT N	1	1	.500	1.69	3	2	1	21.1	12	6	11	1	0	0	0	7	0	0	.000	0	1	0	0	0.3	1.000
1919		0	5	.000	3.99	9	5	0	47.1	55	6	6	0	0	0	0	15	2	0	.133	1	12	3	0	1.8	.813
1920		11	15	.423	2.62	33	23	13	196	182	40	62	2	3	3	0	59	7	0	.119	13	55	3	2	2.2	.958
1921	2 teams PIT N (8G 2–0) CHI N (16G 3–6)																									
"	total	5	6	.455	4.18	24	12	6	114	146	20	34	0	1	0	0	43	4	0	.093	3	38	2	3	1.8	.953
4 yrs.		17	27	.386	3.21	69	42	20	378.2	395	72	113	3	4	3	0	124	13	0	.105	17	106	8	5	1.9	.939

Ed Poole

POOLE, EDWARD T. BR TR 5′10″ 175 lbs.
B. Sept. 7, 1874, Canton, Ohio D. Mar. 11, 1919, Malvern, Ohio.

Year	Team	W	L	PCT	ERA	G	GS	CG	IP	H	BB	SO	ShO	Relief W	Relief L	Relief SV	Batting AB	Batting H	HR	BA	PO	A	E	DP	TC/G	FA
1900	PIT N	1	0	1.000	1.29	1	0	0	7	4	0	3	0	1	0	0	4	2	1	.500	3	3	2	0	4.0	.750
1901		5	4	.556	3.60	12	10	8	80	78	30	26	1	0	0	0	78	16	1	.205	26	23	2	1	2.0	.961
1902	2 teams PIT N (1G 0–0) CIN N (16G 12–4)																									
"	total	12	4	.750	2.10	17	16	16	146	136	57	57	2	0	0	0	65	8	0	.123	6	35	2	1	2.4	.953
1903	CIN N	8	13	.381	3.28	25	21	18	184	188	77	73	1	0	0	0	70	17	0	.243	3	62	5	3	2.8	.929
1904	BKN N	8	13	.381	3.39	25	23	19	178	178	74	67	1	1	0	1	62	8	0	.129	6	65	2	2	2.9	.973
5 yrs.		34	34	.500	3.04	80	70	61	595	584	238	226	5	2	0	1	279	51	2	.183	44	188	13	7	2.6	.947

Jim Poole

POOLE, JAMES RICHARD BL TL 6′ 2″ 190 lbs.
B. Apr. 28, 1966, Rochester, N. Y.

Year	Team	W	L	PCT	ERA	G	GS	CG	IP	H	BB	SO	ShO	Relief W	Relief L	Relief SV	Batting AB	Batting H	HR	BA	PO	A	E	DP	TC/G	FA
1990	LA N	0	0	—	4.22	16	0	0	10.2	7	8	6	0	0	0	0	0	0	0	—	0	1	0	0	0.1	1.000
1991	2 teams TEX A (5G 0–0) BAL A (24G 3–2)																									
"	total	3	2	.600	2.36	29	0	0	42	29	12	38	0	3	2	1	0	0	0		2	6	1	0	0.3	.889
1992	BAL A	0	0	—	0.00	6	0	0	3.1	3	1	3	0	0	0	0	0	0	0	—	0	2	0	0	0.3	1.000
1993		2	1	.667	2.15	55	0	0	50.1	30	21	29	0	2	1	2	0	0	0	—	4	7	1	0	0.2	.917
1994		1	0	1.000	6.64	38	0	0	20.1	32	11	18	0	1	0	0	0	0	0	—	3	4	0	0	0.2	1.000
1995	CLE A	3	3	.500	3.75	42	0	0	50.1	40	17	41	0	3	3	0	0	0	0	—	2	9	1	0	0.3	.917
6 yrs.		9	6	.600	3.25	186	0	0	177	141	70	135	0	9	6	3	0	0	0		11	29	3	0	0.2	.930
DIVISIONAL PLAYOFF SERIES																										
1995	CLE A	0	0	—	5.40	1	0	0	1.2	2	1	2	0	0	0	0	0	0	0	—	0	1	0	0	1.0	1.000
LEAGUE CHAMPIONSHIP SERIES																										
1995	CLE A	0	0	—	0.00	1	0	0	1	0	0	2	0	0	0	0	0	0	0	—	0	0	0	0	0.0	.000
WORLD SERIES																										
1995	CLE A	0	1	.000	3.86	2	0	0	2.1	1	0	1	0	0	1	0	1	0	0	.000	0	0	0	0	0.0	.000

Tom Poorman

POORMAN, THOMAS IVERSON BL TR 5′10½″ 170 lbs.
B. Oct. 14, 1857, Lock Haven, Pa. D. Feb. 18, 1905, Lock Haven, Pa.

Year	Team	W	L	PCT	ERA	G	GS	CG	IP	H	BB	SO	ShO	Relief W	Relief L	Relief SV	Batting AB	Batting H	HR	BA	PO	A	E	DP	TC/G	FA
1880	2 teams BUF N (11G 1–8) CHI N (2G 2–0)																									
"	total	3	8	.273	3.87	13	10	9	100	129	27	13	0	1	0	1	95	16	0	.168	19	25	9	0	1.8	.830
1884	TOL AA	0	1	.000	3.00	1	1	1	9	13	2	0	0	0	0	0	382	89	0	.233	130	31	30	5	2.0	.843
1887	PHI AA	0	0	—	*40.50*	1	0	0	0.2	5	1	1	0	0	0	0	585	155	4	.265	82	9	14	1	1.9	.867
3 yrs.		3	9	.250	4.02	15	11	10	109.2	147	30	14	0	1	0	1	*				728	112	110	19	1.9	.884

Bill Popp

POPP, WILLIAM PETER TR 5′10½″ 170 lbs.
B. June 7, 1877, St. Louis, Mo. D. Sept. 5, 1909, St. Louis, Mo.

Year	Team	W	L	PCT	ERA	G	GS	CG	IP	H	BB	SO	ShO	Relief W	Relief L	Relief SV	Batting AB	Batting H	HR	BA	PO	A	E	DP	TC/G	FA
1902	STL N	2	6	.250	4.92	9	7	5	60.1	87	26	20	0	0	1	0	21	1	0	.048	2	19	2	0	2.6	.913

Ed Porray

PORRAY, EDMUND JOSEPH BR TR 5′11″ 170 lbs.
B. Dec. 5, 1888, Atlantic Ocean D. July 13, 1954, Lackawaxen, Pa.

Year	Team	W	L	PCT	ERA	G	GS	CG	IP	H	BB	SO	ShO	Relief W	Relief L	Relief SV	Batting AB	Batting H	HR	BA	PO	A	E	DP	TC/G	FA
1914	BUF F	1	1	.500	4.35	3	3	0	10.1	18	7	0	0	0	0	0	4	0	0	.000	0	7	2	0	3.0	.778

Chuck Porter

PORTER, CHARLES WILLIAM
B. Jan. 12, 1955, Baltimore, Md.
BR TR 6′ 3″ 188 lbs.

Year	Team	W	L	PCT	ERA	G	GS	CG	IP	H	BB	SO	ShO	Relief Pitching W	Relief Pitching L	Relief Pitching SV	Batting AB	Batting H	HR	BA	PO	A	E	DP	TC/G	FA
1981	MIL A	0	0	—	4.50	3	0	0	4	6	1	1	0	0	0	0	0	0	0	—	0	0	0	0	0.0	.000
1982		0	0	—	4.91	3	0	0	3.2	3	1	3	0	0	0	0	0	0	0	—	0	0	0	0	0.0	.000
1983		7	9	.438	4.50	25	21	6	134	162	38	76	1	0	1	0	0	0	0	—	11	18	0	2	1.2	1.000
1984		6	4	.600	3.87	17	12	1	81.1	92	12	48	0	0	0	0	0	0	0	—	7	10	1	2	1.1	.944
1985		0	0	—	1.98	6	1	0	13.2	15	2	8	0	0	0	0	0	0	0	—	2	0	1	0	0.5	.667
5 yrs.		13	13	.500	4.15	54	34	7	236.2	278	54	136	1	0	1	0	0	0	0		20	28	2	4	0.9	.960

Henry Porter

PORTER, HENRY
B. June 1858, Vergennes, Vt. D. Dec. 30, 1906, Brockton, Mass.
BR TR

Year	Team	W	L	PCT	ERA	G	GS	CG	IP	H	BB	SO	ShO	Relief Pitching W	Relief Pitching L	Relief Pitching SV	Batting AB	Batting H	HR	BA	PO	A	E	DP	TC/G	FA
1884	MIL U	3	3	.500	3.00	6	6	6	51	32	9	71	1	0	0	0	40	11	0	.275	10	10	0	2	1.8	1.000
1885	BKN AA	33	21	.611	*2.78*	54	54	53	481.2	427	107	197	2	0	0	0	195	40	0	.205	13	93	7	0	2.1	.938
1886		27	19	.587	*3.42*	48	48	48	424	439	120	163	1	0	0	0	184	33	0	.179	17	70	15	0	2.1	.853
1887		15	24	.385	*4.21*	40	40	38	339.2	416	96	74	1	0	0	0	146	29	1	.199	8	66	12	1	2.1	.860
1888	KC AA	18	**37**	.327	4.16	55	54	53	474	**527**	120	145	4	**1**	0	0	195	28	0	.144	11	133	16	3	2.8	.900
1889		0	3	.000	12.52	4	4	3	23	52	14	9	0	0	0	0	10	1	0	.100	0	9	2	0	2.8	.818
6 yrs.		96	107	.473	3.70	207	206	201	1793.1	1893	466	659	9	1	0	0	770	142	1	.184	59	381	52	6	2.3	.894

Jim Porter

PORTER, ODIE OSCAR
B. May 24, 1877, Borden, Ind. D. May 2, 1903, Borden, Ind.
TL

Year	Team	W	L	PCT	ERA	G	GS	CG	IP	H	BB	SO	ShO	Relief Pitching W	Relief Pitching L	Relief Pitching SV	Batting AB	Batting H	HR	BA	PO	A	E	DP	TC/G	FA
1902	PHI A	0	1	.000	3.38	1	1	1	8	12	5	2	0	0	0	0	3	0	0	.000	0	4	1	0	5.0	.800

Ned Porter

PORTER, NED SWINDELL
B. May 6, 1905, Apalachicola, Fla. D. June 30, 1968, Gainesville, Fla.
BR TR 6′ 173 lbs.

Year	Team	W	L	PCT	ERA	G	GS	CG	IP	H	BB	SO	ShO	Relief Pitching W	Relief Pitching L	Relief Pitching SV	Batting AB	Batting H	HR	BA	PO	A	E	DP	TC/G	FA
1926	NY N	0	0	—	4.50	2	0	0	2	2	0	1	0	0	0	0	0	0	0	—	0	0	0	0	0.0	.000
1927		0	0	—	0.00	1	0	0	2	3	1	0	0	0	0	0	0	0	0	—	0	0	1	0	1.0	.000
2 yrs.		0	0		2.25	3	0	0	4	5	1	1	0	0	0	0	0	0	0		0	0	1	0	0.3	.000

Bob Porterfield

PORTERFIELD, ERWIN COOLEDGE
B. Aug. 10, 1923, Newport, Va. D. Apr. 28, 1980, Charlotte, N. C.
BR TR 6′ 190 lbs.

Year	Team	W	L	PCT	ERA	G	GS	CG	IP	H	BB	SO	ShO	Relief Pitching W	Relief Pitching L	Relief Pitching SV	Batting AB	Batting H	HR	BA	PO	A	E	DP	TC/G	FA
1948	NY A	5	3	.625	4.50	16	12	2	78	85	34	30	1	1	0	0	24	6	0	.250	4	8	0	0	0.8	1.000
1949		2	5	.286	4.06	12	8	3	57.2	53	29	25	0	0	2	0	19	1	0	.053	1	10	3	1	1.2	.786
1950		1	1	.500	8.69	10	2	0	19.2	28	8	9	0	1	0	1	3	1	0	.333	1	3	0	0	0.4	1.000
1951	2 teams NY A (2G 0–0) WAS A (19G 9–8)																									
″	total	9	8	.529	3.50	21	19	10	136.1	114	57	55	3	0	0	0	46	6	0	.130	8	24	2	0	1.6	.941
1952	WAS A	13	14	.481	2.72	31	29	15	231.1	222	85	80	3	1	0	0	79	15	0	.190	4	34	0	0	1.2	1.000
1953		**22**	10	.688	3.35	34	32	**24**	255	243	73	77	**9**	1	0	0	98	25	3	.255	16	50	0	4	1.9	1.000
1954		13	15	.464	3.32	32	31	**21**	244	**249**	77	82	2	1	0	0	88	9	1	.102	10	61	3	4	2.3	.959
1955		10	17	.370	4.45	30	27	8	178	197	55	74	2	0	1	0	63	12	0	.190	8	28	1	2	1.2	.973
1956	BOS A	3	12	.200	5.14	25	18	4	126	127	64	53	1	0	2	0	43	14	1	.326	8	14	2	1	1.0	.917
1957		4	4	.500	4.05	28	9	3	102.1	107	30	28	1	1	0	1	29	5	0	.172	7	23	3	1	1.2	.909
1958	2 teams BOS A (2G 0–0) PIT N (37G 4–6)																									
″	total	4	6	.400	3.34	39	6	2	91.2	81	19	40	1	2	3	5	20	1	1	.050	8	13	0	0	0.5	1.000
1959	2 teams PIT N (36G 1–2) CHI N (4G 0–0)																									
″	total	1	2	.333	5.29	40	0	0	47.2	65	22	19	0	1	2	1	4	0	0	.000	5	12	1	2	0.4	.944
12 yrs.		87	97	.473	3.79	318	193	92	1567.2	1571	553	572	23	9	10	8	516	95	6	.184	80	280	15	15	1.2	.960

Al Porto

PORTO, ALFRED (Lefty)
B. June 27, 1926, Heilwood, Pa.
BL TL 5′11″ 176 lbs.

Year	Team	W	L	PCT	ERA	G	GS	CG	IP	H	BB	SO	ShO	Relief Pitching W	Relief Pitching L	Relief Pitching SV	Batting AB	Batting H	HR	BA	PO	A	E	DP	TC/G	FA
1948	PHI N	0	0	—	0.00	3	0	0	4	2	1	1	0	0	0	0	0	0	0	—	0	0	0	0	0.0	.000

Arnie Portocarrero

PORTOCARRERO, ARNOLD MARIO
B. July 5, 1931, New York, N. Y. D. July 21, 1986, Kansas City, Kans.
BR TR 6′ 3″ 196 lbs.

Year	Team	W	L	PCT	ERA	G	GS	CG	IP	H	BB	SO	ShO	Relief Pitching W	Relief Pitching L	Relief Pitching SV	Batting AB	Batting H	HR	BA	PO	A	E	DP	TC/G	FA
1954	PHI A	9	18	.333	4.06	34	33	16	248	233	114	132	1	0	0	0	75	8	1	.107	15	22	4	0	1.2	.902
1955	KC A	5	9	.357	4.77	24	20	4	111.1	109	67	34	1	0	0	0	37	4	1	.108	7	15	1	0	1.0	.957
1956		0	1	.000	10.13	3	1	0	8	9	7	2	0	0	0	0	1	0	0	.000	0	1	0	0	0.3	1.000
1957		4	9	.308	3.92	33	17	1	114.2	103	34	42	0	2	0	0	28	3	0	.107	6	16	1	1	0.7	.957
1958	BAL A	15	11	.577	3.25	32	27	10	204.2	173	57	90	3	0	1	2	67	11	1	.164	7	21	0	3	0.9	1.000
1959		2	7	.222	6.80	27	14	1	90	107	32	23	0	0	0	0	21	0	0	.000	6	20	1	0	1.0	.963
1960		3	2	.600	4.43	13	5	1	40.2	44	9	15	0	1	1	0	11	0	0	.000	2	3	0	0	0.4	1.000
7 yrs.		38	57	.400	4.32	166	117	33	817.1	778	320	338	5	3	2	2	240	26	3	.108	43	98	7	4	0.9	.953

Mark Portugal

PORTUGAL, MARK STEVEN
B. Oct. 30, 1962, Los Angeles, Calif.
BR TR 6′ 170 lbs.

Year	Team	W	L	PCT	ERA	G	GS	CG	IP	H	BB	SO	ShO	Relief Pitching W	Relief Pitching L	Relief Pitching SV	Batting AB	Batting H	HR	BA	PO	A	E	DP	TC/G	FA
1985	MIN A	1	3	.250	5.55	6	4	0	24.1	24	14	12	0	0	0	0	0	0	0	—	4	7	1	1	2.0	.917
1986		6	10	.375	4.31	27	15	3	112.2	112	50	67	0	2	4	1	0	0	0	—	5	14	1	3	0.7	.950
1987		1	3	.250	7.77	13	7	0	44	58	24	28	0	0	1	0	0	0	0	—	1	6	0	2	0.5	1.000
1988		3	3	.500	4.53	26	0	0	57.2	60	17	31	0	3	3	3	0	0	0	—	2	1	1	0	0.2	.750
1989	HOU N	7	1	.875	2.75	20	15	2	108	91	37	86	1	0	0	0	34	7	1	.206	11	15	2	0	1.4	.929
1990		11	10	.524	3.62	32	32	1	196.2	187	67	136	0	0	0	0	66	9	0	.136	23	19	1	2	1.3	.977
1991		10	12	.455	4.49	32	27	1	168.1	163	59	120	0	0	2	1	46	9	0	.196	16	17	3	1	1.1	.917
1992		6	3	.667	2.66	18	16	1	101.1	76	41	62	1	1	0	0	28	3	0	.107	16	13	3	1	1.8	.906
1993		18	4	**.818**	2.77	33	33	1	208	194	77	131	1	0	0	0	65	15	1	.231	21	28	2	2	1.5	.961
1994	SF N	10	8	.556	3.93	21	21	1	137.1	135	45	87	0	0	0	0	48	17	0	.354	10	12	1	1	1.1	.957
1995	2 teams SF N (17G 5–5) CIN N (14G 6–5)																									
″	total	11	10	.524	4.01	31	**31**	1	181.2	185	56	96	0	0	0	0	58	8	0	.138	9	21	1	2	1.0	.968
11 yrs.		84	67	.556	3.81	259	201	11	1340	1285	487	856	3	6	10	5	345	68	2	.197	118	153	16	15	1.1	.944
LEAGUE CHAMPIONSHIP SERIES																										
1995	CIN N	0	1	.000	36.00	1	0	0	1	3	1	0	0	0	1	0	0	0	0	—	0	0	0	0	0.0	.000

Bill Posedel

POSEDEL, WILLIAM JOHN (Sailor Bill)
B. Aug. 2, 1906, San Francisco, Calif. D. Nov. 28, 1989, Livermore, Calif.
BR TR 5′11″ 175 lbs.

Year	Team	W	L	PCT	ERA	G	GS	CG	IP	H	BB	SO	ShO	Relief Pitching W	Relief Pitching L	Relief Pitching SV	Batting AB	Batting H	HR	BA	PO	A	E	DP	TC/G	FA
1938	BKN N	8	9	.471	5.66	33	17	6	140	178	46	49	1	0	3	1	44	10	0	.227	5	23	2	2	0.9	.933
1939	BOS N	15	13	.536	3.92	33	29	18	220.2	221	78	73	5	1	0	0	73	8	0	.110	10	40	4	0	1.6	.926

Bill Posedel *continued*

Year	Team	W	L	PCT	ERA	G	GS	CG	IP	H	BB	SO	ShO	Relief W	Relief L	Relief SV	AB	H	HR	BA	PO	A	E	DP	TC/G	FA
1940		12	17	.414	4.13	35	32	18	233	263	81	86	0	1	0	1	82	14	0	.171	17	42	3	3	1.8	.952
1941		4	4	.500	4.87	18	9	3	57.1	61	30	10	0	1	0	0	25	8	0	.320	3	11	1	2	0.8	.933
1946		2	0	1.000	6.99	19	0	0	28.1	34	13	9	0	2	0	4	3	0	0	.000	1	4	0	0	0.3	1.000
5 yrs.		41	43	.488	4.56	138	87	45	679.1	757	248	227	6	5	3	6	227	40	0	.176	36	120	10	7	1.2	.940

Bob Poser

POSER, JOHN FALK — BL TR 6' 173 lbs.
B. Mar. 16, 1910, Columbus, Wis.

Year	Team	W	L	PCT	ERA	G	GS	CG	IP	H	BB	SO	ShO	Relief W	Relief L	Relief SV	AB	H	HR	BA	PO	A	E	DP	TC/G	FA
1932	CHI A	0	0	—	27.00	1	0	0	0.2	3	2	1	0	0	0	0	3	0	0	.000	0	0	0	0	0.0	.000
1935	STL A	1	1	.500	9.22	4	1	0	13.2	26	4	1	0	1	0	0	4	1	0	.250	0	1	0	0	0.3	1.000
2 yrs.		1	1	.500	10.05	5	1	0	14.1	29	6	2	0	1	0	0	7	1	0	.143	0	1	0	0	0.2	1.000

Lou Possehl

POSSEHL, LOUIS THOMAS — BR TR 6' 2" 180 lbs.
B. Apr. 12, 1926, Chicago, Ill.

Year	Team	W	L	PCT	ERA	G	GS	CG	IP	H	BB	SO	ShO	Relief W	Relief L	Relief SV	AB	H	HR	BA	PO	A	E	DP	TC/G	FA
1946	PHI N	1	2	.333	5.93	4	4	0	13.2	19	10	4	0	0	0	0	3	0	0	.000	1	3	0	0	1.0	1.000
1947		0	0	—	4.15	2	0	0	4.1	5	0	1	0	0	0	0	0	0	0	—	0	3	0	0	1.5	1.000
1948		1	1	.500	4.91	3	2	1	14.2	17	4	7	0	0	0	0	4	1	0	.250	1	2	0	1	1.0	1.000
1951		0	1	.000	6.00	2	1	0	6	9	3	6	0	0	0	0	1	0	0	.000	1	1	0	0	1.0	1.000
1952		0	1	.000	4.97	4	1	0	12.2	12	7	4	0	0	0	0	2	0	0	.000	0	1	0	0	0.3	1.000
5 yrs.		2	5	.286	5.26	15	8	1	51.1	62	24	22	0	0	0	0	10	1	0	.100	3	10	0	1	0.9	1.000

Nellie Pott

POTT, NELSON ADOLPH (Lefty) — BL TL 6' 185 lbs.
B. July 16, 1899, Cincinnati, Ohio D. Dec. 3, 1963, Cincinnati, Ohio.

Year	Team	W	L	PCT	ERA	G	GS	CG	IP	H	BB	SO	ShO	Relief W	Relief L	Relief SV	AB	H	HR	BA	PO	A	E	DP	TC/G	FA
1922	CLE A	0	0	—	31.50	2	0	0	2	7	2	0	0	0	0	0	0	0	0	—	0	0	0	0	0.0	.000

Dykes Potter

POTTER, MARYLAND DYKES — BR TR 6' 185 lbs.
Brother of Squire Potter.
B. Sept. 7, 1910, Ashland, Ky.

Year	Team	W	L	PCT	ERA	G	GS	CG	IP	H	BB	SO	ShO	Relief W	Relief L	Relief SV	AB	H	HR	BA	PO	A	E	DP	TC/G	FA
1938	BKN N	0	0	—	4.50	2	0	0	2	4	0	1	0	0	0	0	0	0	0	—	0	0	0	0	0.0	.000

Nels Potter

POTTER, NELSON THOMAS — BL TR 5'11" 180 lbs.
B. Aug. 23, 1911, Mt. Morris, Ill. D. Sept. 30, 1990, Mt. Morris, Ill.

Year	Team	W	L	PCT	ERA	G	GS	CG	IP	H	BB	SO	ShO	Relief W	Relief L	Relief SV	AB	H	HR	BA	PO	A	E	DP	TC/G	FA
1936	STL N	0	0	—	0.00	1	0	0	1	0	0	0	0	0	0	0	0	0	0	—	0	0	0	0	0.0	.000
1938	PHI A	2	12	.143	6.47	35	9	4	111.1	139	49	43	0	1	**5**	5	39	10	0	.256	8	16	1	0	0.7	.960
1939		8	12	.400	6.60	41	25	9	196.1	258	88	60	0	0	2	2	67	12	0	.179	8	34	1	0	1.0	.977
1940		9	14	.391	4.44	31	25	13	200.2	213	71	73	0	1	1	0	71	18	0	.254	17	30	0	2	1.5	1.000
1941	2 teams PHI A (10G 1–1) BOS A (10G 2–0)																									
"	total	3	1	.750	7.06	20	3	1	43.1	56	32	13	0	2	0	2	9	1	0	.111	5	6	1	1	0.6	.917
1943	STL A	10	5	.667	2.78	33	13	8	168.1	146	54	80	0	2	0	1	55	8	0	.145	10	36	1	2	1.4	.979
1944		19	7	.731	2.83	32	29	16	232	211	70	91	3	0	2	0	82	13	0	.159	11	52	3	3	2.1	.955
1945		15	11	.577	2.47	32	32	21	255.1	212	68	129	3	0	0	0	92	28	0	.304	13	43	3	4	1.8	.949
1946		8	9	.471	3.72	23	19	10	145	152	59	72	0	0	0	0	52	12	0	.231	11	18	1	3	1.3	.967
1947		4	10	.286	4.04	32	10	3	122.2	130	44	65	0	2	2	2	35	9	0	.257	6	27	3	1	1.1	.917
1948	3 teams STL A (2G 1–1) PHI A (8G 2–2) BOS N (18G 5–2)																									
"	total	8	5	.615	2.86	28	9	3	113.1	105	17	64	0	3	2	3	37	14	0	.378	7	25	3	1	1.3	.914
1949	BOS N	6	11	.353	4.19	41	3	1	96.2	99	30	57	0	5	**11**	7	23	3	0	.130	2	20	1	1	0.6	.957
12 yrs.		92	97	.487	3.99	349	177	89	1686	1721	582	747	6	16	25	22	562	128	0	.228	98	307	18	18	1.2	.957
WORLD SERIES																										
1944	STL A	0	1	.000	0.93	2	2	0	9.2	10	3	6	0	0	0	0	4	0	0	.000	2	2	2	0	3.0	.667
1948	BOS N	0	0	—	8.44	2	1	0	5.1	6	2	1	0	0	0	0	2	1	0	.500	1	0	0	0	0.5	1.000
2 yrs.		0	1	.000	3.60	4	3	0	15	16	5	7	0	0	0	0	6	1	0	.167	3	2	2	0	1.8	.714

Squire Potter

POTTER, ROBERT — BR TR 6' 1" 185 lbs.
Brother of Dykes Potter.
B. Mar. 18, 1902, Flatwoods, Ky. D. Jan. 27, 1983, Ashland, Ky.

Year	Team	W	L	PCT	ERA	G	GS	CG	IP	H	BB	SO	ShO	Relief W	Relief L	Relief SV	AB	H	HR	BA	PO	A	E	DP	TC/G	FA
1923	WAS A	0	0	—	21.00	1	0	0	3	11	4	1	0	0	0	0	0	0	0	—	0	0	0	0	0.0	.000

Bill Pounds

POUNDS, JEARED WELLS — BR TR 5'10½" 178 lbs.
B. Mar. 11, 1878, Paterson, N. J. D. July 7, 1936, Paterson, N. J.

Year	Team	W	L	PCT	ERA	G	GS	CG	IP	H	BB	SO	ShO	Relief W	Relief L	Relief SV	AB	H	HR	BA	PO	A	E	DP	TC/G	FA
1903	2 teams CLE A (1G 0–0) BKN N (1G 0–0)																									
"	total	0	0		8.18	2	0	0	11	16	2	4	0	0	0	0	5	3	0	.600	0	4	0	0	2.0	1.000

Abner Powell

POWELL, CHARLES ABNER — BL TR 5' 7" 160 lbs.
B. Dec. 15, 1860, Shenandoah, Pa. D. Aug. 7, 1953, New Orleans, La.

Year	Team	W	L	PCT	ERA	G	GS	CG	IP	H	BB	SO	ShO	Relief W	Relief L	Relief SV	AB	H	HR	BA	PO	A	E	DP	TC/G	FA
1884	WAS U	6	12	.333	*3.43*	18	17	14	134	135	19	78	1	1	0	0	191	54	0	.283	55	46	18	0	2.3	.849
1886	2 teams BAL AA (7G 2–5) CIN AA (4G 0–1)																									
"	total	2	6	.250	5.02	11	8	8	75.1	82	35	19	0	0	0	0	113	24	0	.212	30	48	17	4	2.8	.821
2 yrs.		8	18	.308	4.00	29	25	22	209.1	217	54	97	1	1	0	0	*				85	94	35	4	2.5	.836

Bill Powell

POWELL, WILLIAM BURRIS — BR TR 6' 2½" 182 lbs.
B. May 8, 1885, Richmond, Va. D. Sept. 28, 1967, East Liverpool, Ohio.

Year	Team	W	L	PCT	ERA	G	GS	CG	IP	H	BB	SO	ShO	Relief W	Relief L	Relief SV	AB	H	HR	BA	PO	A	E	DP	TC/G	FA
1909	PIT N	0	1	.000	3.68	3	1	0	7.1	7	6	2	0	0	0	0	4	1	0	.250	0	2	0	1	0.7	1.000
1910		4	6	.400	2.40	12	9	4	75	65	34	23	2	1	0	0	23	6	0	.261	6	27	1	1	2.8	.971
1912	CHI N	0	0	—	9.00	1	0	0	2	2	1	0	0	0	0	0	0	0	0	—	0	1	0	0	1.0	1.000
1913	CIN N	0	1	.000	54.00	1	1	0	0.1	2	2	0	0	0	0	0	0	0	0	—	0	0	0	0	0.0	.000
4 yrs.		4	8	.333	2.87	17	11	4	84.2	76	43	25	2	1	0	0	27	7	0	.259	6	30	1	2	2.2	.973

Dennis Powell

POWELL, DENNIS CLAY — BR TL 6' 3" 175 lbs.
B. Aug. 13, 1963, Moultrie, Ga.

Year	Team	W	L	PCT	ERA	G	GS	CG	IP	H	BB	SO	ShO	Relief W	Relief L	Relief SV	AB	H	HR	BA	PO	A	E	DP	TC/G	FA
1985	LA N	1	1	.500	5.22	16	2	0	29.1	30	13	19	0	1	0	1	3	0	0	.000	0	6	0	2	0.4	1.000
1986		2	7	.222	4.27	27	6	0	65.1	65	25	31	0	1	2	0	14	3	0	.214	7	6	1	1	0.5	.929
1987	SEA A	1	3	.250	3.15	16	3	0	34.1	32	15	17	0	1	2	0	0	0	0	—	2	6	0	0	0.5	1.000
1988		1	3	.250	8.68	12	2	0	18.2	29	11	15	0	1	2	0	0	0	0	—	1	3	0	0	0.3	1.000
1989		2	2	.500	5.00	43	1	0	45	49	21	27	0	2	1	2	0	0	0	—	2	11	0	0	0.3	1.000

Dennis Powell *continued*

Year	Team	W	L	PCT	ERA	G	GS	CG	IP	H	BB	SO	ShO	Relief Pitching W	L	SV	Batting AB	H	HR	BA	PO	A	E	DP	TC/G	FA
1990	2 teams SEA A (2G 0–0) MIL A (9G 0–4)																									
"	total	0	4	.000	7.02	11	7	0	42.1	64	21	23	0	0	0	0	0	0	0		2	9	0	0	1.0	1.000
1992	SEA A	4	2	.667	4.58	49	0	0	57	49	29	35	0	4	2	0	0	0	0	—	3	5	0	1	0.2	1.000
1993		0	0	—	4.15	33	2	0	47.2	42	24	32	0	0	0	0	0	0	0	—	3	5	0	0	0.3	1.000
8 yrs.		11	22	.333	4.95	207	23	0	339.2	360	159	199	0	10	9	3	17	3	0	.176	20	51	1	4	0.3	.986

Grover Powell

POWELL, GROVER DAVID
B. Oct. 10, 1940, Sayre, Pa. D. May 21, 1985, Raleigh, N. C.
BL TL 5'10" 175 lbs.

Year	Team	W	L	PCT	ERA	G	GS	CG	IP	H	BB	SO	ShO	Relief Pitching W	L	SV	Batting AB	H	HR	BA	PO	A	E	DP	TC/G	FA
1963	NY N	1	1	.500	2.72	20	4	1	49.2	37	32	39	1	0	0	0	10	2	0	.200	7	7	2	1	0.8	.875

Jack Powell

POWELL, JOHN JOSEPH
B. July 9, 1874, Bloomington, Ill. D. Oct. 17, 1944, Chicago, Ill.
BR TR 5'11" 195 lbs.

Year	Team	W	L	PCT	ERA	G	GS	CG	IP	H	BB	SO	ShO	Relief Pitching W	L	SV	Batting AB	H	HR	BA	PO	A	E	DP	TC/G	FA
1897	CLE N	15	10	.600	3.16	27	26	24	225	245	62	61	2	0	0	0	97	20	0	.206	7	45	4	2	2.0	.929
1898		23	15	.605	3.00	42	41	36	342	328	112	93	**6**	0	1	0	136	18	0	.132	11	70	3	2	2.0	.964
1899	STL N	23	21	.523	3.52	48	**43**	**40**	373	433	85	87	2	2	0	0	134	27	0	.201	12	78	6	2	2.0	.938
1900		17	17	.500	4.44	38	37	28	287.2	325	77	77	3	1	0	0	109	31	1	.284	11	70	6	2	2.3	.931
1901		19	19	.500	3.54	**45**	37	33	338.1	351	50	133	2	2	**2**	**3**	119	21	2	.176	15	64	7	4	1.9	.919
1902	STL A	22	17	.564	3.21	42	39	36	328.1	320	93	137	3	1	0	**2**	127	26	1	.205	24	66	9	6	2.2	.909
1903		15	19	.441	2.91	38	34	33	306.1	294	58	169	4	1	0	**2**	120	25	0	.208	10	85	6	1	2.7	.941
1904	NY A	23	19	.548	2.44	47	45	38	390.1	340	92	202	3	1	0	0	146	26	0	.178	9	100	4	3	2.4	.965
1905	2 teams NY A (37G 8–13) STL A (3G 2–1)																									
"	total	10	14	.417	3.29	40	26	16	230	236	62	96	1	2	**3**	1	75	13	1	.173	2	40	2	2	1.1	.955
1906	STL A	13	14	.481	1.77	28	26	25	244	196	55	132	3	1	0	1	94	22	1	.234	8	53	3	3	2.3	.953
1907		13	16	.448	2.68	32	31	27	255.2	229	62	96	4	0	0	1	91	12	0	.132	2	69	4	2	2.3	.947
1908		16	13	.552	2.11	33	32	23	256	208	47	85	6	0	0	1	89	21	0	.236	2	56	3	0	1.8	.951
1909		12	16	.429	2.11	34	27	18	239	221	42	82	4	2	0	3	78	14	0	.179	9	58	4	0	2.1	.944
1910		7	11	.389	2.30	21	18	8	129.1	121	28	52	3	2	1	0	43	7	0	.163	5	25	3	1	1.6	.909
1911		8	**19**	.296	3.29	31	27	18	207.2	224	44	52	1	0	2	1	73	12	0	.164	5	40	6	1	1.6	.882
1912		9	17	.346	3.10	32	28	19	235.1	248	52	67	0	0	0	0	82	15	1	.183	3	52	5	4	1.9	.917
16 yrs.		245	257 **7th**	.488	2.97	578	517	422	4388	4319	1021	1621	47	15	9	15	1613	310	7	.192	135	971	75	35	2.0	.936

Jack Powell

POWELL, REGINALD BERTRAND
B. Aug. 17, 1891, Holcomb, Mo. D. Mar. 12, 1930, Memphis, Tenn.
TR 6' 2"

Year	Team	W	L	PCT	ERA	G	GS	CG	IP	H	BB	SO	ShO	Relief Pitching W	L	SV	Batting AB	H	HR	BA	PO	A	E	DP	TC/G	FA
1913	STL A	0	0	—	0.00	2	0	0	2	1	2	0	0	0	0	0	0	0	0	—	0	3	0	0	1.5	1.000

Jay Powell

POWELL, JAMES WILLARD
B. Jan. 9, 1972, Meridian, Miss.
BR TR 6' 4" 220 lbs.

Year	Team	W	L	PCT	ERA	G	GS	CG	IP	H	BB	SO	ShO	Relief Pitching W	L	SV	Batting AB	H	HR	BA	PO	A	E	DP	TC/G	FA
1995	FLA N	0	0	—	1.08	9	0	0	8.1	7	6	4	0	0	0	0	0	0	0	—	1	3	0	0	0.4	1.000

Ross Powell

POWELL, ROSS JOHN
B. Jan. 24, 1968, Grand Rapids, Mich.
BL TL 6' 180 lbs.

Year	Team	W	L	PCT	ERA	G	GS	CG	IP	H	BB	SO	ShO	Relief Pitching W	L	SV	Batting AB	H	HR	BA	PO	A	E	DP	TC/G	FA
1993	CIN N	0	3	.000	4.41	9	1	0	16.1	13	6	17	0	0	2	0	1	0	0	.000	0	2	1	0	0.3	.667
1994	HOU N	0	0	—	1.23	12	0	0	7.1	6	5	5	0	0	0	0	0	0	0	—	0	2	0	0	0.2	1.000
1995	2 teams HOU N (15G 0–0) PIT N (12G 0–2)																									
"	total	0	2	.000	6.98	27	3	0	29.2	36	21	20	0	0	1	0	3	0	0	.000	1	5	0	0	0.2	1.000
3 yrs.		0	5	.000	5.40	48	4	0	53.1	55	32	42	0	0	3	0	4	0	0	.000	1	9	1	0	0.2	.909

Ted Power

POWER, TED HENRY
B. Jan. 31, 1955, Guthrie, Okla.
BR TR 6' 4" 220 lbs.

Year	Team	W	L	PCT	ERA	G	GS	CG	IP	H	BB	SO	ShO	Relief Pitching W	L	SV	Batting AB	H	HR	BA	PO	A	E	DP	TC/G	FA
1981	LA N	1	3	.250	3.21	5	2	0	14	16	7	7	0	1	1	0	3	0	0	.000	1	0	1	0	0.4	.500
1982		1	1	.500	6.68	12	4	0	33.2	38	23	15	0	0	0	0	6	0	0	.000	3	5	0	0	0.7	1.000
1983	CIN N	5	6	.455	4.54	49	6	1	111	120	49	57	0	4	3	2	16	0	0	.000	4	8	0	1	0.2	1.000
1984		9	7	.563	2.82	**78**	0	0	108.2	93	46	81	0	9	7	11	5	0	0	.000	6	16	1	3	0.3	.957
1985		8	6	.571	2.70	64	0	0	80	65	45	42	0	8	6	27	0	0	0	—	3	4	1	0	0.1	.875
1986		10	6	.625	3.70	56	10	0	129	115	52	95	0	4	5	1	24	3	0	.125	7	18	1	1	0.5	.962
1987		10	13	.435	4.50	34	34	2	204	213	71	133	1	0	0	0	59	7	1	.119	9	17	2	0	0.8	.929
1988	2 teams KC A (22G 5–6) DET A (4G 1–1)																									
"	total	6	7	.462	5.91	26	14	2	99	121	38	57	2	3	2	0	0	0	0		8	10	1	1	0.7	.947
1989	STL N	7	7	.500	3.71	23	15	0	97	96	21	43	0	2	0	0	33	3	0	.091	5	8	0	0	0.6	1.000
1990	PIT N	1	3	.250	3.66	40	0	0	51.2	50	17	42	0	1	3	7	8	1	0	.125	3	4	0	0	0.2	1.000
1991	CIN N	5	3	.625	3.62	68	0	0	87	87	31	51	0	5	3	3	3	0	0	.000	8	10	0	1	0.3	1.000
1992	CLE A	3	3	.500	2.54	64	0	0	99.1	88	35	51	0	3	3	6	0	0	0	—	4	14	0	1	0.3	1.000
1993	2 teams CLE A (20G 0–2) SEA A (25G 2–2)																									
"	total	2	4	.333	5.36	45	0	0	45.1	57	17	27	0	2	4	13	0	0	0		0	5	0	0	0.1	1.000
13 yrs.		68	69	.496	4.00	564	85	5	1159.2	1159	452	701	3	42	37	70	157	14	1	.089	61	119	7	8	0.3	.963
LEAGUE CHAMPIONSHIP SERIES																										
1990	PIT N	0	0	—	3.60	3	1	0	5	6	2	3	0	0	0	1	1	0	0	.000	0	1	0	0	0.3	1.000

Ike Powers

POWERS, JOHN LLOYD
B. Mar. 13, 1906, Hancock, Md. D. Dec. 22, 1968, Hancock, Md.
BR TR 6'½" 188 lbs.

Year	Team	W	L	PCT	ERA	G	GS	CG	IP	H	BB	SO	ShO	Relief Pitching W	L	SV	Batting AB	H	HR	BA	PO	A	E	DP	TC/G	FA
1927	PHI A	1	1	.500	4.50	11	1	0	26	26	7	3	0	1	0	0	5	2	0	.400	2	6	1	0	0.8	.889
1928		1	0	1.000	4.50	9	0	0	12	8	10	4	0	1	0	2	0	0	0	—	2	4	0	1	0.7	1.000
2 yrs.		2	1	.667	4.50	20	1	0	38	34	17	7	0	2	0	2	5	2	0	.400	4	10	1	1	0.8	.933

Jim Powers

POWERS, JAMES T.
B. 1868, New York, N. Y. Deceased.
5'10" 150 lbs.

Year	Team	W	L	PCT	ERA	G	GS	CG	IP	H	BB	SO	ShO	Relief Pitching W	L	SV	Batting AB	H	HR	BA	PO	A	E	DP	TC/G	FA
1890	BKN AA	1	2	.333	5.70	4	2	2	30	38	16	3	0	1	0	0	13	2	0	.154	0	5	0	0	1.3	1.000

Willie Prall

PRALL, WILFRED ANTHONY — BL TL 6′ 3″ 200 lbs.
B. Apr. 20, 1950, Hackensack, N. J.

Year	Team	W	L	PCT	ERA	G	GS	CG	IP	H	BB	SO	ShO	Relief W	Relief L	Relief SV	AB	H	HR	BA	PO	A	E	DP	TC/G	FA
1975	CHI N	0	2	.000	8.40	3	3	0	15	21	8	7	0	0	0	0	4	0	0	.000	0	3	0	0	1.0	1.000

John Pregenzer

PREGENZER, JOHN ARTHUR — BR TR 6′ 5″ 220 lbs.
B. Aug. 2, 1935, Burlington, Wis.

Year	Team	W	L	PCT	ERA	G	GS	CG	IP	H	BB	SO	ShO	Relief W	Relief L	Relief SV	AB	H	HR	BA	PO	A	E	DP	TC/G	FA
1963	SF N	0	0	—	4.82	6	0	0	9.1	8	8	5	0	0	0	1	0	0	0	—	0	2	0	1	0.3	1.000
1964		2	0	1.000	4.91	13	0	0	18.1	21	11	8	0	2	0	0	0	0	0	—	2	2	0	0	0.3	1.000
2 yrs.		2	0	1.000	4.88	19	0	0	27.2	29	19	13	0	2	0	1	0	0	0		2	4	0	1	0.3	1.000

Jim Prendergast

PRENDERGAST, JAMES BARTHOLOMEW — BL TL 6′ 1″ 208 lbs.
B. Aug. 23, 1917, Brooklyn, N. Y. D. Aug. 23, 1994, Amherst, N. Y.

Year	Team	W	L	PCT	ERA	G	GS	CG	IP	H	BB	SO	ShO	Relief W	Relief L	Relief SV	AB	H	HR	BA	PO	A	E	DP	TC/G	FA
1948	BOS N	1	1	.500	10.26	10	2	0	16.2	30	5	3	0	0	0	1	5	0	0	.000	4	4	0	0	0.8	1.000

Mike Prendergast

PRENDERGAST, MICHAEL THOMAS (Iron Mike) — BR TR 5′ 9½″ 165 lbs.
B. Dec. 15, 1888, Arlington, Ill. D. Nov. 18, 1967, Omaha, Neb.

Year	Team	W	L	PCT	ERA	G	GS	CG	IP	H	BB	SO	ShO	Relief W	Relief L	Relief SV	AB	H	HR	BA	PO	A	E	DP	TC/G	FA
1914	CHI F	5	9	.357	2.38	30	19	7	136	131	40	71	1	0	1	0	37	4	0	.108	1	32	1	0	1.1	.971
1915		14	12	.538	2.48	42	30	16	253.2	220	67	95	3	2	3	0	80	6	0	.075	3	68	3	3	1.8	.959
1916	CHI N	6	11	.353	2.31	35	10	4	152	127	23	56	2	3	4	2	46	7	0	.152	2	40	2	1	1.3	.955
1917		3	6	.333	3.35	35	8	1	99.1	112	21	43	0	1	1	1	28	7	0	.250	3	25	2	2	0.9	.933
1918	PHI N	13	14	.481	2.89	33	30	20	252.1	257	46	41	0	0	0	1	85	7	0	.082	6	70	3	3	2.4	.962
1919		0	1	.000	8.40	5	1	0	15	20	10	5	0	0	1	0	3	1	0	.333	1	5	1	1	1.4	.857
6 yrs.		41	53	.436	2.74	180	98	48	908.1	867	207	311	6	6	10	4	279	32	0	.115	16	240	12	10	1.5	.955

George Prentiss

PRENTISS, GEORGE PEPPER (Kitten) — BB TR 5′11″ 175 lbs.
Played as George Pepper Wilson In 1901.
Born George Pepper Wilson.
B. June 10, 1876, Wilmington, Del. D. Sept. 8, 1902, Wilmington, Del.

Year	Team	W	L	PCT	ERA	G	GS	CG	IP	H	BB	SO	ShO	Relief W	Relief L	Relief SV	AB	H	HR	BA	PO	A	E	DP	TC/G	FA
1901	BOS A	1	0	1.000	1.80	2	1	1	10	7	6	0	0	0	0	0	3	1	0	.333	0	3	0	0	1.5	1.000
1902	2 teams BOS A (7G 2–2) BAL A (2G 0–1)																									
″	total	2	3	.400	6.04	9	6	3	47.2	69	15	10	0	0	0	0	20	5	0	.250	1	13	0	0	1.6	1.000
2 yrs.		3	3	.500	5.31	11	7	4	57.2	76	21	10	0	0	0	0	23	6	0	.261	1	16	0	0	1.5	1.000

Joe Presko

PRESKO, JOSEPH EDWARD (Little Joe) — BR TR 5′ 9½″ 165 lbs.
B. Oct. 7, 1928, Kansas City, Mo.

Year	Team	W	L	PCT	ERA	G	GS	CG	IP	H	BB	SO	ShO	Relief W	Relief L	Relief SV	AB	H	HR	BA	PO	A	E	DP	TC/G	FA
1951	STL N	7	4	.636	3.45	15	12	5	88.2	86	20	38	0	1	0	2	37	6	0	.162	4	11	1	0	1.1	.938
1952		7	10	.412	4.05	28	18	5	146.2	140	57	63	1	2	1	0	43	4	0	.093	6	24	2	3	1.1	.938
1953		6	13	.316	5.01	34	25	4	161.2	165	65	56	0	0	0	1	59	13	0	.220	13	21	1	2	1.0	.971
1954		4	9	.308	6.91	37	6	1	71.2	97	41	36	1	3	5	0	16	4	0	.250	5	9	0	2	0.4	1.000
1957	DET A	1	1	.500	1.64	7	0	0	11	10	4	3	0	1	1	0	1	0	0	.000	0	1	0	0	0.1	1.000
1958		0	0	—	3.38	7	0	0	10.2	13	1	6	0	0	0	2	0	0	0	—	1	1	0	0	0.3	1.000
6 yrs.		25	37	.403	4.61	128	61	15	490.1	511	188	202	2	7	7	5	156	27	0	.173	29	67	4	7	0.8	.960

Tot Pressnell

PRESSNELL, FOREST CHARLES — BR TR 5′10½″ 175 lbs.
B. Aug. 8, 1906, Findlay, Ohio.

Year	Team	W	L	PCT	ERA	G	GS	CG	IP	H	BB	SO	ShO	Relief W	Relief L	Relief SV	AB	H	HR	BA	PO	A	E	DP	TC/G	FA
1938	BKN N	11	14	.440	3.56	43	19	6	192	209	56	57	1	4	3	3	63	9	0	.143	10	36	2	0	1.1	.958
1939		9	7	.563	4.02	31	18	10	156.2	171	33	43	2	0	0	2	51	10	0	.196	5	36	3	2	1.4	.932
1940		6	5	.545	3.69	24	4	1	68.1	58	17	21	1	4	4	2	17	0	0	.000	4	9	1	0	0.6	.929
1941	CHI N	5	3	.625	3.09	29	1	0	70	69	23	27	0	5	2	1	15	3	0	.200	0	13	1	1	0.5	.929
1942		1	1	.500	5.49	27	0	0	39.1	40	5	9	0	1	1	4	3	2	0	.667	2	7	0	0	0.3	1.000
5 yrs.		32	30	.516	3.80	154	42	17	526.1	547	134	157	4	14	10	12	149	24	0	.161	21	101	7	3	0.8	.946

Bill Price

PRICE, WILLIAM
B. Philadelphia, Pa. Deceased.

Year	Team	W	L	PCT	ERA	G	GS	CG	IP	H	BB	SO	ShO	Relief W	Relief L	Relief SV	AB	H	HR	BA	PO	A	E	DP	TC/G	FA
1890	PHI AA	1	0	1.000	2.00	1	1	1	9	6	7	1	0	0	0	0	4	1	0	.250	0	2	0	0	2.0	1.000

Joe Price

PRICE, JOSEPH WALTER — BR TL 6′ 4″ 220 lbs.
B. Nov. 29, 1956, Inglewood, Calif.

Year	Team	W	L	PCT	ERA	G	GS	CG	IP	H	BB	SO	ShO	Relief W	Relief L	Relief SV	AB	H	HR	BA	PO	A	E	DP	TC/G	FA
1980	CIN N	7	3	.700	3.57	24	13	2	111	95	37	44	0	2	0	0	39	5	0	.128	3	16	2	0	0.9	.905
1981		6	1	.857	2.50	41	0	0	54	42	18	41	0	6	1	4	3	0	0	.000	1	13	2	0	0.4	.875
1982		3	4	.429	2.85	59	1	0	72.2	73	32	71	0	3	3	3	3	1	0	.333	1	8	2	0	0.2	.818
1983		10	6	.625	2.88	21	21	5	144	118	46	83	0	0	0	0	41	4	0	.098	8	21	4	3	1.6	.879
1984		7	13	.350	4.19	30	30	3	171.2	176	61	129	1	0	0	0	48	7	0	.146	4	14	0	0	0.6	1.000
1985		2	2	.500	3.90	26	8	0	64.2	59	23	52	0	0	0	1	14	0	0	.000	1	4	0	1	0.2	1.000
1986		1	2	.333	5.40	25	2	0	41.2	49	22	30	0	1	1	0	7	1	0	.143	2	2	0	0	0.2	1.000
1987	SF N	2	2	.500	2.57	20	0	0	35	19	13	42	0	2	2	1	6	1	0	.167	1	2	0	0	0.2	1.000
1988		1	6	.143	3.94	38	3	0	61.2	59	27	49	0	1	6	4	8	0	0	.000	3	8	0	0	0.3	1.000
1989	2 teams SF N (7G 1–1) BOS A (31G 2–5)																									
″	total	3	6	.333	4.59	38	6	0	84.1	87	34	62	0	1	3	0	2	0	0	.000	2	8	0	1	0.3	1.000
1990	BAL A	3	4	.429	3.58	50	0	0	65.1	62	24	54	0	3	4	0	0	0	0	—	1	8	2	0	0.2	.818
11 yrs.		45	49	.479	3.65	372	84	10	906	839	337	657	1	19	20	13	171	19	0	.111	27	104	12	5	0.4	.916
LEAGUE CHAMPIONSHIP SERIES																										
1987	SF N	1	0	1.000	0.00	2	0	0	5.2	3	1	7	0	1	0	0	1	0	0	.000	0	0	0	0	0.0	.000

Bob Priddy

PRIDDY, ROBERT SIMPSON — BR TR 6′ 1″ 200 lbs.
B. Dec. 10, 1939, Pittsburgh, Pa.

Year	Team	W	L	PCT	ERA	G	GS	CG	IP	H	BB	SO	ShO	Relief W	Relief L	Relief SV	AB	H	HR	BA	PO	A	E	DP	TC/G	FA
1962	PIT N	1	0	1.000	3.00	2	0	0	3	4	1	1	0	1	0	0	0	0	0	—	0	0	0	0	0.0	.000
1964		1	2	.333	3.93	19	0	0	34.1	35	15	23	0	1	2	1	3	0	0	.000	3	1	0	0	0.2	1.000
1965	SF N	1	0	1.000	1.74	8	0	0	10.1	6	2	7	0	1	0	0	1	0	0	.000	1	2	0	0	0.4	1.000
1966		6	3	.667	3.96	38	3	0	91	88	28	51	0	6	0	1	17	3	0	.176	4	10	3	2	0.4	.824
1967	WAS A	3	7	.300	3.44	46	8	1	110	98	33	57	0	0	3	4	22	4	0	.182	13	21	1	0	0.8	.971
1968	CHI A	3	11	.214	3.63	35	18	2	114	106	41	66	0	0	2	0	24	1	1	.042	5	10	1	0	0.5	.938
1969	3 teams CHI A (4G 0–0) CAL A (15G 0–1) ATL N (1G 0–0)																									
″	total	0	1	.000	4.46	20	0	0	36.1	35	10	21	0	0	1	0	2	0	0	.000	3	5	0	1	0.4	1.000

Bob Priddy *continued*

Year	Team	Lg	W	L	PCT	ERA	G	GS	CG	IP	H	BB	SO	ShO	Relief Pitching W	Relief Pitching L	Relief Pitching SV	Batting AB	Batting H	Batting HR	BA	PO	A	E	DP	TC/G	FA
1970	ATL	N	5	5	.500	5.42	41	0	0	73	75	24	32	0	5	5	8	15	3	0	.200	7	14	1	0	0.5	.955
1971			4	9	.308	4.22	40	0	0	64	71	44	36	0	4	**9**	4	11	2	0	.182	6	11	1	2	0.4	.944
9 yrs.			24	38	.387	4.00	249	29	3	536	518	198	294	0	18	22	18	95	13	1	.137	42	74	7	5	0.5	.943

Ariel Prieto

PRIETO, ARIEL BR TR 6′ 3″ 220 lbs.
B. Oct. 22, 1969, Havana, Cuba.

Year	Team	Lg	W	L	PCT	ERA	G	GS	CG	IP	H	BB	SO	ShO	Relief Pitching W	Relief Pitching L	Relief Pitching SV	Batting AB	Batting H	Batting HR	BA	PO	A	E	DP	TC/G	FA
1995	OAK	A	2	6	.250	4.97	14	9	1	58	57	32	37	0	0	0	0	0	0	0	—	0	8	1	0	0.6	.889

Ray Prim

PRIM, RAYMOND LEE (Pop) BR TL 6′ 178 lbs.
B. Dec. 30, 1906, Salitpa, Ala. D. Apr. 29, 1995, Monte Rio, Calif.

Year	Team	Lg	W	L	PCT	ERA	G	GS	CG	IP	H	BB	SO	ShO	Relief Pitching W	Relief Pitching L	Relief Pitching SV	Batting AB	Batting H	Batting HR	BA	PO	A	E	DP	TC/G	FA
1933	WAS	A	0	1	.000	3.14	2	1	0	14.1	13	2	6	0	0	0	0	5	0	0	.000	1	7	0	0	4.0	1.000
1934			0	2	.000	6.75	8	1	0	14.2	19	8	3	0	0	1	0	3	0	0	.000	0	5	1	1	0.8	.833
1935	PHI	N	3	4	.429	5.77	29	6	1	73.1	110	15	27	0	3	1	0	24	2	0	.083	4	13	0	2	0.6	1.000
1943	CHI	N	4	3	.571	2.55	29	5	0	60	67	14	27	0	2	1	1	12	2	0	.167	3	21	1	1	0.9	.960
1945			13	8	.619	2.40	34	19	9	165.1	142	23	88	2	3	2	2	51	13	0	.255	7	25	1	2	1.0	.970
1946			2	3	.400	5.79	14	2	0	23.1	28	10	10	0	2	2	1	5	1	0	.200	1	8	0	0	0.6	1.000
6 yrs.			22	21	.512	3.56	116	34	10	351	379	72	161	2	10	7	4	100	18	0	.180	16	79	3	6	0.8	.969
WORLD SERIES																											
1945	CHI	N	0	1	.000	9.00	2	1	0	4	4	1	1	0	0	0	0	0	0	0	—	0	1	0	0	0.5	1.000

Don Prince

PRINCE, DONALD MARK BR TR 6′ 4″ 200 lbs.
B. Apr. 5, 1938, Clarkton, N. C.

Year	Team	Lg	W	L	PCT	ERA	G	GS	CG	IP	H	BB	SO	ShO	Relief Pitching W	Relief Pitching L	Relief Pitching SV	Batting AB	Batting H	Batting HR	BA	PO	A	E	DP	TC/G	FA
1962	CHI	N	0	0	—	0.00	1	0	0	1	0	1	0	0	0	0	0	0	0	0	—	0	1	0	1	1.0	1.000

Jim Proctor

PROCTOR, JAMES ARTHUR BR TR 6′ 165 lbs.
B. Sept. 9, 1935, Brandywine, Md.

Year	Team	Lg	W	L	PCT	ERA	G	GS	CG	IP	H	BB	SO	ShO	Relief Pitching W	Relief Pitching L	Relief Pitching SV	Batting AB	Batting H	Batting HR	BA	PO	A	E	DP	TC/G	FA
1959	DET	A	0	1	.000	16.88	2	1	0	2.2	8	3	0	0	0	1	0	0	0	0	—	0	1	0	0	0.5	1.000

Red Proctor

PROCTOR, NOAH RICHARD BR TR 6′ 1″ 165 lbs.
B. Oct. 27, 1900, Williamsburg, Va. D. Dec. 17, 1954, Richmond, Va.

Year	Team	Lg	W	L	PCT	ERA	G	GS	CG	IP	H	BB	SO	ShO	Relief Pitching W	Relief Pitching L	Relief Pitching SV	Batting AB	Batting H	Batting HR	BA	PO	A	E	DP	TC/G	FA
1923	CHI	A	0	0	—	13.50	2	0	0	4	11	2	0	0	0	0	0	0	0	0	—	0	0	0	0	0.0	.000

George Proeser

PROESER, GEORGE (White Wings) BL TL 5′10″ 190 lbs.
B. May 30, 1864, Cincinnati, Ohio D. Oct. 14, 1941, New Burlington, Ohio.

Year	Team	Lg	W	L	PCT	ERA	G	GS	CG	IP	H	BB	SO	ShO	Relief Pitching W	Relief Pitching L	Relief Pitching SV	Batting AB	Batting H	Batting HR	BA	PO	A	E	DP	TC/G	FA
1888	CLE	AA	3	4	.429	3.81	7	7	7	59	53	30	20	1	0	0	0	*				0	11	2	0	1.9	.846

Mike Proly

PROLY, MICHAEL JAMES BR TR 6′ 185 lbs.
B. Dec. 15, 1950, Jamaica, N. Y.

Year	Team	Lg	W	L	PCT	ERA	G	GS	CG	IP	H	BB	SO	ShO	Relief Pitching W	Relief Pitching L	Relief Pitching SV	Batting AB	Batting H	Batting HR	BA	PO	A	E	DP	TC/G	FA
1976	STL	N	1	0	1.000	3.71	14	0	0	17	21	6	4	0	1	0	0	0	0	0	—	3	3	0	0	0.4	1.000
1978	CHI	A	5	2	.714	2.74	14	6	2	65.2	63	12	19	0	1	0	1	0	0	0	—	1	10	1	0	0.9	.917
1979			3	8	.273	3.89	38	6	0	88	89	40	32	0	3	4	9	0	0	0	—	5	17	1	2	0.6	.957
1980			5	10	.333	3.06	62	3	0	147	136	58	56	0	4	8	8	0	0	0	—	10	29	0	2	0.6	1.000
1981	PHI	N	2	1	.667	3.86	35	2	0	63	66	19	19	0	2	1	2	7	0	0	.000	9	14	1	0	0.7	.958
1982	CHI	N	5	3	.625	2.30	44	1	0	82	77	22	24	0	4	3	1	14	4	0	.286	1	18	0	1	0.4	1.000
1983			1	5	.167	3.58	60	0	0	83	79	38	31	0	1	5	1	11	1	0	.091	6	14	1	0	0.3	.952
7 yrs.			22	29	.431	3.23	267	18	2	545.2	531	195	185	0	16	21	22	32	5	0	.156	35	105	4	5	0.5	.972

Bill Prough

PROUGH, HERSCHEL CLINTON BR TR 6′ 3″ 185 lbs.
B. Nov. 28, 1887, Martle, Ind. D. Dec. 29, 1936, Richmond, Ind.

Year	Team	Lg	W	L	PCT	ERA	G	GS	CG	IP	H	BB	SO	ShO	Relief Pitching W	Relief Pitching L	Relief Pitching SV	Batting AB	Batting H	Batting HR	BA	PO	A	E	DP	TC/G	FA
1912	CIN	N	0	0	—	6.00	1	0	0	3	7	1	1	0	0	0	0	1	0	0	.000	0	0	0	0	0.0	.000

Augie Prudhomme

PRUDHOMME, JOHN OLGUS BR TR 6′ 2″ 186 lbs.
B. Nov. 20, 1902, Frierson, La. D. Oct. 4, 1992, Shreveport, La.

Year	Team	Lg	W	L	PCT	ERA	G	GS	CG	IP	H	BB	SO	ShO	Relief Pitching W	Relief Pitching L	Relief Pitching SV	Batting AB	Batting H	Batting HR	BA	PO	A	E	DP	TC/G	FA
1929	DET	A	1	6	.143	6.22	34	6	2	94	119	53	26	0	0	3	1	21	5	0	.238	3	24	1	3	0.8	.964

Hub Pruett

PRUETT, HUBERT SHELBY (Shucks) BL TL 5′10½″ 165 lbs.
B. Sept. 1, 1900, Malden, Mo. D. Jan. 28, 1982, Ladue, Mo.

Year	Team	Lg	W	L	PCT	ERA	G	GS	CG	IP	H	BB	SO	ShO	Relief Pitching W	Relief Pitching L	Relief Pitching SV	Batting AB	Batting H	Batting HR	BA	PO	A	E	DP	TC/G	FA
1922	STL	A	7	7	.500	2.33	39	8	4	119.2	99	59	70	0	4	4	7	34	5	0	.147	7	37	1	1	1.2	.978
1923			4	7	.364	4.31	32	8	3	104.1	109	64	59	0	1	1	2	23	3	0	.130	2	30	1	1	1.0	.970
1924			3	4	.429	4.57	33	1	0	65	64	42	27	0	3	3	0	15	3	0	.200	6	16	1	0	0.7	.957
1927	PHI	N	7	17	.292	6.05	31	28	12	186	238	89	90	1	0	0	1	60	13	0	.217	9	55	7	1	2.3	.901
1928			2	4	.333	4.54	13	9	4	71.1	78	49	35	0	0	0	0	24	5	0	.208	5	16	3	1	1.8	.875
1930	NY	N	5	4	.556	4.78	45	8	1	135.2	152	63	49	0	4	0	3	37	5	0	.135	7	30	1	1	0.8	.974
1932	BOS	N	1	5	.167	5.14	18	7	4	63	76	30	27	0	0	0	0	19	2	0	.105	5	21	1	0	1.5	.963
7 yrs.			29	48	.377	4.63	211	69	28	745	816	396	357	1	12	8	13	212	36	0	.170	41	205	15	5	1.2	.943

Tex Pruiett

PRUIETT, CHARLES LeROY BL TR
B. Apr. 10, 1883, Osgood, Ind. D. Mar. 6, 1953, Ventura, Calif.

Year	Team	Lg	W	L	PCT	ERA	G	GS	CG	IP	H	BB	SO	ShO	Relief Pitching W	Relief Pitching L	Relief Pitching SV	Batting AB	Batting H	Batting HR	BA	PO	A	E	DP	TC/G	FA
1907	BOS	A	3	11	.214	3.11	35	17	6	173.2	166	59	54	2	0	1	3	51	8	0	.157	7	64	7	3	2.2	.910
1908			1	7	.125	1.99	13	6	1	58.2	55	21	28	1	0	2	2	16	1	0	.063	2	21	3	0	2.0	.885
2 yrs.			4	18	.182	2.83	48	23	7	232.1	221	80	82	3	0	3	5	67	9	0	.134	9	85	10	3	2.2	.904

Troy Puckett

PUCKETT, TROY LEVI BL TR 6′ 2″ 186 lbs.
B. Dec. 10, 1889, Winchester, Ind. D. Apr. 13, 1971, Winchester, Ind.

Year	Team	Lg	W	L	PCT	ERA	G	GS	CG	IP	H	BB	SO	ShO	Relief Pitching W	Relief Pitching L	Relief Pitching SV	Batting AB	Batting H	Batting HR	BA	PO	A	E	DP	TC/G	FA
1911	PHI	N	0	0	—	13.50	1	0	0	2	4	2	1	0	0	0	0	0	0	0	—	0	1	0	0	1.0	1.000

Miguel Puente

PUENTE, MIGUEL ANTONIO BR TR 6′ 160 lbs.
Born Miguel Antonio Puente (Aguilar).
B. May 8, 1948, San Luis Potosi, Mexico.

Year	Team	Lg	W	L	PCT	ERA	G	GS	CG	IP	H	BB	SO	ShO	Relief Pitching W	Relief Pitching L	Relief Pitching SV	Batting AB	Batting H	Batting HR	BA	PO	A	E	DP	TC/G	FA
1970	SF	N	1	3	.250	8.05	6	4	1	19	25	11	14	0	0	1	0	7	0	0	.000	1	4	1	0	1.0	.833

Tim Pugh

PUGH, TIMOTHY DEAN
B. Jan. 26, 1967, Lake Tahoe, Calif.
BR TR 6′ 6″ 225 lbs.

Year	Team		W	L	PCT	ERA	G	GS	CG	IP	H	BB	SO	ShO	Relief Pitching W	Relief Pitching L	Relief Pitching SV	Batting AB	Batting H	Batting HR	BA	PO	A	E	DP	TC/G	FA
1992	CIN	N	4	2	.667	2.58	7	7	0	45.1	47	13	18	0	0	0	0	13	1	0	.077	2	6	0	0	1.1	1.000
1993			10	15	.400	5.26	31	27	3	164.1	200	59	94	1	0	1	0	54	12	0	.222	9	23	1	1	1.1	.970
1994			3	3	.500	6.04	10	9	1	47.2	60	26	24	0	0	0	0	14	5	0	.357	5	7	1	0	1.3	.923
1995			6	5	.545	3.84	28	12	0	98.1	100	32	38	0	1	1	0	28	4	0	.143	10	9	1	0	0.7	.950
4 yrs.			23	25	.479	4.63	76	55	4	355.2	407	130	174	1	1	2	0	109	22	0	.202	26	45	3	1	1.0	.959

Charlie Puleo

PULEO, CHARLES MICHAEL
B. Feb. 7, 1955, Glen Ridge, N. J.
BR TR 6′ 2″ 190 lbs.

Year	Team		W	L	PCT	ERA	G	GS	CG	IP	H	BB	SO	ShO	Relief Pitching W	Relief Pitching L	Relief Pitching SV	Batting AB	Batting H	Batting HR	BA	PO	A	E	DP	TC/G	FA
1981	NY	N	0	0	—	0.00	4	1	0	13	8	8	8	0	0	0	0	2	0	0	.000	1	2	0	0	0.8	1.000
1982			9	9	.500	4.47	36	24	1	171	179	90	98	1	2	1	1	48	6	0	.125	9	43	5	5	1.6	.912
1983	CIN	N	6	12	.333	4.89	27	24	0	143.2	145	91	71	0	0	0	0	50	5	0	.100	11	14	2	1	1.0	.926
1984			1	2	.333	5.73	5	4	0	22	27	15	6	0	0	0	0	5	1	0	.200	0	1	0	0	0.2	1.000
1986	ATL	N	1	2	.333	2.96	5	3	1	24.1	13	12	18	0	0	1	0	6	2	0	.333	0	3	0	0	0.6	1.000
1987			6	8	.429	4.23	35	16	1	123.1	122	40	99	0	2	0	0	28	5	1	.179	6	10	0	0	0.5	1.000
1988			5	5	.500	3.47	53	3	0	106.1	101	47	70	0	5	3	1	13	3	0	.231	5	16	1	0	0.4	.955
1989			1	1	.500	4.66	15	1	0	29	26	16	17	0	1	0	0	1	0	0	.000	2	1	0	0	0.2	1.000
8 yrs.			29	39	.426	4.25	180	76	3	632.2	621	319	387	1	10	5	2	153	22	1	.144	34	90	8	6	0.7	.939

Alfonso Pulido

PULIDO, ALFONSO
Born Alfonso Pulido (Manzo).
B. Jan. 23, 1957, Veracruz, Mexico.
BL TL 5′11″ 170 lbs.

Year	Team		W	L	PCT	ERA	G	GS	CG	IP	H	BB	SO	ShO	Relief Pitching W	Relief Pitching L	Relief Pitching SV	Batting AB	Batting H	Batting HR	BA	PO	A	E	DP	TC/G	FA
1983	PIT	N	0	0	—	9.00	1	1	0	2	4	1	1	0	0	0	0	0	0	0	—	0	0	0	0	0.0	.000
1984			0	0	—	9.00	1	0	0	2	3	1	2	0	0	0	0	0	0	0	—	0	0	0	0	0.0	.000
1986	NY	A	1	1	.500	4.70	10	3	0	30.2	38	9	13	0	0	0	1	0	0	0	—	1	4	0	1	0.5	1.000
3 yrs.			1	1	.500	5.19	12	4	0	34.2	45	11	16	0	0	0	1	0	0	0		1	4	0	1	0.4	1.000

Carlos Pulido

PULIDO, JUAN CARLOS
Born Juan Carlos Pulido (Valera).
B. Aug. 5, 1971, Caracas, Venezuela.
BL TL 6′ 194 lbs.

Year	Team		W	L	PCT	ERA	G	GS	CG	IP	H	BB	SO	ShO	Relief Pitching W	Relief Pitching L	Relief Pitching SV	Batting AB	Batting H	Batting HR	BA	PO	A	E	DP	TC/G	FA
1994	MIN	A	3	7	.300	5.98	19	14	0	84.1	87	40	32	0	0	0	0	0	0	0	—	2	11	1	2	0.7	.929

Bill Pulsipher

PULSIPHER, WILLIAM THOMAS
B. Oct. 9, 1973, Fort Benning, Ga.
BL TL 6′ 3″ 210 lbs.

Year	Team		W	L	PCT	ERA	G	GS	CG	IP	H	BB	SO	ShO	Relief Pitching W	Relief Pitching L	Relief Pitching SV	Batting AB	Batting H	Batting HR	BA	PO	A	E	DP	TC/G	FA
1995	NY	N	5	7	.417	3.98	17	17	2	126.2	122	45	81	0	0	0	0	38	4	0	.105	5	18	0	1	1.4	1.000

Spence Pumpelly

PUMPELLY, SPENCER ARMSTRONG
B. Apr. 11, 1893, Owego, N. Y. D. Dec. 5, 1973, Sayre, Pa.
5′11″ 175 lbs.

Year	Team		W	L	PCT	ERA	G	GS	CG	IP	H	BB	SO	ShO	Relief Pitching W	Relief Pitching L	Relief Pitching SV	Batting AB	Batting H	Batting HR	BA	PO	A	E	DP	TC/G	FA
1925	WAS	A	0	0	—	9.00	1	0	0	1	1	1	0	0	0	0	0	0	0	0	—	0	0	0	0	0.0	.000

Blondie Purcell

PURCELL, WILLIAM ALOYSIUS
B. Mar. 16, 1854, Paterson, N. J. D. Feb. 20, 1912, Trenton, N. J.
Manager 1883.
BR TR 5′ 9½″ 159 lbs.

Year	Team		W	L	PCT	ERA	G	GS	CG	IP	H	BB	SO	ShO	Relief Pitching W	Relief Pitching L	Relief Pitching SV	Batting AB	Batting H	Batting HR	BA	PO	A	E	DP	TC/G	FA
1879	2 teams	SYR N	(22G 4–15)		CIN N	(2G 0–2)																					
″	total		4	17	.190	3.78	24	19	17	197.2	272	21	31	0	1	1	0	327	83	0	.254	98	41	33	0	2.1	.808
1880	CIN	N	3	17	.150	3.21	25	21	21	196	235	32	47	0	0	0	0	325	95	1	.292	88	54	25	1	2.1	.850
1881	BUF	N	4	1	.800	2.77	9	5	5	61.2	62	9	15	0	0	0	0	193	47	0	.244	74	24	29	0	2.4	.772
1882			2	1	.667	4.94	6	3	2	31	44	4	9	0	0	0	0	380	105	2	.276	144	21	35	0	2.3	.825
1883	PHI	N	2	6	.250	*4.39*	11	9	7	80	110	12	30	0	0	0	0	425	114	1	.268	130	146	66	9	3.4	.807
1884			0	0	—	*2.25*	1	0	0	4	3	0	1	0	0	0	0	428	108	1	.252	182	12	28	1	2.1	.874
1885	PHI	AA	0	1	.000	6.00	1	0	0	6	11	2	3	0	0	1	0	391	109	0	.279	97	16	19	1	1.5	.856
1886	BAL	AA	0	0	—	*9.00*	1	0	0	1	1	0	0	0	0	0	0	85	19	0	.224	35	4	6	0	1.6	.867
1887			0	0	—	15.75	1	0	0	4	8	4	2	0	0	0	0	567	142	4	.250	203	18	18	5	1.7	.925
9 yrs.			15	43	.259	3.73	79	57	52	581.1	746	84	138	0	1	2	0	*				1565	382	309	27	2.0	.863

John Purdin

PURDIN, JOHN NOLAN
B. July 16, 1942, Lynx, Ohio.
BR TR 6′ 2″ 185 lbs.

Year	Team		W	L	PCT	ERA	G	GS	CG	IP	H	BB	SO	ShO	Relief Pitching W	Relief Pitching L	Relief Pitching SV	Batting AB	Batting H	Batting HR	BA	PO	A	E	DP	TC/G	FA
1964	LA	N	2	0	1.000	0.56	3	2	1	16	6	6	8	1	0	0	0	5	1	0	.200	0	2	0	0	0.7	1.000
1965			2	1	.667	6.75	11	2	0	22.2	26	13	16	0	2	0	0	3	0	0	.000	1	0	0	0	0.1	1.000
1968			2	3	.400	3.07	35	1	0	55.2	42	21	38	0	2	3	2	6	3	0	.500	2	8	0	0	0.3	1.000
1969			0	0	—	6.19	9	0	0	16	19	12	6	0	0	0	0	2	0	0	.000	1	3	0	0	0.4	1.000
4 yrs.			6	4	.600	3.92	58	5	1	110.1	93	52	68	1	4	3	2	16	4	0	.250	4	13	0	0	0.3	1.000

Bob Purkey

PURKEY, ROBERT THOMAS
B. July 14, 1929, Pittsburgh, Pa.
BR TR 6′ 2″ 175 lbs.

Year	Team		W	L	PCT	ERA	G	GS	CG	IP	H	BB	SO	ShO	Relief Pitching W	Relief Pitching L	Relief Pitching SV	Batting AB	Batting H	Batting HR	BA	PO	A	E	DP	TC/G	FA
1954	PIT	N	3	8	.273	5.07	36	11	0	131.1	145	62	38	0	1	1	0	26	2	0	.077	16	40	0	6	1.6	1.000
1955			2	7	.222	5.32	14	10	2	67.2	77	25	24	0	0	0	1	19	6	1	.316	2	16	1	0	1.4	.947
1956			0	0	—	2.25	2	0	0	4	2	0	1	0	0	0	0	0	0	0	—	0	1	0	0	0.5	1.000
1957			11	14	.440	3.86	48	21	6	179.2	194	38	51	1	5	3	2	45	5	0	.111	13	30	3	3	1.0	.935
1958	CIN	N	17	11	.607	3.60	37	34	17	250	259	49	70	3	0	0	0	81	9	1	.111	10	56	1	2	1.8	.985
1959			13	18	.419	4.25	38	33	9	218	241	43	78	1	2	1	1	66	11	1	.167	19	35	2	1	1.5	.964
1960			17	11	.607	3.60	41	33	11	252.2	259	59	97	1	0	0	0	83	11	0	.133	30	47	1	5	1.9	.987
1961			16	12	.571	3.73	36	34	13	246.1	245	51	116	1	0	0	1	80	8	1	.100	29	69	2	2	2.8	.980
1962			23	5	**.821**	2.81	37	37	18	288.1	260	64	141	2	0	0	0	107	11	2	.103	25	59	4	7	2.4	.955
1963			6	10	.375	3.55	21	21	4	137	143	33	55	1	0	0	0	41	4	0	.098	15	29	3	0	2.2	.936
1964			11	9	.550	3.04	34	25	9	195.2	181	49	78	2	1	1	1	58	3	0	.052	17	44	4	4	1.9	.938
1965	STL	N	10	9	.526	5.79	32	17	3	124.1	148	33	39	1	3	2	2	35	1	0	.029	8	28	1	1	1.2	.973
1966	PIT	N	0	1	.000	1.37	10	0	0	19.2	16	4	5	0	0	1	1	4	0	0	.000	0	10	1	1	1.1	.909
13 yrs.			129	115	.529	3.79	386	276	92	2114.2	2170	510	793	13	12	9	9	645	71	6	.110	184	464	23	32	1.7	.966
WORLD SERIES																											
1961	CIN	N	0	1	.000	1.64	2	1	1	11	6	3	5	0	0	0	0	3	0	0	.000	4	3	1	0	4.0	.875

Oscar Purner

PURNER, OSCAR E.
B. 1873, Washington, D. C.

Year	Team	W	L	PCT	ERA	G	GS	CG	IP	H	BB	SO	ShO	Relief Pitching W	Relief Pitching L	Relief Pitching SV	Batting AB	Batting H	Batting HR	BA	PO	A	E	DP	TC/G	FA
1895	WAS N	0	0	—	9.00	1	0	0	2	4	3	0	0	0	0	0	1	0	0	.000	0	0	0	0	0.0	.000

Ambrose Puttmann

PUTTMANN, AMBROSE NICHOLAS (Putt)
B. Sept. 9, 1880, Cincinnati, Ohio D. June 21, 1936, Jamaica, N. Y.
TL 6′ 4″ 185 lbs.

Year	Team	W	L	PCT	ERA	G	GS	CG	IP	H	BB	SO	ShO	Relief Pitching W	Relief Pitching L	Relief Pitching SV	Batting AB	Batting H	Batting HR	BA	PO	A	E	DP	TC/G	FA
1903	NY A	2	0	1.000	0.95	3	2	1	19	16	4	8	0	0	0	0	7	1	0	.143	0	12	2	0	4.7	.857
1904		2	0	1.000	2.74	9	3	2	49.1	40	17	26	1	0	0	0	18	5	0	.278	2	17	1	0	2.2	.950
1905		2	7	.222	4.27	17	9	5	86.1	79	37	39	1	1	0	1	32	10	0	.313	3	28	5	0	2.1	.861
1906	STL N	1	2	.333	5.30	4	4	0	18.2	23	9	12	0	0	0	0	6	2	0	.333	1	6	0	0	1.8	1.000
4 yrs.		7	9	.438	3.58	33	18	8	173.1	158	67	85	2	1	0	1	63	18	0	.286	6	63	8	0	2.3	.896

John Pyecha

PYECHA, JOHN NICHOLAS
B. Nov. 25, 1931, Aliquippa, Pa.
BR TR 6′ 5″ 200 lbs.

Year	Team	W	L	PCT	ERA	G	GS	CG	IP	H	BB	SO	ShO	Relief Pitching W	Relief Pitching L	Relief Pitching SV	Batting AB	Batting H	Batting HR	BA	PO	A	E	DP	TC/G	FA
1954	CHI N	0	1	.000	10.13	1	0	0	2.2	4	2	2	0	0	1	0	1	0	0	.000	0	0	0	0	0.0	.000

Ewald Pyle

PYLE, HERBERT EWALD (Lefty)
B. Aug. 27, 1910, St. Louis, Mo.
BL TL 6′½″ 175 lbs.

Year	Team	W	L	PCT	ERA	G	GS	CG	IP	H	BB	SO	ShO	Relief Pitching W	Relief Pitching L	Relief Pitching SV	Batting AB	Batting H	Batting HR	BA	PO	A	E	DP	TC/G	FA
1939	STL A	0	2	.000	12.96	6	1	0	8.1	17	11	5	0	0	1	0	2	0	0	.000	1	3	0	1	0.7	1.000
1942		0	0	—	6.75	2	0	0	5.1	6	4	1	0	0	0	0	3	0	0	.000	0	0	0	0	0.0	.000
1943	WAS A	4	8	.333	4.09	18	11	2	72.2	70	45	25	0	0	2	1	20	2	0	.100	3	13	2	0	1.0	.889
1944	NY N	7	10	.412	4.34	31	21	3	164	152	68	79	1	1	1	0	51	8	0	.157	10	28	1	2	1.3	.974
1945	2 teams NY N (6G 0–0) BOS N (4G 0–1)																									
″	total	0	1	.000	10.35	10	3	0	20	32	22	12	0	0	1	0	8	2	0	.250	0	5	0	1	0.5	1.000
5 yrs.		11	21	.344	5.03	67	36	5	270.1	277	150	122	1	1	5	1	84	12	0	.143	14	49	3	4	1.0	.955

Harlan Pyle

PYLE, HARLAN ALBERT (Firpo)
B. Nov. 29, 1905, Burchard, Neb. D. Jan. 13, 1993, Beatrice, Neb.
BR TR 6′ 2″ 180 lbs.

Year	Team	W	L	PCT	ERA	G	GS	CG	IP	H	BB	SO	ShO	Relief Pitching W	Relief Pitching L	Relief Pitching SV	Batting AB	Batting H	Batting HR	BA	PO	A	E	DP	TC/G	FA
1928	CIN N	0	0	—	20.25	2	1	0	1.1	1	4	1	0	0	0	0	1	0	0	.000	0	0	0	0	0.0	.000

Shadow Pyle

PYLE, HARRY THOMAS
B. Nov. 29, 1861, Reading, Pa. D. Dec. 26, 1908, Reading, Pa.
TL 5′ 8″ 136 lbs.

Year	Team	W	L	PCT	ERA	G	GS	CG	IP	H	BB	SO	ShO	Relief Pitching W	Relief Pitching L	Relief Pitching SV	Batting AB	Batting H	Batting HR	BA	PO	A	E	DP	TC/G	FA
1884	PHI N	0	1	.000	*4.00*	1	1	1	9	9	6	4	0	0	0	0	4	0	0	.000	0	1	0	0	1.0	1.000
1887	CHI N	1	3	.250	4.72	4	4	3	26.2	32	21	5	0	0	0	0	16	3	1	.188	1	9	1	0	2.2	.909
2 yrs.		1	4	.200	4.54	5	5	4	35.2	41	27	9	0	0	0	0	20	3	1	.150	1	10	1	0	2.0	.917

Tom Qualters

QUALTERS, THOMAS FRANCIS (Money Bags)
B. Apr. 1, 1935, McKeesport, Pa.
BR TR 6′½″ 190 lbs.

Year	Team	W	L	PCT	ERA	G	GS	CG	IP	H	BB	SO	ShO	Relief Pitching W	Relief Pitching L	Relief Pitching SV	Batting AB	Batting H	Batting HR	BA	PO	A	E	DP	TC/G	FA
1953	PHI N	0	0	—	162.00	1	0	0	0.1	4	1	0	0	0	0	0	0	0	0	—	0	0	0	0	0.0	.000
1957		0	0	—	8.10	6	0	0	6.2	12	4	6	0	0	0	0	0	0	0	—	1	2	0	1	0.5	1.000
1958	2 teams PHI N (1G 0–0) CHI A (26G 0–0)																									
″	total	0	0		4.20	27	0	0	45	47	21	14	0	0	0	0	2	0	0	.000	2	11	0	2	0.5	1.000
3 yrs.		0	0		5.71	34	0	0	52	63	26	20	0	0	0	0	2	0	0	.000	3	13	0	3	0.5	1.000

Paul Quantrill

QUANTRILL, PAUL JOHN
B. Nov. 3, 1968, London, Ont., Canada.
BL TR 6′ 1″ 175 lbs.

Year	Team	W	L	PCT	ERA	G	GS	CG	IP	H	BB	SO	ShO	Relief Pitching W	Relief Pitching L	Relief Pitching SV	Batting AB	Batting H	Batting HR	BA	PO	A	E	DP	TC/G	FA
1992	BOS A	2	3	.400	2.19	27	0	0	49.1	55	15	24	0	2	3	1	0	0	0	—	4	6	2	0	0.4	.833
1993		6	12	.333	3.91	49	14	1	138	151	44	66	1	4	5	1	0	0	0	—	4	18	1	3	0.5	.957
1994	2 teams BOS A (17G 1–1) PHI N (18G 2–2)																									
″	total	3	3	.500	4.92	35	1	0	53	64	15	28	0	3	2	1	3	0	0	.000	2	8	1	1	0.3	.909
1995	PHI N	11	12	.478	4.67	33	29	0	179.1	212	44	103	0	1	0	0	57	6	0	.105	9	32	1	2	1.3	.976
4 yrs.		22	30	.423	4.16	144	44	1	419.2	482	118	221	1	10	10	3	60	6	0	.100	19	64	5	6	0.6	.943

Bill Quarles

QUARLES, WILLIAM H.
B. 1869, Petersburg, Va. D. Mar. 25, 1897, Petersburg, Va.
6′ 3″

Year	Team	W	L	PCT	ERA	G	GS	CG	IP	H	BB	SO	ShO	Relief Pitching W	Relief Pitching L	Relief Pitching SV	Batting AB	Batting H	Batting HR	BA	PO	A	E	DP	TC/G	FA
1891	WAS AA	1	1	.500	8.18	3	2	2	22	32	12	10	0	0	0	0	11	0	0	.000	2	2	0	0	1.3	1.000
1893	BOS N	2	1	.667	4.67	3	3	3	27	31	5	6	0	0	0	0	9	2	0	.222	0	6	1	0	2.3	.857
2 yrs.		3	2	.600	6.24	6	5	5	49	63	17	16	0	0	0	0	20	2	0	.100	2	8	1	0	1.8	.909

Mel Queen

QUEEN, MELVIN DOUGLAS
Son of Mel Queen.
B. Mar. 26, 1942, Johnson City, N. Y.
BL TR 6′ 1″ 189 lbs.

Year	Team	W	L	PCT	ERA	G	GS	CG	IP	H	BB	SO	ShO	Relief Pitching W	Relief Pitching L	Relief Pitching SV	Batting AB	Batting H	Batting HR	BA	PO	A	E	DP	TC/G	FA
1966	CIN N	0	0	—	6.43	7	0	0	7	11	6	9	0	0	0	1	55	7	0	.127	42	0	1	0	2.2	.977
1967		14	8	.636	2.76	31	24	6	195.2	155	52	154	2	3	1	0	81	17	0	.210	15	17	2	2	1.1	.941
1968		0	1	.000	5.89	5	4	0	18.1	25	6	20	0	0	0	0	8	1	0	.125	0	4	0	0	0.8	1.000
1969		1	0	1.000	2.25	2	2	0	12	7	3	7	0	0	0	0	6	1	0	.167	0	1	0	0	0.5	1.000
1970	CAL A	3	6	.333	4.20	34	3	0	60	58	28	44	0	2	5	9	16	4	0	.250	1	5	0	0	0.2	1.000
1971		2	2	.500	1.77	44	0	0	66	49	29	53	0	2	2	4	8	0	0	.000	1	8	1	0	0.2	.900
1972		0	0	—	4.35	17	0	0	31	31	19	19	0	0	0	0	2	0	0	.000	1	4	0	0	0.3	1.000
7 yrs.		20	17	.541	3.14	140	33	6	390	336	143	306	2	7	8	14	*				96	41	4	2	0.7	.972

Mel Queen

QUEEN, MELVIN JOSEPH
Father of Mel Queen.
B. Mar. 4, 1918, Maxwell, Pa. D. Apr. 4, 1982, Fort Smith, Ark.
BR TR 6′½″ 204 lbs.

Year	Team	W	L	PCT	ERA	G	GS	CG	IP	H	BB	SO	ShO	Relief Pitching W	Relief Pitching L	Relief Pitching SV	Batting AB	Batting H	Batting HR	BA	PO	A	E	DP	TC/G	FA
1942	NY A	1	0	1.000	0.00	4	0	0	5.2	6	3	0	0	1	0	0	0	0	0	—	0	2	0	0	0.5	1.000
1944		6	3	.667	3.31	10	10	4	81.2	68	34	30	1	0	0	0	31	6	0	.194	1	7	0	0	0.8	1.000
1946		1	1	.500	6.53	14	3	1	30.1	40	21	26	0	0	0	0	7	1	0	.143	2	2	0	0	0.3	1.000
1947	2 teams NY A (5G 0–0) PIT N (14G 3–7)																									
″	total	3	7	.300	4.46	19	12	2	80.2	79	55	36	0	0	0	0	27	2	0	.074	5	7	1	1	0.7	.923
1948	PIT N	4	4	.500	6.65	25	8	0	66.1	82	40	34	0	2	0	1	17	1	0	.059	6	8	1	0	0.6	.933
1950		5	14	.263	5.98	33	21	4	120.1	135	73	76	1	0	0	0	35	2	0	.057	9	13	0	0	0.7	1.000
1951		7	9	.438	4.44	39	21	4	168.1	149	99	123	1	0	1	0	47	5	0	.106	4	12	1	2	0.4	.941
1952		0	2	.000	29.70	2	2	0	3.1	8	4	3	0	0	0	0	0	0	0	—	0	0	0	0	0.0	.000
8 yrs.		27	40	.403	5.09	146	77	15	556.2	567	329	328	3	3	1	1	164	17	0	.104	27	51	3	3	0.6	.963

Ed Quick

QUICK, EDWIN S. TR 5'11"
Born Edwin S. Stillwell.
B. Dec. 1881, Baltimore, Md. D. June 19, 1913, Rocky Ford, Colo.

Year	Team	W	L	PCT	ERA	G	GS	CG	IP	H	BB	SO	ShO	Relief W	Relief L	Relief SV	AB	H	HR	BA	PO	A	E	DP	TC/G	FA
1903	NY A	0	0	—	9.00	1	1	0	2	5	1	0	0	0	0	0	1	0	0	.000	0	1	0	0	1.0	1.000

Frank Quinn

QUINN, FRANK WILLIAM BR TR 6' 2" 180 lbs.
B. Nov. 27, 1927, Springfield, Mass. D. Jan. 11, 1993, Boynton Beach, Fla.

Year	Team	W	L	PCT	ERA	G	GS	CG	IP	H	BB	SO	ShO	Relief W	Relief L	Relief SV	AB	H	HR	BA	PO	A	E	DP	TC/G	FA
1949	BOS A	0	0	—	2.86	8	0	0	22	18	9	4	0	0	0	0	6	1	0	.167	3	3	0	0	0.8	1.000
1950		0	0	—	9.00	1	0	0	2	2	1	0	0	0	0	0	0	0	0	—	1	1	0	0	2.0	1.000
2 yrs.		0	0		3.38	9	0	0	24	20	10	4	0	0	0	0	6	1	0	.167	4	4	0	0	0.9	1.000

Jack Quinn

QUINN, JOHN PICUS BR TR 6' 196 lbs.
Born John Quinn Picus.
B. July 5, 1883, Jeanesville, Pa. D. Apr. 17, 1946, Pottsville, Pa.

Year	Team	W	L	PCT	ERA	G	GS	CG	IP	H	BB	SO	ShO	Relief W	Relief L	Relief SV	AB	H	HR	BA	PO	A	E	DP	TC/G	FA
1909	NY A	9	5	.643	1.97	23	11	8	118.2	110	24	36	0	**4**	0	1	45	7	0	.156	5	52	2	3	2.6	.966
1910		18	12	.600	2.36	35	31	20	236.2	214	58	82	0	3	0	0	82	19	0	.232	8	111	3	5	3.5	.975
1911		8	10	.444	3.76	40	16	7	174.2	203	41	71	0	4	2	2	61	10	1	.164	4	65	2	2	1.8	.972
1912		5	7	.417	5.79	18	11	7	102.2	139	23	47	0	2	0	0	39	8	0	.205	4	39	1	0	2.4	.977
1913	BOS N	4	3	.571	2.40	8	7	6	56.1	55	7	33	1	0	0	0	20	4	0	.200	0	24	0	1	3.0	1.000
1914	BAL F	26	14	.650	2.60	46	42	27	342.2	**335**	65	164	4	2	1	1	121	33	2	.273	19	104	8	1	2.7	.939
1915		9	**22**	.290	3.45	44	31	21	273.2	289	63	118	0	2	2	1	110	29	0	.264	10	98	3	1	2.5	.973
1918	CHI A	5	1	.833	2.29	6	5	5	51	38	7	22	0	1	0	0	18	4	0	.222	30	13	0	1	7.2	1.000
1919	NY A	15	14	.517	2.63	38	31	18	264	242	65	97	4	3	1	0	91	19	0	.209	6	79	4	2	2.3	.955
1920		18	10	.643	3.20	41	31	16	253.1	271	48	101	2	1	0	3	88	8	2	.091	14	75	5	1	2.3	.947
1921		8	7	.533	3.48	33	13	6	129.1	158	32	44	0	3	2	0	41	9	1	.220	2	33	1	2	1.1	.972
1922	BOS A	13	15	.464	3.48	40	32	16	256	263	59	67	4	1	3	0	91	9	1	.099	12	89	1	2	2.5	.990
1923		13	17	.433	3.89	42	28	16	243	302	53	71	1	2	2	7	80	18	0	.225	11	59	3	1	1.7	.959
1924		12	13	.480	3.20	43	25	13	227.2	237	51	64	2	3	0	7	77	14	0	.182	9	73	3	3	2.0	.965
1925	2 teams BOS A (19G 7–8) PHI A (18G 6–3)																									
"	total	13	11	.542	4.13	37	28	12	204.2	259	42	43	0	1	2	0	63	6	0	.095	12	67	2	3	2.2	.975
1926	PHI A	10	11	.476	3.41	31	21	8	163.2	191	36	58	3	1	2	1	46	8	0	.174	8	47	4	3	1.9	.932
1927		15	10	.600	3.17	34	25	11	207.1	211	37	43	3	1	2	1	66	6	0	.091	4	47	0	2	1.5	1.000
1928		18	7	.720	2.90	31	28	18	211.1	239	34	43	4	0	0	1	79	13	0	.165	7	55	1	2	2.0	.984
1929		11	9	.550	3.97	35	18	7	161	182	39	41	0	4	2	2	60	8	0	.133	3	38	1	1	1.2	.976
1930		9	7	.563	4.42	35	7	0	89.2	109	22	28	0	8	3	6	34	9	1	.265	1	29	0	2	0.9	1.000
1931	BKN N	5	4	.556	2.66	39	1	0	64.1	65	24	25	0	5	3	**15**	15	3	0	.200	0	17	1	2	0.5	.944
1932		3	7	.300	3.30	42	0	0	87.1	102	24	28	0	3	7	**8**	20	4	0	.200	1	20	0	0	0.5	1.000
1933	CIN N	0	1	.000	4.02	14	0	0	15.2	20	5	3	0	0	1	1	1	0	0	.000	1	6	0	0	0.5	1.000
23 yrs.		247	217	.532	3.27	755	442	242	3934.2	4234	859	1329	28	54	35	57	1348	248	8	.184	171	1240	45	40	1.9	.969
WORLD SERIES																										
1921	NY A	0	1	.000	9.82	1	0	0	3.2	8	2	2	0	0	1	0	2	0	0	.000	0	1	0	1	1.0	1.000
1929	PHI A	0	0	—	9.00	1	1	0	5	7	2	2	0	0	0	0	2	0	0	.000	0	0	0	0	0.0	.000
1930		0	0	—	4.50	1	0	0	2	3	0	1	0	0	0	0	0	0	0	—	0	1	0	0	1.0	1.000
3 yrs.		0	1	.000	8.44	3	1	0	10.2	18	4	5	0	0	1	0	4	0	0	.000	0	2	0	1	0.7	1.000

Tad Quinn

QUINN, CLARENCE CARR TR 6' 1" 210 lbs.
B. Sept. 21, 1882, Torrington, Conn. D. Aug. 7, 1946, Westbury, Conn.

Year	Team	W	L	PCT	ERA	G	GS	CG	IP	H	BB	SO	ShO	Relief W	Relief L	Relief SV	AB	H	HR	BA	PO	A	E	DP	TC/G	FA
1902	PHI A	0	1	.000	4.50	1	1	1	8	12	1	3	0	0	0	0	3	0	0	.000	0	1	1	0	2.0	.500
1903		0	0	—	5.00	2	0	0	9	11	5	1	0	0	0	0	3	2	0	.667	1	5	0	0	3.0	1.000
2 yrs.		0	1	.000	4.76	3	1	1	17	23	6	4	0	0	0	0	6	2	0	.333	1	6	1	0	2.7	.875

Wimpy Quinn

QUINN, WELLINGTON HUNT BR TR 6' 2" 187 lbs.
B. May 12, 1918, Birmingham, Ala. D. Sept. 1, 1954, Santa Monica, Calif.

Year	Team	W	L	PCT	ERA	G	GS	CG	IP	H	BB	SO	ShO	Relief W	Relief L	Relief SV	AB	H	HR	BA	PO	A	E	DP	TC/G	FA
1941	CHI N	0	0	—	7.20	3	0	0	5	3	3	2	0	0	0	0	2	1	0	.500	1	0	0	0	0.3	1.000

Luis Quintana

QUINTANA, LUIS JOAQUIN BL TL 6' 2" 175 lbs.
Born Luis Joaquin Quintana (Santos).
B. Dec. 25, 1951, Vega Baja, Puerto Rico.

Year	Team	W	L	PCT	ERA	G	GS	CG	IP	H	BB	SO	ShO	Relief W	Relief L	Relief SV	AB	H	HR	BA	PO	A	E	DP	TC/G	FA
1974	CAL A	2	1	.667	4.15	18	0	0	13	17	14	11	0	2	1	0	0	0	0	—	0	1	0	0	0.1	1.000
1975		0	2	.000	6.43	4	0	0	7	13	6	5	0	0	2	0	0	0	0	—	0	0	0	0	0.0	.000
2 yrs.		2	3	.400	4.95	22	0	0	20	30	20	16	0	2	3	0	0	0	0		0	1	0	0	0.0	1.000

Art Quirk

QUIRK, ARTHUR LINCOLN BR TL 5'11" 170 lbs.
B. Apr. 11, 1938, Providence, R. I.

Year	Team	W	L	PCT	ERA	G	GS	CG	IP	H	BB	SO	ShO	Relief W	Relief L	Relief SV	AB	H	HR	BA	PO	A	E	DP	TC/G	FA
1962	BAL A	2	2	.500	5.93	7	5	0	27.1	36	18	18	0	0	0	0	7	1	0	.143	2	7	0	0	1.3	1.000
1963	WAS A	1	0	1.000	4.29	7	3	0	21	23	8	12	0	0	0	0	4	1	0	.250	1	3	1	0	0.7	.800
2 yrs.		3	2	.600	5.21	14	8	0	48.1	59	26	30	0	0	0	0	11	2	0	.182	3	10	1	0	1.0	.929

Dan Quisenberry

QUISENBERRY, DANIEL RAYMOND (Quiz) BR TR 6' 2" 170 lbs.
B. Feb. 7, 1953, Santa Monica, Calif.

Year	Team	W	L	PCT	ERA	G	GS	CG	IP	H	BB	SO	ShO	Relief W	Relief L	Relief SV	AB	H	HR	BA	PO	A	E	DP	TC/G	FA
1979	KC A	3	2	.600	3.15	32	0	0	40	42	7	13	0	3	2	5	0	0	0	—	0	10	1	2	0.3	.909
1980		12	7	.632	3.09	**75**	0	0	128	129	27	37	0	12	7	**33**	0	0	0	—	17	29	2	4	0.6	.958
1981		1	4	.200	1.74	40	0	0	62	59	15	20	0	1	4	18	0	0	0	—	8	23	1	1	0.8	.969
1982		9	7	.563	2.57	72	0	0	136.2	126	12	46	0	9	7	**35**	0	0	0	—	18	46	2	3	0.9	.970
1983		5	3	.625	1.94	**69**	0	0	139	118	11	48	0	5	3	**45**	0	0	0	—	8	30	3	1	0.6	.927
1984		6	3	.667	2.64	72	0	0	129.1	121	12	41	0	6	3	**44**	0	0	0	—	15	29	0	1	0.6	1.000
1985		8	9	.471	2.37	**84**	0	0	129	142	16	54	0	8	9	**37**	0	0	0	—	8	24	2	2	0.4	.941
1986		3	7	.300	2.77	62	0	0	81.1	92	24	36	0	3	7	12	0	0	0	—	9	19	1	3	0.5	.966
1987		4	1	.800	2.76	47	0	0	49	58	10	17	0	4	1	8	0	0	0	—	6	13	0	3	0.4	1.000
1988	2 teams KC A (20G 0–1) STL N (33G 2–0)																									
"	total	2	1	.667	5.12	53	0	0	63.1	86	11	28	0	2	1	1	1	0	0	.000	1	18	1	1	0.4	.950

Dan Quisenberry *continued*

Year	Team	Lg	W	L	PCT	ERA	G	GS	CG	IP	H	BB	SO	ShO	Relief Pitching W	Relief Pitching L	Relief Pitching SV	Batting AB	Batting H	Batting HR	BA	PO	A	E	DP	TC/G	FA
1989	STL	N	3	1	.750	2.64	63	0	0	78.1	78	14	37	0	3	1	6	4	1	0	.250	7	22	0	1	0.5	1.000
1990	SF	N	0	1	.000	13.50	5	0	0	6.2	13	3	2	0	0	1	0	1	0	0	.000	0	1	0	0	0.2	1.000
12 yrs.			56	46	.549	2.76	674	0	0	1042.2	1064	162	379	0	56	46	244	6	1	0	.167	97	264	13	22	0.6	.965
																	10th										
DIVISIONAL PLAYOFF SERIES																											
1981	KC	A	0	0	—	0.00	1	0	0	1	1	0	0	0	0	0	0	0	0	0	—	0	0	0	0	0.0	.000
LEAGUE CHAMPIONSHIP SERIES																											
1980	KC	A	1	0	1.000	0.00	2	0	0	4.2	4	2	1	0	1	0	1	0	0	0	—	1	0	0	0	0.5	1.000
1984			0	1	.000	3.00	1	0	0	3	2	1	1	0	0	1	0	0	0	0	—	1	1	0	0	2.0	1.000
1985			0	1	.000	3.86	4	0	0	4.2	7	0	3	0	0	1	1	0	0	0	—	1	1	0	0	0.5	1.000
3 yrs.			1	2	.333	2.19	7	0	0	12.1	13	3	5	0	1	2	2	0	0	0		3	2	0	0	0.7	1.000
WORLD SERIES																											
1980	KC	A	1	2	.333	5.23	6	0	0	10.1	10	3	0	0	1	2	1	0	0	0	—	1	1	0	0	0.3	1.000
1985			1	0	1.000	2.08	4	0	0	4.1	5	3	3	0	1	0	0	0	0	0	—	1	1	0	0	0.5	1.000
2 yrs.			2	2	.500	4.30	10	0	0	14.2	15	6	3	0	2	2	1	0	0	0		2	2	0	0	0.4	1.000

Charlie Rabe

RABE, CHARLES HENRY
B. May 6, 1932, Boyce, Tex.
BL TL 6′ 1″ 180 lbs.

Year	Team	Lg	W	L	PCT	ERA	G	GS	CG	IP	H	BB	SO	ShO	Relief Pitching W	Relief Pitching L	Relief Pitching SV	Batting AB	Batting H	Batting HR	BA	PO	A	E	DP	TC/G	FA
1957	CIN	N	0	1	.000	2.16	2	1	0	8.1	5	0	6	0	0	0	0	2	0	0	.000	0	0	0	0	0.0	.000
1958			0	3	.000	4.34	9	1	0	18.2	25	9	10	0	0	2	0	4	0	0	.000	1	5	0	0	0.7	1.000
2 yrs.			0	4	.000	3.67	11	2	0	27	30	9	16	0	0	2	0	6	0	0	.000	1	5	0	0	0.5	1.000

Steve Rachunok

RACHUNOK, STEPHEN STEPANOVICH (The Mad Russian)
B. Dec. 5, 1916, Rittman, Ohio
BR TR 6′ 3½″ 200 lbs.

Year	Team	Lg	W	L	PCT	ERA	G	GS	CG	IP	H	BB	SO	ShO	Relief Pitching W	Relief Pitching L	Relief Pitching SV	Batting AB	Batting H	Batting HR	BA	PO	A	E	DP	TC/G	FA
1940	BKN	N	0	1	.000	4.50	2	1	1	10	9	5	10	0	0	0	0	2	0	0	.000	0	3	0	0	1.5	1.000

Mike Raczka

RACZKA, MICHAEL
B. Nov. 16, 1962, New Britain, Conn.
BL TL 6′ 2″ 180 lbs.

Year	Team	Lg	W	L	PCT	ERA	G	GS	CG	IP	H	BB	SO	ShO	Relief Pitching W	Relief Pitching L	Relief Pitching SV	Batting AB	Batting H	Batting HR	BA	PO	A	E	DP	TC/G	FA
1992	OAK	A	0	0	—	8.53	8	0	0	6.1	8	5	2	0	0	0	0	0	0	0	—	1	0	0	0	0.1	1.000

Dick Radatz

RADATZ, RICHARD RAYMOND (The Monster)
B. Apr. 2, 1937, Detroit, Mich.
BR TR 6′ 6″ 230 lbs.

Year	Team	Lg	W	L	PCT	ERA	G	GS	CG	IP	H	BB	SO	ShO	Relief Pitching W	Relief Pitching L	Relief Pitching SV	Batting AB	Batting H	Batting HR	BA	PO	A	E	DP	TC/G	FA
1962	BOS	A	9	6	.600	2.24	**62**	0	0	124.2	95	40	144	0	**9**	6	**24**	31	3	0	.097	5	8	1	0	0.2	.929
1963			15	6	.714	1.97	66	0	0	132.1	94	51	162	0	**15**	6	25	29	2	0	.069	4	9	2	0	0.2	.867
1964			16	9	.640	2.29	79	0	0	157	103	58	181	0	**16**	**9**	**29**	37	6	0	.162	5	11	2	0	0.2	.889
1965			9	11	.450	3.91	63	0	0	124.1	104	53	121	0	9	**11**	22	27	5	1	.185	5	14	1	1	0.3	.950
1966	2 teams	BOS A (16G 0–2) CLE A (39G 0–3)																									
″	total		0	5	.000	4.64	55	0	0	75.2	73	45	68	0	0	5	14	11	1	0	.091	1	5	1	0	0.1	.857
1967	2 teams	CLE A (3G 0–0) CHI N (20G 1–0)																									
″	total		1	0	1.000	6.49	23	0	0	26.1	17	26	19	0	1	0	5	4	1	0	.250	2	2	0	0	0.2	1.000
1969	2 teams	DET A (11G 2–2) MON N (22G 0–4)																									
″	total		2	6	.250	4.89	33	0	0	53.1	46	23	50	0	2	6	3	6	1	0	.167	3	6	0	0	0.3	1.000
7 yrs.			52	43	.547	3.13	381	0	0	693.2	532	296	745	0	52	43	122	145	19	1	.131	25	55	7	1	0.2	.920

George Radbourn

RADBOURN, GEORGE B. (Dordy)
B. Apr. 8, 1856, Bloomington, Ill. D. Jan. 1, 1904, Bloomington, Ill.
160 lbs.

Year	Team	Lg	W	L	PCT	ERA	G	GS	CG	IP	H	BB	SO	ShO	Relief Pitching W	Relief Pitching L	Relief Pitching SV	Batting AB	Batting H	Batting HR	BA	PO	A	E	DP	TC/G	FA
1883	DET	N	1	2	.333	*6.55*	3	3	2	22	38	7	2	0	0	0	0	12	2	0	.167	2	4	0	0	1.5	1.000

Old Hoss Radbourn

RADBOURN, CHARLES GARDNER
B. Dec. 11, 1854, Rochester, N. Y. D. Feb. 5, 1897, Bloomington, Ill.
Hall of Fame 1939.
BR TR 5′ 9″ 168 lbs.
BB 1886

Year	Team	Lg	W	L	PCT	ERA	G	GS	CG	IP	H	BB	SO	ShO	Relief Pitching W	Relief Pitching L	Relief Pitching SV	Batting AB	Batting H	Batting HR	BA	PO	A	E	DP	TC/G	FA
1881	PRO	N	25	11	**.694**	*2.43*	41	36	34	325.1	309	64	117	3	**1**	**1**	0	270	59	0	.219	15	16	3	2	5.7	.912
1882			33	19	.635	*2.09*	55	52	51	474	429	51	**201**	**6**	**1**	0	0	326	78	1	.239	71	105	16	5	2.2	.917
1883			**49**	25	.662	*2.05*	**76**	68	66	632.1	563	56	315	4	3	**2**	1	381	108	3	.283	74	142	22	8	2.4	.908
1884			**60**	12	**.833**	***1.38***	**75**	**73**	**73**	**678.2**	528	98	**441**	11	**1**	0	1	361	83	1	.230	69	131	25	4	2.5	.889
1885			28	21	.571	*2.20*	49	49	49	445.2	423	83	154	2	0	0	0	249	58	0	.233	40	122	22	9	2.7	.880
1886	BOS	N	27	31	.466	*3.00*	58	58	57	509.1	521	111	218	3	0	0	0	253	60	2	.237	39	107	12	8	2.7	.924
1887			24	23	.511	4.55	50	50	48	425	505	**133**	87	1	0	0	0	175	40	1	.229	15	69	16	3	1.9	.840
1888			7	16	.304	2.87	24	24	24	207	187	45	64	1	0	0	0	79	17	0	.215	14	37	6	1	2.4	.895
1889			20	11	.645	3.67	33	31	28	277	282	72	99	1	1	0	0	122	23	1	.189	19	58	2	6	2.2	.975
1890	BOS	P	27	12	.692	3.31	41	38	36	343	352	100	80	1	1	1	0	154	39	0	.253	16	99	8	4	2.7	.935
1891	CIN	N	11	13	.458	4.25	26	24	23	218	236	62	54	2	0	1	0	96	17	0	.177	9	40	7	1	1.9	.875
11 yrs.			311	194	.616	2.67	528	503	489	4535.1	4335	875	1830	35	8	5	2	*				438	1047	169	59	2.5	.898
									7th																		

Roy Radebaugh

RADEBAUGH, ROY
B. Feb. 22, 1884, Champaign, Ill. D. Jan. 17, 1945, Cedar Rapids, Iowa.
BR TR 5′ 7″ 160 lbs.

Year	Team	Lg	W	L	PCT	ERA	G	GS	CG	IP	H	BB	SO	ShO	Relief Pitching W	Relief Pitching L	Relief Pitching SV	Batting AB	Batting H	Batting HR	BA	PO	A	E	DP	TC/G	FA
1911	STL	N	0	0	—	2.70	2	1	0	10	6	4	1	0	0	0	0	3	0	0	.000	0	4	0	0	2.0	1.000

Drew Rader

RADER, DREW LEON (Lefty)
B. May 14, 1901, Elmira, N. Y. D. June 5, 1975, Catskill, N. Y.
BR TL 6′ 190 lbs.

Year	Team	Lg	W	L	PCT	ERA	G	GS	CG	IP	H	BB	SO	ShO	Relief Pitching W	Relief Pitching L	Relief Pitching SV	Batting AB	Batting H	Batting HR	BA	PO	A	E	DP	TC/G	FA
1921	PIT	N	0	0	—	0.00	1	0	0	2	2	0	0	0	0	0	0	1	0	0	.000	0	0	0	0	0.0	.000

Paul Radford

RADFORD, PAUL REVERE
B. Oct. 14, 1861, Roxbury, Mass. D. Feb. 21, 1945, Boston, Mass.
BR TR 5′ 6″ 148 lbs.

Year	Team	Lg	W	L	PCT	ERA	G	GS	CG	IP	H	BB	SO	ShO	Relief Pitching W	Relief Pitching L	Relief Pitching SV	Batting AB	Batting H	Batting HR	BA	PO	A	E	DP	TC/G	FA
1884	PRO	N	0	2	.000	*7.62*	2	2	1	13	27	3	2	0	0	0	0	355	70	1	.197	86	16	20	2	1.7	.836
1885			0	2	.000	*7.85*	3	2	2	18.1	34	8	3	0	0	0	0	371	90	0	.243	156	73	40	7	2.5	.851
1887	NY	AA	0	0	—	*18.00*	2	0	0	5	15	3	4	0	0	0	0	486	129	4	.265	179	136	46	13	2.9	.873
1890	CLE	P	0	0	—	3.60	1	0	0	5	7	1	3	0	0	0	0	466	136	2	.292	226	294	89	36	4.6	.854
1891	BOS	AA	0	0	—	0.00	1	0	0	1	0	0	0	0	0	0	0	456	118	0	.259	239	455	71	52	5.6	.907
1893	WAS	N	0	0	—	18.00	1	0	0	1	2	2	1	0	0	0	0	464	106	2	.228	186	198	66	22	3.3	.853
6 yrs.			0	4	.000	8.52	10	4	3	43.1	85	17	13	0	0	0	0	*				2254	1709	522	191	3.2	.884

Scott Radinsky

RADINSKY, SCOTT DAVID — BL TL 6′ 3″ 190 lbs.
B. Mar. 3, 1968, Glendale, Calif.

Year	Team	W	L	PCT	ERA	G	GS	CG	IP	H	BB	SO	ShO	Relief W	Relief L	Relief SV	Batting AB	Batting H	Batting HR	BA	PO	A	E	DP	TC/G	FA
1990	CHI A	6	1	.857	4.82	62	0	0	52.1	47	36	46	0	6	1	4	0	0	0	—	7	4	0	0	0.2	1.000
1991		5	5	.500	2.02	67	0	0	71.1	53	23	49	0	5	5	8	0	0	0	—	6	11	0	0	0.3	1.000
1992		3	7	.300	2.73	68	0	0	59.1	54	34	48	0	3	7	15	0	0	0	—	2	9	0	1	0.2	1.000
1993		8	2	.800	4.28	73	0	0	54.2	61	19	44	0	**8**	2	4	0	0	0	—	1	9	2	0	0.2	.833
1995		2	1	.667	5.45	46	0	0	38	46	17	14	0	2	1	1	0	0	0	—	3	5	0	1	0.2	1.000
5 yrs.		24	16	.600	3.62	316	0	0	275.2	261	129	201	0	24	16	32	0	0	0		19	38	2	2	0.2	.966
LEAGUE CHAMPIONSHIP SERIES																										
1993	CHI A	0	0	—	10.80	4	0	0	1.2	3	1	1	0	0	0	0	0	0	0	—	0	0	1	0	0.3	.000

Brad Radke

RADKE, BRAD WILLIAM — BR TR 6′ 2″ 180 lbs.
B. Oct. 27, 1972, Eau Claire, Wis.

Year	Team	W	L	PCT	ERA	G	GS	CG	IP	H	BB	SO	ShO	Relief W	Relief L	Relief SV	Batting AB	Batting H	Batting HR	BA	PO	A	E	DP	TC/G	FA
1995	MIN A	11	14	.440	5.32	29	28	2	181	195	47	75	1	0	0	0	0	0	0	—	17	20	0	1	1.3	1.000

Hal Raether

RAETHER, HAROLD HERMAN (Bud) — BR TR 6′ 1″ 185 lbs.
B. Oct. 10, 1932, Lake Mills, Wis.

Year	Team	W	L	PCT	ERA	G	GS	CG	IP	H	BB	SO	ShO	Relief W	Relief L	Relief SV	Batting AB	Batting H	Batting HR	BA	PO	A	E	DP	TC/G	FA
1954	PHI A	0	0	—	4.50	1	0	0	2	1	4	0	0	0	0	0	0	0	0	—	0	1	0	1	1.0	1.000
1957	KC A	0	0	—	9.00	1	0	0	2	2	0	0	0	0	0	0	0	0	0	—	0	0	0	0	0.0	.000
2 yrs.		0	0		6.75	2	0	0	4	3	4	0	0	0	0	0	0	0	0		0	1	0	1	0.5	1.000

Ken Raffensberger

RAFFENSBERGER, KENNETH DAVID — BR TL 6′ 2″ 185 lbs.
B. Aug. 8, 1917, York, Pa.

Year	Team	W	L	PCT	ERA	G	GS	CG	IP	H	BB	SO	ShO	Relief W	Relief L	Relief SV	Batting AB	Batting H	Batting HR	BA	PO	A	E	DP	TC/G	FA
1939	STL N	0	0	—	0.00	1	0	0	1	2	0	1	0	0	0	0	0	0	0	—	0	0	0	0	0.0	.000
1940	CHI N	7	9	.438	3.38	43	10	3	114.2	120	29	55	0	4	4	3	30	5	0	.167	6	18	0	2	0.6	1.000
1941		0	1	.000	4.50	10	1	0	18	17	7	5	0	0	1	0	5	0	0	.000	2	7	0	1	0.9	1.000
1943	PHI N	0	1	.000	1.13	1	1	1	8	7	2	3	0	0	0	0	3	0	0	.000	0	2	1	0	3.0	.667
1944		13	**20**	.394	3.06	37	31	18	258.2	257	45	136	3	1	2	0	80	11	0	.138	10	33	2	1	1.2	.956
1945		0	3	.000	4.44	5	4	1	24.1	28	14	6	0	0	0	0	8	0	0	.000	1	6	1	0	1.6	.875
1946		8	15	.348	3.63	39	23	14	196	203	39	73	2	0	0	**6**	60	10	0	.167	7	26	0	0	0.8	1.000
1947	2 teams PHI N (10G 2–6) CIN N (19G 6–5)																									
″	total	8	11	.421	4.51	29	22	10	147.2	182	37	54	1	1	2	1	52	10	0	.192	7	28	2	4	1.3	.946
1948	CIN N	11	12	.478	3.84	40	24	7	180.1	187	37	57	4	3	0	0	62	7	0	.113	4	28	3	0	0.9	.914
1949		18	17	.514	3.39	41	**38**	20	284	**289**	80	103	**5**	1	1	0	90	16	1	.178	6	41	1	2	1.2	.979
1950		14	19	.424	4.26	38	35	18	239	271	40	87	4	0	0	0	82	11	1	.134	7	36	1	0	1.2	.977
1951		16	**17**	.485	3.44	42	33	14	248.2	232	38	81	5	2	2	5	82	10	0	.122	5	31	3	1	0.9	.923
1952		17	13	.567	2.81	38	33	18	247	247	45	93	**6**	0	2	1	75	8	1	.107	9	38	1	2	1.3	.979
1953		7	14	.333	3.93	26	26	9	174	200	33	47	1	0	0	0	57	8	1	.140	7	41	2	3	1.9	.960
1954		0	2	.000	7.84	6	1	0	10.1	15	3	5	0	0	2	0	2	1	0	.500	0	0	0	0	0.0	.000
15 yrs.		119	154	.436	3.60	396	282	133	2151.2	2257	449	806	31	12	16	16	688	97	4	.141	71	335	17	16	1.1	.960

Al Raffo

RAFFO, ALBERT MARTIN — BR TR 6′ 5″ 210 lbs.
B. Nov. 27, 1941, San Francisco, Calif.

Year	Team	W	L	PCT	ERA	G	GS	CG	IP	H	BB	SO	ShO	Relief W	Relief L	Relief SV	Batting AB	Batting H	Batting HR	BA	PO	A	E	DP	TC/G	FA
1969	PHI N	1	3	.250	4.13	45	0	0	72	81	25	38	0	1	3	1	6	1	0	.167	5	14	0	2	0.4	1.000

Pat Ragan

RAGAN, DON CARLOS PATRICK — BR TR 5′10½″ 185 lbs.
B. Nov. 15, 1888, Blanchard, Iowa D. Sept. 4, 1956, Los Angeles, Calif.

Year	Team	W	L	PCT	ERA	G	GS	CG	IP	H	BB	SO	ShO	Relief W	Relief L	Relief SV	Batting AB	Batting H	Batting HR	BA	PO	A	E	DP	TC/G	FA
1909	2 teams CIN N (2G 0–1) CHI N (2G 0–0)																									
″	total	0	1	.000	3.09	4	0	0	11.2	11	5	4	0	0	1	0	4	1	0	.250	1	1	0	0	0.5	1.000
1911	BKN N	4	3	.571	2.11	22	7	5	93.2	81	31	39	2	0	0	1	29	4	0	.138	4	21	2	1	1.2	.926
1912		7	18	.280	3.63	36	26	12	208	211	65	101	1	1	2	1	67	4	0	.060	11	40	3	3	1.5	.944
1913		15	18	.455	3.77	44	32	14	264.2	284	64	109	0	3	3	0	91	15	0	.165	7	76	3	3	2.0	.965
1914		10	15	.400	2.98	38	26	14	208.1	214	85	106	1	1	2	3	75	10	0	.133	8	51	3	3	1.6	.952
1915	2 teams BKN N (5G 1–0) BOS N (33G 15–12)																									
″	total	16	12	.571	2.34	38	26	13	246.2	219	67	88	3	4	1	0	86	13	0	.151	8	56	3	2	1.8	.955
1916	BOS N	9	9	.500	2.08	28	23	14	182	143	47	94	3	0	0	0	60	13	0	.217	3	52	2	2	2.0	.965
1917		6	9	.400	2.93	30	13	5	147.2	138	35	61	1	3	2	1	48	6	1	.125	6	42	1	1	1.6	.980
1918		8	17	.320	3.23	30	25	15	206.1	212	54	68	2	0	2	0	71	13	0	.183	6	60	2	1	2.3	.971
1919	3 teams BOS N (4G 0–2) NY N (7G 1–0) CHI A (1G 0–0)																									
″	total	1	2	.333	3.44	12	4	1	36.2	36	17	10	0	0	0	0	11	4	0	.364	2	12	1	0	1.3	.933
1923	PHI N	0	0	—	6.00	1	0	0	3	6	0	0	0	0	0	0	2	1	0	.500	0	0	0	0	0.0	.000
11 yrs.		76	104	.422	2.99	283	182	93	1608.2	1555	470	680	13	12	13	6	544	84	1	.154	56	411	20	16	1.7	.959

Frank Ragland

RAGLAND, FRANK ROLAND — BR TR 6′ 1″ 186 lbs.
B. May 26, 1904, Water Valley, Miss. D. July 28, 1959, Paris, Miss.

Year	Team	W	L	PCT	ERA	G	GS	CG	IP	H	BB	SO	ShO	Relief W	Relief L	Relief SV	Batting AB	Batting H	Batting HR	BA	PO	A	E	DP	TC/G	FA
1932	WAS A	1	0	1.000	7.41	12	1	0	37.2	54	21	11	0	1	0	0	11	3	0	.273	3	8	0	1	0.9	1.000
1933	PHI N	0	4	.000	6.81	11	5	0	38.1	51	10	4	0	0	1	0	10	2	0	.200	4	11	0	0	1.4	1.000
2 yrs.		1	4	.200	7.11	23	6	0	76	105	31	15	0	1	1	0	21	5	0	.238	7	19	0	1	1.1	1.000

Eric Raich

RAICH, ERIC JAMES — BR TR 6′ 4″ 225 lbs.
B. Nov. 1, 1951, Detroit, Mich.

Year	Team	W	L	PCT	ERA	G	GS	CG	IP	H	BB	SO	ShO	Relief W	Relief L	Relief SV	Batting AB	Batting H	Batting HR	BA	PO	A	E	DP	TC/G	FA
1975	CLE A	7	8	.467	5.54	18	17	2	92.2	118	31	34	0	1	0	0	0	0	0	—	5	11	1	0	0.9	.941
1976		0	0	—	15.00	1	0	0	3	7	0	1	0	0	0	0	0	0	0	—	0	0	0	0	0.0	.000
2 yrs.		7	8	.467	5.83	19	17	2	95.2	125	31	35	0	1	0	0	0	0	0		5	11	1	0	0.9	.941

Chuck Rainey

RAINEY, CHARLES DAVID — BR TR 5′11″ 190 lbs.
B. July 14, 1954, San Diego, Calif.

Year	Team	W	L	PCT	ERA	G	GS	CG	IP	H	BB	SO	ShO	Relief W	Relief L	Relief SV	Batting AB	Batting H	Batting HR	BA	PO	A	E	DP	TC/G	FA
1979	BOS A	8	5	.615	3.81	20	16	4	104	97	41	41	1	0	0	1	0	0	0	—	10	18	1	2	1.5	.966
1980		8	3	.727	4.86	16	13	2	87	92	41	43	1	0	0	0	0	0	0	—	4	10	2	2	1.0	.875
1981		0	1	.000	2.70	11	2	0	40	39	13	20	0	0	0	0	0	0	0	—	5	9	2	0	1.5	.875
1982		7	5	.583	5.02	27	25	3	129	146	63	57	3	0	0	0	0	0	0	—	17	19	1	0	1.4	.973
1983	CHI N	14	13	.519	4.48	34	34	1	191	219	74	84	1	0	0	0	56	9	0	.161	28	38	7	2	2.1	.904
1984	2 teams CHI N (17G 5–7) OAK A (16G 1–1)																									
″	total	6	8	.429	4.92	33	16	0	119	145	55	55	0	1	1	1	31	3	0	.097	13	17	0	1	0.9	1.000
6 yrs.		43	35	.551	4.50	141	106	10	670	738	287	300	6	1	1	2	87	12	0	.138	77	111	13	7	1.4	.935

Dave Rajsich

RAJSICH, DAVID CHRISTOPHER — BL TL 6′ 5″ 175 lbs.
Brother of Gary Rajsich.
B. Sept. 28, 1951, Youngstown, Ohio.

Year	Team		W	L	PCT	ERA	G	GS	CG	IP	H	BB	SO	ShO	Relief W	Relief L	Relief SV	Batting AB	Batting H	HR	BA	PO	A	E	DP	TC/G	FA
1978	NY	A	0	0	—	4.05	4	2	0	13.1	16	6	9	0	0	0	0	0	0	0	—	0	1	0	0	0.3	1.000
1979	TEX	A	1	3	.250	3.50	27	3	0	54	56	18	32	0	1	1	0	0	0	0	—	1	13	0	0	0.5	1.000
1980			2	1	.667	6.00	24	1	0	48	56	22	35	0	2	0	2	0	0	0	—	0	7	0	1	0.3	1.000
3 yrs.			3	4	.429	4.60	55	6	0	115.1	128	46	76	0	3	1	2	0	0	0		1	21	0	1	0.4	1.000

Ed Rakow

RAKOW, EDWARD CHARLES (Rock) — BB TR 5′11″ 178 lbs. BR 1960–1961
B. May 30, 1936, Pittsburgh, Pa.

Year	Team		W	L	PCT	ERA	G	GS	CG	IP	H	BB	SO	ShO	Relief W	Relief L	Relief SV	Batting AB	Batting H	HR	BA	PO	A	E	DP	TC/G	FA
1960	LA	N	0	1	.000	7.36	9	2	0	22	30	11	9	0	0	0	0	6	2	0	.333	1	4	0	0	0.6	1.000
1961	KC	A	2	8	.200	4.76	45	11	1	124.2	131	49	81	0	1	3	1	29	3	0	.103	12	19	1	3	0.7	.969
1962			14	**17**	.452	4.25	42	35	11	235.1	232	98	159	2	1	2	1	82	8	0	.098	17	45	5	3	1.6	.925
1963			9	10	.474	3.92	34	26	7	174.1	173	61	104	1	0	0	0	57	6	0	.105	15	30	1	3	1.4	.978
1964	DET	A	8	9	.471	3.72	42	13	1	152.1	155	59	96	0	5	1	3	39	0	0	.000	16	28	0	2	1.0	1.000
1965			0	0	—	6.08	6	0	0	13.1	14	11	10	0	0	0	0	3	0	0	.000	0	0	1	0	0.2	.000
1967	ATL	N	3	2	.600	5.26	17	3	0	39.1	36	15	25	0	1	2	0	10	0	0	.000	1	5	1	0	0.4	.857
7 yrs.			36	47	.434	4.33	195	90	20	761.1	771	304	484	3	8	8	5	226	19	0	.084	62	131	9	11	1.0	.955

John Raleigh

RALEIGH, JOHN AUSTIN — BR TL
B. Apr. 21, 1890, Elkhorn, Wis. D. Aug. 24, 1955, Escondido, Calif.

Year	Team		W	L	PCT	ERA	G	GS	CG	IP	H	BB	SO	ShO	Relief W	Relief L	Relief SV	Batting AB	Batting H	HR	BA	PO	A	E	DP	TC/G	FA
1909	STL	N	1	10	.091	3.79	15	10	3	80.2	85	21	26	0	0	1	0	23	2	0	.087	4	24	3	0	2.1	.903
1910			0	0	—	9.00	3	1	0	5	8	0	2	0	0	0	0	1	0	0	.000	0	2	0	0	0.7	1.000
2 yrs.			1	10	.091	4.10	18	11	3	85.2	93	21	28	0	0	1	0	24	2	0	.083	4	26	3	0	1.8	.909

Pep Rambert

RAMBERT, ELMER DONALD — BR TR 6′ 195 lbs.
B. Aug. 1, 1916, Cleveland, Ohio D. Nov. 16, 1974, West Palm Beach, Fla.

Year	Team		W	L	PCT	ERA	G	GS	CG	IP	H	BB	SO	ShO	Relief W	Relief L	Relief SV	Batting AB	Batting H	HR	BA	PO	A	E	DP	TC/G	FA
1939	PIT	N	0	0	—	9.82	2	0	0	3.2	7	1	4	0	0	0	0	0	0	0	—	0	1	0	0	0.5	1.000
1940			0	1	.000	7.56	3	1	0	8.1	12	4	0	0	0	0	0	2	0	0	.000	0	2	0	0	0.7	1.000
2 yrs.			0	1	.000	8.25	5	1	0	12	19	5	4	0	0	0	0	2	0	0	.000	0	3	0	0	0.6	1.000

Pete Rambo

RAMBO, WARREN DAWSON — BR TR 5′ 9″ 150 lbs.
B. Nov. 1, 1906, Thoroughfare, N. J. D. June 19, 1991, Camden, N. J.

Year	Team		W	L	PCT	ERA	G	GS	CG	IP	H	BB	SO	ShO	Relief W	Relief L	Relief SV	Batting AB	Batting H	HR	BA	PO	A	E	DP	TC/G	FA
1926	PHI	N	0	0	—	14.73	1	0	0	3.2	6	4	4	0	0	0	0	1	1	0	1.000	0	1	0	0	1.0	1.000

Allan Ramirez

RAMIREZ, DANIEL ALLAN — BR TR 5′10″ 190 lbs.
B. May 1, 1957, Victoria, Tex.

Year	Team		W	L	PCT	ERA	G	GS	CG	IP	H	BB	SO	ShO	Relief W	Relief L	Relief SV	Batting AB	Batting H	HR	BA	PO	A	E	DP	TC/G	FA
1983	BAL	A	4	4	.500	3.47	11	10	1	57	46	30	20	0	0	0	0	0	0	0	—	6	9	0	0	1.4	1.000

Pedro Ramos

RAMOS, PEDRO (Pete) — BB TR 6′ 175 lbs. BR 1955–1959
Born Pedro Ramos (Guerra).
B. Apr. 28, 1935, Pinar del Rio, Cuba.

Year	Team		W	L	PCT	ERA	G	GS	CG	IP	H	BB	SO	ShO	Relief W	Relief L	Relief SV	Batting AB	Batting H	HR	BA	PO	A	E	DP	TC/G	FA
1955	WAS	A	5	11	.313	3.88	45	9	3	130	121	39	34	1	3	4	5	38	3	0	.079	7	20	1	1	0.6	.964
1956			12	10	.545	5.27	37	18	4	152	178	76	54	0	6	2	0	44	9	0	.205	9	23	0	2	0.9	1.000
1957			12	16	.429	4.79	43	30	7	231	251	69	91	1	4	2	0	76	13	1	.171	8	41	0	4	1.1	1.000
1958			14	**18**	.438	4.23	43	**37**	10	259.1	**277**	77	132	4	1	0	3	88	21	0	.239	20	34	1	7	1.3	.982
1959			13	**19**	.406	4.16	37	35	11	233.2	233	52	95	0	1	1	0	75	11	1	.147	20	32	0	8	1.4	1.000
1960			11	**18**	.379	3.45	43	**36**	14	**274**	254	99	160	1	1	0	2	86	10	2	.116	16	44	0	2	1.4	1.000
1961	MIN	A	11	**20**	.355	3.95	42	34	9	264.1	**265**	79	174	3	1	2	2	93	16	3	.172	14	28	2	2	1.0	.955
1962	CLE	A	10	12	.455	3.71	37	27	7	201.1	189	85	96	2	0	1	1	68	10	3	.147	21	30	2	3	1.4	.962
1963			9	8	.529	3.12	36	22	5	184.2	156	41	169	0	2	1	0	55	6	3	.109	7	19	1	2	0.8	.963
1964	2 teams CLE A (36G 7–10) NY A (13G 1–0)																										
"	total		8	10	.444	4.60	49	19	3	154.2	157	26	119	1	4	1	8	44	7	2	.159	8	16	1	0	0.5	.960
1965	NY	A	5	5	.500	2.92	65	0	0	92.1	80	27	68	0	5	5	19	12	1	0	.083	6	11	2	0	0.3	.895
1966			3	9	.250	3.61	52	1	0	89.2	98	18	58	0	3	8	13	13	2	0	.154	7	13	1	0	0.4	.952
1967	PHI	N	0	0	—	9.00	6	0	0	8	14	8	1	0	0	0	0	1	0	0	.000	1	4	0	1	0.8	1.000
1969	2 teams PIT N (5G 0–1) CIN N (38G 4–3)																										
"	total		4	4	.500	5.23	43	0	0	72.1	81	24	44	0	4	4	2	9	0	0	.000	2	12	0	1	0.3	1.000
1970	WAS	A	0	0	—	7.88	4	0	0	8	10	4	10	0	0	0	0	1	0	0	.000	0	1	0	0	0.3	1.000
15 yrs.			117	160	.422	4.08	582	268	73	2355.1	2364	724	1305	13	35	31	55	703	109	15	.155	146	328	11	33	0.8	.977

Willie Ramsdell

RAMSDELL, JAMES WILLARD (Willie the Knuck) — BR TR 5′11″ 165 lbs.
B. Apr. 4, 1916, Williamsburg, Kans. D. Oct. 8, 1969, Wichita, Kans.

Year	Team		W	L	PCT	ERA	G	GS	CG	IP	H	BB	SO	ShO	Relief W	Relief L	Relief SV	Batting AB	Batting H	HR	BA	PO	A	E	DP	TC/G	FA
1947	BKN	N	1	1	.500	6.75	2	0	0	2.2	4	3	3	0	1	1	0	1	1	0	1.000	1	1	0	0	1.0	1.000
1948			4	4	.500	5.19	27	1	0	50.1	48	41	34	0	4	3	4	11	1	0	.091	4	13	0	0	0.6	1.000
1950	2 teams BKN N (5G 1–2) CIN N (27G 7–12)																										
"	total		8	14	.364	3.68	32	22	8	163.2	158	77	85	1	1	3	1	53	10	0	.189	8	24	1	0	1.0	.970
1951	CIN	N	9	**17**	.346	4.04	31	31	10	196	204	70	88	1	0	0	0	58	9	0	.155	7	29	3	3	1.3	.923
1952	CHI	N	2	3	.400	2.42	19	4	0	67	41	24	30	0	2	0	0	18	1	0	.056	6	10	4	1	1.1	.800
5 yrs.			24	39	.381	3.83	111	58	18	479.2	455	215	240	2	8	7	5	141	22	0	.156	26	77	8	4	1.0	.928

Toad Ramsey

RAMSEY, THOMAS A. — BR TL
B. Aug. 8, 1864, Indianapolis, Ind. D. Mar. 27, 1906, Indianapolis, Ind.

Year	Team		W	L	PCT	ERA	G	GS	CG	IP	H	BB	SO	ShO	Relief W	Relief L	Relief SV	Batting AB	Batting H	HR	BA	PO	A	E	DP	TC/G	FA
1885	LOU	AA	3	6	.333	*1.94*	9	9	9	79	44	28	83	0	0	0	0	31	4	0	.129	1	11	5	1	1.9	.706
1886			38	27	.585	*2.45*	67	67	**66**	**588.2**	447	**207**	499	3	0	0	0	241	58	0	.241	14	78	23	1	1.7	.800
1887			37	27	.578	*3.43*	65	64	61	561	544	167	**355**	0	**1**	0	0	225	43	0	.191	7	88	31	0	1.9	.754
1888			8	30	.211	3.42	40	40	37	342.1	362	86	228	1	0	0	0	142	17	0	.120	10	58	18	1	2.0	.791
1889	2 teams LOU AA (18G 1–16) STL AA (5G 3–1)																										
"	total		4	17	.190	5.22	23	21	18	181	219	81	93	0	1	0	0	74	20	0	.270	2	36	14	0	2.3	.731
1890	STL	AA	24	17	.585	*3.69*	44	40	34	348.2	325	102	257	1	2	1	0	145	33	0	.228	12	31	16	2	1.3	.729
6 yrs.			114	124	.479	3.29	248	241	225	2100.2	1941	671	1515	5	4	1	0	858	175	0	.204	46	302	107	5	1.8	.765

Ribs Raney

RANEY, FRANK ROBERT DONALD
Born Frank Robert Donald Raniszewski.
B. Feb. 16, 1923, Detroit, Mich.

BR TR 6′ 4″ 190 lbs.

Year	Team	W	L	PCT	ERA	G	GS	CG	IP	H	BB	SO	ShO	Relief Pitching W	Relief Pitching L	Relief Pitching SV	Batting AB	Batting H	HR	BA	PO	A	E	DP	TC/G	FA
1949	STL A	1	2	.333	7.71	3	3	1	16.1	23	12	5	0	0	0	0	6	0	0	.000	1	2	0	0	1.0	1.000
1950		0	1	.000	4.50	1	0	0	2	2	2	2	0	0	1	0	1	0	0	.000	0	1	0	0	1.0	1.000
2 yrs.		1	3	.250	7.36	4	3	1	18.1	25	14	7	0	0	1	0	7	0	0	.000	1	3	0	0	1.0	1.000

Pat Rapp

RAPP, PATRICK LELAND
B. July 13, 1967, Jennings, La.

BR TR 6′ 3″ 195 lbs.

Year	Team	W	L	PCT	ERA	G	GS	CG	IP	H	BB	SO	ShO	Relief Pitching W	Relief Pitching L	Relief Pitching SV	Batting AB	Batting H	HR	BA	PO	A	E	DP	TC/G	FA
1992	SF N	0	2	.000	7.20	3	2	0	10	8	6	3	0	0	0	0	2	0	0	.000	2	2	0	0	1.3	1.000
1993	FLA N	4	6	.400	4.02	16	16	1	94	101	39	57	0	0	0	0	31	6	0	.194	5	15	1	0	1.3	.952
1994		7	8	.467	3.85	24	23	2	133.1	132	69	75	1	0	0	0	41	5	0	.122	8	15	0	1	1.0	1.000
1995		14	7	.667	3.44	28	28	3	167.1	158	76	102	2	0	0	0	56	6	0	.107	13	20	1	1	1.2	.971
4 yrs.		25	23	.521	3.80	71	69	6	404.2	399	190	237	3	0	0	0	130	17	0	.131	28	52	2	2	1.2	.976

Vic Raschi

RASCHI, VICTOR JOHN ANGELO (The Springfield Rifle)
B. Mar. 28, 1919, West Springfield, Mass. D. Oct. 14, 1988, Groveland, N. Y.

BR TR 6′ 1″ 205 lbs.

Year	Team	W	L	PCT	ERA	G	GS	CG	IP	H	BB	SO	ShO	Relief Pitching W	Relief Pitching L	Relief Pitching SV	Batting AB	Batting H	HR	BA	PO	A	E	DP	TC/G	FA
1946	NY A	2	0	1.000	3.94	2	2	2	16	14	5	11	0	0	0	0	4	1	0	.250	1	3	0	0	2.0	1.000
1947		7	2	.778	3.87	15	14	6	104.2	89	38	51	1	0	0	0	40	10	0	.250	4	15	0	1	1.3	1.000
1948		19	8	.704	3.84	36	31	18	222.2	208	74	124	6	0	1	1	81	19	0	.235	12	28	0	3	1.1	1.000
1949		21	10	.677	3.34	38	**37**	21	274.2	247	138	124	3	1	0	0	83	13	0	.157	12	53	1	3	1.7	.985
1950		21	8	**.724**	4.00	33	32	17	256.2	232	116	155	2	0	0	1	86	17	1	.198	10	29	1	3	1.2	.975
1951		21	10	.677	3.27	35	**34**	15	258.1	233	103	**164**	4	0	0	0	85	15	0	.176	8	30	2	1	1.1	.950
1952		16	6	.727	2.78	31	31	13	223	174	91	127	4	0	0	0	69	13	0	.188	6	22	1	3	0.9	.966
1953		13	6	.684	3.33	28	26	7	181	150	55	76	4	1	0	1	63	9	0	.143	5	23	1	2	1.0	.966
1954	STL N	8	9	.471	4.73	30	29	6	179	182	71	73	2	0	0	0	64	9	0	.141	16	35	1	3	1.7	.981
1955	2 teams STL N (1G 0–1) KC A (20G 4–6)																									
″	total	4	7	.364	5.68	21	19	1	103	137	36	39	0	0	0	0	33	6	0	.182	10	21	1	1	1.5	.969
10 yrs.		132	66	.667	3.72	269	255	106	1819	1666	727	944	26	2	1	3	608	112	1	.184	84	259	8	20	1.3	.977
				5th																						
WORLD SERIES																										
1947	NY A	0	0	—	6.75	2	0	0	1.1	2	0	1	0	0	0	0	0	0	0	—	0	0	0	0	0.0	.000
1949		1	1	.500	4.30	2	2	0	14.2	15	5	11	0	0	0	0	5	1	0	.200	0	0	0	0	0.0	.000
1950		1	0	1.000	0.00	1	1	1	9	2	1	5	1	0	0	0	3	1	0	.333	0	3	0	0	3.0	1.000
1951		1	1	.500	0.87	2	2	0	10.1	12	8	4	0	0	0	0	2	0	0	.000	0	0	0	0	0.0	.000
1952		2	0	1.000	1.59	3	2	1	17	12	8	18	0	0	0	0	6	1	0	.167	0	1	0	0	0.3	1.000
1953		0	1	.000	3.38	1	1	1	8	9	3	4	0	0	0	0	2	0	0	.000	1	1	0	0	2.0	1.000
6 yrs.		5	3	.625	2.24	11	8	3	60.1	52	25	43	1	0	0	0	18	3	0	.167	1	5	0	0	0.5	1.000
		8th				10th	10th				10th															

Dennis Rasmussen

RASMUSSEN, DENNIS LEE
B. Apr. 18, 1959, Los Angeles, Calif.

BL TL 6′ 7″ 230 lbs.

Year	Team	W	L	PCT	ERA	G	GS	CG	IP	H	BB	SO	ShO	Relief Pitching W	Relief Pitching L	Relief Pitching SV	Batting AB	Batting H	HR	BA	PO	A	E	DP	TC/G	FA
1983	SD N	0	0	—	1.98	4	1	0	13.2	10	8	13	0	0	0	0	3	0	0	.000	0	4	0	1	1.0	1.000
1984	NY A	9	6	.600	4.57	24	24	1	147.2	127	60	110	0	0	0	0	0	0	0	—	7	14	2	1	1.0	.913
1985		3	5	.375	3.98	22	16	2	101.2	97	42	63	0	0	0	0	0	0	0	—	7	13	0	2	0.9	1.000
1986		18	6	.750	3.88	31	31	3	202	160	74	131	1	0	0	0	0	0	0	—	6	26	0	0	1.0	1.000
1987	2 teams NY A (26G 9–7) CIN N (7G 4–1)																									
″	total	13	8	.619	4.56	33	32	2	191.1	184	67	128	0	0	0	0	15	1	0	.067	6	30	2	0	1.2	.947
1988	2 teams CIN N (11G 2–6) SD N (20G 14–4)																									
″	total	16	10	.615	3.43	31	31	7	204.2	199	58	112	1	0	0	0	70	14	0	.200	3	45	0	1	1.5	1.000
1989	SD N	10	10	.500	4.26	33	33	1	183.2	190	72	87	0	0	0	0	65	11	0	.169	6	27	0	3	1.0	1.000
1990		11	15	.423	4.51	32	32	3	187.2	217	62	86	1	0	0	0	62	18	0	.290	8	31	3	2	1.3	.929
1991		6	13	.316	3.74	24	24	1	146.2	155	49	75	1	0	0	0	44	6	0	.136	5	34	1	0	1.7	.975
1992	2 teams CHI N (3G 0–0) KC A (5G 4–1)																									
″	total	4	1	.800	2.53	8	6	1	42.2	32	8	12	1	0	0	0	0	0	0		1	13	0	0	1.8	1.000
1993	KC A	1	2	.333	7.45	9	4	0	29	40	14	12	0	0	1	0	0	0	0	—	0	5	0	0	0.6	1.000
1995		0	1	.000	9.00	5	1	0	10	13	8	6	0	0	0	0	0	0	0	—	0	0	0	0	0.0	.000
12 yrs.		91	77	.542	4.15	256	235	21	1460.2	1424	522	835	5	0	1	0	259	50	0	.193	49	242	8	10	1.2	.973

Eric Rasmussen

RASMUSSEN, ERIC RALPH
Born Harold Ralph Rasmussen.
B. Mar. 22, 1952, Racine, Wis.

BR TR 6′ 3″ 205 lbs.

Year	Team	W	L	PCT	ERA	G	GS	CG	IP	H	BB	SO	ShO	Relief Pitching W	Relief Pitching L	Relief Pitching SV	Batting AB	Batting H	HR	BA	PO	A	E	DP	TC/G	FA
1975	STL N	5	5	.500	3.78	14	13	2	81	86	20	59	1	0	0	0	26	4	0	.154	2	11	0	0	0.9	1.000
1976		6	12	.333	3.53	43	17	2	150.1	139	54	76	1	3	5	0	38	4	0	.105	15	34	1	2	1.2	.980
1977		11	17	.393	3.48	34	34	11	233	223	63	120	3	0	0	0	72	10	0	.139	8	30	1	4	1.1	.974
1978	2 teams STL N (10G 2–5) SD N (27G 12–10)																									
″	total	14	15	.483	4.09	37	34	5	206.2	215	63	91	3	0	0	0	64	9	0	.141	14	37	2	3	1.4	.962
1979	SD N	6	9	.400	3.27	45	20	5	157	142	42	54	3	0	0	3	36	2	0	.056	6	24	1	1	0.7	.968
1980		4	11	.267	4.38	40	14	0	111	130	33	50	0	3	2	1	21	2	0	.095	8	15	2	2	0.6	.920
1982	STL N	1	2	.333	4.42	8	3	0	18.1	21	8	15	0	1	0	0	3	0	0	.000	0	4	0	0	0.5	1.000
1983	2 teams STL N (6G 0–0) KC A (11G 3–6)																									
″	total	3	6	.333	5.67	17	9	2	60.1	77	26	24	1	0	0	1	0	0	0		2	8	0	2	0.6	1.000
8 yrs.		50	77	.394	3.85	238	144	27	1017.2	1033	309	489	12	7	7	5	260	31	0	.119	55	163	7	14	0.9	.969

Hans Rasmussen

RASMUSSEN, HENRY FLORIAN
B. Apr. 18, 1895, Chicago, Ill. D. Jan. 1, 1949, Chicago, Ill.

BR TR 6′ 6″ 220 lbs.

Year	Team	W	L	PCT	ERA	G	GS	CG	IP	H	BB	SO	ShO	Relief Pitching W	Relief Pitching L	Relief Pitching SV	Batting AB	Batting H	HR	BA	PO	A	E	DP	TC/G	FA
1915	CHI F	0	0	—	13.50	2	0	0	2	3	2	2	0	0	0	0	1	0	0	.000	0	2	0	0	1.0	1.000

Fred Rath

RATH, FREDERICK HELSHER
B. Sept. 1, 1943, Little Rock, Ark.

BR TR 6′ 3″ 200 lbs.

Year	Team	W	L	PCT	ERA	G	GS	CG	IP	H	BB	SO	ShO	Relief Pitching W	Relief Pitching L	Relief Pitching SV	Batting AB	Batting H	HR	BA	PO	A	E	DP	TC/G	FA
1968	CHI A	0	0	—	1.59	5	0	0	11.1	8	3	3	0	0	0	0	0	0	0	—	0	3	1	0	0.8	.750
1969		0	2	.000	7.71	3	2	0	11.2	11	8	4	0	0	0	0	3	0	0	.000	2	2	0	0	1.3	1.000
2 yrs.		0	2	.000	4.70	8	2	0	23	19	11	7	0	0	0	0	3	0	0	.000	2	5	1	0	1.0	.875

Steve Ratzer

RATZER, STEPHEN WAYNE
B. Sept. 9, 1953, Paterson, N. J.
BR TR 6′ 180 lbs.

Year	Team	W	L	PCT	ERA	G	GS	CG	IP	H	BB	SO	ShO	Relief W	Relief L	Relief SV	Batting AB	Batting H	HR	BA	PO	A	E	DP	TC/G	FA
1980	MON N	0	0	—	11.25	1	1	0	4	9	2	0	0	0	0	0	1	0	0	.000	1	2	0	0	3.0	1.000
1981		1	1	.500	6.35	12	0	0	17	23	7	4	0	1	1	0	2	0	0	.000	1	6	0	0	0.6	1.000
2 yrs.		1	1	.500	7.29	13	1	0	21	32	9	4	0	1	1	0	3	0	0	.000	2	8	0	0	0.8	1.000

Doug Rau

RAU, DOUGLAS JAMES
B. Dec. 15, 1948, Columbus, Tex.
BL TL 6′ 2″ 175 lbs.

Year	Team	W	L	PCT	ERA	G	GS	CG	IP	H	BB	SO	ShO	Relief W	Relief L	Relief SV	Batting AB	Batting H	HR	BA	PO	A	E	DP	TC/G	FA
1972	LA N	2	2	.500	2.20	7	3	2	32.2	18	11	19	0	1	0	0	7	1	0	.143	0	6	0	1	0.9	1.000
1973		4	2	.667	3.96	31	3	0	63.2	64	28	51	0	4	1	3	11	1	0	.091	1	8	0	0	0.3	1.000
1974		13	11	.542	3.73	36	35	3	198	191	70	126	1	0	0	0	64	9	0	.141	8	27	0	3	1.0	1.000
1975		15	9	.625	3.10	38	38	8	258	227	61	151	2	0	0	0	87	17	0	.195	6	40	5	1	1.3	.902
1976		16	12	.571	2.57	34	32	8	231	221	69	98	3	0	1	0	60	9	0	.150	5	39	1	1	1.3	.978
1977		14	8	.636	3.44	32	32	4	212	232	49	126	2	0	0	0	71	10	0	.141	3	30	0	0	1.0	1.000
1978		15	9	.625	3.26	30	30	7	199	219	68	95	2	0	0	0	63	9	0	.143	3	24	1	2	0.9	.964
1979		1	5	.167	5.30	11	11	1	56	73	22	28	1	0	0	0	14	2	0	.143	2	10	0	0	1.1	1.000
1981	CAL A	1	2	.333	9.00	3	3	0	10	14	4	3	0	0	0	0	0	0	0	—	1	0	0	0	0.3	1.000
9 yrs.		81	60	.574	3.35	222	187	33	1260.1	1259	382	697	11	5	2	3	377	58	0	.154	29	184	7	8	1.0	.968
LEAGUE CHAMPIONSHIP SERIES																										
1974	LA N	0	1	.000	40.50	1	1	0	0.2	3	1	0	0	0	0	0	0	0	0	—	0	0	0	0	0.0	.000
1977		0	0	—	0.00	1	0	0	1	0	0	1	0	0	0	0	0	0	0	—	0	0	0	0	0.0	.000
1978		0	0	—	3.60	1	1	0	5	5	2	1	0	0	0	0	1	0	0	.000	1	0	0	0	1.0	1.000
3 yrs.		0	1	.000	6.75	3	2	0	6.2	8	3	2	0	0	0	0	1	0	0	.000	1	0	0	0	0.3	1.000
WORLD SERIES																										
1977	LA N	0	1	.000	11.57	2	1	0	2.1	4	0	1	0	0	0	0	0	0	0	—	0	0	0	0	0.0	.000
1978		0	0	—	0.00	1	0	0	2	1	0	3	0	0	0	0	0	0	0	—	0	1	0	0	1.0	1.000
2 yrs.		0	1	.000	6.23	3	1	0	4.1	5	0	4	0	0	0	0	0	0	0		0	1	0	0	0.3	1.000

Bob Rauch

RAUCH, ROBERT JOHN
B. June 16, 1949, Brookings, S. D.
BR TR 6′ 4″ 200 lbs.

Year	Team	W	L	PCT	ERA	G	GS	CG	IP	H	BB	SO	ShO	Relief W	Relief L	Relief SV	Batting AB	Batting H	HR	BA	PO	A	E	DP	TC/G	FA
1972	NY N	0	1	.000	5.00	19	0	0	27	27	21	23	0	0	1	1	3	0	0	.000	1	5	0	0	0.3	1.000

Lance Rautzhan

RAUTZHAN, CLARENCE GEORGE
B. Aug. 20, 1952, Pottsville, Pa.
BR TL 6′ 1″ 195 lbs.

Year	Team	W	L	PCT	ERA	G	GS	CG	IP	H	BB	SO	ShO	Relief W	Relief L	Relief SV	Batting AB	Batting H	HR	BA	PO	A	E	DP	TC/G	FA
1977	LA N	4	1	.800	4.29	25	0	0	21	25	7	13	0	4	1	2	1	0	0	.000	0	5	1	1	0.2	.833
1978		2	1	.667	2.95	43	0	0	61	61	19	25	0	2	1	4	4	0	0	.000	9	15	1	0	0.6	.960
1979	2 teams LA N (12G 0–2) MIL A (3G 0–0)																									
″	total	0	2	.000	7.62	15	0	0	13	12	21	7	0	0	2	1	0	0	0		4	3	0	0	0.5	1.000
3 yrs.		6	4	.600	3.88	83	0	0	95	98	47	45	0	6	4	7	5	0	0	.000	13	23	2	1	0.5	.947
LEAGUE CHAMPIONSHIP SERIES																										
1977	LA N	1	0	1.000	0.00	1	0	0	0.1	0	0	0	0	1	0	0	0	0	0	—	0	0	0	0	0.0	.000
1978		0	0	—	6.75	1	0	0	1.1	3	2	0	0	0	0	0	0	0	0	—	0	1	0	0	1.0	1.000
2 yrs.		1	0	1.000	5.40	2	0	0	1.2	3	2	0	0	1	0	0	0	0	0		0	1	0	0	0.5	1.000
WORLD SERIES																										
1977	LA N	0	0	—	0.00	1	0	0	0.1	0	2	0	0	0	0	0	0	0	0	—	0	1	0	0	1.0	1.000
1978		0	0	—	13.50	2	0	0	2	4	0	0	0	0	0	0	0	0	0	—	0	0	0	0	0.0	.000
2 yrs.		0	0		11.57	3	0	0	2.1	4	2	0	0	0	0	0	0	0	0		0	1	0	0	0.3	1.000

Shane Rawley

RAWLEY, SHANE WILLIAM
B. July 27, 1955, Racine, Wis.
BR TL 6′ 170 lbs.

Year	Team	W	L	PCT	ERA	G	GS	CG	IP	H	BB	SO	ShO	Relief W	Relief L	Relief SV	Batting AB	Batting H	HR	BA	PO	A	E	DP	TC/G	FA
1978	SEA A	4	9	.308	4.12	52	2	0	111.1	114	51	66	0	4	7	4	0	0	0	—	8	20	1	1	0.6	.966
1979		5	9	.357	3.86	48	3	0	84	88	40	48	0	5	9	11	0	0	0	—	4	15	0	1	0.4	1.000
1980		7	7	.500	3.32	59	0	0	114	103	63	68	0	7	7	13	0	0	0	—	4	28	1	3	0.6	.970
1981		4	6	.400	3.97	46	0	0	68	64	38	35	0	4	6	8	0	0	0	—	1	15	0	1	0.3	1.000
1982	NY A	11	10	.524	4.06	47	17	3	164	165	54	111	0	4	5	3	0	0	0	—	5	29	1	1	0.7	.971
1983		14	14	.500	3.78	34	33	13	238.1	246	79	124	2	0	0	1	0	0	0	—	14	33	2	3	1.4	.959
1984	2 teams NY A (11G 2–3) PHI N (18G 10–6)																									
″	total	12	9	.571	4.44	29	28	3	162.1	163	54	82	0	0	0	0	0	0	0	—	9	17	2	1	1.0	.929
1985	PHI N	13	8	.619	3.31	36	31	6	198.2	188	81	106	2	1	0	0	43	5	0	.116	12	36	1	2	1.4	.980
1986		11	7	.611	3.54	23	23	7	157.2	166	50	73	1	0	0	0	58	8	0	.138	4	28	4	3	1.6	.889
1987		17	11	.607	4.39	36	**36**	4	229.2	250	86	123	1	0	0	0	52	9	0	.173	6	34	1	2	1.1	.976
1988		8	16	.333	4.18	32	32	4	198	220	78	87	1	0	0	0	79	12	0	.152	9	33	2	2	1.4	.955
1989	MIN A	5	12	.294	5.21	27	25	1	145	167	60	68	0	0	0	0	57	6	0	.105	4	20	2	2	1.0	.923
12 yrs.		111	118	.485	4.02	469	230	41	1871	1934	734	991	7	25	34	40	289	40	0	.138	80	308	17	22	0.9	.958

Carl Ray

RAY, CARL GRADY
B. Jan. 31, 1889, Danbury, N. C. D. Apr. 3, 1970, Walnut Cove, N. C.
BL TL 5′11″ 170 lbs.

Year	Team	W	L	PCT	ERA	G	GS	CG	IP	H	BB	SO	ShO	Relief W	Relief L	Relief SV	Batting AB	Batting H	HR	BA	PO	A	E	DP	TC/G	FA
1915	PHI A	0	1	.000	4.91	2	1	0	7.1	11	6	6	0	0	0	0	2	0	0	.000	0	0	0	0	0.0	.000
1916		0	1	.000	4.82	3	1	0	9.1	9	14	5	0	0	0	0	3	0	0	.000	1	1	0	0	0.7	1.000
2 yrs.		0	2	.000	4.86	5	2	0	16.2	20	20	11	0	0	0	0	5	0	0	.000	1	1	0	0	0.4	1.000

Farmer Ray

RAY, ROBERT HENRY
B. Sept. 17, 1886, Ft. Lyon, Colo. D. Mar. 11, 1963, Electra, Tex.
BL TR 5′11″ 160 lbs.

Year	Team	W	L	PCT	ERA	G	GS	CG	IP	H	BB	SO	ShO	Relief W	Relief L	Relief SV	Batting AB	Batting H	HR	BA	PO	A	E	DP	TC/G	FA
1910	STL A	4	10	.286	3.58	21	16	11	140.2	146	49	35	0	0	0	0	40	7	0	.175	4	34	5	1	2.0	.884

Jim Ray

RAY, JAMES FRANCIS (Sting)
B. Dec. 1, 1944, Rock Hill, S. C.
BR TR 6′ 1″ 185 lbs.

Year	Team	W	L	PCT	ERA	G	GS	CG	IP	H	BB	SO	ShO	Relief W	Relief L	Relief SV	Batting AB	Batting H	HR	BA	PO	A	E	DP	TC/G	FA
1965	HOU N	0	2	.000	10.57	3	2	0	7.2	11	6	7	0	0	0	0	2	0	0	.000	1	2	0	0	1.0	1.000
1966		0	0	—	∞	1	0	0		0	1	0	0	0	0	0	0	0	0	—	0	0	0	0	0.0	.000
1968		2	3	.400	2.67	41	2	1	81	65	25	71	0	1	2	1	15	1	0	.067	2	9	1	0	0.3	.917
1969		8	2	.800	3.91	40	13	0	115	105	48	115	0	4	0	0	26	3	0	.115	5	11	0	0	0.4	1.000
1970		6	3	.667	3.26	52	2	0	105	97	49	67	0	6	2	5	27	5	0	.185	4	17	1	1	0.4	.955
1971		10	4	.714	2.11	47	1	0	98	72	31	46	0	10	3	3	18	3	0	.167	2	7	0	0	0.2	1.000
1972		10	9	.526	4.30	54	0	0	90	77	44	50	0	10	**9**	8	16	1	0	.063	6	6	0	0	0.2	1.000

Jim Ray *continued*

Year	Team		W	L	PCT	ERA	G	GS	CG	IP	H	BB	SO	ShO	Relief Pitching W	L	SV	Batting AB	H	HR	BA	PO	A	E	DP	TC/G	FA
1973			6	4	.600	4.43	42	0	0	69	65	38	25	0	6	4	6	13	3	0	.231	4	9	0	0	0.3	1.000
1974	DET	A	1	3	.250	4.50	28	0	0	52	49	29	26	0	1	3	2	0	0	0	—	2	9	0	0	0.4	1.000
9 yrs.			43	30	.589	3.61	308	20	1	617.2	541	271	407	0	38	23	25	117	16	0	.137	26	70	2	1	0.3	.980

Curt Raydon

RAYDON, CURTIS LOWELL
B. Nov. 18, 1933, Bloomington, Ill.
BR TR 6′4″ 190 lbs.

Year	Team		W	L	PCT	ERA	G	GS	CG	IP	H	BB	SO	ShO	Relief W	L	SV	AB	H	HR	BA	PO	A	E	DP	TC/G	FA
1958	PIT	N	8	4	.667	3.62	31	20	2	134.1	118	61	85	1	0	1	1	38	1	0	.026	8	9	2	0	0.6	.895

Bugs Raymond

RAYMOND, ARTHUR LAWRENCE
B. Feb. 24, 1882, Chicago, Ill. D. Sept. 7, 1912, Chicago, Ill.
BR TR 5′10″ 180 lbs.

Year	Team		W	L	PCT	ERA	G	GS	CG	IP	H	BB	SO	ShO	Relief W	L	SV	AB	H	HR	BA	PO	A	E	DP	TC/G	FA
1904	DET	A	0	1	.000	3.07	5	2	1	14.2	14	6	7	0	0	0	0	5	0	0	.000	3	10	0	0	2.6	1.000
1907	STL	N	2	4	.333	1.67	8	6	6	64.2	56	21	34	1	0	0	0	22	2	0	.091	5	16	1	2	2.8	.955
1908			15	**25**	.375	2.03	48	37	23	324.1	236	95	145	5	2	1	2	90	17	0	.189	12	108	8	1	2.7	.938
1909	NY	N	18	12	.600	2.47	39	30	18	270	239	87	121	2	3	1	0	89	13	0	.146	8	86	9	2	2.6	.913
1910			4	11	.267	3.81	19	11	6	99.1	106	40	55	0	1	4	0	32	5	0	.156	3	36	1	3	2.1	.975
1911			6	4	.600	3.31	17	9	4	81.2	73	33	39	1	2	1	0	25	5	0	.200	6	23	1	0	1.8	.967
6 yrs.			45	57	.441	2.49	136	95	58	854.2	724	282	401	9	8	7	2	263	42	0	.160	37	279	20	8	2.5	.940

Claude Raymond

RAYMOND, JEAN CLAUDE MARC (Frenchy)
B. May 7, 1937, St. Jean, Que., Canada.
BR TR 5′10″ 175 lbs.

Year	Team		W	L	PCT	ERA	G	GS	CG	IP	H	BB	SO	ShO	Relief W	L	SV	AB	H	HR	BA	PO	A	E	DP	TC/G	FA
1959	CHI	A	0	0	—	9.00	3	0	0	4	5	2	1	0	0	0	0	0	0	0	—	0	1	0	1	0.3	1.000
1961	MIL	N	1	0	1.000	3.98	13	0	0	20.1	22	9	13	0	1	0	2	3	0	0	.000	2	5	0	0	0.5	1.000
1962			5	5	.500	2.74	26	0	0	42.2	37	15	40	0	5	5	10	8	0	0	.000	2	3	0	0	0.2	1.000
1963			4	6	.400	5.40	45	0	0	53.1	57	27	44	0	4	6	5	4	2	0	.500	4	12	0	1	0.4	1.000
1964	HOU	N	5	5	.500	2.82	38	0	0	79.2	64	22	56	0	5	5	0	14	1	0	.071	4	20	1	3	0.7	.960
1965			7	4	.636	2.90	33	7	2	96.1	87	16	79	0	3	2	5	26	3	0	.115	5	15	3	1	0.7	.870
1966			7	5	.583	3.13	62	0	0	92	85	25	73	0	7	5	16	9	1	0	.111	7	4	1	0	0.2	.917
1967	2 teams	HOU N (21G 0–4)	ATL N (28G 4–1)																								
″	total		4	5	.444	2.89	49	0	0	65.1	64	18	31	0	4	5	10	7	1	0	.143	4	10	0	0	0.3	1.000
1968	ATL	N	3	5	.375	2.83	36	0	0	60.1	56	18	37	0	3	5	10	7	1	0	.143	4	12	2	0	0.5	.889
1969	2 teams	ATL N (33G 2–2)	MON N (15G 1–2)																								
″	total		3	4	.429	4.89	48	0	0	70	77	21	26	0	3	4	2	11	2	0	.182	7	11	3	2	0.4	.857
1970	MON	N	6	7	.462	4.45	59	0	0	83	76	27	68	0	6	7	23	11	0	0	.000	6	7	4	0	0.3	.765
1971			1	7	.125	4.67	37	0	0	54	81	25	29	0	1	7	0	1	0	0	.000	4	13	0	0	0.5	1.000
12 yrs.			46	53	.465	3.66	449	7	2	721	711	225	497	0	42	51	83	101	11	0	.109	49	113	14	8	0.4	.920

Harry Raymond

RAYMOND, HARRY H.
B. Feb. 20, 1862, Utica, N. Y. D. Mar. 21, 1925, San Diego, Calif.
5′9″ 179 lbs.

Year	Team		W	L	PCT	ERA	G	GS	CG	IP	H	BB	SO	ShO	Relief W	L	SV	AB	H	HR	BA	PO	A	E	DP	TC/G	FA
1889	LOU	AA	1	0	1.000	1.00	1	1	1	9	8	11	1	0	0	0	0	*				59	55	15	1	4.0	.884

Barry Raziano

RAZIANO, BARRY JOHN
B. Feb. 5, 1947, New Orleans, La.
BB TR 5′10″ 175 lbs.

Year	Team		W	L	PCT	ERA	G	GS	CG	IP	H	BB	SO	ShO	Relief W	L	SV	AB	H	HR	BA	PO	A	E	DP	TC/G	FA
1973	KC	A	0	0	—	5.40	2	0	0	5	6	1	0	0	0	0	0	0	0	0	—	0	2	0	0	1.0	1.000
1974	CAL	A	1	2	.333	6.35	13	0	0	17	15	8	9	0	1	2	1	0	0	0	—	1	1	0	0	0.2	1.000
2 yrs.			1	2	.333	6.14	15	0	0	22	21	9	9	0	1	2	1	0	0	0		1	3	0	0	0.3	1.000

Rip Reagan

REAGAN, ARTHUR EDGAR
Born Arthur Edgar Ragan.
B. June 5, 1878, Lincoln, Ill. D. June 8, 1953, Kansas City, Mo.
BR TR 5′11″ 170 lbs.

Year	Team		W	L	PCT	ERA	G	GS	CG	IP	H	BB	SO	ShO	Relief W	L	SV	AB	H	HR	BA	PO	A	E	DP	TC/G	FA
1903	CIN	N	0	2	.000	6.00	3	2	2	18	40	7	7	0	0	0	0	8	2	0	.250	1	4	0	0	1.7	1.000

Jeff Reardon

REARDON, JEFFREY JAMES
B. Oct. 1, 1955, Pittsfield, Mass.
BR TR 6′ 190 lbs.

Year	Team		W	L	PCT	ERA	G	GS	CG	IP	H	BB	SO	ShO	Relief W	L	SV	AB	H	HR	BA	PO	A	E	DP	TC/G	FA
1979	NY	N	1	2	.333	1.71	18	0	0	21	12	9	10	0	1	2	2	0	0	0	—	1	1	0	1	0.1	1.000
1980			8	7	.533	2.62	61	0	0	110	96	47	101	0	8	7	6	8	0	0	.000	1	7	4	0	0.2	.667
1981	2 teams	NY N (18G 1–0)	MON N (25G 2–0)																								
″	total		3	0	1.000	2.18	43	0	0	70.1	48	21	49	0	3	0	8	5	0	0	.000	1	4	0	0	0.1	1.000
1982	MON	N	7	4	.636	2.06	75	0	0	109	87	36	86	0	7	4	26	10	1	0	.100	6	9	1	0	0.2	.938
1983			7	9	.438	3.03	66	0	0	92	87	44	78	0	7	9	21	8	1	0	.125	3	4	2	0	0.1	.778
1984			7	7	.500	2.90	68	0	0	87	70	37	79	0	7	7	23	9	0	0	.000	2	5	1	0	0.1	.875
1985			2	8	.200	3.18	63	0	0	87.2	68	26	67	0	2	8	**41**	7	2	0	.286	9	8	0	0	0.3	1.000
1986			7	9	.438	3.94	62	0	0	89	83	26	67	0	7	9	35	8	1	0	.125	8	10	0	1	0.3	1.000
1987	MIN	A	8	8	.500	4.48	63	0	0	80.1	70	28	83	0	8	**8**	31	0	0	0	—	2	6	0	1	0.1	1.000
1988			2	4	.333	2.47	63	0	0	73	68	15	56	0	2	4	42	0	0	0	—	1	2	0	0	0.0	1.000
1989			5	4	.556	4.07	65	0	0	73	68	12	46	0	5	4	31	0	0	0	—	1	3	0	0	0.1	1.000
1990	BOS	A	5	3	.625	3.16	47	0	0	51.1	39	19	33	0	5	3	21	0	0	0	—	1	4	1	0	0.1	.833
1991			1	4	.200	3.03	57	0	0	59.1	54	16	44	0	1	4	40	0	0	0	—	2	1	0	0	0.1	1.000
1992	2 teams	BOS A (46G 2–2)	ATL N (14G 3–0)																								
″	total		5	2	.714	3.41	60	0	0	58	67	9	39	0	5	2	30	0	0	0		2	4	0	1	0.1	1.000
1993	CIN	N	4	6	.400	4.09	58	0	0	61.2	66	10	35	0	4	6	8	2	0	0	.000	4	6	2	0	0.2	.833
1994	NY	A	1	0	1.000	8.38	11	0	0	9.2	17	3	4	0	1	0	2	0	0	0	—	0	1	0	0	0.1	1.000
16 yrs.			73	77	.487	3.16	880	0	0	1132.1	1000	358	877	0	73	77	367 **2nd**	57	5	0	.088	44	75	11	4	0.1	.915
DIVISIONAL PLAYOFF SERIES																											
1981	MON	N	0	1	.000	2.08	3	0	0	4.1	1	1	2	0	0	1	2	1	0	0	.000	0	0	0	0	0.0	.000
LEAGUE CHAMPIONSHIP SERIES																											
1981	MON	N	0	0	—	27.00	1	0	0	1	3	0	0	0	0	0	0	0	0	0	—	0	0	0	0	0.0	.000
1987	MIN	A	1	1	.500	5.06	4	0	0	5.1	7	3	5	0	1	1	2	0	0	0	—	0	1	0	0	0.3	1.000
1990	BOS	A	0	0	—	9.00	1	0	0	2	3	1	0	0	0	0	0	0	0	0	—	0	0	0	0	0.0	.000
1992	ATL	N	1	0	1.000	0.00	3	0	0	3	0	2	3	0	1	0	1	0	0	0	—	0	0	0	0	0.0	.000
4 yrs.			2	1	.667	6.35	9	0	0	11.1	13	6	8	0	2	1	3 **6th**	0	0	0		0	1	0	0	0.1	1.000

Jeff Reardon *continued*

Year	Team	Lg	W	L	PCT	ERA	G	GS	CG	IP	H	BB	SO	ShO	Relief Pitching W	Relief Pitching L	Relief Pitching SV	Batting AB	Batting H	Batting HR	BA	PO	A	E	DP	TC/G	FA
WORLD SERIES																											
1987	MIN	A	0	0	—	0.00	4	0	0	4.2	5	0	3	0	0	0	1	0	0	0	—	0	0	0	0	0.0	.000
1992	ATL	N	0	1	.000	13.50	2	0	0	1.1	2	1	1	0	0	1	0	0	0	0	—	0	0	0	0	0.0	.000
2 yrs.			0	1	.000	3.00	6	0	0	6	7	1	4	0	0	1	1	0	0	0		0	0	0	0	0.0	

Jerry Reardon

REARDON, JEREMIAH
B. 1866, St. Louis, Mo. Deceased.

Year	Team	Lg	W	L	PCT	ERA	G	GS	CG	IP	H	BB	SO	ShO	Relief Pitching W	Relief Pitching L	Relief Pitching SV	Batting AB	Batting H	Batting HR	BA	PO	A	E	DP	TC/G	FA
1886	2 teams	STL N (1G 0–1)	CIN AA (1G 0–1)																								
"	total		0	2	.000	9.00	2	2	1	10	15	9	0	0	0	0	0	7	1	0	.143	1	1	0	0	0.7	1.000

Frank Reberger

REBERGER, FRANK BEALL (Crane)
B. June 7, 1944, Caldwell, Ida.
BL TR 6′ 5″ 200 lbs.

Year	Team	Lg	W	L	PCT	ERA	G	GS	CG	IP	H	BB	SO	ShO	Relief Pitching W	Relief Pitching L	Relief Pitching SV	Batting AB	Batting H	Batting HR	BA	PO	A	E	DP	TC/G	FA
1968	CHI	N	0	1	.000	4.50	3	1	0	6	9	2	3	0	0	1	0	0	0	0	—	0	2	0	0	0.7	1.000
1969	SD	N	1	2	.333	3.58	67	0	0	88	83	41	65	0	1	2	6	5	1	0	.200	6	23	1	0	0.4	.967
1970	SF	N	7	8	.467	5.57	45	18	3	152	178	98	117	0	1	2	2	47	11	0	.234	15	19	4	1	0.8	.895
1971			3	0	1.000	3.89	13	7	0	44	37	19	21	0	0	0	0	13	3	0	.231	6	6	0	3	0.9	1.000
1972			3	4	.429	4.00	20	11	2	99	97	37	52	0	0	0	0	35	8	0	.229	4	22	1	0	1.4	.963
5 yrs.			14	15	.483	4.51	148	37	5	389	404	197	258	0	2	5	8	100	23	0	.230	31	72	6	4	0.7	.945

John Reccius

RECCIUS, JOHN
Brother of Phil Reccius.
B. Oct. 29, 1859, Louisville, Ky. D. Sept. 1, 1930, Louisville, Ky.
5′ 6½″

Year	Team	Lg	W	L	PCT	ERA	G	GS	CG	IP	H	BB	SO	ShO	Relief Pitching W	Relief Pitching L	Relief Pitching SV	Batting AB	Batting H	Batting HR	BA	PO	A	E	DP	TC/G	FA
1882	LOU	AA	4	6	.400	*3.03*	13	10	9	95	106	22	31	1	0	0	0	266	63	1	.237	91	40	23	3	2.0	.851
1883			0	0	—	2.25	1	0	0	4	10	0	0	0	0	0	0	63	9	0	.143	35	3	7	1	2.4	.844
2 yrs.			4	6	.400	3.00	14	10	9	99	116	22	31	1	0	0	0	*				126	43	30	4	2.1	.849

Phil Reccius

RECCIUS, PHILIP
Brother of John Reccius.
B. June 7, 1862, Louisville, Ky. D. Feb. 15, 1903, Louisville, Ky.
5′ 9″ 163 lbs.

Year	Team	Lg	W	L	PCT	ERA	G	GS	CG	IP	H	BB	SO	ShO	Relief Pitching W	Relief Pitching L	Relief Pitching SV	Batting AB	Batting H	Batting HR	BA	PO	A	E	DP	TC/G	FA
1884	LOU	AA	6	7	.462	*2.71*	18	11	11	129.1	118	19	46	0	2	0	0	263	63	3	.240	6	1	2	0	2.3	.778
1885			0	4	.000	*3.83*	7	5	4	40	46	11	10	0	0	0	1	402	97	1	.241	107	193	59	18	3.5	.836
1886			0	1	.000	9.00	1	1	0	3	7	3	0	0	0	0	0	13	4	0	.308	6	2	1	0	1.5	.889
1887	CLE	AA	0	0	—	7.71	1	0	0	7	8	5	0	0	0	0	0	266	56	0	.211	109	144	34	18	3.9	.882
4 yrs.			6	12	.333	3.26	27	17	15	179.1	179	38	56	0	2	0	1	*				285	490	128	43	3.3	.858

Phil Redding

REDDING, PHILIP HAYDEN
B. Jan. 25, 1890, Crystal Springs, Miss. D. Mar. 31, 1929, Greenwood, Miss.
BL TR 5′11½″ 190 lbs.

Year	Team	Lg	W	L	PCT	ERA	G	GS	CG	IP	H	BB	SO	ShO	Relief Pitching W	Relief Pitching L	Relief Pitching SV	Batting AB	Batting H	Batting HR	BA	PO	A	E	DP	TC/G	FA
1912	STL	N	2	1	.667	4.97	3	3	2	25.1	31	11	9	0	0	0	0	8	0	0	.000	1	4	0	1	1.7	1.000
1913			0	0	—	6.75	1	0	0	2.2	2	1	1	0	0	0	0	1	0	0	.000	0	1	0	0	1.0	1.000
2 yrs.			2	1	.667	5.14	4	3	2	28	33	12	10	0	0	0	0	9	0	0	.000	1	5	0	1	1.5	1.000

Pete Redfern

REDFERN, PETER IRVINE
B. Aug. 25, 1954, Glendale, Calif.
BR TR 6′ 2″ 195 lbs.

Year	Team	Lg	W	L	PCT	ERA	G	GS	CG	IP	H	BB	SO	ShO	Relief Pitching W	Relief Pitching L	Relief Pitching SV	Batting AB	Batting H	Batting HR	BA	PO	A	E	DP	TC/G	FA
1976	MIN	A	8	8	.500	3.51	23	23	1	118	105	63	74	1	0	0	0	0	0	0	—	8	14	3	1	1.1	.880
1977			6	9	.400	5.19	30	28	1	137	164	66	73	0	1	0	0	0	0	0	—	11	23	1	1	1.2	.971
1978			0	2	.000	6.52	3	2	0	9.2	10	6	4	0	0	0	0	0	0	0	—	0	3	0	0	1.0	1.000
1979			7	3	.700	3.50	40	6	0	108	106	35	85	0	4	3	1	0	0	0	—	7	9	1	2	0.4	.941
1980			7	7	.500	4.54	23	16	2	105	117	33	73	0	1	1	2	0	0	0	—	9	10	2	0	0.9	.905
1981			9	8	.529	4.06	24	23	3	142	140	52	77	0	0	0	0	0	0	0	—	6	18	0	0	1.0	1.000
1982			5	11	.313	6.58	27	13	2	94.1	122	51	40	0	2	3	0	0	0	0	—	8	13	0	2	0.8	1.000
7 yrs.			42	48	.467	4.54	170	111	9	714	764	306	426	1	8	7	3	0	0	0		49	90	7	6	0.9	.952

Bob Reed

REED, ROBERT EDWARD
B. Jan. 12, 1945, Boston, Mass.
BR TR 5′10″ 175 lbs.

Year	Team	Lg	W	L	PCT	ERA	G	GS	CG	IP	H	BB	SO	ShO	Relief Pitching W	Relief Pitching L	Relief Pitching SV	Batting AB	Batting H	Batting HR	BA	PO	A	E	DP	TC/G	FA
1969	DET	A	0	0	—	1.84	8	1	0	14.2	9	8	9	0	0	0	0	2	1	0	.500	1	3	0	0	0.5	1.000
1970			2	4	.333	4.89	16	4	0	46	54	14	26	0	1	2	2	12	1	0	.083	2	4	0	0	0.4	1.000
2 yrs.			2	4	.333	4.15	24	5	0	60.2	63	22	35	0	1	2	2	14	2	0	.143	3	7	0	0	0.4	1.000

Howie Reed

REED, HOWARD DEAN (Diz)
B. Dec. 21, 1936, Dallas, Tex. D. Dec. 7, 1984, Corpus Christi, Tex.
BR TR 6′ 1″ 195 lbs.

Year	Team	Lg	W	L	PCT	ERA	G	GS	CG	IP	H	BB	SO	ShO	Relief Pitching W	Relief Pitching L	Relief Pitching SV	Batting AB	Batting H	Batting HR	BA	PO	A	E	DP	TC/G	FA
1958	KC	A	1	0	1.000	0.87	3	1	1	10.1	5	4	5	0	0	0	0	2	0	0	.000	0	1	0	0	0.3	1.000
1959			0	3	.000	7.40	6	3	0	20.2	26	10	11	0	0	1	0	3	0	0	.000	0	2	1	0	0.5	.667
1960			0	0	—	0.00	1	0	0	1.2	2	0	1	0	0	0	0	0	0	0	—	0	0	0	0	0.0	.000
1964	LA	N	3	4	.429	3.20	26	7	0	90	79	36	52	0	0	1	1	20	2	0	.100	5	20	1	2	1.0	.962
1965			7	5	.583	3.12	38	5	0	78	73	27	47	0	6	3	1	12	0	0	.000	3	18	2	2	0.6	.913
1966	2 teams	LA N (1G 0–0)	CAL A (19G 0–1)																								
"	total		0	1	.000	2.82	20	1	0	44.2	40	15	17	0	0	0	1	7	0	0	.000	4	6	0	0	0.5	1.000
1967	HOU	N	1	1	.500	3.44	4	2	0	18.1	19	2	9	0	1	0	0	4	0	0	.000	0	2	0	0	0.5	1.000
1969	MON	N	6	7	.462	4.84	31	15	2	106	119	50	59	1	0	0	1	32	4	1	.125	10	27	0	0	1.2	1.000
1970			6	5	.545	3.13	57	1	0	89	81	40	42	0	6	4	5	10	0	0	.000	7	13	0	2	0.4	1.000
1971			2	3	.400	4.26	43	0	0	57	66	24	25	0	2	3	0	1	0	0	.000	3	9	0	2	0.3	1.000
10 yrs.			26	29	.473	3.72	229	35	3	515.2	510	208	268	1	15	12	9	91	6	1	.066	32	98	4	8	0.6	.970
WORLD SERIES																											
1965	LA	N	0	0	—	8.10	2	0	0	3.1	2	2	4	0	0	0	0	0	0	0	—	1	0	0	0	0.5	1.000

Jerry Reed

REED, JERRY MAXWELL
B. Oct. 8, 1955, Bryson City, N. C.
BR TR 6′ 1″ 190 lbs.

Year	Team	Lg	W	L	PCT	ERA	G	GS	CG	IP	H	BB	SO	ShO	Relief Pitching W	Relief Pitching L	Relief Pitching SV	Batting AB	Batting H	Batting HR	BA	PO	A	E	DP	TC/G	FA
1981	PHI	N	0	1	.000	7.20	4	0	0	5	7	6	5	0	0	1	0	0	0	0	—	3	0	0	0	0.8	1.000
1982	2 teams	PHI N (7G 1–0)	CLE A (6G 1–1)																								
"	total		2	1	.667	4.07	13	1	0	24.1	26	6	11	0	2	0	0	0	0	0		1	3	1	0	0.4	.800
1983	CLE	A	0	0	—	7.17	7	0	0	21.1	26	9	11	0	0	0	0	0	0	0	—	3	8	1	0	1.7	.917
1985			3	5	.375	4.11	33	5	0	72.1	67	19	37	0	3	2	8	0	0	0	—	13	8	0	1	0.6	1.000
1986	SEA	A	4	0	1.000	3.12	11	4	0	34.2	38	13	16	0	1	0	0	0	0	0	—	4	3	0	0	0.6	1.000

Year	Team	W	L	PCT	ERA	G	GS	CG	IP	H	BB	SO	ShO	Relief Pitching W	Relief Pitching L	Relief Pitching SV	Batting AB	Batting H	Batting HR	BA	PO	A	E	DP	TC/G	FA
Jerry Reed *continued*																										
1987		1	2	.333	3.42	39	1	0	81.2	79	24	51	0	1	2	7	0	0	0	—	10	8	0	1	0.5	1.000
1988		1	1	.500	3.96	46	0	0	86.1	82	33	48	0	1	1	1	0	0	0	—	6	14	1	2	0.5	.952
1989		7	7	.500	3.19	52	1	0	101.2	89	43	50	0	7	6	0	0	0	0	—	10	12	0	1	0.4	1.000
1990	2 teams SEA A (4G 0–1) BOS A (29G 2–1)																									
"	total	2	2	.500	4.82	33	0	0	52.1	63	19	19	0	2	2	2	0	0	0		8	5	0	2	0.4	1.000
9 yrs.		20	19	.513	3.94	238	12	0	479.2	477	172	248	0	17	14	18	0	0	0		58	61	3	7	0.5	.975
Rick Reed	REED, RICHARD ALLEN B. Aug. 16, 1964, Huntington, W. Va.																				BR TR 6′ 195 lbs.					
1988	PIT N	1	0	1.000	3.00	2	2	0	12	10	2	6	0	0	0	0	4	0	0	.000	0	3	0	1	1.5	1.000
1989		1	4	.200	5.60	15	7	0	54.2	62	11	34	0	0	0	0	13	1	0	.077	6	5	0	0	0.7	1.000
1990		2	3	.400	4.36	13	8	1	53.2	62	12	27	1	0	0	1	16	4	0	.250	6	4	1	0	0.8	.909
1991		0	0	—	10.38	1	1	0	4.1	8	1	2	0	0	0	0	2	1	0	.500	0	0	0	0	0.0	.000
1992	KC A	3	7	.300	3.68	19	18	1	100.1	105	20	49	1	1	0	0	0	0	0	—	6	18	1	0	1.3	.960
1993	2 teams KC A (1G 0–0) TEX A (2G 1–0)																									
"	total	1	0	1.000	5.87	3	0	0	7.2	12	2	5	0	1	0	0	0	0	0		3	1	0	0	1.3	1.000
1994	TEX A	1	1	.500	5.94	4	3	0	16.2	17	7	12	0	0	0	0	0	0	0	—	2	2	0	0	1.0	1.000
1995	CIN N	0	0	—	5.82	4	3	0	17	18	3	10	0	0	0	0	3	0	0	.000	2	1	0	0	0.8	1.000
8 yrs.		9	15	.375	4.63	61	42	2	266.1	294	58	145	2	2	0	1	38	6	0	.158	25	34	2	1	1.0	.967
Ron Reed	REED, RONALD LEE B. Nov. 2, 1942, La Porte, Ind.																				BR TR 6′ 6″ 215 lbs.					
1966	ATL N	1	1	.500	2.16	2	2	0	8.1	7	4	6	0	0	0	0	2	0	0	.000	0	0	0	0	0.0	.000
1967		1	1	.500	2.95	3	3	0	21.1	21	3	11	0	0	0	0	8	0	0	.000	1	7	0	0	2.7	1.000
1968		11	10	.524	3.35	35	28	6	201.2	189	49	111	1	0	0	0	62	10	0	.161	16	32	1	3	1.4	.980
1969		18	10	.643	3.47	36	33	7	241	227	56	160	1	0	0	0	80	10	0	.125	20	30	2	3	1.4	.962
1970		7	10	.412	4.40	21	18	6	135	140	39	68	0	0	1	0	44	4	0	.091	10	24	1	2	1.7	.971
1971		13	14	.481	3.73	32	32	8	222	221	54	129	1	0	0	0	74	11	0	.149	19	27	0	1	1.4	1.000
1972		11	15	.423	3.93	31	30	11	213	222	60	111	1	0	0	0	73	13	0	.178	15	36	3	3	1.7	.944
1973		4	11	.267	4.42	20	19	2	116	133	31	64	0	0	0	1	45	9	0	.200	15	20	1	1	1.8	.972
1974		10	11	.476	3.39	28	28	6	186	171	41	78	2	0	0	0	57	6	0	.105	11	21	0	2	1.1	1.000
1975	2 teams ATL N (10G 4–5) STL N (24G 9–8)																									
"	total	13	13	.500	3.52	34	34	8	250.1	274	53	139	2	0	0	0	82	15	0	.183	15	33	1	0	1.4	.980
1976	PHI N	8	7	.533	2.46	59	4	1	128	88	32	96	0	6	7	14	24	4	0	.167	7	13	2	1	0.4	.909
1977		7	5	.583	2.76	60	3	0	124	101	37	84	0	7	5	15	18	2	0	.111	6	16	0	0	0.4	1.000
1978		3	4	.429	2.23	66	0	0	109	87	23	85	0	3	4	17	6	0	0	.000	6	8	1	0	0.2	.933
1979		13	8	.619	4.15	61	0	0	102	110	32	58	0	**13**	8	5	10	3	0	.300	3	13	0	3	0.3	1.000
1980		7	5	.583	4.05	55	0	0	91	88	30	54	0	7	5	9	10	3	0	.300	14	15	0	1	0.5	1.000
1981		5	3	.625	3.10	39	0	0	61	54	17	40	0	5	3	8	6	3	0	.500	0	8	0	0	0.2	1.000
1982		5	5	.500	2.66	57	2	0	98	85	24	57	0	4	4	14	12	4	0	.333	8	21	0	2	0.5	1.000
1983		9	1	.900	3.48	61	0	0	95.2	89	34	73	0	9	1	8	6	1	0	.167	2	7	0	0	0.1	1.000
1984	CHI A	0	6	.000	3.08	51	0	0	73	67	14	57	0	0	6	12	1	0	0	.000	2	11	1	3	0.3	.929
19 yrs.		146	140	.510	3.46	751	236	55	2476.1	2374	633	1481	8	54	44	103	620	98	0	.158	170	342	13	25	0.7	.975
DIVISIONAL PLAYOFF SERIES																										
1981	PHI N	0	0	—	3.00	4	0	0	6	5	3	4	0	0	0	0	0	0	0	—	0	0	0	0	0.0	.000
LEAGUE CHAMPIONSHIP SERIES																										
1969	ATL N	0	1	.000	21.60	1	1	0	1.2	5	3	3	0	0	0	0	0	0	0	—	0	1	0	0	1.0	1.000
1976	PHI N	0	0	—	7.71	2	0	0	4.2	6	2	2	0	0	0	0	1	0	0	.000	0	0	0	0	0.0	.000
1977		0	0	—	1.80	3	0	0	5	3	2	5	0	0	0	0	0	0	0	—	0	0	0	0	0.0	.000
1978		0	0	—	2.25	2	0	0	4	6	0	2	0	0	0	0	0	0	0	—	0	0	0	0	0.0	.000
1980		0	1	.000	18.00	3	0	0	2	3	1	1	0	0	1	0	0	0	0	—	1	0	0	0	0.3	1.000
1983		0	0	—	2.70	2	0	0	3.1	4	1	3	0	0	0	0	0	0	0	—	0	1	0	0	0.5	1.000
6 yrs.		0	2	.000	6.53	13 **5th**	1	0	20.2	27	9	16	0	0	1	0	1	0	0	.000	1	2	0	0	0.2	1.000
WORLD SERIES																										
1980	PHI N	0	0	—	0.00	2	0	0	2	2	0	2	0	0	0	1	0	0	0	—	0	0	0	0	0.0	.000
1983		0	0	—	2.70	3	0	0	3.1	4	2	4	0	0	0	0	0	0	0	—	0	0	0	0	0.0	.000
2 yrs.		0	0		1.69	5	0	0	5.1	6	2	6	0	0	0	1	0	0	0		0	0	0	0	0.0	
Steve Reed	REED, STEVEN VINCENT B. Mar. 11, 1966, Los Angeles, Calif.																				BR TR 6′ 2″ 200 lbs.					
1992	SF N	1	0	1.000	2.30	18	0	0	15.2	13	3	11	0	1	0	0	0	0	0	—	3	4	0	0	0.4	1.000
1993	CLR N	9	5	.643	4.48	64	0	0	84.1	80	30	51	0	9	5	3	9	0	0	.000	3	14	1	1	0.3	.944
1994		3	2	.600	3.94	**61**	0	0	64	79	26	51	0	3	2	3	2	0	0	.000	0	5	0	0	0.1	1.000
1995		5	2	.714	2.14	71	0	0	84	61	21	79	0	5	2	3	3	1	0	.333	4	16	1	1	0.3	.952
4 yrs.		18	9	.667	3.41	214	0	0	248	233	80	192	0	18	9	9	14	1	0	.071	10	39	2	2	0.2	.961
DIVISIONAL PLAYOFF SERIES																										
1995	CLR N	0	0	—	0.00	3	0	0	2.2	2	1	3	0	0	0	0	0	0	0	—	0	1	0	0	0.3	1.000
Bill Reeder	REEDER, WILLIAM EDGAR B. Feb. 20, 1922, Dike, Tex.																				BR TR 6′ 5″ 205 lbs.					
1949	STL N	1	1	.500	5.08	21	1	0	33.2	33	30	21	0	1	0	0	3	0	0	.000	1	6	1	0	0.4	.875
Stan Rees	REES, STANLEY MILTON B. Feb. 25, 1899, Cynthiana, Ky. D. Aug. 30, 1937, Lexington, Ky.																				BL TL 6′ 3″ 190 lbs.					
1918	WAS A	1	0	1.000	0.00	2	0	0	2	3	4	1	0	1	0	0	0	0	0	—	0	1	0	0	0.5	1.000
Bobby Reeves	REEVES, ROBERT EDWIN (Gunner) B. June 24, 1904, Hill City, Tenn. D. June 4, 1993, Chattanooga, Tenn.																				BR TR 5′11″ 170 lbs.					
1931	BOS A	0	0	—	3.68	1	0	0	7.1	6	1	0	0	0	0	0	*				23	29	3	4	3.1	.945

Mike Regan

REGAN, MICHAEL JOSEPH BR TR 5′11″ 165 lbs.
B. Nov. 19, 1887, Phoenix, N. Y. D. May 22, 1961, Albany, N. Y.

Year	Team	W	L	PCT	ERA	G	GS	CG	IP	H	BB	SO	ShO	Relief W	Relief L	Relief SV	AB	H	HR	BA	PO	A	E	DP	TC/G	FA
1917	CIN N	11	10	.524	2.71	32	26	16	216	228	41	50	1	0	0	0	75	15	0	.200	10	77	4	1	2.8	.956
1918		5	5	.500	3.26	22	6	4	80	77	29	15	3	3	2	2	27	8	0	.296	6	21	3	0	1.4	.900
1919		0	0	—	0.00	1	0	0	2.1	1	0	1	0	0	0	0	1	0	0	.000	0	0	0	0	0.0	.000
3 yrs.		16	15	.516	2.84	55	32	20	298.1	306	70	66	4	3	2	2	103	23	0	.223	16	98	7	1	2.2	.942

Phil Regan

REGAN, PHILIP RAYMOND (The Vulture) BR TR 6′ 3″ 200 lbs.
B. Apr. 6, 1937, Otsego, Mich.
Manager 1995.

Year	Team	W	L	PCT	ERA	G	GS	CG	IP	H	BB	SO	ShO	Relief W	Relief L	Relief SV	AB	H	HR	BA	PO	A	E	DP	TC/G	FA
1960	DET A	0	4	.000	4.50	17	7	0	68	70	25	38	0	0	0	1	17	1	0	.059	1	8	0	1	0.5	1.000
1961		10	7	.588	5.25	32	16	6	120	134	41	46	0	2	2	2	40	3	0	.075	7	8	0	0	0.5	1.000
1962		11	9	.550	4.04	35	23	6	171.1	169	64	87	0	1	2	0	63	13	0	.206	15	17	0	1	0.9	1.000
1963		15	9	.625	3.86	38	27	5	189	179	59	115	1	2	1	1	63	9	1	.143	6	20	1	0	0.7	.963
1964		5	10	.333	5.03	32	21	2	146.2	162	49	91	0	1	0	1	41	13	0	.317	13	20	0	1	1.0	1.000
1965		1	5	.167	5.05	16	7	1	51.2	57	20	37	0	0	0	0	12	1	0	.083	3	5	0	3	0.5	1.000
1966	LA N	14	1	.933	1.62	65	0	0	116.2	85	24	88	0	**14**	1	**21**	21	3	0	.143	12	17	0	1	0.4	1.000
1967		6	9	.400	2.99	55	3	0	96.1	108	32	53	0	5	7	6	10	1	0	.100	3	23	2	1	0.5	.929
1968	2 teams LA N (5G 2–0) CHI N (68G 10–5)																									
″	total	12	5	.706	2.27	73	0	0	134.2	119	25	67	0	**12**	5	**25**	21	3	0	.143	9	23	2	1	0.5	.941
1969	CHI N	12	6	.667	3.70	71	0	0	112	120	35	56	0	12	6	17	15	1	0	.067	8	20	0	1	0.4	1.000
1970		5	9	.357	4.74	54	0	0	76	81	32	31	0	5	**9**	12	9	0	0	.000	7	18	0	3	0.5	1.000
1971		5	5	.500	3.95	48	1	0	73	84	33	28	0	4	5	6	8	0	0	.000	5	18	2	1	0.5	.920
1972	2 teams CHI N (5G 0–1) CHI A (10G 0–1)																									
″	total	0	2	.000	3.63	15	0	0	17.1	24	8	6	0	0	2	0	1	1	0	1.000	1	3	0	1	0.3	1.000
13 yrs.		96	81	.542	3.84	551	105	20	1372.2	1392	447	743	1	58	40	92	321	49	1	.153	90	200	7	15	0.5	.976
WORLD SERIES																										
1966	LA N	0	0	—	0.00	2	0	0	1.2	0	1	2	0	0	0	0	0	0	0	—	0	1	0	0	0.5	1.000

Earl Reid

REID, EARL PERCY BL TR 6′ 3″ 190 lbs.
B. June 8, 1913, Bangor, Ala. D. May 11, 1984, Cullman, Ala.

Year	Team	W	L	PCT	ERA	G	GS	CG	IP	H	BB	SO	ShO	Relief W	Relief L	Relief SV	AB	H	HR	BA	PO	A	E	DP	TC/G	FA
1946	BOS N	1	0	1.000	3.00	2	0	0	3	4	3	2	0	1	0	0	0	0	0	—	0	0	0	0	0.0	.000

Bill Reidy

REIDY, WILLIAM JOSEPH (Wee Willie) BR TR 5′10″ 175 lbs.
B. Oct. 9, 1873, Cleveland, Ohio D. Oct. 14, 1915, Cleveland, Ohio.

Year	Team	W	L	PCT	ERA	G	GS	CG	IP	H	BB	SO	ShO	Relief W	Relief L	Relief SV	AB	H	HR	BA	PO	A	E	DP	TC/G	FA
1896	NY N	0	1	.000	7.62	2	1	1	13	24	2	1	0	0	0	0	5	0	0	.000	1	3	0	0	2.0	1.000
1899	BKN N	1	0	1.000	2.57	2	1	1	7	9	2	2	0	0	0	1	3	0	0	.000	2	2	0	0	2.0	1.000
1901	MIL A	16	20	.444	4.21	37	33	28	301.1	364	62	50	2	2	2	0	112	16	0	.143	10	72	4	2	2.3	.953
1902	STL A	3	5	.375	4.45	12	9	7	95	111	13	16	0	0	1	0	41	8	0	.195	11	30	2	3	3.3	.953
1903	2 teams STL A (5G 1–4) BKN N (15G 7–6)																									
″	total	8	10	.444	3.61	20	18	16	147	183	21	29	1	0	1	0	52	10	0	.192	3	33	2	2	1.9	.947
1904	BKN N	0	4	.000	4.46	6	4	2	38.1	49	6	11	0	0	0	1	32	5	0	.156	4	20	7	1	2.8	.774
6 yrs.		28	40	.412	4.17	79	66	55	601.2	740	106	109	3	2	4	2	245	39	0	.159	31	160	15	8	2.4	.927

Art Reinhart

REINHART, ARTHUR CONRAD BL TL 6′ 1″ 170 lbs.
B. May 29, 1899, Ackley, Iowa D. Nov. 11, 1946, Houston, Tex.

Year	Team	W	L	PCT	ERA	G	GS	CG	IP	H	BB	SO	ShO	Relief W	Relief L	Relief SV	AB	H	HR	BA	PO	A	E	DP	TC/G	FA
1919	STL N	0	0	—	0.00	1	0	0		0	0	0	0	0	0	0	0	0	0	—	0	0	0	0	0.0	.000
1925		11	5	.688	3.05	20	16	15	144.2	149	47	26	1	0	0	0	67	22	0	.328	5	35	2	0	2.1	.952
1926		10	5	.667	4.22	27	11	9	143	159	47	26	0	2	2	0	63	20	0	.317	5	40	0	4	1.7	1.000
1927		5	2	.714	4.19	21	9	4	81.2	82	36	15	2	0	0	1	32	10	0	.313	3	13	0	3	0.7	1.000
1928		4	6	.400	2.87	23	9	3	75.1	80	27	12	1	2	2	2	24	4	0	.167	5	15	0	0	0.9	1.000
5 yrs.		30	18	.625	3.60	92	45	31	444.2	470	157	79	4	4	4	3	186	56	0	.301	18	103	2	7	1.3	.984
WORLD SERIES																										
1926	STL N	0	1	.000	∞	1	0	0		1	4	0	0	0	1	0	0	0	0	—	0	0	0	0	0.0	.000

Bobby Reis

REIS, ROBERT JOSEPH THOMAS BR TR 6′ 1″ 175 lbs.
B. Jan. 2, 1909, Woodside, N. Y. D. May 1, 1973, St. Paul, Minn.

Year	Team	W	L	PCT	ERA	G	GS	CG	IP	H	BB	SO	ShO	Relief W	Relief L	Relief SV	AB	H	HR	BA	PO	A	E	DP	TC/G	FA
1935	BKN N	3	2	.600	2.83	14	2	1	41.1	46	24	7	0	1	2	2	85	21	0	.247	7	7	1	0	2.5	.933
1936	BOS N	6	5	.545	4.48	35	5	3	138.2	152	74	25	0	5	1	0	60	13	0	.217	14	47	0	2	1.6	1.000
1937		0	0	—	1.80	4	0	0	5	3	5	0	0	0	0	0	86	21	0	.244	74	2	1	1	3.0	.987
1938		1	6	.143	4.99	16	2	1	57.2	61	41	20	0	1	4	0	49	9	0	.184	17	17	1	0	1.1	.971
4 yrs.		10	13	.435	4.27	69	9	5	242.2	262	144	52	0	7	7	2	*				154	102	6	9	1.8	.977

Jack Reis

REIS, HARRIE CRANE BR TR 5′10½″ 160 lbs.
B. June 14, 1890, Cincinnati, Ohio D. July 20, 1939, Cincinnati, Ohio.

Year	Team	W	L	PCT	ERA	G	GS	CG	IP	H	BB	SO	ShO	Relief W	Relief L	Relief SV	AB	H	HR	BA	PO	A	E	DP	TC/G	FA
1911	STL N	0	0	—	0.96	3	0	0	9.1	5	8	4	0	0	0	0	2	0	0	.000	1	3	0	0	1.3	1.000

Laurie Reis

REIS, LAWRENCE P. BR TR 160 lbs.
B. Nov. 20, 1858, Chicago, Ill. D. Jan. 24, 1921, Chicago, Ill.

Year	Team	W	L	PCT	ERA	G	GS	CG	IP	H	BB	SO	ShO	Relief W	Relief L	Relief SV	AB	H	HR	BA	PO	A	E	DP	TC/G	FA
1877	CHI N	3	1	.750	0.75	4	4	4	36	29	6	11	1	0	0	0	16	2	0	.125	1	4	0	0	1.3	1.000
1878		1	3	.250	3.25	4	4	4	36	55	4	8	0	0	0	0	20	3	0	.150	2	3	4	0	1.8	.556
2 yrs.		4	4	.500	2.00	8	8	8	72	84	10	19	1	0	0	0	36	5	0	.139	3	7	4	0	1.6	.714

Tommy Reis

REIS, THOMAS EDWARD BR TR 6′ 2″ 180 lbs.
B. Aug. 6, 1914, Newport, Ky.

Year	Team	W	L	PCT	ERA	G	GS	CG	IP	H	BB	SO	ShO	Relief W	Relief L	Relief SV	AB	H	HR	BA	PO	A	E	DP	TC/G	FA
1938	2 teams PHI N (4G 0–1) BOS N (4G 0–0)																									
″	total	0	1	.000	12.27	8	0	0	11	16	9	6	0	0	1	0	2	0	0	.000	1	1	0	0	0.3	1.000

Bugs Reisigl

REISIGL, JACOB BR TR 5′10½″ 175 lbs.
B. Dec. 12, 1887, Brooklyn, N. Y. D. Feb. 24, 1957, Amsterdam, N. Y.

Year	Team	W	L	PCT	ERA	G	GS	CG	IP	H	BB	SO	ShO	Relief W	Relief L	Relief SV	AB	H	HR	BA	PO	A	E	DP	TC/G	FA
1911	CLE A	0	1	.000	6.23	2	1	1	13	13	3	6	0	0	0	0	5	0	0	.000	0	3	0	0	1.5	1.000

Doc Reisling

REISLING, FRANK CARL BR TR 5′10″ 180 lbs.
B. July 25, 1874, Martins Ferry, Ohio D. Mar. 4, 1955, Tulsa, Okla.

Year	Team	W	L	PCT	ERA	G	GS	CG	IP	H	BB	SO	ShO	Relief Pitching W	Relief Pitching L	Relief Pitching SV	Batting AB	Batting H	Batting HR	BA	PO	A	E	DP	TC/G	FA
1904	BKN N	3	4	.429	2.12	7	7	6	51	45	10	19	1	0	0	0	13	2	0	.154	5	14	2	1	3.0	.905
1905		0	1	.000	3.00	2	0	0	3	3	4	2	0	0	1	0	1	0	0	.000	0	1	0	0	0.5	1.000
1909	WAS A	2	4	.333	2.43	10	6	6	66.2	70	17	22	1	0	0	0	24	4	0	.167	3	14	0	0	1.7	1.000
1910		10	10	.500	2.54	30	20	13	191	185	44	57	2	1	2	1	60	12	0	.200	7	65	3	1	2.5	.960
4 yrs.		15	19	.441	2.45	49	33	25	311.2	303	75	100	4	1	3	1	98	18	0	.184	15	94	5	2	2.3	.956

Bryan Rekar

REKAR, BRYAN ROBERT BR TR 6′ 3″ 205 lbs.
B. June 3, 1972, Oaklawn, Ill.

Year	Team	W	L	PCT	ERA	G	GS	CG	IP	H	BB	SO	ShO	Relief Pitching W	Relief Pitching L	Relief Pitching SV	Batting AB	Batting H	Batting HR	BA	PO	A	E	DP	TC/G	FA
1995	CLR N	4	6	.400	4.98	15	14	1	85	95	24	60	0	0	0	0	26	1	0	.038	9	16	1	0	1.7	.962

Mike Remlinger

REMLINGER, MICHAEL JOHN BL TL 6′ 195 lbs.
B. Mar. 23, 1966, Middletown, N. Y.

Year	Team	W	L	PCT	ERA	G	GS	CG	IP	H	BB	SO	ShO	Relief Pitching W	Relief Pitching L	Relief Pitching SV	Batting AB	Batting H	Batting HR	BA	PO	A	E	DP	TC/G	FA
1991	SF N	2	1	.667	4.37	8	6	1	35	36	20	19	1	0	0	0	7	0	0	.000	1	6	1	0	1.0	.875
1994	NY N	1	5	.167	4.61	10	9	0	54.2	55	35	33	0	0	0	0	16	0	0	.000	1	4	0	0	0.5	1.000
1995	2 teams NY N (5G 0–1) CIN N (2G 0–0)																									
″	total	0	1	.000	6.75	7	0	0	6.2	9	5	7	0	0	1	0	1	0	0	.000	0	0	0	0	0.0	
3 yrs.		3	7	.300	4.67	25	15	1	96.1	100	60	59	1	0	1	0	24	0	0	.000	2	10	1	0	0.5	.923

Win Remmerswaal

REMMERSWAAL, WILHELMUS ABRAHAM BR TR 6′ 2″ 160 lbs.
B. Mar. 8, 1954, The Hague, Netherlands.

Year	Team	W	L	PCT	ERA	G	GS	CG	IP	H	BB	SO	ShO	Relief Pitching W	Relief Pitching L	Relief Pitching SV	Batting AB	Batting H	Batting HR	BA	PO	A	E	DP	TC/G	FA
1979	BOS A	1	0	1.000	7.20	8	0	0	20	26	12	16	0	1	0	0	0	0	0	—	1	1	0	0	0.3	1.000
1980		2	1	.667	4.63	14	0	0	35	39	9	20	0	2	1	0	0	0	0	—	1	1	0	0	0.1	1.000
2 yrs.		3	1	.750	5.56	22	0	0	55	65	21	36	0	3	1	0	0	0	0		2	2	0	0	0.2	1.000

Alex Remneas

REMNEAS, ALEXANDER NORMAN BR TR 6′ 1″ 180 lbs.
B. Feb. 21, 1886, Minneapolis, Minn. D. Aug. 27, 1975, Phoenix, Ariz.

Year	Team	W	L	PCT	ERA	G	GS	CG	IP	H	BB	SO	ShO	Relief Pitching W	Relief Pitching L	Relief Pitching SV	Batting AB	Batting H	Batting HR	BA	PO	A	E	DP	TC/G	FA
1912	DET A	0	0	—	27.00	1	0	0	1.2	5	0	0	0	0	0	0	0	0	0	—	0	1	0	0	1.0	1.000
1915	STL A	0	0	—	1.50	2	0	0	6	3	3	5	0	0	0	0	1	0	0	.000	0	2	0	0	1.0	1.000
2 yrs.		0	0		7.04	3	0	0	7.2	8	3	5	0	0	0	0	1	0	0	.000	0	3	0	0	1.0	1.000

Erwin Renfer

RENFER, ERWIN ARTHUR BR TR 6′ 180 lbs.
B. Dec. 11, 1895, Elgin, Ill. D. Oct. 26, 1958, Sycamore, Ill.

Year	Team	W	L	PCT	ERA	G	GS	CG	IP	H	BB	SO	ShO	Relief Pitching W	Relief Pitching L	Relief Pitching SV	Batting AB	Batting H	Batting HR	BA	PO	A	E	DP	TC/G	FA
1913	DET A	0	1	.000	6.00	1	1	0	6	5	3	1	0	0	0	0	2	0	0	.000	0	2	0	1	2.0	1.000

Laddie Renfroe

RENFROE, COHEN WILLAMS BB TR 5′11″ 200 lbs.
B. May 9, 1962, Natchez, Miss.

Year	Team	W	L	PCT	ERA	G	GS	CG	IP	H	BB	SO	ShO	Relief Pitching W	Relief Pitching L	Relief Pitching SV	Batting AB	Batting H	Batting HR	BA	PO	A	E	DP	TC/G	FA
1991	CHI N	0	1	.000	13.50	4	0	0	4.2	11	2	4	0	0	1	0	1	0	0	.000	0	1	0	0	0.3	1.000

Marshall Renfroe

RENFROE, MARSHALL DANIEL BL TL 6′ 180 lbs.
B. May 25, 1936, Century, Fla. D. Dec. 10, 1970, Pensacola, Fla.

Year	Team	W	L	PCT	ERA	G	GS	CG	IP	H	BB	SO	ShO	Relief Pitching W	Relief Pitching L	Relief Pitching SV	Batting AB	Batting H	Batting HR	BA	PO	A	E	DP	TC/G	FA
1959	SF N	0	0	—	27.00	1	1	0	2	3	3	3	0	0	0	0	1	0	0	.000	0	0	0	0	0.0	.000

Hal Reniff

RENIFF, HAROLD EUGENE (Porky) BR TR 6′ 215 lbs.
B. July 2, 1938, Warren, Ohio.

Year	Team	W	L	PCT	ERA	G	GS	CG	IP	H	BB	SO	ShO	Relief Pitching W	Relief Pitching L	Relief Pitching SV	Batting AB	Batting H	Batting HR	BA	PO	A	E	DP	TC/G	FA
1961	NY A	2	0	1.000	2.58	25	0	0	45.1	31	31	21	0	2	0	2	5	0	0	.000	3	5	1	0	0.4	.889
1962		0	0	—	7.36	2	0	0	3.2	6	5	1	0	0	0	0	0	0	0	—	0	0	0	0	0.0	.000
1963		4	3	.571	2.62	48	0	0	89.1	63	42	56	0	4	3	18	15	0	0	.000	8	25	2	2	0.7	.943
1964		6	4	.600	3.12	41	0	0	69.1	47	30	38	0	6	4	9	10	1	0	.100	4	13	1	1	0.4	.944
1965		3	4	.429	3.80	51	0	0	85.1	74	48	74	0	3	4	3	2	0	0	.000	11	8	0	0	0.4	1.000
1966		3	7	.300	3.21	56	0	0	95.1	80	49	79	0	3	7	9	14	4	0	.286	12	6	0	1	0.3	1.000
1967	2 teams NY A (24G 0–2) NY N (29G 3–3)																									
″	total	3	5	.375	3.80	53	0	0	83	82	37	45	0	3	5	4	6	0	0	.000	6	7	0	1	0.2	1.000
7 yrs.		21	23	.477	3.27	276	0	0	471.1	383	242	314	0	21	23	45	52	5	0	.096	44	64	4	5	0.4	.964
WORLD SERIES																										
1963	NY A	0	0	—	0.00	3	0	0	3	0	1	1	0	0	0	0	0	0	0	—	1	1	0	0	0.7	1.000
1964		0	0	—	0.00	1	0	0	0.1	2	0	0	0	0	0	0	0	0	0	—	0	0	0	0	0.0	.000
2 yrs.		0	0		0.00	4	0	0	3.1	2	1	1	0	0	0	0	0	0	0		1	1	0	0	0.5	1.000

Jim Reninger

RENINGER, JAMES DAVID BR TR 6′ 3″ 210 lbs.
B. Mar. 7, 1913, Aurora, Ill.

Year	Team	W	L	PCT	ERA	G	GS	CG	IP	H	BB	SO	ShO	Relief Pitching W	Relief Pitching L	Relief Pitching SV	Batting AB	Batting H	Batting HR	BA	PO	A	E	DP	TC/G	FA
1938	PHI A	0	2	.000	6.85	4	4	1	23.2	28	14	9	0	0	0	0	7	0	0	.000	0	6	0	0	1.5	1.000
1939		0	2	.000	7.71	4	2	0	16.1	24	12	3	0	0	0	0	6	1	0	.167	3	2	0	0	1.3	1.000
2 yrs.		0	4	.000	7.20	8	6	1	40	52	26	12	0	0	0	0	13	1	0	.077	3	8	0	0	1.4	1.000

Steve Renko

RENKO, STEVEN BR TR 6′ 5″ 230 lbs.
B. Dec. 10, 1944, Kansas City, Kans.

Year	Team	W	L	PCT	ERA	G	GS	CG	IP	H	BB	SO	ShO	Relief Pitching W	Relief Pitching L	Relief Pitching SV	Batting AB	Batting H	Batting HR	BA	PO	A	E	DP	TC/G	FA
1969	MON N	6	7	.462	4.02	18	15	4	103	94	50	68	0	0	0	0	36	6	1	.167	7	13	1	0	1.2	.952
1970		13	11	.542	4.32	41	33	7	223	203	104	142	1	0	0	1	80	16	1	.200	17	31	7	3	1.3	.873
1971		15	14	.517	3.75	40	37	9	276	256	135	129	3	0	0	0	100	21	2	.210	17	36	3	2	1.4	.946
1972		1	10	.091	5.20	30	12	0	97	96	67	66	0	0	0	0	24	7	0	.292	9	17	1	1	0.9	.963
1973		15	11	.577	2.81	36	34	9	249.2	201	108	164	0	0	0	1	88	24	0	.273	13	28	1	0	1.2	.976
1974		12	16	.429	4.03	37	35	8	228	222	81	138	1	0	0	0	81	17	1	.210	20	46	2	2	1.8	.971
1975		6	12	.333	4.08	31	25	3	170	175	76	99	1	0	0	1	54	15	1	.278	13	24	3	0	1.3	.925
1976	2 teams MON N (5G 0–1) CHI N (28G 8–11)																									
″	total	8	12	.400	3.98	33	28	4	176.1	179	46	116	0	0	0	0	56	6	0	.107	9	17	1	1	0.8	.963
1977	2 teams CHI N (13G 2–2) CHI A (8G 5–0)																									
″	total	7	2	.778	4.07	21	16	0	104	106	38	70	0	0	0	1	12	2	0	.167	9	8	1	0	0.9	.944
1978	OAK A	6	12	.333	4.29	27	25	3	151	152	67	89	1	0	0	0	0	0	0	—	5	22	1	3	1.0	.964
1979	BOS A	11	9	.550	4.11	27	27	4	171	174	53	99	1	0	0	0	0	0	0	—	14	20	2	0	1.3	.944
1980		9	9	.500	4.20	32	23	1	165	180	56	90	0	2	0	0	0	0	0	—	14	17	0	1	1.0	1.000
1981	CAL A	8	4	.667	3.44	22	15	0	102	93	42	50	0	1	0	1	0	0	0	—	2	10	0	0	0.5	1.000

Steve Renko *continued*

Year	Team	W	L	PCT	ERA	G	GS	CG	IP	H	BB	SO	ShO	Relief Pitching W	Relief Pitching L	Relief Pitching SV	Batting AB	Batting H	Batting HR	BA	PO	A	E	DP	TC/G	FA
1982		11	6	.647	4.44	31	23	4	156	163	51	81	0	3	1	0	0	0	0	—	9	14	3	4	0.8	.885
1983	**KC A**	6	11	.353	4.30	25	17	1	121.1	144	36	54	0	0	3	1	0	0	0	—	8	13	0	1	0.8	1.000
15 yrs.		134	146	.479	4.00	451	365	57	2493.1	2438	1010	1455	8	6	4	6	531	114	6	.215	166	316	26	18	1.1	.949

Andy Replogle

REPLOGLE, ANDREW DAVID BR TR 6′ 5″ 205 lbs.
B. Oct. 7, 1953, South Bend, Ind.

Year	Team	W	L	PCT	ERA	G	GS	CG	IP	H	BB	SO	ShO	Relief Pitching W	Relief Pitching L	Relief Pitching SV	Batting AB	Batting H	Batting HR	BA	PO	A	E	DP	TC/G	FA
1978	**MIL A**	9	5	.643	3.92	32	18	3	149.1	177	47	41	2	3	0	0	0	0	0	—	11	12	2	1	0.8	.920
1979		0	0	—	5.63	3	0	0	8	13	2	2	0	0	0	0	0	0	0	—	0	2	0	0	0.7	1.000
2 yrs.		9	5	.643	4.00	35	18	3	157.1	190	49	43	2	3	0	0	0	0	0		11	14	2	1	0.8	.926

Xavier Rescigno

RESCIGNO, XAVIER FREDERICK (Mr. X) BR TR 5′10½″ 175 lbs.
B. Oct. 13, 1913, New York, N. Y.

Year	Team	W	L	PCT	ERA	G	GS	CG	IP	H	BB	SO	ShO	Relief Pitching W	Relief Pitching L	Relief Pitching SV	Batting AB	Batting H	Batting HR	BA	PO	A	E	DP	TC/G	FA
1943	**PIT N**	6	9	.400	3.05	37	14	5	132.2	125	45	41	1	3	3	2	35	5	0	.143	8	16	3	1	0.7	.889
1944		10	8	.556	4.35	48	6	2	124	146	34	45	0	**8**	5	5	22	2	0	.091	7	21	1	2	0.6	.966
1945		3	5	.375	5.72	44	1	0	78.2	95	34	29	0	3	4	9	15	2	0	.133	4	14	0	0	0.4	1.000
3 yrs.		19	22	.463	4.16	129	21	7	335.1	366	113	115	1	14	12	16	72	9	0	.125	19	51	4	3	0.6	.946

George Rettger

RETTGER, GEORGE EDWARD BR TR 5′11″ 175 lbs.
B. July 29, 1868, Cleveland, Ohio D. June 5, 1921, Lakewood, Ohio.

Year	Team	W	L	PCT	ERA	G	GS	CG	IP	H	BB	SO	ShO	Relief Pitching W	Relief Pitching L	Relief Pitching SV	Batting AB	Batting H	Batting HR	BA	PO	A	E	DP	TC/G	FA
1891	**STL AA**	7	3	.700	3.40	14	12	10	92.2	85	51	49	1	1	0	1	42	3	1	.071	7	17	3	0	1.8	.889
1892	**2 teams CLE N** (6G 1–3) **CIN N** (1G 1–0)																									
″	**total**	2	3	.400	4.21	7	6	4	47	40	41	13	0	0	0	0	23	3	0	.130	3	9	2	0	1.8	.857
2 yrs.		9	6	.600	3.67	21	18	14	139.2	125	92	62	1	1	0	1	65	6	1	.092	10	26	5	0	1.8	.878

Otto Rettig

RETTIG, ADOLPH JOHN BR TR 5′11″ 165 lbs.
B. Jan. 29, 1894, New York, N. Y. D. June 16, 1977, Stuart, Fla.

Year	Team	W	L	PCT	ERA	G	GS	CG	IP	H	BB	SO	ShO	Relief Pitching W	Relief Pitching L	Relief Pitching SV	Batting AB	Batting H	Batting HR	BA	PO	A	E	DP	TC/G	FA
1922	**PHI A**	1	2	.333	4.91	4	4	1	18.1	18	12	3	0	0	0	0	6	0	0	.000	1	5	0	0	1.5	1.000

Ed Reulbach

REULBACH, EDWARD MARVIN (Big Ed) BR TR 6′ 1″ 190 lbs.
B. Dec. 1, 1882, Detroit, Mich. D. July 17, 1961, Glens Falls, N. Y.

Year	Team	W	L	PCT	ERA	G	GS	CG	IP	H	BB	SO	ShO	Relief Pitching W	Relief Pitching L	Relief Pitching SV	Batting AB	Batting H	Batting HR	BA	PO	A	E	DP	TC/G	FA
1905	**CHI N**	18	14	.563	1.42	34	29	28	292	208	73	152	5	2	1	1	110	14	0	.127	14	71	4	4	2.6	.955
1906		19	4	**.826**	1.65	33	24	20	218	129	92	94	6	1	0	2	83	13	0	.157	18	75	3	3	2.8	.969
1907		17	4	**.810**	1.69	27	22	16	192	147	64	96	4	2	0	0	63	11	1	.175	13	53	5	3	2.6	.930
1908		24	7	**.774**	2.03	46	35	25	297.2	227	106	133	7	3	0	1	99	23	0	.232	15	77	7	7	2.2	.929
1909		19	10	.655	1.78	35	32	23	262.2	194	82	105	6	0	1	0	86	12	0	.140	15	91	5	4	3.2	.955
1910		12	8	.600	3.12	24	23	13	173.1	161	49	55	1	0	1	0	56	6	0	.107	6	53	4	1	2.6	.937
1911		16	9	.640	2.96	33	29	15	221.2	191	103	79	2	1	0	0	67	6	0	.090	5	77	5	2	2.6	.943
1912		10	6	.625	3.78	39	19	8	169	161	60	75	0	3	1	3	55	6	0	.109	8	60	3	4	1.8	.958
1913	**2 teams CHI N** (10G 1–3) **BKN N** (15G 7–6)																									
″	**total**	8	9	.471	2.66	25	15	9	148.2	118	55	56	2	1	2	0	41	6	0	.146	9	35	3	1	2.0	.936
1914	**BKN N**	11	18	.379	2.64	44	29	14	256	228	83	119	3	1	3	3	74	9	0	.122	11	71	6	2	2.0	.932
1915	**NWK F**	20	10	.667	2.23	33	30	23	270	233	69	117	4	1	0	1	92	18	0	.196	11	90	7	2	3.3	.935
1916	**BOS N**	7	6	.538	2.47	21	11	6	109.1	99	41	47	0	2	1	0	33	3	0	.091	11	50	1	3	3.0	.984
1917		0	1	.000	2.82	5	2	0	22.1	21	15	9	0	0	0	0	3	0	0	.000	1	12	1	1	2.8	.929
13 yrs.		181	106	.631	2.28	399	300	200	2632.2	2117	892	1137	40	17	10	11	862	127	1	.147	137	815	54	37	2.5	.946
WORLD SERIES																										
1906	**CHI N**	1	0	1.000	2.45	2	2	1	11	6	8	4	0	0	0	0	3	0	0	.000	0	4	0	0	2.0	1.000
1907		1	0	1.000	0.75	2	1	1	12	6	3	4	0	0	0	0	5	1	0	.200	1	2	0	0	1.5	1.000
1908		0	0	—	4.70	2	1	0	7.2	9	1	5	0	0	0	0	3	0	0	.000	0	5	0	0	2.5	1.000
1910		0	0	—	13.50	1	1	0	2	3	2	0	0	0	0	0	0	0	0	—	0	1	0	0	1.0	1.000
4 yrs.		2	0	1.000 **1st**	3.03	7	5	2	32.2	24	14	13	0	0	0	0	11	1	0	.091	1	12	0	0	1.9	1.000

Paul Reuschel

REUSCHEL, PAUL RICHARD BR TR 6′ 4″ 225 lbs.
Brother of Rick Reuschel.
B. Jan. 12, 1947, Quincy, Ill.

Year	Team	W	L	PCT	ERA	G	GS	CG	IP	H	BB	SO	ShO	Relief Pitching W	Relief Pitching L	Relief Pitching SV	Batting AB	Batting H	Batting HR	BA	PO	A	E	DP	TC/G	FA
1975	**CHI N**	1	3	.250	3.50	28	0	0	36	44	13	12	0	1	3	5	4	0	0	.000	1	7	1	0	0.3	.889
1976		4	2	.667	4.55	50	2	0	87	94	33	55	0	4	1	3	13	2	0	.154	4	19	1	2	0.5	.958
1977		5	6	.455	4.37	69	0	0	107	105	40	62	0	5	6	4	11	0	0	.000	7	25	1	5	0.5	.970
1978	**2 teams CHI N** (16G 2–0) **CLE A** (18G 2–4)																									
″	**total**	4	4	.500	3.59	34	6	1	117.2	124	35	37	0	4	0	0	4	0	0	.000	7	20	0	4	0.8	1.000
1979	**CLE A**	2	1	.667	8.00	17	1	0	45	73	11	22	0	2	1	1	0	0	0	—	2	10	1	2	0.8	.923
5 yrs.		16	16	.500	4.52	198	9	1	392.2	440	132	188	0	16	11	13	32	2	0	.063	21	81	4	13	0.5	.962

Rick Reuschel

REUSCHEL, RICKEY EUGENE (Big Daddy) BR TR 6′ 3″ 215 lbs.
Brother of Paul Reuschel.
B. May 16, 1949, Quincy, Ill.

Year	Team	W	L	PCT	ERA	G	GS	CG	IP	H	BB	SO	ShO	Relief Pitching W	Relief Pitching L	Relief Pitching SV	Batting AB	Batting H	Batting HR	BA	PO	A	E	DP	TC/G	FA
1972	**CHI N**	10	8	.556	2.93	21	18	5	129	127	29	87	4	1	0	0	44	6	0	.136	9	15	1	1	1.2	.960
1973		14	15	.483	3.00	36	36	7	237	244	62	168	3	0	0	0	73	9	0	.123	24	49	3	0	2.1	.961
1974		13	12	.520	4.29	41	38	8	241	262	83	160	2	1	0	0	86	19	0	.221	28	51	5	4	2.0	.940
1975		11	**17**	.393	3.73	38	37	6	234	244	67	155	0	0	0	1	77	16	1	.208	23	39	0	5	1.6	1.000
1976		14	12	.538	3.46	38	37	9	260	260	64	146	2	0	0	1	83	19	0	.229	23	53	4	0	2.1	.950
1977		20	10	.667	2.79	39	37	8	252	233	74	166	4	1	0	1	87	18	1	.207	27	45	1	4	1.9	.986
1978		14	15	.483	3.41	35	35	9	243	235	54	115	1	0	0	0	73	10	0	.137	24	44	2	1	2.0	.971
1979		18	12	.600	3.62	36	36	5	239	251	75	125	1	0	0	0	79	13	0	.165	27	49	3	9	2.2	.962
1980		11	13	.458	3.40	38	**38**	6	257	**281**	76	140	0	0	0	0	82	13	0	.159	28	56	2	5	2.3	.977
1981	**2 teams CHI N** (13G 4–7) **NY A** (12G 4–4)																									
″	**total**	8	11	.421	3.10	25	24	4	157	162	33	75	0	0	0	0	25	2	0	.080	10	35	2	2	1.9	.957
1983	**CHI N**	1	1	.500	3.92	4	4	0	20.2	18	10	9	0	0	0	0	7	1	0	.143	4	7	0	0	2.8	1.000
1984		5	5	.500	5.17	19	14	1	92.1	123	23	43	0	1	0	0	29	7	0	.241	6	20	1	1	1.4	.963
1985	**PIT N**	14	8	.636	2.27	31	26	9	194	153	52	138	1	2	0	1	59	10	1	.169	24	40	0	2	2.1	1.000
1986		9	16	.360	3.96	35	34	4	215.2	232	57	125	2	0	0	0	70	11	0	.157	24	44	2	0	2.0	.971
1987	**2 teams PIT N** (25G 8–6) **SF N** (9G 5–3)																									
″	**total**	13	9	.591	3.09	34	33	**12**	227	207	42	107	4	0	1	0	79	11	1	.139	25	38	2	2	1.9	.969

Rick Reuschel *continued*

Year	Team	Lg	W	L	PCT	ERA	G	GS	CG	IP	H	BB	SO	ShO	Relief Pitching W	Relief Pitching L	Relief Pitching SV	Batting AB	Batting H	Batting HR	BA	PO	A	E	DP	TC/G	FA
1988	SF	N	19	11	.633	3.12	36	**36**	7	245	242	42	92	2	0	0	0	73	8	0	.110	12	32	0	2	1.2	1.000
1989			17	8	.680	2.94	32	32	2	208.1	195	54	111	0	0	0	0	61	10	0	.164	8	33	0	0	1.3	1.000
1990			3	6	.333	3.93	15	13	0	87	102	31	49	0	0	0	1	26	4	0	.154	2	16	1	1	1.3	.947
1991			0	2	.000	4.22	4	1	0	10.2	17	7	4	0	0	1	0	2	0	0	.000	0	1	0	0	0.3	1.000
19 yrs.			214	191	.528	3.37	557	529	102	3549.2	3588	935	2015	26	6	2	5	1115	187	4	.168	328	667	29	39	1.8	.972
DIVISIONAL PLAYOFF SERIES																											
1981	NY	A	0	1	.000	3.00	1	1	0	6	4	1	3	0	0	0	0	0	0	0	—	0	0	0	0	0.0	.000
LEAGUE CHAMPIONSHIP SERIES																											
1987	SF	N	0	1	.000	6.30	2	2	0	10	15	2	2	0	0	0	0	2	0	0	.000	0	3	1	0	2.0	.750
1989			1	1	.500	5.19	2	2	0	8.2	12	2	5	0	0	0	0	2	0	0	.000	0	3	0	0	1.5	1.000
2 yrs.			1	2	.333	5.79	4	4	0	18.2	27	4	7	0	0	0	0	4	0	0	.000	0	6	1	0	1.8	.857
WORLD SERIES																											
1981	NY	A	0	0	—	4.91	2	1	0	3.2	7	3	2	0	0	0	0	2	0	0	.000	0	0	0	0	0.0	.000
1989	SF	N	0	1	.000	11.25	1	1	0	4	5	4	2	0	0	0	0	0	0	0	—	0	0	0	0	0.0	.000
2 yrs.			0	1	.000	8.22	3	2	0	7.2	12	7	4	0	0	0	0	2	0	0	.000	0	0	0	0	0.0	

Jerry Reuss

REUSS, JERRY
B. June 19, 1949, St. Louis, Mo.
BL TL 6′ 5″ 200 lbs.

Year	Team	Lg	W	L	PCT	ERA	G	GS	CG	IP	H	BB	SO	ShO	Relief Pitching W	Relief Pitching L	Relief Pitching SV	Batting AB	Batting H	Batting HR	BA	PO	A	E	DP	TC/G	FA
1969	STL	N	1	0	1.000	0.00	1	1	0	7	2	3	3	0	0	0	0	3	1	0	.333	0	2	0	0	2.0	1.000
1970			7	8	.467	4.11	20	20	5	127	132	49	74	2	0	0	0	40	2	0	.050	8	18	1	0	1.4	.963
1971			14	14	.500	4.78	36	35	7	211	228	109	131	2	0	0	0	65	8	0	.123	6	26	2	0	0.9	.941
1972	HOU	N	9	13	.409	4.17	33	30	4	192	177	83	174	1	0	0	1	66	7	0	.106	4	25	4	0	1.0	.879
1973			16	13	.552	3.74	41	**40**	12	279.1	271	**117**	177	3	1	0	0	95	13	0	.137	4	37	3	2	1.1	.932
1974	PIT	N	16	11	.593	3.50	35	35	14	260	259	101	105	1	0	0	0	86	13	0	.151	11	37	5	1	1.5	.906
1975			18	11	.621	2.54	32	32	15	237	224	78	131	6	0	0	0	71	14	0	.197	6	48	0	1	1.7	1.000
1976			14	9	.609	3.53	31	29	11	209.1	209	51	108	3	0	0	2	66	16	0	.242	8	26	2	2	1.2	.944
1977			10	13	.435	4.11	33	33	8	208	225	71	116	2	0	0	0	70	12	0	.171	7	40	3	2	1.5	.940
1978			3	2	.600	4.88	23	12	3	83	97	23	42	1	0	0	0	27	5	0	.185	4	10	0	4	0.6	1.000
1979	LA	N	7	14	.333	3.54	39	21	4	160	178	60	83	1	2	4	3	42	7	0	.167	2	35	3	1	1.0	.925
1980			18	6	.750	2.52	37	29	10	229	193	40	111	**6**	3	0	3	68	6	1	.088	18	40	5	5	1.7	.921
1981			10	4	.714	2.29	22	22	8	153	138	27	51	2	0	0	0	51	10	0	.196	10	38	1	4	2.2	.980
1982			18	11	.621	3.11	39	37	8	254.2	232	50	138	4	1	0	0	77	17	0	.221	21	46	3	4	1.8	.957
1983			12	11	.522	2.94	32	31	7	223.1	233	50	143	0	0	0	0	71	20	0	.282	17	52	4	4	2.3	.945
1984			5	7	.417	3.82	30	15	2	99	102	31	44	0	0	2	1	24	4	0	.167	4	16	1	0	0.7	.952
1985			14	10	.583	2.92	34	33	5	212.2	210	58	84	3	0	0	0	74	10	0	.135	12	27	3	0	1.2	.929
1986			2	6	.250	5.84	19	13	0	74	96	17	29	0	0	0	1	20	5	0	.250	5	16	0	1	1.1	1.000
1987	3 teams	LA N	(1G 0–0)		CIN N	(7G 0–5)	CAL A	(17G 4–5)																			
″	total		4	10	.286	5.97	25	23	1	119	166	29	49	1	0	0	0	8	1	0	.125	8	21	1	4	1.2	.967
1988	CHI	A	13	9	.591	3.44	32	29	2	183	183	43	73	0	0	0	0	0	0	0	—	10	27	1	2	1.2	.974
1989	2 teams	CHI A	(23G 8–5)		MIL A	(7G 1–4)																					
″	total		9	9	.500	5.13	30	26	1	140.1	171	34	40	1	0	0	0	0	0	0		4	14	0	1	0.6	1.000
1990	PIT	N	0	0	—	3.52	4	1	0	7.2	8	3	1	0	0	0	0	0	0	0	—	1	2	0	0	0.8	1.000
22 yrs.			220	191	.535	3.64	628	547	127	3669.1	3734	1127	1907	39	7	6	11	1024	171	1	.167	170	603	42	38	1.3	.948
DIVISIONAL PLAYOFF SERIES																											
1981	LA	N	1	0	1.000	0.00	2	2	1	18	10	5	7	1	0	0	0	8	0	0	.000	0	0	0	0	0.0	.000
LEAGUE CHAMPIONSHIP SERIES																											
1974	PIT	N	0	2	.000	3.72	2	2	0	9.2	7	8	3	0	0	0	0	2	0	0	.000	0	0	0	0	0.0	.000
1975			0	1	.000	13.50	1	1	0	2.2	4	4	1	0	0	0	0	1	0	0	.000	0	1	0	0	1.0	1.000
1981	LA	N	0	1	.000	5.14	1	1	0	7	7	1	2	0	0	0	0	2	0	0	.000	0	0	0	0	0.0	.000
1983			0	2	.000	4.50	2	2	0	12	14	3	4	0	0	0	0	3	0	0	.000	0	1	0	0	0.5	1.000
1985			0	1	.000	10.80	1	1	0	1.2	5	1	0	0	0	0	0	0	0	0	—	0	0	1	0	1.0	.000
5 yrs.			0	7	.000	5.45	7	7	0	33	37	17	10	0	0	0	0	8	0	0	.000	0	2	1	0	0.4	.667
				1st								**9th**															
WORLD SERIES																											
1981	LA	N	1	1	.500	3.86	2	2	1	11.2	10	3	8	0	0	0	0	3	0	0	.000	1	3	0	0	2.0	1.000

Todd Revenig

REVENIG, TODD MICHAEL
B. June 28, 1969, Brainerd, Minn.
BR TR 6′ 1″ 185 lbs.

Year	Team	Lg	W	L	PCT	ERA	G	GS	CG	IP	H	BB	SO	ShO	Relief Pitching W	Relief Pitching L	Relief Pitching SV	Batting AB	Batting H	Batting HR	BA	PO	A	E	DP	TC/G	FA
1992	OAK	A	0	0	—	0.00	2	0	0	2	2	0	1	0	0	0	0	0	0	0	—	0	0	0	0	0.0	.000

Alberto Reyes

REYES, RAFAEL ALBERTO
B. Apr. 10, 1971, San Cristobal, Dominican Republic.
BR TR 6′ 1″ 193 lbs.

Year	Team	Lg	W	L	PCT	ERA	G	GS	CG	IP	H	BB	SO	ShO	Relief Pitching W	Relief Pitching L	Relief Pitching SV	Batting AB	Batting H	Batting HR	BA	PO	A	E	DP	TC/G	FA
1995	MIL	A	1	1	.500	2.43	27	0	0	33.1	19	18	29	0	1	1	1	0	0	0	—	0	6	0	0	0.2	1.000

Carlos Reyes

REYES, CARLOS ALBERTO, JR.
B. Apr. 4, 1969, Miami, Fla.
BR TR 6′ 1″ 190 lbs.

Year	Team	Lg	W	L	PCT	ERA	G	GS	CG	IP	H	BB	SO	ShO	Relief Pitching W	Relief Pitching L	Relief Pitching SV	Batting AB	Batting H	Batting HR	BA	PO	A	E	DP	TC/G	FA
1994	OAK	A	0	3	.000	4.15	27	9	0	78	71	44	57	0	0	1	1	0	0	0	—	3	7	0	1	0.4	1.000
1995			4	6	.400	5.09	40	1	0	69	71	28	48	0	4	5	0	0	0	0	—	3	13	0	0	0.4	1.000
2 yrs.			4	9	.308	4.59	67	10	0	147	142	72	105	0	4	6	1	0	0	0		6	20	0	1	0.4	1.000

Allie Reynolds

REYNOLDS, ALLIE PIERCE (Superchief)
B. Feb. 10, 1915, Bethany, Okla. D. Dec. 26, 1994, Oklahoma City, Okla.
BR TR 6′ 195 lbs.

Year	Team	Lg	W	L	PCT	ERA	G	GS	CG	IP	H	BB	SO	ShO	Relief Pitching W	Relief Pitching L	Relief Pitching SV	Batting AB	Batting H	Batting HR	BA	PO	A	E	DP	TC/G	FA
1942	CLE	A	0	0	—	0.00	2	0	0	5	5	4	2	0	0	0	0	2	0	0	.000	0	0	0	0	0.0	.000
1943			11	12	.478	2.99	34	21	11	198.2	140	109	**151**	3	1	6	3	67	10	0	.149	5	35	2	3	1.2	.952
1944			11	8	.579	3.30	28	21	5	158	141	91	84	1	0	3	1	57	7	0	.123	8	21	1	3	1.1	.967
1945			18	12	.600	3.20	44	30	16	247.1	227	**130**	112	2	2	1	4	85	8	0	.094	11	44	5	3	1.4	.917
1946			11	15	.423	3.88	31	28	9	183.1	180	108	107	3	0	0	0	63	14	0	.222	8	27	5	1	1.3	.875
1947	NY	A	19	8	**.704**	3.20	34	30	17	241.2	207	123	129	4	1	1	2	89	13	0	.146	9	31	2	1	1.2	.952
1948			16	7	.696	3.77	39	31	11	236.1	240	111	101	1	0	0	3	83	16	1	.193	10	27	1	1	1.0	.974
1949			17	6	.739	4.00	35	31	4	213.2	200	123	105	2	2	0	1	78	17	0	.218	7	39	2	3	1.4	.958
1950			16	12	.571	3.74	35	29	14	240.2	215	138	160	2	1	3	2	81	15	0	.185	8	36	3	1	1.3	.936
1951			17	8	.680	3.05	40	26	16	221	171	100	126	**7**	1	2	7	76	14	0	.184	17	19	5	2	1.0	.878

Allie Reynolds *continued*

Year	Team	W	L	PCT	ERA	G	GS	CG	IP	H	BB	SO	ShO	Relief Pitching W	Relief Pitching L	Relief Pitching SV	Batting AB	Batting H	Batting HR	BA	PO	A	E	DP	TC/G	FA
1952		20	8	.714	**2.06**	35	29	24	244.1	194	97	**160**	**6**	0	0	6	85	13	0	.153	13	35	2	1	1.4	.960
1953		13	7	.650	3.41	41	15	5	145	140	61	86	1	7	1	13	41	5	0	.122	7	13	4	1	0.6	.833
1954		13	4	.765	3.32	36	18	5	157.1	133	66	100	4	3	2	7	50	8	0	.160	8	22	0	2	0.8	1.000
13 yrs.		182	107	.630	3.30	434	309	137	2492.1	2193	1261	1423	36	18	19	49	857	140	1	.163	111	349	32	22	1.1	.935
WORLD SERIES																										
1947	**NY A**	1	0	1.000	4.76	2	2	1	11.1	15	3	6	0	0	0	0	4	2	0	.500	1	0	0	0	0.5	1.000
1949		1	0	1.000	0.00	2	1	1	12.1	2	4	14	1	0	0	1	4	2	0	.500	0	1	0	1	0.5	1.000
1950		1	0	1.000	0.87	2	1	1	10.1	7	4	7	0	0	0	1	3	1	0	.333	1	2	0	0	1.5	1.000
1951		1	1	.500	4.20	2	2	1	15	16	11	8	0	0	0	0	6	2	0	.333	0	5	0	2	2.5	1.000
1952		2	1	.667	1.77	4	2	1	20.1	12	6	18	1	1	0	1	7	0	0	.000	2	1	2	0	1.3	.600
1953		1	0	1.000	6.75	3	1	0	8	9	4	9	0	1	0	1	2	1	0	.500	0	0	0	0	0.0	.000
6 yrs.		7	2	.778	2.79	15	9	5	77.1	61	32	62	2	2	0	4	26	8	0	.308	4	9	2	3	1.0	.867
		2nd				**3rd**	**6th**		**8th**		**2nd**	**3rd**	**4th**			**2nd**										

Archie Reynolds

REYNOLDS, ARCHIE EDWARD BR TR 6′ 2″ 205 lbs.
B. Jan. 3, 1946, Glendale, Calif.

Year	Team	W	L	PCT	ERA	G	GS	CG	IP	H	BB	SO	ShO	Relief Pitching W	Relief Pitching L	Relief Pitching SV	Batting AB	Batting H	Batting HR	BA	PO	A	E	DP	TC/G	FA
1968	**CHI N**	0	1	.000	6.75	7	1	0	13.1	14	7	6	0	0	1	0	2	1	0	.500	1	0	0	0	0.1	1.000
1969		0	1	.000	2.57	2	2	0	7	11	7	4	0	0	0	0	1	0	0	.000	1	1	0	1	1.0	1.000
1970		0	2	.000	6.60	7	1	0	15	17	9	9	0	0	1	0	2	0	0	.000	0	1	0	1	0.1	1.000
1971	**CAL A**	0	3	.000	4.67	15	1	0	27	32	18	15	0	0	3	0	2	0	0	.000	3	5	0	1	0.5	1.000
1972	**MIL A**	0	1	.000	7.11	5	2	0	19	26	8	13	0	0	1	0	4	2	0	.500	1	0	0	0	0.2	1.000
5 yrs.		0	8	.000	5.75	36	7	0	81.1	100	49	47	0	0	6	0	11	3	0	.273	6	7	0	3	0.4	1.000

Bob Reynolds

REYNOLDS, ROBERT ALLEN (Bullet) BR TR 6′ 205 lbs.
B. Jan. 21, 1947, Seattle, Wash.

Year	Team	W	L	PCT	ERA	G	GS	CG	IP	H	BB	SO	ShO	Relief Pitching W	Relief Pitching L	Relief Pitching SV	Batting AB	Batting H	Batting HR	BA	PO	A	E	DP	TC/G	FA
1969	**MON N**	0	0	—	20.25	1	1	0	1.1	3	3	2	0	0	0	0	0	0	0	—	0	0	0	0	0.0	.000
1971	**2 teams**	**MIL A** (3G 0–1)		**STL N** (4G 0–0)																						
″	**total**	0	1	.000	6.92	7	0	0	13	19	9	8	0	0	1	0	2	0	0	.000	0	2	0	0	0.3	1.000
1972	**BAL A**	0	0	—	1.80	3	0	0	10	8	7	5	0	0	0	0	2	0	0	.000	0	1	0	0	0.3	1.000
1973		7	5	.583	1.95	42	1	0	111	88	31	77	0	7	5	9	0	0	0	—	5	7	5	1	0.4	.706
1974		7	5	.583	2.74	54	0	0	69	75	14	43	0	7	5	7	0	0	0	—	4	8	0	0	0.2	1.000
1975	**3 teams**	**BAL A** (7G 0–1)		**DET A** (21G 0–2)		**CLE A** (5G 0–2)																				
″	**total**	0	5	.000	5.19	33	0	0	50.1	62	18	32	0	0	5	5	0	0	0		4	6	0	0	0.3	1.000
6 yrs.		14	16	.467	3.15	140	2	0	254.2	255	82	167	0	14	16	21	4	0	0	.000	13	24	5	1	0.3	.881
LEAGUE CHAMPIONSHIP SERIES																										
1973	**BAL A**	0	0	—	3.18	2	0	0	5.2	5	3	5	0	0	0	0	0	0	0	—	1	0	0	0	0.5	1.000
1974		0	0	—	0.00	1	0	0	1.1	0	3	1	0	0	0	0	0	0	0	—	0	0	0	0	0.0	.000
2 yrs.		0	0		2.57	3	0	0	7	5	6	6	0	0	0	0	0	0	0		1	0	0	0	0.3	1.000

Charlie Reynolds

REYNOLDS, CHARLES E.
B. July 31, 1857, Allegany, N. Y. D. May 1, 1913, Buffalo, N. Y.

Year	Team	W	L	PCT	ERA	G	GS	CG	IP	H	BB	SO	ShO	Relief Pitching W	Relief Pitching L	Relief Pitching SV	Batting AB	Batting H	Batting HR	BA	PO	A	E	DP	TC/G	FA
1882	**PHI AA**	1	1	.500	*5.25*	2	2	1	12	18	3	4	0	0	0	0	8	1	0	.125	1	1	1	0	1.0	.667

Craig Reynolds

REYNOLDS, GORDON CRAIG BL TR 6′ 1″ 175 lbs.
B. Dec. 27, 1952, Houston, Tex.

Year	Team	W	L	PCT	ERA	G	GS	CG	IP	H	BB	SO	ShO	Relief Pitching W	Relief Pitching L	Relief Pitching SV	Batting AB	Batting H	Batting HR	BA	PO	A	E	DP	TC/G	FA
1986	**HOU N**	0	0	—	27.00	1	0	0	1	3	2	1	0	0	0	0	313	78	6	.249	43	82	4	12	4.3	.969
1989		0	0	—	27.00	1	0	0	1	3	1	0	0	0	0	0	189	38	2	.201	2	6	1	1	1.8	.889
2 yrs.		0	0		27.00	2	0	0	2	6	3	1	0	0	0	0	*				1905	3662	196	695	4.1	.966

Ken Reynolds

REYNOLDS, KENNETH LEE BL TL 6′ 180 lbs.
B. Jan. 4, 1947, Trevose, Pa.

Year	Team	W	L	PCT	ERA	G	GS	CG	IP	H	BB	SO	ShO	Relief Pitching W	Relief Pitching L	Relief Pitching SV	Batting AB	Batting H	Batting HR	BA	PO	A	E	DP	TC/G	FA
1970	**PHI N**	0	0	—	0.00	4	0	0	2	3	4	1	0	0	0	0	0	0	0	—	1	1	1	0	0.8	.667
1971		5	9	.357	4.50	35	25	2	162	163	82	81	1	0	0	0	50	10	0	.200	5	25	2	1	0.9	.938
1972		2	15	.118	4.26	33	23	2	154.1	149	60	87	0	0	1	0	40	8	0	.200	4	23	1	1	0.8	.964
1973	**MIL A**	0	1	.000	7.36	2	1	0	7.1	5	10	3	0	0	0	0	0	0	0	—	0	3	0	2	1.5	1.000
1975	**STL N**	0	1	.000	1.59	10	0	0	17	12	11	7	0	0	1	0	2	0	0	.000	4	6	0	0	1.0	1.000
1976	**SD N**	0	3	.000	6.40	19	2	0	32.1	38	29	18	0	0	2	1	5	0	0	.000	2	3	1	0	0.3	.833
6 yrs.		7	29	.194	4.46	103	51	4	375	370	196	197	1	0	4	1	97	18	0	.186	16	61	5	4	0.8	.939

Ross Reynolds

REYNOLDS, ROSS ERNEST BR TR 6′ 2″ 175 lbs.
B. Aug. 20, 1887, Barksdale, Tex. D. June 23, 1970, Ada, Okla.

Year	Team	W	L	PCT	ERA	G	GS	CG	IP	H	BB	SO	ShO	Relief Pitching W	Relief Pitching L	Relief Pitching SV	Batting AB	Batting H	Batting HR	BA	PO	A	E	DP	TC/G	FA
1914	**DET A**	5	3	.625	2.08	26	7	3	78	62	39	31	1	1	1	0	21	1	0	.048	5	19	4	0	1.1	.857
1915		0	1	.000	6.35	4	2	0	11.1	17	5	2	0	0	0	0	3	0	0	.000	1	5	0	0	1.5	1.000
2 yrs.		5	4	.556	2.62	30	9	3	89.1	79	44	33	1	1	1	0	24	1	0	.042	6	24	4	0	1.1	.882

Shane Reynolds

REYNOLDS, RICHARD SHANE BR TR 6′ 3″ 210 lbs.
B. Mar. 26, 1968, Bastrop, La.

Year	Team	W	L	PCT	ERA	G	GS	CG	IP	H	BB	SO	ShO	Relief Pitching W	Relief Pitching L	Relief Pitching SV	Batting AB	Batting H	Batting HR	BA	PO	A	E	DP	TC/G	FA
1992	**HOU N**	1	3	.250	7.11	8	5	0	25.1	42	6	10	0	0	0	0	4	2	0	.500	0	7	1	0	1.0	.875
1993		0	0	—	0.82	5	1	0	11	11	6	10	0	0	0	0	2	1	0	.500	0	1	0	0	0.2	1.000
1994		8	5	.615	3.05	33	14	1	124	128	21	110	1	3	1	0	33	3	0	.091	10	16	0	0	0.8	1.000
1995		10	11	.476	3.47	30	30	3	189.1	196	37	175	2	0	0	0	63	8	0	.127	13	38	1	0	1.7	.981
4 yrs.		19	19	.500	3.50	76	50	4	349.2	377	70	305	3	3	1	0	102	14	0	.137	23	62	2	0	1.1	.977

Armando Reynoso

REYNOSO, ARMANDO MARTIN BR TR 6′ 186 lbs.
Born Armando Martin Reynoso (Gutierrez).
B. May 1, 1966, San Luis Potosi, Mexico.

Year	Team	W	L	PCT	ERA	G	GS	CG	IP	H	BB	SO	ShO	Relief Pitching W	Relief Pitching L	Relief Pitching SV	Batting AB	Batting H	Batting HR	BA	PO	A	E	DP	TC/G	FA
1991	**ATL N**	2	1	.667	6.17	6	5	0	23.1	26	10	10	0	0	0	0	7	0	0	.000	3	12	0	0	2.5	1.000
1992		1	0	1.000	4.70	3	1	0	7.2	11	2	2	0	0	0	1	2	0	0	.000	0	2	0	1	0.7	1.000
1993	**CLR N**	12	11	.522	4.00	30	30	4	189	206	63	117	0	0	0	0	63	8	2	.127	16	35	6	5	1.9	.895
1994		3	4	.429	4.82	9	9	1	52.1	54	22	25	0	0	0	0	17	3	0	.176	1	20	0	0	2.3	1.000
1995		7	7	.500	5.32	20	18	0	93	116	36	40	0	0	0	0	30	4	0	.133	7	29	2	2	1.9	.947
5 yrs.		25	23	.521	4.61	68	63	5	365.1	413	133	194	0	0	0	1	119	15	2	.126	27	98	8	8	2.0	.940

Armando Reynoso *continued*

Year	Team		W	L	PCT	ERA	G	GS	CG	IP	H	BB	SO	ShO	Relief Pitching W	Relief Pitching L	Relief Pitching SV	Batting AB	Batting H	Batting HR	BA	PO	A	E	DP	TC/G	FA
DIVISIONAL PLAYOFF SERIES																											
1995	CLR	N	0	0	—	0.00	1	0	0	1	2	0	0	0	0	0	0	0	0	0	—	0	0	0	0	0.0	.000

Flint Rhem

RHEM, CHARLES FLINT (Shad)
B. Jan. 24, 1901, Rhems, S. C. D. July 30, 1969, Columbia, S. C.
BR TR 6′ 2″ 180 lbs.

Year	Team		W	L	PCT	ERA	G	GS	CG	IP	H	BB	SO	ShO	Relief Pitching W	Relief Pitching L	Relief Pitching SV	Batting AB	Batting H	Batting HR	BA	PO	A	E	DP	TC/G	FA
1924	STL	N	2	2	.500	4.45	6	3	3	32.1	31	17	20	0	0	1	1	12	2	0	.167	0	9	0	0	1.5	1.000
1925			8	13	.381	4.92	30	24	8	170	204	58	66	1	0	0	1	59	14	1	.237	9	38	5	3	1.7	.904
1926			**20**	7	.741	3.21	34	34	20	258	241	75	72	1	0	0	0	96	18	1	.188	1	76	6	6	2.4	.928
1927			10	12	.455	4.41	27	26	9	169.1	189	54	51	2	0	0	0	59	4	0	.068	2	27	1	0	1.1	.967
1928			11	8	.579	4.14	28	22	9	169.2	199	71	47	0	0	0	3	67	11	1	.164	3	48	0	5	1.8	1.000
1930			12	8	.600	4.45	26	19	9	139.2	173	37	47	0	1	4	0	52	12	0	.231	1	19	4	1	0.9	.833
1931			11	10	.524	3.56	33	26	10	207.1	214	60	72	2	1	0	1	69	9	0	.130	4	38	3	4	1.4	.933
1932	2 teams	STL N	(6G 4–2)		PHI N	(26G 11–7)																					
″	total		15	9	.625	3.58	32	26	15	218.2	225	59	53	1	1	0	1	78	10	0	.128	6	49	3	1	1.8	.948
1933	PHI	N	5	14	.263	6.57	28	19	3	126	182	33	27	0	1	2	2	46	4	0	.087	2	30	2	1	1.2	.941
1934	2 teams	STL N	(5G 1–0)		BOS N	(25G 8–8)																					
″	total		9	8	.529	3.69	30	21	5	168.1	190	45	62	1	3	0	1	54	3	0	.056	3	42	1	2	1.5	.978
1935	BOS	N	0	5	.000	5.31	10	6	0	40.2	61	11	10	0	0	0	0	10	0	0	.000	1	10	0	0	1.1	1.000
1936	STL	N	2	1	.667	6.75	10	4	0	26.2	49	49	9	0	1	0	0	8	1	0	.125	1	3	0	1	0.4	1.000
12 yrs.			105	97	.520	4.20	294	230	91	1726.2	1958	569	536	8	8	7	10	610	88	3	.144	33	389	25	24	1.5	.944
WORLD SERIES																											
1926	STL	N	0	0	—	6.75	1	1	0	4	7	2	4	0	0	0	0	1	0	0	.000	0	1	0	0	1.0	1.000
1928			0	0	—	0.00	1	0	0	2	0	0	1	0	0	0	0	0	0	0	—	0	0	0	0	0.0	.000
1930			0	1	.000	10.80	1	1	0	3.1	7	2	3	0	0	0	0	1	0	0	.000	0	0	1	0	1.0	.000
1931			0	0	—	0.00	1	0	0	1	1	0	1	0	0	0	0	0	0	0	—	0	0	0	0	0.0	.000
4 yrs.			0	1	.000	6.10	4	2	0	10.1	15	4	9	0	0	0	0	2	0	0	.000	0	1	1	0	0.5	.500

Billy Rhines

RHINES, WILLIAM PEARL
B. Mar. 14, 1869, Ridgway, Pa. D. Jan. 30, 1922, Ridgway, Pa.
BR TR 5′11″ 168 lbs.

Year	Team		W	L	PCT	ERA	G	GS	CG	IP	H	BB	SO	ShO	Relief Pitching W	Relief Pitching L	Relief Pitching SV	Batting AB	Batting H	Batting HR	BA	PO	A	E	DP	TC/G	FA
1890	CIN	N	28	17	.622	**1.95**	46	45	45	401.1	337	113	182	6	0	0	0	154	29	0	.188	23	77	7	3	2.3	.935
1891			17	24	.415	2.87	48	43	40	372.2	364	124	138	1	2	0	1	148	18	0	.122	8	95	7	3	2.3	.936
1892			4	7	.364	5.06	12	9	8	83.2	113	36	12	0	1	0	0	30	5	1	.167	4	14	2	1	1.5	.900
1893	LOU	N	1	4	.200	8.71	5	5	3	31	49	19	0	0	0	0	0	11	1	0	.091	0	8	0	0	1.6	1.000
1895	CIN	N	19	10	.655	4.81	38	33	25	267.2	322	76	72	0	1	0	0	113	25	0	.221	17	56	9	3	2.2	.890
1896			8	6	.571	**2.45**	19	17	11	143	128	48	32	3	0	1	0	52	10	0	.192	8	35	3	2	2.4	.935
1897			21	15	.583	4.08	41	32	26	288.2	311	86	65	1	**5**	0	0	107	17	0	.159	16	53	8	2	1.9	.896
1898	PIT	N	12	16	.429	3.52	31	29	27	258	289	61	48	2	0	0	0	100	15	0	.150	11	88	3	0	3.3	.971
1899			4	4	.500	6.00	9	9	4	54	59	13	6	0	0	0	0	23	10	0	.435	2	7	0	1	1.0	1.000
9 yrs.			114	103	.525	3.47	249	222	189	1900	1972	576	555	13	9	1	1	738	130	1	.176	89	433	39	15	2.2	.930

Bob Rhoads

RHOADS, ROBERT BARTON (Dusty)
B. Oct. 4, 1879, Wooster, Ohio D. Feb. 12, 1967, San Bernardino, Calif.
BR TR 6′ 1″ 215 lbs.

Year	Team		W	L	PCT	ERA	G	GS	CG	IP	H	BB	SO	ShO	Relief Pitching W	Relief Pitching L	Relief Pitching SV	Batting AB	Batting H	Batting HR	BA	PO	A	E	DP	TC/G	FA
1902	CHI	N	4	8	.333	3.20	16	12	12	118	131	42	43	1	0	0	1	45	10	0	.222	7	28	3	0	2.4	.921
1903	2 teams	STL N	(17G 5–8)		CLE A	(5G 2–3)																					
″	total		7	11	.389	4.76	22	18	17	170	209	50	73	1	0	0	0	67	9	1	.134	7	40	4	1	2.2	.922
1904	CLE	A	10	9	.526	2.87	22	19	18	175.1	175	48	72	0	0	0	0	92	18	0	.196	20	53	5	4	2.9	.936
1905			16	9	.640	2.83	28	26	24	235	219	55	61	4	1	0	0	95	21	1	.221	6	78	1	3	2.9	.988
1906			22	10	.688	1.80	38	34	31	315	259	92	89	7	1	0	0	118	19	0	.161	17	88	4	5	2.9	.963
1907			15	14	.517	2.29	35	31	23	275	258	84	76	5	1	0	1	92	17	0	.185	13	83	5	6	2.9	.950
1908			18	12	.600	1.77	37	30	20	270	229	73	62	1	2	2	0	90	20	0	.222	18	96	2	2	3.1	.983
1909			5	9	.357	2.90	20	15	9	133.1	124	50	46	2	0	1	0	43	7	0	.163	6	44	4	2	2.7	.926
8 yrs.			97	82	.542	2.61	218	185	154	1691.2	1604	494	522	21	5	3	2	642	121	2	.188	94	510	28	23	2.8	.956

Rick Rhoden

RHODEN, RICHARD ALAN
B. May 16, 1953, Boynton Beach, Fla.
BR TR 6′ 3″ 195 lbs.

Year	Team		W	L	PCT	ERA	G	GS	CG	IP	H	BB	SO	ShO	Relief Pitching W	Relief Pitching L	Relief Pitching SV	Batting AB	Batting H	Batting HR	BA	PO	A	E	DP	TC/G	FA
1974	LA	N	1	0	1.000	2.00	4	0	0	9	5	4	7	0	1	0	0	2	1	0	.500	0	1	0	0	0.3	1.000
1975			3	3	.500	3.09	26	11	1	99	94	32	40	0	0	1	0	28	2	0	.071	5	16	1	1	0.8	.955
1976			12	3	.800	2.98	27	26	10	181	165	53	77	3	0	0	0	65	20	1	.308	9	20	1	0	1.1	.967
1977			16	10	.615	3.75	31	31	4	216	223	63	122	1	0	0	0	78	18	3	.231	8	22	0	1	1.0	1.000
1978			10	8	.556	3.65	30	23	6	165	160	51	79	3	0	2	0	52	7	0	.135	5	23	0	0	0.9	1.000
1979	PIT	N	0	1	.000	7.20	1	1	0	5	5	2	2	0	0	0	0	1	1	0	1.000	1	1	0	0	2.0	1.000
1980			7	5	.583	3.83	20	19	2	127	133	40	70	0	0	0	0	40	15	1	.375	6	22	1	1	1.5	.966
1981			9	4	.692	3.90	21	21	4	136	147	53	76	2	0	0	0	48	9	0	.188	8	25	0	4	1.6	1.000
1982			11	14	.440	4.14	35	35	6	230.1	239	70	128	1	0	0	0	83	22	3	.265	21	44	0	1	1.9	1.000
1983			13	13	.500	3.09	36	35	7	244.1	256	68	153	2	0	0	1	86	13	0	.151	14	38	0	4	1.4	1.000
1984			14	9	.609	2.72	33	33	6	238.1	216	62	136	3	0	0	0	84	28	0	.333	14	44	2	2	1.8	.967
1985			10	15	.400	4.47	35	35	2	213.1	254	69	128	0	0	0	0	74	14	0	.189	13	30	0	1	1.2	1.000
1986			15	12	.556	2.84	34	34	12	253.2	211	76	159	1	0	0	0	90	25	1	.278	32	34	0	4	1.9	1.000
1987	NY	A	16	10	.615	3.86	30	29	4	181.2	184	61	107	0	0	0	0	0	0	0	—	14	24	1	2	1.3	.974
1988			12	12	.500	4.29	30	30	5	197	206	56	94	1	0	0	0	1	0	0	.000	17	22	0	2	1.3	1.000
1989	HOU	N	2	6	.250	4.28	20	17	0	96.2	108	41	41	0	0	0	0	29	6	0	.207	6	20	0	0	1.3	1.000
16 yrs.			151	125	.547	3.60	413	380	69	2593.1	2606	801	1419	17	1	3	1	761	181	9	.238	173	386	6	23	1.4	.989
LEAGUE CHAMPIONSHIP SERIES																											
1977	LA	N	0	0	—	0.00	1	0	0	4.1	2	2	0	0	0	0	0	1	0	0	.000	0	0	0	0	0.0	.000
1978			0	0	—	2.25	1	0	0	4	2	1	3	0	0	0	0	1	0	0	.000	0	2	0	0	2.0	1.000
2 yrs.			0	0		1.08	2	0	0	8.1	4	3	3	0	0	0	0	2	0	0	.000	0	2	0	0	1.0	1.000
WORLD SERIES																											
1977	LA	N	0	1	.000	2.57	2	0	0	7	4	1	5	0	0	1	0	2	1	0	.500	1	1	0	0	1.0	1.000

Arthur Rhodes

RHODES, ARTHUR LEE
B. Oct. 24, 1969, Waco, Tex.
BL TL 6′ 2″ 190 lbs.

Year	Team	W	L	PCT	ERA	G	GS	CG	IP	H	BB	SO	ShO	Relief Pitching W	Relief Pitching L	Relief Pitching SV	Batting AB	Batting H	Batting HR	BA	PO	A	E	DP	TC/G	FA
1991	BAL A	0	3	.000	8.00	8	8	0	36	47	23	23	0	0	0	0	0	0	0	—	0	1	0	0	0.1	1.000
1992		7	5	.583	3.63	15	15	2	94.1	87	38	77	1	0	0	0	0	0	0	—	1	13	0	2	0.9	1.000
1993		5	6	.455	6.51	17	17	0	85.2	91	49	49	0	0	0	0	0	0	0	—	2	9	1	0	0.7	.917
1994		3	5	.375	5.81	10	10	3	52.2	51	30	47	2	0	0	0	0	0	0	—	0	2	1	0	0.3	.667
1995		2	5	.286	6.21	19	9	0	75.1	68	48	77	0	0	2	0	0	0	0	—	3	7	2	0	0.6	.833
5 yrs.		17	24	.415	5.70	69	59	5	344	344	188	273	3	0	2	0	0	0	0		6	32	4	2	0.6	.905

Bill Rhodes

RHODES, WILLIAM CLARENCE (Dusty)
B. Pottstown, Pa. Deceased.

Year	Team	W	L	PCT	ERA	G	GS	CG	IP	H	BB	SO	ShO	Relief Pitching W	Relief Pitching L	Relief Pitching SV	Batting AB	Batting H	Batting HR	BA	PO	A	E	DP	TC/G	FA
1893	LOU N	5	12	.294	7.60	20	19	17	151.2	244	66	22	0	0	0	0	70	9	0	.129	3	26	5	0	1.7	.853

Charlie Rhodes

RHODES, CHARLES ANDERSON
B. Apr. 7, 1885, Caney, Kans. D. Oct. 26, 1918, Caney, Kans.
BR TR 5′ 7″ 180 lbs.

Year	Team	W	L	PCT	ERA	G	GS	CG	IP	H	BB	SO	ShO	Relief Pitching W	Relief Pitching L	Relief Pitching SV	Batting AB	Batting H	Batting HR	BA	PO	A	E	DP	TC/G	FA
1906	STL N	3	4	.429	3.40	9	6	3	45	37	20	32	0	1	0	0	16	3	0	.188	2	14	2	0	2.0	.889
1908	2 teams CIN N (1G 0–0) STL N (4G 1–2)																									
″	total	1	2	.333	2.68	5	4	3	37	24	14	19	0	0	0	0	13	3	0	.231	2	16	1	0	3.8	.947
1909	STL N	3	5	.375	3.98	12	10	4	61	55	33	25	0	1	0	0	19	4	0	.211	2	28	3	0	2.8	.909
3 yrs.		7	11	.389	3.46	26	20	10	143	116	67	76	0	2	0	0	48	10	0	.208	6	58	6	0	2.7	.914

Gordon Rhodes

RHODES, JOHN GORDON (Dusty)
B. Aug. 11, 1907, Winnemucca, Nev. D. Mar. 24, 1960, Long Beach, Calif.
BR TR 6′ 187 lbs.

Year	Team	W	L	PCT	ERA	G	GS	CG	IP	H	BB	SO	ShO	Relief Pitching W	Relief Pitching L	Relief Pitching SV	Batting AB	Batting H	Batting HR	BA	PO	A	E	DP	TC/G	FA
1929	NY A	0	4	.000	4.85	10	4	0	42.2	57	16	13	0	0	0	0	10	3	0	.300	2	7	2	1	1.1	.818
1930		0	0	—	9.00	3	0	0	2	3	4	1	0	0	0	0	0	0	0	—	0	1	0	0	0.3	1.000
1931		6	3	.667	3.41	18	11	4	87	82	52	36	0	1	0	0	28	6	0	.214	2	20	3	0	1.4	.880
1932	2 teams NY A (10G 1–2) BOS A (12G 1–8)																									
″	total	2	10	.167	5.75	22	13	5	103.1	104	52	37	0	0	2	0	34	4	0	.118	7	26	1	0	1.5	.971
1933	BOS A	12	15	.444	4.03	34	29	14	232	242	93	85	0	1	1	0	86	23	1	.267	8	46	4	2	1.7	.931
1934		12	12	.500	4.56	44	31	10	219	247	98	79	0	3	1	2	75	10	1	.133	5	47	0	1	1.2	1.000
1935		2	10	.167	5.41	34	19	1	146.1	195	60	44	0	0	1	2	48	7	0	.146	6	28	4	1	1.1	.895
1936	PHI A	9	**20**	.310	5.74	35	28	13	216.1	266	102	61	1	2	0	1	75	16	0	.213	4	29	3	1	1.0	.917
8 yrs.		43	74	.368	4.85	200	135	47	1048.2	1196	477	356	1	7	5	5	356	69	2	.194	34	204	17	6	1.3	.933

Dennis Ribant

RIBANT, DENNIS JOSEPH
B. Sept. 20, 1941, Detroit, Mich.
BR TR 5′11″ 165 lbs.

Year	Team	W	L	PCT	ERA	G	GS	CG	IP	H	BB	SO	ShO	Relief Pitching W	Relief Pitching L	Relief Pitching SV	Batting AB	Batting H	Batting HR	BA	PO	A	E	DP	TC/G	FA
1964	NY N	1	5	.167	5.15	14	7	1	57.2	65	9	35	1	0	0	1	20	2	0	.100	2	7	0	0	0.6	1.000
1965		1	3	.250	3.82	19	1	0	35.1	29	6	13	0	1	3	3	6	0	0	.000	0	5	0	1	0.3	1.000
1966		11	9	.550	3.20	39	26	10	188.1	184	40	84	1	0	0	3	61	12	0	.197	12	34	2	1	1.2	.958
1967	PIT N	9	8	.529	4.08	38	22	2	172	186	40	75	0	3	2	0	60	16	0	.267	18	34	1	3	1.4	.981
1968	2 teams DET A (14G 2–2) CHI A (17G 0–2)																									
″	total	2	4	.333	4.37	31	0	0	55.2	62	27	27	0	2	4	2	12	1	0	.083	6	8	3	0	0.5	.824
1969	2 teams STL N (1G 0–0) CIN N (7G 0–0)																									
″	total	0	0		2.79	8	0	0	9.2	10	4	7	0	0	0	0	0	0	0		1	0	1	0	0.3	.500
6 yrs.		24	29	.453	3.87	149	56	13	518.2	536	126	241	2	6	9	9	159	31	0	.195	39	88	7	5	0.9	.948

Frank Riccelli

RICCELLI, FRANK JOSEPH
B. Feb. 24, 1953, Syracuse, N. Y.
BL TL 6′ 3″ 205 lbs.

Year	Team	W	L	PCT	ERA	G	GS	CG	IP	H	BB	SO	ShO	Relief Pitching W	Relief Pitching L	Relief Pitching SV	Batting AB	Batting H	Batting HR	BA	PO	A	E	DP	TC/G	FA
1976	SF N	1	1	.500	5.63	4	3	0	16	16	5	11	0	0	0	0	6	1	0	.167	0	1	0	1	0.3	1.000
1978	HOU N	0	0	—	0.00	2	0	0	3	1	0	1	0	0	0	0	0	0	0	—	0	0	0	0	0.0	.000
1979		2	2	.500	4.09	11	2	0	22	22	18	20	0	1	1	0	6	2	0	.333	0	6	0	0	0.5	1.000
3 yrs.		3	3	.500	4.39	17	5	0	41	39	23	32	0	1	1	0	12	3	0	.250	0	7	0	1	0.4	1.000

Chuck Ricci

RICCI, CHARLES MARK
B. Nov. 20, 1968, Abington, Pa.
BR TR 6′ 2″ 180 lbs.

Year	Team	W	L	PCT	ERA	G	GS	CG	IP	H	BB	SO	ShO	Relief Pitching W	Relief Pitching L	Relief Pitching SV	Batting AB	Batting H	Batting HR	BA	PO	A	E	DP	TC/G	FA
1995	PHI N	1	0	1.000	1.80	7	0	0	10	9	3	9	0	1	0	0	0	0	0	—	2	0	0	0	0.3	1.000

Pat Rice

RICE, PATRICK EDWARD
B. Nov. 2, 1963, Rapid City, S. D.
BR TR 6′ 2″ 200 lbs.

Year	Team	W	L	PCT	ERA	G	GS	CG	IP	H	BB	SO	ShO	Relief Pitching W	Relief Pitching L	Relief Pitching SV	Batting AB	Batting H	Batting HR	BA	PO	A	E	DP	TC/G	FA
1991	SEA A	1	1	.500	3.00	7	2	0	21	18	10	12	0	0	0	0	0	0	0	—	2	1	0	0	0.4	1.000

Sam Rice

RICE, EDGAR CHARLES
B. Feb. 20, 1890, Morocco, Ind. D. Oct. 13, 1974, Rossmor, Md.
Hall of Fame 1963.
BL TR 5′ 9″ 150 lbs.

Year	Team	W	L	PCT	ERA	G	GS	CG	IP	H	BB	SO	ShO	Relief Pitching W	Relief Pitching L	Relief Pitching SV	Batting AB	Batting H	Batting HR	BA	PO	A	E	DP	TC/G	FA
1915	WAS A	1	0	1.000	2.00	4	2	1	18	13	9	9	0	0	0	0	8	3	0	.375	1	7	1	1	2.3	.889
1916		0	1	.000	2.95	5	1	0	21.1	18	10	3	0	0	1	0	197	59	1	.299	83	11	4	1	1.9	.959
2 yrs.		1	1	.500	2.52	9	3	1	39.1	31	19	12	0	0	1	0	*				4773	291	185	68	2.3	.965

Woody Rich

RICH, WOODROW EARL
B. Mar. 9, 1916, Morganton, N. C. D. Apr. 18, 1983, Morganton, N. C.
BL TR 6′ 2″ 185 lbs.

Year	Team	W	L	PCT	ERA	G	GS	CG	IP	H	BB	SO	ShO	Relief Pitching W	Relief Pitching L	Relief Pitching SV	Batting AB	Batting H	Batting HR	BA	PO	A	E	DP	TC/G	FA
1939	BOS A	4	3	.571	4.91	21	12	3	77	78	35	24	0	0	0	1	27	7	0	.259	3	22	3	0	1.3	.893
1940		1	0	1.000	0.77	3	1	1	11.2	9	1	8	0	0	0	0	4	0	0	.000	0	1	0	0	0.3	1.000
1941		0	0	—	17.18	2	1	0	3.2	8	2	4	0	0	0	0	0	0	0	—	0	2	0	0	1.0	1.000
1944	BOS N	1	1	.500	5.76	7	2	1	25	32	12	6	0	0	0	0	8	1	0	.125	1	5	0	1	0.9	1.000
4 yrs.		6	4	.600	5.06	33	16	5	117.1	127	50	42	0	0	0	1	39	8	0	.205	4	30	3	1	1.1	.919

J. R. Richard

RICHARD, JAMES RODNEY
B. Mar. 7, 1950, Vienna, La.
BR TR 6′ 8″ 222 lbs.

Year	Team	W	L	PCT	ERA	G	GS	CG	IP	H	BB	SO	ShO	Relief Pitching W	Relief Pitching L	Relief Pitching SV	Batting AB	Batting H	Batting HR	BA	PO	A	E	DP	TC/G	FA
1971	HOU N	2	1	.667	3.43	4	4	1	21	17	16	29	0	0	0	0	7	0	0	.000	1	3	0	0	1.0	1.000
1972		1	0	1.000	13.50	4	1	0	6	10	8	8	0	1	0	0	0	0	0	—	0	2	0	1	0.5	1.000
1973		6	2	.750	4.00	16	10	2	72	54	38	75	1	0	1	0	28	5	0	.179	5	3	1	0	0.6	.889
1974		2	3	.400	4.15	15	9	0	65	58	36	42	0	0	0	0	21	3	1	.143	5	5	0	0	0.7	1.000
1975		12	10	.545	4.39	33	31	7	203	178	**138**	176	1	1	0	0	74	15	1	.203	8	19	1	0	0.8	.964
1976		20	15	.571	2.75	39	39	14	291	221	**151**	214	3	0	0	0	100	14	2	.140	19	39	10	2	1.7	.853
1977		18	12	.600	2.97	36	36	13	267	212	104	214	3	0	0	0	87	20	2	.230	26	44	0	2	1.9	1.000
1978		18	11	.621	3.11	36	36	16	275	192	**141**	**303**	3	0	0	0	101	18	1	.178	29	38	3	0	1.9	.957

J. R. Richard *continued*

Year	Team	Lg	W	L	PCT	ERA	G	GS	CG	IP	H	BB	SO	ShO	Relief W	Relief L	Relief SV	AB	H	HR	BA	PO	A	E	DP	TC/G	FA
1979			18	13	.581	**2.71**	38	38	19	292	220	98	**313**	4	0	0	0	95	12	2	.126	14	32	5	0	1.3	.902
1980			10	4	.714	1.89	17	17	4	114	65	40	119	4	0	0	0	39	6	1	.154	6	10	0	1	0.9	1.000
10 yrs.			107	71	.601	3.15	238	221	76	1606	1227	770	1493	19	2	1	0	552	93	10	.168	113	195	20	6	1.4	.939

Duane Richards

RICHARDS, DUANE LEE BR TR 6′ 3″ 200 lbs.
B. Dec. 16, 1936, Spartanburg, Ind.

Year	Team	Lg	W	L	PCT	ERA	G	GS	CG	IP	H	BB	SO	ShO	Relief W	Relief L	Relief SV	AB	H	HR	BA	PO	A	E	DP	TC/G	FA
1960	CIN	N	0	0	—	9.00	2	0	0	3	5	2	2	0	0	0	0	0	0	0	—	0	1	0	0	0.5	1.000

Rusty Richards

RICHARDS, RUSSELL EARL BL TR 6′ 4″ 200 lbs.
B. Jan. 27, 1965, Houston, Tex.

Year	Team	Lg	W	L	PCT	ERA	G	GS	CG	IP	H	BB	SO	ShO	Relief W	Relief L	Relief SV	AB	H	HR	BA	PO	A	E	DP	TC/G	FA
1989	ATL	N	0	0	—	4.82	2	2	0	9.1	10	6	4	0	0	0	0	3	0	0	.000	1	3	0	0	2.0	1.000
1990			0	0	—	27.00	1	0	0	1	2	1	0	0	0	0	0	0	0	0	—	0	0	0	0	0.0	.000
2 yrs.			0	0		6.97	3	2	0	10.1	12	7	4	0	0	0	0	3	0	0	.000	1	3	0	0	1.3	1.000

Danny Richardson

RICHARDSON, DANIEL BR TR 5′ 8″ 165 lbs.
B. Jan. 25, 1863, Elmira, N. Y. D. Sept. 12, 1926, New York, N. Y.
Manager 1892.

Year	Team	Lg	W	L	PCT	ERA	G	GS	CG	IP	H	BB	SO	ShO	Relief W	Relief L	Relief SV	AB	H	HR	BA	PO	A	E	DP	TC/G	FA
1885	NY	N	7	1	.875	*2.40*	9	8	7	75	58	18	21	1	**1**	0	0	198	52	0	.263	110	54	24	9	2.5	.872
1886			0	2	.000	*5.76*	5	1	1	25	33	11	17	0	1	0	0	237	55	1	.232	103	26	6	3	1.9	.956
1887			0	0	—	0.00	1	0	0		0	1	0	0	0	0	0	450	125	3	.278	273	413	59	47	6.1	.921
3 yrs.			7	3	.700	3.24	15	9	8	100	91	30	38	1	2	0	0	*				2636	3339	442	435	5.6	.931

Gordie Richardson

RICHARDSON, GORDON CLARK BR TL 6′ 185 lbs.
B. July 19, 1939, Colquitt, Ga.

Year	Team	Lg	W	L	PCT	ERA	G	GS	CG	IP	H	BB	SO	ShO	Relief W	Relief L	Relief SV	AB	H	HR	BA	PO	A	E	DP	TC/G	FA
1964	STL	N	4	2	.667	2.30	19	6	1	47	40	15	28	0	1	0	1	13	1	0	.077	1	3	0	0	0.2	1.000
1965	NY	N	2	2	.500	3.78	35	0	0	52.1	41	16	43	0	2	2	2	7	0	0	.000	4	6	1	0	0.3	.909
1966			0	2	.000	9.16	15	1	0	18.2	24	6	15	0	0	1	1	1	0	0	.000	2	2	0	0	0.3	1.000
3 yrs.			6	6	.500	4.04	69	7	1	118	105	37	86	0	3	3	4	21	1	0	.048	7	11	1	0	0.3	.947
WORLD SERIES																											
1964	STL	N	0	0	—	40.50	2	0	0	0.2	3	2	0	0	0	0	0	0	0	0	—	0	0	0	0	0.0	.000

Hardy Richardson

RICHARDSON, ABRAM HARDING (Old True Blue) BR TR 5′ 9½″ 170 lbs.
B. Apr. 21, 1855, Clarksboro, N. J. D. Jan. 14, 1931, Utica, N. Y.

Year	Team	Lg	W	L	PCT	ERA	G	GS	CG	IP	H	BB	SO	ShO	Relief W	Relief L	Relief SV	AB	H	HR	BA	PO	A	E	DP	TC/G	FA
1885	BUF	N	0	0	—	*2.25*	1	0	0	4	5	3	1	0	0	0	0	426	136	6	.319	94	153	44	13	3.7	.849
1886	DET	N	3	0	1.000	*4.50*	4	0	0	12	11	10	5	0	2	0	0	538	189	11	.351	242	153	32	17	3.3	.925
2 yrs.			3	0	1.000	3.94	5	0	0	16	16	13	6	0	2	0	0	*				3236	2529	554	266	4.7	.912

Jack Richardson

RICHARDSON, JOHN WILLIAMSON BB TR 6′ 3″ 197 lbs.
B. Oct. 3, 1891, Central City, Ill. D. Jan. 18, 1970, Marion, Ill.

Year	Team	Lg	W	L	PCT	ERA	G	GS	CG	IP	H	BB	SO	ShO	Relief W	Relief L	Relief SV	AB	H	HR	BA	PO	A	E	DP	TC/G	FA
1915	PHI	A	0	1	.000	2.63	3	3	2	24	21	14	11	0	0	0	0	8	0	0	.000	0	7	1	0	2.7	.875
1916			0	0	—	40.50	1	0	0	0.2	2	1	1	0	0	0	0	0	0	0	—	0	0	0	0	0.0	.000
2 yrs.			0	1	.000	3.65	4	3	2	24.2	23	15	12	0	0	0	0	8	0	0	.000	0	7	1	0	2.0	.875

Jeff Richardson

RICHARDSON, JEFFREY SCOTT BR TR 6′ 3″ 185 lbs.
B. Aug. 29, 1963, Wichita, Kans.

Year	Team	Lg	W	L	PCT	ERA	G	GS	CG	IP	H	BB	SO	ShO	Relief W	Relief L	Relief SV	AB	H	HR	BA	PO	A	E	DP	TC/G	FA
1990	CAL	A	0	0	—	0.00	1	0	0	0.1	1	0	0	0	0	0	0	0	0	0	—	0	1	0	0	1.0	1.000

Pete Richert

RICHERT, PETER GERARD BL TL 5′11″ 165 lbs.
B. Oct. 29, 1939, Floral Park, N. Y.

Year	Team	Lg	W	L	PCT	ERA	G	GS	CG	IP	H	BB	SO	ShO	Relief W	Relief L	Relief SV	AB	H	HR	BA	PO	A	E	DP	TC/G	FA
1962	LA	N	5	4	.556	3.87	19	12	1	81.1	77	45	75	0	1	1	0	25	2	0	.080	2	16	1	2	1.0	.947
1963			5	3	.625	4.50	20	12	1	78	80	28	54	0	1	1	0	22	4	0	.182	3	8	0	0	0.6	1.000
1964			2	3	.400	4.15	8	6	1	34.2	38	18	25	1	0	0	0	11	1	0	.091	2	9	2	1	1.6	.846
1965	WAS	A	15	12	.556	2.60	34	29	6	194	146	84	161	0	1	0	0	64	10	0	.156	5	30	1	3	1.1	.972
1966			14	14	.500	3.37	36	34	7	245.2	196	69	195	0	0	0	0	86	14	1	.163	13	29	5	0	1.3	.894
1967	2 teams WAS A (11G 2–6) BAL A (26G 7–10)																										
″	total		9	16	.360	3.47	37	29	6	186.2	156	56	131	2	2	0	2	54	5	0	.093	8	28	3	2	1.1	.923
1968	BAL	A	6	3	.667	3.47	36	0	0	62.1	51	12	47	0	6	3	6	10	2	0	.200	4	12	1	1	0.5	.941
1969			7	4	.636	2.20	44	0	0	57.1	42	14	54	0	7	4	12	8	1	0	.125	3	5	0	0	0.2	1.000
1970			7	2	.778	1.96	50	0	0	55	36	24	66	0	7	2	13	4	0	0	.000	0	8	0	0	0.2	1.000
1971			3	5	.375	3.50	35	0	0	36	26	22	35	0	3	5	4	2	0	0	.000	4	5	1	1	0.3	.900
1972	LA	N	2	3	.400	2.25	37	0	0	52	42	18	38	0	2	3	6	6	3	0	.500	3	5	2	2	0.3	.800
1973			3	3	.500	3.18	39	0	0	51	44	19	31	0	3	3	7	5	1	0	.200	4	10	0	2	0.4	1.000
1974	2 teams STL N (13G 0–0) PHI N (21G 2–1)																										
″	total		2	1	.667	2.27	34	0	0	31.2	25	15	13	0	2	1	1	0	0	0		2	3	2	0	0.2	.714
13 yrs.			80	73	.523	3.19	429	122	22	1165.2	959	424	925	3	35	23	51	297	43	1	.145	53	168	18	14	0.6	.925
LEAGUE CHAMPIONSHIP SERIES																											
1969	BAL	A	0	0	—	0.00	1	0	0	1	0	2	2	0	0	0	0	0	0	0	—	0	0	0	0	0.0	.000
WORLD SERIES																											
1969	BAL	A	0	0	—	0.00	1	0	0		0	0	0	0	0	0	0	0	0	0	—	0	0	1	0	1.0	.000
1970			0	0	—	0.00	1	0	0	0.1	0	0	0	0	0	0	1	0	0	0	—	0	0	0	0	0.0	.000
1971			0	0	—	0.00	1	0	0	0.2	0	0	1	0	0	0	0	0	0	0	—	0	0	0	0	0.0	.000
3 yrs.			0	0		0.00	3	0	0	1	0	0	1	0	0	0	1	0	0	0		0	0	1	0	0.3	.000

Lew Richie

RICHIE, LEWIS A. BR TR 5′ 8″ 165 lbs.
B. Aug. 23, 1883, Ambler, Pa. D. Aug. 15, 1936, Ambler, Pa.

Year	Team	Lg	W	L	PCT	ERA	G	GS	CG	IP	H	BB	SO	ShO	Relief W	Relief L	Relief SV	AB	H	HR	BA	PO	A	E	DP	TC/G	FA
1906	PHI	N	9	11	.450	2.41	33	22	14	205.2	170	79	65	3	0	1	0	60	3	0	.050	10	44	0	0	1.6	1.000
1907			6	6	.500	1.77	25	12	9	117	88	38	40	2	2	0	0	43	7	0	.163	7	26	2	0	1.4	.943
1908			7	10	.412	1.83	25	15	13	157.2	125	49	58	2	1	1	1	52	11	0	.212	7	40	6	4	2.1	.887
1909	2 teams PHI N (11G 1–1) BOS N (22G 7–7)																										
″	total		8	8	.500	2.24	33	14	9	176.2	158	62	53	2	3	2	3	60	9	0	.150	8	31	4	2	1.3	.907
1910	2 teams BOS N (4G 0–3) CHI N (30G 11–4)																										
″	total		11	7	.611	2.71	34	13	8	146.1	137	60	60	3	5	2	3	44	9	0	.205	8	45	3	2	1.6	.946

Lew Richie *continued*

Year	Team		W	L	PCT	ERA	G	GS	CG	IP	H	BB	SO	ShO	Relief Pitching W	L	SV	Batting AB	H	HR	BA	PO	A	E	DP	TC/G	FA
1911	CHI	N	15	11	.577	2.31	36	28	18	253	213	103	78	4	0	1	1	91	14	0	.154	13	70	3	2	2.4	.965
1912			16	8	.667	2.95	39	27	15	238	222	74	69	4	2	2	0	76	10	0	.132	2	57	5	0	1.6	.922
1913			2	4	.333	5.82	16	6	1	65	77	30	15	0	0	1	0	17	2	0	.118	2	14	3	0	1.2	.842
8 yrs.			74	65	.532	2.54	241	137	87	1359.1	1190	495	438	20	13	10	8	443	65	0	.147	57	327	26	10	1.7	.937
WORLD SERIES																											
1910	CHI	N	0	0	—	0.00	1	0	0	1	1	0	0	0	0	0	0	0	0	0	—	0	0	0	0	0.0	.000

Beryl Richmond

RICHMOND, BERYL JUSTICE
B. Aug. 24, 1907, Glen Easton, W. Va. D. Apr. 24, 1980, Cameron, W. Va.
BB TL 6′ 1″ 185 lbs.
BR 1933

Year	Team		W	L	PCT	ERA	G	GS	CG	IP	H	BB	SO	ShO	Relief Pitching W	L	SV	Batting AB	H	HR	BA	PO	A	E	DP	TC/G	FA
1933	CHI	N	0	0	—	1.93	4	0	0	4.2	10	2	2	0	0	0	0	1	0	0	.000	0	0	0	0	0.0	.000
1934	CIN	N	1	2	.333	3.72	6	2	1	19.1	23	10	9	0	0	1	0	5	0	0	.000	0	3	0	0	0.5	1.000
2 yrs.			1	2	.333	3.38	10	2	1	24	33	12	11	0	0	1	0	6	0	0	.000	0	3	0	0	0.3	1.000

Lee Richmond

RICHMOND, J. LEE
B. May 5, 1857, Sheffield, Ohio D. Oct. 1, 1929, Toledo, Ohio.
TL 5′10″ 155 lbs.

Year	Team		W	L	PCT	ERA	G	GS	CG	IP	H	BB	SO	ShO	Relief Pitching W	L	SV	Batting AB	H	HR	BA	PO	A	E	DP	TC/G	FA
1879	BOS	N	1	0	1.000	2.00	1	1	1	9	4	1	11	0	0	0	0	6	2	0	.333	0	2	0	0	2.0	1.000
1880	WOR	N	32	32	.500	2.15	**74**	66	57	590.2	541	74	243	5	1	0	**3**	309	70	0	.227	17	99	26	1	1.5	.817
1881			25	26	.490	*3.39*	53	52	50	462.1	547	68	156	3	0	0	0	252	63	0	.250	26	101	13	4	2.2	.907
1882			14	**33**	.298	*3.74*	48	46	44	411	525	88	123	0	**1**	0	0	228	64	2	.281	23	101	19	2	2.4	.867
1883	PRO	N	3	7	.300	*3.33*	12	12	8	92	122	27	13	0	0	0	0	194	55	1	.284	49	22	22	0	1.8	.763
1886	CIN	AA	0	2	.000	*8.00*	3	2	1	18	24	11	6	0	0	0	0	29	8	0	.276	6	2	6	0	1.4	.571
6 yrs.			75	100	.429	3.06	191	179	161	1583	1763	269	552	8	2	0	3	*				121	327	86	7	1.9	.839

Ray Richmond

RICHMOND, RAYMOND SINCLAIR (Bud)
B. June 5, 1896, Fillmore, Ill. D. Dec. 21, 1969, DeSoto, Mo.
BR TR 6′ 175 lbs.

Year	Team		W	L	PCT	ERA	G	GS	CG	IP	H	BB	SO	ShO	Relief Pitching W	L	SV	Batting AB	H	HR	BA	PO	A	E	DP	TC/G	FA
1920	STL	A	2	0	1.000	6.35	2	2	1	17	18	9	4	0	0	0	0	6	1	0	.167	3	4	0	0	3.5	1.000
1921			0	1	.000	11.66	7	1	0	14.2	23	14	7	0	0	1	0	4	0	0	.000	3	2	0	0	0.7	1.000
2 yrs.			2	1	.667	8.81	9	3	1	31.2	41	23	11	0	0	1	0	10	1	0	.100	6	6	0	0	1.3	1.000

Reggie Richter

RICHTER, EMIL HENRY
B. Sept. 14, 1888, Dusseldorf, Germany D. Aug. 2, 1934, Winfield, Ill.
BR TR 6′ 2″ 180 lbs.

Year	Team		W	L	PCT	ERA	G	GS	CG	IP	H	BB	SO	ShO	Relief Pitching W	L	SV	Batting AB	H	HR	BA	PO	A	E	DP	TC/G	FA
1911	CHI	N	1	3	.250	3.13	22	5	0	54.2	62	20	34	0	0	1	2	10	1	0	.100	3	11	1	2	0.7	.933

Dick Ricketts

RICKETTS, RICHARD JAMES
Brother of Dave Ricketts.
B. Dec. 4, 1933, Pottstown, Pa. D. Mar. 6, 1988, Rochester, N. Y.
BL TR 6′ 7″ 215 lbs.

Year	Team		W	L	PCT	ERA	G	GS	CG	IP	H	BB	SO	ShO	Relief Pitching W	L	SV	Batting AB	H	HR	BA	PO	A	E	DP	TC/G	FA
1959	STL	N	1	6	.143	5.82	12	9	0	55.2	68	30	25	0	0	0	0	18	1	0	.056	2	2	3	0	0.6	.571

Elmer Riddle

RIDDLE, ELMER RAY
Brother of Johnny Riddle.
B. July 31, 1914, Columbus, Ga. D. May 14, 1984, Columbus, Ga.
BR TR 5′11½″ 170 lbs.

Year	Team		W	L	PCT	ERA	G	GS	CG	IP	H	BB	SO	ShO	Relief Pitching W	L	SV	Batting AB	H	HR	BA	PO	A	E	DP	TC/G	FA
1939	CIN	N	0	0	—	0.00	1	0	0	2	1	0	0	0	0	0	0	0	0	0	—	0	0	0	0	0.0	.000
1940			1	2	.333	1.87	15	1	1	33.2	30	17	9	0	1	1	2	7	1	0	.143	0	7	0	2	0.5	1.000
1941			19	4	**.826**	**2.24**	33	22	15	216.2	180	59	80	4	3	0	1	71	16	0	.225	7	43	0	2	1.5	1.000
1942			7	11	.389	3.69	29	19	7	158.1	157	79	78	1	1	2	0	58	15	0	.259	7	28	0	3	1.2	1.000
1943			**21**	11	.656	2.63	36	33	19	260.1	235	107	69	5	0	0	3	93	18	0	.194	16	48	1	4	1.8	.985
1944			2	2	.500	4.05	4	4	2	26.2	25	12	6	0	0	0	0	8	1	0	.125	2	8	0	0	2.5	1.000
1945			1	4	.200	8.19	12	3	0	29.2	39	27	5	0	1	1	0	11	3	0	.273	1	7	0	1	0.7	1.000
1947			1	0	1.000	8.31	16	3	0	30.1	42	31	8	0	0	0	0	5	0	0	.000	1	2	0	0	0.2	1.000
1948	PIT	N	12	10	.545	3.49	28	27	12	191	184	81	63	3	0	0	1	64	12	1	.188	9	37	2	3	1.7	.958
1949			1	8	.111	5.33	16	12	1	74.1	81	45	24	0	0	1	1	22	3	0	.136	6	4	0	0	0.6	1.000
10 yrs.			65	52	.556	3.40	190	124	57	1023	974	458	342	13	6	5	8	339	69	1	.204	49	184	3	15	1.2	.987
WORLD SERIES																											
1940	CIN	N	0	0	—	0.00	1	0	0	1	0	0	2	0	0	0	0	0	0	0	—	0	0	0	0	0.0	.000

Denny Riddleberger

RIDDLEBERGER, DENNIS MICHAEL
B. Nov. 22, 1945, Clifton Forge, Va.
BR TL 6′ 3″ 195 lbs.

Year	Team		W	L	PCT	ERA	G	GS	CG	IP	H	BB	SO	ShO	Relief Pitching W	L	SV	Batting AB	H	HR	BA	PO	A	E	DP	TC/G	FA
1970	WAS	A	0	0	—	1.00	8	0	0	9	7	2	5	0	0	0	0	0	0	0	—	0	0	0	0	0.0	.000
1971			3	1	.750	3.21	57	0	0	70	67	32	56	0	3	1	1	4	0	0	.000	6	8	0	1	0.2	1.000
1972	CLE	A	1	3	.250	2.50	38	0	0	54	45	22	34	0	1	3	0	4	0	0	.000	0	9	0	0	0.2	1.000
3 yrs.			4	4	.500	2.77	103	0	0	133	119	56	95	0	4	4	1	8	0	0	.000	6	17	0	1	0.2	1.000

Dorsey Riddlemoser

RIDDLEMOSER, DORSEY LEE
B. Mar. 25, 1875, Frederick, Md. D. May 11, 1954, Frederick, Md.
BR TR

Year	Team		W	L	PCT	ERA	G	GS	CG	IP	H	BB	SO	ShO	Relief Pitching W	L	SV	Batting AB	H	HR	BA	PO	A	E	DP	TC/G	FA
1899	WAS	N	0	0	—	18.00	1	0	0	2	7	2	0	0	0	0	0	1	0	0	.000	0	1	0	0	1.0	1.000

Jack Ridgway

RIDGWAY, JACOB AUGUSTUS
B. July 23, 1888, Philadelphia, Pa. D. Feb. 23, 1928, Philadelphia, Pa.
BL TR 5′11″ 174 lbs.

Year	Team		W	L	PCT	ERA	G	GS	CG	IP	H	BB	SO	ShO	Relief Pitching W	L	SV	Batting AB	H	HR	BA	PO	A	E	DP	TC/G	FA
1914	BAL	F	0	1	.000	11.00	4	1	0	9	20	3	2	0	0	0	0	1	0	0	.000	0	3	0	1	0.8	1.000

Steve Ridzik

RIDZIK, STEPHEN GEORGE
B. Apr. 29, 1929, Yonkers, N. Y.
BR TR 5′11″ 170 lbs.

Year	Team		W	L	PCT	ERA	G	GS	CG	IP	H	BB	SO	ShO	Relief Pitching W	L	SV	Batting AB	H	HR	BA	PO	A	E	DP	TC/G	FA
1950	PHI	N	0	0	—	6.00	1	0	0	3	3	1	2	0	0	0	0	0	0	0	—	0	0	0	0	0.0	.000
1952			4	2	.667	3.01	24	9	2	92.2	74	37	43	0	2	0	0	22	3	0	.136	4	7	1	1	0.5	.917
1953			9	6	.600	3.77	42	12	1	124	119	48	53	0	7	1	0	36	7	1	.194	7	17	0	4	0.6	1.000
1954			4	5	.444	4.13	35	6	0	80.2	72	44	45	0	4	1	0	22	5	0	.227	6	13	0	0	0.5	1.000
1955	2 teams	PHI N (3G 0–1) CIN N (13G 0–3)																									
″	total		0	4	.000	3.95	16	3	0	41	42	22	12	0	0	1	0	10	1	0	.100	3	5	2	0	0.6	.800
1956	NY	N	6	2	.750	3.80	41	5	1	92.1	80	65	53	1	3	1	0	28	7	0	.250	8	12	2	1	0.5	.909
1957			0	2	.000	4.72	15	0	0	26.2	19	19	13	0	0	2	0	5	1	0	.200	2	5	0	2	0.5	1.000
1958	CLE	A	0	2	.000	2.08	6	0	0	8.2	9	5	6	0	0	0	0	1	0	0	.000	0	3	0	0	0.5	1.000
1963	WAS	A	5	6	.455	4.82	20	10	0	89.2	82	35	47	0	2	2	1	29	5	0	.172	9	13	1	0	1.1	.957
1964			5	5	.500	2.89	49	3	0	112	96	31	60	0	5	3	2	27	6	0	.222	7	13	2	2	0.4	.909

Steve Ridzik *continued*

Year	Team	W	L	PCT	ERA	G	GS	CG	IP	H	BB	SO	ShO	Relief Pitching W	Relief Pitching L	Relief Pitching SV	Batting AB	Batting H	Batting HR	BA	PO	A	E	DP	TC/G	FA
1965		6	4	.600	4.02	63	0	0	109.2	108	43	72	0	6	4	8	18	3	0	.167	5	19	1	3	0.4	.960
1966	PHI N	0	0	—	7.71	2	0	0	2.1	5	1	0	0	0	0	0	0	0	0	—	0	0	0	0	0.0	.000
12 yrs.		39	38	.506	3.79	314	48	4	782.2	709	351	406	1	29	17	11	198	38	1	.192	51	107	9	13	0.5	.946

Elmer Rieger

RIEGER, ELMER JAY BB TR 6′ 175 lbs.
B. Feb. 25, 1889, Perris, Calif. D. Oct. 21, 1959, Los Angeles, Calif.

Year	Team	W	L	PCT	ERA	G	GS	CG	IP	H	BB	SO	ShO	Relief Pitching W	Relief Pitching L	Relief Pitching SV	Batting AB	Batting H	Batting HR	BA	PO	A	E	DP	TC/G	FA
1910	STL N	0	2	.000	5.48	13	2	0	21.1	26	7	9	0	0	1	0	3	0	0	.000	0	7	1	0	0.6	.875

Dave Righetti

RIGHETTI, DAVID ALLAN (Rags) BL TL 6′ 4″ 195 lbs.
B. Nov. 28, 1958, San Jose, Calif.

Year	Team	W	L	PCT	ERA	G	GS	CG	IP	H	BB	SO	ShO	Relief Pitching W	Relief Pitching L	Relief Pitching SV	Batting AB	Batting H	Batting HR	BA	PO	A	E	DP	TC/G	FA
1979	NY A	0	1	.000	3.71	3	3	0	17	10	10	13	0	0	0	0	0	0	0	—	1	3	0	1	1.3	1.000
1981		8	4	.667	2.06	15	15	2	105	75	38	89	0	0	0	0	0	0	0	—	6	9	1	0	1.1	.938
1982		11	10	.524	3.79	33	27	4	183	155	**108**	163	0	0	0	1	0	0	0	—	5	18	3	1	0.8	.885
1983		14	8	.636	3.44	31	31	7	217	194	67	169	2	0	0	0	0	0	0	—	3	24	1	2	0.9	.964
1984		5	6	.455	2.34	64	0	0	96.1	79	37	90	0	5	6	31	0	0	0	—	2	13	2	0	0.3	.882
1985		12	7	.632	2.78	74	0	0	107	96	45	92	0	**12**	7	29	0	0	0	—	1	12	1	2	0.2	.929
1986		8	8	.500	2.45	74	0	0	106.2	88	35	83	0	8	8	**46**	0	0	0	—	1	10	0	2	0.1	1.000
1987		8	6	.571	3.51	60	0	0	95	95	44	77	0	8	6	31	0	0	0	—	3	12	1	0	0.3	.938
1988		5	4	.556	3.52	60	0	0	87	86	37	70	0	5	4	25	0	0	0	—	2	8	0	0	0.2	1.000
1989		2	6	.250	3.00	55	0	0	69	73	26	51	0	2	6	25	0	0	0	—	0	9	0	0	0.2	1.000
1990		1	1	.500	3.57	53	0	0	53	48	26	43	0	1	1	36	0	0	0	—	3	1	1	0	0.1	.800
1991	SF N	2	7	.222	3.39	61	0	0	71.2	64	28	51	0	2	7	24	3	0	0	.000	3	13	0	1	0.3	1.000
1992		2	7	.222	5.06	54	4	0	78.1	79	36	47	0	2	5	3	7	1	0	.143	3	5	1	0	0.2	.889
1993		1	1	.500	5.70	51	0	0	47.1	58	17	31	0	1	1	1	1	1	0	1.000	2	5	0	0	0.1	1.000
1994	2 teams OAK A (7G 0–0) TOR A (13G 0–1)																									
″	total	0	1	.000	10.18	20	0	0	20.1	22	19	14	0	0	1	0	0	0	0		0	3	0	0	0.2	1.000
1995	CHI A	3	2	.600	4.20	10	9	0	49.1	65	18	29	0	0	0	0	0	0	0	—	0	5	1	1	0.6	.833
16 yrs.		82	79	.509	3.46	718	89	13	1403	1287	591	1112	2	46	52	252 **9th**	11	2	0	.182	35	150	12	10	0.3	.939
DIVISIONAL PLAYOFF SERIES																										
1981	NY A	2	0	1.000	1.00	2	1	0	9	8	3	13	0	1	0	0	0	0	0	—	0	0	0	0	0.0	.000
LEAGUE CHAMPIONSHIP SERIES																										
1981	NY A	1	0	1.000	0.00	1	1	0	6	4	2	4	0	0	0	0	0	0	0	—	0	1	0	0	1.0	1.000
WORLD SERIES																										
1981	NY A	0	0	—	13.50	1	1	0	2	5	2	1	0	0	0	0	1	0	0	.000	0	0	0	0	0.0	.000

Ron Rightnowar

RIGHTNOWAR, RONALD GENE BR TR 6′ 3″ 190 lbs.
B. Sept. 5, 1964, Toledo, Ohio

Year	Team	W	L	PCT	ERA	G	GS	CG	IP	H	BB	SO	ShO	Relief Pitching W	Relief Pitching L	Relief Pitching SV	Batting AB	Batting H	Batting HR	BA	PO	A	E	DP	TC/G	FA
1995	MIL A	2	1	.667	5.40	34	0	0	36.2	35	18	22	0	2	1	1	0	0	0	—	0	8	0	1	0.2	1.000

Johnny Rigney

RIGNEY, JOHN DUNGAN BR TR 6′ 2″ 190 lbs.
B. Oct. 28, 1914, Oak Park, Ill. D. Oct. 21, 1984, Lombard, Ill.

Year	Team	W	L	PCT	ERA	G	GS	CG	IP	H	BB	SO	ShO	Relief Pitching W	Relief Pitching L	Relief Pitching SV	Batting AB	Batting H	Batting HR	BA	PO	A	E	DP	TC/G	FA
1937	CHI A	2	5	.286	4.96	22	4	0	90.2	107	46	38	0	2	2	1	30	5	0	.167	3	14	2	0	0.9	.895
1938		9	9	.500	3.56	38	12	7	167	164	72	84	1	5	3	1	55	8	0	.145	4	32	2	4	1.0	.947
1939		15	8	.652	3.70	35	29	11	218.2	208	84	119	2	0	0	0	80	16	0	.200	3	30	3	1	1.0	.917
1940		14	18	.438	3.11	39	33	19	280.2	240	90	141	2	2	1	3	93	20	0	.215	4	46	0	2	1.3	1.000
1941		13	13	.500	3.84	30	29	18	237	224	92	119	3	0	0	0	84	17	0	.202	13	42	3	2	1.9	.948
1942		3	3	.500	3.20	7	7	6	59	40	16	34	0	0	0	0	19	1	0	.053	1	12	0	1	1.9	1.000
1946		5	5	.500	4.03	15	11	3	82.2	76	35	51	2	0	1	0	26	4	0	.154	2	11	0	0	0.9	1.000
1947		2	3	.400	1.95	11	7	2	50.2	42	15	19	0	0	0	0	14	0	0	.000	2	15	1	2	1.6	.944
8 yrs.		63	64	.496	3.59	197	132	66	1186.1	1101	450	605	10	9	7	5	401	71	0	.177	32	202	11	12	1.2	.955

Jose Rijo

RIJO, JOSE ANTONIO BR TR 6′ 1″ 200 lbs.
Born Jose Antonio Rijo (Abreu).
B. May 13, 1965, San Cristobal, Dominican Republic.

Year	Team	W	L	PCT	ERA	G	GS	CG	IP	H	BB	SO	ShO	Relief Pitching W	Relief Pitching L	Relief Pitching SV	Batting AB	Batting H	Batting HR	BA	PO	A	E	DP	TC/G	FA
1984	NY A	2	8	.200	4.76	24	5	0	62.1	74	33	47	0	2	4	2	0	0	0	—	2	12	1	0	0.6	.933
1985	OAK A	6	4	.600	3.53	12	9	0	63.2	57	28	65	0	2	1	0	0	0	0	—	2	5	0	0	0.6	1.000
1986		9	11	.450	4.65	39	26	4	193.2	172	108	176	0	0	4	1	0	0	0	—	13	18	3	0	0.9	.912
1987		2	7	.222	5.90	21	14	1	82.1	106	41	67	0	0	0	0	0	0	0	—	10	10	1	0	1.0	.952
1988	CIN N	13	8	.619	2.39	49	19	0	162	120	63	160	0	6	1	0	37	2	1	.054	7	23	1	1	0.6	.968
1989		7	6	.538	2.84	19	19	1	111	101	48	86	1	0	0	0	38	8	0	.211	6	14	0	0	1.1	1.000
1990		14	8	.636	2.70	29	29	7	197	151	78	152	1	0	0	0	62	10	0	.161	19	27	2	0	1.7	.958
1991		15	6	**.714**	2.51	30	30	3	204.1	165	55	172	1	0	0	0	67	14	0	.209	17	22	3	2	1.4	.929
1992		15	10	.600	2.56	33	33	2	211	185	44	171	0	0	0	0	72	14	0	.194	19	31	2	1	1.6	.962
1993		14	9	.609	2.48	36	**36**	2	257.1	218	62	**227**	1	0	0	0	82	22	1	.268	27	35	0	8	1.7	1.000
1994		9	6	.600	3.08	26	**26**	2	172.1	177	52	171	0	0	0	0	49	10	0	.204	14	27	0	0	1.6	1.000
1995		5	4	.556	4.17	14	14	0	69	76	22	62	0	0	0	0	22	3	0	.136	4	9	0	0	1.0	1.000
12 yrs.		111	87	.561	3.16	332	260	22	1786	1602	634	1556	4	10	10	3	429	83	2	.193	140	233	13	12	1.2	.966
LEAGUE CHAMPIONSHIP SERIES																										
1990	CIN N	1	0	1.000	4.38	2	2	0	12.1	10	7	15	0	0	0	0	5	0	0	.000	0	0	0	0	0.0	.000
WORLD SERIES																										
1990	CIN N	2	0	1.000	0.59	2	2	0	15.1	9	5	14	0	0	0	0	3	1	0	.333	0	2	0	0	1.0	1.000

George Riley

RILEY, GEORGE MICHAEL BL TL 6′ 2″ 210 lbs.
B. Oct. 6, 1956, Philadelphia, Pa.

Year	Team	W	L	PCT	ERA	G	GS	CG	IP	H	BB	SO	ShO	Relief Pitching W	Relief Pitching L	Relief Pitching SV	Batting AB	Batting H	Batting HR	BA	PO	A	E	DP	TC/G	FA
1979	CHI N	0	1	.000	5.54	4	1	0	13	16	6	5	0	0	0	0	2	0	0	.000	1	3	0	0	1.0	1.000
1980		0	4	.000	5.75	22	0	0	36	41	20	18	0	0	4	0	1	0	0	.000	1	12	2	1	0.7	.867
1984	SF N	1	0	1.000	3.99	5	4	0	29.1	39	7	12	0	0	0	0	10	1	0	.100	1	4	0	0	1.0	1.000
1986	MON N	0	0	—	4.15	10	0	0	8.2	7	8	5	0	0	0	0	0	0	0	—	0	0	0	0	0.0	.000
4 yrs.		1	5	.167	4.97	41	5	0	87	103	41	40	0	0	4	0	13	1	0	.077	3	19	2	1	0.6	.917

Andy Rincon

RINCON, ANDREW JOHN BR TR 6′ 3″ 195 lbs.
B. Mar. 5, 1959, Monterey Park, Calif.

Year	Team	Lg	W	L	PCT	ERA	G	GS	CG	IP	H	BB	SO	ShO	Relief Pitching W	Relief Pitching L	Relief Pitching SV	Batting AB	Batting H	Batting HR	BA	PO	A	E	DP	TC/G	FA
1980	STL	N	3	1	.750	2.61	4	4	1	31	23	7	22	0	0	0	0	12	3	0	.250	3	5	0	1	2.0	1.000
1981			3	1	.750	1.75	5	5	1	36	27	5	13	1	0	0	0	13	3	0	.231	2	5	0	0	1.4	1.000
1982			2	3	.400	4.72	11	6	1	40	35	25	11	0	1	0	0	10	1	0	.100	5	3	0	1	0.7	1.000
3 yrs.			8	5	.615	3.11	20	15	3	107	85	37	46	1	1	0	0	35	7	0	.200	10	13	0	2	1.1	1.000

Jeff Rineer

RINEER, JEFFREY ALAN BL TL 6′ 4″ 205 lbs.
B. July 3, 1955, Lancaster, Pa.

Year	Team	Lg	W	L	PCT	ERA	G	GS	CG	IP	H	BB	SO	ShO	Relief Pitching W	Relief Pitching L	Relief Pitching SV	Batting AB	Batting H	Batting HR	BA	PO	A	E	DP	TC/G	FA
1979	BAL	A	0	0	—	0.00	1	0	0	1	0	0	0	0	0	0	0	0	0	0	—	0	0	0	0	0.0	.000

Jimmy Ring

RING, JAMES JOSEPH BR TR 6′ 1″ 170 lbs.
B. Feb. 15, 1895, Brooklyn, N. Y. D. July 6, 1965, New York, N. Y.

Year	Team	Lg	W	L	PCT	ERA	G	GS	CG	IP	H	BB	SO	ShO	Relief Pitching W	Relief Pitching L	Relief Pitching SV	Batting AB	Batting H	Batting HR	BA	PO	A	E	DP	TC/G	FA
1917	CIN	N	3	7	.300	4.40	24	7	3	88	90	35	33	0	0	3	2	26	2	0	.077	2	27	0	1	1.2	1.000
1918			9	5	.643	2.85	21	18	13	142.1	130	48	26	4	0	0	0	50	6	0	.120	2	29	3	1	1.6	.912
1919			10	9	.526	2.26	32	18	12	183	150	51	61	2	1	1	3	62	6	0	.097	7	64	0	5	2.2	1.000
1920			17	16	.515	3.23	42	33	18	292.2	268	92	73	1	2	1	1	96	19	0	.198	10	80	3	2	2.2	.968
1921	PHI	N	10	19	.345	4.24	34	30	21	246	258	88	88	0	1	1	1	83	12	0	.145	6	76	3	4	2.5	.965
1922			12	18	.400	4.58	40	33	17	249.1	292	**103**	116	0	2	1	1	88	13	1	.148	6	75	3	4	2.1	.964
1923			18	16	.529	3.76	39	36	23	313.1	336	**115**	112	0	1	2	0	113	12	1	.106	11	83	2	2	2.5	.979
1924			10	12	.455	3.97	32	31	16	215.1	236	**108**	72	1	0	0	0	74	17	0	.230	10	61	3	4	2.3	.959
1925			14	16	.467	4.37	38	37	21	270	**325**	**119**	93	1	0	0	0	101	11	2	.109	11	71	4	3	2.3	.953
1926	NY	N	11	10	.524	4.57	39	23	5	183.1	207	74	76	0	2	0	2	56	8	0	.143	5	37	2	3	1.1	.955
1927	STL	N	0	4	.000	6.55	13	3	1	33	39	17	13	0	0	2	0	8	3	0	.375	2	12	2	1	1.2	.875
1928	PHI	N	4	17	.190	6.40	35	25	4	173	214	103	72	0	0	0	1	60	11	0	.183	6	44	0	0	1.4	1.000
12 yrs.			118	149	.442	4.06	389	294	154	2389.1	2545	953	835	9	9	11	11	817	120	4	.147	78	659	25	30	2.0	.967
WORLD SERIES																											
1919	CIN	N	1	1	.500	0.64	2	1	1	14	7	6	4	1	0	1	0	5	0	0	.000	1	3	0	0	2.0	1.000

Allen Ripley

RIPLEY, ALLEN STEVENS BR TR 6′ 3″ 190 lbs.
Son of Walt Ripley.
B. Oct. 18, 1952, Norwood, Mass.

Year	Team	Lg	W	L	PCT	ERA	G	GS	CG	IP	H	BB	SO	ShO	Relief Pitching W	Relief Pitching L	Relief Pitching SV	Batting AB	Batting H	Batting HR	BA	PO	A	E	DP	TC/G	FA
1978	BOS	A	2	5	.286	5.55	15	11	1	73	92	22	26	0	1	0	0	0	0	0	—	3	8	0	0	0.7	1.000
1979			3	1	.750	5.12	16	3	0	65	77	25	34	0	2	0	1	0	0	0	—	2	5	1	0	0.5	.875
1980	SF	N	9	10	.474	4.14	23	20	2	113	119	36	65	0	1	1	0	40	6	0	.150	9	19	2	0	1.3	.933
1981			4	4	.500	4.05	19	14	1	91	103	27	47	0	0	0	0	30	4	0	.133	6	18	1	1	1.3	.960
1982	CHI	N	5	7	.417	4.26	28	19	0	122.2	130	38	57	0	0	1	0	38	5	0	.132	12	22	3	0	1.3	.919
5 yrs.			23	27	.460	4.51	101	67	4	464.2	521	148	229	0	4	2	1	108	15	0	.139	32	72	7	1	1.1	.937

Walt Ripley

RIPLEY, WALTER FRANKLIN BR TR 6′ 168 lbs.
Father of Allen Ripley.
B. Nov. 26, 1916, Worcester, Mass. D. Oct. 7, 1990, Attleboro, Mass.

Year	Team	Lg	W	L	PCT	ERA	G	GS	CG	IP	H	BB	SO	ShO	Relief Pitching W	Relief Pitching L	Relief Pitching SV	Batting AB	Batting H	Batting HR	BA	PO	A	E	DP	TC/G	FA
1935	BOS	A	0	0	—	9.00	2	0	0	4	7	3	0	0	0	0	0	0	0	0	—	0	0	0	0	0.0	.000

Ray Rippelmeyer

RIPPELMEYER, RAYMOND ROY BR TR 6′ 3″ 200 lbs.
B. July 9, 1933, Valmeyer, Ill.

Year	Team	Lg	W	L	PCT	ERA	G	GS	CG	IP	H	BB	SO	ShO	Relief Pitching W	Relief Pitching L	Relief Pitching SV	Batting AB	Batting H	Batting HR	BA	PO	A	E	DP	TC/G	FA
1962	WAS	A	1	2	.333	5.49	18	1	0	39.1	47	17	17	0	1	1	0	6	3	1	.500	3	15	1	1	1.1	.947

Charlie Ripple

RIPPLE, CHARLES DAWSON BL TL 6′ 2″ 210 lbs.
B. Dec. 1, 1921, Bolton, N. C. D. May 6, 1979, Wilmington, N. C.

Year	Team	Lg	W	L	PCT	ERA	G	GS	CG	IP	H	BB	SO	ShO	Relief Pitching W	Relief Pitching L	Relief Pitching SV	Batting AB	Batting H	Batting HR	BA	PO	A	E	DP	TC/G	FA
1944	PHI	N	0	0	—	15.43	1	1	0	2.1	6	4	2	0	0	0	0	1	1	0	1.000	0	0	0	0	0.0	.000
1945			0	1	.000	7.04	4	0	0	7.2	7	10	5	0	0	1	0	1	0	0	.000	0	1	0	0	0.3	1.000
1946			1	0	1.000	10.80	6	0	0	3.1	5	6	3	0	1	0	0	0	0	0	—	0	0	0	0	0.0	.000
3 yrs.			1	1	.500	9.45	11	1	0	13.1	18	20	10	0	1	1	0	2	1	0	.500	0	1	0	0	0.1	1.000

Bill Risley

RISLEY, WILLIAM CHARLES BR TR 6′ 2″ 215 lbs.
B. May 29, 1967, Chicago, Ill.

Year	Team	Lg	W	L	PCT	ERA	G	GS	CG	IP	H	BB	SO	ShO	Relief Pitching W	Relief Pitching L	Relief Pitching SV	Batting AB	Batting H	Batting HR	BA	PO	A	E	DP	TC/G	FA
1992	MON	N	1	0	1.000	1.80	1	1	0	5	4	1	2	0	0	0	0	2	0	0	.000	0	1	0	0	1.0	1.000
1993			0	0	—	6.00	2	0	0	3	2	2	2	0	0	0	0	0	0	0	—	1	0	0	0	0.5	1.000
1994	SEA	A	9	6	.600	3.44	37	0	0	52.1	31	19	61	0	**9**	**6**	0	0	0	0	—	5	2	1	1	0.2	.875
1995			2	1	.667	3.13	45	0	0	60.1	55	18	65	0	2	1	1	0	0	0	—	2	3	0	0	0.1	1.000
4 yrs.			12	7	.632	3.28	85	1	0	120.2	92	40	130	0	11	7	1	2	0	0	.000	8	6	1	1	0.2	.933
DIVISIONAL PLAYOFF SERIES																											
1995	SEA	A	0	0	—	6.00	4	0	0	3	2	0	1	0	0	0	1	0	0	0	—	0	0	0	0	0.0	.000
LEAGUE CHAMPIONSHIP SERIES																											
1995	SEA	A	0	0	—	0.00	3	0	0	2.2	2	1	2	0	0	0	0	0	0	0	—	0	0	0	1	0.0	.000

Jay Ritchie

RITCHIE, JAY SEAY BR TR 6′ 4″ 175 lbs.
B. Nov. 20, 1936, Salisbury, N. C.

Year	Team	Lg	W	L	PCT	ERA	G	GS	CG	IP	H	BB	SO	ShO	Relief Pitching W	Relief Pitching L	Relief Pitching SV	Batting AB	Batting H	Batting HR	BA	PO	A	E	DP	TC/G	FA
1964	BOS	A	1	1	.500	2.74	21	0	0	46	43	14	35	0	1	1	0	9	1	0	.111	1	7	0	0	0.4	1.000
1965			1	2	.333	3.17	44	0	0	71	83	26	55	0	1	2	2	5	1	0	.200	4	12	2	1	0.4	.889
1966	ATL	N	0	1	.000	4.08	22	0	0	35.1	32	12	33	0	0	1	4	4	2	0	.500	2	6	0	0	0.4	1.000
1967			4	6	.400	3.17	52	0	0	82.1	75	29	57	0	4	6	2	10	3	0	.300	8	16	2	1	0.5	.923
1968	CIN	N	2	3	.400	4.61	28	2	0	56.2	68	13	32	0	2	1	0	7	0	0	.000	0	7	0	0	0.3	1.000
5 yrs.			8	13	.381	3.49	167	2	0	291.1	301	94	212	0	8	11	8	35	7	0	.200	15	48	4	2	0.4	.940

Wally Ritchie

RITCHIE, WALLACE REID BL TL 6′ 2″ 180 lbs.
B. July 12, 1965, Glendale, Calif.

Year	Team	Lg	W	L	PCT	ERA	G	GS	CG	IP	H	BB	SO	ShO	Relief Pitching W	Relief Pitching L	Relief Pitching SV	Batting AB	Batting H	Batting HR	BA	PO	A	E	DP	TC/G	FA
1987	PHI	N	3	2	.600	3.75	49	0	0	62.1	60	29	45	0	3	2	3	4	1	0	.250	1	9	0	0	0.2	1.000
1988			0	0	—	3.12	19	0	0	26	19	17	8	0	0	0	0	0	0	0	—	0	4	0	0	0.2	1.000
1991			1	2	.333	2.50	39	0	0	50.1	44	17	26	0	1	2	0	3	0	0	.000	1	8	0	0	0.2	1.000
1992			2	1	.667	3.00	40	0	0	39	44	17	19	0	2	1	1	1	0	0	.000	1	5	0	0	0.2	1.000
4 yrs.			6	5	.545	3.14	147	0	0	177.2	167	80	98	0	6	5	4	8	1	0	.125	3	26	0	0	0.2	1.000

Hank Ritter

RITTER, WILLIAM HERBERT BR TR 6′ 180 lbs.
B. Oct. 12, 1893, McCoysville, Pa. D. Sept. 3, 1964, Akron, Ohio.

Year	Team	W	L	PCT	ERA	G	GS	CG	IP	H	BB	SO	ShO	Relief Pitching W	Relief Pitching L	Relief Pitching SV	Batting AB	Batting H	Batting HR	BA	PO	A	E	DP	TC/G	FA
1912	PHI N	0	0	—	4.50	3	0	0	6	5	5	1	0	0	0	0	1	0	0	.000	0	0	0	0	0.0	.000
1914	NY N	1	0	1.000	1.13	1	0	0	8	4	4	4	0	1	0	0	3	0	0	.000	0	1	0	0	1.0	1.000
1915		2	1	.667	4.63	22	2	0	58.1	66	15	35	0	1	0	1	16	2	0	.125	2	13	2	0	0.8	.882
1916		1	0	1.000	0.00	3	0	0	5	3	0	3	0	1	0	0	0	0	0	—	0	2	0	0	0.7	1.000
4 yrs.		4	1	.800	3.96	29	2	0	77.1	78	24	43	0	3	0	1	20	2	0	.100	2	16	2	0	0.7	.900

Reggie Ritter

RITTER, REGGIE BLAKE BL TR 6′ 2″ 195 lbs.
B. Jan. 23, 1960, Malvern, Ark.

Year	Team	W	L	PCT	ERA	G	GS	CG	IP	H	BB	SO	ShO	Relief Pitching W	Relief Pitching L	Relief Pitching SV	Batting AB	Batting H	Batting HR	BA	PO	A	E	DP	TC/G	FA
1986	CLE A	0	0	—	6.30	5	0	0	10	14	4	6	0	0	0	0	0	0	0	—	3	2	0	0	1.0	1.000
1987		1	1	.500	6.08	14	0	0	26.2	33	16	11	0	1	1	0	0	0	0	—	4	5	1	0	0.7	.900
2 yrs.		1	1	.500	6.14	19	0	0	36.2	47	20	17	0	1	1	0	0	0	0		7	7	1	0	0.8	.933

Jim Rittwage

RITTWAGE, JAMES MICHAEL BR TR 6′ 3″ 190 lbs.
B. Oct. 23, 1944, Cleveland, Ohio.

Year	Team	W	L	PCT	ERA	G	GS	CG	IP	H	BB	SO	ShO	Relief Pitching W	Relief Pitching L	Relief Pitching SV	Batting AB	Batting H	Batting HR	BA	PO	A	E	DP	TC/G	FA
1970	CLE A	1	1	.500	4.15	8	3	1	26	18	21	16	0	0	0	0	8	3	0	.375	2	4	0	1	0.8	1.000

Kevin Ritz

RITZ, KEVIN D. BR TR 6′ 4″ 195 lbs.
B. June 8, 1965, Eatontown, N. J.

Year	Team	W	L	PCT	ERA	G	GS	CG	IP	H	BB	SO	ShO	Relief Pitching W	Relief Pitching L	Relief Pitching SV	Batting AB	Batting H	Batting HR	BA	PO	A	E	DP	TC/G	FA
1989	DET A	4	6	.400	4.38	12	12	1	74	75	44	56	0	0	0	0	0	0	0	—	4	10	0	0	1.2	1.000
1990		0	4	.000	11.05	4	4	0	7.1	14	14	3	0	0	0	0	0	0	0	—	2	4	1	0	1.8	.857
1991		0	3	.000	11.74	11	5	0	15.1	17	22	9	0	0	0	0	0	0	0	—	1	4	1	0	0.5	.833
1992		2	5	.286	5.60	23	11	0	80.1	88	44	57	0	0	0	0	0	0	0	—	4	10	0	1	0.6	1.000
1994	CLR N	5	6	.455	5.62	15	15	0	73.2	88	35	53	0	0	0	0	20	0	0	.000	6	13	0	3	1.3	1.000
1995		11	11	.500	4.21	31	28	0	173.1	171	65	120	0	0	0	2	48	9	0	.188	10	39	0	1	1.6	1.000
6 yrs.		22	35	.386	5.14	96	75	1	424	453	224	298	0	0	0	2	68	9	0	.132	27	80	2	5	1.1	.982
DIVISIONAL PLAYOFF SERIES																										
1995	CLR N	0	0	—	7.71	2	1	0	7	12	3	5	0	0	0	0	2	0	0	.000	0	1	1	0	1.0	.500

Ben Rivera

RIVERA, BIENVENIDO BR TR 6′ 6″ 210 lbs.
Born Bienvenido Rivera (Santana).
B. Jan. 11, 1968, San Pedro de Macoris, Dominican Republic.

Year	Team	W	L	PCT	ERA	G	GS	CG	IP	H	BB	SO	ShO	Relief Pitching W	Relief Pitching L	Relief Pitching SV	Batting AB	Batting H	Batting HR	BA	PO	A	E	DP	TC/G	FA
1992	**2 teams** ATL N (8G 0–1) PHI N (20G 7–3)																									
″	**total**	7	4	.636	3.07	28	14	4	117.1	99	45	77	1	0	1	0	33	3	0	.091	3	19	0	0	0.8	1.000
1993	PHI N	13	9	.591	5.02	30	28	1	163	175	85	123	1	0	0	0	51	5	0	.098	8	14	1	1	0.8	.957
1994		3	4	.429	6.87	9	7	0	38	40	22	19	0	1	1	0	9	0	0	.000	1	6	0	1	0.8	1.000
3 yrs.		23	17	.575	4.52	67	49	5	318.1	314	152	219	2	1	2	0	93	8	0	.086	12	39	1	2	0.8	.981
LEAGUE CHAMPIONSHIP SERIES																										
1993	PHI N	0	0	—	4.50	1	0	0	2	1	1	2	0	0	0	0	0	0	0	—	0	0	0	0	0.0	.000
WORLD SERIES																										
1993	PHI N	0	0	—	27.00	1	0	0	1.1	4	2	3	0	0	0	0	0	0	0	—	0	0	0	0	0.0	.000

Mariano Rivera

RIVERA, MARIANO BR TR 6′ 4″ 168 lbs.
B. Nov. 29, 1969, Panama City, Panama.

Year	Team	W	L	PCT	ERA	G	GS	CG	IP	H	BB	SO	ShO	Relief Pitching W	Relief Pitching L	Relief Pitching SV	Batting AB	Batting H	Batting HR	BA	PO	A	E	DP	TC/G	FA
1995	NY A	5	3	.625	5.51	19	10	0	67	71	30	51	0	2	0	0	0	0	0	—	2	14	0	1	0.8	1.000
DIVISIONAL PLAYOFF SERIES																										
1995	NY A	1	0	1.000	0.00	3	0	0	5.1	3	1	8	0	1	0	0	0	0	0	—	0	0	0	0	0.0	.000

Roberto Rivera

RIVERA, ROBERTO BL TL 6′ 175 lbs.
Born Roberto Rivera (Diaz).
B. Jan. 1, 1969, Bayamon, Puerto Rico.

Year	Team	W	L	PCT	ERA	G	GS	CG	IP	H	BB	SO	ShO	Relief Pitching W	Relief Pitching L	Relief Pitching SV	Batting AB	Batting H	Batting HR	BA	PO	A	E	DP	TC/G	FA
1995	CHI N	0	0	—	5.40	7	0	0	5	8	2	2	0	0	0	0	0	0	0	—	0	1	0	0	0.1	1.000

Tink Riviere

RIVIERE, ARTHUR BERNARD BR TR 5′10″ 167 lbs.
B. Aug. 2, 1899, Liberty, Tex. D. Sept. 27, 1965, Liberty, Tex.

Year	Team	W	L	PCT	ERA	G	GS	CG	IP	H	BB	SO	ShO	Relief Pitching W	Relief Pitching L	Relief Pitching SV	Batting AB	Batting H	Batting HR	BA	PO	A	E	DP	TC/G	FA
1921	STL N	1	0	1.000	6.10	18	2	0	38.1	45	20	15	0	1	0	0	8	3	0	.375	1	1	2	0	0.2	.500
1925	CHI A	0	0	—	13.50	3	0	0	4.2	6	7	1	0	0	0	0	1	0	0	.000	1	4	0	0	1.7	1.000
2 yrs.		1	0	1.000	6.91	21	2	0	43	51	27	16	0	1	0	0	9	3	0	.333	2	5	2	0	0.4	.778

Eppa Rixey

RIXEY, EPPA (Eppa Jephtha) BR TL 6′ 5″ 210 lbs.
B. May 3, 1891, Culpeper, Va. D. Feb. 28, 1963, Terrace Park, Ohio.
Hall of Fame 1963.

Year	Team	W	L	PCT	ERA	G	GS	CG	IP	H	BB	SO	ShO	Relief Pitching W	Relief Pitching L	Relief Pitching SV	Batting AB	Batting H	Batting HR	BA	PO	A	E	DP	TC/G	FA
1912	PHI N	10	10	.500	2.50	23	20	10	162	147	54	59	3	1	0	0	53	9	0	.170	4	35	0	2	1.7	1.000
1913		9	5	.643	3.12	35	19	9	155.2	148	56	75	2	0	0	2	47	9	0	.191	1	39	0	1	1.1	1.000
1914		2	11	.154	4.37	24	15	2	103	124	45	41	0	0	2	0	26	1	0	.038	5	29	6	4	1.7	.850
1915		11	12	.478	2.39	29	22	10	176.2	163	64	88	2	1	2	1	55	9	0	.164	7	47	4	3	2.0	.931
1916		22	10	.688	1.85	38	33	20	287	239	74	134	3	2	0	0	97	15	0	.155	5	90	1	4	2.5	.990
1917		16	**21**	.432	2.27	39	36	23	281.1	249	67	121	4	1	0	1	94	18	0	.191	15	93	0	3	2.8	1.000
1919		6	12	.333	3.97	23	18	11	154	160	50	63	1	0	1	0	47	7	0	.149	5	51	1	3	2.5	.982
1920		11	**22**	.333	3.48	41	34	25	284.1	288	69	109	1	0	2	2	101	25	1	.248	13	90	4	4	2.6	.963
1921	CIN N	19	18	.514	2.78	40	36	21	301	324	66	76	2	1	1	1	101	13	0	.129	4	97	2	4	2.6	.981
1922		**25**	13	.658	3.53	40	**38**	26	**313.1**	**337**	45	80	2	1	0	0	109	21	0	.193	10	72	2	3	2.1	.976
1923		20	15	.571	2.80	42	37	23	309	334	65	97	3	2	0	1	107	17	0	.159	12	78	1	4	2.2	.989
1924		15	14	.517	2.76	35	29	15	238.1	219	47	57	**4**	2	1	1	84	18	1	.214	7	58	3	4	1.9	.956
1925		21	11	.656	2.88	39	36	22	287.1	302	47	69	2	1	1	1	103	22	0	.214	4	64	1	3	1.8	.986
1926		14	8	.636	3.40	37	29	14	233	231	58	61	3	0	1	0	84	19	0	.226	3	52	1	3	1.5	.982
1927		12	10	.545	3.48	34	29	11	219.2	240	43	42	1	0	0	1	81	20	0	.247	4	50	1	1	1.6	.982
1928		19	18	.514	3.43	43	**37**	17	291.1	**317**	67	58	3	4	0	2	104	18	1	.173	10	69	1	3	1.9	.988
1929		10	13	.435	4.16	35	24	11	201	235	60	37	0	2	1	1	65	15	0	.231	6	43	0	1	1.4	1.000
1930		9	13	.409	5.10	32	21	5	164	207	47	37	0	1	2	0	55	11	0	.200	7	34	0	1	1.3	1.000

Eppa Rixey *continued*

Year	Team	W	L	PCT	ERA	G	GS	CG	IP	H	BB	SO	ShO	Relief Pitching W	L	SV	Batting AB	H	HR	BA	PO	A	E	DP	TC/G	FA
1931		4	7	.364	3.91	22	17	4	126.2	143	30	22	0	0	0	0	40	6	0	.150	4	45	0	2	2.2	1.000
1932		5	5	.500	2.66	25	11	6	111.2	108	16	14	2	1	3	0	34	9	0	.265	4	29	1	0	1.4	.971
1933		6	3	.667	3.15	16	12	5	94.1	118	12	10	1	0	0	0	35	9	0	.257	1	30	1	2	2.0	.969
21 yrs.		266	251 9th	.515	3.15	692	553	290	4494.2	4633	1082	1350	39	20	17	14	1522	291	3	.191	131	1195	30	55	2.0	.978
WORLD SERIES																										
1915	PHI N	0	1	.000	4.05	1	0	0	6.2	4	2	2	0	0	1	0	2	1	0	.500	0	1	0	0	1.0	1.000

Joe Roa

ROA, JOSEPH RODGER
B. Oct. 11, 1971, Southfield, Mich.
BR TR 6′ 1″ 195 lbs.

Year	Team	W	L	PCT	ERA	G	GS	CG	IP	H	BB	SO	ShO	Relief Pitching W	L	SV	Batting AB	H	HR	BA	PO	A	E	DP	TC/G	FA
1995	CLE A	0	1	.000	6.00	1	1	0	6	9	2	0	0	0	0	0	0	0	0	—	2	2	0	0	4.0	1.000

John Roach

ROACH, JOHN F.
B. Farrensville, Pa. Deceased.
TL 5′ 9″ 175 lbs.

Year	Team	W	L	PCT	ERA	G	GS	CG	IP	H	BB	SO	ShO	Relief Pitching W	L	SV	Batting AB	H	HR	BA	PO	A	E	DP	TC/G	FA
1887	NY N	0	1	.000	11.25	1	1	1	8	18	4	3	0	0	0	0	4	1	0	.250	2	0	0	0	2.0	1.000

Skel Roach

ROACH, RUDOLPH CHARLES
Born Rudolph Charles Weichbrodt.
B. Oct. 20, 1871, Danzig, Germany D. Mar. 9, 1958, Oak Park, Ill.
BR TR 6′ 2″

Year	Team	W	L	PCT	ERA	G	GS	CG	IP	H	BB	SO	ShO	Relief Pitching W	L	SV	Batting AB	H	HR	BA	PO	A	E	DP	TC/G	FA
1899	CHI N	1	0	1.000	3.00	1	1	1	9	13	1	0	0	0	0	0	4	0	0	.000	0	1	0	0	1.0	1.000

Bruce Robbins

ROBBINS, BRUCE DUANE
B. Sept. 10, 1959, Portland, Ind.
BL TL 6′ 1″ 190 lbs.

Year	Team	W	L	PCT	ERA	G	GS	CG	IP	H	BB	SO	ShO	Relief Pitching W	L	SV	Batting AB	H	HR	BA	PO	A	E	DP	TC/G	FA
1979	DET A	3	3	.500	3.91	10	8	0	46	45	21	22	0	0	0	0	0	0	0	—	1	5	0	1	0.6	1.000
1980		4	2	.667	6.58	15	6	0	52	60	28	23	0	2	0	0	0	0	0	—	2	9	0	0	0.7	1.000
2 yrs.		7	5	.583	5.33	25	14	0	98	105	49	45	0	2	0	0	0	0	0		3	14	0	1	0.7	1.000

Bert Roberge

ROBERGE, BERTRAND ROLAND
B. Oct. 3, 1954, Lewiston, Me.
BR TR 6′ 4″ 190 lbs.

Year	Team	W	L	PCT	ERA	G	GS	CG	IP	H	BB	SO	ShO	Relief Pitching W	L	SV	Batting AB	H	HR	BA	PO	A	E	DP	TC/G	FA
1979	HOU N	3	0	1.000	1.69	26	0	0	32	20	17	13	0	3	0	4	2	0	0	.000	3	3	0	0	0.2	1.000
1980		2	0	1.000	6.00	14	0	0	24	24	10	9	0	2	0	0	3	0	0	.000	2	5	0	0	0.5	1.000
1982		1	2	.333	4.21	22	0	0	25.2	29	6	18	0	1	2	3	1	0	0	.000	2	4	0	0	0.3	1.000
1984	CHI A	3	3	.500	3.76	21	0	0	40.2	36	15	25	0	3	3	0	0	0	0	—	5	9	0	1	0.7	1.000
1985	MON N	3	3	.500	3.44	42	0	0	68	58	22	34	0	3	3	2	1	0	0	.000	5	12	0	0	0.4	1.000
1986		0	4	.000	6.28	21	0	0	28.2	33	10	20	0	0	4	1	2	0	0	.000	3	3	0	0	0.3	1.000
6 yrs.		12	12	.500	3.99	146	0	0	219	200	80	119	0	12	12	10	9	0	0	.000	20	36	0	1	0.4	1.000

Sid Roberson

ROBERSON, SIDNEY DEAN
B. Sept. 9, 1971, Jacksonville, Fla.
BL TL 5′ 9″ 170 lbs.

Year	Team	W	L	PCT	ERA	G	GS	CG	IP	H	BB	SO	ShO	Relief Pitching W	L	SV	Batting AB	H	HR	BA	PO	A	E	DP	TC/G	FA
1995	MIL A	6	4	.600	5.76	26	13	0	84.1	102	37	40	0	0	0	0	0	0	0	—	2	5	3	0	0.4	.700

Dale Roberts

ROBERTS, DALE (Mountain Man)
B. Apr. 12, 1942, Owenton, Ky.
BR TL 6′ 4″ 180 lbs.

Year	Team	W	L	PCT	ERA	G	GS	CG	IP	H	BB	SO	ShO	Relief Pitching W	L	SV	Batting AB	H	HR	BA	PO	A	E	DP	TC/G	FA
1967	NY A	0	0	—	9.00	2	0	0	2	3	2	0	0	0	0	0	0	0	0	—	0	1	0	0	0.5	1.000

Dave Roberts

ROBERTS, DAVID ARTHUR
B. Sept. 11, 1944, Gallipolis, Ohio.
BL TL 6′ 3″ 195 lbs.

Year	Team	W	L	PCT	ERA	G	GS	CG	IP	H	BB	SO	ShO	Relief Pitching W	L	SV	Batting AB	H	HR	BA	PO	A	E	DP	TC/G	FA
1969	SD N	0	3	.000	4.78	22	5	0	49	65	19	19	0	0	0	1	15	4	0	.267	5	9	0	1	0.6	1.000
1970		8	14	.364	3.81	43	21	3	182	182	43	102	2	4	0	1	59	9	2	.153	5	29	1	3	0.8	.971
1971		14	17	.452	2.10	37	34	14	270	238	61	135	2	0	1	0	86	19	0	.221	10	47	1	2	1.6	.983
1972	HOU N	12	7	.632	4.50	35	28	7	192	227	57	111	3	1	0	2	67	16	2	.239	0	31	1	0	0.9	.969
1973		17	11	.607	2.85	39	36	12	249.1	264	62	119	6	0	0	0	85	11	0	.129	9	39	1	1	1.3	.980
1974		10	12	.455	3.40	34	30	8	204	216	65	72	2	1	0	1	73	16	1	.219	15	43	3	5	1.7	.951
1975		8	14	.364	4.27	32	27	7	198	182	73	101	0	2	0	1	63	9	0	.143	13	36	0	0	1.5	1.000
1976	DET A	16	17	.485	4.00	36	36	18	252	254	63	79	4	0	0	0	0	0	0	—	6	53	4	6	1.8	.937
1977	2 teams DET A (22G 4–10) CHI N (17G 1–1)																									
"	total	5	11	.313	4.60	39	28	6	182	198	53	69	0	0	0	1	17	1	0	.059	7	39	1	1	1.2	.979
1978	CHI N	6	8	.429	5.26	35	20	2	142	159	56	54	1	1	0	1	52	17	2	.327	8	29	0	2	1.1	1.000
1979	2 teams SF N (26G 0–2) PIT N (21G 5–2)																									
"	total	5	4	.556	2.90	47	4	0	80.2	89	30	38	0	5	2	4	10	0	0	.000	2	18	2	2	0.5	.909
1980	2 teams PIT N (2G 0–1) SEA A (37G 2–3)																									
"	total	2	4	.333	4.39	39	4	0	82	88	28	48	0	0	2	3	0	0	0		3	6	1	0	0.3	.900
1981	NY N	0	3	.000	9.60	7	4	0	15	26	5	10	0	0	0	0	4	1	0	.250	0	4	1	0	0.7	.800
13 yrs.		103	125	.452	3.78	445	277	77	2098	2188	615	957	20	14	5	15	531	103	7	.194	83	383	16	23	1.1	.967
LEAGUE CHAMPIONSHIP SERIES																										
1979	PIT N	0	0	—	0.00	1	0	0		0	1	0	0	0	0	0	0	0	0	—	0	0	0	0	0.0	.000

Jim Roberts

ROBERTS, JAMES NEWSON (Big Jim)
B. Oct. 13, 1895, Artesia, Miss. D. June 24, 1984, Columbus, Miss.
BR TR 6′ 3″ 205 lbs.

Year	Team	W	L	PCT	ERA	G	GS	CG	IP	H	BB	SO	ShO	Relief Pitching W	L	SV	Batting AB	H	HR	BA	PO	A	E	DP	TC/G	FA
1924	BKN N	0	3	.000	7.46	11	5	0	25.1	41	8	10	0	0	0	0	7	1	0	.143	0	6	0	0	0.5	1.000
1925		0	0	—	0.00	1	0	0	1	1	0	0	0	0	0	0	0	0	0	—	0	1	1	0	2.0	.500
2 yrs.		0	3	.000	7.18	12	5	0	26.1	42	8	10	0	0	0	0	7	1	0	.143	0	7	1	0	0.7	.875

Leon Roberts

ROBERTS, LEON KAUFFMAN
B. Jan. 22, 1951, Vicksburg, Mich.
BR TR 6′ 3″ 200 lbs.

Year	Team	W	L	PCT	ERA	G	GS	CG	IP	H	BB	SO	ShO	Relief Pitching W	L	SV	Batting AB	H	HR	BA	PO	A	E	DP	TC/G	FA
1984	KC A	0	0	—	27.00	1	0	0	1	4	1	1	0	0	0	0	*				25	0	2	0	1.6	.926

Ray Roberts

ROBERTS, RAYMOND
B. Aug. 24, 1895, Cruger, Miss. D. Jan. 30, 1962, Cruger, Miss.
BL TR 5′11″ 180 lbs.

Year	Team	W	L	PCT	ERA	G	GS	CG	IP	H	BB	SO	ShO	Relief Pitching W	L	SV	Batting AB	H	HR	BA	PO	A	E	DP	TC/G	FA
1919	PHI A	0	2	.000	7.71	3	2	0	14	21	3	2	0	0	0	0	4	1	0	.250	1	2	0	0	1.0	1.000

Robin Roberts

ROBERTS, ROBIN EVAN BB TR 6′ 190 lbs.
B. Sept. 30, 1926, Springfield, Ill. BL 1948–1952
Hall of Fame 1976.

Year	Team		W	L	PCT	ERA	G	GS	CG	IP	H	BB	SO	ShO	Relief W	Relief L	Relief SV	AB	H	HR	BA	PO	A	E	DP	TC/G	FA
1948	PHI	N	7	9	.438	3.19	20	20	9	146.2	148	61	84	0	0	0	0	44	11	1	.250	2	17	2	1	1.0	.905
1949			15	15	.500	3.69	43	31	11	226.2	229	75	95	3	3	2	4	67	5	0	.075	10	23	1	4	0.8	.971
1950			20	11	.645	3.02	40	**39**	21	304.1	282	77	146	**5**	0	0	1	102	12	0	.118	22	50	2	6	1.9	.973
1951			21	15	.583	3.03	44	**39**	22	**315**	284	64	127	6	0	1	2	87	15	0	.172	24	37	2	3	1.4	.968
1952			**28**	7	.800	2.59	39	**37**	**30**	**330**	**292**	45	148	3	0	0	2	112	14	0	.125	26	44	1	1	1.8	.986
1953			**23**	16	.590	2.75	44	**41**	**33**	**346.2**	**324**	61	**198**	5	0	0	2	123	22	1	.179	16	51	3	7	1.6	.957
1954			**23**	15	.605	2.97	45	**38**	**29**	**336.2**	**289**	56	**185**	4	3	0	4	122	15	0	.123	15	38	1	3	1.2	.981
1955			**23**	14	.622	3.28	41	**38**	**26**	**305**	**292**	53	160	1	0	0	3	107	27	2	.252	19	26	2	1	1.1	.957
1956			19	**18**	.514	4.45	43	37	**22**	297.1	**328**	40	157	1	2	0	3	100	20	1	.200	12	50	2	4	1.5	.969
1957			10	**22**	.313	4.07	39	32	14	249.2	246	43	128	2	1	2	2	80	13	0	.163	26	38	0	1	1.6	1.000
1958			17	14	.548	3.24	35	34	21	269.2	270	51	130	1	0	0	2	99	20	0	.202	17	34	0	0	1.5	1.000
1959			15	17	.469	4.27	35	35	19	257.1	267	35	137	2	0	0	0	89	17	0	.191	22	38	1	2	1.7	.984
1960			12	16	.429	4.02	35	33	13	237.1	256	34	122	2	0	0	1	79	12	0	.152	21	24	2	2	1.3	.957
1961			1	10	.091	5.85	26	18	2	117	154	23	54	0	0	0	0	33	3	0	.091	6	15	0	1	0.8	1.000
1962	BAL	A	10	9	.526	2.78	27	25	6	191.1	176	41	102	0	0	0	0	52	10	0	.192	24	21	2	4	1.7	.957
1963			14	13	.519	3.33	35	35	9	251.1	230	40	124	2	0	0	0	79	16	0	.203	24	31	3	1	1.7	.948
1964			13	7	.650	2.91	31	31	8	204	203	52	109	4	0	0	0	68	9	0	.132	9	26	1	2	1.2	.972
1965	2 teams	BAL A	(20G 5–7)		HOU N	(10G 5–2)																					
″	total		10	9	.526	2.78	30	25	8	190.2	171	30	97	3	1	0	0	56	11	0	.196	14	21	4	1	1.3	.897
1966	2 teams	HOU N	(13G 3–5)		CHI N	(11G 2–3)																					
″	total		5	8	.385	4.82	24	21	2	112	141	21	54	1	1	0	1	26	3	0	.115	7	17	2	1	1.1	.923
19 yrs.			286	245	.539	3.41	676	609	305	4688.2	4582	902	2357	45	11	5	25	1525	255	5	.167	316	601	31	45	1.4	.967
WORLD SERIES																											
1950	PHI	N	0	1	.000	1.64	2	1	1	11	11	3	5	0	0	0	0	2	0	0	.000	0	0	0	0	0.0	.000

Charlie Robertson

ROBERTSON, CHARLES CULBERTSON BL TR 6′ 175 lbs.
B. Jan. 31, 1896, Dexter, Tex. D. Aug. 23, 1984, Fort Worth, Tex.

Year	Team		W	L	PCT	ERA	G	GS	CG	IP	H	BB	SO	ShO	Relief W	Relief L	Relief SV	AB	H	HR	BA	PO	A	E	DP	TC/G	FA
1919	CHI	A	0	1	.000	9.00	1	1	0	2	5	0	1	0	0	0	0	0	0	0	—	0	0	0	0	0.0	.000
1922			14	15	.483	3.64	37	34	21	272	294	89	83	3	1	1	0	87	16	0	.184	6	48	1	1	1.5	.982
1923			13	18	.419	3.81	38	34	18	255	262	104	91	1	0	3	0	85	21	0	.247	8	54	0	2	1.6	1.000
1924			4	10	.286	4.99	17	14	5	97.1	108	54	29	0	2	0	0	33	6	0	.182	0	15	2	1	1.0	.882
1925			8	12	.400	5.26	24	23	6	137	181	47	27	2	0	0	0	45	10	0	.222	6	28	1	0	1.5	.971
1926	STL	A	1	2	.333	8.36	8	7	1	28	38	21	13	0	0	0	0	10	3	0	.300	6	2	0	0	1.0	1.000
1927	BOS	N	7	17	.292	4.72	28	22	6	154.1	188	46	49	0	1	1	0	50	12	0	.240	3	28	1	1	1.1	.969
1928			2	5	.286	5.31	13	7	3	59.1	73	16	17	0	0	1	1	17	0	0	.000	1	11	0	0	0.9	1.000
8 yrs.			49	80	.380	4.44	166	142	60	1005	1149	377	310	6	4	6	1	327	68	0	.208	30	186	5	5	1.3	.977

Dick Robertson

ROBERTSON, PRESTON BR TR 5′ 9″ 160 lbs.
B. 1891, Washington, D. C. D. Oct. 2, 1944, New Orleans, La.

Year	Team		W	L	PCT	ERA	G	GS	CG	IP	H	BB	SO	ShO	Relief W	Relief L	Relief SV	AB	H	HR	BA	PO	A	E	DP	TC/G	FA
1913	CIN	N	0	1	.000	7.20	2	1	1	10	13	9	1	0	0	0	0	3	0	0	.000	0	1	0	0	0.5	1.000
1918	BKN	N	3	6	.333	2.59	13	9	7	87	87	28	18	1	1	0	0	30	9	0	.300	4	24	1	1	2.2	.966
1919	WAS	A	0	1	.000	2.28	7	4	0	27.2	25	9	7	0	0	0	0	7	0	0	.000	3	8	0	0	1.6	1.000
3 yrs.			3	8	.273	2.89	22	14	8	124.2	125	46	26	1	1	0	0	40	9	0	.225	7	33	1	1	1.9	.976

Jerry Robertson

ROBERTSON, JERRY LEE BB TR 6′ 2″ 205 lbs.
B. Oct. 13, 1943, Winchester, Kans.

Year	Team		W	L	PCT	ERA	G	GS	CG	IP	H	BB	SO	ShO	Relief W	Relief L	Relief SV	AB	H	HR	BA	PO	A	E	DP	TC/G	FA
1969	MON	N	5	16	.238	3.96	38	27	3	179.2	186	81	133	0	0	0	1	56	5	0	.089	8	16	1	0	0.7	.960
1970	DET	A	0	0	—	3.60	11	0	0	15	19	5	11	0	0	0	0	0	0	0	—	0	1	1	0	0.2	.500
2 yrs.			5	16	.238	3.93	49	27	3	194.2	205	86	144	0	0	0	1	56	5	0	.089	8	17	2	0	0.6	.926

Rich Robertson

ROBERTSON, RICHARD PAUL BR TR 6′ 2″ 210 lbs.
B. Oct. 14, 1944, Albany, Calif.

Year	Team		W	L	PCT	ERA	G	GS	CG	IP	H	BB	SO	ShO	Relief W	Relief L	Relief SV	AB	H	HR	BA	PO	A	E	DP	TC/G	FA
1966	SF	N	0	0	—	7.71	1	0	0	2.1	3	2	2	0	0	0	0	0	0	0	—	0	0	0	0	0.0	.000
1967			0	0	—	4.50	1	0	0	2	3	0	1	0	0	0	0	0	0	0	—	1	0	0	0	1.0	1.000
1968			2	0	1.000	6.00	3	1	0	9	9	3	8	0	1	0	0	2	1	0	.500	0	3	0	0	1.0	1.000
1969			1	3	.250	5.52	17	7	1	44	53	21	20	1	0	0	0	10	0	0	.000	0	10	1	1	0.6	.909
1970			8	9	.471	4.84	41	26	6	184	199	96	121	0	1	1	1	59	6	2	.102	14	23	2	3	1.0	.949
1971			2	2	.500	4.57	23	6	1	61	66	31	32	0	1	0	1	15	1	0	.067	5	5	2	0	0.5	.833
6 yrs.			13	14	.481	4.94	86	40	8	302.1	333	153	184	1	3	1	2	86	8	2	.093	20	41	5	4	0.8	.924

Rich Robertson

ROBERTSON, RICHARD WAYNE BL TL 6′ 4″ 175 lbs.
B. Sept. 15, 1968, Nacogdoches, Tex.

Year	Team		W	L	PCT	ERA	G	GS	CG	IP	H	BB	SO	ShO	Relief W	Relief L	Relief SV	AB	H	HR	BA	PO	A	E	DP	TC/G	FA
1993	PIT	N	0	1	.000	6.00	9	0	0	9	15	4	5	0	0	1	0	0	0	0	—	0	0	0	0	0.0	.000
1994			0	0	—	6.89	8	0	0	15.2	20	10	8	0	0	0	0	4	1	0	.250	0	2	0	0	0.3	1.000
1995	MIN	A	2	0	1.000	3.83	25	4	1	51.2	48	31	38	0	0	0	0	0	0	0	—	3	4	1	0	0.3	.875
3 yrs.			2	1	.667	4.72	42	4	1	76.1	83	45	51	0	0	1	0	4	1	0	.250	3	6	1	0	0.2	.900

Bill Robinson

ROBINSON, WILLIAM
Born William Anderson.
B. Taylorsville, Ky. Deceased.

Year	Team		W	L	PCT	ERA	G	GS	CG	IP	H	BB	SO	ShO	Relief W	Relief L	Relief SV	AB	H	HR	BA	PO	A	E	DP	TC/G	FA
1889	LOU	AA	0	1	.000	10.13	1	1	1	8	10	6	2	0	0	0	0	3	1	0	.333	0	2	0	0	2.0	1.000

Dewey Robinson

ROBINSON, DEWEY EVERETT BR TR 6′ 180 lbs.
B. Apr. 28, 1955, Evanston, Ill.

Year	Team		W	L	PCT	ERA	G	GS	CG	IP	H	BB	SO	ShO	Relief W	Relief L	Relief SV	AB	H	HR	BA	PO	A	E	DP	TC/G	FA
1979	CHI	A	0	1	.000	6.43	11	0	0	14	11	9	5	0	0	1	0	0	0	0	—	0	1	0	0	0.1	1.000
1980			1	1	.500	3.09	15	0	0	35	26	16	28	0	1	1	0	0	0	0	—	3	4	0	0	0.5	1.000
1981			1	0	1.000	4.50	4	0	0	4	5	3	2	0	1	0	0	0	0	0	—	1	0	0	0	0.3	1.000
3 yrs.			2	2	.500	4.08	30	0	0	53	42	28	35	0	2	2	0	0	0	0		4	5	0	0	0.3	1.000

Don Robinson

ROBINSON, DON ALLEN BR TR 6′ 4″ 225 lbs.
B. June 8, 1957, Ashland, Ky.

Year	Team	Lg	W	L	PCT	ERA	G	GS	CG	IP	H	BB	SO	ShO	Relief Pitching W	Relief Pitching L	Relief Pitching SV	Batting AB	Batting H	Batting HR	BA	PO	A	E	DP	TC/G	FA
1978	PIT	N	14	6	.700	3.47	35	32	9	228	203	57	135	1	0	0	1	85	20	0	.235	10	32	1	1	1.2	.977
1979			8	8	.500	3.86	29	25	4	161	171	52	96	0	0	1	0	49	10	0	.204	7	10	2	1	0.7	.895
1980			7	10	.412	3.99	29	24	3	160	157	45	103	2	0	0	1	57	19	1	.333	13	23	2	2	1.3	.947
1981			0	3	.000	5.92	16	2	0	38	47	23	17	0	0	2	2	12	3	0	.250	7	8	0	1	0.9	1.000
1982			15	13	.536	4.28	38	30	6	227	213	103	165	0	2	0	0	85	24	2	.282	14	25	4	0	1.1	.907
1983			2	2	.500	4.46	9	6	0	36.1	43	21	28	0	1	0	0	13	2	1	.154	1	6	0	1	0.8	1.000
1984			5	6	.455	3.02	51	1	0	122	99	49	110	0	5	5	10	31	9	1	.290	10	18	0	0	0.5	1.000
1985			5	11	.313	3.87	44	6	0	95.1	95	42	65	0	4	7	3	21	5	1	.238	7	11	0	2	0.4	1.000
1986			3	4	.429	3.38	50	0	0	69.1	61	27	53	0	3	4	14	6	4	0	.667	6	9	0	0	0.3	1.000
1987	2 teams	PIT N	(42G 6–6)	SF N	(25G 5–1)																						
″	total		11	7	.611	3.42	67	0	0	108	105	40	79	0	11	7	19	18	4	1	.222	8	12	0	0	0.3	1.000
1988	SF	N	10	5	.667	2.45	51	19	3	176.2	152	49	122	2	2	1	6	52	9	1	.173	12	19	3	1	0.7	.912
1989			12	11	.522	3.43	34	32	5	197	184	37	96	1	0	1	0	81	15	3	.185	6	12	0	1	0.5	1.000
1990			10	7	.588	4.57	26	25	4	157.2	173	41	78	0	0	0	0	63	9	2	.143	4	18	0	0	0.8	1.000
1991			5	9	.357	4.38	34	16	0	121.1	123	50	78	0	0	1	1	40	6	0	.150	7	16	0	0	0.7	1.000
1992	2 teams	CAL A	(3G 1–0)	PHI N	(8G 1–4)																						
″	total		2	4	.333	5.10	11	11	0	60	68	7	26	0	0	0	0	18	7	0	.389	2	3	0	0	0.5	1.000
15 yrs.			109	106	.507	3.79	524	229	34	1957.2	1894	643	1251	6	28	29	57	631	146	13	.231	114	222	12	10	0.7	.966
LEAGUE CHAMPIONSHIP SERIES																											
1979	PIT	N	1	0	1.000	0.00	2	0	0	2	0	1	3	0	1	0	1	0	0	0	—	0	0	0	0	0.0	.000
1987	SF	N	0	1	.000	9.00	3	0	0	3	3	0	3	0	0	1	0	0	0	0	—	0	0	0	0	0.0	.000
1989			1	0	1.000	0.00	1	0	0	1.2	3	0	0	0	1	0	0	0	0	0	—	0	0	0	0	0.0	.000
3 yrs.			2	1	.667	4.05	6	0	0	6.2	6	1	6	0	2	1	1	0	0	0		0	0	0	0	0.0	
WORLD SERIES																											
1979	PIT	N	1	0	1.000	5.40	4	0	0	5	4	6	3	0	1	0	0	0	0	0	—	0	1	0	0	0.3	1.000
1989	SF	N	0	1	.000	21.60	1	1	0	1.2	4	1	0	0	0	0	0	0	0	0	—	0	0	0	0	0.0	.000
2 yrs.			1	1	.500	9.45	5	1	0	6.2	8	7	3	0	1	0	0	0	0	0		0	1	0	0	0.2	1.000

Hank Robinson

ROBINSON, JOHN HENRY (Rube) BR TL 5′11½″ 160 lbs.
Born John Henry Roberson.
B. Aug. 16, 1889, Floyd, Ark. D. July 3, 1965, North Little Rock, Ark.

Year	Team	Lg	W	L	PCT	ERA	G	GS	CG	IP	H	BB	SO	ShO	Relief Pitching W	Relief Pitching L	Relief Pitching SV	Batting AB	Batting H	Batting HR	BA	PO	A	E	DP	TC/G	FA
1911	PIT	N	0	1	.000	2.77	5	0	0	13	13	5	8	0	0	1	0	3	0	0	.000	0	5	0	2	1.0	1.000
1912			12	7	.632	2.26	33	16	11	175	146	30	79	0	3	1	2	59	15	0	.254	5	40	0	1	1.4	1.000
1913			14	9	.609	2.38	43	23	8	196.1	184	41	50	1	4	4	0	61	11	0	.180	5	45	1	2	1.2	.980
1914	STL	N	6	8	.429	3.00	26	16	6	126	128	32	30	1	2	1	0	35	6	0	.171	1	47	1	0	1.9	.980
1915			7	8	.467	2.45	32	15	6	143	128	35	57	1	3	4	0	47	5	0	.106	3	43	0	4	1.4	1.000
1918	NY	A	2	4	.333	3.00	11	3	1	48	47	16	14	0	1	3	0	13	0	0	.000	1	13	0	0	1.3	1.000
6 yrs.			41	37	.526	2.53	150	73	32	701.1	646	159	238	3	13	14	2	218	37	0	.170	15	193	2	9	1.4	.990

Humberto Robinson

ROBINSON, HUMBERTO VALENTINO BR TR 6′ 1″ 155 lbs.
B. June 25, 1930, Colon, Panama.

Year	Team	Lg	W	L	PCT	ERA	G	GS	CG	IP	H	BB	SO	ShO	Relief Pitching W	Relief Pitching L	Relief Pitching SV	Batting AB	Batting H	Batting HR	BA	PO	A	E	DP	TC/G	FA
1955	MIL	N	3	1	.750	3.08	13	2	1	38	31	25	19	0	2	0	2	13	1	0	.077	1	7	0	1	0.6	1.000
1956			0	0	—	0.00	1	0	0	2	1	2	0	0	0	0	0	0	0	0	—	1	1	0	0	2.0	1.000
1958			2	4	.333	3.02	19	0	0	41.2	30	13	26	0	2	4	1	6	1	0	.167	4	9	0	1	0.7	1.000
1959	2 teams	CLE A	(5G 1–0)	PHI N	(31G 2–4)																						
″	total		3	4	.429	3.42	36	4	1	81.2	79	28	38	0	2	2	1	13	3	0	.231	3	18	2	0	0.6	.913
1960	PHI	N	0	4	.000	3.44	33	1	0	49.2	48	22	31	0	0	3	0	6	1	0	.167	5	8	1	0	0.4	.929
5 yrs.			8	13	.381	3.25	102	7	2	213	189	90	114	0	6	9	4	38	6	0	.158	14	43	3	2	0.6	.950

Jack Robinson

ROBINSON, JOHN EDWARD BR TR 6′ 175 lbs.
B. Feb. 20, 1921, Orange, N. J.

Year	Team	Lg	W	L	PCT	ERA	G	GS	CG	IP	H	BB	SO	ShO	Relief Pitching W	Relief Pitching L	Relief Pitching SV	Batting AB	Batting H	Batting HR	BA	PO	A	E	DP	TC/G	FA
1949	BOS	A	0	0	—	2.25	3	0	0	4	4	1	1	0	0	0	0	0	0	0	—	1	2	0	0	1.0	1.000

Jeff Robinson

ROBINSON, JEFFREY DANIEL BR TR 6′ 4″ 195 lbs.
B. Dec. 13, 1960, Santa Ana, Calif.

Year	Team	Lg	W	L	PCT	ERA	G	GS	CG	IP	H	BB	SO	ShO	Relief Pitching W	Relief Pitching L	Relief Pitching SV	Batting AB	Batting H	Batting HR	BA	PO	A	E	DP	TC/G	FA
1984	SF	N	7	15	.318	4.56	34	33	1	171.2	195	52	102	1	0	0	0	61	7	0	.115	14	24	1	1	1.1	.974
1985			0	0	—	5.11	8	0	0	12.1	16	10	8	0	0	0	0	0	0	0	—	0	0	0	0	0.0	.000
1986			6	3	.667	3.36	64	1	0	104.1	92	32	90	0	6	3	8	15	1	0	.067	10	10	1	1	0.3	.952
1987	2 teams	SF N	(63G 6–8)	PIT N	(18G 2–1)																						
″	total		8	9	.471	2.85	81	0	0	123.1	89	54	101	0	8	9	14	22	3	1	.136	14	18	0	6	0.4	1.000
1988	PIT	N	11	5	.688	3.03	75	0	0	124.2	113	39	87	0	11	5	9	16	3	0	.188	13	17	0	0	0.4	1.000
1989			7	13	.350	4.58	50	19	0	141.1	161	59	95	0	2	6	4	35	8	1	.229	13	26	5	2	0.9	.886
1990	NY	A	3	6	.333	3.45	54	4	1	88.2	82	34	43	0	1	5	0	0	0	0	—	5	23	3	1	0.6	.903
1991	CAL	A	0	3	.000	5.37	39	0	0	57	56	29	57	0	0	3	3	0	0	0	—	3	7	0	0	0.3	1.000
1992	CHI	N	4	3	.571	3.00	49	5	0	78	76	40	46	0	3	2	1	12	0	0	.000	7	13	0	1	0.4	1.000
9 yrs.			46	57	.447	3.79	454	62	2	901.1	880	349	629	1	31	33	39	161	22	2	.137	79	138	10	12	0.5	.956

Jeff Robinson

ROBINSON, JEFFREY MARK BR TR 6′ 6″ 210 lbs.
B. Dec. 14, 1961, Ventura, Calif.

Year	Team	Lg	W	L	PCT	ERA	G	GS	CG	IP	H	BB	SO	ShO	Relief Pitching W	Relief Pitching L	Relief Pitching SV	Batting AB	Batting H	Batting HR	BA	PO	A	E	DP	TC/G	FA
1987	DET	A	9	6	.600	5.37	29	21	2	127.1	132	54	98	1	1	1	0	0	0	0	—	14	9	2	2	0.9	.920
1988			13	6	.684	2.98	24	23	6	172	121	72	114	2	0	0	0	0	0	0	—	16	19	1	1	1.5	.972
1989			4	5	.444	4.73	16	16	1	78	76	46	40	1	0	0	0	0	0	0	—	3	6	0	1	0.6	1.000
1990			10	9	.526	5.96	27	27	1	145	141	88	76	1	0	0	0	0	0	0	—	14	15	3	1	1.2	.906
1991	BAL	A	4	9	.308	5.18	21	19	0	104.1	119	51	65	0	0	0	0	0	0	0	—	5	10	2	0	0.8	.882
1992	2 teams	TEX A	(16G 4–4)	PIT N	(8G 3–1)																						
″	total		7	5	.583	5.16	24	11	0	82	83	36	32	0	4	3	0	11	1	0	.091	8	9	0	2	0.7	1.000
6 yrs.			47	40	.540	4.79	141	117	10	708.2	672	347	425	5	5	4	0	11	1	0	.091	60	68	8	7	1.0	.941
LEAGUE CHAMPIONSHIP SERIES																											
1987	DET	A	0	0	—	0.00	1	0	0	0.1	1	0	0	0	0	0	0	0	0	0	—	0	1	0	0	1.0	1.000

Kenny Robinson

ROBINSON, KENNETH NEAL, JR. BR TR 5′ 9″ 175 lbs.
B. Nov. 3, 1969, Barberton, Ohio

Year	Team	W	L	PCT	ERA	G	GS	CG	IP	H	BB	SO	ShO	Relief Pitching W	Relief Pitching L	Relief Pitching SV	Batting AB	Batting H	Batting HR	BA	PO	A	E	DP	TC/G	FA
1995	TOR A	1	2	.333	3.69	21	0	0	39	25	22	31	0	1	2	0	0	0	0	—	2	1	0	0	0.1	1.000

Ron Robinson

ROBINSON, RONALD DEAN BR TR 6′ 4″ 235 lbs.
B. Mar. 24, 1962, Exeter, Calif.

Year	Team	W	L	PCT	ERA	G	GS	CG	IP	H	BB	SO	ShO	Relief Pitching W	Relief Pitching L	Relief Pitching SV	Batting AB	Batting H	Batting HR	BA	PO	A	E	DP	TC/G	FA
1984	CIN N	1	2	.333	2.72	12	5	1	39.2	35	13	24	0	0	0	0	8	0	0	.000	1	7	0	0	0.7	1.000
1985		7	7	.500	3.99	33	12	0	108.1	107	32	76	0	3	1	1	22	2	0	.091	9	17	2	4	0.8	.929
1986		10	3	.769	3.24	70	0	0	116.2	110	43	117	0	10	3	14	14	1	0	.071	8	20	0	2	0.4	1.000
1987		7	5	.583	3.68	48	18	0	154	148	43	99	0	1	2	4	36	7	0	.194	5	18	5	1	0.6	.821
1988		3	7	.300	4.12	17	16	0	78.2	88	26	38	0	0	0	0	25	5	0	.200	10	11	3	0	1.4	.875
1989		5	3	.625	3.35	15	15	0	83.1	80	28	36	0	0	0	0	28	6	0	.214	4	13	1	0	1.2	.944
1990	2 teams CIN N (6G 2–2) MIL A (22G 12–5)																									
″	total	14	7	.667	3.26	28	27	7	179.2	194	51	71	2	0	1	0	11	1	0	.091	19	21	0	0	1.4	1.000
1991	MIL A	0	1	.000	6.23	1	1	0	4.1	6	3	0	0	0	0	0	0	0	0	—	0	2	0	0	2.0	1.000
1992		1	4	.200	5.86	8	8	0	35.1	51	14	12	0	0	0	0	0	0	0	—	5	2	1	0	1.0	.875
9 yrs.		48	39	.552	3.63	232	102	8	800	819	253	473	2	14	7	19	144	22	0	.153	61	111	12	7	0.8	.935

Yank Robinson

ROBINSON, WILLIAM H. BR TR 5′ 6½″ 170 lbs.
B. Sept. 19, 1859, Philadelphia, Pa. D. Aug. 25, 1894, St. Louis, Mo.

Year	Team	W	L	PCT	ERA	G	GS	CG	IP	H	BB	SO	ShO	Relief Pitching W	Relief Pitching L	Relief Pitching SV	Batting AB	Batting H	Batting HR	BA	PO	A	E	DP	TC/G	FA
1882	DET N	0	0	—	0.00	1	0	0	2	0	1	0	0	0	0	0	39	7	0	.179	11	23	8	2	3.5	.810
1884	BAL U	3	3	.500	*3.48*	11	3	3	75	96	18	61	0	**2**	1	0	415	111	2	.267	219	238	90	14	5.0	.835
1886	STL AA	0	1	.000	3.00	1	1	1	9	10	7	1	0	0	0	0	481	132	3	.274	155	76	32	7	3.3	.878
1887		0	0	—	3.00	1	0	0	3	3	3	0	0	0	0	1	430	131	1	.305	332	368	83	52	6.1	.894
4 yrs.		3	4	.429	3.34	14	4	4	89	109	29	62	0	2	1	1	*				2172	2525	655	313	5.4	.878

Chick Robitaille

ROBITAILLE, JOSEPH ANTHONY BR TR 5′ 8″ 150 lbs.
B. Mar. 2, 1879, Whitehall, N. Y. D. July 30, 1947, Waterford, N. Y.

Year	Team	W	L	PCT	ERA	G	GS	CG	IP	H	BB	SO	ShO	Relief Pitching W	Relief Pitching L	Relief Pitching SV	Batting AB	Batting H	Batting HR	BA	PO	A	E	DP	TC/G	FA
1904	PIT N	4	3	.571	1.91	9	8	8	66	52	13	34	0	0	0	0	21	2	0	.095	4	10	0	0	1.6	1.000
1905		8	5	.615	2.92	17	12	10	120	126	28	32	0	2	0	0	45	6	0	.133	3	35	0	1	2.2	1.000
2 yrs.		12	8	.600	2.56	26	20	18	186	178	41	66	0	2	0	0	66	8	0	.121	7	45	0	1	2.0	1.000

Armando Roche

ROCHE, ARMANDO BR TR 6′ 190 lbs.
Born Armando Roche (Baez).
B. Dec. 7, 1926, Havana, Cuba.

Year	Team	W	L	PCT	ERA	G	GS	CG	IP	H	BB	SO	ShO	Relief Pitching W	Relief Pitching L	Relief Pitching SV	Batting AB	Batting H	Batting HR	BA	PO	A	E	DP	TC/G	FA
1945	WAS A	0	0	—	6.00	2	0	0	6	10	2	0	0	0	0	0	1	0	0	.000	0	3	0	0	1.5	1.000

Mike Rochford

ROCHFORD, MICHAEL JOSEPH BL TL 6′ 4″ 205 lbs.
B. Mar. 14, 1963, Methuen, Mass.

Year	Team	W	L	PCT	ERA	G	GS	CG	IP	H	BB	SO	ShO	Relief Pitching W	Relief Pitching L	Relief Pitching SV	Batting AB	Batting H	Batting HR	BA	PO	A	E	DP	TC/G	FA
1988	BOS A	0	0	—	0.00	2	0	0	2.1	4	1	1	0	0	0	0	0	0	0	—	1	2	0	0	1.5	1.000
1989		0	0	—	6.75	4	0	0	4	4	4	1	0	0	0	0	0	0	0	—	0	0	0	0	0.0	.000
1990		0	1	.000	18.00	2	1	0	4	10	4	0	0	0	0	0	0	0	0	—	0	0	0	0	0.0	.000
3 yrs.		0	1	.000	9.58	8	1	0	10.1	18	9	2	0	0	0	0	0	0	0		1	2	0	0	0.4	1.000

Rich Rodas

RODAS, RICHARD MARTIN BL TL 6′ 2″ 180 lbs.
B. Nov. 7, 1959, Roseville, Calif.

Year	Team	W	L	PCT	ERA	G	GS	CG	IP	H	BB	SO	ShO	Relief Pitching W	Relief Pitching L	Relief Pitching SV	Batting AB	Batting H	Batting HR	BA	PO	A	E	DP	TC/G	FA
1983	LA N	0	0	—	1.93	7	0	0	4.2	4	3	5	0	0	0	0	0	0	0	—	1	0	0	0	0.1	1.000
1984		0	0	—	5.40	3	0	0	5	5	1	1	0	0	0	0	1	0	0	.000	1	1	0	0	0.7	1.000
2 yrs.		0	0		3.72	10	0	0	9.2	9	4	6	0	0	0	0	1	0	0	.000	2	1	0	0	0.3	1.000

Ed Rodriguez

RODRIGUEZ, EDUARDO BR TR 6′ 180 lbs.
Born Eduardo Rodriguez (Reyes).
B. Mar. 6, 1952, Barceloneta, Puerto Rico.

Year	Team	W	L	PCT	ERA	G	GS	CG	IP	H	BB	SO	ShO	Relief Pitching W	Relief Pitching L	Relief Pitching SV	Batting AB	Batting H	Batting HR	BA	PO	A	E	DP	TC/G	FA
1973	MIL A	9	7	.563	3.30	30	6	2	76.1	71	47	49	0	6	6	5	1	1	0	1.000	5	9	1	2	0.5	.933
1974		7	4	.636	3.62	43	6	0	112	97	51	58	0	6	1	4	0	0	0	—	9	15	1	1	0.6	.960
1975		7	0	1.000	3.49	43	1	0	87.2	77	44	65	0	7	0	7	0	0	0	—	4	6	3	0	0.3	.769
1976		5	13	.278	3.64	45	12	3	136	124	65	77	0	2	6	8	0	0	0	—	8	16	4	2	0.6	.857
1977		5	6	.455	4.34	42	5	1	143	126	56	104	1	4	3	4	0	0	0	—	11	14	1	1	0.6	.962
1978		5	5	.500	3.93	32	8	0	105.1	107	26	51	0	2	3	2	0	0	0	—	10	12	0	0	0.7	1.000
1979	KC A	4	1	.800	4.86	29	1	1	74	79	34	26	0	3	1	2	0	0	0	—	0	8	1	0	0.3	.889
7 yrs.		42	36	.538	3.89	264	39	7	734.1	681	323	430	1	30	20	32	1	1	0	1.000	47	80	11	6	0.5	.920

Felix Rodriguez

RODRIGUEZ, FELIX ANTONIO BR TR 6′ 1″ 170 lbs.
B. Dec. 5, 1972, Monte Cristi, Domincan Republic.

Year	Team	W	L	PCT	ERA	G	GS	CG	IP	H	BB	SO	ShO	Relief Pitching W	Relief Pitching L	Relief Pitching SV	Batting AB	Batting H	Batting HR	BA	PO	A	E	DP	TC/G	FA
1995	LA N	1	1	.500	2.53	11	0	0	10.2	11	5	5	0	1	1	0	0	0	0	—	0	1	0	1	0.1	1.000

Frank Rodriguez

RODRIGUEZ, FRANCISCO BR TR 6′ 193 lbs.
B. Dec. 11, 1972, Brooklyn, N. Y.

Year	Team	W	L	PCT	ERA	G	GS	CG	IP	H	BB	SO	ShO	Relief Pitching W	Relief Pitching L	Relief Pitching SV	Batting AB	Batting H	Batting HR	BA	PO	A	E	DP	TC/G	FA
1995	2 teams BOS A (9G 0–2) MIN A (16G 5–6)																									
″	total	5	8	.385	6.13	25	18	0	105.2	114	57	59	0	0	1	0	0	0	0	—	12	23	0	3	1.4	1.000

Freddy Rodriguez

RODRIGUEZ, FERNANDO PEDRO BR TR 6′ 180 lbs.
Born Fernando Pedro Rodriguez (Borrego).
B. Apr. 29, 1924, Havana, Cuba.

Year	Team	W	L	PCT	ERA	G	GS	CG	IP	H	BB	SO	ShO	Relief Pitching W	Relief Pitching L	Relief Pitching SV	Batting AB	Batting H	Batting HR	BA	PO	A	E	DP	TC/G	FA
1958	CHI N	0	0	—	7.36	7	0	0	7.1	8	5	5	0	0	0	2	1	0	0	.000	0	0	0	0	0.0	.000
1959	PHI N	0	0	—	13.50	1	0	0	2	4	0	1	0	0	0	0	0	0	0	—	0	0	0	0	0.0	.000
2 yrs.		0	0		8.68	8	0	0	9.1	12	5	6	0	0	0	2	1	0	0	.000	0	0	0	0	0.0	

Rich Rodriguez

RODRIGUEZ, RICHARD ANTHONY BL TL 5′10″ 185 lbs.
B. Mar. 1, 1963, Downey, Calif.

Year	Team	W	L	PCT	ERA	G	GS	CG	IP	H	BB	SO	ShO	Relief Pitching W	Relief Pitching L	Relief Pitching SV	Batting AB	Batting H	Batting HR	BA	PO	A	E	DP	TC/G	FA
1990	SD N	1	1	.500	2.83	32	0	0	47.2	52	16	22	0	1	1	1	3	0	0	.000	1	10	0	1	0.3	1.000
1991		3	1	.750	3.26	64	1	0	80	66	44	40	0	3	1	0	5	0	0	.000	2	13	0	1	0.2	1.000
1992		6	3	.667	2.37	61	1	0	91	77	29	64	0	6	2	0	6	0	0	.000	4	17	1	2	0.4	.955

Rich Rodriguez *continued*

Year	Team	W	L	PCT	ERA	G	GS	CG	IP	H	BB	SO	ShO	Relief W	Relief L	Relief SV	Batting AB	Batting H	HR	BA	PO	A	E	DP	TC/G	FA
1993	2 teams SD N (34G 2–3) FLA N (36G 0–1)																									
"	total	2	4	.333	3.79	70	0	0	76	73	33	43	0	2	4	3	2	0	0	.000	6	10	1	2	0.2	.941
1994	STL N	3	5	.375	4.03	56	0	0	60.1	62	26	43	0	3	5	0	1	0	0	.000	1	3	1	0	0.1	.800
1995		0	0	—	0.00	1	0	0	1.2	0	0	0	0	0	0	0	0	0	0	—	0	0	0	0	0.0	.000
6 yrs.		15	14	.517	3.20	284	2	0	356.2	330	148	212	0	15	13	4	17	0	0	.000	14	53	3	6	0.2	.957

Rick Rodriguez

RODRIGUEZ, RICARDO
B. Sept. 21, 1960, Oakland, Calif.
BR TR 6′ 3″ 190 lbs.

Year	Team	W	L	PCT	ERA	G	GS	CG	IP	H	BB	SO	ShO	Relief W	Relief L	Relief SV	Batting AB	Batting H	HR	BA	PO	A	E	DP	TC/G	FA
1986	OAK A	1	2	.333	6.61	3	3	0	16.1	17	7	2	0	0	0	0	0	0	0	—	1	4	0	0	1.7	1.000
1987		1	0	1.000	2.96	15	0	0	24.1	32	15	9	0	1	0	0	0	0	0	—	2	6	0	1	0.5	1.000
1988	CLE A	1	2	.333	7.09	10	5	0	33	43	17	9	0	0	0	0	0	0	0	—	4	8	0	1	1.2	1.000
1990	SF N	0	0	—	8.10	3	0	0	3.1	5	2	2	0	0	0	0	0	0	0	—	1	0	0	0	0.3	1.000
4 yrs.		3	4	.429	5.73	31	8	0	77	97	41	22	0	1	0	0	0	0	0		8	18	0	2	0.8	1.000

Roberto Rodriguez

RODRIGUEZ, ROBERTO (Bobby)
Born Roberto Rodriguez (Munoz).
B. Nov. 29, 1941, Caracas, Venezuela.
BR TR 6′ 3″ 185 lbs.

Year	Team	W	L	PCT	ERA	G	GS	CG	IP	H	BB	SO	ShO	Relief W	Relief L	Relief SV	Batting AB	Batting H	HR	BA	PO	A	E	DP	TC/G	FA
1967	KC A	1	1	.500	3.57	15	5	0	40.1	42	14	29	0	0	0	2	9	0	0	.000	0	5	0	0	0.3	1.000
1970	3 teams OAK A (6G 0–0) SD N (10G 0–0) CHI N (26G 3–2)																									
"	total	3	2	.600	5.53	42	0	0	71.2	86	23	62	0	3	2	5	12	1	1	.083	3	9	0	1	0.3	1.000
2 yrs.		4	3	.571	4.82	57	5	0	112	128	37	91	0	3	2	7	21	1	1	.048	3	14	0	1	0.3	1.000

Rosario Rodriguez

RODRIGUEZ, ROSARIO ISABEL
Born Rosario Isabel Rodriguez (Echavarria).
B. July 8, 1969, Los Mochis, Mexico.
BR TL 6′ 185 lbs.

Year	Team	W	L	PCT	ERA	G	GS	CG	IP	H	BB	SO	ShO	Relief W	Relief L	Relief SV	Batting AB	Batting H	HR	BA	PO	A	E	DP	TC/G	FA
1989	CIN N	1	1	.500	4.15	7	0	0	4.1	3	3	0	0	1	1	0	0	0	0	—	1	1	0	0	0.3	1.000
1990		0	0	—	6.10	9	0	0	10.1	15	2	8	0	0	0	0	0	0	0	—	0	3	0	0	0.3	1.000
1991	PIT N	1	1	.500	4.11	18	0	0	15.1	14	8	10	0	1	1	6	1	0	0	.000	2	2	0	0	0.2	1.000
3 yrs.		2	2	.500	4.80	34	0	0	30	32	13	18	0	2	2	6	1	0	0	.000	3	6	0	0	0.3	1.000
LEAGUE CHAMPIONSHIP SERIES																										
1991	PIT N	0	0	—	27.00	1	0	0	1	1	2	1	0	0	0	0	0	0	0	—	0	0	0	0	0.0	.000

Clay Roe

ROE, JAMES CLAY (Shad)
B. Jan. 7, 1904, Greenbrier, Tenn. D. Apr. 3, 1956, Cleveland, Miss.
BL TL 6′ 1″ 180 lbs.

Year	Team	W	L	PCT	ERA	G	GS	CG	IP	H	BB	SO	ShO	Relief W	Relief L	Relief SV	Batting AB	Batting H	HR	BA	PO	A	E	DP	TC/G	FA
1923	WAS A	0	1	.000	0.00	1	1	0	1.2	0	6	2	0	0	0	0	0	0	0	—	0	0	0	0	0.0	.000

Preacher Roe

ROE, ELWIN CHARLES
B. Feb. 26, 1915, Ashflat, Ark.
BR TL 6′ 2″ 170 lbs.

Year	Team	W	L	PCT	ERA	G	GS	CG	IP	H	BB	SO	ShO	Relief W	Relief L	Relief SV	Batting AB	Batting H	HR	BA	PO	A	E	DP	TC/G	FA
1938	STL N	0	0	—	13.50	1	0	0	2.2	6	2	1	0	0	0	0	1	0	0	.000	0	0	0	0	0.0	.000
1944	PIT N	13	11	.542	3.11	39	25	7	185.1	182	59	88	1	5	1	1	53	7	0	.132	11	27	2	0	1.0	.950
1945		14	13	.519	2.87	33	31	15	235	228	46	**148**	3	0	0	1	75	8	0	.107	16	40	0	3	1.7	1.000
1946		3	8	.273	5.14	21	10	1	70	83	25	28	0	2	1	2	15	1	0	.067	4	13	1	1	0.9	.944
1947		4	15	.211	5.25	38	22	4	144	156	63	59	1	1	0	2	40	5	0	.125	6	20	1	2	0.7	.963
1948	BKN N	12	8	.600	2.63	34	22	8	177.2	156	33	86	2	2	0	2	51	5	0	.098	4	30	0	2	1.0	1.000
1949		15	6	**.714**	2.79	30	27	13	212.2	201	44	109	3	0	1	1	70	8	0	.114	5	29	2	4	1.2	.944
1950		19	11	.633	3.30	36	32	16	250.2	245	66	125	2	2	0	1	91	14	0	.154	12	34	1	3	1.3	.979
1951		22	3	**.880**	3.04	34	33	19	257.2	247	64	113	2	1	0	0	89	10	0	.112	18	39	3	6	1.8	.950
1952		11	2	.846	3.12	27	25	8	158.2	163	39	83	2	1	0	0	57	4	0	.070	9	23	0	0	1.2	1.000
1953		11	3	.786	4.36	25	24	9	157	171	40	85	1	0	0	0	57	3	1	.053	4	30	0	3	1.4	1.000
1954		3	4	.429	5.00	15	10	1	63	69	23	31	0	0	0	0	21	3	0	.143	1	10	0	2	0.7	1.000
12 yrs.		127	84	.602	3.43	333	261	101	1914.1	1907	504	956	17	14	3	10	620	68	1	.110	90	295	10	26	1.2	.975
WORLD SERIES																										
1949	BKN N	1	0	1.000	0.00	1	1	1	9	6	0	3	1	0	0	0	3	0	0	.000	1	1	1	0	3.0	.667
1952		1	0	1.000	3.18	3	1	1	11.1	9	6	7	0	0	0	0	2	0	0	.000	1	0	0	0	0.3	1.000
1953		0	1	.000	4.50	1	1	1	8	5	4	4	0	0	0	0	3	0	0	.000	1	1	0	0	2.0	1.000
3 yrs.		2	1	.667	2.54	5	3	3	28.1	20	10	14	1	0	0	0	8	0	0	.000	3	2	1	0	1.2	.833

Ed Roebuck

ROEBUCK, EDWARD JACK
B. July 3, 1931, East Millsboro, Pa.
BR TR 6′ 2″ 185 lbs.

Year	Team	W	L	PCT	ERA	G	GS	CG	IP	H	BB	SO	ShO	Relief W	Relief L	Relief SV	Batting AB	Batting H	HR	BA	PO	A	E	DP	TC/G	FA
1955	BKN N	5	6	.455	4.71	47	0	0	84	96	24	33	0	5	6	12	18	2	0	.111	7	20	2	0	0.6	.931
1956		5	4	.556	3.93	43	0	0	89.1	83	29	60	0	5	4	1	18	6	0	.333	6	17	0	1	0.5	1.000
1957		8	2	.800	2.71	44	1	0	96.1	70	46	73	0	8	1	8	21	5	2	.238	8	26	3	2	0.8	.919
1958	LA N	0	1	.000	3.48	32	0	0	44	45	15	26	0	0	1	5	4	2	0	.500	4	6	1	0	0.3	.909
1960		8	3	.727	2.78	58	0	0	116.2	109	38	77	0	8	3	8	24	4	0	.167	8	28	1	3	0.6	.973
1961		2	0	1.000	5.00	5	0	0	9	12	2	9	0	2	0	0	2	0	0	.000	2	1	1	0	0.8	.750
1962		10	2	.833	3.09	64	0	0	119.1	102	54	72	0	10	2	9	28	6	0	.214	7	22	1	2	0.5	.967
1963	2 teams LA N (29G 2–4) WAS A (26G 2–1)																									
"	total	4	5	.444	3.69	55	0	0	97.2	117	50	51	0	4	5	4	15	3	0	.200	3	24	1	0	0.5	.964
1964	2 teams WAS A (2G 0–0) PHI N (60G 5–3)																									
"	total	5	3	.625	2.30	62	0	0	78.1	55	27	42	0	5	3	12	6	0	0	.000	6	19	3	1	0.5	.893
1965	PHI N	5	3	.625	3.40	44	0	0	50.1	55	15	29	0	5	3	3	1	0	0	.000	1	3	1	1	0.1	.800
1966		0	2	.000	6.00	6	0	0	6	9	2	5	0	0	2	0	0	0	0	—	0	0	0	0	0.0	.000
11 yrs.		52	31	.627	3.35	460	1	0	791	753	302	477	0	52	30	62	137	28	2	.204	52	166	14	10	0.5	.940
WORLD SERIES																										
1955	BKN N	0	0	—	0.00	1	0	0	2	1	0	0	0	0	0	0	0	0	0	—	2	0	0	0	2.0	1.000
1956		0	0	—	2.08	3	0	0	4.1	1	0	5	0	0	0	0	0	0	0	—	0	0	0	0	0.0	.000
2 yrs.		0	0		1.42	4	0	0	6.1	2	0	5	0	0	0	0	0	0	0		2	0	0	0	0.5	1.000

Mike Roesler

ROESLER, MICHAEL JOSEPH — BR TR 6′ 5″ 195 lbs.
B. Sept. 12, 1963, Fort Wayne, Ind.

Year	Team	Lg	W	L	PCT	ERA	G	GS	CG	IP	H	BB	SO	ShO	Relief W	Relief L	SV	AB	H	HR	BA	PO	A	E	DP	TC/G	FA
1989	CIN	N	0	1	.000	3.96	17	0	0	25	22	9	14	0	0	1	0	0	0	0	—	0	1	0	0	0.1	1.000
1990	PIT	N	1	0	1.000	3.00	5	0	0	6	5	2	4	0	1	0	0	1	0	0	.000	0	0	0	0	0.0	.000
2 yrs.			1	1	.500	3.77	22	0	0	31	27	11	18	0	1	1	0	1	0	0	.000	0	1	0	0	0.0	1.000

Oscar Roettger

ROETTGER, OSCAR FREDERICK LOUIS — BR TR 6′ 170 lbs.
Brother of Wally Roettger.
B. Feb. 19, 1900, St. Louis, Mo. D. July 4, 1986, St. Louis, Mo.

Year	Team	Lg	W	L	PCT	ERA	G	GS	CG	IP	H	BB	SO	ShO	Relief W	Relief L	SV	AB	H	HR	BA	PO	A	E	DP	TC/G	FA
1923	NY	A	0	0	—	8.49	5	0	0	11.2	16	12	7	0	0	0	1	2	0	0	.000	3	2	0	0	1.0	1.000
1924			0	0	—	0.00	1	0	0		1	2	0	0	0	0	0	0	0	0	—	0	0	0	0	0.0	.000
2 yrs.			0	0		8.49	6	0	0	11.2	17	14	7	0	0	0	1	*				133	7	3	6	6.5	.979

Joe Rogalski

ROGALSKI, JOSEPH ANTHONY — BR TR 6′ 2″ 187 lbs.
B. July 15, 1912, Ashland, Wis. D. Nov. 20, 1951, Ashland, Wis.

Year	Team	Lg	W	L	PCT	ERA	G	GS	CG	IP	H	BB	SO	ShO	Relief W	Relief L	SV	AB	H	HR	BA	PO	A	E	DP	TC/G	FA
1938	DET	A	0	0	—	2.57	2	0	0	7	12	0	2	0	0	0	0	2	0	0	.000	1	0	0	0	0.5	1.000

Buck Rogers

ROGERS, ORLIN WOODROW (Lefty) — BR TL 5′ 8½″ 164 lbs.
B. Nov. 5, 1912, Spring Garden, Va.

Year	Team	Lg	W	L	PCT	ERA	G	GS	CG	IP	H	BB	SO	ShO	Relief W	Relief L	SV	AB	H	HR	BA	PO	A	E	DP	TC/G	FA
1935	WAS	A	0	1	.000	7.20	2	1	0	10	16	6	7	0	0	0	0	3	0	0	.000	0	0	0	0	0.0	.000

Jimmy Rogers

ROGERS, JAMES RANDALL — BR TR 6′ 2″ 200 lbs.
B. Jan. 3, 1967, Tulsa, Okla.

Year	Team	Lg	W	L	PCT	ERA	G	GS	CG	IP	H	BB	SO	ShO	Relief W	Relief L	SV	AB	H	HR	BA	PO	A	E	DP	TC/G	FA
1995	TOR	A	2	4	.333	5.70	19	0	0	23.2	21	18	13	0	2	4	0	0	0	0	—	0	2	0	0	0.1	1.000

Kenny Rogers

ROGERS, KENNETH SCOTT — BL TL 6′ 1″ 200 lbs.
B. Nov. 10, 1964, Savannah, Ga.

Year	Team	Lg	W	L	PCT	ERA	G	GS	CG	IP	H	BB	SO	ShO	Relief W	Relief L	SV	AB	H	HR	BA	PO	A	E	DP	TC/G	FA
1989	TEX	A	3	4	.429	2.93	73	0	0	73.2	60	42	63	0	3	4	2	0	0	0	—	1	22	0	0	0.3	1.000
1990			10	6	.625	3.13	69	3	0	97.2	93	42	74	0	9	4	15	0	0	0	—	5	22	2	1	0.4	.931
1991			10	10	.500	5.42	63	9	0	109.2	121	61	73	0	6	6	5	0	0	0	—	5	15	3	1	0.4	.870
1992			3	6	.333	3.09	**81**	0	0	78.2	80	26	70	0	3	6	6	0	0	0	—	4	17	2	0	0.3	.913
1993			16	10	.615	4.10	35	33	5	208.1	210	71	140	0	0	0	0	0	0	0	—	18	46	4	4	1.9	.941
1994			11	8	.579	4.46	24	24	6	167.1	169	52	120	2	0	0	0	0	0	0	—	9	33	4	4	1.9	.913
1995			17	7	.708	3.38	31	31	3	208	192	76	140	1	0	0	0	0	0	0	—	10	35	2	2	1.5	.957
7 yrs.			70	51	.579	3.88	376	100	14	943.1	925	370	680	3	21	20	28	0	0	0		52	190	17	12	0.7	.934

Kevin Rogers

ROGERS, CHARLES KEVIN — BB TL 6′ 2″ 190 lbs.
B. Aug. 20, 1968, Cleveland, Miss.

Year	Team	Lg	W	L	PCT	ERA	G	GS	CG	IP	H	BB	SO	ShO	Relief W	Relief L	SV	AB	H	HR	BA	PO	A	E	DP	TC/G	FA
1992	SF	N	0	2	.000	4.24	6	6	0	34	37	13	26	0	0	0	0	9	2	0	.222	1	3	0	0	0.7	1.000
1993			2	2	.500	2.68	64	0	0	80.2	71	28	62	0	2	2	0	3	0	0	.000	2	7	1	1	0.2	.900
1994			0	0	—	3.48	9	0	0	10.1	10	6	7	0	0	0	0	0	0	0	—	0	1	0	0	0.1	1.000
3 yrs.			2	4	.333	3.17	79	6	0	125	118	47	95	0	2	2	0	12	2	0	.167	3	11	1	1	0.2	.933

Lee Rogers

ROGERS, LEE OTIS (Buck, Lefty) — BR TL 5′11″ 170 lbs.
B. Oct. 8, 1913, Tuscaloosa, Ala. D. Nov. 23, 1995, Little Rock, Ark.

Year	Team	Lg	W	L	PCT	ERA	G	GS	CG	IP	H	BB	SO	ShO	Relief W	Relief L	SV	AB	H	HR	BA	PO	A	E	DP	TC/G	FA
1938	2 teams BOS A (14G 1–1) BKN N (12G 0–2)																										
″	total		1	3	.250	6.14	26	4	0	51.1	55	28	18	0	1	0	0	7	0	0	.000	6	19	2	1	1.0	.926

Steve Rogers

ROGERS, STEPHEN DOUGLAS — BR TR 6′ 2″ 175 lbs.
B. Oct. 26, 1949, Jefferson City, Mo.

Year	Team	Lg	W	L	PCT	ERA	G	GS	CG	IP	H	BB	SO	ShO	Relief W	Relief L	SV	AB	H	HR	BA	PO	A	E	DP	TC/G	FA
1973	MON	N	10	5	.667	1.54	17	17	7	134	93	49	64	3	0	0	0	41	4	0	.098	14	22	1	2	2.2	.973
1974			15	**22**	.405	4.46	38	38	11	254	255	80	154	1	0	0	0	79	11	0	.139	30	40	1	4	1.9	.986
1975			11	12	.478	3.29	35	35	12	252	248	88	137	3	0	0	0	77	13	0	.169	18	41	7	2	1.9	.894
1976			7	**17**	.292	3.21	33	32	8	230	212	69	150	4	0	0	1	74	11	0	.149	26	50	3	3	2.4	.962
1977			17	16	.515	3.10	40	40	17	302	272	81	206	4	0	0	0	96	10	0	.104	20	63	7	5	2.3	.922
1978			13	10	.565	2.47	30	29	11	219	186	64	126	1	0	0	1	71	8	0	.113	16	38	1	1	1.8	.982
1979			13	12	.520	3.00	37	37	13	249	232	78	143	**5**	0	0	0	77	12	0	.156	14	46	3	7	1.7	.952
1980			16	11	.593	2.98	37	37	**14**	281	247	85	147	4	0	0	0	81	13	0	.160	21	37	3	3	1.6	.951
1981			12	8	.600	3.41	22	22	7	161	149	41	87	3	0	0	0	55	8	0	.145	10	20	0	1	1.4	1.000
1982			19	8	.704	**2.40**	35	35	14	277	245	65	179	4	0	0	0	85	11	0	.129	18	41	1	3	1.7	.983
1983			17	12	.586	3.23	36	36	13	273	258	78	146	**5**	0	0	0	82	12	0	.146	28	28	0	1	1.6	1.000
1984			6	15	.286	4.31	31	28	1	169.1	171	78	64	0	0	0	0	49	7	0	.143	17	25	3	5	1.5	.933
1985			2	4	.333	5.68	8	7	1	38	51	20	18	0	0	0	0	14	2	0	.143	5	11	1	0	2.1	.941
13 yrs.			158	152	.510	3.17	399	393	129	2839.1	2619	876	1621	37	0	0	2	881	122	0	.138	237	462	31	37	1.8	.958
DIVISIONAL PLAYOFF SERIES																											
1981	MON	N	2	0	1.000	0.51	2	2	1	17.2	16	3	5	1	0	0	0	5	2	0	.400	0	0	0	0	0.0	.000
LEAGUE CHAMPIONSHIP SERIES																											
1981	MON	N	1	1	.500	1.80	2	1	1	10	8	1	6	0	0	0	0	2	0	0	.000	0	1	0	0	0.5	1.000

Tom Rogers

ROGERS, THOMAS ANDREW (Shotgun) — BR TR 6′½″ 180 lbs.
B. Feb. 12, 1892, Sparta, Tenn. D. Mar. 7, 1936, Nashville, Tenn.

Year	Team	Lg	W	L	PCT	ERA	G	GS	CG	IP	H	BB	SO	ShO	Relief W	Relief L	SV	AB	H	HR	BA	PO	A	E	DP	TC/G	FA
1917	STL	A	3	6	.333	3.89	24	8	3	108.2	112	44	27	0	1	0	0	29	5	0	.172	1	34	3	0	1.6	.921
1918			8	10	.444	3.27	29	16	11	154	148	49	29	0	3	1	2	53	13	0	.245	8	52	3	1	2.2	.952
1919	2 teams STL A (2G 0–1) PHI A (23G 4–12)																										
″	total		4	13	.235	4.47	25	18	7	141	159	60	38	1	0	1	0	49	11	1	.224	13	52	4	2	2.8	.942
1921	NY	A	0	1	.000	7.36	5	0	0	11	12	9	0	0	0	1	1	3	1	0	.333	0	6	0	1	1.0	1.000
4 yrs.			15	30	.333	3.95	83	42	21	414.2	431	162	94	1	4	3	3	134	30	1	.224	22	144	10	4	2.1	.943
WORLD SERIES																											
1921	NY	A	0	0	—	6.75	1	0	0	1.1	3	0	1	0	0	0	0	0	0	0	—	0	1	0	0	1.0	1.000

Clint Rogge

ROGGE, FRANCIS CLINTON BL TR 5′10″ 185 lbs.
B. July 19, 1889, Memphis, Mich. D. Jan. 6, 1969, Mount Clemens, Mich.

Year	Team	W	L	PCT	ERA	G	GS	CG	IP	H	BB	SO	ShO	Relief Pitching W	L	SV	Batting AB	H	HR	BA	PO	A	E	DP	TC/G	FA
1915	PIT F	17	12	.586	2.55	37	31	17	254.1	240	93	93	5	2	1	0	81	14	0	.173	8	85	4	2	2.6	.959
1921	CIN N	1	2	.333	4.08	6	3	0	35.1	43	9	12	0	0	0	0	10	1	0	.100	0	10	0	0	1.7	1.000
2 yrs.		18	14	.563	2.73	43	34	17	289.2	283	102	105	5	2	1	0	91	15	0	.165	8	95	4	2	2.5	.963

Garry Roggenburk

ROGGENBURK, GARRY EARL BR TL 6′ 6″ 195 lbs.
B. Apr. 16, 1940, Cleveland, Ohio.

Year	Team	W	L	PCT	ERA	G	GS	CG	IP	H	BB	SO	ShO	Relief Pitching W	L	SV	Batting AB	H	HR	BA	PO	A	E	DP	TC/G	FA
1963	MIN A	2	4	.333	2.16	36	2	0	50	47	22	24	0	2	2	4	7	1	0	.143	3	12	1	0	0.4	.938
1965		1	0	1.000	3.43	12	0	0	21	21	12	6	0	1	0	2	3	0	0	.000	0	3	1	0	0.3	.750
1966	2 teams MIN A (12G 1–2) BOS A (1G 0–0)																									
″	total	1	2	.333	5.68	13	0	0	12.2	15	11	3	0	1	2	1	0	0	0		1	2	0	0	0.2	1.000
1968	BOS A	0	0	—	2.16	4	0	0	8.1	9	3	4	0	0	0	0	0	0	0	—	1	0	0	0	0.3	1.000
1969	2 teams BOS A (7G 0–1) SEA A (7G 2–2)																									
″	total	2	3	.400	5.56	14	4	1	34	40	16	19	0	0	1	0	10	1	0	.100	3	5	0	0	0.6	1.000
5 yrs.		6	9	.400	3.64	79	6	1	126	132	64	56	0	4	5	7	20	2	0	.100	8	22	2	0	0.4	.938

Saul Rogovin

ROGOVIN, SAUL WALTER BR TR 6′ 2″ 205 lbs.
B. Oct. 10, 1923, Brooklyn, N. Y. D. Jan. 23, 1995, New York, N. Y.

Year	Team	W	L	PCT	ERA	G	GS	CG	IP	H	BB	SO	ShO	Relief Pitching W	L	SV	Batting AB	H	HR	BA	PO	A	E	DP	TC/G	FA
1949	DET A	0	1	.000	14.29	5	0	0	5.2	13	7	2	0	0	1	0	0	0	0	—	1	0	0	1	0.2	1.000
1950		2	1	.667	4.50	11	5	1	40	39	26	11	0	1	0	0	16	3	1	.188	1	5	1	1	0.6	.857
1951	2 teams DET A (5G 1–1) CHI A (22G 11–7)																									
″	total	12	8	.600	**2.78**	27	26	17	216.2	189	74	82	3	1	0	0	81	17	0	.210	16	35	3	4	2.0	.944
1952	CHI A	14	9	.609	3.85	33	30	12	231.2	224	79	121	3	0	0	1	84	17	1	.202	11	39	2	4	1.6	.962
1953		7	12	.368	5.22	22	19	4	131	151	48	62	1	1	0	1	37	5	0	.135	10	20	3	1	1.5	.909
1955	2 teams BAL A (14G 1–8) PHI N (12G 5–3)																									
″	total	6	11	.353	3.81	26	23	6	144	139	44	62	2	0	0	0	46	8	1	.174	6	20	3	2	1.1	.897
1956	PHI N	7	6	.538	4.98	22	18	3	106.2	122	27	48	0	0	0	0	36	4	0	.111	10	12	1	1	1.0	.957
1957		0	0	—	9.00	4	0	0	8	11	3	0	0	0	0	0	0	0	0	—	2	0	1	0	0.8	.667
8 yrs.		48	48	.500	4.06	150	121	43	883.2	888	308	388	9	3	1	2	300	54	3	.180	57	131	14	14	1.3	.931

Billy Rohr

ROHR, WILLIAM JOSEPH BL TL 6′ 3″ 170 lbs.
B. July 1, 1945, San Diego, Calif.

Year	Team	W	L	PCT	ERA	G	GS	CG	IP	H	BB	SO	ShO	Relief Pitching W	L	SV	Batting AB	H	HR	BA	PO	A	E	DP	TC/G	FA
1967	BOS A	2	3	.400	5.10	10	8	2	42.1	43	22	16	1	0	0	0	10	0	0	.000	1	7	1	0	0.9	.889
1968	CLE A	1	0	1.000	6.87	17	0	0	18.1	18	10	5	0	1	0	1	1	0	0	.000	1	4	1	0	0.4	.833
2 yrs.		3	3	.500	5.64	27	8	2	60.2	61	32	21	1	1	0	1	11	0	0	.000	2	11	2	0	0.6	.867

Les Rohr

ROHR, LESLIE NORVIN BL TL 6′ 5″ 205 lbs.
B. Mar. 5, 1946, Lowestoft, England.

Year	Team	W	L	PCT	ERA	G	GS	CG	IP	H	BB	SO	ShO	Relief Pitching W	L	SV	Batting AB	H	HR	BA	PO	A	E	DP	TC/G	FA
1967	NY N	2	1	.667	2.12	3	3	0	17	13	9	15	0	0	0	0	6	0	0	.000	0	1	2	0	1.0	.333
1968		0	2	.000	4.50	2	1	0	6	9	7	5	0	0	1	0	0	0	0	—	0	1	0	0	0.5	1.000
1969		0	0	—	20.25	1	0	0	1.1	5	1	0	0	0	0	0	0	0	0	—	0	0	0	0	0.0	.000
3 yrs.		2	3	.400	3.70	6	4	0	24.1	27	17	20	0	0	1	0	6	0	0	.000	0	2	2	0	0.7	.500

Cookie Rojas

ROJAS, OCTAVIO VICTOR BR TR 5′10″ 160 lbs.
Born Octavio Victor Rojas (Rivas).
B. Mar. 6, 1939, Havana, Cuba.
Manager 1988.

Year	Team	W	L	PCT	ERA	G	GS	CG	IP	H	BB	SO	ShO	Relief Pitching W	L	SV	Batting AB	H	HR	BA	PO	A	E	DP	TC/G	FA
1967	PHI N	0	0	—	0.00	1	0	0	1	1	0	0	0	0	0	0	*				60	52	6	13	3.8	.949

Mel Rojas

ROJAS, MELQUIADES BR TR 5′11″ 175 lbs.
Born Melquiades Rojas (Medrano).
B. Dec. 10, 1966, Haina, Dominican Republic.

Year	Team	W	L	PCT	ERA	G	GS	CG	IP	H	BB	SO	ShO	Relief Pitching W	L	SV	Batting AB	H	HR	BA	PO	A	E	DP	TC/G	FA
1990	MON N	3	1	.750	3.60	23	0	0	40	34	24	26	0	3	1	1	3	0	0	.000	2	4	1	0	0.3	.857
1991		3	3	.500	3.75	37	0	0	48	42	13	37	0	3	3	6	4	0	0	.000	2	5	0	0	0.2	1.000
1992		7	1	.875	1.43	68	0	0	100.2	71	34	70	0	7	1	10	15	1	0	.067	9	12	2	1	0.3	.913
1993		5	8	.385	2.95	66	0	0	88.1	80	30	48	0	5	8	10	12	1	0	.083	7	9	0	1	0.2	1.000
1994		3	2	.600	3.32	58	0	0	84	71	21	84	0	3	2	16	10	2	0	.200	8	10	0	1	0.3	1.000
1995		1	4	.200	4.12	59	0	0	67.2	69	29	61	0	1	4	30	6	0	0	.000	4	7	0	1	0.2	1.000
6 yrs.		22	19	.537	3.00	311	0	0	428.2	367	151	326	0	22	19	73	50	4	0	.080	32	47	3	4	0.3	.963

Minnie Rojas

ROJAS, MINERVINO ALEJANDRO BR TR 6′ 1″ 170 lbs.
Born Minervino Alejandro (Landin).
B. Nov. 26, 1938, Remedios Las Villas, Cuba.

Year	Team	W	L	PCT	ERA	G	GS	CG	IP	H	BB	SO	ShO	Relief Pitching W	L	SV	Batting AB	H	HR	BA	PO	A	E	DP	TC/G	FA
1966	CAL A	7	4	.636	2.88	47	2	0	84.1	83	15	37	0	5	4	10	14	1	0	.071	2	10	0	2	0.3	1.000
1967		12	9	.571	2.52	72	0	0	121.2	106	38	83	0	**12**	9	**27**	17	1	0	.059	1	13	0	0	0.2	1.000
1968		4	3	.571	4.25	38	0	0	55	55	15	33	0	4	3	6	10	1	0	.100	2	5	1	0	0.2	.875
3 yrs.		23	16	.590	3.00	157	2	0	261	244	68	153	0	21	16	43	41	3	0	.073	5	28	1	2	0.2	.971

Jim Roland

ROLAND, JAMES IVAN BR TL 6′ 3″ 175 lbs.
B. Dec. 14, 1942, Franklin, N. C.

Year	Team	W	L	PCT	ERA	G	GS	CG	IP	H	BB	SO	ShO	Relief Pitching W	L	SV	Batting AB	H	HR	BA	PO	A	E	DP	TC/G	FA
1962	MIN A	0	0	—	0.00	1	0	0	2	1	0	1	0	0	0	0	0	0	0	—	0	0	0	0	0.0	.000
1963		4	1	.800	2.57	10	7	2	49	32	27	34	1	1	0	0	15	0	0	.000	4	9	1	0	1.4	.929
1964		2	6	.250	4.10	30	13	1	94.1	76	55	63	0	0	0	3	27	4	0	.148	1	11	0	1	0.4	1.000
1966		0	0	—	0.00	1	0	0	2	0	0	1	0	0	0	0	0	0	0	—	0	0	0	0	0.0	.000
1967		0	1	.000	3.03	25	0	0	35.2	33	17	16	0	0	1	2	3	0	0	.000	4	4	0	0	0.3	1.000
1968		4	1	.800	3.50	28	4	1	61.2	55	24	36	0	2	0	0	8	0	0	.000	2	14	1	1	0.6	.941
1969	OAK A	5	1	.833	2.19	39	3	2	86.1	59	46	48	0	2	1	1	21	2	0	.095	4	13	0	3	0.4	1.000
1970		3	3	.500	2.72	28	2	0	43	28	23	26	0	3	2	2	6	0	0	.000	3	9	0	0	0.4	1.000
1971		1	3	.250	3.20	31	0	0	45	34	19	30	0	1	3	1	3	0	0	.000	0	6	0	0	0.2	1.000
1972	3 teams OAK A (2G 0–0) NY A (16G 0–1) TEX A (5G 0–0)																									
″	total	0	1	.000	5.28	23	0	0	30.2	39	18	17	0	0	1	0	1	0	0	.000	1	4	1	1	0.3	.833
10 yrs.		19	17	.528	3.22	216	29	6	449.2	357	229	272	1	9	8	9	84	6	0	.071	19	70	3	6	0.4	.967

Jose Roman

ROMAN, JOSE RAFAEL — BR TR 6′ 175 lbs.
Born Jose Rafael Roman (Sarita).
B. May 21, 1963, Puerto Plata, Dominican Republic.

Year	Team		W	L	PCT	ERA	G	GS	CG	IP	H	BB	SO	ShO	Relief Pitching W	L	SV	Batting AB	H	HR	BA	PO	A	E	DP	TC/G	FA
1984	**CLE**	**A**	0	2	.000	18.00	3	2	0	6	9	11	3	0	0	0	0	0	0	0	—	0	0	0	0	0.0	.000
1985			0	4	.000	6.61	5	3	0	16.1	13	14	12	0	0	1	0	0	0	0	—	3	1	1	0	1.0	.800
1986			1	2	.333	6.55	6	5	0	22	23	17	9	0	0	0	0	0	0	0	—	2	0	1	1	0.5	.667
3 yrs.			1	8	.111	8.12	14	10	0	44.1	45	42	24	0	0	1	0	0	0	0		5	1	2	1	0.6	.750

Ron Romanick

ROMANICK, RONALD JAMES — BR TR 6′ 4″ 195 lbs.
B. Nov. 6, 1960, Burley, Ida.

Year	Team		W	L	PCT	ERA	G	GS	CG	IP	H	BB	SO	ShO	Relief Pitching W	L	SV	Batting AB	H	HR	BA	PO	A	E	DP	TC/G	FA
1984	**CAL**	**A**	12	12	.500	3.76	33	33	8	229.2	240	61	87	2	0	0	0	0	0	0	—	18	24	6	3	1.5	.875
1985			14	9	.609	4.11	31	31	6	195	210	62	64	1	0	0	0	0	0	0	—	10	18	1	0	0.9	.966
1986			5	8	.385	5.50	18	18	1	106.1	124	44	38	1	0	0	0	0	0	0	—	13	8	0	1	1.2	1.000
3 yrs.			31	29	.517	4.24	82	82	15	531	574	167	189	4	0	0	0	0	0	0		41	50	7	4	1.2	.929

Jim Romano

ROMANO, JAMES KING — BR TR 6′ 4″ 190 lbs.
B. Apr. 6, 1927, Brooklyn, N. Y. D. Sept. 12, 1990, New York, N. Y.

Year	Team		W	L	PCT	ERA	G	GS	CG	IP	H	BB	SO	ShO	Relief Pitching W	L	SV	Batting AB	H	HR	BA	PO	A	E	DP	TC/G	FA
1950	**BKN**	**N**	0	0	—	5.68	3	1	0	6.1	8	2	8	0	0	0	0	1	0	0	.000	0	3	0	0	1.0	1.000

Dutch Romberger

ROMBERGER, ALLEN ISAIAH — BR TR 6′ 185 lbs.
B. May 26, 1927, Klingerstown, Pa. D. May 26, 1983, Weikert, Pa.

Year	Team		W	L	PCT	ERA	G	GS	CG	IP	H	BB	SO	ShO	Relief Pitching W	L	SV	Batting AB	H	HR	BA	PO	A	E	DP	TC/G	FA
1954	**PHI**	**A**	1	1	.500	11.49	10	0	0	15.2	28	12	6	0	1	1	0	2	0	0	.000	0	2	0	0	0.2	1.000

Ramon Romero

ROMERO, RAMON — BL TL 6′ 4″ 170 lbs.
Born Ramon Romero (De Los Santos).
B. Jan. 8, 1959, San Pedro de Macoris, Dominican Republic.

Year	Team		W	L	PCT	ERA	G	GS	CG	IP	H	BB	SO	ShO	Relief Pitching W	L	SV	Batting AB	H	HR	BA	PO	A	E	DP	TC/G	FA
1984	**CLE**	**A**	0	0	—	0.00	1	0	0	3	0	0	3	0	0	0	0	0	0	0	—	0	0	0	0	0.0	.000
1985			2	3	.400	6.58	19	10	0	64.1	69	38	38	0	0	0	0	0	0	0	—	0	6	0	0	0.3	1.000
2 yrs.			2	3	.400	6.28	20	10	0	67.1	69	38	41	0	0	0	0	0	0	0		0	6	0	0	0.3	1.000

Eddie Rommel

ROMMEL, EDWIN AMERICUS — BR TR 6′ 2″ 197 lbs.
B. Sept. 13, 1897, Baltimore, Md. D. Aug. 26, 1970, Baltimore, Md.

Year	Team		W	L	PCT	ERA	G	GS	CG	IP	H	BB	SO	ShO	Relief Pitching W	L	SV	Batting AB	H	HR	BA	PO	A	E	DP	TC/G	FA
1920	**PHI**	**A**	7	7	.500	2.85	33	12	8	173.2	165	43	43	2	3	1	1	51	11	0	.216	13	66	1	4	2.4	.988
1921			16	**23**	.410	3.94	46	32	20	285.1	312	87	71	0	4	7	3	94	18	0	.191	12	92	7	5	2.4	.937
1922			**27**	13	.675	3.28	**51**	33	22	294	294	63	54	3	**8**	1	2	94	17	0	.181	12	92	5	5	2.1	.954
1923			18	**19**	.486	3.27	**56**	31	19	297.2	306	108	76	3	3	4	5	101	24	0	.238	17	109	7	4	2.4	.947
1924			18	15	.545	3.95	43	34	21	278	302	94	72	3	1	1	1	95	15	0	.158	20	97	3	12	2.8	.975
1925			**21**	10	.677	3.69	52	28	14	261	285	95	67	1	7	2	3	81	15	1	.185	21	86	2	4	2.1	.982
1926			11	11	.500	3.08	37	26	12	219	225	54	52	3	2	1	0	61	6	0	.098	15	67	3	1	2.3	.965
1927			11	3	.786	4.36	30	17	8	146.2	166	48	33	2	0	1	1	51	8	0	.157	16	44	0	5	2.0	1.000
1928			13	5	.722	3.06	43	11	6	173.2	177	26	37	0	**8**	1	4	47	12	0	.255	8	51	0	5	1.4	1.000
1929			12	2	.857	2.85	32	6	4	113.2	135	34	25	0	**8**	2	4	39	8	0	.205	9	26	1	3	1.1	.972
1930			9	4	.692	4.28	35	9	5	130.1	142	27	35	0	5	3	3	38	10	0	.263	8	32	0	1	1.1	1.000
1931			7	5	.583	2.97	25	10	8	118	136	27	18	1	1	2	0	54	14	0	.259	8	25	2	1	1.2	.943
1932			1	2	.333	5.51	17	0	0	65.1	84	18	16	0	1	2	2	20	6	0	.300	3	23	1	1	1.6	.963
13 yrs.			171	119	.590	3.54	500	249	147	2556.1	2729	724	599	18	51	28	29	826	164	1	.199	162	810	32	51	2.0	.968
WORLD SERIES																											
1929	**PHI**	**A**	1	0	1.000	9.00	1	0	0	1	2	1	0	0	1	0	0	0	0	0	—	0	0	0	0	0.0	.000
1931			0	0	—	9.00	1	0	0	1	3	0	0	0	0	0	0	0	0	0	—	0	0	0	0	0.0	.000
2 yrs.			1	0	1.000	9.00	2	0	0	2	5	1	0	0	1	0	0	0	0	0		0	0	0	0	0.0	

Enrique Romo

ROMO, ENRIQUE — BR TR 5′11″ 185 lbs.
Born Enrique Romo (Navarro).
Brother of Vicente Romo.
B. July 15, 1947, Santa Rosalia, Mexico.

Year	Team		W	L	PCT	ERA	G	GS	CG	IP	H	BB	SO	ShO	Relief Pitching W	L	SV	Batting AB	H	HR	BA	PO	A	E	DP	TC/G	FA
1977	**SEA**	**A**	8	10	.444	2.84	58	3	0	114	93	39	105	0	8	9	16	0	0	0	—	5	19	1	3	0.4	.960
1978			11	7	.611	3.69	56	0	0	107.1	88	39	62	0	11	7	10	0	0	0	—	6	9	0	1	0.3	1.000
1979	**PIT**	**N**	10	5	.667	3.00	84	0	0	129	122	43	106	0	10	5	5	12	2	0	.167	10	25	1	3	0.4	.972
1980			5	5	.500	3.27	74	0	0	124	117	28	82	0	5	5	11	11	5	1	.455	10	20	1	1	0.4	.968
1981			1	3	.250	4.50	33	0	0	42	47	18	23	0	1	3	9	4	0	0	.000	5	3	0	1	0.2	1.000
1982			9	3	.750	4.36	45	0	0	86.2	81	36	58	0	9	3	1	10	3	0	.300	7	10	0	0	0.4	1.000
6 yrs.			44	33	.571	3.45	350	3	0	603	548	203	436	0	44	32	52	37	10	1	.270	43	86	3	9	0.4	.977
LEAGUE CHAMPIONSHIP SERIES																											
1979	**PIT**	**N**	0	0	—	0.00	2	0	0	0.1	3	1	1	0	0	0	0	0	0	0	—	0	0	0	0	0.0	.000
WORLD SERIES																											
1979	**PIT**	**N**	0	0	—	3.86	2	0	0	4.2	5	3	4	0	0	0	0	1	0	0	.000	0	1	0	0	0.5	1.000

Vicente Romo

ROMO, VICENTE (Huevo) — BR TR 6′ 1″ 180 lbs.
Born Vicente Romo (Navarro).
Brother of Enrique Romo.
B. Apr. 12, 1943, Santa Rosalia, Mexico.

Year	Team		W	L	PCT	ERA	G	GS	CG	IP	H	BB	SO	ShO	Relief Pitching W	L	SV	Batting AB	H	HR	BA	PO	A	E	DP	TC/G	FA
1968	**2 teams**	**LA N** (1G 0–0) **CLE A** (40G 5–3)																									
″	**total**		5	3	.625	1.60	41	1	0	84.1	44	32	54	0	5	2	12	14	2	0	.143	6	11	1	1	0.4	.944
1969	**2 teams**	**CLE A** (3G 1–1) **BOS A** (52G 7–9)																									
″	**total**		8	10	.444	3.13	55	11	4	135.1	123	53	96	1	3	8	11	33	5	0	.152	4	22	1	1	0.5	.963
1970	**BOS**	**A**	7	3	.700	4.08	48	10	0	108	115	43	71	0	6	0	6	27	4	1	.148	7	20	3	1	0.6	.900
1971	**CHI**	**A**	1	7	.125	3.38	45	2	0	72	52	37	48	0	1	5	5	11	4	0	.364	0	19	0	1	0.4	1.000
1972			3	0	1.000	3.31	28	0	0	51.2	47	18	46	0	3	0	1	9	0	0	.000	3	11	1	1	0.5	.933
1973	**SD**	**N**	2	3	.400	3.70	49	1	0	87.2	85	46	51	0	2	2	7	16	2	0	.125	5	15	2	1	0.4	.909
1974			5	5	.500	4.56	54	1	0	71	78	37	26	0	5	5	9	6	0	0	.000	2	21	2	1	0.5	.920
1982	**LA**	**N**	1	2	.333	3.03	15	6	0	35.2	25	14	24	0	0	1	1	5	1	0	.200	2	8	0	0	0.7	1.000
8 yrs.			32	33	.492	3.36	335	32	4	645.2	569	280	416	1	25	23	52	121	18	1	.149	29	127	10	7	0.5	.940

John Romonosky

ROMONOSKY, JOHN
B. July 7, 1929, Harrisburg, Ill.
BR TR 6′ 2″ 195 lbs.

Year	Team	W	L	PCT	ERA	G	GS	CG	IP	H	BB	SO	ShO	Relief Pitching W	Relief Pitching L	Relief Pitching SV	Batting AB	Batting H	Batting HR	BA	PO	A	E	DP	TC/G	FA
1953	STL N	0	0	—	4.70	2	2	0	7.2	9	4	3	0	0	0	0	2	0	0	.000	0	0	0	0	0.0	.000
1958	WAS A	2	4	.333	6.51	18	5	1	55.1	52	28	38	0	1	0	0	13	4	1	.308	2	10	0	0	0.7	1.000
1959		1	0	1.000	3.29	12	2	0	38.1	36	19	22	0	0	0	0	11	2	0	.182	1	6	0	1	0.6	1.000
3 yrs.		3	4	.429	5.15	32	9	1	101.1	97	51	63	0	1	0	0	26	6	1	.231	3	16	0	1	0.6	1.000

Gil Rondon

RONDON, GILBERTO
B. Nov. 18, 1953, Bronx, N. Y.
BR TR 6′ 2″ 200 lbs.

Year	Team	W	L	PCT	ERA	G	GS	CG	IP	H	BB	SO	ShO	Relief Pitching W	Relief Pitching L	Relief Pitching SV	Batting AB	Batting H	Batting HR	BA	PO	A	E	DP	TC/G	FA
1976	HOU N	2	2	.500	5.67	19	7	0	54	70	39	21	0	0	0	0	14	4	0	.286	5	4	0	0	0.5	1.000
1979	CHI A	0	0	—	3.60	4	0	0	10	11	6	3	0	0	0	0	0	0	0	—	0	1	0	0	0.3	1.000
2 yrs.		2	2	.500	5.34	23	7	0	64	81	45	24	0	0	0	0	14	4	0	.286	5	5	0	0	0.4	1.000

Jim Rooker

ROOKER, JAMES PHILLIP
B. Sept. 23, 1942, Lakeview, Ore.
BR TL 6′ 195 lbs.

Year	Team	W	L	PCT	ERA	G	GS	CG	IP	H	BB	SO	ShO	Relief Pitching W	Relief Pitching L	Relief Pitching SV	Batting AB	Batting H	Batting HR	BA	PO	A	E	DP	TC/G	FA
1968	DET A	0	0	—	3.86	2	0	0	4.2	4	1	4	0	0	0	0	2	0	0	.000	0	2	0	0	1.0	1.000
1969	KC A	4	16	.200	3.75	28	22	8	158.1	136	73	108	1	0	1	0	57	16	4	.281	3	24	4	0	1.1	.871
1970		10	15	.400	3.53	38	29	6	204	190	102	117	3	0	0	1	70	14	1	.200	6	32	2	4	1.0	.950
1971		2	7	.222	5.33	20	7	1	54	59	24	31	1	1	1	0	10	0	0	.000	1	5	1	1	0.3	.857
1972		5	6	.455	4.38	18	10	4	72	78	24	44	2	1	0	0	20	2	0	.100	3	16	0	1	1.1	1.000
1973	PIT N	10	6	.625	2.85	41	18	6	170.1	143	52	122	3	1	1	5	49	12	0	.245	6	29	2	3	0.9	.946
1974		15	11	.577	2.77	33	33	15	263	228	83	139	1	0	0	0	95	29	0	.305	14	45	1	3	1.8	.983
1975		13	11	.542	2.97	28	28	7	197	177	76	102	1	0	0	0	63	6	0	.095	10	32	4	1	1.6	.913
1976		15	8	.652	3.35	30	29	10	198.2	201	72	92	1	0	0	1	74	16	1	.216	8	29	2	1	1.3	.949
1977		14	9	.609	3.09	30	30	7	204	196	64	89	2	0	0	0	70	13	0	.186	6	27	2	2	1.2	.943
1978		9	11	.450	4.25	28	28	1	163	160	81	76	0	0	0	0	56	9	0	.161	14	24	0	5	1.4	1.000
1979		4	7	.364	4.59	19	17	1	104	106	39	44	0	0	1	0	33	4	0	.121	8	13	2	1	1.2	.913
1980		2	2	.500	3.50	4	4	0	18	16	12	8	0	0	0	0	7	1	1	.143	1	4	0	0	1.3	1.000
13 yrs.		103	109	.486	3.46	319	255	66	1811	1694	703	976	15	3	4	7	606	122	7	.201	80	282	20	22	1.2	.948
LEAGUE CHAMPIONSHIP SERIES																										
1974	PIT N	0	0	—	2.57	1	1	0	7	6	5	4	0	0	0	0	2	1	0	.500	0	3	1	0	4.0	.750
1975		0	1	.000	9.00	1	1	0	4	7	0	5	0	0	0	0	1	0	0	.000	0	0	0	0	0.0	.000
2 yrs.		0	1	.000	4.91	2	2	0	11	13	5	9	0	0	0	0	3	1	0	.333	0	3	1	0	2.0	.750
WORLD SERIES																										
1979	PIT N	0	0	—	1.04	2	1	0	8.2	5	3	4	0	0	0	0	2	0	0	.000	1	2	0	0	1.5	1.000

Charlie Root

ROOT, CHARLES HENRY (Chinski)
B. Mar. 17, 1899, Middletown, Ohio D. Nov. 5, 1970, Hollister, Calif.
BR TR 5′10½″ 190 lbs.

Year	Team	W	L	PCT	ERA	G	GS	CG	IP	H	BB	SO	ShO	Relief Pitching W	Relief Pitching L	Relief Pitching SV	Batting AB	Batting H	Batting HR	BA	PO	A	E	DP	TC/G	FA
1923	STL A	0	4	.000	5.70	27	2	0	60	68	18	27	0	0	2	0	13	1	0	.077	1	13	0	0	0.5	1.000
1926	CHI N	18	**17**	.514	2.82	42	32	21	271.1	267	62	127	2	2	3	2	91	13	1	.143	8	58	4	4	1.7	.943
1927		**26**	15	.634	3.76	**48**	36	21	**309**	296	**117**	145	4	5	2	2	122	27	0	.221	6	49	2	2	1.2	.965
1928		14	18	.438	3.57	40	30	13	237	214	73	122	1	1	2	2	73	13	0	.178	6	39	1	2	1.1	.978
1929		19	6	**.760**	3.47	43	31	19	272	286	83	124	4	2	0	5	96	15	1	.156	12	35	1	2	1.1	.979
1930		16	14	.533	4.33	37	30	15	220.1	247	63	124	**4**	0	1	3	80	21	1	.263	9	27	0	1	1.0	1.000
1931		17	14	.548	3.48	39	31	19	251	240	71	131	3	2	1	2	90	20	0	.222	3	38	1	0	1.1	.976
1932		15	10	.600	3.58	39	23	11	216.1	211	55	96	0	3	2	3	76	13	1	.171	8	32	0	0	1.0	1.000
1933		15	10	.600	2.60	35	30	20	242.1	232	61	86	2	1	1	0	85	8	0	.094	11	36	1	4	1.4	.979
1934		4	7	.364	4.28	34	9	2	117.2	141	53	46	0	3	2	0	40	7	2	.175	2	23	0	1	0.7	1.000
1935		15	8	.652	3.08	38	18	11	201.1	193	47	94	1	**5**	3	2	69	14	1	.203	7	27	1	0	0.9	.971
1936		3	6	.333	4.15	33	4	0	73.2	81	20	32	0	2	5	1	15	5	0	.333	2	10	0	1	0.4	1.000
1937		13	5	.722	3.38	43	15	5	178.2	173	32	74	0	**8**	0	5	67	12	1	.179	8	36	1	2	1.0	.978
1938		8	7	.533	2.86	44	11	5	160.2	163	30	70	0	4	1	8	48	8	0	.167	5	23	1	0	0.7	.966
1939		8	8	.500	4.03	35	16	8	167.1	189	34	65	0	1	1	4	57	10	2	.175	2	22	2	0	0.7	.923
1940		2	4	.333	3.82	36	8	1	113	118	33	50	0	2	0	1	31	4	0	.129	3	22	0	0	0.7	1.000
1941		8	7	.533	5.40	19	15	6	106.2	133	37	46	0	1	0	0	33	5	1	.152	2	16	0	2	0.9	1.000
17 yrs.		201	160	.557	3.58	632	341	177	3198.1	3252	889	1459	21	42	26	40	1086	196	11	.180	95	506	15	21	1.0	.976
WORLD SERIES																										
1929	CHI N	0	1	.000	4.72	2	2	0	13.1	12	2	8	0	0	0	0	5	0	0	.000	0	0	0	0	0.0	.000
1932		0	1	.000	10.38	1	1	0	4.1	6	3	4	0	0	0	0	2	0	0	.000	0	0	0	0	0.0	.000
1935		0	1	.000	18.00	2	1	0	2	5	1	2	0	0	0	0	0	0	0	—	0	1	0	0	0.5	1.000
1938		0	0	—	3.00	1	0	0	3	3	0	1	0	0	0	0	0	0	0	—	0	0	0	0	0.0	.000
4 yrs.		0	3	.000	6.75	6	4	0	22.2	26	6	15	0	0	0	0	7	0	0	.000	0	1	0	0	0.2	1.000

John Roper

ROPER, JOHN CHRISTOPHER
B. Nov. 21, 1971, Southern Pines, N. C.
BR TR 6′ 175 lbs.

Year	Team	W	L	PCT	ERA	G	GS	CG	IP	H	BB	SO	ShO	Relief Pitching W	Relief Pitching L	Relief Pitching SV	Batting AB	Batting H	Batting HR	BA	PO	A	E	DP	TC/G	FA
1993	CIN N	2	5	.286	5.63	16	15	0	80	92	36	54	0	0	0	0	28	5	0	.179	7	8	0	0	0.9	1.000
1994		6	2	.750	4.50	16	15	0	92	90	30	51	0	0	0	0	33	6	0	.182	5	13	2	2	1.3	.900
1995	2 teams	CIN N (2G 0–0)	SF N (1G 0–0)																							
"	total	0	0		12.38	3	2	0	8	15	6	6	0	0	0	0	1	0	0	.000	0	1	0	0	0.3	1.000
3 yrs.		8	7	.533	5.35	35	32	0	180	197	72	111	0	0	0	0	62	11	0	.177	12	22	2	2	1.0	.944

Chuck Rose

ROSE, CHARLES ALFRED
B. Sept. 1, 1885, Macon, Mo. D. Aug. 4, 1961, Salina, Kans.
BL TL 5′ 8½″ 158 lbs.

Year	Team	W	L	PCT	ERA	G	GS	CG	IP	H	BB	SO	ShO	Relief Pitching W	Relief Pitching L	Relief Pitching SV	Batting AB	Batting H	Batting HR	BA	PO	A	E	DP	TC/G	FA
1909	STL A	1	2	.333	5.40	3	3	3	25	32	7	6	0	0	0	0	7	1	1	.143	1	4	2	0	2.3	.714

Don Rose

ROSE, DONALD GARY
B. Mar. 19, 1947, Covina, Calif.
BR TR 6′ 3″ 195 lbs.

Year	Team	W	L	PCT	ERA	G	GS	CG	IP	H	BB	SO	ShO	Relief Pitching W	Relief Pitching L	Relief Pitching SV	Batting AB	Batting H	Batting HR	BA	PO	A	E	DP	TC/G	FA
1971	NY N	0	0	—	0.00	1	0	0	2	2	0	1	0	0	0	0	0	0	0	—	0	0	0	0	0.0	.000
1972	CAL A	1	4	.200	4.19	16	4	0	43	49	19	39	0	0	2	0	10	2	1	.200	3	3	0	0	0.4	1.000
1974	SF N	0	0	—	9.00	2	0	0	1	4	1	0	0	0	0	0	0	0	0	—	0	0	0	0	0.0	.000
3 yrs.		1	4	.200	4.11	19	4	0	46	55	20	40	0	0	2	0	10	2	1	.200	3	3	0	0	0.3	1.000

Zeke Rosebraugh

ROSEBRAUGH, ELI ETHELBERT TL
B. Sept. 8, 1870, Charleston, Ill. D. July 16, 1930, Fresno, Calif.

Year	Team		W	L	PCT	ERA	G	GS	CG	IP	H	BB	SO	ShO	Relief Pitching W	L	SV	Batting AB	H	HR	BA	PO	A	E	DP	TC/G	FA
1898	PIT	N	0	2	.000	3.32	4	2	2	21.2	23	9	6	0	0	0	0	8	3	0	.375	1	4	0	0	1.3	1.000
1899			0	1	.000	9.00	2	2	0	6	14	3	2	0	0	0	0	2	0	0	.000	0	1	0	0	0.5	1.000
2 yrs.			0	3	.000	4.55	6	4	2	27.2	37	12	8	0	0	0	0	10	3	0	.300	1	5	0	0	1.0	1.000

Chief Roseman

ROSEMAN, JAMES JOHN BR TR 5′ 7″ 167 lbs.
B. July 4, 1856, Brooklyn, N. Y. D. July 4, 1938, Brooklyn, N. Y.
Manager 1890.

Year	Team		W	L	PCT	ERA	G	GS	CG	IP	H	BB	SO	ShO	Relief Pitching W	L	SV	Batting AB	H	HR	BA	PO	A	E	DP	TC/G	FA
1885	NY	AA	0	1	.000	*27.00*	1	1	0	1	3	2	0	0	0	0	0	410	114	3	.278	107	21	22	6	1.8	.853
1886			0	0	—	*5.14*	1	0	0	7	6	0	0	0	0	0	0	559	127	5	.227	203	20	27	6	1.9	.892
1887			0	0	—	*7.88*	2	0	0	8	11	5	1	0	0	0	0	317	72	0	.227	166	11	27	4	2.4	.868
3 yrs.			0	1	.000	7.88	4	1	0	16	20	7	1	0	0	0	0	*				1229	109	173	39	2.2	.886

Steve Rosenberg

ROSENBERG, STEVEN ALLEN BL TL 6′ 186 lbs.
B. Oct. 31, 1964, Brooklyn, N. Y.

Year	Team		W	L	PCT	ERA	G	GS	CG	IP	H	BB	SO	ShO	Relief Pitching W	L	SV	Batting AB	H	HR	BA	PO	A	E	DP	TC/G	FA
1988	CHI	A	0	1	.000	4.30	33	0	0	46	53	19	28	0	0	1	1	0	0	0	—	0	6	0	0	0.2	1.000
1989			4	13	.235	4.94	38	21	2	142	148	58	77	0	1	2	0	0	0	0	—	8	20	3	5	0.8	.903
1990			1	0	1.000	5.40	6	0	0	10	10	5	4	0	1	0	0	0	0	0	—	1	2	0	0	0.5	1.000
1991	SD	N	1	1	.500	6.94	10	0	0	11.2	11	5	6	0	1	1	0	1	0	0	.000	0	1	0	0	0.1	1.000
4 yrs.			6	15	.286	4.94	87	21	2	209.2	222	87	115	0	3	4	1	1	0	0	.000	9	29	3	5	0.5	.927

Wayne Rosenthal

ROSENTHAL, WAYNE SCOTT BR TR 6′ 5″ 220 lbs.
B. Feb. 19, 1965, Brooklyn, N. Y.

Year	Team		W	L	PCT	ERA	G	GS	CG	IP	H	BB	SO	ShO	Relief Pitching W	L	SV	Batting AB	H	HR	BA	PO	A	E	DP	TC/G	FA
1991	TEX	A	1	4	.200	5.25	36	0	0	70.1	72	36	61	0	1	4	1	0	0	0	—	4	4	1	0	0.3	.889
1992			0	0	—	7.71	6	0	0	4.2	7	2	1	0	0	0	0	0	0	0	—	0	1	0	0	0.2	1.000
2 yrs.			1	4	.200	5.40	42	0	0	75	79	38	62	0	1	4	1	0	0	0		4	5	1	0	0.2	.900

Steve Roser

ROSER, EMERSON COREY BR TR 6′ 4″ 220 lbs.
B. Jan. 25, 1918, Rome, N. Y.

Year	Team		W	L	PCT	ERA	G	GS	CG	IP	H	BB	SO	ShO	Relief Pitching W	L	SV	Batting AB	H	HR	BA	PO	A	E	DP	TC/G	FA
1944	NY	A	4	3	.571	3.86	16	6	1	84	80	34	34	0	2	1	1	30	3	0	.100	4	13	1	1	1.1	.944
1945			0	0	—	3.67	11	0	0	27	27	8	11	0	0	0	0	8	1	0	.125	2	6	0	0	0.7	1.000
1946	2 teams	NY A	(4G 1–1)		BOS N	(14G 1–1)																					
″	total		2	2	.500	4.70	18	2	0	38.1	40	22	19	0	2	0	1	5	0	0	.000	2	6	0	0	0.4	1.000
3 yrs.			6	5	.545	4.04	45	8	1	149.1	147	64	64	0	4	1	2	43	4	0	.093	8	25	1	1	0.8	.971

Bob Ross

ROSS, FLOYD ROBERT BR TL 6′ 165 lbs.
B. Nov. 2, 1928, Fullerton, Calif.

Year	Team		W	L	PCT	ERA	G	GS	CG	IP	H	BB	SO	ShO	Relief Pitching W	L	SV	Batting AB	H	HR	BA	PO	A	E	DP	TC/G	FA
1950	WAS	A	0	1	.000	8.53	6	2	0	12.2	15	15	2	0	0	0	0	3	0	0	.000	0	4	0	0	0.7	1.000
1951			0	1	.000	6.54	11	1	0	31.2	36	21	23	0	0	0	0	9	1	0	.111	0	2	1	0	0.3	.667
1956	PHI	N	0	0	—	8.10	3	0	0	3.1	4	2	4	0	0	0	0	0	0	0	—	0	2	0	0	0.7	1.000
3 yrs.			0	2	.000	7.17	20	3	0	47.2	55	38	29	0	0	0	0	12	1	0	.083	0	8	1	0	0.4	.889

Buck Ross

ROSS, LEE RAVON BR TR 6′ 2″ 170 lbs.
B. Feb. 2, 1915, Norwood, N. C. D. Nov. 23, 1978, Charlotte, N. C.

Year	Team		W	L	PCT	ERA	G	GS	CG	IP	H	BB	SO	ShO	Relief Pitching W	L	SV	Batting AB	H	HR	BA	PO	A	E	DP	TC/G	FA
1936	PHI	A	9	14	.391	5.83	30	27	12	200.2	253	83	47	1	0	0	0	71	12	0	.169	6	30	3	4	1.3	.923
1937			5	10	.333	4.89	28	22	7	147.1	183	63	37	1	0	0	0	49	5	0	.102	7	28	1	2	1.3	.972
1938			9	16	.360	5.32	29	28	10	184.1	218	80	54	0	0	0	0	63	12	1	.190	5	36	2	2	1.5	.953
1939			6	14	.300	6.00	29	28	6	174	216	95	43	1	0	0	0	58	12	0	.207	9	20	2	1	1.1	.935
1940			5	10	.333	4.38	24	19	10	156.1	160	60	43	0	0	0	1	53	7	1	.132	12	23	3	0	1.6	.921
1941	2 teams	PHI A	(1G 0–1)		CHI A	(20G 3–8)																					
″	total		3	9	.250	3.69	21	12	7	112.1	109	45	30	0	1	0	0	33	7	0	.212	4	15	2	2	1.0	.905
1942	CHI	A	5	7	.417	5.00	22	14	4	113.1	118	39	37	2	0	2	1	38	6	0	.158	4	12	0	0	0.7	1.000
1943			11	7	.611	3.19	21	21	7	149.1	140	56	41	1	0	0	0	46	4	1	.087	5	26	0	1	1.5	1.000
1944			2	7	.222	5.18	20	9	2	90.1	97	35	20	0	1	3	0	26	2	0	.077	1	8	0	0	0.4	1.000
1945			1	1	.500	5.79	13	2	0	37.1	51	17	8	0	1	0	0	11	2	0	.182	0	6	0	0	0.5	1.000
10 yrs.			56	95	.371	4.94	237	182	65	1365.1	1545	573	360	6	3	5	2	448	69	3	.154	53	204	13	12	1.1	.952

Buster Ross

ROSS, CHESTER FRANKLIN BL TL 6′ 1″ 195 lbs.
B. Mar. 11, 1903, Kuttawa, Ky. D. Apr. 24, 1982, Mayfield, Ky.

Year	Team		W	L	PCT	ERA	G	GS	CG	IP	H	BB	SO	ShO	Relief Pitching W	L	SV	Batting AB	H	HR	BA	PO	A	E	DP	TC/G	FA
1924	BOS	A	4	3	.571	3.47	30	2	1	93.1	109	30	16	1	3	2	1	25	5	0	.200	4	16	0	0	0.7	1.000
1925			3	8	.273	6.20	33	8	0	94.1	119	40	15	0	2	2	0	24	3	0	.125	1	24	5	0	0.9	.833
1926			0	1	.000	16.88	1	0	0	2.2	5	4	0	0	0	1	0	1	0	0	.000	0	1	0	0	1.0	1.000
3 yrs.			7	12	.368	5.01	64	10	1	190.1	233	74	31	1	5	5	1	50	8	0	.160	5	41	5	0	0.8	.902

Cliff Ross

ROSS, CLIFFORD DAVIS BL TL 6′ 4″ 195 lbs.
B. Aug. 3, 1928, Philadelphia, Pa.

Year	Team		W	L	PCT	ERA	G	GS	CG	IP	H	BB	SO	ShO	Relief Pitching W	L	SV	Batting AB	H	HR	BA	PO	A	E	DP	TC/G	FA
1954	CIN	N	0	0	—	0.00	4	0	0	2.2	0	0	1	0	0	0	1	0	0	0	—	0	1	0	0	0.3	1.000

Ernie Ross

ROSS, ERNEST BERTRAM (Curly) BL TL 5′ 8″ 150 lbs.
B. Mar. 31, 1880, Toronto, Ont., Canada D. Mar. 28, 1950, Toronto, Ont., Canada.

Year	Team		W	L	PCT	ERA	G	GS	CG	IP	H	BB	SO	ShO	Relief Pitching W	L	SV	Batting AB	H	HR	BA	PO	A	E	DP	TC/G	FA
1902	BAL	A	1	1	.500	7.41	2	2	2	17	20	12	2	0	0	0	0	8	0	0	.000	1	1	2	0	2.0	.500

Gary Ross

ROSS, GARY DOUGLAS BR TR 6′ 1″ 185 lbs.
B. Sept. 16, 1947, McKeesport, Pa.

Year	Team		W	L	PCT	ERA	G	GS	CG	IP	H	BB	SO	ShO	Relief Pitching W	L	SV	Batting AB	H	HR	BA	PO	A	E	DP	TC/G	FA
1968	CHI	N	1	1	.500	4.17	13	5	1	41	44	25	31	0	0	0	0	11	1	0	.091	2	7	0	0	0.7	1.000
1969	2 teams	CHI N	(2G 0–0)		SD N	(46G 3–12)																					
″	total		3	12	.200	4.35	48	8	0	111.2	105	58	60	0	3	6	3	23	0	0	.000	6	27	2	2	0.7	.943
1970	SD	N	2	3	.400	5.23	33	2	0	62	72	36	39	0	2	3	1	8	4	0	.500	3	12	0	1	0.5	1.000
1971			1	3	.250	3.00	13	0	0	24	27	11	13	0	1	3	0	1	0	0	.000	3	3	0	0	0.5	1.000
1972			4	3	.571	2.45	60	0	0	91.2	87	49	46	0	4	3	3	13	2	0	.154	10	16	1	3	0.4	.963
1973			4	4	.500	5.42	58	0	0	76.1	93	33	44	0	4	4	0	4	0	0	.000	8	10	0	2	0.3	1.000
1974			0	0	—	4.50	9	0	0	18	23	6	11	0	0	0	0	1	0	0	.000	1	4	0	0	0.6	1.000
1975	CAL	A	0	1	.000	5.40	1	1	0	5	6	1	4	0	0	0	0	0	0	0	—	0	0	0	0	0.0	.000

Gary Ross *continued*

Year	Team	W	L	PCT	ERA	G	GS	CG	IP	H	BB	SO	ShO	Relief Pitching W	L	SV	Batting AB	H	HR	BA	PO	A	E	DP	TC/G	FA
1976		8	16	.333	3.00	34	31	7	225	224	58	100	2	0	0	0	0	0	0	—	23	55	1	1	2.3	.987
1977		2	4	.333	5.59	14	12	0	58	83	11	30	0	0	0	0	0	0	0	—	9	10	2	0	1.5	.905
10 yrs.		25	47	.347	3.93	283	59	8	712.2	764	288	378	2	14	19	7	61	7	0	.115	65	144	6	9	0.8	.972

George Ross

ROSS, GEORGE SIDNEY BL TL 5′10½″ 175 lbs.
B. June 27, 1892, San Rafael, Calif. D. Apr. 22, 1935, Amityville, N. Y.

Year	Team	W	L	PCT	ERA	G	GS	CG	IP	H	BB	SO	ShO	Relief Pitching W	L	SV	Batting AB	H	HR	BA	PO	A	E	DP	TC/G	FA
1918	NY N	0	0	—	0.00	1	0	0	2.1	2	3	2	0	0	0	1	1	0	0	.000	1	1	0	0	2.0	1.000

Mark Ross

ROSS, MARK JOSEPH BR TR 6′ 195 lbs.
B. Aug. 8, 1954, Galveston, Tex.

Year	Team	W	L	PCT	ERA	G	GS	CG	IP	H	BB	SO	ShO	Relief Pitching W	L	SV	Batting AB	H	HR	BA	PO	A	E	DP	TC/G	FA
1982	HOU N	0	0	—	1.50	4	0	0	6	3	0	4	0	0	0	0	0	0	0	—	0	1	0	0	0.3	1.000
1984		1	0	1.000	0.00	2	0	0	2.1	1	0	1	0	1	0	0	0	0	0	—	0	0	0	0	0.0	.000
1985		0	2	.000	4.85	8	0	0	13	12	2	3	0	0	2	1	1	0	0	.000	2	2	0	0	0.5	1.000
1987	PIT N	0	0	—	9.00	1	0	0	1	1	0	0	0	0	0	0	0	0	0	—	0	1	0	0	1.0	1.000
1988	TOR A	0	0	—	4.91	3	0	0	7.1	5	4	4	0	0	0	0	0	0	0	—	0	0	0	0	0.0	.000
1990	PIT N	1	0	1.000	3.55	9	0	0	12.2	11	4	5	0	1	0	0	1	0	0	.000	1	3	0	0	0.4	1.000
6 yrs.		2	2	.500	3.83	27	0	0	42.1	33	10	17	0	2	2	1	2	0	0	.000	3	7	0	0	0.4	1.000

Joe Rosselli

ROSSELLI, JOSEPH DONALD BR TL 6′ 1″ 170 lbs.
B. May 28, 1972, Burbank, Calif.

Year	Team	W	L	PCT	ERA	G	GS	CG	IP	H	BB	SO	ShO	Relief Pitching W	L	SV	Batting AB	H	HR	BA	PO	A	E	DP	TC/G	FA
1995	SF N	2	1	.667	8.70	9	5	0	30	39	20	7	0	0	0	0	10	2	0	.200	0	5	0	1	0.6	1.000

Frank Rosso

ROSSO, FRANCIS JAMES BR TR 5′11″ 180 lbs.
B. Mar. 1, 1921, Agawam, Mass. D. Jan. 26, 1980, Springfield, Mass.

Year	Team	W	L	PCT	ERA	G	GS	CG	IP	H	BB	SO	ShO	Relief Pitching W	L	SV	Batting AB	H	HR	BA	PO	A	E	DP	TC/G	FA
1944	NY N	0	0	—	9.00	2	0	0	4	11	3	1	0	0	0	0	0	0	0	—	0	3	0	0	1.5	1.000

Marv Rotblatt

ROTBLATT, MARVIN (Rotty) BB TL 5′ 7″ 160 lbs.
B. Oct. 18, 1927, Chicago, Ill.

Year	Team	W	L	PCT	ERA	G	GS	CG	IP	H	BB	SO	ShO	Relief Pitching W	L	SV	Batting AB	H	HR	BA	PO	A	E	DP	TC/G	FA
1948	CHI A	0	1	.000	7.85	7	2	0	18.1	19	23	4	0	0	0	0	4	0	0	.000	0	1	0	0	0.1	1.000
1950		0	0	—	6.23	2	0	0	8.2	11	5	6	0	0	0	0	2	0	0	.000	1	3	0	0	2.0	1.000
1951		4	2	.667	3.40	26	2	0	47.2	44	23	20	0	3	2	2	9	0	0	.000	5	11	0	1	0.6	1.000
3 yrs.		4	3	.571	4.82	35	4	0	74.2	74	51	30	0	3	2	2	15	0	0	.000	6	15	0	1	0.6	1.000

Jack Rothrock

ROTHROCK, JOHN HOUSTON BB TR 5′11½″ 165 lbs.
B. Mar. 14, 1905, Long Beach, Calif. D. Feb. 2, 1980, San Bernardino, Calif.

Year	Team	W	L	PCT	ERA	G	GS	CG	IP	H	BB	SO	ShO	Relief Pitching W	L	SV	Batting AB	H	HR	BA	PO	A	E	DP	TC/G	FA
1928	BOS A	0	0	—	0.00	1	0	0	1	0	0	0	0	0	0	0	*				37	38	9	6	3.8	.893

Larry Rothschild

ROTHSCHILD, LAWRENCE LEE BL TR 6′ 2″ 180 lbs.
B. Mar. 12, 1954, Chicago, Ill.

Year	Team	W	L	PCT	ERA	G	GS	CG	IP	H	BB	SO	ShO	Relief Pitching W	L	SV	Batting AB	H	HR	BA	PO	A	E	DP	TC/G	FA
1981	DET A	0	0	—	1.50	5	0	0	6	4	6	1	0	0	0	1	0	0	0	—	1	3	0	0	0.8	1.000
1982		0	0	—	13.50	2	0	0	2.2	4	2	0	0	0	0	0	0	0	0	—	0	0	0	0	0.0	.000
2 yrs.		0	0		5.19	7	0	0	8.2	8	8	1	0	0	0	1	0	0	0		1	3	0	0	0.6	1.000

Virle Rounsaville

ROUNSAVILLE, VIRLE GENE BR TR 6′ 3″ 205 lbs.
B. Sept. 27, 1944, Konawa, Okla.

Year	Team	W	L	PCT	ERA	G	GS	CG	IP	H	BB	SO	ShO	Relief Pitching W	L	SV	Batting AB	H	HR	BA	PO	A	E	DP	TC/G	FA
1970	CHI A	0	1	.000	10.50	8	0	0	6	10	2	3	0	0	1	0	0	0	0	—	0	1	1	0	0.3	.500

Jack Rowan

ROWAN, JOHN ALBERT BR TR 6′ 1″ 210 lbs.
B. June 16, 1887, New Castle, Pa. D. Sept. 29, 1966, Dayton, Ohio.

Year	Team	W	L	PCT	ERA	G	GS	CG	IP	H	BB	SO	ShO	Relief Pitching W	L	SV	Batting AB	H	HR	BA	PO	A	E	DP	TC/G	FA
1906	DET A	0	1	.000	11.00	1	1	1	9	15	6	0	0	0	0	0	4	1	0	.250	1	1	0	0	2.0	1.000
1908	CIN N	3	3	.500	1.82	8	7	4	49.1	46	16	24	1	1	0	0	14	1	0	.071	1	17	1	0	2.4	.947
1909		11	12	.478	2.79	38	23	14	225.2	185	104	81	0	3	0	0	65	6	0	.092	7	40	3	2	1.3	.940
1910		14	13	.519	2.93	42	30	18	261	242	105	108	4	3	3	1	83	19	0	.229	3	56	6	1	1.5	.908
1911	2 teams PHI N (12G 2–4) CHI N (1G 0–0)																									
″	total	2	4	.333	4.72	13	6	2	47.2	60	22	17	0	0	1	0	14	1	0	.071	0	17	0	1	1.3	1.000
1913	CIN N	0	4	.000	3.00	5	5	5	39	37	9	21	0	0	0	0	11	2	0	.182	0	9	1	0	2.0	.900
1914		1	3	.250	3.46	12	2	0	39	38	10	16	0	1	1	1	8	0	0	.000	0	8	0	0	0.7	1.000
7 yrs.		31	40	.437	3.07	119	74	44	670.2	623	272	267	5	8	5	2	199	30	0	.151	12	148	11	4	1.4	.936

Dave Rowe

ROWE, DAVID ELWOOD (Eli) BR TR 5′ 9″ 180 lbs.
Brother of Jack Rowe.
B. Oct. 9, 1854, Harrisburg, Pa. D. Dec. 9, 1930, Glendale, Calif.
Manager 1886, 1888.

Year	Team	W	L	PCT	ERA	G	GS	CG	IP	H	BB	SO	ShO	Relief Pitching W	L	SV	Batting AB	H	HR	BA	PO	A	E	DP	TC/G	FA
1877	CHI N	0	1	.000	18.00	1	1	0	1	3	2	0	0	0	0	0	7	2	0	.286	2	0	1	0	1.0	.667
1882	CLE N	0	1	.000	12.00	1	1	1	9	29	7	0	0	0	0	0	97	25	1	.258	33	4	7	1	1.8	.841
1883	BAL AA	0	0	—	20.25	1	0	0	4	12	2	1	0	0	0	0	256	80	0	.313	98	21	23	2	2.3	.838
1884	STL U	1	0	1.000	*2.00*	1	1	1	9	10	0	2	0	0	0	0	485	142	3	.293	174	62	30	6	2.4	.887
4 yrs.		1	2	.333	9.78	4	3	2	23	54	11	3	0	0	0	0	*				574	160	114	22	2.4	.866

Don Rowe

ROWE, DONALD HOWARD BL TL 6′ 180 lbs.
B. Apr. 3, 1936, Brawley, Calif.

Year	Team	W	L	PCT	ERA	G	GS	CG	IP	H	BB	SO	ShO	Relief Pitching W	L	SV	Batting AB	H	HR	BA	PO	A	E	DP	TC/G	FA
1963	NY N	0	0	—	4.28	26	1	0	54.2	59	21	27	0	0	0	0	13	3	0	.231	3	5	2	1	0.4	.800

Ken Rowe

ROWE, KENNETH DARRELL BR TR 6′ 2″ 185 lbs.
B. Dec. 31, 1933, Ferndale, Mich.

Year	Team	W	L	PCT	ERA	G	GS	CG	IP	H	BB	SO	ShO	Relief Pitching W	L	SV	Batting AB	H	HR	BA	PO	A	E	DP	TC/G	FA
1963	LA N	1	1	.500	2.93	14	0	0	27.2	28	11	12	0	1	1	1	5	0	0	.000	0	6	3	1	0.6	.667
1964	BAL A	1	0	1.000	8.31	6	0	0	4.1	10	1	4	0	1	0	0	0	0	0	—	1	2	1	0	0.7	.750
1965		0	0	—	3.38	6	0	0	13.1	17	2	3	0	0	0	0	1	1	0	1.000	0	0	1	0	0.2	.000
3 yrs.		2	1	.667	3.57	26	0	0	45.1	55	14	19	0	2	1	1	6	1	0	.167	1	8	5	1	0.5	.643

Schoolboy Rowe

ROWE, LYNWOOD THOMAS BR TR 6′ 4½″ 210 lbs.
B. Jan. 11, 1910, Waco, Tex. D. Jan. 8, 1961, El Dorado, Ark.

Year	Team	W	L	PCT	ERA	G	GS	CG	IP	H	BB	SO	ShO	Relief Pitching W	Relief Pitching L	Relief Pitching SV	Batting AB	Batting H	Batting HR	BA	PO	A	E	DP	TC/G	FA
1933	DET A	7	4	.636	3.58	19	15	8	123.1	129	31	75	1	1	0	0	50	11	0	.220	1	33	0	1	1.8	1.000
1934		24	8	.750	3.45	45	30	20	266	259	81	149	4	6	1	1	109	33	2	.303	9	46	0	3	1.2	1.000
1935		19	13	.594	3.69	42	34	21	275.2	272	68	140	**6**	3	0	3	109	34	3	.312	11	42	1	1	1.3	.981
1936		19	10	.655	4.51	41	35	19	245.1	266	64	115	4	1	0	3	90	23	1	.256	10	50	1	3	1.5	.984
1937		1	4	.200	8.62	10	2	1	31.1	49	9	6	0	1	2	0	10	2	0	.200	6	6	0	0	1.2	1.000
1938		0	2	.000	3.00	4	3	0	21	20	11	4	0	0	0	0	6	1	0	.167	0	8	1	0	2.3	.889
1939		10	12	.455	4.99	28	24	8	164	192	61	51	1	1	1	0	61	15	1	.246	9	27	2	5	1.4	.947
1940		16	3	**.842**	3.46	27	23	11	169	170	43	61	1	1	0	0	67	18	1	.269	10	28	0	2	1.4	1.000
1941		8	6	.571	4.14	27	14	4	139	155	33	54	0	4	2	1	55	15	1	.273	9	29	3	2	1.5	.927
1942	2 teams DET A (2G 1–0) BKN N (9G 1–0)																									
″	total	2	0	1.000	3.98	11	3	0	40.2	45	14	13	0	0	0	0	23	4	0	.174	2	11	0	0	1.2	1.000
1943	PHI N	14	8	.636	2.94	27	25	11	199	194	29	52	3	0	0	1	120	36	4	.300	9	42	1	4	1.9	.981
1946		11	4	.733	2.12	17	16	9	136	112	21	51	2	0	0	0	61	11	1	.180	2	20	0	0	1.3	1.000
1947		14	10	.583	4.32	31	28	15	195.2	232	45	74	1	0	0	1	79	22	2	.278	6	32	1	0	1.3	.974
1948		10	10	.500	4.07	30	20	8	148	167	31	46	0	1	2	2	52	10	1	.192	9	31	1	0	1.4	.976
1949		3	7	.300	4.82	23	6	2	65.1	68	17	22	0	3	2	0	17	4	1	.235	4	16	3	1	1.0	.870
15 yrs.		158	101	.610	3.87	382	278	137	2219.1	2330	558	913	23	22	10	12	*				97	421	14	22	1.4	.974
WORLD SERIES																										
1934	DET A	1	1	.500	2.95	3	2	2	21.1	19	0	12	0	0	0	0	7	0	0	.000	1	1	0	0	0.7	1.000
1935		1	2	.333	2.57	3	2	2	21	19	1	14	0	1	0	0	8	2	0	.250	3	5	1	0	3.0	.889
1940		0	2	.000	17.18	2	2	0	3.2	12	1	1	0	0	0	0	1	0	0	.000	0	1	0	0	0.5	1.000
3 yrs.		2	5	.286	3.91	8	6	4	46	50	2	27	0	1	0	0	*				4	7	1	0	1.5	.917
			2nd																							

Mike Rowland

ROWLAND, MICHAEL EVAN BR TR 6′ 3″ 205 lbs.
B. Jan. 31, 1953, Chicago, Ill.

Year	Team	W	L	PCT	ERA	G	GS	CG	IP	H	BB	SO	ShO	Relief Pitching W	Relief Pitching L	Relief Pitching SV	Batting AB	Batting H	Batting HR	BA	PO	A	E	DP	TC/G	FA
1980	SF N	1	1	.500	2.33	19	0	0	27	20	8	8	0	1	1	0	0	0	0	—	1	4	0	0	0.3	1.000
1981		0	1	.000	3.38	9	1	0	16	13	6	8	0	0	0	0	1	1	0	1.000	1	2	0	0	0.3	1.000
2 yrs.		1	2	.333	2.72	28	1	0	43	33	14	16	0	1	1	0	1	1	0	1.000	2	6	0	0	0.3	1.000

Charlie Roy

ROY, CHARLES ROBERT BR TR 5′10″ 190 lbs.
Brother of Luther Roy.
B. June 22, 1884, Beaulieu, Minn. D. Feb. 10, 1950, Blackfoot, Ida.

Year	Team	W	L	PCT	ERA	G	GS	CG	IP	H	BB	SO	ShO	Relief Pitching W	Relief Pitching L	Relief Pitching SV	Batting AB	Batting H	Batting HR	BA	PO	A	E	DP	TC/G	FA
1906	PHI N	0	1	.000	4.91	7	1	0	18.1	24	5	6	0	0	0	0	7	0	0	.000	5	6	2	0	1.6	.846

Emile Roy

ROY, EMILE ARTHUR BR TR 5′11″ 180 lbs.
B. May 26, 1907, Brighton, Mass.

Year	Team	W	L	PCT	ERA	G	GS	CG	IP	H	BB	SO	ShO	Relief Pitching W	Relief Pitching L	Relief Pitching SV	Batting AB	Batting H	Batting HR	BA	PO	A	E	DP	TC/G	FA
1933	PHI A	0	1	.000	27.00	1	1	0	2.1	4	4	3	0	0	0	0	0	0	0	—	1	0	1	0	2.0	.500

Jean Pierre Roy

ROY, JEAN-PIERRE BB TR 5′10″ 160 lbs.
B. June 26, 1920, Montreal, Que., Canada.

Year	Team	W	L	PCT	ERA	G	GS	CG	IP	H	BB	SO	ShO	Relief Pitching W	Relief Pitching L	Relief Pitching SV	Batting AB	Batting H	Batting HR	BA	PO	A	E	DP	TC/G	FA
1946	BKN N	0	0	—	9.95	3	1	0	6.1	5	5	6	0	0	0	0	2	0	0	.000	0	0	0	0	0.0	.000

Luther Roy

ROY, LUTHER FRANKLIN BR TR 5′10½″ 161 lbs.
Brother of Charlie Roy.
B. July 29, 1902, Ooltewah, Tenn. D. July 24, 1963, Grand Rapids, Mich.

Year	Team	W	L	PCT	ERA	G	GS	CG	IP	H	BB	SO	ShO	Relief Pitching W	Relief Pitching L	Relief Pitching SV	Batting AB	Batting H	Batting HR	BA	PO	A	E	DP	TC/G	FA
1924	CLE A	0	5	.000	7.77	16	5	2	48.2	62	31	14	0	0	1	0	15	4	0	.267	5	12	0	1	1.1	1.000
1925		0	0	—	3.60	6	1	0	10	14	11	1	0	0	0	0	2	0	0	.000	0	1	0	0	0.2	1.000
1927	CHI N	3	1	.750	2.29	11	0	0	19.2	14	11	5	0	3	1	0	3	1	0	.333	0	6	2	1	0.7	.750
1929	2 teams PHI N (21G 3–6) BKN N (2G 0–0)																									
″	total	3	6	.333	8.29	23	12	1	92.1	141	39	16	0	1	1	0	33	9	0	.273	3	25	0	2	1.2	1.000
4 yrs.		6	12	.333	7.17	56	18	3	170.2	231	92	36	0	4	3	0	53	14	0	.264	8	44	2	4	1.0	.963

Norm Roy

ROY, NORMAN BROOKS (Jumbo) BR TR 6′ 200 lbs.
B. Nov. 15, 1928, Newton, Mass.

Year	Team	W	L	PCT	ERA	G	GS	CG	IP	H	BB	SO	ShO	Relief Pitching W	Relief Pitching L	Relief Pitching SV	Batting AB	Batting H	Batting HR	BA	PO	A	E	DP	TC/G	FA
1950	BOS N	4	3	.571	5.13	19	6	2	59.2	72	39	25	0	1	0	1	18	3	0	.167	3	0	0	1	0.2	1.000

Dick Rozek

ROZEK, RICHARD LOUIS BL TL 6′½″ 190 lbs.
B. Mar. 27, 1927, Cedar Rapids, Iowa.

Year	Team	W	L	PCT	ERA	G	GS	CG	IP	H	BB	SO	ShO	Relief Pitching W	Relief Pitching L	Relief Pitching SV	Batting AB	Batting H	Batting HR	BA	PO	A	E	DP	TC/G	FA
1950	CLE A	0	0	—	4.97	12	2	0	25.1	28	19	14	0	0	0	0	5	0	0	.000	0	2	0	0	0.2	1.000
1951		0	0	—	2.93	7	1	0	15.1	18	11	5	0	0	0	0	3	1	0	.333	0	1	1	0	0.3	.500
1952		1	0	1.000	4.97	10	1	0	12.2	11	13	5	0	0	0	0	2	0	0	.000	0	2	0	0	0.2	1.000
1953	PHI A	0	0	—	5.06	2	0	0	10.2	8	9	2	0	0	0	0	2	0	0	.000	0	1	0	0	0.5	1.000
1954		0	0	—	6.75	2	0	0	1.1	0	3	0	0	0	0	0	0	0	0	—	0	0	0	0	0.0	.000
5 yrs.		1	0	1.000	4.55	33	4	0	65.1	65	55	26	0	0	0	0	12	1	0	.083	0	6	1	0	0.2	.857

Dave Rozema

ROZEMA, DAVID SCOTT BR TR 6′ 4″ 185 lbs.
B. Aug. 5, 1956, Grand Rapids, Mich.

Year	Team	W	L	PCT	ERA	G	GS	CG	IP	H	BB	SO	ShO	Relief Pitching W	Relief Pitching L	Relief Pitching SV	Batting AB	Batting H	Batting HR	BA	PO	A	E	DP	TC/G	FA
1977	DET A	15	7	.682	3.10	28	28	16	218	222	34	92	1	0	0	0	0	0	0	—	24	33	3	2	2.1	.950
1978		9	12	.429	3.14	28	28	11	209.1	205	41	57	2	0	0	0	0	0	0	—	17	29	0	0	1.6	1.000
1979		4	4	.500	3.53	16	16	4	97	101	30	33	1	0	0	0	0	0	0	—	7	17	1	1	1.6	.960
1980		6	9	.400	3.91	42	13	2	145	152	49	49	1	2	4	4	0	0	0	—	17	21	1	2	0.9	.974
1981		5	5	.500	3.63	28	9	2	104	99	25	46	2	3	0	3	0	0	0	—	5	15	1	1	0.8	.952
1982		3	0	1.000	1.63	8	2	0	27.2	17	7	15	0	2	0	1	0	0	0	—	7	5	0	0	1.5	1.000
1983		8	3	.727	3.43	29	16	1	105	100	29	63	0	1	0	2	0	0	0	—	12	17	2	1	1.1	.935
1984		7	6	.538	3.74	29	16	0	101	110	18	48	0	0	1	0	0	0	0	—	17	10	0	3	0.9	1.000
1985	TEX A	3	7	.300	4.19	34	4	0	88	100	22	42	0	1	5	7	0	0	0	—	2	18	0	0	0.6	1.000
1986		0	0	—	5.91	6	0	0	10.2	19	3	3	0	0	0	0	0	0	0	—	0	3	0	0	0.5	1.000
10 yrs.		60	53	.531	3.47	248	132	36	1105.2	1125	258	448	7	9	10	17	0	0	0		108	168	8	10	1.1	.972

Jorge Rubio

RUBIO, JORGE JESUS
Born Jorge Jesus Rubio (Chavez).
B. Apr. 23, 1945, Mexicali, Mexico.
BR TR 6′ 3″ 200 lbs.

Year	Team	Lg	W	L	PCT	ERA	G	GS	CG	IP	H	BB	SO	ShO	Relief W	Relief L	Relief SV	Bat AB	Bat H	HR	BA	PO	A	E	DP	TC/G	FA
1966	CAL	A	2	1	.667	2.96	7	4	1	27.1	22	16	27	1	0	0	0	8	0	0	.000	3	1	0	0	0.6	1.000
1967			0	2	.000	3.60	3	3	0	15	18	9	4	0	0	0	0	3	1	0	.333	1	3	0	0	1.3	1.000
2 yrs.			2	3	.400	3.19	10	7	1	42.1	40	25	31	1	0	0	0	11	1	0	.091	4	4	0	0	0.8	1.000

Dave Rucker

RUCKER, DAVID MICHAEL
B. Sept. 1, 1957, San Bernardino, Calif.
BL TL 6′ 1″ 185 lbs.

Year	Team	Lg	W	L	PCT	ERA	G	GS	CG	IP	H	BB	SO	ShO	Relief W	Relief L	Relief SV	Bat AB	Bat H	HR	BA	PO	A	E	DP	TC/G	FA
1981	DET	A	0	0	—	6.75	2	0	0	4	3	1	2	0	0	0	0	0	0	0	—	1	0	0	0	0.5	1.000
1982			5	6	.455	3.38	27	4	1	64	62	23	31	0	4	4	0	0	0	0	—	4	10	3	2	0.6	.824
1983	2 teams	DET A (4G 1–2) STL N (34G 5–3)																									
″	total		6	5	.545	5.28	38	3	0	46	54	26	28	0	5	4	0	4	0	0	.000	6	8	1	1	0.4	.933
1984	STL	N	2	3	.400	2.10	50	0	0	73	62	34	38	0	2	3	0	7	1	0	.143	4	10	5	1	0.4	.737
1985	PHI	N	3	2	.600	4.31	39	3	0	79.1	83	40	41	0	2	1	1	12	4	0	.333	5	14	0	1	0.5	1.000
1986			0	2	.000	5.76	19	0	0	25	34	14	14	0	0	2	0	1	0	0	.000	1	5	0	1	0.3	1.000
1988	PIT	N	0	2	.000	4.76	31	0	0	28.1	39	9	16	0	0	2	0	2	0	0	.000	1	4	1	0	0.2	.833
7 yrs.			16	20	.444	3.94	206	10	1	319.2	337	147	170	0	13	16	1	26	5	0	.192	22	51	10	6	0.4	.880

Nap Rucker

RUCKER, GEORGE
B. Sept. 30, 1884, Crabapple, Ga. D. Dec. 19, 1970, Alpharetta, Ga.
BR TL 5′11″ 190 lbs.

Year	Team	Lg	W	L	PCT	ERA	G	GS	CG	IP	H	BB	SO	ShO	Relief W	Relief L	Relief SV	Bat AB	Bat H	HR	BA	PO	A	E	DP	TC/G	FA
1907	BKN	N	15	13	.536	2.06	37	30	26	275.1	242	80	131	4	1	0	0	97	15	0	.155	5	73	7	4	2.3	.918
1908			17	19	.472	2.08	42	35	30	333.1	265	**125**	199	6	1	1	0	117	21	0	.179	13	109	4	1	3.0	.968
1909			13	19	.406	2.24	38	33	28	309.1	245	101	201	6	0	2	1	101	12	0	.119	3	67	4	3	1.9	.946
1910			17	18	.486	2.58	41	**39**	**27**	**320.1**	**293**	84	147	6	1	0	0	110	23	0	.209	6	80	2	0	2.1	.977
1911			22	18	.550	2.71	48	33	23	315.2	255	110	190	5	5	4	4	104	21	1	.202	7	88	3	1	2.0	.969
1912			18	21	.462	2.21	45	34	23	297.2	272	72	151	**6**	3	4	4	102	25	0	.245	5	82	1	3	2.0	.989
1913			14	15	.483	2.87	41	33	16	260	236	67	111	4	1	1	3	87	21	0	.241	5	50	2	1	1.4	.965
1914			7	6	.538	3.39	16	16	5	103.2	113	27	35	0	0	0	0	34	9	0	.265	4	29	0	1	2.1	1.000
1915			9	4	.692	2.42	19	15	7	122.2	134	28	38	1	2	0	1	42	9	0	.214	6	40	1	2	2.5	.979
1916			2	1	.667	1.69	9	3	1	37.1	34	7	14	0	1	0	0	11	1	0	.091	1	9	0	2	1.1	1.000
10 yrs.			134	134	.500	2.42	336	271	186	2375.1	2089	701	1217	38	15	12	13	805	157	1	.195	55	627	24	18	2.1	.966
WORLD SERIES																											
1916	BKN	N	0	0	—	0.00	1	0	0	2	1	0	3	0	0	0	0	0	0	0	—	0	0	0	0	0.0	.000

Dick Rudolph

RUDOLPH, RICHARD (Baldy)
B. Aug. 25, 1887, New York, N. Y. D. Oct. 20, 1949, Bronx, N. Y.
Manager 1924.
BR TR 5′ 9½″ 160 lbs.
BB 1919–1920, 1922–1923, 1927

Year	Team	Lg	W	L	PCT	ERA	G	GS	CG	IP	H	BB	SO	ShO	Relief W	Relief L	Relief SV	Bat AB	Bat H	HR	BA	PO	A	E	DP	TC/G	FA
1910	NY	N	0	1	.000	7.50	3	1	1	12	21	2	9	0	0	0	2	4	1	0	.250	1	1	0	0	0.7	1.000
1911			0	0	—	9.00	1	0	0	2	2	0	0	0	0	0	0	1	1	0	1.000	0	0	0	0	0.0	.000
1913	BOS	N	14	13	.519	2.92	33	22	17	249.1	258	59	109	1	3	3	0	88	21	0	.239	16	81	2	2	3.0	.980
1914			26	10	.722	2.35	42	36	31	336.1	288	61	138	6	2	2	0	120	15	0	.125	13	96	3	5	2.7	.973
1915			22	**19**	.537	2.37	44	**43**	30	341.1	**304**	64	147	3	0	0	1	116	23	1	.198	8	92	3	6	2.3	.971
1916			19	12	.613	2.16	41	38	27	312	266	38	133	5	0	0	3	101	16	0	.158	6	113	5	3	3.0	.960
1917			13	13	.500	3.41	32	30	22	242.2	252	54	96	5	0	0	0	87	20	0	.230	7	75	5	0	2.7	.943
1918			9	10	.474	2.57	21	20	15	154	144	30	48	3	0	0	0	54	10	0	.185	8	49	1	3	2.8	.983
1919			13	18	.419	2.17	37	32	24	273.2	**282**	54	76	2	0	2	2	88	17	1	.193	15	81	3	0	2.7	.970
1920			4	8	.333	4.04	18	11	3	89	104	24	24	0	2	1	0	27	5	0	.185	4	26	0	0	1.7	1.000
1922			0	2	.000	5.06	3	3	1	16	22	5	3	0	0	0	0	5	2	0	.400	0	4	0	0	1.3	1.000
1923			1	2	.333	3.72	4	4	1	19.1	27	10	3	1	0	0	0	7	0	0	.000	1	6	0	0	1.8	1.000
1927			0	0	—	0.00	1	0	0	1.1	1	1	0	0	0	0	0	0	0	0	—	0	0	0	0	0.0	.000
13 yrs.			121	108	.528	2.66	280	240	172	2049	1971	402	786	26	7	8	8	698	131	2	.188	79	624	22	19	2.6	.970
WORLD SERIES																											
1914	BOS	N	2	0	1.000	0.50	2	2	2	18	12	4	15	0	0	0	0	6	2	0	.333	0	3	0	0	1.5	1.000

Don Rudolph

RUDOLPH, FREDERICK DONALD
B. Aug. 16, 1931, Baltimore, Md. D. Sept. 12, 1968, Granada Hills, Calif.
BL TL 5′11″ 195 lbs.

Year	Team	Lg	W	L	PCT	ERA	G	GS	CG	IP	H	BB	SO	ShO	Relief W	Relief L	Relief SV	Bat AB	Bat H	HR	BA	PO	A	E	DP	TC/G	FA
1957	CHI	A	1	0	1.000	2.25	5	0	0	12	6	2	2	0	1	0	0	2	1	0	.500	0	1	0	0	0.2	1.000
1958			1	0	1.000	2.57	7	0	0	7	4	5	2	0	1	0	1	0	0	0	—	0	3	0	1	0.4	1.000
1959	2 teams	CHI A (4G 0–0) CIN N (5G 0–0)																									
″	total		0	0	—	3.48	9	0	0	10.1	17	5	8	0	0	0	1	1	0	0	.000	1	2	0	1	0.3	1.000
1962	2 teams	CLE A (1G 0–0) WAS A (37G 8–10)																									
″	total		8	10	.444	3.62	38	23	6	176.2	188	42	68	2	0	2	0	57	10	0	.175	6	32	2	0	1.1	.950
1963	WAS	A	7	19	.269	4.55	37	26	4	174	189	36	70	0	0	2	1	45	8	1	.178	9	27	0	2	1.0	1.000
1964			1	3	.250	4.09	28	8	0	70.1	81	12	32	0	0	0	0	15	1	0	.067	4	10	0	0	0.5	1.000
6 yrs.			18	32	.360	4.00	124	57	10	450.1	485	102	182	2	2	4	3	120	20	1	.167	20	75	2	4	0.8	.979

Ernie Rudolph

RUDOLPH, ERNEST WILLIAM
B. Feb. 13, 1909, Black River Falls, Wis.
BL TR 5′ 8″ 165 lbs.

Year	Team	Lg	W	L	PCT	ERA	G	GS	CG	IP	H	BB	SO	ShO	Relief W	Relief L	Relief SV	Bat AB	Bat H	HR	BA	PO	A	E	DP	TC/G	FA
1945	BKN	N	1	0	1.000	5.19	7	0	0	8.2	12	7	3	0	1	0	0	0	0	0	—	0	2	0	0	0.3	1.000

Kirk Rueter

RUETER, KIRK WESLEY
B. Dec. 1, 1970, Hoyleton, Ill.
BL TL 6′ 3″ 190 lbs.

Year	Team	Lg	W	L	PCT	ERA	G	GS	CG	IP	H	BB	SO	ShO	Relief W	Relief L	Relief SV	Bat AB	Bat H	HR	BA	PO	A	E	DP	TC/G	FA
1993	MON	N	8	0	1.000	2.73	14	14	1	85.2	85	18	31	0	0	0	0	26	2	0	.077	7	19	1	4	1.9	.963
1994			7	3	.700	5.17	20	20	0	92.1	106	23	50	0	0	0	0	34	4	0	.118	4	17	1	0	1.1	.955
1995			5	3	.625	3.23	9	9	1	47.1	38	9	28	1	0	0	0	16	0	0	.000	8	9	0	1	1.9	1.000
3 yrs.			20	6	.769	3.83	43	43	2	225.1	229	50	109	1	0	0	0	76	6	0	.079	19	45	2	5	1.5	.970

Dutch Ruether

RUETHER, WALTER HENRY
B. Sept. 13, 1893, Alameda, Calif. D. May 16, 1970, Phoenix, Ariz.
BL TL 6′ 1½″ 180 lbs.

Year	Team	Lg	W	L	PCT	ERA	G	GS	CG	IP	H	BB	SO	ShO	Relief W	Relief L	Relief SV	Bat AB	Bat H	HR	BA	PO	A	E	DP	TC/G	FA
1917	2 teams	CHI N (10G 2–0) CIN N (7G 1–2)																									
″	total		3	2	.600	3.00	17	8	2	72	80	26	35	1	0	0	0	68	17	0	.250	43	23	2	3	3.1	.971
1918	CIN	N	0	1	.000	2.70	2	2	1	10	10	3	10	0	0	0	0	3	0	0	.000	0	2	0	0	1.0	1.000
1919			19	6	**.760**	1.82	33	29	20	242.2	195	83	78	3	0	0	0	92	24	0	.261	10	57	2	1	2.1	.971
1920			16	12	.571	2.47	37	33	23	265.2	235	96	99	5	0	1	3	104	20	0	.192	10	74	4	6	2.3	.955
1921	BKN	N	10	13	.435	4.26	36	27	12	211.1	247	67	78	1	0	0	2	97	34	2	.351	6	51	2	3	1.6	.966

Dutch Ruether *continued*

Year	Team		W	L	PCT	ERA	G	GS	CG	IP	H	BB	SO	ShO	Relief Pitching W	Relief Pitching L	Relief Pitching SV	Batting AB	Batting H	Batting HR	BA	PO	A	E	DP	TC/G	FA
1922			21	12	.636	3.53	35	35	26	267.1	290	92	89	2	0	0	0	125	26	2	.208	9	56	0	6	1.9	1.000
1923			15	14	.517	4.22	34	34	20	275	308	86	87	0	0	0	0	117	32	0	.274	9	53	2	7	1.8	.969
1924			8	13	.381	3.94	30	21	13	166.2	189	45	65	2	1	1	3	62	15	0	.242	5	46	1	3	1.7	.981
1925	**WAS**	**A**	18	7	.720	3.87	30	29	16	223.1	241	105	68	1	0	1	0	108	36	1	.333	7	46	2	2	1.8	.964
1926	**2 teams**	**WAS A** (23G 12–6) **NY A** (5G 2–3)																									
"	**total**		14	9	.609	4.60	28	28	10	205.1	246	84	56	0	0	0	0	113	25	1	.221	4	41	2	2	1.7	.957
1927	**NY**	**A**	13	6	.684	3.38	27	26	12	184	202	52	45	3	0	0	0	80	21	1	.263	7	47	0	2	2.0	1.000
11 yrs.			137	95	.591	3.50	309	272	155	2123.1	2243	739	710	18	1	3	8	*				110	496	17	35	2.0	.973
WORLD SERIES																											
1919	**CIN**	**N**	1	0	1.000	2.57	2	2	1	14	12	4	1	0	0	0	0	6	4	0	.667	0	2	0	0	1.0	1.000
1926	**NY**	**A**	0	1	.000	8.31	1	1	0	4.1	7	2	1	0	0	0	0	4	0	0	.000	0	2	0	0	2.0	1.000
2 yrs.			1	1	.500	3.93	3	3	1	18.1	19	6	2	0	0	0	0	*				0	4	0	0	1.3	1.000

Scott Ruffcorn

RUFFCORN, SCOTT PATRICK
B. Dec. 29, 1969, New Braunfels, Tex.
BR TR 6′ 4″ 215 lbs.

Year	Team		W	L	PCT	ERA	G	GS	CG	IP	H	BB	SO	ShO	Relief Pitching W	Relief Pitching L	Relief Pitching SV	Batting AB	Batting H	Batting HR	BA	PO	A	E	DP	TC/G	FA
1993	**CHI**	**A**	0	2	.000	8.10	3	2	0	10	9	10	2	0	0	0	0	0	0	0	—	0	0	3	0	1.0	.000
1994			0	2	.000	12.79	2	2	0	6.1	15	5	3	0	0	0	0	0	0	0	—	0	0	0	0	0.0	.000
1995			0	0	—	7.88	4	0	0	8	10	13	5	0	0	0	0	0	0	0	—	1	2	0	0	0.8	1.000
3 yrs.			0	4	.000	9.25	9	4	0	24.1	34	28	10	0	0	0	0	0	0	0		1	2	3	0	0.7	.500

Bruce Ruffin

RUFFIN, BRUCE WAYNE
B. Oct. 4, 1963, Lubbock, Tex.
BB TL 6′ 2″ 205 lbs.
BR 1986–1987

Year	Team		W	L	PCT	ERA	G	GS	CG	IP	H	BB	SO	ShO	Relief Pitching W	Relief Pitching L	Relief Pitching SV	Batting AB	Batting H	Batting HR	BA	PO	A	E	DP	TC/G	FA
1986	**PHI**	**N**	9	4	.692	2.46	21	21	6	146.1	138	44	70	0	0	0	0	55	4	0	.073	8	20	1	0	1.4	.966
1987			11	14	.440	4.35	35	35	3	204.2	236	73	93	1	0	0	0	73	4	0	.055	7	32	2	3	1.2	.951
1988			6	10	.375	4.43	55	15	3	144.1	151	80	82	0	2	4	3	33	4	0	.121	11	25	2	2	0.7	.947
1989			6	10	.375	4.44	24	23	1	125.2	152	62	70	0	0	0	0	34	6	0	.176	3	34	4	0	1.7	.902
1990			6	13	.316	5.38	32	25	2	149	178	62	79	1	0	0	0	44	3	0	.068	5	23	0	2	0.9	1.000
1991			4	7	.364	3.78	31	15	1	119	125	38	85	1	1	0	0	24	0	0	.000	8	15	2	1	0.8	.920
1992	**MIL**	**A**	1	6	.143	6.67	25	6	1	58	66	41	45	0	1	2	0	0	0	0	—	4	5	0	0	0.4	1.000
1993	**CLR**	**N**	6	5	.545	3.87	59	12	0	139.2	145	69	126	0	3	1	2	25	2	0	.080	7	16	1	3	0.4	.958
1994			4	5	.444	4.04	56	0	0	55.2	55	30	65	0	4	5	16	4	1	0	.250	2	10	0	0	0.2	1.000
1995			0	1	.000	2.12	37	0	0	34	26	19	23	0	0	1	11	2	0	0	.000	0	8	0	0	0.2	1.000
10 yrs.			53	75	.414	4.19	375	152	17	1176.1	1272	518	738	3	11	13	32	294	24	0	.082	55	188	12	11	0.7	.953
DIVISIONAL PLAYOFF SERIES																											
1995	**CLR**	**N**	0	0	—	2.70	4	0	0	3.1	3	2	2	0	0	0	0	0	0	0	—	0	0	0	0	0.0	.000

Johnny Ruffin

RUFFIN, JOHNNY RENANDO
B. July 29, 1971, Butler, Ala.
BR TR 6′ 3″ 172 lbs.

Year	Team		W	L	PCT	ERA	G	GS	CG	IP	H	BB	SO	ShO	Relief Pitching W	Relief Pitching L	Relief Pitching SV	Batting AB	Batting H	Batting HR	BA	PO	A	E	DP	TC/G	FA
1993	**CIN**	**N**	2	1	.667	3.58	21	0	0	37.2	36	11	30	0	2	1	2	3	1	0	.333	4	5	0	0	0.4	1.000
1994			7	2	.778	3.09	51	0	0	70	57	27	44	0	**7**	2	1	8	0	0	.000	10	2	0	0	0.2	1.000
1995			0	0	—	1.35	10	0	0	13.1	4	11	11	0	0	0	0	2	0	0	.000	2	1	0	1	0.3	1.000
3 yrs.			9	3	.750	3.05	82	0	0	121	97	49	85	0	9	3	3	13	1	0	.077	16	8	0	1	0.3	1.000

Red Ruffing

RUFFING, CHARLES HERBERT
B. May 3, 1904, Granville, Ill. D. Feb. 17, 1986, Mayfield Heights, Ohio.
Hall of Fame 1967.
BR TR 6′ 1½″ 205 lbs.

Year	Team		W	L	PCT	ERA	G	GS	CG	IP	H	BB	SO	ShO	Relief Pitching W	Relief Pitching L	Relief Pitching SV	Batting AB	Batting H	Batting HR	BA	PO	A	E	DP	TC/G	FA
1924	**BOS**	**A**	0	0	—	6.65	8	2	0	23	29	9	10	0	0	0	0	7	1	0	.143	0	3	0	0	0.4	1.000
1925			9	18	.333	5.01	37	27	13	217.1	253	75	64	3	1	1	1	79	17	0	.215	7	50	1	3	1.6	.983
1926			6	15	.286	4.39	37	22	6	166	169	68	58	0	1	2	2	51	10	1	.196	8	42	0	3	1.4	1.000
1927			5	13	.278	4.66	26	18	10	158.1	160	87	77	0	1	1	2	55	14	0	.255	8	36	1	1	1.7	.978
1928			10	**25**	.286	3.89	42	34	**25**	289.1	303	96	118	1	0	2	2	121	38	2	.314	7	51	3	4	1.5	.951
1929			9	**22**	.290	4.86	35	30	18	244.1	280	118	109	2	0	3	1	114	35	2	.307	7	46	3	1	1.5	.946
1930	**2 teams**	**BOS A** (4G 0–3) **NY A** (34G 15–5)																									
"	**total**		15	8	.652	4.38	38	28	13	221.2	242	68	131	2	2	1	1	110	40	4	.364	3	29	3	0	0.9	.914
1931	**NY**	**A**	16	14	.533	4.41	37	30	19	237	240	87	132	1	1	2	2	109	36	3	.330	5	32	0	1	1.0	1.000
1932			18	7	.720	3.09	35	29	22	259	219	115	**190**	3	1	1	2	124	38	3	.306	4	38	2	4	1.3	.955
1933			9	14	.391	3.91	35	28	18	235	230	93	122	0	1	0	3	115	29	2	.252	8	45	2	5	1.6	.964
1934			19	11	.633	3.93	36	31	19	256.1	232	104	149	5	1	1	0	113	28	2	.248	10	32	3	2	1.3	.933
1935			16	11	.593	3.12	30	29	19	222	201	76	81	2	0	1	0	109	37	2	.339	17	26	0	3	1.4	1.000
1936			20	12	.625	3.85	33	33	25	271	274	90	102	3	0	0	0	127	37	5	.291	13	56	1	6	2.1	.986
1937			20	7	.741	2.98	31	31	22	256.1	242	68	131	5	0	0	0	129	26	1	.202	9	28	1	2	1.2	.974
1938			**21**	7	**.750**	3.31	31	31	22	247.1	246	82	127	**4**	0	0	0	107	24	3	.224	11	34	0	2	1.5	1.000
1939			21	7	.750	2.93	28	28	22	233.1	211	75	95	**5**	0	0	0	114	35	1	.307	8	32	2	2	1.5	.952
1940			15	12	.556	3.38	30	30	20	226	218	76	97	3	0	0	0	89	11	1	.124	6	30	2	2	1.3	.947
1941			15	6	.714	3.54	23	23	13	185.2	177	54	60	2	0	0	0	89	27	2	.303	7	21	0	3	1.2	1.000
1942			14	7	.667	3.21	24	24	16	193.2	183	41	80	4	0	0	0	80	20	1	.250	8	30	1	5	1.6	.974
1945			7	3	.700	2.89	11	11	8	87.1	85	20	24	1	0	0	0	46	10	1	.217	2	11	1	1	1.3	.929
1946			5	1	.833	1.77	8	8	4	61	37	23	19	2	0	0	0	25	3	0	.120	2	5	0	0	0.9	1.000
1947	**CHI**	**A**	3	5	.375	6.11	9	9	1	53	63	16	11	0	0	0	0	24	5	0	.208	2	7	0	1	1.0	1.000
22 yrs.			273	225	.548	3.80	624	536	335	4344	4294	1541	1987	48	9	15	16	*				152	684	26	51	1.4	.970
												10th															
WORLD SERIES																											
1932	**NY**	**A**	1	0	1.000	4.00	1	1	1	9	10	6	10	0	0	0	0	4	0	0	.000	1	3	0	0	4.0	1.000
1936			0	1	.000	4.50	2	2	0	14	16	5	12	0	0	0	0	5	0	0	.000	1	3	0	0	2.0	1.000
1937			1	0	1.000	1.00	1	1	1	9	7	3	8	0	0	0	0	4	2	0	.500	0	0	0	0	0.0	.000
1938			2	0	1.000	1.50	2	2	2	18	17	2	11	0	0	0	0	6	1	0	.167	2	4	0	0	3.0	1.000
1939			1	0	1.000	1.00	1	1	1	9	4	1	4	0	0	0	0	3	1	0	.333	0	3	0	1	3.0	1.000
1941			1	0	1.000	1.00	1	1	1	9	6	3	5	0	0	0	0	3	0	0	.000	0	0	0	0	0.0	.000
1942			1	1	.500	4.08	2	2	1	17.2	14	7	11	0	0	0	0	9	2	0	.222	0	1	0	0	0.5	1.000
7 yrs.			7	2	.778	2.63	10	10	7	85.2	74	27	61	0	0	0	0	*				4	14	0	1	1.8	1.000
			2nd					**4th**	**4th**	**3rd**		**6th**	**4th**														

Vern Ruhle

RUHLE, VERNON GERALD BR TR 6′ 1″ 185 lbs.
B. Jan. 25, 1951, Coleman, Mich.

Year	Team	Lg	W	L	PCT	ERA	G	GS	CG	IP	H	BB	SO	ShO	Relief W	Relief L	Relief SV	AB	H	HR	BA	PO	A	E	DP	TC/G	FA
1974	DET	A	2	0	1.000	2.73	5	3	1	33	35	6	10	0	0	0	0	0	0	0	—	4	1	0	0	1.0	1.000
1975			11	12	.478	4.03	32	31	8	190	199	65	67	3	0	0	0	0	0	0	—	15	19	5	1	1.2	.872
1976			9	12	.429	3.92	32	32	5	200	227	59	88	1	0	0	0	0	0	0	—	14	28	0	1	1.3	1.000
1977			3	5	.375	5.73	14	10	0	66	83	15	27	0	0	1	0	0	0	0	—	5	7	1	1	0.9	.923
1978	HOU	N	3	3	.500	2.12	13	10	2	68	57	20	27	2	0	0	0	18	1	0	.056	4	7	0	0	0.8	1.000
1979			2	6	.250	4.09	13	10	2	66	64	8	33	2	0	1	0	19	1	0	.053	3	5	0	0	0.6	1.000
1980			12	4	.750	2.38	28	22	6	159	148	29	55	2	0	0	0	49	12	0	.245	15	17	2	2	1.2	.941
1981			4	6	.400	2.91	20	15	1	102	97	20	39	0	0	1	1	24	6	0	.250	4	9	0	2	0.6	1.000
1982			9	13	.409	3.93	31	21	3	149	169	24	56	2	3	0	1	41	4	0	.098	9	23	2	1	1.1	.941
1983			8	5	.615	3.69	41	9	0	114.2	107	36	43	0	7	3	3	19	2	0	.105	12	19	0	0	0.8	1.000
1984			1	9	.100	4.58	40	6	0	90.1	112	29	60	0	0	5	2	12	1	0	.083	4	18	2	1	0.6	.917
1985	CLE	A	2	10	.167	4.32	42	16	1	125	139	30	54	0	0	3	3	0	0	0	—	15	13	0	0	0.7	1.000
1986	CAL	A	1	3	.250	4.15	16	3	0	47.2	46	7	23	0	0	1	1	0	0	0	—	7	8	1	1	1.0	.938
13 yrs.			67	88	.432	3.73	327	188	29	1410.2	1483	348	582	12	10	15	11	182	27	0	.148	111	174	13	10	0.9	.956
DIVISIONAL PLAYOFF SERIES																											
1981	HOU	N	0	1	.000	2.25	1	1	1	8	4	2	1	0	0	0	0	1	0	0	.000	0	0	0	0	0.0	.000
LEAGUE CHAMPIONSHIP SERIES																											
1980	HOU	N	0	0	—	3.86	1	1	0	7	8	1	3	0	0	0	0	3	0	0	.000	1	1	0	1	2.0	1.000
1986	CAL	A	0	0	—	13.50	1	0	0	0.2	2	0	0	0	0	0	0	0	0	0	—	0	0	0	0	0.0	.000
2 yrs.			0	0		4.70	2	1	0	7.2	10	1	3	0	0	0	0	3	0	0	.000	1	1	0	1	1.0	1.000

Andy Rush

RUSH, JESSE HOWARD BR TR 6′ 3″ 180 lbs.
B. Dec. 26, 1889, Longton, Kans. D. Mar. 16, 1969, Fresno, Calif.

Year	Team	Lg	W	L	PCT	ERA	G	GS	CG	IP	H	BB	SO	ShO	Relief W	Relief L	Relief SV	AB	H	HR	BA	PO	A	E	DP	TC/G	FA
1925	BKN	N	0	1	.000	9.31	4	2	0	9.2	16	5	4	0	0	0	0	3	0	0	.000	1	2	0	0	0.8	1.000

Bob Rush

RUSH, ROBERT RANSOM BR TR 6′ 4″ 205 lbs.
B. Dec. 21, 1925, Battle Creek, Mich.

Year	Team	Lg	W	L	PCT	ERA	G	GS	CG	IP	H	BB	SO	ShO	Relief W	Relief L	Relief SV	AB	H	HR	BA	PO	A	E	DP	TC/G	FA
1948	CHI	N	5	11	.313	3.92	36	16	4	133.1	153	37	72	0	2	0	0	39	5	0	.128	3	31	3	0	1.0	.919
1949			10	18	.357	4.07	35	27	9	201	197	79	80	1	2	0	4	63	2	0	.032	17	37	2	1	1.6	.964
1950			13	**20**	.394	3.71	39	34	19	254.2	261	93	93	1	0	2	1	90	15	1	.167	24	51	1	4	1.9	.987
1951			11	12	.478	3.83	37	29	12	211.1	212	68	129	2	2	0	2	68	13	0	.191	18	39	5	2	1.7	.919
1952			17	13	.567	2.70	34	32	17	250.1	205	81	157	4	0	2	0	96	28	0	.292	13	54	4	5	2.1	.944
1953			9	14	.391	4.54	29	28	8	166.2	177	66	84	1	0	0	0	54	6	0	.111	13	28	0	3	1.4	1.000
1954			13	15	.464	3.77	33	32	11	236.1	213	103	124	0	0	0	0	83	23	2	.277	15	54	3	4	2.2	.958
1955			13	11	.542	3.50	33	33	14	234	204	73	130	3	0	0	0	82	9	1	.110	16	43	1	1	1.8	.983
1956			13	10	.565	3.19	32	32	13	239.2	210	59	104	1	0	0	0	82	8	0	.098	14	34	2	2	1.6	.960
1957			6	16	.273	4.38	31	29	5	205.1	211	66	103	0	0	0	0	69	14	0	.203	15	25	3	1	1.4	.930
1958	MIL	N	10	6	.625	3.42	28	20	5	147.1	142	31	84	2	3	1	0	45	9	0	.200	12	14	1	1	1.0	.963
1959			5	6	.455	2.40	31	9	1	101.1	102	23	64	1	3	2	0	32	6	0	.188	9	13	3	0	0.8	.880
1960	2 teams	MIL N (10G 2–0) CHI A (9G 0–0)																									
″	total		2	0	1.000	4.91	19	0	0	29.1	40	10	20	0	2	0	1	4	2	0	.500	2	5	0	1	0.4	1.000
13 yrs.			127	152	.455	3.65	417	321	118	2410.2	2327	789	1244	16	14	7	8	807	140	4	.173	171	428	28	25	1.5	.955
WORLD SERIES																											
1958	MIL	N	0	1	.000	3.00	1	1	0	6	3	5	2	0	0	0	0	2	0	0	.000	0	3	0	0	3.0	1.000

Amos Rusie

RUSIE, AMOS WILSON (The Hoosier Thunderbolt) BR TR 6′ 1″ 210 lbs.
B. May 30, 1871, Mooresville, Ind. D. Dec. 6, 1942, Seattle, Wash.
Hall of Fame 1977.

Year	Team	Lg	W	L	PCT	ERA	G	GS	CG	IP	H	BB	SO	ShO	Relief W	Relief L	Relief SV	AB	H	HR	BA	PO	A	E	DP	TC/G	FA
1889	IND	N	12	10	.545	5.32	33	22	19	225	246	116	109	1	2	0	0	103	18	0	.175	9	32	6	2	1.4	.872
1890	NY	N	29	**34**	.460	2.56	67	63	56	548.2	436	**289**	**341**	4	1	**1**	1	284	79	0	.278	39	131	23	5	2.4	.881
1891			33	20	.623	2.55	61	57	52	500.1	391	**262**	**337**	**6**	2	1	1	220	54	0	.245	10	106	14	4	2.1	.892
1892			31	31	.500	2.88	64	62	58	532	405	**267**	288	2	0	2	0	252	53	1	.210	30	133	22	5	2.7	.881
1893			33	21	.611	3.23	**56**	**52**[1]	**50**[1]	**482**	**451**	**218**[1]	**208**	**4**	2	1	1	212	57	3	.269	23	114	15	5	2.7	.901
1894			**36**	13	.735	**2.78**	54	**50**	45	444	426	**200**	**195**	**3**	2	0	1	186	52	3	.280	28	113	14	4	2.9	.910
1895			23	23	.500	3.73	49	47	42	393.1	384	159	**201**	**4**	1	1	0	179	44	1	.246	22	93	11	4	2.5	.913
1897			28	10	.737	**2.54**	38	37	35	322.1	314	87	135	2	0	1	0	144	40	0	.278	19	77	8	3	2.7	.923
1898			20	11	.645	3.03	37	36	33	300	288	103	114	4	0	0	1	138	29	0	.210	20	68	12	3	2.6	.880
1901	CIN	N	0	1	.000	8.59	3	2	2	22	43	3	6	0	0	0	0	8	1	0	.125	1	8	1	0	3.3	.900
10 yrs.			245	174	.585	3.07	462	428	392	3769.2	3384	1704 **7th**	1934	30	10	7	5	*				201	875	126	35	2.5	.895

Scott Ruskin

RUSKIN, SCOTT DREW BB TL 6′ 2″ 185 lbs.
B. June 8, 1963, Jacksonville, Fla.

Year	Team	Lg	W	L	PCT	ERA	G	GS	CG	IP	H	BB	SO	ShO	Relief W	Relief L	Relief SV	AB	H	HR	BA	PO	A	E	DP	TC/G	FA
1990	2 teams	PIT N (44G 2–2) MON N (23G 1–0)																									
″	total		3	2	.600	2.75	67	0	0	75.1	75	38	57	0	3	2	2	8	2	0	.250	1	14	2	2	0.3	.882
1991	MON	N	4	4	.500	4.24	64	0	0	63.2	57	30	46	0	4	4	6	2	0	0	.000	1	10	1	1	0.2	.917
1992	CIN	N	4	3	.571	5.03	57	0	0	53.2	56	20	43	0	4	3	0	3	0	0	.000	2	10	0	0	0.2	1.000
1993			0	0	—	18.00	4	0	0	1	3	2	0	0	0	0	0	0	0	0	—	0	0	0	0	0.0	.000
4 yrs.			11	9	.550	3.95	192	0	0	193.2	191	90	146	0	11	9	8	13	2	0	.154	4	34	3	3	0.2	.927

John Russ

RUSS, JOHN
B. Apr. 1, 1858, Cannelton, Ind. D. Jan. 18, 1912, Louisville, Ky.

Year	Team	Lg	W	L	PCT	ERA	G	GS	CG	IP	H	BB	SO	ShO	Relief W	Relief L	Relief SV	AB	H	HR	BA	PO	A	E	DP	TC/G	FA
1882	BAL	AA	0	1	.000	*7.20*	1	1	0	5	10	1	0	0	0	0	0	*				0	1	0	0	0.5	1.000

Allan Russell

RUSSELL, ALLAN E. BB TR 5′11″ 165 lbs.
Brother of Lefty Russell.
B. July 31, 1893, Baltimore, Md. D. Oct. 20, 1972, Baltimore, Md.

Year	Team	Lg	W	L	PCT	ERA	G	GS	CG	IP	H	BB	SO	ShO	Relief W	Relief L	Relief SV	AB	H	HR	BA	PO	A	E	DP	TC/G	FA
1915	NY	A	1	2	.333	2.67	5	3	1	27	21	21	21	0	0	0	0	8	2	0	.250	1	6	1	0	1.6	.875
1916			6	10	.375	3.20	34	19	8	171.1	138	75	104	1	1	0	6	45	2	0	.044	4	49	3	1	1.6	.946
1917			7	8	.467	2.24	25	10	6	104.1	89	39	55	0	4	2	2	31	10	0	.323	3	26	5	1	1.4	.853
1918			7	11	.389	3.26	27	18	7	141	139	73	54	2	0	3	4	42	7	0	.167	6	33	2	0	1.5	.951
1919	2 teams	NY A (23G 5–5) BOS A (21G 10–4)																									
″	total		15	9	.625	2.94	44	20	13	211	194	71	113	2	5	1	**5**	71	12	0	.169	9	53	6	1	1.5	.912

Allan Russell *continued*

Year	Team		W	L	PCT	ERA	G	GS	CG	IP	H	BB	SO	ShO	Relief Pitching W	Relief Pitching L	Relief Pitching SV	Batting AB	Batting H	Batting HR	BA	PO	A	E	DP	TC/G	FA
1920	BOS	A	5	6	.455	3.01	16	10	7	107.2	100	38	53	0	1	1	1	41	5	0	.122	3	34	4	2	2.6	.902
1921			7	11	.389	4.11	39	14	8	173	204	77	60	0	4	2	3	57	7	0	.123	12	44	5	1	1.6	.918
1922			6	7	.462	5.01	34	11	1	125.2	152	57	34	0	3	2	2	38	3	0	.079	6	41	0	1	1.4	1.000
1923	WAS	A	10	8	.556	3.03	52	6	3	181.1	177	77	67	0	**9**	**7**	**9**	50	10	0	.200	5	34	3	2	0.8	.929
1924			5	1	.833	4.37	37	0	0	82.1	83	45	17	0	5	1	8	18	5	0	.278	2	20	3	0	0.7	.880
1925			2	4	.333	5.77	32	2	0	68.2	85	37	25	0	2	2	2	14	2	0	.143	5	24	2	2	1.0	.935
11 yrs.			71	77	.480	3.52	345	113	54	1393.1	1382	610	603	5	34	21	42	415	65	0	.157	56	364	34	11	1.3	.925
WORLD SERIES																											
1924	WAS	A	0	0	—	3.00	1	0	0	3	4	0	0	0	0	0	0	0	0	0	—	0	1	0	0	1.0	1.000

Jack Russell

RUSSELL, JACK ERWIN BR TR 6′ 1½″ 178 lbs.
B. Oct. 24, 1905, Paris, Tex. D. Nov. 3, 1990, Clearwater, Fla.

Year	Team		W	L	PCT	ERA	G	GS	CG	IP	H	BB	SO	ShO	Relief Pitching W	Relief Pitching L	Relief Pitching SV	Batting AB	Batting H	Batting HR	BA	PO	A	E	DP	TC/G	FA
1926	BOS	A	0	5	.000	3.58	36	5	1	98	94	24	17	0	0	2	0	21	4	0	.190	10	34	1	2	1.3	.978
1927			4	9	.308	4.10	34	15	4	147	172	40	25	1	1	1	0	48	6	0	.125	13	44	6	1	1.9	.905
1928			11	14	.440	3.84	32	26	10	201.1	233	41	27	2	1	0	0	62	13	0	.210	13	50	4	6	2.1	.940
1929			6	18	.250	3.94	35	32	13	226.1	263	40	37	0	0	0	0	70	9	0	.129	15	69	0	1	2.4	1.000
1930			9	**20**	.310	5.45	35	30	15	229.2	302	53	35	0	0	0	0	79	14	1	.177	11	59	4	3	2.1	.946
1931			10	18	.357	5.16	36	31	13	232	298	65	45	0	0	1	0	82	16	0	.195	16	63	2	1	2.3	.975
1932	2 teams	BOS A	(11G 1–7)	CLE A	(18G 5–7)																						
″	total		6	14	.300	5.25	29	17	7	152.2	207	42	34	0	0	3	1	51	13	0	.255	13	39	4	1	1.9	.929
1933	WAS	A	12	6	.667	2.69	50	3	2	124	119	32	28	0	**11**	4	**13**	34	5	0	.147	6	46	0	5	1.0	1.000
1934			5	10	.333	4.17	**54**	9	3	157.2	179	56	38	0	2	**7**	**7**	44	7	0	.159	8	44	2	3	1.0	.963
1935			4	9	.308	5.71	43	7	2	126	170	37	30	0	4	5	3	35	7	0	.200	6	39	2	2	1.1	.957
1936	2 teams	WAS A	(18G 3–2)	BOS A	(23G 0–3)																						
″	total		3	5	.375	6.02	41	7	1	89.2	123	41	15	0	1	4	3	22	2	0	.091	3	32	2	1	0.9	.946
1937	DET	A	2	5	.286	7.59	25	0	0	40.1	63	20	10	0	2	5	4	7	0	0	.000	1	13	0	0	0.6	1.000
1938	CHI	N	6	1	.857	3.34	42	0	0	102.1	100	30	29	0	6	1	3	32	7	0	.219	12	32	1	1	1.1	.978
1939			4	3	.571	3.67	39	0	0	68.2	78	24	32	0	4	3	3	17	0	0	.000	3	23	1	0	0.7	.963
1940	STL	N	3	4	.429	2.50	26	0	0	54	53	26	16	0	3	4	1	13	0	0	.000	4	15	0	2	0.7	1.000
15 yrs.			85	141	.376	4.47	557	182	71	2049.2	2454	571	418	3	35	40	38	617	103	1	.167	134	602	29	29	1.4	.962
WORLD SERIES																											
1933	WAS	A	0	1	.000	0.87	3	0	0	10.1	8	0	7	0	0	1	0	2	0	0	.000	2	3	0	0	1.7	1.000
1938	CHI	N	0	0	—	0.00	2	0	0	1.2	1	1	0	0	0	0	0	0	0	0	—	0	0	0	0	0.0	.000
2 yrs.			0	1	.000	0.75	5	0	0	12	9	1	7	0	0	1	0	2	0	0	.000	2	3	0	0	1.0	1.000

Jeff Russell

RUSSELL, JEFFREY LEE BR TR 6′ 4″ 200 lbs.
B. Sept. 2, 1961, Cincinnati, Ohio.

Year	Team		W	L	PCT	ERA	G	GS	CG	IP	H	BB	SO	ShO	Relief Pitching W	Relief Pitching L	Relief Pitching SV	Batting AB	Batting H	Batting HR	BA	PO	A	E	DP	TC/G	FA
1983	CIN	N	4	5	.444	3.03	10	10	2	68.1	58	22	40	0	0	0	0	21	3	1	.143	2	10	1	0	1.3	.923
1984			6	**18**	.250	4.26	33	30	4	181.2	186	65	101	2	0	0	0	57	8	0	.140	7	34	2	4	1.3	.953
1985	TEX	A	3	6	.333	7.55	13	13	0	62	85	27	44	0	0	0	0	0	0	0	—	6	10	0	1	1.2	1.000
1986			5	2	.714	3.40	37	0	0	82	74	31	54	0	5	2	2	0	0	0	—	6	17	0	3	0.6	1.000
1987			5	4	.556	4.44	52	2	0	97.1	109	52	56	0	5	3	3	0	0	0	—	11	17	0	2	0.5	1.000
1988			10	9	.526	3.82	34	24	5	188.2	183	66	88	0	1	0	0	1	0	0	.000	12	37	5	3	1.6	.907
1989			6	4	.600	1.98	71	0	0	72.2	45	24	77	0	6	4	**38**	0	0	0	—	6	14	0	3	0.3	1.000
1990			1	5	.167	4.26	27	0	0	25.1	23	16	16	0	1	5	10	0	0	0	—	1	5	1	0	0.3	.857
1991			6	4	.600	3.29	68	0	0	79.1	71	26	52	0	6	4	30	0	0	0	—	6	18	1	1	0.4	.960
1992	2 teams	TEX A	(51G 2–3)	OAK A	(8G 2–0)																						
″	total		4	3	.571	1.63	59	0	0	66.1	55	25	48	0	4	3	30	0	0	0		8	8	0	0	0.3	1.000
1993	BOS	A	1	4	.200	2.70	51	0	0	46.2	39	14	45	0	1	4	33	0	0	0	—	2	10	0	0	0.2	1.000
1994	2 teams	BOS A	(29G 0–5)	CLE A	(13G 1–1)																						
″	total		1	6	.143	5.09	42	0	0	40.2	43	16	28	0	1	**6**	17	0	0	0		1	2	0	0	0.1	1.000
1995	TEX	A	1	0	1.000	3.03	37	0	0	32.2	36	9	21	0	1	0	20	0	0	0	—	2	2	0	0	0.1	1.000
13 yrs.			53	70	.431	3.77	534	79	11	1043.2	1007	393	670	2	31	31	183	79	11	1	.139	70	184	10	17	0.5	.962
LEAGUE CHAMPIONSHIP SERIES																											
1992	OAK	A	1	0	1.000	9.00	3	0	0	2	2	4	0	0	1	0	0	0	0	0	—	0	0	0	0	0.0	.000

John Russell

RUSSELL, JOHN ALBERT BL TL 6′ 2″ 195 lbs.
B. Oct. 20, 1895, San Mateo, Calif. D. Nov. 19, 1930, Ely, Nev.

Year	Team		W	L	PCT	ERA	G	GS	CG	IP	H	BB	SO	ShO	Relief Pitching W	Relief Pitching L	Relief Pitching SV	Batting AB	Batting H	Batting HR	BA	PO	A	E	DP	TC/G	FA
1917	BKN	N	0	1	.000	4.50	5	1	1	16	12	6	1	0	0	0	0	4	1	0	.250	1	3	0	0	0.8	1.000
1918			0	0	—	18.00	1	0	0	1	2	1	0	0	0	0	0	0	0	0	—	0	0	0	0	0.0	.000
1921	CHI	A	2	5	.286	5.29	11	8	4	66.1	82	35	15	0	0	0	0	25	10	0	.400	3	14	0	0	1.5	1.000
1922			0	1	.000	6.75	4	1	0	6.2	7	4	3	0	0	0	1	1	0	0	.000	1	2	0	0	0.8	1.000
4 yrs.			2	7	.222	5.40	21	10	5	90	103	46	19	0	0	0	1	30	11	0	.367	5	19	0	0	1.1	1.000

John Russell

RUSSELL, JOHN WILLIAM BR TR 6′ 195 lbs.
B. Jan. 5, 1961, Oklahoma City, Okla.

Year	Team		W	L	PCT	ERA	G	GS	CG	IP	H	BB	SO	ShO	Relief Pitching W	Relief Pitching L	Relief Pitching SV	Batting AB	Batting H	Batting HR	BA	PO	A	E	DP	TC/G	FA
1989	ATL	N	0	0	—	0.00	1	0	0	0.1	0	0	0	0	0	0	0	*				51	1	0	0	1.7	1.000

Lefty Russell

RUSSELL, CLARENCE DICKSON BL TL 6′ 1″ 165 lbs.
Brother of Allan Russell.
B. July 8, 1890, Baltimore, Md. D. Jan. 22, 1962, Baltimore, Md.

Year	Team		W	L	PCT	ERA	G	GS	CG	IP	H	BB	SO	ShO	Relief Pitching W	Relief Pitching L	Relief Pitching SV	Batting AB	Batting H	Batting HR	BA	PO	A	E	DP	TC/G	FA
1910	PHI	A	1	0	1.000	0.00	1	1	1	9	8	2	5	1	0	0	0	3	0	0	.000	1	4	1	0	3.0	.833
1911			0	3	.000	7.67	7	2	0	31.2	45	18	7	0	0	1	0	13	5	0	.385	7	11	0	1	2.6	1.000
1912			0	2	.000	7.27	5	2	2	17.1	18	14	9	0	0	1	0	4	0	0	.000	0	5	0	0	1.0	1.000
3 yrs.			1	5	.167	6.36	13	5	3	58	71	34	21	1	0	2	0	20	5	0	.250	8	20	1	1	2.1	.966

Reb Russell

RUSSELL, EWELL ALBERT BL TL 5′11″ 185 lbs.
B. Apr. 12, 1889, Jackson, Miss. D. Sept. 30, 1973, Indianapolis, Ind.

Year	Team		W	L	PCT	ERA	G	GS	CG	IP	H	BB	SO	ShO	Relief Pitching W	Relief Pitching L	Relief Pitching SV	Batting AB	Batting H	Batting HR	BA	PO	A	E	DP	TC/G	FA
1913	CHI	A	22	16	.579	1.91	**51**	36	26	316	249	79	122	8	3	1	4	106	20	0	.189	10	71	4	3	1.7	.953
1914			8	12	.400	2.90	38	23	8	167.1	168	33	79	1	1	0	1	64	17	0	.266	3	50	3	0	1.5	.946
1915			11	10	.524	2.59	41	25	10	229.1	215	47	90	3	1	1	2	86	21	0	.244	11	56	2	1	1.7	.971
1916			18	11	.621	2.42	56	25	16	264.1	207	42	112	5	5	1	3	91	13	0	.143	4	71	2	2	1.4	.974
1917			15	5	**.750**	1.95	35	24	11	189.1	170	32	54	5	2	1	3	68	19	0	.279	14	51	1	2	1.8	.985

Reb Russell *continued*

Year	Team	Lg	W	L	PCT	ERA	G	GS	CG	IP	H	BB	SO	ShO	Relief Pitching W	Relief Pitching L	Relief Pitching SV	Batting AB	Batting H	Batting HR	BA	PO	A	E	DP	TC/G	FA
1918			7	5	.583	2.60	19	14	10	124.2	117	33	38	2	0	0	0	50	7	0	.140	4	28	0	1	1.6	1.000
1919			0	0	—	0.00	1	0	0		1	1	0	0	0	0	0	0	0	0	—	0	0	0	0	0.0	.000
7 yrs.			81	59	.579	2.34	241	147	81	1291	1127	267	495	24	12	4	13	*				317	336	21	11	1.8	.969
WORLD SERIES																											
1917	**CHI**	**A**	0	0	—	∞	1	1	0		2	1	0	0	0	0	0	*				0	0	0	0	0.0	.000

Marius Russo

RUSSO, MARIUS UGO (Lefty)
B. July 19, 1914, Brooklyn, N. Y.

BR TL 6′ 1″ 190 lbs.

Year	Team	Lg	W	L	PCT	ERA	G	GS	CG	IP	H	BB	SO	ShO	Relief Pitching W	Relief Pitching L	Relief Pitching SV	Batting AB	Batting H	Batting HR	BA	PO	A	E	DP	TC/G	FA
1939	**NY**	**A**	8	3	.727	2.41	21	11	9	116	86	41	55	2	0	1	2	41	10	0	.244	7	26	1	6	1.6	.971
1940			14	8	.636	3.28	30	24	15	189.1	181	55	87	0	0	0	1	64	12	0	.188	9	48	0	4	1.9	1.000
1941			14	10	.583	3.09	28	27	17	209.2	195	87	105	3	0	0	1	78	18	0	.231	14	42	4	7	2.1	.933
1942			4	1	.800	2.78	9	5	2	45.1	41	14	15	0	1	0	0	17	4	0	.235	3	9	0	1	1.3	1.000
1943			5	10	.333	3.72	24	14	5	101.2	89	45	42	1	1	2	1	31	6	0	.194	2	24	2	3	1.2	.929
1946			0	2	.000	4.34	8	3	0	18.2	26	11	7	0	0	0	0	4	0	0	.000	2	6	0	1	1.0	1.000
6 yrs.			45	34	.570	3.13	120	84	48	680.2	618	253	311	6	2	3	5	235	50	0	.213	37	155	7	22	1.7	.965
WORLD SERIES																											
1941	**NY**	**A**	1	0	1.000	1.00	1	1	1	9	4	2	5	0	0	0	0	4	0	0	.000	0	4	0	0	4.0	1.000
1943			1	0	1.000	0.00	1	1	1	9	7	1	2	0	0	0	0	3	2	0	.667	0	2	0	0	2.0	1.000
2 yrs.			2	0	1.000	0.50	2	2	2	18	11	3	7	0	0	0	0	7	2	0	.286	0	6	0	0	3.0	1.000

Dick Rusteck

RUSTECK, RICHARD FRANK
B. July 12, 1941, Chicago, Ill.

BR TL 6′ 1″ 175 lbs.

Year	Team	Lg	W	L	PCT	ERA	G	GS	CG	IP	H	BB	SO	ShO	Relief Pitching W	Relief Pitching L	Relief Pitching SV	Batting AB	Batting H	Batting HR	BA	PO	A	E	DP	TC/G	FA
1966	**NY**	**N**	1	2	.333	3.00	8	3	1	24	24	8	9	1	0	0	0	5	0	0	.000	1	4	1	0	0.8	.833

Babe Ruth

RUTH, GEORGE HERMAN (The Bambino, The Sultan of Swat)
B. Feb. 6, 1895, Baltimore, Md. D. Aug. 16, 1948, New York, N. Y.
Hall of Fame 1936.

BL TL 6′ 2″ 215 lbs.

Year	Team	Lg	W	L	PCT	ERA	G	GS	CG	IP	H	BB	SO	ShO	Relief Pitching W	Relief Pitching L	Relief Pitching SV	Batting AB	Batting H	Batting HR	BA	PO	A	E	DP	TC/G	FA
1914	**BOS**	**A**	2	1	.667	3.91	4	3	1	23	21	7	3	0	0	0	0	10	2	0	.200	0	7	0	0	1.8	1.000
1915			18	8	.692	2.44	32	28	16	217.2	166	85	112	1	0	0	0	92	29	4	.315	17	63	2	3	2.6	.976
1916			23	12	.657	**1.75**	44	**41**	23	323.2	230	118	170	**9**	0	1	1	136	37	3	.272	24	83	3	6	2.5	.973
1917			24	13	.649	2.01	41	38	**35**	326.1	244	108	128	6	0	0	2	123	40	2	.325	19	101	2	4	3.0	.984
1918			13	7	.650	2.22	20	19	18	166.1	125	49	40	1	0	1	0	317	95	11	.300	270	72	18	16	3.9	.950
1919			9	5	.643	2.97	17	15	12	133.1	148	58	30	0	1	0	1	432	139	29	.322	270	53	4	11	2.5	.988
1920	**NY**	**A**	1	0	1.000	4.50	1	1	0	4	3	2	0	0	0	0	0	458	172	54	.376	270	21	20	4	2.2	.936
1921			2	0	1.000	9.00	2	1	0	9	14	9	2	0	1	0	0	540	204	59	.378	357	19	13	6	2.5	.967
1930			1	0	1.000	3.00	1	1	1	9	11	2	3	0	0	0	0	518	186	49	.359	226	14	9	4	2.2	.964
1933			1	0	1.000	5.00	1	1	1	9	12	3	0	0	0	0	0	459	138	34	.301	419	21	12	4	3.0	.973
10 yrs.			94	46	.671	2.28	163	148	107	1221.1	974	441	488	17	2	2	4	*				4787	569	179	85	2.3	.968
WORLD SERIES																											
1916	**BOS**	**A**	1	0	1.000	0.64	1	1	1	14	6	3	4	0	0	0	0	5	0	0	.000	2	4	0	0	6.0	1.000
1918			2	0	1.000	1.06	2	2	1	17	13	7	4	1	0	0	0	5	1	0	.200	1	5	0	1	1.5	1.000
2 yrs.			3	0	1.000	0.87	3	3	2	31	19	10	8	1	0	0	0	*				73	12	2	1	2.1	.977
					1st	**3rd**																					

Johnny Rutherford

RUTHERFORD, JOHN WILLIAM (Doc)
B. May 5, 1925, Belleville, Ont., Canada.

BL TR 5′10½″ 170 lbs.

Year	Team	Lg	W	L	PCT	ERA	G	GS	CG	IP	H	BB	SO	ShO	Relief Pitching W	Relief Pitching L	Relief Pitching SV	Batting AB	Batting H	Batting HR	BA	PO	A	E	DP	TC/G	FA
1952	**BKN**	**N**	7	7	.500	4.25	22	11	4	97.1	97	29	29	0	2	2	2	31	9	0	.290	3	24	0	1	1.2	1.000
WORLD SERIES																											
1952	**BKN**	**N**	0	0	—	9.00	1	0	0	1	1	1	1	0	0	0	0	0	0	0	—	0	0	0	0	0.0	.000

Dick Ruthven

RUTHVEN, RICHARD DAVID
B. Mar. 27, 1951, Sacramento, Calif.

BR TR 6′ 3″ 190 lbs.

Year	Team	Lg	W	L	PCT	ERA	G	GS	CG	IP	H	BB	SO	ShO	Relief Pitching W	Relief Pitching L	Relief Pitching SV	Batting AB	Batting H	Batting HR	BA	PO	A	E	DP	TC/G	FA
1973	**PHI**	**N**	6	9	.400	4.21	25	23	3	128.1	125	75	98	1	1	0	1	38	5	0	.132	6	23	6	2	1.4	.829
1974			9	13	.409	4.01	35	35	6	213	182	116	153	0	0	0	0	68	13	0	.191	7	30	7	2	1.3	.841
1975			2	2	.500	4.17	11	7	0	41	37	22	26	0	0	0	0	13	2	0	.154	2	5	2	1	0.8	.778
1976	**ATL**	**N**	14	**17**	.452	4.20	36	36	8	240	255	90	142	4	0	0	0	76	13	0	.171	18	44	1	2	1.8	.984
1977			7	13	.350	4.23	25	23	6	151	158	62	84	2	0	0	0	45	12	1	.267	10	16	5	1	1.2	.839
1978	**2 teams**	**ATL N**	(13G 2–6)	**PHI N**	(20G 13–5)																						
″	**total**		15	11	.577	3.38	33	33	11	231.2	214	56	120	3	0	0	0	77	17	0	.221	17	36	8	0	1.8	.869
1979	**PHI**	**N**	7	5	.583	4.28	20	20	3	122	121	37	58	2	0	0	0	41	6	0	.146	6	9	1	1	0.8	.938
1980			17	10	.630	3.55	33	33	6	223	241	74	86	1	0	0	0	68	16	0	.235	21	33	6	3	1.8	.900
1981			12	7	.632	5.14	23	22	5	147	162	54	80	0	0	0	0	50	7	0	.140	11	20	1	0	1.4	.969
1982			11	11	.500	3.79	33	31	8	204.1	189	59	115	2	0	0	0	64	7	0	.109	22	16	1	1	1.2	.974
1983	**2 teams**	**PHI N**	(7G 1–3)	**CHI N**	(25G 12–9)																						
″	**total**		13	12	.520	4.38	32	32	5	183	202	38	99	2	0	0	0	62	13	0	.210	16	35	2	4	1.7	.962
1984	**CHI**	**N**	6	10	.375	5.04	23	22	0	126.2	154	41	55	0	0	0	0	44	7	0	.159	8	19	0	1	1.2	1.000
1985			4	7	.364	4.53	20	15	0	87.1	103	37	26	0	0	0	0	24	5	0	.208	5	11	1	1	0.9	.941
1986			0	0	—	5.06	6	0	0	10.2	12	6	3	0	0	0	0	1	0	0	.000	0	1	0	0	0.2	1.000
14 yrs.			123	127	.492	4.14	355	332	61	2109	2155	767	1145	17	1	0	1	671	123	1	.183	149	298	41	19	1.4	.916
DIVISIONAL PLAYOFF SERIES																											
1981	**PHI**	**N**	0	1	.000	4.50	1	1	0	4	3	1	0	0	0	0	0	1	0	0	.000	0	0	0	0	0.0	.000
LEAGUE CHAMPIONSHIP SERIES																											
1978	**PHI**	**N**	0	1	.000	5.79	1	1	0	4.2	6	0	3	0	0	0	0	1	0	0	.000	0	0	0	0	0.0	.000
1980			1	0	1.000	2.00	2	1	0	9	3	5	4	0	1	0	0	2	0	0	.000	2	0	0	0	1.0	1.000
2 yrs.			1	1	.500	3.29	3	2	0	13.2	9	5	7	0	1	0	0	3	0	0	.000	2	0	0	0	0.7	1.000
WORLD SERIES																											
1980	**PHI**	**N**	0	0	—	3.00	1	1	0	9	9	0	7	0	0	0	0	0	0	0	—	0	0	0	0	0.0	.000

Cyclone Ryan

RYAN, DANIEL R. TR 6′ 200 lbs.
B. 1866, Capperwhite, Ireland D. Jan. 30, 1917, Medfield, Mass.

Year	Team		W	L	PCT	ERA	G	GS	CG	IP	H	BB	SO	ShO	Relief Pitching W	Relief Pitching L	Relief Pitching SV	Batting AB	Batting H	Batting HR	BA	PO	A	E	DP	TC/G	FA
1887	**NY**	**AA**	0	1	.000	*23.14*	2	1	0	2.1	5	6	0	0	0	0	0	32	7	0	.219	72	4	5	7	8.1	.938
1891	**BOS**	**N**	0	0	—	0.00	1	0	0	3	2	1	0	0	0	0	0	1	0	0	.000	0	1	0	0	1.0	1.000
2 yrs.			0	1	.000	10.13	3	1	0	5.1	7	7	0	0	0	0	0	*				72	5	5	7	7.5	.939

Jack Ryan

RYAN, JACK (Gulfport) BR TR 5′10″ 165 lbs.
B. Sept. 19, 1884, Lawrenceville, Ill. D. Oct. 16, 1949, Mondsboro, Miss.

Year	Team		W	L	PCT	ERA	G	GS	CG	IP	H	BB	SO	ShO	Relief Pitching W	Relief Pitching L	Relief Pitching SV	Batting AB	Batting H	Batting HR	BA	PO	A	E	DP	TC/G	FA
1908	**CLE**	**A**	1	1	.500	2.27	8	1	1	35.2	27	2	7	0	0	1	1	11	1	0	.091	0	12	0	1	1.5	1.000
1909	**BOS**	**A**	4	3	.571	3.23	13	8	2	61.1	65	20	24	0	1	0	0	19	4	0	.211	2	17	1	0	1.5	.950
1911	**BKN**	**N**	0	1	.000	3.00	3	1	0	6	9	4	1	0	0	0	0	1	0	0	.000	0	3	0	0	1.0	1.000
3 yrs.			5	5	.500	2.88	24	10	3	103	101	26	32	0	1	1	1	31	5	0	.161	2	32	1	1	1.5	.971

Jimmy Ryan

RYAN, JAMES EDWARD (Pony) BR TL 5′ 9″ 162 lbs.
B. Feb. 11, 1863, Clinton, Mass. D. Oct. 26, 1923, Chicago, Ill.

Year	Team		W	L	PCT	ERA	G	GS	CG	IP	H	BB	SO	ShO	Relief Pitching W	Relief Pitching L	Relief Pitching SV	Batting AB	Batting H	Batting HR	BA	PO	A	E	DP	TC/G	FA
1886	**CHI**	**N**	0	0	—	*4.63*	5	0	0	23.1	19	13	15	0	0	0	1	327	100	4	.306	6	11	7	0	8.0	.708
1887			2	1	.667	4.20	8	3	2	45	53	17	14	0	1	0	0	508	145	11	.285	172	54	39	8	2.0	.853
1888			4	0	1.000	3.05	8	2	1	38.1	47	12	11	0	**3**	0	0	549	182	16	.332	219	43	38	6	2.2	.873
1891			0	0	—	1.59	2	0	0	5.2	11	2	2	0	0	0	1	505	140	9	.277	286	133	57	19	3.5	.880
1893			0	0	—	0.00	1	0	0	4.2	3	0	1	0	0	0	0	341	102	3	.299	257	25	25	5	2.6	.919
5 yrs.			6	1	.857	3.62	24	5	3	117	133	44	43	0	4	0	2	*				3808	603	434	88	2.4	.910

John Ryan

RYAN, JOHN A. BL TR
Born Daniel Ryan.
B. Birmingham, Mich. Deceased.

Year	Team		W	L	PCT	ERA	G	GS	CG	IP	H	BB	SO	ShO	Relief Pitching W	Relief Pitching L	Relief Pitching SV	Batting AB	Batting H	Batting HR	BA	PO	A	E	DP	TC/G	FA
1884	**BAL**	**U**	3	2	.600	3.35	6	6	5	51	61	16	33	0	0	0	0	25	2	0	.080	2	12	4	1	2.3	.778

Johnny Ryan

RYAN, JOHN JOSEPH 5′ 7½″ 150 lbs.
B. Oct. 1853, Philadelphia, Pa. D. Mar. 22, 1902, Philadelphia, Pa.

Year	Team		W	L	PCT	ERA	G	GS	CG	IP	H	BB	SO	ShO	Relief Pitching W	Relief Pitching L	Relief Pitching SV	Batting AB	Batting H	Batting HR	BA	PO	A	E	DP	TC/G	FA
1876	**LOU**	**N**	0	0	—	5.63	1	0	0	8	22	0	1	0	0	0	0	*				132	2	17	1	2.3	.887

Ken Ryan

RYAN, KENNETH FREDERICK BR TR 6′ 3″ 200 lbs.
B. Oct. 24, 1968, Pawtucket, R. I.

Year	Team		W	L	PCT	ERA	G	GS	CG	IP	H	BB	SO	ShO	Relief Pitching W	Relief Pitching L	Relief Pitching SV	Batting AB	Batting H	Batting HR	BA	PO	A	E	DP	TC/G	FA
1992	**BOS**	**A**	0	0	—	6.43	7	0	0	7	4	5	5	0	0	0	1	0	0	0	—	1	2	0	0	0.4	1.000
1993			7	2	.778	3.60	47	0	0	50	43	29	49	0	7	2	1	0	0	0	—	3	7	1	0	0.2	.909
1994			2	3	.400	2.44	42	0	0	48	46	17	32	0	2	3	13	0	0	0	—	2	4	0	0	0.1	1.000
1995			0	4	.000	4.96	28	0	0	32.2	34	24	34	0	0	4	7	0	0	0	—	1	1	1	1	0.1	.667
4 yrs.			9	9	.500	3.66	124	0	0	137.2	127	75	120	0	9	9	22	0	0	0		7	14	2	1	0.2	.913

Nolan Ryan

RYAN, LYNN NOLAN (The Express) BR TR 6′ 2″ 170 lbs.
B. Jan. 31, 1947, Refugio, Tex.

Year	Team		W	L	PCT	ERA	G	GS	CG	IP	H	BB	SO	ShO	Relief Pitching W	Relief Pitching L	Relief Pitching SV	Batting AB	Batting H	Batting HR	BA	PO	A	E	DP	TC/G	FA
1966	**NY**	**N**	0	1	.000	15.00	2	1	0	3	5	3	6	0	0	0	0	0	0	0	—	1	0	0	0	0.5	1.000
1968			6	9	.400	3.09	21	18	3	134	93	75	133	0	0	0	0	44	5	0	.114	5	11	4	0	1.0	.800
1969			6	3	.667	3.53	25	10	2	89.1	60	53	92	0	3	0	1	29	3	0	.103	0	4	1	0	0.2	.800
1970			7	11	.389	3.41	27	19	5	132	86	97	125	2	0	0	1	45	8	0	.178	11	10	4	2	0.9	.840
1971			10	14	.417	3.97	30	26	3	152	125	116	137	0	1	0	0	47	6	0	.128	5	15	3	2	0.8	.870
1972	**CAL**	**A**	19	16	.543	2.28	39	39	20	284	166	**157**	**329**	**9**	0	0	0	96	13	0	.135	7	28	6	2	1.1	.854
1973			21	16	.568	2.87	41	39	26	326	238	**162**	**383**[1]	4	0	0	1	0	0	0	—	10	27	2	1	1.0	.949
1974			22	16	.579	2.89	42	41	26	**333**	221	**202**	**367**	3	1	0	0	0	0	0	—	12	48	6	1	1.6	.909
1975			14	12	.538	3.45	28	28	10	198	152	132	186	5	0	0	0	0	0	0	—	12	18	7	3	1.3	.811
1976			17	**18**	.486	3.36	39	39	21	284	193	**183**	**327**	**7**	0	0	0	0	0	0	—	14	34	7	1	1.4	.873
1977			19	16	.543	2.77	37	37	**22**	299	198	**204**	**341**	4	0	0	0	0	0	0	—	20	35	8	1	1.7	.873
1978			10	13	.435	3.71	31	31	14	235	183	**148**	**260**	3	0	0	0	0	0	0	—	13	33	8	3	1.7	.852
1979			16	14	.533	3.59	34	34	17	223	169	114	**223**	**5**	0	0	0	0	0	0	—	8	29	4	1	1.2	.902
1980	**HOU**	**N**	11	10	.524	3.35	35	35	4	234	205	**98**	200	2	0	0	0	70	6	1	.086	13	27	5	0	1.3	.889
1981			11	5	.688	**1.69**	21	21	5	149	99	68	140	3	0	0	0	51	11	0	.216	5	16	1	3	1.0	.955
1982			16	12	.571	3.16	35	35	10	250.1	196	**109**	245	3	0	0	0	83	10	0	.120	9	33	2	1	1.3	.955
1983			14	9	.609	2.98	29	29	5	196.1	134	101	183	2	0	0	0	69	5	0	.072	4	28	2	0	1.2	.941
1984			12	11	.522	3.04	30	30	5	183.2	143	69	197	2	0	0	0	61	6	0	.098	7	11	2	0	0.7	.900
1985			10	12	.455	3.80	35	35	4	232	205	95	209	0	0	0	0	63	7	0	.111	6	20	2	0	0.8	.929
1986			12	8	.600	3.34	30	30	1	178	119	82	194	0	0	0	0	59	6	0	.102	10	17	2	2	1.0	.931
1987			8	16	.333	**2.76**	34	34	0	211.2	154	87	**270**	0	0	0	0	65	4	1	.062	11	18	1	1	0.9	.967
1988			12	11	.522	3.52	33	33	4	220	186	87	**228**	1	0	0	0	70	4	0	.057	8	18	4	0	0.9	.867
1989	**TEX**	**A**	16	10	.615	3.20	32	32	6	239.1	162	98	**301**	2	0	0	0	0	0	0	—	11	19	3	0	1.0	.909
1990			13	9	.591	3.44	30	30	5	204	137	74	**232**	2	0	0	0	0	0	0	—	7	13	0	1	0.7	1.000
1991			12	6	.667	2.91	27	27	2	173	102	72	203	2	0	0	0	0	0	0	—	7	14	0	1	0.8	1.000
1992			5	9	.357	3.72	27	27	2	157.1	138	69	157	0	0	0	0	0	0	0	—	2	16	3	1	0.8	.857
1993			5	5	.500	4.88	13	13	0	66.1	54	40	46	0	0	0	0	0	0	0	—	1	4	3	0	0.6	.625
27 yrs.			324	292	.526	3.19	807	773	222	5387.1	3923	2795	5714	61	5	0	3	852	94	2	.110	219	546	90	27	1.1	.895
				3rd						**5th**		**1st**	**1st**	**7th**													
DIVISIONAL PLAYOFF SERIES																											
1981	**HOU**	**N**	1	1	.500	1.80	2	2	1	15	6	3	14	0	0	0	0	4	1	0	.250	0	0	0	0	0.0	.000
LEAGUE CHAMPIONSHIP SERIES																											
1969	**NY**	**N**	1	0	1.000	2.57	1	0	0	7	3	2	7	0	1	0	0	4	2	0	.500	1	0	0	0	1.0	1.000
1979	**CAL**	**A**	0	0	—	1.29	1	1	0	7	4	3	8	0	0	0	0	0	0	0	—	0	0	0	0	0.0	.000
1980	**HOU**	**N**	0	0	—	5.40	2	2	0	13.1	16	3	14	0	0	0	0	4	0	0	.000	1	3	0	0	2.0	1.000
1986			0	1	.000	3.86	2	2	0	14	9	1	17	0	0	0	0	4	0	0	.000	0	0	0	0	0.0	.000
4 yrs.			1	1	.500	3.70	6	5	0	41.1	32	9	46	0	1	0	0	12	2	0	.167	2	3	0	0	0.8	1.000
													1st														
WORLD SERIES																											
1969	**NY**	**N**	0	0	—	0.00	1	0	0	2.1	1	2	3	0	0	0	1	0	0	0	—	0	0	0	0	0.0	.000

Rosy Ryan

RYAN, WILFRED PATRICK DOLAN BL TR 6′ 185 lbs.
B. Mar. 15, 1898, Worcester, Mass. D. Dec. 10, 1980, Scottsdale, Ariz.

Year	Team		W	L	PCT	ERA	G	GS	CG	IP	H	BB	SO	ShO	Relief Pitching W	Relief Pitching L	Relief Pitching SV	Batting AB	Batting H	Batting HR	BA	PO	A	E	DP	TC/G	FA
1919	NY	N	1	2	.333	3.10	4	3	1	20.1	20	9	7	0	1	0	0	6	0	0	.000	1	3	0	0	1.0	1.000
1920			0	1	.000	1.76	3	1	1	15.1	14	4	5	0	0	0	0	5	0	0	.000	0	5	0	0	1.7	1.000
1921			7	10	.412	3.73	36	16	5	147.1	140	32	58	0	1	4	3	45	9	0	.200	5	33	0	1	1.1	1.000
1922			17	12	.586	**3.01**	46	22	12	191.2	194	74	75	1	**7**	3	3	62	12	0	.194	9	35	1	3	1.0	.978
1923			16	5	.762	3.49	**45**	15	7	172.2	169	46	58	0	**9**	2	4	53	11	0	.208	8	40	1	2	1.1	.980
1924			8	6	.571	4.26	37	9	2	124.2	137	37	36	0	6	2	5	36	5	0	.139	8	21	0	0	0.8	1.000
1925	BOS	N	2	8	.200	6.31	37	7	1	122.2	152	52	48	0	2	**5**	2	39	11	1	.282	4	25	5	0	0.9	.853
1926			0	2	.000	7.58	7	2	0	19	29	7	1	0	0	0	0	5	1	0	.200	1	4	0	0	0.7	1.000
1928	NY	A	0	0	—	16.50	3	0	0	6	17	1	5	0	0	0	0	4	0	0	.000	0	0	0	0	0.0	.000
1933	BKN	N	1	1	.500	4.55	30	0	0	61.1	69	16	22	0	1	1	2	13	2	0	.154	1	12	0	0	0.4	1.000
10 yrs.			52	47	.525	4.14	248	75	29	881	941	278	315	1	27	17	19	268	51	1	.190	37	178	7	6	0.9	.968
WORLD SERIES																											
1922	NY	N	1	0	1.000	0.00	1	0	0	2	1	0	2	0	1	0	0	0	0	0	—	0	0	0	0	0.0	.000
1923			1	0	1.000	0.96	3	0	0	9.1	11	3	3	0	1	0	0	2	0	0	.000	1	2	0	1	1.0	1.000
1924			1	0	1.000	3.18	2	0	0	5.2	7	4	3	0	1	0	0	2	1	1	.500	0	1	0	0	0.5	1.000
3 yrs.			3	0	1.000	1.59	6	0	0	17	19	7	8	0	3	0	0	4	1	1	.250	1	3	0	1	0.7	1.000

Mike Ryba

RYBA, DOMINIC JOSEPH BR TR 5′11½″ 190 lbs.
B. June 9, 1903, DeLancey, Pa. D. Dec. 13, 1971, Brookline Station, Mo.

Year	Team		W	L	PCT	ERA	G	GS	CG	IP	H	BB	SO	ShO	Relief Pitching W	Relief Pitching L	Relief Pitching SV	Batting AB	Batting H	Batting HR	BA	PO	A	E	DP	TC/G	FA
1935	STL	N	1	1	.500	3.38	2	1	1	16	15	1	6	0	1	0	0	5	2	0	.400	1	4	0	0	2.5	1.000
1936			5	1	.833	5.40	14	0	0	45	55	16	25	0	5	1	0	18	3	0	.167	16	6	0	0	1.2	1.000
1937			9	6	.600	4.13	38	8	5	135	152	40	57	0	6	3	0	48	15	0	.313	10	31	1	1	1.0	.976
1938			1	1	.500	5.40	3	0	0	5	8	1	0	0	1	1	0	0	0	0	—	0	1	0	1	0.3	1.000
1941	BOS	A	7	3	.700	4.46	40	3	0	121	143	42	54	0	6	2	6	37	8	0	.216	10	30	2	3	1.0	.952
1942			3	3	.500	3.86	18	0	0	44.1	49	13	16	0	3	3	3	17	5	0	.294	12	16	0	0	1.3	1.000
1943			7	5	.583	3.26	40	8	4	143.2	142	57	50	1	4	4	2	43	8	0	.186	9	25	1	1	0.9	.971
1944			12	7	.632	3.33	42	7	2	138	119	39	50	0	9	5	2	41	6	0	.146	8	38	3	3	1.2	.939
1945			7	6	.538	2.49	34	9	4	123	122	33	44	1	4	2	2	36	9	0	.250	8	19	0	2	0.8	1.000
1946			0	1	.000	3.55	9	0	0	12.2	12	5	5	0	0	1	1	2	2	0	1.000	0	1	0	0	0.1	1.000
10 yrs.			52	34	.605	3.66	240	36	16	783.2	817	247	307	2	39	22	16	247	58	0	.235	74	171	7	11	1.0	.972
WORLD SERIES																											
1946	BOS	A	0	0	—	13.50	1	0	0	0.2	2	1	0	0	0	0	0	0	0	0	—	0	0	1	0	1.0	.000

Gary Ryerson

RYERSON, GARY LAWRENCE BL TL 6′ 1″ 175 lbs.
B. June 7, 1948, Los Angeles, Calif.

Year	Team		W	L	PCT	ERA	G	GS	CG	IP	H	BB	SO	ShO	Relief Pitching W	Relief Pitching L	Relief Pitching SV	Batting AB	Batting H	Batting HR	BA	PO	A	E	DP	TC/G	FA
1972	MIL	A	3	8	.273	3.62	20	14	4	102	119	21	45	1	0	0	0	24	1	0	.042	2	15	4	0	1.0	.810
1973			0	1	.000	7.83	9	4	0	23	32	7	10	0	0	0	0	0	0	0	—	1	5	2	0	0.9	.750
2 yrs.			3	9	.250	4.39	29	18	4	125	151	28	55	1	0	0	0	24	1	0	.042	3	20	6	0	1.0	.793

Bret Saberhagen

SABERHAGEN, BRET WILLIAM BR TR 6′ 1″ 160 lbs.
B. Apr. 11, 1964, Chicago Heights, Ill.

Year	Team		W	L	PCT	ERA	G	GS	CG	IP	H	BB	SO	ShO	Relief Pitching W	Relief Pitching L	Relief Pitching SV	Batting AB	Batting H	Batting HR	BA	PO	A	E	DP	TC/G	FA
1984	KC	A	10	11	.476	3.48	38	18	2	157.2	138	36	73	1	4	1	1	0	0	0	—	15	22	1	1	1.0	.974
1985			20	6	.769	2.87	32	32	10	235.1	211	38	158	1	0	0	0	0	0	0	—	22	38	2	4	1.9	.968
1986			7	12	.368	4.15	30	25	4	156	165	29	112	2	1	0	0	0	0	0	—	14	26	2	0	1.4	.952
1987			18	10	.643	3.36	33	33	15	257	246	53	163	4	0	0	0	0	0	0	—	21	34	2	5	1.7	.965
1988			14	16	.467	3.80	35	35	9	260.2	**271**	59	171	0	0	0	0	0	0	0	—	15	34	3	3	1.5	.942
1989			**23**	6	**.793**	**2.16**	36	35	**12**	**262.1**	209	43	193	4	0	1	0	0	0	0	—	21	36	4	1	1.7	.934
1990			5	9	.357	3.27	20	20	5	135	146	28	87	0	0	0	0	0	0	0	—	16	28	1	2	2.3	.978
1991			13	8	.619	3.07	28	28	7	196.1	165	45	136	2	0	0	0	0	0	0	—	17	30	2	2	1.8	.959
1992	NY	N	3	5	.375	3.50	17	15	1	97.2	84	27	81	1	0	1	0	28	3	0	.107	7	26	0	2	1.9	1.000
1993			7	7	.500	3.29	19	19	4	139.1	131	17	93	1	0	0	0	45	5	0	.111	14	30	2	0	2.4	.957
1994			14	4	**.778**	2.74	24	24	4	177.1	169	13	143	0	0	0	0	58	10	0	.172	13	34	2	1	2.0	.959
1995	2 teams	NY N (16G 5–5)	CLR N (9G 2–1)																								
″	total		7	6	.538	4.18	25	25	3	153	165	33	100	0	0	0	0	49	5	0	.102	8	34	1	3	1.7	.977
12 yrs.			141	100	.585	3.26	337	309	76	2227.2	2100	421	1510	16	5	3	1	180	23	0	.128	183	372	22	24	1.7	.962
DIVISIONAL PLAYOFF SERIES																											
1995	CLR	N	0	1	.000	11.25	1	1	0	4	7	1	3	0	0	0	0	1	0	0	.000	0	1	0	0	1.0	1.000
LEAGUE CHAMPIONSHIP SERIES																											
1984	KC	A	0	0	—	2.25	1	1	0	8	6	1	5	0	0	0	0	0	0	0	—	1	1	1	0	3.0	.667
1985			0	0	—	6.14	2	2	0	7.1	12	2	6	0	0	0	0	0	0	0	—	2	1	0	0	1.5	1.000
2 yrs.			0	0		4.11	3	3	0	15.1	18	3	11	0	0	0	0	0	0	0		3	2	1	0	2.0	.833
WORLD SERIES																											
1985	KC	A	2	0	1.000	0.50	2	2	2	18	11	1	10	1	0	0	0	7	0	0	.000	0	0	0	0	0.0	.000

Ray Sadecki

SADECKI, RAYMOND MICHAEL BL TL 5′11″ 180 lbs.
B. Dec. 26, 1940, Kansas City, Kans.

Year	Team		W	L	PCT	ERA	G	GS	CG	IP	H	BB	SO	ShO	Relief Pitching W	Relief Pitching L	Relief Pitching SV	Batting AB	Batting H	Batting HR	BA	PO	A	E	DP	TC/G	FA
1960	STL	N	9	9	.500	3.78	26	26	7	157.1	148	86	95	1	0	0	0	57	12	0	.211	6	19	2	3	1.0	.926
1961			14	10	.583	3.72	31	31	13	222.2	196	102	114	0	0	0	0	87	22	0	.253	3	24	7	1	1.1	.794
1962			6	8	.429	5.54	22	17	4	102.1	121	43	50	1	1	0	1	37	3	1	.081	2	13	5	2	0.9	.750
1963			10	10	.500	4.10	36	28	4	193.1	198	78	136	1	1	0	1	64	9	0	.141	3	22	2	4	0.8	.926
1964			20	11	.645	3.68	37	32	9	220	232	60	119	2	0	2	1	75	12	0	.160	1	34	5	2	1.1	.875
1965			6	15	.286	5.21	36	28	4	172.2	192	64	122	0	0	0	1	55	11	0	.200	5	22	3	2	0.8	.900
1966	2 teams	STL N (5G 2–1)	SF N (26G 3–7)																								
″	total		5	8	.385	4.80	31	22	4	129.1	141	48	83	1	0	0	0	41	14	3	.341	4	14	0	0	0.6	1.000
1967	SF	N	12	6	.667	2.78	35	24	10	188	165	58	145	2	1	0	0	73	18	0	.247	7	30	5	3	1.2	.881
1968			12	**18**	.400	2.91	38	36	13	253.2	225	70	206	6	0	0	0	85	8	0	.094	5	34	6	1	1.2	.867
1969			5	8	.385	4.24	29	17	4	138	137	53	104	3	0	0	0	40	5	1	.125	9	29	2	1	1.4	.950
1970	NY	N	8	4	.667	3.88	28	19	4	139	134	52	89	0	0	0	0	39	8	0	.205	3	13	4	0	0.7	.800
1971			7	7	.500	2.93	34	20	5	163	139	44	120	2	1	0	0	50	10	0	.200	5	17	1	1	0.7	.957
1972			2	1	.667	3.09	34	2	0	75.2	73	31	38	0	1	0	0	13	2	0	.154	1	8	2	0	0.3	.818
1973			5	4	.556	3.39	31	11	1	116.2	109	41	87	0	1	0	1	31	7	0	.226	1	7	1	0	0.3	.889
1974			8	8	.500	3.48	34	10	3	101	107	35	46	1	4	3	0	27	7	0	.259	3	16	3	3	0.6	.864

Ray Sadecki *continued*

Year	Team	Lg	W	L	PCT	ERA	G	GS	CG	IP	H	BB	SO	ShO	Relief Pitching W	Relief Pitching L	Relief Pitching SV	Batting AB	Batting H	Batting HR	BA	PO	A	E	DP	TC/G	FA
1975	**3 teams**	**STL N** (8G 1–0) **ATL N** (25G 2–3) **KC A** (5G 1–0)																									
″	**total**		4	3	.571	4.03	38	5	0	80.1	91	31	32	0	3	1	1	15	3	0	.200	3	8	2	0	0.3	.846
1976	**2 teams**	**KC A** (3G 0–0) **MIL A** (36G 2–0)																									
″	**total**		2	0	1.000	3.86	39	0	0	42	45	23	28	0	2	0	1	0	0	0	—	1	2	2	0	0.1	.600
1977	**NY**	**N**	0	1	.000	6.00	4	0	0	3	3	3	0	0	0	1	0	0	0	0	—	0	0	0	0	0.0	.000
18 yrs.			135	131	.508	3.79	563	328	85	2498	2456	922	1614	20	15	7	7	789	151	5	.191	62	312	52	23	0.8	.878
WORLD SERIES																											
1964	**STL**	**N**	1	0	1.000	8.53	2	2	0	6.1	12	5	2	0	0	0	0	2	1	0	.500	0	1	0	0	0.5	1.000
1973	**NY**	**N**	0	0	—	1.93	4	0	0	4.2	5	1	6	0	0	0	1	0	0	0	—	0	1	0	0	0.3	1.000
2 yrs.			1	0	1.000	5.73	6	2	0	11	17	6	8	0	0	0	1	2	1	0	.500	0	2	0	0	0.3	1.000

Bob Sadowski

SADOWSKI, ROBERT BR TR 6′ 2″ 195 lbs.
Brother of Ted Sadowski. Brother of Eddie Sadowski.
B. Feb. 19, 1938, Pittsburgh, Pa.

Year	Team	Lg	W	L	PCT	ERA	G	GS	CG	IP	H	BB	SO	ShO	Relief Pitching W	Relief Pitching L	Relief Pitching SV	Batting AB	Batting H	Batting HR	BA	PO	A	E	DP	TC/G	FA
1963	**MIL**	**N**	5	7	.417	2.62	19	18	5	116.2	99	30	72	1	0	0	0	35	2	0	.057	7	23	0	2	1.6	1.000
1964			9	10	.474	4.10	51	18	5	166.2	159	56	96	0	3	2	5	52	8	0	.154	9	43	1	1	1.0	.981
1965			5	9	.357	4.32	34	13	3	123	117	35	78	0	2	1	3	35	3	0	.086	4	17	0	1	0.6	1.000
1966	**BOS**	**A**	1	1	.500	5.40	11	5	0	33.1	41	9	11	0	0	0	0	7	0	0	.000	1	7	3	1	1.0	.727
4 yrs.			20	27	.426	3.87	115	54	13	439.2	416	130	257	1	5	3	8	129	13	0	.101	21	90	4	5	1.0	.965

Jim Sadowski

SADOWSKI, JAMES MICHAEL BR TR 6′ 3″ 195 lbs.
B. Aug. 7, 1951, Pittsburgh, Pa.

Year	Team	Lg	W	L	PCT	ERA	G	GS	CG	IP	H	BB	SO	ShO	Relief Pitching W	Relief Pitching L	Relief Pitching SV	Batting AB	Batting H	Batting HR	BA	PO	A	E	DP	TC/G	FA
1974	**PIT**	**N**	0	1	.000	6.00	4	0	0	9	7	9	1	0	0	1	0	1	0	0	.000	2	4	0	0	1.5	1.000

Ted Sadowski

SADOWSKI, THEODORE BR TR 6′ 1½″ 190 lbs.
Brother of Bob Sadowski. Brother of Eddie Sadowski.
B. Apr. 1, 1936, Pittsburgh, Pa. D. July 18, 1993, Pittsburgh, Pa.

Year	Team	Lg	W	L	PCT	ERA	G	GS	CG	IP	H	BB	SO	ShO	Relief Pitching W	Relief Pitching L	Relief Pitching SV	Batting AB	Batting H	Batting HR	BA	PO	A	E	DP	TC/G	FA
1960	**WAS**	**A**	1	0	1.000	5.19	9	1	0	17.1	17	9	12	0	1	0	1	3	0	0	.000	0	2	0	0	0.2	1.000
1961	**MIN**	**A**	0	2	.000	6.82	15	1	0	33	49	11	12	0	0	1	0	6	0	0	.000	1	9	0	0	0.7	1.000
1962			1	1	.500	5.03	19	0	0	34	37	11	15	0	1	1	0	4	2	0	.500	2	7	0	0	0.5	1.000
3 yrs.			2	3	.400	5.76	43	2	0	84.1	103	31	39	0	2	2	1	13	2	0	.154	3	18	0	0	0.5	1.000

A. J. Sager

SAGER, ANTHONY JOSEPH BR TR 6′ 4″ 220 lbs.
B. Mar. 3, 1965, Columbus, Ohio.

Year	Team	Lg	W	L	PCT	ERA	G	GS	CG	IP	H	BB	SO	ShO	Relief Pitching W	Relief Pitching L	Relief Pitching SV	Batting AB	Batting H	Batting HR	BA	PO	A	E	DP	TC/G	FA
1994	**SD**	**N**	1	4	.200	5.98	22	3	0	46.2	62	16	26	0	1	3	0	10	1	0	.100	6	15	0	1	1.0	1.000
1995	**CLR**	**N**	0	0	—	7.36	10	0	0	14.2	19	7	10	0	0	0	0	3	0	0	.000	1	5	0	1	0.6	1.000
2 yrs.			1	4	.200	6.31	32	3	0	61.1	81	23	36	0	1	3	0	13	1	0	.077	7	20	0	2	0.8	1.000

Johnny Sain

SAIN, JOHN FRANKLIN BR TR 6′ 2″ 185 lbs.
B. Sept. 25, 1917, Havana, Ark.

Year	Team	Lg	W	L	PCT	ERA	G	GS	CG	IP	H	BB	SO	ShO	Relief Pitching W	Relief Pitching L	Relief Pitching SV	Batting AB	Batting H	Batting HR	BA	PO	A	E	DP	TC/G	FA
1942	**BOS**	**N**	4	7	.364	3.90	40	3	0	97	79	63	68	0	3	**6**	6	27	2	0	.074	1	25	0	0	0.6	1.000
1946			20	14	.588	2.21	37	34	**24**	265	225	87	129	3	1	0	2	94	28	0	.298	20	61	1	0	2.2	.988
1947			21	12	.636	3.52	38	35	22	266	**265**	79	132	3	0	0	1	107	37	0	.346	11	55	3	1	1.8	.957
1948			**24**	15	.615	2.60	42	**39**	**28**	**314.2**	**297**	83	137	4	1	0	1	115	25	0	.217	21	48	2	3	1.7	.972
1949			10	17	.370	4.81	37	36	16	243	285	75	73	1	0	0	0	97	20	0	.206	14	35	3	2	1.4	.942
1950			20	13	.606	3.94	37	37	25	278.1	**294**	70	96	3	0	0	0	102	21	1	.206	14	42	4	3	1.6	.933
1951	**2 teams**	**BOS N** (26G 5–13) **NY A** (7G 2–1)																									
″	**total**		7	14	.333	4.20	33	26	7	197.1	236	53	84	1	0	0	2	66	15	1	.227	14	38	1	4	1.6	.981
1952	**NY**	**A**	11	6	.647	3.46	35	16	8	148.1	149	38	57	0	3	1	7	71	19	1	.268	15	18	3	0	1.0	.917
1953			14	7	.667	3.00	40	19	10	189	189	45	84	1	4	1	9	68	17	0	.250	8	32	2	1	1.0	.952
1954			6	6	.500	3.16	45	0	0	77	66	15	33	0	6	6	**22**	17	6	0	.353	6	11	0	0	0.4	1.000
1955	**2 teams**	**NY A** (3G 0–0) **KC A** (25G 2–5)																									
″	**total**		2	5	.286	5.58	28	0	0	50	60	11	17	0	2	5	1	10	0	0	.000	3	6	0	0	0.3	1.000
11 yrs.			139	116	.545	3.49	412	245	140	2125.2	2145	619	910	16	20	19	51	774	190	3	.245	127	371	19	14	1.3	.963
WORLD SERIES																											
1948	**BOS**	**N**	1	1	.500	1.06	2	2	2	17	9	0	9	1	0	0	0	5	1	0	.200	2	2	0	0	2.0	1.000
1951	**NY**	**A**	0	0	—	9.00	1	0	0	2	4	2	2	0	0	0	0	1	0	0	.000	0	0	0	0	0.0	.000
1952			0	1	.000	3.00	1	0	0	6	6	3	3	0	0	1	0	3	0	0	.000	0	2	0	0	2.0	1.000
1953			1	0	1.000	4.76	2	0	0	5.2	8	1	1	0	1	0	0	2	1	0	.500	0	0	0	0	0.0	.000
4 yrs.			2	2	.500	2.64	6	2	2	30.2	27	6	15	1	1	1	0	11	2	0	.182	2	4	0	0	1.0	1.000

Luis Salazar

SALAZAR, LUIS ERNESTO BR TR 5′ 9″ 185 lbs.
Born Luis Ernesto Salazar (Garacia).
B. May 19, 1956, Barcelona, Venezuela.

Year	Team	Lg	W	L	PCT	ERA	G	GS	CG	IP	H	BB	SO	ShO	Relief Pitching W	Relief Pitching L	Relief Pitching SV	Batting AB	Batting H	Batting HR	BA	PO	A	E	DP	TC/G	FA
1987	**SD**	**N**	0	0	—	4.50	2	0	0	2	2	1	0	0	0	0	0	*				39	88	7	7	2.9	.948

Freddy Sale

SALE, FREDERICK LINK BR TR 5′ 9″ 160 lbs.
B. May 2, 1902, Chester, S. C. D. May 27, 1956, Hermosa Beach, Calif.

Year	Team	Lg	W	L	PCT	ERA	G	GS	CG	IP	H	BB	SO	ShO	Relief Pitching W	Relief Pitching L	Relief Pitching SV	Batting AB	Batting H	Batting HR	BA	PO	A	E	DP	TC/G	FA
1924	**PIT**	**N**	0	0	—	0.00	1	0	0	1	2	0	0	0	0	0	0	0	0	0	—	0	0	0	0	0.0	.000

Harry Salisbury

SALISBURY, HENRY H. BL 5′ 8½″ 162 lbs.
B. May 15, 1855, Providence, R. I. D. Mar. 29, 1933, Chicago, Ill.

Year	Team	Lg	W	L	PCT	ERA	G	GS	CG	IP	H	BB	SO	ShO	Relief Pitching W	Relief Pitching L	Relief Pitching SV	Batting AB	Batting H	Batting HR	BA	PO	A	E	DP	TC/G	FA
1879	**TRO**	**N**	4	6	.400	2.22	10	10	9	89	103	11	31	0	0	0	0	36	2	0	.056	3	27	2	0	2.9	.938
1882	**PIT**	**AA**	20	18	.526	*2.63*	38	38	38	335	315	37	135	1	0	0	0	145	22	0	.152	10	99	13	1	3.1	.893
2 yrs.			24	24	.500	2.55	48	48	47	424	418	48	166	1	0	0	0	181	24	0	.133	13	126	15	1	3.1	.903

Solly Salisbury

SALISBURY, WILLIAM ANSEL BR TR 6′ 180 lbs.
B. Nov. 12, 1876, Algona, Iowa D. Jan. 17, 1952, Rowena, Ore.

Year	Team	Lg	W	L	PCT	ERA	G	GS	CG	IP	H	BB	SO	ShO	Relief Pitching W	Relief Pitching L	Relief Pitching SV	Batting AB	Batting H	Batting HR	BA	PO	A	E	DP	TC/G	FA
1902	**PHI**	**N**	0	0	—	13.50	2	1	0	6	15	2	0	0	0	0	0	1	0	0	.000	0	0	1	0	0.5	.000

Roger Salkeld

SALKELD, ROGER WILLIAM BR TR 6′ 5″ 215 lbs.
B. Mar. 6, 1971, Burbank, Calif.

Year	Team	W	L	PCT	ERA	G	GS	CG	IP	H	BB	SO	ShO	Relief W	Relief L	Relief SV	AB	H	HR	BA	PO	A	E	DP	TC/G	FA
1993	SEA A	0	0	—	2.51	3	2	0	14.1	13	4	13	0	0	0	0	0	0	0	—	0	2	0	0	0.7	1.000
1994		2	5	.286	7.17	13	13	0	59	76	45	46	0	0	0	0	0	0	0	—	1	3	0	0	0.3	1.000
2 yrs.		2	5	.286	6.26	16	15	0	73.1	89	49	59	0	0	0	0	0	0	0		1	5	0	0	0.4	1.000

Slim Sallee

SALLEE, HARRY FRANKLIN BL TL 6′ 3″ 180 lbs.
B. Feb. 3, 1885, Higginsport, Ohio D. Mar. 22, 1950, Higginsport, Ohio.

Year	Team	W	L	PCT	ERA	G	GS	CG	IP	H	BB	SO	ShO	Relief W	Relief L	Relief SV	AB	H	HR	BA	PO	A	E	DP	TC/G	FA
1908	STL N	3	8	.273	3.15	25	12	7	128.2	144	36	39	1	1	0	0	41	2	0	.049	5	37	1	0	1.7	.977
1909		10	11	.476	2.42	32	27	12	219	223	59	55	1	0	2	0	71	8	0	.113	7	63	3	2	2.3	.959
1910		7	8	.467	2.97	18	13	9	115	112	24	46	1	1	1	2	37	4	0	.108	2	34	0	0	2.0	1.000
1911		15	9	.625	2.76	36	30	18	245	234	64	74	1	1	1	2	89	15	0	.169	7	55	2	0	1.8	.969
1912		16	17	.485	2.60	48	32	20	294	289	72	108	3	4	3	**6**	103	14	0	.136	17	61	3	0	1.7	.963
1913		18	15	.545	2.70	49	31	17	273	254	59	105	3	2	1	5	94	19	2	.202	12	72	2	1	1.8	.977
1914		18	17	.514	2.10	46	30	18	282.1	252	72	105	3	2	**5**	**6**	91	21	0	.231	3	71	2	2	1.7	.974
1915		13	17	.433	2.84	46	33	17	275.1	245	57	91	2	0	2	3	92	11	0	.120	7	74	4	1	1.8	.953
1916	2 teams STL N (16G 5–5) NY N (15G 9–4)																									
″	total	14	9	.609	2.18	31	18	11	181.2	171	33	63	4	4	1	1	53	12	0	.226	5	28	0	3	1.1	1.000
1917	NY N	18	7	.720	2.17	34	24	18	215.2	199	34	54	1	2	3	**4**	77	17	0	.221	4	46	0	5	1.5	1.000
1918		8	8	.500	2.25	18	16	12	132	122	12	33	1	0	0	2	41	5	0	.122	9	28	0	0	2.1	1.000
1919	CIN N	21	7	.750	2.06	29	28	22	227.2	221	20	24	4	1	0	0	74	14	0	.189	3	50	2	2	1.9	.964
1920	2 teams CIN N (21G 5–6) NY N (5G 1–0)																									
″	total	6	6	.500	3.11	26	14	7	133	145	16	15	0	0	1	2	38	7	0	.184	1	25	2	0	1.1	.929
1921	NY N	6	4	.600	3.64	37	0	0	96.1	115	14	23	0	**6**	4	2	22	8	0	.364	4	17	0	1	0.6	1.000
14 yrs.		173	143	.547	2.56	475	308	188	2818.2	2726	572	835	25	24	24	35	923	157	2	.170	86	661	21	17	1.6	.973
WORLD SERIES																										
1917	NY N	0	2	.000	4.70	2	2	1	15.1	20	4	4	0	0	0	0	6	1	0	.167	0	8	0	0	4.0	1.000
1919	CIN N	1	1	.500	1.35	2	2	1	13.1	19	1	2	0	0	0	0	4	0	0	.000	1	4	0	0	2.5	1.000
2 yrs.		1	3	.250	3.14	4	4	2	28.2	39	5	6	0	0	0	0	10	1	0	.100	1	12	0	0	3.3	1.000

Roger Salmon

SALMON, ROGER ELLIOTT BL TL 6′ 2″ 170 lbs.
B. May 11, 1891, Newark, N. J. D. June 17, 1974, Belfast, Me.

Year	Team	W	L	PCT	ERA	G	GS	CG	IP	H	BB	SO	ShO	Relief W	Relief L	Relief SV	AB	H	HR	BA	PO	A	E	DP	TC/G	FA
1912	PHI A	1	0	1.000	9.00	2	1	0	5	7	4	5	0	0	0	0	1	0	0	.000	0	0	0	0	0.0	.000

Gus Salve

SALVE, AUGUSTUS WILLIAM BL TL 6′ 190 lbs.
B. Dec. 29, 1885, Boston, Mass. D. Mar. 29, 1971, Providence, R. I.

Year	Team	W	L	PCT	ERA	G	GS	CG	IP	H	BB	SO	ShO	Relief W	Relief L	Relief SV	AB	H	HR	BA	PO	A	E	DP	TC/G	FA
1908	PHI A	0	1	.000	1.93	1	1	1	9.1	9	8	5	0	0	0	0	4	0	0	.000	1	1	0	0	2.0	1.000

Jack Salveson

SALVESON, JOHN THEODORE BR TR 6′½″ 180 lbs.
B. Jan. 5, 1914, Fullerton, Calif. D. Dec. 28, 1974, Norwalk, Calif.

Year	Team	W	L	PCT	ERA	G	GS	CG	IP	H	BB	SO	ShO	Relief W	Relief L	Relief SV	AB	H	HR	BA	PO	A	E	DP	TC/G	FA
1933	NY N	0	2	.000	3.82	8	2	2	30.2	30	14	8	0	0	0	0	9	1	0	.111	5	7	1	0	1.6	.923
1934		3	1	.750	3.52	12	4	0	38.1	43	13	18	0	2	0	0	10	3	0	.300	5	8	0	0	1.1	1.000
1935	2 teams PIT N (5G 0–1) CHI A (20G 1–2)																									
″	total	1	3	.250	5.25	25	2	2	73.2	90	28	24	0	1	3	1	22	6	1	.273	3	15	1	1	0.8	.947
1943	CLE A	5	3	.625	3.35	23	11	4	86	87	26	24	3	1	1	3	26	6	1	.231	2	19	0	4	0.9	1.000
1945		0	0	—	3.68	19	0	0	44	52	6	11	0	0	0	0	10	4	1	.400	4	13	0	0	0.9	1.000
5 yrs.		9	9	.500	3.99	87	19	8	272.2	302	87	85	3	4	4	4	77	20	3	.260	19	62	2	5	1.0	.976

Manny Salvo

SALVO, MANUEL (Gyp) BR TR 6′ 4″ 210 lbs.
B. June 30, 1913, Sacramento, Calif.

Year	Team	W	L	PCT	ERA	G	GS	CG	IP	H	BB	SO	ShO	Relief W	Relief L	Relief SV	AB	H	HR	BA	PO	A	E	DP	TC/G	FA
1939	NY N	4	10	.286	4.63	32	18	4	136	150	76	69	0	1	0	1	41	4	1	.098	8	31	3	2	1.3	.929
1940	BOS N	10	9	.526	3.08	21	20	14	160.2	151	43	60	**5**	0	0	0	58	6	0	.103	7	26	2	1	1.7	.943
1941		7	16	.304	4.06	35	27	11	195	192	93	67	2	1	1	0	62	7	0	.113	11	37	1	2	1.4	.980
1942		7	8	.467	3.03	25	14	6	130.2	129	41	25	1	2	1	0	41	5	0	.122	6	26	2	0	1.4	.941
1943	3 teams BOS N (1G 0–1) PHI N (1G 0–0) BOS N (20G 5–6)																									
″	total	5	7	.417	3.55	22	14	5	99	101	32	26	1	0	0	0	30	8	0	.267	6	17	2	2	1.1	.920
5 yrs.		33	50	.398	3.69	135	93	40	721.1	723	285	247	9	4	2	1	232	30	1	.129	38	137	10	7	1.4	.946

Joe Sambito

SAMBITO, JOSEPH CHARLES BL TL 6′ 1″ 185 lbs.
B. June 28, 1952, Brooklyn, N. Y.

Year	Team	W	L	PCT	ERA	G	GS	CG	IP	H	BB	SO	ShO	Relief W	Relief L	Relief SV	AB	H	HR	BA	PO	A	E	DP	TC/G	FA
1976	HOU N	3	2	.600	3.57	20	4	1	53	45	14	26	1	1	0	1	9	2	0	.222	4	10	0	1	0.7	1.000
1977		5	5	.500	2.33	54	1	0	89	77	24	67	0	5	4	7	13	2	0	.154	4	17	2	1	0.4	.913
1978		4	9	.308	3.07	62	0	0	88	85	32	96	0	4	9	11	6	1	0	.167	6	16	2	3	0.4	.917
1979		8	7	.533	1.78	63	0	0	91	80	23	83	0	8	7	22	7	2	0	.286	5	14	2	2	0.3	.905
1980		8	4	.667	2.20	64	0	0	90	65	22	75	0	8	4	17	9	0	0	.000	7	13	2	2	0.3	.909
1981		5	5	.500	1.83	49	0	0	64	43	22	41	0	5	5	10	5	0	0	.000	5	12	0	2	0.3	1.000
1982		0	0	—	0.71	9	0	0	12.2	7	2	7	0	0	0	4	1	0	0	.000	0	4	1	1	0.6	.800
1984		0	0	—	3.02	32	0	0	47.2	39	16	26	0	0	0	0	2	0	0	.000	1	3	0	0	0.1	1.000
1985	NY N	0	0	—	12.66	8	0	0	10.2	21	8	3	0	0	0	0	0	0	0	—	1	3	0	0	0.5	1.000
1986	BOS A	2	0	1.000	4.84	53	0	0	44.2	54	16	30	0	2	0	12	0	0	0	—	1	8	0	1	0.2	1.000
1987		2	6	.250	6.93	47	0	0	37.2	46	16	35	0	2	6	0	0	0	0	—	1	4	0	0	0.1	1.000
11 yrs.		37	38	.493	3.04	461	5	1	628.1	562	195	489	1	35	35	84	52	7	0	.135	35	104	9	13	0.3	.939
DIVISIONAL PLAYOFF SERIES																										
1981	HOU N	1	0	1.000	16.20	2	0	0	1.2	5	2	2	0	1	0	0	0	0	0	—	0	0	0	0	0.0	.000
LEAGUE CHAMPIONSHIP SERIES																										
1980	HOU N	0	1	.000	4.91	3	0	0	3.2	4	2	6	0	0	1	0	0	0	0	—	0	0	0	0	0.0	.000
1986	BOS A	0	0	—	0.00	3	0	0	0.2	1	1	0	0	0	0	0	0	0	0	—	0	0	0	0	0.0	.000
2 yrs.		0	1	.000	4.15	6	0	0	4.1	5	3	6	0	0	1	0	0	0	0		0	0	0	0	0.0	
WORLD SERIES																										
1986	BOS A	0	0	—	27.00	2	0	0	0.1	2	2	0	0	0	0	0	0	0	0	—	0	0	0	0	0.0	.000

Bill Sampen

SAMPEN, WILLIAM ALBERT
B. Jan. 18, 1963, Lincoln, Ill.
BR TR 6′ 1″ 185 lbs.

Year	Team	Lg	W	L	PCT	ERA	G	GS	CG	IP	H	BB	SO	ShO	Relief W	Relief L	Relief SV	AB	H	HR	BA	PO	A	E	DP	TC/G	FA
1990	MON	N	12	7	.632	2.99	59	4	0	90.1	94	33	69	0	**11**	6	2	8	0	0	.000	5	9	0	0	0.2	1.000
1991			9	5	.643	4.00	43	8	0	92.1	96	46	52	0	6	3	0	13	3	0	.231	3	9	1	0	0.3	.923
1992	2 teams	MON N	(44G 1–4)		KC A	(8G 0–2)																					
″	total		1	6	.143	3.25	52	2	0	83	83	32	37	0	1	4	0	6	0	0	.000	10	15	0	1	0.5	1.000
1993	KC	A	2	2	.500	5.89	18	0	0	18.1	25	9	9	0	2	2	0	0	0	0	—	2	2	0	0	0.2	1.000
1994	CAL	A	1	1	.500	6.46	10	0	0	15.1	14	13	9	0	1	1	0	0	0	0	—	1	3	0	0	0.4	1.000
5 yrs.			25	21	.543	3.73	182	14	0	299.1	312	133	176	0	21	16	2	27	3	0	.111	21	38	1	1	0.3	.983

Joe Samuels

SAMUELS, JOSEPH JONAS (Skabotch)
B. Mar. 21, 1905, Scranton, Pa.
BR TR 6′ 1½″ 196 lbs.

Year	Team	Lg	W	L	PCT	ERA	G	GS	CG	IP	H	BB	SO	ShO	Relief W	Relief L	Relief SV	AB	H	HR	BA	PO	A	E	DP	TC/G	FA
1930	DET	A	0	0	—	16.50	2	0	0	6	10	6	1	0	0	0	0	1	0	0	.000	1	0	0	0	0.5	1.000

Roger Samuels

SAMUELS, ROGER HOWARD
B. Jan. 5, 1961, San Jose, Calif.
BL TL 6′ 5″ 210 lbs.

Year	Team	Lg	W	L	PCT	ERA	G	GS	CG	IP	H	BB	SO	ShO	Relief W	Relief L	Relief SV	AB	H	HR	BA	PO	A	E	DP	TC/G	FA
1988	SF	N	1	2	.333	3.47	15	0	0	23.1	17	7	22	0	1	2	0	3	0	0	.000	1	4	0	0	0.3	1.000
1989	PIT	N	0	0	—	9.82	5	0	0	3.2	9	4	2	0	0	0	0	0	0	0	—	0	0	0	0	0.0	.000
2 yrs.			1	2	.333	4.33	20	0	0	27	26	11	24	0	1	2	0	3	0	0	.000	1	4	0	0	0.3	1.000

Alex Sanchez

SANCHEZ, ALEX ANTHONY
B. Apr. 8, 1966, Concord, Calif.
BR TR 6′ 2″ 185 lbs.

Year	Team	Lg	W	L	PCT	ERA	G	GS	CG	IP	H	BB	SO	ShO	Relief W	Relief L	Relief SV	AB	H	HR	BA	PO	A	E	DP	TC/G	FA
1989	TOR	A	0	1	.000	10.03	4	3	0	11.2	16	14	4	0	0	0	0	0	0	0	—	1	6	0	1	1.8	1.000

Israel Sanchez

SANCHEZ, ISRAEL
Born Israel Sanchez (Matos).
B. Aug. 20, 1963, Falcon Lasvias, Cuba.
BL TL 5′ 9″ 170 lbs.

Year	Team	Lg	W	L	PCT	ERA	G	GS	CG	IP	H	BB	SO	ShO	Relief W	Relief L	Relief SV	AB	H	HR	BA	PO	A	E	DP	TC/G	FA
1988	KC	A	3	2	.600	4.54	19	1	0	35.2	36	18	14	0	3	2	1	0	0	0	—	2	7	1	0	0.5	.900
1990			0	0	—	8.38	11	0	0	9.2	16	3	5	0	0	0	0	0	0	0	—	1	1	1	0	0.3	.667
2 yrs.			3	2	.600	5.36	30	1	0	45.1	52	21	19	0	3	2	1	0	0	0		3	8	2	0	0.4	.846

Luis Sanchez

SANCHEZ, LUIS MERCEDES
Born Luis Mercedes Escoba (Sanchez).
B. Aug. 24, 1953, Cariaco, Venezuela.
BR TR 6′ 2″ 170 lbs.

Year	Team	Lg	W	L	PCT	ERA	G	GS	CG	IP	H	BB	SO	ShO	Relief W	Relief L	Relief SV	AB	H	HR	BA	PO	A	E	DP	TC/G	FA
1981	CAL	A	0	2	.000	2.91	17	0	0	34	39	11	13	0	0	2	2	0	0	0	—	1	6	2	0	0.5	.778
1982			7	4	.636	3.21	46	0	0	92.2	89	34	58	0	7	4	5	0	0	0	—	1	19	1	1	0.5	.952
1983			10	8	.556	3.66	56	1	0	98.1	92	40	49	0	10	7	7	0	0	0	—	1	24	0	2	0.4	1.000
1984			9	7	.563	3.33	49	0	0	83.2	84	33	62	0	9	7	11	0	0	0	—	3	10	2	2	0.3	.867
1985			2	0	1.000	5.72	26	0	0	61.1	67	27	34	0	2	0	2	0	0	0	—	3	11	1	1	0.6	.933
5 yrs.			28	21	.571	3.75	194	1	0	370	371	145	216	0	28	20	27	0	0	0		9	70	6	6	0.4	.929
LEAGUE CHAMPIONSHIP SERIES																											
1982	CAL	A	0	1	.000	6.75	2	0	0	2.2	4	1	1	0	0	1	0	0	0	0	—	0	0	0	0	0.0	.000

Raul Sanchez

SANCHEZ, RAUL GUADALUPE
Born Raul Guadalupe Sanchez (Rodriguez).
B. Dec. 12, 1930, Marianao, Cuba.
BR TR 6′ 150 lbs.

Year	Team	Lg	W	L	PCT	ERA	G	GS	CG	IP	H	BB	SO	ShO	Relief W	Relief L	Relief SV	AB	H	HR	BA	PO	A	E	DP	TC/G	FA
1952	WAS	A	1	1	.500	3.55	3	2	1	12.2	13	7	6	1	0	0	0	5	0	0	.000	1	2	0	0	1.0	1.000
1957	CIN	N	3	2	.600	4.76	38	0	0	62.1	61	25	37	0	3	2	5	7	2	0	.286	6	12	3	2	0.6	.857
1960			1	0	1.000	4.91	8	0	0	14.2	12	11	5	0	1	0	0	2	1	0	.500	2	3	0	0	0.6	1.000
3 yrs.			5	3	.625	4.62	49	2	1	89.2	86	43	48	1	4	2	5	14	3	0	.214	9	17	3	2	0.6	.897

Ben Sanders

SANDERS, ALEXANDER BENNETT
B. Feb. 16, 1865, Catharpin, Va. D. Aug. 29, 1930, Memphis, Tenn.
BR TR 6′ 210 lbs.

Year	Team	Lg	W	L	PCT	ERA	G	GS	CG	IP	H	BB	SO	ShO	Relief W	Relief L	Relief SV	AB	H	HR	BA	PO	A	E	DP	TC/G	FA
1888	PHI	N	19	10	.655	1.90	31	29	28	275.1	240	33	121	**8**	0	1	0	236	58	1	.246	55	79	10	1	2.5	.931
1889			19	18	.514	3.55	44	39	34	349.2	406	96	123	1	1	0	1	169	47	0	.278	24	58	11	1	2.0	.882
1890	PHI	P	19	18	.514	3.76	43	40	37	346.2	412	69	107	2	0	0	1	189	59	0	.312	30	95	11	6	2.6	.919
1891	PHI	AA	11	5	.688	3.79	19	18	15	145	157	37	40	0	0	0	0	156	39	1	.250	32	31	8	1	1.7	.887
1892	LOU	N	12	19	.387	3.22	31	31	30	268.1	281	62	77	3	0	0	0	198	54	3	.273	172	61	12	7	4.5	.951
5 yrs.			80	70	.533	3.24	168	157	144	1385	1496	297	468	14	1	1	2	*				313	324	52	16	2.7	.925

Dee Sanders

SANDERS, DEE WILMA
B. Apr. 8, 1921, Quitman, Tex.
BR TR 6′ 3″ 195 lbs.

Year	Team	Lg	W	L	PCT	ERA	G	GS	CG	IP	H	BB	SO	ShO	Relief W	Relief L	Relief SV	AB	H	HR	BA	PO	A	E	DP	TC/G	FA
1945	STL	A	0	0	—	40.50	2	0	0	1.1	7	1	1	0	0	0	0	0	0	0	—	0	1	0	0	0.5	1.000

Ken Sanders

SANDERS, KENNETH GEORGE (Daffy)
B. July 8, 1941, St. Louis, Mo.
BR TR 5′11″ 168 lbs.

Year	Team	Lg	W	L	PCT	ERA	G	GS	CG	IP	H	BB	SO	ShO	Relief W	Relief L	Relief SV	AB	H	HR	BA	PO	A	E	DP	TC/G	FA
1964	KC	A	0	2	.000	3.67	21	0	0	27	23	17	18	0	0	2	1	0	0	0	—	2	7	1	2	0.5	.900
1966	2 teams	BOS A	(24G 3–6)		KC A	(38G 3–4)																					
″	total		6	10	.375	3.75	62	1	0	112.2	95	76	74	0	6	**10**	3	14	2	0	.143	8	20	3	2	0.5	.903
1968	OAK	A	0	1	.000	3.38	7	0	0	10.2	8	8	6	0	0	1	0	0	0	0	—	0	2	0	0	0.3	1.000
1970	MIL	A	5	2	.714	1.76	50	0	0	92	64	25	64	0	5	2	13	13	3	0	.231	5	19	1	1	0.5	.960
1971			7	12	.368	1.92	**83**	0	0	136	111	34	80	0	7	**12**	**31**	14	0	0	.000	12	30	1	1	0.5	.977
1972			2	9	.182	3.13	62	0	0	92	88	31	51	0	2	**9**	17	7	1	0	.143	7	18	1	1	0.4	.962
1973	2 teams	MIN A	(27G 2–4)		CLE A	(15G 5–1)																					
″	total		7	5	.583	4.40	42	0	0	71.2	71	30	33	0	7	5	13	0	0	0		5	13	1	1	0.5	.947
1974	2 teams	CLE A	(9G 0–1)		CAL A	(9G 0–0)																					
″	total		0	1	.000	6.53	18	0	0	20.2	31	8	8	0	0	1	2	0	0	0		0	7	0	0	0.4	1.000
1975	NY	N	1	1	.500	2.30	29	0	0	43	31	14	8	0	1	1	5	2	0	0	.000	7	5	0	0	0.4	1.000
1976	2 teams	NY N	(31G 1–2)		KC A	(3G 0–0)																					
″	total		1	2	.333	2.70	34	0	0	50	42	15	18	0	1	2	1	2	0	0	.000	8	8	0	0	0.5	1.000
10 yrs.			29	45	.392	2.98	408	1	0	655.2	564	258	360	0	29	45	86	52	6	0	.115	54	129	8	8	0.5	.958

Roy Sanders

SANDERS, ROY GARVIN (Butch, Pep) BR TR 6′½″ 195 lbs.
B. Aug. 1, 1892, Stafford, Kans. D. Jan. 17, 1950, Kansas City, Mo.

Year	Team	Lg	W	L	PCT	ERA	G	GS	CG	IP	H	BB	SO	ShO	Relief W	Relief L	Relief SV	AB	H	HR	BA	PO	A	E	DP	TC/G	FA
1917	CIN	N	0	1	.000	4.50	2	2	1	14	12	16	3	0	0	0	0	6	0	0	.000	1	6	0	1	3.5	1.000
1918	PIT	N	7	9	.438	2.60	28	14	6	156	135	52	55	1	3	3	1	53	8	0	.151	5	51	2	5	2.1	.966
2 yrs.			7	10	.412	2.75	30	16	7	170	147	68	58	1	3	3	1	59	8	0	.136	6	57	2	6	2.2	.969

Roy Sanders

SANDERS, ROY LEE (Simon) BR TR 6′ 185 lbs.
B. June 10, 1894, Mo. D. July 8, 1963, Louisville, Ky.

Year	Team	Lg	W	L	PCT	ERA	G	GS	CG	IP	H	BB	SO	ShO	Relief W	Relief L	Relief SV	AB	H	HR	BA	PO	A	E	DP	TC/G	FA
1918	NY	A	0	2	.000	4.21	6	2	0	25.2	28	16	8	0	0	0	0	7	0	0	.000	0	5	2	0	1.2	.714
1920	STL	A	1	1	.500	5.19	8	1	0	17.1	20	17	2	0	0	1	0	4	0	0	.000	0	2	0	0	0.3	1.000
2 yrs.			1	3	.250	4.60	14	3	0	43	48	33	10	0	0	1	0	11	0	0	.000	0	7	2	0	0.6	.778

Scott Sanders

SANDERS, SCOTT GERALD BR TR 6′ 4″ 210 lbs.
B. Mar. 25, 1969, Hannibal, Mo.

Year	Team	Lg	W	L	PCT	ERA	G	GS	CG	IP	H	BB	SO	ShO	Relief W	Relief L	Relief SV	AB	H	HR	BA	PO	A	E	DP	TC/G	FA
1993	SD	N	3	3	.500	4.13	9	9	0	52.1	54	23	37	0	0	0	0	16	1	0	.063	3	2	0	0	0.6	1.000
1994			4	8	.333	4.78	23	20	0	111	103	48	109	0	0	0	1	32	4	0	.125	9	15	0	0	1.0	1.000
1995			5	5	.500	4.30	17	15	1	90	79	31	88	0	0	0	0	27	8	0	.296	6	3	0	0	0.5	1.000
3 yrs.			12	16	.429	4.48	49	44	1	253.1	236	102	234	0	0	0	1	75	13	0	.173	18	20	0	0	0.8	1.000

War Sanders

SANDERS, WARREN WILLIAMS BR TL 5′10″ 160 lbs.
B. Aug. 2, 1877, Maynardville, Tenn. D. Aug. 3, 1962, Chattanooga, Tenn.

Year	Team	Lg	W	L	PCT	ERA	G	GS	CG	IP	H	BB	SO	ShO	Relief W	Relief L	Relief SV	AB	H	HR	BA	PO	A	E	DP	TC/G	FA
1903	STL	N	1	5	.167	6.08	8	6	3	40	48	21	9	0	0	1	0	15	1	0	.067	1	9	1	0	1.4	.909
1904			1	2	.333	4.74	4	3	1	19	25	1	11	0	0	0	0	6	0	0	.000	2	6	0	0	2.0	1.000
2 yrs.			2	7	.222	5.64	12	9	4	59	73	22	20	0	0	1	0	21	1	0	.048	3	15	1	0	1.6	.947

Scott Sanderson

SANDERSON, SCOTT DOUGLAS BR TR 6′ 5″ 195 lbs.
B. July 22, 1956, Dearborn, Mich.

Year	Team	Lg	W	L	PCT	ERA	G	GS	CG	IP	H	BB	SO	ShO	Relief W	Relief L	Relief SV	AB	H	HR	BA	PO	A	E	DP	TC/G	FA
1978	MON	N	4	2	.667	2.51	10	9	1	61	52	21	50	1	0	0	0	19	2	0	.105	2	6	1	0	0.9	.889
1979			9	8	.529	3.43	34	24	5	168	148	54	138	3	1	1	1	50	8	0	.160	9	13	1	1	0.7	.957
1980			16	11	.593	3.11	33	33	7	211	206	56	125	3	0	0	0	64	5	0	.078	14	21	1	0	1.1	.972
1981			9	7	.563	2.96	22	22	4	137	122	31	77	1	0	0	0	35	4	0	.114	6	14	0	0	0.9	1.000
1982			12	12	.500	3.46	32	32	7	224	212	58	158	0	0	0	0	57	8	1	.140	13	16	1	1	0.9	.967
1983			6	7	.462	4.65	18	16	0	81.1	98	20	55	0	0	0	1	28	4	0	.143	4	6	2	0	0.7	.833
1984	CHI	N	8	5	.615	3.14	24	24	3	140.2	140	24	76	0	0	0	0	42	5	0	.119	11	24	1	0	1.5	.972
1985			5	6	.455	3.12	19	19	2	121	100	27	80	0	0	0	0	31	2	0	.065	11	21	0	2	1.7	1.000
1986			9	11	.450	4.19	37	28	1	169.2	165	37	124	1	2	0	1	51	3	0	.059	11	20	2	3	0.9	.939
1987			8	9	.471	4.29	32	22	0	144.2	156	50	106	0	1	2	2	40	3	1	.075	10	14	2	3	0.8	.923
1988			1	2	.333	5.28	11	0	0	15.1	13	3	6	0	1	2	0	0	0	0	—	0	1	0	0	0.1	1.000
1989			11	9	.550	3.94	37	23	2	146.1	155	31	86	0	1	2	0	43	2	0	.047	10	12	0	1	0.6	1.000
1990	OAK	A	17	11	.607	3.88	34	34	2	206.1	205	66	128	1	0	0	0	0	0	0	—	11	18	2	2	0.9	.935
1991	NY	A	16	10	.615	3.81	34	34	2	208	200	29	130	2	0	0	0	0	0	0	—	15	13	1	0	0.9	.966
1992			12	11	.522	4.93	33	33	2	193.1	220	64	104	1	0	0	0	0	0	0	—	4	18	2	1	0.7	.917
1993	**2 teams**	**CAL A**	(21G 7–11)	**SF N**	(11G 4–2)																						
"	**total**		11	13	.458	4.21	32	29	4	184	201	34	102	1	0	0	0	14	0	0	.000	13	23	2	1	1.2	.947
1994	CHI	A	8	4	.667	5.09	18	14	1	92	110	12	36	0	0	1	0	0	0	0	—	4	18	0	1	1.2	1.000
1995	CAL	A	1	3	.250	4.12	7	7	0	39.1	48	4	23	0	0	0	0	0	0	0	—	3	4	0	1	1.0	1.000
18 yrs.			163	141	.536	3.82	467	403	43	2543	2551	621	1604	14	6	8	5	474	46	2	.097	151	262	18	17	0.9	.958
DIVISIONAL PLAYOFF SERIES																											
1981	MON	N	0	0	—	6.75	1	1	0	2.2	4	2	2	0	0	0	0	1	0	0	.000	0	0	0	0	0.0	.000
LEAGUE CHAMPIONSHIP SERIES																											
1984	CHI	N	0	0	—	5.79	1	1	0	4.2	6	1	2	0	0	0	0	2	0	0	.000	0	1	0	0	1.0	1.000
1989			0	0	—	0.00	1	0	0	2	2	0	1	0	0	0	0	0	0	0	—	0	0	0	0	0.0	.000
2 yrs.			0	0		4.05	2	1	0	6.2	8	1	3	0	0	0	0	2	0	0	.000	0	1	0	0	0.5	1.000
WORLD SERIES																											
1990	OAK	A	0	0	—	10.80	2	0	0	1.2	4	1	0	0	0	0	0	0	0	0	—	0	0	0	0	0.0	.000

Fred Sanford

SANFORD, JOHN FREDERICK BB TR 6′ 1″ 200 lbs.
B. Aug. 9, 1919, Garfield, Utah BR 1948

Year	Team	Lg	W	L	PCT	ERA	G	GS	CG	IP	H	BB	SO	ShO	Relief W	Relief L	Relief SV	AB	H	HR	BA	PO	A	E	DP	TC/G	FA
1943	STL	A	0	0	—	1.93	3	0	0	9.1	7	4	2	0	0	0	0	0	0	0	—	0	3	0	0	1.0	1.000
1946			2	1	.667	2.05	3	3	2	22	19	9	8	2	0	0	0	7	2	0	.286	1	3	0	1	1.3	1.000
1947			7	16	.304	3.71	34	23	9	186.2	186	76	62	0	0	2	4	54	11	0	.204	7	26	1	0	1.0	.971
1948			12	**21**	.364	4.64	42	33	9	227	250	91	79	1	2	2	2	73	11	1	.151	9	46	4	1	1.4	.932
1949	NY	A	7	3	.700	3.87	29	11	3	95.1	100	57	51	0	2	0	0	34	4	0	.118	2	17	2	1	0.7	.905
1950			5	4	.556	4.55	26	12	2	112.2	103	79	54	0	1	1	0	35	8	0	.229	9	30	0	5	1.5	1.000
1951	**3 teams**	**NY A**	(11G 0–3)	**WAS A**	(7G 2–3)	**STL A**	(9G 2–4)																				
"	**total**		4	10	.286	6.82	27	16	1	91	103	75	29	0	0	1	0	26	3	0	.115	5	15	0	0	0.7	1.000
7 yrs.			37	55	.402	4.45	164	98	26	744	768	391	285	3	5	6	6	229	39	1	.170	33	140	7	8	1.1	.961

Jack Sanford

SANFORD, JOHN STANLEY BR TR 6′ 190 lbs.
B. May 18, 1929, Wellesley Hills, Mass.

Year	Team	Lg	W	L	PCT	ERA	G	GS	CG	IP	H	BB	SO	ShO	Relief W	Relief L	Relief SV	AB	H	HR	BA	PO	A	E	DP	TC/G	FA
1956	PHI	N	1	0	1.000	1.38	3	1	0	13	7	13	6	0	0	0	0	3	1	0	.333	0	2	0	1	0.7	1.000
1957			19	8	.704	3.08	33	33	15	236.2	194	94	**188**	3	0	0	0	89	15	0	.169	15	30	2	2	1.4	.957
1958			10	13	.435	4.44	38	27	7	186.1	197	81	106	2	2	1	0	59	10	0	.169	12	23	2	0	1.0	.946
1959	SF	N	15	12	.556	3.16	36	31	10	222.1	198	70	132	0	0	1	1	72	8	0	.111	10	31	1	1	1.2	.976
1960			12	14	.462	3.82	37	34	11	219	199	99	125	**6**	0	1	0	74	13	0	.176	13	33	1	3	1.3	.979
1961			13	9	.591	4.22	38	33	6	217.1	203	87	112	0	0	0	0	74	16	3	.216	9	41	3	1	1.4	.943
1962			24	7	.774	3.43	39	38	13	265.1	233	92	147	2	0	0	0	98	15	0	.153	21	52	4	4	2.0	.948
1963			16	13	.552	3.51	42	**42**	11	284.1	273	76	158	0	0	0	0	94	13	0	.138	16	65	2	4	2.0	.976
1964			5	7	.417	3.30	18	17	3	106.1	91	37	64	1	0	0	1	30	4	0	.133	8	22	2	0	1.8	.938
1965	**2 teams**	**SF N**	(23G 4–5)	**CAL A**	(9G 1–2)																						
"	**total**		5	7	.417	4.11	32	21	0	120.1	127	40	56	0	0	0	3	32	4	0	.125	7	23	2	1	1.0	.938

Jack Sanford *continued*

Year	Team	Lg	W	L	PCT	ERA	G	GS	CG	IP	H	BB	SO	ShO	Relief Pitching W	Relief Pitching L	Relief Pitching SV	Batting AB	Batting H	Batting HR	BA	PO	A	E	DP	TC/G	FA
1966	CAL	A	13	7	.650	3.83	50	6	0	108	108	27	54	0	**12**	4	5	22	3	0	.136	7	23	2	1	0.6	.938
1967	2 teams	CAL A (12G 3–2) KC A (10G 1–2)																									
″	total		4	4	.500	5.12	22	10	0	70.1	77	21	34	0	1	1	1	18	3	0	.167	4	20	0	1	1.1	1.000
12 yrs.			137	101	.576	3.69	388	293	76	2049.1	1907	737	1182	14	15	8	11	665	105	3	.158	122	365	21	19	1.3	.959
WORLD SERIES																											
1962	SF	N	1	2	.333	1.93	3	3	1	23.1	16	8	19	1	0	0	0	7	3	0	.429	3	3	0	1	2.0	1.000

Mo Sanford

SANFORD, MEREDITH LEROY BR TR 6′ 6″ 220 lbs.
B. Dec. 1, 1967, Americus, Ga.

Year	Team	Lg	W	L	PCT	ERA	G	GS	CG	IP	H	BB	SO	ShO	Relief Pitching W	Relief Pitching L	Relief Pitching SV	Batting AB	Batting H	Batting HR	BA	PO	A	E	DP	TC/G	FA
1991	CIN	N	1	2	.333	3.86	5	5	0	28	19	15	31	0	0	0	0	8	0	0	.000	2	1	0	0	0.6	1.000
1993	CLR	N	1	2	.333	5.30	11	6	0	35.2	37	27	36	0	0	0	0	8	0	0	.000	3	2	3	0	0.7	.625
1995	MIN	A	0	0	—	5.30	11	0	0	18.2	16	16	17	0	0	0	0	0	0	0	—	0	0	0	0	0.0	.000
3 yrs.			2	4	.333	4.81	27	11	0	82.1	72	58	84	0	0	0	0	16	0	0	.000	5	3	3	0	0.4	.727

Jose Santiago

SANTIAGO, JOSE GUILLERMO (Pants) BR TR 5′10″ 175 lbs.
Born Jose Guillermo Santiago (Guzman).
B. Sept. 4, 1928, Coamo, Puerto Rico.

Year	Team	Lg	W	L	PCT	ERA	G	GS	CG	IP	H	BB	SO	ShO	Relief Pitching W	Relief Pitching L	Relief Pitching SV	Batting AB	Batting H	Batting HR	BA	PO	A	E	DP	TC/G	FA
1954	CLE	A	0	0	—	0.00	1	0	0	1.2	0	2	1	0	0	0	0	0	0	0	—	0	0	1	0	1.0	.000
1955			2	0	1.000	2.48	17	0	0	32.2	31	14	19	0	2	0	0	4	2	0	.500	1	6	1	0	0.5	.875
1956	KC	A	1	2	.333	8.31	9	5	0	21.2	36	17	9	0	0	0	0	5	2	0	.400	1	5	0	1	0.7	1.000
3 yrs.			3	2	.600	4.66	27	5	0	56	67	33	29	0	2	0	0	9	4	0	.444	2	11	2	1	0.6	.867

Jose Santiago

SANTIAGO, JOSE RAFAEL BR TR 6′ 2″ 185 lbs.
Born Jose Rafael Santiago (Alfonso).
B. Aug. 15, 1940, Juana Diaz, Puerto Rico.

Year	Team	Lg	W	L	PCT	ERA	G	GS	CG	IP	H	BB	SO	ShO	Relief Pitching W	Relief Pitching L	Relief Pitching SV	Batting AB	Batting H	Batting HR	BA	PO	A	E	DP	TC/G	FA
1963	KC	A	1	0	1.000	9.00	4	0	0	7	8	2	6	0	1	0	0	0	0	0	—	2	1	0	0	0.8	1.000
1964			0	6	.000	4.73	34	8	0	83.2	84	35	64	0	0	1	0	18	0	0	.000	10	9	4	0	0.7	.826
1965			0	0	—	9.00	4	0	0	5	8	4	8	0	0	0	0	0	0	0	—	0	1	0	0	0.3	1.000
1966	BOS	A	12	13	.480	3.66	35	28	7	172	155	58	119	1	0	1	2	56	11	0	.196	9	22	0	1	0.9	1.000
1967			12	4	.750	3.59	50	11	2	145.1	138	47	109	0	8	3	5	42	8	1	.190	9	22	0	2	0.6	1.000
1968			9	4	.692	2.25	18	18	7	124	96	42	86	2	0	0	0	43	7	0	.163	7	16	1	2	1.3	.958
1969			0	0	—	3.52	10	0	0	7.2	11	4	4	0	0	0	0	0	0	0	—	0	0	0	0	0.0	.000
1970			0	2	.000	10.64	8	0	0	11	18	8	8	0	0	2	1	3	2	0	.667	2	0	0	0	0.3	1.000
8 yrs.			34	29	.540	3.74	163	65	16	555.2	518	200	404	3	9	7	8	162	28	1	.173	39	71	5	5	0.7	.957
WORLD SERIES																											
1967	BOS	A	0	2	.000	5.59	3	2	0	9.2	16	3	6	0	0	0	0	2	1	1	.500	0	0	0	0	0.0	.000

Al Santorini

SANTORINI, ALAN JOEL BR TR 6′ 190 lbs.
B. May 19, 1948, Irvington, N. J.

Year	Team	Lg	W	L	PCT	ERA	G	GS	CG	IP	H	BB	SO	ShO	Relief Pitching W	Relief Pitching L	Relief Pitching SV	Batting AB	Batting H	Batting HR	BA	PO	A	E	DP	TC/G	FA
1968	ATL	N	0	1	.000	0.00	1	1	0	3	4	0	0	0	0	0	0	0	0	0	—	0	1	1	0	2.0	.500
1969	SD	N	8	14	.364	3.94	32	30	2	185	194	73	111	1	0	0	0	63	7	1	.111	9	34	2	2	1.4	.956
1970			1	8	.111	6.04	21	12	0	76	91	43	41	0	0	0	1	18	0	0	.000	2	7	0	1	0.4	1.000
1971	2 teams	SD N (18G 0–2) STL N (19G 0–2)																									
″	total		0	4	.000	3.78	37	8	0	88	94	30	42	0	0	0	2	15	5	0	.333	6	9	3	0	0.5	.833
1972	STL	N	8	11	.421	4.11	30	19	3	133.2	136	46	72	3	2	3	0	40	3	0	.075	10	12	1	1	0.8	.957
1973			0	0	—	5.40	6	0	0	8.1	14	2	2	0	0	0	0	1	0	0	.000	1	0	0	0	0.2	1.000
6 yrs.			17	38	.309	4.28	127	70	5	494	533	194	268	4	2	3	3	137	15	1	.109	28	63	7	4	0.8	.929

Manny Sarmiento

SARMIENTO, MANUEL EDUARDO BR TR 6′ 170 lbs.
Born Manuel Eduardo Sarmiento (Aponte).
B. Feb. 2, 1956, Cagua, Venezuela.

Year	Team	Lg	W	L	PCT	ERA	G	GS	CG	IP	H	BB	SO	ShO	Relief Pitching W	Relief Pitching L	Relief Pitching SV	Batting AB	Batting H	Batting HR	BA	PO	A	E	DP	TC/G	FA
1976	CIN	N	5	1	.833	2.05	22	0	0	44	36	12	20	0	5	1	0	7	0	0	.000	2	2	0	0	0.2	1.000
1977			0	0	—	2.48	24	0	0	40	28	11	23	0	0	0	1	1	0	0	.000	0	2	0	0	0.1	1.000
1978			9	7	.563	4.39	63	4	0	127	109	54	72	0	7	5	5	16	0	0	.000	10	15	0	1	0.4	1.000
1979			0	4	.000	4.62	23	1	0	39	47	7	23	0	0	3	0	6	0	0	.000	1	4	0	0	0.2	1.000
1980	SEA	A	0	1	.000	3.60	9	0	0	15	14	6	15	0	0	1	1	0	0	0	—	1	0	0	0	0.1	1.000
1982	PIT	N	9	4	.692	3.39	35	17	4	164.2	153	46	81	0	2	0	1	47	9	0	.191	8	17	2	3	0.8	.926
1983			3	5	.375	2.99	52	0	0	84.1	74	36	49	0	3	5	4	10	0	0	.000	5	9	0	0	0.3	1.000
7 yrs.			26	22	.542	3.48	228	22	4	514	461	172	283	0	17	15	12	87	9	0	.103	27	49	2	4	0.3	.974
LEAGUE CHAMPIONSHIP SERIES																											
1976	CIN	N	0	0	—	18.00	1	0	0	1	2	1	0	0	0	0	0	1	0	0	.000	0	0	0	0	0.0	.000

Kevin Saucier

SAUCIER, KEVIN ANDREW (Hot Sauce) BL TL 6′ 1″ 190 lbs.
B. Aug. 9, 1956, Pensacola, Fla.

Year	Team	Lg	W	L	PCT	ERA	G	GS	CG	IP	H	BB	SO	ShO	Relief Pitching W	Relief Pitching L	Relief Pitching SV	Batting AB	Batting H	Batting HR	BA	PO	A	E	DP	TC/G	FA
1978	PHI	N	0	1	.000	18.00	1	0	0	2	4	1	2	0	0	1	0	0	0	0	—	0	0	0	0	0.0	.000
1979			1	4	.200	4.21	29	2	0	62	68	33	21	0	1	2	1	10	1	0	.100	2	12	1	1	0.5	.933
1980			7	3	.700	3.42	40	0	0	50	50	20	25	0	7	3	0	8	0	0	.000	3	10	1	0	0.3	.929
1981	DET	A	4	2	.667	1.65	38	0	0	49	26	21	23	0	4	2	13	0	0	0	—	3	10	2	1	0.4	.867
1982			3	1	.750	3.12	31	1	0	40.1	35	29	23	0	3	1	5	0	0	0	—	6	4	2	4	0.4	.833
5 yrs.			15	11	.577	3.32	139	3	0	203.1	183	104	94	0	15	9	19	18	1	0	.056	14	36	6	6	0.4	.893
LEAGUE CHAMPIONSHIP SERIES																											
1980	PHI	N	0	0	—	0.00	2	0	0	0.2	1	2	0	0	0	0	0	0	0	0	—	0	0	0	0	0.0	.000
WORLD SERIES																											
1980	PHI	N	0	0	—	0.00	1	0	0	0.2	0	2	0	0	0	0	0	0	0	0	—	0	0	0	0	0.0	.000

Dennis Saunders

SAUNDERS, DENNIS JAMES BB TR 6′ 3″ 195 lbs.
B. Jan. 4, 1949, Alhambra, Calif.

Year	Team	Lg	W	L	PCT	ERA	G	GS	CG	IP	H	BB	SO	ShO	Relief Pitching W	Relief Pitching L	Relief Pitching SV	Batting AB	Batting H	Batting HR	BA	PO	A	E	DP	TC/G	FA
1970	DET	A	1	1	.500	3.21	8	0	0	14	16	5	8	0	1	1	1	5	0	0	.000	2	5	0	0	0.9	1.000

Rich Sauveur

SAUVEUR, RICHARD DANIEL BL TL 6′ 4″ 163 lbs.
B. Nov. 23, 1963, Arlington, Va.

Year	Team		W	L	PCT	ERA	G	GS	CG	IP	H	BB	SO	ShO	Relief Pitching W	Relief Pitching L	Relief Pitching SV	Batting AB	Batting H	Batting HR	BA	PO	A	E	DP	TC/G	FA
1986	PIT	N	0	0	—	6.00	3	3	0	12	17	6	6	0	0	0	0	3	1	0	.333	1	5	0	1	2.0	1.000
1988	MON	N	0	0	—	6.00	4	0	0	3	3	2	3	0	0	0	0	0	0	0	—	0	1	0	0	0.3	1.000
1991	NY	N	0	0	—	10.80	6	0	0	3.1	7	2	4	0	0	0	0	0	0	0	—	0	2	0	0	0.3	1.000
1992	KC	A	0	1	.000	4.40	8	0	0	14.1	15	8	7	0	0	1	0	0	0	0	—	0	1	0	0	0.1	1.000
4 yrs.			0	1	.000	5.79	21	3	0	32.2	42	18	20	0	0	1	0	3	1	0	.333	1	9	0	1	0.5	1.000

Bob Savage

SAVAGE, JOHN ROBERT BR TR 6′ 2″ 180 lbs.
B. Dec. 1, 1921, Manchester, N. H.

Year	Team		W	L	PCT	ERA	G	GS	CG	IP	H	BB	SO	ShO	Relief Pitching W	Relief Pitching L	Relief Pitching SV	Batting AB	Batting H	Batting HR	BA	PO	A	E	DP	TC/G	FA
1942	PHI	A	0	1	.000	3.23	8	3	0	30.2	24	31	10	0	0	0	0	9	1	0	.111	4	4	0	0	1.0	1.000
1946			3	15	.167	4.06	40	19	7	164	164	93	78	1	0	1	2	41	5	0	.122	4	14	1	1	0.5	.947
1947			8	10	.444	3.76	44	8	2	146	135	55	56	1	6	**7**	2	40	2	0	.050	6	16	2	0	0.5	.917
1948			5	1	.833	6.21	33	1	1	75.1	98	33	26	0	5	0	5	13	1	0	.077	1	11	0	0	0.4	1.000
1949	STL	A	0	0	—	6.43	4	0	0	7	12	3	1	0	0	0	0	1	0	0	.000	0	2	0	0	0.5	1.000
5 yrs.			16	27	.372	4.32	129	31	10	423	433	215	171	2	11	8	9	104	9	0	.087	15	47	3	1	0.5	.954

Jack Savage

SAVAGE, JOHN JOSEPH BR TR 6′ 3″ 190 lbs.
B. Apr. 22, 1964, Louisville, Ky.

Year	Team		W	L	PCT	ERA	G	GS	CG	IP	H	BB	SO	ShO	Relief Pitching W	Relief Pitching L	Relief Pitching SV	Batting AB	Batting H	Batting HR	BA	PO	A	E	DP	TC/G	FA
1987	LA	N	0	0	—	2.70	3	0	0	3.1	4	0	0	0	0	0	0	0	0	0	—	0	0	0	0	0.0	.000
1990	MIN	A	0	2	.000	8.31	17	0	0	26	37	11	12	0	0	2	1	0	0	0	—	0	4	0	0	0.2	1.000
2 yrs.			0	2	.000	7.67	20	0	0	29.1	41	11	12	0	0	2	1	0	0	0		0	4	0	0	0.2	1.000

Don Savidge

SAVIDGE, DONALD SNYDER BR TR 6′ 1″ 180 lbs.
Son of Ralph Savidge.
B. Aug. 28, 1908, Berwick, Pa. D. Mar. 22, 1983, Santa Barbara, Calif.

Year	Team		W	L	PCT	ERA	G	GS	CG	IP	H	BB	SO	ShO	Relief Pitching W	Relief Pitching L	Relief Pitching SV	Batting AB	Batting H	Batting HR	BA	PO	A	E	DP	TC/G	FA
1929	WAS	A	0	0	—	9.00	3	0	0	6	12	2	2	0	0	0	0	0	0	0	—	0	2	0	0	0.7	1.000

Ralph Savidge

SAVIDGE, RALPH AUSTIN (The Human Whipcord) BR TR 6′ 2″ 210 lbs.
Father of Don Savidge.
B. Feb. 3, 1879, Jerseytown, Pa. D. July 22, 1959, Berwick, Pa.

Year	Team		W	L	PCT	ERA	G	GS	CG	IP	H	BB	SO	ShO	Relief Pitching W	Relief Pitching L	Relief Pitching SV	Batting AB	Batting H	Batting HR	BA	PO	A	E	DP	TC/G	FA
1908	CIN	N	0	1	.000	2.57	4	1	1	21	18	8	7	0	0	0	0	7	0	0	.000	0	3	0	0	0.8	1.000
1909			0	0	—	22.50	1	0	0	4	10	3	2	0	0	0	0	1	0	0	.000	0	2	1	0	3.0	.667
2 yrs.			0	1	.000	5.76	5	1	1	25	28	11	9	0	0	0	0	8	0	0	.000	0	5	1	0	1.2	.833

Moe Savransky

SAVRANSKY, MORRIS BL TL 5′11″ 175 lbs.
B. Jan. 13, 1929, Cleveland, Ohio.

Year	Team		W	L	PCT	ERA	G	GS	CG	IP	H	BB	SO	ShO	Relief Pitching W	Relief Pitching L	Relief Pitching SV	Batting AB	Batting H	Batting HR	BA	PO	A	E	DP	TC/G	FA
1954	CIN	N	0	2	.000	4.88	16	0	0	24	23	8	7	0	0	2	0	2	1	0	.500	2	7	0	1	0.6	1.000

Rick Sawyer

SAWYER, RICHARD CLYDE BR TR 6′ 2″ 205 lbs.
B. Apr. 7, 1948, Bakersfield, Calif.

Year	Team		W	L	PCT	ERA	G	GS	CG	IP	H	BB	SO	ShO	Relief Pitching W	Relief Pitching L	Relief Pitching SV	Batting AB	Batting H	Batting HR	BA	PO	A	E	DP	TC/G	FA
1974	NY	A	0	0	—	13.50	1	0	0	2	2	1	1	0	0	0	0	0	0	0	—	0	2	0	0	2.0	1.000
1975			0	0	—	3.00	4	0	0	6	7	2	3	0	0	0	0	0	0	0	—	0	0	0	0	0.0	.000
1976	SD	N	5	3	.625	2.53	13	11	4	81.2	84	38	33	2	0	1	0	24	5	0	.208	3	12	0	0	1.2	1.000
1977			7	6	.538	5.84	56	9	0	111	136	55	45	0	6	2	0	20	3	0	.150	3	24	2	2	0.5	.931
4 yrs.			12	9	.571	4.49	74	20	4	200.2	229	96	82	2	6	3	0	44	8	0	.182	6	38	2	2	0.6	.957

Will Sawyer

SAWYER, WILLARD NEWTON BL TL
B. July 29, 1864, Brimfield, Ohio D. Jan. 5, 1936, Kent, Ohio.

Year	Team		W	L	PCT	ERA	G	GS	CG	IP	H	BB	SO	ShO	Relief Pitching W	Relief Pitching L	Relief Pitching SV	Batting AB	Batting H	Batting HR	BA	PO	A	E	DP	TC/G	FA
1883	CLE	N	4	10	.286	2.36	17	15	15	141	119	47	76	0	0	0	0	47	1	0	.021	6	11	4	0	1.2	.810

Bill Sayles

SAYLES, WILLIAM NISBETH BR TR 6′ 2″ 175 lbs.
B. July 27, 1917, Portland, Ore.

Year	Team		W	L	PCT	ERA	G	GS	CG	IP	H	BB	SO	ShO	Relief Pitching W	Relief Pitching L	Relief Pitching SV	Batting AB	Batting H	Batting HR	BA	PO	A	E	DP	TC/G	FA
1939	BOS	A	0	0	—	7.07	5	0	0	14	14	13	9	0	0	0	0	7	1	0	.143	0	3	0	0	0.6	1.000
1943	2 teams	NY N	(18G 1–3)		BKN N	(5G 0–0)																					
″	total		1	3	.250	5.29	23	3	1	64.2	73	33	43	0	0	2	0	15	5	0	.333	3	10	2	0	0.7	.867
2 yrs.			1	3	.250	5.61	28	3	1	78.2	87	46	52	0	0	2	0	22	6	0	.273	3	13	2	0	0.6	.889

Phil Saylor

SAYLOR, PHILIP ANDREW (Lefty) TL
B. Jan. 2, 1871, Van Wert County, Ohio D. July 23, 1937, West Alexandria, Ohio.

Year	Team		W	L	PCT	ERA	G	GS	CG	IP	H	BB	SO	ShO	Relief Pitching W	Relief Pitching L	Relief Pitching SV	Batting AB	Batting H	Batting HR	BA	PO	A	E	DP	TC/G	FA
1891	PHI	N	0	0	—	6.00	1	0	0	3	2	0	0	0	0	0	0	1	0	0	.000	0	0	0	0	0.0	.000

Bob Scanlan

SCANLAN, ROBERT GUY BR TR 6′ 7″ 215 lbs.
B. Aug. 9, 1966, Los Angeles, Calif.

Year	Team		W	L	PCT	ERA	G	GS	CG	IP	H	BB	SO	ShO	Relief Pitching W	Relief Pitching L	Relief Pitching SV	Batting AB	Batting H	Batting HR	BA	PO	A	E	DP	TC/G	FA
1991	CHI	N	7	8	.467	3.89	40	13	0	111	114	40	44	0	5	4	1	24	1	0	.042	9	16	2	0	0.7	.926
1992			3	6	.333	2.89	69	0	0	87.1	76	30	42	0	3	6	14	4	0	0	.000	5	22	2	0	0.4	.931
1993			4	5	.444	4.54	70	0	0	75.1	79	28	44	0	4	5	0	2	1	0	.500	3	6	0	0	0.1	1.000
1994	MIL	A	2	6	.250	4.11	30	12	0	103	117	28	65	0	0	3	2	0	0	0	—	8	12	1	1	0.7	.952
1995			4	7	.364	6.59	17	14	0	83.1	101	44	29	0	1	0	0	0	0	0	—	6	14	2	1	1.3	.909
5 yrs.			20	32	.385	4.34	226	39	0	460	487	170	224	0	13	18	17	30	2	0	.067	31	70	7	2	0.5	.935

Doc Scanlan

SCANLAN, WILLIAM DENNIS BL TR 5′ 8″ 165 lbs.
Brother of Frank Scanlan.
B. Mar. 7, 1881, Syracuse, N. Y. D. May 29, 1949, Brooklyn, N. Y.

Year	Team		W	L	PCT	ERA	G	GS	CG	IP	H	BB	SO	ShO	Relief Pitching W	Relief Pitching L	Relief Pitching SV	Batting AB	Batting H	Batting HR	BA	PO	A	E	DP	TC/G	FA
1903	PIT	N	0	1	.000	4.00	1	1	1	9	5	6	0	0	0	0	0	2	0	0	.000	0	1	0	0	1.0	1.000
1904	2 teams	PIT N	(4G 1–3)		BKN N	(13G 7–6)																					
″	total		8	9	.471	2.64	17	15	12	126	115	60	50	3	0	1	0	41	5	0	.122	11	20	1	1	1.9	.969
1905	BKN	N	14	12	.538	2.92	33	28	22	250	220	104	135	2	0	2	0	96	16	0	.167	6	57	5	3	2.1	.926
1906			18	13	.581	3.19	38	33	28	288	230	**127**	120	6	1	0	1	97	18	0	.186	5	50	5	0	1.6	.917
1907			6	8	.429	3.20	17	15	10	107	90	61	59	2	0	0	0	34	9	0	.265	1	21	3	2	1.5	.880
1909			8	7	.533	2.93	19	17	12	141.1	125	65	72	2	0	0	0	44	12	0	.273	0	33	1	2	1.8	.971
1910			9	11	.450	2.61	34	25	14	217.1	175	116	103	0	0	0	2	69	14	0	.203	4	49	0	1	1.6	1.000
1911			3	10	.231	3.64	22	15	3	113.2	101	69	45	0	1	1	1	33	4	0	.121	1	31	4	1	1.6	.889
8 yrs.			66	71	.482	3.00	181	149	102	1252.1	1061	608	584	15	2	4	4	416	78	0	.188	28	262	19	10	1.7	.939

Frank Scanlan

SCANLAN, FRANK ALOYSIUS (Dreamy) BL TL 6′ 1½″ 175 lbs.
Brother of Doc Scanlan.
B. Apr. 28, 1890, Syracuse, N. Y. D. Apr. 9, 1969, Brooklyn, N. Y.

Year	Team		W	L	PCT	ERA	G	GS	CG	IP	H	BB	SO	ShO	Relief Pitching W	Relief Pitching L	Relief Pitching SV	Batting AB	Batting H	Batting HR	BA	PO	A	E	DP	TC/G	FA
1909	PHI	N	0	0	—	1.64	6	0	0	11	8	5	5	0	0	0	1	4	0	0	.000	1	1	0	1	0.3	1.000

Pat Scantlebury

SCANTLEBURY, PATRICIO ATHELSTAN BL TL 6′ 1″ 180 lbs.
B. Nov. 11, 1917, Gatun, Canal Zone D. May 24, 1991, Glen Ridge, N. J.

Year	Team		W	L	PCT	ERA	G	GS	CG	IP	H	BB	SO	ShO	Relief Pitching W	Relief Pitching L	Relief Pitching SV	Batting AB	Batting H	Batting HR	BA	PO	A	E	DP	TC/G	FA
1956	CIN	N	0	1	.000	6.63	6	2	0	19	24	5	10	0	0	0	0	3	0	0	.000	1	3	0	0	0.7	1.000

Randy Scarbery

SCARBERY, RANDY JAMES BB TR 6′ 1″ 185 lbs.
B. June 22, 1952, Fresno, Calif.

Year	Team		W	L	PCT	ERA	G	GS	CG	IP	H	BB	SO	ShO	Relief Pitching W	Relief Pitching L	Relief Pitching SV	Batting AB	Batting H	Batting HR	BA	PO	A	E	DP	TC/G	FA
1979	CHI	A	2	8	.200	4.63	45	5	0	101	102	34	45	0	2	3	4	0	0	0	—	5	17	2	1	0.5	.917
1980			1	2	.333	4.03	15	0	0	29	24	7	18	0	1	2	2	0	0	0	—	2	2	0	0	0.3	1.000
2 yrs.			3	10	.231	4.50	60	5	0	130	126	41	63	0	3	5	6	0	0	0		7	19	2	1	0.5	.929

Ray Scarborough

SCARBOROUGH, RAE WILSON BR TR 6′ 185 lbs.
B. July 23, 1917, Mt. Gilead, N. C. D. July 1, 1982, Mount Olive, N. C.

Year	Team		W	L	PCT	ERA	G	GS	CG	IP	H	BB	SO	ShO	Relief Pitching W	Relief Pitching L	Relief Pitching SV	Batting AB	Batting H	Batting HR	BA	PO	A	E	DP	TC/G	FA
1942	WAS	A	2	1	.667	4.12	17	5	1	63.1	68	32	16	1	0	0	0	21	4	0	.190	6	15	0	1	1.2	1.000
1943			4	4	.500	2.83	24	6	2	86	93	46	43	0	2	2	3	24	8	0	.333	3	18	2	1	1.0	.913
1946			7	11	.389	4.05	32	20	6	155.2	176	74	46	1	3	1	1	50	7	0	.140	13	35	3	5	1.6	.941
1947			6	13	.316	3.41	33	18	8	161	165	67	63	2	1	2	0	50	6	0	.120	7	24	2	3	1.0	.939
1948			15	8	.652	2.82	31	26	9	185.1	166	72	76	0	1	1	1	64	14	0	.219	13	35	3	3	1.6	.941
1949			13	11	.542	4.60	34	27	11	199.2	204	88	81	1	3	0	0	67	13	0	.194	11	41	5	3	1.7	.912
1950	2 teams	WAS A (8G 3–5) CHI A (27G 10–13)																									
″	total		13	18	.419	4.94	35	31	12	207.2	222	84	94	3	1	1	1	66	10	0	.152	13	33	4	4	1.4	.920
1951	BOS	A	12	9	.571	5.09	37	22	8	184	201	61	71	0	2	2	0	68	13	0	.191	18	30	1	4	1.3	.980
1952	2 teams	BOS A (28G 1–5) NY A (9G 5–1)																									
″	total		6	6	.500	4.23	37	12	2	110.2	106	50	42	1	2	1	4	32	9	0	.281	13	17	1	0	0.8	.968
1953	2 teams	NY A (25G 2–2) DET A (13G 0–2)																									
″	total		2	4	.333	4.66	38	1	0	75.1	86	37	32	0	1	4	4	14	1	1	.071	3	15	4	0	0.6	.818
10 yrs.			80	85	.485	4.13	318	168	59	1428.2	1487	611	564	9	16	14	14	456	85	1	.186	100	263	25	24	1.2	.936
WORLD SERIES																											
1952	NY	A	0	0	—	9.00	1	0	0	1	1	0	1	0	0	0	0	0	0	0	—	0	1	0	0	1.0	1.000

Mac Scarce

SCARCE, GUERRAND McCURDY BL TL 6′ 3″ 180 lbs.
B. Apr. 8, 1949, Danville, Va.

Year	Team		W	L	PCT	ERA	G	GS	CG	IP	H	BB	SO	ShO	Relief Pitching W	Relief Pitching L	Relief Pitching SV	Batting AB	Batting H	Batting HR	BA	PO	A	E	DP	TC/G	FA
1972	PHI	N	1	2	.333	3.44	31	0	0	36.2	30	20	40	0	1	2	4	6	0	0	.000	2	7	0	1	0.3	1.000
1973			1	8	.111	2.42	52	0	0	70.2	54	47	57	0	1	8	12	5	0	0	.000	2	6	1	0	0.2	.889
1974			3	8	.273	5.01	58	0	0	70	72	35	50	0	3	8	5	6	0	0	.000	2	4	0	0	0.1	1.000
1975	NY	N	0	0	—	0.00	1	0	0		1	0	0	0	0	0	0	0	0	0	—	0	0	0	0	0.0	.000
1978	MIN	A	1	1	.500	3.94	17	0	0	32	35	15	17	0	1	1	0	0	0	0	—	0	2	1	0	0.2	.667
5 yrs.			6	19	.240	3.70	159	0	0	209.1	192	117	164	0	6	19	21	17	0	0	.000	6	19	2	1	0.2	.926

Al Schacht

SCHACHT, ALEXANDER (The Clown Prince of Baseball) BR TR 5′11″ 142 lbs.
B. Nov. 11, 1892, New York, N. Y. D. July 14, 1984, Waterbury, Conn.

Year	Team		W	L	PCT	ERA	G	GS	CG	IP	H	BB	SO	ShO	Relief Pitching W	Relief Pitching L	Relief Pitching SV	Batting AB	Batting H	Batting HR	BA	PO	A	E	DP	TC/G	FA
1919	WAS	A	2	0	1.000	2.40	2	2	1	15	14	4	4	0	0	0	0	3	0	0	.000	2	2	0	0	2.0	1.000
1920			6	4	.600	4.44	22	11	5	99.1	130	30	19	1	0	2	1	26	5	0	.192	8	33	2	2	2.0	.953
1921			6	6	.500	4.90	29	5	2	82.2	110	27	15	0	4	4	1	23	5	0	.217	3	7	2	0	0.4	.833
3 yrs.			14	10	.583	4.48	53	18	8	197	254	61	38	1	4	6	2	52	10	0	.192	13	42	4	2	1.1	.932

Sid Schacht

SCHACHT, SIDNEY BR TR 5′11″ 170 lbs.
B. Feb. 3, 1918, Bogota, N. J. D. Mar. 30, 1991, Ft. Lauderdale, Fla.

Year	Team		W	L	PCT	ERA	G	GS	CG	IP	H	BB	SO	ShO	Relief Pitching W	Relief Pitching L	Relief Pitching SV	Batting AB	Batting H	Batting HR	BA	PO	A	E	DP	TC/G	FA
1950	STL	A	0	0	—	16.03	8	1	0	10.2	24	14	7	0	0	0	0	2	0	0	.000	2	0	0	0	0.3	1.000
1951	2 teams	STL A (6G 0–0) BOS N (5G 0–2)																									
″	total		0	2	.000	12.66	11	0	0	10.2	20	7	5	0	0	2	1	0	0	0		0	0	0	0	0.0	
2 yrs.			0	2	.000	14.34	19	1	0	21.1	44	21	12	0	0	2	1	2	0	0	.000	2	0	0	0	0.1	1.000

Hal Schacker

SCHACKER, HAROLD BR TR 6′ 190 lbs.
B. Apr. 6, 1925, Brooklyn, N. Y.

Year	Team		W	L	PCT	ERA	G	GS	CG	IP	H	BB	SO	ShO	Relief Pitching W	Relief Pitching L	Relief Pitching SV	Batting AB	Batting H	Batting HR	BA	PO	A	E	DP	TC/G	FA
1945	BOS	N	0	1	.000	5.28	6	0	0	15.1	14	9	6	0	0	1	0	2	0	0	.000	0	2	1	0	0.5	.667

Germany Schaefer

SCHAEFER, HERMAN A. BR TR 5′ 9″ 175 lbs.
B. Feb. 4, 1877, Chicago, Ill. D. May 16, 1919, Saranac Lake, N. Y.

Year	Team		W	L	PCT	ERA	G	GS	CG	IP	H	BB	SO	ShO	Relief Pitching W	Relief Pitching L	Relief Pitching SV	Batting AB	Batting H	Batting HR	BA	PO	A	E	DP	TC/G	FA
1912	WAS	A	0	0	—	0.00	1	0	0	0.2	1	0	0	0	0	0	0	166	41	0	.247	6	4	0	1	5.0	1.000
1913			0	0	—	54.00	1	0	0	0.1	2	0	0	0	0	0	0	100	32	0	.320	91	40	7	6	5.3	.949
2 yrs.			0	0		18.00	2	0	0	1	3	0	0	0	0	0	0	*				3273	2319	286	316	5.6	.951

Harry Schaeffer

SCHAEFFER, HARRY EDWARD (Lefty) BL TL 6′ 2½″ 175 lbs.
B. June 23, 1924, Reading, Pa.

Year	Team		W	L	PCT	ERA	G	GS	CG	IP	H	BB	SO	ShO	Relief Pitching W	Relief Pitching L	Relief Pitching SV	Batting AB	Batting H	Batting HR	BA	PO	A	E	DP	TC/G	FA
1952	NY	A	0	1	.000	5.29	5	2	0	17	18	18	15	0	0	0	0	3	0	0	.000	0	5	0	0	1.0	1.000

Mark Schaeffer

SCHAEFFER, MARK PHILIP BL TL 6′ 5″ 215 lbs.
B. June 5, 1948, Santa Monica, Calif.

Year	Team		W	L	PCT	ERA	G	GS	CG	IP	H	BB	SO	ShO	Relief Pitching W	Relief Pitching L	Relief Pitching SV	Batting AB	Batting H	Batting HR	BA	PO	A	E	DP	TC/G	FA
1972	SD	N	2	0	1.000	4.61	41	0	0	41	52	28	25	0	2	0	1	3	0	0	.000	5	6	0	3	0.3	1.000

Joe Schaffernoth

SCHAFFERNOTH, JOSEPH ARTHUR BR TR 6′ 4½″ 195 lbs.
B. Aug. 6, 1937, Trenton, N. J.

Year	Team		W	L	PCT	ERA	G	GS	CG	IP	H	BB	SO	ShO	Relief Pitching W	Relief Pitching L	Relief Pitching SV	Batting AB	Batting H	Batting HR	BA	PO	A	E	DP	TC/G	FA
1959	CHI	N	1	0	1.000	8.22	5	1	0	7.2	11	4	3	0	1	0	0	3	0	0	.000	0	1	0	0	0.2	1.000
1960			2	3	.400	2.78	33	0	0	55	46	17	33	0	2	3	3	7	2	0	.286	4	10	0	2	0.4	1.000
1961	2 teams	CHI N (21G 0–4) CLE A (15G 0–1)																									
″	total		0	5	.000	5.86	36	0	0	55.1	59	32	32	0	0	5	0	6	0	0	.000	1	14	1	0	0.4	.938
3 yrs.			3	8	.273	4.58	74	1	0	118	116	53	68	0	3	8	3	16	2	0	.125	5	25	1	2	0.4	.968

Art Schallock

SCHALLOCK, ARTHUR LAWRENCE BL TL 5′ 9″ 160 lbs.
B. Apr. 25, 1924, Mill Valley, Calif.

Year	Team	Lg	W	L	PCT	ERA	G	GS	CG	IP	H	BB	SO	ShO	Relief W	Relief L	Relief SV	Batting AB	Batting H	Batting HR	BA	PO	A	E	DP	TC/G	FA
1951	NY	A	3	1	.750	3.88	11	6	1	46.1	50	20	19	0	0	0	0	17	5	0	.294	3	9	1	1	1.2	.923
1952			0	0	—	9.00	2	0	0	2	3	2	1	0	0	0	0	0	0	0	—	0	0	0	0	0.0	.000
1953			0	0	—	2.95	7	1	0	21.1	30	15	13	0	0	0	1	6	2	0	.333	1	2	0	1	0.4	1.000
1954			0	1	.000	4.15	6	1	1	17.1	20	11	9	0	0	0	0	3	0	0	.000	0	1	0	0	0.2	1.000
1955	2 teams	NY A (2G 0–0) BAL A (30G 3–5)																									
″	total		3	5	.375	4.21	32	6	1	83.1	96	43	35	0	2	1	0	19	2	0	.105	11	8	2	0	0.7	.905
5 yrs.			6	7	.462	4.02	58	14	3	170.1	199	91	77	0	2	1	1	45	9	0	.200	15	20	3	2	0.7	.921
WORLD SERIES																											
1953	NY	A	0	0	—	4.50	1	0	0	2	2	1	1	0	0	0	0	0	0	0	—	0	1	0	0	1.0	1.000

Charley Schanz

SCHANZ, CHARLES MURRELL BR TR 6′ 3½″ 215 lbs.
B. June 8, 1919, Anacortes, Wash. D. May 28, 1992, Sacramento, Calif.

Year	Team	Lg	W	L	PCT	ERA	G	GS	CG	IP	H	BB	SO	ShO	Relief W	Relief L	Relief SV	Batting AB	Batting H	Batting HR	BA	PO	A	E	DP	TC/G	FA
1944	PHI	N	13	16	.448	3.32	40	30	13	241.1	231	103	84	2	4	0	3	81	12	1	.148	10	47	5	4	1.5	.919
1945			4	15	.211	4.35	35	21	5	144.2	165	87	56	1	0	0	5	39	6	0	.154	4	34	4	0	1.2	.905
1946			6	6	.500	5.80	32	15	4	116.1	130	71	47	0	1	1	4	36	3	0	.083	4	28	3	0	1.1	.914
1947			2	4	.333	4.16	34	6	1	101.2	107	47	42	0	1	3	2	27	4	0	.148	5	19	1	0	0.7	.960
1950	BOS	A	3	2	.600	8.34	14	0	0	22.2	25	24	14	0	3	2	0	11	1	0	.091	0	5	1	0	0.4	.833
5 yrs.			28	43	.394	4.34	155	72	23	626.2	658	332	243	3	9	6	14	194	26	1	.134	23	133	14	4	1.1	.918

Jack Schappert

SCHAPPERT, JOHN BR TR 5′10″ 170 lbs.
B. Brooklyn, N. Y. D. July 29, 1916, Rockaway Beach, N. Y.

Year	Team	Lg	W	L	PCT	ERA	G	GS	CG	IP	H	BB	SO	ShO	Relief W	Relief L	Relief SV	Batting AB	Batting H	Batting HR	BA	PO	A	E	DP	TC/G	FA
1882	STL	AA	8	7	.533	*3.52*	15	14	13	128	131	32	38	0	0	**1**	0	50	9	0	.180	5	31	7	1	2.5	.837

Bill Schardt

SCHARDT, WILBURT (Big Bill) BR TR 6′ 4″ 210 lbs.
B. Jan. 20, 1886, Cleveland, Ohio D. July 20, 1964, Vermilion, Ohio.

Year	Team	Lg	W	L	PCT	ERA	G	GS	CG	IP	H	BB	SO	ShO	Relief W	Relief L	Relief SV	Batting AB	Batting H	Batting HR	BA	PO	A	E	DP	TC/G	FA
1911	BKN	N	5	15	.250	3.59	39	22	10	195.1	190	91	77	1	2	0	4	59	10	0	.169	7	57	7	0	1.8	.901
1912			0	1	.000	4.35	7	0	0	20.2	25	6	7	0	0	1	1	6	0	0	.000	1	15	0	1	2.3	1.000
2 yrs.			5	16	.238	3.67	46	22	10	216	215	97	84	1	2	1	5	65	10	0	.154	8	72	7	1	1.9	.920

Jeff Schattinger

SCHATTINGER, JEFFREY CHARLES BL TR 6′ 5″ 200 lbs.
B. Oct. 25, 1955, Fresno, Calif.

Year	Team	Lg	W	L	PCT	ERA	G	GS	CG	IP	H	BB	SO	ShO	Relief W	Relief L	Relief SV	Batting AB	Batting H	Batting HR	BA	PO	A	E	DP	TC/G	FA
1981	KC	A	0	0	—	0.00	1	0	0	3	2	1	1	0	0	0	0	0	0	0	—	0	0	0	0	0.0	.000

Dan Schatzeder

SCHATZEDER, DANIEL ERNEST BL TL 6′ 185 lbs.
B. Dec. 1, 1954, Elmhurst, Ill.

Year	Team	Lg	W	L	PCT	ERA	G	GS	CG	IP	H	BB	SO	ShO	Relief W	Relief L	Relief SV	Batting AB	Batting H	Batting HR	BA	PO	A	E	DP	TC/G	FA
1977	MON	N	2	1	.667	2.45	6	3	1	22	16	13	14	1	0	0	0	6	2	0	.333	1	3	0	0	0.7	1.000
1978			7	7	.500	3.06	29	18	2	144	108	68	69	0	2	0	0	45	10	1	.222	4	17	2	0	0.8	.913
1979			10	5	.667	2.83	32	21	3	162	136	59	106	0	1	1	1	51	11	1	.216	5	13	4	0	0.7	.818
1980	DET	A	11	13	.458	4.01	32	26	9	193	178	58	94	2	2	0	0	0	0	0	—	7	21	3	3	1.0	.903
1981			6	8	.429	6.08	17	14	1	71	74	29	20	0	0	0	0	0	0	0	—	6	12	3	0	1.2	.857
1982	2 teams	SF N (13G 1–4) MON N (26G 0–2)																									
″	total		1	6	.143	5.32	39	4	0	69.1	84	24	33	0	1	3	0	13	3	0	.231	3	11	1	2	0.4	.933
1983	MON	N	5	2	.714	3.21	58	2	0	87	88	25	48	0	4	1	2	10	2	0	.200	9	8	1	0	0.3	.944
1984			7	7	.500	2.71	36	14	1	136	112	36	89	1	1	1	1	35	11	0	.314	9	8	5	0	0.6	.773
1985			3	5	.375	3.80	24	15	1	104.1	101	31	64	0	0	0	0	31	6	2	.194	3	20	4	1	1.1	.852
1986	2 teams	MON N (30G 3–2) PHI N (25G 3–3)																									
″	total		6	5	.545	3.26	55	1	0	88.1	81	35	47	0	6	5	2	26	10	1	.385	3	9	0	0	0.2	1.000
1987	2 teams	PHI N (26G 3–1) MIN A (30G 3–1)																									
″	total		6	2	.750	5.31	56	1	0	81.1	104	32	58	0	6	2	0	12	2	0	.167	4	7	1	0	0.2	.917
1988	2 teams	CLE A (15G 0–2) MIN A (10G 0–1)																									
″	total		0	3	.000	6.49	25	0	0	26.1	34	7	17	0	0	3	3	0	0	0		3	1	0	0	0.2	1.000
1989	HOU	N	4	1	.800	4.45	36	0	0	56.2	64	28	46	0	4	1	1	9	0	0	.000	2	9	2	1	0.4	.846
1990	2 teams	HOU N (45G 1–3) NY N (6G 0–0)																									
″	total		1	3	.250	2.20	51	2	0	69.2	66	23	39	0	1	1	0	4	1	0	.250	1	10	1	0	0.2	.917
1991	KC	A	0	0	—	9.45	8	0	0	6.2	11	7	4	0	0	0	0	0	0	0	—	0	0	0	0	0.0	.000
15 yrs.			69	68	.504	3.74	504	121	18	1317.2	1257	475	748	4	28	18	10	242	58	5	.240	60	149	27	7	0.5	.886
LEAGUE CHAMPIONSHIP SERIES																											
1987	MIN	A	0	0	—	0.00	2	0	0	4.1	2	0	5	0	0	0	0	0	0	0	—	1	1	0	0	1.0	1.000
WORLD SERIES																											
1987	MIN	A	1	0	1.000	6.23	3	0	0	4.1	4	3	3	0	1	0	0	0	0	0	—	0	0	0	0	0.0	.000

Rube Schauer

SCHAUER, ALEXANDER JOHN BR TR 6′ 2″ 192 lbs.
Born Dimitri Ivanovich Dimitrihoff.
B. Mar. 19, 1891, Odessa, Russia D. Apr. 15, 1957, Minneapolis, Minn.

Year	Team	Lg	W	L	PCT	ERA	G	GS	CG	IP	H	BB	SO	ShO	Relief W	Relief L	Relief SV	Batting AB	Batting H	Batting HR	BA	PO	A	E	DP	TC/G	FA
1913	NY	N	0	1	.000	7.50	3	1	1	12	14	9	7	0	0	0	0	3	0	0	.000	0	3	0	0	1.0	1.000
1914			0	0	—	3.22	6	0	0	22.1	16	8	6	0	0	0	0	7	1	0	.143	1	4	1	0	1.0	.833
1915			2	8	.200	3.50	32	7	4	105.1	101	35	65	0	2	3	0	26	2	0	.077	4	24	2	0	0.9	.933
1916			1	4	.200	2.96	19	3	1	45.2	44	16	24	0	1	2	0	9	2	0	.222	1	11	2	0	0.7	.857
1917	PHI	A	7	16	.304	3.14	33	21	10	215	209	69	62	0	3	2	1	76	11	0	.145	14	62	0	0	2.3	1.000
5 yrs.			10	29	.256	3.35	93	32	16	400.1	384	137	164	0	6	7	1	121	16	0	.132	20	104	5	0	1.4	.961

Owen Scheetz

SCHEETZ, OWEN FRANKLIN BR TR 6′ 190 lbs.
B. Dec. 24, 1913, New Bedford, Ohio.

Year	Team	Lg	W	L	PCT	ERA	G	GS	CG	IP	H	BB	SO	ShO	Relief W	Relief L	Relief SV	Batting AB	Batting H	Batting HR	BA	PO	A	E	DP	TC/G	FA
1943	WAS	A	0	0	—	7.00	6	0	0	9	16	4	5	0	0	0	1	2	0	0	.000	0	3	0	0	0.5	1.000

Lefty Schegg

SCHEGG, GILBERT EUGENE BL TL 5′11″ 180 lbs.
Born Gilbert Eugene Price.
B. Aug. 29, 1889, Leesville, Ohio D. Feb. 27, 1963, Niles, Ohio.

Year	Team	Lg	W	L	PCT	ERA	G	GS	CG	IP	H	BB	SO	ShO	Relief W	Relief L	Relief SV	Batting AB	Batting H	Batting HR	BA	PO	A	E	DP	TC/G	FA
1912	WAS	A	0	0	—	3.38	2	1	0	5.1	7	4	3	0	0	0	0	2	0	0	.000	0	0	2	0	1.0	.000

Carl Scheib

SCHEIB, CARL ALVIN BR TR 6′ 1″ 192 lbs.
B. Jan. 1, 1927, Gratz, Pa.

Year	Team	Lg	W	L	PCT	ERA	G	GS	CG	IP	H	BB	SO	ShO	Relief W	Relief L	Relief SV	Batting AB	Batting H	Batting HR	BA	PO	A	E	DP	TC/G	FA
1943	PHI	A	0	1	.000	4.34	6	0	0	18.2	24	3	3	0	0	1	0	5	0	0	.000	1	1	0	0	0.3	1.000
1944			0	0	—	4.10	15	0	0	37.1	36	11	13	0	0	0	0	10	3	0	.300	0	13	0	0	0.9	1.000

Carl Scheib *continued*

Year	Team	W	L	PCT	ERA	G	GS	CG	IP	H	BB	SO	ShO	Relief W	Relief L	Relief SV	Batting AB	Batting H	HR	BA	PO	A	E	DP	TC/G	FA
1945		0	0	—	3.12	4	0	0	8.2	6	4	2	0	0	0	0	2	0	0	.000	1	2	0	0	0.8	1.000
1947		4	6	.400	5.04	21	12	6	116	121	55	26	2	1	0	0	45	6	0	.133	3	13	1	2	0.8	.941
1948		14	8	.636	3.94	32	24	15	198.2	219	76	44	1	3	1	0	104	31	2	.298	16	36	1	5	1.6	.981
1949		9	12	.429	5.12	38	23	11	182.2	191	118	43	2	2	2	0	72	17	0	.236	6	24	3	3	0.9	.909
1950		3	10	.231	7.22	43	8	1	106	138	70	37	0	1	**9**	3	52	13	1	.250	3	16	0	2	0.4	1.000
1951		1	12	.077	4.47	46	11	3	143	132	71	49	0	1	3	10	53	21	2	.396	14	43	1	3	1.3	.983
1952		11	7	.611	4.39	30	19	8	158	153	50	42	1	2	3	2	82	18	0	.220	19	26	2	3	1.6	.957
1953		3	7	.300	4.88	28	8	3	96	99	29	25	0	1	3	2	41	8	0	.195	4	16	1	1	0.8	.952
1954	**2 teams** **PHI A** (1G 0–1) **STL N** (3G 0–1)																									
"	**total**	0	2	.000	14.85	4	2	0	6.2	11	6	6	0	0	0	0	2	0	0	.000	1	1	0	0	0.5	1.000
11 yrs.		45	65	.409	4.88	267	107	47	1071.2	1130	493	290	6	11	22	17	*				68	191	9	19	1.0	.966

Frank Scheibeck

SCHEIBECK, FRANK S. (Archer) BR TR 5′ 7″ 145 lbs.
B. June 28, 1865, Detroit, Mich. D. Oct. 22, 1956, Detroit, Mich.

Year	Team	W	L	PCT	ERA	G	GS	CG	IP	H	BB	SO	ShO	Relief W	Relief L	Relief SV	Batting AB	Batting H	HR	BA	PO	A	E	DP	TC/G	FA
1887	**CLE AA**	0	1	.000	12.00	1	1	1	9	17	4	3	0	0	0	0	*				1	3	4	0	2.7	.500

John Scheible

SCHEIBLE, JOHN G. TL
B. Feb. 16, 1866, Youngstown, Ohio D. Aug. 9, 1897, Youngstown, Ohio.

Year	Team	W	L	PCT	ERA	G	GS	CG	IP	H	BB	SO	ShO	Relief W	Relief L	Relief SV	Batting AB	Batting H	HR	BA	PO	A	E	DP	TC/G	FA
1893	**CLE N**	1	1	.500	2.00	2	2	2	18	15	11	1	1	0	0	0	7	1	0	.143	4	2	1	1	3.5	.857
1894	**PHI N**	0	1	.000	189.00	1	1	0	0.1	6	2	0	0	0	0	0	0	0	0	—	0	0	1	0	1.0	.000
2 yrs.		1	2	.333	5.40	3	3	2	18.1	21	13	1	1	0	0	0	7	1	0	.143	4	2	2	1	2.7	.750

Rich Scheid

SCHEID, RICHARD PAUL BL TL 6′ 3″ 185 lbs.
B. Feb. 3, 1965, Staten Island, N. Y.

Year	Team	W	L	PCT	ERA	G	GS	CG	IP	H	BB	SO	ShO	Relief W	Relief L	Relief SV	Batting AB	Batting H	HR	BA	PO	A	E	DP	TC/G	FA
1992	**HOU N**	0	1	.000	6.00	7	1	0	12	14	6	8	0	0	0	0	1	0	0	.000	1	1	0	0	0.3	1.000
1994	**FLA N**	1	3	.250	3.34	8	5	0	32.1	35	8	17	0	1	0	0	7	0	0	.000	0	4	1	0	0.6	.800
1995		0	0	—	6.10	6	0	0	10.1	14	7	10	0	0	0	0	1	0	0	.000	1	5	0	0	1.0	1.000
3 yrs.		1	4	.200	4.45	21	6	0	54.2	63	21	35	0	1	0	0	9	0	0	.000	2	10	1	0	0.6	.923

Jim Schelle

SCHELLE, GERARD ANTHONY BR TR 6′ 3″ 190 lbs.
B. Apr. 13, 1917, Baltimore, Md. D. May 4, 1990, Weymouth, Mass.

Year	Team	W	L	PCT	ERA	G	GS	CG	IP	H	BB	SO	ShO	Relief W	Relief L	Relief SV	Batting AB	Batting H	HR	BA	PO	A	E	DP	TC/G	FA
1939	**PHI A**	0	0	—	∞	1	0	0		1	3	0	0	0	0	0	0	0	0	—	0	0	0	0	0.0	.000

Fred Schemanske

SCHEMANSKE, FREDERICK GEORGE (Buck) BR TR 6′ 2″ 190 lbs.
B. Apr. 28, 1903, Detroit, Mich. D. Feb. 18, 1960, Detroit, Mich.

Year	Team	W	L	PCT	ERA	G	GS	CG	IP	H	BB	SO	ShO	Relief W	Relief L	Relief SV	Batting AB	Batting H	HR	BA	PO	A	E	DP	TC/G	FA
1923	**WAS A**	0	0	—	27.00	1	0	0	1	3	0	0	0	0	0	0	*				0	0	0	0	0.0	.000

Bill Schenck

SCHENCK, WILLIAM G. 5′ 7″ 171 lbs.
B. Brooklyn, N. Y. Deceased.

Year	Team	W	L	PCT	ERA	G	GS	CG	IP	H	BB	SO	ShO	Relief W	Relief L	Relief SV	Batting AB	Batting H	HR	BA	PO	A	E	DP	TC/G	FA
1882	**LOU AA**	1	0	1.000	*0.90*	2	1	1	10	6	1	4	0	0	0	0	*				70	114	45	5	3.7	.803

John Scheneberg

SCHENEBERG, JOHN BLUFORD BB TR 6′ 1″ 180 lbs.
B. Nov. 20, 1887, Guyandotte, W. Va. D. Sept. 26, 1950, Huntington, W. Va.

Year	Team	W	L	PCT	ERA	G	GS	CG	IP	H	BB	SO	ShO	Relief W	Relief L	Relief SV	Batting AB	Batting H	HR	BA	PO	A	E	DP	TC/G	FA
1913	**PIT N**	0	1	.000	6.00	1	1	0	6	10	2	1	0	0	0	0	2	1	0	.500	1	3	1	0	5.0	.800
1920	**STL A**	0	0	—	27.00	1	0	0	2	7	1	0	0	0	0	0	0	0	0	—	0	0	0	0	0.0	.000
2 yrs.		0	1	.000	11.25	2	1	0	8	17	3	1	0	0	0	0	2	1	0	.500	1	3	1	0	2.5	.800

Fred Scherman

SCHERMAN, FREDERICK JOHN BL TL 6′ 1″ 195 lbs.
B. July 25, 1944, Dayton, Ohio.

Year	Team	W	L	PCT	ERA	G	GS	CG	IP	H	BB	SO	ShO	Relief W	Relief L	Relief SV	Batting AB	Batting H	HR	BA	PO	A	E	DP	TC/G	FA
1969	**DET A**	1	0	1.000	6.75	4	0	0	4	6	0	3	0	1	0	0	0	0	0	—	0	1	0	0	0.3	1.000
1970		4	4	.500	3.21	48	0	0	70	61	28	58	0	4	4	1	12	2	0	.167	8	7	1	2	0.3	.938
1971		11	6	.647	2.71	69	1	1	113	91	49	46	0	**10**	6	20	24	5	0	.208	7	23	0	1	0.4	1.000
1972		7	3	.700	3.64	57	3	0	94	91	53	53	0	7	1	12	22	2	0	.091	5	12	2	1	0.3	.895
1973		2	2	.500	4.21	34	0	0	62	59	30	28	0	2	2	1	0	0	0	—	2	5	0	0	0.2	1.000
1974	**HOU N**	2	5	.286	4.13	53	0	0	61	67	26	35	0	2	5	4	3	0	0	.000	6	7	1	0	0.3	.929
1975	**2 teams** **HOU N** (16G 0–1) **MON N** (34G 4–3)																									
"	**total**	4	4	.500	3.79	50	7	0	92.2	105	45	56	0	4	1	0	17	1	0	.059	5	16	0	2	0.4	1.000
1976	**MON N**	2	2	.500	4.95	31	0	0	40	42	14	18	0	2	2	1	4	1	0	.250	2	4	0	0	0.2	1.000
8 yrs.		33	26	.559	3.66	346	11	1	536.2	522	245	297	0	32	21	39	82	11	0	.134	35	75	4	6	0.3	.965
LEAGUE CHAMPIONSHIP SERIES																										
1972	**DET A**	0	0	—	0.00	1	0	0	0.2	1	0	1	0	0	0	0	0	0	0	—	0	0	0	0	0.0	.000

Bill Scherrer

SCHERRER, WILLIAM JOSEPH BL TL 6′ 4″ 180 lbs.
B. Jan. 20, 1958, Tonawanda, N. Y.

Year	Team	W	L	PCT	ERA	G	GS	CG	IP	H	BB	SO	ShO	Relief W	Relief L	Relief SV	Batting AB	Batting H	HR	BA	PO	A	E	DP	TC/G	FA
1982	**CIN N**	0	1	.000	2.60	5	2	0	17.1	17	0	7	0	0	0	0	2	1	0	.500	0	3	1	0	0.8	.750
1983		2	3	.400	2.74	73	0	0	92	73	33	57	0	2	3	10	11	1	0	.091	2	18	0	1	0.3	1.000
1984	**2 teams** **CIN N** (36G 1–1) **DET A** (18G 1–0)																									
"	**total**	2	1	.667	4.16	54	0	0	71.1	78	23	51	0	2	1	1	3	0	0	.000	1	12	1	0	0.3	.929
1985	**DET A**	3	2	.600	4.36	48	0	0	66	62	41	46	0	3	2	0	0	0	0	—	7	11	2	2	0.4	.900
1986		0	1	.000	7.29	13	0	0	21	19	22	16	0	0	1	0	0	0	0	—	1	3	0	0	0.3	1.000
1987	**CIN N**	1	1	.500	4.36	23	0	0	33	43	16	24	0	1	1	0	1	0	0	.000	3	3	0	0	0.3	1.000
1988	**2 teams** **BAL A** (4G 0–1) **PHI N** (8G 0–0)																									
"	**total**	0	1	.000	8.44	12	0	0	10.2	15	5	6	0	0	1	0	0	0	0		0	1	0	1	0.1	1.000
7 yrs.		8	10	.444	4.08	228	2	0	311.1	307	140	207	0	8	9	11	17	2	0	.118	14	51	4	4	0.3	.942
WORLD SERIES																										
1984	**DET A**	0	0	—	3.00	3	0	0	3	5	0	0	0	0	0	0	0	0	0	—	0	2	0	0	0.7	1.000

Dutch Schesler

SCHESLER, CHARLES BR TR 6′ 2″ 180 lbs.
B. June 1, 1900, Frankfurt, Germany D. Nov. 19, 1953, Harrisburg, Pa.

Year	Team	W	L	PCT	ERA	G	GS	CG	IP	H	BB	SO	ShO	Relief W	Relief L	Relief SV	Batting AB	Batting H	HR	BA	PO	A	E	DP	TC/G	FA
1931	**PHI N**	0	0	—	7.28	17	0	0	38.1	65	18	14	0	0	0	0	9	1	0	.111	0	11	1	0	0.7	.917

Lou Schettler

SCHETTLER, LOUIS MARTIN BR TR 5′11″ 160 lbs.
B. June 12, 1886, Pittsburgh, Pa. D. May 1, 1960, Youngstown, Ohio.

Year	Team	Lg	W	L	PCT	ERA	G	GS	CG	IP	H	BB	SO	ShO	Relief W	Relief L	Relief SV	Batting AB	Batting H	Batting HR	BA	PO	A	E	DP	TC/G	FA
1910	PHI	N	2	6	.250	3.20	27	7	3	107	96	51	62	0	1	2	1	41	7	0	.171	4	24	5	0	1.2	.848

Curt Schilling

SCHILLING, CURTIS MONTAGUE BR TR 6′ 5″ 205 lbs.
B. Nov. 14, 1966, Anchorage, Alaska.

Year	Team	Lg	W	L	PCT	ERA	G	GS	CG	IP	H	BB	SO	ShO	Relief W	Relief L	Relief SV	Batting AB	Batting H	Batting HR	BA	PO	A	E	DP	TC/G	FA
1988	BAL	A	0	3	.000	9.82	4	4	0	14.2	22	10	4	0	0	0	0	0	0	0	—	0	0	1	0	0.3	.000
1989			0	1	.000	6.23	5	1	0	8.2	10	3	6	0	0	0	0	0	0	0	—	1	0	0	0	0.2	1.000
1990			1	2	.333	2.54	35	0	0	46	38	19	32	0	1	2	3	0	0	0	—	1	4	0	0	0.1	1.000
1991	HOU	N	3	5	.375	3.81	56	0	0	75.2	79	39	71	0	3	5	8	3	1	0	.333	6	4	1	0	0.2	.909
1992	PHI	N	14	11	.560	2.35	42	26	10	226.1	165	59	147	4	2	2	2	64	10	0	.156	14	21	3	1	0.9	.921
1993			16	7	.696	4.02	34	34	7	235.1	234	57	186	2	0	0	0	75	11	0	.147	6	36	0	1	1.2	1.000
1994			2	8	.200	4.48	13	13	1	82.1	87	28	58	0	0	0	0	28	3	0	.107	2	11	1	0	1.1	.929
1995			7	5	.583	3.57	17	17	1	116	96	26	114	0	0	0	0	40	7	0	.175	2	8	1	1	0.6	.909
8 yrs.			43	42	.506	3.56	206	95	19	805	731	241	618	6	6	9	13	210	32	0	.152	32	84	7	3	0.6	.943
LEAGUE CHAMPIONSHIP SERIES																											
1993	PHI	N	0	0	—	1.69	2	2	0	16	11	5	19	0	0	0	0	5	0	0	.000	0	0	0	0	0.0	.000
WORLD SERIES																											
1993	PHI	N	1	1	.500	3.52	2	2	1	15.1	13	5	9	1	0	0	0	2	1	0	.500	0	3	0	0	1.5	1.000

Red Schillings

SCHILLINGS, ELBERT ISAIAH BR TR 5′10″ 180 lbs.
B. Mar. 29, 1900, Deport, Tex. D. Jan. 7, 1954, Oklahoma City, Okla.

Year	Team	Lg	W	L	PCT	ERA	G	GS	CG	IP	H	BB	SO	ShO	Relief W	Relief L	Relief SV	Batting AB	Batting H	Batting HR	BA	PO	A	E	DP	TC/G	FA
1922	PHI	A	0	0	—	6.75	4	0	0	8	10	11	4	0	0	0	0	2	0	0	.000	0	1	0	0	0.3	1.000

Calvin Schiraldi

SCHIRALDI, CALVIN DREW BR TR 6′ 5″ 215 lbs.
B. June 16, 1962, Houston, Tex.

Year	Team	Lg	W	L	PCT	ERA	G	GS	CG	IP	H	BB	SO	ShO	Relief W	Relief L	Relief SV	Batting AB	Batting H	Batting HR	BA	PO	A	E	DP	TC/G	FA
1984	NY	N	0	2	.000	5.71	5	3	0	17.1	20	10	16	0	0	0	0	3	0	0	.000	0	3	0	1	0.6	1.000
1985			2	1	.667	8.89	10	4	0	26.1	43	11	21	0	0	0	0	8	1	0	.125	2	3	0	2	0.5	1.000
1986	BOS	A	4	2	.667	1.41	25	0	0	51	36	15	55	0	4	2	9	0	0	0	—	2	3	0	0	0.2	1.000
1987			8	5	.615	4.41	62	1	0	83.2	75	40	93	0	8	5	6	0	0	0	—	3	10	1	0	0.2	.929
1988	CHI	N	9	13	.409	4.38	29	27	2	166.1	166	63	140	1	0	0	1	60	6	0	.100	13	12	4	0	1.0	.862
1989	2 teams	CHI N (54G 3–6)	SD N (5G 3–1)																								
″	total		6	7	.462	3.51	59	4	0	100	72	63	71	0	3	7	4	16	1	1	.063	9	5	0	0	0.2	1.000
1990	SD	N	3	8	.273	4.41	42	8	0	104	105	60	74	0	2	3	1	21	4	1	.190	5	11	3	0	0.5	.842
1991	TEX	A	0	1	.000	11.57	3	0	0	4.2	5	5	1	0	0	1	0	0	0	0	—	1	1	0	0	0.7	1.000
8 yrs.			32	39	.451	4.28	235	47	2	553.1	522	267	471	1	17	18	21	108	12	2	.111	35	48	8	3	0.4	.912
LEAGUE CHAMPIONSHIP SERIES																											
1986	BOS	A	0	1	.000	1.50	4	0	0	6	5	3	9	0	0	1	1	0	0	0	—	0	0	0	0	0.0	.000
WORLD SERIES																											
1986	BOS	A	0	2	.000	13.50	3	0	0	4	7	3	2	0	0	2	1	1	0	0	.000	0	1	0	0	0.3	1.000

Biff Schlitzer

SCHLITZER, VICTOR JOSEPH BR TR 5′11″ 175 lbs.
B. Dec. 4, 1884, Rochester, N. Y. D. Jan. 4, 1948, Wellesley Hills, Mass.

Year	Team	Lg	W	L	PCT	ERA	G	GS	CG	IP	H	BB	SO	ShO	Relief W	Relief L	Relief SV	Batting AB	Batting H	Batting HR	BA	PO	A	E	DP	TC/G	FA
1908	PHI	A	6	8	.429	3.16	24	18	11	131	110	45	57	2	0	0	0	46	9	0	.196	2	31	1	0	1.4	.971
1909	2 teams	PHI A (4G 0–3)	BOS A (13G 4–4)																								
″	total		4	7	.364	3.54	17	11	5	89	94	26	30	0	1	1	1	33	6	0	.182	6	37	6	0	2.9	.878
1914	BUF	F	0	0	—	16.20	3	0	0	3.1	7	2	1	0	0	0	0	1	1	0	1.000	0	1	0	0	0.3	1.000
3 yrs.			10	15	.400	3.51	44	29	16	223.1	211	73	88	2	1	1	1	80	16	0	.200	8	69	7	0	1.9	.917

George Schmees

SCHMEES, GEORGE EDWARD (Rocky) BL TL 6′ 190 lbs.
B. Sept. 6, 1924, Cincinnati, Ohio.

Year	Team	Lg	W	L	PCT	ERA	G	GS	CG	IP	H	BB	SO	ShO	Relief W	Relief L	Relief SV	Batting AB	Batting H	Batting HR	BA	PO	A	E	DP	TC/G	FA
1952	BOS	A	0	0	—	3.00	2	1	0	6	9	2	2	0	0	0	0	*				91	7	4	1	1.9	.961

Al Schmelz

SCHMELZ, ALAN GEORGE BR TR 6′ 4″ 210 lbs.
B. Nov. 12, 1943, Whittier, Calif.

Year	Team	Lg	W	L	PCT	ERA	G	GS	CG	IP	H	BB	SO	ShO	Relief W	Relief L	Relief SV	Batting AB	Batting H	Batting HR	BA	PO	A	E	DP	TC/G	FA
1967	NY	N	0	0	—	3.00	2	0	0	3	4	1	2	0	0	0	0	0	0	0	—	1	1	0	1	1.0	1.000

Butch Schmidt

SCHMIDT, CHARLES JOHN BL TL 6′ 1½″ 200 lbs.
B. July 19, 1886, Baltimore, Md. D. Sept. 4, 1952, Baltimore, Md.

Year	Team	Lg	W	L	PCT	ERA	G	GS	CG	IP	H	BB	SO	ShO	Relief W	Relief L	Relief SV	Batting AB	Batting H	Batting HR	BA	PO	A	E	DP	TC/G	FA
1909	NY	A	0	0	—	7.20	1	0	0	5	10	1	2	0	0	0	0	*				0	1	1	0	2.0	.500

Curt Schmidt

SCHMIDT, CURTIS ALLEN BR TR 6′ 5″ 200 lbs.
B. Mar. 16, 1970, Miles City, Mont.

Year	Team	Lg	W	L	PCT	ERA	G	GS	CG	IP	H	BB	SO	ShO	Relief W	Relief L	Relief SV	Batting AB	Batting H	Batting HR	BA	PO	A	E	DP	TC/G	FA
1995	MON	N	0	0	—	6.97	11	0	0	10.1	15	9	7	0	0	0	0	0	0	0	—	0	1	0	0	0.1	1.000

Dave Schmidt

SCHMIDT, DAVID JOSEPH BR TR 6′ 1″ 185 lbs.
B. Apr. 22, 1957, Niles, Mich.

Year	Team	Lg	W	L	PCT	ERA	G	GS	CG	IP	H	BB	SO	ShO	Relief W	Relief L	Relief SV	Batting AB	Batting H	Batting HR	BA	PO	A	E	DP	TC/G	FA
1981	TEX	A	0	1	.000	3.09	14	1	0	32	31	11	13	0	0	0	1	0	0	0	—	1	6	0	0	0.5	1.000
1982			4	6	.400	3.20	33	8	0	109.2	118	25	69	0	3	1	6	0	0	0	—	2	16	2	2	0.6	.900
1983			3	3	.500	3.88	31	0	0	46.1	42	14	29	0	3	3	2	0	0	0	—	6	4	0	1	0.3	1.000
1984			6	6	.500	2.56	43	0	0	70.1	69	20	46	0	6	6	12	0	0	0	—	6	13	1	2	0.5	.950
1985			7	6	.538	3.15	51	4	1	85.2	81	22	46	1	5	4	5	0	0	0	—	3	19	3	3	0.5	.880
1986	CHI	A	3	6	.333	3.31	49	1	0	92.1	94	27	67	0	3	5	8	0	0	0	—	7	7	3	0	0.3	.824
1987	BAL	A	10	5	.667	3.77	35	14	2	124	128	26	70	2	6	1	1	0	0	0	—	6	14	1	2	0.6	.952
1988			8	5	.615	3.40	41	9	0	129.2	129	38	67	0	3	3	2	0	0	0	—	18	20	1	2	1.0	.974
1989			10	13	.435	5.69	38	26	2	156.2	196	36	46	0	1	0	0	0	0	0	—	18	28	3	2	1.3	.939
1990	MON	N	3	3	.500	4.31	34	0	0	48	58	13	22	0	3	3	13	3	0	0	.000	2	10	2	0	0.4	.857
1991			0	1	.000	10.38	4	0	0	4.1	9	2	3	0	0	1	0	0	0	0	—	0	1	0	0	0.3	1.000
1992	SEA	A	0	0	—	18.90	3	0	0	3.1	7	3	1	0	0	0	0	0	0	0	—	0	0	0	0	0.0	.000
12 yrs.			54	55	.495	3.88	376	63	5	902.1	962	237	479	3	33	27	50	3	0	0	.000	69	138	16	14	0.6	.928

Freddy Schmidt

SCHMIDT, FREDERICK ALBERT BR TR 6′ 1″ 185 lbs.
B. Feb. 9, 1916, Hartford, Conn.

Year	Team	Lg	W	L	PCT	ERA	G	GS	CG	IP	H	BB	SO	ShO	Relief Pitching W	Relief Pitching L	Relief Pitching SV	Batting AB	Batting H	Batting HR	BA	PO	A	E	DP	TC/G	FA
1944	STL	N	7	3	.700	3.15	37	9	3	114.1	94	58	58	2	3	0	5	34	7	0	.206	3	17	0	2	0.5	1.000
1946			1	0	1.000	3.29	16	0	0	27.1	27	15	14	0	1	0	0	1	0	0	.000	1	7	0	0	0.5	1.000
1947	3 teams STL N (2G 0–0) PHI N (29G 5–8) CHI N (1G 0–0)																										
″	total		5	8	.385	4.73	32	6	0	83.2	85	49	26	0	5	4	0	22	1	0	.045	1	13	1	1	0.5	.933
3 yrs.			13	11	.542	3.75	85	15	3	225.1	206	122	98	2	9	4	5	57	8	0	.140	5	37	1	3	0.5	.977
WORLD SERIES																											
1944	STL	N	0	0	—	0.00	1	0	0	3.1	1	1	1	0	0	0	0	1	0	0	.000	0	0	0	0	0.0	.000

Henry Schmidt

SCHMIDT, HENRY MARTIN BR TR 5′11″ 170 lbs.
B. June 26, 1873, Brownsville, Tex. D. Apr. 23, 1926, Nashville, Tenn.

Year	Team	Lg	W	L	PCT	ERA	G	GS	CG	IP	H	BB	SO	ShO	Relief Pitching W	Relief Pitching L	Relief Pitching SV	Batting AB	Batting H	Batting HR	BA	PO	A	E	DP	TC/G	FA
1903	BKN	N	21	13	.618	3.83	40	36	29	301	321	120	96	5	1	0	2	107	21	1	.196	14	110	4	5	3.1	.969

Jason Schmidt

SCHMIDT, JASON DAVID BR TR 6′ 5″ 185 lbs.
B. Jan. 29, 1973, Kelson, Wash.

Year	Team	Lg	W	L	PCT	ERA	G	GS	CG	IP	H	BB	SO	ShO	Relief Pitching W	Relief Pitching L	Relief Pitching SV	Batting AB	Batting H	Batting HR	BA	PO	A	E	DP	TC/G	FA
1995	ATL	N	2	2	.500	5.76	9	2	0	25	27	18	19	0	1	1	0	5	1	0	.200	3	3	0	1	0.7	1.000

Pete Schmidt

SCHMIDT, FREDERICH CHRISTOPH HERMAN BR TR 5′11″ 175 lbs.
B. July 23, 1890, Lowden, Iowa D. Mar. 11, 1973, Pembroke, Ont., Canada.

Year	Team	Lg	W	L	PCT	ERA	G	GS	CG	IP	H	BB	SO	ShO	Relief Pitching W	Relief Pitching L	Relief Pitching SV	Batting AB	Batting H	Batting HR	BA	PO	A	E	DP	TC/G	FA
1913	STL	A	0	0	—	4.50	1	0	0	2	3	2	0	0	0	0	1	0	0	0	—	0	0	0	0	0.0	.000

Willard Schmidt

SCHMIDT, WILLARD RAYMOND BR TR 6′ 1″ 187 lbs.
B. May 29, 1928, Hays, Kans.

Year	Team	Lg	W	L	PCT	ERA	G	GS	CG	IP	H	BB	SO	ShO	Relief Pitching W	Relief Pitching L	Relief Pitching SV	Batting AB	Batting H	Batting HR	BA	PO	A	E	DP	TC/G	FA
1952	STL	N	2	3	.400	5.19	18	3	0	34.2	36	18	30	0	1	1	1	8	1	0	.125	2	11	1	0	0.8	.929
1953			0	2	.000	9.17	6	2	0	17.2	21	13	11	0	0	0	0	4	0	0	.000	2	2	0	0	0.7	1.000
1955			7	6	.538	2.78	20	15	8	129.2	89	57	86	1	0	0	0	42	5	0	.119	12	20	2	5	1.7	.941
1956			6	8	.429	3.84	33	21	2	147.2	131	78	52	0	0	0	1	43	10	0	.233	6	34	0	3	1.2	1.000
1957			10	3	.769	4.78	40	8	1	116.2	146	49	63	0	5	3	0	33	7	0	.212	8	22	1	1	0.8	.968
1958	CIN	N	3	5	.375	2.86	41	2	0	69.1	60	33	41	0	3	5	0	11	1	0	.091	5	17	2	0	0.6	.917
1959			3	2	.600	3.95	36	4	0	70.2	80	30	40	0	2	0	0	12	1	0	.083	5	16	0	2	0.6	1.000
7 yrs.			31	29	.517	3.93	194	55	11	586.1	563	278	323	1	11	9	2	153	25	0	.163	40	122	6	11	0.9	.964

Crazy Schmit

SCHMIT, FREDERICK M. (Germany) BL TL 5′10½″ 165 lbs.
B. Feb. 13, 1866, Chicago, Ill. D. Oct. 5, 1940, Chicago, Ill.

Year	Team	Lg	W	L	PCT	ERA	G	GS	CG	IP	H	BB	SO	ShO	Relief Pitching W	Relief Pitching L	Relief Pitching SV	Batting AB	Batting H	Batting HR	BA	PO	A	E	DP	TC/G	FA
1890	PIT	N	1	9	.100	5.83	11	10	9	83.1	108	42	35	1	0	**1**	0	33	2	0	.061	2	16	5	1	2.1	.783
1892	BAL	N	1	4	.200	3.23	6	6	6	47.1	37	26	17	0	0	0	0	19	2	0	.105	0	15	1	0	2.3	.938
1893	2 teams BAL N (9G 3–2) NY N (4G 0–2)																										
″	total		3	4	.429	6.85	13	10	5	69.2	97	39	15	0	0	0	0	30	9	0	.300	0	14	3	0	1.3	.824
1899	CLE	N	2	17	.105	5.86	20	19	16	138.1	197	62	24	0	0	0	0	70	11	0	.157	18	43	7	0	2.6	.897
1901	BAL	A	0	2	.000	1.99	4	3	1	22.2	25	16	2	0	0	0	0	9	2	0	.222	0	11	0	0	2.8	1.000
5 yrs.			7	36	.163	5.45	54	48	37	361.1	464	185	93	1	0	1	0	161	26	0	.161	20	99	16	1	2.2	.881

Johnny Schmitz

SCHMITZ, JOHN ALBERT (Bear Tracks) BR TL 6′ 170 lbs.
B. Nov. 27, 1920, Wausau, Wis.

Year	Team	Lg	W	L	PCT	ERA	G	GS	CG	IP	H	BB	SO	ShO	Relief Pitching W	Relief Pitching L	Relief Pitching SV	Batting AB	Batting H	Batting HR	BA	PO	A	E	DP	TC/G	FA
1941	CHI	N	2	0	1.000	1.31	5	3	1	20.2	12	9	11	0	1	0	0	7	4	0	.571	0	10	0	1	2.0	1.000
1942			3	7	.300	3.43	23	10	1	86.2	70	45	51	0	1	0	2	26	4	0	.154	5	38	1	2	1.9	.977
1946			11	11	.500	2.61	41	31	14	224.1	184	94	**135**	3	1	1	2	70	9	1	.129	12	49	0	2	1.5	1.000
1947			13	**18**	.419	3.22	38	28	10	207	209	80	97	3	1	3	4	68	9	0	.132	12	45	2	2	1.6	.966
1948			18	13	.581	2.64	34	30	18	242	186	97	100	2	3	0	1	84	11	0	.131	17	68	4	3	2.6	.955
1949			11	13	.458	4.35	36	31	9	207	227	92	75	3	1	1	3	70	10	0	.143	13	59	4	8	2.1	.947
1950			10	16	.385	4.99	39	27	8	193	217	91	75	3	1	1	0	67	8	0	.119	14	61	6	5	2.1	.926
1951	2 teams CHI N (8G 1–2) BKN N (16G 1–4)																										
″	total		2	6	.250	5.99	24	10	0	73.2	77	43	26	0	0	2	0	24	5	1	.208	8	23	0	2	1.3	1.000
1952	3 teams BKN N (10G 1–1) NY A (5G 1–1) CIN N (3G 1–0)																										
″	total		3	2	.600	3.71	18	5	2	53.1	47	30	17	0	1	1	1	13	4	0	.308	3	18	0	1	1.2	1.000
1953	2 teams NY A (3G 0–0) WAS A (24G 2–7)																										
″	total		2	7	.222	3.62	27	13	5	112	120	40	39	0	1	1	4	34	2	0	.059	5	22	3	4	1.1	.900
1954	WAS	A	11	8	.579	2.91	29	23	12	185.1	176	64	56	2	0	1	1	60	7	0	.117	12	40	2	9	1.9	.963
1955			7	10	.412	3.71	32	21	6	165	187	54	49	1	0	0	1	54	10	0	.185	8	40	0	3	1.5	1.000
1956	2 teams BOS A (2G 0–0) BAL A (18G 0–3)																										
″	total		0	3	.000	3.59	20	3	0	42.2	54	18	15	0	0	1	0	10	0	0	.000	4	10	1	1	0.8	.933
13 yrs.			93	114	.449	3.55	366	235	86	1812.2	1766	757	746	17	11	12	19	587	83	2	.141	113	483	23	43	1.7	.963

Charlie Schmutz

SCHMUTZ, CHARLES OTTO (King) BR TR 6′ 1½″ 195 lbs.
B. Jan. 1, 1890, San Diego, Calif. D. June 27, 1962, Seattle, Wash.

Year	Team	Lg	W	L	PCT	ERA	G	GS	CG	IP	H	BB	SO	ShO	Relief Pitching W	Relief Pitching L	Relief Pitching SV	Batting AB	Batting H	Batting HR	BA	PO	A	E	DP	TC/G	FA
1914	BKN	N	1	3	.250	3.30	18	5	1	57.1	57	13	21	0	1	0	0	16	3	0	.188	2	15	1	2	1.0	.944
1915			0	0	—	6.75	1	0	0	4	7	1	1	0	0	0	0	1	0	0	.000	0	3	0	0	3.0	1.000
2 yrs.			1	3	.250	3.52	19	5	1	61.1	64	14	22	0	1	0	0	17	3	0	.176	2	18	1	2	1.1	.952

Frank Schneiberg

SCHNEIBERG, FRANK FREDERICK TR
B. Mar. 12, 1882, Milwaukee, Wis. D. May 18, 1948, Milwaukee, Wis.

Year	Team	Lg	W	L	PCT	ERA	G	GS	CG	IP	H	BB	SO	ShO	Relief Pitching W	Relief Pitching L	Relief Pitching SV	Batting AB	Batting H	Batting HR	BA	PO	A	E	DP	TC/G	FA
1910	BKN	N	0	0	—	63.00	1	0	0	1	5	4	0	0	0	0	0	0	0	0	—	0	0	0	0	0.0	.000

Dan Schneider

SCHNEIDER, DANIEL LOUIS BL TL 6′ 3″ 170 lbs.
B. Aug. 29, 1942, Evansville, Ind.

Year	Team	Lg	W	L	PCT	ERA	G	GS	CG	IP	H	BB	SO	ShO	Relief Pitching W	Relief Pitching L	Relief Pitching SV	Batting AB	Batting H	Batting HR	BA	PO	A	E	DP	TC/G	FA
1963	MIL	N	1	0	1.000	3.09	30	3	0	43.2	36	20	19	0	0	0	0	7	0	0	.000	4	3	1	0	0.3	.875
1964			1	2	.333	5.45	13	5	0	36.1	38	13	14	0	1	1	0	8	0	0	.000	3	11	0	0	1.1	1.000
1966	ATL	N	0	0	—	3.42	14	0	0	26.1	35	5	11	0	0	0	0	8	4	0	.500	0	4	1	0	0.4	.800
1967	HOU	N	0	2	.000	4.96	54	0	0	52.2	60	27	39	0	0	2	2	5	1	0	.200	4	14	0	1	0.3	1.000
1969			0	1	.000	14.14	6	0	0	7	16	5	3	0	0	1	0	1	0	0	.000	0	3	1	0	0.7	.750
5 yrs.			2	5	.286	4.72	117	8	0	166	185	70	86	0	1	4	2	29	5	0	.172	11	35	3	1	0.4	.939

Jeff Schneider

SCHNEIDER, JEFFREY THEODORE — BB TL 6′ 3″ 195 lbs.
B. Dec. 6, 1952, Bremerton, Wash.

Year	Team	Lg	W	L	PCT	ERA	G	GS	CG	IP	H	BB	SO	ShO	Relief Pitching W	Relief Pitching L	Relief Pitching SV	Batting AB	Batting H	Batting HR	BA	PO	A	E	DP	TC/G	FA
1981	BAL	A	0	0	—	4.88	11	0	0	24	27	12	17	0	0	0	1	0	0	0	—	2	2	2	0	0.5	.667

Pete Schneider

SCHNEIDER, PETER JOSEPH — BR TR 6′ 1″ 194 lbs.
B. Aug. 20, 1895, Los Angeles, Calif. D. June 1, 1957, Los Angeles, Calif.

Year	Team	Lg	W	L	PCT	ERA	G	GS	CG	IP	H	BB	SO	ShO	Relief Pitching W	Relief Pitching L	Relief Pitching SV	Batting AB	Batting H	Batting HR	BA	PO	A	E	DP	TC/G	FA
1914	CIN	N	5	13	.278	2.81	29	20	11	144.1	143	56	62	1	1	3	1	45	8	1	.178	6	32	4	4	1.4	.905
1915			13	**19**	.406	2.48	48	35	16	275.2	254	104	108	5	2	0	2	94	23	2	.245	7	75	8	3	1.9	.911
1916			10	19	.345	2.69	44	31	16	274.1	259	82	117	3	2	2	1	89	21	0	.236	4	63	3	0	1.6	.957
1917			20	19	.513	1.98	46	42	25	341.2	316	**119**	142	0	1	0	0	114	19	1	.167	14	67	3	4	1.8	.964
1918			10	15	.400	3.51	33	30	17	217.2	213	**117**	51	2	0	0	0	83	24	1	.289	4	54	6	1	1.9	.906
1919	NY	A	0	1	.000	3.41	7	4	0	29	19	22	11	0	0	0	0	9	1	0	.111	0	5	2	0	1.0	.714
6 yrs.			58	86	.403	2.62	207	162	85	1282.2	1204	500	491	11	6	5	4	434	96	5	.221	35	296	26	12	1.7	.927

Karl Schnell

SCHNELL, KARL OTTO — BR TR 6′ 1″ 176 lbs.
B. Sept. 20, 1899, Los Angeles, Calif. D. May 31, 1992, Palo Alto, Calif.

Year	Team	Lg	W	L	PCT	ERA	G	GS	CG	IP	H	BB	SO	ShO	Relief Pitching W	Relief Pitching L	Relief Pitching SV	Batting AB	Batting H	Batting HR	BA	PO	A	E	DP	TC/G	FA
1922	CIN	N	0	0	—	2.70	10	0	0	20	21	18	5	0	0	0	0	4	1	0	.250	0	6	1	0	0.7	.857
1923			0	0	—	36.00	1	0	0	1	2	2	0	0	0	0	0	0	0	0	—	0	0	0	0	0.0	.000
2 yrs.			0	0		4.29	11	0	0	21	23	20	5	0	0	0	0	4	1	0	.250	0	6	1	0	0.6	.857

Gerry Schoen

SCHOEN, GERALD THOMAS — BR TR 6′ 3″ 215 lbs.
B. Jan. 15, 1947, New Orleans, La.

Year	Team	Lg	W	L	PCT	ERA	G	GS	CG	IP	H	BB	SO	ShO	Relief Pitching W	Relief Pitching L	Relief Pitching SV	Batting AB	Batting H	Batting HR	BA	PO	A	E	DP	TC/G	FA
1968	WAS	A	0	1	.000	7.36	1	1	0	3.2	6	1	1	0	0	0	0	1	0	0	.000	0	0	0	0	0.0	.000

Jumbo Schoeneck

SCHOENECK, LEWIS W. (Lon) — BR TR 6′ 2″ 223 lbs.
B. Mar. 3, 1862, Chicago, Ill. D. Jan. 20, 1930, Chicago, Ill.

Year	Team	Lg	W	L	PCT	ERA	G	GS	CG	IP	H	BB	SO	ShO	Relief Pitching W	Relief Pitching L	Relief Pitching SV	Batting AB	Batting H	Batting HR	BA	PO	A	E	DP	TC/G	FA
1888	IND	N	0	0	—	0.00	2	0	0	4.1	5	1	1	0	0	0	0	*				1063	31	49	30	10.8	.957

Mike Schooler

SCHOOLER, MICHAEL RALPH — BR TR 6′ 3″ 220 lbs.
B. Aug. 10, 1962, Anaheim, Calif.

Year	Team	Lg	W	L	PCT	ERA	G	GS	CG	IP	H	BB	SO	ShO	Relief Pitching W	Relief Pitching L	Relief Pitching SV	Batting AB	Batting H	Batting HR	BA	PO	A	E	DP	TC/G	FA
1988	SEA	A	5	8	.385	3.54	40	0	0	48.1	45	24	54	0	5	**8**	15	0	0	0	—	2	4	0	0	0.2	1.000
1989			1	7	.125	2.81	67	0	0	77	81	19	69	0	1	7	33	0	0	0	—	4	14	0	3	0.3	1.000
1990			1	4	.200	2.25	49	0	0	56	47	16	45	0	1	4	30	1	0	0	.000	3	9	1	0	0.3	.923
1991			3	3	.500	3.67	34	0	0	34.1	25	10	31	0	3	3	7	0	0	0	—	2	2	0	0	0.1	1.000
1992			2	7	.222	4.70	53	0	0	51.2	55	24	33	0	2	7	13	0	0	0	—	1	10	0	1	0.2	1.000
1993	TEX	A	3	0	1.000	5.55	17	0	0	24.1	30	10	16	0	3	0	0	0	0	0	—	1	3	0	0	0.2	1.000
6 yrs.			15	29	.341	3.49	260	0	0	291.2	283	103	248	0	15	29	98	1	0	0	.000	13	42	1	4	0.2	.982

Ed Schorr

SCHORR, EDWARD WALTER — BR TR 6′ 2½″ 180 lbs.
B. Feb. 14, 1891, Bremen, Ohio D. Sept. 12, 1969, Atlantic City, N. J.

Year	Team	Lg	W	L	PCT	ERA	G	GS	CG	IP	H	BB	SO	ShO	Relief Pitching W	Relief Pitching L	Relief Pitching SV	Batting AB	Batting H	Batting HR	BA	PO	A	E	DP	TC/G	FA
1915	CHI	N	0	0	—	7.50	2	0	0	6	9	5	3	0	0	0	0	2	1	0	.500	1	1	0	0	1.0	1.000

Gene Schott

SCHOTT, ARTHUR EUGENE — BR TR 6′ 2″ 185 lbs.
B. July 14, 1913, Batavia, Ohio D. Nov. 16, 1992, Sun City Center, Fla.

Year	Team	Lg	W	L	PCT	ERA	G	GS	CG	IP	H	BB	SO	ShO	Relief Pitching W	Relief Pitching L	Relief Pitching SV	Batting AB	Batting H	Batting HR	BA	PO	A	E	DP	TC/G	FA
1935	CIN	N	8	11	.421	3.91	33	19	9	159	153	64	49	1	0	1	0	60	12	0	.200	6	49	2	0	1.7	.965
1936			11	11	.500	3.80	31	22	8	180	184	73	65	0	3	1	1	60	18	1	.300	10	44	3	3	1.8	.947
1937			4	13	.235	2.97	37	16	7	154.1	150	48	56	2	0	3	1	49	7	0	.143	9	40	2	1	1.4	.961
1938			5	5	.500	4.45	31	4	0	83	89	32	21	0	4	3	2	24	3	0	.125	5	21	0	2	0.8	1.000
1939	PHI	N	0	1	.000	4.91	4	0	0	11	14	5	1	0	0	1	0	6	2	0	.333	1	0	1	0	0.5	.500
5 yrs.			28	41	.406	3.72	136	61	24	587.1	590	222	192	3	7	9	4	199	42	1	.211	31	154	8	6	1.4	.959

Pete Schourek

SCHOUREK, PETER ALAN — BL TL 6′ 5″ 195 lbs.
B. May 10, 1969, Austin, Tex.

Year	Team	Lg	W	L	PCT	ERA	G	GS	CG	IP	H	BB	SO	ShO	Relief Pitching W	Relief Pitching L	Relief Pitching SV	Batting AB	Batting H	Batting HR	BA	PO	A	E	DP	TC/G	FA
1991	NY	N	5	4	.556	4.27	35	8	1	86.1	82	43	67	1	2	1	2	22	3	0	.136	6	14	0	1	0.6	1.000
1992			6	8	.429	3.64	22	21	0	136	137	44	60	0	1	0	0	42	2	0	.048	7	13	0	1	0.9	1.000
1993			5	12	.294	5.96	41	18	0	128.1	168	45	72	0	0	1	0	32	7	0	.219	5	17	0	2	0.5	1.000
1994	CIN	N	7	2	.778	4.09	22	10	0	81.1	90	29	69	0	3	0	0	23	4	1	.174	1	13	0	2	0.6	1.000
1995			18	7	.720	3.22	29	29	2	190.1	158	45	160	0	0	0	0	59	13	0	.220	7	29	1	2	1.3	.973
5 yrs.			41	33	.554	4.14	149	86	3	622.1	635	206	428	1	6	2	2	178	29	1	.163	26	86	1	8	0.8	.991
DIVISIONAL PLAYOFF SERIES																											
1995	CIN	N	1	0	1.000	2.57	1	1	0	7	5	3	5	0	0	0	0	2	0	0	.000	0	2	0	1	2.0	1.000
LEAGUE CHAMPIONSHIP SERIES																											
1995	CIN	N	0	1	.000	1.26	2	2	0	14.1	14	3	13	0	0	0	0	5	0	0	.000	1	3	0	1	2.0	1.000

Barney Schreiber

SCHREIBER, DAVID HENRY — BL TL 6′ 185 lbs.
B. May 8, 1882, Waverly, Ohio D. Oct. 6, 1964, Chillicothe, Ohio.

Year	Team	Lg	W	L	PCT	ERA	G	GS	CG	IP	H	BB	SO	ShO	Relief Pitching W	Relief Pitching L	Relief Pitching SV	Batting AB	Batting H	Batting HR	BA	PO	A	E	DP	TC/G	FA
1911	CIN	N	0	0	—	5.40	3	0	0	10	19	2	5	0	0	0	0	3	0	0	.000	0	1	0	0	0.3	1.000

Paul Schreiber

SCHREIBER, PAUL FREDERICK (Von) — BR TR 6′ 2″ 180 lbs.
B. Oct. 8, 1902, Jacksonville, Fla. D. Jan. 28, 1982, Sarasota, Fla.

Year	Team	Lg	W	L	PCT	ERA	G	GS	CG	IP	H	BB	SO	ShO	Relief Pitching W	Relief Pitching L	Relief Pitching SV	Batting AB	Batting H	Batting HR	BA	PO	A	E	DP	TC/G	FA
1922	BKN	N	0	0	—	0.00	1	0	0	1	2	0	0	0	0	0	0	0	0	0	—	1	1	0	0	2.0	1.000
1923			0	0	—	4.20	9	0	0	15	16	8	4	0	0	0	1	2	0	0	.000	0	3	1	0	0.4	.750
1945	NY	A	0	0	—	4.15	2	0	0	4.1	4	2	1	0	0	0	0	1	0	0	.000	0	4	0	1	2.0	1.000
3 yrs.			0	0		3.98	12	0	0	20.1	22	10	5	0	0	0	1	3	0	0	.000	1	8	1	1	0.8	.900

Al Schroll

SCHROLL, ALBERT BRINGHURST (Bull) — BR TR 6′ 2″ 210 lbs.
B. Mar. 22, 1932, New Orleans, La.

Year	Team	Lg	W	L	PCT	ERA	G	GS	CG	IP	H	BB	SO	ShO	Relief Pitching W	Relief Pitching L	Relief Pitching SV	Batting AB	Batting H	Batting HR	BA	PO	A	E	DP	TC/G	FA
1958	BOS	A	0	0	—	4.50	5	0	0	10	6	4	7	0	0	0	0	1	1	0	1.000	0	3	0	0	0.6	1.000
1959	2 teams	PHI N	(3G 1–1)	BOS A	(14G 1–4)																						
″	total		2	5	.286	5.37	17	5	1	55.1	59	28	30	0	1	2	0	13	2	0	.154	0	9	1	0	0.6	.900
1960	CHI	N	0	0	—	10.13	2	0	0	2.2	3	5	2	0	0	0	0	1	1	0	1.000	0	0	0	0	0.0	.000
1961	MIN	A	4	4	.500	5.22	11	8	2	50	53	27	24	0	1	0	0	18	5	1	.278	2	8	0	0	0.9	1.000
4 yrs.			6	9	.400	5.34	35	13	3	118	121	64	63	0	2	2	0	33	9	1	.273	2	20	1	0	0.7	.957

Ken Schrom

SCHROM, KENNETH MARVIN BR TR 6′ 2″ 195 lbs.
B. Nov. 23, 1954, Grangeville, Ida.

Year	Team	W	L	PCT	ERA	G	GS	CG	IP	H	BB	SO	ShO	Relief W	Relief L	SV	AB	H	HR	BA	PO	A	E	DP	TC/G	FA
1980	TOR A	1	0	1.000	5.23	17	0	0	31	32	19	13	0	1	0	1	0	0	0	—	3	6	0	0	0.5	1.000
1982		1	0	1.000	5.87	6	0	0	15.1	13	15	8	0	1	0	0	0	0	0	—	0	0	0	0	0.0	.000
1983	MIN A	15	8	.652	3.71	33	28	6	196.1	196	80	80	1	1	0	0	0	0	0	—	8	15	2	1	0.8	.920
1984		5	11	.313	4.47	25	21	3	137	156	41	49	0	0	0	0	0	0	0	—	8	9	1	0	0.7	.944
1985		9	12	.429	4.99	29	26	6	160.2	164	59	74	0	0	0	0	0	0	0	—	23	20	3	3	1.6	.935
1986	CLE A	14	7	.667	4.54	34	33	3	206	217	49	87	1	0	0	0	0	0	0	—	16	15	4	1	1.0	.886
1987		6	13	.316	6.50	32	29	4	153.2	185	57	61	1	0	0	0	0	0	0	—	11	13	1	1	0.8	.960
7 yrs.		51	51	.500	4.81	176	137	22	900	963	320	372	3	3	0	1	0	0	0		69	78	11	6	0.9	.930

Ron Schueler

SCHUELER, RONALD RICHARD BR TR 6′ 4″ 205 lbs.
B. Apr. 18, 1948, Catherine, Kans.

Year	Team	W	L	PCT	ERA	G	GS	CG	IP	H	BB	SO	ShO	Relief W	Relief L	SV	AB	H	HR	BA	PO	A	E	DP	TC/G	FA
1972	ATL N	5	8	.385	3.66	37	18	3	145	122	60	96	0	3	0	2	42	8	0	.190	14	11	0	1	0.7	1.000
1973		8	7	.533	3.86	39	20	4	186.1	179	66	124	2	2	3	2	62	11	0	.177	11	23	1	1	0.9	.971
1974	PHI N	11	16	.407	3.72	44	27	5	203	202	98	109	0	4	2	1	51	6	0	.118	16	18	3	0	0.8	.919
1975		4	4	.500	5.23	46	6	1	93	88	40	69	0	2	1	0	13	2	0	.154	11	14	2	3	0.6	.926
1976		1	0	1.000	2.90	35	0	0	49.2	44	16	43	0	1	0	3	2	0	0	.000	2	5	1	0	0.2	.875
1977	MIN A	8	7	.533	4.40	52	7	0	135	131	61	77	0	7	6	3	0	0	0	—	11	26	0	1	0.7	1.000
1978	CHI A	3	5	.375	4.30	30	7	0	81.2	76	39	39	0	1	1	0	0	0	0	—	5	13	1	1	0.6	.947
1979		0	1	.000	7.20	8	1	0	20	19	13	6	0	0	0	0	0	0	0	—	0	3	0	0	0.4	1.000
8 yrs.		40	48	.455	4.08	291	86	13	913.2	861	393	563	2	20	13	11	170	27	0	.159	70	113	8	7	0.7	.958

Dave Schuler

SCHULER, DAVID PAUL BR TL 6′ 4″ 210 lbs.
B. Oct. 4, 1953, Framingham, Mass.

Year	Team	W	L	PCT	ERA	G	GS	CG	IP	H	BB	SO	ShO	Relief W	Relief L	SV	AB	H	HR	BA	PO	A	E	DP	TC/G	FA
1979	CAL A	0	0	—	9.00	1	0	0	2	2	0	0	0	0	0	0	0	0	0	—	0	0	0	0	0.0	.000
1980		0	1	.000	3.46	8	0	0	13	13	2	7	0	0	1	0	0	0	0	—	0	1	0	0	0.1	1.000
1985	ATL N	0	0	—	6.75	9	0	0	10.2	19	3	10	0	0	0	0	0	0	0	—	1	0	0	0	0.1	1.000
3 yrs.		0	1	.000	5.26	18	0	0	25.2	34	5	17	0	0	1	0	0	0	0		1	1	0	0	0.1	1.000

Erik Schullstrom

SCHULLSTROM, ERIK PAUL BR TR 6′ 5″ 220 lbs.
B. Mar. 25, 1969, San Diego, Calif.

Year	Team	W	L	PCT	ERA	G	GS	CG	IP	H	BB	SO	ShO	Relief W	Relief L	SV	AB	H	HR	BA	PO	A	E	DP	TC/G	FA
1994	MIN A	0	0	—	2.77	9	0	0	13	13	5	13	0	0	0	1	0	0	0	—	1	0	1	0	0.2	.500
1995		0	0	—	6.89	37	0	0	47	66	22	21	0	0	0	0	0	0	0	—	1	6	0	0	0.2	1.000
2 yrs.		0	0		6.00	46	0	0	60	79	27	34	0	0	0	1	0	0	0		2	6	1	0	0.2	.889

Barney Schultz

SCHULTZ, GEORGE WARREN BR TR 6′ 2″ 200 lbs.
B. Aug. 15, 1926, Beverly, N. J.

Year	Team	W	L	PCT	ERA	G	GS	CG	IP	H	BB	SO	ShO	Relief W	Relief L	SV	AB	H	HR	BA	PO	A	E	DP	TC/G	FA
1955	STL N	1	2	.333	7.89	19	0	0	29.2	28	15	19	0	1	2	4	4	0	0	.000	6	7	0	0	0.7	1.000
1959	DET A	1	2	.333	4.42	13	0	0	18.1	17	14	17	0	1	2	0	2	2	0	1.000	1	2	2	0	0.4	.600
1961	CHI N	7	6	.538	2.70	41	0	0	66.2	57	25	59	0	7	6	7	10	1	0	.100	4	9	0	0	0.3	1.000
1962		5	5	.500	3.82	51	0	0	77.2	66	23	58	0	5	5	5	5	0	0	.000	5	12	1	2	0.4	.944
1963	2 teams	CHI N (15G 1–0)		STL N (24G 2–0)																						
″	total	3	0	1.000	3.59	39	0	0	62.2	61	17	44	0	3	0	3	4	0	0	.000	4	11	0	0	0.4	1.000
1964	STL N	1	3	.250	1.64	30	0	0	49.1	35	11	29	0	1	3	14	6	1	0	.167	0	7	1	0	0.3	.875
1965		2	2	.500	3.83	34	0	0	42.1	39	11	38	0	2	2	2	2	0	0	.000	1	8	0	0	0.3	1.000
7 yrs.		20	20	.500	3.63	227	0	0	346.2	303	116	264	0	20	20	35	33	4	0	.121	21	56	4	2	0.4	.951
WORLD SERIES																										
1964	STL N	0	1	.000	18.00	4	0	0	4	9	3	1	0	0	1	1	1	0	0	.000	0	0	0	0	0.0	.000

Bob Schultz

SCHULTZ, ROBERT DUFFY (Bill) BR TL 6′ 3″ 200 lbs.
B. Nov. 27, 1923, Louisville, Ky. D. Mar. 31, 1979, Nashville, Tenn.

Year	Team	W	L	PCT	ERA	G	GS	CG	IP	H	BB	SO	ShO	Relief W	Relief L	SV	AB	H	HR	BA	PO	A	E	DP	TC/G	FA
1951	CHI N	3	6	.333	5.24	17	10	2	77.1	75	51	27	0	1	0	0	29	4	0	.138	5	11	3	0	1.1	.842
1952		6	3	.667	4.01	29	5	1	74	63	51	31	0	4	0	0	18	4	0	.222	3	5	1	0	0.3	.889
1953	2 teams	CHI N (7G 0–2)		PIT N (11G 0–2)																						
″	total	0	4	.000	7.12	18	4	0	30.1	39	21	9	0	0	1	0	5	0	0	.000	1	2	1	0	0.2	.750
1955	DET A	0	0	—	20.25	1	0	0	1.1	2	2	0	0	0	0	0	0	0	0	—	0	0	0	0	0.0	.000
4 yrs.		9	13	.409	5.16	65	19	3	183	179	125	67	0	5	1	0	52	8	0	.154	9	18	5	0	0.5	.844

Buddy Schultz

SCHULTZ, CHARLES BUDD BR TL 6′ 170 lbs.
B. Sept. 19, 1950, Cleveland, Ohio.

Year	Team	W	L	PCT	ERA	G	GS	CG	IP	H	BB	SO	ShO	Relief W	Relief L	SV	AB	H	HR	BA	PO	A	E	DP	TC/G	FA
1975	CHI N	2	0	1.000	6.00	6	0	0	6	11	5	4	0	2	0	0	0	0	0	—	1	0	0	0	0.2	1.000
1976		1	1	.500	6.00	29	0	0	24	37	9	15	0	1	1	2	4	0	0	.000	5	4	0	0	0.3	1.000
1977	STL N	6	1	.857	2.33	40	3	0	85	76	24	66	0	5	1	1	12	2	0	.167	3	10	1	1	0.3	.929
1978		2	4	.333	3.80	62	0	0	83	68	36	70	0	2	4	6	5	1	0	.200	4	6	0	1	0.2	1.000
1979		4	3	.571	4.50	31	0	0	42	40	14	38	0	4	3	3	4	0	0	.000	1	5	0	0	0.2	1.000
5 yrs.		15	9	.625	3.67	168	3	0	240	232	88	193	0	14	9	12	25	3	0	.120	14	25	1	2	0.2	.975

Mike Schultz

SCHULTZ, WILLIAM MICHAEL BL TL 6′ 1″ 175 lbs.
B. Dec. 17, 1920, Syracuse, N. Y.

Year	Team	W	L	PCT	ERA	G	GS	CG	IP	H	BB	SO	ShO	Relief W	Relief L	SV	AB	H	HR	BA	PO	A	E	DP	TC/G	FA
1947	CIN N	0	0	—	4.50	1	0	0	2	4	2	0	0	0	0	0	0	0	0	—	0	0	0	0	0.0	.000

Webb Schultz

SCHULTZ, WEBB CARL BR TR 5′11″ 172 lbs.
B. Jan. 31, 1898, Wautoma, Wis. D. July 26, 1986, Delevan, Wis.

Year	Team	W	L	PCT	ERA	G	GS	CG	IP	H	BB	SO	ShO	Relief W	Relief L	SV	AB	H	HR	BA	PO	A	E	DP	TC/G	FA
1924	CHI A	0	0	—	9.00	1	0	0	1	1	0	0	0	0	0	0	0	0	0	—	0	0	0	0	0.0	.000

John Schultze

SCHULTZE, JOHN F. 6′½″ 165 lbs.
B. Burlington, N. J. Deceased.

Year	Team	W	L	PCT	ERA	G	GS	CG	IP	H	BB	SO	ShO	Relief W	Relief L	SV	AB	H	HR	BA	PO	A	E	DP	TC/G	FA
1891	PHI N	0	1	.000	6.60	6	1	0	15	18	11	4	0	0	0	0	6	1	0	.167	0	1	0	0	0.2	1.000

Al Schulz

SCHULZ, ALBERT CHRISTOPHER (Lefty) BR TL 6′ 182 lbs.
B. May 12, 1889, Toledo, Ohio D. Dec. 13, 1931, Gallipolis, Ohio.

Year	Team	W	L	PCT	ERA	G	GS	CG	IP	H	BB	SO	ShO	Relief W	Relief L	SV	AB	H	HR	BA	PO	A	E	DP	TC/G	FA
1912	NY A	1	1	.500	2.20	3	1	1	16.1	11	11	8	0	1	0	0	5	0	0	.000	3	7	1	0	3.7	.909
1913		7	13	.350	3.73	38	22	9	193	197	69	77	0	1	0	0	63	11	0	.175	8	52	4	2	1.7	.938

Al Schulz *continued*

Year	Team	Lg	W	L	PCT	ERA	G	GS	CG	IP	H	BB	SO	ShO	Relief Pitching W	Relief Pitching L	Relief Pitching SV	Batting AB	Batting H	Batting HR	BA	PO	A	E	DP	TC/G	FA
1914	2 teams	NY A (6G 1–3) BUF F (27G 10–11)																									
″	total		11	14	.440	3.57	33	27	11	199.1	187	87	105	0	3	0	1	63	10	1	.159	14	66	5	1	2.6	.941
1915	BUF	F	21	14	.600	3.08	42	38	25	309.2	264	**149**	160	5	0	0	0	109	18	0	.165	10	94	2	3	2.5	.981
1916	CIN	N	8	19	.296	3.14	44	22	10	215	208	93	95	0	4	4	2	64	8	0	.125	10	57	3	2	1.6	.957
5 yrs.			48	61	.440	3.32	160	110	56	933.1	867	409	445	5	9	4	3	304	47	1	.155	45	276	15	8	2.1	.955

Walt Schulz

SCHULZ, WALTER FREDERICK BR TR 6′ 170 lbs.
B. Apr. 16, 1900, St. Louis, Mo. D. Feb. 27, 1928, Prescott, Ariz.

Year	Team	Lg	W	L	PCT	ERA	G	GS	CG	IP	H	BB	SO	ShO	Relief Pitching W	Relief Pitching L	Relief Pitching SV	Batting AB	Batting H	Batting HR	BA	PO	A	E	DP	TC/G	FA
1920	STL	N	0	0	—	6.00	2	0	0	6	10	2	0	0	0	0	0	2	0	0	.000	0	3	0	0	1.5	1.000

Don Schulze

SCHULZE, DONALD ARTHUR BR TR 6′ 3″ 215 lbs.
B. Sept. 27, 1962, Roselle, Ill.

Year	Team	Lg	W	L	PCT	ERA	G	GS	CG	IP	H	BB	SO	ShO	Relief Pitching W	Relief Pitching L	Relief Pitching SV	Batting AB	Batting H	Batting HR	BA	PO	A	E	DP	TC/G	FA
1983	CHI	N	0	1	.000	7.07	4	3	0	14	19	7	8	0	0	0	0	1	0	0	.000	1	2	0	0	0.8	1.000
1984	2 teams	CHI N (1G 0–0) CLE A (19G 3–6)																									
″	total		3	6	.333	5.08	20	15	2	88.2	113	28	41	0	0	0	0	0	0	0		10	9	0	0	0.9	1.000
1985	CLE	A	4	10	.286	6.01	19	18	1	94.1	128	19	37	0	0	0	0	0	0	0	—	8	16	2	2	1.4	.923
1986			4	4	.500	5.00	19	13	1	84.2	88	34	33	0	1	0	0	0	0	0	—	7	7	0	0	0.7	1.000
1987	NY	N	1	2	.333	6.23	5	4	0	21.2	24	6	5	0	0	0	0	2	0	0	.000	6	6	0	0	2.4	1.000
1989	2 teams	NY A (2G 1–1) SD N (7G 2–1)																									
″	total		3	2	.600	5.09	9	6	0	35.1	50	11	20	0	0	0	0	4	0	0	.000	5	6	1	0	1.3	.917
6 yrs.			15	25	.375	5.47	76	59	4	338.2	422	105	144	0	1	0	0	7	0	0	.000	37	46	3	2	1.1	.965

Hal Schumacher

SCHUMACHER, HAROLD HENRY (Prince Hal) BR TR 6′ 190 lbs.
B. Nov. 23, 1910, Hinckley, N. Y. D. Apr. 21, 1993, Cooperstown, N. Y.

Year	Team	Lg	W	L	PCT	ERA	G	GS	CG	IP	H	BB	SO	ShO	Relief Pitching W	Relief Pitching L	Relief Pitching SV	Batting AB	Batting H	Batting HR	BA	PO	A	E	DP	TC/G	FA
1931	NY	N	1	0	1.000	10.80	8	2	1	18.1	31	14	11	0	0	0	1	7	1	0	.143	2	7	1	1	1.3	.900
1932			5	6	.455	3.55	27	13	2	101.1	119	39	38	1	0	1	0	31	7	0	.226	9	31	3	1	1.6	.930
1933			19	12	.613	2.16	35	33	21	258.2	199	84	96	7	0	1	1	98	21	0	.214	15	70	1	3	2.5	.988
1934			23	10	.697	3.18	41	36	18	297	299	89	112	2	2	2	0	117	28	6	.239	21	71	3	4	2.3	.968
1935			19	9	.679	2.89	33	33	19	261.2	235	70	79	3	0	0	0	107	21	2	.196	14	89	0	4	3.1	1.000
1936			11	13	.458	3.49	35	30	9	214.1	234	69	75	3	0	0	1	74	16	1	.216	12	63	4	6	2.3	.949
1937			13	12	.520	3.60	38	29	10	217.2	222	89	100	1	2	1	1	81	18	2	.222	17	46	2	2	1.7	.969
1938			13	8	.619	3.50	28	28	12	185	178	50	54	4	0	0	0	67	16	2	.239	9	49	2	1	2.1	.967
1939			13	10	.565	4.81	29	27	8	181.2	199	89	58	0	0	0	0	69	14	0	.203	4	37	3	4	1.5	.932
1940			13	13	.500	3.25	34	30	12	227	218	96	123	1	1	0	1	78	15	1	.192	14	61	1	2	2.2	.987
1941			12	10	.545	3.36	30	26	12	206	187	79	63	3	1	1	1	66	10	0	.152	12	39	2	2	1.7	.962
1942			12	13	.480	3.04	29	29	12	216	208	82	49	3	0	0	0	75	13	1	.173	13	56	1	3	2.4	.986
1946			4	4	.500	3.91	24	13	2	96.2	95	52	48	0	0	0	1	26	1	0	.038	12	27	1	1	1.7	.975
13 yrs.			158	120	.568	3.36	391	329	138	2481.1	2424	902	906	28	6	6	7	896	181	15	.202	154	646	24	34	2.1	.971
WORLD SERIES																											
1933	NY	N	1	0	1.000	2.45	2	2	1	14.2	13	5	3	0	0	0	0	7	2	0	.286	0	2	0	0	1.0	1.000
1936			1	1	.500	5.25	2	2	1	12	13	10	11	0	0	0	0	4	0	0	.000	0	2	0	1	1.0	1.000
1937			0	1	.000	6.00	1	1	0	6	9	4	3	0	0	0	0	1	0	0	.000	0	1	0	0	1.0	1.000
3 yrs.			2	2	.500	4.13	5	5	2	32.2	35	19	17	0	0	0	0	12	2	0	.167	0	5	0	1	1.0	1.000

Hack Schumann

SCHUMANN, CARL J. TR 6′ 2″ 230 lbs.
B. Aug. 13, 1884, Buffalo, N. Y. D. Mar. 25, 1946, Millgrove, N. Y.

Year	Team	Lg	W	L	PCT	ERA	G	GS	CG	IP	H	BB	SO	ShO	Relief Pitching W	Relief Pitching L	Relief Pitching SV	Batting AB	Batting H	Batting HR	BA	PO	A	E	DP	TC/G	FA
1906	PHI	A	0	2	.000	4.00	4	2	1	18	21	8	9	0	0	0	0	6	0	0	.000	0	4	0	0	1.0	1.000

Ferdie Schupp

SCHUPP, FERDINAND MAURICE BR TL 5′10″ 150 lbs.
B. Jan. 16, 1891, Louisville, Ky. D. Dec. 16, 1971, Los Angeles, Calif.

Year	Team	Lg	W	L	PCT	ERA	G	GS	CG	IP	H	BB	SO	ShO	Relief Pitching W	Relief Pitching L	Relief Pitching SV	Batting AB	Batting H	Batting HR	BA	PO	A	E	DP	TC/G	FA
1913	NY	N	0	0	—	0.75	5	1	0	12	10	3	2	0	0	0	0	3	1	0	.333	2	2	0	0	0.8	1.000
1914			0	0	—	5.82	8	0	0	17	19	9	9	0	0	0	1	2	0	0	.000	0	4	1	0	0.6	.800
1915			1	0	1.000	5.10	23	1	0	54.2	57	29	28	0	1	0	0	10	2	0	.200	1	15	0	0	0.7	1.000
1916			9	3	.750	0.90	30	11	8	140.1	79	37	86	4	2	1	1	41	4	0	.098	1	24	4	0	1.0	.862
1917			21	7	**.750**	1.95	36	32	25	272	202	70	147	6	0	1	0	93	15	0	.161	6	60	3	3	1.9	.957
1918			0	1	.000	7.56	10	2	1	33.1	42	27	22	0	0	0	0	9	1	0	.111	1	9	1	0	1.1	.909
1919	2 teams	NY N (9G 1–3) STL N (10G 4–4)																									
″	total		5	7	.417	4.34	19	14	6	101.2	87	48	54	0	1	0	1	26	3	1	.115	5	19	2	0	1.4	.923
1920	STL	N	16	13	.552	3.52	38	37	17	250.2	246	**127**	119	0	0	0	0	86	22	0	.256	5	57	3	4	1.7	.954
1921	2 teams	STL N (9G 2–0) BKN N (20G 3–4)																									
″	total		5	4	.556	4.39	29	11	2	98.1	117	48	48	0	3	0	3	26	5	0	.192	1	23	0	1	0.8	1.000
1922	CHI	A	4	4	.500	6.08	18	12	3	74	79	66	38	1	1	0	0	25	5	0	.200	1	18	1	0	1.1	.950
10 yrs.			61	39	.610	3.32	216	121	62	1054	938	464	553	11	8	2	6	321	58	1	.181	23	231	15	8	1.2	.944
WORLD SERIES																											
1917	NY	N	1	0	1.000	1.74	2	2	1	10.1	11	2	9	1	0	0	0	4	1	0	.250	1	4	0	0	2.5	1.000

Wayne Schurr

SCHURR, WAYNE ALLEN BR TR 6′ 4″ 185 lbs.
B. Aug. 6, 1937, Garrett, Ind.

Year	Team	Lg	W	L	PCT	ERA	G	GS	CG	IP	H	BB	SO	ShO	Relief Pitching W	Relief Pitching L	Relief Pitching SV	Batting AB	Batting H	Batting HR	BA	PO	A	E	DP	TC/G	FA
1964	CHI	N	0	0	—	3.72	26	0	0	48.1	57	11	29	0	0	0	0	5	0	0	.000	2	7	0	0	0.3	1.000

Mike Schwabe

SCHWABE, MICHAEL SCOTT BR TR 6′ 4″ 200 lbs.
B. July 12, 1964, Fort Dodge, Iowa.

Year	Team	Lg	W	L	PCT	ERA	G	GS	CG	IP	H	BB	SO	ShO	Relief Pitching W	Relief Pitching L	Relief Pitching SV	Batting AB	Batting H	Batting HR	BA	PO	A	E	DP	TC/G	FA
1989	DET	A	2	4	.333	6.04	13	4	0	44.2	58	16	13	0	1	1	0	0	0	0	—	7	8	0	1	1.2	1.000
1990			0	0	—	2.45	1	0	0	3.2	5	0	1	0	0	0	0	0	0	0	—	0	3	0	0	3.0	1.000
2 yrs.			2	4	.333	5.77	14	4	0	48.1	63	16	14	0	1	1	0	0	0	0		7	11	0	1	1.3	1.000

Don Schwall

SCHWALL, DONALD BERNARD BR TR 6′ 6″ 200 lbs.
B. Mar. 2, 1936, Wilkes-Barre, Pa.

Year	Team	Lg	W	L	PCT	ERA	G	GS	CG	IP	H	BB	SO	ShO	Relief Pitching W	Relief Pitching L	Relief Pitching SV	Batting AB	Batting H	Batting HR	BA	PO	A	E	DP	TC/G	FA
1961	BOS	A	15	7	.682	3.22	25	25	10	178.2	167	110	91	2	0	0	0	61	11	0	.180	8	33	3	4	1.8	.932
1962			9	15	.375	4.94	33	32	5	182.1	180	121	89	1	0	0	0	66	9	0	.136	8	34	2	4	1.3	.955
1963	PIT	N	6	12	.333	3.33	33	24	3	167.2	158	74	86	2	0	2	0	50	8	0	.160	15	35	1	3	1.5	.980
1964			4	3	.571	4.35	15	9	0	49.2	53	15	36	0	1	0	0	19	5	0	.263	2	10	1	0	0.9	.923
1965			9	6	.600	2.92	43	1	0	77	77	30	55	0	9	5	4	15	0	0	.000	8	16	0	5	0.6	1.000

Don Schwall *continued*

Year	Team		W	L	PCT	ERA	G	GS	CG	IP	H	BB	SO	ShO	Relief Pitching W	Relief Pitching L	Relief Pitching SV	Batting AB	Batting H	Batting HR	BA	PO	A	E	DP	TC/G	FA
1966	**2 teams**	**PIT N**	(11G 3–2)	**ATL N**	(11G 3–3)																						
″	**total**		6	5	.545	3.31	22	12	0	87	75	40	51	0	2	1	0	23	1	0	.043	11	9	0	2	0.9	1.000
1967	**ATL**	**N**	0	0	—	0.00	1	0	0	0.2	0	1	0	0	0	0	0	0	0	0	—	0	0	0	0	0.0	.000
7 yrs.			49	48	.505	3.72	172	103	18	743	710	391	408	5	12	8	4	234	34	0	.145	52	137	7	18	1.1	.964

Blackie Schwamb

SCHWAMB, RALPH RICHARD BR TR 6′ 5½″ 198 lbs.
B. Aug. 6, 1926, Los Angeles, Calif. D. Dec. 21, 1989, Lancaster, Calif.

Year	Team		W	L	PCT	ERA	G	GS	CG	IP	H	BB	SO	ShO	Relief Pitching W	Relief Pitching L	Relief Pitching SV	Batting AB	Batting H	Batting HR	BA	PO	A	E	DP	TC/G	FA
1948	**STL**	**A**	1	1	.500	8.53	12	5	0	31.2	44	21	7	0	0	0	0	10	3	0	.300	2	8	0	0	0.8	1.000

Jeff Schwarz

SCHWARZ, JEFFREY WILLIAM BR TR 6′ 5″ 190 lbs.
B. May 20, 1964, Fort Pierce, Fla.

Year	Team		W	L	PCT	ERA	G	GS	CG	IP	H	BB	SO	ShO	Relief Pitching W	Relief Pitching L	Relief Pitching SV	Batting AB	Batting H	Batting HR	BA	PO	A	E	DP	TC/G	FA
1993	**CHI**	**A**	2	2	.500	3.71	41	0	0	51	35	38	41	0	2	2	0	0	0	0	—	3	1	1	0	0.1	.800
1994	**2 teams**	**CHI A**	(9G 0–0)	**CAL A**	(4G 0–0)																						
″	**total**		0	0		5.50	13	0	0	18	14	22	18	0	0	0	0	0	0	0		0	1	0	0	0.1	1.000
2 yrs.			2	2	.500	4.17	54	0	0	69	49	60	59	0	2	2	0	0	0	0		3	2	1	0	0.1	.833

Rudy Schwenck

SCHWENCK, RUDOLPH CHRISTIAN BL TL 6′ 174 lbs.
B. Apr. 6, 1884, Louisville, Ky. D. Nov. 27, 1941, Anchorage, Ky.

Year	Team		W	L	PCT	ERA	G	GS	CG	IP	H	BB	SO	ShO	Relief Pitching W	Relief Pitching L	Relief Pitching SV	Batting AB	Batting H	Batting HR	BA	PO	A	E	DP	TC/G	FA
1909	**CHI**	**N**	1	1	.500	13.50	3	2	0	4	16	3	3	0	0	0	0	4	1	0	.250	2	5	0	1	2.3	1.000

Hal Schwenk

SCHWENK, HAROLD EDWARD BL TL 6′ 185 lbs.
B. Aug. 23, 1890, Schuylkill Haven, Pa. D. Sept. 3, 1955, Kansas City, Mo.

Year	Team		W	L	PCT	ERA	G	GS	CG	IP	H	BB	SO	ShO	Relief Pitching W	Relief Pitching L	Relief Pitching SV	Batting AB	Batting H	Batting HR	BA	PO	A	E	DP	TC/G	FA
1913	**STL**	**A**	1	0	1.000	3.27	1	1	1	11	12	4	3	0	0	0	0	3	1	0	.333	1	2	0	0	3.0	1.000

Jim Scoggins

SCOGGINS, LYNN J. (Lefty) BL TL 5′11″ 165 lbs.
B. July 19, 1891, Killeen, Tex. D. Aug. 16, 1923, Columbia, S. C.

Year	Team		W	L	PCT	ERA	G	GS	CG	IP	H	BB	SO	ShO	Relief Pitching W	Relief Pitching L	Relief Pitching SV	Batting AB	Batting H	Batting HR	BA	PO	A	E	DP	TC/G	FA
1913	**CHI**	**A**	0	1	.000	0.00	1	1	0		0	1	0	0	0	0	0	0	0	0	—	0	0	0	0	0.0	.000

Herb Score

SCORE, HERBERT JUDE BL TL 6′ 2″ 185 lbs.
B. June 7, 1933, Rosedale, N. Y.

Year	Team		W	L	PCT	ERA	G	GS	CG	IP	H	BB	SO	ShO	Relief Pitching W	Relief Pitching L	Relief Pitching SV	Batting AB	Batting H	Batting HR	BA	PO	A	E	DP	TC/G	FA
1955	**CLE**	**A**	16	10	.615	2.85	33	32	11	227.1	158	154	**245**	2	0	0	0	84	10	0	.119	4	15	4	2	0.7	.826
1956			20	9	.690	2.53	35	33	16	249.1	162	129	**263**	**5**	0	0	0	87	16	1	.184	1	19	2	0	0.6	.909
1957			2	1	.667	2.00	5	5	3	36	18	26	39	1	0	0	0	11	1	0	.091	0	6	1	0	1.4	.857
1958			2	3	.400	3.95	12	5	2	41	29	34	48	1	1	1	3	11	1	0	.091	0	2	3	0	0.4	.400
1959			9	11	.450	4.71	30	25	9	160.2	123	115	147	1	0	0	0	52	5	0	.096	1	15	5	1	0.7	.762
1960	**CHI**	**A**	5	10	.333	3.72	23	22	5	113.2	91	87	78	1	0	0	0	30	3	0	.100	1	16	0	0	0.7	1.000
1961			1	2	.333	6.66	8	5	1	24.1	22	24	14	0	0	0	0	6	0	0	.000	1	5	0	0	0.8	1.000
1962			0	0	—	4.50	4	0	0	6	6	4	3	0	0	0	0	0	0	0	—	0	2	0	0	0.5	1.000
8 yrs.			55	46	.545	3.36	150	127	47	858.1	609	573	837	11	1	1	3	281	36	1	.128	8	80	15	3	0.7	.854

Darryl Scott

SCOTT, DARRYL NELSON BR TR 6′ 1″ 185 lbs.
B. Aug. 6, 1968, Fresno, Calif.

Year	Team		W	L	PCT	ERA	G	GS	CG	IP	H	BB	SO	ShO	Relief Pitching W	Relief Pitching L	Relief Pitching SV	Batting AB	Batting H	Batting HR	BA	PO	A	E	DP	TC/G	FA
1993	**CAL**	**A**	1	2	.333	5.85	16	0	0	20	19	11	13	0	1	2	0	0	0	0	—	0	0	0	0	0.0	.000

Dick Scott

SCOTT, AMOS RICHARD BR TR 6′ 180 lbs.
B. Feb. 5, 1883, Bethel, Ohio D. Jan. 18, 1911, Chicago, Ill.

Year	Team		W	L	PCT	ERA	G	GS	CG	IP	H	BB	SO	ShO	Relief Pitching W	Relief Pitching L	Relief Pitching SV	Batting AB	Batting H	Batting HR	BA	PO	A	E	DP	TC/G	FA
1901	**CIN**	**N**	0	2	.000	5.14	3	2	2	21	26	9	7	0	0	0	0	9	0	0	.000	1	3	2	0	2.0	.667

Dick Scott

SCOTT, RICHARD LEWIS BR TL 6′ 2″ 185 lbs.
B. Mar. 15, 1933, Portsmouth, N. H.

Year	Team		W	L	PCT	ERA	G	GS	CG	IP	H	BB	SO	ShO	Relief Pitching W	Relief Pitching L	Relief Pitching SV	Batting AB	Batting H	Batting HR	BA	PO	A	E	DP	TC/G	FA
1963	**LA**	**N**	0	0	—	6.75	9	0	0	12	17	3	6	0	0	0	2	0	0	0	—	0	3	0	0	0.3	1.000
1964	**CHI**	**N**	0	0	—	12.46	3	0	0	4.1	10	1	1	0	0	0	0	0	0	0	—	0	2	0	0	0.7	1.000
2 yrs.			0	0		8.27	12	0	0	16.1	27	4	7	0	0	0	2	0	0	0		0	5	0	0	0.4	1.000

Ed Scott

SCOTT, EDWARD BR TR 6′ 3″
B. Aug. 12, 1870, Walbridge, Ohio D. Nov. 1, 1933, Toledo, Ohio.

Year	Team		W	L	PCT	ERA	G	GS	CG	IP	H	BB	SO	ShO	Relief Pitching W	Relief Pitching L	Relief Pitching SV	Batting AB	Batting H	Batting HR	BA	PO	A	E	DP	TC/G	FA
1900	**CIN**	**N**	17	**21**	.447	3.82	43	36	32	323	380	66	92	0	1	2	1	127	20	1	.157	21	120	14	7	3.6	.910
1901	**CLE**	**A**	7	6	.538	4.40	17	16	11	124.2	149	38	23	0	0	0	1	48	10	1	.208	5	43	2	1	2.9	.960
2 yrs.			24	27	.471	3.98	60	52	43	447.2	529	104	115	0	1	2	2	175	30	2	.171	26	163	16	8	3.4	.922

George Scott

SCOTT, GEORGE WILLIAM BR TR 6′ 1″ 175 lbs.
B. Nov. 17, 1896, Trenton, Mo.

Year	Team		W	L	PCT	ERA	G	GS	CG	IP	H	BB	SO	ShO	Relief Pitching W	Relief Pitching L	Relief Pitching SV	Batting AB	Batting H	Batting HR	BA	PO	A	E	DP	TC/G	FA
1920	**STL**	**N**	0	0	—	4.50	2	0	0	6	4	3	1	0	0	0	0	1	0	0	.000	0	0	0	0	0.0	.000

Jack Scott

SCOTT, JOHN WILLIAM BL TR 6′ 2½″ 199 lbs.
B. Apr. 18, 1892, Ridgeway, N. C. D. Nov. 30, 1959, Durham, N. C.

Year	Team		W	L	PCT	ERA	G	GS	CG	IP	H	BB	SO	ShO	Relief Pitching W	Relief Pitching L	Relief Pitching SV	Batting AB	Batting H	Batting HR	BA	PO	A	E	DP	TC/G	FA
1916	**PIT**	**N**	0	0	—	10.80	1	0	0	5	5	3	4	0	0	0	0	2	0	0	.000	1	1	0	0	2.0	1.000
1917	**BOS**	**N**	1	2	.333	1.82	7	3	3	39.2	36	5	21	0	1	0	0	16	2	0	.125	1	8	1	0	1.4	.900
1919			6	6	.500	3.13	19	12	7	103.2	109	39	44	0	0	1	1	40	7	0	.175	4	16	1	0	1.0	.952
1920			10	21	.323	3.53	44	33	22	291	308	85	94	3	0	1	1	99	21	0	.212	8	65	6	1	1.8	.924
1921			15	13	.536	3.70	**47**	28	16	233.2	258	57	83	2	1	2	3	88	30	1	.341	4	56	3	2	1.3	.952
1922	**2 teams**	**CIN N**	(1G 0–0)	**NY N**	(17G 8–2)																						
″	**total**		8	2	.800	4.46	18	10	5	80.2	85	24	37	0	1	1	2	31	8	0	.258	0	14	1	0	0.8	.933
1923	**NY**	**N**	16	7	.696	3.89	40	25	9	220	223	65	79	3	3	2	1	79	25	1	.316	6	43	2	1	1.3	.961
1925			14	15	.483	3.15	36	28	18	239.2	251	55	87	2	1	2	3	87	21	1	.241	11	63	1	3	2.1	.987
1926			13	15	.464	4.34	**50**	22	13	226	242	53	82	0	5	3	5	83	28	1	.337	12	49	2	4	1.3	.968
1927	**PHI**	**N**	9	**21**	.300	5.09	**48**	25	17	233.1	304	69	69	1	2	**7**	1	114	33	1	.289	7	51	3	1	1.3	.951
1928	**NY**	**N**	4	1	.800	3.58	16	3	3	50.1	59	11	17	0	1	1	1	15	4	0	.267	3	11	1	2	0.9	.933
1929			7	6	.538	3.53	30	6	2	91.2	89	27	40	0	4	4	1	26	8	0	.308	6	22	0	1	0.9	1.000
12 yrs.			103	109	.486	3.85	356	195	115	1814.2	1969	493	657	11	19	24	19	*				63	399	21	15	1.4	.957

Jack Scott *continued*

Year	Team	W	L	PCT	ERA	G	GS	CG	IP	H	BB	SO	ShO	Relief Pitching W	Relief Pitching L	Relief Pitching SV	Batting AB	Batting H	Batting HR	BA	PO	A	E	DP	TC/G	FA
WORLD SERIES																										
1922	**NY** N	1	0	1.000	0.00	1	1	1	9	4	1	2	1	0	0	0	4	1	0	.250	1	1	0	0	2.0	1.000
1923		0	1	.000	12.00	2	1	0	3	9	1	2	0	0	0	0	1	0	0	.000	0	1	0	0	1.0	1.000
2 yrs.		1	1	.500	3.00	3	2	1	12	13	2	4	1	0	0	0	*				1	2	0	0	1.5	1.000

Jim Scott

SCOTT, JAMES (Death Valley Jim) BR TR 6′ 1″ 235 lbs.
B. Apr. 23, 1888, Deadwood, S. D. D. Apr. 7, 1957, Jacumba, Calif.

Year	Team	W	L	PCT	ERA	G	GS	CG	IP	H	BB	SO	ShO	Relief W	Relief L	Relief SV	AB	H	HR	BA	PO	A	E	DP	TC/G	FA
1909	**CHI** A	12	12	.500	2.30	36	29	19	250.1	194	93	135	4	1	0	0	85	9	0	.106	6	70	4	2	2.2	.950
1910		8	18	.308	2.43	41	23	14	229.2	182	86	135	2	2	**4**	1	74	15	0	.203	11	84	3	4	2.4	.969
1911		14	11	.560	2.63	39	26	14	202	195	81	128	3	4	2	0	71	11	0	.155	7	43	8	3	1.5	.862
1912		2	2	.500	2.15	6	4	2	37.2	36	15	23	1	1	0	0	12	0	0	.000	0	11	1	0	2.0	.917
1913		20	**20**	.500	1.90	48	**38**	25	312.1	252	86	158	4	1	4	1	97	7	1	.072	7	90	9	2	2.2	.915
1914		14	18	.438	2.84	43	33	12	253.1	228	75	138	2	2	3	1	86	14	0	.163	6	87	7	1	2.3	.930
1915		24	11	.686	2.03	48	35	23	296.1	256	78	120	**7**	4	2	2	95	12	0	.126	6	103	5	2	2.4	.956
1916		7	14	.333	2.72	32	21	8	165.1	155	53	71	1	0	4	3	52	6	0	.115	4	45	1	3	1.6	.980
1917		6	7	.462	1.87	24	17	6	125	126	42	37	2	2	2	1	42	5	0	.119	7	37	2	1	1.9	.957
9 yrs.		107	113	.486	2.32	317	226	123	1872	1624	609	945	26	17	21	9	614	79	1	.129	54	570	40	18	2.1	.940

Lefty Scott

SCOTT, MARSHALL BR TL 6′½″ 165 lbs.
B. July 15, 1915, Roswell, N. M. D. Mar. 3, 1964, Houston, Tex.

Year	Team	W	L	PCT	ERA	G	GS	CG	IP	H	BB	SO	ShO	Relief W	Relief L	Relief SV	AB	H	HR	BA	PO	A	E	DP	TC/G	FA
1945	**PHI** N	0	2	.000	4.43	8	2	0	22.1	29	12	5	0	0	0	0	3	0	0	.000	1	2	0	0	0.4	1.000

Mickey Scott

SCOTT, RALPH ROBERT BL TL 6′ 1″ 155 lbs.
B. July 25, 1947, Weimar, Germany.

Year	Team	W	L	PCT	ERA	G	GS	CG	IP	H	BB	SO	ShO	Relief W	Relief L	Relief SV	AB	H	HR	BA	PO	A	E	DP	TC/G	FA
1972	**BAL** A	0	1	.000	2.74	15	0	0	23	23	5	11	0	0	1	0	1	0	0	.000	3	1	0	0	0.3	1.000
1973	**2 teams** **BAL A** (1G 0–0) **MON N** (22G 1–2)																									
″	**total**	1	2	.333	5.19	23	0	0	26	29	11	13	0	1	2	0	3	0	0	.000	2	4	0	0	0.3	1.000
1975	**CAL** A	4	2	.667	3.29	50	0	0	68.1	59	18	31	0	4	2	1	0	0	0	—	2	9	0	0	0.2	1.000
1976		3	0	1.000	3.23	33	0	0	39	47	12	10	0	3	0	3	0	0	0	—	2	4	0	0	0.2	1.000
1977		0	2	.000	5.63	12	0	0	16	19	4	5	0	0	2	0	0	0	0	—	1	4	0	0	0.4	1.000
5 yrs.		8	7	.533	3.71	133	0	0	172.1	177	50	70	0	8	7	4	4	0	0	.000	10	22	0	0	0.2	1.000

Mike Scott

SCOTT, MICHAEL WARREN BR TR 6′ 2″ 210 lbs.
B. Apr. 26, 1955, Santa Monica, Calif.

Year	Team	W	L	PCT	ERA	G	GS	CG	IP	H	BB	SO	ShO	Relief W	Relief L	Relief SV	AB	H	HR	BA	PO	A	E	DP	TC/G	FA
1979	**NY** N	1	3	.250	5.37	18	9	0	52	59	20	21	0	0	0	0	12	0	0	.000	3	7	2	0	0.7	.833
1980		1	1	.500	4.34	6	6	1	29	40	8	13	1	0	0	0	9	1	0	.111	1	5	2	1	1.3	.750
1981		5	10	.333	3.90	23	23	1	136	130	34	54	0	0	0	0	41	3	0	.073	14	35	1	2	2.2	.980
1982		7	13	.350	5.14	37	22	1	147	185	60	63	0	1	3	3	48	7	0	.146	7	43	4	3	1.5	.926
1983	**HOU** N	10	6	.625	3.72	24	24	2	145	143	46	73	2	0	0	0	48	8	0	.167	20	20	2	0	1.8	.952
1984		5	11	.313	4.68	31	29	0	154	179	43	83	0	0	0	0	47	6	0	.128	10	23	1	1	1.1	.971
1985		18	8	.692	3.29	36	35	4	221.2	194	80	137	2	0	0	0	72	11	1	.153	21	22	2	1	1.3	.956
1986		18	10	.643	**2.22**	37	37	7	**275.1**	182	72	**306**	**5**	0	0	0	95	12	0	.126	24	39	2	2	1.8	.969
1987		16	13	.552	3.23	36	**36**	8	247.2	199	79	233	3	0	0	0	80	10	0	.125	17	32	2	2	1.4	.961
1988		14	8	.636	2.92	32	32	8	218.2	162	53	190	5	0	0	0	71	6	0	.085	14	27	0	0	1.3	1.000
1989		**20**	10	.667	3.10	33	32	9	229	180	62	172	2	1	0	0	75	10	1	.133	15	25	4	0	1.3	.909
1990		9	13	.409	3.81	32	32	4	205.2	194	66	121	2	0	0	0	54	7	0	.130	10	20	1	0	1.0	.968
1991		0	2	.000	12.86	2	2	0	7	11	4	3	0	0	0	0	1	0	0	.000	0	1	0	0	0.5	1.000
13 yrs.		124	108	.534	3.54	347	319	45	2068	1858	627	1469	22	2	3	3	653	81	2	.124	156	299	23	12	1.4	.952
LEAGUE CHAMPIONSHIP SERIES																										
1986	**HOU** N	2	0	1.000	0.50	2	2	2	18	8	1	19	1	0	0	0	6	0	0	.000	0	0	1	0	0.5	.000
								4th					**1st**													

Milt Scott

SCOTT, MILTON PARKER (Mikado Milt) BR 5′ 9″ 160 lbs.
B. Jan. 17, 1866, Chicago, Ill. D. Nov. 3, 1938, Baltimore, Md.

Year	Team	W	L	PCT	ERA	G	GS	CG	IP	H	BB	SO	ShO	Relief W	Relief L	Relief SV	AB	H	HR	BA	PO	A	E	DP	TC/G	FA
1886	**BAL** AA	0	0	—	*3.00*	1	0	0	3	2	2	0	0	0	0	0	*				3	0	0	0	3.0	1.000

Tim Scott

SCOTT, TIMOTHY DALE BR TR 6′ 2″ 185 lbs.
B. Nov. 16, 1966, Hanford, Calif.

Year	Team	W	L	PCT	ERA	G	GS	CG	IP	H	BB	SO	ShO	Relief W	Relief L	Relief SV	AB	H	HR	BA	PO	A	E	DP	TC/G	FA
1991	**SD** N	0	0	—	9.00	2	0	0	1	2	0	1	0	0	0	0	0	0	0	—	0	0	0	0	0.0	.000
1992		4	1	.800	5.26	34	0	0	37.2	39	21	30	0	4	1	0	0	0	0	—	0	4	0	0	0.1	1.000
1993	**2 teams** **SD N** (24G 2–0) **MON N** (32G 5–2)																									
″	**total**	7	2	.778	3.01	56	0	0	71.2	69	34	65	0	7	2	1	4	0	0	.000	3	8	1	1	0.2	.917
1994	**MON** N	5	2	.714	2.70	40	0	0	53.1	51	18	37	0	5	2	1	2	0	0	.000	2	0	0	0	0.1	1.000
1995		2	0	1.000	3.98	62	0	0	63.1	52	23	57	0	2	0	2	4	1	0	.250	3	4	0	1	0.1	1.000
5 yrs.		18	5	.783	3.61	194	0	0	227	213	96	190	0	18	5	4	10	1	0	.100	8	16	1	2	0.1	.960

Scott Scudder

SCUDDER, WILLIAM SCOTT BR TR 6′ 2″ 180 lbs.
B. Feb. 14, 1968, Paris, Tex.

Year	Team	W	L	PCT	ERA	G	GS	CG	IP	H	BB	SO	ShO	Relief W	Relief L	Relief SV	AB	H	HR	BA	PO	A	E	DP	TC/G	FA
1989	**CIN** N	4	9	.308	4.49	23	17	0	100.1	91	61	66	0	0	0	0	24	4	0	.167	5	9	1	0	0.7	.933
1990		5	5	.500	4.90	21	10	0	71.2	74	30	42	0	2	1	0	18	1	0	.056	5	6	1	0	0.6	.917
1991		6	9	.400	4.35	27	14	0	101.1	91	56	51	0	0	2	1	29	3	1	.103	10	11	0	0	0.8	1.000
1992	**CLE** A	6	10	.375	5.28	23	22	0	109	134	55	66	0	0	0	0	0	0	0	—	14	11	0	0	1.1	1.000
1993		0	1	.000	9.00	2	1	0	4	5	4	1	0	0	0	0	0	0	0	—	0	0	0	0	0.0	.000
5 yrs.		21	34	.382	4.80	96	64	0	386.1	395	206	226	0	2	3	1	71	8	1	.113	34	37	2	0	0.8	.973
LEAGUE CHAMPIONSHIP SERIES																										
1990	**CIN** N	0	0	—	0.00	1	0	0	1	1	0	1	0	0	0	0	0	0	0	—	0	0	0	0	0.0	.000

Rod Scurry

SCURRY, RODNEY GRANT BL TL 6′ 2″ 180 lbs.
B. Mar. 17, 1956, Sacramento, Calif. D. Nov. 5, 1992, Reno, Nev.

Year	Team	W	L	PCT	ERA	G	GS	CG	IP	H	BB	SO	ShO	Relief W	Relief L	Relief SV	AB	H	HR	BA	PO	A	E	DP	TC/G	FA
1980	**PIT** N	0	2	.000	2.13	20	0	0	38	23	17	28	0	0	2	0	4	1	0	.250	2	5	0	0	0.3	1.000
1981		4	5	.444	3.77	27	7	0	74	74	40	65	0	1	2	7	19	3	0	.158	0	8	0	1	0.3	1.000
1982		4	5	.444	1.74	76	0	0	103.2	79	64	94	0	4	5	14	21	5	0	.238	11	9	0	0	0.3	1.000
1983		4	9	.308	5.56	61	0	0	68	63	53	67	0	4	9	7	5	0	0	.000	2	8	0	0	0.2	1.000
1984		5	6	.455	2.53	43	0	0	46.1	28	22	48	0	5	6	4	2	0	0	.000	0	9	1	0	0.2	.900

Rod Scurry *continued*

Year	Team	Lg	W	L	PCT	ERA	G	GS	CG	IP	H	BB	SO	ShO	Relief W	Relief L	Relief SV	AB	H	HR	BA	PO	A	E	DP	TC/G	FA
1985	2 teams PIT N (30G 0–1) NY A (5G 1–0)																										
"	total		1	1	.500	3.13	35	0	0	60.1	47	38	60	0	1	1	3	4	0	0	.000	1	10	0	0	0.3	1.000
1986	NY	A	1	2	.333	3.66	31	0	0	39.1	38	22	36	0	1	2	2	0	0	0	—	4	5	0	1	0.3	1.000
1988	SEA	A	0	2	.000	4.02	39	0	0	31.1	32	18	33	0	0	2	2	0	0	0	—	4	4	1	0	0.2	.889
8 yrs.			19	32	.373	3.24	332	7	0	461	384	274	431	0	16	29	39	55	9	0	.164	24	58	2	2	0.3	.976

Johnnie Seale

SEALE, JOHNNY RAY (Durango Kid)
B. Nov. 14, 1938, Edgewater, Colo.
BL TL 5′10″ 155 lbs.

Year	Team	Lg	W	L	PCT	ERA	G	GS	CG	IP	H	BB	SO	ShO	Relief W	Relief L	Relief SV	AB	H	HR	BA	PO	A	E	DP	TC/G	FA
1964	DET	A	1	0	1.000	3.60	4	0	0	10	6	4	5	0	1	0	0	1	0	0	.000	0	4	0	1	1.0	1.000
1965			0	0	—	12.00	4	0	0	3	7	2	3	0	0	0	0	0	0	0	—	0	0	0	0	0.0	.000
2 yrs.			1	0	1.000	5.54	8	0	0	13	13	6	8	0	1	0	0	1	0	0	.000	0	4	0	1	0.5	1.000

Kim Seaman

SEAMAN, KIM MICHAEL
B. May 6, 1957, Pascagoula, Miss.
BL TL 6′ 4″ 205 lbs.

Year	Team	Lg	W	L	PCT	ERA	G	GS	CG	IP	H	BB	SO	ShO	Relief W	Relief L	Relief SV	AB	H	HR	BA	PO	A	E	DP	TC/G	FA
1979	STL	N	0	0	—	0.00	1	0	0	2	0	2	3	0	0	0	0	0	0	0	—	0	0	0	0	0.0	.000
1980			3	2	.600	3.38	26	0	0	24	16	13	10	0	3	2	4	1	0	0	.000	1	3	0	0	0.2	1.000
2 yrs.			3	2	.600	3.12	27	0	0	26	16	15	13	0	3	2	4	1	0	0	.000	1	3	0	0	0.1	1.000

Rudy Seanez

SEANEZ, RUDY CABALLERO
B. Oct. 20, 1968, Brawley, Calif.
BR TR 5′10″ 185 lbs.

Year	Team	Lg	W	L	PCT	ERA	G	GS	CG	IP	H	BB	SO	ShO	Relief W	Relief L	Relief SV	AB	H	HR	BA	PO	A	E	DP	TC/G	FA
1989	CLE	A	0	0	—	3.60	5	0	0	5	1	4	7	0	0	0	0	0	0	0	—	0	0	0	0	0.0	.000
1990			2	1	.667	5.60	24	0	0	27.1	22	25	24	0	2	1	0	0	0	0	—	1	1	0	0	0.1	1.000
1991			0	0	—	16.20	5	0	0	5	10	7	7	0	0	0	0	0	0	0	—	0	0	0	0	0.0	.000
1993	SD	N	0	0	—	13.50	3	0	0	3.1	8	2	1	0	0	0	0	0	0	0	—	0	1	0	0	0.3	1.000
1994	LA	N	1	1	.500	2.66	17	0	0	23.2	24	9	18	0	1	1	0	1	0	0	.000	0	4	0	0	0.2	1.000
1995			1	3	.250	6.75	37	0	0	34.2	39	18	29	0	1	3	3	1	0	0	.000	3	3	1	0	0.2	.857
6 yrs.			4	5	.444	6.00	91	0	0	99	104	65	86	0	4	5	3	2	0	0	.000	4	9	1	0	0.2	.929

Ray Searage

SEARAGE, RAYMOND MARK
B. May 1, 1955, Freeport, N. Y.
BL TL 6′ 1″ 180 lbs.

Year	Team	Lg	W	L	PCT	ERA	G	GS	CG	IP	H	BB	SO	ShO	Relief W	Relief L	Relief SV	AB	H	HR	BA	PO	A	E	DP	TC/G	FA
1981	NY	N	1	0	1.000	3.65	26	0	0	37	34	17	16	0	1	0	1	1	1	0	1.000	2	5	0	0	0.3	1.000
1984	MIL	A	2	1	.667	0.70	21	0	0	38.1	20	16	29	0	2	1	6	0	0	0	—	1	5	1	0	0.3	.857
1985			1	4	.200	5.92	33	0	0	38	54	24	36	0	1	4	1	0	0	0	—	1	2	1	0	0.1	.750
1986	2 teams MIL A (17G 0–1) CHI A (29G 1–0)																										
"	total		1	1	.500	3.35	46	0	0	51	44	28	36	0	1	1	1	0	0	0		3	8	0	0	0.2	1.000
1987	CHI	A	2	3	.400	4.20	58	0	0	55.2	56	24	33	0	2	3	2	0	0	0	—	1	9	0	0	0.2	1.000
1989	LA	N	3	4	.429	3.53	41	0	0	35.2	29	18	24	0	3	4	0	0	0	0	—	5	8	1	0	0.3	.929
1990			1	0	1.000	2.78	29	0	0	32.1	30	10	19	0	1	0	0	2	0	0	.000	2	8	0	0	0.3	1.000
7 yrs.			11	13	.458	3.50	254	0	0	288	267	137	193	0	11	13	11	3	1	0	.333	15	45	3	0	0.2	.952

Steve Searcy

SEARCY, WILLIAM STEVEN
B. June 4, 1964, Knoxville, Tenn.
BL TL 6′ 1″ 190 lbs.

Year	Team	Lg	W	L	PCT	ERA	G	GS	CG	IP	H	BB	SO	ShO	Relief W	Relief L	Relief SV	AB	H	HR	BA	PO	A	E	DP	TC/G	FA
1988	DET	A	0	2	.000	5.63	2	2	0	8	8	4	5	0	0	0	0	0	0	0	—	0	1	0	0	0.5	1.000
1989			1	1	.500	6.04	8	2	0	22.1	27	12	11	0	0	1	0	0	0	0	—	2	2	1	0	0.6	.800
1990			2	7	.222	4.66	16	12	1	75.1	76	51	66	0	0	0	0	0	0	0	—	3	7	0	0	0.6	1.000
1991	2 teams DET A (16G 1–2) PHI N (18G 2–1)																										
"	total		3	3	.500	6.59	34	5	0	71	81	44	53	0	2	2	0	4	0	0	.000	1	10	0	0	0.3	1.000
1992	PHI	N	0	0	—	6.10	10	0	0	10.1	13	8	5	0	0	0	0	0	0	0	—	0	2	0	0	0.2	1.000
5 yrs.			6	13	.316	5.68	70	21	1	187	205	119	140	0	2	3	0	4	0	0	.000	6	22	1	0	0.4	.966

Tom Seaton

SEATON, THOMAS GORDON
B. Aug. 30, 1887, Blair, Neb. D. Apr. 10, 1940, El Paso, Tex.
BB TR 6′ 175 lbs.

Year	Team	Lg	W	L	PCT	ERA	G	GS	CG	IP	H	BB	SO	ShO	Relief W	Relief L	Relief SV	AB	H	HR	BA	PO	A	E	DP	TC/G	FA
1912	PHI	N	16	12	.571	3.28	44	27	16	255	246	106	118	2	3	1	2	83	18	0	.217	9	55	5	2	1.6	.928
1913			**27**	12	.692	2.60	52	35	21	**322.1**	262	**136**	**168**	6	5	5	1	110	12	1	.109	15	86	2	1	2.0	.981
1914	BKN	F	25	13	.658	3.03	44	38	26	302.2	299	102	172	7	2	0	2	107	22	1	.206	18	84	8	3	2.5	.927
1915	2 teams BKN F (32G 12–11) NWK F (12G 3–6)																										
"	total		15	17	.469	3.92	44	33	20	264.1	260	120	114	0	1	1	4	92	20	2	.217	5	92	3	4	2.3	.970
1916	CHI	N	6	6	.500	3.27	31	12	4	121	108	43	45	0	3	2	1	38	7	0	.184	5	36	1	0	1.4	.976
1917			5	4	.556	2.53	16	9	3	74.2	60	23	27	1	1	1	1	21	5	0	.238	2	25	1	0	1.8	.964
6 yrs.			94	64	.595	3.14	231	154	90	1340	1235	530	644	16	15	10	11	451	84	4	.186	54	378	20	10	2.0	.956

Tom Seats

SEATS, THOMAS EDWARD
B. Sept. 24, 1910, Farmington, N. C. D. May 10, 1992, San Ramon, Calif.
BR TL 5′11″ 190 lbs.
BB 1940

Year	Team	Lg	W	L	PCT	ERA	G	GS	CG	IP	H	BB	SO	ShO	Relief W	Relief L	Relief SV	AB	H	HR	BA	PO	A	E	DP	TC/G	FA
1940	DET	A	2	2	.500	4.69	26	2	0	55.2	67	21	25	0	2	1	1	12	1	0	.083	4	11	0	0	0.6	1.000
1945	BKN	N	10	7	.588	4.36	31	18	6	121.2	127	37	44	2	2	1	0	43	9	0	.209	5	25	2	0	1.0	.938
2 yrs.			12	9	.571	4.47	57	20	6	177.1	194	58	69	2	4	2	1	55	10	0	.182	9	36	2	0	0.8	.957

Tom Seaver

SEAVER, GEORGE THOMAS (The Franchise, Tom Terrific)
B. Nov. 17, 1944, Fresno, Calif.
Hall of Fame 1992.
BR TR 6′ 1″ 195 lbs.

Year	Team	Lg	W	L	PCT	ERA	G	GS	CG	IP	H	BB	SO	ShO	Relief W	Relief L	Relief SV	AB	H	HR	BA	PO	A	E	DP	TC/G	FA
1967	NY	N	16	13	.552	2.76	35	34	18	251	224	78	170	2	0	1	0	77	11	0	.143	17	38	1	3	1.6	.982
1968			16	12	.571	2.20	36	35	14	278	224	48	205	5	0	0	1	95	15	0	.158	21	48	1	4	1.9	.986
1969			**25**	7	**.781**	2.21	36	35	18	273.1	202	82	208	5	0	0	0	91	11	0	.121	18	48	2	7	1.9	.971
1970			18	12	.600	**2.81**	37	36	19	291	230	83	**283**	2	0	0	0	95	17	1	.179	19	46	3	3	1.8	.956
1971			20	10	.667	**1.76**	36	35	21	286	210	61	**289**	4	0	1	0	92	18	1	.196	17	38	1	3	1.6	.982
1972			21	12	.636	2.92	35	35	13	262	215	77	249	3	0	0	0	89	13	3	.146	17	40	3	3	1.7	.950
1973			19	10	.655	**2.08**	36	36	**18**	290	219	64	**251**	3	0	0	0	93	15	1	.161	26	35	5	1	1.8	.924
1974			11	11	.500	3.20	32	32	12	236	199	75	201	5	0	0	0	71	7	0	.099	9	42	1	7	1.6	.981
1975			**22**	9	.710	2.38	36	36	15	280	217	88	**243**	5	0	0	0	95	17	0	.179	21	43	4	6	1.9	.941
1976			14	11	.560	2.59	35	34	13	271	211	77	**235**	5	0	0	0	82	7	0	.085	12	41	1	3	1.5	.981

Tom Seaver *continued*

Year	Team	W	L	PCT	ERA	G	GS	CG	IP	H	BB	SO	ShO	Relief Pitching W	L	SV	Batting AB	H	HR	BA	PO	A	E	DP	TC/G	FA
1977	**2 teams** **NY N** (13G 7–3) **CIN N** (20G 14–3)																									
"	**total**	21	6	.778	2.58	33	33	19	261.1	199	66	196	7	0	0	0	86	17	3	.198	13	33	1	3	1.4	.979
1978	**CIN N**	16	14	.533	2.87	36	36	8	260	218	89	226	1	0	0	0	74	9	0	.122	15	28	6	2	1.4	.878
1979		16	6	**.727**	3.14	32	32	9	215	187	61	131	**5**	0	0	0	76	12	2	.158	22	26	2	2	1.6	.960
1980		10	8	.556	3.64	26	26	5	168	140	59	101	1	0	0	0	46	6	0	.130	16	26	0	0	1.6	1.000
1981		**14**	2	**.875**	2.55	23	23	6	166	120	66	87	1	0	0	0	55	11	1	.200	8	22	1	1	1.3	.968
1982		5	13	.278	5.50	21	21	0	111.1	136	44	62	0	0	0	0	34	6	0	.176	7	11	2	1	1.0	.900
1983	**NY N**	9	14	.391	3.55	34	34	5	231	201	86	135	2	0	0	0	64	10	0	.156	22	28	4	0	1.6	.926
1984	**CHI A**	15	11	.577	3.95	34	33	10	236.2	216	61	131	4	1	0	0	0	0	0	—	11	40	0	2	1.5	1.000
1985		16	11	.593	3.17	35	33	6	238.2	223	69	134	1	0	0	0	0	0	0	—	20	43	2	2	1.9	.969
1986	**2 teams** **CHI A** (12G 2–6) **BOS A** (16G 5–7)																									
"	**total**	7	13	.350	4.03	28	28	2	176.1	180	56	103	0	0	0	0	0	0	0		17	16	2	1	1.3	.943
20 yrs.		311	205	.603	2.86	656	647	231	4782.2	3971	1390	3640	61	1	2	1	1315	202	12	.154	328	692	42	54	1.6	.960
												4th	**7th**													
LEAGUE CHAMPIONSHIP SERIES																										
1969	**NY N**	1	0	1.000	6.43	1	1	0	7	8	3	2	0	0	0	0	3	0	0	.000	1	1	0	0	2.0	1.000
1973		1	1	.500	1.62	2	2	1	16.2	13	5	17	0	0	0	0	6	2	0	.333	0	3	0	0	1.5	1.000
1979	**CIN N**	0	0	—	2.25	1	1	0	8	5	2	5	0	0	0	0	2	0	0	.000	0	0	0	0	0.0	.000
3 yrs.		2	1	.667	2.84	4	4	1	31.2	26	10	24	0	0	0	0	11	2	0	.182	1	4	0	0	1.3	1.000
WORLD SERIES																										
1969	**NY N**	1	1	.500	3.00	2	2	1	15	12	3	9	0	0	0	0	4	0	0	.000	2	1	0	0	1.5	1.000
1973		0	1	.000	2.40	2	2	0	15	13	3	18	0	0	0	0	5	0	0	.000	0	2	0	0	1.0	1.000
2 yrs.		1	2	.333	2.70	4	4	1	30	25	6	27	0	0	0	0	9	0	0	.000	2	3	0	0	1.3	1.000

Bob Sebra

SEBRA, ROBERT BUSH BR TR 6′ 2″ 200 lbs.
B. Dec. 11, 1961, Ridgewood, N. J.

Year	Team	W	L	PCT	ERA	G	GS	CG	IP	H	BB	SO	ShO	Relief Pitching W	L	SV	Batting AB	H	HR	BA	PO	A	E	DP	TC/G	FA
1985	**TEX A**	0	2	.000	7.52	7	4	0	20.1	26	14	13	0	0	0	0	0	0	0	—	1	1	0	1	0.3	1.000
1986	**MON N**	5	5	.500	3.55	17	13	3	91.1	82	25	66	1	1	1	0	29	6	0	.207	8	8	0	2	0.9	1.000
1987		6	15	.286	4.42	36	27	4	177.1	184	67	156	1	0	0	0	51	8	0	.157	11	21	2	0	0.9	.941
1988	**PHI N**	1	2	.333	7.94	3	3	0	11.1	15	10	7	0	0	0	0	5	0	0	.000	0	1	0	0	0.3	1.000
1989	**2 teams** **PHI N** (6G 2–3) **CIN N** (15G 0–0)																									
"	**total**	2	3	.400	5.20	21	5	0	55.1	65	28	35	0	0	1	1	11	0	0	.000	2	8	3	0	0.6	.769
1990	**MIL A**	1	2	.333	8.18	10	0	0	11	20	5	4	0	1	2	0	0	0	0	—	2	4	0	1	0.6	1.000
6 yrs.		15	29	.341	4.71	94	52	7	366.2	392	149	281	2	2	4	1	96	14	0	.146	24	43	5	4	0.8	.931

Doc Sechrist

SECHRIST, THEODORE O'HARA BR TR 5′ 9″ 160 lbs.
B. Feb. 10, 1876, Williamstown, Ky. D. Apr. 2, 1950, Louisville, Ky.

Year	Team	W	L	PCT	ERA	G	GS	CG	IP	H	BB	SO	ShO	Relief Pitching W	L	SV	Batting AB	H	HR	BA	PO	A	E	DP	TC/G	FA
1899	**NY N**	0	0	—	0.00	1	0	0		0	2	0	0	0	0	0	0	0	0	—	0	0	0	0	0.0	.000

Don Secrist

SECRIST, DONALD LAVERNE BL TL 6′ 2″ 195 lbs.
B. Feb. 26, 1944, Seattle, Wash.

Year	Team	W	L	PCT	ERA	G	GS	CG	IP	H	BB	SO	ShO	Relief Pitching W	L	SV	Batting AB	H	HR	BA	PO	A	E	DP	TC/G	FA
1969	**CHI A**	0	1	.000	6.08	19	0	0	40	35	14	23	0	0	1	0	7	1	0	.143	2	7	1	0	0.5	.900
1970		0	0	—	5.40	9	0	0	15	19	12	9	0	0	0	0	0	0	0	—	0	2	0	0	0.2	1.000
2 yrs.		0	1	.000	5.89	28	0	0	55	54	26	32	0	0	1	0	7	1	0	.143	2	9	1	0	0.4	.917

Duke Sedgwick

SEDGWICK, HENRY KENNETH BR TR 6′ 175 lbs.
B. June 1, 1898, Martins Ferry, Ohio D. Nov. 4, 1982, Clearwater, Fla.

Year	Team	W	L	PCT	ERA	G	GS	CG	IP	H	BB	SO	ShO	Relief Pitching W	L	SV	Batting AB	H	HR	BA	PO	A	E	DP	TC/G	FA
1921	**PHI N**	1	3	.250	4.92	16	5	1	71.1	81	32	21	0	0	0	0	24	5	0	.208	2	14	3	0	1.2	.842
1923	**WAS A**	0	1	.000	7.88	5	2	1	16	27	6	4	0	0	0	0	5	0	0	.000	0	8	1	1	1.8	.889
2 yrs.		1	4	.200	5.46	21	7	2	87.1	108	38	25	0	0	0	0	29	5	0	.172	2	22	4	1	1.3	.857

Charlie See

SEE, CHARLES HENRY (Chad) BL TR 5′10½″ 175 lbs.
B. Oct. 13, 1896, Pleasantville, N. Y. D. July 19, 1948, Bridgeport, Conn.

Year	Team	W	L	PCT	ERA	G	GS	CG	IP	H	BB	SO	ShO	Relief Pitching W	L	SV	Batting AB	H	HR	BA	PO	A	E	DP	TC/G	FA
1920	**CIN N**	0	0	—	6.00	1	0	0	6	6	4	3	0	0	0	0	*				5	0	1	0	1.5	.833

Chuck Seelbach

SEELBACH, CHARLES FREDERICK III BR TR 6′ 180 lbs.
B. Mar. 20, 1948, Lakewood, Ohio

Year	Team	W	L	PCT	ERA	G	GS	CG	IP	H	BB	SO	ShO	Relief Pitching W	L	SV	Batting AB	H	HR	BA	PO	A	E	DP	TC/G	FA
1971	**DET A**	0	0	—	13.50	5	0	0	4	6	7	1	0	0	0	0	0	0	0	—	0	0	0	0	0.0	.000
1972		9	8	.529	2.89	61	3	0	112	96	39	76	0	9	5	14	21	3	0	.143	1	17	3	1	0.3	.857
1973		1	0	1.000	3.86	5	0	0	7	7	2	2	0	1	0	0	0	0	0	—	1	4	0	0	1.0	1.000
1974		0	0	—	4.50	4	0	0	8	9	3	0	0	0	0	0	0	0	0	—	0	1	0	0	0.3	1.000
4 yrs.		10	8	.556	3.37	75	3	0	131	118	51	79	0	10	5	14	21	3	0	.143	2	22	3	1	0.4	.889
LEAGUE CHAMPIONSHIP SERIES																										
1972	**DET A**	0	0	—	18.00	2	0	0	1	4	0	0	0	0	0	0	0	0	0	—	0	0	0	0	0.0	.000

Emmett Seery

SEERY, JOHN EMMETT BL TR
B. Feb. 13, 1861, Princeville, Ill. D. Aug. 7, 1930, Saranac Lake, N. Y.

Year	Team	W	L	PCT	ERA	G	GS	CG	IP	H	BB	SO	ShO	Relief Pitching W	L	SV	Batting AB	H	HR	BA	PO	A	E	DP	TC/G	FA
1886	**STL N**	0	0	—	7.71	2	0	0	7	8	3	2	0	0	0	0	*				166	30	39	4	2.1	.834

Herman Segelke

SEGELKE, HERMAN NEILS BR TR 6′ 4″ 215 lbs.
B. Apr. 24, 1958, San Mateo, Calif.

Year	Team	W	L	PCT	ERA	G	GS	CG	IP	H	BB	SO	ShO	Relief Pitching W	L	SV	Batting AB	H	HR	BA	PO	A	E	DP	TC/G	FA
1982	**CHI N**	0	0	—	8.31	3	0	0	4.1	6	6	4	0	0	0	0	0	0	0	—	1	0	0	0	0.3	1.000

Diego Segui

SEGUI, DIEGO PABLO BR TR 6′ 190 lbs.
Born Diego Pablo Segui (Gonzalez).
Father of David Segui.
B. Aug. 17, 1937, Holguin, Cuba.

Year	Team	W	L	PCT	ERA	G	GS	CG	IP	H	BB	SO	ShO	Relief Pitching W	L	SV	Batting AB	H	HR	BA	PO	A	E	DP	TC/G	FA
1962	**KC A**	8	5	.615	3.86	37	13	2	116.2	89	46	71	0	3	2	6	34	8	1	.235	11	17	1	2	0.8	.966
1963		9	6	.600	3.77	38	23	4	167	173	73	116	1	1	0	0	55	12	0	.218	7	33	6	1	1.2	.870
1964		8	**17**	.320	4.56	40	35	5	217	219	94	155	2	0	0	0	71	11	1	.155	24	38	2	0	1.6	.969
1965		5	15	.250	4.64	40	25	5	163	166	67	119	1	0	2	0	47	9	1	.191	13	20	1	1	0.9	.971
1966	**WAS A**	3	7	.300	5.00	21	13	1	72	82	24	54	1	1	0	0	18	2	0	.111	6	8	1	0	0.7	.933

Diego Segui *continued*

Year	Team	W	L	PCT	ERA	G	GS	CG	IP	H	BB	SO	ShO	Relief Pitching W	Relief Pitching L	Relief Pitching SV	Batting AB	Batting H	Batting HR	BA	PO	A	E	DP	TC/G	FA
1967	KC A	3	4	.429	3.09	36	3	0	70	62	31	52	0	3	1	1	9	0	0	.000	5	8	0	0	0.4	1.000
1968	OAK A	6	5	.545	2.39	52	0	0	83	51	32	72	0	6	5	6	9	1	0	.111	4	8	0	0	0.2	1.000
1969	SEA A	12	6	.667	3.35	66	8	2	142.1	127	61	113	0	8	4	12	27	4	0	.148	8	23	0	0	0.5	1.000
1970	OAK A	10	10	.500	**2.56**	47	19	3	162	130	68	95	2	2	3	2	43	5	0	.116	17	14	2	2	0.7	.939
1971		10	8	.556	3.14	26	21	5	146	122	63	81	0	1	0	0	47	4	1	.085	11	20	1	0	1.2	.969
1972	2 teams OAK A (7G 0–1) STL N (33G 3–1)																									
"	total	3	2	.600	3.20	40	3	0	78.2	72	39	65	0	3	2	9	14	2	0	.143	5	12	2	1	0.5	.895
1973	STL N	7	6	.538	2.78	65	0	0	100.1	78	53	93	0	7	6	17	10	0	0	.000	4	8	1	0	0.2	.923
1974	BOS A	6	8	.429	4.00	58	0	0	108	106	49	76	0	6	8	10	0	0	0	—	5	12	0	1	0.3	1.000
1975		2	5	.286	4.82	33	1	1	71	71	43	45	0	2	4	6	0	0	0	—	2	8	0	1	0.3	1.000
1977	SEA A	0	7	.000	5.68	40	7	0	111	108	43	91	0	0	3	2	0	0	0	—	6	14	0	2	0.5	1.000
15 yrs.		92	111	.453	3.81	639	171	28	1808	1656	786	1298	7	43	40	71	384	58	4	.151	128	243	17	11	0.6	.956
LEAGUE CHAMPIONSHIP SERIES																										
1971	OAK A	0	1	.000	5.79	1	1	0	4.2	6	6	4	0	0	0	0	2	0	0	.000	0	0	0	0	0.0	.000
WORLD SERIES																										
1975	BOS A	0	0	—	0.00	1	0	0	1	0	0	0	0	0	0	0	0	0	0	—	0	0	0	0	0.0	.000

Jose Segura

SEGURA, JOSE ALTAGRACIA BR TR 5′11″ 180 lbs.
Born Jose Altagracia Segura (Mota).
B. Jan. 26, 1963, Fundacion, Dominican Republic.

Year	Team	W	L	PCT	ERA	G	GS	CG	IP	H	BB	SO	ShO	Relief Pitching W	Relief Pitching L	Relief Pitching SV	Batting AB	Batting H	Batting HR	BA	PO	A	E	DP	TC/G	FA
1988	CHI A	0	0	—	13.50	4	0	0	8.2	19	8	2	0	0	0	0	0	0	0	—	0	3	0	0	0.8	1.000
1989		0	1	.000	15.00	7	0	0	6	13	3	4	0	0	1	0	0	0	0	—	0	2	0	0	0.3	1.000
1991	SF N	0	1	.000	4.41	11	0	0	16.1	20	5	10	0	0	1	0	0	0	0	—	1	1	1	0	0.3	.667
3 yrs.		0	2	.000	9.00	22	0	0	31	52	16	16	0	0	2	0	0	0	0		1	6	1	0	0.4	.875

Socks Seibold

SEIBOLD, HARRY BR TR 5′ 8½″ 162 lbs.
B. Apr. 3, 1896, Philadelphia, Pa. D. Sept. 21, 1965, Philadelphia, Pa.

Year	Team	W	L	PCT	ERA	G	GS	CG	IP	H	BB	SO	ShO	Relief Pitching W	Relief Pitching L	Relief Pitching SV	Batting AB	Batting H	Batting HR	BA	PO	A	E	DP	TC/G	FA
1916	PHI A	1	2	.333	4.15	3	2	1	21.2	22	9	5	1	0	1	0	12	2	0	.167	6	19	10	1	5.0	.714
1917		4	16	.200	3.94	33	15	9	160	141	85	55	1	1	**5**	1	59	13	0	.220	6	41	1	2	1.4	.979
1919		2	3	.400	5.32	14	4	1	45.2	58	26	19	0	1	0	0	13	2	0	.154	5	11	1	1	1.2	.941
1929	BOS N	12	17	.414	4.73	33	27	16	205.2	228	80	54	1	1	1	1	70	20	0	.286	11	40	0	3	1.5	1.000
1930		15	16	.484	4.12	36	33	20	251	288	85	70	1	0	1	2	90	19	1	.211	10	38	3	3	1.4	.941
1931		10	18	.357	4.67	33	29	10	206.1	226	65	50	3	1	1	0	70	9	0	.129	5	44	0	5	1.5	1.000
1932		3	10	.231	4.68	28	20	6	136.2	173	41	33	1	0	1	0	46	7	0	.152	12	35	0	4	1.7	1.000
1933		1	4	.200	3.68	11	5	1	36.2	43	14	10	0	0	1	1	9	1	0	.111	1	10	0	0	1.0	1.000
8 yrs.		48	86	.358	4.43	191	135	64	1063.2	1179	405	296	8	4	11	5	395	76	1	.192	61	249	15	19	1.6	.954

Kevin Seitzer

SEITZER, KEVIN LEE BR TR 5′11″ 180 lbs.
B. Mar. 26, 1962, Springfield, Ill.

Year	Team	W	L	PCT	ERA	G	GS	CG	IP	H	BB	SO	ShO	Relief Pitching W	Relief Pitching L	Relief Pitching SV	Batting AB	Batting H	Batting HR	BA	PO	A	E	DP	TC/G	FA
1993	OAK A	0	0	—	0.00	1	0	0	0.1	0	0	1	0	0	0	0	*				224	19	3	17	8.2	.988

Aaron Sele

SELE, AARON HELMER BR TR 6′ 5″ 205 lbs.
B. June 25, 1970, Golden Valley, Minn.

Year	Team	W	L	PCT	ERA	G	GS	CG	IP	H	BB	SO	ShO	Relief Pitching W	Relief Pitching L	Relief Pitching SV	Batting AB	Batting H	Batting HR	BA	PO	A	E	DP	TC/G	FA
1993	BOS A	7	2	.778	2.74	18	18	0	111.2	100	48	93	0	0	0	0	0	0	0	—	3	9	5	1	0.9	.706
1994		8	7	.533	3.83	22	22	2	143.1	140	60	105	0	0	0	0	0	0	0	—	6	14	0	0	0.9	1.000
1995		3	1	.750	3.06	6	6	0	32.1	32	14	21	0	0	0	0	0	0	0	—	2	5	3	0	1.7	.700
3 yrs.		18	10	.643	3.32	46	46	2	287.1	272	122	219	0	0	0	0	0	0	0		11	28	8	1	1.0	.830

Epp Sell

SELL, LESTER ELWOOD BR TR 6′ 175 lbs.
B. Apr. 26, 1897, Llewellyn, Pa. D. Feb. 19, 1961, Reading, Pa.

Year	Team	W	L	PCT	ERA	G	GS	CG	IP	H	BB	SO	ShO	Relief Pitching W	Relief Pitching L	Relief Pitching SV	Batting AB	Batting H	Batting HR	BA	PO	A	E	DP	TC/G	FA
1922	STL N	4	2	.667	6.82	7	5	0	33	47	6	5	0	2	0	0	12	4	0	.333	0	11	0	0	1.6	1.000
1923		0	1	.000	6.00	5	1	0	15	16	8	2	0	0	1	0	7	0	0	.000	0	3	0	0	0.6	1.000
2 yrs.		4	3	.571	6.56	12	6	0	48	63	14	7	0	2	1	0	19	4	0	.211	0	14	0	0	1.2	1.000

Jeff Sellers

SELLERS, JEFFREY DOYLE BR TR 6′ 1″ 195 lbs.
B. May 11, 1964, Compton, Calif.

Year	Team	W	L	PCT	ERA	G	GS	CG	IP	H	BB	SO	ShO	Relief Pitching W	Relief Pitching L	Relief Pitching SV	Batting AB	Batting H	Batting HR	BA	PO	A	E	DP	TC/G	FA
1985	BOS A	2	0	1.000	3.63	4	4	1	22.1	24	7	6	0	0	0	0	0	0	0	—	2	4	2	0	2.0	.750
1986		3	7	.300	4.94	14	13	1	82	90	40	51	0	0	0	0	0	0	0	—	9	9	0	1	1.3	1.000
1987		7	8	.467	5.28	25	22	4	139.2	161	61	99	2	0	0	0	0	0	0	—	13	20	2	0	1.4	.943
1988		1	7	.125	4.83	18	12	1	85.2	89	56	70	0	1	0	0	0	0	0	—	4	10	1	0	0.8	.933
4 yrs.		13	22	.371	4.97	61	51	7	329.2	364	164	226	2	1	0	0	0	0	0		28	43	5	1	1.2	.934

Dave Sells

SELLS, DAVID WAYNE BR TR 5′11″ 175 lbs.
B. Sept. 18, 1946, Vacaville, Calif.

Year	Team	W	L	PCT	ERA	G	GS	CG	IP	H	BB	SO	ShO	Relief Pitching W	Relief Pitching L	Relief Pitching SV	Batting AB	Batting H	Batting HR	BA	PO	A	E	DP	TC/G	FA
1972	CAL A	2	0	1.000	2.81	10	0	0	16	11	5	2	0	2	0	0	0	0	0	—	2	4	0	0	0.6	1.000
1973		7	2	.778	3.71	51	0	0	68	72	35	25	0	7	2	10	0	0	0	—	1	13	1	1	0.3	.933
1974		2	3	.400	3.69	20	0	0	39	48	16	14	0	2	3	2	0	0	0	—	2	8	1	1	0.6	.909
1975	2 teams CAL A (4G 0–0) LA N (5G 0–2)																									
"	total	0	2	.000	6.46	9	0	0	15.1	15	11	8	0	0	2	0	1	1	0	1.000	1	3	0	0	0.4	1.000
4 yrs.		11	7	.611	3.90	90	0	0	138.1	146	67	49	0	11	7	12	1	1	0	1.000	6	28	2	2	0.4	.944

Dick Selma

SELMA, RICHARD JAY BR TR 5′11″ 160 lbs.
B. Nov. 4, 1943, Santa Ana, Calif. BB 1966

Year	Team	W	L	PCT	ERA	G	GS	CG	IP	H	BB	SO	ShO	Relief Pitching W	Relief Pitching L	Relief Pitching SV	Batting AB	Batting H	Batting HR	BA	PO	A	E	DP	TC/G	FA
1965	NY N	2	1	.667	3.71	4	4	1	26.2	22	9	26	1	0	0	0	9	2	0	.222	4	5	0	0	2.3	1.000
1966		4	6	.400	4.24	30	7	0	80.2	84	39	58	0	4	2	1	14	1	0	.071	4	20	1	1	0.8	.960
1967		2	4	.333	2.77	38	4	0	81.1	71	36	52	0	2	3	2	22	2	0	.091	7	16	1	1	0.6	.958
1968		9	10	.474	2.75	33	23	4	170.1	148	54	117	3	0	0	0	58	12	0	.207	12	35	1	0	1.5	.979
1969	2 teams SD N (4G 2–2) CHI N (36G 10–8)																									
"	total	12	10	.545	3.68	40	28	5	190.2	156	81	181	2	3	1	1	59	10	0	.169	8	25	2	2	0.9	.943
1970	PHI N	8	9	.471	2.75	73	0	0	134	108	59	153	0	8	**9**	22	20	3	0	.150	8	24	1	3	0.4	.970
1971		0	2	.000	3.24	17	0	0	25	21	8	15	0	0	2	1	1	1	0	1.000	2	5	1	0	0.5	.875
1972		2	9	.182	5.56	46	10	1	98.2	91	73	58	0	1	0	3	20	4	0	.200	3	18	0	1	0.5	1.000

Year	Team	W	L	PCT	ERA	G	GS	CG	IP	H	BB	SO	ShO	Relief Pitching W	Relief Pitching L	Relief Pitching SV	Batting AB	Batting H	Batting HR	BA	PO	A	E	DP	TC/G	FA

Dick Selma *continued*

Year	Team	W	L	PCT	ERA	G	GS	CG	IP	H	BB	SO	ShO	Relief W	Relief L	SV	AB	H	HR	BA	PO	A	E	DP	TC/G	FA
1973		1	1	.500	5.63	6	0	0	8	6	5	4	0	1	1	0	0	0	0	—	2	3	0	0	0.8	1.000
1974	**2 teams** **CAL A** (18G 2–2) **MIL A** (2G 0–0)																									
"	**total**	2	2	.500	6.48	20	0	0	25	27	17	17	0	2	2	1	0	0	0		2	6	0	1	0.4	1.000
10 yrs.		42	54	.438	3.62	307	76	11	840.1	734	381	681	6	21	20	31	203	35	0	.172	52	157	7	9	0.7	.968

Carroll Sembera

SEMBERA, CARROLL WILLIAM BR TR 6′ 155 lbs.
B. July 26, 1941, Shiner, Tex.

Year	Team	W	L	PCT	ERA	G	GS	CG	IP	H	BB	SO	ShO	Relief W	Relief L	SV	AB	H	HR	BA	PO	A	E	DP	TC/G	FA
1965	**HOU N**	0	1	.000	3.68	2	1	0	7.1	5	3	4	0	0	0	0	1	0	0	.000	0	2	0	0	1.0	1.000
1966		1	2	.333	3.00	24	0	0	33	36	16	21	0	1	2	1	3	0	0	.000	3	6	0	0	0.4	1.000
1967		2	6	.250	4.83	45	0	0	59.2	66	19	48	0	2	6	3	7	1	0	.143	2	15	0	0	0.4	1.000
1969	**MON N**	0	2	.000	3.55	23	0	0	33	28	24	15	0	0	2	2	4	1	0	.250	0	6	1	1	0.3	.857
1970		0	0	—	18.00	5	0	0	7	14	11	6	0	0	0	0	0	0	0	—	0	1	0	0	0.2	1.000
5 yrs.		3	11	.214	4.69	99	1	0	140	149	73	94	0	3	10	6	15	2	0	.133	5	30	1	1	0.4	.972

Frank Seminara

SEMINARA, FRANK PETER BR TR 6′ 2″ 205 lbs.
B. May 16, 1967, Brooklyn, N. Y.

Year	Team	W	L	PCT	ERA	G	GS	CG	IP	H	BB	SO	ShO	Relief W	Relief L	SV	AB	H	HR	BA	PO	A	E	DP	TC/G	FA
1992	**SD N**	9	4	.692	3.68	19	18	0	100.1	98	46	61	0	0	0	0	34	4	0	.118	9	23	2	1	1.8	.941
1993		3	3	.500	4.47	18	7	0	46.1	53	21	22	0	2	1	0	10	2	0	.200	8	6	2	0	0.9	.875
1994	**NY N**	0	2	.000	5.82	10	1	0	17	20	8	7	0	0	2	0	3	0	0	.000	2	0	2	0	0.4	.500
3 yrs.		12	9	.571	4.12	47	26	0	163.2	171	75	90	0	2	3	0	47	6	0	.128	19	29	6	1	1.1	.889

Ray Semproch

SEMPROCH, ROMAN ANTHONY (Baby) BR TR 5′11″ 180 lbs.
B. Jan. 7, 1931, Cleveland, Ohio.

Year	Team	W	L	PCT	ERA	G	GS	CG	IP	H	BB	SO	ShO	Relief W	Relief L	SV	AB	H	HR	BA	PO	A	E	DP	TC/G	FA
1958	**PHI N**	13	11	.542	3.92	36	30	12	204.1	211	58	92	2	2	2	0	74	7	0	.095	13	31	0	0	1.2	1.000
1959		3	10	.231	5.40	30	18	2	111.2	119	59	54	0	1	0	3	34	6	0	.176	6	21	1	4	0.9	.964
1960	**DET A**	3	0	1.000	4.00	17	0	0	27	29	16	9	0	3	0	0	4	0	0	.000	0	11	2	1	0.8	.846
1961	**LA A**	0	0	—	9.00	2	0	0	1	1	3	1	0	0	0	0	0	0	0	—	0	1	0	0	0.5	1.000
4 yrs.		19	21	.475	4.42	85	48	14	344	360	136	156	2	6	2	3	112	13	0	.116	19	64	3	5	1.0	.965

Steve Senteney

SENTENEY, STEPHEN LEONARD BR TR 6′ 2″ 205 lbs.
B. Aug. 7, 1955, Indianapolis, Ind. D. June 19, 1989, Colusa, Calif.

Year	Team	W	L	PCT	ERA	G	GS	CG	IP	H	BB	SO	ShO	Relief W	Relief L	SV	AB	H	HR	BA	PO	A	E	DP	TC/G	FA
1982	**TOR A**	0	0	—	4.91	11	0	0	22	23	6	20	0	0	0	0	0	0	0	—	1	1	0	0	0.2	1.000

Manny Seoane

SEOANE, MANUEL MODESTO BR TR 6′ 3″ 187 lbs.
B. June 26, 1955, Tampa, Fla.

Year	Team	W	L	PCT	ERA	G	GS	CG	IP	H	BB	SO	ShO	Relief W	Relief L	SV	AB	H	HR	BA	PO	A	E	DP	TC/G	FA
1977	**PHI N**	0	0	—	6.00	2	1	0	6	11	3	4	0	0	0	0	2	1	0	.500	0	0	0	0	0.0	.000
1978	**CHI N**	1	0	1.000	5.63	7	1	0	8	11	6	5	0	1	0	0	0	0	0	—	0	0	0	0	0.0	.000
2 yrs.		1	0	1.000	5.79	9	2	0	14	22	9	9	0	1	0	0	2	1	0	.500	0	0	0	0	0.0	

Billy Serad

SERAD, WILLIAM I. BR TR 5′ 7″ 156 lbs.
B. 1863, Philadelphia, Pa. D. Nov. 1, 1925, Chester, Pa.

Year	Team	W	L	PCT	ERA	G	GS	CG	IP	H	BB	SO	ShO	Relief W	Relief L	SV	AB	H	HR	BA	PO	A	E	DP	TC/G	FA
1884	**BUF N**	16	20	.444	*4.27*	37	37	34	308	373	111	150	2	0	0	0	137	24	0	.175	4	57	14	1	1.9	.813
1885		7	21	.250	*4.10*	30	29	27	241.1	299	80	90	0	0	0	0	104	16	0	.154	9	38	9	2	1.9	.839
1887	**CIN AA**	10	11	.476	*4.08*	22	21	20	187.1	201	80	34	2	0	0	1	79	14	0	.177	7	37	6	1	2.2	.880
1888		2	3	.400	3.55	6	5	5	50.2	62	19	4	0	**1**	0	0	23	3	0	.130	2	10	3	1	2.5	.800
4 yrs.		35	55	.389	4.13	95	92	86	787.1	935	290	278	4	1	0	1	343	57	0	.166	22	142	32	5	2.0	.837

Gary Serum

SERUM, GARY WAYNE BR TR 6′ 1″ 180 lbs.
B. Oct. 24, 1956, Fargo, N. D.

Year	Team	W	L	PCT	ERA	G	GS	CG	IP	H	BB	SO	ShO	Relief W	Relief L	SV	AB	H	HR	BA	PO	A	E	DP	TC/G	FA
1977	**MIN A**	0	0	—	4.30	8	0	0	23	22	10	14	0	0	0	0	0	0	0	—	0	2	0	0	0.3	1.000
1978		9	9	.500	4.10	34	23	6	184.1	188	44	80	1	1	1	1	0	0	0	—	17	25	0	2	1.2	1.000
1979		1	3	.250	6.61	20	5	0	64	93	20	31	0	1	0	0	0	0	0	—	5	10	1	0	0.8	.938
3 yrs.		10	12	.455	4.71	62	28	6	271.1	303	74	125	1	2	1	1	0	0	0		22	37	1	2	1.0	.983

Scott Service

SERVICE, DAVID SCOTT BR TR 6′ 6″ 225 lbs.
B. Feb. 26, 1967, Cincinnati, Ohio.

Year	Team	W	L	PCT	ERA	G	GS	CG	IP	H	BB	SO	ShO	Relief W	Relief L	SV	AB	H	HR	BA	PO	A	E	DP	TC/G	FA
1988	**PHI N**	0	0	—	1.69	5	0	0	5.1	7	1	6	0	0	0	0	0	0	0	—	0	0	0	0	0.0	.000
1992	**MON N**	0	0	—	14.14	5	0	0	7	15	5	11	0	0	0	0	2	0	0	.000	0	0	0	0	0.0	.000
1993	**2 teams** **CLR N** (3G 0–0) **CIN N** (26G 2–2)																									
"	**total**	2	2	.500	4.30	29	0	0	46	44	16	43	0	2	2	2	7	1	0	.143	6	5	0	0	0.4	1.000
1994	**CIN N**	1	2	.333	7.36	6	0	0	7.1	8	3	5	0	1	2	0	0	0	0	—	0	3	0	0	0.5	1.000
1995	**SF N**	3	1	.750	3.19	28	0	0	31	18	20	30	0	3	1	0	1	0	0	.000	2	2	0	0	0.1	1.000
5 yrs.		6	5	.545	4.75	73	0	0	96.2	92	45	95	0	6	5	2	10	1	0	.100	8	10	0	0	0.2	1.000

Merle Settlemire

SETTLEMIRE, EDGAR MERLE (Lefty) BL TL 5′ 9″ 156 lbs.
B. Jan. 19, 1903, Santa Fe, Ohio D. June 12, 1988, Russells Point, Ohio.

Year	Team	W	L	PCT	ERA	G	GS	CG	IP	H	BB	SO	ShO	Relief W	Relief L	SV	AB	H	HR	BA	PO	A	E	DP	TC/G	FA
1928	**BOS A**	0	6	.000	5.47	30	9	0	82.1	116	34	12	0	0	5	0	17	3	0	.176	1	30	2	3	1.1	.939

Al Severinsen

SEVERINSEN, ALBERT HENRY BR TR 6′ 3″ 220 lbs.
B. Nov. 9, 1944, Brooklyn, N. Y.

Year	Team	W	L	PCT	ERA	G	GS	CG	IP	H	BB	SO	ShO	Relief W	Relief L	SV	AB	H	HR	BA	PO	A	E	DP	TC/G	FA
1969	**BAL A**	1	1	.500	2.29	12	0	0	19.2	14	10	13	0	1	1	0	3	1	0	.333	2	4	0	1	0.5	1.000
1971	**SD N**	2	5	.286	3.47	59	0	0	70	77	30	31	0	2	5	8	1	0	0	.000	5	17	0	2	0.4	1.000
1972		0	1	.000	2.53	17	0	0	21.1	13	7	9	0	0	1	1	1	0	0	.000	0	5	0	0	0.3	1.000
3 yrs.		3	7	.300	3.08	88	0	0	111	104	47	53	0	3	7	9	5	1	0	.200	7	26	0	3	0.4	1.000

Ed Seward

SEWARD, EDWARD WILLIAM TR 5′ 7″ 175 lbs.
Born Edward William Sourhardt.
B. June 29, 1867, Cleveland, Ohio D. July 30, 1947, Cleveland, Ohio.

Year	Team	W	L	PCT	ERA	G	GS	CG	IP	H	BB	SO	ShO	Relief W	Relief L	SV	AB	H	HR	BA	PO	A	E	DP	TC/G	FA
1885	**PRO N**	0	0	—	0.00	1	0	0	6	2	0	1	0	0	0	0	3	0	0	.000	0	4	0	0	4.0	1.000
1887	**PHI AA**	25	25	.500	*4.13*	55	52	52	470.2	445	140	155	3	**1**	0	0	266	50	5	.188	63	83	18	2	2.2	.890
1888		35	19	.648	2.01	57	57	57	518.2	388	127	**272**	**6**	0	0	0	225	32	2	.142	32	127	19	5	2.8	.893

Ed Seward *continued*

Year	Team	Lg	W	L	PCT	ERA	G	GS	CG	IP	H	BB	SO	ShO	Relief Pitching W	Relief Pitching L	Relief Pitching SV	Batting AB	Batting H	Batting HR	BA	PO	A	E	DP	TC/G	FA
1889			21	15	.583	3.97	39	38	35	320	353	101	102	3	0	0	0	143	31	2	.217	25	67	9	1	2.1	.911
1890			5	12	.294	*4.73*	21	19	15	154	165	72	55	1	0	1	0	72	10	0	.139	19	27	10	2	2.1	.821
1891	CLE	N	2	1	.667	3.86	3	3	0	16.1	16	11	4	0	0	0	0	19	4	0	.211	8	1	1	0	1.4	.900
6 yrs.			88	72	.550	3.40	176	169	159	1485.2	1369	451	589	13	1	1	0	*				147	309	57	10	2.3	.889

Frank Seward

SEWARD, FRANK MARTIN BR TR 6′ 3″ 200 lbs.
B. Apr. 7, 1921, Pennsauken, N. J.

Year	Team	Lg	W	L	PCT	ERA	G	GS	CG	IP	H	BB	SO	ShO	Relief Pitching W	Relief Pitching L	Relief Pitching SV	Batting AB	Batting H	Batting HR	BA	PO	A	E	DP	TC/G	FA
1943	NY	N	0	1	.000	3.00	1	1	1	9	12	5	2	0	0	0	0	4	0	0	.000	0	2	0	0	2.0	1.000
1944			3	2	.600	5.40	25	7	2	78.1	98	32	16	0	2	2	0	24	2	0	.083	5	8	0	0	0.5	1.000
2 yrs.			3	3	.500	5.15	26	8	3	87.1	110	37	18	0	2	2	0	28	2	0	.071	5	10	0	0	0.6	1.000

Rip Sewell

SEWELL, TRUETT BANKS BR TR 6′ 1″ 180 lbs.
B. May 11, 1907, Decatur, Ala. D. Sept. 3, 1989, Plant City, Fla.

Year	Team	Lg	W	L	PCT	ERA	G	GS	CG	IP	H	BB	SO	ShO	Relief Pitching W	Relief Pitching L	Relief Pitching SV	Batting AB	Batting H	Batting HR	BA	PO	A	E	DP	TC/G	FA
1932	DET	A	0	0	—	12.66	5	0	0	10.2	19	8	2	0	0	0	0	2	1	0	.500	1	3	0	0	0.8	1.000
1938	PIT	N	0	1	.000	4.23	17	0	0	38.1	41	21	17	0	0	1	1	12	1	0	.083	0	13	1	3	0.8	.929
1939			10	9	.526	4.08	52	12	5	176.1	177	73	69	1	4	3	2	55	11	1	.200	9	47	1	3	1.1	.982
1940			16	5	.762	2.80	33	23	14	189.2	169	67	60	2	3	1	1	73	14	1	.192	17	46	5	0	2.1	.926
1941			14	**17**	.452	3.72	39	32	18	249	225	84	76	2	2	0	2	92	16	1	.174	21	56	2	6	2.0	.975
1942			17	15	.531	3.41	40	33	18	248	259	72	69	5	2	2	2	87	13	0	.149	19	51	3	3	1.8	.959
1943			**21**	9	.700	2.54	35	31	**25**	265.1	267	75	65	2	0	1	3	105	30	0	.286	13	60	4	4	2.2	.948
1944			21	12	.636	3.18	38	33	24	286	263	99	87	3	3	0	2	112	25	1	.223	21	49	4	1	1.9	.946
1945			11	9	.550	4.07	33	24	9	188	212	91	60	1	2	1	1	64	20	0	.313	10	35	1	2	1.4	.978
1946			8	12	.400	3.68	25	20	11	149.1	140	53	33	2	1	1	0	50	9	0	.180	8	26	2	1	1.4	.944
1947			6	4	.600	3.57	24	12	4	121	121	36	36	1	2	0	0	40	5	1	.125	10	26	1	3	1.5	.973
1948			13	3	.813	3.48	21	17	7	121.2	126	37	36	0	2	0	0	42	6	1	.143	10	21	3	1	1.6	.912
1949			6	1	.857	3.91	28	6	2	76	82	32	26	1	4	1	1	16	1	0	.063	3	12	2	0	0.6	.882
13 yrs.			143	97	.596	3.48	390	243	137	2119.1	2101	748	636	20	25	11	15	750	152	6	.203	142	445	29	27	1.6	.953

Elmer Sexauer

SEXAUER, ELMER GEORGE BR TR 6′ 4″ 220 lbs.
B. May 21, 1926, St. Louis County, Mo.

Year	Team	Lg	W	L	PCT	ERA	G	GS	CG	IP	H	BB	SO	ShO	Relief Pitching W	Relief Pitching L	Relief Pitching SV	Batting AB	Batting H	Batting HR	BA	PO	A	E	DP	TC/G	FA
1948	BKN	N	0	0	—	13.50	2	0	0	0.2	0	2	0	0	0	0	0	0	0	0	—	0	0	0	0	0.0	.000

Frank Sexton

SEXTON, FRANK JOSEPH 160 lbs.
B. July 8, 1872, Brockton, Mass. D. Jan. 4, 1938, Brighton, Mass.

Year	Team	Lg	W	L	PCT	ERA	G	GS	CG	IP	H	BB	SO	ShO	Relief Pitching W	Relief Pitching L	Relief Pitching SV	Batting AB	Batting H	Batting HR	BA	PO	A	E	DP	TC/G	FA
1895	BOS	N	1	5	.167	5.69	7	5	4	49	59	22	14	0	0	1	0	22	5	0	.227	4	10	0	0	1.6	1.000

Gordon Seyfried

SEYFRIED, GORDON CLAY BR TR 6′ 185 lbs.
B. July 4, 1937, Long Beach, Calif.

Year	Team	Lg	W	L	PCT	ERA	G	GS	CG	IP	H	BB	SO	ShO	Relief Pitching W	Relief Pitching L	Relief Pitching SV	Batting AB	Batting H	Batting HR	BA	PO	A	E	DP	TC/G	FA
1963	CLE	A	0	1	.000	1.23	3	1	0	7.1	9	3	1	0	0	0	0	2	0	0	.000	1	3	0	0	1.3	1.000
1964			0	0	—	0.00	2	0	0	2.1	4	0	0	0	0	0	0	0	0	0	—	0	0	0	0	0.0	.000
2 yrs.			0	1	.000	0.93	5	1	0	9.2	13	3	1	0	0	0	0	2	0	0	.000	1	3	0	0	0.8	1.000

Cy Seymour

SEYMOUR, JAMES BENTLEY BL TL 6′ 200 lbs.
B. Dec. 9, 1872, Albany, N. Y. D. Sept. 20, 1919, New York, N. Y.

Year	Team	Lg	W	L	PCT	ERA	G	GS	CG	IP	H	BB	SO	ShO	Relief Pitching W	Relief Pitching L	Relief Pitching SV	Batting AB	Batting H	Batting HR	BA	PO	A	E	DP	TC/G	FA
1896	NY	N	2	4	.333	6.40	11	8	4	70.1	75	51	33	0	0	0	0	32	7	0	.219	5	19	4	1	2.3	.857
1897			18	14	.563	3.37	38	33	28	277.2	254	**164**	149	2	1	1	1	137	33	2	.241	24	98	20	5	3.2	.859
1898			25	19	.568	3.18	45	43	39	356.2	313	**213**	**239**	4	2	0	0	297	82	4	.276	72	120	25	9	2.7	.885
1899			14	18	.438	3.56	32	32	31	268.1	247	**170**	142	0	0	0	0	159	52	2	.327	50	92	30	3	3.9	.826
1900			2	1	.667	6.96	13	7	2	53	58	54	19	0	0	0	0	40	12	0	.300	9	20	7	0	2.1	.806
1902	CIN	N	0	0	—	9.00	1	0	0	3	4	3	2	0	0	0	0	515	157	5	.305	278	24	18	5	2.4	.944
6 yrs.			61	56	.521	3.76	140	123	104	1029	951	655	584	6	3	1	1	*				2951	533	252	69	2.5	.933

Jake Seymour

SEYMOUR, JACOB
Born Jacob Semer.
B. 1854, Pittsburgh, Pa. D. Aug. 1, 1897, Allegheny, Pa.

Year	Team	Lg	W	L	PCT	ERA	G	GS	CG	IP	H	BB	SO	ShO	Relief Pitching W	Relief Pitching L	Relief Pitching SV	Batting AB	Batting H	Batting HR	BA	PO	A	E	DP	TC/G	FA
1882	PIT	AA	0	1	.000	*7.88*	1	1	1	8	16	2	2	0	0	0	0	4	0	0	.000	1	2	1	0	4.0	.750

John Shaffer

SHAFFER, JOHN W. (Cannon Ball)
B. Feb. 18, 1864, Lock Haven, Pa. D. Nov. 21, 1926, Endicott, N. Y.

Year	Team	Lg	W	L	PCT	ERA	G	GS	CG	IP	H	BB	SO	ShO	Relief Pitching W	Relief Pitching L	Relief Pitching SV	Batting AB	Batting H	Batting HR	BA	PO	A	E	DP	TC/G	FA
1886	NY	AA	5	3	.625	*1.96*	8	8	8	69	40	29	36	1	0	0	0	25	6	0	.240	2	7	2	1	1.4	.818
1887			2	11	.154	*6.19*	13	13	13	112	148	53	22	0	0	0	0	48	8	0	.167	7	33	4	0	3.4	.909
2 yrs.			7	14	.333	4.57	21	21	21	181	188	82	58	1	0	0	0	73	14	0	.192	9	40	6	1	2.6	.891

Gus Shallix

SHALLIX, AUGUST BR TR 5′11″ 165 lbs.
Born August Schallick.
B. Mar. 29, 1858, Paderborn, Germany D. Oct. 28, 1937, Cincinnati, Ohio.

Year	Team	Lg	W	L	PCT	ERA	G	GS	CG	IP	H	BB	SO	ShO	Relief Pitching W	Relief Pitching L	Relief Pitching SV	Batting AB	Batting H	Batting HR	BA	PO	A	E	DP	TC/G	FA
1884	CIN	AA	11	10	.524	*3.70*	23	23	23	199.2	163	53	78	0	0	0	0	84	3	0	.036	13	42	4	2	2.6	.932
1885			6	4	.600	*3.25*	13	12	7	91.1	95	33	15	0	**1**	0	0	39	5	0	.128	4	28	4	3	2.3	.889
2 yrs.			17	14	.548	3.56	36	35	30	291	258	86	93	0	1	0	0	123	8	0	.065	17	70	8	5	2.4	.916

Greg Shanahan

SHANAHAN, PAUL GREGORY, JR. BR TR 6′ 2″ 190 lbs.
B. Dec. 11, 1947, Eureka, Calif.

Year	Team	Lg	W	L	PCT	ERA	G	GS	CG	IP	H	BB	SO	ShO	Relief Pitching W	Relief Pitching L	Relief Pitching SV	Batting AB	Batting H	Batting HR	BA	PO	A	E	DP	TC/G	FA
1973	LA	N	0	0	—	3.45	7	0	0	15.2	14	4	11	0	0	0	1	1	0	0	.000	1	2	0	0	0.4	1.000
1974			0	0	—	3.86	4	0	0	7	7	5	2	0	0	0	0	0	0	0	—	0	2	0	0	0.5	1.000
2 yrs.			0	0		3.57	11	0	0	22.2	21	9	13	0	0	0	1	1	0	0	.000	1	4	0	0	0.5	1.000

Harvey Shank

SHANK, HARVEY TILLMAN BR TR 6′ 4″ 220 lbs.
B. July 29, 1946, Toronto, Ont., Canada.

Year	Team	Lg	W	L	PCT	ERA	G	GS	CG	IP	H	BB	SO	ShO	Relief Pitching W	Relief Pitching L	Relief Pitching SV	Batting AB	Batting H	Batting HR	BA	PO	A	E	DP	TC/G	FA
1970	CAL	A	0	0	—	0.00	1	0	0	3	2	2	1	0	0	0	0	0	0	0	—	0	0	0	0	0.0	.000

Bill Shanner

SHANNER, WILFRED WILLIAM BL TR
B. Nov. 4, 1894, Oakland City, Ind. D. Dec. 18, 1986, Evansville, Ind.

Year	Team	W	L	PCT	ERA	G	GS	CG	IP	H	BB	SO	ShO	Relief Pitching W	Relief Pitching L	Relief Pitching SV	Batting AB	Batting H	Batting HR	BA	PO	A	E	DP	TC/G	FA
1920	PHI A	0	0	—	6.75	1	0	0	4	6	1	1	0	0	0	0	1	0	0	.000	0	1	0	0	1.0	1.000

Bobby Shantz

SHANTZ, ROBERT CLAYTON BR TL 5′ 6″ 139 lbs.
Brother of Billy Shantz.
B. Sept. 26, 1925, Pottstown, Pa.

Year	Team	W	L	PCT	ERA	G	GS	CG	IP	H	BB	SO	ShO	Relief Pitching W	Relief Pitching L	Relief Pitching SV	Batting AB	Batting H	Batting HR	BA	PO	A	E	DP	TC/G	FA
1949	PHI A	6	8	.429	3.40	33	7	4	127	100	74	58	1	3	4	2	37	7	0	.189	12	36	0	5	1.5	1.000
1950		8	14	.364	4.61	36	23	6	214.2	251	85	93	1	2	0	0	66	11	1	.167	13	52	2	6	1.9	.970
1951		18	10	.643	3.94	32	25	13	205.1	213	70	77	4	2	1	0	72	18	0	.250	20	44	2	7	2.1	.970
1952		**24**	7	**.774**	2.48	33	33	27	279.2	230	63	152	5	0	0	0	96	19	0	.198	29	49	0	3	2.4	1.000
1953		5	9	.357	4.09	16	16	6	105.2	107	26	58	0	0	0	0	38	9	0	.237	10	21	1	3	2.0	.969
1954		1	0	1.000	7.88	2	1	0	8	12	3	3	0	0	0	0	3	1	0	.333	1	2	1	0	2.0	.750
1955	KC A	5	10	.333	4.54	23	17	4	125	124	66	58	1	2	0	0	41	6	0	.146	9	26	2	2	1.6	.946
1956		2	7	.222	4.35	45	2	1	101.1	95	37	67	0	1	6	9	22	2	0	.091	10	20	2	2	0.7	.938
1957	NY A	11	5	.688	**2.45**	30	21	9	173	157	40	72	1	1	0	5	56	10	0	.179	14	57	1	8	2.4	.986
1958		7	6	.538	3.36	33	13	3	126	127	35	80	0	5	5	0	35	8	0	.229	7	35	0	4	1.2	1.000
1959		7	3	.700	2.38	33	4	2	94.2	64	33	66	2	5	1	3	23	5	0	.217	8	20	2	1	0.9	.933
1960		5	4	.556	2.79	42	0	0	67.2	57	24	54	0	5	4	11	10	1	0	.100	4	13	0	1	0.4	1.000
1961	PIT N	6	3	.667	3.32	43	6	2	89.1	91	26	61	1	3	1	2	16	7	0	.438	13	18	0	2	0.7	1.000
1962	2 teams HOU N (3G 1–1) STL N (28G 5–3)																									
″	total	6	4	.600	1.95	31	3	1	78.1	60	25	61	0	5	3	4	21	2	0	.095	10	25	1	2	1.2	.972
1963	STL N	6	4	.600	2.61	55	0	0	79.1	55	17	70	0	6	4	11	7	1	0	.143	9	22	1	2	0.6	.969
1964	3 teams STL N (16G 1–3) CHI N (20G 0–1) PHI N (14G 1–1)																									
″	total	2	5	.286	3.12	50	0	0	60.2	52	19	42	0	2	5	1	5	0	0	.000	6	28	1	0	0.7	.971
16 yrs.		119	99	.546	3.38	537	171	78	1935.2	1795	643	1072	16	42	34	48	548	107	1	.195	175	468	16	48	1.2	.976
WORLD SERIES																										
1957	NY A	0	1	.000	4.05	3	1	0	6.2	8	2	7	0	0	0	0	1	0	0	.000	0	1	0	0	0.3	1.000
1960		0	0	—	4.26	3	0	0	6.1	4	1	1	0	0	0	1	3	1	0	.333	3	2	0	1	1.7	1.000
2 yrs.		0	1	.000	4.15	6	1	0	13	12	3	8	0	0	0	1	4	1	0	.250	3	3	0	1	1.0	1.000

George Sharrott

SHARROTT, GEORGE OSCAR BL TL 5′ 8″ 164 lbs.
B. Nov. 2, 1869, West New Brighton, N. Y. D. Jan. 6, 1932, Jamaica, N. Y.

Year	Team	W	L	PCT	ERA	G	GS	CG	IP	H	BB	SO	ShO	Relief Pitching W	Relief Pitching L	Relief Pitching SV	Batting AB	Batting H	Batting HR	BA	PO	A	E	DP	TC/G	FA
1893	BKN N	4	6	.400	5.87	13	10	10	95	114	58	24	0	0	0	1	39	9	1	.231	5	17	4	1	2.0	.846
1894		0	1	.000	7.00	2	2	1	9	7	5	2	0	0	0	0	3	1	0	.333	0	1	0	0	0.5	1.000
2 yrs.		4	7	.364	5.97	15	12	11	104	121	63	26	0	0	0	1	42	10	1	.238	5	18	4	1	1.8	.852

John Sharrott

SHARROTT, JOHN HENRY BL TL 5′ 9″ 165 lbs.
B. Aug. 13, 1869, Bangor, Me. D. Dec. 31, 1927, Los Angeles, Calif.

Year	Team	W	L	PCT	ERA	G	GS	CG	IP	H	BB	SO	ShO	Relief Pitching W	Relief Pitching L	Relief Pitching SV	Batting AB	Batting H	Batting HR	BA	PO	A	E	DP	TC/G	FA
1890	NY N	11	10	.524	2.89	25	20	18	184	162	88	84	0	1	**1**	0	109	22	0	.202	11	46	15	0	2.1	.792
1891		4	5	.444	2.60	10	9	6	69.1	47	35	41	0	0	0	1	30	10	1	.333	4	15	1	0	2.0	.950
1892		0	0	—	4.50	1	0	0	2	2	1	1	0	0	0	0	8	1	0	.125	1	0	2	0	0.8	.333
1893	PHI N	4	2	.667	4.50	12	4	2	56	53	33	11	0	4	0	0	152	38	1	.250	52	19	14	0	1.9	.835
4 yrs.		19	17	.528	3.12	48	33	26	311.1	264	157	137	0	5	1	1	*				68	80	32	0	1.9	.822

Joe Shaute

SHAUTE, JOSEPH BENJAMIN (Lefty) BL TL 6′ 190 lbs.
B. Aug. 1, 1899, Peckville, Pa. D. Feb. 21, 1970, Scranton, Pa.

Year	Team	W	L	PCT	ERA	G	GS	CG	IP	H	BB	SO	ShO	Relief Pitching W	Relief Pitching L	Relief Pitching SV	Batting AB	Batting H	Batting HR	BA	PO	A	E	DP	TC/G	FA
1922	CLE A	0	0	—	19.64	2	0	0	3.2	7	3	3	0	0	0	0	5	0	0	.000	0	0	0	0	0.0	
1923		10	8	.556	3.51	33	16	7	172	176	53	61	0	2	2	0	68	11	0	.162	6	37	2	2	1.4	.956
1924		20	**17**	.541	3.75	46	34	21	283	317	83	68	2	3	2	2	107	34	1	.318	12	59	5	1	1.7	.934
1925		4	12	.250	5.43	26	17	10	131	160	44	34	1	0	2	4	53	16	0	.302	4	26	0	1	1.2	1.000
1926		14	10	.583	3.53	34	25	15	206.2	215	65	47	1	2	1	1	73	20	0	.274	7	30	0	0	1.1	1.000
1927		9	16	.360	4.22	45	28	14	230.1	255	75	63	0	1	0	2	83	27	0	.325	15	45	0	2	1.3	1.000
1928		13	17	.433	4.04	36	32	21	253.2	295	68	81	1	1	0	2	92	21	0	.228	16	60	2	3	2.2	.974
1929		8	8	.500	4.28	26	24	8	162	211	52	43	0	1	0	0	58	17	0	.293	9	23	3	1	1.3	.914
1930		0	0	—	15.43	4	0	0	4.2	8	4	2	0	0	0	0	0	0	0	—	0	2	0	0	0.5	1.000
1931	BKN N	11	8	.579	4.83	25	19	6	128.2	162	32	50	0	1	0	0	45	8	0	.178	7	27	1	1	1.4	.971
1932		7	7	.500	4.62	34	9	1	117	147	21	32	0	6	4	4	45	9	0	.200	6	18	2	1	0.8	.923
1933		3	4	.429	3.49	41	4	0	108.1	125	31	26	0	3	2	2	27	6	0	.222	5	28	2	0	0.9	.943
1934	CIN N	0	2	.000	4.15	8	1	0	17.1	19	3	2	0	0	1	1	4	1	0	.250	0	1	0	0	0.1	1.000
13 yrs.		99	109	.476	4.15	360	209	103	1818.1	2097	534	512	5	20	14	18	660	170	1	.258	87	356	17	12	1.3	.963

Jeff Shaver

SHAVER, JEFFREY THOMAS BR TR 6′ 3″ 195 lbs.
B. July 30, 1963, Beaver, Pa.

Year	Team	W	L	PCT	ERA	G	GS	CG	IP	H	BB	SO	ShO	Relief Pitching W	Relief Pitching L	Relief Pitching SV	Batting AB	Batting H	Batting HR	BA	PO	A	E	DP	TC/G	FA
1988	OAK A	0	0	—	0.00	1	0	0	1	0	0	0	0	0	0	0	0	0	0	—	0	0	0	0	0.0	.000

Bob Shaw

SHAW, ROBERT JOHN BR TR 6′ 2″ 195 lbs.
B. June 29, 1933, Bronx, N. Y.

Year	Team	W	L	PCT	ERA	G	GS	CG	IP	H	BB	SO	ShO	Relief Pitching W	Relief Pitching L	Relief Pitching SV	Batting AB	Batting H	Batting HR	BA	PO	A	E	DP	TC/G	FA
1957	DET A	0	1	.000	7.45	7	0	0	9.2	11	7	4	0	0	1	0	2	0	0	.000	1	1	0	0	0.3	1.000
1958	2 teams DET A (11G 1–2) CHI A (29G 4–2)																									
″	total	5	4	.556	4.76	40	5	0	90.2	99	41	35	0	5	1	1	22	3	0	.136	1	29	1	2	0.8	.968
1959	CHI A	18	6	**.750**	2.69	47	26	8	230.2	217	54	89	3	2	0	3	73	9	0	.123	17	46	2	3	1.4	.969
1960		13	13	.500	4.06	36	32	7	192.2	221	62	46	1	1	1	0	58	8	0	.138	14	33	5	0	1.4	.904
1961	2 teams CHI A (14G 3–4) KC A (26G 9–10)																									
″	total	12	14	.462	4.14	40	34	9	221.2	250	78	91	0	1	0	0	73	11	0	.151	19	35	3	2	1.4	.947
1962	MIL N	15	9	.625	2.80	38	29	12	225	223	44	124	3	1	0	2	73	10	0	.137	16	38	5	0	1.6	.915
1963		7	11	.389	2.66	48	16	3	159	144	55	105	3	3	5	13	41	5	0	.122	8	20	2	3	0.6	.933
1964	SF N	7	6	.538	3.76	61	1	0	93.1	105	31	57	0	7	5	11	13	0	0	.000	4	10	0	1	0.2	1.000
1965		16	9	.640	2.64	42	33	6	235	213	53	148	1	1	1	2	79	8	0	.101	15	45	4	1	1.5	.938
1966	2 teams SF N (13G 1–4) NY N (26G 11–10)																									
″	total	12	14	.462	4.29	39	31	7	199.1	216	49	125	2	0	1	0	56	13	0	.232	12	31	0	3	1.1	1.000
1967	2 teams NY N (23G 3–9) CHI N (9G 0–2)																									
″	total	3	11	.214	4.61	32	16	3	121	138	37	56	1	1	2	0	29	2	0	.069	7	11	2	1	0.6	.900
11 yrs.		108	98	.524	3.52	430	223	55	1778	1837	511	880	14	22	17	32	519	69	0	.133	114	299	24	16	1.0	.945

Bob Shaw *continued*

Year	Team	Lg	W	L	PCT	ERA	G	GS	CG	IP	H	BB	SO	ShO	Relief Pitching W	Relief Pitching L	Relief Pitching SV	Batting AB	Batting H	Batting HR	BA	PO	A	E	DP	TC/G	FA
WORLD SERIES																											
1959	CHI	A	1	1	.500	2.57	2	2	0	14	17	2	2	0	0	0	0	4	1	0	.250	0	4	0	0	2.0	1.000

Don Shaw

SHAW, DONALD WELLINGTON BL TL 6′ 180 lbs.
B. Feb. 23, 1944, Pittsburgh, Pa.

Year	Team	Lg	W	L	PCT	ERA	G	GS	CG	IP	H	BB	SO	ShO	Relief Pitching W	Relief Pitching L	Relief Pitching SV	Batting AB	Batting H	Batting HR	BA	PO	A	E	DP	TC/G	FA
1967	NY	N	4	5	.444	2.98	40	0	0	51.1	40	23	44	0	4	5	3	3	0	0	.000	3	5	0	0	0.2	1.000
1968			0	0	—	0.75	7	0	0	12	3	5	11	0	0	0	0	0	0	0	—	1	2	0	0	0.4	1.000
1969	MON	N	2	5	.286	5.21	35	1	0	65.2	61	37	45	0	2	4	0	10	0	0	.000	2	15	1	0	0.5	.944
1971	STL	N	7	2	.778	2.65	45	0	0	51	45	31	19	0	7	2	2	1	0	0	.000	3	8	2	0	0.3	.846
1972	2 teams STL N (8G 0–1) OAK A (3G 0–1)																										
″	total		0	2	.000	14.63	11	0	0	8	17	5	4	0	0	2	0	1	0	0	.000	0	0	0	0	0.0	
5 yrs.			13	14	.481	4.02	138	1	0	188	166	101	123	0	13	13	5	15	0	0	.000	9	30	3	0	0.3	.929

Dupee Shaw

SHAW, FREDERICK LANDER BL TL 5′ 8″ 165 lbs.
B. May 31, 1859, Charlestown, Mass. D. June 11, 1938, Everett, Mass.

Year	Team	Lg	W	L	PCT	ERA	G	GS	CG	IP	H	BB	SO	ShO	Relief Pitching W	Relief Pitching L	Relief Pitching SV	Batting AB	Batting H	Batting HR	BA	PO	A	E	DP	TC/G	FA
1883	DET	N	10	15	.400	*2.50*	26	25	23	227	238	44	73	1	0	0	0	141	29	0	.206	21	50	7	5	1.9	.910
1884	2 teams DET N (28G 9–18) BOS U (39G 21–15)																										
″	total		30	33	.476	2.30	67	66	60	543.1	446	109	451	5	0	0	0	289	63	1	.218	39	116	34	3	2.2	.820
1885	PRO	N	23	26	.469	*2.57*	49	49	47	399.2	343	99	194	6	0	0	0	165	22	0	.133	11	76	8	2	1.9	.916
1886	WAS	N	13	31	.295	*3.34*	45	44	43	385.2	384	91	177	1	0	0	0	148	13	0	.088	13	70	3	1	1.9	.965
1887			7	13	.350	6.45	21	20	20	181.1	263	46	47	0	1	0	0	70	13	0	.186	4	24	2	0	1.4	.933
1888			0	3	.000	6.48	3	3	3	25	36	7	8	0	0	0	0	10	0	0	.000	0	2	0	0	0.7	1.000
6 yrs.			83	121	.407	3.10	211	207	196	1762	1710	396	950	13	1	0	0	*				88	338	54	11	1.9	.887

Jeff Shaw

SHAW, JEFFREY LEE BR TR 6′ 2″ 185 lbs.
B. July 7, 1966, Washington Court House, Ohio.

Year	Team	Lg	W	L	PCT	ERA	G	GS	CG	IP	H	BB	SO	ShO	Relief Pitching W	Relief Pitching L	Relief Pitching SV	Batting AB	Batting H	Batting HR	BA	PO	A	E	DP	TC/G	FA
1990	CLE	A	3	4	.429	6.66	12	9	0	48.2	73	20	25	0	0	0	0	0	0	0	—	4	7	0	0	0.9	1.000
1991			0	5	.000	3.36	29	1	0	72.1	72	27	31	0	0	4	1	0	0	0	—	4	11	2	2	0.6	.882
1992			0	1	.000	8.22	2	1	0	7.2	7	4	3	0	0	0	0	0	0	0	—	0	2	1	0	1.5	.667
1993	MON	N	2	7	.222	4.14	55	8	0	95.2	91	32	50	0	1	3	0	15	1	0	.067	8	16	0	1	0.4	1.000
1994			5	2	.714	3.88	46	0	0	67.1	67	15	47	0	5	2	1	7	2	0	.286	8	12	0	0	0.4	1.000
1995	2 teams MON N (50G 1–6) CHI A (9G 0–0)																										
″	total		1	6	.143	4.88	59	0	0	72	70	27	51	0	1	6	3	6	0	0	.000	7	13	0	1	0.3	1.000
6 yrs.			11	25	.306	4.50	203	19	0	363.2	380	125	207	0	7	15	5	28	3	0	.107	31	61	3	4	0.5	.968

Jim Shaw

SHAW, JOHN ALOYSIUS (Grunting Jim) BR TR 6′ 180 lbs.
B. Aug. 13, 1893, Pittsburgh, Pa. D. Jan. 27, 1962, Washington, D. C.

Year	Team	Lg	W	L	PCT	ERA	G	GS	CG	IP	H	BB	SO	ShO	Relief Pitching W	Relief Pitching L	Relief Pitching SV	Batting AB	Batting H	Batting HR	BA	PO	A	E	DP	TC/G	FA
1913	WAS	A	0	1	.000	2.08	2	1	0	13	8	7	14	0	0	0	0	2	0	0	.000	0	8	0	0	4.0	1.000
1914			15	17	.469	2.70	48	31	15	257	198	**137**	164	5	2	3	**4**	85	10	1	.118	18	72	9	4	2.1	.909
1915			6	11	.353	2.50	25	18	7	133	102	76	78	1	1	1	1	43	10	0	.233	5	32	3	2	1.6	.925
1916			3	8	.273	2.62	26	9	5	106.1	86	50	44	2	1	2	1	32	5	0	.156	4	16	3	2	0.9	.870
1917			15	14	.517	3.21	47	31	15	266.1	233	**123**	118	2	1	1	1	91	14	0	.154	16	54	3	6	1.6	.959
1918			16	12	.571	2.42	41	30	14	241.1	201	90	129	4	2	1	1	83	11	0	.133	10	41	6	2	1.4	.895
1919			17	17	.500	2.73	**45**	38	23	**306.2**	274	101	128	3	0	1	**5**	106	17	3	.160	9	53	3	1	1.4	.954
1920			11	18	.379	4.27	38	32	17	236.1	285	87	88	0	0	3	1	74	14	0	.189	7	42	1	1	1.3	.980
1921			1	0	1.000	7.36	15	5	0	40.1	59	17	4	0	0	0	3	12	5	0	.417	2	12	1	0	1.0	.933
9 yrs.			84	98	.462	3.07	287	195	96	1600.1	1446	688	767	17	7	12	17	528	86	4	.163	71	330	29	18	1.5	.933

Sam Shaw

SHAW, SAMUEL E. BR TR 5′ 5″ 140 lbs.
B. May 1864, Baltimore, Md. Deceased.

Year	Team	Lg	W	L	PCT	ERA	G	GS	CG	IP	H	BB	SO	ShO	Relief Pitching W	Relief Pitching L	Relief Pitching SV	Batting AB	Batting H	Batting HR	BA	PO	A	E	DP	TC/G	FA
1888	BAL	AA	2	4	.333	3.40	6	6	6	53	65	15	22	0	0	0	0	20	3	0	.150	2	10	5	0	2.8	.706
1893	CHI	N	1	0	1.000	5.63	2	2	1	16	12	13	1	0	0	0	0	7	2	0	.286	0	3	0	0	1.5	1.000
2 yrs.			3	4	.429	3.91	8	8	7	69	77	28	23	0	0	0	0	27	5	0	.185	2	13	5	0	2.5	.750

Bob Shawkey

SHAWKEY, JAMES ROBERT BR TR 5′11″ 168 lbs.
B. Dec. 4, 1890, Sigel, Pa. D. Dec. 31, 1980, Syracuse, N. Y.
Manager 1930.

Year	Team	Lg	W	L	PCT	ERA	G	GS	CG	IP	H	BB	SO	ShO	Relief Pitching W	Relief Pitching L	Relief Pitching SV	Batting AB	Batting H	Batting HR	BA	PO	A	E	DP	TC/G	FA
1913	PHI	A	6	5	.545	2.34	18	15	8	111.1	92	50	52	1	1	0	0	44	6	0	.136	3	40	4	0	2.6	.915
1914			16	8	.667	2.73	38	31	18	237	223	75	89	5	0	0	2	83	17	0	.205	6	63	5	1	1.9	.932
1915	2 teams PHI A (17G 6–6) NY A (16G 4–7)																										
″	total		10	13	.435	3.68	33	22	12	185.2	181	73	87	2	2	1	0	60	11	0	.183	5	49	3	3	1.7	.947
1916	NY	A	24	14	.632	2.21	53	27	21	276.2	204	81	122	4	**7**	4	**8**	93	17	0	.183	12	79	3	2	1.8	.968
1917			13	15	.464	2.44	32	26	16	236.1	207	72	97	2	2	2	0	84	16	0	.190	18	79	4	5	3.2	.960
1918			1	1	.500	1.13	3	2	1	16	7	10	3	1	0	0	0	4	3	0	.750	6	4	0	0	3.3	1.000
1919			20	11	.645	2.72	41	27	22	261.1	218	92	122	3	4	1	4	94	22	0	.234	22	59	4	1	2.1	.953
1920			20	13	.606	**2.45**	38	32	20	267.2	246	85	126	5	1	0	2	100	23	0	.230	15	48	1	0	1.7	.984
1921			18	12	.600	4.08	38	31	18	245	245	86	126	3	1	3	2	90	27	1	.300	14	35	3	1	1.4	.942
1922			20	12	.625	2.91	39	33	19	299.2	286	98	130	3	1	0	1	115	21	1	.183	13	70	4	4	2.2	.954
1923			16	11	.593	3.51	36	31	17	258.2	232	102	125	1	0	0	1	99	20	0	.202	9	61	2	3	2.0	.972
1924			16	11	.593	4.12	38	25	10	207.2	226	74	114	1	2	4	0	69	22	1	.319	11	39	6	1	1.5	.893
1925			6	14	.300	4.11	33	19	9	186	209	67	81	1	1	2	0	68	10	0	.147	7	37	0	1	1.3	1.000
1926			8	7	.533	3.62	29	10	3	104.1	102	37	63	1	4	3	3	35	9	0	.257	2	23	1	0	0.9	.962
1927			2	3	.400	2.89	19	2	0	43.2	44	16	23	0	2	2	4	11	1	0	.091	3	11	1	0	0.8	.933
15 yrs.			196	150	.566	3.09	488	333	194	2937	2722	1018	1360	33	28	22	27	1049	225	3	.214	146	697	41	22	1.8	.954
WORLD SERIES																											
1914	PHI	A	0	1	.000	5.40	1	1	0	5	4	2	0	0	0	0	0	2	1	0	.500	0	3	0	0	3.0	1.000
1921	NY	A	0	1	.000	7.00	2	1	0	9	13	6	5	0	0	1	0	4	2	0	.500	0	0	0	0	0.0	.000
1922			0	0	—	2.70	1	1	1	10	8	2	4	0	0	0	0	4	0	0	.000	0	2	0	0	2.0	1.000
1923			1	0	1.000	3.52	1	1	0	7.2	12	4	2	0	0	0	0	3	1	0	.333	1	2	0	1	3.0	1.000
1926			0	1	.000	5.40	3	1	0	10	8	2	7	0	0	0	0	2	0	0	.000	0	1	0	0	0.3	1.000
5 yrs.			1	3	.250	4.75	8	5	1	41.2	45	16	18	0	0	1	0	15	4	0	.267	1	8	0	1	1.1	1.000

John Shea

SHEA, JOHN MICHAEL JOSEPH BL TL 5′10½″ 171 lbs.
B. Dec. 27, 1904, Everett, Mass. D. Nov. 30, 1956, Malden, Mass.

Year	Team	Lg	W	L	PCT	ERA	G	GS	CG	IP	H	BB	SO	ShO	Relief W	Relief L	Relief SV	Batting AB	Batting H	Batting HR	BA	PO	A	E	DP	TC/G	FA
1928	BOS	A	0	0	—	18.00	1	0	0	1	1	1	0	0	0	0	0	0	0	0	—	0	1	0	0	1.0	1.000

Mike Shea

SHEA, MICHAEL JOSEPH TR 5′10″ 170 lbs.
B. Mar. 10, 1867, New Orleans, La. D. Aug. 22, 1927, New Orleans, La.

Year	Team	Lg	W	L	PCT	ERA	G	GS	CG	IP	H	BB	SO	ShO	Relief W	Relief L	Relief SV	Batting AB	Batting H	Batting HR	BA	PO	A	E	DP	TC/G	FA
1887	CIN	AA	1	1	.500	7.02	2	2	2	16.2	26	10	0	0	0	0	0	8	2	0	.250	1	8	2	0	5.5	.818

Red Shea

SHEA, PATRICK HENRY BR TR 6′ 160 lbs.
B. Nov. 29, 1898, Ware, Mass. D. Nov. 17, 1981, Stafford Springs, Conn.

Year	Team	Lg	W	L	PCT	ERA	G	GS	CG	IP	H	BB	SO	ShO	Relief W	Relief L	Relief SV	Batting AB	Batting H	Batting HR	BA	PO	A	E	DP	TC/G	FA
1918	PHI	A	0	0	—	4.00	3	0	0	9	14	2	2	0	0	0	0	3	0	0	.000	0	1	0	0	0.3	1.000
1921	NY	N	5	2	.714	3.09	9	2	1	32	28	2	10	0	4	1	0	9	1	0	.111	2	5	1	0	0.9	.875
1922			0	3	.000	4.70	11	2	0	23	22	11	5	0	0	2	0	7	0	0	.000	0	10	0	0	0.9	1.000
3 yrs.			5	5	.500	3.80	23	4	1	64	64	15	17	0	4	3	0	19	1	0	.053	2	16	1	0	0.8	.947

Spec Shea

SHEA, FRANCIS JOSEPH (The Naugatuck Nugget) BR TR 6′ 195 lbs.
Born Francis Joseph O'Shea.
B. Oct. 2, 1920, Naugatuck, Conn.

Year	Team	Lg	W	L	PCT	ERA	G	GS	CG	IP	H	BB	SO	ShO	Relief W	Relief L	Relief SV	Batting AB	Batting H	Batting HR	BA	PO	A	E	DP	TC/G	FA
1947	NY	A	14	5	.737	3.07	27	23	13	178.2	127	89	89	3	0	1	1	56	11	0	.196	9	14	0	0	0.9	1.000
1948			9	10	.474	3.41	28	22	8	155.2	117	87	71	3	1	1	1	47	7	0	.149	4	17	1	0	0.8	.955
1949			1	1	.500	5.33	20	3	0	52.1	48	43	22	0	1	0	1	12	3	0	.250	2	9	1	1	0.6	.917
1951			5	5	.500	4.33	25	11	2	95.2	112	50	38	2	2	2	0	28	6	1	.214	7	14	1	3	0.9	.955
1952	WAS	A	11	7	.611	2.93	22	21	12	169	144	92	65	2	0	0	0	63	15	0	.238	14	23	0	1	1.7	1.000
1953			12	7	.632	3.94	23	23	11	164.2	151	75	38	1	0	0	0	62	11	0	.177	5	24	0	2	1.3	1.000
1954			2	9	.182	6.18	23	11	1	71.1	97	34	22	0	1	1	0	20	1	0	.050	5	17	1	1	1.0	.957
1955			2	2	.500	3.99	27	4	1	56.1	53	27	16	1	1	0	2	10	4	0	.400	3	7	2	0	0.4	.833
8 yrs.			56	46	.549	3.80	195	118	48	943.2	849	497	361	12	6	5	5	298	58	1	.195	49	125	6	8	0.9	.967
WORLD SERIES																											
1947	NY	A	2	0	1.000	2.35	3	3	1	15.1	10	8	10	0	0	0	0	5	2	0	.400	1	3	0	0	1.3	1.000

Steve Shea

SHEA, STEVEN FRANCIS BR TR 6′ 3″ 215 lbs.
B. Dec. 5, 1942, Worcester, Mass.

Year	Team	Lg	W	L	PCT	ERA	G	GS	CG	IP	H	BB	SO	ShO	Relief W	Relief L	Relief SV	Batting AB	Batting H	Batting HR	BA	PO	A	E	DP	TC/G	FA
1968	HOU	N	4	4	.500	3.38	30	0	0	34.2	27	11	15	0	4	4	6	6	0	0	.000	2	9	0	1	0.4	1.000
1969	MON	N	0	0	—	2.87	10	0	0	15.2	18	8	11	0	0	0	0	0	0	0	—	1	2	0	1	0.3	1.000
2 yrs.			4	4	.500	3.22	40	0	0	50.1	45	19	26	0	4	4	6	6	0	0	.000	3	11	0	2	0.3	1.000

Al Shealy

SHEALY, ALBERT BERLY BR TR 5′11″ 175 lbs.
B. May 20, 1900, Chapin, S. C. D. Mar. 7, 1967, Hagerstown, Md.

Year	Team	Lg	W	L	PCT	ERA	G	GS	CG	IP	H	BB	SO	ShO	Relief W	Relief L	Relief SV	Batting AB	Batting H	Batting HR	BA	PO	A	E	DP	TC/G	FA
1928	NY	A	8	6	.571	5.06	23	12	3	96	124	42	39	0	2	1	2	38	9	1	.237	4	22	1	0	1.2	.963
1930	CHI	N	0	0	—	8.00	24	0	0	27	37	14	14	0	0	0	0	5	3	0	.600	1	4	0	0	0.2	1.000
2 yrs.			8	6	.571	5.71	47	12	3	123	161	56	53	0	2	1	2	43	12	1	.279	5	26	1	0	0.7	.969

John Shearon

SHEARON, JOHN M.
B. 1870, Pittsburgh, Pa. D. Feb. 1, 1923, Bradford, Pa.

Year	Team	Lg	W	L	PCT	ERA	G	GS	CG	IP	H	BB	SO	ShO	Relief W	Relief L	Relief SV	Batting AB	Batting H	Batting HR	BA	PO	A	E	DP	TC/G	FA
1891	CLE	N	1	3	.250	3.52	6	5	4	46	57	24	19	0	0	0	0	*				32	13	8	1	1.6	.849

George Shears

SHEARS, GEORGE PENFIELD BR TL 6′ 3″ 180 lbs.
B. Apr. 13, 1890, Marshall, Mo. D. Nov. 12, 1978, Loveland, Colo.

Year	Team	Lg	W	L	PCT	ERA	G	GS	CG	IP	H	BB	SO	ShO	Relief W	Relief L	Relief SV	Batting AB	Batting H	Batting HR	BA	PO	A	E	DP	TC/G	FA
1912	NY	A	0	0	—	5.40	4	0	0	15	24	11	9	0	0	0	0	6	1	0	.167	0	5	0	0	1.3	1.000

Tom Sheehan

SHEEHAN, THOMAS CLANCY BR TR 6′ 2½″ 190 lbs.
B. Mar. 31, 1894, Grand Ridge, Ill. D. Oct. 29, 1982, Chillicothe, Ohio.
Manager 1960.

Year	Team	Lg	W	L	PCT	ERA	G	GS	CG	IP	H	BB	SO	ShO	Relief W	Relief L	Relief SV	Batting AB	Batting H	Batting HR	BA	PO	A	E	DP	TC/G	FA
1915	PHI	A	4	9	.308	4.15	15	13	8	102	131	38	22	1	0	0	0	34	4	0	.118	2	30	3	0	2.3	.914
1916			1	16	.059	3.69	38	17	8	188	197	94	54	0	1	2	0	56	7	0	.125	10	71	6	3	2.3	.931
1921	NY	A	1	0	1.000	5.45	12	1	0	33	43	19	7	0	0	0	1	8	5	0	.625	2	16	0	0	1.5	1.000
1924	CIN	N	9	11	.450	3.24	39	14	8	166.2	170	54	52	2	5	4	1	58	18	0	.310	7	31	1	1	1.0	.974
1925	2 teams	CIN N (10G 1–0) PIT N (23G 1–1)																									
″	total		2	1	.667	4.48	33	3	1	86.1	100	25	18	0	1	1	3	25	4	0	.160	8	15	1	2	0.7	.958
1926	PIT	N	0	2	.000	6.68	9	4	1	31	36	12	16	0	0	0	0	9	1	0	.111	0	7	1	0	0.9	.875
6 yrs.			17	39	.304	4.00	146	52	26	607	677	242	169	3	7	7	5	190	39	0	.205	29	170	12	6	1.4	.943

Rollie Sheldon

SHELDON, ROLAND FRANK BR TR 6′ 4″ 185 lbs.
B. Dec. 17, 1936, Putnam, Conn.

Year	Team	Lg	W	L	PCT	ERA	G	GS	CG	IP	H	BB	SO	ShO	Relief W	Relief L	Relief SV	Batting AB	Batting H	Batting HR	BA	PO	A	E	DP	TC/G	FA
1961	NY	A	11	5	.688	3.60	35	21	6	162.2	149	55	84	2	2	0	0	56	7	0	.125	11	30	0	3	1.2	1.000
1962			7	8	.467	5.49	34	16	2	118	136	28	54	0	3	1	1	26	2	0	.077	7	10	1	1	0.5	.944
1964			5	2	.714	3.61	19	12	3	102.1	92	18	57	0	0	0	1	34	3	0	.088	7	20	0	2	1.4	1.000
1965	2 teams	NY A (3G 0–0) KC A (32G 10–8)																									
″	total		10	8	.556	3.86	35	29	4	193.1	185	57	112	1	0	0	0	52	4	0	.077	14	31	2	4	1.3	.957
1966	2 teams	KC A (14G 4–7) BOS A (23G 1–6)																									
″	total		5	13	.278	4.12	37	23	2	148.2	179	49	64	1	0	2	0	41	4	0	.098	9	28	0	2	1.0	1.000
5 yrs.			38	36	.514	4.08	160	101	17	725	741	207	371	4	5	3	2	209	20	0	.096	48	119	3	12	1.1	.982
WORLD SERIES																											
1964	NY	A	0	0	—	0.00	2	0	0	2.2	0	2	2	0	0	0	0	0	0	0	—	1	1	0	1	1.0	1.000

Frank Shellenback

SHELLENBACK, FRANK VICTOR BR TR 6′ 2″ 192 lbs.
B. Dec. 16, 1898, Joplin, Mo. D. Aug. 17, 1969, Newton, Mass.

Year	Team	Lg	W	L	PCT	ERA	G	GS	CG	IP	H	BB	SO	ShO	Relief W	Relief L	Relief SV	Batting AB	Batting H	Batting HR	BA	PO	A	E	DP	TC/G	FA
1918	CHI	A	9	12	.429	2.66	28	20	10	182.2	180	74	47	2	3	0	2	54	7	0	.130	5	28	3	0	1.2	.917
1919			1	3	.250	5.14	8	4	2	35	40	16	10	0	0	1	0	11	1	0	.091	1	9	0	0	1.3	1.000
2 yrs.			10	15	.400	3.06	36	24	12	217.2	220	90	57	2	3	1	2	65	8	0	.123	6	37	3	0	1.2	.935

Jim Shellenback

SHELLENBACK, JAMES PHILIP BL TL 6′ 2″ 200 lbs.
B. Nov. 18, 1943, Riverside, Calif.

Year	Team	Lg	W	L	PCT	ERA	G	GS	CG	IP	H	BB	SO	ShO	Relief W	Relief L	Relief SV	Batting AB	Batting H	Batting HR	BA	PO	A	E	DP	TC/G	FA
1966	PIT	N	0	0	—	9.00	2	0	0	3	3	3	0	0	0	0	0	0	0	0	—	0	2	0	0	1.0	1.000
1967			1	1	.500	2.70	6	2	1	23.1	23	12	11	0	0	0	0	6	1	0	.167	1	4	0	0	0.8	1.000

Jim Shellenback *continued*

Year	Team	Lg	W	L	PCT	ERA	G	GS	CG	IP	H	BB	SO	ShO	Relief Pitching W	L	SV	Batting AB	H	HR	BA	PO	A	E	DP	TC/G	FA
1969	2 teams PIT N (8G 0–0) WAS A (30G 4–7)																										
″	total		4	7	.364	3.90	38	11	2	101.2	101	52	57	0	0	3	1	28	5	0	.179	6	33	2	1	1.1	.951
1970	WAS	A	6	7	.462	3.69	39	14	2	117	107	51	57	1	3	1	0	30	2	0	.067	5	16	1	1	0.6	.955
1971			3	11	.214	3.52	40	15	3	120	123	49	47	1	0	1	0	30	5	0	.167	2	26	2	4	0.8	.933
1972	TEX	A	2	4	.333	3.47	22	6	0	57	46	16	30	0	1	1	1	10	1	0	.100	4	5	0	0	0.4	1.000
1973			0	0	—	0.00	2	0	0	2	0	0	3	0	0	0	0	0	0	0	—	0	1	0	0	0.5	1.000
1974			0	0	—	5.76	11	0	0	25	30	12	14	0	0	0	0	0	0	0	—	1	4	0	0	0.5	1.000
1977	MIN	A	0	0	—	7.50	5	0	0	6	10	5	3	0	0	0	0	0	0	0	—	2	0	0	0	0.4	1.000
9 yrs.			16	30	.348	3.80	165	48	8	455	443	200	222	2	4	6	2	104	14	0	.135	21	91	5	6	0.7	.957

Bert Shepard

SHEPARD, BERT ROBERT BL TL 5′11″ 185 lbs.
B. June 28, 1920, Dana, Ind.

Year	Team	Lg	W	L	PCT	ERA	G	GS	CG	IP	H	BB	SO	ShO	Relief Pitching W	L	SV	Batting AB	H	HR	BA	PO	A	E	DP	TC/G	FA
1945	WAS	A	0	0	—	1.69	1	0	0	5.1	3	1	2	0	0	0	0	3	0	0	.000	0	2	0	0	2.0	1.000

Keith Shepherd

SHEPHERD, KEITH WAYNE BR TR 6′2″ 205 lbs.
B. Jan. 21, 1968, Wabash, Ind.

Year	Team	Lg	W	L	PCT	ERA	G	GS	CG	IP	H	BB	SO	ShO	Relief Pitching W	L	SV	Batting AB	H	HR	BA	PO	A	E	DP	TC/G	FA
1992	PHI	N	1	1	.500	3.27	12	0	0	22	19	6	10	0	1	1	2	0	0	0	—	0	5	0	0	0.4	1.000
1993	CLR	N	1	3	.250	6.98	14	1	0	19.1	26	4	7	0	1	3	1	2	0	0	.000	3	2	2	0	0.5	.714
1995	BOS	A	0	0	—	36.00	2	0	0	1	4	2	0	0	0	0	0	0	0	0	—	0	1	0	0	0.5	1.000
3 yrs.			2	4	.333	5.74	28	1	0	42.1	49	12	17	0	2	4	3	2	0	0	.000	3	8	2	0	0.5	.846

Bill Sherdel

SHERDEL, WILLIAM HENRY (Wee Willie) BL TL 5′10″ 160 lbs.
B. Aug. 15, 1896, McSherrystown, Pa. D. Nov. 14, 1968, McSherrystown, Pa.

Year	Team	Lg	W	L	PCT	ERA	G	GS	CG	IP	H	BB	SO	ShO	Relief Pitching W	L	SV	Batting AB	H	HR	BA	PO	A	E	DP	TC/G	FA
1918	STL	N	6	12	.333	2.71	35	16	9	182.1	174	49	40	1	1	**4**	0	62	15	1	.242	6	46	0	2	1.5	1.000
1919			5	9	.357	3.47	36	11	7	137.1	137	42	52	0	3	1	1	48	13	0	.271	5	45	4	0	1.5	.926
1920			11	10	.524	3.28	43	7	4	170	183	40	74	0	**8**	**8**	**6**	63	14	1	.222	7	50	1	4	1.3	.983
1921			9	8	.529	3.18	38	8	5	144.1	137	38	57	1	4	**6**	1	44	5	0	.114	7	40	3	0	1.3	.940
1922			17	13	.567	3.88	47	31	15	241.1	298	62	79	3	2	1	2	88	17	1	.193	5	41	5	1	1.1	.902
1923			15	13	.536	4.32	39	26	14	225	270	59	78	0	3	2	2	83	28	1	.337	6	41	5	3	1.3	.904
1924			8	9	.471	3.42	35	10	6	168.2	188	38	57	0	6	3	1	75	15	0	.200	9	30	0	2	1.1	1.000
1925			15	6	**.714**	3.11	32	21	17	200	216	42	53	2	0	0	1	73	15	1	.205	6	42	0	4	1.5	1.000
1926			16	12	.571	3.49	34	29	17	234.2	255	49	59	3	1	2	0	90	22	1	.244	9	44	1	0	1.6	.981
1927			17	12	.586	3.53	39	28	18	232.1	241	48	59	0	3	0	**6**	72	14	1	.194	3	36	5	5	1.1	.886
1928			21	10	.677	2.86	38	27	20	248.2	251	56	72	0	3	2	**5**	84	19	1	.226	6	36	2	1	1.2	.955
1929			10	15	.400	5.93	33	22	11	195.2	278	58	69	1	3	2	0	70	16	1	.229	1	36	1	0	1.2	.974
1930	2 teams STL N (13G 3–2) BOS N (21G 6–5)																										
″	total		9	7	.563	4.71	34	21	8	183.1	217	43	55	1	1	0	1	61	6	0	.098	7	31	2	4	1.2	.950
1931	BOS	N	6	10	.375	4.25	27	16	8	137.2	163	35	34	0	1	1	0	46	14	0	.304	4	20	0	0	0.9	1.000
1932	2 teams BOS N (1G 0–0) STL N (3G 0–0)																										
″	total		0	0		3.68	4	0	0	7.1	10	2	1	0	0	0	0	1	1	0	1.000	1	2	0	0	0.8	1.000
15 yrs.			165	146	.531	3.72	514	273	159	2708.2	3018	661	839	12	39	32	26	960	214	9	.223	82	540	29	26	1.3	.955
WORLD SERIES																											
1926	STL	N	0	2	.000	2.12	2	2	1	17	15	8	3	0	0	0	0	5	0	0	.000	2	5	0	0	3.5	1.000
1928			0	2	.000	4.72	2	2	0	13.1	15	3	3	0	0	0	0	5	0	0	.000	0	3	0	0	1.5	1.000
2 yrs.			0	4	.000	3.26	4	4	1	30.1	30	11	6	0	0	0	0	10	0	0	.000	2	8	0	0	2.5	1.000

Roy Sherid

SHERID, ROYDEN RICHARD BR TR 6′2″ 185 lbs.
B. Jan. 25, 1907, Norristown, Pa. D. Feb. 28, 1982, Parker Ford, Pa.

Year	Team	Lg	W	L	PCT	ERA	G	GS	CG	IP	H	BB	SO	ShO	Relief Pitching W	L	SV	Batting AB	H	HR	BA	PO	A	E	DP	TC/G	FA
1929	NY	A	6	6	.500	3.49	33	15	9	159.2	165	55	51	0	0	0	1	50	9	0	.180	8	29	3	3	1.2	.925
1930			12	13	.480	5.23	37	21	8	184	214	87	59	0	2	3	4	69	7	0	.101	11	30	2	4	1.2	.953
1931			5	5	.500	5.69	17	8	3	74.1	94	24	39	0	1	3	2	30	10	0	.333	3	14	0	0	1.0	1.000
3 yrs.			23	24	.489	4.65	87	44	20	418	473	166	149	0	3	6	7	149	26	0	.174	22	73	5	7	1.1	.950

Babe Sherman

SHERMAN, LESTER DANIEL (General) BR TR 5′6″ 145 lbs.
B. May 9, 1890, Hubbardsville, N. Y. D. Sept. 16, 1955, Highland Park, Mich.

Year	Team	Lg	W	L	PCT	ERA	G	GS	CG	IP	H	BB	SO	ShO	Relief Pitching W	L	SV	Batting AB	H	HR	BA	PO	A	E	DP	TC/G	FA
1914	CHI	F	0	1	.000	0.00	1	1	0	0.1	0	2	0	0	0	0	0	0	0	0	—	0	0	0	0	0.0	.000

Joe Sherman

SHERMAN, JOEL POWERS BR TR 6′ 165 lbs.
B. Nov. 4, 1890, Yarmouth, Mass. D. Dec. 21, 1987, Cape Coral, Fla.

Year	Team	Lg	W	L	PCT	ERA	G	GS	CG	IP	H	BB	SO	ShO	Relief Pitching W	L	SV	Batting AB	H	HR	BA	PO	A	E	DP	TC/G	FA
1915	PHI	A	1	0	1.000	2.40	2	1	1	15	15	1	5	0	0	0	0	6	2	0	.333	0	3	0	0	1.5	1.000

Tim Sherrill

SHERRILL, TIMOTHY SHAWN BL TL 5′11″ 170 lbs.
B. Sept. 10, 1965, Harrison, Ark.

Year	Team	Lg	W	L	PCT	ERA	G	GS	CG	IP	H	BB	SO	ShO	Relief Pitching W	L	SV	Batting AB	H	HR	BA	PO	A	E	DP	TC/G	FA
1990	STL	N	0	0	—	6.23	8	0	0	4.1	10	3	3	0	0	0	0	0	0	0	—	1	0	0	0	0.1	1.000
1991			0	0	—	8.16	10	0	0	14.1	20	3	4	0	0	0	0	0	0	0	—	1	3	0	0	0.4	1.000
2 yrs.			0	0		7.71	18	0	0	18.2	30	6	7	0	0	0	0	0	0	0		2	3	0	0	0.3	1.000

Fred Sherry

SHERRY, FRED PETER BR TR 6′ 170 lbs.
Born Fred Peter Schuerholz.
B. June 13, 1889, Honesdale, Pa. D. July 27, 1975, Honesdale, Pa.

Year	Team	Lg	W	L	PCT	ERA	G	GS	CG	IP	H	BB	SO	ShO	Relief Pitching W	L	SV	Batting AB	H	HR	BA	PO	A	E	DP	TC/G	FA
1911	WAS	A	0	4	.000	4.30	10	3	2	52.1	63	19	20	0	0	1	0	19	3	0	.158	3	15	2	1	2.0	.900

Larry Sherry

SHERRY, LAWRENCE BR TR 6′2″ 180 lbs.
Brother of Norm Sherry.
B. July 25, 1935, Los Angeles, Calif.

Year	Team	Lg	W	L	PCT	ERA	G	GS	CG	IP	H	BB	SO	ShO	Relief Pitching W	L	SV	Batting AB	H	HR	BA	PO	A	E	DP	TC/G	FA
1958	LA	N	0	0	—	12.46	5	0	0	4.1	10	7	2	0	0	0	0	0	0	0	—	0	1	0	0	0.2	1.000
1959			7	2	.778	2.19	23	9	1	94.1	75	43	72	1	2	0	3	32	7	2	.219	3	11	1	1	0.7	.933
1960			14	10	.583	3.79	57	3	1	142.1	125	82	114	0	**13**	8	7	37	6	1	.162	18	21	0	0	0.7	1.000
1961			4	4	.500	3.90	53	1	0	94.2	90	39	79	0	4	3	15	13	2	0	.154	8	5	3	0	0.3	.813
1962			7	3	.700	3.20	58	0	0	90	81	44	71	0	7	3	11	17	2	0	.118	2	13	0	1	0.3	1.000
1963			2	6	.250	3.73	36	3	0	79.2	82	24	47	0	2	4	3	9	1	0	.111	1	15	1	1	0.5	.941
1964	DET	A	7	5	.583	3.66	38	0	0	66.1	52	37	58	0	7	5	11	14	0	0	.000	4	9	4	2	0.4	.765

Larry Sherry *continued*

Year	Team	Lg	W	L	PCT	ERA	G	GS	CG	IP	H	BB	SO	ShO	Relief Pitching W	L	SV	Batting AB	H	HR	BA	PO	A	E	DP	TC/G	FA
1965			3	6	.333	3.10	39	0	0	78.1	71	40	46	0	3	6	5	10	3	0	.300	4	15	0	1	0.5	1.000
1966			8	5	.615	3.82	55	0	0	77.2	66	36	63	0	8	5	20	10	4	0	.400	4	9	2	2	0.3	.867
1967	**2 teams**	**DET A**	(20G 0–1)		**HOU N**	(29G 1–2)																					
″	**total**		1	3	.250	5.50	49	0	0	68.2	88	20	52	0	1	3	7	6	0	0	.000	7	14	2	1	0.5	.913
1968	**CAL**	**A**	0	0	—	6.00	3	0	0	3	7	2	2	0	0	0	0	0	0	0	—	0	0	0	0	0.0	.000
11 yrs.			53	44	.546	3.67	416	16	2	799.1	747	374	606	1	47	37	82	148	25	3	.169	51	113	13	9	0.4	.927
WORLD SERIES																											
1959	**LA**	**N**	2	0	1.000	0.71	4	0	0	12.2	8	2	5	0	2	0	2	4	2	0	.500	1	3	0	0	1.0	1.000

Ben Shields

SHIELDS, BENJAMIN COWAN (Big Ben, Lefty) BR TL 6′ 1½″ 195 lbs.
B. June 17, 1903, Huntersville, N. C. D. Jan. 24, 1982, Woodruff, S. C. BB 1930–1931

Year	Team	Lg	W	L	PCT	ERA	G	GS	CG	IP	H	BB	SO	ShO	Relief Pitching W	L	SV	Batting AB	H	HR	BA	PO	A	E	DP	TC/G	FA
1924	**NY**	**A**	0	0	—	27.00	2	0	0	2	6	2	3	0	0	0	0	0	0	0	—	0	0	0	0	0.0	.000
1925			3	0	1.000	4.88	4	2	2	24	24	12	5	0	1	0	0	8	1	0	.125	2	3	0	0	1.3	1.000
1930	**BOS**	**A**	0	0	—	9.00	3	0	0	10	16	6	1	0	0	0	0	3	0	0	.000	0	3	0	0	1.0	1.000
1931	**PHI**	**N**	1	0	1.000	15.19	4	0	0	5.1	9	7	0	0	1	0	0	2	0	0	.000	0	1	0	0	0.3	1.000
4 yrs.			4	0	1.000	8.27	13	2	2	41.1	55	27	9	0	2	0	0	13	1	0	.077	2	7	0	0	0.7	1.000

Charlie Shields

SHIELDS, CHARLES JESSAMINE BL TL 5′ 8″
B. Dec. 10, 1879, Jackson, Tenn. D. Aug. 27, 1953, Memphis, Tenn.

Year	Team	Lg	W	L	PCT	ERA	G	GS	CG	IP	H	BB	SO	ShO	Relief Pitching W	L	SV	Batting AB	H	HR	BA	PO	A	E	DP	TC/G	FA
1902	**2 teams**	**BAL A**	(23G 4–11)		**STL A**	(4G 3–0)																					
″	**total**		7	11	.389	4.07	27	19	13	172.1	238	39	34	1	1	1	1	61	14	0	.230	4	30	6	2	1.4	.850
1907	**STL**	**N**	0	2	.000	9.45	3	2	0	6.2	12	7	1	0	0	0	0	2	0	0	.000	0	3	0	0	1.0	1.000
2 yrs.			7	13	.350	4.27	30	21	13	179	250	46	35	1	1	1	1	63	14	0	.222	4	33	6	2	1.4	.860

Steve Shields

SHIELDS, STEPHEN MACK BR TR 6′ 5″ 220 lbs.
B. Nov. 30, 1958, Gadsden, Ala.

Year	Team	Lg	W	L	PCT	ERA	G	GS	CG	IP	H	BB	SO	ShO	Relief Pitching W	L	SV	Batting AB	H	HR	BA	PO	A	E	DP	TC/G	FA
1985	**ATL**	**N**	1	2	.333	5.16	23	6	0	68	86	32	29	0	0	0	0	18	2	0	.111	6	6	1	0	0.6	.923
1986	**2 teams**	**ATL N**	(6G 0–0)		**KC A**	(3G 0–0)																					
″	**total**		0	0	—	5.06	9	0	0	21.1	16	11	8	0	0	0	0	1	0	0	.000	2	2	0	0	0.4	1.000
1987	**SEA**	**A**	2	0	1.000	6.60	20	0	0	30	43	12	22	0	2	0	3	0	0	0	—	1	5	0	0	0.3	1.000
1988	**NY**	**A**	5	5	.500	4.37	39	0	0	82.1	96	30	55	0	5	5	0	0	0	0	—	9	8	1	2	0.5	.944
1989	**MIN**	**A**	0	1	.000	7.79	11	0	0	17.1	28	6	12	0	0	1	0	0	0	0	—	0	3	0	1	0.3	1.000
5 yrs.			8	8	.500	5.26	102	6	0	219	269	91	126	0	7	6	3	19	2	0	.105	18	24	2	3	0.4	.955

Vince Shields

SHIELDS, VINCENT WILLIAM BL TR 5′11″ 185 lbs.
B. Nov. 18, 1900, Fredericton, N. B., Canada
D. Oct. 17, 1952, Plaster Rock, N. B., Canada.

Year	Team	Lg	W	L	PCT	ERA	G	GS	CG	IP	H	BB	SO	ShO	Relief Pitching W	L	SV	Batting AB	H	HR	BA	PO	A	E	DP	TC/G	FA
1924	**STL**	**N**	1	1	.500	3.00	2	1	0	12	10	3	4	0	1	0	0	5	2	0	.400	0	1	1	0	1.0	.500

Garland Shifflett

SHIFFLETT, GARLAND JESSIE (Duck) BR TR 5′10½″ 165 lbs.
B. Mar. 28, 1935, Elkton, Va.

Year	Team	Lg	W	L	PCT	ERA	G	GS	CG	IP	H	BB	SO	ShO	Relief Pitching W	L	SV	Batting AB	H	HR	BA	PO	A	E	DP	TC/G	FA
1957	**WAS**	**A**	0	0	—	10.13	6	1	0	8	6	10	2	0	0	0	0	0	0	0	—	0	1	0	0	0.2	1.000
1964	**MIN**	**A**	0	2	.000	4.58	10	0	0	17.2	22	7	8	0	0	2	1	4	0	0	.000	0	5	1	2	0.6	.833
2 yrs.			0	2	.000	6.31	16	1	0	25.2	28	17	10	0	0	2	1	4	0	0	.000	0	6	1	2	0.4	.857

Steve Shifflett

SHIFFLETT, STEPHEN EARL BR TR 6′ 1″ 205 lbs.
B. Jan. 5, 1966, Kansas City, Mo.

Year	Team	Lg	W	L	PCT	ERA	G	GS	CG	IP	H	BB	SO	ShO	Relief Pitching W	L	SV	Batting AB	H	HR	BA	PO	A	E	DP	TC/G	FA
1992	**KC**	**A**	1	4	.200	2.60	34	0	0	52	55	17	25	0	1	4	0	0	0	0	—	5	7	1	0	0.4	.923

Zak Shinall

SHINALL, ZAKARY SEBASTIEN BR TR 6′ 3″ 215 lbs.
B. Oct. 14, 1968, St. Louis, Mo.

Year	Team	Lg	W	L	PCT	ERA	G	GS	CG	IP	H	BB	SO	ShO	Relief Pitching W	L	SV	Batting AB	H	HR	BA	PO	A	E	DP	TC/G	FA
1993	**SEA**	**A**	0	0	—	3.38	1	0	0	2.2	4	2	0	0	0	0	0	0	0	0	—	1	0	0	0	1.0	1.000

Razor Shines

SHINES, ANTHONY RAYMOND BB TR 6′ 1″ 210 lbs.
B. July 18, 1956, Durham, N. C.

Year	Team	Lg	W	L	PCT	ERA	G	GS	CG	IP	H	BB	SO	ShO	Relief Pitching W	L	SV	Batting AB	H	HR	BA	PO	A	E	DP	TC/G	FA
1985	**MON**	**N**	0	0	—	0.00	1	0	0	1	1	0	0	0	0	0	0	*				0	0	0	0	0.0	.000

Dave Shipanoff

SHIPANOFF, DAVID NOEL BR TR 6′ 2″ 185 lbs.
B. Nov. 13, 1959, Edmonton, Alta., Canada.

Year	Team	Lg	W	L	PCT	ERA	G	GS	CG	IP	H	BB	SO	ShO	Relief Pitching W	L	SV	Batting AB	H	HR	BA	PO	A	E	DP	TC/G	FA
1985	**PHI**	**N**	1	2	.333	3.22	26	0	0	36.1	33	16	26	0	1	2	3	3	0	0	.000	2	2	1	0	0.2	.800

Joe Shipley

SHIPLEY, JOSEPH CLARK (Moses) BR TR 6′ 4″ 210 lbs.
B. May 9, 1935, Morristown, Tenn.

Year	Team	Lg	W	L	PCT	ERA	G	GS	CG	IP	H	BB	SO	ShO	Relief Pitching W	L	SV	Batting AB	H	HR	BA	PO	A	E	DP	TC/G	FA
1958	**SF**	**N**	0	0	—	33.75	1	0	0	1.1	3	3	0	0	0	0	0	0	0	0	—	0	0	0	0	0.0	.000
1959			0	0	—	4.50	10	1	0	18	16	17	11	0	0	0	0	3	0	0	.000	0	2	1	0	0.3	.667
1960			0	0	—	5.40	15	0	0	20	20	9	9	0	0	0	0	0	0	0	—	0	7	0	0	0.5	1.000
1963	**CHI**	**A**	0	1	.000	5.79	3	0	0	4.2	9	6	3	0	0	1	0	2	0	0	.000	0	1	0	0	0.3	1.000
4 yrs.			0	1	.000	5.93	29	1	0	44	48	35	23	0	0	1	0	5	0	0	.000	0	10	1	0	0.4	.909

Duke Shirey

SHIREY, CLAIR LEE BR TR 6′ 1″ 175 lbs.
B. June 20, 1898, Jersey Shore, Pa. D. Sept. 1, 1962, Hagerstown, Md.

Year	Team	Lg	W	L	PCT	ERA	G	GS	CG	IP	H	BB	SO	ShO	Relief Pitching W	L	SV	Batting AB	H	HR	BA	PO	A	E	DP	TC/G	FA
1920	**WAS**	**A**	0	1	.000	6.75	2	1	0	4	5	2	0	0	0	0	0	1	0	0	.000	0	0	0	0	0.0	.000

Bob Shirley

SHIRLEY, ROBERT CHARLES BR TL 5′11″ 180 lbs.
B. June 25, 1954, Cushing, Okla.

Year	Team	Lg	W	L	PCT	ERA	G	GS	CG	IP	H	BB	SO	ShO	Relief Pitching W	L	SV	Batting AB	H	HR	BA	PO	A	E	DP	TC/G	FA
1977	**SD**	**N**	12	18	.400	3.70	39	35	1	214	215	100	146	0	0	1	0	74	9	0	.122	10	37	3	2	1.3	.940
1978			8	11	.421	3.69	50	20	2	166	164	61	102	0	2	2	5	40	5	0	.125	6	35	0	1	0.8	1.000
1979			8	16	.333	3.38	49	25	4	205	196	59	117	1	2	4	0	55	5	0	.091	13	30	1	1	0.9	.977
1980			11	12	.478	3.55	59	12	3	137	143	54	67	0	7	6	7	30	1	0	.033	7	32	1	1	0.7	.975
1981	**STL**	**N**	6	4	.600	4.10	28	11	1	79	78	34	36	0	1	0	1	22	3	0	.136	1	10	0	0	0.4	1.000
1982	**CIN**	**N**	8	13	.381	3.60	41	20	1	152.2	138	73	89	0	2	3	0	42	6	0	.143	4	31	2	1	0.9	.946
1983	**NY**	**A**	5	8	.385	5.08	25	17	1	108	122	36	53	1	1	0	0	0	0	0	—	5	20	0	1	1.0	1.000
1984			3	3	.500	3.38	41	7	1	114.1	119	38	48	0	1	0	0	0	0	0	—	6	16	1	4	0.6	.957

Bob Shirley *continued*

Year	Team	Lg	W	L	PCT	ERA	G	GS	CG	IP	H	BB	SO	ShO	Relief Pitching W	Relief Pitching L	Relief Pitching SV	Batting AB	Batting H	Batting HR	BA	PO	A	E	DP	TC/G	FA
1985			5	5	.500	2.64	48	8	2	109	103	26	55	0	3	2	2	0	0	0	—	4	15	3	1	0.5	.864
1986			0	4	.000	5.04	39	6	0	105.1	108	40	64	0	0	1	3	0	0	0	—	4	20	1	1	0.6	.960
1987	**2 teams**	**NY A** (12G 1–0)	**KC A** (3G 0–0)																								
″	**total**		1	0	1.000	6.31	15	1	0	41.1	46	22	13	0	0	0	0	0	0	0		2	3	0	0	0.3	1.000
11 yrs.			67	94	.416	3.82	434	162	16	1431.2	1432	543	790	2	19	19	18	263	29	0	.110	62	249	12	13	0.7	.963

Steve Shirley

SHIRLEY, STEVEN BRIAN BL TL 6′ 185 lbs.
B. Oct. 12, 1956, San Francisco, Calif.

Year	Team	Lg	W	L	PCT	ERA	G	GS	CG	IP	H	BB	SO	ShO	Relief W	Relief L	Relief SV	AB	H	HR	BA	PO	A	E	DP	TC/G	FA
1982	**LA**	**N**	1	1	.500	4.26	11	0	0	12.2	15	7	8	0	1	1	0	1	1	0	1.000	0	4	0	0	0.4	1.000

Tex Shirley

SHIRLEY, ALVIS NEWMAN BB TR 6′ 1″ 175 lbs.
B. Apr. 25, 1918, Birthright, Tex. D. Nov. 7, 1993, DeSoto, Tex. BR 1941–1942

Year	Team	Lg	W	L	PCT	ERA	G	GS	CG	IP	H	BB	SO	ShO	Relief W	Relief L	Relief SV	AB	H	HR	BA	PO	A	E	DP	TC/G	FA
1941	**PHI**	**A**	0	1	.000	2.45	5	0	0	7.1	8	6	1	0	0	1	1	1	0	0	.000	0	3	0	0	0.6	1.000
1942			0	1	.000	5.30	15	1	0	35.2	37	22	10	0	0	0	1	9	0	0	.000	1	5	0	0	0.4	1.000
1944	**STL**	**A**	5	4	.556	4.15	23	11	2	80.1	59	64	35	1	2	0	0	28	4	0	.143	6	7	2	1	0.7	.867
1945			8	12	.400	3.63	32	24	10	183.2	191	93	77	2	0	2	0	70	20	0	.286	8	31	2	3	1.3	.951
1946			6	12	.333	4.96	27	18	7	139.2	148	105	45	0	1	2	0	51	10	0	.196	6	23	2	1	1.1	.935
5 yrs.			19	30	.388	4.25	102	54	19	446.2	443	290	168	3	3	5	2	159	34	0	.214	21	69	6	5	0.9	.938
WORLD SERIES																											
1944	**STL**	**A**	0	0	—	0.00	1	0	0	2	2	1	1	0	0	0	0	0	0	0	—	0	1	0	0	1.0	1.000

George Shoch

SHOCH, GEORGE QUINTUS BR TR 5′ 6″ 158 lbs.
B. Jan. 6, 1859, Philadelphia, Pa. D. Sept. 30, 1937, Philadelphia, Pa.

Year	Team	Lg	W	L	PCT	ERA	G	GS	CG	IP	H	BB	SO	ShO	Relief W	Relief L	Relief SV	AB	H	HR	BA	PO	A	E	DP	TC/G	FA
1888	**WAS**	**N**	0	0	—	0.00	1	0	0	3	2	1	0	0	0	0	0	*				29	3	5	0	1.4	.865

Urban Shocker

SHOCKER, URBAN JAMES BR TR 5′10″ 170 lbs.
Born Urbain Jacques Shockcor.
B. Aug. 22, 1890, Cleveland, Ohio D. Sept. 9, 1928, Denver, Colo.

Year	Team	Lg	W	L	PCT	ERA	G	GS	CG	IP	H	BB	SO	ShO	Relief W	Relief L	Relief SV	AB	H	HR	BA	PO	A	E	DP	TC/G	FA
1916	**NY**	**A**	4	3	.571	2.62	12	9	4	82.1	67	32	43	1	0	1	0	21	4	0	.190	9	18	1	0	2.3	.964
1917			8	5	.615	2.61	26	13	7	145	124	46	68	0	1	1	1	45	8	0	.178	6	50	2	2	2.2	.966
1918	**STL**	**A**	6	5	.545	1.81	14	9	7	94.2	69	40	33	0	2	0	2	34	11	0	.324	8	25	0	3	2.4	1.000
1919			13	11	.542	2.69	30	25	13	211	193	55	86	5	1	1	0	58	8	0	.138	11	48	3	2	2.1	.952
1920			20	10	.667	2.71	38	28	22	245.2	224	70	107	5	2	1	**5**	80	18	0	.225	13	58	1	0	1.9	.986
1921			**27**	12	.692	3.55	47	39	31	326.2	345	86	132	4	2	2	4	104	27	0	.260	21	91	2	1	2.4	.982
1922			24	17	.585	2.97	48	38	29	348	**365**	59	**149**	2	4	1	3	115	22	1	.191	33	59	1	1	1.9	.989
1923			20	12	.625	3.41	43	35	24	277.1	292	49	109	3	0	0	5	80	16	0	.200	11	56	3	3	1.6	.957
1924			16	13	.552	4.17	39	33	17	239.1	262	49	84	4	2	0	1	66	15	0	.227	11	42	0	3	1.4	1.000
1925	**NY**	**A**	12	12	.500	3.65	41	30	15	244.1	278	58	74	2	0	1	2	64	11	0	.172	11	50	0	5	1.5	1.000
1926			19	11	.633	3.38	41	33	19	258.1	272	71	59	0	1	0	2	76	13	0	.171	11	59	1	0	1.7	.986
1927			18	6	.750	2.84	31	27	13	200	207	41	35	2	1	0	0	54	13	0	.241	10	42	1	2	1.7	.981
1928			0	0	—	0.00	1	0	0	2	3	0	0	0	0	0	0	0	0	0	—	0	0	0	0	0.0	.000
13 yrs.			187	117	.615	3.17	411	319	201	2674.2	2701	656	979	28	16	8	25	797	166	1	.208	155	598	15	22	1.9	.980
WORLD SERIES																											
1926	**NY**	**A**	0	1	.000	5.87	2	1	0	7.2	13	0	3	0	0	0	0	2	0	0	.000	0	2	0	0	1.0	1.000

Milt Shoffner

SHOFFNER, MILBURN JAMES BL TL 6′ 1½″ 184 lbs.
B. Nov. 13, 1905, Sherman, Tex. D. Jan. 19, 1978, Madison, Ohio.

Year	Team	Lg	W	L	PCT	ERA	G	GS	CG	IP	H	BB	SO	ShO	Relief W	Relief L	Relief SV	AB	H	HR	BA	PO	A	E	DP	TC/G	FA
1929	**CLE**	**A**	2	3	.400	5.04	11	3	1	44.2	46	22	15	0	2	0	0	15	0	0	.000	1	10	0	1	1.0	1.000
1930			3	4	.429	7.97	24	10	1	84.2	129	50	17	0	1	1	0	33	7	1	.212	3	17	2	2	0.9	.909
1931			2	3	.400	7.24	12	4	1	41	55	26	12	0	1	0	0	13	1	0	.077	3	7	0	0	0.8	1.000
1937	**BOS**	**N**	3	1	.750	2.53	6	5	3	42.2	38	9	13	1	0	0	1	16	2	1	.125	2	12	0	1	2.3	1.000
1938			8	7	.533	3.54	26	15	9	139.2	147	36	49	1	2	1	1	57	12	0	.211	8	19	2	0	1.1	.931
1939	**2 teams**	**BOS N** (25G 4–6)	**CIN N** (10G 2–2)																								
″	**total**		6	8	.429	3.18	35	14	7	170	176	53	57	0	3	0	1	55	8	0	.145	3	37	2	0	1.2	.952
1940	**CIN**	**N**	1	0	1.000	5.63	20	0	0	54.1	56	18	17	0	1	0	0	16	2	0	.125	0	10	0	0	0.5	1.000
7 yrs.			25	26	.490	4.59	134	51	22	577	647	214	180	2	10	2	3	205	32	2	.156	20	112	6	4	1.0	.957

Ernie Shore

SHORE, ERNEST GRADY BR TR 6′ 4″ 220 lbs.
B. Mar. 24, 1891, East Bend, N. C. D. Sept. 24, 1980, Winston-Salem, N. C.

Year	Team	Lg	W	L	PCT	ERA	G	GS	CG	IP	H	BB	SO	ShO	Relief W	Relief L	Relief SV	AB	H	HR	BA	PO	A	E	DP	TC/G	FA
1912	**NY**	**N**	0	0	—	27.00	1	0	0	1	8	1	1	0	0	0	1	0	0	0	—	0	0	1	0	1.0	.000
1914	**BOS**	**A**	10	5	.667	1.89	20	17	10	147.2	111	38	53	1	1	0	1	49	5	0	.102	2	52	2	1	2.8	.964
1915			19	8	.704	1.64	38	32	17	247	207	66	102	4	2	0	0	79	8	0	.101	10	95	7	3	2.9	.938
1916			16	10	.615	2.63	38	28	10	225.2	221	49	62	3	2	2	1	77	7	0	.091	18	90	5	2	3.0	.956
1917			13	10	.565	2.22	29	27	14	226.2	201	55	57	1	1	0	1	78	13	0	.167	19	77	4	5	3.4	.960
1919	**NY**	**A**	5	8	.385	4.17	20	13	3	95	105	44	24	0	2	1	0	28	4	0	.143	5	27	0	0	1.6	1.000
1920			2	2	.500	4.87	14	5	2	44.1	61	21	12	0	0	0	1	11	2	0	.182	1	16	1	0	1.3	.944
7 yrs.			65	43	.602	2.45	160	122	56	987.1	914	274	311	9	8	3	5	322	39	0	.121	55	357	20	11	2.7	.954
WORLD SERIES																											
1915	**BOS**	**A**	1	1	.500	2.12	2	2	2	17	12	8	6	0	0	0	0	5	1	0	.200	0	5	1	0	3.0	.833
1916			2	0	1.000	1.53	2	2	1	17.2	12	4	9	0	0	0	0	7	0	0	.000	2	6	0	1	4.0	1.000
2 yrs.			3	1	.750	1.82	4	4	3	34.2	24	12	15	0	0	0	0	12	1	0	.083	2	11	1	1	3.5	.929

Ray Shore

SHORE, RAYMOND EVERETT BR TR 6′ 3″ 210 lbs.
B. June 9, 1921, Cincinnati, Ohio.

Year	Team	Lg	W	L	PCT	ERA	G	GS	CG	IP	H	BB	SO	ShO	Relief W	Relief L	Relief SV	AB	H	HR	BA	PO	A	E	DP	TC/G	FA
1946	**STL**	**A**	0	0	—	18.00	1	0	0	1	3	1	1	0	0	0	0	0	0	0	—	0	0	0	0	0.0	.000
1948			1	2	.333	6.39	17	4	0	38	40	35	12	0	1	0	0	9	0	0	.000	2	8	0	0	0.6	1.000
1949			0	1	.000	10.80	13	0	0	23.1	27	31	13	0	0	1	0	5	0	0	.000	0	7	0	0	0.5	1.000
3 yrs.			1	3	.250	8.23	31	4	0	62.1	70	67	26	0	1	1	0	14	0	0	.000	2	15	0	0	0.5	1.000

Bill Shores

SHORES, WILLIAM DAVID BR TR 6′ 210 lbs.
B. May 26, 1904, Abilene, Tex. D. Feb. 19, 1984, Purcell, Okla.

Year	Team	Lg	W	L	PCT	ERA	G	GS	CG	IP	H	BB	SO	ShO	Relief Pitching W	L	SV	Batting AB	H	HR	BA	PO	A	E	DP	TC/G	FA
1928	**PHI**	**A**	1	1	.500	3.21	3	2	1	14	13	7	5	0	0	0	0	5	0	0	.000	0	2	0	0	0.7	1.000
1929			11	6	.647	3.60	39	13	5	152.2	150	59	49	1	6	2	7	40	5	0	.125	7	28	3	2	1.0	.921
1930			12	4	.750	4.19	31	19	7	159	169	70	48	1	2	0	0	57	11	0	.193	8	35	3	1	1.5	.935
1931			0	3	.000	5.06	6	2	0	16	26	10	2	0	0	2	0	3	1	0	.333	1	4	1	0	1.0	.833
1933	**NY**	**N**	2	1	.667	3.93	8	3	1	36.2	41	14	20	0	1	0	0	11	3	0	.273	2	13	0	0	1.9	1.000
1936	**CHI**	**A**	0	0	—	9.53	9	0	0	17	26	8	5	0	0	0	0	5	1	0	.200	2	4	0	0	0.7	1.000
6 yrs.			26	15	.634	4.17	96	39	14	395.1	425	168	129	2	9	4	7	121	21	0	.174	20	86	7	3	1.2	.938
WORLD SERIES																											
1930	**PHI**	**A**	0	0	—	13.50	1	0	0	1.1	3	0	0	0	0	0	0	0	0	0	—	0	0	0	0	0.0	.000

Bill Short

SHORT, WILLIAM ROSS BL TL 5′ 9″ 170 lbs.
B. Nov. 27, 1937, Kingston, N. Y.

Year	Team	Lg	W	L	PCT	ERA	G	GS	CG	IP	H	BB	SO	ShO	Relief Pitching W	L	SV	Batting AB	H	HR	BA	PO	A	E	DP	TC/G	FA
1960	**NY**	**A**	3	5	.375	4.79	10	10	2	47	49	30	14	0	0	0	0	15	3	0	.200	7	4	1	1	1.2	.917
1962	**BAL**	**A**	0	0	—	15.75	5	0	0	4	8	6	3	0	0	0	0	1	0	0	.000	0	1	0	0	0.2	1.000
1966	**2 teams**	**BAL A** (6G 2–3)	**BOS A** (8G 0–0)																								
″	**total**		2	3	.400	3.13	14	6	1	46	44	12	29	1	0	0	0	12	1	0	.083	4	11	0	0	1.1	1.000
1967	**PIT**	**N**	0	0	—	3.86	6	0	0	2.1	1	1	1	0	0	0	1	1	0	0	.000	2	1	0	0	0.5	1.000
1968	**NY**	**N**	0	3	.000	4.85	34	0	0	29.2	24	14	24	0	0	3	1	2	0	0	.000	2	9	0	0	0.3	1.000
1969	**CIN**	**N**	0	0	—	15.43	4	0	0	2.1	4	1	0	0	0	0	0	1	0	0	.000	0	0	0	0	0.0	.000
6 yrs.			5	11	.313	4.73	73	16	3	131.1	130	64	71	1	0	3	2	32	4	0	.125	15	26	1	1	0.6	.976

Chris Short

SHORT, CHRISTOPHER JOSEPH BR TL 6′ 4″ 205 lbs.
B. Sept. 19, 1937, Milford, Del. D. Aug. 1, 1991, Wilmington, Del. BB 1970–1971

Year	Team	Lg	W	L	PCT	ERA	G	GS	CG	IP	H	BB	SO	ShO	Relief Pitching W	L	SV	Batting AB	H	HR	BA	PO	A	E	DP	TC/G	FA
1959	**PHI**	**N**	0	0	—	8.16	3	2	0	14.1	19	10	8	0	0	0	0	6	0	0	.000	0	2	0	0	0.7	1.000
1960			6	9	.400	3.94	42	10	2	107.1	101	52	54	0	4	1	3	25	0	0	.000	8	18	1	2	0.6	.963
1961			6	12	.333	5.94	39	16	1	127.1	157	71	80	0	3	4	1	37	6	0	.162	6	20	1	1	0.7	.963
1962			11	9	.550	3.42	47	12	4	142	149	56	91	0	5	4	3	36	8	0	.222	11	22	1	2	0.7	.971
1963			9	12	.429	2.95	38	27	6	198	185	69	160	3	1	1	0	66	7	0	.106	15	46	0	3	1.6	1.000
1964			17	9	.654	2.20	42	31	12	220.2	174	51	181	4	0	0	2	65	7	0	.108	7	35	1	1	1.0	.977
1965			18	11	.621	2.82	47	40	15	297.1	260	89	237	5	0	0	2	99	13	0	.131	9	39	4	3	1.1	.923
1966			20	10	.667	3.54	42	39	19	272	257	68	177	4	1	0	0	106	22	0	.208	14	45	2	3	1.5	.967
1967			9	11	.450	2.39	29	26	8	199.1	163	74	142	2	0	0	1	66	6	0	.091	7	35	0	1	1.4	1.000
1968			19	13	.594	2.94	42	36	9	269.2	236	81	202	2	3	0	1	79	12	0	.152	11	38	2	4	1.2	.961
1969			0	0	—	7.20	2	2	0	10	11	4	5	0	0	0	0	3	0	0	.000	2	1	0	1	1.5	1.000
1970			9	16	.360	4.30	36	34	7	199	211	66	133	2	0	0	1	61	3	0	.049	10	18	1	1	0.8	.966
1971			7	14	.333	3.85	31	26	5	173	182	63	95	2	0	0	1	48	4	0	.083	10	26	3	0	1.3	.923
1972			1	1	.500	3.91	19	0	0	23	24	8	20	0	1	1	1	0	0	0	—	1	2	1	0	0.2	.750
1973	**MIL**	**A**	3	5	.375	5.13	42	7	0	72	86	44	44	0	2	4	2	0	0	0	—	1	11	0	0	0.3	1.000
15 yrs.			135	132	.506	3.43	501	308	88	2325	2215	806	1629	24	20	15	18	697	88	0	.126	112	358	17	22	1.0	.965

Clyde Shoun

SHOUN, CLYDE MITCHELL (Hardrock) BL TL 6′ 1″ 188 lbs.
B. Mar. 20, 1912, Mountain City, Tenn. D. Mar. 20, 1968, Mountain Home, Tenn.

Year	Team	Lg	W	L	PCT	ERA	G	GS	CG	IP	H	BB	SO	ShO	Relief Pitching W	L	SV	Batting AB	H	HR	BA	PO	A	E	DP	TC/G	FA
1935	**CHI**	**N**	1	0	1.000	2.84	5	1	0	12.2	14	5	5	0	0	0	0	3	0	0	.000	0	1	0	0	0.2	1.000
1936			0	0	—	12.46	4	0	0	4.1	3	6	1	0	0	0	0	0	0	0	—	0	2	0	0	0.5	1.000
1937			7	7	.500	5.61	37	9	2	93	118	45	43	0	3	3	0	29	4	0	.138	3	18	2	0	0.6	.913
1938	**STL**	**N**	6	6	.500	4.14	40	12	3	117.1	130	43	37	0	2	2	1	31	8	0	.258	5	19	1	1	0.6	.960
1939			3	1	.750	3.76	**53**	2	0	103	98	42	50	0	3	1	**9**	26	3	0	.115	2	19	1	0	0.4	.955
1940			13	11	.542	3.92	**54**	19	13	197.1	193	46	82	1	3	4	5	63	12	0	.190	11	36	1	3	0.9	.979
1941			3	5	.375	5.66	26	6	0	70	98	20	34	0	3	1	0	22	4	0	.182	1	20	2	2	0.9	.913
1942	**2 teams**	**STL N** (2G 0–0)	**CIN N** (34G 1–3)																								
″	**total**		1	3	.250	2.18	36	0	0	74.1	56	24	32	0	1	3	0	13	4	0	.308	3	21	1	0	0.7	.960
1943	**CIN**	**N**	14	5	.737	3.06	45	5	2	147	131	46	61	0	**13**	3	7	42	13	0	.310	6	32	2	5	0.9	.950
1944			13	10	.565	3.02	38	21	12	202.2	193	42	55	1	3	2	2	67	15	0	.224	3	29	1	1	0.9	.970
1946			1	6	.143	4.10	27	5	0	79	87	26	20	0	1	3	0	21	2	0	.095	0	7	0	0	0.3	1.000
1947	**2 teams**	**CIN N** (10G 0–0)	**BOS N** (26G 5–3)																								
″	**total**		5	3	.625	4.50	36	3	1	88	89	26	30	1	4	1	1	19	3	0	.158	3	12	0	0	0.4	1.000
1948	**BOS**	**N**	5	1	.833	4.01	36	2	1	74	77	20	25	0	4	1	4	21	4	0	.190	5	4	3	1	0.3	.750
1949	**2 teams**	**BOS N** (1G 0–0)	**CHI A** (16G 1–1)																								
″	**total**		1	1	.500	5.55	17	0	0	24.1	38	13	8	0	1	1	0	5	1	0	.200	1	5	0	0	0.4	1.000
14 yrs.			73	59	.553	3.91	454	85	34	1287	1325	404	483	3	41	25	29	362	73	0	.202	43	225	14	13	0.6	.950

Brian Shouse

SHOUSE, BRIAN DOUGLAS BL TL 5′11″ 180 lbs.
B. Sept. 26, 1968, Effingham, Ill.

Year	Team	Lg	W	L	PCT	ERA	G	GS	CG	IP	H	BB	SO	ShO	Relief Pitching W	L	SV	Batting AB	H	HR	BA	PO	A	E	DP	TC/G	FA
1993	**PIT**	**N**	0	0	—	9.00	6	0	0	4	7	2	3	0	0	0	0	0	0	0	—	0	1	0	0	0.2	1.000

Eric Show

SHOW, ERIC VAUGHN BR TR 6′ 1″ 185 lbs.
B. May 19, 1956, Riverside, Calif. D. Mar. 16, 1994, Dulzura, Calif.

Year	Team	Lg	W	L	PCT	ERA	G	GS	CG	IP	H	BB	SO	ShO	Relief Pitching W	L	SV	Batting AB	H	HR	BA	PO	A	E	DP	TC/G	FA
1981	**SD**	**N**	1	3	.250	3.13	15	0	0	23	17	9	22	0	1	3	3	0	0	0	—	0	4	1	0	0.3	.800
1982			10	6	.625	2.64	47	14	2	150	117	48	88	2	6	3	3	41	6	0	.146	4	35	3	1	0.9	.929
1983			15	12	.556	4.17	35	33	4	200.2	201	74	120	2	0	0	0	64	11	0	.172	7	27	4	0	1.1	.895
1984			15	9	.625	3.40	32	32	3	206.2	175	88	104	1	0	0	0	69	17	3	.246	14	28	2	2	1.4	.955
1985			12	11	.522	3.09	35	35	5	233	212	87	141	2	0	0	0	79	10	1	.127	14	24	4	2	1.2	.905
1986			9	5	.643	2.97	24	22	2	136.1	109	69	94	0	1	0	0	43	7	0	.163	6	14	1	1	0.9	.952
1987			8	16	.333	3.84	34	34	5	206.1	188	85	117	3	0	0	0	70	5	0	.071	10	27	3	2	1.2	.925
1988			16	11	.593	3.26	32	32	13	234.2	201	53	144	1	0	0	0	81	12	0	.148	5	21	1	0	0.8	.963
1989			8	6	.571	4.23	16	16	1	106.1	113	39	66	0	0	0	0	34	8	0	.235	4	10	1	1	0.9	.933
1990			6	8	.429	5.76	39	12	0	106.1	131	41	55	0	3	1	1	25	5	0	.200	7	12	1	1	0.5	.950
1991	**OAK**	**A**	1	2	.333	5.92	23	5	0	51.2	62	17	20	0	0	0	0	0	0	0	—	3	4	2	0	0.4	.778
11 yrs.			101	89	.532	3.66	332	235	35	1655	1526	610	971	11	11	7	7	506	81	4	.160	74	206	23	10	0.9	.924

Eric Show *continued*

Year	Team	W	L	PCT	ERA	G	GS	CG	IP	H	BB	SO	ShO	Relief Pitching W	Relief Pitching L	Relief Pitching SV	Batting AB	Batting H	Batting HR	BA	PO	A	E	DP	TC/G	FA
LEAGUE CHAMPIONSHIP SERIES																										
1984	SD N	0	1	.000	13.50	2	2	0	5.1	8	4	2	0	0	0	0	1	0	0	.000	0	0	0	0	0.0	.000
WORLD SERIES																										
1984	SD N	0	1	.000	10.13	1	1	0	2.2	4	1	2	0	0	0	0	0	0	0	—	0	0	0	0	0.0	.000

Lev Shreve

SHREVE, LEVEN LAWRENCE BR TR 5′11″ 150 lbs.
B. Jan. 14, 1869, Louisville, Ky. D. Oct. 18, 1942, Detroit, Mich.

Year	Team	W	L	PCT	ERA	G	GS	CG	IP	H	BB	SO	ShO	Relief W	Relief L	Relief SV	AB	H	HR	BA	PO	A	E	DP	TC/G	FA
1887	2 teams BAL AA (5G 3–1) IND N (14G 5–9)																									
″	total	8	10	.444	4.50	19	19	18	160	174	84	35	2	0	0	0	73	17	0	.233	5	25	5	0	1.7	.857
1888	IND N	11	24	.314	4.63	35	35	34	297.2	352	93	101	1	0	0	0	115	21	0	.183	9	74	16	0	2.8	.838
1889		0	3	.000	13.79	3	3	1	15.2	25	12	5	0	0	0	0	7	0	0	.000	1	5	0	0	2.0	1.000
3 yrs.		19	37	.339	4.89	57	57	53	473.1	551	189	141	3	0	0	0	195	38	0	.195	15	104	21	0	2.3	.850

Harry Shriver

SHRIVER, HARRY GRAYDON (Pop) BR TR 6′ 2″ 180 lbs.
B. Sept. 2, 1896, Wadestown, W. Va. D. Jan. 21, 1970, Morgantown, W. Va.

Year	Team	W	L	PCT	ERA	G	GS	CG	IP	H	BB	SO	ShO	Relief W	Relief L	Relief SV	AB	H	HR	BA	PO	A	E	DP	TC/G	FA
1922	BKN N	4	6	.400	2.99	25	13	4	108.1	114	48	38	2	0	0	0	27	1	0	.037	4	13	1	0	0.7	.944
1923		0	0	—	6.75	1	1	0	4	8	0	1	0	0	0	0	1	0	0	.000	0	0	0	0	0.0	.000
2 yrs.		4	6	.400	3.12	26	14	4	112.1	122	48	39	2	0	0	0	28	1	0	.036	4	13	1	0	0.7	.944

Paul Shuey

SHUEY, PAUL KENNETH BR TR 6′ 3″ 215 lbs.
B. Sept. 16, 1970, Lima, Ohio.

Year	Team	W	L	PCT	ERA	G	GS	CG	IP	H	BB	SO	ShO	Relief W	Relief L	Relief SV	AB	H	HR	BA	PO	A	E	DP	TC/G	FA
1994	CLE A	0	1	.000	8.49	14	0	0	11.2	14	12	16	0	0	1	5	0	0	0	—	0	0	0	0	0.0	.000
1995		0	2	.000	4.26	7	0	0	6.1	5	5	5	0	0	2	0	0	0	0	—	0	2	0	0	0.3	1.000
2 yrs.		0	3	.000	7.00	21	0	0	18	19	17	21	0	0	3	5	0	0	0		0	2	0	0	0.1	1.000

Toots Shultz

SHULTZ, WALLACE LUTHER BR TR 5′10″ 175 lbs.
B. Oct. 10, 1888, Homestead, Pa. D. Jan. 30, 1959, McKeesport, Pa.

Year	Team	W	L	PCT	ERA	G	GS	CG	IP	H	BB	SO	ShO	Relief W	Relief L	Relief SV	AB	H	HR	BA	PO	A	E	DP	TC/G	FA
1911	PHI N	0	3	.000	9.36	5	3	2	25	30	15	9	0	0	0	0	8	2	0	.250	0	9	1	1	2.0	.900
1912		1	4	.200	4.58	22	4	1	59	75	35	20	0	1	2	1	21	5	0	.238	4	17	4	0	1.1	.840
2 yrs.		1	7	.125	6.00	27	7	3	84	105	50	29	0	1	2	1	29	7	0	.241	4	26	5	1	1.3	.857

Harry Shuman

SHUMAN, HARRY BR TR 6′ 2″ 195 lbs.
B. Mar. 5, 1916, Philadelphia, Pa.

Year	Team	W	L	PCT	ERA	G	GS	CG	IP	H	BB	SO	ShO	Relief W	Relief L	Relief SV	AB	H	HR	BA	PO	A	E	DP	TC/G	FA
1942	PIT N	0	0	—	0.00	1	0	0	2	0	1	1	0	0	0	0	0	0	0	—	0	0	0	0	0.0	.000
1943		0	0	—	5.32	11	0	0	22	30	8	5	0	0	0	0	2	0	0	.000	0	7	0	1	0.6	1.000
1944	PHI N	0	0	—	4.05	18	0	0	26.2	26	11	4	0	0	0	0	1	0	0	.000	0	8	3	0	0.6	.727
3 yrs.		0	0		4.44	30	0	0	50.2	56	20	10	0	0	0	0	3	0	0	.000	0	15	3	1	0.6	.833

Paul Siebert

SIEBERT, PAUL EDWARD BL TL 6′ 2″ 205 lbs.
Son of Dick Siebert.
B. June 5, 1953, Minneapolis, Minn.

Year	Team	W	L	PCT	ERA	G	GS	CG	IP	H	BB	SO	ShO	Relief W	Relief L	Relief SV	AB	H	HR	BA	PO	A	E	DP	TC/G	FA
1974	HOU N	1	1	.500	3.60	5	5	1	25	21	11	10	1	0	0	0	6	0	0	.000	1	9	0	0	2.0	1.000
1975		0	2	.000	3.00	7	2	0	18	20	6	6	0	0	1	2	3	0	0	.000	3	4	0	0	1.0	1.000
1976		0	2	.000	3.12	19	0	0	26	29	18	10	0	0	2	0	2	0	0	.000	3	1	1	0	0.3	.800
1977	2 teams SD N (4G 0–0) NY N (25G 2–1)																									
″	total	2	1	.667	3.69	29	0	0	31.2	30	17	21	0	2	1	0	1	0	0	.000	3	2	0	0	0.2	1.000
1978	NY N	0	2	.000	5.14	27	0	0	28	30	21	12	0	0	2	1	1	0	0	.000	3	5	0	0	0.3	1.000
5 yrs.		3	8	.273	3.78	87	7	1	128.2	130	73	59	1	2	6	3	13	0	0	.000	13	21	1	0	0.4	.971

Sonny Siebert

SIEBERT, WILFRED CHARLES BR TR 6′ 3″ 190 lbs.
B. Jan. 14, 1937, St. Mary, Mo.

Year	Team	W	L	PCT	ERA	G	GS	CG	IP	H	BB	SO	ShO	Relief W	Relief L	Relief SV	AB	H	HR	BA	PO	A	E	DP	TC/G	FA
1964	CLE A	7	9	.438	3.23	41	14	3	156	142	57	144	1	1	2	3	49	13	2	.265	6	16	3	1	0.6	.880
1965		16	8	.667	2.43	39	27	4	188.2	139	46	191	1	4	0	1	66	7	1	.106	15	29	2	4	1.2	.957
1966		16	8	**.667**	2.80	34	32	11	241	193	62	163	1	0	0	1	85	11	0	.129	19	46	4	4	2.0	.942
1967		10	12	.455	2.38	34	26	7	185.1	136	54	136	1	1	1	4	52	7	1	.135	8	21	2	2	0.9	.935
1968		12	10	.545	2.97	31	30	8	206	145	88	146	4	0	0	0	70	11	0	.157	18	33	4	2	1.8	.927
1969	2 teams CLE A (2G 0–1) BOS A (43G 14–10)																									
″	total	14	11	.560	3.76	45	24	2	177.1	161	76	133	0	5	1	5	57	9	1	.158	6	36	1	6	1.0	.977
1970	BOS A	15	8	.652	3.43	33	33	7	223	207	60	142	2	0	0	0	77	10	0	.130	25	26	2	3	1.6	.962
1971		16	10	.615	2.91	32	32	12	235	220	60	131	4	0	0	0	79	21	6	.266	15	42	4	0	1.9	.934
1972		12	12	.500	3.80	32	30	7	196.1	204	59	123	3	0	0	0	72	17	1	.236	24	30	2	2	1.8	.964
1973	2 teams BOS A (2G 0–1) TEX A (25G 7–11)																									
″	total	7	12	.368	4.06	27	20	1	122	125	38	81	1	0	2	2	0	0	0		13	25	0	0	1.4	1.000
1974	STL N	8	8	.500	3.83	28	20	5	134	150	51	68	3	1	0	0	44	5	0	.114	6	16	0	3	0.8	1.000
1975	2 teams SD N (6G 3–2) OAK A (17G 4–4)																									
″	total	7	6	.538	3.89	23	19	0	88	97	41	54	0	0	0	0	9	3	0	.333	4	9	2	1	0.7	.867
12 yrs.		140	114	.551	3.21	399	307	67	2152.2	1919	692	1512	21	12	6	16	660	114	12	.173	159	329	26	28	1.3	.949

Dwight Siebler

SIEBLER, DWIGHT LEROY BR TR 6′ 2″ 184 lbs.
B. Aug. 5, 1937, Columbus, Neb.

Year	Team	W	L	PCT	ERA	G	GS	CG	IP	H	BB	SO	ShO	Relief W	Relief L	Relief SV	AB	H	HR	BA	PO	A	E	DP	TC/G	FA
1963	MIN A	2	1	.667	2.79	7	5	2	38.2	25	12	22	0	0	0	0	15	2	0	.133	2	2	0	0	0.6	1.000
1964		0	0	—	4.91	9	0	0	11	10	6	10	0	0	0	0	0	0	0	—	0	1	0	0	0.1	1.000
1965		0	0	—	4.20	7	1	0	15	11	11	15	0	0	0	0	1	0	0	.000	1	2	0	0	0.4	1.000
1966		2	2	.500	3.44	23	2	0	49.2	47	14	24	0	2	2	1	11	0	0	.000	3	5	1	0	0.4	.889
1967		0	0	—	3.00	2	0	0	3	4	1	0	0	0	0	0	0	0	0	—	0	0	0	0	0.0	.000
5 yrs.		4	3	.571	3.45	48	8	2	117.1	97	44	71	0	2	2	1	27	2	0	.074	6	10	1	0	0.4	.941

Candy Sierra

SIERRA, ULISES BR TR 6′ 2″ 190 lbs.
Born Ulises Sierra (Pizarro).
B. Mar. 27, 1967, Rio Piedras, Puerto Rico.

Year	Team	W	L	PCT	ERA	G	GS	CG	IP	H	BB	SO	ShO	Relief W	Relief L	Relief SV	AB	H	HR	BA	PO	A	E	DP	TC/G	FA
1988	2 teams SD N (15G 0–1) CIN N (1G 0–0)																									
″	total	0	1	.000	5.53	16	0	0	27.2	41	12	24	0	0	1	0	4	0	0	.000	1	3	0	0	0.3	1.000

Ed Siever

SIEVER, EDWARD TILDEN BL TL 5′11½″ 190 lbs.
B. Apr. 2, 1877, Goodard, Kans. D. Feb. 5, 1920, Detroit, Mich.

Year	Team	W	L	PCT	ERA	G	GS	CG	IP	H	BB	SO	ShO	Relief Pitching W	Relief Pitching L	Relief Pitching SV	Batting AB	Batting H	HR	BA	PO	A	E	DP	TC/G	FA
1901	DET A	18	15	.545	3.24	38	33	30	288.2	334	65	85	2	1	1	0	107	18	0	.168	16	74	9	5	2.6	.909
1902		8	11	.421	**1.91**	25	23	17	188.1	166	32	36	4	0	0	1	66	10	0	.152	5	40	8	1	2.1	.849
1903	STL A	13	14	.481	2.48	31	27	24	254	245	39	90	1	1	0	0	93	13	0	.140	17	87	8	3	3.6	.929
1904		10	15	.400	2.65	29	24	19	217	235	65	77	2	1	1	0	71	11	0	.155	11	77	4	2	3.1	.957
1906	DET A	14	11	.560	2.71	30	25	20	222.2	240	45	71	1	1	0	0	77	12	0	.156	7	59	1	0	2.2	.985
1907		18	11	.621	2.16	39	33	22	274.2	256	52	88	3	1	0	1	91	14	0	.154	11	69	3	2	2.1	.964
1908		2	6	.250	3.50	11	9	4	61.2	74	13	23	1	0	1	0	18	3	0	.167	5	16	2	0	2.1	.913
7 yrs.		83	83	.500	2.60	203	174	136	1507	1550	311	470	14	5	3	2	523	81	0	.155	72	422	35	13	2.6	.934
WORLD SERIES																										
1907	DET A	0	1	.000	4.50	1	1	0	4	7	0	1	0	0	0	0	1	0	0	.000	1	0	0	0	1.0	1.000

Walter Signer

SIGNER, WALTER DONALD ALOYSIUS BR TR 6′ 165 lbs.
B. Oct. 12, 1910, New York, N. Y. D. July 23, 1974, Greenwich, Conn.

Year	Team	W	L	PCT	ERA	G	GS	CG	IP	H	BB	SO	ShO	Relief Pitching W	Relief Pitching L	Relief Pitching SV	Batting AB	Batting H	HR	BA	PO	A	E	DP	TC/G	FA
1943	CHI N	2	1	.667	2.88	4	2	1	25	24	4	5	0	1	0	0	8	2	0	.250	2	4	0	1	1.5	1.000
1945		0	0	—	3.38	6	0	0	8	11	5	0	0	0	0	1	1	0	0	.000	0	1	0	0	0.2	1.000
2 yrs.		2	1	.667	3.00	10	2	1	33	35	9	5	0	1	0	1	9	2	0	.222	2	5	0	1	0.7	1.000

Seth Sigsby

SIGSBY, SETH DeWITT 6′ 175 lbs.
Born Seth DeWitt.
B. Apr. 30, 1874, Cobleskill, N. Y. D. Sept. 15, 1953, Schenectady, N. Y.

Year	Team	W	L	PCT	ERA	G	GS	CG	IP	H	BB	SO	ShO	Relief Pitching W	Relief Pitching L	Relief Pitching SV	Batting AB	Batting H	HR	BA	PO	A	E	DP	TC/G	FA
1893	NY N	0	0	—	9.00	1	0	0	3	1	4	2	0	0	0	0	1	0	0	.000	0	0	0	0	0.0	.000

Al Sima

SIMA, ALBERT BR TL 6′ 187 lbs.
B. Oct. 7, 1921, Mahwah, N. J. D. Aug. 17, 1993, Suffern, N. Y.

Year	Team	W	L	PCT	ERA	G	GS	CG	IP	H	BB	SO	ShO	Relief Pitching W	Relief Pitching L	Relief Pitching SV	Batting AB	Batting H	HR	BA	PO	A	E	DP	TC/G	FA
1950	WAS A	4	5	.444	4.79	17	9	1	77	89	26	23	0	1	0	0	26	3	0	.115	1	10	0	0	0.6	1.000
1951		3	7	.300	4.79	18	8	1	77	79	41	26	0	1	2	0	17	3	1	.176	1	14	2	0	0.9	.882
1953		2	3	.400	3.42	31	5	1	68.1	63	31	25	0	2	0	1	17	2	0	.118	3	15	0	2	0.6	1.000
1954	2 teams CHI A (5G 0–1) PHI A (29G 2–5)																									
″	total	2	6	.250	5.21	34	8	1	86.1	112	34	37	0	1	1	3	22	1	0	.045	2	13	2	0	0.5	.882
4 yrs.		11	21	.344	4.61	100	30	4	308.2	343	132	111	0	5	3	4	82	9	1	.110	7	52	4	2	0.6	.937

Bill Simas

SIMAS, WILLIAM ANTHONY BL TR 6′ 3″ 200 lbs.
B. Nov. 28, 1971, Hanford, Calif.

Year	Team	W	L	PCT	ERA	G	GS	CG	IP	H	BB	SO	ShO	Relief Pitching W	Relief Pitching L	Relief Pitching SV	Batting AB	Batting H	HR	BA	PO	A	E	DP	TC/G	FA
1995	CHI A	1	1	.500	2.57	14	0	0	14	15	10	16	0	1	1	0	0	0	0	—	0	0	0	0	0.0	.000

Curt Simmons

SIMMONS, CURTIS THOMAS BL TL 5′11″ 175 lbs.
B. May 19, 1929, Egypt, Pa.

Year	Team	W	L	PCT	ERA	G	GS	CG	IP	H	BB	SO	ShO	Relief Pitching W	Relief Pitching L	Relief Pitching SV	Batting AB	Batting H	HR	BA	PO	A	E	DP	TC/G	FA
1947	PHI N	1	0	1.000	1.00	1	1	1	9	5	6	9	0	0	0	0	2	1	0	.500	0	0	0	0	0.0	.000
1948		7	12	.368	4.87	31	23	7	170	169	108	86	0	0	0	0	51	7	0	.137	4	34	2	4	1.3	.950
1949		4	10	.286	4.59	38	14	2	131.1	133	55	83	0	1	3	1	41	7	0	.171	5	22	2	0	0.8	.931
1950		17	8	.680	3.40	31	27	11	214.2	178	88	146	2	2	0	1	77	12	0	.156	12	32	0	2	1.4	1.000
1952		14	8	.636	2.82	28	28	15	201.1	170	70	141	**6**	0	0	0	67	11	1	.164	3	25	0	0	1.0	1.000
1953		16	13	.552	3.21	32	30	19	238	211	82	138	4	0	0	0	93	13	0	.140	3	30	2	2	1.1	.943
1954		14	15	.483	2.81	34	33	21	253	226	98	125	3	0	0	1	91	16	0	.176	6	33	3	1	1.2	.929
1955		8	8	.500	4.92	25	22	3	130	148	50	58	0	1	1	0	46	8	0	.174	8	17	1	1	1.0	.962
1956		15	10	.600	3.36	33	27	14	198	186	65	88	0	1	0	0	72	17	0	.236	4	35	1	3	1.2	.975
1957		12	11	.522	3.44	32	29	9	212	214	50	92	2	0	0	0	71	17	0	.239	8	26	0	0	1.1	1.000
1958		7	14	.333	4.38	29	27	7	168.1	196	40	78	1	0	0	1	59	12	0	.203	14	21	2	1	1.3	.946
1959		0	0	—	4.50	7	0	0	10	16	0	4	0	0	0	0	0	0	0	—	0	2	0	0	0.3	1.000
1960	2 teams PHI N (4G 0–0) STL N (23G 7–4)																									
″	total	7	4	.636	3.06	27	19	3	156	162	37	67	1	0	0	0	47	10	0	.213	7	30	1	5	1.4	.974
1961	STL N	9	10	.474	3.13	30	29	6	195.2	203	64	99	2	0	0	0	66	20	0	.303	6	36	1	4	1.4	.977
1962		10	10	.500	3.51	31	22	9	154	167	32	74	4	0	3	0	50	8	0	.160	6	26	1	2	1.1	.970
1963		15	9	.625	2.48	32	32	11	232.2	209	48	127	6	0	0	0	81	13	0	.160	12	23	0	0	1.1	1.000
1964		18	9	.667	3.43	34	34	12	244	233	49	104	3	0	0	0	94	10	0	.106	12	45	2	0	1.7	.966
1965		9	15	.375	4.08	34	32	5	203	229	54	96	0	0	0	0	64	3	0	.047	8	32	1	0	1.2	.976
1966	2 teams STL N (10G 1–1) CHI N (19G 4–7)																									
″	total	5	8	.385	4.23	29	15	4	110.2	114	35	38	1	2	2	0	26	3	0	.115	5	26	2	0	1.1	.939
1967	2 teams CHI N (17G 3–7) CAL A (14G 2–1)																									
″	total	5	8	.385	4.24	31	18	4	116.2	144	32	44	1	1	0	1	37	6	0	.162	4	19	2	1	0.8	.920
20 yrs.		193	182	.515	3.54	569	462	163	3348.1	3313	1063	1697	36	8	9	5	1135	194	1	.171	127	514	23	26	1.2	.965
WORLD SERIES																										
1964	STL N	0	1	.000	2.51	2	2	0	14.1	11	3	8	0	0	0	0	4	2	0	.500	2	1	0	0	1.5	1.000

Pat Simmons

SIMMONS, PATRICK CLEMENT BR TR 5′11″ 172 lbs.
Born Patrick Clement Simoni.
B. Nov. 29, 1908, Watervliet, N. Y. D. July 3, 1968, Albany, N. Y.

Year	Team	W	L	PCT	ERA	G	GS	CG	IP	H	BB	SO	ShO	Relief Pitching W	Relief Pitching L	Relief Pitching SV	Batting AB	Batting H	HR	BA	PO	A	E	DP	TC/G	FA
1928	BOS A	0	2	.000	4.04	31	3	0	69	69	38	16	0	0	0	1	15	2	0	.133	3	15	1	0	0.6	.947
1929		0	0	—	0.00	2	0	0	7	6	3	2	0	0	0	1	1	0	0	.000	1	0	0	0	0.5	1.000
2 yrs.		0	2	.000	3.67	33	3	0	76	75	41	18	0	0	0	2	16	2	0	.125	4	15	1	0	0.6	.950

Doug Simons

SIMONS, DOUGLAS EUGENE BL TL 6′ 160 lbs.
B. Sept. 15, 1966, Bakersfield, Calif.

Year	Team	W	L	PCT	ERA	G	GS	CG	IP	H	BB	SO	ShO	Relief Pitching W	Relief Pitching L	Relief Pitching SV	Batting AB	Batting H	HR	BA	PO	A	E	DP	TC/G	FA
1991	NY N	2	3	.400	5.19	42	1	0	60.2	55	19	38	0	2	2	1	3	0	0	.000	6	16	0	0	0.5	1.000
1992	MON N	0	0	—	23.63	7	0	0	5.1	15	2	6	0	0	0	0	0	0	0	—	0	0	1	0	0.1	.000
2 yrs.		2	3	.400	6.68	49	1	0	66	70	21	44	0	2	2	1	3	0	0	.000	6	16	1	0	0.5	.957

Duke Simpson

SIMPSON, THOMAS LEO BR TR 6′ 1½″ 190 lbs.
B. Sept. 15, 1927, Columbus, Ohio.

Year	Team	W	L	PCT	ERA	G	GS	CG	IP	H	BB	SO	ShO	Relief Pitching W	Relief Pitching L	Relief Pitching SV	Batting AB	Batting H	HR	BA	PO	A	E	DP	TC/G	FA
1953	CHI N	1	2	.333	8.00	30	1	0	45	60	25	21	0	1	1	0	8	2	0	.250	4	6	0	2	0.3	1.000

Year	Team		W	L	PCT	ERA	G	GS	CG	IP	H	BB	SO	ShO	Relief Pitching W	Relief Pitching L	Relief Pitching SV	Batting AB	Batting H	Batting HR	BA	PO	A	E	DP	TC/G	FA

Joe Simpson

SIMPSON, JOE ALLEN BL TL 6′ 3″ 175 lbs.
B. Dec. 31, 1951, Purcell, Okla.

Year	Team		W	L	PCT	ERA	G	GS	CG	IP	H	BB	SO	ShO	W	L	SV	AB	H	HR	BA	PO	A	E	DP	TC/G	FA
1983	KC	A	0	0	—	3.00	2	0	0	3	4	2	1	0	0	0	0	*				5	0	0	0	0.8	1.000

Steve Simpson

SIMPSON, STEVEN EDWARD BR TR 6′ 3″ 200 lbs.
B. Aug. 30, 1948, St. Joseph, Mo. D. Nov. 2, 1989, Omaha, Neb.

Year	Team		W	L	PCT	ERA	G	GS	CG	IP	H	BB	SO	ShO	W	L	SV	AB	H	HR	BA	PO	A	E	DP	TC/G	FA
1972	SD	N	0	2	.000	4.76	9	0	0	11.1	10	8	9	0	0	2	2	0	0	0	—	0	1	0	0	0.1	1.000

Wayne Simpson

SIMPSON, WAYNE KIRBY BR TR 6′ 3″ 220 lbs.
B. Dec. 2, 1948, Los Angeles, Calif.

Year	Team		W	L	PCT	ERA	G	GS	CG	IP	H	BB	SO	ShO	W	L	SV	AB	H	HR	BA	PO	A	E	DP	TC/G	FA
1970	CIN	N	14	3	.824	3.02	26	26	10	176	125	81	119	2	0	0	0	64	6	0	.094	22	30	2	2	2.1	.963
1971			4	7	.364	4.77	22	21	1	117	106	77	61	0	0	0	0	32	1	0	.031	4	30	1	0	1.6	.971
1972			8	5	.615	4.14	24	22	1	130.1	124	49	70	0	0	0	0	48	3	0	.063	3	8	1	1	0.5	.917
1973	KC	A	3	4	.429	5.70	16	10	1	60	66	35	29	0	0	0	0	0	0	0	—	6	7	1	0	0.9	.929
1975	PHI	N	1	0	1.000	3.19	7	5	0	31	31	11	19	0	0	0	0	9	2	0	.222	6	4	0	0	1.4	1.000
1977	CAL	A	6	12	.333	5.83	27	23	0	122	154	62	55	0	0	1	0	0	0	0	—	7	13	1	1	0.8	.952
6 yrs.			36	31	.537	4.37	122	107	13	636.1	606	315	353	2	0	1	0	153	12	0	.078	48	92	6	4	1.2	.959

Pete Sims

SIMS, CLARENCE BR TR 5′11½″ 165 lbs.
B. May 24, 1891, Crown City, Ohio D. Dec. 2, 1968, Dallas, Tex.

Year	Team		W	L	PCT	ERA	G	GS	CG	IP	H	BB	SO	ShO	W	L	SV	AB	H	HR	BA	PO	A	E	DP	TC/G	FA
1915	STL	A	1	0	1.000	4.32	3	2	0	8.1	6	6	4	0	0	0	0	1	1	0	1.000	2	1	2	0	1.7	.600

Bert Sincock

SINCOCK, HERBERT SYLVESTER BL TL 5′10½″ 165 lbs.
B. Sept. 8, 1887, Barkerville, B. C., Canada D. Aug. 1, 1946, Houghton, Mich.

Year	Team		W	L	PCT	ERA	G	GS	CG	IP	H	BB	SO	ShO	W	L	SV	AB	H	HR	BA	PO	A	E	DP	TC/G	FA
1908	CIN	N	0	0	—	3.86	1	0	0	4.2	3	0	1	0	0	0	0	2	0	0	.000	0	1	0	0	1.0	1.000

Bill Singer

SINGER, WILLIAM ROBERT (The Singer Throwing Machine) BR TR 6′ 4″ 184 lbs.
B. Apr. 24, 1944, Los Angeles, Calif.

Year	Team		W	L	PCT	ERA	G	GS	CG	IP	H	BB	SO	ShO	W	L	SV	AB	H	HR	BA	PO	A	E	DP	TC/G	FA
1964	LA	N	0	1	.000	3.21	2	2	0	14	11	12	3	0	0	0	0	6	1	0	.167	0	3	0	0	1.5	1.000
1965			0	0	—	0.00	2	0	0	1	2	2	1	0	0	0	0	0	0	0	—	0	0	0	0	0.0	.000
1966			0	0	—	0.00	3	0	0	4	4	2	4	0	0	0	0	0	0	0	—	0	1	0	0	0.3	1.000
1967			12	8	.600	2.64	32	29	7	204.1	185	61	169	3	0	1	0	67	6	0	.090	10	37	5	0	1.6	.904
1968			13	17	.433	2.88	37	36	12	256.1	227	78	227	6	0	1	0	81	12	0	.148	13	41	7	0	1.6	.885
1969			20	12	.625	2.34	41	40	16	316	244	74	247	2	0	0	1	108	11	0	.102	14	41	2	0	1.4	.965
1970			8	5	.615	3.14	16	16	5	106	79	32	93	3	0	0	0	38	5	0	.132	8	12	3	0	1.4	.870
1971			10	17	.370	4.17	31	31	8	203	195	71	144	1	0	0	0	58	6	0	.103	8	24	1	2	1.1	.970
1972			6	16	.273	3.67	26	25	4	169.1	148	60	101	3	0	1	0	55	4	0	.073	7	28	2	2	1.4	.946
1973	CAL	A	20	14	.588	3.22	40	40	19	315.2	280	130	241	2	0	0	0	0	0	0	—	13	38	5	1	1.4	.911
1974			7	4	.636	2.97	14	14	8	109	102	43	77	0	0	0	0	0	0	0	—	6	16	1	0	1.6	.957
1975			7	15	.318	4.98	29	27	8	179	171	81	78	0	0	0	1	0	0	0	—	7	28	3	1	1.3	.921
1976	2 teams	TEX A (10G 4–1)	MIN A (26G 9–9)																								
"	total		13	10	.565	3.69	36	36	7	236.2	233	96	97	4	0	0	0	0	0	0		7	31	3	0	1.1	.927
1977	TOR	A	2	8	.200	6.75	13	12	0	60	71	39	33	0	0	0	0	0	0	0	—	2	10	2	10	1.1	.857
14 yrs.			118	127	.482	3.39	322	308	94	2174.1	1952	781	1515	24	0	3	2	413	45	0	.109	95	310	34	16	1.4	.923

Elmer Singleton

SINGLETON, BERT ELMER (Smoky) BR TR 6′ 2″ 174 lbs.
B. June 26, 1918, Ogden, Utah D. Jan. 5, 1996, Ogden, Utah. BB 1957–1958

Year	Team		W	L	PCT	ERA	G	GS	CG	IP	H	BB	SO	ShO	W	L	SV	AB	H	HR	BA	PO	A	E	DP	TC/G	FA
1945	BOS	N	1	4	.200	4.82	7	5	1	37.1	35	14	14	0	0	0	0	11	0	0	.000	0	8	1	0	1.3	.889
1946			0	1	.000	3.74	15	2	0	33.2	27	21	17	0	0	0	1	4	0	0	.000	3	6	0	0	0.6	1.000
1947	PIT	N	2	2	.500	6.31	36	3	0	67	70	39	24	0	2	0	1	13	4	0	.308	9	11	1	1	0.6	.952
1948			4	6	.400	4.97	38	5	1	92.1	90	40	53	0	3	4	2	23	2	0	.087	13	18	0	1	0.8	1.000
1950	WAS	A	1	2	.333	5.20	21	1	0	36.1	39	17	19	0	1	2	0	7	3	0	.429	5	7	0	1	0.6	1.000
1957	CHI	N	0	1	.000	6.75	5	2	0	13.1	20	2	6	0	0	1	0	3	0	0	.000	2	4	2	1	1.6	.750
1958			1	0	1.000	0.00	2	0	0	4.2	1	1	2	0	1	0	0	1	0	0	.000	1	0	0	0	0.5	1.000
1959			2	1	.667	2.72	21	1	0	43	40	12	25	0	1	1	0	6	0	0	.000	5	10	1	1	0.8	.938
8 yrs.			11	17	.393	4.83	145	19	2	327.2	322	146	160	0	8	8	4	68	9	0	.132	38	64	5	5	0.7	.953

John Singleton

SINGLETON, JOHN EDWARD (Sheriff) BR TR 5′11″ 171 lbs.
B. Nov. 27, 1896, Gallipolis, Ohio D. Oct. 23, 1937, Dayton, Ohio.

Year	Team		W	L	PCT	ERA	G	GS	CG	IP	H	BB	SO	ShO	W	L	SV	AB	H	HR	BA	PO	A	E	DP	TC/G	FA
1922	PHI	N	1	10	.091	5.90	22	9	3	93	127	38	27	1	0	3	0	36	5	0	.139	2	19	3	1	1.1	.875

Mike Sirotka

SIROTKA, MICHAEL ROBERT BL TL 6′ 1″ 190 lbs.
B. May 13, 1971, Houston, Tex.

Year	Team		W	L	PCT	ERA	G	GS	CG	IP	H	BB	SO	ShO	W	L	SV	AB	H	HR	BA	PO	A	E	DP	TC/G	FA
1995	CHI	A	1	2	.333	4.19	6	6	0	34.1	39	17	19	0	0	0	0	0	0	0	—	1	5	0	0	1.0	1.000

Doug Sisk

SISK, DOUGLAS RANDALL BR TR 6′ 2″ 210 lbs.
B. Sept. 26, 1957, Renton, Wash.

Year	Team		W	L	PCT	ERA	G	GS	CG	IP	H	BB	SO	ShO	W	L	SV	AB	H	HR	BA	PO	A	E	DP	TC/G	FA
1982	NY	N	0	1	.000	1.04	8	0	0	8.2	5	4	4	0	0	1	1	0	0	0	—	0	2	0	0	0.3	1.000
1983			5	4	.556	2.24	67	0	0	104.1	88	59	33	0	5	4	11	6	3	0	.500	7	14	1	1	0.3	.955
1984			1	3	.250	2.09	50	0	0	77.2	57	54	32	0	1	3	15	11	1	0	.091	5	13	1	1	0.4	.947
1985			4	5	.444	5.30	42	0	0	73	86	40	26	0	4	5	2	12	0	0	.000	3	15	0	0	0.4	1.000
1986			4	2	.667	3.06	41	0	0	70.2	77	31	31	0	4	2	1	4	0	0	.000	10	6	0	0	0.4	1.000
1987			3	1	.750	3.46	55	0	0	78	83	22	37	0	3	1	3	5	0	0	.000	5	19	0	0	0.4	1.000
1988	BAL	A	3	3	.500	3.72	52	0	0	94.1	109	45	26	0	3	3	0	0	0	0	—	9	16	3	1	0.5	.893
1990	ATL	N	0	0	—	3.86	3	0	0	2.1	1	4	1	0	0	0	0	0	0	0	—	0	1	0	0	0.3	1.000
1991			2	1	.667	5.02	14	0	0	14.1	21	8	5	0	2	1	0	0	0	0	—	3	2	0	1	0.4	1.000
9 yrs.			22	20	.524	3.27	332	0	0	523.1	527	267	195	0	22	20	33	38	4	0	.105	42	88	5	4	0.4	.963
LEAGUE CHAMPIONSHIP SERIES																											
1986	NY	N	0	0	—	0.00	1	0	0	1	1	1	0	0	0	0	0	0	0	0	—	0	0	0	0	0.0	.000
WORLD SERIES																											
1986	NY	N	0	0	—	0.00	1	0	0	0.2	0	1	1	0	0	0	0	0	0	0	—	0	0	0	0	0.0	.000

Tommie Sisk

SISK, TOMMIE WAYNE BR TR 6′ 3″ 195 lbs.
B. Apr. 12, 1942, Ardmore, Okla.

Year	Team	Lg	W	L	PCT	ERA	G	GS	CG	IP	H	BB	SO	ShO	Relief Pitching W	Relief Pitching L	Relief Pitching SV	Batting AB	Batting H	Batting HR	BA	PO	A	E	DP	TC/G	FA
1962	PIT	N	0	2	.000	4.08	5	3	1	17.2	18	8	6	0	0	0	0	5	1	0	.200	1	2	1	0	0.8	.750
1963			1	3	.250	2.92	57	4	1	108	85	45	73	0	1	1	1	16	1	0	.063	3	24	1	2	0.5	.964
1964			1	4	.200	6.16	42	1	0	61.1	91	29	35	0	1	4	0	8	0	0	.000	7	17	0	0	0.6	1.000
1965			7	3	.700	3.40	38	12	1	111.1	103	50	66	1	3	0	0	33	2	0	.061	4	17	1	0	0.6	.955
1966			10	5	.667	4.14	34	23	4	150	146	52	60	1	2	0	1	51	5	0	.098	9	27	2	3	1.1	.947
1967			13	13	.500	3.34	37	31	11	207.2	196	78	85	2	0	0	1	69	7	0	.101	18	38	2	4	1.6	.966
1968			5	5	.500	3.28	33	11	0	96	101	35	41	0	3	1	1	24	2	0	.083	11	16	3	3	0.9	.900
1969	SD	N	2	13	.133	4.78	53	13	1	143	160	48	59	0	1	3	6	25	3	0	.120	15	24	0	0	0.7	1.000
1970	CHI	A	1	1	.500	5.45	17	1	0	33	37	13	16	0	1	1	0	4	1	0	.250	1	8	1	1	0.6	.900
9 yrs.			40	49	.449	3.92	316	99	19	928	937	358	441	4	12	10	10	235	22	0	.094	69	173	11	13	0.8	.957

Dave Sisler

SISLER, DAVID MICHAEL BR TR 6′ 4″ 200 lbs.
Brother of Dick Sisler. Son of George Sisler.
B. Oct. 16, 1931, St. Louis, Mo.

Year	Team	Lg	W	L	PCT	ERA	G	GS	CG	IP	H	BB	SO	ShO	Relief Pitching W	Relief Pitching L	Relief Pitching SV	Batting AB	Batting H	Batting HR	BA	PO	A	E	DP	TC/G	FA
1956	BOS	A	9	8	.529	4.62	39	14	3	142.1	120	72	93	0	3	3	3	42	5	0	.119	9	22	0	0	0.8	1.000
1957			7	8	.467	4.71	22	19	5	122.1	135	61	55	0	0	0	1	42	7	0	.167	13	22	1	3	1.6	.972
1958			8	9	.471	4.94	30	25	4	149.1	157	79	71	1	1	1	0	46	9	0	.196	7	22	2	1	1.0	.935
1959	2 teams	BOS A	(3G 0–0)		DET A	(32G 1–3)																					
″	total		1	3	.250	4.32	35	0	0	58.1	55	37	32	0	1	3	7	7	2	0	.286	1	7	0	0	0.2	1.000
1960	DET	A	7	5	.583	2.48	41	0	0	80	56	45	47	0	7	5	6	16	2	0	.125	5	18	1	2	0.6	.958
1961	WAS	A	2	8	.200	4.18	45	1	0	60.1	55	48	30	0	2	7	11	6	0	0	.000	4	11	0	1	0.3	1.000
1962	CIN	N	4	3	.571	3.92	35	0	0	43.2	44	26	27	0	4	3	1	0	0	0	—	3	5	0	0	0.2	1.000
7 yrs.			38	44	.463	4.33	247	59	12	656.1	622	368	355	1	18	22	29	159	25	0	.157	42	107	4	7	0.6	.974

George Sisler

SISLER, GEORGE HAROLD (Gorgeous George) BL TL 5′11″ 170 lbs.
Father of Dick Sisler. Father of Dave Sisler.
B. Mar. 24, 1893, Manchester, Ohio D. Mar. 26, 1973, Richmond Heights, Mo.
Manager 1924–26.
Hall of Fame 1939.

Year	Team	Lg	W	L	PCT	ERA	G	GS	CG	IP	H	BB	SO	ShO	Relief Pitching W	Relief Pitching L	Relief Pitching SV	Batting AB	Batting H	Batting HR	BA	PO	A	E	DP	TC/G	FA
1915	STL	A	4	4	.500	2.83	15	8	6	70	62	38	41	0	1	1	0	274	78	3	.285	413	38	7	21	5.7	.985
1916			1	2	.333	1.00	3	3	3	27	18	6	12	1	0	0	0	580	177	4	.305	1523	97	24	87	11.2	.985
1918			0	0	—	4.50	2	1	0	8	10	4	4	0	0	0	1	452	154	2	.341	1386	106	24	97	11.2	.984
1920			0	0	—	0.00	1	0	0	1	0	0	2	0	0	0	1	631	257	19	.407	1244	97	13	65	11.7	.990
1925			0	0	—	0.00	1	0	0	2	1	1	1	0	0	0	0	649	224	12	.345	1249	120	13	62	10.5	.991
1926			0	0	—	0.00	1	0	0	2	0	2	3	0	0	0	1	613	178	7	.290	1467	88	21	141	10.5	.987
1928	BOS	N	0	0	—	0.00	1	0	0	1	0	1	0	0	0	0	0	540	179	4	.331	1374	131	24	138	10.3	.984
7 yrs.			5	6	.455	2.35	24	12	9	111	91	52	63	1	1	1	3	*				18896	1572	274	1471	10.2	.987

Carl Sitton

SITTON, CARL VETTER BR TR 5′10½″ 170 lbs.
B. Sept. 22, 1882, Pendleton, S. C. D. Sept. 11, 1931, Valdosta, Ga.

Year	Team	Lg	W	L	PCT	ERA	G	GS	CG	IP	H	BB	SO	ShO	Relief Pitching W	Relief Pitching L	Relief Pitching SV	Batting AB	Batting H	Batting HR	BA	PO	A	E	DP	TC/G	FA
1909	CLE	A	3	2	.600	2.88	14	5	3	50	50	16	16	0	0	0	0	13	2	0	.154	3	11	1	1	1.1	.933

Pete Sivess

SIVESS, PETER BR TR 6′ 3½″ 195 lbs.
B. Sept. 23, 1913, South River, N. J.

Year	Team	Lg	W	L	PCT	ERA	G	GS	CG	IP	H	BB	SO	ShO	Relief Pitching W	Relief Pitching L	Relief Pitching SV	Batting AB	Batting H	Batting HR	BA	PO	A	E	DP	TC/G	FA
1936	PHI	N	3	4	.429	4.57	17	6	2	65	84	36	22	0	1	0	0	25	3	0	.120	3	6	0	1	0.5	1.000
1937			1	1	.500	8.10	6	2	1	20	30	11	4	0	0	0	0	6	0	0	.000	1	2	0	0	0.5	1.000
1938			3	6	.333	5.51	39	8	2	116	143	69	32	0	2	1	3	32	6	0	.188	5	21	2	2	0.7	.929
3 yrs.			7	11	.389	5.46	62	16	5	201	257	116	58	0	3	1	3	63	9	0	.143	9	29	2	3	0.6	.950

Jim Siwy

SIWY, JAMES GERARD BR TR 6′ 4″ 200 lbs.
B. Sept. 20, 1958, Pawtucket, R. I.

Year	Team	Lg	W	L	PCT	ERA	G	GS	CG	IP	H	BB	SO	ShO	Relief Pitching W	Relief Pitching L	Relief Pitching SV	Batting AB	Batting H	Batting HR	BA	PO	A	E	DP	TC/G	FA
1982	CHI	A	0	0	—	10.29	2	1	0	7	10	5	3	0	0	0	0	0	0	0	—	0	0	0	0	0.0	.000
1984			0	0	—	2.08	1	0	0	4.1	3	2	1	0	0	0	0	0	0	0	—	0	1	0	0	1.0	1.000
2 yrs.			0	0		7.15	3	1	0	11.1	13	7	4	0	0	0	0	0	0	0		0	1	0	0	0.3	1.000

Joe Skalski

SKALSKI, JOSEPH DOUGLAS BR TR 6′ 3″ 190 lbs.
B. Sept. 26, 1964, Burnham, Ill.

Year	Team	Lg	W	L	PCT	ERA	G	GS	CG	IP	H	BB	SO	ShO	Relief Pitching W	Relief Pitching L	Relief Pitching SV	Batting AB	Batting H	Batting HR	BA	PO	A	E	DP	TC/G	FA
1989	CLE	A	0	2	.000	6.75	2	1	0	6.2	7	4	3	0	0	1	0	0	0	0	—	0	1	0	0	0.5	1.000

Dave Skaugstad

SKAUGSTAD, DAVID WENDELL BL TL 6′ 1″ 179 lbs.
B. Jan. 10, 1940, Algona, Iowa.

Year	Team	Lg	W	L	PCT	ERA	G	GS	CG	IP	H	BB	SO	ShO	Relief Pitching W	Relief Pitching L	Relief Pitching SV	Batting AB	Batting H	Batting HR	BA	PO	A	E	DP	TC/G	FA
1957	CIN	N	0	0	—	1.59	2	0	0	5.2	4	6	4	0	0	0	0	1	0	0	.000	1	2	0	0	1.5	1.000

Dave Skeels

SKEELS, DAVID BL TR 6′ 1″ 187 lbs.
B. Dec. 29, 1892, Addy, Wash. D. Dec. 3, 1926, Spokane, Wash.

Year	Team	Lg	W	L	PCT	ERA	G	GS	CG	IP	H	BB	SO	ShO	Relief Pitching W	Relief Pitching L	Relief Pitching SV	Batting AB	Batting H	Batting HR	BA	PO	A	E	DP	TC/G	FA
1910	DET	A	0	0	—	12.00	1	1	0	6	9	4	2	0	0	0	0	3	0	0	.000	0	4	0	0	4.0	1.000

Craig Skok

SKOK, CRAIG RICHARD BR TL 6′ 190 lbs.
B. Sept. 1, 1947, Dobbs Ferry, N. Y.

Year	Team	Lg	W	L	PCT	ERA	G	GS	CG	IP	H	BB	SO	ShO	Relief Pitching W	Relief Pitching L	Relief Pitching SV	Batting AB	Batting H	Batting HR	BA	PO	A	E	DP	TC/G	FA
1973	BOS	A	0	1	.000	6.21	11	0	0	29	35	11	22	0	0	1	1	0	0	0	—	1	2	0	0	0.3	1.000
1976	TEX	A	0	1	.000	12.60	9	0	0	5	13	3	5	0	0	1	0	0	0	0	—	0	1	0	0	0.1	1.000
1978	ATL	N	3	2	.600	4.35	43	0	0	62	64	27	28	0	3	2	2	8	2	0	.250	3	9	0	0	0.3	1.000
1979			1	3	.250	4.00	44	0	0	54	58	17	30	0	1	3	2	3	0	0	.000	0	10	0	1	0.2	1.000
4 yrs.			4	7	.364	4.86	107	0	0	150	170	58	85	0	4	7	5	11	2	0	.182	4	22	0	1	0.2	1.000

John Skopec

SKOPEC, JOHN S. (Buckshot) BR TL 5′10″ 190 lbs.
B. May 8, 1880, Chicago, Ill. D. Oct. 12, 1912, Chicago, Ill.

Year	Team	Lg	W	L	PCT	ERA	G	GS	CG	IP	H	BB	SO	ShO	Relief Pitching W	Relief Pitching L	Relief Pitching SV	Batting AB	Batting H	Batting HR	BA	PO	A	E	DP	TC/G	FA
1901	CHI	A	6	3	.667	3.16	9	9	6	68.1	62	45	24	0	0	0	0	30	10	1	.333	3	32	3	1	4.2	.921
1903	DET	A	2	2	.500	3.43	6	5	3	39.1	46	13	14	0	0	0	0	13	2	0	.154	0	14	2	0	2.7	.875
2 yrs.			8	5	.615	3.26	15	14	9	107.2	108	58	38	0	0	0	0	43	12	1	.279	3	46	5	1	3.6	.907

John Slagle

SLAGLE, JOHN A. BL TR
B. Lawrence, Ind. Deceased.

Year	Team	W	L	PCT	ERA	G	GS	CG	IP	H	BB	SO	ShO	Relief Pitching W	Relief Pitching L	Relief Pitching SV	Batting AB	Batting H	Batting HR	BA	PO	A	E	DP	TC/G	FA
1891	**CIN AA**	0	0	—	0.00	1	0	0	1.1	3	1	1	0	0	0	1	1	0	0	.000	0	0	0	0	0.0	.000

Roger Slagle

SLAGLE, ROGER LEE BR TR 6′ 3″ 190 lbs.
B. Nov. 4, 1953, Wichita., Kans.

Year	Team	W	L	PCT	ERA	G	GS	CG	IP	H	BB	SO	ShO	Relief Pitching W	Relief Pitching L	Relief Pitching SV	Batting AB	Batting H	Batting HR	BA	PO	A	E	DP	TC/G	FA
1979	**NY A**	0	0	—	0.00	1	0	0	2	0	0	2	0	0	0	0	0	0	0	—	1	0	0	0	1.0	1.000

Walt Slagle

SLAGLE, WALTER JENNINGS BB TR 6′ 165 lbs.
B. Dec. 15, 1878, Kenton, Ohio D. June 17, 1974, San Gabriel, Calif.

Year	Team	W	L	PCT	ERA	G	GS	CG	IP	H	BB	SO	ShO	Relief Pitching W	Relief Pitching L	Relief Pitching SV	Batting AB	Batting H	Batting HR	BA	PO	A	E	DP	TC/G	FA
1910	**CIN N**	0	0	—	9.00	1	0	0	1	0	3	0	0	0	0	0	0	0	0	—	0	0	0	0	0.0	.000

Cy Slapnicka

SLAPNICKA, CYRIL CHARLES BB TR 5′10″ 165 lbs.
B. Mar. 23, 1886, Cedar Rapids, Iowa D. Oct. 20, 1979, Cedar Rapids, Iowa.

Year	Team	W	L	PCT	ERA	G	GS	CG	IP	H	BB	SO	ShO	Relief Pitching W	Relief Pitching L	Relief Pitching SV	Batting AB	Batting H	Batting HR	BA	PO	A	E	DP	TC/G	FA
1911	**CHI N**	0	2	.000	3.38	3	2	1	24	21	7	10	0	0	0	0	9	2	0	.222	5	9	0	0	4.7	1.000
1918	**PIT N**	1	4	.200	4.74	7	6	4	49.1	50	22	3	0	0	0	1	14	1	0	.071	3	14	2	0	2.7	.895
2 yrs.		1	6	.143	4.30	10	8	5	73.1	71	29	13	0	0	0	1	23	3	0	.130	8	23	2	0	3.3	.939

John Slappey

SLAPPEY, JOHN HENRY BL TL 6′ 4″ 170 lbs.
B. Aug. 8, 1898, Albany, Ga. D. June 10, 1957, Marietta, Ga.

Year	Team	W	L	PCT	ERA	G	GS	CG	IP	H	BB	SO	ShO	Relief Pitching W	Relief Pitching L	Relief Pitching SV	Batting AB	Batting H	Batting HR	BA	PO	A	E	DP	TC/G	FA
1920	**PHI A**	0	1	.000	7.11	3	1	0	6.1	15	4	1	0	0	0	0	2	1	0	.500	0	1	0	0	0.3	1.000

Jim Slaton

SLATON, JAMES MICHAEL BR TR 6′ 185 lbs.
B. June 19, 1950, Long Beach, Calif.

Year	Team	W	L	PCT	ERA	G	GS	CG	IP	H	BB	SO	ShO	Relief Pitching W	Relief Pitching L	Relief Pitching SV	Batting AB	Batting H	Batting HR	BA	PO	A	E	DP	TC/G	FA
1971	**MIL A**	10	8	.556	3.77	26	23	5	148	140	71	63	4	0	0	0	46	5	0	.109	12	12	2	1	1.0	.923
1972		1	6	.143	5.52	9	8	0	44	50	21	17	0	0	1	0	11	1	0	.091	1	11	0	0	1.3	1.000
1973		13	15	.464	3.71	38	38	13	276.1	266	99	134	3	0	0	0	0	0	0	—	19	27	6	4	1.4	.885
1974		13	16	.448	3.92	40	35	10	250	255	102	126	3	1	0	0	0	0	0	—	16	36	1	3	1.3	.981
1975		11	18	.379	4.52	37	33	10	217	238	90	119	3	0	0	0	0	0	0	—	16	34	4	3	1.5	.926
1976		14	15	.483	3.44	38	38	12	292.2	**287**	94	138	2	0	0	0	0	0	0	—	18	43	3	2	1.7	.953
1977		10	14	.417	3.58	32	31	7	221	223	77	104	1	1	0	0	0	0	0	—	21	34	4	1	1.8	.932
1978	**DET A**	17	11	.607	4.12	35	34	11	233.2	235	85	92	2	0	1	0	0	0	0	—	9	32	2	6	1.2	.953
1979	**MIL A**	15	9	.625	3.63	32	31	12	213	229	54	80	3	0	0	0	0	0	0	—	16	35	1	3	1.6	.981
1980		1	1	.500	4.50	3	3	0	16	17	5	4	0	0	0	0	0	0	0	—	0	3	0	0	1.0	1.000
1981		5	7	.417	4.38	24	21	0	117	120	50	47	0	0	0	0	0	0	0	—	14	14	0	3	1.2	1.000
1982		10	6	.625	3.29	39	7	0	117.2	117	41	59	0	7	4	6	0	0	0	—	6	16	0	0	0.6	1.000
1983		14	6	.700	4.33	46	0	0	112.1	112	56	38	0	**14**	6	5	0	0	0	—	4	16	0	1	0.4	1.000
1984	**CAL A**	7	10	.412	4.97	32	22	5	163	192	56	67	1	1	0	0	0	0	0	—	9	25	0	3	1.1	1.000
1985		6	10	.375	4.37	29	24	1	148.1	162	63	60	0	0	0	1	0	0	0	—	6	22	1	4	1.0	.966
1986	**2 teams**	**CAL A** (14G 4–6)		**DET A** (22G 0–0)																						
″	**total**	4	6	.400	5.08	36	12	0	113.1	130	40	43	0	1	0	2	0	0	0		13	18	0	2	0.9	1.000
16 yrs.		151	158	.489	4.03	496	360	86	2683.1	2773	1004	1191	22	25	12	14	57	6	0	.105	180	378	24	36	1.2	.959
DIVISIONAL PLAYOFF SERIES																										
1981	**MIL A**	0	0	—	3.00	4	0	0	6	6	0	2	0	0	0	0	0	0	0	—	0	0	0	0	0.0	.000
LEAGUE CHAMPIONSHIP SERIES																										
1982	**MIL A**	0	0	—	1.93	2	0	0	4.2	3	1	3	0	0	0	1	0	0	0	—	1	0	0	0	0.5	1.000
WORLD SERIES																										
1982	**MIL A**	1	0	1.000	0.00	2	0	0	2.2	1	2	1	0	1	0	0	0	0	0	—	0	0	0	0	0.0	.000

Phil Slattery

SLATTERY, PHILIP RYAN BR TL 5′11″ 160 lbs.
B. Feb. 25, 1893, Harper, Iowa D. Mar. 10, 1968, Long Beach, Calif.

Year	Team	W	L	PCT	ERA	G	GS	CG	IP	H	BB	SO	ShO	Relief Pitching W	Relief Pitching L	Relief Pitching SV	Batting AB	Batting H	Batting HR	BA	PO	A	E	DP	TC/G	FA
1915	**PIT N**	0	0	—	0.00	3	0	0	8	5	1	1	0	0	0	0	1	0	0	.000	0	0	0	0	0.0	.000

Barney Slaughter

SLAUGHTER, BYRON ATKINS BR TR 5′11½″ 165 lbs.
B. Oct. 6, 1884, Smyrna, Del. D. May 17, 1961, Philadelphia, Pa.

Year	Team	W	L	PCT	ERA	G	GS	CG	IP	H	BB	SO	ShO	Relief Pitching W	Relief Pitching L	Relief Pitching SV	Batting AB	Batting H	Batting HR	BA	PO	A	E	DP	TC/G	FA
1910	**PHI N**	0	1	.000	5.50	8	1	0	18	21	11	7	0	0	1	1	5	1	0	.200	0	6	0	0	0.8	1.000

Sterling Slaughter

SLAUGHTER, STERLING FEORE BR TR 5′11″ 165 lbs.
B. Nov. 18, 1941, Danville, Ill.

Year	Team	W	L	PCT	ERA	G	GS	CG	IP	H	BB	SO	ShO	Relief Pitching W	Relief Pitching L	Relief Pitching SV	Batting AB	Batting H	Batting HR	BA	PO	A	E	DP	TC/G	FA
1964	**CHI N**	2	4	.333	5.75	20	6	1	51.2	64	32	32	0	0	2	0	12	1	0	.083	3	3	0	0	0.3	1.000

Bill Slayback

SLAYBACK, WILLIAM GROVER BR TR 6′ 4″ 200 lbs.
B. Feb. 21, 1948, Hollywood, Calif.

Year	Team	W	L	PCT	ERA	G	GS	CG	IP	H	BB	SO	ShO	Relief Pitching W	Relief Pitching L	Relief Pitching SV	Batting AB	Batting H	Batting HR	BA	PO	A	E	DP	TC/G	FA
1972	**DET A**	5	6	.455	3.18	23	13	3	82	74	25	65	1	1	0	0	23	4	0	.174	5	15	2	0	1.0	.909
1973		0	0	—	4.50	3	0	0	2	5	0	1	0	0	0	0	0	0	0	—	0	0	0	0	0.0	.000
1974		1	3	.250	4.75	16	4	0	55	57	26	23	0	0	0	0	0	0	0	—	1	8	1	0	0.6	.900
3 yrs.		6	9	.400	3.82	42	17	3	139	136	51	89	1	1	0	0	23	4	0	.174	6	23	3	0	0.8	.906

Steve Slayton

SLAYTON, FOSTER HERBERT BR TR 6′ 163 lbs.
B. Apr. 26, 1902, Barre, Vt. D. Dec. 20, 1984, Manchester, N. H.

Year	Team	W	L	PCT	ERA	G	GS	CG	IP	H	BB	SO	ShO	Relief Pitching W	Relief Pitching L	Relief Pitching SV	Batting AB	Batting H	Batting HR	BA	PO	A	E	DP	TC/G	FA
1928	**BOS A**	0	0	—	3.86	3	0	0	7	6	3	2	0	0	0	0	2	0	0	.000	0	1	0	0	0.3	1.000

Lou Sleater

SLEATER, LOUIS MORTIMER BL TL 5′10″ 185 lbs.
B. Sept. 8, 1926, St. Louis, Mo.

Year	Team	W	L	PCT	ERA	G	GS	CG	IP	H	BB	SO	ShO	Relief Pitching W	Relief Pitching L	Relief Pitching SV	Batting AB	Batting H	Batting HR	BA	PO	A	E	DP	TC/G	FA
1950	**STL A**	0	0	—	0.00	1	0	0	1	0	0	1	0	0	0	0	0	0	0	—	0	0	0	0	0.0	.000
1951		1	9	.100	5.11	20	8	4	81	88	53	33	0	1	1	1	31	7	0	.226	2	10	1	1	0.6	.923
1952	**2 teams**	**STL A** (4G 0–1)		**WAS A** (14G 4–2)																						
″	**total**	4	3	.571	4.11	18	11	3	65.2	65	35	23	1	1	0	0	22	1	0	.045	0	8	1	0	0.5	.889
1955	**KC A**	1	1	.500	7.71	16	1	0	25.2	33	21	11	0	1	0	0	13	2	0	.154	2	3	0	0	0.3	1.000
1956	**MIL N**	2	2	.500	3.15	25	1	0	45.2	42	27	32	0	2	2	2	10	5	0	.500	4	11	0	0	0.6	1.000
1957	**DET A**	3	3	.500	3.76	41	0	0	69.1	61	28	43	0	3	3	2	20	5	3	.250	2	11	3	2	0.4	.813
1958	**2 teams**	**DET A** (4G 0–0)		**BAL A** (6G 1–0)																						
″	**total**	1	0	1.000	10.22	10	0	0	12.1	17	8	9	0	1	0	0	7	1	1	.143	1	4	1	0	0.6	.833
7 yrs.		12	18	.400	4.70	131	21	7	300.2	306	172	152	1	9	6	5	103	21	4	.204	11	47	6	3	0.5	.906

Dwain Sloat

SLOAT, DWAIN CLIFFORD (Lefty) BR TL 6′ 168 lbs.
B. Dec. 1, 1918, Nokomis, Ill.

Year	Team		W	L	PCT	ERA	G	GS	CG	IP	H	BB	SO	ShO	Relief Pitching W	Relief Pitching L	Relief Pitching SV	Batting AB	Batting H	Batting HR	BA	PO	A	E	DP	TC/G	FA
1948	BKN	N	0	1	.000	6.14	4	1	0	7.1	7	8	1	0	0	0	0	1	0	0	.000	3	3	0	0	1.5	1.000
1949	CHI	N	0	0	—	7.00	5	1	0	9	14	3	3	0	0	0	0	0	0	0	—	0	2	0	0	0.4	1.000
2 yrs.			0	1	.000	6.61	9	2	0	16.1	21	11	4	0	0	0	0	1	0	0	.000	3	5	0	0	0.9	1.000

Heathcliff Slocumb

SLOCUMB, HEATH BR TR 6′ 3″ 180 lbs.
B. June 7, 1966, Jamaica, N. Y.

Year	Team		W	L	PCT	ERA	G	GS	CG	IP	H	BB	SO	ShO	Relief Pitching W	Relief Pitching L	Relief Pitching SV	Batting AB	Batting H	Batting HR	BA	PO	A	E	DP	TC/G	FA
1991	CHI	N	2	1	.667	3.45	52	0	0	62.2	53	30	34	0	2	1	1	1	0	0	.000	5	10	1	0	0.3	.938
1992			0	3	.000	6.50	30	0	0	36	52	21	27	0	0	3	1	4	0	0	.000	3	4	2	0	0.3	.778
1993	2 teams	CHI N	(10G 1–0)		CLE A	(20G 3–1)																					
″	total		4	1	.800	4.03	30	0	0	38	35	20	22	0	4	1	0	1	0	0	.000	3	4	0	2	0.2	1.000
1994	PHI	N	5	1	.833	2.86	52	0	0	72.1	75	28	58	0	5	1	0	4	1	0	.250	2	13	3	1	0.3	.833
1995			5	6	.455	2.89	61	0	0	65.1	64	35	63	0	5	6	32	1	0	0	.000	4	17	1	3	0.4	.955
5 yrs.			16	12	.571	3.64	225	0	0	274.1	279	134	204	0	16	12	34	11	1	0	.091	17	48	7	6	0.3	.903

Joe Slusarski

SLUSARSKI, JOSEPH ANDREW BR TR 6′ 4″ 195 lbs.
B. Dec. 19, 1966, Indianapolis, Ind.

Year	Team		W	L	PCT	ERA	G	GS	CG	IP	H	BB	SO	ShO	Relief Pitching W	Relief Pitching L	Relief Pitching SV	Batting AB	Batting H	Batting HR	BA	PO	A	E	DP	TC/G	FA
1991	OAK	A	5	7	.417	5.27	20	19	1	109.1	121	52	60	0	0	0	0	0	0	0	—	7	10	1	0	0.9	.944
1992			5	5	.500	5.45	15	14	0	76	85	27	38	0	0	0	0	0	0	0	—	2	6	0	0	0.5	1.000
1993			0	0	—	5.19	2	1	0	8.2	9	11	1	0	0	0	0	0	0	0	—	1	2	0	1	1.5	1.000
1995	MIL	A	1	1	.500	5.40	12	0	0	15	21	6	6	0	1	1	0	0	0	0	—	2	1	0	0	0.3	1.000
4 yrs.			11	13	.458	5.34	49	34	1	209	236	96	105	0	1	1	0	0	0	0		12	19	1	1	0.7	.969

Aaron Small

SMALL, AARON JAMES BR TR 6′ 5″ 200 lbs.
B. Nov. 23, 1971, Oxnard, Calif.

Year	Team		W	L	PCT	ERA	G	GS	CG	IP	H	BB	SO	ShO	Relief Pitching W	Relief Pitching L	Relief Pitching SV	Batting AB	Batting H	Batting HR	BA	PO	A	E	DP	TC/G	FA
1994	TOR	A	0	0	—	9.00	1	0	0	2	5	2	0	0	0	0	0	0	0	0	—	0	1	0	0	1.0	1.000
1995	FLA	N	1	0	1.000	1.42	7	0	0	6.1	7	6	5	0	1	0	0	0	0	0	—	0	1	0	0	0.1	1.000
2 yrs.			1	0	1.000	3.24	8	0	0	8.1	12	8	5	0	1	0	0	0	0	0		0	2	0	0	0.3	1.000

Walt Smallwood

SMALLWOOD, WALTER CLAYTON BR TR 6′ 2″ 190 lbs.
B. Apr. 24, 1893, Dayton, Md. D. Apr. 29, 1967, Baltimore, Md.

Year	Team		W	L	PCT	ERA	G	GS	CG	IP	H	BB	SO	ShO	Relief Pitching W	Relief Pitching L	Relief Pitching SV	Batting AB	Batting H	Batting HR	BA	PO	A	E	DP	TC/G	FA
1917	NY	A	0	0	—	0.00	2	0	0	2	1	1	1	0	0	0	0	0	0	0	—	0	1	0	0	0.5	1.000
1919			0	0	—	4.98	6	0	0	21.2	20	9	6	0	0	0	0	5	0	0	.000	1	4	0	1	0.8	1.000
2 yrs.			0	0		4.56	8	0	0	23.2	21	10	7	0	0	0	0	5	0	0	.000	1	5	0	1	0.8	1.000

John Smiley

SMILEY, JOHN PATRICK BL TL 6′ 4″ 180 lbs.
B. Mar. 17, 1965, Phoenixville, Pa.

Year	Team		W	L	PCT	ERA	G	GS	CG	IP	H	BB	SO	ShO	Relief Pitching W	Relief Pitching L	Relief Pitching SV	Batting AB	Batting H	Batting HR	BA	PO	A	E	DP	TC/G	FA
1986	PIT	N	1	0	1.000	3.86	12	0	0	11.2	4	4	9	0	1	0	0	0	0	0	—	1	2	0	0	0.3	1.000
1987			5	5	.500	5.76	63	0	0	75	69	50	58	0	5	5	4	7	1	0	.143	7	9	0	2	0.3	1.000
1988			13	11	.542	3.25	34	32	5	205	185	46	129	1	0	0	0	63	5	0	.079	14	27	0	3	1.2	1.000
1989			12	8	.600	2.81	28	28	8	205.1	174	49	123	1	0	0	0	65	9	0	.138	7	23	4	2	1.2	.882
1990			9	10	.474	4.64	26	25	2	149.1	161	36	86	0	0	0	0	49	6	0	.122	8	24	2	1	1.3	.941
1991			**20**	8	**.714**	3.08	33	32	2	207.2	194	44	129	1	1	0	0	70	7	0	.100	5	34	1	0	1.2	.975
1992	MIN	A	16	9	.640	3.21	34	34	5	241	205	65	163	2	0	0	0	0	0	0	—	4	35	0	2	1.1	1.000
1993	CIN	N	3	9	.250	5.62	18	18	2	105.2	117	31	60	0	0	0	0	32	8	0	.250	7	16	0	0	1.3	1.000
1994			11	10	.524	3.86	24	24	1	158.2	169	37	112	1	0	0	0	55	11	0	.200	8	19	2	1	1.2	.931
1995			12	5	.706	3.46	28	27	1	176.2	173	39	124	0	0	0	0	55	9	2	.164	3	27	0	3	1.1	1.000
10 yrs.			102	75	.576	3.67	300	220	26	1536	1451	401	993	6	7	5	4	396	56	2	.141	64	216	9	14	1.0	.969
DIVISIONAL PLAYOFF SERIES																											
1995	CIN	N	0	0	—	3.00	1	1	0	6	9	0	1	0	0	0	0	2	0	0	.000	0	1	0	0	1.0	1.000
LEAGUE CHAMPIONSHIP SERIES																											
1990	PIT	N	0	0	—	0.00	1	0	0	2	2	0	0	0	0	0	0	0	0	0	—	0	0	0	0	0.0	.000
1991			0	2	.000	23.63	2	2	0	2.2	8	1	3	0	0	0	0	0	0	0	—	0	1	0	0	0.5	1.000
1995	CIN	N	0	0	—	3.60	1	1	0	5	5	0	1	0	0	0	0	1	0	0	.000	1	1	0	0	2.0	1.000
3 yrs.			0	2	.000	8.38	4	3	0	9.2	15	1	4	0	0	0	0	1	0	0	.000	1	2	0	0	0.8	1.000

Smith

SMITH
Deceased.

Year	Team		W	L	PCT	ERA	G	GS	CG	IP	H	BB	SO	ShO	Relief Pitching W	Relief Pitching L	Relief Pitching SV	Batting AB	Batting H	Batting HR	BA	PO	A	E	DP	TC/G	FA
1884	BAL	U	0	1	.000	1.00	1	1	1	9	15	3	5	0	0	0	0	4	1	0	.250	1	7	0	0	8.0	1.000

Smith

SMITH
Deceased.

Year	Team		W	L	PCT	ERA	G	GS	CG	IP	H	BB	SO	ShO	Relief Pitching W	Relief Pitching L	Relief Pitching SV	Batting AB	Batting H	Batting HR	BA	PO	A	E	DP	TC/G	FA
1886	CIN	AA	0	1	.000	2.00	1	1	1	9	8	10	1	0	0	0	0	4	1	0	.250	0	1	0	0	1.0	1.000

Al Smith

SMITH, ALFRED JOHN BL TL 5′11″ 180 lbs.
B. Oct. 12, 1907, Belleville, Ill. D. Apr. 28, 1977, Brownsville, Tex.

Year	Team		W	L	PCT	ERA	G	GS	CG	IP	H	BB	SO	ShO	Relief Pitching W	Relief Pitching L	Relief Pitching SV	Batting AB	Batting H	Batting HR	BA	PO	A	E	DP	TC/G	FA
1934	NY	N	3	5	.375	4.32	30	5	0	66.2	70	21	27	0	3	1	5	14	4	0	.286	1	14	1	2	0.5	.938
1935			10	8	.556	3.41	40	10	4	124	125	32	44	1	**5**	4	5	34	4	1	.118	5	24	2	2	0.8	.935
1936			14	13	.519	3.78	43	30	9	209.1	217	69	89	**4**	4	1	2	73	10	0	.137	4	44	5	4	1.2	.906
1937			5	4	.556	4.20	33	9	2	85.2	91	30	41	0	3	2	0	25	3	0	.120	3	15	0	1	0.5	1.000
1938	PHI	N	1	4	.200	6.28	37	1	0	86	115	40	46	0	0	4	1	21	0	0	.000	5	16	1	1	0.6	.955
1939			0	0	—	4.00	5	0	0	9	11	5	2	0	0	0	0	2	0	0	.000	1	2	0	0	0.6	1.000
1940	CLE	A	15	7	.682	3.44	31	24	11	183	187	55	46	1	1	1	2	62	19	0	.306	6	44	0	5	1.6	1.000
1941			12	13	.480	3.83	29	27	13	206.2	204	75	76	2	0	0	0	71	11	1	.155	9	46	3	5	2.0	.948
1942			10	15	.400	3.96	30	24	7	168.1	163	71	66	1	2	2	0	60	15	0	.250	5	34	1	0	1.3	.975
1943			17	7	.708	2.55	29	27	14	208.1	186	72	72	3	0	0	1	68	14	0	.206	6	45	2	1	1.8	.962
1944			7	13	.350	3.42	28	26	7	181.2	197	69	44	1	1	1	0	64	10	0	.156	4	46	1	2	1.8	.980
1945			5	12	.294	3.84	21	19	8	133.2	141	48	34	3	0	0	1	41	12	0	.293	6	37	1	3	2.1	.977
12 yrs.			99	101	.495	3.72	356	202	75	1662.1	1707	587	587	16	19	16	17	535	102	2	.191	55	367	17	26	1.2	.961
WORLD SERIES																											
1936	NY	N	0	0	—	81.00	1	0	0	0.1	2	1	0	0	0	0	0	0	0	0	—	0	0	0	0	0.0	.000
1937			0	0	—	3.00	2	0	0	3	2	0	1	0	0	0	0	0	0	0	—	0	1	0	0	0.5	1.000
2 yrs.			0	0		10.80	3	0	0	3.1	4	1	1	0	0	0	0	0	0	0		0	1	0	0	0.3	1.000

Al Smith

SMITH, ALFRED KENDRICKS BR TR 6′ 170 lbs.
B. Dec. 13, 1903, Norristown, Pa.

Year	Team	W	L	PCT	ERA	G	GS	CG	IP	H	BB	SO	ShO	Relief Pitching W	Relief Pitching L	Relief Pitching SV	Batting AB	Batting H	Batting HR	BA	PO	A	E	DP	TC/G	FA
1926	NY N	0	0	—	9.00	1	0	0	2	4	2	0	0	0	0	0	0	0	0	—	0	0	0	0	0.0	.000

Art Smith

SMITH, ARTHUR LAIRD BR TR 6′ 175 lbs.
B. June 21, 1906, Boston, Mass.

Year	Team	W	L	PCT	ERA	G	GS	CG	IP	H	BB	SO	ShO	Relief Pitching W	Relief Pitching L	Relief Pitching SV	Batting AB	Batting H	Batting HR	BA	PO	A	E	DP	TC/G	FA
1932	CHI A	0	1	.000	11.57	3	2	0	7	17	4	1	0	0	0	0	1	0	0	.000	1	4	0	0	1.7	1.000

Bill Smith

SMITH, F. WILLIAM TR 5′ 8″ 152 lbs.
B. 1863, New Orleans, La. Deceased.

Year	Team	W	L	PCT	ERA	G	GS	CG	IP	H	BB	SO	ShO	Relief Pitching W	Relief Pitching L	Relief Pitching SV	Batting AB	Batting H	Batting HR	BA	PO	A	E	DP	TC/G	FA
1886	DET N	5	4	.556	4.09	9	9	9	77	81	30	36	0	0	0	0	38	7	0	.184	5	12	3	0	2.0	.850

Bill Smith

SMITH, WILLIAM GARLAND BL TL 6′ 190 lbs.
B. June 8, 1934, Washington, D. C.

Year	Team	W	L	PCT	ERA	G	GS	CG	IP	H	BB	SO	ShO	Relief Pitching W	Relief Pitching L	Relief Pitching SV	Batting AB	Batting H	Batting HR	BA	PO	A	E	DP	TC/G	FA
1958	STL N	0	1	.000	6.52	2	1	0	9.2	12	4	4	0	0	0	0	2	0	0	.000	1	2	0	0	1.5	1.000
1959		0	0	—	1.08	6	0	0	8.1	11	3	4	0	0	0	1	1	0	0	.000	0	1	0	0	0.2	1.000
1962	PHI N	1	5	.167	4.29	24	5	0	50.1	59	10	26	0	1	1	0	11	2	0	.182	6	6	2	1	0.6	.857
3 yrs.		1	6	.143	4.21	32	6	0	68.1	82	17	34	0	1	1	1	14	2	0	.143	7	9	2	1	0.6	.889

Billy Smith

SMITH, BILLY LAVERN BR TR 6′ 7″ 200 lbs.
B. Sept. 13, 1954, La Marque, Tex.

Year	Team	W	L	PCT	ERA	G	GS	CG	IP	H	BB	SO	ShO	Relief Pitching W	Relief Pitching L	Relief Pitching SV	Batting AB	Batting H	Batting HR	BA	PO	A	E	DP	TC/G	FA
1981	HOU N	1	1	.500	3.00	10	1	0	21	20	3	3	0	0	1	1	2	0	0	.000	2	3	0	1	0.5	1.000
DIVISIONAL PLAYOFF SERIES																										
1981	HOU N	0	0	—	0.00	1	0	0	0.1	0	0	0	0	0	0	0	0	0	0	—	0	0	0	0	0.0	.000

Bob Smith

SMITH, ROBERT ASHLEY BR TR 5′11″ 160 lbs.
Played as Bob Brown in 1914.
B. July 20, 1890, Woodbury, Vt. D. Dec. 27, 1965, West Los Angeles, Calif.

Year	Team	W	L	PCT	ERA	G	GS	CG	IP	H	BB	SO	ShO	Relief Pitching W	Relief Pitching L	Relief Pitching SV	Batting AB	Batting H	Batting HR	BA	PO	A	E	DP	TC/G	FA
1913	CHI A	0	0	—	13.50	1	0	0	2	3	3	1	0	0	0	0	0	0	0	—	0	0	0	0	0.0	.000
1914	BUF F	1	0	1.000	3.44	15	1	0	36.2	39	16	13	0	1	0	2	9	2	0	.222	1	14	1	1	1.1	.938
1915		0	0	—	18.00	1	0	0	1	1	2	0	0	0	0	0	0	0	0	—	0	1	0	0	1.0	1.000
3 yrs.		1	0	1.000	4.31	17	1	0	39.2	43	21	14	0	1	0	2	9	2	0	.222	1	15	1	1	1.0	.941

Bob Smith

SMITH, ROBERT ELDRIDGE BR TR 5′10″ 175 lbs.
B. Apr. 22, 1895, Rogersville, Tenn. D. July 19, 1987, Waycross, Ga.

Year	Team	W	L	PCT	ERA	G	GS	CG	IP	H	BB	SO	ShO	Relief Pitching W	Relief Pitching L	Relief Pitching SV	Batting AB	Batting H	Batting HR	BA	PO	A	E	DP	TC/G	FA
1925	BOS N	5	3	.625	4.47	13	10	6	92.2	110	36	19	0	0	1	0	174	49	0	.282	256	388	35	78	6.2	.948
1926		10	13	.435	3.91	33	23	14	193.1	199	75	44	4	2	0	1	84	25	0	.298	9	60	2	6	2.2	.972
1927		10	18	.357	3.76	41	32	16	260.2	297	75	81	1	2	2	3	109	27	1	.248	22	63	3	3	2.1	.966
1928		13	17	.433	3.87	38	28	14	244.1	274	74	59	0	2	2	2	92	23	1	.250	16	66	3	5	2.2	.965
1929		11	17	.393	4.68	34	29	19	231	256	71	65	1	0	1	3	99	17	1	.172	21	75	2	7	2.5	.980
1930		10	14	.417	4.26	38	24	14	219.2	247	85	84	2	2	0	5	81	19	0	.235	16	47	1	3	1.7	.984
1931	CHI N	15	12	.556	3.22	36	29	18	240.1	239	62	63	2	0	0	2	87	19	0	.218	8	55	0	4	1.8	1.000
1932		4	3	.571	4.61	34	11	4	119	148	36	35	1	0	1	2	42	10	0	.238	8	36	0	4	1.2	1.000
1933	2 teams CIN N (16G 4–4) BOS N (14G 4–3)																									
″	total	8	7	.533	2.65	30	10	7	132.1	143	18	34	1	3	2	1	45	9	0	.200	1	34	2	4	1.2	.946
1934	BOS N	6	9	.400	4.66	39	5	3	121.2	133	36	26	0	4	**6**	5	36	9	0	.250	7	30	0	2	0.9	1.000
1935		8	18	.308	3.94	46	20	8	203.1	232	61	58	2	3	3	5	63	17	0	.270	10	39	1	1	1.1	.980
1936		6	7	.462	3.77	35	11	5	136	142	35	36	2	2	1	8	45	10	0	.222	8	34	0	2	1.2	1.000
1937		0	1	.000	4.09	18	0	0	44	52	6	14	0	0	1	3	10	2	0	.200	1	6	0	0	0.4	1.000
13 yrs.		106	139	.433	3.95	435	232	128	2238.1	2472	670	618	16	20	20	40	*				659	1391	89	198	3.1	.958
WORLD SERIES																										
1932	CHI N	0	0	—	9.00	1	0	0	1	2	0	1	0	0	0	0	*				0	0	0	0	0.0	.000

Bob Smith

SMITH, ROBERT GILCHRIST BR TL 6′ 1½″ 190 lbs.
B. Feb. 1, 1931, Woodsville, N. H.

Year	Team	W	L	PCT	ERA	G	GS	CG	IP	H	BB	SO	ShO	Relief Pitching W	Relief Pitching L	Relief Pitching SV	Batting AB	Batting H	Batting HR	BA	PO	A	E	DP	TC/G	FA
1955	BOS A	0	0	—	0.00	1	0	0	1.2	1	1	1	0	0	0	0	0	0	0	—	0	0	0	0	0.0	.000
1957	2 teams STL N (6G 0–0) PIT N (20G 2–4)																									
″	total	2	4	.333	3.34	26	4	2	64.2	60	31	46	0	0	3	1	15	1	0	.067	3	7	1	0	0.4	.909
1958	PIT N	2	2	.500	4.43	35	4	0	61	61	31	24	0	2	0	1	11	1	0	.091	5	14	2	1	0.6	.905
1959	2 teams PIT N (20G 0–0) DET A (9G 0–3)																									
″	total	0	3	.000	4.81	29	0	0	39.1	52	20	22	0	0	3	0	3	0	0	.000	1	6	1	0	0.3	.875
4 yrs.		4	9	.308	4.05	91	8	2	166.2	174	83	93	0	2	6	2	29	2	0	.069	9	27	4	1	0.4	.900

Bryn Smith

SMITH, BRYN NELSON BR TR 6′ 2″ 200 lbs.
B. Aug. 11, 1955, Marietta, Ga.

Year	Team	W	L	PCT	ERA	G	GS	CG	IP	H	BB	SO	ShO	Relief Pitching W	Relief Pitching L	Relief Pitching SV	Batting AB	Batting H	Batting HR	BA	PO	A	E	DP	TC/G	FA
1981	MON N	1	0	1.000	2.77	7	0	0	13	14	3	9	0	1	0	0	1	0	0	.000	0	1	1	0	0.3	.500
1982		2	4	.333	4.20	47	1	0	79.1	81	23	50	0	2	3	3	8	0	0	.000	2	15	1	0	0.4	.944
1983		6	11	.353	2.49	49	12	5	155.1	142	43	101	3	1	4	3	30	5	0	.167	10	22	0	3	0.7	1.000
1984		12	13	.480	3.32	28	28	4	179	178	51	101	2	0	0	0	53	7	0	.132	25	28	4	3	2.0	.930
1985		18	5	.783	2.91	32	32	4	222.1	193	41	127	2	0	0	0	72	14	1	.194	24	27	5	2	1.8	.911
1986		10	8	.556	3.94	30	30	1	187.1	182	63	105	0	0	0	0	58	8	1	.138	11	44	2	5	1.9	.965
1987		10	9	.526	4.37	26	26	2	150.1	164	31	94	0	0	0	0	44	6	0	.136	10	21	1	2	1.2	.969
1988		12	10	.545	3.00	32	32	1	198	179	32	122	0	0	0	0	55	6	0	.109	7	26	2	1	1.1	.943
1989		10	11	.476	2.84	33	32	3	215.2	177	54	129	1	0	0	0	62	4	0	.065	16	42	1	2	1.8	.983
1990	STL N	9	8	.529	4.27	26	25	0	141.1	160	30	78	0	0	0	0	39	10	1	.256	10	16	2	2	1.1	.929
1991		12	9	.571	3.85	31	31	3	198.2	188	45	94	0	0	0	0	65	16	0	.246	12	26	0	2	1.2	1.000
1992		4	2	.667	4.64	13	1	0	21.1	20	5	9	0	4	2	0	3	0	0	.000	3	3	0	0	0.5	1.000
1993	CLR N	2	4	.333	8.49	11	5	0	29.2	47	11	9	0	1	0	0	6	0	0	.000	2	8	0	1	0.9	1.000
13 yrs.		108	94	.535	3.53	365	255	23	1791.1	1725	432	1028	8	9	9	6	496	76	3	.153	132	279	19	23	1.2	.956

Charlie Smith

SMITH, CHARLES EDWIN BR TR 6′ 1″ 185 lbs.
Brother of Fred Smith.
B. Apr. 20, 1880, Cleveland, Ohio D. Jan. 3, 1929, Wickliffe, Ohio.

Year	Team	W	L	PCT	ERA	G	GS	CG	IP	H	BB	SO	ShO	Relief Pitching W	Relief Pitching L	Relief Pitching SV	Batting AB	Batting H	HR	BA	PO	A	E	DP	TC/G	FA
1902	CLE A	2	1	.667	4.05	3	3	2	20	23	5	5	1	0	0	0	8	1	0	.125	0	6	0	0	2.0	1.000
1906	WAS A	9	16	.360	2.91	33	22	17	235.1	250	75	105	2	3	**2**	0	87	16	1	.184	5	60	5	0	2.1	.929
1907		10	20	.333	2.61	36	31	21	258.2	254	51	119	3	0	**3**	0	84	12	0	.143	10	95	6	2	3.1	.946
1908		9	13	.409	2.40	26	22	13	184	166	60	83	1	0	1	1	65	8	0	.123	2	53	1	2	2.1	.982
1909	2 teams WAS A (23G 3–12) BOS A (3G 3–0)																									
″	total	6	12	.333	3.11	26	18	9	170.2	163	39	83	1	0	2	0	55	10	0	.182	6	54	2	0	2.4	.968
1910	BOS A	11	6	.647	2.30	24	18	11	156.1	141	35	53	0	1	1	1	44	5	0	.114	5	44	7	1	2.3	.875
1911	2 teams BOS A (1G 0–0) CHI N (7G 3–2)																									
″	total	3	2	.600	1.80	8	6	3	40	33	8	11	1	0	0	0	13	1	0	.077	4	9	2	0	1.9	.867
1912	CHI N	7	4	.636	4.21	21	5	1	94	92	31	47	0	**6**	1	1	35	9	0	.257	2	29	0	2	1.5	1.000
1913		7	9	.438	2.55	20	17	8	137.2	138	34	47	1	1	0	0	45	4	0	.089	1	38	1	0	2.0	.975
1914		2	4	.333	3.86	16	5	1	53.2	49	15	17	0	1	0	0	11	1	0	.091	1	10	0	0	0.7	1.000
10 yrs.		66	87	.431	2.81	213	147	86	1350.1	1309	353	570	10	12	10	3	447	67	1	.150	36	398	24	7	2.1	.948

Chick Smith

SMITH, JOHN WILLIAM BL TL 5′ 8″ 165 lbs.
Born Jan Smadt.
B. Dec. 2, 1892, Dayton, Ky. D. Oct. 11, 1935, Dayton, Ky.

Year	Team	W	L	PCT	ERA	G	GS	CG	IP	H	BB	SO	ShO	Relief Pitching W	Relief Pitching L	Relief Pitching SV	Batting AB	Batting H	HR	BA	PO	A	E	DP	TC/G	FA
1913	CIN N	0	1	.000	3.57	5	1	0	17.2	15	11	11	0	0	0	0	4	0	0	.000	0	5	0	0	1.0	1.000

Clay Smith

SMITH, CLAY JAMIESON BR TR 6′ 2″ 190 lbs.
B. Sept. 11, 1914, Cambridge, Kans.

Year	Team	W	L	PCT	ERA	G	GS	CG	IP	H	BB	SO	ShO	Relief Pitching W	Relief Pitching L	Relief Pitching SV	Batting AB	Batting H	HR	BA	PO	A	E	DP	TC/G	FA
1938	CLE A	0	0	—	6.55	4	0	0	11	18	2	3	0	0	0	0	4	0	0	.000	1	2	0	0	0.8	1.000
1940	DET A	1	1	.500	5.08	14	1	0	28.1	32	13	14	0	1	0	0	7	0	0	.000	1	10	0	0	0.8	1.000
2 yrs.		1	1	.500	5.49	18	1	0	39.1	50	15	17	0	1	0	0	11	0	0	.000	2	12	0	0	0.8	1.000
WORLD SERIES																										
1940	DET A	0	0	—	2.25	1	0	0	4	1	3	1	0	0	0	0	1	0	0	.000	0	1	0	0	1.0	1.000

Dan Smith

SMITH, DANIEL SCOTT BL TL 6′ 5″ 190 lbs.
B. Apr. 20, 1969, St. Paul, Minn.

Year	Team	W	L	PCT	ERA	G	GS	CG	IP	H	BB	SO	ShO	Relief Pitching W	Relief Pitching L	Relief Pitching SV	Batting AB	Batting H	HR	BA	PO	A	E	DP	TC/G	FA
1992	TEX A	0	3	.000	5.02	4	2	0	14.1	18	8	5	0	0	1	0	0	0	0	—	1	1	0	0	0.5	1.000
1994		1	2	.333	4.30	13	0	0	14.2	18	12	9	0	1	2	0	0	0	0	—	0	1	0	0	0.1	1.000
2 yrs.		1	5	.167	4.66	17	2	0	29	36	20	14	0	1	3	0	0	0	0		1	2	0	0	0.2	1.000

Daryl Smith

SMITH, DARYL CLINTON BR TR 6′ 4″ 185 lbs.
B. July 29, 1960, Baltimore, Md.

Year	Team	W	L	PCT	ERA	G	GS	CG	IP	H	BB	SO	ShO	Relief Pitching W	Relief Pitching L	Relief Pitching SV	Batting AB	Batting H	HR	BA	PO	A	E	DP	TC/G	FA
1990	KC A	0	1	.000	4.05	2	1	0	6.2	5	4	6	0	0	0	0	0	0	0	—	0	0	0	0	0.0	.000

Dave Smith

SMITH, DAVID MERWIN BR TR 5′10″ 170 lbs.
B. Dec. 17, 1914, Sellers, S. C.

Year	Team	W	L	PCT	ERA	G	GS	CG	IP	H	BB	SO	ShO	Relief Pitching W	Relief Pitching L	Relief Pitching SV	Batting AB	Batting H	HR	BA	PO	A	E	DP	TC/G	FA
1938	PHI A	2	1	.667	5.08	21	0	0	44.1	50	28	13	0	2	1	0	12	0	0	.000	2	8	0	0	0.5	1.000
1939		0	0	—	0.00	1	0	0		1	2	0	0	0	0	0	0	0	0	—	0	0	0	0	0.0	.000
2 yrs.		2	1	.667	5.08	22	0	0	44.1	51	30	13	0	2	1	0	12	0	0	.000	2	8	0	0	0.5	1.000

Dave Smith

SMITH, DAVID STANLEY BR TR 6′ 1″ 195 lbs.
B. Jan. 21, 1955, Richmond, Calif.

Year	Team	W	L	PCT	ERA	G	GS	CG	IP	H	BB	SO	ShO	Relief Pitching W	Relief Pitching L	Relief Pitching SV	Batting AB	Batting H	HR	BA	PO	A	E	DP	TC/G	FA
1980	HOU N	7	5	.583	1.92	57	0	0	103	90	32	85	0	7	5	10	12	0	0	.000	3	11	1	0	0.3	.933
1981		5	3	.625	2.76	42	0	0	75	54	23	52	0	5	3	8	8	2	0	.250	3	11	1	0	0.4	.933
1982		5	4	.556	3.84	49	1	0	63.1	69	31	28	0	5	4	11	2	0	0	.000	3	7	2	2	0.2	.833
1983		3	1	.750	3.10	42	0	0	72.2	72	36	41	0	3	1	6	5	0	0	.000	3	4	2	0	0.2	.778
1984		5	4	.556	2.21	53	0	0	77.1	60	20	45	0	5	4	5	4	0	0	.000	5	9	1	1	0.3	.933
1985		9	5	.643	2.27	64	0	0	79.1	69	17	40	0	9	5	27	3	0	0	.000	4	7	3	1	0.2	.786
1986		4	7	.364	2.73	54	0	0	56	39	22	46	0	4	7	33	2	0	0	.000	7	6	0	0	0.2	1.000
1987		2	3	.400	1.65	50	0	0	60	39	21	73	0	2	3	24	2	1	0	.500	4	4	0	0	0.2	1.000
1988		4	5	.444	2.67	51	0	0	57.1	60	19	38	0	4	5	27	2	0	0	.000	3	8	0	0	0.2	1.000
1989		3	4	.429	2.64	52	0	0	58	49	19	31	0	3	4	25	1	0	0	.000	6	10	0	1	0.3	1.000
1990		6	6	.500	2.39	49	0	0	60.1	45	20	50	0	6	6	23	2	0	0	.000	1	3	1	1	0.1	.800
1991	CHI N	0	6	.000	6.00	35	0	0	33	39	19	16	0	0	6	17	1	0	0	.000	0	5	0	0	0.1	1.000
1992		0	0	—	2.51	11	0	0	14.1	15	4	3	0	0	0	0	0	0	0	—	0	2	0	0	0.2	1.000
13 yrs.		53	53	.500	2.67	609	1	0	809.2	700	283	548	0	53	53	216	44	3	0	.068	42	87	11	6	0.2	.921
DIVISIONAL PLAYOFF SERIES																										
1981	HOU N	0	0	—	3.86	2	0	0	2.1	2	0	4	0	0	0	0	0	0	0	—	0	0	0	0	0.0	.000
LEAGUE CHAMPIONSHIP SERIES																										
1980	HOU N	1	0	1.000	3.86	3	0	0	2.1	4	2	4	0	1	0	0	0	0	0	—	0	0	0	0	0.0	.000
1986		0	1	.000	9.00	2	0	0	2	2	3	2	0	0	1	0	0	0	0	—	0	0	0	0	0.0	.000
2 yrs.		1	1	.500	6.23	5	0	0	4.1	6	5	6	0	1	1	0	0	0	0		0	0	0	0	0.0	

Dave Smith

SMITH, DAVID WAYNE BR TR 6′ 1″ 190 lbs.
B. Aug. 30, 1957, Tomball, Tex.

Year	Team	W	L	PCT	ERA	G	GS	CG	IP	H	BB	SO	ShO	Relief Pitching W	Relief Pitching L	Relief Pitching SV	Batting AB	Batting H	HR	BA	PO	A	E	DP	TC/G	FA
1984	CAL A	0	0	—	18.00	1	0	0	1	4	0	0	0	0	0	0	0	0	0	—	0	0	0	0	0.0	.000
1985		0	0	—	7.20	4	0	0	5	5	1	3	0	0	0	0	0	0	0	—	0	1	0	0	0.3	1.000
2 yrs.		0	0		9.00	5	0	0	6	9	1	3	0	0	0	0	0	0	0		0	1	0	0	0.2	1.000

Doug Smith

SMITH, DOUGLASS WELDON BL TL 5′10″ 168 lbs.
B. May 25, 1892, Millers Falls, Mass. D. Sept. 18, 1973, Greenfield, Mass.

Year	Team	W	L	PCT	ERA	G	GS	CG	IP	H	BB	SO	ShO	Relief Pitching W	Relief Pitching L	Relief Pitching SV	Batting AB	Batting H	HR	BA	PO	A	E	DP	TC/G	FA
1912	BOS A	0	0	—	3.00	1	0	0	3	4	0	1	0	0	0	0	0	0	0	—	0	0	0	0	0.0	.000

Ed Smith

SMITH, RHESA EDWARD BR TR 5′11″ 170 lbs.
B. Feb. 21, 1879, Mentone, Ind. D. Mar. 20, 1955, Tarpon Springs, Fla.

Year	Team	W	L	PCT	ERA	G	GS	CG	IP	H	BB	SO	ShO	Relief Pitching W	Relief Pitching L	Relief Pitching SV	Batting AB	Batting H	HR	BA	PO	A	E	DP	TC/G	FA
1906	STL A	8	11	.421	3.72	19	18	13	154.2	153	53	45	0	1	0	0	54	11	0	.204	7	54	6	2	3.5	.910

Eddie Smith

SMITH, EDGAR BB TL 5′10″ 174 lbs.
B. Dec. 14, 1913, Mansfield, N. J. D. Jan. 2, 1994, Willingboro, N. J.

Year	Team	W	L	PCT	ERA	G	GS	CG	IP	H	BB	SO	ShO	Relief W	Relief L	Relief SV	AB	H	HR	BA	PO	A	E	DP	TC/G	FA
1936	PHI A	1	1	.500	1.89	2	2	2	19	22	8	7	0	0	0	0	8	1	0	.125	0	4	0	0	2.0	1.000
1937		4	17	.190	3.94	38	23	14	196.2	178	90	79	1	0	1	5	73	17	0	.233	9	28	0	1	0.9	1.000
1938		3	10	.231	5.92	43	7	0	130.2	151	76	78	0	3	**5**	4	42	12	0	.286	10	20	1	1	0.7	.968
1939	2 teams PHI A (3G 1–0) CHI A (29G 9–11)																									
″	total	10	11	.476	3.79	32	22	7	180.1	168	92	70	1	2	0	0	52	6	0	.115	7	23	3	1	1.0	.909
1940	CHI A	14	9	.609	3.21	32	28	12	207.1	179	95	119	0	0	1	0	69	15	0	.217	6	32	2	2	1.3	.950
1941		13	17	.433	3.18	34	33	21	263.1	243	114	111	1	0	0	1	88	19	0	.216	10	51	1	3	1.8	.984
1942		7	**20**	.259	3.98	29	28	18	215	223	86	78	2	0	0	1	73	9	0	.123	7	55	2	3	2.2	.969
1943		11	11	.500	3.69	25	25	14	187.2	197	76	66	2	0	0	0	69	11	1	.159	6	43	1	4	2.0	.980
1946		8	11	.421	2.85	24	21	3	145.1	135	60	59	1	1	0	1	45	8	0	.178	2	29	6	1	1.5	.838
1947	2 teams CHI A (15G 1–3) BOS A (8G 1–3)																									
″	total	2	6	.250	7.33	23	8	0	50.1	58	42	27	0	0	1	0	12	2	0	.167	2	5	3	0	0.4	.700
10 yrs.		73	113	.392	3.82	282	197	91	1595.2	1554	739	694	8	6	8	12	531	100	1	.188	59	290	19	16	1.3	.948

Edgar Smith

SMITH, EDGAR EUGENE BR TR 5′10″ 160 lbs.
B. June 12, 1862, Providence, R. I. D. Nov. 3, 1892, Providence, R. I.

Year	Team	W	L	PCT	ERA	G	GS	CG	IP	H	BB	SO	ShO	Relief W	Relief L	Relief SV	AB	H	HR	BA	PO	A	E	DP	TC/G	FA
1883	PHI N	0	1	.000	15.43	1	1	0	7	18	3	2	0	0	0	0	13	5	0	.385	3	0	1	0	0.7	.750
1884	WAS AA	0	2	.000	***4.91***	3	2	2	22	27	5	4	0	0	0	0	57	5	0	.088	19	14	9	4	2.8	.786
1885	PRO N	1	0	1.000	1.00	1	1	1	9	9	0	1	0	0	0	0	4	1	0	.250	0	3	1	0	4.0	.750
1890	CLE N	1	4	.200	4.30	6	6	5	44	42	10	11	0	0	0	0	24	7	0	.292	3	14	2	1	2.4	.895
4 yrs.		2	7	.222	5.05	11	10	8	82	96	18	18	0	0	0	0	*				25	31	13	5	2.3	.812

Elmer Smith

SMITH, ELMER ELLSWORTH BL TL 5′11″ 178 lbs.
B. Mar. 23, 1868, Pittsburgh, Pa. D. Nov. 3, 1945, Pittsburgh, Pa.

Year	Team	W	L	PCT	ERA	G	GS	CG	IP	H	BB	SO	ShO	Relief W	Relief L	Relief SV	AB	H	HR	BA	PO	A	E	DP	TC/G	FA
1886	CIN AA	4	4	.500	*3.96*	9	9	8	72.2	57	44	40	0	0	0	0	28	8	0	.286	1	3	2	0	0.6	.667
1887		34	18	.654	***2.94***	52	52	49	447.1	400	126	176	3	0	0	0	186	47	0	.253	9	67	13	2	1.6	.854
1888		22	17	.564	2.74	40	40	37	348.1	309	89	154	5	0	0	0	129	29	0	.225	4	58	12	0	1.8	.838
1889		9	12	.429	4.88	29	22	16	203	253	101	104	0	2	0	0	83	23	2	.277	2	21	5	0	1.0	.821
1892	PIT N	6	7	.462	3.63	17	13	12	134	140	58	51	1	0	1	0	511	140	4	.274	232	38	37	0	2.2	.879
1894		0	0	—	4.50	1	0	0	4	6	1	0	0	0	0	0	489	174	6	.356	271	20	25	7	2.5	.921
1898	CIN N	0	0	—	18.00	1	0	0	1	2	3	0	0	0	0	0	486	166	1	.342	275	18	21	8	2.5	.933
7 yrs.		75	58	.564	3.36	149	136	122	1210.1	1167	422	525	9	2	1	0	*				2224	315	238	37	2.2	.914

Frank Smith

SMITH, FRANK ELMER (Piano Mover) BR TR 5′10½″ 194 lbs.
Born Frank Elmer Schmidt.
B. Oct. 28, 1879, Pittsburgh, Pa. D. Nov. 3, 1952, Pittsburgh, Pa.

Year	Team	W	L	PCT	ERA	G	GS	CG	IP	H	BB	SO	ShO	Relief W	Relief L	Relief SV	AB	H	HR	BA	PO	A	E	DP	TC/G	FA
1904	CHI A	16	9	.640	2.09	26	23	22	202.1	157	58	107	4	2	0	0	72	18	0	.250	15	53	7	2	2.9	.907
1905		19	13	.594	2.13	39	31	27	291.2	215	107	171	4	2	1	0	106	24	1	.226	27	77	3	3	2.7	.972
1906		5	5	.500	3.39	20	13	8	122	124	37	53	1	0	0	1	41	12	0	.293	6	42	2	1	2.5	.960
1907		23	10	.697	2.47	41	37	29	310	280	**111**	139	3	0	0	0	92	18	0	.196	20	109	5	2	3.3	.963
1908		16	17	.485	2.03	41	35	24	297.2	213	73	129	3	1	1	1	106	20	0	.189	23	101	2	4	3.1	.984
1909		25	17	.595	1.80	**51**	**40**	**37**	**365**	**278**	70	**177**	7	3	2	1	127	22	0	.173	26	154	4	3	3.6	.978
1910	2 teams CHI A (19G 4–9) BOS A (4G 1–2)																									
″	total	5	11	.313	2.53	23	18	11	156.2	113	51	58	3	0	0	0	52	9	0	.173	14	68	4	0	3.7	.953
1911	2 teams BOS A (1G 0–0) CIN N (34G 10–14)																									
″	total	10	14	.417	4.13	35	19	10	178.2	204	58	68	0	4	**5**	1	56	12	0	.214	16	68	6	4	2.6	.933
1912	CIN N	1	1	.500	6.35	7	3	1	22.2	34	15	5	0	1	0	0	6	0	0	.000	3	3	1	1	1.0	.857
1914	BAL F	10	8	.556	2.99	39	22	9	174.2	180	47	83	1	1	2	2	59	12	0	.203	11	57	2	2	1.8	.971
1915	2 teams BAL F (17G 4–4) BKN F (15G 5–2)																									
″	total	9	6	.600	4.04	32	14	6	151.2	177	49	61	1	3	0	0	49	9	1	.184	7	50	1	0	1.8	.983
11 yrs.		139	111	.556	2.59	354	255	184	2273	1975	676	1051	27	17	11	6	766	156	2	.204	168	782	37	22	2.8	.963

Frank Smith

SMITH, FRANK THOMAS BR TR 6′ 3″ 195 lbs.
B. Apr. 4, 1928, Pierrepont Manor, N. Y.

Year	Team	W	L	PCT	ERA	G	GS	CG	IP	H	BB	SO	ShO	Relief W	Relief L	Relief SV	AB	H	HR	BA	PO	A	E	DP	TC/G	FA
1950	CIN N	2	7	.222	3.87	38	4	0	90.2	73	39	55	0	2	4	3	21	2	0	.095	0	14	2	0	0.4	.875
1951		5	5	.500	3.20	50	0	0	76	65	22	34	0	5	5	11	10	0	0	.000	3	17	1	0	0.4	.952
1952		12	11	.522	3.75	53	2	1	122.1	109	41	77	0	12	**9**	7	29	5	0	.172	1	16	3	2	0.4	.850
1953		8	1	.889	5.49	50	1	0	83.2	89	25	42	0	8	1	2	13	2	0	.154	1	19	2	2	0.4	.909
1954		5	8	.385	2.67	50	0	0	81	60	29	51	0	5	**8**	20	10	1	0	.100	1	15	0	0	0.3	1.000
1955	STL N	3	1	.750	3.23	28	0	0	39	27	23	17	0	3	1	1	4	0	0	.000	1	7	1	0	0.3	.889
1956	CIN N	0	0	—	12.00	2	0	0	3	3	2	1	0	0	0	0	0	0	0	—	0	0	0	0	0.0	.000
7 yrs.		35	33	.515	3.81	271	7	1	495.2	426	181	277	0	35	28	44	87	10	0	.115	7	88	9	4	0.4	.913

Fred Smith

SMITH, FREDERICK BR TR 6′ 186 lbs.
B. Nov. 24, 1878, New Diggings, Wis. D. Feb. 4, 1964, Los Angeles, Calif.

Year	Team	W	L	PCT	ERA	G	GS	CG	IP	H	BB	SO	ShO	Relief W	Relief L	Relief SV	AB	H	HR	BA	PO	A	E	DP	TC/G	FA
1907	CIN N	2	7	.222	2.85	18	9	5	85.1	90	24	19	0	0	3	1	28	3	0	.107	6	25	2	0	1.8	.939

Fred Smith

SMITH, FREDERICK C. BL TR 5′11″ 156 lbs.
B. Mar. 25, 1863, Greene, N. Y. D. Jan. 9, 1941, Syracuse, N. Y.

Year	Team	W	L	PCT	ERA	G	GS	CG	IP	H	BB	SO	ShO	Relief W	Relief L	Relief SV	AB	H	HR	BA	PO	A	E	DP	TC/G	FA
1890	TOL AA	19	13	.594	*3.27*	35	34	31	286	273	90	116	2	0	0	0	126	21	0	.167	19	70	6	1	2.5	.937

George Smith

SMITH, GEORGE ALLEN (Columbia George) BR TR 5′11″ 156 lbs.
B. May 31, 1892, Byram, Conn. D. Jan. 7, 1965, Greenwich, Conn.

Year	Team	W	L	PCT	ERA	G	GS	CG	IP	H	BB	SO	ShO	Relief W	Relief L	Relief SV	AB	H	HR	BA	PO	A	E	DP	TC/G	FA
1916	NY N	1	0	1.000	2.61	9	1	0	20.2	14	6	9	0	0	0	0	2	0	0	.000	1	8	1	0	1.1	.900
1917		0	3	.000	2.84	14	1	1	38	38	11	16	0	0	2	0	9	0	0	.000	2	10	0	0	0.9	1.000
1918	3 teams CIN N (10G 2–3) NY N (5G 2–3) BKN N (8G 4–1)																									
″	total	8	7	.533	3.41	23	13	9	132	140	22	41	1	2	1	0	40	5	0	.125	2	40	1	1	1.9	.977
1919	2 teams NY N (3G 0–2) PHI N (31G 5–11)																									
″	total	5	13	.278	3.36	34	21	11	195.2	212	50	42	1	1	1	0	63	8	0	.127	9	55	4	0	2.0	.941
1920	PHI N	13	18	.419	3.45	43	28	10	250.2	265	51	51	2	3	5	2	72	7	0	.097	8	65	4	1	1.8	.948

George Smith *continued*

Year	Team	Lg	W	L	PCT	ERA	G	GS	CG	IP	H	BB	SO	ShO	Relief W	Relief L	Relief SV	Batting AB	Batting H	Batting HR	BA	PO	A	E	DP	TC/G	FA
1921			4	**20**	.167	4.76	39	28	12	221.1	303	52	45	1	1	1	1	71	4	0	.056	5	54	4	0	1.6	.937
1922			5	14	.263	4.78	42	16	6	194	250	35	44	1	1	3	0	66	5	0	.076	4	41	4	1	1.2	.918
1923	BKN	N	3	6	.333	3.66	25	7	3	91	99	28	15	0	0	3	1	26	5	0	.192	2	13	1	0	0.6	.938
8 yrs.			39	81	.325	3.89	229	115	52	1143.1	1321	255	263	6	8	16	4	349	34	0	.097	33	286	19	3	1.5	.944

George Smith

SMITH, GEORGE SHELBY BR TR 6′ 1″ 175 lbs.
B. Oct. 27, 1901, Louisville, Ky. D. May 26, 1981, Richmond, Va.

Year	Team	Lg	W	L	PCT	ERA	G	GS	CG	IP	H	BB	SO	ShO	Relief W	Relief L	Relief SV	Batting AB	Batting H	Batting HR	BA	PO	A	E	DP	TC/G	FA
1926	DET	A	1	2	.333	6.95	23	1	0	44	55	33	15	0	1	1	0	5	0	0	.000	5	6	2	0	0.6	.846
1927			4	1	.800	3.91	29	0	0	71.1	62	50	32	0	4	1	0	19	7	2	.368	4	15	3	0	0.8	.864
1928			1	1	.500	4.42	39	2	0	106	103	50	54	0	0	1	3	27	3	0	.111	8	13	2	0	0.6	.913
1929			3	2	.600	5.80	14	2	1	35.2	42	36	13	0	2	2	0	12	5	0	.417	3	11	3	2	1.2	.824
1930	BOS	A	1	2	.333	6.84	27	2	0	73.2	92	49	21	0	1	2	0	24	8	0	.333	5	15	1	1	0.8	.952
5 yrs.			10	8	.556	5.33	132	7	1	330.2	354	218	135	0	8	7	3	87	23	2	.264	25	60	11	3	0.7	.885

Germany Smith

SMITH, GEORGE J. BR TR 6′ 175 lbs.
B. Apr. 21, 1863, Pittsburgh, Pa. D. Dec. 1, 1927, Altoona, Pa.

Year	Team	Lg	W	L	PCT	ERA	G	GS	CG	IP	H	BB	SO	ShO	Relief W	Relief L	Relief SV	Batting AB	Batting H	Batting HR	BA	PO	A	E	DP	TC/G	FA
1884	ALT	U	0	0	—	*9.00*	1	0	0	1	3	0	1	0	0	0	0	*				155	331	69	27	6.1	.884

Hal Smith

SMITH, HAROLD LAVERNE BR TR 6′ 3″ 195 lbs.
B. June 30, 1902, Creston, Iowa D. Sept. 27, 1992, Ft. Lauderdale, Fla.

Year	Team	Lg	W	L	PCT	ERA	G	GS	CG	IP	H	BB	SO	ShO	Relief W	Relief L	Relief SV	Batting AB	Batting H	Batting HR	BA	PO	A	E	DP	TC/G	FA
1932	PIT	N	1	0	1.000	0.75	2	1	1	12	9	2	4	1	0	0	0	3	0	0	.000	0	3	0	0	1.5	1.000
1933			8	7	.533	2.86	28	19	8	145	149	31	40	2	1	0	1	47	6	0	.128	3	25	2	1	1.1	.933
1934			3	4	.429	7.20	20	5	1	50	72	18	15	0	1	2	0	17	1	0	.059	1	10	1	0	0.6	.917
1935			0	0	—	3.00	1	0	0	3	2	1	0	0	0	0	0	0	0	0	—	0	0	0	0	0.0	.000
4 yrs.			12	11	.522	3.77	51	25	10	210	232	52	59	3	2	2	1	67	7	0	.104	4	38	3	1	0.9	.933

Harry Smith

SMITH, HARRISON MORTON BR TR 5′ 9″ 160 lbs.
B. Aug. 15, 1889, Union, Neb. D. July 26, 1964, Dunbar, Neb.

Year	Team	Lg	W	L	PCT	ERA	G	GS	CG	IP	H	BB	SO	ShO	Relief W	Relief L	Relief SV	Batting AB	Batting H	Batting HR	BA	PO	A	E	DP	TC/G	FA
1912	CHI	A	1	0	1.000	1.80	1	1	0	5	6	0	1	0	0	0	0	1	0	0	.000	0	1	0	0	1.0	1.000

Heinie Smith

SMITH, GEORGE HENRY BR TR 5′ 9½″ 160 lbs.
B. Oct. 24, 1871, Pittsburgh, Pa. D. June 25, 1939, Buffalo, N. Y.
Manager 1902.

Year	Team	Lg	W	L	PCT	ERA	G	GS	CG	IP	H	BB	SO	ShO	Relief W	Relief L	Relief SV	Batting AB	Batting H	Batting HR	BA	PO	A	E	DP	TC/G	FA
1901	NY	N	0	1	.000	8.10	2	1	1	13.1	24	5	5	0	0	0	0	*				46	57	8	8	5.3	.928

Jack Smith

SMITH, JACK HATFIELD BR TR 6′ 185 lbs.
B. Nov. 15, 1935, Pikeville, Ky.

Year	Team	Lg	W	L	PCT	ERA	G	GS	CG	IP	H	BB	SO	ShO	Relief W	Relief L	Relief SV	Batting AB	Batting H	Batting HR	BA	PO	A	E	DP	TC/G	FA
1962	LA	N	0	0	—	4.50	8	0	0	10	10	4	7	0	0	0	1	1	0	0	.000	0	0	0	0	0.0	.000
1963			0	0	—	7.56	4	0	0	8.1	10	2	5	0	0	0	0	2	0	0	.000	0	3	0	0	0.8	1.000
1964	MIL	N	2	2	.500	3.77	22	0	0	31	28	11	19	0	2	2	0	3	1	0	.333	1	11	1	1	0.6	.923
3 yrs.			2	2	.500	4.56	34	0	0	49.1	48	17	31	0	2	2	1	6	1	0	.167	1	14	1	1	0.5	.938

Jake Smith

SMITH, JACOB BB TL 6′ 5″ 200 lbs.
Born Jacob Schmidt.
B. June 10, 1887, Dravosburg, Pa. D. Nov. 7, 1948, East McKeesport, Pa.

Year	Team	Lg	W	L	PCT	ERA	G	GS	CG	IP	H	BB	SO	ShO	Relief W	Relief L	Relief SV	Batting AB	Batting H	Batting HR	BA	PO	A	E	DP	TC/G	FA
1911	PHI	N	0	0	—	0.00	2	0	0	5	3	2	1	0	0	0	0	3	0	0	.000	0	2	0	0	1.0	1.000

Lee Smith

SMITH, LEE ARTHUR, JR. BR TR 6′ 5″ 220 lbs.
B. Dec. 4, 1957, Jamestown, La.

Year	Team	Lg	W	L	PCT	ERA	G	GS	CG	IP	H	BB	SO	ShO	Relief W	Relief L	Relief SV	Batting AB	Batting H	Batting HR	BA	PO	A	E	DP	TC/G	FA
1980	CHI	N	2	0	1.000	2.86	18	0	0	22	21	14	17	0	2	0	0	0	0	0	—	0	3	0	0	0.2	1.000
1981			3	6	.333	3.49	40	1	0	67	57	31	50	0	3	5	1	9	0	0	.000	3	9	0	0	0.3	1.000
1982			2	5	.286	2.69	72	5	0	117	105	37	99	0	2	1	17	16	1	1	.063	9	10	1	2	0.3	.950
1983			4	10	.286	1.65	66	0	0	103.1	70	41	91	0	4	10	**29**	9	1	0	.111	8	9	0	0	0.3	1.000
1984			9	7	.563	3.65	69	0	0	101	98	35	86	0	9	7	33	13	1	0	.077	6	13	0	2	0.3	1.000
1985			7	4	.636	3.04	65	0	0	97.2	87	32	112	0	7	4	33	6	0	0	.000	3	9	0	1	0.2	1.000
1986			9	9	.500	3.09	66	0	0	90.1	69	42	93	0	9	9	31	5	0	0	.000	1	12	0	2	0.2	1.000
1987			4	10	.286	3.12	62	0	0	83.2	84	32	96	0	4	**10**	36	2	0	0	.000	3	8	0	0	0.2	1.000
1988	BOS	A	4	5	.444	2.80	64	0	0	83.2	72	37	96	0	4	5	29	0	0	0	—	5	4	1	0	0.2	.900
1989			6	1	.857	3.57	64	0	0	70.2	53	33	96	0	6	1	25	0	0	0	—	1	1	0	0	0.0	1.000
1990	2 teams	BOS A	(11G 2–1)	STL N	(53G 3–4)																						
″	total		5	5	.500	2.06	64	0	0	83	71	29	87	0	5	5	31	2	0	0	.000	2	3	0	0	0.1	1.000
1991	STL	N	6	3	.667	2.34	67	0	0	73	70	13	67	0	6	3	**47**	0	0	0	—	3	6	0	0	0.1	1.000
1992			4	9	.308	3.12	70	0	0	75	62	26	60	0	4	9	**43**	0	0	0	—	1	7	1	1	0.1	.889
1993	2 teams	STL N	(55G 2–4)	NY A	(8G 0–0)																						
″	total		2	4	.333	3.88	63	0	0	58	53	14	60	0	2	4	46	2	0	0	.000	0	2	0	0	0.0	1.000
1994	BAL	A	1	4	.200	3.29	41	0	0	38.1	34	11	42	0	1	4	**33**	0	0	0	—	2	2	1	0	0.1	.800
1995	CAL	A	0	5	.000	3.47	52	0	0	49.1	42	25	43	0	0	5	37	0	0	0	—	1	4	0	0	0.1	1.000
16 yrs.			68	87	.439	2.95	943	6	0	1213	1048	452	1195	0	68	82	471	64	3	1	.047	48	102	4	8	0.2	.974
							6th										**1st**										

LEAGUE CHAMPIONSHIP SERIES

Year	Team	Lg	W	L	PCT	ERA	G	GS	CG	IP	H	BB	SO	ShO	Relief W	Relief L	Relief SV	Batting AB	Batting H	Batting HR	BA	PO	A	E	DP	TC/G	FA
1984	CHI	N	0	1	.000	9.00	2	0	0	2	3	0	3	0	0	1	1	0	0	0	—	0	0	0	0	0.0	.000
1988	BOS	A	0	1	.000	8.10	2	0	0	3.1	6	1	4	0	0	1	0	0	0	0	—	0	0	0	0	0.0	.000
2 yrs.			0	2	.000	8.44	4	0	0	5.1	9	1	7	0	0	2	1	0	0	0	—	0	0	0	0	0.0	

Mark Smith

SMITH, MARK CHRISTOPHER BL TR 6′ 2″ 215 lbs.
B. Nov. 23, 1955, Alexandria, Va.

Year	Team	Lg	W	L	PCT	ERA	G	GS	CG	IP	H	BB	SO	ShO	Relief W	Relief L	Relief SV	Batting AB	Batting H	Batting HR	BA	PO	A	E	DP	TC/G	FA
1983	OAK	A	1	0	1.000	6.75	8	1	0	14.2	24	6	10	0	1	0	0	0	0	0	—	0	1	0	0	0.1	1.000

Mike Smith

SMITH, MICHAEL ANTHONY BR TR 6′ 3″ 180 lbs.
B. Oct. 31, 1963, San Antonio, Tex.

Year	Team	Lg	W	L	PCT	ERA	G	GS	CG	IP	H	BB	SO	ShO	Relief W	Relief L	Relief SV	Batting AB	Batting H	Batting HR	BA	PO	A	E	DP	TC/G	FA
1989	BAL	A	2	0	1.000	7.65	13	1	0	20	25	14	12	0	2	0	0	0	0	0	—	1	4	0	0	0.4	1.000
1990			0	0	—	12.00	2	0	0	3	4	1	2	0	0	0	0	0	0	0	—	0	0	0	0	0.0	.000
2 yrs.			2	0	1.000	8.22	15	1	0	23	29	15	14	0	2	0	0	0	0	0	—	1	4	0	0	0.3	1.000

Mike Smith

SMITH, MICHAEL ANTHONY BR TR 6′ 1″ 195 lbs.
B. Feb. 23, 1961, Jackson, Miss.

Year	Team	W	L	PCT	ERA	G	GS	CG	IP	H	BB	SO	ShO	Relief Pitching W	Relief Pitching L	Relief Pitching SV	Batting AB	Batting H	Batting HR	BA	PO	A	E	DP	TC/G	FA
1984	CIN N	1	0	1.000	5.23	8	0	0	10.1	12	5	7	0	1	0	0	0	0	0	—	1	0	0	0	0.1	1.000
1985		0	0	—	5.40	2	0	0	3.1	2	1	2	0	0	0	0	0	0	0	—	0	1	0	0	0.5	1.000
1986		0	0	—	13.50	2	1	0	3.1	7	1	1	0	0	0	0	0	0	0	—	0	0	0	0	0.0	.000
1988	MON N	0	0	—	3.12	5	0	0	8.2	6	5	4	0	0	0	1	2	0	0	.000	0	1	0	0	0.2	1.000
1989	PIT N	0	1	.000	3.75	16	0	0	24	28	10	12	0	0	1	0	3	0	0	.000	2	8	0	0	0.6	1.000
5 yrs.		1	1	.500	4.71	33	1	0	49.2	55	22	26	0	1	1	1	5	0	0	.000	3	10	0	0	0.4	1.000

Pete Smith

SMITH, PETER JOHN BR TR 6′ 2″ 185 lbs.
B. Feb. 27, 1966, Abington, Mass.

Year	Team	W	L	PCT	ERA	G	GS	CG	IP	H	BB	SO	ShO	Relief Pitching W	Relief Pitching L	Relief Pitching SV	Batting AB	Batting H	Batting HR	BA	PO	A	E	DP	TC/G	FA
1987	ATL N	1	2	.333	4.83	6	6	0	31.2	39	14	11	0	0	0	0	11	1	0	.091	1	2	1	0	0.7	.750
1988		7	15	.318	3.69	32	32	5	195.1	183	88	124	3	0	0	0	53	6	0	.113	12	19	3	0	1.1	.912
1989		5	14	.263	4.75	28	27	1	142	144	57	115	0	0	0	0	41	4	0	.098	11	11	1	2	0.8	.957
1990		5	6	.455	4.79	13	13	3	77	77	24	56	0	0	0	0	23	2	0	.087	5	5	0	0	0.8	1.000
1991		1	3	.250	5.06	14	10	0	48	48	22	29	0	0	0	0	12	2	0	.167	3	6	0	0	0.6	1.000
1992		7	0	1.000	2.05	12	11	2	79	63	28	43	1	0	0	0	26	1	0	.038	3	13	1	1	1.4	.941
1993		4	8	.333	4.37	20	14	0	90.2	92	36	53	0	1	0	0	27	6	0	.222	7	14	0	0	1.0	1.000
1994	NY N	4	10	.286	5.55	21	21	1	131.1	145	42	62	0	0	0	0	37	5	0	.135	12	21	0	1	1.6	1.000
1995	CIN N	1	2	.333	6.66	11	2	0	24.1	30	7	14	0	1	1	0	3	0	0	.000	1	6	0	0	0.6	1.000
9 yrs.		35	60	.368	4.40	157	136	12	819.1	821	318	507	4	2	1	0	233	27	0	.116	55	97	6	4	1.0	.962
LEAGUE CHAMPIONSHIP SERIES																										
1992	ATL N	0	0	—	2.45	2	0	0	3.2	2	3	3	0	0	0	0	1	0	0	.000	0	1	0	0	0.5	1.000
WORLD SERIES																										
1992	ATL N	0	0	—	0.00	1	0	0	3	3	0	0	0	0	0	0	1	0	0	.000	0	0	0	0	0.0	.000

Pete Smith

SMITH, PETER LUKE BR TR 6′ 2″ 190 lbs.
B. Mar. 19, 1940, Natick, Mass.

Year	Team	W	L	PCT	ERA	G	GS	CG	IP	H	BB	SO	ShO	Relief Pitching W	Relief Pitching L	Relief Pitching SV	Batting AB	Batting H	Batting HR	BA	PO	A	E	DP	TC/G	FA
1962	BOS A	0	1	.000	19.64	1	1	0	3.2	7	2	1	0	0	0	0	1	0	0	.000	0	1	0	0	1.0	1.000
1963		0	0	—	3.60	6	1	0	15	11	6	6	0	0	0	0	2	0	0	.000	1	3	0	0	0.7	1.000
2 yrs.		0	1	.000	6.75	7	2	0	18.2	18	8	7	0	0	0	0	3	0	0	.000	1	4	0	0	0.7	1.000

Phenomenal Smith

SMITH, JOHN FRANCIS BL TL 5′ 6½″ 161 lbs.
Born John Francis Gammon.
B. Dec. 12, 1864, Philadelphia, Pa. D. Apr. 3, 1952, Manchester, N. H.

Year	Team	W	L	PCT	ERA	G	GS	CG	IP	H	BB	SO	ShO	Relief Pitching W	Relief Pitching L	Relief Pitching SV	Batting AB	Batting H	Batting HR	BA	PO	A	E	DP	TC/G	FA
1884	3 teams BAL U (9G 3–3) PHI AA (1G 0–1) PIT AA (1G 0–1)																									
″	total	3	5	.375	4.86	11	10	6	76	108	19	17	0	0	0	0	43	7	0	.163	7	7	7	1	1.3	.667
1885	2 teams BKN AA (1G 0–1) PHI AA (1G 0–1)																									
″	total	0	2	.000	11.25	2	2	1	12	19	10	9	0	0	0	0	5	1	0	.200	3	3	1	0	3.5	.857
1886	DET N	1	1	.500	2.16	3	3	3	25	16	8	15	0	0	0	0	9	1	0	.111	1	2	0	0	1.0	1.000
1887	BAL AA	25	30	.455	*3.79*	58	55	54	491.1	526	176	206	1	0	**2**	0	205	48	1	.234	16	108	24	1	2.3	.838
1888	2 teams BAL AA (35G 14–19) PHI AA (3G 2–1)																									
″	total	16	20	.444	3.55	38	35	34	314	270	147	171	0	**1**	0	0	118	30	1	.254	9	53	17	1	2.0	.785
1889	PHI AA	2	3	.400	4.40	5	5	5	43	53	25	12	0	0	0	0	16	3	0	.188	0	4	1	1	1.0	.800
1890	2 teams PHI N (24G 8–12) PIT N (5G 1–3)																									
″	total	9	15	.375	4.06	29	25	24	248	248	102	96	1	1	0	0	103	31	0	.301	9	32	6	5	1.5	.872
1891	PHI N	1	1	.500	4.26	3	2	0	19	20	8	3	0	0	0	0	8	3	0	.375	1	0	1	0	0.7	.500
8 yrs.		57	77	.425	3.92	149	137	127	1228.1	1260	495	529	2	2	2	0	507	124	2	.245	46	209	57	9	1.9	.817

Pop Smith

SMITH, CHARLES MARVIN BR TR 5′11″ 170 lbs.
B. Oct. 12, 1856, Digby, Nova Scotia, Canada D. Apr. 18, 1927, Boston, Mass.

Year	Team	W	L	PCT	ERA	G	GS	CG	IP	H	BB	SO	ShO	Relief Pitching W	Relief Pitching L	Relief Pitching SV	Batting AB	Batting H	Batting HR	BA	PO	A	E	DP	TC/G	FA
1883	COL AA	0	0	—	*6.35*	3	0	0	5.2	10	0	0	0	0	0	0	*				282	243	89	32	7.4	.855

Pop Boy Smith

SMITH, CLARENCE OSSIE BR TR 6′ 1″ 176 lbs.
B. May 23, 1892, Newport, Tenn. D. Feb. 16, 1924, Sweetwater, Tex.

Year	Team	W	L	PCT	ERA	G	GS	CG	IP	H	BB	SO	ShO	Relief Pitching W	Relief Pitching L	Relief Pitching SV	Batting AB	Batting H	Batting HR	BA	PO	A	E	DP	TC/G	FA
1913	CHI A	0	1	.000	3.38	15	2	0	32	31	11	13	0	0	0	0	5	0	0	.000	2	15	0	0	1.1	1.000
1916	CLE A	1	2	.333	3.86	5	3	0	25.2	25	11	4	0	0	1	1	7	2	0	.286	4	5	1	0	2.0	.900
1917		0	1	.000	8.31	6	0	0	8.2	14	4	3	0	0	1	0	1	0	0	.000	0	9	0	0	1.5	1.000
3 yrs.		1	4	.200	4.21	26	5	0	66.1	70	26	20	0	0	2	1	13	2	0	.154	6	29	1	0	1.4	.972

Rex Smith

SMITH, REX
Born Henry W. Schmidt.
B. 16, 1864, Louisville, Ky. D. June 21, 1895, Louisville, Ky.

Year	Team	W	L	PCT	ERA	G	GS	CG	IP	H	BB	SO	ShO	Relief Pitching W	Relief Pitching L	Relief Pitching SV	Batting AB	Batting H	Batting HR	BA	PO	A	E	DP	TC/G	FA
1886	PHI AA	0	1	.000	*7.00*	1	1	1	9	15	5	4	0	0	0	0	4	0	0	.000	1	1	1	0	3.0	.667

Riverboat Smith

SMITH, ROBERT WALKAY BL TL 6′ 185 lbs.
BB 1959
B. May 13, 1928, Clarence, Mo.

Year	Team	W	L	PCT	ERA	G	GS	CG	IP	H	BB	SO	ShO	Relief Pitching W	Relief Pitching L	Relief Pitching SV	Batting AB	Batting H	Batting HR	BA	PO	A	E	DP	TC/G	FA
1958	BOS A	4	3	.571	3.78	17	7	1	66.2	61	45	43	0	1	1	0	19	2	0	.105	3	14	1	1	1.1	.944
1959	2 teams CHI N (1G 0–0) CLE A (12G 0–1)																									
″	total	0	1	.000	6.90	13	3	0	30	36	14	17	0	0	0	0	6	0	0	.000	1	6	0	2	0.5	1.000
2 yrs.		4	4	.500	4.75	30	10	1	96.2	97	59	60	0	1	1	0	25	2	0	.080	4	20	1	3	0.8	.960

Roy Smith

SMITH, LEROY PURDY III BR TR 6′ 3″ 205 lbs.
B. Sept. 6, 1961, Mt. Vernon, N. Y.

Year	Team	W	L	PCT	ERA	G	GS	CG	IP	H	BB	SO	ShO	Relief Pitching W	Relief Pitching L	Relief Pitching SV	Batting AB	Batting H	Batting HR	BA	PO	A	E	DP	TC/G	FA
1984	CLE A	5	5	.500	4.59	22	14	0	86.1	91	40	55	0	0	0	0	0	0	0	—	4	6	3	0	0.6	.769
1985		1	4	.200	5.34	12	11	1	62.1	84	17	28	0	0	0	0	0	0	0	—	6	3	0	0	0.8	1.000
1986	MIN A	0	2	.000	6.97	5	0	0	10.1	13	5	8	0	0	2	0	0	0	0	—	0	1	0	0	0.2	1.000
1987		1	0	1.000	4.96	7	1	0	16.1	20	6	8	0	0	0	0	0	0	0	—	0	2	0	0	0.3	1.000
1988		3	0	1.000	2.68	9	4	0	37	29	12	17	0	1	0	0	0	0	0	—	3	2	0	0	0.6	1.000
1989		10	6	.625	3.92	32	26	2	172.1	180	51	92	0	0	0	1	0	0	0	—	9	13	0	1	0.7	1.000
1990		5	10	.333	4.81	32	23	1	153.1	191	47	87	1	0	0	0	0	0	0	—	10	9	1	0	0.6	.950
1991	BAL A	5	4	.556	5.60	17	14	0	80.1	99	24	25	0	0	1	0	0	0	0	—	9	8	0	0	1.0	1.000
8 yrs.		30	31	.492	4.60	136	93	4	618.1	707	202	320	1	1	3	1	0	0	0		41	44	4	1	0.7	.955

Rufus Smith

SMITH, RUFUS FRAZIER BR TL 5′ 8″ 165 lbs.
B. Jan. 24, 1905, Guilford College, N. C. D. Aug. 22, 1984, Aiken, S. C.

Year	Team	W	L	PCT	ERA	G	GS	CG	IP	H	BB	SO	ShO	Relief Pitching W	Relief Pitching L	Relief Pitching SV	Batting AB	Batting H	Batting HR	BA	PO	A	E	DP	TC/G	FA
1927	DET A	0	0	—	3.38	1	1	0	8	8	3	2	0	0	0	0	3	0	0	.000	0	1	0	0	1.0	1.000

Sherry Smith

SMITH, SHERROD MALONE BR TL 6′ 1″ 170 lbs.
B. Feb. 18, 1891, Monticello, Ga. D. Sept. 12, 1949, Reidsville, Ga.

Year	Team	W	L	PCT	ERA	G	GS	CG	IP	H	BB	SO	ShO	Relief Pitching W	Relief Pitching L	Relief Pitching SV	Batting AB	Batting H	Batting HR	BA	PO	A	E	DP	TC/G	FA
1911	PIT N	0	0	—	54.00	1	0	0	0.2	4	1	0	0	0	0	0	0	0	0	—	0	0	0	0	0.0	.000
1912		0	0	—	6.75	3	0	0	4	6	1	3	0	0	0	0	0	0	0	—	0	0	0	0	0.0	.000
1915	BKN N	14	8	.636	2.59	29	20	11	173.2	169	42	52	2	3	1	2	57	14	0	.246	5	49	3	1	2.0	.947
1916		14	10	.583	2.34	36	25	15	219	193	45	67	4	2	4	1	77	21	0	.273	3	67	4	0	2.1	.946
1917		12	12	.500	3.32	38	23	15	211.1	210	51	58	0	2	1	3	77	15	0	.195	7	81	3	2	2.2	.967
1919		7	12	.368	2.24	30	19	13	173	181	29	40	2	0	1	1	54	8	0	.148	5	66	2	3	2.4	.973
1920		11	9	.550	1.85	33	13	6	136.1	134	27	33	2	6	3	3	43	10	0	.233	10	63	3	3	2.3	.961
1921		7	11	.389	3.90	35	17	9	175.1	232	34	36	0	1	2	4	57	13	1	.228	8	70	3	1	2.3	.963
1922	2 teams BKN N (28G 4–8) CLE A (2G 1–0)																									
″	total	5	8	.385	4.42	30	10	4	124.1	146	38	19	1	2	3	2	41	11	1	.268	6	40	4	2	1.7	.920
1923	CLE A	9	6	.600	3.27	30	16	10	124	129	37	23	1	1	0	1	45	11	1	.244	4	42	0	5	1.5	1.000
1924		12	14	.462	3.02	39	27	20	247.2	267	42	34	2	2	0	1	89	18	1	.202	21	72	7	4	2.6	.930
1925		11	14	.440	4.86	31	30	**22**	237	**296**	48	30	1	0	0	1	92	28	1	.304	8	64	3	1	2.4	.960
1926		11	10	.524	3.73	27	24	16	188.1	214	31	25	2	1	0	0	65	14	1	.215	10	62	0	6	2.7	1.000
1927		1	4	.200	5.45	11	2	1	38	53	14	8	0	1	2	1	12	2	0	.167	5	10	1	0	1.5	.938
14 yrs.		114	118	.491	3.32	373	226	142	2052.2	2234	440	428	17	21	17	20	709	165	6	.233	92	686	33	28	2.2	.959
WORLD SERIES																										
1916	BKN N	0	1	.000	1.35	1	1	1	13.1	7	6	2	0	0	0	0	5	1	0	.200	1	7	0	0	8.0	1.000
1920		1	1	.500	0.53	2	2	2	17	10	3	3	0	0	0	0	6	0	0	.000	2	4	0	0	3.0	1.000
2 yrs.		1	2	.333	0.89 **4th**	3	3	3	30.1	17	9	5	0	0	0	0	11	1	0	.091	3	11	0	0	4.7	1.000

Tom Smith

SMITH, THOMAS EDWARD BR TR 5′ 7½″ 165 lbs.
B. Dec. 5, 1871, Boston, Mass. D. Mar. 2, 1929, Dorchester, Mass.

Year	Team	W	L	PCT	ERA	G	GS	CG	IP	H	BB	SO	ShO	Relief Pitching W	Relief Pitching L	Relief Pitching SV	Batting AB	Batting H	Batting HR	BA	PO	A	E	DP	TC/G	FA
1894	BOS N	0	0	—	15.00	2	0	0	6	8	6	2	0	0	0	1	2	0	0	.000	0	0	0	0	0.0	.000
1895	PHI N	2	3	.400	6.88	11	7	4	68	76	53	21	0	0	0	0	33	8	0	.242	1	11	1	0	1.2	.923
1896	LOU N	2	3	.400	5.40	11	5	4	55	73	25	14	0	1	0	0	39	8	0	.205	36	18	1	2	3.7	.982
1898	STL N	0	1	.000	2.00	1	1	1	9	9	5	1	0	0	0	0	2	1	0	.500	0	3	0	0	3.0	1.000
4 yrs.		4	7	.364	6.33	25	13	9	138	166	89	38	0	1	0	1	76	17	0	.224	37	32	2	2	2.4	.972

Willie Smith

SMITH, WILLIE (Wonderful Willie) BL TL 6′ 182 lbs.
B. Feb. 11, 1939, Anniston, Ala.

Year	Team	W	L	PCT	ERA	G	GS	CG	IP	H	BB	SO	ShO	Relief Pitching W	Relief Pitching L	Relief Pitching SV	Batting AB	Batting H	Batting HR	BA	PO	A	E	DP	TC/G	FA
1963	DET A	1	0	1.000	4.57	11	2	0	21.2	24	13	16	0	1	0	2	8	1	0	.125	1	4	0	0	0.5	1.000
1964	LA A	1	4	.200	2.84	15	1	0	31.2	34	10	20	0	1	4	0	359	108	11	.301	129	8	3	1	1.4	.979
1968	2 teams CLE A (2G 0–0) CHI N (1G 0–0)																									
″	total	0	0		0.00	3	0	0	7.2	2	1	3	0	0	0	0	184	45	5	.245	196	12	5	2	1.7	.977
3 yrs.		2	4	.333	3.10	29	3	0	61	60	24	39	0	2	4	2	*				1105	63	16	66	2.6	.986

Willie Smith

SMITH, WILLIE EVERETT BR TR 6′ 6″ 250 lbs.
B. Aug. 27, 1967, Savannah, Ga.

Year	Team	W	L	PCT	ERA	G	GS	CG	IP	H	BB	SO	ShO	Relief Pitching W	Relief Pitching L	Relief Pitching SV	Batting AB	Batting H	Batting HR	BA	PO	A	E	DP	TC/G	FA
1994	STL N	1	1	.500	9.00	8	0	0	7	9	3	7	0	1	1	0	0	0	0	—	0	0	0	0	0.0	.000

Zane Smith

SMITH, ZANE WILLIAM BL TL 6′ 2″ 195 lbs.
B. Dec. 28, 1960, Madison, Wis.

Year	Team	W	L	PCT	ERA	G	GS	CG	IP	H	BB	SO	ShO	Relief Pitching W	Relief Pitching L	Relief Pitching SV	Batting AB	Batting H	Batting HR	BA	PO	A	E	DP	TC/G	FA
1984	ATL N	1	0	1.000	2.25	3	3	0	20	16	13	16	0	0	0	0	9	5	0	.556	2	3	1	1	2.0	.833
1985		9	10	.474	3.80	42	18	2	147	135	80	85	2	3	4	0	37	6	0	.162	7	35	3	2	1.1	.933
1986		8	16	.333	4.05	38	32	3	204.2	209	105	139	1	1	0	1	59	5	0	.085	7	45	1	4	1.4	.981
1987		15	10	.600	4.09	36	**36**	9	242	245	91	130	3	0	0	0	76	10	0	.132	15	43	0	4	1.6	1.000
1988		5	10	.333	4.30	23	22	3	140.1	159	44	59	0	0	0	0	42	7	0	.167	16	33	1	6	2.2	.980
1989	2 teams ATL N (17G 1–12) MON N (31G 0–1)																									
″	total	1	13	.071	3.49	48	17	0	147	141	52	93	0	0	1	2	32	6	0	.188	7	39	3	0	1.0	.939
1990	2 teams MON N (22G 6–7) PIT N (11G 6–2)																									
″	total	12	9	.571	2.55	33	31	4	215.1	196	50	130	2	0	0	0	68	11	0	.162	10	35	3	5	1.5	.938
1991	PIT N	16	10	.615	3.20	35	35	6	228	234	29	120	3	0	0	0	71	13	0	.183	12	39	3	5	1.5	.944
1992		8	8	.500	3.06	23	22	4	141	138	19	56	3	0	0	0	49	6	0	.122	6	29	0	2	1.5	1.000
1993		3	7	.300	4.55	14	14	1	83	97	22	32	0	0	0	0	25	2	0	.080	8	8	0	2	1.1	1.000
1994		10	8	.556	3.27	25	24	2	157	162	34	57	1	0	0	0	57	12	0	.211	8	40	0	1	1.9	1.000
1995	BOS A	8	8	.500	5.61	24	21	0	110.2	144	23	47	0	0	0	0	0	0	0	—	5	18	1	1	1.0	.958
12 yrs.		96	109	.468	3.68	344	275	34	1836	1876	562	964	15	4	5	3	525	83	0	.158	103	367	16	33	1.4	.967
DIVISIONAL PLAYOFF SERIES																										
1995	BOS A	0	1	.000	6.75	1	0	0	1.1	1	0	0	0	0	1	0	0	0	0	—	0	0	0	0	0.0	.000
LEAGUE CHAMPIONSHIP SERIES																										
1990	PIT N	0	2	.000	6.00	2	1	0	9	14	1	8	0	0	1	0	3	0	0	.000	0	1	0	0	0.5	1.000
1991		1	1	.500	0.61	2	2	0	14.2	15	3	10	0	0	0	0	5	0	0	.000	0	3	0	0	1.5	1.000
2 yrs.		1	3 **5th**	.250	2.66	4	3	0	23.2	29	4	18	0	0	1	0	8	0	0	.000	0	4	0	0	1.0	1.000

Roger Smithberg

SMITHBERG, ROGER CRAIG BR TR 6′ 3″ 205 lbs.
B. Mar. 21, 1966, Elgin, Ill.

Year	Team	W	L	PCT	ERA	G	GS	CG	IP	H	BB	SO	ShO	Relief Pitching W	Relief Pitching L	Relief Pitching SV	Batting AB	Batting H	Batting HR	BA	PO	A	E	DP	TC/G	FA
1993	OAK A	1	2	.333	2.75	13	0	0	19.2	13	7	4	0	1	2	3	0	0	0	—	2	6	0	0	0.6	1.000
1994		0	0	—	15.43	2	0	0	2.1	6	1	3	0	0	0	0	0	0	0	—	0	0	0	0	0.0	.000
2 yrs.		1	2	.333	4.09	15	0	0	22	19	8	7	0	1	2	3	0	0	0	—	2	6	0	0	0.5	1.000

Mike Smithson

SMITHSON, BILLY MIKE BL TR 6′ 8″ 200 lbs.
B. Jan. 21, 1955, Centerville, Tenn.

Year	Team	W	L	PCT	ERA	G	GS	CG	IP	H	BB	SO	ShO	Relief Pitching W	Relief Pitching L	Relief Pitching SV	Batting AB	Batting H	Batting HR	BA	PO	A	E	DP	TC/G	FA
1982	TEX A	3	4	.429	5.01	8	8	3	46.2	51	13	24	0	0	0	0	0	0	0	—	2	3	0	0	0.6	1.000
1983		10	14	.417	3.91	33	33	10	223.1	233	71	135	0	0	0	0	0	0	0	—	19	33	2	3	1.6	.963
1984	MIN A	15	13	.536	3.68	36	**36**	10	252	246	54	144	1	0	0	0	0	0	0	—	17	29	2	2	1.3	.958
1985		15	14	.517	4.34	37	**37**	8	257	264	78	127	3	0	0	0	0	0	0	—	16	28	2	4	1.2	.957
1986		13	14	.481	4.77	34	33	8	198	234	57	114	1	0	1	0	0	0	0	—	10	32	2	4	1.3	.955

Lary Sorensen *continued*

Year	Team	W	L	PCT	ERA	G	GS	CG	IP	H	BB	SO	ShO	Relief Pitching W	Relief Pitching L	Relief Pitching SV	Batting AB	Batting H	Batting HR	BA	PO	A	E	DP	TC/G	FA
1985	CHI N	3	7	.300	4.26	45	3	0	82.1	86	24	34	0	3	5	0	6	0	0	.000	4	14	2	1	0.4	.900
1987	MON N	3	4	.429	4.72	23	5	0	47.2	56	12	21	0	1	1	1	8	0	0	.000	3	5	1	0	0.4	.889
1988	SF N	0	0	—	4.86	12	0	0	16.2	24	3	9	0	0	0	2	1	0	0	.000	0	2	0	0	0.2	1.000
11 yrs.		93	103	.474	4.15	346	235	69	1735.2	1960	402	569	10	5	10	6	61	3	0	.049	151	263	22	23	1.3	.950

Vic Sorrell

SORRELL, VICTOR GARLAND BR TR 5′10″ 180 lbs.
B. Apr. 9, 1901, Morrisville, N. C. D. May 4, 1972, Raleigh, N. C.

Year	Team	W	L	PCT	ERA	G	GS	CG	IP	H	BB	SO	ShO	Relief Pitching W	Relief Pitching L	Relief Pitching SV	Batting AB	Batting H	Batting HR	BA	PO	A	E	DP	TC/G	FA
1928	DET A	8	11	.421	4.79	29	23	8	171	182	83	67	0	0	0	0	55	6	0	.109	3	28	6	2	1.3	.838
1929		14	15	.483	5.18	36	31	13	226	270	106	81	1	2	0	1	83	12	0	.145	7	41	0	2	1.3	1.000
1930		16	11	.593	3.86	35	30	14	233.1	245	106	97	2	2	1	1	80	15	0	.188	3	33	1	2	1.1	.973
1931		13	14	.481	4.12	35	32	19	247	267	114	99	1	0	0	1	88	14	0	.159	12	52	3	4	1.9	.955
1932		14	14	.500	4.03	32	31	13	234.1	234	77	84	1	1	0	0	76	9	0	.118	9	40	1	0	1.6	.980
1933		11	15	.423	3.79	36	28	13	232.2	233	78	75	2	2	1	1	74	11	0	.149	14	48	2	1	1.8	.969
1934		6	9	.400	4.79	28	19	6	129.2	146	45	46	0	0	2	2	37	4	0	.108	7	34	3	2	1.6	.932
1935		4	3	.571	4.03	12	6	4	51.1	65	25	22	0	0	2	0	18	0	0	.000	3	11	0	0	1.2	1.000
1936		6	7	.462	5.28	30	14	5	131.1	153	64	37	1	2	3	3	39	6	0	.154	9	31	0	4	1.3	1.000
1937		0	2	.000	9.00	7	2	0	17	25	8	11	0	0	0	1	3	0	0	.000	1	3	1	0	0.7	.800
10 yrs.		92	101	.477	4.43	280	216	95	1673.2	1820	706	619	8	9	9	10	553	77	0	.139	68	321	17	17	1.5	.958

Elias Sosa

SOSA, ELIAS BR TR 6′ 2″ 186 lbs.
Born Elias Sosa (Martinez).
B. June 10, 1950, La Vega, Dominican Republic.

Year	Team	W	L	PCT	ERA	G	GS	CG	IP	H	BB	SO	ShO	Relief Pitching W	Relief Pitching L	Relief Pitching SV	Batting AB	Batting H	Batting HR	BA	PO	A	E	DP	TC/G	FA
1972	SF N	0	1	.000	2.25	8	0	0	16	10	12	10	0	0	1	3	4	0	0	.000	0	2	0	0	0.3	1.000
1973		10	4	.714	3.28	71	1	0	107	95	41	70	0	10	3	18	14	1	0	.071	7	12	0	0	0.3	1.000
1974		9	7	.563	3.48	68	0	0	101	94	45	48	0	9	7	6	15	1	0	.067	4	14	3	2	0.3	.857
1975	2 teams STL N (14G 0–3) ATL N (43G 2–2)																									
″	total	2	5	.286	4.32	57	1	0	89.2	92	43	46	0	2	4	2	15	2	0	.133	3	14	2	1	0.3	.895
1976	2 teams ATL N (21G 4–4) LA N (24G 2–4)																									
″	total	6	8	.429	4.43	45	0	0	69	71	25	52	0	6	8	4	7	1	0	.143	1	10	2	0	0.3	.846
1977	LA N	2	2	.500	1.97	44	0	0	64	42	12	47	0	2	2	1	4	1	0	.250	3	9	0	0	0.3	1.000
1978	OAK A	8	2	.800	2.64	68	0	0	109	106	44	61	0	8	2	14	0	0	0	—	9	15	0	1	0.4	1.000
1979	MON N	8	7	.533	1.95	62	0	0	97	77	37	59	0	8	7	18	13	2	0	.154	8	8	2	0	0.3	.889
1980		9	6	.600	3.06	67	0	0	94	104	19	58	0	9	6	9	11	1	0	.091	4	13	1	0	0.3	.944
1981		1	2	.333	3.69	32	0	0	39	46	8	18	0	1	2	3	2	2	0	1.000	3	8	0	0	0.3	1.000
1982	DET A	3	3	.500	4.43	38	0	0	61	64	18	24	0	3	3	4	0	0	0	—	3	13	0	0	0.4	1.000
1983	SD N	1	4	.200	4.35	41	1	0	72.1	72	30	45	0	1	4	1	7	1	0	.143	7	5	0	0	0.3	1.000
12 yrs.		59	51	.536	3.32	601	3	0	919	873	334	538	0	59	49	83	92	12	0	.130	52	123	10	4	0.3	.946
DIVISIONAL PLAYOFF SERIES																										
1981	MON N	0	0	—	3.00	2	0	0	3	4	0	1	0	0	0	0	0	0	0	—	0	0	1	0	0.5	.000
LEAGUE CHAMPIONSHIP SERIES																										
1977	LA N	0	1	.000	10.13	2	0	0	2.2	5	0	0	0	0	1	0	1	0	0	.000	0	1	0	0	0.5	1.000
1981	MON N	0	0	—	0.00	1	0	0	0.1	1	1	0	0	0	0	0	0	0	0	—	0	0	0	0	0.0	.000
2 yrs.		0	1	.000	9.00	3	0	0	3	6	1	0	0	0	1	0	1	0	0	.000	0	1	0	0	0.3	1.000
WORLD SERIES																										
1977	LA N	0	0	—	11.57	2	0	0	2.1	3	1	1	0	0	0	0	0	0	0	—	0	0	0	0	0.0	.000

Jose Sosa

SOSA, JOSE BR TR 5′11″ 158 lbs.
Born Jose Ynocencio (Sosa).
B. Dec. 28, 1952, Santo Domingo, Dominican Republic.

Year	Team	W	L	PCT	ERA	G	GS	CG	IP	H	BB	SO	ShO	Relief Pitching W	Relief Pitching L	Relief Pitching SV	Batting AB	Batting H	Batting HR	BA	PO	A	E	DP	TC/G	FA
1975	HOU N	1	3	.250	4.02	25	2	0	47	51	23	31	0	1	3	1	9	3	1	.333	1	1	0	0	0.1	1.000
1976		0	0	—	6.75	9	0	0	12	16	6	5	0	0	0	0	0	0	0	—	2	5	0	0	0.8	1.000
2 yrs.		1	3	.250	4.58	34	2	0	59	67	29	36	0	1	3	1	9	3	1	.333	3	6	0	0	0.3	1.000

Allen Sothoron

SOTHORON, ALLEN SUTTON BB TR 5′11″ 182 lbs.
BR 1924–1926
B. Apr. 27, 1893, Bradford, Ohio D. June 17, 1939, St. Louis, Mo.
Manager 1933.

Year	Team	W	L	PCT	ERA	G	GS	CG	IP	H	BB	SO	ShO	Relief Pitching W	Relief Pitching L	Relief Pitching SV	Batting AB	Batting H	Batting HR	BA	PO	A	E	DP	TC/G	FA
1914	STL A	0	0	—	6.00	1	0	0	6	6	4	3	0	0	0	0	2	0	0	.000	0	1	0	0	1.0	1.000
1915		0	1	.000	7.36	3	1	0	3.2	8	5	2	0	0	0	0	1	0	0	.000	0	3	0	0	1.0	1.000
1917		14	**19**	.424	2.83	48	33	17	276.2	259	96	85	3	2	3	4	91	19	0	.209	13	81	11	0	2.2	.895
1918		12	12	.500	1.94	29	24	14	209	152	67	71	2	0	1	0	63	10	0	.159	10	43	8	0	2.1	.869
1919		20	13	.606	2.20	40	30	21	270	256	87	106	3	5	0	3	97	17	0	.175	17	39	13	2	1.7	.812
1920		8	15	.348	4.70	36	26	12	218.1	263	89	81	1	0	1	2	72	16	0	.222	12	49	14	0	2.1	.813
1921	3 teams STL A (5G 1–2) BOS A (2G 0–2) CLE A (22G 12–4)																									
″	total	13	8	.619	3.89	29	22	11	178.1	194	71	72	2	2	0	0	69	18	0	.261	8	34	4	0	1.6	.913
1922	CLE A	1	3	.250	6.39	6	4	2	25.1	26	14	8	0	0	1	0	9	4	0	.444	0	5	1	0	1.0	.833
1924	STL N	10	16	.385	3.57	29	28	16	196.2	209	84	62	**4**	0	1	0	72	14	0	.194	2	35	0	1	1.3	1.000
1925		10	10	.500	4.05	28	22	8	155.2	173	63	67	2	1	1	0	56	11	0	.196	4	15	3	0	0.8	.864
1926		3	3	.500	4.22	15	4	1	42.2	37	16	19	0	2	2	0	13	3	0	.231	0	7	2	0	0.6	.778
11 yrs.		91	100	.476	3.31	264	194	102	1582.1	1583	596	576	17	12	10	9	545	112	0	.206	66	312	56	3	1.6	.871

Mario Soto

SOTO, MARIO MELVIN BR TR 6′ 174 lbs.
B. July 12, 1956, Bani, Dominican Republic.

Year	Team	W	L	PCT	ERA	G	GS	CG	IP	H	BB	SO	ShO	Relief Pitching W	Relief Pitching L	Relief Pitching SV	Batting AB	Batting H	Batting HR	BA	PO	A	E	DP	TC/G	FA
1977	CIN N	2	6	.250	5.31	12	10	2	61	60	26	44	1	0	0	0	13	1	0	.077	5	9	0	1	1.2	1.000
1978		1	0	1.000	2.50	5	1	0	18	13	13	13	0	1	0	0	2	0	0	.000	0	1	0	0	0.2	1.000
1979		3	2	.600	5.35	25	0	0	37	33	30	32	0	3	2	0	7	4	0	.571	1	2	0	0	0.1	1.000
1980		10	8	.556	3.08	53	12	3	190	126	84	182	1	3	8	4	46	2	0	.043	12	25	3	2	0.8	.925
1981		12	9	.571	3.29	25	**25**	10	175	142	61	151	3	0	0	0	59	4	0	.068	10	19	2	1	1.2	.935
1982		14	13	.519	2.79	35	34	13	257.2	202	71	274	2	1	0	0	84	14	0	.167	10	29	3	1	1.2	.929
1983		17	13	.567	2.70	34	34	**18**	273.2	207	95	242	3	0	0	0	88	11	0	.125	22	28	5	1	1.6	.909
1984		18	7	.720	3.53	33	33	**13**	237.1	181	87	185	0	0	0	0	87	18	1	.207	12	22	3	1	1.1	.919

Mario Soto *continued*

Year	Team	Lg	W	L	PCT	ERA	G	GS	CG	IP	H	BB	SO	ShO	Relief W	Relief L	Relief SV	Batting AB	Batting H	HR	BA	PO	A	E	DP	TC/G	FA
1985			12	15	.444	3.58	36	36	9	256.2	196	104	214	1	0	0	0	83	11	0	.133	13	34	2	0	1.4	.959
1986			5	10	.333	4.71	19	19	1	105	113	46	67	1	0	0	0	27	3	0	.111	3	16	1	1	1.1	.950
1987			3	2	.600	5.12	6	6	0	31.2	34	12	11	0	0	0	0	12	1	0	.083	2	6	0	0	1.3	1.000
1988			3	7	.300	4.66	14	14	3	87	88	28	34	1	0	0	0	22	1	0	.045	5	12	3	1	1.4	.850
12 yrs.			100	92	.521	3.47	297	224	72	1730	1395	657	1449	13	8	10	4	530	70	1	.132	95	203	22	9	1.1	.931
LEAGUE CHAMPIONSHIP SERIES																											
1979	CIN	N	0	0	—	0.00	1	0	0	2	0	0	1	0	0	0	0	0	0	0	—	0	0	0	0	0.0	.000

Mark Souza

SOUZA, KENNETH MARK
B. Feb. 1, 1954, Redwood City, Calif.
BL TL 6′ 180 lbs.

Year	Team	Lg	W	L	PCT	ERA	G	GS	CG	IP	H	BB	SO	ShO	Relief W	Relief L	Relief SV	Batting AB	Batting H	HR	BA	PO	A	E	DP	TC/G	FA
1980	OAK	A	0	0	—	7.71	5	0	0	7	9	5	2	0	0	0	0	0	0	0	—	1	0	0	0	0.2	1.000

Bill Sowders

SOWDERS, WILLIAM JEFFERSON
Brother of Len Sowders. Brother of John Sowders.
B. Nov. 29, 1864, Louisville, Ky. D. Feb. 2, 1951, Indianapolis, Ind.
BR TR 6′ 155 lbs.

Year	Team	Lg	W	L	PCT	ERA	G	GS	CG	IP	H	BB	SO	ShO	Relief W	Relief L	Relief SV	Batting AB	Batting H	HR	BA	PO	A	E	DP	TC/G	FA
1888	BOS	N	19	15	.559	2.07	36	35	34	317	278	73	132	2	0	0	0	122	18	0	.148	23	69	8	1	2.8	.920
1889	2 teams	BOS N (7G 1–2) PIT N (13G 6–5)																									
″	total		7	7	.500	6.37	20	15	12	94.2	147	52	43	0	0	0	**3**	65	17	0	.262	13	30	3	0	2.1	.935
1890	PIT	N	3	8	.273	4.42	15	11	9	106	117	24	30	0	1	**1**	0	50	9	0	.180	12	9	3	0	1.4	.875
3 yrs.			29	30	.492	3.34	71	61	55	517.2	542	149	205	2	1	1	3	237	44	0	.186	48	108	14	1	2.3	.918

John Sowders

SOWDERS, JOHN
Brother of Bill Sowders. Brother of Len Sowders.
B. Dec. 10, 1866, Louisville, Ky. D. July 29, 1939, Indianapolis, Ind.
BR TL 6′

Year	Team	Lg	W	L	PCT	ERA	G	GS	CG	IP	H	BB	SO	ShO	Relief W	Relief L	Relief SV	Batting AB	Batting H	HR	BA	PO	A	E	DP	TC/G	FA
1887	IND	N	0	0	—	21.00	1	0	0	3	11	5	0	0	0	0	0	2	0	0	.000	1	0	2	0	1.5	.333
1889	KC	AA	6	16	.273	4.82	25	23	20	185	204	105	104	0	0	0	1	87	19	0	.218	7	27	7	0	1.5	.829
1890	BKN	P	19	16	.543	3.82	39	37	28	309	358	161	91	1	0	0	0	132	25	1	.189	7	76	7	1	2.1	.922
3 yrs.			25	32	.439	4.29	65	60	48	497	573	271	195	1	0	0	1	221	44	1	.199	15	103	16	1	1.9	.881

Bob Spade

SPADE, ROBERT
B. Jan. 4, 1877, Akron, Ohio D. Sept. 7, 1924, Cincinnati, Ohio.
BR TR 5′10″ 190 lbs.

Year	Team	Lg	W	L	PCT	ERA	G	GS	CG	IP	H	BB	SO	ShO	Relief W	Relief L	Relief SV	Batting AB	Batting H	HR	BA	PO	A	E	DP	TC/G	FA
1907	CIN	N	1	2	.333	1.00	3	3	3	27	21	9	7	1	0	0	0	7	2	0	.286	0	5	1	1	2.0	.833
1908			17	12	.586	2.74	35	28	22	249.1	230	85	74	2	1	1	1	87	17	0	.195	4	57	6	2	1.9	.910
1909			5	5	.500	2.85	14	13	8	98	91	39	31	0	1	0	0	34	10	0	.294	2	9	2	0	0.9	.846
1910	2 teams	CIN N (3G 1–2) STL A (7G 1–3)																									
″	total		2	5	.286	5.19	10	8	3	52	69	26	9	1	0	0	0	16	3	0	.188	1	14	0	0	1.5	1.000
4 yrs.			25	24	.510	2.96	62	52	36	426.1	411	159	121	4	2	1	1	144	32	0	.222	7	85	9	3	1.6	.911

Warren Spahn

SPAHN, WARREN EDWARD
B. Apr. 23, 1921, Buffalo, N. Y.
Hall of Fame 1973.
BL TL 6′ 172 lbs.

Year	Team	Lg	W	L	PCT	ERA	G	GS	CG	IP	H	BB	SO	ShO	Relief W	Relief L	Relief SV	Batting AB	Batting H	HR	BA	PO	A	E	DP	TC/G	FA
1942	BOS	N	0	0	—	5.74	4	2	1	15.2	25	11	7	0	0	0	0	6	1	0	.167	1	2	0	0	0.8	1.000
1946			8	5	.615	2.94	24	16	8	125.2	107	36	67	0	0	1	1	43	7	0	.163	2	16	2	0	0.8	.900
1947			21	10	.677	**2.33**	40	35	22	**289.2**	245	84	123	**7**	0	0	3	98	16	0	.163	5	48	1	1	1.4	.981
1948			15	12	.556	3.71	36	35	16	257	237	77	114	3	0	0	1	90	15	1	.167	4	52	1	3	1.6	.982
1949			**21**	14	.600	3.07	38	**38**	**25**	**302.1**	283	86	**151**	4	0	0	0	111	18	2	.162	14	41	4	2	1.6	.932
1950			**21**	17	.553	3.16	41	**39**	25	293	248	111	**191**	1	0	1	1	106	23	1	.217	9	55	8	3	1.8	.889
1951			22	14	.611	2.98	39	36	**26**	310.2	278	**109**	**164**	**7**	0	3	0	116	22	1	.190	7	50	3	1	1.5	.950
1952			14	19	.424	2.98	40	35	19	290	263	73	**183**	5	0	1	3	112	18	2	.161	18	56	5	4	2.0	.937
1953	MIL	N	**23**	7	.767	**2.10**	35	32	24	265.2	211	70	148	5	0	0	3	105	23	2	.219	12	53	4	7	2.0	.942
1954			21	12	.636	3.14	39	34	23	283.1	262	86	136	1	1	1	3	101	21	1	.208	12	57	4	4	1.9	.945
1955			17	14	.548	3.26	39	32	16	245.2	249	65	110	1	0	3	1	81	17	4	.210	13	44	3	4	1.5	.950
1956			20	11	.645	2.78	39	35	20	281.1	249	52	128	3	0	0	3	105	22	3	.210	16	41	1	7	1.5	.983
1957			**21**	11	.656	2.69	39	35	**18**	271	241	78	111	4	1	0	3	94	13	2	.138	18	47	0	4	1.7	1.000
1958			**22**	11	**.667**	3.07	38	36	**23**	**290**	257	76	150	2	0	0	1	108	36	2	.333	11	67	2	7	2.1	.975
1959			**21**	15	.583	2.96	40	36	**21**	**292**	282	70	143	**4**	0	3	0	104	24	2	.231	14	45	3	4	1.5	.952
1960			**21**	10	.677	3.50	40	33	**18**	267.2	254	74	154	4	2	2	2	95	14	3	.147	14	59	3	7	1.9	.961
1961			**21**	13	.618	**3.02**	38	34	**21**	262.2	236	64	115	**4**	1	3	0	94	21	4	.223	16	63	2	7	2.1	.975
1962			18	14	.563	3.04	34	34	**22**	269.1	248	55	118	0	0	0	0	98	18	2	.184	13	55	1	5	2.0	.986
1963			23	7	.767	2.60	33	33	**22**	259.2	241	49	102	7	0	0	0	90	16	2	.178	11	71	3	8	2.6	.965
1964			6	13	.316	5.29	38	25	4	173.2	204	52	78	1	0	0	4	59	11	1	.186	4	36	6	2	1.2	.870
1965	2 teams	NY N (20G 4–12) SF N (16G 3–4)																									
″	total		7	16	.304	4.01	36	30	8	197.2	210	56	90	0	0	0	0	56	7	0	.125	8	41	2	2	1.4	.961
21 yrs.			363 **5th**	245	.597	3.09	750	665	382	5243.2 **8th**	4830	1434	2583	63 **6th**	5	18	29	1872	363	35	.194	222	999	58	82	1.7	.955
WORLD SERIES																											
1948	BOS	N	1	1	.500	3.00	3	1	0	12	10	3	12	0	1	0	0	4	0	0	.000	0	3	0	0	1.0	1.000
1957	MIL	N	1	1	.500	4.70	2	2	1	15.1	18	2	2	0	0	0	0	4	0	0	.000	1	3	0	0	2.0	1.000
1958			2	1	.667	2.20	3	3	2	28.2	19	8	18	1	0	0	0	12	4	0	.333	2	6	0	0	2.7	1.000
3 yrs.			4	3	.571	3.05	8	6	3	56	47	13	32	1	1	0	0	20	4	0	.200	3	12	0	0	1.9	1.000

Al Spalding

SPALDING, ALBERT GOODWILL
B. Sept. 2, 1850, Byron, Ill. D. Sept. 9, 1915, San Diego, Calif.
Manager 1876–77.
Hall of Fame 1939.
BR TR 6′ 1″ 170 lbs.

Year	Team	Lg	W	L	PCT	ERA	G	GS	CG	IP	H	BB	SO	ShO	Relief W	Relief L	Relief SV	Batting AB	Batting H	HR	BA	PO	A	E	DP	TC/G	FA
1876	CHI	N	**47**	13	**.783**	1.75	61	60	53	528.2	542	26	39	8	0	0	0	292	91	0	.312	58	94	10	7	2.2	.938
1877			1	0	1.000	3.27	4	1	0	11	17	0	2	0	1	0	1	254	65	0	.256	511	82	33	29	9.8	.947
2 yrs.			48	13	.787	1.78	65	61	53	539.2	559	26	41	8	1	0	1	*				572	176	47	36	5.7	.941

Bill Spanswick

SPANSWICK, WILLIAM HENRY
B. July 8, 1938, Springfield, Mass.
BL TL 6′ 3″ 195 lbs.

Year	Team	Lg	W	L	PCT	ERA	G	GS	CG	IP	H	BB	SO	ShO	Relief W	Relief L	Relief SV	Batting AB	Batting H	HR	BA	PO	A	E	DP	TC/G	FA
1964	BOS	A	2	3	.400	6.89	29	7	0	65.1	75	44	55	0	1	0	0	14	4	0	.286	3	13	0	1	0.6	1.000

Steve Sparks

SPARKS, STEVEN WILLIAM BR TR 6′ 187 lbs.
B. July 2, 1965, Tulsa, Okla.

Year	Team		W	L	PCT	ERA	G	GS	CG	IP	H	BB	SO	ShO	Relief W	Relief L	Relief SV	Batting AB	Batting H	Batting HR	BA	PO	A	E	DP	TC/G	FA
1995	MIL	A	9	11	.450	4.63	33	27	3	202	210	86	96	0	0	0	0	0	0	0	—	25	43	2	5	2.1	.971

Tully Sparks

SPARKS, THOMAS FRANK BR TR
B. Dec. 12, 1874, Etna, Ga. D. July 15, 1937, Anniston, Ala.

Year	Team		W	L	PCT	ERA	G	GS	CG	IP	H	BB	SO	ShO	Relief W	Relief L	Relief SV	Batting AB	Batting H	Batting HR	BA	PO	A	E	DP	TC/G	FA
1897	PHI	N	0	1	.000	10.13	1	1	1	8	12	4	0	0	0	0	0	3	0	0	.000	0	3	0	0	3.0	1.000
1899	PIT	N	8	6	.571	3.86	28	17	8	170	180	82	53	0	2	1	0	62	8	0	.129	5	41	8	1	1.9	.852
1901	MIL	A	7	16	.304	3.51	29	26	18	210	228	93	62	0	0	0	0	71	12	0	.169	9	60	8	1	2.7	.896
1902	2 teams	NY N (15G 4–10)	BOS A (17G 7–9)																								
″	total		11	19	.367	3.60	32	28	26	257.2	274	80	77	1	1	1	1	89	13	0	.146	13	84	5	4	3.2	.951
1903	PHI	N	11	15	.423	2.72	28	28	27	248	248	56	88	0	0	0	0	92	10	0	.109	14	59	8	0	2.9	.901
1904			7	18	.280	2.65	26	25	19	200.2	208	43	67	3	0	1	0	76	8	0	.105	11	35	4	3	1.9	.920
1905			14	11	.560	2.18	34	26	20	260	217	73	98	3	1	1	1	94	12	0	.128	9	45	0	3	1.6	1.000
1906			19	16	.543	2.16	42	37	29	316.2	244	62	114	6	1	0	3	104	16	0	.154	20	66	3	4	2.1	.966
1907			22	8	.733	2.00	33	31	24	265	221	51	90	3	1	0	1	89	3	0	.034	10	50	4	1	1.9	.938
1908			16	15	.516	2.60	33	31	24	263.1	251	51	85	2	0	0	2	77	4	0	.052	15	65	6	3	2.6	.930
1909			6	11	.353	2.96	24	16	6	121.2	126	32	40	1	2	0	0	36	5	0	.139	4	31	0	0	1.5	1.000
1910			0	2	.000	6.00	3	3	0	15	22	2	4	0	0	0	0	5	0	0	.000	0	5	0	0	1.7	1.000
12 yrs.			121	138	.467	2.79	313	269	202	2336	2231	629	778	19	8	4	8	798	91	0	.114	110	544	46	20	2.2	.934

Joe Sparma

SPARMA, JOSEPH BLASE BR TR 6′ 1″ 190 lbs.
B. Feb. 4, 1942, Massillon, Ohio D. May 14, 1986, Columbus, Ohio.

Year	Team		W	L	PCT	ERA	G	GS	CG	IP	H	BB	SO	ShO	Relief W	Relief L	Relief SV	Batting AB	Batting H	Batting HR	BA	PO	A	E	DP	TC/G	FA
1964	DET	A	5	6	.455	3.00	21	11	3	84	62	45	71	2	1	1	0	25	4	0	.160	5	16	1	2	1.0	.955
1965			13	8	.619	3.18	30	28	6	167	142	75	127	0	1	0	0	52	7	0	.135	11	25	6	1	1.4	.857
1966			2	7	.222	5.30	29	13	0	91.2	103	52	61	0	0	0	0	23	5	0	.217	5	8	2	1	0.5	.867
1967			16	9	.640	3.76	37	37	11	217.2	186	85	153	5	0	0	0	74	4	0	.054	16	20	2	1	1.0	.947
1968			10	10	.500	3.70	34	31	7	182.1	169	77	110	1	1	0	0	60	8	0	.133	9	19	2	0	0.9	.933
1969			6	8	.429	4.76	23	16	3	92.2	78	77	41	2	0	1	0	29	4	0	.138	9	7	0	2	0.7	1.000
1970	MON	N	0	4	.000	7.14	9	6	1	29	34	25	23	0	0	0	0	6	0	0	.000	2	3	2	0	0.8	.714
7 yrs.			52	52	.500	3.95	183	142	31	864.1	774	436	586	10	3	2	0	269	32	0	.119	57	98	15	7	0.9	.912
WORLD SERIES																											
1968	DET	A	0	0	—	54.00	1	0	0	0.1	2	0	0	0	0	0	0	0	0	0	—	0	0	0	0	0.0	.000

Tris Speaker

SPEAKER, TRISTRAM E. (Spoke, The Grey Eagle) BL TL 5′11½″ 193 lbs.
B. Apr. 4, 1888, Hubbard, Tex. D. Dec. 8, 1958, Lake Whitney, Tex.
Manager 1919–26.
Hall of Fame 1937.

Year	Team		W	L	PCT	ERA	G	GS	CG	IP	H	BB	SO	ShO	Relief W	Relief L	Relief SV	Batting AB	Batting H	Batting HR	BA	PO	A	E	DP	TC/G	FA
1914	BOS	A	0	0	—	9.00	1	0	0	1	2	0	0	0	0	0	0	*				4	2	0	1	1.5	1.000

Cliff Speck

SPECK, ROBERT CLIFFORD BR TR 6′ 4″ 196 lbs.
B. Aug. 8, 1956, Portland, Ore.

Year	Team		W	L	PCT	ERA	G	GS	CG	IP	H	BB	SO	ShO	Relief W	Relief L	Relief SV	Batting AB	Batting H	Batting HR	BA	PO	A	E	DP	TC/G	FA
1986	ATL	N	2	1	.667	4.13	13	1	0	28.1	25	15	21	0	1	1	0	3	0	0	.000	1	5	0	0	0.5	1.000

Byron Speece

SPEECE, BYRON FRANKLIN BR TR 5′11″ 170 lbs.
B. Jan. 6, 1897, West Baden, Ind. D. Sept. 29, 1974, Elgin, Ore.

Year	Team		W	L	PCT	ERA	G	GS	CG	IP	H	BB	SO	ShO	Relief W	Relief L	Relief SV	Batting AB	Batting H	Batting HR	BA	PO	A	E	DP	TC/G	FA
1924	WAS	A	2	1	.667	2.65	21	1	0	54.1	60	27	15	0	2	0	0	20	3	0	.150	2	19	1	0	1.0	.955
1925	CLE	A	3	5	.375	4.28	28	3	3	90.1	106	28	26	0	2	3	1	31	5	0	.161	4	23	1	2	1.0	.964
1926			0	0	—	0.00	2	0	0	3	1	2	1	0	0	0	0	0	0	0	—	0	2	0	1	1.0	1.000
1930	PHI	N	0	0	—	13.27	11	0	0	19.2	41	4	9	0	0	0	0	3	1	0	.333	2	3	0	0	0.5	1.000
4 yrs.			5	6	.455	4.73	62	4	3	167.1	208	61	51	0	4	3	1	54	9	0	.167	8	47	2	3	0.9	.965
WORLD SERIES																											
1924	WAS	A	0	0	—	9.00	1	0	0	1	3	0	0	0	0	0	0	0	0	0	—	0	2	0	0	2.0	1.000

Floyd Speer

SPEER, FLOYD VERNIE BR TR 6′ 180 lbs.
B. Jan. 27, 1913, Booneville, Ark. D. Mar. 22, 1969, Little Rock, Ark.

Year	Team		W	L	PCT	ERA	G	GS	CG	IP	H	BB	SO	ShO	Relief W	Relief L	Relief SV	Batting AB	Batting H	Batting HR	BA	PO	A	E	DP	TC/G	FA
1943	CHI	A	0	0	—	9.00	1	0	0	1	1	2	1	0	0	0	0	0	0	0	—	0	1	0	0	1.0	1.000
1944			0	0	—	9.00	2	0	0	2	4	0	1	0	0	0	0	0	0	0	—	0	0	0	0	0.0	.000
2 yrs.			0	0		9.00	3	0	0	3	5	2	2	0	0	0	0	0	0	0		0	1	0	0	0.3	1.000

George Speer

SPEER, GEORGE NATHAN BL TL 5′ 9″ 152 lbs.
B. June 16, 1886, Corning, Mo. D. Jan. 13, 1946, Edmonton, Alta., Canada.

Year	Team		W	L	PCT	ERA	G	GS	CG	IP	H	BB	SO	ShO	Relief W	Relief L	Relief SV	Batting AB	Batting H	Batting HR	BA	PO	A	E	DP	TC/G	FA
1909	DET	A	4	4	.500	2.83	12	8	4	76.1	88	13	12	0	1	1	1	25	3	0	.120	4	30	2	2	3.0	.944

George Spencer

SPENCER, GEORGE ELWELL BR TR 6′ 1″ 215 lbs.
B. July 7, 1926, Columbus, Ohio.

Year	Team		W	L	PCT	ERA	G	GS	CG	IP	H	BB	SO	ShO	Relief W	Relief L	Relief SV	Batting AB	Batting H	Batting HR	BA	PO	A	E	DP	TC/G	FA
1950	NY	N	1	0	1.000	2.49	10	1	1	25.1	12	7	5	0	0	0	0	4	0	0	.000	0	6	0	0	0.6	1.000
1951			10	4	.714	3.75	57	4	2	132	125	56	36	0	8	2	6	32	4	0	.125	13	29	4	2	0.8	.913
1952			3	5	.375	5.55	35	4	0	60	57	21	27	0	3	4	3	10	2	0	.200	5	10	1	1	0.5	.938
1953			0	0	—	7.71	1	0	0	2.1	3	2	1	0	0	0	0	0	0	0	—	0	0	0	0	0.0	.000
1954			1	0	1.000	3.65	6	0	0	12.1	9	8	4	0	1	0	0	3	0	0	.000	2	4	0	1	1.0	1.000
1955			0	0	—	5.40	1	0	0	1.2	1	3	0	0	0	0	0	0	0	0	—	0	1	0	0	1.0	1.000
1958	DET	A	1	0	1.000	2.70	7	0	0	10	11	4	5	0	1	0	0	0	0	0	—	0	3	0	0	0.4	1.000
1960			0	1	.000	3.52	5	0	0	7.2	10	5	4	0	0	1	0	1	0	0	.000	0	1	0	0	0.2	1.000
8 yrs.			16	10	.615	4.05	122	9	3	251.1	228	106	82	0	13	7	9	50	6	0	.120	20	54	5	4	0.6	.937
WORLD SERIES																											
1951	NY	N	0	0	—	18.90	2	0	0	3.1	6	3	0	0	0	0	0	0	0	0	—	0	1	0	0	0.5	1.000

Glenn Spencer

SPENCER, GLENN EDWARD BR TR 5′11″ 155 lbs.
B. Sept. 11, 1905, Corning, N. Y. D. Dec. 30, 1958, Binghamton, N. Y.

Year	Team		W	L	PCT	ERA	G	GS	CG	IP	H	BB	SO	ShO	Relief W	Relief L	Relief SV	Batting AB	Batting H	Batting HR	BA	PO	A	E	DP	TC/G	FA
1928	PIT	N	0	0	—	1.59	4	0	0	5.2	4	3	2	0	0	0	0	1	0	0	.000	0	0	1	0	0.3	.000
1930			8	9	.471	5.40	41	10	5	156.2	185	63	60	0	3	5	4	53	6	0	.113	4	25	3	1	0.8	.906
1931			11	12	.478	3.42	38	18	11	186.2	180	65	51	1	3	3	3	52	5	0	.096	7	39	3	2	1.3	.939

Glenn Spencer *continued*

Year	Team	W	L	PCT	ERA	G	GS	CG	IP	H	BB	SO	ShO	Relief Pitching W	L	SV	Batting AB	H	HR	BA	PO	A	E	DP	TC/G	FA
1932		4	8	.333	4.97	39	13	5	137.2	167	44	35	1	2	1	1	37	6	0	.162	4	25	2	2	0.8	.935
1933	NY N	0	2	.000	5.13	17	3	1	47.1	52	26	14	0	0	0	0	12	2	0	.167	5	10	0	2	0.9	1.000
5 yrs.		23	31	.426	4.53	139	44	22	534	588	201	162	2	8	9	8	155	19	0	.123	20	99	9	7	0.9	.930

Hack Spencer

SPENCER, FRED CALVIN
B. Apr. 25, 1885, Minneapolis, Minn. D. Feb. 5, 1969, St. Anthony, Minn.
BR TR 5′10½″ 172 lbs.

Year	Team	W	L	PCT	ERA	G	GS	CG	IP	H	BB	SO	ShO	Relief Pitching W	L	SV	Batting AB	H	HR	BA	PO	A	E	DP	TC/G	FA
1912	STL A	0	0	—	0.00	1	0	0	1.2	2	0	0	0	0	0	0	0	0	0	—	0	1	0	0	1.0	1.000

Bob Spicer

SPICER, ROBERT OBERTON
B. Apr. 11, 1925, Richmond, Va.
BL TR 5′10″ 173 lbs.

Year	Team	W	L	PCT	ERA	G	GS	CG	IP	H	BB	SO	ShO	Relief Pitching W	L	SV	Batting AB	H	HR	BA	PO	A	E	DP	TC/G	FA
1955	KC A	0	0	—	33.75	2	0	0	2.2	9	4	2	0	0	0	0	1	0	0	.000	0	0	0	0	0.0	.000
1956		0	0	—	19.29	2	0	0	2.1	6	1	0	0	0	0	0	0	0	0	—	0	1	0	0	0.5	1.000
2 yrs.		0	0	—	27.00	4	0	0	5	15	5	2	0	0	0	0	1	0	0	.000	0	1	0	0	0.3	1.000

Dan Spillner

SPILLNER, DANIEL RAY
B. Nov. 27, 1951, Casper, Wyo.
BR TR 6′ 1″ 190 lbs.

Year	Team	W	L	PCT	ERA	G	GS	CG	IP	H	BB	SO	ShO	Relief Pitching W	L	SV	Batting AB	H	HR	BA	PO	A	E	DP	TC/G	FA
1974	SD N	9	11	.450	4.01	30	25	5	148	153	70	95	2	1	0	0	43	1	0	.023	6	16	0	0	0.7	1.000
1975		5	13	.278	4.26	37	25	3	167	194	63	104	0	0	0	1	45	6	0	.133	13	21	3	2	1.0	.919
1976		2	11	.154	5.06	32	14	0	106.2	120	55	57	0	1	1	0	25	1	0	.040	7	21	3	3	1.0	.903
1977		7	6	.538	3.73	76	0	0	123	130	60	74	0	7	6	6	17	2	0	.118	5	9	1	1	0.2	.933
1978	2 teams SD N (17G 1–0) CLE A (36G 3–1)																									
″	total	4	1	.800	3.94	53	0	0	82.1	86	28	64	0	4	1	3	0	0	0		1	6	0	1	0.1	1.000
1979	CLE A	9	5	.643	4.61	49	13	3	158	153	64	97	0	3	3	1	0	0	0	—	9	18	0	0	0.6	1.000
1980		16	11	.593	5.29	34	30	7	194	225	74	100	1	1	0	0	0	0	0	—	9	17	0	2	0.8	1.000
1981		4	4	.500	3.15	32	5	1	97	86	39	59	0	3	0	7	0	0	0	—	6	16	1	1	0.7	.957
1982		12	10	.545	2.49	65	0	0	133.2	117	45	90	0	12	**10**	21	0	0	0	—	6	7	1	0	0.2	.929
1983		2	9	.182	5.07	60	0	0	92.1	117	38	48	0	2	9	8	0	0	0	—	4	8	1	0	0.2	.923
1984	2 teams CLE A (14G 0–5) CHI A (22G 1–0)																									
″	total	1	5	.167	4.89	36	8	0	99.1	121	36	49	0	1	0	2	0	0	0		11	16	0	0	0.8	1.000
1985	CHI A	4	3	.571	3.44	52	3	0	91.2	83	33	41	0	4	3	1	0	0	0	—	4	2	1	0	0.1	.857
12 yrs.		75	89	.457	4.21	556	123	19	1493	1585	605	878	3	39	33	50	130	10	0	.077	81	157	11	10	0.4	.956

Scipio Spinks

SPINKS, SCIPIO RONALD
B. July 12, 1947, Chicago, Ill.
BR TR 6′ 1″ 183 lbs.

Year	Team	W	L	PCT	ERA	G	GS	CG	IP	H	BB	SO	ShO	Relief Pitching W	L	SV	Batting AB	H	HR	BA	PO	A	E	DP	TC/G	FA
1969	HOU N	0	0	—	0.00	1	0	0	2	1	1	4	0	0	0	0	0	0	0	—	0	0	0	0	0.0	.000
1970		0	1	.000	9.64	5	2	0	14	17	9	6	0	0	0	0	3	0	0	.000	0	0	0	0	0.0	.000
1971		1	0	1.000	3.72	5	3	1	29	22	13	26	0	0	0	0	9	2	0	.222	1	4	0	0	1.0	1.000
1972	STL N	5	5	.500	2.67	16	16	6	118	96	59	93	0	0	0	0	42	7	0	.167	2	21	1	1	1.5	.958
1973		1	5	.167	4.89	8	8	0	38.2	39	25	25	0	0	0	0	11	2	1	.182	5	7	0	0	1.5	1.000
5 yrs.		7	11	.389	3.70	35	29	7	201.2	175	107	154	0	0	0	0	65	11	1	.169	8	32	1	1	1.2	.976

Paul Splittorff

SPLITTORFF, PAUL WILLIAM, JR.
B. Oct. 8, 1946, Evansville, Ind.
BL TL 6′ 3″ 205 lbs.

Year	Team	W	L	PCT	ERA	G	GS	CG	IP	H	BB	SO	ShO	Relief Pitching W	L	SV	Batting AB	H	HR	BA	PO	A	E	DP	TC/G	FA
1970	KC A	0	1	.000	7.00	2	1	0	9	16	5	10	0	0	0	0	2	1	0	.500	0	1	0	1	0.5	1.000
1971		8	9	.471	2.69	22	22	6	144	129	35	80	3	0	0	0	48	5	0	.104	7	32	2	3	1.9	.951
1972		12	12	.500	3.12	35	33	12	216.1	189	67	140	2	0	0	0	71	16	0	.225	6	51	0	5	1.6	1.000
1973		20	11	.645	3.99	38	38	12	261.2	279	78	110	3	0	0	0	0	0	0	—	9	46	1	7	1.5	.982
1974		13	19	.406	4.10	36	36	8	226	252	75	90	1	0	0	0	0	0	0	—	8	39	2	2	1.4	.959
1975		9	10	.474	3.17	35	23	6	159	156	56	76	3	1	0	1	0	0	0	—	10	33	1	4	1.3	.977
1976		11	8	.579	3.96	26	23	5	159	169	59	59	1	0	0	0	0	0	0	—	9	30	0	5	1.5	1.000
1977		16	6	**.727**	3.69	37	37	6	229	243	83	99	2	0	0	0	0	0	0	—	9	38	2	3	1.3	.959
1978		19	13	.594	3.40	39	38	13	262	244	60	76	2	0	0	0	0	0	0	—	18	45	2	4	1.7	.969
1979		15	17	.469	4.24	36	35	11	240	248	77	77	0	0	0	0	0	0	0	—	15	27	3	3	1.3	.933
1980		14	11	.560	4.15	34	33	4	204	236	43	53	0	0	0	0	0	0	0	—	14	30	0	4	1.3	1.000
1981		5	5	.500	4.36	21	15	1	99	111	23	48	0	1	0	0	0	0	0	—	2	22	0	2	1.1	1.000
1982		10	10	.500	4.28	29	28	0	162	166	57	74	0	0	0	0	0	0	0	—	7	24	1	4	1.1	.969
1983		13	8	.619	3.63	27	27	4	156	159	52	61	0	0	0	0	0	0	0	—	9	23	1	2	1.2	.970
1984		1	3	.250	7.71	12	3	0	28	47	10	4	0	1	0	0	0	0	0	—	2	9	0	0	0.9	1.000
15 yrs.		166	143	.537	3.81	429	392	88	2555	2644	780	1057	17	3	0	1	121	22	0	.182	125	450	15	49	1.4	.975
LEAGUE CHAMPIONSHIP SERIES																										
1976	KC A	1	0	1.000	1.93	2	0	0	9.1	7	5	2	0	1	0	0	0	0	0	—	0	1	0	0	0.5	1.000
1977		1	0	1.000	2.40	2	2	0	15	14	3	4	0	0	0	0	0	0	0	—	0	3	0	0	1.5	1.000
1978		0	0	—	4.91	1	1	0	7.1	9	0	2	0	0	0	0	0	0	0	—	0	0	0	0	0.0	.000
1980		0	0	—	1.69	1	1	0	5.1	5	2	3	0	0	0	0	0	0	0	—	0	1	0	1	1.0	1.000
4 yrs.		2	0	1.000 1st	2.68	6	4	0	37	35	10	11	0	1	0	0	0	0	0		0	5	0	1	0.8	1.000
WORLD SERIES																										
1980	KC A	0	0	—	5.40	1	0	0	1.2	4	0	0	0	0	0	0	0	0	0	—	0	1	0	1	1.0	1.000

Paul Spoljaric

SPOLJARIC, PAUL NIKOLA
B. Sept. 24, 1970, Kelowna, B. C., Canada.
BR TL 6′ 3″ 205 lbs.

Year	Team	W	L	PCT	ERA	G	GS	CG	IP	H	BB	SO	ShO	Relief Pitching W	L	SV	Batting AB	H	HR	BA	PO	A	E	DP	TC/G	FA
1994	TOR A	0	1	.000	38.57	2	1	0	2.1	5	9	2	0	0	0	0	0	0	0	—	0	2	1	0	1.5	.667

Carl Spongberg

SPONGBERG, CARL GUSTAV
B. May 21, 1884, Idaho Falls, Ida. D. July 21, 1938, Los Angeles, Calif.
BR TR 6′ 2″ 208 lbs.

Year	Team	W	L	PCT	ERA	G	GS	CG	IP	H	BB	SO	ShO	Relief Pitching W	L	SV	Batting AB	H	HR	BA	PO	A	E	DP	TC/G	FA
1908	CHI N	0	0	—	9.00	1	0	0	7	9	6	4	0	0	0	0	3	2	0	.667	0	3	0	0	3.0	1.000

Karl Spooner

SPOONER, KARL BENJAMIN
B. June 23, 1931, Oriskany Falls, N. Y. D. Apr. 10, 1984, Vero Beach, Fla.
BR TL 6′ 185 lbs.

Year	Team	W	L	PCT	ERA	G	GS	CG	IP	H	BB	SO	ShO	Relief Pitching W	L	SV	Batting AB	H	HR	BA	PO	A	E	DP	TC/G	FA
1954	BKN N	2	0	1.000	0.00	2	2	2	18	7	6	27	2	0	0	0	6	1	0	.167	1	0	0	0	0.5	1.000
1955		8	6	.571	3.65	29	14	2	98.2	79	41	78	1	5	1	2	28	8	0	.286	9	11	0	0	0.7	1.000
2 yrs.		10	6	.625	3.09	31	16	4	116.2	86	47	105	3	5	1	2	34	9	0	.265	10	11	0	0	0.7	1.000

Karl Spooner *continued*

Year	Team	W	L	PCT	ERA	G	GS	CG	IP	H	BB	SO	ShO	Relief W	Relief L	Relief SV	AB	H	HR	BA	PO	A	E	DP	TC/G	FA
WORLD SERIES																										
1955	BKN N	0	1	.000	13.50	2	1	0	3.1	4	3	6	0	0	0	0	0	0	0	—	0	1	0	0	0.5	1.000

Jerry Spradlin

SPRADLIN, JERRY CARL BB TR 6′ 7″ 230 lbs.
B. June 14, 1967, Fullerton, Calif.

Year	Team	W	L	PCT	ERA	G	GS	CG	IP	H	BB	SO	ShO	Relief W	Relief L	Relief SV	AB	H	HR	BA	PO	A	E	DP	TC/G	FA
1993	CIN N	2	1	.667	3.49	37	0	0	49	44	9	24	0	2	1	2	2	0	0	.000	2	2	0	0	0.1	1.000
1994		0	0	—	10.13	6	0	0	8	12	2	4	0	0	0	0	0	0	0	—	1	1	0	0	0.3	1.000
2 yrs.		2	1	.667	4.42	43	0	0	57	56	11	28	0	2	1	2	2	0	0	.000	3	3	0	0	0.1	1.000

Homer Spragins

SPRAGINS, HOMER FRANKLIN BR TR 6′ 1″ 190 lbs.
B. Nov. 9, 1920, Grenada, Miss.

Year	Team	W	L	PCT	ERA	G	GS	CG	IP	H	BB	SO	ShO	Relief W	Relief L	Relief SV	AB	H	HR	BA	PO	A	E	DP	TC/G	FA
1947	PHI N	0	0	—	6.75	4	0	0	5.1	3	3	3	0	0	0	0	0	0	0	—	2	0	0	0	0.5	1.000

Charlie Sprague

SPRAGUE, CHARLES WELLINGTON BL TL 5′11″ 150 lbs.
B. Oct. 10, 1864, Cleveland, Ohio D. Dec. 31, 1912, Des Moines, Iowa.

Year	Team	W	L	PCT	ERA	G	GS	CG	IP	H	BB	SO	ShO	Relief W	Relief L	Relief SV	AB	H	HR	BA	PO	A	E	DP	TC/G	FA
1887	CHI N	1	0	1.000	4.91	3	3	2	22	24	13	9	0	0	0	0	13	2	0	.154	0	2	1	0	0.8	.667
1889	CLE N	0	2	.000	8.47	2	2	2	17	27	10	8	0	0	0	0	7	1	0	.143	0	6	1	1	3.5	.857
1890	TOL AA	9	5	.643	*3.89*	19	12	9	122.2	111	78	59	0	1	**2**	0	199	47	1	.236	60	18	8	1	1.5	.907
3 yrs.		10	7	.588	4.51	24	17	13	161.2	162	101	76	0	1	2	0	*				60	26	10	2	1.5	.896

Ed Sprague

SPRAGUE, EDWARD NELSON, SR. BR TR 6′ 4″ 195 lbs.
Father of Ed Sprague.
B. Sept. 16, 1945, Boston, Mass.

Year	Team	W	L	PCT	ERA	G	GS	CG	IP	H	BB	SO	ShO	Relief W	Relief L	Relief SV	AB	H	HR	BA	PO	A	E	DP	TC/G	FA
1968	OAK A	3	4	.429	3.28	47	1	0	68.2	51	34	34	0	3	3	4	7	0	0	.000	8	15	2	0	0.5	.920
1969		1	1	.500	4.47	27	0	0	46.1	47	31	20	0	1	1	2	5	1	0	.200	5	17	1	1	0.9	.957
1971	CIN N	1	0	1.000	0.00	7	0	0	11	8	1	7	0	1	0	0	1	0	0	.000	0	0	1	0	0.1	.000
1972		3	3	.500	4.13	33	1	0	56.2	55	26	25	0	2	3	0	7	0	0	.000	2	6	1	1	0.3	.889
1973	3 teams CIN N (28G 1–3) STL N (8G 0–0) MIL A (7G 0–1)																									
″	total	1	4	.200	5.43	43	0	0	56.1	56	40	24	0	1	4	2	2	0	0	.000	6	11	2	1	0.4	.895
1974	MIL A	7	2	.778	2.39	20	10	3	94	94	31	57	0	0	0	0	0	0	0	—	8	9	2	2	0.9	.895
1975		1	7	.125	4.68	18	11	0	67.1	81	40	21	0	0	2	1	0	0	0	—	7	8	3	0	1.0	.833
1976		0	2	.000	6.75	3	0	0	8	14	3	0	0	0	2	0	0	0	0	—	0	4	0	1	1.3	1.000
8 yrs.		17	23	.425	3.84	198	23	3	408.1	406	206	188	0	8	15	9	22	1	0	.045	36	70	12	6	0.6	.898

Jack Spring

SPRING, JACK RUSSELL BR TL 6′ 1″ 175 lbs.
B. Mar. 11, 1933, Spokane, Wash.

Year	Team	W	L	PCT	ERA	G	GS	CG	IP	H	BB	SO	ShO	Relief W	Relief L	Relief SV	AB	H	HR	BA	PO	A	E	DP	TC/G	FA
1955	PHI N	0	1	.000	6.75	2	0	0	2.2	2	1	2	0	0	1	0	1	0	0	.000	0	0	0	0	0.0	.000
1957	BOS A	0	0	—	0.00	1	0	0	1	0	0	2	0	0	0	0	0	0	0	—	0	0	0	0	0.0	.000
1958	WAS A	0	0	—	14.14	3	1	0	7	16	7	1	0	0	0	0	2	0	0	.000	0	1	0	1	0.3	1.000
1961	LA A	3	0	1.000	4.26	18	4	0	38	35	15	27	0	0	0	0	8	0	0	.000	2	6	1	0	0.5	.889
1962		4	2	.667	4.02	57	0	0	65	66	30	31	0	4	2	6	11	1	0	.091	4	16	2	2	0.4	.909
1963		3	0	1.000	3.05	45	0	0	38.1	40	9	13	0	3	0	2	3	1	0	.333	2	10	0	0	0.3	1.000
1964	3 teams LA A (6G 1–0) CHI N (7G 0–0) STL N (2G 0–0)																									
″	total	1	0	1.000	4.38	15	0	0	12.1	15	6	1	0	1	0	0	0	0	0		0	4	1	1	0.3	.800
1965	CLE A	1	2	.333	3.74	14	0	0	21.2	21	10	9	0	1	2	0	3	1	0	.333	1	2	0	0	0.2	1.000
8 yrs.		12	5	.706	4.26	155	5	0	186	195	78	86	0	9	5	8	28	3	0	.107	9	39	4	4	0.3	.923

Brad Springer

SPRINGER, BRADFORD LOUIS BL TL 6′ 155 lbs.
B. May 9, 1904, Detroit, Mich. D. Jan. 4, 1970, Birmingham, Mich.

Year	Team	W	L	PCT	ERA	G	GS	CG	IP	H	BB	SO	ShO	Relief W	Relief L	Relief SV	AB	H	HR	BA	PO	A	E	DP	TC/G	FA
1925	STL A	0	0	—	3.00	2	0	0	3	1	7	0	0	0	0	0	0	0	0	—	0	2	0	0	1.0	1.000
1926	CIN N	0	0	—	6.75	1	0	0	1.1	2	2	1	0	0	0	0	1	0	0	.000	0	0	0	0	0.0	.000
2 yrs.		0	0		4.15	3	0	0	4.1	3	9	1	0	0	0	0	1	0	0	.000	0	2	0	0	0.7	1.000

Dennis Springer

SPRINGER, DENNIS LEROY BR TR 5′10″ 185 lbs.
B. Feb. 12, 1965, Fresno, Calif.

Year	Team	W	L	PCT	ERA	G	GS	CG	IP	H	BB	SO	ShO	Relief W	Relief L	Relief SV	AB	H	HR	BA	PO	A	E	DP	TC/G	FA
1995	PHI N	0	3	.000	4.84	4	4	0	22.1	21	9	15	0	0	0	0	8	1	0	.125	2	1	1	0	1.0	.750

Ed Springer

SPRINGER, EDWARD H. 6′ 2″ 187 lbs.
B. Feb. 8, 1861, California D. Apr. 24, 1926, Los Angeles, Calif.

Year	Team	W	L	PCT	ERA	G	GS	CG	IP	H	BB	SO	ShO	Relief W	Relief L	Relief SV	AB	H	HR	BA	PO	A	E	DP	TC/G	FA
1889	LOU AA	0	1	.000	9.00	1	1	1	5	8	2	1	0	0	0	0	2	0	0	.000	1	0	2	0	3.0	.333

Russ Springer

SPRINGER, RUSSELL PAUL BR TR 6′ 4″ 195 lbs.
B. Nov. 7, 1968, Alexandria, La.

Year	Team	W	L	PCT	ERA	G	GS	CG	IP	H	BB	SO	ShO	Relief W	Relief L	Relief SV	AB	H	HR	BA	PO	A	E	DP	TC/G	FA
1992	NY A	0	0	—	6.19	14	0	0	16	18	10	12	0	0	0	0	0	0	0	—	0	1	0	0	0.1	1.000
1993	CAL A	1	6	.143	7.20	14	9	1	60	73	32	31	0	0	0	0	0	0	0	—	3	2	0	0	0.4	1.000
1994		2	2	.500	5.52	18	5	0	45.2	53	14	28	0	1	0	2	0	0	0	—	2	3	0	1	0.3	1.000
1995	2 teams CAL A (19G 1–2) PHI N (14G 0–0)																									
″	total	1	2	.333	5.29	33	6	0	78.1	82	35	70	0	0	0	1	1	0	0	.000	3	10	0	2	0.4	1.000
4 yrs.		4	10	.286	5.99	79	20	1	200	226	91	141	0	1	0	3	1	0	0	.000	8	16	0	3	0.3	1.000

Charlie Sproull

SPROULL, CHARLES WILLIAM BR TR 6′ 3″ 185 lbs.
B. Jan. 9, 1919, Taylorsville, Ga. D. Jan. 13, 1980, Rockford, Ill.

Year	Team	W	L	PCT	ERA	G	GS	CG	IP	H	BB	SO	ShO	Relief W	Relief L	Relief SV	AB	H	HR	BA	PO	A	E	DP	TC/G	FA
1945	PHI N	4	10	.286	5.94	34	19	2	130.1	158	80	47	0	1	0	1	35	5	0	.143	7	21	3	1	0.9	.903

Bob Sprout

SPROUT, ROBERT SAMUEL BL TL 6′ 165 lbs.
B. Dec. 5, 1941, Florian, Pa.

Year	Team	W	L	PCT	ERA	G	GS	CG	IP	H	BB	SO	ShO	Relief W	Relief L	Relief SV	AB	H	HR	BA	PO	A	E	DP	TC/G	FA
1961	LA A	0	0	—	4.50	1	1	0	4	4	3	2	0	0	0	0	0	0	0	—	0	0	1	0	1.0	.000

Bobby Sprowl

SPROWL, ROBERT JOHN, JR. BL TL 6′ 2″ 190 lbs.
B. Apr. 14, 1956, Sandusky, Ohio.

Year	Team	W	L	PCT	ERA	G	GS	CG	IP	H	BB	SO	ShO	Relief W	Relief L	Relief SV	AB	H	HR	BA	PO	A	E	DP	TC/G	FA
1978	BOS A	0	2	.000	6.39	3	3	0	12.2	12	10	10	0	0	0	0	0	0	0	—	0	1	0	0	0.3	1.000
1979	HOU N	0	0	—	0.00	3	0	0	4	1	2	3	0	0	0	0	0	0	0	—	0	0	0	0	0.0	.000

Bobby Sprowl *continued*

Year	Team	Lg	W	L	PCT	ERA	G	GS	CG	IP	H	BB	SO	ShO	Relief Pitching W	Relief Pitching L	Relief Pitching SV	Batting AB	Batting H	Batting HR	BA	PO	A	E	DP	TC/G	FA
1980			0	0	—	0.00	1	0	0	1	1	1	3	0	0	0	0	0	0	0	—	0	0	0	0	0.0	.000
1981			0	1	.000	5.90	15	1	0	29	40	14	18	0	0	1	0	6	1	0	.167	2	3	0	0	0.3	1.000
4 yrs.			0	3	.000	5.40	22	4	0	46.2	54	27	34	0	0	1	0	6	1	0	.167	2	4	0	0	0.3	1.000

Mike Squires

SQUIRES, MICHAEL LYNN
B. Mar. 5, 1952, Kalamazoo, Mich.
BL TL 5′11″ 185 lbs.

Year	Team	Lg	W	L	PCT	ERA	G	GS	CG	IP	H	BB	SO	ShO	Relief Pitching W	Relief Pitching L	Relief Pitching SV	Batting AB	Batting H	Batting HR	BA	PO	A	E	DP	TC/G	FA
1984	CHI	A	0	0	—	0.00	1	0	0	0.1	0	0	0	0	0	0	0	*				155	12	2	14	8.4	.988

George Stablein

STABLEIN, GEORGE CHARLES
B. Oct. 29, 1957, Inglewood, Calif.
BR TR 6′ 4″ 185 lbs.

Year	Team	Lg	W	L	PCT	ERA	G	GS	CG	IP	H	BB	SO	ShO	Relief Pitching W	Relief Pitching L	Relief Pitching SV	Batting AB	Batting H	Batting HR	BA	PO	A	E	DP	TC/G	FA
1980	SD	N	0	1	.000	3.00	4	2	0	12	16	3	4	0	0	0	0	3	0	0	.000	1	1	0	0	0.5	1.000

Eddie Stack

STACK, WILLIAM EDWARD
B. Oct. 24, 1887, Chicago, Ill. D. Aug. 28, 1958, Chicago, Ill.
BR TR 6′ 175 lbs.

Year	Team	Lg	W	L	PCT	ERA	G	GS	CG	IP	H	BB	SO	ShO	Relief Pitching W	Relief Pitching L	Relief Pitching SV	Batting AB	Batting H	Batting HR	BA	PO	A	E	DP	TC/G	FA
1910	PHI	N	6	7	.462	4.00	20	16	7	117	115	34	48	1	0	0	0	36	3	0	.083	3	27	2	0	1.6	.938
1911			5	5	.500	3.59	13	10	5	77.2	67	41	36	0	0	0	0	24	2	0	.083	1	24	1	0	2.0	.962
1912	BKN	N	7	5	.583	3.36	28	17	4	142	139	55	45	0	2	1	1	52	7	0	.135	2	34	2	1	1.4	.947
1913	2 teams BKN N (23G 4–4) CHI N (11G 4–2)																										
"	total		8	6	.571	3.07	34	16	7	138	135	47	62	2	0	1	1	41	5	0	.122	3	22	2	0	0.8	.926
1914	CHI	N	0	1	.000	4.96	7	1	0	16.1	13	11	9	0	0	0	0	4	0	0	.000	0	6	0	0	0.9	1.000
5 yrs.			26	24	.520	3.52	102	60	23	491	469	188	200	3	2	2	2	157	17	0	.108	9	113	7	1	1.3	.946

Bill Stafford

STAFFORD, WILLIAM CHARLES
B. Aug. 13, 1939, Catskill, N. Y.
BR TR 6′ 1″ 188 lbs.

Year	Team	Lg	W	L	PCT	ERA	G	GS	CG	IP	H	BB	SO	ShO	Relief Pitching W	Relief Pitching L	Relief Pitching SV	Batting AB	Batting H	Batting HR	BA	PO	A	E	DP	TC/G	FA
1960	NY	A	3	1	.750	2.25	11	8	2	60	50	18	36	1	0	0	0	22	1	0	.045	7	10	0	2	1.5	1.000
1961			14	9	.609	2.68	36	25	8	195	168	59	101	3	0	2	2	67	12	0	.179	7	29	1	5	1.0	.973
1962			14	9	.609	3.67	35	33	7	213.1	188	77	109	2	0	1	0	78	17	0	.218	12	33	0	1	1.3	1.000
1963			4	8	.333	6.02	28	14	0	89.2	104	42	52	0	2	1	3	24	7	0	.292	5	12	0	1	0.6	1.000
1964			5	0	1.000	2.67	31	1	0	60.2	50	22	39	0	5	0	4	13	1	0	.077	3	10	0	2	0.4	1.000
1965			3	8	.273	3.56	22	15	1	111.1	93	31	71	0	0	1	0	29	0	0	.000	10	16	1	2	1.2	.963
1966	KC	A	0	4	.000	4.99	9	8	0	39.2	42	12	31	0	0	0	0	11	0	0	.000	0	4	0	0	0.4	1.000
1967			0	1	.000	1.69	14	0	0	16	12	9	10	0	0	1	0	1	0	0	.000	1	3	0	0	0.3	1.000
8 yrs.			43	40	.518	3.52	186	104	18	785.2	707	270	449	6	7	6	9	245	38	0	.155	45	117	2	13	0.9	.988
WORLD SERIES																											
1960	NY	A	0	0	—	1.50	2	0	0	6	5	1	2	0	0	0	0	1	0	0	.000	0	2	0	2	1.0	1.000
1961			0	0	—	2.70	1	1	0	6.2	7	2	5	0	0	0	0	2	0	0	.000	1	0	1	0	2.0	.500
1962			1	0	1.000	2.00	1	1	1	9	4	2	5	0	0	0	0	3	0	0	.000	0	1	0	0	1.0	1.000
3 yrs.			1	0	1.000	2.08	4	2	1	21.2	16	5	12	0	0	0	0	6	0	0	.000	1	3	1	2	1.3	.800

General Stafford

STAFFORD, JAMES JOSEPH
Brother of John Stafford.
B. July 9, 1868, Webster, Mass. D. Sept. 18, 1923, Worcester, Mass.
BR TR 5′ 8″ 165 lbs.

Year	Team	Lg	W	L	PCT	ERA	G	GS	CG	IP	H	BB	SO	ShO	Relief Pitching W	Relief Pitching L	Relief Pitching SV	Batting AB	Batting H	Batting HR	BA	PO	A	E	DP	TC/G	FA
1890	BUF	P	3	9	.250	5.14	12	12	11	98	123	43	21	0	0	0	0	*				9	21	5	2	2.2	.857

John Stafford

STAFFORD, JOHN HENRY (Doc)
Brother of General Stafford.
B. Apr. 8, 1870, Dudley, Mass. D. July 3, 1940, Worcester, Mass.
BR TR 5′10″ 170 lbs.

Year	Team	Lg	W	L	PCT	ERA	G	GS	CG	IP	H	BB	SO	ShO	Relief Pitching W	Relief Pitching L	Relief Pitching SV	Batting AB	Batting H	Batting HR	BA	PO	A	E	DP	TC/G	FA
1893	CLE	N	0	1	.000	14.14	2	0	0	7	12	7	4	0	0	1	0	4	0	0	.000	0	1	2	0	1.0	.333

Chick Stahl

STAHL, CHARLES SYLVESTER
B. Jan. 10, 1873, Avila, Ind. D. Mar. 28, 1907, West Baden, Ind.
Manager 1906.
BL TL 5′10″ 160 lbs.

Year	Team	Lg	W	L	PCT	ERA	G	GS	CG	IP	H	BB	SO	ShO	Relief Pitching W	Relief Pitching L	Relief Pitching SV	Batting AB	Batting H	Batting HR	BA	PO	A	E	DP	TC/G	FA
1899	BOS	N	0	0	—	9.00	1	0	0	2	2	3	0	0	0	0	0	*				164	17	14	4	1.8	.928

Gerry Staley

STALEY, GERALD LEE
B. Aug. 21, 1920, Brush Prairie, Wash.
BR TR 6′ 195 lbs.

Year	Team	Lg	W	L	PCT	ERA	G	GS	CG	IP	H	BB	SO	ShO	Relief Pitching W	Relief Pitching L	Relief Pitching SV	Batting AB	Batting H	Batting HR	BA	PO	A	E	DP	TC/G	FA
1947	STL	N	1	0	1.000	2.76	18	1	1	29.1	33	8	14	0	0	0	0	6	0	0	.000	0	10	0	1	0.6	1.000
1948			4	4	.500	6.92	31	3	0	52	61	21	23	0	4	3	0	9	2	1	.222	0	15	1	1	0.5	.938
1949			10	10	.500	2.73	45	17	5	171.1	154	41	55	2	4	2	6	41	5	0	.122	11	46	1	2	1.3	.983
1950			13	13	.500	4.99	42	22	7	169.2	201	61	62	1	6	1	3	55	8	0	.145	10	46	0	4	1.3	1.000
1951			19	13	.594	3.81	42	30	10	227	244	74	67	4	6	1	3	81	13	0	.160	14	54	1	2	1.6	.986
1952			17	14	.548	3.27	35	33	15	239.2	238	52	93	0	0	2	0	85	13	0	.153	27	55	2	5	2.4	.976
1953			18	9	.667	3.99	40	32	10	230	243	54	88	1	0	0	4	78	8	0	.103	13	52	4	2	1.7	.942
1954			7	13	.350	5.26	48	20	3	155.2	198	47	50	1	3	6	2	36	5	0	.139	26	32	1	2	1.2	.983
1955	2 teams CIN N (30G 5–8) NY A (2G 0–0)																										
"	total		5	8	.385	4.81	32	18	2	121.2	151	29	40	0	0	1	0	36	2	0	.056	9	25	3	3	1.2	.919
1956	2 teams NY A (1G 0–0) CHI A (26G 8–3)																										
"	total		8	3	.727	3.26	27	10	5	102	102	20	26	0	1	1	0	33	3	0	.091	4	23	0	2	1.0	1.000
1957	CHI	A	5	1	.833	2.06	47	0	0	105	95	27	44	0	5	1	7	22	1	0	.045	5	31	2	0	0.8	.947
1958			4	5	.444	3.16	50	0	0	85.1	81	24	27	0	4	5	8	11	0	0	.000	6	28	0	3	0.7	1.000
1959			8	5	.615	2.24	**67**	0	0	116.1	111	25	54	0	8	5	14	13	2	0	.154	7	19	2	3	0.4	.929
1960			13	8	.619	2.42	64	0	0	115.1	94	25	52	0	**13**	**8**	10	17	4	0	.235	10	31	2	1	0.7	.953
1961	3 teams CHI A (16G 0–3) KC A (23G 1–1) DET A (13G 1–1)																										
"	total		2	5	.286	3.96	52	0	0	61.1	64	21	32	0	2	5	4	2	0	0	.000	4	14	0	2	0.3	1.000
15 yrs.			134	111	.547	3.70	640	186	58	1981.2	2070	529	727	9	56	41	61	525	66	1	.126	146	481	19	33	1.0	.971
WORLD SERIES																											
1959	CHI	A	0	1	.000	2.16	4	0	0	8.1	8	0	3	0	0	1	1	1	0	0	.000	1	1	0	0	0.5	1.000

Harry Staley

STALEY, HENRY ELI
B. Nov. 3, 1866, Jacksonville, Ill. D. Jan. 12, 1910, Battle Creek, Mich.
BR TR 5′10″ 175 lbs.

Year	Team	Lg	W	L	PCT	ERA	G	GS	CG	IP	H	BB	SO	ShO	Relief Pitching W	Relief Pitching L	Relief Pitching SV	Batting AB	Batting H	Batting HR	BA	PO	A	E	DP	TC/G	FA
1888	PIT	N	12	12	.500	2.69	25	24	24	207.1	185	53	89	2	0	0	0	85	11	0	.129	8	41	5	0	2.2	.907
1889			21	**26**	.447	3.51	49	47	46	420	433	116	159	1	0	0	1	186	30	0	.161	20	90	7	3	2.3	.940

Harry Staley *continued*

Year	Team	W	L	PCT	ERA	G	GS	CG	IP	H	BB	SO	ShO	Relief W	Relief L	Relief SV	Batting AB	Batting H	HR	BA	PO	A	E	DP	TC/G	FA
1890	PIT P	21	25	.457	3.23	46	46	44	387.2	392	74	145	3	0	0	0	164	34	1	.207	11	86	6	5	2.2	.942
1891	2 teams PIT N (9G 4–5) BOS N (31G 20–8)																									
"	total	24	13	.649	2.58	40	37	32	324	313	80	139	1	2	1	0	133	24	1	.180	9	61	5	2	1.9	.933
1892	BOS N	22	10	.688	3.03	37	35	31	299.2	273	97	93	3	0	0	0	122	16	1	.131	0	63	3	5	1.7	.955
1893		18	10	.643	5.13	36	31	23	263	344	81	61	0	2	0	0	113	30	2	.265	3	60	9	2	2.0	.875
1894		12	10	.545	6.81	27	21	18	208.2	305	61	32	0	0	3	1	85	20	2	.235	5	28	6	0	1.4	.846
1895	STL N	6	13	.316	5.22	23	16	13	158.2	223	39	28	0	2	1	0	67	9	0	.134	1	27	1	0	1.3	.966
8 yrs.		136	119	.533	3.80	283	257	231	2269	2468	601	746	10	6	5	2	955	174	7	.182	57	456	42	17	1.9	.924

Tracy Stallard

STALLARD, EVAN TRACY — BR TR 6′ 5″ 204 lbs.
B. Aug. 31, 1937, Coeburn, Va.

Year	Team	W	L	PCT	ERA	G	GS	CG	IP	H	BB	SO	ShO	Relief W	Relief L	Relief SV	Batting AB	Batting H	HR	BA	PO	A	E	DP	TC/G	FA
1960	BOS A	0	0	—	0.00	4	0	0	4	0	2	6	0	0	0	0	0	0	0	—	1	0	0	0	0.3	1.000
1961		2	7	.222	4.88	43	14	1	132.2	110	96	109	0	0	0	2	36	3	0	.083	3	14	0	0	0.4	1.000
1962		0	0	—	0.00	1	0	0	1	0	0	0	0	0	0	0	0	0	0	—	0	0	0	0	0.0	.000
1963	NY N	6	17	.261	4.71	39	23	5	154.2	156	77	110	0	0	3	1	48	3	0	.063	12	20	0	0	0.8	1.000
1964		10	**20**	.333	3.79	36	34	11	225.2	213	73	118	2	0	1	0	79	15	0	.190	18	29	3	0	1.4	.940
1965	STL N	11	8	.579	3.38	40	26	4	194.1	172	70	99	1	0	0	0	68	6	0	.088	12	26	1	1	1.0	.974
1966		1	5	.167	5.68	20	7	0	52.1	65	25	35	0	0	2	1	14	0	0	.000	5	8	1	0	0.7	.929
7 yrs.		30	57	.345	4.17	183	104	21	764.2	716	343	477	3	0	6	4	245	27	0	.110	51	97	5	1	0.8	.967

Charley Stanceu

STANCEU, CHARLES — BR TR 6′ 2″ 190 lbs.
B. Jan. 9, 1916, Canton, Ohio D. Apr. 3, 1969, Canton, Ohio.

Year	Team	W	L	PCT	ERA	G	GS	CG	IP	H	BB	SO	ShO	Relief W	Relief L	Relief SV	Batting AB	Batting H	HR	BA	PO	A	E	DP	TC/G	FA
1941	NY A	3	3	.500	5.63	22	2	0	48	58	35	21	0	2	2	0	12	0	0	.000	1	5	0	0	0.3	1.000
1946	2 teams NY A (3G 0–0) PHI N (14G 2–4)																									
"	total	2	4	.333	4.48	17	11	1	74.1	77	44	26	0	0	0	0	19	0	0	.000	1	12	0	0	0.8	1.000
2 yrs.		5	7	.417	4.93	39	13	1	122.1	135	79	47	0	2	2	0	31	0	0	.000	2	17	0	0	0.5	1.000

Pete Standridge

STANDRIDGE, ALFRED PETER — BR TR 5′10½″ 165 lbs.
B. Apr. 25, 1891, Black Diamond, Wash. D. Aug. 2, 1963, San Francisco, Calif.

Year	Team	W	L	PCT	ERA	G	GS	CG	IP	H	BB	SO	ShO	Relief W	Relief L	Relief SV	Batting AB	Batting H	HR	BA	PO	A	E	DP	TC/G	FA
1911	STL N	0	0	—	9.64	2	0	0	4.2	10	4	3	0	0	0	0	1	0	0	.000	0	2	0	0	1.0	1.000
1915	CHI N	4	1	.800	3.61	29	3	2	112.1	120	36	42	0	2	1	0	40	9	0	.225	2	33	2	1	1.3	.946
2 yrs.		4	1	.800	3.85	31	3	2	117	130	40	45	0	2	1	0	41	9	0	.220	2	35	2	1	1.3	.949

Al Stanek

STANEK, ALBERT WILFRED (Lefty) — BL TL 5′11½″ 190 lbs.
B. Dec. 24, 1943, Springfield, Mass.

Year	Team	W	L	PCT	ERA	G	GS	CG	IP	H	BB	SO	ShO	Relief W	Relief L	Relief SV	Batting AB	Batting H	HR	BA	PO	A	E	DP	TC/G	FA
1963	SF N	0	0	—	4.72	11	0	0	13.1	10	12	5	0	0	0	0	1	0	0	.000	1	6	0	1	0.6	1.000

Kevin Stanfield

STANFIELD, KEVIN BRUCE — BL TL 6′ 190 lbs.
B. Dec. 19, 1955, Huron, S. D.

Year	Team	W	L	PCT	ERA	G	GS	CG	IP	H	BB	SO	ShO	Relief W	Relief L	Relief SV	Batting AB	Batting H	HR	BA	PO	A	E	DP	TC/G	FA
1979	MIN A	0	0	—	6.00	3	0	0	3	2	0	0	0	0	0	0	0	0	0	—	1	0	0	0	0.3	1.000

Lee Stange

STANGE, ALBERT LEE — BR TR 5′10″ 165 lbs.
B. Oct. 27, 1936, Chicago, Ill.

Year	Team	W	L	PCT	ERA	G	GS	CG	IP	H	BB	SO	ShO	Relief W	Relief L	Relief SV	Batting AB	Batting H	HR	BA	PO	A	E	DP	TC/G	FA
1961	MIN A	1	0	1.000	2.92	7	0	0	12.1	15	10	10	0	1	0	0	1	0	0	.000	1	2	0	0	0.4	1.000
1962		4	3	.571	4.45	44	6	1	95	98	39	70	0	2	3	3	17	1	0	.059	7	14	2	0	0.5	.913
1963		12	5	.706	2.62	32	20	7	164.2	145	43	100	2	0	0	0	52	5	0	.096	14	22	1	2	1.2	.973
1964	2 teams MIN A (14G 3–6) CLE A (23G 4–8)																									
"	total	7	14	.333	4.41	37	25	2	171.1	176	50	132	0	0	3	0	50	3	0	.060	10	27	2	2	1.1	.949
1965	CLE A	8	4	.667	3.34	41	12	4	132	122	26	80	2	2	1	0	28	3	0	.107	5	14	1	0	0.5	.950
1966	2 teams CLE A (8G 1–0) BOS A (28G 7–9)																									
"	total	8	9	.471	3.30	36	21	9	169.1	157	46	85	2	0	2	0	52	4	0	.077	12	21	0	0	0.9	1.000
1967	BOS A	8	10	.444	2.77	35	24	6	181.2	171	32	101	2	0	2	1	49	3	0	.061	13	17	1	1	0.9	.968
1968		5	5	.500	3.93	50	2	1	103	89	25	53	0	5	3	12	15	2	0	.133	3	12	2	0	0.3	.882
1969		6	9	.400	3.68	41	15	2	137	137	56	59	0	2	1	3	35	3	0	.086	12	12	0	2	0.6	1.000
1970	2 teams BOS A (20G 2–2) CHI A (16G 1–0)																									
"	total	3	2	.600	5.44	36	0	0	49.2	62	17	28	0	3	2	2	6	0	0	.000	4	7	2	0	0.4	.846
10 yrs.		62	61	.504	3.56	359	125	32	1216	1172	344	718	8	15	17	21	305	24	0	.079	81	148	11	7	0.7	.954
WORLD SERIES																										
1967	BOS A	0	0	—	0.00	1	0	0	2	3	0	0	0	0	0	0	0	0	0	—	0	0	1	0	1.0	.000

Don Stanhouse

STANHOUSE, DONALD JOSEPH (Stan The Man Unusual) — BR TR 6′ 2½″ 185 lbs.
B. Feb. 12, 1951, DuQuoin, Ill.

Year	Team	W	L	PCT	ERA	G	GS	CG	IP	H	BB	SO	ShO	Relief W	Relief L	Relief SV	Batting AB	Batting H	HR	BA	PO	A	E	DP	TC/G	FA
1972	TEX A	2	9	.182	3.77	24	16	1	105	83	73	78	0	0	0	0	31	4	0	.129	8	23	2	1	1.4	.939
1973		1	7	.125	4.76	21	5	1	70	70	44	42	0	1	3	1	0	0	0	—	11	18	1	2	1.4	.967
1974		1	1	.500	4.94	18	0	0	31	38	17	26	0	1	1	0	0	0	0	—	0	7	1	2	0.4	.875
1975	MON N	0	0	—	8.31	4	3	0	13	19	11	5	0	0	0	0	3	1	0	.333	2	1	0	0	0.8	1.000
1976		9	12	.429	3.77	34	26	8	184	182	92	79	1	2	0	1	52	11	0	.212	24	33	1	4	1.7	.983
1977		10	10	.500	3.42	47	16	1	158	147	84	89	1	6	2	10	47	9	1	.191	7	21	2	1	0.6	.933
1978	BAL A	6	9	.400	2.89	56	0	0	74.2	60	52	42	0	6	9	24	0	0	0	—	6	11	2	2	0.3	.895
1979		7	3	.700	2.84	52	0	0	73	49	51	34	0	7	3	21	0	0	0	—	3	16	1	2	0.4	.950
1980	LA N	2	2	.500	5.04	21	0	0	25	30	16	5	0	2	2	7	2	0	0	.000	2	7	0	2	0.4	1.000
1982	BAL A	0	1	.000	5.40	17	0	0	26.2	29	15	8	0	0	1	0	0	0	0	—	2	5	0	1	0.4	1.000
10 yrs.		38	54	.413	3.84	294	66	11	760.1	707	455	408	2	25	21	64	135	25	1	.185	65	142	10	17	0.7	.954
LEAGUE CHAMPIONSHIP SERIES																										
1979	BAL A	1	1	.500	6.00	3	0	0	3	5	3	0	0	1	1	0	0	0	0	—	0	0	0	0	0.0	.000
WORLD SERIES																										
1979	BAL A	0	1	.000	13.50	3	0	0	2	6	3	0	0	0	1	0	0	0	0	—	0	0	1	0	0.3	.000

Joe Stanka

STANKA, JOE DONALD — BR TR 6′ 5″ 201 lbs.
B. July 23, 1931, Hammon, Okla.

Year	Team	W	L	PCT	ERA	G	GS	CG	IP	H	BB	SO	ShO	Relief W	Relief L	Relief SV	Batting AB	Batting H	HR	BA	PO	A	E	DP	TC/G	FA
1959	CHI A	1	0	1.000	3.38	2	0	0	5.1	2	4	3	0	1	0	0	3	1	0	.333	0	0	0	0	0.0	.000

Bob Stanley

STANLEY, ROBERT WILLIAM (Bigfoot)
B. Nov. 10, 1954, Portland, Me.
BR TR 6′ 4″ 210 lbs.

Year	Team	Lg	W	L	PCT	ERA	G	GS	CG	IP	H	BB	SO	ShO	Relief W	Relief L	Relief SV	Batting AB	Batting H	Batting HR	BA	PO	A	E	DP	TC/G	FA
1977	BOS	A	8	7	.533	3.99	41	13	3	151	176	43	44	1	3	2	3	0	0	0	—	6	43	2	6	1.2	.961
1978			15	2	.882	2.60	52	3	0	141.2	142	34	38	0	**13**	2	10	0	0	0	—	10	34	1	2	0.9	.978
1979			16	12	.571	3.98	40	30	9	217	250	44	56	4	3	1	1	0	0	0	—	19	43	3	2	1.6	.954
1980			10	8	.556	3.39	52	17	5	175	186	52	71	1	4	2	14	0	0	0	—	9	42	2	8	1.0	.962
1981			10	8	.556	3.82	35	1	0	99	110	38	28	0	**10**	**7**	0	0	0	0	—	10	29	2	6	1.2	.951
1982			12	7	.632	3.10	48	0	0	168.1	161	50	83	0	12	7	14	0	0	0	—	13	43	2	4	1.2	.966
1983			8	10	.444	2.85	64	0	0	145.1	145	38	65	0	8	**10**	33	0	0	0	—	9	18	3	3	0.5	.900
1984			9	10	.474	3.54	57	0	0	106.2	113	23	52	0	9	10	22	0	0	0	—	7	28	2	0	0.6	.946
1985			6	6	.500	2.87	48	0	0	87.2	76	30	46	0	6	6	10	0	0	0	—	8	12	1	1	0.4	.952
1986			6	6	.500	4.37	66	1	0	82.1	109	22	54	0	6	5	16	0	0	0	—	6	14	2	0	0.3	.909
1987			4	15	.211	5.01	34	20	4	152.2	198	42	67	1	0	3	0	0	0	0	—	15	22	1	4	1.1	.974
1988			6	4	.600	3.19	57	0	0	101.2	90	29	57	0	6	4	5	0	0	0	—	7	12	2	2	0.4	.905
1989			5	2	.714	4.88	43	0	0	79.1	102	26	32	0	5	2	4	0	0	0	—	3	17	1	0	0.5	.952
13 yrs.			115	97	.542	3.64	637	85	21	1707.2	1858	471	693	7	85	61	132	0	0	0		122	357	24	38	0.8	.952
LEAGUE CHAMPIONSHIP SERIES																											
1986	BOS	A	0	0	—	4.76	3	0	0	5.2	7	3	1	0	0	0	0	0	0	0	—	0	1	0	0	0.3	1.000
1988			0	0	—	9.00	2	0	0	1	2	1	0	0	0	0	0	0	0	0	—	0	0	0	0	0.0	.000
2 yrs.			0	0		5.40	5	0	0	6.2	9	4	1	0	0	0	0	0	0	0		0	1	0	0	0.2	1.000
WORLD SERIES																											
1986	BOS	A	0	0	—	0.00	5	0	0	6.1	5	1	4	0	0	0	1	1	0	0	.000	1	2	0	0	0.6	1.000

Buck Stanley

STANLEY, JOHN LEONARD
Brother of Joe Stanley.
B. Nov. 13, 1889, Washington, D. C. D. Aug. 13, 1940, Norfolk, Va.
BL TL 5′10″ 160 lbs.

Year	Team	Lg	W	L	PCT	ERA	G	GS	CG	IP	H	BB	SO	ShO	Relief W	Relief L	Relief SV	Batting AB	Batting H	Batting HR	BA	PO	A	E	DP	TC/G	FA
1911	PHI	N	0	0	—	6.35	4	0	0	11.1	14	9	5	0	0	0	0	4	0	0	.000	1	0	1	0	0.5	.500

Joe Stanley

STANLEY, JOSEPH BERNARD
Brother of Buck Stanley.
B. Apr. 2, 1881, Washington, D. C. D. Sept. 13, 1967, Detroit, Mich.
BB TR 5′ 9½″ 150 lbs.

Year	Team	Lg	W	L	PCT	ERA	G	GS	CG	IP	H	BB	SO	ShO	Relief W	Relief L	Relief SV	Batting AB	Batting H	Batting HR	BA	PO	A	E	DP	TC/G	FA
1897	WAS	N	0	0	—	0.00	1	0	0	0.2	0	0	0	0	0	0	0	1	0	0	.000	0	0	0	0	0.0	.000
1903	BOS	N	0	0	—	9.00	1	0	0	4	4	4	4	0	0	0	0	308	77	1	.250	5	0	1	0	2.0	.833
1906	WAS	A	0	0	—	12.00	1	0	0	3	3	1	0	0	0	0	0	221	36	0	.163	119	23	19	2	2.0	.882
3 yrs.			0	0		9.39	3	0	0	7.2	7	5	4	0	0	0	0	*				268	37	31	2	1.7	.908

Mike Stanton

STANTON, MICHAEL THOMAS
B. Sept. 25, 1952, Phenix City, Ala.
BB TR 6′ 2″ 205 lbs.

Year	Team	Lg	W	L	PCT	ERA	G	GS	CG	IP	H	BB	SO	ShO	Relief W	Relief L	Relief SV	Batting AB	Batting H	Batting HR	BA	PO	A	E	DP	TC/G	FA
1975	HOU	N	0	2	.000	7.41	7	2	0	17	20	20	16	0	0	0	1	4	1	0	.250	2	3	0	0	0.7	1.000
1980	CLE	A	1	3	.250	5.44	51	0	0	86	98	44	74	0	1	3	5	0	0	0	—	4	15	0	2	0.4	1.000
1981			3	3	.500	4.40	24	0	0	43	43	18	34	0	3	3	2	0	0	0	—	3	3	0	0	0.3	1.000
1982	SEA	A	2	4	.333	4.16	56	1	0	71.1	70	21	49	0	2	3	7	0	0	0	—	10	13	2	1	0.4	.920
1983			2	3	.400	3.32	50	0	0	65	65	28	47	0	2	3	7	0	0	0	—	1	7	0	1	0.2	1.000
1984			4	4	.500	3.54	54	0	0	61	55	22	55	0	4	4	8	0	0	0	—	4	4	1	0	0.2	.889
1985	2 teams	SEA A (24G 1–2)	CHI A (11G 0–1)																								
″	total		1	3	.250	6.42	35	0	0	40.2	47	29	29	0	1	3	1	0	0	0		4	7	1	1	0.3	.917
7 yrs.			13	22	.371	4.62	277	3	0	384	398	182	304	0	13	19	31	4	1	0	.250	28	52	4	5	0.3	.952

Mike Stanton

STANTON, WILLIAM MICHAEL
B. June 2, 1967, Houston, Tex.
BL TL 6′ 1″ 190 lbs.

Year	Team	Lg	W	L	PCT	ERA	G	GS	CG	IP	H	BB	SO	ShO	Relief W	Relief L	Relief SV	Batting AB	Batting H	Batting HR	BA	PO	A	E	DP	TC/G	FA
1989	ATL	N	0	1	.000	1.50	20	0	0	24	17	8	27	0	0	1	7	0	0	0	—	1	2	1	0	0.2	.750
1990			0	3	.000	18.00	7	0	0	7	16	4	7	0	0	3	2	0	0	0	—	0	2	0	0	0.3	1.000
1991			5	5	.500	2.88	74	0	0	78	62	21	54	0	5	5	7	6	3	0	.500	6	16	0	0	0.3	1.000
1992			5	4	.556	4.10	65	0	0	63.2	59	20	44	0	5	4	8	2	1	0	.500	3	10	0	2	0.2	1.000
1993			4	6	.400	4.67	63	0	0	52	51	29	43	0	4	6	27	0	0	0	—	1	9	1	1	0.2	.909
1994			3	1	.750	3.55	49	0	0	45.2	41	26	35	0	3	1	3	3	2	0	.667	2	10	0	1	0.2	1.000
1995	2 teams	ATL N (26G 1–1)	BOS A (22G 1–0)																								
″	total		2	1	.667	4.24	48	0	0	40.1	48	14	23	0	2	1	1	0	0	0	—	1	9	4	0	0.3	.714
7 yrs.			19	21	.475	3.94	326	0	0	310.2	294	122	233	0	19	21	55	11	6	0	.545	14	58	6	4	0.2	.923
DIVISIONAL PLAYOFF SERIES																											
1995	BOS	A	0	0	—	0.00	1	0	0	2.1	1	0	4	0	0	0	0	0	0	0	—	0	1	0	0	1.0	1.000
LEAGUE CHAMPIONSHIP SERIES																											
1991	ATL	N	0	0	—	2.45	3	0	0	3.2	4	3	3	0	0	0	0	0	0	0	—	0	2	0	0	0.7	1.000
1992			0	0	—	0.00	5	0	0	4.1	2	2	5	0	0	0	0	1	1	0	1.000	0	1	0	0	0.2	1.000
1993			0	0	—	0.00	1	0	0	1	1	1	0	0	0	0	0	0	0	0	—	0	0	0	0	0.0	.000
3 yrs.			0	0		1.00	9	0	0	9	7	6	8	0	0	0	0	1	1	0	1.000	0	3	0	0	0.3	1.000
WORLD SERIES																											
1991	ATL	N	1	0	1.000	0.00	5	0	0	7.1	5	2	7	0	1	0	0	0	0	0	—	0	0	0	0	0.0	.000
1992			0	0	—	0.00	4	0	0	5	3	2	1	0	0	0	1	0	0	0	—	0	0	0	0	0.0	.000
2 yrs.			1	0	1.000	0.00	9	0	0	12.1	8	4	8	0	1	0	1	0	0	0		0	0	0	0	0.0	

Dave Stapleton

STAPLETON, DAVID EARL
B. Oct. 16, 1961, Miami, Ariz.
BL TL 6′ 1″ 185 lbs.

Year	Team	Lg	W	L	PCT	ERA	G	GS	CG	IP	H	BB	SO	ShO	Relief W	Relief L	Relief SV	Batting AB	Batting H	Batting HR	BA	PO	A	E	DP	TC/G	FA
1987	MIL	A	2	0	1.000	1.84	4	0	0	14.2	13	3	14	0	2	0	0	0	0	0	—	0	2	0	0	0.5	1.000
1988			0	0	—	5.93	6	0	0	13.2	20	9	6	0	0	0	0	0	0	0	—	0	2	0	0	0.3	1.000
2 yrs.			2	0	1.000	3.81	10	0	0	28.1	33	12	20	0	2	0	0	0	0	0		0	4	0	0	0.4	1.000

Con Starkell

STARKELL, CONRAD
B. Nov. 16, 1880, Germany D. Jan. 19, 1933, Tacoma, Wash.
BR TR 6′ 200 lbs.

Year	Team	Lg	W	L	PCT	ERA	G	GS	CG	IP	H	BB	SO	ShO	Relief W	Relief L	Relief SV	Batting AB	Batting H	Batting HR	BA	PO	A	E	DP	TC/G	FA
1906	WAS	A	0	0	—	18.00	1	0	0	3	7	2	1	0	0	0	0	0	0	0	—	0	1	0	0	1.0	1.000

Dick Starr

STARR, RICHARD EUGENE BR TR 6′ 3″ 190 lbs.
B. Mar. 2, 1921, Kittanning, Pa.

Year	Team	W	L	PCT	ERA	G	GS	CG	IP	H	BB	SO	ShO	Relief W	Relief L	Relief SV	Batting AB	Batting H	HR	BA	PO	A	E	DP	TC/G	FA
1947	NY A	1	0	1.000	1.46	4	1	1	12.1	12	8	1	0	0	0	0	3	1	0	.333	1	2	0	0	0.8	1.000
1948		0	0	—	4.50	1	0	0	2	0	2	2	0	0	0	0	0	0	0	—	0	0	0	0	0.0	.000
1949	STL A	1	7	.125	4.32	30	8	1	83.1	96	48	44	1	0	1	0	23	2	0	.087	3	9	0	1	0.4	1.000
1950		7	5	.583	5.02	32	16	4	123.2	140	74	30	1	1	0	2	36	5	0	.139	2	21	3	3	0.8	.885
1951	2 teams STL A (15G 2–5) WAS A (11G 1–7)																									
″	total	3	12	.200	6.49	26	20	1	123.1	142	66	43	0	0	0	0	35	7	0	.200	7	11	0	1	0.7	1.000
5 yrs.		12	24	.333	5.25	93	45	7	344.2	390	198	120	2	1	1	2	97	15	0	.155	13	43	3	5	0.6	.949

Ray Starr

STARR, RAYMOND FRANCIS (Iron Man) BR TR 6′ 1″ 178 lbs.
B. Apr. 23, 1906, Nowata, Okla. D. Feb. 9, 1963, Baylis, Ill.

Year	Team	W	L	PCT	ERA	G	GS	CG	IP	H	BB	SO	ShO	Relief W	Relief L	Relief SV	Batting AB	Batting H	HR	BA	PO	A	E	DP	TC/G	FA
1932	STL N	1	1	.500	2.70	3	2	1	20	19	10	6	1	0	0	0	4	1	0	.250	2	6	1	0	3.0	.889
1933	2 teams NY N (6G 0–1) BOS N (9G 0–1)																									
″	total	0	2	.000	4.35	15	3	0	41.1	51	19	17	0	0	1	0	10	1	0	.100	4	9	0	0	0.9	1.000
1941	CIN N	3	2	.600	2.65	7	4	3	34	28	6	11	2	1	1	0	11	2	0	.182	2	8	1	0	1.6	.909
1942		15	13	.536	2.67	37	33	17	276.2	228	106	83	4	0	0	0	88	8	0	.091	12	55	1	3	1.8	.985
1943		11	10	.524	3.64	36	33	9	217.1	201	91	42	2	1	0	1	74	9	0	.122	4	50	1	2	1.5	.982
1944	PIT N	6	5	.545	5.02	27	12	5	89.2	116	36	25	0	2	2	3	22	3	0	.136	1	16	1	0	0.7	.944
1945	2 teams PIT N (4G 0–2) CHI N (9G 1–0)																									
″	total	1	2	.333	8.10	13	1	0	20	27	11	5	0	1	2	0	3	2	0	.667	0	6	0	0	0.5	1.000
7 yrs.		37	35	.514	3.53	138	88	35	699	670	279	189	9	5	6	4	212	26	0	.123	25	150	5	5	1.3	.972

Herm Starrette

STARRETTE, HERMAN PAUL BR TR 6′ 175 lbs.
B. Nov. 20, 1938, Statesville, N. C.

Year	Team	W	L	PCT	ERA	G	GS	CG	IP	H	BB	SO	ShO	Relief W	Relief L	Relief SV	Batting AB	Batting H	HR	BA	PO	A	E	DP	TC/G	FA
1963	BAL A	0	1	.000	3.46	18	0	0	26	26	7	13	0	0	1	0	1	0	0	.000	2	7	0	0	0.5	1.000
1964		1	0	1.000	1.64	5	0	0	11	9	6	5	0	1	0	0	3	0	0	.000	0	1	0	0	0.2	1.000
1965		0	0	—	1.00	4	0	0	9	8	3	3	0	0	0	0	1	0	0	.000	0	4	1	0	1.3	.800
3 yrs.		1	1	.500	2.54	27	0	0	46	43	16	21	0	1	1	0	5	0	0	.000	2	12	1	0	0.6	.933

Ed Stauffer

STAUFFER, CHARLES EDWARD BR TR 5′11″ 185 lbs.
B. Jan. 10, 1898, Emsworth, Pa. D. July 2, 1979, St. Petersburg, Fla.

Year	Team	W	L	PCT	ERA	G	GS	CG	IP	H	BB	SO	ShO	Relief W	Relief L	Relief SV	Batting AB	Batting H	HR	BA	PO	A	E	DP	TC/G	FA
1923	CHI N	0	0	—	13.50	1	0	0	2	5	1	0	0	0	0	0	0	0	0	—	0	1	0	0	1.0	1.000
1925	STL A	0	1	.000	5.34	20	1	0	30.1	34	21	13	0	0	0	0	4	1	0	.250	2	1	0	1	0.2	1.000
2 yrs.		0	1	.000	5.85	21	1	0	32.1	39	22	13	0	0	0	0	4	1	0	.250	2	2	0	1	0.2	1.000

Charlie Stecher

STECHER, CHARLES
B. Bordentown, N. J. Deceased.

Year	Team	W	L	PCT	ERA	G	GS	CG	IP	H	BB	SO	ShO	Relief W	Relief L	Relief SV	Batting AB	Batting H	HR	BA	PO	A	E	DP	TC/G	FA
1890	PHI AA	0	10	.000	*10.32*	10	10	9	68	111	60	18	0	0	0	0	29	7	0	.241	3	23	3	0	2.6	.897

Bill Steele

STEELE, WILLIAM MITCHELL (Big Bill) BR TR 5′11″ 200 lbs.
B. Oct. 5, 1885, Milford, Pa. D. Oct. 19, 1949, Overland, Mo.

Year	Team	W	L	PCT	ERA	G	GS	CG	IP	H	BB	SO	ShO	Relief W	Relief L	Relief SV	Batting AB	Batting H	HR	BA	PO	A	E	DP	TC/G	FA
1910	STL N	4	4	.500	3.27	9	8	8	71.2	71	24	25	0	0	0	1	31	8	0	.258	2	24	0	0	2.9	1.000
1911		18	**19**	.486	3.73	43	34	23	287.1	287	113	115	1	2	2	3	101	21	0	.208	14	88	2	5	2.4	.981
1912		9	13	.409	4.69	40	25	7	194	245	66	67	0	4	2	1	61	11	0	.180	10	66	2	2	2.0	.974
1913		4	4	.500	5.00	12	9	2	54	58	18	10	0	0	0	0	18	1	0	.056	5	9	0	2	1.2	1.000
1914	2 teams STL N (17G 2–2) BKN N (8G 0–1)																									
″	total	2	3	.400	3.36	25	3	0	69.2	72	14	19	0	2	3	0	20	6	0	.300	1	24	2	0	1.1	.926
5 yrs.		37	43	.463	4.02	129	79	40	676.2	733	235	236	1	8	7	5	231	47	0	.203	32	211	6	9	1.9	.976

Bob Steele

STEELE, ROBERT WESLEY BB TL 5′10½″ 175 lbs.
B. Mar. 29, 1894, Cassburn, Ont., Canada D. Jan. 27, 1962, Ocala, Fla.

Year	Team	W	L	PCT	ERA	G	GS	CG	IP	H	BB	SO	ShO	Relief W	Relief L	Relief SV	Batting AB	Batting H	HR	BA	PO	A	E	DP	TC/G	FA
1916	STL N	5	15	.250	3.41	29	21	7	148	156	42	67	1	0	1	0	51	10	0	.196	3	26	3	0	1.1	.906
1917	2 teams STL N (12G 1–3) PIT N (27G 5–11)																									
″	total	6	14	.300	2.84	39	25	14	221.2	191	72	105	1	2	1	1	89	22	0	.247	5	52	7	3	1.6	.891
1918	2 teams PIT N (10G 2–3) NY N (12G 3–5)																									
″	total	5	8	.385	2.90	22	11	7	115	100	28	45	2	1	3	2	37	8	0	.216	2	21	2	0	1.1	.920
1919	NY N	0	1	.000	6.00	1	0	0	3	3	2	0	0	0	1	0	1	0	0	.000	0	0	0	0	0.0	.000
4 yrs.		16	38	.296	3.05	91	57	28	487.2	450	144	217	4	3	6	3	178	40	0	.225	10	99	12	3	1.3	.901

Elmer Steele

STEELE, ELMER RAE BB TR 5′11″ 200 lbs.
B. May 17, 1884, Muitzeskill, N. Y. D. Mar. 9, 1966, Poughkeepsie, N. Y.

Year	Team	W	L	PCT	ERA	G	GS	CG	IP	H	BB	SO	ShO	Relief W	Relief L	Relief SV	Batting AB	Batting H	HR	BA	PO	A	E	DP	TC/G	FA
1907	BOS A	0	1	.000	1.59	4	1	0	11.1	11	1	10	0	0	0	0	4	0	0	.000	0	4	0	0	1.0	1.000
1908		5	7	.417	1.83	16	13	9	118	85	13	37	1	1	0	0	39	2	0	.051	11	30	2	1	2.7	.953
1909		4	4	.500	2.85	16	8	2	75.2	75	15	32	0	1	0	1	24	6	0	.250	4	27	2	0	2.1	.939
1910	PIT N	0	3	.000	2.25	3	3	2	24	19	3	7	0	0	0	0	7	0	0	.000	3	11	0	0	4.7	1.000
1911	2 teams PIT N (31G 9–9) BKN N (5G 0–0)																									
″	total	9	9	.500	2.67	36	18	7	189	177	36	61	2	3	2	2	70	11	0	.157	11	61	3	1	2.1	.960
5 yrs.		18	24	.429	2.41	75	43	20	418	367	68	147	3	5	2	3	144	19	0	.132	29	133	7	2	2.3	.959

Bill Steen

STEEN, WILLIAM JOHN BR TR 6′½″ 180 lbs.
B. Nov. 11, 1887, Pittsburgh, Pa. D. Mar. 13, 1979, Signal Hill, Calif.

Year	Team	W	L	PCT	ERA	G	GS	CG	IP	H	BB	SO	ShO	Relief W	Relief L	Relief SV	Batting AB	Batting H	HR	BA	PO	A	E	DP	TC/G	FA
1912	CLE A	9	8	.529	3.77	26	16	6	143.1	163	45	61	1	1	2	0	49	13	0	.265	7	36	2	0	1.7	.956
1913		4	5	.444	2.45	22	13	8	128.1	113	49	57	2	0	1	2	41	7	0	.171	3	38	5	0	2.1	.891
1914		9	14	.391	2.60	30	22	13	200.2	201	68	97	1	2	2	0	70	14	0	.200	11	57	9	2	2.5	.883
1915	2 teams CLE A (10G 1–4) DET A (20G 5–1)																									
″	total	6	5	.545	3.54	30	14	5	124.2	134	37	50	0	0	1	4	44	8	0	.182	8	54	3	0	2.2	.954
4 yrs.		28	32	.467	3.05	108	65	32	597	611	199	265	4	3	6	6	204	42	0	.206	29	185	19	2	2.1	.918

Milt Steengrafe

STEENGRAFE, MILTON HENRY BR TR 6′ 170 lbs.
B. May 26, 1900, San Francisco, Calif. D. June 2, 1977, Oklahoma City, Okla.

Year	Team	W	L	PCT	ERA	G	GS	CG	IP	H	BB	SO	ShO	Relief W	Relief L	Relief SV	Batting AB	Batting H	HR	BA	PO	A	E	DP	TC/G	FA
1924	CHI A	0	0	—	12.71	3	0	0	5.2	15	4	3	0	0	0	0	1	0	0	.000	1	1	0	1	0.7	1.000
1926		1	1	.500	3.99	13	1	0	38.1	43	19	10	0	1	1	0	14	0	0	.000	2	7	2	1	0.8	.818
2 yrs.		1	1	.500	5.11	16	1	0	44	58	23	13	0	1	1	0	15	0	0	.000	3	8	2	2	0.8	.846

Morrie Steevens

STEEVENS, MORRIS DALE — BL TL 6′ 2″ 175 lbs.
B. Oct. 7, 1940, Salem, Ill.

Year	Team	Lg	W	L	PCT	ERA	G	GS	CG	IP	H	BB	SO	ShO	Relief W	Relief L	Relief SV	Batting AB	Batting H	HR	BA	PO	A	E	DP	TC/G	FA
1962	CHI	N	0	1	.000	2.40	12	1	0	15	10	11	5	0	0	0	0	1	0	0	.000	0	5	1	0	0.5	.833
1964	PHI	N	0	0	—	3.38	4	0	0	2.2	5	1	3	0	0	0	0	0	0	0	—	0	1	0	0	0.3	1.000
1965			0	1	.000	16.88	6	0	0	2.2	5	4	3	0	0	1	0	0	0	0	—	0	0	0	0	0.0	.000
3 yrs.			0	2	.000	4.43	22	1	0	20.1	20	16	11	0	0	1	0	1	0	0	.000	0	6	1	0	0.3	.857

Ed Stein

STEIN, EDWARD F. — BR TR 5′11″ 170 lbs.
B. Sept. 5, 1869, Detroit, Mich. D. May 10, 1928, Detroit, Mich.

Year	Team	Lg	W	L	PCT	ERA	G	GS	CG	IP	H	BB	SO	ShO	Relief W	Relief L	Relief SV	Batting AB	Batting H	HR	BA	PO	A	E	DP	TC/G	FA
1890	CHI	N	12	6	.667	3.81	20	18	14	160.2	147	83	65	1	0	**1**	0	59	9	0	.153	3	21	2	0	1.3	.923
1891			7	6	.538	3.74	14	10	9	101	99	57	38	1	2	1	0	43	7	0	.163	10	27	3	2	2.9	.925
1892	BKN	N	27	16	.628	2.84	48	42	38	377.1	310	150	190	6	3	0	1	144	31	0	.215	36	78	5	2	2.5	.958
1893			19	15	.559	3.77	37	34	28	298.1	294	119	81	1	2	0	0	118	25	0	.212	25	67	6	2	2.6	.939
1894			27	14	.659	4.54	45	41	38	359	396	171	84	2	2	0	1	146	38	2	.260	20	64	7	1	2.0	.923
1895			15	13	.536	4.72	32	27	24	255.1	282	93	55	1	1	0	1	104	26	0	.250	12	62	2	1	2.4	.974
1896			3	6	.333	4.88	17	10	6	90.1	130	51	16	0	1	0	0	39	10	0	.256	3	24	2	0	1.7	.931
1898			0	2	.000	5.48	3	2	2	23	39	9	6	0	0	0	0	10	4	0	.400	1	4	1	0	2.0	.833
8 yrs.			110	78	.585	3.96	216	184	159	1665	1697	733	535	12	11	2	3	663	150	2	.226	110	347	28	8	2.2	.942

Irv Stein

STEIN, IRVIN MICHAEL — BR TR 6′ 2″ 170 lbs.
B. May 21, 1911, Madisonville, La. D. Jan. 7, 1981, Covington, La.

Year	Team	Lg	W	L	PCT	ERA	G	GS	CG	IP	H	BB	SO	ShO	Relief W	Relief L	Relief SV	Batting AB	Batting H	HR	BA	PO	A	E	DP	TC/G	FA
1932	PHI	A	0	0	—	12.00	1	0	0	3	7	1	0	0	0	0	0	1	0	0	.000	0	2	0	0	2.0	1.000

Randy Stein

STEIN, WILLIAM RANDOLPH — BR TR 6′ 4″ 210 lbs.
B. Mar. 7, 1953, Pomona, Calif.

Year	Team	Lg	W	L	PCT	ERA	G	GS	CG	IP	H	BB	SO	ShO	Relief W	Relief L	Relief SV	Batting AB	Batting H	HR	BA	PO	A	E	DP	TC/G	FA
1978	MIL	A	3	2	.600	5.33	31	1	0	72.2	78	39	42	0	3	1	1	0	0	0	—	9	10	3	0	0.7	.864
1979	SEA	A	2	3	.400	5.93	23	1	0	41	48	27	39	0	2	2	0	0	0	0	—	1	3	1	0	0.2	.800
1981			0	1	.000	11.00	5	0	0	9	18	8	6	0	0	1	0	0	0	0	—	0	2	0	1	0.4	1.000
1982	CHI	N	0	0	—	3.48	6	0	0	10.1	7	7	6	0	0	0	0	0	0	0	—	1	0	0	0	0.2	1.000
4 yrs.			5	6	.455	5.75	65	2	0	133	151	81	93	0	5	4	1	0	0	0		11	15	4	1	0.5	.867

Ray Steineder

STEINEDER, RAYMOND — BR TR 6′½″ 160 lbs.
B. Nov. 13, 1895, Salem, N. J. D. Aug. 25, 1982, Vineland, N. J.

Year	Team	Lg	W	L	PCT	ERA	G	GS	CG	IP	H	BB	SO	ShO	Relief W	Relief L	Relief SV	Batting AB	Batting H	HR	BA	PO	A	E	DP	TC/G	FA
1923	PIT	N	2	0	1.000	4.75	15	2	1	55	58	18	23	0	1	0	0	15	7	0	.467	1	8	1	0	0.7	.900
1924	2 teams	PIT N (5G 0–1)	PHI N (9G 1–1)																								
″	total		1	2	.333	5.17	14	0	0	31.1	37	21	11	0	1	2	0	10	3	0	.300	1	9	0	0	0.7	1.000
2 yrs.			3	2	.600	4.90	29	2	1	86.1	95	39	34	0	2	2	0	25	10	0	.400	2	17	1	0	0.7	.950

Ricky Steirer

STEIRER, RICKY FRANCIS — BR TR 6′ 4″ 200 lbs.
B. Aug. 27, 1956, Baltimore, Md.

Year	Team	Lg	W	L	PCT	ERA	G	GS	CG	IP	H	BB	SO	ShO	Relief W	Relief L	Relief SV	Batting AB	Batting H	HR	BA	PO	A	E	DP	TC/G	FA
1982	CAL	A	1	0	1.000	3.76	10	1	0	26.1	25	11	14	0	1	0	0	0	0	0	—	2	5	0	0	0.7	1.000
1983			3	2	.600	4.82	19	5	0	61.2	77	18	25	0	2	1	0	0	0	0	—	5	11	1	1	0.9	.941
1984			0	1	.000	16.88	1	1	0	2.2	6	2	2	0	0	0	0	0	0	0	—	1	0	0	1	1.0	1.000
3 yrs.			4	3	.571	4.86	30	7	0	90.2	108	31	41	0	3	1	0	0	0	0		8	16	1	2	0.8	.960

Bill Stellberger

STELLBERGER, WILLIAM F. — BL TL
B. Apr. 22, 1865, Detroit, Mich. D. Nov. 9, 1936, Detroit, Mich.

Year	Team	Lg	W	L	PCT	ERA	G	GS	CG	IP	H	BB	SO	ShO	Relief W	Relief L	Relief SV	Batting AB	Batting H	HR	BA	PO	A	E	DP	TC/G	FA
1885	PRO	N	0	1	.000	7.88	1	1	1	8	14	4	0	0	0	0	0	4	0	0	.000	0	4	0	0	4.0	1.000

Jeff Stember

STEMBER, JEFFREY ALAN — BR TR 6′ 5″ 220 lbs.
B. Mar. 2, 1958, Elizabeth, N. J.

Year	Team	Lg	W	L	PCT	ERA	G	GS	CG	IP	H	BB	SO	ShO	Relief W	Relief L	Relief SV	Batting AB	Batting H	HR	BA	PO	A	E	DP	TC/G	FA
1980	SF	N	0	0	—	3.00	1	1	0	3	2	2	0	0	0	0	0	1	0	0	.000	0	0	0	0	0.0	.000

Bill Stemmeyer

STEMMEYER, WILLIAM (Cannon Ball Bill) — BR TR 6′ 2″ 190 lbs.
B. May 6, 1865, Cleveland, Ohio D. May 3, 1945, Cleveland, Ohio.

Year	Team	Lg	W	L	PCT	ERA	G	GS	CG	IP	H	BB	SO	ShO	Relief W	Relief L	Relief SV	Batting AB	Batting H	HR	BA	PO	A	E	DP	TC/G	FA
1885	BOS	N	1	1	.500	0.00	2	2	2	11	7	11	8	1	0	0	0	7	3	0	.429	0	4	0	0	2.0	1.000
1886			22	18	.550	*3.02*	41	41	41	348.2	300	144	239	0	0	0	0	148	41	0	.277	6	61	17	0	2.0	.798
1887			6	8	.429	5.20	15	14	14	119.1	138	41	41	0	0	0	**1**	47	12	1	.255	1	16	3	0	1.3	.850
1888	CLE	AA	0	2	.000	9.00	2	2	2	16	37	9	7	0	0	0	0	10	4	0	.400	6	5	3	1	4.7	.786
4 yrs.			29	29	.500	3.67	60	59	59	495	482	205	295	1	0	0	1	212	60	1	.283	13	86	23	1	2.0	.811

Dave Stenhouse

STENHOUSE, DAVID ROTCHFORD — BR TR 6′ 195 lbs.
Father of Mike Stenhouse.
B. Sept. 12, 1933, Westerly, R. I.

Year	Team	Lg	W	L	PCT	ERA	G	GS	CG	IP	H	BB	SO	ShO	Relief W	Relief L	Relief SV	Batting AB	Batting H	HR	BA	PO	A	E	DP	TC/G	FA
1962	WAS	A	11	12	.478	3.65	34	26	9	197	169	90	123	2	0	1	0	58	3	0	.052	21	33	0	3	1.6	1.000
1963			3	9	.250	4.55	16	16	2	87	90	45	47	1	0	0	0	25	2	0	.080	4	14	0	2	1.1	1.000
1964			2	7	.222	4.81	26	14	1	88	80	39	44	0	0	1	1	20	6	0	.300	7	13	1	0	0.8	.952
3 yrs.			16	28	.364	4.14	76	56	12	372	339	174	214	3	0	2	1	103	11	0	.107	32	60	1	5	1.2	.989

Buzz Stephen

STEPHEN, LOUIS ROBERTS — BR TR 6′ 4″ 205 lbs.
B. July 13, 1944, Porterville, Calif.

Year	Team	Lg	W	L	PCT	ERA	G	GS	CG	IP	H	BB	SO	ShO	Relief W	Relief L	Relief SV	Batting AB	Batting H	HR	BA	PO	A	E	DP	TC/G	FA
1968	MIN	A	1	1	.500	4.76	2	2	0	11.1	11	7	4	0	0	0	0	3	0	0	.000	1	2	1	0	2.0	.750

Bryan Stephens

STEPHENS, BRYAN MARIS — BR TR 6′ 4″ 175 lbs.
B. July 14, 1920, Fayetteville, Ark. D. Nov. 21, 1991, Santa Ana, Calif.

Year	Team	Lg	W	L	PCT	ERA	G	GS	CG	IP	H	BB	SO	ShO	Relief W	Relief L	Relief SV	Batting AB	Batting H	HR	BA	PO	A	E	DP	TC/G	FA
1947	CLE	A	5	10	.333	4.01	31	5	1	92	79	39	34	0	4	6	1	27	3	0	.111	5	10	1	0	0.5	.938
1948	STL	A	3	6	.333	6.02	43	12	2	122.2	141	67	35	0	2	1	3	32	4	0	.125	2	22	2	2	0.6	.923
2 yrs.			8	16	.333	5.16	74	17	3	214.2	220	106	69	0	6	7	4	59	7	0	.119	7	32	3	2	0.6	.929

Clarence Stephens

STEPHENS, CLARENCE WRIGHT — TR
B. Aug. 19, 1863, Cincinnati, Ohio D. Feb. 28, 1945, Cincinnati, Ohio.

Year	Team	Lg	W	L	PCT	ERA	G	GS	CG	IP	H	BB	SO	ShO	Relief W	Relief L	Relief SV	Batting AB	Batting H	HR	BA	PO	A	E	DP	TC/G	FA
1886	CIN	AA	1	0	1.000	*5.63*	1	1	1	8	9	5	6	0	0	0	0	5	3	0	.600	0	3	0	0	3.0	1.000
1891	CIN	N	0	1	.000	7.88	1	1	1	8	9	3	3	0	0	0	0	3	0	0	.000	0	0	0	0	0.0	.000
1892			0	1	.000	1.29	1	1	0	7	12	4	1	0	0	0	0	2	0	0	.000	0	4	0	0	4.0	1.000
3 yrs.			1	2	.333	5.09	3	3	2	23	30	12	10	0	0	0	0	10	3	0	.300	0	7	0	0	2.3	1.000

George Stephens

STEPHENS, GEORGE BENJAMIN 5′10½″ 170 lbs.
B. Sept. 28, 1867, Romeo, Mich. D. Aug. 5, 1896, Armada, Mich.

Year	Team	W	L	PCT	ERA	G	GS	CG	IP	H	BB	SO	ShO	Relief Pitching W	Relief Pitching L	Relief Pitching SV	Batting AB	Batting H	Batting HR	BA	PO	A	E	DP	TC/G	FA
1892	BAL N	1	1	.500	2.79	5	2	2	29	37	9	7	0	0	0	1	13	0	0	.000	2	6	2	0	2.0	.800
1893	WAS N	0	6	.000	5.80	9	6	6	63.2	83	31	14	0	0	0	0	29	3	0	.103	2	17	2	1	2.3	.905
1894		0	1	.000	4.91	3	2	1	11	19	8	1	1	0	0	0	4	1	0	.250	1	3	1	0	1.7	.800
3 yrs.		1	8	.111	4.86	17	10	9	103.2	139	48	22	1	0	0	1	46	4	0	.087	5	26	5	1	2.1	.861

Earl Stephenson

STEPHENSON, CHESTER EARL BL TL 6′ 3″ 175 lbs.
B. July 31, 1947, Benson, N. C.

Year	Team	W	L	PCT	ERA	G	GS	CG	IP	H	BB	SO	ShO	Relief Pitching W	Relief Pitching L	Relief Pitching SV	Batting AB	Batting H	Batting HR	BA	PO	A	E	DP	TC/G	FA
1971	CHI N	1	0	1.000	4.50	16	0	0	20	24	11	11	0	1	0	1	2	0	0	.000	2	4	0	1	0.4	1.000
1972	MIL A	3	5	.375	3.26	35	8	1	80	79	33	33	0	1	0	0	18	0	0	.000	4	14	1	0	0.5	.947
1977	BAL A	0	0	—	9.00	1	0	0	3	5	0	2	0	0	0	0	0	0	0	—	0	0	0	0	0.0	.000
1978		0	0	—	2.79	2	0	0	9.2	10	5	4	0	0	0	0	0	0	0	—	0	0	0	0	0.0	.000
4 yrs.		4	5	.444	3.59	54	8	1	112.2	118	49	50	0	2	0	1	20	0	0	.000	6	18	1	1	0.5	.960

Jerry Stephenson

STEPHENSON, JERRY JOSEPH BL TR 6′ 2″ 185 lbs.
Son of Joe Stephenson.
B. Oct. 6, 1943, Detroit, Mich.

Year	Team	W	L	PCT	ERA	G	GS	CG	IP	H	BB	SO	ShO	Relief Pitching W	Relief Pitching L	Relief Pitching SV	Batting AB	Batting H	Batting HR	BA	PO	A	E	DP	TC/G	FA
1963	BOS A	0	0	—	7.71	1	1	0	2.1	5	2	3	0	0	0	0	1	0	0	.000	0	0	0	0	0.0	.000
1965		1	5	.167	6.23	15	8	0	52	62	33	49	0	0	0	0	13	3	0	.231	3	9	0	0	0.8	1.000
1966		2	5	.286	5.83	15	11	1	66.1	68	44	50	0	0	0	0	17	2	0	.118	3	11	1	0	1.0	.933
1967		3	1	.750	3.86	8	6	0	39.2	32	16	24	0	0	0	1	16	4	0	.250	1	7	0	1	1.0	1.000
1968		2	8	.200	5.64	23	7	2	68.2	81	42	51	0	0	3	0	17	6	0	.353	2	15	1	0	0.8	.944
1969	SEA A	0	0	—	10.13	2	0	0	2.2	6	3	1	0	0	0	0	0	0	0	—	0	1	0	0	0.5	1.000
1970	LA N	0	0	—	9.00	3	0	0	7	11	5	6	0	0	0	0	1	0	0	.000	0	0	0	0	0.0	.000
7 yrs.		8	19	.296	5.69	67	33	3	238.2	265	145	184	0	0	3	1	65	15	0	.231	9	43	2	1	0.8	.963
WORLD SERIES																										
1967	BOS A	0	0	—	9.00	1	0	0	2	3	1	0	0	0	0	0	0	0	0	—	0	0	0	0	0.0	.000

John Sterling

STERLING, JOHN A.
B. Philadelphia, Pa. Deceased.

Year	Team	W	L	PCT	ERA	G	GS	CG	IP	H	BB	SO	ShO	Relief Pitching W	Relief Pitching L	Relief Pitching SV	Batting AB	Batting H	Batting HR	BA	PO	A	E	DP	TC/G	FA
1890	PHI AA	0	1	.000	21.60	1	1	1	5	16	4	1	0	0	0	0	2	0	0	.000	0	0	0	0	0.0	.000

Randy Sterling

STERLING, RANDALL WAYNE BB TR 6′ 2″ 195 lbs.
B. Apr. 21, 1951, Key West, Fla.

Year	Team	W	L	PCT	ERA	G	GS	CG	IP	H	BB	SO	ShO	Relief Pitching W	Relief Pitching L	Relief Pitching SV	Batting AB	Batting H	Batting HR	BA	PO	A	E	DP	TC/G	FA
1974	NY N	1	1	.500	5.00	3	2	0	9	13	3	2	0	0	0	0	2	0	0	.000	0	2	0	0	0.7	1.000

Dave Stevens

STEVENS, DAVID JAMES BR TR 6′ 3″ 210 lbs.
B. Mar. 4, 1970, Fullerton, Calif.

Year	Team	W	L	PCT	ERA	G	GS	CG	IP	H	BB	SO	ShO	Relief Pitching W	Relief Pitching L	Relief Pitching SV	Batting AB	Batting H	Batting HR	BA	PO	A	E	DP	TC/G	FA
1994	MIN A	5	2	.714	6.80	24	0	0	45	55	23	24	0	5	2	0	0	0	0	—	2	5	0	0	0.3	1.000
1995		5	4	.556	5.07	56	0	0	65.2	74	32	47	0	5	4	10	0	0	0	—	9	7	1	1	0.3	.941
2 yrs.		10	6	.625	5.77	80	0	0	110.2	129	55	71	0	10	6	10	0	0	0		11	12	1	1	0.3	.958

Jim Stevens

STEVENS, JAMES ARTHUR (Harry) BR TR 5′11″ 180 lbs.
B. Aug. 25, 1889, Williamsburg, Md. D. Sept. 25, 1966, Baltimore, Md.

Year	Team	W	L	PCT	ERA	G	GS	CG	IP	H	BB	SO	ShO	Relief Pitching W	Relief Pitching L	Relief Pitching SV	Batting AB	Batting H	Batting HR	BA	PO	A	E	DP	TC/G	FA
1914	WAS A	0	0	—	9.00	2	0	0	3	4	2	0	0	0	0	0	1	0	0	.000	0	0	0	0	0.0	.000

Bunky Stewart

STEWART, VESTON GOFF BL TL 6′ 154 lbs.
B. Jan. 7, 1931, Jasper, N. C.

Year	Team	W	L	PCT	ERA	G	GS	CG	IP	H	BB	SO	ShO	Relief Pitching W	Relief Pitching L	Relief Pitching SV	Batting AB	Batting H	Batting HR	BA	PO	A	E	DP	TC/G	FA
1952	WAS A	0	0	—	18.00	1	0	0	1	2	1	1	0	0	0	0	0	0	0	—	0	1	0	0	1.0	1.000
1953		0	2	.000	4.70	2	2	1	15.1	17	11	3	0	0	0	0	5	1	0	.200	0	1	0	0	0.5	1.000
1954		0	2	.000	7.64	29	2	0	50.2	67	27	27	0	0	1	1	3	0	0	.000	1	15	2	1	0.6	.889
1955		0	0	—	4.11	7	1	0	15.1	18	6	10	0	0	0	0	2	0	0	.000	0	3	0	1	0.4	1.000
1956		5	7	.417	5.57	33	9	1	105	111	82	36	0	4	2	2	28	7	0	.250	5	22	2	2	0.9	.931
5 yrs.		5	11	.313	6.01	72	14	2	187.1	215	127	77	0	4	3	3	38	8	0	.211	6	42	4	4	0.7	.923

Dave Stewart

STEWART, DAVID KEITH BR TR 6′ 2″ 200 lbs.
B. Feb. 19, 1957, Oakland, Calif.

Year	Team	W	L	PCT	ERA	G	GS	CG	IP	H	BB	SO	ShO	Relief Pitching W	Relief Pitching L	Relief Pitching SV	Batting AB	Batting H	Batting HR	BA	PO	A	E	DP	TC/G	FA
1978	LA N	0	0	—	0.00	1	0	0	2	1	0	1	0	0	0	0	0	0	0	—	0	0	0	0	0.0	.000
1981		4	3	.571	2.51	32	0	0	43	40	14	29	0	4	3	6	5	2	0	.400	4	7	0	0	0.3	1.000
1982		9	8	.529	3.81	45	14	0	146.1	137	49	80	0	6	3	1	39	7	0	.179	15	16	3	2	0.8	.912
1983	2 teams LA N (46G 5–2) TEX A (8G 5–2)																									
″	total	10	4	.714	2.60	54	9	2	135	117	50	78	0	5	2	8	7	1	0	.143	9	17	1	2	0.5	.963
1984	TEX A	7	14	.333	4.73	32	27	3	192.1	193	87	119	0	0	1	0	0	0	0	—	11	19	3	2	1.0	.909
1985	2 teams TEX A (42G 0–6) PHI N (4G 0–0)																									
″	total	0	6	.000	5.46	46	5	0	85.2	91	41	66	0	0	4	4	0	0	0		6	10	3	2	0.4	.842
1986	2 teams PHI N (8G 0–0) OAK A (29G 9–5)																									
″	total	9	5	.643	3.95	37	17	4	161.2	152	69	111	1	0	0	0	0	0	0		10	18	1	2	0.8	.966
1987	OAK A	**20**	13	.606	3.68	37	37	8	261.1	224	105	205	1	0	0	0	0	0	0	—	18	20	1	0	1.1	.974
1988		21	12	.636	3.23	37	**37**	**14**	**275.2**	240	110	192	2	0	0	0	0	0	0	—	26	16	5	2	1.3	.894
1989		21	9	.700	3.32	36	**36**	8	257.2	**260**	69	155	0	0	0	0	0	0	0	—	22	28	4	4	1.5	.926
1990		22	11	.667	2.56	36	**36**	**11**	**267**	226	83	166	**4**	0	0	0	0	0	0	—	25	23	0	2	1.3	1.000
1991		11	11	.500	5.18	35	**35**	2	226	245	105	144	1	0	0	0	0	0	0	—	14	19	2	0	1.0	.943
1992		12	10	.545	3.66	31	31	2	199.1	175	79	130	0	0	0	0	0	0	0	—	8	13	3	2	0.8	.875
1993	TOR A	12	8	.600	4.44	26	26	0	162	146	72	96	0	0	0	0	0	0	0	—	13	9	0	1	0.8	1.000
1994		7	8	.467	5.87	22	22	1	133.1	151	62	111	0	0	0	0	0	0	0	—	11	6	0	0	0.8	1.000
1995	OAK A	3	7	.300	6.89	16	16	0	81	101	39	58	0	0	0	0	0	0	0	—	5	11	0	0	1.0	1.000
16 yrs.		168	129	.566	3.95	523	348	55	2629.1	2499	1034	1741	9	15	13	19	51	10	0	.196	197	232	26	21	0.9	.943
DIVISIONAL PLAYOFF SERIES																										
1981	LA N	0	2	.000	40.50	2	0	0	0.2	4	0	1	0	0	2	0	0	0	0	—	0	0	0	0	0.0	.000
LEAGUE CHAMPIONSHIP SERIES																										
1988	OAK A	1	0	1.000	1.35	2	2	0	13.1	9	6	11	0	0	0	0	0	0	0	—	0	2	0	0	1.0	1.000
1989		2	0	1.000	2.81	2	2	0	16	13	3	9	0	0	0	0	0	0	0	—	0	1	0	0	0.5	1.000
1990		2	0	1.000	1.13	2	2	0	16	8	2	4	0	0	0	0	0	0	0	—	0	3	0	0	1.5	1.000

Dave Stewart *continued*

Year	Team	Lg	W	L	PCT	ERA	G	GS	CG	IP	H	BB	SO	ShO	Relief Pitching W	Relief Pitching L	Relief Pitching SV	Batting AB	Batting H	Batting HR	BA	PO	A	E	DP	TC/G	FA
1992			1	0	1.000	2.70	2	2	1	16.2	14	6	7	0	0	0	0	0	0	0	—	1	1	0	0	1.0	1.000
1993	**TOR**	**A**	2	0	1.000	2.02	2	2	0	13.1	8	8	8	0	0	0	0	0	0	0	—	2	0	0	0	1.0	1.000
5 yrs.			8	0	1.000	2.03	10	10	1	75.1	52	25	39	0	0	0	0	0	0	0		3	7	0	0	1.0	1.000
			1st		**1st**	**9th**		**1st**		**1st**		**2nd**	**4th**														
WORLD SERIES																											
1981	**LA**	**N**	0	0	—	0.00	2	0	0	1.2	1	2	1	0	0	0	0	0	0	0	—	0	0	1	0	0.5	.000
1988	**OAK**	**A**	0	1	.000	3.14	2	2	0	14.1	12	5	5	0	0	0	0	3	0	0	.000	0	1	0	0	0.5	1.000
1989			2	0	1.000	1.69	2	2	1	16	10	2	14	1	0	0	0	3	0	0	.000	3	0	1	0	2.0	.750
1990			0	2	.000	3.46	2	2	1	13	10	6	5	0	0	0	0	1	0	0	.000	2	1	1	0	2.0	.750
1993	**TOR**	**A**	0	1	.000	6.75	2	2	0	12	10	8	8	0	0	0	0	0	0	0	—	1	1	0	0	1.0	1.000
5 yrs.			2	4	.333	3.47	10	8	2	57	43	23	33	1	0	0	0	7	0	0	.000	6	3	3	0	1.2	.750
								10th																			

Frank Stewart

STEWART, FRANK (Stewy)
B. Sept. 8, 1906, Minneapolis, Minn.
BR TR 6′ 1½″ 180 lbs.

Year	Team	Lg	W	L	PCT	ERA	G	GS	CG	IP	H	BB	SO	ShO	Relief Pitching W	Relief Pitching L	Relief Pitching SV	Batting AB	Batting H	Batting HR	BA	PO	A	E	DP	TC/G	FA
1927	**CHI**	**A**	0	1	.000	9.00	1	1	0	4	5	4	0	0	0	0	0	1	0	0	.000	1	3	0	0	4.0	1.000

Joe Stewart

STEWART, JOSEPH LAWRENCE
B. Mar. 11, 1879, Monroe, N. C. D. Feb. 9, 1913, Youngstown, Ohio.
TR 5′11″ 175 lbs.

Year	Team	Lg	W	L	PCT	ERA	G	GS	CG	IP	H	BB	SO	ShO	Relief Pitching W	Relief Pitching L	Relief Pitching SV	Batting AB	Batting H	Batting HR	BA	PO	A	E	DP	TC/G	FA
1904	**BOS**	**N**	0	0	—	9.64	2	0	0	9.1	12	4	1	0	0	0	0	5	1	0	.200	1	1	0	0	1.0	1.000

Lefty Stewart

STEWART, WALTER CLEVELAND
B. Sept. 23, 1900, Sparta, Tenn. D. Sept. 26, 1974, Knoxville, Tenn.
BR TL 5′10″ 160 lbs.

Year	Team	Lg	W	L	PCT	ERA	G	GS	CG	IP	H	BB	SO	ShO	Relief Pitching W	Relief Pitching L	Relief Pitching SV	Batting AB	Batting H	Batting HR	BA	PO	A	E	DP	TC/G	FA
1921	**DET**	**A**	0	0	—	12.00	5	0	0	9	20	5	4	0	0	0	1	1	0	0	.000	1	3	0	0	0.8	1.000
1927	**STL**	**A**	8	11	.421	4.28	27	19	11	155.2	187	43	43	0	0	1	1	49	15	0	.306	7	45	0	2	1.9	1.000
1928			7	9	.438	4.67	29	17	7	142.2	173	32	25	1	2	0	3	51	14	0	.275	3	33	0	2	1.2	1.000
1929			9	6	.600	3.25	23	18	8	149.1	137	49	47	1	1	1	0	51	6	0	.118	8	30	2	1	1.7	.950
1930			20	12	.625	3.45	35	33	23	271	281	70	79	1	1	1	0	90	22	0	.244	13	56	2	3	2.0	.972
1931			14	17	.452	4.40	36	33	20	258	287	85	89	1	1	1	0	88	22	0	.250	17	52	3	3	2.0	.958
1932			14	19	.424	4.61	41	32	18	259.2	269	99	86	2	0	3	1	82	12	0	.146	8	50	0	3	1.4	1.000
1933	**WAS**	**A**	15	6	.714	3.82	34	31	11	230.2	227	60	69	1	0	0	0	77	11	0	.143	5	56	1	2	1.8	.984
1934			7	11	.389	4.03	24	22	7	152	184	36	36	1	0	1	0	45	7	0	.156	4	30	1	2	1.5	.971
1935	**2 teams**		**WAS A**	(1G 0–1)	**CLE A**	(24G 6–6)																					
″	**total**		6	7	.462	5.67	25	11	2	93.2	130	19	25	1	2	2	2	31	6	0	.194	2	15	3	0	0.8	.850
10 yrs.			100	98	.505	4.19	279	216	107	1721.2	1895	498	503	9	7	10	8	565	115	0	.204	68	370	12	18	1.6	.973
WORLD SERIES																											
1933	**WAS**	**A**	0	1	.000	9.00	1	1	0	2	6	0	0	0	0	0	0	1	0	0	.000	0	0	0	0	0.0	.000

Mack Stewart

STEWART, WILLIAM MACKLIN
B. Sept. 23, 1914, Stevenson, Ala. D. Mar. 21, 1960, Macon, Ga.
BR TR 6′ 167 lbs.

Year	Team	Lg	W	L	PCT	ERA	G	GS	CG	IP	H	BB	SO	ShO	Relief Pitching W	Relief Pitching L	Relief Pitching SV	Batting AB	Batting H	Batting HR	BA	PO	A	E	DP	TC/G	FA
1944	**CHI**	**N**	0	0	—	1.46	8	0	0	12.1	11	4	3	0	0	0	0	1	0	0	.000	0	1	0	0	0.1	1.000
1945			0	1	.000	4.76	16	1	0	28.1	37	14	9	0	0	0	0	3	1	0	.333	1	6	0	1	0.4	1.000
2 yrs.			0	1	.000	3.76	24	1	0	40.2	48	18	12	0	0	0	0	4	1	0	.250	1	7	0	1	0.3	1.000

Sammy Stewart

STEWART, SAMUEL LEE
B. Oct. 28, 1954, Asheville, N. C.
BR TR 6′ 3″ 200 lbs.

Year	Team	Lg	W	L	PCT	ERA	G	GS	CG	IP	H	BB	SO	ShO	Relief Pitching W	Relief Pitching L	Relief Pitching SV	Batting AB	Batting H	Batting HR	BA	PO	A	E	DP	TC/G	FA
1978	**BAL**	**A**	1	1	.500	3.18	2	2	0	11.1	10	3	11	0	0	0	0	0	0	0	—	1	2	1	0	2.0	.750
1979			8	5	.615	3.51	31	3	1	118	96	71	71	0	6	4	1	0	0	0	—	10	27	1	3	1.2	.974
1980			7	7	.500	3.55	33	3	2	119	103	60	78	0	6	6	3	0	0	0	—	5	16	2	1	0.7	.913
1981			4	8	.333	2.33	29	3	0	112	89	57	57	0	4	5	4	0	0	0	—	12	14	1	3	0.9	.963
1982			10	9	.526	4.14	38	12	1	139	140	62	69	1	7	4	5	0	0	0	—	10	21	1	3	0.8	.969
1983			9	4	.692	3.62	58	1	0	144.1	138	67	95	0	9	3	7	0	0	0	—	6	17	0	1	0.4	1.000
1984			7	4	.636	3.29	60	0	0	93	81	47	56	0	7	4	13	0	0	0	—	2	14	0	0	0.3	1.000
1985			5	7	.417	3.61	56	1	0	129.2	117	66	77	0	5	6	9	0	0	0	—	12	13	0	0	0.4	1.000
1986	**BOS**	**A**	4	1	.800	4.38	27	0	0	63.2	64	48	47	0	4	1	0	0	0	0	—	6	5	0	0	0.4	1.000
1987	**CLE**	**A**	4	2	.667	5.67	25	0	0	27	25	21	25	0	4	2	3	0	0	0	—	1	3	0	2	0.2	1.000
10 yrs.			59	48	.551	3.59	359	25	4	957	863	502	586	1	52	35	45	0	0	0		65	132	6	13	0.6	.970
LEAGUE CHAMPIONSHIP SERIES																											
1983	**BAL**	**A**	0	0	—	0.00	1	0	0	4.1	2	1	2	0	0	0	1	0	0	0	—	0	1	0	0	1.0	1.000
WORLD SERIES																											
1979	**BAL**	**A**	0	0	—	0.00	1	0	0	2.2	4	1	0	0	0	0	0	1	0	0	.000	1	2	0	0	3.0	1.000
1983			0	0	—	0.00	3	0	0	5	2	2	6	0	0	0	0	2	0	0	.000	0	0	0	0	0.0	.000
2 yrs.			0	0		0.00	4	0	0	7.2	6	3	6	0	0	0	0	3	0	0	.000	1	2	0	0	0.8	1.000

Phil Stidham

STIDHAM, PHILLIP WAYNE
B. Nov. 18, 1968, Tulsa, Okla.
BR TR 6′ 180 lbs.

Year	Team	Lg	W	L	PCT	ERA	G	GS	CG	IP	H	BB	SO	ShO	Relief Pitching W	Relief Pitching L	Relief Pitching SV	Batting AB	Batting H	Batting HR	BA	PO	A	E	DP	TC/G	FA
1994	**DET**	**A**	0	0	—	24.92	5	0	0	4.1	12	4	4	0	0	0	0	0	0	0	—	0	0	0	0	0.0	.000

Dave Stieb

STIEB, DAVID ANDREW
B. July 22, 1957, Santa Ana, Calif.
BR TR 6′ 185 lbs.

Year	Team	Lg	W	L	PCT	ERA	G	GS	CG	IP	H	BB	SO	ShO	Relief Pitching W	Relief Pitching L	Relief Pitching SV	Batting AB	Batting H	Batting HR	BA	PO	A	E	DP	TC/G	FA
1979	**TOR**	**A**	8	8	.500	4.33	18	18	7	129	139	48	52	1	0	0	0	0	0	0	—	12	31	1	1	2.4	.977
1980			12	15	.444	3.70	34	32	14	243	232	83	108	4	0	0	0	1	0	0	.000	20	58	1	8	2.3	.987
1981			11	10	.524	3.18	25	25	11	184	148	61	89	2	0	0	0	0	0	0	—	11	38	1	3	2.0	.980
1982			17	14	.548	3.25	38	38	**19**	**288.1**	**271**	75	141	**5**	0	0	0	0	0	0	—	27	53	2	6	2.2	.976
1983			17	12	.586	3.04	36	36	14	278	223	93	187	4	0	0	0	0	0	0	—	28	33	2	1	1.8	.968
1984			16	8	.667	2.83	35	35	11	**267**	215	88	198	2	0	0	0	0	0	0	—	22	34	1	4	1.6	.982
1985			14	13	.519	**2.48**	36	36	8	265	206	96	167	2	0	0	0	0	0	0	—	34	53	5	5	2.6	.946
1986			7	12	.368	4.74	37	34	1	205	239	87	127	1	0	0	1	0	0	0	—	15	33	1	4	1.3	.980
1987			13	9	.591	4.09	33	31	3	185	164	87	115	1	0	0	0	0	0	0	—	24	25	2	2	1.5	.961
1988			16	8	.667	3.04	32	31	8	207.1	157	79	147	4	0	0	0	0	0	0	—	19	26	0	3	1.4	1.000
1989			17	8	.680	3.35	33	33	3	206.2	164	76	101	2	0	0	0	0	0	0	—	18	29	0	1	1.4	1.000
1990			18	6	.750	2.93	33	33	2	208.2	179	64	125	2	0	0	0	0	0	0	—	24	40	4	3	2.1	.941

Dave Stieb *continued*

Year	Team		W	L	PCT	ERA	G	GS	CG	IP	H	BB	SO	ShO	Relief Pitching W	L	SV	Batting AB	H	HR	BA	PO	A	E	DP	TC/G	FA
1991			4	3	.571	3.17	9	9	1	59.2	52	23	29	0	0	0	0	0	0	0	—	5	12	1	2	2.0	.944
1992			4	6	.400	5.04	21	14	1	96.1	98	43	45	0	1	0	0	0	0	0	—	8	21	0	1	1.4	1.000
1993	CHI	A	1	3	.250	6.04	4	4	0	22.1	27	14	11	0	0	0	0	0	0	0	—	0	2	1	1	0.8	.667
15 yrs.			175	135	.565	3.41	424	409	103	2845.1	2514	1017	1642	30	1	0	1	1	0	0	.000	267	488	22	45	1.8	.972
LEAGUE CHAMPIONSHIP SERIES																											
1985	TOR	A	1	1	.500	3.10	3	3	0	20.1	11	10	18	0	0	0	0	0	0	0	—	1	3	0	0	1.3	1.000
1989			0	2	.000	6.35	2	2	0	11.1	12	6	10	0	0	0	0	0	0	0	—	0	1	0	0	0.5	1.000
2 yrs.			1	3	.250	4.26	5	5	0	31.2	23	16	28	0	0	0	0	0	0	0		1	4	0	0	1.0	1.000
				5th								**10th**															

Fred Stiely

STIELY, FRED WARREN BL TL 5′ 8″ 170 lbs.
B. June 1, 1901, Pillow, Pa. D. Jan. 6, 1981, Valley View, Pa.

Year	Team		W	L	PCT	ERA	G	GS	CG	IP	H	BB	SO	ShO	Relief W	L	SV	AB	H	HR	BA	PO	A	E	DP	TC/G	FA
1929	STL	A	1	0	1.000	0.00	1	1	1	9	11	3	2	0	0	0	0	3	2	0	.667	1	1	0	1	2.0	1.000
1930			0	1	.000	8.53	4	2	1	19	27	8	5	0	0	0	0	7	3	0	.429	0	3	0	0	0.8	1.000
1931			0	0	—	6.75	4	0	0	6.2	7	3	2	0	0	0	0	0	0	0	—	1	0	0	0	0.3	1.000
3 yrs.			1	1	.500	5.97	9	3	2	34.2	45	14	9	0	0	0	0	10	5	0	.500	2	4	0	1	0.7	1.000

Dick Stigman

STIGMAN, RICHARD LEWIS BR TL 6′ 3″ 200 lbs.
B. Jan. 24, 1936, Nimrod, Minn.

Year	Team		W	L	PCT	ERA	G	GS	CG	IP	H	BB	SO	ShO	Relief W	L	SV	AB	H	HR	BA	PO	A	E	DP	TC/G	FA
1960	CLE	A	5	11	.313	4.51	41	18	3	133.2	118	87	104	0	2	3	9	36	8	0	.222	8	11	0	0	0.5	1.000
1961			2	5	.286	4.62	22	6	0	64.1	65	25	48	0	1	1	0	16	2	0	.125	2	12	0	0	0.6	1.000
1962	MIN	A	12	5	.706	3.66	40	15	6	142.2	122	64	116	0	3	2	3	45	2	0	.044	5	12	0	0	0.4	1.000
1963			15	15	.500	3.25	33	33	15	241	210	81	193	3	0	0	0	84	9	0	.107	6	17	0	0	0.7	1.000
1964			6	15	.286	4.03	32	29	5	190	160	70	159	1	1	0	0	69	7	0	.101	5	17	4	2	0.8	.846
1965			4	2	.667	4.37	33	8	0	70	59	33	70	0	4	2	4	15	2	0	.133	1	8	1	0	0.3	.900
1966	BOS	A	2	1	.667	5.44	34	10	1	81	85	46	65	1	1	0	0	17	2	0	.118	0	9	2	1	0.3	.818
7 yrs.			46	54	.460	4.03	235	119	30	922.2	819	406	755	5	12	8	16	282	32	0	.113	27	86	7	3	0.5	.942

Rollie Stiles

STILES, ROLLAND MAYS BR TR 6′ 1½″ 180 lbs.
B. Nov. 17, 1906, Ratcliff, Ark.

Year	Team		W	L	PCT	ERA	G	GS	CG	IP	H	BB	SO	ShO	Relief W	L	SV	AB	H	HR	BA	PO	A	E	DP	TC/G	FA
1930	STL	A	3	6	.333	5.89	20	7	3	102.1	136	41	25	0	1	3	0	37	10	0	.270	5	18	1	0	1.2	.958
1931			3	1	.750	7.22	34	2	0	81	112	60	32	0	2	0	0	22	1	0	.045	3	16	2	1	0.6	.905
1933			3	7	.300	5.01	31	9	6	115	154	47	29	1	1	3	1	33	2	0	.061	5	22	3	0	1.0	.900
3 yrs.			9	14	.391	5.91	85	18	9	298.1	402	148	86	1	4	6	1	92	13	0	.141	13	56	6	1	0.9	.920

Archie Stimmel

STIMMEL, ARCHIBALD RAY (Lumbago) BR TR 6′ 175 lbs.
B. May 30, 1873, Woodsboro, Md. D. Aug. 18, 1958, Frederick, Md.

Year	Team		W	L	PCT	ERA	G	GS	CG	IP	H	BB	SO	ShO	Relief W	L	SV	AB	H	HR	BA	PO	A	E	DP	TC/G	FA
1900	CIN	N	1	1	.500	6.92	2	1	1	13	18	4	2	0	1	0	0	5	1	0	.200	0	2	0	0	1.0	1.000
1901			4	14	.222	4.11	20	18	14	153.1	170	44	55	1	0	0	0	62	5	0	.081	6	28	2	2	1.6	.944
1902			0	4	.000	3.46	4	3	3	26	37	12	7	0	0	1	0	10	2	0	.200	0	6	1	0	1.8	.857
3 yrs.			5	19	.208	4.21	26	22	18	192.1	225	60	64	1	1	1	0	77	8	0	.104	6	36	3	2	1.6	.933

Carl Stimson

STIMSON, CARL REMUS BB TR 6′ 5″ 190 lbs.
B. July 18, 1894, Hamburg, Iowa D. Nov. 9, 1936, Omaha, Neb.

Year	Team		W	L	PCT	ERA	G	GS	CG	IP	H	BB	SO	ShO	Relief W	L	SV	AB	H	HR	BA	PO	A	E	DP	TC/G	FA
1923	BOS	A	0	0	—	22.50	2	0	0	4	12	5	1	0	0	0	0	2	0	0	.000	0	2	0	1	1.0	1.000

Harry Stine

STINE, HARRY C. TL 5′ 6″ 150 lbs.
B. Feb. 20, 1864, Shenandoah, Pa. D. June 5, 1924, Niagara Falls, N. Y.

Year	Team		W	L	PCT	ERA	G	GS	CG	IP	H	BB	SO	ShO	Relief W	L	SV	AB	H	HR	BA	PO	A	E	DP	TC/G	FA
1890	PHI	AA	0	1	.000	9.00	1	1	1	8	17	4	1	0	0	0	0	3	0	0	.000	0	0	0	0	0.0	.000

Lee Stine

STINE, LEE ELBERT BR TR 5′11″ 185 lbs.
B. Nov. 17, 1913, Stillwater, Okla.

Year	Team		W	L	PCT	ERA	G	GS	CG	IP	H	BB	SO	ShO	Relief W	L	SV	AB	H	HR	BA	PO	A	E	DP	TC/G	FA
1934	CHI	A	0	0	—	8.18	4	0	0	11	11	10	8	0	0	0	0	1	0	0	.000	1	0	0	0	0.3	1.000
1935			0	0	—	9.00	1	0	0	2	2	3	1	0	0	0	0	0	0	0	—	0	3	0	1	3.0	1.000
1936	CIN	N	3	8	.273	5.03	40	13	5	121.2	157	41	26	1	0	1	2	27	8	0	.296	8	33	0	1	1.0	1.000
1938	NY	A	0	0	—	1.04	4	0	0	8.2	9	1	4	0	0	0	0	2	1	0	.500	0	1	0	0	0.3	1.000
4 yrs.			3	8	.273	5.09	49	13	5	143.1	179	55	39	1	0	1	2	30	9	0	.300	9	37	0	2	0.9	1.000

Jack Stivetts

STIVETTS, JOHN ELMER (Happy Jack) BR TR 6′ 2″ 185 lbs.
B. Mar. 31, 1868, Ashland, Pa. D. Apr. 18, 1930, Ashland, Pa.

Year	Team		W	L	PCT	ERA	G	GS	CG	IP	H	BB	SO	ShO	Relief W	L	SV	AB	H	HR	BA	PO	A	E	DP	TC/G	FA
1889	STL	AA	13	7	.650	**2.25**	26	20	18	191.2	153	68	143	2	3	1	1	79	18	0	.228	12	43	6	0	2.3	.902
1890			27	21	.563	*3.52*	54	46	41	419.1	399	179	289	3	**3**	**2**	0	226	65	7	.288	65	89	17	6	2.6	.901
1891			33	22	.600	2.86	**64**	56	40	440	357	**232**	**259**	3	4	1	1	302	92	7	.305	51	113	17	4	2.1	.906
1892	BOS	N	35	16	.686	3.04	53	48	45	414.2	346	171	180	3	2	1	1	240	71	3	.296	53	97	16	8	2.3	.904
1893			20	12	.625	4.41	38	34	29	283.2	315	115	61	1	2	0	1	172	51	3	.297	31	55	7	3	1.9	.925
1894			26	14	.650	4.90	45	39	30	338	429	127	76	0	3	1	0	244	80	8	.328	79	53	13	5	2.2	.910
1895			17	17	.500	4.64	38	34	30	291	341	89	111	0	1	0	0	158	30	0	.190	76	53	4	5	3.0	.970
1896			21	14	.600	4.10	42	36	31	329	353	99	71	2	0	1	0	221	76	3	.344	90	62	15	4	2.8	.910
1897			11	4	.733	3.41	18	15	10	129.1	147	43	27	0	1	0	0	199	73	2	.367	68	45	8	3	2.4	.934
1898			0	1	.000	8.25	2	1	1	12	17	7	1	0	0	0	0	111	28	2	.252	97	22	10	4	4.0	.922
1899	CLE	N	0	4	.000	5.68	7	4	3	38	48	25	5	0	0	0	0	39	8	0	.205	14	20	1	0	2.2	.971
11 yrs.			203	132	.606	3.74	387	333	278	2886.2	2905	1155	1223	14	19	7	4	*				636	652	114	42	2.5	.919

Chuck Stobbs

STOBBS, CHARLES KLEIN BL TL 6′ 1″ 185 lbs.
B. July 2, 1929, Wheeling, W. Va.

Year	Team		W	L	PCT	ERA	G	GS	CG	IP	H	BB	SO	ShO	Relief W	L	SV	AB	H	HR	BA	PO	A	E	DP	TC/G	FA
1947	BOS	A	0	1	.000	6.00	4	1	0	9	10	10	5	0	0	0	0	1	0	0	.000	1	0	0	0	0.3	1.000
1948			0	0	—	6.43	6	0	0	7	9	7	4	0	0	0	0	1	0	0	.000	0	3	0	0	0.5	1.000
1949			11	6	.647	4.03	26	19	10	152	145	75	70	0	0	2	0	53	11	0	.208	5	25	3	4	1.3	.909
1950			12	7	.632	5.10	32	21	6	169.1	158	88	78	0	1	1	1	57	14	0	.246	12	33	0	0	1.4	1.000
1951			10	9	.526	4.76	34	25	6	170	180	74	75	0	0	0	0	61	11	0	.180	9	20	1	1	0.9	.967
1952	CHI	A	7	12	.368	3.13	38	17	2	135	118	72	73	0	3	1	1	38	3	0	.079	8	26	1	2	0.9	.971
1953	WAS	A	11	8	.579	3.29	27	20	8	153	146	44	67	0	0	0	0	44	10	0	.227	12	21	1	0	1.3	.971
1954			11	11	.500	4.10	31	24	10	182	189	67	67	3	1	0	0	51	7	0	.137	8	35	2	5	1.5	.956

Chuck Stobbs *continued*

Year	Team	W	L	PCT	ERA	G	GS	CG	IP	H	BB	SO	ShO	Relief Pitching W	Relief Pitching L	Relief Pitching SV	Batting AB	Batting H	Batting HR	BA	PO	A	E	DP	TC/G	FA
1955		4	14	.222	5.00	41	16	2	140.1	169	57	60	0	3	3	3	35	6	0	.171	12	28	0	1	1.0	1.000
1956		15	15	.500	3.60	37	33	15	240	264	54	97	1	1	0	1	84	15	0	.179	19	39	1	5	1.6	.983
1957		8	**20**	.286	5.36	42	31	5	211.2	235	80	114	2	1	2	1	76	16	0	.211	9	24	0	1	0.8	1.000
1958	**2 teams WAS A** (19G 2–6) **STL N** (17G 1–3)																									
″	**total**	3	9	.250	5.04	36	8	0	96.1	127	30	48	0	2	3	1	16	1	0	.063	8	19	1	0	0.8	.964
1959	**WAS A**	1	8	.111	2.98	41	7	0	90.2	82	24	50	0	0	3	7	19	2	0	.105	6	14	0	1	0.5	1.000
1960		12	7	.632	3.32	40	13	1	119.1	115	38	72	1	6	2	2	34	3	0	.088	4	11	0	1	0.4	1.000
1961	**MIN A**	2	3	.400	7.46	24	3	0	44.2	56	15	17	0	2	1	2	8	3	0	.375	3	3	0	0	0.3	1.000
15 yrs.		107	130	.451	4.29	459	238	65	1920.1	2003	735	897	7	20	18	19	578	102	0	.176	116	301	10	21	0.9	.977

Wes Stock

STOCK, WESLEY GAY BR TR 6′ 2″ 188 lbs.
B. Apr. 10, 1934, Longview, Wash.

Year	Team	W	L	PCT	ERA	G	GS	CG	IP	H	BB	SO	ShO	Relief Pitching W	Relief Pitching L	Relief Pitching SV	Batting AB	Batting H	Batting HR	BA	PO	A	E	DP	TC/G	FA
1959	**BAL A**	0	0	—	3.55	7	0	0	12.2	16	2	8	0	0	0	1	2	0	0	.000	0	2	1	0	0.4	.667
1960		2	2	.500	2.88	17	0	0	34.1	26	14	23	0	2	2	2	6	0	0	.000	1	8	0	1	0.5	1.000
1961		5	0	1.000	3.01	35	1	0	71.2	58	27	47	0	5	0	3	11	0	0	.000	5	22	0	1	0.8	1.000
1962		3	2	.600	4.43	53	0	0	65	50	36	34	0	3	2	3	3	0	0	.000	4	23	0	4	0.5	1.000
1963		7	0	1.000	3.94	47	0	0	75.1	69	31	55	0	7	0	1	10	0	0	.000	6	13	1	1	0.4	.950
1964	**2 teams BAL A** (14G 2–0) **KC A** (50G 6–3)																									
″	**total**	8	3	.727	2.30	64	0	0	113.2	86	42	115	0	8	3	5	19	3	0	.158	8	12	0	0	0.3	1.000
1965	**KC A**	0	4	.000	5.24	62	2	0	99.2	96	40	52	0	0	3	4	6	0	0	.000	9	25	1	0	0.6	.971
1966		2	2	.500	2.66	35	0	0	44	30	21	31	0	2	2	3	2	0	0	.000	1	5	0	1	0.2	1.000
1967		0	0	—	18.00	1	0	0	1	3	2	0	0	0	0	0	0	0	0	—	0	1	0	0	1.0	1.000
9 yrs.		27	13	.675	3.60	321	3	0	517.1	434	215	365	0	27	12	22	59	3	0	.051	34	111	3	8	0.5	.980

Otis Stocksdale

STOCKSDALE, OTIS HINKLEY BL TR 5′10½″ 180 lbs.
B. Aug. 7, 1871, Arcadia, Md. D. Mar. 15, 1933, Pennsville, N. J.

Year	Team	W	L	PCT	ERA	G	GS	CG	IP	H	BB	SO	ShO	Relief Pitching W	Relief Pitching L	Relief Pitching SV	Batting AB	Batting H	Batting HR	BA	PO	A	E	DP	TC/G	FA
1893	**WAS N**	2	8	.200	8.22	11	11	7	69	111	32	12	0	0	0	0	40	12	0	.300	14	17	1	2	2.5	.969
1894		5	9	.357	5.06	18	14	11	117.1	176	42	10	0	0	1	0	71	23	0	.324	15	29	2	0	1.8	.957
1895	**2 teams WAS N** (20G 6–11) **BOS N** (4G 2–2)																									
″	**total**	8	13	.381	6.06	24	21	12	159	230	60	25	0	0	0	1	89	27	0	.303	24	30	6	2	2.1	.900
1896	**BAL N**	0	1	.000	16.20	1	0	0	1.2	4	2	1	0	0	1	0	3	1	0	.333	0	0	0	0	0.0	.000
4 yrs.		15	31	.326	6.20	54	46	30	347	521	136	48	0	0	2	1	203	63	0	.310	53	76	9	4	2.0	.935

Bob Stoddard

STODDARD, ROBERT LYLE BR TR 6′ 1″ 190 lbs.
B. Mar. 8, 1957, San Jose, Calif.

Year	Team	W	L	PCT	ERA	G	GS	CG	IP	H	BB	SO	ShO	Relief Pitching W	Relief Pitching L	Relief Pitching SV	Batting AB	Batting H	Batting HR	BA	PO	A	E	DP	TC/G	FA
1981	**SEA A**	2	1	.667	2.57	5	5	1	35	35	9	22	0	0	0	0	0	0	0	—	0	6	0	0	1.2	1.000
1982		3	3	.500	2.41	9	9	2	67.1	48	18	24	1	0	0	0	0	0	0	—	0	14	0	1	1.6	1.000
1983		9	17	.346	4.41	35	23	2	175.2	182	58	87	1	1	4	0	0	0	0	—	15	36	2	2	1.5	.962
1984		2	3	.400	5.13	27	6	0	79	86	37	39	0	2	1	0	0	0	0	—	3	14	0	1	0.6	1.000
1985	**DET A**	0	0	—	6.75	8	0	0	13.1	15	5	11	0	0	0	1	0	0	0	—	2	3	0	1	0.6	1.000
1986	**SD N**	1	0	1.000	2.31	18	0	0	23.1	20	11	17	0	1	0	1	1	0	0	.000	0	3	0	0	0.2	1.000
1987	**KC A**	1	3	.250	4.28	17	2	0	40	51	22	23	0	1	2	1	0	0	0	—	4	10	0	1	0.8	1.000
7 yrs.		18	27	.400	4.03	119	45	5	433.2	437	160	223	2	5	7	3	1	0	0	.000	24	86	2	6	0.9	.982

Tim Stoddard

STODDARD, TIMOTHY PAUL BR TR 6′ 7″ 230 lbs.
B. Jan. 24, 1953, East Chicago, Ind.

Year	Team	W	L	PCT	ERA	G	GS	CG	IP	H	BB	SO	ShO	Relief Pitching W	Relief Pitching L	Relief Pitching SV	Batting AB	Batting H	Batting HR	BA	PO	A	E	DP	TC/G	FA
1975	**CHI A**	0	0	—	9.00	1	0	0	1	2	0	0	0	0	0	0	0	0	0	—	0	1	0	0	1.0	1.000
1978	**BAL A**	0	1	.000	6.00	8	0	0	18	22	8	14	0	0	1	0	0	0	0	—	0	3	0	0	0.4	1.000
1979		3	1	.750	1.71	29	0	0	58	44	19	47	0	3	1	3	0	0	0	—	9	5	1	0	0.5	.933
1980		5	3	.625	2.51	64	0	0	86	72	38	64	0	5	3	26	0	0	0	—	4	9	0	0	0.2	1.000
1981		4	2	.667	3.89	31	0	0	37	38	18	32	0	4	2	7	0	0	0	—	4	3	0	1	0.2	1.000
1982		3	4	.429	4.02	50	0	0	56	53	29	42	0	3	4	12	0	0	0	—	2	6	1	0	0.2	.889
1983		4	3	.571	6.09	47	0	0	57.2	65	29	50	0	4	3	9	0	0	0	—	3	7	0	1	0.2	1.000
1984	**CHI N**	10	6	.625	3.82	58	0	0	92	77	57	87	0	10	6	7	11	1	0	.091	4	8	1	0	0.2	.923
1985	**SD N**	1	6	.143	4.65	44	0	0	60	63	37	42	0	1	6	1	5	0	0	.000	3	5	0	0	0.2	1.000
1986	**2 teams SD N** (30G 1–3) **NY A** (24G 4–1)																									
″	**total**	5	4	.556	3.80	54	0	0	94.2	74	57	81	0	5	4	0	4	1	1	.250	3	14	2	2	0.4	.895
1987	**NY A**	4	3	.571	3.50	57	0	0	92.2	83	30	78	0	4	3	8	0	0	0	—	8	8	1	0	0.3	.941
1988		2	2	.500	6.38	28	0	0	55	62	27	33	0	2	2	3	0	0	0	—	4	7	0	2	0.4	1.000
1989	**CLE A**	0	0	—	2.95	14	0	0	21.1	25	7	12	0	0	0	0	0	0	0	—	0	4	0	0	0.3	1.000
13 yrs.		41	35	.539	3.95	485	0	0	729.1	680	356	582	0	41	35	76	20	2	1	.100	44	80	6	6	0.3	.954
LEAGUE CHAMPIONSHIP SERIES																										
1984	**CHI N**	0	0	—	4.50	2	0	0	2	1	2	2	0	0	0	0	0	0	0	—	1	1	0	0	1.0	1.000
WORLD SERIES																										
1979	**BAL A**	1	0	1.000	5.40	4	0	0	5	6	1	3	0	1	0	0	1	1	0	1.000	1	4	1	0	1.5	.833

Art Stokes

STOKES, ARTHUR MILTON BR TR 5′10½″ 155 lbs.
B. Sept. 13, 1896, Emmitsburg, Md. D. June 3, 1962, Titusville, Pa.

Year	Team	W	L	PCT	ERA	G	GS	CG	IP	H	BB	SO	ShO	Relief Pitching W	Relief Pitching L	Relief Pitching SV	Batting AB	Batting H	Batting HR	BA	PO	A	E	DP	TC/G	FA
1925	**PHI A**	1	1	.500	4.07	12	0	0	24.1	24	10	7	0	1	1	0	4	0	0	.000	1	6	2	0	0.8	.778

Arnie Stone

STONE, EDWIN ARNOLD BR TL 6′ 180 lbs.
B. Dec. 19, 1892, North Creek, N. Y. D. July 29, 1948, Hudson Falls, N. Y.

Year	Team	W	L	PCT	ERA	G	GS	CG	IP	H	BB	SO	ShO	Relief Pitching W	Relief Pitching L	Relief Pitching SV	Batting AB	Batting H	Batting HR	BA	PO	A	E	DP	TC/G	FA
1923	**PIT N**	0	1	.000	8.03	9	0	0	12.1	19	4	2	0	0	1	0	1	0	0	.000	0	1	1	0	0.2	.500
1924		4	2	.667	2.95	26	2	1	64	57	15	7	0	3	1	0	15	2	0	.133	1	18	0	0	0.7	1.000
2 yrs.		4	3	.571	3.77	35	2	1	76.1	76	19	9	0	3	2	0	16	2	0	.125	1	19	1	0	0.6	.952

Dean Stone

STONE, DARRAGH DEAN BL TL 6′ 4″ 205 lbs.
B. Sept. 1, 1930, Moline, Ill.

Year	Team	W	L	PCT	ERA	G	GS	CG	IP	H	BB	SO	ShO	Relief Pitching W	Relief Pitching L	Relief Pitching SV	Batting AB	Batting H	Batting HR	BA	PO	A	E	DP	TC/G	FA
1953	**WAS A**	0	1	.000	8.31	3	1	0	8.2	13	5	5	0	0	0	0	2	0	0	.000	2	0	0	0	0.7	1.000
1954		12	10	.545	3.22	31	23	10	178.2	161	69	87	2	1	0	0	52	5	1	.096	5	17	0	3	0.7	1.000
1955		6	13	.316	4.15	43	24	5	180	180	114	84	1	0	2	1	46	2	0	.043	4	23	0	2	0.6	1.000
1956		5	7	.417	6.27	41	21	2	132	148	93	86	0	0	1	3	34	3	0	.088	4	20	5	2	0.7	.828
1957	**2 teams WAS A** (3G 0–0) **BOS A** (17G 1–3)																									
″	**total**	1	3	.250	5.27	20	8	0	54.2	61	37	35	0	0	0	1	14	0	0	.000	2	11	0	1	0.6	1.000

Dean Stone *continued*

Year	Team		W	L	PCT	ERA	G	GS	CG	IP	H	BB	SO	ShO	Relief Pitching W	L	SV	Batting AB	H	HR	BA	PO	A	E	DP	TC/G	FA
1959	STL	N	0	1	.000	4.20	18	1	0	30	30	16	17	0	0	0	1	4	0	0	.000	2	4	1	0	0.4	.857
1962	2 teams	HOU N	(15G 3–2)		CHI A	(27G 1–0)																					
"	total		4	2	.667	4.03	42	7	2	82.2	89	29	54	2	2	0	5	18	5	0	.278	5	13	1	0	0.5	.947
1963	BAL	A	1	2	.333	5.12	17	0	0	19.1	23	10	12	0	1	2	1	0	0	0	—	1	5	0	0	0.4	1.000
8 yrs.			29	39	.426	4.47	215	85	19	686	705	373	380	5	4	5	12	170	15	1	.088	25	93	7	8	0.6	.944

Dick Stone

STONE, CHARLES RICHARD BL TL 5′ 9″ 153 lbs.
B. Dec. 5, 1911, Oklahoma City, Okla. D. Feb. 18, 1980, Oklahoma City, Okla.

Year	Team		W	L	PCT	ERA	G	GS	CG	IP	H	BB	SO	ShO	Relief Pitching W	L	SV	Batting AB	H	HR	BA	PO	A	E	DP	TC/G	FA
1945	WAS	A	0	0	—	0.00	3	0	0	5	6	2	0	0	0	0	0	0	0	0	—	0	1	0	1	0.3	1.000

Dwight Stone

STONE, DWIGHT ELY BR TR 6′ 1½″ 170 lbs.
B. Aug. 2, 1886, Holt County, Neb. D. July 3, 1976, Glendale, Calif.

Year	Team		W	L	PCT	ERA	G	GS	CG	IP	H	BB	SO	ShO	Relief Pitching W	L	SV	Batting AB	H	HR	BA	PO	A	E	DP	TC/G	FA
1913	STL	A	2	6	.250	3.56	18	7	4	91	94	46	37	1	1	0	0	33	9	0	.273	4	33	1	1	2.1	.974
1914	KC	F	7	14	.333	4.34	39	22	6	186.2	205	77	88	0	2	1	0	58	7	1	.121	9	57	4	4	1.8	.943
2 yrs.			9	20	.310	4.08	57	29	10	277.2	299	123	125	1	3	1	0	91	16	1	.176	13	90	5	5	1.9	.954

George Stone

STONE, GEORGE HEARD BL TL 6′ 3″ 205 lbs.
B. July 9, 1946, Ruston, La.

Year	Team		W	L	PCT	ERA	G	GS	CG	IP	H	BB	SO	ShO	Relief Pitching W	L	SV	Batting AB	H	HR	BA	PO	A	E	DP	TC/G	FA
1967	ATL	N	0	0	—	4.91	2	1	0	7.1	8	1	5	0	0	0	0	2	0	0	.000	1	1	0	0	1.0	1.000
1968			7	4	.636	2.76	17	10	2	75	63	19	52	0	1	1	0	27	9	0	.333	4	6	2	1	0.7	.833
1969			13	10	.565	3.65	36	20	3	165	166	48	102	0	4	3	3	59	11	1	.186	7	24	0	3	0.9	1.000
1970			11	11	.500	3.87	35	30	9	207	218	50	131	2	0	0	0	72	17	0	.236	14	42	3	3	1.7	.949
1971			6	8	.429	3.59	27	24	4	173	186	35	110	2	0	0	0	62	11	0	.177	5	26	1	4	1.2	.969
1972			6	11	.353	5.51	31	16	2	111	143	44	63	1	2	2	1	25	5	0	.200	3	23	1	2	0.9	.963
1973	NY	N	12	3	.800	2.80	27	20	2	148	157	31	77	0	1	0	1	48	13	0	.271	6	27	0	2	1.2	1.000
1974			2	7	.222	5.03	15	13	1	77	103	21	29	0	0	0	0	26	3	0	.115	6	13	1	1	1.3	.950
1975			3	3	.500	5.05	13	11	1	57	75	21	21	0	0	0	0	18	3	0	.167	1	15	0	1	1.2	1.000
9 yrs.			60	57	.513	3.89	203	145	24	1020.1	1119	270	590	5	8	6	5	339	72	1	.212	47	177	8	17	1.1	.966
LEAGUE CHAMPIONSHIP SERIES																											
1969	ATL	N	0	0	—	9.00	1	0	0	1	2	0	0	0	0	0	0	1	0	0	.000	1	1	0	0	2.0	1.000
1973	NY	N	0	0	—	1.35	1	1	0	6.2	3	2	4	0	0	0	0	1	0	0	.000	1	2	0	0	3.0	1.000
2 yrs.			0	0		2.35	2	1	0	7.2	5	2	4	0	0	0	0	2	0	0	.000	2	3	0	0	2.5	1.000
WORLD SERIES																											
1973	NY	N	0	0	—	0.00	2	0	0	3	4	1	3	0	0	0	1	0	0	0	—	0	0	0	0	0.0	.000

Rocky Stone

STONE, JOHN VERNON BR TR 6′ 200 lbs.
B. Aug. 23, 1918, Redding, Calif. D. Nov. 12, 1986, Fountain Valley, Calif.

Year	Team		W	L	PCT	ERA	G	GS	CG	IP	H	BB	SO	ShO	Relief Pitching W	L	SV	Batting AB	H	HR	BA	PO	A	E	DP	TC/G	FA
1943	CIN	N	0	1	.000	4.38	13	0	0	24.2	23	8	11	0	0	1	0	4	1	0	.250	1	3	1	0	0.4	.800

Steve Stone

STONE, STEVEN MICHAEL BR TR 5′10″ 175 lbs.
B. July 14, 1947, Euclid, Ohio.

Year	Team		W	L	PCT	ERA	G	GS	CG	IP	H	BB	SO	ShO	Relief Pitching W	L	SV	Batting AB	H	HR	BA	PO	A	E	DP	TC/G	FA
1971	SF	N	5	9	.357	4.14	24	19	2	111	110	55	63	2	0	0	0	34	0	0	.000	12	21	1	2	1.4	.971
1972			6	8	.429	2.98	27	16	4	124	97	49	85	1	1	0	0	34	4	0	.118	6	21	3	0	1.1	.900
1973	CHI	A	6	11	.353	4.24	36	22	3	176.1	163	82	138	0	0	1	1	0	0	0	—	13	24	2	2	1.1	.949
1974	CHI	N	8	6	.571	4.13	38	23	1	170	185	64	90	0	1	1	0	58	7	0	.121	15	30	3	0	1.3	.938
1975			12	8	.600	3.95	33	32	6	214	198	80	139	1	0	0	0	72	8	0	.111	21	27	3	1	1.5	.941
1976			3	6	.333	4.08	17	15	1	75	70	21	33	1	0	0	0	21	3	0	.143	3	6	1	1	0.6	.900
1977	CHI	A	15	12	.556	4.52	31	31	8	207	228	80	124	0	0	0	0	0	0	0	—	5	34	2	2	1.3	.951
1978			12	12	.500	4.37	30	30	6	212	196	84	118	1	0	0	0	0	0	0	—	12	28	4	1	1.5	.909
1979	BAL	A	11	7	.611	3.77	32	32	3	186	173	73	96	0	0	0	0	0	0	0	—	21	27	1	3	1.5	.980
1980			**25**	7	**.781**	3.23	37	37	9	251	224	101	149	1	0	0	0	0	0	0	—	14	26	2	1	1.1	.952
1981			4	7	.364	4.57	15	12	0	63	63	27	30	0	0	1	0	0	0	0	—	3	10	0	0	0.9	1.000
11 yrs.			107	93	.535	3.96	320	269	43	1789.1	1707	716	1065	7	2	3	1	219	22	0	.100	125	254	22	13	1.3	.945
WORLD SERIES																											
1979	BAL	A	0	0	—	9.00	1	0	0	2	4	2	2	0	0	0	0	0	0	0	—	0	0	0	0	0.0	.000

Tige Stone

STONE, WILLIAM ARTHUR BR TR 5′ 8″ 145 lbs.
B. Sept. 18, 1901, Macon, Ga. D. Jan. 1, 1960, Jacksonville, Fla.

Year	Team		W	L	PCT	ERA	G	GS	CG	IP	H	BB	SO	ShO	Relief Pitching W	L	SV	Batting AB	H	HR	BA	PO	A	E	DP	TC/G	FA
1923	STL	N	0	0	—	12.00	1	0	0	3	5	3	1	0	0	0	0	*				0	2	0	0	0.4	1.000

Bill Stoneman

STONEMAN, WILLIAM HAMBLY BR TR 5′10″ 170 lbs.
B. Apr. 7, 1944, Oak Park, Ill.

Year	Team		W	L	PCT	ERA	G	GS	CG	IP	H	BB	SO	ShO	Relief Pitching W	L	SV	Batting AB	H	HR	BA	PO	A	E	DP	TC/G	FA
1967	CHI	N	2	4	.333	3.29	28	2	0	63	51	22	52	0	2	4	4	13	0	0	.000	2	5	0	0	0.3	1.000
1968			0	1	.000	5.52	18	0	0	29.1	35	14	18	0	0	1	0	4	0	0	.000	2	4	1	0	0.4	.857
1969	MON	N	11	19	.367	4.39	42	36	8	235.2	233	**123**	185	5	0	0	0	73	4	0	.055	22	26	1	3	1.2	.980
1970			7	15	.318	4.59	40	30	5	208	209	109	176	3	0	0	0	60	6	0	.100	10	22	0	1	0.8	1.000
1971			17	16	.515	3.14	39	**39**	20	295	243	**146**	251	3	0	0	0	93	12	0	.129	18	39	1	2	1.5	.983
1972			12	14	.462	2.98	36	35	13	250.2	213	102	171	4	0	0	0	75	6	0	.080	20	32	3	2	1.5	.945
1973			4	8	.333	6.80	29	17	0	96.2	120	55	48	0	1	0	1	20	1	0	.050	5	16	1	0	0.8	.955
1974	CAL	A	1	8	.111	6.10	13	11	0	59	78	31	33	0	0	0	0	0	0	0	—	3	9	0	0	0.9	1.000
8 yrs.			54	85	.388	4.08	245	170	46	1237.1	1182	602	934	15	3	5	5	338	29	0	.086	82	153	7	8	1.0	.971

Lil Stoner

STONER, ULYSSES SIMPSON GRANT BR TR 5′ 9½″ 180 lbs.
B. Feb. 28, 1899, Bowie, Tex. D. June 26, 1966, Enid, Okla.

Year	Team		W	L	PCT	ERA	G	GS	CG	IP	H	BB	SO	ShO	Relief Pitching W	L	SV	Batting AB	H	HR	BA	PO	A	E	DP	TC/G	FA
1922	DET	A	4	4	.500	7.04	17	7	2	62.2	76	35	18	0	4	0	0	20	2	0	.100	1	23	2	1	1.5	.923
1924			11	11	.500	4.72	36	25	10	215.2	271	65	66	1	1	2	0	77	15	2	.195	5	50	3	2	1.6	.948
1925			10	9	.526	4.26	34	18	8	152	166	53	51	0	1	3	1	55	16	0	.291	1	24	1	0	0.8	.962
1926			7	10	.412	5.47	32	22	7	159.2	179	63	57	0	2	1	0	53	9	0	.170	7	36	0	2	1.3	1.000
1927			10	13	.435	3.98	38	24	13	215	251	77	63	0	1	2	5	74	8	0	.108	5	47	3	2	1.4	.945
1928			5	8	.385	4.35	36	11	4	126.1	151	42	29	0	1	2	4	39	7	0	.179	4	19	3	2	0.7	.885
1929			3	3	.500	5.26	24	3	1	53	57	31	12	0	3	2	4	15	1	0	.067	3	20	2	2	1.0	.920

Lil Stoner *continued*

Year	Team		W	L	PCT	ERA	G	GS	CG	IP	H	BB	SO	ShO	Relief Pitching W	L	SV	Batting AB	H	HR	BA	PO	A	E	DP	TC/G	FA
1930	PIT	N	0	0	—	4.76	5	0	0	5.2	7	3	1	0	0	0	0	0	0	0	—	0	3	0	0	0.6	1.000
1931	PHI	N	0	0	—	6.59	7	1	0	13.2	22	5	2	0	0	0	0	5	0	0	.000	0	3	0	0	0.4	1.000
9 yrs.			50	58	.463	4.76	229	111	45	1003.2	1180	374	299	1	13	12	14	338	58	2	.172	26	225	14	11	1.2	.947

Mel Stottlemyre

STOTTLEMYRE, MELVIN LEON, JR. BR TR 6′ 190 lbs.
Brother of Todd Stottlemyre. Son of Mel Stottlemyre.
B. Dec. 28, 1963, Prosser, Wash.

Year	Team		W	L	PCT	ERA	G	GS	CG	IP	H	BB	SO	ShO	Relief Pitching W	L	SV	Batting AB	H	HR	BA	PO	A	E	DP	TC/G	FA
1990	KC	A	0	1	.000	4.88	13	2	0	31.1	35	12	14	0	0	0	0	0	0	0	—	1	5	0	0	0.5	1.000

Mel Stottlemyre

STOTTLEMYRE, MELVIN LEON, SR. BR TR 6′ 1″ 178 lbs.
Father of Mel Stottlemyre. Father of Todd Stottlemyre.
B. Nov. 13, 1941, Hazelton, Mo.

Year	Team		W	L	PCT	ERA	G	GS	CG	IP	H	BB	SO	ShO	Relief Pitching W	L	SV	Batting AB	H	HR	BA	PO	A	E	DP	TC/G	FA
1964	NY	A	9	3	.750	2.06	13	12	5	96	77	35	49	2	0	0	0	37	9	0	.243	7	20	2	3	2.2	.931
1965			20	9	.690	2.63	37	37	**18**	**291**	250	88	155	4	0	0	0	99	13	2	.131	30	74	1	3	2.8	.990
1966			12	**20**	.375	3.80	37	35	9	251	239	82	146	3	0	1	1	80	11	1	.138	27	54	3	5	2.3	.964
1967			15	15	.500	2.96	36	36	10	255	235	88	151	4	0	0	0	82	8	0	.098	36	60	5	4	2.8	.950
1968			21	12	.636	2.45	36	36	19	278.2	**243**	65	140	6	0	0	0	91	13	0	.143	20	54	0	0	2.1	1.000
1969			20	14	.588	2.82	39	39	**24**	303	267	97	113	3	0	0	0	101	18	1	.178	24	88	5	3	3.0	.957
1970			15	13	.536	3.09	37	37	14	271	262	84	126	0	0	0	0	85	16	2	.188	22	51	1	3	2.0	.986
1971			16	12	.571	2.87	35	35	19	270	234	69	132	7	0	0	0	94	16	1	.170	23	55	4	6	2.3	.951
1972			14	**18**	.438	3.22	36	36	9	260	250	85	110	7	0	0	0	80	16	0	.200	19	52	0	7	2.0	1.000
1973			16	16	.500	3.07	38	38	19	273	259	79	95	4	0	0	0	0	0	0	—	27	48	5	4	2.1	.938
1974			6	7	.462	3.58	16	15	6	113	119	37	40	0	0	0	0	0	0	0	—	7	14	0	0	1.3	1.000
11 yrs.			164	139	.541	2.97	360	356	152	2661.2	2435	809	1257	40	0	1	1	749	120	7	.160	242	570	26	38	2.3	.969
WORLD SERIES																											
1964	NY	A	1	1	.500	3.15	3	3	1	20	18	6	12	0	0	0	0	8	1	0	.125	2	5	0	0	2.3	1.000

Todd Stottlemyre

STOTTLEMYRE, TODD VERNON BL TR 6′ 3″ 195 lbs.
Brother of Mel Stottlemyre. Son of Mel Stottlemyre.
B. May 20, 1965, Sunnyside, Wash.

Year	Team		W	L	PCT	ERA	G	GS	CG	IP	H	BB	SO	ShO	Relief Pitching W	L	SV	Batting AB	H	HR	BA	PO	A	E	DP	TC/G	FA
1988	TOR	A	4	8	.333	5.69	28	16	0	98	109	46	67	0	2	1	0	0	0	0	—	7	11	0	0	0.6	1.000
1989			7	7	.500	3.88	27	18	0	127.2	137	44	63	0	0	1	0	0	0	0	—	7	16	5	1	1.0	.821
1990			13	17	.433	4.34	33	33	4	203	214	69	115	0	0	0	0	0	0	0	—	17	30	1	5	1.5	.979
1991			15	8	.652	3.78	34	34	1	219	194	75	116	0	0	0	0	0	0	0	—	30	21	2	2	1.6	.962
1992			12	11	.522	4.50	28	27	6	174	175	63	98	2	1	0	0	0	0	0	—	15	17	1	2	1.2	.970
1993			11	12	.478	4.84	30	28	1	176.2	204	69	98	1	0	0	0	0	0	0	—	11	19	1	2	1.0	.968
1994			7	7	.500	4.22	26	19	3	140.2	149	48	105	1	2	0	1	0	0	0	—	10	12	0	0	0.8	1.000
1995	OAK	A	14	7	.667	4.55	31	31	2	209.2	228	80	205	0	0	0	0	1	0	0	.000	16	18	2	1	1.2	.944
8 yrs.			83	77	.519	4.41	237	206	17	1348.2	1410	494	867	4	5	2	1	1	0	0	.000	113	144	12	13	1.1	.955
LEAGUE CHAMPIONSHIP SERIES																											
1989	TOR	A	0	1	.000	7.20	1	1	0	5	7	2	3	0	0	0	0	0	0	0	—	0	0	0	0	0.0	.000
1991			0	1	.000	9.82	1	1	0	3.2	7	1	3	0	0	0	0	0	0	0	—	1	0	0	0	1.0	1.000
1992			0	0	—	2.45	1	0	0	3.2	3	0	1	0	0	0	0	0	0	0	—	0	0	0	0	0.0	.000
1993			0	1	.000	7.50	1	1	0	6	6	4	4	0	0	0	0	0	0	0	—	2	0	0	0	2.0	1.000
4 yrs.			0	3 **5th**	.000	6.87	4	3	0	18.1	23	7	11	0	0	0	0	0	0	0		3	0	0	0	0.8	1.000
WORLD SERIES																											
1992	TOR	A	0	0	—	0.00	4	0	0	3.2	4	0	4	0	0	0	0	0	0	0	—	0	0	0	0	0.0	.000
1993			0	0	—	27.00	1	1	0	2	3	4	1	0	0	0	0	0	0	0	—	0	0	0	0	0.0	.000
2 yrs.			0	0		9.53	5	1	0	5.2	7	4	5	0	0	0	0	0	0	0		0	0	0	0	0.0	

Allyn Stout

STOUT, ALLYN McCLELLAND (Fish Hook) BR TR 5′10″ 167 lbs.
B. Oct. 31, 1904, Peoria, Ill. D. Dec. 22, 1974, Sikeston, Mo.

Year	Team		W	L	PCT	ERA	G	GS	CG	IP	H	BB	SO	ShO	Relief Pitching W	L	SV	Batting AB	H	HR	BA	PO	A	E	DP	TC/G	FA
1931	STL	N	6	0	1.000	4.21	30	3	1	72.2	87	34	40	0	4	0	3	19	2	0	.105	1	18	0	4	0.6	1.000
1932			4	5	.444	4.40	36	3	1	73.2	87	28	32	0	4	3	1	20	2	0	.100	6	16	1	2	0.6	.957
1933	2 teams	STL N	(1G 0–0)		CIN N	(23G 2–3)																					
"	total		2	3	.400	3.68	24	5	2	73.1	86	27	30	0	0	0	0	22	4	0	.182	4	13	3	1	0.8	.850
1934	CIN	N	6	8	.429	4.86	41	16	4	140.2	170	47	51	0	1	3	1	43	8	0	.186	4	29	1	0	0.8	.971
1935	NY	N	1	4	.200	4.91	40	2	0	88	99	37	29	0	1	4	5	15	2	1	.133	6	12	1	1	0.5	.947
1943	BOS	N	1	0	1.000	6.75	9	0	0	9.1	17	4	3	0	1	0	1	2	0	0	.000	1	1	0	0	0.2	1.000
6 yrs.			20	20	.500	4.54	180	29	8	457.2	546	177	185	0	11	10	11	121	18	1	.149	22	89	6	8	0.6	.949

Jesse Stovall

STOVALL, JESSE CRAMER (Scout) BL TR 6′ 175 lbs.
Brother of George Stovall.
B. July 24, 1875, Independence, Mo. D. July 12, 1955, San Diego, Calif.

Year	Team		W	L	PCT	ERA	G	GS	CG	IP	H	BB	SO	ShO	Relief Pitching W	L	SV	Batting AB	H	HR	BA	PO	A	E	DP	TC/G	FA
1903	CLE	A	5	1	.833	2.05	6	6	6	57	44	21	12	2	0	0	0	22	1	0	.045	4	15	1	1	3.3	.950
1904	DET	A	3	13	.188	4.42	22	17	13	146.2	170	45	41	1	0	1	0	56	11	0	.196	16	52	5	1	2.9	.932
2 yrs.			8	14	.364	3.76	28	23	19	203.2	214	66	53	3	0	1	0	78	12	0	.154	20	67	6	2	3.0	.935

Harry Stovey

STOVEY, HARRY DUFFIELD BR TR 5′11½″ 180 lbs.
Born Harry Duffield Stowe.
B. Dec. 20, 1856, Philadelphia, Pa. D. Sept. 20, 1937, New Bedford, Mass.
Manager 1881, 1885.

Year	Team		W	L	PCT	ERA	G	GS	CG	IP	H	BB	SO	ShO	Relief Pitching W	L	SV	Batting AB	H	HR	BA	PO	A	E	DP	TC/G	FA
1880	WOR	N	0	0	—	4.50	2	0	0	6	8	3	3	0	0	0	0	355	94	6	.265	514	18	35	21	6.7	.938
1883	PHI	AA	0	0	—	9.00	1	0	0	3	5	0	4	0	0	0	0	421	127	14	.302	592	17	32	26	8.5	.950
1886			0	0	—	*27.00*	1	0	0	0.1	2	0	0	0	0	0	0	489	144	7	.294	557	25	45	27	7.5	.928
3 yrs.			0	0		6.75	4	0	0	9.1	15	3	7	0	0	0	0	*				7503	329	470	286	5.5	.943

Hal Stowe

STOWE, HAROLD RUDOLPH (Rudy) BL TL 6′ 170 lbs.
B. Aug. 29, 1937, Gastonia, N. C.

Year	Team		W	L	PCT	ERA	G	GS	CG	IP	H	BB	SO	ShO	Relief Pitching W	L	SV	Batting AB	H	HR	BA	PO	A	E	DP	TC/G	FA
1960	NY	A	0	0	—	9.00	1	0	0	1	0	1	0	0	0	0	0	0	0	0	—	0	0	0	0	0.0	.000

Mike Strahler

STRAHLER, MICHAEL WAYNE BR TR 6′ 4″ 180 lbs.
B. Mar. 14, 1947, Chicago, Ill.

Year	Team	Lg	W	L	PCT	ERA	G	GS	CG	IP	H	BB	SO	ShO	Relief Pitching W	L	SV	Batting AB	H	HR	BA	PO	A	E	DP	TC/G	FA
1970	LA	N	1	1	.500	1.42	6	0	0	19	13	10	11	0	1	1	1	8	2	0	.250	3	2	0	0	0.8	1.000
1971			0	0	—	2.77	6	0	0	13	10	8	7	0	0	0	0	1	0	0	.000	1	1	0	0	0.3	1.000
1972			1	2	.333	3.26	19	2	1	47	42	22	25	0	0	1	0	11	2	0	.182	3	6	2	0	0.6	.818
1973	DET	A	4	5	.444	4.39	22	11	1	80	84	39	37	0	0	1	0	0	0	0	—	3	9	0	1	0.5	1.000
4 yrs.			6	8	.429	3.57	53	13	2	159	149	79	80	0	1	3	1	20	4	0	.200	10	18	2	1	0.6	.933

Dick Strahs

STRAHS, RICHARD BERNARD BL TR 6′ 192 lbs.
B. Dec. 4, 1923, Evanston, Ill. D. May 26, 1988, Las Vegas, Nev.

Year	Team	Lg	W	L	PCT	ERA	G	GS	CG	IP	H	BB	SO	ShO	Relief Pitching W	L	SV	Batting AB	H	HR	BA	PO	A	E	DP	TC/G	FA
1954	CHI	A	0	0	—	5.65	9	0	0	14.1	16	8	8	0	0	0	1	1	0	0	.000	0	4	0	0	0.4	1.000

Les Straker

STRAKER, LESTER PAUL BR TR 6′ 1″ 193 lbs.
Born Lester Paul Straker (Bolnalda).
B. Oct. 10, 1959, Ciudad Bolivar, Venezuela.

Year	Team	Lg	W	L	PCT	ERA	G	GS	CG	IP	H	BB	SO	ShO	Relief Pitching W	L	SV	Batting AB	H	HR	BA	PO	A	E	DP	TC/G	FA
1987	MIN	A	8	10	.444	4.37	31	26	1	154.1	150	59	76	0	0	1	0	0	0	0	—	5	18	1	0	0.8	.958
1988			2	5	.286	3.92	16	14	1	82.2	86	25	23	1	0	0	1	0	0	0	—	9	13	1	1	1.4	.957
2 yrs.			10	15	.400	4.22	47	40	2	237	236	84	99	1	0	1	1	0	0	0		14	31	2	1	1.0	.957
LEAGUE CHAMPIONSHIP SERIES																											
1987	MIN	A	0	0	—	16.88	1	1	0	2.2	3	4	1	0	0	0	0	0	0	0	—	0	2	0	0	2.0	1.000
WORLD SERIES																											
1987	MIN	A	0	0	—	4.00	2	2	0	9	9	3	6	0	0	0	0	2	0	0	.000	1	0	0	0	0.5	1.000

Bob Strampe

STRAMPE, ROBERT EDWIN BB TR 6′ 1″ 185 lbs.
B. June 13, 1950, Janesville, Wis.

Year	Team	Lg	W	L	PCT	ERA	G	GS	CG	IP	H	BB	SO	ShO	Relief Pitching W	L	SV	Batting AB	H	HR	BA	PO	A	E	DP	TC/G	FA
1972	DET	A	0	0	—	10.80	7	0	0	5	6	7	4	0	0	0	0	0	0	0	—	0	0	0	0	0.0	.000

Paul Strand

STRAND, PAUL EDWARD BL TL 6′½″ 190 lbs.
B. Dec. 19, 1893, Carbonado, Wash. D. July 2, 1974, Salt Lake City, Utah.

Year	Team	Lg	W	L	PCT	ERA	G	GS	CG	IP	H	BB	SO	ShO	Relief Pitching W	L	SV	Batting AB	H	HR	BA	PO	A	E	DP	TC/G	FA
1913	BOS	N	0	0	—	2.12	7	0	0	17	22	12	6	0	0	0	0	6	1	0	.167	1	6	1	0	1.1	.875
1914			6	2	.750	2.44	16	3	1	55.1	47	23	33	0	**5**	1	0	19	2	0	.105	0	13	3	1	1.0	.813
1915			1	1	.500	2.38	6	2	2	22.2	26	3	13	0	0	0	1	22	2	0	.091	4	3	1	0	0.7	.875
3 yrs.			7	3	.700	2.37	29	5	3	95	95	38	52	0	5	1	1	*				85	25	6	1	1.5	.948

Monty Stratton

STRATTON, MONTY FRANKLIN PIERCE (Gander) BR TR 6′ 5″ 180 lbs.
B. May 21, 1912, Celeste, Tex. D. Sept. 29, 1982, Greenville, Tex.

Year	Team	Lg	W	L	PCT	ERA	G	GS	CG	IP	H	BB	SO	ShO	Relief Pitching W	L	SV	Batting AB	H	HR	BA	PO	A	E	DP	TC/G	FA
1934	CHI	A	0	0	—	5.40	1	0	0	3.1	4	1	0	0	0	0	0	2	0	0	.000	0	0	0	0	0.0	.000
1935			1	2	.333	4.03	5	5	2	38	40	9	8	0	0	0	0	14	2	0	.143	1	9	0	0	2.0	1.000
1936			5	7	.417	5.21	16	14	3	95	117	46	37	0	0	1	0	37	8	1	.216	3	25	1	1	1.8	.966
1937			15	5	.750	2.40	22	21	14	164.2	142	37	69	5	0	0	0	60	12	1	.200	4	35	0	2	1.8	1.000
1938			15	9	.625	4.01	26	22	17	186.1	186	56	82	0	1	1	2	79	21	2	.266	6	36	2	1	1.7	.955
5 yrs.			36	23	.610	3.71	70	62	36	487.1	489	149	196	5	1	2	2	192	43	4	.224	14	105	3	4	1.7	.975

Scott Stratton

STRATTON, C. SCOTT BL TR 6′ 180 lbs.
B. Oct. 2, 1869, Campbellsburg, Ky. D. Mar. 8, 1939, Louisville, Ky.

Year	Team	Lg	W	L	PCT	ERA	G	GS	CG	IP	H	BB	SO	ShO	Relief Pitching W	L	SV	Batting AB	H	HR	BA	PO	A	E	DP	TC/G	FA
1888	LOU	AA	10	17	.370	3.64	33	28	28	269.2	287	53	97	2	0	0	0	249	64	1	.257	66	70	17	1	2.2	.889
1889			3	13	.188	3.23	19	17	13	133.2	157	42	42	0	0	1	1	229	66	4	.288	198	57	21	15	4.2	.924
1890			34	14	**.708**	***2.36***	50	49	44	431	398	61	207	4	0	0	0	189	61	0	.323	29	111	4	2	2.6	.972
1891	2 teams	PIT N (2G 0–2)	LOU AA (20G 6–13)																								
″	total		6	15	.286	3.92	22	22	22	190.1	220	39	57	1	0	0	0	123	28	0	.228	88	70	11	11	4.7	.935
1892	LOU	N	21	19	.525	2.92	42	40	39	351.2	342	70	93	2	0	0	0	219	56	0	.256	83	94	17	8	3.0	.912
1893			12	23	.343	5.45	38	35	35	323.2	**451**	104	44	1	0	0	0	221	50	0	.226	66	96	8	4	2.7	.953
1894	2 teams	LOU N (7G 1–5)	CHI N (15G 8–5)																								
″	total		9	10	.474	6.65	22	17	15	162.1	270	53	26	0	2	1	0	133	48	3	.361	44	33	4	5	2.4	.951
1895	CHI	N	2	3	.400	9.60	5	5	3	30	51	14	4	0	0	0	0	24	7	0	.292	10	10	5	0	2.8	.800
8 yrs.			97	114	.460	3.88	231	213	199	1892.1	2176	436	570	10	2	2	1	*				584	541	87	46	3.1	.928

Joe Strauss

STRAUSS, JOSEPH (The Socker) BR TR
Born Joseph Strasser.
B. Nov. 16, 1858, Cincinnati, Ohio D. June 24, 1906, Cincinnati, Ohio.

Year	Team	Lg	W	L	PCT	ERA	G	GS	CG	IP	H	BB	SO	ShO	Relief Pitching W	L	SV	Batting AB	H	HR	BA	PO	A	E	DP	TC/G	FA
1886	LOU	AA	0	0	—	*4.50*	2	0	0	4	6	3	0	0	0	0	**1**	*				31	17	14	1	3.9	.774

Oscar Streit

STREIT, OSCAR WILLIAM BL TL 6′ 5″ 190 lbs.
B. July 7, 1873, Florence, Ala. D. Oct. 10, 1935, Birmingham, Ala.

Year	Team	Lg	W	L	PCT	ERA	G	GS	CG	IP	H	BB	SO	ShO	Relief Pitching W	L	SV	Batting AB	H	HR	BA	PO	A	E	DP	TC/G	FA
1899	BOS	N	1	0	1.000	6.75	2	1	1	14.2	15	15	0	0	0	0	0	7	0	0	.000	0	5	0	0	2.5	1.000
1902	CLE	A	0	7	.000	5.23	8	7	4	51.2	72	25	10	0	0	0	0	19	4	0	.211	1	13	4	0	2.3	.778
2 yrs.			1	7	.125	5.56	10	8	5	66.1	87	40	10	0	0	0	0	26	4	0	.154	1	18	4	0	2.3	.826

Ed Strelecki

STRELECKI, EDWARD HENRY BR TR 5′11½″ 180 lbs.
B. Apr. 10, 1908, Newark, N. J. D. Jan. 9, 1968, Newark, N. J.

Year	Team	Lg	W	L	PCT	ERA	G	GS	CG	IP	H	BB	SO	ShO	Relief Pitching W	L	SV	Batting AB	H	HR	BA	PO	A	E	DP	TC/G	FA
1928	STL	A	0	2	.000	4.29	22	2	1	50.1	49	17	8	0	0	0	1	10	2	0	.200	0	13	1	0	0.6	.929
1929			1	1	.500	4.91	7	0	0	11	12	6	2	0	1	1	0	2	0	0	.000	1	3	0	0	0.6	1.000
1931	CIN	N	0	0	—	9.25	13	0	0	24.1	37	9	3	0	0	0	0	5	1	0	.200	1	8	1	0	0.8	.900
3 yrs.			1	3	.250	5.78	42	2	1	85.2	98	32	13	0	1	1	1	17	3	0	.176	2	24	2	0	0.7	.929

Phil Stremmel

STREMMEL, PHILIP BR TR 6′ 175 lbs.
B. Apr. 16, 1880, Zanesville, Ohio D. Dec. 26, 1947, Chicago, Ill.

Year	Team	Lg	W	L	PCT	ERA	G	GS	CG	IP	H	BB	SO	ShO	Relief Pitching W	L	SV	Batting AB	H	HR	BA	PO	A	E	DP	TC/G	FA
1909	STL	A	0	2	.000	4.50	2	2	2	18	20	4	6	0	0	0	0	6	0	0	.000	2	7	0	0	4.5	1.000
1910			0	2	.000	3.72	5	2	2	29	31	16	7	0	0	0	0	8	1	0	.125	4	17	1	1	4.4	.955
2 yrs.			0	4	.000	4.02	7	4	4	47	51	20	13	0	0	0	0	14	1	0	.071	6	24	1	1	4.4	.968

Year	Team	W	L	PCT	ERA	G	GS	CG	IP	H	BB	SO	ShO	Relief Pitching W	Relief Pitching L	Relief Pitching SV	Batting AB	Batting H	Batting HR	BA	PO	A	E	DP	TC/G	FA

Cub Stricker

STRICKER, JOHN A. BR TR 5′ 3″ 133 lbs.
Born John A. Streaker.
B. June 8, 1859, Philadelphia, Pa. D. Nov. 19, 1937, Philadelphia, Pa.
Manager 1892.

Year	Team	W	L	PCT	ERA	G	GS	CG	IP	H	BB	SO	ShO	Relief W	Relief L	SV	AB	H	HR	BA	PO	A	E	DP	TC/G	FA
1882	PHI AA	1	0	1.000	1.29	2	0	0	7	3	1	2	0	1	0	0	272	59	0	.217	240	252	52	29	7.3	.904
1884		0	0	—	6.00	1	0	0	3	6	1	1	0	0	0	0	399	92	1	.231	260	226	95	23	6.5	.836
1887	CLE AA	0	0	—	*3.18*	3	0	0	5.2	5	7	2	0	0	0	1	534	141	2	.264	281	257	81	40	5.6	.869
1888		1	0	1.000	4.50	2	0	0	12	16	2	5	0	1	0	0	493	115	1	.233	397	366	58	58	6.3	.929
4 yrs.		2	0	1.000	3.58	8	0	0	27.2	30	11	10	0	2	0	1	*				3545	3529	748	520	6.5	.904

Bill Strickland

STRICKLAND, WILLIAM GOSS BR TR 6′ 2″ 170 lbs.
B. Mar. 29, 1908, Nashville, Ga.

Year	Team	W	L	PCT	ERA	G	GS	CG	IP	H	BB	SO	ShO	Relief W	Relief L	SV	AB	H	HR	BA	PO	A	E	DP	TC/G	FA
1937	STL A	0	0	—	5.91	9	0	0	21.1	28	15	6	0	0	0	0	6	1	0	.167	1	3	0	0	0.4	1.000

Jim Strickland

STRICKLAND, JAMES MICHAEL BL TL 6′ 175 lbs.
B. June 12, 1946, Los Angeles, Calif.

Year	Team	W	L	PCT	ERA	G	GS	CG	IP	H	BB	SO	ShO	Relief W	Relief L	SV	AB	H	HR	BA	PO	A	E	DP	TC/G	FA
1971	MIN A	1	0	1.000	1.45	24	0	0	31	20	18	21	0	1	0	1	1	0	0	.000	4	5	1	0	0.4	.900
1972		3	1	.750	2.50	25	0	0	36	28	19	30	0	3	1	3	3	1	0	.333	3	6	2	1	0.4	.818
1973		0	1	.000	11.81	7	0	0	5.1	11	5	6	0	0	1	0	0	0	0	—	0	1	0	0	0.1	1.000
1975	CLE A	0	0	—	1.93	4	0	0	4.2	4	2	3	0	0	0	0	0	0	0	—	0	0	0	0	0.0	.000
4 yrs.		4	2	.667	2.69	60	0	0	77	63	44	60	0	4	2	4	4	1	0	.250	7	12	3	1	0.4	.864

Elmer Stricklett

STRICKLETT, ELMER GRIFFIN BR TR 5′ 6″ 140 lbs.
B. Aug. 29, 1876, Glasco, Kans. D. June 7, 1964, Santa Cruz, Calif.

Year	Team	W	L	PCT	ERA	G	GS	CG	IP	H	BB	SO	ShO	Relief W	Relief L	SV	AB	H	HR	BA	PO	A	E	DP	TC/G	FA
1904	CHI A	0	1	.000	10.29	1	1	0	7	12	2	3	0	0	0	0	3	0	0	.000	0	3	0	0	3.0	1.000
1905	BKN N	9	18	.333	3.34	33	28	25	237	259	71	77	1	0	0	1	88	13	0	.148	13	112	10	4	4.1	.926
1906		14	18	.438	2.72	41	35	28	291.2	273	77	88	5	0	1	5	97	20	0	.206	22	128	5	2	3.8	.968
1907		12	14	.462	2.27	29	26	25	229.2	211	65	69	4	1	1	0	81	12	0	.148	17	95	2	4	3.8	.982
4 yrs.		35	51	.407	2.85	104	90	78	765.1	755	215	237	10	1	2	6	269	45	0	.167	52	338	17	10	3.9	.958

John Strike

STRIKE, JOHN
B. 1865, Philadelphia, Pa. Deceased.

Year	Team	W	L	PCT	ERA	G	GS	CG	IP	H	BB	SO	ShO	Relief W	Relief L	SV	AB	H	HR	BA	PO	A	E	DP	TC/G	FA
1886	PHI N	1	1	.500	*4.80*	2	2	1	15	19	7	11	0	0	0	0	7	0	0	.000	1	0	0	0	0.3	1.000

Jake Striker

STRIKER, WILBUR SCOTT BL TL 6′ 2″ 200 lbs.
B. Oct. 23, 1933, New Washington, Ohio.

Year	Team	W	L	PCT	ERA	G	GS	CG	IP	H	BB	SO	ShO	Relief W	Relief L	SV	AB	H	HR	BA	PO	A	E	DP	TC/G	FA
1959	CLE A	1	0	1.000	2.70	1	1	0	6.2	8	4	5	0	0	0	0	1	0	0	.000	1	1	0	0	2.0	1.000
1960	CHI A	0	0	—	4.91	2	0	0	3.2	5	1	1	0	0	0	0	0	0	0	—	0	0	0	0	0.0	.000
2 yrs.		1	0	1.000	3.48	3	1	0	10.1	13	5	6	0	0	0	0	1	0	0	.000	1	1	0	0	0.7	1.000

Nick Strincevich

STRINCEVICH, NICHOLAS (Jumbo) BR TR 6′ 1″ 180 lbs.
B. Mar. 1, 1915, Gary, Ind.

Year	Team	W	L	PCT	ERA	G	GS	CG	IP	H	BB	SO	ShO	Relief W	Relief L	SV	AB	H	HR	BA	PO	A	E	DP	TC/G	FA
1940	BOS N	4	8	.333	5.53	32	14	5	128.2	142	63	54	0	0	1	1	43	5	0	.116	11	14	1	1	0.8	.962
1941	2 teams	BOS N (3G 0–0)		PIT N (12G 1–2)																						
″	total	1	2	.333	5.77	15	3	0	34.1	42	19	13	0	1	0	0	7	3	0	.429	3	8	2	0	0.9	.846
1942	PIT N	0	0	—	2.82	7	1	0	22.1	19	9	10	0	0	0	0	4	0	0	.000	4	3	1	0	1.1	.875
1944		14	7	.667	3.08	40	26	11	190	190	37	47	0	2	0	2	57	9	0	.158	19	60	2	2	2.0	.975
1945		16	10	.615	3.31	36	29	18	228.1	235	49	74	1	0	0	2	84	17	0	.202	14	36	2	1	1.4	.962
1946		10	15	.400	3.58	32	22	11	176	185	44	49	3	0	3	1	52	8	0	.154	14	25	1	0	1.3	.975
1947		1	6	.143	5.26	32	7	1	89	111	37	22	0	0	1	0	21	1	0	.048	2	17	0	1	0.6	1.000
1948	2 teams	PIT N (3G 0–0)		PHI N (6G 0–1)																						
″	total	0	1	.000	9.00	9	1	0	21	34	12	5	0	0	0	0	4	0	0	.000	1	3	1	0	0.6	.800
8 yrs.		46	49	.484	4.05	203	103	46	889.2	958	270	274	4	3	5	6	272	43	0	.158	68	166	10	5	1.2	.959

John Strohmayer

STROHMAYER, JOHN EMERY BR TR 6′ 1″ 181 lbs.
B. Oct. 13, 1946, Belle Fourche, S. D.

Year	Team	W	L	PCT	ERA	G	GS	CG	IP	H	BB	SO	ShO	Relief W	Relief L	SV	AB	H	HR	BA	PO	A	E	DP	TC/G	FA
1970	MON N	3	1	.750	4.86	42	0	0	76	85	39	74	0	3	1	0	6	1	0	.167	7	7	0	0	0.3	1.000
1971		7	5	.583	4.34	27	14	2	114	124	31	56	0	1	1	1	35	8	0	.229	12	12	1	0	0.9	.960
1972		1	2	.333	3.52	48	0	0	76.2	73	31	50	0	1	2	3	4	0	0	.000	1	16	0	2	0.4	1.000
1973	2 teams	MON N (17G 0–1)		NY N (7G 0–0)																						
″	total	0	1	.000	5.84	24	3	0	44.2	47	26	20	0	0	0	0	5	1	0	.200	3	6	0	0	0.4	1.000
1974	NY N	0	0	—	0.00	1	0	0	1	0	1	0	0	0	0	0	0	0	0	—	0	0	0	0	0.0	.000
5 yrs.		11	9	.550	4.47	142	17	2	312.1	329	128	200	0	5	4	4	50	10	0	.200	23	41	1	2	0.5	.985

Brent Strom

STROM, BRENT TERRY BR TL 6′ 3″ 189 lbs.
B. Oct. 14, 1948, San Diego, Calif.

Year	Team	W	L	PCT	ERA	G	GS	CG	IP	H	BB	SO	ShO	Relief W	Relief L	SV	AB	H	HR	BA	PO	A	E	DP	TC/G	FA
1972	NY N	0	3	.000	6.82	11	5	0	30.1	34	15	20	0	0	0	0	6	0	0	.000	0	2	0	0	0.2	1.000
1973	CLE A	2	10	.167	4.61	27	18	2	123	134	47	91	0	0	1	0	0	0	0	—	2	23	1	1	1.0	.962
1975	SD N	8	8	.500	2.55	18	16	6	120	103	33	56	2	0	0	0	30	3	0	.100	8	19	1	2	1.6	.964
1976		12	16	.429	3.29	36	33	8	210.2	188	73	103	1	0	0	0	63	4	0	.063	13	32	3	3	1.3	.938
1977		0	2	.000	12.18	8	3	0	17	23	12	8	0	0	0	0	3	1	0	.333	1	2	0	0	0.4	1.000
5 yrs.		22	39	.361	3.95	100	75	16	501	482	180	278	3	0	1	0	102	8	0	.078	24	78	5	6	1.1	.953

Floyd Stromme

STROMME, FLOYD MARVIN (Rock) BR TR 5′11″ 170 lbs.
B. Aug. 1, 1916, Cooperstown, N. D. D. Feb. 7, 1993, Wenatchee, Wash.

Year	Team	W	L	PCT	ERA	G	GS	CG	IP	H	BB	SO	ShO	Relief W	Relief L	SV	AB	H	HR	BA	PO	A	E	DP	TC/G	FA
1939	CLE A	0	1	.000	4.85	5	0	0	13	13	13	4	0	0	1	0	3	1	0	.333	0	2	1	0	0.6	.667

Sailor Stroud

STROUD, RALPH VIVIAN BR TR 6′ 160 lbs.
B. May 15, 1885, Ironia, N. J. D. Apr. 11, 1970, Stockton, Calif.

Year	Team	W	L	PCT	ERA	G	GS	CG	IP	H	BB	SO	ShO	Relief W	Relief L	SV	AB	H	HR	BA	PO	A	E	DP	TC/G	FA
1910	DET A	5	9	.357	3.25	28	15	7	130.1	123	41	63	3	0	0	1	39	1	0	.026	6	21	1	0	1.0	.964
1915	NY N	11	9	.550	2.79	32	22	8	184	194	35	62	0	1	2	1	56	9	0	.161	6	53	3	0	1.9	.952
1916		1	2	.333	2.70	10	4	0	46.2	47	9	16	0	1	1	1	14	1	0	.071	0	12	0	0	1.2	1.000
3 yrs.		17	20	.459	2.94	70	41	15	361	364	85	141	3	2	3	3	109	11	0	.101	12	86	4	0	1.5	.961

Steamboat Struss

STRUSS, CLARENCE HERBERT BR TR 5′11″ 163 lbs.
B. Feb. 24, 1909, Riverdale, Ill. D. Sept. 12, 1985, Grand Rapids, Mich.

Year	Team	W	L	PCT	ERA	G	GS	CG	IP	H	BB	SO	ShO	Relief W	Relief L	Relief SV	Batting AB	Batting H	HR	BA	PO	A	E	DP	TC/G	FA
1934	PIT N	0	1	.000	6.43	1	1	0	7	7	6	3	0	0	0	0	3	1	0	.333	0	2	0	0	2.0	1.000

Dutch Stryker

STRYKER, STERLING ALPA BR TR 5′11½″ 180 lbs.
B. July 29, 1895, Atlantic Highlands, N. J. D. Nov. 5, 1964, Red Bank, N. J.

Year	Team	W	L	PCT	ERA	G	GS	CG	IP	H	BB	SO	ShO	Relief W	Relief L	Relief SV	Batting AB	Batting H	HR	BA	PO	A	E	DP	TC/G	FA
1924	BOS N	3	8	.273	6.01	20	10	2	73.1	90	22	22	0	2	2	0	23	5	0	.217	0	30	1	1	1.5	.968
1926	BKN N	0	0	—	27.00	2	0	0	2	8	1	0	0	0	0	0	0	0	0	—	0	0	0	0	0.0	.000
2 yrs.		3	8	.273	6.57	22	10	2	75.1	98	23	22	0	2	2	0	23	5	0	.217	0	30	1	1	1.4	.968

Johnny Stuart

STUART, JOHN DAVIS (Stud) BR TR 5′11″ 170 lbs.
B. Apr. 27, 1901, Clinton, Tenn. D. May 13, 1970, Charleston, W. Va.

Year	Team	W	L	PCT	ERA	G	GS	CG	IP	H	BB	SO	ShO	Relief W	Relief L	Relief SV	Batting AB	Batting H	HR	BA	PO	A	E	DP	TC/G	FA
1922	STL N	0	0	—	9.00	2	1	0	2	2	2	1	0	0	0	0	0	0	0	—	0	0	0	0	0.0	.000
1923		9	5	.643	4.27	37	10	7	149.2	139	70	55	1	2	3	3	57	14	0	.246	6	29	3	2	1.0	.921
1924		9	11	.450	4.75	28	22	13	159	167	60	54	0	0	1	0	54	11	0	.204	3	23	0	1	0.9	1.000
1925		2	2	.500	6.13	15	1	1	47	52	24	14	0	1	2	0	16	4	0	.250	2	10	1	0	0.9	.923
4 yrs.		20	18	.526	4.76	82	34	21	357.2	360	156	124	1	3	6	3	127	29	0	.228	11	62	4	3	0.9	.948

Marlin Stuart

STUART, MARLIN HENRY BL TR 6′ 2″ 185 lbs.
B. Aug. 8, 1918, Paragould, Ark. D. June 16, 1994, Paragould, Ark.

Year	Team	W	L	PCT	ERA	G	GS	CG	IP	H	BB	SO	ShO	Relief W	Relief L	Relief SV	Batting AB	Batting H	HR	BA	PO	A	E	DP	TC/G	FA
1949	DET A	0	2	.000	9.10	14	2	0	29.2	39	35	14	0	0	1	0	6	2	0	.333	0	7	0	0	0.5	1.000
1950		3	1	.750	5.56	19	1	0	43.2	59	22	19	0	3	0	2	12	1	0	.083	2	8	0	0	0.5	1.000
1951		4	6	.400	3.77	29	15	5	124	119	71	46	0	0	0	1	43	10	1	.233	6	25	1	0	1.1	.969
1952	2 teams DET A (30G 3–2) STL A (12G 1–2)																									
″	total	4	4	.500	4.76	42	11	2	117.1	117	57	45	0	2	1	2	29	2	0	.069	9	17	6	0	0.8	.813
1953	STL A	8	2	.800	3.94	60	2	0	114.1	136	44	46	0	8	1	7	26	5	0	.192	9	15	1	2	0.4	.960
1954	2 teams BAL A (22G 1–2) NY A (10G 3–0)																									
″	total	4	2	.667	4.76	32	0	0	56.2	74	27	15	0	4	2	3	9	2	0	.222	5	13	1	2	0.6	.947
6 yrs.		23	17	.575	4.65	196	31	7	485.2	544	256	185	0	17	5	15	125	22	1	.176	31	85	9	4	0.6	.928

George Stueland

STUELAND, GEORGE ANTON BB TR 6′ 1½″ 174 lbs.
B. Mar. 2, 1899, Algona, Iowa D. Sept. 9, 1964, Onawa, Iowa.

Year	Team	W	L	PCT	ERA	G	GS	CG	IP	H	BB	SO	ShO	Relief W	Relief L	Relief SV	Batting AB	Batting H	HR	BA	PO	A	E	DP	TC/G	FA
1921	CHI N	0	1	.000	5.73	2	1	0	11	11	7	4	0	0	0	0	3	1	0	.333	0	3	0	0	1.5	1.000
1922		9	4	.692	5.92	35	11	4	111	129	48	43	0	3	1	0	31	4	0	.129	3	20	0	0	0.7	1.000
1923		0	1	.000	5.63	6	0	0	8	11	5	2	0	0	1	0	0	0	0	—	0	3	0	0	0.5	1.000
1925		0	0	—	3.00	2	0	0	3	2	3	2	0	0	0	0	1	1	0	1.000	0	1	0	1	0.5	1.000
4 yrs.		9	6	.600	5.82	45	12	4	133	153	63	51	0	3	2	0	35	6	0	.171	3	27	0	1	0.7	1.000

Paul Stuffel

STUFFEL, PAUL HARRINGTON (Stu) BR TR 6′ 2″ 185 lbs.
B. Mar. 22, 1927, Canton, Ohio.

Year	Team	W	L	PCT	ERA	G	GS	CG	IP	H	BB	SO	ShO	Relief W	Relief L	Relief SV	Batting AB	Batting H	HR	BA	PO	A	E	DP	TC/G	FA
1950	PHI N	0	0	—	1.80	3	0	0	5	4	1	3	0	0	0	0	0	0	0	—	0	1	0	0	0.3	1.000
1952		1	0	1.000	3.00	2	1	0	6	5	7	3	0	0	0	0	2	0	0	.000	0	3	0	0	1.5	1.000
1953		0	0	—	∞	2	0	0		0	4	0	0	0	0	0	0	0	0	—	0	0	0	0	0.0	.000
3 yrs.		1	0	1.000	5.73	7	1	0	11	9	12	6	0	0	0	0	2	0	0	.000	0	4	0	0	0.6	1.000

George Stultz

STULTZ, GEORGE IRVIN 5′10″ 150 lbs.
B. June 30, 1873, Louisville, Ky. D. Mar. 19, 1955, Louisville, Ky.

Year	Team	W	L	PCT	ERA	G	GS	CG	IP	H	BB	SO	ShO	Relief W	Relief L	Relief SV	Batting AB	Batting H	HR	BA	PO	A	E	DP	TC/G	FA
1894	BOS N	1	0	1.000	0.00	1	1	1	9	4	5	1	0	0	0	0	3	1	0	.333	0	5	0	0	5.0	1.000

Jim Stump

STUMP, JAMES GILBERT BR TR 6′ 188 lbs.
B. Feb. 10, 1932, Lansing, Mich.

Year	Team	W	L	PCT	ERA	G	GS	CG	IP	H	BB	SO	ShO	Relief W	Relief L	Relief SV	Batting AB	Batting H	HR	BA	PO	A	E	DP	TC/G	FA
1957	DET A	1	0	1.000	2.02	6	0	0	13.1	11	8	2	0	1	0	0	2	1	0	.500	2	3	0	0	0.8	1.000
1959		0	0	—	2.38	5	0	0	11.1	12	4	6	0	0	0	0	1	1	0	1.000	1	2	0	0	0.6	1.000
2 yrs.		1	0	1.000	2.19	11	0	0	24.2	23	12	8	0	1	0	0	3	2	0	.667	3	5	0	0	0.7	1.000

John Stuper

STUPER, JOHN ANTON BR TR 6′ 2″ 200 lbs.
B. May 9, 1957, Butler, Pa.

Year	Team	W	L	PCT	ERA	G	GS	CG	IP	H	BB	SO	ShO	Relief W	Relief L	Relief SV	Batting AB	Batting H	HR	BA	PO	A	E	DP	TC/G	FA
1982	STL N	9	7	.563	3.36	23	21	2	136.2	137	55	53	0	0	0	0	42	5	0	.119	7	10	1	1	0.8	.944
1983		12	11	.522	3.68	40	30	6	198	202	71	81	1	1	1	1	59	8	0	.136	17	24	4	2	1.1	.911
1984		3	5	.375	5.28	15	12	0	61.1	73	20	19	0	0	0	0	16	1	0	.063	5	12	1	0	1.2	.944
1985	CIN N	8	5	.615	4.55	33	13	1	99	116	37	38	0	2	0	0	17	1	0	.059	12	14	0	0	0.8	1.000
4 yrs.		32	28	.533	3.96	111	76	9	495	528	183	191	1	3	1	1	134	15	0	.112	41	60	6	3	1.0	.944
LEAGUE CHAMPIONSHIP SERIES																										
1982	STL N	0	0	—	3.00	1	1	0	6	4	1	4	0	0	0	0	1	0	0	.000	0	0	0	0	0.0	.000
WORLD SERIES																										
1982	STL N	1	0	1.000	3.46	2	2	1	13	10	5	5	0	0	0	0	0	0	0	—	1	1	0	0	1.0	1.000

Tom Sturdivant

STURDIVANT, THOMAS VIRGIL (Snake) BL TR 6′½″ 170 lbs.
B. Apr. 28, 1930, Gordon, Kans.

Year	Team	W	L	PCT	ERA	G	GS	CG	IP	H	BB	SO	ShO	Relief W	Relief L	Relief SV	Batting AB	Batting H	HR	BA	PO	A	E	DP	TC/G	FA
1955	NY A	1	3	.250	3.16	33	1	0	68.1	48	42	48	0	1	2	0	12	1	0	.083	4	8	0	2	0.4	1.000
1956		16	8	.667	3.30	32	17	6	158.1	134	52	110	2	6	2	5	64	20	0	.313	11	13	2	1	0.8	.923
1957		16	6	**.727**	2.54	28	28	7	201.2	170	80	118	2	0	0	0	71	13	0	.183	8	26	2	4	1.3	.944
1958		3	6	.333	4.20	15	10	0	70.2	77	38	41	0	0	0	0	21	4	0	.190	3	4	1	1	0.5	.875
1959	2 teams NY A (7G 0–2) KC A (36G 2–6)																									
″	total	2	8	.200	4.73	43	6	0	97	90	43	73	0	2	4	5	23	1	0	.043	9	21	3	2	0.8	.909
1960	BOS A	3	3	.500	4.97	40	3	0	101.1	106	45	67	0	3	2	1	22	4	0	.182	7	14	1	0	0.6	.955
1961	2 teams WAS A (15G 2–6) PIT N (13G 5–2)																									
″	total	7	8	.467	3.69	28	21	7	165.2	148	57	84	2	0	2	1	58	10	0	.172	11	29	0	0	1.4	1.000
1962	PIT N	9	5	.643	3.73	49	12	2	125.1	120	39	76	1	3	1	2	33	6	0	.182	10	23	3	0	0.7	.917
1963	3 teams PIT N (3G 0–0) DET A (28G 1–2) KC A (17G 1–2)																									
″	total	2	4	.333	3.95	48	3	0	116.1	98	45	68	0	2	3	2	22	0	0	.000	8	21	0	1	0.6	1.000
1964	2 teams KC A (3G 0–0) NY N (16G 0–0)																									
″	total	0	0		6.40	19	0	0	32.1	38	8	19	0	0	0	1	2	1	0	.500	1	4	1	0	0.3	.833
10 yrs.		59	51	.536	3.74	335	101	22	1137	1029	449	704	7	17	16	17	328	60	0	.183	72	163	13	11	0.7	.948

Tom Sturdivant *continued*

Year	Team	Lg	W	L	PCT	ERA	G	GS	CG	IP	H	BB	SO	ShO	Relief Pitching W	Relief Pitching L	Relief Pitching SV	Batting AB	Batting H	Batting HR	BA	PO	A	E	DP	TC/G	FA
WORLD SERIES																											
1955	**NY**	**A**	0	0	—	6.00	2	0	0	3	5	2	0	0	0	0	0	0	0	0	—	0	1	0	0	0.5	1.000
1956			1	0	1.000	2.79	2	1	1	9.2	8	8	9	0	0	0	0	3	1	0	.333	2	0	0	0	1.0	1.000
1957			0	0	—	6.00	2	1	0	6	6	1	2	0	0	0	0	1	0	0	.000	0	1	0	0	0.5	1.000
3 yrs.			1	0	1.000	4.34	6	2	1	18.2	19	11	11	0	0	0	0	4	1	0	.250	2	2	0	0	0.7	1.000

Tanyon Sturtze

STURTZE, TANYON JAMES BR TR 6′ 5″ 190 lbs.
B. Oct. 12, 1970, Worcester, Mass.

Year	Team	Lg	W	L	PCT	ERA	G	GS	CG	IP	H	BB	SO	ShO	Relief W	Relief L	Relief SV	AB	H	HR	BA	PO	A	E	DP	TC/G	FA
1995	**CHI**	**N**	0	0	—	9.00	2	0	0	2	2	1	0	0	0	0	0	0	0	0	—	0	0	0	0	0.0	.000

Dick Such

SUCH, RICHARD STANLEY BL TR 6′ 4″ 190 lbs.
B. Oct. 15, 1944, Sanford, N. C.

Year	Team	Lg	W	L	PCT	ERA	G	GS	CG	IP	H	BB	SO	ShO	Relief W	Relief L	Relief SV	AB	H	HR	BA	PO	A	E	DP	TC/G	FA
1970	**WAS**	**A**	1	5	.167	7.56	21	5	0	50	48	45	41	0	1	0	0	13	3	0	.231	1	7	0	1	0.4	1.000

Charley Suche

SUCHE, CHARLES MORRIS BR TL 6′ 2″ 190 lbs.
B. Aug. 5, 1915, Cranes Mill, Tex. D. Feb. 11, 1984, San Antonio, Tex.

Year	Team	Lg	W	L	PCT	ERA	G	GS	CG	IP	H	BB	SO	ShO	Relief W	Relief L	Relief SV	AB	H	HR	BA	PO	A	E	DP	TC/G	FA
1938	**CLE**	**A**	0	0	—	27.00	1	0	0	1.1	4	3	1	0	0	0	0	1	1	0	1.000	0	0	0	0	0.0	.000

Jim Suchecki

SUCHECKI, JAMES JOSEPH BR TR 6′ 200 lbs.
B. Aug. 25, 1927, Chicago, Ill.

Year	Team	Lg	W	L	PCT	ERA	G	GS	CG	IP	H	BB	SO	ShO	Relief W	Relief L	Relief SV	AB	H	HR	BA	PO	A	E	DP	TC/G	FA
1950	**BOS**	**A**	0	0	—	4.50	4	0	0	4	3	4	3	0	0	0	0	0	0	0	—	0	0	0	0	0.0	.000
1951	**STL**	**A**	0	6	.000	5.42	29	6	0	89.2	113	42	47	0	0	1	0	20	2	0	.100	4	11	1	1	0.6	.938
1952	**PIT**	**N**	0	0	—	5.40	5	0	0	10	14	4	6	0	0	0	0	2	0	0	.000	0	2	1	0	0.6	.667
3 yrs.			0	6	.000	5.38	38	6	0	103.2	130	50	56	0	0	1	0	22	2	0	.091	4	13	2	1	0.5	.895

Willie Sudhoff

SUDHOFF, JOHN WILLIAM (Wee Willie) BR TR 5′ 7″ 165 lbs.
B. Sept. 17, 1874, St. Louis, Mo. D. May 25, 1917, St. Louis, Mo.

Year	Team	Lg	W	L	PCT	ERA	G	GS	CG	IP	H	BB	SO	ShO	Relief W	Relief L	Relief SV	AB	H	HR	BA	PO	A	E	DP	TC/G	FA
1897	**STL**	**N**	2	7	.222	4.47	11	9	9	92.2	126	21	19	0	0	0	0	42	10	0	.238	8	29	3	2	3.6	.925
1898			11	27	.289	4.34	41	38	35	315	355	102	65	0	1	0	1	120	19	0	.158	15	114	12	5	3.4	.915
1899	**2 teams**	**CLE N** (11G 3–8)	**STL N** (26G 13–10)																								
″	**total**		16	18	.471	4.67	37	34	26	275.2	334	92	43	0	2	0	0	99	16	0	.162	11	99	11	3	3.3	.909
1900	**STL**	**N**	6	8	.429	2.76	16	14	13	127	128	37	29	2	0	1	0	106	20	0	.189	26	57	12	1	2.7	.874
1901			17	11	.607	3.52	38	26	25	276.1	281	92	78	1	1	0	2	108	19	1	.176	14	84	5	4	2.7	.951
1902	**STL**	**A**	12	12	.500	2.86	30	25	20	220	213	67	42	1	2	1	0	77	13	0	.169	8	84	10	4	3.3	.902
1903			21	15	.583	2.27	38	35	30	293.2	262	56	104	5	**2**	1	0	110	20	0	.182	15	104	5	0	3.3	.960
1904			8	15	.348	3.76	27	24	20	222.1	232	54	63	1	2	1	0	85	14	0	.165	13	104	3	4	4.0	.975
1905			10	20	.333	2.99	32	30	23	244	222	78	70	1	1	0	0	86	16	0	.186	20	96	4	0	3.8	.967
1906	**WAS**	**A**	0	2	.000	9.15	9	5	0	19.2	30	9	7	0	0	0	0	7	3	0	.429	1	11	1	0	1.4	.923
10 yrs.			103	135	.433	3.56	279	240	201	2086.1	2183	608	520	11	11	4	3	*				131	782	66	23	3.2	.933

Joe Sugden

SUGDEN, JOSEPH BB TR 5′10″ 180 lbs.
B. July 31, 1870, Philadelphia, Pa. D. June 28, 1959, Philadelphia, Pa.

Year	Team	Lg	W	L	PCT	ERA	G	GS	CG	IP	H	BB	SO	ShO	Relief W	Relief L	Relief SV	AB	H	HR	BA	PO	A	E	DP	TC/G	FA
1902	**STL**	**A**	0	0	—	0.00	1	0	0	1	1	0	0	0	0	0	0	*				81	27	5	3	4.2	.956

George Suggs

SUGGS, GEORGE FRANKLIN BR TR 5′ 7½″ 168 lbs.
B. July 7, 1882, Kinston, N. C. D. Apr. 4, 1949, Kinston, N. C.

Year	Team	Lg	W	L	PCT	ERA	G	GS	CG	IP	H	BB	SO	ShO	Relief W	Relief L	Relief SV	AB	H	HR	BA	PO	A	E	DP	TC/G	FA
1908	**DET**	**A**	1	1	.500	1.67	6	1	1	27	32	2	8	0	0	1	1	10	2	0	.200	0	4	0	1	0.7	1.000
1909			1	3	.250	2.03	9	4	2	44.1	34	10	18	0	0	1	1	15	1	0	.067	1	12	0	0	1.4	1.000
1910	**CIN**	**N**	19	11	.633	2.40	35	30	23	266	248	48	91	2	2	0	3	85	14	0	.165	8	81	4	4	2.7	.957
1911			15	13	.536	3.00	36	29	17	260.2	258	79	91	1	2	1	0	90	23	0	.256	13	83	3	9	2.8	.970
1912			19	16	.543	2.94	42	36	25	303	**320**	56	104	5	2	1	3	106	17	1	.160	14	82	4	0	2.4	.960
1913			8	15	.348	4.03	36	22	9	199	220	35	73	2	2	2	2	67	17	0	.254	8	64	1	1	2.0	.986
1914	**BAL**	**F**	24	14	.632	2.90	46	38	26	319.1	322	57	132	6	3	2	3	99	21	0	.212	23	114	3	4	3.0	.979
1915			13	17	.433	4.14	35	25	12	232.2	288	68	71	0	3	2	1	77	17	0	.221	7	81	2	1	2.6	.978
8 yrs.			100	90	.526	3.11	245	185	115	1652	1722	355	588	16	14	10	14	549	112	1	.204	74	521	17	20	2.5	.972

Ed Sukla

SUKLA, EDWARD ANTHONY BR TR 5′11″ 170 lbs.
Born Edward Anthony Suckla.
B. Mar. 3, 1943, Long Beach, Calif.

Year	Team	Lg	W	L	PCT	ERA	G	GS	CG	IP	H	BB	SO	ShO	Relief W	Relief L	Relief SV	AB	H	HR	BA	PO	A	E	DP	TC/G	FA
1964	**LA**	**A**	0	1	.000	6.75	2	0	0	2.2	2	1	3	0	0	1	0	0	0	0	—	1	0	0	0	0.5	1.000
1965	**CAL**	**A**	2	3	.400	4.50	25	0	0	32	32	10	15	0	2	3	3	0	0	0	—	2	9	0	1	0.4	1.000
1966			1	1	.500	6.48	12	0	0	16.2	18	6	8	0	1	1	1	1	0	0	.000	0	1	0	0	0.1	1.000
3 yrs.			3	5	.375	5.26	39	0	0	51.1	52	17	26	0	3	5	4	1	0	0	.000	3	10	0	1	0.3	1.000

Bill Sullivan

SULLIVAN, WILLIAM T.
Deceased.

Year	Team	Lg	W	L	PCT	ERA	G	GS	CG	IP	H	BB	SO	ShO	Relief W	Relief L	Relief SV	AB	H	HR	BA	PO	A	E	DP	TC/G	FA
1890	**SYR**	**AA**	1	4	.200	*7.93*	6	6	4	42	51	27	13	0	0	0	0	22	2	0	.091	0	8	0	0	1.1	1.000

Charlie Sullivan

SULLIVAN, CHARLES EDWARD BL TR 6′ 1″ 185 lbs.
B. May 23, 1903, Yadkin Valley, N. C. D. May 28, 1935, Maiden, N. C.

Year	Team	Lg	W	L	PCT	ERA	G	GS	CG	IP	H	BB	SO	ShO	Relief W	Relief L	Relief SV	AB	H	HR	BA	PO	A	E	DP	TC/G	FA
1928	**DET**	**A**	0	2	.000	6.57	3	2	0	12.1	18	6	2	0	0	0	0	4	0	0	.000	0	3	1	1	1.3	.750
1930			1	5	.167	6.53	40	3	2	93.2	112	53	38	0	1	2	5	24	7	0	.292	6	20	0	4	0.6	1.000
1931			3	2	.600	4.73	31	4	2	99	109	46	28	0	1	0	0	24	4	0	.167	2	20	2	0	0.8	.917
3 yrs.			4	9	.308	5.66	74	9	4	205	239	105	68	0	2	2	5	52	11	0	.212	8	43	3	5	0.7	.944

Fleury Sullivan

SULLIVAN, FLORENCE P.
B. 1862, East St. Louis, Ill. D. Feb. 15, 1897, East St. Louis, Ill.

Year	Team	Lg	W	L	PCT	ERA	G	GS	CG	IP	H	BB	SO	ShO	Relief W	Relief L	Relief SV	AB	H	HR	BA	PO	A	E	DP	TC/G	FA
1884	**PIT**	**AA**	16	35	.314	*4.20*	51	51	51	441	496	96	189	2	0	0	0	189	29	0	.153	28	90	26	2	2.7	.819

Frank Sullivan

SULLIVAN, FRANKLIN LEAL BR TR 6′ 6½″ 215 lbs.
B. Jan. 23, 1930, Hollywood, Calif.

Year	Team	Lg	W	L	PCT	ERA	G	GS	CG	IP	H	BB	SO	ShO	Relief W	Relief L	Relief SV	AB	H	HR	BA	PO	A	E	DP	TC/G	FA
1953	**BOS**	**A**	1	1	.500	5.61	14	0	0	25.2	24	11	17	0	1	1	0	4	1	0	.250	4	2	0	0	0.4	1.000
1954			15	12	.556	3.14	36	26	11	206.1	185	66	124	3	1	3	1	68	7	0	.103	12	36	2	5	1.4	.960

Frank Sullivan *continued*

Year	Team	Lg	W	L	PCT	ERA	G	GS	CG	IP	H	BB	SO	ShO	Relief Pitching W	Relief Pitching L	Relief Pitching SV	Batting AB	Batting H	HR	BA	PO	A	E	DP	TC/G	FA
1955			**18**	13	.581	2.91	35	**35**	16	**260**	235	100	129	3	0	0	0	89	10	0	.112	22	41	1	5	1.8	.984
1956			14	7	.667	3.42	34	33	12	242	253	82	116	1	1	0	0	85	12	0	.141	16	37	1	5	1.6	.981
1957			14	11	.560	2.73	31	30	14	240.2	206	48	127	3	0	0	0	79	13	0	.165	17	48	1	5	2.1	.985
1958			13	9	.591	3.57	32	29	10	199.1	216	49	103	2	0	0	3	67	11	0	.164	13	26	0	5	1.2	1.000
1959			9	11	.450	3.95	30	26	5	177.2	172	67	107	2	0	0	1	60	12	0	.200	15	20	2	4	1.2	.946
1960			6	16	.273	5.10	40	22	4	153.2	164	52	98	0	2	3	1	40	5	0	.125	6	17	0	1	0.6	1.000
1961	PHI	N	3	16	.158	4.29	49	18	1	159.1	161	55	114	1	1	4	6	33	5	0	.152	10	34	2	0	0.9	.957
1962	2 teams	PHI N	(19G 0–2)		MIN A	(21G 4–1)																					
"	total		4	3	.571	4.47	40	0	0	56.1	71	25	22	0	4	3	5	4	0	0	.000	6	10	0	0	0.4	1.000
1963	MIN	A	0	1	.000	5.73	10	0	0	11	15	4	2	0	0	1	1	0	0	0	—	0	4	0	0	0.4	1.000
11 yrs.			97	100	.492	3.60	351	219	73	1732	1702	559	959	15	10	15	18	529	76	0	.144	121	275	9	30	1.2	.978

Harry Sullivan

SULLIVAN, HARRY ANDREW BL TL
B. Apr. 12, 1888, Rockford, Ill. D. Sept. 22, 1919, Rockford, Ill.

Year	Team	Lg	W	L	PCT	ERA	G	GS	CG	IP	H	BB	SO	ShO	Relief W	Relief L	Relief SV	AB	H	HR	BA	PO	A	E	DP	TC/G	FA
1909	STL	N	0	0	—	36.00	2	1	0	1	4	2	1	0	0	0	0	1	0	0	.000	0	0	1	0	0.5	.000

Jim Sullivan

SULLIVAN, JAMES E. BR TR 5′10″ 155 lbs.
B. Apr. 25, 1869, Charlestown, Mass. D. Nov. 30, 1901, Roxbury, Mass.

Year	Team	Lg	W	L	PCT	ERA	G	GS	CG	IP	H	BB	SO	ShO	Relief W	Relief L	Relief SV	AB	H	HR	BA	PO	A	E	DP	TC/G	FA
1891	2 teams	BOS N	(1G 0–0)		COL AA	(1G 0–1)																					
"	total		0	1	.000	7.00	2	1	1	9	12	10	1	0	0	0	0	4	0	0	.000	0	6	2	0	4.0	.750
1895	BOS	N	11	9	.550	4.82	21	19	16	179.1	236	58	46	0	1	0	0	85	15	0	.176	5	31	6	1	1.9	.857
1896			11	12	.478	4.03	31	26	21	225.1	268	68	33	1	0	0	1	88	19	1	.216	7	43	5	2	1.8	.909
1897			4	5	.444	3.94	13	9	8	89	91	26	17	1	0	1	2	33	6	0	.182	4	16	2	1	1.7	.909
4 yrs.			26	27	.491	4.35	67	55	46	502.2	607	162	97	2	1	1	3	210	40	1	.190	16	96	15	4	1.9	.882

Jim Sullivan

SULLIVAN, JAMES RICHARD BR TR 5′11″ 165 lbs.
B. Apr. 5, 1894, Mine Run, Va. D. Feb. 12, 1972, Burtonville, Md.

Year	Team	Lg	W	L	PCT	ERA	G	GS	CG	IP	H	BB	SO	ShO	Relief W	Relief L	Relief SV	AB	H	HR	BA	PO	A	E	DP	TC/G	FA
1921	PHI	A	0	2	.000	3.18	2	2	2	17	20	7	8	0	0	0	0	6	0	0	.000	0	4	0	0	2.0	1.000
1922			0	2	.000	5.44	20	2	1	51.1	76	25	15	0	0	0	0	11	1	0	.091	2	12	3	0	0.9	.824
1923	CLE	A	0	1	.000	14.40	3	0	0	5	10	5	4	0	0	1	0	2	0	0	.000	0	1	0	0	0.3	1.000
3 yrs.			0	5	.000	5.52	25	4	3	73.1	106	37	27	0	0	1	0	19	1	0	.053	2	17	3	0	0.9	.864

Joe Sullivan

SULLIVAN, JOE BL TL 5′11″ 175 lbs.
B. Sept. 26, 1910, Mason City, Ill. D. Apr. 8, 1985, Sequim, Wash.

Year	Team	Lg	W	L	PCT	ERA	G	GS	CG	IP	H	BB	SO	ShO	Relief W	Relief L	Relief SV	AB	H	HR	BA	PO	A	E	DP	TC/G	FA
1935	DET	A	6	6	.500	3.51	25	12	5	125.2	119	71	53	0	2	1	0	43	7	0	.163	7	20	4	5	1.2	.871
1936			2	5	.286	6.78	26	4	1	79.2	111	40	32	0	1	3	1	28	5	0	.179	3	12	1	0	0.6	.938
1939	BOS	N	6	9	.400	3.64	31	11	7	113.2	114	50	46	0	2	**5**	2	40	12	0	.300	6	23	0	0	0.9	1.000
1940			10	14	.417	3.55	36	22	7	177.1	157	89	64	0	3	3	1	71	14	0	.197	8	38	3	1	1.4	.939
1941	2 teams	BOS N	(16G 2–2)		PIT N	(16G 4–1)																					
"	total		6	3	.667	3.63	32	6	0	91.2	100	48	21	0	4	1	1	26	5	0	.192	7	22	0	1	0.9	1.000
5 yrs.			30	37	.448	4.01	150	55	20	588	601	298	216	0	12	13	5	208	43	0	.207	31	115	8	7	1.0	.948

John Sullivan

SULLIVAN, JOHN JEREMIAH (Lefty) BL TL 5′11″ 165 lbs.
B. May 31, 1894, Chicago, Ill. D. July 7, 1958, Chicago, Ill.

Year	Team	Lg	W	L	PCT	ERA	G	GS	CG	IP	H	BB	SO	ShO	Relief W	Relief L	Relief SV	AB	H	HR	BA	PO	A	E	DP	TC/G	FA
1919	CHI	A	0	1	.000	4.20	4	2	1	15	24	8	9	0	0	0	0	3	0	0	.000	0	2	3	1	1.3	.400

Lefty Sullivan

SULLIVAN, PAUL THOMAS BL TL 6′ 3″ 204 lbs.
B. Sept. 7, 1916, Nashville, Tenn. D. Nov. 1, 1988, Scottsdale, Ariz.

Year	Team	Lg	W	L	PCT	ERA	G	GS	CG	IP	H	BB	SO	ShO	Relief W	Relief L	Relief SV	AB	H	HR	BA	PO	A	E	DP	TC/G	FA
1939	CLE	A	0	1	.000	4.26	7	1	0	12.2	9	9	4	0	0	0	0	3	0	0	.000	0	0	1	0	0.1	.000

Marty Sullivan

SULLIVAN, MARTIN C. BR TR
B. Oct. 20, 1862, Lowell, Mass. D. Jan. 6, 1894, Lowell, Mass.

Year	Team	Lg	W	L	PCT	ERA	G	GS	CG	IP	H	BB	SO	ShO	Relief W	Relief L	Relief SV	AB	H	HR	BA	PO	A	E	DP	TC/G	FA
1887	CHI	N	0	0	—	7.71	1	0	0	2.1	6	1	1	0	0	0	0	*				189	10	36	0	2.0	.847

Mike Sullivan

SULLIVAN, MICHAEL JOSEPH (Big Mike) BL 6′ 1″ 210 lbs.
B. Oct. 23, 1866, Boston, Mass. D. June 14, 1906, Boston, Mass.

Year	Team	Lg	W	L	PCT	ERA	G	GS	CG	IP	H	BB	SO	ShO	Relief W	Relief L	Relief SV	AB	H	HR	BA	PO	A	E	DP	TC/G	FA
1889	WAS	N	0	3	.000	7.24	9	3	3	41	47	32	15	0	0	0	0	19	1	0	.053	3	7	4	0	1.6	.714
1890	CHI	N	5	6	.455	4.59	12	12	10	96	108	58	33	0	0	0	0	40	5	0	.125	6	11	1	2	1.5	.944
1891	2 teams	PHI AA	(2G 0–2)		NY N	(3G 1–2)																					
"	total		1	4	.200	3.43	5	5	5	42	41	18	18	0	0	0	0	17	2	0	.118	1	8	2	0	2.2	.818
1892	CIN	N	12	4	.750	3.08	21	16	15	166.1	179	74	56	0	2	0	0	74	13	0	.176	3	31	6	1	1.9	.850
1893			8	11	.421	5.05	27	18	14	183.2	200	103	40	0	2	2	1	79	16	1	.203	11	40	10	4	2.3	.836
1894	2 teams	WAS N	(20G 2–10)		CLE N	(13G 6–5)																					
"	total		8	15	.348	6.48	33	23	20	208.1	294	121	40	0	0	2	1	101	22	1	.218	8	35	5	0	1.4	.896
1895	CLE	N	1	2	.333	8.42	4	3	2	31	42	16	5	0	0	0	0	15	2	0	.133	1	5	1	0	1.8	.857
1896	NY	N	10	13	.435	4.66	25	22	18	185.1	188	71	42	0	**3**	0	0	77	16	0	.208	8	45	6	2	2.4	.898
1897			8	7	.533	5.09	23	16	11	148.2	183	71	35	1	2	1	2	66	18	0	.273	4	39	6	2	2.1	.878
1898	BOS	N	0	1	.000	12.00	3	2	0	12	19	9	1	0	0	0	0	3	1	0	.333	0	3	2	0	1.7	.600
1899			1	0	1.000	5.00	1	1	1	9	10	4	1	0	0	0	0	3	1	0	.333	1	0	0	0	1.0	1.000
11 yrs.			54	66	.450	5.11	163	121	99	1123.1	1311	577	286	1	9	5	4	494	97	2	.196	46	224	43	11	1.9	.863

Pat Sullivan

SULLIVAN, PATRICK J. TR 5′11″ 165 lbs.
B. Dec. 22, 1862, Milwaukee, Wis. Deceased.

Year	Team	Lg	W	L	PCT	ERA	G	GS	CG	IP	H	BB	SO	ShO	Relief W	Relief L	Relief SV	AB	H	HR	BA	PO	A	E	DP	TC/G	FA
1884	KC	U	0	1	.000	*11.57*	1	1	0	7	15	5	1	0	0	0	0	*				47	40	25	5	3.5	.777

Scott Sullivan

SULLIVAN, WILLIAM SCOTT BR TR 6′ 3″ 210 lbs.
B. Mar. 13, 1971, Tuscaloosa, Ala.

Year	Team	Lg	W	L	PCT	ERA	G	GS	CG	IP	H	BB	SO	ShO	Relief W	Relief L	Relief SV	AB	H	HR	BA	PO	A	E	DP	TC/G	FA
1995	CIN	N	0	0	—	4.91	3	0	0	3.2	4	2	2	0	0	0	0	1	0	0	.000	0	1	0	0	0.3	1.000

Sleeper Sullivan

SULLIVAN, THOMAS JEFFERSON BR TR 175 lbs.
B. St. Louis, Mo. D. Sept. 25, 1899, Camden, N. J.

Year	Team		W	L	PCT	ERA	G	GS	CG	IP	H	BB	SO	ShO	Relief Pitching W	L	SV	Batting AB	H	HR	BA	PO	A	E	DP	TC/G	FA
1882	STL	AA	0	1	.000	*8.00*	1	1	1	9	15	1	0	0	0	0	0	188	34	0	.181	111	33	27	1	4.8	.842
1884	STL	U	1	0	1.000	*4.50*	1	1	0	6	10	0	3	0	0	0	0	9	1	0	.111	232	46	53	4	6.5	.840
2 yrs.			1	1	.500	6.60	2	2	1	15	25	1	3	0	0	0	0	*				387	92	86	6	5.8	.848

Suter Sullivan

SULLIVAN, SUTER G. 6′ 170 lbs.
B. Oct. 14, 1872, Baltimore, Md. D. Apr. 19, 1925, Baltimore, Md.

Year	Team		W	L	PCT	ERA	G	GS	CG	IP	H	BB	SO	ShO	Relief Pitching W	L	SV	Batting AB	H	HR	BA	PO	A	E	DP	TC/G	FA
1898	STL	N	0	0	—	1.50	1	0	0	6	10	4	3	0	0	0	0	*				75	78	19	7	4.2	.890

Tom Sullivan

SULLIVAN, THOMAS
B. Mar. 1, 1860, New York, N. Y. D. Apr. 12, 1947, Boston, Mass.

Year	Team		W	L	PCT	ERA	G	GS	CG	IP	H	BB	SO	ShO	Relief Pitching W	L	SV	Batting AB	H	HR	BA	PO	A	E	DP	TC/G	FA
1884	COL	AA	2	2	.500	*4.06*	4	4	4	31	42	3	12	0	0	0	0	11	1	0	.091	0	3	0	0	0.8	1.000
1886	LOU	AA	2	7	.222	*3.96*	9	9	8	75	94	33	27	0	0	0	0	27	3	0	.111	6	13	2	0	2.1	.905
1888	KC	AA	8	16	.333	3.40	24	24	24	214.2	227	68	84	0	0	0	0	92	10	0	.109	18	68	5	2	3.3	.945
1889			2	8	.200	5.67	10	10	10	87.1	111	48	24	0	0	0	0	33	5	0	.152	3	16	5	0	2.4	.792
4 yrs.			14	33	.298	4.04	47	47	46	408	474	152	147	0	0	0	0	163	19	0	.117	27	100	12	2	2.7	.914

Tom Sullivan

SULLIVAN, THOMAS AUGUSTIN BL TL 5′11″ 178 lbs.
B. Oct. 18, 1895, Boston, Mass. D. Sept. 23, 1962, Boston, Mass.

Year	Team		W	L	PCT	ERA	G	GS	CG	IP	H	BB	SO	ShO	Relief Pitching W	L	SV	Batting AB	H	HR	BA	PO	A	E	DP	TC/G	FA
1922	PHI	N	0	0	—	11.25	3	0	0	8	16	5	2	0	0	0	0	4	1	1	.250	0	2	0	1	0.7	1.000

Ed Summers

SUMMERS, ORON EDGAR (Kickapoo Chief) BB TR 6′ 2″ 180 lbs.
B. Dec. 5, 1884, Ladoga, Ind. D. May 12, 1953, Indianapolis, Ind.

Year	Team		W	L	PCT	ERA	G	GS	CG	IP	H	BB	SO	ShO	Relief Pitching W	L	SV	Batting AB	H	HR	BA	PO	A	E	DP	TC/G	FA
1908	DET	A	24	12	.667	1.64	40	32	24	301	271	55	103	5	5	0	1	113	14	0	.124	20	90	7	2	2.9	.940
1909			19	9	.679	2.24	35	32	24	281.2	243	52	107	3	0	0	1	94	10	0	.106	14	89	3	8	3.0	.972
1910			13	12	.520	2.53	30	25	18	220.1	211	60	82	1	1	1	0	76	14	2	.184	14	74	3	1	3.0	.967
1911			11	11	.500	3.66	30	20	13	179.1	189	51	65	0	3	2	0	63	16	0	.254	5	46	1	1	1.7	.981
1912			1	1	.500	4.86	3	3	1	16.2	16	3	5	0	0	0	0	6	3	0	.500	1	5	0	0	2.0	1.000
5 yrs.			68	45	.602	2.42	138	112	80	999	930	221	362	9	9	3	2	352	57	2	.162	54	304	14	12	2.7	.962
WORLD SERIES																											
1908	DET	A	0	2	.000	4.30	2	1	0	14.2	18	4	7	0	0	1	0	5	1	0	.200	0	7	0	0	3.5	1.000
1909			0	2	.000	8.59	2	2	0	7.1	13	4	4	0	0	0	0	3	0	0	.000	0	2	0	0	1.0	1.000
2 yrs.			0	4	.000	5.73	4	3	0	22	31	8	11	0	0	1	0	8	1	0	.125	0	9	0	0	2.3	1.000

Billy Sunday

SUNDAY, WILLIAM ASHLEY (The Evangelist) BL TR 5′10″ 160 lbs.
B. Nov. 19, 1862, Ames, Iowa D. Nov. 6, 1935, Chicago, Ill.

Year	Team		W	L	PCT	ERA	G	GS	CG	IP	H	BB	SO	ShO	Relief Pitching W	L	SV	Batting AB	H	HR	BA	PO	A	E	DP	TC/G	FA
1890	PIT	N	0	0	—	∞	1	0	0		2	0	0	0	0	0	0	*				10	1	6	0	1.2	.647

Gordie Sundin

SUNDIN, GORDON VINCENT BR TR 6′ 4″ 215 lbs.
B. Oct. 10, 1937, Minneapolis, Minn.

Year	Team		W	L	PCT	ERA	G	GS	CG	IP	H	BB	SO	ShO	Relief Pitching W	L	SV	Batting AB	H	HR	BA	PO	A	E	DP	TC/G	FA
1956	BAL	A	0	0	—	∞	1	0	0		0	2	0	0	0	0	0	0	0	0	—	0	0	0	0	0.0	.000

Steve Sundra

SUNDRA, STEPHEN RICHARD (Smokey) BR TR 6′ 2″ 190 lbs.
B. Mar. 27, 1910, Luxor, Pa. D. Mar. 23, 1952, Cleveland, Ohio.
BB 1936, 1938–1940, 1944, 1946

Year	Team		W	L	PCT	ERA	G	GS	CG	IP	H	BB	SO	ShO	Relief Pitching W	L	SV	Batting AB	H	HR	BA	PO	A	E	DP	TC/G	FA
1936	NY	A	0	0	—	0.00	1	0	0	2	2	2	1	0	0	0	0	1	0	0	.000	0	0	0	0	0.0	.000
1938			6	4	.600	4.80	25	8	3	93.2	107	43	33	0	3	2	0	33	6	1	.182	0	25	1	2	1.0	.962
1939			11	1	.917	2.76	24	11	8	120.2	110	56	27	1	3	0	0	49	13	0	.265	2	27	0	1	1.2	1.000
1940			4	6	.400	5.53	27	8	2	99.1	121	42	26	0	2	2	2	29	4	0	.138	3	22	2	1	1.0	.926
1941	WAS	A	9	13	.409	5.29	28	23	11	168.1	203	61	50	0	0	0	0	60	13	0	.217	12	29	3	0	1.6	.932
1942	2 teams	WAS A	(6G 1–3)	STL A	(20G 8–3)																						
″	total		9	6	.600	4.24	26	17	8	144.1	165	44	31	0	1	0	0	52	11	1	.212	11	28	2	3	1.6	.951
1943	STL	A	15	11	.577	3.25	32	29	13	208	212	66	44	3	0	1	0	73	16	0	.219	10	47	4	2	1.9	.934
1944			2	0	1.000	1.42	3	3	2	19	15	4	1	0	0	0	0	5	0	0	.000	0	3	0	0	1.0	1.000
1946			0	0	—	11.25	2	0	0	4	9	3	1	0	0	0	0	0	0	0	—	0	1	0	0	0.5	1.000
9 yrs.			56	41	.577	4.17	168	99	47	859.1	944	321	214	4	9	5	2	302	63	2	.209	38	182	12	9	1.4	.948
WORLD SERIES																											
1939	NY	A	0	0	—	0.00	1	0	0	2.2	4	1	2	0	0	0	0	0	0	0	—	0	0	0	0	0.0	.000

Tom Sunkel

SUNKEL, THOMAS JACOB (Lefty) BL TL 6′ 1″ 190 lbs.
B. Aug. 9, 1912, Paris, Ill.

Year	Team		W	L	PCT	ERA	G	GS	CG	IP	H	BB	SO	ShO	Relief Pitching W	L	SV	Batting AB	H	HR	BA	PO	A	E	DP	TC/G	FA
1937	STL	N	0	0	—	2.06	9	1	0	39.1	24	11	9	0	0	0	1	9	1	0	.111	2	5	0	0	0.8	1.000
1939			4	4	.500	4.22	20	11	2	85.1	79	56	54	1	0	0	0	28	9	0	.321	2	9	1	2	0.6	.917
1941	NY	N	1	1	.500	2.93	2	2	1	15.1	7	12	14	1	0	0	0	6	2	0	.333	1	1	0	0	1.0	1.000
1942			3	6	.333	4.81	19	11	3	63.2	65	41	29	0	0	0	0	19	2	0	.105	1	5	0	0	0.3	1.000
1943			0	1	.000	10.13	1	1	0	2.2	4	3	0	0	0	0	0	0	0	0	—	0	0	0	0	0.0	.000
1944	BKN	N	1	3	.250	7.50	12	3	0	24	39	10	6	0	1	1	1	4	0	0	.000	1	0	1	0	0.2	.500
6 yrs.			9	15	.375	4.34	63	29	6	230.1	218	133	112	2	1	1	2	66	14	0	.212	7	20	2	2	0.5	.931

Jeff Suppan

SUPPAN, JEFFREY SCOT BR TR 6′ 1″ 200 lbs.
B. Jan. 2, 1975, Oklahoma City, Okla.

Year	Team		W	L	PCT	ERA	G	GS	CG	IP	H	BB	SO	ShO	Relief Pitching W	L	SV	Batting AB	H	HR	BA	PO	A	E	DP	TC/G	FA
1995	BOS	A	1	2	.333	5.96	8	3	0	22.2	29	5	19	0	1	0	0	0	0	0	—	2	2	0	0	0.5	1.000

Rich Surhoff

SURHOFF, RICHARD CLIFFORD BR TR 6′ 3″ 210 lbs.
Brother of B. J. Surhoff.
B. Oct. 3, 1962, Bronx, N. Y.

Year	Team		W	L	PCT	ERA	G	GS	CG	IP	H	BB	SO	ShO	Relief Pitching W	L	SV	Batting AB	H	HR	BA	PO	A	E	DP	TC/G	FA
1985	2 teams	PHI N	(2G 1–0)	TEX A	(7G 0–1)																						
″	total		1	1	.500	6.75	9	0	0	9.1	14	3	9	0	1	1	2	0	0	0		0	0	0	0	0.0	

Max Surkont

SURKONT, MATTHEW CONSTANTINE BR TR 6′ 1″ 195 lbs.
B. June 16, 1922, Central Falls, R. I. D. Oct. 8, 1986, Largo, Fla.

Year	Team		W	L	PCT	ERA	G	GS	CG	IP	H	BB	SO	ShO	Relief Pitching W	L	SV	Batting AB	H	HR	BA	PO	A	E	DP	TC/G	FA
1949	CHI	A	3	5	.375	4.78	44	2	0	96	92	60	38	0	3	4	4	22	1	0	.045	4	13	0	0	0.4	1.000
1950	BOS	N	5	2	.714	3.23	9	6	2	55.2	63	20	21	0	2	0	0	23	10	1	.435	1	9	0	0	1.1	1.000
1951			12	16	.429	3.99	37	33	11	237	230	89	110	2	1	0	1	73	11	0	.151	11	31	2	2	1.2	.955

Max Surkont *continued*

Year	Team	Lg	W	L	PCT	ERA	G	GS	CG	IP	H	BB	SO	ShO	Relief Pitching W	Relief Pitching L	Relief Pitching SV	Batting AB	Batting H	Batting HR	BA	PO	A	E	DP	TC/G	FA
1952			12	13	.480	3.77	31	29	12	215	201	76	125	3	0	0	0	63	7	0	.111	9	38	5	3	1.7	.904
1953	MIL	N	11	5	.688	4.18	28	24	11	170	168	64	83	2	0	0	0	56	16	0	.286	11	32	2	3	1.6	.956
1954	PIT	N	9	18	.333	4.41	33	29	11	208.1	216	78	78	0	1	0	0	60	10	0	.167	8	40	1	1	1.5	.980
1955			7	14	.333	5.57	35	22	5	166.1	194	78	84	0	1	1	2	50	7	0	.140	8	21	2	0	0.9	.935
1956	3 teams	PIT N (1G 0–0) STL N (5G 0–0) NY N (8G 2–2)																									
"	total		2	2	.500	5.45	14	4	1	39.2	36	14	24	0	0	0	1	10	1	0	.100	0	5	0	0	0.4	1.000
1957	NY	N	0	1	.000	9.95	5	0	0	6.1	9	2	8	0	0	1	0	0	0	0	—	0	1	0	0	0.2	1.000
9 yrs.			61	76	.445	4.38	236	149	53	1194.1	1209	481	571	7	8	6	8	357	63	1	.176	52	190	12	9	1.1	.953

George Susce

SUSCE, GEORGE DANIEL BR TR 6′ 1″ 180 lbs.
Son of George Susce.
B. Sept. 13, 1931, Pittsburgh, Pa.

Year	Team	Lg	W	L	PCT	ERA	G	GS	CG	IP	H	BB	SO	ShO	Relief Pitching W	Relief Pitching L	Relief Pitching SV	Batting AB	Batting H	Batting HR	BA	PO	A	E	DP	TC/G	FA
1955	BOS	A	9	7	.563	3.06	29	15	6	144.1	123	49	60	1	2	1	1	49	7	0	.143	9	22	0	2	1.1	1.000
1956			2	4	.333	6.20	21	6	0	69.2	71	44	26	0	2	1	0	18	4	0	.222	3	11	1	1	0.7	.933
1957			7	3	.700	4.28	29	5	0	88.1	93	41	40	0	6	1	1	25	3	0	.120	4	11	1	1	0.6	.938
1958	2 teams	BOS A (2G 0–0) DET A (27G 4–3)																									
"	total		4	3	.571	3.98	29	10	2	92.2	96	27	42	0	3	2	1	24	3	0	.125	6	6	1	1	0.4	.923
1959	DET	A	0	0	—	12.89	9	0	0	14.2	24	9	9	0	0	0	0	1	0	0	.000	2	1	0	0	0.3	1.000
5 yrs.			22	17	.564	4.42	117	36	8	409.2	407	170	177	1	13	5	3	117	17	0	.145	24	51	3	5	0.7	.962

Rick Sutcliffe

SUTCLIFFE, RICHARD LEE BL TR 6′ 7″ 215 lbs.
B. June 21, 1956, Independence, Mo.

Year	Team	Lg	W	L	PCT	ERA	G	GS	CG	IP	H	BB	SO	ShO	Relief Pitching W	Relief Pitching L	Relief Pitching SV	Batting AB	Batting H	Batting HR	BA	PO	A	E	DP	TC/G	FA
1976	LA	N	0	0	—	0.00	1	1	0	5	2	1	3	0	0	0	0	1	0	0	.000	0	0	0	0	0.0	.000
1978			0	0	—	0.00	2	0	0	2	2	1	0	0	0	0	0	0	0	0	—	0	1	0	1	0.5	1.000
1979			17	10	.630	3.46	39	30	5	242	217	97	117	1	1	2	0	85	21	1	.247	18	24	0	1	1.1	1.000
1980			3	9	.250	5.56	42	10	1	110	122	55	59	1	2	5	5	27	4	0	.148	6	13	0	0	0.5	1.000
1981			2	2	.500	4.02	14	6	0	47	41	20	16	0	0	0	0	11	2	0	.182	6	8	0	0	1.0	1.000
1982	CLE	A	14	8	.636	**2.96**	34	27	6	216	174	98	142	1	2	1	1	0	0	0	—	14	32	1	1	1.4	.979
1983			17	11	.607	4.29	36	35	10	243.1	251	102	160	2	1	0	0	0	0	0	—	36	29	0	1	1.8	1.000
1984	2 teams	CLE A (15G 4–5) CHI N (20G 16–1)																									
"	total		20	6	**.769**	3.64	35	35	9	244.2	234	85	213	3	0	0	0	56	14	0	.250	19	35	2	1	1.6	.964
1985	CHI	N	8	8	.500	3.18	20	20	6	130	119	44	102	3	0	0	0	43	10	1	.233	12	23	1	0	1.8	.972
1986			5	14	.263	4.64	28	27	4	176.2	166	96	122	1	0	0	0	53	11	1	.208	8	30	1	4	1.4	.974
1987			**18**	10	.643	3.68	34	34	6	237.1	223	106	174	1	0	0	0	81	12	0	.148	12	54	4	4	2.1	.943
1988			13	14	.481	3.86	32	32	12	226	232	70	144	2	0	0	0	75	12	1	.160	21	37	3	2	1.9	.951
1989			16	11	.593	3.66	35	34	5	229	202	69	153	1	0	0	0	70	10	0	.143	22	31	1	3	1.5	.981
1990			0	2	.000	5.91	5	5	0	21.1	25	12	7	0	0	0	0	5	0	0	.000	2	5	0	0	1.4	1.000
1991			6	5	.545	4.10	19	18	0	96.2	96	45	52	0	0	0	0	32	3	0	.094	10	12	0	2	1.2	1.000
1992	BAL	A	16	15	.516	4.47	36	**36**	5	237.1	251	74	109	2	0	0	0	0	0	0	—	11	24	3	2	1.1	.921
1993			10	10	.500	5.75	29	28	3	166	212	74	80	0	0	0	0	0	0	0	—	9	30	1	2	1.4	.975
1994	STL	N	6	4	.600	6.52	16	14	0	67.2	93	32	26	0	0	0	0	23	3	0	.130	5	16	0	1	1.3	1.000
18 yrs.			171	139	.552	4.08	457	392	72	2698	2662	1081	1679	18	6	8	6	562	102	4	.181	211	404	17	25	1.4	.973
LEAGUE CHAMPIONSHIP SERIES																											
1984	CHI	N	1	1	.500	3.38	2	2	0	13.1	9	8	10	0	0	0	0	6	3	1	.500	0	0	0	0	0.0	.000
1989			0	0	—	4.50	1	1	0	6	5	4	2	0	0	0	0	2	1	0	.500	0	2	0	0	2.0	1.000
2 yrs.			1	1	.500	3.72	3	3	0	19.1	14	12	12	0	0	0	0	8	4	1	.500	0	2	0	0	0.7	1.000

Rube Suter

SUTER, HARRY RICHARD BL TL 5′10″ 190 lbs.
B. Sept. 15, 1887, Independence, Mo. D. July 24, 1971, Topeka, Kans.

Year	Team	Lg	W	L	PCT	ERA	G	GS	CG	IP	H	BB	SO	ShO	Relief Pitching W	Relief Pitching L	Relief Pitching SV	Batting AB	Batting H	Batting HR	BA	PO	A	E	DP	TC/G	FA
1909	CHI	A	2	3	.400	2.47	18	7	3	87.1	72	28	53	1	0	0	1	32	3	0	.094	6	19	0	2	1.4	1.000

Darrell Sutherland

SUTHERLAND, DARRELL WAYNE BR TR 6′ 4″ 169 lbs.
Brother of Gary Sutherland.
B. Nov. 14, 1941, Glendale, Calif.

Year	Team	Lg	W	L	PCT	ERA	G	GS	CG	IP	H	BB	SO	ShO	Relief Pitching W	Relief Pitching L	Relief Pitching SV	Batting AB	Batting H	Batting HR	BA	PO	A	E	DP	TC/G	FA
1964	NY	N	0	3	.000	7.76	10	4	0	26.2	32	12	9	0	0	0	0	5	1	0	.200	4	9	1	1	1.4	.929
1965			3	1	.750	2.81	18	2	0	48	33	17	16	0	3	0	0	13	2	0	.154	4	17	1	1	1.2	.955
1966			2	0	1.000	4.87	31	0	0	44.1	60	25	23	0	2	0	1	3	2	0	.667	4	11	0	1	0.5	1.000
1968	CLE	A	0	0	—	8.10	3	0	0	3.1	6	4	2	0	0	0	0	0	0	0	—	0	0	0	0	0.0	.000
4 yrs.			5	4	.556	4.78	62	6	0	122.1	131	58	50	0	5	0	1	21	5	0	.238	12	37	2	3	0.8	.961

Dizzy Sutherland

SUTHERLAND, HOWARD ALVIN BL TL 6′ 200 lbs.
B. Apr. 9, 1922, Washington, D. C. D. Aug. 21, 1979, Washington, D. C.

Year	Team	Lg	W	L	PCT	ERA	G	GS	CG	IP	H	BB	SO	ShO	Relief Pitching W	Relief Pitching L	Relief Pitching SV	Batting AB	Batting H	Batting HR	BA	PO	A	E	DP	TC/G	FA
1949	WAS	A	0	1	.000	45.00	1	1	0	1	2	6	0	0	0	0	0	0	0	0	—	0	1	0	0	1.0	1.000

Suds Sutherland

SUTHERLAND, HARVEY SCOTT BR TR 6′ 180 lbs.
B. Feb. 20, 1894, Beaverton, Ore. D. May 11, 1972, Portland, Ore.

Year	Team	Lg	W	L	PCT	ERA	G	GS	CG	IP	H	BB	SO	ShO	Relief Pitching W	Relief Pitching L	Relief Pitching SV	Batting AB	Batting H	Batting HR	BA	PO	A	E	DP	TC/G	FA
1921	DET	A	6	2	.750	4.97	13	8	3	58	80	18	18	0	2	2	0	27	11	0	.407	2	24	0	1	2.0	1.000

Bruce Sutter

SUTTER, HOWARD BRUCE BR TR 6′ 2″ 190 lbs.
B. Jan. 8, 1953, Lancaster, Pa.

Year	Team	Lg	W	L	PCT	ERA	G	GS	CG	IP	H	BB	SO	ShO	Relief Pitching W	Relief Pitching L	Relief Pitching SV	Batting AB	Batting H	Batting HR	BA	PO	A	E	DP	TC/G	FA
1976	CHI	N	6	3	.667	2.71	52	0	0	83	63	26	73	0	6	3	10	8	0	0	.000	6	9	1	1	0.3	.938
1977			7	3	.700	1.35	62	0	0	107	69	23	129	0	7	3	31	20	3	0	.150	11	14	0	0	0.4	1.000
1978			8	10	.444	3.18	64	0	0	99	82	34	106	0	8	10	27	13	1	0	.077	12	9	0	0	0.3	1.000
1979			6	6	.500	2.23	62	0	0	101	67	32	110	0	6	6	**37**	12	3	0	.250	9	15	3	0	0.4	.889
1980			5	8	.385	2.65	60	0	0	102	90	34	76	0	5	8	**28**	9	1	0	.111	6	14	0	0	0.3	1.000
1981	STL	N	3	5	.375	2.63	48	0	0	82	64	24	57	0	3	5	**25**	9	0	0	.000	7	8	0	0	0.3	1.000
1982			9	8	.529	2.90	70	0	0	102.1	88	34	61	0	9	8	**36**	8	1	0	.125	6	15	1	5	0.3	.955
1983			9	10	.474	4.23	60	0	0	89.1	90	30	64	0	9	10	21	7	0	0	.000	11	19	2	1	0.5	.938
1984			5	7	.417	1.54	71	0	0	122.2	109	23	77	0	5	7	**45**	10	0	0	.000	14	19	0	2	0.5	1.000
1985	ATL	N	7	7	.500	4.48	58	0	0	88.1	91	29	52	0	7	7	23	4	0	0	.000	5	13	0	0	0.3	1.000

Bruce Sutter *continued*

Year	Team	Lg	W	L	PCT	ERA	G	GS	CG	IP	H	BB	SO	ShO	Relief Pitching W	Relief Pitching L	Relief Pitching SV	Batting AB	Batting H	Batting HR	BA	PO	A	E	DP	TC/G	FA
1986			2	0	1.000	4.34	16	0	0	18.2	17	9	16	0	2	0	3	1	0	0	.000	1	3	0	0	0.3	1.000
1988			1	4	.200	4.76	38	0	0	45.1	49	11	40	0	1	4	14	1	0	0	.000	2	7	2	0	0.3	.818
12 yrs.			68	71	.489	2.84	661	0	0	1040.2	879	309	861	0	68	71	300	102	9	0	.088	90	145	9	9	0.4	.963
																	7th										
LEAGUE CHAMPIONSHIP SERIES																											
1982	**STL**	**N**	1	0	1.000	0.00	2	0	0	4.1	0	0	1	0	1	0	1	1	0	0	.000	0	2	0	0	1.0	1.000
WORLD SERIES																											
1982	**STL**	**N**	1	0	1.000	4.70	4	0	0	7.2	6	3	6	0	1	0	2	0	0	0	—	0	1	0	0	0.3	1.000

Jack Sutthoff

SUTTHOFF, JOHN GERHARD (Sunny Jack) BL TR 5′ 9″ 175 lbs.
B. June 29, 1873, Cincinnati, Ohio D. Aug. 3, 1942, Cincinnati, Ohio.

Year	Team	Lg	W	L	PCT	ERA	G	GS	CG	IP	H	BB	SO	ShO	Relief Pitching W	Relief Pitching L	Relief Pitching SV	Batting AB	Batting H	Batting HR	BA	PO	A	E	DP	TC/G	FA
1898	**WAS**	**N**	0	0	—	12.96	2	1	0	8.1	16	8	3	0	0	0	0	3	1	0	.333	0	2	0	0	1.0	1.000
1899	**STL**	**N**	1	1	.500	10.38	2	2	1	13	19	10	4	0	0	0	0	6	0	0	.000	1	6	1	0	4.0	.875
1901	**CIN**	**N**	1	3	.250	5.50	10	4	4	70.1	82	39	12	0	0	0	0	28	3	0	.107	6	15	5	0	2.4	.808
1903			16	10	.615	2.80	30	27	21	224.2	207	79	76	3	0	0	0	84	12	0	.143	10	54	3	2	2.2	.955
1904	**2 teams**	**CIN N**	(12G 5–6)		**PHI N**	(19G 6–13)																					
″	**total**		11	19	.367	3.19	31	28	25	253.2	255	114	73	0	**2**	1	0	94	16	0	.170	11	57	9	6	2.5	.883
1905	**PHI**	**N**	3	4	.429	3.81	13	6	4	78	82	36	26	1	0	1	0	25	2	0	.080	3	23	1	0	2.1	.963
6 yrs.			32	37	.464	3.65	88	68	55	648	661	286	194	4	2	2	0	240	34	0	.142	31	157	19	8	2.3	.908

Don Sutton

SUTTON, DONALD HOWARD BR TR 6′ 1″ 185 lbs.
B. Apr. 2, 1945, Clio, Ala.

Year	Team	Lg	W	L	PCT	ERA	G	GS	CG	IP	H	BB	SO	ShO	Relief Pitching W	Relief Pitching L	Relief Pitching SV	Batting AB	Batting H	Batting HR	BA	PO	A	E	DP	TC/G	FA
1966	**LA**	**N**	12	12	.500	2.99	37	35	6	225.2	192	52	209	2	0	1	0	82	15	0	.183	8	32	2	3	1.1	.952
1967			11	15	.423	3.95	37	34	11	232.2	223	57	169	3	0	1	1	75	10	0	.133	7	31	1	2	1.1	.974
1968			11	15	.423	2.60	35	27	7	207.2	179	59	162	2	1	1	1	62	11	0	.177	12	25	1	0	1.1	.974
1969			17	18	.486	3.47	41	41	11	293	269	91	217	4	0	0	0	98	15	0	.153	19	43	1	3	1.5	.984
1970			15	13	.536	4.08	38	38	10	260	251	78	201	4	0	0	0	84	13	0	.155	21	28	3	1	1.4	.942
1971			17	12	.586	2.55	38	37	12	265	231	55	194	4	0	0	1	88	19	0	.216	27	26	2	5	1.4	.964
1972			19	9	.679	2.08	33	33	18	272.2	186	63	207	**9**	0	0	0	91	13	0	.143	18	34	1	2	1.6	.981
1973			18	10	.643	2.42	33	33	14	256.1	196	56	200	3	0	0	0	84	10	0	.119	12	34	1	2	1.4	.979
1974			19	9	.679	3.23	40	**40**	10	276	241	80	179	5	0	0	0	98	18	0	.184	17	33	0	1	1.3	1.000
1975			16	13	.552	2.87	35	35	11	254	202	62	175	4	0	0	0	80	11	0	.138	24	25	2	0	1.5	.961
1976			21	10	.677	3.06	35	34	15	267.2	231	82	161	4	1	0	0	84	7	0	.083	5	31	1	2	1.1	.973
1977			14	8	.636	3.19	33	33	9	240	207	69	150	3	0	0	0	73	11	0	.151	15	29	1	3	1.4	.978
1978			15	11	.577	3.55	34	34	12	238	228	54	154	2	0	0	0	72	6	0	.083	13	23	0	2	1.1	1.000
1979			12	15	.444	3.82	33	32	6	226	201	61	146	1	0	0	1	77	11	0	.143	16	24	1	2	1.2	.976
1980			13	5	.722	**2.21**	32	31	4	212	163	47	128	2	0	0	1	64	5	0	.078	24	25	2	3	1.6	.961
1981	**HOU**	**N**	11	9	.550	2.60	23	23	6	159	132	29	104	3	0	0	0	51	7	0	.137	11	24	2	3	1.6	.946
1982	**2 teams**	**HOU N**	(27G 13–8)		**MIL A**	(7G 4–1)																					
″	**total**		17	9	.654	3.06	34	34	6	249.2	224	64	175	1	0	0	0	68	11	0	.162	22	28	1	3	1.5	.980
1983	**MIL**	**A**	8	13	.381	4.08	31	31	4	220.1	209	54	134	0	0	0	0	0	0	0	—	13	23	1	1	1.2	.973
1984			14	12	.538	3.77	33	33	1	212.2	224	51	143	0	0	0	0	0	0	0	—	11	19	1	1	0.9	.968
1985	**2 teams**	**OAK A**	(29G 13–8)		**CAL A**	(5G 2–2)																					
″	**total**		15	10	.600	3.86	34	34	1	226	221	59	107	1	0	0	0	0	0	0		8	32	4	1	1.3	.909
1986	**CAL**	**A**	15	11	.577	3.74	34	34	3	207	192	49	116	1	0	0	0	0	0	0	—	18	14	2	1	1.0	.941
1987			11	11	.500	4.70	35	34	1	191.2	199	41	99	0	1	0	0	0	0	0	—	8	18	0	1	0.7	1.000
1988	**LA**	**N**	3	6	.333	3.92	16	16	0	87.1	91	30	44	0	0	0	0	23	2	0	.087	5	12	1	0	1.1	.944
23 yrs.			324	256	.559	3.26	774	756	178	5280.1	4692	1343	3574	58	3	3	5	1354	195	0	.144	334	613	31	42	1.3	.968
				8th						**7th**			**5th**	**10th**													
LEAGUE CHAMPIONSHIP SERIES																											
1974	**LA**	**N**	2	0	1.000	0.53	2	2	1	17	7	2	13	1	0	0	0	7	2	0	.286	2	3	0	1	2.5	1.000
1977			1	0	1.000	1.00	1	1	1	9	9	0	4	0	0	0	0	3	0	0	.000	0	2	0	0	2.0	1.000
1978			0	1	.000	6.35	1	1	0	5.2	7	2	0	0	0	0	0	2	0	0	.000	0	1	0	0	1.0	1.000
1982	**MIL**	**A**	1	0	1.000	3.52	1	1	0	7.2	8	2	9	0	0	0	0	0	0	0	—	0	1	0	0	1.0	1.000
1986	**CAL**	**A**	0	0	—	1.86	2	1	0	9.2	6	1	4	0	0	0	0	0	0	0	—	0	0	0	0	0.0	.000
5 yrs.			4	1	.800	2.02	7	6	2	49	37	7	30	1	0	0	0	12	2	0	.167	2	7	0	1	1.3	1.000
			3rd		**7th**	**7th**		**9th**	**4th**	**6th**			**10th**	**1st**													
WORLD SERIES																											
1974	**LA**	**N**	1	0	1.000	2.77	2	2	0	13	9	3	12	0	0	0	0	3	0	0	.000	0	2	0	0	1.0	1.000
1977			1	0	1.000	3.94	2	2	1	16	17	1	6	0	0	0	0	6	0	0	.000	1	1	0	0	1.0	1.000
1978			0	2	.000	7.50	2	2	0	12	17	4	8	0	0	0	0	0	0	0	—	0	0	0	0	0.0	.000
1982	**MIL**	**A**	0	1	.000	7.84	2	2	0	10.1	12	1	5	0	0	0	0	0	0	0	—	1	2	0	0	1.5	1.000
4 yrs.			2	3	.400	5.26	8	8	1	51.1	55	9	31	0	0	0	0	9	0	0	.000	2	5	0	0	0.9	1.000
								10th																			

Johnny Sutton

SUTTON, JOHNNY IKE BR TR 5′11″ 185 lbs.
B. Nov. 13, 1952, Dallas, Tex.

Year	Team	Lg	W	L	PCT	ERA	G	GS	CG	IP	H	BB	SO	ShO	Relief Pitching W	Relief Pitching L	Relief Pitching SV	Batting AB	Batting H	Batting HR	BA	PO	A	E	DP	TC/G	FA
1977	**STL**	**N**	2	1	.667	2.63	14	0	0	24	28	9	9	0	2	1	0	1	0	0	.000	1	5	0	2	0.4	1.000
1978	**MIN**	**A**	0	0	—	3.48	17	0	0	44	46	15	18	0	0	0	0	0	0	0	—	2	6	2	0	0.6	.800
2 yrs.			2	1	.667	3.18	31	0	0	68	74	24	27	0	2	1	0	1	0	0	.000	3	11	2	2	0.5	.875

Bill Swabach

SWABACH, WILLIAM
Deceased.

Year	Team	Lg	W	L	PCT	ERA	G	GS	CG	IP	H	BB	SO	ShO	Relief Pitching W	Relief Pitching L	Relief Pitching SV	Batting AB	Batting H	Batting HR	BA	PO	A	E	DP	TC/G	FA
1887	**NY**	**N**	0	2	.000	5.06	2	2	2	16	27	6	6	0	0	0	0	7	0	0	.000	0	3	0	0	1.5	1.000

Bill Swaggerty

SWAGGERTY, WILLIAM DAVID BR TR 6′ 2″ 190 lbs.
B. Dec. 5, 1956, Sanford, Fla.

Year	Team	Lg	W	L	PCT	ERA	G	GS	CG	IP	H	BB	SO	ShO	Relief Pitching W	Relief Pitching L	Relief Pitching SV	Batting AB	Batting H	Batting HR	BA	PO	A	E	DP	TC/G	FA
1983	**BAL**	**A**	1	1	.500	2.91	7	2	0	21.2	23	6	7	0	1	1	0	0	0	0	—	4	7	0	0	1.6	1.000
1984			3	2	.600	5.21	23	6	0	57	68	21	18	0	2	0	0	0	0	0	—	3	6	2	1	0.5	.818
1985			0	0	—	5.40	1	0	0	1.2	3	2	2	0	0	0	0	0	0	0	—	0	0	0	0	0.0	.000
1986			0	0	—	18.00	1	0	0	1	6	1	1	0	0	0	0	0	0	0	—	0	0	0	0	0.0	.000
4 yrs.			4	3	.571	4.76	32	8	0	81.1	100	30	28	0	3	1	0	0	0	0		7	13	2	1	0.7	.909

Cy Swaim

SWAIM, JOHN HILLARY 6′ 6″ 180 lbs.
B. Mar. 11, 1874, Cadwallader, Ohio D. Dec. 27, 1945, Eustis, Fla.

Year	Team	Lg	W	L	PCT	ERA	G	GS	CG	IP	H	BB	SO	ShO	Relief Pitching W	Relief Pitching L	Relief Pitching SV	Batting AB	Batting H	Batting HR	BA	PO	A	E	DP	TC/G	FA
1897	WAS	N	10	11	.476	4.41	27	19	16	194	227	61	55	0	1	0	0	75	17	0	.227	12	25	6	1	1.6	.860
1898			3	11	.214	4.26	16	13	9	101.1	119	28	30	0	0	1	1	35	5	0	.143	4	18	4	1	1.6	.846
2 yrs.			13	22	.371	4.36	43	32	25	295.1	346	89	85	0	1	1	1	110	22	0	.200	16	43	10	2	1.6	.855

Craig Swan

SWAN, CRAIG STEVEN BR TR 6′ 3″ 215 lbs.
B. Nov. 30, 1950, Van Nuys, Calif.

Year	Team	Lg	W	L	PCT	ERA	G	GS	CG	IP	H	BB	SO	ShO	Relief Pitching W	Relief Pitching L	Relief Pitching SV	Batting AB	Batting H	Batting HR	BA	PO	A	E	DP	TC/G	FA
1973	NY	N	0	1	.000	8.64	3	1	0	8.1	16	2	4	0	0	0	0	2	0	0	.000	0	1	1	0	0.7	.500
1974			1	3	.250	4.50	7	5	0	30	28	21	10	0	0	1	0	11	4	0	.364	0	7	1	0	1.1	.875
1975			1	3	.250	6.39	6	6	0	31	38	13	19	0	0	0	0	7	0	0	.000	1	1	0	0	0.3	1.000
1976			6	9	.400	3.55	23	22	2	132	129	44	89	1	0	0	0	39	4	0	.103	6	17	2	0	1.1	.920
1977			9	10	.474	4.22	26	24	2	147	153	56	71	1	0	0	0	48	9	0	.188	13	10	2	0	1.0	.920
1978			9	6	.600	**2.43**	29	28	5	207	164	58	125	1	0	0	0	65	10	0	.154	17	30	2	5	1.7	.959
1979			14	13	.519	3.30	35	35	10	251	241	57	145	3	0	0	0	81	10	0	.123	17	29	0	3	1.3	1.000
1980			5	9	.357	3.59	21	21	4	128	117	30	79	1	0	0	0	32	7	0	.219	4	10	3	0	0.8	.824
1981			0	2	.000	3.21	5	3	0	14	10	1	9	0	0	0	0	3	0	0	.000	0	2	0	0	0.4	1.000
1982			11	7	.611	3.35	37	21	2	166.1	165	37	67	0	2	0	1	44	8	1	.182	16	18	0	0	0.9	1.000
1983			2	8	.200	5.51	27	18	0	96.1	112	42	43	0	0	0	1	26	2	0	.077	4	10	0	0	0.5	1.000
1984	2 teams	NY N	(10G 1–0)		CAL A	(2G 0–1)																					
″	total		1	1	.500	8.75	12	1	0	23.2	26	7	12	0	1	0	0	0	0	0		1	3	0	0	0.3	1.000
12 yrs.			59	72	.450	3.75	231	185	25	1234.2	1199	368	673	7	3	1	2	358	54	1	.151	79	138	11	8	1.0	.952

Ducky Swan

SWAN, HARRY GORDON BR TR 5′10″ 165 lbs.
B. Aug. 11, 1887, Lancaster, Pa. D. May 9, 1946, Pittsburgh, Pa.

Year	Team	Lg	W	L	PCT	ERA	G	GS	CG	IP	H	BB	SO	ShO	Relief Pitching W	Relief Pitching L	Relief Pitching SV	Batting AB	Batting H	Batting HR	BA	PO	A	E	DP	TC/G	FA
1914	KC	F	0	0	—	0.00	1	0	0	1	0	1	1	0	0	0	0	0	0	0	—	0	0	0	0	0.0	.000

Russ Swan

SWAN, RUSSELL HOWARD BL TL 6′ 4″ 210 lbs.
B. Jan. 3, 1964, Fremont, Calif.

Year	Team	Lg	W	L	PCT	ERA	G	GS	CG	IP	H	BB	SO	ShO	Relief Pitching W	Relief Pitching L	Relief Pitching SV	Batting AB	Batting H	Batting HR	BA	PO	A	E	DP	TC/G	FA
1989	SF	N	0	2	.000	10.80	2	2	0	6.2	11	4	2	0	0	0	0	2	0	0	.000	1	1	0	0	1.0	1.000
1990	2 teams	SF N	(2G 0–1)		SEA A	(11G 2–3)																					
″	total		2	4	.333	3.65	13	9	0	49.1	48	22	16	0	0	0	0	1	0	0	.000	3	8	0	0	0.8	1.000
1991	SEA	A	6	2	.750	3.43	63	0	0	78.2	81	28	33	0	6	2	2	0	0	0	—	3	16	1	1	0.3	.950
1992			3	10	.231	4.74	55	9	1	104.1	104	45	45	0	1	5	9	0	0	0	—	7	23	1	0	0.6	.968
1993			3	3	.500	9.15	23	0	0	19.2	25	18	10	0	3	3	0	0	0	0	—	0	6	0	0	0.3	1.000
1994	CLE	A	0	1	.000	11.25	12	0	0	8	13	7	2	0	0	1	0	0	0	0	—	0	2	0	0	0.2	1.000
6 yrs.			14	22	.389	4.83	168	20	1	266.2	282	124	108	0	10	11	11	3	0	0	.000	14	56	2	1	0.4	.972

Red Swanson

SWANSON, ARTHUR LEONARD BR TR 6′ 1½″ 175 lbs.
B. Oct. 15, 1936, Baton Rouge, La.

Year	Team	Lg	W	L	PCT	ERA	G	GS	CG	IP	H	BB	SO	ShO	Relief Pitching W	Relief Pitching L	Relief Pitching SV	Batting AB	Batting H	Batting HR	BA	PO	A	E	DP	TC/G	FA
1955	PIT	N	0	0	—	18.00	1	0	0	2	2	3	0	0	0	0	0	0	0	0	—	0	0	0	0	0.0	.000
1956			0	0	—	10.03	9	0	0	11.2	21	8	5	0	0	0	0	0	0	0	—	1	5	0	0	0.7	1.000
1957			3	3	.500	3.72	32	8	1	72.2	68	31	29	0	0	0	0	13	0	0	.000	4	8	0	1	0.4	1.000
3 yrs.			3	3	.500	4.90	42	8	1	86.1	91	42	34	0	0	0	0	13	0	0	.000	5	13	0	1	0.4	1.000

Ed Swartwood

SWARTWOOD, CYRUS EDWARD BL TR 198 lbs.
B. Jan. 12, 1859, Rockford, Ill. D. May 15, 1924, Pittsburgh, Pa.

Year	Team	Lg	W	L	PCT	ERA	G	GS	CG	IP	H	BB	SO	ShO	Relief Pitching W	Relief Pitching L	Relief Pitching SV	Batting AB	Batting H	Batting HR	BA	PO	A	E	DP	TC/G	FA
1884	PIT	AA	0	0	—	*11.57*	1	0	0	2.1	6	1	0	0	0	0	0	399	115	0	.288	1	0	1	0	2.0	.500
1890	TOL	AA	0	0	—	*3.00*	1	0	0	3	2	0	1	0	0	0	0	462	151	3	.327	133	10	32	3	2.3	.817
2 yrs.			0	0		6.75	2	0	0	5.1	8	1	1	0	0	0	0	*				1930	182	257	65	3.2	.892

Bud Swartz

SWARTZ, SHERWIN MERLE BL TL 6′ 2½″ 180 lbs.
B. June 13, 1929, Tulsa, Okla.

Year	Team	Lg	W	L	PCT	ERA	G	GS	CG	IP	H	BB	SO	ShO	Relief Pitching W	Relief Pitching L	Relief Pitching SV	Batting AB	Batting H	Batting HR	BA	PO	A	E	DP	TC/G	FA
1947	STL	A	0	0	—	6.75	5	0	0	5.1	9	7	1	0	0	0	0	1	1	0	1.000	0	0	0	0	0.0	.000

Dazzy Swartz

SWARTZ, VERNON MONROE (Monty) BR TR 5′11″ 182 lbs.
B. Jan. 1, 1897, Farmersville, Ohio D. Jan. 13, 1980, Germantown, Ohio.

Year	Team	Lg	W	L	PCT	ERA	G	GS	CG	IP	H	BB	SO	ShO	Relief Pitching W	Relief Pitching L	Relief Pitching SV	Batting AB	Batting H	Batting HR	BA	PO	A	E	DP	TC/G	FA
1920	CIN	N	0	1	.000	4.50	1	1	1	12	17	2	2	0	0	0	0	4	2	0	.500	0	4	0	0	4.0	1.000

Dave Swartzbaugh

SWARTZBAUGH, DAVID THEODORE BR TR 6′ 2″ 195 lbs.
B. Feb. 11, 1968, Middletown, Ohio

Year	Team	Lg	W	L	PCT	ERA	G	GS	CG	IP	H	BB	SO	ShO	Relief Pitching W	Relief Pitching L	Relief Pitching SV	Batting AB	Batting H	Batting HR	BA	PO	A	E	DP	TC/G	FA
1995	CHI	N	0	0	—	0.00	7	0	0	7.1	5	3	5	0	0	0	0	0	0	0	—	0	0	0	0	0.0	.000

Park Swartzel

SWARTZEL, PARKE B. BR TR
B. Nov. 21, 1865, Knightstown, Ind. D. Jan. 3, 1940, Los Angeles, Calif.

Year	Team	Lg	W	L	PCT	ERA	G	GS	CG	IP	H	BB	SO	ShO	Relief Pitching W	Relief Pitching L	Relief Pitching SV	Batting AB	Batting H	Batting HR	BA	PO	A	E	DP	TC/G	FA
1889	KC	AA	19	27	.413	4.32	48	47	45	410.1	**481**	117	147	0	0	0	1	174	25	0	.144	24	145	12	6	3.5	.934

Bill Sweeney

SWEENEY, WILLIAM J. TR
B. 1858, Philadelphia, Pa. D. Aug. 2, 1903, Philadelphia, Pa.

Year	Team	Lg	W	L	PCT	ERA	G	GS	CG	IP	H	BB	SO	ShO	Relief Pitching W	Relief Pitching L	Relief Pitching SV	Batting AB	Batting H	Batting HR	BA	PO	A	E	DP	TC/G	FA
1882	PHI	AA	9	11	.450	*2.91*	20	20	18	170	178	42	48	0	0	0	0	88	14	0	.159	12	51	9	0	2.9	.875
1884	BAL	U	**40**	21	.656	*2.59*	**62**	**60**	**58**	**538**	**522**	74	374	4	1	1	0	296	71	0	.240	44	162	46	5	3.1	.817
2 yrs.			49	32	.605	2.67	82	80	76	708	700	116	422	4	1	1	0	384	85	0	.221	56	213	55	5	3.1	.830

Charlie Sweeney

SWEENEY, CHARLES J. BR TR 5′10½″ 160 lbs.
B. Apr. 13, 1863, San Francisco, Calif. D. Apr. 4, 1902, San Francisco, Calif.

Year	Team	Lg	W	L	PCT	ERA	G	GS	CG	IP	H	BB	SO	ShO	Relief Pitching W	Relief Pitching L	Relief Pitching SV	Batting AB	Batting H	Batting HR	BA	PO	A	E	DP	TC/G	FA
1883	PRO	N	7	7	.500	*3.13*	20	18	14	146.2	142	28	48	0	0	0	0	87	19	0	.218	0	1	1	0	2.0	.500
1884	2 teams	PRO N	(27G 17–8)		STL U	(33G 24–7)																					
″	total		41	15	.732	1.70	60	56	53	492	360	42	337	6	**1**	**2**	1	339	104	2	.307	92	127	15	5	2.5	.936
1885	STL	N	11	21	.344	*3.93*	35	35	32	275	276	50	84	2	0	0	0	267	55	0	.206	81	67	27	3	2.4	.846
1886			5	6	.455	4.16	11	11	11	93	108	39	28	0	0	0	0	64	16	0	.250	9	26	5	1	2.4	.875
1887	CLE	AA	0	3	.000	8.25	3	3	3	24	42	13	8	0	0	0	0	133	30	0	.226	173	17	20	4	5.7	.905
5 yrs.			64	52	.552	2.87	129	123	113	1030.2	928	172	505	8	1	2	1	*				384	276	78	14	3.0	.894

Leo Sweetland

SWEETLAND, LEO (Sugar) BR TL 5′11½″ 155 lbs.
B. Aug. 15, 1901, St. Ignace, Mich. D. Mar. 4, 1974, Melbourne, Fla. BB 1930–1931

Year	Team		W	L	PCT	ERA	G	GS	CG	IP	H	BB	SO	ShO	Relief Pitching W	Relief Pitching L	Relief Pitching SV	Batting AB	Batting H	HR	BA	PO	A	E	DP	TC/G	FA
1927	PHI	N	2	10	.167	6.16	21	13	6	103.2	147	53	21	0	0	1	0	38	12	0	.316	7	43	1	3	2.4	.980
1928			3	15	.167	6.58	37	18	5	135.1	163	97	23	0	1	3	2	47	9	0	.191	8	44	4	3	1.5	.929
1929			13	11	.542	5.11	43	25	10	204.1	255	87	47	2	2	0	2	89	26	0	.292	14	64	3	1	1.9	.963
1930			7	15	.318	7.71	34	25	8	167	271	60	36	1	0	2	0	57	16	0	.281	10	38	3	2	1.5	.941
1931	CHI	N	8	7	.533	5.04	26	14	9	130.1	156	61	32	0	1	1	0	56	15	0	.268	5	30	4	0	1.5	.897
5 yrs.			33	58	.363	6.10	161	95	38	740.2	992	358	159	3	4	7	4	287	78	0	.272	44	219	15	9	1.7	.946

Steve Swetonic

SWETONIC, STEPHEN ALBERT BR TR 5′11″ 185 lbs.
B. Aug. 13, 1903, Mt. Pleasant, Pa. D. Apr. 22, 1974, Canonsburg, Pa.

Year	Team		W	L	PCT	ERA	G	GS	CG	IP	H	BB	SO	ShO	Relief Pitching W	Relief Pitching L	Relief Pitching SV	Batting AB	Batting H	HR	BA	PO	A	E	DP	TC/G	FA
1929	PIT	N	8	10	.444	4.82	41	12	3	143.2	172	50	35	0	5	**5**	5	48	13	0	.271	7	41	2	0	1.2	.960
1930			6	6	.500	4.47	23	6	3	96.2	107	27	35	1	4	2	5	36	4	0	.111	3	16	0	3	0.8	1.000
1931			0	2	.000	3.90	14	0	0	27.2	28	16	8	0	0	2	1	7	1	0	.143	1	5	0	0	0.4	1.000
1932			11	6	.647	2.82	24	19	11	162.2	134	55	39	**4**	0	0	0	54	5	0	.093	3	31	0	0	1.4	1.000
1933			12	12	.500	3.50	31	21	8	164.2	166	64	37	3	3	3	0	55	11	0	.200	4	34	2	2	1.3	.950
5 yrs.			37	36	.507	3.81	133	58	25	595.1	607	212	154	8	12	12	11	200	34	0	.170	18	127	4	5	1.1	.973

Bill Swift

SWIFT, WILLIAM CHARLES BR TR 6′ 170 lbs.
B. Oct. 27, 1961, Portland, Me.

Year	Team		W	L	PCT	ERA	G	GS	CG	IP	H	BB	SO	ShO	Relief Pitching W	Relief Pitching L	Relief Pitching SV	Batting AB	Batting H	HR	BA	PO	A	E	DP	TC/G	FA
1985	SEA	A	6	10	.375	4.77	23	21	0	120.2	131	48	55	0	1	0	0	0	0	0	—	10	18	1	1	1.3	.966
1986			2	9	.182	5.46	29	17	1	115.1	148	55	55	0	0	0	0	0	0	0	—	13	21	1	1	1.2	.971
1988			8	12	.400	4.59	38	24	6	174.2	199	65	47	1	3	1	0	0	0	0	—	19	33	4	3	1.5	.929
1989			7	3	.700	4.43	37	16	0	130	140	38	45	0	2	0	1	0	0	0	—	18	39	2	5	1.6	.966
1990			6	4	.600	2.39	55	8	0	128	135	21	42	0	3	2	6	0	0	0	—	10	21	2	1	0.6	.939
1991			1	2	.333	1.99	71	0	0	90.1	74	26	48	0	1	2	17	0	0	0	—	6	25	3	4	0.5	.912
1992	SF	N	10	4	.714	**2.08**	30	22	3	164.2	144	43	77	2	1	1	1	51	8	0	.157	18	33	1	3	1.7	.981
1993			21	8	.724	2.82	34	34	1	232.2	195	55	157	1	0	0	0	80	21	0	.263	17	44	6	3	2.0	.910
1994			8	7	.533	3.38	17	17	0	109.1	109	31	62	0	0	0	0	32	6	0	.188	8	12	2	1	1.3	.909
1995	CLR	N	9	3	.750	4.94	19	19	0	105.2	122	43	68	0	0	0	0	36	7	1	.194	9	27	1	2	1.9	.973
10 yrs.			78	62	.557	3.62	353	178	11	1371.1	1397	425	656	4	11	6	25	199	42	1	.211	128	273	23	24	1.2	.946
DIVISIONAL PLAYOFF SERIES																											
1995	CLR	N	0	0	—	6.00	1	1	0	6	7	2	3	0	0	0	0	3	0	0	.000	0	0	0	0	0.0	.000

Bill Swift

SWIFT, WILLIAM VINCENT BR TR 6′ 1½″ 192 lbs.
B. Jan. 10, 1908, Elmira, N. Y. D. Feb. 23, 1969, Bartow, Fla.

Year	Team		W	L	PCT	ERA	G	GS	CG	IP	H	BB	SO	ShO	Relief Pitching W	Relief Pitching L	Relief Pitching SV	Batting AB	Batting H	HR	BA	PO	A	E	DP	TC/G	FA
1932	PIT	N	14	10	.583	3.61	39	23	11	214.1	205	26	64	0	6	1	4	78	15	0	.192	8	27	2	1	0.9	.946
1933			14	10	.583	3.13	37	29	13	218.1	214	36	64	2	2	0	0	82	20	0	.244	11	39	2	1	1.4	.962
1934			11	13	.458	3.98	37	24	13	212.2	244	46	81	1	1	2	0	84	18	0	.214	8	38	2	0	1.3	.958
1935			15	8	.652	2.70	39	21	11	203.2	193	37	74	3	3	4	1	78	19	0	.244	4	23	0	2	0.7	1.000
1936			16	16	.500	4.01	45	31	17	262.1	275	63	92	0	4	1	2	105	31	2	.295	4	36	2	3	0.9	.952
1937			9	10	.474	3.95	36	17	9	164	160	34	84	0	2	2	3	54	9	0	.167	4	36	2	1	1.2	.952
1938			7	5	.583	3.24	36	9	2	150	155	40	77	0	5	2	4	50	10	1	.200	1	26	2	1	0.8	.931
1939			5	7	.417	3.89	36	8	2	129.2	150	28	56	1	2	4	4	42	10	0	.238	2	14	0	0	0.4	1.000
1940	BOS	N	1	1	.500	2.89	4	0	0	9.1	12	7	7	0	1	1	1	3	0	0	.000	0	2	0	0	0.5	1.000
1941	BKN	N	3	0	1.000	3.27	9	0	0	22	26	7	9	0	3	0	1	5	1	0	.200	0	3	0	0	0.3	1.000
1943	CHI	A	0	2	.000	4.21	18	1	0	51.1	48	27	28	0	0	1	0	10	1	0	.100	1	2	1	0	0.2	.750
11 yrs.			95	82	.537	3.58	336	163	78	1637.2	1682	351	636	7	29	18	20	591	134	3	.227	43	246	13	9	0.9	.957

Oad Swigart

SWIGART, OADIS VAUGHN BL TR 6′ 175 lbs.
B. Feb. 13, 1915, Archie, Mo.

Year	Team		W	L	PCT	ERA	G	GS	CG	IP	H	BB	SO	ShO	Relief Pitching W	Relief Pitching L	Relief Pitching SV	Batting AB	Batting H	HR	BA	PO	A	E	DP	TC/G	FA
1939	PIT	N	1	1	.500	4.44	3	3	1	24.1	27	6	8	1	0	0	0	8	2	0	.250	2	3	0	1	1.7	1.000
1940			0	2	.000	4.43	7	2	0	22.1	27	10	9	0	0	1	0	5	1	0	.200	0	6	0	0	0.9	1.000
2 yrs.			1	3	.250	4.44	10	5	1	46.2	54	16	17	1	0	1	0	13	3	0	.231	2	9	0	1	1.1	1.000

Ad Swigler

SWIGLER, ADAM WILLIAM BR TR 5′10″ 180 lbs.
B. Sept. 21, 1895, Philadelphia, Pa. D. Feb. 5, 1975, Philadelphia, Pa.

Year	Team		W	L	PCT	ERA	G	GS	CG	IP	H	BB	SO	ShO	Relief Pitching W	Relief Pitching L	Relief Pitching SV	Batting AB	Batting H	HR	BA	PO	A	E	DP	TC/G	FA
1917	NY	N	0	1	.000	6.00	1	1	0	6	7	8	4	0	0	0	0	2	0	0	.000	0	2	0	0	2.0	1.000

Greg Swindell

SWINDELL, FOREST GREGORY BR TL 6′ 2″ 225 lbs.
B. Jan. 2, 1965, Fort Worth, Tex.

Year	Team		W	L	PCT	ERA	G	GS	CG	IP	H	BB	SO	ShO	Relief Pitching W	Relief Pitching L	Relief Pitching SV	Batting AB	Batting H	HR	BA	PO	A	E	DP	TC/G	FA
1986	CLE	A	5	2	.714	4.23	9	9	1	61.2	57	15	46	0	0	0	0	0	0	0	—	2	12	0	1	1.6	1.000
1987			3	8	.273	5.10	16	15	4	102.1	112	37	97	1	0	0	0	0	0	0	—	0	13	1	1	0.9	.929
1988			18	14	.563	3.20	33	33	12	242	234	45	180	4	0	0	0	0	0	0	—	8	29	1	0	1.2	.974
1989			13	6	.684	3.37	28	28	5	184.1	170	51	129	2	0	0	0	0	0	0	—	7	25	0	1	1.1	1.000
1990			12	9	.571	4.40	34	34	3	214.2	245	47	135	0	0	0	0	0	0	0	—	8	20	1	1	0.9	.966
1991			9	16	.360	3.48	33	33	7	238	241	31	169	0	0	0	0	0	0	0	—	7	30	1	2	1.2	.974
1992	CIN	N	12	8	.600	2.70	31	30	5	213.2	210	41	138	3	0	0	0	80	10	0	.125	6	33	1	2	1.3	.975
1993	HOU	N	12	13	.480	4.16	31	30	1	190.1	215	40	124	1	0	0	0	60	11	0	.183	2	32	1	0	1.1	.971
1994			8	9	.471	4.37	24	24	1	148.1	175	26	74	0	0	0	0	44	11	0	.250	6	13	1	0	0.8	.950
1995			10	9	.526	4.47	33	26	1	153	180	39	96	1	2	0	0	50	12	0	.240	9	31	1	3	1.2	.976
10 yrs.			102	94	.520	3.80	272	262	40	1748.1	1839	372	1188	12	2	0	0	234	44	0	.188	55	238	8	11	1.1	.973

Josh Swindell

SWINDELL, JOSHUA ERNEST BR TR 6′ 180 lbs.
B. July 5, 1885, Rose Hill, Kans. D. Mar. 19, 1969, Fruita, Colo.

Year	Team		W	L	PCT	ERA	G	GS	CG	IP	H	BB	SO	ShO	Relief Pitching W	Relief Pitching L	Relief Pitching SV	Batting AB	Batting H	HR	BA	PO	A	E	DP	TC/G	FA
1911	CLE	A	0	1	.000	2.08	4	1	1	17.1	19	4	6	0	0	0	0	4	1	0	.250	1	3	1	0	1.3	.800

Paul Swingle

SWINGLE, PAUL CHRISTOPHER BR TR 6′ 185 lbs.
B. Dec. 21, 1966, Inglewood, Calif.

Year	Team		W	L	PCT	ERA	G	GS	CG	IP	H	BB	SO	ShO	Relief Pitching W	Relief Pitching L	Relief Pitching SV	Batting AB	Batting H	HR	BA	PO	A	E	DP	TC/G	FA
1993	CAL	A	0	1	.000	8.38	9	0	0	9.2	15	6	6	0	0	1	0	0	0	0	—	0	1	0	0	0.1	1.000

Len Swormstedt

SWORMSTEDT, LEONARD JORDAN BR TR 5′11½″ 165 lbs.
B. Oct. 6, 1878, Cincinnati, Ohio D. July 19, 1964, Salem, Mass.

Year	Team		W	L	PCT	ERA	G	GS	CG	IP	H	BB	SO	ShO	Relief Pitching W	Relief Pitching L	Relief Pitching SV	Batting AB	Batting H	HR	BA	PO	A	E	DP	TC/G	FA
1901	**CIN**	**N**	2	1	.667	1.73	3	3	3	26	19	5	13	0	0	0	0	9	0	0	.000	2	6	0	0	2.7	1.000
1902			0	2	.000	4.00	2	2	2	18	22	5	3	0	0	0	0	6	0	0	.000	1	3	0	0	2.0	1.000
1906	**BOS**	**A**	1	1	.500	1.29	3	2	2	21	17	0	6	0	0	0	0	8	1	0	.125	1	4	1	0	2.0	.833
3 yrs.			3	4	.429	2.22	8	7	7	65	58	10	22	0	0	0	0	23	1	0	.043	4	13	1	0	2.3	.944

Bob Sykes

SYKES, ROBERT JOSEPH BB TL 6′ 1″ 195 lbs.
B. Dec. 11, 1954, Neptune, N. J.

Year	Team		W	L	PCT	ERA	G	GS	CG	IP	H	BB	SO	ShO	Relief Pitching W	Relief Pitching L	Relief Pitching SV	Batting AB	Batting H	HR	BA	PO	A	E	DP	TC/G	FA
1977	**DET**	**A**	5	7	.417	4.40	32	20	3	133	141	50	58	0	0	1	0	0	0	0	—	6	20	2	3	0.9	.929
1978			6	6	.500	3.94	22	10	3	93.2	99	34	58	2	3	1	2	0	0	0	—	1	7	1	0	0.4	.889
1979	**STL**	**N**	4	3	.571	6.18	13	11	0	67	86	34	35	0	0	0	0	21	2	0	.095	0	7	0	0	0.5	1.000
1980			6	10	.375	4.64	27	19	4	126	134	54	50	3	0	3	0	39	4	0	.103	4	14	1	2	0.7	.947
1981			2	0	1.000	4.62	22	1	0	37	37	18	14	0	2	0	0	2	0	0	.000	4	8	0	1	0.5	1.000
5 yrs.			23	26	.469	4.65	116	61	10	456.2	497	190	215	5	5	5	2	62	6	0	.097	15	56	4	6	0.6	.947

Lou Sylvester

SYLVESTER, LOUIS J. BR TR 5′ 3″ 165 lbs.
B. Feb. 14, 1855, Springfield, Ill. Deceased.

Year	Team		W	L	PCT	ERA	G	GS	CG	IP	H	BB	SO	ShO	Relief Pitching W	Relief Pitching L	Relief Pitching SV	Batting AB	Batting H	HR	BA	PO	A	E	DP	TC/G	FA
1884	**CIN**	**U**	0	1	.000	*3.58*	6	1	1	32.2	32	6	7	0	0	0	1	*				111	28	39	2	2.0	.781

Jeff Tabaka

TABAKA, JEFFREY JON BR TL 6′ 2″ 195 lbs.
B. Jan. 17, 1964, Barberton, Ohio

Year	Team		W	L	PCT	ERA	G	GS	CG	IP	H	BB	SO	ShO	Relief Pitching W	Relief Pitching L	Relief Pitching SV	Batting AB	Batting H	HR	BA	PO	A	E	DP	TC/G	FA
1994	**2 teams**	**PIT N** (5G 0–0) **SD N** (34G 3–1)																									
″	**total**		3	1	.750	5.27	39	0	0	41	32	27	32	0	3	1	1	1	1	0	1.000	3	4	1	0	0.2	.875
1995	**2 teams**	**SD N** (10G 0–0) **HOU N** (24G 1–0)																									
″	**total**		1	0	1.000	3.23	34	0	0	30.2	27	17	25	0	1	0	0	1	0	0	.000	1	3	0	0	0.1	1.000
2 yrs.			4	1	.800	4.40	73	0	0	71.2	59	44	57	0	4	1	1	2	1	0	.500	4	7	1	0	0.2	.917

John Taber

TABER, JOHN PARDON BR TR 5′ 8″
B. June 28, 1868, Acushnet, Mass. D. Feb. 21, 1940, Boston, Mass.

Year	Team		W	L	PCT	ERA	G	GS	CG	IP	H	BB	SO	ShO	Relief Pitching W	Relief Pitching L	Relief Pitching SV	Batting AB	Batting H	HR	BA	PO	A	E	DP	TC/G	FA
1890	**BOS**	**N**	0	1	.000	4.15	2	1	1	13	11	8	3	0	0	0	1	6	0	0	.000	0	4	0	0	2.0	1.000

Lefty Taber

TABER, EDWARD TIMOTHY BL TL 6′ 180 lbs.
B. Jan. 11, 1900, Rock Island, Ill. D. Nov. 5, 1983, Lincoln, Neb.

Year	Team		W	L	PCT	ERA	G	GS	CG	IP	H	BB	SO	ShO	Relief Pitching W	Relief Pitching L	Relief Pitching SV	Batting AB	Batting H	HR	BA	PO	A	E	DP	TC/G	FA
1926	**PHI**	**N**	0	0	—	7.56	6	0	0	8.1	8	5	0	0	0	0	0	1	0	0	.000	0	2	0	0	0.3	1.000
1927			0	1	.000	18.90	3	1	0	3.1	8	5	0	0	0	0	0	1	0	0	.000	1	1	0	0	0.7	1.000
2 yrs.			0	1	.000	10.80	9	1	0	11.2	16	10	0	0	0	0	0	2	0	0	.000	1	3	0	0	0.4	1.000

Jeff Tackett

TACKETT, JEFFREY WILSON BR TR 6′ 2″ 200 lbs.
B. Dec. 1, 1965, Fresno, Calif.

Year	Team		W	L	PCT	ERA	G	GS	CG	IP	H	BB	SO	ShO	Relief Pitching W	Relief Pitching L	Relief Pitching SV	Batting AB	Batting H	HR	BA	PO	A	E	DP	TC/G	FA
1993	**BAL**	**A**	0	0	—	0.00	1	0	0	1	1	1	0	0	0	0	0	*				22	0	0	0	3.7	1.000

John Taff

TAFF, JOHN GALLATIN BR TR 6′ 170 lbs.
B. June 3, 1890, Austin, Tex. D. May 15, 1961, Houston, Tex.

Year	Team		W	L	PCT	ERA	G	GS	CG	IP	H	BB	SO	ShO	Relief Pitching W	Relief Pitching L	Relief Pitching SV	Batting AB	Batting H	HR	BA	PO	A	E	DP	TC/G	FA
1913	**PHI**	**A**	0	1	.000	6.62	7	1	0	17.2	22	5	9	0	0	0	1	5	1	0	.200	0	6	0	0	0.9	1.000

Doug Taitt

TAITT, DOUGLAS JOHN (Poco) BL TR 6′ 176 lbs.
B. Aug. 3, 1902, Bay City, Mich. D. Dec. 12, 1970, Portland, Ore.

Year	Team		W	L	PCT	ERA	G	GS	CG	IP	H	BB	SO	ShO	Relief Pitching W	Relief Pitching L	Relief Pitching SV	Batting AB	Batting H	HR	BA	PO	A	E	DP	TC/G	FA
1928	**BOS**	**A**	0	0	—	27.00	1	0	0	1	2	2	1	0	0	0	0	*				252	19	7	8	2.0	.975

Fred Talbot

TALBOT, FREDERICK LEALAND (Bubby) BR TR 6′ 2″ 195 lbs.
B. June 28, 1941, Washington, D. C.

Year	Team		W	L	PCT	ERA	G	GS	CG	IP	H	BB	SO	ShO	Relief Pitching W	Relief Pitching L	Relief Pitching SV	Batting AB	Batting H	HR	BA	PO	A	E	DP	TC/G	FA
1963	**CHI**	**A**	0	0	—	3.00	1	0	0	3	2	4	2	0	0	0	0	1	0	0	.000	1	1	0	1	2.0	1.000
1964			4	5	.444	3.70	17	12	3	75.1	83	20	34	2	1	1	0	19	5	0	.263	4	9	0	0	0.8	1.000
1965	**KC**	**A**	10	12	.455	4.14	39	33	2	198	188	86	117	1	0	1	0	70	14	0	.200	15	30	4	3	1.3	.918
1966	**2 teams**	**KC A** (11G 4–4) **NY A** (23G 7–7)																									
″	**total**		11	11	.500	4.36	34	30	3	192	188	73	85	0	0	0	0	55	8	0	.145	17	30	2	1	1.4	.959
1967	**NY**	**A**	6	8	.429	4.22	29	22	2	138.2	132	54	61	0	1	1	0	38	6	1	.158	14	34	1	0	1.7	.980
1968			1	9	.100	3.36	29	11	1	99	89	42	67	0	1	1	0	17	2	1	.118	8	16	0	2	0.8	1.000
1969	**3 teams**	**NY A** (8G 0–0) **SEA A** (25G 5–8) **OAK A** (12G 1–2)																									
″	**total**		6	10	.375	4.38	45	18	1	146	160	54	83	1	2	2	1	41	7	2	.171	10	22	2	3	0.8	.941
1970	**OAK**	**A**	0	1	.000	9.00	1	0	0	2	2	1	0	0	0	1	0	0	0	0	—	0	1	0	0	1.0	1.000
8 yrs.			38	56	.404	4.12	195	126	12	854	844	334	449	4	5	7	1	241	42	4	.174	69	143	9	10	1.1	.959

Roy Talcott

TALCOTT, LeROY EVERETT BR TR 6′ 1½″ 180 lbs.
B. Jan. 16, 1920, Brookline, Mass.

Year	Team		W	L	PCT	ERA	G	GS	CG	IP	H	BB	SO	ShO	Relief Pitching W	Relief Pitching L	Relief Pitching SV	Batting AB	Batting H	HR	BA	PO	A	E	DP	TC/G	FA
1943	**BOS**	**N**	0	0	—	27.00	1	0	0	0.2	1	2	0	0	0	0	0	0	0	0	—	0	1	0	0	1.0	1.000

Vito Tamulis

TAMULIS, VITAUTRIS CASIMIRUS BL TL 5′ 9″ 170 lbs.
B. July 11, 1911, Cambridge, Mass. D. May 5, 1974, Nashville, Tenn.

Year	Team		W	L	PCT	ERA	G	GS	CG	IP	H	BB	SO	ShO	Relief Pitching W	Relief Pitching L	Relief Pitching SV	Batting AB	Batting H	HR	BA	PO	A	E	DP	TC/G	FA
1934	**NY**	**A**	1	0	1.000	0.00	1	1	1	9	7	1	5	1	0	0	0	4	1	0	.250	2	1	0	0	3.0	1.000
1935			10	5	.667	4.09	30	19	9	160.2	178	55	57	3	2	0	1	57	14	1	.246	7	29	1	0	1.2	.973
1938	**2 teams**	**STL A** (3G 0–3) **BKN N** (38G 12–6)																									
″	**total**		12	9	.571	4.17	41	20	9	175	207	50	81	0	3	3	2	60	9	0	.150	3	28	1	1	0.8	.969
1939	**BKN**	**N**	9	8	.529	4.37	39	17	8	158.2	177	45	83	1	1	1	4	55	10	0	.182	5	31	0	5	0.9	1.000
1940			8	5	.615	3.09	41	12	4	154.1	147	34	55	1	3	5	2	46	6	0	.130	6	28	2	3	0.9	.944
1941	**2 teams**	**PHI N** (6G 0–1) **BKN N** (12G 0–0)																									
″	**total**		0	1	.000	5.56	18	1	0	34	42	17	13	0	0	0	1	7	0	0	.000	2	8	0	0	0.6	1.000
6 yrs.			40	28	.588	3.97	170	70	31	691.2	758	202	294	6	9	9	10	229	40	1	.175	25	125	4	9	0.9	.974

Frank Tanana

TANANA, FRANK DARYL BL TL 6′ 2″ 180 lbs.
B. July 3, 1953, Detroit, Mich.

Year	Team		W	L	PCT	ERA	G	GS	CG	IP	H	BB	SO	ShO	Relief Pitching W	Relief Pitching L	Relief Pitching SV	Batting AB	Batting H	HR	BA	PO	A	E	DP	TC/G	FA
1973	**CAL**	**A**	2	2	.500	3.08	4	4	2	26.1	20	8	22	1	0	0	0	0	0	0	—	0	5	0	0	1.3	1.000
1974			14	19	.424	3.11	39	35	12	269	262	77	180	4	2	0	0	0	0	0	—	9	39	1	4	1.3	.980
1975			16	9	.640	2.62	34	33	16	257.1	211	73	**269**	5	0	0	0	0	0	0	—	9	44	2	5	1.6	.964
1976			19	10	.655	2.44	34	34	23	288	212	73	261	2	0	0	0	0	0	0	—	12	45	1	1	1.7	.983
1977			15	9	.625	**2.54**	31	31	20	241.1	201	61	205	**7**	0	0	0	0	0	0	—	15	37	1	2	1.7	.981

Frank Tanana *continued*

Year	Team		W	L	PCT	ERA	G	GS	CG	IP	H	BB	SO	ShO	Relief Pitching W	Relief Pitching L	Relief Pitching SV	Batting AB	Batting H	Batting HR	BA	PO	A	E	DP	TC/G	FA
1978			18	12	.600	3.65	33	33	10	239	239	60	137	4	0	0	0	0	0	0	—	8	25	0	2	1.0	1.000
1979			7	5	.583	3.90	18	17	2	90	93	25	46	1	0	0	0	0	0	0	—	3	12	1	1	0.9	.938
1980			11	12	.478	4.15	32	31	7	204	223	45	113	0	0	0	0	0	0	0	—	12	24	0	1	1.1	1.000
1981	**BOS**	**A**	4	10	.286	4.02	24	23	5	141	142	43	78	2	0	0	0	0	0	0	—	9	25	1	2	1.5	.971
1982	**TEX**	**A**	7	**18**	.280	4.21	30	30	7	194.1	199	55	87	0	0	0	0	0	0	0	—	8	30	1	0	1.3	.974
1983			7	9	.438	3.16	29	22	3	159.1	144	49	108	0	1	0	0	0	0	0	—	9	37	2	0	1.7	.958
1984			15	15	.500	3.25	35	35	9	246.1	234	81	141	1	0	0	0	0	0	0	—	18	35	0	2	1.5	1.000
1985	**2 teams**	**TEX A** (13G 2–7) **DET A** (20G 10–7)																									
″	**total**		12	14	.462	4.27	33	33	4	215	220	57	159	0	0	0	0	0	0	0		14	31	1	2	1.4	.978
1986	**DET**	**A**	12	9	.571	4.16	32	31	3	188.1	196	65	119	1	0	0	0	0	0	0	—	19	26	2	5	1.5	.957
1987			15	10	.600	3.91	34	34	5	218.2	216	56	146	3	0	0	0	0	0	0	—	14	35	0	2	1.4	1.000
1988			14	11	.560	4.21	32	32	2	203	213	64	127	0	0	0	0	0	0	0	—	11	31	1	4	1.3	.977
1989			10	14	.417	3.58	33	33	6	223.2	227	74	147	1	0	0	0	0	0	0	—	16	41	0	2	1.7	1.000
1990			9	8	.529	5.31	34	29	1	176.1	190	66	114	0	0	0	1	0	0	0	—	9	27	0	0	1.1	1.000
1991			13	12	.520	3.77	33	33	3	217.1	217	78	107	2	0	0	0	1	0	0	.000	12	36	1	3	1.5	.980
1992			13	11	.542	4.39	32	31	3	186.2	188	90	91	0	1	0	0	0	0	0	—	8	30	2	1	1.3	.950
1993	**2 teams**	**NY N** (29G 7–15) **NY A** (3G 0–2)																									
″	**total**		7	17	.292	4.35	32	32	0	202.2	216	55	116	0	0	0	0	58	9	0	.155	11	23	2	1	1.1	.944
21 yrs.			240	236	.504	3.66	638	616	143	4187.2	4063	1255	2773	34	4	0	1	59	9	0	.153	226	638	19	40	1.4	.978
LEAGUE CHAMPIONSHIP SERIES																											
1979	**CAL**	**A**	0	0	—	3.60	1	1	0	5	6	2	3	0	0	0	0	0	0	0	—	0	0	0	0	0.0	.000
1987	**DET**	**A**	0	1	.000	5.06	1	1	0	5.1	6	4	1	0	0	0	0	0	0	0	—	0	1	0	0	1.0	1.000
2 yrs.			0	1	.000	4.35	2	2	0	10.1	12	6	4	0	0	0	0	0	0	0		0	1	0	0	0.5	1.000

Jesse Tannehill

TANNEHILL, JESSE NILES (Tanny)	BB TL 5′ 8″ 150 lbs.
Brother of Lee Tannehill.	BL 1903
B. July 14, 1874, Dayton, Ky. D. Sept. 22, 1956, Dayton, Ky.	

Year	Team		W	L	PCT	ERA	G	GS	CG	IP	H	BB	SO	ShO	Relief Pitching W	Relief Pitching L	Relief Pitching SV	Batting AB	Batting H	Batting HR	BA	PO	A	E	DP	TC/G	FA
1894	**CIN**	**N**	1	0	1.000	7.14	5	2	1	29	37	16	7	0	0	0	1	11	0	0	.000	1	2	2	0	1.0	.600
1897	**PIT**	**N**	9	9	.500	4.25	21	16	11	142	172	24	40	1	1	2	1	184	49	0	.266	89	53	13	1	2.9	.916
1898			25	13	.658	2.95	43	38	34	326.2	338	63	93	5	1	0	2	152	44	1	.289	28	95	5	2	2.6	.961
1899			24	14	.632	2.73	41	35	32	313	354	51	64	3	**3**	1	1	132	34	0	.258	9	95	5	7	2.6	.954
1900			20	6	**.769**	2.88	29	27	23	234	247	43	50	2	0	0	0	110	37	0	.336	14	65	6	1	2.6	.929
1901			18	10	.643	**2.18**	32	30	25	252.1	240	36	118	4	0	0	1	135	33	1	.244	23	53	7	1	2.0	.916
1902			20	6	.769	1.95	26	24	23	231	203	25	100	2	**2**	0	0	148	43	1	.291	25	57	4	3	2.0	.953
1903	**NY**	**A**	15	15	.500	3.27	32	31	22	239.2	258	34	106	2	0	0	0	111	26	1	.234	14	83	3	2	2.7	.970
1904	**BOS**	**A**	21	11	.656	2.04	33	31	30	281.2	256	33	116	4	2	0	0	122	24	0	.197	12	107	1	4	3.4	.992
1905			22	9	.710	2.48	37	31	27	271.2	238	59	113	6	3	1	0	93	21	1	.226	9	97	6	3	3.0	.946
1906			13	11	.542	3.16	27	26	18	196.1	207	39	82	2	0	0	0	79	22	0	.278	15	58	4	1	2.9	.948
1907			6	7	.462	2.47	18	16	10	131	131	20	29	2	0	0	1	51	10	0	.196	9	42	1	3	2.9	.981
1908	**2 teams**	**BOS A** (1G 0–0) **WAS A** (10G 2–4)																									
″	**total**		2	4	.333	3.76	11	10	5	76.2	81	26	16	0	0	0	0	45	12	0	.267	5	34	4	2	3.9	.907
1909	**WAS**	**A**	1	1	.500	3.43	3	2	2	21	19	5	8	1	0	0	0	36	6	0	.167	14	9	0	1	1.9	1.000
1911	**CIN**	**N**	0	0	—	6.23	1	0	0	4.1	6	3	1	0	0	0	0	1	0	0	.000	0	1	0	0	1.0	1.000
15 yrs.			197	116	.629	2.79	359	319	263	2750.1	2787	477	943	34	12	4	7	*				267	851	61	31	2.6	.948

Bruce Tanner

TANNER, BRUCE MATTHEW	BL TR 6′ 3″ 220 lbs.
Son of Chuck Tanner.	
B. Dec. 9, 1961, New Castle, Pa.	

Year	Team		W	L	PCT	ERA	G	GS	CG	IP	H	BB	SO	ShO	Relief Pitching W	Relief Pitching L	Relief Pitching SV	Batting AB	Batting H	Batting HR	BA	PO	A	E	DP	TC/G	FA
1985	**CHI**	**A**	1	2	.333	5.33	10	4	0	27	34	13	9	0	0	0	0	0	0	0	—	3	7	1	1	1.1	.909

Kevin Tapani

TAPANI, KEVIN RAY	BR TR 6′ 180 lbs.
B. Feb. 18, 1964, Des Moines, Iowa	

Year	Team		W	L	PCT	ERA	G	GS	CG	IP	H	BB	SO	ShO	Relief Pitching W	Relief Pitching L	Relief Pitching SV	Batting AB	Batting H	Batting HR	BA	PO	A	E	DP	TC/G	FA
1989	**2 teams**	**NY N** (3G 0–0) **MIN A** (5G 2–2)																									
″	**total**		2	2	.500	3.83	8	5	0	40	39	12	23	0	0	0	0	2	0	0	.000	4	4	0	1	1.0	1.000
1990	**MIN**	**A**	12	8	.600	4.07	28	28	1	159.1	164	29	101	1	0	0	0	0	0	0	—	14	20	1	1	1.3	.971
1991			16	9	.640	2.99	34	34	4	244	225	40	135	1	0	0	0	0	0	0	—	26	26	1	2	1.6	.981
1992			16	11	.593	3.97	34	34	4	220	226	48	138	1	0	0	0	0	0	0	—	17	26	2	0	1.3	.956
1993			12	15	.444	4.43	36	35	3	225.2	243	57	150	1	0	0	0	0	0	0	—	17	32	0	2	1.4	1.000
1994			11	7	.611	4.62	24	24	4	156	181	39	91	1	0	0	0	0	0	0	—	11	27	1	2	1.6	.974
1995	**2 teams**	**MIN A** (20G 6–11) **LA N** (13G 4–2)																									
″	**total**		10	13	.435	4.96	33	31	3	190.2	227	48	131	1	0	0	0	17	3	0	.176	20	21	1	1	1.3	.976
7 yrs.			79	65	.549	4.10	197	191	19	1235.2	1305	273	769	6	0	0	0	19	3	0	.158	109	156	6	9	1.4	.978
DIVISIONAL PLAYOFF SERIES																											
1995	**LA**	**N**	0	0	—	81.00	2	0	0	0.1	0	4	1	0	0	0	0	0	0	0	—	0	0	0	0	0.0	.000
LEAGUE CHAMPIONSHIP SERIES																											
1991	**MIN**	**A**	0	1	.000	7.84	2	2	0	10.1	16	3	9	0	0	0	0	0	0	0	—	3	0	0	0	1.5	1.000
WORLD SERIES																											
1991	**MIN**	**A**	1	1	.500	4.50	2	2	0	12	13	2	7	0	0	0	0	1	0	0	.000	0	2	0	0	1.0	1.000

Al Tate

TATE, WALTER ALVIN	BR TR 6′ 180 lbs.
B. July 1, 1918, Coleman, Okla. D. May 8, 1993, Bountiful, Utah.	

Year	Team		W	L	PCT	ERA	G	GS	CG	IP	H	BB	SO	ShO	Relief Pitching W	Relief Pitching L	Relief Pitching SV	Batting AB	Batting H	Batting HR	BA	PO	A	E	DP	TC/G	FA
1946	**PIT**	**N**	0	1	.000	5.00	2	1	1	9	8	7	2	0	0	0	0	3	1	0	.333	0	3	0	0	1.5	1.000

Randy Tate

TATE, RANDALL LEE	BR TR 6′ 3″ 190 lbs.
B. Oct. 23, 1952, Florence, Ala.	

Year	Team		W	L	PCT	ERA	G	GS	CG	IP	H	BB	SO	ShO	Relief Pitching W	Relief Pitching L	Relief Pitching SV	Batting AB	Batting H	Batting HR	BA	PO	A	E	DP	TC/G	FA
1975	**NY**	**N**	5	13	.278	4.43	26	23	2	138	121	86	99	0	0	0	0	41	0	0	.000	11	19	2	0	1.2	.938

Stu Tate

TATE, STUART DOUGLAS	BR TR 6′ 3″ 205 lbs.
B. June 17, 1962, Huntsville, Ala.	

Year	Team		W	L	PCT	ERA	G	GS	CG	IP	H	BB	SO	ShO	Relief Pitching W	Relief Pitching L	Relief Pitching SV	Batting AB	Batting H	Batting HR	BA	PO	A	E	DP	TC/G	FA
1989	**SF**	**N**	0	0	—	3.38	2	0	0	2.2	3	0	4	0	0	0	0	0	0	0	—	0	0	0	0	0.0	.000

Ken Tatum

TATUM, KENNETH RAY BR TR 6′ 2″ 205 lbs.
B. Apr. 25, 1944, Alexandria, La.

Year	Team	Lg	W	L	PCT	ERA	G	GS	CG	IP	H	BB	SO	ShO	Relief Pitching W	Relief Pitching L	Relief Pitching SV	Batting AB	Batting H	Batting HR	BA	PO	A	E	DP	TC/G	FA
1969	**CAL**	**A**	7	2	.778	1.36	45	0	0	86.1	51	39	65	0	7	2	22	21	6	2	.286	1	12	0	0	0.3	1.000
1970			7	4	.636	2.93	62	0	0	89	68	26	50	0	7	4	17	11	2	1	.182	4	15	1	0	0.3	.950
1971	**BOS**	**A**	2	4	.333	4.17	36	1	0	54	50	25	21	0	2	3	9	10	3	1	.300	2	11	0	2	0.4	1.000
1972			0	2	.000	3.10	22	0	0	29	32	15	15	0	0	2	4	2	0	0	.000	1	4	1	0	0.3	.833
1973			0	0	—	9.00	1	0	0	4	6	3	0	0	0	0	0	0	0	0	—	0	0	0	0	0.0	.000
1974	**CHI**	**A**	0	0	—	4.71	10	1	0	21	23	9	5	0	0	0	0	1	0	0	.000	2	5	0	1	0.7	1.000
6 yrs.			16	12	.571	2.92	176	2	0	283.1	230	117	156	0	16	11	52	45	11	4	.244	10	47	2	3	0.3	.966

Walt Tauscher

TAUSCHER, WALTER EDWARD BR TR 6′ 1″ 186 lbs.
B. Nov. 22, 1901, LaSalle, Ill. D. Nov. 37, 1992, Winter Park, Fla.

Year	Team	Lg	W	L	PCT	ERA	G	GS	CG	IP	H	BB	SO	ShO	Relief Pitching W	Relief Pitching L	Relief Pitching SV	Batting AB	Batting H	Batting HR	BA	PO	A	E	DP	TC/G	FA
1928	**PIT**	**N**	0	0	—	4.91	17	0	0	29.1	28	12	7	0	0	0	1	6	1	0	.167	1	6	0	0	0.4	1.000
1931	**WAS**	**A**	1	0	1.000	7.50	6	0	0	12	24	4	5	0	1	0	0	0	0	0	—	1	9	1	2	1.8	.909
2 yrs.			1	0	1.000	5.66	23	0	0	41.1	52	16	12	0	1	0	1	6	1	0	.167	2	15	1	2	0.8	.944

Julian Tavarez

TAVAREZ, JULIAN BR TR 6′ 2″ 165 lbs.
Born Julian Tavarez (Carmen).
B. May 22, 1973, Santiago, Dominican Republic.

Year	Team	Lg	W	L	PCT	ERA	G	GS	CG	IP	H	BB	SO	ShO	Relief Pitching W	Relief Pitching L	Relief Pitching SV	Batting AB	Batting H	Batting HR	BA	PO	A	E	DP	TC/G	FA
1993	**CLE**	**A**	2	2	.500	6.57	8	7	0	37	53	13	19	0	0	0	0	0	0	0	—	2	3	0	2	0.6	1.000
1994			0	1	.000	21.60	1	1	0	1.2	6	1	0	0	0	0	0	0	0	0	—	0	0	0	0	0.0	.000
1995			10	2	.833	2.44	57	0	0	85	76	21	68	0	10	2	0	0	0	0	—	7	11	2	1	0.4	.900
3 yrs.			12	5	.706	3.93	66	8	0	123.2	135	35	87	0	10	2	0	0	0	0		9	14	2	3	0.4	.920
DIVISIONAL PLAYOFF SERIES																											
1995	**CLE**	**A**	0	0	—	6.75	3	0	0	2.2	5	0	3	0	0	0	0	0	0	0	—	0	0	0	0	0.0	.000
LEAGUE CHAMPIONSHIP SERIES																											
1995	**CLE**	**A**	0	1	.000	2.70	4	0	0	3.1	3	1	2	0	0	1	0	0	0	0	—	0	1	0	0	0.3	1.000
WORLD SERIES																											
1995	**CLE**	**A**	0	0	—	0.00	5	0	0	4.1	3	2	1	0	0	0	0	0	0	0	—	0	2	0	0	0.4	1.000

Arlas Taylor

TAYLOR, ARLAS WALTER (Foxy, Lefty) BR TL 5′11″
B. Mar. 16, 1896, Warrick County, Ind. D. Sept. 10, 1968, Dade City, Fla.

Year	Team	Lg	W	L	PCT	ERA	G	GS	CG	IP	H	BB	SO	ShO	Relief Pitching W	Relief Pitching L	Relief Pitching SV	Batting AB	Batting H	Batting HR	BA	PO	A	E	DP	TC/G	FA
1921	**PHI**	**A**	0	1	.000	22.50	1	1	0	2	7	2	1	0	0	0	0	0	0	0	—	0	0	0	0	0.0	.000

Ben Taylor

TAYLOR, BENJAMIN HARRISON TR 5′11″ 163 lbs.
B. Apr. 2, 1889, Paoli, Ind. D. Nov. 3, 1946, Martin County, Ind.

Year	Team	Lg	W	L	PCT	ERA	G	GS	CG	IP	H	BB	SO	ShO	Relief Pitching W	Relief Pitching L	Relief Pitching SV	Batting AB	Batting H	Batting HR	BA	PO	A	E	DP	TC/G	FA
1912	**CIN**	**N**	0	0	—	3.18	2	0	0	5.2	9	3	2	0	0	0	0	2	0	0	.000	0	1	0	0	0.5	1.000

Bill Taylor

TAYLOR, WILLIAM HOWELL BR TR 6′ 8″ 200 lbs.
B. Oct. 16, 1961, Monticello, Fla.

Year	Team	Lg	W	L	PCT	ERA	G	GS	CG	IP	H	BB	SO	ShO	Relief Pitching W	Relief Pitching L	Relief Pitching SV	Batting AB	Batting H	Batting HR	BA	PO	A	E	DP	TC/G	FA
1994	**OAK**	**A**	1	3	.250	3.50	41	0	0	46.1	38	18	48	0	1	3	1	0	0	0	—	2	3	0	0	0.1	1.000

Billy Taylor

TAYLOR, WILLIAM HENRY (Bollicky) BR TR 5′11½″ 204 lbs.
B. 1855, Washington, D. C. D. May 14, 1900, Jacksonville, Fla.

Year	Team	Lg	W	L	PCT	ERA	G	GS	CG	IP	H	BB	SO	ShO	Relief Pitching W	Relief Pitching L	Relief Pitching SV	Batting AB	Batting H	Batting HR	BA	PO	A	E	DP	TC/G	FA
1881	**2 teams**	**WOR N** (1G 0–1)	**CLE N** (1G 0–0)																								
″	**total**		0	1	.000	5.73	2	1	1	11	15	7	2	0	0	0	0	135	30	0	.222	67	9	15	1	2.8	.835
1882	**PIT**	**AA**	0	1	.000	16.20	1	0	0	5	11	4	1	0	0	**1**	0	299	84	4	.281	377	73	60	7	7.0	.882
1883			4	7	.364	*5.39*	19	9	8	127	166	34	41	0	**1**	**1**	0	369	96	2	.260	263	66	58	4	3.9	.850
1884	**2 teams**	**STL U** (33G 25–4)	**PHI AA** (30G 18–12)																								
″	**total**		43	16	**.729**	2.10	63	59	59	523	454	84	284	3	0	0	**4**	297	96	3	.323	122	118	37	5	3.6	.866
1885	**PHI**	**AA**	1	5	.167	*3.27*	6	6	6	52.1	68	9	11	0	0	0	0	21	4	0	.190	0	5	4	0	1.5	.556
1886	**BAL**	**AA**	1	6	.143	*5.72*	8	8	8	72.1	87	20	37	0	0	0	0	39	12	0	.308	18	14	3	0	3.5	.914
1887	**PHI**	**AA**	1	0	1.000	3.00	1	1	1	9	10	7	0	0	0	0	0	4	1	0	.250	0	1	0	0	1.0	1.000
7 yrs.			50	36	.581	3.17	100	84	83	799.2	811	165	376	3	1	2	4	*				847	286	177	17	4.4	.865

Bruce Taylor

TAYLOR, BRUCE BELL BR TR 6′ 178 lbs.
B. Apr. 16, 1953, Holden, Mass.

Year	Team	Lg	W	L	PCT	ERA	G	GS	CG	IP	H	BB	SO	ShO	Relief Pitching W	Relief Pitching L	Relief Pitching SV	Batting AB	Batting H	Batting HR	BA	PO	A	E	DP	TC/G	FA
1977	**DET**	**A**	1	0	1.000	3.41	19	0	0	29	23	10	19	0	1	0	2	0	0	0	—	2	4	0	0	0.3	1.000
1978			0	0	—	0.00	1	0	0	1	0	0	0	0	0	0	0	0	0	0	—	0	0	0	0	0.0	.000
1979			1	2	.333	4.74	10	0	0	19	16	7	8	0	1	2	0	0	0	0	—	2	3	1	1	0.6	.833
3 yrs.			2	2	.500	3.86	30	0	0	49	39	17	27	0	2	2	2	0	0	0		4	7	1	1	0.4	.917

Chuck Taylor

TAYLOR, CHARLES GILBERT BR TR 6′ 2″ 195 lbs.
B. Apr. 18, 1942, Shelbyville, Tenn.

Year	Team	Lg	W	L	PCT	ERA	G	GS	CG	IP	H	BB	SO	ShO	Relief Pitching W	Relief Pitching L	Relief Pitching SV	Batting AB	Batting H	Batting HR	BA	PO	A	E	DP	TC/G	FA
1969	**STL**	**N**	7	5	.583	2.55	27	13	5	127	108	30	62	1	0	0	0	39	7	0	.179	3	15	0	1	0.7	1.000
1970			6	7	.462	3.12	56	7	1	124	116	31	64	1	3	5	8	26	3	0	.115	7	23	0	1	0.5	1.000
1971			3	1	.750	3.55	43	1	0	71	72	25	46	0	3	1	3	12	2	0	.167	4	11	1	0	0.4	.938
1972	**2 teams**	**NY N** (20G 0–0)	**MIL A** (5G 0–0)																								
″	**total**		0	0		4.40	25	0	0	43	52	12	14	0	0	0	3	5	1	0	.200	5	11	0	2	0.6	1.000
1973	**MON**	**N**	2	0	1.000	1.77	8	0	0	20.1	17	2	10	0	2	0	0	4	0	0	.000	1	6	0	1	0.9	1.000
1974			6	2	.750	2.17	61	0	0	108	101	25	43	0	6	2	11	10	3	0	.300	8	15	1	2	0.4	.958
1975			2	2	.500	3.53	54	0	0	74	72	24	29	0	2	2	6	2	0	0	.000	6	11	0	0	0.3	1.000
1976			2	3	.400	4.50	31	0	0	40	38	13	14	0	2	3	0	3	0	0	.000	2	5	0	1	0.2	1.000
8 yrs.			28	20	.583	3.07	305	21	6	607.1	576	162	282	2	18	13	31	101	16	0	.158	36	97	2	8	0.4	.985

Dorn Taylor

TAYLOR, DONALD CLYDE BR TR 6′ 2″ 180 lbs.
B. Aug. 11, 1958, Abington, Pa.

Year	Team	Lg	W	L	PCT	ERA	G	GS	CG	IP	H	BB	SO	ShO	Relief Pitching W	Relief Pitching L	Relief Pitching SV	Batting AB	Batting H	Batting HR	BA	PO	A	E	DP	TC/G	FA
1987	**PIT**	**N**	2	3	.400	5.74	14	8	0	53.1	48	28	37	0	1	0	0	18	3	0	.167	3	5	2	3	0.7	.800
1989			1	1	.500	5.06	9	0	0	10.2	14	5	3	0	1	1	0	1	0	0	.000	0	1	0	0	0.1	1.000
1990	**BAL**	**A**	0	1	.000	2.45	4	0	0	3.2	4	2	4	0	0	1	0	0	0	0	—	0	0	0	0	0.0	.000
3 yrs.			3	5	.375	5.45	27	8	0	67.2	66	35	44	0	2	2	0	19	3	0	.158	3	6	2	3	0.4	.818

Dummy Taylor

TAYLOR, LUTHER HADEN — BR TR 6′ 1″ 160 lbs.
B. Feb. 21, 1875, Oskaloosa, Kans. D. Aug. 22, 1958, Jacksonville, Ill.

Year	Team	Lg	W	L	PCT	ERA	G	GS	CG	IP	H	BB	SO	ShO	Relief Pitching W	Relief Pitching L	Relief Pitching SV	Batting AB	Batting H	Batting HR	BA	PO	A	E	DP	TC/G	FA
1900	NY	N	4	3	.571	2.45	11	7	6	62.1	74	24	16	0	0	0	0	22	3	0	.136	0	9	2	0	1.0	.818
1901			18	**27**	.400	3.18	**45**	**43**	37	353.1	**377**	112	136	4	1	1	0	136	18	0	.132	19	92	6	2	2.6	.949
1902	2 teams	CLE A (4G 1–3)	NY N (26G 7–15)																								
″	total		8	18	.308	2.19	30	29	22	234.2	231	63	95	1	0	0	0	75	7	0	.093	7	63	5	0	2.5	.933
1903	NY	N	13	13	.500	4.23	33	31	18	244.2	306	89	94	1	0	1	0	82	12	0	.146	10	62	4	2	2.3	.947
1904			21	15	.583	2.34	37	36	29	296.1	231	75	138	5	0	1	0	102	16	0	.157	20	87	1	7	2.8	.991
1905			16	9	.640	2.66	32	28	18	213	200	51	91	4	0	0	0	69	9	0	.130	13	62	5	1	2.5	.938
1906			17	9	.654	2.20	31	27	13	213	186	57	91	2	0	2	0	76	14	0	.184	10	54	4	2	2.2	.941
1907			11	7	.611	2.42	28	21	11	171	145	46	56	3	2	0	1	48	6	0	.125	8	46	4	0	2.0	.931
1908			8	5	.615	2.33	27	15	6	127.2	127	34	50	1	2	0	2	35	8	0	.229	8	35	4	1	1.7	.915
9 yrs.			116	106	.523	2.75	274	237	160	1916	1877	551	767	21	5	5	3	645	93	0	.144	95	510	35	15	2.3	.945

Gary Taylor

TAYLOR, GARY WILLIAM — BR TR 6′ 2″ 190 lbs.
B. Oct. 19, 1945, Detroit, Mich.

Year	Team	Lg	W	L	PCT	ERA	G	GS	CG	IP	H	BB	SO	ShO	Relief Pitching W	Relief Pitching L	Relief Pitching SV	Batting AB	Batting H	Batting HR	BA	PO	A	E	DP	TC/G	FA
1969	DET	A	0	1	.000	5.23	7	0	0	10.1	10	6	3	0	0	1	0	1	0	0	.000	0	2	0	0	0.3	1.000

Harry Taylor

TAYLOR, HARRY EVANS — BR TR 6′ 185 lbs.
B. Dec. 2, 1935, San Angelo, Tex.

Year	Team	Lg	W	L	PCT	ERA	G	GS	CG	IP	H	BB	SO	ShO	Relief Pitching W	Relief Pitching L	Relief Pitching SV	Batting AB	Batting H	Batting HR	BA	PO	A	E	DP	TC/G	FA
1957	KC	A	0	0	—	3.12	2	0	0	8.2	11	4	4	0	0	0	0	4	1	0	.250	0	1	1	0	1.0	.500

Harry Taylor

TAYLOR, JAMES HARRY — BR TR 6′ 1″ 175 lbs.
B. May 20, 1919, East Glenn, Ind.

Year	Team	Lg	W	L	PCT	ERA	G	GS	CG	IP	H	BB	SO	ShO	Relief Pitching W	Relief Pitching L	Relief Pitching SV	Batting AB	Batting H	Batting HR	BA	PO	A	E	DP	TC/G	FA
1946	BKN	N	0	0	—	3.86	4	0	0	4.2	5	1	6	0	0	0	1	0	0	0	—	0	1	0	0	0.3	1.000
1947			10	5	.667	3.11	33	20	10	162	130	83	58	2	0	0	1	62	8	0	.129	5	35	1	4	1.2	.976
1948			2	7	.222	5.36	17	13	2	80.2	90	61	32	0	0	1	0	22	6	0	.273	9	19	0	4	1.6	1.000
1950	BOS	A	2	0	1.000	1.42	3	2	2	19	13	8	8	1	0	0	0	7	2	0	.286	3	3	0	0	2.0	1.000
1951			4	9	.308	5.75	31	8	1	81.1	100	42	22	0	2	5	2	29	3	0	.103	6	20	0	0	0.8	1.000
1952			1	0	1.000	1.80	2	1	1	10	6	6	1	0	0	0	0	4	1	0	.250	1	2	0	0	1.5	1.000
6 yrs.			19	21	.475	4.10	90	44	16	357.2	344	201	127	3	2	6	4	124	20	0	.161	24	80	1	8	1.2	.990
WORLD SERIES																											
1947	BKN	N	0	0	—	0.00	1	1	0		2	1	0	0	0	0	0	0	0	0	—	0	0	0	0	0.0	.000

Jack Taylor

TAYLOR, JOHN BUDD (Brewery Jack) — BR TR 6′ 1″ 190 lbs.
B. May 23, 1873, Staten Island, N. Y. D. Feb. 7, 1900, Staten Island, N. Y.

Year	Team	Lg	W	L	PCT	ERA	G	GS	CG	IP	H	BB	SO	ShO	Relief Pitching W	Relief Pitching L	Relief Pitching SV	Batting AB	Batting H	Batting HR	BA	PO	A	E	DP	TC/G	FA
1891	NY	N	0	1	.000	1.13	1	1	1	8	4	3	3	0	0	0	0	2	0	0	.000	1	0	0	0	1.0	1.000
1892	PHI	N	1	0	1.000	1.38	3	3	2	26	28	10	7	0	0	0	0	12	2	0	.167	0	3	5	0	2.7	.375
1893			10	9	.526	4.24	25	16	14	170	189	77	41	0	3	2	1	93	20	0	.215	16	42	3	4	2.2	.951
1894			23	13	.639	4.08	41	34	31	298	347	96	76	1	1	2	1	144	48	0	.333	13	68	12	3	2.3	.871
1895			26	14	.650	4.49	41	37	33	335	403	83	93	1	1	2	1	155	45	3	.290	19	89	6	3	2.7	.947
1896			20	21	.488	4.79	45	41	35	359	459	112	97	1	0	1	1	157	29	0	.185	19	107	11	3	2.9	.920
1897			16	20	.444	4.23	40	37	35	317.1	376	76	88	2	0	1	2	139	35	1	.252	15	89	17	2	3.0	.860
1898	STL	N	15	**29**	.341	3.90	**50**	**47**	**42**	**397.1**	**465**	83	89	0	0	0	1	157	38	1	.242	19	144	22	2	3.6	.881
1899	CIN	N	9	10	.474	4.12	24	18	15	168.1	197	41	34	2	1	1	2	68	17	0	.250	6	37	4	2	2.0	.915
9 yrs.			120	117	.506	4.23	270	234	208	2079	2468	581	528	7	6	9	9	927	234	5	.252	108	579	80	19	2.7	.896

Jack Taylor

TAYLOR, JOHN W. (Brakeman) — BR TR 5′10″ 170 lbs.
B. Jan. 14, 1874, New Straightsville, Ohio D. Mar. 4, 1938, Columbus, Ohio.

Year	Team	Lg	W	L	PCT	ERA	G	GS	CG	IP	H	BB	SO	ShO	Relief Pitching W	Relief Pitching L	Relief Pitching SV	Batting AB	Batting H	Batting HR	BA	PO	A	E	DP	TC/G	FA
1898	CHI	N	5	0	1.000	2.20	5	5	5	41	32	10	11	0	0	0	0	15	3	0	.200	0	9	0	1	1.8	1.000
1899			18	21	.462	3.76	41	39	39	354.2	380	84	67	1	1	0	0	139	37	0	.266	24	88	8	8	2.9	.933
1900			10	17	.370	2.55	28	26	25	222.1	226	58	57	2	1	0	1	81	19	1	.235	10	42	7	2	2.1	.881
1901			13	19	.406	3.36	33	31	30	275.2	341	44	68	0	1	0	0	106	23	0	.217	24	78	6	3	3.3	.944
1902			22	11	.667	**1.33**	36	33	33	324.2	271	43	83	**8**	1	0	1	186	44	0	.237	42	133	9	5	3.4	.951
1903			21	14	.600	2.45	37	33	33	312.1	277	57	83	1	1	1	1	126	28	0	.222	16	91	7	2	2.9	.939
1904	STL	N	21	19	.525	2.22	41	40	**39**	352	297	82	103	2	0	0	1	133	28	1	.211	14	109	6	1	3.1	.953
1905			15	21	.417	3.44	37	34	34	309	302	85	102	3	1	1	1	121	23	0	.190	12	82	3	1	2.5	.969
1906	2 teams	STL N (17G 8–9)	CHI N (17G 12–3)																								
″	total		20	12	.625	1.99	34	33	32	302.1	249	86	61	3	0	0	0	106	22	0	.208	12	95	2	2	3.2	.982
1907	CHI	N	6	5	.545	3.29	18	13	8	123	127	33	22	0	1	0	0	47	9	0	.191	6	40	0	1	2.6	1.000
10 yrs.			151	139	.521	2.66	310	287	278	2617	2502	582	657	20	7	2	5	*				160	767	48	26	2.9	.951

Kerry Taylor

TAYLOR, KERRY THOMAS — BR TR 6′ 3″ 200 lbs.
B. Jan. 25, 1971, Bemidji, Minn.

Year	Team	Lg	W	L	PCT	ERA	G	GS	CG	IP	H	BB	SO	ShO	Relief Pitching W	Relief Pitching L	Relief Pitching SV	Batting AB	Batting H	Batting HR	BA	PO	A	E	DP	TC/G	FA
1993	SD	N	0	5	.000	6.45	36	7	0	68.1	72	49	45	0	0	0	0	12	0	0	.000	4	7	0	0	0.3	1.000
1994			0	0	—	8.31	1	1	0	4.1	9	1	3	0	0	0	0	2	0	0	.000	0	0	0	0	0.0	.000
2 yrs.			0	5	.000	6.56	37	8	0	72.2	81	50	48	0	0	0	0	14	0	0	.000	4	7	0	0	0.3	1.000

Pete Taylor

TAYLOR, VERNON CHARLES — BR TR 6′ 1″ 170 lbs.
B. Nov. 26, 1927, Severn, Md.

Year	Team	Lg	W	L	PCT	ERA	G	GS	CG	IP	H	BB	SO	ShO	Relief Pitching W	Relief Pitching L	Relief Pitching SV	Batting AB	Batting H	Batting HR	BA	PO	A	E	DP	TC/G	FA
1952	STL	A	0	0	—	13.50	1	0	0	2	4	3	0	0	0	0	0	0	0	0	—	0	1	0	1	1.0	1.000

Ron Taylor

TAYLOR, RONALD WESLEY — BR TR 6′ 1″ 195 lbs.
B. Dec. 13, 1937, Toronto, Ont., Canada.

Year	Team	Lg	W	L	PCT	ERA	G	GS	CG	IP	H	BB	SO	ShO	Relief Pitching W	Relief Pitching L	Relief Pitching SV	Batting AB	Batting H	Batting HR	BA	PO	A	E	DP	TC/G	FA
1962	CLE	A	2	2	.500	5.94	8	4	1	33.1	36	13	15	0	1	0	0	11	3	0	.273	0	5	0	0	0.6	1.000
1963	STL	N	9	7	.563	2.84	54	9	2	133.1	119	30	91	0	7	3	11	32	1	0	.031	2	13	0	0	0.3	1.000
1964			8	4	.667	4.62	63	2	0	101.1	109	33	69	0	**8**	2	7	15	2	0	.133	2	27	1	3	0.5	.967
1965	2 teams	STL N (25G 2–1)	HOU N (32G 1–5)																								
″	total		3	6	.333	5.60	57	1	0	101.1	111	31	63	0	3	5	5	18	2	0	.111	5	15	0	0	0.4	1.000
1966	HOU	N	2	3	.400	5.71	36	1	0	64.2	89	10	29	0	2	3	0	12	2	0	.167	0	7	0	0	0.2	1.000
1967	NY	N	4	6	.400	2.34	50	0	0	73	60	23	46	0	4	6	8	7	0	0	.000	7	11	1	1	0.4	.947
1968			1	5	.167	2.70	58	0	0	76.2	64	18	49	0	1	5	13	9	0	0	.000	9	14	1	1	0.4	.958
1969			9	4	.692	2.72	59	0	0	76	61	24	42	0	9	4	13	4	1	0	.250	6	13	0	1	0.3	1.000

Ron Taylor *continued*

Year	Team	Lg	W	L	PCT	ERA	G	GS	CG	IP	H	BB	SO	ShO	Relief W	Relief L	Relief SV	AB	H	HR	BA	PO	A	E	DP	TC/G	FA
1970			5	4	.556	3.95	57	0	0	66	65	16	28	0	5	4	13	4	0	0	.000	5	12	0	0	0.3	1.000
1971			2	2	.500	3.65	45	0	0	69	71	11	32	0	2	2	2	4	1	0	.250	1	11	0	0	0.3	1.000
1972	**SD**	**N**	0	0	—	12.60	4	0	0	5	9	0	0	0	0	0	0	0	0	0	—	0	1	0	0	0.3	1.000
11 yrs.			45	43	.511	3.93	491	17	3	799.2	794	209	464	0	42	34	72	116	12	0	.103	37	129	3	6	0.3	.982
LEAGUE CHAMPIONSHIP SERIES																											
1969	**NY**	**N**	1	0	1.000	0.00	2	0	0	3.1	3	0	4	0	1	0	1	0	0	0	—	1	0	0	0	0.5	1.000
WORLD SERIES																											
1964	**STL**	**N**	0	0	—	0.00	2	0	0	4.2	0	1	2	0	0	0	1	1	0	0	.000	0	2	0	0	1.0	1.000
1969	**NY**	**N**	0	0	—	0.00	2	0	0	2.1	0	1	3	0	0	0	1	0	0	0	—	0	1	0	0	0.5	1.000
2 yrs.			0	0		0.00	4	0	0	7	0	2	5	0	0	0	2	1	0	0	.000	0	3	0	0	0.8	1.000

Rube Taylor

TAYLOR, EDGAR RUBEN TL
B. Mar. 23, 1877, Palestine, Tex. D. Jan. 31, 1912, Dallas, Tex.

Year	Team	Lg	W	L	PCT	ERA	G	GS	CG	IP	H	BB	SO	ShO	Relief W	Relief L	Relief SV	AB	H	HR	BA	PO	A	E	DP	TC/G	FA
1903	**STL**	**N**	0	0	—	0.00	1	0	0	3	0	0	1	0	0	0	0	1	0	0	.000	0	1	0	0	1.0	1.000

Scott Taylor

TAYLOR, RODNEY SCOTT BL TL 6′ 1″ 185 lbs.
B. Aug. 2, 1967, Defiance, Ohio

Year	Team	Lg	W	L	PCT	ERA	G	GS	CG	IP	H	BB	SO	ShO	Relief W	Relief L	Relief SV	AB	H	HR	BA	PO	A	E	DP	TC/G	FA
1992	**BOS**	**A**	1	1	.500	4.91	4	1	0	14.2	13	4	7	0	1	0	0	0	0	0	—	0	3	0	0	0.8	1.000
1993			0	1	.000	8.18	16	0	0	11	14	12	8	0	0	1	0	0	0	0	—	0	1	0	0	0.1	1.000
2 yrs.			1	2	.333	6.31	20	1	0	25.2	27	16	15	0	1	1	0	0	0	0		0	4	0	0	0.2	1.000

Scott Taylor

TAYLOR, SCOTT MICHAEL BR TR 6′ 3″ 200 lbs.
B. Oct. 3, 1966, Topeka, Kans.

Year	Team	Lg	W	L	PCT	ERA	G	GS	CG	IP	H	BB	SO	ShO	Relief W	Relief L	Relief SV	AB	H	HR	BA	PO	A	E	DP	TC/G	FA
1995	**TEX**	**A**	1	2	.333	9.39	3	3	0	15.1	25	5	10	0	0	0	0	0	0	0	—	1	3	0	2	1.3	1.000

Terry Taylor

TAYLOR, TERRY DERRELL BR TR 6′ 1″ 180 lbs.
B. July 28, 1964, Crestview, Fla.

Year	Team	Lg	W	L	PCT	ERA	G	GS	CG	IP	H	BB	SO	ShO	Relief W	Relief L	Relief SV	AB	H	HR	BA	PO	A	E	DP	TC/G	FA
1988	**SEA**	**A**	0	1	.000	6.26	5	5	0	23	26	11	9	0	0	0	0	0	0	0	—	1	0	0	0	0.2	1.000

Wade Taylor

TAYLOR, WADE ERIC BR TR 6′ 1″ 185 lbs.
B. Oct. 19, 1965, Mobile, Ala.

Year	Team	Lg	W	L	PCT	ERA	G	GS	CG	IP	H	BB	SO	ShO	Relief W	Relief L	Relief SV	AB	H	HR	BA	PO	A	E	DP	TC/G	FA
1991	**NY**	**A**	7	12	.368	6.27	23	22	0	116.1	144	53	72	0	0	0	0	0	0	0	—	2	21	0	3	1.0	1.000

Wiley Taylor

TAYLOR, PHILIP WILEY BR TR 6′ 1″ 175 lbs.
B. Mar. 18, 1888, Wamego, Kans. D. July 8, 1954, Westmoreland, Kans.

Year	Team	Lg	W	L	PCT	ERA	G	GS	CG	IP	H	BB	SO	ShO	Relief W	Relief L	Relief SV	AB	H	HR	BA	PO	A	E	DP	TC/G	FA
1911	**DET**	**A**	0	2	.000	3.79	3	2	1	19	18	10	9	0	0	0	0	6	0	0	.000	0	3	0	0	1.0	1.000
1912	**CHI**	**A**	0	1	.000	4.95	3	3	0	20	21	14	4	0	0	0	0	5	0	0	.000	1	6	0	0	2.3	1.000
1913	**STL**	**A**	0	2	.000	4.83	5	4	1	31.2	33	16	12	0	0	0	0	10	0	0	.000	1	12	2	0	3.0	.867
1914			2	5	.286	3.42	16	8	2	50	41	25	20	1	0	1	0	12	2	0	.167	1	15	3	1	1.2	.842
4 yrs.			2	10	.167	4.10	27	17	4	120.2	113	65	45	1	0	1	0	33	2	0	.061	3	36	5	1	1.6	.886

Bud Teachout

TEACHOUT, ARTHUR JOHN BR TL 6′ 2″ 183 lbs.
B. Feb. 27, 1904, Los Angeles, Calif. D. May 11, 1985, Laguna Beach, Calif.

Year	Team	Lg	W	L	PCT	ERA	G	GS	CG	IP	H	BB	SO	ShO	Relief W	Relief L	Relief SV	AB	H	HR	BA	PO	A	E	DP	TC/G	FA
1930	**CHI**	**N**	11	4	.733	4.06	40	16	6	153	178	48	59	0	4	1	0	63	17	0	.270	10	27	3	2	1.0	.925
1931			1	2	.333	5.72	27	3	1	61.1	79	28	14	0	1	0	0	21	5	0	.238	7	19	2	0	0.9	.929
1932	**STL**	**N**	0	0	—	0.00	1	0	0	1	2	0	0	0	0	0	0	0	0	0	—	0	0	0	0	0.0	.000
3 yrs.			12	6	.667	4.51	68	19	7	215.1	259	76	73	0	5	1	0	84	22	0	.262	17	46	5	2	1.0	.926

Patsy Tebeau

TEBEAU, OLIVER WENDELL BR TR 5′ 8″ 163 lbs.
Brother of White Wings Tebeau.
B. Dec. 5, 1864, St. Louis, Mo. D. May 15, 1918, St. Louis, Mo.
Manager 1890–00.

Year	Team	Lg	W	L	PCT	ERA	G	GS	CG	IP	H	BB	SO	ShO	Relief W	Relief L	Relief SV	AB	H	HR	BA	PO	A	E	DP	TC/G	FA
1896	**CLE**	**N**	0	0	—	0.00	1	0	0		1	0	0	0	0	0	0	*				19	34	9	4	3.1	.855

White Wings Tebeau

TEBEAU, GEORGE E. (Hard Call) BR TR 5′ 9″ 175 lbs.
Brother of Patsy Tebeau.
B. Dec. 26, 1861, St. Louis, Mo. D. Feb. 4, 1923, Denver, Colo.

Year	Team	Lg	W	L	PCT	ERA	G	GS	CG	IP	H	BB	SO	ShO	Relief W	Relief L	Relief SV	AB	H	HR	BA	PO	A	E	DP	TC/G	FA
1887	**CIN**	**AA**	0	1	.000	13.50	1	1	1	8	21	3	1	0	0	0	0	318	94	4	.296	176	17	24	2	2.6	.889
1890	**TOL**	**AA**	0	0	—	*9.00*	1	0	0	5	9	5	0	0	0	0	0	381	102	1	.268	195	20	21	3	2.0	.911
2 yrs.			0	1	.000	11.77	2	1	1	13	30	8	1	0	0	0	0	*				1574	107	141	36	2.9	.923

Al Tedrow

TEDROW, ALLEN SEYMOUR BR TL 6′ 180 lbs.
B. Dec. 14, 1891, Westerville, Ohio D. Jan. 23, 1958, Westerville, Ohio.

Year	Team	Lg	W	L	PCT	ERA	G	GS	CG	IP	H	BB	SO	ShO	Relief W	Relief L	Relief SV	AB	H	HR	BA	PO	A	E	DP	TC/G	FA
1914	**CLE**	**A**	1	2	.333	1.21	4	3	1	22.1	19	14	4	0	0	0	0	6	1	0	.167	0	7	1	0	2.0	.875

Kent Tekulve

TEKULVE, KENTON CHARLES BR TR 6′ 4″ 180 lbs.
B. Mar. 5, 1947, Cincinnati, Ohio.

Year	Team	Lg	W	L	PCT	ERA	G	GS	CG	IP	H	BB	SO	ShO	Relief W	Relief L	Relief SV	AB	H	HR	BA	PO	A	E	DP	TC/G	FA
1974	**PIT**	**N**	1	1	.500	6.00	8	0	0	9	12	5	6	0	1	1	0	0	0	0	—	2	3	0	0	0.6	1.000
1975			1	2	.333	2.25	34	0	0	56	43	23	28	0	1	2	5	11	1	0	.091	5	17	1	1	0.7	.957
1976			5	3	.625	2.45	64	0	0	102.2	91	25	68	0	5	3	9	9	0	0	.000	6	24	1	0	0.5	.968
1977			10	1	.909	3.06	72	0	0	103	89	33	59	0	10	1	7	12	3	0	.250	7	32	0	1	0.5	1.000
1978			8	7	.533	2.33	**91**	0	0	135	115	55	77	0	8	7	31	21	2	0	.095	8	38	4	1	0.5	.920
1979			10	8	.556	2.75	**94**	0	0	134	109	49	75	0	10	8	31	15	2	0	.133	8	28	1	0	0.4	.973
1980			8	12	.400	3.39	78	0	0	93	96	40	47	0	8	**12**	21	9	0	0	.000	5	18	1	1	0.3	.958
1981			5	5	.500	2.49	45	0	0	65	61	17	34	0	5	5	3	2	0	0	.000	4	16	0	2	0.4	1.000
1982			12	8	.600	2.87	**85**	0	0	128.2	113	46	66	0	**12**	8	20	14	1	0	.071	11	27	1	2	0.5	.974
1983			7	5	.583	1.64	76	0	0	99	78	36	52	0	7	5	18	8	0	0	.000	3	20	0	2	0.3	1.000
1984			3	9	.250	2.66	72	0	0	88	86	33	36	0	3	9	13	7	0	0	.000	6	25	0	3	0.4	1.000
1985	**2 teams**	**PIT N** (3G 0–0)	**PHI N** (58G 4–10)																								
″	**total**		4	10	.286	3.57	61	0	0	75.2	74	30	40	0	4	10	14	3	0	0	.000	4	14	0	0	0.3	1.000
1986	**PHI**	**N**	11	5	.688	2.54	73	0	0	110	99	25	57	0	11	5	4	5	0	0	.000	4	22	3	2	0.4	.897

Kent Tekulve *continued*

Year	Team		W	L	PCT	ERA	G	GS	CG	IP	H	BB	SO	ShO	Relief Pitching W	Relief Pitching L	Relief Pitching SV	Batting AB	Batting H	Batting HR	BA	PO	A	E	DP	TC/G	FA
1987			6	4	.600	3.09	**90**	0	0	105	96	29	60	0	6	4	3	1	0	0	.000	11	20	1	0	0.4	.969
1988			3	7	.300	3.60	70	0	0	80	87	22	43	0	3	7	4	2	0	0	.000	7	14	0	1	0.3	1.000
1989	**CIN**	**N**	0	3	.000	5.02	37	0	0	52	56	23	31	0	0	3	1	2	1	0	.500	2	9	0	1	0.3	1.000
16 yrs.			94	90	.511	2.85	1050 **2nd**	0	0	1436	1305	491	779	0	94 **7th**	90	184	121	10	0	.083	93	327	13	17	0.4	.970
LEAGUE CHAMPIONSHIP SERIES																											
1975	**PIT**	**N**	0	0	—	6.75	2	0	0	1.1	3	1	2	0	0	0	0	0	0	0	—	0	0	0	0	0.0	.000
1979			0	0	—	3.00	2	0	0	3	2	2	2	0	0	0	0	1	0	0	.000	0	1	0	0	0.5	1.000
2 yrs.			0	0		4.15	4	0	0	4.1	5	3	4	0	0	0	0	1	0	0	.000	0	1	0	0	0.3	1.000
WORLD SERIES																											
1979	**PIT**	**N**	0	1	.000	2.89	5	0	0	9.1	4	3	10	0	0	1	3 **4th**	2	0	0	.000	1	0	0	0	0.2	1.000

Anthony Telford

TELFORD, ANTHONY CHARLES BR TR 6′ 175 lbs.
B. Mar. 6, 1966, San Jose, Calif.

Year	Team		W	L	PCT	ERA	G	GS	CG	IP	H	BB	SO	ShO	Relief W	Relief L	Relief SV	AB	H	HR	BA	PO	A	E	DP	TC/G	FA
1990	**BAL**	**A**	3	3	.500	4.95	8	8	0	36.1	43	19	20	0	0	0	0	0	0	0	—	3	5	0	0	1.0	1.000
1991			0	0	—	4.05	9	1	0	26.2	27	6	24	0	0	0	0	0	0	0	—	2	2	0	0	0.4	1.000
1993			0	0	—	9.82	3	0	0	7.1	11	1	6	0	0	0	0	0	0	0	—	1	2	0	0	1.0	1.000
3 yrs.			3	3	.500	5.12	20	9	0	70.1	81	26	50	0	0	0	0	0	0	0		6	9	0	0	0.8	1.000

Dave Telgheder

TELGHEDER, DAVID WILLIAM BR TR 6′ 3″ 212 lbs.
B. Nov. 11, 1966, Middletown, N. Y.

Year	Team		W	L	PCT	ERA	G	GS	CG	IP	H	BB	SO	ShO	Relief W	Relief L	Relief SV	AB	H	HR	BA	PO	A	E	DP	TC/G	FA
1993	**NY**	**N**	6	2	.750	4.76	24	7	0	75.2	82	21	35	0	1	0	0	15	1	0	.067	4	9	0	0	0.5	1.000
1994			0	1	.000	7.20	6	0	0	10	11	8	4	0	0	1	0	0	0	0	—	0	0	1	0	0.2	.000
1995			1	2	.333	5.61	7	4	0	25.2	34	7	16	0	0	0	0	6	2	0	.333	2	6	0	0	1.1	1.000
3 yrs.			7	5	.583	5.17	37	11	0	111.1	127	36	55	0	1	1	0	21	3	0	.143	6	15	1	0	0.6	.955

Tom Tellmann

TELLMANN, THOMAS JOHN BR TR 6′ 3″ 195 lbs.
B. Mar. 29, 1954, Warren, Pa.

Year	Team		W	L	PCT	ERA	G	GS	CG	IP	H	BB	SO	ShO	Relief W	Relief L	Relief SV	AB	H	HR	BA	PO	A	E	DP	TC/G	FA
1979	**SD**	**N**	0	0	—	15.00	1	0	0	3	7	0	1	0	0	0	0	1	0	0	.000	1	1	0	0	2.0	1.000
1980			3	0	1.000	1.64	6	2	2	22	23	8	9	0	1	0	1	8	1	0	.125	1	4	0	1	0.8	1.000
1983	**MIL**	**A**	9	4	.692	2.80	44	0	0	99.2	95	35	48	0	9	4	8	0	0	0	—	9	26	0	0	0.8	1.000
1984			6	3	.667	2.78	50	0	0	81	82	31	28	0	6	3	4	0	0	0	—	4	15	0	0	0.4	1.000
1985	**OAK**	**A**	0	0	—	5.06	11	0	0	21.1	33	9	8	0	0	0	0	0	0	0	—	0	4	0	0	0.4	1.000
5 yrs.			18	7	.720	3.05	112	2	2	227	240	83	94	0	16	7	13	9	1	0	.111	15	50	0	1	0.6	1.000

Chuck Templeton

TEMPLETON, CHARLES SHERMAN BR TL 6′ 3″ 210 lbs.
B. June 1, 1932, Detroit, Mich.

Year	Team		W	L	PCT	ERA	G	GS	CG	IP	H	BB	SO	ShO	Relief W	Relief L	Relief SV	AB	H	HR	BA	PO	A	E	DP	TC/G	FA
1955	**BKN**	**N**	0	1	.000	11.57	4	0	0	4.2	5	5	3	0	0	1	0	0	0	0	—	0	1	0	0	0.3	1.000
1956			0	1	.000	6.61	6	2	0	16.1	20	10	8	0	0	0	0	3	0	0	.000	1	1	1	0	0.5	.667
2 yrs.			0	2	.000	7.71	10	2	0	21	25	15	11	0	0	1	0	3	0	0	.000	1	2	1	0	0.4	.750

John Tener

TENER, JOHN KINLEY BR TR 6′ 4″ 180 lbs.
B. July 25, 1863, County Tyrone, Ireland D. May 19, 1946, Pittsburgh, Pa.

Year	Team		W	L	PCT	ERA	G	GS	CG	IP	H	BB	SO	ShO	Relief W	Relief L	Relief SV	AB	H	HR	BA	PO	A	E	DP	TC/G	FA
1888	**CHI**	**N**	7	5	.583	2.74	12	12	11	102	90	25	39	1	0	0	0	46	9	0	.196	0	0	3	0	3.0	.000
1889			15	15	.500	3.64	35	30	28	287	302	105	105	1	1	**2**	0	150	41	1	.273	48	73	10	1	3.0	.924
1890	**PIT**	**P**	3	11	.214	7.31	14	14	13	117	160	70	30	0	0	0	0	63	12	2	.190	15	49	5	2	3.8	.928
3 yrs.			25	31	.446	4.30	61	56	52	506	552	200	174	2	1	2	0	263	62	3	.236	72	146	22	3	3.2	.908

Jim Tennant

TENNANT, JAMES McDONNELL BR TR 6′ 1″ 190 lbs.
B. Mar. 3, 1907, Shepherdstown, W. Va. D. Apr. 16, 1967, Trumbull, Conn.

Year	Team		W	L	PCT	ERA	G	GS	CG	IP	H	BB	SO	ShO	Relief W	Relief L	Relief SV	AB	H	HR	BA	PO	A	E	DP	TC/G	FA
1929	**NY**	**N**	0	0	—	0.00	1	0	0	1	1	0	1	0	0	0	0	0	0	0	—	0	0	0	0	0.0	.000

Fred Tenney

TENNEY, FRED CLAY
B. July 9, 1859, Marlborough, N. H. D. June 15, 1919, Fall River, Mass.

Year	Team		W	L	PCT	ERA	G	GS	CG	IP	H	BB	SO	ShO	Relief W	Relief L	Relief SV	AB	H	HR	BA	PO	A	E	DP	TC/G	FA
1884	**2 teams**	**BOS U** (4G 3–1) **WIL U** (1G 0–1)																									
″	**total**		3	2	.600	2.09	5	5	5	43	37	9	28	0	0	0	0	*				80	11	16	3	2.8	.850

Fred Tenney

TENNEY, FREDERICK BL TL 5′ 9″ 155 lbs.
B. Nov. 26, 1871, Georgetown, Mass. D. July 3, 1952, Boston, Mass.
Manager 1905–07, 1911.

Year	Team		W	L	PCT	ERA	G	GS	CG	IP	H	BB	SO	ShO	Relief W	Relief L	Relief SV	AB	H	HR	BA	PO	A	E	DP	TC/G	FA
1905	**BOS**	**N**	0	0	—	4.50	1	0	0	2	5	1	0	0	0	0	0	*				64	22	11	3	3.6	.887

Bob Terlecki

TERLECKI, ROBERT JOSEPH (Terk) BR TR 5′ 8″ 185 lbs.
B. Feb. 14, 1945, Trenton, N. J.

Year	Team		W	L	PCT	ERA	G	GS	CG	IP	H	BB	SO	ShO	Relief W	Relief L	Relief SV	AB	H	HR	BA	PO	A	E	DP	TC/G	FA
1972	**PHI**	**N**	0	0	—	4.72	9	0	0	13.1	16	10	5	0	0	0	0	0	0	0	—	1	3	1	0	0.6	.800

Greg Terlecky

TERLECKY, GREGORY JOHN BR TR 6′ 3″ 200 lbs.
B. Mar. 20, 1952, Culver City, Calif.

Year	Team		W	L	PCT	ERA	G	GS	CG	IP	H	BB	SO	ShO	Relief W	Relief L	Relief SV	AB	H	HR	BA	PO	A	E	DP	TC/G	FA
1975	**STL**	**N**	0	1	.000	4.50	20	0	0	30	38	12	13	0	0	1	0	3	1	0	.333	2	5	0	0	0.3	1.000

Jeff Terpko

TERPKO, JEFFREY MICHAEL BR TR 6′ 180 lbs.
B. Oct. 16, 1950, Sayre, Pa.

Year	Team		W	L	PCT	ERA	G	GS	CG	IP	H	BB	SO	ShO	Relief W	Relief L	Relief SV	AB	H	HR	BA	PO	A	E	DP	TC/G	FA
1974	**TEX**	**A**	0	0	—	1.29	3	0	0	7	6	4	3	0	0	0	0	0	0	0	—	0	0	0	0	0.0	.000
1976			3	3	.500	2.38	32	0	0	53	42	29	24	0	3	3	0	0	0	0	—	2	8	0	0	0.3	1.000
1977	**MON**	**N**	0	1	.000	5.57	13	0	0	21	28	15	14	0	0	1	0	1	0	0	.000	0	2	2	1	0.3	.500
3 yrs.			3	4	.429	3.11	48	0	0	81	76	48	41	0	3	4	0	1	0	0	.000	2	10	2	1	0.3	.857

Jerry Terrell

TERRELL, JERRY WAYNE BR TR 5′11″ 165 lbs.
B. July 13, 1946, Waseca, Minn. BB 1974

Year	Team		W	L	PCT	ERA	G	GS	CG	IP	H	BB	SO	ShO	Relief W	Relief L	Relief SV	AB	H	HR	BA	PO	A	E	DP	TC/G	FA
1979	**KC**	**A**	0	0	—	0.00	1	0	0	1	0	0	0	0	0	0	0	40	12	1	.300	170	298	18	55	3.1	.963
1980			0	0	—	0.00	1	0	0	1	1	1	0	0	0	0	0	16	1	0	.063	29	7	0	2	2.4	1.000
2 yrs.			0	0		0.00	2	0	0	2	1	1	0	0	0	0	0	*				818	1098	60	218	3.0	.970

Walt Terrell

TERRELL, CHARLES WALTER
B. May 11, 1958, Jeffersonville, Ind.
BL TR 6′ 2″ 205 lbs.

Year	Team	W	L	PCT	ERA	G	GS	CG	IP	H	BB	SO	ShO	Relief Pitching W	Relief Pitching L	Relief Pitching SV	Batting AB	Batting H	Batting HR	BA	PO	A	E	DP	TC/G	FA
1982	**NY N**	0	3	.000	3.43	3	3	0	21	22	14	8	0	0	0	0	5	2	0	.400	2	2	0	0	1.3	1.000
1983		8	8	.500	3.57	21	20	4	133.2	123	55	59	2	0	0	0	44	8	3	.182	16	15	0	2	1.5	1.000
1984		11	12	.478	3.52	33	33	3	215	232	80	114	1	0	0	0	75	6	0	.080	16	32	2	5	1.5	.960
1985	**DET A**	15	10	.600	3.85	34	34	5	229	221	95	130	3	0	0	0	0	0	0	—	21	43	2	8	1.9	.970
1986		15	12	.556	4.56	34	33	9	217.1	199	98	93	2	0	0	0	0	0	0	—	30	29	0	0	1.7	1.000
1987		17	10	.630	4.05	35	35	10	244.2	254	94	143	1	0	0	0	0	0	0	—	24	25	2	3	1.5	.961
1988		7	16	.304	3.97	29	29	11	206.1	199	78	84	1	0	0	0	0	0	0	—	22	29	2	3	1.8	.962
1989	**2 teams SD N** (19G 5–13) **NY A** (13G 6–5)																									
″	**total**	11	18	.379	4.49	32	32	5	206.1	236	50	93	2	0	0	0	40	4	0	.100	19	41	0	4	1.9	1.000
1990	**2 teams PIT N** (16G 2–7) **DET A** (13G 6–4)																									
″	**total**	8	11	.421	5.24	29	28	0	158	184	57	64	0	0	0	0	28	3	0	.107	13	21	1	2	1.2	.971
1991	**DET A**	12	14	.462	4.24	35	33	8	218.2	**257**	79	80	2	1	0	0	0	0	0	—	18	26	0	5	1.3	1.000
1992		7	10	.412	5.20	36	14	1	136.2	163	48	61	0	4	4	0	0	0	0	—	13	22	1	0	1.0	.972
11 yrs.		111	124	.472	4.22	321	294	56	1986.2	2090	748	929	14	5	4	0	192	23	3	.120	194	285	10	32	1.5	.980
LEAGUE CHAMPIONSHIP SERIES																										
1987	**DET A**	0	0	—	9.00	1	1	0	6	7	4	4	0	0	0	0	0	0	0	—	0	1	0	0	1.0	1.000

Adonis Terry

TERRY, WILLIAM H.
B. Aug. 7, 1864, Westfield, Mass. D. Feb. 24, 1915, Milwaukee, Wis.
BR TR 5′11½″ 168 lbs.

Year	Team	W	L	PCT	ERA	G	GS	CG	IP	H	BB	SO	ShO	Relief Pitching W	Relief Pitching L	Relief Pitching SV	Batting AB	Batting H	Batting HR	BA	PO	A	E	DP	TC/G	FA
1884	**BKN AA**	20	35	.364	*3.49*	57	56	55	485	487	75	233	3	0	0	0	240	56	0	.233	56	85	37	2	2.5	.792
1885		6	17	.261	*4.26*	25	23	23	209	213	42	96	0	0	0	1	264	45	1	.170	90	46	15	2	2.1	.901
1886		18	16	.529	*3.09*	34	34	32	288.1	263	115	162	5	0	0	0	299	71	2	.237	99	117	35	3	3.2	.861
1887		16	16	.500	*4.02*	40	35	35	318	331	99	138	1	0	0	**3**	352	103	3	.293	128	90	26	2	2.7	.893
1888		13	8	.619	2.03	23	23	20	195	145	67	138	2	0	0	0	115	29	0	.252	34	44	6	3	2.6	.929
1889		22	15	.595	3.29	41	39	35	326	285	126	186	2	0	0	0	160	48	2	.300	88	88	10	4	3.6	.946
1890	**BKN N**	26	16	.619	2.94	46	44	38	370	362	133	185	1	0	0	0	363	101	4	.278	127	79	19	6	2.2	.916
1891		6	16	.273	4.22	25	22	18	194	207	80	65	1	0	0	1	91	19	0	.209	12	35	4	1	1.7	.922
1892	**2 teams BAL N** (1G 0–1) **PIT N** (30G 18–7)																									
″	**total**	18	8	.692	2.57	31	27	25	249	192	113	98	2	0	0	1	104	16	2	.154	27	51	7	0	2.7	.918
1893	**PIT N**	12	8	.600	4.45	26	19	14	170	177	99	52	0	2	1	0	71	18	0	.254	9	37	4	2	1.9	.920
1894	**2 teams PIT N** (1G 0–1) **CHI N** (23G 5–11)																									
″	**total**	5	12	.294	6.09	24	21	16	164	234	127	39	0	0	0	0	95	33	0	.347	21	27	6	1	1.6	.889
1895	**CHI N**	21	14	.600	4.80	38	34	31	311.1	346	131	88	0	2	0	0	137	30	1	.219	17	83	13	3	2.8	.885
1896		15	13	.536	4.28	30	28	25	235.1	268	88	74	1	1	1	0	99	26	0	.263	18	43	2	0	2.1	.968
1897		0	1	.000	10.13	1	1	1	8	11	6	1	0	0	0	0	3	0	0	.000	0	3	1	0	4.0	.750
14 yrs.		198	195	.504	3.72	441	406	368	3523	3521	1301	1555	18	5	2	6	*				726	828	185	29	2.5	.894

John Terry

TERRY, JOHN BUCHARD
B. Nov. 1, 1879, Waterbury, Conn. D. Apr. 27, 1933, Kansas City, Mo.

Year	Team	W	L	PCT	ERA	G	GS	CG	IP	H	BB	SO	ShO	Relief Pitching W	Relief Pitching L	Relief Pitching SV	Batting AB	Batting H	Batting HR	BA	PO	A	E	DP	TC/G	FA
1902	**DET A**	0	1	.000	3.60	1	1	1	5	8	1	0	0	0	0	0	2	0	0	.000	0	0	0	0	0.0	.000
1903	**STL A**	1	1	.500	2.55	3	1	1	17.2	21	4	2	0	0	1	0	9	0	0	.000	1	5	2	0	2.7	.750
2 yrs.		1	2	.333	2.78	4	2	2	22.2	29	5	2	0	0	1	0	11	0	0	.000	1	5	2	0	2.0	.750

Ralph Terry

TERRY, RALPH WILLARD
B. Jan. 9, 1936, Big Cabin, Okla.
BR TR 6′ 3″ 195 lbs.

Year	Team	W	L	PCT	ERA	G	GS	CG	IP	H	BB	SO	ShO	Relief Pitching W	Relief Pitching L	Relief Pitching SV	Batting AB	Batting H	Batting HR	BA	PO	A	E	DP	TC/G	FA
1956	**NY A**	1	2	.333	9.45	3	3	0	13.1	17	11	8	0	0	0	0	6	1	0	.167	0	1	0	0	0.3	1.000
1957	**2 teams NY A** (7G 1–1) **KC A** (21G 4–11)																									
″	**total**	5	12	.294	3.33	28	21	4	151.1	137	55	87	2	0	1	0	46	7	0	.152	13	24	2	2	1.4	.949
1958	**KC A**	11	13	.458	4.24	40	33	8	216.2	217	61	134	3	0	0	2	71	14	0	.197	13	24	4	3	1.0	.902
1959	**2 teams KC A** (9G 2–4) **NY A** (24G 3–7)																									
″	**total**	5	11	.313	3.89	33	23	7	173.2	186	49	90	1	0	0	0	58	7	0	.121	14	29	3	4	1.4	.935
1960	**NY A**	10	8	.556	3.40	35	23	7	166.2	149	52	92	3	1	1	1	49	6	0	.122	12	24	0	3	1.0	1.000
1961		16	3	.842	3.15	31	27	9	188.1	162	42	86	2	1	0	0	66	15	0	.227	20	30	0	1	1.6	1.000
1962		**23**	12	.657	3.19	43	**39**	14	**298.2**	257	57	176	3	1	0	2	106	20	0	.189	21	31	1	0	1.2	.981
1963		17	15	.531	3.22	40	**37**	**18**	268	246	39	114	3	0	0	1	87	7	0	.080	31	32	1	2	1.6	.984
1964		7	11	.389	4.54	27	14	2	115	130	31	77	1	2	3	4	35	7	0	.200	10	16	0	0	1.0	1.000
1965	**CLE A**	11	6	.647	3.69	30	26	6	165.2	154	23	84	2	0	0	0	49	7	1	.143	11	12	1	1	0.8	.958
1966	**2 teams KC A** (15G 1–5) **NY N** (11G 0–1)																									
″	**total**	1	6	.143	4.06	26	11	0	88.2	92	26	47	0	0	1	1	20	4	0	.200	5	11	1	0	0.7	.941
1967	**NY N**	0	0	—	0.00	2	0	0	3.1	1	0	5	0	0	0	0	0	0	0	—	0	1	0	0	0.5	1.000
12 yrs.		107	99	.519	3.62	338	257	75	1849.1	1748	446	1000	20	5	6	11	593	95	1	.160	150	235	13	16	1.2	.967
WORLD SERIES																										
1960	**NY A**	0	2	.000	5.40	2	1	0	6.2	7	1	5	0	0	1	0	2	0	0	.000	0	3	0	0	1.5	1.000
1961		0	1	.000	4.82	2	2	0	9.1	12	2	7	0	0	0	0	3	0	0	.000	1	2	0	0	1.5	1.000
1962		2	1	.667	1.80	3	3	2	25	17	2	16	1	0	0	0	8	1	0	.125	3	2	0	0	1.7	1.000
1963		0	0	—	3.00	1	0	0	3	3	1	0	0	0	0	0	0	0	0	—	1	1	0	1	2.0	1.000
1964		0	0	—	0.00	1	0	0	2	2	0	3	0	0	0	0	0	0	0	—	0	0	0	0	0.0	.000
5 yrs.		2	4	.333	2.93	9	6	2	46	41	6	31	1	0	1	0	13	1	0	.077	5	8	0	1	1.4	1.000

Scott Terry

TERRY, SCOTT RAY
B. Nov. 21, 1959, Hobbs, N. M.
BR TR 5′11″ 195 lbs.

Year	Team	W	L	PCT	ERA	G	GS	CG	IP	H	BB	SO	ShO	Relief Pitching W	Relief Pitching L	Relief Pitching SV	Batting AB	Batting H	Batting HR	BA	PO	A	E	DP	TC/G	FA
1986	**CIN N**	1	2	.333	6.14	28	3	0	55.2	66	32	32	0	1	1	0	4	1	0	.250	2	9	1	2	0.4	.917
1987	**STL N**	0	0	—	3.38	11	0	0	13.1	13	8	9	0	0	0	0	2	0	0	.000	0	4	0	0	0.4	1.000
1988		9	6	.600	2.92	51	11	1	129.1	119	34	65	0	2	3	3	28	7	0	.250	7	22	0	1	0.6	1.000
1989		8	10	.444	3.57	31	24	1	148.2	142	43	69	0	0	0	2	45	7	2	.156	6	33	2	2	1.3	.951
1990		2	6	.250	4.75	50	2	0	72	75	27	35	0	2	5	2	11	5	0	.455	3	14	1	0	0.4	.944
1991		4	4	.500	2.80	65	0	0	80.1	76	32	52	0	4	4	1	7	1	0	.143	7	16	0	1	0.4	1.000
6 yrs.		24	28	.462	3.73	236	40	2	499.1	491	176	262	0	9	13	8	97	21	2	.216	25	98	4	6	0.5	.969

Yank Terry

TERRY, LANCELOT YANK BR TR 6′ 1″ 180 lbs.
B. Feb. 11, 1911, Bedford, Ind. D. Nov. 4, 1979, Bloomington, Ind.

Year	Team		W	L	PCT	ERA	G	GS	CG	IP	H	BB	SO	ShO	Relief Pitching W	Relief Pitching L	Relief Pitching SV	Batting AB	Batting H	Batting HR	BA	PO	A	E	DP	TC/G	FA
1940	**BOS**	**A**	1	0	1.000	8.84	4	1	0	19.1	24	11	9	0	0	0	0	8	2	0	.250	0	4	0	0	1.0	1.000
1942			6	5	.545	3.92	20	11	3	85	82	43	37	0	1	1	1	27	3	0	.111	3	16	1	1	1.0	.950
1943			7	9	.438	3.52	30	22	7	163.2	147	63	63	0	1	1	1	45	3	0	.067	8	37	2	0	1.6	.957
1944			6	10	.375	4.21	27	17	3	132.2	142	65	30	0	2	1	0	47	11	0	.234	2	28	0	2	1.1	1.000
1945			0	4	.000	4.13	12	4	1	56.2	68	14	28	0	0	1	0	18	2	0	.111	0	9	0	0	0.8	1.000
5 yrs.			20	28	.417	4.09	93	55	14	457.1	463	196	167	0	4	4	2	145	21	0	.145	13	94	3	3	1.2	.973

Dick Terwilliger

TERWILLIGER, RICHARD MARTIN BR TR 5′11″ 178 lbs.
B. June 27, 1906, Sand Lake, Mich. D. Jan. 21, 1969, Greenville, Mich.

Year	Team		W	L	PCT	ERA	G	GS	CG	IP	H	BB	SO	ShO	Relief Pitching W	Relief Pitching L	Relief Pitching SV	Batting AB	Batting H	Batting HR	BA	PO	A	E	DP	TC/G	FA
1932	**STL**	**N**	0	0	—	0.00	1	0	0	3	1	2	2	0	0	0	0	1	0	0	.000	0	2	0	0	2.0	1.000

Jeff Tesreau

TESREAU, CHARLES MONROE BR TR 6′ 2½″ 218 lbs.
B. Mar. 5, 1889, Silver Mine, Mo. D. Sept. 24, 1946, Hanover, N. H.

Year	Team		W	L	PCT	ERA	G	GS	CG	IP	H	BB	SO	ShO	Relief Pitching W	Relief Pitching L	Relief Pitching SV	Batting AB	Batting H	Batting HR	BA	PO	A	E	DP	TC/G	FA
1912	**NY**	**N**	17	7	.708	**1.96**	36	28	19	243	177	106	119	3	1	0	1	82	12	0	.146	9	63	5	2	2.1	.935
1913			22	13	.629	2.17	41	**38**	17	282	222	119	167	1	1	2	0	95	21	0	.221	3	73	2	2	1.9	.974
1914			26	10	.722	2.37	42	**40**	26	322.1	238	128	189	**8**	1	0	1	117	28	0	.239	8	71	6	5	2.0	.929
1915			19	16	.543	2.29	43	38	24	306	235	75	176	8	1	0	3	103	24	1	.233	13	80	4	5	2.3	.959
1916			18	14	.563	2.92	40	32	23	268.1	249	65	113	5	1	0	1	94	18	1	.191	12	67	1	2	2.0	.988
1917			13	8	.619	3.09	33	20	11	183.2	168	58	85	1	4	2	2	61	14	0	.230	6	60	5	2	2.2	.930
1918			4	4	.500	2.32	12	9	3	73.2	61	21	31	1	1	1	0	22	7	0	.318	1	26	0	1	2.3	1.000
7 yrs.			119	72	.623	2.43	247	205	123	1679	1350	572	880	27	10	5	8	574	124	2	.216	52	440	23	19	2.1	.955
WORLD SERIES																											
1912	**NY**	**N**	1	2	.333	3.13	3	3	1	23	19	11	15	0	0	0	0	8	3	0	.375	0	10	0	0	3.3	1.000
1913			0	1	.000	5.40	2	1	0	8.1	11	1	4	0	0	0	0	2	0	0	.000	0	1	0	0	0.5	1.000
1917			0	0	—	0.00	1	0	0	1	0	1	1	0	0	0	0	0	0	0	—	0	0	0	0	0.0	.000
3 yrs.			1	3	.250	3.62	6	4	1	32.1	30	13	20	0	0	0	0	10	3	0	.300	0	11	0	0	1.8	1.000

Bob Tewksbury

TEWKSBURY, ROBERT ALAN BR TR 6′ 4″ 200 lbs.
B. Nov. 30, 1960, Concord, N. H.

Year	Team		W	L	PCT	ERA	G	GS	CG	IP	H	BB	SO	ShO	Relief Pitching W	Relief Pitching L	Relief Pitching SV	Batting AB	Batting H	Batting HR	BA	PO	A	E	DP	TC/G	FA
1986	**NY**	**A**	9	5	.643	3.31	23	20	2	130.1	144	31	49	0	0	0	0	0	0	0	—	7	29	1	2	1.6	.973
1987	**2 teams**	**NY A** (8G 1–4) **CHI N** (7G 0–4)																									
″	**total**		1	8	.111	6.66	15	9	0	51.1	79	20	22	0	0	1	0	5	0	0	.000	3	6	1	1	0.7	.900
1988	**CHI**	**N**	0	0	—	8.10	1	1	0	3.1	6	2	1	0	0	0	0	2	0	0	.000	0	1	0	0	1.0	1.000
1989	**STL**	**N**	1	0	1.000	3.30	7	4	1	30	25	10	17	1	0	0	0	9	1	0	.111	1	3	0	0	0.6	1.000
1990			10	9	.526	3.47	28	20	3	145.1	151	15	50	2	0	0	1	41	7	0	.171	6	20	1	2	1.0	.963
1991			11	12	.478	3.25	30	30	3	191	206	38	75	0	0	0	0	58	9	0	.155	9	34	2	2	1.5	.956
1992			16	5	**.762**	2.16	33	32	5	233	217	20	91	0	1	0	0	70	6	0	.086	14	42	1	2	1.7	.982
1993			17	10	.630	3.83	32	32	2	213.2	**258**	20	97	0	0	0	0	69	14	0	.203	19	46	0	2	2.0	1.000
1994			12	10	.545	5.32	24	24	4	155.2	**190**	22	79	1	0	0	0	54	10	0	.185	12	31	1	1	1.8	.977
1995	**TEX**	**A**	8	7	.533	4.58	21	21	4	129.2	169	20	53	1	0	0	0	1	0	0	.000	12	24	1	3	1.8	.973
10 yrs.			85	66	.563	3.72	214	193	24	1283.1	1445	198	534	5	1	1	1	309	47	0	.152	83	236	8	15	1.5	.976

Grant Thatcher

THATCHER, ULYSSES GRANT TR 5′10½″ 180 lbs.
B. Feb. 23, 1877, Maytown, Pa. D. Mar. 17, 1936, Lancaster, Pa.

Year	Team		W	L	PCT	ERA	G	GS	CG	IP	H	BB	SO	ShO	Relief Pitching W	Relief Pitching L	Relief Pitching SV	Batting AB	Batting H	Batting HR	BA	PO	A	E	DP	TC/G	FA
1903	**BKN**	**N**	3	1	.750	2.89	4	4	4	28	33	7	9	0	0	0	0	11	2	0	.182	0	8	1	0	2.3	.889
1904			1	0	1.000	4.00	1	0	0	9	9	2	4	0	1	0	0	4	1	0	.250	0	1	0	0	1.0	1.000
2 yrs.			4	1	.800	3.16	5	4	4	37	42	9	13	0	1	0	0	15	3	0	.200	0	9	1	0	2.0	.900

Greg Thayer

THAYER, GREGORY ALLEN BR TR 5′11″ 182 lbs.
B. Oct. 23, 1949, Cedar Rapids, Iowa

Year	Team		W	L	PCT	ERA	G	GS	CG	IP	H	BB	SO	ShO	Relief Pitching W	Relief Pitching L	Relief Pitching SV	Batting AB	Batting H	Batting HR	BA	PO	A	E	DP	TC/G	FA
1978	**MIN**	**A**	1	1	.500	3.80	20	0	0	45	40	30	30	0	1	1	0	0	0	0	—	0	7	0	0	0.3	1.000

Jack Theis

THEIS, JOHN LOUIS BR TR 6′ 190 lbs.
B. July 23, 1891, Georgetown, Ohio D. July 6, 1941, Georgetown, Ohio.

Year	Team		W	L	PCT	ERA	G	GS	CG	IP	H	BB	SO	ShO	Relief Pitching W	Relief Pitching L	Relief Pitching SV	Batting AB	Batting H	Batting HR	BA	PO	A	E	DP	TC/G	FA
1920	**CIN**	**N**	0	0	—	0.00	1	0	0	2	1	3	0	0	0	0	0	0	0	0	—	0	0	0	0	0.0	.000

Duane Theiss

THEISS, DUANE CHARLES BR TR 6′ 3″ 185 lbs.
B. Nov. 20, 1953, Zanesville, Ohio.

Year	Team		W	L	PCT	ERA	G	GS	CG	IP	H	BB	SO	ShO	Relief Pitching W	Relief Pitching L	Relief Pitching SV	Batting AB	Batting H	Batting HR	BA	PO	A	E	DP	TC/G	FA
1977	**ATL**	**N**	1	1	.500	6.43	17	0	0	21	26	16	7	0	1	1	0	1	0	0	.000	2	3	0	0	0.3	1.000
1978			0	0	—	1.50	3	0	0	6	3	3	3	0	0	0	0	1	0	0	.000	2	0	0	0	0.7	1.000
2 yrs.			1	1	.500	5.33	20	0	0	27	29	19	10	0	1	1	0	2	0	0	.000	4	3	0	0	0.3	1.000

Jug Thesenga

THESENGA, ARNOLD JOSEPH BR TR 6′ 200 lbs.
B. Apr. 27, 1914, Jefferson, S. D.

Year	Team		W	L	PCT	ERA	G	GS	CG	IP	H	BB	SO	ShO	Relief Pitching W	Relief Pitching L	Relief Pitching SV	Batting AB	Batting H	Batting HR	BA	PO	A	E	DP	TC/G	FA
1944	**WAS**	**A**	0	0	—	5.11	5	1	0	12.1	18	12	2	0	0	0	0	2	0	0	.000	0	3	0	1	0.6	1.000

Bert Thiel

THIEL, MAYNARD BERT BR TR 5′10″ 185 lbs.
B. May 4, 1926, Marion, Wis.

Year	Team		W	L	PCT	ERA	G	GS	CG	IP	H	BB	SO	ShO	Relief Pitching W	Relief Pitching L	Relief Pitching SV	Batting AB	Batting H	Batting HR	BA	PO	A	E	DP	TC/G	FA
1952	**BOS**	**N**	1	1	.500	7.71	4	0	0	7	11	4	6	0	1	1	0	0	0	0	—	0	1	0	0	0.3	1.000

Henry Thielman

THIELMAN, HENRY JOSEPH BR TR 5′11″ 175 lbs.
Brother of Jake Thielman.
B. Oct. 30, 1880, St. Cloud, Minn. D. Sept. 2, 1942, New York, N. Y.

Year	Team		W	L	PCT	ERA	G	GS	CG	IP	H	BB	SO	ShO	Relief Pitching W	Relief Pitching L	Relief Pitching SV	Batting AB	Batting H	Batting HR	BA	PO	A	E	DP	TC/G	FA
1902	**2 teams**	**NY N** (2G 0–1) **CIN N** (25G 8–15)																									
″	**total**		8	16	.333	3.19	27	25	22	217	209	84	54	0	0	0	1	104	13	0	.125	18	58	10	2	2.6	.884
1903	**BKN**	**N**	0	3	.000	4.66	4	3	3	29	31	14	10	0	0	0	0	23	5	1	.217	9	10	2	1	2.3	.905
2 yrs.			8	19	.296	3.37	31	28	25	246	240	98	64	0	0	0	1	127	18	1	.142	27	68	12	3	2.5	.888

Jake Thielman

THIELMAN, JOHN PETER BR TR 5′11″ 175 lbs.
Brother of Henry Thielman.
B. Mar. 20, 1879, St. Cloud, Minn. D. Jan. 28, 1928, Minneapolis, Minn.

Year	Team		W	L	PCT	ERA	G	GS	CG	IP	H	BB	SO	ShO	Relief Pitching W	Relief Pitching L	Relief Pitching SV	Batting AB	Batting H	Batting HR	BA	PO	A	E	DP	TC/G	FA
1905	**STL**	**N**	15	16	.484	3.50	32	29	26	242	265	62	87	0	1	1	0	91	21	0	.231	11	84	3	3	3.0	.969
1906			0	1	.000	3.60	1	1	0	5	5	2	0	0	0	0	0	2	1	0	.500	0	2	1	0	3.0	.667

Jake Thielman *continued*

Year	Team		W	L	PCT	ERA	G	GS	CG	IP	H	BB	SO	ShO	Relief Pitching W	Relief Pitching L	Relief Pitching SV	Batting AB	Batting H	Batting HR	BA	PO	A	E	DP	TC/G	FA
1907	CLE	A	11	8	.579	2.33	20	18	18	166	151	34	56	3	1	0	0	59	12	0	.203	9	42	4	1	2.6	.927
1908	2 teams	CLE A (11G 4–3)		BOS A (1G 0–0)																							
"	total		4	3	.571	4.04	12	8	5	62.1	62	9	15	0	0	0	0	23	8	0	.348	3	28	2	2	2.4	.939
4 yrs.			30	28	.517	3.16	65	56	49	475.1	483	107	158	3	2	1	0	175	42	0	.240	23	156	10	6	2.7	.947

Dave Thies

THIES, DAVID ROBERT BR TR 6′ 4″ 205 lbs.
B. Mar. 21, 1937, Minneapolis, Minn.

Year	Team		W	L	PCT	ERA	G	GS	CG	IP	H	BB	SO	ShO	Relief W	Relief L	SV	AB	H	HR	BA	PO	A	E	DP	TC/G	FA
1963	KC	A	0	1	.000	4.62	9	2	0	25.1	26	12	9	0	0	0	0	6	2	0	.333	0	6	0	0	0.7	1.000

Jake Thies

THIES, VERNON ARTHUR BR TR 5′11″ 170 lbs.
B. Apr. 1, 1926, St. Louis, Mo.

Year	Team		W	L	PCT	ERA	G	GS	CG	IP	H	BB	SO	ShO	Relief W	Relief L	SV	AB	H	HR	BA	PO	A	E	DP	TC/G	FA
1954	PIT	N	3	9	.250	3.87	33	18	3	130.1	120	49	57	1	0	0	0	33	1	0	.030	8	24	4	0	1.1	.889
1955			0	1	.000	4.91	1	1	0	3.2	5	3	0	0	0	0	0	0	0	0	—	0	0	0	0	0.0	.000
2 yrs.			3	10	.231	3.90	34	19	3	134	125	52	57	1	0	0	0	33	1	0	.030	8	24	4	0	1.1	.889

Bobby Thigpen

THIGPEN, ROBERT THOMAS BR TR 6′ 3″ 195 lbs.
B. July 17, 1963, Tallahassee, Fla.

Year	Team		W	L	PCT	ERA	G	GS	CG	IP	H	BB	SO	ShO	Relief W	Relief L	SV	AB	H	HR	BA	PO	A	E	DP	TC/G	FA
1986	CHI	A	2	0	1.000	1.77	20	0	0	35.2	26	12	20	0	2	0	7	0	0	0	—	2	4	0	1	0.3	1.000
1987			7	5	.583	2.73	51	0	0	89	86	24	52	0	7	5	16	0	0	0	—	8	14	2	1	0.5	.917
1988			5	8	.385	3.30	68	0	0	90	96	33	62	0	5	**8**	34	0	0	0	—	5	11	0	2	0.2	1.000
1989			2	6	.250	3.76	61	0	0	79	62	40	47	0	2	6	34	0	0	0	—	7	7	0	0	0.2	1.000
1990			4	6	.400	1.83	**77**	0	0	88.2	60	32	70	0	4	6	**57**ˡ	0	0	0	—	10	8	1	2	0.2	.947
1991			7	5	.583	3.49	67	0	0	69.2	63	38	47	0	7	5	30	0	0	0	—	3	15	1	0	0.3	.947
1992			1	3	.250	4.75	55	0	0	55	58	33	45	0	1	3	22	0	0	0	—	7	6	0	2	0.2	1.000
1993	2 teams	CHI A (25G 0–0)		PHI N (17G 3–1)																							
"	total		3	1	.750	5.83	42	0	0	54	74	21	29	0	3	1	1	1	0	0	.000	1	5	0	2	0.1	1.000
1994	SEA	A	0	2	.000	9.39	7	0	0	7.2	12	5	4	0	0	2	0	0	0	0	—	0	1	0	0	0.1	1.000
9 yrs.			31	36	.463	3.43	448	0	0	568.2	537	238	376	0	31	36	201	1	0	0	.000	43	71	4	10	0.3	.966
LEAGUE CHAMPIONSHIP SERIES																											
1993	PHI	N	0	0	—	5.40	2	0	0	1.2	1	1	3	0	0	0	0	0	0	0	—	0	0	0	0	0.0	.000
WORLD SERIES																											
1993	PHI	N	0	0	—	0.00	2	0	0	2.2	1	1	0	0	0	0	0	0	0	0	—	0	1	0	0	0.5	1.000

J. J. Thobe

THOBE, JOHN JOSEPH BR TR 6′ 6″ 200 lbs.
Brother of Tom Thobe.
B. Nov. 19, 1970, Covington, Ky.

Year	Team		W	L	PCT	ERA	G	GS	CG	IP	H	BB	SO	ShO	Relief W	Relief L	SV	AB	H	HR	BA	PO	A	E	DP	TC/G	FA
1995	MON	N	0	0	—	9.00	4	0	0	4	6	3	0	0	0	0	0	0	0	0	—	0	0	1	0	0.3	.000

Tom Thobe

THOBE, THOMAS NEAL BL TL 6′ 6″ 195 lbs.
Brother of J. J. Thobe.
B. Sept. 3, 1969, Covington, Ky.

Year	Team		W	L	PCT	ERA	G	GS	CG	IP	H	BB	SO	ShO	Relief W	Relief L	SV	AB	H	HR	BA	PO	A	E	DP	TC/G	FA
1995	ATL	N	0	0	—	10.80	3	0	0	3.1	7	0	2	0	0	0	0	0	0	0	—	0	0	0	0	0.0	.000

Dick Thoenen

THOENEN, RICHARD CRISPIN BR TR 6′ 6″ 215 lbs.
B. Jan. 9, 1944, Mexico, Mo.

Year	Team		W	L	PCT	ERA	G	GS	CG	IP	H	BB	SO	ShO	Relief W	Relief L	SV	AB	H	HR	BA	PO	A	E	DP	TC/G	FA
1967	PHI	N	0	0	—	9.00	1	0	0	1	2	0	0	0	0	0	0	0	0	0	—	0	2	0	0	2.0	1.000

Blaine Thomas

THOMAS, BLAINE M. BR TR 5′10″ 165 lbs.
B. Aug. 1888, Glendora, Calif. D. Aug. 21, 1915, Glendora, Calif.

Year	Team		W	L	PCT	ERA	G	GS	CG	IP	H	BB	SO	ShO	Relief W	Relief L	SV	AB	H	HR	BA	PO	A	E	DP	TC/G	FA
1911	BOS	A	0	0	—	0.00	2	2	0	4.2	3	7	0	0	0	0	0	2	1	0	.500	0	3	1	0	2.0	.750

Bud Thomas

THOMAS, LUTHER BAXTER BR TR 6′ 180 lbs.
B. Sept. 9, 1910, Faber, Va.

Year	Team		W	L	PCT	ERA	G	GS	CG	IP	H	BB	SO	ShO	Relief W	Relief L	SV	AB	H	HR	BA	PO	A	E	DP	TC/G	FA
1932	WAS	A	0	0	—	0.00	2	0	0	3	1	2	1	0	0	0	0	0	0	0	—	0	0	0	0	0.0	.000
1933			0	0	—	15.75	2	0	0	4	11	2	1	0	0	0	0	1	0	0	.000	0	3	0	0	1.5	1.000
1937	PHI	A	8	15	.348	4.99	35	26	6	169.2	208	52	54	1	1	1	0	47	6	1	.128	7	17	0	0	0.7	1.000
1938			9	14	.391	4.92	42	29	7	212.1	259	62	48	1	0	0	0	69	9	0	.130	7	39	2	1	1.1	.958
1939	3 teams	PHI A (2G 0–1)		WAS A (4G 0–0)			DET A (27G 7–0)																				
"	total		7	1	.875	5.22	33	2	0	60.1	64	23	14	0	7	0	1	14	1	0	.071	2	13	0	0	0.5	1.000
1940	DET	A	0	1	.000	9.00	3	0	0	4	8	3	0	0	0	1	0	0	0	0	—	0	4	0	0	1.3	1.000
1941			1	3	.250	4.21	26	1	0	72.2	74	22	17	0	1	2	2	19	2	0	.105	6	22	0	0	1.1	1.000
7 yrs.			25	34	.424	4.96	143	58	13	526	625	166	135	2	9	4	3	150	18	1	.120	22	98	2	1	0.9	.984

Carl Thomas

THOMAS, CARL LESLIE BR TR 6′ 5″ 245 lbs.
B. May 28, 1932, Minneapolis, Minn.

Year	Team		W	L	PCT	ERA	G	GS	CG	IP	H	BB	SO	ShO	Relief W	Relief L	SV	AB	H	HR	BA	PO	A	E	DP	TC/G	FA
1960	CLE	A	1	0	1.000	7.45	4	0	0	9.2	8	10	5	0	1	0	0	3	1	0	.333	2	1	0	0	0.8	1.000

Claude Thomas

THOMAS, CLAUDE ALFRED (Lefty) BL TL 6′ 1″ 180 lbs.
B. May 15, 1890, Stanberry, Mo. D. Mar. 6, 1946, Sulphur, Okla.

Year	Team		W	L	PCT	ERA	G	GS	CG	IP	H	BB	SO	ShO	Relief W	Relief L	SV	AB	H	HR	BA	PO	A	E	DP	TC/G	FA
1916	WAS	A	1	2	.333	4.13	7	4	1	28.1	27	12	7	1	0	0	0	10	1	0	.100	2	7	1	0	1.4	.900

Fay Thomas

THOMAS, FAY WESLEY (Scow) BR TR 6′ 2″ 195 lbs.
B. Oct. 10, 1904, Holyrood, Kans. D. Aug. 16, 1990, Chatsworth, Calif.

Year	Team		W	L	PCT	ERA	G	GS	CG	IP	H	BB	SO	ShO	Relief W	Relief L	SV	AB	H	HR	BA	PO	A	E	DP	TC/G	FA
1927	NY	N	0	0	—	3.31	9	0	0	16.1	19	4	11	0	0	0	0	2	0	0	.000	0	1	0	0	0.1	1.000
1931	CLE	A	2	4	.333	5.18	16	2	1	48.2	63	32	25	0	1	3	0	13	2	0	.154	1	6	1	0	0.5	.875
1932	BKN	N	0	1	.000	7.41	7	2	0	17	22	8	9	0	0	0	0	3	0	0	.000	1	4	0	0	0.7	1.000
1935	STL	A	7	15	.318	4.78	49	19	4	147	165	89	67	0	5	2	1	38	4	0	.105	5	41	3	1	1.0	.939
4 yrs.			9	20	.310	4.95	81	23	5	229	269	133	112	0	6	5	1	56	6	0	.107	7	52	4	1	0.8	.937

Frosty Thomas

THOMAS, FORREST BR TR 6′ 185 lbs.
B. May 23, 1881, Faucett, Mo. D. Mar. 18, 1970, St. Joseph, Mo.

Year	Team		W	L	PCT	ERA	G	GS	CG	IP	H	BB	SO	ShO	Relief W	Relief L	SV	AB	H	HR	BA	PO	A	E	DP	TC/G	FA
1905	DET	A	0	1	.000	7.50	2	1	0	6	10	3	5	0	0	0	0	2	0	0	.000	0	2	0	0	1.0	1.000

Larry Thomas

THOMAS, LARRY WAYNE BR TL 6′ 1″ 195 lbs.
B. Oct. 25, 1969, Miami, Fla.

Year	Team	W	L	PCT	ERA	G	GS	CG	IP	H	BB	SO	ShO	Relief Pitching W	Relief Pitching L	Relief Pitching SV	Batting AB	Batting H	Batting HR	BA	PO	A	E	DP	TC/G	FA
1995	CHI A	0	0	—	1.32	17	0	0	13.2	8	6	12	0	0	0	0	0	0	0	—	2	0	0	0	0.1	1.000

Lefty Thomas

THOMAS, CLARENCE FLETCHER BL TL 6′ 183 lbs.
B. Oct. 4, 1903, Glade Springs, Va. D. Mar. 21, 1952, Charlottesville, Va.

Year	Team	W	L	PCT	ERA	G	GS	CG	IP	H	BB	SO	ShO	Relief Pitching W	Relief Pitching L	Relief Pitching SV	Batting AB	Batting H	Batting HR	BA	PO	A	E	DP	TC/G	FA
1925	WAS A	0	2	.000	2.08	2	2	1	13	14	7	10	0	0	0	0	5	0	0	.000	0	3	0	0	1.5	1.000
1926		0	0	—	5.19	6	0	0	8.2	8	10	3	0	0	0	0	2	0	0	.000	0	0	0	0	0.0	.000
2 yrs.		0	2	.000	3.32	8	2	1	21.2	22	17	13	0	0	0	0	7	0	0	.000	0	3	0	0	0.4	1.000

Mike Thomas

THOMAS, MICHAEL STEVEN BL TL 6′ 2″ 205 lbs.
B. Sept. 2, 1969, Sacramento, Calif.

Year	Team	W	L	PCT	ERA	G	GS	CG	IP	H	BB	SO	ShO	Relief Pitching W	Relief Pitching L	Relief Pitching SV	Batting AB	Batting H	Batting HR	BA	PO	A	E	DP	TC/G	FA
1995	MIL A	0	0	—	0.00	1	0	0	1.1	2	1	0	0	0	0	0	0	0	0	—	0	0	0	0	0.0	.000

Myles Thomas

THOMAS, MYLES LEWIS BR TR 5′ 9½″ 170 lbs.
B. Oct. 22, 1897, State College, Pa. D. Dec. 12, 1963, Toledo, Ohio.

Year	Team	W	L	PCT	ERA	G	GS	CG	IP	H	BB	SO	ShO	Relief Pitching W	Relief Pitching L	Relief Pitching SV	Batting AB	Batting H	Batting HR	BA	PO	A	E	DP	TC/G	FA
1926	NY A	6	6	.500	4.23	33	13	3	140.1	140	65	38	0	0	2	0	43	5	0	.116	7	39	2	1	1.5	.958
1927		7	4	.636	4.87	21	9	1	88.2	111	43	25	0	4	1	0	27	9	0	.333	4	22	1	2	1.3	.963
1928		1	0	1.000	3.41	12	1	0	31.2	33	9	10	0	0	0	0	10	4	0	.400	2	7	1	0	0.8	.900
1929	2 teams NY A (5G 0–2) WAS A (22G 7–8)																									
″	total	7	10	.412	4.30	27	15	7	140.1	166	57	36	0	0	2	2	55	15	0	.273	6	34	1	1	1.5	.976
1930	WAS A	2	2	.500	8.29	12	2	0	33.2	49	15	12	0	2	0	0	11	2	0	.182	1	4	1	0	0.5	.833
5 yrs.		23	22	.511	4.64	105	40	11	434.2	499	189	121	0	6	5	2	146	35	0	.240	20	106	6	4	1.3	.955
WORLD SERIES																										
1926	NY A	0	0	—	3.00	2	0	0	3	3	0	0	0	0	0	0	0	0	0	—	0	2	0	0	1.0	1.000

Roy Thomas

THOMAS, ROY ALLEN BL TL 5′11″ 150 lbs.
Brother of Bill Thomas.
B. Mar. 24, 1874, Norristown, Pa. D. Nov. 20, 1959, Norristown, Pa.

Year	Team	W	L	PCT	ERA	G	GS	CG	IP	H	BB	SO	ShO	Relief Pitching W	Relief Pitching L	Relief Pitching SV	Batting AB	Batting H	Batting HR	BA	PO	A	E	DP	TC/G	FA
1900	PHI N	0	0	—	3.38	1	0	0	2.2	4	0	0	0	0	0	0	*				454	23	20	14	3.3	.960

Roy Thomas

THOMAS, ROY JUSTIN BR TR 6′ 5″ 215 lbs.
B. June 22, 1953, Quantico, Va.

Year	Team	W	L	PCT	ERA	G	GS	CG	IP	H	BB	SO	ShO	Relief Pitching W	Relief Pitching L	Relief Pitching SV	Batting AB	Batting H	Batting HR	BA	PO	A	E	DP	TC/G	FA
1977	HOU N	0	0	—	3.00	4	0	0	6	5	3	4	0	0	0	0	0	0	0	—	0	1	0	0	0.3	1.000
1978	STL N	1	1	.500	3.86	16	1	0	28	21	16	16	0	1	0	3	4	1	0	.250	1	7	0	0	0.5	1.000
1979		3	4	.429	2.92	26	6	0	77	66	24	44	0	2	2	1	17	1	0	.059	10	13	0	1	0.9	1.000
1980		2	3	.400	4.75	24	5	0	55	59	25	22	0	0	2	0	13	2	0	.154	7	10	0	1	0.7	1.000
1983	SEA A	3	1	.750	3.45	43	0	0	88.2	95	32	77	0	3	1	1	0	0	0	—	7	8	0	0	0.3	1.000
1984		3	2	.600	5.26	21	1	0	49.2	52	37	42	0	3	1	1	0	0	0	—	4	7	0	1	0.5	1.000
1985		7	0	1.000	3.36	40	0	0	93.2	66	48	70	0	7	0	1	0	0	0	—	7	7	0	1	0.3	1.000
1987		1	0	1.000	5.23	8	0	0	20.2	23	11	14	0	1	0	0	0	0	0	—	0	1	0	0	0.1	1.000
8 yrs.		20	11	.645	3.83	182	13	0	418.2	387	196	289	0	17	6	7	34	4	0	.118	36	54	0	4	0.5	1.000

Stan Thomas

THOMAS, STANLEY BROWN BR TR 6′ 2″ 185 lbs.
B. July 11, 1949, Rumford, Me.

Year	Team	W	L	PCT	ERA	G	GS	CG	IP	H	BB	SO	ShO	Relief Pitching W	Relief Pitching L	Relief Pitching SV	Batting AB	Batting H	Batting HR	BA	PO	A	E	DP	TC/G	FA
1974	TEX A	0	0	—	6.43	12	0	0	14	22	6	8	0	0	0	0	0	0	0	—	1	3	0	0	0.3	1.000
1975		4	4	.500	3.10	46	1	0	81.1	72	34	46	0	4	3	3	0	0	0	—	6	13	0	1	0.4	1.000
1976	CLE A	4	4	.500	2.29	37	7	2	106	88	41	54	0	1	2	6	0	0	0	—	12	26	1	2	1.1	.974
1977	2 teams SEA A (13G 2–6) NY A (3G 1–0)																									
″	total	3	6	.333	6.12	16	9	1	64.2	81	29	15	0	2	1	0	0	0	0		3	10	2	1	0.9	.867
4 yrs.		11	14	.440	3.69	111	17	3	266	263	110	123	0	7	6	9	0	0	0		22	52	3	4	0.7	.961

Tom Thomas

THOMAS, THOMAS R. (Savage Tom) BR TR 6′ 4″ 195 lbs.
B. Dec. 27, 1873, Shawnee, Ohio D. Sept. 23, 1942, Shawnee, Ohio.

Year	Team	W	L	PCT	ERA	G	GS	CG	IP	H	BB	SO	ShO	Relief Pitching W	Relief Pitching L	Relief Pitching SV	Batting AB	Batting H	Batting HR	BA	PO	A	E	DP	TC/G	FA
1899	STL N	1	1	.500	2.52	4	2	2	25	22	4	8	0	0	0	0	12	3	0	.250	0	7	2	0	2.3	.778
1900		1	1	.500	3.76	5	1	1	26.1	38	4	7	0	1	0	0	11	1	0	.091	0	3	1	0	0.8	.750
2 yrs.		2	2	.500	3.16	9	3	3	51.1	60	8	15	0	1	0	0	23	4	0	.174	0	10	3	0	1.4	.769

Tommy Thomas

THOMAS, ALPHONSE BR TR 5′10″ 175 lbs.
B. Dec. 23, 1899, Baltimore, Md. D. Apr. 27, 1988, Dallastown, Pa.

Year	Team	W	L	PCT	ERA	G	GS	CG	IP	H	BB	SO	ShO	Relief Pitching W	Relief Pitching L	Relief Pitching SV	Batting AB	Batting H	Batting HR	BA	PO	A	E	DP	TC/G	FA
1926	CHI A	15	12	.556	3.80	44	32	13	249	225	110	127	2	3	2	2	86	16	0	.186	8	44	0	3	1.2	1.000
1927		19	16	.543	2.98	40	**36**	24	**307.2**	271	94	107	3	1	0	1	95	14	1	.147	6	55	2	4	1.6	.968
1928		17	16	.515	3.08	36	32	24	283	277	76	129	3	1	0	2	96	21	2	.219	9	48	1	2	1.6	.983
1929		14	18	.438	3.19	36	31	**24**	259.2	270	60	62	2	1	0	1	98	25	0	.255	8	44	2	2	1.5	.963
1930		5	13	.278	5.22	34	27	7	169	229	44	58	0	0	0	0	56	7	0	.125	8	34	2	2	1.3	.955
1931		10	14	.417	4.80	42	36	11	242	296	69	71	2	0	0	2	87	21	0	.241	8	47	1	3	1.3	.982
1932	2 teams CHI A (12G 3–3) WAS A (18G 8–7)																									
″	total	11	10	.524	4.26	30	17	8	160.2	169	61	47	1	4	1	0	55	11	0	.200	2	24	1	2	0.9	.963
1933	WAS A	7	7	.500	4.80	35	14	2	135	149	49	35	0	4	4	3	42	10	0	.238	3	22	1	1	0.7	.962
1934		8	9	.471	5.47	33	18	7	133.1	154	58	42	1	2	2	1	38	7	0	.184	1	20	1	1	0.7	.955
1935	2 teams WAS A (1G 0–0) PHI N (4G 0–1)																									
″	total	0	1	.000	6.57	5	1	0	12.1	18	5	3	0	0	1	0	3	0	0	.000	0	2	0	0	0.4	1.000
1936	STL A	11	9	.550	5.26	36	21	8	179.2	219	72	40	1	2	0	0	58	8	0	.138	2	24	0	1	0.7	1.000
1937	2 teams STL A (17G 0–1) BOS A (9G 0–2)																									
″	total	0	3	.000	6.26	26	2	0	41.2	62	14	14	0	0	2	0	8	1	0	.125	1	8	0	0	0.3	1.000
12 yrs.		117	128	.478	4.12	397	267	128	2173	2339	712	735	15	18	12	12	722	141	3	.195	56	372	11	21	1.1	.975
WORLD SERIES																										
1933	WAS A	0	0	—	0.00	2	0	0	1.1	1	0	2	0	0	0	0	0	0	0	—	0	0	0	0	0.0	.000

Erskine Thomason

THOMASON, MELVIN ERSKINE BR TR 6′ 1″ 190 lbs.
B. Aug. 13, 1948, Laurens, S. C.

Year	Team	W	L	PCT	ERA	G	GS	CG	IP	H	BB	SO	ShO	Relief Pitching W	Relief Pitching L	Relief Pitching SV	Batting AB	Batting H	Batting HR	BA	PO	A	E	DP	TC/G	FA
1974	PHI N	0	0	—	0.00	1	0	0	1	0	0	1	0	0	0	0	0	0	0	—	0	0	0	0	0.0	.000

Art Thompson

THOMPSON, ARTHUR J.
Deceased.

Year	Team		W	L	PCT	ERA	G	GS	CG	IP	H	BB	SO	ShO	Relief Pitching W	Relief Pitching L	Relief Pitching SV	Batting AB	Batting H	Batting HR	BA	PO	A	E	DP	TC/G	FA
1884	WAS	U	0	1	.000	6.75	1	1	1	8	10	3	8	0	0	0	0	3	0	0	.000	0	3	0	0	3.0	1.000

Bill Thompson

THOMPSON, WILL McLAIN BR TR 5′11½″ 190 lbs.
B. Aug. 30, 1870, Pittsburgh, Pa. D. June 9, 1962, Pittsburgh, Pa.

Year	Team		W	L	PCT	ERA	G	GS	CG	IP	H	BB	SO	ShO	Relief Pitching W	Relief Pitching L	Relief Pitching SV	Batting AB	Batting H	Batting HR	BA	PO	A	E	DP	TC/G	FA
1892	PIT	N	0	1	.000	3.00	1	1	0	3	3	5	0	0	0	0	0	0	0	0	—	0	1	0	0	1.0	1.000

Dave Thompson

THOMPSON, DAVID FORREST BL TL 5′11″ 195 lbs.
B. Mar. 3, 1918, Mooresville, N. C. D. Feb. 26, 1979, Charlotte, N. C.

Year	Team		W	L	PCT	ERA	G	GS	CG	IP	H	BB	SO	ShO	Relief Pitching W	Relief Pitching L	Relief Pitching SV	Batting AB	Batting H	Batting HR	BA	PO	A	E	DP	TC/G	FA
1948	WAS	A	6	10	.375	3.84	46	7	0	131.1	134	54	40	0	5	5	4	35	10	0	.286	7	22	2	1	0.7	.935
1949			1	3	.250	4.41	9	1	1	16.1	22	9	8	0	1	2	0	5	3	0	.600	0	3	1	1	0.4	.750
2 yrs.			7	13	.350	3.90	55	8	1	147.2	156	63	48	0	6	7	4	40	13	0	.325	7	25	3	2	0.6	.914

Fuller Thompson

THOMPSON, FULLER WEIDNER BR TR 5′11½″ 164 lbs.
B. May 1, 1889, Los Angeles, Calif. D. Feb. 19, 1972, Los Angeles, Calif.

Year	Team		W	L	PCT	ERA	G	GS	CG	IP	H	BB	SO	ShO	Relief Pitching W	Relief Pitching L	Relief Pitching SV	Batting AB	Batting H	Batting HR	BA	PO	A	E	DP	TC/G	FA
1911	BOS	N	0	0	—	3.86	3	0	0	4.2	5	2	0	0	0	0	0	0	0	0	—	0	2	0	1	0.7	1.000

Gus Thompson

THOMPSON, JOHN GUSTAV BR TR 6′2″ 185 lbs.
B. June 22, 1877, Humboldt, Iowa D. Mar. 28, 1958, Kalispell, Mont.

Year	Team		W	L	PCT	ERA	G	GS	CG	IP	H	BB	SO	ShO	Relief Pitching W	Relief Pitching L	Relief Pitching SV	Batting AB	Batting H	Batting HR	BA	PO	A	E	DP	TC/G	FA
1903	PIT	N	2	3	.400	3.56	5	4	3	43	52	16	22	0	0	1	0	16	4	0	.250	2	8	3	0	2.6	.769
1906	STL	N	2	11	.154	4.28	17	12	8	103	111	25	36	0	0	3	0	34	6	0	.176	1	36	1	1	2.2	.974
2 yrs.			4	14	.222	4.07	22	16	11	146	163	41	58	0	0	4	0	50	10	0	.200	3	44	4	1	2.3	.922
WORLD SERIES																											
1903	PIT	N	0	0	—	4.50	1	0	0	2	3	0	1	0	0	0	0	1	0	0	.000	0	1	0	0	1.0	1.000

Harry Thompson

THOMPSON, HAROLD BL TL 5′8″ 150 lbs.
B. Sept. 9, 1889, Nanticoke, Pa. D. Feb. 14, 1951, Reno, Nev.

Year	Team		W	L	PCT	ERA	G	GS	CG	IP	H	BB	SO	ShO	Relief Pitching W	Relief Pitching L	Relief Pitching SV	Batting AB	Batting H	Batting HR	BA	PO	A	E	DP	TC/G	FA
1919	2 teams	WAS A (12G 0–3) PHI A (3G 0–1)																									
″	total		0	4	.000	4.23	15	2	0	55.1	64	11	11	0	0	2	1	38	8	0	.211	11	16	0	1	1.4	1.000

Jocko Thompson

THOMPSON, JOHN SAMUEL BL TL 6′ 185 lbs.
B. Jan. 17, 1917, Beverly, Mass. D. Feb. 3, 1988, Olney, Md.

Year	Team		W	L	PCT	ERA	G	GS	CG	IP	H	BB	SO	ShO	Relief Pitching W	Relief Pitching L	Relief Pitching SV	Batting AB	Batting H	Batting HR	BA	PO	A	E	DP	TC/G	FA
1948	PHI	N	1	0	1.000	2.77	2	2	1	13	10	9	7	0	0	0	0	3	0	0	.000	0	1	0	0	0.5	1.000
1949			1	3	.250	6.89	8	5	1	31.1	38	11	12	0	0	0	0	11	2	0	.182	0	5	0	1	0.6	1.000
1950			0	0	—	0.00	2	0	0	4	1	4	2	0	0	0	0	0	0	0	—	0	1	0	0	0.5	1.000
1951			4	8	.333	3.85	29	14	3	119.1	102	59	60	2	0	1	1	39	4	0	.103	9	16	3	2	1.0	.893
4 yrs.			6	11	.353	4.24	41	21	5	167.2	151	83	81	2	0	1	1	53	6	0	.113	9	23	3	3	0.9	.914

Junior Thompson

THOMPSON, EUGENE EARL BR TR 6′1″ 185 lbs.
B. June 7, 1917, Latham, Ill.

Year	Team		W	L	PCT	ERA	G	GS	CG	IP	H	BB	SO	ShO	Relief Pitching W	Relief Pitching L	Relief Pitching SV	Batting AB	Batting H	Batting HR	BA	PO	A	E	DP	TC/G	FA
1939	CIN	N	13	5	.722	2.54	42	11	5	152.1	130	55	87	3	**8**	1	2	48	11	0	.229	3	25	3	0	0.7	.903
1940			16	9	.640	3.32	33	31	17	225.1	197	96	103	3	1	0	0	79	18	0	.228	12	40	4	1	1.7	.929
1941			6	6	.500	4.87	27	15	4	109	117	57	46	0	2	0	1	30	7	0	.233	6	32	2	0	1.5	.950
1942			4	7	.364	3.36	29	10	1	101.2	86	53	35	0	1	3	0	30	8	0	.267	9	39	4	4	1.8	.923
1946	NY	N	4	6	.400	1.29	39	1	0	62.2	36	40	31	0	4	5	4	7	1	0	.143	5	18	0	0	0.6	1.000
1947			4	2	.667	4.29	15	0	0	35.2	36	27	13	0	4	2	0	6	0	0	.000	5	9	0	1	0.9	1.000
6 yrs.			47	35	.573	3.26	185	68	27	686.2	602	328	315	6	20	11	7	200	45	0	.225	40	163	13	6	1.2	.940
WORLD SERIES																											
1939	CIN	N	0	1	.000	13.50	1	1	0	4.2	5	4	3	0	0	0	0	1	1	0	1.000	0	0	0	0	0.0	.000
1940			0	1	.000	16.20	1	1	0	3.1	8	4	2	0	0	0	0	1	0	0	.000	0	1	0	0	1.0	1.000
2 yrs.			0	2	.000	14.63	2	2	0	8	13	8	5	0	0	0	0	2	1	0	.500	0	1	0	0	0.5	1.000

Lee Thompson

THOMPSON, JOHN DUDLEY (Lefty) BL TL 6′1″ 185 lbs.
B. Feb. 26, 1898, Smithfield, Utah D. Feb. 17, 1963, Santa Barbara, Calif.

Year	Team		W	L	PCT	ERA	G	GS	CG	IP	H	BB	SO	ShO	Relief Pitching W	Relief Pitching L	Relief Pitching SV	Batting AB	Batting H	Batting HR	BA	PO	A	E	DP	TC/G	FA
1921	CHI	A	0	3	.000	8.27	4	4	0	20.2	32	6	4	0	0	0	0	7	2	0	.286	1	2	0	0	0.8	1.000

Mark Thompson

THOMPSON, MARK RADFORD BR TR 6′2″ 205 lbs.
B. Apr. 7, 1971, Russellville, Ky.

Year	Team		W	L	PCT	ERA	G	GS	CG	IP	H	BB	SO	ShO	Relief Pitching W	Relief Pitching L	Relief Pitching SV	Batting AB	Batting H	Batting HR	BA	PO	A	E	DP	TC/G	FA
1994	CLR	N	1	1	.500	9.00	2	2	0	9	16	8	5	0	0	0	0	4	0	0	.000	1	0	0	0	0.5	1.000
1995			2	3	.400	6.53	21	5	0	51	73	22	30	0	1	1	0	13	5	0	.385	3	10	0	1	0.6	1.000
2 yrs.			3	4	.429	6.90	23	7	0	60	89	30	35	0	1	1	0	17	5	0	.294	4	10	0	1	0.6	1.000
DIVISIONAL PLAYOFF SERIES																											
1995	CLR	N	0	0	—	0.00	1	0	0	1	0	0	0	0	0	0	1	0	0	0	—	1	0	0	0	1.0	1.000

Mike Thompson

THOMPSON, MICHAEL WAYNE BR TR 6′3″ 190 lbs.
B. Sept. 6, 1949, Denver, Colo.

Year	Team		W	L	PCT	ERA	G	GS	CG	IP	H	BB	SO	ShO	Relief Pitching W	Relief Pitching L	Relief Pitching SV	Batting AB	Batting H	Batting HR	BA	PO	A	E	DP	TC/G	FA
1971	WAS	A	1	6	.143	4.84	16	12	0	67	53	54	41	0	0	0	0	17	2	0	.118	6	12	1	0	1.2	.947
1973	STL	N	0	0	—	0.00	2	2	0	4	1	5	3	0	0	0	0	1	0	0	.000	0	0	0	0	0.0	.000
1974	2 teams	STL N (19G 0–3) ATL N (1G 0–0)																									
″	total		0	3	.000	5.53	20	5	0	42.1	44	37	27	0	0	0	0	9	1	0	.111	4	6	0	1	0.5	1.000
1975	ATL	N	0	6	.000	4.67	16	10	0	52	60	32	42	0	0	0	0	14	1	0	.071	3	9	0	0	0.8	1.000
4 yrs.			1	15	.063	4.84	54	29	0	165.1	158	128	113	0	0	0	0	41	4	0	.098	13	27	1	1	0.8	.976

Rich Thompson

THOMPSON, RICHARD NEIL BR TR 6′3″ 225 lbs.
B. Nov. 1, 1958, New York, N. Y.

Year	Team		W	L	PCT	ERA	G	GS	CG	IP	H	BB	SO	ShO	Relief Pitching W	Relief Pitching L	Relief Pitching SV	Batting AB	Batting H	Batting HR	BA	PO	A	E	DP	TC/G	FA
1985	CLE	A	3	8	.273	6.30	57	0	0	80	95	48	30	0	3	8	5	0	0	0	—	2	7	3	1	0.2	.750
1989	MON	N	0	2	.000	2.18	19	1	0	33	27	11	15	0	0	1	0	2	0	0	.000	0	4	0	0	0.2	1.000
1990			0	0	—	0.00	1	0	0	1	1	0	0	0	0	0	0	0	0	0	—	0	0	0	0	0.0	.000
3 yrs.			3	10	.231	5.05	77	1	0	114	123	59	45	0	3	9	5	2	0	0	.000	2	11	3	1	0.2	.813

Tommy Thompson

THOMPSON, THOMAS CARL BR TR 5′9½″ 170 lbs.
Brother of Homer Thompson.
B. Nov. 7, 1889, Spring City, Tenn. D. Jan. 16, 1963, La Jolla, Calif.

Year	Team		W	L	PCT	ERA	G	GS	CG	IP	H	BB	SO	ShO	Relief Pitching W	Relief Pitching L	Relief Pitching SV	Batting AB	Batting H	Batting HR	BA	PO	A	E	DP	TC/G	FA
1912	NY	A	0	2	.000	6.06	7	2	1	32.2	43	13	15	0	0	0	0	10	3	0	.300	0	7	1	0	1.1	.875

Hank Thormahlen

THORMAHLEN, HERBERT EHLER (Lefty) BL TL 6′ 180 lbs.
B. July 5, 1896, Jersey City, N. J. D. Feb. 6, 1955, Los Angeles, Calif.

Year	Team		W	L	PCT	ERA	G	GS	CG	IP	H	BB	SO	ShO	Relief Pitching W	Relief Pitching L	Relief Pitching SV	Batting AB	Batting H	Batting HR	BA	PO	A	E	DP	TC/G	FA
1917	NY	A	0	1	.000	2.25	1	1	0	8	9	4	5	0	0	0	0	2	0	0	.000	0	1	1	1	2.0	.500
1918			7	3	.700	2.48	16	12	5	112.2	85	52	22	2	1	1	0	39	3	0	.077	1	34	0	3	2.2	1.000
1919			12	10	.545	2.62	30	25	13	188.2	155	61	62	2	0	1	1	59	11	0	.186	7	47	2	0	1.9	.964
1920			9	6	.600	4.14	29	14	5	143.1	178	43	35	0	3	0	1	45	10	0	.222	6	45	4	1	1.9	.927
1921	BOS	A	1	7	.125	4.48	23	9	3	96.1	101	34	17	0	0	0	0	23	4	0	.174	1	26	1	2	1.2	.964
1925	BKN	N	0	3	.000	3.94	5	2	0	16	22	9	7	0	0	1	0	5	1	0	.200	2	6	2	0	2.0	.800
6 yrs.			29	30	.492	3.33	104	63	26	565	550	203	148	4	4	3	2	173	29	0	.168	17	159	10	7	1.8	.946

Paul Thormodsgard

THORMODSGARD, PAUL GAYTON BR TR 6′ 2″ 190 lbs.
B. Nov. 10, 1953, San Francisco, Calif.

Year	Team		W	L	PCT	ERA	G	GS	CG	IP	H	BB	SO	ShO	Relief Pitching W	Relief Pitching L	Relief Pitching SV	Batting AB	Batting H	Batting HR	BA	PO	A	E	DP	TC/G	FA
1977	MIN	A	11	15	.423	4.62	37	37	8	218	236	65	94	1	0	0	0	0	0	0	—	8	31	2	2	1.1	.951
1978			1	6	.143	5.05	12	12	1	66	81	17	23	0	0	0	0	0	0	0	—	3	9	2	0	1.2	.857
1979			0	0	—	9.00	1	0	0	1	3	0	1	0	0	0	0	0	0	0	—	0	0	0	0	0.0	.000
3 yrs.			12	21	.364	4.74	50	49	9	285	320	82	118	1	0	0	0	0	0	0		11	40	4	2	1.1	.927

John Thornton

THORNTON, JOHN 5′10½″ 175 lbs.
B. 1870, Washington, D. C. Deceased.

Year	Team		W	L	PCT	ERA	G	GS	CG	IP	H	BB	SO	ShO	Relief Pitching W	Relief Pitching L	Relief Pitching SV	Batting AB	Batting H	Batting HR	BA	PO	A	E	DP	TC/G	FA
1889	WAS	N	0	1	.000	5.00	1	1	1	9	8	7	3	0	0	0	0	4	0	0	.000	0	1	0	0	1.0	1.000
1891	PHI	N	15	16	.484	3.68	37	32	23	269	268	115	52	1	0	0	2	123	17	0	.138	28	61	13	4	2.5	.873
1892			0	2	.000	12.75	3	2	1	12	16	17	2	0	0	0	0	16	5	0	.313	3	4	2	0	1.5	.778
3 yrs.			15	19	.441	4.10	41	35	25	290	292	139	57	1	0	0	2	143	22	0	.154	31	66	15	4	2.4	.866

Walter Thornton

THORNTON, WALTER MILLER BL TL 6′ 1″ 180 lbs.
B. Feb. 18, 1875, Lewiston, Me. D. July 14, 1960, Los Angeles, Calif.

Year	Team		W	L	PCT	ERA	G	GS	CG	IP	H	BB	SO	ShO	Relief Pitching W	Relief Pitching L	Relief Pitching SV	Batting AB	Batting H	Batting HR	BA	PO	A	E	DP	TC/G	FA
1895	CHI	N	2	0	1.000	6.08	7	2	2	40	58	31	13	0	0	0	1	22	7	1	.318	7	5	1	0	1.6	.923
1896			2	1	.667	5.70	5	5	2	23.2	30	13	10	0	0	0	0	22	8	0	.364	8	3	3	0	1.8	.786
1897			6	7	.462	4.70	16	16	15	130.1	164	51	55	0	0	0	0	265	85	0	.321	85	33	24	1	1.9	.831
1898			13	10	.565	3.34	28	25	21	215.1	226	56	56	2	0	0	0	210	62	0	.295	74	53	17	5	2.3	.882
4 yrs.			23	18	.561	4.18	56	48	40	409.1	478	151	134	2	0	0	1	*				174	94	45	6	2.0	.856

Bob Thorpe

THORPE, ROBERT JOSEPH BR TR 6′ 1″ 170 lbs.
B. Jan. 12, 1935, San Diego, Calif. D. Mar. 17, 1960, San Diego, Calif.

Year	Team		W	L	PCT	ERA	G	GS	CG	IP	H	BB	SO	ShO	Relief Pitching W	Relief Pitching L	Relief Pitching SV	Batting AB	Batting H	Batting HR	BA	PO	A	E	DP	TC/G	FA
1955	CHI	N	0	0	—	3.00	2	0	0	3	4	0	0	0	0	0	0	0	0	0	—	0	2	0	0	1.0	1.000

George Throop

THROOP, GEORGE LYNFORD III BR TR 6′ 7″ 205 lbs.
B. Nov. 24, 1950, Pasadena, Calif.

Year	Team		W	L	PCT	ERA	G	GS	CG	IP	H	BB	SO	ShO	Relief Pitching W	Relief Pitching L	Relief Pitching SV	Batting AB	Batting H	Batting HR	BA	PO	A	E	DP	TC/G	FA
1975	KC	A	0	0	—	4.00	7	0	0	9	8	2	8	0	0	0	2	0	0	0	—	1	2	0	0	0.4	1.000
1977			0	0	—	3.60	4	0	0	5	1	4	1	0	0	0	1	0	0	0	—	1	2	0	0	0.8	1.000
1978			1	0	1.000	0.00	1	0	0	3	2	3	2	0	1	0	0	0	0	0	—	0	1	0	0	1.0	1.000
1979	2 teams	KC A (4G 0–0)	HOU N (14G 1–0)																								
″	total		1	0	1.000	4.32	18	0	0	25	30	16	16	0	1	0	0	3	0	0	.000	1	2	0	0	0.2	1.000
4 yrs.			2	0	1.000	3.86	30	0	0	42	41	25	27	0	2	0	3	3	0	0	.000	3	7	0	0	0.3	1.000

Lou Thuman

THUMAN, LOUIS CHARLES FRANK BR TR 6′ 2″ 185 lbs.
B. Dec. 13, 1916, Baltimore, Md.

Year	Team		W	L	PCT	ERA	G	GS	CG	IP	H	BB	SO	ShO	Relief Pitching W	Relief Pitching L	Relief Pitching SV	Batting AB	Batting H	Batting HR	BA	PO	A	E	DP	TC/G	FA
1939	WAS	A	0	0	—	9.00	3	0	0	4	5	2	1	0	0	0	0	0	0	0	—	2	2	0	0	1.3	1.000
1940			0	1	.000	14.40	2	0	0	5	10	7	0	0	0	1	0	2	0	0	.000	1	1	1	0	1.5	.667
2 yrs.			0	1	.000	12.00	5	0	0	9	15	9	1	0	0	1	0	2	0	0	.000	3	3	1	0	1.4	.857

Mark Thurmond

THURMOND, MARK ANTHONY BL TL 6′ 190 lbs.
B. Sept. 12, 1956, Houston, Tex.

Year	Team		W	L	PCT	ERA	G	GS	CG	IP	H	BB	SO	ShO	Relief Pitching W	Relief Pitching L	Relief Pitching SV	Batting AB	Batting H	Batting HR	BA	PO	A	E	DP	TC/G	FA
1983	SD	N	7	3	.700	2.65	21	18	2	115.1	104	33	49	0	0	0	0	37	2	0	.054	7	22	0	0	1.4	1.000
1984			14	8	.636	2.97	32	29	1	178.2	174	55	57	1	0	1	0	58	11	0	.190	11	38	0	3	1.5	1.000
1985			7	11	.389	3.97	36	23	1	138.1	154	44	57	1	1	1	2	34	3	0	.088	8	27	1	2	1.0	.972
1986	2 teams	SD N (17G 3–7)	DET A (25G 4–1)																								
″	total		7	8	.467	4.56	42	19	2	122.1	140	44	49	1	2	0	3	24	6	0	.250	10	15	0	0	0.6	1.000
1987	DET	A	0	1	.000	4.23	48	0	0	61.2	83	24	21	0	0	1	5	0	0	0	—	2	9	0	0	0.2	1.000
1988	BAL	A	1	8	.111	4.58	43	6	0	74.2	80	27	29	0	1	2	3	0	0	0	—	3	8	1	0	0.3	.917
1989			2	4	.333	3.90	49	2	0	90	102	17	34	0	2	3	4	0	0	0	—	4	10	0	0	0.3	1.000
1990	SF	N	2	3	.400	3.34	43	0	0	56.2	53	18	24	0	2	3	4	5	0	0	.000	4	15	1	2	0.5	.950
8 yrs.			40	46	.465	3.69	314	97	6	837.2	890	262	320	3	8	11	21	158	22	0	.139	49	144	3	7	0.6	.985
LEAGUE CHAMPIONSHIP SERIES																											
1984	SD	N	0	1	.000	9.82	1	1	0	3.2	7	2	1	0	0	0	0	1	1	0	1.000	0	1	0	0	1.0	1.000
1987	DET	A	0	0	—	0.00	1	0	0	0.1	0	0	0	0	0	0	0	0	0	0	—	0	0	0	0	0.0	.000
2 yrs.			0	1	.000	9.00	2	1	0	4	7	2	1	0	0	0	0	1	1	0	1.000	0	1	0	0	0.5	1.000
WORLD SERIES																											
1984	SD	N	0	1	.000	10.13	2	2	0	5.1	12	3	2	0	0	0	0	0	0	0	—	0	2	0	0	1.0	1.000

Sloppy Thurston

THURSTON, HOLLIS JOHN BR TR 5′11″ 165 lbs.
B. June 2, 1899, Fremont, Neb. D. Sept. 14, 1973, Los Angeles, Calif.

Year	Team		W	L	PCT	ERA	G	GS	CG	IP	H	BB	SO	ShO	Relief Pitching W	Relief Pitching L	Relief Pitching SV	Batting AB	Batting H	Batting HR	BA	PO	A	E	DP	TC/G	FA
1923	2 teams	STL A (2G 0–0)	CHI A (44G 7–8)																								
″	total		7	8	.467	3.13	46	13	8	195.2	231	38	55	0	4	3	4	79	25	0	.316	6	50	2	2	1.3	.966
1924	CHI	A	20	14	.588	3.80	38	36	**28**	291	**330**	60	37	1	0	1	1	122	31	1	.254	15	75	3	1	2.4	.968
1925			10	14	.417	6.17	36	25	9	175	250	47	35	0	1	4	1	84	24	0	.286	15	55	2	4	2.0	.972
1926			6	8	.429	5.02	31	13	6	134.1	164	36	35	1	2	3	3	61	19	0	.311	4	30	1	1	1.1	.971
1927	WAS	A	13	13	.500	4.47	29	28	13	205.1	254	60	38	2	0	1	0	92	29	2	.315	12	46	4	4	2.1	.935
1930	BKN	N	6	4	.600	3.40	24	11	5	106	110	17	26	2	1	0	1	50	10	1	.200	3	30	0	0	1.4	1.000
1931			9	9	.500	3.97	24	17	11	143	175	39	23	0	1	3	0	60	13	1	.217	3	30	2	3	1.5	.943
1932			12	8	.600	4.06	28	20	10	153	174	38	35	2	1	1	0	56	17	0	.304	10	34	0	2	1.6	1.000
1933			6	8	.429	4.52	32	15	5	131.1	171	34	22	0	3	1	3	44	7	0	.159	3	40	1	0	1.4	.977
9 yrs.			89	86	.509	4.26	288	178	95	1534.2	1859	369	306	8	13	17	13	*				71	390	15	17	1.6	.968

Luis Tiant

TIANT, LUIS CLEMENTE
Born Luis Clemente Tiant (Vega).
B. Nov. 23, 1940, Marianao, Cuba.
BR TR 6′ 180 lbs.

Year	Team	W	L	PCT	ERA	G	GS	CG	IP	H	BB	SO	ShO	Relief Pitching W	Relief Pitching L	Relief Pitching SV	Batting AB	Batting H	Batting HR	BA	PO	A	E	DP	TC/G	FA
1964	CLE A	10	4	.714	2.83	19	16	9	127	94	47	105	3	1	1	1	45	5	1	.111	3	21	1	2	1.3	.960
1965		11	11	.500	3.53	41	30	10	196.1	166	66	152	2	0	1	1	68	6	1	.088	17	27	1	2	1.1	.978
1966		12	11	.522	2.79	46	16	7	155	121	50	145	**5**	4	6	8	36	4	0	.111	9	20	4	0	0.7	.879
1967		12	9	.571	2.74	33	29	9	213.2	177	67	219	1	0	0	2	71	18	1	.254	13	17	4	3	1.0	.882
1968		21	9	.700	**1.60**	34	32	19	258.1	152	73	264	**9**	0	1	0	87	7	0	.080	15	19	1	2	1.0	.971
1969		9	**20**	.310	3.71	38	37	9	249.2	229	**129**	156	1	0	0	0	81	19	2	.235	22	31	4	1	1.5	.930
1970	MIN A	7	3	.700	3.39	18	17	2	93	84	41	50	1	0	0	0	32	13	0	.406	3	14	1	2	1.0	.944
1971	BOS A	1	7	.125	4.88	21	10	1	72	73	32	59	0	1	1	0	19	3	0	.158	5	9	1	0	0.7	.933
1972		15	6	.714	**1.91**	43	19	12	179	128	65	123	6	3	1	3	56	6	0	.107	7	24	1	1	0.7	.969
1973		20	13	.606	3.34	35	35	23	272	217	78	206	0	0	0	0	0	0	0	—	17	31	1	4	1.4	.980
1974		22	13	.629	2.92	38	38	25	311	281	82	176	**7**	0	0	0	0	0	0	—	22	31	4	1	1.5	.930
1975		18	14	.563	4.02	35	35	18	260	262	72	142	2	0	0	0	1	0	0	.000	16	22	4	2	1.2	.905
1976		21	12	.636	3.06	38	38	19	279	274	64	131	3	0	0	0	1	0	0	.000	12	34	4	4	1.3	.920
1977		12	8	.600	4.53	32	32	3	188.2	210	51	124	3	0	0	0	0	0	0	—	16	16	0	0	1.0	1.000
1978		13	8	.619	3.31	32	31	12	212.1	185	57	114	5	1	0	0	0	0	0	—	14	20	0	2	1.1	1.000
1979	NY A	13	8	.619	3.90	30	30	5	196	190	53	104	1	0	0	0	0	0	0	—	13	27	2	2	1.4	.952
1980		8	9	.471	4.90	25	25	3	136	139	50	84	0	0	0	0	0	0	0	—	13	21	2	3	1.4	.944
1981	PIT N	2	5	.286	3.95	9	9	1	57	54	19	32	0	0	0	0	16	3	0	.188	3	5	0	0	0.9	1.000
1982	CAL A	2	2	.500	5.76	6	5	0	29.2	39	8	30	0	0	0	0	0	0	0	—	1	0	0	0	0.2	1.000
19 yrs.		229	172	.571	3.30	573	484	187	3485.2	3075	1104	2416	49	10	11	15	513	84	5	.164	221	389	35	31	1.1	.946
LEAGUE CHAMPIONSHIP SERIES																										
1970	MIN A	0	0	—	13.50	1	0	0	0.2	1	0	0	0	0	0	0	0	0	0	—	0	0	0	0	0.0	.000
1975	BOS A	1	0	1.000	0.00	1	1	1	9	3	3	8	0	0	0	0	0	0	0	—	0	1	0	0	1.0	1.000
2 yrs.		1	0	1.000	0.93	2	1	1	9.2	4	3	8	0	0	0	0	0	0	0		0	1	0	0	0.5	1.000
WORLD SERIES																										
1975	BOS A	2	0	1.000 1st	3.60	3	3	2	25	25	8	12	1	0	0	0	8	2	0	.250	0	4	0	0	1.3	1.000

Jay Tibbs

TIBBS, JAY LINDSEY
B. Jan. 4, 1962, Birmingham, Ala.
BR TR 6′ 3″ 185 lbs.

Year	Team	W	L	PCT	ERA	G	GS	CG	IP	H	BB	SO	ShO	Relief Pitching W	Relief Pitching L	Relief Pitching SV	Batting AB	Batting H	Batting HR	BA	PO	A	E	DP	TC/G	FA
1984	CIN N	6	2	.750	2.86	14	14	3	100.2	87	33	40	1	0	0	0	36	5	0	.139	6	10	1	1	1.2	.941
1985		10	16	.385	3.92	35	34	5	218	216	83	98	2	0	1	0	65	6	0	.092	15	40	3	4	1.7	.948
1986	MON N	7	9	.438	3.97	35	31	3	190.1	181	70	117	2	0	0	0	54	7	0	.130	14	24	0	2	1.1	1.000
1987		4	5	.444	4.99	19	12	0	83	95	34	54	0	0	0	0	25	3	0	.120	7	8	0	1	0.8	1.000
1988	BAL A	4	15	.211	5.39	30	24	1	158.2	184	63	82	0	0	1	0	0	0	0	—	17	18	0	0	1.2	1.000
1989		5	0	1.000	2.82	10	8	1	54.1	62	20	30	0	0	0	0	0	0	0	—	5	5	0	0	1.0	1.000
1990	2 teams	BAL A	(10G 2–7)		PIT N	(5G 1–0)																				
″	total	3	7	.300	5.31	15	10	0	57.2	62	16	27	0	1	0	0	0	0	0		7	9	0	0	1.1	1.000
7 yrs.		39	54	.419	4.20	158	133	13	862.2	887	319	448	5	1	2	0	180	21	0	.117	71	114	4	8	1.2	.979

Dick Tidrow

TIDROW, RICHARD WILLIAM (Dirt)
B. May 14, 1947, San Francisco, Calif.
BR TR 6′ 4″ 210 lbs.

Year	Team	W	L	PCT	ERA	G	GS	CG	IP	H	BB	SO	ShO	Relief Pitching W	Relief Pitching L	Relief Pitching SV	Batting AB	Batting H	Batting HR	BA	PO	A	E	DP	TC/G	FA
1972	CLE A	14	15	.483	2.77	39	34	10	237	200	70	123	3	1	0	0	70	7	0	.100	10	23	1	0	0.9	.971
1973		14	16	.467	4.42	42	40	13	274.2	289	95	138	2	0	0	0	0	0	0	—	17	34	2	3	1.3	.962
1974	2 teams	CLE A	(4G 1–3)		NY A	(33G 11–9)																				
″	total	12	12	.500	4.16	37	29	5	210	226	66	108	0	2	0	1	0	0	0		8	27	3	2	1.0	.921
1975	NY A	6	3	.667	3.13	37	0	0	69	65	31	38	0	6	3	5	0	0	0	—	3	6	0	1	0.2	1.000
1976		4	5	.444	2.63	47	2	0	92.1	80	24	65	0	3	5	10	0	0	0	—	2	9	1	0	0.3	.917
1977		11	4	.733	3.16	49	7	0	151	143	41	83	0	6	4	5	0	0	0	—	13	18	2	2	0.7	.939
1978		7	11	.389	3.84	31	25	4	185.1	191	53	73	0	0	1	0	0	0	0	—	12	18	0	0	1.0	1.000
1979	2 teams	NY A	(14G 2–1)		CHI N	(63G 11–5)																				
″	total	13	6	.684	3.64	77	0	0	126	124	46	75	0	13	6	6	10	2	0	.200	9	28	0	2	0.5	1.000
1980	CHI N	6	5	.545	2.79	**84**	0	0	116	97	53	97	0	6	5	6	4	0	0	.000	7	13	1	0	0.3	.952
1981		3	10	.231	5.04	51	0	0	75	73	30	39	0	3	**10**	9	5	0	0	.000	0	10	1	0	0.2	.909
1982		8	3	.727	3.39	65	0	0	103.2	106	29	62	0	8	3	6	6	0	0	.000	6	7	0	0	0.2	1.000
1983	CHI A	2	4	.333	4.22	50	1	0	91.2	86	34	66	0	2	4	7	0	0	0	—	7	16	1	0	0.5	.958
1984	NY N	0	0	—	9.19	11	0	0	15.2	25	7	8	0	0	0	0	0	0	0	—	3	3	0	0	0.5	1.000
13 yrs.		100	94	.515	3.68	620	138	32	1747.1	1705	579	975	5	50	41	55	95	9	0	.095	97	212	12	10	0.5	.963
LEAGUE CHAMPIONSHIP SERIES																										
1976	NY A	1	0	1.000	3.68	3	0	0	7.1	6	4	0	0	1	0	0	0	0	0	—	1	0	0	0	0.3	1.000
1977		0	0	—	3.86	2	0	0	7	6	3	3	0	0	0	0	0	0	0	—	1	2	0	0	1.5	1.000
1978		0	0	—	4.76	1	0	0	5.2	8	2	1	0	0	0	0	0	0	0	—	0	2	0	0	2.0	1.000
1983	CHI A	0	0	—	3.00	1	0	0	3	1	3	3	0	0	0	0	0	0	0	—	0	0	0	0	0.0	.000
4 yrs.		1	0	1.000	3.91	7	0	0	23	21	12	7	0	1	0	0	0	0	0		2	4	0	0	0.9	1.000
WORLD SERIES																										
1976	NY A	0	0	—	7.71	2	0	0	2.1	5	1	1	0	0	0	0	0	0	0	—	0	0	0	0	0.0	.000
1977		0	0	—	4.91	2	0	0	3.2	5	0	1	0	0	0	0	1	0	0	.000	0	1	0	0	0.5	1.000
1978		0	0	—	1.93	2	0	0	4.2	4	0	5	0	0	0	0	0	0	0	—	0	0	0	0	0.0	.000
3 yrs.		0	0		4.22	6	0	0	10.2	14	1	7	0	0	0	0	1	0	0	.000	0	1	0	0	0.2	1.000

Bobby Tiefenauer

TIEFENAUER, BOBBY GENE
B. Oct. 10, 1929, Desloge, Mo.
BR TR 6′ 2″ 185 lbs.

Year	Team	W	L	PCT	ERA	G	GS	CG	IP	H	BB	SO	ShO	Relief Pitching W	Relief Pitching L	Relief Pitching SV	Batting AB	Batting H	Batting HR	BA	PO	A	E	DP	TC/G	FA
1952	STL N	0	0	—	7.88	6	0	0	8	12	7	3	0	0	0	0	1	0	0	.000	0	3	0	0	0.5	1.000
1955		1	4	.200	4.41	18	0	0	32.2	31	10	16	0	1	4	0	5	0	0	.000	3	7	0	0	0.6	1.000
1960	CLE A	0	1	.000	2.00	6	0	0	9	8	3	2	0	1	0	0	1	0	0	.000	0	1	0	1	0.2	1.000
1961	STL N	0	0	—	6.23	3	0	0	4.1	9	4	3	0	0	0	0	0	0	0	—	0	0	0	0	0.0	.000
1962	HOU N	2	4	.333	4.34	43	0	0	85	91	21	60	0	2	4	1	9	1	0	.111	6	6	2	0	0.3	.857
1963	MIL N	1	1	.500	1.21	12	0	0	29.2	20	4	22	0	1	1	2	5	0	0	.000	4	8	0	0	1.0	1.000
1964		4	6	.400	3.21	46	0	0	73	61	15	48	0	4	6	13	14	0	0	.000	4	9	1	0	0.3	.929

Bobby Tiefenauer *continued*

Year	Team	W	L	PCT	ERA	G	GS	CG	IP	H	BB	SO	ShO	Relief Pitching W	Relief Pitching L	Relief Pitching SV	Batting AB	Batting H	Batting HR	BA	PO	A	E	DP	TC/G	FA
1965	3 teams MIL N (6G 0–1) NY A (10G 1–1) CLE A (15G 0–5)																									
"	total	1	7	.125	4.71	31	0	0	49.2	51	18	35	0	1	7	6	3	0	0	.000	5	6	0	0	0.4	1.000
1967	CLE A	0	1	.000	0.79	5	0	0	11.1	9	3	6	0	0	1	0	0	0	0	—	0	0	1	0	0.2	.000
1968	CHI N	0	1	.000	6.08	9	0	0	13.1	20	2	9	0	0	1	1	1	0	0	.000	1	1	0	0	0.2	1.000
10 yrs.		9	25	.265	3.84	179	0	0	316	312	87	204	0	9	25	23	39	1	0	.026	23	41	4	1	0.4	.941

Verle Tiefenthaler

TIEFENTHALER, VERLE MATTHEW BL TR 6′ 1″ 190 lbs.
B. July 11, 1937, Breda, Iowa

Year	Team	W	L	PCT	ERA	G	GS	CG	IP	H	BB	SO	ShO	Relief Pitching W	Relief Pitching L	Relief Pitching SV	Batting AB	Batting H	Batting HR	BA	PO	A	E	DP	TC/G	FA
1962	CHI A	0	0	—	9.82	3	0	0	3.2	6	7	1	0	0	0	0	0	0	0	—	0	0	0	0	0.0	.000

Eddie Tiemeyer

TIEMEYER, EDWARD CARL BR TR 5′11½″ 185 lbs.
B. May 9, 1885, Cincinnati, Ohio D. Sept. 27, 1946, Cincinnati, Ohio.

Year	Team	W	L	PCT	ERA	G	GS	CG	IP	H	BB	SO	ShO	Relief Pitching W	Relief Pitching L	Relief Pitching SV	Batting AB	Batting H	Batting HR	BA	PO	A	E	DP	TC/G	FA
1906	CIN N	0	0	—	0.00	1	0	0	1	1	1	1	0	0	0	0	*				1	6	0	1	1.8	1.000

Mike Tiernan

TIERNAN, MICHAEL JOSEPH (Silent Mike) BL TL 5′11″ 165 lbs.
B. Jan. 21, 1867, Trenton, N. J. D. Nov. 9, 1918, New York, N. Y.

Year	Team	W	L	PCT	ERA	G	GS	CG	IP	H	BB	SO	ShO	Relief Pitching W	Relief Pitching L	Relief Pitching SV	Batting AB	Batting H	Batting HR	BA	PO	A	E	DP	TC/G	FA
1887	NY N	1	2	.333	8.69	5	0	0	19.2	33	7	3	0	1	**2**	**1**	*				150	13	25	3	1.7	.867

Les Tietje

TIETJE, LESLIE WILLIAM (Toots) BR TR 6′½″ 178 lbs.
B. Sept. 11, 1911, Summer, Iowa.

Year	Team	W	L	PCT	ERA	G	GS	CG	IP	H	BB	SO	ShO	Relief Pitching W	Relief Pitching L	Relief Pitching SV	Batting AB	Batting H	Batting HR	BA	PO	A	E	DP	TC/G	FA
1933	CHI A	2	0	1.000	2.42	3	3	1	22.1	16	15	9	0	0	0	0	8	1	0	.125	1	5	0	1	2.0	1.000
1934		5	14	.263	4.81	34	22	6	176	174	96	81	1	1	0	0	59	1	0	.017	3	43	0	1	1.4	1.000
1935		9	15	.375	4.30	30	21	9	169.2	184	81	64	1	1	5	0	61	12	0	.197	4	26	1	0	1.0	.968
1936	2 teams CHI A (2G 0–0) STL A (14G 3–5)																									
"	total	3	5	.375	7.52	16	7	2	52.2	71	35	19	0	1	0	0	15	1	0	.067	1	14	1	0	1.0	.938
1937	STL A	1	2	.333	4.20	5	4	2	30	32	17	5	0	0	0	0	10	0	0	.000	0	3	0	1	0.6	1.000
1938		2	5	.286	7.55	17	8	2	62	83	38	15	1	0	1	0	18	2	0	.111	5	10	0	0	0.9	1.000
6 yrs.		22	41	.349	5.11	105	65	22	512.2	560	282	193	3	3	6	0	171	17	0	.099	14	101	2	3	1.1	.983

Ray Tift

TIFT, RAYMOND FRANK TR
B. June 21, 1884, Fitchburg, Mass. D. Mar. 29, 1945, Verona, N. J.

Year	Team	W	L	PCT	ERA	G	GS	CG	IP	H	BB	SO	ShO	Relief Pitching W	Relief Pitching L	Relief Pitching SV	Batting AB	Batting H	Batting HR	BA	PO	A	E	DP	TC/G	FA
1907	NY A	0	0	—	4.74	4	1	0	19	33	4	6	0	0	0	0	5	0	0	.000	0	4	0	0	1.0	1.000

Johnny Tillman

TILLMAN, JOHN LAWRENCE BB TR 5′11″ 170 lbs.
B. Oct. 6, 1893, Bridgeport, Conn. D. Apr. 7, 1964, Harrisburg, Pa.

Year	Team	W	L	PCT	ERA	G	GS	CG	IP	H	BB	SO	ShO	Relief Pitching W	Relief Pitching L	Relief Pitching SV	Batting AB	Batting H	Batting HR	BA	PO	A	E	DP	TC/G	FA
1915	STL A	1	0	1.000	0.90	2	1	0	10	6	4	6	0	0	0	0	3	0	0	.000	0	3	0	0	1.5	1.000

Thad Tillotson

TILLOTSON, THADDEUS ASA BR TR 6′ 2½″ 195 lbs.
B. Dec. 20, 1940, Merced, Calif.

Year	Team	W	L	PCT	ERA	G	GS	CG	IP	H	BB	SO	ShO	Relief Pitching W	Relief Pitching L	Relief Pitching SV	Batting AB	Batting H	Batting HR	BA	PO	A	E	DP	TC/G	FA
1967	NY A	3	9	.250	4.03	43	5	1	98.1	99	39	62	0	1	6	2	16	1	0	.063	12	14	0	0	0.6	1.000
1968		1	0	1.000	4.35	7	0	0	10.1	11	7	1	0	1	0	0	1	0	0	.000	0	4	0	0	0.6	1.000
2 yrs.		4	9	.308	4.06	50	5	1	108.2	110	46	63	0	2	6	2	17	1	0	.059	12	18	0	0	0.6	1.000

Gary Timberlake

TIMBERLAKE, GARY DALE BR TL 6′ 2″ 205 lbs.
B. Aug. 9, 1948, Laconia, Ind.

Year	Team	W	L	PCT	ERA	G	GS	CG	IP	H	BB	SO	ShO	Relief Pitching W	Relief Pitching L	Relief Pitching SV	Batting AB	Batting H	Batting HR	BA	PO	A	E	DP	TC/G	FA
1969	SEA A	0	0	—	7.50	2	2	0	6	7	9	4	0	0	0	0	1	0	0	.000	0	0	0	0	0.0	.000

Mike Timlin

TIMLIN, MICHAEL AUGUST BR TR 6′ 4″ 205 lbs.
B. Mar. 10, 1966, Midland, Tex.

Year	Team	W	L	PCT	ERA	G	GS	CG	IP	H	BB	SO	ShO	Relief Pitching W	Relief Pitching L	Relief Pitching SV	Batting AB	Batting H	Batting HR	BA	PO	A	E	DP	TC/G	FA
1991	TOR A	11	6	.647	3.16	63	3	0	108.1	94	50	85	0	**10**	5	3	0	0	0	—	9	17	2	0	0.4	.929
1992		0	2	.000	4.12	26	0	0	43.2	45	20	35	0	0	2	1	0	0	0	—	2	5	0	1	0.3	1.000
1993		4	2	.667	4.69	54	0	0	55.2	63	27	49	0	4	2	1	0	0	0	—	7	10	1	1	0.3	.944
1994		0	1	.000	5.17	34	0	0	40	41	20	38	0	0	1	2	0	0	0	—	5	5	0	0	0.3	1.000
1995		4	3	.571	2.14	31	0	0	42	38	17	36	0	4	3	5	0	0	0	—	1	9	0	1	0.3	1.000
5 yrs.		19	14	.576	3.73	208	3	0	289.2	281	134	243	0	18	13	12	0	0	0		24	46	3	3	0.4	.959
LEAGUE CHAMPIONSHIP SERIES																										
1991	TOR A	0	1	.000	3.18	4	0	0	5.2	5	2	5	0	0	1	0	0	0	0	—	0	2	1	0	0.8	.667
1992		0	0	—	6.75	2	0	0	1.1	4	0	1	0	0	0	0	0	0	0	—	0	0	0	0	0.0	.000
1993		0	0	—	3.86	1	0	0	2.1	3	0	2	0	0	0	0	0	0	0	—	1	1	0	0	2.0	1.000
3 yrs.		0	1	.000	3.86	7	0	0	9.1	12	2	8	0	0	1	0	0	0	0		1	3	1	0	0.7	.800
WORLD SERIES																										
1992	TOR A	0	0	—	0.00	2	0	0	1.1	0	0	0	0	0	0	1	0	0	0	—	0	1	0	0	0.5	1.000
1993		0	0	—	0.00	2	0	0	2.1	2	0	4	0	0	0	0	0	0	0	—	0	0	0	0	0.0	.000
2 yrs.		0	0		0.00	4	0	0	3.2	2	0	4	0	0	0	1	0	0	0		0	1	0	0	0.3	1.000

Tom Timmerman

TIMMERMAN, THOMAS HENRY BR TR 6′ 4″ 215 lbs.
B. May 12, 1940, Breese, Ill.

Year	Team	W	L	PCT	ERA	G	GS	CG	IP	H	BB	SO	ShO	Relief Pitching W	Relief Pitching L	Relief Pitching SV	Batting AB	Batting H	Batting HR	BA	PO	A	E	DP	TC/G	FA
1969	DET A	4	3	.571	2.75	31	1	1	55.2	50	26	42	0	3	3	1	9	1	0	.111	2	5	0	0	0.2	1.000
1970		6	7	.462	4.13	61	0	0	85	90	34	49	0	6	7	27	16	0	0	.000	7	10	1	0	0.3	.944
1971		7	6	.538	3.86	52	2	0	84	82	37	51	0	6	5	4	19	1	0	.053	4	14	0	2	0.3	1.000
1972		8	10	.444	2.89	34	25	3	149.2	121	41	88	2	0	0	0	44	6	0	.136	7	16	3	2	0.8	.885
1973	2 teams DET A (17G 1–1) CLE A (29G 8–7)																									
"	total	9	8	.529	4.63	46	16	4	163.1	156	65	83	0	2	1	3	0	0	0		10	22	3	2	0.8	.914
1974	CLE A	1	1	.500	5.40	4	0	0	10	9	5	2	0	1	1	0	0	0	0	—	0	5	0	0	1.3	1.000
6 yrs.		35	35	.500	3.78	228	44	8	547.2	508	208	315	2	18	17	35	88	8	0	.091	30	72	7	6	0.5	.936

Ben Tincup

TINCUP, AUSTIN BEN BL TR 6′ 1″ 180 lbs.
B. Dec. 14, 1890, Adair, Okla. D. July 5, 1980, Claremore, Okla.

Year	Team	W	L	PCT	ERA	G	GS	CG	IP	H	BB	SO	ShO	Relief Pitching W	Relief Pitching L	Relief Pitching SV	Batting AB	Batting H	Batting HR	BA	PO	A	E	DP	TC/G	FA
1914	PHI N	7	10	.412	2.61	28	17	9	155	165	62	108	3	2	1	1	53	9	0	.170	10	40	4	1	1.9	.926
1915		0	0	—	2.03	10	0	0	31	26	9	10	0	0	0	0	9	0	0	.000	0	11	0	0	1.1	1.000
1918		0	1	.000	7.56	8	1	0	16.2	24	6	6	0	0	0	0	8	1	0	.125	4	9	3	1	1.8	.813
1928	CHI N	0	0	—	7.00	2	0	0	9	14	1	3	0	0	0	0	3	0	0	.000	1	3	0	0	2.0	1.000
4 yrs.		7	11	.389	3.10	48	18	9	211.2	229	78	127	3	2	1	1	74	10	0	.135	15	63	7	2	1.7	.918

Bud Tinning

TINNING, LYLE FORREST BB TR 6′ 198 lbs.
B. Mar. 12, 1906, Pilger, Neb. D. Jan. 17, 1961, Evansville, Ind. BR 1934–1935

Year	Team	W	L	PCT	ERA	G	GS	CG	IP	H	BB	SO	ShO	Relief W	Relief L	SV	AB	H	HR	BA	PO	A	E	DP	TC/G	FA
1932	CHI N	5	3	.625	2.80	24	7	2	93.1	93	24	30	0	4	0	0	23	2	0	.087	9	20	5	0	1.4	.853
1933		13	6	.684	3.18	32	21	10	175.1	169	60	59	3	1	0	1	67	14	0	.209	3	28	2	3	1.0	.939
1934		4	6	.400	3.34	39	7	1	129.1	134	46	44	1	3	1	3	39	7	0	.179	4	23	2	0	0.7	.931
1935	STL N	0	0	—	5.87	4	0	0	7.2	9	5	2	0	0	0	0	1	0	0	.000	2	1	0	0	0.8	1.000
4 yrs.		22	15	.595	3.19	99	35	13	405.2	405	135	135	4	8	1	4	130	23	0	.177	18	72	9	3	1.0	.909
WORLD SERIES																										
1932	CHI N	0	0	—	0.00	2	0	0	2.1	0	0	3	0	0	0	0	0	0	0	—	0	1	0	0	0.5	1.000

Dan Tipple

TIPPLE, DANIEL E. (Big Dan, Rusty) BR TR 6′ 176 lbs.
B. Feb. 13, 1890, Rockford, Ill. D. Mar. 26, 1960, Omaha, Neb.

Year	Team	W	L	PCT	ERA	G	GS	CG	IP	H	BB	SO	ShO	Relief W	Relief L	SV	AB	H	HR	BA	PO	A	E	DP	TC/G	FA
1915	NY A	1	1	.500	2.84	3	2	2	19	14	11	14	0	0	0	0	6	0	0	.000	1	1	1	0	1.0	.667

Jack Tising

TISING, JOHNNIE JOSEPH BL TR 6′ 2″ 180 lbs.
B. Oct. 9, 1903, High Point, Mo. D. Sept. 5, 1967, Leadville, Colo.

Year	Team	W	L	PCT	ERA	G	GS	CG	IP	H	BB	SO	ShO	Relief W	Relief L	SV	AB	H	HR	BA	PO	A	E	DP	TC/G	FA
1936	PIT N	1	3	.250	4.21	10	6	1	47	52	24	27	0	0	0	0	11	3	0	.273	2	10	4	0	1.6	.750

Cannonball Titcomb

TITCOMB, LEDELL BL TL 5′ 6″ 157 lbs.
B. Aug. 21, 1866, W. Baldwin, Me. D. June 8, 1950, Kingston, N. H.

Year	Team	W	L	PCT	ERA	G	GS	CG	IP	H	BB	SO	ShO	Relief W	Relief L	SV	AB	H	HR	BA	PO	A	E	DP	TC/G	FA
1886	PHI N	0	5	.000	3.73	5	5	5	41	43	24	24	0	0	0	0	16	1	0	.063	0	13	2	0	3.0	.867
1887	2 teams PHI AA (3G 1–2) NY N (9G 4–3)																									
″	total	5	5	.500	4.59	12	12	12	96	99	56	50	0	0	0	0	39	2	0	.051	0	9	1	1	0.8	.900
1888	NY N	14	8	.636	2.24	23	23	22	197	149	46	129	4	0	0	0	82	10	0	.122	1	26	8	0	1.5	.771
1889		1	2	.333	6.58	3	3	3	26	27	16	7	0	0	0	0	12	1	0	.083	1	3	0	0	1.3	1.000
1890	ROC AA	10	9	.526	*3.74*	20	19	19	168.2	168	97	73	1	1	0	0	75	8	0	.107	8	24	6	0	1.7	.842
5 yrs.		30	29	.508	3.47	63	62	61	528.2	486	239	283	5	1	0	0	224	22	0	.098	10	75	17	1	1.5	.833

Dave Tobik

TOBIK, DAVID VANCE BR TR 6′ 1″ 190 lbs.
B. Mar. 2, 1953, Euclid, Ohio.

Year	Team	W	L	PCT	ERA	G	GS	CG	IP	H	BB	SO	ShO	Relief W	Relief L	SV	AB	H	HR	BA	PO	A	E	DP	TC/G	FA
1978	DET A	0	0	—	3.75	5	0	0	12	12	3	11	0	0	1	0	0	0	0	—	0	1	0	0	0.2	1.000
1979		3	5	.375	4.30	37	0	0	69	59	25	48	0	3	5	3	0	0	0	—	5	5	0	1	0.3	1.000
1980		1	0	1.000	3.98	17	1	0	61	61	21	34	0	0	0	0	0	0	0	—	4	7	0	1	0.6	1.000
1981		2	2	.500	2.70	27	0	0	60	47	33	32	0	2	2	1	0	0	0	—	2	3	0	0	0.2	1.000
1982		4	9	.308	3.56	51	1	0	98.2	86	38	63	0	4	8	9	0	0	0	—	8	8	1	1	0.3	.941
1983	TEX A	2	1	.667	3.68	27	0	0	44	36	13	30	0	2	1	9	0	0	0	—	6	4	0	0	0.4	1.000
1984		1	6	.143	3.61	24	0	0	42.1	44	17	30	0	1	6	5	0	0	0	—	3	7	0	1	0.4	1.000
1985	SEA A	1	0	1.000	6.00	8	0	0	9	10	3	8	0	1	0	1	0	0	0	—	1	0	0	0	0.1	1.000
8 yrs.		14	23	.378	3.70	196	2	0	396	355	153	256	0	13	23	28	0	0	0		29	35	1	4	0.3	.985

Jim Tobin

TOBIN, JAMES ANTHONY (Abba Dabba) BR TR 6′ 185 lbs.
Brother of Johnny Tobin.
B. Dec. 27, 1912, Oakland, Calif. D. May 19, 1969, Oakland, Calif.

Year	Team	W	L	PCT	ERA	G	GS	CG	IP	H	BB	SO	ShO	Relief W	Relief L	SV	AB	H	HR	BA	PO	A	E	DP	TC/G	FA
1937	PIT N	6	3	.667	3.00	20	8	7	87	74	28	37	0	1	0	1	34	15	0	.441	5	10	1	0	0.8	.938
1938		14	12	.538	3.47	40	33	14	241.1	254	66	70	2	4	1	0	103	25	0	.243	11	41	0	1	1.3	1.000
1939		9	9	.500	4.52	25	19	8	145.1	194	33	43	0	2	1	0	74	18	2	.243	2	26	0	2	1.1	1.000
1940	BOS N	7	3	.700	3.83	15	11	9	96.1	102	24	29	0	1	0	0	43	12	0	.279	6	16	1	1	1.5	.957
1941		12	12	.500	3.10	33	26	20	238	229	60	61	3	0	1	0	103	19	0	.184	15	71	3	4	2.7	.966
1942		12	**21**	.364	3.97	37	33	**28**	**287.2**	283	96	71	1	0	3	0	114	28	6	.246	14	93	6	6	3.1	.947
1943		14	14	.500	2.66	33	30	24	250	241	69	52	1	0	1	0	107	30	2	.280	17	67	6	7	2.6	.933
1944		18	19	.486	3.01	43	36	**28**	299.1	271	97	83	5	0	2	3	116	22	2	.190	13	93	3	4	2.5	.972
1945	2 teams BOS N (27G 9–14) DET A (14G 4–5)																									
″	total	13	19	.406	3.78	41	31	18	255	281	84	52	0	2	2	1	102	14	5	.137	20	63	1	6	2.0	.988
9 yrs.		105	112	.484	3.44	287	227	156	1900	1929	557	498	12	10	11	5	*				103	480	21	31	2.1	.965
WORLD SERIES																										
1945	DET A	0	0	—	6.00	1	0	0	3	4	1	0	0	0	0	0	*				0	1	0	0	1.0	1.000

Pat Tobin

TOBIN, MARION BROOKS BR TR 6′ 1″ 198 lbs.
B. Jan. 28, 1916, Hermitage, Ark. D. Jan. 21, 1975, Shreveport, La.

Year	Team	W	L	PCT	ERA	G	GS	CG	IP	H	BB	SO	ShO	Relief W	Relief L	SV	AB	H	HR	BA	PO	A	E	DP	TC/G	FA
1941	PHI A	0	0	—	36.00	1	0	0	1	4	2	0	0	0	0	0	0	0	0	—	0	1	0	0	1.0	1.000

Frank Todd

TODD, GEORGE FRANKLIN TL
Born George Franklin Todd.
B. Oct. 18, 1869, Aberdeen, Md. D. Aug. 11, 1919, Havre de Grace, Md.

Year	Team	W	L	PCT	ERA	G	GS	CG	IP	H	BB	SO	ShO	Relief W	Relief L	SV	AB	H	HR	BA	PO	A	E	DP	TC/G	FA
1898	LOU N	0	2	.000	13.91	4	2	0	11	23	8	5	0	0	0	0	5	1	0	.200	0	0	1	0	0.3	.000

Jackson Todd

TODD, JACKSON A. BR TR 6′ 2″ 180 lbs.
B. Sept. 20, 1951, Tulsa, Okla.

Year	Team	W	L	PCT	ERA	G	GS	CG	IP	H	BB	SO	ShO	Relief W	Relief L	SV	AB	H	HR	BA	PO	A	E	DP	TC/G	FA
1977	NY N	3	6	.333	4.75	19	10	0	72	78	20	39	0	1	0	0	17	1	0	.059	7	10	1	0	0.9	.944
1979	TOR A	0	1	.000	5.91	12	1	0	32	40	7	14	0	0	0	0	0	0	0	—	6	3	0	0	0.8	1.000
1980		5	2	.714	4.02	12	12	4	85	90	30	44	0	0	0	0	0	0	0	—	7	16	2	3	2.1	.920
1981		2	7	.222	3.95	21	13	3	98	94	31	41	0	0	0	0	0	0	0	—	11	20	1	0	1.5	.969
4 yrs.		10	16	.385	4.39	64	36	7	287	302	88	138	0	1	0	0	17	1	0	.059	31	49	4	3	1.3	.952

Jim Todd

TODD, JAMES RICHARD, JR. BL TR 6′ 2″ 190 lbs.
B. Sept. 21, 1947, Lancaster, Pa.

Year	Team	W	L	PCT	ERA	G	GS	CG	IP	H	BB	SO	ShO	Relief W	Relief L	SV	AB	H	HR	BA	PO	A	E	DP	TC/G	FA
1974	CHI N	4	2	.667	3.89	43	6	0	88	82	41	42	0	3	0	3	16	1	0	.063	8	15	0	1	0.5	1.000
1975	OAK A	8	3	.727	2.29	58	0	0	122	104	33	50	0	8	3	12	0	0	0	—	6	37	2	4	0.8	.956
1976		7	8	.467	3.80	49	0	0	83	87	34	22	0	7	8	4	0	0	0	—	7	22	2	1	0.6	.935
1977	CHI N	1	1	.500	9.00	20	0	0	31	47	19	17	0	1	1	0	1	0	0	.000	4	5	0	1	0.4	1.000
1978	SEA A	3	4	.429	3.88	49	2	0	106.2	113	61	37	0	3	3	3	0	0	0	—	11	17	2	0	0.6	.933
1979	OAK A	2	5	.286	6.56	51	0	0	81	108	51	26	0	2	5	2	0	0	0	—	5	14	0	2	0.4	1.000
6 yrs.		25	23	.521	4.22	270	8	0	511.2	541	239	194	0	24	20	24	17	1	0	.059	41	110	6	9	0.6	.962

Jim Todd *continued*

Year	Team	Lg	W	L	PCT	ERA	G	GS	CG	IP	H	BB	SO	ShO	Relief Pitching W	Relief Pitching L	Relief Pitching SV	Batting AB	Batting H	Batting HR	BA	PO	A	E	DP	TC/G	FA
LEAGUE CHAMPIONSHIP SERIES																											
1975	OAK	A	0	0	—	9.00	3	0	0	1	3	0	0	0	0	0	0	0	0	0	—	0	0	0	0	0.0	.000

Hal Toenes

TOENES, WILLIAM HARREL BR TR 5′11½″ 175 lbs.
B. Oct. 8, 1917, Mobile, Ala.

Year	Team	Lg	W	L	PCT	ERA	G	GS	CG	IP	H	BB	SO	ShO	Relief Pitching W	Relief Pitching L	Relief Pitching SV	Batting AB	Batting H	Batting HR	BA	PO	A	E	DP	TC/G	FA
1947	WAS	A	0	1	.000	6.75	3	1	0	6.2	11	2	5	0	0	0	0	1	0	0	.000	0	0	0	0	0.0	.000

Fred Toliver

TOLIVER, FREDDIE LEE BR TR 6′ 1″ 170 lbs.
B. Feb. 3, 1961, Natchez, Miss.

Year	Team	Lg	W	L	PCT	ERA	G	GS	CG	IP	H	BB	SO	ShO	Relief Pitching W	Relief Pitching L	Relief Pitching SV	Batting AB	Batting H	Batting HR	BA	PO	A	E	DP	TC/G	FA
1984	CIN	N	0	0	—	0.90	3	1	0	10	7	7	4	0	0	0	0	1	0	0	.000	0	1	0	0	0.3	1.000
1985	PHI	N	0	4	.000	4.68	11	3	0	25	27	17	23	0	0	1	1	4	2	0	.500	0	4	1	0	0.5	.800
1986			0	2	.000	3.51	5	5	0	25.2	28	11	20	0	0	0	0	6	0	0	.000	1	4	0	1	1.0	1.000
1987			1	1	.500	5.64	10	4	0	30.1	34	17	25	0	0	0	0	5	0	0	.000	1	6	0	0	0.7	1.000
1988	MIN	A	7	6	.538	4.24	21	19	0	114.2	116	52	69	0	0	0	0	0	0	0	—	1	19	2	2	1.0	.909
1989	2 teams	MIN A (7G 1–3)	SD N (9G 0–0)																								
″	total		1	3	.250	7.53	16	5	0	43	56	24	25	0	1	0	0	0	0	0		4	12	0	0	1.0	1.000
1993	PIT	N	1	0	1.000	3.74	12	0	0	21.2	20	8	14	0	1	0	0	2	0	0	.000	1	1	0	0	0.2	1.000
7 yrs.			10	16	.385	4.73	78	37	0	270.1	288	136	180	0	2	1	1	18	2	0	.111	8	47	3	3	0.7	.948

Dick Tomanek

TOMANEK, RICHARD CARL (Bones) BL TL 6′ 1″ 175 lbs.
B. Jan. 6, 1931, Avon Lake, Ohio.

Year	Team	Lg	W	L	PCT	ERA	G	GS	CG	IP	H	BB	SO	ShO	Relief Pitching W	Relief Pitching L	Relief Pitching SV	Batting AB	Batting H	Batting HR	BA	PO	A	E	DP	TC/G	FA
1953	CLE	A	1	0	1.000	2.00	1	1	1	9	6	6	6	0	0	0	0	5	0	0	.000	0	0	1	0	1.0	.000
1954			0	0	—	5.40	1	0	0	1.2	1	1	0	0	0	0	0	0	0	0	—	0	1	0	0	1.0	1.000
1957			2	1	.667	5.68	34	2	0	69.2	67	37	55	0	2	1	0	13	3	0	.231	5	11	0	2	0.5	1.000
1958	2 teams	CLE A (18G 2–3)	KC A (36G 5–5)																								
″	total		7	8	.467	4.50	54	8	3	130	130	56	92	0	6	5	5	30	5	1	.167	5	20	1	3	0.5	.962
1959	KC	A	0	1	.000	6.53	16	0	0	20.2	27	12	13	0	0	1	2	2	1	0	.500	0	6	0	0	0.4	1.000
5 yrs.			10	10	.500	4.95	106	11	4	231	231	112	166	0	8	7	7	50	9	1	.180	10	38	2	5	0.5	.960

Andy Tomasic

TOMASIC, ANDREW JOHN BR TR 6′ 175 lbs.
B. Dec. 10, 1919, Hokendauqua, Pa.

Year	Team	Lg	W	L	PCT	ERA	G	GS	CG	IP	H	BB	SO	ShO	Relief Pitching W	Relief Pitching L	Relief Pitching SV	Batting AB	Batting H	Batting HR	BA	PO	A	E	DP	TC/G	FA
1949	NY	N	0	1	.000	18.00	2	0	0	5	9	5	2	0	0	1	0	1	0	0	.000	0	0	0	0	0.0	.000

Andy Tomberlin

TOMBERLIN, ANDY LEE BL TL 5′11″ 160 lbs.
B. Nov. 7, 1966, Monroe, N. C.

Year	Team	Lg	W	L	PCT	ERA	G	GS	CG	IP	H	BB	SO	ShO	Relief Pitching W	Relief Pitching L	Relief Pitching SV	Batting AB	Batting H	Batting HR	BA	PO	A	E	DP	TC/G	FA
1994	BOS	A	0	0	—	0.00	1	0	0	2	1	1	1	0	0	0	0	*				9	1	0	0	1.4	1.000

Dave Tomlin

TOMLIN, DAVID ALLEN BL TL 6′ 2″ 180 lbs.
B. June 22, 1949, Maysville, Ky.

Year	Team	Lg	W	L	PCT	ERA	G	GS	CG	IP	H	BB	SO	ShO	Relief Pitching W	Relief Pitching L	Relief Pitching SV	Batting AB	Batting H	Batting HR	BA	PO	A	E	DP	TC/G	FA
1972	CIN	N	0	0	—	9.00	3	0	0	4	7	1	2	0	0	0	0	0	0	0	—	0	1	0	0	0.3	1.000
1973			1	2	.333	4.88	16	0	0	27.2	24	15	20	0	1	2	1	3	0	0	.000	2	4	0	0	0.4	1.000
1974	SD	N	2	0	1.000	4.34	47	0	0	58	59	30	29	0	2	0	2	4	0	0	.000	5	11	0	1	0.3	1.000
1975			4	2	.667	3.25	67	0	0	83	87	31	48	0	4	2	1	5	1	0	.200	7	27	3	3	0.6	.919
1976			0	1	.000	2.84	49	1	0	73	62	20	43	0	0	0	0	8	0	0	.000	8	21	2	1	0.6	.935
1977			4	4	.500	3.00	76	0	0	102	98	32	55	0	4	4	3	7	2	0	.286	7	21	0	2	0.4	1.000
1978	CIN	N	9	1	.900	5.81	57	0	0	62	88	30	32	0	9	1	4	5	1	0	.200	5	13	3	0	0.4	.857
1979			2	2	.500	2.64	53	0	0	58	59	18	30	0	2	2	1	2	1	0	.500	4	10	3	1	0.3	.824
1980			3	0	1.000	5.54	27	0	0	26	38	11	6	0	3	0	0	0	0	0	—	1	7	0	0	0.3	1.000
1982	MON	N	0	0	—	4.50	1	0	0	2	1	1	2	0	0	0	0	0	0	0	—	0	0	0	0	0.0	.000
1983	PIT	N	0	0	—	6.75	5	0	0	4	6	1	5	0	0	0	0	0	0	0	—	0	0	0	0	0.0	.000
1985			0	0	—	0.00	1	0	0	1	1	1	0	0	0	0	0	0	0	0	—	0	0	0	0	0.0	.000
1986	MON	N	0	0	—	5.23	7	0	0	10.1	13	7	6	0	0	0	0	0	0	0	—	0	4	0	0	0.6	1.000
13 yrs.			25	12	.676	3.82	409	1	0	511	543	198	278	0	25	11	12	34	5	0	.147	39	119	11	8	0.4	.935
LEAGUE CHAMPIONSHIP SERIES																											
1973	CIN	N	0	0	—	16.20	1	0	0	1.2	5	1	1	0	0	0	0	0	0	0	—	0	0	0	0	0.0	.000
1979			0	0	—	0.00	3	0	0	3	3	2	3	0	0	0	0	0	0	0	—	1	1	0	0	0.7	1.000
2 yrs.			0	0		5.79	4	0	0	4.2	8	3	4	0	0	0	0	0	0	0		1	1	0	0	0.5	1.000

Randy Tomlin

TOMLIN, RANDY LEON BL TL 5′11″ 179 lbs.
B. June 14, 1966, Bainbridge, Md.

Year	Team	Lg	W	L	PCT	ERA	G	GS	CG	IP	H	BB	SO	ShO	Relief Pitching W	Relief Pitching L	Relief Pitching SV	Batting AB	Batting H	Batting HR	BA	PO	A	E	DP	TC/G	FA
1990	PIT	N	4	4	.500	2.55	12	12	2	77.2	62	12	42	0	0	0	0	25	1	0	.040	1	19	0	0	1.7	1.000
1991			8	7	.533	2.98	31	27	4	175	170	54	104	2	0	0	0	52	10	0	.192	9	36	2	0	1.5	.957
1992			14	9	.609	3.41	35	33	1	208.2	226	42	90	1	0	0	0	65	9	0	.138	12	52	1	3	1.9	.985
1993			4	8	.333	4.85	18	18	1	98.1	109	15	44	0	0	0	0	33	6	0	.182	9	18	1	2	1.6	.964
1994			0	3	.000	3.92	10	4	0	20.2	23	10	17	0	0	1	0	6	3	0	.500	1	3	0	0	0.4	1.000
5 yrs.			30	31	.492	3.43	106	94	8	580.1	590	133	297	3	0	1	0	181	29	0	.160	32	128	4	5	1.5	.976
LEAGUE CHAMPIONSHIP SERIES																											
1991	PIT	N	0	0	—	3.00	1	1	0	6	6	2	1	0	0	0	0	2	0	0	.000	1	0	0	0	1.0	1.000
1992			0	0	—	6.75	2	0	0	2.2	5	1	0	0	0	0	0	0	0	0	—	0	1	0	0	0.5	1.000
2 yrs.			0	0		4.15	3	1	0	8.2	11	3	1	0	0	0	0	2	0	0	.000	1	1	0	0	0.7	1.000

Chuck Tompkins

TOMPKINS, CHARLES HERBERT BR TR 6′ 185 lbs.
B. Sept. 1, 1889, Prescott, Ark. D. Sept. 20, 1975, Prescott, Ark.

Year	Team	Lg	W	L	PCT	ERA	G	GS	CG	IP	H	BB	SO	ShO	Relief Pitching W	Relief Pitching L	Relief Pitching SV	Batting AB	Batting H	Batting HR	BA	PO	A	E	DP	TC/G	FA
1912	CIN	N	0	0	—	0.00	1	0	0	3	5	0	1	0	0	0	0	1	1	0	1.000	0	1	1	0	2.0	.500

Ron Tompkins

TOMPKINS, RONALD EVERETT (Stretch) BR TR 6′ 4″ 198 lbs.
B. Nov. 27, 1944, San Diego, Calif.

Year	Team	Lg	W	L	PCT	ERA	G	GS	CG	IP	H	BB	SO	ShO	Relief Pitching W	Relief Pitching L	Relief Pitching SV	Batting AB	Batting H	Batting HR	BA	PO	A	E	DP	TC/G	FA
1965	KC	A	0	0	—	3.48	5	1	0	10.1	9	3	4	0	0	0	0	1	0	0	.000	1	2	0	0	0.6	1.000
1971	CHI	N	0	2	.000	4.05	35	0	0	40	31	21	20	0	0	2	3	0	0	0	—	2	12	0	0	0.4	1.000
2 yrs.			0	2	.000	3.93	40	1	0	50.1	40	24	24	0	0	2	3	1	0	0	.000	3	14	0	0	0.4	1.000

Tommy Toms

TOMS, THOMAS HOWARD BR TR 6′ 4″ 195 lbs.
B. Oct. 15, 1951, Charlottesville, Va.

Year	Team	Lg	W	L	PCT	ERA	G	GS	CG	IP	H	BB	SO	ShO	Relief W	Relief L	Relief SV	AB	H	HR	BA	PO	A	E	DP	TC/G	FA
1975	SF	N	0	1	.000	6.30	7	0	0	10	13	6	6	0	0	1	0	0	0	0	—	2	0	0	0	0.3	1.000
1976			0	1	.000	6.23	7	0	0	8.2	13	1	4	0	0	1	1	0	0	0	—	1	1	0	0	0.3	1.000
1977			0	1	.000	2.25	4	0	0	4	7	2	2	0	0	1	0	0	0	0	—	0	0	0	0	0.0	.000
3 yrs.			0	3	.000	5.56	18	0	0	22.2	33	9	12	0	0	3	1	0	0	0		3	1	0	0	0.2	1.000

Fred Toney

TONEY, FRED ALEXANDRA BR TR 6′ 6″ 245 lbs.
B. Dec. 11, 1888, Nashville, Tenn. D. Mar. 11, 1953, Nashville, Tenn.

Year	Team	Lg	W	L	PCT	ERA	G	GS	CG	IP	H	BB	SO	ShO	Relief W	Relief L	Relief SV	AB	H	HR	BA	PO	A	E	DP	TC/G	FA
1911	CHI	N	1	1	.500	2.42	18	4	1	67	55	35	27	0	0	0	0	18	2	0	.111	0	23	2	0	1.4	.920
1912			1	2	.333	5.25	9	2	0	24	21	11	9	0	1	0	0	5	0	0	.000	0	4	1	0	0.6	.800
1913			2	2	.500	6.00	7	5	2	39	52	22	12	0	0	0	0	12	3	0	.250	1	11	0	0	1.7	1.000
1915	CIN	N	15	6	.714	1.58	36	23	18	222.2	160	73	108	6	1	1	2	74	7	0	.095	6	63	1	2	1.9	.986
1916			14	17	.452	2.28	41	38	21	300	247	78	146	3	0	0	1	99	12	0	.121	7	59	2	2	1.7	.971
1917			24	16	.600	2.20	43	42	31	339.2	300	77	123	7	0	0	1	116	13	0	.112	13	76	7	1	2.2	.927
1918	2 teams CIN N (21G 6–10) NY N (11G 6–2)																										
″	total		12	12	.500	2.43	32	28	16	222	203	38	51	2	0	0	**3**	74	15	0	.203	6	67	4	3	2.4	.948
1919	NY	N	13	6	.684	1.84	24	20	14	181	157	35	40	4	0	1	1	66	15	0	.227	5	39	1	0	1.9	.978
1920			21	11	.656	2.65	42	37	17	278.1	266	57	81	4	2	0	1	96	23	0	.240	6	72	3	0	1.9	.963
1921			18	11	.621	3.61	42	32	16	249.1	274	65	63	1	3	0	3	86	18	3	.209	4	63	2	3	1.6	.971
1922			5	6	.455	4.17	13	12	6	86.1	91	31	10	0	0	0	0	30	2	0	.067	0	15	1	0	1.2	.938
1923	STL	N	11	12	.478	3.84	29	28	16	196.2	211	61	48	1	0	0	0	69	8	0	.116	9	63	2	3	2.6	.973
12 yrs.			137	102	.573	2.69	336	271	158	2206	2037	583	718	28	7	2	12	745	118	3	.158	57	555	26	14	1.9	.959
WORLD SERIES																											
1921	NY	N	0	0	—	23.63	2	2	0	2.2	7	3	1	0	0	0	0	0	0	0	—	0	1	0	0	0.5	1.000

Doc Tonkin

TONKIN, HARRY GLENVILLE BL TL 5′ 9″ 165 lbs.
B. Aug. 11, 1881, Concord, N. H. D. May 30, 1959, Miami, Fla.

Year	Team	Lg	W	L	PCT	ERA	G	GS	CG	IP	H	BB	SO	ShO	Relief W	Relief L	Relief SV	AB	H	HR	BA	PO	A	E	DP	TC/G	FA
1907	WAS	A	0	0	—	6.75	1	0	0	2.2	6	5	0	0	0	0	0	2	2	0	1.000	0	2	0	0	2.0	1.000

Steve Toole

TOOLE, STEPHEN JOHN BL TL 6′ 170 lbs.
B. Apr. 9, 1859, New Orleans, La. D. Mar. 28, 1919, Pittsburgh, Pa.

Year	Team	Lg	W	L	PCT	ERA	G	GS	CG	IP	H	BB	SO	ShO	Relief W	Relief L	Relief SV	AB	H	HR	BA	PO	A	E	DP	TC/G	FA
1886	BKN	AA	6	6	.500	*4.41*	13	12	11	104	100	64	48	0	0	0	0	57	20	0	.351	11	25	6	1	2.6	.857
1887			14	10	.583	*4.31*	24	24	22	194	186	106	48	1	0	0	0	103	24	1	.233	36	32	10	3	2.9	.872
1888	KC	AA	5	6	.455	6.68	12	10	10	91.2	124	50	35	0	**1**	0	0	48	10	0	.208	12	21	3	0	2.6	.917
1890	BKN	AA	2	4	.333	4.08	6	6	6	53	47	39	10	0	0	0	0	20	6	0	.300	5	13	3	1	3.5	.857
4 yrs.			27	26	.509	4.80	55	52	49	442.2	457	259	141	1	1	0	0	228	60	1	.263	64	91	22	5	2.8	.876

Rupe Toppin

TOPPIN, RUPERTO BR TR 6′ 185 lbs.
B. Dec. 7, 1941, Panama City, Panama.

Year	Team	Lg	W	L	PCT	ERA	G	GS	CG	IP	H	BB	SO	ShO	Relief W	Relief L	Relief SV	AB	H	HR	BA	PO	A	E	DP	TC/G	FA
1962	KC	A	0	0	—	13.50	2	0	0	2	1	5	1	0	0	0	0	1	1	0	1.000	0	0	0	0	0.0	.000

Red Torkelson

TORKELSON, CHESTER LeROY BR TR 6′ 175 lbs.
B. Mar. 19, 1894, Chicago, Ill. D. Sept. 22, 1964, Chicago, Ill.

Year	Team	Lg	W	L	PCT	ERA	G	GS	CG	IP	H	BB	SO	ShO	Relief W	Relief L	Relief SV	AB	H	HR	BA	PO	A	E	DP	TC/G	FA
1917	CLE	A	2	1	.667	7.66	4	3	0	22.1	33	13	10	0	0	0	0	9	2	0	.222	1	9	4	0	3.5	.714

Pablo Torrealba

TORREALBA, PABLO ARNOLDO BL TL 5′10″ 173 lbs.
Born Pablo Arnoldo Torrealba (Torrealba).
B. Apr. 28, 1948, Barquisimento, Venezuela.

Year	Team	Lg	W	L	PCT	ERA	G	GS	CG	IP	H	BB	SO	ShO	Relief W	Relief L	Relief SV	AB	H	HR	BA	PO	A	E	DP	TC/G	FA
1975	ATL	N	0	1	.000	1.29	6	0	0	7	7	3	5	0	0	1	0	1	1	0	1.000	1	3	0	0	0.7	1.000
1976			0	2	.000	3.57	36	0	0	53	67	22	33	0	0	2	2	4	0	0	.000	1	13	0	2	0.4	1.000
1977	OAK	A	4	6	.400	2.62	41	10	3	117	127	38	51	0	4	1	2	0	0	0	—	11	26	4	1	1.0	.902
1978	CHI	A	2	4	.333	4.71	25	3	1	57.1	69	39	23	1	1	3	1	0	0	0	—	2	4	1	0	0.3	.857
1979			0	0	—	1.50	3	0	0	6	5	2	1	0	0	0	0	0	0	0	—	0	1	0	0	0.3	1.000
5 yrs.			6	13	.316	3.26	111	13	4	240.1	275	104	113	1	5	7	5	5	1	0	.200	15	47	5	3	0.6	.925

Angel Torres

TORRES, ANGEL RAFAEL BL TL 5′11″ 168 lbs.
Born Angel Rafael Torres (Ruiz).
B. Oct. 24, 1952, Las Ciengas Azua, Dominican Republic.

Year	Team	Lg	W	L	PCT	ERA	G	GS	CG	IP	H	BB	SO	ShO	Relief W	Relief L	Relief SV	AB	H	HR	BA	PO	A	E	DP	TC/G	FA
1977	CIN	N	0	0	—	2.25	5	0	0	8	7	8	8	0	0	0	0	0	0	0	—	0	1	0	0	0.2	1.000

Dilson Torres

TORRES, DILSON DARIO BR TR 6′ 3″ 200 lbs.
B. May 31, 1970, Sur Edo Aragua, Venezuela.

Year	Team	Lg	W	L	PCT	ERA	G	GS	CG	IP	H	BB	SO	ShO	Relief W	Relief L	Relief SV	AB	H	HR	BA	PO	A	E	DP	TC/G	FA
1995	KC	A	1	2	.333	6.09	24	2	0	44.1	56	17	28	0	1	1	0	0	0	0	—	6	12	0	1	0.8	1.000

Gil Torres

TORRES, DON GILBERTO BR TR 6′ 155 lbs.
Born Don Gilberto Torres (Nunez).
Son of Ricardo Torres.
B. Aug. 23, 1915, Regla, Cuba D. Jan. 11, 1983, Regla, Cuba.

Year	Team	Lg	W	L	PCT	ERA	G	GS	CG	IP	H	BB	SO	ShO	Relief W	Relief L	Relief SV	AB	H	HR	BA	PO	A	E	DP	TC/G	FA
1940	WAS	A	0	0	—	0.00	2	0	0	2.2	3	0	1	0	0	0	0	0	0	0	—	0	1	0	0	0.5	1.000
1946			0	0	—	7.71	3	0	0	7	9	3	2	0	0	0	1	185	47	0	.254	167	322	24	35	3.7	.953
2 yrs.			0	0		5.59	5	0	0	9.2	12	3	3	0	0	0	1	*				523	900	70	120	4.3	.953

Hector Torres

TORRES, HECTOR EPITACIO BR TR 6′ 175 lbs.
Born Hector Epitacio Torres (Marroquin).
B. Sept. 16, 1945, Monterrey, Mexico.

Year	Team	Lg	W	L	PCT	ERA	G	GS	CG	IP	H	BB	SO	ShO	Relief W	Relief L	Relief SV	AB	H	HR	BA	PO	A	E	DP	TC/G	FA
1972	MON	N	0	0	—	27.00	1	0	0	0.2	5	0	0	0	0	0	0	*				159	393	24	55	4.5	.958

Salomon Torres

TORRES, SALOMON BR TR 5′11″ 150 lbs.
Born Salomon Torres (Ramirez).
B. Mar. 11, 1972, San Pedro de Macoris, Dominican Republic.

Year	Team	W	L	PCT	ERA	G	GS	CG	IP	H	BB	SO	ShO	Relief W	Relief L	Relief SV	AB	H	HR	BA	PO	A	E	DP	TC/G	FA
1993	SF N	3	5	.375	4.03	8	8	0	44.2	37	27	23	0	0	0	0	13	3	0	.231	4	9	0	0	1.6	1.000
1994		2	8	.200	5.44	16	14	1	84.1	95	34	42	0	0	0	0	26	4	0	.154	4	7	1	0	0.8	.917
1995	2 teams SF N (4G 0–1) SEA A (16G 3–8)																									
″	total	3	9	.250	6.30	20	14	1	80	100	49	47	0	0	1	0	1	0	0	.000	9	16	0	2	1.3	1.000
3 yrs.		8	22	.267	5.47	44	36	2	209	232	110	112	0	0	1	0	40	7	0	.175	17	32	1	2	1.1	.980

Mike Torrez

TORREZ, MICHAEL AUGUSTINE BR TR 6′ 5″ 220 lbs.
B. Aug. 28, 1946, Topeka, Kans.

Year	Team	W	L	PCT	ERA	G	GS	CG	IP	H	BB	SO	ShO	Relief W	Relief L	Relief SV	AB	H	HR	BA	PO	A	E	DP	TC/G	FA
1967	STL N	0	1	.000	3.18	3	1	0	5.2	5	1	5	0	0	1	0	1	0	0	.000	0	0	0	0	0.0	.000
1968		2	1	.667	2.84	5	2	0	19	20	12	6	0	1	0	0	7	2	0	.286	2	4	1	0	1.4	.857
1969		10	4	.714	3.58	24	15	3	108	96	62	61	0	0	0	0	41	3	0	.073	11	17	0	2	1.2	1.000
1970		8	10	.444	4.22	30	28	5	179	168	103	100	1	0	0	0	63	17	0	.270	7	27	1	2	1.2	.971
1971	2 teams STL N (9G 1–2) MON N (1G 0–0)																									
″	total	1	2	.333	5.54	10	6	0	39	45	31	10	0	0	0	0	7	1	0	.143	4	9	1	0	1.4	.929
1972	MON N	16	12	.571	3.33	34	33	13	243.1	215	103	112	0	0	0	0	85	15	0	.176	15	48	1	2	1.9	.984
1973		9	12	.429	4.46	35	34	3	208	207	115	90	1	0	0	0	69	12	0	.174	13	41	2	1	1.6	.964
1974		15	8	.652	3.58	32	30	6	186	184	84	92	1	0	0	0	64	8	0	.125	19	48	2	4	2.2	.971
1975	BAL A	20	9	**.690**	3.06	36	36	16	270.2	238	**133**	119	2	0	0	0	0	0	0	—	19	46	5	3	1.9	.929
1976	OAK A	16	12	.571	2.50	39	39	13	266	231	87	115	4	0	0	0	0	0	0	—	19	37	6	4	1.6	.903
1977	2 teams OAK A (4G 3–1) NY A (31G 14–12)																									
″	total	17	13	.567	3.92	35	35	17	243.1	235	86	102	2	0	0	0	0	0	0		17	29	3	2	1.4	.939
1978	BOS A	16	13	.552	3.96	36	36	15	250	272	99	120	2	0	0	0	0	0	0	—	12	29	2	3	1.2	.953
1979		16	13	.552	4.50	36	36	12	252	254	**121**	125	1	0	0	0	0	0	0	—	19	35	4	3	1.6	.931
1980		9	16	.360	5.09	36	32	6	207	256	75	97	1	0	2	0	0	0	0	—	20	36	6	4	1.7	.903
1981		10	3	.769	3.69	22	22	2	127	130	51	54	0	0	0	0	0	0	0	—	12	13	3	2	1.3	.893
1982		9	9	.500	5.23	31	31	1	175.2	196	74	84	0	0	0	0	0	0	0	—	12	14	1	0	0.9	.963
1983	NY N	10	**17**	.370	4.37	39	34	5	222.1	227	**113**	94	0	0	0	0	65	3	0	.046	20	33	2	4	1.4	.964
1984	2 teams NY N (9G 1–5) OAK A (2G 0–0)																									
″	total	1	5	.167	6.30	11	8	0	40	64	21	18	0	0	0	0	10	3	0	.300	2	6	1	2	0.8	.889
18 yrs.		185	160	.536	3.97	494	458	117	3042	3043	1371	1404	15	1	3	0	412	64	0	.155	223	472	41	38	1.5	.944
LEAGUE CHAMPIONSHIP SERIES																										
1977	NY A	0	1	.000	4.09	2	1	0	11	11	5	5	0	0	0	0	0	0	0	—	2	1	0	0	1.5	1.000
WORLD SERIES																										
1977	NY A	2	0	1.000	2.50	2	2	2	18	16	5	15	0	0	0	0	6	0	0	.000	2	3	0	0	2.5	1.000

Lou Tost

TOST, LOUIS EUGENE BL TL 6′ 175 lbs.
B. June 1, 1911, Cumberland, Wash. D. Feb. 22, 1967, Santa Clara, Calif.

Year	Team	W	L	PCT	ERA	G	GS	CG	IP	H	BB	SO	ShO	Relief W	Relief L	Relief SV	AB	H	HR	BA	PO	A	E	DP	TC/G	FA
1942	BOS N	10	10	.500	3.53	35	22	5	147.2	146	52	43	1	3	2	0	51	9	0	.176	4	27	2	2	0.9	.939
1943		0	1	.000	5.40	3	1	0	6.2	10	4	3	0	0	0	0	1	0	0	.000	0	2	0	0	0.7	1.000
1947	PIT N	0	0	—	9.00	1	0	0	1	3	0	0	0	0	0	0	0	0	0	—	0	1	0	0	1.0	1.000
3 yrs.		10	11	.476	3.65	39	23	5	155.1	159	56	46	1	3	2	0	52	9	0	.173	4	30	2	2	0.9	.944

Paul Toth

TOTH, PAUL LOUIS BR TR 6′ 1″ 175 lbs.
B. June 30, 1935, McRoberts, Ky.

Year	Team	W	L	PCT	ERA	G	GS	CG	IP	H	BB	SO	ShO	Relief W	Relief L	Relief SV	AB	H	HR	BA	PO	A	E	DP	TC/G	FA
1962	2 teams STL N (6G 1–0) CHI N (6G 3–1)																									
″	total	4	1	.800	4.62	12	5	2	50.2	47	14	16	0	0	0	0	16	4	0	.250	4	7	2	0	1.1	.846
1963	CHI N	5	9	.357	3.10	27	14	3	130.2	115	35	66	2	1	3	0	39	1	0	.026	5	18	1	2	0.9	.958
1964		0	2	.000	8.44	4	2	0	10.2	15	5	0	0	0	0	0	3	1	0	.333	2	5	0	0	1.8	1.000
3 yrs.		9	12	.429	3.80	43	21	5	192	177	54	82	2	1	3	0	58	6	0	.103	11	30	3	2	1.0	.932

Clay Touchstone

TOUCHSTONE, CLAYLAND MAFFITT BR TR 5′11½″ 175 lbs.
B. Jan. 24, 1903, Moore, Pa. D. Apr. 28, 1949, Beaumont, Tex.

Year	Team	W	L	PCT	ERA	G	GS	CG	IP	H	BB	SO	ShO	Relief W	Relief L	Relief SV	AB	H	HR	BA	PO	A	E	DP	TC/G	FA
1928	BOS N	0	0	—	4.50	5	0	0	8	15	2	1	0	0	0	0	2	0	0	.000	0	3	0	0	0.6	1.000
1929		0	0	—	16.88	1	0	0	2.2	6	0	1	0	0	0	0	1	1	0	1.000	0	0	0	0	0.0	.000
1945	CHI A	0	0	—	5.40	6	0	0	10	14	6	4	0	0	0	0	1	0	0	.000	1	2	0	0	0.5	1.000
3 yrs.		0	0		6.53	12	0	0	20.2	35	8	6	0	0	0	0	4	1	0	.250	1	5	0	0	0.5	1.000

Cesar Tovar

TOVAR, CESAR LEONARDO (Pepito) BR TR 5′ 9″ 155 lbs.
Born Cesar Leonardo Perez (Tovar).
B. July 3, 1940, Caracas, Venezuela D. July 14, 1994, Caracas, Venezuela.

Year	Team	W	L	PCT	ERA	G	GS	CG	IP	H	BB	SO	ShO	Relief W	Relief L	Relief SV	AB	H	HR	BA	PO	A	E	DP	TC/G	FA
1968	MIN A	0	0	—	0.00	1	1	0	1	0	1	1	0	0	0	0	*				5	14	3	2	2.4	.864

Ira Townsend

TOWNSEND, IRA DANCE (Pat) BR TR 6′ 1″ 180 lbs.
B. Jan. 9, 1894, Weimar, Tex. D. July 21, 1965, Schulenburg, Tex.

Year	Team	W	L	PCT	ERA	G	GS	CG	IP	H	BB	SO	ShO	Relief W	Relief L	Relief SV	AB	H	HR	BA	PO	A	E	DP	TC/G	FA
1920	BOS N	0	0	—	1.35	4	1	0	6.2	10	2	1	0	0	0	0	2	0	0	.000	0	2	1	0	0.8	.667
1921		0	0	—	6.14	4	0	0	7.1	11	4	0	0	0	0	0	2	0	0	.000	0	4	0	0	1.0	1.000
2 yrs.		0	0		3.86	8	1	0	14	21	6	1	0	0	0	0	4	0	0	.000	0	6	1	0	0.9	.857

Jack Townsend

TOWNSEND, JOHN (Happy) BR TR 6′ 190 lbs.
B. Apr. 9, 1879, Townsend, Del. D. Dec. 21, 1963, Wilmington, Del.

Year	Team	W	L	PCT	ERA	G	GS	CG	IP	H	BB	SO	ShO	Relief W	Relief L	Relief SV	AB	H	HR	BA	PO	A	E	DP	TC/G	FA
1901	PHI N	9	6	.600	3.45	19	16	14	143.2	118	64	72	2	0	0	0	64	7	0	.109	5	25	3	2	1.6	.909
1902	WAS A	9	16	.360	4.45	27	26	22	220.1	233	89	71	0	0	0	0	87	23	0	.264	12	57	6	1	2.8	.920
1903		2	11	.154	4.76	20	13	10	126.2	145	48	54	0	0	1	0	44	2	0	.045	6	37	0	2	2.2	1.000
1904		5	**26**	.161	3.58	36	34	31	291.1	319	100	143	2	0	0	0	119	20	1	.168	19	81	4	8	2.7	.962
1905		7	16	.304	2.63	34	24	22	263	247	84	102	0	1	1	0	83	15	0	.181	21	64	5	1	2.6	.944
1906	CLE A	3	7	.300	2.91	17	12	8	92.2	92	31	31	1	0	1	0	30	4	0	.133	2	31	3	0	2.1	.917
6 yrs.		35	82	.299	3.59	153	125	107	1137.2	1154	416	473	5	1	3	0	427	71	1	.166	65	295	21	14	2.4	.945

Leo Townsend

TOWNSEND, LEO ALPHONSE (Lefty) BL TL 5′10″ 160 lbs.
B. Jan. 15, 1891, Mobile, Ala. D. Dec. 3, 1976, Mobile, Ala.

Year	Team		W	L	PCT	ERA	G	GS	CG	IP	H	BB	SO	ShO	Relief Pitching W	L	SV	Batting AB	H	HR	BA	PO	A	E	DP	TC/G	FA
1920	BOS	N	2	2	.500	1.48	7	1	1	24.1	18	2	0	0	2	1	0	6	1	0	.167	0	8	0	0	1.1	1.000
1921			0	1	.000	27.00	1	1	0	1.1	2	3	0	0	0	0	0	0	0	0	—	1	1	0	1	2.0	1.000
2 yrs.			2	3	.400	2.81	8	2	1	25.2	20	5	0	0	2	1	0	6	1	0	.167	1	9	0	1	1.3	1.000

Bill Tozer

TOZER, WILLIAM LOUIS BR TR 6′ 200 lbs.
B. July 3, 1882, St. Louis, Mo. D. Feb. 23, 1955, Belmont, Calif.

Year	Team		W	L	PCT	ERA	G	GS	CG	IP	H	BB	SO	ShO	Relief Pitching W	L	SV	Batting AB	H	HR	BA	PO	A	E	DP	TC/G	FA
1908	CIN	N	0	0	—	1.69	4	0	0	10.2	11	4	5	0	0	0	0	2	0	0	.000	1	4	1	0	1.5	.833

Steve Trachsel

TRACHSEL, STEPHEN CHRISTOPHER BR TR 6′ 3″ 185 lbs.
B. Oct. 31, 1970, Oxnard, Calif.

Year	Team		W	L	PCT	ERA	G	GS	CG	IP	H	BB	SO	ShO	Relief Pitching W	L	SV	Batting AB	H	HR	BA	PO	A	E	DP	TC/G	FA
1993	CHI	N	0	2	.000	4.58	3	3	0	19.2	16	3	14	0	0	0	0	6	1	0	.167	1	5	0	0	2.0	1.000
1994			9	7	.563	3.21	22	22	1	146	133	54	108	0	0	0	0	43	8	0	.186	10	33	2	0	2.0	.956
1995			7	13	.350	5.15	30	29	2	160.2	174	76	117	0	0	0	0	49	13	0	.265	7	13	1	0	0.7	.952
3 yrs.			16	22	.421	4.25	55	54	3	326.1	323	133	239	0	0	0	0	98	22	0	.224	18	51	3	0	1.3	.958

Fred Trautman

TRAUTMAN, FREDERICK ORLANDO BR TR 6′ 1″ 175 lbs.
B. Mar. 24, 1892, Bucyrus, Ohio D. Feb. 15, 1964, Bucyrus, Ohio.

Year	Team		W	L	PCT	ERA	G	GS	CG	IP	H	BB	SO	ShO	Relief Pitching W	L	SV	Batting AB	H	HR	BA	PO	A	E	DP	TC/G	FA
1915	NWK	F	0	0	—	6.00	1	0	0	3	4	1	2	0	0	0	0	1	0	0	.000	0	0	0	0	0.0	.000

John Trautwein

TRAUTWEIN, JOHN HOWARD BR TR 6′ 3″ 205 lbs.
B. Aug. 7, 1962, Lafayette Hills, Pa.

Year	Team		W	L	PCT	ERA	G	GS	CG	IP	H	BB	SO	ShO	Relief Pitching W	L	SV	Batting AB	H	HR	BA	PO	A	E	DP	TC/G	FA
1988	BOS	A	0	1	.000	9.00	9	0	0	16	26	9	8	0	0	1	0	0	0	0	—	2	1	0	1	0.3	1.000

Al Travers

TRAVERS, ALOYSIUS JOSEPH BR TR 6′ 1″ 180 lbs.
B. May 7, 1892, Philadelphia, Pa. D. Apr. 19, 1968, Philadelphia, Pa.

Year	Team		W	L	PCT	ERA	G	GS	CG	IP	H	BB	SO	ShO	Relief Pitching W	L	SV	Batting AB	H	HR	BA	PO	A	E	DP	TC/G	FA
1912	DET	A	0	1	.000	15.75	1	1	1	8	26	7	1	0	0	0	0	3	0	0	.000	0	7	0	0	7.0	1.000

Bill Travers

TRAVERS, WILLIAM EDWARD BL TL 6′ 4″ 187 lbs.
B. Oct. 27, 1952, Norwood, Mass.

Year	Team		W	L	PCT	ERA	G	GS	CG	IP	H	BB	SO	ShO	Relief Pitching W	L	SV	Batting AB	H	HR	BA	PO	A	E	DP	TC/G	FA
1974	MIL	A	2	3	.400	4.92	23	1	0	53	59	30	31	0	2	3	0	0	0	0	—	2	8	0	0	0.4	1.000
1975			6	11	.353	4.29	28	23	5	136.1	130	60	57	0	0	0	1	0	0	0	—	2	19	2	5	0.8	.913
1976			15	16	.484	2.81	34	34	15	240	211	95	120	3	0	0	0	0	0	0	—	13	31	1	4	1.3	.978
1977			4	12	.250	5.24	19	19	2	122	140	57	49	1	0	0	0	0	0	0	—	6	21	2	3	1.5	.931
1978			12	11	.522	4.41	28	28	8	175.2	184	58	66	3	0	0	0	0	0	0	—	5	36	3	1	1.6	.932
1979			14	8	.636	3.90	30	27	9	187	196	45	74	2	2	0	0	0	0	0	—	7	25	2	0	1.1	.941
1980			12	6	.667	3.92	29	25	7	154	147	47	62	1	0	0	0	0	0	0	—	12	18	1	2	1.1	.968
1981	CAL	A	0	1	.000	8.10	4	4	0	10	14	4	5	0	0	0	0	0	0	0	—	1	1	0	0	0.5	1.000
1983			0	3	.000	5.91	10	7	0	42.2	58	19	24	0	0	0	0	0	0	0	—	0	8	1	1	0.9	.889
9 yrs.			65	71	.478	4.10	205	168	46	1120.2	1139	415	488	10	4	3	1	0	0	0		48	167	12	16	1.1	.947

Harry Trekell

TREKELL, HARRY ROY BR TR 6′ 1½″ 170 lbs.
B. Nov. 18, 1892, Breda, Ill. D. Nov. 4, 1965, Spokane, Wash.

Year	Team		W	L	PCT	ERA	G	GS	CG	IP	H	BB	SO	ShO	Relief Pitching W	L	SV	Batting AB	H	HR	BA	PO	A	E	DP	TC/G	FA
1913	STL	N	0	1	.000	4.50	7	1	1	30	25	8	15	0	0	0	0	9	1	0	.111	2	6	2	0	1.4	.800

Bill Tremel

TREMEL, WILLIAM LEONARD (Mumbles) BR TR 5′11″ 180 lbs.
B. July 4, 1929, Lilly, Pa.

Year	Team		W	L	PCT	ERA	G	GS	CG	IP	H	BB	SO	ShO	Relief Pitching W	L	SV	Batting AB	H	HR	BA	PO	A	E	DP	TC/G	FA
1954	CHI	N	1	2	.333	4.21	33	0	0	51.1	45	28	21	0	1	2	4	8	2	0	.250	1	5	1	0	0.2	.857
1955			3	0	1.000	3.72	23	0	0	38.2	33	18	13	0	3	0	2	7	2	0	.286	2	5	2	0	0.4	.778
1956			0	0	—	13.50	1	0	0	0.2	3	0	0	0	0	0	0	0	0	0	—	0	0	0	0	0.0	.000
3 yrs.			4	2	.667	4.07	57	0	0	90.2	81	46	34	0	4	2	6	15	4	0	.267	3	10	3	0	0.3	.813

Bob Trice

TRICE, ROBERT LEE BR TR 6′ 3″ 190 lbs.
B. Aug. 28, 1926, Newton, Ga. D. Sept. 16, 1988, Weirton, W. Va.

Year	Team		W	L	PCT	ERA	G	GS	CG	IP	H	BB	SO	ShO	Relief Pitching W	L	SV	Batting AB	H	HR	BA	PO	A	E	DP	TC/G	FA
1953	PHI	A	2	1	.667	5.48	3	3	1	23	25	6	4	0	0	0	0	7	1	0	.143	2	8	0	2	3.3	1.000
1954			7	8	.467	5.60	19	18	8	119	146	48	22	1	0	1	0	42	12	1	.286	11	21	3	4	1.8	.914
1955	KC	A	0	0	—	9.00	4	0	0	10	14	6	2	0	0	0	0	3	2	0	.667	3	4	0	0	1.8	1.000
3 yrs.			9	9	.500	5.80	26	21	9	152	185	60	28	1	0	1	0	52	15	1	.288	16	33	3	6	2.0	.942

Joe Trimble

TRIMBLE, JOSEPH GERARD BR TR 6′ 1″ 190 lbs.
B. Oct. 12, 1930, Providence, R. I.

Year	Team		W	L	PCT	ERA	G	GS	CG	IP	H	BB	SO	ShO	Relief Pitching W	L	SV	Batting AB	H	HR	BA	PO	A	E	DP	TC/G	FA
1955	BOS	A	0	0	—	0.00	2	0	0	2	0	3	1	0	0	0	0	0	0	0	—	0	1	0	0	0.5	1.000
1957	PIT	N	0	2	.000	8.24	5	4	0	19.2	23	13	9	0	0	0	0	7	1	0	.143	1	5	1	1	1.4	.857
2 yrs.			0	2	.000	7.48	7	4	0	21.2	23	16	10	0	0	0	0	7	1	0	.143	1	6	1	1	1.1	.875

Ken Trinkle

TRINKLE, KENNETH WAYNE BR TR 6′ 1½″ 175 lbs.
B. Dec. 15, 1919, Paoli, Ind. D. May 10, 1976, Paoli, Ind.

Year	Team		W	L	PCT	ERA	G	GS	CG	IP	H	BB	SO	ShO	Relief Pitching W	L	SV	Batting AB	H	HR	BA	PO	A	E	DP	TC/G	FA
1943	NY	N	1	5	.167	3.74	11	6	1	45.2	51	15	10	0	0	1	0	12	3	0	.250	5	16	1	0	2.0	.955
1946			7	14	.333	3.87	**48**	13	2	151	146	74	49	0	3	5	2	38	3	0	.079	6	30	1	1	0.8	.973
1947			8	4	.667	3.75	**62**	0	0	93.2	100	48	37	0	8	4	10	16	3	0	.188	4	27	0	2	0.5	1.000
1948			4	5	.444	3.18	53	0	0	70.2	66	41	20	0	4	5	7	8	2	0	.250	4	18	0	1	0.4	1.000
1949	PHI	N	1	1	.500	4.00	42	0	0	74.1	79	30	14	0	1	1	2	6	0	0	.000	7	20	1	0	0.7	.964
5 yrs.			21	29	.420	3.74	216	19	3	435.1	442	208	130	0	16	16	21	80	11	0	.138	26	111	3	4	0.6	.979

Rick Trlicek

TRLICEK, RICHARD ALAN BR TR 6′ 3″ 200 lbs.
B. Apr. 26, 1969, Houston, Tex.

Year	Team		W	L	PCT	ERA	G	GS	CG	IP	H	BB	SO	ShO	Relief Pitching W	L	SV	Batting AB	H	HR	BA	PO	A	E	DP	TC/G	FA
1992	TOR	A	0	0	—	10.80	2	0	0	1.2	2	2	1	0	0	0	0	0	0	0	—	0	0	0	0	0.0	.000
1993	LA	N	1	2	.333	4.08	41	0	0	64	59	21	41	0	1	2	1	4	1	0	.250	7	12	0	2	0.5	1.000
1994	BOS	A	1	1	.500	8.06	12	1	0	22.1	32	16	7	0	1	0	0	0	0	0	—	4	1	0	0	0.4	1.000
3 yrs.			2	3	.400	5.22	55	1	0	88	93	39	49	0	2	2	1	4	1	0	.250	11	13	0	2	0.4	1.000

Rich Troedson

TROEDSON, RICHARD LAMONTE
B. May 1, 1950, Palo Alto, Calif.

BL TL 6′ 1″ 170 lbs.

Year	Team	W	L	PCT	ERA	G	GS	CG	IP	H	BB	SO	ShO	Relief Pitching W	Relief Pitching L	Relief Pitching SV	Batting AB	Batting H	Batting HR	BA	PO	A	E	DP	TC/G	FA
1973	SD N	7	9	.438	4.25	50	18	2	152.1	167	59	81	0	2	0	1	40	7	0	.175	5	34	0	0	0.8	1.000
1974		1	1	.500	8.53	15	1	0	19	24	8	11	0	1	0	1	1	0	0	.000	1	5	1	0	0.5	.857
2 yrs.		8	10	.444	4.73	65	19	2	171.1	191	67	92	0	3	0	2	41	7	0	.171	6	39	1	0	0.7	.978

Mike Trombley

TROMBLEY, MICHAEL SCOTT
B. Apr. 14, 1967, Springfield, Mass.

BR TR 6′ 2″ 200 lbs.

Year	Team	W	L	PCT	ERA	G	GS	CG	IP	H	BB	SO	ShO	Relief Pitching W	Relief Pitching L	Relief Pitching SV	Batting AB	Batting H	Batting HR	BA	PO	A	E	DP	TC/G	FA
1992	MIN A	3	2	.600	3.30	10	7	0	46.1	43	17	38	0	0	0	0	0	0	0	—	1	6	0	0	0.7	1.000
1993		6	6	.500	4.88	44	10	0	114.1	131	41	85	0	3	1	2	0	0	0	—	6	19	0	2	0.6	1.000
1994		2	0	1.000	6.33	24	0	0	48.1	56	18	32	0	2	0	0	0	0	0	—	5	3	1	0	0.4	.889
1995		4	8	.333	5.62	20	18	0	97.2	107	42	68	0	0	0	0	0	0	0	—	9	10	1	2	1.0	.950
4 yrs.		15	16	.484	5.11	98	35	0	306.2	337	118	223	0	5	1	2	0	0	0		21	38	2	4	0.6	.967

Hal Trosky

TROSKY, HAROLD ARTHUR, JR. (Hoot)
Born Harold Arthur, Jr. Troyavesky.
Son of Hal Trosky.
B. Sept. 29, 1936, Cleveland, Ohio.

BR TR 6′ 3″ 205 lbs.

Year	Team	W	L	PCT	ERA	G	GS	CG	IP	H	BB	SO	ShO	Relief Pitching W	Relief Pitching L	Relief Pitching SV	Batting AB	Batting H	Batting HR	BA	PO	A	E	DP	TC/G	FA
1958	CHI A	1	0	1.000	6.00	2	0	0	3	5	2	1	0	1	0	0	0	0	0	—	0	1	0	0	0.5	1.000

Bill Trotter

TROTTER, WILLIAM FELIX
B. Aug. 10, 1908, Cisne, Ill. D. Aug. 26, 1984, Arlington, Mass.

BR TR 6′ 2″ 195 lbs.

Year	Team	W	L	PCT	ERA	G	GS	CG	IP	H	BB	SO	ShO	Relief Pitching W	Relief Pitching L	Relief Pitching SV	Batting AB	Batting H	Batting HR	BA	PO	A	E	DP	TC/G	FA
1937	STL A	2	9	.182	5.81	34	12	3	122.1	150	50	37	0	0	2	1	33	1	0	.030	2	18	3	0	0.7	.870
1938		0	1	.000	5.63	1	1	1	8	8	0	1	0	0	0	0	2	0	0	.000	0	5	0	0	5.0	1.000
1939		6	13	.316	5.34	41	13	4	156.2	205	54	61	0	4	2	0	37	4	0	.108	9	29	0	3	0.9	1.000
1940		7	6	.538	3.77	36	4	1	98	117	31	29	0	6	3	2	22	1	0	.045	2	21	0	3	0.6	1.000
1941		4	2	.667	5.98	29	0	0	49.2	68	19	17	0	4	2	0	6	0	0	.000	0	13	0	1	0.4	1.000
1942	2 teams STL A (3G 0–1) WAS A (17G 3–1)																									
″	total	3	2	.600	6.33	20	0	0	42.2	57	16	13	0	3	2	0	8	0	0	.000	2	12	1	0	0.8	.933
1944	STL N	0	1	.000	13.50	2	1	0	6	14	4	0	0	0	0	0	1	0	0	.000	0	2	0	0	1.0	1.000
7 yrs.		22	34	.393	5.40	163	31	9	483.1	619	174	158	0	17	11	3	109	6	0	.055	15	100	4	7	0.7	.966

Dizzy Trout

TROUT, PAUL HOWARD
Father of Steve Trout.
B. June 29, 1915, Sandcut, Ind. D. Feb. 28, 1972, Harvey, Ill.

BR TR 6′ 2½″ 195 lbs.

Year	Team	W	L	PCT	ERA	G	GS	CG	IP	H	BB	SO	ShO	Relief Pitching W	Relief Pitching L	Relief Pitching SV	Batting AB	Batting H	Batting HR	BA	PO	A	E	DP	TC/G	FA
1939	DET A	9	10	.474	3.61	33	22	6	162	168	74	72	0	0	0	2	57	12	0	.211	3	23	4	1	0.9	.867
1940		3	7	.300	4.47	33	10	1	100.2	125	54	64	0	1	2	2	31	4	0	.129	5	25	2	1	1.0	.938
1941		9	9	.500	3.74	37	18	6	151.2	144	84	88	1	2	2	2	50	9	0	.180	7	30	2	3	1.1	.949
1942		12	18	.400	3.43	35	29	13	223	214	89	91	1	2	1	0	75	16	1	.213	24	56	6	6	2.5	.930
1943		**20**	12	.625	2.48	44	30	18	246.2	204	101	111	**5**	3	1	6	91	20	1	.220	20	67	4	1	2.1	.956
1944		27	14	.659	**2.12**	49	**40**	**33**	**352.1**	**314**	83	144	**7**	3	0	0	133	36	5	.271	21	94	4	8	2.4	.966
1945		18	15	.545	3.14	41	31	18	246.1	252	79	97	4	2	0	2	102	25	2	.245	13	65	9	9	2.1	.897
1946		17	13	.567	2.34	38	32	23	276.1	244	97	151	5	0	0	3	103	20	3	.194	17	64	5	6	2.3	.942
1947		10	11	.476	3.48	32	26	9	186.1	186	65	74	2	0	0	2	68	11	3	.162	22	40	3	4	2.0	.954
1948		10	14	.417	3.43	32	23	11	183.2	193	73	91	2	1	1	2	69	15	1	.217	11	37	5	7	1.7	.906
1949		3	6	.333	4.40	33	0	0	59.1	68	21	19	0	3	6	3	14	2	1	.143	4	19	3	4	0.8	.885
1950		13	5	.722	3.75	34	20	11	184.2	190	64	88	1	1	0	4	63	12	1	.190	15	43	0	5	1.7	1.000
1951		9	**14**	.391	4.04	42	22	7	191.2	172	75	89	0	3	1	5	52	14	1	.269	18	47	1	6	1.6	.985
1952	2 teams DET A (10G 1–5) BOS A (26G 9–8)																									
″	total	10	13	.435	3.92	36	19	2	160.2	163	87	77	0	4	3	2	53	9	1	.170	13	35	2	2	1.4	.960
1957	BAL A	0	0	—	81.00	2	0	0	0.1	4	0	0	0	0	0	0	0	0	0	—	0	0	0	0	0.0	.000
15 yrs.		170	161	.514	3.23	521	322	158	2725.2	2641	1046	1256	28	25	17	35	961	205	20	.213	193	645	50	63	1.7	.944
WORLD SERIES																										
1940	DET A	0	1	.000	9.00	1	1	0	2	6	1	1	0	0	0	0	1	0	0	.000	0	1	0	0	1.0	1.000
1945		1	1	.500	0.66	2	1	1	13.2	9	3	9	0	0	1	0	6	1	0	.167	2	5	0	0	3.5	1.000
2 yrs.		1	2	.333	1.72	3	2	1	15.2	15	4	10	0	0	1	0	7	1	0	.143	2	6	0	0	2.7	1.000

Steve Trout

TROUT, STEVEN RUSSELL (Rainbow)
Son of Dizzy Trout.
B. July 30, 1957, Detroit, Mich.

BL TL 6′ 4″ 195 lbs.

Year	Team	W	L	PCT	ERA	G	GS	CG	IP	H	BB	SO	ShO	Relief Pitching W	Relief Pitching L	Relief Pitching SV	Batting AB	Batting H	Batting HR	BA	PO	A	E	DP	TC/G	FA
1978	CHI A	3	0	1.000	4.03	4	3	1	22.1	19	11	11	0	0	0	0	0	0	0	—	0	3	0	1	0.8	1.000
1979		11	8	.579	3.89	34	18	6	155	165	59	76	2	1	2	4	0	0	0	—	6	33	3	2	1.2	.929
1980		9	16	.360	3.69	32	30	7	200	229	49	89	2	0	0	0	0	0	0	—	11	42	2	3	1.7	.964
1981		8	7	.533	3.46	20	18	3	125	122	38	54	0	1	0	0	0	0	0	—	3	23	2	5	1.4	.929
1982		6	9	.400	4.26	25	19	2	120.1	130	50	62	0	0	0	0	0	0	0	—	9	18	4	2	1.2	.871
1983	CHI N	10	14	.417	4.65	34	32	1	180	217	59	80	0	1	0	0	62	12	0	.194	8	40	2	3	1.5	.960
1984		13	7	.650	3.41	32	31	6	190	205	59	81	2	0	1	0	61	8	0	.131	13	48	4	5	2.0	.938
1985		9	7	.563	3.39	24	24	3	140.2	142	63	44	1	0	0	0	46	5	0	.109	6	38	2	0	1.9	.957
1986		5	7	.417	4.75	37	25	0	161	184	78	69	0	1	0	0	43	9	0	.209	7	31	1	3	1.1	.974
1987	2 teams CHI N (11G 6–3) NY A (14G 0–4)																									
″	total	6	7	.462	4.38	25	20	3	121.1	123	64	59	2	0	0	0	26	4	0	.154	7	21	0	1	1.1	1.000
1988	SEA A	4	7	.364	7.83	15	13	0	56.1	86	31	14	0	0	0	0	0	0	0	—	5	8	2	2	1.0	.867
1989		4	3	.571	6.60	19	3	0	30	43	17	17	0	3	2	0	0	0	0	—	2	5	0	1	0.4	1.000
12 yrs.		88	92	.489	4.18	301	236	32	1502	1665	578	656	9	7	5	4	238	38	0	.160	77	310	22	28	1.4	.946
LEAGUE CHAMPIONSHIP SERIES																										
1984	CHI N	1	0	1.000	2.00	2	1	0	9	5	3	3	0	0	0	0	2	1	0	.500	0	1	1	0	1.0	.500

Bob Trowbridge

TROWBRIDGE, ROBERT
B. June 27, 1930, Hudson, N. Y. D. Apr. 3, 1980, Hudson, N. Y.

BR TR 6′ 1″ 180 lbs.

Year	Team	W	L	PCT	ERA	G	GS	CG	IP	H	BB	SO	ShO	Relief Pitching W	Relief Pitching L	Relief Pitching SV	Batting AB	Batting H	Batting HR	BA	PO	A	E	DP	TC/G	FA
1956	MIL N	3	2	.600	2.66	19	4	1	50.2	38	34	40	0	1	2	0	7	0	0	.000	0	11	1	1	0.6	.917
1957		7	5	.583	3.64	32	16	3	126	118	52	75	1	2	0	1	39	4	0	.103	13	15	0	1	0.9	1.000
1958		1	3	.250	3.93	27	4	0	55	53	26	31	0	1	2	1	9	1	0	.111	1	5	1	3	0.3	.857
1959		1	0	1.000	5.93	16	0	0	30.1	45	10	22	0	1	0	1	4	0	0	.000	0	4	0	0	0.3	1.000
1960	KC A	1	3	.250	4.61	22	1	0	68.1	70	34	33	0	1	3	2	18	1	0	.056	4	13	0	0	0.8	1.000
5 yrs.		13	13	.500	3.95	116	25	4	330.1	324	156	201	1	6	7	5	77	6	0	.078	18	48	2	5	0.6	.971

Bob Trowbridge *continued*

Year	Team	Lg	W	L	PCT	ERA	G	GS	CG	IP	H	BB	SO	ShO	Relief Pitching W	Relief Pitching L	Relief Pitching SV	Batting AB	Batting H	Batting HR	BA	PO	A	E	DP	TC/G	FA
WORLD SERIES																											
1957	MIL	N	0	0	—	45.00	1	0	0	1	2	3	1	0	0	0	0	0	0	0	—	0	0	0	0	0.0	.000

Bun Troy

TROY, ROBERT BR TR 6′ 4″ 195 lbs.
B. Aug. 22, 1888, Germany D. Oct. 7, 1918, Meuse, France.

Year	Team	Lg	W	L	PCT	ERA	G	GS	CG	IP	H	BB	SO	ShO	Relief Pitching W	Relief Pitching L	Relief Pitching SV	Batting AB	Batting H	Batting HR	BA	PO	A	E	DP	TC/G	FA
1912	DET	A	0	1	.000	5.40	1	1	0	6.2	9	3	1	0	0	0	0	2	0	0	.000	0	1	0	0	1.0	1.000

Virgil Trucks

TRUCKS, VIRGIL OLIVER (Fire) BR TR 5′11″ 198 lbs.
B. Apr. 26, 1917, Birmingham, Ala.

Year	Team	Lg	W	L	PCT	ERA	G	GS	CG	IP	H	BB	SO	ShO	Relief Pitching W	Relief Pitching L	Relief Pitching SV	Batting AB	Batting H	Batting HR	BA	PO	A	E	DP	TC/G	FA
1941	DET	A	0	0	—	9.00	1	0	0	2	4	0	3	0	0	0	0	0	0	0	—	1	0	0	0	1.0	1.000
1942			14	8	.636	2.74	28	20	8	167.2	147	74	91	2	4	1	0	65	8	0	.123	5	28	3	0	1.3	.917
1943			16	10	.615	2.84	33	25	10	202.2	170	52	118	3	2	1	2	72	13	0	.181	16	24	0	0	1.2	1.000
1945			0	0	—	1.69	1	1	0	5.1	3	2	3	0	0	0	0	2	0	0	.000	1	1	0	0	2.0	1.000
1946			14	9	.609	3.23	32	29	15	236.2	217	75	161	3	1	1	0	95	17	0	.179	11	33	3	1	1.5	.936
1947			10	12	.455	4.53	36	26	8	180.2	186	79	108	2	0	2	2	70	19	0	.271	13	22	2	0	1.0	.946
1948			14	13	.519	3.78	43	26	7	211.2	190	85	123	0	4	2	2	79	13	0	.165	13	28	0	1	1.0	1.000
1949			19	11	.633	2.81	41	32	17	275	209	124	**153**	**6**	2	0	4	100	12	0	.120	13	33	2	2	1.2	.958
1950			3	1	.750	3.54	7	7	2	48.1	45	21	25	1	0	0	0	20	3	0	.150	2	13	1	1	2.3	.938
1951			13	8	.619	4.33	37	18	6	153.2	153	75	89	1	4	2	1	55	13	0	.236	11	32	3	2	1.2	.935
1952			5	19	.208	3.97	35	29	8	197	190	82	129	3	0	1	1	64	12	1	.188	21	37	2	1	1.7	.967
1953	2 teams	STL A	(16G 5–4)		CHI A	(24G 15–6)																					
″	total		20	10	.667	2.93	40	33	17	264.1	234	99	149	5	0	1	3	88	19	1	.216	14	42	6	3	1.5	.903
1954	CHI	A	19	12	.613	2.79	40	33	16	264.2	224	95	152	**5**	3	1	3	93	17	0	.183	10	48	0	1	1.5	1.000
1955			13	8	.619	3.96	32	26	7	175	176	61	91	3	1	0	0	64	8	0	.125	4	33	0	1	1.2	1.000
1956	DET	A	6	5	.545	3.83	22	16	3	120	104	63	43	1	0	1	1	45	11	0	.244	6	18	3	1	1.2	.889
1957	KC	A	9	7	.563	3.03	48	7	0	116	106	62	55	0	8	3	7	28	4	0	.143	8	21	1	0	0.6	.967
1958	2 teams	KC A	(16G 0–1)		NY A	(25G 2–1)																					
″	total		2	2	.500	3.65	41	0	0	61.2	58	39	41	0	2	2	4	9	2	0	.222	7	7	1	0	0.4	.933
17 yrs.			177	135	.567	3.39	517	328	124	2682.1	2416	1088	1534	35	31	18	30	949	171	2	.180	156	420	27	14	1.2	.955
WORLD SERIES																											
1945	DET	A	1	0	1.000	3.38	2	2	1	13.1	14	5	7	0	0	0	0	4	0	0	.000	1	1	0	0	1.0	1.000

Mike Trujillo

TRUJILLO, MICHAEL ANDREW BR TR 6′ 1″ 180 lbs.
B. Jan. 12, 1960, Denver, Colo.

Year	Team	Lg	W	L	PCT	ERA	G	GS	CG	IP	H	BB	SO	ShO	Relief Pitching W	Relief Pitching L	Relief Pitching SV	Batting AB	Batting H	Batting HR	BA	PO	A	E	DP	TC/G	FA
1985	BOS	A	4	4	.500	4.82	27	7	1	84	112	23	19	0	2	1	1	0	0	0	—	11	20	2	1	1.2	.939
1986	2 teams	BOS A	(3G 0–0)		SEA A	(11G 3–2)																					
″	total		3	2	.600	3.26	14	4	1	47	39	21	23	1	1	1	1	0	0	0		5	8	0	0	0.9	1.000
1987	SEA	A	4	4	.500	6.17	28	7	0	65.2	70	26	36	0	2	1	1	0	0	0	—	5	3	0	2	0.3	1.000
1988	DET	A	0	0	—	5.11	6	0	0	12.1	11	5	5	0	0	0	0	0	0	0	—	1	3	0	0	0.7	1.000
1989			1	2	.333	5.96	8	4	1	25.2	35	13	13	0	0	0	0	0	0	0	—	0	5	0	0	0.6	1.000
5 yrs.			12	12	.500	5.02	83	22	3	234.2	267	88	96	1	5	3	3	0	0	0		22	39	2	3	0.8	.968

Ed Trumbull

TRUMBULL, EDWARD J.
Born Edward J. Trembly.
B. Nov. 3, 1860, Chicopee, Mass. D. Jan. 14, 1937, Kingston, Pa.

Year	Team	Lg	W	L	PCT	ERA	G	GS	CG	IP	H	BB	SO	ShO	Relief Pitching W	Relief Pitching L	Relief Pitching SV	Batting AB	Batting H	Batting HR	BA	PO	A	E	DP	TC/G	FA
1884	WAS	AA	1	9	.100	*4.71*	10	10	10	84	108	31	43	0	0	0	0	*				24	24	14	1	2.5	.774

George Tsamis

TSAMIS, GEORGE ALEX BR TL 6′ 2″ 190 lbs.
B. June 14, 1967, Campbell, Calif.

Year	Team	Lg	W	L	PCT	ERA	G	GS	CG	IP	H	BB	SO	ShO	Relief Pitching W	Relief Pitching L	Relief Pitching SV	Batting AB	Batting H	Batting HR	BA	PO	A	E	DP	TC/G	FA
1993	MIN	A	1	2	.333	6.19	41	0	0	68.1	86	27	30	0	1	2	1	0	0	0	—	7	14	0	2	0.5	1.000

John Tsitouris

TSITOURIS, JOHN PHILIP BR TR 6′ 175 lbs.
B. May 4, 1936, Monroe, N. C.

Year	Team	Lg	W	L	PCT	ERA	G	GS	CG	IP	H	BB	SO	ShO	Relief Pitching W	Relief Pitching L	Relief Pitching SV	Batting AB	Batting H	Batting HR	BA	PO	A	E	DP	TC/G	FA
1957	DET	A	1	0	1.000	8.10	2	0	0	3.1	8	2	2	0	1	0	0	1	0	0	.000	1	0	0	0	0.5	1.000
1958	KC	A	0	0	—	3.00	1	1	0	3	2	2	1	0	0	0	0	1	0	0	.000	0	1	0	0	1.0	1.000
1959			4	3	.571	4.97	24	10	0	83.1	90	35	50	0	2	0	0	20	3	0	.150	3	13	2	0	0.8	.889
1960			0	2	.000	6.55	14	2	0	33	38	21	12	0	0	1	0	6	0	0	.000	2	6	0	0	0.6	1.000
1962	CIN	N	1	0	1.000	0.84	4	2	1	21.1	13	7	7	1	0	0	0	5	0	0	.000	1	3	0	0	1.0	1.000
1963			12	8	.600	3.16	30	21	8	191	167	38	113	3	0	1	0	62	5	0	.081	13	16	1	0	1.0	.967
1964			9	13	.409	3.80	37	24	6	175.1	178	75	146	1	0	1	2	58	11	0	.190	14	23	0	1	1.0	1.000
1965			6	9	.400	4.95	31	20	3	131	134	65	91	0	1	0	1	43	3	0	.070	5	19	2	0	0.8	.923
1966			0	0	—	18.00	1	0	0	1	3	1	0	0	0	0	0	0	0	0	—	0	0	0	0	0.0	.000
1967			1	0	1.000	3.38	2	1	0	8	4	6	4	0	0	0	0	0	0	0	—	2	1	0	0	1.5	1.000
1968			0	3	.000	7.11	3	3	0	12.2	16	8	6	0	0	0	0	2	0	0	.000	0	3	0	0	1.0	1.000
11 yrs.			34	38	.472	4.13	149	84	18	663	653	260	432	5	4	3	3	198	22	0	.111	41	85	5	1	0.9	.962

Tommy Tucker

TUCKER, THOMAS JOSEPH BB TR 5′11″ 165 lbs.
B. Oct. 28, 1863, Holyoke, Mass. D. Oct. 22, 1935, Montague, Mass.

Year	Team	Lg	W	L	PCT	ERA	G	GS	CG	IP	H	BB	SO	ShO	Relief Pitching W	Relief Pitching L	Relief Pitching SV	Batting AB	Batting H	Batting HR	BA	PO	A	E	DP	TC/G	FA
1888	BAL	AA	0	0	—	3.86	1	0	0	2.1	4	0	2	0	0	0	0	520	149	6	.287	1346	50	35	49	10.5	.976
1891	BOS	N	0	0	—	9.00	1	0	0	1	3	0	0	0	0	0	0	548	148	2	.270	1365	59	38	64	10.7	.974
2 yrs.			0	0		5.40	2	0	0	3.1	7	0	2	0	0	0	0	*				16425	752	399	925	10.4	.977

Tom Tuckey

TUCKEY, THOMAS H. TL 6′ 3″
B. Oct. 7, 1883, Birmingham, England D. Oct. 17, 1950, New York, N. Y.

Year	Team	Lg	W	L	PCT	ERA	G	GS	CG	IP	H	BB	SO	ShO	Relief Pitching W	Relief Pitching L	Relief Pitching SV	Batting AB	Batting H	Batting HR	BA	PO	A	E	DP	TC/G	FA
1908	BOS	N	3	3	.500	2.50	8	8	3	72	60	20	26	1	0	0	0	20	1	0	.050	4	22	1	1	3.4	.963
1909			0	9	.000	4.27	17	10	4	90.2	104	22	16	0	0	1	0	29	4	0	.138	11	28	3	1	2.5	.929
2 yrs.			3	12	.200	3.49	25	18	7	162.2	164	42	42	1	0	1	0	49	5	0	.102	15	50	4	2	2.8	.942

John Tudor

TUDOR, JOHN THOMAS BL TL 6′ 185 lbs.
B. Feb. 2, 1954, Schenectady, N. Y.

Year	Team	Lg	W	L	PCT	ERA	G	GS	CG	IP	H	BB	SO	ShO	Relief Pitching W	Relief Pitching L	Relief Pitching SV	Batting AB	Batting H	Batting HR	BA	PO	A	E	DP	TC/G	FA
1979	BOS	A	1	2	.333	6.43	6	6	1	28	39	9	11	0	0	0	0	0	0	0	—	1	7	0	1	1.3	1.000
1980			8	5	.615	3.03	16	13	5	92	81	31	45	0	0	1	0	0	0	0	—	5	24	1	1	1.9	.967
1981			4	3	.571	4.56	18	11	2	79	74	28	44	0	1	1	1	0	0	0	—	2	17	0	1	1.1	1.000
1982			13	10	.565	3.63	32	30	6	195.2	215	59	146	1	0	0	0	0	0	0	—	5	39	2	4	1.4	.957
1983			13	12	.520	4.09	34	34	7	242	236	81	136	2	0	0	0	0	0	0	—	12	26	2	4	1.2	.950
1984	PIT	N	12	11	.522	3.27	32	32	6	212	200	56	117	1	0	0	0	76	16	0	.211	11	31	0	0	1.3	1.000
1985	STL	N	21	8	.724	1.93	36	36	14	275	209	49	169	**10**	0	0	0	94	13	0	.138	18	45	3	4	1.8	.955
1986			13	7	.650	2.92	30	30	3	219	197	53	107	0	0	0	0	72	11	0	.153	10	41	2	4	1.8	.962
1987			10	2	.833	3.84	16	16	0	96	100	32	54	0	0	0	0	35	7	0	.200	4	20	0	2	1.5	1.000
1988	2 teams	STL N	(21G 6–5)		LA N	(9G 4–3)																					
″	total		10	8	.556	2.32	30	30	5	197.2	189	41	87	1	0	0	0	59	5	0	.085	7	39	0	4	1.5	1.000
1989	LA	N	0	0	—	3.14	6	3	0	14.1	17	6	9	0	0	0	0	2	0	0	.000	0	3	0	0	0.5	1.000
1990	STL	N	12	4	.750	2.40	25	22	1	146.1	120	30	63	1	1	0	0	46	7	0	.152	10	29	1	2	1.6	.975
12 yrs.			117	72	.619	3.12	281	263	50	1797	1677	475	988	16	2	2	1	384	59	0	.154	85	321	11	27	1.5	.974
LEAGUE CHAMPIONSHIP SERIES																											
1985	STL	N	1	1	.500	2.84	2	2	0	12.2	10	3	8	0	0	0	0	4	0	0	.000	0	1	0	0	0.5	1.000
1987			1	1	.500	1.76	2	2	0	15.1	16	5	12	0	0	0	0	4	0	0	.000	0	4	0	0	2.0	1.000
1988	LA	N	0	0	—	7.20	1	1	0	5	8	1	1	0	0	0	0	2	0	0	.000	1	2	0	0	3.0	1.000
3 yrs.			2	2	.500	3.00	5	5	0	33	34	9	21	0	0	0	0	10	0	0	.000	1	7	0	0	1.6	1.000
WORLD SERIES																											
1985	STL	N	2	1	.667	3.00	3	3	1	18	15	7	14	1	0	0	0	5	0	0	.000	0	3	0	0	1.0	1.000
1987			1	1	.500	5.73	2	2	0	11	15	3	8	0	0	0	0	2	0	0	.000	0	4	0	0	2.0	1.000
1988	LA	N	0	0	—	0.00	1	1	0	1.1	0	0	1	0	0	0	0	0	0	0	—	0	0	0	0	0.0	.000
3 yrs.			3	2	.600	3.86	6	6	1	30.1	30	10	23	1	0	0	0	7	0	0	.000	0	7	0	0	1.2	1.000

Oscar Tuero

TUERO, OSCAR BR TR 5′ 8½″ 158 lbs.
Born Oscar Monzon (Tuero).
B. Dec. 17, 1898, Havana, Cuba D. Oct. 21, 1960, Houston, Tex.

Year	Team	Lg	W	L	PCT	ERA	G	GS	CG	IP	H	BB	SO	ShO	Relief Pitching W	Relief Pitching L	Relief Pitching SV	Batting AB	Batting H	Batting HR	BA	PO	A	E	DP	TC/G	FA
1918	STL	N	1	2	.333	1.02	11	3	2	44.1	32	10	13	0	0	0	0	12	3	0	.250	4	10	1	0	1.4	.933
1919			5	7	.417	3.20	**45**	16	4	154.2	137	42	45	0	1	1	**4**	39	8	0	.205	3	44	2	1	1.1	.959
1920			0	0	—	54.00	2	0	0	0.2	5	1	0	0	0	0	0	0	0	0	—	0	0	0	0	0.0	.000
3 yrs.			6	9	.400	2.88	58	19	6	199.2	174	53	58	0	1	1	4	51	11	0	.216	7	54	3	1	1.1	.953

Bob Tufts

TUFTS, ROBERT MALCOLM BL TL 6′ 5″ 215 lbs.
B. Nov. 2, 1955, Medford, Mass.

Year	Team	Lg	W	L	PCT	ERA	G	GS	CG	IP	H	BB	SO	ShO	Relief Pitching W	Relief Pitching L	Relief Pitching SV	Batting AB	Batting H	Batting HR	BA	PO	A	E	DP	TC/G	FA
1981	SF	N	0	0	—	3.60	11	0	0	15	20	6	12	0	0	0	0	1	0	0	.000	3	4	0	0	0.6	1.000
1982	KC	A	2	0	1.000	4.50	10	0	0	20	24	3	13	0	2	0	2	0	0	0	—	1	0	0	0	0.1	1.000
1983			0	0	—	8.10	6	0	0	6.2	16	5	3	0	0	0	0	0	0	0	—	0	2	0	0	0.3	1.000
3 yrs.			2	0	1.000	4.75	27	0	0	41.2	60	14	28	0	2	0	2	1	0	0	.000	4	6	0	0	0.4	1.000

Lee Tunnell

TUNNELL, BYRON LEE BR TR 6′ 1″ 180 lbs.
B. Oct. 30, 1960, Tyler, Tex.

Year	Team	Lg	W	L	PCT	ERA	G	GS	CG	IP	H	BB	SO	ShO	Relief Pitching W	Relief Pitching L	Relief Pitching SV	Batting AB	Batting H	Batting HR	BA	PO	A	E	DP	TC/G	FA
1982	PIT	N	1	1	.500	3.93	5	3	0	18.1	17	5	4	0	0	1	0	4	0	0	.000	1	4	0	0	1.0	1.000
1983			11	6	.647	3.65	35	25	5	177.2	167	58	95	3	1	0	0	58	7	0	.121	11	35	0	6	1.3	1.000
1984			1	7	.125	5.27	26	6	0	68.1	81	40	51	0	0	5	1	12	1	0	.083	8	14	1	1	0.9	.957
1985			4	10	.286	4.01	24	23	0	132.1	126	57	74	0	0	1	0	47	4	0	.085	7	23	0	1	1.3	1.000
1987	STL	N	4	4	.500	4.84	32	9	0	74.1	90	34	49	0	2	2	0	17	4	0	.235	6	12	0	1	0.6	1.000
1989	MIN	A	1	0	1.000	6.00	10	0	0	12	18	6	7	0	1	0	0	0	0	0	—	0	0	0	0	0.0	.000
6 yrs.			22	28	.440	4.23	132	66	5	483	499	200	280	3	4	9	1	138	16	0	.116	33	88	1	9	0.9	.992
WORLD SERIES																											
1987	STL	N	0	0	—	2.08	2	0	0	4.1	4	2	1	0	0	0	0	0	0	0	—	0	1	0	0	0.5	1.000

George Turbeville

TURBEVILLE, GEORGE ELKINS BR TL 6′ 1″ 175 lbs.
B. Aug. 24, 1914, Turbeville, S. C. D. Oct. 5, 1983, Salisbury, N. C.

Year	Team	Lg	W	L	PCT	ERA	G	GS	CG	IP	H	BB	SO	ShO	Relief Pitching W	Relief Pitching L	Relief Pitching SV	Batting AB	Batting H	Batting HR	BA	PO	A	E	DP	TC/G	FA
1935	PHI	A	0	3	.000	7.63	19	6	2	63.2	74	69	20	0	0	0	0	19	2	0	.105	2	11	2	0	0.8	.867
1936			2	5	.286	6.39	12	6	2	43.2	42	32	10	0	1	0	0	14	2	0	.143	2	7	1	0	0.8	.900
1937			0	4	.000	4.77	31	3	0	77.1	80	56	17	0	0	2	0	26	6	0	.231	2	14	5	0	0.7	.762
3 yrs.			2	12	.143	6.14	62	15	4	184.2	196	157	47	0	1	2	0	59	10	0	.169	6	32	8	0	0.7	.826

Lucas Turk

TURK, LUCAS NEWTON (Chief) BR TR 6′ 165 lbs.
B. May 2, 1898, Homer, Ga. D. Jan. 11, 1994, Homer, Ga.

Year	Team	Lg	W	L	PCT	ERA	G	GS	CG	IP	H	BB	SO	ShO	Relief Pitching W	Relief Pitching L	Relief Pitching SV	Batting AB	Batting H	Batting HR	BA	PO	A	E	DP	TC/G	FA
1922	WAS	A	0	0	—	6.94	5	0	0	11.2	16	5	1	0	0	0	0	4	1	0	.250	0	0	0	0	0.0	.000

Bob Turley

TURLEY, ROBERT LEE (Bullet Bob) BR TR 6′ 2″ 215 lbs.
B. Sept. 19, 1930, Troy, Ill.

Year	Team	Lg	W	L	PCT	ERA	G	GS	CG	IP	H	BB	SO	ShO	Relief Pitching W	Relief Pitching L	Relief Pitching SV	Batting AB	Batting H	Batting HR	BA	PO	A	E	DP	TC/G	FA
1951	STL	A	0	1	.000	7.36	1	1	0	7.1	11	3	5	0	0	0	0	2	0	0	.000	1	1	0	1	2.0	1.000
1953			2	6	.250	3.28	10	7	3	60.1	39	44	61	1	1	1	0	18	5	1	.278	4	3	0	2	0.7	1.000
1954	BAL	A	14	15	.483	3.46	35	35	14	247.1	178	**181**	**185**	0	0	0	0	81	11	0	.136	7	35	1	1	1.2	.977
1955	NY	A	17	13	.567	3.06	36	34	13	246.2	168	**177**	210	6	0	0	1	82	11	0	.134	6	30	4	2	1.1	.900
1956			8	4	.667	5.05	27	21	5	132	138	103	91	1	0	0	1	46	8	0	.174	3	18	1	2	0.8	.955
1957			13	6	.684	2.71	32	23	9	176.1	120	85	152	4	1	0	3	57	5	0	.088	13	22	2	1	1.2	.946
1958			**21**	7	**.750**	2.97	33	31	**19**	245.1	178	**128**	168	6	0	0	1	88	12	2	.136	17	26	0	4	1.3	1.000
1959			8	11	.421	4.32	33	22	7	154.1	141	83	111	3	0	0	0	46	4	0	.087	11	18	1	1	0.9	.967
1960			9	3	.750	3.27	34	24	4	173.1	138	87	87	1	1	0	5	55	4	0	.073	10	21	0	1	0.9	1.000
1961			3	5	.375	5.75	15	12	1	72	74	51	48	0	0	0	0	21	2	0	.095	4	8	0	0	0.8	1.000
1962			3	3	.500	4.57	24	8	0	69	68	47	42	0	3	0	1	12	0	0	.000	3	15	0	0	0.8	1.000
1963	2 teams	LA A	(19G 2–7)		BOS A	(11G 1–4)																					
″	total		3	11	.214	4.20	30	19	3	128.2	113	79	105	2	0	1	0	39	7	1	.179	9	14	0	1	0.8	1.000
12 yrs.			101	85	.543	3.64	310	237	78	1712.2	1366	1068	1265	24	6	2	12	547	69	4	.126	88	211	9	16	1.0	.971

Bob Turley *continued*

Year	Team	Lg	W	L	PCT	ERA	G	GS	CG	IP	H	BB	SO	ShO	Relief W	Relief L	Relief SV	Batting AB	Batting H	Batting HR	BA	PO	A	E	DP	TC/G	FA
WORLD SERIES																											
1955	**NY**	**A**	0	1	.000	8.44	3	1	0	5.1	7	4	7	0	0	0	0	1	0	0	.000	0	1	0	0	0.3	1.000
1956			0	1	.000	0.82	3	1	1	11	4	8	14	0	0	0	0	4	0	0	.000	0	2	0	0	0.7	1.000
1957			1	0	1.000	2.31	3	2	1	11.2	7	6	12	0	0	0	0	4	0	0	.000	2	2	0	1	1.3	1.000
1958			2	1	.667	2.76	4	2	1	16.1	10	7	13	1	1	0	1	5	1	0	.200	0	1	0	0	0.3	1.000
1960			1	0	1.000	4.82	2	2	0	9.1	15	4	0	0	0	0	0	4	1	0	.250	0	2	0	0	1.0	1.000
5 yrs.			4	3	.571	3.19	15	8	3	53.2	43	29	46	1	1	0	1	18	2	0	.111	2	8	0	1	0.7	1.000
							3rd	**10th**				**5th**	**10th**														

Jim Turner

TURNER, JAMES RILEY (Milkman Jim) BL TR 6′ 185 lbs.
B. Aug. 6, 1903, Antioch, Tenn.

Year	Team	Lg	W	L	PCT	ERA	G	GS	CG	IP	H	BB	SO	ShO	Relief W	Relief L	Relief SV	Batting AB	Batting H	Batting HR	BA	PO	A	E	DP	TC/G	FA
1937	**BOS**	**N**	20	11	.645	**2.38**	33	30	**24**	256.2	228	52	69	**5**	0	1	1	96	24	0	.250	12	59	4	3	2.3	.947
1938			14	18	.438	3.46	35	34	22	268	267	54	71	3	0	0	0	96	22	0	.229	17	72	0	4	2.5	1.000
1939			4	11	.267	4.28	25	22	9	157.2	181	51	50	0	0	0	0	55	13	1	.236	8	38	2	0	1.9	.958
1940	**CIN**	**N**	14	7	.667	2.89	24	23	11	187	181	32	53	0	1	0	0	75	18	0	.240	8	35	1	1	1.8	.977
1941			6	4	.600	3.11	23	10	3	113	120	24	34	0	1	0	0	41	6	0	.146	0	33	1	4	1.5	.971
1942	**2 teams** **CIN N** (3G 0–0) **NY A** (5G 1–1)																										
″	**total**		1	1	.500	4.35	8	0	0	10.1	9	4	2	0	1	1	1	2	0	0	.000	2	4	0	1	0.8	1.000
1943	**NY**	**A**	3	0	1.000	3.53	18	0	0	43.1	44	13	15	0	3	0	1	13	1	0	.077	3	8	1	0	0.7	.917
1944			4	4	.500	3.46	35	0	0	41.2	42	22	13	0	4	4	7	10	2	0	.200	2	6	2	0	0.3	.800
1945			3	4	.429	3.64	30	0	0	54.1	45	31	22	0	3	4	**10**	11	1	0	.091	3	14	1	2	0.6	.944
9 yrs.			69	60	.535	3.22	231	119	69	1132	1117	283	329	8	13	10	20	399	87	1	.218	55	269	12	15	1.5	.964
WORLD SERIES																											
1940	**CIN**	**N**	0	1	.000	7.50	1	1	0	6	8	0	4	0	0	0	0	2	0	0	.000	0	1	0	0	1.0	1.000
1942	**NY**	**A**	0	0	—	0.00	1	0	0	1	0	1	0	0	0	0	0	0	0	0	—	0	0	0	0	0.0	.000
2 yrs.			0	1	.000	6.43	2	1	0	7	8	1	4	0	0	0	0	2	0	0	.000	0	1	0	0	0.5	1.000

Ken Turner

TURNER, KENNETH CHARLES BR TL 6′ 2″ 190 lbs.
B. Aug. 17, 1943, Framingham, Mass.

Year	Team	Lg	W	L	PCT	ERA	G	GS	CG	IP	H	BB	SO	ShO	Relief W	Relief L	Relief SV	Batting AB	Batting H	Batting HR	BA	PO	A	E	DP	TC/G	FA
1967	**CAL**	**A**	1	2	.333	4.15	13	1	0	17.1	16	4	6	0	1	1	0	4	0	0	.000	1	4	0	0	0.4	1.000

Matt Turner

TURNER, WILLIAM MATTHEW BR TR 6′ 5″ 215 lbs.
B. Feb. 18, 1967, Lexington, Ky.

Year	Team	Lg	W	L	PCT	ERA	G	GS	CG	IP	H	BB	SO	ShO	Relief W	Relief L	Relief SV	Batting AB	Batting H	Batting HR	BA	PO	A	E	DP	TC/G	FA
1993	**FLA**	**N**	4	5	.444	2.91	55	0	0	68	55	26	59	0	4	5	0	2	0	0	.000	3	11	0	0	0.3	1.000
1994	**CLE**	**A**	1	0	1.000	2.13	9	0	0	12.2	13	7	5	0	1	0	1	0	0	0	—	0	0	0	0	0.0	.000
2 yrs.			5	5	.500	2.79	64	0	0	80.2	68	33	64	0	5	5	1	2	0	0	.000	3	11	0	0	0.2	1.000

Ted Turner

TURNER, THEODORE HOLHOT BR TR 6′ 180 lbs.
B. May 4, 1892, Lawrenceburg, Ky. D. Feb. 4, 1958, Lexington, Ky.

Year	Team	Lg	W	L	PCT	ERA	G	GS	CG	IP	H	BB	SO	ShO	Relief W	Relief L	Relief SV	Batting AB	Batting H	Batting HR	BA	PO	A	E	DP	TC/G	FA
1920	**CHI**	**N**	0	0	—	13.50	1	0	0	1.1	2	1	0	0	0	0	0	1	0	0	.000	0	0	0	0	0.0	.000

Tink Turner

TURNER, THOMAS LOVATT BR TR 6′ 1″ 190 lbs.
B. Feb. 20, 1890, Swarthmore, Pa. D. Feb. 25, 1962, Philadelphia, Pa.

Year	Team	Lg	W	L	PCT	ERA	G	GS	CG	IP	H	BB	SO	ShO	Relief W	Relief L	Relief SV	Batting AB	Batting H	Batting HR	BA	PO	A	E	DP	TC/G	FA
1915	**PHI**	**A**	0	1	.000	22.50	1	1	0	2	5	3	0	0	0	0	0	0	0	0	—	0	1	0	0	1.0	1.000

Tuck Turner

TURNER, GEORGE A. BB TL 5′ 6½″ 155 lbs.
B. Feb. 13, 1873, West Brighton, N. Y. D. July 16, 1945, Staten Island, N. Y.

Year	Team	Lg	W	L	PCT	ERA	G	GS	CG	IP	H	BB	SO	ShO	Relief W	Relief L	Relief SV	Batting AB	Batting H	Batting HR	BA	PO	A	E	DP	TC/G	FA
1894	**PHI**	**N**	0	0	—	7.50	1	0	0	6	9	2	3	0	0	0	0	*				79	5	6	2	2.5	.933

Elmer Tutwiler

TUTWILER, ELMER STRANGE BR TR 5′11″ 158 lbs.
B. Nov. 19, 1905, Carbon Hill, Ala. D. May 3, 1976, Pensacola, Fla.

Year	Team	Lg	W	L	PCT	ERA	G	GS	CG	IP	H	BB	SO	ShO	Relief W	Relief L	Relief SV	Batting AB	Batting H	Batting HR	BA	PO	A	E	DP	TC/G	FA
1928	**PIT**	**N**	0	0	—	4.91	2	0	0	3.2	4	0	1	0	0	0	0	1	0	0	.000	1	0	0	0	0.5	1.000

Twink Twining

TWINING, HOWARD EARLE (Doc) BR TR 6′ 168 lbs.
B. May 30, 1894, Horsham, Pa. D. June 14, 1973, Lansdale, Pa.

Year	Team	Lg	W	L	PCT	ERA	G	GS	CG	IP	H	BB	SO	ShO	Relief W	Relief L	Relief SV	Batting AB	Batting H	Batting HR	BA	PO	A	E	DP	TC/G	FA
1916	**CIN**	**N**	0	0	—	13.50	1	0	0	2	4	1	0	0	0	0	0	0	0	0	—	1	0	0	0	1.0	1.000

Larry Twitchell

TWITCHELL, LAWRENCE GRANT BR TR 6′ 185 lbs.
B. Feb. 18, 1864, Cleveland, Ohio D. Aug. 23, 1930, Cleveland, Ohio.

Year	Team	Lg	W	L	PCT	ERA	G	GS	CG	IP	H	BB	SO	ShO	Relief W	Relief L	Relief SV	Batting AB	Batting H	Batting HR	BA	PO	A	E	DP	TC/G	FA
1886	**DET**	**N**	0	2	.000	6.48	4	4	2	25	35	12	6	0	0	0	0	16	1	0	.063	2	8	0	1	1.7	1.000
1887			11	1	.917	4.33	15	12	11	112.1	120	36	24	0	1	0	**1**	264	88	0	.333	89	16	13	2	1.7	.890
1888			0	0	—	6.75	2	0	0	4	6	0	3	0	0	0	1	524	128	5	.244	195	15	28	4	1.8	.882
1889	**CLE**	**N**	0	0	—	0.00	1	0	0	1	0	1	0	0	0	0	0	549	151	4	.275	220	10	21	0	1.9	.916
1890	**BUF**	**P**	5	7	.417	4.57	12	12	12	104.1	112	72	29	0	0	0	0	405	90	4	.222	125	47	22	2	1.9	.887
1891	**COL**	**AA**	1	1	.500	4.06	6	1	1	31	29	13	8	0	1	0	0	224	62	2	.277	70	10	9	0	1.4	.899
1894	**LOU**	**N**	0	0	—	6.00	1	0	0	3	5	1	0	0	0	0	0	210	56	2	.267	80	11	13	1	2.0	.875
7 yrs.			17	11	.607	4.62	41	29	26	280.2	307	135	70	0	2	0	2	*				975	140	132	14	1.9	.894

Wayne Twitchell

TWITCHELL, WAYNE LEE BR TR 6′ 6″ 215 lbs.
B. Mar. 10, 1948, Portland, Ore.

Year	Team	Lg	W	L	PCT	ERA	G	GS	CG	IP	H	BB	SO	ShO	Relief W	Relief L	Relief SV	Batting AB	Batting H	Batting HR	BA	PO	A	E	DP	TC/G	FA
1970	**MIL**	**A**	0	0	—	9.00	2	0	0	2	3	1	5	0	0	0	0	0	0	0	—	0	0	0	0	0.0	.000
1971	**PHI**	**N**	1	0	1.000	0.00	6	1	0	16	8	10	15	0	1	0	0	3	0	0	.000	0	2	0	0	0.3	1.000
1972			5	9	.357	4.06	49	15	1	139.2	138	56	112	1	2	1	1	28	2	0	.071	8	14	4	1	0.5	.846
1973			13	9	.591	2.50	34	28	10	223.1	172	99	169	5	0	0	0	72	7	0	.097	12	17	4	0	1.0	.879
1974			6	9	.400	5.22	25	18	2	112	122	65	72	0	1	1	0	35	6	0	.171	4	11	3	1	0.7	.833
1975			5	10	.333	4.43	36	20	0	134	132	78	101	0	0	0	0	34	3	0	.088	7	6	4	0	0.5	.765
1976			3	1	.750	1.75	26	2	0	61.2	55	18	67	0	2	0	1	6	1	0	.167	1	9	1	1	0.4	.909
1977	**2 teams** **PHI N** (12G 0–5) **MON N** (22G 6–5)																										
″	**total**		6	10	.375	4.29	34	30	2	184.2	166	74	130	0	0	1	0	50	9	0	.180	10	24	0	3	1.0	1.000
1978	**MON**	**N**	4	12	.250	5.38	33	15	0	112	121	71	69	0	1	4	0	24	2	0	.083	2	15	3	1	0.6	.850
1979	**2 teams** **NY N** (33G 5–3) **SEA A** (4G 0–2)																										
″	**total**		5	5	.500	5.19	37	4	0	78	66	65	49	0	5	2	0	8	3	0	.375	2	10	1	1	0.4	.923
10 yrs.			48	65	.425	3.98	282	133	15	1063.1	983	537	789	6	12	9	2	260	33	0	.127	46	108	20	8	0.6	.885

Jeff Twitty

TWITTY, JEFFREY DEAN — BL TL 6′ 2″ 185 lbs.
B. Nov. 10, 1957, Lancaster, S. C.

Year	Team		W	L	PCT	ERA	G	GS	CG	IP	H	BB	SO	ShO	Relief W	Relief L	Relief SV	AB	H	HR	BA	PO	A	E	DP	TC/G	FA
1980	**KC**	**A**	2	1	.667	6.14	13	0	0	22	33	7	9	0	2	1	0	0	0	0	—	0	5	0	0	0.4	1.000

Cy Twombly

TWOMBLY, EDWIN PARKER — BR TR 5′10½″ 170 lbs.
B. June 15, 1897, Groveland, Mass. D. Dec. 3, 1974, Savannah, Ga.

Year	Team		W	L	PCT	ERA	G	GS	CG	IP	H	BB	SO	ShO	Relief W	Relief L	Relief SV	AB	H	HR	BA	PO	A	E	DP	TC/G	FA
1921	**CHI**	**A**	1	2	.333	5.86	7	4	0	27.2	26	25	7	0	0	0	0	10	0	0	.000	0	10	0	2	1.4	1.000

Lefty Tyler

TYLER, GEORGE ALBERT — BL TL 6′ 175 lbs.
Brother of Fred Tyler.
B. Dec. 14, 1889, Derry, N. H. D. Sept. 29, 1953, Lowell, Mass.

Year	Team		W	L	PCT	ERA	G	GS	CG	IP	H	BB	SO	ShO	Relief W	Relief L	Relief SV	AB	H	HR	BA	PO	A	E	DP	TC/G	FA
1910	**BOS**	**N**	0	0	—	2.38	2	0	0	11.1	11	6	6	0	0	0	0	4	2	0	.500	0	2	0	0	1.0	1.000
1911			7	10	.412	5.06	28	20	10	165.1	150	109	90	1	1	0	0	61	10	0	.164	8	58	8	2	2.6	.892
1912			12	**22**	.353	4.18	42	31	**29**	256.1	262	126	144	1	2	3	0	96	19	0	.198	15	75	5	3	2.3	.947
1913			16	17	.485	2.79	39	34	**28**	290.1	245	108	143	4	1	0	2	102	21	0	.206	13	107	9	1	3.3	.930
1914			16	13	.552	2.69	38	34	21	271.1	247	101	140	5	0	0	2	94	19	0	.202	16	57	5	3	2.1	.936
1915			10	9	.526	2.86	32	24	15	204.2	182	84	89	1	0	0	0	88	23	1	.261	6	50	1	1	1.8	.982
1916			17	9	.654	2.02	34	28	21	249.1	200	58	117	6	2	0	1	93	19	3	.204	9	72	3	3	2.5	.964
1917			14	12	.538	2.52	32	28	22	239	203	86	98	4	1	1	1	134	31	0	.231	105	80	2	10	4.3	.989
1918	**CHI**	**N**	19	9	.679	2.00	33	30	22	269.1	218	67	102	**8**	1	1	1	100	21	0	.210	17	88	3	3	3.3	.972
1919			2	2	.500	2.10	6	5	3	30	20	13	9	0	0	0	0	7	1	0	.143	1	13	0	1	2.3	1.000
1920			11	12	.478	3.31	27	27	18	193	193	57	57	2	0	0	0	65	17	0	.262	15	64	2	3	3.0	.975
1921			3	2	.600	3.24	10	6	4	50	59	14	8	0	1	0	0	26	6	0	.231	3	10	0	1	1.3	1.000
12 yrs.			127	117	.520	2.95	323	267	193	2230	1990	829	1003	32	9	5	7	*				208	676	38	31	2.8	.959
WORLD SERIES																											
1914	**BOS**	**N**	0	0	—	3.60	1	1	0	10	8	3	4	0	0	0	0	3	0	0	.000	1	5	0	0	6.0	1.000
1918	**CHI**	**N**	1	1	.500	1.17	3	3	1	23	14	11	4	0	0	0	0	5	1	0	.200	2	9	1	0	4.0	.917
2 yrs.			1	1	.500	1.91	4	4	1	33	22	14	8	0	0	0	0	*				3	14	1	0	4.5	.944

Jim Tyng

TYNG, JAMES ALEXANDER — 5′ 9″ 155 lbs.
B. Mar. 27, 1856, Philadelphia, Pa. D. Oct. 30, 1931, New York, N. Y.

Year	Team		W	L	PCT	ERA	G	GS	CG	IP	H	BB	SO	ShO	Relief W	Relief L	Relief SV	AB	H	HR	BA	PO	A	E	DP	TC/G	FA
1879	**BOS**	**N**	1	2	.333	5.00	3	3	3	27	35	6	7	0	0	0	0	14	5	0	.357	2	6	0	0	2.7	1.000
1888	**PHI**	**N**	0	0	—	4.50	1	0	0	4	8	2	2	0	0	0	1	1	0	0	.000	0	2	0	0	2.0	1.000
2 yrs.			1	2	.333	4.94	4	3	3	31	43	8	9	0	0	0	1	15	5	0	.333	2	8	0	0	2.5	1.000

Dave Tyriver

TYRIVER, DAVID BURTON — BR TR 6′ 175 lbs.
B. Oct. 31, 1937, Oshkosh, Wis. D. Oct. 28, 1988, Oshkosh, Wis.

Year	Team		W	L	PCT	ERA	G	GS	CG	IP	H	BB	SO	ShO	Relief W	Relief L	Relief SV	AB	H	HR	BA	PO	A	E	DP	TC/G	FA
1962	**CLE**	**A**	0	0	—	4.22	4	0	0	10.2	10	7	7	0	0	0	0	3	0	0	.000	1	2	0	0	0.8	1.000

Jimmy Uchrinsko

UCHRINSKO, JAMES EMERSON — BL TR 6′ 180 lbs.
B. Oct. 20, 1900, West Newton, Pa. D. Mar. 17, 1995, Mount Pleasant, Pa.

Year	Team		W	L	PCT	ERA	G	GS	CG	IP	H	BB	SO	ShO	Relief W	Relief L	Relief SV	AB	H	HR	BA	PO	A	E	DP	TC/G	FA
1926	**WAS**	**A**	0	0	—	10.13	3	0	0	8	13	8	0	0	0	0	0	2	0	0	.000	1	2	0	1	1.0	1.000

Bob Uhl

UHL, ROBERT ELLWOOD (Lefty) — BB TL 5′11″ 175 lbs.
B. Sept. 17, 1913, San Francisco, Calif. D. Aug. 21, 1990, Santa Rosa, Calif.

Year	Team		W	L	PCT	ERA	G	GS	CG	IP	H	BB	SO	ShO	Relief W	Relief L	Relief SV	AB	H	HR	BA	PO	A	E	DP	TC/G	FA
1938	**CHI**	**A**	0	0	—	0.00	1	0	0	2	1	0	0	0	0	0	0	0	0	0	—	0	0	0	0	0.0	.000
1940	**DET**	**A**	0	0	—	∞	1	0	0		4	2	0	0	0	0	0	0	0	0	—	0	0	0	0	0.0	.000
2 yrs.			0	0		18.00	2	0	0	2	5	2	0	0	0	0	0	0	0	0		0	0	0	0	0.0	

George Uhle

UHLE, GEORGE ERNEST (The Bull) — BR TR 6′ 190 lbs.
B. Sept. 18, 1898, Cleveland, Ohio D. Feb. 26, 1985, Lakewood, Ohio.

Year	Team		W	L	PCT	ERA	G	GS	CG	IP	H	BB	SO	ShO	Relief W	Relief L	Relief SV	AB	H	HR	BA	PO	A	E	DP	TC/G	FA
1919	**CLE**	**A**	10	5	.667	2.91	26	12	7	127	129	43	50	1	2	2	0	43	13	0	.302	10	33	4	1	1.8	.915
1920			4	5	.444	5.21	27	6	2	84.2	98	29	27	0	4	1	1	32	11	0	.344	6	21	0	0	1.0	1.000
1921			16	13	.552	4.01	41	28	13	238	288	62	63	2	2	2	2	94	23	1	.245	15	46	4	2	1.5	.938
1922			22	16	.579	4.07	50	**40**	23	287.1	328	89	82	**5**	1	1	3	109	29	0	.266	16	53	5	5	1.5	.932
1923			**26**	16	.619	3.77	54	**44**	**29**	**357.2**	**378**	102	109	1	1	0	5	144	52	0	.361	18	89	2	9	2.0	.982
1924			9	15	.375	4.77	28	25	15	196.1	238	75	57	0	1	1	1	107	33	1	.308	19	42	0	5	2.2	1.000
1925			13	11	.542	4.10	29	26	17	210.2	218	78	68	1	1	1	0	104	29	0	.279	12	39	3	2	1.9	.944
1926			**27**	11	**.711**	2.83	39	**36**	**32**	**318.1**	**300**	**118**	159	3	1	1	1	132	30	1	.227	30	67	7	3	2.7	.933
1927			8	9	.471	4.34	25	22	10	153.1	187	59	69	1	0	1	1	79	21	0	.266	6	31	1	3	1.5	.974
1928			12	17	.414	4.07	31	28	18	214.1	252	48	74	2	1	1	1	98	28	1	.286	10	59	2	4	2.3	.972
1929	**DET**	**A**	15	11	.577	4.08	32	30	23	249	283	58	100	1	1	0	0	108	37	0	.343	13	39	4	2	1.8	.929
1930			12	12	.500	3.65	33	29	18	239	239	75	117	1	0	0	3	117	36	2	.308	10	29	1	2	1.2	.975
1931			11	12	.478	3.50	29	18	15	193	190	49	63	2	4	3	2	90	22	2	.244	3	38	0	1	1.4	1.000
1932			6	6	.500	4.48	33	15	6	146.2	152	42	51	1	1	2	5	55	10	0	.182	5	25	0	2	0.9	1.000
1933	**3 teams**	**DET A**	(1G 0–0)		**NY N**	(6G 1–1)		**NY A**	(12G 6–1)																		
″	**total**		7	2	.778	5.85	19	7	4	75.1	81	26	31	0	2	0	0	25	8	0	.320	1	13	0	1	0.7	1.000
1934	**NY**	**A**	2	4	.333	9.92	10	2	0	16.1	30	7	10	0	2	2	0	5	3	0	.600	1	1	0	0	0.2	1.000
1936	**CLE**	**A**	0	1	.000	8.53	7	0	0	12.2	26	5	5	0	0	1	0	21	8	1	.381	0	0	0	0	0.0	.000
17 yrs.			200	166	.546	3.99	513	368	232	3119.2	3417	965	1135	21	24	19	25	*				175	625	33	42	1.6	.960
WORLD SERIES																											
1920	**CLE**	**A**	0	0	—	0.00	2	0	0	3	1	0	3	0	0	0	0	*				0	1	0	0	1.0	1.000

Jerry Ujdur

UJDUR, GERALD RAYMOND — BR TR 6′ 1″ 195 lbs.
B. Mar. 5, 1957, Duluth, Minn.

Year	Team		W	L	PCT	ERA	G	GS	CG	IP	H	BB	SO	ShO	Relief W	Relief L	Relief SV	AB	H	HR	BA	PO	A	E	DP	TC/G	FA
1980	**DET**	**A**	1	0	1.000	7.71	9	2	0	21	36	10	8	0	0	0	0	0	0	0	—	0	1	0	0	0.1	1.000
1981			0	0	—	6.43	4	4	0	14	19	5	5	0	0	0	0	0	0	0	—	1	3	0	0	1.0	1.000
1982			10	10	.500	3.69	25	25	7	178	150	69	86	0	0	0	0	0	0	0	—	11	21	2	2	1.4	.941
1983			0	4	.000	7.15	11	6	0	34	41	20	13	0	0	0	0	0	0	0	—	3	1	1	0	0.5	.800
1984	**CLE**	**A**	1	2	.333	6.91	4	3	0	14.1	22	6	6	0	1	0	0	0	0	0	—	0	0	1	0	0.3	.000
5 yrs.			12	16	.429	4.79	53	40	7	261.1	268	110	118	0	1	0	0	0	0	0		15	26	4	2	0.8	.911

Sandy Ullrich

ULLRICH, CARLOS SANTIAGO BR TR 6′½″ 175 lbs.
Born Carlos Santiago Ullrich (Castello).
B. July 25, 1921, Havana, Cuba.

Year	Team	Lg	W	L	PCT	ERA	G	GS	CG	IP	H	BB	SO	ShO	Relief W	Relief L	Relief SV	Batting AB	Batting H	HR	BA	PO	A	E	DP	TC/G	FA
1944	WAS	A	0	0	—	9.31	3	0	0	9.2	17	4	2	0	0	0	0	3	1	0	.333	1	2	0	0	1.0	1.000
1945			3	3	.500	4.54	28	6	0	81.1	91	34	26	0	3	1	1	22	6	0	.273	2	24	0	1	0.9	1.000
2 yrs.			3	3	.500	5.04	31	6	0	91	108	38	28	0	3	1	1	25	7	0	.280	3	26	0	1	0.9	1.000

Dutch Ulrich

ULRICH, FRANK W. BR TR 6′ 2″ 195 lbs.
B. Nov. 18, 1899, Baltimore, Md. D. Feb. 11, 1929, Baltimore, Md.

Year	Team	Lg	W	L	PCT	ERA	G	GS	CG	IP	H	BB	SO	ShO	Relief W	Relief L	Relief SV	Batting AB	Batting H	HR	BA	PO	A	E	DP	TC/G	FA
1925	PHI	N	3	3	.500	3.05	21	4	2	65	73	12	29	1	2	0	0	16	2	0	.125	2	18	0	2	1.0	1.000
1926			8	13	.381	4.08	45	17	8	147.2	178	37	52	1	1	**4**	1	49	12	0	.245	7	33	2	3	0.9	.952
1927			8	11	.421	3.17	32	18	14	193.1	201	40	42	1	1	1	1	73	9	0	.123	12	29	0	1	1.3	1.000
3 yrs.			19	27	.413	3.48	98	39	24	406	452	89	123	3	4	5	2	138	23	0	.167	21	80	2	6	1.1	.981

Arnie Umbach

UMBACH, ARNOLD WILLIAM BR TR 6′ 1″ 180 lbs.
B. Dec. 6, 1942, Williamsburg, Va.

Year	Team	Lg	W	L	PCT	ERA	G	GS	CG	IP	H	BB	SO	ShO	Relief W	Relief L	Relief SV	Batting AB	Batting H	HR	BA	PO	A	E	DP	TC/G	FA
1964	MIL	N	1	0	1.000	3.24	1	1	0	8.1	11	4	7	0	0	0	0	3	0	0	.000	0	1	0	0	1.0	1.000
1966	ATL	N	0	2	.000	3.10	22	3	0	40.2	40	18	23	0	0	1	0	5	1	0	.200	4	5	1	0	0.5	.900
2 yrs.			1	2	.333	3.12	23	4	0	49	51	22	30	0	0	1	0	8	1	0	.125	4	6	1	0	0.5	.909

Jim Umbarger

UMBARGER, JAMES HAROLD BL TL 6′ 6″ 200 lbs.
B. Feb. 17, 1953, Burbank, Calif.

Year	Team	Lg	W	L	PCT	ERA	G	GS	CG	IP	H	BB	SO	ShO	Relief W	Relief L	Relief SV	Batting AB	Batting H	HR	BA	PO	A	E	DP	TC/G	FA
1975	TEX	A	8	7	.533	4.12	56	12	3	131	134	59	50	2	3	2	2	0	0	0	—	8	26	1	2	0.6	.971
1976			10	12	.455	3.15	30	30	10	197	208	54	105	3	0	0	0	0	0	0	—	4	30	1	3	1.2	.971
1977	2 teams	OAK A	(12G 1–5)	TEX A	(3G 1–1)																						
″	total		2	6	.250	6.32	15	10	1	57	76	32	29	0	0	1	0	0	0	0		0	11	1	1	0.8	.917
1978	TEX	A	5	8	.385	4.88	32	9	1	97.2	116	36	60	0	3	3	1	0	0	0	—	1	21	2	0	0.8	.917
4 yrs.			25	33	.431	4.14	133	61	15	482.2	534	181	244	5	6	6	3	0	0	0		13	88	5	6	0.8	.953

Jim Umbricht

UMBRICHT, JAMES BR TR 6′ 4″ 215 lbs.
B. Sept. 17, 1930, Chicago, Ill. D. Apr. 8, 1964, Houston, Tex.

Year	Team	Lg	W	L	PCT	ERA	G	GS	CG	IP	H	BB	SO	ShO	Relief W	Relief L	Relief SV	Batting AB	Batting H	HR	BA	PO	A	E	DP	TC/G	FA
1959	PIT	N	0	0	—	6.43	1	1	0	7	7	4	3	0	0	0	0	3	0	0	.000	1	1	0	0	2.0	1.000
1960			1	2	.333	5.09	17	3	0	40.2	40	27	26	0	1	0	1	6	2	0	.333	1	4	2	1	0.4	.714
1961			0	0	—	2.70	1	0	0	3.1	5	2	1	0	0	0	0	1	1	0	1.000	0	0	0	0	0.0	.000
1962	HOU	N	4	0	1.000	2.01	34	0	0	67	51	17	55	0	4	0	2	9	1	0	.111	1	14	0	0	0.4	1.000
1963			4	3	.571	2.61	35	3	0	76	52	21	48	0	4	1	0	9	1	0	.111	7	14	0	2	0.6	1.000
5 yrs.			9	5	.643	3.06	88	7	0	194	155	71	133	0	9	1	3	28	5	0	.179	10	33	2	3	0.5	.956

Willie Underhill

UNDERHILL, WILLIE VERN BR TR 6′ 2″ 185 lbs.
B. Sept. 6, 1904, Yowell, Tex. D. Oct. 26, 1970, Bay City, Tex.

Year	Team	Lg	W	L	PCT	ERA	G	GS	CG	IP	H	BB	SO	ShO	Relief W	Relief L	Relief SV	Batting AB	Batting H	HR	BA	PO	A	E	DP	TC/G	FA
1927	CLE	A	0	2	.000	9.72	4	1	0	8.1	12	11	4	0	0	1	0	1	0	0	.000	0	2	0	0	0.5	1.000
1928			1	2	.333	4.50	11	3	1	28	33	20	16	0	1	0	0	11	4	0	.364	1	6	0	0	0.6	1.000
2 yrs.			1	4	.200	5.70	15	4	1	36.1	45	31	20	0	1	1	0	12	4	0	.333	1	8	0	0	0.6	1.000

Fred Underwood

UNDERWOOD, FREDERICK THEODORE 170 lbs.
B. Oct. 14, 1868, St. Louis County, Mo. D. Jan. 26, 1906, Kansas City, Mo.

Year	Team	Lg	W	L	PCT	ERA	G	GS	CG	IP	H	BB	SO	ShO	Relief W	Relief L	Relief SV	Batting AB	Batting H	HR	BA	PO	A	E	DP	TC/G	FA
1894	BKN	N	2	4	.333	7.85	7	6	5	47	80	30	10	0	0	0	0	18	7	0	.389	2	7	1	0	1.4	.900

Pat Underwood

UNDERWOOD, PATRICK JOHN BL TL 6′ 175 lbs.
Brother of Tom Underwood.
B. Feb. 9, 1957, Kokomo, Ind.

Year	Team	Lg	W	L	PCT	ERA	G	GS	CG	IP	H	BB	SO	ShO	Relief W	Relief L	Relief SV	Batting AB	Batting H	HR	BA	PO	A	E	DP	TC/G	FA
1979	DET	A	6	4	.600	4.57	27	15	1	122	126	29	83	0	0	0	0	0	0	0	—	1	15	1	0	0.6	.941
1980			3	6	.333	3.58	49	7	0	113	121	35	60	0	1	4	5	0	0	0	—	7	16	0	0	0.5	1.000
1982			4	8	.333	4.73	33	12	2	99	108	22	43	0	1	1	3	0	0	0	—	1	21	1	1	0.7	.957
1983			0	0	—	8.71	4	0	0	10.1	11	6	2	0	0	0	0	0	0	0	—	1	0	0	0	0.3	1.000
4 yrs.			13	18	.419	4.42	113	34	3	344.1	366	92	188	0	2	5	8	0	0	0		10	52	2	1	0.6	.969

Tom Underwood

UNDERWOOD, THOMAS GERALD BR TL 5′11″ 170 lbs.
Brother of Pat Underwood.
B. Dec. 22, 1953, Kokomo, Ind.

Year	Team	Lg	W	L	PCT	ERA	G	GS	CG	IP	H	BB	SO	ShO	Relief W	Relief L	Relief SV	Batting AB	Batting H	HR	BA	PO	A	E	DP	TC/G	FA
1974	PHI	N	1	0	1.000	4.85	7	0	0	13	15	5	8	0	1	0	0	1	0	0	.000	0	0	0	0	0.0	.000
1975			14	13	.519	4.15	35	35	7	219	221	84	123	2	0	0	0	74	9	0	.122	2	21	4	1	0.8	.852
1976			10	5	.667	3.53	33	25	3	155.2	154	63	94	0	1	0	2	46	5	0	.109	3	17	1	1	0.6	.952
1977	2 teams	PHI N	(14G 3–2)	STL N	(19G 6–9)																						
″	total		9	11	.450	5.01	33	17	1	133	148	75	86	0	3	3	1	33	4	0	.121	4	14	3	2	0.6	.857
1978	TOR	A	6	14	.300	4.10	31	30	7	197.2	201	87	139	1	0	1	0	0	0	0	—	5	19	5	0	0.9	.828
1979			9	16	.360	3.69	33	32	12	227	213	95	127	1	0	0	0	0	0	0	—	6	36	5	2	1.4	.894
1980	NY	A	13	9	.591	3.66	38	27	2	187	163	66	116	2	2	2	2	0	0	0	—	10	26	2	2	1.0	.947
1981	2 teams	NY A	(9G 1–4)	OAK A	(16G 3–2)																						
″	total		4	6	.400	3.64	25	11	1	84	69	38	75	0	2	2	1	0	0	0		2	13	2	1	0.7	.882
1982	OAK	A	10	6	.625	3.29	56	10	2	153	136	68	79	0	5	3	7	0	0	0	—	9	11	2	0	0.4	.909
1983			9	7	.563	4.04	51	15	0	144.2	156	50	62	0	4	2	4	0	0	0	—	3	11	2	2	0.3	.875
1984	BAL	A	1	0	1.000	3.52	37	1	0	71.2	78	31	39	0	1	0	1	0	0	0	—	5	12	0	2	0.5	1.000
11 yrs.			86	87	.497	3.89	379	203	35	1585.2	1554	662	948	6	19	13	18	154	18	0	.117	49	180	26	13	0.7	.898
DIVISIONAL PLAYOFF SERIES																											
1981	OAK	A	0	0	—	0.00	1	0	0	0.1	0	0	1	0	0	0	0	0	0	0	—	0	0	0	0	0.0	.000
LEAGUE CHAMPIONSHIP SERIES																											
1976	PHI	N	0	0	—	0.00	1	0	0	0.1	1	2	0	0	0	0	0	0	0	0	—	0	0	0	0	0.0	.000
1980	NY	A	0	0	—	0.00	2	0	0	3	3	0	3	0	0	0	0	0	0	0	—	0	2	0	0	1.0	1.000
1981	OAK	A	0	0	—	13.50	2	0	0	1.1	4	2	2	0	0	0	0	0	0	0	—	0	0	0	0	0.0	.000
3 yrs.			0	0		3.86	5	0	0	4.2	8	4	5	0	0	0	0	0	0	0		0	2	0	0	0.4	1.000

Woody Upchurch

UPCHURCH, JEFFERSON WOODROW BR TL 6′ 180 lbs.
B. Apr. 13, 1911, Buies Creek, N. C. D. Oct. 23, 1971, Buies Creek, N. C.

Year	Team		W	L	PCT	ERA	G	GS	CG	IP	H	BB	SO	ShO	Relief Pitching W	Relief Pitching L	Relief Pitching SV	Batting AB	Batting H	Batting HR	BA	PO	A	E	DP	TC/G	FA
1935	PHI	A	0	2	.000	5.06	3	3	1	21.1	23	12	2	0	0	0	0	7	2	0	.286	0	4	1	0	1.7	.800
1936			0	2	.000	9.67	7	2	1	22.1	36	14	6	0	0	0	0	7	1	0	.143	0	1	0	0	0.1	1.000
2 yrs.			0	4	.000	7.42	10	5	2	43.2	59	26	8	0	0	0	0	14	3	0	.214	0	5	1	0	0.6	.833

Bill Upham

UPHAM, WILLIAM LAWRENCE BB TR 6′ 178 lbs.
B. Apr. 4, 1888, Akron, Ohio D. Sept. 14, 1959, Newark, N. J.

Year	Team		W	L	PCT	ERA	G	GS	CG	IP	H	BB	SO	ShO	Relief Pitching W	Relief Pitching L	Relief Pitching SV	Batting AB	Batting H	Batting HR	BA	PO	A	E	DP	TC/G	FA
1915	BKN	F	7	8	.467	3.05	33	11	4	121	129	40	46	2	3	2	4	36	4	0	.111	5	48	3	3	1.7	.946
1918	BOS	N	1	1	.500	5.23	3	2	2	20.2	28	1	8	0	0	0	0	9	2	0	.222	0	6	0	0	2.0	1.000
2 yrs.			8	9	.471	3.37	36	13	6	141.2	157	41	54	2	3	2	4	45	6	0	.133	5	54	3	3	1.7	.952

John Upham

UPHAM, JOHN LESLIE BL TL 6′ 180 lbs.
B. Dec. 29, 1941, Windsor, Ont., Canada.

Year	Team		W	L	PCT	ERA	G	GS	CG	IP	H	BB	SO	ShO	Relief Pitching W	Relief Pitching L	Relief Pitching SV	Batting AB	Batting H	Batting HR	BA	PO	A	E	DP	TC/G	FA
1967	CHI	N	0	1	.000	33.75	5	0	0	1.1	4	2	2	0	0	1	0	3	2	0	.667	0	0	0	0	0.0	.000
1968			0	0	—	0.00	2	0	0	7	2	3	2	0	0	0	0	10	2	0	.200	0	3	0	0	0.8	1.000
2 yrs.			0	1	.000	5.40	7	0	0	8.1	6	5	4	0	0	1	0	*				0	3	0	0	0.3	1.000

Jerry Upp

UPP, GEORGE HENRY TL
B. Dec. 10, 1883, Sandusky, Ohio D. June 30, 1937, Sandusky, Ohio.

Year	Team		W	L	PCT	ERA	G	GS	CG	IP	H	BB	SO	ShO	Relief Pitching W	Relief Pitching L	Relief Pitching SV	Batting AB	Batting H	Batting HR	BA	PO	A	E	DP	TC/G	FA
1909	CLE	A	2	1	.667	1.69	7	4	2	26.2	26	12	13	0	0	0	0	9	2	0	.222	3	11	1	0	2.1	.933

Cecil Upshaw

UPSHAW, CECIL LEE BR TR 6′ 6″ 205 lbs.
B. Oct. 22, 1942, Spearsville, La. D. Feb. 7, 1995, Lawrenceville, Ga.

Year	Team		W	L	PCT	ERA	G	GS	CG	IP	H	BB	SO	ShO	Relief Pitching W	Relief Pitching L	Relief Pitching SV	Batting AB	Batting H	Batting HR	BA	PO	A	E	DP	TC/G	FA
1966	ATL	N	0	0	—	0.00	1	0	0	3	0	3	2	0	0	0	0	1	1	0	1.000	0	0	0	0	0.0	.000
1967			2	3	.400	2.58	30	0	0	45.1	42	8	31	0	2	3	8	6	1	0	.167	2	8	1	0	0.4	.909
1968			8	7	.533	2.47	52	0	0	116.2	98	24	74	0	8	7	13	23	4	0	.174	6	19	1	0	0.5	.962
1969			6	4	.600	2.91	62	0	0	105	102	29	57	0	6	4	27	21	5	1	.238	6	21	1	1	0.5	.964
1971			11	6	.647	3.51	49	0	0	82	95	28	56	0	11	6	17	15	0	0	.000	3	11	1	0	0.3	.933
1972			3	5	.375	3.67	42	0	0	54	50	19	23	0	3	5	13	7	1	0	.143	2	12	1	0	0.4	.933
1973	2 teams	ATL N (5G 0–1)	HOU N (35G 2–3)																								
″	total		2	4	.333	4.93	40	0	0	42	46	17	24	0	2	4	1	2	0	0	.000	3	10	0	0	0.3	1.000
1974	2 teams	CLE A (7G 0–1)	NY A (36G 1–5)																								
″	total		1	6	.143	3.04	43	0	0	68	63	28	34	0	1	6	6	0	0	0		6	13	3	1	0.5	.864
1975	CHI	A	1	1	.500	3.23	29	0	0	47.1	49	21	22	0	1	1	1	0	0	0	—	0	8	2	1	0.3	.800
9 yrs.			34	36	.486	3.13	348	0	0	563.1	545	177	323	0	34	36	86	75	12	1	.160	28	102	10	3	0.4	.929
LEAGUE CHAMPIONSHIP SERIES																											
1969	ATL	N	0	0	—	2.84	3	0	0	6.1	5	1	4	0	0	0	0	1	0	0	.000	0	1	0	1	0.3	1.000

Bill Upton

UPTON, WILLIAM RAY BR TR 6′ 167 lbs.
Brother of Tom Upton.
B. June 18, 1929, Esther, Mo. D. Jan. 2, 1987, San Diego, Calif.

Year	Team		W	L	PCT	ERA	G	GS	CG	IP	H	BB	SO	ShO	Relief Pitching W	Relief Pitching L	Relief Pitching SV	Batting AB	Batting H	Batting HR	BA	PO	A	E	DP	TC/G	FA
1954	PHI	A	0	0	—	1.80	2	0	0	5	6	1	2	0	0	0	1	0	0	0	—	0	1	0	0	0.5	1.000

Jack Urban

URBAN, JACK ELMER BR TR 5′ 8″ 155 lbs.
B. Dec. 5, 1928, Omaha, Neb.

Year	Team		W	L	PCT	ERA	G	GS	CG	IP	H	BB	SO	ShO	Relief Pitching W	Relief Pitching L	Relief Pitching SV	Batting AB	Batting H	Batting HR	BA	PO	A	E	DP	TC/G	FA
1957	KC	A	7	4	.636	3.34	31	13	3	129.1	111	45	55	0	1	0	0	39	11	0	.282	12	27	1	2	1.3	.975
1958			8	11	.421	5.93	30	24	5	132	150	51	54	1	0	0	1	46	7	0	.152	13	14	2	2	1.0	.931
1959	STL	N	0	0	—	9.28	8	0	0	10.2	18	7	4	0	0	0	0	1	0	0	.000	0	1	0	0	0.1	1.000
3 yrs.			15	15	.500	4.83	69	37	8	272	279	103	113	1	1	0	1	86	18	0	.209	25	42	3	4	1.0	.957

Tom Urbani

URBANI, THOMAS JAMES BL TL 6′ 1″ 190 lbs.
B. Jan. 21, 1968, Santa Cruz, Calif.

Year	Team		W	L	PCT	ERA	G	GS	CG	IP	H	BB	SO	ShO	Relief Pitching W	Relief Pitching L	Relief Pitching SV	Batting AB	Batting H	Batting HR	BA	PO	A	E	DP	TC/G	FA
1993	STL	N	1	3	.250	4.65	18	9	0	62	73	26	33	0	0	1	0	16	3	0	.188	2	12	1	1	0.8	.933
1994			3	7	.300	5.15	20	10	0	80.1	98	21	43	0	0	2	0	24	6	0	.250	0	15	0	1	0.8	1.000
1995			3	5	.375	3.70	24	13	0	82.2	99	21	52	0	1	0	0	19	6	1	.316	4	19	0	0	1.0	1.000
3 yrs.			7	15	.318	4.48	62	32	0	225	270	68	128	0	1	3	0	59	15	1	.254	6	46	1	2	0.9	.981

Ugueth Urbina

URBINA, UGUETH URTAIN BR TR 6′ 2″ 185 lbs.
Born Ugueth Urtain Urbina (Villarreal).
B. Feb. 15, 1974, Caracas, Venezuela.

Year	Team		W	L	PCT	ERA	G	GS	CG	IP	H	BB	SO	ShO	Relief Pitching W	Relief Pitching L	Relief Pitching SV	Batting AB	Batting H	Batting HR	BA	PO	A	E	DP	TC/G	FA
1995	MON	N	2	2	.500	6.17	7	4	0	23.1	26	14	15	0	1	0	0	6	2	0	.333	5	4	0	0	1.3	1.000

John Urrea

URREA, JOHN GODOY BR TR 6′ 3″ 200 lbs.
B. Feb. 9, 1955, Los Angeles, Calif.

Year	Team		W	L	PCT	ERA	G	GS	CG	IP	H	BB	SO	ShO	Relief Pitching W	Relief Pitching L	Relief Pitching SV	Batting AB	Batting H	Batting HR	BA	PO	A	E	DP	TC/G	FA
1977	STL	N	7	6	.538	3.15	41	12	2	140	126	35	81	1	2	3	4	29	4	0	.138	7	24	2	2	0.8	.939
1978			4	9	.308	5.36	27	12	1	99	108	47	61	0	0	2	0	24	3	0	.125	3	18	2	0	0.9	.913
1979			0	0	—	4.09	3	2	0	11	13	9	5	0	0	0	0	4	1	0	.250	2	1	0	0	1.0	1.000
1980			4	1	.800	3.46	30	1	0	65	57	41	36	0	3	1	3	13	3	0	.231	2	6	2	0	0.3	.800
1981	SD	N	2	2	.500	2.39	38	0	0	49	43	28	19	0	2	2	2	4	1	0	.250	0	6	1	0	0.2	.857
5 yrs.			17	18	.486	3.73	139	27	3	364	347	160	202	1	7	8	9	74	12	0	.162	14	55	7	2	0.5	.908

Bob Vail

VAIL, ROBERT GARFIELD (Doc) BR TR 5′10″ 165 lbs.
B. Sept. 24, 1881, Linneus, Me. D. May 28, 1948, Pittsburgh, Pa.

Year	Team		W	L	PCT	ERA	G	GS	CG	IP	H	BB	SO	ShO	Relief Pitching W	Relief Pitching L	Relief Pitching SV	Batting AB	Batting H	Batting HR	BA	PO	A	E	DP	TC/G	FA
1908	PIT	N	1	2	.333	6.00	4	1	0	15	15	7	9	0	1	1	0	3	1	0	.333	0	0	0	0	0.0	.000

Ismael Valdes

VALDES, ISMAEL BR TR 6′ 3″ 185 lbs.
Born Ismael Valdes (Alvarez).
B. Aug. 21, 1973, Victoria, Mexico.

Year	Team		W	L	PCT	ERA	G	GS	CG	IP	H	BB	SO	ShO	Relief Pitching W	Relief Pitching L	Relief Pitching SV	Batting AB	Batting H	Batting HR	BA	PO	A	E	DP	TC/G	FA
1994	LA	N	3	1	.750	3.18	21	1	0	28.1	21	10	28	0	3	1	0	2	0	0	.000	1	8	0	0	0.4	1.000
1995			13	11	.542	3.05	33	27	6	197.2	168	51	150	2	0	0	1	62	6	0	.097	16	31	1	0	1.5	.979
2 yrs.			16	12	.571	3.07	54	28	6	226	189	61	178	2	3	1	1	64	6	0	.094	17	39	1	0	1.1	.982
DIVISIONAL PLAYOFF SERIES																											
1995	LA	N	0	0	—	0.00	1	1	0	7	3	1	6	0	0	0	0	3	0	0	.000	0	0	0	0	0.0	.000

Marc Valdes

VALDES, MARC CHRISTOPHER BR TR 6′ 170 lbs.
B. Dec. 20, 1971, Dayton, Ohio.

Year	Team	Lg	W	L	PCT	ERA	G	GS	CG	IP	H	BB	SO	ShO	Relief Pitching W	Relief Pitching L	Relief Pitching SV	Batting AB	Batting H	Batting HR	BA	PO	A	E	DP	TC/G	FA
1995	**FLA**	**N**	0	0	—	14.14	3	3	0	7	17	9	2	0	0	0	0	2	0	0	.000	0	0	0	0	0.0	.000

Carlos Valdez

VALDEZ, CARLOS LUIS BR TR 5′11″ 165 lbs.
Born Carlos Luis Valdez (Lorenzo).
B. Dec. 26, 1971, Bani, Dominican Republic.

Year	Team	Lg	W	L	PCT	ERA	G	GS	CG	IP	H	BB	SO	ShO	Relief Pitching W	Relief Pitching L	Relief Pitching SV	Batting AB	Batting H	Batting HR	BA	PO	A	E	DP	TC/G	FA
1995	**SF**	**N**	0	1	.000	6.14	11	0	0	14.2	19	8	7	0	0	1	0	1	0	0	.000	1	2	0	0	0.3	1.000

Efrain Valdez

VALDEZ, EFRAIN ANTONIO BL TL 5′11″ 180 lbs.
B. July 11, 1966, Nizao Bani, Dominican Republic.

Year	Team	Lg	W	L	PCT	ERA	G	GS	CG	IP	H	BB	SO	ShO	Relief Pitching W	Relief Pitching L	Relief Pitching SV	Batting AB	Batting H	Batting HR	BA	PO	A	E	DP	TC/G	FA
1990	**CLE**	**A**	1	1	.500	3.04	13	0	0	23.2	20	14	13	0	1	1	0	0	0	0	—	2	3	1	0	0.5	.833
1991			0	0	—	1.50	7	0	0	6	5	3	1	0	0	0	0	0	0	0	—	0	1	0	0	0.1	1.000
2 yrs.			1	1	.500	2.73	20	0	0	29.2	25	17	14	0	1	1	0	0	0	0		2	4	1	0	0.3	.857

Rafael Valdez

VALDEZ, RAFAEL EMILIO BR TR 5′11″ 165 lbs.
Born Rafael Emilio Valdez (Diaz).
B. Dec. 17, 1967, Nizao Bani, Dominican Republic.

Year	Team	Lg	W	L	PCT	ERA	G	GS	CG	IP	H	BB	SO	ShO	Relief Pitching W	Relief Pitching L	Relief Pitching SV	Batting AB	Batting H	Batting HR	BA	PO	A	E	DP	TC/G	FA
1990	**SD**	**N**	0	1	.000	11.12	3	0	0	5.2	11	2	3	0	0	1	0	1	0	0	.000	0	0	0	0	0.0	.000

Rene Valdez

VALDEZ, RENE (Latigo) BR TR 6′ 3″ 175 lbs.
Born Rene Valdez (Gutierrez).
B. June 2, 1929, Guanabacoa, Cuba.

Year	Team	Lg	W	L	PCT	ERA	G	GS	CG	IP	H	BB	SO	ShO	Relief Pitching W	Relief Pitching L	Relief Pitching SV	Batting AB	Batting H	Batting HR	BA	PO	A	E	DP	TC/G	FA
1957	**BKN**	**N**	1	1	.500	5.54	5	1	0	13	13	7	10	0	1	1	0	3	0	0	.000	0	1	1	0	0.4	.500

Sergio Valdez

VALDEZ, SERGIO BR TR 6′ 165 lbs.
Born Sergio Sanchez (Valdez).
B. Sept. 7, 1964, Elias Pina, Dominican Republic.

Year	Team	Lg	W	L	PCT	ERA	G	GS	CG	IP	H	BB	SO	ShO	Relief Pitching W	Relief Pitching L	Relief Pitching SV	Batting AB	Batting H	Batting HR	BA	PO	A	E	DP	TC/G	FA
1986	**MON**	**N**	0	4	.000	6.84	5	5	0	25	39	11	20	0	0	0	0	8	1	0	.125	3	1	1	1	1.0	.800
1989	**ATL**	**N**	1	2	.333	6.06	19	1	0	32.2	31	17	26	0	1	1	0	1	1	0	1.000	2	2	0	0	0.2	1.000
1990	**2 teams**	**ATL N** (6G 0–0) **CLE A** (24G 6–6)																									
″	**total**		6	6	.500	4.85	30	13	0	107.2	115	38	66	0	1	1	0	0	0	0		10	12	2	1	0.8	.917
1991	**CLE**	**A**	1	0	1.000	5.51	6	0	0	16.1	15	5	11	0	1	0	0	0	0	0	—	0	0	0	0	0.0	.000
1992	**MON**	**N**	0	2	.000	2.41	27	0	0	37.1	25	12	32	0	0	2	0	3	0	0	.000	9	3	0	0	0.4	1.000
1993			0	0	—	9.00	4	0	0	3	4	1	2	0	0	0	0	0	0	0	—	0	0	0	0	0.0	.000
1994	**BOS**	**A**	0	1	.000	8.16	12	1	0	14.1	25	8	4	0	0	0	0	0	0	0	—	1	4	0	0	0.4	1.000
1995	**SF**	**N**	4	5	.444	4.75	13	11	1	66.1	78	17	29	0	0	0	0	21	2	0	.095	4	14	2	0	1.5	.900
8 yrs.			12	20	.375	5.06	116	31	1	302.2	332	109	190	0	3	4	0	33	4	0	.121	29	36	5	2	0.6	.929

Corky Valentine

VALENTINE, HAROLD LEWIS BR TR 6′ 1″ 203 lbs.
B. Jan. 4, 1929, Troy, Ohio.

Year	Team	Lg	W	L	PCT	ERA	G	GS	CG	IP	H	BB	SO	ShO	Relief Pitching W	Relief Pitching L	Relief Pitching SV	Batting AB	Batting H	Batting HR	BA	PO	A	E	DP	TC/G	FA
1954	**CIN**	**N**	12	11	.522	4.45	36	28	7	194.1	211	60	73	3	2	1	1	65	9	0	.138	9	25	1	6	1.0	.971
1955			2	1	.667	7.42	10	5	0	26.2	29	16	14	0	2	0	0	7	0	0	.000	2	9	1	0	1.2	.917
2 yrs.			14	12	.538	4.81	46	33	7	221	240	76	87	3	4	1	1	72	9	0	.125	11	34	2	6	1.0	.957

John Valentine

VALENTINE, JOHN GILL
B. Nov. 21, 1855, Brooklyn, N. Y. D. Oct. 10, 1903, Central Islip, N. Y.

Year	Team	Lg	W	L	PCT	ERA	G	GS	CG	IP	H	BB	SO	ShO	Relief Pitching W	Relief Pitching L	Relief Pitching SV	Batting AB	Batting H	Batting HR	BA	PO	A	E	DP	TC/G	FA
1883	**COL**	**AA**	2	10	.167	*3.53*	13	12	11	102	130	17	13	0	0	0	0	60	17	0	.283	10	25	7	1	2.5	.833

Vito Valentinetti

VALENTINETTI, VITO JOHN BR TR 6′ 195 lbs.
B. Sept. 16, 1928, West New York, N. J.

Year	Team	Lg	W	L	PCT	ERA	G	GS	CG	IP	H	BB	SO	ShO	Relief Pitching W	Relief Pitching L	Relief Pitching SV	Batting AB	Batting H	Batting HR	BA	PO	A	E	DP	TC/G	FA
1954	**CHI**	**A**	0	0	—	54.00	1	0	0	1	4	2	1	0	0	0	0	0	0	0	—	0	0	0	0	0.0	.000
1956	**CHI**	**N**	6	4	.600	3.78	42	2	0	95.1	84	36	26	0	6	3	1	20	2	0	.100	4	12	1	0	0.4	.941
1957	**2 teams**	**CHI N** (9G 0–0) **CLE A** (11G 2–2)																									
″	**total**		2	2	.500	4.04	20	2	1	35.2	38	20	17	0	1	2	0	7	1	0	.143	2	6	0	0	0.4	1.000
1958	**2 teams**	**DET A** (15G 1–0) **WAS A** (23G 4–6)																									
″	**total**		5	6	.455	4.80	38	10	2	114.1	124	54	43	0	1	1	2	28	9	0	.321	8	23	1	5	0.8	.969
1959	**WAS**	**A**	0	2	.000	10.13	7	1	0	10.2	16	10	7	0	0	1	0	0	0	0	—	2	3	0	0	0.7	1.000
5 yrs.			13	14	.481	4.73	108	15	3	257	266	122	94	0	8	7	3	55	12	0	.218	16	44	2	5	0.6	.968

Fernando Valenzuela

VALENZUELA, FERNANDO BL TL 5′11″ 180 lbs.
Born Fernando Valenzuela (Anguamea).
B. Nov. 1, 1960, Navajoa, Mexico.

Year	Team	Lg	W	L	PCT	ERA	G	GS	CG	IP	H	BB	SO	ShO	Relief Pitching W	Relief Pitching L	Relief Pitching SV	Batting AB	Batting H	Batting HR	BA	PO	A	E	DP	TC/G	FA
1980	**LA**	**N**	2	0	1.000	0.00	10	0	0	18	8	5	16	0	2	0	1	1	0	0	.000	0	3	0	1	0.3	1.000
1981			13	7	.650	2.48	25	**25**	**11**	**192**	140	61	**180**	**8**	0	0	0	64	16	0	.250	12	33	3	2	1.9	.938
1982			19	13	.594	2.87	37	37	18	285	247	83	199	4	0	0	0	95	16	1	.168	20	64	2	4	2.3	.977
1983			15	10	.600	3.75	35	35	9	257	245	99	189	4	0	0	0	91	17	1	.187	20	54	2	5	2.2	.974
1984			12	17	.414	3.03	34	34	12	**261**	218	**106**	240	2	0	0	0	79	15	3	.190	21	48	2	4	2.1	.972
1985			17	10	.630	2.45	35	35	14	272.1	211	101	208	5	0	0	0	97	21	1	.216	18	45	0	0	1.8	1.000
1986			**21**	11	.656	3.14	34	34	**20**	269.1	226	85	242	3	0	0	0	109	24	0	.220	29	47	1	2	2.3	.987
1987			14	14	.500	3.98	34	34	**12**	251	**254**	**124**	190	1	0	0	0	92	13	1	.141	15	53	4	2	2.1	.944
1988			5	8	.385	4.24	23	22	3	142.1	142	76	64	0	0	0	1	44	8	0	.182	6	38	1	2	2.0	.978
1989			10	13	.435	3.43	31	31	3	196.2	185	98	116	0	0	0	0	66	12	0	.182	20	35	5	4	1.9	.917
1990			13	13	.500	4.59	33	33	5	204	223	77	115	2	0	0	0	69	21	1	.304	5	31	3	2	1.2	.923
1991	**CAL**	**A**	0	2	.000	12.15	2	2	0	6.2	14	3	5	0	0	0	0	0	0	0	—	0	1	0	0	0.5	1.000
1993	**BAL**	**A**	8	10	.444	4.94	32	31	5	178.2	179	79	78	2	0	0	0	0	0	0	—	11	37	4	1	1.6	.923
1994	**PHI**	**N**	1	2	.333	3.00	8	7	0	45	42	7	19	0	0	0	0	12	3	0	.250	2	8	0	0	1.3	1.000
1995	**SD**	**N**	8	3	.727	4.98	29	15	0	90.1	101	34	57	0	2	0	0	32	8	2	.250	7	27	0	2	1.2	1.000
15 yrs.			158	133	.543	3.49	402	375	112	2669.1	2435	1038	1918	31	4	0	2	851	174	10	.204	186	524	27	31	1.8	.963
DIVISIONAL PLAYOFF SERIES																											
1981	**LA**	**N**	1	0	1.000	1.06	2	2	1	17	10	3	10	0	0	0	0	4	0	0	.000	0	0	0	0	0.0	.000

Fernando Valenzuela *continued*

Year	Team	W	L	PCT	ERA	G	GS	CG	IP	H	BB	SO	ShO	Relief Pitching W	Relief Pitching L	Relief Pitching SV	Batting AB	Batting H	Batting HR	BA	PO	A	E	DP	TC/G	FA
LEAGUE CHAMPIONSHIP SERIES																										
1981	**LA N**	1	1	.500	2.45	2	2	0	14.2	10	5	10	0	0	0	0	5	0	0	.000	0	2	0	0	1.0	1.000
1983		1	0	1.000	1.13	1	1	0	8	7	4	5	0	0	0	0	3	0	0	.000	1	0	0	0	1.0	1.000
1985		1	0	1.000	1.88	2	2	0	14.1	11	10	13	0	0	0	0	5	1	0	.200	1	3	1	0	2.5	.800
3 yrs.		3	1	.750	1.95	5	5	0	37	28	19	28	0	0	0	0	13	1	0	.077	2	5	1	0	1.6	.875
					5th						**4th**															
WORLD SERIES																										
1981	**LA N**	1	0	1.000	4.00	1	1	1	9	9	7	6	0	0	0	0	3	0	0	.000	0	1	0	0	1.0	1.000

Julio Valera

VALERA, JULIO ENRIQUE BR TR 6′ 2″ 185 lbs.
Born Julio Enrique Valera (Torres).
B. Oct. 13, 1968, Aguadilla, Puerto Rico.

Year	Team	W	L	PCT	ERA	G	GS	CG	IP	H	BB	SO	ShO	Relief W	Relief L	Relief SV	AB	H	HR	BA	PO	A	E	DP	TC/G	FA
1990	**NY N**	1	1	.500	6.92	3	3	0	13	20	7	4	0	0	0	0	5	1	0	.200	1	0	1	0	0.7	.500
1991		0	0	—	0.00	2	0	0	2	1	4	3	0	0	0	0	0	0	0	—	0	0	0	0	0.0	.000
1992	**CAL A**	8	11	.421	3.73	30	28	4	188	188	64	113	2	1	0	0	0	0	0	—	10	13	1	0	0.8	.958
1993		3	6	.333	6.62	19	5	0	53	77	15	28	0	1	3	4	0	0	0	—	4	5	1	1	0.5	.900
4 yrs.		12	18	.400	4.46	54	36	4	256	286	90	148	2	2	3	4	5	1	0	.200	15	18	3	1	0.7	.917

Clay Van Alstyne

VAN ALSTYNE, CLAYTON EMORY (Spike) BR TR 5′11″ 180 lbs.
B. May 24, 1900, Stuyvesant, N. Y. D. Jan. 5, 1960, Hudson, N. Y.

Year	Team	W	L	PCT	ERA	G	GS	CG	IP	H	BB	SO	ShO	Relief W	Relief L	Relief SV	AB	H	HR	BA	PO	A	E	DP	TC/G	FA
1927	**WAS A**	0	0	—	3.00	2	0	0	3	3	0	0	0	0	0	0	0	0	0	—	0	0	0	0	0.0	.000
1928		0	0	—	5.48	4	0	0	21.1	26	13	5	0	0	0	0	8	2	1	.250	0	9	0	1	2.3	1.000
2 yrs.		0	0		5.18	6	0	0	24.1	29	13	5	0	0	0	0	8	2	1	.250	0	9	0	1	1.5	1.000

Russ Van Atta

VAN ATTA, RUSSELL (Sheriff) BL TL 6′ 184 lbs.
B. June 21, 1906, Augusta, N. J. D. Oct. 10, 1986, Andover, N. J.

Year	Team	W	L	PCT	ERA	G	GS	CG	IP	H	BB	SO	ShO	Relief W	Relief L	Relief SV	AB	H	HR	BA	PO	A	E	DP	TC/G	FA
1933	**NY A**	12	4	.750	4.18	26	22	10	157	160	63	76	2	0	0	1	60	17	0	.283	7	32	1	1	1.5	.975
1934		3	5	.375	6.34	28	9	0	88	107	46	39	0	2	0	0	29	6	1	.207	3	13	1	0	0.6	.941
1935	**2 teams NY A** (5G 0–0) **STL A** (53G 9–16)																									
″	**total**	9	16	.360	5.30	**58**	17	1	175	206	90	90	0	**6**	4	3	43	9	0	.209	2	28	5	1	0.6	.857
1936	**STL A**	4	7	.364	6.60	**52**	9	2	122.2	164	68	59	0	4	2	2	29	5	0	.172	3	28	1	0	0.6	.969
1937		1	2	.333	5.52	16	6	1	58.2	74	32	34	0	0	0	0	13	6	1	.462	2	14	2	0	1.1	.889
1938		4	7	.364	6.06	25	12	3	104	118	61	35	1	1	0	0	30	4	0	.133	3	21	2	3	1.0	.923
1939		0	0	—	11.57	2	1	0	7	9	7	6	0	0	0	0	2	0	0	.000	0	0	0	0	0.0	.000
7 yrs.		33	41	.446	5.60	207	76	17	712.1	838	367	339	3	13	6	6	206	47	2	.228	20	136	12	5	0.8	.929

Ozzie Van Brabant

VAN BRABANT, CAMILLE OSCAR BR TR 6′ 1″ 165 lbs.
B. Sept. 28, 1926, Kingsville, Ont., Canada.

Year	Team	W	L	PCT	ERA	G	GS	CG	IP	H	BB	SO	ShO	Relief W	Relief L	Relief SV	AB	H	HR	BA	PO	A	E	DP	TC/G	FA
1954	**PHI A**	0	2	.000	7.09	9	2	0	26.2	35	18	10	0	0	0	0	5	1	0	.200	1	8	0	0	1.0	1.000
1955	**KC A**	0	0	—	18.00	2	0	0	2	4	2	1	0	0	0	0	0	0	0	—	0	0	0	0	0.0	.000
2 yrs.		0	2	.000	7.85	11	2	0	28.2	39	20	11	0	0	0	0	5	1	0	.200	1	8	0	0	0.8	1.000

Dazzy Vance

VANCE, CLARENCE ARTHUR BR TR 6′ 2″ 200 lbs.
B. Mar. 4, 1891, Orient, Iowa D. Feb. 16, 1961, Homosassa Springs, Fla.
Hall of Fame 1955.

Year	Team	W	L	PCT	ERA	G	GS	CG	IP	H	BB	SO	ShO	Relief W	Relief L	Relief SV	AB	H	HR	BA	PO	A	E	DP	TC/G	FA
1915	**2 teams PIT N** (1G 0–1) **NY A** (8G 0–3)																									
″	**total**	0	4	.000	4.11	9	4	1	30.2	26	21	18	0	0	0	0	4	2	0	.500	1	9	2	1	1.3	.833
1918	**NY A**	0	0	—	15.43	2	0	0	2.1	9	2	0	0	0	0	0	0	0	0	—	0	0	0	0	0.0	.000
1922	**BKN N**	18	12	.600	3.70	36	31	16	245.2	259	94	**134**	**5**	0	1	0	89	20	0	.225	10	51	0	2	1.7	1.000
1923		18	15	.545	3.50	37	35	21	280.1	263	100	**197**	3	2	0	0	83	7	1	.084	12	54	2	3	1.8	.971
1924		**28**	6	.824	**2.16**	35	34	**30**	308.2	238	77	**262**	3	1	0	0	106	16	2	.151	16	58	1	3	2.1	.987
1925		**22**	9	.710	3.53	31	31	26	265.1	247	66	**221**	**4**	0	0	0	98	14	3	.143	10	55	1	1	2.1	.985
1926		9	10	.474	3.89	24	22	12	169	172	58	**140**	1	0	0	1	55	10	0	.182	5	41	1	2	2.0	.979
1927		16	15	.516	2.70	34	32	**25**	273.1	242	69	**184**	2	0	0	1	90	15	0	.167	14	42	3	2	1.7	.949
1928		22	10	.688	**2.09**	38	32	24	280.1	226	72	**200**	**4**	1	1	2	96	17	0	.177	17	55	0	6	1.9	1.000
1929		14	13	.519	3.89	31	26	17	231.1	244	47	126	1	1	2	0	74	10	0	.135	13	49	0	1	2.0	1.000
1930		17	15	.531	**2.61**	35	31	20	258.2	241	55	173	**4**	1	1	0	89	12	0	.135	5	44	5	0	1.5	.907
1931		11	13	.458	3.38	30	29	12	218.2	221	53	150	2	1	0	0	67	9	0	.134	4	46	0	0	1.7	1.000
1932		12	11	.522	4.20	27	24	9	175.2	171	57	103	1	1	0	1	56	5	0	.089	7	32	1	3	1.5	.975
1933	**STL N**	6	2	.750	3.55	28	11	2	99	105	28	67	0	3	0	3	28	5	0	.179	5	14	2	0	0.8	.905
1934	**2 teams STL N** (19G 1–1) **CIN N** (6G 0–2)																									
″	**total**	1	3	.250	4.56	25	6	1	77	90	25	42	0	0	0	1	19	3	1	.158	4	12	0	3	0.6	1.000
1935	**BKN N**	3	2	.600	4.41	20	0	0	51	55	16	28	0	3	2	2	17	1	0	.059	3	8	0	1	0.6	1.000
16 yrs.		197	140	.585	3.24	442	348	216	2967	2809	840	2045	30	14	7	11	971	146	7	.150	126	570	18	28	1.6	.975
WORLD SERIES																										
1934	**STL N**	0	0	—	0.00	1	0	0	1.1	2	1	3	0	0	0	0	0	0	0	—	0	0	0	0	0.0	.000

Joe Vance

VANCE, JOSEPH ALBERT (Sandy) BR TR 6′ 1½″ 190 lbs.
B. Sept. 16, 1905, Devine, Tex. D. July 4, 1978, Devine, Tex.

Year	Team	W	L	PCT	ERA	G	GS	CG	IP	H	BB	SO	ShO	Relief W	Relief L	Relief SV	AB	H	HR	BA	PO	A	E	DP	TC/G	FA
1935	**CHI A**	2	2	.500	6.68	10	0	0	31	36	21	12	0	2	2	0	11	2	0	.182	0	9	1	1	1.0	.900
1937	**NY A**	1	0	1.000	3.00	2	2	0	15	11	9	3	0	0	0	0	5	0	0	.000	4	4	0	1	4.0	1.000
1938		0	0	—	7.15	3	1	0	11.1	20	4	2	0	0	0	0	4	3	0	.750	0	3	0	0	1.0	1.000
3 yrs.		3	2	.600	5.81	15	3	0	57.1	67	34	17	0	2	2	0	20	5	0	.250	4	16	1	2	1.4	.952

Sandy Vance

VANCE, GENE COVINGTON BR TR 6′ 2″ 180 lbs.
B. Jan. 5, 1947, Lamar, Colo.

Year	Team	W	L	PCT	ERA	G	GS	CG	IP	H	BB	SO	ShO	Relief W	Relief L	Relief SV	AB	H	HR	BA	PO	A	E	DP	TC/G	FA
1970	**LA N**	7	7	.500	3.13	20	18	2	115	109	37	45	0	0	0	0	37	7	0	.189	6	8	2	0	0.8	.875
1971		2	1	.667	6.92	10	3	0	26	38	9	11	0	1	1	0	5	0	0	.000	2	2	0	0	0.4	1.000
2 yrs.		9	8	.529	3.83	30	21	2	141	147	46	56	0	1	1	0	42	7	0	.167	8	10	2	0	0.7	.900

Chris Van Cuyk

VAN CUYK, CHRISTIAN GERALD BL TL 6′ 6″ 215 lbs.
Brother of Johnny Van Cuyk.
B. Jan. 3, 1927, Kimberly, Wis. D. Nov. 3, 1992, Hudson, Fla.

Year	Team		W	L	PCT	ERA	G	GS	CG	IP	H	BB	SO	ShO	Relief W	Relief L	Relief SV	Batting AB	Batting H	HR	BA	PO	A	E	DP	TC/G	FA
1950	BKN	N	1	3	.250	4.86	12	4	1	33.1	33	12	21	0	0	1	0	10	1	0	.100	1	3	0	0	0.3	1.000
1951			1	2	.333	5.52	9	6	0	29.1	33	11	16	0	0	0	0	8	2	0	.250	2	4	1	2	0.8	.857
1952			5	6	.455	5.16	23	16	4	97.2	104	40	66	0	0	1	1	33	8	0	.242	4	13	1	0	0.8	.944
3 yrs.			7	11	.389	5.16	44	26	5	160.1	170	63	103	0	0	2	1	51	11	0	.216	7	20	2	2	0.7	.931

Johnny Van Cuyk

VAN CUYK, JOHN HENRY BL TL 6′ 1″ 190 lbs.
Brother of Chris Van Cuyk.
B. July 7, 1921, Little Chute, Wis.

Year	Team		W	L	PCT	ERA	G	GS	CG	IP	H	BB	SO	ShO	Relief W	Relief L	Relief SV	Batting AB	Batting H	HR	BA	PO	A	E	DP	TC/G	FA
1947	BKN	N	0	0	—	5.40	2	0	0	3.1	5	1	2	0	0	0	0	0	0	0	—	0	1	0	0	0.5	1.000
1948			0	0	—	3.60	3	0	0	5	4	1	1	0	0	0	0	0	0	0	—	0	2	0	0	0.7	1.000
1949			0	0	—	9.00	2	0	0	2	3	1	0	0	0	0	0	0	0	0	—	0	0	0	0	0.0	.000
3 yrs.			0	0		5.23	7	0	0	10.1	12	3	3	0	0	0	0	0	0	0		0	3	0	0	0.4	1.000

Ed Vande Berg

VANDE BERG, EDWARD JOHN BR TL 6′ 2″ 175 lbs.
B. Oct. 26, 1958, Redlands, Calif.

Year	Team		W	L	PCT	ERA	G	GS	CG	IP	H	BB	SO	ShO	Relief W	Relief L	Relief SV	Batting AB	Batting H	HR	BA	PO	A	E	DP	TC/G	FA
1982	SEA	A	9	4	.692	2.37	**78**	0	0	76	54	32	60	0	9	4	5	0	0	0	—	5	19	1	3	0.3	.960
1983			2	4	.333	3.36	68	0	0	64.1	59	22	49	0	2	4	5	0	0	0	—	3	9	2	0	0.2	.857
1984			8	12	.400	4.76	50	17	2	130.1	165	50	71	0	3	1	7	0	0	0	—	3	20	2	0	0.5	.920
1985			2	1	.667	3.72	76	0	0	67.2	71	31	34	0	2	1	3	0	0	0	—	8	11	0	1	0.3	1.000
1986	LA	N	1	5	.167	3.41	60	0	0	71.1	83	33	42	0	1	5	0	1	0	0	.000	5	16	2	0	0.4	.913
1987	CLE	A	1	0	1.000	5.10	55	0	0	72.1	96	21	40	0	1	0	0	0	0	0	—	7	11	1	1	0.3	.947
1988	TEX	A	2	2	.500	4.14	26	0	0	37	44	11	18	0	2	2	2	0	0	0	—	1	4	1	0	0.2	.833
7 yrs.			25	28	.472	3.92	413	17	2	519	572	200	314	0	20	17	22	1	0	0	.000	32	90	9	5	0.3	.931

Hy Vandenburg

VANDENBURG, HAROLD HARRIS BR TR 6′ 4″ 220 lbs.
B. Mar. 17, 1907, Abilene, Kans. D. July 31, 1994, Bloomington, Minn.

Year	Team		W	L	PCT	ERA	G	GS	CG	IP	H	BB	SO	ShO	Relief W	Relief L	Relief SV	Batting AB	Batting H	HR	BA	PO	A	E	DP	TC/G	FA
1935	BOS	A	0	0	—	20.25	3	0	0	5.1	15	4	2	0	0	0	0	1	1	0	1.000	0	1	0	0	0.3	1.000
1937	NY	N	0	1	.000	7.88	1	1	1	8	10	6	2	0	0	0	0	4	0	0	.000	1	4	0	0	5.0	1.000
1938			0	1	.000	7.50	6	1	0	18	28	12	7	0	0	1	0	4	0	0	.000	2	8	0	1	1.7	1.000
1939			0	0	—	5.68	2	1	0	6.1	10	6	3	0	0	0	0	2	0	0	.000	0	2	0	0	1.0	1.000
1940			1	1	.500	3.90	13	3	1	32.1	27	16	17	0	0	1	1	8	1	0	.125	0	4	0	1	0.3	1.000
1944	CHI	N	7	4	.636	3.63	35	9	2	126.1	123	51	54	0	4	2	2	38	9	0	.237	4	24	1	1	0.8	.966
1945			6	3	.667	3.49	30	7	3	95.1	91	33	35	1	2	1	2	32	4	0	.125	7	18	2	1	0.9	.926
7 yrs.			14	10	.583	4.32	90	22	7	291.2	304	128	120	1	6	5	5	89	15	0	.169	14	61	3	4	0.9	.962
WORLD SERIES																											
1945	CHI	N	0	0	—	0.00	3	0	0	6	1	3	3	0	0	0	0	1	0	0	.000	1	2	0	0	1.0	1.000

Johnny Vander Meer

VANDER MEER, JOHN SAMUEL (The Dutch Master) BB TL 6′ 1″ 190 lbs.
B. Nov. 2, 1914, Prospect Park, N. J.

Year	Team		W	L	PCT	ERA	G	GS	CG	IP	H	BB	SO	ShO	Relief W	Relief L	Relief SV	Batting AB	Batting H	HR	BA	PO	A	E	DP	TC/G	FA
1937	CIN	N	3	5	.375	3.84	19	10	4	84.1	63	69	52	0	0	0	0	23	5	0	.217	7	23	0	1	1.6	1.000
1938			15	10	.600	3.12	32	29	16	225.1	177	103	125	3	0	0	0	83	15	0	.181	8	38	3	0	1.5	.939
1939			5	9	.357	4.67	30	21	8	129	128	95	102	0	0	2	0	36	4	0	.111	5	16	3	5	0.8	.875
1940			3	1	.750	3.75	10	7	2	48	38	41	41	0	0	0	1	20	6	0	.300	0	9	0	0	0.9	1.000
1941			16	13	.552	2.82	33	32	18	226.1	172	126	**202**	6	0	0	0	76	10	0	.132	10	47	2	3	1.8	.966
1942			18	12	.600	2.43	33	33	21	244	188	102	**186**	4	0	0	0	75	11	0	.147	6	51	2	4	1.8	.966
1943			15	16	.484	2.87	36	**36**	21	289	228	**162**	**174**	3	0	0	0	95	13	0	.137	11	67	4	7	2.3	.951
1946			10	12	.455	3.17	29	25	11	204.1	175	78	94	5	1	0	0	73	18	0	.247	6	33	3	2	1.4	.929
1947			9	14	.391	4.40	30	29	9	186	186	87	79	3	0	0	0	57	5	0	.088	8	31	2	1	1.4	.951
1948			17	14	.548	3.41	33	33	14	232	204	**124**	120	3	0	0	0	78	11	1	.141	11	39	5	3	1.7	.909
1949			5	10	.333	4.90	28	24	7	159.2	172	85	76	3	0	0	0	52	4	0	.077	6	33	2	4	1.5	.951
1950	CHI	N	3	4	.429	3.79	32	6	0	73.2	60	59	41	0	3	1	1	16	2	0	.125	4	14	3	0	0.7	.857
1951	CLE	A	0	1	.000	18.00	1	1	0	3	8	1	2	0	0	0	0	1	0	0	.000	0	3	0	0	3.0	1.000
13 yrs.			119	121	.496	3.44	346	286	131	2104.2	1799	1132	1294	30	4	3	2	685	104	1	.152	82	404	29	30	1.5	.944
WORLD SERIES																											
1940	CIN	N	0	0	—	0.00	1	0	0	3	2	3	2	0	0	0	0	0	0	0	—	0	0	0	0	0.0	.000

Ben Van Dyke

VAN DYKE, BENJAMIN HARRISON BR TL 6′ 1″ 150 lbs.
B. Aug. 15, 1888, Clintonville, Pa. D. Oct. 22, 1973, Sarasota, Fla.

Year	Team		W	L	PCT	ERA	G	GS	CG	IP	H	BB	SO	ShO	Relief W	Relief L	Relief SV	Batting AB	Batting H	HR	BA	PO	A	E	DP	TC/G	FA
1909	PHI	N	0	0	—	3.68	2	0	0	7.1	7	4	5	0	0	0	0	3	0	0	.000	0	0	0	0	0.0	.000
1912	BOS	A	0	0	—	3.14	3	1	0	14.1	13	7	8	0	0	0	0	4	1	0	.250	2	1	1	0	1.3	.750
2 yrs.			0	0		3.32	5	1	0	21.2	20	11	13	0	0	0	0	7	1	0	.143	2	1	1	0	0.8	.750

Tim VanEgmond

VanEGMOND, TIMOTHY LAYNE BR TR 6′ 2″ 185 lbs.
B. May 31, 1969, Shreveport, La.

Year	Team		W	L	PCT	ERA	G	GS	CG	IP	H	BB	SO	ShO	Relief W	Relief L	Relief SV	Batting AB	Batting H	HR	BA	PO	A	E	DP	TC/G	FA
1994	BOS	A	2	3	.400	6.34	7	7	1	38.1	38	21	22	0	0	0	0	0	0	0	—	0	2	0	0	0.3	1.000
1995			0	1	.000	9.45	4	1	0	6.2	9	6	5	0	0	0	0	0	0	0	—	1	1	0	0	0.5	1.000
2 yrs.			2	4	.333	6.80	11	8	1	45	47	27	27	0	0	0	0	0	0	0		1	3	0	0	0.4	1.000

Elam Vangilder

VANGILDER, ELAM RUSSELL BR TR 6′ 1″ 192 lbs.
B. Apr. 23, 1896, Cape Girardeau, Mo. D. Apr. 30, 1977, Cape Girardeau, Mo.

Year	Team		W	L	PCT	ERA	G	GS	CG	IP	H	BB	SO	ShO	Relief W	Relief L	Relief SV	Batting AB	Batting H	HR	BA	PO	A	E	DP	TC/G	FA
1919	STL	A	1	0	1.000	2.08	3	1	1	13	15	3	6	0	0	0	0	3	2	0	.667	1	6	0	0	2.3	1.000
1920			3	8	.273	5.50	24	13	4	104.2	131	40	25	0	0	2	0	30	4	0	.133	1	28	2	2	1.3	.935
1921			11	12	.478	3.94	31	21	10	180.1	196	67	48	1	1	1	0	65	13	1	.200	3	47	0	2	1.6	1.000
1922			19	13	.594	3.42	43	30	19	245	248	48	63	3	3	4	4	93	32	2	.344	14	47	1	3	1.4	.984
1923			16	17	.485	3.06	41	35	20	282.1	276	**120**	74	4	1	2	1	110	24	1	.218	4	61	1	4	1.6	.985
1924			5	10	.333	5.76	43	18	5	145.1	183	55	49	0	2	2	1	44	13	1	.295	8	38	3	6	1.1	.939
1925			14	8	.636	4.70	52	16	4	193.1	225	92	61	1	**11**	4	6	71	13	0	.183	11	44	2	3	1.1	.965
1926			9	11	.450	5.17	42	19	8	181	196	98	40	1	3	2	1	58	11	0	.190	5	38	3	1	1.1	.935

Elam Vangilder *continued*

Year	Team		W	L	PCT	ERA	G	GS	CG	IP	H	BB	SO	ShO	Relief Pitching W	Relief Pitching L	Relief Pitching SV	Batting AB	Batting H	Batting HR	BA	PO	A	E	DP	TC/G	FA
1927			10	12	.455	4.79	44	23	12	203	245	102	62	3	0	2	1	68	19	1	.279	9	32	2	0	1.0	.953
1928	DET	A	11	10	.524	3.91	38	11	7	156.1	163	68	43	0	4	6	5	58	15	2	.259	8	37	4	3	1.3	.918
1929			0	1	.000	6.35	6	0	0	11.1	16	7	3	0	0	1	0	1	0	0	.000	3	6	0	0	1.5	1.000
11 yrs.			99	102	.493	4.29	367	187	90	1715.2	1894	700	474	13	25	26	19	601	146	8	.243	67	384	18	24	1.3	.962

George Van Haltren

VAN HALTREN, GEORGE EDWARD MARTIN BL TL 5′11″ 170 lbs.
B. Mar. 30, 1866, St. Louis, Mo. D. Sept. 29, 1945, Oakland, Calif.
Manager 1892.

Year	Team		W	L	PCT	ERA	G	GS	CG	IP	H	BB	SO	ShO	Relief Pitching W	Relief Pitching L	Relief Pitching SV	Batting AB	Batting H	Batting HR	BA	PO	A	E	DP	TC/G	FA
1887	CHI	N	11	7	.611	3.86	20	18	18	161	177	66	76	1	0	0	**1**	172	35	3	.203	47	26	8	2	1.7	.901
1888			13	13	.500	3.52	30	24	24	245.2	263	60	139	4	0	**2**	1	318	90	4	.283	98	62	17	0	2.0	.904
1890	BKN	P	15	10	.600	4.28	28	25	23	223	272	89	48	0	0	0	2	376	126	5	.335	230	35	32	5	2.2	.892
1891	BAL	AA	0	1	.000	5.09	6	1	0	23	38	10	7	0	0	0	0	566	180	9	.318	275	190	82	22	3.7	.850
1892	BAL	N	0	0	—	9.20	4	0	0	14.2	28	7	5	0	0	0	0	611	179	7	.293	270	47	52	9	2.4	.859
1895	NY	N	0	0	—	12.60	1	0	0	5	13	2	1	0	0	0	0	521	177	8	.340	245	69	49	6	2.9	.865
1896			1	0	1.000	2.25	2	0	0	8	5	1	3	0	1	0	0	562	197	5	.351	273	26	15	4	2.3	.952
1900			0	0	—	0.00	1	0	0	3	1	3	0	0	0	0	0	571	180	1	.315	267	31	20	4	2.5	.937
1901			0	0	—	3.00	1	0	0	6	12	6	2	0	0	0	0	544	186	1	.342	263	27	18	5	2.3	.942
9 yrs.			40	31	.563	4.05	93	68	65	689.1	809	244	281	5	1	2	4	*				3749	749	458	94	2.5	.908

William VanLandingham

VanLANDINGHAM, WILLIAM JOSEPH BR TR 6′ 2″ 210 lbs.
B. July 16, 1970, Columbia, Tenn.

Year	Team		W	L	PCT	ERA	G	GS	CG	IP	H	BB	SO	ShO	Relief Pitching W	Relief Pitching L	Relief Pitching SV	Batting AB	Batting H	Batting HR	BA	PO	A	E	DP	TC/G	FA
1994	SF	N	8	2	.800	3.54	16	14	0	84	70	43	56	0	0	0	0	31	2	0	.065	4	9	0	0	0.8	1.000
1995			6	3	.667	3.67	18	18	1	122.2	124	40	95	0	0	0	0	46	7	1	.152	7	19	1	2	1.5	.963
2 yrs.			14	5	.737	3.61	34	32	1	206.2	194	83	151	0	0	0	0	77	9	1	.117	11	28	1	2	1.2	.975

Todd Van Poppel

VAN POPPEL, TODD MATTHEW BR TR 6′ 5″ 210 lbs.
B. Dec. 9, 1971, Hinsdale, Ill.

Year	Team		W	L	PCT	ERA	G	GS	CG	IP	H	BB	SO	ShO	Relief Pitching W	Relief Pitching L	Relief Pitching SV	Batting AB	Batting H	Batting HR	BA	PO	A	E	DP	TC/G	FA
1991	OAK	A	0	0	—	9.64	1	1	0	4.2	7	2	6	0	0	0	0	0	0	0	—	0	1	0	0	1.0	1.000
1993			6	6	.500	5.04	16	16	0	84	76	62	47	0	0	0	0	0	0	0	—	6	4	0	1	0.6	1.000
1994			7	10	.412	6.09	23	23	0	116.2	108	**89**	83	0	0	0	0	0	0	0	—	1	11	0	1	0.5	1.000
1995			4	8	.333	4.88	36	14	1	138.1	125	56	122	0	1	2	0	0	0	0	—	4	11	1	0	0.4	.938
4 yrs.			17	24	.415	5.39	76	54	1	343.2	316	209	258	0	1	2	0	0	0	0		11	27	1	2	0.5	.974

Ike Van Zandt

VAN ZANDT, CHARLES ISAAC BL
B. 1877, Brooklyn, N. Y. D. Sept. 14, 1908, Nashua, N. H.

Year	Team		W	L	PCT	ERA	G	GS	CG	IP	H	BB	SO	ShO	Relief Pitching W	Relief Pitching L	Relief Pitching SV	Batting AB	Batting H	Batting HR	BA	PO	A	E	DP	TC/G	FA
1901	NY	N	0	0	—	7.11	2	0	0	12.2	16	8	2	0	0	0	0	6	1	0	.167	1	0	3	0	1.3	.250
1905	STL	A	0	0	—	0.00	1	0	0	6.2	2	2	3	0	0	0	0	322	75	1	.233	3	0	0	0	1.0	1.000
2 yrs.			0	0		4.66	3	0	0	19.1	18	10	5	0	0	0	0	*				80	9	14	0	1.3	.864

Andy Varga

VARGA, ANDREW WILLIAM BR TL 6′ 4″ 187 lbs.
B. Dec. 11, 1930, Chicago, Ill. D. Nov. 4, 1992, Orlando, Fla.

Year	Team		W	L	PCT	ERA	G	GS	CG	IP	H	BB	SO	ShO	Relief Pitching W	Relief Pitching L	Relief Pitching SV	Batting AB	Batting H	Batting HR	BA	PO	A	E	DP	TC/G	FA
1950	CHI	N	0	0	—	0.00	1	0	0	1	0	1	0	0	0	0	0	0	0	0	—	0	0	0	0	0.0	.000
1951			0	0	—	3.00	2	0	0	3	2	6	1	0	0	0	0	0	0	0	—	0	0	0	0	0.0	.000
2 yrs.			0	0		2.25	3	0	0	4	2	7	1	0	0	0	0	0	0	0		0	0	0	0	0.0	

Roberto Vargas

VARGAS, ROBERTO ENRIQUE BL TL 5′11″ 170 lbs.
Born Roberto Enrique Vargas (Valez).
B. May 29, 1929, Santurce, Puerto Rico.

Year	Team		W	L	PCT	ERA	G	GS	CG	IP	H	BB	SO	ShO	Relief Pitching W	Relief Pitching L	Relief Pitching SV	Batting AB	Batting H	Batting HR	BA	PO	A	E	DP	TC/G	FA
1955	MIL	N	0	0	—	8.76	25	0	0	24.2	39	14	13	0	0	0	2	2	1	0	.500	4	8	0	0	0.5	1.000

Bill Vargus

VARGUS, WILLIAM FAY BL TL 6′ 165 lbs.
B. Nov. 11, 1899, Hyannis, Mass. D. Feb. 12, 1979, Cape Cod, Mass.

Year	Team		W	L	PCT	ERA	G	GS	CG	IP	H	BB	SO	ShO	Relief Pitching W	Relief Pitching L	Relief Pitching SV	Batting AB	Batting H	Batting HR	BA	PO	A	E	DP	TC/G	FA
1925	BOS	N	1	1	.500	3.96	11	2	1	36.1	45	13	5	0	0	0	0	12	3	0	.250	0	11	2	0	1.2	.846
1926			0	0	—	3.00	4	0	0	3	4	1	0	0	0	0	0	0	0	0	—	0	1	0	0	0.3	1.000
2 yrs.			1	1	.500	3.89	15	2	1	39.1	49	14	5	0	0	0	0	12	3	0	.250	0	12	2	0	0.9	.857

Dike Varney

VARNEY, LAWRENCE DELANO BL TL 6′ 165 lbs.
Born Lawrence Delano de Varney.
B. Aug. 9, 1880, Dover, N. H. D. Apr. 23, 1950, Long Island City, N. Y.

Year	Team		W	L	PCT	ERA	G	GS	CG	IP	H	BB	SO	ShO	Relief Pitching W	Relief Pitching L	Relief Pitching SV	Batting AB	Batting H	Batting HR	BA	PO	A	E	DP	TC/G	FA
1902	CLE	A	1	1	.500	6.14	3	3	0	14.2	14	12	7	0	0	0	0	6	1	0	.167	0	5	1	0	2.0	.833

Moses Vasbinder

VASBINDER, MOSES CALHOUN BR TR 6′ 2″
B. July 19, 1880, Scio, Ohio D. Dec. 22, 1950, Cadiz, Ohio.

Year	Team		W	L	PCT	ERA	G	GS	CG	IP	H	BB	SO	ShO	Relief Pitching W	Relief Pitching L	Relief Pitching SV	Batting AB	Batting H	Batting HR	BA	PO	A	E	DP	TC/G	FA
1902	CLE	A	0	0	—	9.00	2	0	0	5	5	8	2	0	0	0	0	2	1	0	.500	0	2	0	0	1.0	1.000

Rafael Vasquez

VASQUEZ, RAFAEL BR TR 6′ 160 lbs.
Born Rafael Vasquez (Santiago).
B. June 28, 1958, La Romana, Dominican Republic.

Year	Team		W	L	PCT	ERA	G	GS	CG	IP	H	BB	SO	ShO	Relief Pitching W	Relief Pitching L	Relief Pitching SV	Batting AB	Batting H	Batting HR	BA	PO	A	E	DP	TC/G	FA
1979	SEA	A	1	0	1.000	5.06	9	0	0	16	23	6	9	0	1	0	0	0	0	0	—	0	1	0	0	0.1	1.000

Charlie Vaughan

VAUGHAN, CHARLES WAYNE BR TL 6′ 1½″ 185 lbs.
B. Oct. 6, 1947, Mercedes, Tex.

Year	Team		W	L	PCT	ERA	G	GS	CG	IP	H	BB	SO	ShO	Relief Pitching W	Relief Pitching L	Relief Pitching SV	Batting AB	Batting H	Batting HR	BA	PO	A	E	DP	TC/G	FA
1966	ATL	N	1	0	1.000	2.57	1	1	0	7	8	3	6	0	0	0	0	4	1	0	.250	0	1	0	0	1.0	1.000
1969			0	0	—	18.00	1	0	0	1	1	3	1	0	0	0	0	0	0	0	—	0	1	0	0	1.0	1.000
2 yrs.			1	0	1.000	4.50	2	1	0	8	9	6	7	0	0	0	0	4	1	0	.250	0	2	0	0	1.0	1.000

Porter Vaughan

VAUGHAN, CECIL PORTER (Lefty) BR TL 6′ 1″ 178 lbs.
B. May 11, 1919, Stevensville, Va.

Year	Team		W	L	PCT	ERA	G	GS	CG	IP	H	BB	SO	ShO	Relief Pitching W	Relief Pitching L	Relief Pitching SV	Batting AB	Batting H	Batting HR	BA	PO	A	E	DP	TC/G	FA
1940	PHI	A	2	9	.182	5.35	18	15	5	99.1	104	61	46	0	0	0	2	34	8	0	.235	2	16	3	0	1.2	.857
1941			0	2	.000	7.94	5	3	1	22.2	32	12	6	0	0	0	0	7	1	0	.143	2	3	1	0	1.2	.833
1946			0	0	—	0.00	1	0	0		1	1	0	0	0	0	0	0	0	0	—	0	0	0	0	0.0	.000
3 yrs.			2	11	.154	5.83	24	18	6	122	137	74	52	0	0	0	2	41	9	0	.220	4	19	4	0	1.1	.852

Clarence Vaughn

VAUGHN, CLARENCE LeROY BB TR 6′½″ 178 lbs.
B. Sept. 4, 1911, Sedalia, Mo. D. Mar. 1, 1937, Martinsville, Va.

Year	Team		W	L	PCT	ERA	G	GS	CG	IP	H	BB	SO	ShO	Relief Pitching W	Relief Pitching L	Relief Pitching SV	Batting AB	Batting H	HR	BA	PO	A	E	DP	TC/G	FA
1934	PHI	A	0	0	—	2.08	2	0	0	4.1	3	3	1	0	0	0	0	2	0	0	.000	0	0	0	0	0.0	.000

DeWayne Vaughn

VAUGHN, DeWAYNE MATHEW BR TR 6′ 1″ 175 lbs.
B. July 22, 1959, Oklahoma City, Okla.

Year	Team		W	L	PCT	ERA	G	GS	CG	IP	H	BB	SO	ShO	Relief Pitching W	Relief Pitching L	Relief Pitching SV	Batting AB	Batting H	HR	BA	PO	A	E	DP	TC/G	FA
1988	TEX	A	0	0	—	7.63	8	0	0	15.1	24	4	8	0	0	0	0	0	0	0	—	0	0	0	0	0.0	.000

Farmer Vaughn

VAUGHN, HENRY FRANCIS BR TR 6′ 3″ 177 lbs.
B. Mar. 1, 1864, Ruraldale, Ohio D. Feb. 21, 1914, Cincinnati, Ohio.

Year	Team		W	L	PCT	ERA	G	GS	CG	IP	H	BB	SO	ShO	Relief Pitching W	Relief Pitching L	Relief Pitching SV	Batting AB	Batting H	HR	BA	PO	A	E	DP	TC/G	FA
1891	CIN	AA	0	0	—	3.86	1	0	0	7	12	1	0	0	0	0	0	*				8	3	1	0	12.0	.917

Hippo Vaughn

VAUGHN, JAMES LESLIE BB TL 6′ 4″ 215 lbs.
B. Apr. 9, 1888, Weatherford, Tex. D. May 29, 1966, Chicago, Ill.

Year	Team		W	L	PCT	ERA	G	GS	CG	IP	H	BB	SO	ShO	Relief Pitching W	Relief Pitching L	Relief Pitching SV	Batting AB	Batting H	HR	BA	PO	A	E	DP	TC/G	FA
1908	NY	A	0	0	—	3.86	2	0	0	2.1	1	4	2	0	0	0	0	1	0	0	.000	0	2	0	0	1.0	1.000
1910			13	11	.542	1.83	30	25	18	221.2	190	58	107	5	4	0	1	75	10	0	.133	5	73	8	2	2.9	.907
1911			8	10	.444	4.39	26	18	11	145.2	158	54	74	0	1	2	0	49	7	0	.143	9	41	4	1	2.1	.926
1912	**2 teams**	**NY A** (15G 2–8)	**WAS A** (12G 4–3)																								
″	**total**		6	11	.353	3.88	27	18	9	144	141	80	95	1	1	2	0	51	8	0	.157	5	53	4	0	2.3	.935
1913	CHI	N	5	1	.833	1.45	7	6	5	56	37	27	36	2	0	0	0	21	4	0	.190	3	13	2	1	2.6	.889
1914			21	13	.618	2.05	42	35	23	293.2	236	109	165	4	0	1	1	97	14	1	.144	11	75	13	1	2.4	.869
1915			20	12	.625	2.87	41	34	18	269.2	240	77	148	4	4	1	1	86	14	0	.163	5	70	8	1	2.0	.904
1916			17	15	.531	2.20	44	35	21	294	269	67	144	4	1	2	1	104	14	0	.135	6	82	4	0	2.1	.957
1917			23	13	.639	2.01	41	38	27	295.2	255	91	195	5	0	0	0	100	16	0	.160	14	89	7	2	2.7	.936
1918			**22**	10	.688	**1.74**	35	**33**	27	**290.1**	216	76	**148**	**8**	0	2	0	96	23	0	.240	14	73	3	2	2.6	.967
1919			21	14	.600	1.79	38	**37**	25	**306.2**	264	62	**141**	4	0	0	1	98	17	0	.173	10	74	9	3	2.4	.903
1920			19	16	.543	2.54	40	38	24	301	301	81	131	4	0	0	0	102	22	1	.216	9	71	10	4	2.3	.889
1921			3	11	.214	6.01	17	14	7	109.1	153	31	30	0	0	2	0	41	10	1	.244	1	24	2	0	1.6	.926
13 yrs.			178	137	.565	2.49	390	331	215	2730	2461	817	1416	41	11	12	5	921	159	3	.173	92	740	74	17	2.3	.918
WORLD SERIES																											
1918	CHI	N	1	2	.333	1.00 **6th**	3	3	3	27	17	5	17	1	0	0	0	10	0	0	.000	6	11	0	1	5.7	1.000

Al Veach

VEACH, ALVIS LINDELL BR TR 5′11″ 178 lbs.
B. Aug. 6, 1909, Maylene, Ala.

Year	Team		W	L	PCT	ERA	G	GS	CG	IP	H	BB	SO	ShO	Relief Pitching W	Relief Pitching L	Relief Pitching SV	Batting AB	Batting H	HR	BA	PO	A	E	DP	TC/G	FA
1935	PHI	A	0	2	.000	11.70	2	2	1	10	20	9	3	0	0	0	0	4	0	0	.000	2	1	0	1	1.5	1.000

Bobby Veach

VEACH, ROBERT HAYES BL TR 5′11″ 160 lbs.
B. June 29, 1888, Island, Ky. D. Aug. 7, 1945, Detroit, Mich.

Year	Team		W	L	PCT	ERA	G	GS	CG	IP	H	BB	SO	ShO	Relief Pitching W	Relief Pitching L	Relief Pitching SV	Batting AB	Batting H	HR	BA	PO	A	E	DP	TC/G	FA
1918	DET	A	0	0	—	4.50	1	0	0	2	2	2	0	0	0	0	1	*				46	5	4	0	2.5	.927

Peek-A-Boo Veach

VEACH, WILLIAM WALTER
B. June 15, 1862, Indianapolis, Ind. D. Nov. 12, 1937, Indianapolis, Ind.

Year	Team		W	L	PCT	ERA	G	GS	CG	IP	H	BB	SO	ShO	Relief Pitching W	Relief Pitching L	Relief Pitching SV	Batting AB	Batting H	HR	BA	PO	A	E	DP	TC/G	FA
1884	KC	U	3	9	.250	*2.42*	12	12	12	104	95	10	62	0	0	0	0	82	11	1	.134	33	28	6	4	2.4	.910
1887	LOU	AA	0	1	.000	4.00	1	1	1	9	5	8	2	0	0	0	0	3	0	0	.000	2	1	1	0	4.0	.750
2 yrs.			3	10	.231	2.55	13	13	13	113	100	18	64	0	0	0	0	*				756	73	30	42	8.5	.965

Bob Veale

VEALE, ROBERT ANDREW BB TL 6′ 6″ 212 lbs.
B. Oct. 28, 1935, Birmingham, Ala.

Year	Team		W	L	PCT	ERA	G	GS	CG	IP	H	BB	SO	ShO	Relief Pitching W	Relief Pitching L	Relief Pitching SV	Batting AB	Batting H	HR	BA	PO	A	E	DP	TC/G	FA
1962	PIT	N	2	2	.500	3.74	11	6	2	45.2	39	25	42	0	0	0	1	16	4	0	.250	0	6	0	0	0.5	1.000
1963			5	2	.714	1.04	34	7	3	77.2	59	40	68	2	1	0	3	23	2	0	.087	1	14	2	2	0.5	.882
1964			18	12	.600	2.74	40	38	14	279.2	222	**124**	**250**	1	0	0	0	96	15	0	.156	14	39	2	4	1.4	.964
1965			17	12	.586	2.84	39	37	14	266	221	**119**	276	7	0	0	0	93	8	0	.086	3	36	2	1	1.1	.951
1966			16	12	.571	3.02	38	37	12	268.1	228	102	229	3	0	0	0	94	13	0	.138	2	34	3	5	1.0	.923
1967			16	8	.667	3.64	33	31	6	203	184	**119**	179	1	0	0	0	69	3	0	.043	6	36	1	3	1.3	.977
1968			13	14	.481	2.05	36	33	13	245.1	187	**94**	171	4	0	1	0	82	9	0	.110	4	37	3	0	1.2	.932
1969			13	14	.481	3.23	34	34	9	226	232	91	213	1	0	0	0	79	4	0	.051	6	33	1	2	1.2	.975
1970			10	15	.400	3.92	34	32	5	202	189	94	178	1	0	0	0	67	11	0	.164	0	23	3	1	0.8	.885
1971			6	0	1.000	7.04	37	0	0	46	59	24	40	0	6	0	2	9	3	0	.333	1	1	3	0	0.1	.400
1972	**2 teams**	**PIT N** (5G 0–0)	**BOS A** (6G 2–0)																								
″	**total**		2	0	1.000	3.18	11	0	0	17	12	10	16	0	2	0	2	2	0	0	.000	0	2	1	0	0.3	.667
1973	BOS	A	2	3	.400	3.50	32	0	0	36	37	12	25	0	2	3	11	0	0	0	—	0	9	0	1	0.3	1.000
1974			0	1	.000	5.54	18	0	0	13	15	4	16	0	0	1	2	0	0	0	—	0	0	0	0	0.0	.000
13 yrs.			120	95	.558	3.08	397	255	78	1925.2	1684	858	1703	20	11	5	21	630	72	0	.114	37	270	21	19	0.8	.936
WORLD SERIES																											
1971	PIT	N	0	0	—	13.50	1	0	0	0.2	1	2	0	0	0	0	0	0	0	0	—	0	1	0	0	1.0	1.000

Lou Vedder

VEDDER, LOUIS EDWARD BR TR 5′10½″ 175 lbs.
B. Apr. 20, 1897, Oakville, Mich. D. Mar. 9, 1990, Lake Placid, Fla.

Year	Team		W	L	PCT	ERA	G	GS	CG	IP	H	BB	SO	ShO	Relief Pitching W	Relief Pitching L	Relief Pitching SV	Batting AB	Batting H	HR	BA	PO	A	E	DP	TC/G	FA
1920	DET	A	0	0	—	0.00	1	0	0	2	0	0	1	0	0	0	0	0	0	0	—	0	2	0	0	2.0	1.000

Al Veigel

VEIGEL, ALLEN FRANCIS BR TR 6′ 1″ 180 lbs.
B. Jan. 30, 1917, Dover, Ohio.

Year	Team		W	L	PCT	ERA	G	GS	CG	IP	H	BB	SO	ShO	Relief Pitching W	Relief Pitching L	Relief Pitching SV	Batting AB	Batting H	HR	BA	PO	A	E	DP	TC/G	FA
1939	BOS	N	0	1	.000	6.75	2	2	0	2.2	3	5	1	0	0	0	0	1	0	0	.000	0	0	1	0	0.5	.000

Bucky Veil

VEIL, FREDERICK WILLIAM BR TR 5′10½″ 165 lbs.
B. Aug. 2, 1881, Tyrone, Pa. D. Apr. 16, 1931, Altoona, Pa.

Year	Team		W	L	PCT	ERA	G	GS	CG	IP	H	BB	SO	ShO	Relief Pitching W	Relief Pitching L	Relief Pitching SV	Batting AB	Batting H	HR	BA	PO	A	E	DP	TC/G	FA
1903	PIT	N	5	4	.556	3.82	12	6	4	70.2	70	36	20	0	**2**	0	0	29	6	0	.207	4	17	0	0	1.8	1.000
1904			0	0	—	5.79	1	1	0	4.2	4	4	1	0	0	0	0	1	1	0	1.000	0	2	0	0	2.0	1.000
2 yrs.			5	4	.556	3.94	13	7	4	75.1	74	40	21	0	2	0	0	30	7	0	.233	4	19	0	0	1.8	1.000
WORLD SERIES																											
1903	PIT	N	0	0	—	1.29	1	0	0	7	6	4	1	0	0	0	0	2	0	0	.000	0	0	1	0	1.0	.000

Carlos Velazquez

VELAZQUEZ, CARLOS BR TR 5′11″ 180 lbs.
Born Carlos Velazquez (Quinones).
B. Mar. 22, 1948, Loiza, Puerto Rico.

Year	Team	Lg	W	L	PCT	ERA	G	GS	CG	IP	H	BB	SO	ShO	Relief W	Relief L	SV	AB	Batting H	HR	BA	PO	A	E	DP	TC/G	FA
1973	MIL	A	2	2	.500	2.58	18	0	0	38.1	46	10	12	0	2	2	2	0	0	0	—	2	7	0	0	0.5	1.000

Joe Verbanic

VERBANIC, JOSEPH MICHAEL BR TR 6′ 155 lbs.
B. Apr. 24, 1943, Washington, Pa.

Year	Team	Lg	W	L	PCT	ERA	G	GS	CG	IP	H	BB	SO	ShO	Relief W	Relief L	SV	AB	Batting H	HR	BA	PO	A	E	DP	TC/G	FA
1966	PHI	N	1	1	.500	5.14	17	0	0	14	12	10	7	0	1	1	0	0	0	0	—	1	2	1	0	0.2	.750
1967	NY	A	4	3	.571	2.80	28	6	1	80.1	74	21	39	1	1	1	2	18	2	0	.111	9	19	0	2	1.0	1.000
1968			6	7	.462	3.15	40	11	2	97	104	41	40	1	3	3	4	25	2	0	.080	6	21	3	4	0.8	.900
1970			1	0	1.000	4.50	7	0	0	16	20	12	8	0	1	0	0	3	1	0	.333	2	7	0	0	1.3	1.000
4 yrs.			12	11	.522	3.26	92	17	3	207.1	210	84	94	2	6	5	6	46	5	0	.109	18	49	4	6	0.8	.944

Al Verdel

VERDEL, ALBERT ALFRED (Stumpy) BR TR 5′ 9½″ 186 lbs.
B. June 10, 1921, Punxsutawney, Pa. D. Apr. 16, 1991, Sarasota, Fla.

Year	Team	Lg	W	L	PCT	ERA	G	GS	CG	IP	H	BB	SO	ShO	Relief W	Relief L	SV	AB	Batting H	HR	BA	PO	A	E	DP	TC/G	FA
1944	PHI	N	0	0	—	0.00	1	0	0	1	0	0	0	0	0	0	0	0	0	0	—	0	0	0	0	0.0	.000

Tommy Vereker

VEREKER, JOHN JAMES 5′10″ 185 lbs.
B. Dec. 2, 1893, Baltimore, Md. D. Apr. 2, 1974, Baltimore, Md.

Year	Team	Lg	W	L	PCT	ERA	G	GS	CG	IP	H	BB	SO	ShO	Relief W	Relief L	SV	AB	Batting H	HR	BA	PO	A	E	DP	TC/G	FA
1915	BAL	F	0	0	—	15.00	2	0	0	3	3	2	1	0	0	0	0	0	0	0	—	0	1	0	0	0.5	1.000

David Veres

VERES, DAVID SCOTT BR TR 6′ 2″ 195 lbs.
B. Oct. 19, 1966, Montgomery, Ala.

Year	Team	Lg	W	L	PCT	ERA	G	GS	CG	IP	H	BB	SO	ShO	Relief W	Relief L	SV	AB	Batting H	HR	BA	PO	A	E	DP	TC/G	FA
1994	HOU	N	3	3	.500	2.41	32	0	0	41	39	7	28	0	3	3	1	2	1	0	.500	5	2	0	0	0.2	1.000
1995			5	1	.833	2.26	72	0	0	103.1	89	30	94	0	5	1	1	5	0	0	.000	6	11	1	0	0.3	.944
2 yrs.			8	4	.667	2.31	104	0	0	144.1	128	37	122	0	8	4	2	7	1	0	.143	11	13	1	0	0.2	.960

Randy Veres

VERES, RANDOLPH RUHLAND BR TR 6′ 3″ 190 lbs.
B. Nov. 25, 1965, San Francisco, Calif.

Year	Team	Lg	W	L	PCT	ERA	G	GS	CG	IP	H	BB	SO	ShO	Relief W	Relief L	SV	AB	Batting H	HR	BA	PO	A	E	DP	TC/G	FA
1989	MIL	A	0	1	.000	4.32	3	1	0	8.1	9	4	8	0	0	0	0	0	0	0	—	0	1	0	0	0.3	1.000
1990			0	3	.000	3.67	26	0	0	41.2	38	16	16	0	0	3	1	0	0	0	—	2	10	0	2	0.5	1.000
1994	CHI	N	1	1	.500	5.59	10	0	0	9.2	12	2	5	0	1	1	0	1	0	0	.000	0	2	0	0	0.2	1.000
1995	FLA	N	4	4	.500	3.88	47	0	0	48.2	46	22	31	0	4	4	1	3	0	0	.000	2	3	1	0	0.1	.833
4 yrs.			5	9	.357	3.99	86	1	0	108.1	105	44	60	0	5	8	2	4	0	0	.000	4	16	1	2	0.2	.952

John Verhoeven

VERHOEVEN, JOHN C. BR TR 6′ 5″ 200 lbs.
B. July 3, 1953, Long Beach, Calif.

Year	Team	Lg	W	L	PCT	ERA	G	GS	CG	IP	H	BB	SO	ShO	Relief W	Relief L	SV	AB	Batting H	HR	BA	PO	A	E	DP	TC/G	FA
1976	CAL	A	0	2	.000	3.41	21	0	0	37	35	14	23	0	0	2	4	0	0	0	—	4	10	0	0	0.7	1.000
1977	2 teams CAL A (3G 0–2) CHI A (6G 0–0)																										
″	total		0	2	.000	2.40	9	0	0	15	13	6	9	0	0	2	0	0	0	0		1	6	0	0	0.8	1.000
1980	MIN	A	3	4	.429	3.96	44	0	0	100	109	29	42	0	3	4	0	0	0	0	—	4	17	3	2	0.5	.875
1981			0	0	—	3.98	25	0	0	52	57	14	16	0	0	0	0	0	0	0	—	0	11	0	1	0.4	1.000
4 yrs.			3	8	.273	3.75	99	0	0	204	214	63	90	0	3	8	4	0	0	0		9	44	3	3	0.6	.946

Joe Vernon

VERNON, JOSEPH HENRY BR TR 5′11″ 160 lbs.
B. Nov. 25, 1889, Mansfield, Mass. D. Mar. 13, 1955, Philadelphia, Pa.

Year	Team	Lg	W	L	PCT	ERA	G	GS	CG	IP	H	BB	SO	ShO	Relief W	Relief L	SV	AB	Batting H	HR	BA	PO	A	E	DP	TC/G	FA
1912	CHI	N	0	0	—	11.25	1	0	0	4	4	6	1	0	0	0	0	2	0	0	.000	0	0	0	0	0.0	.000
1914	BKN	F	0	0	—	10.80	1	1	0	3.1	4	5	0	0	0	0	0	1	0	0	.000	0	1	0	0	1.0	1.000
2 yrs.			0	0		11.05	2	1	0	7.1	8	11	1	0	0	0	0	3	0	0	.000	0	1	0	0	0.5	1.000

Bob Veselic

VESELIC, ROBERT MITCHELL BR TR 6′ 175 lbs.
B. Sept. 27, 1955, Pittsburgh, Pa. D. Dec. 26, 1995, Los Angeles, Calif.

Year	Team	Lg	W	L	PCT	ERA	G	GS	CG	IP	H	BB	SO	ShO	Relief W	Relief L	SV	AB	Batting H	HR	BA	PO	A	E	DP	TC/G	FA
1980	MIN	A	0	0	—	4.50	1	0	0	4	3	1	2	0	0	0	0	0	0	0	—	0	0	0	0	0.0	.000
1981			1	1	.500	3.13	5	0	0	23	22	12	13	0	1	1	0	0	0	0	—	1	1	0	0	0.4	1.000
2 yrs.			1	1	.500	3.33	6	0	0	27	25	13	15	0	1	1	0	0	0	0		1	1	0	0	0.3	1.000

Lee Viau

VIAU, LEON A. BR TR 5′ 4″ 160 lbs.
B. July 5, 1866, Corinth, Vt. D. Dec. 17, 1947, Hopewell, N. J.

Year	Team	Lg	W	L	PCT	ERA	G	GS	CG	IP	H	BB	SO	ShO	Relief W	Relief L	SV	AB	Batting H	HR	BA	PO	A	E	DP	TC/G	FA
1888	CIN	AA	27	14	.659	2.65	42	42	42	387.2	331	110	164	1	0	0	0	149	13	0	.087	18	78	9	0	2.4	.914
1889			22	20	.524	3.79	47	42	38	373	379	136	152	1	1	0	1	147	21	0	.143	9	61	4	2	1.5	.946
1890	2 teams CIN N (13G 7–5) CLE N (13G 4–9)																										
″	total		11	14	.440	3.88	26	23	20	197	198	81	71	2	**2**	0	0	79	12	0	.152	6	51	7	0	2.5	.891
1891	CLE	N	18	17	.514	3.01	45	38	31	343.2	367	138	130	0	2	1	0	144	23	0	.160	12	79	14	2	2.3	.867
1892	3 teams CLE N (1G 0–1) LOU N (16G 4–11) BOS N (1G 1–0)																										
″	total		5	12	.294	3.97	18	17	15	140.2	166	61	37	1	0	0	0	69	13	0	.188	15	43	4	5	2.7	.935
5 yrs.			83	77	.519	3.33	178	162	146	1442	1441	526	554	5	5	1	1	588	82	0	.139	60	312	38	9	2.2	.907

Rube Vickers

VICKERS, HARRY PORTER BL TR 6′ 2″ 225 lbs.
B. May 17, 1878, St. Mary'S, Ont., Canada D. Dec. 9, 1958, Belleville, Mich.

Year	Team	Lg	W	L	PCT	ERA	G	GS	CG	IP	H	BB	SO	ShO	Relief W	Relief L	SV	AB	Batting H	HR	BA	PO	A	E	DP	TC/G	FA
1902	CIN	N	0	3	.000	6.00	3	3	3	21	31	8	6	0	0	0	0	11	4	0	.364	0	4	0	0	1.0	1.000
1903	BKN	N	0	1	.000	10.93	4	1	1	14	27	9	5	0	0	0	0	10	1	0	.100	1	10	1	0	2.4	.917
1907	PHI	A	2	2	.500	3.40	10	4	3	50.1	44	12	21	1	1	0	0	20	3	0	.150	2	17	1	1	2.0	.950
1908			18	19	.486	2.21	53	34	21	317	264	71	156	6	**6**	2	1	106	17	0	.160	10	83	7	0	1.9	.930
1909			2	2	.500	3.40	18	3	1	55.2	60	19	25	0	1	1	1	16	1	0	.063	3	11	1	0	0.8	.933
5 yrs.			22	27	.449	2.93	88	45	29	458	426	119	213	7	8	3	2	163	26	0	.160	16	125	10	1	1.7	.934

Tom Vickery

VICKERY, THOMAS GILL TR 6′ 170 lbs.
B. May 5, 1867, Milford, N. J. D. Mar. 21, 1921, Burlington, N. J.

Year	Team	Lg	W	L	PCT	ERA	G	GS	CG	IP	H	BB	SO	ShO	Relief W	Relief L	SV	AB	Batting H	HR	BA	PO	A	E	DP	TC/G	FA
1890	PHI	N	24	22	.522	3.44	46	46	41	382	405	184	162	1	0	0	0	159	33	0	.208	17	71	20	3	2.3	.815
1891	CHI	N	5	5	.500	4.07	14	12	7	79.2	72	44	39	0	0	0	0	39	7	0	.179	6	21	3	1	2.0	.900
1892	BAL	N	8	10	.444	3.53	24	21	17	176	189	87	49	0	0	0	0	74	18	0	.243	11	30	5	1	1.9	.891
1893	PHI	N	4	5	.444	5.40	13	11	7	80	100	37	15	0	1	1	0	35	11	0	.314	6	28	2	3	2.6	.944
4 yrs.			41	42	.494	3.75	97	90	72	717.2	766	352	265	1	1	1	0	307	69	0	.225	40	150	30	8	2.2	.864

Ron Villone

VILLONE, RONALD THOMAS, JR. BL TL 6′ 3″ 230 lbs.
B. Jan. 16, 1970, Englewood, N. J.

Year	Team	W	L	PCT	ERA	G	GS	CG	IP	H	BB	SO	ShO	Relief W	Relief L	Relief SV	Batting AB	Batting H	HR	BA	PO	A	E	DP	TC/G	FA
1995	2 teams SEA A (19G 0–2) SD N (19G 2–1)																									
″	total	2	3	.400	5.80	38	0	0	45	44	34	63	0	2	3	1	1	0	0	.000	0	4	1	0	0.1	.800

Bob Vines

VINES, ROBERT EARL BR TR 6′ 4″ 184 lbs.
B. Feb. 25, 1897, Waxahachie, Tex. D. Oct. 18, 1982, Orlando, Fla.

Year	Team	W	L	PCT	ERA	G	GS	CG	IP	H	BB	SO	ShO	Relief W	Relief L	Relief SV	Batting AB	Batting H	HR	BA	PO	A	E	DP	TC/G	FA
1924	STL N	0	0	—	9.28	2	0	0	10.2	23	0	0	0	0	0	0	4	0	0	.000	0	2	0	0	1.0	1.000
1925	PHI N	0	0	—	11.25	3	0	0	4	9	3	0	0	0	0	0	0	0	0	—	0	1	0	0	0.3	1.000
2 yrs.		0	0		9.82	5	0	0	14.2	32	3	0	0	0	0	0	4	0	0	.000	0	3	0	0	0.6	1.000

Dave Vineyard

VINEYARD, DAVID KENT BR TR 6′ 3″ 195 lbs.
B. Feb. 25, 1941, Clay, W. Va.

Year	Team	W	L	PCT	ERA	G	GS	CG	IP	H	BB	SO	ShO	Relief W	Relief L	Relief SV	Batting AB	Batting H	HR	BA	PO	A	E	DP	TC/G	FA
1964	BAL A	2	5	.286	4.17	19	6	1	54	57	27	50	0	0	1	0	12	2	0	.167	2	5	0	0	0.4	1.000

Bill Vinton

VINTON, WILLIAM MILLER BR TR 6′ 1″ 170 lbs.
B. Apr. 27, 1865, Winthrop, Mass. D. Sept. 3, 1893, Pawtucket, R. I.

Year	Team	W	L	PCT	ERA	G	GS	CG	IP	H	BB	SO	ShO	Relief W	Relief L	Relief SV	Batting AB	Batting H	HR	BA	PO	A	E	DP	TC/G	FA
1884	PHI N	10	10	.500	*2.23*	21	21	20	182	166	35	105	0	0	0	0	78	9	0	.115	9	50	6	1	3.0	.908
1885	2 teams PHI N (9G 3–6) PHI AA (7G 4–3)																									
″	total	7	9	.438	2.80	16	16	14	132	136	38	55	2	0	0	0	56	6	0	.107	4	30	11	0	2.5	.756
2 yrs.		17	19	.472	2.46	37	37	34	314	302	73	160	2	0	0	0	134	15	0	.112	13	80	17	1	2.8	.845

Frank Viola

VIOLA, FRANK JOHN, JR. (Sweet Music) BL TL 6′ 4″ 195 lbs.
B. Apr. 19, 1960, Hempstead, N. Y.

Year	Team	W	L	PCT	ERA	G	GS	CG	IP	H	BB	SO	ShO	Relief W	Relief L	Relief SV	Batting AB	Batting H	HR	BA	PO	A	E	DP	TC/G	FA
1982	MIN A	4	10	.286	5.21	22	22	3	126	152	38	84	1	0	0	0	0	0	0	—	1	15	2	0	0.8	.889
1983		7	15	.318	5.49	35	34	4	210	242	92	127	0	0	0	0	0	0	0	—	7	23	1	2	0.9	.968
1984		18	12	.600	3.21	35	35	10	257.2	225	73	149	4	0	0	0	0	0	0	—	6	26	1	1	0.9	.970
1985		18	14	.563	4.09	36	36	9	250.2	262	68	135	0	0	0	0	0	0	0	—	6	33	5	0	1.2	.886
1986		16	13	.552	4.51	37	**37**	7	245.2	257	83	191	1	0	0	0	0	0	0	—	8	21	3	1	0.9	.906
1987		17	10	.630	2.90	36	36	7	251.2	230	66	197	1	0	0	0	0	0	0	—	6	34	3	1	1.2	.930
1988		**24**	7	**.774**	2.64	35	35	7	255.1	236	54	193	2	0	0	0	0	0	0	—	5	30	2	1	1.1	.946
1989	2 teams MIN A (24G 8–12) NY N (12G 5–5)																									
″	total	13	17	.433	3.66	36	36	9	261	246	74	211	2	0	0	0	23	3	0	.130	10	35	4	3	1.4	.918
1990	NY N	20	12	.625	2.67	35	**35**	7	**249.2**	227	60	182	3	0	0	0	85	13	0	.153	11	34	1	1	1.3	.978
1991		13	15	.464	3.97	35	35	3	231.1	**259**	54	132	0	0	0	0	71	9	0	.127	6	34	4	1	1.3	.909
1992	BOS A	13	12	.520	3.44	35	35	6	238	214	89	121	1	0	0	0	0	0	0	—	6	47	2	6	1.6	.964
1993		11	8	.579	3.14	29	29	2	183.2	180	72	91	1	0	0	0	0	0	0	—	10	31	4	1	1.6	.911
1994		1	1	.500	4.65	6	6	0	31	34	17	9	0	0	0	0	0	0	0	—	0	4	0	1	0.7	1.000
1995	CIN N	0	1	.000	6.28	3	3	0	14.1	20	3	4	0	0	0	0	6	1	0	.167	0	2	0	0	0.7	1.000
14 yrs.		175	147	.543	3.69	415	414	74	2806	2784	843	1826	16	0	0	0	185	26	0	.141	82	369	32	19	1.2	.934
LEAGUE CHAMPIONSHIP SERIES																										
1987	MIN A	1	0	1.000	5.25	2	2	0	12	14	5	9	0	0	0	0	0	0	0	—	0	1	0	0	0.5	1.000
WORLD SERIES																										
1987	MIN A	2	1	.667	3.72	3	3	0	19.1	17	3	16	0	0	0	0	1	0	0	.000	1	5	0	0	2.0	1.000

Jake Virtue

VIRTUE, JACOB KITCHLINE BB TL 5′ 9½″ 165 lbs.
B. Mar. 2, 1865, Philadelphia, Pa. D. Feb. 3, 1943, Camden, N. J.

Year	Team	W	L	PCT	ERA	G	GS	CG	IP	H	BB	SO	ShO	Relief W	Relief L	Relief SV	Batting AB	Batting H	HR	BA	PO	A	E	DP	TC/G	FA
1893	CLE N	0	0	—	1.80	1	0	0	5	3	3	2	0	0	0	0	378	100	1	.265	633	21	12	33	10.7	.982
1894		0	0	—	0.00	1	0	0		0	1	0	0	0	0	0	89	23	0	.258	65	8	7	0	3.0	.913
2 yrs.		0	0		1.80	2	0	0	5	3	4	2	0	0	0	0	*				4483	210	117	214	10.2	.976

Joe Vitelli

VITELLI, ANTONIO JOSEPH BR TR 6′ 1″ 195 lbs.
B. Apr. 12, 1908, McKees Rocks, Pa. D. Feb. 7, 1967, Pittsburgh, Pa.

Year	Team	W	L	PCT	ERA	G	GS	CG	IP	H	BB	SO	ShO	Relief W	Relief L	Relief SV	Batting AB	Batting H	HR	BA	PO	A	E	DP	TC/G	FA
1944	PIT N	0	0	—	2.57	4	0	0	7	5	7	2	0	0	0	0	3	0	0	.000	1	2	1	0	1.0	.750

Joe Vitko

VITKO, JOSEPH JOHN BR TR 6′ 8″ 210 lbs.
B. Feb. 1, 1970, Somerville, N. J.

Year	Team	W	L	PCT	ERA	G	GS	CG	IP	H	BB	SO	ShO	Relief W	Relief L	Relief SV	Batting AB	Batting H	HR	BA	PO	A	E	DP	TC/G	FA
1992	NY N	0	1	.000	13.50	3	1	0	4.2	12	1	6	0	0	0	0	0	0	0	—	1	0	2	0	1.0	.333

Ollie Voigt

VOIGT, OLEN EDWARD BR TR 6′ 1″ 170 lbs.
B. Jan. 29, 1900, Wheaton, Ill. D. Apr. 7, 1970, Scottsdale, Ariz.

Year	Team	W	L	PCT	ERA	G	GS	CG	IP	H	BB	SO	ShO	Relief W	Relief L	Relief SV	Batting AB	Batting H	HR	BA	PO	A	E	DP	TC/G	FA
1924	STL A	1	0	1.000	5.51	8	1	0	16.1	21	13	4	0	1	0	0	4	1	0	.250	0	9	2	0	1.4	.818

Bill Voiselle

VOISELLE, WILLIAM SYMMES (Big Bill, Ninety-Six) BR TR 6′ 4″ 200 lbs.
B. Jan. 29, 1919, Greenwood, S. C.

Year	Team	W	L	PCT	ERA	G	GS	CG	IP	H	BB	SO	ShO	Relief W	Relief L	Relief SV	Batting AB	Batting H	HR	BA	PO	A	E	DP	TC/G	FA
1942	NY N	0	1	.000	2.00	2	1	0	9	6	4	5	0	0	0	0	2	0	0	.000	1	3	0	0	2.0	1.000
1943		1	2	.333	2.03	4	4	3	31	18	14	19	0	0	0	0	9	1	0	.111	2	2	1	0	1.3	.800
1944		21	16	.568	3.02	43	**41**	25	**312.2**	276	118	**161**	1	1	0	0	105	22	0	.210	9	42	6	4	1.3	.895
1945		14	14	.500	4.49	41	**35**	14	232.1	249	97	115	4	1	0	0	79	10	0	.127	11	41	1	3	1.3	.981
1946		9	15	.375	3.74	36	25	10	178	171	85	89	2	1	1	0	55	9	0	.164	14	29	3	3	1.3	.935
1947	2 teams NY N (11G 1–4) BOS N (22G 8–7)																									
″	total	9	11	.450	4.40	33	25	8	174	190	73	71	0	1	1	0	68	11	0	.162	6	34	1	4	1.2	.976
1948	BOS N	13	13	.500	3.63	37	30	9	215.2	226	90	89	2	2	0	2	72	7	0	.097	6	33	5	0	1.2	.886
1949		7	8	.467	4.04	30	22	5	169.1	170	78	63	4	1	0	1	61	7	0	.115	7	34	2	2	1.4	.953
1950	CHI N	0	4	.000	5.79	19	7	0	51.1	64	29	25	0	0	0	0	13	1	0	.077	3	6	1	0	0.5	.900
9 yrs.		74	84	.468	3.83	245	190	74	1373.1	1370	588	637	13	7	2	3	464	68	0	.147	59	224	20	16	1.2	.934
WORLD SERIES																										
1948	BOS N	0	1	.000	2.53	2	1	0	10.2	8	2	2	0	0	0	0	2	0	0	.000	1	0	0	0	0.5	1.000

Jake Volz

VOLZ, JACOB PHILLIP (Silent Jake) BR TR 5′10″ 175 lbs.
B. Apr. 4, 1878, San Antonio, Tex. D. Aug. 11, 1962, San Antonio, Tex.

Year	Team	W	L	PCT	ERA	G	GS	CG	IP	H	BB	SO	ShO	Relief W	Relief L	Relief SV	Batting AB	Batting H	HR	BA	PO	A	E	DP	TC/G	FA
1901	BOS A	1	0	1.000	9.00	1	1	1	7	6	9	5	0	0	0	0	4	0	0	.000	0	0	2	0	2.0	.000
1905	BOS N	0	2	.000	10.38	3	2	0	8.2	12	8	1	0	0	0	0	2	0	0	.000	0	0	0	0	0.0	.000
1908	CIN N	1	2	.333	3.57	7	4	1	22.2	16	12	6	0	0	0	0	4	1	0	.250	0	2	0	0	0.3	1.000
3 yrs.		2	4	.333	6.10	11	7	2	38.1	34	29	12	0	0	0	0	10	1	0	.100	0	2	2	0	0.4	.500

Hon Von Fricken

VON FRICKEN, ANTHONY BB TR 5′11½″ 160 lbs.
B. May 30, 1870, Brooklyn, N. Y. D. Mar. 22, 1947, Troy, N. Y.

Year	Team	W	L	PCT	ERA	G	GS	CG	IP	H	BB	SO	ShO	Relief W	Relief L	Relief SV	Batting AB	Batting H	HR	BA	PO	A	E	DP	TC/G	FA
1890	**BOS** **N**	0	1	.000	10.13	1	1	1	8	23	8	2	0	0	0	0	3	0	0	.000	0	2	2	0	4.0	.500

Bruce Von Hoff

VON HOFF, BRUCE FREDERICK BR TR 6′ 187 lbs.
B. Nov. 17, 1943, Oakland, Calif.

Year	Team	W	L	PCT	ERA	G	GS	CG	IP	H	BB	SO	ShO	Relief W	Relief L	Relief SV	Batting AB	Batting H	HR	BA	PO	A	E	DP	TC/G	FA
1965	**HOU** **N**	0	0	—	9.00	3	0	0	3	3	2	1	0	0	0	0	0	0	0	—	0	0	0	0	0.0	.000
1967		0	3	.000	4.83	10	10	0	50.1	52	28	22	0	0	0	0	15	1	0	.067	1	5	0	0	0.6	1.000
2 yrs.		0	3	.000	5.06	13	10	0	53.1	55	30	23	0	0	0	0	15	1	0	.067	1	5	0	0	0.5	1.000

Dave Von Ohlen

VON OHLEN, DAVID BL TL 6′ 2″ 200 lbs.
B. Oct. 25, 1958, Flushing, N. Y.

Year	Team	W	L	PCT	ERA	G	GS	CG	IP	H	BB	SO	ShO	Relief W	Relief L	Relief SV	Batting AB	Batting H	HR	BA	PO	A	E	DP	TC/G	FA
1983	**STL** **N**	3	2	.600	3.29	46	0	0	68.1	71	25	21	0	3	2	2	7	1	0	.143	2	11	1	1	0.3	.929
1984		1	0	1.000	3.12	27	0	0	34.2	39	8	19	0	1	0	1	1	1	0	1.000	2	10	0	2	0.4	1.000
1985	**CLE** **A**	3	2	.600	2.91	26	0	0	43.1	47	20	12	0	3	2	0	0	0	0	—	2	9	0	1	0.4	1.000
1986	**OAK** **A**	0	3	.000	3.52	24	0	0	15.1	18	7	4	0	0	3	1	0	0	0	—	0	5	0	0	0.2	1.000
1987		0	0	—	7.50	4	0	0	6	10	1	3	0	0	0	0	0	0	0	—	0	0	0	0	0.0	.000
5 yrs.		7	7	.500	3.33	127	0	0	167.2	185	61	59	0	7	7	4	8	2	0	.250	6	35	1	4	0.3	.976

Cy Vorhees

VORHEES, HENRY BERT 6′ 3″ 200 lbs.
B. Sept. 30, 1874, Lodi, Ohio D. Feb. 8, 1910, Perry, Ohio.

Year	Team	W	L	PCT	ERA	G	GS	CG	IP	H	BB	SO	ShO	Relief W	Relief L	Relief SV	Batting AB	Batting H	HR	BA	PO	A	E	DP	TC/G	FA
1902	**2 teams** **PHI N** (10G 3–3) **WAS A** (1G 0–1)																									
″	**total**	3	4	.429	3.94	11	6	4	61.2	73	22	25	1	1	1	0	23	9	0	.391	2	12	3	0	1.5	.824

Ed Vosberg

VOSBERG, EDWARD JOHN BL TL 6′ 1″ 190 lbs.
B. Sept. 28, 1961, Tucson, Ariz.

Year	Team	W	L	PCT	ERA	G	GS	CG	IP	H	BB	SO	ShO	Relief W	Relief L	Relief SV	Batting AB	Batting H	HR	BA	PO	A	E	DP	TC/G	FA
1986	**SD** **N**	0	1	.000	6.59	5	3	0	13.2	17	9	8	0	0	0	0	2	0	0	.000	0	1	1	0	0.4	.500
1990	**SF** **N**	1	1	.500	5.55	18	0	0	24.1	21	12	12	0	1	1	0	0	0	0	—	1	5	0	0	0.3	1.000
1994	**OAK** **A**	0	2	.000	3.95	16	0	0	13.2	16	5	12	0	0	2	0	0	0	0	—	2	5	0	1	0.4	1.000
1995	**TEX** **A**	5	5	.500	3.00	44	0	0	36	32	16	36	0	5	5	4	0	0	0	—	0	1	1	0	0.0	.500
4 yrs.		6	9	.400	4.41	83	3	0	87.2	86	42	68	0	6	8	4	2	0	0	.000	3	12	2	1	0.2	.882

Alex Voss

VOSS, ALEXANDER BR TR 6′ 1″ 180 lbs.
B. May 16, 1858, Roswell, Ga. D. Aug. 31, 1906, Cincinnati, Ohio.

Year	Team	W	L	PCT	ERA	G	GS	CG	IP	H	BB	SO	ShO	Relief W	Relief L	Relief SV	Batting AB	Batting H	HR	BA	PO	A	E	DP	TC/G	FA
1884	**2 teams** **WAS U** (27G 5–14) **KC U** (7G 0–6)																									
″	**total**	5	20	.200	3.72	34	26	24	239.1	280	39	129	0	0	1	0	*				180	113	36	11	3.8	.891

Rip Vowinkel

VOWINKEL, JOHN HENRY BR TR 5′10″ 195 lbs.
B. Nov. 18, 1884, Oswego, N. Y. D. July 13, 1966, Oswego, N. Y.

Year	Team	W	L	PCT	ERA	G	GS	CG	IP	H	BB	SO	ShO	Relief W	Relief L	Relief SV	Batting AB	Batting H	HR	BA	PO	A	E	DP	TC/G	FA
1905	**CIN** **N**	3	3	.500	4.20	6	6	4	45	52	10	7	0	0	0	0	14	1	0	.071	1	6	1	0	1.3	.875

Pete Vuckovich

VUCKOVICH, PETER DENNIS BR TR 6′ 4″ 215 lbs.
B. Oct. 27, 1952, Johnstown, Pa.

Year	Team	W	L	PCT	ERA	G	GS	CG	IP	H	BB	SO	ShO	Relief W	Relief L	Relief SV	Batting AB	Batting H	HR	BA	PO	A	E	DP	TC/G	FA
1975	**CHI** **A**	0	1	.000	13.06	4	2	0	10.1	17	7	5	0	0	0	0	0	0	0	—	1	2	0	0	0.8	1.000
1976		7	4	.636	4.66	33	7	1	110	122	60	62	0	2	2	0	0	0	0	—	3	19	3	0	0.8	.880
1977	**TOR** **A**	7	7	.500	3.47	53	8	3	148	143	59	123	1	5	3	8	0	0	0	—	9	23	5	3	0.7	.865
1978	**STL** **N**	12	12	.500	2.55	45	23	6	198	187	59	149	2	1	4	1	58	8	0	.138	12	34	2	4	1.1	.958
1979		15	10	.600	3.59	34	32	9	233	229	64	145	0	0	1	0	79	12	0	.152	14	28	5	2	1.4	.894
1980		12	9	.571	3.41	32	30	7	222	203	68	132	3	0	0	1	71	13	0	.183	16	28	1	3	1.4	.978
1981	**MIL** **A**	**14**	4	**.778**	3.54	24	23	2	150	137	57	84	1	0	0	0	0	0	0	—	11	27	0	1	1.6	1.000
1982		18	6	**.750**	3.34	30	30	9	223.2	234	102	105	1	0	0	0	0	0	0	—	13	39	4	1	1.9	.929
1983		0	2	.000	4.91	3	3	0	14.2	15	10	10	0	0	0	0	0	0	0	—	1	1	0	0	0.7	1.000
1985		6	10	.375	5.51	22	22	1	112.2	134	48	55	0	0	0	0	0	0	0	—	5	14	1	1	0.9	.950
1986		2	4	.333	3.06	6	6	0	32.1	33	11	12	0	0	0	0	0	0	0	—	2	7	0	0	1.5	1.000
11 yrs.		93	69	.574	3.66	286	186	38	1454.2	1454	545	882	8	8	10	10	208	33	0	.159	87	222	21	15	1.2	.936
DIVISIONAL PLAYOFF SERIES																										
1981	**MIL** **A**	1	0	1.000	0.00	2	1	0	5.1	2	3	4	0	0	0	0	0	0	0	—	0	0	0	0	0.0	.000
LEAGUE CHAMPIONSHIP SERIES																										
1982	**MIL** **A**	0	1	.000	4.40	2	2	1	14.1	15	7	8	0	0	0	0	0	0	0	—	0	3	0	0	1.5	1.000
WORLD SERIES																										
1982	**MIL** **A**	0	1	.000	4.50	2	2	0	14	16	5	4	0	0	0	0	0	0	0	—	0	2	0	0	1.0	1.000

Paul Wachtel

WACHTEL, PAUL HORINE BR TR 5′11″ 175 lbs.
B. Apr. 30, 1888, Myersville, Md. D. Dec. 15, 1964, San Antonio, Tex.

Year	Team	W	L	PCT	ERA	G	GS	CG	IP	H	BB	SO	ShO	Relief W	Relief L	Relief SV	Batting AB	Batting H	HR	BA	PO	A	E	DP	TC/G	FA
1917	**BKN** **N**	0	0	—	10.50	2	0	0	6	9	4	3	0	0	0	0	3	1	0	.333	0	0	0	0	0.0	.000

Charlie Wacker

WACKER, CHARLES JAMES BL TL 5′ 9″
B. Dec. 8, 1883, Jeffersonville, Ind. D. Aug. 7, 1948, Evansville, Ind.

Year	Team	W	L	PCT	ERA	G	GS	CG	IP	H	BB	SO	ShO	Relief W	Relief L	Relief SV	Batting AB	Batting H	HR	BA	PO	A	E	DP	TC/G	FA
1909	**PIT** **N**	0	0	—	0.00	1	0	0	2	2	1	0	0	0	0	0	0	0	0	—	0	1	0	0	1.0	1.000

Rube Waddell

WADDELL, GEORGE EDWARD BR TL 6′ 1½″ 196 lbs.
B. Oct. 13, 1876, Bradford, Pa. D. Apr. 1, 1914, San Antonio, Tex.
Hall of Fame 1946.

Year	Team	W	L	PCT	ERA	G	GS	CG	IP	H	BB	SO	ShO	Relief W	Relief L	Relief SV	Batting AB	Batting H	HR	BA	PO	A	E	DP	TC/G	FA
1897	**LOU** **N**	0	1	.000	3.21	2	1	1	14	17	6	5	0	0	0	0	6	0	0	.000	0	4	0	0	2.0	1.000
1899		7	2	.778	3.08	10	9	9	79	69	14	44	1	0	0	1	34	8	0	.235	4	14	2	1	2.0	.900
1900	**PIT** **N**	8	13	.381	**2.37**	29	22	16	208.2	176	55	**130**	2	0	**3**	0	81	14	0	.173	12	49	5	1	2.3	.924
1901	**2 teams** **PIT N** (2G 0–2) **CHI N** (29G 13–15)																									
″	**total**	13	17	.433	3.01	31	30	26	251.1	249	75	172	0	0	1	0	101	25	2	.248	38	66	5	1	3.4	.954
1902	**PHI** **A**	24	7	.774	2.05	33	27	26	276.1	224	64	**210**	3	**5**	0	0	112	32	1	.286	15	64	7	1	2.6	.919
1903		21	16	.568	2.44	39	38	**34**	324	274	85	**302**	4	0	0	0	115	14	0	.122	17	77	7	3	2.6	.931
1904		25	19	.568	1.62	46	46	39	383	307	91	**349**	8	0	0	0	139	17	0	.122	27	105	9	2	3.1	.936
1905		**27**	10	**.730**	**1.48**	**46**	34	27	328.2	231	90	**287**	7	**8**	0	0	116	20	0	.172	13	89	15	3	2.5	.872
1906		15	17	.469	2.21	43	34	22	272.2	221	92	**196**	8	2	0	0	86	14	0	.163	15	64	6	0	2.0	.929
1907		19	13	.594	2.15	44	33	20	284.2	234	73	**232**	7	3	0	0	97	12	0	.124	16	67	12	3	2.2	.874

Rube Waddell *continued*

Year	Team	W	L	PCT	ERA	G	GS	CG	IP	H	BB	SO	ShO	Relief Pitching W	L	SV	Batting AB	H	HR	BA	PO	A	E	DP	TC/G	FA
1908	STL A	19	14	.576	1.89	43	36	25	285.2	223	90	232	5	1	1	3	91	10	1	.110	5	79	10	1	2.2	.894
1909		11	14	.440	2.37	31	28	16	220.1	204	57	141	5	1	0	0	75	5	0	.067	13	56	11	1	2.6	.863
1910		3	1	.750	3.55	10	2	0	33	31	11	16	0	2	1	1	9	1	0	.111	0	6	2	0	0.8	.750
13 yrs.		192	144	.571	2.16 6th	407	340	261	2961.1	2460	803	2316	50	22	6	5	1062	172	4	.162	175	740	91	17	2.5	.910

Tom Waddell

WADDELL, THOMAS DAVID BR TR 6′ 1″ 185 lbs.
B. Sept. 17, 1958, Dundee, Scotland.

Year	Team	W	L	PCT	ERA	G	GS	CG	IP	H	BB	SO	ShO	Relief Pitching W	L	SV	Batting AB	H	HR	BA	PO	A	E	DP	TC/G	FA
1984	CLE A	7	4	.636	3.06	58	0	0	97	68	37	59	0	7	4	6	0	0	0	—	8	9	0	1	0.3	1.000
1985		8	6	.571	4.87	49	9	1	112.2	104	39	53	0	4	5	9	0	0	0	—	10	15	0	0	0.5	1.000
1987		0	1	.000	14.29	6	0	0	5.2	7	7	6	0	0	1	0	0	0	0	—	0	0	0	0	0.0	.000
3 yrs.		15	11	.577	4.30	113	9	1	215.1	179	83	118	0	11	10	15	0	0	0		18	24	0	1	0.4	1.000

Ben Wade

WADE, BENJAMIN STYRON BR TR 6′ 3″ 195 lbs.
Brother of Jake Wade.
B. Nov. 26, 1922, Morehead City, N. C.

Year	Team	W	L	PCT	ERA	G	GS	CG	IP	H	BB	SO	ShO	Relief Pitching W	L	SV	Batting AB	H	HR	BA	PO	A	E	DP	TC/G	FA
1948	CHI N	0	1	.000	7.20	2	0	0	5	4	4	1	0	0	1	0	2	0	0	.000	1	1	0	0	1.0	1.000
1952	BKN N	11	9	.550	3.60	37	24	5	180	166	94	118	1	2	0	3	60	7	3	.117	12	20	1	1	0.9	.970
1953		7	5	.583	3.79	32	0	0	90.1	79	33	65	0	7	5	3	24	4	1	.167	4	4	1	2	0.3	.889
1954	2 teams	BKN N	(23G 1–1)	STL N	(13G 0–0)																					
″	total	1	1	.500	7.28	36	0	0	68	89	36	44	0	1	1	3	8	0	0	.000	6	8	2	1	0.4	.875
1955	PIT N	0	1	.000	3.21	11	1	0	28	26	14	7	0	0	1	1	4	0	0	.000	4	3	0	0	0.6	1.000
5 yrs.		19	17	.528	4.34	118	25	5	371.1	364	181	235	1	10	8	10	98	11	4	.112	27	36	4	4	0.6	.940
WORLD SERIES																										
1953	BKN N	0	0	—	15.43	2	0	0	2.1	4	1	2	0	0	0	0	0	0	0	—	0	0	0	0	0.0	.000

Jake Wade

WADE, JACOB FIELDS (Whistlin' Jake) BL TL 6′ 2″ 175 lbs.
Brother of Ben Wade.
B. Apr. 1, 1912, Morehead City, N. C.

Year	Team	W	L	PCT	ERA	G	GS	CG	IP	H	BB	SO	ShO	Relief Pitching W	L	SV	Batting AB	H	HR	BA	PO	A	E	DP	TC/G	FA
1936	DET A	4	5	.444	5.29	13	11	4	78.1	93	52	30	1	0	0	0	29	5	0	.172	1	14	4	0	1.5	.789
1937		7	10	.412	5.39	33	25	7	165.1	160	107	69	1	0	1	0	59	11	0	.186	6	33	0	1	1.2	1.000
1938		3	2	.600	6.56	27	2	0	70	73	48	23	0	3	0	0	21	1	0	.048	2	14	1	1	0.6	.941
1939	2 teams	BOS A	(20G 1–4)	STL A	(4G 0–2)																					
″	total	1	6	.143	7.45	24	8	2	64	94	56	30	0	1	1	0	17	0	0	.000	0	12	0	0	0.5	1.000
1942	CHI A	5	5	.500	4.10	15	10	3	85.2	84	56	32	0	1	0	0	29	7	0	.241	6	23	2	3	2.1	.935
1943		3	7	.300	3.01	21	9	3	83.2	66	54	41	1	0	1	0	27	4	0	.148	2	11	1	2	0.7	.929
1944		2	4	.333	4.82	19	5	1	74.2	75	41	35	0	1	1	2	24	7	0	.292	1	4	1	1	0.3	.833
1946	2 teams	NY A	(13G 2–1)	WAS A	(6G 0–0)																					
″	total	2	1	.667	2.89	19	1	0	46.2	45	26	31	0	2	0	1	10	1	0	.100	4	9	0	0	0.7	1.000
8 yrs.		27	40	.403	5.00	171	71	20	668.1	690	440	291	3	8	4	3	216	36	0	.167	22	120	9	8	0.9	.940

Terrell Wade

WADE, HAWATHA TERRELL BL TL 6′ 3″ 205 lbs.
B. Jan. 25, 1973, Rembert, S. C.

Year	Team	W	L	PCT	ERA	G	GS	CG	IP	H	BB	SO	ShO	Relief Pitching W	L	SV	Batting AB	H	HR	BA	PO	A	E	DP	TC/G	FA
1995	ATL N	0	1	.000	4.50	3	0	0	4	3	4	3	0	0	1	0	0	0	0	—	0	0	0	0	0.0	.000

Jack Wadsworth

WADSWORTH, JOHN L. BL TR 180 lbs.
B. Dec. 17, 1867, Wellington, Ohio D. July 8, 1941, Elyria, Ohio.

Year	Team	W	L	PCT	ERA	G	GS	CG	IP	H	BB	SO	ShO	Relief Pitching W	L	SV	Batting AB	H	HR	BA	PO	A	E	DP	TC/G	FA
1890	CLE N	2	16	.111	5.20	20	19	19	169.2	202	81	26	0	0	0	0	68	12	0	.176	5	35	4	0	2.2	.909
1893	BAL N	0	3	.000	11.25	3	3	0	16	37	8	2	0	0	0	0	7	3	0	.429	3	0	1	0	1.3	.750
1894	LOU N	4	18	.182	7.60	22	22	20	173	261	103	57	0	0	0	0	74	19	0	.257	14	25	2	2	1.9	.951
1895		0	1	.000	16.00	2	0	0	9	24	7	2	0	0	1	0	4	1	0	.250	0	3	0	1	1.5	1.000
4 yrs.		6	38	.136	6.85	47	44	39	367.2	524	199	87	0	0	1	0	153	35	0	.229	22	63	7	3	2.0	.924

Billy Wagner

WAGNER, WILLIAM EDWARD BL TL 5′10″ 180 lbs.
B. July 25, 1971, Tannersville, Va.

Year	Team	W	L	PCT	ERA	G	GS	CG	IP	H	BB	SO	ShO	Relief Pitching W	L	SV	Batting AB	H	HR	BA	PO	A	E	DP	TC/G	FA
1995	HOU N	0	0	—	0.00	1	0	0	0.1	0	0	0	0	0	0	0	0	0	0	—	0	0	0	0	0.0	.000

Bull Wagner

WAGNER, WILLIAM GEORGE BR TR 6′½″ 225 lbs.
B. Dec. 25, 1887, Lilley, Mich. D. Oct. 2, 1967, Muskegon, Mich.

Year	Team	W	L	PCT	ERA	G	GS	CG	IP	H	BB	SO	ShO	Relief Pitching W	L	SV	Batting AB	H	HR	BA	PO	A	E	DP	TC/G	FA
1913	BKN N	4	2	.667	5.48	18	1	0	70.2	77	30	11	0	4	2	0	26	6	0	.231	4	12	1	0	0.9	.941
1914		0	1	.000	6.57	6	0	0	12.1	14	12	4	0	0	1	0	1	0	0	.000	0	3	0	0	0.5	1.000
2 yrs.		4	3	.571	5.64	24	1	0	83	91	42	15	0	4	3	0	27	6	0	.222	4	15	1	0	0.8	.950

Charlie Wagner

WAGNER, CHARLES THOMAS (Broadway) BR TR 5′11″ 170 lbs.
B. Dec. 3, 1912, Reading, Pa.

Year	Team	W	L	PCT	ERA	G	GS	CG	IP	H	BB	SO	ShO	Relief Pitching W	L	SV	Batting AB	H	HR	BA	PO	A	E	DP	TC/G	FA
1938	BOS A	1	3	.250	8.35	13	6	1	36.2	47	24	14	0	0	1	0	12	2	0	.167	2	4	0	0	0.5	1.000
1939		3	1	.750	4.23	9	5	0	38.1	49	14	13	0	0	0	0	14	1	0	.071	2	6	0	0	0.9	1.000
1940		1	0	1.000	5.52	12	1	0	29.1	45	8	13	0	1	0	0	5	1	0	.200	1	5	0	0	0.5	1.000
1941		12	8	.600	3.07	29	25	12	187.1	175	85	51	3	2	0	0	63	10	0	.159	13	33	1	3	1.6	.979
1942		14	11	.560	3.29	29	26	17	205.1	184	95	52	2	2	0	0	65	5	0	.077	9	46	0	3	1.9	1.000
1946		1	0	1.000	5.87	8	4	0	30.2	32	19	14	0	0	0	0	11	1	0	.091	0	5	0	0	0.6	1.000
6 yrs.		32	23	.582	3.91	100	67	30	527.2	532	245	157	5	5	1	0	170	20	0	.118	27	99	1	6	1.3	.992

Gary Wagner

WAGNER, GARY EDWARD BR TR 6′ 4″ 185 lbs.
B. June 28, 1940, Bridgeport, Ill.

Year	Team	W	L	PCT	ERA	G	GS	CG	IP	H	BB	SO	ShO	Relief Pitching W	L	SV	Batting AB	H	HR	BA	PO	A	E	DP	TC/G	FA
1965	PHI N	7	7	.500	3.00	59	0	0	105	87	49	91	0	7	7	7	13	1	0	.077	9	21	2	1	0.5	.938
1966		0	1	.000	8.53	5	1	0	6.1	8	5	2	0	0	1	0	0	0	0	—	0	0	0	0	0.0	.000
1967		0	0	—	0.00	1	0	0	2	1	0	1	0	0	0	0	0	0	0	—	0	1	0	0	1.0	1.000
1968		4	4	.500	3.00	44	0	0	78	69	31	43	0	4	4	8	12	1	0	.083	11	15	2	1	0.6	.929
1969	2 teams	PHI N	(9G 0–3)	BOS A	(6G 1–3)																					
″	total	1	6	.143	7.13	15	3	0	35.1	49	22	17	0	1	4	0	6	0	0	.000	0	5	3	0	0.5	.625
1970	BOS A	3	1	.750	3.38	38	0	0	40	36	19	20	0	3	1	7	6	1	0	.167	5	3	1	0	0.2	.889
6 yrs.		15	19	.441	3.71	162	4	0	266.2	250	126	174	0	15	17	22	37	3	0	.081	25	45	8	2	0.5	.897

Hector Wagner

WAGNER, HECTOR RAUL BR TR 6′ 3″ 185 lbs.
Born Hector Raul Guerrero (Wagner).
B. Nov. 26, 1968, Santo Domingo, Dominican Republic.

Year	Team	W	L	PCT	ERA	G	GS	CG	IP	H	BB	SO	ShO	Relief W	Relief L	Relief SV	Batting AB	Batting H	HR	BA	PO	A	E	DP	TC/G	FA
1990	KC A	0	2	.000	8.10	5	5	0	23.1	32	11	14	0	0	0	0	0	0	0	—	3	3	0	1	1.2	1.000
1991		1	1	.500	7.20	2	2	0	10	16	3	5	0	0	0	0	0	0	0	—	0	0	0	0	0.0	.000
2 yrs.		1	3	.250	7.83	7	7	0	33.1	48	14	19	0	0	0	0	0	0	0		3	3	0	1	0.9	1.000

Honus Wagner

WAGNER, JOHN PETER (The Flying Dutchman) BR TR 5′11″ 200 lbs.
Brother of Butts Wagner.
B. Feb. 24, 1874, Chartiers, Pa. D. Dec. 6, 1955, Carnegie, Pa.
Manager 1917.
Hall of Fame 1936.

Year	Team	W	L	PCT	ERA	G	GS	CG	IP	H	BB	SO	ShO	Relief W	Relief L	Relief SV	Batting AB	Batting H	HR	BA	PO	A	E	DP	TC/G	FA
1900	PIT N	0	0	—	0.00	1	0	0	3	3	4	1	0	0	0	0	527	201	4	.381	124	37	16	7	2.9	.910
1902		0	0	—	0.00	1	0	0	5.1	4	2	5	0	0	0	0	538	177	3	.329	847	192	43	57	7.2	.960
2 yrs.		0	0		0.00	2	0	0	8.1	7	6	6	0	0	0	0	*				7930	6781	824	964	5.6	.947

Mark Wagner

WAGNER, MARK DUANE BR TR 6′ 165 lbs.
B. Mar. 4, 1954, Conneaut, Ohio.

Year	Team	W	L	PCT	ERA	G	GS	CG	IP	H	BB	SO	ShO	Relief W	Relief L	Relief SV	Batting AB	Batting H	HR	BA	PO	A	E	DP	TC/G	FA
1984	OAK A	0	0	—	0.00	1	0	0	1.2	2	1	1	0	0	0	0	*				60	135	11	25	5.3	.947

Paul Wagner

WAGNER, PAUL ALAN BR TR 6′ 3″ 205 lbs.
B. Nov. 14, 1967, Milwaukee, Wis.

Year	Team	W	L	PCT	ERA	G	GS	CG	IP	H	BB	SO	ShO	Relief W	Relief L	Relief SV	Batting AB	Batting H	HR	BA	PO	A	E	DP	TC/G	FA
1992	PIT N	2	0	1.000	0.69	6	1	0	13	9	5	5	0	2	0	0	3	1	0	.333	2	2	0	0	0.7	1.000
1993		8	8	.500	4.27	44	17	1	141.1	143	42	114	1	2	3	2	42	8	0	.190	9	13	0	3	0.5	1.000
1994		7	8	.467	4.59	29	17	1	119.2	136	50	86	0	2	0	0	37	6	0	.162	14	22	0	3	1.2	1.000
1995		5	**16**	.238	4.80	33	25	3	165	174	72	120	1	1	2	1	42	9	0	.214	12	24	0	1	1.1	1.000
4 yrs.		22	32	.407	4.45	112	60	5	439	462	169	325	2	7	5	3	124	24	0	.194	37	61	0	7	0.9	1.000

Dave Wainhouse

WAINHOUSE, DAVID PAUL BL TR 6′ 2″ 190 lbs.
B. Nov. 7, 1967, Toronto, Ont., Canada.

Year	Team	W	L	PCT	ERA	G	GS	CG	IP	H	BB	SO	ShO	Relief W	Relief L	Relief SV	Batting AB	Batting H	HR	BA	PO	A	E	DP	TC/G	FA
1991	MON N	0	1	.000	6.75	2	0	0	2.2	2	4	1	0	0	1	0	0	0	0	—	0	0	0	0	0.0	.000
1993	SEA A	0	0	—	27.00	3	0	0	2.1	7	5	2	0	0	0	0	0	0	0	—	0	0	0	0	0.0	.000
2 yrs.		0	1	.000	16.20	5	0	0	5	9	9	3	0	0	1	0	0	0	0		0	0	0	0	0.0	

Rick Waits

WAITS, MICHAEL RICHARD BL TL 6′ 3″ 194 lbs.
B. May 15, 1952, Atlanta, Ga.

Year	Team	W	L	PCT	ERA	G	GS	CG	IP	H	BB	SO	ShO	Relief W	Relief L	Relief SV	Batting AB	Batting H	HR	BA	PO	A	E	DP	TC/G	FA
1973	TEX A	0	0	—	9.00	1	0	0	1	1	1	0	0	0	0	1	0	0	0	—	0	0	0	0	0.0	.000
1975	CLE A	6	2	.750	2.94	16	7	3	70.1	57	25	34	0	2	0	1	0	0	0	—	5	12	1	1	1.1	.944
1976		7	9	.438	3.99	26	22	4	124	143	54	65	2	0	0	0	0	0	0	—	10	20	2	2	1.2	.938
1977		9	7	.563	4.00	37	16	1	135	132	64	62	0	3	2	2	0	0	0	—	4	24	2	0	0.8	.933
1978		13	15	.464	3.20	34	33	15	230.1	206	86	97	2	0	0	0	0	0	0	—	19	49	1	1	2.0	.986
1979		16	13	.552	4.44	34	34	8	231	230	91	91	3	0	0	0	0	0	0	—	15	43	0	2	1.7	1.000
1980		13	14	.481	4.46	33	33	9	224	231	82	109	2	0	0	0	0	0	0	—	10	30	1	0	1.2	.976
1981		8	10	.444	4.93	22	21	5	126	173	44	51	1	0	0	0	0	0	0	—	12	28	0	2	1.8	1.000
1982		2	13	.133	5.40	25	21	2	115	128	57	44	0	1	1	0	0	0	0	—	6	23	0	1	1.2	1.000
1983	2 teams CLE A (8G 0–1) MIL A (10G 0–2)																									
″	total	0	3	.000	4.89	18	2	0	49.2	62	20	33	0	0	2	0	0	0	0		0	7	1	0	0.4	.875
1984	MIL A	2	4	.333	3.58	47	1	0	73	84	24	49	0	2	3	3	0	0	0	—	2	12	0	0	0.3	1.000
1985		3	2	.600	6.51	24	0	0	47	67	20	24	0	3	2	1	1	0	0	.000	8	4	0	0	0.5	1.000
12 yrs.		79	92	.462	4.25	317	190	47	1426.1	1514	568	659	10	11	10	8	1	0	0	.000	91	252	8	9	1.1	.977

Bill Wakefield

WAKEFIELD, WILLIAM SUMNER BR TR 6′ 175 lbs.
B. May 24, 1941, Kansas City, Mo.

Year	Team	W	L	PCT	ERA	G	GS	CG	IP	H	BB	SO	ShO	Relief W	Relief L	Relief SV	Batting AB	Batting H	HR	BA	PO	A	E	DP	TC/G	FA
1964	NY N	3	5	.375	3.61	62	4	0	119.2	103	61	61	0	3	2	2	24	4	0	.167	4	23	0	2	0.4	1.000

Tim Wakefield

WAKEFIELD, TIMOTHY STEPHEN BR TR 6′ 2″ 195 lbs.
B. Aug. 2, 1966, Melbourne, Fla.

Year	Team	W	L	PCT	ERA	G	GS	CG	IP	H	BB	SO	ShO	Relief W	Relief L	Relief SV	Batting AB	Batting H	HR	BA	PO	A	E	DP	TC/G	FA
1992	PIT N	8	1	.889	2.15	13	13	4	92	76	35	51	1	0	0	0	28	2	0	.071	6	19	0	1	1.9	1.000
1993		6	11	.353	5.61	24	20	3	128.1	145	75	59	2	1	0	0	43	7	1	.163	8	15	4	2	1.1	.852
1995	BOS A	16	8	.667	2.95	27	27	6	195.1	163	68	119	1	0	0	0	0	0	0	—	15	19	2	4	1.3	.944
3 yrs.		30	20	.600	3.59	64	60	13	415.2	384	178	229	4	1	0	0	71	9	1	.127	29	53	6	7	1.4	.932
DIVISIONAL PLAYOFF SERIES																										
1995	BOS A	0	1	.000	11.81	1	1	0	5.1	5	5	4	0	0	0	0	0	0	0	—	0	0	0	0	0.0	.000
LEAGUE CHAMPIONSHIP SERIES																										
1992	PIT N	2	0	1.000	3.00	2	2	2 **4th**	18	14	5	7	0	0	0	0	6	0	0	.000	3	2	0	0	2.5	1.000

Rube Walberg

WALBERG, GEORGE ELVIN BL TL 6′ 1½″ 190 lbs.
B. July 27, 1896, Pine City, Minn. D. Oct. 27, 1978, Tempe, Ariz.

Year	Team	W	L	PCT	ERA	G	GS	CG	IP	H	BB	SO	ShO	Relief W	Relief L	Relief SV	Batting AB	Batting H	HR	BA	PO	A	E	DP	TC/G	FA
1923	2 teams NY N (2G 0–0) PHI A (26G 4–8)																									
″	total	4	8	.333	5.18	28	10	4	120	126	61	39	0	3	1	0	42	13	0	.310	2	35	3	2	1.4	.925
1924	PHI A	0	0	—	12.86	6	2	0	7	10	10	3	0	0	0	0	2	1	0	.500	0	2	0	0	0.3	1.000
1925		8	14	.364	3.99	53	20	7	191.2	197	77	82	0	3	4	7	64	10	0	.156	10	51	2	0	1.2	.968
1926		12	10	.545	2.80	40	19	5	151	168	60	72	2	3	1	2	46	7	0	.152	4	35	4	2	1.1	.907
1927		16	12	.571	3.97	46	34	15	249.1	257	91	136	0	2	2	4	87	18	2	.207	2	62	6	0	1.5	.914
1928		17	12	.586	3.55	38	30	15	235.2	236	64	112	3	3	1	1	86	18	1	.209	9	56	4	3	1.8	.942
1929		18	11	.621	3.60	40	33	20	267.2	256	99	94	3	1	1	4	103	23	1	.223	11	49	0	1	1.5	1.000
1930		13	12	.520	4.69	38	30	12	205.1	207	85	100	2	4	1	1	73	12	0	.164	7	34	3	1	1.2	.932
1931		20	12	.625	3.74	44	35	19	**291**	298	109	106	1	1	0	3	105	13	0	.124	13	52	0	1	1.5	1.000
1932		17	10	.630	4.73	41	34	19	272	305	103	96	3	0	0	1	94	16	0	.170	14	55	4	2	1.8	.945
1933		9	13	.409	4.88	40	20	10	201	224	95	68	1	3	3	4	68	9	0	.132	14	45	2	1	1.5	.967
1934	BOS A	6	7	.462	4.04	30	10	2	104.2	118	41	38	0	4	2	1	32	6	0	.188	5	25	2	0	1.1	.938
1935		5	9	.357	3.91	44	10	4	142.2	152	54	44	0	4	3	3	37	6	0	.162	8	23	2	0	0.8	.939

Rube Walberg *continued*

Year	Team	Lg	W	L	PCT	ERA	G	GS	CG	IP	H	BB	SO	ShO	Relief Pitching W	Relief Pitching L	Relief Pitching SV	Batting AB	Batting H	Batting HR	BA	PO	A	E	DP	TC/G	FA
1936			5	4	.556	4.40	24	9	5	100.1	98	36	49	0	1	2	0	32	5	0	.156	8	17	1	2	1.1	.962
1937			5	7	.417	5.59	32	11	3	104.2	143	46	46	0	2	2	1	34	5	0	.147	6	17	4	3	0.8	.852
15 yrs.			155	141	.524	4.17	544	307	140	2644	2795	1031	1085	15	34	23	32	905	162	4	.179	113	558	37	18	1.3	.948
WORLD SERIES																											
1929	**PHI**	**A**	1	0	1.000	0.00	2	0	0	6.1	3	0	8	0	1	0	0	1	0	0	.000	0	1	1	0	1.0	.500
1930			0	1	.000	3.86	1	1	0	4.2	4	1	3	0	0	0	0	2	0	0	.000	0	0	0	0	0.0	.000
1931			0	0	—	3.00	2	0	0	3	3	2	4	0	0	0	0	0	0	0	—	0	0	0	0	0.0	.000
3 yrs.			1	1	.500	1.93	5	1	0	14	10	3	15	0	1	0	0	3	0	0	.000	0	1	1	0	0.4	.500

Doc Waldbauer

WALDBAUER, ALBERT CHARLES BR TR 6′ 172 lbs.
B. Feb. 22, 1892, Richmond, Va. D. July 16, 1969, Yakima, Wash.

Year	Team	Lg	W	L	PCT	ERA	G	GS	CG	IP	H	BB	SO	ShO	Relief W	Relief L	SV	AB	H	HR	BA	PO	A	E	DP	TC/G	FA
1917	**WAS**	**A**	0	0	—	7.20	2	0	0	5	10	2	2	0	0	0	1	1	0	0	.000	0	3	0	0	1.5	1.000

Bob Walk

WALK, ROBERT VERNON (Whirlybird) BR TR 6′ 3″ 185 lbs.
B. Nov. 26, 1956, Van Nuys, Calif.

Year	Team	Lg	W	L	PCT	ERA	G	GS	CG	IP	H	BB	SO	ShO	Relief W	Relief L	SV	AB	H	HR	BA	PO	A	E	DP	TC/G	FA
1980	**PHI**	**N**	11	7	.611	4.56	27	27	2	152	163	71	94	0	0	0	0	50	7	0	.140	17	15	1	2	1.2	.970
1981	**ATL**	**N**	1	4	.200	4.60	12	8	0	43	41	23	16	0	0	0	0	7	1	0	.143	3	4	0	0	0.6	1.000
1982			11	9	.550	4.87	32	27	3	164.1	179	59	84	1	0	0	0	51	10	0	.196	12	17	6	2	1.1	.829
1983			0	0	—	7.36	1	1	0	3.2	7	2	4	0	0	0	0	1	0	0	.000	0	2	0	0	2.0	1.000
1984	**PIT**	**N**	1	1	.500	2.61	2	2	0	10.1	8	4	10	0	0	0	0	3	0	0	.000	0	0	0	0	0.0	.000
1985			2	3	.400	3.68	9	9	1	58.2	60	18	40	1	0	0	0	17	0	0	.000	7	2	0	0	1.0	1.000
1986			7	8	.467	3.75	44	15	1	141.2	129	64	78	1	2	3	2	39	6	0	.154	21	28	3	4	1.2	.942
1987			8	2	.800	3.31	39	12	1	117	107	51	78	1	2	1	0	26	6	0	.231	9	22	2	2	0.8	.939
1988			12	10	.545	2.71	32	32	1	212.2	183	65	81	1	0	0	0	69	6	0	.087	23	34	3	3	1.9	.950
1989			13	10	.565	4.41	33	31	2	196	208	65	83	0	0	0	0	70	13	0	.186	19	31	3	3	1.6	.943
1990			7	5	.583	3.75	26	24	1	129.2	136	36	73	1	0	0	1	37	6	0	.162	12	11	3	0	1.0	.885
1991			9	2	.818	3.60	25	20	0	115	104	35	67	0	2	0	0	39	8	1	.205	9	15	2	1	1.0	.923
1992			10	6	.625	3.20	36	19	1	135	132	43	60	0	4	0	2	43	4	0	.093	10	28	1	1	1.1	.974
1993			13	14	.481	5.68	32	32	3	187	214	70	80	0	0	0	0	58	7	0	.121	12	23	2	4	1.2	.946
14 yrs.			105	81	.565	4.03	350	259	16	1666	1671	606	848	6	10	4	5	510	74	1	.145	154	232	26	22	1.2	.937
LEAGUE CHAMPIONSHIP SERIES																											
1982	**ATL**	**N**	0	0	—	9.00	1	0	0	1	2	1	1	0	0	0	0	0	0	0	—	0	0	0	0	0.0	.000
1990	**PIT**	**N**	1	1	.500	4.85	2	2	0	13	11	2	8	0	0	0	0	4	0	0	.000	2	1	0	0	1.5	1.000
1991			0	0	—	1.93	3	0	0	9.1	5	3	5	0	0	0	1	2	0	0	.000	0	0	0	0	0.0	.000
1992			1	0	1.000	3.86	2	1	1	11.2	6	7	6	0	0	0	0	5	0	0	.000	1	2	0	0	1.5	1.000
4 yrs.			2	1	.667	3.86	8	3	1	35	24	13	20	0	0	0	1	11	0	0	.000	3	3	0	0	0.8	1.000
WORLD SERIES																											
1980	**PHI**	**N**	1	0	1.000	7.71	1	1	0	7	8	3	3	0	0	0	0	0	0	0	—	2	0	0	0	2.0	1.000

Bill Walker

WALKER, WILLIAM HENRY BR TL 6′ 175 lbs.
B. Oct. 7, 1903, East St. Louis, Ill. D. June 14, 1966, East St. Louis, Ill.

Year	Team	Lg	W	L	PCT	ERA	G	GS	CG	IP	H	BB	SO	ShO	Relief W	Relief L	SV	AB	H	HR	BA	PO	A	E	DP	TC/G	FA
1927	**NY**	**N**	0	0	—	9.00	3	0	0	4	6	5	4	0	0	0	0	0	0	0	—	0	0	0	0	0.0	.000
1928			3	6	.333	4.72	22	8	1	76.1	79	31	39	0	1	1	0	22	2	0	.091	0	17	1	0	0.8	.944
1929			14	7	.667	**3.09**	29	23	13	177.2	188	57	65	1	1	1	0	61	7	1	.115	10	23	3	1	1.2	.917
1930			17	15	.531	3.93	39	34	13	245.1	258	88	105	2	2	1	1	86	16	2	.186	10	44	4	1	1.5	.931
1931			17	9	.654	**2.26**	37	28	19	239.1	212	64	121	**6**	1	0	3	77	5	0	.065	8	31	4	1	1.2	.907
1932			8	12	.400	4.14	31	22	9	163	177	55	74	0	1	1	2	52	7	0	.135	10	39	2	1	1.6	.961
1933	**STL**	**N**	9	10	.474	3.42	29	20	6	158	168	67	41	2	3	1	0	53	7	1	.132	11	40	4	0	1.9	.927
1934			12	4	.750	3.12	24	19	10	153	160	66	76	1	0	0	0	54	5	0	.093	8	23	1	2	1.3	.969
1935			13	8	.619	3.82	37	25	8	193.1	222	78	79	2	4	1	1	59	6	0	.102	4	42	4	0	1.4	.920
1936			5	6	.455	5.87	21	13	4	79.2	106	27	22	1	1	1	1	25	7	0	.280	3	23	1	1	1.3	.963
10 yrs.			98	77	.560	3.59	272	192	83	1489.2	1576	538	626	15	14	7	8	489	62	4	.127	64	282	24	7	1.4	.935
WORLD SERIES																											
1934	**STL**	**N**	0	2	.000	7.11	2	0	0	6.1	6	6	2	0	0	2	0	2	0	0	.000	0	1	1	0	1.0	.500

Dixie Walker

WALKER, EWART GLADSTONE BL TR 6′ 192 lbs.
Father of Harry Walker. Father of Dixie Walker. Brother of Ernie Walker.
B. June 1, 1887, Brownsville, Pa. D. Nov. 14, 1965, Leeds, Ala.

Year	Team	Lg	W	L	PCT	ERA	G	GS	CG	IP	H	BB	SO	ShO	Relief W	Relief L	SV	AB	H	HR	BA	PO	A	E	DP	TC/G	FA
1909	**WAS**	**A**	3	1	.750	2.50	4	4	4	36	31	6	25	0	0	0	0	13	2	0	.154	1	10	2	1	3.3	.846
1910			11	11	.500	3.30	29	26	16	199.1	167	68	85	3	0	0	0	69	9	0	.130	4	60	4	1	2.3	.941
1911			8	13	.381	3.39	32	24	15	185.2	205	50	65	2	1	2	0	66	20	0	.303	11	45	4	0	1.9	.933
1912			3	6	.333	5.25	9	8	5	60	72	18	29	0	1	0	0	16	2	0	.125	5	18	6	0	3.2	.793
4 yrs.			25	31	.446	3.52	74	62	40	481	475	142	204	5	2	2	0	164	33	0	.201	21	133	16	2	2.3	.906

Ed Walker

WALKER, EDWARD HARRISON BL TL 6′ 5″ 242 lbs.
B. Aug. 11, 1874, Cambois, England D. Sept. 29, 1947, Akron, Ohio.

Year	Team	Lg	W	L	PCT	ERA	G	GS	CG	IP	H	BB	SO	ShO	Relief W	Relief L	SV	AB	H	HR	BA	PO	A	E	DP	TC/G	FA
1902	**CLE**	**A**	0	1	.000	3.38	1	1	1	8	11	3	1	0	0	0	0	3	1	0	.333	0	3	1	0	4.0	.750
1903			0	0	—	5.25	3	3	0	12	13	10	4	0	0	0	0	3	0	0	.000	0	1	0	0	0.3	1.000
2 yrs.			0	1	.000	4.50	4	4	1	20	24	13	5	0	0	0	0	6	1	0	.167	0	4	1	0	1.3	.800

George Walker

WALKER, GEORGE A. 5′ 9″ 184 lbs.
B. 1863, Hamilton, Ont., Canada Deceased.

Year	Team	Lg	W	L	PCT	ERA	G	GS	CG	IP	H	BB	SO	ShO	Relief W	Relief L	SV	AB	H	HR	BA	PO	A	E	DP	TC/G	FA
1888	**BAL**	**AA**	1	3	.250	5.91	4	4	4	35	36	14	18	1	0	0	0	13	1	0	.077	0	7	1	0	2.0	.875

Jerry Walker

WALKER, JERRY ALLEN BB TR 6′ 1″ 195 lbs.
B. Feb. 12, 1939, Ada, Okla. BR 1963–1964

Year	Team	Lg	W	L	PCT	ERA	G	GS	CG	IP	H	BB	SO	ShO	Relief W	Relief L	SV	AB	H	HR	BA	PO	A	E	DP	TC/G	FA
1957	**BAL**	**A**	1	0	1.000	2.93	13	3	1	27.2	24	14	13	1	0	0	1	5	0	0	.000	0	5	0	0	0.4	1.000
1958			0	0	—	6.97	6	0	0	10.1	16	5	6	0	0	0	0	2	0	0	.000	2	0	0	0	0.3	1.000
1959			11	10	.524	2.92	30	22	7	182	160	52	100	2	0	1	4	65	11	1	.169	5	32	0	2	1.2	1.000
1960			3	4	.429	3.74	29	18	1	118	107	56	48	0	0	0	5	38	14	0	.368	5	23	0	1	1.0	1.000
1961	**KC**	**A**	8	14	.364	4.82	36	24	4	168	161	96	56	0	2	1	2	64	16	0	.250	9	31	0	4	1.1	1.000

Jerry Walker *continued*

Year	Team	Lg	W	L	PCT	ERA	G	GS	CG	IP	H	BB	SO	ShO	Relief Pitching W	Relief Pitching L	Relief Pitching SV	Batting AB	Batting H	Batting HR	BA	PO	A	E	DP	TC/G	FA
1962			8	9	.471	5.90	31	21	3	143.1	165	78	57	1	0	1	0	57	15	3	.263	15	27	0	3	1.4	1.000
1963	CLE	A	6	6	.500	4.91	39	2	0	88	92	36	41	0	6	4	1	19	2	0	.105	7	14	2	0	0.6	.913
1964			0	1	.000	4.66	6	0	0	9.2	9	4	5	0	0	1	0	2	0	0	.000	0	1	0	0	0.2	1.000
8 yrs.			37	44	.457	4.36	190	90	16	747	734	341	326	4	8	8	13	252	58	4	.230	43	133	2	10	0.9	.989

Luke Walker

WALKER, JAMES LUKE BL TL 6′ 2″ 190 lbs.
B. Sept. 2, 1943, DeKalb, Tex.

Year	Team	Lg	W	L	PCT	ERA	G	GS	CG	IP	H	BB	SO	ShO	Relief Pitching W	Relief Pitching L	Relief Pitching SV	Batting AB	Batting H	Batting HR	BA	PO	A	E	DP	TC/G	FA
1965	PIT	N	0	0	—	0.00	2	0	0	5	2	1	5	0	0	0	0	0	0	0	—	0	1	0	0	0.5	1.000
1966			0	1	.000	4.50	10	1	0	10	8	15	7	0	0	1	0	2	0	0	.000	1	1	1	0	0.3	.667
1968			0	3	.000	2.02	39	2	0	62.1	42	39	66	0	0	2	3	8	0	0	.000	3	12	0	0	0.4	1.000
1969			4	6	.400	3.63	31	15	3	119	98	57	96	1	0	0	0	32	0	0	.000	2	24	2	0	0.9	.929
1970			15	6	.714	3.04	42	19	5	163	129	89	124	3	3	1	3	46	6	0	.130	3	24	1	3	0.7	.964
1971			10	8	.556	3.54	28	24	4	160	157	53	86	2	2	0	0	46	1	0	.022	3	18	1	3	0.8	.955
1972			4	6	.400	3.40	26	12	2	92.2	98	34	48	0	0	1	2	24	2	0	.083	3	13	3	3	0.7	.842
1973			7	12	.368	4.65	37	18	2	122	129	66	74	1	0	2	1	30	2	0	.067	4	16	2	1	0.6	.909
1974	DET	A	5	5	.500	4.99	28	9	0	92	100	54	52	0	2	0	0	0	0	0	—	6	11	1	0	0.6	.944
9 yrs.			45	47	.489	3.64	243	100	16	826	763	408	558	7	7	7	9	188	11	0	.059	25	120	11	10	0.6	.929
LEAGUE CHAMPIONSHIP SERIES																											
1970	PIT	N	0	1	.000	1.29	1	1	0	7	5	1	5	0	0	0	0	2	0	0	.000	0	0	1	0	1.0	.000
1972			0	0	—	18.00	1	0	0	1	3	0	0	0	0	0	0	0	0	0	—	0	0	0	0	0.0	.000
2 yrs.			0	1	.000	3.38	2	1	0	8	8	1	5	0	0	0	0	2	0	0	.000	0	0	1	0	0.5	.000
WORLD SERIES																											
1971	PIT	N	0	0	—	40.50	1	1	0	0.2	3	1	0	0	0	0	0	0	0	0	—	0	0	0	0	0.0	.000

Marty Walker

WALKER, MARTIN VAN BUREN (Buddy) BL TL 6′ 170 lbs.
B. Mar. 27, 1899, Philadelphia, Pa. D. Apr. 24, 1978, Philadelphia, Pa.

Year	Team	Lg	W	L	PCT	ERA	G	GS	CG	IP	H	BB	SO	ShO	Relief Pitching W	Relief Pitching L	Relief Pitching SV	Batting AB	Batting H	Batting HR	BA	PO	A	E	DP	TC/G	FA
1928	PHI	N	0	1	.000	∞	1	1	0		2	3	0	0	0	0	0	0	0	0	—	0	0	0	0	0.0	.000

Mike Walker

WALKER, MICHAEL AARON BR TR 6′ 3″ 205 lbs.
B. June 23, 1965, Houston, Tex.

Year	Team	Lg	W	L	PCT	ERA	G	GS	CG	IP	H	BB	SO	ShO	Relief Pitching W	Relief Pitching L	Relief Pitching SV	Batting AB	Batting H	Batting HR	BA	PO	A	E	DP	TC/G	FA
1992	SEA	A	0	3	.000	7.36	5	3	0	14.2	21	9	5	0	0	1	0	0	0	0	—	1	3	2	0	1.2	.667

Mike Walker

WALKER, MICHAEL CHARLES BR TR 6′ 1″ 175 lbs.
B. Oct. 4, 1966, Chicago, Ill.

Year	Team	Lg	W	L	PCT	ERA	G	GS	CG	IP	H	BB	SO	ShO	Relief Pitching W	Relief Pitching L	Relief Pitching SV	Batting AB	Batting H	Batting HR	BA	PO	A	E	DP	TC/G	FA
1988	CLE	A	0	1	.000	7.27	3	1	0	8.2	8	10	7	0	0	0	0	0	0	0	—	0	3	0	0	1.0	1.000
1990			2	6	.250	4.88	18	11	0	75.2	82	42	34	0	1	0	0	0	0	0	—	4	9	0	1	0.7	1.000
1991			0	1	.000	2.08	5	0	0	4.1	6	2	2	0	0	1	0	0	0	0	—	1	1	0	0	0.4	1.000
1995	CHI	N	1	3	.250	3.22	42	0	0	44.2	45	24	20	0	1	3	1	3	0	0	.000	4	7	1	0	0.3	.917
4 yrs.			3	11	.214	4.39	68	12	0	133.1	141	78	63	0	2	4	1	3	0	0	.000	9	20	1	1	0.4	.967

Mysterious Walker

WALKER, FREDERICK MITCHELL BR TR 5′10½″ 185 lbs.
B. Mar. 21, 1884, Utica, Neb. D. Feb. 1, 1958, Oak Park, Ill.

Year	Team	Lg	W	L	PCT	ERA	G	GS	CG	IP	H	BB	SO	ShO	Relief Pitching W	Relief Pitching L	Relief Pitching SV	Batting AB	Batting H	Batting HR	BA	PO	A	E	DP	TC/G	FA
1910	CIN	N	0	0	—	3.00	1	0	0	3	4	4	1	0	0	0	0	1	0	0	.000	0	3	0	0	3.0	1.000
1912	CLE	A	0	0	—	0.00	1	0	0	1	0	1	0	0	0	0	0	0	0	0	—	0	0	0	0	0.0	.000
1913	BKN	N	1	3	.250	3.55	11	8	3	58.1	44	35	35	0	0	0	0	18	3	0	.167	1	22	0	0	2.1	1.000
1914	PIT	F	3	16	.158	4.31	35	21	12	169.1	197	74	79	0	1	1	0	53	6	0	.113	11	64	7	3	2.3	.915
1915	BKN	F	2	4	.333	3.70	13	7	2	65.2	61	22	28	0	0	1	1	27	6	0	.222	1	28	1	0	2.3	.967
5 yrs.			6	23	.207	4.00	61	36	17	297.1	306	136	143	0	1	2	1	99	15	0	.152	13	117	8	3	2.2	.942

Pete Walker

WALKER, PETER BRIAN BR TR 6′ 2″ 195 lbs.
B. Apr. 8, 1969, Beverly, Mass.

Year	Team	Lg	W	L	PCT	ERA	G	GS	CG	IP	H	BB	SO	ShO	Relief Pitching W	Relief Pitching L	Relief Pitching SV	Batting AB	Batting H	Batting HR	BA	PO	A	E	DP	TC/G	FA
1995	NY	N	1	0	1.000	4.58	13	0	0	17.2	24	5	5	0	1	0	0	0	0	0	—	1	2	0	0	0.2	1.000

Roy Walker

WALKER, JAMES ROY (Dixie) BR TR 6′ 1½″ 180 lbs.
B. Apr. 13, 1893, Lawrenceburg, Tenn. D. Feb. 10, 1962, New Orleans, La. BB 1917–1918, 1922

Year	Team	Lg	W	L	PCT	ERA	G	GS	CG	IP	H	BB	SO	ShO	Relief Pitching W	Relief Pitching L	Relief Pitching SV	Batting AB	Batting H	Batting HR	BA	PO	A	E	DP	TC/G	FA
1912	CLE	A	0	0	—	0.00	1	0	0	2	0	2	1	0	0	0	0	0	0	0	—	0	0	0	0	0.0	.000
1915			4	9	.308	3.98	25	15	4	131	122	65	57	0	0	1	1	38	5	0	.132	6	25	1	1	1.3	.969
1917	CHI	N	0	1	.000	3.86	2	1	0	7	8	5	4	0	0	0	0	1	0	0	.000	0	1	0	0	0.5	1.000
1918			1	3	.250	2.70	13	7	2	43.1	50	15	20	0	0	0	1	11	0	0	.000	1	12	0	1	1.0	1.000
1921	STL	N	11	12	.478	4.22	38	23	11	170.2	194	53	52	0	2	0	3	54	11	0	.204	6	38	3	1	1.2	.936
1922			1	2	.333	4.78	12	2	0	32	34	15	14	0	1	1	0	7	1	0	.143	1	1	2	0	0.3	.500
6 yrs.			17	27	.386	3.99	91	48	17	386	408	155	148	0	3	2	5	111	17	0	.153	14	77	6	3	1.1	.938

Tom Walker

WALKER, ROBERT THOMAS BR TR 6′ 1″ 188 lbs.
B. Nov. 7, 1948, Tampa, Fla.

Year	Team	Lg	W	L	PCT	ERA	G	GS	CG	IP	H	BB	SO	ShO	Relief Pitching W	Relief Pitching L	Relief Pitching SV	Batting AB	Batting H	Batting HR	BA	PO	A	E	DP	TC/G	FA
1972	MON	N	2	2	.500	2.89	46	0	0	74.2	71	22	42	0	2	2	2	3	0	0	.000	6	10	3	1	0.4	.842
1973			7	5	.583	3.63	54	0	0	91.2	95	42	68	0	7	5	4	7	0	0	.000	5	12	1	0	0.3	.944
1974			4	5	.444	3.82	33	8	1	92	96	28	70	0	2	1	2	16	3	0	.188	5	9	0	1	0.4	1.000
1975	DET	A	3	8	.273	4.45	36	9	1	115.1	116	40	60	0	1	3	0	0	0	0	—	3	12	2	0	0.5	.882
1976	STL	N	1	2	.333	4.12	10	0	0	19.2	22	3	11	0	1	2	3	5	2	0	.400	1	0	0	0	0.1	1.000
1977	2 teams	MON N	(11G 1–1)		CAL A	(1G 0–0)																					
″	total		1	1	.500	5.14	12	0	0	21	18	7	11	0	1	1	0	2	0	0	.000	1	2	0	0	0.3	1.000
6 yrs.			18	23	.439	3.87	191	17	2	414.1	418	142	262	0	14	14	11	33	5	0	.152	21	45	6	2	0.4	.917

Tom Walker

WALKER, THOMAS WILLIAM BR TR 5′11″ 170 lbs.
B. Aug. 1, 1881, Philadelphia, Pa. D. July 10, 1944, Woodbury Heights, N. J.

Year	Team	Lg	W	L	PCT	ERA	G	GS	CG	IP	H	BB	SO	ShO	Relief Pitching W	Relief Pitching L	Relief Pitching SV	Batting AB	Batting H	Batting HR	BA	PO	A	E	DP	TC/G	FA
1902	PHI	A	0	1	.000	5.63	1	1	1	8	10	0	2	0	0	0	0	4	1	0	.250	1	5	0	0	6.0	1.000
1904	CIN	N	15	8	.652	2.24	24	24	22	217	196	53	64	2	0	0	0	77	9	0	.117	9	55	3	1	2.8	.955
1905			9	7	.563	3.23	23	19	12	145	171	44	28	1	0	0	0	51	7	0	.137	5	41	0	1	2.0	1.000
3 yrs.			24	16	.600	2.70	48	44	35	370	377	97	94	3	0	0	0	132	17	0	.129	15	101	3	2	2.5	.975

Jim Walkup

WALKUP, JAMES ELTON BR TR 6′ 1″ 170 lbs.
B. Dec. 14, 1909, Havana, Ark.

Year	Team		W	L	PCT	ERA	G	GS	CG	IP	H	BB	SO	ShO	Relief Pitching W	Relief Pitching L	Relief Pitching SV	Batting AB	Batting H	HR	BA	PO	A	E	DP	TC/G	FA
1934	**STL**	**A**	0	0	—	2.16	3	0	0	8.1	6	5	6	0	0	0	0	3	1	0	.333	0	0	0	0	0.0	.000
1935			6	9	.400	6.25	55	20	4	181.1	226	104	44	1	1	1	0	47	6	0	.128	11	28	2	2	0.7	.951
1936			0	3	.000	8.04	5	2	0	15.2	20	6	5	0	0	1	0	4	0	0	.000	1	6	0	1	1.4	1.000
1937			9	12	.429	7.36	27	18	6	150.1	218	83	46	0	2	3	0	58	14	0	.241	7	37	2	1	1.7	.957
1938			1	12	.077	6.80	18	13	1	94	127	53	28	0	1	2	0	29	4	0	.138	3	19	0	2	1.2	1.000
1939	**2 teams**	**STL A**	(1G 0–1)	**DET A**	(7G 0–1)																						
″	**total**		0	2	.000	7.11	8	0	0	12.2	17	9	5	0	0	2	0	2	1	0	.500	1	2	0	0	0.4	1.000
6 yrs.			16	38	.296	6.74	116	53	11	462.1	614	260	134	1	4	9	0	143	26	0	.182	23	92	4	6	1.0	.966

Jim Walkup

WALKUP, JAMES HUEY BR TL 5′ 8″ 150 lbs.
B. Nov. 3, 1895, Havana, Ark. D. June 12, 1990, Duncan, Okla.

Year	Team		W	L	PCT	ERA	G	GS	CG	IP	H	BB	SO	ShO	Relief Pitching W	Relief Pitching L	Relief Pitching SV	Batting AB	Batting H	HR	BA	PO	A	E	DP	TC/G	FA
1927	**DET**	**A**	0	0	—	5.40	2	0	0	1.2	3	0	0	0	0	0	0	1	0	0	.000	0	1	0	0	0.5	1.000

Donne Wall

WALL, DONNELL LEE BR TR 6′ 1″ 180 lbs.
B. July 11, 1967, Potosi, Mo.

Year	Team		W	L	PCT	ERA	G	GS	CG	IP	H	BB	SO	ShO	Relief Pitching W	Relief Pitching L	Relief Pitching SV	Batting AB	Batting H	HR	BA	PO	A	E	DP	TC/G	FA
1995	**HOU**	**N**	3	1	.750	5.55	6	5	0	24.1	33	5	16	0	0	0	0	5	0	0	.000	4	2	1	0	1.2	.857

Murray Wall

WALL, MURRAY WESLEY (Tex) BR TR 6′ 3″ 185 lbs.
B. Sept. 19, 1926, Dallas, Tex. D. Oct. 8, 1971, Lone Oak, Tex.

Year	Team		W	L	PCT	ERA	G	GS	CG	IP	H	BB	SO	ShO	Relief Pitching W	Relief Pitching L	Relief Pitching SV	Batting AB	Batting H	HR	BA	PO	A	E	DP	TC/G	FA
1950	**BOS**	**N**	0	0	—	9.00	1	0	0	4	6	2	2	0	0	0	0	1	0	0	.000	0	0	1	0	1.0	.000
1957	**BOS**	**A**	3	0	1.000	3.33	11	0	0	24.1	21	2	13	0	3	0	1	6	2	0	.333	4	8	0	1	1.1	1.000
1958			8	9	.471	3.62	52	1	0	114.1	109	33	53	0	8	**8**	10	28	3	0	.107	9	32	0	2	0.8	1.000
1959	**3 teams**	**BOS A**	(15G 1–4)	**WAS A**	(1G 0–0)	**BOS A**	(11G 1–1)																				
″	**total**		2	5	.286	5.54	27	0	0	50.1	60	26	14	0	2	5	3	11	0	0	.000	4	14	2	0	0.7	.900
4 yrs.			13	14	.481	4.20	91	1	0	193	196	63	82	0	13	13	14	46	5	0	.109	17	54	3	3	0.8	.959

Stan Wall

WALL, STANLEY ARTHUR BL TL 6′ 1″ 175 lbs.
B. June 16, 1951, Butler, Mo.

Year	Team		W	L	PCT	ERA	G	GS	CG	IP	H	BB	SO	ShO	Relief Pitching W	Relief Pitching L	Relief Pitching SV	Batting AB	Batting H	HR	BA	PO	A	E	DP	TC/G	FA
1975	**LA**	**N**	0	1	.000	1.69	10	0	0	16	12	7	6	0	0	1	0	0	0	0	—	0	3	0	0	0.3	1.000
1976			2	2	.500	3.60	31	0	0	50	50	15	27	0	2	2	1	4	0	0	.000	0	6	0	1	0.2	1.000
1977			2	3	.400	5.34	25	0	0	32	36	13	22	0	2	3	0	1	0	0	.000	0	3	1	0	0.2	.750
3 yrs.			4	6	.400	3.86	66	0	0	98	98	35	55	0	4	6	1	5	0	0	.000	0	12	1	1	0.2	.923

Bobby Wallace

WALLACE, RHODERICK JOHN (Rhody) BR TR 5′ 8″ 170 lbs.
B. Nov. 4, 1873, Pittsburgh, Pa. D. Nov. 3, 1960, Torrance, Calif.
Manager 1911–12, 1937.
Hall of Fame 1953.

Year	Team		W	L	PCT	ERA	G	GS	CG	IP	H	BB	SO	ShO	Relief Pitching W	Relief Pitching L	Relief Pitching SV	Batting AB	Batting H	HR	BA	PO	A	E	DP	TC/G	FA
1894	**CLE**	**N**	2	1	.667	5.47	4	3	3	26.1	28	22	10	0	0	0	0	13	2	0	.154	3	9	0	0	3.0	1.000
1895			12	14	.462	4.09	30	28	22	228.2	271	87	63	1	0	1	1	98	21	0	.214	15	66	8	2	3.0	.910
1896			10	7	.588	3.34	22	16	13	145.1	167	49	46	2	1	1	0	149	35	1	.235	44	35	5	4	1.8	.940
1902	**STL**	**A**	0	0	—	0.00	1	1	0	2	3	0	1	0	0	0	0	495	142	1	.287	191	250	35	10	3.6	.926
4 yrs.			24	22	.522	3.89	57	48	38	402.1	469	158	120	3	1	2	1	*				4919	7465	814	724	5.6	.938

Dave Wallace

WALLACE, DAVID WILLIAM BR TR 5′10″ 185 lbs.
B. Sept. 7, 1947, Waterbury, Conn.

Year	Team		W	L	PCT	ERA	G	GS	CG	IP	H	BB	SO	ShO	Relief Pitching W	Relief Pitching L	Relief Pitching SV	Batting AB	Batting H	HR	BA	PO	A	E	DP	TC/G	FA
1973	**PHI**	**N**	0	0	—	22.09	4	0	0	3.2	13	2	2	0	0	0	0	0	0	0	—	0	2	0	0	0.5	1.000
1974			0	1	.000	9.00	3	0	0	3	4	3	3	0	0	1	0	0	0	0	—	0	1	0	0	0.3	1.000
1978	**TOR**	**A**	0	0	—	3.86	6	0	0	14	12	11	7	0	0	0	0	0	0	0	—	1	1	0	0	0.3	1.000
3 yrs.			0	1	.000	7.84	13	0	0	20.2	29	16	12	0	0	1	0	0	0	0		1	4	0	0	0.4	1.000

Huck Wallace

WALLACE, HARRY CLINTON (Lefty) BL TL 5′ 6″ 160 lbs.
B. July 27, 1882, Richmond, Ind. D. July 6, 1951, Cleveland, Ohio.

Year	Team		W	L	PCT	ERA	G	GS	CG	IP	H	BB	SO	ShO	Relief Pitching W	Relief Pitching L	Relief Pitching SV	Batting AB	Batting H	HR	BA	PO	A	E	DP	TC/G	FA
1912	**PHI**	**N**	0	0	—	0.00	4	0	0	4.2	7	4	4	0	0	0	0	0	0	0	—	0	1	0	0	0.3	1.000

Lefty Wallace

WALLACE, JAMES HAROLD BL TL 5′11″ 160 lbs.
B. Aug. 12, 1921, Evansville, Ind. D. July 28, 1982, Evansville, Ind.

Year	Team		W	L	PCT	ERA	G	GS	CG	IP	H	BB	SO	ShO	Relief Pitching W	Relief Pitching L	Relief Pitching SV	Batting AB	Batting H	HR	BA	PO	A	E	DP	TC/G	FA
1942	**BOS**	**N**	1	3	.250	3.83	19	3	1	49.1	39	24	20	0	0	1	0	14	2	0	.143	0	7	0	0	0.4	1.000
1945			1	0	1.000	4.50	5	3	1	20	18	9	4	0	0	0	0	6	0	0	.000	2	4	0	1	1.2	1.000
1946			3	3	.500	4.18	27	8	2	75.1	76	31	27	0	1	1	0	18	1	0	.056	7	21	0	0	1.0	1.000
3 yrs.			5	6	.455	4.11	51	14	4	144.2	133	64	51	0	1	2	0	38	3	0	.079	9	32	0	1	0.8	1.000

Mike Wallace

WALLACE, MICHAEL SHERMAN BL TL 6′ 2″ 190 lbs.
B. Feb. 3, 1951, Gastonia, N. C.

Year	Team		W	L	PCT	ERA	G	GS	CG	IP	H	BB	SO	ShO	Relief Pitching W	Relief Pitching L	Relief Pitching SV	Batting AB	Batting H	HR	BA	PO	A	E	DP	TC/G	FA
1973	**PHI**	**N**	1	1	.500	3.78	20	3	1	33.1	38	15	20	0	0	0	1	4	0	0	.000	2	3	0	0	0.3	1.000
1974	**2 teams**	**PHI N**	(8G 1–0)	**NY A**	(23G 6–0)																						
″	**total**		7	0	1.000	2.85	31	1	0	60	54	37	35	0	6	0	0	0	0	0		4	3	1	0	0.3	.875
1975	**2 teams**	**NY A**	(3G 0–0)	**STL N**	(9G 0–0)																						
″	**total**		0	0		6.23	12	0	0	13	20	6	8	0	0	0	0	0	0	0		2	2	0	0	0.3	1.000
1976	**STL**	**N**	3	2	.600	4.07	49	0	0	66.1	66	39	40	0	3	2	2	3	1	0	.333	1	12	1	2	0.3	.929
1977	**TEX**	**A**	0	0	—	7.88	5	0	0	8	10	10	2	0	0	0	0	0	0	0	—	0	3	0	0	0.6	1.000
5 yrs.			11	3	.786	3.94	117	4	1	180.2	188	107	105	0	9	2	3	7	1	0	.143	9	23	2	2	0.3	.941

Tim Wallach

WALLACH, TIMOTHY CHARLES BR TR 6′ 3″ 220 lbs.
B. Sept. 14, 1957, Huntington Park, Calif.

Year	Team		W	L	PCT	ERA	G	GS	CG	IP	H	BB	SO	ShO	Relief Pitching W	Relief Pitching L	Relief Pitching SV	Batting AB	Batting H	HR	BA	PO	A	E	DP	TC/G	FA
1987	**MON**	**N**	0	0	—	0.00	1	0	0	1	1	0	0	0	0	0	0	593	177	26	.298	12	0	0	0	3.0	1.000
1989			0	0	—	9.00	1	0	0	1	2	0	0	0	0	0	0	573	159	13	.277	207	31	1	9	3.6	.996
2 yrs.			0	0		4.50	2	0	0	2	3	0	0	0	0	0	0	*				2458	3913	236	361	3.1	.964

Red Waller

WALLER, JOHN FRANCIS
B. June 16, 1883, Washington, D. C. D. Feb. 9, 1915, Secaucus, N. J.

Year	Team		W	L	PCT	ERA	G	GS	CG	IP	H	BB	SO	ShO	Relief Pitching W	Relief Pitching L	Relief Pitching SV	Batting AB	Batting H	HR	BA	PO	A	E	DP	TC/G	FA
1909	**NY**	**N**	0	0	—	0.00	1	0	0	1	3	0	1	0	0	0	0	0	0	0	—	0	1	0	1	1.0	1.000

Year	Team	Lg	W	L	PCT	ERA	G	GS	CG	IP	H	BB	SO	ShO	Relief Pitching W	Relief Pitching L	Relief Pitching SV	Batting AB	Batting H	Batting HR	BA	PO	A	E	DP	TC/G	FA

Augie Walsh

WALSH, AUGUST SOTHLEY BR TR 6′ 175 lbs.
B. Aug. 9, 1904, Wilmington, Del. D. Nov. 12, 1985, San Rafael, Calif.

Year	Team	Lg	W	L	PCT	ERA	G	GS	CG	IP	H	BB	SO	ShO	W	L	SV	AB	H	HR	BA	PO	A	E	DP	TC/G	FA
1927	PHI	N	0	1	.000	4.50	1	1	1	10	12	5	0	0	0	0	0	4	1	0	.250	0	1	0	1	1.0	1.000
1928			4	9	.308	6.18	38	11	2	122.1	160	40	38	0	2	1	2	39	10	1	.256	2	20	0	2	0.6	1.000
2 yrs.			4	10	.286	6.05	39	12	3	132.1	172	45	38	0	2	1	2	43	11	1	.256	2	21	0	3	0.6	1.000

Connie Walsh

WALSH, CORNELIUS R.
B. Apr. 23, 1882, St. Louis, Mo. D. Apr. 5, 1953, St. Louis, Mo.

Year	Team	Lg	W	L	PCT	ERA	G	GS	CG	IP	H	BB	SO	ShO	W	L	SV	AB	H	HR	BA	PO	A	E	DP	TC/G	FA
1907	PIT	N	0	0	—	9.00	1	0	0	1	1	1	0	0	0	0	0	0	0	0	—	0	0	0	0	0.0	.000

David Walsh

WALSH, DAVID PETER BL TL 6′ 1″ 185 lbs.
B. Sept. 25, 1960, Arlington, Mass.

Year	Team	Lg	W	L	PCT	ERA	G	GS	CG	IP	H	BB	SO	ShO	W	L	SV	AB	H	HR	BA	PO	A	E	DP	TC/G	FA
1990	LA	N	1	0	1.000	3.86	20	0	0	16.1	15	6	15	0	1	0	1	0	0	0	—	2	3	0	0	0.3	1.000

Dee Walsh

WALSH, LEO THOMAS BB TR 5′ 9½″ 165 lbs.
B. Mar. 28, 1890, St. Louis, Mo. D. July 14, 1971, St. Louis, Mo.

Year	Team	Lg	W	L	PCT	ERA	G	GS	CG	IP	H	BB	SO	ShO	W	L	SV	AB	H	HR	BA	PO	A	E	DP	TC/G	FA
1915	STL	A	0	0	—	13.50	1	0	0	2	2	2	0	0	0	0	0	*				36	63	7	6	4.6	.934

Ed Walsh

WALSH, EDWARD ARTHUR BR TR 6′ 1″ 180 lbs.
Son of Ed Walsh.
B. Feb. 11, 1905, Meriden, Conn. D. Oct. 31, 1937, Meriden, Conn.

Year	Team	Lg	W	L	PCT	ERA	G	GS	CG	IP	H	BB	SO	ShO	W	L	SV	AB	H	HR	BA	PO	A	E	DP	TC/G	FA
1928	CHI	A	4	7	.364	4.96	14	10	3	78	86	42	32	0	1	0	0	27	3	0	.111	0	14	0	1	1.0	1.000
1929			6	11	.353	5.65	24	20	7	129	156	64	31	0	0	1	0	43	10	0	.233	5	31	1	2	1.5	.973
1930			1	4	.200	5.38	37	4	4	103.2	131	30	37	0	1	3	0	34	9	0	.265	5	25	1	1	0.8	.968
1932			0	2	.000	8.41	4	4	1	20.1	26	13	7	0	0	0	0	7	2	0	.286	2	3	0	0	1.3	1.000
4 yrs.			11	24	.314	5.57	79	38	15	331	399	149	107	0	2	4	0	111	24	0	.216	12	73	2	4	1.1	.977

Ed Walsh

WALSH, EDWARD AUGUSTINE (Big Ed) BR TR 6′ 1″ 193 lbs.
Father of Ed Walsh.
B. May 14, 1881, Plains, Pa. D. May 26, 1959, Pompano Beach, Fla.
Manager 1924.
Hall of Fame 1946.

Year	Team	Lg	W	L	PCT	ERA	G	GS	CG	IP	H	BB	SO	ShO	W	L	SV	AB	H	HR	BA	PO	A	E	DP	TC/G	FA
1904	CHI	A	6	3	.667	2.60	18	8	6	110.2	90	32	57	1	2	0	1	41	9	1	.220	8	35	1	2	2.4	.977
1905			8	3	.727	2.17	22	13	9	136.2	121	29	71	1	1	0	0	58	9	0	.155	13	42	2	1	2.1	.965
1906			17	13	.567	1.88	41	31	24	278.1	215	58	171	**10**	1	1	1	99	14	0	.141	30	108	6	2	3.5	.958
1907			24	18	.571	**1.60**	**56**	**46**	**37**	**422.1**	341	87	206	5	0	1	**4**	154	25	1	.162	35	227	4	2	4.8	.985
1908			**40**	15	**.727**	1.42	**66**	**49**	**42**	**464**	**343**	56	**269**	**11**	5	1	**6**	157	27	1	.172	41	190	6	9	3.6	.975
1909			15	11	.577	1.41	31	28	20	230.1	166	50	127	**8**	0	1	2	84	18	0	.214	23	93	1	2	3.7	.991
1910			18	**20**	.474	**1.27**	**45**	36	33	369.2	242	61	258	7	2	2	**5**	138	30	0	.217	21	154	9	5	4.1	.951
1911			27	18	.600	2.22	**56**	37	33	**368.2**	327	72	**255**	5	**7**	**5**	**4**	155	32	0	.206	27	159	8	5	3.5	.959
1912			27	17	.614	2.15	**62**	**41**	32	**393**	**332**	94	254	6	4	2	**10**	136	33	0	.243	22	143	15	3	2.9	.917
1913			8	3	.727	2.58	16	14	7	97.2	91	39	34	1	0	0	1	32	5	0	.156	6	32	3	1	2.6	.927
1914			2	3	.400	2.82	8	5	3	44.2	33	20	15	1	0	0	0	16	1	0	.063	7	15	1	0	2.9	.957
1915			3	0	1.000	1.33	3	3	3	27	19	7	12	1	0	0	0	11	4	0	.364	3	4	0	0	2.3	1.000
1916			0	1	.000	2.70	2	1	0	3.1	4	3	3	0	0	0	0	0	0	0	—	0	2	0	0	1.0	1.000
1917	BOS	N	0	1	.000	3.50	4	3	1	18	22	9	4	0	0	0	0	4	1	0	.250	1	7	1	0	2.3	.889
14 yrs.			195	126	.607	1.82 **1st**	430	315	250	2964.1	2346	617	1736	57	22	13	34	*				237	1211	57	32	3.5	.962
WORLD SERIES																											
1906	CHI	A	2	0	1.000	1.80	2	2	1	15	7	6	17	1	0	0	0	*				0	5	1	0	3.0	.833

Jim Walsh

WALSH, JAMES THOMAS BL TL 5′11″ 175 lbs.
B. July 10, 1894, Roxbury, Mass. D. May 13, 1967, Boston, Mass.

Year	Team	Lg	W	L	PCT	ERA	G	GS	CG	IP	H	BB	SO	ShO	W	L	SV	AB	H	HR	BA	PO	A	E	DP	TC/G	FA
1921	DET	A	0	0	—	2.25	3	0	0	4	2	1	3	0	0	0	0	0	0	0	—	0	0	1	0	0.3	.000

Jimmy Walsh

WALSH, MICHAEL TIMOTHY (Runt) BR TR 5′ 9″ 174 lbs.
B. Mar. 25, 1886, Lima, Ohio D. Jan. 21, 1947, Baltimore, Md.

Year	Team	Lg	W	L	PCT	ERA	G	GS	CG	IP	H	BB	SO	ShO	W	L	SV	AB	H	HR	BA	PO	A	E	DP	TC/G	FA
1911	PHI	N	0	1	.000	13.50	1	0	0	2.2	7	1	1	0	0	1	0	*				122	101	23	11	3.7	.907

Junior Walsh

WALSH, JAMES GERALD BR TR 5′11″ 185 lbs.
B. Mar. 7, 1919, Newark, N. J. D. Nov. 12, 1990, Olyphant, Pa.

Year	Team	Lg	W	L	PCT	ERA	G	GS	CG	IP	H	BB	SO	ShO	W	L	SV	AB	H	HR	BA	PO	A	E	DP	TC/G	FA
1946	PIT	N	0	1	.000	5.23	4	2	0	10.1	9	10	2	0	0	0	0	4	0	0	.000	0	2	0	0	0.5	1.000
1948			1	0	1.000	10.38	2	0	0	4.1	4	5	0	0	1	0	0	2	0	0	.000	0	2	0	0	1.0	1.000
1949			1	4	.200	5.06	9	7	1	42.2	40	16	24	1	0	0	0	12	0	0	.000	2	5	2	0	1.0	.778
1950			1	1	.500	5.05	38	2	0	62.1	56	34	33	0	1	1	2	6	1	0	.167	4	11	1	1	0.4	.938
1951			1	4	.200	6.87	36	1	0	73.1	92	46	32	0	1	3	0	7	1	0	.143	6	13	2	0	0.6	.905
5 yrs.			4	10	.286	5.88	89	12	1	193	201	111	91	1	3	4	2	31	2	0	.065	12	33	5	1	0.6	.900

Bernie Walter

WALTER, JAMES BERNARD BR TR 6′ 1″ 175 lbs.
B. Aug. 15, 1908, Dover, Tenn. D. Oct. 30, 1988, Nashville, Tenn.

Year	Team	Lg	W	L	PCT	ERA	G	GS	CG	IP	H	BB	SO	ShO	W	L	SV	AB	H	HR	BA	PO	A	E	DP	TC/G	FA
1930	PIT	N	0	0	—	0.00	1	0	0	1	0	0	1	0	0	0	0	0	0	0	—	0	1	0	0	1.0	1.000

Gene Walter

WALTER, GENE WINSTON BL TL 6′ 4″ 200 lbs.
B. Nov. 22, 1960, Chicago, Ill.

Year	Team	Lg	W	L	PCT	ERA	G	GS	CG	IP	H	BB	SO	ShO	W	L	SV	AB	H	HR	BA	PO	A	E	DP	TC/G	FA
1985	SD	N	0	2	.000	2.05	15	0	0	22	12	8	18	0	0	2	3	1	0	0	.000	1	4	0	0	0.3	1.000
1986			2	2	.500	3.86	57	0	0	98	89	49	84	0	2	2	1	10	2	0	.200	8	17	1	1	0.5	.962
1987	NY	N	1	2	.333	3.20	21	0	0	19.2	18	13	11	0	1	2	0	1	0	0	.000	2	2	1	1	0.2	.800
1988	2 teams	NY N (19G 0–1)	SEA A (16G 1–0)																								
″	total		1	1	.500	4.60	35	0	0	43	42	26	27	0	1	1	0	0	0	0		2	3	0	0	0.1	1.000
4 yrs.			4	7	.364	3.74	128	0	0	182.2	161	96	140	0	4	7	4	12	2	0	.167	13	26	2	2	0.3	.951

Bucky Walters

WALTERS, WILLIAM HENRY BR TR 6′ 1″ 180 lbs.
B. Apr. 19, 1909, Philadelphia, Pa. D. Apr. 20, 1991, Abington, Pa.
Manager 1948–49.

Year	Team	W	L	PCT	ERA	G	GS	CG	IP	H	BB	SO	ShO	Relief Pitching W	Relief Pitching L	Relief Pitching SV	Batting AB	Batting H	HR	BA	PO	A	E	DP	TC/G	FA
1934	PHI N	0	0	—	1.29	2	1	0	7	8	2	7	0	0	0	0	388	97	8	.250	7	22	1	0	3.3	.967
1935		9	9	.500	4.17	24	22	8	151	168	68	40	2	0	1	0	96	24	0	.250	15	48	1	4	2.0	.984
1936		11	**21**	.344	4.26	40	33	15	258	284	115	66	**4**	1	1	0	121	29	1	.240	15	98	3	6	2.8	.974
1937		14	15	.483	4.75	37	**34**	15	246.1	292	86	87	3	0	1	0	137	38	1	.277	12	85	1	8	2.2	.990
1938	2 teams PHI N (12G 4–8) CIN N (27G 11–6)																									
″	total	15	14	.517	4.20	39	34	20	251	259	108	93	3	1	0	1	99	19	1	.192	6	66	2	5	1.9	.973
1939	CIN N	**27**	11	.711	**2.29**	39	**36**	**31**	**319**	250	109	**137**	2	0	3	0	120	39	1	.325	16	77	2	10	2.4	.979
1940		**22**	10	.688	**2.48**	36	36	**29**	**305**	241	92	115	3	0	0	0	117	24	1	.205	13	56	4	7	2.0	.945
1941		19	15	.559	2.83	37	35	**27**	**302**	**292**	88	129	5	0	0	2	106	20	0	.189	18	68	2	6	2.4	.977
1942		15	14	.517	2.66	34	32	21	253.2	223	73	109	2	0	1	0	99	24	2	.242	13	60	3	6	2.2	.961
1943		15	15	.500	3.54	34	34	21	246.1	244	109	80	5	0	0	0	90	24	1	.267	19	49	2	7	2.1	.971
1944		**23**	8	.742	2.40	34	32	27	285	233	87	77	6	1	0	1	107	30	0	.280	15	55	0	7	2.1	1.000
1945		10	10	.500	2.68	22	22	12	168	166	51	45	3	0	0	0	61	14	3	.230	6	33	1	3	1.8	.975
1946		10	7	.588	2.56	22	22	10	151.1	146	64	60	2	0	0	0	55	7	0	.127	10	37	3	7	2.3	.940
1947		8	8	.500	5.75	20	20	5	122	137	49	43	2	0	0	0	45	12	0	.267	6	19	1	0	1.3	.962
1948		0	3	.000	4.63	7	5	1	35	42	18	19	0	0	0	0	15	4	0	.267	1	11	0	0	1.7	1.000
1950	BOS N	0	0	—	4.50	1	0	0	4	5	2	0	0	0	0	0	2	0	0	.000	1	0	0	0	1.0	1.000
16 yrs.		198	160	.553	3.30	428	398	242	3104.2	2990	1121	1107	42	3	7	4	*				364	1135	63	117	2.5	.960
WORLD SERIES																										
1939	CIN N	0	2	.000	4.91	2	1	1	11	13	1	6	0	0	1	0	3	0	0	.000	0	3	0	1	1.5	1.000
1940		2	0	1.000	1.50	2	2	2	18	8	6	6	1	0	0	0	7	2	1	.286	0	4	0	0	2.0	1.000
2 yrs.		2	2	.500	2.79	4	3	3	29	21	7	12	1	0	1	0	*				0	7	0	1	1.8	1.000

Charley Walters

WALTERS, CHARLES LEONARD BR TR 6′ 4″ 190 lbs.
B. Feb. 21, 1947, Minneapolis, Minn.

Year	Team	W	L	PCT	ERA	G	GS	CG	IP	H	BB	SO	ShO	Relief Pitching W	Relief Pitching L	Relief Pitching SV	Batting AB	Batting H	HR	BA	PO	A	E	DP	TC/G	FA
1969	MIN A	0	0	—	5.40	6	0	0	6.2	6	3	2	0	0	0	0	0	0	0	—	0	1	0	0	0.2	1.000

Mike Walters

WALTERS, MICHAEL CHARLES BR TR 6′ 5″ 195 lbs.
B. Oct. 18, 1957, St. Louis, Mo.

Year	Team	W	L	PCT	ERA	G	GS	CG	IP	H	BB	SO	ShO	Relief Pitching W	Relief Pitching L	Relief Pitching SV	Batting AB	Batting H	HR	BA	PO	A	E	DP	TC/G	FA
1983	MIN A	1	1	.500	4.12	23	0	0	59	52	20	21	0	1	1	2	0	0	0	—	3	10	0	1	0.6	1.000
1984		0	3	.000	3.72	23	0	0	29	31	14	10	0	0	3	2	0	0	0	—	1	2	0	1	0.1	1.000
2 yrs.		1	4	.200	3.99	46	0	0	88	83	34	31	0	1	4	4	0	0	0		4	12	0	2	0.3	1.000

Bruce Walton

WALTON, BRUCE KENNETH BR TR 6′ 2″ 195 lbs.
B. Dec. 25, 1962, Bakersfield, Calif.

Year	Team	W	L	PCT	ERA	G	GS	CG	IP	H	BB	SO	ShO	Relief Pitching W	Relief Pitching L	Relief Pitching SV	Batting AB	Batting H	HR	BA	PO	A	E	DP	TC/G	FA
1991	OAK A	1	0	1.000	6.23	12	0	0	13	11	6	10	0	1	0	0	0	0	0	—	1	0	0	0	0.1	1.000
1992		0	0	—	9.90	7	0	0	10	17	3	7	0	0	0	0	0	0	0	—	0	1	0	0	0.1	1.000
1993	MON N	0	0	—	9.53	4	0	0	5.2	11	3	0	0	0	0	0	1	0	0	.000	1	1	0	0	0.5	1.000
1994	CLR N	1	0	1.000	8.44	4	0	0	5.1	6	3	1	0	1	0	0	0	0	0	—	0	1	1	0	0.5	.500
4 yrs.		2	0	1.000	8.21	27	0	0	34	45	15	18	0	2	0	0	1	0	0	.000	2	3	1	0	0.2	.833

Zach Walton

Playing record listed under Tom Zachary.

Dick Wantz

WANTZ, RICHARD CARTER BR TR 6′ 5″ 175 lbs.
B. Apr. 11, 1940, South Gate, Calif. D. May 13, 1965, Inglewood, Calif.

Year	Team	W	L	PCT	ERA	G	GS	CG	IP	H	BB	SO	ShO	Relief Pitching W	Relief Pitching L	Relief Pitching SV	Batting AB	Batting H	HR	BA	PO	A	E	DP	TC/G	FA
1965	CAL A	0	0	—	18.00	1	0	0	1	3	0	2	0	0	0	0	0	0	0	—	0	0	0	0	0.0	.000

Steve Wapnick

WAPNICK, STEVEN LEE BR TR 6′ 2″ 200 lbs.
B. Sept. 25, 1965, Panorama City, Calif.

Year	Team	W	L	PCT	ERA	G	GS	CG	IP	H	BB	SO	ShO	Relief Pitching W	Relief Pitching L	Relief Pitching SV	Batting AB	Batting H	HR	BA	PO	A	E	DP	TC/G	FA
1990	DET A	0	0	—	6.43	4	0	0	7	8	10	6	0	0	0	0	0	0	0	—	0	0	1	0	0.3	.000
1991	CHI A	0	1	.000	1.80	6	0	0	5	2	4	1	0	0	1	0	0	0	0	—	1	0	0	0	0.2	1.000
2 yrs.		0	1	.000	4.50	10	0	0	12	10	14	7	0	0	1	0	0	0	0		1	0	1	0	0.2	.500

Colby Ward

WARD, ROBERT COLBY BR TR 6′ 2″ 185 lbs.
B. Jan. 2, 1964, Lansing, Mich.

Year	Team	W	L	PCT	ERA	G	GS	CG	IP	H	BB	SO	ShO	Relief Pitching W	Relief Pitching L	Relief Pitching SV	Batting AB	Batting H	HR	BA	PO	A	E	DP	TC/G	FA
1990	CLE A	1	3	.250	4.25	22	0	0	36	31	21	23	0	1	3	1	0	0	0	—	3	3	0	0	0.3	1.000

Colin Ward

WARD, COLIN NORVAL BL TL 6′ 3″ 190 lbs.
B. Nov. 22, 1960, Los Angeles, Calif.

Year	Team	W	L	PCT	ERA	G	GS	CG	IP	H	BB	SO	ShO	Relief Pitching W	Relief Pitching L	Relief Pitching SV	Batting AB	Batting H	HR	BA	PO	A	E	DP	TC/G	FA
1985	SF N	0	0	—	4.38	6	2	0	12.1	10	7	8	0	0	0	0	2	0	0	.000	0	2	0	0	0.3	1.000

Dick Ward

WARD, RICHARD O. (Ole) BR TR 6′ 1″ 198 lbs.
B. May 21, 1909, Herrick, S. D. D. May 30, 1966, Freeland, Wash.

Year	Team	W	L	PCT	ERA	G	GS	CG	IP	H	BB	SO	ShO	Relief Pitching W	Relief Pitching L	Relief Pitching SV	Batting AB	Batting H	HR	BA	PO	A	E	DP	TC/G	FA
1934	CHI N	0	0	—	3.18	3	0	0	5.2	9	2	1	0	0	0	0	1	0	0	.000	0	1	0	0	0.3	1.000
1935	STL N	0	0	—	0.00	1	0	0		0	1	0	0	0	0	0	0	0	0	—	0	0	0	0	0.0	.000
2 yrs.		0	0		3.18	4	0	0	5.2	9	3	1	0	0	0	0	1	0	0	.000	0	1	0	0	0.3	1.000

Duane Ward

WARD, ROY DUANE BR TR 6′ 4″ 185 lbs.
B. May 28, 1964, Park View, N. M.

Year	Team	W	L	PCT	ERA	G	GS	CG	IP	H	BB	SO	ShO	Relief Pitching W	Relief Pitching L	Relief Pitching SV	Batting AB	Batting H	HR	BA	PO	A	E	DP	TC/G	FA
1986	2 teams ATL N (10G 0–1) TOR A (2G 0–1)																									
″	total	0	2	.000	8.00	12	1	0	18	25	12	9	0	0	1	0	1	0	0	.000	1	6	0	0	0.6	1.000
1987	TOR A	1	0	1.000	6.94	12	1	0	11.2	14	12	10	0	1	0	0	0	0	0	—	2	2	0	0	0.3	1.000
1988		9	3	.750	3.30	64	0	0	111.2	101	60	91	0	**9**	3	15	0	0	0	—	6	12	1	0	0.3	.947
1989		4	10	.286	3.77	66	0	0	114.2	94	58	122	0	4	**10**	15	0	0	0	—	5	21	1	2	0.4	.963
1990		2	8	.200	3.45	73	0	0	127.2	101	42	112	0	2	**8**	11	0	0	0	—	9	18	1	0	0.4	.964
1991		7	6	.538	2.77	**81**	0	0	107.1	80	33	132	0	7	6	23	0	0	0	—	9	11	1	1	0.3	.952
1992		7	4	.636	1.95	79	0	0	101.1	76	39	103	0	7	4	12	0	0	0	—	4	11	1	0	0.2	.938

Duane Ward *continued*

Year	Team	Lg	W	L	PCT	ERA	G	GS	CG	IP	H	BB	SO	ShO	Relief Pitching W	L	SV	Batting AB	H	HR	BA	PO	A	E	DP	TC/G	FA
1993			2	3	.400	2.13	71	0	0	71.2	49	25	97	0	2	3	**45**	0	0	0	—	1	5	0	0	0.1	1.000
1995			0	1	.000	27.00	4	0	0	2.2	11	5	3	0	0	1	0	0	0	0	—	0	0	1	0	0.3	.000
9 yrs.			32	37	.464	3.28	462	2	0	666.2	551	286	679	0	32	36	121	1	0	0	.000	37	86	6	3	0.3	.953
LEAGUE CHAMPIONSHIP SERIES																											
1989	**TOR**	**A**	0	0	—	7.36	2	0	0	3.2	6	3	5	0	0	0	0	0	0	0	—	1	0	0	0	0.5	1.000
1991			0	1	.000	6.23	2	0	0	4.1	4	1	6	0	0	1	1	0	0	0	—	0	0	0	0	0.0	.000
1992			1	0	1.000	6.75	3	0	0	4	6	1	2	0	1	0	0	0	0	0	—	1	0	0	0	0.3	1.000
1993			0	0	—	5.79	4	0	0	4.2	4	3	8	0	0	0	2	0	0	0	—	0	0	0	0	0.0	.000
4 yrs.			1	1	.500	6.48	11	0	0	16.2	20	8	21	0	1	1	3	0	0	0		2	0	0	0	0.2	1.000
							9th										**6th**										
WORLD SERIES																											
1992	**TOR**	**A**	2	0	1.000	0.00	4	0	0	3.1	1	1	6	0	2	0	0	0	0	0	—	0	0	0	0	0.0	.000
1993			1	0	1.000	1.93	4	0	0	4.2	3	0	7	0	1	0	2	0	0	0	—	0	0	0	0	0.0	.000
2 yrs.			3	0	1.000	1.13	8	0	0	8	4	1	13	0	3	0	2	0	0	0		0	0	0	0	0.0	

John Ward

WARD, JOHN
B. East St. Louis, Ill. Deceased.

Year	Team	Lg	W	L	PCT	ERA	G	GS	CG	IP	H	BB	SO	ShO	Relief Pitching W	L	SV	Batting AB	H	HR	BA	PO	A	E	DP	TC/G	FA
1885	**PRO**	**N**	0	1	.000	4.50	1	1	1	8	10	1	3	0	0	0	0	3	0	0	.000	0	1	1	0	2.0	.500

Monte Ward

WARD, JOHN MONTGOMERY BL TR 5′ 9″ 165 lbs.
B. Mar. 3, 1860, Bellefonte, Pa. D. Mar. 4, 1925, Augusta, Ga. BB 1888
Manager 1880, 1884, 1890–94.
Hall of Fame 1964.

Year	Team	Lg	W	L	PCT	ERA	G	GS	CG	IP	H	BB	SO	ShO	Relief Pitching W	L	SV	Batting AB	H	HR	BA	PO	A	E	DP	TC/G	FA
1878	**PRO**	**N**	22	13	.629	**1.51**	37	37	37	334	308	34	116	6	0	0	0	138	27	1	.196	23	74	15	4	3.0	.866
1879			**47**	17	**.734**	2.15	70	60	58	587	571	36	**239**	2	**5**	**1**	**1**	364	104	2	.286	55	167	23	4	2.6	.906
1880			40	23	.635	1.74	70	67	59	595	501	45	230	**8**	1	1	1	356	81	0	.228	74	203	17	5	3.0	.942
1881			18	18	.500	*2.13*	39	35	32	330	326	53	119	3	**1**	**1**	0	357	87	0	.244	110	130	29	11	2.9	.892
1882			19	13	.594	*2.59*	33	32	29	278	261	36	72	4	0	0	**1**	355	87	0	.245	105	105	31	8	2.8	.871
1883	**NY**	**N**	16	13	.552	*2.70*	33	25	24	277	278	31	121	1	**4**	1	0	380	97	7	.255	154	116	42	4	3.2	.865
1884			3	3	.500	*3.41*	9	5	5	60.2	72	18	23	0	0	**1**	0	482	122	2	.253	201	206	58	19	4.0	.875
7 yrs.			165	100	.623	2.10	291	261	244	2461.2	2317	253	920	24	11	5	3	*				3230	5043	950	493	4.9	.897
						4th																					

Jon Warden

WARDEN, JONATHAN EDGAR (Warbler) BB TL 6′ 205 lbs.
B. Oct. 1, 1946, Columbus, Ohio.

Year	Team	Lg	W	L	PCT	ERA	G	GS	CG	IP	H	BB	SO	ShO	Relief Pitching W	L	SV	Batting AB	H	HR	BA	PO	A	E	DP	TC/G	FA
1968	**DET**	**A**	4	1	.800	3.62	28	0	0	37.1	30	15	25	0	4	1	3	2	0	0	.000	0	2	1	0	0.1	.667

Curt Wardle

WARDLE, CURTIS RAY BL TL 6′ 5″ 220 lbs.
B. Nov. 16, 1960, Downey, Calif.

Year	Team	Lg	W	L	PCT	ERA	G	GS	CG	IP	H	BB	SO	ShO	Relief Pitching W	L	SV	Batting AB	H	HR	BA	PO	A	E	DP	TC/G	FA
1984	**MIN**	**A**	0	0	—	4.50	2	0	0	4	3	0	5	0	0	0	0	0	0	0	—	0	1	0	0	0.5	1.000
1985	**2 teams**	**MIN A**	(35G 1–3)		**CLE A**	(15G 7–6)																					
″	**total**		8	9	.471	6.18	50	12	0	115	127	62	84	0	2	3	1	0	0	0		5	15	1	1	0.4	.952
2 yrs.			8	9	.471	6.13	52	12	0	119	130	62	89	0	2	3	1	0	0	0		5	16	1	1	0.4	.955

Jeff Ware

WARE, JEFFREY ALLAN BR TR 6′ 3″ 190 lbs.
B. Nov. 11, 1970, Norfolk, Va.

Year	Team	Lg	W	L	PCT	ERA	G	GS	CG	IP	H	BB	SO	ShO	Relief Pitching W	L	SV	Batting AB	H	HR	BA	PO	A	E	DP	TC/G	FA
1995	**TOR**	**A**	2	1	.667	5.47	5	5	0	26.1	28	21	18	0	0	0	0	0	0	0	—	2	4	0	1	1.2	1.000

Jack Warhop

WARHOP, JOHN MILTON (Chief, Crab) BR TR 5′ 9½″ 168 lbs.
Born John Milton Wauhop.
B. July 4, 1884, Hinton, W. Va. D. Oct. 4, 1960, Freeport, Ill.

Year	Team	Lg	W	L	PCT	ERA	G	GS	CG	IP	H	BB	SO	ShO	Relief Pitching W	L	SV	Batting AB	H	HR	BA	PO	A	E	DP	TC/G	FA
1908	**NY**	**A**	1	2	.333	4.46	5	4	3	36.1	40	8	11	0	0	0	0	16	1	0	.063	1	14	1	0	1.8	.938
1909			13	15	.464	2.40	36	23	21	243.1	197	81	95	3	**4**	2	2	86	11	0	.128	15	80	7	2	2.8	.931
1910			14	14	.500	2.87	37	27	20	254	219	79	75	0	3	2	2	79	14	0	.177	15	65	11	0	2.5	.879
1911			12	13	.480	4.16	31	25	17	209.2	239	44	71	1	1	2	0	77	12	0	.156	7	53	4	1	2.0	.938
1912			10	19	.345	2.86	39	22	16	258	256	59	110	0	4	3	3	92	19	0	.207	3	64	7	1	1.9	.905
1913			4	6	.400	3.75	15	7	1	62.1	69	33	11	0	0	3	0	23	3	0	.130	0	12	4	2	1.1	.750
1914			8	15	.348	2.37	37	23	15	216.2	182	44	56	0	0	3	0	71	10	0	.141	5	60	7	3	1.9	.903
1915			7	9	.438	3.96	21	19	12	143.1	164	52	34	0	1	0	0	51	7	0	.137	4	34	3	1	2.0	.927
8 yrs.			69	93	.426	3.09	221	150	105	1423.2	1366	400	463	4	13	15	7	495	77	0	.156	50	382	44	10	2.1	.908

Cy Warmoth

WARMOTH, WALLACE WALTER BL TL 5′11″ 158 lbs.
B. Feb. 2, 1893, Bone Gap, Ill. D. June 20, 1957, Mt. Carmel, Ill.

Year	Team	Lg	W	L	PCT	ERA	G	GS	CG	IP	H	BB	SO	ShO	Relief Pitching W	L	SV	Batting AB	H	HR	BA	PO	A	E	DP	TC/G	FA
1916	**STL**	**N**	0	0	—	14.40	3	0	0	5	12	4	1	0	0	0	0	2	0	0	.000	1	0	0	0	0.3	1.000
1922	**WAS**	**A**	1	0	1.000	1.42	5	1	1	19	15	9	8	0	1	0	0	7	1	0	.143	2	3	0	0	1.0	1.000
1923			7	4	.636	4.29	21	13	4	105	103	76	45	0	1	0	0	36	8	0	.222	8	25	1	2	1.6	.971
3 yrs.			8	4	.667	4.26	29	14	5	129	130	89	54	0	2	0	0	45	9	0	.200	11	28	1	2	1.4	.975

Lon Warneke

WARNEKE, LONNIE (The Arkansas Humming Bird) BR TR 6′ 2″ 185 lbs.
B. Mar. 28, 1909, Mt. Ida, Ark. D. June 23, 1976, Hot Springs, Ark.

Year	Team	Lg	W	L	PCT	ERA	G	GS	CG	IP	H	BB	SO	ShO	Relief Pitching W	L	SV	Batting AB	H	HR	BA	PO	A	E	DP	TC/G	FA
1930	**CHI**	**N**	0	0	—	33.75	1	0	0	1.1	2	5	0	0	0	0	0	0	0	0	—	0	1	0	0	1.0	1.000
1931			2	4	.333	3.22	20	7	3	64.1	67	37	27	0	0	1	0	19	5	0	.263	1	8	1	0	0.5	.900
1932			**22**	6	**.786**	**2.37**	35	32	25	277	247	64	106	**4**	0	0	0	99	19	0	.192	11	55	1	1	1.9	.985
1933			18	13	.581	2.00	36	34	**26**	287.1	262	75	133	4	0	0	1	100	30	2	.300	8	72	0	7	2.2	1.000
1934			22	10	.688	3.21	43	35	23	291.1	273	66	143	3	2	1	3	113	22	0	.195	15	58	0	1	1.7	1.000
1935			20	13	.606	3.06	42	30	20	261.2	257	50	120	1	4	3	4	91	20	0	.220	15	47	1	1	1.5	.984
1936			16	13	.552	3.44	40	29	13	240.2	246	76	113	**4**	1	5	1	84	17	1	.202	15	44	1	1	1.5	.983
1937	**STL**	**N**	18	11	.621	4.53	36	33	18	238.2	280	69	87	2	0	0	0	80	21	0	.263	10	40	2	0	1.4	.962
1938			13	8	.619	3.97	31	26	12	197	199	64	89	4	2	0	0	71	23	0	.324	4	34	2	0	1.3	.950
1939			13	7	.650	3.78	34	21	6	162	160	49	59	3	3	1	2	52	10	0	.192	9	28	0	4	1.1	1.000
1940			16	10	.615	3.14	33	31	17	232	235	47	85	1	0	0	0	86	18	1	.209	10	50	0	5	1.8	1.000
1941			17	9	.654	3.15	37	30	12	246	227	82	83	4	3	1	0	77	9	0	.117	8	43	0	3	1.4	1.000

Lon Warneke *continued*

Year	Team	Lg	W	L	PCT	ERA	G	GS	CG	IP	H	BB	SO	ShO	Relief Pitching W	Relief Pitching L	Relief Pitching SV	Batting AB	Batting H	Batting HR	BA	PO	A	E	DP	TC/G	FA
1942	**2 teams**	**STL N** (12G 6–4)	**CHI N** (15G 5–7)																								
"	**total**		11	11	.500	2.73	27	24	13	181	173	36	59	1	0	0	2	62	16	0	.258	14	33	0	0	1.7	1.000
1943	**CHI**	**N**	4	5	.444	3.16	21	10	4	88.1	82	18	30	0	1	0	0	26	5	0	.192	3	22	0	2	1.2	1.000
1945			1	1	.500	3.86	9	1	0	14	16	1	6	0	1	0	0	2	0	0	.000	3	3	0	0	0.7	1.000
15 yrs.			193	121	.615	3.18	445	343	192	2782.2	2726	739	1140	31	17	12	13	962	215	4	.223	126	538	8	25	1.5	.988
WORLD SERIES																											
1932	**CHI**	**N**	0	1	.000	5.91	2	1	1	10.2	15	5	8	0	0	0	0	4	0	0	.000	1	2	0	1	1.5	1.000
1935			2	0	1.000	0.54	3	2	1	16.2	9	4	5	1	0	0	0	5	1	0	.200	2	9	0	0	3.7	1.000
2 yrs.			2	1	.667	2.63	5	3	2	27.1	24	9	13	1	0	0	0	9	1	0	.111	3	11	0	1	2.8	1.000

Ed Warner

WARNER, EDWARD EMORY BR TL 5′10½″ 165 lbs.
B. June 20, 1889, Fitchburg, Mass. D. Feb. 2, 1954, Fitchburg, Mass.

Year	Team	Lg	W	L	PCT	ERA	G	GS	CG	IP	H	BB	SO	ShO	Relief Pitching W	Relief Pitching L	Relief Pitching SV	Batting AB	Batting H	Batting HR	BA	PO	A	E	DP	TC/G	FA
1912	**PIT**	**N**	1	1	.500	3.60	11	3	1	45	40	18	13	1	0	1	0	15	2	0	.133	2	15	2	0	1.7	.895

Jack Warner

WARNER, JACK DYER BR TR 5′11″ 190 lbs.
B. July 12, 1940, Brandywine, W. Va.

Year	Team	Lg	W	L	PCT	ERA	G	GS	CG	IP	H	BB	SO	ShO	Relief Pitching W	Relief Pitching L	Relief Pitching SV	Batting AB	Batting H	Batting HR	BA	PO	A	E	DP	TC/G	FA
1962	**CHI**	**N**	0	0	—	7.71	7	0	0	7	9	0	3	0	0	0	0	0	0	0	—	0	3	0	0	0.4	1.000
1963			0	1	.000	2.78	8	0	0	22.2	21	8	7	0	0	1	0	4	1	0	.250	0	4	0	0	0.5	1.000
1964			0	0	—	2.89	7	0	0	9.1	12	4	6	0	0	0	0	0	0	0	—	2	3	0	0	0.7	1.000
1965			0	1	.000	8.62	11	0	0	15.2	22	9	7	0	0	1	0	1	0	0	.000	1	3	0	0	0.4	1.000
4 yrs.			0	2	.000	5.10	33	0	0	54.2	64	21	23	0	0	2	0	5	1	0	.200	3	13	0	0	0.5	1.000

Mike Warren

WARREN, MICHAEL BRUCE BR TR 6′ 1″ 175 lbs.
B. Mar. 26, 1961, Inglewood, Calif.

Year	Team	Lg	W	L	PCT	ERA	G	GS	CG	IP	H	BB	SO	ShO	Relief Pitching W	Relief Pitching L	Relief Pitching SV	Batting AB	Batting H	Batting HR	BA	PO	A	E	DP	TC/G	FA
1983	**OAK**	**A**	5	3	.625	4.11	12	9	3	65.2	51	18	30	1	0	1	0	0	0	0	—	2	7	1	1	0.8	.900
1984			3	6	.333	4.90	24	12	0	90	104	44	61	0	0	0	0	0	0	0	—	1	4	2	0	0.3	.714
1985			1	4	.200	6.61	16	6	0	49	52	38	48	0	1	0	0	0	0	0	—	2	1	1	1	0.3	.750
3 yrs.			9	13	.409	5.06	52	27	3	204.2	207	100	139	1	1	1	0	0	0	0		5	12	4	2	0.4	.810

Tommy Warren

WARREN, THOMAS GENTRY BB TR 6′ 1″ 180 lbs.
B. July 5, 1922, Tulsa, Okla. D. Jan. 2, 1968, Tulsa, Okla.

Year	Team	Lg	W	L	PCT	ERA	G	GS	CG	IP	H	BB	SO	ShO	Relief Pitching W	Relief Pitching L	Relief Pitching SV	Batting AB	Batting H	Batting HR	BA	PO	A	E	DP	TC/G	FA
1944	**BKN**	**N**	1	4	.200	4.98	22	4	2	68.2	74	40	18	0	0	1	0	43	11	0	.256	6	14	2	0	1.0	.909

Dan Warthen

WARTHEN, DANIEL DEAN BB TL 6′ 200 lbs.
B. Dec. 1, 1952, Omaha, Neb.

Year	Team	Lg	W	L	PCT	ERA	G	GS	CG	IP	H	BB	SO	ShO	Relief Pitching W	Relief Pitching L	Relief Pitching SV	Batting AB	Batting H	Batting HR	BA	PO	A	E	DP	TC/G	FA
1975	**MON**	**N**	8	6	.571	3.11	40	18	2	168	130	87	128	0	4	1	3	51	6	0	.118	6	26	1	3	0.8	.970
1976			2	10	.167	5.30	23	16	2	90	76	66	67	1	0	0	0	27	0	0	.000	3	13	0	0	0.7	1.000
1977	**2 teams**	**MON N** (12G 2–3)	**PHI N** (3G 0–1)																								
"	**total**		2	4	.333	7.22	15	6	1	38.2	37	43	27	0	1	1	0	9	1	0	.111	1	8	1	2	0.7	.900
1978	**HOU**	**N**	0	1	.000	4.09	5	1	0	11	10	2	2	0	0	0	0	2	0	0	.000	1	1	0	0	0.4	1.000
4 yrs.			12	21	.364	4.30	83	41	5	307.2	253	198	224	1	5	2	3	89	7	0	.079	11	48	2	5	0.7	.967

John Wasdin

WASDIN, JOHN TRUMAN BR TR 6′ 2″ 190 lbs.
B. Aug. 5, 1972, Fort Belvoir, Va.

Year	Team	Lg	W	L	PCT	ERA	G	GS	CG	IP	H	BB	SO	ShO	Relief Pitching W	Relief Pitching L	Relief Pitching SV	Batting AB	Batting H	Batting HR	BA	PO	A	E	DP	TC/G	FA
1995	**OAK**	**A**	1	1	.500	4.67	5	2	0	17.1	14	3	6	0	0	0	0	0	0	0	—	1	0	0	0	0.2	1.000

George Washburn

WASHBURN, GEORGE EDWARD BL TR 6′ 1″ 175 lbs.
B. Oct. 6, 1914, Solon, Me. D. Jan. 5, 1979, Baton Rouge, La.

Year	Team	Lg	W	L	PCT	ERA	G	GS	CG	IP	H	BB	SO	ShO	Relief Pitching W	Relief Pitching L	Relief Pitching SV	Batting AB	Batting H	Batting HR	BA	PO	A	E	DP	TC/G	FA
1941	**NY**	**A**	0	1	.000	13.50	1	1	0	2	2	5	1	0	0	0	0	1	0	0	.000	1	0	0	0	1.0	1.000

Greg Washburn

WASHBURN, GREGORY JAMES BR TR 6′ 190 lbs.
B. Dec. 3, 1946, Coal City, Ill.

Year	Team	Lg	W	L	PCT	ERA	G	GS	CG	IP	H	BB	SO	ShO	Relief Pitching W	Relief Pitching L	Relief Pitching SV	Batting AB	Batting H	Batting HR	BA	PO	A	E	DP	TC/G	FA
1969	**CAL**	**A**	0	2	.000	7.94	8	2	0	11.1	21	5	4	0	0	0	0	0	0	0	—	2	2	0	0	0.5	1.000

Libe Washburn

WASHBURN, LIBEUS BB TL 5′10″ 180 lbs.
B. June 16, 1874, Lynn, N. H. D. Mar. 22, 1940, Malone, N. Y.

Year	Team	Lg	W	L	PCT	ERA	G	GS	CG	IP	H	BB	SO	ShO	Relief Pitching W	Relief Pitching L	Relief Pitching SV	Batting AB	Batting H	Batting HR	BA	PO	A	E	DP	TC/G	FA
1903	**PHI**	**N**	0	4	.000	4.37	4	4	4	35	44	11	9	0	0	0	0	*				4	0	0	0	1.3	1.000

Ray Washburn

WASHBURN, RAY CLARK BR TR 6′ 1″ 205 lbs.
B. May 31, 1938, Pasco, Wash.

Year	Team	Lg	W	L	PCT	ERA	G	GS	CG	IP	H	BB	SO	ShO	Relief Pitching W	Relief Pitching L	Relief Pitching SV	Batting AB	Batting H	Batting HR	BA	PO	A	E	DP	TC/G	FA
1961	**STL**	**N**	1	1	.500	1.77	3	2	1	20.1	10	7	12	0	0	0	0	8	1	0	.125	0	5	0	0	1.7	1.000
1962			12	9	.571	4.10	34	25	2	175.2	187	58	109	1	1	2	0	56	10	0	.179	9	34	2	1	1.3	.956
1963			5	3	.625	3.08	11	11	4	64.1	50	14	47	2	0	0	0	19	1	0	.053	5	15	0	0	1.8	1.000
1964			3	4	.429	4.05	15	10	0	60	60	17	28	0	0	0	2	15	2	0	.133	4	14	0	3	1.2	1.000
1965			9	11	.450	3.62	28	16	1	119.1	114	28	67	1	5	0	2	33	5	0	.152	7	19	1	0	1.0	.963
1966			11	9	.550	3.76	27	26	4	170	183	44	98	1	0	0	0	54	5	1	.093	10	33	3	2	1.7	.935
1967			10	7	.588	3.53	27	27	3	186.1	190	42	98	1	0	0	0	66	6	0	.091	14	40	2	4	2.1	.964
1968			14	8	.636	2.26	31	30	8	215.1	191	47	124	4	1	0	0	60	5	0	.083	24	20	1	2	1.5	.978
1969			3	8	.273	3.07	28	16	2	132	133	49	80	0	0	0	1	37	3	0	.081	11	23	2	2	1.3	.944
1970	**CIN**	**N**	4	4	.500	6.95	35	3	0	66	90	48	37	0	4	2	0	13	0	0	.000	7	13	2	2	0.6	.909
10 yrs.			72	64	.529	3.54	239	166	25	1209.1	1208	354	700	10	11	4	5	361	38	1	.105	91	216	13	16	1.3	.959
WORLD SERIES																											
1967	**STL**	**N**	0	0	—	0.00	2	0	0	2.1	1	1	2	0	0	0	0	0	0	0	—	0	1	0	0	0.5	1.000
1968			1	1	.500	9.82	2	2	0	7.1	7	7	6	0	0	0	0	3	0	0	.000	0	1	0	0	0.5	1.000
1970	**CIN**	**N**	0	0	—	13.50	1	0	0	1.1	2	2	0	0	0	0	0	0	0	0	—	1	3	0	0	4.0	1.000
3 yrs.			1	1	.500	8.18	5	2	0	11	10	10	8	0	0	0	0	3	0	0	.000	1	5	0	0	1.2	1.000

Buck Washer

WASHER, WILLIAM BR TR 5′10″ 175 lbs.
B. Oct. 11, 1882, Akron, Ohio D. Dec. 8, 1955, Akron, Ohio.

Year	Team	Lg	W	L	PCT	ERA	G	GS	CG	IP	H	BB	SO	ShO	Relief Pitching W	Relief Pitching L	Relief Pitching SV	Batting AB	Batting H	Batting HR	BA	PO	A	E	DP	TC/G	FA
1905	**PHI**	**N**	0	0	—	6.00	1	0	0	3	4	5	0	0	0	0	0	1	0	0	.000	0	1	0	0	1.0	1.000

Gary Waslewski

WASLEWSKI, GARY LEE BR TR 6′ 4″ 190 lbs.
B. July 21, 1941, Meriden, Conn.

Year	Team	W	L	PCT	ERA	G	GS	CG	IP	H	BB	SO	ShO	Relief Pitching W	Relief Pitching L	Relief Pitching SV	Batting AB	Batting H	Batting HR	BA	PO	A	E	DP	TC/G	FA
1967	BOS A	2	2	.500	3.21	12	8	0	42	34	20	20	0	0	0	0	11	1	0	.091	5	7	0	1	1.0	1.000
1968		4	7	.364	3.67	34	11	2	105.1	108	40	59	0	1	1	2	26	1	0	.038	9	23	0	2	0.9	1.000
1969	2 teams STL N (12G 0–2) MON N (30G 3–7)																									
″	total	3	9	.250	3.39	42	14	3	130	121	71	79	1	0	2	2	31	1	0	.032	10	24	1	3	0.8	.971
1970	2 teams MON N (6G 0–2) NY A (26G 2–2)																									
″	total	2	4	.333	3.71	32	9	0	80	65	42	46	0	1	0	0	16	1	0	.063	9	15	1	1	0.8	.960
1971	NY A	0	1	.000	3.25	24	0	0	36	28	16	17	0	0	1	1	1	0	0	.000	3	5	0	0	0.3	1.000
1972	OAK A	0	3	.000	2.00	8	0	0	18	12	8	8	0	0	3	0	3	0	0	.000	2	4	0	0	0.8	1.000
6 yrs.		11	26	.297	3.44	152	42	5	411.1	368	197	229	1	2	7	5	88	4	0	.045	38	78	2	7	0.8	.983
WORLD SERIES																										
1967	BOS A	0	0	—	2.16	2	1	0	8.1	4	2	7	0	0	0	0	1	0	0	.000	2	0	0	0	1.0	1.000

Steve Waterbury

WATERBURY, STEVEN CRAIG BR TR 6′ 5″ 190 lbs.
B. Apr. 6, 1952, Carbondale, Ill.

Year	Team	W	L	PCT	ERA	G	GS	CG	IP	H	BB	SO	ShO	Relief Pitching W	Relief Pitching L	Relief Pitching SV	Batting AB	Batting H	Batting HR	BA	PO	A	E	DP	TC/G	FA
1976	STL N	0	0	—	6.00	5	0	0	6	7	3	4	0	0	0	0	0	0	0	—	1	0	0	0	0.2	1.000

Fred Waters

WATERS, FRED WARREN BL TL 5′11″ 185 lbs.
B. Feb. 2, 1927, Benton, Miss. D. Aug. 28, 1989, Pensacola, Fla.

Year	Team	W	L	PCT	ERA	G	GS	CG	IP	H	BB	SO	ShO	Relief Pitching W	Relief Pitching L	Relief Pitching SV	Batting AB	Batting H	Batting HR	BA	PO	A	E	DP	TC/G	FA
1955	PIT N	0	0	—	3.60	2	0	0	5	7	2	0	0	0	0	0	1	0	0	.000	0	1	0	0	0.5	1.000
1956		2	2	.500	2.82	23	5	1	51	48	30	14	0	0	1	0	20	1	0	.050	2	3	0	0	0.2	1.000
2 yrs.		2	2	.500	2.89	25	5	1	56	55	32	14	0	0	1	0	21	1	0	.048	2	4	0	0	0.2	1.000

Bob Watkins

WATKINS, ROBERT CECIL BR TR 6′ 1″ 170 lbs.
B. Mar. 12, 1948, San Francisco, Calif.

Year	Team	W	L	PCT	ERA	G	GS	CG	IP	H	BB	SO	ShO	Relief Pitching W	Relief Pitching L	Relief Pitching SV	Batting AB	Batting H	Batting HR	BA	PO	A	E	DP	TC/G	FA
1969	HOU N	0	0	—	5.06	5	0	0	16	13	13	11	0	0	0	0	2	0	0	.000	0	1	0	0	0.2	1.000

Scott Watkins

WATKINS, SCOTT ALLEN BL TL 6′ 3″ 180 lbs.
B. May 15, 1970, Tulsa, Okla.

Year	Team	W	L	PCT	ERA	G	GS	CG	IP	H	BB	SO	ShO	Relief Pitching W	Relief Pitching L	Relief Pitching SV	Batting AB	Batting H	Batting HR	BA	PO	A	E	DP	TC/G	FA
1995	MIN A	0	0	—	5.40	27	0	0	21.2	22	11	11	0	0	0	0	0	0	0	—	1	4	0	0	0.2	1.000

Allen Watson

WATSON, ALLEN KENNETH BL TL 6′ 3″ 195 lbs.
B. Nov. 18, 1970, Jamaica, N. Y.

Year	Team	W	L	PCT	ERA	G	GS	CG	IP	H	BB	SO	ShO	Relief Pitching W	Relief Pitching L	Relief Pitching SV	Batting AB	Batting H	Batting HR	BA	PO	A	E	DP	TC/G	FA
1993	STL N	6	7	.462	4.60	16	15	0	86	90	28	49	0	0	1	0	26	6	0	.231	3	10	1	1	0.9	.929
1994		6	5	.545	5.52	22	22	0	115.2	130	53	74	0	0	0	0	38	6	0	.158	4	14	1	0	0.9	.947
1995		7	9	.438	4.96	21	19	0	114.1	126	41	49	0	0	0	0	36	15	0	.417	7	20	0	0	1.3	1.000
3 yrs.		19	21	.475	5.07	59	56	0	316	346	122	172	0	0	1	0	100	27	0	.270	14	44	2	1	1.0	.967

Doc Watson

WATSON, CHARLES JOHN BL TL 6′ 170 lbs.
B. Jan. 30, 1886, Carroll County, Ohio D. Dec. 30, 1949, San Diego, Calif.

Year	Team	W	L	PCT	ERA	G	GS	CG	IP	H	BB	SO	ShO	Relief Pitching W	Relief Pitching L	Relief Pitching SV	Batting AB	Batting H	Batting HR	BA	PO	A	E	DP	TC/G	FA
1913	CHI N	1	0	1.000	1.00	1	1	1	9	8	6	1	0	0	0	0	2	0	0	.000	0	0	0	0	0.0	.000
1914	2 teams CHI F (26G 9–11) STL F (9G 3–4)																									
″	total	12	15	.444	2.01	35	25	14	228	186	73	87	5	1	3	1	70	7	0	.100	7	60	2	0	2.0	.971
1915	STL F	9	9	.500	3.98	33	20	6	135.2	132	58	45	0	2	0	0	40	5	0	.125	2	24	2	1	0.8	.929
3 yrs.		22	24	.478	2.70	69	46	21	372.2	326	137	133	5	3	3	1	112	12	0	.107	9	84	4	1	1.4	.959

Milt Watson

WATSON, MILTON WILSON (Mule) BR TR 6′ 1″ 180 lbs.
B. Jan. 10, 1890, Flovilla, Ga. D. Apr. 20, 1962, Pine Bluff, Ark.

Year	Team	W	L	PCT	ERA	G	GS	CG	IP	H	BB	SO	ShO	Relief Pitching W	Relief Pitching L	Relief Pitching SV	Batting AB	Batting H	Batting HR	BA	PO	A	E	DP	TC/G	FA
1916	STL N	4	6	.400	3.06	18	13	5	103	109	33	27	2	0	0	0	32	7	0	.219	4	26	5	1	1.9	.857
1917		10	13	.435	3.51	41	20	5	161.1	149	51	45	3	3	3	0	51	5	0	.098	3	55	2	2	1.5	.967
1918	PHI N	5	7	.417	3.43	23	11	6	112.2	126	36	29	0	2	1	0	40	3	0	.075	0	31	2	1	1.4	.939
1919		2	4	.333	5.17	8	4	3	47	51	19	12	0	1	1	0	16	1	0	.063	0	17	1	0	2.3	.944
4 yrs.		21	30	.412	3.57	90	48	19	424	435	139	113	5	6	5	0	139	16	0	.115	7	129	10	4	1.6	.932

Mother Watson

WATSON, WALTER L. 5′ 9″ 145 lbs.
B. Jan. 27, 1865, Middleport, Ohio D. Nov. 23, 1898, Middleport, Ohio.

Year	Team	W	L	PCT	ERA	G	GS	CG	IP	H	BB	SO	ShO	Relief Pitching W	Relief Pitching L	Relief Pitching SV	Batting AB	Batting H	Batting HR	BA	PO	A	E	DP	TC/G	FA
1887	CIN AA	0	1	.000	*5.79*	2	2	1	14	22	6	1	0	0	0	0	8	1	0	.125	0	1	2	0	1.0	.333

Mule Watson

WATSON, JOHN REEVES BR TR 6′ 1½″ 185 lbs.
B. Oct. 15, 1896, Homer, La. D. Aug. 25, 1949, Shreveport, La.

Year	Team	W	L	PCT	ERA	G	GS	CG	IP	H	BB	SO	ShO	Relief Pitching W	Relief Pitching L	Relief Pitching SV	Batting AB	Batting H	Batting HR	BA	PO	A	E	DP	TC/G	FA
1918	PHI A	7	10	.412	3.37	21	19	11	141.2	139	44	30	3	0	0	0	52	7	0	.135	5	30	3	3	1.8	.921
1919		0	1	.000	6.91	4	2	0	14.1	17	7	6	0	0	0	0	6	0	0	.000	0	9	0	0	2.3	1.000
1920	2 teams BOS N (13G 5–4) PIT N (5G 0–0)																									
″	total	5	4	.556	4.29	18	10	4	86	94	24	17	2	0	1	0	27	3	0	.111	0	26	1	1	1.5	.963
1921	BOS N	14	13	.519	3.85	44	31	15	259.1	269	57	48	1	2	1	2	87	12	0	.138	7	72	6	1	1.9	.929
1922		8	14	.364	4.70	41	27	8	201	262	59	53	1	1	0	1	66	13	0	.197	4	47	3	1	1.3	.944
1923	2 teams BOS N (11G 1–2) NY N (17G 8–5)																									
″	total	9	7	.563	3.84	28	19	9	138.1	159	41	36	0	1	0	1	54	10	0	.185	5	29	1	0	1.3	.971
1924	NY N	7	4	.636	3.79	22	16	6	99.2	122	24	18	1	1	0	0	35	9	2	.257	1	22	1	3	1.1	.958
7 yrs.		50	53	.485	4.04	178	124	53	940.1	1062	256	208	8	5	2	4	327	54	2	.165	22	235	15	9	1.5	.945
WORLD SERIES																										
1923	NY N	0	0	—	13.50	1	1	0	2	4	1	1	0	0	0	0	0	0	0	—	0	0	1	0	1.0	.000
1924		0	0	—	0.00	1	0	0	0.2	0	0	0	0	0	0	1	0	0	0	—	0	0	0	0	0.0	.000
2 yrs.		0	0	—	10.13	2	1	0	2.2	4	1	1	0	0	0	1	0	0	0		0	0	1	0	0.5	.000

Eddie Watt

WATT, EDWARD DEAN BR TR 5′10″ 183 lbs.
B. Apr. 4, 1942, Lamoni, Iowa.

Year	Team	W	L	PCT	ERA	G	GS	CG	IP	H	BB	SO	ShO	Relief Pitching W	Relief Pitching L	Relief Pitching SV	Batting AB	Batting H	Batting HR	BA	PO	A	E	DP	TC/G	FA
1966	BAL A	9	7	.563	3.83	43	13	1	145.2	123	44	102	0	7	2	4	46	14	2	.304	7	14	1	0	0.5	.955
1967		3	5	.375	2.26	49	0	0	103.2	67	37	93	0	3	5	8	22	4	1	.182	6	15	0	1	0.4	1.000
1968		5	5	.500	2.27	59	0	0	83.1	63	35	72	0	5	5	11	8	0	0	.000	1	14	1	1	0.3	.938
1969		5	2	.714	1.65	56	0	0	71	49	26	46	0	5	2	16	8	0	0	.000	4	10	0	0	0.3	1.000
1970		7	7	.500	3.27	53	0	0	55	44	29	33	0	7	7	12	8	1	0	.125	2	10	0	1	0.2	1.000
1971		3	1	.750	1.80	35	0	0	40	39	8	26	0	3	1	11	5	0	0	.000	2	4	0	0	0.2	1.000
1972		2	3	.400	2.15	38	0	0	46	30	20	23	0	2	3	7	2	0	0	.000	2	7	0	0	0.2	1.000

Eddie Watt *continued*

Year	Team		W	L	PCT	ERA	G	GS	CG	IP	H	BB	SO	ShO	Relief Pitching W	Relief Pitching L	Relief Pitching SV	Batting AB	Batting H	Batting HR	BA	PO	A	E	DP	TC/G	FA
1973			3	4	.429	3.30	30	0	0	71	62	21	38	0	3	4	5	0	0	0	—	3	6	1	0	0.3	.900
1974	PHI	N	1	1	.500	4.03	42	0	0	38	39	26	23	0	1	1	6	1	0	0	.000	0	6	1	2	0.2	.857
1975	CHI	N	0	1	.000	13.50	6	0	0	6	14	8	6	0	0	1	0	0	0	0	—	0	1	0	0	0.2	1.000
10 yrs.			38	36	.514	2.91	411	13	1	659.2	530	254	462	0	36	31	80	100	19	3	.190	27	87	4	5	0.3	.966
LEAGUE CHAMPIONSHIP SERIES																											
1969	BAL	A	0	0	—	0.00	1	0	0	2	0	0	2	0	0	0	0	0	0	0	—	0	0	0	0	0.0	.000
1971			0	0	—	0.00	1	0	0	2	2	0	1	0	0	0	1	0	0	0	—	0	1	0	0	1.0	1.000
1973			0	0	—	0.00	1	0	0	0.1	0	0	0	0	0	0	0	0	0	0	—	0	1	0	0	1.0	1.000
3 yrs.			0	0		0.00	3	0	0	4.1	2	0	3	0	0	0	1	0	0	0		0	2	0	0	0.7	1.000
WORLD SERIES																											
1969	BAL	A	0	1	.000	3.00	2	0	0	3	4	0	3	0	0	1	0	0	0	0	—	0	0	1	0	0.5	.000
1970			0	1	.000	9.00	1	0	0	1	2	1	3	0	0	1	0	0	0	0	—	0	0	0	0	0.0	.000
1971			0	1	.000	3.86	2	0	0	2.1	4	0	2	0	0	0	0	0	0	0	—	0	0	0	0	0.0	.000
3 yrs.			0	3	.000	4.26	5	0	0	6.1	10	1	8	0	0	2	0	0	0	0		0	0	1	0	0.2	.000

Frank Watt

WATT, FRANK MARION (Kilo) BR TR 6′ 1″ 205 lbs.
Brother of Allie Watt.
B. Dec. 15, 1902, Washington, D. C. D. Aug. 31, 1956, Washington, D. C.

Year	Team		W	L	PCT	ERA	G	GS	CG	IP	H	BB	SO	ShO	Relief Pitching W	Relief Pitching L	Relief Pitching SV	Batting AB	Batting H	Batting HR	BA	PO	A	E	DP	TC/G	FA
1931	PHI	N	5	5	.500	4.84	38	12	5	122.2	147	49	25	0	1	0	2	39	8	0	.205	7	19	4	1	0.8	.867

Jim Waugh

WAUGH, JAMES ELDEN BR TR 6′ 3″ 185 lbs.
B. Nov. 25, 1933, Lancaster, Ohio.

Year	Team		W	L	PCT	ERA	G	GS	CG	IP	H	BB	SO	ShO	Relief Pitching W	Relief Pitching L	Relief Pitching SV	Batting AB	Batting H	Batting HR	BA	PO	A	E	DP	TC/G	FA
1952	PIT	N	1	6	.143	6.36	17	7	1	52.1	61	32	18	0	0	1	0	10	1	0	.100	0	11	1	1	0.7	.917
1953			4	5	.444	6.48	29	11	1	90.1	108	56	23	0	0	0	0	22	5	0	.227	5	13	1	1	0.7	.947
2 yrs.			5	11	.313	6.43	46	18	2	142.2	169	88	41	0	0	1	0	32	6	0	.188	5	24	2	2	0.7	.935

Frank Wayenberg

WAYENBERG, FRANK BR TR 6′½″ 172 lbs.
B. Aug. 27, 1898, Franklin, Kans. D. Apr. 16, 1975, Zanesville, Ohio.

Year	Team		W	L	PCT	ERA	G	GS	CG	IP	H	BB	SO	ShO	Relief Pitching W	Relief Pitching L	Relief Pitching SV	Batting AB	Batting H	Batting HR	BA	PO	A	E	DP	TC/G	FA
1924	CLE	A	0	0	—	5.40	2	1	0	6.2	7	5	3	0	0	0	0	2	1	0	.500	0	1	0	0	0.5	1.000

Gary Wayne

WAYNE, GARY ANTHONY BL TL 6′ 3″ 185 lbs.
B. Nov. 30, 1962, Dearborn, Mich.

Year	Team		W	L	PCT	ERA	G	GS	CG	IP	H	BB	SO	ShO	Relief Pitching W	Relief Pitching L	Relief Pitching SV	Batting AB	Batting H	Batting HR	BA	PO	A	E	DP	TC/G	FA
1989	MIN	A	3	4	.429	3.30	60	0	0	71	55	36	41	0	3	4	1	0	0	0	—	2	11	1	1	0.2	.929
1990			1	1	.500	4.19	38	0	0	38.2	38	13	28	0	1	1	1	0	0	0	—	1	4	0	1	0.1	1.000
1991			1	0	1.000	5.11	8	0	0	12.1	11	4	7	0	1	0	1	0	0	0	—	0	1	0	0	0.1	1.000
1992			3	3	.500	2.63	41	0	0	48	46	19	29	0	3	3	0	0	0	0	—	1	13	0	0	0.3	1.000
1993	CLR	N	5	3	.625	5.05	65	0	0	62.1	68	26	49	0	5	3	1	1	1	0	1.000	0	9	0	1	0.1	1.000
1994	LA	N	1	3	.250	4.67	19	0	0	17.1	19	6	10	0	1	3	0	1	0	0	.000	2	3	1	0	0.3	.833
6 yrs.			14	14	.500	3.93	231	0	0	249.2	237	104	164	0	14	14	4	2	1	0	.500	6	41	2	3	0.2	.959

Hal Weafer

WEAFER, KENNETH ALBERT (Al) BR TR 6′½″ 183 lbs.
B. Feb. 6, 1914, Woburn, Mass.

Year	Team		W	L	PCT	ERA	G	GS	CG	IP	H	BB	SO	ShO	Relief Pitching W	Relief Pitching L	Relief Pitching SV	Batting AB	Batting H	Batting HR	BA	PO	A	E	DP	TC/G	FA
1936	BOS	N	0	0	—	12.00	1	0	0	3	6	3	0	0	0	0	0	1	0	0	.000	0	0	0	0	0.0	.000

Dave Weathers

WEATHERS, JOHN DAVID BR TR 6′ 3″ 205 lbs.
B. Sept. 25, 1969, Lawrenceburg, Tenn.

Year	Team		W	L	PCT	ERA	G	GS	CG	IP	H	BB	SO	ShO	Relief Pitching W	Relief Pitching L	Relief Pitching SV	Batting AB	Batting H	Batting HR	BA	PO	A	E	DP	TC/G	FA
1991	TOR	A	1	0	1.000	4.91	15	0	0	14.2	15	17	13	0	1	0	0	0	0	0	—	0	1	0	0	0.1	1.000
1992			0	0	—	8.10	2	0	0	3.1	5	2	3	0	0	0	0	0	0	0	—	0	0	0	0	0.0	.000
1993	FLA	N	2	3	.400	5.12	14	6	0	45.2	57	13	34	0	0	0	0	10	1	0	.100	5	3	0	0	0.6	1.000
1994			8	12	.400	5.27	24	24	0	135	166	59	72	0	0	0	0	44	3	0	.068	2	21	1	0	1.0	.958
1995			4	5	.444	5.98	28	15	0	90.1	104	52	60	0	1	1	0	26	4	0	.154	3	12	2	0	0.6	.882
5 yrs.			15	20	.429	5.48	83	45	0	289	347	143	182	0	2	1	0	80	8	0	.100	10	37	3	0	0.6	.940

Floyd Weaver

WEAVER, DAVID FLOYD BR TR 6′ 4″ 195 lbs.
B. May 12, 1941, Ben Franklin, Tex.

Year	Team		W	L	PCT	ERA	G	GS	CG	IP	H	BB	SO	ShO	Relief Pitching W	Relief Pitching L	Relief Pitching SV	Batting AB	Batting H	Batting HR	BA	PO	A	E	DP	TC/G	FA
1962	CLE	A	1	0	1.000	1.80	1	1	0	5	3	0	8	0	0	0	0	2	1	0	.500	0	0	0	0	0.0	.000
1965			2	2	.500	5.43	32	1	0	61.1	61	24	37	0	2	2	1	11	1	0	.091	6	9	0	0	0.5	1.000
1970	CHI	A	1	2	.333	4.35	31	3	0	62	52	31	51	0	1	2	0	7	0	0	.000	4	4	2	0	0.3	.800
1971	MIL	A	0	1	.000	7.33	21	0	0	27	33	18	12	0	0	1	0	0	0	0	—	1	6	0	1	0.3	1.000
4 yrs.			4	5	.444	5.21	85	5	0	155.1	149	73	108	0	3	5	1	20	2	0	.100	11	19	2	1	0.4	.938

Harry Weaver

WEAVER, HARRY ABRAHAM BR TR 5′11″ 160 lbs.
B. Feb. 26, 1892, Clarendon, Pa. D. May 30, 1983, Rochester, N. Y.

Year	Team		W	L	PCT	ERA	G	GS	CG	IP	H	BB	SO	ShO	Relief Pitching W	Relief Pitching L	Relief Pitching SV	Batting AB	Batting H	Batting HR	BA	PO	A	E	DP	TC/G	FA
1915	PHI	A	0	2	.000	3.00	2	2	2	18	18	10	1	0	0	0	0	6	1	0	.167	2	11	0	0	6.5	1.000
1916			0	0	—	10.13	3	0	0	8	14	5	2	0	0	0	0	2	1	0	.500	1	2	0	0	1.0	1.000
1917	CHI	N	1	1	.500	2.75	4	2	1	19.2	17	7	8	1	0	0	0	5	1	0	.200	0	10	1	0	2.8	.909
1918			2	2	.500	2.20	8	3	1	32.2	27	7	9	1	1	0	1	8	2	0	.250	2	13	0	1	1.9	1.000
1919			0	1	.000	10.80	2	1	0	3.1	6	2	1	0	0	0	0	1	0	0	.000	0	0	0	0	0.0	.000
5 yrs.			3	6	.333	3.64	19	8	4	81.2	82	31	21	2	1	0	1	22	5	0	.227	5	36	1	1	2.2	.976

Jim Weaver

WEAVER, JAMES BRIAN (Fluss) BL TL 6′ 178 lbs.
B. Feb. 19, 1939, Lancaster, Pa.

Year	Team		W	L	PCT	ERA	G	GS	CG	IP	H	BB	SO	ShO	Relief Pitching W	Relief Pitching L	Relief Pitching SV	Batting AB	Batting H	Batting HR	BA	PO	A	E	DP	TC/G	FA
1967	CAL	A	3	0	1.000	2.67	13	2	0	30.1	26	9	20	0	1	0	1	6	0	0	.000	7	9	0	2	1.2	1.000
1968			0	1	.000	2.38	14	0	0	22.2	22	10	8	0	0	1	0	1	0	0	.000	0	2	1	0	0.2	.667
2 yrs.			3	1	.750	2.55	27	2	0	53	48	19	28	0	1	1	1	7	0	0	.000	7	11	1	2	0.7	.947

Jim Weaver

WEAVER, JAMES DEMENT (Big Jim) BR TR 6′ 6″ 230 lbs.
B. Nov. 25, 1903, Obion County, Tenn. D. Dec. 12, 1983, Lakeland, Fla.

Year	Team		W	L	PCT	ERA	G	GS	CG	IP	H	BB	SO	ShO	Relief Pitching W	Relief Pitching L	Relief Pitching SV	Batting AB	Batting H	Batting HR	BA	PO	A	E	DP	TC/G	FA
1928	WAS	A	0	0	—	1.50	3	0	0	6	2	6	2	0	0	0	0	1	0	0	.000	0	2	1	0	1.0	.667
1931	NY	A	2	1	.667	5.31	17	5	2	57.2	66	29	28	0	0	1	0	20	1	0	.050	0	13	1	3	0.8	.929
1934	2 teams	STL A	(5G 2–0)		CHI N	(27G 11–9)																					
″	total		13	9	.591	4.18	32	25	10	178.2	180	74	109	1	2	0	0	59	4	0	.068	10	33	2	1	1.4	.956
1935	PIT	N	14	8	.636	3.42	33	22	11	176.1	177	58	87	**4**	2	0	0	56	4	0	.071	4	40	2	2	1.4	.957
1936			14	8	.636	4.31	38	31	11	225.2	239	74	108	1	0	0	0	79	8	0	.101	7	38	4	1	1.3	.918

Jim Weaver *continued*

Year	Team	W	L	PCT	ERA	G	GS	CG	IP	H	BB	SO	ShO	Relief Pitching W	Relief Pitching L	Relief Pitching SV	Batting AB	Batting H	Batting HR	BA	PO	A	E	DP	TC/G	FA
1937		8	5	.615	3.20	32	9	2	109.2	106	31	44	1	5	4	0	27	4	0	.148	3	16	2	1	0.7	.905
1938	2 teams STL A (1G 0–1) CIN N (30G 6–4)																									
″	total	6	5	.545	3.43	31	16	2	136.1	118	63	68	0	1	0	3	46	9	0	.196	5	25	4	1	1.1	.882
1939	CIN N	0	0	—	3.00	3	0	0	3	3	1	3	0	0	0	0	1	0	0	.000	0	2	0	0	0.7	1.000
8 yrs.		57	36	.613	3.88	189	108	38	893.1	891	336	449	7	10	5	3	289	30	0	.104	29	169	16	9	1.1	.925

Monte Weaver

WEAVER, MONTE MORTON (Prof) BL TR 6′ 170 lbs.
B. June 15, 1906, Helton, N. C. D. June 14, 1994, Orlando, Fla.

Year	Team	W	L	PCT	ERA	G	GS	CG	IP	H	BB	SO	ShO	Relief Pitching W	Relief Pitching L	Relief Pitching SV	Batting AB	Batting H	Batting HR	BA	PO	A	E	DP	TC/G	FA
1931	WAS A	1	0	1.000	4.50	3	1	1	10	11	6	6	0	0	0	0	3	0	0	.000	0	4	0	0	1.3	1.000
1932		22	10	.688	4.08	43	30	13	234	236	112	83	1	2	2	2	94	27	0	.287	8	37	1	3	1.1	.978
1933		10	5	.667	3.25	23	21	12	152.1	147	53	45	1	0	0	0	56	7	0	.125	2	30	1	4	1.4	.970
1934		11	15	.423	4.79	31	31	11	204.2	255	63	51	0	0	0	0	80	13	0	.163	3	37	5	0	1.5	.889
1935		1	1	.500	5.25	5	2	0	12	16	6	4	0	1	0	0	3	1	0	.333	0	3	1	1	0.8	.750
1936		6	4	.600	4.35	26	5	3	91	92	38	15	0	4	1	1	25	5	0	.200	5	15	1	1	0.8	.952
1937		12	9	.571	4.20	30	26	9	188.2	197	70	44	0	2	1	0	68	14	0	.206	3	45	4	3	1.7	.923
1938		7	6	.538	5.24	31	18	7	139	157	74	43	0	2	1	0	45	12	0	.267	6	25	2	0	1.1	.939
1939	BOS A	1	0	1.000	6.64	9	1	1	20.1	26	13	6	0	0	0	1	4	0	0	.000	1	0	0	0	0.1	1.000
9 yrs.		71	50	.587	4.36	201	135	57	1052	1137	435	297	2	11	5	4	378	79	0	.209	28	196	15	12	1.2	.937
WORLD SERIES																										
1933	WAS A	0	1	.000	1.74	1	1	0	10.1	11	4	3	0	0	0	0	4	0	0	.000	0	6	0	0	6.0	1.000

Orlie Weaver

WEAVER, ORVILLE FOREST BR TR 6′ 180 lbs.
B. June 4, 1886, Newport, Ky. D. Nov. 28, 1970, New Orleans, La.

Year	Team	W	L	PCT	ERA	G	GS	CG	IP	H	BB	SO	ShO	Relief Pitching W	Relief Pitching L	Relief Pitching SV	Batting AB	Batting H	Batting HR	BA	PO	A	E	DP	TC/G	FA
1910	CHI N	1	2	.333	3.66	7	2	2	32	34	15	22	0	0	1	0	13	2	0	.154	1	3	0	1	0.6	1.000
1911	2 teams CHI N (6G 3–2) BOS N (27G 3–12)																									
″	total	6	14	.300	5.30	33	21	5	164.2	169	101	70	1	1	1	0	58	6	0	.103	3	34	5	0	1.3	.881
2 yrs.		7	16	.304	5.03	40	23	7	196.2	203	116	92	1	1	2	0	71	8	0	.113	4	37	5	1	1.1	.891

Roger Weaver

WEAVER, ROGER EDWARD BR TR 6′ 3″ 190 lbs.
B. Oct. 6, 1954, Amsterdam, N. Y.

Year	Team	W	L	PCT	ERA	G	GS	CG	IP	H	BB	SO	ShO	Relief Pitching W	Relief Pitching L	Relief Pitching SV	Batting AB	Batting H	Batting HR	BA	PO	A	E	DP	TC/G	FA
1980	DET A	3	4	.429	4.08	19	6	0	64	56	34	42	0	2	0	0	0	0	0	—	8	9	2	2	1.0	.895

Sam Weaver

WEAVER, SAMUEL H. BR TR 5′10″ 185 lbs.
B. July 10, 1855, Philadelphia, Pa. D. Feb. 1, 1914, Philadelphia, Pa.

Year	Team	W	L	PCT	ERA	G	GS	CG	IP	H	BB	SO	ShO	Relief Pitching W	Relief Pitching L	Relief Pitching SV	Batting AB	Batting H	Batting HR	BA	PO	A	E	DP	TC/G	FA
1878	MIL N	12	**31**	.279	1.95	45	43	39	383	371	21	95	1	**1**	0	0	170	34	0	.200	37	80	18	1	2.5	.867
1882	PHI AA	26	15	.634	*2.74*	42	41	41	371	374	35	104	2	0	0	0	155	36	0	.232	18	127	9	1	3.5	.942
1883	LOU AA	24	20	.545	*3.70*	46	44	43	418.2	468	38	116	4	0	0	0	203	39	0	.192	41	82	10	4	2.4	.925
1884	PHI U	5	10	.333	*5.76*	17	17	14	136	206	11	40	0	0	0	0	84	18	0	.214	20	29	11	0	2.6	.817
1886	PHI AA	0	2	.000	*14.73*	2	2	1	11	30	2	2	0	0	0	0	7	1	0	.143	5	1	0	1	2.0	1.000
5 yrs.		67	78	.462	3.23	152	147	138	1319.2	1449	107	357	7	1	0	0	*				121	319	48	7	2.7	.902

Bill Webb

WEBB, WILLIAM FREDERICK BR TR 6′ 2″ 180 lbs.
B. Dec. 12, 1913, Atlanta, Ga. D. June 1, 1994, Austell, Ga.

Year	Team	W	L	PCT	ERA	G	GS	CG	IP	H	BB	SO	ShO	Relief Pitching W	Relief Pitching L	Relief Pitching SV	Batting AB	Batting H	Batting HR	BA	PO	A	E	DP	TC/G	FA
1943	PHI N	0	0	—	9.00	1	0	0	1	1	1	0	0	0	0	0	0	0	0	—	0	0	0	0	0.0	.000

Hank Webb

WEBB, HENRY GAYLON MATTHEW BR TR 6′ 3″ 175 lbs.
B. May 21, 1950, Copiague, N. Y.

Year	Team	W	L	PCT	ERA	G	GS	CG	IP	H	BB	SO	ShO	Relief Pitching W	Relief Pitching L	Relief Pitching SV	Batting AB	Batting H	Batting HR	BA	PO	A	E	DP	TC/G	FA
1972	NY N	0	0	—	4.42	6	2	0	18.1	18	9	15	0	0	0	0	5	0	0	.000	3	4	0	0	1.2	1.000
1973		0	0	—	10.80	2	0	0	1.2	2	2	1	0	0	0	0	0	0	0	—	0	0	0	0	0.0	.000
1974		0	2	.000	7.20	3	2	0	10	15	10	8	0	0	1	0	3	0	0	.000	2	0	1	0	1.0	.667
1975		7	6	.538	4.07	29	15	3	115	102	62	38	1	2	0	0	31	8	0	.258	11	10	0	2	0.7	1.000
1976		0	1	.000	4.50	8	0	0	16	17	7	7	0	0	1	0	1	0	0	.000	0	3	0	0	0.4	1.000
1977	LA N	0	0	—	2.25	5	0	0	8	5	1	2	0	0	0	0	0	0	0	—	0	1	0	0	0.2	1.000
6 yrs.		7	9	.438	4.31	53	19	3	169	159	91	71	1	2	2	0	40	8	0	.200	16	18	1	2	0.7	.971

Lefty Webb

WEBB, CLEON EARL BB TL 5′11″ 165 lbs.
B. Mar. 1, 1885, Mt. Gilead, Ohio D. Jan. 12, 1958, Circleville, Ohio.

Year	Team	W	L	PCT	ERA	G	GS	CG	IP	H	BB	SO	ShO	Relief Pitching W	Relief Pitching L	Relief Pitching SV	Batting AB	Batting H	Batting HR	BA	PO	A	E	DP	TC/G	FA
1910	PIT N	2	1	.667	5.67	7	3	2	27	29	9	6	0	0	0	0	10	2	0	.200	1	8	2	1	1.6	.818

Red Webb

WEBB, SAMUEL HENRY BL TR 6′ 175 lbs.
B. Sept. 25, 1924, Washington, D. C.

Year	Team	W	L	PCT	ERA	G	GS	CG	IP	H	BB	SO	ShO	Relief Pitching W	Relief Pitching L	Relief Pitching SV	Batting AB	Batting H	Batting HR	BA	PO	A	E	DP	TC/G	FA
1948	NY N	2	1	.667	3.21	5	3	2	28	27	10	9	0	0	0	0	9	2	0	.222	3	5	0	1	1.6	1.000
1949		1	1	.500	4.03	20	0	0	44.2	41	21	9	0	1	1	0	10	4	0	.400	3	18	2	2	1.1	.913
2 yrs.		3	2	.600	3.72	25	3	2	72.2	68	31	18	0	1	1	0	19	6	0	.316	6	23	2	3	1.2	.935

Les Webber

WEBBER, LESTER ELMER BR TR 6′½″ 185 lbs.
B. May 6, 1915, Kelseyville, Calif. D. Nov. 13, 1987, Santa Maria, Calif.

Year	Team	W	L	PCT	ERA	G	GS	CG	IP	H	BB	SO	ShO	Relief Pitching W	Relief Pitching L	Relief Pitching SV	Batting AB	Batting H	Batting HR	BA	PO	A	E	DP	TC/G	FA
1942	BKN N	3	2	.600	2.96	19	3	1	51.2	46	22	23	0	1	2	1	14	1	0	.071	2	14	0	1	0.8	1.000
1943		2	2	.500	3.81	54	0	0	115.2	112	69	24	0	2	2	**10**	25	3	0	.120	11	34	2	1	0.9	.957
1944		7	8	.467	4.94	48	9	1	140.1	157	64	42	0	7	2	3	39	8	1	.205	10	43	1	0	1.1	.981
1945		7	3	.700	3.58	17	7	5	75.1	69	25	30	0	2	1	0	22	2	0	.091	6	7	0	0	0.8	1.000
1946	2 teams BKN N (11G 3–3) CLE A (4G 1–1)																									
″	total	4	4	.500	4.66	15	6	0	48.1	47	20	21	0	2	1	0	11	1	0	.091	3	8	0	0	0.7	1.000
1948	CLE A	0	0	—	40.50	1	0	0	0.2	3	1	1	0	0	0	0	0	0	0	—	0	0	0	0	0.0	.000
6 yrs.		23	19	.548	4.19	154	25	7	432	434	201	141	0	14	8	14	111	15	1	.135	32	106	3	2	0.9	.979

Charlie Weber

WEBER, CHARLES P.
B. Oct. 22, 1868, Cincinnati, Ohio D. June 13, 1914, Beaumont, Tex.

Year	Team	W	L	PCT	ERA	G	GS	CG	IP	H	BB	SO	ShO	Relief Pitching W	Relief Pitching L	Relief Pitching SV	Batting AB	Batting H	Batting HR	BA	PO	A	E	DP	TC/G	FA
1898	WAS N	0	1	.000	15.75	1	1	0	4	9	1	0	0	0	0	0	2	0	0	.000	0	1	1	0	2.0	.500

Mike Wegener

WEGENER, MICHAEL DENIS BR TR 6′ 4″ 215 lbs.
B. Oct. 8, 1946, Denver, Colo.

Year	Team	W	L	PCT	ERA	G	GS	CG	IP	H	BB	SO	ShO	Relief Pitching W	Relief Pitching L	Relief Pitching SV	Batting AB	Batting H	Batting HR	BA	PO	A	E	DP	TC/G	FA
1969	MON N	5	14	.263	4.40	32	26	4	165.2	150	96	124	1	0	0	0	54	13	0	.241	11	31	1	1	1.3	.977
1970		3	6	.333	5.28	25	16	1	104	100	56	35	0	0	0	0	34	4	0	.118	7	14	0	0	0.8	1.000
2 yrs.		8	20	.286	4.74	57	42	5	269.2	250	152	159	1	0	0	0	88	17	0	.193	18	45	1	1	1.1	.984

Bill Wegman

WEGMAN, WILLIAM EDWARD BR TR 6′ 5″ 200 lbs.
B. Dec. 19, 1962, Cincinnati, Ohio.

Year	Team	W	L	PCT	ERA	G	GS	CG	IP	H	BB	SO	ShO	Relief Pitching W	Relief Pitching L	Relief Pitching SV	Batting AB	Batting H	Batting HR	BA	PO	A	E	DP	TC/G	FA
1985	MIL A	2	0	1.000	3.57	3	3	0	17.2	17	3	6	0	0	0	0	0	0	0	—	3	0	0	0	1.0	1.000
1986		5	12	.294	5.13	35	32	2	198.1	217	43	82	0	0	0	0	0	0	0	—	20	19	1	4	1.1	.975
1987		12	11	.522	4.24	34	33	7	225	229	53	102	0	0	1	0	0	0	0	—	29	27	2	2	1.7	.966
1988		13	13	.500	4.12	32	31	4	199	207	50	84	1	0	0	0	0	0	0	—	14	24	3	3	1.3	.927
1989		2	6	.250	6.71	11	8	0	51	69	21	27	0	0	1	0	0	0	0	—	3	11	0	0	1.3	1.000
1990		2	2	.500	4.85	8	5	1	29.2	37	6	20	1	0	0	0	0	0	0	—	1	3	2	0	0.8	.667
1991		15	7	.682	2.84	28	28	7	193.1	176	40	89	2	0	0	0	0	0	0	—	28	34	4	1	2.4	.939
1992		13	14	.481	3.20	35	35	7	261.2	251	55	127	0	0	0	0	0	0	0	—	35	43	2	3	2.3	.975
1993		4	14	.222	4.48	20	18	5	120.2	135	34	50	0	0	0	0	0	0	0	—	12	21	2	4	1.8	.943
1994		8	4	.667	4.51	19	19	0	115.2	140	26	59	0	0	0	0	0	0	0	—	12	21	1	4	1.8	.971
1995		5	7	.417	5.35	37	4	0	70.2	89	21	50	0	5	4	2	0	0	0	—	9	5	1	0	0.4	.933
11 yrs.		81	90	.474	4.16	262	216	33	1482.2	1567	352	696	4	5	6	2	0	0	0		166	208	18	21	1.5	.954

Biggs Wehde

WEHDE, WILBUR BR TR 5′10½″ 180 lbs.
B. Nov. 23, 1906, Holstein, Iowa D. Sept. 21, 1970, Sioux Falls, S. D.

Year	Team	W	L	PCT	ERA	G	GS	CG	IP	H	BB	SO	ShO	Relief Pitching W	Relief Pitching L	Relief Pitching SV	Batting AB	Batting H	Batting HR	BA	PO	A	E	DP	TC/G	FA
1930	CHI A	0	0	—	9.95	4	0	0	6.1	7	7	3	0	0	0	0	1	0	0	.000	0	5	0	0	1.3	1.000
1931		1	0	1.000	6.75	8	0	0	16	19	10	3	0	1	0	0	3	0	0	.000	1	6	0	0	0.9	1.000
2 yrs.		1	0	1.000	7.66	12	0	0	22.1	26	17	6	0	1	0	0	4	0	0	.000	1	11	0	0	1.0	1.000

Herm Wehmeier

WEHMEIER, HERMAN RALPH BR TR 6′ 2″ 185 lbs.
B. Feb. 18, 1927, Cincinnati, Ohio D. May 21, 1973, Dallas, Tex.

Year	Team	W	L	PCT	ERA	G	GS	CG	IP	H	BB	SO	ShO	Relief Pitching W	Relief Pitching L	Relief Pitching SV	Batting AB	Batting H	Batting HR	BA	PO	A	E	DP	TC/G	FA
1945	CIN N	0	1	.000	12.60	2	2	0	5	10	4	0	0	0	0	0	1	0	0	.000	0	2	0	1	1.0	1.000
1947		0	0	—	0.00	1	0	0	1	0	0	0	0	0	0	0	0	0	0	—	0	0	0	0	0.0	.000
1948		11	8	.579	5.86	33	24	6	147.1	179	75	56	0	1	1	0	55	5	0	.091	4	29	3	1	1.1	.917
1949		11	12	.478	4.68	33	29	11	213.1	202	**117**	80	1	1	1	0	78	20	0	.256	3	31	2	3	1.1	.944
1950		10	18	.357	5.67	41	32	12	230	255	**135**	121	0	0	0	4	92	14	0	.152	9	27	5	1	1.0	.878
1951		7	10	.412	3.70	39	22	10	184.2	167	89	93	2	0	0	2	59	17	0	.288	14	23	4	3	1.1	.902
1952		9	11	.450	5.15	33	26	6	190.1	197	**103**	83	1	0	2	0	64	12	1	.188	8	18	3	2	0.9	.897
1953		1	6	.143	7.16	28	10	2	81.2	100	47	32	0	0	0	0	20	4	0	.200	2	10	0	0	0.4	1.000
1954	**2 teams** CIN N (12G 0–3) PHI N (25G 10–8)																									
″	**total**	10	11	.476	4.40	37	20	10	171.2	153	72	62	2	1	0	2	59	6	0	.102	7	37	3	2	1.3	.936
1955	PHI N	10	12	.455	4.41	31	29	10	193.2	176	67	85	1	0	0	0	72	20	0	.278	6	29	3	2	1.2	.921
1956	**2 teams** PHI N (3G 0–2) STL N (34G 12–9)																									
″	**total**	12	11	.522	3.73	37	22	7	190.2	168	82	76	2	5	1	1	66	13	2	.197	16	24	2	1	1.1	.952
1957	STL N	10	7	.588	4.31	36	18	5	165	165	54	91	0	2	2	0	59	12	0	.203	18	24	1	0	1.2	.977
1958	**2 teams** STL N (3G 0–1) DET A (7G 1–0)																									
″	**total**	1	1	.500	4.71	10	6	0	28.2	34	7	15	0	0	0	0	8	1	0	.125	0	5	0	0	0.5	1.000
13 yrs.		92	108	.460	4.80	361	240	79	1803	1806	852	794	9	10	7	9	633	124	3	.196	87	259	26	16	1.0	.930

Dave Wehrmeister

WEHRMEISTER, DAVID THOMAS BR TR 6′ 4″ 195 lbs.
B. Nov. 9, 1952, Berwyn, Ill.

Year	Team	W	L	PCT	ERA	G	GS	CG	IP	H	BB	SO	ShO	Relief Pitching W	Relief Pitching L	Relief Pitching SV	Batting AB	Batting H	Batting HR	BA	PO	A	E	DP	TC/G	FA
1976	SD N	0	4	.000	7.45	7	4	0	19.1	27	11	10	0	0	0	0	6	0	0	.000	1	4	0	1	0.7	1.000
1977		1	3	.250	6.04	30	6	0	70	81	44	32	0	1	2	0	12	2	0	.167	7	9	2	1	0.6	.889
1978		1	0	1.000	6.43	4	0	0	7	8	5	2	0	1	0	0	0	0	0	—	0	0	0	0	0.0	.000
1981	NY A	0	0	—	5.14	5	0	0	7	6	7	7	0	0	0	0	0	0	0	—	1	2	0	0	0.6	1.000
1984	PHI N	0	0	—	7.20	7	0	0	15	18	7	13	0	0	0	0	2	0	0	.000	1	3	0	1	0.6	1.000
1985	CHI A	2	2	.500	3.43	23	0	0	39.1	35	10	32	0	2	2	2	0	0	0	—	3	2	0	2	0.2	1.000
6 yrs.		4	9	.308	5.65	76	10	0	157.2	175	84	96	0	4	4	2	20	2	0	.100	13	20	2	5	0.5	.943

Dick Weik

WEIK, RICHARD HENRY (Legs) BR TR 6′ 3½″ 184 lbs.
B. Nov. 17, 1927, Waterloo, Iowa D. Apr. 21, 1991, Harvey, Ill.

Year	Team	W	L	PCT	ERA	G	GS	CG	IP	H	BB	SO	ShO	Relief Pitching W	Relief Pitching L	Relief Pitching SV	Batting AB	Batting H	Batting HR	BA	PO	A	E	DP	TC/G	FA
1948	WAS A	1	2	.333	5.68	3	3	0	12.2	14	22	8	0	0	0	0	4	3	0	.750	0	2	0	0	0.7	1.000
1949		3	12	.200	5.38	27	14	2	95.1	78	103	58	2	1	1	1	28	5	0	.179	5	22	1	0	1.0	.964
1950	**2 teams** WAS A (14G 1–3) CLE A (11G 1–3)																									
″	**total**	2	6	.250	4.11	25	7	1	70	56	73	42	0	1	1	0	18	3	0	.167	1	9	0	1	0.4	1.000
1953	DET A	0	1	.000	13.97	12	1	0	19.1	32	23	6	0	0	1	0	2	1	0	.500	3	3	0	1	0.5	1.000
1954		0	1	.000	7.16	9	1	0	16.1	23	16	9	0	0	1	0	1	0	0	.000	0	1	1	0	0.2	.500
5 yrs.		6	22	.214	5.90	76	26	3	213.2	203	237	123	2	2	4	1	53	12	0	.226	9	37	2	2	0.6	.958

Bob Weiland

WEILAND, ROBERT GEORGE (Lefty) BL TL 6′ 4″ 215 lbs.
Brother of Ed Weiland.
B. Dec. 14, 1905, Chicago, Ill. D. Nov. 9, 1988, Chicago, Ill.

Year	Team	W	L	PCT	ERA	G	GS	CG	IP	H	BB	SO	ShO	Relief Pitching W	Relief Pitching L	Relief Pitching SV	Batting AB	Batting H	Batting HR	BA	PO	A	E	DP	TC/G	FA
1928	CHI A	1	0	1.000	0.00	1	1	1	9	7	5	9	1	0	0	0	3	1	0	.333	1	1	0	0	2.0	1.000
1929		2	4	.333	5.81	15	9	1	62	62	43	25	0	0	0	1	18	2	0	.111	1	8	0	0	0.6	1.000
1930		0	4	.000	6.61	14	3	0	32.2	38	21	15	0	0	0	0	8	0	0	.000	0	6	0	0	0.4	1.000
1931		2	7	.222	5.16	15	8	3	75	75	46	38	0	0	1	0	22	4	0	.182	2	18	0	0	1.3	1.000
1932	BOS A	6	16	.273	4.51	43	27	7	195.2	231	97	63	0	0	1	1	61	9	0	.148	14	49	3	7	1.5	.955
1933		8	14	.364	3.87	39	27	12	216.1	197	100	97	0	0	0	3	65	7	0	.108	5	38	2	3	1.2	.956
1934	**2 teams** BOS A (11G 1–5) CLE A (16G 1–5)																									
″	**total**	2	10	.167	4.73	27	14	4	125.2	134	57	71	0	0	1	0	43	5	1	.116	4	22	1	2	1.0	.963
1935	STL A	0	2	.000	9.56	14	4	0	32	39	31	11	0	0	0	0	8	0	0	.000	0	4	1	0	0.4	.800
1937	STL N	15	14	.517	3.54	41	**34**	21	264.1	283	94	105	2	0	2	0	89	15	2	.169	6	54	4	2	1.6	.938
1938		16	11	.593	3.59	35	29	11	228.1	248	67	117	1	0	0	1	80	11	0	.138	7	41	3	3	1.5	.941
1939		10	12	.455	3.57	32	23	6	146.1	146	50	63	3	2	1	1	46	3	0	.065	4	24	1	2	0.9	.966
1940		0	0	—	40.50	1	0	0	0.2	3	0	0	0	0	0	0	0	0	0	—	0	0	0	0	0.0	.000
12 yrs.		62	94	.397	4.24	277	179	66	1388	1463	611	614	7	2	6	7	443	57	3	.129	44	265	15	19	1.2	.954

Ed Weiland

WEILAND, EDWIN NICHOLAS BL TR 5′11″ 180 lbs.
Brother of Bob Weiland.
B. Nov. 26, 1914, Evanston, Ill. D. July 12, 1971, Chicago, Ill.

Year	Team	Lg	W	L	PCT	ERA	G	GS	CG	IP	H	BB	SO	ShO	Relief Pitching W	Relief Pitching L	Relief Pitching SV	Batting AB	Batting H	Batting HR	BA	PO	A	E	DP	TC/G	FA
1940	**CHI**	**A**	0	0	—	8.79	5	0	0	14.1	15	7	3	0	0	0	0	5	1	0	.200	0	1	0	0	0.2	1.000
1942			0	0	—	7.45	5	0	0	9.2	18	3	4	0	0	0	0	2	0	0	.000	0	1	0	0	0.2	1.000
2 yrs.			0	0		8.25	10	0	0	24	33	10	7	0	0	0	0	7	1	0	.143	0	2	0	0	0.2	1.000

Carl Weilman

WEILMAN, CARL WOOLWORTH (Zeke) BL TL 6′ 5½″ 187 lbs.
Born Carl Woolworth Weilenmann.
B. Nov. 29, 1889, Hamilton, Ohio D. May 25, 1924, Hamilton, Ohio.

Year	Team	Lg	W	L	PCT	ERA	G	GS	CG	IP	H	BB	SO	ShO	Relief Pitching W	Relief Pitching L	Relief Pitching SV	Batting AB	Batting H	Batting HR	BA	PO	A	E	DP	TC/G	FA
1912	**STL**	**A**	2	4	.333	2.79	9	6	5	48.1	42	3	24	2	0	0	1	17	2	0	.118	2	15	0	0	1.9	1.000
1913			10	**20**	.333	3.40	39	28	17	251.2	262	60	79	2	2	2	0	82	12	0	.146	8	83	8	3	2.5	.919
1914			18	13	.581	2.08	44	36	20	299	260	84	119	3	2	1	1	101	15	0	.149	15	88	3	4	2.4	.972
1915			18	19	.486	2.34	47	31	19	295.2	240	83	125	3	**5**	2	4	100	23	0	.230	8	85	5	2	2.1	.949
1916			17	18	.486	2.15	46	31	19	276	237	76	91	1	5	4	2	91	14	0	.154	7	69	7	6	1.8	.916
1917			1	2	.333	1.89	5	3	0	19	19	6	9	0	0	0	0	4	0	0	.000	0	10	1	1	2.2	.909
1919			10	6	.625	2.07	20	20	12	148	133	45	44	3	0	0	0	47	9	0	.191	3	40	0	2	2.2	1.000
1920			9	13	.409	4.47	30	24	13	183.1	201	61	45	1	0	0	2	63	11	0	.175	16	52	4	1	2.4	.944
8 yrs.			85	95	.472	2.67	240	179	105	1521	1394	418	536	15	14	9	10	505	86	0	.170	59	442	28	19	2.2	.947

Jake Weimer

WEIMER, JACOB (Tornado Jake) BR TL 5′11″ 175 lbs.
B. Nov. 29, 1873, Ottumwa, Iowa D. June 19, 1928, Chicago, Ill.

Year	Team	Lg	W	L	PCT	ERA	G	GS	CG	IP	H	BB	SO	ShO	Relief Pitching W	Relief Pitching L	Relief Pitching SV	Batting AB	Batting H	Batting HR	BA	PO	A	E	DP	TC/G	FA
1903	**CHI**	**N**	21	9	.700	2.30	35	33	27	282	241	104	128	3	0	0	0	107	21	0	.196	20	66	9	2	2.7	.905
1904			20	14	.588	1.91	37	37	31	307	229	97	177	5	0	0	0	115	21	0	.183	37	81	5	0	3.3	.959
1905			18	12	.600	2.27	33	30	26	250	212	80	107	2	1	1	1	92	19	0	.207	18	65	7	2	2.7	.922
1906	**CIN**	**N**	20	14	.588	2.22	41	39	31	304.2	263	99	141	6	1	0	1	108	29	0	.269	18	87	4	1	2.7	.963
1907			11	14	.440	2.41	29	26	19	209	165	63	67	3	2	1	0	72	14	1	.194	21	66	7	1	3.2	.926
1908			8	7	.533	2.39	15	15	9	116.2	110	50	36	2	0	0	0	45	11	0	.244	7	37	0	2	2.9	1.000
1909	**NY**	**N**	0	0	—	9.00	1	0	0	3	7	0	1	0	0	0	0	1	0	0	.000	1	0	0	0	1.0	1.000
7 yrs.			98	70	.583	2.23	191	180	143	1472.1	1227	493	657	21	4	2	2	540	115	1	.213	122	402	32	8	2.9	.942

Lefty Weinert

WEINERT, PHILIP WALTER BL TL 6′ 1″ 195 lbs.
B. Apr. 21, 1902, Philadelphia, Pa. D. Apr. 17, 1973, Rockledge, Fla.

Year	Team	Lg	W	L	PCT	ERA	G	GS	CG	IP	H	BB	SO	ShO	Relief Pitching W	Relief Pitching L	Relief Pitching SV	Batting AB	Batting H	Batting HR	BA	PO	A	E	DP	TC/G	FA
1919	**PHI**	**N**	0	0	—	18.00	1	0	0	4	11	2	0	0	0	0	0	2	2	0	1.000	2	1	0	0	3.0	1.000
1920			1	1	.500	6.14	10	2	0	22	27	19	10	0	1	0	0	5	0	0	.000	1	5	0	0	0.6	1.000
1921			1	0	1.000	1.46	8	0	0	12.1	8	5	2	0	1	0	0	1	1	0	1.000	0	1	1	0	0.3	.500
1922			8	11	.421	3.40	34	22	10	166.2	189	70	58	0	3	1	1	58	14	0	.241	3	31	2	1	1.1	.944
1923			4	17	.190	5.42	38	20	8	156	207	81	46	0	0	2	1	59	19	0	.322	1	26	2	1	0.8	.931
1924			0	1	.000	2.45	8	1	0	14.2	10	11	7	0	0	0	0	4	0	0	.000	0	5	1	0	0.8	.833
1927	**CHI**	**N**	1	1	.500	4.58	5	3	1	19.2	21	6	5	0	0	0	0	5	1	0	.200	3	2	1	0	1.2	.833
1928			1	0	1.000	5.29	10	1	0	17	24	9	8	0	1	0	0	2	0	0	.000	0	0	0	0	0.0	.000
1931	**NY**	**A**	2	2	.500	6.20	17	0	0	24.2	31	19	24	0	2	2	0	6	0	0	.000	0	4	0	1	0.2	1.000
9 yrs.			18	33	.353	4.59	131	49	19	437	528	222	160	0	8	5	2	142	37	0	.261	10	75	7	3	0.7	.924

Roy Weir

WEIR, WILLIAM FRANKLIN (Bill) BL TL 5′ 8½″ 170 lbs.
B. Feb. 25, 1911, Portland, Me. D. Sept. 30, 1989, Anaheim, Ca.

Year	Team	Lg	W	L	PCT	ERA	G	GS	CG	IP	H	BB	SO	ShO	Relief Pitching W	Relief Pitching L	Relief Pitching SV	Batting AB	Batting H	Batting HR	BA	PO	A	E	DP	TC/G	FA
1936	**BOS**	**N**	4	3	.571	2.83	12	7	2	57.1	53	24	29	2	1	0	0	18	5	0	.278	3	14	0	2	1.4	1.000
1937			1	1	.500	3.82	10	4	1	33	27	19	8	0	0	0	0	10	0	0	.000	3	0	0	0	1.5	1.000
1938			1	0	1.000	6.75	5	0	0	13.1	14	6	3	0	1	0	0	3	1	0	.333	0	5	0	0	1.0	1.000
1939			0	0	—	0.00	2	0	0	2.2	1	1	2	0	0	0	0	1	0	0	.000	1	1	0	0	1.0	1.000
4 yrs.			6	4	.600	3.55	29	11	3	106.1	95	50	42	2	2	0	0	32	6	0	.188	7	20	0	2	1.3	1.000

Bob Welch

WELCH, ROBERT LYNN BR TR 6′ 3″ 190 lbs.
B. Nov. 3, 1956, Detroit, Mich.

Year	Team	Lg	W	L	PCT	ERA	G	GS	CG	IP	H	BB	SO	ShO	Relief Pitching W	Relief Pitching L	Relief Pitching SV	Batting AB	Batting H	Batting HR	BA	PO	A	E	DP	TC/G	FA
1978	**LA**	**N**	7	4	.636	2.03	23	13	4	111	92	26	66	3	1	0	3	29	5	0	.172	6	12	1	0	0.8	.947
1979			5	6	.455	4.00	25	12	1	81	82	32	64	0	3	1	5	19	3	0	.158	2	8	3	3	0.5	.769
1980			14	9	.609	3.28	32	32	3	214	190	79	141	2	0	0	0	70	17	0	.243	15	26	1	3	1.3	.976
1981			9	5	.643	3.45	23	23	2	141	141	41	88	1	0	0	0	45	10	0	.222	4	18	0	1	1.0	1.000
1982			16	11	.593	3.36	36	36	9	235.2	199	81	176	3	0	0	0	85	12	0	.141	19	26	2	0	1.3	.957
1983			15	12	.556	2.65	31	31	4	204	164	72	156	3	0	0	0	73	7	1	.096	14	27	3	1	1.4	.932
1984			13	13	.500	3.78	31	29	3	178.2	191	58	126	1	0	0	0	51	4	0	.078	20	28	2	5	1.6	.960
1985			14	4	.778	2.31	23	23	8	167.1	141	35	96	3	0	0	0	50	9	0	.180	15	27	3	1	2.0	.933
1986			7	13	.350	3.28	33	33	7	235.2	227	55	183	3	0	0	0	76	8	1	.105	21	26	2	2	1.5	.959
1987			15	9	.625	3.22	35	35	6	251.2	204	86	196	**4**	0	0	0	83	13	0	.157	25	38	0	3	1.8	1.000
1988	**OAK**	**A**	17	9	.654	3.64	36	36	4	244.2	237	81	158	2	0	0	0	0	0	0	—	16	32	1	2	1.4	.980
1989			17	8	.680	3.00	33	33	1	209.2	191	78	137	0	0	0	0	0	0	0	—	26	21	4	3	1.5	.922
1990			**27**	6	**.818**	2.95	35	35	2	238	214	77	127	2	0	0	0	0	0	0	—	20	31	0	2	1.5	1.000
1991			12	13	.480	4.58	35	**35**	7	220	220	91	101	1	0	0	0	0	0	0	—	15	29	2	1	1.3	.957
1992			11	7	.611	3.27	20	20	0	123.2	114	43	47	0	0	0	0	0	0	0	—	5	13	1	1	0.9	.947
1993			9	11	.450	5.29	30	28	0	166.2	208	56	63	0	1	0	0	0	0	0	—	16	26	0	2	1.4	1.000
1994			3	6	.333	7.08	25	8	0	68.2	79	43	44	0	3	1	0	1	0	0	.000	4	6	1	0	0.4	.909
17 yrs.			211	146	.591	3.47	506	462	61	3091.1	2894	1034	1969	28	8	2	8	582	88	2	.151	243	394	26	30	1.3	.961
DIVISIONAL PLAYOFF SERIES																											
1981	**LA**	**N**	0	0	—	0.00	1	0	0	1	0	1	1	0	0	0	0	0	0	0	—	0	0	0	0	0.0	.000
LEAGUE CHAMPIONSHIP SERIES																											
1978	**LA**	**N**	1	0	1.000	2.08	1	0	0	4.1	2	0	5	0	1	0	0	2	0	0	.000	0	1	0	0	1.0	1.000
1981			0	0	—	5.40	3	0	0	1.2	2	0	2	0	0	0	1	0	0	0	—	0	0	0	0	0.0	.000
1983			0	1	.000	6.75	1	1	0	1.1	0	2	0	0	0	0	0	0	0	0	—	0	0	0	0	0.0	.000
1985			0	1	.000	6.75	1	1	0	2.2	5	6	2	0	0	0	0	1	0	0	.000	0	0	1	0	1.0	.000
1988	**OAK**	**A**	0	0	—	27.00	1	1	0	1.2	6	2	0	0	0	0	0	0	0	0	—	1	0	0	0	1.0	1.000

Bob Welch *continued*

Year	Team	Lg	W	L	PCT	ERA	G	GS	CG	IP	H	BB	SO	ShO	Relief Pitching W	Relief Pitching L	Relief Pitching SV	Batting AB	Batting H	Batting HR	BA	PO	A	E	DP	TC/G	FA
1989			1	0	1.000	3.18	1	1	0	5.2	8	1	4	0	0	0	0	0	0	0	—	1	0	0	0	1.0	1.000
1990			1	0	1.000	1.23	1	1	0	7.1	6	3	4	0	0	0	0	0	0	0	—	0	3	0	0	3.0	1.000
1992			0	0	—	2.57	1	1	0	7	7	1	7	0	0	0	0	0	0	0	—	0	1	0	0	1.0	1.000
8 yrs.			3	2	.600	4.26	10	6	0	31.2	36	15	24	0	1	0	1	3	0	0	.000	2	5	1	0	0.8	.875
WORLD SERIES																											
1978	LA	N	0	1	.000	6.23	3	0	0	4.1	4	2	6	0	0	1	1	0	0	0	—	0	0	0	0	0.0	.000
1981			0	0	—	∞	1	1	0		3	1	0	0	0	0	0	0	0	0	—	0	0	0	0	0.0	.000
1988	OAK	A	0	0	—	1.80	1	1	0	5	6	3	8	0	0	0	0	0	0	0	—	1	1	0	0	2.0	1.000
1990			0	0	—	4.91	1	1	0	7.1	9	2	2	0	0	0	0	3	0	0	.000	0	2	0	0	2.0	1.000
4 yrs.			0	1	.000	5.40	6	3	0	16.2	22	8	16	0	0	1	1	3	0	0	.000	1	3	0	0	0.7	1.000

Curt Welch

WELCH, CURTIS BENTON BR TR 5′10″ 175 lbs.
B. Feb. 11, 1862, East Liverpool, Ohio D. Aug. 29, 1896, East Liverpool, Ohio.

Year	Team	Lg	W	L	PCT	ERA	G	GS	CG	IP	H	BB	SO	ShO	Relief Pitching W	Relief Pitching L	Relief Pitching SV	Batting AB	Batting H	Batting HR	BA	PO	A	E	DP	TC/G	FA
1890	PHI	AA	0	0	—	54.00	1	0	0	1	6	0	1	0	0	0	0	*				212	29	31	4	2.4	.886

Johnny Welch

WELCH, JOHN VERNON BL TR 6′ 3″ 184 lbs.
B. Dec. 2, 1906, Washington, D. C. D. Sept. 2, 1940, St. Louis, Mo.

Year	Team	Lg	W	L	PCT	ERA	G	GS	CG	IP	H	BB	SO	ShO	Relief Pitching W	Relief Pitching L	Relief Pitching SV	Batting AB	Batting H	Batting HR	BA	PO	A	E	DP	TC/G	FA
1926	CHI	N	0	0	—	2.08	3	0	0	4.1	5	1	0	0	0	0	0	1	1	0	1.000	0	0	0	0	0.0	.000
1927			0	0	—	9.00	1	0	0	1	0	3	1	0	0	0	0	0	0	0	—	0	0	0	0	0.0	.000
1928			0	0	—	15.75	3	0	0	4	13	0	2	0	0	0	0	0	0	0	—	0	1	0	0	0.3	1.000
1931			2	1	.667	3.74	8	3	1	33.2	39	10	7	0	1	1	0	12	5	0	.417	2	7	0	0	1.1	1.000
1932	BOS	A	4	6	.400	5.23	20	8	3	72.1	93	38	26	1	1	1	0	36	9	1	.250	1	17	1	0	0.9	.947
1933			4	9	.308	4.60	47	7	1	129	142	67	68	0	3	5	3	37	6	0	.162	1	33	1	0	0.7	.971
1934			13	15	.464	4.49	41	22	8	206.1	223	76	91	1	3	6	0	74	15	0	.203	9	40	0	3	1.2	1.000
1935			10	9	.526	4.47	31	19	10	143	155	53	48	1	2	0	2	50	9	0	.180	5	27	1	2	1.1	.970
1936	**2 teams**	**BOS A** (9G 2–1) **PIT N** (9G 0–0)																									
″	**total**		2	1	.667	5.10	18	4	1	54.2	65	14	14	0	0	0	1	18	5	0	.278	2	10	1	0	0.7	.923
9 yrs.			35	41	.461	4.66	172	63	24	648.1	735	262	257	3	10	13	6	228	50	1	.219	20	135	4	5	0.9	.975

Mickey Welch

WELCH, MICHAEL FRANCIS (Smiling Mickey) BR TR 5′ 8″ 160 lbs.
B. July 4, 1859, Brooklyn, N. Y. D. July 30, 1941, Concord, N. H.
Hall of Fame 1973.

Year	Team	Lg	W	L	PCT	ERA	G	GS	CG	IP	H	BB	SO	ShO	Relief Pitching W	Relief Pitching L	Relief Pitching SV	Batting AB	Batting H	Batting HR	BA	PO	A	E	DP	TC/G	FA
1880	TRO	N	34	30	.531	2.54	65	64	64	574	575	80	123	4	0	0	0	251	72	0	.287	36	86	23	4	2.2	.841
1881			21	18	.538	*2.67*	40	40	40	368	371	78	104	4	0	0	0	148	30	0	.203	20	39	7	3	1.6	.894
1882			14	16	.467	*3.46*	33	33	30	281	334	62	53	5	0	0	0	151	37	1	.245	15	46	11	4	1.8	.847
1883	NY	N	25	23	.521	*2.73*	54	52	46	426	431	66	144	4	1	1	0	320	75	3	.234	71	63	38	4	1.9	.779
1884			39	21	.650	*2.50*	65	65	62	557.1	528	**146**	345	4	0	0	0	249	60	3	.241	25	78	14	6	1.6	.880
1885			44	11	**.800**	*1.66*	56	55	55	492	372	**131**	258	7	0	0	1	199	41	2	.206	16	70	14	0	1.8	.860
1886			33	22	.600	*2.99*	59	59	56	500	514	**163**	272	1	0	0	0	213	46	2	.216	19	82	5	0	1.7	.953
1887			22	15	.595	3.36	40	40	39	346	339	91	115	2	0	0	0	148	36	2	.243	17	51	12	0	2.0	.850
1888			26	19	.578	1.93	47	47	47	425.1	328	108	167	5	0	0	0	169	32	2	.189	16	75	17	1	2.3	.843
1889			27	12	.692	3.02	45	41	39	375	340	149	125	3	0	0	2	156	30	0	.192	13	59	4	2	1.7	.947
1890			17	13	.567	2.99	37	37	33	292.1	268	122	97	2	0	0	0	123	22	0	.179	10	43	4	1	1.5	.930
1891			6	9	.400	4.28	22	15	14	160	176	97	46	0	2	1	1	71	10	0	.141	7	21	4	0	1.5	.875
1892			0	0	—	14.40	1	1	0	5	11	4	1	0	0	0	0	3	1	0	.333	0	1	0	0	1.0	1.000
13 yrs.			308	209	.596	2.71	564	549	525 **6th**	4802	4587	1297	1850	41	3	2	4	*				265	714	153	25	1.8	.865

Ted Welch

WELCH, FLOYD JOHN BL TR 5′ 9½″ 160 lbs.
B. Oct. 17, 1892, Coyville, Kans. D. Jan. 6, 1943, Great Bend, Kans.

Year	Team	Lg	W	L	PCT	ERA	G	GS	CG	IP	H	BB	SO	ShO	Relief Pitching W	Relief Pitching L	Relief Pitching SV	Batting AB	Batting H	Batting HR	BA	PO	A	E	DP	TC/G	FA
1914	STL	F	0	0	—	6.00	3	0	0	6	6	3	2	0	0	0	0	1	0	0	.000	1	1	0	0	0.7	1.000

Don Welchel

WELCHEL, DONALD RAY BR TR 6′ 4″ 205 lbs.
B. Feb. 3, 1957, Atlanta, Tex.

Year	Team	Lg	W	L	PCT	ERA	G	GS	CG	IP	H	BB	SO	ShO	Relief Pitching W	Relief Pitching L	Relief Pitching SV	Batting AB	Batting H	Batting HR	BA	PO	A	E	DP	TC/G	FA
1982	BAL	A	1	0	1.000	8.31	2	0	0	4.1	6	2	3	0	1	0	0	0	0	0	—	0	0	0	0	0.0	.000
1983			0	2	.000	5.40	11	0	0	26.2	33	10	16	0	0	2	0	0	0	0	—	2	3	1	0	0.5	.833
2 yrs.			1	2	.333	5.81	13	0	0	31	39	12	19	0	1	2	0	0	0	0		2	3	1	0	0.5	.833

Bob Wells

WELLS, ROBERT LEE BR TR 6′ 180 lbs.
B. Nov. 1, 1966, Yakima, Wash.

Year	Team	Lg	W	L	PCT	ERA	G	GS	CG	IP	H	BB	SO	ShO	Relief Pitching W	Relief Pitching L	Relief Pitching SV	Batting AB	Batting H	Batting HR	BA	PO	A	E	DP	TC/G	FA
1994	**2 teams**	**PHI N** (6G 1–0) **SEA A** (1G 1–0)																									
″	**total**		2	0	1.000	2.00	7	0	0	9	8	4	6	0	2	0	0	0	0	0		0	0	0	0	0.0	
1995	SEA	A	4	3	.571	5.75	30	4	0	76.2	88	39	38	0	4	1	0	0	0	0	—	7	8	0	0	0.5	1.000
2 yrs.			6	3	.667	5.36	37	4	0	85.2	96	43	44	0	6	1	0	0	0	0		7	8	0	0	0.4	1.000
DIVISIONAL PLAYOFF SERIES																											
1995	SEA	A	0	0	—	9.00	1	0	0	1	2	1	0	0	0	0	0	0	0	0	—	0	0	0	0	0.0	.000
LEAGUE CHAMPIONSHIP SERIES																											
1995	SEA	A	0	0	—	3.00	1	0	0	3	2	2	2	0	0	0	0	0	0	0	—	0	1	0	0	1.0	1.000

David Wells

WELLS, DAVID LEE BL TL 6′ 3″ 187 lbs.
B. May 20, 1963, Torrance, Calif.

Year	Team	Lg	W	L	PCT	ERA	G	GS	CG	IP	H	BB	SO	ShO	Relief Pitching W	Relief Pitching L	Relief Pitching SV	Batting AB	Batting H	Batting HR	BA	PO	A	E	DP	TC/G	FA
1987	TOR	A	4	3	.571	3.99	18	2	0	29.1	37	12	32	0	4	1	1	0	0	0	—	2	4	0	1	0.3	1.000
1988			3	5	.375	4.62	41	0	0	64.1	65	31	56	0	3	5	4	0	0	0	—	5	5	0	1	0.2	1.000
1989			7	4	.636	2.40	54	0	0	86.1	66	28	78	0	7	4	2	0	0	0	—	9	11	1	0	0.4	.952
1990			11	6	.647	3.14	43	25	0	189	165	45	115	0	1	1	3	0	0	0	—	7	32	0	1	0.9	1.000
1991			15	10	.600	3.72	40	28	2	198.1	188	49	106	0	1	0	1	0	0	0	—	5	35	2	1	1.0	.952
1992			7	9	.438	5.40	41	14	0	120	138	36	62	0	1	2	2	0	0	0	—	9	14	1	1	0.6	.958
1993	DET	A	11	9	.550	4.19	32	30	0	187	183	42	139	0	0	0	0	0	0	0	—	10	22	1	0	1.0	.970
1994			5	7	.417	3.96	16	16	5	111.1	113	24	71	1	0	0	0	0	0	0	—	6	11	0	0	1.1	1.000
1995	**2 teams**	**DET A** (18G 10–3) **CIN N** (11G 6–5)																									
″	**total**		16	8	.667	3.24	29	29	6	203	194	53	133	0	0	0	0	28	4	0	.143	15	22	2	2	1.3	.949
9 yrs.			79	61	.564	3.77	314	144	13	1188.2	1149	320	792	1	17	13	13	28	4	0	.143	68	156	7	7	0.7	.970

David Wells *continued*

Year	Team		W	L	PCT	ERA	G	GS	CG	IP	H	BB	SO	ShO	Relief W	Relief L	Relief SV	AB	H	HR	BA	PO	A	E	DP	TC/G	FA
DIVISIONAL PLAYOFF SERIES																											
1995	CIN	N	1	0	1.000	0.00	1	1	0	6.1	6	1	8	0	0	0	0	3	1	0	.333	1	1	0	0	2.0	1.000
LEAGUE CHAMPIONSHIP SERIES																											
1989	TOR	A	0	0	—	0.00	1	0	0	1	0	2	1	0	0	0	0	0	0	0	—	0	0	0	0	0.0	.000
1991			0	0	—	2.35	4	0	0	7.2	6	2	9	0	0	0	0	0	0	0	—	1	1	0	0	0.5	1.000
1995	CIN	N	0	1	.000	4.50	1	1	0	6	8	2	3	0	0	0	0	2	1	0	.500	0	0	0	0	0.0	.000
3 yrs.			0	1	.000	3.07	6	1	0	14.2	14	6	13	0	0	0	0	2	1	0	.500	1	1	0	0	0.3	1.000
WORLD SERIES																											
1992	TOR	A	0	0	—	0.00	4	0	0	4.1	1	2	3	0	0	0	0	0	0	0	—	0	0	0	0	0.0	.000

Ed Wells

WELLS, EDWIN LEE BL TL 6′ 1½″ 183 lbs.
B. June 7, 1900, Ashland, Ohio D. May 1, 1986, Montgomery, Ala.

Year	Team		W	L	PCT	ERA	G	GS	CG	IP	H	BB	SO	ShO	Relief W	Relief L	Relief SV	AB	H	HR	BA	PO	A	E	DP	TC/G	FA
1923	DET	A	0	0	—	5.40	7	0	0	10	11	6	6	0	0	0	0	1	0	0	.000	1	1	0	0	0.3	1.000
1924			6	8	.429	4.06	29	15	5	102	117	42	33	0	1	1	4	33	7	0	.212	4	30	1	1	1.2	.971
1925			6	9	.400	6.23	35	14	5	134.1	190	62	45	0	2	3	2	43	12	0	.279	8	34	1	1	1.2	.977
1926			12	10	.545	4.15	36	26	9	178	201	76	58	**4**	2	2	0	73	15	0	.205	9	30	3	3	1.2	.929
1927			0	1	.000	6.75	8	1	0	20	28	5	5	0	0	0	1	7	2	0	.286	1	8	1	0	1.3	.900
1929	NY	A	13	9	.591	4.33	31	23	10	193.1	179	81	78	3	0	0	0	74	17	0	.230	5	21	2	2	0.9	.929
1930			12	3	.800	5.20	27	21	7	150.2	185	49	46	0	1	1	0	58	15	0	.259	6	21	1	1	1.0	.964
1931			9	5	.643	4.32	27	10	6	116.2	130	37	34	0	2	4	2	45	10	0	.222	6	17	2	1	0.9	.920
1932			3	3	.500	4.26	22	0	0	31.2	38	12	13	0	3	3	2	6	0	0	.000	1	6	0	0	0.3	1.000
1933	STL	A	6	14	.300	4.20	36	22	10	203.2	230	63	58	0	2	3	1	71	14	0	.197	11	31	2	0	1.2	.955
1934			1	7	.125	4.79	33	8	2	92	108	35	27	0	1	3	1	22	1	0	.045	5	23	0	2	0.8	1.000
11 yrs.			68	69	.496	4.65	291	140	54	1232.1	1417	468	403	7	14	20	13	433	93	0	.215	57	222	13	11	1.0	.955

John Wells

WELLS, JOHN FREDERICK BR TR 5′11½″ 180 lbs.
B. Nov. 25, 1922, Junction City, Kans. D. Oct. 23, 1993, Olean, N. Y.

Year	Team		W	L	PCT	ERA	G	GS	CG	IP	H	BB	SO	ShO	Relief W	Relief L	Relief SV	AB	H	HR	BA	PO	A	E	DP	TC/G	FA
1944	BKN	N	0	2	.000	5.40	4	2	0	15	18	11	7	0	0	1	0	4	1	0	.250	0	2	0	1	0.5	1.000

Terry Wells

WELLS, TERRY BL TL 6′ 3″ 205 lbs.
B. Sept. 10, 1963, Kankakee, Ill.

Year	Team		W	L	PCT	ERA	G	GS	CG	IP	H	BB	SO	ShO	Relief W	Relief L	Relief SV	AB	H	HR	BA	PO	A	E	DP	TC/G	FA
1990	LA	N	1	2	.333	7.84	5	5	0	20.2	25	14	18	0	0	0	0	7	0	0	.000	1	0	2	0	0.6	.333

Chris Welsh

WELSH, CHRISTOPHER CHARLES BL TL 6′ 2″ 185 lbs.
B. Apr. 14, 1955, Wilmington, Del.

Year	Team		W	L	PCT	ERA	G	GS	CG	IP	H	BB	SO	ShO	Relief W	Relief L	Relief SV	AB	H	HR	BA	PO	A	E	DP	TC/G	FA
1981	SD	N	6	7	.462	3.77	22	19	4	124	122	41	51	2	0	0	0	41	6	0	.146	3	30	0	0	1.5	1.000
1982			8	8	.500	4.91	28	20	3	139.1	146	63	48	1	1	2	0	42	11	0	.262	7	29	2	0	1.4	.947
1983	2 teams	SD N (7G 0–1) MON N (16G 0–1)																									
″	total		0	2	.000	4.42	23	6	0	59	59	20	22	0	0	1	0	18	4	0	.222	3	15	2	2	0.9	.900
1985	TEX	A	2	5	.286	4.13	25	6	0	76.1	101	25	31	0	1	1	0	0	0	0	—	1	10	0	1	0.4	1.000
1986	CIN	N	6	9	.400	4.78	24	24	1	139.1	163	40	40	0	0	0	0	42	5	1	.119	7	23	0	1	1.3	1.000
5 yrs.			22	31	.415	4.45	122	75	8	538	591	189	192	3	2	4	0	143	26	1	.182	21	107	4	4	1.1	.970

Dick Welteroth

WELTEROTH, RICHARD JOHN BR TR 5′11″ 165 lbs.
B. Aug. 3, 1927, Williamsport, Pa.

Year	Team		W	L	PCT	ERA	G	GS	CG	IP	H	BB	SO	ShO	Relief W	Relief L	Relief SV	AB	H	HR	BA	PO	A	E	DP	TC/G	FA
1948	WAS	A	2	1	.667	5.51	33	2	0	65.1	73	50	16	0	1	1	1	10	1	0	.100	1	11	0	0	0.4	1.000
1949			2	5	.286	7.36	52	2	0	95.1	107	89	37	0	2	3	2	17	1	0	.059	3	18	0	1	0.4	1.000
1950			0	0	—	3.00	5	0	0	6	5	6	2	0	0	0	0	0	0	0	—	0	2	0	0	0.4	1.000
3 yrs.			4	6	.400	6.48	90	4	0	166.2	185	145	55	0	3	4	3	27	2	0	.074	4	31	0	1	0.4	1.000

Tony Welzer

WELZER, ANTON FRANK BR TR 5′11″ 160 lbs.
B. Apr. 5, 1899, Germany D. Mar. 18, 1971, Milwaukee, Wis.

Year	Team		W	L	PCT	ERA	G	GS	CG	IP	H	BB	SO	ShO	Relief W	Relief L	Relief SV	AB	H	HR	BA	PO	A	E	DP	TC/G	FA
1926	BOS	A	4	3	.571	4.79	40	6	1	141	167	57	30	1	2	1	0	38	8	0	.211	7	55	1	1	1.6	.984
1927			6	11	.353	4.46	37	19	8	181.2	214	71	56	0	1	2	1	42	4	0	.095	3	45	2	4	1.4	.960
2 yrs.			10	14	.417	4.60	77	25	9	322.2	381	128	86	1	3	3	1	80	12	0	.150	10	100	3	5	1.5	.973

Turk Wendell

WENDELL, STEVEN JOHN BB TR 6′ 2″ 185 lbs.
B. May 19, 1967, Pittsfield, Mass.

Year	Team		W	L	PCT	ERA	G	GS	CG	IP	H	BB	SO	ShO	Relief W	Relief L	Relief SV	AB	H	HR	BA	PO	A	E	DP	TC/G	FA
1993	CHI	N	1	2	.333	4.37	7	4	0	22.2	24	8	15	0	0	0	0	7	1	0	.143	7	1	0	0	1.1	1.000
1994			0	1	.000	11.93	6	2	0	14.1	22	10	9	0	0	0	0	2	0	0	.000	1	3	0	0	0.7	1.000
1995			3	1	.750	4.92	43	0	0	60.1	71	24	50	0	3	1	0	7	0	0	.000	9	12	1	2	0.5	.955
3 yrs.			4	4	.500	5.83	56	6	0	97.1	117	42	74	0	3	1	0	16	1	0	.063	17	16	1	2	0.6	.971

Don Wengert

WENGERT, DONALD PAUL BR TR 6′ 2″ 205 lbs.
B. Nov. 6, 1969, Sioux City, Iowa.

Year	Team		W	L	PCT	ERA	G	GS	CG	IP	H	BB	SO	ShO	Relief W	Relief L	Relief SV	AB	H	HR	BA	PO	A	E	DP	TC/G	FA
1995	OAK	A	1	1	.500	3.34	19	0	0	29.2	30	12	16	0	1	1	0	0	0	0	—	3	1	0	0	0.2	1.000

Butch Wensloff

WENSLOFF, CHARLES WILLIAM BR TR 5′11″ 185 lbs.
B. Dec. 3, 1915, Sausalito, Calif.

Year	Team		W	L	PCT	ERA	G	GS	CG	IP	H	BB	SO	ShO	Relief W	Relief L	Relief SV	AB	H	HR	BA	PO	A	E	DP	TC/G	FA
1943	NY	A	13	11	.542	2.54	29	27	18	223.1	179	70	105	1	0	0	1	79	14	0	.177	4	46	4	2	1.9	.926
1947			3	1	.750	2.61	11	5	1	51.2	41	22	18	0	0	1	0	19	5	0	.263	3	4	0	0	0.6	1.000
1948	CLE	A	0	1	.000	10.80	1	0	0	1.2	2	3	2	0	0	1	0	0	0	0	—	0	0	0	0	0.0	.000
3 yrs.			16	13	.552	2.60	41	32	19	276.2	222	95	125	1	0	2	1	98	19	0	.194	7	50	4	2	1.5	.934
WORLD SERIES																											
1947	NY	A	0	0	—	0.00	1	0	0	2	0	0	0	0	0	0	0	0	0	0	—	0	1	0	0	1.0	1.000

Fred Wenz

WENZ, FREDERICK CHARLES (Fireball) BR TR 6′ 3″ 214 lbs.
B. Aug. 26, 1941, Bound Brook, N. J.

Year	Team		W	L	PCT	ERA	G	GS	CG	IP	H	BB	SO	ShO	Relief W	Relief L	Relief SV	AB	H	HR	BA	PO	A	E	DP	TC/G	FA
1968	BOS	A	0	0	—	0.00	1	0	0	1	0	2	3	0	0	0	0	0	0	0	—	0	0	0	0	0.0	.000
1969			1	0	1.000	5.73	8	0	0	11	9	10	11	0	1	0	0	0	0	0	—	1	1	0	0	0.3	1.000
1970	PHI	N	2	0	1.000	4.50	22	0	0	30	27	13	24	0	2	0	1	5	0	0	.000	1	1	0	0	0.1	1.000
3 yrs.			3	0	1.000	4.71	31	0	0	42	36	25	38	0	3	0	1	5	0	0	.000	2	2	0	0	0.1	1.000

Year	Team		W	L	PCT	ERA	G	GS	CG	IP	H	BB	SO	ShO	Relief Pitching W	L	SV	Batting AB	H	HR	BA	PO	A	E	DP	TC/G	FA

Perry Werden

WERDEN, PERCIVAL WHERITT (Moose) BR TR 6′ 2″ 220 lbs.
B. July 21, 1865, St. Louis, Mo. D. Jan. 9, 1934, Minneapolis, Minn.

1884	STL	U	12	1	.923	*1.97*	16	16	12	141.1	113	22	51	1	0	0	0	*				17	36	6	1	2.7	.898

Bill Werle

WERLE, WILLIAM GEORGE (Bugs) BL TL 6′ 2½″ 182 lbs.
B. Dec. 21, 1920, Oakland, Calif.

1949	PIT	N	12	13	.480	4.24	35	29	10	221	243	51	106	2	2	1	0	77	9	0	.117	7	43	2	3	1.5	.962
1950			8	16	.333	4.60	48	22	6	215.1	249	65	78	0	2	5	8	67	13	0	.194	11	58	2	4	1.5	.972
1951			8	6	.571	5.65	59	9	2	149.2	181	51	59	0	4	2	6	40	12	0	.300	10	42	0	3	0.9	1.000
1952	2 teams	PIT N	(5G 0–0)	STL N	(19G 1–2)																						
″	total		1	2	.333	5.23	24	0	0	43	49	16	24	0	1	2	1	9	1	0	.111	4	14	2	3	0.8	.900
1953	BOS	A	0	1	.000	1.54	5	0	0	11.2	7	1	4	0	0	1	0	2	0	0	.000	0	6	0	1	1.2	1.000
1954			0	1	.000	4.38	14	0	0	24.2	41	10	14	0	0	1	0	4	0	0	.000	0	4	0	0	0.3	1.000
6 yrs.			29	39	.426	4.69	185	60	18	665.1	770	194	285	2	9	12	15	199	35	0	.176	32	167	6	14	1.1	.971

George Werley

WERLEY, GEORGE WILLIAM BR TR 6′ 2″ 196 lbs.
B. Sept. 8, 1938, St. Louis, Mo.

1956	BAL	A	0	0	—	9.00	1	0	0	1	1	2	0	0	0	0	0	0	0	0	—	1	0	0	0	1.0	1.000

Bill Wertz

WERTZ, WILLIAM CHARLES BR TR 6′ 6″ 220 lbs.
B. Jan. 15, 1967, Cleveland, Ohio.

1993	CLE	A	2	3	.400	3.62	34	0	0	59.2	54	32	53	0	2	3	0	0	0	0	—	4	0	1	0	0.1	.800
1994			0	0	—	10.38	1	0	0	4.1	9	1	1	0	0	0	0	0	0	0	—	1	0	0	0	1.0	1.000
2 yrs.			2	3	.400	4.08	35	0	0	64	63	33	54	0	2	3	0	0	0	0		5	0	1	0	0.2	.833

Johnny Wertz

WERTZ, HENRY LEVI BR TR 5′10″ 180 lbs.
Born Henry Levi Werts.
B. Apr. 20, 1898, Pomaria, S. C. D. Sept. 24, 1990, Newberry, S. C.

1926	BOS	N	11	9	.550	3.28	32	23	7	189.1	212	47	65	1	3	0	0	64	17	1	.266	14	54	2	2	2.2	.971
1927			4	10	.286	4.55	42	15	4	164.1	204	52	39	0	1	3	1	43	7	0	.163	8	32	3	1	1.0	.930
1928			0	2	.000	10.31	10	2	0	18.1	31	8	5	0	0	0	0	3	1	0	.333	1	5	0	0	0.6	1.000
1929			0	0	—	10.50	4	0	0	6	13	4	2	0	0	0	1	1	1	0	1.000	0	1	0	0	0.3	1.000
4 yrs.			15	21	.417	4.29	88	40	11	378	460	111	111	1	4	3	2	111	26	1	.234	23	92	5	3	1.4	.958

David West

WEST, DAVID LEE BL TL 6′ 6″ 205 lbs.
B. Sept. 1, 1964, Memphis, Tenn.

1988	NY	N	1	0	1.000	3.00	2	1	0	6	6	3	3	0	0	0	0	2	2	0	1.000	1	0	0	0	0.5	1.000
1989	2 teams	NY N	(11G 0–2)	MIN A	(10G 3–2)																						
″	total		3	4	.429	6.79	21	7	0	63.2	73	33	50	0	0	0	0	5	1	0	.200	2	2	1	0	0.2	.800
1990	MIN	A	7	9	.438	5.10	29	27	2	146.1	142	78	92	0	0	0	0	0	0	0	—	3	16	2	2	0.7	.905
1991			4	4	.500	4.54	15	12	0	71.1	66	28	52	0	0	0	0	0	0	0	—	1	11	1	1	0.9	.923
1992			1	3	.250	6.99	9	3	0	28.1	32	20	19	0	1	0	0	0	0	0	—	0	5	2	0	0.8	.714
1993	PHI	N	6	4	.600	2.92	76	0	0	86.1	60	51	87	0	6	4	3	5	2	0	.400	2	4	2	1	0.1	.750
1994			4	10	.286	3.55	31	14	0	99	74	61	83	0	0	4	0	28	2	0	.071	3	6	0	1	0.3	1.000
1995			3	2	.600	3.79	8	8	0	38	34	19	25	0	0	0	0	8	1	1	.125	1	3	1	0	0.6	.800
8 yrs.			29	36	.446	4.58	191	72	2	539	487	293	411	0	7	8	3	48	8	1	.167	13	47	9	5	0.4	.870
LEAGUE CHAMPIONSHIP SERIES																											
1991	MIN	A	1	0	1.000	0.00	2	0	0	5.2	1	4	4	0	1	0	0	0	0	0	—	0	0	0	0	0.0	.000
1993	PHI	N	0	0	—	13.50	3	0	0	2.2	5	2	5	0	0	0	0	0	0	0	—	0	1	0	0	0.3	1.000
2 yrs.			1	0	1.000	4.32	5	0	0	8.1	6	6	9	0	1	0	0	0	0	0		0	1	0	0	0.2	1.000
WORLD SERIES																											
1991	MIN	A	0	0	—	∞	2	0	0		2	4	0	0	0	0	0	0	0	0	—	0	0	0	0	0.0	.000
1993	PHI	N	0	0	—	27.00	3	0	0	1	5	1	0	0	0	0	0	0	0	0	—	0	0	0	0	0.0	.000
2 yrs.			0	0		63.00	5	0	0	1	7	5	0	0	0	0	0	0	0	0		0	0	0	0	0.0	

Frank West

WEST, J. FRANKLIN 180 lbs.
B. Jan. 1874, Johnstown, Pa. D. Sept. 6, 1932, Wilmerding, Pa.

1894	BOS	N	0	0	—	9.00	1	0	0	3	5	2	1	0	0	0	0	1	0	0	.000	0	0	0	0	0.0	.000

Hi West

WEST, JAMES HIRAM BR TR 6′ 185 lbs.
B. Aug. 8, 1884, Roseville, Ill. D. May 25, 1963, Los Angeles, Calif.

1905	CLE	A	2	2	.500	4.09	6	4	4	33	43	10	15	1	0	0	0	13	1	0	.077	0	3	1	0	0.7	.750
1911			3	4	.429	3.76	13	8	3	64.2	84	18	17	0	0	1	1	23	3	0	.130	3	13	1	1	1.3	.941
2 yrs.			5	6	.455	3.87	19	12	7	97.2	127	28	32	1	0	1	1	36	4	0	.111	3	16	2	1	1.1	.905

Lefty West

WEST, WELDON EDISON BR TL 6′ 165 lbs.
B. Sept. 3, 1915, Gibsonville, N. C. D. July 23, 1979, Hendersonville, N. C.

1944	STL	A	0	0	—	6.29	11	0	0	24.1	34	19	11	0	0	0	0	7	1	0	.143	0	3	0	0	0.3	1.000
1945			3	4	.429	3.63	24	8	1	74.1	71	31	38	0	1	0	0	27	2	0	.074	2	7	0	0	0.4	1.000
2 yrs.			3	4	.429	4.29	35	8	1	98.2	105	50	49	0	1	0	0	34	3	0	.088	2	10	0	0	0.3	1.000

Huyler Westervelt

WESTERVELT, HUYLER 5′ 9″ 170 lbs.
B. Oct. 1, 1870, Piermont, N. Y. Deceased.

1894	NY	N	7	10	.412	5.04	23	18	11	141	170	76	35	1	1	0	0	56	8	0	.143	13	24	6	3	1.9	.860

Mickey Weston

WESTON, MICHAEL LEE BR TR 6′ 1″ 180 lbs.
B. Mar. 26, 1961, Flint, Mich.

1989	BAL	A	1	0	1.000	5.54	7	0	0	13	18	2	7	0	1	0	1	0	0	0	—	0	1	0	0	0.1	1.000
1990			0	1	.000	7.71	9	2	0	21	28	6	9	0	0	0	0	0	0	0	—	3	0	0	0	0.3	1.000
1991	TOR	A	0	0	—	0.00	2	0	0	2	1	1	1	0	0	0	0	0	0	0	—	0	0	0	0	0.0	.000
1992	PHI	N	0	1	.000	12.27	1	1	0	3.2	7	1	0	0	0	0	0	2	0	0	.000	0	0	0	0	0.0	.000
1993	NY	N	0	0	—	7.94	4	0	0	5.2	11	1	2	0	0	0	0	0	0	0	—	0	1	0	0	0.3	1.000
5 yrs.			1	2	.333	7.15	23	3	0	45.1	65	11	19	0	1	0	1	2	0	0	.000	3	2	0	0	0.2	1.000

John Wetteland

WETTELAND, JOHN KARL BR TR 6′ 2″ 195 lbs.
B. Aug. 22, 1966, San Mateo, Calif.

Year	Team	Lg	W	L	PCT	ERA	G	GS	CG	IP	H	BB	SO	ShO	Relief Pitching W	Relief L	Relief SV	Batting AB	Batting H	HR	BA	PO	A	E	DP	TC/G	FA
1989	LA	N	5	8	.385	3.77	31	12	0	102.2	81	34	96	0	3	2	1	21	3	0	.143	5	8	2	0	0.5	.867
1990			2	4	.333	4.81	22	5	0	43	44	17	36	0	2	1	0	7	1	1	.143	1	3	1	0	0.2	.800
1991			1	0	1.000	0.00	6	0	0	9	5	3	9	0	1	0	0	0	0	0	—	1	2	1	0	0.7	.750
1992	MON	N	4	4	.500	2.92	67	0	0	83.1	64	36	99	0	4	4	37	5	1	0	.200	7	6	1	0	0.2	.929
1993			9	3	.750	1.37	70	0	0	85.1	58	28	113	0	9	3	43	4	0	0	.000	1	5	3	0	0.1	.667
1994			4	6	.400	2.83	52	0	0	63.2	46	21	68	0	4	**6**	25	4	1	0	.250	3	4	1	0	0.2	.875
1995	NY	A	1	5	.167	2.93	60	0	0	61.1	40	14	66	0	1	5	31	0	0	0	—	2	3	1	1	0.1	.833
7 yrs.			26	30	.464	2.93	308	17	0	448.1	338	153	487	0	24	21	137	41	6	1	.146	20	31	10	1	0.2	.836
DIVISIONAL PLAYOFF SERIES																											
1995	NY	A	0	1	.000	14.54	3	0	0	4.1	8	2	5	0	0	1	0	0	0	0	—	1	0	0	0	0.3	1.000

Buzz Wetzel

WETZEL, CHARLES EDWARD BR TR 6′ 1″ 162 lbs.
B. Aug. 25, 1894, Jay, Okla. D. Mar. 7, 1941, Globe, Ariz.

Year	Team	Lg	W	L	PCT	ERA	G	GS	CG	IP	H	BB	SO	ShO	Relief Pitching W	Relief L	Relief SV	Batting AB	Batting H	HR	BA	PO	A	E	DP	TC/G	FA
1927	PHI	A	0	0	—	7.71	2	1	0	4.2	8	5	0	0	0	0	0	1	1	0	1.000	0	2	0	1	1.0	1.000

Shorty Wetzel

WETZEL, GEORGE WILLIAM
B. 1868, Philadelphia, Pa. D. Feb. 25, 1899, Dayton, Ohio.

Year	Team	Lg	W	L	PCT	ERA	G	GS	CG	IP	H	BB	SO	ShO	Relief Pitching W	Relief L	Relief SV	Batting AB	Batting H	HR	BA	PO	A	E	DP	TC/G	FA
1885	BAL	AA	0	2	.000	*8.00*	2	2	2	18	27	9	6	0	0	0	0	7	0	0	.000	4	6	0	1	5.0	1.000

Stefan Wever

WEVER, STEFAN MATTHEW BR TR 6′ 8″ 245 lbs.
B. Apr. 22, 1958, Marburg, West Germany.

Year	Team	Lg	W	L	PCT	ERA	G	GS	CG	IP	H	BB	SO	ShO	Relief Pitching W	Relief L	Relief SV	Batting AB	Batting H	HR	BA	PO	A	E	DP	TC/G	FA
1982	NY	A	0	1	.000	27.00	1	1	0	2.2	6	3	2	0	0	0	0	0	0	0	—	0	0	0	0	0.0	.000

Gus Weyhing

WEYHING, AUGUST (Rubber-Winged Gus) BR TR 5′10″ 145 lbs.
Brother of John Weyhing.
B. Sept. 29, 1866, Louisville, Ky. D. Sept. 4, 1955, Louisville, Ky.

Year	Team	Lg	W	L	PCT	ERA	G	GS	CG	IP	H	BB	SO	ShO	Relief Pitching W	Relief L	Relief SV	Batting AB	Batting H	HR	BA	PO	A	E	DP	TC/G	FA
1887	PHI	AA	26	28	.481	*4.27*	55	55	53	466.1	465	167	193	2	0	0	0	209	42	0	.201	21	88	27	5	2.3	.801
1888			28	18	.609	2.25	47	47	45	404	314	111	204	3	0	0	0	184	40	1	.217	22	93	17	1	2.7	.871
1889			30	21	.588	2.95	54	53	50	449	382	212	213	4	0	0	0	191	25	0	.131	12	71	8	2	1.7	.912
1890	BKN	P	30	16	.652	3.60	49	46	38	390	419	179	177	3	1	1	0	165	27	1	.164	12	55	12	2	1.6	.848
1891	PHI	AA	31	20	.608	3.18	52	51	51	450	428	161	219	3	0	0	0	198	22	0	.111	31	73	9	2	2.1	.920
1892	PHI	N	32	21	.604	2.66	59	49	46	469.2	411	168	202	6	**4**	0	**3**	214	29	0	.136	30	63	21	2	1.7	.816
1893			23	16	.590	4.74	42	40	33	345.1	399	145	101	2	1	1	0	147	22	0	.150	31	56	5	3	2.1	.946
1894			16	14	.533	5.81	38	34	25	266.1	365	116	81	2	1	0	1	115	20	0	.174	15	33	4	1	1.4	.923
1895	3 teams	PHI N (2G 0–2) PIT N (1G 1–0) LOU N (28G 7–19)																									
"	total		8	21	.276	5.81	31	28	23	231	318	84	61	1	1	0	0	97	21	1	.216	13	54	7	3	2.4	.905
1896	LOU	N	2	3	.400	6.64	5	5	4	42	62	15	9	0	0	0	0	15	2	0	.133	2	17	2	1	4.2	.905
1898	WAS	N	15	26	.366	4.51	45	42	39	361	428	84	92	0	0	1	0	141	25	0	.177	18	73	8	2	2.2	.919
1899			17	21	.447	4.54	43	38	34	334.2	414	76	96	2	1	0	0	126	26	0	.206	7	50	10	2	1.6	.851
1900	2 teams	STL N (7G 3–4) BKN N (8G 3–3)																									
"	total		6	7	.462	4.47	15	13	6	94.2	126	41	14	0	1	0	0	39	6	0	.154	6	16	3	1	1.7	.880
1901	2 teams	CLE A (2G 0–0) CIN N (1G 0–1)																									
"	total		0	1	.000	5.75	3	2	1	20.1	31	7	3	0	0	0	0	8	0	0	.000	0	4	0	0	1.3	1.000
14 yrs.			264	233	.531	3.89	538	503	448	4324.1	4562	1566 **9th**	1665	28	10	3	4	1849	307	3	.166	220	746	133	27	2.0	.879

John Weyhing

WEYHING, JOHN BL TL 6′ 2″ 185 lbs.
Brother of Gus Weyhing.
B. June 24, 1869, Louisville, Ky. D. June 20, 1890, Louisville, Ky.

Year	Team	Lg	W	L	PCT	ERA	G	GS	CG	IP	H	BB	SO	ShO	Relief Pitching W	Relief L	Relief SV	Batting AB	Batting H	HR	BA	PO	A	E	DP	TC/G	FA
1888	CIN	AA	3	4	.429	1.23	8	8	7	65.2	52	17	30	0	0	0	0	23	3	0	.130	6	9	1	0	2.0	.938
1889	COL	AA	0	0	—	27.00	1	0	0	1	1	4	0	0	0	0	0	0	0	0	—	0	0	0	0	0.0	.000
2 yrs.			3	4	.429	1.62	9	8	7	66.2	53	21	30	0	0	0	0	23	3	0	.130	6	9	1	0	1.8	.938

Lee Wheat

WHEAT, LEROY WILLIAM BR TR 6′ 4″ 200 lbs.
B. Sept. 15, 1929, Edwardsville, Ill.

Year	Team	Lg	W	L	PCT	ERA	G	GS	CG	IP	H	BB	SO	ShO	Relief Pitching W	Relief L	Relief SV	Batting AB	Batting H	HR	BA	PO	A	E	DP	TC/G	FA
1954	PHI	A	0	2	.000	5.72	8	1	0	28.1	38	9	7	0	0	2	0	8	1	0	.125	3	3	0	1	0.8	1.000
1955	KC	A	0	0	—	22.50	3	0	0	2	8	3	1	0	0	0	0	0	0	0	—	0	1	0	0	0.3	1.000
2 yrs.			0	2	.000	6.82	11	1	0	30.1	46	12	8	0	0	2	0	8	1	0	.125	3	4	0	1	0.6	1.000

Charlie Wheatley

WHEATLEY, CHARLES BR TR 5′11″ 174 lbs.
B. June 27, 1893, Rosedale, Kans. D. Dec. 10, 1982, Tulsa, Okla.

Year	Team	Lg	W	L	PCT	ERA	G	GS	CG	IP	H	BB	SO	ShO	Relief Pitching W	Relief L	Relief SV	Batting AB	Batting H	HR	BA	PO	A	E	DP	TC/G	FA
1912	DET	A	1	4	.200	6.17	5	5	2	35	45	17	14	0	0	0	0	12	0	0	.000	1	13	1	0	3.0	.933

Woody Wheaton

WHEATON, ELWOOD PIERCE BL TL 5′ 8½″ 160 lbs.
B. Oct. 3, 1914, Philadelphia, Pa.

Year	Team	Lg	W	L	PCT	ERA	G	GS	CG	IP	H	BB	SO	ShO	Relief Pitching W	Relief L	Relief SV	Batting AB	Batting H	HR	BA	PO	A	E	DP	TC/G	FA
1944	PHI	A	0	1	.000	3.55	11	1	1	38	36	20	15	0	0	0	0	*				20	1	0	0	3.0	1.000

George Wheeler

WHEELER, GEORGE L. BB TB
Born George L. Heroux.
B. Aug. 3, 1869, Methuen, Mass. D. Mar. 23, 1946, Santa Ana, Calif.

Year	Team	Lg	W	L	PCT	ERA	G	GS	CG	IP	H	BB	SO	ShO	Relief Pitching W	Relief L	Relief SV	Batting AB	Batting H	HR	BA	PO	A	E	DP	TC/G	FA
1896	PHI	N	1	1	.500	3.86	3	2	2	16.1	18	5	2	0	0	0	0	9	1	0	.111	0	6	0	0	2.0	1.000
1897			11	10	.524	3.96	26	19	17	191	229	62	35	0	3	0	0	79	16	0	.203	10	48	3	3	2.3	.951
1898			6	8	.429	4.17	15	13	10	112.1	155	36	20	0	1	0	0	43	8	0	.186	8	41	6	0	3.7	.891
1899			3	1	.750	6.00	6	5	3	39	44	13	3	0	0	0	0	17	4	1	.235	1	11	1	0	2.2	.923
4 yrs.			21	20	.512	4.24	50	39	32	358.2	446	116	60	0	4	0	0	148	29	1	.196	19	106	10	3	2.7	.926

Harry Wheeler

WHEELER, HARRY EUGENE BR TR 5′11″ 165 lbs.
B. Mar. 3, 1858, Versailles, Ind. D. Oct. 9, 1900, Cincinnati, Ohio.
Manager 1884.

Year	Team	Lg	W	L	PCT	ERA	G	GS	CG	IP	H	BB	SO	ShO	Relief Pitching W	Relief L	Relief SV	Batting AB	Batting H	HR	BA	PO	A	E	DP	TC/G	FA
1878	PRO	N	6	1	.857	3.48	7	6	6	62	70	25	25	0	**1**	0	0	27	4	0	.148	2	5	1	0	1.1	.875
1879	CIN	N	0	1	.000	81.00	1	1	0	1	6	4	0	0	0	0	0	3	0	0	.000	2	0	0	0	1.0	1.000
1882	CIN	AA	1	2	.333	*5.40*	4	1	1	21.2	21	12	10	0	**1**	**1**	0	344	86	1	.250	39	5	14	1	3.2	.759

Harry Wheeler *continued*

Year	Team	Lg	W	L	PCT	ERA	G	GS	CG	IP	H	BB	SO	ShO	Relief Pitching W	Relief Pitching L	Relief Pitching SV	Batting AB	Batting H	Batting HR	BA	PO	A	E	DP	TC/G	FA
1883	COL	AA	0	1	.000	*7.20*	1	1	0	5	13	2	0	0	0	0	0	371	84	1	.226	131	17	38	2	2.2	.796
1884	KC	U	0	1	.000	1.13	1	1	1	8	7	0	6	0	0	0	0	308	75	1	.244	99	10	32	0	1.9	.773
5 yrs.			7	6	.538	4.70	14	10	8	97.2	117	43	41	0	2	1	0	*				448	56	120	14	2.4	.808

Rip Wheeler

WHEELER, FLOYD CLARK BR TR 6′ 180 lbs.
B. Mar. 2, 1898, Marion, Ky. D. Sept. 18, 1968, Marion, Ky.

Year	Team	Lg	W	L	PCT	ERA	G	GS	CG	IP	H	BB	SO	ShO	Relief Pitching W	Relief Pitching L	Relief Pitching SV	Batting AB	Batting H	Batting HR	BA	PO	A	E	DP	TC/G	FA
1921	PIT	N	0	0	—	9.00	1	0	0	3	6	1	0	0	0	0	0	1	0	0	.000	0	2	0	0	2.0	1.000
1922			0	0	—	0.00	1	0	0	1	1	2	0	0	0	0	0	0	0	0	—	0	1	0	0	1.0	1.000
1923	CHI	N	1	2	.333	4.88	3	3	1	24	28	5	5	0	0	0	0	9	1	0	.111	2	10	0	1	4.0	1.000
1924			3	6	.333	3.91	29	4	0	101.1	103	21	16	0	2	3	0	32	7	0	.219	4	28	0	0	1.1	1.000
4 yrs.			4	8	.333	4.18	34	7	1	129.1	138	29	21	0	2	3	0	42	8	0	.190	6	41	0	1	1.4	1.000

Gary Wheelock

WHEELOCK, GARY RICHARD BR TR 6′ 3″ 205 lbs.
B. Nov. 29, 1951, Bakersfield, Calif.

Year	Team	Lg	W	L	PCT	ERA	G	GS	CG	IP	H	BB	SO	ShO	Relief Pitching W	Relief Pitching L	Relief Pitching SV	Batting AB	Batting H	Batting HR	BA	PO	A	E	DP	TC/G	FA
1976	CAL	A	0	0	—	27.00	2	0	0	2	6	1	2	0	0	0	0	0	0	0	—	0	0	0	0	0.0	.000
1977	SEA	A	6	9	.400	4.91	17	17	2	88	94	26	47	0	0	0	0	0	0	0	—	10	9	2	0	1.2	.905
1980			0	0	—	6.00	1	1	0	3	4	1	1	0	0	0	0	0	0	0	—	0	1	0	0	1.0	1.000
3 yrs.			6	9	.400	5.42	20	18	2	93	104	28	50	0	0	0	0	0	0	0		10	10	2	0	1.1	.909

Jack Whillock

WHILLOCK, JACK FRANKLIN BR TR 6′ 3″ 195 lbs.
B. Nov. 4, 1942, Clinton, Ark.

Year	Team	Lg	W	L	PCT	ERA	G	GS	CG	IP	H	BB	SO	ShO	Relief Pitching W	Relief Pitching L	Relief Pitching SV	Batting AB	Batting H	Batting HR	BA	PO	A	E	DP	TC/G	FA
1971	DET	A	0	2	.000	5.63	7	0	0	8	10	2	6	0	0	2	1	1	0	0	.000	0	2	0	0	0.3	1.000

Pat Whitaker

WHITAKER, WILLIAM H. TR
B. 1865, St. Louis, Mo. D. July 15, 1902, St. Louis, Mo.

Year	Team	Lg	W	L	PCT	ERA	G	GS	CG	IP	H	BB	SO	ShO	Relief Pitching W	Relief Pitching L	Relief Pitching SV	Batting AB	Batting H	Batting HR	BA	PO	A	E	DP	TC/G	FA
1888	BAL	AA	1	1	.500	5.14	2	2	2	14	13	6	5	0	0	0	0	6	0	0	.000	0	11	0	0	5.5	1.000
1889			1	0	1.000	2.00	1	1	1	9	10	4	1	0	0	0	0	4	1	0	.250	1	3	0	0	4.0	1.000
2 yrs.			2	1	.667	3.91	3	3	3	23	23	10	6	0	0	0	0	10	1	0	.100	1	14	0	0	5.0	1.000

Bill Whitby

WHITBY, WILLIAM EDWARD BR TR 6′ 1″ 190 lbs.
B. July 29, 1943, Crewe, Va.

Year	Team	Lg	W	L	PCT	ERA	G	GS	CG	IP	H	BB	SO	ShO	Relief Pitching W	Relief Pitching L	Relief Pitching SV	Batting AB	Batting H	Batting HR	BA	PO	A	E	DP	TC/G	FA
1964	MIN	A	0	0	—	8.53	4	0	0	6.1	8	1	2	0	0	0	0	1	0	0	.000	0	1	0	0	0.3	1.000

Bob Whitcher

WHITCHER, ROBERT ARTHUR BL TL 5′ 8″ 165 lbs.
B. Apr. 29, 1917, Berlin, N. H.

Year	Team	Lg	W	L	PCT	ERA	G	GS	CG	IP	H	BB	SO	ShO	Relief Pitching W	Relief Pitching L	Relief Pitching SV	Batting AB	Batting H	Batting HR	BA	PO	A	E	DP	TC/G	FA
1945	BOS	N	0	2	.000	2.87	6	3	0	15.2	12	12	6	0	0	0	0	3	1	0	.333	1	2	0	1	0.5	1.000

Ade White

WHITE, ADEL BR TL 6′ 185 lbs.
B. May 16, 1904, Winder, Ga. D. Oct. 1, 1978, Atlanta, Ga.

Year	Team	Lg	W	L	PCT	ERA	G	GS	CG	IP	H	BB	SO	ShO	Relief Pitching W	Relief Pitching L	Relief Pitching SV	Batting AB	Batting H	Batting HR	BA	PO	A	E	DP	TC/G	FA
1937	STL	N	0	1	.000	6.75	5	0	0	9.1	14	3	2	0	0	1	0	1	1	0	1.000	0	2	0	0	0.4	1.000

Bill White

WHITE, WILLIAM DIGHTON
B. May 1, 1860, Bridgeport, Ohio D. Dec. 31, 1924, Bellaire, Ohio.

Year	Team	Lg	W	L	PCT	ERA	G	GS	CG	IP	H	BB	SO	ShO	Relief Pitching W	Relief Pitching L	Relief Pitching SV	Batting AB	Batting H	Batting HR	BA	PO	A	E	DP	TC/G	FA
1886	LOU	AA	0	0	—	*9.00*	1	0	0	1	2	2	1	0	0	0	0	*				75	206	69	14	4.7	.803

Deacon White

WHITE, JAMES LAURIE BL TR 5′11″ 175 lbs.
Brother of Will White.
B. Dec. 7, 1847, Caton, N. Y. D. July 7, 1939, Aurora, Ill.
Manager 1879.

Year	Team	Lg	W	L	PCT	ERA	G	GS	CG	IP	H	BB	SO	ShO	Relief Pitching W	Relief Pitching L	Relief Pitching SV	Batting AB	Batting H	Batting HR	BA	PO	A	E	DP	TC/G	FA
1876	CHI	N	0	0	—	0.00	1	0	0	2	1	0	3	0	0	0	1	303	104	1	.343	318	51	69	3	6.2	.842
1890	BUF	P	0	0	—	9.00	1	0	0	8	18	2	0	0	0	0	0	439	114	0	.260	384	22	24	16	7.0	.944
2 yrs.			0	0		7.20	2	0	0	10	19	2	3	0	0	0	1	*				3559	2099	773	215	4.9	.880

Deke White

WHITE, GEORGE FREDERICK BB TL
B. Sept. 8, 1872, Albany, N. Y. D. Nov. 27, 1957, Albany, N. Y.

Year	Team	Lg	W	L	PCT	ERA	G	GS	CG	IP	H	BB	SO	ShO	Relief Pitching W	Relief Pitching L	Relief Pitching SV	Batting AB	Batting H	Batting HR	BA	PO	A	E	DP	TC/G	FA
1895	PHI	N	1	0	1.000	9.87	3	1	1	17.1	17	13	6	0	0	0	1	8	1	0	.125	1	2	0	0	1.0	1.000

Doc White

WHITE, GUY HARRIS BL TL 6′ 1″ 165 lbs.
B. Apr. 9, 1879, Washington, D. C. D. Feb. 19, 1969, Silver Spring, Md.

Year	Team	Lg	W	L	PCT	ERA	G	GS	CG	IP	H	BB	SO	ShO	Relief Pitching W	Relief Pitching L	Relief Pitching SV	Batting AB	Batting H	Batting HR	BA	PO	A	E	DP	TC/G	FA
1901	PHI	N	14	13	.519	3.19	31	27	22	236.2	241	56	132	0	1	1	0	95	26	1	.274	7	72	4	0	2.6	.952
1902			16	**20**	.444	2.53	36	35	34	306	277	72	185	3	0	0	1	179	47	1	.263	35	84	12	0	2.4	.908
1903	CHI	A	17	16	.515	2.13	37	36	29	300	258	69	114	3	0	0	0	99	20	0	.202	27	98	4	5	3.4	.969
1904			16	12	.571	1.78	30	30	23	228	201	68	115	7	0	0	0	76	12	0	.158	33	68	5	2	3.3	.953
1905			17	13	.567	1.76	36	33	25	260.1	204	58	120	4	1	0	0	86	14	0	.163	20	77	4	2	2.7	.960
1906			18	6	.750	**1.52**	28	24	20	219.1	160	38	95	7	2	1	0	65	12	0	.185	17	77	8	1	3.5	.922
1907			**27**	13	.675	2.26	46	35	24	291	270	38	141	7	**5**	1	1	90	20	0	.222	33	103	2	1	2.9	.986
1908			18	13	.581	2.55	41	37	24	296	267	69	126	5	0	0	0	109	25	0	.229	30	116	2	7	3.4	.986
1909			11	9	.550	1.72	24	21	14	177.2	149	31	77	3	1	0	0	192	45	0	.234	71	54	8	1	2.1	.940
1910			15	13	.536	2.56	33	29	20	245.2	219	50	111	2	1	0	1	126	25	0	.198	44	79	3	4	2.7	.976
1911			10	14	.417	2.98	34	29	16	214.1	219	35	72	4	1	0	2	78	20	0	.256	20	57	6	2	2.2	.928
1912			8	10	.444	3.24	32	19	9	172	172	47	57	1	2	2	0	56	7	0	.125	5	46	0	1	1.6	1.000
1913			2	4	.333	3.50	19	8	2	103	106	39	39	0	0	1	0	25	3	0	.120	4	44	2	0	2.5	.960
13 yrs.			189	156	.548	2.38	427	363	262	3050	2743	670	1384	46	14	6	5	*				346	975	60	26	2.7	.957
WORLD SERIES																											
1906	CHI	A	1	1	.500	1.80	3	2	1	15	12	7	4	0	0	0	1	*				1	3	0	0	1.3	1.000

Ernie White

WHITE, ERNEST DANIEL BR TL 5′11½″ 175 lbs.
B. Sept. 5, 1916, Pacolet Mills, S. C. D. May 22, 1974, Augusta, Ga.

Year	Team	Lg	W	L	PCT	ERA	G	GS	CG	IP	H	BB	SO	ShO	Relief Pitching W	Relief Pitching L	Relief Pitching SV	Batting AB	Batting H	Batting HR	BA	PO	A	E	DP	TC/G	FA
1940	STL	N	1	1	.500	4.15	8	1	0	21.2	29	14	15	0	1	0	0	7	3	0	.429	1	7	0	0	1.0	1.000
1941			17	7	.708	2.40	32	25	12	210	169	70	117	3	3	0	2	79	15	0	.190	10	25	3	0	1.2	.921
1942			7	5	.583	2.52	26	19	7	128.1	113	41	67	1	1	0	2	41	8	0	.195	3	16	1	1	0.8	.950
1943			5	5	.500	3.78	14	10	5	78.2	78	33	28	1	0	1	0	28	6	0	.214	3	12	0	1	1.1	1.000
1946	BOS	N	0	1	.000	4.18	12	1	0	23.2	22	12	8	0	0	0	0	4	1	0	.250	2	1	0	0	0.3	1.000

Ernie White *continued*

Year	Team	W	L	PCT	ERA	G	GS	CG	IP	H	BB	SO	ShO	Relief Pitching W	Relief Pitching L	Relief Pitching SV	Batting AB	Batting H	Batting HR	BA	PO	A	E	DP	TC/G	FA
1947		0	0	—	0.00	1	1	0	4	1	1	1	0	0	0	0	1	1	0	1.000	0	0	0	0	0.0	.000
1948		0	2	.000	1.96	15	0	0	23	13	17	8	0	0	2	2	3	0	0	.000	0	2	2	0	0.3	.500
7 yrs.		30	21	.588	2.78	108	57	24	489.1	425	188	244	5	5	3	6	163	34	0	.209	19	63	6	2	0.8	.932
WORLD SERIES																										
1942	STL N	1	0	1.000	0.00	1	1	1	9	6	0	6	1	0	0	0	2	0	0	.000	0	0	0	0	0.0	.000

Gabe White

WHITE, GABRIEL ALLEN BL TL 6′ 2″ 200 lbs.
B. Nov. 20, 1971, Sebring, Fla.

Year	Team	W	L	PCT	ERA	G	GS	CG	IP	H	BB	SO	ShO	Relief Pitching W	Relief Pitching L	Relief Pitching SV	Batting AB	Batting H	Batting HR	BA	PO	A	E	DP	TC/G	FA
1994	MON N	1	1	.500	6.08	7	5	0	23.2	24	11	17	0	0	0	1	4	0	0	.000	0	2	0	0	0.3	1.000
1995		1	2	.333	7.01	19	1	0	25.2	26	9	25	0	1	1	0	3	0	0	.000	0	2	0	0	0.1	1.000
2 yrs.		2	3	.400	6.57	26	6	0	49.1	50	20	42	0	1	1	1	7	0	0	.000	0	4	0	0	0.2	1.000

Hal White

WHITE, HAROLD GEORGE BL TR 5′10″ 165 lbs.
B. Mar. 18, 1919, Utica, N. Y.

Year	Team	W	L	PCT	ERA	G	GS	CG	IP	H	BB	SO	ShO	Relief Pitching W	Relief Pitching L	Relief Pitching SV	Batting AB	Batting H	Batting HR	BA	PO	A	E	DP	TC/G	FA
1941	DET A	0	0	—	6.00	4	0	0	9	11	6	2	0	0	0	0	2	0	0	.000	1	2	0	0	0.8	1.000
1942		12	12	.500	2.91	34	25	12	216.2	212	82	93	4	1	3	1	77	13	0	.169	20	41	6	6	2.0	.910
1943		7	12	.368	3.39	32	24	7	177.2	150	71	58	2	0	2	2	57	8	0	.140	12	38	1	2	1.6	.980
1946		1	1	.500	5.60	11	1	1	27.1	34	15	12	0	0	1	0	7	0	0	.000	3	6	0	1	0.8	1.000
1947		4	5	.444	3.61	35	5	0	84.2	91	47	33	0	4	2	2	18	3	0	.167	4	22	3	0	0.8	.897
1948		2	1	.667	6.12	27	0	0	42.2	46	26	17	0	2	1	1	13	2	0	.154	2	4	0	0	0.2	1.000
1949		1	0	1.000	0.00	9	0	0	12	5	4	4	0	1	0	2	3	1	0	.333	1	5	0	0	0.7	1.000
1950		9	6	.600	4.54	42	8	3	111	96	65	53	1	6	3	1	33	4	0	.121	8	19	1	1	0.7	.964
1951		3	4	.429	4.74	38	4	0	76	74	49	23	0	2	1	4	16	4	0	.250	5	21	2	2	0.7	.929
1952		1	8	.111	3.69	41	0	0	63.1	53	39	18	0	1	**8**	5	11	2	0	.182	3	18	0	0	0.5	1.000
1953	2 teams STL A (10G 0–0) STL N (49G 6–5)																									
"	total	6	5	.545	2.94	59	0	0	95	92	42	34	0	6	5	7	17	0	0	.000	8	21	2	1	0.5	.935
1954	STL N	0	0	—	19.80	4	0	0	5	11	4	2	0	0	0	0	1	0	0	.000	1	0	0	0	0.3	1.000
12 yrs.		46	54	.460	3.78	336	67	23	920.1	875	450	349	7	23	26	25	255	37	0	.145	68	197	15	13	0.8	.946

Kirby White

WHITE, OLIVER KIRBY (Buck, Redbuck) BL TR 6′ 190 lbs.
B. Jan. 3, 1884, Hillsboro, Ohio D. Apr. 22, 1943, Hillsboro, Ohio.

Year	Team	W	L	PCT	ERA	G	GS	CG	IP	H	BB	SO	ShO	Relief Pitching W	Relief Pitching L	Relief Pitching SV	Batting AB	Batting H	Batting HR	BA	PO	A	E	DP	TC/G	FA
1909	BOS N	6	13	.316	3.22	23	19	11	148.1	134	80	53	1	1	0	0	50	8	0	.160	6	37	6	1	2.1	.878
1910	2 teams BOS N (3G 1–2) PIT N (30G 10–9)																									
"	total	11	11	.500	3.16	33	24	10	179.1	157	87	48	3	2	1	2	52	14	0	.269	5	41	6	1	1.6	.885
1911	PIT N	0	1	.000	9.00	2	1	0	3	3	1	1	0	0	0	0	1	0	0	.000	0	1	0	0	0.5	1.000
3 yrs.		17	25	.405	3.24	58	44	21	330.2	294	168	102	4	3	1	2	103	22	0	.214	11	79	12	2	1.8	.882

Larry White

WHITE, LARRY DAVID BR TR 6′ 5″ 190 lbs.
B. Sept. 25, 1958, San Fernando, Calif.

Year	Team	W	L	PCT	ERA	G	GS	CG	IP	H	BB	SO	ShO	Relief Pitching W	Relief Pitching L	Relief Pitching SV	Batting AB	Batting H	Batting HR	BA	PO	A	E	DP	TC/G	FA
1983	LA N	0	0	—	1.29	4	0	0	7	4	3	5	0	0	0	0	0	0	0	—	1	1	0	0	0.5	1.000
1984		0	1	.000	3.00	7	1	0	12	9	6	10	0	0	1	0	1	0	0	.000	1	1	1	0	0.4	.667
2 yrs.		0	1	.000	2.37	11	1	0	19	13	9	15	0	0	1	0	1	0	0	.000	2	2	1	0	0.5	.800

Rick White

WHITE, RICHARD ALLEN BR TR 6′ 4″ 215 lbs.
B. Dec. 23, 1968, Springfield, Ohio.

Year	Team	W	L	PCT	ERA	G	GS	CG	IP	H	BB	SO	ShO	Relief Pitching W	Relief Pitching L	Relief Pitching SV	Batting AB	Batting H	Batting HR	BA	PO	A	E	DP	TC/G	FA
1994	PIT N	4	5	.444	3.82	43	5	0	75.1	79	17	38	0	2	4	6	13	1	0	.077	3	10	2	1	0.3	.867
1995		2	3	.400	4.75	15	9	0	55	66	18	29	0	0	0	0	15	1	0	.067	2	9	1	1	0.8	.917
2 yrs.		6	8	.429	4.21	58	14	0	130.1	145	35	67	0	2	4	6	28	2	0	.071	5	19	3	2	0.5	.889

Steve White

WHITE, STEPHEN VINCENT BR TR 5′10″ 160 lbs.
B. Dec. 21, 1884, Dorchester, Mass. D. Jan. 29, 1975, Braintree, Mass.

Year	Team	W	L	PCT	ERA	G	GS	CG	IP	H	BB	SO	ShO	Relief Pitching W	Relief Pitching L	Relief Pitching SV	Batting AB	Batting H	Batting HR	BA	PO	A	E	DP	TC/G	FA
1912	2 teams WAS A (1G 0–0) BOS N (3G 0–0)																									
"	total	0	0		5.40	4	0	0	6.2	11	5	3	0	0	0	0	3	0	0	.000	0	2	1	0	0.8	.667

Will White

WHITE, WILLIAM HENRY (Whoop-La) BB TR 5′ 9½″ 175 lbs.
Brother of Deacon White.
B. Oct. 11, 1854, Caton, N. Y. D. Aug. 31, 1911, Port Carling, Ont., Canada.
Manager 1884.

Year	Team	W	L	PCT	ERA	G	GS	CG	IP	H	BB	SO	ShO	Relief Pitching W	Relief Pitching L	Relief Pitching SV	Batting AB	Batting H	Batting HR	BA	PO	A	E	DP	TC/G	FA
1877	BOS N	2	1	.667	3.00	3	3	3	27	27	2	7	1	0	0	0	15	3	0	.200	3	1	1	0	1.7	.800
1878	CIN N	30	21	.588	1.79	52	52	52	468	477	45	169	5	0	0	0	197	28	0	.142	13	90	15	2	2.3	.873
1879		43	31	.581	1.99	**76**	**75**	**75**	**680**	**676**	68	232	4	0	0	0	294	40	0	.136	20	114	20	0	2.0	.870
1880		18	**42**	.300	2.14	62	62	58	517.1	550	56	161	3	0	0	0	207	35	0	.169	18	68	10	2	1.5	.896
1881	DET N	0	2	.000	5.00	2	2	2	18	24	2	5	0	0	0	0	7	0	0	.000	0	1	0	0	0.5	1.000
1882	CIN AA	**40**	12	**.769**	*1.54*	54	54	**52**	**480**	411	71	122	**8**	0	0	0	207	55	0	.266	23	223	11	3	4.6	.957
1883		**43**	22	.662	***2.09***	65	64	64	577	473	104	141	**6**	0	**1**	0	240	54	0	.225	23	106	23	1	2.3	.849
1884		34	18	.654	*3.32*	52	52	52	456	479	74	118	**7**	0	0	0	184	35	1	.190	8	72	18	2	1.9	.816
1885		18	15	.545	*3.53*	34	34	33	293.1	295	64	80	2	0	0	0	118	20	0	.169	10	35	6	0	1.5	.882
1886		1	2	.333	4.15	3	3	3	26	28	10	6	0	0	0	0	9	1	0	.111	0	5	2	0	2.3	.714
10 yrs.		229	166	.580	2.28 **10th**	403	401	394	3542.2	3440	496	1041	36	0	1	0	1478	271	1	.183	118	715	106	10	2.3	.887

John Whitehead

WHITEHEAD, JOHN HENDERSON (Silent John) BR TR 6′ 2″ 195 lbs.
B. Apr. 27, 1909, Coleman, Tex. D. Oct. 20, 1964, Bonham, Tex.

Year	Team	W	L	PCT	ERA	G	GS	CG	IP	H	BB	SO	ShO	Relief Pitching W	Relief Pitching L	Relief Pitching SV	Batting AB	Batting H	Batting HR	BA	PO	A	E	DP	TC/G	FA
1935	CHI A	13	13	.500	3.72	28	27	18	222.1	209	101	72	1	0	0	0	82	12	0	.146	7	56	1	6	2.3	.984
1936		13	13	.500	4.64	34	32	15	230.2	254	98	70	1	0	0	1	87	21	0	.241	10	60	5	4	2.2	.933
1937		11	8	.579	4.07	26	24	8	165.2	191	56	45	4	0	0	0	58	13	0	.224	6	27	1	1	1.3	.971
1938		10	11	.476	4.76	32	24	10	183.1	218	80	38	2	1	0	2	60	6	0	.100	4	35	1	3	1.3	.975
1939	2 teams CHI A (7G 0–3) STL A (26G 1–3)																									
"	total	1	6	.143	6.61	33	8	0	98	148	22	18	0	1	1	1	26	1	0	.038	7	20	0	2	0.8	1.000
1940	STL A	1	3	.250	5.40	15	4	1	40	46	14	11	1	0	2	0	12	2	0	.167	1	6	1	0	0.5	.875
1942		0	0	—	6.75	4	0	0	4	8	1	0	0	0	0	0	0	0	0	—	0	2	0	0	0.5	1.000
7 yrs.		49	54	.476	4.60	172	119	52	944	1074	372	254	9	2	3	4	325	55	0	.169	35	206	9	16	1.5	.964

Milt Whitehead

WHITEHEAD, MILTON P. BB
B. 1862 D. Aug. 15, 1901, Highland, Calif.

Year	Team		W	L	PCT	ERA	G	GS	CG	IP	H	BB	SO	ShO	Relief Pitching W	Relief Pitching L	Relief Pitching SV	Batting AB	Batting H	Batting HR	BA	PO	A	E	DP	TC/G	FA
1884	STL	U	0	1	.000	9.00	1	1	1	8	14	2	2	0	0	0	0	*				101	291	93	19	4.6	.808

Earl Whitehill

WHITEHILL, EARL OLIVER BL TL 5′ 9½″ 174 lbs.
B. Feb. 7, 1900, Cedar Rapids, Iowa D. Oct. 22, 1954, Omaha, Neb.

Year	Team		W	L	PCT	ERA	G	GS	CG	IP	H	BB	SO	ShO	Relief Pitching W	Relief Pitching L	Relief Pitching SV	Batting AB	Batting H	Batting HR	BA	PO	A	E	DP	TC/G	FA
1923	DET	A	2	0	1.000	2.73	8	3	2	33	22	15	19	1	2	0	0	11	4	0	.364	1	7	2	0	1.3	.800
1924			17	9	.654	3.86	35	32	16	233	260	79	65	2	0	2	0	89	19	0	.213	14	53	4	3	2.0	.944
1925			11	11	.500	4.66	35	**33**	15	239.1	267	88	83	1	0	0	2	87	19	0	.218	13	52	5	2	2.0	.929
1926			16	13	.552	3.99	36	34	13	252.1	271	79	109	0	2	0	0	91	23	0	.253	12	54	2	2	1.9	.971
1927			16	14	.533	3.36	41	30	17	236	238	**105**	95	3	3	1	3	78	16	0	.205	5	47	7	3	1.4	.881
1928			11	16	.407	4.31	31	30	12	196.1	214	78	93	1	1	0	0	67	13	0	.194	17	40	1	3	1.9	.983
1929			14	15	.483	4.62	38	28	18	245.1	267	96	103	1	4	1	1	90	23	3	.256	15	49	4	0	1.8	.941
1930			17	13	.567	4.24	34	31	16	220.2	248	80	109	0	0	1	1	83	16	0	.193	8	32	1	1	1.2	.976
1931			13	16	.448	4.06	34	34	22	272.1	287	118	81	0	0	0	0	97	15	0	.155	20	62	2	5	2.5	.976
1932			16	12	.571	4.54	33	31	17	244	255	93	81	3	1	0	0	90	22	0	.244	9	44	2	1	1.7	.964
1933	WAS	A	22	8	.733	3.33	39	**37**	19	270	271	100	96	2	0	0	1	108	24	0	.222	8	51	7	2	1.6	.894
1934			14	11	.560	4.52	32	31	15	235	269	94	96	0	0	0	0	85	17	1	.200	2	47	1	2	1.6	.980
1935			14	13	.519	4.29	34	34	19	279.1	318	104	102	1	0	0	0	104	19	0	.183	13	60	3	4	2.2	.961
1936			14	11	.560	4.87	28	28	14	212.1	252	89	63	0	0	0	0	77	13	0	.169	10	35	2	0	1.7	.957
1937	CLE	A	8	8	.500	6.49	33	22	6	147	189	80	53	1	0	0	2	49	11	0	.224	9	33	2	0	1.3	.955
1938			9	8	.529	5.56	26	23	4	160.1	187	83	60	0	1	0	0	56	7	0	.125	9	21	2	3	1.2	.938
1939	CHI	N	4	7	.364	5.14	24	11	2	89.1	102	50	42	1	0	1	1	29	3	0	.103	1	14	0	0	0.6	1.000
17 yrs.			218	185	.541	4.36	541	472	227	3565.2	3917	1431	1350	17	14	6	11	1291	264	4	.204	166	701	47	31	1.7	.949
WORLD SERIES																											
1933	WAS	A	1	0	1.000	0.00	1	1	1	9	5	2	2	1	0	0	0	3	0	0	.000	0	4	0	0	4.0	1.000

Charlie Whitehouse

WHITEHOUSE, CHARLES EVIS (Lefty) BB TL 6′ 152 lbs.
B. Jan. 25, 1894, Charleston, Ill. D. July 19, 1960, Indianapolis, Ind.

Year	Team		W	L	PCT	ERA	G	GS	CG	IP	H	BB	SO	ShO	Relief Pitching W	Relief Pitching L	Relief Pitching SV	Batting AB	Batting H	Batting HR	BA	PO	A	E	DP	TC/G	FA
1914	IND	F	2	0	1.000	4.85	8	2	2	26	34	5	10	0	0	0	0	8	0	0	.000	0	8	0	0	1.0	1.000
1915	NWK	F	2	2	.500	4.31	11	3	1	39.2	46	17	18	0	1	0	0	10	0	0	.000	0	10	1	0	1.0	.909
1919	WAS	A	0	1	.000	4.50	6	1	0	12	13	6	5	0	0	0	0	1	0	0	.000	0	2	0	0	0.3	1.000
3 yrs.			4	3	.571	4.52	25	6	3	77.2	93	28	33	0	1	0	0	19	0	0	.000	0	20	1	0	0.8	.952

Gil Whitehouse

WHITEHOUSE, GILBERT ARTHUR BB TR 5′10½″ 170 lbs.
B. Oct. 15, 1893, Somerville, Mass. D. Feb. 14, 1926, Brewer, Me.

Year	Team		W	L	PCT	ERA	G	GS	CG	IP	H	BB	SO	ShO	Relief Pitching W	Relief Pitching L	Relief Pitching SV	Batting AB	Batting H	Batting HR	BA	PO	A	E	DP	TC/G	FA
1915	NWK	F	0	0	—	0.00	1	0	0	1	0	1	0	0	0	0	0	*				4	0	2	0	3.0	.667

Len Whitehouse

WHITEHOUSE, LEONARD JOSEPH BL TL 5′11″ 175 lbs.
B. Sept. 10, 1957, Burlington, Vt.

Year	Team		W	L	PCT	ERA	G	GS	CG	IP	H	BB	SO	ShO	Relief Pitching W	Relief Pitching L	Relief Pitching SV	Batting AB	Batting H	Batting HR	BA	PO	A	E	DP	TC/G	FA
1981	TEX	A	0	1	.000	18.00	2	1	0	3	8	2	2	0	0	0	0	0	0	0	—	0	0	0	0	0.0	.000
1983	MIN	A	7	1	.875	4.15	60	0	0	73.2	70	44	44	0	7	1	2	0	0	0	—	3	6	0	0	0.2	1.000
1984			2	2	.500	3.16	30	0	0	31.1	29	17	18	0	2	2	1	0	0	0	—	2	3	0	0	0.2	1.000
1985			0	0	—	11.05	5	0	0	7.1	12	2	4	0	0	0	1	0	0	0	—	1	0	0	0	0.2	1.000
4 yrs.			9	4	.692	4.68	97	1	0	115.1	119	65	68	0	9	3	4	0	0	0		6	9	0	0	0.2	1.000

Wally Whitehurst

WHITEHURST, WALTER RICHARD BR TR 6′ 3″ 180 lbs.
B. Apr. 11, 1964, Shreveport, La.

Year	Team		W	L	PCT	ERA	G	GS	CG	IP	H	BB	SO	ShO	Relief Pitching W	Relief Pitching L	Relief Pitching SV	Batting AB	Batting H	Batting HR	BA	PO	A	E	DP	TC/G	FA
1989	NY	N	0	1	.000	4.50	9	1	0	14	17	5	9	0	0	0	0	1	0	0	.000	1	1	0	0	0.2	1.000
1990			1	0	1.000	3.29	38	0	0	65.2	63	9	46	0	1	0	2	8	2	0	.250	4	9	0	1	0.3	1.000
1991			7	12	.368	4.18	36	20	0	133.1	142	25	87	0	2	1	1	33	6	0	.182	11	24	2	2	1.0	.946
1992			3	9	.250	3.62	44	11	0	97	99	33	70	0	2	4	0	22	4	0	.182	6	17	1	1	0.5	.958
1993	SD	N	4	7	.364	3.83	21	19	0	105.2	109	30	57	0	0	0	0	24	2	0	.083	3	18	2	2	1.1	.913
1994			4	7	.364	4.92	13	13	0	64	84	26	43	0	0	0	0	19	2	0	.105	4	10	1	0	1.2	.933
6 yrs.			19	36	.345	3.98	161	64	0	479.2	514	128	312	0	5	5	3	107	16	0	.150	29	79	6	6	0.7	.947

Matt Whiteside

WHITESIDE, MATTHEW CHRISTOPHER BR TR 6′ 185 lbs.
B. Aug. 8, 1967, Charleston, Mo.

Year	Team		W	L	PCT	ERA	G	GS	CG	IP	H	BB	SO	ShO	Relief Pitching W	Relief Pitching L	Relief Pitching SV	Batting AB	Batting H	Batting HR	BA	PO	A	E	DP	TC/G	FA
1992	TEX	A	1	1	.500	1.93	20	0	0	28	26	11	13	0	1	1	4	0	0	0	—	3	2	1	0	0.3	.833
1993			2	1	.667	4.32	60	0	0	73	78	23	39	0	2	1	1	0	0	0	—	5	7	2	3	0.2	.857
1994			2	2	.500	5.02	47	0	0	61	68	28	37	0	2	2	1	0	0	0	—	4	6	1	0	0.2	.909
1995			5	4	.556	4.08	40	0	0	53	48	19	46	0	5	4	3	0	0	0	—	0	4	0	0	0.1	1.000
4 yrs.			10	8	.556	4.14	167	0	0	215	220	81	135	0	10	8	9	0	0	0		12	19	4	3	0.2	.886

Sean Whiteside

WHITESIDE, DAVID SEAN BL TL 6′ 4″ 190 lbs.
B. Apr. 19, 1971, Lakeland, Fla.

Year	Team		W	L	PCT	ERA	G	GS	CG	IP	H	BB	SO	ShO	Relief Pitching W	Relief Pitching L	Relief Pitching SV	Batting AB	Batting H	Batting HR	BA	PO	A	E	DP	TC/G	FA
1995	DET	A	0	0	—	14.73	2	0	0	3.2	7	4	2	0	0	0	0	0	0	0	—	0	0	0	0	0.0	.000

Jesse Whiting

WHITING, JESSE W.
B. May 30, 1879, Philadelphia, Pa. D. Oct. 28, 1937, Philadelphia, Pa.

Year	Team		W	L	PCT	ERA	G	GS	CG	IP	H	BB	SO	ShO	Relief Pitching W	Relief Pitching L	Relief Pitching SV	Batting AB	Batting H	Batting HR	BA	PO	A	E	DP	TC/G	FA
1902	PHI	N	0	1	.000	5.00	1	1	1	9	13	6	0	0	0	0	0	3	1	0	.333	0	4	0	0	4.0	1.000
1906	BKN	N	1	1	.500	2.92	3	2	2	24.2	26	6	7	1	0	0	0	10	3	0	.300	1	11	0	0	4.0	1.000
1907			0	0	—	12.00	1	0	0	3	3	3	2	0	0	0	0	2	0	0	.000	0	1	0	0	1.0	1.000
3 yrs.			1	2	.333	4.17	5	3	3	36.2	42	15	9	1	0	0	0	15	4	0	.267	1	16	0	0	3.4	1.000

Art Whitney

WHITNEY, ARTHUR WILSON BR TR 5′ 8″ 155 lbs.
Brother of Frank Whitney.
B. Jan. 16, 1858, Brockton, Mass. D. Aug. 15, 1943, Lowell, Mass.

Year	Team		W	L	PCT	ERA	G	GS	CG	IP	H	BB	SO	ShO	Relief Pitching W	Relief Pitching L	Relief Pitching SV	Batting AB	Batting H	Batting HR	BA	PO	A	E	DP	TC/G	FA
1882	DET	N	0	1	.000	*6.00*	3	2	1	18	31	8	11	0	0	0	0	155	24	0	.155	83	162	40	6	3.8	.860
1886	PIT	AA	0	0	—	*3.00*	1	0	0	6	7	3	2	0	0	0	0	511	122	0	.239	73	141	38	10	4.3	.849
1889	NY	N	0	1	.000	3.00	1	0	0	6	7	3	3	0	0	1	0	473	103	1	.218	65	100	32	9	4.5	.838
3 yrs.			0	2	.000	4.80	5	2	1	30	45	14	16	0	0	1	0	*				1259	2195	448	165	4.0	.885

Jim Whitney

WHITNEY, JAMES EVANS (Grasshopper Jim) BL TR 6′ 2″ 172 lbs.
B. Nov. 10, 1857, Conklin, N. Y. D. May 21, 1891, Binghamton, N. Y.

Year	Team		W	L	PCT	ERA	G	GS	CG	IP	H	BB	SO	ShO	Relief Pitching W	Relief Pitching L	Relief Pitching SV	Batting AB	Batting H	HR	BA	PO	A	E	DP	TC/G	FA
1881	BOS	N	**31**	**33**	.484	*2.48*	**66**	**63**	**57**	**552.1**	**548**	**90**	162	6	0	**1**	0	282	72	0	.255	40	100	32	3	2.1	.814
1882			24	21	.533	*2.64*	49	48	46	420	404	41	180	3	0	0	0	251	81	5	.323	57	88	19	3	2.6	.884
1883			37	21	.638	*2.24*	62	56	54	514	492	35	**345**	1	3	0	**2**	409	115	5	.281	89	100	27	4	2.1	.875
1884			23	14	.622	*2.09*	41	37	35	336	272	27	270	6	0	**1**	0	270	70	3	.259	135	80	10	3	3.1	.956
1885			18	**32**	.360	*2.98*	51	50	50	441.1	**503**	37	200	2	0	0	0	290	68	0	.234	86	133	26	4	3.4	.894
1886	KC	N	12	32	.273	*4.49*	46	44	42	393	465	55	167	3	0	0	0	247	59	2	.239	39	119	18	6	2.6	.898
1887	WAS	N	24	21	.533	3.22	47	47	46	404.2	430	42	146	3	0	0	0	201	53	2	.264	16	93	13	5	2.3	.893
1888			18	21	.462	3.05	39	39	37	325	317	54	79	3	0	0	0	141	24	1	.170	24	67	12	2	2.4	.883
1889	IND	N	2	7	.222	6.81	9	8	7	70	106	19	16	0	0	1	0	32	12	0	.375	5	9	0	0	1.4	1.000
1890	PHI	AA	2	2	.500	*5.17*	6	4	3	40	61	11	6	0	0	0	0	21	5	0	.238	1	8	1	1	1.4	.900
10 yrs.			191	204	.484	2.97	416	396	377	3496.1	3598	411	1571	27	3	3	2	*				492	797	158	31	2.5	.891

Bill Whitrock

WHITROCK, WILLIAM FRANKLIN TR 5′ 7½″ 170 lbs.
B. Mar. 4, 1870, Cincinnati, Ohio D. July 26, 1935, Derby, Conn.

Year	Team		W	L	PCT	ERA	G	GS	CG	IP	H	BB	SO	ShO	Relief Pitching W	Relief Pitching L	Relief Pitching SV	Batting AB	Batting H	HR	BA	PO	A	E	DP	TC/G	FA
1890	STL	AA	5	6	.455	*3.51*	16	11	10	105	104	40	39	0	0	0	1	48	7	0	.146	6	23	5	0	2.0	.853
1893	LOU	N	2	5	.286	7.88	8	8	4	37.2	54	14	7	0	0	0	0	21	6	0	.286	5	11	2	1	2.6	.889
1894	2 teams	LOU N	(16G 0–1)	CIN N	(10G 2–6)																						
″	total		2	7	.222	6.78	11	9	8	74.1	118	41	9	0	0	0	0	62	13	0	.210	21	18	3	0	2.2	.929
1896	PHI	N	0	1	.000	3.00	2	1	1	9	10	3	1	0	0	0	0	3	0	0	.000	0	1	0	0	0.5	1.000
4 yrs.			9	19	.321	5.30	37	29	23	226	286	98	56	0	0	0	1	134	26	0	.194	32	53	10	1	2.1	.895

Ed Whitson

WHITSON, EDDIE LEE BR TR 6′ 3″ 195 lbs.
B. May 19, 1955, Johnson City, Tenn.

Year	Team		W	L	PCT	ERA	G	GS	CG	IP	H	BB	SO	ShO	Relief Pitching W	Relief Pitching L	Relief Pitching SV	Batting AB	Batting H	HR	BA	PO	A	E	DP	TC/G	FA
1977	PIT	N	1	0	1.000	3.38	5	2	0	16	11	9	10	0	1	0	0	4	0	0	.000	0	2	0	0	0.4	1.000
1978			5	6	.455	3.28	43	0	0	74	66	37	64	0	5	6	4	11	2	0	.182	3	8	1	0	0.3	.917
1979	2 teams	PIT N	(19G 2–3)	SF N	(18G 5–8)																						
″	total		7	11	.389	4.10	37	24	2	158	151	75	93	0	0	3	1	45	5	0	.111	4	21	2	2	0.7	.926
1980	SF	N	11	13	.458	3.10	34	34	6	212	222	56	90	2	0	0	0	66	6	0	.091	8	27	3	0	1.1	.921
1981			6	9	.400	4.02	22	22	2	123	130	47	65	1	0	0	0	33	3	0	.091	10	11	3	1	1.1	.875
1982	CLE	A	4	2	.667	3.26	40	9	1	107.2	91	58	61	1	2	1	2	0	0	0	—	4	8	0	0	0.3	1.000
1983	SD	N	5	7	.417	4.30	31	21	2	144.1	143	50	81	0	0	0	1	44	8	0	.182	4	6	0	0	0.3	1.000
1984			14	8	.636	3.24	31	31	1	189	181	42	103	0	0	0	0	61	3	0	.049	11	35	0	3	1.5	1.000
1985	NY	A	10	8	.556	4.88	30	30	2	158.2	201	43	89	2	0	0	0	0	0	0	—	8	16	3	3	0.9	.889
1986	2 teams	NY A	(14G 5–2)	SD N	(17G 1–7)																						
″	total		6	9	.400	6.23	31	16	0	112.2	139	60	73	0	4	0	0	18	3	0	.167	7	18	2	1	0.9	.926
1987	SD	N	10	13	.435	4.73	36	34	3	205.2	197	64	135	1	0	0	0	65	8	0	.123	14	19	1	0	0.9	.971
1988			13	11	.542	3.77	34	33	3	205.1	202	45	118	1	1	0	0	66	11	0	.167	10	30	4	2	1.3	.909
1989			16	11	.593	2.66	33	33	5	227	198	48	117	1	0	0	0	72	10	0	.139	17	22	2	1	1.2	.951
1990			14	9	.609	2.60	32	32	6	228.2	215	47	127	3	0	0	0	67	10	1	.149	18	42	0	3	1.9	1.000
1991			4	6	.400	5.03	13	12	2	78.2	93	17	40	0	0	0	0	24	3	0	.125	5	9	0	0	1.1	1.000
15 yrs.			126	123	.506	3.79	452	333	35	2240.2	2240	698	1266	12	13	10	8	576	72	1	.125	123	274	21	16	0.9	.950
LEAGUE CHAMPIONSHIP SERIES																											
1984	SD	N	1	0	1.000	1.13	1	1	0	8	5	2	6	0	0	0	0	3	0	0	.000	1	0	0	0	1.0	1.000
WORLD SERIES																											
1984	SD	N	0	0	—	40.50	1	1	0	0.2	5	0	0	0	0	0	0	0	0	0	—	0	0	0	0	0.0	.000

Walt Whittaker

WHITTAKER, WALTER ELTON (Doc) BL TR 5′ 9½″ 165 lbs.
B. June 11, 1894, Chelsea, Mass. D. Aug. 7, 1965, Pembroke, Mass.

Year	Team		W	L	PCT	ERA	G	GS	CG	IP	H	BB	SO	ShO	Relief Pitching W	Relief Pitching L	Relief Pitching SV	Batting AB	Batting H	HR	BA	PO	A	E	DP	TC/G	FA
1916	PHI	A	0	0	—	4.50	1	0	0	2	3	2	0	0	0	0	0	0	0	0	—	0	1	0	0	1.0	1.000

Kevin Wickander

WICKANDER, KEVIN DEAN BL TL 6′ 2″ 202 lbs.
B. Jan. 4, 1965, Fort Dodge, Iowa.

Year	Team		W	L	PCT	ERA	G	GS	CG	IP	H	BB	SO	ShO	Relief Pitching W	Relief Pitching L	Relief Pitching SV	Batting AB	Batting H	HR	BA	PO	A	E	DP	TC/G	FA
1989	CLE	A	0	0	—	3.38	2	0	0	2.2	6	2	0	0	0	0	0	0	0	0	—	0	0	0	0	0.0	.000
1990			0	1	.000	3.65	10	0	0	12.1	14	4	10	0	0	1	0	0	0	0	—	0	1	0	0	0.1	1.000
1992			2	0	1.000	3.07	44	0	0	41	39	28	38	0	2	0	1	0	0	0	—	0	5	0	1	0.1	1.000
1993	2 teams	CLE A	(11G 0–0)	CIN N	(33G 1–0)																						
″	total		1	0	1.000	6.09	44	0	0	34	47	22	23	0	1	0	0	2	0	0	.000	0	3	0	0	0.1	1.000
1995	2 teams	DET A	(21G 0–0)	MIL A	(8G 0–0)																						
″	total		0	0		1.93	29	0	0	23.1	19	12	11	0	0	0	1	0	0	0	—	1	4	0	0	0.2	1.000
5 yrs.			3	1	.750	3.81	129	0	0	113.1	125	68	82	0	3	1	2	2	0	0	.000	1	13	0	1	0.1	1.000

Bob Wicker

WICKER, ROBERT KITRIDGE BR TR 6′ 2″ 180 lbs.
B. May 24, 1878, Bedford, Ind. D. Jan. 22, 1955, Evanston, Ill.

Year	Team		W	L	PCT	ERA	G	GS	CG	IP	H	BB	SO	ShO	Relief Pitching W	Relief Pitching L	Relief Pitching SV	Batting AB	Batting H	HR	BA	PO	A	E	DP	TC/G	FA
1901	STL	N	0	0	—	0.00	1	0	0	3	4	1	2	0	0	0	0	3	1	0	.333	0	0	0	0	0.0	.000
1902			5	13	.278	3.19	22	16	14	152.1	159	45	78	1	1	2	0	77	18	0	.234	22	47	10	3	3.2	.873
1903	2 teams	STL N	(1G 0–0)	CHI N	(32G 19–10)																						
″	total		19	10	.655	2.96	33	27	24	252	240	77	113	1	1	1	1	100	24	0	.240	13	45	9	2	2.0	.866
1904	CHI	N	17	8	.680	2.67	30	27	23	229	201	58	99	4	0	1	0	155	34	0	.219	48	34	7	1	1.8	.921
1905			13	6	.684	2.02	22	22	17	178	139	47	86	4	0	0	0	72	10	0	.139	8	36	2	3	1.8	.957
1906	2 teams	CHI N	(10G 3–5)	CIN N	(20G 6–14)																						
″	total		9	19	.321	2.79	30	25	19	222.1	220	65	94	0	1	3	0	70	11	0	.157	13	38	6	2	1.9	.895
6 yrs.			63	56	.529	2.73	138	117	97	1036.2	963	293	472	10	3	7	1	*				104	200	34	11	2.1	.899

Kemp Wicker

WICKER, KEMP CASWELL BR TL 5′11″ 182 lbs.
Born Kemp Caswell Whicker.
B. Aug. 13, 1906, Kernersville, N. C. D. June 11, 1973, Kernersville, N. C.

Year	Team		W	L	PCT	ERA	G	GS	CG	IP	H	BB	SO	ShO	Relief Pitching W	Relief Pitching L	Relief Pitching SV	Batting AB	Batting H	HR	BA	PO	A	E	DP	TC/G	FA
1936	NY	A	1	2	.333	7.65	7	0	0	20	31	11	5	0	1	2	0	7	1	0	.143	0	5	0	0	0.7	1.000
1937			7	3	.700	4.40	16	10	6	88	107	26	14	1	1	0	0	35	4	0	.114	0	9	1	0	0.6	.900
1938			1	0	1.000	0.00	1	0	0	1	0	1	0	0	1	0	0	0	0	0	—	0	0	0	0	0.0	.000
1941	BKN	N	1	2	.333	3.66	16	2	0	32	30	14	8	0	1	1	1	4	1	0	.250	0	7	0	0	0.4	1.000
4 yrs.			10	7	.588	4.66	40	12	6	141	168	52	27	1	4	3	1	46	6	0	.130	0	21	1	0	0.6	.955
WORLD SERIES																											
1937	NY	A	0	0	—	0.00	1	0	0	1	0	0	0	0	0	0	0	0	0	0	—	0	0	0	0	0.0	.000

Dave Wickersham

WICKERSHAM, DAVID CLIFFORD — B. Sept. 27, 1935, Erie, Pa. — BR TR 6′ 3″ 188 lbs.

Year	Team	Lg	W	L	PCT	ERA	G	GS	CG	IP	H	BB	SO	ShO	Relief Pitching W	Relief Pitching L	Relief Pitching SV	Batting AB	Batting H	Batting HR	BA	PO	A	E	DP	TC/G	FA
1960	**KC**	**A**	0	0	—	1.08	5	0	0	8.1	4	1	3	0	0	0	2	1	0	0	.000	0	2	0	0	0.4	1.000
1961			2	1	.667	5.14	17	0	0	21	25	5	10	0	2	1	2	3	2	0	.667	0	5	1	0	0.4	.833
1962			11	4	.733	4.17	30	9	3	110	105	43	61	0	5	2	1	35	2	0	.057	7	22	0	2	1.0	1.000
1963			12	15	.444	4.09	38	34	4	237.2	244	79	118	1	1	0	1	80	11	0	.138	15	43	2	2	1.6	.967
1964	**DET**	**A**	19	12	.613	3.44	40	36	11	254	224	81	164	1	0	1	1	82	6	0	.073	22	35	2	2	1.5	.966
1965			9	14	.391	3.78	34	27	8	195.1	179	61	109	3	1	0	0	58	4	0	.069	15	37	2	0	1.6	.963
1966			8	3	.727	3.20	38	14	3	140.2	139	54	93	0	4	1	1	45	2	0	.044	11	24	0	2	0.9	1.000
1967			4	5	.444	2.74	36	4	0	85.1	72	33	44	0	4	1	4	15	0	0	.000	8	18	2	1	0.8	.929
1968	**PIT**	**N**	1	0	1.000	3.48	11	0	0	20.2	21	13	9	0	1	0	1	3	1	0	.333	0	4	0	0	0.4	1.000
1969	**KC**	**A**	2	3	.400	3.96	34	0	0	50	58	14	27	0	2	3	5	2	0	0	.000	2	10	1	0	0.4	.923
10 yrs.			68	57	.544	3.66	283	124	29	1123	1071	384	638	5	20	9	18	324	28	0	.086	80	200	10	9	1.0	.966

Bob Wickman

WICKMAN, ROBERT JOE — B. Feb. 6, 1969, Green Bay, Wis. — BR TR 6′ 1″ 207 lbs.

Year	Team	Lg	W	L	PCT	ERA	G	GS	CG	IP	H	BB	SO	ShO	Relief Pitching W	Relief Pitching L	Relief Pitching SV	Batting AB	Batting H	Batting HR	BA	PO	A	E	DP	TC/G	FA
1992	**NY**	**A**	6	1	.857	4.11	8	8	0	50.1	51	20	21	0	0	0	0	0	0	0	—	4	6	0	3	1.3	1.000
1993			14	4	.778	4.63	41	19	1	140	156	69	70	1	6	0	4	0	0	0	—	7	19	2	1	0.7	.929
1994			5	4	.556	3.09	**53**	0	0	70	54	27	56	0	5	4	6	0	0	0	—	3	7	0	0	0.2	1.000
1995			2	4	.333	4.05	63	1	0	80	77	33	51	0	2	3	1	0	0	0	—	4	14	1	1	0.3	.947
4 yrs.			27	13	.675	4.10	165	28	1	340.1	338	149	198	1	13	7	11	0	0	0		18	46	3	5	0.4	.955
DIVISIONAL PLAYOFF SERIES																											
1995	**NY**	**A**	0	0	—	0.00	3	0	0	3	5	0	3	0	0	0	0	0	0	0	—	0	1	0	0	0.3	1.000

Al Widmar

WIDMAR, ALBERT JOSEPH — B. Mar. 20, 1925, Cleveland, Ohio. — BR TR 6′ 3″ 185 lbs.

Year	Team	Lg	W	L	PCT	ERA	G	GS	CG	IP	H	BB	SO	ShO	Relief Pitching W	Relief Pitching L	Relief Pitching SV	Batting AB	Batting H	Batting HR	BA	PO	A	E	DP	TC/G	FA
1947	**BOS**	**A**	0	0	—	13.50	2	0	0	1.1	1	2	1	0	0	0	0	0	0	0	—	0	0	0	0	0.0	.000
1948	**STL**	**A**	2	6	.250	4.46	49	0	0	82.2	88	48	34	0	2	6	1	10	3	0	.300	4	22	0	0	0.5	1.000
1950			7	15	.318	4.76	36	26	8	194.2	211	74	78	1	0	1	4	67	10	0	.149	17	32	0	3	1.4	1.000
1951			4	9	.308	6.52	26	16	4	107.2	157	52	28	0	1	1	0	30	5	0	.167	10	22	1	3	1.3	.970
1952	**CHI**	**A**	0	0	—	4.50	1	0	0	2	4	0	2	0	0	0	0	0	0	0	—	0	0	0	0	0.0	.000
5 yrs.			13	30	.302	5.21	114	42	12	388.1	461	176	143	1	3	8	5	107	18	0	.168	31	76	1	6	0.9	.991

Wild Bill Widner

WIDNER, WILLIAM WATERFIELD — B. June 3, 1867, Cincinnati, Ohio D. Dec. 10, 1908, Cincinnati, Ohio. — BR TR 6′ 180 lbs.

Year	Team	Lg	W	L	PCT	ERA	G	GS	CG	IP	H	BB	SO	ShO	Relief Pitching W	Relief Pitching L	Relief Pitching SV	Batting AB	Batting H	Batting HR	BA	PO	A	E	DP	TC/G	FA
1887	**CIN**	**AA**	1	0	1.000	5.00	1	1	1	9	11	2	0	0	0	0	0	4	1	0	.250	0	3	0	0	3.0	1.000
1888	**WAS**	**N**	5	7	.417	2.82	13	13	13	115	111	22	33	0	0	0	0	60	12	0	.200	16	21	8	0	3.0	.822
1889	**COL**	**AA**	12	20	.375	5.20	41	34	25	294	368	85	63	2	1	1	1	133	28	2	.211	18	63	9	3	2.1	.900
1890			4	8	.333	*3.28*	13	10	8	96	103	24	14	1	0	**2**	0	41	8	0	.195	7	30	3	2	3.1	.925
1891	**CIN**	**AA**	0	1	.000	7.88	1	1	1	8	13	4	0	0	0	0	0	4	1	0	.250	0	2	0	0	2.0	1.000
5 yrs.			22	36	.379	4.36	69	59	48	522	606	137	110	3	1	3	1	242	50	2	.207	41	119	20	5	2.5	.889

Ted Wieand

WIEAND, FRANKLIN DELANO ROOSEVELT — B. Apr. 4, 1933, Walnutport, Pa. — BR TR 6′ 2″ 195 lbs.

Year	Team	Lg	W	L	PCT	ERA	G	GS	CG	IP	H	BB	SO	ShO	Relief Pitching W	Relief Pitching L	Relief Pitching SV	Batting AB	Batting H	Batting HR	BA	PO	A	E	DP	TC/G	FA
1958	**CIN**	**N**	0	0	—	9.00	1	0	0	2	4	0	2	0	0	0	0	0	0	0	—	0	0	0	0	0.0	.000
1960			0	1	.000	10.38	5	0	0	4.1	4	5	3	0	0	1	0	0	0	0	—	0	1	0	1	0.2	1.000
2 yrs.			0	1	.000	9.95	6	0	0	6.1	8	5	5	0	0	1	0	0	0	0		0	1	0	1	0.2	1.000

Charlie Wiedemeyer

WIEDEMEYER, CHARLES JOHN — B. Jan. 31, 1914, Chicago, Ill. D. Oct. 27, 1979, Lake Geneva, Fla. — BL TL 6′ 3″ 180 lbs.

Year	Team	Lg	W	L	PCT	ERA	G	GS	CG	IP	H	BB	SO	ShO	Relief Pitching W	Relief Pitching L	Relief Pitching SV	Batting AB	Batting H	Batting HR	BA	PO	A	E	DP	TC/G	FA
1934	**CHI**	**N**	0	0	—	9.72	4	1	0	8.1	16	4	2	0	0	0	0	1	0	0	.000	0	2	0	1	0.5	1.000

Stump Wiedman

WIEDMAN, GEORGE EDWARD — B. Feb. 17, 1861, Rochester, N. Y. D. Mar. 3, 1905, New York, N. Y. — BR TR 5′ 7½″ 165 lbs.

Year	Team	Lg	W	L	PCT	ERA	G	GS	CG	IP	H	BB	SO	ShO	Relief Pitching W	Relief Pitching L	Relief Pitching SV	Batting AB	Batting H	Batting HR	BA	PO	A	E	DP	TC/G	FA
1880	**BUF**	**N**	0	9	.000	3.40	17	13	9	113.2	141	9	25	0	0	0	0	78	8	0	.103	21	20	5	0	1.5	.891
1881	**DET**	**N**	8	5	.615	**1.80**	13	13	13	115	108	12	26	1	0	0	0	47	12	0	.255	3	15	0	0	1.4	1.000
1882			25	20	.556	2.63	46	45	43	411	391	39	161	4	0	0	0	193	42	0	.218	39	76	12	2	2.4	.906
1883			20	24	.455	*3.53*	52	47	41	402.1	435	72	183	3	0	0	**2**	313	58	1	.185	81	94	26	4	2.2	.871
1884			4	21	.160	*3.72*	26	26	24	212.2	257	57	96	0	0	0	0	300	49	0	.163	89	62	37	3	2.3	.803
1885			14	24	.368	*3.14*	38	38	37	330	343	63	149	3	0	0	0	153	24	1	.157	19	60	18	1	1.3	.814
1886	**KC**	**N**	12	**36**	.250	*4.52*	51	51	48	427.2	**549**	112	168	1	0	0	0	179	30	0	.168	26	106	9	5	2.6	.936
1887	**3 teams**	**DET N** (21G 13–7) **NY AA** (12G 4–8) **NY N** (1G 0–1)																									
"	**total**		17	16	.515	5.00	34	34	32	288	353	87	97	1	0	0	0	131	25	0	.191	20	59	13	0	2.4	.859
1888	**NY**	**N**	0	1	.000	3.50	2	2	2	18	17	8	5	0	0	0	0	7	0	0	.000	3	2	2	0	3.5	.714
9 yrs.			100	156	.391	3.61	279	269	249	2318.1	2594	459	910	13	0	0	2	*				301	494	122	15	2.1	.867

Jack Wieneke

WIENEKE, JOHN — B. Mar. 10, 1894, Saltsburg, Pa. D. Mar. 16, 1933, Pleasant Ridge, Mich. — BR TL 6′ 182 lbs.

Year	Team	Lg	W	L	PCT	ERA	G	GS	CG	IP	H	BB	SO	ShO	Relief Pitching W	Relief Pitching L	Relief Pitching SV	Batting AB	Batting H	Batting HR	BA	PO	A	E	DP	TC/G	FA
1921	**CHI**	**A**	0	1	.000	8.17	10	3	0	25.1	39	17	10	0	0	0	0	9	1	0	.111	0	8	0	0	0.8	1.000

Bob Wiesler

WIESLER, ROBERT GEORGE — B. Aug. 13, 1930, St. Louis, Mo. — BB TL 6′ 3″ 188 lbs.

Year	Team	Lg	W	L	PCT	ERA	G	GS	CG	IP	H	BB	SO	ShO	Relief Pitching W	Relief Pitching L	Relief Pitching SV	Batting AB	Batting H	Batting HR	BA	PO	A	E	DP	TC/G	FA
1951	**NY**	**A**	0	2	.000	13.50	4	3	0	9.1	13	11	3	0	0	0	0	3	0	0	.000	0	3	0	1	0.8	1.000
1954			3	2	.600	4.15	6	5	0	30.1	28	30	25	0	0	0	0	11	3	0	.273	1	2	0	0	0.5	1.000
1955			0	2	.000	3.91	16	7	0	53	39	49	22	0	0	0	0	14	2	0	.143	2	13	0	1	0.9	1.000
1956	**WAS**	**A**	3	12	.200	6.44	37	21	3	123	141	112	49	0	0	0	0	33	3	0	.091	12	24	3	5	1.1	.923
1957			1	1	.500	4.41	3	2	1	16.1	15	11	9	0	0	0	0	6	1	0	.167	2	3	0	0	1.7	1.000
1958			0	0	—	6.75	4	0	0	9.1	14	5	5	0	0	0	0	2	0	0	.000	0	4	0	1	1.0	1.000
6 yrs.			7	19	.269	5.74	70	38	4	241.1	250	218	113	0	0	0	0	69	9	0	.130	17	49	3	8	1.0	.957

Whitey Wietelmann

WIETELMANN, WILLIAM FREDERICK — B. Mar. 15, 1919, Zanesville, Ohio. — BB TR 6′ 170 lbs. BR 1939–1941

Year	Team	Lg	W	L	PCT	ERA	G	GS	CG	IP	H	BB	SO	ShO	Relief Pitching W	Relief Pitching L	Relief Pitching SV	Batting AB	Batting H	Batting HR	BA	PO	A	E	DP	TC/G	FA
1945	**BOS**	**N**	0	0	—	54.00	1	0	0	1	6	2	0	0	0	0	0	428	116	4	.271	38	69	5	12	4.9	.955
1946			0	0	—	8.10	3	0	0	6.2	9	4	2	0	0	0	0	78	16	0	.205	40	39	7	6	2.8	.919
2 yrs.			0	0		14.09	4	0	0	7.2	15	6	2	0	0	0	0	*				1091	1531	121	292	4.9	.956

Jimmy Wiggs

WIGGS, JAMES ALVIN (Big Jim) BB TR 6′ 4″ 200 lbs.
B. Sept. 1, 1876, Trondheim, Norway D. Jan. 20, 1963, Xenia, Ohio.

Year	Team	W	L	PCT	ERA	G	GS	CG	IP	H	BB	SO	ShO	Relief Pitching W	Relief Pitching L	Relief Pitching SV	Batting AB	Batting H	Batting HR	BA	PO	A	E	DP	TC/G	FA
1903	CIN N	0	1	.000	5.40	2	1	0	5	12	2	2	0	0	0	0	1	0	0	.000	0	1	0	0	0.5	1.000
1905	DET A	3	3	.500	3.27	7	7	4	41.1	30	29	37	0	0	0	0	15	2	0	.133	1	11	3	0	2.1	.800
1906		0	0	—	5.23	4	1	0	10.1	11	7	7	0	0	0	0	3	1	0	.333	0	5	1	0	1.5	.833
3 yrs.		3	4	.429	3.81	13	9	4	56.2	53	38	46	0	0	0	0	19	3	0	.158	1	17	4	0	1.7	.818

Bill Wight

WIGHT, WILLIAM ROBERT (Lefty) BL TL 6′ 1″ 180 lbs.
B. Apr. 12, 1922, Rio Vista, Calif.

Year	Team	W	L	PCT	ERA	G	GS	CG	IP	H	BB	SO	ShO	Relief Pitching W	Relief Pitching L	Relief Pitching SV	Batting AB	Batting H	Batting HR	BA	PO	A	E	DP	TC/G	FA
1946	NY A	2	2	.500	4.46	14	4	1	40.1	44	30	11	0	0	0	0	9	0	0	.000	1	11	3	0	1.1	.800
1947		1	0	1.000	1.00	1	1	1	9	8	2	3	0	0	0	0	2	0	0	.000	1	3	0	0	4.0	1.000
1948	CHI A	9	20	.310	4.80	34	32	7	223.1	238	**135**	68	1	0	0	1	73	6	0	.082	4	47	3	2	1.6	.944
1949		15	13	.536	3.31	35	33	14	245	254	96	78	3	0	0	1	85	14	0	.165	10	50	5	3	1.9	.923
1950		10	16	.385	3.58	30	28	13	206	213	79	62	3	0	1	0	61	0	0	.000	5	49	6	2	2.0	.900
1951	BOS A	7	7	.500	5.10	34	17	4	118.1	128	63	38	2	2	0	0	41	3	0	.073	1	29	3	2	1.0	.909
1952	2 teams BOS A (10G 2–1) DET A (23G 5–9)																									
″	total	7	10	.412	3.75	33	21	8	168	181	69	70	3	1	0	0	57	12	0	.211	7	44	4	1	1.7	.927
1953	2 teams DET A (13G 0–3) CLE A (20G 2–1)																									
″	total	2	4	.333	6.23	33	4	0	52	64	30	24	0	2	2	1	12	3	0	.250	1	9	4	1	0.4	.714
1955	2 teams CLE A (17G 0–0) BAL A (19G 6–8)																									
″	total	6	8	.429	2.48	36	14	8	141.1	135	48	63	2	0	1	3	36	3	0	.083	3	49	3	1	1.5	.945
1956	BAL A	9	12	.429	4.02	35	26	7	174.2	198	72	84	1	1	0	0	60	12	0	.200	6	27	4	1	1.1	.892
1957		6	6	.500	3.64	27	17	2	121	122	54	50	0	0	0	0	34	1	0	.029	5	21	3	1	1.1	.897
1958	2 teams CIN N (7G 0–1) STL N (28G 3–0)																									
″	total	3	1	.750	4.92	35	1	1	64	71	36	23	0	2	1	2	10	1	0	.100	3	16	2	2	0.6	.905
12 yrs.		77	99	.438	3.95	347	198	66	1563	1656	714	574	15	8	5	8	480	55	0	.115	47	355	40	16	1.3	.910

Fred Wigington

WIGINGTON, FRED THOMAS BR TR 5′10″ 168 lbs.
B. Dec. 16, 1897, Rogers, Neb. D. May 8, 1980, Mesa, Ariz.

Year	Team	W	L	PCT	ERA	G	GS	CG	IP	H	BB	SO	ShO	Relief Pitching W	Relief Pitching L	Relief Pitching SV	Batting AB	Batting H	Batting HR	BA	PO	A	E	DP	TC/G	FA
1923	STL N	0	0	—	3.24	4	0	0	8.1	11	5	2	0	0	0	0	1	0	0	.000	0	5	2	0	1.8	.714

Sandy Wihtol

WIHTOL, ALEXANDER AMES BR TR 6′ 1″ 195 lbs.
B. June 1, 1955, Palo Alto, Calif.

Year	Team	W	L	PCT	ERA	G	GS	CG	IP	H	BB	SO	ShO	Relief Pitching W	Relief Pitching L	Relief Pitching SV	Batting AB	Batting H	Batting HR	BA	PO	A	E	DP	TC/G	FA
1979	CLE A	0	0	—	3.27	5	0	0	11	10	3	6	0	0	0	0	0	0	0	—	2	2	0	0	0.8	1.000
1980		1	0	1.000	3.60	17	0	0	35	35	14	20	0	1	0	1	0	0	0	—	1	2	0	0	0.2	1.000
1982		0	0	—	4.63	6	0	0	11.2	9	7	8	0	0	0	0	0	0	0	—	0	1	0	0	0.2	1.000
3 yrs.		1	0	1.000	3.75	28	0	0	57.2	54	24	34	0	1	0	1	0	0	0		3	5	0	0	0.3	1.000

Milt Wilcox

WILCOX, MILTON EDWARD BR TR 6′ 2″ 185 lbs.
B. Apr. 20, 1950, Honolulu, Hawaii.

Year	Team	W	L	PCT	ERA	G	GS	CG	IP	H	BB	SO	ShO	Relief Pitching W	Relief Pitching L	Relief Pitching SV	Batting AB	Batting H	Batting HR	BA	PO	A	E	DP	TC/G	FA
1970	CIN N	3	1	.750	2.45	5	2	1	22	19	7	13	1	1	1	1	5	1	0	.200	1	5	0	0	1.2	1.000
1971		2	2	.500	3.35	18	3	0	43	43	17	21	0	2	1	1	9	0	0	.000	1	9	0	0	0.6	1.000
1972	CLE A	7	14	.333	3.40	32	27	4	156	145	72	90	2	0	1	0	45	9	0	.200	9	14	5	1	0.9	.821
1973		8	10	.444	5.83	26	19	4	134.1	143	68	82	0	0	1	0	0	0	0	—	6	26	1	0	1.3	.970
1974		2	2	.500	4.69	41	2	1	71	74	24	33	0	1	1	4	0	0	0	—	5	14	3	1	0.5	.864
1975	CHI N	0	1	.000	5.68	25	0	0	38	50	17	21	0	0	1	0	3	1	0	.333	0	8	1	0	0.4	.889
1977	DET A	6	2	.750	3.65	20	13	1	106	96	37	82	0	1	0	0	0	0	0	—	4	14	2	2	1.0	.900
1978		13	12	.520	3.76	29	27	16	215.1	208	68	132	2	0	1	0	0	0	0	—	10	36	1	0	1.6	.979
1979		12	10	.545	4.36	33	29	7	196	201	73	109	0	1	0	0	0	0	0	—	10	41	0	7	1.5	1.000
1980		13	11	.542	4.48	32	31	13	199	201	68	97	1	1	0	0	0	0	0	—	14	36	4	1	1.7	.926
1981		12	9	.571	3.04	24	24	8	166	152	52	79	1	0	0	0	0	0	0	—	5	33	2	1	1.7	.950
1982		12	10	.545	3.62	29	29	9	193.2	187	85	112	1	0	0	0	0	0	0	—	11	38	2	5	1.8	.961
1983		11	10	.524	3.97	26	26	9	186	164	74	101	2	0	0	0	0	0	0	—	19	34	1	3	2.1	.981
1984		17	8	.680	4.00	33	33	0	193.2	183	66	119	0	0	0	0	0	0	0	—	20	28	3	4	1.5	.941
1985		1	3	.250	4.85	8	8	0	39	51	14	20	0	0	0	0	0	0	0	—	3	12	2	2	2.1	.882
1986	SEA A	0	8	.000	5.50	13	10	0	55.2	74	28	26	0	0	1	0	0	0	0	—	4	9	0	1	1.0	1.000
16 yrs.		119	113	.513	4.08	394	283	73	2014.2	1991	770	1137	10	7	8	6	62	11	0	.177	122	357	27	28	1.3	.947
LEAGUE CHAMPIONSHIP SERIES																										
1970	CIN N	1	0	1.000	0.00	1	0	0	3	1	2	5	0	1	0	0	0	0	0	—	0	1	0	0	1.0	1.000
1984	DET A	1	0	1.000	0.00	1	1	0	8	2	2	8	0	0	0	0	0	0	0	—	2	0	0	0	2.0	1.000
2 yrs.		2	0	1.000	0.00	2	1	0	11	3	4	13	0	1	0	0	0	0	0		2	1	0	0	1.5	1.000
WORLD SERIES																										
1970	CIN N	0	1	.000	9.00	2	0	0	2	3	0	2	0	0	1	0	0	0	0	—	0	1	0	0	0.5	1.000
1984	DET A	1	0	1.000	1.50	1	1	0	6	7	2	4	0	0	0	0	0	0	0	—	1	1	0	0	2.0	1.000
2 yrs.		1	1	.500	3.38	3	1	0	8	10	2	6	0	0	1	0	0	0	0		1	2	0	0	1.0	1.000

Randy Wiles

WILES, RANDALL E. BL TL 6′ 1″ 185 lbs.
B. Sept. 10, 1951, Ft. Belvoir, Va.

Year	Team	W	L	PCT	ERA	G	GS	CG	IP	H	BB	SO	ShO	Relief Pitching W	Relief Pitching L	Relief Pitching SV	Batting AB	Batting H	Batting HR	BA	PO	A	E	DP	TC/G	FA
1977	CHI A	1	1	.500	9.00	5	0	0	3	5	3	0	0	1	1	0	0	0	0	—	0	1	0	0	0.2	1.000

Mark Wiley

WILEY, MARK EUGENE BR TR 6′ 1″ 200 lbs.
B. Feb. 28, 1948, National City, Calif.

Year	Team	W	L	PCT	ERA	G	GS	CG	IP	H	BB	SO	ShO	Relief Pitching W	Relief Pitching L	Relief Pitching SV	Batting AB	Batting H	Batting HR	BA	PO	A	E	DP	TC/G	FA
1975	MIN A	1	3	.250	6.05	15	3	1	38.2	50	13	15	0	0	1	2	0	0	0	—	3	3	1	1	0.5	.857
1978	2 teams SD N (4G 1–0) TOR A (2G 0–0)																									
″	total	1	0	1.000	5.91	6	1	0	10.2	14	2	3	0	0	0	0	2	0	0	.000	0	1	0	0	0.2	1.000
2 yrs.		2	3	.400	6.02	21	4	1	49.1	64	15	18	0	0	1	2	2	0	0	.000	3	4	1	1	0.4	.875

Harry Wilhelm

WILHELM, HARRY LESTER BR TR 5′ 7″ 155 lbs.
B. Apr. 7, 1874, Uniontown, Pa. D. Feb. 20, 1944, Republic, Pa.

Year	Team	W	L	PCT	ERA	G	GS	CG	IP	H	BB	SO	ShO	Relief Pitching W	Relief Pitching L	Relief Pitching SV	Batting AB	Batting H	Batting HR	BA	PO	A	E	DP	TC/G	FA
1899	LOU N	1	1	.500	6.12	5	3	2	25	36	3	6	0	0	0	0	12	3	1	.250	1	8	0	0	1.8	1.000

Hoyt Wilhelm

WILHELM, JAMES HOYT BR TR 6′ 190 lbs.
B. July 26, 1923, Huntersville, N. C.
Hall of Fame 1985.

Year	Team	Lg	W	L	PCT	ERA	G	GS	CG	IP	H	BB	SO	ShO	Relief W	Relief L	Relief SV	AB	H	HR	BA	PO	A	E	DP	TC/G	FA
1952	NY	N	15	3	**.833**	**2.43**	**71**	0	0	159.1	127	57	108	0	**15**	3	11	38	6	1	.158	9	32	2	0	0.6	.953
1953			7	8	.467	3.04	**68**	0	0	145	127	77	71	0	7	**8**	15	33	5	0	.152	11	19	1	1	0.5	.968
1954			12	4	.750	2.10	57	0	0	111.1	77	52	64	0	**12**	4	7	21	1	0	.048	5	25	0	0	0.5	1.000
1955			4	1	.800	3.93	59	0	0	103	104	40	71	0	4	1	0	19	3	0	.158	6	28	1	2	0.6	.971
1956			4	9	.308	3.83	64	0	0	89.1	97	43	71	0	4	9	8	9	2	0	.222	4	20	0	2	0.4	1.000
1957	**2 teams**	**STL N**	(40G 1–4)		**CLE A**	(2G 1–0)																					
″	**total**		2	4	.333	4.14	42	0	0	58.2	54	22	29	0	2	4	12	6	0	0	.000	3	8	0	0	0.3	1.000
1958	**2 teams**	**CLE A**	(30G 2–7)		**BAL A**	(9G 1–3)																					
″	**total**		3	10	.231	2.34	39	10	4	131	95	45	92	1	2	5	5	32	3	0	.094	9	22	0	0	0.8	1.000
1959	BAL	A	15	11	.577	**2.19**	32	27	13	226	178	77	139	3	0	2	0	76	4	0	.053	13	32	0	1	1.4	1.000
1960			11	8	.579	3.31	41	11	3	147	125	39	107	1	8	4	7	42	3	0	.071	4	28	1	2	0.8	.970
1961			9	7	.563	2.30	51	1	0	109.2	89	41	87	0	9	7	18	20	1	0	.050	6	22	2	1	0.6	.933
1962			7	10	.412	1.94	52	0	0	93	64	34	90	0	7	**10**	15	16	2	0	.125	10	12	0	0	0.4	1.000
1963	CHI	A	5	8	.385	2.64	55	3	0	136.1	106	30	111	0	5	7	21	29	2	0	.069	4	24	1	1	0.5	.966
1964			12	9	.571	1.99	73	0	0	131.1	94	30	95	0	12	**9**	27	21	3	0	.143	5	16	0	2	0.3	1.000
1965			7	7	.500	1.81	66	0	0	144	88	32	106	0	7	7	20	22	0	0	.000	7	20	0	2	0.4	1.000
1966			5	2	.714	1.66	46	0	0	81.1	50	17	61	0	5	2	6	8	1	0	.125	2	10	0	1	0.3	1.000
1967			8	3	.727	1.31	49	0	0	89	58	34	76	0	8	3	12	13	1	0	.077	2	11	1	1	0.3	.929
1968			4	4	.500	1.73	72	0	0	93.2	69	24	72	0	4	4	12	3	0	0	.000	3	10	0	1	0.2	1.000
1969	**2 teams**	**CAL A**	(44G 5–7)		**ATL N**	(8G 2–0)																					
″	**total**		7	7	.500	2.20	52	0	0	77.2	50	22	67	0	7	7	14	9	0	0	.000	3	10	1	0	0.3	.929
1970	**2 teams**	**ATL N**	(50G 6–4)		**CHI N**	(3G 0–1)																					
″	**total**		6	5	.545	3.40	53	0	0	82	73	42	68	0	6	5	13	11	1	0	.091	4	16	1	0	0.4	.952
1971	**2 teams**	**ATL N**	(3G 0–0)		**LA N**	(9G 0–1)																					
″	**total**		0	1	.000	2.70	12	0	0	20	12	5	16	0	0	1	3	3	0	0	.000	1	3	0	0	0.3	1.000
1972	LA	N	0	1	.000	4.62	16	0	0	25.1	20	15	9	0	0	1	1	1	0	0	.000	3	5	0	0	0.5	1.000
21 yrs.			143	122	.540	2.52	1070 1st	52	20	2254	1757	778	1610	5	124 1st	103	227	432	38	1	.088	114	373	11	17	0.5	.978
WORLD SERIES																											
1954	NY	N	0	0	—	0.00	2	0	0	2.1	1	0	3	0	0	0	1	1	0	0	.000	0	1	1	0	1.0	.500

Kaiser Wilhelm

WILHELM, IRVIN KEY BR TR 6′ 162 lbs.
B. Jan. 26, 1874, Wooster, Ohio D. May 21, 1936, Rochester, N. Y.
Manager 1921–22.

Year	Team	Lg	W	L	PCT	ERA	G	GS	CG	IP	H	BB	SO	ShO	Relief W	Relief L	Relief SV	AB	H	HR	BA	PO	A	E	DP	TC/G	FA
1903	PIT	N	5	4	.556	3.24	12	9	7	86	88	25	20	1	0	0	0	34	3	0	.088	2	35	2	2	3.0	.949
1904	BOS	N	14	22	.389	3.69	39	36	30	288	316	74	73	3	0	1	0	100	7	0	.070	10	90	7	3	2.7	.935
1905			3	22	.120	4.54	34	28	23	242	287	75	76	0	0	0	1	100	16	0	.160	24	77	7	2	2.8	.935
1908	BKN	N	16	22	.421	1.87	42	36	33	332	266	83	99	6	1	2	0	111	12	0	.108	17	109	6	3	3.1	.955
1909			3	13	.188	3.26	22	17	14	163	176	59	45	1	0	0	0	57	13	0	.228	3	56	6	0	3.0	.908
1910			3	7	.300	4.74	15	5	0	68.1	88	18	17	0	3	2	0	19	6	0	.316	2	24	1	0	1.8	.963
1914	BAL	F	12	17	.414	4.03	47	27	11	243.2	263	81	113	1	5	2	4	84	21	0	.250	14	82	4	1	2.1	.960
1915			0	0	—	0.00	1	0	0	1	0	0	0	0	0	0	0	0	0	0	—	0	0	0	0	0.0	.000
1921	PHI	N	0	0	—	3.38	4	0	0	8	11	3	1	0	0	0	0	2	0	0	.000	1	1	0	0	0.5	1.000
9 yrs.			56	107	.344	3.44	216	158	118	1432	1495	418	444	12	9	7	5	507	78	0	.154	73	474	33	11	2.6	.943

Lefty Wilkie

WILKIE, ALDON JAY BL TL 5′11½″ 175 lbs.
B. Oct. 30, 1914, Zealandia, Sask., Canada D. Aug. 5, 1992, Tualatin, Ore.

Year	Team	Lg	W	L	PCT	ERA	G	GS	CG	IP	H	BB	SO	ShO	Relief W	Relief L	Relief SV	AB	H	HR	BA	PO	A	E	DP	TC/G	FA
1941	PIT	N	2	4	.333	4.56	26	6	2	79	90	40	16	1	2	4	2	24	7	0	.292	2	22	0	1	0.9	1.000
1942			6	7	.462	4.19	35	6	3	107.1	112	37	18	0	3	4	1	38	10	0	.263	3	36	1	0	1.1	.975
1946			0	0	—	10.57	7	0	0	7.2	13	3	3	0	0	0	0	0	0	0	—	0	1	0	0	0.1	1.000
3 yrs.			8	11	.421	4.59	68	12	5	194	215	80	37	1	5	8	3	62	17	0	.274	5	59	1	1	1.0	.985

Dean Wilkins

WILKINS, DEAN ALLAN BR TR 6′1″ 170 lbs.
B. Aug. 24, 1966, Blue Island, Ill.

Year	Team	Lg	W	L	PCT	ERA	G	GS	CG	IP	H	BB	SO	ShO	Relief W	Relief L	Relief SV	AB	H	HR	BA	PO	A	E	DP	TC/G	FA
1989	CHI	N	1	0	1.000	5.17	11	0	0	15.2	13	9	14	0	1	0	0	1	0	0	.000	1	3	0	0	0.4	1.000
1990			0	0	—	9.82	7	0	0	7.1	11	7	3	0	0	0	1	0	0	0	—	0	0	0	0	0.0	.000
1991	HOU	N	2	1	.667	11.25	7	0	0	8	16	10	4	0	2	1	1	1	0	0	.000	1	0	0	0	0.1	1.000
3 yrs.			3	1	.750	7.84	25	0	0	31	40	26	21	0	3	1	2	2	0	0	.000	2	3	0	0	0.2	1.000

Eric Wilkins

WILKINS, ERIC LAMOINE BR TR 6′1″ 190 lbs.
B. Dec. 9, 1956, St. Louis, Mo.

Year	Team	Lg	W	L	PCT	ERA	G	GS	CG	IP	H	BB	SO	ShO	Relief W	Relief L	Relief SV	AB	H	HR	BA	PO	A	E	DP	TC/G	FA
1979	CLE	A	2	4	.333	4.37	16	14	0	70	77	38	52	0	1	0	0	0	0	0	—	4	12	6	2	1.4	.727

Bill Wilkinson

WILKINSON, WILLIAM CARL BR TL 5′10″ 160 lbs.
B. Aug. 10, 1964, Greybull, Wyo.

Year	Team	Lg	W	L	PCT	ERA	G	GS	CG	IP	H	BB	SO	ShO	Relief W	Relief L	Relief SV	AB	H	HR	BA	PO	A	E	DP	TC/G	FA
1985	SEA	A	0	2	.000	13.50	2	2	0	6	8	6	5	0	0	0	0	0	0	0	—	0	2	0	0	1.0	1.000
1987			3	4	.429	3.66	56	0	0	76.1	61	21	73	0	3	4	10	0	0	0	—	1	6	1	0	0.1	.875
1988			2	2	.500	3.48	30	0	0	31	28	15	25	0	2	2	2	0	0	0	—	1	1	0	1	0.1	1.000
3 yrs.			5	8	.385	4.13	88	2	0	113.1	97	42	103	0	5	6	12	0	0	0		2	9	1	1	0.1	.917

Roy Wilkinson

WILKINSON, ROY HAMILTON BR TR 6′1″ 170 lbs.
B. May 8, 1894, Canandaigua, N. Y. D. July 2, 1956, Louisville, Ky.

Year	Team	Lg	W	L	PCT	ERA	G	GS	CG	IP	H	BB	SO	ShO	Relief W	Relief L	Relief SV	AB	H	HR	BA	PO	A	E	DP	TC/G	FA
1918	CLE	A	0	0	—	0.00	1	0	0	1	0	0	0	0	0	0	0	0	0	0	—	0	0	0	0	0.0	.000
1919	CHI	A	1	1	.500	2.05	4	1	1	22	21	10	5	1	0	1	0	8	3	0	.375	0	11	0	1	2.8	1.000
1920			7	9	.438	4.03	34	12	9	145	162	48	30	0	5	0	2	48	7	0	.146	3	27	1	1	0.9	.968
1921			4	20	.167	5.13	36	22	11	198.1	259	78	50	0	0	3	3	65	8	0	.123	12	76	1	1	2.5	.989
1922			0	1	.000	8.79	4	1	0	14.1	24	6	3	0	0	0	1	3	0	0	.000	1	3	0	0	1.0	1.000
5 yrs.			12	31	.279	4.66	79	36	21	380.2	466	142	88	1	5	4	6	124	18	0	.145	16	117	2	3	1.7	.985
WORLD SERIES																											
1919	CHI	A	0	0	—	3.68	2	0	0	7.1	9	4	3	0	0	0	0	2	0	0	.000	0	2	0	0	1.0	1.000

Ted Wilks

WILKS, THEODORE (Cork) BR TR 5′ 9½″ 178 lbs.
B. Nov. 13, 1915, Fulton, N. Y. D. Aug. 21, 1989, Houston, Tex.

Year	Team	W	L	PCT	ERA	G	GS	CG	IP	H	BB	SO	ShO	Relief W	Relief L	Relief SV	Batting AB	Batting H	HR	BA	PO	A	E	DP	TC/G	FA
1944	STL N	17	4	**.810**	2.65	36	21	16	207.1	173	49	70	4	2	1	0	64	9	0	.141	6	20	0	3	0.7	1.000
1945		4	7	.364	2.93	18	16	4	98.1	103	29	28	1	0	0	0	30	4	0	.133	1	12	1	0	0.8	.929
1946		8	0	1.000	3.41	40	4	0	95	88	38	40	0	6	0	1	24	5	0	.208	2	16	1	3	0.5	.947
1947		4	0	1.000	5.01	37	0	0	50.1	57	11	28	0	4	0	5	6	1	0	.167	2	9	1	0	0.3	.917
1948		6	6	.500	2.62	57	2	1	130.2	113	39	71	0	5	6	13	30	5	0	.167	6	19	0	1	0.4	1.000
1949		10	3	.769	3.73	**59**	0	0	118.1	105	38	71	0	**10**	3	**9**	27	1	0	.037	4	10	4	0	0.3	.778
1950		2	0	1.000	6.66	18	0	0	24.1	27	9	15	0	2	0	0	4	0	0	.000	1	4	0	0	0.3	1.000
1951	2 teams STL N	(17G 0–0)	PIT N	(48G 3–5)																						
″	total	3	5	.375	2.86	**65**	1	1	100.2	88	29	48	0	2	5	**13**	13	1	0	.077	5	18	0	1	0.4	1.000
1952	2 teams PIT N	(44G 5–5)	CLE A	(7G 0–0)																						
″	total	5	5	.500	3.64	51	0	0	84	73	38	30	0	5	5	5	8	1	0	.125	3	12	1	1	0.3	.938
1953	CLE A	0	0	—	7.36	4	0	0	3.2	5	3	2	0	0	0	0	0	0	0	—	0	0	0	0	0.0	.000
10 yrs.		59	30	.663	3.26	385	44	22	912.2	832	283	403	5	36	20	46	206	27	0	.131	30	120	8	9	0.4	.949
WORLD SERIES																										
1944	STL N	0	1	.000	5.68	2	1	0	6.1	5	3	7	0	0	0	1	2	0	0	.000	0	1	0	0	0.5	1.000
1946		0	0	—	0.00	1	0	0	1	2	0	0	0	0	0	0	0	0	0	—	0	1	0	0	1.0	1.000
2 yrs.		0	1	.000	4.91	3	1	0	7.1	7	3	7	0	0	0	1	2	0	0	.000	0	2	0	0	0.7	1.000

Ed Willett

WILLETT, ROBERT EDGAR BR TR 6′ 183 lbs.
B. Mar. 7, 1884, Norfolk, Va. D. May 10, 1934, Wellington, Kans.

Year	Team	W	L	PCT	ERA	G	GS	CG	IP	H	BB	SO	ShO	Relief W	Relief L	Relief SV	Batting AB	Batting H	HR	BA	PO	A	E	DP	TC/G	FA
1906	DET A	0	3	.000	3.96	3	3	3	25	24	8	16	0	0	0	0	9	0	0	.000	3	9	0	0	4.0	1.000
1907		1	5	.167	3.70	10	6	1	48.2	47	20	27	0	0	0	0	13	1	0	.077	3	18	1	0	2.2	.955
1908		15	8	.652	2.28	30	22	18	197.1	186	60	77	2	0	1	1	67	11	0	.164	14	81	4	3	3.3	.960
1909		21	10	.677	2.34	41	34	25	292.2	239	76	89	3	0	2	1	112	22	0	.196	14	92	8	2	2.7	.930
1910		16	11	.593	3.60	37	25	18	147.1	175	74	65	4	1	2	0	83	11	0	.133	6	113	7	2	3.3	.944
1911		13	14	.481	3.66	38	27	15	231.1	261	80	86	2	2	3	1	82	22	1	.268	5	84	3	2	2.4	.967
1912		17	15	.531	3.29	37	31	28	284.1	281	84	89	1	2	1	0	115	19	2	.165	12	113	7	2	3.6	.947
1913		13	14	.481	3.09	34	30	19	242	237	89	59	0	1	1	0	92	26	1	.283	8	93	5	3	3.1	.953
1914	STL F	4	16	.200	4.22	27	21	14	175	208	56	73	0	0	1	0	64	15	1	.234	6	76	4	2	3.2	.953
1915		2	3	.400	4.61	17	2	1	52.2	61	18	19	0	1	3	2	15	3	0	.200	2	17	3	2	1.3	.864
10 yrs.		102	99	.507	3.22	274	201	142	1696.1	1719	565	600	12	7	14	5	652	130	5	.199	73	696	42	18	2.9	.948
WORLD SERIES																										
1909	DET A	0	0	—	0.00	2	0	0	7.2	3	0	1	0	0	0	0	2	0	0	.000	1	3	1	0	2.5	.800

Carl Willey

WILLEY, CARLTON FRANCIS BR TR 6′ 175 lbs.
B. June 6, 1931, Cherryfield, Me.

Year	Team	W	L	PCT	ERA	G	GS	CG	IP	H	BB	SO	ShO	Relief W	Relief L	Relief SV	Batting AB	Batting H	HR	BA	PO	A	E	DP	TC/G	FA
1958	MIL N	9	7	.563	2.70	23	19	9	140	110	53	74	**4**	0	1	0	48	5	0	.104	6	15	0	1	0.9	1.000
1959		5	9	.357	4.15	26	15	5	117	126	31	51	2	0	2	0	39	4	0	.103	5	17	1	0	0.9	.957
1960		6	7	.462	4.35	28	21	2	144.2	136	65	109	1	1	0	0	48	7	1	.146	8	18	2	0	1.0	.929
1961		6	12	.333	3.83	35	22	4	159.2	147	65	91	0	2	1	0	54	1	0	.019	9	42	0	3	1.5	1.000
1962		2	5	.286	5.40	30	6	0	73.1	95	20	40	0	2	2	1	11	3	0	.273	3	12	1	0	0.5	.938
1963	NY N	9	14	.391	3.10	30	28	7	183	149	69	101	4	0	0	0	54	6	1	.111	20	29	2	0	1.7	.961
1964		0	2	.000	3.60	14	3	0	30	37	8	14	0	0	0	0	4	0	0	.000	3	0	1	0	0.3	.750
1965		1	2	.333	4.18	13	3	1	28	30	15	13	0	0	0	0	5	0	0	.000	1	5	2	1	0.6	.750
8 yrs.		38	58	.396	3.76	199	117	28	875.2	830	326	493	11	5	6	1	263	26	2	.099	55	138	9	5	1.0	.955
WORLD SERIES																										
1958	MIL N	0	0	—	0.00	1	0	0	1	0	0	2	0	0	0	0	0	0	0	—	0	0	0	0	0.0	.000

Nick Willhite

WILLHITE, JON NICHOLAS BL TL 6′ 2″ 190 lbs.
B. Jan. 27, 1941, Tulsa, Okla.

Year	Team	W	L	PCT	ERA	G	GS	CG	IP	H	BB	SO	ShO	Relief W	Relief L	Relief SV	Batting AB	Batting H	HR	BA	PO	A	E	DP	TC/G	FA
1963	LA N	2	3	.400	3.79	8	8	1	38	44	10	28	1	0	0	0	10	3	0	.300	1	3	1	0	0.6	.800
1964		2	4	.333	3.71	10	7	2	43.2	43	13	24	0	0	0	0	11	0	0	.000	3	12	0	1	1.5	1.000
1965	2 teams WAS A	(5G 0–0)	LA N	(15G 2–2)																						
″	total	2	2	.500	5.59	20	6	0	48.1	57	26	31	0	0	2	1	10	4	0	.400	0	9	0	0	0.4	1.000
1966	LA N	0	0	—	2.08	6	0	0	4.1	3	5	4	0	0	0	0	0	0	0	—	0	2	0	0	0.3	1.000
1967	2 teams CAL A	(10G 0–2)	NY N	(4G 0–1)																						
″	total	0	3	.000	5.10	14	8	0	47.2	48	21	31	0	0	0	0	12	0	0	.000	1	9	0	1	0.7	1.000
5 yrs.		6	12	.333	4.55	58	29	3	182	195	75	118	1	0	2	1	43	7	0	.163	5	35	1	2	0.7	.976

Ace Williams

WILLIAMS, ROBERT FULTON BR TL 6′ 2″ 174 lbs.
B. Mar. 18, 1917, Montclair, N. J.

Year	Team	W	L	PCT	ERA	G	GS	CG	IP	H	BB	SO	ShO	Relief W	Relief L	Relief SV	Batting AB	Batting H	HR	BA	PO	A	E	DP	TC/G	FA
1940	BOS N	0	0	—	16.00	5	0	0	9	21	12	5	0	0	0	0	2	0	0	.000	0	4	0	0	0.8	1.000
1946		0	0	—	0.00	1	0	0		1	1	0	0	0	0	0	0	0	0	—	0	0	0	0	0.0	.000
2 yrs.		0	0		16.00	6	0	0	9	22	13	5	0	0	0	0	2	0	0	.000	0	4	0	0	0.7	1.000

Al Williams

WILLIAMS, ALBERT HAMILTON BR TR 6′ 4″ 190 lbs.
Born Albert Hamilton Williams (DeSouza).
B. May 6, 1954, Pearl Lagoon, Nicaragua.

Year	Team	W	L	PCT	ERA	G	GS	CG	IP	H	BB	SO	ShO	Relief W	Relief L	Relief SV	Batting AB	Batting H	HR	BA	PO	A	E	DP	TC/G	FA
1980	MIN A	6	2	.750	3.51	18	9	3	77	73	30	35	0	1	2	1	0	0	0	—	5	9	2	1	0.9	.875
1981		6	10	.375	4.08	23	22	4	150	160	52	76	0	0	0	0	0	0	0	—	9	13	3	2	1.1	.880
1982		9	7	.563	4.22	26	26	3	153.2	166	55	61	0	0	0	0	0	0	0	—	14	23	3	0	1.5	.925
1983		11	14	.440	4.14	36	29	4	193.1	196	68	68	1	1	2	1	0	0	0	—	11	22	3	1	1.0	.917
1984		3	5	.375	5.77	17	11	1	68.2	75	22	22	0	1	0	0	0	0	0	—	4	10	0	1	0.8	1.000
5 yrs.		35	38	.479	4.24	120	97	15	642.2	670	227	262	1	3	4	2	0	0	0		43	77	11	5	1.1	.916

Al Williams

WILLIAMS, ALMON EDWARD BR TR 6′ 3″ 200 lbs.
B. May 11, 1914, Valhermoso Springs, Ala. D. July 19, 1969, Groves, Tex.

Year	Team	W	L	PCT	ERA	G	GS	CG	IP	H	BB	SO	ShO	Relief W	Relief L	Relief SV	Batting AB	Batting H	HR	BA	PO	A	E	DP	TC/G	FA
1937	PHI A	4	1	.800	5.38	16	8	2	75.1	88	49	27	0	1	0	1	24	2	0	.083	2	14	1	5	1.1	.941
1938		0	7	.000	6.94	30	8	1	93.1	128	54	25	0	0	0	0	25	1	0	.040	4	18	2	0	0.8	.917
2 yrs.		4	8	.333	6.24	46	16	3	168.2	216	103	52	0	1	0	1	49	3	0	.061	6	32	3	5	0.9	.927

Brian Williams

WILLIAMS, BRIAN O'NEAL BR TR 6′ 3″ 205 lbs.
B. Feb. 15, 1969, Lancaster, S. C.

Year	Team		W	L	PCT	ERA	G	GS	CG	IP	H	BB	SO	ShO	Relief Pitching W	Relief Pitching L	Relief Pitching SV	Batting AB	Batting H	Batting HR	BA	PO	A	E	DP	TC/G	FA
1991	HOU	N	0	1	.000	3.75	2	2	0	12	11	4	4	0	0	0	0	3	0	0	.000	1	2	0	0	1.5	1.000
1992			7	6	.538	3.92	16	16	0	96.1	92	42	54	0	0	0	0	30	4	0	.133	8	15	2	0	1.6	.920
1993			4	4	.500	4.83	42	5	0	82	76	38	56	0	1	3	3	10	2	0	.200	7	20	1	0	0.7	.964
1994			6	5	.545	5.74	20	13	0	78.1	112	41	49	0	1	0	0	23	6	0	.261	8	9	4	0	1.0	.810
1995	SD	N	3	10	.231	6.00	44	6	0	72	79	38	75	0	1	**8**	0	14	1	0	.071	6	9	0	0	0.3	1.000
5 yrs.			20	26	.435	4.99	124	42	0	340.2	370	163	238	0	3	11	3	80	13	0	.162	30	55	7	0	0.7	.924

Charlie Williams

WILLIAMS, CHARLES PROSEK BR TR 6′ 2″ 200 lbs.
B. Oct. 11, 1947, Flushing, N. Y.

Year	Team		W	L	PCT	ERA	G	GS	CG	IP	H	BB	SO	ShO	Relief Pitching W	Relief Pitching L	Relief Pitching SV	Batting AB	Batting H	Batting HR	BA	PO	A	E	DP	TC/G	FA
1971	NY	N	5	6	.455	4.80	31	9	1	90	92	41	53	0	2	2	0	23	2	0	.087	6	7	2	1	0.5	.867
1972	SF	N	0	2	.000	9.00	3	2	0	9	14	3	3	0	0	0	0	2	0	0	.000	0	0	1	0	0.3	.000
1973			3	0	1.000	6.65	12	2	0	23	32	7	11	0	3	0	0	3	1	0	.333	2	5	0	0	0.6	1.000
1974			1	3	.250	2.79	39	7	0	100	93	31	48	0	1	0	0	22	3	0	.136	5	27	0	2	0.8	1.000
1975			5	3	.625	3.49	55	2	0	98	94	66	45	0	5	2	3	16	2	0	.125	12	18	1	5	0.6	.968
1976			2	0	1.000	2.96	48	2	0	85	80	39	34	0	1	0	1	8	1	0	.125	1	19	3	2	0.5	.870
1977			6	5	.545	4.01	55	8	1	119	116	60	41	0	4	2	0	18	4	0	.222	6	18	1	2	0.5	.960
1978			1	3	.250	5.44	25	1	0	48	60	28	22	0	1	2	0	5	0	0	.000	2	8	0	0	0.4	1.000
8 yrs.			23	22	.511	3.98	268	33	2	572	581	275	257	0	17	8	4	97	13	0	.134	34	102	8	12	0.5	.944

Dale Williams

WILLIAMS, ELISHA ALPHONSO BR TR 5′ 9″ 175 lbs.
B. Oct. 6, 1855, Ludlow, Ky. D. Oct. 22, 1939, Covington, Ky.

Year	Team		W	L	PCT	ERA	G	GS	CG	IP	H	BB	SO	ShO	Relief Pitching W	Relief Pitching L	Relief Pitching SV	Batting AB	Batting H	Batting HR	BA	PO	A	E	DP	TC/G	FA
1876	CIN	N	1	8	.111	4.23	9	9	9	83	123	4	9	0	0	0	0	35	7	0	.200	10	8	0	0	2.0	1.000

Dave Williams

WILLIAMS, DAVID OWEN BR TL 5′11½″ 167 lbs.
B. Feb. 7, 1881, Scranton, Pa. D. Apr. 25, 1918, Hot Springs, Ark.

Year	Team		W	L	PCT	ERA	G	GS	CG	IP	H	BB	SO	ShO	Relief Pitching W	Relief Pitching L	Relief Pitching SV	Batting AB	Batting H	Batting HR	BA	PO	A	E	DP	TC/G	FA
1902	BOS	A	0	0	—	5.30	3	0	0	18.2	22	11	7	0	0	0	0	9	3	0	.333	0	2	0	0	0.7	1.000

Don Williams

WILLIAMS, DONALD FRED BR TR 6′ 2″ 180 lbs.
B. Sept. 14, 1931, Floyd, Va.

Year	Team		W	L	PCT	ERA	G	GS	CG	IP	H	BB	SO	ShO	Relief Pitching W	Relief Pitching L	Relief Pitching SV	Batting AB	Batting H	Batting HR	BA	PO	A	E	DP	TC/G	FA
1958	PIT	N	0	0	—	6.75	2	0	0	4	6	1	3	0	0	0	0	0	0	0	—	1	0	0	0	0.5	1.000
1959			0	0	—	6.75	6	0	0	12	17	3	3	0	0	0	0	3	1	0	.333	0	0	0	0	0.0	.000
1962	KC	A	0	0	—	9.00	3	0	0	4	6	0	1	0	0	0	0	1	0	0	.000	1	0	0	0	0.3	1.000
3 yrs.			0	0		7.20	11	0	0	20	29	4	7	0	0	0	0	4	1	0	.250	2	0	0	0	0.2	1.000

Don Williams

WILLIAMS, DONALD REID (Dino) BR TR 6′ 5″ 218 lbs.
B. Sept. 2, 1935, Los Angeles, Calif. D. Dec. 20, 1991, La Jolla, Calif.

Year	Team		W	L	PCT	ERA	G	GS	CG	IP	H	BB	SO	ShO	Relief Pitching W	Relief Pitching L	Relief Pitching SV	Batting AB	Batting H	Batting HR	BA	PO	A	E	DP	TC/G	FA
1963	MIN	A	0	0	—	10.38	3	0	0	4.1	8	6	2	0	0	0	0	0	0	0	—	2	2	0	0	1.3	1.000

Frank Williams

WILLIAMS, FRANK LEE BR TR 6′ 1″ 180 lbs.
B. Feb. 13, 1958, Seattle, Wash.

Year	Team		W	L	PCT	ERA	G	GS	CG	IP	H	BB	SO	ShO	Relief Pitching W	Relief Pitching L	Relief Pitching SV	Batting AB	Batting H	Batting HR	BA	PO	A	E	DP	TC/G	FA
1984	SF	N	9	4	.692	3.55	61	1	1	106.1	88	51	91	1	8	4	3	18	4	0	.222	4	35	4	2	0.7	.907
1985			2	4	.333	4.19	49	0	0	73	65	35	54	0	2	4	0	3	0	0	.000	4	12	4	2	0.4	.800
1986			3	1	.750	1.20	36	0	0	52.1	35	21	33	0	3	1	1	2	1	0	.500	1	10	0	3	0.3	1.000
1987	CIN	N	4	0	1.000	2.30	85	0	0	105.2	101	39	60	0	4	0	2	5	0	0	.000	8	19	2	5	0.3	.931
1988			3	2	.600	2.59	60	0	0	62.2	59	35	43	0	3	2	1	1	0	0	.000	2	13	4	1	0.3	.789
1989	DET	A	3	3	.500	3.64	42	0	0	71.2	70	46	33	0	3	3	1	0	0	0	—	3	10	0	0	0.3	1.000
6 yrs.			24	14	.632	3.00	333	1	1	471.2	418	227	314	1	23	14	8	29	5	0	.172	22	99	14	13	0.4	.896

Gus Williams

WILLIAMS, AUGUSTINE H. 5′11″ 170 lbs.
B. 1870, New York, N. Y. D. Oct. 14, 1890, New York, N. Y.

Year	Team		W	L	PCT	ERA	G	GS	CG	IP	H	BB	SO	ShO	Relief Pitching W	Relief Pitching L	Relief Pitching SV	Batting AB	Batting H	Batting HR	BA	PO	A	E	DP	TC/G	FA
1890	BKN	AA	0	1	.000	7.50	2	2	1	12	13	12	2	0	0	0	0	4	2	0	.500	0	0	1	0	0.5	.000

Johnny Williams

WILLIAMS, JOHN BRODIE (Honolulu Johnny) BR TR 6′ 180 lbs.
B. July 16, 1889, Honolulu, Hawaii D. Sept. 8, 1963, Long Beach, Calif.

Year	Team		W	L	PCT	ERA	G	GS	CG	IP	H	BB	SO	ShO	Relief Pitching W	Relief Pitching L	Relief Pitching SV	Batting AB	Batting H	Batting HR	BA	PO	A	E	DP	TC/G	FA
1914	DET	A	0	2	.000	6.35	4	3	1	11.1	17	5	4	0	0	0	0	3	0	0	.000	0	2	1	0	0.8	.667

Lefty Williams

WILLIAMS, CLAUDE PRESTON BR TL 5′ 9″ 160 lbs.
B. Mar. 9, 1893, Aurora, Mo. D. Nov. 4, 1959, Laguna Beach, Calif.

Year	Team		W	L	PCT	ERA	G	GS	CG	IP	H	BB	SO	ShO	Relief Pitching W	Relief Pitching L	Relief Pitching SV	Batting AB	Batting H	Batting HR	BA	PO	A	E	DP	TC/G	FA
1913	DET	A	1	3	.250	4.97	5	4	3	29	34	4	9	0	0	0	1	10	1	0	.100	0	3	0	0	0.6	1.000
1914			0	1	.000	0.00	1	1	0	1	3	2	0	0	0	0	0	0	0	0	—	0	0	0	0	0.0	.000
1916	CHI	A	13	7	.650	2.89	43	26	10	224.1	220	65	138	2	1	1	1	74	10	0	.135	9	37	0	0	1.1	1.000
1917			17	8	.680	2.97	45	29	8	230	221	81	85	1	4	2	1	67	6	0	.090	8	46	4	2	1.3	.931
1918			6	4	.600	2.73	15	14	7	105.2	76	47	30	2	0	0	1	38	5	0	.132	3	20	2	0	1.7	.920
1919			23	11	.676	2.64	41	**40**	27	297	265	58	125	5	0	0	1	94	17	0	.181	8	54	3	1	1.6	.954
1920			22	14	.611	3.91	39	38	26	299	302	90	128	0	1	0	0	101	22	0	.218	8	57	3	5	1.7	.956
7 yrs.			82	48	.631	3.13	189	152	81	1186	1121	347	515	10	6	3	5	384	61	0	.159	36	217	12	8	1.4	.955
WORLD SERIES																											
1917	CHI	A	0	0	—	9.00	1	0	0	1	2	0	3	0	0	0	0	0	0	0	—	0	0	1	0	1.0	.000
1919			0	3	.000	6.61	3	3	1	16.1	12	8	4	0	0	0	0	5	1	0	.200	1	2	0	0	1.0	1.000
2 yrs.			0	3	.000	6.75	4	3	1	17.1	14	8	7	0	0	0	0	5	1	0	.200	1	2	1	0	1.0	.750

Leon Williams

WILLIAMS, LEON THEO BL TL 5′10½″ 154 lbs.
B. Dec. 2, 1905, Macon, Ga. D. Nov. 20, 1984, Atlanta, Ga.

Year	Team		W	L	PCT	ERA	G	GS	CG	IP	H	BB	SO	ShO	Relief Pitching W	Relief Pitching L	Relief Pitching SV	Batting AB	Batting H	Batting HR	BA	PO	A	E	DP	TC/G	FA
1926	BKN	N	0	0	—	5.40	8	0	0	8.1	16	2	3	0	0	0	0	5	1	0	.200	0	5	0	0	0.6	1.000

Marsh Williams

WILLIAMS, MARSHALL McDIARMID (Cap) BR TR 6′ 180 lbs.
B. Feb. 21, 1893, Faison, N. C. D. Feb. 22, 1935, Tucson, Ariz.

Year	Team		W	L	PCT	ERA	G	GS	CG	IP	H	BB	SO	ShO	Relief Pitching W	Relief Pitching L	Relief Pitching SV	Batting AB	Batting H	Batting HR	BA	PO	A	E	DP	TC/G	FA
1916	PHI	A	0	6	.000	7.89	10	4	3	51.1	71	31	17	0	0	2	0	19	2	0	.105	2	11	2	1	1.5	.867

Matt Williams

WILLIAMS, MATTHEW EVAN B. July 25, 1959, Houston, Tex. BR TR 6′ 1″ 200 lbs.

Year	Team	Lg	W	L	PCT	ERA	G	GS	CG	IP	H	BB	SO	ShO	Relief W	Relief L	Relief SV	Batting AB	Batting H	Batting HR	BA	PO	A	E	DP	TC/G	FA
1983	TOR	A	1	1	.500	14.63	4	3	0	8	13	7	5	0	0	0	0	0	0	0	—	0	3	0	0	0.8	1.000
1985	TEX	A	2	1	.667	2.42	6	3	0	26	20	10	22	0	1	0	0	0	0	0	—	0	1	1	0	0.3	.500
2 yrs.			3	2	.600	5.29	10	6	0	34	33	17	27	0	1	0	0	0	0	0		0	4	1	0	0.5	.800

Mike Williams

WILLIAMS, MICHAEL DARREN B. July 29, 1968, Radford, Va. BR TR 6′ 2″ 190 lbs.

Year	Team	Lg	W	L	PCT	ERA	G	GS	CG	IP	H	BB	SO	ShO	Relief W	Relief L	Relief SV	Batting AB	Batting H	Batting HR	BA	PO	A	E	DP	TC/G	FA
1992	PHI	N	1	1	.500	5.34	5	5	1	28.2	29	7	5	0	0	0	0	10	4	0	.400	0	5	0	0	1.0	1.000
1993			1	3	.250	5.29	17	4	0	51	50	22	33	0	1	2	0	12	1	0	.083	2	6	0	1	0.5	1.000
1994			2	4	.333	5.01	12	8	0	50.1	61	20	29	0	0	0	0	12	2	0	.167	3	7	0	3	0.8	1.000
1995			3	3	.500	3.29	33	8	0	87.2	78	29	57	0	1	1	0	16	2	0	.125	4	19	1	0	0.7	.958
4 yrs.			7	11	.389	4.42	67	25	1	217.2	218	78	124	0	2	3	0	50	9	0	.180	9	37	1	4	0.7	.979

Mitch Williams

WILLIAMS, MITCHELL STEVEN (Wild Thing) B. Nov. 17, 1964, Santa Ana, Calif. BL TL 6′ 3″ 180 lbs.

Year	Team	Lg	W	L	PCT	ERA	G	GS	CG	IP	H	BB	SO	ShO	Relief W	Relief L	Relief SV	Batting AB	Batting H	Batting HR	BA	PO	A	E	DP	TC/G	FA
1986	TEX	A	8	6	.571	3.58	**80**	0	0	98	69	79	90	0	8	6	8	0	0	0	—	1	10	2	1	0.2	.846
1987			8	6	.571	3.23	85	1	0	108.2	63	94	129	0	8	5	6	0	0	0	—	5	15	3	3	0.3	.870
1988			2	7	.222	4.63	67	0	0	68	48	47	61	0	2	7	18	0	0	0	—	3	10	1	0	0.2	.929
1989	CHI	N	4	4	.500	2.64	**76**	0	0	81.2	71	52	67	0	4	4	36	5	1	1	.200	0	11	3	0	0.2	.786
1990			1	8	.111	3.93	59	2	0	66.1	60	50	55	0	1	7	16	5	0	0	.000	1	5	0	0	0.1	1.000
1991	PHI	N	12	5	.706	2.34	69	0	0	88.1	56	62	84	0	**12**	5	30	1	0	0	.000	0	8	3	0	0.2	.727
1992			5	8	.385	3.78	66	0	0	81	69	64	74	0	5	8	29	4	1	0	.250	1	11	3	0	0.2	.800
1993			3	7	.300	3.34	65	0	0	62	56	44	60	0	3	7	43	1	1	0	1.000	2	3	2	0	0.1	.714
1994	HOU	N	1	4	.200	7.65	25	0	0	20	21	24	21	0	1	4	6	0	0	0	—	0	1	0	0	0.0	1.000
1995	CAL	A	1	2	.333	6.75	20	0	0	10.2	13	21	9	0	1	2	0	0	0	0	—	1	1	0	0	0.1	1.000
10 yrs.			45	57	.441	3.56	612	3	0	684.2	526	537	650	0	45	55	192	16	3	1	.188	14	75	17	4	0.2	.840
LEAGUE CHAMPIONSHIP SERIES																											
1989	CHI	N	0	0	—	0.00	2	0	0	1	1	0	2	0	0	0	0	0	0	0	—	0	0	0	0	0.0	.000
1993	PHI	N	2	0	1.000	1.69	4	0	0	5.1	6	2	5	0	2	0	2	0	0	0	—	0	1	1	0	0.5	.500
2 yrs.			2	0	1.000	1.42	6	0	0	6.1	7	2	7	0	2	0	2	0	0	0		0	1	1	0	0.3	.500
WORLD SERIES																											
1993	PHI	N	0	2	.000	20.25	3	0	0	2.2	5	4	1	0	0	2	1	0	0	0	—	0	1	0	0	0.3	1.000

Mutt Williams

WILLIAMS, DAVID CARTER B. July 31, 1891, Ozark, Ark. D. Mar. 30, 1962, Fayetteville, Ark. BR TR 6′ 3½″ 195 lbs.

Year	Team	Lg	W	L	PCT	ERA	G	GS	CG	IP	H	BB	SO	ShO	Relief W	Relief L	Relief SV	Batting AB	Batting H	Batting HR	BA	PO	A	E	DP	TC/G	FA
1913	WAS	A	1	0	1.000	4.50	1	1	0	4	4	2	1	0	0	0	0	2	1	0	.500	1	2	1	0	4.0	.750
1914			0	0	—	5.14	5	0	0	7	5	4	3	0	0	0	1	0	0	0	—	0	0	0	0	0.0	.000
2 yrs.			1	0	1.000	4.91	6	1	0	11	9	6	4	0	0	0	1	2	1	0	.500	1	2	1	0	0.7	.750

Pop Williams

WILLIAMS, WALTER MERRILL B. May 19, 1874, Bowdoinham, Me. D. Aug. 4, 1959, Topsham, Me. BL TL 5′11″ 190 lbs.

Year	Team	Lg	W	L	PCT	ERA	G	GS	CG	IP	H	BB	SO	ShO	Relief W	Relief L	Relief SV	Batting AB	Batting H	Batting HR	BA	PO	A	E	DP	TC/G	FA
1898	WAS	N	0	2	.000	8.47	2	2	2	17	32	7	3	0	0	0	0	8	3	0	.375	0	2	1	0	1.5	.667
1902	CHI	N	12	16	.429	2.51	31	31	26	254.1	259	63	94	1	0	0	0	116	23	0	.198	20	78	5	1	2.8	.951
1903	3 teams	CHI N (1G 0–1) PHI N (2G 1–1) BOS N (10G 4–5)																									
″	total		5	7	.417	3.99	13	13	12	106	127	43	30	1	0	0	0	51	12	0	.235	11	29	3	2	2.9	.930
3 yrs.			17	25	.405	3.20	46	46	40	377.1	418	113	127	2	0	0	0	175	38	0	.217	31	109	9	3	2.8	.940

Rick Williams

WILLIAMS, RICHARD ALLEN B. Nov. 9, 1952, Merced, Calif. BR TR 6′ 1″ 180 lbs.

Year	Team	Lg	W	L	PCT	ERA	G	GS	CG	IP	H	BB	SO	ShO	Relief W	Relief L	Relief SV	Batting AB	Batting H	Batting HR	BA	PO	A	E	DP	TC/G	FA
1978	HOU	N	1	2	.333	4.63	17	1	0	35	43	10	17	0	1	1	0	5	0	0	.000	1	7	1	0	0.5	.889
1979			4	7	.364	3.27	31	16	2	121	122	30	37	2	0	0	0	31	8	0	.258	3	23	1	2	0.9	.963
2 yrs.			5	9	.357	3.58	48	17	2	156	165	40	54	2	1	1	0	36	8	0	.222	4	30	2	2	0.8	.944

Stan Williams

WILLIAMS, STANLEY WILSON B. Sept. 14, 1936, Enfield, N. H. BR TR 6′ 5″ 230 lbs.

Year	Team	Lg	W	L	PCT	ERA	G	GS	CG	IP	H	BB	SO	ShO	Relief W	Relief L	Relief SV	Batting AB	Batting H	Batting HR	BA	PO	A	E	DP	TC/G	FA
1958	LA	N	9	7	.563	4.01	27	21	3	119	99	65	80	2	1	1	0	40	2	1	.050	10	16	1	1	1.0	.963
1959			5	5	.500	3.97	35	15	2	124.2	102	86	89	0	2	2	0	36	7	0	.194	6	21	0	1	0.8	1.000
1960			14	10	.583	3.00	38	30	9	207.1	162	72	175	2	0	0	1	64	9	2	.141	15	33	1	2	1.3	.980
1961			15	12	.556	3.90	41	35	6	235.1	213	108	205	2	1	0	0	78	13	0	.167	12	37	7	3	1.4	.875
1962			14	12	.538	4.46	40	28	4	185.2	184	98	108	1	1	1	1	66	5	2	.076	8	28	2	3	0.9	.947
1963	NY	A	9	8	.529	3.20	29	21	6	146.1	137	57	98	1	2	2	0	49	5	0	.102	9	25	2	2	1.2	.944
1964			1	5	.167	3.84	21	10	1	82	76	38	54	0	1	1	0	21	3	0	.143	8	15	2	1	1.2	.920
1965	CLE	A	0	0	—	6.23	3	0	0	4.1	6	3	1	0	0	0	0	0	0	0	—	0	1	0	0	0.3	1.000
1967			6	4	.600	2.62	16	8	2	79	64	24	75	1	3	0	1	22	2	0	.091	4	4	1	0	0.6	.889
1968			13	11	.542	2.50	44	24	6	194.1	163	51	147	2	2	0	9	56	9	0	.161	7	27	1	2	0.8	.971
1969			6	14	.300	3.94	61	15	3	178.1	155	67	139	0	2	9	12	40	4	0	.100	15	19	3	1	0.6	.919
1970	MIN	A	10	1	.909	1.99	68	0	0	113	85	32	76	0	**10**	1	15	19	0	0	.000	8	8	0	0	0.2	1.000
1971	2 teams	MIN A (46G 4–5) STL N (10G 3–0)																									
″	total		7	5	.583	3.76	56	1	0	91	76	46	55	0	7	5	4	11	0	0	.000	7	11	1	1	0.3	.947
1972	BOS	A	0	0	—	6.75	3	0	0	4	5	1	3	0	0	0	0	0	0	0	—	0	1	0	0	0.3	1.000
14 yrs.			109	94	.537	3.48	482	208	42	1764.1	1527	748	1305	11	32	22	43	502	59	5	.118	109	246	21	17	0.8	.944
LEAGUE CHAMPIONSHIP SERIES																											
1970	MIN	A	0	0	—	0.00	2	0	0	6	2	1	2	0	0	0	0	0	0	0	—	0	0	0	0	0.0	.000
WORLD SERIES																											
1959	LA	N	0	0	—	0.00	1	0	0	2	0	2	1	0	0	0	0	0	0	0	—	0	0	0	0	0.0	.000
1963	NY	A	0	0	—	0.00	1	0	0	3	1	0	5	0	0	0	0	0	0	0	—	0	0	0	0	0.0	.000
2 yrs.			0	0		0.00	2	0	0	5	1	2	6	0	0	0	0	0	0	0		0	0	0	0	0.0	

Steamboat Williams

WILLIAMS, REES GEPHARDT B. Jan. 31, 1892, Cascade, Mont. D. June 29, 1979, Deer River, Minn. BL TR 5′11″ 170 lbs.

Year	Team	Lg	W	L	PCT	ERA	G	GS	CG	IP	H	BB	SO	ShO	Relief W	Relief L	Relief SV	Batting AB	Batting H	Batting HR	BA	PO	A	E	DP	TC/G	FA
1914	STL	N	0	1	.000	6.55	5	1	0	11	13	6	2	0	0	0	0	1	0	0	.000	0	3	0	0	0.6	1.000
1916			6	7	.462	4.20	36	8	5	105	121	27	25	0	4	2	1	24	5	0	.208	1	31	5	1	1.0	.865
2 yrs.			6	8	.429	4.42	41	9	5	116	134	33	27	0	4	2	1	25	5	0	.200	1	34	5	1	1.0	.875

Ted Williams

WILLIAMS, THEODORE SAMUEL (The Splendid Splinter, The Thumper) BL TR 6′ 3″ 205 lbs.
B. Aug. 30, 1918, San Diego, Calif.
Manager 1969–72.
Hall of Fame 1966.

Year	Team	Lg	W	L	PCT	ERA	G	GS	CG	IP	H	BB	SO	ShO	Relief Pitching W	Relief Pitching L	Relief Pitching SV	Batting AB	Batting H	Batting HR	BA	PO	A	E	DP	TC/G	FA
1940	**BOS**	**A**	0	0	—	4.50	1	0	0	2	3	0	1	0	0	0	0	*				318	11	19	3	2.3	.945

Todd Williams

WILLIAMS, TODD MICHAEL BR TR 6′ 3″ 185 lbs.
B. Feb. 13, 1971, Syracuse, N. Y.

Year	Team	Lg	W	L	PCT	ERA	G	GS	CG	IP	H	BB	SO	ShO	Relief Pitching W	Relief Pitching L	Relief Pitching SV	Batting AB	Batting H	Batting HR	BA	PO	A	E	DP	TC/G	FA
1995	**LA**	**N**	2	2	.500	5.12	16	0	0	19.1	19	7	8	0	2	2	0	2	1	0	.500	2	5	0	1	0.4	1.000

Tom Williams

WILLIAMS, THOMAS C.
B. Aug. 19, 1870, Minersville, Ohio D. July 27, 1940, Columbus, Ohio.

Year	Team	Lg	W	L	PCT	ERA	G	GS	CG	IP	H	BB	SO	ShO	Relief Pitching W	Relief Pitching L	Relief Pitching SV	Batting AB	Batting H	Batting HR	BA	PO	A	E	DP	TC/G	FA
1892	**CLE**	**N**	1	0	1.000	3.00	2	1	1	9	9	1	3	0	0	0	0	10	1	0	.100	1	2	1	0	1.3	.750
1893			1	1	.500	4.88	5	2	2	24	33	10	6	0	0	0	0	18	5	0	.278	3	7	6	0	2.0	.625
2 yrs.			2	1	.667	4.36	7	3	3	33	42	11	9	0	0	0	0	28	6	0	.214	4	9	7	0	1.8	.650

Wash Williams

WILLIAMS, WASHINGTON J. 5′11″ 180 lbs.
B. Philadelphia, Pa. D. Aug. 9, 1892, Philadelphia, Pa.

Year	Team	Lg	W	L	PCT	ERA	G	GS	CG	IP	H	BB	SO	ShO	Relief Pitching W	Relief Pitching L	Relief Pitching SV	Batting AB	Batting H	Batting HR	BA	PO	A	E	DP	TC/G	FA
1885	**CHI**	**N**	0	0	—	*13.50*	1	1	0	2	2	5	0	0	0	0	0	*				1	0	1	0	1.0	.500

Woody Williams

WILLIAMS, GREGORY SCOTT BR TR 6′ 180 lbs.
B. Aug. 19, 1966, Houston, Tex.

Year	Team	Lg	W	L	PCT	ERA	G	GS	CG	IP	H	BB	SO	ShO	Relief Pitching W	Relief Pitching L	Relief Pitching SV	Batting AB	Batting H	Batting HR	BA	PO	A	E	DP	TC/G	FA
1993	**TOR**	**A**	3	1	.750	4.38	30	0	0	37	40	22	24	0	3	1	0	0	0	0	—	5	6	0	1	0.4	1.000
1994			1	3	.250	3.64	38	0	0	59.1	44	33	56	0	1	3	0	0	0	0	—	2	6	1	2	0.2	.889
1995			1	2	.333	3.69	23	3	0	53.2	44	28	41	0	0	2	0	0	0	0	—	6	6	0	0	0.5	1.000
3 yrs.			5	6	.455	3.84	91	3	0	150	128	83	121	0	4	6	0	0	0	0		13	18	1	3	0.4	.969

Al Williamson

WILLIAMSON, SILAS ALBERT BR TR 5′11″ 160 lbs.
B. Feb. 20, 1900, Buckville, Ark. D. Nov. 29, 1978, Hot Springs, Ark.

Year	Team	Lg	W	L	PCT	ERA	G	GS	CG	IP	H	BB	SO	ShO	Relief Pitching W	Relief Pitching L	Relief Pitching SV	Batting AB	Batting H	Batting HR	BA	PO	A	E	DP	TC/G	FA
1928	**CHI**	**A**	0	0	—	0.00	1	0	0	2	1	0	0	0	0	0	0	0	0	0	—	1	0	0	0	1.0	1.000

Mark Williamson

WILLIAMSON, MARK ALAN BR TR 6′ 155 lbs.
B. July 21, 1959, Corpus Christi, Tex.

Year	Team	Lg	W	L	PCT	ERA	G	GS	CG	IP	H	BB	SO	ShO	Relief Pitching W	Relief Pitching L	Relief Pitching SV	Batting AB	Batting H	Batting HR	BA	PO	A	E	DP	TC/G	FA
1987	**BAL**	**A**	8	9	.471	4.03	61	2	0	125	122	41	73	0	8	**8**	3	0	0	0	—	20	17	2	1	0.6	.949
1988			5	8	.385	4.90	37	10	2	117.2	125	40	69	0	4	2	2	0	0	0	—	9	14	1	0	0.6	.958
1989			10	5	.667	2.93	65	0	0	107.1	105	30	55	0	10	5	9	0	0	0	—	9	10	0	1	0.3	1.000
1990			8	2	.800	2.21	49	0	0	85.1	65	28	60	0	8	2	1	0	0	0	—	14	13	2	2	0.6	.931
1991			5	5	.500	4.48	65	0	0	80.1	87	35	53	0	5	5	4	0	0	0	—	7	9	2	0	0.3	.889
1992			0	0	—	0.96	12	0	0	18.2	16	10	14	0	0	0	1	0	0	0	—	1	0	0	0	0.1	1.000
1993			7	5	.583	4.91	48	1	0	88	106	25	45	0	7	5	0	0	0	0	—	8	10	0	0	0.4	1.000
1994			3	1	.750	4.01	28	2	0	67.1	75	17	28	0	3	0	1	0	0	0	—	8	3	0	0	0.4	1.000
8 yrs.			46	35	.568	3.86	365	15	2	689.2	701	226	397	0	45	27	21	0	0	0		76	76	7	4	0.4	.956

Ned Williamson

WILLIAMSON, EDWARD NAGLE BR TR 5′11″ 210 lbs.
B. Oct. 24, 1857, Philadelphia, Pa. D. Mar. 3, 1894, Willow Springs, Ark.

Year	Team	Lg	W	L	PCT	ERA	G	GS	CG	IP	H	BB	SO	ShO	Relief Pitching W	Relief Pitching L	Relief Pitching SV	Batting AB	Batting H	Batting HR	BA	PO	A	E	DP	TC/G	FA
1881	**CHI**	**N**	1	1	.500	2.00	3	1	1	18	14	0	2	0	0	0	0	343	92	1	.268	88	128	33	6	4.0	.867
1882			0	0	—	6.00	1	0	0	3	9	1	0	0	0	0	0	348	98	3	.282	108	211	43	16	4.3	.881
1883			0	0	—	9.00	1	0	0	1	1	1	1	0	0	0	0	402	111	2	.276	115	257	88	20	4.6	.809
1884			0	0	—	*18.00*	2	0	0	2	8	2	0	0	0	0	0	417	116	27	.278	155	271	67	26	4.4	.864
1885			0	0	—	0.00	2	0	0	6	2	0	3	0	0	0	**2**	407	97	3	.238	120	261	45	18	3.7	.894
1886			0	0	—	0.00	2	0	0	3	2	0	1	0	0	0	1	430	93	6	.216	162	356	79	36	4.7	.868
1887			0	0	—	9.00	1	0	0	2	2	1	0	0	0	0	0	439	117	9	.267	133	362	61	31	4.3	.890
7 yrs.			1	1	.500	3.34	12	1	1	35	38	5	7	0	0	0	3	*				1589	3095	684	257	4.4	.873

Carl Willis

WILLIS, CARL BLAKE BL TR 6′ 4″ 210 lbs.
B. Dec. 28, 1960, Danville, Va.

Year	Team	Lg	W	L	PCT	ERA	G	GS	CG	IP	H	BB	SO	ShO	Relief Pitching W	Relief Pitching L	Relief Pitching SV	Batting AB	Batting H	Batting HR	BA	PO	A	E	DP	TC/G	FA
1984	**2 teams**	**DET A** (10G 0–2)	**CIN N** (7G 0–1)																								
″	**total**		0	3	.000	5.96	17	2	0	25.2	33	7	7	0	0	2	1	0	0	0		1	5	0	1	0.4	1.000
1985	**CIN**	**N**	1	0	1.000	9.22	11	0	0	13.2	21	5	6	0	1	0	1	1	0	0	.000	0	1	1	0	0.2	.500
1986			1	3	.250	4.47	29	0	0	52.1	54	32	24	0	1	3	0	3	1	0	.333	4	10	0	3	0.5	1.000
1988	**CHI**	**A**	0	0	—	8.25	6	0	0	12	17	7	6	0	0	0	0	0	0	0	—	3	0	0	0	0.5	1.000
1991	**MIN**	**A**	8	3	.727	2.63	40	0	0	89	76	19	53	0	8	3	2	0	0	0	—	4	8	1	0	0.3	.923
1992			7	3	.700	2.72	59	0	0	79.1	73	11	45	0	7	3	1	0	0	0	—	6	6	1	1	0.2	.923
1993			3	0	1.000	3.10	53	0	0	58	56	17	44	0	3	0	5	0	0	0	—	2	6	0	0	0.2	1.000
1994			2	4	.333	5.92	49	0	0	59.1	89	12	37	0	2	4	3	0	0	0	—	2	5	0	0	0.1	1.000
1995			0	0	—	94.50	3	0	0	0.2	5	5	0	0	0	0	0	0	0	0	—	0	0	0	0	0.0	.000
9 yrs.			22	16	.579	4.25	267	2	0	390	424	115	222	0	22	15	13	4	1	0	.250	22	41	3	5	0.2	.955
LEAGUE CHAMPIONSHIP SERIES																											
1991	**MIN**	**A**	0	0	—	0.00	3	0	0	5.1	2	0	3	0	0	0	0	0	0	0	—	0	0	0	0	0.0	.000
WORLD SERIES																											
1991	**MIN**	**A**	0	0	—	5.14	4	0	0	7	6	2	2	0	0	0	0	0	0	0	—	1	0	0	0	0.3	1.000

Dale Willis

WILLIS, DALE JEROME BR TR 5′11″ 165 lbs.
B. May 29, 1938, Calhoun, Ga.

Year	Team	Lg	W	L	PCT	ERA	G	GS	CG	IP	H	BB	SO	ShO	Relief Pitching W	Relief Pitching L	Relief Pitching SV	Batting AB	Batting H	Batting HR	BA	PO	A	E	DP	TC/G	FA
1963	**KC**	**A**	0	2	.000	5.04	25	0	0	44.2	46	25	47	0	0	2	1	6	1	0	.167	4	8	1	0	0.5	.923

Jim Willis

WILLIS, JAMES GLADDEN BL TR 6′ 3″ 175 lbs.
B. Mar. 20, 1927, Doyline, La.

Year	Team	Lg	W	L	PCT	ERA	G	GS	CG	IP	H	BB	SO	ShO	Relief Pitching W	Relief Pitching L	Relief Pitching SV	Batting AB	Batting H	Batting HR	BA	PO	A	E	DP	TC/G	FA
1953	**CHI**	**N**	2	1	.667	3.12	13	3	2	43.1	37	17	15	0	0	0	0	9	0	0	.000	4	12	0	0	1.2	1.000
1954			0	1	.000	3.91	14	1	0	23	22	18	5	0	0	0	0	5	0	0	.000	0	8	0	1	0.6	1.000
2 yrs.			2	2	.500	3.39	27	4	2	66.1	59	35	20	0	0	0	0	14	0	0	.000	4	20	0	1	0.9	1.000

Joe Willis

WILLIS, JOSEPH DANK (Big Joe) BR TL 6′ 1″ 185 lbs.
B. Apr. 9, 1890, Coal Grove, Ohio D. Dec. 4, 1966, Ironton, Ohio.

Year	Team	Lg	W	L	PCT	ERA	G	GS	CG	IP	H	BB	SO	ShO	Relief W	Relief L	Relief SV	AB	H	HR	BA	PO	A	E	DP	TC/G	FA
1911	2 teams	STL A (1G 0–1)	STL N (2G 0–1)																								
″	total		0	2	.000	4.50	3	3	1	22	21	7	5	0	0	0	0	7	0	0	.000	0	5	0	0	1.7	1.000
1912	STL	N	4	9	.308	4.44	31	17	4	129.2	143	62	55	0	1	2	2	38	6	0	.158	3	26	0	4	0.9	1.000
1913			0	0	—	7.45	7	0	0	9.2	9	11	6	0	0	0	1	3	0	0	.000	0	2	0	0	0.3	1.000
3 yrs.			4	11	.267	4.63	41	20	5	161.1	173	80	66	0	1	2	3	48	6	0	.125	3	33	0	4	0.9	1.000

Lefty Willis

WILLIS, CHARLES WILLIAM BL TL 6′ 1″ 175 lbs.
B. Nov. 4, 1905, Leetown, W. Va. D. May 10, 1962, Bethesda, Md. BR 1925

Year	Team	Lg	W	L	PCT	ERA	G	GS	CG	IP	H	BB	SO	ShO	Relief W	Relief L	Relief SV	AB	H	HR	BA	PO	A	E	DP	TC/G	FA
1925	PHI	A	0	0	—	10.80	1	1	0	5	9	2	3	0	0	0	0	3	0	0	.000	0	2	0	0	2.0	1.000
1926			0	0	—	1.39	13	1	0	32.1	31	12	13	0	0	0	1	9	2	0	.222	1	6	1	1	0.6	.875
1927			3	1	.750	5.67	15	2	1	27	32	11	7	0	2	0	0	6	0	0	.000	2	11	0	0	0.9	1.000
3 yrs.			3	1	.750	3.92	29	4	1	64.1	72	25	23	0	2	0	1	18	2	0	.111	3	19	1	1	0.8	.957

Les Willis

WILLIS, LESTER EVANS (Lefty, Wimpy) BL TL 5′ 9½″ 195 lbs.
B. Jan. 17, 1908, Nacogdoches, Tex. D. Jan. 22, 1982, Jasper, Tex.

Year	Team	Lg	W	L	PCT	ERA	G	GS	CG	IP	H	BB	SO	ShO	Relief W	Relief L	Relief SV	AB	H	HR	BA	PO	A	E	DP	TC/G	FA
1947	CLE	A	0	2	.000	3.48	22	2	0	44	58	24	10	0	0	1	1	11	1	0	.091	2	4	0	1	0.3	1.000

Mike Willis

WILLIS, MICHAEL HENRY BL TL 6′ 2″ 205 lbs.
B. Dec. 26, 1950, Oklahoma City, Okla.

Year	Team	Lg	W	L	PCT	ERA	G	GS	CG	IP	H	BB	SO	ShO	Relief W	Relief L	Relief SV	AB	H	HR	BA	PO	A	E	DP	TC/G	FA
1977	TOR	A	2	6	.250	3.95	43	3	0	107	105	38	59	0	2	5	5	0	0	0	—	6	19	1	1	0.6	.962
1978			3	7	.300	4.56	44	2	1	100.2	104	39	52	0	2	6	7	0	0	0	—	4	18	1	0	0.5	.957
1979			0	3	.000	8.33	17	1	0	27	35	16	8	0	0	2	0	0	0	0	—	1	5	0	0	0.4	1.000
1980			2	1	.667	1.73	20	0	0	26	25	11	14	0	2	1	3	0	0	0	—	5	2	0	0	0.3	1.000
1981			0	4	.000	5.91	20	0	0	35	43	20	16	0	0	4	0	0	0	0	—	3	5	0	1	0.4	1.000
5 yrs.			7	21	.250	4.60	144	6	1	295.2	312	124	149	0	6	18	15	0	0	0		19	49	2	2	0.5	.971

Ron Willis

WILLIS, RONALD EARL BR TR 6′ 2″ 185 lbs.
B. July 12, 1943, Willisville, Tenn. D. Nov. 21, 1977, Memphis, Tenn.

Year	Team	Lg	W	L	PCT	ERA	G	GS	CG	IP	H	BB	SO	ShO	Relief W	Relief L	Relief SV	AB	H	HR	BA	PO	A	E	DP	TC/G	FA
1966	STL	N	0	0	—	0.00	4	0	0	3	1	1	2	0	0	0	1	0	0	0	—	0	0	0	0	0.0	.000
1967			6	5	.545	2.67	65	0	0	81	76	43	42	0	6	5	10	8	3	0	.375	8	20	0	5	0.4	1.000
1968			2	3	.400	3.39	48	0	0	63.2	50	28	39	0	2	3	4	11	0	0	.000	2	15	0	0	0.4	1.000
1969	2 teams	STL N (26G 1–2)	HOU N (3G 0–0)																								
″	total		1	2	.333	3.89	29	0	0	34.2	29	19	25	0	1	2	0	1	1	0	1.000	5	8	0	0	0.4	1.000
1970	SD	N	2	2	.500	4.02	42	0	0	56	53	28	20	0	2	2	4	5	0	0	.000	9	13	0	1	0.5	1.000
5 yrs.			11	12	.478	3.32	188	0	0	238.1	209	119	128	0	11	12	19	25	4	0	.160	24	56	0	6	0.4	1.000
WORLD SERIES																											
1967	STL	N	0	0	—	27.00	3	0	0	1	2	4	1	0	0	0	0	0	0	0	—	0	0	0	0	0.0	.000
1968			0	0	—	8.31	3	0	0	4.1	2	4	3	0	0	0	0	0	0	0	—	1	0	0	0	0.3	1.000
2 yrs.			0	0		11.81	6	0	0	5.1	4	8	4	0	0	0	0	0	0	0		1	0	0	0	0.2	1.000

Vic Willis

WILLIS, VICTOR GAZAWAY BR TR 6′ 2″ 185 lbs.
B. Apr. 12, 1876, Cecil County, Md. D. Aug. 3, 1947, Elkton, Md.
Hall of Fame 1995.

Year	Team	Lg	W	L	PCT	ERA	G	GS	CG	IP	H	BB	SO	ShO	Relief W	Relief L	Relief SV	AB	H	HR	BA	PO	A	E	DP	TC/G	FA
1898	BOS	N	25	13	.658	2.84	41	38	29	311	264	148	160	1	1	1	0	117	17	0	.145	19	67	11	1	2.4	.887
1899			27	8	.771	2.50	41	38	35	342.2	277	117	120	**5**	0	0	2	134	29	0	.216	17	81	8	2	2.6	.925
1900			10	17	.370	4.19	32	29	22	236	258	106	53	2	1	0	0	88	12	0	.136	10	49	2	0	1.9	.967
1901			20	17	.541	2.36	38	35	33	305.1	262	78	133	**6**	2	0	0	107	20	1	.187	22	66	3	2	2.4	.967
1902			27	**20**	.574	2.20	**51**	**46**	**45**	**410**	**372**	101	**225**	4	1	1	**3**	150	23	0	.153	37	105	4	5	2.9	.973
1903			12	18	.400	2.98	33	32	29	278	256	88	125	2	0	0	0	128	24	0	.188	82	89	8	1	4.6	.955
1904			18	**25**	.419	2.85	43	43	**39**	350	357	109	196	2	0	0	0	148	27	0	.182	88	112	2	6	4.1	.990
1905			12	**29**	.293	3.21	41	41	36	342	**340**	107	149	4	0	0	0	131	20	0	.153	37	115	7	3	3.9	.956
1906	PIT	N	22	13	.629	1.73	41	36	32	322	295	76	124	6	1	0	1	115	20	0	.174	22	117	8	5	3.6	.946
1907			22	11	.667	2.34	39	37	27	292.2	234	69	107	6	1	0	1	103	14	0	.136	17	87	3	2	2.7	.972
1908			23	11	.676	2.07	41	38	25	304.2	239	69	97	7	1	0	0	103	17	0	.165	11	87	1	2	2.4	.990
1909			22	11	.667	2.24	39	**35**	24	289.2	243	83	95	4	2	1	0	103	14	0	.136	16	85	5	1	2.7	.953
1910	STL	N	9	12	.429	3.35	33	23	12	212	224	61	67	1	3	0	3	66	11	0	.167	11	71	4	0	2.6	.953
13 yrs.			249	205	.548	2.63	513	471	388	3996	3621	1212	1651	50	13	3	10	1493	248	1	.166	389	1131	66	30	3.0	.958
WORLD SERIES																											
1909	PIT	N	0	1	.000	4.76	2	1	0	11.1	10	8	3	0	0	0	0	4	0	0	.000	1	2	0	0	1.5	1.000

Claude Willoughby

WILLOUGHBY, CLAUDE WILLIAM (Flunky, Weeping Willie) BR TR 5′ 9½″ 165 lbs.
B. Nov. 14, 1898, Buffalo, Kans. D. Aug. 14, 1973, McPherson, Kans.

Year	Team	Lg	W	L	PCT	ERA	G	GS	CG	IP	H	BB	SO	ShO	Relief W	Relief L	Relief SV	AB	H	HR	BA	PO	A	E	DP	TC/G	FA
1925	PHI	N	2	1	.667	1.96	3	3	1	23	26	11	6	0	0	0	0	8	0	0	.000	1	3	0	0	1.3	1.000
1926			8	12	.400	5.95	47	18	6	168	218	71	37	0	4	1	1	52	11	0	.212	6	54	2	4	1.3	.968
1927			3	7	.300	6.54	35	6	1	97.2	126	53	14	1	2	3	2	26	2	0	.077	4	19	1	2	0.7	.958
1928			6	5	.545	5.30	35	13	5	130.2	180	83	26	1	2	1	1	40	6	0	.150	9	25	2	6	1.0	.944
1929			15	14	.517	4.99	49	34	14	243.1	288	**108**	50	1	0	2	4	91	13	0	.143	8	76	2	6	1.8	.977
1930			4	17	.190	7.59	41	24	5	153	241	68	38	1	0	1	1	48	5	0	.104	3	41	0	7	1.1	1.000
1931	PIT	N	0	2	.000	6.31	9	2	1	25.2	32	12	4	0	0	1	0	7	2	0	.286	0	8	1	0	1.0	.889
7 yrs.			38	58	.396	5.84	219	100	33	841.1	1111	406	175	4	8	9	9	272	39	0	.143	31	226	8	25	1.2	.970

Jim Willoughby

WILLOUGHBY, JAMES ARTHUR BR TR 6′ 2″ 185 lbs.
B. Jan. 31, 1949, Salinas, Calif.

Year	Team	Lg	W	L	PCT	ERA	G	GS	CG	IP	H	BB	SO	ShO	Relief W	Relief L	Relief SV	AB	H	HR	BA	PO	A	E	DP	TC/G	FA
1971	SF	N	0	1	.000	9.00	2	1	0	4	8	1	3	0	0	0	0	1	0	0	.000	0	2	0	0	1.0	1.000
1972			6	4	.600	2.35	11	11	7	88	72	14	40	0	0	0	0	27	5	0	.185	8	12	1	1	1.9	.952
1973			4	5	.444	4.70	39	12	1	122.2	138	37	60	1	1	2	1	28	4	1	.143	7	15	0	1	0.6	1.000
1974			1	4	.200	4.61	18	4	0	41	51	9	12	0	0	1	0	10	1	0	.100	6	10	0	0	0.9	1.000
1975	BOS	A	5	2	.714	3.54	24	0	0	48.1	46	16	29	0	5	2	8	0	0	0	—	3	7	0	0	0.4	1.000
1976			3	12	.200	2.82	54	0	0	99	94	31	37	0	3	**12**	10	1	0	0	.000	7	22	2	1	0.6	.935
1977			6	2	.750	4.94	31	0	0	54.2	54	18	33	0	6	2	2	0	0	0	—	12	10	1	1	0.7	.957
1978	CHI	A	1	6	.143	3.86	59	0	0	93.1	95	19	36	0	1	6	13	0	0	0	—	11	19	1	3	0.5	.968
8 yrs.			26	36	.419	3.79	238	28	8	551	558	145	250	1	16	25	34	67	10	1	.149	54	97	5	7	0.7	.968

Jim Willoughby *continued*

Year	Team	Lg	W	L	PCT	ERA	G	GS	CG	IP	H	BB	SO	ShO	Relief Pitching W	Relief Pitching L	Relief Pitching SV	Batting AB	Batting H	Batting HR	BA	PO	A	E	DP	TC/G	FA
WORLD SERIES																											
1975	BOS	A	0	1	.000	0.00	3	0	0	6.1	3	0	2	0	0	1	0	0	0	0	—	1	0	0	0	0.3	1.000

Frank Wills

WILLS, FRANK LEE, JR. BR TR 6′ 2″ 200 lbs.
B. Oct. 26, 1958, New Orleans, La.

Year	Team	Lg	W	L	PCT	ERA	G	GS	CG	IP	H	BB	SO	ShO	Relief Pitching W	Relief Pitching L	Relief Pitching SV	Batting AB	Batting H	Batting HR	BA	PO	A	E	DP	TC/G	FA
1983	KC	A	2	1	.667	4.15	6	4	0	34.2	35	15	23	0	0	0	0	0	0	0	—	1	3	1	1	0.8	.800
1984			2	3	.400	5.11	10	5	0	37	39	13	21	0	1	0	0	0	0	0	—	3	2	2	0	0.7	.714
1985	SEA	A	5	11	.313	6.00	24	18	1	123	122	68	67	0	0	0	1	0	0	0	—	9	17	0	1	1.1	1.000
1986	CLE	A	4	4	.500	4.91	26	0	0	40.1	43	16	32	0	4	4	4	0	0	0	—	3	6	1	0	0.4	.900
1987			0	1	.000	5.06	6	0	0	5.1	3	7	4	0	0	1	1	0	0	0	—	0	2	0	0	0.3	1.000
1988	TOR	A	0	0	—	5.23	10	0	0	20.2	22	6	19	0	0	0	0	0	0	0	—	1	5	0	0	0.6	1.000
1989			3	1	.750	3.66	24	4	0	71.1	65	30	41	0	3	0	0	0	0	0	—	5	10	0	0	0.6	1.000
1990			6	4	.600	4.73	44	4	0	99	101	38	72	0	5	4	0	0	0	0	—	9	10	0	2	0.4	1.000
1991			0	1	.000	16.62	4	0	0	4.1	8	5	2	0	0	1	0	0	0	0	—	0	2	0	0	0.5	1.000
9 yrs.			22	26	.458	5.06	154	35	1	435.2	438	198	281	0	13	10	6	0	0	0		31	57	4	4	0.6	.957

Ted Wills

WILLS, THEODORE CARL BL TL 6′ 2″ 200 lbs.
B. Feb. 9, 1934, Fresno, Calif.

Year	Team	Lg	W	L	PCT	ERA	G	GS	CG	IP	H	BB	SO	ShO	Relief Pitching W	Relief Pitching L	Relief Pitching SV	Batting AB	Batting H	Batting HR	BA	PO	A	E	DP	TC/G	FA
1959	BOS	A	2	6	.250	5.27	9	8	2	56.1	68	24	24	0	0	0	0	16	4	0	.250	1	9	0	1	1.1	1.000
1960			1	1	.500	7.42	15	0	0	30.1	38	16	28	0	1	1	1	8	2	0	.250	1	7	0	0	0.5	1.000
1961			3	2	.600	5.95	17	0	0	19.2	24	19	11	0	3	2	0	2	0	0	.000	1	4	1	1	0.4	.833
1962	2 teams	BOS A	(1G 0–0)	CIN N	(26G 0–2)																						
″	total		0	2	.000	5.46	27	5	0	61	63	24	58	0	0	1	3	16	5	0	.313	3	8	2	2	0.5	.846
1965	CHI	A	2	0	1.000	2.84	15	0	0	19	17	14	12	0	2	0	1	2	0	0	.000	1	6	1	0	0.5	.875
5 yrs.			8	11	.421	5.51	83	13	2	186.1	210	97	133	0	6	4	5	44	11	0	.250	7	34	4	4	0.5	.911

Paul Wilmet

WILMET, PAUL RICHARD BR TR 5′11″ 170 lbs.
B. Nov. 8, 1958, Green Bay, Wis.

Year	Team	Lg	W	L	PCT	ERA	G	GS	CG	IP	H	BB	SO	ShO	Relief Pitching W	Relief Pitching L	Relief Pitching SV	Batting AB	Batting H	Batting HR	BA	PO	A	E	DP	TC/G	FA
1989	TEX	A	0	0	—	15.43	3	0	0	2.1	5	2	1	0	0	0	0	0	0	0	—	0	1	0	0	0.3	1.000

Whitey Wilshere

WILSHERE, VERNON SPRAGUE BL TL 6′ 180 lbs.
B. Aug. 3, 1912, Poplar Ridge, N. Y. D. May 23, 1985, Cooperstown, N. Y.

Year	Team	Lg	W	L	PCT	ERA	G	GS	CG	IP	H	BB	SO	ShO	Relief Pitching W	Relief Pitching L	Relief Pitching SV	Batting AB	Batting H	Batting HR	BA	PO	A	E	DP	TC/G	FA
1934	PHI	A	0	1	.000	12.05	9	2	0	21.2	39	15	19	0	0	0	0	3	0	0	.000	0	0	0	0	0.0	.000
1935			9	9	.500	4.05	27	18	7	142.1	136	78	80	3	2	1	1	43	4	0	.093	2	25	0	1	1.0	1.000
1936			1	2	.333	6.87	5	3	0	18.1	21	19	4	0	0	0	0	4	0	0	.000	1	3	1	0	1.0	.800
3 yrs.			10	12	.455	5.28	41	23	7	182.1	196	112	103	3	2	1	1	50	4	0	.080	3	28	1	1	0.8	.969

Terry Wilshusen

WILSHUSEN, TERRY WAYNE BR TR 6′ 2″ 210 lbs.
B. Mar. 22, 1949, Atascadero, Calif.

Year	Team	Lg	W	L	PCT	ERA	G	GS	CG	IP	H	BB	SO	ShO	Relief Pitching W	Relief Pitching L	Relief Pitching SV	Batting AB	Batting H	Batting HR	BA	PO	A	E	DP	TC/G	FA
1973	CAL	A	0	0	—	81.00	1	0	0	0.1	0	2	0	0	0	0	0	0	0	0	—	0	0	0	0	0.0	.000

Bill Wilson

WILSON, WILLIAM DONALD BR TR 6′ 2″ 200 lbs.
B. Nov. 6, 1928, Central City, Neb.

Year	Team	Lg	W	L	PCT	ERA	G	GS	CG	IP	H	BB	SO	ShO	Relief Pitching W	Relief Pitching L	Relief Pitching SV	Batting AB	Batting H	Batting HR	BA	PO	A	E	DP	TC/G	FA
1955	KC	A	0	0	—	0.00	1	0	0	1	1	1	1	0	0	0	0	*				3	0	0	0	1.5	1.000

Billy Wilson

WILSON, WILLIAM HARLAN BR TR 6′ 2″ 195 lbs.
B. Sept. 21, 1942, Pomeroy, Ohio D. 1993

Year	Team	Lg	W	L	PCT	ERA	G	GS	CG	IP	H	BB	SO	ShO	Relief Pitching W	Relief Pitching L	Relief Pitching SV	Batting AB	Batting H	Batting HR	BA	PO	A	E	DP	TC/G	FA
1969	PHI	N	2	5	.286	3.34	37	0	0	62	53	36	48	0	2	5	6	6	0	0	.000	2	6	0	0	0.2	1.000
1970			1	0	1.000	4.81	37	0	0	58	57	33	41	0	1	0	0	4	1	0	.250	0	9	1	1	0.3	.900
1971			4	6	.400	3.05	38	0	0	59	39	22	40	0	4	6	7	10	1	0	.100	5	16	1	0	0.6	.955
1972			1	1	.500	3.30	23	0	0	30	26	11	18	0	1	1	0	0	0	0	—	4	4	0	0	0.3	1.000
1973			1	3	.250	6.66	44	0	0	48.2	54	29	24	0	1	3	4	4	0	0	.000	2	6	0	0	0.2	1.000
5 yrs.			9	15	.375	4.23	179	0	0	257.2	229	131	171	0	9	15	17	24	2	0	.083	13	41	2	1	0.3	.964

Chink Wilson

WILSON, WILLIAM BR TR
B. Jan. 7, 1884, Columbus, Ohio D. Oct. 28, 1925, Seattle, Wash.

Year	Team	Lg	W	L	PCT	ERA	G	GS	CG	IP	H	BB	SO	ShO	Relief Pitching W	Relief Pitching L	Relief Pitching SV	Batting AB	Batting H	Batting HR	BA	PO	A	E	DP	TC/G	FA
1906	WAS	A	0	1	.000	2.57	1	1	1	7	3	2	1	0	0	0	0	2	0	0	.000	0	3	0	0	3.0	1.000

Don Wilson

WILSON, DONALD EDWARD BR TR 6′ 2½″ 195 lbs.
B. Feb. 12, 1945, Monroe, La. D. Jan. 5, 1975, Houston, Tex.

Year	Team	Lg	W	L	PCT	ERA	G	GS	CG	IP	H	BB	SO	ShO	Relief Pitching W	Relief Pitching L	Relief Pitching SV	Batting AB	Batting H	Batting HR	BA	PO	A	E	DP	TC/G	FA
1966	HOU	N	1	0	1.000	3.00	1	0	0	6	5	1	7	0	1	0	0	2	1	0	.500	0	1	0	1	1.0	1.000
1967			10	9	.526	2.79	31	28	7	184	141	69	159	3	0	2	0	66	6	0	.091	9	17	2	0	0.9	.929
1968			13	16	.448	3.28	33	30	9	208.2	187	70	175	3	0	2	0	70	15	1	.214	16	22	4	0	1.3	.905
1969			16	12	.571	4.00	34	34	13	225	210	97	235	1	0	0	0	81	8	0	.099	19	25	3	0	1.4	.936
1970			11	6	.647	3.91	29	27	3	184	188	66	94	0	0	0	0	69	8	0	.116	6	17	2	2	0.9	.920
1971			16	10	.615	2.45	35	34	18	268	195	79	180	3	0	0	0	91	14	0	.154	9	26	2	4	1.1	.946
1972			15	10	.600	2.68	33	33	13	228.1	196	66	172	3	0	0	0	76	8	0	.105	8	37	2	1	1.4	.957
1973			11	16	.407	3.20	37	32	10	239.1	187	92	149	3	1	0	2	79	14	0	.177	15	25	4	3	1.2	.909
1974			11	13	.458	3.07	33	27	5	205	170	100	112	4	1	0	0	63	13	0	.206	11	21	5	1	1.1	.865
9 yrs.			104	92	.531	3.15	266	245	78	1748.1	1479	640	1283	20	3	4	2	597	87	1	.146	93	191	24	12	1.2	.922

Duane Wilson

WILSON, DUANE LEWIS BL TL 6′ 1″ 185 lbs.
B. June 29, 1934, Wichita, Kans.

Year	Team	Lg	W	L	PCT	ERA	G	GS	CG	IP	H	BB	SO	ShO	Relief Pitching W	Relief Pitching L	Relief Pitching SV	Batting AB	Batting H	Batting HR	BA	PO	A	E	DP	TC/G	FA
1958	BOS	A	0	0	—	5.68	2	2	0	6.1	10	7	3	0	0	0	0	1	0	0	.000	0	2	0	0	1.0	1.000

Earl Wilson

WILSON, EARL LAWRENCE BR TR 6′ 3″ 216 lbs.
B. Oct. 2, 1934, Ponchatoula, La.

Year	Team	Lg	W	L	PCT	ERA	G	GS	CG	IP	H	BB	SO	ShO	Relief Pitching W	Relief Pitching L	Relief Pitching SV	Batting AB	Batting H	Batting HR	BA	PO	A	E	DP	TC/G	FA
1959	BOS	A	1	1	.500	6.08	9	4	0	23.2	21	31	17	0	1	0	0	8	4	0	.500	2	5	1	0	0.9	.875
1960			3	2	.600	4.71	13	9	2	65	61	48	40	0	0	0	0	23	4	0	.174	6	10	1	1	1.3	.941
1962			12	8	.600	3.90	31	28	4	191.1	163	111	137	1	0	0	0	69	12	3	.174	19	22	3	2	1.4	.932
1963			11	16	.407	3.76	37	34	6	210.2	184	**105**	123	3	0	0	0	72	15	1	.208	17	36	3	1	1.5	.946
1964			11	12	.478	4.49	33	31	5	202.1	213	73	166	0	0	0	0	73	15	5	.205	14	29	2	0	1.4	.956

Earl Wilson *continued*

Year	Team	W	L	PCT	ERA	G	GS	CG	IP	H	BB	SO	ShO	Relief Pitching W	Relief Pitching L	Relief Pitching SV	Batting AB	Batting H	Batting HR	BA	PO	A	E	DP	TC/G	FA
1965		13	14	.481	3.98	36	36	8	230.2	221	77	164	1	0	0	0	79	14	6	.177	24	26	3	2	1.5	.943
1966	2 teams BOS A (15G 5–5) DET A (23G 13–6)																									
"	total	18	11	.621	3.07	38	37	13	264	214	74	200	3	0	0	0	96	23	7	.240	36	39	5	4	2.1	.938
1967	DET A	**22**	11	.667	3.27	39	38	12	264	216	92	184	0	0	0	0	108	20	4	.185	26	42	0	2	1.7	1.000
1968		13	12	.520	2.85	34	33	10	224.1	192	65	168	3	0	0	0	88	20	7	.227	26	30	4	3	1.8	.933
1969		12	10	.545	3.31	35	35	5	214.2	209	69	150	1	0	0	0	76	10	0	.132	8	38	4	3	1.4	.920
1970	2 teams DET A (18G 4–6) SD N (15G 1–6)																									
"	total	5	12	.294	4.58	33	25	4	161	169	51	103	1	1	1	0	48	7	2	.146	7	18	2	1	0.8	.926
11 yrs.		121	109	.526	3.69	338	310	69	2051.2	1863	796	1452	13	2	1	0	*				185	295	28	19	1.5	.945
WORLD SERIES																										
1968	DET A	0	1	.000	6.23	1	1	0	4.1	4	6	3	0	0	0	0	*				0	2	0	0	2.0	1.000

Fin Wilson

WILSON, FINIS ELBERT BL TL 6′ 1″ 194 lbs.
B. Dec. 9, 1889, East Fork, Ky. D. Mar. 9, 1959, Coral Gables, Fla.

Year	Team	W	L	PCT	ERA	G	GS	CG	IP	H	BB	SO	ShO	Relief Pitching W	Relief Pitching L	Relief Pitching SV	Batting AB	Batting H	Batting HR	BA	PO	A	E	DP	TC/G	FA
1914	BKN F	0	1	.000	7.71	2	1	1	7	7	11	4	0	0	0	0	2	1	0	.500	0	0	0	0	0.0	.000
1915		1	7	.125	3.78	18	11	5	102.1	85	53	47	0	0	0	0	35	11	0	.314	11	30	2	2	2.3	.953
2 yrs.		1	8	.111	4.03	20	12	6	109.1	92	64	51	0	0	0	0	37	12	0	.324	11	30	2	2	2.0	.953

Gary Wilson

WILSON, GARY MORRIS BR TR 6′ 3″ 190 lbs.
B. Jan. 1, 1970, Arcata, Calif.

Year	Team	W	L	PCT	ERA	G	GS	CG	IP	H	BB	SO	ShO	Relief Pitching W	Relief Pitching L	Relief Pitching SV	Batting AB	Batting H	Batting HR	BA	PO	A	E	DP	TC/G	FA
1995	PIT N	0	1	.000	5.02	10	0	0	14.1	13	5	8	0	0	1	0	0	0	0	—	0	2	0	0	0.2	1.000

Gary Wilson

WILSON, GARY STEVEN BR TR 6′ 2″ 185 lbs.
B. Nov. 21, 1954, Camden, Ark.

Year	Team	W	L	PCT	ERA	G	GS	CG	IP	H	BB	SO	ShO	Relief Pitching W	Relief Pitching L	Relief Pitching SV	Batting AB	Batting H	Batting HR	BA	PO	A	E	DP	TC/G	FA
1979	HOU N	0	0	—	12.86	6	0	0	7	15	6	6	0	0	0	0	0	0	0	—	0	0	0	0	0.0	.000

George Pepper Wilson

Playing record listed under George Prentiss.

Glenn Wilson

WILSON, GLENN DWIGHT BR TR 6′ 1″ 190 lbs.
B. Dec. 22, 1958, Baytown, Tex.

Year	Team	W	L	PCT	ERA	G	GS	CG	IP	H	BB	SO	ShO	Relief Pitching W	Relief Pitching L	Relief Pitching SV	Batting AB	Batting H	Batting HR	BA	PO	A	E	DP	TC/G	FA
1987	PHI N	0	0	—	0.00	1	0	0	1	0	0	1	0	0	0	0	*				215	8	3	1	2.7	.987

Highball Wilson

WILSON, HOWARD PAUL TR
B. Aug. 9, 1878, Philadelphia, Pa. D. Oct. 16, 1934, Havre de Grace, Md.

Year	Team	W	L	PCT	ERA	G	GS	CG	IP	H	BB	SO	ShO	Relief Pitching W	Relief Pitching L	Relief Pitching SV	Batting AB	Batting H	Batting HR	BA	PO	A	E	DP	TC/G	FA
1899	CLE N	0	1	.000	9.00	1	1	1	8	12	5	1	0	0	0	0	3	1	0	.333	1	1	0	0	2.0	1.000
1902	PHI A	7	5	.583	2.43	13	10	8	96.1	103	19	18	0	1	1	0	35	6	0	.171	5	21	0	1	2.0	1.000
1903	WAS A	7	18	.280	3.31	30	28	25	242.1	269	43	56	1	0	0	0	85	17	0	.200	11	58	2	0	2.3	.972
1904		0	3	.000	4.68	3	3	3	25	33	4	11	0	0	0	0	9	2	0	.222	2	8	1	0	3.7	.909
4 yrs.		14	27	.341	3.29	47	42	37	371.2	417	71	86	1	1	1	0	132	26	0	.197	19	88	3	1	2.3	.973

Jack Wilson

WILSON, JOHN FRANCIS (Black Jack) BR TR 5′11″ 210 lbs.
B. Apr. 12, 1912, Portland, Ore. D. Apr. 19, 1995, Edmonds, Wash.

Year	Team	W	L	PCT	ERA	G	GS	CG	IP	H	BB	SO	ShO	Relief Pitching W	Relief Pitching L	Relief Pitching SV	Batting AB	Batting H	Batting HR	BA	PO	A	E	DP	TC/G	FA
1934	PHI A	0	1	.000	12.00	2	2	1	9	15	9	2	0	0	0	0	3	0	0	.000	1	1	0	0	1.0	1.000
1935	BOS A	3	4	.429	4.22	23	6	2	64	72	36	19	0	1	0	1	16	5	1	.313	4	19	2	0	1.1	.920
1936		6	8	.429	4.42	43	9	2	136.1	152	86	74	0	5	3	3	50	11	0	.220	9	21	1	1	0.7	.968
1937		16	10	.615	3.70	51	21	14	221.1	209	119	137	1	5	4	7	85	14	0	.165	9	41	2	3	1.0	.962
1938		15	15	.500	4.30	37	27	11	194.2	200	91	96	3	6	2	1	68	15	0	.221	15	27	3	2	1.2	.933
1939		11	11	.500	4.67	36	22	6	177.1	198	75	80	0	3	0	2	63	10	0	.159	14	25	1	1	1.1	.975
1940		12	6	.667	5.08	41	16	9	157.2	170	87	102	0	4	4	5	66	18	2	.273	14	12	0	1	0.6	1.000
1941		4	13	.235	5.03	27	12	4	116.1	140	70	55	1	2	4	1	44	7	0	.159	15	26	2	4	1.6	.953
1942	2 teams WAS A (12G 1–4) DET A (9G 0–0)																									
"	total	1	4	.200	6.22	21	6	1	55	77	28	25	0	0	1	0	18	2	0	.111	2	10	1	1	0.6	.923
9 yrs.		68	72	.486	4.59	281	121	50	1131.2	1233	601	590	5	26	18	20	413	82	3	.199	83	182	12	13	1.0	.957

Jim Wilson

WILSON, JAMES ALGER BR TR 6′ 1½″ 200 lbs.
B. Feb. 20, 1922, San Diego, Calif. D. Sept. 2, 1986, Newport Beach, Calif.

Year	Team	W	L	PCT	ERA	G	GS	CG	IP	H	BB	SO	ShO	Relief Pitching W	Relief Pitching L	Relief Pitching SV	Batting AB	Batting H	Batting HR	BA	PO	A	E	DP	TC/G	FA
1945	BOS A	6	8	.429	3.30	23	21	8	144.1	121	88	50	2	0	0	0	53	13	0	.245	4	19	1	0	1.0	.958
1946		0	0	—	27.00	1	0	0	0.2	2	0	0	0	0	0	0	0	0	0	—	0	0	0	0	0.0	.000
1948	STL A	0	0	—	13.50	4	0	0	2.2	5	5	1	0	0	0	0	0	0	0	—	0	2	0	0	0.5	1.000
1949	PHI A	0	0	—	14.40	2	0	0	5	7	5	2	0	0	0	0	3	0	0	.000	0	0	0	0	0.0	.000
1951	BOS N	7	7	.500	5.40	20	15	5	110	131	40	33	0	1	0	1	39	7	0	.179	4	16	0	2	1.0	1.000
1952		12	14	.462	4.23	33	33	14	234	234	90	104	0	0	0	0	86	14	0	.163	21	32	1	4	1.6	.981
1953	MIL N	4	9	.308	4.34	20	18	5	114	107	43	71	0	0	0	0	36	6	1	.167	10	23	0	1	1.6	1.000
1954		8	2	.800	3.52	27	19	6	127.2	129	36	52	4	0	0	0	44	7	0	.159	7	26	0	2	1.2	1.000
1955	BAL A	12	**18**	.400	3.44	34	31	14	235.1	200	87	96	4	0	1	0	89	15	0	.169	15	39	2	0	1.6	.964
1956	2 teams BAL A (7G 4–2) CHI A (28G 9–12)																									
"	total	13	14	.481	4.28	35	28	7	208	198	86	113	3	2	1	0	77	23	1	.299	10	33	0	3	1.2	1.000
1957	CHI A	15	8	.652	3.48	30	29	12	201.2	189	65	100	**5**	0	1	0	68	10	0	.147	14	26	0	0	1.3	1.000
1958		9	9	.500	4.10	28	23	4	155.2	156	63	70	1	1	2	1	51	4	0	.078	9	19	0	1	1.0	1.000
12 yrs.		86	89	.491	4.01	257	217	75	1539	1479	608	692	19	4	5	2	546	99	2	.181	94	235	4	13	1.3	.988

John Wilson

WILSON, JOHN NICODEMUS (Lefty) BR TL 6′ 1″ 185 lbs.
B. June 15, 1890, Boonsboro, Md. D. Sept. 23, 1954, Annapolis, Md.

Year	Team	W	L	PCT	ERA	G	GS	CG	IP	H	BB	SO	ShO	Relief Pitching W	Relief Pitching L	Relief Pitching SV	Batting AB	Batting H	Batting HR	BA	PO	A	E	DP	TC/G	FA
1913	WAS A	0	0	—	4.50	3	0	0	4	4	3	1	0	0	0	0	0	0	0	—	0	2	0	1	0.7	1.000

John Wilson

WILSON, JOHN SAMUEL BR TR 6′ 2″ 164 lbs.
B. Apr. 25, 1905, Coal City, Ala. D. Aug. 27, 1980, Chattanooga, Tenn.

Year	Team	W	L	PCT	ERA	G	GS	CG	IP	H	BB	SO	ShO	Relief Pitching W	Relief Pitching L	Relief Pitching SV	Batting AB	Batting H	Batting HR	BA	PO	A	E	DP	TC/G	FA
1927	BOS A	0	2	.000	3.55	5	2	2	25.1	31	13	8	0	0	0	0	9	1	0	.111	0	5	1	0	1.2	.833
1928		0	0	—	9.00	2	0	0	5	6	6	1	0	0	0	0	1	0	0	.000	0	2	0	0	1.0	1.000
2 yrs.		0	2	.000	4.45	7	2	2	30.1	37	19	9	0	0	0	0	10	1	0	.100	0	7	1	0	1.1	.875

Maxie Wilson

WILSON, MAX BL TL 5′ 7″ 150 lbs.
B. June 3, 1916, Haw River, N. C. D. Jan. 2, 1977, Greensboro, N. C.

Year	Team	Lg	W	L	PCT	ERA	G	GS	CG	IP	H	BB	SO	ShO	Relief W	Relief L	Relief SV	AB	H	HR	BA	PO	A	E	DP	TC/G	FA
1940	PHI	N	0	0	—	12.86	3	0	0	7	16	2	3	0	0	0	0	2	0	0	.000	0	2	0	0	0.7	1.000
1946	WAS	A	0	1	.000	7.11	9	0	0	12.2	16	9	8	0	0	1	0	2	0	0	.000	1	1	0	0	0.2	1.000
2 yrs.			0	1	.000	9.15	12	0	0	19.2	32	11	11	0	0	1	0	4	0	0	.000	1	3	0	0	0.3	1.000

Mutt Wilson

WILSON, WILLIAM CLARENCE BR TR 6′ 3″ 167 lbs.
B. July 20, 1896, Kiser, N. C. D. Aug. 31, 1962, Wildwood, Fla.

Year	Team	Lg	W	L	PCT	ERA	G	GS	CG	IP	H	BB	SO	ShO	Relief W	Relief L	Relief SV	AB	H	HR	BA	PO	A	E	DP	TC/G	FA
1920	DET	A	1	1	.500	3.46	3	2	1	13	12	5	4	0	0	0	0	4	1	0	.250	0	0	0	0	0.0	.000

Pete Wilson

WILSON, PETER ALEX TL
B. Oct. 9, 1885, Springfield, Mass. D. June 5, 1957, St. Petersburg, Fla.

Year	Team	Lg	W	L	PCT	ERA	G	GS	CG	IP	H	BB	SO	ShO	Relief W	Relief L	Relief SV	AB	H	HR	BA	PO	A	E	DP	TC/G	FA
1908	NY	A	3	3	.500	3.46	6	6	4	39	27	33	28	1	0	0	0	13	1	0	.077	1	9	1	1	1.8	.909
1909			6	5	.545	3.17	14	13	7	93.2	82	43	44	1	1	0	0	34	4	0	.118	2	27	4	0	2.4	.879
2 yrs.			9	8	.529	3.26	20	19	11	132.2	109	76	72	2	1	0	0	47	5	0	.106	3	36	5	1	2.2	.886

Roy Wilson

WILSON, ROY EDWARD (Lefty) BL TL 6′ 175 lbs.
B. Sept. 13, 1896, Foster, Iowa D. Dec. 3, 1969, Clarion, Iowa.

Year	Team	Lg	W	L	PCT	ERA	G	GS	CG	IP	H	BB	SO	ShO	Relief W	Relief L	Relief SV	AB	H	HR	BA	PO	A	E	DP	TC/G	FA
1928	CHI	A	0	0	—	0.00	1	0	0	3.1	2	3	2	0	0	0	0	1	0	0	.000	0	2	0	0	2.0	1.000

Steve Wilson

WILSON, STEPHEN DOUGLAS BL TL 6′ 4″ 205 lbs.
B. Dec. 13, 1964, Victoria, B. C., Canada.

Year	Team	Lg	W	L	PCT	ERA	G	GS	CG	IP	H	BB	SO	ShO	Relief W	Relief L	Relief SV	AB	H	HR	BA	PO	A	E	DP	TC/G	FA
1988	TEX	A	0	0	—	5.87	3	0	0	7.2	7	4	1	0	0	0	0	0	0	0	—	0	0	0	0	0.0	.000
1989	CHI	N	6	4	.600	4.20	53	8	0	85.2	83	31	65	0	3	2	2	16	1	0	.063	6	14	2	0	0.4	.909
1990			4	9	.308	4.79	45	15	1	139	140	43	95	0	2	2	1	37	6	0	.162	4	16	2	0	0.5	.909
1991	2 teams	CHI N (8G 0–0) LA N (11G 0–0)																									
″	total		0	0		2.61	19	0	0	20.2	14	9	14	0	0	0	2	2	0	0	.000	0	0	0	0	0.0	
1992	LA	N	2	5	.286	4.18	60	0	0	66.2	74	29	54	0	2	5	0	3	1	0	.333	2	9	1	1	0.2	.917
1993			1	0	1.000	4.56	25	0	0	25.2	30	14	23	0	1	0	1	2	0	0	.000	2	4	1	0	0.3	.857
6 yrs.			13	18	.419	4.40	205	23	1	345.1	348	130	252	0	8	9	6	60	8	0	.133	14	43	6	1	0.3	.905
LEAGUE CHAMPIONSHIP SERIES																											
1989	CHI	N	0	1	.000	4.91	2	0	0	3.2	3	1	4	0	0	1	0	0	0	0	—	0	1	0	0	0.5	1.000

Tex Wilson

WILSON, GOMER RUSSELL BR TL 5′10″ 170 lbs.
B. July 8, 1901, Trenton, Tex. D. Sept. 15, 1946, Sulphur Springs, Tex.

Year	Team	Lg	W	L	PCT	ERA	G	GS	CG	IP	H	BB	SO	ShO	Relief W	Relief L	Relief SV	AB	H	HR	BA	PO	A	E	DP	TC/G	FA
1924	BKN	N	0	0	—	14.73	2	0	0	3.2	7	1	1	0	0	0	0	1	0	0	.000	0	2	0	0	1.0	1.000

Trevor Wilson

WILSON, TREVOR KIRK BL TL 6′ 185 lbs.
B. June 7, 1966, Torrance, Calif.

Year	Team	Lg	W	L	PCT	ERA	G	GS	CG	IP	H	BB	SO	ShO	Relief W	Relief L	Relief SV	AB	H	HR	BA	PO	A	E	DP	TC/G	FA
1988	SF	N	0	2	.000	4.09	4	4	0	22	25	8	15	0	0	0	0	7	2	0	.286	1	1	0	0	0.5	1.000
1989			2	3	.400	4.35	14	4	0	39.1	28	24	22	0	1	1	0	8	2	0	.250	0	7	1	0	0.6	.875
1990			8	7	.533	4.00	27	17	3	110.1	87	49	66	2	1	1	0	29	4	0	.138	9	22	0	1	1.1	1.000
1991			13	11	.542	3.56	44	29	2	202	173	77	139	1	0	3	0	51	12	1	.235	9	42	1	4	1.2	.981
1992			8	14	.364	4.21	26	26	1	154	152	64	88	1	0	0	0	39	3	0	.077	7	30	2	2	1.5	.949
1993			7	5	.583	3.60	22	18	1	110	110	40	57	0	0	0	0	29	4	1	.138	3	13	0	2	0.7	1.000
1995			3	4	.429	3.92	17	17	0	82.2	82	38	38	0	0	0	0	30	7	0	.233	2	18	1	2	1.2	.952
7 yrs.			41	46	.471	3.87	154	115	7	720.1	657	300	425	4	2	5	0	193	34	2	.176	31	133	5	11	1.1	.970

Walter Wilson

WILSON, WALTER WOOD BL TR 6′ 4″ 190 lbs.
B. Nov. 24, 1913, Glenn, Ga. D. Apr. 17, 1994, Bremen, Ga.

Year	Team	Lg	W	L	PCT	ERA	G	GS	CG	IP	H	BB	SO	ShO	Relief W	Relief L	Relief SV	AB	H	HR	BA	PO	A	E	DP	TC/G	FA
1945	DET	A	1	3	.250	4.61	25	4	1	70.1	76	35	28	0	0	1	0	19	1	0	.053	3	20	0	2	0.9	1.000

Zeke Wilson

WILSON, FRANK EALTON BR TR 5′10″ 165 lbs.
B. Dec. 24, 1869, Benton, Ala. D. Apr. 26, 1928, Montgomery, Ala.

Year	Team	Lg	W	L	PCT	ERA	G	GS	CG	IP	H	BB	SO	ShO	Relief W	Relief L	Relief SV	AB	H	HR	BA	PO	A	E	DP	TC/G	FA
1895	2 teams	BOS N (6G 2–4) CLE N (8G 3–1)																									
″	total		5	5	.500	4.72	14	13	7	89.2	117	47	21	0	1	0	0	37	8	1	.216	4	25	0	0	2.1	1.000
1896	CLE	N	17	9	.654	4.01	33	29	20	240	265	81	56	1	1	0	1	100	27	0	.270	23	85	8	3	3.5	.931
1897			16	11	.593	4.16	34	30	26	263.2	323	83	69	1	0	0	0	116	26	0	.224	21	59	4	2	2.3	.952
1898			13	18	.419	3.60	33	31	28	254.2	307	51	45	1	0	0	0	118	21	0	.178	14	83	5	1	2.8	.951
1899	STL	N	1	1	.500	4.50	5	2	2	26	30	4	3	0	0	0	0	10	0	0	.000	3	12	1	0	3.2	.938
5 yrs.			52	44	.542	4.03	119	105	83	874	1042	266	194	3	2	0	1	381	82	1	.215	65	264	18	6	2.8	.948

Hal Wiltse

WILTSE, HAROLD JAMES (Whitey) BL TL 5′ 9″ 168 lbs.
B. Aug. 6, 1903, Clay City, Ill. D. Nov. 2, 1983, Bunkie, La.

Year	Team	Lg	W	L	PCT	ERA	G	GS	CG	IP	H	BB	SO	ShO	Relief W	Relief L	Relief SV	AB	H	HR	BA	PO	A	E	DP	TC/G	FA
1926	BOS	A	8	15	.348	4.22	37	29	9	196.1	201	99	59	1	1	0	0	59	5	0	.085	5	53	5	4	1.7	.921
1927			10	18	.357	5.10	36	29	13	219	276	76	47	1	1	1	1	77	16	0	.208	12	63	5	1	2.2	.938
1928	2 teams	BOS A (2G 0–2) STL A (26G 2–5)																									
″	total		2	7	.222	5.79	28	7	1	84	109	36	28	0	2	0	0	26	5	0	.192	4	19	1	0	0.9	.958
1931	PHI	N	0	0	—	9.00	1	0	0	1	3	0	0	0	0	0	0	0	0	0	—	0	1	0	0	1.0	1.000
4 yrs.			20	40	.333	4.87	102	65	23	500.1	589	211	134	2	4	1	1	162	26	0	.160	21	136	11	5	1.6	.935

Hooks Wiltse

WILTSE, GEORGE LeROY BR TL 6′ 185 lbs.
Brother of Snake Wiltse.
B. Sept. 7, 1880, Hamilton, N. Y. D. Jan. 21, 1959, Long Beach, N. Y.

Year	Team	Lg	W	L	PCT	ERA	G	GS	CG	IP	H	BB	SO	ShO	Relief W	Relief L	Relief SV	AB	H	HR	BA	PO	A	E	DP	TC/G	FA
1904	NY	N	13	3	.813	2.84	24	16	14	164.2	150	61	105	2	0	0	3	67	15	1	.224	11	54	5	2	2.8	.929
1905			15	6	.714	2.47	32	19	18	197	158	61	120	1	2	0	3	72	20	0	.278	20	71	5	3	2.9	.948
1906			16	11	.593	2.27	38	26	21	249.1	227	58	125	4	**4**	0	5	94	18	0	.191	13	65	3	1	2.0	.963
1907			13	12	.520	2.18	33	21	14	190.1	171	48	79	3	2	2	1	67	9	0	.134	11	59	2	2	2.1	.972
1908			23	14	.622	2.24	44	38	30	330	266	73	118	7	0	2	2	110	26	0	.236	28	89	2	1	2.7	.983
1909			20	11	.645	2.00	37	30	22	269.1	228	51	119	4	1	2	3	95	19	1	.200	9	62	2	2	2.0	.973
1910			14	12	.538	2.72	36	30	18	235.1	232	52	88	2	2	1	1	74	13	0	.176	8	52	9	4	1.9	.870
1911			12	9	.571	3.27	30	24	11	187.1	177	39	92	4	2	2	0	69	13	0	.188	19	44	4	2	2.2	.940
1912			9	6	.600	3.16	28	17	5	134	140	28	58	0	2	1	2	46	15	0	.326	5	40	0	2	1.6	1.000
1913			0	0	—	1.56	17	2	0	57.2	53	8	25	0	0	0	3	24	5	0	.208	23	20	2	1	2.3	.956

Hooks Wiltse *continued*

Year	Team	Lg	W	L	PCT	ERA	G	GS	CG	IP	H	BB	SO	ShO	Relief Pitching W	L	SV	Batting AB	H	HR	BA	PO	A	E	DP	TC/G	FA
1914			1	1	.500	2.84	20	0	0	38	41	12	19	0	1	1	1	3	2	0	.667	2	10	1	0	0.6	.923
1915	BKN	F	3	5	.375	2.28	18	3	1	59.1	49	7	17	0	3	2	5	22	1	0	.045	16	16	3	0	1.8	.914
12 yrs.			139	90	.607	2.47	357	226	154	2112.1	1892	498	965	27	19	13	29	743	156	2	.210	165	582	38	20	2.1	.952
WORLD SERIES																											
1911	NY	N	0	0	—	18.90	2	0	0	3.1	8	0	2	0	0	0	0	1	0	0	.000	0	1	0	0	0.5	1.000

Snake Wiltse

WILTSE, LEWIS DeWITT BR TL
Brother of Hooks Wiltse.
B. Dec. 5, 1871, Bouckville, N. Y. D. Aug. 25, 1928, Harrisburg, Pa.

Year	Team	Lg	W	L	PCT	ERA	G	GS	CG	IP	H	BB	SO	ShO	Relief Pitching W	L	SV	Batting AB	H	HR	BA	PO	A	E	DP	TC/G	FA
1901	2 teams	PIT N (7G 1–4) PHI A (19G 13–5)																									
"	total		14	9	.609	3.72	26	24	21	210.1	242	48	50	2	0	0	0	86	28	0	.326	11	68	6	2	3.3	.929
1902	2 teams	PHI A (19G 8–8) BAL A (19G 7–11)																									
"	total		15	19	.441	5.13	38	35	31	302	**397**	92	65	0	1	1	1	189	49	2	.259	177	75	14	11	4.8	.947
1903	NY	A	1	3	.250	5.40	4	3	2	25	35	6	6	0	0	0	1	9	2	0	.222	2	6	0	0	2.0	1.000
3 yrs.			30	31	.492	4.59	68	62	54	537.1	674	146	121	2	1	1	2	284	79	2	.278	190	149	20	13	4.2	.944

Fred Winchell

WINCHELL, FREDERICK RUSSELL TL 5′ 8″
Born Frederick Russell Cook.
B. Jan. 23, 1882, Arlington, Mass. D. Aug. 8, 1958, Toronto, Ont., Canada.

Year	Team	Lg	W	L	PCT	ERA	G	GS	CG	IP	H	BB	SO	ShO	Relief Pitching W	L	SV	Batting AB	H	HR	BA	PO	A	E	DP	TC/G	FA
1909	CLE	A	0	3	.000	6.28	4	3	0	14.1	16	2	7	0	0	0	1	5	1	0	.200	1	2	0	0	0.8	1.000

Ed Wineapple

WINEAPPLE, EDWARD (Lefty) BL TL 6′ 210 lbs.
B. Aug. 10, 1905, Boston, Mass.

Year	Team	Lg	W	L	PCT	ERA	G	GS	CG	IP	H	BB	SO	ShO	Relief Pitching W	L	SV	Batting AB	H	HR	BA	PO	A	E	DP	TC/G	FA
1929	WAS	A	0	0	—	4.50	1	0	0	4	7	3	1	0	0	0	0	2	0	0	.000	0	1	2	0	3.0	.333

Ralph Winegarner

WINEGARNER, RALPH LEE BR TR 6′ 182 lbs.
B. Oct. 29, 1909, Benton, Kans. D. Apr. 14, 1988, Wichita, Kans.

Year	Team	Lg	W	L	PCT	ERA	G	GS	CG	IP	H	BB	SO	ShO	Relief Pitching W	L	SV	Batting AB	H	HR	BA	PO	A	E	DP	TC/G	FA
1932	CLE	A	1	0	1.000	1.04	5	1	1	17.1	7	13	5	0	0	0	0	7	1	0	.143	5	13	3	2	4.2	.857
1934			5	4	.556	5.51	22	6	4	78.1	91	39	32	0	2	1	0	51	10	1	.196	2	17	0	0	0.8	1.000
1935			2	2	.500	5.75	25	4	2	67.1	89	29	41	0	1	1	0	84	26	3	.310	21	21	3	3	1.4	.933
1936			0	0	—	4.91	9	0	0	14.2	18	6	3	0	0	0	0	16	2	0	.125	0	1	0	0	0.1	1.000
1949	STL	A	0	0	—	7.56	9	0	0	16.2	24	2	8	0	0	0	0	5	2	1	.400	1	1	0	0	0.2	1.000
5 yrs.			8	6	.571	5.33	70	11	7	194.1	229	89	89	0	3	2	0	*				29	56	7	6	1.1	.924

Jim Winford

WINFORD, JAMES HEAD (Cowboy) BR TR 6′ 1″ 180 lbs.
B. Oct. 9, 1909, Shelbyville, Tenn. D. Dec. 16, 1970, Miami, Okla.

Year	Team	Lg	W	L	PCT	ERA	G	GS	CG	IP	H	BB	SO	ShO	Relief Pitching W	L	SV	Batting AB	H	HR	BA	PO	A	E	DP	TC/G	FA
1932	STL	N	1	1	.500	6.48	4	1	0	8.1	9	5	4	0	1	0	0	3	2	0	.667	0	2	0	0	0.5	1.000
1934			0	2	.000	7.82	5	1	0	12.2	17	6	3	0	0	1	0	1	0	0	.000	0	3	0	1	0.6	1.000
1935			0	0	—	3.97	2	1	0	11.1	13	5	7	0	0	0	0	2	0	0	.000	0	0	0	0	0.0	.000
1936			11	10	.524	3.80	39	23	10	192	203	68	72	1	1	2	3	59	5	0	.085	5	23	2	0	0.8	.933
1937			2	4	.333	5.83	16	4	0	46.1	56	27	19	0	2	0	0	8	1	0	.125	1	8	0	1	0.6	1.000
1938	BKN	N	0	1	.000	11.12	2	1	0	5.2	9	4	4	0	0	0	0	1	0	0	.000	0	0	0	0	0.0	.000
6 yrs.			14	18	.438	4.56	68	31	10	276.1	307	115	109	1	4	3	3	74	8	0	.108	6	36	2	2	0.6	.955

Ernie Wingard

WINGARD, ERNEST JAMES (Jim) BL TL 6′ 2″ 176 lbs.
B. Oct. 17, 1900, Prattville, Ala. D. Jan. 17, 1977, Prattville, Ala.

Year	Team	Lg	W	L	PCT	ERA	G	GS	CG	IP	H	BB	SO	ShO	Relief Pitching W	L	SV	Batting AB	H	HR	BA	PO	A	E	DP	TC/G	FA
1924	STL	A	13	12	.520	3.51	36	26	14	218	215	85	23	0	2	0	1	76	17	3	.224	10	42	3	1	1.5	.945
1925			9	10	.474	5.06	32	18	8	153	184	77	20	0	2	4	0	52	15	1	.288	6	49	5	3	1.8	.917
1926			5	8	.385	3.57	39	16	7	169	188	76	30	0	1	2	3	61	14	0	.230	11	59	5	3	1.8	.933
1927			2	13	.133	6.56	38	17	7	156.1	213	79	28	0	0	2	0	56	10	3	.179	14	45	3	1	1.6	.952
4 yrs.			29	43	.403	4.55	145	77	36	696.1	800	317	101	0	5	8	4	245	56	7	.229	41	195	16	8	1.7	.937

Ted Wingfield

WINGFIELD, FREDERICK DAVIS BR TR 5′11″ 168 lbs.
B. Aug. 7, 1899, Bedford, Va. D. July 18, 1975, Johnson City, Tenn.

Year	Team	Lg	W	L	PCT	ERA	G	GS	CG	IP	H	BB	SO	ShO	Relief Pitching W	L	SV	Batting AB	H	HR	BA	PO	A	E	DP	TC/G	FA
1923	WAS	A	0	0	—	0.00	1	0	0	1	0	0	1	0	0	0	0	0	0	0	—	0	0	0	0	0.0	.000
1924	2 teams	WAS A (4G 0–0) BOS A (4G 0–2)																									
"	total		0	2	.000	2.48	8	3	2	32.2	32	12	6	0	0	0	0	11	3	0	.273	4	7	2	0	1.6	.846
1925	BOS	A	12	19	.387	3.96	41	27	18	254.1	267	92	30	2	2	4	2	94	23	1	.245	19	94	2	6	2.8	.983
1926			11	16	.407	4.44	43	20	9	190.2	220	50	30	1	5	3	3	69	15	0	.217	13	56	2	3	1.7	.972
1927			1	7	.125	5.06	20	8	2	74.2	105	27	1	0	0	1	0	18	4	0	.222	6	30	1	3	1.9	.973
5 yrs.			24	44	.353	4.18	113	58	31	553.1	624	181	68	3	7	8	5	192	45	1	.234	42	187	7	12	2.1	.970

Lave Winham

WINHAM, LAFAYETTE SHARKEY BL TL 5′11″ 200 lbs.
B. Oct. 23, 1881, Brooklyn, N. Y. D. Sept. 12, 1951, Brooklyn, N. Y.

Year	Team	Lg	W	L	PCT	ERA	G	GS	CG	IP	H	BB	SO	ShO	Relief Pitching W	L	SV	Batting AB	H	HR	BA	PO	A	E	DP	TC/G	FA
1902	BKN	N	0	0	—	0.00	1	0	0	3	4	2	1	0	0	0	0	2	0	0	.000	0	3	0	0	3.0	1.000
1903	PIT	N	3	1	.750	2.25	5	4	3	36	33	21	22	1	0	0	0	14	1	0	.071	3	5	4	0	2.4	.667
2 yrs.			3	1	.750	2.08	6	4	3	39	37	23	23	1	0	0	0	16	1	0	.063	3	8	4	0	2.5	.733

George Winkelman

WINKELMAN, GEORGE EDWARD BL TL
B. June 14, 1861, Philadelphia, Pa. D. May 19, 1960, Washington, D. C.

Year	Team	Lg	W	L	PCT	ERA	G	GS	CG	IP	H	BB	SO	ShO	Relief Pitching W	L	SV	Batting AB	H	HR	BA	PO	A	E	DP	TC/G	FA
1886	WAS	N	0	1	.000	10.50	1	1	0	6	12	5	4	0	0	0	0	*				8	2	6	0	4.0	.625

George Winn

WINN, GEORGE BENJAMIN (Lefty, Breezy) BL TL 5′11″ 170 lbs.
B. Oct. 26, 1897, Perry, Ga. D. Nov. 1, 1969, Roberta, Ga.

Year	Team	Lg	W	L	PCT	ERA	G	GS	CG	IP	H	BB	SO	ShO	Relief Pitching W	L	SV	Batting AB	H	HR	BA	PO	A	E	DP	TC/G	FA
1919	BOS	A	0	0	—	7.71	3	0	0	4.2	6	1	0	0	0	0	0	1	0	0	.000	0	0	0	0	0.0	.000
1922	CLE	A	1	2	.333	4.54	8	3	1	33.2	44	5	7	0	0	1	0	9	3	0	.333	1	9	0	1	1.3	1.000
1923			0	0	—	0.00	1	0	0	2	0	1	0	0	0	0	0	0	0	0	—	0	0	0	0	0.0	.000
3 yrs.			1	2	.333	4.69	12	3	1	40.1	50	7	7	0	0	1	0	10	3	0	.300	1	9	0	1	0.8	1.000

Jim Winn

WINN, JAMES FRANCIS BR TR 6′ 3″ 190 lbs.
B. Sept. 23, 1959, Stockton, Calif.

Year	Team	Lg	W	L	PCT	ERA	G	GS	CG	IP	H	BB	SO	ShO	Relief Pitching W	L	SV	Batting AB	H	HR	BA	PO	A	E	DP	TC/G	FA
1983	PIT	N	0	0	—	7.36	7	0	0	11	12	6	3	0	0	0	0	0	0	0	—	1	2	0	0	0.4	1.000
1984			1	0	1.000	3.86	9	0	0	18.2	19	9	11	0	1	0	1	1	0	0	.000	1	3	0	1	0.4	1.000

Jim Winn *continued*

Year	Team	Lg	W	L	PCT	ERA	G	GS	CG	IP	H	BB	SO	ShO	Relief W	Relief L	Relief SV	Batting AB	Batting H	Batting HR	BA	PO	A	E	DP	TC/G	FA
1985			3	6	.333	5.23	30	7	0	75.2	77	31	22	0	1	4	0	18	2	0	.111	4	21	0	1	0.8	1.000
1986			3	5	.375	3.58	50	3	0	88	85	38	70	0	3	3	3	16	1	0	.063	8	15	1	1	0.5	.958
1987	CHI	A	4	6	.400	4.79	56	0	0	94	95	62	44	0	4	6	6	0	0	0	—	4	28	1	5	0.6	.970
1988	MIN	A	1	0	1.000	6.00	9	0	0	21	33	10	9	0	1	0	0	0	0	0	—	2	4	1	0	0.8	.857
6 yrs.			12	17	.414	4.67	161	10	0	308.1	321	156	159	0	10	13	10	35	3	0	.086	20	73	3	8	0.6	.969

Tom Winsett

WINSETT, JOHN THOMAS (Long Tom) BL TR 6′ 2″ 190 lbs.
B. Nov. 24, 1909, McKenzie, Tenn. D. July 20, 1987, Memphis, Tenn.

Year	Team	Lg	W	L	PCT	ERA	G	GS	CG	IP	H	BB	SO	ShO	Relief W	Relief L	Relief SV	Batting AB	Batting H	Batting HR	BA	PO	A	E	DP	TC/G	FA
1937	BKN	N	0	0	—	18.00	1	0	0	1	3	2	0	0	0	0	0	*				13	1	0	0	1.8	1.000

Hank Winston

WINSTON, HENRY RUDOLPH BL TR 6′ 3½″ 226 lbs.
B. June 15, 1904, Youngsville, N. C. D. Feb. 4, 1974, Jacksonville, Fla.

Year	Team	Lg	W	L	PCT	ERA	G	GS	CG	IP	H	BB	SO	ShO	Relief W	Relief L	Relief SV	Batting AB	Batting H	Batting HR	BA	PO	A	E	DP	TC/G	FA
1933	PHI	A	0	0	—	6.75	1	0	0	6.2	7	6	2	0	0	0	0	3	0	0	.000	0	3	0	0	3.0	1.000
1936	BKN	N	1	3	.250	6.12	14	0	0	32.1	40	16	8	0	1	3	0	11	1	0	.091	0	7	0	0	0.5	1.000
2 yrs.			1	3	.250	6.23	15	0	0	39	47	22	10	0	1	3	0	14	1	0	.071	0	10	0	0	0.7	1.000

George Winter

WINTER, GEORGE LOVINGTON (Sassafras) TR 5′ 8″ 155 lbs.
B. Apr. 27, 1878, New Providence, Pa. D. May 26, 1951, Ramsey, N. J.

Year	Team	Lg	W	L	PCT	ERA	G	GS	CG	IP	H	BB	SO	ShO	Relief W	Relief L	Relief SV	Batting AB	Batting H	Batting HR	BA	PO	A	E	DP	TC/G	FA
1901	BOS	A	16	12	.571	2.80	28	28	26	241	234	66	63	1	0	0	0	100	19	1	.190	15	64	8	4	3.1	.908
1902			11	9	.550	2.99	20	20	18	168.1	149	53	51	0	0	0	0	61	10	0	.164	4	50	5	1	3.0	.915
1903			9	8	.529	3.08	24	19	14	178.1	182	37	64	0	0	0	0	66	7	0	.106	19	47	4	0	2.9	.943
1904			8	4	.667	2.32	20	16	12	135.2	126	27	31	1	0	0	0	43	5	0	.116	7	43	6	1	2.8	.893
1905			16	17	.485	2.96	35	27	24	264.1	249	54	119	2	4	**3**	0	89	24	0	.270	14	81	6	4	2.9	.941
1906			6	18	.250	4.12	29	22	18	207.2	215	38	72	1	0	**2**	2	69	17	0	.246	13	59	2	4	2.6	.973
1907			12	15	.444	2.07	35	27	21	256.2	198	61	88	4	2	1	1	94	21	0	.223	6	77	5	5	2.5	.943
1908	2 teams	BOS A	(22G 4–14)		DET A	(7G 1–5)																					
"	total		5	19	.208	2.65	29	23	13	204	199	43	80	0	1	1	1	67	11	0	.164	16	67	10	2	3.2	.892
8 yrs.			83	102	.449	2.87	220	182	146	1656	1552	379	568	9	7	7	4	589	114	1	.194	94	488	46	21	2.9	.927
WORLD SERIES																											
1908	DET	A	0	0	—	0.00	1	0	0	1	1	1	0	0	0	0	0	0	0	0	—	0	0	0	0	0.0	.000

Clarence Winters

WINTERS, CLARENCE JOHN TR
B. Sept. 7, 1898, Detroit, Mich. D. June 29, 1945, Detroit, Mich.

Year	Team	Lg	W	L	PCT	ERA	G	GS	CG	IP	H	BB	SO	ShO	Relief W	Relief L	Relief SV	Batting AB	Batting H	Batting HR	BA	PO	A	E	DP	TC/G	FA
1924	BOS	A	0	1	.000	20.57	4	2	0	7	22	4	3	0	0	0	0	3	1	0	.333	0	0	0	0	0.0	.000

Jesse Winters

WINTERS, JESSE FRANKLIN (T-Bone) BR TR 6′ 1″ 165 lbs.
B. Dec. 22, 1893, Stephenville, Tex. D. June 5, 1986, Abilene, Tex.

Year	Team	Lg	W	L	PCT	ERA	G	GS	CG	IP	H	BB	SO	ShO	Relief W	Relief L	Relief SV	Batting AB	Batting H	Batting HR	BA	PO	A	E	DP	TC/G	FA
1919	NY	N	1	2	.333	5.46	16	2	0	28	39	13	6	0	1	1	3	3	0	0	.000	0	8	1	0	0.6	.889
1920			0	0	—	3.50	21	0	0	46.1	37	28	14	0	0	0	0	7	0	0	.000	0	18	1	0	0.9	.947
1921	PHI	N	5	10	.333	3.63	18	14	10	114	142	28	22	0	0	1	0	39	5	0	.128	6	37	1	3	2.4	.977
1922			6	6	.500	5.33	34	9	4	138.1	176	56	29	0	4	1	2	43	11	0	.256	5	36	3	2	1.3	.932
1923			1	6	.143	7.35	21	6	1	78.1	116	39	23	0	1	1	1	25	4	0	.160	3	17	4	1	1.1	.833
5 yrs.			13	24	.351	5.04	110	31	15	405	510	164	94	0	6	4	6	117	20	0	.171	14	116	10	6	1.3	.929

Alan Wirth

WIRTH, ALAN LEE BR TR 6′ 4″ 190 lbs.
B. Dec. 8, 1956, Mesa, Ariz.

Year	Team	Lg	W	L	PCT	ERA	G	GS	CG	IP	H	BB	SO	ShO	Relief W	Relief L	Relief SV	Batting AB	Batting H	Batting HR	BA	PO	A	E	DP	TC/G	FA
1978	OAK	A	5	6	.455	3.43	16	14	2	81.1	72	34	31	1	1	0	0	0	0	0	—	2	9	0	2	0.7	1.000
1979			1	0	1.000	6.00	5	1	0	12	14	8	7	0	0	0	0	0	0	0	—	0	3	0	0	0.6	1.000
1980			0	0	—	4.50	2	0	0	2	3	0	1	0	0	0	0	0	0	0	—	0	0	0	0	0.0	.000
3 yrs.			6	6	.500	3.78	23	15	2	95.1	89	42	39	1	1	0	0	0	0	0		2	12	0	2	0.6	1.000

Archie Wise

WISE, ARCHIBALD EDWIN BR TR 6′ 165 lbs.
B. July 31, 1912, Waxahachie, Tex. D. Feb. 2, 1978, Dallas, Tex.

Year	Team	Lg	W	L	PCT	ERA	G	GS	CG	IP	H	BB	SO	ShO	Relief W	Relief L	Relief SV	Batting AB	Batting H	Batting HR	BA	PO	A	E	DP	TC/G	FA
1932	CHI	A	0	0	—	4.91	2	0	0	7.1	8	5	2	0	0	0	0	4	0	0	.000	0	2	0	0	1.0	1.000

Bill Wise

WISE, WILLIAM E.
B. Mar. 15, 1861, Washington, D. C. D. May 5, 1940, Washington, D. C.

Year	Team	Lg	W	L	PCT	ERA	G	GS	CG	IP	H	BB	SO	ShO	Relief W	Relief L	Relief SV	Batting AB	Batting H	Batting HR	BA	PO	A	E	DP	TC/G	FA
1882	BAL	AA	1	2	.333	*2.77*	3	3	3	26	30	4	9	0	0	0	0	20	2	0	.100	4	7	2	1	2.6	.846
1884	WAS	U	23	18	.561	*3.04*	50	41	34	364.1	383	60	268	4	0	**2**	0	339	79	2	.233	80	137	49	7	2.6	.816
1886	WAS	N	0	1	.000	9.00	1	1	0	3	6	2	0	0	0	0	0	3	0	0	.000	0	0	0	0	0.0	.000
3 yrs.			24	21	.533	3.07	54	45	37	393.1	419	66	277	4	0	2	0	*				84	144	51	8	2.5	.817

Rick Wise

WISE, RICHARD CHARLES BR TR 6′ 1″ 180 lbs.
B. Sept. 13, 1945, Jackson, Mich.

Year	Team	Lg	W	L	PCT	ERA	G	GS	CG	IP	H	BB	SO	ShO	Relief W	Relief L	Relief SV	Batting AB	Batting H	Batting HR	BA	PO	A	E	DP	TC/G	FA
1964	PHI	N	5	3	.625	4.04	25	8	0	69	78	25	39	0	1	1	0	17	5	0	.294	2	7	1	0	0.4	.900
1966			5	6	.455	3.71	22	13	3	99.1	100	24	58	0	0	2	0	30	0	0	.000	3	14	0	1	0.8	1.000
1967			11	11	.500	3.28	36	25	6	181.1	177	45	111	3	2	0	0	53	11	0	.208	11	32	0	4	1.2	1.000
1968			9	15	.375	4.54	30	30	7	182.1	210	37	97	1	0	0	0	58	14	2	.241	13	32	0	3	1.5	1.000
1969			15	13	.536	3.23	33	31	14	220	215	61	144	4	0	0	0	74	20	1	.270	7	43	0	3	1.5	1.000
1970			13	14	.481	4.17	35	34	5	220	253	65	113	1	0	0	0	75	15	2	.200	17	35	1	3	1.5	.981
1971			17	14	.548	2.88	38	37	17	272	261	70	155	4	0	0	0	97	23	6	.237	23	36	0	7	1.6	1.000
1972	STL	N	16	16	.500	3.11	35	35	20	269	250	71	142	2	0	0	0	93	16	1	.172	15	48	1	7	1.8	.984
1973			16	12	.571	3.37	35	34	14	259	259	59	144	5	1	0	0	88	17	3	.193	19	34	1	3	1.5	.981
1974	BOS	A	3	4	.429	3.86	9	9	1	49	47	16	25	0	0	0	0	0	0	0	—	3	4	0	2	0.8	1.000
1975			19	12	.613	3.95	35	35	17	255.1	262	72	141	1	0	0	0	0	0	0	—	16	32	4	3	1.5	.923
1976			14	11	.560	3.54	34	34	11	224	218	48	93	4	0	0	0	0	0	0	—	15	39	0	5	1.6	1.000
1977			11	5	.688	4.78	26	20	4	128	151	28	85	2	2	0	0	0	0	0	—	8	23	0	1	1.2	1.000
1978	CLE	A	9	**19**	.321	4.32	33	31	9	212.2	226	59	106	1	0	0	0	0	0	0	—	15	29	2	2	1.4	.957
1979			15	10	.600	3.72	34	34	9	232	229	68	108	2	0	0	0	0	0	0	—	23	53	2	2	2.3	.974

Year	Team	Lg	W	L	PCT	ERA	G	GS	CG	IP	H	BB	SO	ShO	Relief Pitching W	Relief Pitching L	Relief Pitching SV	Batting AB	Batting H	Batting HR	BA	PO	A	E	DP	TC/G	FA

Rick Wise *continued*

Year	Team	Lg	W	L	PCT	ERA	G	GS	CG	IP	H	BB	SO	ShO	Relief W	Relief L	SV	AB	H	HR	BA	PO	A	E	DP	TC/G	FA
1980	SD	N	6	8	.429	3.68	27	27	1	154	172	37	59	0	0	0	0	58	8	0	.138	11	22	1	0	1.3	.971
1981			4	8	.333	3.77	18	18	0	98	116	19	27	0	0	0	0	25	1	0	.040	3	21	0	0	1.3	1.000
1982			0	0	—	9.00	1	0	0	2	3	0	0	0	0	0	0	0	0	0	—	2	0	0	0	2.0	1.000
18 yrs.			188	181	.509	3.69	506	455	138	3127	3227	804	1647	30	6	3	0	668	130	15	.195	206	504	13	46	1.4	.982
LEAGUE CHAMPIONSHIP SERIES																											
1975	BOS	A	1	0	1.000	2.45	1	1	0	7.1	6	3	2	0	0	0	0	0	0	0	—	2	3	0	0	5.0	1.000
WORLD SERIES																											
1975	BOS	A	1	0	1.000	8.44	2	1	0	5.1	6	2	2	0	1	0	0	2	0	0	.000	0	0	0	0	0.0	.000

Roy Wise

WISE, ROY OGDEN
B. Nov. 18, 1924, Springfield, Ill.

BB TR 6′ 2″ 170 lbs.

Year	Team	Lg	W	L	PCT	ERA	G	GS	CG	IP	H	BB	SO	ShO	Relief W	Relief L	SV	AB	H	HR	BA	PO	A	E	DP	TC/G	FA
1944	PIT	N	0	0	—	9.00	2	0	0	3	4	3	1	0	0	0	0	0	0	0	—	0	0	0	0	0.0	.000

John Wisner

WISNER, JOHN HENRY
B. Nov. 5, 1899, Grand Rapids, Mich. D. Dec. 15, 1981, Jackson, Mich.

BR TR 6′ 3″ 195 lbs.

Year	Team	Lg	W	L	PCT	ERA	G	GS	CG	IP	H	BB	SO	ShO	Relief W	Relief L	SV	AB	H	HR	BA	PO	A	E	DP	TC/G	FA
1919	PIT	N	1	0	1.000	0.96	4	1	1	18.2	12	7	4	0	0	0	0	7	0	0	.000	1	6	2	0	2.3	.778
1920			1	3	.250	3.43	17	2	1	44.2	46	10	13	0	1	1	0	7	0	0	.000	5	15	0	0	1.2	1.000
1925	NY	N	0	0	—	3.79	25	0	0	40.1	33	14	13	0	0	0	0	7	0	0	.000	5	9	1	0	0.6	.933
1926			2	2	.500	3.54	5	3	2	28	21	10	5	0	0	1	0	10	2	0	.200	2	6	0	1	1.6	1.000
4 yrs.			4	5	.444	3.21	51	6	4	131.2	112	41	35	0	1	2	0	31	2	0	.065	13	36	3	1	1.0	.942

Whitey Wistert

WISTERT, FRANCIS MICHAEL
B. Feb. 20, 1912, Chicago, Ill. D. Apr. 23, 1985, Painesville, Ohio.

BR TR 6′ 4″ 210 lbs.

Year	Team	Lg	W	L	PCT	ERA	G	GS	CG	IP	H	BB	SO	ShO	Relief W	Relief L	SV	AB	H	HR	BA	PO	A	E	DP	TC/G	FA
1934	CIN	N	0	1	.000	1.13	2	1	0	8	5	5	1	0	0	0	0	3	0	0	.000	0	1	0	0	0.5	1.000

Roy Witherup

WITHERUP, FOSTER LeROY
B. July 26, 1886, N. Washington, Pa. D. Dec. 23, 1941, New Bethlehem, Pa.

BR TR 6′ 185 lbs.

Year	Team	Lg	W	L	PCT	ERA	G	GS	CG	IP	H	BB	SO	ShO	Relief W	Relief L	SV	AB	H	HR	BA	PO	A	E	DP	TC/G	FA
1906	BOS	N	0	3	.000	6.26	8	3	3	46	59	19	14	0	0	0	0	15	2	0	.133	0	12	3	1	1.9	.800
1908	WAS	A	2	4	.333	2.98	6	6	4	48.1	51	8	31	0	0	0	0	18	3	0	.167	1	15	0	0	2.7	1.000
1909			1	5	.167	4.24	12	8	5	68	79	20	26	0	0	0	0	19	1	0	.053	0	15	1	0	1.3	.938
3 yrs.			3	12	.200	4.44	26	17	12	162.1	189	47	71	0	0	0	0	52	6	0	.115	1	42	4	1	1.8	.915

Bobby Witt

WITT, ROBERT ANDREW
B. May 11, 1964, Arlington, Va.

BR TR 6′ 2″ 190 lbs.

Year	Team	Lg	W	L	PCT	ERA	G	GS	CG	IP	H	BB	SO	ShO	Relief W	Relief L	SV	AB	H	HR	BA	PO	A	E	DP	TC/G	FA
1986	TEX	A	11	9	.550	5.48	31	31	0	157.2	130	**143**	174	0	0	0	0	0	0	0	—	8	20	3	1	1.0	.903
1987			8	10	.444	4.91	26	25	1	143	114	**140**	160	0	0	0	0	1	0	0	.000	8	17	0	1	1.0	1.000
1988			8	10	.444	3.92	22	22	13	174.1	134	101	148	2	0	0	0	0	0	0	—	15	15	4	2	1.5	.882
1989			12	13	.480	5.14	31	31	5	194.1	182	**114**	166	1	0	0	0	0	0	0	—	13	22	1	1	1.2	.972
1990			17	10	.630	3.36	33	32	7	222	197	110	221	1	0	0	0	0	0	0	—	18	18	5	2	1.2	.878
1991			3	7	.300	6.09	17	16	1	88.2	84	74	82	1	0	0	0	0	0	0	—	7	6	2	1	0.9	.867
1992	2 teams	TEX A	(25G 9–13)		OAK A	(6G 1–1)																					
″	total		10	14	.417	4.29	31	31	0	193	183	114	125	0	0	0	0	0	0	0		14	20	1	2	1.1	.971
1993	OAK	A	14	13	.519	4.21	35	33	5	220	226	91	131	1	0	0	0	0	0	0	—	12	39	3	5	1.5	.944
1994			8	10	.444	5.04	24	24	5	135.2	151	70	111	3	0	0	0	0	0	0	—	7	13	4	2	1.0	.833
1995	2 teams	FLA N	(19G 2–7)		TEX A	(10G 3–4)																					
″	total		5	11	.313	4.13	29	29	2	172	185	68	141	0	0	0	0	32	2	0	.063	8	20	0	0	1.0	1.000
10 yrs.			96	107	.473	4.52	279	274	39	1700.2	1586	1025	1459	9	0	0	0	33	2	0	.061	110	190	23	17	1.2	.929
LEAGUE CHAMPIONSHIP SERIES																											
1992	OAK	A	0	0	—	18.00	1	0	0	1	2	1	1	0	0	0	0	0	0	0	—	0	0	0	0	0.0	.000

George Witt

WITT, GEORGE ADRIAN (Red)
B. Nov. 9, 1933, Long Beach, Calif.

BR TR 6′ 3″ 185 lbs.

Year	Team	Lg	W	L	PCT	ERA	G	GS	CG	IP	H	BB	SO	ShO	Relief W	Relief L	SV	AB	H	HR	BA	PO	A	E	DP	TC/G	FA
1957	PIT	N	0	1	.000	40.50	1	1	0	1.1	4	5	1	0	0	0	0	0	0	0	—	0	0	0	0	0.0	.000
1958			9	2	.818	1.61	18	15	5	106	78	59	81	3	0	0	0	39	6	0	.154	4	14	1	1	1.1	.947
1959			0	7	.000	6.93	15	11	0	50.2	58	32	30	0	0	0	0	12	0	0	.000	2	7	1	1	0.7	.900
1960			1	2	.333	4.20	10	6	0	30	33	12	15	0	0	0	0	9	0	0	.000	1	4	0	0	0.5	1.000
1961			0	1	.000	6.32	9	1	0	15.2	17	5	9	0	0	0	0	2	1	0	.500	0	1	0	0	0.1	1.000
1962	2 teams	LA A	(5G 1–1)		HOU N	(8G 0–2)																					
″	total		1	3	.250	7.46	13	4	0	25.1	35	14	20	0	1	0	0	7	2	0	.286	1	4	0	0	0.4	1.000
6 yrs.			11	16	.407	4.32	66	38	5	229	225	127	156	3	1	0	0	69	9	0	.130	8	30	2	2	0.6	.950
WORLD SERIES																											
1960	PIT	N	0	0	—	0.00	3	0	0	2.2	5	2	1	0	0	0	0	0	0	0	—	0	0	0	0	0.0	.000

Mike Witt

WITT, MICHAEL ATWATER
B. July 20, 1960, Fullerton, Calif.

BR TR 6′ 7″ 185 lbs.

Year	Team	Lg	W	L	PCT	ERA	G	GS	CG	IP	H	BB	SO	ShO	Relief W	Relief L	SV	AB	H	HR	BA	PO	A	E	DP	TC/G	FA
1981	CAL	A	8	9	.471	3.28	22	21	7	129	123	47	75	1	0	1	0	0	0	0	—	7	16	3	0	1.2	.885
1982			8	6	.571	3.51	33	26	5	179.2	177	47	85	1	0	1	0	0	0	0	—	14	24	4	3	1.3	.905
1983			7	14	.333	4.91	43	19	2	154	173	75	77	0	3	3	5	0	0	0	—	6	24	1	2	0.7	.968
1984			15	11	.577	3.47	34	34	9	246.2	227	84	196	2	0	0	0	0	0	0	—	16	27	2	0	1.3	.956
1985			15	9	.625	3.56	35	35	6	250	228	98	180	1	0	0	0	0	0	0	—	16	33	2	2	1.5	.961
1986			18	10	.643	2.84	34	34	14	269	218	73	208	3	0	0	0	0	0	0	—	22	39	1	5	1.8	.984
1987			16	14	.533	4.01	36	36	10	247	252	84	192	0	0	0	0	0	0	0	—	18	29	3	2	1.4	.940
1988			13	16	.448	4.15	34	34	12	249.2	263	87	133	2	0	0	0	0	0	0	—	19	32	2	2	1.6	.962
1989			9	15	.375	4.54	33	33	5	220	252	48	123	0	0	0	0	0	0	0	—	18	49	4	4	2.2	.944
1990	2 teams	CAL A	(10G 0–3)		NY A	(16G 5–6)																					
″	total		5	9	.357	4.00	26	16	2	117	106	47	74	1	0	3	1	0	0	0		9	18	1	1	1.1	.964
1991	NY	A	0	1	.000	10.13	2	2	0	5.1	8	1	0	0	0	0	0	0	0	0	—	1	1	0	0	1.0	1.000
1993			3	2	.600	5.27	9	9	0	41	39	22	30	0	0	0	0	0	0	0	—	1	6	0	0	0.8	1.000
12 yrs.			117	116	.502	3.83	341	299	72	2108.1	2066	713	1373	11	3	8	6	0	0	0		147	298	23	21	1.4	.951

Mike Witt *continued*

LEAGUE CHAMPIONSHIP SERIES

Year	Team	Lg	W	L	PCT	ERA	G	GS	CG	IP	H	BB	SO	ShO	Relief Pitching W	Relief Pitching L	Relief Pitching SV	Batting AB	Batting H	Batting HR	BA	PO	A	E	DP	TC/G	FA
1982	CAL	A	0	0	—	6.00	1	0	0	3	2	2	3	0	0	0	0	0	0	0	—	0	1	0	0	1.0	1.000
1986			1	0	1.000	2.55	2	2	1	17.2	13	2	8	0	0	0	0	0	0	0	—	2	4	0	0	3.0	1.000
2 yrs.			1	0	1.000	3.05	3	2	1	20.2	15	4	11	0	0	0	0	0	0	0		2	5	0	0	2.3	1.000

Johnnie Wittig

WITTIG, JOHN CARL (Hans) BR TR 6′ 180 lbs.
B. June 16, 1914, Baltimore, Md.

Year	Team	Lg	W	L	PCT	ERA	G	GS	CG	IP	H	BB	SO	ShO	Relief Pitching W	Relief Pitching L	Relief Pitching SV	Batting AB	Batting H	Batting HR	BA	PO	A	E	DP	TC/G	FA
1938	NY	N	2	3	.400	4.81	13	6	2	39.1	41	26	14	0	1	0	0	10	0	0	.000	0	1	0	1	0.1	1.000
1939			0	2	.000	7.56	5	2	1	16.2	18	14	4	0	0	0	0	5	0	0	.000	0	4	0	0	0.8	1.000
1941			3	5	.375	5.59	25	9	0	85.1	111	45	47	0	1	1	0	25	5	0	.200	0	10	0	1	0.4	1.000
1943			5	15	.250	4.23	40	22	4	164	171	76	56	1	0	1	4	51	5	0	.098	3	22	1	1	0.6	.962
1949	BOS	A	0	0	—	9.00	1	0	0	2	2	2	0	0	0	0	0	0	0	0	—	0	1	0	0	1.0	1.000
5 yrs.			10	25	.286	4.89	84	39	7	307.1	343	163	121	1	2	2	4	91	10	0	.110	3	38	1	3	0.5	.976

Mark Wohlers

WOHLERS, MARK EDWARD BR TR 6′ 4″ 207 lbs.
B. Jan. 23, 1970, Holyoke, Mass.

Year	Team	Lg	W	L	PCT	ERA	G	GS	CG	IP	H	BB	SO	ShO	Relief Pitching W	Relief Pitching L	Relief Pitching SV	Batting AB	Batting H	Batting HR	BA	PO	A	E	DP	TC/G	FA
1991	ATL	N	3	1	.750	3.20	17	0	0	19.2	17	13	13	0	3	1	2	1	0	0	.000	0	3	0	1	0.2	1.000
1992			1	2	.333	2.55	32	0	0	35.1	28	14	17	0	1	2	4	2	0	0	.000	2	7	0	0	0.3	1.000
1993			6	2	.750	4.50	46	0	0	48	37	22	45	0	6	2	0	0	0	0	—	6	6	0	1	0.3	1.000
1994			7	2	.778	4.59	51	0	0	51	51	33	58	0	**7**	2	1	1	1	0	1.000	3	7	1	0	0.2	.909
1995			7	3	.700	2.09	65	0	0	64.2	51	24	90	0	7	3	25	3	0	0	.000	4	3	0	0	0.1	1.000
5 yrs.			24	10	.706	3.38	211	0	0	218.2	184	106	223	0	24	10	32	7	1	0	.143	15	26	1	2	0.2	.976

DIVISIONAL PLAYOFF SERIES

Year	Team	Lg	W	L	PCT	ERA	G	GS	CG	IP	H	BB	SO	ShO	Relief Pitching W	Relief Pitching L	Relief Pitching SV	Batting AB	Batting H	Batting HR	BA	PO	A	E	DP	TC/G	FA
1995	ATL	N	0	1	.000	6.75	3	0	0	2.2	6	2	4	0	0	1	2	0	0	0	—	0	0	0	0	0.0	.000

LEAGUE CHAMPIONSHIP SERIES

Year	Team	Lg	W	L	PCT	ERA	G	GS	CG	IP	H	BB	SO	ShO	Relief Pitching W	Relief Pitching L	Relief Pitching SV	Batting AB	Batting H	Batting HR	BA	PO	A	E	DP	TC/G	FA
1991	ATL	N	0	0	—	0.00	3	0	0	1.2	3	1	1	0	0	0	0	0	0	0	—	0	0	0	0	0.0	.000
1992			0	0	—	0.00	3	0	0	3	2	1	2	0	0	0	0	0	0	0	—	1	0	0	0	0.3	1.000
1993			0	1	.000	3.38	4	0	0	5.1	2	3	10	0	0	1	0	0	0	0	—	0	0	0	0	0.0	.000
1995			1	0	1.000	1.80	4	0	0	5	2	0	8	0	1	0	0	0	0	0	—	1	0	0	0	0.3	1.000
4 yrs.			1	1	.500	1.80	14 **4th**	0	0	15	9	5	21	0	1	1	0	0	0	0		2	0	0	0	0.1	1.000

WORLD SERIES

Year	Team	Lg	W	L	PCT	ERA	G	GS	CG	IP	H	BB	SO	ShO	Relief Pitching W	Relief Pitching L	Relief Pitching SV	Batting AB	Batting H	Batting HR	BA	PO	A	E	DP	TC/G	FA
1991	ATL	N	0	0	—	0.00	3	0	0	1.2	2	2	1	0	0	0	0	0	0	0	—	0	0	0	0	0.0	.000
1992			0	0	—	0.00	2	0	0	0.2	0	1	0	0	0	0	0	0	0	0	—	0	0	0	0	0.0	.000
1995			0	0	—	1.80	4	0	0	5	4	3	3	0	0	0	2	0	0	0	—	0	0	0	0	0.0	.000
3 yrs.			0	0		1.23	9	0	0	7.1	6	6	4	0	0	0	2	0	0	0		0	0	0	0	0.0	

Steve Wojciechowski

WOJCIECHOWSKI, STEVEN JOSEPH BL TL 6′ 2″ 185 lbs.
B. July 29, 1970, Blue Island, Ill.

Year	Team	Lg	W	L	PCT	ERA	G	GS	CG	IP	H	BB	SO	ShO	Relief Pitching W	Relief Pitching L	Relief Pitching SV	Batting AB	Batting H	Batting HR	BA	PO	A	E	DP	TC/G	FA
1995	OAK	A	2	3	.400	5.18	14	7	0	48.2	51	28	13	0	0	0	0	0	0	0	—	1	8	0	0	0.6	1.000

Pete Wojey

WOJEY, PETER PAUL BR TR 5′11″ 185 lbs.
B. Dec. 1, 1919, Stowe, Pa.

Year	Team	Lg	W	L	PCT	ERA	G	GS	CG	IP	H	BB	SO	ShO	Relief Pitching W	Relief Pitching L	Relief Pitching SV	Batting AB	Batting H	Batting HR	BA	PO	A	E	DP	TC/G	FA
1954	BKN	N	1	1	.500	3.25	14	1	0	27.2	24	14	21	0	0	0	1	3	0	0	.000	1	8	0	0	0.6	1.000
1956	DET	A	0	0	—	2.25	2	0	0	4	2	1	1	0	0	0	0	0	0	0	—	0	2	0	0	1.0	1.000
1957			0	0	—	0.00	2	0	0	1.1	1	0	0	0	0	0	0	0	0	0	—	0	1	0	0	0.5	1.000
3 yrs.			1	1	.500	3.00	18	1	0	33	27	15	22	0	0	0	1	3	0	0	.000	1	11	0	0	0.7	1.000

Ed Wojna

WOJNA, EDWARD DAVID BR TR 6′ 1″ 195 lbs.
B. Aug. 20, 1960, Bridgeport, Conn.

Year	Team	Lg	W	L	PCT	ERA	G	GS	CG	IP	H	BB	SO	ShO	Relief Pitching W	Relief Pitching L	Relief Pitching SV	Batting AB	Batting H	Batting HR	BA	PO	A	E	DP	TC/G	FA
1985	SD	N	2	4	.333	5.79	15	7	0	42	53	19	18	0	1	1	0	12	2	0	.167	4	8	3	1	1.0	.800
1986			2	2	.500	3.23	7	7	1	39	42	16	19	0	0	0	0	14	2	0	.143	1	5	2	0	1.1	.750
1987			0	3	.000	5.89	5	3	0	18.1	25	6	13	0	0	0	0	5	0	0	.000	3	5	0	0	1.6	1.000
1989	CLE	A	0	1	.000	4.09	9	3	0	33	31	14	10	0	0	0	0	0	0	0	—	4	7	0	1	1.2	1.000
4 yrs.			4	10	.286	4.62	36	20	1	132.1	151	55	60	0	1	1	0	31	4	0	.129	12	25	5	2	1.2	.881

Bob Wolcott

WOLCOTT, ROBERT WILLIAM BR TR 6′ 190 lbs.
B. Sept. 8, 1973, Huntington Beach, Calif.

Year	Team	Lg	W	L	PCT	ERA	G	GS	CG	IP	H	BB	SO	ShO	Relief Pitching W	Relief Pitching L	Relief Pitching SV	Batting AB	Batting H	Batting HR	BA	PO	A	E	DP	TC/G	FA
1995	SEA	A	3	2	.600	4.42	7	6	0	36.2	43	14	19	0	0	0	0	0	0	0	—	4	0	0	0	0.6	1.000

LEAGUE CHAMPIONSHIP SERIES

Year	Team	Lg	W	L	PCT	ERA	G	GS	CG	IP	H	BB	SO	ShO	Relief Pitching W	Relief Pitching L	Relief Pitching SV	Batting AB	Batting H	Batting HR	BA	PO	A	E	DP	TC/G	FA
1995	SEA	A	1	0	1.000	2.57	1	1	0	7	8	5	2	0	0	0	0	0	0	0	—	1	1	0	0	2.0	1.000

Chicken Wolf

WOLF, WILLIAM VAN WINKLE BR TR 5′ 9″ 190 lbs.
B. May 12, 1862, Louisville, Ky. D. May 16, 1903, Louisville, Ky.
Manager 1889.

Year	Team	Lg	W	L	PCT	ERA	G	GS	CG	IP	H	BB	SO	ShO	Relief Pitching W	Relief Pitching L	Relief Pitching SV	Batting AB	Batting H	Batting HR	BA	PO	A	E	DP	TC/G	FA
1882	LOU	AA	0	0	—	*9.00*	1	0	0	6	11	3	1	0	0	0	0	318	95	0	.299	98	45	21	3	2.0	.872
1885			0	0	—	*9.00*	1	0	0	1	1	0	1	0	0	0	0	483	141	1	.292	244	66	42	9	3.4	.881
1886			0	0	—	*15.00*	1	0	0	3	7	0	0	0	0	0	0	545	148	3	.272	267	40	27	13	2.5	.919
3 yrs.			0	0		10.80	3	0	0	10	19	3	2	0	0	0	0	*				2306	580	304	97	2.6	.905

Ernie Wolf

WOLF, ERNEST ADOLPH BR TR 5′11″ 174 lbs.
B. Feb. 2, 1889, Newark, N. J. D. May 23, 1964, Atlantic Highlands, N. J.

Year	Team	Lg	W	L	PCT	ERA	G	GS	CG	IP	H	BB	SO	ShO	Relief Pitching W	Relief Pitching L	Relief Pitching SV	Batting AB	Batting H	Batting HR	BA	PO	A	E	DP	TC/G	FA
1912	CLE	A	0	0	—	6.35	1	0	0	5.2	8	4	1	0	0	0	0	2	0	0	.000	0	0	0	0	0.0	.000

Lefty Wolf

WOLF, WALTER FRANCIS BR TL 5′10″ 163 lbs.
B. June 10, 1900, Hartford, Conn. D. Sept. 25, 1971, New Orleans, La.

Year	Team	Lg	W	L	PCT	ERA	G	GS	CG	IP	H	BB	SO	ShO	Relief Pitching W	Relief Pitching L	Relief Pitching SV	Batting AB	Batting H	Batting HR	BA	PO	A	E	DP	TC/G	FA
1921	PHI	A	0	0	—	7.20	8	0	0	15	15	16	12	0	0	0	0	4	1	0	.250	1	3	2	0	0.8	.667

Wally Wolf

WOLF, WALTER BECK BR TR 6′½″ 191 lbs.
B. Jan. 5, 1942, South Gate, Calif.

Year	Team	Lg	W	L	PCT	ERA	G	GS	CG	IP	H	BB	SO	ShO	Relief Pitching W	Relief Pitching L	Relief Pitching SV	Batting AB	Batting H	Batting HR	BA	PO	A	E	DP	TC/G	FA
1969	CAL	A	0	0	—	11.57	2	0	0	2.1	3	3	2	0	0	0	0	0	0	0	—	0	0	0	0	0.0	.000
1970			0	0	—	5.40	4	0	0	5	3	4	5	0	0	0	0	0	0	0	—	0	0	0	0	0.0	.000
2 yrs.			0	0		7.36	6	0	0	7.1	6	7	7	0	0	0	0	0	0	0		0	0	0	0	0.0	

Bill Wolfe

WOLFE, WILBERT OTTO (Barney)
B. June 7, 1876, Independence, Pa. D. Feb. 27, 1953, Gibsontown, Pa.
BR TR 6′ 1″

Year	Team	Lg	W	L	PCT	ERA	G	GS	CG	IP	H	BB	SO	ShO	Relief W	Relief L	Relief SV	AB	H	HR	BA	PO	A	E	DP	TC/G	FA
1903	NY	A	6	9	.400	2.97	20	16	12	148.1	143	26	48	1	0	1	0	53	4	0	.075	6	45	2	1	2.7	.962
1904	2 teams	NY A (7G 0–3) WAS A (17G 6–9)																									
″	total		6	12	.333	3.26	24	19	15	160.1	162	26	52	2	0	1	0	52	5	0	.096	10	44	2	1	2.3	.964
1905	WAS	A	9	13	.409	2.57	28	24	17	182	162	37	52	1	2	0	**2**	60	8	1	.133	10	48	3	1	2.2	.951
1906			0	3	.000	4.05	4	3	2	20	17	10	8	0	0	0	0	7	2	0	.286	0	7	1	0	2.0	.875
4 yrs.			21	37	.362	2.96	76	62	46	510.2	484	99	160	4	2	2	2	172	19	1	.110	26	144	8	3	2.3	.955

Bill Wolfe

WOLFE, WILLIAM F.
B. Jersey City, N. J. Deceased.

Year	Team	Lg	W	L	PCT	ERA	G	GS	CG	IP	H	BB	SO	ShO	Relief W	Relief L	Relief SV	AB	H	HR	BA	PO	A	E	DP	TC/G	FA
1902	PHI	N	0	1	.000	4.00	1	1	1	9	11	4	3	0	0	0	0	3	1	0	.333	0	3	0	0	3.0	1.000

Chuck Wolfe

WOLFE, CHARLES HUNT
B. Feb. 15, 1897, Wolfsburg, Pa. D. Nov. 27, 1957, Schellsburg, Pa.
BL TR 5′ 7″ 175 lbs.

Year	Team	Lg	W	L	PCT	ERA	G	GS	CG	IP	H	BB	SO	ShO	Relief W	Relief L	Relief SV	AB	H	HR	BA	PO	A	E	DP	TC/G	FA
1923	PHI	A	0	0	—	3.72	3	0	0	9.2	6	8	1	0	0	0	0	3	1	0	.333	0	2	0	0	0.7	1.000

Ed Wolfe

WOLFE, EDWARD ANTHONY
B. Jan. 2, 1929, Los Angeles, Calif.
BR TR 6′ 3″ 185 lbs.

Year	Team	Lg	W	L	PCT	ERA	G	GS	CG	IP	H	BB	SO	ShO	Relief W	Relief L	Relief SV	AB	H	HR	BA	PO	A	E	DP	TC/G	FA
1952	PIT	N	0	0	—	7.36	3	0	0	3.2	7	5	1	0	0	0	0	0	0	0	—	1	1	0	1	0.7	1.000

Roger Wolff

WOLFF, ROGER FRANCIS
B. Apr. 10, 1911, Evansville, Ill. D. Mar. 23, 1994, Chester, Ill.
BR TR 6′½″ 208 lbs.

Year	Team	Lg	W	L	PCT	ERA	G	GS	CG	IP	H	BB	SO	ShO	Relief W	Relief L	Relief SV	AB	H	HR	BA	PO	A	E	DP	TC/G	FA
1941	PHI	A	0	2	.000	3.18	2	2	2	17	15	4	2	0	0	0	0	5	1	0	.200	1	2	0	0	1.5	1.000
1942			12	15	.444	3.32	32	25	15	214.1	206	69	94	2	2	2	3	68	6	0	.088	17	38	2	5	1.8	.965
1943			10	15	.400	3.54	41	26	13	221	232	72	91	2	2	2	6	74	9	0	.122	12	30	1	0	1.0	.977
1944	WAS	A	4	15	.211	4.99	33	21	5	155	186	60	73	0	1	2	2	55	12	0	.218	8	37	0	2	1.4	1.000
1945			20	10	.667	2.12	33	29	21	250	200	53	108	4	0	2	2	84	9	0	.107	6	45	1	2	1.6	.981
1946			5	8	.385	2.58	21	17	6	122	115	30	50	0	1	2	0	39	4	0	.103	9	17	1	0	1.3	.963
1947	2 teams	CLE A (7G 0–0) PIT N (13G 1–4)																									
″	total		1	4	.200	7.04	20	8	1	46	64	28	12	0	0	1	0	12	0	0	.000	4	8	0	1	0.6	1.000
7 yrs.			52	69	.430	3.41	182	128	63	1025.1	1018	316	430	8	6	11	13	337	41	0	.122	57	177	5	10	1.3	.979

Mellie Wolfgang

WOLFGANG, MELDON JOHN (Red)
B. Mar. 20, 1890, Albany, N. Y. D. June 30, 1947, Albany, N. Y.
BR TR 5′ 9″ 160 lbs.

Year	Team	Lg	W	L	PCT	ERA	G	GS	CG	IP	H	BB	SO	ShO	Relief W	Relief L	Relief SV	AB	H	HR	BA	PO	A	E	DP	TC/G	FA
1914	CHI	A	9	5	.643	1.89	24	11	9	119.1	96	32	50	2	4	0	0	40	7	0	.175	7	53	2	1	2.6	.968
1915			2	2	.500	1.84	17	2	0	53.2	39	12	21	0	2	1	0	17	2	0	.118	1	13	3	0	1.0	.824
1916			4	6	.400	1.98	27	14	6	127	103	42	36	1	0	2	0	40	9	0	.225	5	47	5	2	2.0	.912
1917			0	0	—	5.09	5	0	0	17.2	18	6	3	0	0	0	0	4	0	0	.000	0	5	1	0	1.2	.833
1918			0	1	.000	5.40	4	0	0	8.1	12	3	1	0	0	1	0	2	1	0	.500	1	4	0	0	1.0	1.000
5 yrs.			15	14	.517	2.18	77	27	15	326	268	95	111	3	6	4	0	103	19	0	.184	14	122	11	3	1.9	.925

Harry Wolter

WOLTER, HARRY MEIGS
B. July 11, 1884, Monterey, Calif. D. July 7, 1970, Palo Alto, Calif.
BL TL 5′10″ 175 lbs.

Year	Team	Lg	W	L	PCT	ERA	G	GS	CG	IP	H	BB	SO	ShO	Relief W	Relief L	Relief SV	AB	H	HR	BA	PO	A	E	DP	TC/G	FA
1907	2 teams	PIT N (1G 0–0) STL N (3G 1–2)																									
″	total		1	2	.333	4.32	4	3	1	25	30	20	8	0	0	0	0	63	18	0	.286	20	5	1	1	1.5	.962
1909	BOS	A	4	4	.500	3.91	10	6	0	53	53	28	20	0	1	1	0	119	29	2	.244	189	26	9	6	6.2	.960
2 yrs.			5	6	.455	4.04	14	9	1	78	83	48	28	0	1	1	0	*				966	92	59	25	2.1	.947

Dooley Womack

WOMACK, HORACE GUY
B. Aug. 25, 1939, Columbia, S. C.
BL TR 6′ 170 lbs.

Year	Team	Lg	W	L	PCT	ERA	G	GS	CG	IP	H	BB	SO	ShO	Relief W	Relief L	Relief SV	AB	H	HR	BA	PO	A	E	DP	TC/G	FA
1966	NY	A	7	3	.700	2.64	42	1	0	75	52	23	50	0	7	2	4	5	1	0	.200	7	21	1	2	0.7	.966
1967			5	6	.455	2.41	65	0	0	97	80	35	57	0	5	6	18	14	4	0	.286	13	33	2	3	0.7	.958
1968			3	7	.300	3.21	45	0	0	61.2	53	29	27	0	3	7	2	5	1	0	.200	6	19	0	1	0.6	1.000
1969	2 teams	HOU N (30G 2–1) SEA A (9G 2–1)																									
″	total		4	2	.667	3.31	39	0	0	65.1	64	23	40	0	4	2	0	7	1	0	.143	9	20	1	0	0.8	.967
1970	OAK	A	0	0	—	15.00	2	0	0	3	4	1	3	0	0	0	0	0	0	0	—	0	1	0	0	0.5	1.000
5 yrs.			19	18	.514	2.95	193	1	0	302	253	111	177	0	19	17	24	31	7	0	.226	35	94	4	6	0.7	.970

George Wood

WOOD, GEORGE A. (Dandy)
B. Nov. 9, 1858, Boston, Mass. D. Apr. 4, 1924, Harrisburg, Pa.
Manager 1891.
BL TR 5′10½″ 175 lbs.

Year	Team	Lg	W	L	PCT	ERA	G	GS	CG	IP	H	BB	SO	ShO	Relief W	Relief L	Relief SV	AB	H	HR	BA	PO	A	E	DP	TC/G	FA
1883	DET	N	0	0	—	*7.20*	1	0	0	5	8	3	0	0	0	0	0	441	133	5	.302	128	11	17	1	1.9	.891
1885			0	0	—	0.00	1	0	0	4	5	1	1	0	0	0	0	362	105	5	.290	132	18	24	4	2.2	.862
1888	PHI	N	0	0	—	4.50	2	0	0	2	3	1	0	0	0	0	**2**	433	99	6	.229	161	14	23	8	2.4	.884
1889			0	0	—	18.00	1	0	0	1	2	0	2	0	0	0	0	432	108	5	.250	175	27	19	1	2.2	.914
4 yrs.			0	0		5.25	5	0	0	12	18	5	3	0	0	0	2	*				2198	321	305	56	2.2	.892

Joe Wood

WOOD, JOSEPH FRANK
Son of Smoky Joe Wood.
B. May 20, 1916, Shohola, Pa.
BR TR 6′ 190 lbs.

Year	Team	Lg	W	L	PCT	ERA	G	GS	CG	IP	H	BB	SO	ShO	Relief W	Relief L	Relief SV	AB	H	HR	BA	PO	A	E	DP	TC/G	FA
1944	BOS	A	0	1	.000	6.52	3	1	0	9.2	13	3	5	0	0	0	0	2	0	0	.000	3	1	0	1	1.3	1.000

John Wood

WOOD, JOHN B.
B. 1871 Deceased.
5′ 7″ 142 lbs.

Year	Team	Lg	W	L	PCT	ERA	G	GS	CG	IP	H	BB	SO	ShO	Relief W	Relief L	Relief SV	AB	H	HR	BA	PO	A	E	DP	TC/G	FA
1896	STL	N	0	0	—	∞	1	0	0		1	2	0	0	0	0	0	0	0	0	—	0	0	0	0	0.0	.000

Pete Wood

WOOD, PETER BURKE
Brother of Fred Wood.
B. Feb. 1, 1857, Hamilton, Ont., Canada D. Mar. 15, 1923, Chicago, Ill.
TR 5′ 7″ 185 lbs.

Year	Team	Lg	W	L	PCT	ERA	G	GS	CG	IP	H	BB	SO	ShO	Relief W	Relief L	Relief SV	AB	H	HR	BA	PO	A	E	DP	TC/G	FA
1885	BUF	N	8	15	.348	*4.44*	24	22	21	198.2	235	66	38	0	0	**1**	0	104	23	0	.221	28	43	12	0	2.8	.855
1889	PHI	N	1	1	.500	5.21	3	2	2	19	28	3	8	0	0	0	0	8	0	0	.000	0	4	2	1	2.0	.667
2 yrs.			9	16	.360	4.51	27	24	23	217.2	263	69	46	0	0	1	0	112	23	0	.205	28	47	14	1	2.7	.843

Smoky Joe Wood

WOOD, JOE BR TR 5′11″ 180 lbs.
Born Howard Ellsworth Wood.
Father of Joe Wood.
B. Oct. 25, 1889, Kansas City, Mo. D. July 27, 1985, West Haven, Conn.

Year	Team	W	L	PCT	ERA	G	GS	CG	IP	H	BB	SO	ShO	Relief Pitching W	Relief Pitching L	Relief Pitching SV	Batting AB	Batting H	Batting HR	BA	PO	A	E	DP	TC/G	FA
1908	BOS A	1	1	.500	2.38	6	2	1	22.2	14	16	11	1	0	0	0	7	0	0	.000	3	5	1	1	1.5	.889
1909		11	7	.611	2.21	24	19	13	158.2	121	43	88	4	2	0	0	55	9	0	.164	7	27	1	0	1.5	.971
1910		12	13	.480	1.68	35	17	14	197.2	155	56	145	3	**6**	3	0	69	18	1	.261	17	62	2	3	2.3	.975
1911		23	17	.575	2.02	44	33	25	276.2	226	76	231	5	6	2	3	88	23	2	.261	23	67	5	3	2.2	.947
1912		**34**	5	**.872**	1.91	43	38	**35**	344	267	82	258	**10**	1	0	1	124	36	1	.290	41	110	4	2	3.6	.974
1913		11	5	.688	2.29	23	18	12	145.2	120	61	123	1	1	1	2	56	15	0	.268	9	55	3	1	2.9	.955
1914		9	3	.750	2.62	18	14	11	113.1	94	34	67	1	0	0	1	43	6	0	.140	13	28	0	0	2.3	1.000
1915		15	5	**.750**	**1.49**	25	16	10	157.1	120	44	63	3	3	2	2	54	14	1	.259	8	48	1	6	2.3	.982
1917	CLE A	0	1	.000	3.45	5	1	0	15.2	17	7	2	0	0	0	1	6	0	0	.000	2	5	0	0	1.4	1.000
1919		0	0	—	0.00	1	0	0	0.2	0	0	0	0	0	0	1	192	49	1	.255	273	77	17	7	3.1	.954
1920		0	0	—	22.50	1	0	0	2	4	2	1	0	0	0	0	137	37	1	.270	71	6	1	0	1.4	.987
11 yrs.		116	57	.671	2.03	225	158	121	1434.1	1138	421	989	28	19	8	11	*				911	518	56	30	2.2	.962
WORLD SERIES																										
1912	BOS A	3	1	.750	3.68	4	3	2	22	27	3	21	0	1	0	0	*				1	6	0	1	1.8	1.000

Spades Wood

WOOD, CHARLES ASHER BL TL 5′10½″ 150 lbs.
B. Jan. 13, 1909, Spartanburg, S. C. D. May 18, 1986, Wichita, Kans.

Year	Team	W	L	PCT	ERA	G	GS	CG	IP	H	BB	SO	ShO	Relief Pitching W	Relief Pitching L	Relief Pitching SV	Batting AB	Batting H	Batting HR	BA	PO	A	E	DP	TC/G	FA
1930	PIT N	4	3	.571	5.12	9	7	4	58	61	32	23	2	0	1	0	20	5	0	.250	1	4	0	1	0.6	1.000
1931		2	6	.250	6.05	15	10	2	64	69	46	33	0	0	0	0	22	5	0	.227	1	13	1	0	1.0	.933
2 yrs.		6	9	.400	5.61	24	17	6	122	130	78	56	2	0	1	0	42	10	0	.238	2	17	1	1	0.8	.950

Wilbur Wood

WOOD, WILBUR FORRESTER BR TL 6′ 180 lbs.
B. Oct. 22, 1941, Cambridge, Mass.

Year	Team	W	L	PCT	ERA	G	GS	CG	IP	H	BB	SO	ShO	Relief Pitching W	Relief Pitching L	Relief Pitching SV	Batting AB	Batting H	Batting HR	BA	PO	A	E	DP	TC/G	FA
1961	BOS A	0	0	—	5.54	6	1	0	13	14	7	7	0	0	0	0	3	0	0	.000	2	0	0	0	0.3	1.000
1962		0	0	—	3.52	1	1	0	7.2	6	3	3	0	0	0	0	3	0	0	.000	0	3	0	0	3.0	1.000
1963		0	5	.000	3.76	25	6	0	64.2	67	13	28	0	0	1	0	12	0	0	.000	2	10	1	0	0.5	.923
1964	2 teams	BOS A (4G 0–0)	PIT N (3G 0–2)																							
″	total	0	2	.000	7.04	7	2	1	23	29	14	12	0	0	0	0	6	0	0	.000	1	3	0	0	0.6	1.000
1965	PIT N	1	1	.500	3.16	34	1	0	51.1	44	16	29	0	1	0	0	6	0	0	.000	2	6	0	0	0.2	1.000
1967	CHI A	4	2	.667	2.45	51	8	0	95.1	95	28	47	0	0	0	4	16	1	0	.063	7	13	2	2	0.4	.909
1968		13	12	.520	1.87	**88**	2	0	159	127	33	74	0	**12**	**11**	16	22	2	0	.091	7	25	0	1	0.4	1.000
1969		10	11	.476	3.01	**76**	0	0	119.2	113	40	73	0	10	**11**	15	15	0	0	.000	5	22	1	0	0.4	.964
1970		9	13	.409	2.80	**77**	0	0	122	118	36	85	0	9	13	21	18	2	0	.111	7	27	0	3	0.4	1.000
1971		22	13	.629	1.91	44	42	22	334	272	62	210	7	0	0	1	96	5	0	.052	11	65	1	3	1.8	.987
1972		**24**	17	.585	2.51	49	**49**	20	**376.2**	**325**	74	193	8	0	0	0	125	17	0	.136	9	82	4	8	1.9	.958
1973		**24**	20	.545	3.46	49	**48**	21	**359.1**	**381**	91	199	4	1	0	0	0	0	0	—	9	62	1	3	1.5	.986
1974		20	19	.513	3.60	42	**42**	22	320	305	80	169	1	0	0	0	0	0	0	—	8	67	3	1	1.9	.962
1975		16	**20**	.444	4.11	43	**43**	14	291.1	309	92	140	2	0	0	0	0	0	0	—	8	53	1	3	1.4	.984
1976		4	3	.571	2.25	7	7	5	56	51	11	31	1	0	0	0	0	0	0	—	1	12	0	0	1.9	1.000
1977		7	8	.467	4.98	24	18	5	123	139	50	42	1	0	0	0	0	0	0	—	3	33	0	1	1.5	1.000
1978		10	10	.500	5.20	28	27	4	168	187	74	69	0	0	0	0	0	0	0	—	2	40	0	1	1.5	1.000
17 yrs.		164	156	.512	3.24	651	297	114	2684	2582	724	1411	24	33	36	57	322	27	0	.084	84	523	14	26	1.0	.977

Brad Woodall

WOODALL, DAVID BRADLEY BB TL 6′ 175 lbs.
B. June 25, 1969, Atlanta, Ga.

Year	Team	W	L	PCT	ERA	G	GS	CG	IP	H	BB	SO	ShO	Relief Pitching W	Relief Pitching L	Relief Pitching SV	Batting AB	Batting H	Batting HR	BA	PO	A	E	DP	TC/G	FA
1994	ATL N	0	1	.000	4.50	1	1	0	6	5	2	2	0	0	0	0	2	1	0	.500	0	3	0	1	3.0	1.000
1995		1	1	.500	6.10	9	0	0	10.1	13	8	5	0	1	1	0	1	1	0	1.000	0	2	0	1	0.2	1.000
2 yrs.		1	2	.333	5.51	10	1	0	16.1	18	10	7	0	1	1	0	3	2	0	.667	0	5	0	2	0.5	1.000

Gene Woodburn

WOODBURN, EUGENE STEWART BR TR 6′ 175 lbs.
B. Aug. 20, 1886, Bellaire, Ohio D. Jan. 18, 1961, Sandusky, Ohio.

Year	Team	W	L	PCT	ERA	G	GS	CG	IP	H	BB	SO	ShO	Relief Pitching W	Relief Pitching L	Relief Pitching SV	Batting AB	Batting H	Batting HR	BA	PO	A	E	DP	TC/G	FA
1911	STL N	1	5	.167	5.40	11	6	1	38.1	22	40	23	0	0	1	0	6	1	0	.167	1	13	1	1	1.4	.933
1912		1	4	.200	5.59	20	5	1	48.1	60	42	25	0	1	0	0	13	0	0	.000	2	10	5	0	0.9	.706
2 yrs.		2	9	.182	5.50	31	11	2	86.2	82	82	48	0	1	1	0	19	1	0	.053	3	23	6	1	1.0	.813

Fred Woodcock

WOODCOCK, FRED WAYLAND BL TL 6′2″ 190 lbs.
B. May 17, 1868, Winchendon, Mass. D. Aug. 11, 1943, Ashburnham, Mass.

Year	Team	W	L	PCT	ERA	G	GS	CG	IP	H	BB	SO	ShO	Relief Pitching W	Relief Pitching L	Relief Pitching SV	Batting AB	Batting H	Batting HR	BA	PO	A	E	DP	TC/G	FA
1892	PIT N	1	2	.333	3.55	5	4	3	33	42	17	8	0	0	0	0	15	3	0	.200	2	6	0	2	1.6	1.000

George Woodend

WOODEND, GEORGE ANTHONY BR TR 6′ 200 lbs.
B. Dec. 9, 1917, Hartford, Conn. D. May 1, 1980, Hartford, Conn.

Year	Team	W	L	PCT	ERA	G	GS	CG	IP	H	BB	SO	ShO	Relief Pitching W	Relief Pitching L	Relief Pitching SV	Batting AB	Batting H	Batting HR	BA	PO	A	E	DP	TC/G	FA
1944	BOS N	0	0	—	13.50	3	0	0	2	5	5	0	0	0	0	0	0	0	0	—	0	1	0	0	0.3	1.000

Hal Woodeshick

WOODESHICK, HAROLD JOSEPH BR TL 6′3″ 200 lbs.
B. Aug. 24, 1932, Wilkes-Barre, Pa.

Year	Team	W	L	PCT	ERA	G	GS	CG	IP	H	BB	SO	ShO	Relief Pitching W	Relief Pitching L	Relief Pitching SV	Batting AB	Batting H	Batting HR	BA	PO	A	E	DP	TC/G	FA
1956	DET A	0	2	.000	13.50	2	2	0	5.1	12	3	1	0	0	0	0	0	0	0	—	1	1	0	0	1.0	1.000
1958	CLE A	6	6	.500	3.64	14	9	3	71.2	71	25	27	0	3	0	0	24	4	0	.167	4	26	4	4	2.4	.882
1959	WAS A	2	4	.333	3.69	31	3	0	61	58	36	30	0	2	1	0	8	0	0	.000	1	16	2	0	0.6	.895
1960		4	5	.444	4.70	41	14	1	115	131	60	46	0	2	1	4	29	2	0	.069	4	33	4	1	1.0	.902
1961	2 teams	WAS A (7G 3–2)	DET A (12G 1–1)																							
″	total	4	3	.571	5.22	19	8	1	58.2	63	41	37	0	1	0	0	20	2	0	.100	6	19	3	0	1.5	.893
1962	HOU N	5	16	.238	4.39	31	26	2	139.1	161	54	82	1	0	1	0	37	3	0	.081	7	26	3	0	1.2	.917
1963		11	9	.550	1.97	55	0	0	114	75	42	94	0	11	**9**	10	23	3	0	.130	6	33	3	1	0.8	.929
1964		2	9	.182	2.76	61	0	0	78.1	73	32	58	0	2	**9**	**23**	10	0	0	.000	5	23	5	0	0.5	.848
1965	2 teams	HOU N (27G 3–4)	STL N (51G 3–2)																							
″	total	6	6	.500	2.25	78	0	0	92	74	45	59	0	6	6	18	14	1	0	.071	11	24	1	1	0.5	.972
1966	STL N	2	1	.667	1.92	59	0	0	70.1	57	23	30	0	2	1	4	5	1	0	.200	7	26	0	1	0.6	1.000
1967		2	1	.667	5.18	36	0	0	41.2	41	28	20	0	2	1	2	4	0	0	.000	2	12	2	1	0.4	.875
11 yrs.		44	62	.415	3.56	427	62	7	847.1	816	389	484	1	31	29	61	174	16	0	.092	54	239	27	9	0.7	.916

Hal Woodeshick *continued*

Year	Team	Lg	W	L	PCT	ERA	G	GS	CG	IP	H	BB	SO	ShO	Relief W	Relief L	Relief SV	Batting AB	Batting H	HR	BA	PO	A	E	DP	TC/G	FA
WORLD SERIES																											
1967	STL	N	0	0	—	0.00	1	0	0	1	1	0	0	0	0	0	0	0	0	0	—	0	1	0	0	1.0	1.000

Dan Woodman

WOODMAN, DANIEL COURTENAY (Cocoa) BR TR 5′ 8″ 160 lbs.
B. July 8, 1893, Danvers, Mass. D. Dec. 14, 1962, Danvers, Mass.

Year	Team	Lg	W	L	PCT	ERA	G	GS	CG	IP	H	BB	SO	ShO	Relief W	Relief L	Relief SV	Batting AB	Batting H	HR	BA	PO	A	E	DP	TC/G	FA
1914	BUF	F	0	0	—	2.41	13	0	0	33.2	30	11	13	0	0	0	1	7	1	0	.143	1	7	2	0	0.8	.800
1915			0	0	—	4.11	5	1	0	15.1	14	9	1	0	0	0	0	4	1	0	.250	1	10	0	0	2.2	1.000
2 yrs.			0	0		2.94	18	1	0	49	44	20	14	0	0	0	1	11	2	0	.182	2	17	2	0	1.2	.905

Clarence Woods

WOODS, CLARENCE COFIELD BR TR 6′ 5½″ 230 lbs.
B. June 11, 1892, Woods Ridge, Ind. D. July 2, 1969, Rising Sun, Ind.

Year	Team	Lg	W	L	PCT	ERA	G	GS	CG	IP	H	BB	SO	ShO	Relief W	Relief L	Relief SV	Batting AB	Batting H	HR	BA	PO	A	E	DP	TC/G	FA
1914	IND	F	0	0	—	4.50	2	0	0	2	1	2	1	0	0	0	1	0	0	0	—	0	1	0	0	0.5	1.000

John Woods

WOODS, JOHN FULTON (Abe) BR TR 5′11″ 150 lbs.
B. Jan. 18, 1898, Princeton, W. Va. D. Oct. 4, 1946, Norfolk, Va.

Year	Team	Lg	W	L	PCT	ERA	G	GS	CG	IP	H	BB	SO	ShO	Relief W	Relief L	Relief SV	Batting AB	Batting H	HR	BA	PO	A	E	DP	TC/G	FA
1924	BOS	A	0	0	—	0.00	1	0	0	1	0	3	0	0	0	0	0	0	0	0	—	0	0	0	0	0.0	.000

Pinky Woods

WOODS, GEORGE ROWLAND BR TR 6′ 5″ 225 lbs.
B. May 22, 1915, Waterbury, Conn. D. Oct. 30, 1982, Los Angeles, Calif.

Year	Team	Lg	W	L	PCT	ERA	G	GS	CG	IP	H	BB	SO	ShO	Relief W	Relief L	Relief SV	Batting AB	Batting H	HR	BA	PO	A	E	DP	TC/G	FA
1943	BOS	A	5	6	.455	4.92	23	12	2	100.2	109	55	32	0	2	0	1	36	8	0	.222	9	20	2	1	1.3	.935
1944			4	8	.333	3.27	38	20	5	170.2	171	88	56	1	0	1	0	48	7	0	.146	13	37	1	3	1.3	.980
1945			4	7	.364	4.19	24	12	3	107.1	108	63	36	0	1	1	2	42	9	0	.214	8	25	0	3	1.4	1.000
3 yrs.			13	21	.382	3.97	85	44	10	378.2	388	206	124	1	3	2	3	126	24	0	.190	30	82	3	7	1.4	.974

Walt Woods

WOODS, WALTER SYDNEY BR TR 5′ 9½″ 165 lbs.
B. Apr. 28, 1875, Rye, N. H. D. Oct. 30, 1951, Portsmouth, N. H.

Year	Team	Lg	W	L	PCT	ERA	G	GS	CG	IP	H	BB	SO	ShO	Relief W	Relief L	Relief SV	Batting AB	Batting H	HR	BA	PO	A	E	DP	TC/G	FA
1898	CHI	N	9	13	.409	3.14	27	22	18	215	224	59	26	3	0	1	0	154	27	0	.175	42	87	15	3	2.9	.896
1899	LOU	N	9	13	.409	3.28	26	21	17	186.1	216	37	21	0	2	1	0	126	19	1	.151	38	108	12	2	3.8	.924
1900	PIT	N	0	0	—	21.00	1	0	0	3	9	1	1	0	0	0	0	1	0	0	.000	0	0	0	0	0.0	.000
3 yrs.			18	26	.409	3.34	54	43	35	404.1	449	97	48	3	2	2	0	*				80	195	27	5	3.2	.911

Dick Woodson

WOODSON, RICHARD LEE BR TR 6′ 5″ 205 lbs.
B. Mar. 30, 1945, Oelwein, Iowa.

Year	Team	Lg	W	L	PCT	ERA	G	GS	CG	IP	H	BB	SO	ShO	Relief W	Relief L	Relief SV	Batting AB	Batting H	HR	BA	PO	A	E	DP	TC/G	FA
1969	MIN	A	7	5	.583	3.67	44	10	2	110.1	99	49	66	0	3	2	1	27	2	0	.074	3	22	0	3	0.6	1.000
1970			1	2	.333	3.77	21	0	0	31	29	19	22	0	1	2	1	2	0	0	.000	1	6	2	1	0.4	.778
1972			14	14	.500	2.71	36	36	9	252	193	101	150	3	0	0	0	88	7	0	.080	17	43	4	1	1.8	.938
1973			10	8	.556	3.95	23	23	4	141.1	137	68	53	2	0	0	0	0	0	0	—	10	14	1	0	1.1	.960
1974	2 teams	MIN A (5G 1–1) NY A (8G 1–2)																									
"	total		2	3	.400	5.07	13	7	0	55	64	16	24	0	1	0	0	0	0	0		4	8	1	0	1.0	.923
5 yrs.			34	32	.515	3.46	137	76	15	589.2	522	253	315	5	5	4	2	117	9	0	.077	35	93	8	5	1.0	.941
LEAGUE CHAMPIONSHIP SERIES																											
1969	MIN	A	0	0	—	10.80	1	0	0	1.2	3	3	2	0	0	0	0	1	1	0	1.000	0	0	0	0	0.0	.000
1970			0	0	—	9.00	1	0	0	1	2	1	0	0	0	0	0	0	0	0	—	0	0	0	0	0.0	.000
2 yrs.			0	0		10.13	2	0	0	2.2	5	4	2	0	0	0	0	1	1	0	1.000	0	0	0	0	0.0	

Kerry Woodson

WOODSON, WALTER BROWNE BR TR 6′ 2″ 190 lbs.
B. May 18, 1969, Jacksonville, Fla.

Year	Team	Lg	W	L	PCT	ERA	G	GS	CG	IP	H	BB	SO	ShO	Relief W	Relief L	Relief SV	Batting AB	Batting H	HR	BA	PO	A	E	DP	TC/G	FA
1992	SEA	A	0	1	.000	3.29	8	1	0	13.2	12	11	6	0	0	0	0	0	0	0	—	3	2	0	1	0.6	1.000

Frank Woodward

WOODWARD, FRANK RUSSELL BR TR 5′10″ 175 lbs.
B. May 17, 1894, New Haven, Conn. D. June 11, 1961, New Haven, Conn.

Year	Team	Lg	W	L	PCT	ERA	G	GS	CG	IP	H	BB	SO	ShO	Relief W	Relief L	Relief SV	Batting AB	Batting H	HR	BA	PO	A	E	DP	TC/G	FA
1918	PHI	N	0	0	—	6.00	2	0	0	6	6	4	4	0	0	0	0	3	1	0	.333	0	1	0	0	0.5	1.000
1919	2 teams	PHI N (17G 6–9) STL N (17G 3–5)																									
"	total		9	14	.391	3.86	34	19	8	172.2	174	63	45	0	3	2	1	50	7	0	.140	9	39	4	2	1.5	.923
1921	WAS	A	0	0	—	5.91	3	1	0	10.2	11	3	4	0	0	0	0	3	1	0	.333	0	4	0	0	1.3	1.000
1922			0	0	—	11.57	1	0	0	2.1	3	3	2	0	0	0	0	1	0	0	.000	0	1	0	0	1.0	1.000
1923	CHI	A	0	1	.000	13.50	2	1	0	2	5	1	0	0	0	0	0	0	0	0	—	0	2	0	0	1.0	1.000
5 yrs.			9	15	.375	4.23	42	21	8	193.2	199	74	55	0	3	2	1	57	9	0	.158	9	47	4	2	1.4	.933

Rob Woodward

WOODWARD, ROBERT JOHN BR TR 6′ 3″ 185 lbs.
B. Sept. 28, 1962, Hanover, N. H.

Year	Team	Lg	W	L	PCT	ERA	G	GS	CG	IP	H	BB	SO	ShO	Relief W	Relief L	Relief SV	Batting AB	Batting H	HR	BA	PO	A	E	DP	TC/G	FA
1985	BOS	A	1	0	1.000	1.69	5	2	0	26.2	17	9	16	0	0	0	0	0	0	0	—	5	0	2	0	1.4	.714
1986			2	3	.400	5.30	9	6	0	35.2	46	11	14	0	1	0	0	0	0	0	—	5	6	0	0	1.2	1.000
1987			1	1	.500	7.05	9	6	0	37	53	15	15	0	0	0	0	0	0	0	—	2	1	0	0	0.3	1.000
1988			0	0	—	13.50	1	0	0	0.2	2	1	0	0	0	0	0	0	0	0	—	0	0	0	0	0.0	.000
4 yrs.			4	4	.500	5.04	24	14	0	100	118	36	45	0	1	0	0	0	0	0		12	7	2	0	0.9	.905

Floyd Wooldridge

WOOLDRIDGE, FLOYD LEWIS BR TR 6′ 1″ 185 lbs.
B. Aug. 25, 1928, Jerico Springs, Mo.

Year	Team	Lg	W	L	PCT	ERA	G	GS	CG	IP	H	BB	SO	ShO	Relief W	Relief L	Relief SV	Batting AB	Batting H	HR	BA	PO	A	E	DP	TC/G	FA
1955	STL	N	2	4	.333	4.84	18	8	2	57.2	64	27	14	0	0	1	0	18	4	0	.222	2	5	0	0	0.4	1.000

Earl Wooten

WOOTEN, EARL HAZWELL (Junior) BR TL 5′11″ 160 lbs.
B. Jan. 16, 1924, Pelzer, S. C.

Year	Team	Lg	W	L	PCT	ERA	G	GS	CG	IP	H	BB	SO	ShO	Relief W	Relief L	Relief SV	Batting AB	Batting H	HR	BA	PO	A	E	DP	TC/G	FA
1948	WAS	A	0	0	—	9.00	1	0	0	2	2	2	1	0	0	0	0	*				19	0	2	0	3.5	.905

Fred Worden

WORDEN, FREDERICK BAMFORD BR TR
B. Sept. 4, 1894, St. Louis, Mo. D. Nov. 9, 1941, St. Louis, Mo.

Year	Team	Lg	W	L	PCT	ERA	G	GS	CG	IP	H	BB	SO	ShO	Relief W	Relief L	Relief SV	Batting AB	Batting H	HR	BA	PO	A	E	DP	TC/G	FA
1914	PHI	A	0	0	—	18.00	1	0	0	2	8	0	1	0	0	0	0	1	0	0	.000	0	1	0	0	1.0	1.000

Hoge Workman

WORKMAN, HARRY HALL BR TR 5′11″ 170 lbs.
B. Sept. 25, 1899, Huntington, W. Va. D. May 20, 1972, Fort Myers, Fla.

Year	Team	Lg	W	L	PCT	ERA	G	GS	CG	IP	H	BB	SO	ShO	Relief W	Relief L	Relief SV	Batting AB	Batting H	HR	BA	PO	A	E	DP	TC/G	FA
1924	BOS	A	0	0	—	8.50	11	0	0	18	25	11	7	0	0	0	0	2	0	0	.000	2	4	0	0	0.5	1.000

Ralph Works

WORKS, RALPH TALMADGE (Judge) BL TR 6′ 2½″ 185 lbs.
B. Mar. 16, 1888, Payson, Ill. D. Aug. 8, 1941, Pasadena, Calif.

Year	Team		W	L	PCT	ERA	G	GS	CG	IP	H	BB	SO	ShO	Relief Pitching W	L	SV	Batting AB	H	HR	BA	PO	A	E	DP	TC/G	FA
1909	DET	A	4	1	.800	1.97	16	4	4	64	62	17	31	0	1	0	2	17	1	0	.059	2	16	2	1	1.3	.900
1910			3	6	.333	3.57	18	10	5	85.2	73	39	36	0	0	1	1	30	8	0	.267	4	26	5	1	1.9	.857
1911			11	5	.688	3.87	30	15	9	167.1	173	67	68	3	4	0	1	61	9	0	.148	3	28	4	1	1.2	.886
1912	2 teams	DET A	(27G 5–10)		CIN N	(3G 1–1)																					
″	total		6	11	.353	4.16	30	18	10	166.2	189	71	69	1	1	1	1	61	9	0	.148	2	52	6	0	2.0	.900
1913	CIN	N	0	1	.000	7.80	5	2	0	15	15	8	4	0	0	0	0	6	1	0	.167	0	6	0	0	1.2	1.000
5 yrs.			24	24	.500	3.79	99	49	28	498.2	512	202	208	4	6	2	5	175	28	0	.160	11	128	17	3	1.6	.891
WORLD SERIES																											
1909	DET	A	0	0	—	9.00	1	0	0	2	4	0	2	0	0	0	0	0	0	0	—	0	1	0	0	1.0	1.000

Tim Worrell

WORRELL, TIMOTHY HOWARD BR TR 6′ 4″ 210 lbs.
Brother of Todd Worrell.
B. July 5, 1967, Pasadena, Calif.

Year	Team		W	L	PCT	ERA	G	GS	CG	IP	H	BB	SO	ShO	Relief Pitching W	L	SV	Batting AB	H	HR	BA	PO	A	E	DP	TC/G	FA
1993	SD	N	2	7	.222	4.92	21	16	0	100.2	104	43	52	0	0	0	0	31	1	0	.032	6	11	1	0	0.9	.944
1994			0	1	.000	3.68	3	3	0	14.2	9	5	14	0	0	0	0	2	1	0	.500	4	2	0	0	2.0	1.000
1995			1	0	1.000	4.72	9	0	0	13.1	16	6	13	0	1	0	0	1	0	0	.000	0	2	0	0	0.2	1.000
3 yrs.			3	8	.273	4.76	33	19	0	128.2	129	54	79	0	1	0	0	34	2	0	.059	10	15	1	0	0.8	.962

Todd Worrell

WORRELL, SCOTT ROLAND BR TR 6′ 5″ 215 lbs.
Brother of Tim Worrell.
B. Sept. 28, 1959, Arcadia, Calif.

Year	Team		W	L	PCT	ERA	G	GS	CG	IP	H	BB	SO	ShO	Relief Pitching W	L	SV	Batting AB	H	HR	BA	PO	A	E	DP	TC/G	FA
1985	STL	N	3	0	1.000	2.91	17	0	0	21.2	17	7	17	0	3	0	5	1	0	0	.000	3	0	0	0	0.2	1.000
1986			9	10	.474	2.08	74	0	0	103.2	86	41	73	0	9	10	**36**	7	1	0	.143	5	8	2	0	0.2	.867
1987			8	6	.571	2.66	75	0	0	94.2	86	34	92	0	8	6	33	10	1	0	.100	0	17	0	0	0.2	1.000
1988			5	9	.357	3.00	68	0	0	90	69	34	78	0	5	9	32	6	0	0	.000	3	10	0	4	0.2	1.000
1989			3	5	.375	2.96	47	0	0	51.2	42	26	41	0	3	5	20	1	0	0	.000	0	11	0	1	0.2	1.000
1992			5	3	.625	2.11	67	0	0	64	45	25	64	0	5	3	3	0	0	0	—	2	2	0	0	0.1	1.000
1993	LA	N	1	1	.500	6.05	35	0	0	38.2	46	11	31	0	1	1	5	0	0	0	—	1	4	0	0	0.1	1.000
1994			6	5	.545	4.29	38	0	0	42	37	12	44	0	6	5	11	0	0	0	—	3	3	0	0	0.2	1.000
1995			4	1	.800	2.02	59	0	0	62.1	50	19	61	0	4	1	32	2	0	0	.000	6	11	0	2	0.3	1.000
9 yrs.			44	40	.524	2.86	480	0	0	568.2	478	209	501	0	44	40	177	27	2	0	.074	23	66	2	7	0.2	.978
LEAGUE CHAMPIONSHIP SERIES																											
1985	STL	N	1	0	1.000	1.42	4	0	0	6.1	4	2	3	0	1	0	0	0	0	0	—	0	1	0	0	0.3	1.000
1987			0	0	—	2.08	3	0	0	4.1	4	1	6	0	0	0	1	1	0	0	.000	0	0	0	0	0.0	
2 yrs.			1	0	1.000	1.69	7	0	0	10.2	8	3	9	0	1	0	1	1	0	0	.000	0	1	0	0	0.1	1.000
WORLD SERIES																											
1985	STL	N	0	1	.000	3.86	3	0	0	4.2	4	2	6	0	0	1	1	1	0	0	.000	0	1	0	0	0.3	1.000
1987			0	0	—	1.29	4	0	0	7	6	4	3	0	0	0	2	0	0	0	—	0	0	0	0	0.0	.000
2 yrs.			0	1	.000	2.31	7	0	0	11.2	10	6	9	0	0	1	3 **4th**	1	0	0	.000	0	1	0	0	0.1	1.000

Rich Wortham

WORTHAM, RICHARD COOPER (Tex) BR TL 6′ 185 lbs.
B. Oct. 22, 1953, Odessa, Tex.

Year	Team		W	L	PCT	ERA	G	GS	CG	IP	H	BB	SO	ShO	Relief Pitching W	L	SV	Batting AB	H	HR	BA	PO	A	E	DP	TC/G	FA
1978	CHI	A	3	2	.600	3.05	8	8	2	59	59	23	25	0	0	0	0	0	0	0	—	0	9	0	0	1.1	1.000
1979			14	14	.500	4.90	34	33	5	204	195	100	119	0	0	0	0	0	0	0	—	7	27	5	0	1.1	.872
1980			4	7	.364	5.97	41	10	0	92	102	58	45	0	2	2	1	0	0	0	—	7	18	5	1	0.7	.833
1983	OAK	A	0	0	—	∞	1	0	0		3	1	0	0	0	0	0	0	0	0	—	0	0	0	0	0.0	.000
4 yrs.			21	23	.477	4.89	84	51	7	355	359	182	189	0	2	2	1	0	0	0		14	54	10	1	0.9	.872

Al Worthington

WORTHINGTON, ALLAN FULTON (Red) BR TR 6′ 2″ 195 lbs.
B. Feb. 5, 1929, Birmingham, Ala.

Year	Team		W	L	PCT	ERA	G	GS	CG	IP	H	BB	SO	ShO	Relief Pitching W	L	SV	Batting AB	H	HR	BA	PO	A	E	DP	TC/G	FA
1953	NY	N	4	8	.333	3.44	20	17	5	102	103	54	52	2	0	1	0	31	2	0	.065	12	16	2	1	1.5	.933
1954			0	2	.000	3.50	10	1	0	18	21	15	8	0	0	0	0	4	0	0	.000	0	4	1	0	0.5	.800
1956			7	14	.333	3.97	28	24	4	165.2	158	74	95	0	0	1	0	51	12	1	.235	9	35	4	6	1.7	.917
1957			8	11	.421	4.22	55	12	1	157.2	140	56	90	1	7	5	4	40	4	0	.100	10	26	0	0	0.7	1.000
1958	SF	N	11	7	.611	3.63	54	12	1	151.1	152	57	76	0	3	4	6	44	8	0	.182	9	26	2	0	0.7	.946
1959			2	3	.400	3.68	42	3	0	73.1	68	37	45	0	1	2	2	13	1	0	.077	5	15	0	0	0.5	1.000
1960	2 teams	BOS A	(6G 0–1)		CHI A	(4G 1–1)																					
″	total		1	2	.333	6.35	10	0	0	17	20	15	8	0	1	2	0	3	2	0	.667	2	3	0	0	0.5	1.000
1963	CIN	N	4	4	.500	2.99	50	0	0	81.1	75	31	55	0	4	4	10	12	1	0	.083	5	22	0	3	0.5	1.000
1964	2 teams	CIN N	(6G 1–0)		MIN A	(41G 5–6)																					
″	total		6	6	.500	2.16	47	0	0	79.1	61	30	65	0	6	6	14	16	1	0	.063	8	14	4	0	0.6	.846
1965	MIN	A	10	7	.588	2.13	62	0	0	80.1	57	41	59	0	10	7	21	10	1	0	.100	3	24	1	0	0.5	.964
1966			6	3	.667	2.46	65	0	0	91.1	66	27	93	0	6	3	16	11	3	0	.273	8	14	2	0	0.4	.917
1967			8	9	.471	2.84	59	0	0	92	77	38	80	0	8	9	16	8	0	0	.000	4	13	0	1	0.3	1.000
1968			4	5	.444	2.71	54	0	0	76.1	67	32	57	0	4	5	**18**	7	0	0	.000	5	11	1	0	0.3	.941
1969			4	1	.800	4.57	46	0	0	61	65	20	51	0	4	1	3	5	0	0	.000	2	6	0	1	0.2	1.000
14 yrs.			75	82	.478	3.39	602	69	11	1246.2	1130	527	834	3	54	50	110	255	35	1	.137	82	229	17	12	0.5	.948
LEAGUE CHAMPIONSHIP SERIES																											
1969	MIN	A	0	0	—	6.75	1	0	0	1.1	3	0	1	0	0	0	0	0	0	0	—	0	0	0	0	0.0	.000
WORLD SERIES																											
1965	MIN	A	0	0	—	0.00	2	0	0	4	2	2	2	0	0	0	0	0	0	0	—	1	1	1	0	1.5	.667

Bob Wright

WRIGHT, ROBERT CASSIUS BR TR 6′ 1½″ 175 lbs.
B. Dec. 13, 1891, Decatur County, Ind. D. July 30, 1993, Carmichael, Calif.

Year	Team		W	L	PCT	ERA	G	GS	CG	IP	H	BB	SO	ShO	Relief Pitching W	L	SV	Batting AB	H	HR	BA	PO	A	E	DP	TC/G	FA
1915	CHI	N	0	0	—	2.25	2	0	0	4	6	0	3	0	0	0	0	0	0	0	—	0	1	0	0	0.5	1.000

Clarence Wright

WRIGHT, CLARENCE EUGENE BR TR 6′ 2½″ 190 lbs.
B. Dec. 11, 1878, Cleveland, Ohio D. Oct. 29, 1930, Barberton, Ohio.

Year	Team		W	L	PCT	ERA	G	GS	CG	IP	H	BB	SO	ShO	Relief Pitching W	L	SV	Batting AB	H	HR	BA	PO	A	E	DP	TC/G	FA
1901	BKN	N	1	0	1.000	1.00	1	1	1	9	6	1	6	0	0	0	0	3	1	0	.333	0	1	0	0	1.0	1.000
1902	CLE	A	7	11	.389	3.95	21	18	15	148	150	75	52	1	0	1	1	70	10	1	.143	9	35	1	0	2.0	.978

Clarence Wright *continued*

Year	Team		W	L	PCT	ERA	G	GS	CG	IP	H	BB	SO	ShO	Relief Pitching W	Relief Pitching L	Relief Pitching SV	Batting AB	Batting H	HR	BA	PO	A	E	DP	TC/G	FA
1903	2 teams	CLE A (15G 3–9)		STL A (8G 3–5)																							
"	total		6	14	.300	4.98	23	20	15	162.2	195	74	79	1	0	1	0	64	12	0	.188	5	61	3	3	3.0	.957
1904	STL	A	0	1	.000	13.50	1	1	0	4	10	2	3	0	0	0	0	1	0	0	.000	0	4	0	0	4.0	1.000
4 yrs.			14	26	.350	4.50	46	40	31	323.2	361	152	140	2	0	2	1	138	23	1	.167	14	101	4	3	2.5	.966

Clyde Wright

WRIGHT, CLYDE BR TL 6′ 1″ 180 lbs.
B. Feb. 20, 1941, Jefferson City, Tenn.

Year	Team		W	L	PCT	ERA	G	GS	CG	IP	H	BB	SO	ShO	Relief W	Relief L	Relief SV	AB	H	HR	BA	PO	A	E	DP	TC/G	FA
1966	CAL	A	4	7	.364	3.74	20	13	3	91.1	92	25	37	1	1	1	0	29	3	0	.103	7	17	1	1	1.3	.960
1967			5	5	.500	3.26	20	11	1	77.1	76	24	35	0	1	0	0	22	6	0	.273	7	13	0	1	1.0	1.000
1968			10	6	.625	3.94	41	13	2	125.2	123	44	71	1	6	0	3	37	8	0	.216	8	14	0	1	0.5	1.000
1969			1	8	.111	4.10	37	5	0	63.2	66	30	31	0	1	3	0	11	2	0	.182	1	12	0	1	0.4	1.000
1970			22	12	.647	2.83	39	39	7	261	226	88	110	2	0	0	0	105	18	2	.171	18	33	3	1	1.4	.944
1971			16	17	.485	2.99	37	37	10	277	225	82	135	2	0	0	0	91	14	0	.154	18	67	2	6	2.4	.977
1972			18	11	.621	2.98	35	35	15	251	229	80	87	2	0	0	0	83	18	2	.217	8	61	6	4	2.1	.920
1973			11	19	.367	3.68	37	36	13	257	273	76	65	1	0	0	0	0	0	0	—	16	63	3	9	2.2	.963
1974	MIL	A	9	20	.310	4.42	38	32	15	232	264	54	64	0	1	1	0	0	0	0	—	18	42	1	4	1.6	.984
1975	TEX	A	4	6	.400	4.44	25	14	1	93.1	105	47	32	0	1	0	0	0	0	0	—	7	22	2	2	1.2	.935
10 yrs.			100	111	.474	3.50	329	235	67	1729.1	1679	550	667	9	11	5	3	378	69	4	.183	108	344	18	30	1.4	.962

Dave Wright

WRIGHT, DAVID WILLIAM BR TR 6′ 185 lbs.
B. Aug. 27, 1875, Dennison, Ohio D. Jan. 18, 1946, Dennison, Ohio.

Year	Team		W	L	PCT	ERA	G	GS	CG	IP	H	BB	SO	ShO	Relief W	Relief L	Relief SV	AB	H	HR	BA	PO	A	E	DP	TC/G	FA
1895	PIT	N	0	0	—	27.00	1	0	0	2	6	1	0	0	0	0	0	1	0	0	.000	0	1	1	0	2.0	.500
1897	CHI	N	1	0	1.000	15.43	1	1	1	7	17	2	4	0	0	0	0	3	1	0	.333	0	2	1	0	3.0	.667
2 yrs.			1	0	1.000	18.00	2	1	1	9	23	3	4	0	0	0	0	4	1	0	.250	0	3	2	0	2.5	.600

Ed Wright

WRIGHT, HENDERSON EDWARD BR TR 6′ 1″ 180 lbs.
B. May 15, 1919, Dyersburg, Tenn.

Year	Team		W	L	PCT	ERA	G	GS	CG	IP	H	BB	SO	ShO	Relief W	Relief L	Relief SV	AB	H	HR	BA	PO	A	E	DP	TC/G	FA
1945	BOS	N	8	3	.727	2.51	15	12	7	111.1	104	33	24	1	0	0	0	39	5	0	.128	2	20	1	1	1.5	.957
1946			12	9	.571	3.52	36	21	9	176.1	164	71	44	2	2	0	0	59	18	0	.305	12	35	1	0	1.3	.979
1947			3	3	.500	6.40	23	6	1	64.2	80	35	14	0	1	0	0	23	3	0	.130	4	10	0	1	0.6	1.000
1948			0	0	—	1.93	3	0	0	4.2	9	2	2	0	0	0	0	0	0	0	—	0	1	0	0	0.3	1.000
1952	PHI	A	2	1	.667	6.53	24	0	0	41.1	55	20	9	0	2	1	1	7	1	0	.143	1	6	0	1	0.3	1.000
5 yrs.			25	16	.610	4.00	101	39	17	398.1	412	161	93	3	5	1	1	128	27	0	.211	19	72	2	3	0.9	.978

George Wright

WRIGHT, GEORGE BR TR 5′ 9½″ 150 lbs.
Brother of Harry Wright. Brother of Sam Wright.
B. Jan. 28, 1847, Yonkers, N. Y. D. Aug. 21, 1937, Boston, Mass.
Manager 1879.
Hall of Fame 1937.

Year	Team		W	L	PCT	ERA	G	GS	CG	IP	H	BB	SO	ShO	Relief W	Relief L	Relief SV	AB	H	HR	BA	PO	A	E	DP	TC/G	FA
1876	BOS	N	0	0	—	0.00	1	0	0	1	1	0	1	0	0	0	0	*				96	253	44	16	5.5	.888

Jim Wright

WRIGHT, JAMES BR TR 6′ 4″ 195 lbs.
B. Sept. 19, 1900, Hyde, England D. Apr. 10, 1963, Oakland, Calif.

Year	Team		W	L	PCT	ERA	G	GS	CG	IP	H	BB	SO	ShO	Relief W	Relief L	Relief SV	AB	H	HR	BA	PO	A	E	DP	TC/G	FA
1927	STL	A	1	0	1.000	4.50	2	1	1	12	8	4	4	0	0	0	0	4	0	0	.000	1	1	0	0	1.0	1.000
1928			0	0	—	13.50	2	0	0	2	3	2	2	0	0	0	0	0	0	0	—	0	2	0	0	1.0	1.000
2 yrs.			1	0	1.000	5.79	4	1	1	14	11	6	6	0	0	0	0	4	0	0	.000	1	3	0	0	1.0	1.000

Jim Wright

WRIGHT, JAMES CLIFTON BR TR 6′ 1″ 165 lbs.
B. Dec. 21, 1950, Reed City, Mich.

Year	Team		W	L	PCT	ERA	G	GS	CG	IP	H	BB	SO	ShO	Relief W	Relief L	Relief SV	AB	H	HR	BA	PO	A	E	DP	TC/G	FA
1978	BOS	A	8	4	.667	3.57	24	16	5	116	122	24	56	3	0	0	0	0	0	0	—	4	12	1	0	0.7	.941
1979			1	0	1.000	5.09	11	1	0	23	19	7	15	0	0	0	0	0	0	0	—	2	1	0	0	0.3	1.000
2 yrs.			9	4	.692	3.82	35	17	5	139	141	31	71	3	0	0	0	0	0	0		6	13	1	0	0.6	.950

Jim Wright

WRIGHT, JAMES LEON, JR. BR TR 6′ 5″ 205 lbs.
B. Mar. 3, 1955, St. Joseph, Mo.

Year	Team		W	L	PCT	ERA	G	GS	CG	IP	H	BB	SO	ShO	Relief W	Relief L	Relief SV	AB	H	HR	BA	PO	A	E	DP	TC/G	FA
1981	KC	A	2	3	.400	3.46	17	4	0	52	57	21	27	0	1	1	0	0	0	0	—	2	6	0	0	0.5	1.000
1982			0	0	—	5.32	7	0	0	23.2	32	6	9	0	0	0	0	0	0	0	—	1	2	1	0	0.6	.750
2 yrs.			2	3	.400	4.04	24	4	0	75.2	89	27	36	0	1	1	0	0	0	0		3	8	1	0	0.5	.917

Ken Wright

WRIGHT, KENNETH WARREN BR TR 6′ 2″ 210 lbs.
B. Sept. 4, 1946, Pensacola, Fla.

Year	Team		W	L	PCT	ERA	G	GS	CG	IP	H	BB	SO	ShO	Relief W	Relief L	Relief SV	AB	H	HR	BA	PO	A	E	DP	TC/G	FA
1970	KC	A	1	2	.333	5.26	47	0	0	53	49	29	30	0	1	2	3	4	0	0	.000	1	8	1	0	0.2	.900
1971			3	6	.333	3.69	21	12	1	78	66	47	56	0	0	0	1	22	2	0	.091	1	16	1	2	0.9	.944
1972			1	2	.333	5.00	17	0	0	18	15	15	18	0	1	2	4	2	0	0	.000	1	2	0	0	0.2	1.000
1973			6	5	.545	4.89	25	12	1	81	60	82	75	0	1	0	0	0	0	0	—	1	6	2	0	0.4	.778
1974	NY	A	0	0	—	3.00	3	0	0	6	5	7	2	0	0	0	0	0	0	0	—	2	1	0	0	1.0	1.000
5 yrs.			11	15	.423	4.54	113	24	2	236	195	180	181	0	3	4	8	28	2	0	.071	6	33	4	2	0.4	.907

Lucky Wright

WRIGHT, WILLIAM SIMMONS (Deacon, William The Red) BR TR 6′ 178 lbs.
B. Feb. 21, 1880, Tontogany, Ohio D. July 6, 1941, Tontogany, Ohio.

Year	Team		W	L	PCT	ERA	G	GS	CG	IP	H	BB	SO	ShO	Relief W	Relief L	Relief SV	AB	H	HR	BA	PO	A	E	DP	TC/G	FA
1909	CLE	A	0	4	.000	3.97	5	4	3	22.2	20	8	6	0	0	0	0	7	0	0	.000	0	10	1	0	2.2	.909

Mel Wright

WRIGHT, MELVIN JAMES BR TR 6′ 3″ 210 lbs.
B. May 11, 1928, Manila, Ark. D. May 16, 1983, Houston, Tex.

Year	Team		W	L	PCT	ERA	G	GS	CG	IP	H	BB	SO	ShO	Relief W	Relief L	Relief SV	AB	H	HR	BA	PO	A	E	DP	TC/G	FA
1954	STL	N	0	0	—	10.45	9	0	0	10.1	16	11	4	0	0	0	0	1	0	0	.000	2	1	0	1	0.3	1.000
1955			2	2	.500	6.19	29	0	0	36.1	44	9	18	0	2	2	1	6	0	0	.000	5	6	0	0	0.4	1.000
1960	CHI	N	0	1	.000	4.96	9	0	0	16.1	17	3	8	0	0	1	2	2	0	0	.000	2	0	0	0	0.2	1.000
1961			0	1	.000	10.71	11	0	0	21	42	4	6	0	0	1	0	2	0	0	.000	3	7	0	1	0.9	1.000
4 yrs.			2	4	.333	7.61	58	0	0	84	119	27	36	0	2	4	3	11	0	0	.000	12	14	0	2	0.4	1.000

Rasty Wright

WRIGHT, WAYNE BROMLEY BR TR 5′11″ 160 lbs.
B. Nov. 5, 1895, Ceredo, W. Va. D. June 12, 1948, Columbus, Ohio.

Year	Team		W	L	PCT	ERA	G	GS	CG	IP	H	BB	SO	ShO	Relief W	Relief L	Relief SV	AB	H	HR	BA	PO	A	E	DP	TC/G	FA
1917	STL	A	0	1	.000	5.45	16	1	0	39.2	48	10	5	0	0	0	0	10	2	0	.200	3	13	0	0	1.0	1.000
1918			8	2	.800	2.51	18	13	6	111.1	99	18	25	1	0	0	0	34	10	0	.294	8	25	1	0	1.9	.971

Rasty Wright *continued*

Year	Team	W	L	PCT	ERA	G	GS	CG	IP	H	BB	SO	ShO	Relief Pitching W	Relief Pitching L	Relief Pitching SV	Batting AB	Batting H	Batting HR	BA	PO	A	E	DP	TC/G	FA
1919		0	5	.000	5.54	24	5	2	63.1	79	20	14	0	0	0	0	12	1	0	.083	4	18	0	0	0.9	1.000
1922		9	7	.563	2.92	31	16	5	154	148	50	44	0	3	2	5	50	7	0	.140	6	40	1	4	1.5	.979
1923		7	4	.636	6.42	20	8	4	82.2	107	34	26	0	4	1	0	27	6	0	.222	4	23	2	1	1.5	.931
5 yrs.		24	19	.558	4.05	109	43	17	451	481	132	114	1	7	3	5	133	26	0	.195	25	119	4	5	1.4	.973

Ricky Wright

WRIGHT, JAMES RICHARD BL TL 6′ 3″ 175 lbs.
B. Nov. 22, 1958, Paris, Tex.

Year	Team	W	L	PCT	ERA	G	GS	CG	IP	H	BB	SO	ShO	Relief Pitching W	Relief Pitching L	Relief Pitching SV	Batting AB	Batting H	Batting HR	BA	PO	A	E	DP	TC/G	FA
1982	LA N	2	1	.667	3.03	14	5	0	32.2	28	20	24	0	1	1	0	8	1	0	.125	3	6	0	0	0.6	1.000
1983	2 teams LA N (6G 0–0) TEX A (1G 0–0)																									
″	total	0	0		2.16	7	0	0	8.1	5	3	7	0	0	0	0	0	0	0		0	0	1	0	0.1	.000
1984	TEX A	0	2	.000	6.14	8	1	0	14.2	20	11	6	0	0	2	0	0	0	0	—	1	4	0	0	0.6	1.000
1985		0	0	—	4.70	5	0	0	7.2	5	5	7	0	0	0	0	0	0	0	—	0	1	0	0	0.2	1.000
1986		1	0	1.000	5.03	21	1	0	39.1	44	21	23	0	1	0	0	0	0	0	—	3	7	0	1	0.5	1.000
5 yrs.		3	3	.500	4.30	55	7	0	102.2	102	60	67	0	2	3	0	8	1	0	.125	7	18	1	1	0.5	.962

Roy Wright

WRIGHT, ROY EARL BR TR 6′ 2″ 170 lbs.
B. Sept. 26, 1933, Buchtel, Ohio.

Year	Team	W	L	PCT	ERA	G	GS	CG	IP	H	BB	SO	ShO	Relief Pitching W	Relief Pitching L	Relief Pitching SV	Batting AB	Batting H	Batting HR	BA	PO	A	E	DP	TC/G	FA
1956	NY N	0	1	.000	16.88	1	1	0	2.2	8	2	0	0	0	0	0	1	0	0	.000	1	0	0	0	1.0	1.000

Frank Wurm

WURM, FRANK JAMES BB TL 6′ 1″ 175 lbs.
B. Apr. 27, 1924, Cambridge, N. Y. D. Sept. 19, 1993, Glens Falls, N. Y.

Year	Team	W	L	PCT	ERA	G	GS	CG	IP	H	BB	SO	ShO	Relief Pitching W	Relief Pitching L	Relief Pitching SV	Batting AB	Batting H	Batting HR	BA	PO	A	E	DP	TC/G	FA
1944	BKN N	0	0	—	108.00	1	1	0	0.1	1	5	1	0	0	0	0	0	0	0	—	0	0	0	0	0.0	.000

John Wyatt

WYATT, JOHN THOMAS BR TR 5′11½″ 200 lbs.
B. Apr. 19, 1935, Chicago, Ill.

Year	Team	W	L	PCT	ERA	G	GS	CG	IP	H	BB	SO	ShO	Relief Pitching W	Relief Pitching L	Relief Pitching SV	Batting AB	Batting H	Batting HR	BA	PO	A	E	DP	TC/G	FA
1961	KC A	0	0	—	2.45	5	0	0	7.1	8	4	6	0	0	0	1	0	0	0	—	0	2	1	0	0.6	.667
1962		10	7	.588	4.46	59	9	0	125	121	80	106	0	7	4	11	29	3	0	.103	8	14	3	0	0.4	.880
1963		6	4	.600	3.13	63	0	0	92	83	43	81	0	6	4	21	9	0	0	.000	3	12	2	1	0.3	.882
1964		9	8	.529	3.59	**81**	0	0	128	111	52	74	0	9	8	20	14	0	0	.000	8	16	1	0	0.3	.960
1965		2	6	.250	3.25	65	0	0	88.2	78	53	70	0	2	6	18	4	0	0	.000	2	16	0	0	0.3	1.000
1966	2 teams KC A (19G 0–3) BOS A (42G 3–4)																									
″	total	3	7	.300	3.68	61	0	0	95.1	78	43	88	0	3	7	10	11	0	0	.000	3	11	1	0	0.2	.933
1967	BOS A	10	7	.588	2.60	60	0	0	93.1	71	39	68	0	10	7	20	12	1	0	.083	1	21	0	0	0.4	1.000
1968	3 teams BOS A (8G 1–2) NY A (7G 0–2) DET A (22G 1–0)																									
″	total	2	4	.333	2.74	37	0	0	49.1	42	26	42	0	2	4	2	3	0	0	.000	5	7	1	1	0.4	.923
1969	OAK A	0	1	.000	5.40	4	0	0	8.1	8	6	5	0	0	1	0	1	0	0	.000	0	1	0	0	0.3	1.000
9 yrs.		42	44	.488	3.47	435	9	0	687.1	600	346	540	0	39	41	103	83	4	0	.048	30	100	9	2	0.3	.935
WORLD SERIES																										
1967	BOS A	1	0	1.000	4.91	2	0	0	3.2	1	3	1	0	1	0	0	0	0	0	—	0	0	0	0	0.0	.000

Whit Wyatt

WYATT, JOHN WHITLOW BR TR 6′ 1″ 185 lbs.
B. Sept. 27, 1907, Kensington, Ga.

Year	Team	W	L	PCT	ERA	G	GS	CG	IP	H	BB	SO	ShO	Relief Pitching W	Relief Pitching L	Relief Pitching SV	Batting AB	Batting H	Batting HR	BA	PO	A	E	DP	TC/G	FA
1929	DET A	0	1	.000	6.75	4	4	1	25.1	30	18	14	0	0	0	0	10	1	0	.100	0	8	1	2	2.3	.889
1930		4	5	.444	3.57	21	7	2	85.2	76	35	68	0	3	2	2	34	12	1	.353	4	15	1	0	1.0	.950
1931		0	2	.000	8.44	4	1	1	21.1	30	12	8	0	0	1	0	7	2	0	.286	0	1	1	0	0.5	.500
1932		9	13	.409	5.03	43	22	10	205.2	228	102	82	0	3	1	1	78	15	2	.192	7	35	1	3	1.0	.977
1933	2 teams DET A (10G 0–1) CHI A (26G 3–4)																									
″	total	3	5	.375	4.56	36	7	2	104.2	111	54	40	0	1	2	1	30	6	0	.200	3	23	0	0	0.7	1.000
1934	CHI A	4	11	.267	7.18	23	6	2	67.2	83	37	36	0	3	6	2	26	6	0	.231	3	14	3	2	0.9	.850
1935		4	3	.571	6.75	30	1	0	52	65	25	22	0	4	3	5	13	3	0	.231	2	13	0	0	0.5	1.000
1936		0	0	—	0.00	3	0	0	3	3	0	0	0	0	0	1	0	0	0	—	0	0	0	0	0.0	.000
1937	CLE A	2	3	.400	4.44	29	4	2	73	67	40	52	0	2	2	0	18	7	0	.389	2	12	1	1	0.5	.933
1939	BKN N	8	3	.727	2.31	16	14	6	109	88	39	52	2	2	0	0	36	6	0	.167	5	28	3	1	2.3	.917
1940		15	14	.517	3.46	37	34	16	239.1	233	62	124	**5**	1	1	0	80	14	1	.175	8	37	1	0	1.2	.978
1941		**22**	10	.688	2.34	38	35	23	288.1	223	82	176	**7**	0	1	1	109	26	3	.239	11	47	2	5	1.6	.967
1942		19	7	.731	2.73	31	30	16	217.1	185	63	104	0	1	0	0	77	14	0	.182	11	39	3	1	1.7	.943
1943		14	5	.737	2.49	26	26	13	180.2	139	43	80	3	0	0	0	60	17	0	.283	9	27	1	0	1.4	.973
1944		2	6	.250	7.17	9	9	1	37.2	51	16	4	0	0	0	0	13	2	0	.154	4	5	0	1	1.0	1.000
1945	PHI N	0	7	.000	5.26	10	10	2	51.1	72	14	10	0	0	0	0	16	2	0	.125	5	12	0	0	1.7	1.000
16 yrs.		106	95	.527	3.78	360	210	97	1762	1684	642	872	17	20	19	13	607	133	7	.219	74	316	18	16	1.1	.956
WORLD SERIES																										
1941	BKN N	1	1	.500	2.50	2	2	2	18	15	10	14	0	0	0	0	6	1	0	.167	1	2	0	0	1.5	1.000

John Wyckoff

WYCKOFF, JOHN WELDON BR TR 6′ 1″ 175 lbs.
B. Feb. 19, 1892, Williamsport, Pa. D. May 8, 1961, Sheboygan Falls, Wis.

Year	Team	W	L	PCT	ERA	G	GS	CG	IP	H	BB	SO	ShO	Relief Pitching W	Relief Pitching L	Relief Pitching SV	Batting AB	Batting H	Batting HR	BA	PO	A	E	DP	TC/G	FA
1913	PHI A	2	4	.333	4.38	17	7	3	61.2	56	46	31	0	0	1	0	21	4	0	.190	3	19	1	0	1.4	.957
1914		11	7	.611	3.02	32	20	11	185	153	103	86	0	1	1	2	75	11	1	.147	5	34	4	0	1.3	.907
1915		10	**22**	.313	3.52	43	34	20	276	238	**165**	157	1	1	1	0	96	12	0	.125	11	85	10	2	2.5	.906
1916	2 teams PHI A (7G 0–1) BOS A (8G 0–0)																									
″	total	0	1	.000	5.11	15	2	1	44	39	38	22	0	0	0	1	14	4	0	.286	0	9	0	1	0.6	1.000
1917	BOS A	0	0	—	1.80	1	0	0	5	4	4	1	0	0	0	0	1	0	0	.000	0	3	0	0	3.0	1.000
1918		0	0	—	0.00	1	0	0	2	4	1	2	0	0	0	0	1	0	0	.000	0	0	0	0	0.0	.000
6 yrs.		23	34	.404	3.55	109	63	35	573.2	494	357	299	1	2	3	3	208	31	1	.149	19	150	15	3	1.7	.918
WORLD SERIES																										
1914	PHI A	0	0	—	2.45	1	0	0	3.2	3	1	2	0	0	0	0	1	1	0	1.000	1	0	0	0	1.0	1.000

Frank Wyman

WYMAN, FRANK C.
B. May 10, 1862, Haverhill, Mass. D. Feb. 4, 1916, Everett, Mass.

Year	Team	W	L	PCT	ERA	G	GS	CG	IP	H	BB	SO	ShO	Relief Pitching W	Relief Pitching L	Relief Pitching SV	Batting AB	Batting H	Batting HR	BA	PO	A	E	DP	TC/G	FA
1884	KC U	0	1	.000	*6.86*	3	1	1	21	37	3	9	0	0	0	0	*				90	19	26	4	3.8	.807

Early Wynn

WYNN, EARLY (Gus)
B. Jan. 6, 1920, Hartford, Ala.
Hall of Fame 1972.

BB TR 6′ 190 lbs.
BR 1941–1944

Year	Team	Lg	W	L	PCT	ERA	G	GS	CG	IP	H	BB	SO	ShO	Relief Pitching W	Relief Pitching L	Relief Pitching SV	Batting AB	Batting H	Batting HR	BA	PO	A	E	DP	TC/G	FA
1939	WAS	A	0	2	.000	5.75	3	3	1	20.1	26	10	1	0	0	0	0	6	1	0	.167	1	0	0	0	0.3	1.000
1941			3	1	.750	1.58	5	5	4	40	35	10	15	0	0	0	0	15	2	0	.133	2	9	1	1	2.4	.917
1942			10	16	.385	5.12	30	28	10	190	246	73	58	1	0	2	0	69	15	0	.217	5	36	2	3	1.4	.953
1943			18	12	.600	2.91	37	**33**	12	256.2	232	83	89	3	2	0	0	98	29	1	.296	5	49	3	3	1.5	.947
1944			8	**17**	.320	3.38	33	25	19	207.2	221	67	65	2	0	2	2	92	19	1	.207	4	31	1	4	1.1	.972
1946			8	5	.615	3.11	17	12	9	107	112	33	36	0	1	0	0	47	15	1	.319	7	18	1	2	1.5	.962
1947			17	15	.531	3.64	33	31	22	247	251	90	73	2	1	0	0	120	33	2	.275	15	33	1	3	1.5	.980
1948			8	19	.296	5.82	33	31	15	198	236	94	49	1	0	0	0	106	23	0	.217	6	32	2	1	1.2	.950
1949	CLE	A	11	7	.611	4.15	26	23	6	164.2	186	57	62	0	0	0	0	70	10	1	.143	16	31	0	3	1.8	1.000
1950			18	8	.692	**3.20**	32	28	14	213.2	166	101	143	2	1	2	0	77	18	2	.234	5	36	3	5	1.4	.932
1951			20	13	.606	3.02	37	**34**	21	**274.1**	227	107	133	3	1	0	1	108	20	1	.185	13	42	1	2	1.5	.982
1952			23	12	.657	2.90	42	33	19	285.2	239	**132**	153	4	3	1	3	99	22	0	.222	20	46	4	2	1.7	.943
1953			17	12	.586	3.93	36	34	16	251.2	234	107	138	1	2	0	0	91	25	3	.275	11	36	0	2	1.3	1.000
1954			**23**	11	.676	2.73	40	**36**	20	**270.2**	225	83	155	3	0	1	2	93	17	0	.183	17	27	2	1	1.1	.957
1955			17	11	.607	2.82	32	31	16	230	207	80	122	6	0	0	0	84	15	1	.179	7	27	2	0	1.1	.944
1956			20	9	.690	2.72	38	35	18	277.2	233	91	158	4	0	0	2	101	23	1	.228	15	48	3	3	1.7	.955
1957			14	17	.452	4.31	40	**37**	13	263	**270**	104	**184**	1	0	1	1	86	10	0	.116	10	38	0	5	1.2	1.000
1958	CHI	A	14	16	.467	4.13	40	34	11	239.2	214	104	**179**	4	0	2	2	75	15	0	.200	12	25	0	2	0.9	1.000
1959			**22**	10	.688	3.17	37	**37**	14	**255.2**	202	**119**	179	5	0	0	0	90	22	2	.244	6	39	2	2	1.3	.957
1960			13	12	.520	3.49	36	35	13	237.1	220	112	158	**4**	0	0	1	75	15	1	.200	7	28	1	1	1.0	.972
1961			8	2	.800	3.51	17	16	5	110.1	88	47	64	0	0	0	0	37	6	0	.162	4	11	0	0	0.9	1.000
1962			7	15	.318	4.46	27	26	11	167.2	171	56	91	3	0	0	0	54	7	0	.130	3	20	0	2	0.9	1.000
1963	CLE	A	1	2	.333	2.28	20	5	1	55.1	50	15	29	0	0	1	1	11	3	0	.273	2	8	0	0	0.5	1.000
23 yrs.			300	244	.551	3.54	691	612	290	4564	4291	1775 **4th**	2334	49	11	12	15	*				193	670	29	47	1.3	.967
WORLD SERIES																											
1954	CLE	A	0	1	.000	3.86	1	1	0	7	4	2	5	0	0	0	0	2	1	0	.500	1	1	0	0	2.0	1.000
1959	CHI	A	1	1	.500	5.54	3	3	0	13	19	4	10	0	0	0	0	5	1	0	.200	1	3	0	0	1.3	1.000
2 yrs.			1	2	.333	4.95	4	4	0	20	23	6	15	0	0	0	0	*				2	4	0	0	1.5	1.000

Bill Wynne

WYNNE, WILLIAM ANDREW
B. Mar. 27, 1869, Neuse, N. C. D. Aug. 7, 1951, Raleigh, N. C.

BR TR 5′11½″ 161 lbs.

Year	Team	Lg	W	L	PCT	ERA	G	GS	CG	IP	H	BB	SO	ShO	Relief Pitching W	Relief Pitching L	Relief Pitching SV	Batting AB	Batting H	Batting HR	BA	PO	A	E	DP	TC/G	FA
1894	WAS	N	0	1	.000	6.75	1	1	1	8	10	8	2	0	0	0	0	3	0	0	.000	0	1	0	0	1.0	1.000

Billy Wynne

WYNNE, BILLY VERNON
B. July 31, 1943, Williamston, N. C.

BR TR 6′ 3″ 205 lbs.
BB 1967

Year	Team	Lg	W	L	PCT	ERA	G	GS	CG	IP	H	BB	SO	ShO	Relief Pitching W	Relief Pitching L	Relief Pitching SV	Batting AB	Batting H	Batting HR	BA	PO	A	E	DP	TC/G	FA
1967	NY	N	0	0	—	3.12	6	1	0	8.2	12	2	4	0	0	0	0	1	0	0	.000	1	0	0	0	0.2	1.000
1968	CHI	A	0	0	—	4.50	1	0	0	2	2	2	1	0	0	0	0	0	0	0	—	0	0	0	0	0.0	.000
1969			7	7	.500	4.06	20	20	6	128.2	143	50	67	1	0	0	0	41	5	0	.122	11	19	0	2	1.5	1.000
1970			1	4	.200	5.32	12	9	0	44	54	22	19	0	0	0	0	13	1	0	.077	1	11	1	1	1.1	.923
1971	CAL	A	0	0	—	4.50	3	0	0	4	6	2	6	0	0	0	0	0	0	0	—	0	1	0	0	0.3	1.000
5 yrs.			8	11	.421	4.32	42	30	6	187.1	217	78	97	1	0	0	0	55	6	0	.109	13	31	1	3	1.1	.978

Hank Wyse

WYSE, HENRY WASHINGTON (Hooks)
B. Mar. 1, 1918, Lunsford, Ark.

BR TR 5′11½″ 185 lbs.

Year	Team	Lg	W	L	PCT	ERA	G	GS	CG	IP	H	BB	SO	ShO	Relief Pitching W	Relief Pitching L	Relief Pitching SV	Batting AB	Batting H	Batting HR	BA	PO	A	E	DP	TC/G	FA
1942	CHI	N	2	1	.667	1.93	4	4	1	28	33	6	8	1	0	0	0	8	1	0	.125	0	5	0	1	1.3	1.000
1943			9	7	.563	2.94	38	15	8	156	160	34	45	2	1	2	5	50	4	0	.080	9	47	1	4	1.5	.982
1944			16	15	.516	3.15	41	34	14	257.1	**277**	57	86	3	2	1	1	90	16	0	.178	7	51	1	3	1.4	.983
1945			22	10	.688	2.68	38	34	23	278.1	272	55	77	2	1	0	0	101	17	0	.168	10	67	2	5	2.1	.975
1946			14	12	.538	2.68	40	27	12	201.1	206	52	52	2	0	0	1	74	18	0	.243	9	50	1	4	1.5	.983
1947			6	9	.400	4.31	37	19	5	142	158	64	53	1	1	0	1	45	5	0	.111	7	33	5	5	1.2	.889
1950	PHI	A	9	14	.391	5.85	41	23	4	170.2	192	87	33	0	1	4	0	59	9	0	.153	13	34	5	1	1.3	.904
1951	2 teams	PHI A (9G 1–2) WAS A (3G 0–0)																									
″	total		1	2	.333	8.63	12	3	0	24	41	18	8	0	1	1	0	8	1	0	.125	1	4	0	1	0.4	1.000
8 yrs.			79	70	.530	3.52	251	159	67	1257.2	1339	373	362	11	7	8	8	435	71	0	.163	56	291	15	24	1.4	.959
WORLD SERIES																											
1945	CHI	N	0	1	.000	7.04	3	1	0	7.2	8	4	1	0	0	0	0	3	0	0	.000	0	0	0	0	0.0	.000

Biff Wysong

WYSONG, HARLIN
B. Apr. 13, 1905, Clarksville, Ohio D. Aug. 8, 1951, Xenia, Ohio.

BL TL 6′ 3″ 195 lbs.

Year	Team	Lg	W	L	PCT	ERA	G	GS	CG	IP	H	BB	SO	ShO	Relief Pitching W	Relief Pitching L	Relief Pitching SV	Batting AB	Batting H	Batting HR	BA	PO	A	E	DP	TC/G	FA
1930	CIN	N	0	1	.000	19.29	1	1	0	2.1	6	3	1	0	0	0	0	0	0	0	—	0	0	0	0	0.0	.000
1931			0	2	.000	7.89	12	2	0	21.2	25	23	5	0	0	0	0	4	1	0	.250	0	3	1	0	0.3	.750
1932			1	0	1.000	3.65	7	0	0	12.1	13	8	5	0	1	0	0	2	0	0	.000	1	3	1	1	0.7	.800
3 yrs.			1	3	.250	7.18	20	3	0	36.1	44	34	11	0	1	0	0	6	1	0	.167	1	6	2	1	0.4	.778

Rusty Yarnall

YARNALL, WALDO WILLIAM
B. Oct. 22, 1902, Chicago, Ill. D. Oct. 9, 1985, Lowell, Mass.

BR TR 6′ 175 lbs.

Year	Team	Lg	W	L	PCT	ERA	G	GS	CG	IP	H	BB	SO	ShO	Relief Pitching W	Relief Pitching L	Relief Pitching SV	Batting AB	Batting H	Batting HR	BA	PO	A	E	DP	TC/G	FA
1926	PHI	N	0	1	.000	18.00	1	0	0	1	3	1	0	0	0	1	0	1	0	0	.000	0	1	0	0	1.0	1.000

Rube Yarrison

YARRISON, BYRON WARDSWORTH
B. Mar. 9, 1896, Montgomery, Pa. D. Apr. 22, 1977, Williamsport, Pa.

BR TR 5′11″ 165 lbs.

Year	Team	Lg	W	L	PCT	ERA	G	GS	CG	IP	H	BB	SO	ShO	Relief Pitching W	Relief Pitching L	Relief Pitching SV	Batting AB	Batting H	Batting HR	BA	PO	A	E	DP	TC/G	FA
1922	PHI	A	1	2	.333	8.29	18	1	0	33.2	50	12	10	0	1	1	0	6	1	0	.167	0	8	0	1	0.4	1.000
1924	BKN	N	0	2	.000	6.55	3	2	0	11	12	3	2	0	0	0	0	2	0	0	.000	0	5	1	0	2.0	.833
2 yrs.			1	4	.200	7.86	21	3	0	44.2	62	15	12	0	1	1	0	8	1	0	.125	0	13	1	1	0.7	.929

Emil Yde

YDE, EMIL OGDEN
B. Jan. 28, 1900, Great Lakes, Ill. D. Dec. 4, 1968, Leesburg, Fla.

BB TL 5′11″ 165 lbs.
BL 1925

Year	Team	Lg	W	L	PCT	ERA	G	GS	CG	IP	H	BB	SO	ShO	Relief Pitching W	Relief Pitching L	Relief Pitching SV	Batting AB	Batting H	Batting HR	BA	PO	A	E	DP	TC/G	FA
1924	PIT	N	16	3	**.842**	2.83	33	22	14	194	171	62	53	**4**	1	0	0	88	21	1	.239	5	57	6	4	2.1	.912
1925			17	9	.654	4.13	33	28	13	207	254	75	41	0	2	0	0	89	17	0	.191	8	46	4	8	1.8	.931
1926			8	7	.533	3.65	37	22	12	187.1	181	81	34	1	0	0	0	74	17	0	.230	10	47	4	3	1.6	.934

Emil Yde *continued*

Year	Team	W	L	PCT	ERA	G	GS	CG	IP	H	BB	SO	ShO	Relief W	Relief L	Relief SV	Batting AB	Batting H	Batting HR	BA	PO	A	E	DP	TC/G	FA
1927		1	3	.250	9.71	9	2	0	29.2	45	15	9	0	1	1	0	18	3	0	.167	2	11	1	0	1.6	.929
1929	**DET A**	7	3	.700	5.30	29	6	4	86.2	100	63	23	1	3	1	0	48	16	0	.333	5	16	2	0	0.8	.913
5 yrs.		49	25	.662	4.02	141	80	43	704.2	751	296	160	6	7	2	0	*				30	177	17	15	1.6	.924
WORLD SERIES																										
1925	**PIT N**	0	1	.000	11.57	1	1	0	2.1	5	3	1	0	0	0	0	*				0	0	0	0	0.0	.000

Joe Yeager

YEAGER, JOSEPH F. (Little Joe) BR TR 5′10″ 160 lbs.
B. Aug. 28, 1875, Philadelphia, Pa. D. July 2, 1937, Detroit, Mich.

Year	Team	W	L	PCT	ERA	G	GS	CG	IP	H	BB	SO	ShO	Relief W	Relief L	Relief SV	Batting AB	Batting H	Batting HR	BA	PO	A	E	DP	TC/G	FA
1898	**BKN N**	12	22	.353	3.65	36	33	32	291.1	333	80	70	0	1	**2**	0	134	23	0	.172	21	107	11	3	3.2	.921
1899		2	2	.500	4.72	10	4	2	47.2	56	16	6	1	1	1	1	47	9	0	.191	21	50	5	10	3.3	.934
1900		1	1	.500	6.88	2	2	2	17	21	5	2	0	0	0	0	9	3	0	.333	0	3	0	0	1.0	1.000
1901	**DET A**	12	11	.522	2.61	26	25	22	199.2	209	46	38	3	0	0	1	125	37	2	.296	33	104	13	12	3.8	.913
1902		6	12	.333	4.82	19	15	14	140	171	41	28	0	1	**2**	0	161	39	1	.242	59	94	9	3	3.4	.944
1903		0	1	.000	4.00	1	1	1	9	15	0	1	0	0	0	0	402	103	0	.256	130	186	27	10	3.1	.921
6 yrs.		33	49	.402	3.74	94	80	73	704.2	805	188	145	4	3	5	2	*				657	1171	137	84	3.7	.930

Jim Yeargin

YEARGIN, JAMES ALMOND (Grapefruit) BR TR 5′11″ 170 lbs.
B. Oct. 16, 1901, Mauldin, S. C. D. May 8, 1937, Greenville, S. C.

Year	Team	W	L	PCT	ERA	G	GS	CG	IP	H	BB	SO	ShO	Relief W	Relief L	Relief SV	Batting AB	Batting H	Batting HR	BA	PO	A	E	DP	TC/G	FA
1922	**BOS N**	0	1	.000	1.29	1	1	1	7	5	2	1	0	0	0	0	3	0	0	.000	0	2	0	0	2.0	1.000
1924		1	11	.083	5.09	32	12	6	141.1	162	42	34	0	0	1	0	42	6	0	.143	11	50	2	2	2.0	.968
2 yrs.		1	12	.077	4.91	33	13	7	148.1	167	44	35	0	0	1	0	45	6	0	.133	11	52	2	2	2.0	.969

Larry Yellen

YELLEN, LAWRENCE ALAN BR TR 5′11″ 190 lbs.
B. Jan. 4, 1943, Brooklyn, N. Y.

Year	Team	W	L	PCT	ERA	G	GS	CG	IP	H	BB	SO	ShO	Relief W	Relief L	Relief SV	Batting AB	Batting H	Batting HR	BA	PO	A	E	DP	TC/G	FA
1963	**HOU N**	0	0	—	3.60	1	1	0	5	7	1	3	0	0	0	0	2	0	0	.000	0	2	0	0	2.0	1.000
1964		0	0	—	6.86	13	1	0	21	27	10	9	0	0	0	0	3	0	0	.000	0	4	0	0	0.3	1.000
2 yrs.		0	0		6.23	14	2	0	26	34	11	12	0	0	0	0	5	0	0	.000	0	6	0	0	0.4	1.000

Chief Yellowhorse

YELLOWHORSE, MOSES J. BR TR 5′10″ 180 lbs.
B. Jan. 28, 1898, Pawnee, Okla. D. Apr. 10, 1964, Pawnee, Okla.

Year	Team	W	L	PCT	ERA	G	GS	CG	IP	H	BB	SO	ShO	Relief W	Relief L	Relief SV	Batting AB	Batting H	Batting HR	BA	PO	A	E	DP	TC/G	FA
1921	**PIT N**	5	3	.625	2.98	10	4	1	48.1	45	13	19	0	3	0	1	17	0	0	.000	1	3	1	0	0.5	.800
1922		3	1	.750	4.52	28	4	2	77.2	92	20	24	0	2	0	0	19	6	0	.316	4	15	1	0	0.7	.950
2 yrs.		8	4	.667	3.93	38	8	3	126	137	33	43	0	5	0	1	36	6	0	.167	5	18	2	0	0.7	.920

Carroll Yerkes

YERKES, CHARLES CARROLL (Lefty) BR TL 5′11″ 180 lbs.
B. June 13, 1903, McSherrystown, Pa. D. Dec. 20, 1950, Oakland, Calif.

Year	Team	W	L	PCT	ERA	G	GS	CG	IP	H	BB	SO	ShO	Relief W	Relief L	Relief SV	Batting AB	Batting H	Batting HR	BA	PO	A	E	DP	TC/G	FA
1927	**PHI A**	0	0	—	0.00	1	0	0	1	0	1	0	0	0	0	0	0	0	0	—	0	2	0	0	2.0	1.000
1928		0	1	.000	2.08	2	1	1	8.2	7	2	1	0	0	0	0	3	0	0	.000	0	5	0	1	2.5	1.000
1929		1	0	1.000	4.58	19	2	0	37.1	47	13	11	0	1	0	1	10	0	0	.000	3	18	0	3	1.1	1.000
1932	**CHI N**	0	0	—	3.00	2	0	0	9	5	3	4	0	0	0	0	3	1	0	.333	0	0	0	0	0.0	.000
1933		0	0	—	4.50	1	0	0	2	2	1	0	0	0	0	0	0	0	0	—	0	1	0	0	1.0	1.000
5 yrs.		1	1	.500	3.88	25	3	1	58	61	20	16	0	1	0	1	16	1	0	.063	3	26	0	4	1.2	1.000

Stan Yerkes

YERKES, STANLEY LEWIS BR TR 5′10″ 165 lbs.
B. Nov. 28, 1874, Cheltenham, Pa. D. July 28, 1940, Boston, Mass.

Year	Team	W	L	PCT	ERA	G	GS	CG	IP	H	BB	SO	ShO	Relief W	Relief L	Relief SV	Batting AB	Batting H	Batting HR	BA	PO	A	E	DP	TC/G	FA
1901	**2 teams** **BAL A** (1G 0–1) **STL N** (4G 3–1)																									
″	**total**	3	2	.600	3.86	5	5	5	42	47	8	19	0	0	0	0	15	2	0	.133	0	10	0	0	2.0	1.000
1902	**STL N**	11	**20**	.355	3.66	39	37	27	272.2	341	79	81	1	0	0	0	91	12	0	.132	11	61	7	0	2.0	.911
1903		0	1	.000	1.80	1	1	0	5	8	0	3	0	0	0	0	2	0	0	.000	0	0	0	0	0.0	.000
3 yrs.		14	23	.378	3.66	45	43	32	319.2	396	87	103	1	0	0	0	108	14	0	.130	11	71	7	0	2.0	.921

Rich Yett

YETT, RICHARD MARTIN BR TR 6′ 2″ 187 lbs.
B. Oct. 6, 1962, Pomona, Calif.

Year	Team	W	L	PCT	ERA	G	GS	CG	IP	H	BB	SO	ShO	Relief W	Relief L	Relief SV	Batting AB	Batting H	Batting HR	BA	PO	A	E	DP	TC/G	FA
1985	**MIN A**	0	0	—	27.00	1	1	0	0.1	1	2	0	0	0	0	0	0	0	0	—	0	0	0	0	0.0	.000
1986	**CLE A**	5	3	.625	5.15	39	3	1	78.2	84	37	50	1	4	2	1	0	0	0	—	2	7	0	0	0.2	1.000
1987		3	9	.250	5.25	37	11	2	97.2	96	49	59	0	1	5	1	0	0	0	—	6	9	0	0	0.4	1.000
1988		9	6	.600	4.62	23	22	0	134.1	146	55	71	0	0	0	0	0	0	0	—	8	9	0	1	0.7	1.000
1989		5	6	.455	5.00	32	12	1	99	111	47	47	0	1	1	0	0	0	0	—	9	7	0	0	0.5	1.000
1990	**MIN A**	0	0	—	2.08	4	0	0	4.1	6	1	2	0	0	0	0	0	0	0	—	2	1	1	1	1.0	.750
6 yrs.		22	24	.478	4.95	136	49	4	414.1	444	191	229	1	6	8	2	0	0	0		27	33	1	2	0.4	.984

Earl Yingling

YINGLING, EARL HERSHEY (Chink) BL TL 5′11½″ 180 lbs.
B. Oct. 29, 1888, Chillicothe, Ohio D. Oct. 2, 1962, Columbus, Ohio.

Year	Team	W	L	PCT	ERA	G	GS	CG	IP	H	BB	SO	ShO	Relief W	Relief L	Relief SV	Batting AB	Batting H	Batting HR	BA	PO	A	E	DP	TC/G	FA
1911	**CLE A**	1	0	1.000	4.43	4	3	1	22.1	30	9	6	0	0	0	0	11	3	0	.273	2	6	0	1	2.0	1.000
1912	**BKN N**	6	11	.353	3.59	25	16	12	163	186	56	51	0	1	3	0	64	16	0	.250	7	36	5	0	1.9	.896
1913		8	8	.500	2.58	26	13	8	146.2	158	10	40	2	3	3	0	60	23	0	.383	8	34	4	2	1.8	.913
1914	**CIN N**	8	13	.381	3.45	34	27	8	198	207	54	80	3	0	0	0	120	23	1	.192	22	45	8	2	1.6	.893
1918	**WAS A**	1	2	.333	2.13	5	2	2	38	30	12	15	0	1	0	0	15	7	0	.467	4	12	0	3	3.2	1.000
5 yrs.		24	34	.414	3.22	94	61	31	568	611	141	192	5	5	6	0	*				43	133	17	8	1.8	.912

Joe Yingling

YINGLING, JOSEPH GRANVILLE BR TL 5′ 7½″ 145 lbs.
B. July 23, 1866, Baltimore, Md. D. Oct. 24, 1946, Baltimore, Md.

Year	Team	W	L	PCT	ERA	G	GS	CG	IP	H	BB	SO	ShO	Relief W	Relief L	Relief SV	Batting AB	Batting H	Batting HR	BA	PO	A	E	DP	TC/G	FA
1886	**WAS N**	0	0	—	*12.00*	1	0	0	3	7	1	1	0	0	0	0	*				0	1	1	1	2.0	.500

Len Yochim

YOCHIM, LEONARD JOSEPH BL TL 6′ 2″ 200 lbs.
Brother of Ray Yochim.
B. Oct. 16, 1928, New Orleans, La.

Year	Team	W	L	PCT	ERA	G	GS	CG	IP	H	BB	SO	ShO	Relief W	Relief L	Relief SV	Batting AB	Batting H	Batting HR	BA	PO	A	E	DP	TC/G	FA
1951	**PIT N**	1	1	.500	8.31	2	2	0	8.2	10	11	5	0	0	0	0	3	0	0	.000	2	1	0	0	1.5	1.000
1954		0	1	.000	7.32	10	1	0	19.2	30	8	7	0	0	0	0	2	1	0	.500	4	6	1	0	1.1	.909
2 yrs.		1	2	.333	7.62	12	3	0	28.1	40	19	12	0	0	0	0	5	1	0	.200	6	7	1	0	1.2	.929

Ray Yochim

YOCHIM, RAYMOND AUSTIN ALOYSIUS BR TR 6′ 1″ 170 lbs.
Brother of Len Yochim.
B. July 19, 1922, New Orleans, La.

Year	Team		W	L	PCT	ERA	G	GS	CG	IP	H	BB	SO	ShO	Relief Pitching W	Relief Pitching L	Relief Pitching SV	Batting AB	Batting H	Batting HR	BA	PO	A	E	DP	TC/G	FA
1948	STL	N	0	0	—	0.00	1	0	0	1	0	3	1	0	0	0	0	0	0	0	—	0	0	0	0	0.0	.000
1949			0	0	—	15.43	3	0	0	2.1	3	4	3	0	0	0	0	0	0	0	—	1	0	1	0	0.7	.500
2 yrs.			0	0		10.80	4	0	0	3.1	3	7	4	0	0	0	0	0	0	0		1	0	1	0	0.5	.500

Jim York

YORK, JAMES HARLAN BR TR 6′ 3″ 200 lbs.
B. Aug. 27, 1947, Maywood, Calif.

Year	Team		W	L	PCT	ERA	G	GS	CG	IP	H	BB	SO	ShO	Relief Pitching W	Relief Pitching L	Relief Pitching SV	Batting AB	Batting H	Batting HR	BA	PO	A	E	DP	TC/G	FA
1970	KC	A	1	1	.500	3.38	4	0	0	8	5	2	6	0	1	1	0	2	0	0	.000	0	0	0	0	0.0	.000
1971			5	5	.500	2.90	53	0	0	93	70	44	103	0	5	5	3	17	2	1	.118	6	10	2	1	0.3	.889
1972	HOU	N	0	1	.000	5.25	26	0	0	36	45	18	25	0	0	1	0	1	0	0	.000	0	6	0	0	0.2	1.000
1973			3	4	.429	4.42	41	0	0	53	65	20	22	0	3	4	6	5	0	0	.000	1	12	2	0	0.4	.867
1974			2	2	.500	3.32	28	0	0	38	48	19	15	0	2	2	1	4	0	0	.000	4	6	0	0	0.4	1.000
1975			4	4	.500	3.83	19	4	0	47	43	25	17	0	1	3	0	11	1	0	.091	3	2	1	0	0.3	.833
1976	NY	A	1	0	1.000	5.59	3	0	0	9.2	14	4	6	0	1	0	0	0	0	0	—	0	1	0	0	0.3	1.000
7 yrs.			16	17	.485	3.79	174	4	0	284.2	290	132	194	0	13	16	10	40	3	1	.075	14	37	5	1	0.3	.911

Lefty York

YORK, JAMES EDWARD BL TL 5′10″ 185 lbs.
B. Nov. 1, 1892, West Fork, Ark. D. Apr. 9, 1961, York, Pa.

Year	Team		W	L	PCT	ERA	G	GS	CG	IP	H	BB	SO	ShO	Relief Pitching W	Relief Pitching L	Relief Pitching SV	Batting AB	Batting H	Batting HR	BA	PO	A	E	DP	TC/G	FA
1919	PHI	A	0	2	.000	24.92	2	2	0	4.1	13	5	2	0	0	0	0	1	0	0	.000	0	1	0	0	0.5	1.000
1921	CHI	N	5	9	.357	4.73	40	11	4	139	170	63	57	1	4	0	1	39	5	0	.128	1	22	4	0	0.7	.852
2 yrs.			5	11	.313	5.34	42	13	4	143.1	183	68	59	1	4	0	1	40	5	0	.125	1	23	4	0	0.7	.857

Mike York

YORK, MICHAEL DAVID BR TR 6′ 1″ 187 lbs.
B. Sept. 6, 1964, Oak Park, Ill.

Year	Team		W	L	PCT	ERA	G	GS	CG	IP	H	BB	SO	ShO	Relief Pitching W	Relief Pitching L	Relief Pitching SV	Batting AB	Batting H	Batting HR	BA	PO	A	E	DP	TC/G	FA
1990	PIT	N	1	1	.500	2.84	4	1	0	12.2	13	5	4	0	0	1	0	3	1	0	.333	1	3	0	0	1.0	1.000
1991	CLE	A	1	4	.200	6.75	14	4	0	34.2	45	19	19	0	1	2	0	0	0	0	—	2	3	0	0	0.4	1.000
2 yrs.			2	5	.286	5.70	18	5	0	47.1	58	24	23	0	1	3	0	3	1	0	.333	3	6	0	0	0.5	1.000

Gus Yost

YOST, AUGUST 6′ 5″
Deceased.

Year	Team		W	L	PCT	ERA	G	GS	CG	IP	H	BB	SO	ShO	Relief Pitching W	Relief Pitching L	Relief Pitching SV	Batting AB	Batting H	Batting HR	BA	PO	A	E	DP	TC/G	FA
1893	CHI	N	0	1	.000	13.50	1	1	0	2.2	3	8	1	0	0	0	0	1	0	0	.000	1	1	0	1	2.0	1.000

Floyd Youmans

YOUMANS, FLOYD EVERETT BR TR 6′ 2″ 180 lbs.
B. May 11, 1964, Tampa, Fla.

Year	Team		W	L	PCT	ERA	G	GS	CG	IP	H	BB	SO	ShO	Relief Pitching W	Relief Pitching L	Relief Pitching SV	Batting AB	Batting H	Batting HR	BA	PO	A	E	DP	TC/G	FA
1985	MON	N	4	3	.571	2.45	14	12	0	77	57	49	54	0	1	0	0	19	1	0	.053	6	1	0	0	0.5	1.000
1986			13	12	.520	3.53	33	32	6	219	145	**118**	202	2	0	1	0	75	12	1	.160	11	16	3	1	0.9	.900
1987			9	8	.529	4.64	23	23	3	116.1	112	47	94	3	0	0	0	40	6	1	.150	16	10	0	1	1.1	1.000
1988			3	6	.333	3.21	14	13	1	84	64	41	54	1	0	0	0	26	4	0	.154	7	10	1	0	1.3	.944
1989	PHI	N	1	5	.167	5.70	10	10	0	42.2	50	25	20	0	0	0	0	13	1	0	.077	4	6	0	1	1.0	1.000
5 yrs.			30	34	.469	3.74	94	90	10	539	428	280	424	6	1	1	0	173	24	2	.139	44	43	4	3	1.0	.956

Anthony Young

YOUNG, ANTHONY WAYNE BR TR 6′ 2″ 200 lbs.
B. Jan. 19, 1966, Houston, Tex.

Year	Team		W	L	PCT	ERA	G	GS	CG	IP	H	BB	SO	ShO	Relief Pitching W	Relief Pitching L	Relief Pitching SV	Batting AB	Batting H	Batting HR	BA	PO	A	E	DP	TC/G	FA
1991	NY	N	2	5	.286	3.10	10	8	0	49.1	48	12	20	0	0	0	0	14	2	0	.143	4	4	1	0	0.9	.889
1992			2	14	.125	4.17	52	13	1	121	134	31	64	0	1	7	15	27	3	0	.111	13	15	2	1	0.6	.933
1993			1	16	.059	3.77	39	10	1	100.1	103	42	62	0	1	8	3	14	2	0	.143	9	14	3	1	0.7	.885
1994	CHI	N	4	6	.400	3.92	20	19	0	114.2	103	46	65	0	0	0	0	34	6	0	.176	13	18	1	1	1.6	.969
1995			3	4	.429	3.70	32	1	0	41.1	47	14	15	0	3	3	2	3	2	0	.667	5	3	2	1	0.3	.800
5 yrs.			12	45	.211	3.84	153	51	2	426.2	435	145	226	0	5	18	20	92	15	0	.163	44	54	9	4	0.7	.916

Charlie Young

YOUNG, CHARLES (Cy) BB TR 5′10½″ 155 lbs.
B. Jan. 12, 1893, Philadelphia, Pa. D. May 12, 1952, Riverside, N. J.

Year	Team		W	L	PCT	ERA	G	GS	CG	IP	H	BB	SO	ShO	Relief Pitching W	Relief Pitching L	Relief Pitching SV	Batting AB	Batting H	Batting HR	BA	PO	A	E	DP	TC/G	FA
1915	BAL	F	1	3	.250	5.91	9	5	1	35	39	21	13	0	0	0	0	9	2	0	.222	3	17	0	2	2.2	1.000

Cliff Young

YOUNG, CLIFFORD RAPHAEL BL TL 6′ 4″ 200 lbs.
B. Aug. 8, 1964, Willis, Tex. D. Nov. 4, 1993, Willis, Tex.

Year	Team		W	L	PCT	ERA	G	GS	CG	IP	H	BB	SO	ShO	Relief Pitching W	Relief Pitching L	Relief Pitching SV	Batting AB	Batting H	Batting HR	BA	PO	A	E	DP	TC/G	FA
1990	CAL	A	1	1	.500	3.52	17	0	0	30.2	40	7	19	0	1	1	0	0	0	0	—	0	5	1	0	0.4	.833
1991			1	0	1.000	4.26	11	0	0	12.2	12	3	6	0	1	0	0	0	0	0	—	0	3	0	0	0.3	1.000
1993	CLE	A	3	3	.500	4.62	21	7	0	60.1	74	18	31	0	2	1	1	0	0	0	—	4	5	0	1	0.4	1.000
3 yrs.			5	4	.556	4.25	49	7	0	103.2	126	28	56	0	4	2	1	0	0	0		4	13	1	1	0.4	.944

Curt Young

YOUNG, CURTIS ALLEN BR TL 6′ 175 lbs.
B. Apr. 16, 1960, Saginaw, Mich.

Year	Team		W	L	PCT	ERA	G	GS	CG	IP	H	BB	SO	ShO	Relief Pitching W	Relief Pitching L	Relief Pitching SV	Batting AB	Batting H	Batting HR	BA	PO	A	E	DP	TC/G	FA
1983	OAK	A	0	1	.000	16.00	8	2	0	9	17	5	5	0	0	0	0	0	0	0	—	0	0	0	0	0.0	.000
1984			9	4	.692	4.06	20	17	2	108.2	118	31	41	1	0	0	0	0	0	0	—	6	13	0	1	0.9	1.000
1985			0	4	.000	7.24	19	7	0	46	57	22	19	0	0	0	0	0	0	0	—	4	4	0	0	0.4	1.000
1986			13	9	.591	3.45	29	27	5	198	176	57	116	2	1	0	0	0	0	0	—	9	32	4	1	1.6	.911
1987			13	7	.650	4.08	31	31	6	203	194	44	124	0	0	0	0	1	0	0	.000	15	28	1	2	1.4	.977
1988			11	8	.579	4.14	26	26	1	156.1	162	50	69	0	0	0	0	0	0	0	—	11	16	0	0	1.0	1.000
1989			5	9	.357	3.73	25	20	1	111	117	47	55	0	0	0	0	0	0	0	—	2	14	0	0	0.6	1.000
1990			9	6	.600	4.85	26	21	0	124.1	124	53	56	0	0	0	0	0	0	0	—	6	25	1	3	1.2	.969
1991			4	2	.667	5.00	41	1	0	68.1	74	34	27	0	4	1	0	0	0	0	—	4	12	0	2	0.4	1.000
1992	2 teams	KC A (10G 1–2)	NY A (13G 3–0)																								
″	total		4	2	.667	3.99	23	7	0	67.2	80	17	20	0	0	1	0	0	0	0		4	10	1	1	0.7	.933
1993	OAK	A	1	1	.500	4.30	3	3	0	14.2	14	6	4	0	0	0	0	0	0	0	—	0	3	0	0	1.0	1.000
11 yrs.			69	53	.566	4.31	251	162	15	1107	1133	366	536	3	5	2	0	1	0	0	.000	61	157	7	10	0.9	.969
LEAGUE CHAMPIONSHIP SERIES																											
1988	OAK	A	0	0	—	0.00	1	0	0	1.1	1	0	2	0	0	0	0	0	0	0	—	0	0	0	0	0.0	.000
WORLD SERIES																											
1988	OAK	A	0	0	—	0.00	1	0	0	1	1	0	0	0	0	0	0	0	0	0	—	0	1	0	0	1.0	1.000
1990			0	0	—	0.00	1	0	0	1	1	0	0	0	0	0	0	0	0	0	—	0	0	0	0	0.0	.000
2 yrs.			0	0		0.00	2	0	0	2	2	0	0	0	0	0	0	0	0	0		0	1	0	0	0.5	1.000

Cy Young

YOUNG, DENTON TRUE (Foxy Grandpa) BR TR 6′ 2″ 210 lbs.
B. Mar. 29, 1867, Gilmore, Ohio D. Nov. 4, 1955, Newcomerstown, Ohio.
Manager 1907.
Hall of Fame 1937.

Year	Team	W	L	PCT	ERA	G	GS	CG	IP	H	BB	SO	ShO	Relief W	Relief L	Relief SV	Batting AB	Batting H	Batting HR	BA	PO	A	E	DP	TC/G	FA
1890	CLE N	9	7	.563	3.47	17	16	16	147.2	145	30	39	0	**1**	1	0	65	8	0	.123	6	39	5	0	2.9	.900
1891		27	22	.551	2.85	55	46	43	423.2	431	140	147	0	1	**3**	2	174	29	1	.167	10	89	9	0	2.0	.917
1892		36	12	**.750**	**1.93**	53	49	48	453	363	118	168	**9**	1	1	0	196	31	1	.158	19	122	8	7	2.8	.946
1893		34	16	.680	3.36	53	46	42	422.2	442	103	102	1	4	1	1	187	44	1	.235	27	112	8	1	2.8	.946
1894		26	21	.553	3.94	52	47	44	408.2	488	106	108	2	1	1	1	186	40	2	.215	16	108	7	4	2.5	.947
1895		**35**	10	.778	3.24	47	40	36	369.2	363	75	121	**4**	**7**	0	0	140	30	0	.214	15	120	6	2	3.0	.957
1896		28	15	.651	3.24	51	46	42	414.1	**477**	62	**140**	**5**	0	1	**3**	180	52	3	.289	17	146	12	3	3.2	.931
1897		21	19	.525	3.79	**46**	38	35	335	391	49	88	2	1	**4**	0	153	34	0	.222	29	88	11	1	2.7	.914
1898		25	13	.658	2.53	46	41	40	377.2	387	41	101	1	0	1	0	154	39	2	.253	12	122	4	2	3.0	.971
1899	STL N	26	16	.619	2.58	44	42	**40**	369.1	368	44	111	4	0	1	1	148	32	1	.216	13	117	9	0	3.2	.935
1900		19	19	.500	3.00	41	35	32	321.1	337	36	115	**4**	2	2	0	124	22	1	.177	12	79	11	1	2.5	.892
1901	BOS A	**33**	10	.767	**1.62**	43	41	38	371.1	324	37	**158**	**5**	2	0	0	153	32	0	.209	12	105	3	3	2.8	.975
1902		**32**	11	.744	2.15	**45**	**43**	**41**	**384.2**	350	53	160	3	0	0	0	148	34	1	.230	10	82	7	4	2.2	.929
1903		**28**	9	**.757**	2.08	40	35	**34**	**341.2**	294	37	176	**7**	**2**	1	**2**	137	44	1	.321	6	86	5	4	2.4	.948
1904		26	16	.619	1.97	43	41	40	380	327	29	200	**10**	1	0	1	148	33	1	.223	7	103	7	0	2.7	.940
1905		18	19	.486	1.82	38	33	32	320.2	248	30	210	4	5	0	0	120	18	2	.150	2	87	3	1	2.4	.967
1906		13	**21**	.382	3.19	39	34	28	287.2	288	25	140	0	0	1	2	104	16	0	.154	8	81	6	1	2.4	.937
1907		21	15	.583	1.99	43	37	33	343.1	286	51	147	6	2	0	2	125	27	1	.216	5	83	6	2	2.2	.936
1908		21	11	.656	1.26	36	33	30	299	230	37	150	3	0	0	2	115	26	0	.226	5	62	3	2	1.9	.957
1909	CLE A	19	15	.559	2.26	35	34	30	295	267	59	109	3	0	1	0	107	21	0	.196	10	88	10	1	3.1	.907
1910		7	10	.412	2.53	21	20	14	163.1	149	27	58	1	0	0	0	55	8	0	.145	6	62	6	0	3.5	.919
1911	2 teams CLE A (7G 3–4) BOS N (11G 4–5)																									
″	total	7	9	.438	3.78	18	18	12	126.1	137	28	55	2	0	0	0	41	3	0	.073	4	33	2	2	2.2	.949
22 yrs.		511	316	.618	2.63	906	815	750	7356	7092	1217	2803	76	29	19	17	2960	623	18	.210	251	2014	148	41	2.6	.939
		1st	1st			8th		1st	1st				4th													
WORLD SERIES																										
1903	BOS A	2	1	.667	1.59	4	3	3	34	31	4	17	0	0	0	0	15	2	0	.133	0	7	1	0	2.0	.875

Harley Young

YOUNG, HARLAN EDWARD (Cy the Third) BR TR 6′ 2″
B. Sept. 28, 1883, Portland, Ind. D. Mar. 26, 1975, Jacksonville, Fla.

Year	Team	W	L	PCT	ERA	G	GS	CG	IP	H	BB	SO	ShO	Relief W	Relief L	Relief SV	Batting AB	Batting H	Batting HR	BA	PO	A	E	DP	TC/G	FA
1908	2 teams PIT N (8G 0–2) BOS N (6G 0–1)																									
″	total	0	3	.000	2.62	14	5	1	75.2	69	14	29	0	0	0	0	22	3	0	.136	2	27	4	1	2.4	.879

Irv Young

YOUNG, IRVING MELROSE (Cy the Second, Young Cy) BL TL 5′10″ 170 lbs.
B. July 21, 1877, Columbia Falls, Me. D. Jan. 14, 1935, Brewer, Me.

Year	Team	W	L	PCT	ERA	G	GS	CG	IP	H	BB	SO	ShO	Relief W	Relief L	Relief SV	Batting AB	Batting H	Batting HR	BA	PO	A	E	DP	TC/G	FA
1905	BOS N	20	21	.488	2.90	43	**42**	**41**	**378**	337	71	156	7	0	0	0	136	14	0	.103	33	115	3	1	3.5	.980
1906		16	25	.390	2.91	43	**41**	**37**	**358.1**	**349**	83	151	4	0	1	0	125	12	0	.096	27	108	8	5	3.3	.944
1907		10	23	.303	3.96	40	32	22	245.1	287	58	86	3	2	1	1	80	13	0	.163	20	69	3	4	2.3	.967
1908	2 teams BOS N (16G 4–8) PIT N (16G 4–3)																									
″	total	8	11	.421	2.42	32	18	10	174.2	167	40	63	2	1	2	1	62	11	0	.177	10	42	7	2	1.8	.881
1910	CHI A	4	8	.333	2.72	27	17	7	135.2	122	39	64	4	0	0	0	44	5	0	.114	11	38	0	1	1.8	1.000
1911		5	6	.455	4.37	24	11	3	92.2	99	25	40	1	2	0	2	28	5	0	.179	4	28	1	1	1.4	.970
6 yrs.		63	94	.401	3.11	209	161	120	1384.2	1361	316	560	21	5	4	4	475	60	0	.126	105	400	22	14	2.5	.958

Joe Young

YOUNG, JOSEPH B.
B. June 1857, Mt. Carmel, Pa. Deceased.

Year	Team	W	L	PCT	ERA	G	GS	CG	IP	H	BB	SO	ShO	Relief W	Relief L	Relief SV	Batting AB	Batting H	Batting HR	BA	PO	A	E	DP	TC/G	FA
1892	STL N	0	0	—	22.50	1	0	0	2	9	2	1	0	0	0	0	1	0	0	.000	0	0	0	0	0.0	.000

Kip Young

YOUNG, KIP LANE BR TR 5′11″ 175 lbs.
B. Oct. 29, 1954, Georgetown, Ohio.

Year	Team	W	L	PCT	ERA	G	GS	CG	IP	H	BB	SO	ShO	Relief W	Relief L	Relief SV	Batting AB	Batting H	Batting HR	BA	PO	A	E	DP	TC/G	FA
1978	DET A	6	7	.462	2.81	14	13	7	105.2	94	30	49	0	0	1	0	0	0	0	—	4	10	1	1	1.1	.933
1979		2	2	.500	6.34	13	7	0	44	60	11	22	0	0	1	0	0	0	0	—	3	10	0	0	1.0	1.000
2 yrs.		8	9	.471	3.85	27	20	7	149.2	154	41	71	0	0	2	0	0	0	0		7	20	1	1	1.0	.964

Matt Young

YOUNG, MATTHEW JOHN BL TL 6′ 3″ 205 lbs.
B. Aug. 9, 1958, Pasadena, Calif.

Year	Team	W	L	PCT	ERA	G	GS	CG	IP	H	BB	SO	ShO	Relief W	Relief L	Relief SV	Batting AB	Batting H	Batting HR	BA	PO	A	E	DP	TC/G	FA
1983	SEA A	11	15	.423	3.27	33	32	5	203.2	178	79	130	2	0	0	0	0	0	0	—	9	39	3	0	1.5	.941
1984		6	8	.429	5.72	22	22	1	113.1	141	57	73	0	0	0	0	0	0	0	—	3	21	2	3	1.2	.923
1985		12	**19**	.387	4.91	37	35	5	218.1	242	76	136	2	0	0	1	0	0	0	—	6	24	1	1	0.8	.968
1986		8	6	.571	3.82	65	5	1	103.2	108	46	82	0	6	3	13	0	0	0	—	4	9	4	0	0.3	.765
1987	LA N	5	8	.385	4.47	47	0	0	54.1	62	17	42	0	5	8	11	3	0	0	.000	3	1	2	0	0.1	.667
1989	OAK A	1	4	.200	6.75	26	4	0	37.1	42	31	27	0	1	2	0	0	0	0	—	3	6	0	0	0.3	1.000
1990	SEA A	8	18	.308	3.51	34	33	7	225.1	198	107	176	1	0	0	0	0	0	0	—	12	31	9	1	1.5	.827
1991	BOS A	3	7	.300	5.18	19	16	0	88.2	92	53	69	0	0	1	0	0	0	0	—	4	10	1	1	0.8	.933
1992		0	4	.000	4.58	28	8	1	70.2	69	42	57	0	0	0	0	0	0	0	—	2	8	6	0	0.6	.625
1993	CLE A	1	6	.143	5.21	22	8	0	74.1	75	57	65	0	1	2	0	0	0	0	—	4	10	1	0	0.7	.933
10 yrs.		55	95	.367	4.40	333	163	20	1189.2	1207	565	857	5	13	16	25	3	0	0	.000	50	159	29	6	0.7	.878
LEAGUE CHAMPIONSHIP SERIES																										
1989	OAK A	0	0	—	0.00	1	0	0	0.1	0	2	0	0	0	0	0	0	0	0	—	0	0	0	0	0.0	.000

Pete Young

YOUNG, BRYAN OWEN BR TR 6′ 225 lbs.
B. Mar. 19, 1968, Meadville, Miss.

Year	Team	W	L	PCT	ERA	G	GS	CG	IP	H	BB	SO	ShO	Relief W	Relief L	Relief SV	Batting AB	Batting H	Batting HR	BA	PO	A	E	DP	TC/G	FA
1992	MON N	0	0	—	3.98	13	0	0	20.1	18	9	11	0	0	0	0	0	0	0	—	3	1	0	0	0.3	1.000
1993		1	0	1.000	3.38	4	0	0	5.1	4	0	3	0	1	0	0	1	0	0	.000	0	1	0	0	0.3	1.000
2 yrs.		1	0	1.000	3.86	17	0	0	25.2	22	9	14	0	1	0	0	1	0	0	.000	3	2	0	0	0.3	1.000

Chief Youngblood

YOUNGBLOOD, ALBERT CLYDE BL TR 6′ 3″ 202 lbs.
B. June 13, 1900, Hillsboro, Tex. D. July 6, 1968, Amarillo, Tex.

Year	Team	W	L	PCT	ERA	G	GS	CG	IP	H	BB	SO	ShO	Relief W	Relief L	Relief SV	Batting AB	Batting H	Batting HR	BA	PO	A	E	DP	TC/G	FA
1922	WAS A	0	0	—	14.54	2	0	0	4.1	9	7	0	0	0	0	0	2	0	0	.000	0	1	0	0	0.5	1.000

Ducky Yount

YOUNT, HENRY MACON (Hub) BR TR 6′ 2″ 178 lbs.
B. Dec. 7, 1885, Iredell County, N. C. D. May 9, 1970, Winston-Salem, N. C.

Year	Team	W	L	PCT	ERA	G	GS	CG	IP	H	BB	SO	ShO	Relief Pitching W	Relief L	Relief SV	Batting AB	Batting H	HR	BA	PO	A	E	DP	TC/G	FA
1914	BAL F	1	1	.500	4.14	13	1	1	41.1	44	19	19	0	1	2	0	12	1	0	.083	2	15	2	1	1.5	.895

Larry Yount

YOUNT, LAWRENCE KING BR TR 6′ 2″ 185 lbs.
Brother of Robin Yount.
B. Feb. 15, 1950, Houston, Tex.

Year	Team	W	L	PCT	ERA	G	GS	CG	IP	H	BB	SO	ShO	Relief Pitching W	Relief L	Relief SV	Batting AB	Batting H	HR	BA	PO	A	E	DP	TC/G	FA
1971	HOU N	0	0	—	0.00	1	0	0		0	0	0	0	0	0	0	0	0	0	—	0	0	0	0	0.0	.000

Carl Yowell

YOWELL, CARL COLUMBUS (Sundown) BL TL 6′ 4″ 180 lbs.
B. Dec. 20, 1902, Madison, Va. D. July 27, 1985, Jacksonville, Tex.

Year	Team	W	L	PCT	ERA	G	GS	CG	IP	H	BB	SO	ShO	Relief Pitching W	Relief L	Relief SV	Batting AB	Batting H	HR	BA	PO	A	E	DP	TC/G	FA
1924	CLE A	1	1	.500	6.67	4	2	2	27	37	13	8	0	0	0	0	11	2	0	.182	2	4	0	0	1.5	1.000
1925		2	3	.400	4.46	12	4	1	36.1	40	17	12	0	1	0	0	8	1	0	.125	1	11	0	0	1.0	1.000
2 yrs.		3	4	.429	5.40	16	6	3	63.1	77	30	20	0	1	0	0	19	3	0	.158	3	15	0	0	1.1	1.000

Eddie Yuhas

YUHAS, JOHN EDWARD BR TR 6′ 1″ 180 lbs.
B. Aug. 5, 1924, Youngstown, Ohio D. July 6, 1986, Winston-Salem, N. C.

Year	Team	W	L	PCT	ERA	G	GS	CG	IP	H	BB	SO	ShO	Relief Pitching W	Relief L	Relief SV	Batting AB	Batting H	HR	BA	PO	A	E	DP	TC/G	FA
1952	STL N	12	2	.857	2.72	54	2	0	99.1	90	35	39	0	11	1	6	21	4	0	.190	3	15	1	1	0.4	.947
1953		0	0	—	18.00	2	0	0	1	3	0	0	0	0	0	0	0	0	0	—	0	0	0	0	0.0	.000
2 yrs.		12	2	.857	2.87	56	2	0	100.1	93	35	39	0	11	1	6	21	4	0	.190	3	15	1	1	0.3	.947

Adrian Zabala

ZABALA, ADRIAN BL TL 5′11″ 165 lbs.
Born Adrian Zabala (Rodriguez)Rodriguez.
B. Aug. 26, 1916, San Antonio de los Banos, Cuba.

Year	Team	W	L	PCT	ERA	G	GS	CG	IP	H	BB	SO	ShO	Relief Pitching W	Relief L	Relief SV	Batting AB	Batting H	HR	BA	PO	A	E	DP	TC/G	FA
1945	NY N	2	4	.333	4.78	11	5	1	43.1	46	20	14	0	1	1	0	13	3	0	.231	3	8	1	1	1.1	.917
1949		2	3	.400	5.27	15	4	2	41	44	10	13	1	0	2	1	13	1	0	.077	0	2	1	1	0.2	.667
2 yrs.		4	7	.364	5.02	26	9	3	84.1	90	30	27	1	1	3	1	26	4	0	.154	3	10	2	2	0.6	.867

Zip Zabel

ZABEL, GEORGE WASHINGTON BR TR 6′ 1½″ 185 lbs.
B. Feb. 18, 1891, Wetmore, Kans. D. May 31, 1970, Beloit, Wis.

Year	Team	W	L	PCT	ERA	G	GS	CG	IP	H	BB	SO	ShO	Relief Pitching W	Relief L	Relief SV	Batting AB	Batting H	HR	BA	PO	A	E	DP	TC/G	FA
1913	CHI N	1	0	1.000	0.00	1	1	0	5	3	1	0	0	0	0	0	2	0	0	.000	0	2	0	0	2.0	1.000
1914		4	4	.500	2.18	29	7	2	128	104	45	50	0	2	0	1	38	7	0	.184	5	29	2	0	1.2	.944
1915		7	10	.412	3.20	36	17	8	163	124	84	60	3	2	2	0	54	4	0	.074	6	62	4	1	2.0	.944
3 yrs.		12	14	.462	2.71	66	25	10	296	231	130	110	3	4	2	1	94	11	0	.117	11	93	6	1	1.7	.945

Chink Zachary

ZACHARY, ALBERT MYRON BR TR 5′11″ 182 lbs.
Born Albert Myron Zarski.
B. Oct. 19, 1917, Brooklyn, N. Y.

Year	Team	W	L	PCT	ERA	G	GS	CG	IP	H	BB	SO	ShO	Relief Pitching W	Relief L	Relief SV	Batting AB	Batting H	HR	BA	PO	A	E	DP	TC/G	FA
1944	BKN N	0	2	.000	9.58	4	2	0	10.1	10	7	3	0	0	2	0	3	0	0	.000	0	1	0	0	0.3	1.000

Chris Zachary

ZACHARY, WILLIAM CHRISTOPHER BL TR 6′ 2″ 200 lbs.
B. Feb. 19, 1944, Knoxville, Tenn.

Year	Team	W	L	PCT	ERA	G	GS	CG	IP	H	BB	SO	ShO	Relief Pitching W	Relief L	Relief SV	Batting AB	Batting H	HR	BA	PO	A	E	DP	TC/G	FA
1963	HOU N	2	2	.500	4.89	22	7	0	57	62	22	42	0	0	0	0	13	0	0	.000	3	14	0	0	0.8	1.000
1964		0	1	.000	9.00	1	1	0	4	6	1	2	0	0	0	0	1	0	0	.000	0	2	0	0	2.0	1.000
1965		0	2	.000	4.22	4	2	0	10.2	12	6	4	0	0	0	0	2	0	0	.000	2	1	0	0	0.8	1.000
1966		3	5	.375	3.44	10	8	0	55	44	32	37	0	0	1	0	18	4	0	.222	5	6	2	0	1.3	.846
1967		1	6	.143	5.70	9	7	0	36.1	42	12	18	0	0	0	0	10	1	0	.100	2	5	2	1	1.0	.778
1969	KC A	0	1	.000	7.85	8	2	0	18.1	27	7	6	0	0	0	0	2	1	0	.500	0	2	0	0	0.3	1.000
1971	STL N	3	10	.231	5.30	23	12	1	90	114	26	48	1	1	2	0	33	8	0	.242	4	14	1	2	0.8	.947
1972	DET A	1	1	.500	1.42	25	1	0	38	27	15	21	0	1	0	1	2	1	0	.500	2	5	0	0	0.3	1.000
1973	PIT N	0	1	.000	3.00	6	0	0	12	10	1	6	0	0	1	1	2	0	0	.000	1	0	0	0	0.2	1.000
9 yrs.		10	29	.256	4.57	108	40	1	321.1	344	122	184	1	2	4	2	83	15	0	.181	19	49	5	3	0.7	.932
LEAGUE CHAMPIONSHIP SERIES																										
1972	DET A	0	0	—	∞	1	0	0		0	1	0	0	0	0	0	0	0	0	—	0	0	0	0	0.0	.000

Tom Zachary

ZACHARY, JONATHAN THOMPSON WALTON BL TL 6′ 1″ 187 lbs.
Played as Zach Walton in 1918.
B. May 7, 1896, Graham, N. C. D. Jan. 24, 1969, Burlington, N. C.

Year	Team	W	L	PCT	ERA	G	GS	CG	IP	H	BB	SO	ShO	Relief Pitching W	Relief L	Relief SV	Batting AB	Batting H	HR	BA	PO	A	E	DP	TC/G	FA
1918	PHI A	2	0	1.000	5.63	2	2	0	8	9	7	1	0	0	0	0	4	2	0	.500	1	2	1	0	2.0	.750
1919	WAS A	1	5	.167	2.92	17	7	0	61.2	68	20	9	0	0	1	0	15	5	0	.333	3	15	0	0	1.1	1.000
1920		15	16	.484	3.77	44	30	18	262.2	289	78	53	3	3	0	2	111	29	0	.261	5	74	2	2	1.8	.975
1921		18	16	.529	3.96	39	30	17	250	314	59	53	2	3	3	1	90	23	0	.256	6	68	5	1	2.0	.937
1922		15	10	.600	3.12	32	25	13	184.2	190	43	37	1	1	1	1	71	21	1	.296	4	48	0	2	1.6	1.000
1923		10	16	.385	4.49	35	29	10	204.1	270	63	40	0	1	2	0	78	15	0	.192	9	50	0	3	1.7	1.000
1924		15	9	.625	2.75	33	27	13	202.2	198	53	45	1	1	0	2	72	22	0	.306	3	58	0	2	1.8	1.000
1925		12	15	.444	3.85	38	**33**	11	217.2	247	74	58	1	1	2	2	69	12	1	.174	17	50	1	1	1.8	.985
1926	STL A	14	15	.483	3.60	34	31	18	247.1	264	97	53	3	0	3	0	86	23	1	.267	5	80	5	4	2.6	.944
1927	2 teams STL A (13G 4–6) WAS A (15G 4–7)																									
″	total	8	13	.381	3.96	28	26	11	188.2	236	57	26	1	0	2	0	64	8	0	.125	3	32	2	3	1.3	.946
1928	2 teams WAS A (20G 6–9) NY A (7G 3–3)																									
″	total	9	12	.429	4.98	27	20	8	148.1	184	55	26	1	0	1	1	48	12	1	.250	4	46	1	2	1.9	.980
1929	NY A	12	0	1.000	2.48	26	11	7	119.2	131	30	35	2	3	0	2	42	10	0	.238	2	15	2	1	0.7	.895
1930	2 teams NY A (3G 1–1) BOS N (24G 11–5)																									
″	total	12	6	.667	4.77	27	25	10	168	210	59	58	1	1	0	0	62	15	2	.242	5	31	3	2	1.4	.923
1931	BOS N	11	15	.423	3.10	33	28	16	229	243	53	64	3	0	3	2	84	14	0	.167	2	65	2	1	2.1	.971
1932		12	11	.522	3.10	32	24	12	212	231	55	67	1	2	1	0	77	21	0	.273	4	39	1	1	1.4	.977
1933		7	9	.438	3.53	26	20	6	125	134	35	22	2	0	0	2	42	5	0	.119	1	32	0	0	1.3	1.000
1934	2 teams BOS N (5G 1–2) BKN N (22G 5–6)																									
″	total	6	8	.429	4.23	27	16	6	125.2	149	29	32	1	1	1	2	46	7	0	.152	5	23	2	0	1.1	.933
1935	BKN N	7	12	.368	3.59	25	21	9	158	193	35	33	1	0	0	4	52	7	0	.135	5	38	2	2	1.8	.956
1936	2 teams BKN N (1G 0–0) PHI N (7G 0–3)																									
″	total	0	3	.000	8.71	8	2	0	20.2	30	12	8	0	0	0	1	9	3	0	.333	0	5	0	0	0.6	1.000
19 yrs.		186	191	.493	3.72	533	407	185	3134	3590	914	720	24	17	20	22	1122	254	6	.226	84	771	29	27	1.7	.967

Tom Zachary *continued*

Year	Team	W	L	PCT	ERA	G	GS	CG	IP	H	BB	SO	ShO	Relief W	Relief L	Relief SV	Batting AB	Batting H	Batting HR	BA	PO	A	E	DP	TC/G	FA
WORLD SERIES																										
1924	**WAS A**	2	0	1.000	2.04	2	2	1	17.2	13	3	3	0	0	0	0	5	0	0	.000	1	4	0	0	2.5	1.000
1925		0	0	—	10.80	1	0	0	1.2	3	1	0	0	0	0	0	0	0	0	—	0	0	0	0	0.0	.000
1928	**NY A**	1	0	1.000	3.00	1	1	1	9	9	1	7	0	0	0	0	4	0	0	.000	0	1	0	0	1.0	1.000
3 yrs.		3	0	1.000 **1st**	2.86	4	3	2	28.1	25	5	10	0	0	0	0	9	0	0	.000	1	5	0	0	1.5	1.000

Pat Zachry

ZACHRY, PATRICK PAUL BR TR 6′5″ 180 lbs.
B. Apr. 24, 1952, Richmond, Tex.

Year	Team	W	L	PCT	ERA	G	GS	CG	IP	H	BB	SO	ShO	Relief W	Relief L	Relief SV	Batting AB	Batting H	Batting HR	BA	PO	A	E	DP	TC/G	FA
1976	**CIN N**	14	7	.667	2.74	38	28	6	204	170	83	143	1	2	0	0	62	7	0	.113	13	20	1	2	0.9	.971
1977	**2 teams** **CIN N** (12G 3–7) **NY N** (19G 7–6)																									
″	**total**	10	13	.435	4.25	31	31	5	194.2	207	77	99	2	0	0	0	64	9	0	.141	6	30	1	4	1.2	.973
1978	**NY N**	10	6	.625	3.33	21	21	5	138	120	60	78	2	0	0	0	43	3	0	.070	9	24	2	4	1.7	.943
1979		5	1	.833	3.56	7	7	1	43	44	21	17	0	0	0	0	16	2	0	.125	3	7	0	0	1.4	1.000
1980		6	10	.375	3.00	28	26	7	165	145	58	88	3	0	1	0	46	2	0	.043	5	20	1	1	0.9	.962
1981		7	**14**	.333	4.14	24	24	3	139	151	56	76	0	0	0	0	38	6	0	.158	4	26	3	4	1.4	.909
1982		6	9	.400	4.05	36	16	2	137.2	149	57	69	0	2	3	1	38	3	0	.079	10	19	1	1	0.8	.967
1983	**LA N**	6	1	.857	2.49	40	1	0	61.1	63	21	36	0	5	1	0	4	2	0	.500	6	9	2	1	0.4	.882
1984		5	6	.455	3.81	58	0	0	82.2	84	51	55	0	5	6	2	6	2	0	.333	4	16	2	2	0.4	.909
1985	**PHI N**	0	0	—	4.26	10	0	0	12.2	14	11	8	0	0	0	0	1	0	0	.000	0	5	0	0	0.5	1.000
10 yrs.		69	67	.507	3.52	293	154	29	1178	1147	495	669	8	14	11	3	318	36	0	.113	60	176	13	19	0.8	.948
LEAGUE CHAMPIONSHIP SERIES																										
1976	**CIN N**	1	0	1.000	3.60	1	1	0	5	6	3	3	0	0	0	0	1	0	0	.000	1	3	0	0	4.0	1.000
1983	**LA N**	0	0	—	2.25	2	0	0	4	4	2	2	0	0	0	0	0	0	0	—	1	0	0	0	0.5	1.000
2 yrs.		1	0	1.000	3.00	3	1	0	9	10	5	5	0	0	0	0	1	0	0	.000	2	3	0	0	1.7	1.000
WORLD SERIES																										
1976	**CIN N**	1	0	1.000	2.70	1	1	1	6.2	6	5	6	0	0	0	0	0	0	0	—	0	2	1	0	3.0	.667

George Zackert

ZACKERT, GEORGE CARL (Zeke) BL TL 6′ 177 lbs.
B. Dec. 24, 1884, Buchanan County, Mo. D. Feb. 18, 1977, Burlington, Iowa.

Year	Team	W	L	PCT	ERA	G	GS	CG	IP	H	BB	SO	ShO	Relief W	Relief L	Relief SV	Batting AB	Batting H	Batting HR	BA	PO	A	E	DP	TC/G	FA
1911	**STL N**	0	2	.000	11.05	4	1	0	7.1	17	6	6	0	0	1	0	1	0	0	.000	0	4	0	0	1.0	1.000
1912		0	0	—	18.00	1	0	0	1	2	1	0	0	0	0	0	1	0	0	.000	0	1	0	0	1.0	1.000
2 yrs.		0	2	.000	11.88	5	1	0	8.1	19	7	6	0	0	1	0	2	0	0	.000	0	5	0	0	1.0	1.000

Geoff Zahn

ZAHN, GEOFFREY CLAYTON BL TL 6′1″ 180 lbs.
B. Dec. 19, 1945, Baltimore, Md.

Year	Team	W	L	PCT	ERA	G	GS	CG	IP	H	BB	SO	ShO	Relief W	Relief L	Relief SV	Batting AB	Batting H	Batting HR	BA	PO	A	E	DP	TC/G	FA
1973	**LA N**	1	0	1.000	1.35	6	1	0	13.1	5	2	9	0	0	0	0	2	0	0	.000	0	4	1	0	0.8	.800
1974		3	5	.375	2.02	21	10	1	80	78	16	33	0	0	1	0	23	4	0	.174	2	15	2	1	0.9	.895
1975	**2 teams** **LA N** (2G 0–1) **CHI N** (16G 2–7)																									
″	**total**	2	8	.200	4.66	18	10	0	65.2	69	31	22	0	2	1	1	15	2	0	.133	6	16	2	0	1.3	.917
1976	**CHI N**	0	1	.000	11.25	3	2	0	8	16	2	4	0	0	0	0	3	0	0	.000	0	3	1	0	1.3	.750
1977	**MIN A**	12	14	.462	4.68	34	32	7	198	234	66	88	1	2	0	0	0	0	0	—	16	40	2	5	1.7	.966
1978		14	14	.500	3.03	35	35	12	252.1	260	81	106	1	0	0	0	0	0	0	—	9	41	2	2	1.5	.962
1979		13	7	.650	3.57	26	24	4	169	181	41	58	0	0	0	0	0	0	0	—	8	37	4	2	1.9	.918
1980		14	18	.438	4.40	38	35	13	233	273	66	96	5	0	1	0	0	0	0	—	12	37	1	3	1.3	.980
1981	**CAL A**	10	11	.476	4.42	25	25	9	161	181	43	52	0	0	0	0	0	0	0	—	7	31	3	2	1.6	.927
1982		18	8	.692	3.73	34	34	12	229.1	225	65	81	4	0	0	0	0	0	0	—	3	35	2	1	1.2	.950
1983		9	11	.450	3.33	29	28	11	203	212	51	81	3	0	0	0	0	0	0	—	9	25	3	2	1.3	.919
1984		13	10	.565	3.12	28	27	9	199.1	200	48	61	**5**	0	0	0	0	0	0	—	14	33	1	1	1.7	.979
1985		2	2	.500	4.38	7	7	1	37	44	14	14	1	0	0	0	0	0	0	—	1	9	0	0	1.4	1.000
13 yrs.		111	109	.505	3.74	304	270	79	1849	1978	526	705	20	4	3	1	43	6	0	.140	87	326	24	19	1.4	.945
LEAGUE CHAMPIONSHIP SERIES																										
1982	**CAL A**	0	1	.000	7.36	1	1	0	3.2	4	1	2	0	0	0	0	0	0	0	—	0	0	0	0	0.0	.000

Paul Zahniser

ZAHNISER, PAUL VERNON BR TR 5′10½″ 170 lbs.
B. Sept. 6, 1896, Sac City, Iowa D. Sept. 26, 1964, Klamath Falls, Ore.

Year	Team	W	L	PCT	ERA	G	GS	CG	IP	H	BB	SO	ShO	Relief W	Relief L	Relief SV	Batting AB	Batting H	Batting HR	BA	PO	A	E	DP	TC/G	FA
1923	**WAS A**	9	10	.474	3.86	33	21	10	177	201	76	52	1	2	2	0	52	5	0	.096	8	38	3	1	1.5	.939
1924		5	7	.417	4.40	24	14	5	92	98	49	28	1	1	0	0	30	4	0	.133	4	14	0	0	0.8	1.000
1925	**BOS A**	5	12	.294	5.15	37	21	7	176.2	232	89	30	1	1	0	1	58	8	0	.138	6	34	0	0	1.1	1.000
1926		6	**18**	.250	4.97	30	24	7	172	213	69	35	1	0	2	0	49	8	0	.163	11	57	2	1	2.3	.971
1929	**CIN N**	0	0	—	27.00	1	0	0	1	2	1	0	0	0	0	0	0	0	0	—	0	0	0	0	0.0	.000
5 yrs.		25	47	.347	4.66	125	80	29	618.2	746	284	145	4	4	4	1	189	25	0	.132	29	143	5	2	1.4	.972

Carl Zamloch

ZAMLOCH, CARL EUGENE BR TR 6′1″ 176 lbs.
B. Oct. 6, 1889, Oakland, Calif. D. Aug. 19, 1963, Santa Barbara, Calif.

Year	Team	W	L	PCT	ERA	G	GS	CG	IP	H	BB	SO	ShO	Relief W	Relief L	Relief SV	Batting AB	Batting H	Batting HR	BA	PO	A	E	DP	TC/G	FA
1913	**DET A**	1	6	.143	2.45	17	5	3	69.2	66	23	28	0	1	2	1	22	4	0	.182	3	16	2	1	1.2	.905

Oscar Zamora

ZAMORA, OSCAR JOSE BR TR 5′10″ 178 lbs.
Born Oscar Jose Zamora (Sosa).
B. Sept. 23, 1944, Camaguey, Cuba.

Year	Team	W	L	PCT	ERA	G	GS	CG	IP	H	BB	SO	ShO	Relief W	Relief L	Relief SV	Batting AB	Batting H	Batting HR	BA	PO	A	E	DP	TC/G	FA
1974	**CHI N**	3	9	.250	3.11	56	0	0	84	82	19	38	0	3	9	10	11	2	0	.182	5	13	1	0	0.3	.947
1975		5	2	.714	5.07	52	0	0	71	84	15	28	0	5	2	10	6	1	0	.167	3	10	1	0	0.3	.929
1976		5	3	.625	5.24	40	2	0	55	70	17	27	0	5	2	3	9	0	0	.000	1	7	2	0	0.3	.800
1978	**HOU N**	0	0	—	7.20	10	0	0	15	20	7	6	0	0	0	0	2	0	0	.000	1	2	0	1	0.3	1.000
4 yrs.		13	14	.481	4.52	158	2	0	225	256	58	99	0	13	13	23	28	3	0	.107	10	32	4	1	0.3	.913

Dom Zanni

ZANNI, DOMINICK THOMAS BR TR 5′11″ 180 lbs.
B. Mar. 1, 1932, Bronx, N. Y.

Year	Team	W	L	PCT	ERA	G	GS	CG	IP	H	BB	SO	ShO	Relief W	Relief L	Relief SV	Batting AB	Batting H	Batting HR	BA	PO	A	E	DP	TC/G	FA
1958	**SF N**	1	0	1.000	2.25	1	0	0	4	7	1	3	0	1	0	0	2	0	0	.000	0	0	0	0	0.0	.000
1959		0	0	—	6.55	9	0	0	11	12	8	11	0	0	0	0	0	0	0	—	3	5	0	1	0.9	1.000
1961		1	0	1.000	3.95	8	0	0	13.2	13	12	11	0	1	0	0	0	0	0	—	0	3	0	0	0.4	1.000
1962	**CHI A**	6	5	.545	3.75	44	2	0	86.1	67	31	66	0	6	3	5	18	5	0	.278	6	22	0	1	0.6	1.000
1963	**2 teams** **CHI A** (5G 0–0) **CIN N** (31G 1–1)																									
″	**total**	1	1	.500	4.56	36	1	0	47.1	44	25	42	0	1	1	5	3	1	0	.333	6	10	1	1	0.5	.941

Dom Zanni *continued*

Year	Team	Lg	W	L	PCT	ERA	G	GS	CG	IP	H	BB	SO	ShO	Relief W	Relief L	Relief SV	AB	H	HR	BA	PO	A	E	DP	TC/G	FA
1965	CIN	N	0	0	—	1.35	8	0	0	13.1	7	5	10	0	0	0	0	1	0	0	.000	1	2	0	0	0.4	1.000
1966			0	0	—	0.00	5	0	0	7.1	5	3	5	0	0	0	0	1	1	0	1.000	0	0	0	0	0.0	.000
7 yrs.			9	6	.600	3.79	111	3	0	183	155	85	148	0	9	4	10	25	7	0	.280	16	42	1	3	0.5	.983

Jeff Zaske

ZASKE, LLOYD JEFFREY BR TR 6′ 5″ 180 lbs.
B. Oct. 6, 1960, Seattle, Wash.

Year	Team	Lg	W	L	PCT	ERA	G	GS	CG	IP	H	BB	SO	ShO	Relief W	Relief L	Relief SV	AB	H	HR	BA	PO	A	E	DP	TC/G	FA
1984	PIT	N	0	0	—	0.00	3	0	0	5	4	1	2	0	0	0	0	0	0	0	—	0	2	0	0	0.7	1.000

Clint Zavaras

ZAVARAS, CLINTON WAYNE BR TR 6′ 1″ 175 lbs.
B. Jan. 4, 1967, Denver, Colo.

Year	Team	Lg	W	L	PCT	ERA	G	GS	CG	IP	H	BB	SO	ShO	Relief W	Relief L	Relief SV	AB	H	HR	BA	PO	A	E	DP	TC/G	FA
1989	SEA	A	1	6	.143	5.19	10	10	0	52	49	30	31	0	0	0	0	0	0	0	—	0	8	1	0	0.9	.889

Zay

ZAY
B. Pittsburgh, Pa. Deceased.

Year	Team	Lg	W	L	PCT	ERA	G	GS	CG	IP	H	BB	SO	ShO	Relief W	Relief L	Relief SV	AB	H	HR	BA	PO	A	E	DP	TC/G	FA
1886	BAL	AA	0	1	.000	9.00	1	1	0	2	4	4	2	0	0	0	0	*				1	0	1	0	1.0	.500

Matt Zeiser

ZEISER, MATTHEW J. BR TR 5′10″ 170 lbs.
B. Sept. 25, 1888, Chicago, Ill. D. June 10, 1942, Chicago, Ill.

Year	Team	Lg	W	L	PCT	ERA	G	GS	CG	IP	H	BB	SO	ShO	Relief W	Relief L	Relief SV	AB	H	HR	BA	PO	A	E	DP	TC/G	FA
1914	BOS	A	0	0	—	1.80	2	0	0	10	9	8	0	0	0	0	0	3	0	0	.000	1	1	1	0	1.5	.667

Bill Zepp

ZEPP, WILLIAM CLINTON BR TR 6′ 2″ 185 lbs.
B. July 22, 1946, Detroit, Mich.

Year	Team	Lg	W	L	PCT	ERA	G	GS	CG	IP	H	BB	SO	ShO	Relief W	Relief L	Relief SV	AB	H	HR	BA	PO	A	E	DP	TC/G	FA
1969	MIN	A	0	0	—	6.75	4	0	0	5.1	6	4	2	0	0	0	0	1	0	0	.000	1	0	0	0	0.3	1.000
1970			9	4	.692	3.22	43	20	1	151	154	51	64	1	3	0	2	44	6	0	.136	8	17	2	1	0.6	.926
1971	DET	A	1	1	.500	5.06	16	4	0	32	41	17	15	0	0	1	2	4	0	0	.000	3	6	0	0	0.6	1.000
3 yrs.			10	5	.667	3.63	63	24	1	188.1	201	72	81	1	3	1	4	49	6	0	.122	12	23	2	1	0.6	.946
LEAGUE CHAMPIONSHIP SERIES																											
1970	MIN	A	0	0	—	6.75	2	0	0	1.1	2	2	2	0	0	0	0	0	0	0	—	0	0	0	0	0.0	.000

George Zettlein

ZETTLEIN, GEORGE (The Charmer) BR TR 5′ 9″ 162 lbs.
B. July 18, 1844, Brooklyn, N. Y. D. May 23, 1905, Patchogue, N. Y.

Year	Team	Lg	W	L	PCT	ERA	G	GS	CG	IP	H	BB	SO	ShO	Relief W	Relief L	Relief SV	AB	H	HR	BA	PO	A	E	DP	TC/G	FA
1876	PHI	N	4	20	.167	3.88	28	25	23	234	358	6	10	1	0	0	2	128	27	0	.211	70	39	11	6	3.2	.908

Bob Zick

ZICK, ROBERT GEORGE BL TR 6′ 168 lbs.
B. Apr. 26, 1927, Chicago, Ill.

Year	Team	Lg	W	L	PCT	ERA	G	GS	CG	IP	H	BB	SO	ShO	Relief W	Relief L	Relief SV	AB	H	HR	BA	PO	A	E	DP	TC/G	FA
1954	CHI	N	0	0	—	8.27	8	0	0	16.1	23	7	9	0	0	0	0	4	1	0	.250	1	2	1	0	0.5	.750

George Ziegler

ZIEGLER, GEORGE J.
B. 1872, Chicago, Ill. D. July 22, 1916, Kankakee, Ill.

Year	Team	Lg	W	L	PCT	ERA	G	GS	CG	IP	H	BB	SO	ShO	Relief W	Relief L	Relief SV	AB	H	HR	BA	PO	A	E	DP	TC/G	FA
1890	PIT	N	0	1	.000	10.50	1	1	0	6	12	0	1	0	0	0	0	2	0	0	.000	0	1	0	0	1.0	1.000

Steve Ziem

ZIEM, STEPHEN GRAELING BR TR 6′ 2″ 210 lbs.
B. Oct. 24, 1961, Milwaukee, Wis.

Year	Team	Lg	W	L	PCT	ERA	G	GS	CG	IP	H	BB	SO	ShO	Relief W	Relief L	Relief SV	AB	H	HR	BA	PO	A	E	DP	TC/G	FA
1987	ATL	N	0	1	.000	7.71	2	0	0	2.1	4	1	0	0	0	1	0	0	0	0	—	0	0	0	0	0.0	.000

Walt Zink

ZINK, WALTER NOBLE BR TR 6′ 165 lbs.
B. Nov. 21, 1899, Pittsfield, Mass. D. June 12, 1964, Quincy, Mass.

Year	Team	Lg	W	L	PCT	ERA	G	GS	CG	IP	H	BB	SO	ShO	Relief W	Relief L	Relief SV	AB	H	HR	BA	PO	A	E	DP	TC/G	FA
1921	NY	N	0	0	—	2.25	2	0	0	4	4	3	1	0	0	0	0	1	0	0	.000	0	0	0	0	0.0	.000

Jimmy Zinn

ZINN, JAMES EDWARD BR TR 6′½″ 195 lbs.
B. Jan. 21, 1895, Benton, Ark. D. Feb. 26, 1991, Memphis, Tenn. BB 1929

Year	Team	Lg	W	L	PCT	ERA	G	GS	CG	IP	H	BB	SO	ShO	Relief W	Relief L	Relief SV	AB	H	HR	BA	PO	A	E	DP	TC/G	FA
1919	PHI	A	1	3	.250	6.31	5	3	2	25.2	38	10	9	0	0	1	0	13	4	1	.308	0	7	0	0	1.4	1.000
1920	PIT	N	1	1	.500	3.48	6	3	2	31	32	5	18	0	0	0	0	15	3	0	.200	3	6	0	0	1.3	1.000
1921			7	6	.538	3.68	32	9	5	127.1	159	30	49	1	3	1	4	49	11	0	.224	5	26	3	2	1.0	.912
1922			0	0	—	1.86	5	0	0	9.2	11	2	3	0	0	0	1	1	0	0	.000	1	1	1	0	0.6	.667
1929	CLE	A	4	6	.400	5.04	18	11	6	105.1	150	33	29	1	0	1	2	42	16	1	.381	11	19	3	2	1.8	.909
5 yrs.			13	16	.448	4.30	66	26	15	299	390	80	108	2	3	3	7	120	34	2	.283	20	59	7	4	1.3	.919

Bill Zinser

ZINSER, WILLIAM FRANCIS BR TR 6′ 1″ 185 lbs.
B. Jan. 6, 1918, Astoria, N. Y.

Year	Team	Lg	W	L	PCT	ERA	G	GS	CG	IP	H	BB	SO	ShO	Relief W	Relief L	Relief SV	AB	H	HR	BA	PO	A	E	DP	TC/G	FA
1944	WAS	A	0	0	—	27.00	2	0	0	0.2	1	5	1	0	0	0	0	0	0	0	—	0	0	0	0	0.0	.000

Ed Zmich

ZMICH, EDWARD ALBERT (Ike) BL TL 6′ 180 lbs.
B. Oct. 1, 1884, Cleveland, Ohio D. Aug. 20, 1950, Cleveland, Ohio.

Year	Team	Lg	W	L	PCT	ERA	G	GS	CG	IP	H	BB	SO	ShO	Relief W	Relief L	Relief SV	AB	H	HR	BA	PO	A	E	DP	TC/G	FA
1910	STL	N	0	5	.000	6.25	9	6	2	36	38	29	19	0	0	0	0	13	1	0	.077	2	13	0	0	1.7	1.000
1911			1	0	1.000	2.13	4	0	0	12.2	8	8	4	0	1	0	0	4	0	0	.000	0	0	0	0	0.0	.000
2 yrs.			1	5	.167	5.18	13	6	2	48.2	46	37	23	0	1	0	0	17	1	0	.059	2	13	0	0	1.2	1.000

Sam Zoldak

ZOLDAK, SAMUEL WALTER (Sad Sam) BL TL 5′11½″ 185 lbs.
B. Dec. 8, 1918, Brooklyn, N. Y. D. Aug. 25, 1966, New Hyde Park, N. Y.

Year	Team	Lg	W	L	PCT	ERA	G	GS	CG	IP	H	BB	SO	ShO	Relief W	Relief L	Relief SV	AB	H	HR	BA	PO	A	E	DP	TC/G	FA
1944	STL	A	0	0	—	3.72	18	0	0	38.2	49	19	15	0	0	0	0	6	2	0	.333	0	8	0	2	0.4	1.000
1945			3	2	.600	3.36	26	1	1	69.2	74	18	19	0	2	2	0	20	1	0	.050	3	9	1	0	0.5	.923
1946			9	11	.450	3.43	35	21	9	170.1	166	57	51	2	1	1	2	52	9	0	.173	10	32	1	3	1.2	.977
1947			9	10	.474	3.47	35	19	6	171	162	76	36	1	2	1	1	58	10	0	.172	6	44	1	2	1.5	.980
1948	2 teams	STL A	(11G 2–4)		CLE A	(23G 9–6)																					
″	total		11	10	.524	3.44	34	21	4	159.2	168	43	30	1	4	2	0	58	11	0	.190	7	39	1	4	1.4	.979
1949	CLE	A	1	2	.333	4.25	27	0	0	53	60	18	11	0	1	2	0	8	3	0	.375	12	19	0	1	1.1	1.000
1950			4	2	.667	3.96	33	3	0	63.2	64	21	15	0	4	0	4	16	3	0	.188	4	10	0	0	0.4	1.000
1951	PHI	A	6	10	.375	3.16	26	18	8	128	127	24	18	1	0	1	0	45	7	0	.156	6	17	0	0	0.9	1.000
1952			0	6	.000	4.06	16	10	2	75.1	86	25	12	0	0	0	1	23	4	0	.174	6	22	0	2	1.8	1.000
9 yrs.			43	53	.448	3.54	250	93	30	929.1	956	301	207	5	14	9	8	286	50	0	.175	54	200	4	14	1.0	.984

PART TEN

Trades

Chronological Listing by Player
Of Every Trade, Sale,
Or Free Agent Signing

Trades

The Trades section is a listing, for each player, of every trade, sale, or free agent signing he was involved in during the course of his career. Players are listed alphabetically, with no separation of pitchers and nonpitchers. At present, trades and sales are included from 1900 through January 1, 1996.

Date	Traded To		Traded With	Traded By		In Exchange For
Doyle Alexander						
Dec. 2, 1971	**BAL**	**A**	Bob O'Brien Sergio Robles Royle Stillman	**LA**	**N**	Frank Robinson Pete Richert
June 15, 1976	**NY**	**A**	—	**BAL**	**A**	See *Tippy Martinez*
Nov. 23, 1976	**TEX**	**A**	—	**NY**	**A**	No compensation (free agent signing)

The name given for each player is the shortened version of his full name that will be most familiar to fans. This is the same name as that used in the Player and Pitcher registers. If more specific biographical information is needed, consult those registers.

For each player, all trades in which he was involved are listed chronologically. Player-for-player, player-for-cash, and re-entry free agent signings are listed; the movement of a player from one team to another following his outright release is not listed. Selection of a player by a new expansion franchise in a stocking draft, or by an existing club in a minor league free-agent draft, is also not included in his record. Dollar amounts, where known, are included for player sales; if the dollar amount is not known, "cash" or "waiver price" is listed.

Players to Be Named Later. Transactions involving "a player to be named later" have, for the most part, been rewritten to reflect the players who were ultimately exchanged (or cash, in those cases where money was accepted in lieu of a player). If there was a delay between the announcement of a trade and the final transfer of players, that fact has been noted in an explanatory note.

See John Doe. For many particularly large transactions, the entire transaction is listed under the primary players only. Minor players involved in the deal are listed with the date of the trade, the teams involved, and the notation "See Player X" in italic type. The entire deal will be listed under that player on the appropriate date.

Three-Team Trades. Three-team or four-team trades have been rewritten as a series of two-team transactions: a player from Team A is traded to Team B, and then traded on to Team C in a separate transaction on the same date. In any such series, each step is noted with the explanatory comment, "Part of a three-team trade involving Team A, Team B, and Team C."

Minor League Players. Any player involved in a transaction who never played in the major leagues (or has not through the 1995 season) is listed in the "Traded With" or "In Exchange For" columns but does not have a separate entry in this section. Minor leaguers are so noted in the listing, along with their primary positions. (Players involved in a transaction who later played in the major leagues are simply listed by name, with no "minor league" reference.)

Date	Traded To	Traded With	Traded By	In Exchange For

Hank Aaron

Date	Traded To	Traded With	Traded By	In Exchange For
Nov. 2, 1974	MIL A	—	ATL N	Dave May minor league P Roger Alexander

Don Aase

Date	Traded To	Traded With	Traded By	In Exchange For
Dec. 8, 1977	CAL A	Cash	BOS A	Jerry Remy
Dec. 13, 1984	BAL A	—	CAL A	No compensation (free agent signing)

Ed Abbaticchio

Date	Traded To	Traded With	Traded By	In Exchange For
Dec. 1906	PIT N	—	BOS N	Ginger Beaumont Claude Ritchey Patsy Flaherty
May 1910	BOS N	—	PIT N	Cash

Glenn Abbott

Date	Traded To	Traded With	Traded By	In Exchange For
Aug. 23, 1983	DET A	—	SEA A	$100,000.

Jim Abbott

Date	Traded To	Traded With	Traded By	In Exchange For
Dec. 6, 1992	NY A	—	CAL A	J. T. Snow Russ Springer Jerry Nielsen
Apr. 8, 1995	CHI A	—	NY A	No compensation (free agent signing)
July 27, 1995	CAL A	Tim Fortugno	CHI A	Andrew Lorraine Bill Simas Minor league OF McKay Christensen Minor league P John Snyder

Kurt Abbott

Date	Traded To	Traded With	Traded By	In Exchange For
Dec. 20, 1993	FLA N	—	OAK A	Minor league OF Kerwin Moore

Kyle Abbott

Date	Traded To	Traded With	Traded By	In Exchange For
Dec. 8, 1991	PHI N	Ruben Amaro	CAL A	Von Hayes

Al Aber

Date	Traded To	Traded With	Traded By	In Exchange For
June 15, 1953	DET A	*see Ray Boone*	CLE A	—
Aug. 27, 1957	KC A	—	DET A	Waiver price

Ted Abernathy

Date	Traded To	Traded With	Traded By	In Exchange For
Apr. 14, 1965	CHI N	—	CLE A	Cash
May 28, 1966	ATL N	—	CHI N	Lee Thomas
Jan. 9, 1969	CHI N	—	CIN N	Bill Plummer Clarence Jones minor league P Ken Myette
May 29, 1970	STL N	—	CHI N	Phil Gagliano
July 1, 1970	KC A	—	STL N	Chris Zachary

Shawn Abner

Date	Traded To	Traded With	Traded By	In Exchange For
Dec. 11, 1986	SD N	—	NY N	*see Kevin McReynolds*
July 30, 1991	CAL A	—	SD N	Jack Howell

Cal Abrams

Date	Traded To	Traded With	Traded By	In Exchange For
June 9, 1952	CIN N	—	BKN N	Rudy Rufer Cash
Oct. 14, 1952	PIT N	Joe Rossi Gail Henley	CIN N	Gus Bell
May 25, 1954	BAL A	—	PIT N	Dick Littlefield
Oct. 18, 1955	CHI A	—	BAL A	Bobby Adams

Bill Abstein

Date	Traded To	Traded With	Traded By	In Exchange For
Jan. 1910	STL A	—	PIT N	Cash

Juan Acevedo

Date	Traded To	Traded With	Traded By	In Exchange For
July 31, 1995	NY N	Minor league P Arnold Gooch	CLR N	Bret Saberhagen Player to be named

(Colorado received P David Swanson on August 4, 1995.)

Jim Acker

Date	Traded To	Traded With	Traded By	In Exchange For
July 6, 1986	ATL N	—	TOR A	Joe Johnson

Date	Traded To	Traded With	Traded By	In Exchange For

Jim Acker *continued*

Date	Traded To	Traded With	Traded By	In Exchange For
Aug. 24, 1989	TOR A	—	ATL N	Tony Castillo Francisco Cabrera

(Atlanta received Cabrera on Aug. 29, 1989.)

Tom Acker

Date	Traded To	Traded With	Traded By	In Exchange For
Nov. 21, 1959	KC A	—	CIN N	Frank House

Fritz Ackley

Date	Traded To	Traded With	Traded By	In Exchange For
Nov. 24, 1964	STL N	—	CHI A	Cash

Cy Acosta

Date	Traded To	Traded With	Traded By	In Exchange For
Mar. 17, 1975	PHI N	—	CHI A	Cash

Ed Acosta

Date	Traded To	Traded With	Traded By	In Exchange For
Aug. 10, 1971	SD N	John Jeter	PIT N	Bob Miller

Jose Acosta

Date	Traded To	Traded With	Traded By	In Exchange For
Jan. 10, 1922	PHI A	Bing Miller	WAS A	Joe Dugan
(Part of three-team trade involving Boston, Philadelphia, and Washington.)				
Feb. 4, 1922	CHI A	—	PHI A	Cash

Merito Acosta

Date	Traded To	Traded With	Traded By	In Exchange For
May 25, 1918	PHI A	—	WAS A	Cash

Jerry Adair

Date	Traded To	Traded With	Traded By	In Exchange For
June 12, 1966	CHI A	minor league OF Johnny Riddle	BAL A	Eddie Fisher
June 3, 1967	BOS A	—	CHI A	Don McMahon minor league P Bob Snow

Babe Adams

Date	Traded To	Traded With	Traded By	In Exchange For
Oct. 1907	PIT N	—	STL N	Cash

Bert Adams

Date	Traded To	Traded With	Traded By	In Exchange For
Jan. 1915	PHI N	Al Demaree Milt Stock	NY N	Hans Lobert

Bob Adams

Date	Traded To	Traded With	Traded By	In Exchange For
Mar. 29, 1971	MIN A	Minor League P Art Clifford	DET A	Bill Zepp

Bobby Adams

Date	Traded To	Traded With	Traded By	In Exchange For
July 26, 1955	CHI A	—	CIN N	Cash
Oct. 18, 1955	BAL A	—	CHI A	Cal Abrams

Buster Adams

Date	Traded To	Traded With	Traded By	In Exchange For
June 1, 1943	PHI N	Coaker Triplett Dain Clay	STL N	Danny Litwhiler Earl Naylor
May 8, 1945	STL N	—	PHI N	John Antonelli Glenn Crawford
Mar. 21, 1947	PHI N	—	STL N	Cash

Glenn Adams

Date	Traded To	Traded With	Traded By	In Exchange For
Dec. 6, 1976	MIN A	—	SF N	Cash

Herb Adams

Date	Traded To	Traded With	Traded By	In Exchange For
Sept. 11, 1950	CLE A	—	CHI A	Waiver price

Mike Adams

Date	Traded To	Traded With	Traded By	In Exchange For
Apr. 1, 1978	OAK A	—	CHI N	Cash

Sparky Adams

Date	Traded To	Traded With	Traded By	In Exchange For
Nov. 28, 1927	PIT N	Pete Scott	CHI N	Kiki Cuyler
Nov. 1929	STL N	—	PIT N	Cash
May 7, 1933	CIN N	Paul Derringer Allyn Stout	STL N	Leo Durocher Dutch Henry Jack Ogden

Spencer Adams

Date	Traded To	Traded With	Traded By	In Exchange For
Jan. 20, 1926	NY A	—	WAS A	Cash

Joe Adcock

Date	Traded To	Traded With	Traded By	In Exchange For
Feb. 16, 1953	MIL N	—	CIN N	Rocky Bridges Cash

(Part of four-team trade involving Milwaukee Braves, Philadelphia Phillies, Brooklyn, and Cincinnati.)

Date	Traded To	Traded With	Traded By	In Exchange For
Nov. 27, 1962	CLE A	Jack Curtis	MIL N	Ty Cline Don Dillard Frank Funk
Dec. 2, 1963	LA A	Barry Latman	CLE A	Leon Wagner

Bob Addis

Date	Traded To	Traded With	Traded By	In Exchange For
Oct. 11, 1951	CHI N	—	BOS N	Jack Cusick
June 4, 1953	PIT N	—	CHI N	*see Ralph Kiner*

Jim Adduci

Date	Traded To	Traded With	Traded By	In Exchange For
Oct. 3, 1984	MIL A	Paul Householder	STL N	Minor leaguers P Rich Buonantony C Jim Koontz IF Ron Koenigsfeld
Apr. 19, 1987	SF N	—	MIL A	Cash

(Deal was cancelled and Adduci returned to Milwaukee on April 26.)

Steve Adkins

Date	Traded To	Traded With	Traded By	In Exchange For
June 26, 1991	CHI A	—	NY A	Minor league P David Rosario

Dave Adlesh

Date	Traded To	Traded With	Traded By	In Exchange For
Oct. 11, 1968	STL N	Dave Giusti	HOU N	Johnny Edwards minor league C Tommy Smith
Mar. 25, 1969	ATL N	—	STL N	Bob Johnson

Troy Afenir

Date	Traded To	Traded With	Traded By	In Exchange For
Apr. 6, 1989	OAK A	—	HOU N	Matt Sinatro

Tommie Agee

Date	Traded To	Traded With	Traded By	In Exchange For
Jan. 20, 1965	CHI A	Tommy John Johnny Romano	CLE A	Rocky Colavito Camilo Carreon

(Part of three-team trade involving Kansas City, Cleveland, and Chicago White Sox.)

Date	Traded To	Traded With	Traded By	In Exchange For
Dec. 15, 1967	NY N	Al Weis	CHI A	Tommy Davis Jack Fisher Billy Wynne Buddy Booker
Nov. 27, 1972	HOU N	—	NY N	Rich Chiles Buddy Harris
Aug. 18, 1973	STL N	—	HOU N	Dave Campbell Cash
Dec. 5, 1973	LA N	—	STL N	Pete Richert

Joe Agler

Date	Traded To	Traded With	Traded By	In Exchange For
May 1915	BAL F	—	BUF F	Cash

Sam Agnew

Date	Traded To	Traded With	Traded By	In Exchange For
Dec. 1915	BOS A	—	STL A	Cash
Jan. 1919	WAS A	—	BOS A	Cash

Juan Agosto

Date	Traded To	Traded With	Traded By	In Exchange For
Apr. 30, 1986	MIN A	—	CHI A	Cash
Dec. 14, 1990	STL N	—	HOU N	No compensation (free agent signing)

Luis Aguayo

Date	Traded To	Traded With	Traded By	In Exchange For
July 15, 1988	NY A	—	PHI N	Amalio Carreno
Dec. 2, 1988	CLE A	—	NY A	No compensation (free agent signing)

Rick Aguilera

Date	Traded To	Traded With	Traded By	In Exchange For
July 31, 1989	MIN A	David West Tim Drummond Kevin Tapani Jack Savage	NY N	Frank Viola

(Minnesota received Savage on October 16, 1989.)

Date	Traded To	Traded With	Traded By	In Exchange For
July 6, 1995	BOS A	—	MIN A	Frank Rodriguez Player to be named

(Minnesota received OF J.J. Johnson on October 11, 1995.)

Rick Aguilera *continued*

Date	Traded To	Traded With	Traded By	In Exchange For
Dec. 11, 1995	MIN A	—	BOS A	No compensation (free agent signing)

Hank Aguirre

Date	Traded To	Traded With	Traded By	In Exchange For
Feb. 18, 1958	DET A	Jim Hegan	CLE A	Hal Woodeshick J. W. Porter
Apr. 3, 1968	LA N	—	DET A	Minor league IF Fred Moulder and cash

Willie Aikens

Date	Traded To	Traded With	Traded By	In Exchange For
Dec. 6, 1979	KC A	Rance Mulliniks	CAL A	Al Cowens Todd Cruz Craig Eaton
Dec. 20, 1983	TOR A	—	KC A	Jorge Orta

Eddie Ainsmith

Date	Traded To	Traded With	Traded By	In Exchange For
Jan. 17, 1919	BOS A	George Dumont	WAS A	Hal Janvrin Cash
Jan. 17, 1919	DET A	Chick Shorten Slim Love	BOS A	Ossie Vitt

Jack Aker

Date	Traded To	Traded With	Traded By	In Exchange For
May 20, 1969	NY A	—	SEA A	Fred Talbot
Jan. 20, 1972	CHI N	—	NY A	Johnny Callison

(Chicago received Aker on May 17, 1972.)

Date	Traded To	Traded With	Traded By	In Exchange For
June 14, 1974	NY N	—	ATL N	Cash

Darrel Akerfelds

Date	Traded To	Traded With	Traded By	In Exchange For
Nov. 21, 1983	OAK A	*see Bill Caudill*	SEA A	—
July 15, 1987	CLE A	Brian Dorsett	OAK A	Tony Bernazard
Mar. 31, 1990	PHI N	—	TEX A	Cash

Butch Alberts

Date	Traded To	Traded With	Traded By	In Exchange For
Dec. 8, 1977	TOR A	Dale Kelly	CAL A	Ron Fairly

Santo Alcala

Date	Traded To	Traded With	Traded By	In Exchange For
May 21, 1977	MON N	—	CIN N	Shane Rawley Angel Torres
Mar. 23, 1978	SEA A	—	MON N	Cash

(Alcala was returned to Montreal before the start of the 1979 season.)

Luis Alcaraz

Date	Traded To	Traded With	Traded By	In Exchange For
Mar. 24, 1971	CHI A	Cash	KC A	Bobby Knoop

Scott Aldred

Date	Traded To	Traded With	Traded By	In Exchange For
Apr. 29, 1993	MON N	—	CLR N	Waiver price

Mike Aldrete

Date	Traded To	Traded With	Traded By	In Exchange For
Dec. 8, 1988	MON N	—	SF N	Tracy Jones
Aug. 24, 1995	CAL A	—	OAK A	Minor league OF Demond Smith

Jay Aldrich

Date	Traded To	Traded With	Traded By	In Exchange For
Aug. 23, 1989	ATL N	—	MIL A	Ed Romero

Vic Aldridge

Date	Traded To	Traded With	Traded By	In Exchange For
Oct. 27, 1924	PIT N	George Grantham Al Niehaus	CHI N	Charlie Grimm Rabbit Maranville Wilbur Cooper
Feb. 11, 1928	NY N	—	PIT N	Burleigh Grimes
Dec. 9, 1928	BKN N	—	NY N	Waiver price

(Aldridge refused to report and retired.)

Dale Alexander

Date	Traded To	Traded With	Traded By	In Exchange For
June 12, 1932	BOS A	Roy Johnson	DET A	Earl Webb

Doyle Alexander

Date	Traded To	Traded With	Traded By	In Exchange For
Dec. 2, 1971	BAL A	Bob O'Brien Sergio Robles Royle Stillman	LA N	Frank Robinson Pete Richert

Doyle Alexander *continued*

Date	Traded To	Traded With	Traded By	In Exchange For
June 15, 1976	NY A	—	BAL A	*see Tippy Martinez*
Nov. 23, 1976	TEX A	—	NY A	No compensation (free agent signing)
Dec. 6, 1979	ATL N	Larvell Blanks $50,000.	TEX A	Adrian Devine Pepe Frias
Dec. 12, 1980	SF N	—	ATL N	John Montefusco minor league OF Craig Landis
Mar. 30, 1982	NY A	—	SF N	Andy McGaffigan Ted Wilborn
July 6, 1986	ATL N	—	TOR A	Duane Ward
Aug. 12, 1987	DET A	—	ATL N	John Smoltz

Gary Alexander

Date	Traded To	Traded With	Traded By	In Exchange For
Mar. 15, 1978	OAK A	Gary Thomasson Dave Heaverlo Alan Wirth John Henry Johnson Phil Huffman Mario Guerrero $390,000.	SF N	Vida Blue
June 15, 1978	CLE A	—	OAK A	Joe Wallis
Dec. 9, 1980	PIT N	Victor Cruz Rafael Vasquez Bob Owchinko	CLE A	Bert Blyleven Manny Sanguillen

Gerald Alexander

Date	Traded To	Traded With	Traded By	In Exchange For
Aug. 4, 1993	CLE A	Allan Anderson	TEX A	Dave Eiland

Grover Alexander

Date	Traded To	Traded With	Traded By	In Exchange For
Dec. 11, 1917	CHI N	Bill Killefer	PHI N	Mike Prendergast Pickles Dillhoefer $55,000.
June 22, 1926	STL N	—	CHI N	Waiver price
Dec. 11, 1929	PHI N	Harry McCurdy	STL N	Homer Peel Bob McGraw

Matt Alexander

Date	Traded To	Traded With	Traded By	In Exchange For
Apr. 28, 1975	OAK A	—	CHI N	Minor league P Howell Copeland

Walt Alexander

Date	Traded To	Traded With	Traded By	In Exchange For
July 30, 1915	NY A	—	STL A	Cash

Luis Alicea

Date	Traded To	Traded With	Traded By	In Exchange For
Dec. 7, 1994	BOS A	—	STL N	Nate Minchey Jeff McNeely

Andy Allanson

Date	Traded To	Traded With	Traded By	In Exchange For
Mar. 30, 1991	DET A	—	KC A	Minor league C Jim Baxter

Brian Allard

Date	Traded To	Traded With	Traded By	In Exchange For
Dec. 12, 1980	SEA A	—	TEX A	*see Rick Honeycutt*

Bernie Allen

Date	Traded To	Traded With	Traded By	In Exchange For
Dec. 3, 1966	WAS A	Camilo Pascual	MIN A	Ron Kline
Dec. 2, 1971	NY A	—	TEX A	Gary Jones Terry Ley
Aug. 13, 1973	MON N	—	NY A	Cash

Bob Allen

Date	Traded To	Traded With	Traded By	In Exchange For
Dec. 14, 1963	PIT N	—	CLE A	Cash

Dick Allen

Date	Traded To	Traded With	Traded By	In Exchange For
Oct. 7, 1969	STL N	Cookie Rojas Jerry Johnson	PHI N	Curt Flood Tim McCarver Joe Hoerner Byron Browne

(Flood refused to report to the Philadelphia Phillies, and the Cardinals sent Willie Montanez and Bob Browning on April 8, 1970 to complete the trade.)

Date	Traded To	Traded With	Traded By	In Exchange For
Oct. 5, 1970	LA N	—	STL N	Ted Sizemore Bob Stinson
Dec. 2, 1971	CHI A	—	LA N	Tommy John Steve Huntz
Dec. 3, 1974	ATL N	—	CHI A	Jim Essian Cash

(Chicago received Essian on May 15, 1975.)

Dick Allen *continued*

Date	Traded To	Traded With	Traded By	In Exchange For
May 7, 1975	PHI N	Johnny Oates	ATL N	Jim Essian Barry Bonnell Cash
Mar. 15, 1977	OAK A	—	PHI N	No compensation (free agent signing)

Ethan Allen

Date	Traded To	Traded With	Traded By	In Exchange For
May 27, 1930	NY N	Pete Donohue	CIN N	Pat Crawford
Oct. 10, 1932	STL N	Bob O'Farrell Bill Walker Jim Mooney	NY N	Gus Mancuso Ray Starr
Jan. 1934	PHI N	—	STL N	Cash
May 21, 1936	CHI N	Curt Davis	PHI N	Chuck Klein Fabian Kowalik
Dec. 2, 1936	STL A	—	CHI N	Cash

Frank Allen

Date	Traded To	Traded With	Traded By	In Exchange For
Sept. 1914	PIT F	—	BKN F	Cash
Feb. 10, 1916	BOS N	Elmer Knetzer	PIT F	Cash

Hank Allen

Date	Traded To	Traded With	Traded By	In Exchange For
May 11, 1970	MIL A	Ron Theobald	WAS A	Wayne Comer
Dec. 2, 1970	ATL N	minor leaguers P Paul Click and IF John Ryan	MIL A	Bob Tillman

Johnny Allen

Date	Traded To	Traded With	Traded By	In Exchange For
Dec. 11, 1935	CLE A	—	NY A	Monte Pearson Steve Sundra
Dec. 24, 1940	STL A	—	CLE A	$20,000.
July 30, 1941	BKN N	—	STL A	Waiver price
Dec. 12, 1942	PHI N	$30,000.	BKN N	Rube Melton
Apr. 22, 1943	BKN N	George Washburn	PHI N	Cash
July 31, 1943	NY N	Dolf Camilli	BKN N	Bill Lohrman Bill Sayles Joe Orengo

(Camilli refused to report to New York and retired.)

Lloyd Allen

Date	Traded To	Traded With	Traded By	In Exchange For
May 20, 1973	TEX A	—	CAL A	*see Mike Epstein*
July 1, 1974	CHI A	—	TEX A	Cash
Aug. 1, 1975	STL N	—	CHI A	Cash

Neil Allen

Date	Traded To	Traded With	Traded By	In Exchange For
June 15, 1983	STL N	Rick Ownbey	NY N	Keith Hernandez
July 16, 1985	NY A	—	STL N	Cash
Feb. 13, 1986	CHI A	—	NY A	*see Ron Hassey*

Nick Allen

Date	Traded To	Traded With	Traded By	In Exchange For
Feb. 10, 1916	CHI N	—	BUF F	Cash

Rod Allen

Date	Traded To	Traded With	Traded By	In Exchange For
Dec. 11, 1981	SEA A	Todd Cruz Jim Essian	CHI A	Tom Paciorek

Gary Allenson

Date	Traded To	Traded With	Traded By	In Exchange For
Feb. 25, 1985	TOR A	—	BOS A	No compensation (free agent signing)

Mel Almada

Date	Traded To	Traded With	Traded By	In Exchange For
June 11, 1937	WAS A	Wes Ferrell Rick Ferrell	BOS A	Ben Chapman Bobo Newsom
June 15, 1938	STL A	—	WAS A	Sammy West
June 15, 1939	BKN N	—	STL A	$25,000.

Bill Almon

Date	Traded To	Traded With	Traded By	In Exchange For
Nov. 27, 1979	MON N	Dan Briggs	SD N	Dave Cash
Jan. 18, 1983	OAK A	—	CHI A	No compensation (free agent signing)
Apr. 8, 1985	PIT N	—	OAK A	No compensation (free agent signing)
May 29, 1987	NY N	—	PIT N	Al Pedrique Scott Little

Bill Almon *continued*

Date	Traded To	Traded With	Traded By	In Exchange For
Mar. 21, 1988	PHI N	—	NY N	Shawn Barton Minor league P Vladimir Perez

Roberto Alomar

Date	Traded To	Traded With	Traded By	In Exchange For
Dec. 5, 1990	TOR A	Joe Carter	SD N	Fred McGriff Tony Fernandez
Dec. 21, 1995	BAL A	—	TOR A	No compensation (free agent signing)

Sandy Alomar

Date	Traded To	Traded With	Traded By	In Exchange For
Dec. 31, 1966	HOU N	Eddie Mathews Arnie Umbach	ATL N	Dave Nicholson Bob Bruce
Mar. 24, 1967	NY N	—	HOU N	Derrell Griffith
Aug. 15, 1967	CHI A	—	NY N	Cash
May 14, 1969	CAL A	Bob Priddy	CHI A	Bobby Knoop
July 8, 1974	NY A	—	CAL A	Cash
Feb. 17, 1977	TEX A	—	NY A	Greg Pryor Brian Doyle Cash

Sandy Alomar

Date	Traded To	Traded With	Traded By	In Exchange For
Dec. 6, 1989	CLE A	Chris James Carlos Baerga	SD N	Joe Carter

Felipe Alou

Date	Traded To	Traded With	Traded By	In Exchange For
Dec. 3, 1963	MIL N	Billy Hoeft Ed Bailey Ernie Bowman	SF N	Del Crandall Bob Shaw Bob Hendley
Dec. 3, 1969	OAK A	—	ATL N	Jim Nash
Apr. 9, 1971	NY A	—	OAK A	Ron Klimkowski Rob Gardner
Sept. 6, 1973	MON N	—	NY A	Cash
Dec. 7, 1973	MIL A	—	MON N	Cash

Jesus Alou

Date	Traded To	Traded With	Traded By	In Exchange For
Jan. 22, 1969	HOU N	Donn Clendenon Jack Billingham Skip Guinn $100,000.	MON N	Rusty Staub

(Clendenon refused to report, and Houston sent Billingham, Guinn, and cash on April 8, 1969.)

Date	Traded To	Traded With	Traded By	In Exchange For
July 31, 1973	OAK A	—	HOU N	Cash

Matty Alou

Date	Traded To	Traded With	Traded By	In Exchange For
Oct. 1, 1965	PIT N	—	SF N	Joe Gibbon Ozzie Virgil
Jan. 29, 1971	STL N	George Brunet	PIT N	Nellie Briles Vic Davalillo
Aug. 27, 1972	OAK A	—	STL N	Bill Voss minor league P Steve Easton
Nov. 24, 1972	NY A	—	OAK A	Rob Gardner Rich McKinney
Sept. 6, 1973	STL N	—	NY A	Cash
Oct. 25, 1973	SD N	—	STL N	Cash

Moises Alou

Date	Traded To	Traded With	Traded By	In Exchange For
Aug. 8, 1990	MON N	Scott Ruskin Willie Greene	PIT N	Zane Smith

(Montreal received Alou on August 16, 1990.)

Dell Alston

Date	Traded To	Traded With	Traded By	In Exchange For
June 15, 1978	OAK A	Mickey Klutts $50,000.	NY A	Gary Thomasson

Porfi Altamirano

Date	Traded To	Traded With	Traded By	In Exchange For
Mar. 26, 1984	CHI N	Gary Matthews Bob Dernier	PHI N	Bill Campbell Mike Diaz
Dec. 4, 1984	NY A	Henry Cotto Ron Hassey Rich Bordi	CHI N	Ray Fontenot Brian Dayett

Dave Altizer

Date	Traded To	Traded With	Traded By	In Exchange For
Aug. 1908	CLE A	Cy Falkenberg	WAS A	Cash

George Altman

Date	Traded To	Traded With	Traded By	In Exchange For
Oct. 17, 1962	STL N	Don Cardwell Moe Thacker	CHI N	Larry Jackson Jimmie Schaffer Lindy McDaniel
Nov. 4, 1963	NY N	Bill Wakefield	STL N	Roger Craig
Jan. 15, 1965	CHI N	—	NY N	Billy Cowan

Nick Altrock

Date	Traded To	Traded With	Traded By	In Exchange For
Apr. 1903	CHI A	—	BOS A	Cash
May 16, 1909	WAS A	Gavvy Cravath Jiggs Donahue	CHI A	Bill Burns

George Alusik

Date	Traded To	Traded With	Traded By	In Exchange For
May 7, 1962	KC A	—	DET A	Cash

Luis Alvarado

Date	Traded To	Traded With	Traded By	In Exchange For
Dec. 1, 1970	CHI A	Mike Andrews	BOS A	Luis Aparicio
Apr. 27, 1974	STL N	—	CHI A	Ken Tatum
June 1, 1974	CLE A	Ed Crosby	STL N	Jack Heidemann
Sept. 30, 1975	STL N	—	CLE A	Doug Howard
Nov. 6, 1976	DET A	—	STL N	Cash
Feb. 25, 1977	NY N	—	DET A	Cash

(Alvarado was returned to Detroit on April 27, 1977.)

Jose Alvarez

Date	Traded To	Traded With	Traded By	In Exchange For
Feb. 14, 1984	HOU N	—	ATL N	Ron Meridith

Orlando Alvarez

Date	Traded To	Traded With	Traded By	In Exchange For
Mar. 21, 1976	CAL A	Cash	LA N	Ellie Rodriguez

Ossie Alvarez

Date	Traded To	Traded With	Traded By	In Exchange For
Oct. 27, 1958	CLE A	—	WAS A	J. W. Porter
Nov. 20, 1958	DET A	Don Mossi Ray Narleski	CLE A	Billy Martin Al Cicotte

Rogelio Alvarez

Date	Traded To	Traded With	Traded By	In Exchange For
Nov. 24, 1962	WAS A	—	CIN N	Harry Bright

Wilson Alvarez

Date	Traded To	Traded With	Traded By	In Exchange For
July 29, 1989	CHI A	Scott Fletcher Sammy Sosa	TEX A	Harold Baines Fred Manrique

Max Alvis

Date	Traded To	Traded With	Traded By	In Exchange For
Apr. 4, 1970	MIL A	Russ Snyder	CLE A	Roy Foster Frank Coggins Cash

Brant Alyea

Date	Traded To	Traded With	Traded By	In Exchange For
Mar. 21, 1970	MIN A	—	WAS A	Joe Grzenda Charley Walters
May 18, 1972	STL N	—	OAK A	Marty Martinez

(Alyea was returned to Oakland on July 23.)

Date	Traded To	Traded With	Traded By	In Exchange For
Oct. 30, 1972	TEX A	Bill McNulty	OAK A	Paul Lindblad

Joey Amalfitano

Date	Traded To	Traded With	Traded By	In Exchange For
Nov. 30, 1962	SF N	—	HOU N	Dick LeMay Manny Mota

Ruben Amaro

Date	Traded To	Traded With	Traded By	In Exchange For
Dec. 3, 1958	PHI N	—	STL N	Chuck Essegian
Nov. 29, 1965	NY A	—	PHI N	Phil Linz
Nov. 6, 1968	CAL A	—	NY A	Cash

Ruben Amaro

Date	Traded To	Traded With	Traded By	In Exchange For
Dec. 8, 1991	PHI N	Kyle Abbott	CAL A	Von Hayes
Nov. 2, 1993	CLE A	—	PHI N	Heathcliff Slocumb

Red Ames

Date	Traded To		Traded With	Traded By		In Exchange For
May 22, 1913	CIN	N	Heinie Groh Josh Devore $20,000.	NY	N	Art Fromme Eddie Grant
July 24, 1915	STL	N	—	CIN	N	Cash
Sept. 5, 1919	PHI	N	—	STL	N	Cash

(Ames was returned to St. Louis in October.)

Sandy Amoros

Date	Traded To		Traded With	Traded By		In Exchange For
May 7, 1960	DET	A	—	LA	N	Gail Harris

Larry Andersen

Date	Traded To		Traded With	Traded By		In Exchange For
Dec. 21, 1979	PIT	N	—	CLE	A	Larry Littleton minor league P John Burden
Apr. 1, 1980	SEA	A	Cash	PIT	N	Odell Jones
July 29, 1983	PHI	N	—	SEA	A	Cash
Aug. 31, 1990	BOS	A	—	HOU	N	Jeff Bagwell
Dec. 21, 1990	SD	N	—	BOS	A	No compensation (free agent signing)

Allan Anderson

Date	Traded To		Traded With	Traded By		In Exchange For
Aug. 4, 1993	CLE	A	Gerald Alexander	TEX	A	Dave Eiland

Bob Anderson

Date	Traded To		Traded With	Traded By		In Exchange For
Nov. 28, 1962	DET	A	—	CHI	N	Steve Boros
Nov. 18, 1963	KC	A	*see Rocky Colavito*	DET	A	—

Brady Anderson

Date	Traded To		Traded With	Traded By		In Exchange For
July 29, 1988	BAL	A	Curt Schilling	BOS	A	Mike Boddicker

Bud Anderson

Date	Traded To		Traded With	Traded By		In Exchange For
Dec. 6, 1979	CLE	A	Rafael Vasquez minor league P Bob Pietroburgo	SEA	A	Ted Cox

Dave Anderson

Date	Traded To		Traded With	Traded By		In Exchange For
Nov. 28, 1989	SF	N	—	LA	N	No compensation (free agent signing)
Jan. 15, 1993	SF	N	—	LA	N	No compensation (free agent signing)

Dwain Anderson

Date	Traded To		Traded With	Traded By		In Exchange For
May 15, 1972	STL	N	—	OAK	A	Don Shaw
June 7, 1973	SD	N	—	STL	N	Dave Campbell

Fred Anderson

Date	Traded To		Traded With	Traded By		In Exchange For
Feb. 10, 1916	NY	N	—	BUF	F	Cash

Harry Anderson

Date	Traded To		Traded With	Traded By		In Exchange For
June 15, 1960	CIN	N	Wally Post minor league 1B Fred Hopke	PHI	N	Tony Gonzalez Lee Walls

Jim Anderson

Date	Traded To		Traded With	Traded By		In Exchange For
Aug. 29, 1979	SEA	A	—	CAL	A	John Montague
Nov. 2, 1985	MON	N	—	TEX	A	*see Pete Incaviglia*

John Anderson

Date	Traded To		Traded With	Traded By		In Exchange For
Oct. 26, 1903	NY	A	—	STL	A	Jack O'Connor
Feb. 1904	NY	A	—	STL	A	Cash
June 3, 1905	WAS	A	—	NY	A	Waiver price
Jan. 1908	CHI	A	—	WAS	A	Cash

John Anderson

Date	Traded To		Traded With	Traded By		In Exchange For
May 7, 1962	HOU	N	Carl Warwick	STL	N	Bobby Shantz

Larry Anderson

Date	Traded To		Traded With	Traded By		In Exchange For
Oct. 21, 1976	CHI	A	—	TOR	A	Phil Roof

(Chicago received Anderson on January 5, 1977.)

Date	Traded To		Traded With	Traded By		In Exchange For
Aug. 18, 1977	CHI	N	Cash	CHI	A	Steve Renko
Aug. 6, 1978	PHI	N	—	CHI	N	Davey Johnson

Mike Anderson

Date	Traded To		Traded With	Traded By		In Exchange For
Dec. 9, 1975	STL	N	—	PHI	N	Ron Reed

Mike Anderson

Date	Traded To		Traded With	Traded By		In Exchange For
Dec. 10, 1993	CHI	N	Larry Luebbers Minor league C Darron Cox	CIN	N	Chuck McElroy

Rick Anderson

Date	Traded To		Traded With	Traded By		In Exchange For
Nov. 1, 1979	SEA	A	*see Jim Beattie*	NY	A	—

Rick Anderson

Date	Traded To		Traded With	Traded By		In Exchange For
Mar. 27, 1987	KC	A	Ed Hearn Mauro Gozzo	NY	N	David Cone Chris Jelic

Sparky Anderson

Date	Traded To		Traded With	Traded By		In Exchange For
Dec. 23, 1958	PHI	N	—	LA	N	Rip Repulski Jim Golden Gene Snyder

Fred Andrews

Date	Traded To		Traded With	Traded By		In Exchange For
Mar. 24, 1978	NY	N	Cash	PHI	N	Bud Harrelson

Ivy Andrews

Date	Traded To		Traded With	Traded By		In Exchange For
June 5, 1932	BOS	A	Hank Johnson $50,000.	NY	A	Danny MacFayden
Dec. 14, 1933	STL	A	Smead Jolley Cash	BOS	A	Carl Reynolds
Jan. 17, 1937	CLE	A	Lyn Lary Moose Solters	STL	A	Bill Knickerbocker Joe Vosmik Oral Hildebrand
Aug. 14, 1937	NY	A	—	CLE	A	$7,500.

John Andrews

Date	Traded To		Traded With	Traded By		In Exchange For
Dec. 6, 1973	CAL	A	—	STL	N	Jeff Torborg

Mike Andrews

Date	Traded To		Traded With	Traded By		In Exchange For
Dec. 1, 1970	CHI	A	Luis Alvarado	BOS	A	Luis Aparicio

Nate Andrews

Date	Traded To		Traded With	Traded By		In Exchange For
Sept. 25, 1939	STL	A	—	STL	N	Cash
June 10, 1940	CLE	A	—	STL	A	Cash
Dec. 4, 1942	BOS	N	Eddie Joost $25,000.	CIN	N	Eddie Miller
Aug. 22, 1945	CIN	N	—	BOS	N	Cash

Rob Andrews

Date	Traded To		Traded With	Traded By		In Exchange For
Dec. 3, 1974	HOU	N	Enos Cabell	BAL	A	Lee May Jay Schlueter
Mar. 26, 1977	SF	N	Cash	HOU	N	Willie Crawford Rob Sperring

Joaquin Andujar

Date	Traded To		Traded With	Traded By		In Exchange For
Oct. 24, 1975	HOU	N	—	CIN	N	Luis Sanchez minor league P Carlos Alfonso
June 7, 1981	STL	N	—	HOU	N	Tony Scott
Dec. 10, 1985	OAK	A	—	STL	N	Mike Heath Tim Conroy
Jan. 8, 1988	HOU	N	—	OAK	A	No compensation (free agent signing)

Norm Angelini

Date	Traded To		Traded With	Traded By		In Exchange For
June 30, 1975	ATL	N	Bruce Dal Canton Al Autry	KC	A	Ray Sadecki Cash

(Atlanta received Angelini and Autry on September 4,1975.)

Eric Anthony

Date	Traded To		Traded With	Traded By		In Exchange For
Dec. 10, 1993	SEA	A	—	HOU	N	Mike Felder Mike Hampton

John Antonelli

Date	Traded To	Traded With	Traded By	In Exchange For
May 8, 1945	PHI N	Glenn Crawford	STL N	Buster Adams

Johnny Antonelli

Date	Traded To	Traded With	Traded By	In Exchange For
Feb. 1, 1954	NY N	Don Liddle Ebba St. Claire Billy Klaus $50,000.	MIL N	Bobby Thomson Sammy Calderone
Dec. 3, 1960	CLE A	Willie Kirkland	SF N	Harvey Kuenn
July 4, 1961	MIL N	—	CLE A	Cash
Oct. 11, 1961	NY N	Ken MacKenzie	MIL N	Cash

Luis Aparicio

Date	Traded To	Traded With	Traded By	In Exchange For
Jan. 14, 1963	BAL A	Al Smith	CHI A	Hoyt Wilhelm Pete Ward Ron Hansen Dave Nicholson
Nov. 29, 1967	CHI A	Russ Snyder John Matias	BAL A	Don Buford Bruce Howard Roger Nelson
Dec. 1, 1970	BOS A	—	CHI A	Mike Andrews Luis Alvarado

Luis Aponte

Date	Traded To	Traded With	Traded By	In Exchange For
Mar. 24, 1984	CLE A	—	BOS A	Minor league Ps Mike Poindexter Paul Perry

Pete Appleton

Date	Traded To	Traded With	Traded By	In Exchange For
June 10, 1932	BOS A	—	CLE A	Jack Russell
Dec. 8, 1939	CHI A	Taffy Wright	WAS A	Gee Walker

Luis Aquino

Date	Traded To	Traded With	Traded By	In Exchange For
July 14, 1987	KC A	—	TOR A	Juan Beniquez
Mar. 27, 1993	FLA N	—	KC A	Cash
July 24, 1995	SF N	—	MON N	Minor league P Lou Pote

Jim Archer

Date	Traded To	Traded With	Traded By	In Exchange For
Jan. 24, 1961	KC A	—	BAL A	*see Russ Snyder*

Jimmy Archer

Date	Traded To	Traded With	Traded By	In Exchange For
Dec. 1917	PIT N	—	CHI N	Cash
Sept. 1918	CIN N	—	BKN N	Cash

George Archie

Date	Traded To	Traded With	Traded By	In Exchange For
Sept. 10, 1941	STL A	—	WAS A	Bobby Estalella

Alex Arias

Date	Traded To	Traded With	Traded By	In Exchange For
Nov. 17, 1992	FLA N	Gary Scott	CHI N	Greg Hibbard

Steve Arlin

Date	Traded To	Traded With	Traded By	In Exchange For
June 15, 1974	CLE A	—	SD N	Brent Strom minor league P Jerry Lee

Tony Armas

Date	Traded To	Traded With	Traded By	In Exchange For
Mar. 15, 1977	OAK A	Dave Giusti Doc Medich Doug Bair Rick Langford Mitchell Page	PIT N	Phil Garner Tommy Helms Chris Batton
Dec. 6, 1982	BOS A	Jeff Newman	OAK A	Carney Lansford Garry Hancock minor league P Jerry King

Ed Armbrister

Date	Traded To	Traded With	Traded By	In Exchange For
Nov. 29, 1971	CIN N	*see Joe Morgan*	HOU N	—

Charlie Armbruster

Date	Traded To	Traded With	Traded By	In Exchange For
Sept. 1, 1907	CHI A	—	BOS A	Cash

Jack Armstrong

Date	Traded To	Traded With	Traded By	In Exchange For
Nov. 15, 1991	CLE A	Scott Scudder Minor league P Joe Turek	CIN N	Greg Swindell
Jan. 7, 1994	TEX A	—	FLA N	No compensation (free agent signing)

Mike Armstrong

Date	Traded To	Traded With	Traded By	In Exchange For
Apr. 4, 1982	KC A	—	SD N	Cash
Dec. 7, 1983	NY A	minor league C Duane Dewey	KC A	Steve Balboni Roger Erickson

Harry Arndt

Date	Traded To	Traded With	Traded By	In Exchange For
May 1902	BAL A	—	DET A	Cash

Morrie Arnovich

Date	Traded To	Traded With	Traded By	In Exchange For
June 15, 1940	CIN N	—	PHI N	Johnny Rizzo
Dec. 10, 1940	NY N	—	CIN N	Cash

Brad Arnsberg

Date	Traded To	Traded With	Traded By	In Exchange For
Nov. 2, 1987	TEX A	—	NY A	Don Slaught

(Texas received Arnsberg on November 10, 1987.)

Jerry Arrigo

Date	Traded To	Traded With	Traded By	In Exchange For
Dec. 4, 1964	CIN N	—	MIN A	Cesar Tovar
May 20, 1966	NY N	—	CIN N	Cash
Aug. 16, 1966	CIN N	—	NY N	Cash
Dec. 15, 1969	CHI A	—	CIN N	Angel Bravo

Fernando Arroyo

Date	Traded To	Traded With	Traded By	In Exchange For
Dec. 5, 1979	MIN A	—	DET A	Jeff Holly

Luis Arroyo

Date	Traded To	Traded With	Traded By	In Exchange For
May 5, 1956	PIT N	—	STL N	Max Surkont

Rudy Arroyo

Date	Traded To	Traded With	Traded By	In Exchange For
Oct. 26, 1972	LA N	minor league P Greg Millikan	STL N	Larry Hisle

Randy Asadoor

Date	Traded To	Traded With	Traded By	In Exchange For
Apr. 6, 1985	SD N	—	TEX A	Mitch Williams

Richie Ashburn

Date	Traded To	Traded With	Traded By	In Exchange For
Jan. 11, 1960	CHI N	—	PHI N	John Buzhardt Alvin Dark Jim Woods
Dec. 8, 1961	NY N	—	CHI N	Cash

Alan Ashby

Date	Traded To	Traded With	Traded By	In Exchange For
Nov. 5, 1976	TOR A	Doug Howard	CLE A	Al Fitzmorris
Nov. 27, 1978	HOU N	—	TOR A	Joe Cannon Pedro Hernandez Mark Lemongello

Andy Ashby

Date	Traded To	Traded With	Traded By	In Exchange For
July 26, 1993	SD N	Brad Ausmus Doug Bochtler	CLR N	Bruce Hurst Greg Harris

Tucker Ashford

Date	Traded To	Traded With	Traded By	In Exchange For
Feb. 15, 1980	TEX A	Gaylord Perry minor league P Joe Carroll	SD N	Willie Montanez
Oct. 24, 1980	NY A	Cash	TEX A	Roger Holt
Oct. 27, 1982	TOR A	—	NY A	Cash

(Ashford was returned to the Yankees on April 5, 1983.)

Date	Traded To	Traded With	Traded By	In Exchange For
Apr. 18, 1983	NY N	—	NY A	Minor leaguers P Steve Ray and IF Felix Perdomo
Apr. 1, 1984	KC A	—	NY N	Tom Edens

Bob Aspromonte

Date	Traded To	Traded With	Traded By	In Exchange For
Dec. 4, 1968	ATL N	—	HOU N	Marty Martinez
Dec. 1, 1970	NY N	—	ATL N	Ron Herbel

Ken Aspromonte

Date	Traded To	Traded With	Traded By	In Exchange For
May 1, 1958	WAS A	—	BOS A	Lou Berberet
May 15, 1960	CLE A	—	WAS A	Pete Whisenant
July 3, 1961	CLE A	—	LA A	Waiver price
June 24, 1962	MIL N	Cash	CLE A	Bob Hartman
Dec. 3, 1962	CHI N	—	MIL N	Jim McKnight

Paul Assenmacher

Date	Traded To	Traded With	Traded By	In Exchange For
Aug. 24, 1989	CHI N	—	ATL N	Rick Luecken Pat Gomez
July 30, 1993	NY A	—	CHI N	Karl Rhodes
(Part of three team trade involving New York Yankees, Chicago Cubs, and Kansas City Royals.)				
Mar. 21, 1994	CHI A	—	NY A	Brian Boehringer

Keith Atherton

Date	Traded To	Traded With	Traded By	In Exchange For
May 20, 1986	MIN A	—	OAK A	Cash and player to be named
(Oakland received P Eric Broersma on May 23, 1985.)				
Mar. 26, 1989	CLE A	—	MIN A	Carmen Castillo

Bill Atkinson

Date	Traded To	Traded With	Traded By	In Exchange For
Dec. 12, 1979	CHI A	—	MON N	Cash

Toby Atwell

Date	Traded To	Traded With	Traded By	In Exchange For
June 4, 1953	PIT N	—	CHI N	*see Ralph Kiner*

Rick Auerbach

Date	Traded To	Traded With	Traded By	In Exchange For
Oct. 27, 1973	LA N	—	MIL A	Cash
Feb. 7, 1977	NY N	—	LA N	Hank Webb minor league P Dick Sander
Apr. 26, 1977	TEX A	Cash	NY N	Lenny Randle
June 15, 1977	CIN N	—	TEX A	Cash
July 19, 1980	TEX A	—	CIN N	Cash
(Auerbach refused to report and was suspended.)				
Dec. 12, 1980	SEA A	—	TEX A	*see Rick Honeycutt*

Don August

Date	Traded To	Traded With	Traded By	In Exchange For
Aug. 19, 1986	MIL A	Mark Knudson	HOU N	Danny Darwin

Eldon Auker

Date	Traded To	Traded With	Traded By	In Exchange For
Dec. 15, 1938	BOS A	Jake Wade Chet Morgan	DET A	Pinky Higgins Archie McKain
Feb. 8, 1940	STL A	—	BOS A	Cash

Rich Aurilia

Date	Traded To	Traded With	Traded By	In Exchange For
Dec. 22, 1994	SF N	Minor league OF Desi Wilson	TEX A	John Burkett

Brad Ausmus

Date	Traded To	Traded With	Traded By	In Exchange For
July 26, 1993	SD N	Andy Ashby Doug Bochtler	CLR N	Bruce Hurst Greg Harris

Jimmy Austin

Date	Traded To	Traded With	Traded By	In Exchange For
Jan. 1911	STL A	Frank LaPorte	NY A	Roy Hartzell

Al Autry

Date	Traded To	Traded With	Traded By	In Exchange For
June 30, 1975	ATL N	Bruce Dal Canton Norm Angelini	KC A	Ray Sadecki Cash
(Atlanta received Angelini and Autry on September 4,1975.)				

Chick Autry

Date	Traded To	Traded With	Traded By	In Exchange For
June 10, 1909	BOS N	—	CIN N	Cash

Martin Autry

Date	Traded To	Traded With	Traded By	In Exchange For
Feb. 28, 1929	CHI A	—	CLE A	Bibb Falk

Earl Averill

Date	Traded To	Traded With	Traded By	In Exchange For
June 14, 1939	DET A	—	CLE A	Harry Eisenstat Cash

Earl Averill

Date	Traded To	Traded With	Traded By	In Exchange For
Jan. 23, 1959	CHI N	—	CLE A	Johnny Briggs Jim Bolger

Earl Averill *continued*

Date	Traded To	Traded With	Traded By	In Exchange For
Aug. 13, 1960	CHI A	—	CHI N	Minor league C Don Prohovich Cash
Dec. 11, 1962	PHI N	—	LA A	Jacke Davis

Bobby Avila

Date	Traded To	Traded With	Traded By	In Exchange For
Dec. 2, 1958	BAL A	—	CLE A	Russ Heman $30,000.
May 21, 1959	BOS A	—	BAL A	Waiver price
July 21, 1959	MIL N	—	BOS A	Waiver price

Ramon Aviles

Date	Traded To	Traded With	Traded By	In Exchange For
Apr. 5, 1978	PHI N	—	BOS A	Cash
Oct. 20, 1981	TEX A	—	PHI N	Dave Rajsich

Benny Ayala

Date	Traded To	Traded With	Traded By	In Exchange For
Mar. 30, 1977	STL N	—	NY N	Doug Clarey
Apr. 19, 1985	CLE A	—	BAL A	No compensation (free agent signing)

Bobby Ayala

Date	Traded To	Traded With	Traded By	In Exchange For
Nov. 2, 1993	SEA A	Dan Wilson	CIN N	Erik Hanson Bret Boone

Doc Ayers

Date	Traded To	Traded With	Traded By	In Exchange For
July 5, 1919	DET A	—	WAS A	Eric Erickson

Bob Ayrault

Date	Traded To	Traded With	Traded By	In Exchange For
June 12, 1993	SEA A	—	PHI N	Kevin Foster
Aug. 9, 1993	LA N	—	SEA A	Waiver price

Joe Azcue

Date	Traded To	Traded With	Traded By	In Exchange For
Dec. 15, 1961	KC A	Ed Charles Manny Jimenez	MIL N	Bob Shaw Lou Klimchock
May 25, 1963	CLE A	Dick Howser	KC A	Doc Edwards $100,000.
Apr. 19, 1969	BOS A	—	CLE A	*see Ken Harrelson*
June 15, 1969	CAL A	—	BOS A	Tom Satriano
July 28, 1972	MIL A	Syd O'Brien	CAL A	Paul Ratliff Ron Clark

Oscar Azocar

Date	Traded To	Traded With	Traded By	In Exchange For
Dec. 3, 1990	SD N	—	NY A	Mike Humphreys
(New York received Humphreys on February 7, 1991.)				

Charlie Babb

Date	Traded To	Traded With	Traded By	In Exchange For
Dec. 12, 1903	NY N	John Cronin	BKN N	Bill Dahlen

Bob Babcock

Date	Traded To	Traded With	Traded By	In Exchange For
Jan. 27, 1983	SEA A	—	TEX A	Vance McHenry

Loren Babe

Date	Traded To	Traded With	Traded By	In Exchange For
Apr. 27, 1953	PHI A	—	NY A	Cash
Dec. 16, 1953	NY A	*see Harry Byrd*	PHI A	—

Johnny Babich

Date	Traded To	Traded With	Traded By	In Exchange For
Feb. 6, 1936	BOS N	Gene Moore	BKN N	Fred Frankhouse
Aug. 10, 1938	CIN N	Tommy Reis Gil English Johnny Riddle Vince DiMaggio Cash	BOS N	Eddie Miller

Wally Backman

Date	Traded To	Traded With	Traded By	In Exchange For
Dec. 7, 1988	MIN A	Minor league P Mike Santiago	NY N	Minor league Ps Jeff Bumgarner Steve Gasser Toby Nivens
Jan. 31, 1990	PIT N	—	MIN A	No compensation (free agent signing)

Wally Backman *continued*

Date	Traded To	Traded With	Traded By	In Exchange For
Jan. 10, 1991	PHI N	—	PIT N	No compensation (free agent signing)

Mike Bacsik

Date	Traded To	Traded With	Traded By	In Exchange For
Dec. 13, 1978	MIN A	—	TEX A	Mac Scarce
Dec. 19, 1980	SEA A	—	MIN A	Steve Stroughter

Fred Baczewski

Date	Traded To	Traded With	Traded By	In Exchange For
June 12, 1953	CIN N	Bob Kelly	CHI N	Bubba Church

Carlos Baerga

Date	Traded To	Traded With	Traded By	In Exchange For
Dec. 6, 1989	CLE A	Sandy Alomar Chris James	SD N	Joe Carter

Jose Baez

Date	Traded To	Traded With	Traded By	In Exchange For
Oct. 22, 1976	SEA A	—	LA N	Cash
June 26, 1978	STL N	—	SEA A	Mike Potter

Kevin Baez

Date	Traded To	Traded With	Traded By	In Exchange For
Mar. 27, 1994	BAL A	Minor league P Tom Wegmann	NY N	David Segui

Jim Bagby

Date	Traded To	Traded With	Traded By	In Exchange For
Nov. 5, 1922	PIT N	—	CLE A	Waiver price

Jim Bagby

Date	Traded To	Traded With	Traded By	In Exchange For
Dec. 12, 1940	CLE A	Gene Desautels Gee Walker	BOS A	Frankie Pytlak Odell Hale Joe Dobson
Dec. 12, 1945	BOS A	—	CLE A	Vic Johnson Cash
Feb. 10, 1947	PIT N	—	BOS A	Cash

Jeff Bagwell

Date	Traded To	Traded With	Traded By	In Exchange For
Aug. 31, 1990	HOU N	—	BOS A	Larry Andersen

Stan Bahnsen

Date	Traded To	Traded With	Traded By	In Exchange For
Dec. 2, 1971	CHI A	—	NY A	Rich McKinney
June 15, 1975	OAK A	Skip Pitlock	CHI A	Dave Hamilton Chet Lemon
May 22, 1977	MON N	—	OAK A	Mike Jorgensen

Scott Bailes

Date	Traded To	Traded With	Traded By	In Exchange For
May 30, 1985	CLE A	—	PIT N	Johnnie LeMaster
		(Cleveland received Bailes on July 3, 1985.)		
Jan. 9, 1990	CAL A	—	CLE A	Jeff Manto Minor league P Colin Charland

Bill Bailey

Date	Traded To	Traded With	Traded By	In Exchange For
Sept. 1915	CHI F	—	BAL F	Jimmy Smith Adam Johnson

Bob Bailey

Date	Traded To	Traded With	Traded By	In Exchange For
Dec. 1, 1966	LA N	Gene Michael	PIT N	Maury Wills
Oct. 21, 1968	MON N	—	LA N	Cash
Dec. 12, 1975	CIN N	—	MON N	Clay Kirby
Sept. 19, 1977	BOS A	—	CIN N	Minor league P Frank Newcomer Cash

Cory Bailey

Date	Traded To	Traded With	Traded By	In Exchange For
Apr. 8, 1995	STL N	*see Scott Cooper*	BOS A	—

Ed Bailey

Date	Traded To	Traded With	Traded By	In Exchange For
Apr. 27, 1961	SF N	—	CIN N	Bob Schmidt Don Blasingame Sherman Jones
Dec. 3, 1963	MIL N	*see Felipe Alou*	SF N	—
Feb. 1, 1965	SF N	—	MIL N	Billy O'Dell
May 29, 1965	CHI N	Harvey Kuenn Bob Hendley	SF N	Dick Bertell Len Gabrielson

Ed Bailey *continued*

Date	Traded To	Traded With	Traded By	In Exchange For
Feb. 15, 1966	CAL A	—	CHI N	Cash

Gene Bailey

Date	Traded To	Traded With	Traded By	In Exchange For
May 1920	BOS A	—	BOS N	Cash

Mark Bailey

Date	Traded To	Traded With	Traded By	In Exchange For
July 23, 1988	MON N	—	HOU N	Casey Candaele
Mar. 28, 1989	NY N	Tom O'Malley	MON N	Steve Frey

Sweetbreads Bailey

Date	Traded To	Traded With	Traded By	In Exchange For
May 1921	BKN N	—	CHI N	Cash

Bob Bailor

Date	Traded To	Traded With	Traded By	In Exchange For
Dec. 12, 1980	NY N	—	TOR A	Roy Lee Jackson
Dec. 8, 1983	LA N	Carlos Diaz	NY N	Sid Fernandez Ross Jones

Harold Baines

Date	Traded To	Traded With	Traded By	In Exchange For
July 29, 1989	TEX A	Fred Manrique	CHI A	Scott Fletcher Wilson Alvarez Sammy Sosa
Aug. 29, 1990	OAK A	—	TEX A	Joe Bitker Scott Chiamparino
		(Texas received Bitker and Chiamparino on September 4, 1990.)		
Jan. 14, 1993	BAL A	—	OAK A	Minor league Ps Bobby Chouinard and Allen Plaster
Dec. 11, 1995	CHI A	—	BAL A	No compensation (free agent signing)

Doug Bair

Date	Traded To	Traded With	Traded By	In Exchange For
Mar. 15, 1977	OAK A	—	PIT N	*see Phil Garner*
Feb. 25, 1978	CIN N	—	OAK A	Dave Revering Cash
Sept. 10, 1981	STL N	—	CIN N	Neil Fiala Joe Edelen
June 22, 1983	DET A	—	STL N	Dave Rucker

Doug Baird

Date	Traded To	Traded With	Traded By	In Exchange For
June 14, 1917	STL N	—	PIT N	Bob Steele
Jan. 21, 1919	PHI N	Stuffy Stewart Gene Packard	STL N	Milt Stock Pickles Dillhoefer Dixie Davis
July 14, 1919	STL N	Elmer Jacobs Frank Woodward	PHI N	Lee Meadows Gene Paulette
Aug. 1919	BKN N	—	STL N	Cash
July 27, 1920	NY N	—	BKN N	Cash

Bill Baker

Date	Traded To	Traded With	Traded By	In Exchange For
May 12, 1941	PIT N	—	CIN N	Cash

Bock Baker

Date	Traded To	Traded With	Traded By	In Exchange For
Apr. 28, 1901	PHI A	—	CLE A	Cash

Chuck Baker

Date	Traded To	Traded With	Traded By	In Exchange For
Dec. 8, 1980	MIN A	—	SD N	Dave Edwards

Dave Baker

Date	Traded To	Traded With	Traded By	In Exchange For
Dec. 10, 1982	MIN A	—	TOR A	Don Cooper

Doug Baker

Date	Traded To	Traded With	Traded By	In Exchange For
Feb. 24, 1988	MIN A	—	DET A	Minor league SS Julius McDougal

Dusty Baker

Date	Traded To	Traded With	Traded By	In Exchange For
Nov. 17, 1975	LA N	Ed Goodson	ATL N	Jimmy Wynn Tom Paciorek Lee Lacy Jerry Royster

Dusty Baker *continued*

Date	Traded To		Traded With	Traded By		In Exchange For
Apr. 3, 1984	SF	N	—	LA	N	No compensation (free agent signing)
Mar. 24, 1985	OAK	A	—	SF	N	Minor league P Ed Puikunas Minor league C Dan Winters

Floyd Baker

Date	Traded To		Traded With	Traded By		In Exchange For
Dec. 30, 1944	CHI	A	—	STL	A	Cash
Oct. 24, 1951	WAS	A	—	CHI	A	Willie Miranda
May 12, 1953	BOS	A	—	WAS	A	Cash
July 18, 1954	PHI	N	—	BOS	A	Cash

Frank Baker

Date	Traded To		Traded With	Traded By		In Exchange For
Oct. 5, 1971	CAL	A	—	CLE	A	*see Alex Johnson*

Frank Baker

Date	Traded To		Traded With	Traded By		In Exchange For
Apr. 5, 1973	BAL	A	—	NY	A	Tom Matchick

Frank Baker

Date	Traded To		Traded With	Traded By		In Exchange For
Feb. 15, 1916	NY	A	—	PHI	A	$37,500.

Gene Baker

Date	Traded To		Traded With	Traded By		In Exchange For
May 1, 1957	PIT	N	Dee Fondy	CHI	N	Dale Long Lee Walls

Howard Baker

Date	Traded To		Traded With	Traded By		In Exchange For
July 1915	NY	N	—	CHI	A	Cash

Jack Baker

Date	Traded To		Traded With	Traded By		In Exchange For
Dec. 9, 1977	CLE	A	—	BOS	A	Garry Hancock

Kirtley Baker

Date	Traded To		Traded With	Traded By		In Exchange For
Jan. 10, 1900	BOS	N	Shad Barry Bill Dinneen	WAS	N	Cash

Scott Baker

Date	Traded To		Traded With	Traded By		In Exchange For
Nov. 17, 1992	OAK	A	Eric Helfand	FLA	N	Walt Weiss

(Oakland received Baker on November 20, 1992.)

Steve Baker

Date	Traded To		Traded With	Traded By		In Exchange For
Sept. 2, 1983	STL	N	—	OAK	A	Minor league Ps Tom Dozier Jim Strichek

Tom Baker

Date	Traded To		Traded With	Traded By		In Exchange For
June 11, 1937	NY	N	—	BKN	N	Freddie Fitzsimmons
Dec. 11, 1938	WAS	A	Jim Carlin $20,000.	NY	N	Zeke Bonura

John Balaz

Date	Traded To		Traded With	Traded By		In Exchange For
Mar. 3, 1976	BOS	A	Dick Sharon Dave Machemer	CAL	A	Dick Drago

Steve Balboni

Date	Traded To		Traded With	Traded By		In Exchange For
Dec. 7, 1983	KC	A	Roger Erickson	NY	A	Mike Armstrong minor league C Duane Dewey
Mar. 27, 1989	NY	A	—	SEA	A	Minor league P Dana Ridenour

Jack Baldschun

Date	Traded To		Traded With	Traded By		In Exchange For
Dec. 6, 1965	BAL	A	—	PHI	N	Jackie Brandt Darold Knowles
Dec. 9, 1965	CIN	N	Milt Pappas Dick Simpson	BAL	A	Frank Robinson

Billy Baldwin

Date	Traded To		Traded With	Traded By		In Exchange For
Dec. 12, 1975	NY	N	Mickey Lolich	DET	A	Rusty Staub Bill Laxton

Dave Baldwin

Date	Traded To		Traded With	Traded By		In Exchange For
Dec. 4, 1969	SEA	A	—	WAS	A	George Brunet

Reggie Baldwin

Date	Traded To		Traded With	Traded By		In Exchange For
Feb. 20, 1980	NY	N	—	HOU	N	Minor league OF Keith Bodie

Lee Bales

Date	Traded To		Traded With	Traded By		In Exchange For
Oct. 13, 1966	HOU	N	*see Tom Dukes*	ATL	N	—

Neal Ball

Date	Traded To		Traded With	Traded By		In Exchange For
May 1909	CLE	A	—	NY	A	Cash
May 1912	BOS	A	—	CLE	A	Cash

Jay Baller

Date	Traded To		Traded With	Traded By		In Exchange For
Dec. 9, 1982	CLE	A	Manny Trillo George Vukovich Julio Franco Jerry Willard	PHI	N	Von Hayes
Apr. 1, 1985	CHI	N	—	CLE	A	Dan Rohn

Win Ballou

Date	Traded To		Traded With	Traded By		In Exchange For
Feb. 1926	STL	A	Tom Zachary	WAS	A	Joe Bush Jack Tobin

Dave Bancroft

Date	Traded To		Traded With	Traded By		In Exchange For
June 8, 1920	NY	N	—	PHI	N	Art Fletcher Bill Hubbell Cash
Nov. 12, 1923	BOS	N	Casey Stengel Bill Cunningham	NY	N	Billy Southworth Joe Oeschger

(Bancroft was named Boston manager.)

Sal Bando

Date	Traded To		Traded With	Traded By		In Exchange For
Nov. 19, 1976	MIL	A	—	OAK	A	No compensation (free agent signing)

Eddie Bane

Date	Traded To		Traded With	Traded By		In Exchange For
Jan. 15, 1980	KC	A	—	CHI	A	Joe Zdeb

Dick Baney

Date	Traded To		Traded With	Traded By		In Exchange For
June 15, 1970	BAL	A	Buzz Stephen	MIL	A	Dave May

Scott Bankhead

Date	Traded To		Traded With	Traded By		In Exchange For
Dec. 10, 1986	SEA	A	Mike Kingery Steve Shields	KC	A	Danny Tartabull Rick Luecken
Dec. 8, 1992	BOS	A	—	CIN	N	No compensation (free agent signing)
Sept. 1, 1994	NY	A	—	BOS	A	Player to be named Cash

(Boston received P Steve Munda on February 14, 1995.)

George Banks

Date	Traded To		Traded With	Traded By		In Exchange For
June 15, 1964	CLE	A	Lee Stange	MIN	A	Mudcat Grant

Willie Banks

Date	Traded To		Traded With	Traded By		In Exchange For
Nov. 24, 1993	CHI	N	—	MIN	A	Matt Walbeck Dave Stevens
June 20, 1995	LA	N	—	CHI	N	Minor league P Dax Winslett
Aug. 10, 1995	FLA	N	—	LA	N	Waiver price
Oct. 4, 1995	PHI	N	—	LA	N	Waiver price

Alan Bannister

Date	Traded To		Traded With	Traded By		In Exchange For
Dec. 10, 1975	CHI	A	Dick Ruthven Roy Thomas	PHI	N	Jim Kaat Mike Buskey
June 13, 1980	CLE	A	—	CHI	A	Ron Pruitt

Alan Bannister *continued*

Date	Traded To	Traded With	Traded By	In Exchange For
Mar. 25, 1984	HOU N	—	CLE A	Cash
May 25, 1984	TEX A	—	HOU N	Mike Richardt

Floyd Bannister

Date	Traded To	Traded With	Traded By	In Exchange For
Dec. 8, 1978	SEA A	—	HOU N	Craig Reynolds
Dec. 13, 1982	CHI A	—	SEA A	No compensation (free agent signing)
Dec. 10, 1987	KC A	Dave Cochrane	CHI A	Melido Perez John Davis Greg Hibbard Minor league P Chuck Mount

Walter Barbare

Date	Traded To	Traded With	Traded By	In Exchange For
Jan. 1919	PIT N	—	BOS A	Cash
Feb. 23, 1921	BOS N	Billy Southworth Fred Nicholson $15,000.	PIT N	Rabbit Maranville

Jap Barbeau

Date	Traded To	Traded With	Traded By	In Exchange For
Aug. 19, 1909	STL N	Alan Storke	PIT N	Bobby Byrne

Steve Barber

Date	Traded To	Traded With	Traded By	In Exchange For
July 5, 1967	NY A	—	BAL A	Ray Barker minor league IFs Chet Trail and Joe Brady Cash
Oct. 22, 1973	MIL A	Clyde Wright Ken Berry Art Kusnyer Cash	CAL A	Ellie Rodriguez Skip Lockwood Gary Ryerson Ollie Brown Joe Lahoud

Turner Barber

Date	Traded To	Traded With	Traded By	In Exchange For
Jan. 2, 1923	BKN N	—	CHI N	Cash

Bret Barberie

Date	Traded To	Traded With	Traded By	In Exchange For
Dec. 6, 1994	BAL A	—	FLA N	Jay Powell

George Barclay

Date	Traded To	Traded With	Traded By	In Exchange For
Sept. 11, 1904	BOS N	—	STL N	Cash

Ray Bare

Date	Traded To	Traded With	Traded By	In Exchange For
Apr. 4, 1975	DET A	—	STL N	Cash

Jesse Barfield

Date	Traded To	Traded With	Traded By	In Exchange For
Apr. 30, 1989	NY A	—	TOR A	Al Leiter

Len Barker

Date	Traded To	Traded With	Traded By	In Exchange For
Oct. 3, 1978	CLE A	Bobby Bonds	TEX A	Jim Kern Larvell Blanks
Aug. 28, 1983	ATL N	—	CLE A	Rick Behenna Brett Butler Brook Jacoby $150,000.

(Cleveland received Butler and Jacoby on October 21, 1983.)

Ray Barker

Date	Traded To	Traded With	Traded By	In Exchange For
Nov. 16, 1961	CLE A	Harry Chiti minor leaguer Art Kay	BAL A	Johnny Temple
May 10, 1965	NY A	—	CLE A	Pedro Gonzalez
July 5, 1967	BAL A	minor league IFs Chet Trail and Joe Brady Cash	NY A	Steve Barber

Mike Barlow

Date	Traded To	Traded With	Traded By	In Exchange For
May 18, 1975	STL N	Minor league P Steve Staniland	OAK A	Teddy Martinez
Sept. 30, 1975	HOU N	—	STL N	Mike Easler
June 6, 1976	CAL A	Terry Humphrey	HOU N	Ed Herrmann

Brian Barnes

Date	Traded To	Traded With	Traded By	In Exchange For
Dec. 13, 1993	CLE A	—	MON N	Randy Milligan

(Cleveland received Barnes on December 17.)

Date	Traded To	Traded With	Traded By	In Exchange For
June 16, 1994	LA N	—	CLE A	Minor league IF Eduardo Lantigua
Oct. 18, 1994	FLA N	—	LA N	Waiver price

Frank Barnes

Date	Traded To	Traded With	Traded By	In Exchange For
May 19, 1960	CHI A	—	STL N	Cash
Dec. 15, 1961	PHI N	Andy Carey Cal McLish	CHI A	Bob Sadowski Taylor Phillips minor league IF Lou Vassie

(Carey refused to report, and the Phillies received McLish in exchange for Vassie to complete the trade on March 24, 1962.)

Jesse Barnes

Date	Traded To	Traded With	Traded By	In Exchange For
Jan. 8, 1918	NY N	Larry Doyle	BOS N	Buck Herzog
June 7, 1923	BOS N	Earl Smith	NY N	Hank Gowdy Mule Watson
Oct. 7, 1925	BKN N	Mickey O'Neil Gus Felix	BOS N	Zack Taylor Jimmy Johnston Eddie Brown

Red Barnes

Date	Traded To	Traded With	Traded By	In Exchange For
June 13, 1930	CHI A	—	WAS A	Dave Harris

Rich Barnes

Date	Traded To	Traded With	Traded By	In Exchange For
Aug. 25, 1983	CLE A	—	CHI A	Miguel Dilone

Skeeter Barnes

Date	Traded To	Traded With	Traded By	In Exchange For
Apr. 26, 1985	MON N	—	CIN N	Max Venable
July 24, 1986	PHI N	*see Dan Schatzeder*	MON N	—

Virgil Barnes

Date	Traded To	Traded With	Traded By	In Exchange For
June 15, 1928	BOS N	Ben Cantwell Al Spohrer Bill Clarkson	NY N	Joe Genewich

Ed Barney

Date	Traded To	Traded With	Traded By	In Exchange For
Aug. 19, 1915	PIT N	—	NY A	Waiver price

Salome Barojas

Date	Traded To	Traded With	Traded By	In Exchange For
June 29, 1984	SEA A	—	CHI A	Gene Nelson Jerry Don Gleaton

Jim Barr

Date	Traded To	Traded With	Traded By	In Exchange For
Dec. 3, 1978	CAL A	—	SF N	No compensation (free agent signing)

Steve Barr

Date	Traded To	Traded With	Traded By	In Exchange For
Nov. 17, 1975	TEX A	Juan Beniquez Craig Skok	BOS A	Ferguson Jenkins

Cuno Barragan

Date	Traded To	Traded With	Traded By	In Exchange For
Dec. 13, 1963	LA N	Jim Brewer	CHI N	Dick Scott

German Barranca

Date	Traded To	Traded With	Traded By	In Exchange For
Jan. 21, 1981	CIN N	—	KC A	Cesar Geronimo
Sept. 7, 1982	DET A	—	CIN N	Cash

Bill Barrett

Date	Traded To	Traded With	Traded By	In Exchange For
May 23, 1929	BOS A	—	CHI A	Doug Taitt
Apr. 30, 1930	WAS A	—	BOS A	Earl Webb

Bob Barrett

Date	Traded To	Traded With	Traded By	In Exchange For
May 10, 1925	BKN N	—	CHI N	Tommy Griffith

Dick Barrett

Date	Traded To	Traded With	Traded By	In Exchange For
Dec. 1933	BOS N	—	PHI A	Cash
July 1943	PHI N	—	CHI N	Cash

Jimmy Barrett

Date	Traded To	Traded With	Traded By	In Exchange For
Feb. 1906	CIN N	—	DET A	Waiver price

Johnny Barrett

Date	Traded To	Traded With	Traded By	In Exchange For
June 12, 1946	BOS N	—	PIT N	Chuck Workman

Red Barrett

Date	Traded To	Traded With	Traded By	In Exchange For
May 23, 1945	STL N	$60,000.	BOS N	Mort Cooper
Dec. 9, 1946	BOS N	—	STL N	Cash

Tom Barrett

Date	Traded To	Traded With	Traded By	In Exchange For
Dec. 11, 1986	PHI N	—	NY A	*see Charles Hudson*

Jack Barry

Date	Traded To	Traded With	Traded By	In Exchange For
July 2, 1915	BOS A	—	PHI A	$8,000.
June 27, 1919	PHI A	Amos Strunk	BOS A	Braggo Roth Red Shannon

(Barry refused to report, and retired.)

Jeff Barry

Date	Traded To	Traded With	Traded By	In Exchange For
Dec. 9, 1991	NY N	—	MON N	Blaine Beatty
Dec. 15, 1995	SD N	—	NY N	Pedro Martinez

Shad Barry

Date	Traded To	Traded With	Traded By	In Exchange For
Jan. 10, 1900	BOS N	Kirtley Baker Bill Dinneen	WAS N	Cash
June 1901	PHI N	—	BOS N	Jimmy Slagle
July 20, 1904	CHI N	—	PHI N	Frank Corridon Jack Sutthoff
May 20, 1905	CIN N	—	CHI N	Cash
July 25, 1906	STL N	Carl Druhot	CIN N	Homer Smoot
July 1908	NY N	—	STL N	Cash

Dick Bartell

Date	Traded To	Traded With	Traded By	In Exchange For
Nov. 6, 1930	PHI N	—	PIT N	Tommy Thevenow Claude Willoughby
Nov. 1, 1934	NY N	—	PHI N	Pretzels Pezzullo Blondy Ryan Johnny Vergez George Watkins Cash
Dec. 6, 1938	CHI N	Hank Leiber Gus Mancuso	NY N	Frank Demaree Bill Jurges Ken O'Dea
Dec. 6, 1939	DET A	—	CHI N	Billy Rogell

Bob Barton

Date	Traded To	Traded With	Traded By	In Exchange For
Dec. 5, 1969	SD N	Ron Herbel Bobby Etheridge	SF N	Frank Reberger
June 11, 1972	CIN N	—	SD N	Pat Corrales

Shawn Barton

Date	Traded To	Traded With	Traded By	In Exchange For
Mar. 21, 1988	NY N	Minor league P Vladimir Perez	PHI N	Bill Almon

Eddie Basinski

Date	Traded To	Traded With	Traded By	In Exchange For
Dec. 5, 1946	PIT N	—	BKN N	Al Gerheauser

Kevin Bass

Date	Traded To	Traded With	Traded By	In Exchange For
Aug. 30, 1982	HOU N	Frank DiPino Mike Madden Cash	MIL A	Don Sutton
Nov. 16, 1989	SF N	—	HOU N	No compensation (free agent signing)
Aug. 7, 1992	NY N	—	SF N	Player to be named

(San Francisco received OF Rob Katzaroff on October 1, 1992.)

Date	Traded To	Traded With	Traded By	In Exchange For
Jan. 7, 1993	HOU N	—	NY N	No compensation (free agent signing)

Randy Bass

Date	Traded To	Traded With	Traded By	In Exchange For
Aug. 11, 1980	SD N	—	MON N	John D'Acquisto Cash
May 17, 1982	TEX A	—	SD N	Cash

Richard Batchelor

Date	Traded To	Traded With	Traded By	In Exchange For
Aug. 31, 1993	STL N	—	NY A	Lee Smith

John Bateman

Date	Traded To	Traded With	Traded By	In Exchange For
June 14, 1972	PHI N	—	MON N	Tim McCarver

Billy Bates

Date	Traded To	Traded With	Traded By	In Exchange For
June 9, 1990	CIN N	Glenn Braggs	MIL A	Ron Robinson Bob Sebra

Bud Bates

Date	Traded To	Traded With	Traded By	In Exchange For
Dec. 5, 1939	BOS N	—	PHI N	Waiver price

Johnny Bates

Date	Traded To	Traded With	Traded By	In Exchange For
July 16, 1909	PHI N	Charlie Starr	BOS N	Buster Brown Lew Richie Dave Shean
Feb. 1911	CIN N	—	PHI N	*see Dode Paskert*
Aug. 1914	CHI N	—	CIN N	Elmer Koestner

Bill Bathe

Date	Traded To	Traded With	Traded By	In Exchange For
Dec. 17, 1986	CHI N	—	OAK A	Minor league OF Joe Hicks

Kevin Batiste

Date	Traded To	Traded With	Traded By	In Exchange For
Dec. 17, 1989	ATL N	Ernie Whitt	TOR A	Rick Trlicek

Earl Battey

Date	Traded To	Traded With	Traded By	In Exchange For
Apr. 4, 1960	WAS A	Don Mincher $150,000.	CHI A	Roy Sievers

Howard Battle

Date	Traded To	Traded With	Traded By	In Exchange For
Dec. 6, 1995	PHI N	Ricardo Jordan	TOR A	Paul Quantrill

Chris Batton

Date	Traded To	Traded With	Traded By	In Exchange For
Mar. 15, 1977	PIT N	*see Phil Garner*	OAK A	—

Matt Batts

Date	Traded To	Traded With	Traded By	In Exchange For
May 17, 1951	STL A	Jim Suchecki Jim McDonald $100,000.	BOS A	Les Moss
May 29, 1954	CHI A	—	DET A	Red Wilson
Dec. 6, 1954	BAL A	—	CHI A	*see Clint Courtney*

Hank Bauer

Date	Traded To	Traded With	Traded By	In Exchange For
Dec. 11, 1959	KC A	Don Larsen Norm Siebern Marv Throneberry	NY A	Roger Maris Joe De Maestri Kent Hadley

Frank Baumann

Date	Traded To	Traded With	Traded By	In Exchange For
Nov. 3, 1959	CHI A	—	BOS A	Ron Jackson
Dec. 1, 1964	CHI N	—	CHI A	Jimmie Schaffer

Jim Baumer

Date	Traded To	Traded With	Traded By	In Exchange For
May 10, 1961	DET A	—	CIN N	Dick Gernert

Ross Baumgarten

Date	Traded To	Traded With	Traded By	In Exchange For
Mar. 21, 1982	PIT N	Butch Edge	CHI A	Vance Law Ernie Camacho

Frankie Baumholtz

Date	Traded To	Traded With	Traded By	In Exchange For
June 15, 1949	CHI N	Hank Sauer	CIN N	Harry Walker Peanuts Lowrey
Dec. 9, 1955	PHI N	—	CHI N	Cash

Ed Bauta

Date	Traded To	Traded With	Traded By	In Exchange For
May 28, 1960	STL N	Julian Javier	PIT N	Vinegar Bend Mizell Dick Gray
Aug. 5, 1963	NY N	—	STL N	Ken MacKenzie

Mike Baxes

Date	Traded To		Traded With	Traded By		In Exchange For
Apr. 12, 1959	NY	A	Bob Martyn	KC	A	Russ Snyder Tommy Carroll

Don Baylor

Date	Traded To		Traded With	Traded By		In Exchange For
Apr. 2, 1976	OAK	A	Mike Torrez Paul Mitchell	BAL	A	Reggie Jackson Ken Holtzman minor leaguer Bill Van Bommell
Nov. 16, 1976	CAL	A	—	OAK	A	No compensation (free agent signing)
Dec. 1, 1982	NY	A	—	CAL	A	No compensation (free agent signing)
Mar. 28, 1986	BOS	A	—	NY	A	Mike Easler
Aug. 31, 1987	MIN	A	—	BOS	A	Minor league P Enrique Rios

(Boston recieved Rios on December 18, 1987.)

Bill Bayne

Date	Traded To		Traded With	Traded By		In Exchange For
Nov. 22, 1928	BOS	A	—	CLE	A	Cash

Bob Beall

Date	Traded To		Traded With	Traded By		In Exchange For
Dec. 4, 1973	ATL	N	—	PHI	N	Gil Garrido

Belve Bean

Date	Traded To		Traded With	Traded By		In Exchange For
May 14, 1935	WAS	A	—	CLE	A	Lefty Stewart

Billy Bean

Date	Traded To		Traded With	Traded By		In Exchange For
July 17, 1989	LA	N	—	DET	A	Minor league OF Steve Green Minor league 1B-OF Domingo Michel

Billy Beane

Date	Traded To		Traded With	Traded By		In Exchange For
Jan. 16, 1986	MIN	A	Bill Latham Joe Klink	NY	N	Tim Teufel Minor league OF Pat Crosby
Mar. 24, 1988	DET	A	—	MIN	A	Balvino Galvez

Dave Beard

Date	Traded To		Traded With	Traded By		In Exchange For
Nov. 21, 1983	SEA	A	Bob Kearney	OAK	A	Bill Caudill Darrel Akerfelds
July 26, 1985	CHI	N	—	CLE	A	Minor league OF Tom Grant

Gene Bearden

Date	Traded To		Traded With	Traded By		In Exchange For
Dec. 20, 1946	CLE	A	Hal Peck Al Gettel	NY	A	Sherm Lollar Ray Mack
Aug. 2, 1950	WAS	A	—	CLE	A	Waiver price
Apr. 26, 1951	DET	A	—	WAS	A	Waiver price
Feb. 14, 1952	STL	A	Bob Cain Dick Kryhoski	DET	A	Dick Littlefield Ben Taylor Cliff Mapes
Mar. 18, 1953	CHI	A	—	STL	A	Waiver price

Gary Beare

Date	Traded To		Traded With	Traded By		In Exchange For
Mar. 28, 1979	PHI	N	—	MIL	A	Danny Boitano

Kevin Bearse

Date	Traded To		Traded With	Traded By		In Exchange For
Sept. 4, 1990	MON	N	—	CLE	A	Waiver price

Jim Beattie

Date	Traded To		Traded With	Traded By		In Exchange For
Nov. 1, 1979	SEA	A	Rick Anderson Juan Beniquez Jerry Narron	NY	A	Ruppert Jones Jim Lewis

Blaine Beatty

Date	Traded To		Traded With	Traded By		In Exchange For
Dec. 8, 1987	NY	N	Minor league P Greg Talamantez	BAL	A	Doug Sisk
Dec. 9, 1991	MON	N	—	NY	N	Jeff Barry

Jim Beauchamp

Date	Traded To		Traded With	Traded By		In Exchange For
Feb. 17, 1964	HOU	N	Chuck Taylor	STL	N	Carl Warwick
May 13, 1965	MIL	N	Ken Johnson	HOU	N	Lee Maye
Oct. 10, 1967	CIN	N	Mack Jones Jay Ritchie	ATL	N	Deron Johnson
June 13, 1970	STL	N	Leon McFadden	HOU	N	George Culver
Oct. 18, 1971	NY	N	—	STL	N	*see Jim Bibby*

Ginger Beaumont

Date	Traded To		Traded With	Traded By		In Exchange For
Dec. 1906	BOS	N	Claude Ritchey Patsy Flaherty	PIT	N	Ed Abbaticchio
Feb. 1910	CHI	N	—	BOS	N	Fred Liese

Johnny Beazley

Date	Traded To		Traded With	Traded By		In Exchange For
Apr. 18, 1947	BOS	N	—	STL	N	Cash

Clyde Beck

Date	Traded To		Traded With	Traded By		In Exchange For
Jan. 1931	CIN	N	—	CHI	N	Waiver price

Fred Beck

Date	Traded To		Traded With	Traded By		In Exchange For
Mar. 1911	CIN	N	—	BOS	N	Cash
July 15, 1911	PHI	N	Bill Burns	CIN	N	Bert Humphries

Heinie Beckendorf

Date	Traded To		Traded With	Traded By		In Exchange For
Apr. 1910	WAS	A	—	DET	A	Cash

Beals Becker

Date	Traded To		Traded With	Traded By		In Exchange For
June 1908	BOS	N	—	PIT	N	Cash
Dec. 1909	NY	N	—	BOS	N	Buck Herzog
June 5, 1913	PHI	N	Josh Devore	CIN	N	John Dodge Red Nelson

Heinz Becker

Date	Traded To		Traded With	Traded By		In Exchange For
May 1946	CLE	A	—	CHI	N	Mickey Rocco

Glenn Beckert

Date	Traded To		Traded With	Traded By		In Exchange For
Nov. 7, 1973	SD	N	Bobby Fenwick	CHI	N	Jerry Morales

Jake Beckley

Date	Traded To		Traded With	Traded By		In Exchange For
Feb. 1904	STL	N	—	CIN	N	Cash

Joe Beckwith

Date	Traded To		Traded With	Traded By		In Exchange For
Dec. 7, 1983	KC	A	—	LA	N	Minor leaguers C Joe Szekeley P Jose Torres and P John Serritella

Steve Bedrosian

Date	Traded To		Traded With	Traded By		In Exchange For
Dec. 10, 1985	PHI	N	Milt Thompson	ATL	N	Ozzie Virgil Pete Smith
June 18, 1989	SF	N	Rick Parker	PHI	N	Dennis Cook Terry Mulholland Charlie Hayes
Dec. 5, 1990	MIN	A	—	SF	N	Minor league P Johnny Ard Player to be named

(San Francisco received P Jimmy Williams on December 18, 1990.)

Fred Beebe

Date	Traded To		Traded With	Traded By		In Exchange For
July 1, 1906	STL	N	Pete Noonan Cash	CHI	N	Jack Taylor
Feb. 1910	CIN	N	Alan Storke	STL	N	Miller Huggins Rebel Oakes Frank Corridon
Feb. 1911	PHI	N	*see Dode Paskert*	CIN	N	—

Fred Beene

Date	Traded To		Traded With	Traded By		In Exchange For
Dec. 1, 1970	SD	N	—	BAL	A	*see Pat Dobson*
Apr. 27, 1974	CLE	A	—	NY	A	*see Chris Chambliss*

Joe Beggs

Date	Traded To		Traded With	Traded By		In Exchange For
Jan. 4, 1940	CIN	N	—	NY	A	Lee Grissom
June 7, 1947	NY	N	—	CIN	N	Babe Young

Rick Behenna

Date	Traded To		Traded With	Traded By		In Exchange For
Aug. 28, 1983	CLE	A	Brett Butler Brook Jacoby $150,000.	ATL	N	Len Barker

(Cleveland received Butler and Jacoby on October 21, 1983.)

Mel Behney

Date	Traded To		Traded With	Traded By		In Exchange For
Mar. 27, 1973	BOS	A	—	CIN	N	Phil Gagliano Andy Kosco

Hank Behrman

Date	Traded To		Traded With	Traded By		In Exchange For
May 3, 1947	PIT	N	Kirby Higbe Cal McLish Gene Mauch Dixie Howell	BKN	N	Al Gionfriddo $100,000.
June 14, 1947	BKN	N	—	PIT	N	Cash
Feb. 26, 1949	NY	N	—	BKN	N	Cash

Mark Belanger

Date	Traded To		Traded With	Traded By		In Exchange For
Dec. 11, 1981	LA	N	—	BAL	A	No compensation (free agent signing)

Wayne Belardi

Date	Traded To		Traded With	Traded By		In Exchange For
June 9, 1954	DET	A	—	BKN	N	Charlie Kress Johnny Bucha Ernie Nevel Cash
Dec. 5, 1956	KC	A	*see Ned Garver*	DET	A	—
Feb. 19, 1957	NY	A	—	KC	A	*see Billy Hunter*

Tim Belcher

Date	Traded To		Traded With	Traded By		In Exchange For
Feb. 8, 1984	OAK	A	—	NY	A	
			(Claimed in compensation draft after Oakland lost free agent P Tom Underwood to Baltimore.)			
Aug. 29, 1987	LA	N	—	OAK	A	Rick Honeycutt
			(Los Angeles received Belcher on September 3, 1987.)			
Nov. 27, 1991	CIN	N	John Wetteland	LA	N	Eric Davis Kip Gross
July 31, 1993	CHI	A	—	CIN	N	Johnny Ruffin Jeff Pierce
May 15, 1995	SEA	A	—	CIN	N	Roger Salkeld

Stan Belinda

Date	Traded To		Traded With	Traded By		In Exchange For
July 31, 1993	KC	A	—	PIT	N	Dan Miceli Jon Lieber

Bo Belinsky

Date	Traded To		Traded With	Traded By		In Exchange For
Dec. 3, 1964	PHI	N	—	LA	A	Costen Shockley Rudy May

Beau Bell

Date	Traded To		Traded With	Traded By		In Exchange For
May 13, 1939	DET	A	Bobo Newsom Red Kress Jim Walkup	STL	A	Vern Kennedy Bob Harris George Gill Roxie Lawson Chet Laabs Mark Christman
Jan. 20, 1940	CLE	A	—	DET	A	Bruce Campbell

Buddy Bell

Date	Traded To		Traded With	Traded By		In Exchange For
Dec. 8, 1978	TEX	A	—	CLE	A	Toby Harrah
July 19, 1985	CIN	N	—	TEX	A	Jeff Russell Duane Walker
June 19, 1988	HOU	N	—	CIN	N	player to be named

(Cincinnati received P Carl Grovam on October 20, 1988.)

David Bell

Date	Traded To		Traded With	Traded By		In Exchange For
July 27, 1995	STL	N	Minor league P Rick Heiserman Minor league C Pepe McNeal	CLE	A	Ken Hill

Derek Bell

Date	Traded To		Traded With	Traded By		In Exchange For
Mar. 30, 1993	SD	N	Minor league OF Stoney Briggs	TOR	A	Darrin Jackson

Derek Bell *continued*

Date	Traded To		Traded With	Traded By		In Exchange For
Dec. 28, 1994	HOU	N	Phil Plantier Pedro Martinez Doug Brocail Craig Shipley Ricky Gutierrez	SD	N	Ken Caminiti Steve Finley Andujar Cedeno Brian Williams Roberto Petagine Player to be named

(San Diego received P Sean Fesh on May 1, 1995.)

Gary Bell

Date	Traded To		Traded With	Traded By		In Exchange For
June 4, 1967	BOS	A	—	CLE	A	Tony Horton Don Demeter
June 8, 1969	CHI	A	—	SEA	A	Bob Locker

George Bell

Date	Traded To		Traded With	Traded By		In Exchange For
Dec. 6, 1990	CHI	N	—	TOR	A	No compensation (free agent signing)
Mar. 30, 1992	CHI	A	—	CHI	N	Sammy Sosa Ken Patterson

Gus Bell

Date	Traded To		Traded With	Traded By		In Exchange For
Oct. 14, 1952	CIN	N	—	PIT	N	Cal Abrams Joe Rossi Gail Henley
Nov. 28, 1961	MIL	N	Cash	NY	N	Frank Thomas

(Milwaukee received Bell on May 21, 1962.)

Jay Bell

Date	Traded To		Traded With	Traded By		In Exchange For
Aug. 1, 1985	CLE	A	Jim Weaver Curt Wardle Rich Yett	MIN	A	Bert Blyleven
			(Cleveland received Yett on September 17, 1985.)			
Mar. 25, 1989	PIT	N	—	CLE	A	Felix Fermin Denny Gonzalez

(Completion of deal in which Cleveland acquired Gonzalez on November 28, 1988 for a player to be named.)

Juan Bell

Date	Traded To		Traded With	Traded By		In Exchange For
Dec. 4, 1988	BAL	A	Brian Holton Ken Howell	LA	N	Eddie Murray
Aug. 11, 1992	PHI	N	—	BAL	A	Steve Scarsone
June 1, 1993	MIL	A	—	PHI	N	Waiver price

Kevin Bell

Date	Traded To		Traded With	Traded By		In Exchange For
Mar. 27, 1981	OAK	A	Tony Phillips minor league P Eric Mustard	SD	N	Bob Lacey minor league P Ray Moretti

Les Bell

Date	Traded To		Traded With	Traded By		In Exchange For
Mar. 25, 1928	BOS	N	—	STL	N	Andy High $25,000.
Oct. 29, 1929	CHI	N	—	BOS	N	Waiver price

Terry Bell

Date	Traded To		Traded With	Traded By		In Exchange For
May 21, 1986	KC	A	—	SEA	A	Mark Huismann
Aug. 31, 1987	ATL	N	—	KC	A	Gene Garber

(Atlanta received Bell on September 3, 1987.)

Zeke Bella

Date	Traded To		Traded With	Traded By		In Exchange For
Aug. 22, 1958	KC	A	Cash	NY	A	Murry Dickson

Rafael Belliard

Date	Traded To		Traded With	Traded By		In Exchange For
Dec. 18, 1990	ATL	N	—	PIT	N	No compensation (free agent signing)

Rob Belloir

Date	Traded To		Traded With	Traded By		In Exchange For
June 7, 1975	ATL	N	Blue Moon Odom	CLE	A	Roric Harrison

Esteban Beltre

Date	Traded To		Traded With	Traded By		In Exchange For
May 23, 1991	CHI	A	—	MIL	A	John Cangelosi
Mar. 28, 1994	TEX	A	—	CHI	A	Minor league P Scott Eyre

Freddie Benavides

Date	Traded To		Traded With	Traded By		In Exchange For
Jan. 7, 1994	MON	N	—	CLR	N	Minor league Ps Ivan Arteaga and Rodney Pedraza

Chief Bender

Date	Traded To		Traded With	Traded By		In Exchange For
Feb. 10, 1916	PHI	N	—	BAL	F	Cash

Andy Benes

Date	Traded To		Traded With	Traded By		In Exchange For
July 31, 1995	SEA	A	Player to be named	SD	N	Ron Villone Marc Newfield

(Seattle received P Greg Keagle on September 16, 1995.)

Date	Traded To		Traded With	Traded By		In Exchange For
Dec. 23, 1995	STL	N	—	SEA	A	No compensation (free agent signing)

Ray Benge

Date	Traded To		Traded With	Traded By		In Exchange For
Dec. 15, 1932	BKN	N	$15,000.	PHI	N	Cy Moore Mickey Finn Jack Warner
Dec. 12, 1935	BOS	N	Tony Cuccinello Al Lopez Bobby Reis	BKN	N	Ed Brandt Randy Moore
Aug. 4, 1936	PHI	N	—	BOS	N	Fabian Kowalik

Juan Beniquez

Date	Traded To		Traded With	Traded By		In Exchange For
Nov. 17, 1975	TEX	A	Steve Barr Craig Skok	BOS	A	Ferguson Jenkins
Nov. 10, 1978	NY	A	*see Dave Righetti*	TEX	A	—
Nov. 1, 1979	SEA	A	Jim Beattie Rick Anderson Jerry Narron	NY	A	Ruppert Jones Jim Lewis
Dec. 29, 1980	CAL	A	—	SEA	A	No compensation (free agent signing)
Jan. 28, 1986	BAL	A	—	CAL	A	No compensation (free agent signing)
Dec. 17, 1986	KC	A	—	BAL	A	Minor league SS Joe Jarrell Minor league P Jimmy Daniels
July 14, 1987	TOR	A	—	KC	A	Luis Aquino

Mike Benjamin

Date	Traded To		Traded With	Traded By		In Exchange For
June 10, 1995	PHI	N	—	SF	N	Jeff Juden Minor league C-1B Tommy Eason

Dennis Bennett

Date	Traded To		Traded With	Traded By		In Exchange For
Nov. 29, 1964	BOS	A	—	PHI	N	Dick Stuart
June 24, 1967	NY	N	—	BOS	A	Al Yates Cash

Joe Bennett

Date	Traded To		Traded With	Traded By		In Exchange For
May 1921	STL	A	—	CHI	A	Cash

Jack Bentley

Date	Traded To		Traded With	Traded By		In Exchange For
Dec. 30, 1925	PHI	N	Wayland Dean	NY	N	Jimmy Ring
Sept. 15, 1926	NY	N	—	PHI	N	Waiver price

Al Benton

Date	Traded To		Traded With	Traded By		In Exchange For
Jan. 1938	DET	A	—	PHI	A	Cash
Apr. 20, 1949	CLE	A	—	DET	A	Cash

Butch Benton

Date	Traded To		Traded With	Traded By		In Exchange For
Apr. 6, 1981	CHI	N	—	NY	N	Cash

Larry Benton

Date	Traded To		Traded With	Traded By		In Exchange For
July 30, 1922	BOS	N	Fred Toney $100,000.	NY	N	Hugh McQuillan

(Toney refused to report and remained Giants' property.)

Date	Traded To		Traded With	Traded By		In Exchange For
June 12, 1927	NY	N	Zack Taylor Herb Thomas	BOS	N	Hugh McQuillan Kent Greenfield Doc Farrell

Larry Benton *continued*

Date	Traded To		Traded With	Traded By		In Exchange For
May 21, 1930	CIN	N	—	NY	N	Hughie Critz

Rube Benton

Date	Traded To		Traded With	Traded By		In Exchange For
Aug. 19, 1915	NY	N	—	CIN	N	$3,000.
July 30, 1922	CIN	N	—	NY	N	Cash

Todd Benzinger

Date	Traded To		Traded With	Traded By		In Exchange For
Dec. 13, 1988	CIN	N	Jeff Sellers player to be named	BOS	A	Nick Esasky Rob Murphy

(Cincinnati received P Luis Vasquez on January 12, 1989.)

Date	Traded To		Traded With	Traded By		In Exchange For
July 11, 1991	KC	A	—	CIN	N	Carmelo Martinez
Dec. 11, 1991	LA	N	—	KC	A	Chris Gwynn Minor league 2B Domingo Mota
Jan. 14, 1993	SF	N	—	LA	N	No compensation (free agent signing)

Johnny Berardino

Date	Traded To		Traded With	Traded By		In Exchange For
Nov. 22, 1947	WAS	A	—	STL	A	Gerry Priddy

(Berardino announced his retirement to go into movies. Commissioner Chandler cancelled the trade. Berardino then unretired.)

Date	Traded To		Traded With	Traded By		In Exchange For
Dec. 9, 1947	CLE	A	—	STL	A	Catfish Metkovich $50,000.

(Metkovich was returned to Cleveland because of a broken finger and the St. Louis Browns received another $15,000 to complete the trade.)

Date	Traded To		Traded With	Traded By		In Exchange For
Aug. 18, 1952	PIT	N	minor league P Charlie Sipple $50,000.	CLE	A	George Strickland Ted Wilks

Lou Berberet

Date	Traded To		Traded With	Traded By		In Exchange For
Feb. 8, 1956	WAS	A	*see Whitey Herzog*	NY	A	—
May 1, 1958	BOS	A	—	WAS	A	Ken Aspromonte
Dec. 2, 1958	DET	A	—	BOS	A	Herb Moford

Juan Berenguer

Date	Traded To		Traded With	Traded By		In Exchange For
Mar. 31, 1981	KC	A	—	NY	N	Marvell Wynne minor league P John Skinner
Aug. 8, 1981	TOR	A	—	KC	A	Cash
Oct. 7, 1985	SF	N	Bob Melvin Scott Medvin	DET	A	Dave LaPoint Matt Nokes Eric King

(San Francisco received Medvin on Dec. 11, 1985.)

Date	Traded To		Traded With	Traded By		In Exchange For
Jan. 11, 1987	MIN	A	—	SF	N	No compensation (free agent signing)
Jan. 29, 1991	ATL	N	—	MIN	A	No compensation (free agent signing)
July 21, 1992	KC	A	—	ATL	N	Mark Davis

Bruce Berenyi

Date	Traded To		Traded With	Traded By		In Exchange For
June 15, 1984	NY	N	—	CIN	N	Jay Tibbs Eddie Williams Minor league P Matt Bullinger

Moe Berg

Date	Traded To		Traded With	Traded By		In Exchange For
Aug. 1925	CHI	A	—	BKN	N	Cash
Apr. 2, 1931	CLE	A	—	CHI	A	Waiver price

Bill Bergen

Date	Traded To		Traded With	Traded By		In Exchange For
Feb. 1904	BKN	N	—	CIN	N	Cash

Boze Berger

Date	Traded To		Traded With	Traded By		In Exchange For
Apr. 1937	CHI	A	—	CLE	A	Cash
Dec. 21, 1938	BOS	A	—	CHI	A	Eric McNair
Dec. 26, 1939	BKN	N	—	BOS	A	Waiver price

Wally Berger

Date	Traded To		Traded With	Traded By		In Exchange For
June 15, 1937	NY	N	—	BOS	N	Frank Gabler $35,000.
June 6, 1938	CIN	N	—	NY	N	Alex Kampouris

Dave Bergman

Date	Traded To		Traded With	Traded By		In Exchange For
June 15, 1977	HOU	N	Randy Niemann Mike Fischlin	NY	A	Cliff Johnson

(Houston received Bergman on November 23.)

Dave Bergman *continued*

Date	Traded To	Traded With	Traded By	In Exchange For
Apr. 20, 1981	SF N	Jeffrey Leonard	HOU N	Mike Ivie
Mar. 24, 1984	PHI N	—	SF N	Alejandro Sanchez
Mar. 24, 1984	DET A	Guillermo Hernandez	PHI N	John Wockenfuss Glenn Wilson

Dwight Bernard

Date	Traded To	Traded With	Traded By	In Exchange For
Oct. 26, 1979	MIL A	—	NY N	Mark Bomback

Tony Bernazard

Date	Traded To	Traded With	Traded By	In Exchange For
Dec. 12, 1980	CHI A	—	MON N	Rich Wortham
June 15, 1983	SEA A	—	CHI A	Julio Cruz
Dec. 7, 1983	CLE A	—	SEA A	Gorman Thomas Jack Perconte
July 15, 1987	OAK A	—	CLE A	Darrel Akerfelds Brian Dorsett

Bill Bernhard

Date	Traded To	Traded With	Traded By	In Exchange For
June 1902	CLE A	—	PHI A	Ossee Schreckengost Frank Bonner

Juan Bernhardt

Date	Traded To	Traded With	Traded By	In Exchange For
July 6, 1979	CHI A	—	SEA A	Rich Hinton

Dale Berra

Date	Traded To	Traded With	Traded By	In Exchange For
Dec. 20, 1984	NY A	Jay Buhner	PIT N	Steve Kemp Tim Foli $400,000.

Ray Berres

Date	Traded To	Traded With	Traded By	In Exchange For
June 14, 1940	BOS N	$40,000.	PIT N	Al Lopez
Feb. 6, 1942	NY N	—	BOS N	Cash

Charlie Berry

Date	Traded To	Traded With	Traded By	In Exchange For
Apr. 29, 1932	CHI A	—	BOS A	Bennie Tate Smead Jolley Cliff Watwood
Dec. 12, 1933	PHI A	$20,000.	CHI A	George Earnshaw Johnny Pasek

Joe Berry

Date	Traded To	Traded With	Traded By	In Exchange For
May 1946	CLE A	—	PHI A	Cash

Ken Berry

Date	Traded To	Traded With	Traded By	In Exchange For
Nov. 30, 1970	CAL A	Syd O'Brien Billy Wynne	CHI A	Jay Johnstone Tom Egan Tom Bradley
Oct. 22, 1973	MIL A	Clyde Wright Steve Barber Art Kusnyer Cash	CAL A	Ellie Rodriguez Skip Lockwood Gary Ryerson Ollie Brown Joe Lahoud

Neil Berry

Date	Traded To	Traded With	Traded By	In Exchange For
Oct. 27, 1952	STL A	Cliff Mapes $25,000.	DET A	Rufus Crawford
Sept. 1, 1953	CHI A	—	STL A	Waiver price
Feb. 5, 1954	BAL A	Sam Mele	CHI A	Johnny Groth Johnny Lipon

Sean Berry

Date	Traded To	Traded With	Traded By	In Exchange For
Aug. 29, 1992	MON N	Archie Corbin	KC A	Bill Sampen Chris Haney
Dec. 20, 1995	HOU N	—	MON N	David Veres Minor league C Raul Chavez

Damon Berryhill

Date	Traded To	Traded With	Traded By	In Exchange For
Sept. 29, 1991	ATL N	Mike Bielecki	CHI N	Yorkis Perez Turk Wendell
Feb. 1, 1994	BOS A	—	ATL N	No compensation (free agent signing)
Nov. 8, 1994	CIN N	—	BOS A	No compensation (free agent signing)

Frank Bertaina

Date	Traded To	Traded With	Traded By	In Exchange For
May 29, 1967	WAS A	Mike Epstein	BAL A	Pete Richert
June 16, 1969	BAL A	—	WAS A	Minor league P Paul Campbell
Aug. 14, 1970	STL N	—	BAL A	Cash

Dick Bertell

Date	Traded To	Traded With	Traded By	In Exchange For
May 29, 1965	SF N	Len Gabrielson	CHI N	Harvey Kuenn Ed Bailey Bob Hendley

Reno Bertoia

Date	Traded To	Traded With	Traded By	In Exchange For
Dec. 6, 1958	WAS A	—	DET A	*see Eddie Yost*
June 1, 1961	KC A	Paul Giel	MIN A	Bill Tuttle
Aug. 2, 1961	DET A	Gerry Staley	KC A	Ozzie Virgil Bill Fischer

(Giel was returned to Minnesota for a cash payment.)

Andres Berumen

Date	Traded To	Traded With	Traded By	In Exchange For
June 24, 1993	SD N	—	FLA N	*see Gary Sheffield*

Bob Bescher

Date	Traded To	Traded With	Traded By	In Exchange For
Dec. 12, 1913	NY N	—	CIN N	Buck Herzog Grover Hartley

(Hartley jumped to the Federal League and Herzog was made Cincinnati manager.)

Karl Best

Date	Traded To	Traded With	Traded By	In Exchange For
June 22, 1987	DET A	—	SEA A	Bryan Kelly
Mar. 28, 1988	MIN A	—	DET A	Don Schulze
Aug. 12, 1988	SF N	—	MIN A	Minor league OF Alan Cockrell

Kurt Bevacqua

Date	Traded To	Traded With	Traded By	In Exchange For
May 8, 1971	CLE A	—	CIN N	Buddy Bradford
Nov. 2, 1972	KC A	—	CLE A	Mike Hedlund
Dec. 4, 1973	PIT N	Ed Kirkpatrick minor league 1B Winston Cole	KC A	Nellie Briles Fernando Gonzalez
July 8, 1974	KC A	—	PIT N	Minor league IF Cal Meier Cash
Mar. 6, 1975	MIL A	—	KC A	Cash
Oct. 22, 1976	SEA A	—	MIL A	Cash
Oct. 25, 1978	SD N	Mike Hargrove Bill Fahey	TEX A	Oscar Gamble Dave Roberts $300,000.
Aug. 5, 1980	PIT N	Mark Lee	SD N	Rick Lancellotti Luis Salazar

Hal Bevan

Date	Traded To	Traded With	Traded By	In Exchange For
May 3, 1952	PHI A	—	BOS A	Waiver price

Bill Bevens

Date	Traded To	Traded With	Traded By	In Exchange For
Jan. 17, 1949	CHI A	—	NY A	Cash

(Bevens was returned to New York Yankees on March 28, 1949.)

Monte Beville

Date	Traded To	Traded With	Traded By	In Exchange For
July 25, 1904	DET A	—	NY A	Frank McManus

Buddy Biancalana

Date	Traded To	Traded With	Traded By	In Exchange For
July 30, 1987	HOU N	—	KC A	Mel Stottlemyre

Jim Bibby

Date	Traded To	Traded With	Traded By	In Exchange For
Oct. 18, 1971	STL N	Art Shamsky Rich Folkers Charles Hudson	NY N	Jim Beauchamp Chuck Taylor Harry Parker Tom Coulter
June 6, 1973	TEX A	—	STL N	Mike Nagy John Wockenfuss

Jim Bibby *continued*

Date	Traded To	Traded With	Traded By	In Exchange For
June 13, 1975	CLE A	Jackie Brown Rick Waits $100,000.	TEX A	Gaylord Perry
Mar. 15, 1978	PIT N	—	CLE A	No compensation (free agent signing)
Feb. 7, 1984	TEX A	—	PIT N	No compensation (free agent signing)

Dante Bichette

Date	Traded To	Traded With	Traded By	In Exchange For
Mar. 14, 1991	MIL A	—	CAL A	Dave Parker
Nov. 17, 1992	CLR N	—	MIL A	Kevin Reimer

Vern Bickford

Date	Traded To	Traded With	Traded By	In Exchange For
Feb. 10, 1954	BAL A	—	MIL N	Charlie White $10,000.

Mike Bielecki

Date	Traded To	Traded With	Traded By	In Exchange For
Mar. 31, 1988	CHI N	—	PIT N	Minor league P Mike Curtis
Sept. 29, 1991	ATL N	Damon Berryhill	CHI N	Yorkis Perez Turk Wendell

Elliott Bigelow

Date	Traded To	Traded With	Traded By	In Exchange For
Dec. 15, 1928	BOS A	Milt Gaston Hod Lisenbee Bobby Reeves Grant Gillis	WAS A	Buddy Myer

Larry Biittner

Date	Traded To	Traded With	Traded By	In Exchange For
Dec. 20, 1973	MON N	—	TEX A	Pat Jarvis
May 17, 1976	CHI N	Steve Renko	MON N	Andre Thornton
Jan. 8, 1981	CIN N	—	CHI N	No compensation (free agent signing)

Dann Bilardello

Date	Traded To	Traded With	Traded By	In Exchange For
Dec. 19, 1985	MON N	—	CIN N	*see Bill Gullickson*
Mar. 20, 1987	PIT N	—	MON N	Cash
July 23, 1987	KC A	—	PIT N	Cash

Steve Bilko

Date	Traded To	Traded With	Traded By	In Exchange For
Apr. 30, 1954	CHI N	—	STL N	$12,500.
June 15, 1958	LA N	Johnny Klippstein	CIN N	Don Newcombe

Jack Billingham

Date	Traded To	Traded With	Traded By	In Exchange For
Jan. 22, 1969	HOU N	Jesus Alou Donn Clendenon Skip Guinn $100,000.	MON N	Rusty Staub

(Clendenon refused to report, and Houston sent Billingham, Guinn, and cash on April 8, 1969.)

Date	Traded To	Traded With	Traded By	In Exchange For
Nov. 29, 1971	CIN N	*see Joe Morgan*	HOU N	—
Mar. 6, 1978	DET A	—	CIN N	George Cappuzzello minor league OF John Valle
May 12, 1980	BOS A	—	DET A	Cash

Dick Billings

Date	Traded To	Traded With	Traded By	In Exchange For
Aug. 12, 1974	STL N	—	TEX A	Cash

Josh Billings

Date	Traded To	Traded With	Traded By	In Exchange For
Mar. 1919	STL A	—	CLE A	Les Nunamaker

George Binks

Date	Traded To	Traded With	Traded By	In Exchange For
Feb. 14, 1947	PHI A	—	WAS A	Lou Knerr
June 4, 1948	STL A	$20,000.	PHI A	Ray Coleman

Doug Bird

Date	Traded To	Traded With	Traded By	In Exchange For
Apr. 3, 1979	PHI N	—	KC A	Todd Cruz
June 12, 1981	CHI N	Mike Griffin $400,000.	NY A	Rick Reuschel
Dec. 10, 1982	BOS A	—	CHI N	Chuck Rainey

Ralph Birkofer

Date	Traded To	Traded With	Traded By	In Exchange For
Dec. 4, 1936	BKN N	Cookie Lavagetto	PIT N	Ed Brandt

Babe Birrer

Date	Traded To	Traded With	Traded By	In Exchange For
Apr. 5, 1956	BAL A	—	DET A	Waiver price

Tim Birtsas

Date	Traded To	Traded With	Traded By	In Exchange For
Dec. 8, 1984	OAK A	—	NY A	*see Rickey Henderson*
Dec. 8, 1987	CIN N	—	OAK A	*see Dave Parker*

John Bischoff

Date	Traded To	Traded With	Traded By	In Exchange For
July 11, 1925	BOS A	—	CHI A	Cash

Max Bishop

Date	Traded To	Traded With	Traded By	In Exchange For
Dec. 12, 1933	BOS A	Lefty Grove Rube Walberg	PHI A	Bob Kline Rabbit Warstler $125,000.

Rivington Bisland

Date	Traded To	Traded With	Traded By	In Exchange For
Mar. 1913	STL A	—	PIT N	Waiver price

Hi Bithorn

Date	Traded To	Traded With	Traded By	In Exchange For
Jan. 25, 1947	PIT N	—	CHI N	Cash
Mar. 22, 1947	CHI A	—	PIT N	Waiver price

Joe Bitker

Date	Traded To	Traded With	Traded By	In Exchange For
Aug. 29, 1990	TEX A	Scott Chiamparino	OAK A	Harold Baines

(Texas received Bitker and Chiamparino on September 4, 1990.)

Jeff Bittiger

Date	Traded To	Traded With	Traded By	In Exchange For
Jan. 16, 1986	PHI N	*see Ronn Reynolds*	NY N	—
Nov. 9, 1989	LA N	—	CHI A	Tracy Woodson

George Bjorkman

Date	Traded To	Traded With	Traded By	In Exchange For
Mar. 16, 1983	HOU N	—	STL N	Minor league P Jeff Meadows
Feb. 24, 1984	MON N	—	HOU N	Tom Wieghaus

(Montreal received Bjorkman on March 26, 1984.)

Bill Black

Date	Traded To	Traded With	Traded By	In Exchange For
Aug. 14, 1952	DET A	—	STL A	*see Vic Wertz*

Bud Black

Date	Traded To	Traded With	Traded By	In Exchange For
Oct. 23, 1981	KC A	—	SEA A	Manny Castillo
June 3, 1988	CLE A	—	KC A	Pat Tabler
Sept. 16, 1990	TOR A	—	CLE A	Mauro Gozzo Steve Cummings Alex Sanchez

(Cleveland received Cummings on September 21 and Sanchez on September 24, 1990.)

Date	Traded To	Traded With	Traded By	In Exchange For
Nov. 9, 1990	SF N	—	TOR A	No compensation (free agent signing)

Don Black

Date	Traded To	Traded With	Traded By	In Exchange For
Oct. 2, 1945	CLE A	—	PHI A	Cash

Joe Black

Date	Traded To	Traded With	Traded By	In Exchange For
June 9, 1955	CIN N	—	BKN N	Bob Borkowski Cash

Earl Blackburn

Date	Traded To	Traded With	Traded By	In Exchange For
June 1912	CIN N	—	PIT N	Cash

Lena Blackburne

Date	Traded To	Traded With	Traded By	In Exchange For
Feb. 1919	BOS N	—	CIN N	Wally Rehg
July 9, 1919	PHI N	—	BOS N	Cash

Ewell Blackwell

Date	Traded To	Traded With	Traded By	In Exchange For
Aug. 28, 1952	NY A	—	CIN N	Jim Greengrass Johnny Schmitz Ernie Nevel Bob Marquis $35,000.

Ewell Blackwell *continued*

Date	Traded To	Traded With	Traded By	In Exchange For
Mar. 30, 1955	KC A	Dick Kryhoski Tom Gorman	NY A	$50,000.

Tim Blackwell

Date	Traded To	Traded With	Traded By	In Exchange For
Apr. 19, 1976	PHI N	—	BOS A	Cash
June 15, 1977	MON N	Wayne Twitchell	PHI N	Barry Foote Dan Warthen
Jan. 14, 1982	MON N	—	CHI N	No compensation (free agent signing)

Rick Bladt

Date	Traded To	Traded With	Traded By	In Exchange For
Jan. 20, 1977	BAL A	Elliott Maddox	NY A	Paul Blair

George Blaeholder

Date	Traded To	Traded With	Traded By	In Exchange For
May 21, 1935	PHI A	—	STL A	Ed Coleman Sugar Cain
Jan. 27, 1936	CLE A	—	PHI A	Waiver price

Dennis Blair

Date	Traded To	Traded With	Traded By	In Exchange For
July 14, 1977	BAL A	—	MON N	Fred Holdsworth

Paul Blair

Date	Traded To	Traded With	Traded By	In Exchange For
Jan. 20, 1977	NY A	—	BAL A	Elliott Maddox Rick Bladt

Willie Blair

Date	Traded To	Traded With	Traded By	In Exchange For
Nov. 6, 1990	CLE A	—	TOR A	Alex Sanchez
Dec. 10, 1991	HOU N	Eddie Taubensee	CLE A	Kenny Lofton Dave Rohde

Sheriff Blake

Date	Traded To	Traded With	Traded By	In Exchange For
July 27, 1931	PHI N	—	CHI N	Waiver price

Johnny Blanchard

Date	Traded To	Traded With	Traded By	In Exchange For
May 3, 1965	KC A	Rollie Sheldon	NY A	Doc Edwards
Sept. 9, 1965	MIL N	—	KC A	Cash

Gil Blanco

Date	Traded To	Traded With	Traded By	In Exchange For
June 10, 1966	KC A	Roger Repoz Bill Stafford	NY A	Fred Talbot Billy Bryan

Ossie Blanco

Date	Traded To	Traded With	Traded By	In Exchange For
Nov. 30, 1970	CHI N	Jose Ortiz	CHI A	Pat Jacquez Dave Lemonds Roe Skidmore

Kevin Blankenship

Date	Traded To	Traded With	Traded By	In Exchange For
Sept. 29, 1988	CHI N	—	ATL N	*see Jody Davis*

Larvell Blanks

Date	Traded To	Traded With	Traded By	In Exchange For
Dec. 12, 1975	CHI A	Ralph Garr	ATL N	Ken Henderson Dick Ruthven Danny Osborn
Dec. 12, 1975	CLE A	—	CHI A	Jack Brohamer
Oct. 3, 1978	TEX A	Jim Kern	CLE A	Bobby Bonds Len Barker
Dec. 6, 1979	ATL N	Doyle Alexander $50,000.	TEX A	Adrian Devine Pepe Frias

Don Blasingame

Date	Traded To	Traded With	Traded By	In Exchange For
Dec. 15, 1959	SF N	—	STL N	Daryl Spencer Leon Wagner
Apr. 27, 1961	CIN N	Bob Schmidt Sherman Jones	SF N	Ed Bailey
July 1, 1963	WAS A	—	CIN N	Cash
Aug. 22, 1966	KC A	—	WAS A	Cash

Wade Blasingame

Date	Traded To	Traded With	Traded By	In Exchange For
June 15, 1967	HOU N	—	ATL N	Claude Raymond
June 6, 1972	NY A	—	HOU N	Cash

Steve Blateric

Date	Traded To	Traded With	Traded By	In Exchange For
Sept. 16, 1972	NY A	—	CIN N	Cash
Dec. 12, 1973	CLE A	—	CIN N	Roger Freed

Johnny Blatnik

Date	Traded To	Traded With	Traded By	In Exchange For
Apr. 27, 1950	STL N	—	PHI N	Ken Johnson

Gary Blaylock

Date	Traded To	Traded With	Traded By	In Exchange For
July 26, 1959	NY A	—	STL N	Waiver price

Curt Blefary

Date	Traded To	Traded With	Traded By	In Exchange For
Dec. 4, 1968	HOU N	Minor leaguer John Mason	BAL A	Mike Cuellar Enzo Hernandez Minor League IF Elijah Johnson
Dec. 4, 1969	NY A	—	HOU N	Joe Pepitone
May 26, 1971	OAK A	—	NY A	Rob Gardner
May 17, 1972	SD N	Mike Kilkenny minor league OF Greg Schubert	OAK A	Ollie Brown

Terry Blocker

Date	Traded To	Traded With	Traded By	In Exchange For
Nov. 11, 1987	ATL N	—	NY N	Kevin Brown

(New York received Brown on December 8, 1987.)

Ron Blomberg

Date	Traded To	Traded With	Traded By	In Exchange For
Nov. 17, 1977	CHI A	—	NY A	No compensation (free agent signing)

Jimmy Bloodworth

Date	Traded To	Traded With	Traded By	In Exchange For
Dec. 12, 1941	DET A	Doc Cramer	WAS A	Frank Croucher Bruce Campbell
Dec. 12, 1946	PIT N	—	DET A	Cash
May 10, 1950	PHI N	—	CIN N	Cash

Mike Blowers

Date	Traded To	Traded With	Traded By	In Exchange For
Aug. 29, 1989	NY A	—	MON N	John Candelaria
May 17, 1991	SEA A	—	NY A	Player to be named

(New York received P Jim Blueberg on June 22, 1991.)

Date	Traded To	Traded With	Traded By	In Exchange For
Nov. 29, 1995	LA N	—	SEA A	Minor league 2B Miguel Cairo Minor league 3B Willie Otanez

Bert Blue

Date	Traded To	Traded With	Traded By	In Exchange For
July 1908	PHI A	—	STL A	Syd Smith

Lu Blue

Date	Traded To	Traded With	Traded By	In Exchange For
Dec. 2, 1927	STL A	Heinie Manush	DET A	Chick Galloway Elam Vangilder Harry Rice
Apr. 3, 1931	CHI A	—	STL A	$15,000.

Vida Blue

Date	Traded To	Traded With	Traded By	In Exchange For
Mar. 15, 1978	SF N	—	OAK A	Gary Alexander Gary Thomasson Dave Heaverlo Alan Wirth John Henry Johnson Phil Huffman Mario Guerrero $390,000.
Mar. 30, 1982	KC A	Bob Tufts	SF N	Renie Martin Craig Chamberlain Atlee Hammaker Brad Wellman
Jan. 20, 1987	OAK A	—	SF N	No compensation (free agent signing)

Date	Traded To		Traded With	Traded By		In Exchange For
Otto Bluege						
Dec. 20, 1933	PHI	N	Irv Jeffries	CIN	N	Mark Koenig
Jim Bluejacket						
Feb. 10, 1916	CIN	N	—	BKN	F	Cash
Bert Blyleven						
June 1, 1976	TEX	A	Danny Thompson	MIN	A	Bill Singer Roy Smalley Mike Cubbage Jim Gideon $250,000.
Dec. 8, 1977	PIT	N	John Milner	TEX	A	Al Oliver Nelson Norman
(Part of four-team trade involving Texas, New York Mets, Pittsburgh, and Atlanta.)						
Dec. 9, 1980	CLE	A	Manny Sanguillen	PIT	N	Gary Alexander Victor Cruz Rafael Vasquez Bob Owchinko
Aug. 1, 1985	MIN	A	—	CLE	A	Jim Weaver Jay Bell Curt Wardle Rich Yett
(Cleveland received Yett on September 17, 1985.)						
Nov. 3, 1988	CAL	A	Minor league P Kevin Trudeau	MIN	A	Mike Cook Paul Sorrento Minor league P Rob Wassenaar
Mike Blyzka						
Dec. 1, 1954	NY	A	*see Dick Kryhoski*	BAL	A	—
Randy Bobb						
Mar. 29, 1970	NY	N	—	CHI	N	J. C. Martin
John Boccabella						
Apr. 1, 1974	SF	N	—	MON	N	Don Carrithers
Bruce Bochte						
May 11, 1977	CLE	A	Sid Monge $250,000.	CAL	A	Dave LaRoche Dave Schuler
Dec. 20, 1977	SEA	A	—	CLE	A	No compensation (free agent signing)
Doug Bochtler						
July 26, 1993	SD	N	—	CLR	N	*see Bruce Hurst*
Bruce Bochy						
Feb. 11, 1981	NY	N	—	HOU	N	Minor leaguers C Stan Hough and IF Randy Rogers
Eddie Bockman						
Oct. 19, 1946	CLE	A	Joe Gordon	NY	A	Allie Reynolds
Jan. 16, 1948	PIT	N	—	CLE	A	Cash
Mike Boddicker						
July 29, 1988	BOS	A	—	BAL	A	Brady Anderson Curt Schilling
Nov. 21, 1990	KC	A	—	BOS	A	No compensation (free agent signing)
Apr. 26, 1993	MIL	A	—	KC	A	Cash
Ping Bodie						
Mar. 8, 1918	NY	A	—	PHI	A	George Burns
Tony Boeckel						
June 12, 1919	BOS	N	—	PIT	N	Waiver price
Joe Boehling						
Aug. 18, 1916	CLE	A	Danny Moeller	WAS	A	Elmer Smith Joe Leonard
Len Boehmer						
Sept. 18, 1967	NY	A	—	CIN	N	Bill Henry

Date	Traded To		Traded With	Traded By		In Exchange For
Brian Boehringer						
Mar. 21, 1994	NY	A	—	CHI	A	Paul Assenmacher
Joe Boever						
July 23, 1987	ATL	N	—	STL	N	Randy O'Neal
July 23, 1990	PHI	N	—	ATL	N	Marvin Freeman
Jan. 21, 1993	OAK	A	—	HOU	N	No compensation (free agent signing)
Tommy Boggs						
Dec. 8, 1977	ATL	N	Adrian Devine Eddie Miller	TEX	A	Willie Montanez
(Part of four-team trade involving Texas, Atlanta, Pittsburgh, and New York Mets.)						
Wade Boggs						
Dec. 15, 1992	NY	A	—	BOS	A	No compensation (free agent signing)
Pat Bohen						
Jan. 1914	PIT	N	—	PHI	A	Waiver price
Sammy Bohne						
June 15, 1926	BKN	N	—	CIN	N	Cash
Danny Boitano						
Mar. 28, 1979	MIL	A	—	PHI	N	Gary Beare
Apr. 5, 1981	NY	N	—	MIL	A	Cash
Dec. 11, 1981	TEX	A	Doug Flynn	NY	N	Jim Kern
Bob Boken						
May 12, 1934	CHI	A	—	WAS	A	Red Kress
Joe Boley						
June 6, 1932	CLE	A	—	PHI	A	Cash
Jim Bolger						
Oct. 1, 1954	CHI	N	Ted Tappe Harry Perkowski	CIN	N	Johnny Klippstein Jim Willis
Jan. 23, 1959	CLE	A	Johnny Briggs	CHI	N	Earl Averill
June 6, 1959	PHI	N	Cash	CLE	A	Willie Jones
Nov. 30, 1962	HOU	N	Connie Grob	MIL	N	Norm Larker
Frank Bolick						
June 6, 1990	SEA	A	—	MIL	A	Mickey Brantley
Nov. 20, 1992	MON	N	Player to be named	SEA	A	Dave Wainhouse Kevin Foster
(Montreal received C Miah Bradbury on December 8, 1992.)						
Bobby Bolin						
Dec. 12, 1969	SEA	A	—	SF	N	Steve Whitaker Dick Simpson
Sept. 10, 1970	BOS	A	—	MIL	A	Cash
Frank Bolling						
Dec. 7, 1960	MIL	N	Neil Chrisley	DET	A	Bill Bruton Terry Fox Dick Brown Chuck Cottier
Milt Bolling						
Apr. 29, 1957	WAS	A	Russ Kemmerer Faye Throneberry	BOS	A	Dean Stone Bob Chakales
Feb. 25, 1958	CLE	A	—	WAS	A	Minor league P Pete Mesa
Mar. 27, 1958	DET	A	Vito Valentinetti	CLE	A	Pete Wojey $20,000.
Don Bollweg						
May 14, 1951	NY	A	$15,000.	STL	N	Billy Johnson
Dec. 16, 1953	PHI	A	—	NY	A	*see Harry Byrd*

Cliff Bolton

Date	Traded To		Traded With	Traded By		In Exchange For
June 10, 1937	DET	A	—	WAS	A	Waiver price

Tom Bolton

Date	Traded To		Traded With	Traded By		In Exchange For
July 9, 1992	CIN	N	—	BOS	A	Billy Hatcher
Dec. 10, 1992	DET	A	—	CIN	N	No compensation (free agent signing)

Mark Bomback

Date	Traded To		Traded With	Traded By		In Exchange For
Oct. 26, 1979	NY	N	—	MIL	A	Dwight Bernard
Apr. 6, 1981	TOR	A	—	NY	N	Charlie Puleo Cash

Barry Bonds

Date	Traded To		Traded With	Traded By		In Exchange For
Dec. 8, 1992	SF	N	—	PIT	N	No compensation (free agent signing)

Bobby Bonds

Date	Traded To		Traded With	Traded By		In Exchange For
Oct. 22, 1974	NY	A	—	SF	N	Bobby Murcer
Dec. 11, 1975	CAL	A	—	NY	A	Mickey Rivers Ed Figueroa
Dec. 5, 1977	CHI	A	Thad Bosley Richard Dotson	CAL	A	Brian Downing Chris Knapp Dave Frost
May 16, 1978	TEX	A	—	CHI	A	Claudell Washington Rusty Torres
Oct. 3, 1978	CLE	A	Len Barker	TEX	A	Jim Kern Larvell Blanks
Dec. 7, 1979	STL	N	—	CLE	A	Jerry Mumphrey John Denny
June 4, 1981	CHI	N	—	TEX	A	Cash

Ricky Bones

Date	Traded To		Traded With	Traded By		In Exchange For
Mar. 27, 1992	MIL	A	—	SD	N	*see Gary Sheffield*

Bill Bonham

Date	Traded To		Traded With	Traded By		In Exchange For
Oct. 31, 1977	CIN	N	—	CHI	N	Woodie Fryman Bill Caudill

Ernie Bonham

Date	Traded To		Traded With	Traded By		In Exchange For
Oct. 21, 1946	PIT	N	—	NY	A	Cookie Cuccurullo

Bobby Bonilla

Date	Traded To		Traded With	Traded By		In Exchange For
July 23, 1986	PIT	N	—	CHI	A	Jose DeLeon
Dec. 2, 1991	NY	N	—	PIT	N	No compensation (free agent signing)
July 28, 1995	BAL	A	Player to be named	NY	N	Alex Ochoa Damon Buford

(Baltimore received P Jimmy Williams on August 16, 1995.)

Juan Bonilla

Date	Traded To		Traded With	Traded By		In Exchange For
Apr. 1, 1981	SD	N	—	CLE	A	Bob Lacey

Barry Bonnell

Date	Traded To		Traded With	Traded By		In Exchange For
May 7, 1975	ATL	N	Jim Essian Cash	PHI	N	Dick Allen Johnny Oates
Dec. 5, 1979	TOR	A	Pat Rockett Joey McLaughlin	ATL	N	Chris Chambliss Luis Gomez
Dec. 8, 1983	SEA	A	—	TOR	A	Bryan Clark

Frank Bonner

Date	Traded To		Traded With	Traded By		In Exchange For
June 1902	PHI	A	Ossee Schreckengost	CLE	A	Bill Bernhard

Zeke Bonura

Date	Traded To		Traded With	Traded By		In Exchange For
Mar. 18, 1938	WAS	A	—	CHI	A	Joe Kuhel
Dec. 11, 1938	NY	N	—	WAS	A	Jim Carlin Tom Baker $20,000.
Apr. 26, 1940	WAS	A	—	NY	N	$20,000.
July 22, 1940	CHI	N	—	WAS	A	Cash

Everitt Booe

Date	Traded To		Traded With	Traded By		In Exchange For
June 1914	BUF	F	—	IND	F	Cash

Buddy Booker

Date	Traded To		Traded With	Traded By		In Exchange For
Dec. 15, 1967	CHI	A	—	NY	N	*see Tommie Agee*

Greg Booker

Date	Traded To		Traded With	Traded By		In Exchange For
June 29, 1989	MIN	A	—	SD	N	Fred Toliver

Al Bool

Date	Traded To		Traded With	Traded By		In Exchange For
Nov. 12, 1930	BOS	N	—	PIT	N	Waiver price

Bob Boone

Date	Traded To		Traded With	Traded By		In Exchange For
Dec. 6, 1981	CAL	A	—	PHI	N	Cash
Nov. 30, 1988	KC	A	—	CAL	A	No compensation (free agent signing)

Bret Boone

Date	Traded To		Traded With	Traded By		In Exchange For
Nov. 2, 1993	CIN	N	Erik Hanson	SEA	A	Dan Wilson Bobby Ayala

Danny Boone

Date	Traded To		Traded With	Traded By		In Exchange For
June 8, 1982	HOU	N	—	SD	N	Joe Pittman

Danny Boone

Date	Traded To		Traded With	Traded By		In Exchange For
Jan. 7, 1924	BOS	A	Steve O'Neill Joe Connolly Bill Wambsganss	CLE	A	George Burns Roxy Walters Chick Fewster

Ray Boone

Date	Traded To		Traded With	Traded By		In Exchange For
June 15, 1953	DET	A	Al Aber Steve Gromek Dick Weik	CLE	A	Art Houtteman Owen Friend Bill Wight Joe Ginsberg
June 15, 1958	CHI	A	Bob Shaw	DET	A	Bill Fischer Tito Francona
May 2, 1959	KC	A	—	CHI	A	Harry Simpson
Aug. 20, 1959	MIL	N	—	KC	A	Waiver price
May 17, 1960	BOS	A	—	MIL	N	Ron Jackson

Pedro Borbon

Date	Traded To		Traded With	Traded By		In Exchange For
Nov. 25, 1969	CIN	N	Jim McGlothlin Vern Geishert	CAL	A	Alex Johnson Chico Ruiz
June 28, 1979	SF	N	—	CIN	N	Hector Cruz

Frenchy Bordagaray

Date	Traded To		Traded With	Traded By		In Exchange For
Dec. 3, 1936	STL	N	Dutch Leonard Jimmy Jordan	BKN	N	Tom Winsett
Dec. 8, 1938	CIN	N	—	STL	N	Dusty Cooke
Apr. 4, 1942	BOS	N	—	NY	A	Cash

Pat Borders

Date	Traded To		Traded With	Traded By		In Exchange For
Apr. 7, 1995	KC	A	—	TOR	A	No compensation (free agent signing)
Aug. 11, 1995	HOU	N	—	KC	A	Rick Huisman

(Kansas City received Huisman on August 17, 1995.)

Rich Bordi

Date	Traded To		Traded With	Traded By		In Exchange For
Dec. 9, 1981	SEA	A	—	OAK	A	Dan Meyer
Dec. 9, 1982	CHI	N	—	SEA	A	Steve Henderson
Dec. 4, 1984	NY	A	Henry Cotto Porfi Altamirano Ron Hassey	CHI	N	Ray Fontenot Brian Dayett
Dec. 12, 1985	BAL	A	Rex Hudler	NY	A	Gary Roenicke Leo Hernandez

Glenn Borgmann

Date	Traded To		Traded With	Traded By		In Exchange For
Jan. 29, 1980	CHI	A	—	MIN	A	No compensation (free agent signing)
Mar. 24, 1981	CLE	A	—	CHI	A	No compensation (free agent signing)

Paul Boris

Date	Traded To		Traded With	Traded By		In Exchange For
Apr. 10, 1982	MIN	A	Ron Davis Greg Gagne	NY	A	Roy Smalley

Bob Borkowski

Date	Traded To		Traded With	Traded By		In Exchange For
Oct. 4, 1951	CIN	N	Smoky Burgess	CHI	N	Johnny Pramesa Bob Usher
June 9, 1955	BKN	N	Cash	CIN	N	Joe Black

Tom Borland

Date	Traded To		Traded With	Traded By		In Exchange For
Mar. 24, 1962	HOU	N	—	BOS	A	Dave Philley

Steve Boros

Date	Traded To		Traded With	Traded By		In Exchange For
Nov. 28, 1962	CHI	N	—	DET	A	Bob Anderson

Joe Borowski

Date	Traded To		Traded With	Traded By		In Exchange For
Dec. 17, 1995	ATL	N	Minor league P Rachaad Stewart	BAL	A	Kent Mercker

Hank Borowy

Date	Traded To		Traded With	Traded By		In Exchange For
July 27, 1945	CHI	N	—	NY	A	$97,000.
Dec. 14, 1948	PHI	N	Eddie Waitkus	CHI	N	Monk Dubiel Dutch Leonard
June 12, 1950	PIT	N	—	PHI	N	$10,000.
Aug. 3, 1950	DET	A	—	PIT	N	$15,000.

Babe Borton

Date	Traded To		Traded With	Traded By		In Exchange For
June 1, 1913	NY	A	Rollie Zeider	CHI	A	Hal Chase
Feb. 10, 1916	STL	A	*see Eddie Plank*	STL	F	—

Don Bosch

Date	Traded To		Traded With	Traded By		In Exchange For
Dec. 6, 1966	NY	N	Don Cardwell	PIT	N	Dennis Ribant Gary Kolb
Oct. 16, 1968	MON	N	—	NY	N	Cash

Rick Bosetti

Date	Traded To		Traded With	Traded By		In Exchange For
June 15, 1977	STL	N	Tom Underwood Dane Iorg	PHI	N	Bake McBride Steve Waterbury
Mar. 15, 1978	TOR	A	—	STL	N	Cash
June 10, 1981	OAK	A	—	TOR	A	Cash

Chris Bosio

Date	Traded To		Traded With	Traded By		In Exchange For
Dec. 3, 1992	SEA	A	—	MIL	A	No compensation (free agent signing)

Shawn Boskie

Date	Traded To		Traded With	Traded By		In Exchange For
Apr. 12, 1994	PHI	N	—	CHI	N	Kevin Foster
July 21, 1994	SEA	A	—	PHI	N	Player to be named

(Philadelphia received 1B Fred McNair on September 7, 1994.)

Thad Bosley

Date	Traded To		Traded With	Traded By		In Exchange For
Dec. 5, 1977	CHI	A	—	CAL	A	*see Brian Downing*
Apr. 1, 1981	MIL	A	—	CHI	A	John Poff
Mar. 5, 1982	SEA	A	—	MIL	A	Mike Parrott
Mar. 30, 1983	CHI	N	—	OAK	A	Cash
Mar. 30, 1987	KC	A	Dave Gumpert	CHI	N	Jim Sundberg

Dick Bosman

Date	Traded To		Traded With	Traded By		In Exchange For
May 10, 1973	CLE	A	Ted Ford	TEX	A	Steve Dunning
May 20, 1975	OAK	A	Jim Perry	CLE	A	Blue Moon Odom Cash

Harley Boss

Date	Traded To		Traded With	Traded By		In Exchange For
Dec. 15, 1932	CLE	A	—	WAS	A	Jack Russell Bruce Connatser

Lyman Bostock

Date	Traded To		Traded With	Traded By		In Exchange For
Nov. 21, 1976	CAL	A	—	MIN	A	No compensation (free agent signing)

Daryl Boston

Date	Traded To		Traded With	Traded By		In Exchange For
Apr. 30, 1990	NY	N	—	CHI	A	Waiver price
Jan. 13, 1994	NY	A	—	CLR	N	No compensation (free agent signing)

Ken Boswell

Date	Traded To		Traded With	Traded By		In Exchange For
Oct. 29, 1974	HOU	N	—	NY	N	Bob Gallagher

Derek Botelho

Date	Traded To		Traded With	Traded By		In Exchange For
Feb. 23, 1979	CHI	N	Barry Foote Ted Sizemore Jerry Martin minor league P Henry Mack	PHI	N	Manny Trillo Dave Rader Greg Gross
Mar. 30, 1984	CHI	N	—	KC	A	Alan Hargesheimer

Kent Bottenfield

Date	Traded To		Traded With	Traded By		In Exchange For
July 16, 1993	CLR	N	—	MON	N	Butch Henry

Jim Bottomley

Date	Traded To		Traded With	Traded By		In Exchange For
Dec. 17, 1932	CIN	N	—	STL	N	Estel Crabtree Ownie Carroll
Mar. 21, 1936	STL	A	—	CIN	N	Johnny Burnett

Ed Bouchee

Date	Traded To		Traded With	Traded By		In Exchange For
May 13, 1960	CHI	N	Don Cardwell	PHI	N	Tony Taylor Cal Neeman

Denis Boucher

Date	Traded To		Traded With	Traded By		In Exchange For
June 27, 1991	CLE	A	—	TOR	A	*see Tom Candiotti*
Mar. 21, 1993	SD	N	—	CLR	N	Jay Gainer
July 10, 1993	MON	N	—	SD	N	Minor league IF Austin Manahan Cash

Medric Boucher

Date	Traded To		Traded With	Traded By		In Exchange For
Aug. 1914	PIT	F	—	BAL	F	Doc Kerr

Carl Bouldin

Date	Traded To		Traded With	Traded By		In Exchange For
July 13, 1964	CHI	A	Bill Skowron	WAS	A	Joe Cunningham Frank Kreutzer

Chris Bourjos

Date	Traded To		Traded With	Traded By		In Exchange For
Dec. 8, 1980	HOU	N	Bob Knepper	SF	N	Enos Cabell
Apr. 1, 1981	BAL	A	Cash	HOU	N	Kiko Garcia

Rafael Bournigal

Date	Traded To		Traded With	Traded By		In Exchange For
June 9, 1995	MON	N	—	LA	N	Minor league P John Foster

Pat Bourque

Date	Traded To		Traded With	Traded By		In Exchange For
Aug. 29, 1973	OAK	A	—	CHI	N	Gonzalo Marquez
Aug. 19, 1974	MIN	A	—	OAK	A	Jim Holt
Oct. 23, 1974	OAK	A	—	MIN	A	Dan Ford minor league P Denny Myers

Jim Bouton

Date	Traded To		Traded With	Traded By		In Exchange For
Oct. 21, 1968	SEA	A	—	NY	A	Cash
Aug. 24, 1969	HOU	N	—	SEA	A	Dooley Womack Roric Harrison

Larry Bowa

Date	Traded To		Traded With	Traded By		In Exchange For
Jan. 27, 1982	CHI	N	Ryne Sandberg	PHI	N	Ivan DeJesus

Sam Bowens

Date	Traded To		Traded With	Traded By		In Exchange For
Nov. 28, 1967	WAS	A	—	BAL	A	Cash

Frank Bowerman

Date	Traded To		Traded With	Traded By		In Exchange For
Feb. 1900	NY	N	—	PIT	N	Cash
Dec. 3, 1907	BOS	N	—	NY	N	*see Fred Tenney*

Bob Bowman

Date	Traded To		Traded With	Traded By		In Exchange For
Dec. 5, 1940	NY	N	—	STL	N	Cash
Dec. 4, 1941	CHI	N	—	NY	N	Hank Leiber

Ernie Bowman

Date	Traded To	Traded With	Traded By	In Exchange For
Dec. 3, 1963	MIL N	*see Felipe Alou*	SF N	—

Joe Bowman

Date	Traded To	Traded With	Traded By	In Exchange For
Dec. 13, 1934	PHI N	—	NY N	Kiddo Davis
Apr. 16, 1937	PIT N	—	PHI N	Earl Browne

Roger Bowman

Date	Traded To	Traded With	Traded By	In Exchange For
May 12, 1953	PIT N	—	NY N	Waiver price

Ted Bowsfield

Date	Traded To	Traded With	Traded By	In Exchange For
June 13, 1960	CLE A	Marty Keough	BOS A	Russ Nixon Carroll Hardy
July 23, 1962	KC A	Gordie Windhorn	LA A	Dan Osinski

(Kansas City received Bowsfield on November 30.)

Bob Boyd

Date	Traded To	Traded With	Traded By	In Exchange For
Jan. 24, 1961	KC A	—	BAL A	*see Russ Snyder*
June 10, 1961	MIL N	—	KC A	Cash

Oil Can Boyd

Date	Traded To	Traded With	Traded By	In Exchange For
Dec. 7, 1989	MON N	—	BOS A	No compensation (free agent signing)
July 21, 1991	TEX A	—	MON N	Jonathan Hurst Joey Eischen Player to be named

(Montreal received P Travis Buckley on September 1, 1991.)

Clete Boyer

Date	Traded To	Traded With	Traded By	In Exchange For
Feb. 19, 1957	NY A	Art Ditmar Bobby Shantz Jack McMahan Wayne Belardi Curt Roberts	KC A	Billy Hunter Rip Coleman Tom Morgan Mickey McDermott Milt Graff Irv Noren

(New York received Roberts on April 4, and Boyer on June 4, 1957.)

Date	Traded To	Traded With	Traded By	In Exchange For
Nov. 29, 1966	ATL N	—	NY A	Bill Robinson Chi Chi Olivo

Ken Boyer

Date	Traded To	Traded With	Traded By	In Exchange For
Oct. 20, 1965	NY N	—	STL N	Charley Smith Al Jackson
July 22, 1967	CHI A	—	NY N	J. C. Martin Bill Southworth

Doe Boyland

Date	Traded To	Traded With	Traded By	In Exchange For
Dec. 11, 1981	SF N	—	PIT N	Tom Griffin

Gene Brabender

Date	Traded To	Traded With	Traded By	In Exchange For
Mar. 31, 1969	SEA A	Gordon Lund	BAL A	Chico Salmon
Jan. 28, 1971	CAL A	—	MIL A	Bill Voss

Gib Brack

Date	Traded To	Traded With	Traded By	In Exchange For
July 11, 1938	PHI N	—	BKN N	Tuck Stainback

Buddy Bradford

Date	Traded To	Traded With	Traded By	In Exchange For
June 15, 1970	CLE A	—	CHI A	Barry Moore Bob Miller
May 8, 1971	CIN N	—	CLE A	Kurt Bevacqua
June 30, 1975	STL N	—	CHI A	Bill Parsons Cash
Dec. 12, 1975	CHI A	Greg Terlecky	STL N	Lee Richard

Bert Bradley

Date	Traded To	Traded With	Traded By	In Exchange For
Dec. 8, 1984	NY A	*see Rickey Henderson*	OAK A	—

Fred Bradley

Date	Traded To	Traded With	Traded By	In Exchange For
Feb. 24, 1948	CHI A	Aaron Robinson Bill Wight	NY A	Ed Lopat

Hugh Bradley

Date	Traded To	Traded With	Traded By	In Exchange For
Feb. 1915	NWK F	Larry Pratt Tom Seaton	BKN F	Cy Falkenberg

Mark Bradley

Date	Traded To	Traded With	Traded By	In Exchange For
Mar. 29, 1983	NY N	—	LA N	Minor league Ps Steve Walker Jody Johnston Cash

Phil Bradley

Date	Traded To	Traded With	Traded By	In Exchange For
Dec. 9, 1987	PHI N	Tim Fortugno	SEA A	Glenn Wilson Mike Jackson Minor league OF Dave Brundage
Dec. 8, 1988	BAL A	—	PHI N	Ken Howell Gordon Dillard
July 30, 1990	CHI A	—	BAL A	Ron Kittle

Scott Bradley

Date	Traded To	Traded With	Traded By	In Exchange For
Feb. 13, 1986	CHI A	—	NY A	*see Ron Hassey*
June 26, 1986	SEA A	—	CHI A	Ivan Calderon

(Chicago received Calderon on July 1, 1986.)

Date	Traded To	Traded With	Traded By	In Exchange For
July 28, 1992	NY N	—	CIN N	Player to be named

(Cincinnati received P Joe McCann on September 15, 1992.)

Tom Bradley

Date	Traded To	Traded With	Traded By	In Exchange For
Nov. 30, 1970	CHI A	—	CAL A	*see Ken Berry*
Nov. 28, 1972	SF N	—	CHI A	Ken Henderson Steve Stone

King Brady

Date	Traded To	Traded With	Traded By	In Exchange For
Oct. 1905	PIT N	—	PHI N	Cash

Bobby Bragan

Date	Traded To	Traded With	Traded By	In Exchange For
Mar. 24, 1943	BKN N		PHI N	Tex Kraus Cash

Glenn Braggs

Date	Traded To	Traded With	Traded By	In Exchange For
June 9, 1990	CIN N	Billy Bates	MIL A	Ron Robinson Bob Sebra

Dave Brain

Date	Traded To	Traded With	Traded By	In Exchange For
July 4, 1905	PIT N	—	STL N	George McBride
Dec. 15, 1905	BOS N	Del Howard Vive Lindaman	PIT N	Vic Willis
Feb. 1908	CIN N	—	BOS N	Cash
July 1908	NY N	—	CIN N	Cash

Ralph Branca

Date	Traded To	Traded With	Traded By	In Exchange For
July 10, 1953	DET A	—	BKN N	Waiver price

Harvey Branch

Date	Traded To	Traded With	Traded By	In Exchange For
Sept. 1, 1962	STL N	—	CHI N	Paul Toth

Darrell Brandon

Date	Traded To	Traded With	Traded By	In Exchange For
Sept. 14, 1965	BOS A	—	HOU N	Jack Lamabe
July 8, 1969	MIN A	—	SEA A	Cash

Ed Brandt

Date	Traded To	Traded With	Traded By	In Exchange For
Dec. 12, 1935	BKN N	Randy Moore	BOS N	Tony Cuccinello Ray Benge Al Lopez Bobby Reis
Dec. 4, 1936	PIT N	—	BKN N	Cookie Lavagetto Ralph Birkofer

Jackie Brandt

Date	Traded To	Traded With	Traded By	In Exchange For
June 14, 1956	NY N	Red Schoendienst Bobby Stephenson Dick Littlefield Bill Sarni	STL N	Alvin Dark Ray Katt Don Liddle Whitey Lockman
Nov. 30, 1959	BAL A	Gordon Jones Roger McCardell	SF N	Billy O'Dell Billy Loes
Dec. 6, 1965	PHI N	Darold Knowles	BAL A	Jack Baldschun
June 3, 1967	HOU N	—	PHI N	Cash

Kitty Bransfield

Date	Traded To	Traded With	Traded By	In Exchange For
Dec. 20, 1904	PHI N	Otto Krueger Moose McCormick	PIT N	Del Howard
Aug. 9, 1911	CHI N	—	PHI N	Cash

Marshall Brant

Date	Traded To	Traded With	Traded By	In Exchange For
Apr. 1, 1980	NY A	—	NY N	Cash
June 15, 1983	OAK A	Ben Callahan Cash	NY A	Matt Keough

Cliff Brantley

Date	Traded To	Traded With	Traded By	In Exchange For
May 27, 1993	MON N	—	PHI N	Waiver price

Jeff Brantley

Date	Traded To	Traded With	Traded By	In Exchange For
Jan. 4, 1994	CIN N	—	SF N	No compensation (free agent signing)

Mickey Brantley

Date	Traded To	Traded With	Traded By	In Exchange For
June 6, 1990	MIL A	—	SEA A	Frank Bolick

Steve Braun

Date	Traded To	Traded With	Traded By	In Exchange For
June 1, 1978	KC A	—	SEA A	Jim Colborn

Angel Bravo

Date	Traded To	Traded With	Traded By	In Exchange For
Dec. 15, 1969	CIN N	—	CHI A	Jerry Arrigo
May 13, 1971	SD N	—	CIN N	Al Ferrara

Garland Braxton

Date	Traded To	Traded With	Traded By	In Exchange For
Aug. 27, 1926	WAS A	Nick Cullop	NY A	Dutch Ruether
	(New York sent Braxton and Cullop to Washington on October 19, 1926.)			
June 16, 1930	CHI A	Bennie Tate	WAS A	Art Shires
July 13, 1931	STL A	—	CHI A	Waiver price

Sid Bream

Date	Traded To	Traded With	Traded By	In Exchange For
Aug. 31, 1985	PIT N	R. J. Reynolds Cecil Espy	LA N	Bill Madlock
	(Pittsburgh received Reynolds on Sept. 3 and Bream and Espy on September 9, 1985.)			
Dec. 5, 1990	ATL N	—	PIT N	No compensation (free agent signing)

Danny Breeden

Date	Traded To	Traded With	Traded By	In Exchange For
Dec. 3, 1968	SD N	Ed Spiezio Ron Davis minor league P Phil Knuckles	STL N	Dave Giusti
June 30, 1969	CIN N	—	SD N	Cash
Nov. 30, 1970	CHI N	—	CIN N	Willie Smith
Nov. 18, 1974	STL N	Ed Brinkman	SD N	Alan Foster Rich Folkers Sonny Siebert
	(Part of three-team trade involving San Diego, Detroit, and St. Louis Cardinals.)			

Hal Breeden

Date	Traded To	Traded With	Traded By	In Exchange For
Nov. 30, 1970	CHI N	—	ATL N	Hoyt Wilhelm
Apr. 7, 1972	MON N	Hector Torres	CHI N	Dan McGinn

Marv Breeding

Date	Traded To	Traded With	Traded By	In Exchange For
Dec. 5, 1962	WAS A	Barry Shetrone minor league P Art Quick	BAL A	Bob Johnson Pete Burnside
July 20, 1963	LA N	—	WAS A	Ed Roebuck

Fred Breining

Date	Traded To	Traded With	Traded By	In Exchange For
June 28, 1979	SF N	—	PIT N	*see Bill Madlock*
Feb. 27, 1984	MON N	Max Venable Andy McGaffigan	SF N	Al Oliver
	(San Francisco sent McGaffigan to Montreal on April 1, 1984, after Breining reported to the Expos with a sore arm.)			

Bob Brenly

Date	Traded To	Traded With	Traded By	In Exchange For
Jan. 18, 1989	TOR A	—	SF N	No compensation (free agent signing)

Ad Brennan

Date	Traded To	Traded With	Traded By	In Exchange For
Jan. 20, 1910	PHI N	—	CIN N	Harry Coveleski
June 1918	CLE A	—	WAS A	Cash

Tom Brennan

Date	Traded To	Traded With	Traded By	In Exchange For
Jan. 21, 1984	CHI A	—	CLE A	Craig Smajstrla
	(Cleveland received Smajstrla on July 8, 1985.)			

Roger Bresnahan

Date	Traded To	Traded With	Traded By	In Exchange For
Dec. 12, 1908	STL N	—	NY N	Admiral Schlei Bugs Raymond Red Murray
June 8, 1913	CHI N	—	STL N	Cash

Rube Bressler

Date	Traded To	Traded With	Traded By	In Exchange For
Mar. 13, 1928	BKN N	—	CIN N	Waiver price
June 28, 1932	STL N	—	PHI N	Waiver price

Ed Bressoud

Date	Traded To	Traded With	Traded By	In Exchange For
Nov. 26, 1961	BOS A	—	HOU N	Don Buddin
Nov. 30, 1965	NY N	—	BOS A	Joe Christopher
Apr. 1, 1967	STL N	Danny Napoleon Cash	NY N	Jerry Buchek Art Mahaffey Tony Martinez

Ken Brett

Date	Traded To	Traded With	Traded By	In Exchange For
Oct. 11, 1971	MIL A	*see George Scott*	BOS A	—
Oct. 31, 1972	PHI N	—	MIL A	*see Don Money*
Oct. 18, 1973	PIT N	—	PHI N	Dave Cash
Dec. 11, 1975	NY A	Willie Randolph Dock Ellis	PIT N	Doc Medich
May 18, 1976	CHI A	Rich Coggins	NY A	Carlos May
June 15, 1977	CAL A	—	CHI A	Don Kirkwood John Verhoeven John Flannery

Billy Brewer

Date	Traded To	Traded With	Traded By	In Exchange For
Dec. 17, 1995	LA N	—	KC A	Jose Offerman

Jim Brewer

Date	Traded To	Traded With	Traded By	In Exchange For
Dec. 13, 1963	LA N	Cuno Barragan	CHI N	Dick Scott
July 15, 1975	CAL A	—	LA N	Cash

Mike Brewer

Date	Traded To	Traded With	Traded By	In Exchange For
Apr. 4, 1985	CLE A	—	KC A	player to be named
	(Brewer returned to Kansas City on Sept. 17, 1985.)			

Charlie Brewster

Date	Traded To	Traded With	Traded By	In Exchange For
June 6, 1943	PHI N	—	CIN N	Dain Clay

Fred Brickell

Date	Traded To	Traded With	Traded By	In Exchange For
Aug. 7, 1930	PHI N	—	PIT N	Denny Sothern

Fritzie Brickell

Date	Traded To	Traded With	Traded By	In Exchange For
Apr. 4, 1961	LA A	—	NY A	Duke Maas

Jim Brideweser

Date	Traded To	Traded With	Traded By	In Exchange For
May 11, 1954	BAL A	—	NY A	Waiver price
Dec. 6, 1954	CHI A	*see Clint Courtney*	BAL A	—
May 15, 1956	DET A	Harry Byrd Bob Kennedy	CHI A	Fred Hatfield Jim Delsing
Feb. 8, 1957	BAL A	—	DET A	Cash
Oct. 14, 1958	STL N	Art Ceccarelli	BAL A	Jim Finigan

Marshall Bridges

Date	Traded To	Traded With	Traded By	In Exchange For
Aug. 2, 1960	CIN N	—	STL N	Waiver price
Nov. 27, 1963	WAS A	—	NY A	Cash

Rocky Bridges

Date	Traded To	Traded With	Traded By	In Exchange For
Feb. 16, 1953	MIL N	Jim Pendleton	BKN N	Russ Meyer
	(Part of four-team trade involving Milwaukee, Philadelphia Phillies, Brooklyn, and Cincinnati.)			

Date	Traded To		Traded With	Traded By		In Exchange For

Rocky Bridges *continued*

Date	Traded To		Traded With	Traded By		In Exchange For
Feb. 16, 1953	CIN	N	Cash	MIL	N	Joe Adcock
(Part of four-team trade involving Milwaukee Braves, Philadelphia Phillies, Brooklyn, and Cincinnati.)						
May 20, 1957	WAS	A	—	CIN	N	Waiver price
Dec. 6, 1958	DET	A	Eddie Yost Neil Chrisley	WAS	A	Reno Bertoia Ron Samford Jim Delsing
July 26, 1960	CLE	A	Red Wilson	DET	A	Hank Foiles
Sept. 2, 1960	STL	N	—	CLE	A	Cash

Al Bridwell

Date	Traded To		Traded With	Traded By		In Exchange For
Mar. 1906	BOS	N	—	CIN	N	Jim Delahanty Chick Fraser
Dec. 3, 1907	NY	N	Fred Tenney Tom Needham	BOS	N	Dan McGann Frank Bowerman Bill Dahlen George Browne George Ferguson
July 22, 1911	BOS	N	Hank Gowdy	NY	N	Buck Herzog
Nov. 1912	CHI	N	—	BOS	N	Cash

Buttons Briggs

Date	Traded To		Traded With	Traded By		In Exchange For
Dec. 30, 1905	BKN	N	Billy Maloney Jack McCarthy Doc Casey $2,000.	CHI	N	Jimmy Sheckard

Dan Briggs

Date	Traded To		Traded With	Traded By		In Exchange For
Mar. 30, 1979	SD	N	—	CLE	A	Mike Champion
Nov. 27, 1979	MON	N	Bill Almon	SD	N	Dave Cash
Mar. 16, 1982	CHI	N	—	MON	N	Mike Griffin

John Briggs

Date	Traded To		Traded With	Traded By		In Exchange For
Apr. 22, 1971	MIL	A	—	PHI	N	Ray Peters Pete Koegel
June 14, 1975	MIN	A	—	MIL	A	Bobby Darwin

Johnny Briggs

Date	Traded To		Traded With	Traded By		In Exchange For
Jan. 23, 1959	CLE	A	Jim Bolger	CHI	N	Earl Averill
July 30, 1960	KC	A	—	CLE	A	Cash
Jan. 25, 1961	CIN	N	John Tsitouris	KC	A	Joe Nuxhall

Harry Bright

Date	Traded To		Traded With	Traded By		In Exchange For
Dec. 16, 1960	WAS	A	Bennie Daniels R C Stevens	PIT	N	Bobby Shantz
Nov. 24, 1962	CIN	N	—	WAS	A	Rogelio Alvarez
Apr. 21, 1963	NY	A	—	CIN	N	Cash

Nellie Briles

Date	Traded To		Traded With	Traded By		In Exchange For
Jan. 29, 1971	PIT	N	Vic Davalillo	STL	N	Matty Alou George Brunet
Dec. 4, 1973	KC	A	Fernando Gonzalez	PIT	N	Ed Kirkpatrick Kurt Bevacqua minor league 1B Winston Cole
Nov. 12, 1975	TEX	A	—	KC	A	Dave Nelson
Sept. 19, 1977	BAL	A	—	TEX	A	Cash

Brad Brink

Date	Traded To		Traded With	Traded By		In Exchange For
Mar. 31, 1994	SF	N	—	PHI	N	Waiver price

Chuck Brinkman

Date	Traded To		Traded With	Traded By		In Exchange For
July 11, 1974	PIT	N	—	CHI	A	Cash

Ed Brinkman

Date	Traded To		Traded With	Traded By		In Exchange For
Oct. 9, 1970	DET	A	Joe Coleman Aurelio Rodriguez Jim Hannan	WAS	A	Denny McLain Don Wert Norm McRae Elliott Maddox

Ed Brinkman *continued*

Date	Traded To		Traded With	Traded By		In Exchange For
Nov. 18, 1974	SD	N	Bob Strampe Dick Sharon	DET	A	Nate Colbert
(Part of three-team trade involving San Diego, Detroit, and St. Louis Cardinals.)						
Nov. 18, 1974	STL	N	Danny Breeden	SD	N	Alan Foster Rich Folkers Sonny Siebert
(Part of three-team trade involving San Diego, Detroit, and St. Louis Cardinals.)						
June 4, 1975	TEX	A	Tommy Moore	STL	N	Willie Davis
June 13, 1975	NY	A	—	TEX	A	Cash

Lou Brissie

Date	Traded To		Traded With	Traded By		In Exchange For
Apr. 30, 1951	CLE	A	—	PHI	A	Sam Zoldak Ray Murray Minnie Minoso
(Part of three-team trade involving Cleveland, Philadelphia A's, and Chicago White Sox.)						

Jim Britton

Date	Traded To		Traded With	Traded By		In Exchange For
Dec. 2, 1969	MON	N	minor league C Don Johnson	ATL	N	Larry Jaster

Johnny Broaca

Date	Traded To		Traded With	Traded By		In Exchange For
Nov. 1938	CLE	A	—	NY	A	Waiver price

Pete Broberg

Date	Traded To		Traded With	Traded By		In Exchange For
Dec. 5, 1974	MIL	A	—	TEX	A	Clyde Wright
Apr. 20, 1977	CHI	N	—	SEA	A	Jim Todd
Mar. 29, 1978	OAK	A	—	CHI	N	Rodney Scott Cash

Doug Brocail

Date	Traded To		Traded With	Traded By		In Exchange For
Dec. 28, 1994	HOU	N	—	SD	N	*see Ken Caminiti*

Greg Brock

Date	Traded To		Traded With	Traded By		In Exchange For
Dec. 10, 1986	MIL	A	—	LA	N	Tim Leary Tim Crews

Lou Brock

Date	Traded To		Traded With	Traded By		In Exchange For
June 15, 1964	STL	N	Jack Spring Paul Toth	CHI	N	Ernie Broglio Bobby Shantz Doug Clemens

Dick Brodowski

Date	Traded To		Traded With	Traded By		In Exchange For
Nov. 8, 1955	WAS	A	—	BOS	A	*see Mickey Vernon*

Ernie Broglio

Date	Traded To		Traded With	Traded By		In Exchange For
Oct. 8, 1958	STL	N	Marv Grissom	SF	N	Hobie Landrith Billy Muffett Benny Valenzuela
June 15, 1964	CHI	N	Bobby Shantz Doug Clemens	STL	N	Lou Brock Jack Spring Paul Toth

Rico Brogna

Date	Traded To		Traded With	Traded By		In Exchange For
Mar. 31, 1994	NY	N	—	DET	A	Minor league 1B Alan Zinter

Jack Brohamer

Date	Traded To		Traded With	Traded By		In Exchange For
Dec. 12, 1975	CHI	A	—	CLE	A	Larvell Blanks
June 20, 1980	CLE	A	—	BOS	A	Cash

Jeff Bronkey

Date	Traded To		Traded With	Traded By		In Exchange For
Jan. 13, 1994	TEX	A	—	MIL	A	Minor league P David Pike

Jim Bronstad

Date	Traded To		Traded With	Traded By		In Exchange For
Mar. 21, 1963	WAS	A	—	NY	A	Cash

Tom Brookens

Date	Traded To		Traded With	Traded By		In Exchange For
Mar. 23, 1989	NY	A	—	DET	A	Charles Hudson
Dec. 8, 1989	CLE	A	—	NY	A	No compensation (free agent signing)

Hubie Brooks

Date	Traded To	Traded With	Traded By	In Exchange For
Dec. 10, 1984	MON N	Mike Fitzgerald Herm Winningham Floyd Youmans	NY N	Gary Carter
Dec. 21, 1989	LA N	—	MON N	No compensation (free agent signing)
Dec. 15, 1990	NY N	—	LA N	Bob Ojeda Greg Hansell
Dec. 10, 1991	CAL A	—	NY N	Dave Gallagher

Jim Brosnan

Date	Traded To	Traded With	Traded By	In Exchange For
May 20, 1958	STL N	—	CHI N	Alvin Dark
June 8, 1959	CIN N	—	STL N	Hal Jeffcoat
May 5, 1963	CHI A	—	CIN N	Dom Zanni

Terry Bross

Date	Traded To	Traded With	Traded By	In Exchange For
Mar. 30, 1992	SD N	—	NY N	Minor league 3B Craig Bullock
Dec. 16, 1992	TEX A	—	SD N	Minor league P Pat Gomez
Dec. 12, 1994	CHI A	—	CIN N	Waiver price

Tony Brottem

Date	Traded To	Traded With	Traded By	In Exchange For
July 1921	PIT N	—	WAS A	Cash

Bob Brower

Date	Traded To	Traded With	Traded By	In Exchange For
Dec. 5, 1988	NY A	—	TEX A	Bobby Meacham

Frank Brower

Date	Traded To	Traded With	Traded By	In Exchange For
Jan. 8, 1923	CLE A	—	WAS A	Joe Evans

Boardwalk Brown

Date	Traded To	Traded With	Traded By	In Exchange For
June 1914	NY A	—	PHI A	Cash

Bobby Brown

Date	Traded To	Traded With	Traded By	In Exchange For
June 14, 1978	NY A	Jay Johnstone	PHI N	Rawly Eastwick
Mar. 25, 1979	TOR A	—	NY N	Cash
Apr. 1, 1982	SEA A	Bill Caudill Gene Nelson	NY A	Shane Rawley

Buster Brown

Date	Traded To	Traded With	Traded By	In Exchange For
July 16, 1909	BOS N	Lew Richie Dave Shean	PHI N	Johnny Bates Charlie Starr

Charlie Brown

Date	Traded To	Traded With	Traded By	In Exchange For
June 10, 1907	PHI N	—	STL N	Johnny Lush

Chris Brown

Date	Traded To	Traded With	Traded By	In Exchange For
July 5, 1987	SD N	Mark Davis Keith Comstock Mark Grant	SF N	Kevin Mitchell Craig Lefferts Dave Dravecky
Oct. 28, 1988	DET A	Keith Moreland	SD N	Walt Terrell

Clint Brown

Date	Traded To	Traded With	Traded By	In Exchange For
Apr. 11, 1936	CHI A	—	CLE A	Cash
Feb. 7, 1941	CLE A	—	CHI A	John Humphries

Curt Brown

Date	Traded To	Traded With	Traded By	In Exchange For
Dec. 19, 1983	NY A	—	CAL A	Minor league P Mike Browning
June 30, 1987	MIL A	—	MON N	player to be named
July 2, 1987	OAK A	—	MIL A	Minor league P Eric Broersma

(Oakland received Brown on August 5, 1987.)

Darrell Brown

Date	Traded To	Traded With	Traded By	In Exchange For
Mar. 1, 1982	OAK A	minor league Ps Mark Fellows Jack Smith	DET A	Jeff Cox Scott Meyer

Dick Brown

Date	Traded To	Traded With	Traded By	In Exchange For
Dec. 6, 1959	CHI A	—	CLE A	*see Norm Cash*
Nov. 28, 1960	MIL N	—	CHI A	Cash
Dec. 7, 1960	DET A	*see Bill Bruton*	MIL N	—
Nov. 26, 1962	BAL A	—	DET A	Gus Triandos Whitey Herzog

Eddie Brown

Date	Traded To	Traded With	Traded By	In Exchange For
Oct. 7, 1925	BOS N	Zack Taylor Jimmy Johnston	BKN N	Jesse Barnes Mickey O'Neil Gus Felix

Elmer Brown

Date	Traded To	Traded With	Traded By	In Exchange For
Nov. 1912	BKN N	—	STL A	Cash

Hal Brown

Date	Traded To	Traded With	Traded By	In Exchange For
Feb. 9, 1953	BOS A	Marv Grissom Bill Kennedy	CHI A	Vern Stephens
Sept. 7, 1962	NY A	—	BAL A	Cash
Apr. 21, 1963	HOU N	—	NY A	Cash

Jackie Brown

Date	Traded To	Traded With	Traded By	In Exchange For
June 13, 1975	CLE A	Jim Bibby Rick Waits $100,000.	TEX A	Gaylord Perry
Dec. 10, 1976	MON N	—	CLE A	Andre Thornton

Jake Brown

Date	Traded To	Traded With	Traded By	In Exchange For
June 13, 1976	ATL N	—	SF N	*see Darrell Evans*

Jarvis Brown

Date	Traded To	Traded With	Traded By	In Exchange For
Nov. 18, 1993	ATL N	—	SD N	Waiver price

Jimmy Brown

Date	Traded To	Traded With	Traded By	In Exchange For
Jan. 5, 1946	PIT N	—	STL N	$30,000.

Jumbo Brown

Date	Traded To	Traded With	Traded By	In Exchange For
June 1937	NY N	—	CIN N	Cash

Kevin Brown

Date	Traded To	Traded With	Traded By	In Exchange For
Nov. 11, 1987	NY N	—	ATL N	Terry Blocker

(New York received Brown on December 8, 1987.)

Date	Traded To	Traded With	Traded By	In Exchange For
Aug. 31, 1990	MIL A	Julio Machado	NY N	Charlie O'Brien Player to be named

(Machado and Brown were assigned to Milwaukee on September 7 and New York received P Kevin Carmody on September 11, 1990.)

Date	Traded To	Traded With	Traded By	In Exchange For
Apr. 2, 1992	SEA A	—	MIL A	Waiver price

Kevin Brown

Date	Traded To	Traded With	Traded By	In Exchange For
Apr. 8, 1995	BAL A	—	TEX A	No compensation (free agent signing)
Dec. 22, 1995	FLA N	—	BAL A	No compensation (free agent signing)

Larry Brown

Date	Traded To	Traded With	Traded By	In Exchange For
Apr. 24, 1971	OAK A	—	CLE A	Cash

Leon Brown

Date	Traded To	Traded With	Traded By	In Exchange For
Dec. 9, 1976	STL N	Brock Pemberton	NY N	Minor league 1B Ed Kurpiel

Lloyd Brown

Date	Traded To	Traded With	Traded By	In Exchange For
Dec. 14, 1932	STL A	Sammy West Carl Reynolds $20,000.	WAS A	Goose Goslin Fred Schulte Lefty Stewart
May 9, 1933	BOS A	Rick Ferrell	STL A	Merv Shea Cash
Oct. 12, 1933	CLE A	—	BOS A	Bill Cissell

Mace Brown

Date	Traded To	Traded With	Traded By	In Exchange For
Apr. 22, 1941	BKN N	—	PIT N	Cash
Dec. 10, 1941	BOS A	—	BKN N	Cash

Mark Brown

Date	Traded To	Traded With	Traded By	In Exchange For
Mar. 27, 1985	MIN A	—	BAL A	Brad Havens

Mike Brown

Date	Traded To	Traded With	Traded By	In Exchange For
Aug. 19, 1986	SEA A	—	BOS A	*see Dave Henderson*
Aug. 11, 1987	BAL A	—	SEA A	Nelson Simmons

(Baltimore received Brown on August 26, 1987.)

Mike Brown

Date	Traded To	Traded With	Traded By	In Exchange For
Aug. 2, 1985	PIT N	Pat Clements Bob Kipper	CAL A	John Candelaria Al Holland George Hendrick

(Pittsburgh received Kipper on Aug. 16, 1985.)

Ollie Brown

Date	Traded To	Traded With	Traded By	In Exchange For
May 17, 1972	OAK A	—	SD N	Curt Blefary Mike Kilkenny minor league OF Greg Schubert
June 29, 1972	MIL A	—	OAK A	Cash
Oct. 22, 1973	CAL A	Ellie Rodriguez Skip Lockwood Gary Ryerson Joe Lahoud	MIL A	Clyde Wright Steve Barber Ken Berry Art Kusnyer Cash
Mar. 28, 1974	HOU N	—	CAL A	Cash
June 24, 1974	PHI N	—	HOU N	Cash

Scott Brown

Date	Traded To	Traded With	Traded By	In Exchange For
Dec. 11, 1981	KC A	—	CIN N	Clint Hurdle

Three Finger Brown

Date	Traded To	Traded With	Traded By	In Exchange For
Dec. 12, 1903	CHI N	Jack O'Neill	STL N	Jack Taylor Larry McLean
Feb. 10, 1916	CHI N	Clem Clemens Mickey Doolan Bill Fischer Max Flack Claude Hendrix Les Mann Dykes Potter Joe Tinker Rollie Zeider George McConnell	CHI F	Cash

Tommy Brown

Date	Traded To	Traded With	Traded By	In Exchange For
June 8, 1951	PHI N	—	BKN N	Dick Whitman Cash
June 15, 1952	CHI N	—	PHI N	Cash

Byron Browne

Date	Traded To	Traded With	Traded By	In Exchange For
May 4, 1968	HOU N	—	CHI N	Aaron Pointer
Oct. 7, 1969	PHI N	*see Curt Flood*	STL N	—

Earl Browne

Date	Traded To	Traded With	Traded By	In Exchange For
Apr. 16, 1937	PHI N	—	PIT N	Joe Bowman

George Browne

Date	Traded To	Traded With	Traded By	In Exchange For
July 1902	NY N	—	PHI N	Cash
Dec. 3, 1907	BOS N	Dan McGann Frank Bowerman Bill Dahlen George Ferguson	NY N	Fred Tenney Al Bridwell Tom Needham
Sept. 1908	CHI N	—	BOS N	Cash
May 21, 1909	WAS A	—	CHI N	Waiver price
May 1910	CHI A	—	WAS A	Cash

Jerry Browne

Date	Traded To	Traded With	Traded By	In Exchange For
Dec. 6, 1988	CLE A	—	TEX A	*see Julio Franco*
Jan. 5, 1994	FLA N	—	OAK A	No compensation (free agent signing)

Cal Browning

Date	Traded To	Traded With	Traded By	In Exchange For
Jan. 26, 1961	LA A	Leon Wagner Ellis Burton Cash	STL N	Al Cicotte

Bob Bruce

Date	Traded To	Traded With	Traded By	In Exchange For
Dec. 1, 1961	HOU N	Manny Montejo	DET A	Sam Jones
Dec. 31, 1966	ATL N	Dave Nicholson	HOU N	Sandy Alomar Eddie Mathews Arnie Umbach

J. T. Bruett

Date	Traded To	Traded With	Traded By	In Exchange For
June 22, 1995	CLE A	—	MIN A	Cash

Frank Bruggy

Date	Traded To	Traded With	Traded By	In Exchange For
Dec. 1921	PHI A	—	PHI N	Cash

Mike Bruhert

Date	Traded To	Traded With	Traded By	In Exchange For
June 15, 1979	TEX A	Bob Myrick	NY N	Dock Ellis

Jacob Brumfield

Date	Traded To	Traded With	Traded By	In Exchange For
Oct. 13, 1994	PIT N	—	CIN N	Minor league OF Danny Clyburn

Duff Brumley

Date	Traded To	Traded With	Traded By	In Exchange For
July 22, 1993	TEX A	—	STL N	Todd Burns

(Texas received Brumley on July 30, 1993.)

Mike Brumley

Date	Traded To	Traded With	Traded By	In Exchange For
Oct. 14, 1963	WAS A	—	LA N	Cash

Mike Brumley

Date	Traded To	Traded With	Traded By	In Exchange For
May 25, 1984	CHI N	—	BOS A	*see Bill Buckner*
Feb. 12, 1988	SD N	—	CHI N	*see Goose Gossage*
Mar. 23, 1989	DET A	—	SD N	Luis Salazar
Jan. 10, 1990	BAL A	—	DET A	Larry Sheets
Oct. 4, 1993	CAL A	—	HOU N	Waiver price

Greg Brummett

Date	Traded To	Traded With	Traded By	In Exchange For
Aug. 28, 1993	MIN A	Minor league P Aaron Fultz Minor league SS Andres Duncan	SF N	Jim Deshaies

(Minnesota received Brummett on September 1, 1993.)

Date	Traded To	Traded With	Traded By	In Exchange For
June 30, 1994	BOS A	—	MIN A	Waiver price

Tom Brunansky

Date	Traded To	Traded With	Traded By	In Exchange For
May 12, 1982	MIN A	Mike Walters $400,000.	CAL A	Doug Corbett Rob Wilfong
Apr. 22, 1988	STL N	—	MIN A	Tommy Herr
May 4, 1990	BOS A	—	STL N	Lee Smith
Jan. 28, 1993	MIL A	—	BOS A	No compensation (free agent signing)
June 16, 1994	BOS A	—	MIL A	Dave Valle

Jack Bruner

Date	Traded To	Traded With	Traded By	In Exchange For
July 1, 1950	STL A	—	CHI A	Cash

George Brunet

Date	Traded To	Traded With	Traded By	In Exchange For
May 11, 1960	MIL N	—	KC A	Bob Giggie
July 14, 1963	BAL A	—	HOU N	Cash
May 12, 1964	HOU N	—	BAL A	Cash
Aug. 18, 1964	LA A	—	HOU N	Cash
July 31, 1969	SEA A	—	CAL A	Cash
Dec. 4, 1969	WAS A	—	SEA A	Dave Baldwin
Aug. 31, 1970	PIT N	—	WAS A	Denny Riddleberger Cash
Jan. 29, 1971	STL N	Matty Alou	PIT N	Nellie Briles Vic Davalillo

Warren Brusstar

Date	Traded To	Traded With	Traded By	In Exchange For
Aug. 30, 1982	CHI A	—	PHI N	Cash
Jan. 25, 1983	CHI N	Steve Trout	CHI A	Scott Fletcher Pat Tabler Randy Martz Dick Tidrow

Bill Bruton

Date	Traded To		Traded With	Traded By		In Exchange For
Dec. 7, 1960	DET	A	Terry Fox Dick Brown Chuck Cottier	MIL	N	Frank Bolling Neil Chrisley

Billy Bryan

Date	Traded To		Traded With	Traded By		In Exchange For
June 10, 1966	NY	A	Fred Talbot	KC	A	Gil Blanco Roger Repoz Bill Stafford

Don Bryant

Date	Traded To		Traded With	Traded By		In Exchange For
Apr. 3, 1967	SF	N	—	CHI	N	Cash

Ron Bryant

Date	Traded To		Traded With	Traded By		In Exchange For
May 9, 1975	STL	N	—	SF	N	Larry Herndon minor league P Luis Gonzalez

Steve Brye

Date	Traded To		Traded With	Traded By		In Exchange For
Mar. 21, 1977	MIL	A	—	MIN	A	Cash
Feb. 7, 1979	SD	N	—	PIT	N	No compensation (free agent signing)

Johnny Bucha

Date	Traded To		Traded With	Traded By		In Exchange For
June 9, 1954	BKN	N	Charlie Kress Ernie Nevel Cash	DET	A	Wayne Belardi

Bob Buchanan

Date	Traded To		Traded With	Traded By		In Exchange For
Nov. 11, 1985	CIN	N	—	SF	N	Colin Ward

Jerry Buchek

Date	Traded To		Traded With	Traded By		In Exchange For
Apr. 1, 1967	NY	N	Art Mahaffey Tony Martinez	STL	N	Ed Bressoud Danny Napoleon Cash
Apr. 3, 1969	PHI	N	Jim Hutto	STL	N	Bill White

Jim Bucher

Date	Traded To		Traded With	Traded By		In Exchange For
Oct. 4, 1937	STL	N	Johnny Cooney Joe Stripp Roy Henshaw	BKN	N	Leo Durocher

Kevin Buckley

Date	Traded To		Traded With	Traded By		In Exchange For
Apr. 4, 1985	CLE	A	—	TEX	A	Jeff Moronko

(Texas received Moronko on April 29, 1985.)

Bill Buckner

Date	Traded To		Traded With	Traded By		In Exchange For
Jan. 11, 1977	CHI	N	Ivan DeJesus minor league P Jeff Albert	LA	N	Rick Monday Mike Garman
May 25, 1984	BOS	A	—	CHI	N	Dennis Eckersley Mike Brumley

Don Buddin

Date	Traded To		Traded With	Traded By		In Exchange For
Nov. 26, 1961	HOU	N	—	BOS	A	Ed Bressoud
July 20, 1962	DET	A	—	HOU	N	Cash

Steve Buechele

Date	Traded To		Traded With	Traded By		In Exchange For
Aug. 30, 1991	PIT	N	—	TEX	A	Hector Fajardo Kurt Miller
			(Texas received Fajardo on September 6, 1991.)			
July 10, 1992	CHI	N	—	PIT	N	Danny Jackson

Fritz Buelow

Date	Traded To		Traded With	Traded By		In Exchange For
Aug. 7, 1904	CLE	A	Charlie Carr	DET	A	Piano Legs Hickman
Dec. 1906	STL	A	—	CLE	A	Pete O'Brien

Damon Buford

Date	Traded To		Traded With	Traded By		In Exchange For
July 28, 1995	NY	N	Alex Ochoa	BAL	A	Bobby Bonilla Player to be named

(Baltimore received P Jimmy Williams on August 16, 1995.)

Don Buford

Date	Traded To		Traded With	Traded By		In Exchange For
Nov. 29, 1967	BAL	A	Bruce Howard Roger Nelson	CHI	A	Luis Aparicio Russ Snyder John Matias

Bob Buhl

Date	Traded To		Traded With	Traded By		In Exchange For
Apr. 30, 1962	CHI	N	—	MIL	N	Jack Curtis
Apr. 21, 1966	PHI	N	Larry Jackson	CHI	N	Adolfo Phillips John Herrnstein Ferguson Jenkins

Jay Buhner

Date	Traded To		Traded With	Traded By		In Exchange For
Dec. 20, 1984	NY	A	Dale Berra	PIT	N	Steve Kemp Tim Foli $400,000.
July 21, 1988	SEA	A	Minor league P Rich Balabon player to be named	NY	A	Ken Phelps

(Seattle received P Troy Evers on October 12, 1988.)

DeWayne Buice

Date	Traded To		Traded With	Traded By		In Exchange For
Mar. 9, 1989	TOR	A	—	CAL	A	Cliff Young

Scott Bullett

Date	Traded To		Traded With	Traded By		In Exchange For
Mar. 29, 1994	CHI	N	—	PIT	N	Minor league P Travis Willis

Terry Bulling

Date	Traded To		Traded With	Traded By		In Exchange For
Mar. 29, 1979	SEA	A	—	MIN	A	Cash

Eric Bullock

Date	Traded To		Traded With	Traded By		In Exchange For
June 2, 1987	MIN	A	—	HOU	N	Clay Christiansen
Oct. 24, 1988	PHI	N	*see Tommy Herr*	MIN	A	—

Al Bumbry

Date	Traded To		Traded With	Traded By		In Exchange For
Mar. 28, 1985	SD	N	—	BAL	A	No compensation (free agent signing)

Jim Bunning

Date	Traded To		Traded With	Traded By		In Exchange For
Dec. 4, 1963	PHI	N	Gus Triandos	DET	A	Don Demeter Jack Hamilton
Dec. 15, 1967	PIT	N	—	PHI	N	Don Money Woodie Fryman Bill Laxton minor league P Hal Clem
Aug. 15, 1969	LA	N	—	PIT	N	Minor leaguers OF Ron Mitchell and IF Chuck Coggin Cash

Dave Burba

Date	Traded To		Traded With	Traded By		In Exchange For
Dec. 11, 1991	SF	N	—	SEA	A	*see Kevin Mitchell*
July 21, 1995	CIN	N	—	SF	N	*see Deion Sanders*

Bill Burbach

Date	Traded To		Traded With	Traded By		In Exchange For
May 28, 1971	BAL	A	—	NY	A	Jim Hardin

Al Burch

Date	Traded To		Traded With	Traded By		In Exchange For
July 5, 1907	BKN	N	—	STL	N	Cash

Bob Burda

Date	Traded To		Traded With	Traded By		In Exchange For
Feb. 11, 1965	SF	N	Bob Priddy	PIT	N	Del Crandall
June 9, 1970	MIL	A	—	SF	N	Cash
Feb. 2, 1971	STL	N	—	MIL	A	Minor league P Fred Reahm
Mar. 20, 1972	BOS	A	—	STL	N	Mike Fiore

Lew Burdette

Date	Traded To		Traded With	Traded By		In Exchange For
Aug. 30, 1951	BOS	N	$50,000.	NY	A	Johnny Sain
June 15, 1963	STL	N	—	MIL	N	Gene Oliver Bob Sadowski
June 2, 1964	CHI	N	—	STL	N	Glen Hobbie
May 30, 1965	PHI	N	—	CHI	N	Cash

Smoky Burgess

Date	Traded To		Traded With	Traded By		In Exchange For
Oct. 4, 1951	CIN	N	Bob Borkowski	CHI	N	Johnny Pramesa Bob Usher
Dec. 10, 1951	PHI	N	Howie Fox Connie Ryan	CIN	N	Andy Seminick Eddie Pellagrini Dick Sisler Niles Jordan
Apr. 30, 1955	CIN	N	Steve Ridzik Stan Palys	PHI	N	Andy Seminick Glen Gorbous Jim Greengrass
Jan. 30, 1959	PIT	N	Harvey Haddix Don Hoak	CIN	N	Whammy Douglas Jim Pendleton Frank Thomas Johnny Powers
Sept. 12, 1964	CHI	A	—	PIT	N	Waiver price

Tom Burgmeier

Date	Traded To		Traded With	Traded By		In Exchange For
Oct. 24, 1973	MIN	A	—	KC	A	Minor leaguer Ken Gill
Nov. 15, 1982	OAK	A	—	BOS	A	No compensation (free agent signing)

Enrique Burgos

Date	Traded To		Traded With	Traded By		In Exchange For
Apr. 22, 1995	SF	N	—	KC	A	Brent Cookson

(Kansas City received Cookson on June 26, 1995.)

Sandy Burk

Date	Traded To		Traded With	Traded By		In Exchange For
Apr. 1912	STL	N	—	BKN	N	Cash

Glenn Burke

Date	Traded To		Traded With	Traded By		In Exchange For
May 17, 1978	OAK	A	—	LA	N	Billy North

Jimmy Burke

Date	Traded To		Traded With	Traded By		In Exchange For
July 1901	CHI	A	—	MIL	A	Cash
Sept. 1901	PIT	N	—	CHI	A	Cash
Jan. 1903	STL	N	—	PIT	N	Otto Krueger

Leo Burke

Date	Traded To		Traded With	Traded By		In Exchange For
Jan. 4, 1961	LA	A	—	WAS	A	Cash
Mar. 25, 1963	STL	N	—	LA	A	Cash
June 24, 1963	CHI	N	—	STL	N	Barney Schultz

Tim Burke

Date	Traded To		Traded With	Traded By		In Exchange For
Dec. 22, 1982	NY	A	Minor league P John Holland Minor league 1B Jose Rivera Minor league OF Don Aubin	PIT	N	Lee Mazzilli
Dec. 20, 1983	MON	N	—	NY	A	Pat Rooney
July 15, 1991	NY	N	—	MON	N	Ron Darling Mike Thomas
June 9, 1992	NY	A	—	NY	N	Lee Guetterman

Jesse Burkett

Date	Traded To		Traded With	Traded By		In Exchange For
Jan. 16, 1905	BOS	A	—	STL	A	George Stone

John Burkett

Date	Traded To		Traded With	Traded By		In Exchange For
Dec. 22, 1994	TEX	A	—	SF	N	Rich Aurilia Minor league OF Desi Wilson
Apr. 8, 1995	FLA	N	—	TEX	A	No compensation (free agent signing)

Ken Burkhart

Date	Traded To		Traded With	Traded By		In Exchange For
July 26, 1948	CIN	N	—	STL	N	Cash

Ellis Burks

Date	Traded To		Traded With	Traded By		In Exchange For
Jan. 4, 1993	CHI	A	—	BOS	A	No compensation (free agent signing)
Nov. 30, 1993	CLR	N	—	CHI	A	No compensation (free agent signing)

Rick Burleson

Date	Traded To		Traded With	Traded By		In Exchange For
Dec. 10, 1980	CAL	A	Butch Hobson	BOS	A	Carney Lansford Rick Miller Mark Clear

Rick Burleson *continued*

Date	Traded To		Traded With	Traded By		In Exchange For
Jan. 7, 1987	BAL	A	—	CAL	A	No compensation (free agent signing)

Johnny Burnett

Date	Traded To		Traded With	Traded By		In Exchange For
Nov. 20, 1934	STL	A	Bob Weiland Cash	CLE	A	Bruce Campbell
Mar. 21, 1936	CIN	N	—	STL	A	Jim Bottomley

Jeromy Burnitz

Date	Traded To		Traded With	Traded By		In Exchange For
Nov. 18, 1994	CLE	A	Joe Roa	NY	N	Jerry DiPoto Dave Mlicki Paul Byrd

Bill Burns

Date	Traded To		Traded With	Traded By		In Exchange For
May 16, 1909	CHI	A	—	WAS	A	Nick Altrock Gavvy Cravath Jiggs Donahue
June 7, 1910	CIN	N	—	CHI	A	Cash
July 15, 1911	PHI	N	Fred Beck	CIN	N	Bert Humphries

Britt Burns

Date	Traded To		Traded With	Traded By		In Exchange For
Dec. 12, 1985	NY	A	Minor league SS Mike Soper Minor league OF Glen Braxton	CHI	A	Joe Cowley Ron Hassey

George Burns

Date	Traded To		Traded With	Traded By		In Exchange For
Dec. 6, 1921	CIN	N	Mike Gonzalez $150,000.	NY	N	Heinie Groh
Apr. 2, 1925	PHI	N	—	CIN	N	Waiver price

George Burns

Date	Traded To		Traded With	Traded By		In Exchange For
Mar. 8, 1918	NY	A	—	DET	A	Cash
Mar. 8, 1918	PHI	A	—	NY	A	Ping Bodie
May 29, 1920	CLE	A	—	PHI	A	Cash
Dec. 24, 1921	BOS	A	Joe Harris Elmer Smith	CLE	A	Stuffy McInnis
Jan. 7, 1924	CLE	A	Roxy Walters Chick Fewster	BOS	A	Danny Boone Steve O'Neill Joe Connolly Bill Wambsganss
June 19, 1929	PHI	A	—	NY	A	Cash

Jack Burns

Date	Traded To		Traded With	Traded By		In Exchange For
Apr. 30, 1936	DET	A	—	STL	A	Chief Hogsett

Todd Burns

Date	Traded To		Traded With	Traded By		In Exchange For
July 22, 1993	STL	N	—	TEX	A	Duff Brumley

(Texas received Brumley on July 30, 1993.)

Pete Burnside

Date	Traded To		Traded With	Traded By		In Exchange For
Oct. 5, 1958	DET	A	—	SF	N	Cash
Dec. 5, 1962	BAL	A	Bob Johnson	WAS	A	Barry Shetrone Marv Breeding minor league P Art Quick

Sheldon Burnside

Date	Traded To		Traded With	Traded By		In Exchange For
May 25, 1979	CIN	N	—	DET	A	Champ Summers

Larry Burright

Date	Traded To		Traded With	Traded By		In Exchange For
Nov. 30, 1962	NY	N	Tim Harkness	LA	N	Bob Miller

Ray Burris

Date	Traded To		Traded With	Traded By		In Exchange For
May 23, 1979	NY	A	—	CHI	N	Dick Tidrow
Aug. 20, 1979	NY	N	—	NY	A	Cash
Feb. 18, 1981	MON	N	—	NY	N	No compensation (free agent signing)
Dec. 7, 1983	OAK	A	—	MON	N	Rusty McNealy Cash

Ray Burris *continued*

Date	Traded To	Traded With	Traded By	In Exchange For
Dec. 7, 1984	MIL A	minor league P Eric Barry Player to be named	OAK A	Don Sutton

(Milwaukee received P Ed Myers on March 25, 1985.)

Jeff Burroughs

Date	Traded To	Traded With	Traded By	In Exchange For
Dec. 9, 1976	ATL N	—	TEX A	Ken Henderson Dave May Carl Morton Roger Moret Adrian Devine $250,000.
Mar. 7, 1981	SEA A	—	ATL N	Carlos Diaz
Apr. 7, 1982	OAK A	—	SEA A	No compensation (free agent signing)
Dec. 22, 1984	TOR A	—	OAK A	Cash

Ellis Burton

Date	Traded To	Traded With	Traded By	In Exchange For
Jan. 26, 1961	LA A	Leon Wagner Cal Browning Cash	STL N	Al Cicotte
Apr. 2, 1963	CLE A	—	HOU N	Cash

Jim Burton

Date	Traded To	Traded With	Traded By	In Exchange For
Mar. 29, 1978	NY N	—	BOS A	Leo Foster

Moe Burtschy

Date	Traded To	Traded With	Traded By	In Exchange For
June 14, 1956	NY A	Bill Renna Cash	KC A	Lou Skizas Eddie Robinson

Jim Busby

Date	Traded To	Traded With	Traded By	In Exchange For
May 3, 1952	WAS A	Mel Hoderlein	CHI A	Sam Mele
June 7, 1955	CHI A	—	WAS A	Bob Chakales Clint Courtney Johnny Groth
Oct. 25, 1955	CLE A	Chico Carrasquel	CHI A	Larry Doby
June 13, 1957	BAL A	—	CLE A	Dick Williams
Dec. 15, 1958	BOS A	—	BAL A	Billy Klaus

Donie Bush

Date	Traded To	Traded With	Traded By	In Exchange For
Aug. 20, 1921	WAS A	—	DET A	Waiver price

Guy Bush

Date	Traded To	Traded With	Traded By	In Exchange For
Nov. 22, 1934	PIT N	Jim Weaver Babe Herman	CHI N	Larry French Freddie Lindstrom
Feb. 2, 1938	STL N	—	BOS N	Cash

Joe Bush

Date	Traded To	Traded With	Traded By	In Exchange For
Dec. 14, 1917	BOS A	Amos Strunk Wally Schang	PHI A	Vean Gregg Merlin Kopp Pinch Thomas $60,000.
Dec. 20, 1921	NY A	Everett Scott Sad Sam Jones	BOS A	Roger Peckinpaugh Jack Quinn Rip Collins Bill Piercy
Dec. 17, 1924	STL A	Milt Gaston Joe Giard	NY A	Urban Shocker
Feb. 1926	WAS A	Jack Tobin	STL A	Tom Zachary Win Ballou
July 1, 1926	PIT N	—	WAS A	Cash

Mike Buskey

Date	Traded To	Traded With	Traded By	In Exchange For
Dec. 10, 1975	PHI N	Jim Kaat	CHI A	Dick Ruthven Alan Bannister Roy Thomas
Sept. 11, 1978	HOU N	—	PHI N	Cash

Tom Buskey

Date	Traded To	Traded With	Traded By	In Exchange For
Apr. 27, 1974	CLE A	—	NY A	*see Chris Chambliss*

Tom Buskey *continued*

Date	Traded To	Traded With	Traded By	In Exchange For
Feb. 28, 1978	TEX A	John Lowenstein	CLE A	Willie Horton David Clyde

Ray Busse

Date	Traded To	Traded With	Traded By	In Exchange For
Nov. 28, 1972	STL N	Bobby Fenwick	HOU N	Skip Jutze Milt Ramirez
June 8, 1973	HOU N	—	STL N	Stan Papi

John Butcher

Date	Traded To	Traded With	Traded By	In Exchange For
Dec. 7, 1983	MIN A	Mike Smithson minor league C Sam Sorce	TEX A	Gary Ward
June 20, 1986	CLE A	—	MIN A	Neal Heaton

Max Butcher

Date	Traded To	Traded With	Traded By	In Exchange For
Aug. 8, 1938	PHI N	—	BKN N	Wayne LaMaster
July 28, 1939	PIT N	—	PHI N	Gus Suhr

Sal Butera

Date	Traded To	Traded With	Traded By	In Exchange For
Mar. 25, 1983	DET A	—	MIN A	Minor league C Stine Poole Cash
Dec. 19, 1985	CIN N	Bill Gullickson	MON N	Jay Tibbs Andy McGaffigan Dann Bilardello John Stuper

Art Butler

Date	Traded To	Traded With	Traded By	In Exchange For
Jan. 1912	PIT N	—	BOS N	Cash
Dec. 12, 1913	STL N	—	PIT N	*see Ed Konetchy*

Bill Butler

Date	Traded To	Traded With	Traded By	In Exchange For
July 11, 1972	CLE A	—	KC A	Cash

Brett Butler

Date	Traded To	Traded With	Traded By	In Exchange For
Aug. 28, 1983	CLE A	Rick Behenna Brook Jacoby $150,000.	ATL N	Len Barker

(Cleveland received Butler and Jacoby on October 21, 1983.)

Date	Traded To	Traded With	Traded By	In Exchange For
Dec. 1, 1987	SF N	—	CLE A	No compensation (free agent signing)
Dec. 14, 1990	LA N	—	SF N	No compensation (free agent signing)
Apr. 11, 1995	NY N	—	LA N	No compensation (free agent signing)
Aug. 18, 1995	LA N	—	NY N	Minor league OFs Scott Hunter and Dwight Maness

Johnny Butler

Date	Traded To	Traded With	Traded By	In Exchange For
Dec. 1927	CHI N	—	BKN N	Howard Freigau

Rob Butler

Date	Traded To	Traded With	Traded By	In Exchange For
Dec. 5, 1994	PHI N	—	TOR A	Player to be named

John Buzhardt

Date	Traded To	Traded With	Traded By	In Exchange For
Jan. 11, 1960	PHI N	Alvin Dark Jim Woods	CHI N	Richie Ashburn
Nov. 28, 1961	CHI A	Charley Smith	PHI N	Roy Sievers
Aug. 21, 1967	BAL A	—	CHI A	Cash
Sept. 23, 1967	HOU N	—	BAL A	Cash

Bud Byerly

Date	Traded To	Traded With	Traded By	In Exchange For
June 15, 1952	BKN N	Cash	CIN N	Bud Podbielan
June 24, 1958	BOS A	—	WAS A	Jack Spring

Harry Byrd

Date	Traded To	Traded With	Traded By	In Exchange For
Dec. 16, 1953	NY A	Eddie Robinson Tom Hamilton Carmen Mauro Loren Babe	PHI A	Don Bollweg John Gray Jim Robertson Jim Finigan Vic Power Bill Renna
Nov. 18, 1954	BAL A	—	NY A	*see Bob Turley*

Harry Byrd *continued*

Date	Traded To	Traded With	Traded By	In Exchange For
June 15, 1955	CHI A	—	BAL A	Waiver price
May 15, 1956	DET A	Jim Brideweser Bob Kennedy	CHI A	Fred Hatfield Jim Delsing

Paul Byrd

Date	Traded To	Traded With	Traded By	In Exchange For
Nov. 18, 1994	NY N	—	CLE A	*see Jeromy Burnitz*

Sammy Byrd

Date	Traded To	Traded With	Traded By	In Exchange For
Dec. 19, 1934	CIN N	—	NY A	Cash

Bobby Byrne

Date	Traded To	Traded With	Traded By	In Exchange For
Aug. 19, 1909	PIT N	—	STL N	Jap Barbeau Alan Storke
Aug. 20, 1913	PHI N	Howie Camnitz	PIT N	Cozy Dolan Cash
Sept. 1917	CHI A	—	PHI N	Waiver price

Tommy Byrne

Date	Traded To	Traded With	Traded By	In Exchange For
June 15, 1951	STL A	$25,000.	NY A	Stubby Overmire
Oct. 16, 1952	CHI A	Joe De Maestri	STL A	Willie Miranda Hank Edwards
June 11, 1953	WAS A	—	CHI A	Cash

Marty Bystrom

Date	Traded To	Traded With	Traded By	In Exchange For
June 30, 1984	NY A	Keith Hughes	PHI N	Shane Rawley

Enos Cabell

Date	Traded To	Traded With	Traded By	In Exchange For
Dec. 3, 1974	HOU N	Rob Andrews	BAL A	Lee May Jay Schlueter
Dec. 8, 1980	SF N	—	HOU N	Bob Knepper Chris Bourjos
Mar. 4, 1982	DET A	Cash	SF N	Champ Summers
Feb. 14, 1984	HOU N	—	DET A	No compensation (free agent signing)
July 10, 1985	LA N	—	HOU N	Rafael Montalvo German Rivera

Francisco Cabrera

Date	Traded To	Traded With	Traded By	In Exchange For
Aug. 24, 1989	ATL N	Tony Castillo	TOR A	Jim Acker

(Atlanta received Cabrera on Aug. 29, 1989.)

Craig Cacek

Date	Traded To	Traded With	Traded By	In Exchange For
Dec. 17, 1981	CAL A	—	PIT N	Cash

Edgar Caceres

Date	Traded To	Traded With	Traded By	In Exchange For
Apr. 13, 1988	CHI A	—	MON N	Tim Hulett

Greg Cadaret

Date	Traded To	Traded With	Traded By	In Exchange For
June 21, 1989	NY A	Eric Plunk Luis Polonia	OAK A	Rickey Henderson
Nov. 6, 1992	CIN N	—	NY A	Cash

Leon Cadore

Date	Traded To	Traded With	Traded By	In Exchange For
July 6, 1923	CHI A	—	BKN N	Waiver price

Hick Cady

Date	Traded To	Traded With	Traded By	In Exchange For
Jan. 10, 1918	PHI A	Larry Gardner Tilly Walker	BOS A	Stuffy McInnis

Wayne Cage

Date	Traded To	Traded With	Traded By	In Exchange For
Mar. 26, 1981	SEA A	—	CLE A	Rodney Craig

Bob Cain

Date	Traded To	Traded With	Traded By	In Exchange For
May 15, 1951	DET A	—	CHI A	Saul Rogovin
Feb. 14, 1952	STL A	Gene Bearden Dick Kryhoski	DET A	Dick Littlefield Ben Taylor Cliff Mapes

Bob Cain *continued*

Date	Traded To	Traded With	Traded By	In Exchange For
Dec. 17, 1953	PHI A	—	BAL A	Frank Fanovich Joe Coleman

Sugar Cain

Date	Traded To	Traded With	Traded By	In Exchange For
May 21, 1935	STL A	Ed Coleman	PHI A	George Blaeholder
May 5, 1936	CHI A	—	STL A	Les Tietje

Ivan Calderon

Date	Traded To	Traded With	Traded By	In Exchange For
June 26, 1986	CHI A	—	SEA A	Scott Bradley

(Chicago received Calderon on July 1, 1986.)

Date	Traded To	Traded With	Traded By	In Exchange For
Dec. 24, 1990	MON N	Barry Jones	CHI A	Tim Raines Minor league P Jeff Carter Player to be named

(Chicago received P Mario Brito on February 15, 1991.)

Date	Traded To	Traded With	Traded By	In Exchange For
Dec. 8, 1992	BOS A	—	MON N	Mike Gardiner Minor league P Terry Powers

Sammy Calderone

Date	Traded To	Traded With	Traded By	In Exchange For
Feb. 1, 1954	MIL N	—	NY N	*see Johnny Antonelli*

Mike Caldwell

Date	Traded To	Traded With	Traded By	In Exchange For
Oct. 25, 1973	SF N	—	SD N	Willie McCovey Bernie Williams
Oct. 20, 1976	STL N	John D'Acquisto Dave Rader	SF N	Willie Crawford Vic Harris John Curtis
Mar. 29, 1977	CIN N	—	STL N	Pat Darcy
June 15, 1977	MIL A	—	CIN N	Minor leaguers P Dick O'Keefe and IF Garry Pyka

Ray Caldwell

Date	Traded To	Traded With	Traded By	In Exchange For
Dec. 18, 1918	BOS A	Frank Gilhooley Slim Love Roxy Walters $15,000.	NY A	Ernie Shore Duffy Lewis Dutch Leonard

Jeff Calhoun

Date	Traded To	Traded With	Traded By	In Exchange For
Apr. 2, 1987	PHI N	—	HOU N	Ronn Reynolds

Ben Callahan

Date	Traded To	Traded With	Traded By	In Exchange For
June 15, 1983	OAK A	Marshall Brant Cash	NY A	Matt Keough

Johnny Callison

Date	Traded To	Traded With	Traded By	In Exchange For
Dec. 9, 1959	PHI N	—	CHI A	Gene Freese
Nov. 17, 1969	CHI N	—	PHI N	Dick Selma Oscar Gamble
Jan. 20, 1972	NY A	—	CHI N	Jack Aker

(Chicago received Aker on May 17, 1972.)

Paul Calvert

Date	Traded To	Traded With	Traded By	In Exchange For
Feb. 15, 1950	DET A	—	WAS A	Waiver price

Ernie Camacho

Date	Traded To	Traded With	Traded By	In Exchange For
Apr. 6, 1981	PIT N	Cash	OAK A	Bob Owchinko
Mar. 21, 1982	CHI A	Vance Law	PIT N	Ross Baumgarten Butch Edge
June 6, 1983	CLE A	Gorman Thomas Jamie Easterly	MIL A	Rick Manning Rick Waits

Hank Camelli

Date	Traded To	Traded With	Traded By	In Exchange For
Sept. 30, 1946	BOS N	Bob Elliott	PIT N	Billy Herman Elmer Singleton Stan Wentzel Whitey Wietelmann

Dolf Camilli

Date	Traded To		Traded With	Traded By		In Exchange For
June 11, 1934	PHI	N	—	CHI	N	Don Hurst
Mar. 6, 1938	BKN	N	—	PHI	N	Eddie Morgan $45,000.
July 31, 1943	NY	N	Johnny Allen	BKN	N	Bill Lohrman Bill Sayles Joe Orengo

(Camilli refused to report to New York and retired.)

Doug Camilli

Date	Traded To		Traded With	Traded By		In Exchange For
Nov. 30, 1964	WAS	A	—	LA	N	Cash

Ken Caminiti

Date	Traded To		Traded With	Traded By		In Exchange For
Dec. 28, 1994	SD	N	Steve Finley Andujar Cedeno Brian Williams Roberto Petagine Player to be named	HOU	N	Phil Plantier Derek Bell Pedro Martinez Doug Brocail Craig Shipley Ricky Gutierrez

(San Diego received P Sean Fesh on May 1, 1995.)

Howie Camnitz

Date	Traded To		Traded With	Traded By		In Exchange For
Aug. 20, 1913	PHI	N	Bobby Byrne	PIT	N	Cozy Dolan Cash

Bert Campaneris

Date	Traded To		Traded With	Traded By		In Exchange For
Nov. 17, 1976	TEX	A	—	OAK	A	No compensation (free agent signing)
May 4, 1979	CAL	A	—	TEX	A	Dave Chalk

Jim Campanis

Date	Traded To		Traded With	Traded By		In Exchange For
Dec. 15, 1968	KC	A	—	LA	N	Two minor leaguers
Dec. 2, 1970	PIT	N	—	KC	A	*see Freddie Patek*

Bill Campbell

Date	Traded To		Traded With	Traded By		In Exchange For
Nov. 6, 1976	BOS	A	—	MIN	A	No compensation (free agent signing)
Dec. 8, 1981	CHI	N	—	BOS	A	No compensation (free agent signing)
Mar. 26, 1984	PHI	N	Mike Diaz	CHI	N	Gary Matthews Porfi Altamirano Bob Dernier
Apr. 6, 1985	STL	N	Ivan DeJesus	PHI	N	Dave Rucker
Jan. 31, 1986	DET	A	—	STL	N	No compensation (free agent signing)

Bruce Campbell

Date	Traded To		Traded With	Traded By		In Exchange For
Apr. 27, 1932	STL	A	Bump Hadley	CHI	A	Red Kress
Nov. 20, 1934	CLE	A	—	STL	A	Johnny Burnett Bob Weiland Cash
Jan. 20, 1940	DET	A	—	CLE	A	Beau Bell
Dec. 12, 1941	WAS	A	Frank Croucher	DET	A	Jimmy Bloodworth Doc Cramer

Dave Campbell

Date	Traded To		Traded With	Traded By		In Exchange For
Mar. 31, 1979	MON	N	—	ATL	N	Pepe Frias

Dave Campbell

Date	Traded To		Traded With	Traded By		In Exchange For
Dec. 4, 1969	SD	N	Pat Dobson	DET	A	Joe Niekro
June 7, 1973	STL	N	—	SD	N	Dwain Anderson
Aug. 18, 1973	HOU	N	Cash	STL	N	Tommie Agee

Jim Campbell

Date	Traded To		Traded With	Traded By		In Exchange For
Oct. 21, 1970	BOS	A	—	STL	N	Dick Schofield

Jim Campbell

Date	Traded To		Traded With	Traded By		In Exchange For
Oct. 9, 1963	CIN	N	—	HOU	N	Cash

Kevin Campbell

Date	Traded To		Traded With	Traded By		In Exchange For
Jan. 15, 1991	OAK	A	—	LA	N	David Veres

Mike Campbell

Date	Traded To		Traded With	Traded By		In Exchange For
May 25, 1989	MON	N	Mark Langston	SEA	A	Randy Johnson Brian Holman Gene Harris

(Montreal received Campbell on July 31, 1989.)

Date	Traded To		Traded With	Traded By		In Exchange For
Apr. 5, 1990	CHI	A	—	MON	N	Minor league 2B Rob Fletcher

Ron Campbell

Date	Traded To		Traded With	Traded By		In Exchange For
Jan. 15, 1969	PIT	N	Chuck Hartenstein	CHI	N	Manny Jimenez

Vin Campbell

Date	Traded To		Traded With	Traded By		In Exchange For
Jan. 1910	PIT	N	—	CHI	N	Cash
Feb. 1912	BOS	N	—	PIT	N	Mike Donlin

Card Camper

Date	Traded To		Traded With	Traded By		In Exchange For
May 28, 1976	CLE	A	—	STL	N	Cash

Sal Campisi

Date	Traded To		Traded With	Traded By		In Exchange For
Oct. 20, 1970	MIN	A	Jim Kennedy	STL	N	Herman Hill minor league OF Charlie Wissler

George Canale

Date	Traded To		Traded With	Traded By		In Exchange For
Oct. 15, 1991	MON	N	—	MIL	A	Alex Diaz

Willie Canate

Date	Traded To		Traded With	Traded By		In Exchange For
Apr. 13, 1993	TOR	A	—	CIN	N	Waiver price

Casey Candaele

Date	Traded To		Traded With	Traded By		In Exchange For
July 23, 1988	HOU	N	—	MON	N	Mark Bailey

John Candelaria

Date	Traded To		Traded With	Traded By		In Exchange For
Aug. 2, 1985	CAL	A	Al Holland George Hendrick	PIT	N	Pat Clements Mike Brown Bob Kipper

(Pittsburgh received Kipper on Aug. 16, 1985.)

Date	Traded To		Traded With	Traded By		In Exchange For
Sept. 15, 1987	NY	N	—	CAL	A	Jeff Richardson Minor league P Shane Young
Jan. 15, 1988	NY	A	—	NY	N	No compensation (free agent signing)
Aug. 29, 1989	MON	N	—	NY	A	Mike Blowers
July 27, 1990	TOR	A	—	MIN	A	Nelson Liriano Pedro Munoz
Dec. 16, 1992	PIT	N	—	LA	N	No compensation (free agent signing)

Milo Candini

Date	Traded To		Traded With	Traded By		In Exchange For
Jan. 29, 1943	WAS	A	Gerry Priddy	NY	A	Bill Zuber Cash

Tom Candiotti

Date	Traded To		Traded With	Traded By		In Exchange For
June 27, 1991	TOR	A	Turner Ward	CLE	A	Glenallen Hill Mark Whiten Denis Boucher Cash
Dec. 3, 1991	LA	N	—	TOR	A	No compensation (free agent signing)

John Cangelosi

Date	Traded To		Traded With	Traded By		In Exchange For
Mar. 27, 1987	PIT	N	—	CHI	A	Jim Winn

(Pittsburgh received Cangelosi on March 30, 1987.)

Date	Traded To		Traded With	Traded By		In Exchange For
May 23, 1991	MIL	A	—	CHI	A	Esteban Beltre

Chris Cannizzaro

Date	Traded To		Traded With	Traded By		In Exchange For
Dec. 19, 1966	DET	A	—	NY	N	Cash
Nov. 29, 1967	PIT	N	—	DET	A	Cash
Mar. 28, 1969	SD	N	Tommie Sisk	PIT	N	Ron Davis Bobby Klaus
May 19, 1971	CHI	N	—	SD	N	Garry Jestadt
Dec. 17, 1971	LA	N	—	CHI	N	Cash

Joe Cannon

Date	Traded To	Traded With	Traded By	In Exchange For
Nov. 27, 1978	TOR A	Pedro Hernandez Mark Lemongello	HOU N	Alan Ashby

Jose Canseco

Date	Traded To	Traded With	Traded By	In Exchange For
Aug. 31, 1992	TEX A	—	OAK A	Ruben Sierra Bobby Witt Jeff Russell Cash
Dec. 9, 1994	BOS A	—	TEX A	Otis Nixon Luis Ortiz

Ozzie Canseco

Date	Traded To	Traded With	Traded By	In Exchange For
Dec. 14, 1993	MIL A	—	STL N	Minor league OF Tony Diggs

Ben Cantwell

Date	Traded To	Traded With	Traded By	In Exchange For
June 15, 1928	BOS N	Virgil Barnes Al Spohrer Bill Clarkson	NY N	Joe Genewich
Jan. 27, 1937	NY N	Hal Lee	BOS N	Cash
Aug. 9, 1937	BKN N	—	NY N	Cash

Doug Capilla

Date	Traded To	Traded With	Traded By	In Exchange For
June 15, 1977	CIN N	—	STL N	Rawly Eastwick
May 3, 1979	CHI N	—	CIN N	Minor league P Mark Gilbert
Dec. 7, 1981	SF N	—	CHI N	Allen Ripley

George Cappuzzello

Date	Traded To	Traded With	Traded By	In Exchange For
Mar. 6, 1978	CIN N	minor league OF John Valle	DET A	Jack Billingham

Buzz Capra

Date	Traded To	Traded With	Traded By	In Exchange For
Mar. 26, 1974	ATL N	—	NY N	Cash

Ralph Capron

Date	Traded To	Traded With	Traded By	In Exchange For
Jan. 1913	PHI N	—	PIT N	Cash

Ramon Caraballo

Date	Traded To	Traded With	Traded By	In Exchange For
Nov. 28, 1994	STL N	—	ATL N	Player to be named

(Atlanta received 1B Aldo Pecorilli on December 9, 1994.)

Bernie Carbo

Date	Traded To	Traded With	Traded By	In Exchange For
May 19, 1972	STL N	—	CIN N	Joe Hague
Oct. 26, 1973	BOS A	Rick Wise	STL N	Reggie Smith Ken Tatum
June 3, 1976	MIL A	—	BOS A	Tom Murphy Bobby Darwin
Dec. 6, 1976	BOS A	George Scott	MIL A	Cecil Cooper
June 15, 1978	CLE A	—	BOS A	Cash
Mar. 10, 1979	STL N	—	BOS A	No compensation (free agent signing)

Jose Cardenal

Date	Traded To	Traded With	Traded By	In Exchange For
Nov. 21, 1964	LA A	—	SF N	Jack Hiatt
Nov. 29, 1967	CLE A	—	CAL A	Chuck Hinton
Nov. 21, 1969	STL N	—	CLE A	Vada Pinson
July 29, 1971	MIL A	Dick Schofield Bob Reynolds	STL N	Ted Kubiak minor league P Charlie Loseth
Dec. 3, 1971	CHI N	—	MIL A	Brock Davis Jim Colborn Earl Stephenson
Oct. 25, 1977	PHI N	—	CHI N	Manny Seoane
Aug. 2, 1979	NY N	—	PHI N	Cash

Leo Cardenas

Date	Traded To	Traded With	Traded By	In Exchange For
Nov. 21, 1968	MIN A	—	CIN N	Jim Merritt
Nov. 30, 1971	CAL A	—	MIN A	Dave LaRoche
Apr. 2, 1973	CLE A	—	CAL A	Tom McCraw minor league 2B Bob Marcano

Leo Cardenas *continued*

Date	Traded To	Traded With	Traded By	In Exchange For
Feb. 12, 1974	TEX A	—	CLE A	Ken Suarez

Don Cardwell

Date	Traded To	Traded With	Traded By	In Exchange For
May 13, 1960	CHI N	Ed Bouchee	PHI N	Tony Taylor Cal Neeman
Oct. 17, 1962	STL N	George Altman Moe Thacker	CHI N	Larry Jackson Jimmie Schaffer Lindy McDaniel
Nov. 19, 1962	PIT N	Julio Gotay	STL N	Dick Groat Diomedes Olivo
Dec. 6, 1966	NY N	Don Bosch	PIT N	Dennis Ribant Gary Kolb
July 12, 1970	ATL N	—	NY N	Cash

Rod Carew

Date	Traded To	Traded With	Traded By	In Exchange For
Feb. 3, 1979	CAL A	—	MIN A	Ken Landreaux Dave Engle Paul Hartzell Brad Havens

Andy Carey

Date	Traded To	Traded With	Traded By	In Exchange For
May 19, 1960	KC A	—	NY A	Bob Cerv
June 10, 1961	CHI A	—	KC A	*see Wes Covington*
Dec. 15, 1961	PHI N	Frank Barnes Cal McLish	CHI A	Bob Sadowski Taylor Phillips minor league IF Lou Vassie

(Carey refused to report, and the Phillies received McLish in exchange for Vassie to complete the trade on March 24, 1962.)

Date	Traded To	Traded With	Traded By	In Exchange For
Mar. 24, 1962	LA N	—	CHI A	Minor leaguers IF Ramon Conde and 1B Jim Koranda

Max Carey

Date	Traded To	Traded With	Traded By	In Exchange For
Aug. 13, 1926	BKN N	—	PIT N	Waiver price

Paul Carey

Date	Traded To	Traded With	Traded By	In Exchange For
Dec. 19, 1995	BOS A	—	BAL A	Player to be named

Tom Carey

Date	Traded To	Traded With	Traded By	In Exchange For
Dec. 6, 1938	BOS A	—	STL A	Johnny Marcum

Tex Carleton

Date	Traded To	Traded With	Traded By	In Exchange For
Nov. 21, 1934	CHI N	—	STL N	Bud Tinning Dick Ward Cash

Jim Carlin

Date	Traded To	Traded With	Traded By	In Exchange For
Dec. 11, 1938	WAS A	Tom Baker $20,000.	NY N	Zeke Bonura

Cisco Carlos

Date	Traded To	Traded With	Traded By	In Exchange For
Aug. 25, 1969	WAS A	—	CHI A	Cash

Hal Carlson

Date	Traded To	Traded With	Traded By	In Exchange For
June 7, 1927	CHI N	—	PHI N	Jimmy Cooney Tony Kaufmann

Steve Carlton

Date	Traded To	Traded With	Traded By	In Exchange For
Feb. 25, 1972	PHI N	—	STL N	Rick Wise
Apr. 3, 1987	CLE A	—	CHI A	No compensation (free agent signing)
July 31, 1987	MIN A	—	CLE A	Minor league P Jeff Perry

(Cleveland received Perry on August 18, 1987.)

Roy Carlyle

Date	Traded To	Traded With	Traded By	In Exchange For
Apr. 26, 1925	BOS A	Paul Zahniser	WAS A	Joe Harris
June 15, 1926	NY A	—	BOS A	Waiver price

Duke Carmel

Date	Traded To	Traded With	Traded By	In Exchange For
July 29, 1963	NY N	—	STL N	Jacke Davis Cash

Eddie Carnett

Date	Traded To	Traded With	Traded By	In Exchange For
Dec. 12, 1944	CLE A	—	CHI A	Oris Hockett

Cris Carpenter

Date	Traded To	Traded With	Traded By	In Exchange For
July 17, 1993	TEX A	—	FLA N	Robb Nen Minor league P Kurt Miller

Charlie Carr

Date	Traded To	Traded With	Traded By	In Exchange For
Aug. 7, 1904	CLE A	Fritz Buelow	DET A	Piano Legs Hickman
Feb. 1906	CIN N	—	CLE A	Cash

Chuck Carr

Date	Traded To	Traded With	Traded By	In Exchange For
Nov. 17, 1988	NY N	—	SEA A	Minor league P Reggie Dobie
Dec. 13, 1991	STL N	—	NY N	Minor league P Clyde Keller
Dec. 4, 1995	MIL A	—	FLA N	Minor league P Juan Gonzalez

Hector Carrasco

Date	Traded To	Traded With	Traded By	In Exchange For
Nov. 17, 1992	FLA N	Minor league P Brian Griffiths	HOU N	Tom Edens
Mar. 27, 1993	CIN N	Gary Scott	FLA N	Chris Hammond

(Cincinnati received Carrasco on September 10, 1993.)

Alex Carrasquel

Date	Traded To	Traded With	Traded By	In Exchange For
Jan. 2, 1946	CHI A	Fred Vaughn	WAS A	Cash

Chico Carrasquel

Date	Traded To	Traded With	Traded By	In Exchange For
Oct. 25, 1955	CLE A	Jim Busby	CHI A	Larry Doby
June 12, 1958	KC A	—	CLE A	Billy Hunter
Oct. 2, 1958	BAL A	—	KC A	Dick Williams

Amalio Carreno

Date	Traded To	Traded With	Traded By	In Exchange For
July 15, 1988	PHI N	—	NY A	Luis Aguayo

Camilo Carreon

Date	Traded To	Traded With	Traded By	In Exchange For
Jan. 20, 1965	CLE A	Rocky Colavito	CHI A	Tommy John Tommie Agee Johnny Romano

(Part of three-team trade involving Kansas City, Cleveland, and Chicago White Sox.)

Mark Carreon

Date	Traded To	Traded With	Traded By	In Exchange For
Jan. 22, 1992	DET A	Tony Castillo	NY N	Paul Gibson Minor league P Randy Marshall
Jan. 13, 1993	SF N	—	DET A	No compensation (free agent signing)

Don Carrithers

Date	Traded To	Traded With	Traded By	In Exchange For
Apr. 1, 1974	MON N	—	SF N	John Boccabella
Apr. 6, 1977	MIN A	—	MON N	Cash

Clay Carroll

Date	Traded To	Traded With	Traded By	In Exchange For
June 11, 1968	CIN N	Woody Woodward Tony Cloninger	ATL N	Milt Pappas Ted Davidson Bob Johnson
Dec. 12, 1975	CHI A	—	CIN N	Rich Hinton minor league C Jeff Sovern
Mar. 23, 1977	STL N	—	CHI A	Lerrin LaGrow
Aug. 31, 1977	CHI A	—	STL N	Nyls Nyman Dave Hamilton Silvio Martinez

Ownie Carroll

Date	Traded To	Traded With	Traded By	In Exchange For
May 30, 1930	NY A	Yats Wuestling Harry Rice	DET A	Waite Hoyt Mark Koenig
Sept. 13, 1930	CIN N	—	NY A	Cash
Dec. 17, 1932	STL N	Estel Crabtree	CIN N	Jim Bottomley
Feb. 1933	BKN N	Jake Flowers	STL N	Dazzy Vance Gordon Slade

Tom Carroll

Date	Traded To	Traded With	Traded By	In Exchange For
Nov. 6, 1976	PIT N	—	CIN N	Jim Sadowski

Tommy Carroll

Date	Traded To	Traded With	Traded By	In Exchange For
Apr. 12, 1959	KC A	Russ Snyder	NY A	Mike Baxes Bob Martyn

Gary Carter

Date	Traded To	Traded With	Traded By	In Exchange For
Dec. 10, 1984	NY N	—	MON N	Hubie Brooks Mike Fitzgerald Herm Winningham Floyd Youmans
Mar. 26, 1991	LA N	—	SF N	No compensation (free agent signing)
Nov. 15, 1991	MON N	—	LA N	Waiver price

Joe Carter

Date	Traded To	Traded With	Traded By	In Exchange For
June 13, 1984	CLE A	Mel Hall Don Schulze Minor league P Darryl Banks	CHI N	Rick Sutcliffe George Frazier Ron Hassey
Dec. 6, 1989	SD N	—	CLE A	Sandy Alomar Chris James Carlos Baerga
Dec. 5, 1990	TOR A	Roberto Alomar	SD N	Fred McGriff Tony Fernandez

Steve Carter

Date	Traded To	Traded With	Traded By	In Exchange For
Mar. 29, 1991	CHI N	—	PIT N	Gary Varsho
July 12, 1993	HOU N	—	CIN N	Jack Daugherty

Rico Carty

Date	Traded To	Traded With	Traded By	In Exchange For
Oct. 27, 1972	TEX A	—	ATL N	Jim Panther
Aug. 13, 1973	CHI N	—	TEX A	Cash
Sept. 11, 1973	OAK A	—	CHI N	Cash
Dec. 6, 1976	CLE A	—	TOR A	John Lowenstein Rick Cerone
Mar. 15, 1978	TOR A	—	CLE A	Denny DeBarr
Aug. 15, 1978	OAK A	—	TOR A	Willie Horton Phil Huffman
Oct. 3, 1978	TOR A	—	OAK A	Cash

Chuck Cary

Date	Traded To	Traded With	Traded By	In Exchange For
Jan. 27, 1987	ATL N	—	DET A	*see Terry Harper*

Jerry Casale

Date	Traded To	Traded With	Traded By	In Exchange For
June 7, 1961	DET A	—	LA A	Jim Donohue

Paul Casanova

Date	Traded To	Traded With	Traded By	In Exchange For
Dec. 2, 1971	ATL N	—	TEX A	Hal King

Joe Cascarella

Date	Traded To	Traded With	Traded By	In Exchange For
June 30, 1935	BOS A	—	PHI A	Cash
June 13, 1936	WAS A	—	BOS A	Jack Russell
July 3, 1937	CIN N	—	WAS A	Cash

George Case

Date	Traded To	Traded With	Traded By	In Exchange For
Dec. 14, 1945	CLE A	—	WAS A	Jeff Heath
Mar. 4, 1947	WAS A	—	CLE A	Roger Wolff

Doc Casey

Date	Traded To	Traded With	Traded By	In Exchange For
Dec. 30, 1905	BKN N	Billy Maloney Buttons Briggs Jack McCarthy $2,000.	CHI N	Jimmy Sheckard

Dave Cash

Date	Traded To	Traded With	Traded By	In Exchange For
Oct. 18, 1973	PHI N	—	PIT N	Ken Brett
Nov. 17, 1976	MON N	—	PHI N	No compensation (free agent signing)
Nov. 27, 1979	SD N	—	MON N	Bill Almon Dan Briggs

Norm Cash

Date	Traded To	Traded With	Traded By	In Exchange For
Dec. 6, 1959	CLE A	Johnny Romano Bubba Phillips	CHI A	Dick Brown Don Ferrarese Jake Striker Minnie Minoso
Apr. 12, 1960	DET A	—	CLE A	Steve Demeter

Larry Casian

Date	Traded To	Traded With	Traded By	In Exchange For
July 14, 1994	CLE A	—	MIN A	Waiver price

Harry Cassady

Date	Traded To	Traded With	Traded By	In Exchange For
Mar. 1905	WAS A	—	PIT N	Waiver price

George Caster

Date	Traded To	Traded With	Traded By	In Exchange For
Nov. 16, 1940	STL A	—	PHI A	Waiver price
Aug. 8, 1945	DET A	—	STL A	Waiver price

Pete Castiglione

Date	Traded To	Traded With	Traded By	In Exchange For
June 14, 1953	STL N	—	PIT N	Hal Rice Cash

Bobby Castillo

Date	Traded To	Traded With	Traded By	In Exchange For
Jan. 6, 1982	MIN A	Bobby Mitchell	LA N	Scotti Madison Minor League P Paul Voigt
Feb. 11, 1985	LA N	—	MIN A	No compensation (free agent signing)

Braulio Castillo

Date	Traded To	Traded With	Traded By	In Exchange For
July 31, 1991	PHI N	Mike Hartley	LA N	Roger McDowell
May 20, 1993	HOU N	—	CLR N	Mark Grant

Carmen Castillo

Date	Traded To	Traded With	Traded By	In Exchange For
Mar. 26, 1989	MIN A	—	CLE A	Keith Atherton

Juan Castillo

Date	Traded To	Traded With	Traded By	In Exchange For
Nov. 28, 1994	HOU N	Minor league P Andy Beckerman	NY N	Pete Harnisch

(Houston received Beckerman on December 6, 1994 and Castillo on April 12, 1995.)

Manny Castillo

Date	Traded To	Traded With	Traded By	In Exchange For
Oct. 23, 1981	SEA A	—	KC A	Bud Black

Tony Castillo

Date	Traded To	Traded With	Traded By	In Exchange For
Aug. 24, 1989	ATL N	Francisco Cabrera (Atlanta received Cabrera on Aug. 29, 1989.)	TOR A	Jim Acker
Aug. 28, 1991	NY N	Joe Roa	ATL N	Alejandro Pena
Jan. 22, 1992	DET A	Mark Carreon	NY N	Paul Gibson Minor league P Randy Marshall

Foster Castleman

Date	Traded To	Traded With	Traded By	In Exchange For
Mar. 24, 1958	BAL A	—	SF N	$30,000.

Bill Castro

Date	Traded To	Traded With	Traded By	In Exchange For
Feb. 17, 1981	NY A	—	MIL A	No compensation (free agent signing)
Mar. 24, 1982	CAL A	—	NY A	Butch Hobson

Danny Cater

Date	Traded To	Traded With	Traded By	In Exchange For
Dec. 1, 1964	CHI A	Lee Elia	PHI N	Ray Herbert Jeoff Long
May 27, 1966	KC A	—	CHI A	Wayne Causey
Dec. 5, 1969	NY A	Ossie Chavarria	OAK A	Al Downing Frank Fernandez
Mar. 22, 1972	BOS A	—	NY A	Sparky Lyle

Danny Cater *continued*

Date	Traded To	Traded With	Traded By	In Exchange For
Mar. 29, 1975	STL N	—	BOS A	Danny Godby

Ted Cather

Date	Traded To	Traded With	Traded By	In Exchange For
June 1914	BOS N	Possum Whitted	STL N	Hub Perdue

Keefe Cato

Date	Traded To	Traded With	Traded By	In Exchange For
Nov. 1, 1984	SD N	—	CIN N	Minor league P Darren Burroughs

Bill Caudill

Date	Traded To	Traded With	Traded By	In Exchange For
Mar. 28, 1977	CIN N	—	STL N	Joel Youngblood
Oct. 31, 1977	CHI N	Woodie Fryman	CIN N	Bill Bonham
Aug. 19, 1981	NY A	Jay Howell	CHI N	Pat Tabler

(New York received Caudill on April 1, 1982, and Howell on August 2, 1982.)

Date	Traded To	Traded With	Traded By	In Exchange For
Apr. 1, 1982	SEA A	Bobby Brown Gene Nelson	NY A	Shane Rawley
Nov. 21, 1983	OAK A	Darrel Akerfelds	SEA A	Dave Beard Bob Kearney
Dec. 8, 1984	TOR A	—	OAK A	Alfredo Griffin Dave Collins Cash

Red Causey

Date	Traded To	Traded With	Traded By	In Exchange For
Aug. 15, 1919	BOS N	Joe Oeschger Johnny Jones Mickey O'Neil $55,000.	NY N	Art Nehf
July 1, 1921	NY N	Casey Stengel Johnny Rawlings	PHI N	Goldie Rapp Lee King Lance Richbourg

Wayne Causey

Date	Traded To	Traded With	Traded By	In Exchange For
Jan. 24, 1961	KC A	Jim Archer Bob Boyd Al Pilarcik	BAL A	Whitey Herzog Russ Snyder
May 27, 1966	CHI A	—	KC A	Danny Cater
July 20, 1968	CAL A	—	CHI A	Woodie Held
July 29, 1968	ATL N	—	CAL A	Cash

Art Ceccarelli

Date	Traded To	Traded With	Traded By	In Exchange For
Oct. 11, 1956	BAL A	Al Pilarcik	KC A	Ryne Duren Jim Pisoni
Oct. 14, 1958	STL N	Jim Brideweser	BAL A	Jim Finigan
May 19, 1960	NY A	minor league IF Ray Bellino and $20,000.	CHI N	Mark Freeman

Andujar Cedeno

Date	Traded To	Traded With	Traded By	In Exchange For
Dec. 28, 1994	SD N	*see Ken Caminiti*	HOU N	—

Cesar Cedeno

Date	Traded To	Traded With	Traded By	In Exchange For
Dec. 18, 1981	CIN N	—	HOU N	Ray Knight
Aug. 29, 1985	STL N	—	CIN N	Minor league OF Mark Jackson

Orlando Cepeda

Date	Traded To	Traded With	Traded By	In Exchange For
May 8, 1966	STL N	—	SF N	Ray Sadecki
Mar. 17, 1969	ATL N	—	STL N	Joe Torre
June 29, 1972	OAK A	—	ATL N	Denny McLain

Rick Cerone

Date	Traded To	Traded With	Traded By	In Exchange For
Dec. 6, 1976	TOR A	John Lowenstein	CLE A	Rico Carty
Nov. 1, 1979	NY A	Tom Underwood Ted Wilborn	TOR A	Chris Chambliss Damaso Garcia Paul Mirabella
Dec. 5, 1984	ATL N	—	NY A	Brian Fisher
Mar. 5, 1986	MIL A	Minor league SS Flavio Alfaro	ATL N	Ted Simmons
Feb. 13, 1987	NY A	—	MIL A	No compensation (free agent signing)

Rick Cerone *continued*

Date	Traded To	Traded With	Traded By	In Exchange For
Dec. 21, 1989	NY A	—	BOS A	No compensation (free agent signing)

John Cerutti

Date	Traded To	Traded With	Traded By	In Exchange For
Jan. 14, 1991	DET A	—	TOR A	No compensation (free agent signing)

Bob Cerv

Date	Traded To	Traded With	Traded By	In Exchange For
Oct. 16, 1956	KC A	—	NY A	Cash
May 19, 1960	NY A	—	KC A	Andy Carey
May 8, 1961	NY A	Tex Clevenger	LA A	Lee Thomas Ryne Duren Johnny James
June 26, 1962	HOU N	—	NY A	Cash

Ron Cey

Date	Traded To	Traded With	Traded By	In Exchange For
Jan. 20, 1983	CHI N	—	LA N	Vance Lovelace Minor league OF Dan Cataline
Jan. 30, 1987	OAK A	—	CHI N	Luis Quinones

Elio Chacon

Date	Traded To	Traded With	Traded By	In Exchange For
Dec. 7, 1964	STL N	Tracy Stallard	NY N	Johnny Lewis Gordie Richardson

Ray Chadwick

Date	Traded To	Traded With	Traded By	In Exchange For
Aug. 2, 1989	BOS A	—	CHI A	Dana Williams

Leon Chagnon

Date	Traded To	Traded With	Traded By	In Exchange For
Dec. 1934	NY N	—	PIT N	Cash

Bob Chakales

Date	Traded To	Traded With	Traded By	In Exchange For
June 1, 1954	BAL A	—	CLE A	Vic Wertz
Dec. 6, 1954	CHI A	*see Clint Courtney*	BAL A	—
June 7, 1955	WAS A	Clint Courtney Johnny Groth	CHI A	Jim Busby
Apr. 29, 1957	BOS A	Dean Stone	WAS A	Milt Bolling Russ Kemmerer Faye Throneberry

Dave Chalk

Date	Traded To	Traded With	Traded By	In Exchange For
May 4, 1979	TEX A	—	CAL A	Bert Campaneris
June 15, 1979	OAK A	Mike Heath Cash	TEX A	John Henry Johnson
Feb. 29, 1980	KC A	—	OAK A	No compensation (free agent signing)

Craig Chamberlain

Date	Traded To	Traded With	Traded By	In Exchange For
Mar. 30, 1982	SF N	—	KC A	*see Vida Blue*

Icebox Chamberlain

Date	Traded To	Traded With	Traded By	In Exchange For
Jan. 1900	PIT N	*see Honus Wagner*	LOU N	—

Wes Chamberlain

Date	Traded To	Traded With	Traded By	In Exchange For
Aug. 30, 1990	PHI N	Julio Peguero Tony Longmire	PIT N	Carmelo Martinez
		(Philadelphia received Longmire on September 28, 1990.)		
May 31, 1994	BOS A	Minor league P Mike Sullivan	PHI N	Paul Quantrill Billy Hatcher
Aug. 14, 1995	KC A	—	BOS A	Chris James

Cliff Chambers

Date	Traded To	Traded With	Traded By	In Exchange For
Dec. 8, 1948	PIT N	Clyde McCullough	CHI N	Cal McLish Frankie Gustine
June 15, 1951	STL N	—	PIT N	*see Joe Garagiola*

Chris Chambliss

Date	Traded To	Traded With	Traded By	In Exchange For
Apr. 27, 1974	NY A	Dick Tidrow Cecil Upshaw	CLE A	Fritz Peterson Steve Kline Fred Beene Tom Buskey

Chris Chambliss *continued*

Date	Traded To	Traded With	Traded By	In Exchange For
Nov. 1, 1979	TOR A	Damaso Garcia Paul Mirabella	NY A	Tom Underwood Rick Cerone Ted Wilborn
Dec. 5, 1979	ATL N	Luis Gomez	TOR A	Barry Bonnell Pat Rockett Joey McLaughlin

Billy Champion

Date	Traded To	Traded With	Traded By	In Exchange For
Oct. 31, 1972	MIL A	*see Don Money*	PHI N	—

Mike Champion

Date	Traded To	Traded With	Traded By	In Exchange For
Mar. 30, 1979	CLE A	—	SD N	Dan Briggs

Bob Chance

Date	Traded To	Traded With	Traded By	In Exchange For
Dec. 1, 1964	WAS A	Woodie Held	CLE A	Chuck Hinton

Dean Chance

Date	Traded To	Traded With	Traded By	In Exchange For
Dec. 2, 1966	MIN A	Jackie Hernandez	CAL A	Jimmie Hall Don Mincher Pete Cimino
Dec. 10, 1969	CLE A	*see Graig Nettles*	MIN A	—
Sept. 18, 1970	NY N	—	CLE A	Cash
Mar. 30, 1971	DET A	Bill Denehy	NY N	Jerry Robertson

Darrel Chaney

Date	Traded To	Traded With	Traded By	In Exchange For
Dec. 12, 1975	ATL N	—	CIN N	Mike Lum

Charlie Chant

Date	Traded To	Traded With	Traded By	In Exchange For
Oct. 28, 1975	STL N	—	OAK A	Larry Lintz

Darrin Chapin

Date	Traded To	Traded With	Traded By	In Exchange For
Jan. 8, 1992	PHI N	—	NY A	Charlie Hayes
		(New York received Hayes on February 19, 1992.)		

Tiny Chaplin

Date	Traded To	Traded With	Traded By	In Exchange For
Jan. 17, 1936	BOS N	—	NY N	Cash

Ben Chapman

Date	Traded To	Traded With	Traded By	In Exchange For
June 14, 1936	WAS A	—	NY A	Jake Powell
June 11, 1937	BOS A	Bobo Newsom	WAS A	Wes Ferrell Mel Almada Rick Ferrell
Dec. 15, 1938	CLE A	—	BOS A	Denny Galehouse Tommy Irwin
Dec. 24, 1940	WAS A	—	CLE A	Joe Krakauskas
June 15, 1945	PHI N	—	BKN N	Johnny Peacock

Harry Chapman

Date	Traded To	Traded With	Traded By	In Exchange For
Dec. 15, 1912	CIN N	*see Joe Tinker*	CHI N	—
Feb. 10, 1916	STL A	*see Eddie Plank*	STL F	—

Sam Chapman

Date	Traded To	Traded With	Traded By	In Exchange For
May 10, 1951	CLE A	—	PHI A	Allie Clark Lou Klein

Larry Chappell

Date	Traded To	Traded With	Traded By	In Exchange For
Aug. 21, 1915	CLE A	Braggo Roth Ed Klepfer $31,500.	CHI A	Joe Jackson
May 1916	BOS N	—	CLE A	Cash

Bill Chappelle

Date	Traded To	Traded With	Traded By	In Exchange For
May 24, 1909	CIN N	—	BOS N	Cash

Chappy Charles

Date	Traded To	Traded With	Traded By	In Exchange For
Aug. 22, 1909	CIN N	—	STL N	Mike Mowrey

Ed Charles

Date	Traded To	Traded With	Traded By	In Exchange For
Dec. 15, 1961	KC A	Joe Azcue Manny Jimenez	MIL N	Bob Shaw Lou Klimchock

Ed Charles *continued*

Date	Traded To	Traded With	Traded By	In Exchange For
May 10, 1967	NY N	—	KC A	Larry Elliot $50,000.

Norm Charlton

Date	Traded To	Traded With	Traded By	In Exchange For
Mar. 31, 1986	CIN N	Minor league 2B Tim Barker	MON N	Wayne Krenchicki
Nov. 17, 1992	SEA A	—	CIN N	Kevin Mitchell

Mike Chartak

Date	Traded To	Traded With	Traded By	In Exchange For
June 7, 1942	STL A	Steve Sundra	WAS A	Roy Cullenbine Bill Trotter

Hal Chase

Date	Traded To	Traded With	Traded By	In Exchange For
June 1, 1913	CHI A	—	NY A	Rollie Zeider Babe Borton
Feb. 2, 1919	NY N	—	CIN N	Bill Rariden

Ken Chase

Date	Traded To	Traded With	Traded By	In Exchange For
Dec. 13, 1941	BOS A	Johnny Welaj	WAS A	Stan Spence Jack Wilson

Ossie Chavarria

Date	Traded To	Traded With	Traded By	In Exchange For
Dec. 5, 1969	NY A	Danny Cater	OAK A	Al Downing Frank Fernandez

Dave Cheadle

Date	Traded To	Traded With	Traded By	In Exchange For
June 7, 1973	ATL N	Frank Tepedino Wayne Nordhagen Al Closter	NY A	Pat Dobson

Charlie Chech

Date	Traded To	Traded With	Traded By	In Exchange For
Feb. 18, 1909	BOS A	Jack Ryan $12,500.	CLE A	Cy Young

Larry Cheney

Date	Traded To	Traded With	Traded By	In Exchange For
Aug. 1915	BKN N	—	CHI N	Joe Schultz $3,000.
June 1919	BOS N	—	BKN N	Waiver price
Aug. 1919	PHI N	—	BOS N	Waiver price

Tom Cheney

Date	Traded To	Traded With	Traded By	In Exchange For
Dec. 21, 1959	PIT N	Gino Cimoli	STL N	Ron Kline
June 29, 1961	WAS A	—	PIT N	Tom Sturdivant

Jack Chesbro

Date	Traded To	Traded With	Traded By	In Exchange For
Jan. 1900	LOU N	—	PIT N	*see Honus Wagner*
Sept. 11, 1909	BOS A	—	NY A	Waiver price

Scott Chiamparino

Date	Traded To	Traded With	Traded By	In Exchange For
Aug. 29, 1990	TEX A	Joe Bitker	OAK A	Harold Baines

(Texas received Bitker and Chiamparino on September 4, 1990.)

Floyd Chiffer

Date	Traded To	Traded With	Traded By	In Exchange For
Dec. 7, 1984	MIN A	—	SD N	Ray Smith

Rocky Childress

Date	Traded To	Traded With	Traded By	In Exchange For
Nov. 16, 1986	HOU N	—	PHI N	Cash

Cupid Childs

Date	Traded To	Traded With	Traded By	In Exchange For
Jan. 1900	CHI N	—	STL N	Cash

Rich Chiles

Date	Traded To	Traded With	Traded By	In Exchange For
Nov. 27, 1972	NY N	Buddy Harris	HOU N	Tommie Agee

Lou Chiozza

Date	Traded To	Traded With	Traded By	In Exchange For
Dec. 8, 1936	NY N	—	PHI N	George Scharein Cash

Bob Chipman

Date	Traded To	Traded With	Traded By	In Exchange For
June 6, 1944	CHI N	—	BKN N	Eddie Stanky

Bob Chipman *continued*

Date	Traded To	Traded With	Traded By	In Exchange For
Apr. 18, 1950	BOS N	—	CHI N	Cash

Tom Chism

Date	Traded To	Traded With	Traded By	In Exchange For
Dec. 7, 1979	MIN A	—	BAL A	Dan Graham

Harry Chiti

Date	Traded To	Traded With	Traded By	In Exchange For
July 26, 1960	DET A	—	KC A	Cash
Nov. 16, 1961	CLE A	Ray Barker minor leaguer Art Kay	BAL A	Johnny Temple
Apr. 26, 1962	NY N	—	CLE A	Cash

Nels Chittum

Date	Traded To	Traded With	Traded By	In Exchange For
Mar. 15, 1959	BOS A	—	STL N	Dean Stone
May 6, 1960	LA N	—	BOS A	Rip Repulski

Bob Chlupsa

Date	Traded To	Traded With	Traded By	In Exchange For
June 20, 1972	SD N	Mike Fiore	STL N	Rafael Robles

(Fiore was returned to St. Louis on July 3.)

Don Choate

Date	Traded To	Traded With	Traded By	In Exchange For
Mar. 25, 1959	SF N	Sam Jones	STL N	Bill White Ray Jablonski

Mike Chris

Date	Traded To	Traded With	Traded By	In Exchange For
Dec. 9, 1981	SF N	Dan Schatzeder	DET A	Larry Herndon
Sept. 30, 1983	CHI N	—	SF N	Cash

Neil Chrisley

Date	Traded To	Traded With	Traded By	In Exchange For
Nov. 8, 1955	WAS A	—	BOS A	*see Mickey Vernon*
Dec. 6, 1958	DET A	*see Eddie Yost*	WAS A	—
Dec. 7, 1960	MIL N	—	DET A	*see Bill Bruton*
Oct. 16, 1961	NY N	—	MIL N	Cash

John Christensen

Date	Traded To	Traded With	Traded By	In Exchange For
Nov. 13, 1985	BOS A	Calvin Schiraldi Wes Gardner LaSchelle Tarver	NY N	Bob Ojeda John Mitchell Tom McCarthy Minor league P Chris Bayer
Aug. 19, 1986	SEA A	—	BOS A	*see Dave Henderson*

Bob Christian

Date	Traded To	Traded With	Traded By	In Exchange For
Sept. 30, 1968	CHI A	—	DET A	Cash

Clay Christiansen

Date	Traded To	Traded With	Traded By	In Exchange For
June 2, 1987	HOU N	—	MIN A	Eric Bullock

Mark Christman

Date	Traded To	Traded With	Traded By	In Exchange For
May 13, 1939	STL A	—	DET A	*see Beau Bell*
Apr. 9, 1947	WAS A	—	STL A	Cash

Steve Christmas

Date	Traded To	Traded With	Traded By	In Exchange For
Nov. 21, 1983	CHI A	—	CIN N	Fran Mullins

Joe Christopher

Date	Traded To	Traded With	Traded By	In Exchange For
Nov. 30, 1965	BOS A	—	NY N	Ed Bressoud
June 14, 1966	DET A	Earl Wilson	BOS A	Julio Navarro Don Demeter

Mike Christopher

Date	Traded To	Traded With	Traded By	In Exchange For
Dec. 10, 1991	CLE A	Dennis Cook	LA N	Rudy Seanez

Russ Christopher

Date	Traded To	Traded With	Traded By	In Exchange For
Apr. 3, 1948	CLE A	—	PHI A	Cash

Date	Traded To	Traded With	Traded By	In Exchange For
Bubba Church				
May 23, 1952	CIN N	—	PHI N	Johnny Wyrostek Kent Peterson
June 12, 1953	CHI N	—	CIN N	Fred Baczewski Bob Kelly
Chuck Churn				
Mar. 26, 1958	CLE A	—	BOS A	Waiver price
Archi Cianfrocco				
June 23, 1993	SD N	—	MON N	Tim Scott
Al Cicotte				
May 14, 1958	WAS A	—	NY A	Cash
June 23, 1958	DET A	—	WAS A	Vito Valentinetti
Nov. 20, 1958	CLE A	Billy Martin	DET A	Don Mossi Ossie Alvarez Ray Narleski
Jan. 26, 1961	STL N	—	LA A	Leon Wagner Cal Browning Ellis Burton Cash
Oct. 13, 1961	HOU N	—	STL N	Cash
Eddie Cicotte				
July 22, 1912	CHI A	—	BOS A	Cash
Pete Cimino				
Dec. 2, 1966	CAL A	—	MIN A	*see Dean Chance*
Gino Cimoli				
Dec. 4, 1958	STL N	—	LA N	Wally Moon Phil Paine
Dec. 21, 1959	PIT N	Tom Cheney	STL N	Ron Kline
June 15, 1961	MIL N	—	PIT N	Johnny Logan
Galen Cisco				
Sept. 7, 1962	NY N	—	BOS A	Waiver price
Bill Cissell				
Apr. 24, 1932	CLE A	Jim Moore	CHI A	Johnny Hodapp Bob Seeds
Oct. 12, 1933	BOS A	—	CLE A	Lloyd Brown
Mar. 1938	NY N	—	PHI A	Cash
Ralph Citarella				
Jan. 23, 1985	PHI N	—	STL N	Cash
Jim Clancy				
Dec. 16, 1988	HOU N	—	TOR A	No compensation (free agent signing)
July 31, 1991	ATL N	—	HOU N	Matt Turner Player to be named
(Houston received P Earl Sanders on November 15, 1991.)				
Doug Clarey				
Mar. 30, 1977	NY N	—	STL N	Benny Ayala
Allie Clark				
Oct. 10, 1947	CLE A	—	NY A	Red Embree
May 10, 1951	PHI A	Lou Klein	CLE A	Sam Chapman
May 12, 1953	CHI A	—	PHI A	Waiver price
Bobby Clark				
Dec. 20, 1983	MIL A	—	CAL A	Jim Slaton
Bryan Clark				
Dec. 8, 1983	TOR A	—	SEA A	Barry Bonnell
Cap Clark				
Dec. 8, 1937	PHI N	—	STL A	Earl Grace

Date	Traded To	Traded With	Traded By	In Exchange For
Danny Clark				
Oct. 30, 1922	BOS A	Carl Holling Howard Ehmke Babe Herman $25,000.	DET A	Del Pratt Rip Collins
Dave Clark				
Nov. 20, 1989	CHI N	—	CLE A	Mitch Webster
Jack Clark				
Feb. 1, 1985	STL N	—	SF N	David Green Jose Uribe Dave LaPoint Gary Rajsich
Jan. 6, 1988	NY A	—	STL N	No compensation (free agent signing)
Oct. 24, 1988	SD N	Pat Clements	NY A	Lance McCullers Jimmy Jones Stan Jefferson
Dec. 15, 1990	BOS A	—	SD N	No compensation (free agent signing)
Jim Clark				
July 10, 1972	KC A	—	CLE A	Tom Hilgendorf
Mark Clark				
Mar. 31, 1993	CLE A	—	STL N	Mark Whiten Minor league SS Juan Andujar
Phil Clark				
Apr. 2, 1993	SD N	—	DET A	Waiver price
Rickey Clark				
Jan. 29, 1973	PHI N	—	CAL A	Cash
Ron Clark				
Jan. 15, 1970	OAK A	*see Don Mincher*	MIL A	—
June 20, 1972	MIL A	—	OAK A	Bill Voss
July 28, 1972	CAL A	Paul Ratliff	MIL A	Syd O'Brien Joe Azcue
Watty Clark				
June 16, 1933	NY N	Lefty O'Doul	BKN N	Sam Leslie
Will Clark				
Nov. 22, 1993	TEX A	—	SF N	No compensation (free agent signing)
Fred Clarke				
Jan. 1900	PIT N	*see Honus Wagner*	LOU N	—
Horace Clarke				
May 31, 1974	SD N	—	NY A	Cash
Nig Clarke				
Aug. 1, 1905	DET A	—	CLE A	Cash
Aug. 11, 1905	CLE A	—	DET A	Cash
Oct. 1910	STL A	—	CLE A	Art Griggs
Nov. 1919	PIT N	—	PHI N	Waiver price
Stan Clarke				
Oct. 5, 1987	DET A	—	SEA A	Bruce Fields
Tommy Clarke				
Apr. 28, 1918	NY A	—	CIN N	Lee Magee
Bill Clarkson				
June 15, 1928	BOS N	Ben Cantwell Virgil Barnes Al Spohrer	NY N	Joe Genewich

Walter Clarkson

Date	Traded To	Traded With	Traded By	In Exchange For
May 16, 1907	CLE A	—	NY A	Earl Moore

Ellis Clary

Date	Traded To	Traded With	Traded By	In Exchange For
Aug. 18, 1943	STL A	Ox Miller Cash	WAS A	Harlond Clift Johnny Niggeling

Dain Clay

Date	Traded To	Traded With	Traded By	In Exchange For
June 1, 1943	PHI N	Buster Adams Coaker Triplett	STL N	Danny Litwhiler Earl Naylor
June 6, 1943	CIN N	—	PHI N	Charlie Brewster

Ken Clay

Date	Traded To	Traded With	Traded By	In Exchange For
Aug. 14, 1980	TEX A	minor league OF Marvin Thompson	NY A	Gaylord Perry
Dec. 12, 1980	SEA A	—	TEX A	*see Rick Honeycutt*

Royce Clayton

Date	Traded To	Traded With	Traded By	In Exchange For
Dec. 14, 1995	STL N	—	SF N	Allen Watson Rich DeLucia Doug Creek

Mark Clear

Date	Traded To	Traded With	Traded By	In Exchange For
Dec. 10, 1980	BOS A	Carney Lansford Rick Miller	CAL A	Rick Burleson Butch Hobson
Dec. 11, 1985	MIL A	—	BOS A	Ed Romero

Clem Clemens

Date	Traded To	Traded With	Traded By	In Exchange For
Feb. 10, 1916	CHI N	*see Three Finger Brown*	CHI F	—

Doug Clemens

Date	Traded To	Traded With	Traded By	In Exchange For
June 15, 1964	CHI N	—	STL N	*see Lou Brock*
Jan. 10, 1966	PHI N	—	CHI N	Wes Covington

Jack Clements

Date	Traded To	Traded With	Traded By	In Exchange For
Jan. 1900	BOS N	—	CLE N	Cash

Pat Clements

Date	Traded To	Traded With	Traded By	In Exchange For
Aug. 2, 1985	PIT N	—	CAL A	*see John Candelaria*
Nov. 26, 1986	NY A	*see Rick Rhoden*	PIT N	—
Oct. 24, 1988	SD N	Jack Clark	NY A	Lance McCullers Jimmy Jones Stan Jefferson
July 9, 1992	BAL A	—	SD N	Waiver price

Lance Clemons

Date	Traded To	Traded With	Traded By	In Exchange For
Dec. 2, 1971	HOU N	Jim York	KC A	John Mayberry minor league IF Dave Grangaard
Apr. 15, 1972	STL N	Scipio Spinks	HOU N	Jerry Reuss
Jan. 24, 1973	BOS A	—	STL N	Mike Nagy

Donn Clendenon

Date	Traded To	Traded With	Traded By	In Exchange For
Jan. 22, 1969	HOU N	Jesus Alou Jack Billingham Skip Guinn $100,000.	MON N	Rusty Staub

(Clendenon refused to report, and Houston sent Billingham, Guinn, and cash on April 8, 1969.)

Date	Traded To	Traded With	Traded By	In Exchange For
June 15, 1969	NY N	—	MON N	Steve Renko Kevin Collins minor league Ps Bill Carden and Dave Colon

Reggie Cleveland

Date	Traded To	Traded With	Traded By	In Exchange For
Dec. 7, 1973	BOS A	Diego Segui Terry Hughes	STL N	Lynn McGlothen John Curtis Mike Garman
Apr. 18, 1978	TEX A	—	BOS A	Cash
Dec. 15, 1978	MIL A	—	TEX A	Ed Farmer Gary Holle Cash

Tex Clevenger

Date	Traded To	Traded With	Traded By	In Exchange For
Nov. 8, 1955	WAS A	—	BOS A	*see Mickey Vernon*
May 8, 1961	NY A	Bob Cerv	LA A	Lee Thomas Ryne Duren Johnny James

Harlond Clift

Date	Traded To	Traded With	Traded By	In Exchange For
Aug. 18, 1943	WAS A	Johnny Niggeling	STL A	Ellis Clary Ox Miller Cash

Ty Cline

Date	Traded To	Traded With	Traded By	In Exchange For
Nov. 27, 1962	MIL N	Don Dillard Frank Funk	CLE A	Joe Adcock Jack Curtis
May 31, 1967	SF N	—	ATL N	Cash
June 15, 1970	CIN N	—	MON N	Clyde Mashore

Gene Clines

Date	Traded To	Traded With	Traded By	In Exchange For
Oct. 22, 1974	NY N	—	PIT N	Duffy Dyer
Dec. 12, 1975	TEX A	—	NY N	Joe Lovitto
Feb. 5, 1977	CHI N	Cash	TEX A	Darold Knowles

Billy Clingman

Date	Traded To	Traded With	Traded By	In Exchange For
Jan. 1900	CHI N	—	WAS N	Cash

Lu Clinton

Date	Traded To	Traded With	Traded By	In Exchange For
June 4, 1964	LA A	—	BOS A	Lee Thomas
Sept. 9, 1965	CLE A	—	CAL A	Waiver price

(Clinton was claimed on waivers by Kansas City and played one game for them before Cleveland's claim was upheld.)

Date	Traded To	Traded With	Traded By	In Exchange For
Jan. 14, 1966	NY A	—	CLE A	Doc Edwards

Tony Cloninger

Date	Traded To	Traded With	Traded By	In Exchange For
June 11, 1968	CIN N	Woody Woodward Clay Carroll	ATL N	Milt Pappas Ted Davidson Bob Johnson
Mar. 24, 1972	STL N	—	CIN N	Julian Javier

Al Closter

Date	Traded To	Traded With	Traded By	In Exchange For
Apr. 5, 1966	WAS A	—	CLE A	Cash
May 3, 1966	NY A	—	WAS A	Cash
June 7, 1973	ATL N	Frank Tepedino Dave Cheadle Wayne Nordhagen	NY A	Pat Dobson

David Clyde

Date	Traded To	Traded With	Traded By	In Exchange For
Feb. 28, 1978	CLE A	Willie Horton	TEX A	Tom Buskey John Lowenstein
Jan. 4, 1980	TEX A	Jim Norris	CLE A	Larry McCall Gary Gray minor league 3B-OF Mike Bucci

Otis Clymer

Date	Traded To	Traded With	Traded By	In Exchange For
June 26, 1907	WAS A	—	PIT N	Cash
July 1913	BOS N	—	CHI N	Cash

Andy Coakley

Date	Traded To	Traded With	Traded By	In Exchange For
Sept. 1908	CHI N	—	CIN N	Cash

Gil Coan

Date	Traded To	Traded With	Traded By	In Exchange For
Feb. 18, 1954	BAL A	—	WAS A	Roy Sievers
July 17, 1955	CHI A	—	BAL A	Waiver price
Aug. 26, 1955	NY N	—	CHI A	Waiver price

Jim Coates

Date	Traded To	Traded With	Traded By	In Exchange For
Apr. 21, 1963	WAS A	—	NY A	Steve Hamilton

Dave Cochrane

Date	Traded To	Traded With	Traded By	In Exchange For
July 12, 1985	CHI A	—	NY N	Tom Paciorek
Dec. 10, 1987	KC A	*see Floyd Bannister*	CHI A	—
Feb. 3, 1988	SEA A	—	KC A	Minor league P Ken Spratke

Mickey Cochrane

Date	Traded To	Traded With	Traded By	In Exchange For
Dec. 12, 1933	DET A	—	PHI A	Johnny Pasek $100,000.

Jack Coffey

Date	Traded To	Traded With	Traded By	In Exchange For
July 1918	BOS A	—	DET A	Cash

Dick Coffman

Date	Traded To	Traded With	Traded By	In Exchange For
Oct. 19, 1927	STL A	Earl McNeely	WAS A	Milt Gaston
June 9, 1932	WAS A	—	STL A	Carl Fischer
Dec. 13, 1932	STL A	—	WAS A	Carl Fischer
Nov. 14, 1935	NY N	—	STL A	Cash

Kevin Coffman

Date	Traded To	Traded With	Traded By	In Exchange For
Sept. 29, 1988	CHI N	Kevin Blankenship	ATL N	Jody Davis

Slick Coffman

Date	Traded To	Traded With	Traded By	In Exchange For
Dec. 9, 1939	PHI A	Benny McCoy	DET A	Wally Moses

(Commissioner Landis ruled that Detroit had kept McCoy covered up in the minors and declared him a free agent, cancelling the deal. McCoy then signed with Philadelphia for a $10,000 bonus.)

Date	Traded To	Traded With	Traded By	In Exchange For
Jan. 30, 1940	STL A	—	DET A	Billy Sullivan

Frank Coggins

Date	Traded To	Traded With	Traded By	In Exchange For
Apr. 4, 1970	CLE A	Roy Foster Cash	MIL A	Max Alvis Russ Snyder

Rich Coggins

Date	Traded To	Traded With	Traded By	In Exchange For
Dec. 4, 1974	MON N	Dave McNally minor league P Bill Kirkpatrick	BAL A	Ken Singleton Mike Torrez
June 20, 1975	NY A	—	MON N	Cash
May 18, 1976	CHI A	Ken Brett	NY A	Carlos May
July 14, 1976	PHI N	—	CHI A	Wayne Nordhagen

Jimmie Coker

Date	Traded To	Traded With	Traded By	In Exchange For
Nov. 21, 1962	BAL A	—	PHI N	Cash
Dec. 15, 1962	SF N	—	BAL A	*see Mike McCormick*
Oct. 1, 1963	STL N	—	SF N	Ken MacKenzie
Apr. 9, 1964	MIL N	Gary Kolb	STL N	Bob Uecker

Rocky Colavito

Date	Traded To	Traded With	Traded By	In Exchange For
Apr. 17, 1960	DET A	—	CLE A	Harvey Kuenn
Nov. 18, 1963	KC A	Bob Anderson $50,000.	DET A	Jerry Lumpe Ed Rakow Dave Wickersham
Jan. 20, 1965	CHI A	—	KC A	Jim Landis Mike Hershberger Fred Talbot

(Part of three-team trade involving Kansas City, Cleveland, and the Chicago White Sox.)

Date	Traded To	Traded With	Traded By	In Exchange For
Jan. 20, 1965	CLE A	Camilo Carreon	CHI A	Tommy John Tommie Agee Johnny Romano

(Part of three-team trade involving Kansas City, Cleveland, and Chicago White Sox.)

Date	Traded To	Traded With	Traded By	In Exchange For
July 29, 1967	CHI A	—	CLE A	Jim King Marv Staehle
Mar. 26, 1968	LA N	—	CHI A	Cash

Nate Colbert

Date	Traded To	Traded With	Traded By	In Exchange For
Nov. 18, 1974	DET A	—	SD N	Ed Brinkman Bob Strampe Dick Sharon

(Part of three-team trade involving San Diego, Detroit, and St. Louis Cardinals.)

Date	Traded To	Traded With	Traded By	In Exchange For
June 15, 1975	MON N	—	DET A	Cash

Vince Colbert

Date	Traded To	Traded With	Traded By	In Exchange For
Nov. 30, 1972	TEX A	—	CLE A	Tom Ragland
Mar. 8, 1973	CLE A	Rich Hinton	TEX A	Alex Johnson

Jim Colborn

Date	Traded To	Traded With	Traded By	In Exchange For
Dec. 3, 1971	MIL A	Brock Davis Earl Stephenson	CHI N	Jose Cardenal
Dec. 6, 1976	KC A	Darrell Porter	MIL A	Jim Wohlford Jamie Quirk Bob McClure

Jim Colborn *continued*

Date	Traded To	Traded With	Traded By	In Exchange For
June 1, 1978	SEA A	—	KC A	Steve Braun

Greg Colbrunn

Date	Traded To	Traded With	Traded By	In Exchange For
Oct. 7, 1993	FLA N	—	MON N	Waiver price

Alex Cole

Date	Traded To	Traded With	Traded By	In Exchange For
Feb. 27, 1990	SD N	Steve Peters	STL N	Omar Olivares
July 11, 1990	CLE A	—	SD N	Tom Lampkin
July 3, 1992	PIT N	—	CLE A	Minor league OF Tony Mitchell Minor league P John Carter
Feb. 16, 1994	MIN N	—	CLR N	No compensation (free agent signing)

Bert Cole

Date	Traded To	Traded With	Traded By	In Exchange For
July 1925	CLE A	—	DET A	Cash

Dave Cole

Date	Traded To	Traded With	Traded By	In Exchange For
Mar. 20, 1954	CHI N	Cash	MIL N	Roy Smalley
Mar. 19, 1955	PHI N	—	CHI N	Cash

Dick Cole

Date	Traded To	Traded With	Traded By	In Exchange For
June 15, 1951	PIT N	*see Joe Garagiola*	STL N	—
Apr. 3, 1957	MIL N	—	PIT N	Jim Pendleton

Ed Cole

Date	Traded To	Traded With	Traded By	In Exchange For
Feb. 10, 1938	STL A	Roy Hughes Billy Sullivan	CLE A	Rollie Hemsley

King Cole

Date	Traded To	Traded With	Traded By	In Exchange For
June 22, 1912	PIT N	Solly Hofman	CHI N	Tommy Leach Lefty Leifield

Victor Cole

Date	Traded To	Traded With	Traded By	In Exchange For
May 3, 1991	PIT N	—	KC A	Carmelo Martinez

Dave Coleman

Date	Traded To	Traded With	Traded By	In Exchange For
Feb. 3, 1979	MIN A	—	BOS A	Larry Wolfe

Ed Coleman

Date	Traded To	Traded With	Traded By	In Exchange For
May 21, 1935	STL A	Sugar Cain	PHI A	George Blaeholder

Gordy Coleman

Date	Traded To	Traded With	Traded By	In Exchange For
Dec. 15, 1959	CIN N	Cal McLish Billy Martin	CLE A	Johnny Temple

Joe Coleman

Date	Traded To	Traded With	Traded By	In Exchange For
Oct. 9, 1970	DET A	Ed Brinkman Aurelio Rodriguez Jim Hannan	WAS A	Denny McLain Don Wert Norm McRae Elliott Maddox
June 8, 1976	CHI N	—	DET A	Cash
Mar. 15, 1977	OAK A	—	CHI N	Jim Todd
May 22, 1978	TOR A	—	OAK A	Cash

Joe Coleman

Date	Traded To	Traded With	Traded By	In Exchange For
Dec. 17, 1953	BAL A	Frank Fanovich	PHI A	Bob Cain

Ray Coleman

Date	Traded To	Traded With	Traded By	In Exchange For
June 4, 1948	PHI A	—	STL A	George Binks $20,000.
Dec. 13, 1949	STL A	Frankie Gustine Billy DeMars minor league OF Ray Ippolito $100,000.	PHI A	Bob Dillinger Paul Lehner
July 31, 1951	CHI A	—	STL A	Waiver price
July 28, 1952	STL A	J. W. Porter	CHI A	Jim Rivera Darrell Johnson

Ray Coleman *continued*

Date	Traded To	Traded With	Traded By	In Exchange For
Oct. 14, 1952	BKN N	Bob Mahoney Stan Rojek $90,000.	STL A	Billy Hunter

Rip Coleman

Date	Traded To	Traded With	Traded By	In Exchange For
Feb. 19, 1957	KC A	*see Billy Hunter*	NY A	—
Sept. 6, 1959	BAL A	—	KC A	Waiver price

Vince Coleman

Date	Traded To	Traded With	Traded By	In Exchange For
Dec. 5, 1990	NY N	—	STL N	No compensation (free agent signing)
Jan. 5, 1994	KC A	—	NY N	Kevin McReynolds
Aug. 15, 1995	SEA A	—	KC A	Jim Converse

(Kansas City received Converse on August 18, 1995.)

Darnell Coles

Date	Traded To	Traded With	Traded By	In Exchange For
Dec. 12, 1985	DET A	—	SEA A	Rich Monteleone
Aug. 7, 1987	PIT N	Morris Madden	DET A	Jim Morrison

(Pittsburgh received Madden on August 12, 1987.)

Date	Traded To	Traded With	Traded By	In Exchange For
July 22, 1988	SEA A	—	PIT N	Glenn Wilson
June 18, 1990	DET A	—	SEA A	Tracy Jones
Nov. 25, 1992	TOR A	—	CIN N	No compensation (free agent signing)

Chris Coletta

Date	Traded To	Traded With	Traded By	In Exchange For
Aug. 15, 1972	CAL A	—	BOS A	Andy Kosco
Aug. 14, 1973	PHI N	Aurelio Monteagudo Billy Grabarkewitz	CAL A	Denny Doyle

Bill Collins

Date	Traded To	Traded With	Traded By	In Exchange For
June 10, 1911	CHI N	—	BOS N	*see Johnny Kling*

Dave Collins

Date	Traded To	Traded With	Traded By	In Exchange For
Dec. 9, 1977	CIN N	—	SEA A	Shane Rawley
Dec. 23, 1981	NY A	—	CIN N	No compensation (free agent signing)
Dec. 9, 1982	TOR A	Fred McGriff Mike Morgan $400,000	NY A	Dale Murray Tom Dodd
Dec. 8, 1984	OAK A	Alfredo Griffin Cash	TOR A	Bill Caudill
Nov. 13, 1985	DET A	—	OAK A	Barbaro Garbey

Don Collins

Date	Traded To	Traded With	Traded By	In Exchange For
Feb. 15, 1980	CLE A	—	ATL N	Minor league P Gary Melson

Eddie Collins

Date	Traded To	Traded With	Traded By	In Exchange For
Dec. 8, 1914	CHI A	—	PHI A	$50,000.

Jimmy Collins

Date	Traded To	Traded With	Traded By	In Exchange For
June 7, 1907	PHI A	—	BOS A	Jack Knight

Joe Collins

Date	Traded To	Traded With	Traded By	In Exchange For
Mar. 20, 1958	PHI N	—	NY A	Cash

(Collins refused to report and retired.)

Kevin Collins

Date	Traded To	Traded With	Traded By	In Exchange For
June 15, 1969	MON N	Steve Renko minor league Ps Bill Carden and Dave Colon	NY N	Donn Clendenon
June 15, 1973	CLE A	Tom Timmerman	DET A	Ed Farmer

Pat Collins

Date	Traded To	Traded With	Traded By	In Exchange For
Dec. 13, 1928	BOS N	—	NY A	$7,500.

Phil Collins

Date	Traded To	Traded With	Traded By	In Exchange For
May 18, 1935	STL N	—	PHI N	Cash

Rip Collins

Date	Traded To	Traded With	Traded By	In Exchange For
Dec. 20, 1921	BOS A	Roger Peckinpaugh Jack Quinn Bill Piercy	NY A	Everett Scott Joe Bush Sad Sam Jones
Oct. 30, 1922	DET A	Del Pratt	BOS A	Carl Holling Danny Clark Howard Ehmke Babe Herman $25,000.

Ripper Collins

Date	Traded To	Traded With	Traded By	In Exchange For
Oct. 8, 1936	CHI N	Roy Parmelee	STL N	Lon Warneke

Shano Collins

Date	Traded To	Traded With	Traded By	In Exchange For
Mar. 4, 1921	BOS A	Nemo Leibold	CHI A	Harry Hooper

Zip Collins

Date	Traded To	Traded With	Traded By	In Exchange For
Sept. 3, 1915	BOS N	—	PIT N	Cash

Jackie Collum

Date	Traded To	Traded With	Traded By	In Exchange For
May 23, 1953	CIN N	—	STL N	Eddie Erautt
Jan. 31, 1956	STL N	—	CIN N	Brooks Lawrence Sonny Senerchia
Dec. 11, 1956	CHI N	*see Tom Poholsky*	STL N	—
May 23, 1957	CHI N	Vito Valentinetti	BKN N	Don Elston
Aug. 20, 1962	CLE A	Georges Maranda Cash	MIN A	Ruben Gomez

Bob Coluccio

Date	Traded To	Traded With	Traded By	In Exchange For
May 8, 1975	CHI A	—	MIL A	Bill Sharp
June 8, 1978	STL N	—	HOU N	Frank Riccelli
Oct. 2, 1978	NY N	—	STL N	Paul Siebert

Merrill Combs

Date	Traded To	Traded With	Traded By	In Exchange For
May 8, 1950	WAS A	Tommy O'Brien	BOS A	Clyde Vollmer
Apr. 1, 1951	CLE A	Snuffy Stirnweiss	STL A	Freddie Marsh $35,000.

Wayne Comer

Date	Traded To	Traded With	Traded By	In Exchange For
Mar. 23, 1963	DET A	—	WAS A	Bobo Osborne
May 11, 1970	WAS A	—	MIL A	Hank Allen Ron Theobald

Adam Comorosky

Date	Traded To	Traded With	Traded By	In Exchange For
Nov. 17, 1933	CIN N	Tony Piet	PIT N	Red Lucas Wally Roettger

Pete Compton

Date	Traded To	Traded With	Traded By	In Exchange For
June 1916	PIT N	—	BOS N	Cash

(Pittsburgh returned Compton to Boston ten days later.)

Keith Comstock

Date	Traded To	Traded With	Traded By	In Exchange For
July 5, 1987	SD N	—	SF N	*see Kevin Mitchell*

David Cone

Date	Traded To	Traded With	Traded By	In Exchange For
Mar. 27, 1987	NY N	Chris Jelic	KC A	Ed Hearn Rick Anderson Mauro Gozzo
Aug. 27, 1992	TOR A	—	NY N	Jeff Kent Ryan Thompson

(New York received Thompson on September 1, 1992.)

Date	Traded To	Traded With	Traded By	In Exchange For
Dec. 8, 1992	KC A	—	TOR A	No compensation (free agent signing)
Apr. 6, 1995	TOR A	—	KC A	Chris Stynes Minor league P David Sinnes Minor league SS Anthony Medrano

David Cone *continued*

Date	Traded To	Traded With	Traded By	In Exchange For
July 28, 1995	NY A	—	TOR A	Minor league Ps Marty Janzen Jason Jarvis Mike Gordon

Bunk Congalton

Date	Traded To	Traded With	Traded By	In Exchange For
May 20, 1907	BOS A	—	CLE A	Cash

Billy Conigliaro

Date	Traded To	Traded With	Traded By	In Exchange For
Oct. 11, 1971	MIL A	*see George Scott*	BOS A	—
Feb. 14, 1973	OAK A	—	MIL A	Cash

Tony Conigliaro

Date	Traded To	Traded With	Traded By	In Exchange For
Oct. 11, 1970	CAL A	Ray Jarvis Gerry Moses	BOS A	Ken Tatum Jarvis Tatum Doug Griffin

Gene Conley

Date	Traded To	Traded With	Traded By	In Exchange For
Mar. 31, 1959	PHI N	Joe Koppe Harry Hanebrink	MIL N	Stan Lopata Ted Kazanski Johnny O'Brien
Dec. 15, 1960	BOS A	—	PHI N	Frank Sullivan

Fritz Connally

Date	Traded To	Traded With	Traded By	In Exchange For
Dec. 7, 1983	SD N	Carmelo Martinez Craig Lefferts	CHI N	Scott Sanderson
Feb. 7, 1985	BAL A	—	SD N	Vic Rodriguez

(Part of three-team trade involving Chicago Cubs, San Diego, and Montreal.) [printed below the Dec. 7, 1983 trade]

Bruce Connatser

Date	Traded To	Traded With	Traded By	In Exchange For
Dec. 15, 1932	WAS A	Jack Russell	CLE A	Harley Boss

Joe Connolly

Date	Traded To	Traded With	Traded By	In Exchange For
Jan. 7, 1924	BOS A	*see Bill Wambsganss*	CLE A	—

Joe Connolly

Date	Traded To	Traded With	Traded By	In Exchange For
Apr. 10, 1913	BOS N	—	WAS A	Cash

Joe Connor

Date	Traded To	Traded With	Traded By	In Exchange For
June 1901	CLE A	—	MIL A	Cash

Bill Connors

Date	Traded To	Traded With	Traded By	In Exchange For
Aug. 20, 1967	NY N	—	CHI N	Cash

Chuck Connors

Date	Traded To	Traded With	Traded By	In Exchange For
Oct. 10, 1950	CHI N	Dee Fondy	BKN N	Hank Edwards Cash

Tim Conroy

Date	Traded To	Traded With	Traded By	In Exchange For
Dec. 10, 1985	STL N	—	OAK A	*see Joaquin Andujar*

Billy Consolo

Date	Traded To	Traded With	Traded By	In Exchange For
June 11, 1959	WAS A	Murray Wall	BOS A	Dick Hyde Herb Plews
June 1, 1961	MIL N	—	MIN A	Billy Martin
May 8, 1962	LA A	—	PHI N	Cash
June 26, 1962	KC A	—	LA A	Cash

(Hyde was returned to Washington and Wall was returned to Boston.) [printed below the June 11, 1959 trade]

Jim Constable

Date	Traded To	Traded With	Traded By	In Exchange For
June 7, 1958	CLE A	—	SF N	Waiver price
July 12, 1958	WAS A	—	CLE A	Waiver price

Sandy Consuegra

Date	Traded To	Traded With	Traded By	In Exchange For
May 12, 1953	CHI A	—	WAS A	Cash
May 14, 1956	BAL A	—	CHI A	Cash
May 14, 1957	NY N	—	BAL A	Waiver price

Jim Converse

Date	Traded To	Traded With	Traded By	In Exchange For
Aug. 15, 1995	KC A	—	SEA A	Vince Coleman

(Kansas City received Converse on August 18, 1995.)

Jack Conway

Date	Traded To	Traded With	Traded By	In Exchange For
Jan. 16, 1948	NY N	—	CLE A	Cash

Cliff Cook

Date	Traded To	Traded With	Traded By	In Exchange For
May 7, 1962	NY N	Bob Miller	CIN N	Don Zimmer

Dennis Cook

Date	Traded To	Traded With	Traded By	In Exchange For
June 18, 1989	PHI N	Terry Mulholland Charlie Hayes	SF N	Steve Bedrosian Rick Parker
Sept. 13, 1990	LA N	—	PHI N	Darrin Fletcher
Dec. 10, 1991	CLE A	Mike Christopher	LA N	Rudy Seanez
Jan. 5, 1994	CHI A	—	CLE A	No compensation (free agent signing)
Oct. 17, 1994	CLE A	—	CHI A	Waiver price
June 22, 1995	TEX A	—	CLE A	Minor league SS Guillermo Mercedes

Mike Cook

Date	Traded To	Traded With	Traded By	In Exchange For
Nov. 3, 1988	MIN A	Paul Sorrento Minor league P Rob Wassenaar	CAL A	Bert Blyleven Minor league P Kevin Trudeau

Dusty Cooke

Date	Traded To	Traded With	Traded By	In Exchange For
Dec. 8, 1938	STL N	—	CIN N	Frenchy Bordagaray

Brent Cookson

Date	Traded To	Traded With	Traded By	In Exchange For
Apr. 22, 1995	KC A	—	SF N	Enrique Burgos
June 10, 1995	BOS A	—	KC A	Waiver price

(Kansas City received Cookson on June 26, 1995.) [printed below the Apr. 22, 1995 trade]

Scott Coolbaugh

Date	Traded To	Traded With	Traded By	In Exchange For
Dec. 12, 1990	SD N	—	TEX A	Mark Parent

Duff Cooley

Date	Traded To	Traded With	Traded By	In Exchange For
Feb. 1900	PIT N	—	PHI N	Tully Sparks Heinie Reitz
May 1901	BOS N	—	PIT N	Cash
Oct. 1904	DET A	—	BOS N	Waiver price
Dec. 1905	DET A	—	BOS N	Cash

Danny Coombs

Date	Traded To	Traded With	Traded By	In Exchange For
Oct. 22, 1969	SD N	—	HOU N	Cash

Ron Coomer

Date	Traded To	Traded With	Traded By	In Exchange For
July 31, 1995	MIN A	—	LA N	*see Kevin Tapani*

Jimmy Cooney

Date	Traded To	Traded With	Traded By	In Exchange For
Dec. 11, 1925	CHI N	—	STL N	Vic Keen
June 7, 1927	PHI N	Tony Kaufmann	CHI N	Hal Carlson
Dec. 13, 1927	STL N	Johnny Mokan Bubber Jonnard	PHI N	Johnny Schulte Jimmy Ring
Feb. 3, 1928	BOS N	—	STL N	Waiver price

Johnny Cooney

Date	Traded To	Traded With	Traded By	In Exchange For
Oct. 4, 1937	STL N	Jim Bucher Joe Stripp Roy Henshaw	BKN N	Leo Durocher

Cecil Cooper

Date	Traded To	Traded With	Traded By	In Exchange For
Dec. 6, 1976	MIL A	—	BOS A	George Scott Bernie Carbo

Claude Cooper

Date	Traded To	Traded With	Traded By	In Exchange For
Feb. 10, 1916	PHI N	—	BKN F	Cash

Don Cooper

Date	Traded To	Traded With	Traded By	In Exchange For
Dec. 10, 1982	TOR A	—	MIN A	Dave Baker

Guy Cooper

Date	Traded To	Traded With	Traded By	In Exchange For
May 27, 1914	BOS A	—	NY A	Cash

Mort Cooper

Date	Traded To	Traded With	Traded By	In Exchange For
May 23, 1945	BOS N	—	STL N	Red Barrett $60,000.
June 13, 1947	NY N	—	BOS N	Bill Voiselle Cash

Scott Cooper

Date	Traded To	Traded With	Traded By	In Exchange For
Apr. 8, 1995	STL N	Cory Bailey Player to be named	BOS A	Mark Whiten Rheal Cormier

Walker Cooper

Date	Traded To	Traded With	Traded By	In Exchange For
Jan. 5, 1946	NY N	—	STL N	$175,000.
June 13, 1949	CIN N	—	NY N	Ray Mueller
May 10, 1950	BOS N	—	CIN N	Connie Ryan
May 19, 1954	CHI N	—	PIT N	Waiver price

Wilbur Cooper

Date	Traded To	Traded With	Traded By	In Exchange For
Oct. 27, 1924	CHI N	Charlie Grimm Rabbit Maranville	PIT N	Vic Aldridge George Grantham Al Niehaus
June 7, 1926	DET A	—	CHI N	Waiver price

Joey Cora

Date	Traded To	Traded With	Traded By	In Exchange For
Mar. 31, 1991	CHI A	Warren Newson Minor league IF Kevin Garner	SD N	Adam Peterson Steve Rosenberg
Apr. 6, 1995	SEA A	—	CHI A	No Compensation (free agent signing)

Doug Corbett

Date	Traded To	Traded With	Traded By	In Exchange For
May 12, 1982	CAL A	Rob Wilfong	MIN A	Tom Brunansky Mike Walters $400,000.

Archie Corbin

Date	Traded To	Traded With	Traded By	In Exchange For
Aug. 30, 1990	KC A	—	NY N	Pat Tabler
Aug. 29, 1992	MON N	Sean Berry	KC A	Bill Sampen Chris Haney
Nov. 20, 1992	MIL A	—	MON N	Player to be named
Feb. 5, 1993	MON N	—	MIL A	Cash

Claude Corbitt

Date	Traded To	Traded With	Traded By	In Exchange For
Mar. 18, 1946	CIN N	—	BKN N	Cash

Tim Corcoran

Date	Traded To	Traded With	Traded By	In Exchange For
Aug. 23, 1981	MIN A	—	DET A	Ron Jackson

Rheal Cormier

Date	Traded To	Traded With	Traded By	In Exchange For
Apr. 8, 1995	BOS A	—	STL N	*see Scott Cooper*

Mardie Cornejo

Date	Traded To	Traded With	Traded By	In Exchange For
Mar. 13, 1979	DET A	—	NY N	Ed Glynn

Reid Cornelius

Date	Traded To	Traded With	Traded By	In Exchange For
June 8, 1995	NY N	—	MON N	David Segui

Pat Corrales

Date	Traded To	Traded With	Traded By	In Exchange For
Oct. 27, 1965	STL N	Art Mahaffey Alex Johnson	PHI N	Bill White Dick Groat Bob Uecker
Feb. 8, 1968	CIN N	Jimy Williams	STL N	Johnny Edwards
June 11, 1972	SD N	—	CIN N	Bob Barton

Ed Correa

Date	Traded To	Traded With	Traded By	In Exchange For
Nov. 25, 1985	TEX A	Scott Fletcher Jose Mota	CHI A	Wayne Tolleson Dave Schmidt

(Texas received Mota on December 12, 1985)

Rod Correia

Date	Traded To	Traded With	Traded By	In Exchange For
Jan. 17, 1992	CAL A	—	OAK A	Minor league OF Dan Grunhard

Vic Correll

Date	Traded To	Traded With	Traded By	In Exchange For
Mar. 26, 1974	ATL N	—	BOS A	Chuck Goggin

Red Corriden

Date	Traded To	Traded With	Traded By	In Exchange For
Nov. 16, 1912	CIN N	—	DET A	Cash
Dec. 15, 1912	CHI N	—	CIN N	*see Joe Tinker*

Frank Corridon

Date	Traded To	Traded With	Traded By	In Exchange For
July 20, 1904	PHI N	Jack Sutthoff	CHI N	Shad Barry
Jan. 20, 1910	CIN N	—	PHI N	Bob Ewing
Feb. 1910	STL N	Miller Huggins Rebel Oakes	CIN N	Fred Beebe Alan Storke

Pete Coscarart

Date	Traded To	Traded With	Traded By	In Exchange For
Dec. 12, 1941	PIT N	Luke Hamlin Babe Phelps Jimmy Wasdell	BKN N	Arky Vaughan

Dan Costello

Date	Traded To	Traded With	Traded By	In Exchange For
Jan. 1914	PIT N	—	NY A	Waiver price

John Costello

Date	Traded To	Traded With	Traded By	In Exchange For
Apr. 23, 1990	MON N	—	STL N	Rex Hudler
Nov. 9, 1990	SD N	—	MON N	Minor league P Brian Harrison

Tim Costo

Date	Traded To	Traded With	Traded By	In Exchange For
June 14, 1991	CIN N	—	CLE A	Reggie Jefferson
Dec. 14, 1994	CLE A	—	CIN N	Mark Lewis

Dick Cotter

Date	Traded To	Traded With	Traded By	In Exchange For
Oct. 1911	CHI N	—	PHI N	Peaches Graham

Chuck Cottier

Date	Traded To	Traded With	Traded By	In Exchange For
Dec. 7, 1960	DET A	Bill Bruton Terry Fox Dick Brown	MIL N	Frank Bolling Neil Chrisley
June 5, 1961	WAS A	—	DET A	Hal Woodeshick
Feb. 16, 1967	CAL A	—	WAS A	Cash

Henry Cotto

Date	Traded To	Traded With	Traded By	In Exchange For
Dec. 4, 1984	NY A	Porfi Altamirano Ron Hassey Rich Bordi	CHI N	Ray Fontenot Brian Dayett
Dec. 22, 1987	SEA A	Steve Trout	NY A	Lee Guetterman Clay Parker Wade Taylor
June 27, 1993	FLA N	Jeff Darwin	SEA A	Dave Magadan

Ensign Cottrell

Date	Traded To	Traded With	Traded By	In Exchange For
Jan. 1912	CHI N	—	PIT N	Cash
Apr. 18, 1915	NY A	—	BOS N	Cash

Johnny Couch

Date	Traded To	Traded With	Traded By	In Exchange For
Aug. 2, 1923	PHI N	—	CIN N	Waiver price

Bill Coughlin

Date	Traded To	Traded With	Traded By	In Exchange For
Aug. 10, 1904	DET A	Lew Drill	WAS A	$7,500.

Marlan Coughtry

Date	Traded To	Traded With	Traded By	In Exchange For
May 12, 1962	KC A	—	LA A	Gordie Windhorn
July 2, 1962	CLE A	—	KC A	Cash

Tom Coulter

Date	Traded To	Traded With	Traded By	In Exchange For
Oct. 18, 1971	NY N	—	STL N	*see Jim Bibby*

Fritz Coumbe

Date	Traded To	Traded With	Traded By	In Exchange For
July 28, 1914	CLE A	Adam Johnson Ben Egan	BOS A	Vean Gregg

Clint Courtney

Date	Traded To	Traded With	Traded By	In Exchange For
Nov. 23, 1951	STL A	—	NY A	Jim McDonald
Dec. 6, 1954	CHI A	Jim Brideweser Bob Chakales	BAL A	Don Ferrarese Don Johnson Matt Batts Freddie Marsh
June 7, 1955	WAS A	Bob Chakales Johnny Groth	CHI A	Jim Busby
Apr. 3, 1960	BAL A	Ron Samford	WAS A	Billy Gardner

Ernie Courtney

Date	Traded To	Traded With	Traded By	In Exchange For
June 10, 1903	DET A	Herman Long	NY A	Kid Elberfeld

Henry Courtney

Date	Traded To	Traded With	Traded By	In Exchange For
May 1922	CHI A	—	WAS A	Cash

John Courtright

Date	Traded To	Traded With	Traded By	In Exchange For
June 8, 1995	MIN N	—	CIN N	David McCarty
June 8, 1995	MIN A	—	CIN N	David McCarty

Harry Coveleski

Date	Traded To	Traded With	Traded By	In Exchange For
Jan. 20, 1910	CIN N	—	PHI N	Ad Brennan

Stan Coveleski

Date	Traded To	Traded With	Traded By	In Exchange For
Dec. 12, 1924	WAS A	—	CLE A	Byron Speece Carr Smith

Wes Covington

Date	Traded To	Traded With	Traded By	In Exchange For
May 10, 1961	CHI A	—	MIL N	Waiver price
June 10, 1961	KC A	Bob Shaw Gerry Staley Stan Johnson	CHI A	Ray Herbert Don Larsen Andy Carey Al Pilarcik
July 2, 1961	PHI N	—	KC A	Bobby Del Greco
Jan. 10, 1966	CHI N	—	PHI N	Doug Clemens

Billy Cowan

Date	Traded To	Traded With	Traded By	In Exchange For
Jan. 15, 1965	NY N	—	CHI N	George Altman
Apr. 28, 1966	CHI N	—	ATL N	Cash
July 26, 1969	CAL A	—	NY A	Cash

Al Cowens

Date	Traded To	Traded With	Traded By	In Exchange For
Dec. 6, 1979	CAL A	Todd Cruz Craig Eaton	KC A	Rance Mulliniks Willie Aikens
May 27, 1980	DET A	—	CAL A	Jason Thompson
Mar. 28, 1982	SEA A	—	DET A	Cash

Joe Cowley

Date	Traded To	Traded With	Traded By	In Exchange For
Dec. 12, 1985	CHI A	Ron Hassey	NY A	Britt Burns Minor league SS Mike Soper Minor league OF Glen Braxton
Mar. 26, 1987	PHI N	Cash	CHI A	Gary Redus

Billy Cox

Date	Traded To	Traded With	Traded By	In Exchange For
June 11, 1938	STL A	—	CHI A	Jack Knott
Dec. 8, 1947	BKN N	Preacher Roe Gene Mauch	PIT N	Dixie Walker Hal Gregg Vic Lombardi
Dec. 13, 1954	BAL A	Preacher Roe	BKN N	Minor leaguers John Jancse and Harry Schwegeman $50,000.

(Roe retired; Erv Palica trade of March 17, 1955 was additional compensation.)

Date	Traded To	Traded With	Traded By	In Exchange For
June 15, 1955	CLE A	Gene Woodling	BAL A	Dave Pope Wally Westlake

(Cox refused to report and announced retirement. Cleveland received $15,000 to complete trade.)

Bobby Cox

Date	Traded To	Traded With	Traded By	In Exchange For
Dec. 7, 1967	NY A	—	ATL N	Bob Tillman Dale Roberts

Casey Cox

Date	Traded To	Traded With	Traded By	In Exchange For
Aug. 30, 1972	NY A	—	TEX A	Jim Roland

Glenn Cox

Date	Traded To	Traded With	Traded By	In Exchange For
Sept. 12, 1955	KC A	—	BKN N	Waiver price

Jeff Cox

Date	Traded To	Traded With	Traded By	In Exchange For
Mar. 1, 1982	DET A	Scott Meyer	OAK A	Darrell Brown minor league Ps Mark Fellows Jack Smith

Larry Cox

Date	Traded To	Traded With	Traded By	In Exchange For
Oct. 24, 1975	MIN A	—	PHI N	Sergio Ferrer
Oct. 22, 1976	SEA A	—	MIN A	Cash
Oct. 25, 1977	CHI N	—	SEA A	Minor league P Steve Hamrick
Mar. 20, 1979	SEA A	—	CHI N	Luis Delgado
Dec. 12, 1980	TEX A	*see Rick Honeycutt*	SEA A	—

Ted Cox

Date	Traded To	Traded With	Traded By	In Exchange For
Mar. 30, 1978	CLE A	—	BOS A	*see Dennis Eckersley*
Dec. 6, 1979	SEA A	—	CLE A	Rafael Vasquez Bud Anderson minor league P Bob Pietroburgo

Jim Crabb

Date	Traded To	Traded With	Traded By	In Exchange For
May 1912	PHI A	—	CHI A	Cash

Estel Crabtree

Date	Traded To	Traded With	Traded By	In Exchange For
Dec. 17, 1932	STL N	Ownie Carroll	CIN N	Jim Bottomley

Rodney Craig

Date	Traded To	Traded With	Traded By	In Exchange For
Mar. 26, 1981	CLE A	—	SEA A	Wayne Cage

Roger Craig

Date	Traded To	Traded With	Traded By	In Exchange For
Nov. 4, 1963	STL N	—	NY N	George Altman Bill Wakefield
Dec. 14, 1964	CIN N	Charlie James	STL N	Bob Purkey

Doc Cramer

Date	Traded To	Traded With	Traded By	In Exchange For
Jan. 4, 1936	BOS A	Eric McNair	PHI A	Hank Johnson Al Niemiec $75,000.
Dec. 12, 1940	WAS A	—	BOS A	Gee Walker
Dec. 12, 1941	DET A	Jimmy Bloodworth	WAS A	Frank Croucher Bruce Campbell

Del Crandall

Date	Traded To	Traded With	Traded By	In Exchange For
Dec. 3, 1963	SF N	Bob Shaw Bob Hendley	MIL N	Felipe Alou Billy Hoeft Ed Bailey Ernie Bowman
Feb. 11, 1965	PIT N	—	SF N	Bob Priddy Bob Burda

Doc Crandall

Date	Traded To	Traded With	Traded By	In Exchange For
Aug. 6, 1913	STL N	—	NY N	Larry McLean
Aug. 13, 1913	NY N	—	STL N	Cash
Feb. 10, 1916	STL A	*see Eddie Plank*	STL F	—

Sam Crane

Date	Traded To	Traded With	Traded By	In Exchange For
Feb. 3, 1917	WAS A	—	PHI A	Cash
Jan. 24, 1922	BKN N	—	CIN N	Cash

Gavvy Cravath

Date	Traded To	Traded With	Traded By	In Exchange For
Aug. 1908	CHI A	—	BOS A	Cash
May 16, 1909	WAS A	Nick Altrock Jiggs Donahue	CHI A	Bill Burns

Glenn Crawford

Date	Traded To	Traded With	Traded By	In Exchange For
May 8, 1945	PHI N	John Antonelli	STL N	Buster Adams

Jim Crawford

Date	Traded To	Traded With	Traded By	In Exchange For
Dec. 6, 1975	DET A	*see Milt May*	HOU N	—

Pat Crawford

Date	Traded To	Traded With	Traded By	In Exchange For
May 27, 1930	CIN N	—	NY N	Ethan Allen Pete Donohue

Rufus Crawford

Date	Traded To	Traded With	Traded By	In Exchange For
Oct. 27, 1952	DET A	—	STL A	Neil Berry Cliff Mapes $25,000.

Willie Crawford

Date	Traded To	Traded With	Traded By	In Exchange For
Mar. 2, 1976	STL N	—	LA N	Ted Sizemore
Oct. 20, 1976	SF N	Vic Harris John Curtis	STL N	John D'Acquisto Mike Caldwell Dave Rader
Mar. 26, 1977	HOU N	Rob Sperring	SF N	Rob Andrews Cash
June 15, 1977	OAK A	—	HOU N	Denny Walling Cash

Birdie Cree

Date	Traded To	Traded With	Traded By	In Exchange For
Mar. 1908	NY A	—	PHI A	Cash

Doug Creek

Date	Traded To	Traded With	Traded By	In Exchange For
Dec. 14, 1995	SF N	Allen Watson Rich DeLucia	STL N	Royce Clayton

Keith Creel

Date	Traded To	Traded With	Traded By	In Exchange For
Mar. 19, 1985	CLE A	—	KC A	player to be named

(Kansas City received OF Dwight Taylor on Oct. 3, 1985.)

Tim Crews

Date	Traded To	Traded With	Traded By	In Exchange For
Dec. 10, 1986	LA N	—	MIL A	*see Greg Brock*

Lou Criger

Date	Traded To	Traded With	Traded By	In Exchange For
Dec. 12, 1908	STL A	—	BOS A	Tubby Spencer
Dec. 1909	NY A	—	STL A	Joe Lake

Chuck Crim

Date	Traded To	Traded With	Traded By	In Exchange For
Dec. 10, 1991	CAL A	—	MIL A	Mike Fetters Minor league P Glenn Carter

Jack Crimian

Date	Traded To	Traded With	Traded By	In Exchange For
Dec. 2, 1953	CIN N	$100,000.	STL N	Alex Grammas
Dec. 5, 1956	DET A	—	KC A	*see Ned Garver*

Leo Cristante

Date	Traded To	Traded With	Traded By	In Exchange For
Dec. 6, 1954	DET A	*see Ferris Fain*	CHI A	—

Hughie Critz

Date	Traded To	Traded With	Traded By	In Exchange For
May 21, 1930	NY N	—	CIN N	Larry Benton

Fred Crolius

Date	Traded To	Traded With	Traded By	In Exchange For
Feb. 1902	PIT N	—	BOS N	Cash

Ray Crone

Date	Traded To	Traded With	Traded By	In Exchange For
June 15, 1957	NY N	Danny O'Connell Bobby Thomson	MIL N	Red Schoendienst

Joe Cronin

Date	Traded To	Traded With	Traded By	In Exchange For
Oct. 26, 1934	BOS A	—	WAS A	Lyn Lary $225,000.

John Cronin

Date	Traded To	Traded With	Traded By	In Exchange For
June 1902	BAL A	—	DET A	Cash
Dec. 12, 1903	NY N	Charlie Babb	BKN N	Bill Dahlen

Ed Crosby

Date	Traded To	Traded With	Traded By	In Exchange For
July 27, 1973	CIN N	minor league C Gene Dusan	STL N	Ed Sprague Roe Skidmore
Mar. 29, 1974	STL N	—	PHI N	Cash
June 1, 1974	CLE A	Luis Alvarado	STL N	Jack Heidemann

Ken Crosby

Date	Traded To	Traded With	Traded By	In Exchange For
Aug. 7, 1973	STL N	Cash	NY A	Wayne Granger

Jeff Cross

Date	Traded To	Traded With	Traded By	In Exchange For
May 2, 1948	CHI N	—	STL N	Cash

Lave Cross

Date	Traded To	Traded With	Traded By	In Exchange For
May 1900	BKN N	—	STL N	Cash
Jan. 1905	WAS A	—	PHI A	Cash

Bill Crouch

Date	Traded To	Traded With	Traded By	In Exchange For
Nov. 11, 1940	PHI N	Vito Tamulis Mickey Livingston $100,000.	BKN N	Kirby Higbe

Jack Crouch

Date	Traded To	Traded With	Traded By	In Exchange For
Sept. 1, 1933	CIN N	—	STL A	Waiver price

Frank Croucher

Date	Traded To	Traded With	Traded By	In Exchange For
Dec. 12, 1941	WAS A	Bruce Campbell	DET A	Jimmy Bloodworth Doc Cramer

General Crowder

Date	Traded To	Traded With	Traded By	In Exchange For
July 7, 1927	STL A	—	WAS A	Tom Zachary
June 13, 1930	WAS A	Heinie Manush	STL A	Goose Goslin
Aug. 4, 1934	DET A	—	WAS A	Waiver price

George Crowe

Date	Traded To	Traded With	Traded By	In Exchange For
Apr. 9, 1956	CIN N	—	MIL N	Bob Hazle Corky Valentine
Oct. 3, 1958	STL N	Alex Kellner Alex Grammas	CIN N	Bob Mabe Eddie Kasko Del Ennis

Terry Crowley

Date	Traded To	Traded With	Traded By	In Exchange For
Dec. 6, 1973	TEX A	—	BAL A	Cash
Mar. 19, 1974	CIN N	—	TEX A	Cash
Apr. 7, 1976	ATL N	—	CIN N	Mike Thompson

Walt Cruise

Date	Traded To	Traded With	Traded By	In Exchange For
May 1919	BOS N	—	STL N	Cash

Hector Cruz

Date	Traded To	Traded With	Traded By	In Exchange For
Dec. 8, 1977	CHI N	Dave Rader	STL N	Jerry Morales Steve Swisher Cash
June 15, 1978	SF N	—	CHI N	Lynn McGlothen
June 28, 1979	CIN N	—	SF N	Pedro Borbon
Dec. 12, 1980	CHI N	—	CIN N	Mike Vail

Henry Cruz

Date	Traded To	Traded With	Traded By	In Exchange For
Sept. 2, 1977	CHI A	—	LA N	Cash

Jose Cruz

Date	Traded To	Traded With	Traded By	In Exchange For
Oct. 24, 1974	HOU N	—	STL N	Cash
Feb. 25, 1988	NY A	—	HOU N	No compensation (free agent signing)

Julio Cruz

Date	Traded To	Traded With	Traded By	In Exchange For
June 15, 1983	CHI A	—	SEA A	Tony Bernazard

Todd Cruz

Date	Traded To	Traded With	Traded By	In Exchange For
Apr. 3, 1979	KC A	—	PHI N	Doug Bird
Dec. 6, 1979	CAL A	Al Cowens Craig Eaton	KC A	Rance Mulliniks Willie Aikens

Todd Cruz *continued*

Date	Traded To	Traded With	Traded By	In Exchange For
June 12, 1980	CHI A	—	CAL A	Randy Scarbery
Dec. 11, 1981	SEA A	Rod Allen Jim Essian	CHI A	Tom Paciorek
June 30, 1983	BAL A	—	SEA A	Cash

Tommy Cruz

Date	Traded To	Traded With	Traded By	In Exchange For
Oct. 26, 1973	TEX A	Cash	STL N	Sonny Siebert
Dec. 12, 1977	NY A	Jim Spencer minor league P Bob Polinsky	CHI A	Stan Thomas minor league P Ed Ricks and cash

Victor Cruz

Date	Traded To	Traded With	Traded By	In Exchange For
Dec. 6, 1977	TOR A	Tom Underwood	STL N	Pete Vuckovich John Scott
Dec. 5, 1978	CLE A	—	TOR A	Alfredo Griffin minor league 3B Phil Lansford
Dec. 9, 1980	PIT N	Gary Alexander Rafael Vasquez Bob Owchinko	CLE A	Bert Blyleven Manny Sanguillen

Mike Cubbage

Date	Traded To	Traded With	Traded By	In Exchange For
June 1, 1976	MIN A	*see Roy Smalley*	TEX A	—
Dec. 19, 1980	NY N	—	MIN A	No compensation (free agent signing)

Tony Cuccinello

Date	Traded To	Traded With	Traded By	In Exchange For
Mar. 14, 1932	BKN N	Joe Stripp Clyde Sukeforth	CIN N	Babe Herman Wally Gilbert Ernie Lombardi
Dec. 12, 1935	BOS N	Ray Benge Al Lopez Bobby Reis	BKN N	Ed Brandt Randy Moore
June 15, 1940	NY N	—	BOS N	Manny Salvo Al Glossop

Cookie Cuccurullo

Date	Traded To	Traded With	Traded By	In Exchange For
Oct. 21, 1946	NY A	—	PIT N	Ernie Bonham

Bobby Cuellar

Date	Traded To	Traded With	Traded By	In Exchange For
Aug. 31, 1978	CLE A	minor league OF Dave Rivera	TEX A	Johnny Grubb

Mike Cuellar

Date	Traded To	Traded With	Traded By	In Exchange For
June 15, 1965	HOU N	Ron Taylor	STL N	Hal Woodeshick Chuck Taylor
Dec. 4, 1968	BAL A	Enzo Hernandez Minor League IF Elijah Johnson	HOU N	Curt Blefary Minor leaguer John Mason

Leon Culberson

Date	Traded To	Traded With	Traded By	In Exchange For
Dec. 10, 1947	WAS A	Al Kozar	BOS A	Stan Spence
May 13, 1948	NY A	$15,000.	WAS A	Bud Stewart

Jack Cullen

Date	Traded To	Traded With	Traded By	In Exchange For
Apr. 3, 1967	LA N	John Miller $25,000.	NY A	John Kennedy

Tim Cullen

Date	Traded To	Traded With	Traded By	In Exchange For
Feb. 13, 1968	CHI A	Buster Narum Bob Priddy	WAS A	Dennis Higgins Steve Jones Ron Hansen
Aug. 2, 1968	WAS A	—	CHI A	Ron Hansen

Roy Cullenbine

Date	Traded To	Traded With	Traded By	In Exchange For
May 27, 1940	STL A	—	BKN N	Joe Gallagher
June 7, 1942	WAS A	Bill Trotter	STL A	Mike Chartak Steve Sundra
Aug. 31, 1942	NY A	—	WAS A	Waiver price
Dec. 17, 1942	CLE A	Buddy Rosar	NY A	Roy Weatherly Oscar Grimes

Roy Cullenbine *continued*

Date	Traded To	Traded With	Traded By	In Exchange For
Apr. 27, 1945	DET A	—	CLE A	Don Ross Dutch Meyer

Dick Culler

Date	Traded To	Traded With	Traded By	In Exchange For
Mar. 1, 1948	CHI N	—	BOS N	Bobby Sturgeon

Nick Cullop

Date	Traded To	Traded With	Traded By	In Exchange For
Dec. 23, 1915	NY A	—	KC F	Cash
Jan. 22, 1918	STL A	—	NY A	*see Eddie Plank*

Nick Cullop

Date	Traded To	Traded With	Traded By	In Exchange For
Aug. 27, 1926	WAS A	Garland Braxton	NY A	Dutch Ruether

(New York sent Braxton and Cullop to Washington on October 19, 1926.)

Date	Traded To	Traded With	Traded By	In Exchange For
Dec. 2, 1931	STL N	Cash	CIN N	Andy High

Wil Culmer

Date	Traded To	Traded With	Traded By	In Exchange For
Sept. 12, 1982	CLE A	Jerry Reed Roy Smith	PHI N	John Denny

Ray Culp

Date	Traded To	Traded With	Traded By	In Exchange For
Dec. 7, 1966	CHI N	Cash	PHI N	Dick Ellsworth
Nov. 30, 1967	BOS A	—	CHI N	Rudy Schlesinger Cash

George Culver

Date	Traded To	Traded With	Traded By	In Exchange For
Nov. 21, 1967	CIN N	Fred Whitfield Bob Raudman	CLE A	Tommy Harper
Nov. 5, 1969	STL N	—	CIN N	Ray Washburn
June 13, 1970	HOU N	—	STL N	Jim Beauchamp Leon McFadden
Mar. 26, 1973	LA N	—	HOU N	Cash
Aug. 10, 1973	PHI N	—	LA N	Cash

John Cumberland

Date	Traded To	Traded With	Traded By	In Exchange For
July 20, 1970	SF N	—	NY A	Mike McCormick
June 16, 1972	STL N	—	SF N	Cash
Nov. 29, 1972	MIN A	Larry Hisle	STL N	Wayne Granger

Jack Cummings

Date	Traded To	Traded With	Traded By	In Exchange For
July 14, 1929	BOS N	—	NY N	Cash

John Cummings

Date	Traded To	Traded With	Traded By	In Exchange For
May 25, 1995	LA N	—	SEA A	Waiver price

Midre Cummings

Date	Traded To	Traded With	Traded By	In Exchange For
Mar. 17, 1992	PIT N	Denny Neagle	MIN A	John Smiley

Steve Cummings

Date	Traded To	Traded With	Traded By	In Exchange For
Sept. 16, 1990	CLE A	—	TOR A	*see Bud Black*
May 21, 1991	DET A	—	CLE A	Player to be named

(Cleveland received P Eric Stone on July 8, 1991.)

Bert Cunningham

Date	Traded To	Traded With	Traded By	In Exchange For
Jan. 1900	CHI N	—	PIT N	Cash

Bill Cunningham

Date	Traded To	Traded With	Traded By	In Exchange For
Nov. 12, 1923	BOS N	Casey Stengel Dave Bancroft	NY N	Billy Southworth Joe Oeschger

(Bancroft was named Boston manager.)

Bruce Cunningham

Date	Traded To	Traded With	Traded By	In Exchange For
Nov. 7, 1928	BOS N	Socks Seibold Percy Jones Lou Legett Freddie Maguire $200,000.	CHI N	Rogers Hornsby

Joe Cunningham

Date	Traded To	Traded With	Traded By	In Exchange For
Nov. 27, 1961	CHI A	—	STL N	Minnie Minoso
July 13, 1964	WAS A	Frank Kreutzer	CHI A	Bill Skowron Carl Bouldin

Nig Cuppy

Date	Traded To	Traded With	Traded By	In Exchange For
Jan. 1900	BOS N	—	STL N	Cash

Clarence Currie

Date	Traded To	Traded With	Traded By	In Exchange For
Aug. 1902	STL N	—	CIN N	Cash
July 1903	CHI N	—	STL N	Cash

Tony Curry

Date	Traded To	Traded With	Traded By	In Exchange For
Mar. 20, 1962	CLE A	Ken Lehman	PHI N	Mel Roach
July 19, 1966	HOU N	—	CLE A	Jim Gentile

Chad Curtis

Date	Traded To	Traded With	Traded By	In Exchange For
Apr. 13, 1995	DET A	—	CAL A	Tony Phillips

Cliff Curtis

Date	Traded To	Traded With	Traded By	In Exchange For
June 10, 1911	CHI N	—	BOS N	*see Johnny Kling*
Aug. 1911	PHI N	—	CHI N	Jack Rowan
May 1912	BKN N	—	PHI N	Cash

Jack Curtis

Date	Traded To	Traded With	Traded By	In Exchange For
Apr. 30, 1962	MIL N	—	CHI N	Bob Buhl
Nov. 27, 1962	CLE A	Joe Adcock	MIL N	Ty Cline Don Dillard Frank Funk

John Curtis

Date	Traded To	Traded With	Traded By	In Exchange For
Dec. 7, 1973	STL N	Lynn McGlothen Mike Garman	BOS A	Reggie Cleveland Diego Segui Terry Hughes
Oct. 20, 1976	SF N	Willie Crawford Vic Harris	STL N	John D'Acquisto Mike Caldwell Dave Rader
Nov. 26, 1979	SD N	—	SF N	No compensation (free agent signing)
Aug. 31, 1982	CAL A	—	SD N	Cash

Jack Cusick

Date	Traded To	Traded With	Traded By	In Exchange For
Oct. 11, 1951	BOS N	—	CHI N	Bob Addis

George Cutshaw

Date	Traded To	Traded With	Traded By	In Exchange For
Jan. 9, 1918	PIT N	Casey Stengel	BKN N	Chuck Ward Burleigh Grimes Al Mamaux
Dec. 29, 1921	DET A	—	PIT N	Waiver price

Kiki Cuyler

Date	Traded To	Traded With	Traded By	In Exchange For
Nov. 28, 1927	CHI N	—	PIT N	Sparky Adams Pete Scott

Mike Cvengros

Date	Traded To	Traded With	Traded By	In Exchange For
Dec. 1927	CHI N	—	PIT N	Fred Fussell

Omar Daal

Date	Traded To	Traded With	Traded By	In Exchange For
Dec. 15, 1995	MON N	—	LA N	Minor league P Rick Clelland

John D'Acquisto

Date	Traded To	Traded With	Traded By	In Exchange For
Oct. 20, 1976	STL N	*see Mike Caldwell*	SF N	—
May 17, 1977	SD N	Pat Scanlon	STL N	Butch Metzger
Aug. 11, 1980	MON N	Cash	SD N	Randy Bass
Dec. 11, 1980	CAL A	—	MON N	No compensation (free agent signing)

Paul Dade

Date	Traded To	Traded With	Traded By	In Exchange For
June 14, 1979	SD N	—	CLE A	Mike Hargrove

Bill Dahlen

Date	Traded To	Traded With	Traded By	In Exchange For
Dec. 12, 1903	BKN N	—	NY N	John Cronin Charlie Babb

Bill Dahlen *continued*

Date	Traded To	Traded With	Traded By	In Exchange For
Dec. 3, 1907	BOS N	Dan McGann Frank Bowerman George Browne George Ferguson	NY N	Fred Tenney Al Bridwell Tom Needham

Babe Dahlgren

Date	Traded To	Traded With	Traded By	In Exchange For
Feb. 17, 1937	NY A	—	BOS A	Cash
Feb. 25, 1941	BOS N	—	NY A	Cash
June 15, 1941	CHI N	—	BOS N	Cash
May 13, 1942	STL A	—	CHI N	Cash

(Ten-day conditional sale; Dahlgren was returned to the Cubs on May 19, 1940.)

Date	Traded To	Traded With	Traded By	In Exchange For
May 19, 1942	BKN N	—	CHI N	Cash
Mar. 9, 1943	PHI N	—	BKN N	Lloyd Waner Al Glossop
Dec. 30, 1943	PIT N	—	PHI N	Babe Phelps Cash
Apr. 23, 1946	STL A	—	PIT N	Cash

Bill Dailey

Date	Traded To	Traded With	Traded By	In Exchange For
Apr. 8, 1963	MIN A	—	CLE A	Cash

Bruce Dal Canton

Date	Traded To	Traded With	Traded By	In Exchange For
Dec. 2, 1970	KC A	*see Freddie Patek*	PIT N	—
June 30, 1975	ATL N	Norm Angelini Al Autry	KC A	Ray Sadecki Cash

(Atlanta received Angelini and Autry on September 4,1975.)

Bud Daley

Date	Traded To	Traded With	Traded By	In Exchange For
Apr. 1, 1958	BAL A	Dick Williams Gene Woodling	CLE A	Larry Doby Don Ferrarese
Apr. 17, 1958	KC A	—	BAL A	Arnie Portocarrero
June 14, 1961	NY A	—	KC A	Art Ditmar Deron Johnson
Sept. 5, 1964	CLE A	Ralph Terry $75,000.	NY A	Pedro Ramos

Pete Daley

Date	Traded To	Traded With	Traded By	In Exchange For
Dec. 3, 1959	KC A	—	BOS A	Tom Sturdivant

Tom Daley

Date	Traded To	Traded With	Traded By	In Exchange For
June 10, 1914	NY A	—	PHI A	Jimmy Walsh

Clay Dalrymple

Date	Traded To	Traded With	Traded By	In Exchange For
Jan. 20, 1969	BAL A	—	PHI N	Ron Stone

Jack Dalton

Date	Traded To	Traded With	Traded By	In Exchange For
Feb. 10, 1916	DET A	Howard Ehmke	BUF F	Cash

Tom Daly

Date	Traded To	Traded With	Traded By	In Exchange For
Dec. 1915	CLE A	—	CHI A	Cash

Tom Daly

Date	Traded To	Traded With	Traded By	In Exchange For
June 9, 1903	CIN N	Cozy Dolan	CHI A	George Magoon

Bennie Daniels

Date	Traded To	Traded With	Traded By	In Exchange For
Dec. 16, 1960	WAS A	Harry Bright R C Stevens	PIT N	Bobby Shantz

Bert Daniels

Date	Traded To	Traded With	Traded By	In Exchange For
Oct. 1913	CIN N	—	NY A	Cash

Kal Daniels

Date	Traded To	Traded With	Traded By	In Exchange For
July 18, 1989	LA N	Lenny Harris	CIN N	Tim Leary Mariano Duncan
June 27, 1992	CHI N	—	LA N	Player to be named

(Los Angeles received P Mike Sodders on July 28, 1992.)

Pat Darcy

Date	Traded To	Traded With	Traded By	In Exchange For
Feb. 18, 1974	CIN N	Cash	HOU N	Denis Menke

Pat Darcy *continued*

Date	Traded To	Traded With	Traded By	In Exchange For
Mar. 29, 1977	STL N	—	CIN N	Mike Caldwell

Alvin Dark

Date	Traded To	Traded With	Traded By	In Exchange For
Dec. 14, 1949	NY N	Eddie Stanky	BOS N	Sid Gordon Buddy Kerr Willard Marshall Red Webb
June 14, 1956	STL N	Ray Katt Don Liddle Whitey Lockman	NY N	Jackie Brandt Red Schoendienst Bobby Stephenson Dick Littlefield Bill Sarni
May 20, 1958	CHI N	—	STL N	Jim Brosnan
Jan. 11, 1960	PHI N	John Buzhardt Jim Woods	CHI N	Richie Ashburn
June 23, 1960	MIL N	—	PHI N	Joe Morgan
Oct. 31, 1960	SF N	—	MIL N	Andre Rodgers

Ron Darling

Date	Traded To	Traded With	Traded By	In Exchange For
Apr. 1, 1982	NY N	Walt Terrell	TEX A	Lee Mazzilli
July 15, 1991	MON N	Mike Thomas	NY N	Tim Burke
July 31, 1991	OAK A	—	MON N	Matt Grott Minor league P Russell Cormier

Bobby Darwin

Date	Traded To	Traded With	Traded By	In Exchange For
Oct. 22, 1971	MIN A	—	LA N	Paul Ray Powell
June 14, 1975	MIL A	—	MIN A	John Briggs
June 3, 1976	BOS A	Tom Murphy	MIL A	Bernie Carbo
May 28, 1977	CHI N	—	BOS A	Ramon Hernandez

Danny Darwin

Date	Traded To	Traded With	Traded By	In Exchange For
Jan. 18, 1985	MIL A	Minor league C Bill Hance	TEX A	Don Slaught

(Part of a four-team trade involving Texas, Milwaukee, Kansas City, and New York Mets.)

Date	Traded To	Traded With	Traded By	In Exchange For
Aug. 19, 1986	HOU N	—	MIL A	Don August Mark Knudson
Dec. 19, 1990	BOS A	—	HOU N	No compensation (free agent signing)
Apr. 10, 1995	TOR A	—	BOS A	No compensation (free agent signing)

Jeff Darwin

Date	Traded To	Traded With	Traded By	In Exchange For
June 27, 1993	FLA N	Henry Cotto	SEA A	Dave Magadan
Nov. 9, 1993	SEA A	Cash	FLA N	Dave Magadan
July 18, 1995	CHI A	—	SEA A	Warren Newson

(Chicago received Darwin on October 9, 1995.)

Jake Daubert

Date	Traded To	Traded With	Traded By	In Exchange For
Mar. 1919	CIN N	—	BKN N	Tommy Griffith

Jack Daugherty

Date	Traded To	Traded With	Traded By	In Exchange For
Sept. 1, 1988	TEX A	—	MON N	Tom O'Malley

(Texas received Daugherty on Sept. 13, 1988.)

Date	Traded To	Traded With	Traded By	In Exchange For
July 12, 1993	CIN N	—	HOU N	Steve Carter

Vic Davalillo

Date	Traded To	Traded With	Traded By	In Exchange For
June 15, 1968	CAL A	—	CLE A	Jimmie Hall
May 30, 1969	STL N	—	CAL A	Jim Hicks
Jan. 29, 1971	PIT N	Nellie Briles	STL N	Matty Alou George Brunet
Aug. 1, 1973	OAK A	—	PIT N	Cash

Jerry DaVanon

Date	Traded To	Traded With	Traded By	In Exchange For
May 22, 1969	STL N	Bill Davis	SD N	John Sipin Sonny Ruberto
Nov. 30, 1970	BAL A	—	STL N	Moe Drabowsky
June 10, 1972	CAL A	—	BAL A	Roger Repoz
Nov. 23, 1976	STL N	Larry Dierker	HOU N	Joe Ferguson Bob Detherage

Mike Davey

Date	Traded To	Traded With	Traded By	In Exchange For
Feb. 23, 1979	SEA A	—	ATL N	Cash

Mark Davidson

Date	Traded To	Traded With	Traded By	In Exchange For
May 16, 1989	HOU N	—	MIN A	Player to be named

(Minnesota received P Greg Johnson on September 6, 1989.)

Ted Davidson

Date	Traded To	Traded With	Traded By	In Exchange For
June 11, 1968	ATL N	*see Milt Pappas*	CIN N	—

Alvin Davis

Date	Traded To	Traded With	Traded By	In Exchange For
Feb. 13, 1992	CAL A	—	SEA A	No compensation (free agent signing)

Bill Davis

Date	Traded To	Traded With	Traded By	In Exchange For
Oct. 21, 1968	SD N	—	CLE A	Zoilo Versalles
May 22, 1969	STL N	Jerry DaVanon	SD N	John Sipin Sonny Ruberto

Brock Davis

Date	Traded To	Traded With	Traded By	In Exchange For
Dec. 3, 1971	MIL A	Jim Colborn Earl Stephenson	CHI N	Jose Cardenal
Feb. 25, 1975	CLE A	Dave LaRoche	CHI N	Milt Wilcox

Chili Davis

Date	Traded To	Traded With	Traded By	In Exchange For
Dec. 1, 1987	CAL A	—	SF N	No compensation (free agent signing)
Jan. 29, 1991	MIN A	—	CAL A	No compensation (free agent signing)
Dec. 11, 1992	CAL A	—	MIN A	No compensation (free agent signing)

Curt Davis

Date	Traded To	Traded With	Traded By	In Exchange For
May 21, 1936	CHI N	Ethan Allen	PHI N	Chuck Klein Fabian Kowalik
Apr. 16, 1938	STL N	Clyde Shoun Tuck Stainback $185,000.	CHI N	Dizzy Dean
June 12, 1940	BKN N	Joe Medwick	STL N	Ernie Koy Carl Doyle Sam Nahem Bert Haas $125,000.

Dick Davis

Date	Traded To	Traded With	Traded By	In Exchange For
Mar. 1, 1981	PHI N	—	MIL A	Randy Lerch
June 15, 1982	TOR A	—	PHI N	Wayne Nordhagen
June 22, 1982	PIT N	—	TOR A	Wayne Nordhagen

Dixie Davis

Date	Traded To	Traded With	Traded By	In Exchange For
Jan. 21, 1919	STL N	Milt Stock Pickles Dillhoefer	PHI N	Doug Baird Stuffy Stewart Gene Packard

Eric Davis

Date	Traded To	Traded With	Traded By	In Exchange For
Nov. 27, 1991	LA N	Kip Gross	CIN N	Tim Belcher John Wetteland
Aug. 31, 1993	DET A	—	LA N	John DeSilva

(Los Angeles received DeSilva on September 7, 1993.)

George Davis

Date	Traded To	Traded With	Traded By	In Exchange For
Dec. 1912	BOS N	Guy Zinn	NY A	Cash

Glenn Davis

Date	Traded To	Traded With	Traded By	In Exchange For
Jan. 10, 1991	BAL A	—	HOU N	Pete Harnisch Curt Schilling Steve Finley

Jacke Davis

Date	Traded To	Traded With	Traded By	In Exchange For
Dec. 11, 1962	LA A	—	PHI N	Earl Averill
Mar. 29, 1963	SF N	—	LA A	Charlie Dees
July 29, 1963	STL N	Cash	NY N	Duke Carmel

Jim Davis

Date	Traded To	Traded With	Traded By	In Exchange For
Dec. 11, 1956	STL N	—	CHI N	*see Tom Poholsky*
June 4, 1957	NY N	—	STL N	Waiver price

Jody Davis

Date	Traded To	Traded With	Traded By	In Exchange For
Dec. 10, 1979	STL N	—	NY N	Ray Searage
Sept. 29, 1988	ATL N	—	CHI N	Kevin Coffman Kevin Blankenship

Joel Davis

Date	Traded To	Traded With	Traded By	In Exchange For
Jan. 23, 1989	CLE A	—	CHI A	*see Eddie Williams*

John Davis

Date	Traded To	Traded With	Traded By	In Exchange For
Dec. 10, 1987	CHI A	—	KC A	*see Floyd Bannister*

Kiddo Davis

Date	Traded To	Traded With	Traded By	In Exchange For
Dec. 12, 1932	NY N	—	PHI N	Gus Dugas Chick Fullis

(Part of three-team trade involving New York, Philadelphia, and Pittsburgh.)

Date	Traded To	Traded With	Traded By	In Exchange For
Feb. 1934	STL N	—	NY N	George Watkins
June 15, 1934	PHI N	—	STL N	Chick Fullis
Dec. 13, 1934	NY N	—	PHI N	Joe Bowman
Aug. 4, 1937	CIN N	—	NY N	Cash

Lefty Davis

Date	Traded To	Traded With	Traded By	In Exchange For
May 1901	PIT N	—	BKN N	Tom McCreery

Mark Davis

Date	Traded To	Traded With	Traded By	In Exchange For
Dec. 14, 1982	SF N	Mike Krukow minor league OF Charles Penigar	PHI N	Joe Morgan Al Holland
July 5, 1987	SD N	—	SF N	*see Kevin Mitchell*
Dec. 11, 1989	KC A	—	SD N	No compensation (free agent signing)
July 21, 1992	ATL N	—	KC A	Juan Berenguer
Apr. 13, 1993	PHI N	—	ATL N	Minor league P Brad Hassinger

Mike Davis

Date	Traded To	Traded With	Traded By	In Exchange For
Dec. 15, 1987	LA N	—	OAK A	No compensation (free agent signing)

Peaches Davis

Date	Traded To	Traded With	Traded By	In Exchange For
Aug. 19, 1939	PHI N	—	CIN N	Cash

Ron Davis

Date	Traded To	Traded With	Traded By	In Exchange For
June 10, 1978	NY A	—	CHI N	Ken Holtzman
Apr. 10, 1982	MIN A	Paul Boris Greg Gagne	NY A	Roy Smalley
Aug. 13, 1986	CHI N	Minor league P Dewayne Coleman	MIN A	George Frazier Ray Fontenot Minor league SS Julius McDougal

Ron Davis

Date	Traded To	Traded With	Traded By	In Exchange For
June 15, 1968	STL N	—	HOU N	Dick Simpson Hal Gilson
Dec. 3, 1968	SD N	Danny Breeden Ed Spiezio minor league P Phil Knuckles	STL N	Dave Giusti
Mar. 28, 1969	PIT N	Bobby Klaus	SD N	Chris Cannizzaro Tommie Sisk

Russ Davis

Date	Traded To	Traded With	Traded By	In Exchange For
Dec. 6, 1995	SEA A	Sterling Hitchcock	NY A	Tino Martinez Jeff Nelson Jim Mecir

Spud Davis

Date	Traded To	Traded With	Traded By	In Exchange For
May 11, 1928	PHI N	Homer Peel	STL N	Jimmie Wilson
Nov. 15, 1933	STL N	Eddie Delker	PHI N	Jimmie Wilson

(Wilson was named manager of the Phillies.)

Spud Davis *continued*

Date	Traded To	Traded With	Traded By	In Exchange For
Dec. 2, 1936	CIN N	—	STL N	Cash
June 13, 1938	PHI N	Al Hollingsworth $50,000.	CIN N	Bucky Walters
Oct. 27, 1939	PIT N	—	PHI N	Cash

Steve Davis

Date	Traded To	Traded With	Traded By	In Exchange For
Dec. 12, 1989	LA N	—	CLE A	Minor league IF Manny Francois Minor league OF Joe Kesselmark

Storm Davis

Date	Traded To	Traded With	Traded By	In Exchange For
Oct. 30, 1986	SD N	—	BAL A	Terry Kennedy Mark Williamson
Aug. 30, 1987	OAK A	—	SD N	Dave Leiper Rob Nelson

(San Diego received Nelson on September 8, 1987.)

Date	Traded To	Traded With	Traded By	In Exchange For
Dec. 7, 1989	KC A	—	OAK A	No compensation (free agent signing)
Dec. 11, 1991	BAL A	—	KC A	Bob Melvin
Dec. 8, 1992	OAK A	—	BAL A	No compensation (free agent signing)

Tommy Davis

Date	Traded To	Traded With	Traded By	In Exchange For
Nov. 29, 1966	NY N	Derrell Griffith	LA N	Ron Hunt Jim Hickman
Dec. 15, 1967	CHI A	Jack Fisher Billy Wynne Buddy Booker	NY N	Tommie Agee Al Weis
Aug. 30, 1969	HOU N	—	SEA A	Danny Walton Sandy Valdespino
June 22, 1970	OAK A	—	HOU N	Cash
Sept. 16, 1970	CHI N	—	OAK A	Cash
Aug. 18, 1972	BAL A	—	CHI N	Ellie Hendricks
Sept. 20, 1976	KC A	—	CAL A	Cash

Willie Davis

Date	Traded To	Traded With	Traded By	In Exchange For
Dec. 5, 1973	MON N	—	LA N	Mike Marshall
Dec. 5, 1974	TEX A	—	MON N	Don Stanhouse Pete Mackanin
June 4, 1975	STL N	—	TEX A	Ed Brinkman Tommy Moore
Oct. 20, 1975	SD N	—	STL N	Dick Sharon

Bill Dawley

Date	Traded To	Traded With	Traded By	In Exchange For
Mar. 31, 1983	HOU N	Tony Walker	CIN N	Alan Knicely
Dec. 22, 1986	STL N	—	CHI A	Fred Manrique

Andre Dawson

Date	Traded To	Traded With	Traded By	In Exchange For
Mar. 6, 1987	CHI N	—	MON N	No compensation (free agent signing)
Dec. 9, 1992	BOS A	—	CHI N	No compensation (free agent signing)
Apr. 8, 1995	FLA N	—	BOS A	No compensation (free agent signing)

Boots Day

Date	Traded To	Traded With	Traded By	In Exchange For
Dec. 4, 1969	CHI N	—	STL N	Rich Nye
May 12, 1970	MON N	—	CHI N	Jack Hiatt

Brian Dayett

Date	Traded To	Traded With	Traded By	In Exchange For
Dec. 4, 1984	CHI N	Ray Fontenot	NY A	Henry Cotto Porfi Altamirano Ron Hassey Rich Bordi

Ken Dayley

Date	Traded To	Traded With	Traded By	In Exchange For
June 15, 1984	STL N	Mike Jorgensen	ATL N	Ken Oberkfell
Nov. 26, 1990	TOR A	—	STL N	No compensation (free agent signing)

Charlie Deal

Date	Traded To	Traded With	Traded By	In Exchange For
June 1913	BOS N	—	DET A	Cash
Feb. 10, 1916	STL A	*see Eddie Plank*	STL F	—

Charlie Deal *continued*

Date	Traded To		Traded With	Traded By		In Exchange For
June 2, 1916	CHI	N	—	STL	A	Cash

Chubby Dean

Date	Traded To		Traded With	Traded By		In Exchange For
Aug. 9, 1941	CLE	A	—	PHI	A	Waiver price

Dizzy Dean

Date	Traded To		Traded With	Traded By		In Exchange For
Apr. 16, 1938	CHI	N	—	STL	N	Curt Davis Clyde Shoun Tuck Stainback $185,000.

Paul Dean

Date	Traded To		Traded With	Traded By		In Exchange For
May 14, 1941	STL	N	Harry Gumbert Cash	NY	N	Bill McGee
Feb. 1, 1943	WAS	A	—	STL	A	Cash

Tommy Dean

Date	Traded To		Traded With	Traded By		In Exchange For
Apr. 17, 1969	SD	N	Leon Everitt	LA	N	Al McBean

Wayland Dean

Date	Traded To		Traded With	Traded By		In Exchange For
Dec. 30, 1925	PHI	N	Jack Bentley	NY	N	Jimmy Ring
June 14, 1927	CHI	N	—	PHI	N	Cash

Denny DeBarr

Date	Traded To		Traded With	Traded By		In Exchange For
Mar. 15, 1978	CLE	A	—	TOR	A	Rico Carty
June 26, 1978	CHI	N	—	CLE	A	Paul Reuschel

Art Decatur

Date	Traded To		Traded With	Traded By		In Exchange For
May 1, 1925	PHI	N	—	BKN	N	Bill Hubbell

Doug DeCinces

Date	Traded To		Traded With	Traded By		In Exchange For
Jan. 28, 1982	CAL	A	Jeff Schneider	BAL	A	Dan Ford

Joe Decker

Date	Traded To		Traded With	Traded By		In Exchange For
Nov. 30, 1972	MIN	A	Bill Hands minor league P Bob Maneely	CHI	N	Dave LaRoche

Marty Decker

Date	Traded To		Traded With	Traded By		In Exchange For
Aug. 31, 1983	SD	N	—	PHI	N	*see Sixto Lezcano*

Jeff Dedmon

Date	Traded To		Traded With	Traded By		In Exchange For
Mar. 28, 1988	CLE	A	—	ATL	N	player to be named

(Atlanta received P Tommy Kurczewski on June 22, 1988.)

Rob Deer

Date	Traded To		Traded With	Traded By		In Exchange For
Dec. 17, 1985	MIL	A	—	SF	N	Minor league P Dean Freeland Minor league P Eric Pilkington
Nov. 21, 1990	DET	A	—	MIL	A	No compensation (free agent signing)
Aug. 21, 1993	BOS	A	—	DET	A	Cash

Charlie Dees

Date	Traded To		Traded With	Traded By		In Exchange For
Mar. 29, 1963	LA	A	—	SF	N	Jacke Davis

Tony DeFate

Date	Traded To		Traded With	Traded By		In Exchange For
Sept. 1917	DET	A	—	STL	N	Waiver price

Ivan DeJesus

Date	Traded To		Traded With	Traded By		In Exchange For
Jan. 11, 1977	CHI	N	Bill Buckner minor league P Jeff Albert	LA	N	Rick Monday Mike Garman
Jan. 27, 1982	PHI	N	—	CHI	N	Larry Bowa Ryne Sandberg
Apr. 6, 1985	STL	N	Bill Campbell	PHI	N	Dave Rucker
Feb. 4, 1986	MON	N	—	STL	N	No compensation (free agent signing)
June 5, 1987	SF	N	—	STL	N	Cash

Jose DeJesus

Date	Traded To		Traded With	Traded By		In Exchange For
Mar. 31, 1990	PHI	N	—	KC	A	Steve Jeltz

Frank Delahanty

Date	Traded To		Traded With	Traded By		In Exchange For
Nov. 1907	NY	A	—	CLE	A	Cash
Aug. 1914	PIT	F	—	BUF	F	Tex McDonald

Jim Delahanty

Date	Traded To		Traded With	Traded By		In Exchange For
Feb. 1902	NY	N	Jack Doyle	CHI	N	Cash
Mar. 1906	CIN	N	Chick Fraser	BOS	N	Al Bridwell
June 11, 1907	WAS	A	—	STL	A	$2,000.
Sept. 1907	STL	A	—	CIN	N	Cash
Aug. 13, 1909	DET	A	—	WAS	A	Germany Schaefer Red Killefer

Mike de la Hoz

Date	Traded To		Traded With	Traded By		In Exchange For
Apr. 1, 1964	MIL	N	—	CLE	A	Chico Salmon

Francisco de la Rosa

Date	Traded To		Traded With	Traded By		In Exchange For
Feb. 29, 1992	NY	A	Minor league P Mark Carper	BAL	A	Alan Mills

(New York received de la Rosa on March 5, and Carper on June 8, 1992.)

Jose DeLeon

Date	Traded To		Traded With	Traded By		In Exchange For
July 23, 1986	CHI	A	—	PIT	N	Bobby Bonilla
Feb. 9, 1988	STL	N	—	CHI	A	Ricky Horton Lance Johnson Cash
Aug. 10, 1993	CHI	A	—	PHI	N	Bobby Thigpen
Aug. 28, 1995	MON	N	—	CHI	A	Jeff Shaw

Luis DeLeon

Date	Traded To		Traded With	Traded By		In Exchange For
Dec. 10, 1981	SD	N	Sixto Lezcano Garry Templeton	STL	N	Ozzie Smith Steve Mura Al Olmsted

(Templeton and Smith were exchanged on February 11, 1982; Olmsted and DeLeon were exchanged on February 19.)

Luis Delgado

Date	Traded To		Traded With	Traded By		In Exchange For
Mar. 20, 1979	CHI	N	—	SEA	A	Larry Cox

Bobby Del Greco

Date	Traded To		Traded With	Traded By		In Exchange For
May 17, 1956	STL	N	Dick Littlefield	PIT	N	Bill Virdon
Apr. 20, 1957	CHI	N	Ed Mayer	STL	N	Jim King
Sept. 10, 1957	NY	A	—	CHI	N	Cash
July 2, 1961	KC	A	—	PHI	N	Wes Covington

Eddie Delker

Date	Traded To		Traded With	Traded By		In Exchange For
May 30, 1932	PHI	N	Flint Rhem	STL	N	Cash
Nov. 15, 1933	STL	N	Spud Davis	PHI	N	Jimmie Wilson

(Wilson was named manager of the Phillies.)

Luis de los Santos

Date	Traded To		Traded With	Traded By		In Exchange For
Apr. 5, 1991	DET	A	—	KC	A	Waiver price

Garton Del Savio

Date	Traded To		Traded With	Traded By		In Exchange For
Apr. 2, 1943	PHI	N	—	CIN	N	Cash

Jim Delsing

Date	Traded To		Traded With	Traded By		In Exchange For
Dec. 14, 1948	NY	A	—	CHI	A	Steve Souchock
June 15, 1950	STL	A	Don Johnson Duane Pillette Snuffy Stirnweiss $50,000.	NY	A	Tom Ferrick Joe Ostrowski Leo Thomas Sid Schacht
Aug. 14, 1952	DET	A	—	STL	A	*see Vic Wertz*
May 15, 1956	CHI	A	Fred Hatfield	DET	A	Jim Brideweser Harry Byrd Bob Kennedy
Dec. 6, 1958	WAS	A	—	DET	A	*see Eddie Yost*

Rich DeLucia

Date	Traded To		Traded With	Traded By		In Exchange For
Dec. 14, 1995	SF	N	Allen Watson Doug Creek	STL	N	Royce Clayton

Joe De Maestri

Date	Traded To	Traded With	Traded By	In Exchange For
Nov. 27, 1951	STL A	Dick Littlefield Gus Niarhos Gordon Goldsberry Jim Rivera	CHI A	Al Widmar Sherm Lollar Tom Upton
Oct. 16, 1952	CHI A	Tommy Byrne	STL A	Willie Miranda Hank Edwards
Jan. 27, 1953	PHI A	Eddie Robinson Ed McGhee	CHI A	Ferris Fain minor league 2B Bob Wilson
Dec. 11, 1959	NY A	*see Roger Maris*	KC A	—

Al Demaree

Date	Traded To	Traded With	Traded By	In Exchange For
Jan. 1915	PHI N	Bert Adams Milt Stock	NY N	Hans Lobert
Jan. 16, 1917	CHI N	—	PHI N	Jimmy Lavender $5,000.
July 31, 1917	NY N	—	CHI N	Pete Kilduff
Feb. 1919	BOS N	—	NY N	Cash

Frank Demaree

Date	Traded To	Traded With	Traded By	In Exchange For
Dec. 6, 1938	NY N	Bill Jurges Ken O'Dea	CHI N	Dick Bartell Hank Leiber Gus Mancuso
July 21, 1941	BOS N	—	NY N	Waiver price
Jan. 1943	STL N	—	BOS N	Cash

Billy DeMars

Date	Traded To	Traded With	Traded By	In Exchange For
Dec. 13, 1949	STL A	Ray Coleman Frankie Gustine minor league OF Ray Ippolito $100,000.	PHI A	Bob Dillinger Paul Lehner

Larry Demery

Date	Traded To	Traded With	Traded By	In Exchange For
Mar. 27, 1978	TOR A	—	PIT N	Cash

(Demery was returned on March 31.)

Don Demeter

Date	Traded To	Traded With	Traded By	In Exchange For
May 4, 1961	PHI N	Charley Smith	LA N	Dick Farrell Joe Koppe
Dec. 4, 1963	DET A	Jack Hamilton	PHI N	Jim Bunning Gus Triandos
June 14, 1966	BOS A	Julio Navarro	DET A	Earl Wilson Joe Christopher
June 4, 1967	CLE A	Tony Horton	BOS A	Gary Bell

Steve Demeter

Date	Traded To	Traded With	Traded By	In Exchange For
Apr. 12, 1960	CLE A	—	DET A	Norm Cash

Ray Demmitt

Date	Traded To	Traded With	Traded By	In Exchange For
Apr. 1914	CHI A	—	DET A	Cash

Gene DeMontreville

Date	Traded To	Traded With	Traded By	In Exchange For
Jan. 1900	BKN N	—	BAL N	Cash
Feb. 1901	BOS N	—	BKN N	Cash

Rick Dempsey

Date	Traded To	Traded With	Traded By	In Exchange For
Oct. 27, 1972	NY A	—	MIN A	Danny Walton
June 15, 1976	BAL A	Rudy May Tippy Martinez Dave Pagan Scott McGregor	NY A	Ken Holtzman Doyle Alexander Grant Jackson Ellie Hendricks Jimmy Freeman
Feb. 3, 1987	CLE A	—	BAL A	No compensation (free agent signing)

Bill Denehy

Date	Traded To	Traded With	Traded By	In Exchange For
Nov. 27, 1967	WAS A	$100,000.	NY N	Gil Hodges
		(Hodges was named New York manager.)		
June 20, 1969	CLE A	Cash	WAS A	Lee Maye
Mar. 30, 1971	DET A	Dean Chance	NY N	Jerry Robertson

Don Dennis

Date	Traded To	Traded With	Traded By	In Exchange For
Dec. 14, 1966	CHI A	Walt Williams	STL N	Johnny Romano minor league P Lee White

John Denny

Date	Traded To	Traded With	Traded By	In Exchange For
Dec. 7, 1979	CLE A	Jerry Mumphrey	STL N	Bobby Bonds
Sept. 12, 1982	PHI N	—	CLE A	Wil Culmer Jerry Reed Roy Smith
Dec. 11, 1985	CIN N	Jeff Gray	PHI N	Gary Redus Tom Hume

Bucky Dent

Date	Traded To	Traded With	Traded By	In Exchange For
Apr. 5, 1977	NY A	—	CHI A	Oscar Gamble LaMarr Hoyt minor league P Bob Polinsky $200,000.
Aug. 8, 1982	TEX A	—	NY A	Lee Mazzilli

Sam Dente

Date	Traded To	Traded With	Traded By	In Exchange For
Nov. 18, 1947	STL A	Clem Dreisewerd Bill Sommers $65,000.	BOS A	Ellis Kinder Billy Hitchcock
Oct. 4, 1948	WAS A	—	STL A	Tom Ferrick John Sullivan $25,000.
Nov. 27, 1951	CHI A	—	WAS A	Tom Upton

Bob Dernier

Date	Traded To	Traded With	Traded By	In Exchange For
Mar. 26, 1984	CHI N	Gary Matthews Porfi Altamirano	PHI N	Bill Campbell Mike Diaz
Dec. 8, 1987	PHI N	—	CHI N	No compensation (free agent signing)

Claud Derrick

Date	Traded To	Traded With	Traded By	In Exchange For
Nov. 1912	NY A	—	PHI A	Cash
July 20, 1914	CHI N	—	CIN N	Fritz Mollwitz

Paul Derringer

Date	Traded To	Traded With	Traded By	In Exchange For
May 7, 1933	CIN N	Sparky Adams Allyn Stout	STL N	Leo Durocher Dutch Henry Jack Ogden
Jan. 27, 1943	CHI N	—	CIN N	Cash

Gene Desautels

Date	Traded To	Traded With	Traded By	In Exchange For
Dec. 12, 1940	CLE A	Jim Bagby Gee Walker	BOS A	Frankie Pytlak Odell Hale Joe Dobson
Sept. 17, 1945	PHI A	—	CLE A	Waiver price

Jim Deshaies

Date	Traded To	Traded With	Traded By	In Exchange For
Sept. 15, 1985	HOU N	Two players to be named	NY A	Joe Niekro
		(Houston received IF Neder Horta and P Dody Rather on Jan. 11, 1986.)		
Dec. 8, 1992	MIN A	—	SD N	No compensation (free agent signing)
Aug. 28, 1993	SF N	—	MIN A	Greg Brummett Minor league P Aaron Fultz Minor league SS Andres Duncan
		(Minnesota received Brummett on September 1, 1993.)		
Jan. 13, 1994	MIN A	—	SF N	No compensation (free agent signing)

Delino DeShields

Date	Traded To	Traded With	Traded By	In Exchange For
Nov. 19, 1993	LA N	—	MON N	Pedro Martinez

Jimmie DeShong

Date	Traded To	Traded With	Traded By	In Exchange For
Jan. 17, 1936	WAS A	Jesse Hill	NY A	Bump Hadley Roy Johnson
June 20, 1939	NY A	—	WAS A	Waiver price

John DeSilva

Date	Traded To	Traded With	Traded By	In Exchange For
Aug. 31, 1993	LA N	—	DET A	Eric Davis

(Los Angeles received DeSilva on September 7, 1993.)

Orestes Destrade

Date	Traded To	Traded With	Traded By	In Exchange For
Mar. 30, 1988	PIT N	—	NY A	Hipolito Pena

Bob Detherage

Date	Traded To	Traded With	Traded By	In Exchange For
June 15, 1976	STL N	Joe Ferguson minor league IF Fred Tisdale	LA N	Reggie Smith
Nov. 23, 1976	HOU N	Joe Ferguson	STL N	Larry Dierker Jerry DaVanon

John Dettmer

Date	Traded To	Traded With	Traded By	In Exchange For
May 16, 1995	BAL A	—	TEX A	Jack Voigt

Tom Dettore

Date	Traded To	Traded With	Traded By	In Exchange For
Apr. 1, 1974	CHI N	Cash	PIT N	Paul Popovich

Mike Devereaux

Date	Traded To	Traded With	Traded By	In Exchange For
Mar. 11, 1989	BAL A	—	LA N	Mike Morgan
Apr. 8, 1995	CHI A	—	BAL A	No compensation (free agent signing)
Aug. 25, 1995	ATL N	—	CHI A	Minor league OF Andre King

Adrian Devine

Date	Traded To	Traded With	Traded By	In Exchange For
Dec. 9, 1976	TEX A	Ken Henderson Dave May Carl Morton Roger Moret $250,000.	ATL N	Jeff Burroughs
Dec. 8, 1977	ATL N	Tommy Boggs Eddie Miller	TEX A	Willie Montanez

(Part of four-team trade involving Texas, Atlanta, Pittsburgh, and New York Mets.)

Date	Traded To	Traded With	Traded By	In Exchange For
Dec. 6, 1979	TEX A	Pepe Frias	ATL N	Doyle Alexander Larvell Blanks $50,000.

Art Devlin

Date	Traded To	Traded With	Traded By	In Exchange For
Dec. 1911	BOS N	—	NY N	Cash

Josh Devore

Date	Traded To	Traded With	Traded By	In Exchange For
May 22, 1913	CIN N	Red Ames Heinie Groh $20,000.	NY N	Art Fromme Eddie Grant
June 5, 1913	PHI N	Beals Becker	CIN N	John Dodge Red Nelson
July 3, 1914	BOS N	—	PHI N	Jack Martin

Al DeVormer

Date	Traded To	Traded With	Traded By	In Exchange For
Jan. 3, 1923	BOS A	Cash	NY A	George Pipgras Harvey Hendrick

Mark Dewey

Date	Traded To	Traded With	Traded By	In Exchange For
May 9, 1991	NY N	—	SF N	Waiver price
May 11, 1993	PIT N	—	NY N	Waiver price

Charlie Dexter

Date	Traded To	Traded With	Traded By	In Exchange For
Jan. 1900	CHI N	—	LOU N	Cash
July 1902	BOS N	—	CHI N	Bobby Lowe

Alex Diaz

Date	Traded To	Traded With	Traded By	In Exchange For
Apr. 2, 1991	MON N	Darren Reed	NY N	Minor league OF-1B Terrell Hansen Minor league P David Sommer
Oct. 15, 1991	MIL A	—	MON N	George Canale
Oct. 14, 1994	SEA A	—	MIL A	Waiver price

Bo Diaz

Date	Traded To	Traded With	Traded By	In Exchange For
Mar. 30, 1978	CLE A	Rick Wise Mike Paxton Ted Cox	BOS A	Dennis Eckersley Fred Kendall
Nov. 20, 1981	PHI N	—	CLE A	Lonnie Smith Scott Munninghoff

(Part of three-team trade involving Cleveland, Philadelphia, and St. Louis.)

Date	Traded To	Traded With	Traded By	In Exchange For
Aug. 8, 1985	CIN N	Minor league P Greg Simpson	PHI N	Tom Foley Alan Knicely Fred Toliver

(Philadelphia received Toliver on August 27, 1985.)

Carlos Diaz

Date	Traded To	Traded With	Traded By	In Exchange For
Mar. 7, 1981	ATL N	—	SEA A	Jeff Burroughs
Sept. 10, 1982	NY N	—	ATL N	Tom Hausman
Dec. 8, 1983	LA N	Bob Bailor	NY N	Sid Fernandez Ross Jones

Mario Diaz

Date	Traded To	Traded With	Traded By	In Exchange For
June 19, 1990	NY N	—	SEA A	Brian Givens

Mike Diaz

Date	Traded To	Traded With	Traded By	In Exchange For
Mar. 26, 1984	PHI N	Bill Campbell	CHI N	Gary Matthews Porfi Altamirano Bob Dernier
Apr. 27, 1985	PIT N	—	PHI N	Minor league C Steve Herz
Aug. 19, 1988	CHI A	—	PIT N	Gary Redus

Leo Dickerman

Date	Traded To	Traded With	Traded By	In Exchange For
June 13, 1924	STL N	—	BKN N	Bill Doak

Johnny Dickshot

Date	Traded To	Traded With	Traded By	In Exchange For
Dec. 16, 1938	BOS N	Al Todd Cash	PIT N	Ray Mueller

Jim Dickson

Date	Traded To	Traded With	Traded By	In Exchange For
Jan. 20, 1964	CIN N	Wally Wolf Cash	HOU N	Eddie Kasko

Murry Dickson

Date	Traded To	Traded With	Traded By	In Exchange For
Jan. 29, 1949	PIT N	—	STL N	$125,000.
Jan. 13, 1954	PHI N	—	PIT N	Andy Hansen Lucky Lohrke $70,000.
May 11, 1956	STL N	Herm Wehmeier	PHI N	Harvey Haddix Ben Flowers Stu Miller
Aug. 22, 1958	NY A	—	KC A	Zeke Bella Cash
May 9, 1959	KC A	—	NY A	Cash

Bob Didier

Date	Traded To	Traded With	Traded By	In Exchange For
May 14, 1973	DET A	—	ATL N	Gene Lamont
Mar. 26, 1974	BOS A	—	DET A	Cash

Chuck Diering

Date	Traded To	Traded With	Traded By	In Exchange For
Dec. 11, 1951	NY N	Max Lanier	STL N	Eddie Stanky

(Stanky was named St. Louis manager.)

Larry Dierker

Date	Traded To	Traded With	Traded By	In Exchange For
Nov. 23, 1976	STL N	Jerry DaVanon	HOU N	Joe Ferguson Bob Detherage

Bill Dietrich

Date	Traded To	Traded With	Traded By	In Exchange For
July 1, 1936	WAS A	—	PHI A	Waiver price
July 20, 1936	CHI A	—	WAS A	Waiver price

Dick Dietz

Date	Traded To	Traded With	Traded By	In Exchange For
Apr. 14, 1972	LA N	—	SF N	Cash
Mar. 27, 1973	ATL N	—	LA N	Cash

Dutch Dietz

Date	Traded To	Traded With	Traded By	In Exchange For
Aug. 1940	PIT N	—	CIN N	Cash
June 15, 1943	PHI N	—	PIT N	Johnny Podgajny

Don Dillard

Date	Traded To	Traded With	Traded By	In Exchange For
Nov. 27, 1962	MIL N	Ty Cline Frank Funk	CLE A	Joe Adcock Jack Curtis

Gordon Dillard

Date	Traded To	Traded With	Traded By	In Exchange For
Dec. 8, 1988	PHI N	—	BAL A	*see Phil Bradley*

Steve Dillard

Date	Traded To	Traded With	Traded By	In Exchange For
Jan. 30, 1978	DET A	—	BOS A	Minor league Ps Mike Burns Frank Harris Cash
Mar. 20, 1979	CHI N	—	DET A	Ed Putman

Pickles Dillhoefer

Date	Traded To	Traded With	Traded By	In Exchange For
Dec. 11, 1917	PHI N	Mike Prendergast $55,000.	CHI N	Grover Alexander Bill Killefer
Jan. 21, 1919	STL N	Milt Stock Dixie Davis	PHI N	Doug Baird Stuffy Stewart Gene Packard

Bob Dillinger

Date	Traded To	Traded With	Traded By	In Exchange For
Dec. 13, 1949	PHI A	Paul Lehner	STL A	Ray Coleman Frankie Gustine Billy DeMars minor league OF Ray Ippolito $100,000.
July 20, 1950	PIT N	—	PHI A	$35,000.
May 16, 1951	CHI A	—	PIT N	Cash

Bill Dillman

Date	Traded To	Traded With	Traded By	In Exchange For
Dec. 5, 1969	STL N	—	BAL A	Cash

Pop Dillon

Date	Traded To	Traded With	Traded By	In Exchange For
Jan. 1901	DET A	—	PIT N	Cash
July 1902	BAL A	—	DET A	Cash

Miguel Dilone

Date	Traded To	Traded With	Traded By	In Exchange For
Apr. 4, 1978	OAK A	Elias Sosa Mike Edwards	PIT N	Manny Sanguillen
July 4, 1979	CHI N	—	OAK A	Cash
May 7, 1980	CLE A	—	CHI N	Cash
Aug. 25, 1983	CHI A	—	CLE A	Rich Barnes
Sept. 7, 1983	PIT N	minor league P Mike Maitland	CHI A	Randy Niemann
Jan. 19, 1984	MON N	—	PIT N	No compensation (free agent signing)

Vince DiMaggio

Date	Traded To	Traded With	Traded By	In Exchange For
Aug. 10, 1938	CIN N	Tommy Reis Johnny Babich Gil English Johnny Riddle Cash	BOS N	Eddie Miller
May 8, 1940	PIT N	—	CIN N	Johnny Rizzo
Mar. 31, 1945	PHI N	—	PIT N	Al Gerheauser
May 1, 1946	NY N	—	PHI N	Clyde Kluttz

Kerry Dineen

Date	Traded To	Traded With	Traded By	In Exchange For
Mar. 26, 1977	PHI N	—	NY A	Sergio Ferrer

Bill Dinneen

Date	Traded To	Traded With	Traded By	In Exchange For
Jan. 10, 1900	BOS N	Kirtley Baker Shad Barry	WAS N	Cash
June 22, 1907	STL A	—	BOS A	Beany Jacobson $1,000.

Frank DiPino

Date	Traded To	Traded With	Traded By	In Exchange For
Aug. 30, 1982	HOU N	Kevin Bass Mike Madden Cash	MIL A	Don Sutton

Frank DiPino *continued*

Date	Traded To	Traded With	Traded By	In Exchange For
July 21, 1986	CHI N	—	HOU N	Davey Lopes
Dec. 21, 1988	STL N	—	CHI N	No compensation (free agent signing)

Jerry DiPoto

Date	Traded To	Traded With	Traded By	In Exchange For
Nov. 18, 1994	NY N	Dave Mlicki Paul Byrd	CLE A	Jeromy Burnitz Joe Roa

Art Ditmar

Date	Traded To	Traded With	Traded By	In Exchange For
Feb. 19, 1957	NY A	Clete Boyer Bobby Shantz Jack McMahan Wayne Belardi Curt Roberts	KC A	Billy Hunter Rip Coleman Tom Morgan Mickey McDermott Milt Graff Irv Noren

(New York received Roberts on April 4, and Boyer on June 4, 1957.)

Date	Traded To	Traded With	Traded By	In Exchange For
June 14, 1961	KC A	Deron Johnson	NY A	Bud Daley

Jack Dittmer

Date	Traded To	Traded With	Traded By	In Exchange For
Feb. 12, 1957	DET A	—	MIL N	Charlie King Cash

Ken Dixon

Date	Traded To	Traded With	Traded By	In Exchange For
Dec. 9, 1987	SEA A	—	BAL A	Mike Morgan

Sonny Dixon

Date	Traded To	Traded With	Traded By	In Exchange For
June 11, 1954	CHI A	—	WAS A	Gus Keriazakos
June 11, 1954	PHI A	Al Sima Bill Wilson $20,000.	CHI A	Ed McGhee Morrie Martin
May 11, 1955	NY A	Cash	KC A	Johnny Sain Enos Slaughter

Steve Dixon

Date	Traded To	Traded With	Traded By	In Exchange For
Nov. 17, 1994	CLE A	—	STL N	Waiver price
Apr. 12, 1995	CHI N	—	CLE A	Waiver price

Bill Doak

Date	Traded To	Traded With	Traded By	In Exchange For
June 13, 1924	BKN N	—	STL N	Leo Dickerman

Dan Dobbek

Date	Traded To	Traded With	Traded By	In Exchange For
Jan. 30, 1962	CIN N	—	MIN A	Jerry Zimmerman

John Dobbs

Date	Traded To	Traded With	Traded By	In Exchange For
July 1902	CHI N	—	CIN N	Cash
May 1903	BKN N	—	CHI N	Cash

Joe Dobson

Date	Traded To	Traded With	Traded By	In Exchange For
Dec. 12, 1940	BOS A	Frankie Pytlak Odell Hale	CLE A	Gene Desautels Jim Bagby Gee Walker
Dec. 10, 1950	CHI A	Dick Littlefield Al Zarilla	BOS A	Ray Scarborough Bill Wight

Pat Dobson

Date	Traded To	Traded With	Traded By	In Exchange For
Dec. 4, 1969	SD N	Dave Campbell	DET A	Joe Niekro
Dec. 1, 1970	BAL A	Tom Dukes	SD N	Tom Phoebus Al Severinsen Fred Beene Enzo Hernandez
Nov. 30, 1972	ATL N	Roric Harrison Davey Johnson Johnny Oates	BAL A	Earl Williams Taylor Duncan
June 7, 1973	NY A	—	ATL N	Frank Tepedino Dave Cheadle Wayne Nordhagen Al Closter
Nov. 22, 1975	CLE A	—	NY A	Oscar Gamble

Larry Doby

Date	Traded To	Traded With	Traded By	In Exchange For
Oct. 25, 1955	CHI A	—	CLE A	Jim Busby Chico Carrasquel

Larry Doby *continued*

Date	Traded To	Traded With	Traded By	In Exchange For
Dec. 3, 1957	BAL A	Jack Harshman Russ Heman Jim Marshall	CHI A	Tito Francona Ray Moore Billy Goodman
Apr. 1, 1958	CLE A	Don Ferrarese	BAL A	Bud Daley Dick Williams Gene Woodling
Mar. 21, 1959	DET A	—	CLE A	Tito Francona
May 13, 1959	CHI A	—	DET A	$30,000.

Tom Dodd

Date	Traded To	Traded With	Traded By	In Exchange For
Dec. 9, 1982	NY A	—	TOR A	*see Dave Collins*

John Dodge

Date	Traded To	Traded With	Traded By	In Exchange For
June 5, 1913	CIN N	Red Nelson	PHI N	Josh Devore Beals Becker

Ed Doheny

Date	Traded To	Traded With	Traded By	In Exchange For
June 1901	PIT N	—	NY N	Heinie Smith

Cozy Dolan

Date	Traded To	Traded With	Traded By	In Exchange For
June 1901	BKN N	—	CHI N	Cash
June 9, 1903	CIN N	Tom Daly	CHI A	George Magoon
June 6, 1905	BOS N	—	CIN N	Cash

Cozy Dolan

Date	Traded To	Traded With	Traded By	In Exchange For
May 1912	PHI N	—	NY A	Cash
Aug. 20, 1913	PIT N	Cash	PHI N	Bobby Byrne Howie Camnitz
Dec. 12, 1913	STL N	—	PIT N	*see Ed Konetchy*

Joe Dolan

Date	Traded To	Traded With	Traded By	In Exchange For
May 1901	PHI A	—	PHI N	Cash

Jiggs Donahue

Date	Traded To	Traded With	Traded By	In Exchange For
Apr. 1901	MIL A	—	PIT N	Cash
Aug. 1908	WAS A	—	CHI A	Cash
May 16, 1909	WAS A	Nick Altrock Gavvy Cravath	CHI A	Bill Burns

Pat Donahue

Date	Traded To	Traded With	Traded By	In Exchange For
May 1910	PHI A	—	BOS A	Cash
Sept. 1910	CLE A	—	PHI A	Cash

Red Donahue

Date	Traded To	Traded With	Traded By	In Exchange For
June 1903	CLE A	—	STL A	Completes Charlie Hemphill trade of May, 1902.
Dec. 1905	DET A	—	CLE A	Cash

John Donaldson

Date	Traded To	Traded With	Traded By	In Exchange For
June 14, 1969	SEA A	—	OAK A	Larry Haney
May 18, 1970	OAK A	—	MIL A	Roberto Pena
May 22, 1971	DET A	—	OAK A	Daryl Patterson

Mike Donlin

Date	Traded To	Traded With	Traded By	In Exchange For
July 3, 1904	NY N	—	CIN N	Moose McCormick
Aug. 1, 1911	BOS N	—	NY N	Cash
Feb. 1912	PIT N	—	BOS N	Vin Campbell
Dec. 1912	PHI N	—	PIT N	Waiver price

(Donlin refused to report and announced his retirement.)

Blix Donnelly

Date	Traded To	Traded With	Traded By	In Exchange For
July 6, 1946	PHI N	—	STL N	Cash
Apr. 16, 1951	BOS N	—	PHI N	Waiver price

Chris Donnels

Date	Traded To	Traded With	Traded By	In Exchange For
June 10, 1995	BOS A	—	HOU N	Player to be named

Jim Donohue

Date	Traded To	Traded With	Traded By	In Exchange For
June 15, 1960	LA N	—	STL N	John Glenn
June 7, 1961	LA A	—	DET A	Jerry Casale
May 29, 1962	MIN A	—	LA A	Don Lee

Pete Donohue

Date	Traded To	Traded With	Traded By	In Exchange For
May 27, 1930	NY N	Ethan Allen	CIN N	Pat Crawford

Dick Donovan

Date	Traded To	Traded With	Traded By	In Exchange For
Oct. 5, 1961	CLE A	Gene Green Jim Mahoney	WAS A	Jimmy Piersall

Mike Donovan

Date	Traded To	Traded With	Traded By	In Exchange For
Jan. 1908	NY A	—	CLE A	Cash

Patsy Donovan

Date	Traded To	Traded With	Traded By	In Exchange For
Jan. 1900	STL N	—	PIT N	$1,000.

Red Dooin

Date	Traded To	Traded With	Traded By	In Exchange For
Nov. 1914	CIN N	—	PHI N	Bert Niehoff
July 6, 1915	NY N	—	CIN N	Waiver price

Mickey Doolan

Date	Traded To	Traded With	Traded By	In Exchange For
Feb. 10, 1916	CHI N	*see Three Finger Brown*	CHI F	—
Aug. 28, 1916	NY N	Heinie Zimmerman	CHI N	Larry Doyle Herb Hunter Merwin Jacobson

John Dopson

Date	Traded To	Traded With	Traded By	In Exchange For
Dec. 8, 1988	BOS A	Luis Rivera	MON N	Spike Owen Dan Gakeler
Feb. 2, 1994	CAL A	—	BOS A	No compensation (free agent signing)

Bill Doran

Date	Traded To	Traded With	Traded By	In Exchange For
Aug. 31, 1990	CIN N	—	HOU N	Terry McGriff Butch Henry Minor league P Keith Kaiser

(McGriff, Henry, and Kaiser were assigned to Houston on September 7, 1990.)

Date	Traded To	Traded With	Traded By	In Exchange For
Jan. 13, 1993	MIL A	—	CIN N	Cash

Tom Doran

Date	Traded To	Traded With	Traded By	In Exchange For
May 18, 1905	DET A	—	BOS A	Waiver price

Harry Dorish

Date	Traded To	Traded With	Traded By	In Exchange For
May 9, 1950	STL A	—	BOS A	Cash
June 6, 1955	BAL A	—	CHI A	Les Moss
June 25, 1956	BOS A	—	BAL A	Cash

Gus Dorner

Date	Traded To	Traded With	Traded By	In Exchange For
May 13, 1906	BOS N	—	CIN N	Cash

Brian Dorsett

Date	Traded To	Traded With	Traded By	In Exchange For
July 15, 1987	CLE A	—	OAK A	*see Tony Bernazard*
June 7, 1988	CAL A	—	CLE A	Cash
Nov. 17, 1988	NY A	—	CAL A	Minor league P Eric Schmidt

Jim Dorsey

Date	Traded To	Traded With	Traded By	In Exchange For
Jan. 23, 1981	BOS A	Frank Tanana Joe Rudi	CAL A	Fred Lynn Steve Renko

Jack Doscher

Date	Traded To	Traded With	Traded By	In Exchange For
June 1903	BKN N	—	CHI N	Cash

Richard Dotson

Date	Traded To	Traded With	Traded By	In Exchange For
Dec. 5, 1977	CHI A	Bobby Bonds Thad Bosley	CAL A	Brian Downing Chris Knapp Dave Frost
Nov. 12, 1987	NY A	Scott Nielsen	CHI A	Dan Pasqua Mark Salas Steve Rosenberg

Richard Dotson *continued*

Date	Traded To	Traded With	Traded By	In Exchange For
Dec. 5, 1989	KC A	—	CHI A	No compensation (free agent signing)

Patsy Dougherty

Date	Traded To	Traded With	Traded By	In Exchange For
June 18, 1904	NY A	—	BOS A	Bob Unglaub
June 6, 1906	CHI A	—	NY A	Cash

Phil Douglas

Date	Traded To	Traded With	Traded By	In Exchange For
June 13, 1915	BKN N	—	CIN N	Cash
Sept. 8, 1915	CHI N	—	BKN N	Cash
July 25, 1919	NY N	—	CHI N	Dave Robertson

Whammy Douglas

Date	Traded To	Traded With	Traded By	In Exchange For
Jan. 30, 1959	CIN N	—	PIT N	*see Harvey Haddix*

Taylor Douthit

Date	Traded To	Traded With	Traded By	In Exchange For
June 15, 1931	CIN N	—	STL N	Wally Roettger
Apr. 29, 1933	CHI N	—	CIN N	Waiver price

Snooks Dowd

Date	Traded To	Traded With	Traded By	In Exchange For
Apr. 1919	PHI A	—	DET A	Cash

Dave Dowling

Date	Traded To	Traded With	Traded By	In Exchange For
May 11, 1965	CHI N	—	STL N	Waiver price
Apr. 22, 1968	STL N	Pete Mikkelsen	CHI N	Jack Lamabe Ron Piche

Pete Dowling

Date	Traded To	Traded With	Traded By	In Exchange For
May 1901	CLE A	—	MIL A	Cash

Tom Downey

Date	Traded To	Traded With	Traded By	In Exchange For
Jan. 18, 1909	CIN N	Kid Durbin	CHI N	John Kane
Aug. 1912	CHI N	—	PHI N	Cash

Al Downing

Date	Traded To	Traded With	Traded By	In Exchange For
Dec. 5, 1969	OAK A	Frank Fernandez	NY A	Danny Cater Ossie Chavarria
June 11, 1970	MIL A	Tito Francona	OAK A	Steve Hovley
Feb. 10, 1971	LA N	—	MIL A	Andy Kosco

Brian Downing

Date	Traded To	Traded With	Traded By	In Exchange For
Dec. 5, 1977	CAL A	Chris Knapp Dave Frost	CHI A	Bobby Bonds Thad Bosley Richard Dotson

Kelly Downs

Date	Traded To	Traded With	Traded By	In Exchange For
Aug. 20, 1984	SF N	George Riley	PHI N	Al Oliver Renie Martin

Red Downs

Date	Traded To	Traded With	Traded By	In Exchange For
May 1912	CHI N	—	BKN N	Cash

Brian Doyle

Date	Traded To	Traded With	Traded By	In Exchange For
Feb. 17, 1977	NY A	Greg Pryor Cash	TEX A	Sandy Alomar
Nov. 3, 1980	OAK A	Fred Stanley	NY A	Mike Morgan

Carl Doyle

Date	Traded To	Traded With	Traded By	In Exchange For
June 12, 1940	STL N	Ernie Koy Sam Nahem Bert Haas $125,000.	BKN N	Joe Medwick Curt Davis

Conny Doyle

Date	Traded To	Traded With	Traded By	In Exchange For
Jan. 1900	PIT N	*see Honus Wagner*	LOU N	—

Denny Doyle

Date	Traded To	Traded With	Traded By	In Exchange For
Aug. 14, 1973	CAL A	—	PHI N	Aurelio Monteagudo Chris Coletta Billy Grabarkewitz
June 14, 1975	BOS A	—	CAL A	Cash

(California also received minor league P Chuck Ross on March 5, 1976.)

Jack Doyle

Date	Traded To	Traded With	Traded By	In Exchange For
Feb. 1901	CHI N	—	NY N	Sammy Strang
Feb. 1902	NY N	Jim Delahanty	CHI N	Cash
Jan. 30, 1903	BKN N	—	WAS A	Cash
Apr. 30, 1904	PHI N	Deacon Van Buren	BKN N	Cash

Larry Doyle

Date	Traded To	Traded With	Traded By	In Exchange For
Aug. 28, 1916	CHI N	Herb Hunter Merwin Jacobson	NY N	Heinie Zimmerman Mickey Doolan
Jan. 4, 1918	BOS N	Art Wilson $15,000.	CHI N	Lefty Tyler
Jan. 8, 1918	NY N	Jesse Barnes	BOS N	Buck Herzog

Paul Doyle

Date	Traded To	Traded With	Traded By	In Exchange For
Nov. 27, 1969	CAL A	—	ATL N	Cash
Aug. 25, 1970	SD N	—	CAL A	Cash

Slow Joe Doyle

Date	Traded To	Traded With	Traded By	In Exchange For
May 1910	CIN N	—	NY A	Cash

D. J. Dozier

Date	Traded To	Traded With	Traded By	In Exchange For
Oct. 27, 1992	SD N	Wally Whitehurst Player to be named	NY N	Tony Fernandez

(San Diego received C Raul Casanova on December 7, 1992.)

Doug Drabek

Date	Traded To	Traded With	Traded By	In Exchange For
July 17, 1984	NY A	Kevin Hickey	CHI A	Roy Smalley
Nov. 26, 1986	PIT N	Logan Easley Brian Fisher	NY A	Rick Rhoden Cecilio Guante Pat Clements
Dec. 1, 1992	HOU N	—	PIT N	No compensation (free agent signing)

Moe Drabowsky

Date	Traded To	Traded With	Traded By	In Exchange For
Mar. 31, 1961	MIL N	Seth Morehead	CHI N	Andre Rodgers Daryl Robertson
Aug. 13, 1962	KC A	—	CIN N	Cash
June 15, 1970	BAL A	—	KC A	Bobby Floyd
Nov. 30, 1970	STL N	—	BAL A	Jerry DaVanon

Dick Drago

Date	Traded To	Traded With	Traded By	In Exchange For
Oct. 24, 1973	BOS A	—	KC A	Marty Pattin
Mar. 3, 1976	CAL A	—	BOS A	John Balaz Dick Sharon Dave Machemer
June 13, 1977	BAL A	—	CAL A	Dyar Miller
Apr. 8, 1981	SEA A	—	BOS A	Manny Sarmiento

Brian Drahman

Date	Traded To	Traded With	Traded By	In Exchange For
Nov. 10, 1993	FLA N	—	CHI A	Cash

Solly Drake

Date	Traded To	Traded With	Traded By	In Exchange For
June 9, 1959	PHI N	—	LA N	Waiver price

Dave Dravecky

Date	Traded To	Traded With	Traded By	In Exchange For
Apr. 5, 1981	SD N	—	PIT N	Bobby Mitchell
July 5, 1987	SF N	*see Kevin Mitchell*	SD N	—

Clem Dreisewerd

Date	Traded To	Traded With	Traded By	In Exchange For
Nov. 18, 1947	STL A	—	BOS A	*see Ellis Kinder*

Rob Dressler

Date	Traded To	Traded With	Traded By	In Exchange For
July 18, 1978	STL N	—	SF N	John Tamargo
June 7, 1979	SEA A	—	STL N	Cash

Karl Drews

Date	Traded To	Traded With	Traded By	In Exchange For
Aug. 9, 1948	STL A	—	NY A	Cash
June 15, 1954	CIN N	—	PHI N	Cash

Dan Driessen

Date	Traded To	Traded With	Traded By	In Exchange For
July 26, 1984	MON N	—	CIN N	Andy McGaffigan minor league P Jim Jefferson
Aug. 1, 1985	SF N	—	MON N	Scot Thompson player to be named

(Montreal returned Bill Laskey on Oct. 24 to complete deal.)

Lew Drill

Date	Traded To	Traded With	Traded By	In Exchange For
Sept. 1902	WAS A	—	BAL A	Cash
Aug. 10, 1904	DET A	Bill Coughlin	WAS A	$7,500.

Walt Dropo

Date	Traded To	Traded With	Traded By	In Exchange For
June 3, 1952	DET A	Bill Wight Fred Hatfield Johnny Pesky Don Lenhardt	BOS A	Dizzy Trout George Kell Johnny Lipon Hoot Evers
Dec. 6, 1954	CHI A	Ted Gray Bob Nieman	DET A	Leo Cristante Ferris Fain Jack Phillips
June 24, 1958	CIN N	—	CHI A	Waiver price
June 23, 1959	BAL A	—	CIN N	Whitey Lockman

Carl Druhot

Date	Traded To	Traded With	Traded By	In Exchange For
July 25, 1906	STL N	Shad Barry	CIN N	Homer Smoot

Tim Drummond

Date	Traded To	Traded With	Traded By	In Exchange For
Mar. 26, 1988	NY N	*see Mackey Sasser*	PIT N	—
July 31, 1989	MIN A	Rick Aguilera David West Kevin Tapani Jack Savage	NY N	Frank Viola

(Minnesota received Savage on October 16, 1989.)

Keith Drumright

Date	Traded To	Traded With	Traded By	In Exchange For
Apr. 27, 1979	KC A	—	HOU N	George Throop
Dec. 11, 1980	OAK A	Cliff Johnson	CHI N	Minor league P Mike King

Monk Dubiel

Date	Traded To	Traded With	Traded By	In Exchange For
Dec. 14, 1948	CHI N	Dutch Leonard	PHI N	Hank Borowy Eddie Waitkus
Dec. 20, 1952	BOS N	—	CHI N	Sheldon Jones

Brian Dubois

Date	Traded To	Traded With	Traded By	In Exchange For
July 28, 1989	DET A	—	BAL A	Keith Moreland
Aug. 29, 1990	BAL A	—	DET A	Waiver price

Rob Ducey

Date	Traded To	Traded With	Traded By	In Exchange For
July 30, 1992	CAL A	Greg Myers	TOR A	Mark Eichhorn

Jim Duckworth

Date	Traded To	Traded With	Traded By	In Exchange For
June 23, 1966	KC A	—	WAS A	Ken Harrelson
July 30, 1966	WAS A	—	KC A	Diego Segui

Clise Dudley

Date	Traded To	Traded With	Traded By	In Exchange For
Oct. 14, 1930	PHI N	Jumbo Elliott Hal Lee Cash	BKN N	Lefty O'Doul Fresco Thompson

Jim Duffalo

Date	Traded To	Traded With	Traded By	In Exchange For
May 4, 1965	CIN N	—	SF N	Bill Henry

Frank Duffy

Date	Traded To	Traded With	Traded By	In Exchange For
May 29, 1971	SF N	Vern Geishert	CIN N	George Foster
Nov. 29, 1971	CLE A	Gaylord Perry	SF N	Sam McDowell
Mar. 24, 1978	BOS A	—	CLE A	Rick Kreuger

Joe Dugan

Date	Traded To	Traded With	Traded By	In Exchange For
Jan. 10, 1922	WAS A	—	PHI A	Jose Acosta Bing Miller

(Part of three-team trade involving Boston, Philadelphia, and Washington.)

Date	Traded To	Traded With	Traded By	In Exchange For
Jan. 10, 1922	BOS A	Frank O'Rourke	WAS A	Roger Peckinpaugh

(Part of three-team trade involving Boston, Philadelphia, and Washington.)

Date	Traded To	Traded With	Traded By	In Exchange For
July 23, 1922	NY A	Elmer Smith	BOS A	Chick Fewster Elmer Miller Johnny Mitchell Lefty O'Doul $50,000.
Dec. 29, 1928	BOS N	—	NY A	Waiver price

Gus Dugas

Date	Traded To	Traded With	Traded By	In Exchange For
Dec. 12, 1932	NY N	Glenn Spencer	PIT N	Freddie Lindstrom

(Part of three-team trade involving New York, Philadelphia, and Pittsburgh.)

Date	Traded To	Traded With	Traded By	In Exchange For
Dec. 12, 1932	PHI N	Chick Fullis	NY N	Kiddo Davis

(Part of three-team trade involving New York, Philadelphia, and Pittsburgh.)

Oscar Dugey

Date	Traded To	Traded With	Traded By	In Exchange For
Feb. 10, 1915	PHI N	Possum Whitted	BOS N	Cash

Bill Duggleby

Date	Traded To	Traded With	Traded By	In Exchange For
July 15, 1907	PIT N	—	PHI N	Cash

Tom Dukes

Date	Traded To	Traded With	Traded By	In Exchange For
Oct. 13, 1966	HOU N	Dan Schneider Lee Bales	ATL N	Gene Ratliff John Hoffman minor league IF Ed Pacheco
Dec. 1, 1970	BAL A	*see Pat Dobson*	SD N	—

George Dumont

Date	Traded To	Traded With	Traded By	In Exchange For
Jan. 17, 1919	BOS A	Eddie Ainsmith	WAS A	Hal Janvrin Cash

Dave Duncan

Date	Traded To	Traded With	Traded By	In Exchange For
Mar. 24, 1973	CLE A	George Hendrick	OAK A	Ray Fosse Jack Heidemann
Feb. 25, 1975	BAL A	minor league OF Al McGrew	CLE A	Boog Powell Don Hood
Nov. 18, 1976	CHI A	—	BAL A	Pat Kelly

Mariano Duncan

Date	Traded To	Traded With	Traded By	In Exchange For
July 18, 1989	CIN N	Tim Leary	LA N	Kal Daniels Lenny Harris
Dec. 10, 1991	PHI N	—	CIN N	No compensation (free agent signing)
Aug. 8, 1995	CIN N	—	PHI N	Brian Koelling
Dec. 11, 1995	NY A	—	CIN N	No compensation (free agent signing)

Pat Duncan

Date	Traded To	Traded With	Traded By	In Exchange For
Oct. 1924	WAS A	—	CIN N	Waiver price

Taylor Duncan

Date	Traded To	Traded With	Traded By	In Exchange For
Nov. 30, 1972	BAL A	*see Earl Williams*	ATL N	—
Sept. 7, 1977	STL N	—	BAL A	Cash

Davey Dunkle

Date	Traded To	Traded With	Traded By	In Exchange For
June 1903	WAS A	—	CHI A	Ducky Holmes

Jack Dunn

Date	Traded To	Traded With	Traded By	In Exchange For
June 1900	PHI N	—	BKN N	Cash

Mike Dunne

Date	Traded To	Traded With	Traded By	In Exchange For
Apr. 1, 1987	PIT N	—	STL N	*see Tony Pena*
Apr. 21, 1989	SEA A	Mike Walker Minor league OF Mark Merchant	PIT N	Rey Quinones Bill Wilkinson

Steve Dunning

Date	Traded To	Traded With	Traded By	In Exchange For
May 10, 1973	TEX A	—	CLE A	Dick Bosman Ted Ford

Steve Dunning *continued*

Date	Traded To		Traded With	Traded By		In Exchange For
Feb. 25, 1975	CHI	A	—	TEX	A	Stan Perzanowski
Dec. 11, 1975	CAL	A	Bill Melton	CHI	A	Jim Spencer Morris Nettles
Nov. 6, 1976	STL	N	Pat Scanlon Tony Scott	MON	N	Bill Greif Angel Torres Sam Mejias
Aug. 12, 1977	OAK	A	—	STL	N	Randy Scarbery

Kid Durbin

Date	Traded To		Traded With	Traded By		In Exchange For
Jan. 18, 1909	CIN	N	Tom Downey	CHI	N	John Kane
May 28, 1909	PIT	N	—	CIN	N	Ward Miller Cash

Ryne Duren

Date	Traded To		Traded With	Traded By		In Exchange For
Oct. 11, 1956	KC	A	Jim Pisoni	BAL	A	Art Ceccarelli Al Pilarcik
June 15, 1957	NY	A	Jim Pisoni Milt Graff Harry Simpson	KC	A	Billy Martin Woodie Held Ralph Terry Bob Martyn
May 8, 1961	LA	A	Lee Thomas Johnny James	NY	A	Tex Clevenger Bob Cerv
Mar. 14, 1963	PHI	N	—	LA	A	Cash
May 13, 1964	CIN	N	—	PHI	N	Cash

Don Durham

Date	Traded To		Traded With	Traded By		In Exchange For
July 16, 1973	TEX	A	—	STL	N	Jim Kremmel

Ed Durham

Date	Traded To		Traded With	Traded By		In Exchange For
Dec. 15, 1932	CHI	A	Hal Rhyne	BOS	A	Johnny Hodapp Greg Mulleavy Bob Fothergill Bob Seeds

Leon Durham

Date	Traded To		Traded With	Traded By		In Exchange For
Dec. 9, 1980	CHI	N	Ken Reitz Tye Waller	STL	N	Bruce Sutter
May 19, 1988	CIN	N	—	CHI	N	Pat Perry Cash

Leo Durocher

Date	Traded To		Traded With	Traded By		In Exchange For
Feb. 2, 1930	CIN	N	—	NY	A	Waiver price
May 7, 1933	STL	N	Dutch Henry Jack Ogden	CIN	N	Paul Derringer Sparky Adams Allyn Stout
Oct. 4, 1937	BKN	N	—	STL	N	Johnny Cooney Jim Bucher Joe Stripp Roy Henshaw

Cedric Durst

Date	Traded To		Traded With	Traded By		In Exchange For
Feb. 8, 1927	NY	A	Joe Giard	STL	A	Sad Sam Jones
May 6, 1930	BOS	A	$50,000.	NY	A	Red Ruffing

Erv Dusak

Date	Traded To		Traded With	Traded By		In Exchange For
May 17, 1951	PIT	N	Rocky Nelson	STL	N	Stan Rojek

Jim Dwyer

Date	Traded To		Traded With	Traded By		In Exchange For
July 25, 1975	MON	N	—	STL	N	Larry Lintz
July 21, 1976	NY	N	Pepe Mangual	MON	N	Del Unser Wayne Garrett
Dec. 8, 1976	CHI	N	—	NY	N	Sheldon Mallory

(Part of three-team trade involving Chicago Cubs, New York Mets, and Kansas City.)

Date	Traded To		Traded With	Traded By		In Exchange For
Oct. 25, 1977	SF	N	—	STL	N	Frank Riccelli

(San Francisco received Dwyer on June 15, 1978.)

Date	Traded To		Traded With	Traded By		In Exchange For
Mar. 15, 1979	BOS	A	—	SF	N	Cash
Dec. 23, 1980	BAL	A	—	BOS	A	No compensation (free agent signing)
Aug. 29, 1988	MIN	A	—	BAL	A	player to be named

(Baltimore received P Doug Cline on August 31, 1988.)

Date	Traded To		Traded With	Traded By		In Exchange For
Aug. 28, 1989	MON	N	—	MIN	A	Alonzo Powell

(Minnesota received Powell on Sept. 15, 1989.)

Jim Dwyer *continued*

Date	Traded To		Traded With	Traded By		In Exchange For
Jan. 12, 1990	MIN	A	—	MON	N	Minor league P Jim Davins

Jerry Dybzinski

Date	Traded To		Traded With	Traded By		In Exchange For
Apr. 1, 1983	CHI	A	—	CLE	A	Pat Tabler

Jim Dyck

Date	Traded To		Traded With	Traded By		In Exchange For
Apr. 17, 1954	CLE	A	—	BAL	A	Bob Kennedy
July 16, 1955	BAL	A	—	CLE	A	Cash
May 11, 1956	CIN	N	—	BAL	A	$25,000.

Duffy Dyer

Date	Traded To		Traded With	Traded By		In Exchange For
Oct. 22, 1974	PIT	N	—	NY	N	Gene Clines
Nov. 28, 1978	MON	N	—	PIT	N	No compensation (free agent signing)
Mar. 15, 1980	DET	A	—	MON	N	Jerry Manuel

Jimmy Dykes

Date	Traded To		Traded With	Traded By		In Exchange For
Sept. 28, 1932	CHI	A	Al Simmons Mule Haas	PHI	A	$100,000.
Aug. 10, 1960	CLE	A	—	DET	A	Joe Gordon

Len Dykstra

Date	Traded To		Traded With	Traded By		In Exchange For
June 18, 1989	PHI	N	Roger McDowell Tom Edens	NY	N	Juan Samuel

(Philadelphia received Edens on July 26, 1989.)

Arnold Earley

Date	Traded To		Traded With	Traded By		In Exchange For
Dec. 15, 1965	MIL	N	Lee Thomas Jay Ritchie	BOS	A	Bob Sadowski Dan Osinski

Jake Early

Date	Traded To		Traded With	Traded By		In Exchange For
Dec. 16, 1946	WAS	A	—	STL	A	Frank Mancuso
Mar. 26, 1948	WAS	A	—	STL	A	Cash

George Earnshaw

Date	Traded To		Traded With	Traded By		In Exchange For
Dec. 12, 1933	CHI	A	Johnny Pasek	PHI	A	Charlie Berry $20,000.
May 16, 1935	BKN	N	—	CHI	A	Cash
July 1936	STL	N	—	BKN	N	Cash

Mike Easler

Date	Traded To		Traded With	Traded By		In Exchange For
Sept. 30, 1975	STL	N	—	HOU	N	Mike Barlow
Sept. 3, 1976	CAL	A	—	STL	N	Minor league IF Ron Farkas
Apr. 4, 1977	PIT	N	—	CAL	A	Minor league P Randy Sealy
Oct. 27, 1978	BOS	A	—	PIT	N	Cash
Mar. 15, 1979	PIT	N	—	BOS	A	Minor league OF George Hill and P Martin Rivas Cash
Dec. 6, 1983	BOS	A	—	PIT	N	John Tudor
Mar. 28, 1986	NY	A	—	BOS	A	Don Baylor
Dec. 11, 1986	PHI	N	Tom Barrett	NY	A	Charles Hudson Minor league P Jeff Knox
June 10, 1987	NY	A	—	PHI	N	Keith Hughes Shane Turner

Logan Easley

Date	Traded To		Traded With	Traded By		In Exchange For
Nov. 26, 1986	PIT	N	—	NY	A	*see Rick Rhoden*

Mal Eason

Date	Traded To		Traded With	Traded By		In Exchange For
Apr. 1902	BOS	N	—	CHI	N	Cash

Jamie Easterly

Date	Traded To		Traded With	Traded By		In Exchange For
Oct. 19, 1979	MON	N	—	ATL	N	Cash
Sept. 22, 1980	MIL	A	—	MON	N	Cash
June 6, 1983	CLE	A	Gorman Thomas Ernie Camacho	MIL	A	Rick Manning Rick Waits

Ted Easterly

Date	Traded To	Traded With	Traded By	In Exchange For
Jan. 1912	CHI A	—	CLE A	Cash

Rawly Eastwick

Date	Traded To	Traded With	Traded By	In Exchange For
June 15, 1977	STL N	—	CIN N	Doug Capilla
Dec. 12, 1977	NY A	—	STL N	No compensation (free agent signing)
June 14, 1978	PHI N	—	NY A	Jay Johnstone Bobby Brown

Craig Eaton

Date	Traded To	Traded With	Traded By	In Exchange For
Dec. 6, 1979	CAL A	Al Cowens Todd Cruz	KC A	Rance Mulliniks Willie Aikens

Gary Eave

Date	Traded To	Traded With	Traded By	In Exchange For
Jan. 24, 1990	SEA A	Minor league 3B Ken Pennington	ATL N	Jim Presley
May 24, 1990	SF N	—	SEA A	Russ Swan

Eddie Eayrs

Date	Traded To	Traded With	Traded By	In Exchange For
Aug. 31, 1921	BKN N	—	BOS N	Cash

Dennis Eckersley

Date	Traded To	Traded With	Traded By	In Exchange For
Mar. 30, 1978	BOS A	Fred Kendall	CLE A	Bo Diaz Rick Wise Mike Paxton Ted Cox
May 25, 1984	CHI N	Mike Brumley	BOS A	Bill Buckner
Apr. 3, 1987	OAK A	Dan Rohn	CHI N	Minor league OF David Wilder Minor league IF Brian Guinn Minor league P Mark Leonette

Don Eddy

Date	Traded To	Traded With	Traded By	In Exchange For
July 9, 1972	SD N	Cash	CHI A	Ed Spiezio

Joe Edelen

Date	Traded To	Traded With	Traded By	In Exchange For
Sept. 10, 1981	CIN N	Neil Fiala	STL N	Doug Bair

Mike Eden

Date	Traded To	Traded With	Traded By	In Exchange For
June 13, 1976	ATL N	—	SF N	*see Darrell Evans*

Tom Edens

Date	Traded To	Traded With	Traded By	In Exchange For
Apr. 1, 1984	NY N	—	KC A	Tucker Ashford
June 18, 1989	PHI N	—	NY N	*see Juan Samuel*
Nov. 17, 1992	HOU N	—	FLA N	Hector Carrasco Minor league P Brian Griffiths
July 31, 1994	PHI N	—	HOU N	Milt Thompson

Butch Edge

Date	Traded To	Traded With	Traded By	In Exchange For
Mar. 21, 1982	PIT N	Ross Baumgarten	CHI A	Vance Law Ernie Camacho

Bill Edgerton

Date	Traded To	Traded With	Traded By	In Exchange For
Feb. 15, 1965	CLE A	—	KC A	Waiver price
Apr. 9, 1965	KC A	—	CLE A	Waiver price

Bruce Edwards

Date	Traded To	Traded With	Traded By	In Exchange For
June 15, 1951	CHI N	—	BKN N	*see Andy Pafko*

Dave Edwards

Date	Traded To	Traded With	Traded By	In Exchange For
Dec. 8, 1980	SD N	—	MIN A	Chuck Baker

Doc Edwards

Date	Traded To	Traded With	Traded By	In Exchange For
May 25, 1963	KC A	$100,000.	CLE A	Joe Azcue Dick Howser
May 3, 1965	NY A	—	KC A	Johnny Blanchard Rollie Sheldon
Jan. 14, 1966	CLE A	—	NY A	Lu Clinton

Doc Edwards *continued*

Date	Traded To	Traded With	Traded By	In Exchange For
Jan. 4, 1967	HOU N	Jim Landis Jim Weaver	CLE A	Lee Maye Ken Retzer

Hank Edwards

Date	Traded To	Traded With	Traded By	In Exchange For
May 7, 1949	CHI N	—	CLE A	Waiver price
Oct. 10, 1950	BKN N	Cash	CHI N	Chuck Connors Dee Fondy
July 21, 1951	CIN N	—	BKN N	Waiver price
Sept. 1, 1952	CHI A	—	CIN N	Howie Judson
		(Cincinnati received Judson on December 9.)		
Oct. 16, 1952	STL A	Willie Miranda	CHI A	Joe De Maestri Tommy Byrne

Jim Joe Edwards

Date	Traded To	Traded With	Traded By	In Exchange For
July 1925	CHI A	—	CLE A	Cash

Johnny Edwards

Date	Traded To	Traded With	Traded By	In Exchange For
Feb. 8, 1968	STL N	—	CIN N	Pat Corrales Jimy Williams
Oct. 11, 1968	HOU N	minor league C Tommy Smith	STL N	Dave Giusti Dave Adlesh

Mike Edwards

Date	Traded To	Traded With	Traded By	In Exchange For
Apr. 4, 1978	OAK A	Miguel Dilone Elias Sosa	PIT N	Manny Sanguillen

Ben Egan

Date	Traded To	Traded With	Traded By	In Exchange For
July 28, 1914	CLE A	Adam Johnson Fritz Coumbe	BOS A	Vean Gregg

Dick Egan

Date	Traded To	Traded With	Traded By	In Exchange For
May 27, 1966	LA N	minor league IF John Butler	CAL A	Howie Reed

Dick Egan

Date	Traded To	Traded With	Traded By	In Exchange For
Dec. 1913	CIN N	$6,500.	BKN N	Joe Tinker

(Tinker demanded $2,000 of the purchase price; when this was refused, he jumped to the Federal League and the deal was cancelled.)

Date	Traded To	Traded With	Traded By	In Exchange For
Apr. 1914	BKN N	—	CIN N	Herbie Moran Earl Yingling
Apr. 23, 1915	BOS N	—	BKN N	Cash

Tom Egan

Date	Traded To	Traded With	Traded By	In Exchange For
Nov. 30, 1970	CHI A	—	CAL A	*see Ken Berry*

Howard Ehmke

Date	Traded To	Traded With	Traded By	In Exchange For
Feb. 10, 1916	DET A	Jack Dalton	BUF F	Cash
Oct. 30, 1922	BOS A	Carl Holling Danny Clark Babe Herman $25,000.	DET A	Del Pratt Rip Collins
June 15, 1926	PHI A	Tom Jenkins	BOS A	Fred Heimach Slim Harriss Baby Doll Jacobson

Rube Ehrhardt

Date	Traded To	Traded With	Traded By	In Exchange For
Apr. 18, 1929	CIN N	Johnny Gooch	BKN N	Val Picinich

Juan Eichelberger

Date	Traded To	Traded With	Traded By	In Exchange For
Nov. 18, 1982	CLE A	Broderick Perkins	SD N	Ed Whitson

Mark Eichhorn

Date	Traded To	Traded With	Traded By	In Exchange For
Mar. 28, 1989	ATL N	—	TOR A	Cash
July 30, 1992	TOR A	—	CAL A	Rob Ducey Greg Myers

Date	Traded To	Traded With	Traded By	In Exchange For

Dave Eiland

Date	Traded To	Traded With	Traded By	In Exchange For
Aug. 4, 1993	TEX A	—	CLE A	Allan Anderson Gerald Alexander

Dave Eilers

Date	Traded To	Traded With	Traded By	In Exchange For
Aug. 18, 1965	NY N	—	MIL N	Cash

Joey Eischen

Date	Traded To	Traded With	Traded By	In Exchange For
July 21, 1991	MON N	—	TEX A	*see Oil Can Boyd*
May 23, 1995	LA N	Roberto Kelly	MON N	Henry Rodriguez Jeff Treadway

Jim Eisenreich

Date	Traded To	Traded With	Traded By	In Exchange For
Jan. 20, 1993	PHI N	—	KC A	No compensation (free agent signing)

Harry Eisenstat

Date	Traded To	Traded With	Traded By	In Exchange For
June 14, 1939	CLE A	Cash	DET A	Earl Averill

Kid Elberfeld

Date	Traded To	Traded With	Traded By	In Exchange For
June 10, 1903	NY A	—	DET A	Herman Long Ernie Courtney
Dec. 16, 1909	WAS A	—	NY A	$5,000.

Lee Elia

Date	Traded To	Traded With	Traded By	In Exchange For
Dec. 1, 1964	CHI A	Danny Cater	PHI N	Ray Herbert Jeoff Long
Apr. 19, 1969	NY A	—	CHI N	Nate Oliver

Frank Ellerbe

Date	Traded To	Traded With	Traded By	In Exchange For
May 31, 1921	STL A	—	WAS A	Earl Smith
June 3, 1924	CLE A	—	STL A	Cash

Bruce Ellingsen

Date	Traded To	Traded With	Traded By	In Exchange For
Apr. 3, 1974	CLE A	—	LA N	Pedro Guerrero

Larry Elliot

Date	Traded To	Traded With	Traded By	In Exchange For
May 10, 1967	KC A	$50,000.	NY N	Ed Charles

Bob Elliott

Date	Traded To	Traded With	Traded By	In Exchange For
Sept. 30, 1946	BOS N	Hank Camelli	PIT N	Billy Herman Elmer Singleton Stan Wentzel Whitey Wietelmann
Apr. 8, 1952	NY N	—	BOS N	Sheldon Jones $50,000.
June 13, 1953	CHI A	Virgil Trucks	STL A	Darrell Johnson Lou Kretlow $75,000.

Claude Elliott

Date	Traded To	Traded With	Traded By	In Exchange For
Aug. 1904	NY N	—	CIN N	Cash

Donnie Elliott

Date	Traded To	Traded With	Traded By	In Exchange For
May 28, 1992	ATL N	—	PHI N	Ben Rivera
July 18, 1993	SD N	Melvin Nieves Minor league OF Vince Moore	ATL N	Fred McGriff

Jumbo Elliott

Date	Traded To	Traded With	Traded By	In Exchange For
Oct. 14, 1930	PHI N	Clise Dudley Hal Lee Cash	BKN N	Lefty O'Doul Fresco Thompson
May 16, 1934	BOS N	—	PHI N	Cash

Dock Ellis

Date	Traded To	Traded With	Traded By	In Exchange For
Dec. 11, 1975	NY A	Willie Randolph Ken Brett	PIT N	Doc Medich
Apr. 27, 1977	OAK A	Marty Perez Larry Murray	NY A	Mike Torrez
June 15, 1977	TEX A	—	OAK A	Cash

Dock Ellis *continued*

Date	Traded To	Traded With	Traded By	In Exchange For
June 15, 1979	NY N	—	TEX A	Bob Myrick Mike Bruhert
Sept. 21, 1979	PIT N	—	NY N	Cash

Jim Ellis

Date	Traded To	Traded With	Traded By	In Exchange For
Apr. 23, 1968	LA N	Ted Savage	CHI N	Jim Hickman Phil Regan
Oct. 20, 1970	MIL A	Carl Taylor	STL N	Jerry McNertney George Lauzerique minor league P Jesse Higgins

John Ellis

Date	Traded To	Traded With	Traded By	In Exchange For
Nov. 27, 1972	CLE A	Jerry Kenney Charlie Spikes Rusty Torres	NY A	Graig Nettles Gerry Moses
Dec. 9, 1975	TEX A	—	CLE A	Stan Thomas Ron Pruitt

Sammy Ellis

Date	Traded To	Traded With	Traded By	In Exchange For
Nov. 29, 1967	CAL A	—	CIN N	Bill Kelso Jorge Rubio
Jan. 20, 1969	CHI A	—	CAL A	Bill Voss minor league P Andy Rubicotta
June 13, 1969	CLE A	—	CHI A	Jack Hamilton

Dick Ellsworth

Date	Traded To	Traded With	Traded By	In Exchange For
Dec. 7, 1966	PHI N	—	CHI N	Ray Culp Cash
Dec. 15, 1967	BOS A	Gene Oliver	PHI N	Mike Ryan Cash
Apr. 19, 1969	CLE A	*see Ken Harrelson*	BOS A	—
Aug. 7, 1970	MIL A	—	CLE A	Cash

Don Elston

Date	Traded To	Traded With	Traded By	In Exchange For
Dec. 9, 1955	BKN N	Randy Jackson	CHI N	Don Hoak Russ Meyer Walt Moryn
May 23, 1957	BKN N	—	CHI N	Jackie Collum Vito Valentinetti

Red Embree

Date	Traded To	Traded With	Traded By	In Exchange For
Oct. 10, 1947	NY A	—	CLE A	Allie Clark
Dec. 13, 1948	STL A	Sherm Lollar Dick Starr $100,000.	NY A	Fred Sanford Roy Partee

Steve Engel

Date	Traded To	Traded With	Traded By	In Exchange For
Dec. 16, 1985	HOU N	*see Billy Hatcher*	CHI N	—

Clyde Engle

Date	Traded To	Traded With	Traded By	In Exchange For
May 10, 1910	BOS A	—	NY A	Waiver price
Feb. 10, 1916	CLE A	—	BUF F	Cash

Dave Engle

Date	Traded To	Traded With	Traded By	In Exchange For
Feb. 3, 1979	MIN A	Ken Landreaux Paul Hartzell Brad Havens	CAL A	Rod Carew
Jan. 18, 1986	DET A	—	MIN A	Chris Pittaro Alejandro Sanchez

Gil English

Date	Traded To	Traded With	Traded By	In Exchange For
June 1937	BOS N	—	DET A	Cash
Aug. 10, 1938	CIN N	Tommy Reis Johnny Babich Johnny Riddle Vince DiMaggio Cash	BOS N	Eddie Miller

Woody English

Date	Traded To	Traded With	Traded By	In Exchange For
Dec. 5, 1936	BKN N	Roy Henshaw	CHI N	Lonny Frey
July 8, 1938	CIN N	—	BKN N	Cash

Del Ennis

Date	Traded To	Traded With	Traded By	In Exchange For
Nov. 19, 1956	STL N	—	PHI N	Bobby Morgan Rip Repulski
Oct. 3, 1958	CIN N	Bob Mabe Eddie Kasko	STL N	George Crowe Alex Kellner Alex Grammas
May 1, 1959	CHI A	—	CIN N	Don Rudolph Lou Skizas

Johnny Enzmann

Date	Traded To	Traded With	Traded By	In Exchange For
Dec. 1919	PHI N	—	CLE A	Cash

Jim Eppard

Date	Traded To	Traded With	Traded By	In Exchange For
Jan. 12, 1987	CAL A	—	OAK A	Cash

Mike Epstein

Date	Traded To	Traded With	Traded By	In Exchange For
May 29, 1967	WAS A	Frank Bertaina	BAL A	Pete Richert
May 8, 1971	OAK A	Darold Knowles	WAS A	Frank Fernandez Don Mincher Paul Lindblad Cash
Nov. 30, 1972	TEX A	—	OAK A	Horacio Pina
May 20, 1973	CAL A	Rich Hand Rick Stelmaszek	TEX A	Jim Spencer Lloyd Allen

Eddie Erautt

Date	Traded To	Traded With	Traded By	In Exchange For
May 23, 1953	STL N	—	CIN N	Jackie Collum

Eric Erickson

Date	Traded To	Traded With	Traded By	In Exchange For
July 5, 1919	WAS A	—	DET A	Doc Ayers

Paul Erickson

Date	Traded To	Traded With	Traded By	In Exchange For
May 20, 1948	PHI N	—	CHI N	Waiver price
July 1, 1948	NY N	—	PHI N	Waiver price
July 30, 1948	PIT N	—	NY N	Cash

Roger Erickson

Date	Traded To	Traded With	Traded By	In Exchange For
May 12, 1982	NY A	Butch Wynegar	MIN A	John Pacella Larry Milbourne Pete Filson Cash
Dec. 7, 1983	KC A	Steve Balboni	NY A	Mike Armstrong minor league C Duane Dewey

Scott Erickson

Date	Traded To	Traded With	Traded By	In Exchange For
July 7, 1995	BAL A	—	MIN A	Scott Klingenbeck Player to be named

(Minnesota received OF Kimera Bartee on September 19, 1995.)

Tex Erwin

Date	Traded To	Traded With	Traded By	In Exchange For
June 1914	CIN N	—	BKN N	Cash

Nick Esasky

Date	Traded To	Traded With	Traded By	In Exchange For
Dec. 13, 1988	BOS A	Rob Murphy	CIN N	Todd Benzinger Jeff Sellers player to be named

(Cincinnati received P Luis Vasquez on January 12, 1989.)

Date	Traded To	Traded With	Traded By	In Exchange For
Nov. 17, 1989	ATL N	—	BOS A	No compensation (free agent signing)

Angel Escobar

Date	Traded To	Traded With	Traded By	In Exchange For
Nov. 20, 1988	MON N	—	SF N	Wil Tejada

Juan Espino

Date	Traded To	Traded With	Traded By	In Exchange For
Apr. 1, 1984	CLE A	—	NY A	Cash

Nino Espinosa

Date	Traded To	Traded With	Traded By	In Exchange For
Mar. 27, 1979	PHI N	—	NY N	Richie Hebner Jose Moreno

Cecil Espy

Date	Traded To	Traded With	Traded By	In Exchange For
Mar. 30, 1982	LA N	Minor league P Bert Geiger	CHI A	Rudy Law
Aug. 31, 1985	PIT N	—	LA N	*see Bill Madlock*
Apr. 2, 1987	TEX A	—	PIT N	Minor league C Mike Dotzler

Chuck Essegian

Date	Traded To	Traded With	Traded By	In Exchange For
Dec. 3, 1958	STL N	—	PHI N	Ruben Amaro
June 15, 1959	LA N	Lloyd Merritt	STL N	Dick Gray
Apr. 12, 1961	KC A	Jerry Walker	BAL A	Dick Hall Dick Williams
May 3, 1961	CLE A	—	KC A	Cash
Feb. 27, 1963	KC A	—	CLE A	Jerry Walker

Jim Essian

Date	Traded To	Traded With	Traded By	In Exchange For
Dec. 3, 1974	CHI A	Cash	ATL N	Dick Allen

(Chicago received Essian on May 15, 1975.)

Date	Traded To	Traded With	Traded By	In Exchange For
May 7, 1975	ATL N	Barry Bonnell Cash	PHI N	Dick Allen Johnny Oates
Mar. 30, 1978	OAK A	Steve Renko	CHI A	Pablo Torrealba
Nov. 20, 1980	CHI A	—	OAK A	No compensation (free agent signing)
Dec. 11, 1981	SEA A	Todd Cruz Rod Allen	CHI A	Tom Paciorek
Jan. 21, 1983	CLE A	—	SEA A	Cash
Dec. 6, 1983	OAK A	—	CLE A	Luis Quinones

Bobby Estalella

Date	Traded To	Traded With	Traded By	In Exchange For
Sept. 10, 1941	WAS A	—	STL A	George Archie
Mar. 21, 1943	PHI A	Cash	WAS A	Bob Johnson

Shawn Estes

Date	Traded To	Traded With	Traded By	In Exchange For
May 20, 1995	SF N	Minor league IF Wilson Delgado	SEA A	Salomon Torres

Francisco Estrada

Date	Traded To	Traded With	Traded By	In Exchange For
Dec. 10, 1971	CAL A	Nolan Ryan Don Rose Leroy Stanton	NY N	Jim Fregosi
June 12, 1972	BAL A	—	CAL A	Cash
Oct. 27, 1972	CHI N	—	BAL A	Ellie Hendricks

Andy Etchebarren

Date	Traded To	Traded With	Traded By	In Exchange For
June 15, 1975	CAL A	—	BAL A	Cash
Dec. 15, 1977	MIL A	—	CAL A	Cash

Bobby Etheridge

Date	Traded To	Traded With	Traded By	In Exchange For
Dec. 5, 1969	SD N	Bob Barton Ron Herbel	SF N	Frank Reberger

Nick Etten

Date	Traded To	Traded With	Traded By	In Exchange For
Jan. 22, 1943	NY A	—	PHI N	Tom Padden Al Gerheauser Ed Levy Al Gettel $10,000.

Al Evans

Date	Traded To	Traded With	Traded By	In Exchange For
Feb. 5, 1951	BOS A	—	WAS A	Waiver price

Barry Evans

Date	Traded To	Traded With	Traded By	In Exchange For
Feb. 22, 1982	NY A	—	SD N	Cash

Darrell Evans

Date	Traded To	Traded With	Traded By	In Exchange For
June 13, 1976	SF N	Marty Perez	ATL N	Willie Montanez Craig Robinson Mike Eden Jake Brown
Dec. 19, 1983	DET A	—	SF N	No compensation (free agent signing)
Dec. 23, 1988	ATL N	—	DET A	No compensation (free agent signing)

Joe Evans

Date	Traded To	Traded With	Traded By	In Exchange For
Jan. 8, 1923	WAS A	—	CLE A	Frank Brower
Jan. 1924	STL A	—	WAS A	Cash

Roy Evans

Date	Traded To	Traded With	Traded By	In Exchange For
July 1902	BKN N	Joe Wall	NY N	Cash
July 1903	STL A	—	BKN N	Cash

Steve Evans

Date	Traded To	Traded With	Traded By	In Exchange For
June 1915	BAL F	—	BKN F	Frank Smith

Carl Everett

Date	Traded To	Traded With	Traded By	In Exchange For
Nov. 29, 1994	NY N	—	FLA N	Quilvio Veras

Leon Everitt

Date	Traded To	Traded With	Traded By	In Exchange For
Apr. 17, 1969	SD N	Tommy Dean	LA N	Al McBean

Hoot Evers

Date	Traded To	Traded With	Traded By	In Exchange For
June 3, 1952	BOS A	Dizzy Trout George Kell Johnny Lipon	DET A	Walt Dropo Bill Wight Fred Hatfield Johnny Pesky Don Lenhardt
May 18, 1954	NY N	—	BOS A	Waiver price
July 29, 1954	DET A	—	NY N	Waiver price
Jan. 3, 1955	BAL A	—	DET A	Cash
July 13, 1955	CLE A	—	BAL A	Bill Wight
May 13, 1956	BAL A	—	CLE A	Dave Pope

Johnny Evers

Date	Traded To	Traded With	Traded By	In Exchange For
Feb. 1914	BOS N	—	CHI N	Bill Sweeney Cash
July 12, 1917	PHI N	—	BOS N	Waiver price

Bryan Eversgerd

Date	Traded To	Traded With	Traded By	In Exchange For
Apr. 5, 1995	MON N	Minor league P Kirk Bullinger Minor league OF Darond Stovall	STL N	Ken Hill

Bob Ewing

Date	Traded To	Traded With	Traded By	In Exchange For
Jan. 20, 1910	PHI N	—	CIN N	Frank Corridon

Homer Ezzell

Date	Traded To	Traded With	Traded By	In Exchange For
Dec. 1923	BOS A	—	STL A	Norm McMillan
Dec. 9, 1925	DET A	Tex Vache	BOS A	Fred Haney

Roy Face

Date	Traded To	Traded With	Traded By	In Exchange For
Aug. 31, 1968	DET A	—	PIT N	Cash

Bill Fahey

Date	Traded To	Traded With	Traded By	In Exchange For
Oct. 25, 1978	SD N	Mike Hargrove Kurt Bevacqua	TEX A	Oscar Gamble Dave Roberts $300,000.
Mar. 24, 1981	DET A	—	SD N	Cash

Ferris Fain

Date	Traded To	Traded With	Traded By	In Exchange For
Jan. 27, 1953	CHI A	minor league 2B Bob Wilson	PHI A	Joe De Maestri Eddie Robinson Ed McGhee
Dec. 6, 1954	DET A	Leo Cristante Jack Phillips	CHI A	Walt Dropo Ted Gray Bob Nieman

Ron Fairly

Date	Traded To	Traded With	Traded By	In Exchange For
June 11, 1969	MON N	Paul Popovich	LA N	Maury Wills Manny Mota
Dec. 6, 1974	STL N	—	MON N	Minor leaguers IF Rudy Kinard and 1B Ed Kurpiel
Sept. 14, 1976	OAK A	—	STL N	Cash
Feb. 24, 1977	TOR A	—	OAK A	Minor league IF Mike Weathers Cash
Dec. 8, 1977	CAL A	—	TOR A	Dale Kelly Butch Alberts

Hector Fajardo

Date	Traded To	Traded With	Traded By	In Exchange For
Aug. 30, 1991	TEX A	Kurt Miller	PIT N	Steve Buechele

(Texas received Fajardo on September 6, 1991.)

Date	Traded To	Traded With	Traded By	In Exchange For
July 30, 1995	MON N	—	TEX A	Lou Frazier

(Montreal received Fajardo on August 5, 1995.)

Pete Falcone

Date	Traded To	Traded With	Traded By	In Exchange For
Dec. 8, 1975	STL N	—	SF N	Ken Reitz
Dec. 5, 1978	NY N	—	STL N	Tom Grieve Kim Seaman
Jan. 25, 1983	ATL N	—	NY N	No compensation (free agent signing)

Bibb Falk

Date	Traded To	Traded With	Traded By	In Exchange For
Feb. 28, 1929	CLE A	—	CHI A	Martin Autry

Cy Falkenberg

Date	Traded To	Traded With	Traded By	In Exchange For
Aug. 1908	CLE A	Dave Altizer	WAS A	Cash
Feb. 1915	BKN F	—	NWK F	Hugh Bradley Larry Pratt Tom Seaton

Rikkert Faneyte

Date	Traded To	Traded With	Traded By	In Exchange For
Dec. 1, 1995	TEX A	—	SF N	Player to be named

Frank Fanovich

Date	Traded To	Traded With	Traded By	In Exchange For
Dec. 17, 1953	BAL A	Joe Coleman	PHI A	Bob Cain

Carmen Fanzone

Date	Traded To	Traded With	Traded By	In Exchange For
Dec. 3, 1970	CHI N	—	BOS A	Phil Gagliano

Paul Faries

Date	Traded To	Traded With	Traded By	In Exchange For
Dec. 10, 1992	SF N	—	SD N	Jim Pena

Bob Farley

Date	Traded To	Traded With	Traded By	In Exchange For
Nov. 30, 1961	CHI A	—	SF N	*see Billy Pierce*
June 25, 1962	DET A	—	CHI A	Charlie Maxwell

Ed Farmer

Date	Traded To	Traded With	Traded By	In Exchange For
June 15, 1973	DET A	—	CLE A	Tom Timmerman Kevin Collins
Mar. 19, 1974	NY A	Rick Sawyer Walt Williams	DET A	Gerry Moses

(Part of three-team trade involving Detroit, New York Yankees, and Cleveland.)

Date	Traded To	Traded With	Traded By	In Exchange For
Mar. 21, 1974	PHI N	—	NY A	Cash
Dec. 3, 1974	MIL A	—	PHI N	Minor league IF Steve McCartney
Dec. 15, 1978	TEX A	Gary Holle Cash	MIL A	Reggie Cleveland
June 15, 1979	CHI A	Gary Holle	TEX A	Eric Soderholm
Jan. 28, 1982	PHI N	—	CHI A	

(Chicago selected Joel Skinner of Pittsburgh from the compensation pool.)

Steve Farr

Date	Traded To	Traded With	Traded By	In Exchange For
June 8, 1983	CLE A	—	PIT N	Minor league C John Malkin
Nov. 26, 1990	NY A	—	KC A	No compensation (free agent signing)
Feb. 10, 1994	CLE A	—	NY A	No compensation (free agent signing)

Steve Farr *continued*

Date	Traded To		Traded With	Traded By		In Exchange For
July 1, 1994	BOS	A	Chris Nabholz	CLE	A	Jeff Russell

Dick Farrell

Date	Traded To		Traded With	Traded By		In Exchange For
May 4, 1961	LA	N	Joe Koppe	PHI	N	Don Demeter Charley Smith
May 8, 1967	PHI	N	—	HOU	N	Cash

Doc Farrell

Date	Traded To		Traded With	Traded By		In Exchange For
June 12, 1927	BOS	N	Hugh McQuillan Kent Greenfield	NY	N	Zack Taylor Larry Benton Herb Thomas
June 14, 1929	NY	N	—	BOS	N	Jimmy Welsh
Apr. 10, 1930	STL	N	Showboat Fisher	NY	N	Wally Roettger
June 29, 1930	CHI	N	—	STL	N	Waiver price

Bill Faul

Date	Traded To		Traded With	Traded By		In Exchange For
Mar. 27, 1965	CHI	N	—	DET	A	Cash

Ernie Fazio

Date	Traded To		Traded With	Traded By		In Exchange For
June 4, 1965	KC	A	Jess Hickman $100,000.	HOU	N	Jim Gentile

(Kansas City received Fazio on October 15.)

Mike Felder

Date	Traded To		Traded With	Traded By		In Exchange For
Nov. 29, 1992	SEA	A	—	SF	N	No compensation (free agent signing)
Dec. 10, 1993	HOU	N	Mike Hampton	SEA	A	Eric Anthony

Gus Felix

Date	Traded To		Traded With	Traded By		In Exchange For
Oct. 7, 1925	BKN	N	Jesse Barnes Mickey O'Neil	BOS	N	Zack Taylor Jimmy Johnston Eddie Brown

Junior Felix

Date	Traded To		Traded With	Traded By		In Exchange For
Dec. 2, 1990	CAL	A	Luis Sojo Minor league C Ken Rivers	TOR	A	Devon White Willie Fraser Marcus Moore

Bobby Fenwick

Date	Traded To		Traded With	Traded By		In Exchange For
Nov. 28, 1972	STL	N	Ray Busse	HOU	N	Skip Jutze Milt Ramirez
Nov. 7, 1973	SD	N	Glenn Beckert	CHI	N	Jerry Morales

Alex Ferguson

Date	Traded To		Traded With	Traded By		In Exchange For
Feb. 24, 1922	BOS	A	—	NY	A	Waiver price
May 5, 1925	NY	A	Bobby Veach	BOS	A	Ray Francis $9,000.
Aug. 19, 1925	WAS	A	—	NY	A	Cash
Oct. 1926	PHI	N	—	WAS	A	Cash
May 14, 1929	BKN	N	—	PHI	N	Cash

George Ferguson

Date	Traded To		Traded With	Traded By		In Exchange For
Dec. 3, 1907	BOS	N	—	NY	N	*see Fred Tenney*

Joe Ferguson

Date	Traded To		Traded With	Traded By		In Exchange For
June 15, 1976	STL	N	Bob Detherage minor league IF Fred Tisdale	LA	N	Reggie Smith
Nov. 23, 1976	HOU	N	Bob Detherage	STL	N	Larry Dierker Jerry DaVanon
July 1, 1978	LA	N	Cash	HOU	N	Rafael Landestoy Jeffrey Leonard

Felix Fermin

Date	Traded To		Traded With	Traded By		In Exchange For
Mar. 25, 1989	CLE	A	Denny Gonzalez	PIT	N	Jay Bell

(Completion of deal in which Cleveland acquired Gonzalez on November 28, 1988 for a player to be named.)

Date	Traded To		Traded With	Traded By		In Exchange For
Dec. 20, 1993	SEA	A	Reggie Jefferson Cash	CLE	A	Omar Vizquel

Chico Fernandez

Date	Traded To		Traded With	Traded By		In Exchange For
Apr. 5, 1957	PHI	N	—	BKN	N	Ron Negray Tim Harkness Elmer Valo Ben Flowers minor league SS Mel Geho and $75,000.
Dec. 5, 1959	DET	A	Ray Semproch	PHI	N	Ken Walters Ted Lepcio minor league P Alex Cosmidis
May 8, 1963	MIL	N	—	DET	A	Lou Johnson Cash
May 8, 1963	NY	N	—	MIL	N	Larry Foss
Apr. 23, 1964	CHI	A	minor league C Bobby Catton Cash	NY	N	Charley Smith

Frank Fernandez

Date	Traded To		Traded With	Traded By		In Exchange For
Dec. 5, 1969	OAK	A	Al Downing	NY	A	Danny Cater Ossie Chavarria
May 8, 1971	WAS	A	Don Mincher Paul Lindblad Cash	OAK	A	Mike Epstein Darold Knowles
June 23, 1971	OAK	A	—	WAS	A	Cash
Aug. 31, 1971	CHI	N	Bill McNulty	OAK	A	Adrian Garrett

Sid Fernandez

Date	Traded To		Traded With	Traded By		In Exchange For
Dec. 8, 1983	NY	N	Ross Jones	LA	N	Carlos Diaz Bob Bailor
Nov. 22, 1993	BAL	A	—	NY	N	No compensation (free agent signing)

Tony Fernandez

Date	Traded To		Traded With	Traded By		In Exchange For
Dec. 5, 1990	SD	N	Fred McGriff	TOR	A	Joe Carter Roberto Alomar
Oct. 27, 1992	NY	N	—	SD	N	Wally Whitehurst D. J. Dozier Player to be named

(San Diego received C Raul Casanova on December 7, 1992.)

Date	Traded To		Traded With	Traded By		In Exchange For
June 11, 1993	TOR	A	—	NY	N	Darrin Jackson
Mar. 8, 1994	CIN	N	—	TOR	A	No compensation (free agent signing)
Dec. 15, 1994	NY	A	—	CIN	N	No compensation (free agent signing)

Al Ferrara

Date	Traded To		Traded With	Traded By		In Exchange For
May 13, 1971	CIN	N	—	SD	N	Angel Bravo

Don Ferrarese

Date	Traded To		Traded With	Traded By		In Exchange For
Dec. 6, 1954	BAL	A	—	CHI	A	*see Clint Courtney*
Apr. 1, 1958	CLE	A	Larry Doby	BAL	A	Bud Daley Dick Williams Gene Woodling
Dec. 6, 1959	CHI	A	—	CLE	A	*see Norm Cash*
Apr. 28, 1962	STL	N	—	PHI	N	Bobby Locke Cash

Mike Ferraro

Date	Traded To		Traded With	Traded By		In Exchange For
Apr. 30, 1969	BAL	A	Gerry Schoen	SEA	A	John O'Donoghue Tom Fisher minor league P Lloyd Fourroux
Mar. 27, 1973	MIN	A	—	MIL	A	Ken Reynolds

Tony Ferreira

Date	Traded To		Traded With	Traded By		In Exchange For
Apr. 1, 1986	NY	N	—	KC	A	Angel Salazar

Rick Ferrell

Date	Traded To		Traded With	Traded By		In Exchange For
May 9, 1933	BOS	A	Lloyd Brown	STL	A	Merv Shea Cash
June 11, 1937	WAS	A	Wes Ferrell Mel Almada	BOS	A	Ben Chapman Bobo Newsom
May 15, 1941	STL	A	—	WAS	A	Vern Kennedy

Rick Ferrell *continued*

Date	Traded To	Traded With	Traded By	In Exchange For
Mar. 1, 1944	WAS A	—	STL A	Tony Giuliani Gene Moore Cash

(Giuliani announced his retirement, and St. Louis received Moore to complete the trade.)

Wes Ferrell

Date	Traded To	Traded With	Traded By	In Exchange For
May 25, 1934	BOS A	Dick Porter	CLE A	Bob Weiland Bob Seeds $25,000.
June 11, 1937	WAS A	Mel Almada Rick Ferrell	BOS A	Ben Chapman Bobo Newsom

Sergio Ferrer

Date	Traded To	Traded With	Traded By	In Exchange For
Oct. 24, 1975	PHI N	—	MIN A	Larry Cox
Mar. 26, 1977	NY A	—	PHI N	Kerry Dineen
Dec. 9, 1977	NY N	—	NY A	Roy Staiger

Tom Ferrick

Date	Traded To	Traded With	Traded By	In Exchange For
Sept. 22, 1941	CLE A	—	PHI A	Waiver price
June 24, 1946	STL A	—	CLE A	Cash
Jan. 14, 1947	WAS A	—	STL A	Cash
Oct. 4, 1948	STL A	John Sullivan $25,000.	WAS A	Sam Dente
June 15, 1950	NY A	Joe Ostrowski Leo Thomas Sid Schacht	STL A	Jim Delsing Don Johnson Duane Pillette Snuffy Stirnweiss $50,000.
June 15, 1951	WAS A	Fred Sanford Bob Porterfield	NY A	Bob Kuzava

Hobe Ferris

Date	Traded To	Traded With	Traded By	In Exchange For
Oct. 1907	STL A	—	BOS A	Cash
Feb. 1908	STL A	Jimmy Williams Danny Hoffman	NY A	Fred Glade Charlie Hemphill

Lou Fette

Date	Traded To	Traded With	Traded By	In Exchange For
July 1940	BKN N	—	BOS N	Cash

Mike Fetters

Date	Traded To	Traded With	Traded By	In Exchange For
Dec. 10, 1991	MIL A	Minor league P Glenn Carter	CAL A	Chuck Crim

Chick Fewster

Date	Traded To	Traded With	Traded By	In Exchange For
July 23, 1922	BOS A	Elmer Miller Johnny Mitchell Lefty O'Doul $50,000.	NY A	Joe Dugan Elmer Smith
Jan. 7, 1924	CLE A	—	BOS A	*see Bill Wambsganss*
Jan. 1926	BKN N	—	CLE A	Cash

Neil Fiala

Date	Traded To	Traded With	Traded By	In Exchange For
Sept. 10, 1981	CIN N	Joe Edelen	STL N	Doug Bair

Cecil Fielder

Date	Traded To	Traded With	Traded By	In Exchange For
Feb. 5, 1983	TOR A	—	KC A	Leon Roberts

Bruce Fields

Date	Traded To	Traded With	Traded By	In Exchange For
Oct. 5, 1987	SEA A	—	DET A	Stan Clarke

Dan Fife

Date	Traded To	Traded With	Traded By	In Exchange For
Mar. 27, 1973	MIN A	Cash	DET A	Jim Perry

Ed Figueroa

Date	Traded To	Traded With	Traded By	In Exchange For
Dec. 11, 1975	NY A	Mickey Rivers	CAL A	Bobby Bonds
July 28, 1980	TEX A	—	NY A	Cash

Jesus Figueroa

Date	Traded To	Traded With	Traded By	In Exchange For
Dec. 12, 1980	SF N	Jerry Martin minor league IF Mike Turgeon	CHI N	Joe Strain Phil Nastu

Tom Filer

Date	Traded To	Traded With	Traded By	In Exchange For
Apr. 27, 1981	CHI N	Cash	NY A	Barry Foote
Oct. 6, 1987	MIL A	—	TOR A	Cash

Pete Filson

Date	Traded To	Traded With	Traded By	In Exchange For
May 12, 1982	MIN A	John Pacella Larry Milbourne Cash	NY A	Butch Wynegar Roger Erickson
Apr. 30, 1986	CHI A	—	MIN A	Minor league P Kurt Walker
Jan. 5, 1987	NY A	Randy Velarde	CHI A	Scott Nielsen Minor league IF Mike Soper

Jack Fimple

Date	Traded To	Traded With	Traded By	In Exchange For
Dec. 9, 1981	LA N	Jorge Orta Larry White	CLE A	Rick Sutcliffe Jack Perconte

Rollie Fingers

Date	Traded To	Traded With	Traded By	In Exchange For
Dec. 14, 1976	SD N	—	OAK A	No compensation (free agent signing)
Dec. 8, 1980	STL N	Bob Shirley Gene Tenace Bob Geren	SD N	Terry Kennedy Steve Swisher Mike Phillips John Littlefield John Urrea Kim Seaman Al Olmsted
Dec. 12, 1980	MIL A	Pete Vuckovich Ted Simmons	STL N	Sixto Lezcano David Green Lary Sorensen Dave LaPoint

Jim Finigan

Date	Traded To	Traded With	Traded By	In Exchange For
Dec. 16, 1953	PHI A	Don Bollweg John Gray Jim Robertson Vic Power Bill Renna	NY A	Harry Byrd Eddie Robinson Tom Hamilton Carmen Mauro Loren Babe
Dec. 5, 1956	DET A	Jack Crimian Bill Harrington Eddie Robinson	KC A	Ned Garver Gene Host Virgil Trucks Wayne Belardi $20,000.
Jan. 28, 1958	SF N	$25,000.	DET A	Gail Harris Ozzie Virgil
Oct. 14, 1958	BAL A	—	STL N	Jim Brideweser Art Ceccarelli

Steve Finley

Date	Traded To	Traded With	Traded By	In Exchange For
Jan. 10, 1991	HOU N	Pete Harnisch Curt Schilling	BAL A	Glenn Davis
Dec. 28, 1994	SD N	Ken Caminiti Andujar Cedeno Brian Williams Roberto Petagine Player to be named	HOU N	Phil Plantier Derek Bell Pedro Martinez Doug Brocail Craig Shipley Ricky Gutierrez

(San Diego received P Sean Fesh on May 1, 1995.)

Mickey Finn

Date	Traded To	Traded With	Traded By	In Exchange For
Dec. 15, 1932	PHI N	Cy Moore Jack Warner	BKN N	Ray Benge $15,000.

Happy Finneran

Date	Traded To	Traded With	Traded By	In Exchange For
May 1918	NY A	—	DET A	Cash

Lou Finney

Date	Traded To	Traded With	Traded By	In Exchange For
May 8, 1939	BOS A	—	PHI A	Cash
July 27, 1945	STL A	—	BOS A	Cash

Mike Fiore

Date	Traded To	Traded With	Traded By	In Exchange For
May 28, 1970	BOS A	—	KC A	Tom Matchick
Mar. 20, 1972	STL N	—	BOS A	Bob Burda
June 20, 1972	SD N	Bob Chlupsa	STL N	Rafael Robles

(Fiore was returned to St. Louis on July 3.)

Date	Traded To		Traded With	Traded By		In Exchange For

Steve Fireovid

Date	Traded To		Traded With	Traded By		In Exchange For
Aug. 31, 1983	PHI	N	*see Sixto Lezcano*	SD	N	—

Bill Fischer

Date	Traded To		Traded With	Traded By		In Exchange For
June 15, 1958	DET	A	Tito Francona	CHI	A	Ray Boone Bob Shaw
Sept. 11, 1958	WAS	A	—	DET	A	Waiver price
July 22, 1960	DET	A	—	WAS	A	Tom Morgan
Aug. 2, 1961	KC	A	Ozzie Virgil	DET	A	Gerry Staley Reno Bertoia

Bill Fischer

Date	Traded To		Traded With	Traded By		In Exchange For
Feb. 10, 1916	CHI	N	*see Three Finger Brown*	CHI	F	—
July 29, 1916	PIT	N	Wildfire Schulte	CHI	N	Art Wilson Otto Knabe

Carl Fischer

Date	Traded To		Traded With	Traded By		In Exchange For
June 9, 1932	STL	A	—	WAS	A	Dick Coffman
Dec. 13, 1932	WAS	A	—	STL	A	Dick Coffman
Dec. 14, 1932	DET	A	Firpo Marberry	WAS	A	Earl Whitehill
May 17, 1935	CHI	A	—	DET	A	Cash
May 1937	WAS	A	—	CLE	A	Cash

Hank Fischer

Date	Traded To		Traded With	Traded By		In Exchange For
June 15, 1966	CIN	N	—	ATL	N	Joey Jay
Aug. 15, 1966	BOS	A	—	CIN	N	Dick Stigman Rollie Sheldon

(Cincinnati received Stigman and Sheldon on December 15, 1966.)

Jeff Fischer

Date	Traded To		Traded With	Traded By		In Exchange For
Mar. 27, 1989	LA	N	—	MON	N	Gilberto Reyes

Mike Fischlin

Date	Traded To		Traded With	Traded By		In Exchange For
June 15, 1977	HOU	N	Randy Niemann Dave Bergman	NY	A	Cliff Johnson

(Houston received Bergman on November 23.)

Date	Traded To		Traded With	Traded By		In Exchange For
Apr. 3, 1981	CLE	A	—	HOU	N	Jim Lentine Cash
Dec. 15, 1985	NY	A	—	CLE	A	Minor league P Kevin Trudeau

(Cleveland received Trudeau on Apr. 7, 1986.)

John Fishel

Date	Traded To		Traded With	Traded By		In Exchange For
Jan. 10, 1989	NY	A	—	HOU	N	*see Rick Rhoden*

Bob Fisher

Date	Traded To		Traded With	Traded By		In Exchange For
Jan. 1916	CIN	N	—	CHI	N	Cash

Brian Fisher

Date	Traded To		Traded With	Traded By		In Exchange For
Dec. 5, 1984	NY	A	—	ATL	N	Rick Cerone
Nov. 26, 1986	PIT	N	—	NY	A	*see Rick Rhoden*
June 29, 1992	SEA	A	—	CIN	N	Player to be named

Chauncey Fisher

Date	Traded To		Traded With	Traded By		In Exchange For
May 1901	STL	N	—	NY	N	Bill Magee

Eddie Fisher

Date	Traded To		Traded With	Traded By		In Exchange For
Nov. 30, 1961	CHI	A	Dom Zanni Verle Tiefenthaler Bob Farley	SF	N	Billy Pierce Don Larsen
June 12, 1966	BAL	A	—	CHI	A	Jerry Adair minor league OF Johnny Riddle
Nov. 28, 1967	CLE	A	minor leaguers P Bob Scott and IF John Scruggs	BAL	A	John O'Donoghue Gordon Lund
Oct. 8, 1968	CAL	A	—	CLE	A	Jack Hamilton
Aug. 17, 1972	CHI	A	—	CAL	A	Bruce Miller Bruce Kimm
Aug. 29, 1973	STL	N	—	CHI	A	Cash

Gus Fisher

Date	Traded To		Traded With	Traded By		In Exchange For
Mar. 1912	NY	A	—	CLE	A	Waiver price

Jack Fisher

Date	Traded To		Traded With	Traded By		In Exchange For
Dec. 15, 1962	SF	N	Jimmie Coker Billy Hoeft	BAL	A	Mike McCormick Stu Miller John Orsino
Oct. 10, 1963	NY	N	—	SF	N	$30,000.
Dec. 15, 1967	CHI	A	Tommy Davis Billy Wynne Buddy Booker	NY	N	Tommie Agee Al Weis
Dec. 5, 1968	CIN	N	—	CHI	A	Don Pavletich Don Secrist
Jan. 14, 1970	CAL	A	—	CIN	N	Bill Harrelson minor league IF Dan Loomer

Ray Fisher

Date	Traded To		Traded With	Traded By		In Exchange For
Mar. 15, 1919	CIN	N	—	NY	A	Waiver price

Showboat Fisher

Date	Traded To		Traded With	Traded By		In Exchange For
Apr. 10, 1930	STL	N	Doc Farrell	NY	N	Wally Roettger

Tom Fisher

Date	Traded To		Traded With	Traded By		In Exchange For
Apr. 30, 1969	SEA	A	John O'Donoghue minor league P Lloyd Fourroux	BAL	A	Gerry Schoen Mike Ferraro

Carlton Fisk

Date	Traded To		Traded With	Traded By		In Exchange For
Mar. 18, 1981	CHI	A	—	BOS	A	No compensation (free agent signing)

Ed Fitz Gerald

Date	Traded To		Traded With	Traded By		In Exchange For
May 13, 1953	WAS	A	—	PIT	N	Cash
May 25, 1959	CLE	A	—	WAS	A	Hal Woodeshick Hal Naragon

Mike Fitzgerald

Date	Traded To		Traded With	Traded By		In Exchange For
Dec. 10, 1984	MON	N	Hubie Brooks Herm Winningham Floyd Youmans	NY	N	Gary Carter

Al Fitzmorris

Date	Traded To		Traded With	Traded By		In Exchange For
Nov. 5, 1976	CLE	A	—	TOR	A	Alan Ashby Doug Howard

Freddie Fitzsimmons

Date	Traded To		Traded With	Traded By		In Exchange For
June 11, 1937	BKN	N	—	NY	N	Tom Baker

Max Flack

Date	Traded To		Traded With	Traded By		In Exchange For
Feb. 10, 1916	CHI	N	*see Three Finger Brown*	CHI	F	—
May 30, 1922	STL	N	—	CHI	N	Cliff Heathcote

Ira Flagstead

Date	Traded To		Traded With	Traded By		In Exchange For
Apr. 20, 1923	BOS	A	—	DET	A	Cash
May 25, 1929	WAS	A	—	BOS	A	Waiver price
July 12, 1929	PIT	N	—	WAS	A	Waiver price

John Flaherty

Date	Traded To		Traded With	Traded By		In Exchange For
Apr. 1, 1994	DET	A	—	BOS	A	Rich Rowland

Patsy Flaherty

Date	Traded To		Traded With	Traded By		In Exchange For
Jan. 1900	PIT	N	*see Honus Wagner*	LOU	N	—
Dec. 1906	BOS	N	Ginger Beaumont Claude Ritchey	PIT	N	Ed Abbaticchio

Mike Flanagan

Date	Traded To		Traded With	Traded By		In Exchange For
Aug. 31, 1987	TOR	A	—	BAL	A	Jose Mesa Oswald Peraza

(Baltimore received Mesa on September 4, 1987.)

John Flannery

Date	Traded To		Traded With	Traded By		In Exchange For
June 15, 1977	CHI	A	Don Kirkwood John Verhoeven	CAL	A	Ken Brett

Dave Fleming

Date	Traded To		Traded With	Traded By		In Exchange For
July 7, 1995	KC	A	—	SEA	A	Bob Milacki

Les Fleming

Date	Traded To	Traded With	Traded By	In Exchange For
Dec. 4, 1947	PIT N	—	CLE A	Cash

Art Fletcher

Date	Traded To	Traded With	Traded By	In Exchange For
June 8, 1920	PHI N	Bill Hubbell Cash	NY N	Dave Bancroft

Darrin Fletcher

Date	Traded To	Traded With	Traded By	In Exchange For
Sept. 13, 1990	PHI N	—	LA N	Dennis Cook
Dec. 9, 1991	MON N	Cash	PHI N	Barry Jones

Elbie Fletcher

Date	Traded To	Traded With	Traded By	In Exchange For
June 15, 1939	PIT N	—	BOS N	Bill Schuster Cash
Dec. 4, 1947	CLE A	—	PIT N	Cash

Scott Fletcher

Date	Traded To	Traded With	Traded By	In Exchange For
Jan. 25, 1983	CHI A	Pat Tabler Randy Martz Dick Tidrow	CHI N	Steve Trout Warren Brusstar
Nov. 25, 1985	TEX A	Ed Correa Jose Mota	CHI A	Wayne Tolleson Dave Schmidt

(Texas received Mota on December 12, 1985)

Date	Traded To	Traded With	Traded By	In Exchange For
July 29, 1989	CHI A	Wilson Alvarez Sammy Sosa	TEX A	Harold Baines Fred Manrique
Nov. 30, 1992	BOS A	—	MIL A	No compensation (free agent signing)

Elmer Flick

Date	Traded To	Traded With	Traded By	In Exchange For
May 16, 1902	CLE A	—	PHI A	Cash

John Flinn

Date	Traded To	Traded With	Traded By	In Exchange For
Dec. 6, 1979	MIL A	—	BAL A	Lenn Sakata

Curt Flood

Date	Traded To	Traded With	Traded By	In Exchange For
Dec. 5, 1957	STL N	Joe Taylor	CIN N	Marty Kutyna Ted Wieand Willard Schmidt
Oct. 7, 1969	PHI N	Tim McCarver Joe Hoerner Byron Browne	STL N	Dick Allen Cookie Rojas Jerry Johnson

(Flood refused to report to the Philadelphia Phillies, and the Cardinals sent Willie Montanez and Bob Browning on April 8, 1970 to complete the trade.)

Date	Traded To	Traded With	Traded By	In Exchange For
Nov. 3, 1970	WAS A	—	PHI N	Greg Goossen Jeff Terpko Gene Martin

Kevin Flora

Date	Traded To	Traded With	Traded By	In Exchange For
Aug. 8, 1995	PHI N	Russ Springer	CAL A	Dave Gallagher

(Philadelphia received Springer on August 15, 1995.)

Gil Flores

Date	Traded To	Traded With	Traded By	In Exchange For
July 28, 1978	NY N	—	CAL A	Cash

Ben Flowers

Date	Traded To	Traded With	Traded By	In Exchange For
Sept. 8, 1955	STL N	—	DET A	Bobby Tiefenauer
May 11, 1956	PHI N	Harvey Haddix Stu Miller	STL N	Murry Dickson Herm Wehmeier
Oct. 15, 1956	KC A	—	PHI N	Waiver price
Apr. 5, 1957	BKN N	—	PHI N	*see Chico Fernandez*

Jake Flowers

Date	Traded To	Traded With	Traded By	In Exchange For
May 1927	BKN N	—	STL N	Bob McGraw
June 15, 1931	STL N	—	BKN N	Waiver price
Feb. 1933	BKN N	Ownie Carroll	STL N	Dazzy Vance Gordon Slade

Bobby Floyd

Date	Traded To	Traded With	Traded By	In Exchange For
June 15, 1970	KC A	—	BAL A	Moe Drabowsky

Doug Flynn

Date	Traded To	Traded With	Traded By	In Exchange For
June 15, 1977	NY N	Pat Zachry Steve Henderson Dan Norman	CIN N	Tom Seaver
Dec. 11, 1981	TEX A	Danny Boitano	NY N	Jim Kern
Aug. 2, 1982	MON N	—	TEX A	Cash

John Flynn

Date	Traded To	Traded With	Traded By	In Exchange For
Feb. 1912	WAS A	—	PIT N	Waiver price

Lee Fohl

Date	Traded To	Traded With	Traded By	In Exchange For
Oct. 1903	CIN N	—	PIT N	Waiver price

Hank Foiles

Date	Traded To	Traded With	Traded By	In Exchange For
May 3, 1953	CLE A	—	CIN N	Cash
May 15, 1956	PIT N	—	CLE A	Preston Ward
Dec. 15, 1959	KC A	—	PIT N	Cash
June 1, 1960	PIT N	Cash	KC A	Danny Kravitz
June 2, 1960	CLE A	—	PIT N	Johnny Powers
July 26, 1960	DET A	—	CLE A	Rocky Bridges Red Wilson
Apr. 20, 1962	CIN N	—	BAL A	Cash

Tom Foley

Date	Traded To	Traded With	Traded By	In Exchange For
Aug. 8, 1985	PHI N	Alan Knicely Fred Toliver	CIN N	Bo Diaz Minor league P Greg Simpson

(Philadelphia received Toliver on August 27, 1985.)

Date	Traded To	Traded With	Traded By	In Exchange For
July 24, 1986	MON N	Lary Sorensen	PHI N	Dan Schatzeder Skeeter Barnes

Tim Foli

Date	Traded To	Traded With	Traded By	In Exchange For
Apr. 5, 1972	MON N	Ken Singleton Mike Jorgensen	NY N	Rusty Staub
Apr. 27, 1977	SF N	—	MON N	Chris Speier
Dec. 7, 1977	NY N	—	SF N	Cash
Apr. 19, 1979	PIT N	minor league P Greg Field	NY N	Frank Taveras
Dec. 11, 1981	CAL A	—	PIT N	Brian Harper
Dec. 7, 1983	NY A	—	CAL A	Curt Kaufman Cash
Dec. 20, 1984	PIT N	Steve Kemp $400,000.	NY A	Dale Berra Jay Buhner

Rich Folkers

Date	Traded To	Traded With	Traded By	In Exchange For
Oct. 18, 1971	STL N	*see Jim Bibby*	NY N	—
Nov. 18, 1974	SD N	Alan Foster Sonny Siebert	STL N	Ed Brinkman Danny Breeden

(Part of three-team trade involving San Diego, Detroit, and St. Louis Cardinals.)

Date	Traded To	Traded With	Traded By	In Exchange For
Mar. 23, 1977	MIL A	—	SD N	Cash
Dec. 9, 1977	DET A	Jim Slaton	MIL A	Ben Oglivie

Dee Fondy

Date	Traded To	Traded With	Traded By	In Exchange For
Oct. 10, 1950	CHI N	Chuck Connors	BKN N	Hank Edwards Cash
May 1, 1957	PIT N	Gene Baker	CHI N	Dale Long Lee Walls
Dec. 28, 1957	CIN N	—	PIT N	Ted Kluszewski

Lew Fonseca

Date	Traded To	Traded With	Traded By	In Exchange For
Mar. 30, 1925	PHI N	—	CIN N	Cash
May 17, 1931	CHI A	—	CLE A	Willie Kamm

Ray Fontenot

Date	Traded To	Traded With	Traded By	In Exchange For
Aug. 1, 1979	NY A	Oscar Gamble Gene Nelson minor league 3B Amos Lewis	TEX A	Mickey Rivers minor league Ps Bob Polinsky Neil Mersch and Mark Softy
Dec. 4, 1984	CHI N	Brian Dayett	NY A	Henry Cotto Porfi Altamirano Ron Hassey Rich Bordi

Ray Fontenot *continued*

Date	Traded To	Traded With	Traded By	In Exchange For
Aug. 13, 1986	MIN A	—	CHI N	*see Ron Davis*

Chad Fonville

Date	Traded To	Traded With	Traded By	In Exchange For
May 31, 1995	LA N	—	MON N	Waiver price

Jim Foor

Date	Traded To	Traded With	Traded By	In Exchange For
Nov. 30, 1972	PIT N	Norm McRae	DET A	Dick Sharon
Mar. 28, 1974	KC A	—	PIT N	Wayne Simpson

Barry Foote

Date	Traded To	Traded With	Traded By	In Exchange For
June 15, 1977	PHI N	Dan Warthen	MON N	Wayne Twitchell Tim Blackwell
Feb. 23, 1979	CHI N	Derek Botelho Ted Sizemore Jerry Martin minor league P Henry Mack	PHI N	Manny Trillo Dave Rader Greg Gross
Apr. 27, 1981	NY A	—	CHI N	Tom Filer Cash

Curt Ford

Date	Traded To	Traded With	Traded By	In Exchange For
Dec. 16, 1988	PHI N	Steve Lake	STL N	Milt Thompson

Dan Ford

Date	Traded To	Traded With	Traded By	In Exchange For
Oct. 23, 1974	MIN A	minor league P Denny Myers	OAK A	Pat Bourque
Dec. 4, 1978	CAL A	—	MIN A	Ron Jackson Danny Goodwin
Jan. 28, 1982	BAL A	—	CAL A	Doug DeCinces Jeff Schneider

Hod Ford

Date	Traded To	Traded With	Traded By	In Exchange For
Dec. 15, 1923	PHI N	Ray Powell	BOS N	Cotton Tierney

(Powell announced his intention to retire after the 1924 season. He remained with Boston, and Philadelphia received cash instead.)

Date	Traded To	Traded With	Traded By	In Exchange For
May 16, 1925	BKN N	—	PHI N	Waiver price
Jan. 26, 1932	STL N	—	CIN N	Cash

Ted Ford

Date	Traded To	Traded With	Traded By	In Exchange For
Apr. 3, 1972	TEX A	—	CLE A	Roy Foster Tom McCraw
May 10, 1973	CLE A	Dick Bosman	TEX A	Steve Dunning

Brook Fordyce

Date	Traded To	Traded With	Traded By	In Exchange For
May 15, 1995	CLE A	—	NY N	Waiver price

Frank Foreman

Date	Traded To	Traded With	Traded By	In Exchange For
Apr. 1901	BAL A	—	BOS A	Cash

Mike Fornieles

Date	Traded To	Traded With	Traded By	In Exchange For
Dec. 10, 1952	CHI A	—	WAS A	Chuck Stobbs
May 21, 1956	BAL A	Bob Nieman Connie Johnson George Kell	CHI A	Jim Wilson Dave Philley
June 14, 1957	BOS A	—	BAL A	Billy Goodman
June 14, 1963	MIN A	—	BOS A	Cash

Bob Forsch

Date	Traded To	Traded With	Traded By	In Exchange For
Aug. 31, 1988	HOU N	—	STL N	Denny Walling

Ken Forsch

Date	Traded To	Traded With	Traded By	In Exchange For
Apr. 1, 1981	CAL A	—	HOU N	Dickie Thon

Terry Forster

Date	Traded To	Traded With	Traded By	In Exchange For
Dec. 10, 1976	PIT N	Goose Gossage	CHI A	Richie Zisk Silvio Martinez
Nov. 22, 1977	LA N	—	PIT N	No compensation (free agent signing)
Dec. 1, 1982	ATL N	—	LA N	No compensation (free agent signing)

Tim Fortugno

Date	Traded To	Traded With	Traded By	In Exchange For
Dec. 9, 1987	PHI N	*see Phil Bradley*	SEA A	—
Jan. 6, 1995	CHI A	—	CIN N	Waiver price
July 27, 1995	CAL A	*see Jim Abbott*	CHI A	—

Larry Foss

Date	Traded To	Traded With	Traded By	In Exchange For
Sept. 6, 1962	NY N	—	PIT N	Waiver price
May 8, 1963	MIL N	—	NY N	Chico Fernandez

Ray Fosse

Date	Traded To	Traded With	Traded By	In Exchange For
Mar. 24, 1973	OAK A	Jack Heidemann	CLE A	George Hendrick Dave Duncan
Dec. 9, 1975	CLE A	—	OAK A	Cash
Sept. 9, 1977	SEA A	—	CLE A	Bill Laxton Cash

Alan Foster

Date	Traded To	Traded With	Traded By	In Exchange For
Dec. 11, 1970	CLE A	Ray Lamb	LA N	Duke Sims
Oct. 5, 1971	CAL A	—	CLE A	*see Alex Johnson*
Apr. 5, 1973	STL N	—	CAL A	Cash
Nov. 18, 1974	SD N	Rich Folkers Sonny Siebert	STL N	Ed Brinkman Danny Breeden

(Part of three-team trade involving San Diego, Detroit, and St. Louis Cardinals.)

Eddie Foster

Date	Traded To	Traded With	Traded By	In Exchange For
Jan. 20, 1920	BOS A	Mike Menosky Harry Harper	WAS A	Braggo Roth Red Shannon
Aug. 15, 1922	STL A	—	BOS A	Waiver price

George Foster

Date	Traded To	Traded With	Traded By	In Exchange For
May 29, 1971	CIN N	—	SF N	Frank Duffy Vern Geishert
Feb. 10, 1982	NY N	—	CIN N	Alex Trevino Jim Kern Greg Harris

Kevin Foster

Date	Traded To	Traded With	Traded By	In Exchange For
Nov. 20, 1992	SEA A	Dave Wainhouse	MON N	Frank Bolick Player to be named

(Montreal received C Miah Bradbury on December 8, 1992.)

Date	Traded To	Traded With	Traded By	In Exchange For
June 12, 1993	PHI N	—	SEA A	Bob Ayrault
Apr. 12, 1994	CHI N	—	PHI N	Shawn Boskie

Leo Foster

Date	Traded To	Traded With	Traded By	In Exchange For
Mar. 29, 1978	BOS A	—	NY N	Jim Burton

Pop Foster

Date	Traded To	Traded With	Traded By	In Exchange For
Sept. 4, 1901	CHI A	—	WAS A	Cash

Roy Foster

Date	Traded To	Traded With	Traded By	In Exchange For
Apr. 4, 1970	CLE A	Frank Coggins Cash	MIL A	Max Alvis Russ Snyder
Dec. 2, 1971	TEX A	—	CLE A	*see Del Unser*
Apr. 3, 1972	CLE A	Tom McCraw	TEX A	Ted Ford

Rube Foster

Date	Traded To	Traded With	Traded By	In Exchange For
Apr. 1918	CIN N	—	BOS A	Dave Shean

(Foster refused to report to Cincinnati; Cincinnati received cash instead.)

Steve Foster

Date	Traded To	Traded With	Traded By	In Exchange For
Oct. 11, 1994	SF N	—	CIN N	Waiver price

Bob Fothergill

Date	Traded To	Traded With	Traded By	In Exchange For
July 18, 1930	CHI A	—	DET A	Waiver price
Dec. 15, 1932	BOS A	Johnny Hodapp Greg Mulleavy Bob Seeds	CHI A	Ed Durham Hal Rhyne

Steve Foucault

Date	Traded To	Traded With	Traded By	In Exchange For
Apr. 12, 1977	DET A	—	TEX A	Willie Horton
Aug. 16, 1978	KC A	—	DET A	Cash

Jack Fournier

Date	Traded To	Traded With	Traded By	In Exchange For
May 8, 1912	CHI A	—	BOS A	Cash
Feb. 15, 1923	BKN N	—	STL N	Hy Myers Ray Schmandt
Nov. 5, 1926	BOS N	—	BKN N	Cash

Howie Fox

Date	Traded To	Traded With	Traded By	In Exchange For
Dec. 10, 1951	PHI N	*see Smoky Burgess*	CIN N	—

Nellie Fox

Date	Traded To	Traded With	Traded By	In Exchange For
Oct. 19, 1949	CHI A	—	PHI A	Joe Tipton
Dec. 10, 1963	HOU N	—	CHI A	Jim Golden Danny Murphy Cash

Paddy Fox

Date	Traded To	Traded With	Traded By	In Exchange For
Jan. 1900	LOU N	—	PIT N	*see Honus Wagner*

Pete Fox

Date	Traded To	Traded With	Traded By	In Exchange For
Dec. 12, 1940	BOS A	—	DET A	Cash

Terry Fox

Date	Traded To	Traded With	Traded By	In Exchange For
Dec. 7, 1960	DET A	*see Bill Bruton*	MIL N	—
May 10, 1966	PHI N	—	DET A	Cash

Bill Foxen

Date	Traded To	Traded With	Traded By	In Exchange For
July 1910	CHI N	—	PHI N	Fred Luderus

Jimmie Foxx

Date	Traded To	Traded With	Traded By	In Exchange For
Dec. 10, 1935	BOS A	Johnny Marcum	PHI A	Gordon Rhodes minor league C George Savino $150,000.
June 1, 1942	CHI N	—	BOS A	Waiver price

Joe Foy

Date	Traded To	Traded With	Traded By	In Exchange For
Dec. 3, 1969	NY N	—	KC A	Amos Otis Bob Johnson

Paul Foytack

Date	Traded To	Traded With	Traded By	In Exchange For
June 15, 1963	LA A	Frank Kostro	DET A	George Thomas Cash

Ken Frailing

Date	Traded To	Traded With	Traded By	In Exchange For
Dec. 11, 1973	CHI N	Steve Stone Steve Swisher Jim Kremmel	CHI A	Ron Santo

Ray Francis

Date	Traded To	Traded With	Traded By	In Exchange For
Nov. 24, 1922	DET A	—	WAS A	Chick Gagnon
May 5, 1925	BOS A	$9,000.	NY A	Bobby Veach Alex Ferguson

John Franco

Date	Traded To	Traded With	Traded By	In Exchange For
May 9, 1983	CIN N	minor league P Brett Wise	LA N	Rafael Landestoy
Dec. 6, 1989	NY N	Minor league OF Don Brown	CIN N	Randy Myers Kip Gross

Julio Franco

Date	Traded To	Traded With	Traded By	In Exchange For
Dec. 9, 1982	CLE A	Manny Trillo Jay Baller George Vukovich Jerry Willard	PHI N	Von Hayes
Dec. 6, 1988	TEX A	—	CLE A	Pete O'Brien Oddibe McDowell Jerry Browne
Dec. 15, 1993	CHI A	—	TEX A	No compensation (free agent signing)

Terry Francona

Date	Traded To	Traded With	Traded By	In Exchange For
Mar. 23, 1987	CIN N	—	CHI N	No compensation (free agent signing)

Tito Francona

Date	Traded To	Traded With	Traded By	In Exchange For
Dec. 3, 1957	CHI A	Ray Moore Billy Goodman	BAL A	Jack Harshman Larry Doby Russ Heman Jim Marshall
June 15, 1958	DET A	Bill Fischer	CHI A	Ray Boone Bob Shaw
Mar. 21, 1959	CLE A	—	DET A	Larry Doby
Dec. 15, 1964	STL N	—	CLE A	Cash
Apr. 10, 1967	PHI N	—	STL N	Cash
June 12, 1967	ATL N	—	PHI N	Cash
Aug. 22, 1969	OAK A	—	ATL N	Cash
June 11, 1970	MIL A	Al Downing	OAK A	Steve Hovley

Fred Frankhouse

Date	Traded To	Traded With	Traded By	In Exchange For
June 16, 1930	BOS N	Bill Sherdel	STL N	Burleigh Grimes
Feb. 6, 1936	BKN N	—	BOS N	Johnny Babich Gene Moore
Dec. 13, 1938	BOS N	—	BKN N	Joe Stripp

Herman Franks

Date	Traded To	Traded With	Traded By	In Exchange For
Feb. 6, 1940	BKN N	—	STL N	Cash

Chick Fraser

Date	Traded To	Traded With	Traded By	In Exchange For
Dec. 20, 1904	BOS N	Harry Wolverton	PHI N	Togie Pittinger
Mar. 1906	CIN N	Jim Delahanty	BOS N	Al Bridwell
Oct. 1906	CIN N	—	CHI N	Jack Harper

Willie Fraser

Date	Traded To	Traded With	Traded By	In Exchange For
Dec. 2, 1990	TOR A	*see Devon White*	CAL A	—
June 26, 1991	STL N	—	TOR A	Waiver price

Vic Frasier

Date	Traded To	Traded With	Traded By	In Exchange For
June 2, 1933	DET A	—	CHI A	Whit Wyatt

George Frazier

Date	Traded To	Traded With	Traded By	In Exchange For
Dec. 8, 1977	STL N	—	MIL A	Buck Martinez
June 7, 1981	NY A	—	STL N	Cash
Feb. 5, 1984	CLE A	Otis Nixon Minor league P Guy Elston	NY A	Toby Harrah Minor league P Rick Browne
June 13, 1984	CHI N	Rick Sutcliffe Ron Hassey	CLE A	Mel Hall Joe Carter Don Schulze Minor league P Darryl Banks
Aug. 13, 1986	MIN A	Ray Fontenot Minor league SS Julius McDougal	CHI N	Ron Davis Minor league P Dewayne Coleman

Joe Frazier

Date	Traded To	Traded With	Traded By	In Exchange For
Nov. 20, 1947	STL A	Dick Kokos Bryan Stephens $25,000.	CLE A	Bob Muncrief Walt Judnich
May 16, 1956	CIN N	Alex Grammas	STL N	Chuck Harmon
June 26, 1956	BAL A	—	CIN N	Cash

Lou Frazier

Date	Traded To	Traded With	Traded By	In Exchange For
July 30, 1995	TEX A	—	MON N	Hector Fajardo

(Montreal received Fajardo on August 5, 1995.)

Roger Freed

Date	Traded To	Traded With	Traded By	In Exchange For
Dec. 16, 1970	PHI N	—	BAL A	Grant Jackson Jim Hutto Sam Parrilla
Nov. 30, 1972	CLE A	Oscar Gamble	PHI N	Del Unser minor league IF Terry Wedgewood

Roger Freed *continued*

Date	Traded To	Traded With	Traded By	In Exchange For
Dec. 12, 1973	CIN N	—	CLE A	Steve Blateric

Hersh Freeman

Date	Traded To	Traded With	Traded By	In Exchange For
May 10, 1955	CIN N	—	BOS A	Cash
May 8, 1958	CHI N	—	CIN N	Turk Lown

Jimmy Freeman

Date	Traded To	Traded With	Traded By	In Exchange For
Apr. 17, 1975	BAL A	$75,000.	ATL N	Earl Williams
June 15, 1976	NY A	—	BAL A	*see Tippy Martinez*

LaVel Freeman

Date	Traded To	Traded With	Traded By	In Exchange For
June 29, 1989	TEX A	Minor league P Todd Simmons	MIL A	Scott May Minor league OF Mike Wilson

Mark Freeman

Date	Traded To	Traded With	Traded By	In Exchange For
Apr. 8, 1959	KC A	—	NY A	Jack Urban
	(Freeman was returned to the Yankees on May 8, 1959.)			
May 19, 1960	CHI N	—	NY A	Art Ceccarelli minor league IF Ray Bellino and $20,000.

Marvin Freeman

Date	Traded To	Traded With	Traded By	In Exchange For
July 23, 1990	ATL N	—	PHI N	Joe Boever

Gene Freese

Date	Traded To	Traded With	Traded By	In Exchange For
June 15, 1958	STL N	Johnny O'Brien	PIT N	Dick Schofield Cash
Sept. 29, 1958	PHI N	—	STL N	Solly Hemus
	(Hemus was named St. Louis manager.)			
Dec. 9, 1959	CHI A	—	PHI N	Johnny Callison
Dec. 15, 1960	CIN N	—	CHI A	Juan Pizarro Cal McLish
Nov. 26, 1963	PIT N	—	CIN N	Cash
Aug. 25, 1965	CHI A	—	PIT N	Cash
July 20, 1966	HOU N	—	CHI A	Jim Mahoney Cash

George Freese

Date	Traded To	Traded With	Traded By	In Exchange For
Apr. 7, 1953	DET A	—	STL A	Cash
June 4, 1953	PIT N	—	CHI N	*see Ralph Kiner*

Jim Fregosi

Date	Traded To	Traded With	Traded By	In Exchange For
Dec. 10, 1971	NY N	—	CAL A	Nolan Ryan Francisco Estrada Don Rose Leroy Stanton
July 11, 1973	TEX A	—	NY N	Cash
June 15, 1977	PIT N	—	TEX A	Ed Kirkpatrick

Howard Freigau

Date	Traded To	Traded With	Traded By	In Exchange For
May 23, 1925	CHI N	Mike Gonzalez	STL N	Bob O'Farrell
Dec. 1927	BKN N	—	CHI N	Johnny Butler
June 23, 1928	BOS N	—	BKN N	Cash

Dave Freisleben

Date	Traded To	Traded With	Traded By	In Exchange For
June 22, 1978	CLE A	—	SD N	Bill Laxton
Nov. 3, 1978	TOR A	—	CLE A	Sheldon Mallory

Tony Freitas

Date	Traded To	Traded With	Traded By	In Exchange For
Dec. 1933	CIN N	—	PHI A	Cash

Charlie French

Date	Traded To	Traded With	Traded By	In Exchange For
May 1910	CHI A	—	BOS A	Cash

Larry French

Date	Traded To	Traded With	Traded By	In Exchange For
Nov. 22, 1934	CHI N	Freddie Lindstrom	PIT N	Guy Bush Jim Weaver Babe Herman
Aug. 20, 1941	BKN N	—	CHI N	Waiver price

Benny Frey

Date	Traded To	Traded With	Traded By	In Exchange For
Apr. 11, 1932	STL N	Harvey Hendrick Cash	CIN N	Chick Hafey
May 10, 1932	CIN N	—	STL N	Cash

Lonny Frey

Date	Traded To	Traded With	Traded By	In Exchange For
Dec. 5, 1936	CHI N	—	BKN N	Roy Henshaw Woody English
Feb. 4, 1938	CIN N	—	CHI N	Cash
Apr. 16, 1947	CHI N	—	CIN N	Cash
June 25, 1947	NY A	—	CHI N	Cash

Steve Frey

Date	Traded To	Traded With	Traded By	In Exchange For
Dec. 11, 1987	NY N	Phil Lombardi Darren Reed	NY A	Rafael Santana Minor league P Victor Garcia
Mar. 28, 1989	MON N	—	NY N	Tom O'Malley Mark Bailey
Mar. 29, 1992	CAL A	—	MON N	Cash
Jan. 5, 1994	SF N	—	CAL A	No compensation (free agent signing)
May 20, 1995	SEA A	—	SF N	Future considerations

Pepe Frias

Date	Traded To	Traded With	Traded By	In Exchange For
Mar. 31, 1979	ATL N	—	MON N	Dave Campbell
Dec. 6, 1979	TEX A	Adrian Devine	ATL N	Doyle Alexander Larvell Blanks $50,000.
Sept. 13, 1980	LA N	—	TEX A	Dennis Lewallyn

Barney Friberg

Date	Traded To	Traded With	Traded By	In Exchange For
June 15, 1925	PHI N	—	CHI N	Waiver price
Jan. 7, 1932	BOS A	—	PHI N	Waiver price
Jan. 7, 1933	BOS A	—	PHI N	Waiver price

Jim Fridley

Date	Traded To	Traded With	Traded By	In Exchange For
Apr. 6, 1953	STL A	—	CLE A	Waiver price
Dec. 1, 1954	NY A	*see Dick Kryhoski*	BAL A	—

Bob Friend

Date	Traded To	Traded With	Traded By	In Exchange For
Dec. 10, 1965	NY A	—	PIT N	Pete Mikkelsen Cash
June 15, 1966	NY N	—	NY A	Cash

Owen Friend

Date	Traded To	Traded With	Traded By	In Exchange For
Dec. 4, 1952	DET A	—	STL A	*see Virgil Trucks*
June 15, 1953	CLE A	—	DET A	*see Ray Boone*

John Frill

Date	Traded To	Traded With	Traded By	In Exchange For
Jan. 1912	CIN N	—	STL A	Waiver price

Charlie Frisbee

Date	Traded To	Traded With	Traded By	In Exchange For
Feb. 17, 1900	NY N	—	BOS N	Cash

Frankie Frisch

Date	Traded To	Traded With	Traded By	In Exchange For
Dec. 20, 1926	STL N	Jimmy Ring	NY N	Rogers Hornsby

Danny Frisella

Date	Traded To	Traded With	Traded By	In Exchange For
Nov. 2, 1972	ATL N	Gary Gentry	NY N	Felix Millan George Stone
Nov. 8, 1974	SD N	—	ATL N	Cito Gaston
Apr. 8, 1976	STL N	—	SD N	Ken Reynolds minor leaguer Bob Stewart
June 7, 1976	MIL A	—	STL N	Sam Mejias

Sam Frock

Date	Traded To	Traded With	Traded By	In Exchange For
June 1, 1910	BOS N	—	PIT N	Kirby White

Art Fromme

Date	Traded To	Traded With	Traded By	In Exchange For
Dec. 12, 1908	CIN N	Ed Karger	STL N	Admiral Schlei
May 22, 1913	NY N	Eddie Grant	CIN N	Red Ames Heinie Groh Josh Devore $20,000.

Dave Frost

Date	Traded To	Traded With	Traded By	In Exchange For
Dec. 5, 1977	CAL A	*see Brian Downing*	CHI A	—
Feb. 3, 1982	KC A	—	CAL A	No compensation (free agent signing)

Woodie Fryman

Date	Traded To	Traded With	Traded By	In Exchange For
Dec. 15, 1967	PHI N	Don Money Bill Laxton minor league P Hal Clem	PIT N	Jim Bunning
Aug. 2, 1972	DET A	—	PHI N	Cash
Dec. 4, 1974	MON N	—	DET A	Tom Walker Terry Humphrey
Dec. 16, 1976	CIN N	Dale Murray	MON N	Tony Perez Will McEnaney
Oct. 31, 1977	CHI N	Bill Caudill	CIN N	Bill Bonham
June 9, 1978	MON N	—	CHI N	Jerry White

Tito Fuentes

Date	Traded To	Traded With	Traded By	In Exchange For
Dec. 6, 1974	SD N	Butch Metzger	SF N	Derrel Thomas
Feb. 23, 1977	DET A	—	SD N	No compensation (free agent signing)
Jan. 30, 1978	MON N	—	DET A	Cash

Chick Fullis

Date	Traded To	Traded With	Traded By	In Exchange For
Dec. 12, 1932	PHI N	Gus Dugas	NY N	Kiddo Davis

(Part of three-team trade involving New York, Philadelphia, and Pittsburgh.)

Date	Traded To	Traded With	Traded By	In Exchange For
June 15, 1934	STL N	—	PHI N	Kiddo Davis

Dave Fultz

Date	Traded To	Traded With	Traded By	In Exchange For
Mar. 1903	NY A	—	PHI A	Cash

Frank Funk

Date	Traded To	Traded With	Traded By	In Exchange For
Nov. 27, 1962	MIL N	Ty Cline Don Dillard	CLE A	Joe Adcock Jack Curtis

Fred Fussell

Date	Traded To	Traded With	Traded By	In Exchange For
Dec. 1927	PIT N	—	CHI N	Mike Cvengros

Frank Gabler

Date	Traded To	Traded With	Traded By	In Exchange For
June 15, 1937	BOS N	$35,000.	NY N	Wally Berger
May 2, 1938	CHI A	—	BOS N	Cash

Len Gabrielson

Date	Traded To	Traded With	Traded By	In Exchange For
June 3, 1964	CHI N	—	MIL N	Merritt Ranew $40,000.
May 29, 1965	SF N	Dick Bertell	CHI N	Harvey Kuenn Ed Bailey Bob Hendley
Dec. 14, 1966	CAL A	—	SF N	Norm Siebern
May 10, 1967	LA N	—	CAL A	Johnny Werhas

Gary Gaetti

Date	Traded To	Traded With	Traded By	In Exchange For
Jan. 23, 1991	CAL A	—	MIN A	No compensation (free agent signing)
Dec. 18, 1995	STL N	—	KC A	No compensation (free agent signing)

Phil Gagliano

Date	Traded To	Traded With	Traded By	In Exchange For
May 29, 1970	CHI N	—	STL N	Ted Abernathy
Dec. 3, 1970	BOS A	—	CHI N	Carmen Fanzone
Mar. 27, 1973	CIN N	Andy Kosco	BOS A	Mel Behney

Greg Gagne

Date	Traded To	Traded With	Traded By	In Exchange For
Apr. 10, 1982	MIN A	Ron Davis Paul Boris	NY A	Roy Smalley

Greg Gagne *continued*

Date	Traded To	Traded With	Traded By	In Exchange For
Dec. 8, 1992	KC A	—	MIN A	No compensation (free agent signing)
Nov. 30, 1995	LA N	—	KC A	No compensation (free agent signing)

Ed Gagnier

Date	Traded To	Traded With	Traded By	In Exchange For
July 1915	BUF F	Ed Lafitte	BKN F	Fred Smith

Chick Gagnon

Date	Traded To	Traded With	Traded By	In Exchange For
Nov. 24, 1922	WAS A	—	DET A	Ray Francis

Del Gainer

Date	Traded To	Traded With	Traded By	In Exchange For
June 2, 1911	BOS A	—	DET A	Waiver price
June 2, 1914	BOS A	—	DET A	Waiver price

Jay Gainer

Date	Traded To	Traded With	Traded By	In Exchange For
Mar. 21, 1993	CLR N	—	SD N	Denis Boucher

Joe Gaines

Date	Traded To	Traded With	Traded By	In Exchange For
Dec. 15, 1962	BAL A	—	CIN N	Dick Luebke minor league IF Willard Oplinger
June 15, 1964	HOU N	—	BAL A	Johnny Weekly Cash

Dan Gakeler

Date	Traded To	Traded With	Traded By	In Exchange For
Dec. 8, 1988	MON N	*see Spike Owen*	BOS A	—

Augie Galan

Date	Traded To	Traded With	Traded By	In Exchange For
Dec. 4, 1946	CIN N	—	BKN N	Ed Heusser

Andres Galarraga

Date	Traded To	Traded With	Traded By	In Exchange For
Nov. 25, 1991	STL N	—	MON N	Ken Hill
Nov. 16, 1992	CLR N	—	STL N	No compensation (free agent signing)

Rich Gale

Date	Traded To	Traded With	Traded By	In Exchange For
Dec. 11, 1981	SF N	Bill Laskey	KC A	Jerry Martin
Jan. 5, 1983	CIN N	—	SF N	Mike Vail

Denny Galehouse

Date	Traded To	Traded With	Traded By	In Exchange For
Dec. 15, 1938	BOS A	Tommy Irwin	CLE A	Ben Chapman
Dec. 3, 1940	STL A	—	BOS A	Cash
June 20, 1947	BOS A	—	STL A	Cash

Alan Gallagher

Date	Traded To	Traded With	Traded By	In Exchange For
Apr. 14, 1973	CAL A	—	SF N	Bruce Miller

Bob Gallagher

Date	Traded To	Traded With	Traded By	In Exchange For
Oct. 29, 1974	NY N	—	HOU N	Ken Boswell

Dave Gallagher

Date	Traded To	Traded With	Traded By	In Exchange For
May 12, 1987	SEA A	—	CLE A	Mark Huismann
Aug. 1, 1990	BAL A	—	CHI A	Waiver price
Dec. 4, 1990	CAL A	—	BAL A	Minor league Ps David Martinez and Mike Hook
Dec. 10, 1991	NY N	—	CAL A	Hubie Brooks
Nov. 24, 1993	ATL N	—	NY N	Pete Smith
Aug. 8, 1995	CAL A	—	PHI N	Russ Springer Kevin Flora

(Philadelphia received Springer on August 15, 1995.)

Joe Gallagher

Date	Traded To	Traded With	Traded By	In Exchange For
June 13, 1939	STL A	—	NY A	Roy Hughes Cash
May 27, 1940	BKN N	—	STL A	Roy Cullenbine

Mike Gallego

Date	Traded To	Traded With	Traded By	In Exchange For
Jan. 7, 1992	NY A	—	OAK A	No compensation (free agent signing)

Bert Gallia

Date	Traded To	Traded With	Traded By	In Exchange For
Dec. 15, 1917	STL A	$15,000.	WAS A	Burt Shotton Doc Lavan
Apr. 1920	PHI N	—	STL A	Cash

Chick Galloway

Date	Traded To	Traded With	Traded By	In Exchange For
Dec. 2, 1927	STL A	—	PHI A	Cash
Dec. 2, 1927	DET A	Elam Vangilder Harry Rice	STL A	Heinie Manush Lu Blue

Balvino Galvez

Date	Traded To	Traded With	Traded By	In Exchange For
May 5, 1987	LA N	—	DET A	Orlando Mercado
Mar. 24, 1988	MIN A	—	DET A	Billy Beane
Mar. 20, 1989	NY A	—	MIN A	Steve Shields

Oscar Gamble

Date	Traded To	Traded With	Traded By	In Exchange For
Nov. 17, 1969	PHI N	Dick Selma	CHI N	Johnny Callison
Nov. 30, 1972	CLE A	Roger Freed	PHI N	Del Unser minor league IF Terry Wedgewood
Nov. 22, 1975	NY A	—	CLE A	Pat Dobson
Apr. 5, 1977	CHI A	LaMarr Hoyt minor league P Bob Polinsky $200,000.	NY A	Bucky Dent
Nov. 29, 1977	SD N	—	CHI A	No compensation (free agent signing)
Oct. 25, 1978	TEX A	Dave Roberts $300,000.	SD N	Mike Hargrove Kurt Bevacqua Bill Fahey
Aug. 1, 1979	NY A	Ray Fontenot Gene Nelson minor league 3B Amos Lewis	TEX A	Mickey Rivers minor league Ps Bob Polinsky Neil Mersch and Mark Softy
Mar. 23, 1985	CHI A	—	NY A	No compensation (free agent signing)

Chick Gandil

Date	Traded To	Traded With	Traded By	In Exchange For
Feb. 15, 1916	CLE A	—	WAS A	$7,500.
Feb. 25, 1917	CHI A	—	CLE A	$3,500.

Bob Ganley

Date	Traded To	Traded With	Traded By	In Exchange For
Feb. 1907	WAS A	—	PIT N	Cash
May 1909	PHI A	—	WAS A	Cash

Ron Gant

Date	Traded To	Traded With	Traded By	In Exchange For
Dec. 23, 1995	STL N	—	CIN N	No compensation (free agent signing)

John Ganzel

Date	Traded To	Traded With	Traded By	In Exchange For
Feb. 1901	NY N	—	CHI N	Cash

Joe Garagiola

Date	Traded To	Traded With	Traded By	In Exchange For
June 15, 1951	PIT N	Bill Howerton Howie Pollet Ted Wilks Dick Cole	STL N	Cliff Chambers Wally Westlake
June 4, 1953	CHI N	Ralph Kiner Howie Pollet Catfish Metkovich	PIT N	Toby Atwell Bob Schultz Preston Ward George Freese Bob Addis Gene Hermanski $150,000.
Sept. 8, 1954	NY N	—	CHI N	Waiver price

Gene Garber

Date	Traded To	Traded With	Traded By	In Exchange For
Oct. 25, 1972	KC A	—	PIT N	Jim Rooker
June 15, 1978	ATL N	—	PHI N	Dick Ruthven
Aug. 31, 1987	KC A	—	ATL N	Terry Bell

(Atlanta received Bell on September 3, 1987.)

Barbaro Garbey

Date	Traded To	Traded With	Traded By	In Exchange For
Nov. 13, 1985	OAK A	—	DET A	Dave Collins

Rich Garces

Date	Traded To	Traded With	Traded By	In Exchange For
Aug. 9, 1995	FLA N	—	CHI N	Waiver price

Damaso Garcia

Date	Traded To	Traded With	Traded By	In Exchange For
Nov. 1, 1979	TOR A	Chris Chambliss Paul Mirabella	NY A	Tom Underwood Rick Cerone Ted Wilborn
Feb. 2, 1987	ATL N	Luis Leal	TOR A	Craig McMurtry
Dec. 22, 1989	NY A	—	MON N	No compensation (free agent signing)

Kiko Garcia

Date	Traded To	Traded With	Traded By	In Exchange For
Apr. 1, 1981	HOU N	—	BAL A	Chris Bourjos Cash

Leo Garcia

Date	Traded To	Traded With	Traded By	In Exchange For
Aug. 23, 1982	CIN N	—	CHI A	*see Jim Kern*

Miguel Garcia

Date	Traded To	Traded With	Traded By	In Exchange For
Aug. 29, 1987	PIT N	Minor league IF Bill Merrifield	CAL A	Johnny Ray

Pedro Garcia

Date	Traded To	Traded With	Traded By	In Exchange For
June 10, 1976	DET A	—	MIL A	Gary Sutherland

Ron Gardenhire

Date	Traded To	Traded With	Traded By	In Exchange For
Nov. 12, 1986	MIN A	—	NY N	Minor league P Dom Iasparro

Mike Gardiner

Date	Traded To	Traded With	Traded By	In Exchange For
Apr. 1, 1991	BOS A	—	SEA A	Rob Murphy
Dec. 8, 1992	MON N	Minor league P Terry Powers	BOS A	Ivan Calderon

Billy Gardner

Date	Traded To	Traded With	Traded By	In Exchange For
Apr. 21, 1956	BAL A	—	NY N	$20,000.
Apr. 3, 1960	WAS A	—	BAL A	Clint Courtney Ron Samford
June 14, 1961	NY A	—	MIN A	Danny McDevitt
June 12, 1962	BOS A	—	NY A	Tommy Umphlett Cash

Jeff Gardner

Date	Traded To	Traded With	Traded By	In Exchange For
Dec. 11, 1991	SD N	—	NY N	Steve Rosenberg

Larry Gardner

Date	Traded To	Traded With	Traded By	In Exchange For
Jan. 10, 1918	PHI A	Hick Cady Tilly Walker	BOS A	Stuffy McInnis
Mar. 1, 1919	CLE A	Elmer Myers Charlie Jamieson	PHI A	Braggo Roth

Mark Gardner

Date	Traded To	Traded With	Traded By	In Exchange For
Dec. 9, 1992	KC A	Doug Piatt	MON N	Tim Spehr Jeff Shaw

Rob Gardner

Date	Traded To	Traded With	Traded By	In Exchange For
June 12, 1967	CHI N	Johnny Stephenson	NY N	Bob Hendley
Mar. 30, 1968	CLE A	—	CHI N	Bobby Tiefenauer
Apr. 9, 1971	OAK A	Ron Klimkowski	NY A	Felipe Alou
May 26, 1971	NY A	—	OAK A	Curt Blefary
Nov. 24, 1972	OAK A	Rich McKinney	NY A	Matty Alou
May 31, 1973	MIL A	—	OAK A	Cash

(Deal was cancelled and Gardner was returned to Oakland on July 16.)

Wes Gardner

Date	Traded To	Traded With	Traded By	In Exchange For
Nov. 13, 1985	BOS A	Calvin Schiraldi John Christensen LaSchelle Tarver	NY N	Bob Ojeda John Mitchell Tom McCarthy Minor league P Chris Bayer
Dec. 15, 1990	SD N	—	BOS A	Minor league 1B-OF Steve Hendricks Minor league P Brad Hoyer

Wayne Garland

Date	Traded To	Traded With	Traded By	In Exchange For
Nov. 19, 1976	CLE A	—	BAL A	No compensation (free agent signing)

Mike Garman

Date	Traded To	Traded With	Traded By	In Exchange For
Dec. 7, 1973	STL N	Lynn McGlothen John Curtis	BOS A	Reggie Cleveland Diego Segui Terry Hughes
Oct. 28, 1975	CHI N	minor league IF Bobby Hrapmann	STL N	Don Kessinger
Jan. 11, 1977	LA N	Rick Monday	CHI N	Bill Buckner Ivan DeJesus minor league P Jeff Albert
May 20, 1978	MON N	—	LA N	Larry Landreth Gerald Hannahs

Debs Garms

Date	Traded To	Traded With	Traded By	In Exchange For
Mar. 3, 1940	PIT N	—	BOS N	Cash

Phil Garner

Date	Traded To	Traded With	Traded By	In Exchange For
Mar. 15, 1977	PIT N	Tommy Helms Chris Batton	OAK A	Dave Giusti Tony Armas Doc Medich Doug Bair Rick Langford Mitchell Page
Aug. 31, 1981	HOU N	—	PIT N	Johnny Ray minor league OF Kevin Houston Randy Niemann
June 19, 1987	LA N	—	HOU N	Minor league P Jeff Edwards
		(Houston received Edwards on June 26, 1987.)		
Jan. 28, 1988	SF N	—	LA N	No compensation (free agent signing)

Ralph Garr

Date	Traded To	Traded With	Traded By	In Exchange For
Dec. 12, 1975	CHI A	Larvell Blanks	ATL N	Ken Henderson Dick Ruthven Danny Osborn
Sept. 20, 1979	CAL A	—	CHI A	Cash

Adrian Garrett

Date	Traded To	Traded With	Traded By	In Exchange For
May 8, 1964	MIL N	Jay Hook	NY N	Roy McMillan
Aug. 31, 1971	OAK A	—	CHI N	Frank Fernandez Bill McNulty
July 31, 1975	CAL A	—	CHI N	Cash

Greg Garrett

Date	Traded To	Traded With	Traded By	In Exchange For
Dec. 15, 1970	CIN N	—	CAL A	Jim Maloney

Wayne Garrett

Date	Traded To	Traded With	Traded By	In Exchange For
July 21, 1976	MON N	Del Unser	NY N	Jim Dwyer Pepe Mangual
July 21, 1978	STL N	—	MON N	Cash

Gil Garrido

Date	Traded To	Traded With	Traded By	In Exchange For
May 16, 1966	ATL N	—	SF N	Cash
Dec. 4, 1973	PHI N	—	ATL N	Bob Beall

Ford Garrison

Date	Traded To	Traded With	Traded By	In Exchange For
May 7, 1944	PHI A	—	BOS A	Hal Wagner

Ned Garver

Date	Traded To	Traded With	Traded By	In Exchange For
Aug. 14, 1952	DET A	Jim Delsing Dave Madison Bill Black	STL A	Dick Littlefield Marlin Stuart Don Lenhardt Vic Wertz
Dec. 5, 1956	KC A	Gene Host Virgil Trucks Wayne Belardi $20,000.	DET A	Jim Finigan Jack Crimian Bill Harrington Eddie Robinson

Steve Garvey

Date	Traded To	Traded With	Traded By	In Exchange For
Dec. 21, 1982	SD N	—	LA N	No compensation (free agent signing)

Jerry Garvin

Date	Traded To	Traded With	Traded By	In Exchange For
Jan. 18, 1983	STL N	—	TOR A	Cash

Ned Garvin

Date	Traded To	Traded With	Traded By	In Exchange For
Sept. 1904	NY A	—	BKN N	Waiver price

Rod Gaspar

Date	Traded To	Traded With	Traded By	In Exchange For
Sept. 1, 1970	SD N	—	NY N	Ron Herbel
		(San Diego received Gaspar on October 20.)		

Cito Gaston

Date	Traded To	Traded With	Traded By	In Exchange For
Nov. 8, 1974	ATL N	—	SD N	Danny Frisella
Sept. 22, 1978	PIT N	—	ATL N	Cash

Milt Gaston

Date	Traded To	Traded With	Traded By	In Exchange For
Dec. 17, 1924	STL A	Joe Bush Joe Giard	NY A	Urban Shocker
Oct. 19, 1927	WAS A	—	STL A	Dick Coffman Earl McNeely
Dec. 15, 1928	BOS A	Elliott Bigelow Hod Lisenbee Bobby Reeves Grant Gillis	WAS A	Buddy Myer
Dec. 2, 1931	CHI A	—	BOS A	Bob Weiland

Doc Gautreau

Date	Traded To	Traded With	Traded By	In Exchange For
July 1, 1925	BOS N	—	PHI A	Cash

Dinty Gearin

Date	Traded To	Traded With	Traded By	In Exchange For
June 5, 1924	BOS N	—	NY N	Cash

Joe Gedeon

Date	Traded To	Traded With	Traded By	In Exchange For
Jan. 22, 1918	STL A	Les Nunamaker Fritz Maisel Nick Cullop Urban Shocker	NY A	Eddie Plank Del Pratt $15,000.

Rich Gedman

Date	Traded To	Traded With	Traded By	In Exchange For
June 8, 1990	HOU N	—	BOS A	Cash

Johnny Gee

Date	Traded To	Traded With	Traded By	In Exchange For
June 12, 1944	NY N	—	PIT N	Cash

Phil Geier

Date	Traded To	Traded With	Traded By	In Exchange For
June 1901	MIL A	—	PHI A	Tom Leahy

Gary Geiger

Date	Traded To	Traded With	Traded By	In Exchange For
Dec. 2, 1958	BOS A	Vic Wertz	CLE A	Jimmy Piersall

Dave Geisel

Date	Traded To	Traded With	Traded By	In Exchange For
Dec. 28, 1981	TOR A	—	CHI N	Paul Mirabella

Vern Geishert

Date	Traded To	Traded With	Traded By	In Exchange For
Nov. 25, 1969	CIN N	Pedro Borbon Jim McGlothlin	CAL A	Alex Johnson Chico Ruiz
May 29, 1971	SF N	Frank Duffy	CIN N	George Foster

Charley Gelbert

Date	Traded To		Traded With	Traded By		In Exchange For
Dec. 2, 1936	CIN	N	—	STL	N	Cash
July 9, 1937	DET	A	—	CIN	N	Waiver price
Aug. 30, 1940	BOS	A	—	WAS	A	Waiver price

John Gelnar

Date	Traded To		Traded With	Traded By		In Exchange For
Oct. 18, 1968	KC	A	—	PIT	N	Cash
Apr. 1, 1969	SEA	A	Steve Whitaker	KC	A	Lou Piniella
May 11, 1971	DET	A	Jose Herrera	MIL	A	Jim Hannan

Joe Genewich

Date	Traded To		Traded With	Traded By		In Exchange For
June 15, 1928	NY	N	—	BOS	N	Ben Cantwell Virgil Barnes Al Spohrer Bill Clarkson

Jim Gentile

Date	Traded To		Traded With	Traded By		In Exchange For
Nov. 27, 1963	KC	A	Cash	BAL	A	Norm Siebern
June 4, 1965	HOU	N	—	KC	A	Jess Hickman Ernie Fazio $100,000.
			(Kansas City received Fazio on October 15.)			
July 19, 1966	CLE	A	—	HOU	N	Tony Curry

Gary Gentry

Date	Traded To		Traded With	Traded By		In Exchange For
Nov. 2, 1972	ATL	N	Danny Frisella	NY	N	Felix Millan George Stone

Lefty George

Date	Traded To		Traded With	Traded By		In Exchange For
Jan. 1912	CLE	A	—	STL	A	George Stovall

Dave Gerard

Date	Traded To		Traded With	Traded By		In Exchange For
Mar. 28, 1963	HOU	N	Danny Murphy	CHI	N	Merritt Ranew Hal Haydel Dick LeMay

Wally Gerber

Date	Traded To		Traded With	Traded By		In Exchange For
Apr. 25, 1928	BOS	A	—	STL	A	Hal Wiltse

Bob Geren

Date	Traded To		Traded With	Traded By		In Exchange For
Dec. 8, 1980	STL	N	*see Rollie Fingers*	SD	N	—
Dec. 2, 1991	CIN	N	—	NY	A	Waiver price

Ken Gerhart

Date	Traded To		Traded With	Traded By		In Exchange For
Mar. 24, 1989	SF	N	—	BAL	A	Francisco Melendez

Al Gerheauser

Date	Traded To		Traded With	Traded By		In Exchange For
Jan. 22, 1943	PHI	N	Tom Padden Ed Levy Al Gettel $10,000.	NY	A	Nick Etten
Mar. 31, 1945	PIT	N	—	PHI	N	Vince DiMaggio
Dec. 5, 1946	BKN	N	—	PIT	N	Eddie Basinski

Dick Gernert

Date	Traded To		Traded With	Traded By		In Exchange For
Nov. 21, 1959	CHI	N	—	BOS	A	Dave Hillman Jim Marshall
Aug. 31, 1960	DET	A	—	CHI	N	Cash
May 10, 1961	CIN	N	—	DET	A	Jim Baumer

Cesar Geronimo

Date	Traded To		Traded With	Traded By		In Exchange For
Nov. 29, 1971	CIN	N	Joe Morgan Denis Menke Jack Billingham Ed Armbrister	HOU	N	Lee May Tommy Helms Jimmy Stewart
Jan. 21, 1981	KC	A	—	CIN	N	German Barranca

Doc Gessler

Date	Traded To		Traded With	Traded By		In Exchange For
May 8, 1906	CHI	N	—	BKN	N	Cash
Sept. 1909	WAS	A	—	BOS	A	Charlie Smith

Al Gettel

Date	Traded To		Traded With	Traded By		In Exchange For
Jan. 22, 1943	PHI	N	Tom Padden Al Gerheauser Ed Levy $10,000.	NY	A	Nick Etten
Dec. 20, 1946	CLE	A	Hal Peck Gene Bearden	NY	A	Sherm Lollar Ray Mack
June 2, 1948	CHI	A	Pat Seerey	CLE	A	Bob Kennedy
July 12, 1949	WAS	A	—	CHI	A	Cash

Gus Getz

Date	Traded To		Traded With	Traded By		In Exchange For
June 1918	PIT	N	—	CLE	A	Waiver price

Joe Giard

Date	Traded To		Traded With	Traded By		In Exchange For
Dec. 17, 1924	STL	A	Joe Bush Milt Gaston	NY	A	Urban Shocker
Feb. 8, 1927	NY	A	Cedric Durst	STL	A	Sad Sam Jones

Joe Gibbon

Date	Traded To		Traded With	Traded By		In Exchange For
Oct. 1, 1965	SF	N	Ozzie Virgil	PIT	N	Matty Alou
June 10, 1969	PIT	N	—	SF	N	Ron Kline

John Gibbons

Date	Traded To		Traded With	Traded By		In Exchange For
Apr. 1, 1988	LA	N	—	NY	N	Craig Shipley

Frank Gibson

Date	Traded To		Traded With	Traded By		In Exchange For
Dec. 15, 1927	STL	N	—	BOS	N	Cash

George Gibson

Date	Traded To		Traded With	Traded By		In Exchange For
Aug. 5, 1916	NY	N	—	PIT	N	Waiver price
Jan. 1917	NY	N	—	PIT	N	Waiver price

Kirk Gibson

Date	Traded To		Traded With	Traded By		In Exchange For
Jan. 29, 1988	LA	N	—	DET	A	No compensation (free agent signing)
Dec. 1, 1990	KC	A	—	LA	N	No compensation (free agent signing)
Mar. 10, 1992	PIT	N	—	KC	A	Neal Heaton

Paul Gibson

Date	Traded To		Traded With	Traded By		In Exchange For
Jan. 22, 1992	NY	N	Minor league P Randy Marshall	DET	A	Mark Carreon Tony Castillo
Sept. 1, 1994	MIL	A	—	NY	A	Player to be named

Russ Gibson

Date	Traded To		Traded With	Traded By		In Exchange For
Apr. 4, 1970	SF	N	—	BOS	A	Cash

Brett Gideon

Date	Traded To		Traded With	Traded By		In Exchange For
Mar. 28, 1989	MON	N	—	PIT	N	Neal Heaton

Jim Gideon

Date	Traded To		Traded With	Traded By		In Exchange For
June 1, 1976	MIN	A	*see Roy Smalley*	TEX	A	—

Paul Giel

Date	Traded To		Traded With	Traded By		In Exchange For
Apr. 13, 1959	PIT	N	—	SF	N	Waiver price
June 1, 1961	KC	A	Reno Bertoia	MIN	A	Bill Tuttle
			(Giel was returned to Minnesota for a cash payment.)			

Bob Giggie

Date	Traded To		Traded With	Traded By		In Exchange For
May 11, 1960	KC	A	—	MIL	N	George Brunet

Gus Gil

Date	Traded To		Traded With	Traded By		In Exchange For
Oct. 15, 1966	CLE	A	—	CIN	N	Cash

Charlie Gilbert

Date	Traded To		Traded With	Traded By		In Exchange For
May 6, 1941	CHI	N	Johnny Hudson $65,000.	BKN	N	Billy Herman
June 15, 1946	PHI	N	—	CHI	N	Cash

Wally Gilbert

Date	Traded To		Traded With	Traded By		In Exchange For
Mar. 14, 1932	CIN	N	Babe Herman Ernie Lombardi	BKN	N	Tony Cuccinello Joe Stripp Clyde Sukeforth

Bill Gilbreth

Date	Traded To		Traded With	Traded By		In Exchange For
Sept. 6, 1972	CAL	A	—	DET	A	Cash
Sept. 12, 1974	CLE	A	—	CAL	A	Charles Hudson

Frank Gilhooley

Date	Traded To		Traded With	Traded By		In Exchange For
Aug. 25, 1913	NY	A	—	STL	N	Cash
Dec. 18, 1918	BOS	A	—	NY	A	*see Duffy Lewis*

George Gill

Date	Traded To		Traded With	Traded By		In Exchange For
May 13, 1939	STL	A	—	DET	A	*see Beau Bell*

Grant Gillis

Date	Traded To		Traded With	Traded By		In Exchange For
Dec. 15, 1928	BOS	A	Milt Gaston Elliott Bigelow Hod Lisenbee Bobby Reeves	WAS	A	Buddy Myer

Hal Gilson

Date	Traded To		Traded With	Traded By		In Exchange For
June 15, 1968	HOU	N	Dick Simpson	STL	N	Ron Davis

Joe Ginsberg

Date	Traded To		Traded With	Traded By		In Exchange For
June 15, 1953	CLE	A	—	DET	A	*see Ray Boone*
Aug. 17, 1956	BAL	A	—	KC	A	Hal Smith

Al Gionfriddo

Date	Traded To		Traded With	Traded By		In Exchange For
May 3, 1947	BKN	N	$100,000.	PIT	N	Kirby Higbe Hank Behrman Cal McLish Gene Mauch Dixie Howell

Joe Girardi

Date	Traded To		Traded With	Traded By		In Exchange For
Nov. 20, 1995	NY	A	—	CLR	N	Minor league P Mike DeJean Player to be named

(Colorado received P Steve Shoemaker on December 6, 1995.)

Tony Giuliani

Date	Traded To		Traded With	Traded By		In Exchange For
Mar. 24, 1938	WAS	A	—	STL	A	Cash
Mar. 1, 1944	STL	A	Gene Moore Cash	WAS	A	Rick Ferrell

(Giuliani announced his retirement, and St. Louis received Moore to complete the trade.)

Dave Giusti

Date	Traded To		Traded With	Traded By		In Exchange For
Oct. 11, 1968	STL	N	Dave Adlesh	HOU	N	Johnny Edwards minor league C Tommy Smith
Dec. 3, 1968	STL	N	—	SD	N	Danny Breeden Ed Spiezio Ron Davis minor league P Phil Knuckles
Oct. 21, 1969	PIT	N	Dave Ricketts	STL	N	Carl Taylor minor league OF Frank Vanzin
Mar. 15, 1977	OAK	A	—	PIT	N	*see Phil Garner*
Aug. 5, 1977	CHI	N	—	OAK	A	Cash

Brian Givens

Date	Traded To		Traded With	Traded By		In Exchange For
June 19, 1990	SEA	A	—	NY	N	Mario Diaz

Dan Gladden

Date	Traded To		Traded With	Traded By		In Exchange For
Mar. 31, 1987	MIN	A	Minor league P David Blakley	SF	N	Bryan Hickerson Minor league P Jose Dominguez Minor league P Ray Velasquez

(San Francisco received Hickerson on June 16, 1987.)

Dan Gladden *continued*

Date	Traded To		Traded With	Traded By		In Exchange For
Dec. 20, 1991	DET	A	—	MIN	A	No compensation (free agent signing)

Fred Gladding

Date	Traded To		Traded With	Traded By		In Exchange For
Aug. 17, 1967	HOU	N	Cash	DET	A	Eddie Mathews

Fred Glade

Date	Traded To		Traded With	Traded By		In Exchange For
Feb. 1908	NY	A	Charlie Hemphill	STL	A	Jimmy Williams Hobe Ferris Danny Hoffman

Tommy Glaviano

Date	Traded To		Traded With	Traded By		In Exchange For
Sept. 30, 1952	PHI	N	—	STL	N	Waiver price

Whitey Glazner

Date	Traded To		Traded With	Traded By		In Exchange For
May 22, 1923	PHI	N	Cotton Tierney $50,000.	PIT	N	Lee Meadows Johnny Rawlings

Jerry Don Gleaton

Date	Traded To		Traded With	Traded By		In Exchange For
Dec. 12, 1980	SEA	A	—	TEX	A	*see Rick Honeycutt*
June 29, 1984	CHI	A	Gene Nelson	SEA	A	Salome Barojas
Apr. 2, 1990	DET	A	—	KC	A	Minor league P Greg Everson

Jim Gleeson

Date	Traded To		Traded With	Traded By		In Exchange For
Jan. 24, 1939	CHI	N	—	NY	A	$25,000.
Dec. 4, 1940	CIN	N	Bobby Mattick	CHI	N	Billy Myers

Joe Glenn

Date	Traded To		Traded With	Traded By		In Exchange For
Oct. 26, 1938	STL	A	Myril Hoag	NY	A	Oral Hildebrand Buster Mills

John Glenn

Date	Traded To		Traded With	Traded By		In Exchange For
June 15, 1960	STL	N	—	LA	N	Jim Donohue

Al Glossop

Date	Traded To		Traded With	Traded By		In Exchange For
June 15, 1940	BOS	N	Manny Salvo	NY	N	Tony Cuccinello
Mar. 9, 1943	BKN	N	Lloyd Waner	PHI	N	Babe Dahlgren
Sept. 28, 1943	CHI	N	—	BKN	N	Cash

Ed Glynn

Date	Traded To		Traded With	Traded By		In Exchange For
Mar. 13, 1979	NY	N	—	DET	A	Mardie Cornejo
Apr. 6, 1981	CLE	A	—	NY	N	Minor league P Dominick Bullinger
June 24, 1984	NY	N	—	CLE	A	Minor league P Rich Miles
Nov. 9, 1984	BOS	A	—	NY	N	Cash
Apr. 27, 1985	MON	N	—	BOS	A	Cash

Danny Godby

Date	Traded To		Traded With	Traded By		In Exchange For
Mar. 29, 1975	BOS	A	—	STL	N	Danny Cater

Ed Goebel

Date	Traded To		Traded With	Traded By		In Exchange For
Feb. 10, 1923	BOS	A	Val Picinich Howard Shanks	WAS	A	Muddy Ruel Allan Russell

Jerry Goff

Date	Traded To		Traded With	Traded By		In Exchange For
Feb. 27, 1990	MON	N	—	SEA	A	Pat Pacillo

Chuck Goggin

Date	Traded To		Traded With	Traded By		In Exchange For
May 24, 1973	ATL	N	—	PIT	N	Cash
Mar. 26, 1974	BOS	A	—	ATL	N	Vic Correll

Bill Gogolewski

Date	Traded To		Traded With	Traded By		In Exchange For
Mar. 23, 1974	CLE	A	—	TEX	A	Steve Hargan

Jim Golden

Date	Traded To		Traded With	Traded By		In Exchange For
Dec. 23, 1958	LA	N	Rip Repulski Gene Snyder	PHI	N	Sparky Anderson
Dec. 10, 1963	CHI	A	Danny Murphy Cash	HOU	N	Nellie Fox

Gordon Goldsberry

Date	Traded To		Traded With	Traded By		In Exchange For
Nov. 27, 1951	STL	A	—	CHI	A	*see Sherm Lollar*

Mike Goliat

Date	Traded To		Traded With	Traded By		In Exchange For
Sept. 12, 1951	STL	A	—	PHI	N	Waiver price

Dave Goltz

Date	Traded To		Traded With	Traded By		In Exchange For
Nov. 15, 1979	LA	N	—	MIN	A	No compensation (free agent signing)

Lefty Gomez

Date	Traded To		Traded With	Traded By		In Exchange For
Jan. 25, 1943	BOS	N	—	NY	A	Cash

Luis Gomez

Date	Traded To		Traded With	Traded By		In Exchange For
Dec. 5, 1979	ATL	N	Chris Chambliss	TOR	A	Barry Bonnell Pat Rockett Joey McLaughlin

Pat Gomez

Date	Traded To		Traded With	Traded By		In Exchange For
Aug. 24, 1989	ATL	N	Rick Luecken	CHI	N	Paul Assenmacher
Dec. 9, 1992	TEX	A	Charlie Leibrandt	ATL	N	Jose Oliva

Ruben Gomez

Date	Traded To		Traded With	Traded By		In Exchange For
Dec. 3, 1958	PHI	N	Valmy Thomas	SF	N	Jack Sanford
Aug. 20, 1962	MIN	A	—	CLE	A	Georges Maranda Jackie Collum Cash

Jesse Gonder

Date	Traded To		Traded With	Traded By		In Exchange For
July 1, 1963	NY	N	—	CIN	N	Charlie Neal Sammy Taylor
July 21, 1965	MIL	N	—	NY	N	Gary Kolb

Rene Gonzales

Date	Traded To		Traded With	Traded By		In Exchange For
June 16, 1986	BAL	A	—	MON	N	Dennis Martinez

(Baltimore received Gonzales on Dec. 16, 1986.)

Date	Traded To		Traded With	Traded By		In Exchange For
Dec. 8, 1986	BAL	A	—	MON	N	John Stefero

(Baltimore received Gonzales on Dec. 16, 1986, also completing Dennis Martinez deal.)

Date	Traded To		Traded With	Traded By		In Exchange For
Jan. 15, 1991	TOR	A	—	BAL	A	Minor league P Rob Blumberg

Denny Gonzalez

Date	Traded To		Traded With	Traded By		In Exchange For
Mar. 25, 1989	CLE	A	Felix Fermin	PIT	N	Jay Bell

(Completion of deal in which Cleveland acquired Gonzalez on November 28, 1988 for a player to be named.)

Fernando Gonzalez

Date	Traded To		Traded With	Traded By		In Exchange For
Dec. 4, 1973	KC	A	Nellie Briles	PIT	N	Ed Kirkpatrick Kurt Bevacqua minor league 1B Winston Cole
May 5, 1974	NY	A	—	KC	A	Cash
June 5, 1978	SD	N	—	PIT	N	Cash

Jose Gonzalez

Date	Traded To		Traded With	Traded By		In Exchange For
July 3, 1991	PIT	N	—	LA	N	Mitch Webster
Aug. 15, 1991	CLE	A	—	PIT	N	Waiver price

Julio Gonzalez

Date	Traded To		Traded With	Traded By		In Exchange For
Dec. 8, 1976	HOU	N	—	CHI	N	Greg Gross

Luis Gonzalez

Date	Traded To		Traded With	Traded By		In Exchange For
June 28, 1995	CHI	N	Scott Servais	HOU	N	Rick Wilkins

Mike Gonzalez

Date	Traded To		Traded With	Traded By		In Exchange For
Apr. 8, 1915	STL	N	—	CIN	N	Ivy Wingo
May 1919	NY	N	—	STL	N	Waiver price
Dec. 6, 1921	CIN	N	George Burns $150,000.	NY	N	Heinie Groh
Apr. 27, 1924	STL	N	—	BKN	N	Milt Stock
May 23, 1925	CHI	N	Howard Freigau	STL	N	Bob O'Farrell

Orlando Gonzalez

Date	Traded To		Traded With	Traded By		In Exchange For
July 25, 1980	OAK	A	—	PHI	N	Cash

Pedro Gonzalez

Date	Traded To		Traded With	Traded By		In Exchange For
May 10, 1965	CLE	A	—	NY	A	Ray Barker

Tony Gonzalez

Date	Traded To		Traded With	Traded By		In Exchange For
June 15, 1960	PHI	N	Lee Walls	CIN	N	Harry Anderson Wally Post minor league 1B Fred Hopke
June 12, 1969	ATL	N	—	SD	N	Walt Hriniak Van Kelly minor league OF Andy Finlay
Aug. 31, 1970	CAL	A	—	ATL	N	Cash

Johnny Gooch

Date	Traded To		Traded With	Traded By		In Exchange For
June 8, 1928	BKN	N	Joe Harris	PIT	N	Charlie Hargreaves
Apr. 18, 1929	CIN	N	Rube Ehrhardt	BKN	N	Val Picinich

Wilbur Good

Date	Traded To		Traded With	Traded By		In Exchange For
June 10, 1911	CHI	N	Cliff Curtis Bill Collins Peaches Graham	BOS	N	Johnny Kling Al Kaiser Orlie Weaver Hank Griffin
Feb. 3, 1916	PHI	N	—	CHI	N	Cash

Billy Goodman

Date	Traded To		Traded With	Traded By		In Exchange For
June 14, 1957	BAL	A	—	BOS	A	Mike Fornieles
Dec. 3, 1957	CHI	A	Tito Francona Ray Moore	BAL	A	Jack Harshman Larry Doby Russ Heman Jim Marshall

Ival Goodman

Date	Traded To		Traded With	Traded By		In Exchange For
Nov. 3, 1934	CIN	N	—	STL	N	$25,000.
Nov. 14, 1942	CHI	N	—	CIN	N	Cash

Ed Goodson

Date	Traded To		Traded With	Traded By		In Exchange For
June 11, 1975	ATL	N	—	SF	N	Craig Robinson
Nov. 17, 1975	LA	N	Dusty Baker	ATL	N	Jimmy Wynn Tom Paciorek Lee Lacy Jerry Royster

Curtis Goodwin

Date	Traded To		Traded With	Traded By		In Exchange For
Dec. 26, 1995	CIN	N	Minor league OF Trovin Valdez	BAL	A	David Wells

Danny Goodwin

Date	Traded To		Traded With	Traded By		In Exchange For
Dec. 4, 1978	MIN	A	Ron Jackson	CAL	A	Dan Ford

Tom Goodwin

Date	Traded To		Traded With	Traded By		In Exchange For
Jan. 6, 1994	KC	A	—	LA	N	Waiver price

Greg Goossen

Date	Traded To		Traded With	Traded By		In Exchange For
Nov. 3, 1970	PHI	N	Jeff Terpko Gene Martin	WAS	A	Curt Flood

Glen Gorbous

Date	Traded To		Traded With	Traded By		In Exchange For
Apr. 30, 1955	PHI	N	*see Andy Seminick*	CIN	N	—
May 10, 1957	STL	N	—	PHI	N	Chuck Harmon

Don Gordon

Date	Traded To		Traded With	Traded By		In Exchange For
Aug. 7, 1987	CLE	A	Minor league OF Darryl Landrum	TOR	A	Phil Niekro

Joe Gordon

Date	Traded To		Traded With	Traded By		In Exchange For
Oct. 19, 1946	CLE	A	Eddie Bockman	NY	A	Allie Reynolds

Date	Traded To	Traded With	Traded By	In Exchange For

Joe Gordon *continued*

Date	Traded To	Traded With	Traded By	In Exchange For
Aug. 10, 1960	DET A	—	CLE A	Jimmy Dykes

Sid Gordon

Date	Traded To	Traded With	Traded By	In Exchange For
Dec. 14, 1949	BOS N	Buddy Kerr Willard Marshall Red Webb	NY N	Eddie Stanky Alvin Dark
Dec. 26, 1953	PIT N	Max Surkont Sam Jethroe Curt Raydon Fred Walters minor league P Larry Lasalle and $100,000.	MIL N	Danny O'Connell
May 23, 1955	NY N	—	PIT N	Cash

Tom Gordon

Date	Traded To	Traded With	Traded By	In Exchange For
Dec. 21, 1995	BOS A	—	KC A	No compensation (free agent signing)

Tom Gorman

Date	Traded To	Traded With	Traded By	In Exchange For
Aug. 4, 1982	NY N	—	MON N	Joel Youngblood

Tom Gorman

Date	Traded To	Traded With	Traded By	In Exchange For
Mar. 30, 1955	KC A	Ewell Blackwell Dick Kryhoski	NY A	$50,000.

Hank Gornicki

Date	Traded To	Traded With	Traded By	In Exchange For
Sept. 2, 1941	CHI N	—	STL N	Cash
(Gornicki was returned to St. Louis after the season.)				
Dec. 1, 1941	PIT N	—	STL N	Waiver price

John Goryl

Date	Traded To	Traded With	Traded By	In Exchange For
Apr. 8, 1960	LA N	Ron Perranoski minor league OF Lee Handley $25,000.	CHI N	Don Zimmer

Jim Gosger

Date	Traded To	Traded With	Traded By	In Exchange For
June 13, 1966	KC A	Ken Sanders Guido Grilli	BOS A	John Wyatt Rollie Sheldon Jose Tartabull
Dec. 12, 1969	SF N	Bob Heise	NY N	Ray Sadecki Dave Marshall
Apr. 20, 1970	MON N	—	SF N	Cash

Goose Goslin

Date	Traded To	Traded With	Traded By	In Exchange For
June 13, 1930	STL A	—	WAS A	General Crowder Heinie Manush
Dec. 14, 1932	WAS A	Fred Schulte Lefty Stewart	STL A	Sammy West Lloyd Brown Carl Reynolds $20,000.
Dec. 20, 1933	DET A	—	WAS A	John Stone

Howie Goss

Date	Traded To	Traded With	Traded By	In Exchange For
Apr. 4, 1963	HOU N	Cash	PIT N	Manny Mota

Goose Gossage

Date	Traded To	Traded With	Traded By	In Exchange For
Dec. 10, 1976	PIT N	Terry Forster	CHI A	Richie Zisk Silvio Martinez
Nov. 23, 1977	NY A	—	PIT N	No compensation (free agent signing)
Jan. 12, 1984	SD N	—	NY A	No compensation (free agent signing)
Feb. 12, 1988	CHI N	Ray Hayward	SD N	Keith Moreland Mike Brumley
Aug. 11, 1989	NY A	—	SF N	Waiver price

Julio Gotay

Date	Traded To	Traded With	Traded By	In Exchange For
Nov. 19, 1962	PIT N	Don Cardwell	STL N	Dick Groat Diomedes Olivo

Jim Gott

Date	Traded To	Traded With	Traded By	In Exchange For
Jan. 26, 1985	SF N	Minor league IF Augie Schmidt Minor league P Jack McKnight	TOR A	Gary Lavelle
Aug. 3, 1987	PIT N	—	SF N	Waiver price
Dec. 7, 1989	LA N	—	PIT N	No compensation (free agent signing)

Hank Gowdy

Date	Traded To	Traded With	Traded By	In Exchange For
July 22, 1911	BOS N	Al Bridwell	NY N	Buck Herzog
June 7, 1923	NY N	Mule Watson	BOS N	Jesse Barnes Earl Smith

Mauro Gozzo

Date	Traded To	Traded With	Traded By	In Exchange For
Mar. 27, 1987	KC A	Ed Hearn Rick Anderson	NY N	David Cone Chris Jelic
Sept. 16, 1990	CLE A	—	TOR A	*see Bud Black*

Billy Grabarkewitz

Date	Traded To	Traded With	Traded By	In Exchange For
Nov. 28, 1972	CAL A	—	LA N	*see Andy Messersmith*
Aug. 14, 1973	PHI N	Aurelio Monteagudo Chris Coletta	CAL A	Denny Doyle
July 10, 1974	CHI N	—	PHI N	Cash

Johnny Grabowski

Date	Traded To	Traded With	Traded By	In Exchange For
Jan. 13, 1927	NY A	Ray Morehart	CHI A	Aaron Ward

Earl Grace

Date	Traded To	Traded With	Traded By	In Exchange For
June 13, 1931	PIT N	—	CHI N	Rollie Hemsley
Nov. 21, 1935	PHI N	Claude Passeau	PIT N	Al Todd
Dec. 8, 1937	STL A	—	PHI N	Cap Clark

Joe Grace

Date	Traded To	Traded With	Traded By	In Exchange For
June 15, 1946	WAS A	Al LaMacchia	STL A	Jeff Heath
Dec. 1947	PIT N	—	WAS A	Cash

Milt Graff

Date	Traded To	Traded With	Traded By	In Exchange For
Feb. 19, 1957	KC A	*see Billy Hunter*	NY A	—
June 15, 1957	NY A	—	KC A	*see Ralph Terry*

Dan Graham

Date	Traded To	Traded With	Traded By	In Exchange For
Dec. 7, 1979	BAL A	—	MIN A	Tom Chism

Jack Graham

Date	Traded To	Traded With	Traded By	In Exchange For
May 1946	NY N	—	BKN N	Cash

Peaches Graham

Date	Traded To	Traded With	Traded By	In Exchange For
June 10, 1911	CHI N	—	BOS N	*see Johnny Kling*
Oct. 1911	PHI N	—	CHI N	Dick Cotter

Wayne Graham

Date	Traded To	Traded With	Traded By	In Exchange For
Aug. 7, 1964	NY N	Gary Kroll Cash	PHI N	Frank Thomas
Feb. 22, 1966	PHI N	Jimmie Schaffer Bobby Klaus	NY N	Dick Stuart

Alex Grammas

Date	Traded To	Traded With	Traded By	In Exchange For
Dec. 2, 1953	STL N	—	CIN N	Jack Crimian $100,000.
May 16, 1956	CIN N	Joe Frazier	STL N	Chuck Harmon
Oct. 3, 1958	STL N	George Crowe Alex Kellner	CIN N	Bob Mabe Eddie Kasko Del Ennis
June 5, 1962	CHI N	Don Landrum	STL N	Bobby Gene Smith Daryl Robertson

Wayne Granger

Date	Traded To		Traded With	Traded By		In Exchange For
Oct. 11, 1968	CIN	N	Bobby Tolan	STL	N	Vada Pinson
Dec. 3, 1971	MIN	A	—	CIN	N	Tom Hall
Nov. 29, 1972	STL	N	—	MIN	A	Larry Hisle John Cumberland
Aug. 7, 1973	NY	A	—	STL	N	Ken Crosby Cash

Eddie Grant

Date	Traded To		Traded With	Traded By		In Exchange For
Feb. 1911	CIN	N	Johnny Bates George McQuillan Lew Moren	PHI	N	Fred Beebe Jack Rowan Dode Paskert Hans Lobert
May 22, 1913	NY	N	Art Fromme	CIN	N	Red Ames Heinie Groh Josh Devore $20,000.
June 1913	NY	N	—	CIN	N	Cash

Jimmy Grant

Date	Traded To		Traded With	Traded By		In Exchange For
Aug. 11, 1943	CLE	A	—	CHI	A	Cash

Mark Grant

Date	Traded To		Traded With	Traded By		In Exchange For
July 5, 1987	SD	N	—	SF	N	*see Kevin Mitchell*
July 12, 1990	ATL	N	—	SD	N	Derek Lilliquist
May 20, 1993	CLR	N	—	HOU	N	Braulio Castillo

Mudcat Grant

Date	Traded To		Traded With	Traded By		In Exchange For
June 15, 1964	MIN	A	—	CLE	A	George Banks Lee Stange
Nov. 28, 1967	LA	N	Zoilo Versalles	MIN	A	Johnny Roseboro Ron Perranoski Bob Miller
June 3, 1969	STL	N	—	MON	N	Gary Waslewski
Dec. 5, 1969	OAK	A	—	STL	N	Cash
Sept. 14, 1970	PIT	N	—	OAK	A	Angel Mangual
Aug. 10, 1971	OAK	A	—	PIT	N	Cash

(Oakland received Mangual on October 20.)

George Grantham

Date	Traded To		Traded With	Traded By		In Exchange For
Oct. 27, 1924	PIT	N	Vic Aldridge Al Niehaus	CHI	N	Charlie Grimm Rabbit Maranville Wilbur Cooper
Feb. 4, 1932	CIN	N	—	PIT	N	Cash
Nov. 15, 1933	NY	N	—	CIN	N	Glenn Spencer

Mickey Grasso

Date	Traded To		Traded With	Traded By		In Exchange For
Jan. 20, 1954	CLE	A	—	WAS	A	Joe Tipton

Dick Gray

Date	Traded To		Traded With	Traded By		In Exchange For
June 15, 1959	STL	N	—	LA	N	Chuck Essegian Lloyd Merritt
May 28, 1960	PIT	N	Vinegar Bend Mizell	STL	N	Julian Javier Ed Bauta

Gary Gray

Date	Traded To		Traded With	Traded By		In Exchange For
Jan. 4, 1980	CLE	A	Larry McCall minor league 3B-OF Mike Bucci	TEX	A	David Clyde Jim Norris
Feb. 17, 1983	CAL	A	—	SEA	A	Cash

Jeff Gray

Date	Traded To		Traded With	Traded By		In Exchange For
Dec. 11, 1985	CIN	N	*see John Denny*	PHI	N	—
July 13, 1989	PHI	N	—	CIN	N	Bob Sebra

(Philadelphia received Gray on Sept. 6, 1989.)

John Gray

Date	Traded To		Traded With	Traded By		In Exchange For
Dec. 16, 1953	PHI	A	—	NY	A	*see Harry Byrd*

Sam Gray

Date	Traded To		Traded With	Traded By		In Exchange For
Dec. 13, 1927	STL	A	—	PHI	A	Bing Miller

Ted Gray

Date	Traded To		Traded With	Traded By		In Exchange For
Dec. 6, 1954	CHI	A	Walt Dropo Bob Nieman	DET	A	Leo Cristante Ferris Fain Jack Phillips

Dallas Green

Date	Traded To		Traded With	Traded By		In Exchange For
Apr. 11, 1965	WAS	A	—	PHI	N	Cash
July 22, 1966	NY	N	—	PHI	N	Cash

(Green was returned to Philadelphia on May 11.)

(Green was returned to Philadelphia on Aug. 10.)

David Green

Date	Traded To		Traded With	Traded By		In Exchange For
Dec. 12, 1980	STL	N	Sixto Lezcano Lary Sorensen Dave LaPoint	MIL	A	Pete Vuckovich Rollie Fingers Ted Simmons
Feb. 1, 1985	SF	N	Jose Uribe Dave LaPoint Gary Rajsich	STL	N	Jack Clark
Dec. 4, 1985	MIL	A	—	SF	N	player to be named

(San Francisco received SS Hector Quinones on Dec. 11, 1985.)

Freddie Green

Date	Traded To		Traded With	Traded By		In Exchange For
Sept. 25, 1961	WAS	A	—	PIT	N	Waiver price

Gene Green

Date	Traded To		Traded With	Traded By		In Exchange For
Dec. 2, 1959	BAL	A	minor league C Charles Staniland	STL	N	Bob Nieman
Oct. 5, 1961	CLE	A	Dick Donovan Jim Mahoney	WAS	A	Jimmy Piersall
Aug. 1, 1963	CIN	N	—	CLE	A	Sammy Taylor

Lenny Green

Date	Traded To		Traded With	Traded By		In Exchange For
May 26, 1959	WAS	A	—	BAL	A	Albie Pearson
June 11, 1964	LA	A	Vic Power	MIN	A	Jerry Kindall Frank Kostro
Sept. 5, 1964	BAL	A	—	LA	A	Cash

(Part of three-team trade involving Los Angeles Angels, Minnesota, and Cleveland.)

Pumpsie Green

Date	Traded To		Traded With	Traded By		In Exchange For
Dec. 11, 1962	NY	N	Tracy Stallard Al Moran	BOS	A	Felix Mantilla

Hank Greenberg

Date	Traded To		Traded With	Traded By		In Exchange For
Jan. 18, 1947	PIT	N	—	DET	A	$75,000.

Al Greene

Date	Traded To		Traded With	Traded By		In Exchange For
June 2, 1980	STL	N	John Martin	DET	A	Jim Lentine

Tommy Greene

Date	Traded To		Traded With	Traded By		In Exchange For
Aug. 3, 1990	PHI	N	Dale Murphy	ATL	N	Jeff Parrett Jim Vatcher Victor Rosario

(Greene and Vatcher were exhanged on August 9, and Atlanta received Rosario on September 4, 1990.)

Willie Greene

Date	Traded To		Traded With	Traded By		In Exchange For
Aug. 8, 1990	MON	N	—	PIT	N	*see Zane Smith*
Dec. 11, 1991	CIN	N	—	MON	N	*see John Wetteland*

Kent Greenfield

Date	Traded To		Traded With	Traded By		In Exchange For
June 12, 1927	BOS	N	Hugh McQuillan Doc Farrell	NY	N	Zack Taylor Larry Benton Herb Thomas
July 4, 1929	BKN	N	—	BOS	N	Cash

Jim Greengrass

Date	Traded To		Traded With	Traded By		In Exchange For
Aug. 28, 1952	CIN	N	Johnny Schmitz Ernie Nevel Bob Marquis $35,000.	NY	A	Ewell Blackwell
Apr. 30, 1955	PHI	N	*see Andy Seminick*	CIN	N	—

Kenny Greer

Date	Traded To	Traded With	Traded By	In Exchange For
Sept. 17, 1993	NY N	—	NY A	Frank Tanana

Hal Gregg

Date	Traded To	Traded With	Traded By	In Exchange For
Dec. 8, 1947	PIT N	Dixie Walker Vic Lombardi	BKN N	Preacher Roe Billy Cox Gene Mauch

Tommy Gregg

Date	Traded To	Traded With	Traded By	In Exchange For
Aug. 28, 1988	ATL N	—	PIT N	Ken Oberkfell

(Atlanta received Gregg on September 1, 1988.)

Date	Traded To	Traded With	Traded By	In Exchange For
Dec. 1, 1992	CIN N	—	ATL N	Waiver price

Vean Gregg

Date	Traded To	Traded With	Traded By	In Exchange For
July 28, 1914	BOS A	—	CLE A	Adam Johnson Fritz Coumbe Ben Egan
Dec. 14, 1917	PHI A	Merlin Kopp Pinch Thomas $60,000.	BOS A	Amos Strunk Joe Bush Wally Schang

Bill Greif

Date	Traded To	Traded With	Traded By	In Exchange For
Dec. 3, 1971	SD N	Derrel Thomas Mark Schaeffer	HOU N	Dave Roberts
May 19, 1976	STL N	—	SD N	Luis Melendez
Nov. 6, 1976	MON N	Angel Torres Sam Mejias	STL N	Steve Dunning Pat Scanlon Tony Scott

Ed Gremminger

Date	Traded To	Traded With	Traded By	In Exchange For
July 24, 1904	DET A	—	BOS N	Cash

Bobby Grich

Date	Traded To	Traded With	Traded By	In Exchange For
Nov. 24, 1976	CAL A	—	BAL A	No compensation (free agent signing)

Tom Grieve

Date	Traded To	Traded With	Traded By	In Exchange For
Dec. 8, 1977	NY N	Willie Montanez Ken Henderson	TEX A	Jon Matlack John Milner

(Part of four-team trade involving Texas, New York Mets, Pittsburgh, and Atlanta.)

Date	Traded To	Traded With	Traded By	In Exchange For
Dec. 5, 1978	STL N	Kim Seaman	NY N	Pete Falcone

Ken Griffey

Date	Traded To	Traded With	Traded By	In Exchange For
Nov. 4, 1981	NY A	—	CIN N	Fred Toliver minor league P Bryan Ryder
June 29, 1986	ATL N	Andre Robertson	NY A	Claudell Washington Paul Zuvella

(Atlanta received Robertson on July 3, 1986.)

Alfredo Griffin

Date	Traded To	Traded With	Traded By	In Exchange For
Dec. 5, 1978	TOR A	minor league 3B Phil Lansford	CLE A	Victor Cruz
Dec. 8, 1984	OAK A	Dave Collins Cash	TOR A	Bill Caudill
Dec. 11, 1987	LA N	Jay Howell	OAK A	Bob Welch Matt Young

(Part of three-team trade involving Oakland, Los Angeles and New York Mets.)

Doug Griffin

Date	Traded To	Traded With	Traded By	In Exchange For
Oct. 11, 1970	BOS A	—	CAL A	*see Tony Conigliaro*

Hank Griffin

Date	Traded To	Traded With	Traded By	In Exchange For
June 10, 1911	BOS N	*see Johnny Kling*	CHI N	—

Mike Griffin

Date	Traded To	Traded With	Traded By	In Exchange For
Nov. 10, 1978	NY A	*see Dave Righetti*	TEX A	—
June 12, 1981	CHI N	Doug Bird $400,000.	NY A	Rick Reuschel
Mar. 16, 1982	MON N	—	CHI N	Dan Briggs
June 8, 1982	SD N	—	MON N	Jerry Manuel

Tom Griffin

Date	Traded To	Traded With	Traded By	In Exchange For
Aug. 3, 1976	SD N	—	HOU N	Cash
Dec. 11, 1981	PIT N	—	SF N	Doe Boyland

Bart Griffith

Date	Traded To	Traded With	Traded By	In Exchange For
Dec. 1923	WAS A	—	BKN N	Bonnie Hollingsworth

Derrell Griffith

Date	Traded To	Traded With	Traded By	In Exchange For
Nov. 29, 1966	NY N	Tommy Davis	LA N	Ron Hunt Jim Hickman
Mar. 24, 1967	HOU N	—	NY N	Sandy Alomar

Tommy Griffith

Date	Traded To	Traded With	Traded By	In Exchange For
Mar. 1919	BKN N	—	CIN N	Jake Daubert
May 10, 1925	CHI N	—	BKN N	Bob Barrett

Art Griggs

Date	Traded To	Traded With	Traded By	In Exchange For
Oct. 1910	CLE A	—	STL A	Nig Clarke

Guido Grilli

Date	Traded To	Traded With	Traded By	In Exchange For
June 13, 1966	KC A	—	BOS A	*see John Wyatt*

Steve Grilli

Date	Traded To	Traded With	Traded By	In Exchange For
Feb. 23, 1978	TOR A	—	DET A	Cash

Bob Grim

Date	Traded To	Traded With	Traded By	In Exchange For
June 15, 1958	KC A	Harry Simpson	NY A	Duke Maas Virgil Trucks
Apr. 5, 1960	CLE A	—	KC A	Leo Kiely
May 18, 1960	CIN N	—	CLE A	Cash
July 29, 1960	STL N	—	CIN N	Cash

Burleigh Grimes

Date	Traded To	Traded With	Traded By	In Exchange For
Jan. 9, 1918	BKN N	Chuck Ward Al Mamaux	PIT N	Casey Stengel George Cutshaw
Jan. 9, 1927	NY N	—	BKN N	Butch Henline

(Part of three-team trade involving Brooklyn, New York, and Philadelphia.)

Date	Traded To	Traded With	Traded By	In Exchange For
Feb. 11, 1928	PIT N	—	NY N	Vic Aldridge
Apr. 9, 1930	BOS N	—	PIT N	Percy Jones Cash
June 16, 1930	STL N	—	BOS N	Fred Frankhouse Bill Sherdel
Dec. 1931	CHI N	—	STL N	Bud Teachout Hack Wilson
Aug. 4, 1933	STL N	—	CHI N	Waiver price
May 15, 1934	PIT N	—	STL N	Waiver price
May 26, 1934	NY A	—	PIT N	Cash

Oscar Grimes

Date	Traded To	Traded With	Traded By	In Exchange For
Dec. 17, 1942	NY A	Roy Weatherly	CLE A	Roy Cullenbine Buddy Rosar

Charlie Grimm

Date	Traded To	Traded With	Traded By	In Exchange For
Oct. 27, 1924	CHI N	Rabbit Maranville Wilbur Cooper	PIT N	Vic Aldridge George Grantham Al Niehaus

Jason Grimsley

Date	Traded To	Traded With	Traded By	In Exchange For
Apr. 2, 1992	HOU N	—	PHI N	Curt Schilling

Ross Grimsley

Date	Traded To	Traded With	Traded By	In Exchange For
Dec. 4, 1973	BAL A	minor league C Wally Williams	CIN N	Merv Rettenmund Junior Kennedy minor league C Bill Wood
Dec. 21, 1977	MON N	—	BAL A	No compensation (free agent signing)
July 11, 1980	CLE A	—	MON N	Dave Oliver

Lee Grissom

Date	Traded To	Traded With	Traded By	In Exchange For
Jan. 4, 1940	NY A	—	CIN N	Joe Beggs
May 15, 1940	BKN N	—	NY A	Waiver price
May 6, 1941	PHI N	—	BKN N	Vito Tamulis

Marquis Grissom

Date	Traded To	Traded With	Traded By	In Exchange For
Apr. 6, 1995	ATL N	—	MON N	Roberto Kelly Tony Tarasco Minor league P Esteban Yan

Marv Grissom

Date	Traded To	Traded With	Traded By	In Exchange For
Feb. 9, 1953	BOS A	Hal Brown Bill Kennedy	CHI A	Vern Stephens
July 1, 1953	NY N	—	BOS A	Waiver price
Oct. 8, 1958	STL N	Ernie Broglio	SF N	Hobie Landrith Billy Muffett Benny Valenzuela

Dick Groat

Date	Traded To	Traded With	Traded By	In Exchange For
Nov. 19, 1962	STL N	Diomedes Olivo	PIT N	Julio Gotay Don Cardwell
Oct. 27, 1965	PHI N	Bill White Bob Uecker	STL N	Pat Corrales Art Mahaffey Alex Johnson
June 22, 1967	SF N	—	PHI N	Cash

Connie Grob

Date	Traded To	Traded With	Traded By	In Exchange For
Nov. 30, 1962	HOU N	Jim Bolger	MIL N	Norm Larker

Heinie Groh

Date	Traded To	Traded With	Traded By	In Exchange For
May 22, 1913	CIN N	Red Ames Josh Devore $20,000.	NY N	Art Fromme Eddie Grant
Dec. 6, 1921	NY N	—	CIN N	Mike Gonzalez George Burns $150,000.

Steve Gromek

Date	Traded To	Traded With	Traded By	In Exchange For
June 15, 1953	DET A	Ray Boone Al Aber Dick Weik	CLE A	Art Houtteman Owen Friend Bill Wight Joe Ginsberg

Bob Groom

Date	Traded To	Traded With	Traded By	In Exchange For
Feb. 10, 1916	STL A	*see Eddie Plank*	STL F	—
Feb. 15, 1918	CLE A	—	STL A	Waiver price

Buddy Groom

Date	Traded To	Traded With	Traded By	In Exchange For
Aug. 7, 1995	FLA N	—	DET A	Mike Myers

Don Gross

Date	Traded To	Traded With	Traded By	In Exchange For
Dec. 9, 1957	PIT N	—	CIN N	Bob Purkey

Greg Gross

Date	Traded To	Traded With	Traded By	In Exchange For
Dec. 8, 1976	CHI N	—	HOU N	Julio Gonzalez
Feb. 23, 1979	PHI N	*see Manny Trillo*	CHI N	—

Kevin Gross

Date	Traded To	Traded With	Traded By	In Exchange For
Dec. 6, 1988	MON N	—	PHI N	Floyd Youmans Jeff Parrett
Dec. 3, 1990	LA N	—	MON N	No compensation (free agent signing)
Dec. 13, 1994	TEX A	—	LA N	No compensation (free agent signing)

Kip Gross

Date	Traded To	Traded With	Traded By	In Exchange For
Dec. 6, 1989	CIN N	—	NY N	*see John Franco*
Nov. 27, 1991	LA N	Eric Davis	CIN N	Tim Belcher John Wetteland

Wayne Gross

Date	Traded To	Traded With	Traded By	In Exchange For
Dec. 8, 1983	BAL A	—	OAK A	Tim Stoddard

Jerry Grote

Date	Traded To	Traded With	Traded By	In Exchange For
Oct. 19, 1965	NY N	—	HOU N	Tom Parsons Cash

Jerry Grote *continued*

Date	Traded To	Traded With	Traded By	In Exchange For
Aug. 31, 1977	LA N	—	NY N	Minor leaguers P Dan Smith and IF Randy Rogers
Feb. 5, 1981	KC A	—	LA N	No compensation (free agent signing)

Ernie Groth

Date	Traded To	Traded With	Traded By	In Exchange For
Dec. 2, 1948	CHI A	Bob Kuzava	CLE A	Frank Papish

Johnny Groth

Date	Traded To	Traded With	Traded By	In Exchange For
Dec. 4, 1952	STL A	Virgil Trucks Hal White	DET A	Owen Friend Bob Nieman J. W. Porter
Feb. 5, 1954	CHI A	Johnny Lipon	BAL A	Neil Berry Sam Mele
June 7, 1955	WAS A	Bob Chakales Clint Courtney	CHI A	Jim Busby
Apr. 16, 1956	KC A	—	WAS A	Cash
Aug. 1, 1957	DET A	—	KC A	Cash

Matt Grott

Date	Traded To	Traded With	Traded By	In Exchange For
July 31, 1991	MON N	Minor league P Russell Cormier	OAK A	Ron Darling

Lefty Grove

Date	Traded To	Traded With	Traded By	In Exchange For
Dec. 12, 1933	BOS A	Max Bishop Rube Walberg	PHI A	Bob Kline Rabbit Warstler $125,000.

Roy Grover

Date	Traded To	Traded With	Traded By	In Exchange For
June 1919	WAS A	—	PHI A	Cash

Johnny Grubb

Date	Traded To	Traded With	Traded By	In Exchange For
Dec. 8, 1976	CLE A	Fred Kendall Hector Torres	SD N	George Hendrick
Aug. 31, 1978	TEX A	—	CLE A	Bobby Cuellar minor league OF Dave Rivera
Mar. 24, 1983	DET A	—	TEX A	Dave Tobik

Frank Grube

Date	Traded To	Traded With	Traded By	In Exchange For
Dec. 15, 1933	STL A	—	CHI A	Cash
Sept. 20, 1935	CHI A	—	STL A	Cash

Kelly Gruber

Date	Traded To	Traded With	Traded By	In Exchange For
Dec. 8, 1992	CAL A	—	TOR A	Luis Sojo cash

Joe Grzenda

Date	Traded To	Traded With	Traded By	In Exchange For
Aug. 14, 1967	NY N	—	KC A	Cash
Nov. 29, 1967	MIN A	—	NY N	Cash
Mar. 21, 1970	WAS A	Charley Walters	MIN A	Brant Alyea
Nov. 3, 1971	STL N	—	TEX A	Ted Kubiak

Cecilio Guante

Date	Traded To	Traded With	Traded By	In Exchange For
Nov. 26, 1986	NY A	Rick Rhoden Pat Clements	PIT N	Doug Drabek Logan Easley Brian Fisher
Aug. 30, 1988	TEX A	—	NY A	Dale Mohorcic
Nov. 21, 1989	CLE A	—	TEX A	No compensation (free agent signing)

Mike Guerra

Date	Traded To	Traded With	Traded By	In Exchange For
Dec. 2, 1946	PHI A	—	WAS A	Cash
Dec. 13, 1950	BOS A	—	PHI A	Cash
May 7, 1951	WAS A	—	BOS A	Cash

Mario Guerrero

Date	Traded To	Traded With	Traded By	In Exchange For
Apr. 4, 1975	STL N	—	BOS A	Jim Willoughby
May 29, 1976	CAL A	—	STL N	Minor leaguers C Ed Jordan and 1B Ed Kurpiel

Mario Guerrero *continued*

Date	Traded To	Traded With	Traded By	In Exchange For
Mar. 15, 1978	OAK A	—	SF N	*see Vida Blue*
Dec. 8, 1980	SEA A	—	OAK A	Cash

Pedro Guerrero

Date	Traded To	Traded With	Traded By	In Exchange For
Apr. 3, 1974	LA N	—	CLE A	Bruce Ellingsen
Aug. 16, 1988	STL N	—	LA N	John Tudor

Lee Guetterman

Date	Traded To	Traded With	Traded By	In Exchange For
Dec. 22, 1987	NY A	Clay Parker Wade Taylor	SEA A	Steve Trout Henry Cotto
June 9, 1992	NY N	—	NY A	Tim Burke

Ozzie Guillen

Date	Traded To	Traded With	Traded By	In Exchange For
Dec. 6, 1984	CHI A	Tim Lollar Luis Salazar Bill Long	SD N	LaMarr Hoyt Minor league Ps Todd Simmons and Kevin Kristan

Skip Guinn

Date	Traded To	Traded With	Traded By	In Exchange For
Jan. 22, 1969	HOU N	Jesus Alou Donn Clendenon Jack Billingham $100,000.	MON N	Rusty Staub

(Clendenon refused to report, and Houston sent Billingham, Guinn, and cash on April 8, 1969.)

Brad Gulden

Date	Traded To	Traded With	Traded By	In Exchange For
Feb. 15, 1979	NY A	—	LA N	Gary Thomasson
Nov. 18, 1980	SEA A	$150,000.	NY A	Larry Milbourne
Apr. 5, 1982	MON N	—	NY A	Bobby Ramos
Oct. 26, 1982	NY A	—	MON N	Cash
June 12, 1985	HOU N	—	CIN N	Cash

Don Gullett

Date	Traded To	Traded With	Traded By	In Exchange For
Nov. 18, 1976	NY A	—	CIN N	No compensation (free agent signing)

Bill Gullickson

Date	Traded To	Traded With	Traded By	In Exchange For
Dec. 19, 1985	CIN N	Sal Butera	MON N	Jay Tibbs Andy McGaffigan Dann Bilardello John Stuper
Aug. 26, 1987	NY A	—	CIN N	Dennis Rasmussen

Glenn Gulliver

Date	Traded To	Traded With	Traded By	In Exchange For
July 5, 1984	STL N	—	BAL A	Player to be named

Harry Gumbert

Date	Traded To	Traded With	Traded By	In Exchange For
May 14, 1941	STL N	Paul Dean Cash	NY N	Bill McGee
June 15, 1944	CIN N	—	STL N	Cash
July 27, 1949	PIT N	—	CIN N	Waiver price

Dave Gumpert

Date	Traded To	Traded With	Traded By	In Exchange For
Mar. 30, 1987	KC A	—	CHI N	*see Jim Sundberg*

Randy Gumpert

Date	Traded To	Traded With	Traded By	In Exchange For
July 28, 1948	CHI A	—	NY A	Cash
Nov. 13, 1951	BOS A	Don Lenhardt	CHI A	Mel Hoderlein Chuck Stobbs
June 10, 1952	WAS A	Walt Masterson	BOS A	Sid Hudson

Eric Gunderson

Date	Traded To	Traded With	Traded By	In Exchange For
Aug. 4, 1995	SEA A	—	NY N	Waiver price
Aug. 10, 1995	BOS A	—	SEA A	Waiver price

Larry Gura

Date	Traded To	Traded With	Traded By	In Exchange For
Aug. 31, 1973	TEX A	—	CHI N	Mike Paul
May 8, 1974	NY A	Cash	TEX A	Duke Sims
May 16, 1976	KC A	—	NY A	Fran Healy

Frankie Gustine

Date	Traded To	Traded With	Traded By	In Exchange For
Dec. 8, 1948	CHI N	Cal McLish	PIT N	Clyde McCullough Cliff Chambers
Sept. 14, 1949	PHI A	—	CHI N	Waiver price
Dec. 13, 1949	STL A	Ray Coleman Billy DeMars minor league OF Ray Ippolito $100,000.	PHI A	Bob Dillinger Paul Lehner

Mark Guthrie

Date	Traded To	Traded With	Traded By	In Exchange For
July 31, 1995	LA N	*see Kevin Tapani*	MIN A	—

Cesar Gutierrez

Date	Traded To	Traded With	Traded By	In Exchange For
Sept. 2, 1969	DET A	—	SF N	Cash
Mar. 24, 1972	MON N	—	DET A	Cash

Jackie Gutierrez

Date	Traded To	Traded With	Traded By	In Exchange For
Dec. 17, 1985	BAL A	—	BOS A	Sammy Stewart

Ricky Gutierrez

Date	Traded To	Traded With	Traded By	In Exchange For
Aug. 31, 1992	SD N	Erik Schullstrom	BAL A	Craig Lefferts

(San Diego received Gutierrez on Sept. 4, 1992.)

Date	Traded To	Traded With	Traded By	In Exchange For
Dec. 28, 1994	HOU N	—	SD N	*see Ken Caminiti*

Don Gutteridge

Date	Traded To	Traded With	Traded By	In Exchange For
Mar. 26, 1948	PIT N	—	BOS A	Cash

Jose Guzman

Date	Traded To	Traded With	Traded By	In Exchange For
Dec. 1, 1992	CHI N	—	TEX A	No compensation (free agent signing)

Juan Guzman

Date	Traded To	Traded With	Traded By	In Exchange For
Sept. 22, 1987	TOR A	—	LA N	Mike Sharperson

Doug Gwosdz

Date	Traded To	Traded With	Traded By	In Exchange For
Dec. 17, 1986	SEA A	—	NY N	Ricky Nelson

Chris Gwynn

Date	Traded To	Traded With	Traded By	In Exchange For
Dec. 11, 1991	KC A	Minor league 2B Domingo Mota	LA N	Todd Benzinger

Bert Haas

Date	Traded To	Traded With	Traded By	In Exchange For
June 12, 1940	STL N	Ernie Koy Carl Doyle Sam Nahem $125,000.	BKN N	Joe Medwick Curt Davis
Dec. 11, 1947	PHI N	—	CIN N	Tommy Hughes

Eddie Haas

Date	Traded To	Traded With	Traded By	In Exchange For
Dec. 5, 1957	MIL N	Don Kaiser Bob Rush	CHI N	Taylor Phillips Sammy Taylor

Moose Haas

Date	Traded To	Traded With	Traded By	In Exchange For
Mar. 30, 1986	OAK A	—	MIL A	Steve Kiefer Charlie O'Brien Minor league P Mike Fulmer Minor league P Pete Kendrick

Mule Haas

Date	Traded To	Traded With	Traded By	In Exchange For
Sept. 28, 1932	CHI A	Jimmy Dykes Al Simmons	PHI A	$100,000.

Bob Habenicht

Date	Traded To	Traded With	Traded By	In Exchange For
Oct. 1, 1952	STL A	—	STL N	Waiver price

John Habyan

Date	Traded To	Traded With	Traded By	In Exchange For
July 20, 1989	NY A	—	BAL A	Stan Jefferson
July 30, 1993	KC A	—	NY A	Karl Rhodes

(Part of three team trade involving New York Yankees, Chicago Cubs, and Kansas City Royals.)

John Habyan *continued*

Date	Traded To		Traded With	Traded By		In Exchange For
Jan. 5, 1994	STL	N	—	KC	A	No compensation (free agent signing)
July 8, 1995	CAL	A	—	STL	N	Mark Sweeney Player to be named

Rich Hacker

Date	Traded To		Traded With	Traded By		In Exchange For
Mar. 31, 1971	MON	N	Ron Swoboda	NY	N	Don Hahn

Warren Hacker

Date	Traded To		Traded With	Traded By		In Exchange For
Nov. 13, 1956	CIN	N	Don Hoak Pete Whisenant	CHI	N	Elmer Singleton Ray Jablonski
June 26, 1957	PHI	N	—	CIN	N	Waiver price

Harvey Haddix

Date	Traded To		Traded With	Traded By		In Exchange For
May 11, 1956	PHI	N	Ben Flowers Stu Miller	STL	N	Murry Dickson Herm Wehmeier
Dec. 16, 1957	CIN	N	—	PHI	N	Wally Post
Jan. 30, 1959	PIT	N	Smoky Burgess Don Hoak	CIN	N	Whammy Douglas Jim Pendleton Frank Thomas Johnny Powers
Dec. 14, 1963	BAL	A	—	PIT	N	Minor league SS Dick Yencha Cash

Bump Hadley

Date	Traded To		Traded With	Traded By		In Exchange For
Dec. 4, 1931	CHI	A	Jackie Hayes Sad Sam Jones	WAS	A	Carl Reynolds John Kerr
Apr. 27, 1932	STL	A	Bruce Campbell	CHI	A	Red Kress
Jan. 22, 1935	WAS	A	—	STL	A	Luke Sewell
Jan. 17, 1936	NY	A	Roy Johnson	WAS	A	Jimmie DeShong Jesse Hill
Jan. 2, 1941	NY	N	—	NY	A	Cash
May 29, 1941	PHI	A	—	NY	N	Cash

Kent Hadley

Date	Traded To		Traded With	Traded By		In Exchange For
Nov. 20, 1957	KC	A	—	DET	A	*see Billy Martin*
Dec. 11, 1959	NY	A	*see Roger Maris*	KC	A	—

Mickey Haefner

Date	Traded To		Traded With	Traded By		In Exchange For
July 21, 1949	CHI	A	—	WAS	A	Cash
Aug. 8, 1950	BOS	N	—	CHI	A	Cash

Bud Hafey

Date	Traded To		Traded With	Traded By		In Exchange For
Aug. 5, 1939	PHI	N	—	CIN	N	Cash

Chick Hafey

Date	Traded To		Traded With	Traded By		In Exchange For
Apr. 11, 1932	CIN	N	—	STL	N	Harvey Hendrick Benny Frey Cash

Casey Hageman

Date	Traded To		Traded With	Traded By		In Exchange For
June 1914	BKN	N	—	STL	N	Joe Riggert
June 1914	CHI	N	—	BKN	N	Cash

Joe Hague

Date	Traded To		Traded With	Traded By		In Exchange For
May 19, 1972	CIN	N	—	STL	N	Bernie Carbo

Don Hahn

Date	Traded To		Traded With	Traded By		In Exchange For
Mar. 31, 1971	NY	N	—	MON	N	Ron Swoboda Rich Hacker
Dec. 3, 1974	PHI	N	Tug McGraw Dave Schneck	NY	N	Del Unser John Stearns Mac Scarce
June 24, 1975	SD	N	—	STL	N	Cash

Ed Hahn

Date	Traded To		Traded With	Traded By		In Exchange For
May 9, 1906	CHI	A	—	NY	A	Cash

Noodles Hahn

Date	Traded To		Traded With	Traded By		In Exchange For
Apr. 1906	NY	A	—	CIN	N	Waiver price

Hal Haid

Date	Traded To		Traded With	Traded By		In Exchange For
Jan. 1931	BOS	N	—	STL	N	Waiver price

Jerry Hairston

Date	Traded To		Traded With	Traded By		In Exchange For
June 13, 1977	PIT	N	—	CHI	A	Cash

Bob Hale

Date	Traded To		Traded With	Traded By		In Exchange For
July 26, 1961	NY	A	—	CLE	A	Cash

John Hale

Date	Traded To		Traded With	Traded By		In Exchange For
Sept. 2, 1977	TOR	A	—	LA	N	Cash
Sept. 14, 1977	SEA	A	—	TOR	A	Cash

Odell Hale

Date	Traded To		Traded With	Traded By		In Exchange For
Dec. 12, 1940	BOS	A	Frankie Pytlak Joe Dobson	CLE	A	Gene Desautels Jim Bagby Gee Walker
June 19, 1941	NY	N	—	BOS	A	Waiver price

Sammy Hale

Date	Traded To		Traded With	Traded By		In Exchange For
Dec. 11, 1929	STL	A	—	PHI	A	Wally Schang

Ray Haley

Date	Traded To		Traded With	Traded By		In Exchange For
Sept. 2, 1916	PHI	A	—	BOS	A	Jimmy Walsh

Ed Halicki

Date	Traded To		Traded With	Traded By		In Exchange For
June 20, 1980	CAL	A	—	SF	N	Cash

Bob Hall

Date	Traded To		Traded With	Traded By		In Exchange For
Apr. 1905	BKN	N	—	NY	N	Cash

Dick Hall

Date	Traded To		Traded With	Traded By		In Exchange For
Dec. 15, 1959	KC	A	Ken Hamlin	PIT	N	Hal Smith
Apr. 12, 1961	BAL	A	Dick Williams	KC	A	Jerry Walker Chuck Essegian
Dec. 15, 1966	PHI	N	—	BAL	A	John Morris

Drew Hall

Date	Traded To		Traded With	Traded By		In Exchange For
Dec. 5, 1988	TEX	A	*see Rafael Palmeiro*	CHI	N	—
Apr. 2, 1990	MON	N	—	TEX	A	Jeff Huson

Jimmie Hall

Date	Traded To		Traded With	Traded By		In Exchange For
Dec. 2, 1966	CAL	A	Don Mincher Pete Cimino	MIN	A	Dean Chance Jackie Hernandez
June 15, 1968	CLE	A	—	CAL	A	Vic Davalillo
Apr. 14, 1969	NY	A	—	CLE	A	Cash
Sept. 11, 1969	CHI	N	—	NY	A	Minor league P Terry Bongiovanni Cash
June 29, 1970	ATL	N	—	CHI	N	Cash

Mel Hall

Date	Traded To		Traded With	Traded By		In Exchange For
June 13, 1984	CLE	A	Joe Carter Don Schulze Minor league P Darryl Banks	CHI	N	Rick Sutcliffe George Frazier Ron Hassey
Mar. 19, 1989	NY	A	—	CLE	A	Joel Skinner Turner Ward

Tom Hall

Date	Traded To		Traded With	Traded By		In Exchange For
Dec. 3, 1971	CIN	N	—	MIN	A	Wayne Granger
Apr. 15, 1975	NY	N	—	CIN	N	Mac Scarce
May 7, 1976	KC	A	—	NY	N	Minor league IF Bryan Jones Cash

Bill Hallahan

Date	Traded To		Traded With	Traded By		In Exchange For
May 31, 1936	CIN	N	—	STL	N	Cash

Tom Haller

Date	Traded To		Traded With	Traded By		In Exchange For
Feb. 13, 1968	LA	N	minor league P Frank Kasmeta	SF	N	Ron Hunt Nate Oliver
Dec. 2, 1971	DET	A	—	LA	N	Minor league P Bernie Beckman Cash
Oct. 25, 1972	PHI	N	Don Leshnock	DET	A	Cash

Jack Hallett

Date	Traded To		Traded With	Traded By		In Exchange For
Dec. 9, 1941	PHI	A	Mike Kreevich	CHI	A	Wally Moses

Darryl Hamilton

Date	Traded To		Traded With	Traded By		In Exchange For
Dec. 14, 1995	TEX	A	—	MIL	A	No compensation (free agent signing)

Dave Hamilton

Date	Traded To		Traded With	Traded By		In Exchange For
June 15, 1975	CHI	A	Chet Lemon	OAK	A	Stan Bahnsen Skip Pitlock
Aug. 31, 1977	STL	N	Nyls Nyman Silvio Martinez	CHI	A	Clay Carroll
May 28, 1978	PIT	N	—	STL	N	Cash

Earl Hamilton

Date	Traded To		Traded With	Traded By		In Exchange For
May 30, 1916	DET	A	—	STL	A	Cash
June 22, 1916	STL	A	—	DET	A	Waiver price
1918	PIT	N	—	STL	A	Cash
Dec. 1923	PHI	N	—	PIT	N	Waiver price

Jack Hamilton

Date	Traded To		Traded With	Traded By		In Exchange For
Dec. 4, 1963	DET	A	Don Demeter	PHI	N	Jim Bunning Gus Triandos
Oct. 14, 1965	NY	N	—	DET	A	Cash
June 10, 1967	CAL	A	—	NY	N	Nick Willhite
Oct. 8, 1968	CLE	A	—	CAL	A	Eddie Fisher
June 13, 1969	CHI	A	—	CLE	A	Sammy Ellis

Steve Hamilton

Date	Traded To		Traded With	Traded By		In Exchange For
May 3, 1962	WAS	A	Don Rudolph	CLE	A	Willie Tasby
Apr. 21, 1963	NY	A	—	WAS	A	Jim Coates
Sept. 9, 1970	CHI	A	—	NY	A	Cash
Mar. 23, 1971	SF	N	—	CHI	A	Steve Huntz

Tom Hamilton

Date	Traded To		Traded With	Traded By		In Exchange For
Dec. 16, 1953	NY	A	*see Harry Byrd*	PHI	A	—

Ken Hamlin

Date	Traded To		Traded With	Traded By		In Exchange For
Dec. 15, 1959	KC	A	Dick Hall	PIT	N	Hal Smith

Luke Hamlin

Date	Traded To		Traded With	Traded By		In Exchange For
Dec. 12, 1941	PIT	N	Pete Coscarart Babe Phelps Jimmy Wasdell	BKN	N	Arky Vaughan

Pete Hamm

Date	Traded To		Traded With	Traded By		In Exchange For
Feb. 5, 1972	CHI	A	—	MIN	A	Cash

Atlee Hammaker

Date	Traded To		Traded With	Traded By		In Exchange For
Mar. 30, 1982	SF	N	Renie Martin Craig Chamberlain Brad Wellman	KC	A	Vida Blue Bob Tufts

Chris Hammond

Date	Traded To		Traded With	Traded By		In Exchange For
Mar. 27, 1993	FLA	N	—	CIN	N	Gary Scott Hector Carrasco

(Cincinnati received Carrasco on September 10, 1993.)

Jack Hammond

Date	Traded To		Traded With	Traded By		In Exchange For
May 13, 1922	PIT	N	—	CLE	A	Cash

Steve Hammond

Date	Traded To		Traded With	Traded By		In Exchange For
Apr. 28, 1982	KC	A	—	ATL	N	Cash

Granny Hamner

Date	Traded To		Traded With	Traded By		In Exchange For
May 16, 1959	CLE	A	—	PHI	N	Humberto Robinson

Ike Hampton

Date	Traded To		Traded With	Traded By		In Exchange For
Mar. 22, 1975	CAL	A	—	NY	N	Ken Sanders

Mike Hampton

Date	Traded To		Traded With	Traded By		In Exchange For
Dec. 10, 1993	HOU	N	Mike Felder	SEA	A	Eric Anthony

Garry Hancock

Date	Traded To		Traded With	Traded By		In Exchange For
Dec. 9, 1977	BOS	A	—	CLE	A	Jack Baker
Dec. 6, 1982	OAK	A	Carney Lansford minor league P Jerry King	BOS	A	Tony Armas Jeff Newman

Rich Hand

Date	Traded To		Traded With	Traded By		In Exchange For
Dec. 2, 1971	TEX	A	Roy Foster Ken Suarez Mike Paul	CLE	A	Del Unser Denny Riddleberger Gary Jones minor league P Terry Ley
May 20, 1973	CAL	A	Mike Epstein Rick Stelmaszek	TEX	A	Jim Spencer Lloyd Allen
Sept. 5, 1974	STL	N	—	CAL	A	Orlando Pena

(St. Louis received Hand on October 15, 1974.)

Bill Hands

Date	Traded To		Traded With	Traded By		In Exchange For
Dec. 2, 1965	CHI	N	Randy Hundley	SF	N	Lindy McDaniel Don Landrum Jim Rittwage
Nov. 30, 1972	MIN	A	Joe Decker minor league P Bob Maneely	CHI	N	Dave LaRoche
Sept. 9, 1974	TEX	A	—	MIN	A	Cash
Feb. 24, 1976	NY	N	—	TEX	A	George Stone

Harry Hanebrink

Date	Traded To		Traded With	Traded By		In Exchange For
Mar. 31, 1959	PHI	N	Gene Conley Joe Koppe	MIL	N	Stan Lopata Ted Kazanski Johnny O'Brien

Chris Haney

Date	Traded To		Traded With	Traded By		In Exchange For
Aug. 29, 1992	KC	A	Bill Sampen	MON	N	Sean Berry Archie Corbin

Fred Haney

Date	Traded To		Traded With	Traded By		In Exchange For
Dec. 9, 1925	BOS	A	—	DET	A	Tex Vache Homer Ezzell
July 12, 1927	CHI	N	—	BOS	A	Cash

Larry Haney

Date	Traded To		Traded With	Traded By		In Exchange For
June 14, 1969	OAK	A	—	SEA	A	John Donaldson
Sept. 6, 1972	OAK	A	—	SD	N	Cash
Sept. 1, 1973	STL	N	Lew Krausse	OAK	A	Cash
Mar. 26, 1974	OAK	A	—	STL	N	Cash
Dec. 6, 1976	MIL	A	—	OAK	A	Cash

Gerald Hannahs

Date	Traded To		Traded With	Traded By		In Exchange For
May 20, 1978	LA	N	Larry Landreth	MON	N	Mike Garman

Jim Hannan

Date	Traded To		Traded With	Traded By		In Exchange For
Oct. 9, 1970	DET	A	—	WAS	A	*see Denny McLain*
May 11, 1971	MIL	A	—	DET	A	John Gelnar Jose Herrera

Jack Hannifin

Date	Traded To		Traded With	Traded By		In Exchange For
June 1906	NY	N	—	PHI	A	Waiver price
Apr. 1908	BOS	N	—	NY	N	Cash

Greg Hansell

Date	Traded To		Traded With	Traded By		In Exchange For
July 27, 1990	NY	N	Minor league IF Ed Perozo Player to be named	BOS	A	Mike Marshall

(New York received C Paul Williams on November 19, 1990.)

Date	Traded To		Traded With	Traded By		In Exchange For
Dec. 15, 1990	LA	N	Bob Ojeda	NY	N	Hubie Brooks
July 31, 1995	MIN	A	—	LA	N	*see Kevin Tapani*

Andy Hansen

Date	Traded To		Traded With	Traded By		In Exchange For
Jan. 13, 1954	PIT	N	Lucky Lohrke $70,000.	PHI	N	Murry Dickson

Ron Hansen

Date	Traded To		Traded With	Traded By		In Exchange For
Jan. 14, 1963	CHI	A	Hoyt Wilhelm Pete Ward Dave Nicholson	BAL	A	Luis Aparicio Al Smith
Feb. 13, 1968	WAS	A	Dennis Higgins Steve Jones	CHI	A	Tim Cullen Buster Narum Bob Priddy
Aug. 2, 1968	CHI	A	—	WAS	A	Tim Cullen
Feb. 28, 1970	NY	A	—	CHI	A	Cash

Snipe Hansen

Date	Traded To		Traded With	Traded By		In Exchange For
June 22, 1935	STL	A	—	PHI	N	Cash

Erik Hanson

Date	Traded To		Traded With	Traded By		In Exchange For
Nov. 2, 1993	CIN	N	Bret Boone	SEA	A	Dan Wilson Bobby Ayala
Apr. 11, 1994	BOS	A	—	CIN	N	No compensation (free agent signing)
Dec. 22, 1995	TOR	A	—	BOS	A	No compensation (free agent signing)

Jim Hardin

Date	Traded To		Traded With	Traded By		In Exchange For
May 28, 1971	NY	A	—	BAL	A	Bill Burbach

Carroll Hardy

Date	Traded To		Traded With	Traded By		In Exchange For
June 13, 1960	BOS	A	Russ Nixon	CLE	A	Marty Keough Ted Bowsfield
Dec. 10, 1962	HOU	N	—	BOS	A	Dick Williams

Larry Hardy

Date	Traded To		Traded With	Traded By		In Exchange For
Dec. 11, 1975	HOU	N	Joe McIntosh	SD	N	Doug Rader

Shawn Hare

Date	Traded To		Traded With	Traded By		In Exchange For
May 12, 1994	NY	N	—	DET	A	Waiver price

Steve Hargan

Date	Traded To		Traded With	Traded By		In Exchange For
Mar. 23, 1974	TEX	A	—	CLE	A	Bill Gogolewski
May 9, 1977	TEX	A	Jim Mason $200,000.	TOR	A	Roy Howell
June 15, 1977	ATL	N	—	TEX	A	Cash

Alan Hargesheimer

Date	Traded To		Traded With	Traded By		In Exchange For
Oct. 15, 1982	CHI	N	—	SF	N	Herman Segelke
Mar. 30, 1984	KC	A	—	CHI	N	Derek Botelho

Pinky Hargrave

Date	Traded To		Traded With	Traded By		In Exchange For
June 8, 1925	STL	A	George Mogridge	WAS	A	Hank Severeid
Jan. 15, 1927	DET	A	Marty McManus Bobby LaMotte	STL	A	Lefty Stewart Frank O'Rourke Billy Mullen Otto Miller
Sept. 10, 1930	WAS	A	—	DET	A	Cash
Dec. 1931	BOS	N	—	WAS	A	Waiver price

Charlie Hargreaves

Date	Traded To		Traded With	Traded By		In Exchange For
June 8, 1928	PIT	N	—	BKN	N	Joe Harris Johnny Gooch

Mike Hargrove

Date	Traded To		Traded With	Traded By		In Exchange For
Oct. 25, 1978	SD	N	Kurt Bevacqua Bill Fahey	TEX	A	Oscar Gamble Dave Roberts $300,000.
June 14, 1979	CLE	A	—	SD	N	Paul Dade

Mike Harkey

Date	Traded To		Traded With	Traded By		In Exchange For
July 19, 1995	CAL	A	—	OAK	A	Waiver price

Tim Harkness

Date	Traded To		Traded With	Traded By		In Exchange For
Apr. 5, 1957	BKN	N	Ron Negray Elmer Valo Ben Flowers minor league SS Mel Geho and $75,000.	PHI	N	Chico Fernandez
Nov. 30, 1962	NY	N	Larry Burright	LA	N	Bob Miller

Dick Harley

Date	Traded To		Traded With	Traded By		In Exchange For
Apr. 1900	CIN	N	—	CLE	N	Cash

Larry Harlow

Date	Traded To		Traded With	Traded By		In Exchange For
June 5, 1979	CAL	A	—	BAL	A	Floyd Rayford Cash

Bob Harmon

Date	Traded To		Traded With	Traded By		In Exchange For
Dec. 12, 1913	PIT	N	Ed Konetchy Mike Mowrey	STL	N	Art Butler Dots Miller Cozy Dolan Owen Wilson Hank Robinson

Chuck Harmon

Date	Traded To		Traded With	Traded By		In Exchange For
May 16, 1956	STL	N	—	CIN	N	Joe Frazier Alex Grammas
May 10, 1957	PHI	N	—	STL	N	Glen Gorbous

Pete Harnisch

Date	Traded To		Traded With	Traded By		In Exchange For
Jan. 10, 1991	HOU	N	Curt Schilling Steve Finley	BAL	A	Glenn Davis
Nov. 28, 1994	NY	N	—	HOU	N	Juan Castillo Minor league P Andy Beckerman

(Houston received Beckerman on December 6, 1994 and Castillo on April 12, 1995.)

Brian Harper

Date	Traded To		Traded With	Traded By		In Exchange For
Dec. 11, 1981	PIT	N	—	CAL	A	Tim Foli
Dec. 12, 1984	STL	N	John Tudor	PIT	N	George Hendrick minor league C Steve Barnard
Feb. 13, 1994	MIL	A	—	MIN	A	No compensation (free agent signing)

George Harper

Date	Traded To		Traded With	Traded By		In Exchange For
May 30, 1924	PHI	N	—	CIN	N	Curt Walker
Jan. 9, 1927	NY	N	Butch Henline	PHI	N	Jack Scott Fresco Thompson

(Part of three-team trade involving Philadelphia, New York, and Brooklyn.)

Date	Traded To		Traded With	Traded By		In Exchange For
May 1, 1928	STL	N	—	NY	N	Bob O'Farrell
Dec. 8, 1928	BOS	N	—	STL	N	Cash

Harry Harper

Date	Traded To		Traded With	Traded By		In Exchange For
Jan. 20, 1920	BOS	A	Mike Menosky Eddie Foster	WAS	A	Braggo Roth Red Shannon
Dec. 15, 1920	NY	A	*see Waite Hoyt*	BOS	A	—

Jack Harper

Date	Traded To		Traded With	Traded By		In Exchange For
Jan. 1900	STL	N	Otto Krueger Joe Quinn Jim Hughey	CLE	N	Cash
Oct. 1906	CHI	N	—	CIN	N	Chick Fraser

Terry Harper

Date	Traded To	Traded With	Traded By	In Exchange For
Jan. 27, 1987	DET A	Minor league OF Freddie Tiburcio	ATL N	Randy O'Neal Chuck Cary
June 28, 1987	PIT N	—	DET A	Shawn Holman Minor league IF Pete Rice

Tommy Harper

Date	Traded To	Traded With	Traded By	In Exchange For
Nov. 21, 1967	CLE A	—	CIN N	George Culver Fred Whitfield Bob Raudman
Oct. 11, 1971	BOS A	Marty Pattin Lew Krausse Minor leaguer Pat Skrable	MIL A	George Scott Billy Conigliaro Joe Lahoud Jim Lonborg Ken Brett Don Pavletich
Dec. 2, 1974	CAL A	—	BOS A	Bob Heise
Aug. 13, 1975	OAK A	—	CAL A	Cash

Toby Harrah

Date	Traded To	Traded With	Traded By	In Exchange For
Dec. 8, 1978	CLE A	—	TEX A	Buddy Bell
Feb. 5, 1984	NY A	Minor league P Rick Browne	CLE A	George Frazier Otis Nixon Minor league P Guy Elston
Feb. 27, 1985	TEX A	—	NY A	Billy Sample player to be named

(New York received P Eric Dersin on July 14, 1985.)

Billy Harrell

Date	Traded To	Traded With	Traded By	In Exchange For
Feb. 2, 1959	STL N	—	CLE A	Waiver price

Ray Harrell

Date	Traded To	Traded With	Traded By	In Exchange For
Dec. 8, 1938	CHI N	—	STL N	Cash
May 29, 1939	PHI N	Joe Marty Kirby Higbe	CHI N	Claude Passeau
Jan. 22, 1940	PIT N	—	PHI N	Waiver price

Bill Harrelson

Date	Traded To	Traded With	Traded By	In Exchange For
Jan. 14, 1970	CIN N	minor league IF Dan Loomer	CAL A	Jack Fisher

Bud Harrelson

Date	Traded To	Traded With	Traded By	In Exchange For
Mar. 24, 1978	PHI N	—	NY N	Fred Andrews Cash

Ken Harrelson

Date	Traded To	Traded With	Traded By	In Exchange For
June 23, 1966	WAS A	—	KC A	Jim Duckworth
June 9, 1967	KC A	—	WAS A	Cash
Apr. 19, 1969	CLE A	Juan Pizarro Dick Ellsworth	BOS A	Sonny Siebert Joe Azcue Vicente Romo

Bill Harrington

Date	Traded To	Traded With	Traded By	In Exchange For
Dec. 5, 1956	DET A	—	KC A	*see Ned Garver*

Bob Harris

Date	Traded To	Traded With	Traded By	In Exchange For
May 13, 1939	STL A	—	DET A	*see Beau Bell*
June 1, 1942	PHI A	Bob Swift	STL A	Frankie Hayes

Bucky Harris

Date	Traded To	Traded With	Traded By	In Exchange For
Dec. 19, 1928	DET A	—	WAS A	Jack Warner

(Harris was named Detroit manager.)

Buddy Harris

Date	Traded To	Traded With	Traded By	In Exchange For
Nov. 27, 1972	NY N	Rich Chiles	HOU N	Tommie Agee

Charlie Harris

Date	Traded To	Traded With	Traded By	In Exchange For
May 2, 1951	CLE A	—	PHI A	Cash

Dave Harris

Date	Traded To	Traded With	Traded By	In Exchange For
June 13, 1930	WAS A	—	CHI A	Red Barnes

Gail Harris

Date	Traded To	Traded With	Traded By	In Exchange For
Jan. 28, 1958	DET A	Ozzie Virgil	SF N	Jim Finigan $25,000.
May 7, 1960	LA N	—	DET A	Sandy Amoros

Gene Harris

Date	Traded To	Traded With	Traded By	In Exchange For
May 25, 1989	SEA A	Randy Johnson Brian Holman	MON N	Mark Langston Mike Campbell

(Montreal received Campbell on July 31, 1989.)

Date	Traded To	Traded With	Traded By	In Exchange For
May 11, 1992	SD N	—	SEA A	Minor league OF Will Taylor
May 11, 1994	DET A	—	SD N	Scott Livingstone
June 18, 1995	BAL A	—	PHI N	Andy Van Slyke

Greg Harris

Date	Traded To	Traded With	Traded By	In Exchange For
July 26, 1993	CLR N	Bruce Hurst	SD N	Brad Ausmus Andy Ashby Doug Bochtler

Greg Harris

Date	Traded To	Traded With	Traded By	In Exchange For
Feb. 10, 1982	CIN N	Alex Trevino Jim Kern	NY N	George Foster
Sept. 27, 1983	MON N	—	CIN N	Cash
July 21, 1984	SD N	—	MON N	Al Newman
Feb. 13, 1985	TEX A	—	SD N	Cash
Aug. 7, 1989	BOS A	—	PHI N	Waiver price

Joe Harris

Date	Traded To	Traded With	Traded By	In Exchange For
Dec. 24, 1921	BOS A	George Burns Elmer Smith	CLE A	Stuffy McInnis
Apr. 26, 1925	WAS A	—	BOS A	Paul Zahniser Roy Carlyle
Feb. 4, 1927	PIT N	—	WAS A	Waiver price
June 8, 1928	BKN N	Johnny Gooch	PIT N	Charlie Hargreaves

John Harris

Date	Traded To	Traded With	Traded By	In Exchange For
Jan. 10, 1983	CIN N	—	CAL A	Mike O'Berry

Lenny Harris

Date	Traded To	Traded With	Traded By	In Exchange For
July 18, 1989	LA N	Kal Daniels	CIN N	Tim Leary Mariano Duncan
Dec. 1, 1993	CIN N	—	LA N	No compensation (free agent signing)

Lum Harris

Date	Traded To	Traded With	Traded By	In Exchange For
Feb. 14, 1947	WAS A	—	PHI A	Waiver price

Mickey Harris

Date	Traded To	Traded With	Traded By	In Exchange For
June 13, 1949	WAS A	Sam Mele	BOS A	Walt Masterson
Apr. 22, 1952	CLE A	—	WAS A	Waiver price

Vic Harris

Date	Traded To	Traded With	Traded By	In Exchange For
July 20, 1972	TEX A	Marty Martinez Steve Lawson	OAK A	Don Mincher Ted Kubiak
Oct. 25, 1973	CHI N	Bill Madlock	TEX A	Ferguson Jenkins
Dec. 22, 1975	STL N	—	CHI N	Mick Kelleher
Oct. 20, 1976	SF N	—	STL N	*see Mike Caldwell*

Chuck Harrison

Date	Traded To	Traded With	Traded By	In Exchange For
Oct. 8, 1967	ATL N	Sonny Jackson	HOU N	Denny Lemaster Denis Menke
Oct. 17, 1968	KC A	—	HOU N	Cash

Roric Harrison

Date	Traded To	Traded With	Traded By	In Exchange For
Aug. 24, 1969	SEA A	Dooley Womack	HOU N	Jim Bouton
Apr. 5, 1971	BAL A	minor leaguer Marion Jackson	MIL A	Marcelino Lopez
Nov. 30, 1972	ATL N	—	BAL A	*see Earl Williams*
June 7, 1975	CLE A	—	ATL N	Blue Moon Odom Rob Belloir

Roric Harrison *continued*

Date	Traded To	Traded With	Traded By	In Exchange For
Apr. 7, 1976	STL N	—	CLE A	Harry Parker

Slim Harriss

Date	Traded To	Traded With	Traded By	In Exchange For
June 15, 1926	BOS A	Fred Heimach Baby Doll Jacobson	PHI A	Tom Jenkins Howard Ehmke

Earl Harrist

Date	Traded To	Traded With	Traded By	In Exchange For
June 9, 1948	WAS A	—	CHI A	Marino Pieretti
Mar. 7, 1953	CHI A	—	STL A	Cash
May 23, 1953	DET A	—	CHI A	Waiver price

Jack Harshman

Date	Traded To	Traded With	Traded By	In Exchange For
Dec. 3, 1957	BAL A	*see Larry Doby*	CHI A	—
June 15, 1959	BOS A	—	BAL A	Billy Hoeft
July 30, 1959	CLE A	—	BOS A	Waiver price

Jim Ray Hart

Date	Traded To	Traded With	Traded By	In Exchange For
Apr. 17, 1973	NY A	—	SF N	Cash

Mike Hart

Date	Traded To	Traded With	Traded By	In Exchange For
Dec. 8, 1978	TEX A	—	MON N	Jim Mason

Chuck Hartenstein

Date	Traded To	Traded With	Traded By	In Exchange For
Jan. 15, 1969	PIT N	Ron Campbell	CHI N	Manny Jimenez
June 22, 1970	STL N	—	PIT N	Cash
Nov. 5, 1976	TOR A	—	SD N	Cash

Grover Hartley

Date	Traded To	Traded With	Traded By	In Exchange For
Dec. 12, 1913	CIN N	Buck Herzog	NY N	Bob Bescher
(Hartley jumped to the Federal League and Herzog was made Cincinnati manager.)				
Feb. 10, 1916	STL A	*see Eddie Plank*	STL F	—
Dec. 1927	CLE A	—	BOS A	Waiver price

Mike Hartley

Date	Traded To	Traded With	Traded By	In Exchange For
July 31, 1991	PHI N	Braulio Castillo	LA N	Roger McDowell
Dec. 5, 1992	MIN A	—	PHI N	David West

Bob Hartman

Date	Traded To	Traded With	Traded By	In Exchange For
June 24, 1962	CLE A	—	MIL N	Ken Aspromonte Cash

Topsy Hartsel

Date	Traded To	Traded With	Traded By	In Exchange For
Apr. 1901	CHI N	Mike Kahoe	CIN N	Cash

Roy Hartsfield

Date	Traded To	Traded With	Traded By	In Exchange For
Jan. 17, 1953	BKN N	$50,000.	MIL N	Andy Pafko

Jeff Hartsock

Date	Traded To	Traded With	Traded By	In Exchange For
Sept. 6, 1991	CHI N	—	LA N	Steve Wilson

Paul Hartzell

Date	Traded To	Traded With	Traded By	In Exchange For
Feb. 3, 1979	MIN A	Ken Landreaux Dave Engle Brad Havens	CAL A	Rod Carew

Roy Hartzell

Date	Traded To	Traded With	Traded By	In Exchange For
Jan. 1911	NY A	—	STL A	Jimmy Austin Frank LaPorte

Bryan Harvey

Date	Traded To	Traded With	Traded By	In Exchange For
Dec. 20, 1995	CAL A	—	FLA N	No compensation (free agent signing)

Ervin Harvey

Date	Traded To	Traded With	Traded By	In Exchange For
Aug. 1901	CLE A	—	CHI A	Cash

Bill Haselman

Date	Traded To	Traded With	Traded By	In Exchange For
May 29, 1992	SEA A	—	TEX A	Waiver price

Mickey Haslin

Date	Traded To	Traded With	Traded By	In Exchange For
Apr. 30, 1936	BOS N	—	PHI N	Pinky Whitney
Dec. 4, 1936	NY N	—	BOS N	Eddie Mayo

Buddy Hassett

Date	Traded To	Traded With	Traded By	In Exchange For
Jan. 1936	BKN N	—	NY A	Cash
Dec. 13, 1938	BOS N	Jimmy Outlaw	BKN N	Gene Moore Ira Hutchinson
Feb. 5, 1942	NY A	Gene Moore	BOS N	Tommy Holmes

Ron Hassey

Date	Traded To	Traded With	Traded By	In Exchange For
June 13, 1984	CHI N	*see Rick Sutcliffe*	CLE A	—
Dec. 4, 1984	NY A	Henry Cotto Porfi Altamirano Rich Bordi	CHI N	Ray Fontenot Brian Dayett
Dec. 12, 1985	CHI A	Joe Cowley	NY A	Britt Burns Minor league SS Mike Soper Minor league OF Glen Braxton
Feb. 13, 1986	NY A	Matt Winters Minor league P Eric Schmidt Minor league C Chris Alvarez	CHI A	Neil Allen Scott Bradley Minor league OF Glen Braxton Cash
July 30, 1986	CHI A	Carlos Martinez Bill Lindsey	NY A	Ron Kittle Joel Skinner Wayne Tolleson
(Chicago received Lindsey on Dec. 24, 1986.)				
Dec. 9, 1987	OAK A	—	CHI A	No compensation (free agent signing)

Andy Hassler

Date	Traded To	Traded With	Traded By	In Exchange For
July 5, 1976	KC A	—	CAL A	Cash
July 24, 1978	BOS A	—	KC A	Cash
June 15, 1979	NY N	—	BOS A	Cash
Nov. 19, 1979	PIT N	—	NY N	No compensation (free agent signing)
June 10, 1980	CAL A	—	PIT N	Cash

Billy Hatcher

Date	Traded To	Traded With	Traded By	In Exchange For
Dec. 16, 1985	HOU N	Steve Engel	CHI N	Jerry Mumphrey
Aug. 18, 1989	PIT N	—	HOU N	Glenn Wilson
Apr. 3, 1990	CIN N	—	PIT N	Mike Roesler Jeff Richardson
July 9, 1992	BOS A	—	CIN N	Tom Bolton
May 31, 1994	PHI N	Paul Quantrill	BOS A	Wes Chamberlain Minor league P Mike Sullivan

Mickey Hatcher

Date	Traded To	Traded With	Traded By	In Exchange For
Mar. 30, 1981	MIN A	Minor leaguers P Matt Reeves and 1B Kelly Snider	LA N	Ken Landreaux

Fred Hatfield

Date	Traded To	Traded With	Traded By	In Exchange For
June 3, 1952	DET A	—	BOS A	*see George Kell*
May 15, 1956	CHI A	Jim Delsing	DET A	Jim Brideweser Harry Byrd Bob Kennedy
Dec. 4, 1957	CLE A	Minnie Minoso	CHI A	Early Wynn Al Smith
Apr. 23, 1958	CIN N	—	CLE A	Bob Kelly

Hilly Hathaway

Date	Traded To	Traded With	Traded By	In Exchange For
Mar. 29, 1994	SD N	—	CAL A	Harold Reynolds

Joe Hatten

Date	Traded To	Traded With	Traded By	In Exchange For
June 15, 1951	CHI N	Bruce Edwards Eddie Miksis Gene Hermanski	BKN N	Johnny Schmitz Rube Walker Andy Pafko Wayne Terwilliger

Grady Hatton

Date	Traded To	Traded With	Traded By	In Exchange For
Apr. 18, 1954	CHI A	—	CIN N	Johnny Lipon
May 23, 1954	BOS A	$100,000.	CHI A	George Kell
May 11, 1956	STL N	—	BOS A	Cash
Aug. 1, 1956	BAL A	—	STL N	Cash

Phil Haugstad

Date	Traded To	Traded With	Traded By	In Exchange For
May 25, 1952	CIN N	—	BKN N	Waiver price

Joe Hauser

Date	Traded To	Traded With	Traded By	In Exchange For
June 7, 1929	CLE A	—	PHI A	Waiver price

Tom Hausman

Date	Traded To	Traded With	Traded By	In Exchange For
Nov. 21, 1977	NY N	—	MIL A	No compensation (free agent signing)
Sept. 10, 1982	ATL N	—	NY N	Carlos Diaz

Brad Havens

Date	Traded To	Traded With	Traded By	In Exchange For
Feb. 3, 1979	MIN A	Ken Landreaux Dave Engle Paul Hartzell	CAL A	Rod Carew
Mar. 27, 1985	BAL A	—	MIN A	Mark Brown
May 22, 1987	LA N	*see John Shelby*	BAL A	—

Andy Hawkins

Date	Traded To	Traded With	Traded By	In Exchange For
Dec. 8, 1988	NY A	—	SD N	No compensation (free agent signing)

Wynn Hawkins

Date	Traded To	Traded With	Traded By	In Exchange For
Nov. 27, 1962	NY N	—	CLE A	Cash

Pink Hawley

Date	Traded To	Traded With	Traded By	In Exchange For
Feb. 27, 1900	NY N	—	CIN N	Cash

Hal Haydel

Date	Traded To	Traded With	Traded By	In Exchange For
Mar. 28, 1963	CHI N	Merritt Ranew Dick LeMay	HOU N	Dave Gerard Danny Murphy

Charlie Hayes

Date	Traded To	Traded With	Traded By	In Exchange For
June 18, 1989	PHI N	—	SF N	*see Steve Bedrosian*
Jan. 8, 1992	NY A	—	PHI N	Darrin Chapin
		(New York received Hayes on February 19, 1992.)		
Apr. 6, 1995	PHI N	—	CLR N	No compensation (free agent signing)
Dec. 28, 1995	PIT N	—	PHI N	No compensation (free agent signing)

Frankie Hayes

Date	Traded To	Traded With	Traded By	In Exchange For
June 1, 1942	STL A	—	PHI A	Bob Harris Bob Swift
Feb. 17, 1944	PHI A	—	STL A	Sam Zoldak minor league OF Barney Lutz
May 29, 1945	CLE A	—	PHI A	Buddy Rosar
June 1946	CHI A	—	CLE A	Tom Jordan

Jackie Hayes

Date	Traded To	Traded With	Traded By	In Exchange For
Dec. 4, 1931	CHI A	Bump Hadley Sad Sam Jones	WAS A	Carl Reynolds John Kerr

Von Hayes

Date	Traded To	Traded With	Traded By	In Exchange For
Dec. 9, 1982	PHI N	—	CLE A	Manny Trillo Jay Baller George Vukovich Julio Franco Jerry Willard
Dec. 8, 1991	CAL A	—	PHI N	Ruben Amaro Kyle Abbott

Heath Haynes

Date	Traded To	Traded With	Traded By	In Exchange For
Nov. 17, 1994	BOS A	—	MON N	Waiver price
Dec. 9, 1994	OAK A	—	BOS A	Waiver price

Joe Haynes

Date	Traded To	Traded With	Traded By	In Exchange For
Jan. 4, 1941	CHI A	—	WAS A	Cash
Nov. 22, 1948	CLE A	—	CHI A	Joe Tipton
Dec. 14, 1948	WAS A	Eddie Klieman Eddie Robinson	CLE A	Mickey Vernon Early Wynn

Ray Hayward

Date	Traded To	Traded With	Traded By	In Exchange For
Feb. 12, 1988	CHI N	*see Goose Gossage*	SD N	—
Mar. 17, 1988	TEX A	—	CHI N	Dave Meier Greg Tabor

Ray Hayworth

Date	Traded To	Traded With	Traded By	In Exchange For
Sept. 14, 1938	BKN N	—	DET A	Waiver price
Aug. 23, 1939	NY N	—	BKN N	Jimmy Ripple

Bob Hazle

Date	Traded To	Traded With	Traded By	In Exchange For
Apr. 9, 1956	MIL N	Corky Valentine	CIN N	George Crowe
May 24, 1958	DET A	—	MIL N	Cash

Fran Healy

Date	Traded To	Traded With	Traded By	In Exchange For
Apr. 2, 1973	KC A	—	SF N	Greg Minton
May 16, 1976	NY A	—	KC A	Larry Gura

Francis Healy

Date	Traded To	Traded With	Traded By	In Exchange For
May 4, 1934	STL N	—	NY N	Cash

Ed Hearn

Date	Traded To	Traded With	Traded By	In Exchange For
Mar. 27, 1987	KC A	Rick Anderson Mauro Gozzo	NY N	David Cone Chris Jelic

Jim Hearn

Date	Traded To	Traded With	Traded By	In Exchange For
July 10, 1950	NY N	—	STL N	Cash
Oct. 11, 1956	PHI N	—	NY N	Stu Miller

Bill Heath

Date	Traded To	Traded With	Traded By	In Exchange For
Oct. 15, 1964	CHI A	minor league P Joel Gibson	PHI N	Rudy May
Dec. 1, 1965	HOU N	Dave Nicholson	CHI A	Jack Lamabe minor league P Ray Cordeiro Cash
May 8, 1967	DET A	—	HOU N	Cash

Jeff Heath

Date	Traded To	Traded With	Traded By	In Exchange For
Dec. 14, 1945	WAS A	—	CLE A	George Case
June 15, 1946	STL A	—	WAS A	Joe Grace Al LaMacchia
Dec. 4, 1947	BOS N	—	STL A	Cash

Mickey Heath

Date	Traded To	Traded With	Traded By	In Exchange For
May 7, 1931	BKN N	—	CIN N	Harvey Hendrick

Mike Heath

Date	Traded To	Traded With	Traded By	In Exchange For
Nov. 10, 1978	TEX A	—	NY A	*see Dave Righetti*
June 15, 1979	OAK A	Dave Chalk Cash	TEX A	John Henry Johnson
Dec. 10, 1985	STL N	Tim Conroy	OAK A	Joaquin Andujar
Aug. 10, 1986	DET A	—	STL N	Mike Laga Ken Hill
		(St. Louis received Laga on Sept. 2, 1986.)		
Jan. 22, 1991	ATL N	—	DET A	No compensation (free agent signing)

Cliff Heathcote

Date	Traded To	Traded With	Traded By	In Exchange For
May 30, 1922	CHI N	—	STL N	Max Flack
May 1931	CIN N	—	CHI N	Waiver price
June 25, 1932	PHI N	—	CIN N	Waiver price

Neal Heaton

Date	Traded To	Traded With	Traded By	In Exchange For
June 20, 1986	MIN A	—	CLE A	John Butcher

Neal Heaton *continued*

Date	Traded To		Traded With	Traded By		In Exchange For
Feb. 3, 1987	MON	N	Jeff Reed Yorkis Perez Minor league P Al Cardwood	MIN	A	Jeff Reardon Tom Nieto
Mar. 28, 1989	PIT	N	—	MON	N	Brett Gideon
Mar. 10, 1992	KC	A	—	PIT	N	Kirk Gibson

Dave Heaverlo

Date	Traded To		Traded With	Traded By		In Exchange For
Mar. 15, 1978	OAK	A	—	SF	N	*see Vida Blue*
Apr. 9, 1980	SEA	A	—	OAK	A	Cash

Richie Hebner

Date	Traded To		Traded With	Traded By		In Exchange For
Dec. 15, 1976	PHI	N	—	PIT	N	No compensation (free agent signing)
Mar. 27, 1979	NY	N	Jose Moreno	PHI	N	Nino Espinosa
Oct. 31, 1979	DET	A	—	NY	N	Jerry Morales Phil Mankowski
Aug. 16, 1982	PIT	N	—	DET	A	Cash
Jan. 5, 1984	CHI	N	—	PIT	N	No compensation (free agent signing)

Mike Hechinger

Date	Traded To		Traded With	Traded By		In Exchange For
May 1913	BKN	N	—	CHI	N	Waiver price

Mike Hedlund

Date	Traded To		Traded With	Traded By		In Exchange For
Nov. 2, 1972	CLE	A	—	KC	A	Kurt Bevacqua

Danny Heep

Date	Traded To		Traded With	Traded By		In Exchange For
Dec. 10, 1982	NY	N	—	HOU	N	Mike Scott
June 12, 1987	LA	N	—	NY	N	No compensation (free agent signing)
May 6, 1991	ATL	N	—	CHI	A	Minor league IF Kevin Castleberry

Bert Heffernan

Date	Traded To		Traded With	Traded By		In Exchange For
Dec. 20, 1990	LA	N	—	MIL	A	Darren Holmes

Bob Heffner

Date	Traded To		Traded With	Traded By		In Exchange For
Oct. 15, 1966	NY	N	—	CLE	A	Cash

Don Heffner

Date	Traded To		Traded With	Traded By		In Exchange For
Feb. 15, 1938	STL	A	$10,000.	NY	A	Bill Knickerbocker
June 14, 1943	PHI	A	—	STL	A	Cash
Oct. 11, 1943	DET	A	Bob Swift	PHI	A	Rip Radcliff

Jim Hegan

Date	Traded To		Traded With	Traded By		In Exchange For
Feb. 18, 1958	DET	A	Hank Aguirre	CLE	A	Hal Woodeshick J. W. Porter
July 27, 1958	PHI	N	—	DET	A	Minor league OF John Turk Cash
June 14, 1959	SF	N	—	PHI	N	Cash

Mike Hegan

Date	Traded To		Traded With	Traded By		In Exchange For
June 14, 1968	SEA	A	—	NY	A	Cash
June 14, 1971	OAK	A	—	MIL	A	Cash
Aug. 18, 1973	NY	A	—	OAK	A	Cash
May 13, 1974	MIL	A	—	NY	A	Cash

Jack Heidemann

Date	Traded To		Traded With	Traded By		In Exchange For
Mar. 24, 1973	OAK	A	Ray Fosse	CLE	A	George Hendrick Dave Duncan
Mar. 25, 1974	CLE	A	—	OAK	A	Cash
June 1, 1974	STL	N	—	CLE	A	Luis Alvarado Ed Crosby
Dec. 11, 1974	NY	N	Mike Vail	STL	N	Teddy Martinez
June 22, 1976	MIL	A	—	NY	N	Minor league P Tom Deidel

Harry Heilmann

Date	Traded To		Traded With	Traded By		In Exchange For
Oct. 14, 1929	CIN	N	—	DET	A	Cash

Fred Heimach

Date	Traded To		Traded With	Traded By		In Exchange For
June 15, 1926	BOS	A	Slim Harriss Baby Doll Jacobson	PHI	A	Tom Jenkins Howard Ehmke

Ken Heintzelman

Date	Traded To		Traded With	Traded By		In Exchange For
May 9, 1947	PHI	N	—	PIT	N	Cash

Tom Heintzelman

Date	Traded To		Traded With	Traded By		In Exchange For
Oct. 14, 1974	SF	N	—	STL	N	Jim Willoughby

Bob Heise

Date	Traded To		Traded With	Traded By		In Exchange For
Dec. 12, 1969	SF	N	Jim Gosger	NY	N	Ray Sadecki Dave Marshall
June 1, 1971	MIL	A	—	SF	N	Floyd Wicker
Dec. 8, 1973	STL	N	—	MIL	A	Tom Murphy
July 31, 1974	CAL	A	—	STL	N	Doug Howard
Dec. 2, 1974	BOS	A	—	CAL	A	Tommy Harper
Dec. 6, 1976	KC	A	—	BOS	A	Cash

Woodie Held

Date	Traded To		Traded With	Traded By		In Exchange For
June 15, 1957	KC	A	*see Ralph Terry*	NY	A	—
June 15, 1958	CLE	A	Vic Power	KC	A	Roger Maris Dick Tomanek Preston Ward
Dec. 1, 1964	WAS	A	Bob Chance	CLE	A	Chuck Hinton
Oct. 12, 1965	BAL	A	—	WAS	A	John Orsino
June 15, 1967	CAL	A	—	BAL	A	Marcelino Lopez minor league P Tom Arruda
July 20, 1968	CHI	A	—	CAL	A	Wayne Causey

Eric Helfand

Date	Traded To		Traded With	Traded By		In Exchange For
Nov. 17, 1992	OAK	A	Scott Baker	FLA	N	Walt Weiss

(Oakland received Baker on November 20, 1992.)

Tommy Helms

Date	Traded To		Traded With	Traded By		In Exchange For
Nov. 29, 1971	HOU	N	—	CIN	N	*see Joe Morgan*
Dec. 12, 1975	PIT	N	—	HOU	N	Art Howe
Nov. 5, 1976	OAK	A	—	PIT	N	Cash
Mar. 15, 1977	PIT	N	*see Phil Garner*	OAK	A	—

Russ Heman

Date	Traded To		Traded With	Traded By		In Exchange For
Dec. 3, 1957	BAL	A	*see Larry Doby*	CHI	A	—
Dec. 2, 1958	CLE	A	$30,000.	BAL	A	Bobby Avila
June 5, 1961	LA	A	—	CLE	A	Cash

Scott Hemond

Date	Traded To		Traded With	Traded By		In Exchange For
Aug. 6, 1992	CHI	A	—	OAK	A	Waiver price
Mar. 29, 1993	OAK	A	—	CHI	A	Waiver price

Charlie Hemphill

Date	Traded To		Traded With	Traded By		In Exchange For
May 30, 1902	STL	A	—	CLE	A	Player to be named later
			(Cleveland received P Red Donahue in June, 1903.)			
Feb. 1908	NY	A	Fred Glade	STL	A	Jimmy Williams Hobe Ferris Danny Hoffman

Rollie Hemsley

Date	Traded To		Traded With	Traded By		In Exchange For
June 13, 1931	CHI	N	—	PIT	N	Earl Grace
Nov. 30, 1932	CIN	N	Bob Smith Johnny Moore Lance Richbourg	CHI	N	Babe Herman
Aug. 3, 1933	STL	A	—	CIN	N	Waiver price
Feb. 10, 1938	CLE	A	—	STL	A	Ed Cole Roy Hughes Billy Sullivan
Dec. 4, 1941	CIN	N	—	CLE	A	Cash
Mar. 25, 1946	PHI	N	—	NY	A	Cash

Solly Hemus

Date	Traded To		Traded With	Traded By		In Exchange For
May 14, 1956	PHI	N	—	STL	N	Bobby Morgan

Solly Hemus *continued*

Date	Traded To		Traded With	Traded By		In Exchange For
Sept. 29, 1958	STL	N	—	PHI	N	Gene Freese

(Hemus was named St. Louis manager.)

Dave Henderson

Date	Traded To		Traded With	Traded By		In Exchange For
Aug. 19, 1986	BOS	A	Spike Owen	SEA	A	Rey Quinones Mike Trujillo John Christensen Mike Brown

(Seattle received Trujillo and Brown on August 22 and Christensen on September 25, 1986.)

Date	Traded To		Traded With	Traded By		In Exchange For
Sept. 1, 1987	SF	N	—	BOS	A	Randy Kutcher

(Boston received Kutcher on December 9, 1987.)

Date	Traded To		Traded With	Traded By		In Exchange For
Dec. 21, 1987	OAK	A	—	SF	A	No compensation (free agent signing)
Jan. 27, 1994	KC	A	—	OAK	A	No compensation (free agent signing)

Joe Henderson

Date	Traded To		Traded With	Traded By		In Exchange For
Oct. 31, 1977	TOR	A	—	CIN	N	Cash

Ken Henderson

Date	Traded To		Traded With	Traded By		In Exchange For
Nov. 28, 1972	CHI	A	Steve Stone	SF	N	Tom Bradley
Dec. 12, 1975	ATL	N	Dick Ruthven Danny Osborn	CHI	A	Ralph Garr Larvell Blanks
Dec. 9, 1976	TEX	A	Dave May Carl Morton Roger Moret Adrian Devine $250,000.	ATL	N	Jeff Burroughs
Dec. 8, 1977	NY	N	Willie Montanez Tom Grieve	TEX	A	Jon Matlack John Milner

(Part of four-team trade involving Texas, New York Mets, Pittsburgh, and Atlanta.)

Date	Traded To		Traded With	Traded By		In Exchange For
May 19, 1978	CIN	N	—	NY	N	Dale Murray
June 28, 1979	CHI	N	—	CIN	N	Cash

Rickey Henderson

Date	Traded To		Traded With	Traded By		In Exchange For
Dec. 8, 1984	NY	A	Bert Bradley Cash	OAK	A	Jay Howell Jose Rijo Stan Javier Tim Birtsas Eric Plunk
June 21, 1989	OAK	A	—	NY	A	Eric Plunk Greg Cadaret Luis Polonia
July 31, 1993	TOR	A	—	OAK	A	Steve Karsay Jose Herrera

(Oakland received Herrera on August 6, 1993.)

Date	Traded To		Traded With	Traded By		In Exchange For
Dec. 17, 1993	OAK	A	—	TOR	A	No compensation (free agent signing)
Dec. 29, 1995	SD	N	—	OAK	A	No compensation (free agent signing)

Steve Henderson

Date	Traded To		Traded With	Traded By		In Exchange For
June 15, 1977	NY	N	Pat Zachry Doug Flynn Dan Norman	CIN	N	Tom Seaver
Feb. 28, 1981	CHI	N	Cash	NY	N	Dave Kingman
Dec. 9, 1982	SEA	A	—	CHI	N	Rich Bordi
Mar. 31, 1985	OAK	A	—	SEA	A	No compensation (free agent signing)
Mar. 10, 1988	HOU	N	—	OAK	A	No compensation (free agent signing)

Bob Hendley

Date	Traded To		Traded With	Traded By		In Exchange For
Dec. 3, 1963	SF	N	Del Crandall Bob Shaw	MIL	N	Felipe Alou Billy Hoeft Ed Bailey Ernie Bowman
May 29, 1965	CHI	N	Harvey Kuenn Ed Bailey	SF	N	Dick Bertell Len Gabrielson
June 12, 1967	NY	N	—	CHI	N	Johnny Stephenson Rob Gardner

George Hendrick

Date	Traded To		Traded With	Traded By		In Exchange For
Mar. 24, 1973	CLE	A	Dave Duncan	OAK	A	Ray Fosse Jack Heidemann
Dec. 8, 1976	SD	N	—	CLE	A	Johnny Grubb Fred Kendall Hector Torres
May 26, 1978	STL	N	—	SD	N	Eric Rasmussen
Dec. 12, 1984	PIT	N	minor league C Steve Barnard	STL	N	John Tudor Brian Harper
Aug. 2, 1985	CAL	A	John Candelaria Al Holland	PIT	N	Pat Clements Mike Brown Bob Kipper

(Pittsburgh received Kipper on Aug. 16, 1985.)

Harvey Hendrick

Date	Traded To		Traded With	Traded By		In Exchange For
Jan. 3, 1923	NY	A	George Pipgras	BOS	A	Al DeVormer Cash
May 7, 1931	CIN	N	—	BKN	N	Mickey Heath
Apr. 11, 1932	STL	N	Benny Frey Cash	CIN	N	Chick Hafey
June 5, 1932	CIN	N	—	STL	N	Cash
Nov. 21, 1933	PHI	N	Ted Kleinhans Mark Koenig $65,000.	CHI	N	Chuck Klein

Ellie Hendricks

Date	Traded To		Traded With	Traded By		In Exchange For
Aug. 18, 1972	CHI	N	—	BAL	A	Tommy Davis
Oct. 27, 1972	BAL	A	—	CHI	N	Francisco Estrada
June 15, 1976	NY	A	—	BAL	A	*see Tippy Martinez*

Jack Hendricks

Date	Traded To		Traded With	Traded By		In Exchange For
July 1902	CHI	N	—	NY	N	Hal O'Hagen

Claude Hendrix

Date	Traded To		Traded With	Traded By		In Exchange For
Feb. 10, 1916	CHI	N	*see Three Finger Brown*	CHI	F	—

Tim Hendryx

Date	Traded To		Traded With	Traded By		In Exchange For
Apr. 28, 1918	STL	A	—	NY	A	Lee Magee
Jan. 1920	BOS	A	—	STL	A	Cash

Dave Hengel

Date	Traded To		Traded With	Traded By		In Exchange For
Apr. 2, 1989	CLE	A	—	SEA	A	Paul Noce Minor League IF Chuck Baldwin

Tom Henke

Date	Traded To		Traded With	Traded By		In Exchange For
Jan. 24, 1985	TOR	A	—	TEX	A	

(Claimed in compensation draft after Toronto lost free agent DH Cliff Johnson to Texas.)

Date	Traded To		Traded With	Traded By		In Exchange For
Dec. 15, 1992	TEX	A	—	TOR	A	No compensation (free agent signing)
Dec. 12, 1994	STL	N	—	TEX	A	No compensation (free agent signing)

Gail Henley

Date	Traded To		Traded With	Traded By		In Exchange For
Oct. 13, 1952	CIN	N	—	NY	N	Frank Hiller
Oct. 14, 1952	PIT	N	Cal Abrams Joe Rossi	CIN	N	Gus Bell

Butch Henline

Date	Traded To		Traded With	Traded By		In Exchange For
July 25, 1921	PHI	N	Curt Walker Jesse Winters $30,000.	NY	N	Irish Meusel
Jan. 9, 1927	NY	N	George Harper	PHI	N	Jack Scott Fresco Thompson

(Part of three-team trade involving Philadelphia, New York, and Brooklyn.)

Date	Traded To		Traded With	Traded By		In Exchange For
Jan. 9, 1927	BKN	N	—	NY	N	Burleigh Grimes

(Part of three-team trade involving Brooklyn, New York, and Philadelphia.)

Mike Henneman

Date	Traded To		Traded With	Traded By		In Exchange For
Aug. 8, 1995	HOU	N	—	DET	A	Phil Nevin

(Detroit received Nevin on August 15, 1995.)

Mike Henneman *continued*

Date	Traded To	Traded With	Traded By	In Exchange For
Dec. 22, 1995	TEX A	—	HOU N	No compensation (free agent signing)

Phil Hennigan

Date	Traded To	Traded With	Traded By	In Exchange For
Nov. 27, 1972	NY N	—	CLE A	Brent Strom Bob Rauch

Bill Henry

Date	Traded To	Traded With	Traded By	In Exchange For
Dec. 6, 1959	CIN N	Lou Jackson Lee Walls	CHI N	Frank Thomas
May 4, 1965	SF N	—	CIN N	Jim Duffalo
June 27, 1968	PIT N	—	SF N	Cash

Bill Henry

Date	Traded To	Traded With	Traded By	In Exchange For
Sept. 18, 1967	CIN N	—	NY A	Len Boehmer

Butch Henry

Date	Traded To	Traded With	Traded By	In Exchange For
Aug. 31, 1990	HOU N	—	CIN N	*see Bill Doran*
July 16, 1993	MON N	—	CLR N	Kent Bottenfield
Oct. 13, 1995	BOS A	—	MON N	Waiver price

Doug Henry

Date	Traded To	Traded With	Traded By	In Exchange For
Nov. 30, 1994	NY N	—	MIL A	Fernando Vina Minor league C Javier Gonzalez

(Milwaukee received Gonzalez on December 6, and Vina on December 22, 1994.)

Dutch Henry

Date	Traded To	Traded With	Traded By	In Exchange For
Sept. 27, 1929	CHI A	—	NY N	Waiver price
May 7, 1933	STL N	*see Leo Durocher*	CIN N	—

Dwayne Henry

Date	Traded To	Traded With	Traded By	In Exchange For
July 1, 1984	CHI N	minor league IF Jorge Gomez	TEX A	Dickie Noles

(Chicago received Henry and Gomez on December 22.)

Date	Traded To	Traded With	Traded By	In Exchange For
Mar. 30, 1989	ATL N	—	TEX A	Minor league P David Miller Cash
Nov. 26, 1991	CIN N	—	HOU N	Waiver price
Apr. 13, 1993	SEA A	—	CIN N	Waiver price

John Henry

Date	Traded To	Traded With	Traded By	In Exchange For
Feb. 14, 1918	BOS N	—	WAS A	Cash

Roy Henshaw

Date	Traded To	Traded With	Traded By	In Exchange For
Dec. 5, 1936	BKN N	Woody English	CHI N	Lonny Frey
Oct. 4, 1937	STL N	Johnny Cooney Jim Bucher Joe Stripp	BKN N	Leo Durocher

Ron Herbel

Date	Traded To	Traded With	Traded By	In Exchange For
Dec. 5, 1969	SD N	Bob Barton Bobby Etheridge	SF N	Frank Reberger
Sept. 1, 1970	NY N	—	SD N	Rod Gaspar

(San Diego received Gaspar on October 20.)

Date	Traded To	Traded With	Traded By	In Exchange For
Dec. 1, 1970	ATL N	—	NY N	Bob Aspromonte

Ray Herbert

Date	Traded To	Traded With	Traded By	In Exchange For
May 11, 1955	KC A	—	DET A	Cash
June 10, 1961	CHI A	—	KC A	*see Wes Covington*
Dec. 1, 1964	PHI N	Jeoff Long	CHI A	Danny Cater Lee Elia

Gil Heredia

Date	Traded To	Traded With	Traded By	In Exchange For
Aug. 18, 1992	MON N	—	SF N	Minor league IF Brett Jenkins

Wilson Heredia

Date	Traded To	Traded With	Traded By	In Exchange For
Aug. 8, 1995	FLA N	Player to be named	TEX A	Bobby Witt

(Florida received Heredia on August 11 and OF Scott Podsednik on October 2, 1995.)

Babe Herman

Date	Traded To	Traded With	Traded By	In Exchange For
Oct. 30, 1922	BOS A	Carl Holling Danny Clark Howard Ehmke $25,000.	DET A	Del Pratt Rip Collins
Mar. 14, 1932	CIN N	Wally Gilbert Ernie Lombardi	BKN N	Tony Cuccinello Joe Stripp Clyde Sukeforth
Nov. 30, 1932	CHI N	—	CIN N	Bob Smith Rollie Hemsley Johnny Moore Lance Richbourg
Nov. 22, 1934	PIT N	Guy Bush Jim Weaver	CHI N	Larry French Freddie Lindstrom
June 21, 1935	CIN N	—	PIT N	Cash
Apr. 1, 1937	DET A	—	CIN N	Cash

Billy Herman

Date	Traded To	Traded With	Traded By	In Exchange For
May 6, 1941	BKN N	—	CHI N	Johnny Hudson Charlie Gilbert $65,000.
June 15, 1946	BOS N	—	BKN N	Stew Hofferth
Sept. 30, 1946	PIT N	Elmer Singleton Stan Wentzel Whitey Wietelmann	BOS N	Bob Elliott Hank Camelli

Gene Hermanski

Date	Traded To	Traded With	Traded By	In Exchange For
June 15, 1951	CHI N	Bruce Edwards Joe Hatten Eddie Miksis	BKN N	Johnny Schmitz Rube Walker Andy Pafko Wayne Terwilliger
June 4, 1953	PIT N	—	CHI N	*see Ralph Kiner*

Enzo Hernandez

Date	Traded To	Traded With	Traded By	In Exchange For
Dec. 4, 1968	BAL A	—	HOU N	*see Curt Blefary*
Dec. 1, 1970	SD N	—	BAL A	*see Pat Dobson*

Guillermo Hernandez

Date	Traded To	Traded With	Traded By	In Exchange For
May 22, 1983	PHI N	—	CHI N	Dick Ruthven Bill Johnson
Mar. 24, 1984	DET A	Dave Bergman	PHI N	John Wockenfuss Glenn Wilson

Jackie Hernandez

Date	Traded To	Traded With	Traded By	In Exchange For
Dec. 2, 1966	MIN A	*see Dean Chance*	CAL A	—
Dec. 2, 1970	PIT N	—	KC A	*see Freddie Patek*
Jan. 31, 1974	PHI N	—	PIT N	Mike Ryan

Jeremy Hernandez

Date	Traded To	Traded With	Traded By	In Exchange For
June 1, 1993	CLE A	—	SD N	Minor league OF Tracy Sanders Minor league P Fernando Hernandez
Apr. 3, 1994	FLA N	—	CLE A	Matt Turner

Jose Hernandez

Date	Traded To	Traded With	Traded By	In Exchange For
Apr. 3, 1992	CLE A	—	TEX A	Waiver price
June 1, 1993	CHI N	—	CLE A	Heathcliff Slocumb

Keith Hernandez

Date	Traded To	Traded With	Traded By	In Exchange For
June 15, 1983	NY N	—	STL N	Neil Allen Rick Ownbey
Dec. 7, 1989	CLE A	—	NY N	No compensation (free agent signing)

Leo Hernandez

Date	Traded To	Traded With	Traded By	In Exchange For
Apr. 28, 1982	BAL A	—	LA N	Jose Morales
Dec. 12, 1985	NY A	*see Gary Roenicke*	BAL A	—

Manny Hernandez

Date	Traded To	Traded With	Traded By	In Exchange For
Aug. 1, 1989	NY N	—	MIN A	Cash

Date	Traded To	Traded With	Traded By	In Exchange For

Pedro Hernandez

Date	Traded To	Traded With	Traded By	In Exchange For
Nov. 27, 1978	TOR A	Joe Cannon Mark Lemongello	HOU N	Alan Ashby
Aug. 23, 1982	NY A	—	TOR A	Cash

Ramon Hernandez

Date	Traded To	Traded With	Traded By	In Exchange For
Sept. 8, 1976	CHI N	—	PIT N	Cash
May 28, 1977	BOS A	—	CHI N	Bobby Darwin

Xavier Hernandez

Date	Traded To	Traded With	Traded By	In Exchange For
Nov. 27, 1993	NY A	—	HOU N	Domingo Jean Andy Stankiewicz
Dec. 1, 1994	CIN N	—	NY A	No compensation (free agent signing)

Larry Herndon

Date	Traded To	Traded With	Traded By	In Exchange For
May 9, 1975	SF N	minor league P Luis Gonzalez	STL N	Ron Bryant
Dec. 9, 1981	DET A	—	SF N	Dan Schatzeder Mike Chris

Tommy Herr

Date	Traded To	Traded With	Traded By	In Exchange For
Apr. 22, 1988	MIN A	—	STL N	Tom Brunansky
Oct. 24, 1988	PHI N	Tom Nieto Eric Bullock	MIN A	Shane Rawley Cash
Aug. 31, 1990	NY N	—	PHI N	Nikco Riesgo Minor league P Rocky Elli

Jose Herrera

Date	Traded To	Traded With	Traded By	In Exchange For
May 11, 1971	DET A	John Gelnar	MIL A	Jim Hannan

Jose Herrera

Date	Traded To	Traded With	Traded By	In Exchange For
July 31, 1993	OAK A	Steve Karsay	TOR A	Rickey Henderson

(Oakland received Herrera on August 6, 1993.)

Pancho Herrera

Date	Traded To	Traded With	Traded By	In Exchange For
Nov. 28, 1962	PIT N	Ted Savage	PHI N	Don Hoak

Art Herring

Date	Traded To	Traded With	Traded By	In Exchange For
Dec. 1933	BKN N	—	DET A	Cash
Oct. 19, 1946	PIT N	—	BKN N	Cash

Ed Herrmann

Date	Traded To	Traded With	Traded By	In Exchange For
Apr. 1, 1975	NY A	—	CHI A	Minor leaguers Ken Bennett Terry Quinn Fred Anyzeski John Narron Cash
Feb. 20, 1976	CAL A	—	NY A	Cash
June 6, 1976	HOU N	—	CAL A	Terry Humphrey Mike Barlow
June 9, 1978	MON N	—	HOU N	Cash

John Herrnstein

Date	Traded To	Traded With	Traded By	In Exchange For
Apr. 21, 1966	CHI N	Adolfo Phillips Ferguson Jenkins	PHI N	Larry Jackson Bob Buhl
May 29, 1966	ATL N	—	CHI N	Marty Keough

Mike Hershberger

Date	Traded To	Traded With	Traded By	In Exchange For
Jan. 20, 1965	KC A	Jim Landis Fred Talbot	CHI A	Rocky Colavito

(Part of three-team trade involving Kansas City, Cleveland, and the Chicago White Sox.)

Date	Traded To	Traded With	Traded By	In Exchange For
Jan. 15, 1970	MIL A	Lew Krausse Phil Roof Ken Sanders	OAK A	Don Mincher Ron Clark

Orel Hershiser

Date	Traded To	Traded With	Traded By	In Exchange For
Apr. 8, 1995	CLE A	—	LA N	No compensation (free agent signing)

Buck Herzog

Date	Traded To	Traded With	Traded By	In Exchange For
Dec. 1909	BOS N	—	NY N	Beals Becker
July 22, 1911	NY N	—	BOS N	Al Bridwell Hank Gowdy
Dec. 12, 1913	CIN N	Grover Hartley	NY N	Bob Bescher

(Hartley jumped to the Federal League and Herzog was made Cincinnati manager.)

Date	Traded To	Traded With	Traded By	In Exchange For
July 20, 1916	NY N	Red Killefer	CIN N	Christy Mathewson Edd Roush Bill McKechnie
Jan. 8, 1918	BOS N	—	NY N	Larry Doyle Jesse Barnes
Aug. 1919	CHI N	—	BOS N	Les Mann Charlie Pick

Whitey Herzog

Date	Traded To	Traded With	Traded By	In Exchange For
Feb. 8, 1956	WAS A	Lou Berberet Bob Wiesler Herb Plews Dick Tettelbach	NY A	Mickey McDermott Bobby Kline
May 14, 1958	KC A	—	WAS A	Cash
Jan. 24, 1961	BAL A	Russ Snyder	KC A	Wayne Causey Jim Archer Bob Boyd Al Pilarcik
Nov. 26, 1962	DET A	Gus Triandos	BAL A	Dick Brown

Joe Hesketh

Date	Traded To	Traded With	Traded By	In Exchange For
Apr. 30, 1990	ATL N	—	MON N	Waiver price

Ed Heusser

Date	Traded To	Traded With	Traded By	In Exchange For
Dec. 4, 1946	BKN N	—	CIN N	Augie Galan

Joe Heving

Date	Traded To	Traded With	Traded By	In Exchange For
Aug. 1938	BOS A	—	CLE A	Cash
Feb. 3, 1941	CLE A	—	BOS A	Cash

Johnnie Heving

Date	Traded To	Traded With	Traded By	In Exchange For
Jan. 1931	PHI A	—	BOS A	Waiver price

Jack Hiatt

Date	Traded To	Traded With	Traded By	In Exchange For
Nov. 21, 1964	SF N	—	LA A	Jose Cardenal
Apr. 6, 1970	MON N	—	SF N	Cash
May 12, 1970	CHI N	—	MON N	Boots Day
Dec. 1, 1970	HOU N	—	CHI N	Cash
July 29, 1972	CAL A	—	HOU N	Cash

Phil Hiatt

Date	Traded To	Traded With	Traded By	In Exchange For
Sept. 8, 1995	DET A	—	KC A	Juan Samuel

(Detroit received Hiatt on September 14, 1995.)

Greg Hibbard

Date	Traded To	Traded With	Traded By	In Exchange For
Dec. 10, 1987	CHI A	Melido Perez John Davis Minor league P Chuck Mount	KC A	Floyd Bannister Dave Cochrane
Nov. 17, 1992	CHI N	—	FLA N	Alex Arias Gary Scott
Jan. 14, 1994	SEA A	—	CHI N	No compensation (free agent signing)

Bryan Hickerson

Date	Traded To	Traded With	Traded By	In Exchange For
Mar. 31, 1987	SF N	—	MIN A	*see Dan Gladden*
Nov. 22, 1994	CHI N	—	SF N	Waiver price
July 31, 1995	CLR N	—	CHI N	Player to be named

Kevin Hickey

Date	Traded To	Traded With	Traded By	In Exchange For
July 17, 1984	NY A	—	CHI A	*see Roy Smalley*

Jess Hickman

Date	Traded To	Traded With	Traded By	In Exchange For
June 4, 1965	KC A	Ernie Fazio $100,000.	HOU N	Jim Gentile

(Kansas City received Fazio on October 15.)

Jim Hickman

Date	Traded To	Traded With	Traded By	In Exchange For
Feb. 10, 1916	BKN N	—	BAL F	Cash

Jim Hickman

Date	Traded To	Traded With	Traded By	In Exchange For
Nov. 29, 1966	LA N	Ron Hunt	NY N	Tommy Davis Derrell Griffith
Apr. 23, 1968	CHI N	Phil Regan	LA N	Ted Savage Jim Ellis
Mar. 23, 1974	STL N	—	CHI N	Scipio Spinks

Piano Legs Hickman

Date	Traded To	Traded With	Traded By	In Exchange For
Feb. 17, 1900	NY N	—	BOS N	Cash
Aug. 7, 1904	DET A	—	CLE A	Charlie Carr Fritz Buelow
July 6, 1905	WAS A	—	DET A	Cash
Aug. 1, 1907	CHI A	—	WAS A	Cash
Nov. 1907	CLE A	—	CHI A	Cash

Jim Hicks

Date	Traded To	Traded With	Traded By	In Exchange For
Oct. 13, 1967	STL N	—	CHI N	Cash
May 30, 1969	CAL A	—	STL N	Vic Davalillo

Kirby Higbe

Date	Traded To	Traded With	Traded By	In Exchange For
May 29, 1939	PHI N	Joe Marty Ray Harrell	CHI N	Claude Passeau
Nov. 11, 1940	BKN N	—	PHI N	Vito Tamulis Bill Crouch Mickey Livingston $100,000.
May 3, 1947	PIT N	Hank Behrman Cal McLish Gene Mauch Dixie Howell	BKN N	Al Gionfriddo $100,000.
June 6, 1949	NY N	—	PIT N	Ray Poat Bobby Rhawn

Dennis Higgins

Date	Traded To	Traded With	Traded By	In Exchange For
Feb. 13, 1968	WAS A	*see Ron Hansen*	CHI A	—
Dec. 5, 1969	CLE A	Barry Moore	WAS A	Dave Nelson Horacio Pina Ron Law
July 15, 1971	STL N	—	CLE A	Cash
Sept. 1, 1972	SD N	—	STL N	Cash

Pinky Higgins

Date	Traded To	Traded With	Traded By	In Exchange For
Dec. 9, 1936	BOS A	—	PHI A	Bill Werber
Dec. 15, 1938	DET A	Archie McKain	BOS A	Eldon Auker Jake Wade Chet Morgan
May 19, 1946	BOS A	—	DET A	Cash

Andy High

Date	Traded To	Traded With	Traded By	In Exchange For
July 25, 1925	BOS N	—	BKN N	Waiver price
Mar. 25, 1928	STL N	$25,000.	BOS N	Les Bell
Dec. 2, 1931	CIN N	—	STL N	Nick Cullop Cash

Hugh High

Date	Traded To	Traded With	Traded By	In Exchange For
Jan. 7, 1915	NY A	—	DET A	Waiver price

Oral Hildebrand

Date	Traded To	Traded With	Traded By	In Exchange For
Jan. 17, 1937	STL A	Bill Knickerbocker Joe Vosmik	CLE A	Ivy Andrews Lyn Lary Moose Solters
Oct. 26, 1938	NY A	Buster Mills	STL A	Joe Glenn Myril Hoag

Tom Hilgendorf

Date	Traded To	Traded With	Traded By	In Exchange For
July 10, 1972	CLE A	—	KC A	Jim Clark
Mar. 6, 1975	PHI N	—	CLE A	Minor league OF Nelson Garcia

Carmen Hill

Date	Traded To	Traded With	Traded By	In Exchange For
Aug. 28, 1929	STL N	—	PIT N	Waiver price

Donnie Hill

Date	Traded To	Traded With	Traded By	In Exchange For
Dec. 11, 1986	CHI A	—	OAK A	Gene Nelson Bruce Tanner

(Oakland received Tanner on Dec. 18, 1986.)

Glenallen Hill

Date	Traded To	Traded With	Traded By	In Exchange For
June 27, 1991	CLE A	Mark Whiten Denis Boucher Cash	TOR A	Tom Candiotti Turner Ward
Aug. 19, 1993	CHI N	—	CLE A	Candy Maldonado

Herman Hill

Date	Traded To	Traded With	Traded By	In Exchange For
Oct. 20, 1970	STL N	minor league OF Charlie Wissler	MIN A	Sal Campisi Jim Kennedy

Hunter Hill

Date	Traded To	Traded With	Traded By	In Exchange For
July 14, 1904	WAS A	Frank Huelsman	STL A	Charlie Moran

(Huelsman went to Washington on loan.)

Jesse Hill

Date	Traded To	Traded With	Traded By	In Exchange For
Jan. 17, 1936	WAS A	Jimmie DeShong	NY A	Bump Hadley Roy Johnson
July 13, 1937	PHI A	—	WAS A	Cash

Ken Hill

Date	Traded To	Traded With	Traded By	In Exchange For
Aug. 10, 1986	STL N	—	DET A	*see Mike Heath*
Nov. 25, 1991	MON N	—	STL N	Andres Galarraga
Apr. 5, 1995	STL N	—	MON N	Bryan Eversgerd Minor league P Kirk Bullinger Minor league OF Darond Stovall
July 27, 1995	CLE A	—	STL N	David Bell Minor league P Rick Heiserman Minor league C Pepe McNeal
Dec. 22, 1995	TEX A	—	CLE A	No compensation (free agent signing)

Marc Hill

Date	Traded To	Traded With	Traded By	In Exchange For
Oct. 14, 1974	SF N	—	STL N	Elias Sosa Ken Rudolph
June 20, 1980	SEA A	—	SF N	Cash
Feb. 12, 1981	CHI A	—	SEA A	No compensation (free agent signing)

Milt Hill

Date	Traded To	Traded With	Traded By	In Exchange For
Oct. 5, 1993	ATL N	—	CIN N	Waiver price
June 6, 1994	SEA A	—	ATL N	Waiver price

Shawn Hillegas

Date	Traded To	Traded With	Traded By	In Exchange For
Aug. 30, 1988	CHI A	—	LA N	Ricky Horton

(Chicago received Hillegas on September 1, 1988.)

Date	Traded To	Traded With	Traded By	In Exchange For
Dec. 4, 1990	CLE A	Eric King	CHI A	Cory Snyder Minor league IF Lindsay Foster

Chuck Hiller

Date	Traded To	Traded With	Traded By	In Exchange For
May 12, 1965	NY N	—	SF N	Cash
July 11, 1967	PHI N	—	NY N	Phil Linz

Frank Hiller

Date	Traded To	Traded With	Traded By	In Exchange For
Jan. 3, 1952	CIN N	—	CHI N	Willie Ramsdell
Oct. 13, 1952	NY N	—	CIN N	Gail Henley

Dave Hillman

Date	Traded To	Traded With	Traded By	In Exchange For
Nov. 21, 1959	BOS A	Jim Marshall	CHI N	Dick Gernert

Dave Hilton

Date	Traded To	Traded With	Traded By	In Exchange For
Nov. 22, 1976	TOR A	Dave Roberts John Scott	SD N	Cash

Date	Traded To	Traded With	Traded By	In Exchange For

Chuck Hinton

Date	Traded To	Traded With	Traded By	In Exchange For
Dec. 1, 1964	CLE A	—	WAS A	Bob Chance Woodie Held
Nov. 29, 1967	CAL A	—	CLE A	Jose Cardenal
Apr. 4, 1969	CLE A	—	CAL A	Lou Johnson

Rich Hinton

Date	Traded To	Traded With	Traded By	In Exchange For
Oct. 13, 1971	NY A	—	CHI A	Jim Lyttle
Sept. 6, 1972	TEX A	—	NY A	Cash
Mar. 8, 1973	CLE A	Vince Colbert	TEX A	Alex Johnson
Dec. 12, 1975	CIN N	minor league C Jeff Sovern	CHI A	Clay Carroll
July 6, 1979	SEA A	—	CHI A	Juan Bernhardt

Tommy Hinzo

Date	Traded To	Traded With	Traded By	In Exchange For
Mar. 18, 1990	ATL N	—	CLE A	Jeff Wetherby Minor league OF Miguel Sabino

Larry Hisle

Date	Traded To	Traded With	Traded By	In Exchange For
Oct. 21, 1971	LA N	—	PHI N	Tom Hutton
Oct. 26, 1972	STL N	—	LA N	Rudy Arroyo minor league P Greg Millikan
Nov. 29, 1972	MIN A	John Cumberland	STL N	Wayne Granger
Nov. 17, 1977	MIL A	—	MIN A	No compensation (free agent signing)

Billy Hitchcock

Date	Traded To	Traded With	Traded By	In Exchange For
May 16, 1946	WAS A	—	DET A	Cash
Feb. 8, 1947	STL A	—	WAS A	Cash
Nov. 18, 1947	BOS A	Ellis Kinder	STL A	Sam Dente Clem Dreisewerd Bill Sommers $65,000.
Oct. 8, 1949	PHI A	—	BOS A	Buddy Rosar
Jan. 29, 1953	DET A	—	PHI A	Don Kolloway

Sterling Hitchcock

Date	Traded To	Traded With	Traded By	In Exchange For
Dec. 6, 1995	SEA A	Russ Davis	NY A	Tino Martinez Jeff Nelson Jim Mecir

Myril Hoag

Date	Traded To	Traded With	Traded By	In Exchange For
Oct. 26, 1938	STL A	Joe Glenn	NY A	Oral Hildebrand Buster Mills
Apr. 30, 1940	CHI A	—	STL A	Cash
June 27, 1944	CLE A	—	CHI A	Cash

Don Hoak

Date	Traded To	Traded With	Traded By	In Exchange For
Dec. 9, 1955	CHI N	Russ Meyer Walt Moryn	BKN N	Randy Jackson Don Elston
Nov. 13, 1956	CIN N	Warren Hacker Pete Whisenant	CHI N	Elmer Singleton Ray Jablonski
Jan. 30, 1959	PIT N	Smoky Burgess Harvey Haddix	CIN N	Whammy Douglas Jim Pendleton Frank Thomas Johnny Powers
Nov. 28, 1962	PHI N	—	PIT N	Pancho Herrera Ted Savage

Glen Hobbie

Date	Traded To	Traded With	Traded By	In Exchange For
June 2, 1964	STL N	—	CHI N	Lew Burdette

Dick Hoblitzell

Date	Traded To	Traded With	Traded By	In Exchange For
July 16, 1914	BOS A	—	CIN N	Waiver price

Butch Hobson

Date	Traded To	Traded With	Traded By	In Exchange For
Dec. 10, 1980	CAL A	Rick Burleson	BOS A	Carney Lansford Rick Miller Mark Clear
Mar. 24, 1982	NY A	—	CAL A	Bill Castro

Oris Hockett

Date	Traded To	Traded With	Traded By	In Exchange For
Dec. 12, 1944	CHI A	—	CLE A	Eddie Carnett

Johnny Hodapp

Date	Traded To	Traded With	Traded By	In Exchange For
Apr. 24, 1932	CHI A	Bob Seeds	CLE A	Bill Cissell Jim Moore
Dec. 15, 1932	BOS A	Greg Mulleavy Bob Fothergill Bob Seeds	CHI A	Ed Durham Hal Rhyne

Mel Hoderlein

Date	Traded To	Traded With	Traded By	In Exchange For
Nov. 13, 1951	CHI A	Chuck Stobbs	BOS A	Randy Gumpert Don Lenhardt
May 3, 1952	WAS A	Jim Busby	CHI A	Sam Mele
June 14, 1954	DET A	—	WAS A	Johnny Pesky

Gil Hodges

Date	Traded To	Traded With	Traded By	In Exchange For
May 23, 1963	WAS A	—	NY N	Jimmy Piersall
		(Hodges was named Washington manager.)		
Nov. 27, 1967	NY N	—	WAS A	Bill Denehy $100,000.
		(Hodges was named New York manager.)		

Billy Hoeft

Date	Traded To	Traded With	Traded By	In Exchange For
May 2, 1959	BOS A	—	DET A	Dave Sisler Ted Lepcio
June 15, 1959	BAL A	—	BOS A	Jack Harshman
Dec. 15, 1962	SF N	Jack Fisher Jimmie Coker	BAL A	Mike McCormick Stu Miller John Orsino
Dec. 3, 1963	MIL N	Felipe Alou Ed Bailey Ernie Bowman	SF N	Del Crandall Bob Shaw Bob Hendley

Joe Hoerner

Date	Traded To	Traded With	Traded By	In Exchange For
Oct. 7, 1969	PHI N	*see Curt Flood*	STL N	—
June 15, 1972	ATL N	Andre Thornton	PHI N	Jim Nash Gary Neibauer
July 18, 1973	KC A	—	ATL N	Cash

Bill Hoffer

Date	Traded To	Traded With	Traded By	In Exchange For
Jan. 1901	CLE A	—	PIT N	Cash

Stew Hofferth

Date	Traded To	Traded With	Traded By	In Exchange For
June 15, 1946	BKN N	—	BOS N	Billy Herman

Danny Hoffman

Date	Traded To	Traded With	Traded By	In Exchange For
May 11, 1906	NY A	—	PHI A	Cash
Feb. 1908	STL A	Jimmy Williams Hobe Ferris	NY A	Fred Glade Charlie Hemphill

Glenn Hoffman

Date	Traded To	Traded With	Traded By	In Exchange For
Aug. 21, 1987	LA N	—	BOS A	Player to be named
		(Red Sox received P Billy Bartels on Dec. 8, 1987.)		

Guy Hoffman

Date	Traded To	Traded With	Traded By	In Exchange For
Feb. 17, 1987	CIN N	—	CHI N	Wade Rowdon
		(Chicago received Rowdon on Feb. 23, 1987.)		

John Hoffman

Date	Traded To	Traded With	Traded By	In Exchange For
Oct. 13, 1966	ATL N	—	HOU N	*see Tom Dukes*

Trevor Hoffman

Date	Traded To	Traded With	Traded By	In Exchange For
June 24, 1993	SD N	Jose Martinez Andres Berumen	FLA N	Gary Sheffield Rich Rodriguez

Solly Hofman

Date	Traded To	Traded With	Traded By	In Exchange For
Jan. 1904	CHI N	—	PIT N	Cash
June 22, 1912	PIT N	King Cole	CHI N	Tommy Leach Lefty Leifield

Happy Hogan

Date	Traded To	Traded With	Traded By	In Exchange For
May 1911	STL A	—	PHI A	Cash

Shanty Hogan

Date	Traded To	Traded With	Traded By	In Exchange For
Jan. 10, 1928	NY N	Jimmy Welsh	BOS N	Rogers Hornsby
Dec. 29, 1932	BOS N	—	NY N	$25,000.
Dec. 1935	WAS A	—	BOS N	Cash

Chief Hogsett

Date	Traded To	Traded With	Traded By	In Exchange For
Apr. 30, 1936	STL A	—	DET A	Jack Burns
Dec. 1, 1937	WAS A	—	STL A	Ed Linke

Bobby Hogue

Date	Traded To	Traded With	Traded By	In Exchange For
May 14, 1951	STL A	—	BOS N	Waiver price
July 31, 1951	NY A	Kermit Wahl Tom Upton Lou Sleater	STL A	Cliff Mapes
Aug. 4, 1952	STL A	—	NY A	Waiver price

Chris Hoiles

Date	Traded To	Traded With	Traded By	In Exchange For
Aug. 31, 1988	BAL A	Minor league P Robinson Garces Minor league P Cesar Mejia	DET A	Fred Lynn

Ray Holbert

Date	Traded To	Traded With	Traded By	In Exchange For
Oct. 10, 1995	HOU N	—	SD N	Pedro Martinez

Ken Holcombe

Date	Traded To	Traded With	Traded By	In Exchange For
June 16, 1952	STL A	—	CHI A	Cash

Bill Holden

Date	Traded To	Traded With	Traded By	In Exchange For
Aug. 1914	CIN N	—	NY A	Waiver price

Fred Holdsworth

Date	Traded To	Traded With	Traded By	In Exchange For
May 29, 1975	BAL A	—	DET A	Bob Reynolds
July 14, 1977	MON N	—	BAL A	Dennis Blair

Walter Holke

Date	Traded To	Traded With	Traded By	In Exchange For
Feb. 1919	BOS N	—	NY N	Jimmy Smith
Dec. 1922	PHI N	—	BOS N	Cash
July 9, 1925	CIN N	—	PHI N	Waiver price

Al Holland

Date	Traded To	Traded With	Traded By	In Exchange For
June 28, 1979	SF N	Ed Whitson Fred Breining	PIT N	Bill Madlock Lenny Randle Dave Roberts
Dec. 14, 1982	PHI N	Joe Morgan	SF N	Mike Krukow Mark Davis minor league OF Charles Penigar
Apr. 20, 1985	PIT N	Minor league P Frankie Griffin	PHI N	Kent Tekulve
Aug. 2, 1985	CAL A	John Candelaria George Hendrick	PIT N	Pat Clements Mike Brown Bob Kipper
		(Pittsburgh received Kipper on Aug. 16, 1985.)		
Feb. 6, 1986	NY A	—	CAL A	No compensation (free agent signing)

Gary Holle

Date	Traded To	Traded With	Traded By	In Exchange For
Dec. 15, 1978	TEX A	Ed Farmer Cash	MIL A	Reggie Cleveland
June 15, 1979	CHI A	Ed Farmer	TEX A	Eric Soderholm
Oct. 30, 1981	PHI N	Dewey Robinson	CHI A	Minor league IF Jose Castro

Ed Holley

Date	Traded To	Traded With	Traded By	In Exchange For
July 12, 1934	PIT N	—	PHI N	Cash

Carl Holling

Date	Traded To	Traded With	Traded By	In Exchange For
Oct. 30, 1922	BOS A	Danny Clark Howard Ehmke Babe Herman $25,000.	DET A	Del Pratt Rip Collins

Al Hollingsworth

Date	Traded To	Traded With	Traded By	In Exchange For
June 13, 1938	PHI N	Spud Davis $50,000.	CIN N	Bucky Walters
July 13, 1939	NY A	—	PHI N	Roy Hughes
Aug. 12, 1939	BKN N	—	NY A	Cash
June 6, 1946	CHI A	—	STL A	Waiver price

Bonnie Hollingsworth

Date	Traded To	Traded With	Traded By	In Exchange For
Dec. 1923	BKN N	—	WAS A	Bart Griffith

Dave Hollins

Date	Traded To	Traded With	Traded By	In Exchange For
July 24, 1995	BOS A	—	PHI N	Mark Whiten
Dec. 23, 1995	MIN A	—	BOS A	No compensation (free agent signing)

Ken Holloway

Date	Traded To	Traded With	Traded By	In Exchange For
Dec. 11, 1928	CLE A	Jackie Tavener	DET A	George Uhle
June 30, 1930	NY A	—	CLE A	Cash

Jeff Holly

Date	Traded To	Traded With	Traded By	In Exchange For
Dec. 5, 1979	DET A	—	MIN A	Fernando Arroyo

Billy Holm

Date	Traded To	Traded With	Traded By	In Exchange For
Dec. 1944	BOS A	—	CHI N	Cash

Brian Holman

Date	Traded To	Traded With	Traded By	In Exchange For
May 25, 1989	SEA A	Randy Johnson Gene Harris	MON N	Mark Langston Mike Campbell
		(Montreal received Campbell on July 31, 1989.)		
Oct. 14, 1993	CIN N	—	SEA A	Waiver price

Shawn Holman

Date	Traded To	Traded With	Traded By	In Exchange For
June 28, 1987	DET A	Minor league IF Pete Rice	PIT N	Terry Harper

Darren Holmes

Date	Traded To	Traded With	Traded By	In Exchange For
Dec. 20, 1990	MIL A	—	LA N	Bert Heffernan

Ducky Holmes

Date	Traded To	Traded With	Traded By	In Exchange For
Feb. 1903	WAS A	—	DET A	Cash
June 1903	CHI A	—	WAS A	Davey Dunkle

Tommy Holmes

Date	Traded To	Traded With	Traded By	In Exchange For
Feb. 5, 1942	BOS N	—	NY A	Buddy Hassett Gene Moore

Jim Holt

Date	Traded To	Traded With	Traded By	In Exchange For
Aug. 19, 1974	OAK A	—	MIN A	Pat Bourque

Roger Holt

Date	Traded To	Traded With	Traded By	In Exchange For
Oct. 24, 1980	TEX A	—	NY A	Tucker Ashford Cash

Brian Holton

Date	Traded To	Traded With	Traded By	In Exchange For
Dec. 4, 1988	BAL A	Juan Bell Ken Howell	LA N	Eddie Murray

Ken Holtzman

Date	Traded To	Traded With	Traded By	In Exchange For
Nov. 29, 1971	OAK A	—	CHI N	Rick Monday
Apr. 2, 1976	BAL A	Reggie Jackson minor leaguer Bill Van Bommell	OAK A	Don Baylor Mike Torrez Paul Mitchell

Date	Traded To		Traded With	Traded By		In Exchange For
Ken Holtzman *continued*						
June 15, 1976	NY	A	Doyle Alexander Grant Jackson Ellie Hendricks Jimmy Freeman	BAL	A	Rudy May Rick Dempsey Tippy Martinez Dave Pagan Scott McGregor
June 10, 1978	CHI	N	—	NY	A	Ron Davis
Rick Honeycutt						
July 27, 1977	SEA	A	—	PIT	N	Dave Pagan
Dec. 12, 1980	TEX	A	Mario Mendoza Larry Cox Leon Roberts Willie Horton	SEA	A	Richie Zisk Rick Auerbach Ken Clay Jerry Don Gleaton Brian Allard Minor league P Steve Finch
Aug. 19, 1983	LA	N	—	TEX	A	Dave Stewart Ricky Wright $200,000.
Aug. 29, 1987	OAK	A	—	LA	N	Tim Belcher
(Los Angeles received Belcher on September 3, 1987.)						
Nov. 24, 1993	TEX	A	—	OAK	A	No compensation (free agent signing)
Sept. 25, 1995	NY	A	—	OAK	A	Cash
Dec. 21, 1995	STL	N	—	NY	A	Cash
Don Hood						
Feb. 25, 1975	CLE	A	Boog Powell	BAL	A	Dave Duncan minor league OF Al McGrew
June 15, 1979	NY	A	—	CLE	A	Cliff Johnson
Mar. 13, 1980	STL	N	—	NY	A	No compensation (free agent signing)
Wally Hood						
July 1920	PIT	N	—	BKN	N	Cash
Jay Hook						
May 8, 1964	MIL	N	Adrian Garrett	NY	N	Roy McMillan
Bob Hooper						
Dec. 19, 1952	CLE	A	—	PHI	A	Dick Rozek minor league 2B Bob Wilson
Apr. 13, 1955	CIN	N	—	CLE	A	Cash
Harry Hooper						
Mar. 4, 1921	CHI	A	—	BOS	A	Shano Collins Nemo Leibold
Burt Hooton						
May 2, 1975	LA	N	—	CHI	N	Geoff Zahn Eddie Solomon
Dec. 20, 1984	TEX	A	—	LA	N	No compensation (free agent signing)
John Hoover						
Feb. 16, 1988	MON	N	—	BAL	A	*see Jay Tibbs*
Don Hopkins						
Mar. 26, 1975	OAK	A	—	MON	N	Cash
Gail Hopkins						
Oct. 13, 1970	KC	A	John Matias	CHI	A	Pat Kelly Don O'Riley
July 11, 1974	LA	N	—	SD	N	Cash
Marty Hopkins						
June 27, 1934	CHI	A	—	PHI	N	Waiver price

Date	Traded To		Traded With	Traded By		In Exchange For
Paul Hopkins						
June 26, 1929	STL	A	—	WAS	A	Cash
Johnny Hopp						
Feb. 5, 1946	BOS	N	—	STL	N	Eddie Joost $40,000.
Nov. 18, 1947	PIT	N	Danny Murtaugh	BOS	N	Jim Russell Bill Salkeld Al Lyons
May 18, 1949	BKN	N	$25,000.	PIT	N	Marv Rackley
(Trade was cancelled on June 7, 1949.)						
Sept. 5, 1950	NY	A	—	PIT	N	Cash
Bob Horner						
Jan. 14, 1988	STL	N	—	ATL	N	No compensation (free agent signing)
Rogers Hornsby						
Dec. 20, 1926	NY	N	—	STL	N	Frankie Frisch Jimmy Ring
Jan. 10, 1928	BOS	N	—	NY	N	Shanty Hogan Jimmy Welsh
Nov. 7, 1928	CHI	N	—	BOS	N	Socks Seibold Bruce Cunningham Percy Jones Lou Legett Freddie Maguire $200,000.
Vince Horsman						
Mar. 20, 1992	OAK	A	—	TOR	A	Waiver price
Ricky Horton						
Feb. 9, 1988	CHI	A	Lance Johnson Cash	STL	N	Jose DeLeon
Aug. 30, 1988	LA	N	—	CHI	A	Shawn Hillegas
(Chicago received Hillegas on September 1, 1988.)						
Tony Horton						
June 4, 1967	CLE	A	Don Demeter	BOS	A	Gary Bell
Willie Horton						
Apr. 12, 1977	TEX	A	—	DET	A	Steve Foucault
Feb. 28, 1978	CLE	A	David Clyde	TEX	A	Tom Buskey John Lowenstein
Aug. 15, 1978	TOR	A	Phil Huffman	OAK	A	Rico Carty
Jan. 27, 1979	SEA	A	—	TOR	A	No compensation (free agent signing)
Dec. 12, 1980	TEX	A	Rick Honeycutt Mario Mendoza Larry Cox Leon Roberts	SEA	A	Richie Zisk Rick Auerbach Ken Clay Jerry Don Gleaton Brian Allard Minor league P Steve Finch
Dwayne Hosey						
Aug. 31, 1995	BOS	A	—	KC	A	Waiver price
Steve Hosey						
Mar. 25, 1994	CAL	A	—	SF	N	Minor league P Bob Gamez
Tim Hosley						
Apr. 19, 1976	OAK	A	—	CHI	N	Cash
Gene Host						
Dec. 5, 1956	KC	A	*see Ned Garver*	DET	A	—
Dave Hostetler						
Mar. 31, 1982	TEX	A	Larry Parrish	MON	N	Al Oliver
Nov. 8, 1984	MON	N	—	TEX	A	Chris Welsh
Charlie Hough						
July 11, 1980	TEX	A	—	LA	N	Cash

Charlie Hough *continued*

Date	Traded To		Traded With	Traded By		In Exchange For
Dec. 20, 1990	CHI	A	—	TEX	A	No compensation (free agent signing)
Dec. 8, 1992	FLA	N	—	CHI	A	No compensation (free agent signing)

Frank House

Date	Traded To		Traded With	Traded By		In Exchange For
Nov. 20, 1957	KC	A	—	DET	A	*see Billy Martin*
Nov. 21, 1959	CIN	N	—	KC	A	Tom Acker

Tom House

Date	Traded To		Traded With	Traded By		In Exchange For
Dec. 12, 1975	BOS	A	—	ATL	N	Roger Moret
May 28, 1977	SEA	A	—	BOS	A	Cash

Paul Householder

Date	Traded To		Traded With	Traded By		In Exchange For
Sept. 10, 1984	STL	N	—	CIN	N	John Stuper
Oct. 3, 1984	MIL	A	Jim Adduci	STL	N	Minor leaguers P Rich Buonantony C Jim Koontz IF Ron Koenigsfeld
May 16, 1987	HOU	N	—	MIL	A	No compensation (free agent signing)

Wayne Housie

Date	Traded To		Traded With	Traded By		In Exchange For
June 12, 1993	MIL	A	—	NY	N	Josias Manzanillo

Art Houtteman

Date	Traded To		Traded With	Traded By		In Exchange For
June 15, 1953	CLE	A	Owen Friend Bill Wight Joe Ginsberg	DET	A	Ray Boone Al Aber Steve Gromek Dick Weik
May 20, 1957	BAL	A	—	CLE	A	Cash

Steve Hovley

Date	Traded To		Traded With	Traded By		In Exchange For
June 11, 1970	OAK	A	—	MIL	A	Al Downing Tito Francona

Bruce Howard

Date	Traded To		Traded With	Traded By		In Exchange For
Nov. 29, 1967	BAL	A	—	CHI	A	*see Luis Aparicio*
June 15, 1968	WAS	A	—	BAL	A	Fred Valentine

Chris Howard

Date	Traded To		Traded With	Traded By		In Exchange For
Aug. 31, 1995	TEX	A	—	BOS	A	Jack Voigt

Del Howard

Date	Traded To		Traded With	Traded By		In Exchange For
Dec. 20, 1904	PIT	N	—	PHI	N	Kitty Bransfield Otto Krueger Moose McCormick
Dec. 15, 1905	BOS	N	Dave Brain Vive Lindaman	PIT	N	Vic Willis
June 24, 1907	CHI	N	—	BOS	N	Bill Sweeney Newt Randall

Doug Howard

Date	Traded To		Traded With	Traded By		In Exchange For
July 31, 1974	STL	N	—	CAL	A	Bob Heise
Sept. 30, 1975	CLE	A	—	STL	N	Luis Alvarado
Nov. 5, 1976	TOR	A	Alan Ashby	CLE	A	Al Fitzmorris

Elston Howard

Date	Traded To		Traded With	Traded By		In Exchange For
Aug. 3, 1967	BOS	A	—	NY	A	Ron Klimkowski Pete Magrini

Frank Howard

Date	Traded To		Traded With	Traded By		In Exchange For
Dec. 4, 1964	WAS	A	Phil Ortega Pete Richert Dick Nen Ken McMullen	LA	N	Claude Osteen John Kennedy $100,000.
Aug. 31, 1972	DET	A	—	TEX	A	Cash

Ivon Howard

Date	Traded To		Traded With	Traded By		In Exchange For
July 14, 1914	STL	A	—	DET	A	Waiver price
Jan. 1916	CLE	A	—	STL	A	Cash

Larry Howard

Date	Traded To		Traded With	Traded By		In Exchange For
May 22, 1973	ATL	N	—	HOU	N	Minor league C Tom Heierle

Thomas Howard

Date	Traded To		Traded With	Traded By		In Exchange For
Apr. 15, 1992	CLE	A	—	SD	N	Minor league SS Jason Hardtke Minor league P Chris Maffett
Aug. 17, 1993	CIN	N	—	CLE	A	Randy Milligan

(Cincinnati received Howard on August 20, 1993.)

Art Howe

Date	Traded To		Traded With	Traded By		In Exchange For
Dec. 12, 1975	HOU	N	—	PIT	N	Tommy Helms
Feb. 22, 1984	STL	N	—	HOU	N	No compensation (free agent signing)

Dixie Howell

Date	Traded To		Traded With	Traded By		In Exchange For
May 3, 1947	PIT	N	Kirby Higbe Hank Behrman Cal McLish Gene Mauch	BKN	N	Al Gionfriddo $100,000.

Harry Howell

Date	Traded To		Traded With	Traded By		In Exchange For
Jan. 1900	BKN	N	Jimmy Sheckard Jerry Nops Broadway Aleck Smith Frank Kitson Joe McGinnity	BAL	N	Cash
Jan. 1904	STL	A	Jack O'Connor	NY	A	Jack Powell

Jack Howell

Date	Traded To		Traded With	Traded By		In Exchange For
July 30, 1991	SD	N	—	CAL	A	Shawn Abner

Jay Howell

Date	Traded To		Traded With	Traded By		In Exchange For
Oct. 17, 1980	CHI	N	—	CIN	N	Mike O'Berry
Aug. 19, 1981	NY	A	Bill Caudill	CHI	N	Pat Tabler

(New York received Caudill on April 1, 1982, and Howell on August 2, 1982.)

Date	Traded To		Traded With	Traded By		In Exchange For
Dec. 8, 1984	OAK	A	Jose Rijo Stan Javier Tim Birtsas Eric Plunk	NY	A	Rickey Henderson Bert Bradley Cash
Dec. 11, 1987	LA	N	Alfredo Griffin	OAK	A	Bob Welch Matt Young

(Part of three-team trade involving Oakland, Los Angeles and New York Mets.)

Date	Traded To		Traded With	Traded By		In Exchange For
Jan. 6, 1994	TEX	A	—	ATL	N	No compensation (free agent signing)

Ken Howell

Date	Traded To		Traded With	Traded By		In Exchange For
Dec. 4, 1988	BAL	A	Brian Holton Juan Bell	LA	N	Eddie Murray
Dec. 8, 1988	PHI	N	Gordon Dillard	BAL	A	Phil Bradley

Pat Howell

Date	Traded To		Traded With	Traded By		In Exchange For
Nov. 18, 1992	MIN	A	—	NY	N	Darren Reed

Roy Howell

Date	Traded To		Traded With	Traded By		In Exchange For
May 9, 1977	TOR	A	—	TEX	A	Steve Hargan Jim Mason $200,000.
Dec. 23, 1980	MIL	A	—	TOR	A	No compensation (free agent signing)

Bill Howerton

Date	Traded To		Traded With	Traded By		In Exchange For
June 15, 1951	PIT	N	*see Joe Garagiola*	STL	N	—
May 7, 1952	NY	N	—	PIT	N	Waiver price

Dick Howser

Date	Traded To		Traded With	Traded By		In Exchange For
May 25, 1963	CLE	A	Joe Azcue	KC	A	Doc Edwards $100,000.
Dec. 20, 1966	NY	A	—	CLE	A	Minor league P Gil Downs

LaMarr Hoyt

Date	Traded To		Traded With	Traded By		In Exchange For
Apr. 5, 1977	CHI	A	Oscar Gamble minor league P Bob Polinsky $200,000.	NY	A	Bucky Dent
Dec. 6, 1984	SD	N	Minor league Ps Todd Simmons and Kevin Kristan	CHI	A	Ozzie Guillen Tim Lollar Luis Salazar Bill Long

Waite Hoyt

Date	Traded To		Traded With	Traded By		In Exchange For
Dec. 15, 1920	NY	A	Harry Harper Wally Schang Mike McNally	BOS	A	Muddy Ruel Del Pratt Sammy Vick Hank Thormahlen
May 30, 1930	DET	A	Mark Koenig	NY	A	Ownie Carroll Yats Wuestling Harry Rice
June 30, 1931	PHI	A	—	DET	A	Cash
Nov. 1932	PIT	N	—	NY	N	Waiver price

Al Hrabosky

Date	Traded To		Traded With	Traded By		In Exchange For
Dec. 8, 1977	KC	A	—	STL	N	Mark Littell Buck Martinez
Nov. 20, 1979	ATL	N	—	KC	A	No compensation (free agent signing)

Walt Hriniak

Date	Traded To		Traded With	Traded By		In Exchange For
June 12, 1969	SD	N	Van Kelly minor league OF Andy Finlay	ATL	N	Tony Gonzalez

Glenn Hubbard

Date	Traded To		Traded With	Traded By		In Exchange For
Jan. 11, 1988	OAK	A	—	ATL	N	No compensation (free agent signing)

Bill Hubbell

Date	Traded To		Traded With	Traded By		In Exchange For
June 8, 1920	PHI	N	Art Fletcher Cash	NY	N	Dave Bancroft
May 1, 1925	BKN	N	—	PHI	N	Art Decatur

John Hudek

Date	Traded To		Traded With	Traded By		In Exchange For
July 29, 1993	HOU	N	—	DET	A	Waiver price

Rex Hudler

Date	Traded To		Traded With	Traded By		In Exchange For
Dec. 12, 1985	BAL	A	Rich Bordi	NY	A	Gary Roenicke Leo Hernandez
Apr. 23, 1990	STL	N	—	MON	N	John Costello

Charles Hudson

Date	Traded To		Traded With	Traded By		In Exchange For
Oct. 18, 1971	STL	N	*see Jim Bibby*	NY	N	—
Feb. 1, 1973	TEX	A	Mike Nagy	STL	N	Mike Thompson
Sept. 12, 1974	CAL	A	—	CLE	A	Bill Gilbreth

(Thompson and Nagy were exchanged on March 31.) [This note follows the Feb. 1, 1973 trade.]

Charles Hudson

Date	Traded To		Traded With	Traded By		In Exchange For
Dec. 11, 1986	NY	A	Minor league P Jeff Knox	PHI	N	Mike Easler Tom Barrett
Mar. 23, 1989	DET	A	—	NY	A	Tom Brookens

Hal Hudson

Date	Traded To		Traded With	Traded By		In Exchange For
Aug. 27, 1952	CHI	A	—	STL	A	Waiver price

Johnny Hudson

Date	Traded To		Traded With	Traded By		In Exchange For
May 6, 1941	CHI	N	Charlie Gilbert $65,000.	BKN	N	Billy Herman

Sid Hudson

Date	Traded To		Traded With	Traded By		In Exchange For
June 10, 1952	BOS	A	—	WAS	A	Randy Gumpert Walt Masterson

Frank Huelsman

Date	Traded To		Traded With	Traded By		In Exchange For
May 30, 1904	DET	A	—	CHI	A	Cash
June 16, 1904	STL	A	—	DET	A	Cash
July 14, 1904	WAS	A	Hunter Hill	STL	A	Charlie Moran

(Huelsman went to Washington on loan.)

Frank Huelsman *continued*

Date	Traded To		Traded With	Traded By		In Exchange For
Jan. 16, 1905	WAS	A	—	BOS	A	See note

(St. Louis reclaimed Huelsman, who was with Washington on loan, and traded him to Boston. Boston then sent him to Washington as payment for George Stone.)

Mike Huff

Date	Traded To		Traded With	Traded By		In Exchange For
July 12, 1991	CHI	A	—	CLE	A	Waiver price
Mar. 29, 1994	TOR	A	—	CHI	A	Domingo Martinez

Phil Huffman

Date	Traded To		Traded With	Traded By		In Exchange For
Mar. 15, 1978	OAK	A	—	SF	N	*see Vida Blue*
Aug. 15, 1978	TOR	A	Willie Horton	OAK	A	Rico Carty
Mar. 25, 1982	KC	A	—	TOR	A	Rance Mulliniks

Miller Huggins

Date	Traded To		Traded With	Traded By		In Exchange For
Feb. 1910	STL	N	Rebel Oakes Frank Corridon	CIN	N	Fred Beebe Alan Storke

Jim Hughes

Date	Traded To		Traded With	Traded By		In Exchange For
May 15, 1956	CHI	N	—	BKN	N	Cash

Keith Hughes

Date	Traded To		Traded With	Traded By		In Exchange For
June 30, 1984	NY	A	Marty Bystrom	PHI	N	Shane Rawley
June 10, 1987	PHI	N	Shane Turner	NY	A	Mike Easler
Mar. 21, 1988	BAL	A	*see Rick Schu*	PHI	N	—
Dec. 5, 1989	NY	N	Minor league P Cesar Mejia	BAL	A	John Mitchell Minor league OF Joaquin Contreras

Long Tom Hughes

Date	Traded To		Traded With	Traded By		In Exchange For
July 1902	BOS	A	—	BAL	A	Cash
Dec. 1903	NY	A	—	BOS	A	Jesse Tannehill
July 13, 1904	WAS	A	Bill Wolfe	NY	A	Al Orth

Roy Hughes

Date	Traded To		Traded With	Traded By		In Exchange For
Feb. 10, 1938	STL	A	Ed Cole Billy Sullivan	CLE	A	Rollie Hemsley
June 13, 1939	NY	A	Cash	STL	A	Joe Gallagher
July 13, 1939	PHI	N	—	NY	A	Al Hollingsworth
Jan. 21, 1946	PHI	N	—	CHI	N	Cash

Terry Hughes

Date	Traded To		Traded With	Traded By		In Exchange For
Dec. 7, 1973	BOS	A	*see Reggie Cleveland*	STL	N	—
Jan. 9, 1976	STL	N	—	BOS	A	Cash

Tommy Hughes

Date	Traded To		Traded With	Traded By		In Exchange For
Dec. 11, 1947	CIN	N	—	PHI	N	Bert Haas

Jim Hughey

Date	Traded To		Traded With	Traded By		In Exchange For
Jan. 1900	STL	N	Jack Harper Otto Krueger Joe Quinn	CLE	N	Cash

Emil Huhn

Date	Traded To		Traded With	Traded By		In Exchange For
Feb. 10, 1916	CIN	N	—	NWK	F	Cash

Rick Huisman

Date	Traded To		Traded With	Traded By		In Exchange For
Aug. 11, 1995	KC	A	—	HOU	N	Pat Borders

(Kansas City received Huisman on August 17, 1995.)

Mark Huismann

Date	Traded To		Traded With	Traded By		In Exchange For
May 21, 1986	SEA	A	—	KC	A	Terry Bell
May 12, 1987	CLE	A	—	SEA	A	Dave Gallagher

Tim Hulett

Date	Traded To		Traded With	Traded By		In Exchange For
Apr. 13, 1988	MON	N	—	CHI	A	Edgar Caceres

David Hulse

Date	Traded To		Traded With	Traded By		In Exchange For
Apr. 14, 1995	MIL	A	—	TEX	A	Scott Taylor

Rudy Hulswitt

Date	Traded To		Traded With	Traded By		In Exchange For
Dec. 1908	STL	N	—	CIN	N	Cash

Tom Hume

Date	Traded To	Traded With	Traded By	In Exchange For
Dec. 11, 1985	PHI N	Gary Redus	CIN N	John Denny Jeff Gray

Terry Humphrey

Date	Traded To	Traded With	Traded By	In Exchange For
Dec. 4, 1974	DET A	Tom Walker	MON N	Woodie Fryman
Dec. 6, 1975	HOU N	Leon Roberts Gene Pentz Mark Lemongello	DET A	Milt May Dave Roberts Jim Crawford
June 6, 1976	CAL A	Mike Barlow	HOU N	Ed Herrmann

Bob Humphreys

Date	Traded To	Traded With	Traded By	In Exchange For
Mar. 25, 1963	STL N	—	DET A	Cash
Apr. 10, 1965	CHI N	—	STL N	Bobby Pfeil minor league P Hal Gibson
Apr. 2, 1966	WAS A	—	CHI N	Ken Hunt Cash

Mike Humphreys

Date	Traded To	Traded With	Traded By	In Exchange For
Dec. 3, 1990	NY A	—	SD N	Oscar Azocar

(New York received Humphreys on February 7, 1991.)

Bert Humphries

Date	Traded To	Traded With	Traded By	In Exchange For
July 15, 1911	CIN N	—	PHI N	Fred Beck Bill Burns
Dec. 15, 1912	CHI N	Red Corriden Pete Knisely Art Phelan Mike Mitchell	CIN N	Joe Tinker Grover Lowdermilk Harry Chapman
Aug. 8, 1915	PHI N	—	CHI N	Cash

John Humphries

Date	Traded To	Traded With	Traded By	In Exchange For
Feb. 7, 1941	CHI A	—	CLE A	Clint Brown
Dec. 7, 1945	PHI N	—	CHI A	Cash

Randy Hundley

Date	Traded To	Traded With	Traded By	In Exchange For
Dec. 2, 1965	CHI N	Bill Hands	SF N	Lindy McDaniel Don Landrum Jim Rittwage
Dec. 6, 1973	MIN A	—	CHI N	George Mitterwald
Apr. 13, 1976	CHI N	—	SD N	Cash

Bill Hunnefield

Date	Traded To	Traded With	Traded By	In Exchange For
Nov. 1930	CLE A	—	CHI A	Cash
May 28, 1931	BOS N	—	CLE A	Waiver price
June 30, 1931	NY N	—	BOS N	Waiver price

Ken Hunt

Date	Traded To	Traded With	Traded By	In Exchange For
Sept. 12, 1963	WAS A	—	LA A	Cash
Apr. 2, 1966	CHI N	Cash	WAS A	Bob Humphreys

Randy Hunt

Date	Traded To	Traded With	Traded By	In Exchange For
Feb. 27, 1986	MON N	—	STL N	Cash

Ron Hunt

Date	Traded To	Traded With	Traded By	In Exchange For
Nov. 29, 1966	LA N	Jim Hickman	NY N	Tommy Davis Derrell Griffith
Feb. 13, 1968	SF N	Nate Oliver	LA N	Tom Haller minor league P Frank Kasmeta
Dec. 30, 1970	MON N	—	SF N	Dave McDonald
Sept. 5, 1974	STL N	—	MON N	Cash

Billy Hunter

Date	Traded To	Traded With	Traded By	In Exchange For
Oct. 14, 1952	STL A	—	BKN N	Bob Mahoney Ray Coleman Stan Rojek $90,000.
Nov. 18, 1954	NY A	*see Bob Turley*	BAL A	—

Billy Hunter *continued*

Date	Traded To	Traded With	Traded By	In Exchange For
Feb. 19, 1957	KC A	Rip Coleman Tom Morgan Mickey McDermott Milt Graff Irv Noren	NY A	Art Ditmar Clete Boyer Bobby Shantz Jack McMahan Wayne Belardi Curt Roberts

(New York received Roberts on April 4, and Boyer on June 4, 1957.)

Date	Traded To	Traded With	Traded By	In Exchange For
June 12, 1958	CLE A	—	KC A	Chico Carrasquel

Brian Hunter

Date	Traded To	Traded With	Traded By	In Exchange For
Nov. 17, 1993	PIT N	—	ATL N	Player to be named

(Atlanta received SS Jose Delgado on June 6, 1994.)

Date	Traded To	Traded With	Traded By	In Exchange For
July 27, 1994	CIN N	—	PIT N	Player to be named

(Pittsburgh received OF Micah Franklin on October 13, 1994.)

Buddy Hunter

Date	Traded To	Traded With	Traded By	In Exchange For
Dec. 10, 1973	KC A	—	BOS A	Cash

Catfish Hunter

Date	Traded To	Traded With	Traded By	In Exchange For
Dec. 31, 1974	NY A	—	OAK A	No compensation (free agent signing)

Herb Hunter

Date	Traded To	Traded With	Traded By	In Exchange For
Aug. 28, 1916	CHI N	Larry Doyle Merwin Jacobson	NY N	Heinie Zimmerman Mickey Doolan

Steve Huntz

Date	Traded To	Traded With	Traded By	In Exchange For
Apr. 2, 1970	SD N	—	STL N	Billy McCool
Dec. 4, 1970	SF N	—	SD N	Don Mason minor league P Bill Frost
Mar. 23, 1971	CHI A	—	SF N	Steve Hamilton
Dec. 2, 1971	LA N	Tommy John	CHI A	Dick Allen

Walter Huntzinger

Date	Traded To	Traded With	Traded By	In Exchange For
June 21, 1926	CHI N	—	STL N	Waiver price

Clint Hurdle

Date	Traded To	Traded With	Traded By	In Exchange For
Dec. 11, 1981	CIN N	—	KC A	Scott Brown

Bruce Hurst

Date	Traded To	Traded With	Traded By	In Exchange For
Dec. 8, 1988	SD N	—	BOS A	No compensation (free agent signing)
July 26, 1993	CLR N	Greg Harris	SD N	Brad Ausmus Andy Ashby Doug Bochtler
Dec. 20, 1993	TEX A	—	CLR N	No compensation (free agent signing)

Don Hurst

Date	Traded To	Traded With	Traded By	In Exchange For
June 11, 1934	CHI N	—	PHI N	Dolf Camilli

Jonathan Hurst

Date	Traded To	Traded With	Traded By	In Exchange For
July 21, 1991	MON N	—	TEX A	*see Oil Can Boyd*
June 2, 1993	LA N	—	MON N	Waiver price

Edwin Hurtado

Date	Traded To	Traded With	Traded By	In Exchange For
Dec. 18, 1995	SEA A	Paul Menhart	TOR A	Bill Risley Minor league 2B Miguel Cairo

Jeff Huson

Date	Traded To	Traded With	Traded By	In Exchange For
Apr. 2, 1990	TEX A	—	MON N	Drew Hall

Bert Husting

Date	Traded To	Traded With	Traded By	In Exchange For
June 1902	PHI A	—	BOS A	Cash

Johnny Hutchings

Date	Traded To	Traded With	Traded By	In Exchange For
June 12, 1941	BOS N	—	CIN N	Lloyd Waner

Hal Janvrin

Date	Traded To		Traded With	Traded By		In Exchange For
Jan. 17, 1919	WAS	A	Cash	BOS	A	Eddie Ainsmith George Dumont
Sept. 10, 1919	STL	N	—	WAS	A	Waiver price
June 18, 1921	BKN	N	Ferdie Schupp	STL	N	Jeff Pfeffer

Pat Jarvis

Date	Traded To		Traded With	Traded By		In Exchange For
Feb. 28, 1973	MON	N	—	ATL	N	Carl Morton
Dec. 20, 1973	TEX	A	—	MON	N	Larry Biittner

Ray Jarvis

Date	Traded To		Traded With	Traded By		In Exchange For
Oct. 11, 1970	CAL	A	*see Tony Conigliaro*	BOS	A	—

Larry Jaster

Date	Traded To		Traded With	Traded By		In Exchange For
Dec. 2, 1969	ATL	N	—	MON	N	Jim Britton minor league C Don Johnson

Julian Javier

Date	Traded To		Traded With	Traded By		In Exchange For
May 28, 1960	STL	N	Ed Bauta	PIT	N	Vinegar Bend Mizell Dick Gray
Mar. 24, 1972	CIN	N	—	STL	N	Tony Cloninger

Stan Javier

Date	Traded To		Traded With	Traded By		In Exchange For
Dec. 14, 1982	NY	A	Bobby Meacham	STL	N	Minor league P Marty Mason Minor league P Steve Fincher Minor league OF Bob Helson
Dec. 8, 1984	OAK	A	—	NY	A	*see Rickey Henderson*
May 13, 1990	LA	N	—	OAK	A	Willie Randolph
July 2, 1992	PHI	N	—	LA	N	Steve Searcy Julio Peguero
			(Los Angeles received Peguero on July 28, 1992.)			
Dec. 7, 1993	OAK	A	—	CAL	A	No compensation (free agent signing)
Dec. 8, 1995	SF	N	—	OAK	A	No compensation (free agent signing)

Joey Jay

Date	Traded To		Traded With	Traded By		In Exchange For
Dec. 15, 1960	CIN	N	Juan Pizarro	MIL	N	Roy McMillan
June 15, 1966	ATL	N	—	CIN	N	Hank Fischer

Domingo Jean

Date	Traded To		Traded With	Traded By		In Exchange For
Jan. 10, 1992	NY	A	Melido Perez Bob Wickman	CHI	A	Steve Sax
Nov. 27, 1993	HOU	N	Andy Stankiewicz	NY	A	Xavier Hernandez
May 18, 1995	TEX	A	—	HOU	N	Minor league C Roger Luce
Aug. 31, 1995	CIN	N	—	TEX	A	Waiver price

Hal Jeffcoat

Date	Traded To		Traded With	Traded By		In Exchange For
Nov. 28, 1955	CIN	N	—	CHI	N	Hobie Landrith
June 8, 1959	STL	N	—	CIN	N	Jim Brosnan

Mike Jeffcoat

Date	Traded To		Traded With	Traded By		In Exchange For
May 7, 1985	SF	N	Luis Quinones	CLE	A	Johnnie LeMaster

Gregg Jefferies

Date	Traded To		Traded With	Traded By		In Exchange For
Dec. 11, 1991	KC	A	Kevin McReynolds Keith Miller	NY	N	Bret Saberhagen Bill Pecota
Feb. 22, 1993	STL	N	Minor league OF Ed Gerald	KC	A	Felix Jose Craig Wilson
Dec. 14, 1994	PHI	N	—	STL	N	No compensation (free agent signing)

Jesse Jefferson

Date	Traded To		Traded With	Traded By		In Exchange For
June 15, 1975	CHI	A	—	BAL	A	Tony Muser
Sept. 11, 1980	PIT	N	—	TOR	A	Cash
Jan. 23, 1981	CAL	A	—	PIT	N	No compensation (free agent signing)
Feb. 19, 1982	BAL	A	—	TOR	A	No compensation (free agent signing)

Reggie Jefferson

Date	Traded To		Traded With	Traded By		In Exchange For
June 14, 1991	CLE	A	—	CIN	N	Tim Costo
Dec. 20, 1993	SEA	A	Felix Fermin Cash	CLE	A	Omar Vizquel

Stan Jefferson

Date	Traded To		Traded With	Traded By		In Exchange For
Dec. 11, 1986	SD	N	Kevin Mitchell Shawn Abner Minor league Ps Kevin Armstrong and Kevin Brown	NY	N	Kevin McReynolds Gene Walter Minor league IF Adam Ging
Oct. 24, 1988	NY	A	—	SD	N	*see Jack Clark*
July 20, 1989	BAL	A	—	NY	A	John Habyan
May 7, 1990	CLE	A	—	BAL	A	Waiver price

Irv Jeffries

Date	Traded To		Traded With	Traded By		In Exchange For
Dec. 20, 1933	PHI	N	Otto Bluege	CIN	N	Mark Koenig

Chris Jelic

Date	Traded To		Traded With	Traded By		In Exchange For
Mar. 27, 1987	NY	N	*see David Cone*	KC	A	—

Steve Jeltz

Date	Traded To		Traded With	Traded By		In Exchange For
Mar. 31, 1990	KC	A	—	PHI	N	Jose DeJesus

Ferguson Jenkins

Date	Traded To		Traded With	Traded By		In Exchange For
Apr. 21, 1966	CHI	N	Adolfo Phillips John Herrnstein	PHI	N	Larry Jackson Bob Buhl
Oct. 25, 1973	TEX	A	—	CHI	N	Bill Madlock Vic Harris
Nov. 17, 1975	BOS	A	—	TEX	A	Juan Beniquez Steve Barr Craig Skok
Dec. 14, 1977	TEX	A	—	BOS	A	John Poloni Cash
Dec. 8, 1981	CHI	N	—	TEX	A	No compensation (free agent signing)

Jack Jenkins

Date	Traded To		Traded With	Traded By		In Exchange For
Sept. 1, 1969	LA	N	—	WAS	A	Cash

Tom Jenkins

Date	Traded To		Traded With	Traded By		In Exchange For
June 15, 1926	PHI	A	Howard Ehmke	BOS	A	Fred Heimach Slim Harriss Baby Doll Jacobson

Bill Jennings

Date	Traded To		Traded With	Traded By		In Exchange For
July 16, 1951	STL	A	—	NY	N	Waiver price

Hughie Jennings

Date	Traded To		Traded With	Traded By		In Exchange For
Feb. 1901	PHI	N	—	BKN	N	$3,000.

Jackie Jensen

Date	Traded To		Traded With	Traded By		In Exchange For
May 3, 1952	WAS	A	Spec Shea Jerry Snyder Archie Wilson	NY	A	Irv Noren Tom Upton
Dec. 9, 1953	BOS	A	—	WAS	A	Mickey McDermott Tommy Umphlett

Garry Jestadt

Date	Traded To		Traded With	Traded By		In Exchange For
May 19, 1971	SD	N	—	CHI	N	Chris Cannizzaro

John Jeter

Date	Traded To		Traded With	Traded By		In Exchange For
Aug. 10, 1971	SD	N	Ed Acosta	PIT	N	Bob Miller
Oct. 28, 1972	CHI	A	—	SD	N	Vicente Romo

Shawn Jeter

Date	Traded To		Traded With	Traded By		In Exchange For
July 14, 1991	CHI	A	Steve Wapnick	TOR	A	Cory Snyder
			(Chicago received Wapnick on September 4, 1991.)			

Sam Jethroe

Date	Traded To	Traded With	Traded By	In Exchange For
Dec. 26, 1953	PIT N	Sid Gordon Max Surkont Curt Raydon Fred Walters minor league P Larry Lasalle and $100,000.	MIL N	Danny O'Connell

Manny Jimenez

Date	Traded To	Traded With	Traded By	In Exchange For
Dec. 15, 1961	KC A	—	MIL N	*see Bob Shaw*
Jan. 15, 1969	CHI N	—	PIT N	Ron Campbell Chuck Hartenstein

Tommy John

Date	Traded To	Traded With	Traded By	In Exchange For
Jan. 20, 1965	CHI A	Tommie Agee Johnny Romano	CLE A	Rocky Colavito Camilo Carreon

(Part of three-team trade involving Kansas City, Cleveland, and Chicago White Sox.)

Date	Traded To	Traded With	Traded By	In Exchange For
Dec. 2, 1971	LA N	Steve Huntz	CHI A	Dick Allen
Nov. 21, 1978	NY A	—	LA N	No compensation (free agent signing)
Aug. 31, 1982	CAL A	—	NY A	Dennis Rasmussen
May 2, 1986	NY A	—	OAK A	No compensation (free agent signing)

Adam Johnson

Date	Traded To	Traded With	Traded By	In Exchange For
July 28, 1914	CLE A	Fritz Coumbe Ben Egan	BOS A	Vean Gregg
Sept. 1915	BAL F	Jimmy Smith	CHI F	Bill Bailey

Alex Johnson

Date	Traded To	Traded With	Traded By	In Exchange For
Oct. 27, 1965	STL N	Pat Corrales Art Mahaffey	PHI N	Bill White Dick Groat Bob Uecker
Jan. 11, 1968	CIN N	—	STL N	Dick Simpson
Nov. 25, 1969	CAL A	Chico Ruiz	CIN N	Pedro Borbon Jim McGlothlin Vern Geishert
Oct. 5, 1971	CLE A	Gerry Moses	CAL A	Vada Pinson Frank Baker Alan Foster
Mar. 8, 1973	TEX A	—	CLE A	Rich Hinton Vince Colbert
Sept. 9, 1974	NY A	—	TEX A	Cash

Ben Johnson

Date	Traded To	Traded With	Traded By	In Exchange For
Nov. 10, 1957	CHI N	Charlie King minor league OF Len Williams and cash	MIL N	Casey Wise

Bill Johnson

Date	Traded To	Traded With	Traded By	In Exchange For
May 22, 1983	CHI N	Dick Ruthven	PHI N	Guillermo Hernandez

Billy Johnson

Date	Traded To	Traded With	Traded By	In Exchange For
May 14, 1951	STL N	—	NY A	Don Bollweg $15,000.

Bob Johnson

Date	Traded To	Traded With	Traded By	In Exchange For
Mar. 21, 1943	WAS A	—	PHI A	Bobby Estalella Cash
Dec. 4, 1943	BOS A	—	WAS A	Cash

Bob Johnson

Date	Traded To	Traded With	Traded By	In Exchange For
Dec. 3, 1969	KC A	Amos Otis	NY N	Joe Foy
Dec. 2, 1970	PIT N	—	KC A	*see Freddie Patek*
Dec. 7, 1973	CLE A	—	PIT N	Minor league OF Burnel Flowers
July 1, 1974	TEX A	—	CLE A	Cash

Bob Johnson

Date	Traded To	Traded With	Traded By	In Exchange For
Dec. 5, 1962	BAL A	Pete Burnside	WAS A	Barry Shetrone Marv Breeding minor league P Art Quick

Bob Johnson *continued*

Date	Traded To	Traded With	Traded By	In Exchange For
May 10, 1967	NY N	—	BAL A	Cash
Nov. 8, 1967	CIN N	—	NY N	Art Shamsky
June 11, 1968	ATL N	*see Milt Pappas*	CIN N	—
Mar. 25, 1969	STL N	—	ATL N	Dave Adlesh
July 12, 1969	OAK A	—	STL N	Joe Nossek

Cliff Johnson

Date	Traded To	Traded With	Traded By	In Exchange For
June 15, 1977	NY A	—	HOU N	Randy Niemann Dave Bergman Mike Fischlin

(Houston received Bergman on November 23.)

Date	Traded To	Traded With	Traded By	In Exchange For
June 15, 1979	CLE A	—	NY A	Don Hood
June 23, 1980	CHI N	—	CLE A	Karl Pagel Cash
Dec. 11, 1980	OAK A	Keith Drumright	CHI N	Minor league P Mike King
Nov. 5, 1982	TOR A	—	OAK A	Al Woods
Dec. 4, 1984	TEX A	—	TOR A	Free agent signing

(Toronto selected Tom Henke from Texas as compensation.)

Date	Traded To	Traded With	Traded By	In Exchange For
Aug. 28, 1985	TOR A	—	TEX A	Matt Williams Minor league Ps Jeff Mays and Greg Ferlenda

(Texas received Williams and Mays on August 29, and Ferlenda on November 14, 1985)

Connie Johnson

Date	Traded To	Traded With	Traded By	In Exchange For
May 21, 1956	BAL A	*see George Kell*	CHI A	—

Darrell Johnson

Date	Traded To	Traded With	Traded By	In Exchange For
July 28, 1952	CHI A	Jim Rivera	STL A	J. W. Porter Ray Coleman
June 13, 1953	STL A	Lou Kretlow $75,000.	CHI A	Virgil Trucks Bob Elliott
Dec. 1, 1954	NY A	*see Dick Kryhoski*	BAL A	—
Aug. 14, 1961	CIN N	—	PHI N	Cash

Dave Johnson

Date	Traded To	Traded With	Traded By	In Exchange For
Mar. 31, 1989	BAL A	Minor league OF Victor Hithe	HOU N	Carl Nichols

Dave Johnson

Date	Traded To	Traded With	Traded By	In Exchange For
Sept. 29, 1976	SEA A	—	BAL A	Cash
May 2, 1977	MIN A	—	SEA A	Cash

Davey Johnson

Date	Traded To	Traded With	Traded By	In Exchange For
Nov. 30, 1972	ATL N	Pat Dobson Roric Harrison Johnny Oates	BAL A	Earl Williams Taylor Duncan
Aug. 6, 1978	CHI N	—	PHI N	Larry Anderson

Deron Johnson

Date	Traded To	Traded With	Traded By	In Exchange For
June 14, 1961	KC A	Art Ditmar	NY A	Bud Daley
Oct. 10, 1967	ATL N	—	CIN N	Jim Beauchamp Mack Jones Jay Ritchie
Dec. 3, 1968	PHI N	—	ATL N	Cash
May 2, 1973	OAK A	—	PHI N	Minor league UT Jack Bastable
June 24, 1974	MIL A	—	OAK A	Bill Parsons Cash
Sept. 7, 1974	BOS A	—	MIL A	Cash
Sept. 22, 1975	BOS A	—	CHI A	Minor league C Chuck Erickson Cash

Don Johnson

Date	Traded To	Traded With	Traded By	In Exchange For
June 15, 1950	STL A	*see Snuffy Stirnweiss*	NY A	—
May 29, 1951	WAS A	—	STL A	$12,500.
Dec. 6, 1954	BAL A	—	CHI A	*see Clint Courtney*

Ernie Johnson

Date	Traded To	Traded With	Traded By	In Exchange For
Feb. 10, 1916	STL A	*see Eddie Plank*	STL F	—
May 31, 1923	NY A	—	CHI A	Waiver price

Hank Johnson

Date	Traded To	Traded With	Traded By	In Exchange For
June 5, 1932	BOS A	Ivy Andrews $50,000.	NY A	Danny MacFayden
Jan. 4, 1936	PHI A	Al Niemiec $75,000.	BOS A	Doc Cramer Eric McNair

Howard Johnson

Date	Traded To	Traded With	Traded By	In Exchange For
Dec. 7, 1984	NY N	—	DET A	Walt Terrell
Nov. 19, 1993	CLR N	—	NY N	No compensation (free agent signing)

Jerry Johnson

Date	Traded To	Traded With	Traded By	In Exchange For
Oct. 7, 1969	STL N	—	PHI N	*see Curt Flood*
May 19, 1970	SF N	—	STL N	Frank Linzy
Mar. 6, 1973	CLE A	—	SF N	Cash
Dec. 3, 1973	HOU N	—	CLE A	Cecil Upshaw
Feb. 16, 1977	TOR A	—	SD N	Dave Roberts

Joe Johnson

Date	Traded To	Traded With	Traded By	In Exchange For
July 6, 1986	TOR A	—	ATL N	Jim Acker

John Henry Johnson

Date	Traded To	Traded With	Traded By	In Exchange For
Mar. 15, 1978	OAK A	—	SF N	*see Vida Blue*
June 15, 1979	TEX A	—	OAK A	Dave Chalk Mike Heath Cash
Apr. 9, 1982	BOS A	—	TEX A	Mike Smithson

Johnny Johnson

Date	Traded To	Traded With	Traded By	In Exchange For
Dec. 15, 1944	CHI A	—	NY A	Jake Wade

Ken Johnson

Date	Traded To	Traded With	Traded By	In Exchange For
Apr. 27, 1950	PHI N	—	STL N	Johnny Blatnik
Mar. 21, 1952	DET A	—	PHI N	Waiver price

Ken Johnson

Date	Traded To	Traded With	Traded By	In Exchange For
July 21, 1961	CIN N	—	KC A	Cash
May 13, 1965	MIL N	Jim Beauchamp	HOU N	Lee Maye
June 10, 1969	NY A	—	ATL N	Cash
Aug. 11, 1969	CHI N	—	NY A	Cash

Lamar Johnson

Date	Traded To	Traded With	Traded By	In Exchange For
Jan. 15, 1982	TEX A	—	CHI A	No compensation (free agent signing)

Lance Johnson

Date	Traded To	Traded With	Traded By	In Exchange For
Feb. 9, 1988	CHI A	Ricky Horton Cash	STL N	Jose DeLeon
Dec. 14, 1995	NY N	—	CHI A	No compensation (free agent signing)

Lou Johnson

Date	Traded To	Traded With	Traded By	In Exchange For
Apr. 1, 1961	LA A	—	CHI N	Jim McAnany
May 8, 1963	DET A	Cash	MIL N	Chico Fernandez
Apr. 9, 1964	LA N	$10,000.	DET A	Larry Sherry
Nov. 30, 1967	CHI N	—	LA N	Paul Popovich Jim Williams
June 28, 1968	CLE A	—	CHI N	Willie Smith
Apr. 4, 1969	CAL A	—	CLE A	Chuck Hinton

Mike Johnson

Date	Traded To	Traded With	Traded By	In Exchange For
June 12, 1973	SD N	Gene Locklear Cash	CIN N	Fred Norman

Randy Johnson

Date	Traded To	Traded With	Traded By	In Exchange For
May 25, 1989	SEA A	Brian Holman Gene Harris	MON N	Mark Langston Mike Campbell

(Montreal received Campbell on July 31, 1989.)

Randy Johnson

Date	Traded To	Traded With	Traded By	In Exchange For
Aug. 30, 1981	MIN A	minor leaguers SS Ivan Mesa and 3B Ronnie Perry Cash	CHI A	Jerry Koosman
Feb. 19, 1985	CHI A	Minor league OF Ron Scheer	MIN A	Roy Smalley

Roy Johnson

Date	Traded To	Traded With	Traded By	In Exchange For
June 12, 1932	BOS A	Dale Alexander	DET A	Earl Webb
Dec. 17, 1935	WAS A	Carl Reynolds	BOS A	Heinie Manush
Jan. 17, 1936	NY A	Bump Hadley	WAS A	Jimmie DeShong Jesse Hill
May 11, 1937	BOS N	—	NY A	Waiver price

Si Johnson

Date	Traded To	Traded With	Traded By	In Exchange For
Aug. 6, 1936	STL N	—	CIN N	Bill Walker
Apr. 24, 1946	BOS N	—	PHI N	Cash

Stan Johnson

Date	Traded To	Traded With	Traded By	In Exchange For
June 10, 1961	KC A	*see Wes Covington*	CHI A	—

Syl Johnson

Date	Traded To	Traded With	Traded By	In Exchange For
Jan. 11, 1934	CIN N	Bob O'Farrell	STL N	Glenn Spencer

(O'Farrell was named Cincinnati manager.)

Date	Traded To	Traded With	Traded By	In Exchange For
May 16, 1934	PHI N	Johnny Moore	CIN N	Ted Kleinhans Wes Schulmerich Art Ruble

Tim Johnson

Date	Traded To	Traded With	Traded By	In Exchange For
Apr. 24, 1973	MIL A	—	LA N	Cash
Apr. 29, 1978	TOR A	—	MIL A	Tim Nordbrook

Vic Johnson

Date	Traded To	Traded With	Traded By	In Exchange For
Dec. 12, 1945	CLE A	Cash	BOS A	Jim Bagby

Wallace Johnson

Date	Traded To	Traded With	Traded By	In Exchange For
May 25, 1983	SF N	—	MON N	Mike Vail

Doc Johnston

Date	Traded To	Traded With	Traded By	In Exchange For
Feb. 22, 1915	PIT N	—	CLE A	$7,500.
Feb. 16, 1922	PHI A	—	CLE A	Cash

Greg Johnston

Date	Traded To	Traded With	Traded By	In Exchange For
Apr. 3, 1980	MIN A	—	SF N	Cash

Jimmy Johnston

Date	Traded To	Traded With	Traded By	In Exchange For
Oct. 7, 1925	BOS N	Zack Taylor Eddie Brown	BKN N	Jesse Barnes Mickey O'Neil Gus Felix
July 1926	NY N	—	BOS N	Waiver price

Joel Johnston

Date	Traded To	Traded With	Traded By	In Exchange For
Nov. 19, 1992	PIT N	Dennis Moeller	KC A	Jose Lind

Jay Johnstone

Date	Traded To	Traded With	Traded By	In Exchange For
Nov. 30, 1970	CHI A	Tom Egan Tom Bradley	CAL A	Ken Berry Syd O'Brien Billy Wynne
Jan. 9, 1974	STL N	—	OAK A	Cash
June 14, 1978	NY A	Bobby Brown	PHI N	Rawly Eastwick
June 15, 1979	SD N	—	NY A	Dave Wehrmeister
Dec. 4, 1979	LA N	—	SD N	No compensation (free agent signing)

Stan Jok

Date	Traded To	Traded With	Traded By	In Exchange For
May 10, 1954	CHI A	—	PHI N	Waiver price

Smead Jolley

Date	Traded To	Traded With	Traded By	In Exchange For
Apr. 29, 1932	BOS A	Bennie Tate Cliff Watwood	CHI A	Charlie Berry
Dec. 14, 1933	STL A	Ivy Andrews Cash	BOS A	Carl Reynolds

Dave Jolly

Date	Traded To		Traded With	Traded By		In Exchange For
Oct. 15, 1957	NY	N	—	MIL	N	Waiver price

Al Jones

Date	Traded To		Traded With	Traded By		In Exchange For
July 23, 1986	MIL	A	—	CHI	A	*see Ray Searage*

Barry Jones

Date	Traded To		Traded With	Traded By		In Exchange For
Aug. 13, 1988	CHI	A	—	PIT	N	Dave LaPoint
Dec. 24, 1990	MON	N	—	CHI	A	*see Tim Raines*
Dec. 9, 1991	PHI	N	—	MON	N	Darrin Fletcher Cash

Charlie Jones

Date	Traded To		Traded With	Traded By		In Exchange For
Oct. 5, 1907	STL	A	—	WAS	A	Ollie Pickering

Clarence Jones

Date	Traded To		Traded With	Traded By		In Exchange For
Jan. 9, 1969	CIN	N	Bill Plummer minor league P Ken Myette	CHI	N	Ted Abernathy

Dalton Jones

Date	Traded To		Traded With	Traded By		In Exchange For
Dec. 13, 1969	DET	A	—	BOS	A	Tom Matchick
May 30, 1972	TEX	A	—	DET	A	Norm McRae

Davy Jones

Date	Traded To		Traded With	Traded By		In Exchange For
Dec. 1912	CHI	A	—	DET	A	Cash

Doug Jones

Date	Traded To		Traded With	Traded By		In Exchange For
Dec. 2, 1993	PHI	N	Jeff Juden	HOU	N	Mitch Williams
Apr. 8, 1995	BAL	A	—	PHI	N	No compensation (free agent signing)
Dec. 28, 1995	CHI	N	—	BAL	A	No compensation (free agent signing)

Gary Jones

Date	Traded To		Traded With	Traded By		In Exchange For
Dec. 2, 1971	TEX	A	Terry Ley	NY	A	Bernie Allen
Dec. 2, 1971	CLE	A	Del Unser Denny Riddleberger minor league P Terry Ley	TEX	A	Roy Foster Rich Hand Ken Suarez Mike Paul

Gordon Jones

Date	Traded To		Traded With	Traded By		In Exchange For
Oct. 1, 1956	NY	N	—	STL	N	Cash
Nov. 30, 1959	BAL	A	Jackie Brandt Roger McCardell	SF	N	Billy O'Dell Billy Loes

Jake Jones

Date	Traded To		Traded With	Traded By		In Exchange For
June 14, 1947	BOS	A	—	CHI	A	Rudy York

Jimmy Jones

Date	Traded To		Traded With	Traded By		In Exchange For
Oct. 24, 1988	NY	A	Lance McCullers Stan Jefferson	SD	N	Jack Clark Pat Clements

Johnny Jones

Date	Traded To		Traded With	Traded By		In Exchange For
Aug. 15, 1919	BOS	N	Joe Oeschger Red Causey Mickey O'Neil $55,000.	NY	N	Art Nehf

Mack Jones

Date	Traded To		Traded With	Traded By		In Exchange For
Oct. 10, 1967	CIN	N	Jim Beauchamp Jay Ritchie	ATL	N	Deron Johnson

Odell Jones

Date	Traded To		Traded With	Traded By		In Exchange For
Dec. 5, 1978	SEA	A	Rafael Vasquez Mario Mendoza	PIT	N	Enrique Romo Rick Jones Tommy McMillan
Apr. 1, 1980	PIT	N	—	SEA	A	Larry Andersen Cash

Percy Jones

Date	Traded To		Traded With	Traded By		In Exchange For
Nov. 7, 1928	BOS	N	Socks Seibold Bruce Cunningham Lou Legett Freddie Maguire $200,000.	CHI	N	Rogers Hornsby
Apr. 9, 1930	PIT	N	Cash	BOS	N	Burleigh Grimes

Randy Jones

Date	Traded To		Traded With	Traded By		In Exchange For
Dec. 15, 1980	NY	N	—	SD	N	John Pacella Jose Moreno

Rick Jones

Date	Traded To		Traded With	Traded By		In Exchange For
Dec. 5, 1978	PIT	N	—	SEA	A	*see Mario Mendoza*

Ross Jones

Date	Traded To		Traded With	Traded By		In Exchange For
Dec. 8, 1983	NY	N	Sid Fernandez	LA	N	Carlos Diaz Bob Bailor

Ruppert Jones

Date	Traded To		Traded With	Traded By		In Exchange For
Nov. 1, 1979	NY	A	Jim Lewis	SEA	A	Jim Beattie Rick Anderson Juan Beniquez Jerry Narron
Apr. 1, 1981	SD	N	Joe Lefebvre Tim Lollar Chris Welsh	NY	A	Jerry Mumphrey John Pacella
Jan. 30, 1985	CAL	A	—	DET	A	No compensation (free agent signing)

Sad Sam Jones

Date	Traded To		Traded With	Traded By		In Exchange For
Apr. 12, 1916	BOS	A	Fred Thomas $55,000.	CLE	A	Tris Speaker
Dec. 20, 1921	NY	A	Everett Scott Joe Bush	BOS	A	Roger Peckinpaugh Jack Quinn Rip Collins Bill Piercy
Feb. 8, 1927	STL	A	—	NY	A	Cedric Durst Joe Giard
Sept. 28, 1927	WAS	A	—	STL	A	Waiver price
Dec. 4, 1931	CHI	A	Jackie Hayes Bump Hadley	WAS	A	Carl Reynolds John Kerr

Sam Jones

Date	Traded To		Traded With	Traded By		In Exchange For
Nov. 16, 1954	CHI	N	Gale Wade $60,000.	CLE	A	Ralph Kiner
Dec. 11, 1956	STL	N	Hobie Landrith Jim Davis Eddie Miksis	CHI	N	Tom Poholsky Jackie Collum Ray Katt minor league P Wally Lammers
Mar. 25, 1959	SF	N	Don Choate	STL	N	Bill White Ray Jablonski
Dec. 1, 1961	DET	A	—	HOU	N	Bob Bruce Manny Montejo

Sheldon Jones

Date	Traded To		Traded With	Traded By		In Exchange For
Apr. 8, 1952	BOS	N	$50,000.	NY	N	Bob Elliott
Dec. 20, 1952	CHI	N	—	BOS	N	Monk Dubiel

Sherman Jones

Date	Traded To		Traded With	Traded By		In Exchange For
Apr. 27, 1961	CIN	N	Bob Schmidt Don Blasingame	SF	N	Ed Bailey

Steve Jones

Date	Traded To		Traded With	Traded By		In Exchange For
Feb. 13, 1968	WAS	A	*see Ron Hansen*	CHI	A	—

Tim Jones

Date	Traded To		Traded With	Traded By		In Exchange For
Mar. 29, 1978	MON	N	—	PIT	N	Will McEnaney

Tom Jones

Date	Traded To		Traded With	Traded By		In Exchange For
Aug. 20, 1909	DET	A	—	STL	A	Claude Rossman

Tracy Jones

Date	Traded To	Traded With	Traded By	In Exchange For
July 13, 1988	MON N	Pat Pacillo	CIN N	Jeff Reed Herm Winningham Randy St. Claire
Dec. 8, 1988	SF N	—	MON N	Mike Aldrete
June 16, 1989	DET A	—	SF N	Pat Sheridan
June 18, 1990	SEA A	—	DET A	Darnell Coles

Willie Jones

Date	Traded To	Traded With	Traded By	In Exchange For
June 6, 1959	CLE A	—	PHI N	Jim Bolger Cash
July 1, 1959	CIN N	—	CLE A	Cash

Bubber Jonnard

Date	Traded To	Traded With	Traded By	In Exchange For
Dec. 13, 1927	STL N	Johnny Mokan Jimmy Cooney	PHI N	Johnny Schulte Jimmy Ring

Eddie Joost

Date	Traded To	Traded With	Traded By	In Exchange For
Dec. 4, 1942	BOS N	Nate Andrews $25,000.	CIN N	Eddie Miller
Feb. 5, 1946	STL N	$40,000.	BOS N	Johnny Hopp

Buck Jordan

Date	Traded To	Traded With	Traded By	In Exchange For
May 12, 1937	CIN N	—	BOS N	Cash
June 10, 1938	PHI N	—	CIN N	Justin Stein

Jimmy Jordan

Date	Traded To	Traded With	Traded By	In Exchange For
Dec. 3, 1936	STL N	Frenchy Bordagaray Dutch Leonard	BKN N	Tom Winsett

Kevin Jordan

Date	Traded To	Traded With	Traded By	In Exchange For
Feb. 9, 1994	PHI N	—	NY A	*see Terry Mulholland*

Niles Jordan

Date	Traded To	Traded With	Traded By	In Exchange For
Dec. 10, 1951	CIN N	—	PHI N	*see Smoky Burgess*

Ricardo Jordan

Date	Traded To	Traded With	Traded By	In Exchange For
Dec. 6, 1995	PHI N	Howard Battle	TOR A	Paul Quantrill

Tim Jordan

Date	Traded To	Traded With	Traded By	In Exchange For
May 1901	BAL A	—	WAS A	Cash

Tom Jordan

Date	Traded To	Traded With	Traded By	In Exchange For
June 1946	CLE A	—	CHI A	Frankie Hayes

Mike Jorgensen

Date	Traded To	Traded With	Traded By	In Exchange For
Apr. 5, 1972	MON N	Tim Foli Ken Singleton	NY N	Rusty Staub
May 22, 1977	OAK A	—	MON N	Stan Bahnsen
Jan. 21, 1978	TEX A	—	OAK A	No compensation (free agent signing)
Aug. 12, 1979	NY N	Ed Lynch	TEX A	Willie Montanez
June 15, 1983	ATL N	—	NY N	$75,000.
June 15, 1984	STL N	Ken Dayley	ATL N	Ken Oberkfell

Felix Jose

Date	Traded To	Traded With	Traded By	In Exchange For
Aug. 29, 1990	STL N	Stan Royer Minor league P Daryl Green	OAK A	Willie McGee
Feb. 22, 1993	KC A	Craig Wilson	STL N	Gregg Jefferies Minor league OF Ed Gerald

Duane Josephson

Date	Traded To	Traded With	Traded By	In Exchange For
Mar. 31, 1971	BOS A	Danny Murphy	CHI A	Vicente Romo Tony Muser

Von Joshua

Date	Traded To	Traded With	Traded By	In Exchange For
Jan. 29, 1975	SF N	—	LA N	Cash
June 2, 1976	MIL A	—	SF N	Cash

Von Joshua *continued*

Date	Traded To	Traded With	Traded By	In Exchange For
Dec. 3, 1979	SD N	—	LA N	Cash

Mike Joyce

Date	Traded To	Traded With	Traded By	In Exchange For
Mar. 31, 1964	NY N	—	CHI A	Cash

Wally Joyner

Date	Traded To	Traded With	Traded By	In Exchange For
Dec. 9, 1991	KC A	—	CAL A	No compensation (free agent signing)
Dec. 21, 1995	SD N	Minor league P Aaron Dorlarque	KC A	Bip Roberts Minor league P Bryan Wolff

Oscar Judd

Date	Traded To	Traded With	Traded By	In Exchange For
May 31, 1945	PHI N	—	BOS A	Waiver price

Ralph Judd

Date	Traded To	Traded With	Traded By	In Exchange For
May 15, 1930	STL N	—	NY N	Clarence Mitchell

Jeff Juden

Date	Traded To	Traded With	Traded By	In Exchange For
Dec. 2, 1993	PHI N	Doug Jones	HOU N	Mitch Williams
June 10, 1995	SF N	Minor league C-1B Tommy Eason	PHI N	Mike Benjamin

Walt Judnich

Date	Traded To	Traded With	Traded By	In Exchange For
Jan. 30, 1940	STL A	—	NY A	Cash
Nov. 20, 1947	CLE A	Bob Muncrief	STL A	Dick Kokos Joe Frazier Bryan Stephens $25,000.
Feb. 9, 1949	PIT N	—	CLE A	Waiver price

Howie Judson

Date	Traded To	Traded With	Traded By	In Exchange For
Sept. 1, 1952	CIN N	—	CHI A	Hank Edwards

(Cincinnati received Judson on December 9.)

Bill Jurges

Date	Traded To	Traded With	Traded By	In Exchange For
Dec. 6, 1938	NY N	Frank Demaree Ken O'Dea	CHI N	Dick Bartell Hank Leiber Gus Mancuso

Al Jurisich

Date	Traded To	Traded With	Traded By	In Exchange For
Feb. 5, 1946	PHI N	—	STL N	Cash

Skip Jutze

Date	Traded To	Traded With	Traded By	In Exchange For
Nov. 28, 1972	HOU N	Milt Ramirez	STL N	Ray Busse Bobby Fenwick
Jan. 12, 1977	SEA A	—	HOU N	Minor league P Alan Griffin Cash

Jim Kaat

Date	Traded To	Traded With	Traded By	In Exchange For
Aug. 15, 1973	CHI A	—	MIN A	Cash
Dec. 10, 1975	PHI N	Mike Buskey	CHI A	Dick Ruthven Alan Bannister Roy Thomas
May 11, 1979	NY A	—	PHI N	Cash
Apr. 30, 1980	STL N	—	NY A	Cash

Mike Kahoe

Date	Traded To	Traded With	Traded By	In Exchange For
Apr. 1901	CHI N	Topsy Hartsel	CIN N	Cash
Mar. 1905	PHI N	—	STL A	Cash
June 27, 1907	WAS A	—	CHI N	Cash

Al Kaiser

Date	Traded To	Traded With	Traded By	In Exchange For
June 10, 1911	BOS N	*see Johnny Kling*	CHI N	—

Don Kaiser

Date	Traded To	Traded With	Traded By	In Exchange For
Dec. 5, 1957	MIL N	Eddie Haas Bob Rush	CHI N	Taylor Phillips Sammy Taylor

Don Kaiser *continued*

Date	Traded To	Traded With	Traded By	In Exchange For
Oct. 15, 1959	DET A	Mike Roarke Casey Wise	MIL N	Charlie Lau Don Lee

Jeff Kaiser

Date	Traded To	Traded With	Traded By	In Exchange For
Feb. 23, 1987	CLE A	—	OAK A	Curt Wardle
Apr. 23, 1993	NY N	—	CIN N	Waiver price

Willie Kamm

Date	Traded To	Traded With	Traded By	In Exchange For
May 17, 1931	CLE A	—	CHI A	Lew Fonseca

Alex Kampouris

Date	Traded To	Traded With	Traded By	In Exchange For
June 6, 1938	NY N	—	CIN N	Wally Berger
May 20, 1943	WAS A	—	BKN N	Cash

John Kane

Date	Traded To	Traded With	Traded By	In Exchange For
Jan. 18, 1909	CHI N	—	CIN N	Kid Durbin Tom Downey

Erv Kantlehner

Date	Traded To	Traded With	Traded By	In Exchange For
Sept. 2, 1916	PHI N	—	PIT N	Cash

Ed Karger

Date	Traded To	Traded With	Traded By	In Exchange For
June 3, 1906	STL N	—	PIT N	Cash
Dec. 12, 1908	CIN N	Art Fromme	STL N	Admiral Schlei
June 1909	BOS A	—	CIN N	Waiver price

Andy Karl

Date	Traded To	Traded With	Traded By	In Exchange For
Mar. 27, 1947	BOS N	—	PHI N	Don Padgett

Ryan Karp

Date	Traded To	Traded With	Traded By	In Exchange For
Feb. 9, 1994	PHI N	Bobby Munoz Kevin Jordan	NY A	Terry Mulholland Jeff Patterson

(New York received Patterson on November 8, 1994.)

Steve Karsay

Date	Traded To	Traded With	Traded By	In Exchange For
July 31, 1993	OAK A	Jose Herrera	TOR A	Rickey Henderson

(Oakland received Herrera on August 6, 1993.)

Eddie Kasko

Date	Traded To	Traded With	Traded By	In Exchange For
Oct. 3, 1958	CIN N	Bob Mabe Del Ennis	STL N	George Crowe Alex Kellner Alex Grammas
Jan. 20, 1964	HOU N	—	CIN N	Jim Dickson Wally Wolf Cash
Apr. 3, 1966	BOS A	—	HOU N	Felix Mantilla

John Katoll

Date	Traded To	Traded With	Traded By	In Exchange For
May 5, 1902	BAL A	Herm McFarland	CHI A	Cash

Ray Katt

Date	Traded To	Traded With	Traded By	In Exchange For
June 14, 1956	STL N	—	NY N	*see Red Schoendienst*
Dec. 11, 1956	CHI N	*see Tom Poholsky*	STL N	—
Apr. 16, 1957	NY N	Ray Jablonski	CHI N	Dick Littlefield Bob Lennon
Apr. 2, 1958	STL N	—	SF N	Jim King

Benny Kauff

Date	Traded To	Traded With	Traded By	In Exchange For
Dec. 23, 1915	NY N	—	BKN F	$35,000.

Curt Kaufman

Date	Traded To	Traded With	Traded By	In Exchange For
Dec. 7, 1983	CAL A	Cash	NY A	Tim Foli

Tony Kaufmann

Date	Traded To	Traded With	Traded By	In Exchange For
June 7, 1927	PHI N	Jimmy Cooney	CHI N	Hal Carlson
Sept. 10, 1927	STL N	—	PHI N	Cash

Marty Kavanagh

Date	Traded To	Traded With	Traded By	In Exchange For
May 1916	CLE A	—	DET A	Cash
June 1918	STL N	—	CLE A	Cash

Marty Kavanagh *continued*

Date	Traded To	Traded With	Traded By	In Exchange For
Aug. 1918	DET A	—	STL N	Cash

Eddie Kazak

Date	Traded To	Traded With	Traded By	In Exchange For
May 13, 1952	CIN N	Wally Westlake	STL N	Dick Sisler Virgil Stallcup

Ted Kazanski

Date	Traded To	Traded With	Traded By	In Exchange For
Mar. 31, 1959	MIL N	Stan Lopata Johnny O'Brien	PHI N	Gene Conley Joe Koppe Harry Hanebrink

Steve Kealey

Date	Traded To	Traded With	Traded By	In Exchange For
Mar. 15, 1971	CHI A	—	CAL A	Cash
Aug. 29, 1973	CIN N	—	CHI A	Jim McGlothlin

Bob Kearney

Date	Traded To	Traded With	Traded By	In Exchange For
Nov. 21, 1983	SEA A	Dave Beard	OAK A	Bill Caudill Darrel Akerfelds

Ray Keating

Date	Traded To	Traded With	Traded By	In Exchange For
Mar. 6, 1919	BOS N	—	NY A	Cash

Dave Keefe

Date	Traded To	Traded With	Traded By	In Exchange For
June 2, 1921	CLE A	—	PHI A	Waiver price

Vic Keen

Date	Traded To	Traded With	Traded By	In Exchange For
Dec. 11, 1925	STL N	—	CHI N	Jimmy Cooney

Buster Keeton

Date	Traded To	Traded With	Traded By	In Exchange For
Oct. 23, 1981	HOU N	—	MIL A	Pete Ladd

Bill Keister

Date	Traded To	Traded With	Traded By	In Exchange For
Feb. 11, 1900	STL N	John McGraw Wilbert Robinson	BAL N	Cash

Mike Kekich

Date	Traded To	Traded With	Traded By	In Exchange For
Dec. 4, 1968	NY A	—	LA N	Andy Kosco
June 12, 1973	CLE A	—	NY A	Lowell Palmer

George Kell

Date	Traded To	Traded With	Traded By	In Exchange For
May 18, 1946	DET A	—	PHI A	Barney McCosky
June 3, 1952	BOS A	Dizzy Trout Johnny Lipon Hoot Evers	DET A	Walt Dropo Bill Wight Fred Hatfield Johnny Pesky Don Lenhardt
May 23, 1954	CHI A	—	BOS A	Grady Hatton $100,000.
May 21, 1956	BAL A	Bob Nieman Mike Fornieles Connie Johnson	CHI A	Jim Wilson Dave Philley

Frankie Kelleher

Date	Traded To	Traded With	Traded By	In Exchange For
July 16, 1942	CIN N	—	NY A	Jim Turner

John Kelleher

Date	Traded To	Traded With	Traded By	In Exchange For
Dec. 13, 1923	BOS N	—	CHI N	Cash

Mick Kelleher

Date	Traded To	Traded With	Traded By	In Exchange For
Oct. 23, 1973	HOU N	—	STL N	Cash
Dec. 13, 1974	STL N	—	HOU N	Cash
Dec. 22, 1975	CHI N	—	STL N	Vic Harris
Apr. 1, 1981	DET A	—	CHI N	Cash
Apr. 21, 1982	CAL A	—	DET A	Cash

Frank Kellert

Date	Traded To	Traded With	Traded By	In Exchange For
Mar. 17, 1955	BKN N	Cash	BAL A	Erv Palica
Oct. 11, 1955	CHI N	—	BKN N	Waiver price

Harry Kelley

Date	Traded To	Traded With	Traded By	In Exchange For
May 4, 1938	WAS A	—	PHI A	Waiver price

Alex Kellner

Date	Traded To	Traded With	Traded By	In Exchange For
June 23, 1958	CIN N	—	KC A	Waiver price
Oct. 3, 1958	STL N	George Crowe Alex Grammas	CIN N	Bob Mabe Eddie Kasko Del Ennis

Win Kellum

Date	Traded To	Traded With	Traded By	In Exchange For
Feb. 1905	STL N	—	CIN N	Cash

Bill Kelly

Date	Traded To	Traded With	Traded By	In Exchange For
Jan. 1911	PIT N	—	STL N	Cash

Bob Kelly

Date	Traded To	Traded With	Traded By	In Exchange For
June 12, 1953	CIN N	Fred Baczewski	CHI N	Bubba Church
Apr. 23, 1958	CLE A	—	CIN N	Fred Hatfield

Bryan Kelly

Date	Traded To	Traded With	Traded By	In Exchange For
June 22, 1987	SEA A	—	DET A	Karl Best

Dale Kelly

Date	Traded To	Traded With	Traded By	In Exchange For
Dec. 8, 1977	TOR A	Butch Alberts	CAL A	Ron Fairly

George Kelly

Date	Traded To	Traded With	Traded By	In Exchange For
July 25, 1917	PIT N	—	NY N	Waiver price
Aug. 4, 1917	NY N	—	PIT N	Waiver price
Feb. 9, 1927	CIN N	$100,000	NY N	Edd Roush

Joe Kelly

Date	Traded To	Traded With	Traded By	In Exchange For
Dec. 14, 1916	BOS N	—	CHI N	Fred Mitchell

Mike Kelly

Date	Traded To	Traded With	Traded By	In Exchange For
Jan. 1900	PIT N	*see Honus Wagner*	LOU N	—

Pat Kelly

Date	Traded To	Traded With	Traded By	In Exchange For
Oct. 13, 1970	CHI A	Don O'Riley	KC A	Gail Hopkins John Matias
Nov. 18, 1976	BAL A	—	CHI A	Dave Duncan
Dec. 29, 1980	CLE A	—	BAL A	No compensation (free agent signing)

Roberto Kelly

Date	Traded To	Traded With	Traded By	In Exchange For
Nov. 3, 1992	CIN N	—	NY A	Paul O'Neill Minor league 1B Joe DeBerry
May 29, 1994	ATL N	Minor league P Roger Etheridge	CIN N	Deion Sanders
Apr. 6, 1995	MON N	Tony Tarasco Minor league P Esteban Yan	ATL N	Marquis Grissom
May 23, 1995	LA N	Joey Eischen	MON N	Henry Rodriguez Jeff Treadway

Van Kelly

Date	Traded To	Traded With	Traded By	In Exchange For
June 12, 1969	SD N	Walt Hriniak minor league OF Andy Finlay	ATL N	Tony Gonzalez

Bill Kelso

Date	Traded To	Traded With	Traded By	In Exchange For
Nov. 29, 1967	CIN N	Jorge Rubio	CAL A	Sammy Ellis
Mar. 18, 1969	BOS A	—	CIN N	Cash

(Kelso was returned to Cincinnati on March 29.)

Russ Kemmerer

Date	Traded To	Traded With	Traded By	In Exchange For
Apr. 29, 1957	WAS A	Milt Bolling Faye Throneberry	BOS A	Dean Stone Bob Chakales
May 18, 1960	CHI A	—	WAS A	Cash
June 22, 1962	HOU N	—	CHI A	Dean Stone

Steve Kemp

Date	Traded To	Traded With	Traded By	In Exchange For
Nov. 27, 1981	CHI A	—	DET A	Chet Lemon
Dec. 9, 1982	NY A	—	CHI A	

(Chicago claimed P Steve Mura from St. Louis as compensation.)

Date	Traded To	Traded With	Traded By	In Exchange For
Dec. 20, 1984	PIT N	Tim Foli $400,000.	NY A	Dale Berra Jay Buhner

Fred Kendall

Date	Traded To	Traded With	Traded By	In Exchange For
Dec. 8, 1976	CLE A	Johnny Grubb Hector Torres	SD N	George Hendrick
Mar. 30, 1978	BOS A	*see Dennis Eckersley*	CLE A	—

Bill Kennedy

Date	Traded To	Traded With	Traded By	In Exchange For
June 15, 1948	STL A	$100,000.	CLE A	Sam Zoldak
Mar. 13, 1952	CHI A	—	STL A	Cash
Feb. 9, 1953	BOS A	Hal Brown Marv Grissom	CHI A	Vern Stephens

Bob Kennedy

Date	Traded To	Traded With	Traded By	In Exchange For
June 2, 1948	CLE A	—	CHI A	Al Gettel Pat Seerey
Apr. 17, 1954	BAL A	—	CLE A	Jim Dyck
May 30, 1955	CHI A	—	BAL A	Cash
May 15, 1956	DET A	Jim Brideweser Harry Byrd	CHI A	Fred Hatfield Jim Delsing
May 20, 1957	BKN N	—	CHI A	Cash

Brickyard Kennedy

Date	Traded To	Traded With	Traded By	In Exchange For
Jan. 1903	PIT N	—	NY N	Cash

Jim Kennedy

Date	Traded To	Traded With	Traded By	In Exchange For
Oct. 20, 1970	MIN A	Sal Campisi	STL N	Herman Hill minor league OF Charlie Wissler

John Kennedy

Date	Traded To	Traded With	Traded By	In Exchange For
Dec. 4, 1964	LA N	—	WAS A	*see Frank Howard*
Apr. 3, 1967	NY A	—	LA N	Jack Cullen John Miller $25,000.
Nov. 13, 1968	SEA A	—	NY A	Cash
June 26, 1970	BOS A	—	MIL A	Cash

Junior Kennedy

Date	Traded To	Traded With	Traded By	In Exchange For
Dec. 4, 1973	CIN N	Merv Rettenmund minor league C Bill Wood	BAL A	Ross Grimsley minor league C Wally Williams
Oct. 20, 1977	CIN N	—	SF N	Cash
Oct. 23, 1981	CHI N	—	CIN N	$50,000.

Terry Kennedy

Date	Traded To	Traded With	Traded By	In Exchange For
Dec. 8, 1980	SD N	Steve Swisher Mike Phillips John Littlefield John Urrea Kim Seaman Al Olmsted	STL N	Rollie Fingers Bob Shirley Gene Tenace Bob Geren
Oct. 30, 1986	BAL A	Mark Williamson	SD N	Storm Davis
Jan. 24, 1989	SF N	—	BAL A	Bob Melvin

Vern Kennedy

Date	Traded To	Traded With	Traded By	In Exchange For
Dec. 2, 1937	DET A	Tony Piet Dixie Walker	CHI A	Marv Owen Mike Tresh Gee Walker
May 13, 1939	STL A	Bob Harris George Gill Roxie Lawson Chet Laabs Mark Christman	DET A	Beau Bell Bobo Newsom Red Kress Jim Walkup
May 15, 1941	WAS A	—	STL A	Rick Ferrell
Dec. 11, 1941	CLE A	—	WAS A	Cash
July 28, 1944	PHI N	—	CLE A	Cash

Jerry Kenney

Date	Traded To	Traded With	Traded By	In Exchange For
Nov. 27, 1972	CLE A	—	NY A	*see Graig Nettles*

Jeff Kent

Date	Traded To	Traded With	Traded By	In Exchange For
Aug. 27, 1992	NY N	Ryan Thompson	TOR A	David Cone

(New York received Thompson on September 1, 1992.)

Joe Keough

Date	Traded To	Traded With	Traded By	In Exchange For
Feb. 1, 1973	CHI A	—	KC A	Jim Lyttle

Date	Traded To	Traded With	Traded By	In Exchange For

Marty Keough

Date	Traded To	Traded With	Traded By	In Exchange For
June 13, 1960	CLE A	Ted Bowsfield	BOS A	Russ Nixon Carroll Hardy
Dec. 15, 1961	CIN N	Johnny Klippstein	WAS A	Dave Stenhouse Bob Schmidt
Apr. 4, 1966	ATL N	—	CIN N	Cash and minor league player to be named later
May 29, 1966	CHI N	—	ATL N	John Herrnstein

Matt Keough

Date	Traded To	Traded With	Traded By	In Exchange For
June 15, 1983	NY A	—	OAK A	Ben Callahan Marshall Brant Cash
Feb. 1, 1986	CHI N	—	STL N	No compensation (free agent signing)

Charlie Kerfeld

Date	Traded To	Traded With	Traded By	In Exchange For
Apr. 28, 1990	ATL N	—	HOU N	Minor league OF Kevin Dean Player to be named

(Houston received P Lee Ellis Johnson on October 29, 1990.)

Gus Keriazakos

Date	Traded To	Traded With	Traded By	In Exchange For
June 11, 1954	WAS A	—	CHI A	Sonny Dixon

Bill Kerksieck

Date	Traded To	Traded With	Traded By	In Exchange For
June 15, 1939	BOS N	—	PHI N	Cash

Jim Kern

Date	Traded To	Traded With	Traded By	In Exchange For
Oct. 3, 1978	TEX A	Larvell Blanks	CLE A	Bobby Bonds Len Barker
Dec. 11, 1981	NY N	—	TEX A	Doug Flynn Danny Boitano
Feb. 10, 1982	CIN N	Alex Trevino Greg Harris	NY N	George Foster
Aug. 23, 1982	CHI A	—	CIN N	Wade Rowdon Leo Garcia

George Kernek

Date	Traded To	Traded With	Traded By	In Exchange For
Oct. 13, 1967	CHI A	—	STL N	Cash

Buddy Kerr

Date	Traded To	Traded With	Traded By	In Exchange For
Dec. 14, 1949	BOS N	Sid Gordon Willard Marshall Red Webb	NY N	Eddie Stanky Alvin Dark

Doc Kerr

Date	Traded To	Traded With	Traded By	In Exchange For
Aug. 1914	BAL F	—	PIT F	Medric Boucher

John Kerr

Date	Traded To	Traded With	Traded By	In Exchange For
Dec. 4, 1931	WAS A	Carl Reynolds	CHI A	Jackie Hayes Bump Hadley Sad Sam Jones

Joe Kerrigan

Date	Traded To	Traded With	Traded By	In Exchange For
Dec. 7, 1977	BAL A	Don Stanhouse Gary Roenicke	MON N	Rudy May Randy Miller Bryn Smith

Don Kessinger

Date	Traded To	Traded With	Traded By	In Exchange For
Oct. 28, 1975	STL N	—	CHI N	Mike Garman minor league IF Bobby Hrapmann
Aug. 20, 1977	CHI A	—	STL N	Minor league P Steve Staniland

Keith Kessinger

Date	Traded To	Traded With	Traded By	In Exchange For
Jan. 11, 1995	CHI N	—	CIN N	Minor league P Greg Hillman

Jimmy Key

Date	Traded To	Traded With	Traded By	In Exchange For
Dec. 10, 1992	NY A	—	TOR A	No compensation (free agent signing)

Steve Kiefer

Date	Traded To	Traded With	Traded By	In Exchange For
Mar. 30, 1986	MIL A	Charlie O'Brien Minor league P Mike Fulmer Minor league P Pete Kendrick	OAK A	Moose Haas

Leo Kiely

Date	Traded To	Traded With	Traded By	In Exchange For
Jan. 8, 1960	CLE A	—	BOS A	Ray Webster
Apr. 5, 1960	KC A	—	CLE A	Bob Grim

Pete Kilduff

Date	Traded To	Traded With	Traded By	In Exchange For
July 31, 1917	CHI N	—	NY N	Al Demaree
June 2, 1919	BKN N	—	CHI N	Lee Magee

Paul Kilgus

Date	Traded To	Traded With	Traded By	In Exchange For
Dec. 5, 1988	CHI N	Mitch Williams Steve Wilson Curtis Wilkerson Minor league IF Luis Benitez Minor league OF Pablo Delgado	TEX A	Rafael Palmeiro Jamie Moyer Drew Hall
Dec. 7, 1989	TOR A	—	CHI N	Jose Nunez
Dec. 14, 1990	BAL A	—	TOR A	Mickey Weston

Mike Kilkenny

Date	Traded To	Traded With	Traded By	In Exchange For
May 9, 1972	OAK A	—	DET A	Reggie Sanders
May 17, 1972	SD N	Curt Blefary minor league OF Greg Schubert	OAK A	Ollie Brown
June 11, 1972	CLE A	—	SD N	Fred Stanley

Bill Killefer

Date	Traded To	Traded With	Traded By	In Exchange For
Dec. 11, 1917	CHI N	Grover Alexander	PHI N	Mike Prendergast Pickles Dillhoefer $55,000.

Red Killefer

Date	Traded To	Traded With	Traded By	In Exchange For
Aug. 13, 1909	WAS A	Germany Schaefer	DET A	Jim Delahanty
July 20, 1916	NY N	Buck Herzog	CIN N	Christy Mathewson Edd Roush Bill McKechnie

Frank Killen

Date	Traded To	Traded With	Traded By	In Exchange For
1900	CHI N	—	BOS N	Cash

Ed Killian

Date	Traded To	Traded With	Traded By	In Exchange For
Jan. 1904	DET A	Jesse Stovall	CLE A	Billy Lush

Newt Kimball

Date	Traded To	Traded With	Traded By	In Exchange For
Dec. 8, 1939	BKN N	Gus Mancuso	CHI N	Al Todd
Sept. 1940	STL N	—	BKN N	Cash

(Sale was cancelled by Commissioner Landis.)

Date	Traded To	Traded With	Traded By	In Exchange For
May 20, 1943	PHI N	—	BKN N	Cash

Bruce Kimm

Date	Traded To	Traded With	Traded By	In Exchange For
Aug. 17, 1972	CAL A	Bruce Miller	CHI A	Eddie Fisher
Aug. 30, 1979	CHI N	—	DET A	Cash

Chad Kimsey

Date	Traded To	Traded With	Traded By	In Exchange For
Sept. 9, 1932	CHI A	—	STL A	Cash

Jerry Kindall

Date	Traded To	Traded With	Traded By	In Exchange For
Nov. 27, 1961	CLE A	—	CHI N	Bobby Locke

Jerry Kindall *continued*

Date	Traded To	Traded With	Traded By	In Exchange For
June 11, 1964	LA A	—	CLE A	Billy Moran
(Part of three-team trade involving Los Angeles Angels, Cleveland, and Minnesota.)				
June 11, 1964	MIN A	Frank Kostro	LA A	Lenny Green Vic Power
(Part of three-team trade involving Los Angeles Angels, Minnesota, and Cleveland.)				

Ellis Kinder

Date	Traded To	Traded With	Traded By	In Exchange For
Nov. 18, 1947	BOS A	Billy Hitchcock	STL A	Sam Dente Clem Dreisewerd Bill Sommers $65,000.
Dec. 4, 1955	STL N	—	BOS A	Waiver price
July 11, 1956	CHI A	—	STL N	Waiver price

Ralph Kiner

Date	Traded To	Traded With	Traded By	In Exchange For
June 4, 1953	CHI N	Joe Garagiola Howie Pollet Catfish Metkovich	PIT N	Toby Atwell Bob Schultz Preston Ward George Freese Bob Addis Gene Hermanski $150,000.
Nov. 16, 1954	CLE A	—	CHI N	Sam Jones Gale Wade $60,000.

Charlie King

Date	Traded To	Traded With	Traded By	In Exchange For
Feb. 12, 1957	MIL N	Cash	DET A	Jack Dittmer
Nov. 10, 1957	CHI N	Ben Johnson minor league OF Len Williams and cash	MIL N	Casey Wise
May 19, 1959	STL N	—	CHI N	Irv Noren

Clyde King

Date	Traded To	Traded With	Traded By	In Exchange For
Oct. 10, 1952	CIN N	—	BKN N	Cash

Eric King

Date	Traded To	Traded With	Traded By	In Exchange For
Oct. 7, 1985	DET A	*see Dave LaPoint*	SF N	—
Mar. 23, 1989	CHI A	—	DET A	Kenny Williams
Dec. 4, 1990	CLE A	Shawn Hillegas	CHI A	Cory Snyder Minor league IF Lindsay Foster

Hal King

Date	Traded To	Traded With	Traded By	In Exchange For
Dec. 2, 1971	TEX A	—	ATL N	Paul Casanova
Dec. 1, 1972	CIN N	Minor leaguer Jim Driscoll	TEX A	Jim Merritt

Jim King

Date	Traded To	Traded With	Traded By	In Exchange For
Apr. 20, 1957	STL N	—	CHI N	Ed Mayer Bobby Del Greco
Apr. 2, 1958	SF N	—	STL N	Ray Katt
June 15, 1967	CHI A	—	WAS A	Ed Stroud
July 29, 1967	CLE A	Marv Staehle	CHI A	Rocky Colavito

Lee King

Date	Traded To	Traded With	Traded By	In Exchange For
July 1921	PHI N	—	NY N	Waiver price
July 1, 1921	PHI N	Goldie Rapp Lance Richbourg	NY N	Casey Stengel Red Causey Johnny Rawlings

Lee King

Date	Traded To	Traded With	Traded By	In Exchange For
Jan. 1919	NY N	—	PIT N	Cash

Mike Kingery

Date	Traded To	Traded With	Traded By	In Exchange For
Dec. 10, 1986	SEA A	Scott Bankhead Steve Shields	KC A	Danny Tartabull Rick Luecken
Dec. 14, 1995	PIT N	—	CLR N	No compensation (free agent signing)

Brian Kingman

Date	Traded To	Traded With	Traded By	In Exchange For
Jan. 17, 1983	BOS A	—	OAK A	Cash

Dave Kingman

Date	Traded To	Traded With	Traded By	In Exchange For
Feb. 28, 1975	NY N	—	SF N	$150,000.
June 15, 1977	SD N	—	NY N	Bobby Valentine Paul Siebert
Sept. 6, 1977	CAL A	—	SD N	Cash
Sept. 15, 1977	NY A	—	CAL A	Cash
Nov. 30, 1977	CHI N	—	NY A	No compensation (free agent signing)
Feb. 28, 1981	NY N	—	CHI N	Steve Henderson Cash

Dennis Kinney

Date	Traded To	Traded With	Traded By	In Exchange For
June 14, 1978	SD N	—	CLE A	Dan Spillner
Dec. 12, 1980	DET A	—	SD N	Dave Stegman

Mike Kinnunen

Date	Traded To	Traded With	Traded By	In Exchange For
Jan. 7, 1985	KC A	Minor League OF Ken Baker	MON N	U. L. Washington

Matt Kinzer

Date	Traded To	Traded With	Traded By	In Exchange For
Dec. 6, 1989	DET A	Jim Lindeman	STL N	Minor league 2B Pat Austin Minor league C Bill Henderson Minor league P Marcos Betances

Fred Kipp

Date	Traded To	Traded With	Traded By	In Exchange For
Apr. 5, 1960	NY A	—	LA N	Gordie Windhorn minor league 1B Dick Sanders

Bob Kipper

Date	Traded To	Traded With	Traded By	In Exchange For
Aug. 2, 1985	PIT N	—	CAL A	*see John Candelaria*
Dec. 17, 1991	MIN A	—	PIT N	No compensation (free agent signing)

Clay Kirby

Date	Traded To	Traded With	Traded By	In Exchange For
Nov. 9, 1973	CIN N	—	SD N	Bobby Tolan Dave Tomlin
Dec. 12, 1975	MON N	—	CIN N	Bob Bailey

Willie Kirkland

Date	Traded To	Traded With	Traded By	In Exchange For
Dec. 3, 1960	CLE A	Johnny Antonelli	SF N	Harvey Kuenn
Dec. 4, 1963	BAL A	—	CLE A	Al Smith $25,000.
Aug. 12, 1964	WAS A	—	BAL A	Cash

Ed Kirkpatrick

Date	Traded To	Traded With	Traded By	In Exchange For
Dec. 12, 1968	KC A	Dennis Paepke	CAL A	Hoyt Wilhelm
Dec. 4, 1973	PIT N	Kurt Bevacqua minor league 1B Winston Cole	KC A	Nellie Briles Fernando Gonzalez
June 15, 1977	TEX A	—	PIT N	Jim Fregosi
Aug. 20, 1977	MIL A	—	TEX A	Gorman Thomas

Don Kirkwood

Date	Traded To	Traded With	Traded By	In Exchange For
June 15, 1977	CHI A	John Verhoeven John Flannery	CAL A	Ken Brett
Apr. 11, 1978	TOR A	—	CHI A	Cash

Bruce Kison

Date	Traded To	Traded With	Traded By	In Exchange For
Nov. 16, 1979	CAL A	—	PIT N	No compensation (free agent signing)
Jan. 14, 1985	BOS A	—	CAL A	No compensation (free agent signing)

Frank Kitson

Date	Traded To	Traded With	Traded By	In Exchange For
Jan. 1900	BKN N	Harry Howell Jimmy Sheckard Jerry Nops Broadway Aleck Smith Joe McGinnity	BAL N	Cash
Dec. 1905	WAS A	—	DET A	Cash
July 1907	NY A	—	WAS A	Cash

Ron Kittle

Date	Traded To	Traded With	Traded By	In Exchange For
July 30, 1986	NY A	Joel Skinner Wayne Tolleson	CHI A	Ron Hassey Carlos Martinez Bill Lindsey

(Chicago received Lindsey on Dec. 24, 1986.)

Date	Traded To	Traded With	Traded By	In Exchange For
Feb. 9, 1988	CLE A	—	NY A	No compensation (free agent signing)
Nov. 26, 1988	CHI A	—	CLE A	No compensation (free agent signing)
July 30, 1990	BAL A	—	CHI A	Phil Bradley
Jan. 20, 1991	CLE A	—	BAL A	No compensation (free agent signing)

Mal Kittridge

Date	Traded To	Traded With	Traded By	In Exchange For
June 1903	WAS A	—	BOS N	Cash
Aug. 15, 1906	CLE A	—	WAS A	Cash

Billy Klaus

Date	Traded To	Traded With	Traded By	In Exchange For
Feb. 1, 1954	NY N	*see Johnny Antonelli*	MIL N	—
Dec. 14, 1954	BOS A	—	NY N	Del Wilber
Dec. 15, 1958	BAL A	—	BOS A	Jim Busby
Apr. 5, 1962	PHI N	—	WAS A	Cash

Bobby Klaus

Date	Traded To	Traded With	Traded By	In Exchange For
July 19, 1964	NY N	—	CIN N	Cash
Feb. 22, 1966	PHI N	Jimmie Schaffer Wayne Graham	NY N	Dick Stuart
Mar. 28, 1969	PIT N	Ron Davis	SD N	Chris Cannizzaro Tommie Sisk

Chuck Klein

Date	Traded To	Traded With	Traded By	In Exchange For
Nov. 21, 1933	CHI N	—	PHI N	Ted Kleinhans Harvey Hendrick Mark Koenig $65,000.
May 21, 1936	PHI N	Fabian Kowalik	CHI N	Ethan Allen Curt Davis

Lou Klein

Date	Traded To	Traded With	Traded By	In Exchange For
Dec. 14, 1949	CIN N	Ron Northey	STL N	Harry Walker
May 10, 1951	PHI A	Allie Clark	CLE A	Sam Chapman

Ted Kleinhans

Date	Traded To	Traded With	Traded By	In Exchange For
Nov. 21, 1933	PHI N	Harvey Hendrick Mark Koenig $65,000.	CHI N	Chuck Klein
May 16, 1934	CIN N	Wes Schulmerich Art Ruble	PHI N	Syl Johnson Johnny Moore

Red Kleinow

Date	Traded To	Traded With	Traded By	In Exchange For
May 1910	BOS A	—	NY A	Cash
June 1911	PHI N	—	BOS A	Waiver price

Ed Klepfer

Date	Traded To	Traded With	Traded By	In Exchange For
Aug. 21, 1915	CLE A	Braggo Roth Larry Chappell $31,500.	CHI A	Joe Jackson

Eddie Klieman

Date	Traded To	Traded With	Traded By	In Exchange For
Dec. 14, 1948	WAS A	Joe Haynes Eddie Robinson	CLE A	Mickey Vernon Early Wynn
May 3, 1949	NY A	—	WAS A	Waiver price
May 16, 1949	CHI A	—	NY A	Cash
Dec. 14, 1949	PHI A	—	CHI A	Hank Majeski

Lou Klimchock

Date	Traded To	Traded With	Traded By	In Exchange For
Dec. 15, 1961	MIL N	*see Bob Shaw*	KC A	—

Ron Klimkowski

Date	Traded To	Traded With	Traded By	In Exchange For
Aug. 3, 1967	NY A	Pete Magrini	BOS A	Elston Howard
Apr. 9, 1971	OAK A	Rob Gardner	NY A	Felipe Alou

Bob Kline

Date	Traded To	Traded With	Traded By	In Exchange For
Dec. 12, 1933	PHI A	Rabbit Warstler $125,000.	BOS A	Lefty Grove Max Bishop Rube Walberg
June 23, 1934	WAS A	—	PHI A	Cash

Bobby Kline

Date	Traded To	Traded With	Traded By	In Exchange For
Feb. 8, 1956	NY A	—	WAS A	*see Whitey Herzog*

Ron Kline

Date	Traded To	Traded With	Traded By	In Exchange For
Dec. 21, 1959	STL N	—	PIT N	Gino Cimoli Tom Cheney
Apr. 10, 1961	LA A	—	STL N	Cash
Aug. 10, 1961	DET A	—	LA A	Waiver price
Mar. 18, 1963	WAS A	—	DET A	Cash
Dec. 3, 1966	MIN A	—	WAS A	Bernie Allen Camilo Pascual
Dec. 2, 1967	PIT N	—	MIN A	Bob Oliver
June 10, 1969	SF N	—	PIT N	Joe Gibbon
July 5, 1969	BOS A	—	SF N	Cash

Steve Kline

Date	Traded To	Traded With	Traded By	In Exchange For
Apr. 27, 1974	CLE A	—	NY A	*see Chris Chambliss*
Dec. 13, 1976	ATL N	—	CLE A	Cash

Johnny Kling

Date	Traded To	Traded With	Traded By	In Exchange For
June 10, 1911	BOS N	Al Kaiser Orlie Weaver Hank Griffin	CHI N	Cliff Curtis Wilbur Good Bill Collins Peaches Graham
Feb. 1913	CIN N	—	BOS N	Cash

Scott Klingenbeck

Date	Traded To	Traded With	Traded By	In Exchange For
July 7, 1995	MIN A	Player to be named	BAL A	Scott Erickson

(Minnesota received OF Kimera Bartee on September 19, 1995.)

Joe Klink

Date	Traded To	Traded With	Traded By	In Exchange For
Jan. 16, 1986	MIN A	Billy Beane Bill Latham	NY N	Tim Teufel Minor league OF Pat Crosby

Johnny Klippstein

Date	Traded To	Traded With	Traded By	In Exchange For
Oct. 1, 1954	CIN N	Jim Willis	CHI N	Ted Tappe Jim Bolger Harry Perkowski
June 15, 1958	LA N	Steve Bilko	CIN N	Don Newcombe
Apr. 11, 1960	CLE A	—	LA N	$25,000.
Dec. 15, 1961	CIN N	Marty Keough	WAS A	Dave Stenhouse Bob Schmidt
Mar. 25, 1963	PHI N	—	CIN N	Cash
June 29, 1964	MIN A	—	PHI N	Cash

Ted Kluszewski

Date	Traded To	Traded With	Traded By	In Exchange For
Dec. 28, 1957	PIT N	—	CIN N	Dee Fondy
Aug. 25, 1959	CHI A	—	PIT N	Harry Simpson minor league IF Bob Sagers

Mickey Klutts

Date	Traded To	Traded With	Traded By	In Exchange For
June 15, 1978	OAK A	Dell Alston $50,000.	NY A	Gary Thomasson

Clyde Klutz

Date	Traded To	Traded With	Traded By	In Exchange For
June 16, 1945	NY N	—	BOS N	Ewald Pyle Joe Medwick
May 1, 1946	PHI N	—	NY N	Vince DiMaggio
May 2, 1946	STL N	—	PHI N	Emil Verban
Dec. 26, 1946	PIT N	—	STL N	Cash
June 12, 1951	WAS A	—	STL A	Waiver price

Date	Traded To		Traded With	Traded By		In Exchange For
Joe Kmak						
Nov. 18, 1993	NY	N	—	MIL	A	Waiver price
Otto Knabe						
Feb. 10, 1916	PIT	N	Jimmy Smith	BAL	F	Cash
July 29, 1916	CHI	N	Art Wilson	PIT	N	Wildfire Schulte Bill Fischer
Brent Knackert						
Apr. 5, 1990	SEA	A	—	NY	N	Waiver price
Chris Knapp						
Dec. 5, 1977	CAL	A	*see Brian Downing*	CHI	A	—
Bob Knepper						
Dec. 8, 1980	HOU	N	Chris Bourjos	SF	N	Enos Cabell
Lou Knerr						
Feb. 14, 1947	WAS	A	—	PHI	A	George Binks
Elmer Knetzer						
Feb. 10, 1916	BOS	N	Frank Allen	PIT	F	Cash
Apr. 1916	CIN	N	—	BOS	N	Cash
Alan Knicely						
Mar. 31, 1983	CIN	N	—	HOU	N	Bill Dawley Tony Walker
Aug. 8, 1985	PHI	N	—	CIN	N	*see Bo Diaz*
Bill Knickerbocker						
Jan. 17, 1937	STL	A	Joe Vosmik Oral Hildebrand	CLE	A	Ivy Andrews Lyn Lary Moose Solters
Feb. 15, 1938	NY	A	—	STL	A	Don Heffner $10,000.
Dec. 31, 1940	CHI	A	—	NY	A	Ken Silvestri
Apr. 3, 1942	PHI	A	—	CHI	A	Waiver price
Jack Knight						
June 7, 1907	BOS	A	—	PHI	A	Jimmy Collins
John Knight						
Feb. 1909	NY	A	—	BOS	A	Waiver price
Dec. 1911	WAS	A	Roxy Roach	NY	A	Gabby Street Jack Lelivelt
July 7, 1913	NY	A	—	WAS	A	Cash
Ray Knight						
Dec. 18, 1981	HOU	N	—	CIN	N	Cesar Cedeno
Aug. 28, 1984	NY	N	—	HOU	N	Gerald Young Manny Lee Minor league P Mitch Cook
Feb. 11, 1987	BAL	A	—	NY	N	No compensation (free agent signing)
Feb. 27, 1988	DET	A	—	BAL	A	Mark Thurmond
Pete Knisely						
Dec. 15, 1912	CHI	N	—	CIN	N	*see Joe Tinker*
Bobby Knoop						
May 14, 1969	CHI	A	—	CAL	A	Sandy Alomar Bob Priddy
Mar. 24, 1971	KC	A	—	CHI	A	Luis Alcaraz Cash
Fritz Knothe						
June 17, 1933	PHI	N	Wes Schulmerich Cash	BOS	N	Hal Lee Pinky Whitney
Jack Knott						
June 11, 1938	CHI	A	—	STL	A	Billy Cox
Dec. 16, 1940	PHI	A	—	CHI	A	Dario Lodigiani
Darold Knowles						
Dec. 6, 1965	PHI	N	Jackie Brandt	BAL	A	Jack Baldschun
Nov. 30, 1966	WAS	A	Cash	PHI	N	Don Lock
May 8, 1971	OAK	A	Mike Epstein	WAS	A	Frank Fernandez Don Mincher Paul Lindblad Cash
Oct. 23, 1974	CHI	N	Bob Locker Manny Trillo	OAK	A	Billy Williams
Feb. 5, 1977	TEX	A	—	CHI	N	Gene Clines Cash
Nov. 10, 1977	MON	N	—	TEX	A	Cash
Jan. 16, 1979	STL	N	—	MON	N	No compensation (free agent signing)
Mark Knudson						
Aug. 19, 1986	MIL	A	—	HOU	N	*see Danny Darwin*
Kevin Kobel						
June 17, 1980	KC	A	—	NY	N	Randy McGilberry
Alan Koch						
May 9, 1964	WAS	A	—	DET	A	Cash
Pete Koegel						
Aug. 29, 1969	SEA	A	Bob Meyer	OAK	A	Fred Talbot
Apr. 22, 1971	PHI	N	Ray Peters	MIL	A	John Briggs
Brian Koelling						
Aug. 8, 1995	PHI	N	—	CIN	N	Mariano Duncan
Mark Koenig						
May 30, 1930	DET	A	Waite Hoyt	NY	A	Ownie Carroll Yats Wuestling Harry Rice
Nov. 21, 1933	PHI	N	Ted Kleinhans Harvey Hendrick $65,000.	CHI	N	Chuck Klein
Dec. 20, 1933	CIN	N	—	PHI	N	Otto Bluege Irv Jeffries
Dec. 14, 1934	NY	N	Allyn Stout	CIN	N	Billy Myers Cash
Elmer Koestner						
Aug. 1914	CIN	N	—	CHI	N	Johnny Bates
Dick Kokos						
Nov. 20, 1947	STL	A	Joe Frazier Bryan Stephens $25,000.	CLE	A	Bob Muncrief Walt Judnich
Gary Kolb						
Apr. 9, 1964	MIL	N	Jimmie Coker	STL	N	Bob Uecker
July 21, 1965	NY	N	—	MIL	N	Jesse Gonder
Dec. 6, 1966	PIT	N	Dennis Ribant	NY	N	Don Bosch Don Cardwell
Don Kolloway						
May 7, 1949	DET	A	—	CHI	A	Vern Rapp
Jan. 29, 1953	PHI	A	—	DET	A	Billy Hitchcock
Fred Kommers						
Aug. 1914	BAL	F	—	STL	F	Cash
Brad Komminsk						
Jan. 19, 1987	MIL	A	—	ATL	N	Dion James
Apr. 5, 1990	SF	N	—	CLE	A	Waiver price
May 2, 1990	BAL	A	—	SF	N	Waiver price

Ed Konetchy

Date	Traded To	Traded With	Traded By	In Exchange For
Dec. 12, 1913	PIT N	Bob Harmon Mike Mowrey	STL N	Art Butler Dots Miller Cozy Dolan Owen Wilson Hank Robinson
Feb. 10, 1916	BOS N	—	PIT N	Cash
Apr. 14, 1919	BKN N	—	BOS N	Cash
July 4, 1921	PHI N	—	BKN N	Waiver price

Jim Konstanty

Date	Traded To	Traded With	Traded By	In Exchange For
Apr. 18, 1946	BOS N	Cash	CIN N	Max West
Aug. 22, 1954	NY A	—	PHI N	Cash

Cal Koonce

Date	Traded To	Traded With	Traded By	In Exchange For
Aug. 2, 1967	NY N	—	CHI N	Cash
June 8, 1970	BOS A	—	NY N	Cash

Jerry Koosman

Date	Traded To	Traded With	Traded By	In Exchange For
Dec. 8, 1978	MIN A	—	NY N	Jesse Orosco minor league P Greg Field
Aug. 30, 1981	CHI A	—	MIN A	Randy Johnson minor leaguers SS Ivan Mesa and 3B Ronnie Perry Cash
Dec. 5, 1983	PHI N	—	CHI A	Ron Reed

Larry Kopf

Date	Traded To	Traded With	Traded By	In Exchange For
Dec. 1915	CIN N	—	PHI A	Cash
Feb. 18, 1922	CIN N	Jack Scott	BOS N	Rube Marquard

Merlin Kopp

Date	Traded To	Traded With	Traded By	In Exchange For
Dec. 14, 1917	PHI A	Vean Gregg Pinch Thomas $60,000.	BOS A	Amos Strunk Joe Bush Wally Schang

Joe Koppe

Date	Traded To	Traded With	Traded By	In Exchange For
Mar. 31, 1959	PHI N	Gene Conley Harry Hanebrink	MIL N	Stan Lopata Ted Kazanski Johnny O'Brien
May 4, 1961	LA N	Dick Farrell	PHI N	Don Demeter Charley Smith

Andy Kosco

Date	Traded To	Traded With	Traded By	In Exchange For
Dec. 4, 1968	LA N	—	NY A	Mike Kekich
Feb. 10, 1971	MIL A	—	LA N	Al Downing
Jan. 26, 1972	CAL A	—	MIL A	Tommie Reynolds
Aug. 15, 1972	BOS A	—	CAL A	Chris Coletta
Mar. 27, 1973	CIN N	Phil Gagliano	BOS A	Mel Behney

Dave Koslo

Date	Traded To	Traded With	Traded By	In Exchange For
Apr. 8, 1954	BAL A	—	NY N	Cash

Frank Kostro

Date	Traded To	Traded With	Traded By	In Exchange For
June 15, 1963	LA A	Paul Foytack	DET A	George Thomas Cash
June 11, 1964	MIN A	Jerry Kindall	LA A	Lenny Green Vic Power

(Part of three-team trade involving Los Angeles Angels, Minnesota, and Cleveland.)

Lou Koupal

Date	Traded To	Traded With	Traded By	In Exchange For
July 24, 1929	PHI N	—	BKN N	Luther Roy

Fabian Kowalik

Date	Traded To	Traded With	Traded By	In Exchange For
May 21, 1936	PHI N	Chuck Klein	CHI N	Ethan Allen Curt Davis
Aug. 4, 1936	BOS N	—	PHI N	Ray Benge

Ernie Koy

Date	Traded To	Traded With	Traded By	In Exchange For
Apr. 15, 1938	BKN N	—	NY A	Cash

Ernie Koy *continued*

Date	Traded To	Traded With	Traded By	In Exchange For
June 12, 1940	STL N	Carl Doyle Sam Nahem Bert Haas $125,000.	BKN N	Joe Medwick Curt Davis
May 14, 1941	CIN N	—	STL N	Cash
May 2, 1942	PHI N	—	CIN N	Cash

Al Kozar

Date	Traded To	Traded With	Traded By	In Exchange For
Dec. 10, 1947	WAS A	Leon Culberson	BOS A	Stan Spence
May 31, 1950	CHI A	*see Eddie Robinson*	WAS A	—

Joe Krakauskas

Date	Traded To	Traded With	Traded By	In Exchange For
Dec. 24, 1940	CLE A	—	WAS A	Ben Chapman

Jack Kralick

Date	Traded To	Traded With	Traded By	In Exchange For
May 2, 1963	CLE A	—	MIN A	Jim Perry
May 1, 1967	NY N	—	CLE A	Cash

Jack Kramer

Date	Traded To	Traded With	Traded By	In Exchange For
Nov. 17, 1947	BOS A	Vern Stephens	STL A	Roy Partee Jim Wilson Al Widmar Eddie Pellagrini Pete Layden Joe Ostrowski $310,000.
Mar. 26, 1950	NY N	—	BOS A	Cash

Randy Kramer

Date	Traded To	Traded With	Traded By	In Exchange For
Sept. 30, 1986	PIT N	—	TEX A	Jeff Zaske
Sept. 3, 1990	CHI N	—	PIT N	Minor league P Greg Kallevig

Tom Kramer

Date	Traded To	Traded With	Traded By	In Exchange For
May 17, 1994	CIN N	—	CLE A	Minor league P John Hrusovsky

Tex Kraus

Date	Traded To	Traded With	Traded By	In Exchange For
Mar. 24, 1943	PHI N	Cash	BKN N	Bobby Bragan

Harry Krause

Date	Traded To	Traded With	Traded By	In Exchange For
July 1912	CLE A	—	PHI A	Cash

Lew Krausse

Date	Traded To	Traded With	Traded By	In Exchange For
Jan. 15, 1970	MIL A	—	OAK A	*see Don Mincher*
Oct. 11, 1971	BOS A	—	MIL A	*see George Scott*
Sept. 1, 1973	STL N	Larry Haney	OAK A	Cash

Lew Krausse

Date	Traded To	Traded With	Traded By	In Exchange For
Dec. 13, 1938	CIN N	Cash	BKN N	Jimmy Outlaw

Ken Kravec

Date	Traded To	Traded With	Traded By	In Exchange For
Mar. 28, 1981	CHI N	—	CHI A	Dennis Lamp

Danny Kravitz

Date	Traded To	Traded With	Traded By	In Exchange For
June 1, 1960	KC A	—	PIT N	Hank Foiles Cash

Mike Kreevich

Date	Traded To	Traded With	Traded By	In Exchange For
Dec. 9, 1941	PHI A	Jack Hallett	CHI A	Wally Moses
Aug. 8, 1945	WAS A	—	STL A	Waiver price

Jimmy Kremers

Date	Traded To	Traded With	Traded By	In Exchange For
Apr. 1, 1991	MON N	Player to be named	ATL N	Otis Nixon Minor league 3B Boi Rodriguez

(Montreal received P Keith Morrison on June 3, 1991.)

Jim Kremmel

Date	Traded To	Traded With	Traded By	In Exchange For
July 16, 1973	STL N	—	TEX A	Don Durham
Oct. 26, 1973	CHI A	—	STL N	Denny O'Toole

Jim Kremmel *continued*

Date	Traded To	Traded With	Traded By	In Exchange For
Dec. 11, 1973	CHI N	Steve Stone Ken Frailing Steve Swisher	CHI A	Ron Santo

Wayne Krenchicki

Date	Traded To	Traded With	Traded By	In Exchange For
Feb. 9, 1982	CIN N	—	BAL A	Paul Moskau
June 30, 1983	DET A	—	CIN N	Pat Underwood
Nov. 21, 1983	CIN N	—	DET A	Cash
Mar. 31, 1986	MON N	—	CIN N	Norm Charlton Minor league 2B Tim Barker

Charlie Kress

Date	Traded To	Traded With	Traded By	In Exchange For
June 8, 1949	CHI A	—	CIN N	Cash
June 9, 1954	BKN N	Johnny Bucha Ernie Nevel Cash	DET A	Wayne Belardi

Red Kress

Date	Traded To	Traded With	Traded By	In Exchange For
Apr. 27, 1932	CHI A	—	STL A	Bruce Campbell Bump Hadley
May 12, 1934	WAS A	—	CHI A	Bob Boken
Dec. 2, 1937	STL A	Bobo Newsom Buster Mills	BOS A	Joe Vosmik
May 13, 1939	DET A	Beau Bell Bobo Newsom Jim Walkup	STL A	Vern Kennedy Bob Harris George Gill Roxie Lawson Chet Laabs Mark Christman

Lou Kretlow

Date	Traded To	Traded With	Traded By	In Exchange For
Dec. 14, 1949	STL A	$100,000.	DET A	Gerry Priddy
July 5, 1950	CHI A	—	STL A	Waiver price
June 13, 1953	STL A	Darrell Johnson $75,000.	CHI A	Virgil Trucks Bob Elliott

Rick Kreuger

Date	Traded To	Traded With	Traded By	In Exchange For
Mar. 24, 1978	CLE A	—	BOS A	Frank Duffy

Frank Kreutzer

Date	Traded To	Traded With	Traded By	In Exchange For
July 13, 1964	WAS A	Joe Cunningham	CHI A	Bill Skowron Carl Bouldin
May 17, 1969	PIT N	—	WAS A	Jim Shellenback

Gary Kroll

Date	Traded To	Traded With	Traded By	In Exchange For
Aug. 7, 1964	NY N	Wayne Graham Cash	PHI N	Frank Thomas
Jan. 6, 1966	HOU N	—	NY N	Johnny Weekly Cash
July 20, 1967	CLE A	—	HOU N	Cash

John Kroner

Date	Traded To	Traded With	Traded By	In Exchange For
Dec. 1936	CLE A	—	BOS A	Cash

Marc Kroon

Date	Traded To	Traded With	Traded By	In Exchange For
Dec. 10, 1993	SD N	Minor league OF Randy Curtis	NY N	Frank Seminara Minor league OF Tracy Sanders Minor league SS Pablo Martinez

(Martinez and Kroon were exchanged on December 13.)

Rocky Krsnich

Date	Traded To	Traded With	Traded By	In Exchange For
Dec. 10, 1953	CIN N	Saul Rogovin Connie Ryan	CHI A	Willard Marshall

Bill Krueger

Date	Traded To	Traded With	Traded By	In Exchange For
June 23, 1987	LA N	—	OAK A	Minor league P Tim Meeks

Bill Krueger *continued*

Date	Traded To	Traded With	Traded By	In Exchange For
Oct. 3, 1988	PIT N	—	LA N	Jim Neidlinger
Dec. 19, 1990	SEA A	—	MIL A	No compensation (free agent signing)
Aug. 31, 1992	MON N	—	MIN A	Darren Reed
Dec. 11, 1992	DET A	—	MON N	No compensation (free agent signing)

Ernie Krueger

Date	Traded To	Traded With	Traded By	In Exchange For
May 1917	BKN N	—	NY N	Waiver price
Feb. 17, 1922	CIN N	—	BKN N	Cash

Otto Krueger

Date	Traded To	Traded With	Traded By	In Exchange For
Jan. 1900	STL N	Jack Harper Joe Quinn Jim Hughey	CLE N	Cash
Jan. 1903	PIT N	—	STL N	Jimmy Burke
Dec. 20, 1904	PHI N	Kitty Bransfield Moose McCormick	PIT N	Del Howard
Jan. 1905	PHI N	—	PIT N	Waiver price

Art Kruger

Date	Traded To	Traded With	Traded By	In Exchange For
Sept. 1910	BOS N	—	CLE A	Cash

John Kruk

Date	Traded To	Traded With	Traded By	In Exchange For
June 2, 1989	PHI N	Randy Ready	SD N	Chris James
May 12, 1995	CHI A	—	PHI N	No compensation (free agent signing)

Mike Krukow

Date	Traded To	Traded With	Traded By	In Exchange For
Dec. 8, 1981	PHI N	Cash	CHI N	Keith Moreland Dan Larson Dickie Noles
Dec. 14, 1982	SF N	Mark Davis minor league OF Charles Penigar	PHI N	Joe Morgan Al Holland

Dick Kryhoski

Date	Traded To	Traded With	Traded By	In Exchange For
Dec. 17, 1949	DET A	—	NY A	Dick Wakefield
Feb. 14, 1952	STL A	*see Gene Bearden*	DET A	—
Dec. 1, 1954	NY A	Mike Blyzka Darrell Johnson Jim Fridley	BAL A	Bill Miller Kal Segrist Don Leppert minor league OF Ted Del Guercio player to be named later

(Second part of 18-player trade begun on November 18, 1954; see Bob Turley.)

Date	Traded To	Traded With	Traded By	In Exchange For
Mar. 30, 1955	KC A	Ewell Blackwell Tom Gorman	NY A	$50,000.

Ted Kubiak

Date	Traded To	Traded With	Traded By	In Exchange For
Dec. 7, 1969	SEA A	George Lauzerique	OAK A	Diego Segui Ray Oyler
July 29, 1971	STL N	minor league P Charlie Loseth	MIL A	Jose Cardenal Dick Schofield Bob Reynolds
Nov. 3, 1971	TEX A	—	STL N	Joe Grzenda
July 20, 1972	OAK A	Don Mincher	TEX A	Marty Martinez Vic Harris Steve Lawson
May 16, 1975	SD N	—	OAK A	Sonny Siebert

Jack Kubiszyn

Date	Traded To	Traded With	Traded By	In Exchange For
Dec. 15, 1962	STL N	Ron Taylor	CLE A	Fred Whitfield

Gil Kubski

Date	Traded To	Traded With	Traded By	In Exchange For
May 10, 1981	MIL A	—	TOR A	Buck Martinez

Jack Kucek

Date	Traded To	Traded With	Traded By	In Exchange For
Apr. 13, 1979	PHI N	—	CHI A	Jim Morrison

Johnny Kucks

Date	Traded To		Traded With	Traded By		In Exchange For
May 26, 1959	KC	A	Tom Sturdivant Jerry Lumpe	NY	A	Hector Lopez Ralph Terry
Oct. 11, 1961	BAL	A	—	KC	A	Cash
Dec. 1, 1961	STL	N	—	BAL	A	Minor leaguer Ron Kabbes

Harvey Kuenn

Date	Traded To		Traded With	Traded By		In Exchange For
Apr. 17, 1960	CLE	A	—	DET	A	Rocky Colavito
Dec. 3, 1960	SF	N	—	CLE	A	Johnny Antonelli Willie Kirkland
May 29, 1965	CHI	N	Ed Bailey Bob Hendley	SF	N	Dick Bertell Len Gabrielson
Apr. 23, 1966	PHI	N	—	CHI	N	Cash

Joe Kuhel

Date	Traded To		Traded With	Traded By		In Exchange For
Mar. 18, 1938	CHI	A	—	WAS	A	Zeke Bonura
Nov. 24, 1943	WAS	A	—	CHI	A	Cash
June 13, 1946	CHI	A	—	WAS	A	Cash

Duane Kuiper

Date	Traded To		Traded With	Traded By		In Exchange For
Nov. 14, 1981	SF	N	—	CLE	A	Ed Whitson

Jeff Kunkel

Date	Traded To		Traded With	Traded By		In Exchange For
July 7, 1992	CHI	N	—	MIL	A	Ced Landrum

Rusty Kuntz

Date	Traded To		Traded With	Traded By		In Exchange For
June 21, 1983	MIN	A	—	CHI	A	Minor league IF Mike Sodders
Dec. 8, 1983	DET	A	—	MIN	A	Larry Pashnick

Craig Kusick

Date	Traded To		Traded With	Traded By		In Exchange For
July 25, 1979	TOR	A	—	MIN	A	Cash

Art Kusnyer

Date	Traded To		Traded With	Traded By		In Exchange For
Oct. 22, 1973	MIL	A	*see Clyde Wright*	CAL	A	—

Randy Kutcher

Date	Traded To		Traded With	Traded By		In Exchange For
Sept. 1, 1987	BOS	A	—	SF	N	Dave Henderson

(Boston received Kutcher on December 9, 1987.)

Marty Kutyna

Date	Traded To		Traded With	Traded By		In Exchange For
Dec. 5, 1957	CIN	N	Ted Wieand Willard Schmidt	STL	N	Curt Flood Joe Taylor
Dec. 29, 1960	WAS	A	Cash	KC	A	Haywood Sullivan

Bob Kuzava

Date	Traded To		Traded With	Traded By		In Exchange For
Dec. 2, 1948	CHI	A	Ernie Groth	CLE	A	Frank Papish
May 31, 1950	WAS	A	Cass Michaels John Ostrowski	CHI	A	Al Kozar Ray Scarborough Eddie Robinson
June 15, 1951	NY	A	—	WAS	A	Fred Sanford Tom Ferrick Bob Porterfield
Aug. 7, 1954	BAL	A	—	NY	A	Waiver price
May 23, 1955	PHI	N	—	BAL	A	Waiver price

Chet Laabs

Date	Traded To		Traded With	Traded By		In Exchange For
May 13, 1939	STL	A	Vern Kennedy Bob Harris George Gill Roxie Lawson Mark Christman	DET	A	Beau Bell Bobo Newsom Red Kress Jim Walkup
Apr. 9, 1947	PHI	A	—	STL	A	Cash

Clem Labine

Date	Traded To		Traded With	Traded By		In Exchange For
June 15, 1960	DET	A	—	LA	N	Ray Semproch Cash

Bob Lacey

Date	Traded To		Traded With	Traded By		In Exchange For
Mar. 27, 1981	SD	N	minor league P Ray Moretti	OAK	A	Kevin Bell Tony Phillips minor league P Eric Mustard
Apr. 1, 1981	CLE	A	—	SD	N	Juan Bonilla
Sept. 8, 1981	TEX	A	—	CLE	A	Cash

George LaClaire

Date	Traded To		Traded With	Traded By		In Exchange For
June 15, 1915	BUF	F	—	PIT	F	Cash
June 30, 1915	BAL	F	—	BUF	F	Cash

Pete LaCock

Date	Traded To		Traded With	Traded By		In Exchange For
Dec. 8, 1976	KC	A	—	CHI	N	Sheldon Mallory

(Part of three-team trade involving Kansas City, Chicago Cubs, and New York Mets.)

Frank LaCorte

Date	Traded To		Traded With	Traded By		In Exchange For
May 25, 1979	HOU	N	—	ATL	N	Bo McLaughlin
Dec. 8, 1983	CAL	A	—	HOU	N	No compensation (free agent signing)

Mike LaCoss

Date	Traded To		Traded With	Traded By		In Exchange For
Apr. 6, 1982	HOU	N	—	CIN	N	Cash
Feb. 19, 1985	KC	A	—	HOU	N	No compensation (free agent signing)

Lee Lacy

Date	Traded To		Traded With	Traded By		In Exchange For
Nov. 17, 1975	ATL	N	Jimmy Wynn Tom Paciorek Jerry Royster	LA	N	Dusty Baker Ed Goodson
June 23, 1976	LA	N	Elias Sosa	ATL	N	Mike Marshall
Jan. 18, 1979	PIT	N	—	LA	N	No compensation (free agent signing)
Dec. 7, 1984	BAL	A	—	PIT	N	No compensation (free agent signing)

Pete Ladd

Date	Traded To		Traded With	Traded By		In Exchange For
June 13, 1979	HOU	N	Bobby Sprowl Cash	BOS	A	Bob Watson
Oct. 23, 1981	MIL	A	—	HOU	N	Buster Keeton

Ed Lafitte

Date	Traded To		Traded With	Traded By		In Exchange For
July 1915	BUF	F	Ed Gagnier	BKN	F	Fred Smith

Mike Laga

Date	Traded To		Traded With	Traded By		In Exchange For
Aug. 10, 1986	STL	N	Ken Hill	DET	A	Mike Heath

(St. Louis received Laga on Sept. 2, 1986.)

Lerrin LaGrow

Date	Traded To		Traded With	Traded By		In Exchange For
Apr. 2, 1976	STL	N	—	DET	A	Cash
Mar. 23, 1977	CHI	A	—	STL	N	Clay Carroll
May 11, 1979	LA	N	—	CHI	A	Cash
Jan. 31, 1980	PHI	N	—	LA	N	No compensation (free agent signing)

Joe Lahoud

Date	Traded To		Traded With	Traded By		In Exchange For
Oct. 11, 1971	MIL	A	*see George Scott*	BOS	A	—
Oct. 22, 1973	CAL	A	—	MIL	A	*see Clyde Wright*
June 15, 1976	TEX	A	—	CAL	A	Cash

Jeff Lahti

Date	Traded To		Traded With	Traded By		In Exchange For
Apr. 1, 1982	STL	N	minor league P Jose Brito	CIN	N	Bob Shirley

Nap Lajoie

Date	Traded To		Traded With	Traded By		In Exchange For
June 1902	CLE	A	—	PHI	A	Cash
Jan. 1915	PHI	A	—	CLE	A	Waiver price

Eddie Lake

Date	Traded To		Traded With	Traded By		In Exchange For
Jan. 3, 1946	DET	A	—	BOS	A	Rudy York

Joe Lake

Date	Traded To		Traded With	Traded By		In Exchange For
Dec. 1909	STL	A	—	NY	A	Lou Criger
May 1912	DET	A	—	STL	A	Cash

Steve Lake

Date	Traded To	Traded With	Traded By	In Exchange For
Apr. 1, 1983	CHI N	—	MIL A	Minor league P Rich Buonantony Cash
Dec. 16, 1988	PHI N	Curt Ford	STL N	Milt Thompson
Dec. 2, 1992	CHI N	—	PHI N	No compensation (free agent signing)

Al Lakeman

Date	Traded To	Traded With	Traded By	In Exchange For
June 14, 1947	PHI N	—	CIN N	Ken Raffensberger Hugh Poland

Jack Lamabe

Date	Traded To	Traded With	Traded By	In Exchange For
Nov. 20, 1962	BOS A	Dick Stuart	PIT N	Jim Pagliaroni Don Schwall
Sept. 14, 1965	HOU N	—	BOS A	Darrell Brandon
Dec. 1, 1965	CHI A	minor league P Ray Cordeiro Cash	HOU N	Dave Nicholson Bill Heath
Apr. 26, 1967	NY N	—	CHI A	Cash
July 16, 1967	STL N	—	NY N	Al Jackson
Apr. 22, 1968	CHI N	Ron Piche	STL N	Pete Mikkelsen Dave Dowling
June 11, 1969	MON N	Adolfo Phillips	CHI N	Paul Popovich

Al LaMacchia

Date	Traded To	Traded With	Traded By	In Exchange For
June 15, 1946	WAS A	Joe Grace	STL A	Jeff Heath

Bill Lamar

Date	Traded To	Traded With	Traded By	In Exchange For
May 1919	BOS A	—	NY A	Cash
Mar. 1920	BKN N	—	BOS A	Cash

Wayne LaMaster

Date	Traded To	Traded With	Traded By	In Exchange For
Aug. 8, 1938	BKN N	—	PHI N	Max Butcher

Ray Lamb

Date	Traded To	Traded With	Traded By	In Exchange For
Dec. 11, 1970	CLE A	Alan Foster	LA N	Duke Sims

Gene Lamont

Date	Traded To	Traded With	Traded By	In Exchange For
May 14, 1973	ATL N	—	DET A	Bob Didier

Bobby LaMotte

Date	Traded To	Traded With	Traded By	In Exchange For
Jan. 15, 1927	DET A	*see Marty McManus*	STL A	—

Dennis Lamp

Date	Traded To	Traded With	Traded By	In Exchange For
Mar. 28, 1981	CHI A	—	CHI N	Ken Kravec
Jan. 10, 1984	TOR A	—	CHI A	Free agent signing

(Chicago selected Tom Seaver from the New York Mets as compensation.)

Date	Traded To	Traded With	Traded By	In Exchange For
Feb. 5, 1987	CLE A	—	TOR A	No compensation (free agent signing)

Tom Lampkin

Date	Traded To	Traded With	Traded By	In Exchange For
July 11, 1990	SD N	—	CLE A	Alex Cole
Mar. 25, 1993	MIL A	—	SD N	Cash

Les Lancaster

Date	Traded To	Traded With	Traded By	In Exchange For
Jan. 13, 1993	STL N	—	DET A	No compensation (free agent signing)

Gary Lance

Date	Traded To	Traded With	Traded By	In Exchange For
June 5, 1978	SEA A	—	KC A	Minor league P Steve Hamrick

Rick Lancellotti

Date	Traded To	Traded With	Traded By	In Exchange For
Aug. 5, 1980	SD N	Luis Salazar	PIT N	Kurt Bevacqua Mark Lee
Oct. 7, 1982	MON N	—	SD N	Cash
Mar. 31, 1985	NY N	—	SD N	Rusty Tillman

Rafael Landestoy

Date	Traded To	Traded With	Traded By	In Exchange For
July 1, 1978	HOU N	Jeffrey Leonard	LA N	Joe Ferguson Cash
June 8, 1981	CIN N	—	HOU N	Harry Spilman
May 9, 1983	LA N	—	CIN N	John Franco minor league P Brett Wise

Jim Landis

Date	Traded To	Traded With	Traded By	In Exchange For
Jan. 20, 1965	KC A	Mike Hershberger Fred Talbot	CHI A	Rocky Colavito

(Part of three-team trade involving Kansas City, Cleveland, and the Chicago White Sox.)

Date	Traded To	Traded With	Traded By	In Exchange For
Dec. 1, 1965	CLE A	Jim Rittwage	KC A	Phil Roof Joe Rudi
Jan. 4, 1967	HOU N	Doc Edwards Jim Weaver	CLE A	Lee Maye Ken Retzer
June 29, 1967	DET A	—	HOU N	Larry Sherry

Ken Landreaux

Date	Traded To	Traded With	Traded By	In Exchange For
Feb. 3, 1979	MIN A	Dave Engle Paul Hartzell Brad Havens	CAL A	Rod Carew
Mar. 30, 1981	LA N	—	MIN A	Mickey Hatcher Minor leaguers P Matt Reeves and 1B Kelly Snider

Larry Landreth

Date	Traded To	Traded With	Traded By	In Exchange For
May 20, 1978	LA N	Gerald Hannahs	MON N	Mike Garman

Hobie Landrith

Date	Traded To	Traded With	Traded By	In Exchange For
Nov. 28, 1955	CHI N	—	CIN N	Hal Jeffcoat
Dec. 11, 1956	STL N	—	CHI N	*see Tom Poholsky*
Oct. 8, 1958	SF N	Billy Muffett Benny Valenzuela	STL N	Ernie Broglio Marv Grissom
May 9, 1962	BAL A	Cash	NY N	Marv Throneberry
May 8, 1963	WAS A	—	BAL A	Cash

Bill Landrum

Date	Traded To	Traded With	Traded By	In Exchange For
Apr. 1, 1988	CIN N	—	CHI N	Luis Quinones

Ced Landrum

Date	Traded To	Traded With	Traded By	In Exchange For
July 7, 1992	MIL A	—	CHI N	Jeff Kunkel

Don Landrum

Date	Traded To	Traded With	Traded By	In Exchange For
June 5, 1962	CHI N	Alex Grammas	STL N	Bobby Gene Smith Daryl Robertson
Dec. 2, 1965	SF N	—	CHI N	*see Randy Hundley*

Tito Landrum

Date	Traded To	Traded With	Traded By	In Exchange For
June 15, 1983	BAL A	—	STL N	Floyd Rayford
Mar. 25, 1984	STL N	—	BAL A	Minor league P Jose Brito

Don Lang

Date	Traded To	Traded With	Traded By	In Exchange For
Dec. 30, 1940	NY A	$20,000.	CIN N	Monte Pearson

Rick Langford

Date	Traded To	Traded With	Traded By	In Exchange For
Mar. 15, 1977	OAK A	—	PIT N	*see Phil Garner*

Mark Langston

Date	Traded To	Traded With	Traded By	In Exchange For
May 25, 1989	MON N	Mike Campbell	SEA A	Randy Johnson Brian Holman Gene Harris

(Montreal received Campbell on July 31, 1989.)

Date	Traded To	Traded With	Traded By	In Exchange For
Dec. 1, 1989	CAL A	—	MON N	No compensation (free agent signing)

Hal Lanier

Date	Traded To	Traded With	Traded By	In Exchange For
Feb. 2, 1972	NY A	—	SF N	Cash

Max Lanier

Date	Traded To	Traded With	Traded By	In Exchange For
Dec. 11, 1951	NY N	Chuck Diering	STL N	Eddie Stanky

(Stanky was named St. Louis manager.)

Johnny Lanning

Date	Traded To	Traded With	Traded By	In Exchange For
Dec. 6, 1939	PIT N	—	BOS N	Jim Tobin Cash

Carney Lansford

Date	Traded To	Traded With	Traded By	In Exchange For
Dec. 10, 1980	BOS A	Rick Miller Mark Clear	CAL A	Rick Burleson Butch Hobson
Dec. 6, 1982	OAK A	Garry Hancock minor league P Jerry King	BOS A	Tony Armas Jeff Newman

Paul LaPalme

Date	Traded To	Traded With	Traded By	In Exchange For
Jan. 11, 1955	STL N	—	PIT N	Ben Wade Cash
May 1, 1956	CIN N	—	STL N	Milt Smith
June 22, 1956	CHI A	—	CIN N	Waiver price

Dave LaPoint

Date	Traded To	Traded With	Traded By	In Exchange For
Dec. 12, 1980	STL N	Sixto Lezcano David Green Lary Sorensen	MIL A	Pete Vuckovich Rollie Fingers Ted Simmons
Feb. 1, 1985	SF N	David Green Jose Uribe Gary Rajsich	STL N	Jack Clark
Oct. 7, 1985	DET A	Matt Nokes Eric King	SF N	Juan Berenguer Bob Melvin Scott Medvin

(San Francisco received Medvin on Dec. 11, 1985.)

Date	Traded To	Traded With	Traded By	In Exchange For
July 9, 1986	SD N	—	DET A	Mark Thurmond
July 30, 1987	CHI A	—	STL N	Minor league P Bryce Hulstrom
Aug. 13, 1988	PIT N	—	CHI A	Barry Jones
Dec. 3, 1988	NY A	—	PIT N	No compensation (free agent signing)

Ralph LaPointe

Date	Traded To	Traded With	Traded By	In Exchange For
Apr. 7, 1948	STL N	$30,000.	PHI N	Dick Sisler

Frank LaPorte

Date	Traded To	Traded With	Traded By	In Exchange For
Dec. 1907	BOS A	—	NY A	Cash
Aug. 17, 1908	NY A	—	BOS A	Harry Niles
Jan. 1911	STL A	Jimmy Austin	NY A	Roy Hartzell
July 1912	WAS A	—	STL A	Cash

Jack Lapp

Date	Traded To	Traded With	Traded By	In Exchange For
Jan. 7, 1916	CHI A	—	PHI A	Cash

Norm Larker

Date	Traded To	Traded With	Traded By	In Exchange For
Nov. 30, 1962	MIL N	—	HOU N	Connie Grob Jim Bolger
Aug. 8, 1963	SF N	—	MIL N	Cash

Dave LaRoche

Date	Traded To	Traded With	Traded By	In Exchange For
Nov. 30, 1971	MIN A	—	CAL A	Leo Cardenas
Nov. 30, 1972	CHI N	—	MIN A	Bill Hands Joe Decker minor league P Bob Maneely
Feb. 25, 1975	CLE A	Brock Davis	CHI N	Milt Wilcox
May 11, 1977	CAL A	Dave Schuler	CLE A	Bruce Bochte Sid Monge $250,000.

Don Larsen

Date	Traded To	Traded With	Traded By	In Exchange For
Nov. 18, 1954	NY A	Bob Turley Billy Hunter	BAL A	Harry Byrd Jim McDonald Hal Smith Gus Triandos Gene Woodling Willie Miranda

(First part of 18-player trade completed on December 1, 1954; see Dick Kryhoski.)

Date	Traded To	Traded With	Traded By	In Exchange For
Dec. 11, 1959	KC A	Hank Bauer Norm Siebern Marv Throneberry	NY A	Roger Maris Joe De Maestri Kent Hadley

Don Larsen *continued*

Date	Traded To	Traded With	Traded By	In Exchange For
June 10, 1961	CHI A	Ray Herbert Andy Carey Al Pilarcik	KC A	Wes Covington Bob Shaw Gerry Staley Stan Johnson
Nov. 30, 1961	SF N	Billy Pierce	CHI A	Eddie Fisher Dom Zanni Verle Tiefenthaler Bob Farley
May 20, 1964	HOU N	—	SF N	Cash
Apr. 24, 1965	BAL A	—	HOU N	Bob Saverine Cash

Dan Larson

Date	Traded To	Traded With	Traded By	In Exchange For
Aug. 15, 1974	HOU N	Minor league P Ron Selak	STL N	Claude Osteen
Dec. 8, 1981	CHI N	Keith Moreland Dickie Noles	PHI N	Mike Krukow Cash

Tony LaRussa

Date	Traded To	Traded With	Traded By	In Exchange For
Aug. 14, 1971	ATL N	—	OAK A	Cash
Oct. 20, 1972	CHI N	—	ATL N	Tom Phoebus

Frank Lary

Date	Traded To	Traded With	Traded By	In Exchange For
May 30, 1964	NY N	—	DET A	Cash
Aug. 8, 1964	MIL N	—	NY N	Dennis Ribant Cash
Mar. 20, 1965	NY N	—	MIL N	Cash
July 8, 1965	CHI A	—	NY N	Jimmie Schaffer

Lyn Lary

Date	Traded To	Traded With	Traded By	In Exchange For
May 15, 1934	BOS A	—	NY A	Freddie Muller $20,000.
Oct. 26, 1934	WAS A	$225,000.	BOS A	Joe Cronin
June 29, 1935	STL A	—	WAS A	Alan Strange
Jan. 17, 1937	CLE A	Ivy Andrews Moose Solters	STL A	Bill Knickerbocker Joe Vosmik Oral Hildebrand
May 3, 1939	BKN N	—	CLE A	Cash
Aug. 14, 1939	STL N	—	BKN N	Waiver price

Fred Lasher

Date	Traded To	Traded With	Traded By	In Exchange For
May 22, 1970	CLE A	—	DET A	Russ Nagelson Billy Rohr

Bill Laskey

Date	Traded To	Traded With	Traded By	In Exchange For
Dec. 11, 1981	SF N	Rich Gale	KC A	Jerry Martin
Oct. 24, 1985	SF N	—	MON N	Alonzo Powell George Riley

Bill Latham

Date	Traded To	Traded With	Traded By	In Exchange For
Jan. 16, 1986	MIN A	Billy Beane Joe Klink	NY N	Tim Teufel Minor league OF Pat Crosby

Tacks Latimer

Date	Traded To	Traded With	Traded By	In Exchange For
Jan. 1900	PIT N	*see Honus Wagner*	LOU N	—

Barry Latman

Date	Traded To	Traded With	Traded By	In Exchange For
Apr. 18, 1960	CLE A	—	CHI A	Herb Score
Dec. 2, 1963	LA A	Joe Adcock	CLE A	Leon Wagner
Dec. 15, 1965	HOU N	—	CAL A	Minor league C Ed Pacheco Cash

Charlie Lau

Date	Traded To	Traded With	Traded By	In Exchange For
Oct. 15, 1959	MIL N	Don Lee	DET A	Don Kaiser Mike Roarke Casey Wise
July 1, 1963	KC A	—	BAL A	Cash
June 15, 1964	BAL A	—	KC A	Wes Stock
May 31, 1967	ATL N	—	BAL A	Cash

George Lauzerique

Date	Traded To	Traded With	Traded By	In Exchange For
Dec. 7, 1969	SEA A	Ted Kubiak	OAK A	Diego Segui Ray Oyler

Date	Traded To	Traded With	Traded By	In Exchange For

George Lauzerique *continued*

Date	Traded To	Traded With	Traded By	In Exchange For
Oct. 20, 1970	STL N	Jerry McNertney minor league P Jesse Higgins	MIL A	Carl Taylor Jim Ellis

Cookie Lavagetto

Date	Traded To	Traded With	Traded By	In Exchange For
Dec. 4, 1936	BKN N	Ralph Birkofer	PIT N	Ed Brandt

Mike LaValliere

Date	Traded To	Traded With	Traded By	In Exchange For
Apr. 1, 1987	PIT N	—	STL N	*see Tony Pena*

Doc Lavan

Date	Traded To	Traded With	Traded By	In Exchange For
Aug. 24, 1913	PHI A	—	STL A	Cash
Feb. 5, 1914	STL A	—	PHI A	Cash
Dec. 15, 1917	WAS A	Burt Shotton	STL A	Bert Gallia $15,000.
Jan. 1919	STL N	—	WAS A	Cash

Gary Lavelle

Date	Traded To	Traded With	Traded By	In Exchange For
Jan. 26, 1985	TOR A	—	SF N	Jim Gott Minor league IF Augie Schmidt Minor league P Jack McKnight

Jimmy Lavender

Date	Traded To	Traded With	Traded By	In Exchange For
Jan. 16, 1917	PHI N	$5,000.	CHI N	Al Demaree

Ron Law

Date	Traded To	Traded With	Traded By	In Exchange For
Dec. 5, 1969	WAS A	Dave Nelson Horacio Pina	CLE A	Dennis Higgins Barry Moore

Rudy Law

Date	Traded To	Traded With	Traded By	In Exchange For
Mar. 30, 1982	CHI A	—	LA N	Cecil Espy Minor league P Bert Geiger

Vance Law

Date	Traded To	Traded With	Traded By	In Exchange For
Mar. 21, 1982	CHI A	Ernie Camacho	PIT N	Ross Baumgarten Butch Edge
Dec. 7, 1984	MON N	Bert Roberge	CHI A	Bob James Bryan Little
Dec. 14, 1987	CHI N	—	MON N	No compensation (free agent signing)

Tom Lawless

Date	Traded To	Traded With	Traded By	In Exchange For
Aug. 16, 1984	MON N	—	CIN N	Pete Rose
(Rose was named Cincinnati manager.)				
Feb. 6, 1985	STL N	—	MON N	Mickey Mahler
(St. Louis received Lawless on March 25, 1985.)				

Brooks Lawrence

Date	Traded To	Traded With	Traded By	In Exchange For
Jan. 31, 1956	CIN N	Sonny Senerchia	STL N	Jackie Collum

Roxie Lawson

Date	Traded To	Traded With	Traded By	In Exchange For
May 13, 1939	STL A	—	DET A	*see Beau Bell*

Steve Lawson

Date	Traded To	Traded With	Traded By	In Exchange For
July 20, 1972	TEX A	Marty Martinez Vic Harris	OAK A	Don Mincher Ted Kubiak

Marcus Lawton

Date	Traded To	Traded With	Traded By	In Exchange For
July 10, 1989	NY A	—	NY N	Scott Nielsen

Bill Laxton

Date	Traded To	Traded With	Traded By	In Exchange For
Dec. 15, 1967	PHI N	Don Money Woodie Fryman minor league P Hal Clem	PIT N	Jim Bunning

Bill Laxton *continued*

Date	Traded To	Traded With	Traded By	In Exchange For
Dec. 12, 1975	DET A	Rusty Staub	NY N	Mickey Lolich Billy Baldwin
Sept. 9, 1977	CLE A	Cash	SEA A	Ray Fosse
June 22, 1978	SD N	—	CLE A	Dave Freisleben

Pete Layden

Date	Traded To	Traded With	Traded By	In Exchange For
Nov. 17, 1947	STL A	—	BOS A	*see Vern Stephens*

Charlie Lea

Date	Traded To	Traded With	Traded By	In Exchange For
Feb. 4, 1988	MIN A	—	MON N	No compensation (free agent signing)

Freddy Leach

Date	Traded To	Traded With	Traded By	In Exchange For
Oct. 29, 1928	NY N	—	PHI N	Lefty O'Doul Cash
Mar. 19, 1932	BOS N	—	NY N	$10,000.

Rick Leach

Date	Traded To	Traded With	Traded By	In Exchange For
Jan. 23, 1989	TEX A	—	TOR A	No compensation (free agent signing)

Terry Leach

Date	Traded To	Traded With	Traded By	In Exchange For
Sept. 26, 1983	CHI N	Minor league 1B Mike Anicich	NY N	Minor league P Mitch Cook Minor league P Jim Adamczak
Apr. 9, 1984	ATL N	—	CHI N	Ron Meridith
June 9, 1989	KC A	—	NY N	Player to be named later
(New York received P Aguedo Vasquez on Sept. 29, 1989.)				

Tommy Leach

Date	Traded To	Traded With	Traded By	In Exchange For
Jan. 1900	PIT N	*see Honus Wagner*	LOU N	—
June 22, 1912	CHI N	Lefty Leifield	PIT N	King Cole Solly Hofman

Tom Leahy

Date	Traded To	Traded With	Traded By	In Exchange For
June 1901	PHI A	—	MIL A	Phil Geier

Luis Leal

Date	Traded To	Traded With	Traded By	In Exchange For
Feb. 2, 1987	ATL N	*see Damaso Garcia*	TOR A	—

Fred Lear

Date	Traded To	Traded With	Traded By	In Exchange For
Feb. 1920	NY N	—	CHI N	Cash

Tim Leary

Date	Traded To	Traded With	Traded By	In Exchange For
Jan. 18, 1985	MIL A	—	NY N	Frank Wills
(Part of a four-team trade involving Texas, Milwaukee, Kansas City, and New York Mets.)				
Dec. 10, 1986	LA N	Tim Crews	MIL A	Greg Brock
July 18, 1989	CIN N	Mariano Duncan	LA N	Kal Daniels Lenny Harris
Dec. 12, 1989	NY A	Van Snider	CIN N	Hal Morris Minor league P Rodney Imes
Aug. 22, 1992	SEA A	Cash	NY A	Minor league OF Sean Twitty

Bevo LeBourveau

Date	Traded To	Traded With	Traded By	In Exchange For
Feb. 8, 1923	PHI A	—	PHI N	Cash

Bill Lee

Date	Traded To	Traded With	Traded By	In Exchange For
Aug. 5, 1943	PHI N	—	CHI N	Mickey Livingston
July 14, 1945	BOS N	—	PHI N	Cash

Bill Lee

Date	Traded To	Traded With	Traded By	In Exchange For
Dec. 7, 1978	MON N	—	BOS A	Stan Papi

Bob Lee

Date	Traded To	Traded With	Traded By	In Exchange For
Dec. 15, 1966	LA N	—	CAL A	Nick Willhite
May 31, 1967	CIN N	—	LA N	Cash

Cliff Lee

Date	Traded To	Traded With	Traded By	In Exchange For
May 1921	PHI N	—	PIT N	Waiver price

Cliff Lee *continued*

Date	Traded To	Traded With	Traded By	In Exchange For
June 20, 1924	CIN N	—	PHI N	Cash

Derek Lee

Date	Traded To	Traded With	Traded By	In Exchange For
Oct. 5, 1992	MIN A	—	CHI A	Waiver price
Jan. 24, 1994	MON N	—	MIN A	Minor league P Joe Norris

Don Lee

Date	Traded To	Traded With	Traded By	In Exchange For
Oct. 15, 1959	MIL N	Charlie Lau	DET A	Don Kaiser Mike Roarke Casey Wise
May 29, 1962	LA A	—	MIN A	Jim Donohue
June 1, 1965	HOU N	—	CAL A	Al Spangler

Hal Lee

Date	Traded To	Traded With	Traded By	In Exchange For
Oct. 14, 1930	PHI N	Clise Dudley Jumbo Elliott Cash	BKN N	Lefty O'Doul Fresco Thompson
June 17, 1933	BOS N	Pinky Whitney	PHI N	Fritz Knothe Wes Schulmerich Cash
Jan. 27, 1937	NY N	Ben Cantwell	BOS N	Cash

Leron Lee

Date	Traded To	Traded With	Traded By	In Exchange For
June 11, 1971	SD N	Fred Norman	STL N	Al Santorini
Mar. 28, 1974	CLE A	—	SD N	Cash

Manny Lee

Date	Traded To	Traded With	Traded By	In Exchange For
Aug. 28, 1984	HOU N	—	NY N	*see Ray Knight*

Mark Lee

Date	Traded To	Traded With	Traded By	In Exchange For
Aug. 31, 1988	KC A	—	DET A	*see Ted Power*

Mark Lee

Date	Traded To	Traded With	Traded By	In Exchange For
Aug. 5, 1980	PIT N	Kurt Bevacqua	SD N	Rick Lancellotti Luis Salazar

Mike Lee

Date	Traded To	Traded With	Traded By	In Exchange For
May 10, 1961	STL N	Joe Morgan Cash	CLE A	Bob Nieman

(St. Louis received Lee on September 25.)

Thornton Lee

Date	Traded To	Traded With	Traded By	In Exchange For
Dec. 10, 1936	CHI A	—	CLE A	Jack Salveson

(Part of three-team trade involving Chicago, Cleveland, and Washington.)

Joe Lefebvre

Date	Traded To	Traded With	Traded By	In Exchange For
Apr. 1, 1981	SD N	Ruppert Jones Tim Lollar Chris Welsh	NY A	Jerry Mumphrey John Pacella
May 22, 1983	PHI N	—	SD N	Sid Monge

Craig Lefferts

Date	Traded To	Traded With	Traded By	In Exchange For
Dec. 7, 1983	SD N	Carmelo Martinez Fritz Connally	CHI N	Scott Sanderson

(Part of three-team trade involving Chicago Cubs, San Diego, and Montreal.)

Date	Traded To	Traded With	Traded By	In Exchange For
July 5, 1987	SF N	Kevin Mitchell Dave Dravecky	SD N	Chris Brown Mark Davis Keith Comstock Mark Grant
Dec. 7, 1989	SD N	—	SF N	No compensation (free agent signing)
Aug. 31, 1992	BAL A	—	SD N	Ricky Gutierrez Erik Schullstrom

(San Diego received Gutierrez on Sept. 4, 1992.)

Date	Traded To	Traded With	Traded By	In Exchange For
Jan. 13, 1993	TEX A	—	BAL A	No compensation (free agent signing)
Jan. 13, 1994	CAL A	—	TEX A	No compensation (free agent signing)

Ron LeFlore

Date	Traded To	Traded With	Traded By	In Exchange For
Dec. 7, 1979	MON N	—	DET A	Dan Schatzeder
Dec. 6, 1980	CHI A	—	MON N	No compensation (free agent signing)

Lou Legett

Date	Traded To	Traded With	Traded By	In Exchange For
Nov. 7, 1928	BOS N	Socks Seibold Bruce Cunningham Percy Jones Freddie Maguire $200,000.	CHI N	Rogers Hornsby

Ken Lehman

Date	Traded To	Traded With	Traded By	In Exchange For
June 4, 1957	BAL A	—	BKN N	$30,000.
Oct. 2, 1958	PHI N	—	BAL A	Waiver price
Mar. 20, 1962	CLE A	Tony Curry	PHI N	Mel Roach

Paul Lehner

Date	Traded To	Traded With	Traded By	In Exchange For
Dec. 13, 1949	PHI A	Bob Dillinger	STL A	Ray Coleman Frankie Gustine Billy DeMars minor league OF Ray Ippolito $100,000.
Apr. 30, 1951	CHI A	Minnie Minoso	PHI A	Gus Zernial Dave Philley

(Part of three-team trade involving Chicago White Sox, Philadelphia A's, and Cleveland.)

Date	Traded To	Traded With	Traded By	In Exchange For
June 4, 1951	STL A	Kermit Wahl Cash	CHI A	Don Lenhardt
July 19, 1951	CLE A	—	STL A	Waiver price
June 25, 1952	BOS A	—	CLE A	Waiver price

Hank Leiber

Date	Traded To	Traded With	Traded By	In Exchange For
Dec. 6, 1938	CHI N	Dick Bartell Gus Mancuso	NY N	Frank Demaree Bill Jurges Ken O'Dea
Dec. 4, 1941	NY N	—	CHI N	Bob Bowman

Nemo Leibold

Date	Traded To	Traded With	Traded By	In Exchange For
July 7, 1915	CHI A	—	CLE A	Waiver price
Mar. 4, 1921	BOS A	Shano Collins	CHI A	Harry Hooper
May 26, 1923	WAS A	—	BOS A	Waiver price

Charlie Leibrandt

Date	Traded To	Traded With	Traded By	In Exchange For
June 7, 1983	KC A	—	CIN N	Bob Tufts
Dec. 15, 1989	ATL N	Rick Luecken	KC A	Gerald Perry Minor league P Jim Lemasters
Dec. 9, 1992	TEX A	Pat Gomez	ATL N	Jose Oliva

Lefty Leifield

Date	Traded To	Traded With	Traded By	In Exchange For
May 1911	CHI N	—	PIT N	Cash
June 22, 1912	CHI N	Tommy Leach	PIT N	King Cole Solly Hofman

Ed Leip

Date	Traded To	Traded With	Traded By	In Exchange For
Apr. 1940	PIT N	—	WAS A	Cash

Dave Leiper

Date	Traded To	Traded With	Traded By	In Exchange For
Aug. 30, 1987	SD N	Rob Nelson	OAK A	Storm Davis

(San Diego received Nelson on September 8, 1987.)

Date	Traded To	Traded With	Traded By	In Exchange For
July 26, 1995	MON N	—	OAK A	Minor league OF Kevin Northrup

Al Leiter

Date	Traded To	Traded With	Traded By	In Exchange For
Apr. 30, 1989	TOR A	—	NY A	Jesse Barfield
Dec. 14, 1995	FLA N	—	TOR A	No compensation (free agent signing)

Mark Leiter

Date	Traded To	Traded With	Traded By	In Exchange For
Mar. 19, 1991	DET A	—	NY A	Torey Lovullo

Dummy Leitner

Date	Traded To	Traded With	Traded By	In Exchange For
May 1902	CHI A	—	CLE A	Cash

Frank Leja

Date	Traded To	Traded With	Traded By	In Exchange For
Mar. 30, 1962	LA A	—	STL N	Cash

Jack Lelivelt

Date	Traded To		Traded With	Traded By		In Exchange For
Dec. 1911	NY	A	Gabby Street	WAS	A	John Knight Roxy Roach
May 20, 1913	CLE	A	Bill Stumpf	NY	A	Roger Peckinpaugh

Dave Lemanczyk

Date	Traded To		Traded With	Traded By		In Exchange For
June 3, 1980	CAL	A	—	TOR	A	Ken Schrom

Denny Lemaster

Date	Traded To		Traded With	Traded By		In Exchange For
Oct. 8, 1967	HOU	N	Denis Menke	ATL	N	Sonny Jackson Chuck Harrison
Oct. 14, 1971	MON	N	—	HOU	N	Cash

Johnnie LeMaster

Date	Traded To		Traded With	Traded By		In Exchange For
May 7, 1985	CLE	A	—	SF	N	Mike Jeffcoat Luis Quinones
May 30, 1985	PIT	N	—	CLE	A	Scott Bailes

(Cleveland received Bailes on July 3, 1985.)

Dick LeMay

Date	Traded To		Traded With	Traded By		In Exchange For
Nov. 30, 1962	HOU	N	Manny Mota	SF	N	Joey Amalfitano
Mar. 28, 1963	CHI	N	Merritt Ranew Hal Haydel	HOU	N	Dave Gerard Danny Murphy

Chet Lemon

Date	Traded To		Traded With	Traded By		In Exchange For
June 15, 1975	CHI	A	Dave Hamilton	OAK	A	Stan Bahnsen Skip Pitlock
Nov. 27, 1981	DET	A	—	CHI	A	Steve Kemp

Jim Lemon

Date	Traded To		Traded With	Traded By		In Exchange For
May 12, 1954	WAS	A	—	CLE	A	Cash
May 4, 1963	PHI	N	—	MIN	A	Cash
June 28, 1963	CHI	A	—	PHI	N	Cash

Dave Lemonds

Date	Traded To		Traded With	Traded By		In Exchange For
Nov. 30, 1970	CHI	A	Pat Jacquez Roe Skidmore	CHI	N	Jose Ortiz Ossie Blanco

Mark Lemongello

Date	Traded To		Traded With	Traded By		In Exchange For
Dec. 6, 1975	HOU	N	—	DET	A	*see Milt May*
Nov. 27, 1978	TOR	A	Joe Cannon Pedro Hernandez	HOU	N	Alan Ashby
Apr. 7, 1980	CHI	N	—	TOR	A	Cash

Don Lenhardt

Date	Traded To		Traded With	Traded By		In Exchange For
June 4, 1951	CHI	A	—	STL	A	Paul Lehner Kermit Wahl Cash
Nov. 13, 1951	BOS	A	Randy Gumpert	CHI	A	Mel Hoderlein Chuck Stobbs
June 3, 1952	DET	A	—	BOS	A	*see George Kell*
Aug. 14, 1952	STL	A	*see Vic Wertz*	DET	A	—
Feb. 12, 1954	BOS	A	—	BAL	A	Cash

Bob Lennon

Date	Traded To		Traded With	Traded By		In Exchange For
Apr. 16, 1957	CHI	N	Dick Littlefield	NY	N	Ray Jablonski Ray Katt

Jim Lentine

Date	Traded To		Traded With	Traded By		In Exchange For
June 2, 1980	DET	A	—	STL	N	John Martin Al Greene
Apr. 3, 1981	HOU	N	Cash	CLE	A	Mike Fischlin

Eddie Leon

Date	Traded To		Traded With	Traded By		In Exchange For
Oct. 19, 1972	CHI	A	—	CLE	A	Walt Williams
Dec. 5, 1974	NY	A	—	CHI	A	Cecil Upshaw

Dutch Leonard

Date	Traded To		Traded With	Traded By		In Exchange For
Dec. 18, 1918	NY	A	Ernie Shore Duffy Lewis	BOS	A	Frank Gilhooley Ray Caldwell Slim Love Roxy Walters $15,000.
May 18, 1919	DET	A	—	NY	A	Cash

Dutch Leonard

Date	Traded To		Traded With	Traded By		In Exchange For
Dec. 3, 1936	STL	N	Frenchy Bordagaray Jimmy Jordan	BKN	N	Tom Winsett
Dec. 9, 1946	PHI	N	—	WAS	A	Cash
Dec. 14, 1948	CHI	N	Monk Dubiel	PHI	N	Hank Borowy Eddie Waitkus

Jeffrey Leonard

Date	Traded To		Traded With	Traded By		In Exchange For
July 1, 1978	HOU	N	Rafael Landestoy	LA	N	Joe Ferguson Cash
Apr. 20, 1981	SF	N	Dave Bergman	HOU	N	Mike Ivie
June 8, 1988	MIL	A	—	SF	N	Ernest Riles
Dec. 7, 1988	SEA	A	—	MIL	A	No compensation (free agent signing)

Joe Leonard

Date	Traded To		Traded With	Traded By		In Exchange For
Aug. 18, 1916	WAS	A	Elmer Smith	CLE	A	Joe Boehling Danny Moeller

Mark Leonard

Date	Traded To		Traded With	Traded By		In Exchange For
Mar. 20, 1993	BAL	A	—	SF	N	Steve Scarsone

Ted Lepcio

Date	Traded To		Traded With	Traded By		In Exchange For
May 2, 1959	DET	A	Dave Sisler	BOS	A	Billy Hoeft
Dec. 5, 1959	PHI	N	Ken Walters minor league P Alex Cosmidis	DET	A	Chico Fernandez Ray Semproch
Apr. 3, 1961	CHI	A	—	PHI	N	Cash

Don Leppert

Date	Traded To		Traded With	Traded By		In Exchange For
Dec. 15, 1962	WAS	A	—	PIT	N	Minor league P Ron Honeycutt Cash

Don Leppert

Date	Traded To		Traded With	Traded By		In Exchange For
Dec. 1, 1954	BAL	A	—	NY	A	*see Dick Kryhoski*

Randy Lerch

Date	Traded To		Traded With	Traded By		In Exchange For
Mar. 1, 1981	MIL	A	—	PHI	N	Dick Davis
Aug. 14, 1982	MON	N	—	MIL	A	Cash

Barry Lersch

Date	Traded To		Traded With	Traded By		In Exchange For
Dec. 3, 1973	ATL	N	Craig Robinson	PHI	N	Ron Schueler
Sept. 14, 1974	STL	N	—	ATL	N	Cash

Don Leshnock

Date	Traded To		Traded With	Traded By		In Exchange For
Oct. 25, 1972	PHI	N	Tom Haller	DET	A	Cash

Curtis Leskanic

Date	Traded To		Traded With	Traded By		In Exchange For
Mar. 28, 1992	MIN	A	Oscar Munoz	CLE	A	Paul Sorrento

Brad Lesley

Date	Traded To		Traded With	Traded By		In Exchange For
Nov. 13, 1984	MIL	A	—	CIN	N	Cash

Sam Leslie

Date	Traded To		Traded With	Traded By		In Exchange For
June 16, 1933	BKN	N	—	NY	N	Lefty O'Doul Watty Clark
Feb. 20, 1936	NY	N	—	BKN	N	Cash

Ed Levy

Date	Traded To		Traded With	Traded By		In Exchange For
Jan. 22, 1943	PHI	N	Tom Padden Al Gerheauser Al Gettel $10,000.	NY	A	Nick Etten

Dennis Lewallyn

Date	Traded To	Traded With	Traded By	In Exchange For
Nov. 23, 1977	MIN A	—	LA N	Cash

(Lewallyn was returned to the Dodgers on March 15, 1978.)

Date	Traded To	Traded With	Traded By	In Exchange For
Sept. 13, 1980	TEX A	—	LA N	Pepe Frias
Aug. 25, 1981	CLE A	—	TEX A	Cash

Darren Lewis

Date	Traded To	Traded With	Traded By	In Exchange For
Dec. 4, 1990	SF N	Player to be named	OAK A	Ernest Riles

(San Francisco received P Pedro Pena on December 17, 1990.)

Date	Traded To	Traded With	Traded By	In Exchange For
July 21, 1995	CIN N	—	SF N	*see Deion Sanders*
Dec. 6, 1995	TEX A	—	CIN N	Waiver price

Duffy Lewis

Date	Traded To	Traded With	Traded By	In Exchange For
Dec. 18, 1918	NY A	Ernie Shore Dutch Leonard	BOS A	Frank Gilhooley Ray Caldwell Slim Love Roxy Walters $15,000.
Jan. 20, 1921	WAS A	George Mogridge	NY A	Braggo Roth

Jim Lewis

Date	Traded To	Traded With	Traded By	In Exchange For
Feb. 17, 1992	BAL A	Minor league OF Steve Martin	SD N	Craig Worthington Minor league P Tom Martin

Jim Lewis

Date	Traded To	Traded With	Traded By	In Exchange For
Nov. 1, 1979	NY A	—	SEA A	*see Jim Beattie*

Johnny Lewis

Date	Traded To	Traded With	Traded By	In Exchange For
Dec. 7, 1964	NY N	Gordie Richardson	STL N	Tracy Stallard Elio Chacon

Mark Lewis

Date	Traded To	Traded With	Traded By	In Exchange For
Dec. 14, 1994	CIN N	—	CLE A	Tim Costo
July 31, 1995	DET A	C. J. Nitkowski Minor league P Dave Tuttle	CIN N	David Wells

(Detroit received Lewis on November 16, 1995.)

Richie Lewis

Date	Traded To	Traded With	Traded By	In Exchange For
Aug. 24, 1991	BAL A	—	MON N	Minor league P Chris Myers

Terry Ley

Date	Traded To	Traded With	Traded By	In Exchange For
Dec. 2, 1971	TEX A	Gary Jones	NY A	Bernie Allen

Sixto Lezcano

Date	Traded To	Traded With	Traded By	In Exchange For
Dec. 12, 1980	STL N	David Green Lary Sorensen Dave LaPoint	MIL A	Pete Vuckovich Rollie Fingers Ted Simmons
Dec. 10, 1981	SD N	Luis DeLeon Garry Templeton	STL N	Ozzie Smith Steve Mura Al Olmsted

(Templeton and Smith were exchanged on February 11, 1982; Olmsted and DeLeon were exchanged on February 19.)

Date	Traded To	Traded With	Traded By	In Exchange For
Aug. 31, 1983	PHI N	Steve Fireovid	SD N	Lance McCullers Ed Wojna Marty Decker Minor league P Darren Burroughs
Jan. 22, 1985	PIT N	—	PHI N	No compensation (free agent signing)

Francisco Libran

Date	Traded To	Traded With	Traded By	In Exchange For
Apr. 25, 1969	SD N	Joe Niekro Gary Ross	CHI N	Dick Selma

Dave Liddell

Date	Traded To	Traded With	Traded By	In Exchange For
June 30, 1986	NY N	Minor league P Dave Lenderman	CHI N	Ed Lynch

Don Liddle

Date	Traded To	Traded With	Traded By	In Exchange For
Feb. 1, 1954	NY N	*see Johnny Antonelli*	MIL N	—
June 14, 1956	STL N	—	NY N	*see Red Schoendienst*

Jon Lieber

Date	Traded To	Traded With	Traded By	In Exchange For
July 31, 1993	PIT N	Dan Miceli	KC A	Stan Belinda

Fred Liese

Date	Traded To	Traded With	Traded By	In Exchange For
Feb. 1910	BOS N	—	CHI N	Ginger Beaumont

Gene Lillard

Date	Traded To	Traded With	Traded By	In Exchange For
Dec. 27, 1939	STL N	Steve Mesner Cash	CHI N	Ken Raffensberger

Derek Lilliquist

Date	Traded To	Traded With	Traded By	In Exchange For
July 12, 1990	SD N	—	ATL N	Mark Grant
Nov. 20, 1991	CLE A	—	SD N	Waiver price
Nov. 9, 1994	ATL N	—	CLE A	Waiver price

Bob Lillis

Date	Traded To	Traded With	Traded By	In Exchange For
May 30, 1961	STL N	Carl Warwick	LA N	Daryl Spencer

Jose Lind

Date	Traded To	Traded With	Traded By	In Exchange For
Nov. 19, 1992	KC A	—	PIT N	Dennis Moeller Joel Johnston

Vive Lindaman

Date	Traded To	Traded With	Traded By	In Exchange For
Dec. 15, 1905	BOS N	Dave Brain Del Howard	PIT N	Vic Willis

Paul Lindblad

Date	Traded To	Traded With	Traded By	In Exchange For
May 8, 1971	WAS A	Frank Fernandez Don Mincher Cash	OAK A	Mike Epstein Darold Knowles
Oct. 30, 1972	OAK A	—	TEX A	Bill McNulty Brant Alyea
Feb. 19, 1977	TEX A	—	OAK A	$400,000.
Aug. 2, 1978	NY A	—	TEX A	Cash
Nov. 30, 1978	SEA A	—	NY A	Cash

Johnny Lindell

Date	Traded To	Traded With	Traded By	In Exchange For
May 15, 1950	STL N	—	NY A	Cash
Aug. 31, 1953	PHI N	—	PIT N	Cash

Jim Lindeman

Date	Traded To	Traded With	Traded By	In Exchange For
Dec. 6, 1989	DET A	Matt Kinzer	STL N	Minor league 2B Pat Austin Minor league C Bill Henderson Minor league P Marcos Betances

Bill Lindsey

Date	Traded To	Traded With	Traded By	In Exchange For
July 30, 1986	CHI A	—	NY A	*see Ron Kittle*

Doug Lindsey

Date	Traded To	Traded With	Traded By	In Exchange For
Sept. 1, 1993	CHI A	—	PHI N	Donn Pall

(Chicago received Lindsey on September 8, 1993.)

Jim Lindsey

Date	Traded To	Traded With	Traded By	In Exchange For
May 30, 1934	STL N	—	CIN N	Cash

Freddie Lindstrom

Date	Traded To	Traded With	Traded By	In Exchange For
Dec. 12, 1932	PIT N	—	NY N	Glenn Spencer Gus Dugas

(Part of three-team trade involving New York, Philadelphia, and Pittsburgh.)

Date	Traded To	Traded With	Traded By	In Exchange For
Nov. 22, 1934	CHI N	Larry French	PIT N	Guy Bush Jim Weaver Babe Herman

Fred Link

Date	Traded To	Traded With	Traded By	In Exchange For
Sept. 1910	STL A	—	CLE A	Cash

Ed Linke

Date	Traded To	Traded With	Traded By	In Exchange For
Dec. 1, 1937	STL A	—	WAS A	Chief Hogsett

Doug Linton

Date	Traded To	Traded With	Traded By	In Exchange For
June 17, 1993	CAL A	—	TOR A	Waiver price

Larry Lintz

Date	Traded To	Traded With	Traded By	In Exchange For
July 25, 1975	STL N	—	MON N	Jim Dwyer
Oct. 28, 1975	OAK A	—	STL N	Charlie Chant

Phil Linz

Date	Traded To	Traded With	Traded By	In Exchange For
Nov. 29, 1965	PHI N	—	NY A	Ruben Amaro
July 11, 1967	NY N	—	PHI N	Chuck Hiller

Frank Linzy

Date	Traded To	Traded With	Traded By	In Exchange For
May 19, 1970	STL N	—	SF N	Jerry Johnson
Mar. 26, 1972	MIL A	—	STL N	Minor league P Rich Stonum
Nov. 7, 1973	PHI N	—	MIL A	Billy Wilson

Johnny Lipon

Date	Traded To	Traded With	Traded By	In Exchange For
June 3, 1952	BOS A	*see George Kell*	DET A	—
Sept. 8, 1953	STL A	—	BOS A	Cash
Feb. 5, 1954	CHI A	Johnny Groth	BAL A	Neil Berry Sam Mele
Apr. 18, 1954	CIN N	—	CHI A	Grady Hatton

Nelson Liriano

Date	Traded To	Traded With	Traded By	In Exchange For
July 27, 1990	MIN A	Pedro Munoz	TOR A	John Candelaria
Oct. 14, 1994	PIT N	—	CLR N	Waiver price

Joe Lis

Date	Traded To	Traded With	Traded By	In Exchange For
Nov. 30, 1972	MIN A	Ken Sanders Ken Reynolds	PHI N	Cesar Tovar
June 5, 1974	CLE A	—	MIN A	Cash

Hod Lisenbee

Date	Traded To	Traded With	Traded By	In Exchange For
Dec. 15, 1928	BOS A	Milt Gaston Elliott Bigelow Bobby Reeves Grant Gillis	WAS A	Buddy Myer

Rick Lisi

Date	Traded To	Traded With	Traded By	In Exchange For
Feb. 19, 1982	BAL A	—	TEX A	Steve Luebber

Mark Littell

Date	Traded To	Traded With	Traded By	In Exchange For
Dec. 8, 1977	STL N	Buck Martinez	KC A	Al Hrabosky

Bryan Little

Date	Traded To	Traded With	Traded By	In Exchange For
Dec. 7, 1984	CHI A	Bob James	MON N	Vance Law Bert Roberge
July 2, 1986	NY A	—	CHI A	Cash

Scott Little

Date	Traded To	Traded With	Traded By	In Exchange For
May 29, 1987	PIT N	Al Pedrique	NY N	Bill Almon

Dick Littlefield

Date	Traded To	Traded With	Traded By	In Exchange For
Dec. 10, 1950	CHI A	Joe Dobson Al Zarilla	BOS A	Ray Scarborough Bill Wight
Nov. 27, 1951	STL A	Joe De Maestri Gus Niarhos Gordon Goldsberry Jim Rivera	CHI A	Al Widmar Sherm Lollar Tom Upton
Feb. 14, 1952	DET A	Ben Taylor Cliff Mapes	STL A	Gene Bearden Bob Cain Dick Kryhoski
Aug. 14, 1952	STL A	Marlin Stuart Don Lenhardt Vic Wertz	DET A	Jim Delsing Ned Garver Dave Madison Bill Black
May 25, 1954	PIT N	—	BAL A	Cal Abrams
May 17, 1956	STL N	Bobby Del Greco	PIT N	Bill Virdon

Dick Littlefield *continued*

Date	Traded To	Traded With	Traded By	In Exchange For
June 14, 1956	NY N	*see Red Schoendienst*	STL N	—
Dec. 13, 1956	BKN N	$30,000.	NY N	Jackie Robinson
		(Trade was cancelled when Robinson retired.)		
Apr. 16, 1957	CHI N	Bob Lennon	NY N	Ray Jablonski Ray Katt
Mar. 30, 1958	MIL N	—	CHI N	Cash

John Littlefield

Date	Traded To	Traded With	Traded By	In Exchange For
Dec. 8, 1980	SD N	—	STL N	*see Rollie Fingers*

Larry Littleton

Date	Traded To	Traded With	Traded By	In Exchange For
Dec. 21, 1979	CLE A	minor league P John Burden	PIT N	Larry Andersen
July 3, 1982	MIN A	—	CLE A	Larry Milbourne

Danny Litwhiler

Date	Traded To	Traded With	Traded By	In Exchange For
June 1, 1943	STL N	Earl Naylor	PHI N	Buster Adams Coaker Triplett Dain Clay
June 9, 1946	BOS N	—	STL N	Cash
May 11, 1948	CIN N	—	BOS N	Marv Rickert

Mickey Livingston

Date	Traded To	Traded With	Traded By	In Exchange For
Nov. 11, 1940	PHI N	Vito Tamulis Bill Crouch $100,000.	BKN N	Kirby Higbe
Aug. 5, 1943	CHI N	—	PHI N	Bill Lee
July 7, 1947	NY N	—	CHI N	Waiver price

Paddy Livingston

Date	Traded To	Traded With	Traded By	In Exchange For
Dec. 6, 1911	CLE A	—	PHI A	Cash

Scott Livingstone

Date	Traded To	Traded With	Traded By	In Exchange For
May 11, 1994	SD N	—	DET A	Gene Harris

Graeme Lloyd

Date	Traded To	Traded With	Traded By	In Exchange For
Dec. 8, 1992	MIL A	—	PHI N	Minor league P John Trisler

Hans Lobert

Date	Traded To	Traded With	Traded By	In Exchange For
Mar. 1906	CIN N	Jake Weimer	CHI N	Harry Steinfeldt
Feb. 1911	PHI N	Fred Beebe Jack Rowan Dode Paskert	CIN N	Johnny Bates Eddie Grant George McQuillan Lew Moren
Jan. 1915	NY N	—	PHI N	Al Demaree Bert Adams Milt Stock

Harry Lochhead

Date	Traded To	Traded With	Traded By	In Exchange For
Apr. 1901	PHI A	—	DET A	Cash

Don Lock

Date	Traded To	Traded With	Traded By	In Exchange For
July 11, 1962	WAS A	—	NY A	Dale Long
Nov. 30, 1966	PHI N	—	WAS A	Darold Knowles Cash
May 5, 1969	BOS A	—	PHI N	Rudy Schlesinger

Bobby Locke

Date	Traded To	Traded With	Traded By	In Exchange For
Nov. 27, 1961	CHI N	—	CLE A	Jerry Kindall
Apr. 7, 1962	STL N	—	CLE A	Minor league OF Al Herring
Apr. 28, 1962	PHI N	Cash	STL N	Don Ferrarese
Oct. 15, 1964	LA A	—	PHI N	Cash
July 28, 1965	CIN N	—	CAL A	Cash
June 3, 1966	CAL A	—	CIN N	Cash

Bob Locker

Date	Traded To	Traded With	Traded By	In Exchange For
June 8, 1969	SEA A	—	CHI A	Gary Bell
June 15, 1970	OAK A	—	MIL A	Cash
Nov. 21, 1972	CHI N	—	OAK A	Billy North

Bob Locker *continued*

Date	Traded To	Traded With	Traded By	In Exchange For
Dec. 3, 1973	OAK A	—	CHI N	Horacio Pina
Oct. 23, 1974	CHI N	Darold Knowles Manny Trillo	OAK A	Billy Williams

Gene Locklear

Date	Traded To	Traded With	Traded By	In Exchange For
June 12, 1973	SD N	Mike Johnson Cash	CIN N	Fred Norman
July 10, 1976	NY A	—	SD N	Rick Sawyer

Whitey Lockman

Date	Traded To	Traded With	Traded By	In Exchange For
June 14, 1956	STL N	Alvin Dark Ray Katt Don Liddle	NY N	Jackie Brandt Red Schoendienst Bobby Stephenson Dick Littlefield Bill Sarni
Feb. 26, 1957	NY N	—	STL N	Hoyt Wilhelm
Feb. 14, 1959	BAL A	—	SF N	Cash
June 23, 1959	CIN N	—	BAL A	Walt Dropo

Skip Lockwood

Date	Traded To	Traded With	Traded By	In Exchange For
Oct. 22, 1973	CAL A	Ellie Rodriguez Gary Ryerson Ollie Brown Joe Lahoud	MIL A	Clyde Wright Steve Barber Ken Berry Art Kusnyer Cash
Dec. 3, 1974	NY A	—	CAL A	Bill Sudakis
July 28, 1975	NY N	—	OAK A	Cash
Nov. 27, 1979	BOS A	—	NY N	No compensation (free agent signing)

Dario Lodigiani

Date	Traded To	Traded With	Traded By	In Exchange For
Dec. 16, 1940	CHI A	—	PHI A	Jack Knott

Billy Loes

Date	Traded To	Traded With	Traded By	In Exchange For
May 14, 1956	BAL A	—	BKN N	$20,000.
Apr. 1, 1959	WAS A	—	BAL A	Vito Valentinetti
(Trade was cancelled on April 8, 1959, by Commissioner Frick due to Loes's sore arm.)				
Nov. 30, 1959	SF N	Billy O'Dell	BAL A	Jackie Brandt Gordon Jones Roger McCardell
Oct. 16, 1961	NY N	—	SF N	Cash

Kenny Lofton

Date	Traded To	Traded With	Traded By	In Exchange For
Dec. 10, 1991	CLE A	Dave Rohde	HOU N	Eddie Taubensee Willie Blair

Johnny Logan

Date	Traded To	Traded With	Traded By	In Exchange For
June 15, 1961	PIT N	—	MIL N	Gino Cimoli

Lucky Lohrke

Date	Traded To	Traded With	Traded By	In Exchange For
Dec. 13, 1951	PHI N	—	NY N	Minor league C Jake Schmitt
Jan. 13, 1954	PIT N	Andy Hansen $70,000.	PHI N	Murry Dickson

Bill Lohrman

Date	Traded To	Traded With	Traded By	In Exchange For
Dec. 11, 1941	STL N	Ken O'Dea Johnny McCarthy $50,000.	NY N	Johnny Mize
May 5, 1942	NY N	—	STL N	Cash
July 31, 1943	BKN N	Bill Sayles Joe Orengo	NY N	Dolf Camilli Johnny Allen
(Camilli refused to report to New York and retired.)				

Mickey Lolich

Date	Traded To	Traded With	Traded By	In Exchange For
Dec. 12, 1975	NY N	Billy Baldwin	DET A	Rusty Staub Bill Laxton

Sherm Lollar

Date	Traded To	Traded With	Traded By	In Exchange For
Dec. 20, 1946	NY A	Ray Mack	CLE A	Hal Peck Gene Bearden Al Gettel

Sherm Lollar *continued*

Date	Traded To	Traded With	Traded By	In Exchange For
Dec. 13, 1948	STL A	Red Embree Dick Starr $100,000.	NY A	Fred Sanford Roy Partee
Nov. 27, 1951	CHI A	Al Widmar Tom Upton	STL A	Joe De Maestri Dick Littlefield Gus Niarhos Gordon Goldsberry Jim Rivera

Tim Lollar

Date	Traded To	Traded With	Traded By	In Exchange For
Apr. 1, 1981	SD N	Ruppert Jones Joe Lefebvre Chris Welsh	NY A	Jerry Mumphrey John Pacella
Dec. 6, 1984	CHI A	—	SD N	*see LaMarr Hoyt*
July 11, 1985	BOS A	—	CHI A	Reid Nichols

Ernie Lombardi

Date	Traded To	Traded With	Traded By	In Exchange For
Mar. 14, 1932	CIN N	Babe Herman Wally Gilbert	BKN N	Tony Cuccinello Joe Stripp Clyde Sukeforth
Feb. 7, 1942	BOS N	—	CIN N	Cash
Apr. 27, 1943	NY N	—	BOS N	Hugh Poland Connie Ryan

Phil Lombardi

Date	Traded To	Traded With	Traded By	In Exchange For
Dec. 11, 1987	NY N	Steve Frey Darren Reed	NY A	Rafael Santana Minor league P Victor Garcia
Apr. 4, 1990	ATL N	—	NY N	Waiver price

Vic Lombardi

Date	Traded To	Traded With	Traded By	In Exchange For
Dec. 8, 1947	PIT N	Dixie Walker Hal Gregg	BKN N	Preacher Roe Billy Cox Gene Mauch

Steve Lombardozzi

Date	Traded To	Traded With	Traded By	In Exchange For
Mar. 21, 1989	HOU N	—	MIN A	Two players to be named
(Minnesota received P Gordon Farmer and OF Ramon Cedeno on Sept. 15, 1989.)				

Jim Lonborg

Date	Traded To	Traded With	Traded By	In Exchange For
Oct. 11, 1971	MIL A	George Scott Billy Conigliaro Joe Lahoud Ken Brett Don Pavletich	BOS A	Marty Pattin Tommy Harper Lew Krausse Minor leaguer Pat Skrable
Oct. 31, 1972	PHI N	Ken Sanders Ken Brett Earl Stephenson	MIL A	Don Money John Vukovich Billy Champion

Bill Long

Date	Traded To	Traded With	Traded By	In Exchange For
Dec. 6, 1984	CHI A	—	SD N	*see LaMarr Hoyt*
Apr. 30, 1990	CHI N	—	CHI A	Minor league P Frank Campos

Dale Long

Date	Traded To	Traded With	Traded By	In Exchange For
June 1, 1951	STL A	—	PIT N	Waiver price
May 1, 1957	CHI N	Lee Walls	PIT N	Gene Baker Dee Fondy
Apr. 5, 1960	SF N	—	CHI N	Cash
Aug. 22, 1960	NY A	—	SF N	Cash
July 11, 1962	NY A	—	WAS A	Don Lock

Herman Long

Date	Traded To	Traded With	Traded By	In Exchange For
June 10, 1903	DET A	Ernie Courtney	NY A	Kid Elberfeld

Jeoff Long

Date	Traded To	Traded With	Traded By	In Exchange For
July 7, 1964	CHI A	—	STL N	Cash
Dec. 1, 1964	PHI N	Ray Herbert	CHI A	Danny Cater Lee Elia

Tony Longmire

Date	Traded To		Traded With	Traded By		In Exchange For
Aug. 30, 1990	PHI	N	Wes Chamberlain Julio Peguero	PIT	N	Carmelo Martinez

(Philadelphia received Longmire on September 28, 1990.)

Joe Lonnett

Date	Traded To		Traded With	Traded By		In Exchange For
June 13, 1958	MIL	N	—	PHI	N	Carl Sawatski

Brian Looney

Date	Traded To		Traded With	Traded By		In Exchange For
Nov. 9, 1994	BOS	A	—	MON	N	Player to be named

Ed Lopat

Date	Traded To		Traded With	Traded By		In Exchange For
Feb. 24, 1948	NY	A	—	CHI	A	Aaron Robinson Fred Bradley Bill Wight
July 30, 1955	BAL	A	—	NY	A	Jim McDonald

Stan Lopata

Date	Traded To		Traded With	Traded By		In Exchange For
Mar. 31, 1959	MIL	N	Ted Kazanski Johnny O'Brien	PHI	N	Gene Conley Joe Koppe Harry Hanebrink

Davey Lopes

Date	Traded To		Traded With	Traded By		In Exchange For
Feb. 8, 1982	OAK	A	—	LA	N	Minor league 2B Lance Hudson
July 15, 1984	CHI	N	—	OAK	A	Chuck Rainey Minor league OF Damon Farmar

(Chicago received Lopes on August 31, 1984, and Oakland received Farmar on March 18, 1985.)

Date	Traded To		Traded With	Traded By		In Exchange For
July 21, 1986	HOU	N	—	CHI	N	Frank DiPino

Al Lopez

Date	Traded To		Traded With	Traded By		In Exchange For
Dec. 12, 1935	BOS	N	Tony Cuccinello Ray Benge Bobby Reis	BKN	N	Ed Brandt Randy Moore
June 14, 1940	PIT	N	—	BOS	N	Ray Berres $40,000.
Dec. 7, 1946	CLE	A	—	PIT	N	Gene Woodling

Aurelio Lopez

Date	Traded To		Traded With	Traded By		In Exchange For
Dec. 4, 1978	DET	A	Jerry Morales	STL	N	Bob Sykes minor league P Jack Murphy
June 3, 1986	HOU	N	—	DET	A	No compensation (free agent signing)

Carlos Lopez

Date	Traded To		Traded With	Traded By		In Exchange For
Dec. 7, 1977	BAL	A	Tommy Moore	SEA	A	Mike Parrott

Hector Lopez

Date	Traded To		Traded With	Traded By		In Exchange For
May 26, 1959	NY	A	Ralph Terry	KC	A	Johnny Kucks Tom Sturdivant Jerry Lumpe

Marcelino Lopez

Date	Traded To		Traded With	Traded By		In Exchange For
Sept. 9, 1964	LA	A	Cash	PHI	N	Vic Power
June 15, 1967	BAL	A	minor league P Tom Arruda	CAL	A	Woodie Held
Apr. 5, 1971	MIL	A	—	BAL	A	Roric Harrison minor leaguer Marion Jackson
Mar. 29, 1972	CLE	A	—	MIL	A	Cash

Bris Lord

Date	Traded To		Traded With	Traded By		In Exchange For
July 23, 1910	PHI	A	—	CLE	A	Morrie Rath
Dec. 1912	BOS	N	—	PHI	A	Cash

Harry Lord

Date	Traded To		Traded With	Traded By		In Exchange For
Aug. 9, 1910	CHI	A	Amby McConnell	BOS	A	Frank Smith Billy Purtell

Andrew Lorraine

Date	Traded To		Traded With	Traded By		In Exchange For
July 27, 1995	CHI	A	Bill Simas Minor league OF McKay Christensen Minor league P John Snyder	CAL	A	Jim Abbott Tim Fortugno

Baldy Louden

Date	Traded To		Traded With	Traded By		In Exchange For
Dec. 23, 1915	CIN	N	—	BUF	F	Cash

Slim Love

Date	Traded To		Traded With	Traded By		In Exchange For
Dec. 18, 1918	BOS	A	—	NY	A	*see Duffy Lewis*
Jan. 17, 1919	DET	A	Eddie Ainsmith Chick Shorten	BOS	A	Ossie Vitt

Vance Lovelace

Date	Traded To		Traded With	Traded By		In Exchange For
Jan. 20, 1983	LA	N	Minor league OF Dan Cataline	CHI	N	Ron Cey

Jay Loviglio

Date	Traded To		Traded With	Traded By		In Exchange For
Apr. 1, 1981	CHI	A	—	PHI	N	Mike Proly
Nov. 29, 1982	CHI	N	—	CHI	A	Cash

Joe Lovitto

Date	Traded To		Traded With	Traded By		In Exchange For
Dec. 12, 1975	NY	N	—	TEX	A	Gene Clines

Torey Lovullo

Date	Traded To		Traded With	Traded By		In Exchange For
Mar. 19, 1991	NY	A	—	DET	A	Mark Leiter
Apr. 1, 1994	SEA	A	—	CAL	A	Waiver price

Grover Lowdermilk

Date	Traded To		Traded With	Traded By		In Exchange For
Dec. 15, 1912	CIN	N	Joe Tinker Harry Chapman	CHI	N	Bert Humphries Red Corriden Pete Knisely Art Phelan Mike Mitchell
Aug. 18, 1915	DET	A	Bill James	STL	A	Baby Doll Jacobson
Aug. 1916	CLE	A	—	DET	A	Cash
Oct. 1917	STL	A	—	CLE	A	Waiver price
May 1919	CHI	A	—	STL	A	Cash

Bobby Lowe

Date	Traded To		Traded With	Traded By		In Exchange For
July 1902	CHI	N	—	BOS	N	Charlie Dexter
Apr. 20, 1904	PIT	N	—	CHI	N	Cash
Apr. 30, 1904	DET	A	—	PIT	N	Cash

John Lowenstein

Date	Traded To		Traded With	Traded By		In Exchange For
Dec. 6, 1976	TOR	A	Rick Cerone	CLE	A	Rico Carty
Mar. 29, 1977	CLE	A	—	TOR	A	Hector Torres
Feb. 28, 1978	TEX	A	Tom Buskey	CLE	A	Willie Horton David Clyde
Nov. 27, 1978	BAL	A	—	TEX	A	Cash

Turk Lown

Date	Traded To		Traded With	Traded By		In Exchange For
May 8, 1958	CIN	N	—	CHI	N	Hersh Freeman
June 23, 1958	CHI	A	—	CIN	N	Waiver price

Peanuts Lowrey

Date	Traded To		Traded With	Traded By		In Exchange For
June 15, 1949	CIN	N	Harry Walker	CHI	N	Frankie Baumholtz Hank Sauer
Sept. 7, 1950	STL	N	—	CIN	N	Cash

Mike Loynd

Date	Traded To		Traded With	Traded By		In Exchange For
Mar. 25, 1988	HOU	N	—	TEX	A	Robbie Wine

Johnny Lucadello

Date	Traded To		Traded With	Traded By		In Exchange For
Mar. 1, 1947	NY	A	—	STL	A	Waiver price

Gary Lucas

Date	Traded To		Traded With	Traded By		In Exchange For
Dec. 7, 1983	MON	N	—	SD	N	Scott Sanderson
Dec. 27, 1985	MON	N	—	CAL	A	Luis Sanchez Minor league P Tim Arnold

Red Lucas

Date	Traded To		Traded With	Traded By		In Exchange For
Nov. 17, 1933	PIT	N	Wally Roettger	CIN	N	Adam Comorosky Tony Piet

Fred Luderus

Date	Traded To		Traded With	Traded By		In Exchange For
July 1910	PHI	N	—	CHI	N	Bill Foxen

Steve Luebber

Date	Traded To		Traded With	Traded By		In Exchange For
Feb. 19, 1982	TEX	A	—	BAL	A	Rick Lisi

Larry Luebbers

Date	Traded To		Traded With	Traded By		In Exchange For
Dec. 10, 1993	CHI	N	Mike Anderson Minor league C Darron Cox	CIN	N	Chuck McElroy
Nov. 18, 1994	CIN	N	—	CHI	N	Waiver price

Dick Luebke

Date	Traded To		Traded With	Traded By		In Exchange For
Dec. 15, 1962	CIN	N	minor league IF Willard Oplinger	BAL	A	Joe Gaines

Rick Luecken

Date	Traded To		Traded With	Traded By		In Exchange For
Dec. 10, 1986	KC	A	Danny Tartabull	SEA	A	Scott Bankhead Mike Kingery Steve Shields
Aug. 24, 1989	ATL	N	Pat Gomez	CHI	N	Paul Assenmacher
Dec. 15, 1989	ATL	N	Charlie Leibrandt	KC	A	Gerald Perry Minor league P Jim Lemasters
Sept. 24, 1990	TOR	A	—	ATL	N	Cash

Mike Lum

Date	Traded To		Traded With	Traded By		In Exchange For
Dec. 12, 1975	CIN	N	—	ATL	N	Darrel Chaney
Feb. 15, 1979	ATL	N	—	CIN	N	No compensation (free agent signing)

Jerry Lumpe

Date	Traded To		Traded With	Traded By		In Exchange For
May 26, 1959	KC	A	Johnny Kucks Tom Sturdivant	NY	A	Hector Lopez Ralph Terry
Nov. 18, 1963	DET	A	Ed Rakow Dave Wickersham	KC	A	Rocky Colavito Bob Anderson $50,000.

Don Lund

Date	Traded To		Traded With	Traded By		In Exchange For
June 28, 1948	STL	A	—	BKN	N	Waiver price
Jan. 20, 1949	DET	A	—	STL	A	$15,000.

Gordon Lund

Date	Traded To		Traded With	Traded By		In Exchange For
Nov. 28, 1967	BAL	A	John O'Donoghue	CLE	A	Eddie Fisher minor leaguers P Bob Scott and IF John Scruggs
Mar. 31, 1969	SEA	A	Gene Brabender	BAL	A	Chico Salmon

Tony Lupien

Date	Traded To		Traded With	Traded By		In Exchange For
Apr. 13, 1944	PHI	N	—	BOS	A	Waiver price
Jan. 26, 1949	DET	A	—	CHI	A	Waiver price

Al Luplow

Date	Traded To		Traded With	Traded By		In Exchange For
Nov. 29, 1965	NY	N	—	CLE	A	Cash
June 21, 1967	PIT	N	—	NY	N	Cash

Dolf Luque

Date	Traded To		Traded With	Traded By		In Exchange For
Feb. 1930	BKN	N	—	CIN	N	Doug McWeeny

Scott Lusader

Date	Traded To		Traded With	Traded By		In Exchange For
Apr. 5, 1991	NY	A	—	DET	A	Waiver price

Billy Lush

Date	Traded To		Traded With	Traded By		In Exchange For
Jan. 1904	CLE	A	—	DET	A	Jesse Stovall Ed Killian

Johnny Lush

Date	Traded To		Traded With	Traded By		In Exchange For
June 10, 1907	STL	N	—	PHI	N	Charlie Brown

Greg Luzinski

Date	Traded To		Traded With	Traded By		In Exchange For
Mar. 30, 1981	CHI	A	—	PHI	N	Cash

Sparky Lyle

Date	Traded To		Traded With	Traded By		In Exchange For
Mar. 22, 1972	NY	A	—	BOS	A	Danny Cater
Nov. 10, 1978	TEX	A	Domingo Ramos Mike Heath Larry McCall Dave Rajsich Cash	NY	A	Dave Righetti Juan Beniquez Mike Griffin Paul Mirabella minor league P Greg Jemison
Sept. 13, 1980	PHI	N	—	TEX	A	Kevin Saucier
Aug. 21, 1982	CHI	A	—	PHI	N	Cash

Ed Lynch

Date	Traded To		Traded With	Traded By		In Exchange For
Aug. 12, 1979	NY	N	Mike Jorgensen	TEX	A	Willie Montanez
June 30, 1986	CHI	N	—	NY	N	Dave Liddell Minor league P Dave Lenderman

Jerry Lynch

Date	Traded To		Traded With	Traded By		In Exchange For
May 23, 1963	PIT	N	—	CIN	N	Bob Skinner

Fred Lynn

Date	Traded To		Traded With	Traded By		In Exchange For
Jan. 23, 1981	CAL	A	Steve Renko	BOS	A	Frank Tanana Jim Dorsey Joe Rudi
Dec. 11, 1984	BAL	A	—	CAL	A	Free agent signing

(California selected Donnie Moore from Atlanta as compensation.)

Date	Traded To		Traded With	Traded By		In Exchange For
Aug. 31, 1988	DET	A	—	BAL	A	Chris Hoiles Minor league P Robinson Garces Minor league P Cesar Mejia
Dec. 6, 1989	SD	N	—	DET	A	No compensation (free agent signing)

Red Lynn

Date	Traded To		Traded With	Traded By		In Exchange For
May 9, 1939	NY	N	—	DET	A	Cash

Al Lyons

Date	Traded To		Traded With	Traded By		In Exchange For
Aug. 4, 1947	PIT	N	—	NY	A	Cash
Nov. 18, 1947	BOS	N	Jim Russell Bill Salkeld	PIT	N	Johnny Hopp Danny Murtaugh

Steve Lyons

Date	Traded To		Traded With	Traded By		In Exchange For
June 29, 1986	CHI	A	—	BOS	A	Tom Seaver
Jan. 8, 1992	ATL	N	—	CHI	A	No compensation (free agent signing)
June 29, 1992	BOS	A	—	MON	N	Cash

Rick Lysander

Date	Traded To		Traded With	Traded By		In Exchange For
Feb. 10, 1981	HOU	N	—	OAK	A	Jimmy Sexton
Jan. 12, 1983	MIN	A	—	HOU	N	Bob Veselic

Jim Lyttle

Date	Traded To		Traded With	Traded By		In Exchange For
Oct. 13, 1971	CHI	A	—	NY	A	Rich Hinton
Feb. 1, 1973	KC	A	—	CHI	A	Joe Keough
July 10, 1973	MON	N	—	KC	A	Cash
July 18, 1975	MON	N	—	CHI	A	Cash

Duke Maas

Date	Traded To		Traded With	Traded By		In Exchange For
Nov. 20, 1957	KC	A	—	DET	A	*see Billy Martin*
June 15, 1958	NY	A	Virgil Trucks	KC	A	Bob Grim Harry Simpson
Apr. 4, 1961	NY	A	—	LA	A	Fritzie Brickell

Bob Mabe

Date	Traded To		Traded With	Traded By		In Exchange For
Oct. 3, 1958	CIN	N	—	STL	N	*see George Crowe*

Bob MacDonald

Date	Traded To		Traded With	Traded By		In Exchange For
Mar. 30, 1993	DET	A	—	TOR	A	Cash

Mike Macfarlane

Date	Traded To	Traded With	Traded By	In Exchange For
Apr. 8, 1995	BOS A	—	KC A	No compensation (free agent signing)
Dec. 16, 1995	KC A	—	BOS A	No compensation (free agent signing)

Danny MacFayden

Date	Traded To	Traded With	Traded By	In Exchange For
June 5, 1932	NY A	—	BOS A	Ivy Andrews Hank Johnson $50,000.
Nov. 13, 1934	CIN N	—	NY A	Cash
June 15, 1935	BOS N	—	CIN N	Waiver price
Dec. 8, 1939	PIT N	—	BOS N	Bill Swift Cash

Ken Macha

Date	Traded To	Traded With	Traded By	In Exchange For
Jan. 15, 1981	TOR A	—	MON N	Cash

Julio Machado

Date	Traded To	Traded With	Traded By	In Exchange For
Aug. 31, 1990	MIL A	Kevin Brown	NY N	Charlie O'Brien Player to be named

(Machado and Brown were assigned to Milwaukee on September 7 and New York received P Kevin Carmody on September 11, 1990.)

Dave Machemer

Date	Traded To	Traded With	Traded By	In Exchange For
Mar. 3, 1976	BOS A	John Balaz Dick Sharon	CAL A	Dick Drago

Ray Mack

Date	Traded To	Traded With	Traded By	In Exchange For
Dec. 20, 1946	NY A	Sherm Lollar	CLE A	Hal Peck Gene Bearden Al Gettel

Pete Mackanin

Date	Traded To	Traded With	Traded By	In Exchange For
Dec. 5, 1974	MON N	Don Stanhouse	TEX A	Willie Davis
Sept. 5, 1978	PHI N	—	MON N	Cash
Dec. 7, 1979	MIN A	—	PHI N	Paul Thormodsgard
Feb. 11, 1982	CHI A	—	MIN A	No compensation (free agent signing)

Ken MacKenzie

Date	Traded To	Traded With	Traded By	In Exchange For
Oct. 11, 1961	NY N	Johnny Antonelli	MIL N	Cash
Aug. 5, 1963	STL N	—	NY N	Ed Bauta
Oct. 1, 1963	SF N	—	STL N	Jimmie Coker

Max Macon

Date	Traded To	Traded With	Traded By	In Exchange For
Sept. 1939	BKN N	—	STL N	Cash

Mike Madden

Date	Traded To	Traded With	Traded By	In Exchange For
Aug. 30, 1982	HOU N	Kevin Bass Frank DiPino Cash	MIL A	Don Sutton

Morris Madden

Date	Traded To	Traded With	Traded By	In Exchange For
Aug. 7, 1987	PIT N	—	DET A	*see Jim Morrison*

Tom Madden

Date	Traded To	Traded With	Traded By	In Exchange For
May 1911	PHI N	—	BOS A	Waiver price

Elliott Maddox

Date	Traded To	Traded With	Traded By	In Exchange For
Oct. 9, 1970	WAS A	*see Denny McLain*	DET A	—
Mar. 23, 1974	NY A	—	TEX A	Cash
Jan. 20, 1977	BAL A	Rick Bladt	NY A	Paul Blair
Nov. 30, 1977	NY A	—	BAL A	No compensation (free agent signing)

Garry Maddox

Date	Traded To	Traded With	Traded By	In Exchange For
May 4, 1975	PHI N	—	SF N	Willie Montanez

Greg Maddux

Date	Traded To	Traded With	Traded By	In Exchange For
Dec. 9, 1992	ATL N	—	CHI N	No compensation (free agent signing)

Mike Maddux

Date	Traded To	Traded With	Traded By	In Exchange For
Dec. 17, 1992	NY N	—	SD N	Roger Mason Minor league P Mike Freitas

Art Madison

Date	Traded To	Traded With	Traded By	In Exchange For
Jan. 1900	LOU N	—	PIT N	*see Honus Wagner*

Dave Madison

Date	Traded To	Traded With	Traded By	In Exchange For
Apr. 7, 1952	STL A	—	NY A	Cash
Aug. 14, 1952	DET A	—	STL A	*see Vic Wertz*

Scotti Madison

Date	Traded To	Traded With	Traded By	In Exchange For
Jan. 6, 1982	LA N	—	MIN A	*see Bobby Castillo*

Ed Madjeski

Date	Traded To	Traded With	Traded By	In Exchange For
May 15, 1934	CHI A	—	PHI A	Cash

Bill Madlock

Date	Traded To	Traded With	Traded By	In Exchange For
Oct. 25, 1973	CHI N	Vic Harris	TEX A	Ferguson Jenkins
Feb. 11, 1977	SF N	Rob Sperring	CHI N	Bobby Murcer Steve Ontiveros minor league P Andy Muhlstock
June 28, 1979	PIT N	Lenny Randle Dave Roberts	SF N	Ed Whitson Al Holland Fred Breining
Aug. 31, 1985	LA N	—	PIT N	R. J. Reynolds Sid Bream Cecil Espy

(Pittsburgh received Reynolds on Sept. 3 and Bream and Espy on September 9, 1985.)

Alex Madrid

Date	Traded To	Traded With	Traded By	In Exchange For
Aug. 24, 1988	PHI N	—	MIL A	Mike Young

Dave Magadan

Date	Traded To	Traded With	Traded By	In Exchange For
Dec. 8, 1992	FLA N	—	NY N	No compensation (free agent signing)
June 27, 1993	SEA A	—	FLA N	Henry Cotto Jeff Darwin
Nov. 9, 1993	FLA N	—	SEA A	Jeff Darwin Cash
Apr. 13, 1995	HOU N	—	FLA N	No compensation (free agent signing)
Dec. 26, 1995	CHI N	—	HOU N	No compensation (free agent signing)

Bill Magee

Date	Traded To	Traded With	Traded By	In Exchange For
May 1901	NY N	—	STL N	Chauncey Fisher
May 1902	PHI N	—	NY N	Cash

Lee Magee

Date	Traded To	Traded With	Traded By	In Exchange For
Feb. 10, 1916	NY A	—	BKN F	Cash
July 15, 1917	STL A	—	NY A	Armando Marsans
Apr. 28, 1918	NY A	—	STL A	Tim Hendryx
Apr. 28, 1918	CIN N	—	NY A	Tommy Clarke
Apr. 18, 1919	BKN N	—	CIN N	Cash
June 2, 1919	CHI N	—	BKN N	Pete Kilduff

Sherry Magee

Date	Traded To	Traded With	Traded By	In Exchange For
Dec. 24, 1914	BOS N	—	PHI N	Cash
Aug. 1, 1917	CIN N	—	BOS N	Waiver price

Sal Maglie

Date	Traded To	Traded With	Traded By	In Exchange For
July 31, 1955	CLE A	—	NY N	Waiver price
May 15, 1956	BKN N	—	CLE A	Cash
Sept. 1, 1957	NY A	—	BKN N	Waiver price
June 14, 1958	STL N	—	NY A	Joe McClain $25,000.

George Magoon

Date	Traded To	Traded With	Traded By	In Exchange For
June 9, 1903	CHI A	—	CIN N	Cozy Dolan Tom Daly

Tom Magrann

Date	Traded To		Traded With	Traded By		In Exchange For
Nov. 15, 1988	CLE	A	Minor league OF Gary Holtz	BAL	A	Minor league 1B Don Lovell Minor league P John Githens

Pete Magrini

Date	Traded To		Traded With	Traded By		In Exchange For
Aug. 3, 1967	NY	A	Ron Klimkowski	BOS	A	Elston Howard

Freddie Maguire

Date	Traded To		Traded With	Traded By		In Exchange For
Nov. 7, 1928	BOS	N	Socks Seibold Bruce Cunningham Percy Jones Lou Legett $200,000.	CHI	N	Rogers Hornsby

Jack Maguire

Date	Traded To		Traded With	Traded By		In Exchange For
June 5, 1951	PIT	N	—	NY	N	Waiver price
July 16, 1951	STL	A	—	PIT	N	Waiver price

Art Mahaffey

Date	Traded To		Traded With	Traded By		In Exchange For
Oct. 27, 1965	STL	N	Pat Corrales Alex Johnson	PHI	N	Bill White Dick Groat Bob Uecker
Apr. 1, 1967	NY	N	Jerry Buchek Tony Martinez	STL	N	Ed Bressoud Danny Napoleon Cash

Roy Mahaffey

Date	Traded To		Traded With	Traded By		In Exchange For
Jan. 29, 1936	STL	A	—	PHI	A	Waiver price

Greg Mahlberg

Date	Traded To		Traded With	Traded By		In Exchange For
Dec. 15, 1980	CIN	N	*see Danny Walton*	TEX	A	—

Mickey Mahler

Date	Traded To		Traded With	Traded By		In Exchange For
Apr. 1, 1981	CAL	A	Ed Ott	PIT	N	Jason Thompson
Feb. 6, 1985	MON	N	—	STL	N	Tom Lawless

(St. Louis received Lawless on March 25, 1985.)

Rick Mahler

Date	Traded To		Traded With	Traded By		In Exchange For
Dec. 4, 1988	CIN	N	—	ATL	N	No compensation (free agent signing)

Bob Mahoney

Date	Traded To		Traded With	Traded By		In Exchange For
May 29, 1951	STL	A	—	CHI	A	Waiver price
Oct. 14, 1952	BKN	N	Ray Coleman Stan Rojek $90,000.	STL	A	Billy Hunter

Jim Mahoney

Date	Traded To		Traded With	Traded By		In Exchange For
Oct. 5, 1961	CLE	A	Dick Donovan Gene Green	WAS	A	Jimmy Piersall
July 20, 1966	CHI	A	Cash	HOU	N	Gene Freese

Duster Mails

Date	Traded To		Traded With	Traded By		In Exchange For
May 10, 1917	PIT	N	—	BKN	N	Waiver price

Fritz Maisel

Date	Traded To		Traded With	Traded By		In Exchange For
Jan. 22, 1918	STL	A	—	NY	A	*see Eddie Plank*

Hank Majeski

Date	Traded To		Traded With	Traded By		In Exchange For
Sept. 25, 1942	NY	A	—	BOS	N	Cash
June 14, 1946	PHI	A	—	NY	A	Cash
Dec. 14, 1949	CHI	A	—	PHI	A	Eddie Klieman
June 4, 1951	PHI	A	—	CHI	A	Kermit Wahl
June 10, 1952	CLE	A	—	PHI	A	Cash
June 27, 1955	BAL	A	—	CLE	A	Bobby Young

Mike Maksudian

Date	Traded To		Traded With	Traded By		In Exchange For
Aug. 4, 1988	NY	N	Minor league OF Vince Harris	CHI	A	Tom McCarthy Steve Springer
Oct. 27, 1992	MIN	A	—	TOR	A	Waiver price

Candy Maldonado

Date	Traded To		Traded With	Traded By		In Exchange For
Dec. 11, 1985	SF	N	—	LA	N	Alex Trevino
Nov. 28, 1989	CLE	A	—	SF	N	No compensation (free agent signing)
Aug. 9, 1991	TOR	A	—	MIL	A	William Suero Minor league P Rob Wishnevski

(Milwaukee received Suero on August 14, 1991.)

Date	Traded To		Traded With	Traded By		In Exchange For
Dec. 11, 1992	CHI	N	—	TOR	A	No compensation (free agent signing)
Aug. 19, 1993	CLE	A	—	CHI	N	Glenallen Hill
Aug. 31, 1995	TEX	A	—	TOR	A	Cash

Carlos Maldonado

Date	Traded To		Traded With	Traded By		In Exchange For
Dec. 10, 1992	MIL	A	—	KC	A	Minor league SS Mike Guerrero

Jim Maler

Date	Traded To		Traded With	Traded By		In Exchange For
Jan. 15, 1984	NY	N	—	SEA	A	Minor league P John Semprini

Sheldon Mallory

Date	Traded To		Traded With	Traded By		In Exchange For
Dec. 8, 1976	CHI	N	—	KC	A	Pete LaCock

(Part of three-team trade involving Kansas City, Chicago Cubs, and New York Mets.)

Date	Traded To		Traded With	Traded By		In Exchange For
Dec. 8, 1976	NY	N	—	CHI	N	Jim Dwyer

(Part of three-team trade involving Chicago Cubs, New York Mets, and Kansas City.)

Date	Traded To		Traded With	Traded By		In Exchange For
Apr. 4, 1977	OAK	A	—	NY	N	Cash
Mar. 25, 1978	TOR	A	—	OAK	A	Steve Staggs
Nov. 3, 1978	CLE	A	—	TOR	A	Dave Freisleben

Bob Malloy

Date	Traded To		Traded With	Traded By		In Exchange For
Apr. 28, 1947	PIT	N	—	CIN	N	Waiver price

Harry Malmberg

Date	Traded To		Traded With	Traded By		In Exchange For
Apr. 7, 1955	DET	A	—	CLE	A	Waiver price

Pat Malone

Date	Traded To		Traded With	Traded By		In Exchange For
Oct. 26, 1934	STL	N	—	CHI	N	Ken O'Dea
Mar. 26, 1935	NY	A	—	STL	N	$15,000.

Billy Maloney

Date	Traded To		Traded With	Traded By		In Exchange For
Dec. 30, 1905	BKN	N	Buttons Briggs Jack McCarthy Doc Casey $2,000.	CHI	N	Jimmy Sheckard

Jim Maloney

Date	Traded To		Traded With	Traded By		In Exchange For
Dec. 15, 1970	CAL	A	—	CIN	N	Greg Garrett

Al Mamaux

Date	Traded To		Traded With	Traded By		In Exchange For
Jan. 9, 1918	BKN	N	Chuck Ward Burleigh Grimes	PIT	N	Casey Stengel George Cutshaw

Frank Mancuso

Date	Traded To		Traded With	Traded By		In Exchange For
Dec. 16, 1946	STL	A	—	WAS	A	Jake Early

Gus Mancuso

Date	Traded To		Traded With	Traded By		In Exchange For
Oct. 10, 1932	NY	N	Ray Starr	STL	N	Ethan Allen Bob O'Farrell Bill Walker Jim Mooney
Dec. 6, 1938	CHI	N	Dick Bartell Hank Leiber	NY	N	Frank Demaree Bill Jurges Ken O'Dea
Dec. 8, 1939	BKN	N	Newt Kimball	CHI	N	Al Todd
Dec. 4, 1940	STL	N	Minor league P John Pintar $65,000.	BKN	N	Mickey Owen
May 5, 1942	NY	N	—	STL	N	Cash

Jim Mangan

Date	Traded To		Traded With	Traded By		In Exchange For
Mar. 5, 1956	NY	N	—	PIT	N	Cash

Angel Mangual

Date	Traded To	Traded With	Traded By	In Exchange For
Sept. 14, 1970	OAK A	—	PIT N	Mudcat Grant

(Oakland received Mangual on October 20.)

Pepe Mangual

Date	Traded To	Traded With	Traded By	In Exchange For
July 21, 1976	NY N	Jim Dwyer	MON N	Del Unser Wayne Garrett

Leo Mangum

Date	Traded To	Traded With	Traded By	In Exchange For
Jan. 15, 1927	WAS A	Sloppy Thurston	CHI A	Roger Peckinpaugh

Phil Mankowski

Date	Traded To	Traded With	Traded By	In Exchange For
Oct. 31, 1979	NY N	Jerry Morales	DET A	Richie Hebner

Les Mann

Date	Traded To	Traded With	Traded By	In Exchange For
Feb. 10, 1916	CHI N	*see Three Finger Brown*	CHI F	—
Aug. 1919	BOS N	Charlie Pick	CHI N	Buck Herzog
Nov. 9, 1920	STL N	—	BOS N	Cash
July 18, 1927	NY N	—	BOS N	Waiver price

Rick Manning

Date	Traded To	Traded With	Traded By	In Exchange For
June 6, 1983	MIL A	Rick Waits	CLE A	Gorman Thomas Ernie Camacho Jamie Easterly

Fred Manrique

Date	Traded To	Traded With	Traded By	In Exchange For
Apr. 7, 1985	MON N	—	TOR A	Cash
Mar. 31, 1986	STL N	—	MON N	Tom Nieto
Dec. 22, 1986	CHI A	—	STL N	Bill Dawley
July 29, 1989	TEX A	Harold Baines	CHI A	Scott Fletcher Wilson Alvarez Sammy Sosa
Apr. 13, 1990	MIN A	—	TEX A	Minor league P Jeff Satzinger

Felix Mantilla

Date	Traded To	Traded With	Traded By	In Exchange For
Dec. 11, 1962	BOS A	—	NY N	Tracy Stallard Pumpsie Green Al Moran
Apr. 3, 1966	HOU N	—	BOS A	Eddie Kasko

Jeff Manto

Date	Traded To	Traded With	Traded By	In Exchange For
Jan. 9, 1990	CLE A	Minor league P Colin Charland	CAL A	Scott Bailes

Barry Manuel

Date	Traded To	Traded With	Traded By	In Exchange For
Aug. 9, 1993	BAL A	—	TEX A	Waiver price

Jerry Manuel

Date	Traded To	Traded With	Traded By	In Exchange For
Mar. 15, 1980	MON N	—	DET A	Duffy Dyer
May 22, 1982	SD N	—	MON N	Kim Seaman
June 8, 1982	MON N	—	SD N	Mike Griffin
Apr. 10, 1984	CHI A	—	CHI N	Minor league IF Tim Gourley

Heinie Manush

Date	Traded To	Traded With	Traded By	In Exchange For
Dec. 2, 1927	STL A	Lu Blue	DET A	Chick Galloway Elam Vangilder Harry Rice
June 13, 1930	WAS A	General Crowder	STL A	Goose Goslin
Dec. 17, 1935	BOS A	—	WAS A	Carl Reynolds Roy Johnson
May 1938	PIT N	—	BKN N	Waiver price

Dick Manville

Date	Traded To	Traded With	Traded By	In Exchange For
Dec. 3, 1952	PIT N	$25,000.	CHI N	Clyde McCullough

Josias Manzanillo

Date	Traded To	Traded With	Traded By	In Exchange For
June 12, 1993	NY N	—	MIL A	Wayne Housie

Josias Manzanillo *continued*

Date	Traded To	Traded With	Traded By	In Exchange For
June 5, 1995	NY A	—	NY N	Waiver price

Cliff Mapes

Date	Traded To	Traded With	Traded By	In Exchange For
July 31, 1951	STL A	—	NY A	Bobby Hogue Kermit Wahl Tom Upton Lou Sleater
Feb. 14, 1952	DET A	—	STL A	*see Gene Bearden*
Oct. 27, 1952	STL A	Neil Berry $25,000.	DET A	Rufus Crawford

Georges Maranda

Date	Traded To	Traded With	Traded By	In Exchange For
Aug. 20, 1962	CLE A	Jackie Collum Cash	MIN A	Ruben Gomez

Rabbit Maranville

Date	Traded To	Traded With	Traded By	In Exchange For
Feb. 23, 1921	PIT N	—	BOS N	Billy Southworth Walter Barbare Fred Nicholson $15,000.
Oct. 27, 1924	CHI N	Charlie Grimm Wilbur Cooper	PIT N	Vic Aldridge George Grantham Al Niehaus
Nov. 9, 1925	BKN N	—	CHI N	Waiver price
Dec. 8, 1928	BOS N	—	STL N	Cash

Firpo Marberry

Date	Traded To	Traded With	Traded By	In Exchange For
Dec. 14, 1932	DET A	Carl Fischer	WAS A	Earl Whitehill

Johnny Marcum

Date	Traded To	Traded With	Traded By	In Exchange For
Dec. 10, 1935	BOS A	Jimmie Foxx	PHI A	Gordon Rhodes minor league C George Savino $150,000.
Dec. 6, 1938	STL A	—	BOS A	Tom Carey
June 2, 1939	CHI A	—	STL A	John Whitehead

Leo Marentette

Date	Traded To	Traded With	Traded By	In Exchange For
Apr. 3, 1969	MON N	Howie Reed	HOU N	Cash

Juan Marichal

Date	Traded To	Traded With	Traded By	In Exchange For
Dec. 7, 1973	BOS A	—	SF N	Cash

Roger Maris

Date	Traded To	Traded With	Traded By	In Exchange For
June 15, 1958	KC A	Dick Tomanek Preston Ward	CLE A	Woodie Held Vic Power
Dec. 11, 1959	NY A	Joe De Maestri Kent Hadley	KC A	Hank Bauer Don Larsen Norm Siebern Marv Throneberry
Dec. 8, 1966	STL N	—	NY A	Charley Smith

Dick Marlowe

Date	Traded To	Traded With	Traded By	In Exchange For
Sept. 17, 1956	CHI A	—	DET A	Waiver price

Rube Marquard

Date	Traded To	Traded With	Traded By	In Exchange For
Aug. 31, 1915	BKN N	—	NY N	Waiver price
Dec. 15, 1920	CIN N	—	BKN N	Dutch Ruether
Feb. 18, 1922	BOS N	—	CIN N	Larry Kopf Jack Scott

Gonzalo Marquez

Date	Traded To	Traded With	Traded By	In Exchange For
Aug. 29, 1973	CHI N	—	OAK A	Pat Bourque

Isidro Marquez

Date	Traded To	Traded With	Traded By	In Exchange For
Dec. 27, 1993	CHI A	—	LA N	Minor league 3B Ron Coomer

Luis Marquez

Date	Traded To	Traded With	Traded By	In Exchange For
June 14, 1954	PIT N	—	CHI N	Hal Rice

Bob Marquis

Date	Traded To	Traded With	Traded By	In Exchange For
Aug. 28, 1952	CIN N	—	NY A	*see Ewell Blackwell*

Oreste Marrero

Date	Traded To	Traded With	Traded By	In Exchange For
Jan. 20, 1993	MON N	Charlie Montoyo	MIL A	Minor league OF Todd Samples Minor league P Ron Gerstein

Bill Marriott

Date	Traded To	Traded With	Traded By	In Exchange For
Apr. 1926	BKN N	—	BOS N	Cash

Armando Marsans

Date	Traded To	Traded With	Traded By	In Exchange For
Feb. 10, 1916	STL A	*see Eddie Plank*	STL F	—
July 15, 1917	NY A	—	STL A	Lee Magee

Freddie Marsh

Date	Traded To	Traded With	Traded By	In Exchange For
Apr. 1, 1951	STL A	$35,000.	CLE A	Snuffy Stirnweiss Merrill Combs
May 12, 1952	WAS A	Lou Sleater	STL A	Cass Michaels
June 10, 1952	STL A	—	WAS A	Earl Rapp
Jan. 20, 1953	CHI A	—	STL A	Dixie Upright $25,000.
Dec. 6, 1954	BAL A	—	CHI A	*see Clint Courtney*

Cuddles Marshall

Date	Traded To	Traded With	Traded By	In Exchange For
May 15, 1950	STL A	—	NY A	Cash

Dave Marshall

Date	Traded To	Traded With	Traded By	In Exchange For
Dec. 12, 1969	NY N	Ray Sadecki	SF N	Bob Heise Jim Gosger
Nov. 30, 1972	SD N	—	NY N	Al Severinsen

Doc Marshall

Date	Traded To	Traded With	Traded By	In Exchange For
May 1904	NY N	—	PHI N	Cash
Aug. 7, 1904	BOS N	—	NY N	Cash
July 13, 1906	STL N	Sam Mertes	NY N	Spike Shannon
June 1908	CHI N	—	STL N	Cash
Nov. 1908	BKN N	—	CHI N	Waiver price

Jim Marshall

Date	Traded To	Traded With	Traded By	In Exchange For
Dec. 3, 1957	BAL A	Jack Harshman Larry Doby Russ Heman	CHI A	Tito Francona Ray Moore Billy Goodman
Aug. 23, 1958	CHI N	—	BAL A	Waiver price
Nov. 21, 1959	BOS A	Dave Hillman	CHI N	Dick Gernert
Mar. 16, 1960	CLE A	Sammy White	BOS A	Russ Nixon
		(Trade was cancelled when White decided to retire.)		
Mar. 29, 1960	SF N	—	BOS A	Al Worthington
Oct. 13, 1961	NY N	—	SF N	Cash
May 7, 1962	PIT N	—	NY N	Vinegar Bend Mizell

Mike Marshall

Date	Traded To	Traded With	Traded By	In Exchange For
Dec. 20, 1989	NY N	Alejandro Pena	LA N	Juan Samuel
July 27, 1990	BOS A	—	NY N	Greg Hansell Minor league IF Ed Perozo Player to be named
		(New York received C Paul Williams on November 19, 1990.)		

Mike Marshall

Date	Traded To	Traded With	Traded By	In Exchange For
Dec. 5, 1973	LA N	—	MON N	Willie Davis
June 23, 1976	ATL N	—	LA N	Elias Sosa Lee Lacy
Apr. 30, 1977	TEX A	—	ATL N	Cash

Willard Marshall

Date	Traded To	Traded With	Traded By	In Exchange For
Dec. 14, 1949	BOS N	Sid Gordon Buddy Kerr Red Webb	NY N	Eddie Stanky Alvin Dark
June 4, 1952	CIN N	—	BOS N	Cash
Dec. 10, 1953	CHI A	—	CIN N	Saul Rogovin Rocky Krsnich Connie Ryan

Billy Martin

Date	Traded To	Traded With	Traded By	In Exchange For
June 15, 1957	KC A	Woodie Held Ralph Terry Bob Martyn	NY A	Ryne Duren Jim Pisoni Milt Graff Harry Simpson
Nov. 20, 1957	DET A	Gus Zernial Tom Morgan Lou Skizas Mickey McDermott Tim Thompson	KC A	Bill Tuttle Jim Small Duke Maas John Tsitouris Frank House Kent Hadley Jim McManus
Nov. 20, 1958	CLE A	Al Cicotte	DET A	Don Mossi Ossie Alvarez Ray Narleski
Dec. 15, 1959	CIN N	Cal McLish Gordy Coleman	CLE A	Johnny Temple
Dec. 3, 1960	MIL N	—	CIN N	Cash
June 1, 1961	MIN A	—	MIL N	Billy Consolo

Gene Martin

Date	Traded To	Traded With	Traded By	In Exchange For
Nov. 3, 1970	PHI N	Greg Goossen Jeff Terpko	WAS A	Curt Flood

J. C. Martin

Date	Traded To	Traded With	Traded By	In Exchange For
July 22, 1967	NY N	Bill Southworth	CHI A	Ken Boyer
Mar. 29, 1970	CHI N	—	NY N	Randy Bobb

Jack Martin

Date	Traded To	Traded With	Traded By	In Exchange For
July 3, 1914	PHI N	—	BOS N	Josh Devore

Jerry Martin

Date	Traded To	Traded With	Traded By	In Exchange For
Feb. 23, 1979	CHI N	Barry Foote Derek Botelho Ted Sizemore minor league P Henry Mack	PHI N	Manny Trillo Dave Rader Greg Gross
Dec. 12, 1980	SF N	Jesus Figueroa minor league IF Mike Turgeon	CHI N	Joe Strain Phil Nastu
Dec. 11, 1981	KC A	—	SF N	Rich Gale Bill Laskey
Mar. 17, 1984	NY N	—	KC A	No compensation (free agent signing)

Joe Martin

Date	Traded To	Traded With	Traded By	In Exchange For
July 1903	STL A	—	WAS A	Barry McCormick

John Martin

Date	Traded To	Traded With	Traded By	In Exchange For
June 2, 1980	STL N	Al Greene	DET A	Jim Lentine
Aug. 4, 1983	DET A	—	STL N	Cash

Morrie Martin

Date	Traded To	Traded With	Traded By	In Exchange For
June 11, 1954	CHI A	Ed McGhee	PHI A	Sonny Dixon Al Sima Bill Wilson $20,000.
July 13, 1956	BAL A	—	CHI A	Waiver price
July 2, 1958	CLE A	—	STL N	Waiver price

Renie Martin

Date	Traded To	Traded With	Traded By	In Exchange For
Mar. 30, 1982	SF N	Craig Chamberlain Atlee Hammaker Brad Wellman	KC A	Vida Blue Bob Tufts
Aug. 20, 1984	PHI N	Al Oliver	SF N	Kelly Downs George Riley

Speed Martin

Date	Traded To	Traded With	Traded By	In Exchange For
July 14, 1917	STL A	—	CHI A	Cash

Stu Martin

Date	Traded To	Traded With	Traded By	In Exchange For
Dec. 2, 1940	PIT N	—	STL N	Cash

Buck Martinez

Date	Traded To	Traded With	Traded By	In Exchange For
Dec. 16, 1968	KC A	Tommy Smith minor league IF Mickey Sinnerud	HOU N	Minor league C John Jones
Dec. 8, 1977	STL N	Mark Littell	KC A	Al Hrabosky
Dec. 8, 1977	MIL A	—	STL N	George Frazier
May 10, 1981	TOR A	—	MIL A	Gil Kubski

Carlos Martinez

Date	Traded To	Traded With	Traded By	In Exchange For
July 30, 1986	CHI A	—	NY A	*see Ron Kittle*

Carmelo Martinez

Date	Traded To	Traded With	Traded By	In Exchange For
Dec. 7, 1983	SD N	Fritz Connally Craig Lefferts	CHI N	Scott Sanderson

(Part of three-team trade involving Chicago Cubs, San Diego, and Montreal.)

Date	Traded To	Traded With	Traded By	In Exchange For
Dec. 1, 1989	PHI N	—	SD N	No compensation (free agent signing)
Aug. 30, 1990	PIT N	—	PHI N	Wes Chamberlain Julio Peguero Tony Longmire

(Philadelphia received Longmire on September 28, 1990.)

Date	Traded To	Traded With	Traded By	In Exchange For
May 3, 1991	KC A	—	PIT N	Victor Cole
July 11, 1991	CIN N	—	KC A	Todd Benzinger

Dave Martinez

Date	Traded To	Traded With	Traded By	In Exchange For
July 14, 1988	MON N	—	CHI N	Mitch Webster
Dec. 11, 1991	CIN N	Scott Ruskin Willie Greene	MON N	John Wetteland Bill Risley
Dec. 9, 1992	SF N	—	CIN N	No compensation (free agent signing)
Apr. 4, 1995	CHI A	—	SF N	No compensation (free agent signing)

Dennis Martinez

Date	Traded To	Traded With	Traded By	In Exchange For
June 16, 1986	MON N	—	BAL A	Rene Gonzales

(Baltimore received Gonzales on Dec. 16, 1986.)

Date	Traded To	Traded With	Traded By	In Exchange For
Dec. 2, 1993	CLE A	—	MON N	No compensation (free agent signing)

Domingo Martinez

Date	Traded To	Traded With	Traded By	In Exchange For
Mar. 29, 1994	CHI A	—	TOR A	Mike Huff

Jose Martinez

Date	Traded To	Traded With	Traded By	In Exchange For
June 24, 1993	SD N	Trevor Hoffman Andres Berumen	FLA N	Gary Sheffield Rich Rodriguez

Marty Martinez

Date	Traded To	Traded With	Traded By	In Exchange For
Dec. 4, 1968	HOU N	—	ATL N	Bob Aspromonte
Nov. 3, 1971	STL N	—	HOU N	Bob Stinson
May 18, 1972	OAK A	—	STL N	Brant Alyea

(Alyea was returned to Oakland on July 23.)

Date	Traded To	Traded With	Traded By	In Exchange For
July 20, 1972	TEX A	Vic Harris Steve Lawson	OAK A	Don Mincher Ted Kubiak

Pedro Martinez

Date	Traded To	Traded With	Traded By	In Exchange For
Nov. 19, 1993	MON N	—	LA N	Delino DeShields

Pedro Martinez

Date	Traded To	Traded With	Traded By	In Exchange For
Dec. 28, 1994	HOU N	—	SD N	*see Ken Caminiti*

Pedro Martinez *continued*

Date	Traded To	Traded With	Traded By	In Exchange For
Oct. 10, 1995	SD N	—	HOU N	Ray Holbert
Dec. 15, 1995	NY N	—	SD N	Jeff Barry

Silvio Martinez

Date	Traded To	Traded With	Traded By	In Exchange For
Dec. 10, 1976	CHI A	Richie Zisk	PIT N	Terry Forster Goose Gossage
Aug. 31, 1977	STL N	Nyls Nyman Dave Hamilton	CHI A	Clay Carroll
Nov. 20, 1981	CLE A	Lary Sorensen	STL N	Lonnie Smith

(Part of three-team trade involving Cleveland, Philadelphia, and St. Louis.)

Teddy Martinez

Date	Traded To	Traded With	Traded By	In Exchange For
Dec. 11, 1974	STL N	—	NY N	Jack Heidemann Mike Vail
May 18, 1975	OAK A	—	STL N	Mike Barlow Minor league P Steve Staniland

Tino Martinez

Date	Traded To	Traded With	Traded By	In Exchange For
Dec. 6, 1995	NY A	Jeff Nelson Jim Mecir	SEA A	Sterling Hitchcock Russ Davis

Tippy Martinez

Date	Traded To	Traded With	Traded By	In Exchange For
June 15, 1976	BAL A	Rudy May Rick Dempsey Dave Pagan Scott McGregor	NY A	Ken Holtzman Doyle Alexander Grant Jackson Ellie Hendricks Jimmy Freeman

Tony Martinez

Date	Traded To	Traded With	Traded By	In Exchange For
Apr. 1, 1967	NY N	Jerry Buchek Art Mahaffey	STL N	Ed Bressoud Danny Napoleon Cash

Joe Marty

Date	Traded To	Traded With	Traded By	In Exchange For
May 29, 1939	PHI N	Ray Harrell Kirby Higbe	CHI N	Claude Passeau

Bob Martyn

Date	Traded To	Traded With	Traded By	In Exchange For
June 15, 1957	KC A	*see Ralph Terry*	NY A	—
Apr. 12, 1959	NY A	Mike Baxes	KC A	Russ Snyder Tommy Carroll

Randy Martz

Date	Traded To	Traded With	Traded By	In Exchange For
Jan. 25, 1983	CHI A	Scott Fletcher Pat Tabler Dick Tidrow	CHI N	Steve Trout Warren Brusstar

Clyde Mashore

Date	Traded To	Traded With	Traded By	In Exchange For
June 15, 1970	MON N	—	CIN N	Ty Cline

Phil Masi

Date	Traded To	Traded With	Traded By	In Exchange For
June 15, 1949	PIT N	—	BOS N	Ed Sauer
Feb. 2, 1950	CHI A	—	PIT N	Cash

Don Mason

Date	Traded To	Traded With	Traded By	In Exchange For
Dec. 4, 1970	SD N	minor league P Bill Frost	SF N	Steve Huntz

Jim Mason

Date	Traded To	Traded With	Traded By	In Exchange For
Dec. 6, 1973	NY A	—	TEX A	Cash
May 9, 1977	TEX A	Steve Hargan $200,000.	TOR A	Roy Howell
Dec. 8, 1978	MON N	—	TEX A	Mike Hart

Mike Mason

Date	Traded To		Traded With	Traded By		In Exchange For
May 16, 1987	CHI	N	—	TEX	A	Dave Pavlas

(Texas received Pavlas on June 6, 1987.)

Roger Mason

Date	Traded To		Traded With	Traded By		In Exchange For
Apr. 5, 1985	SF	N	—	DET	A	Alejandro Sanchez
Dec. 2, 1992	NY	N	—	SD	N	No compensation (free agent signing)
Dec. 17, 1992	SD	N	Minor league P Mike Freitas	NY	N	Mike Maddux
July 3, 1993	PHI	N	—	SD	N	Tim Mauser

Walt Masterson

Date	Traded To		Traded With	Traded By		In Exchange For
June 13, 1949	BOS	A	—	WAS	A	Sam Mele Mickey Harris
June 10, 1952	WAS	A	Randy Gumpert	BOS	A	Sid Hudson

Tom Matchick

Date	Traded To		Traded With	Traded By		In Exchange For
Dec. 13, 1969	BOS	A	—	DET	A	Dalton Jones
May 28, 1970	KC	A	—	BOS	A	Mike Fiore
May 11, 1971	MIL	A	—	KC	A	Ted Savage
Apr. 5, 1973	NY	A	—	BAL	A	Frank Baker

Eddie Mathews

Date	Traded To		Traded With	Traded By		In Exchange For
Dec. 31, 1966	HOU	N	Sandy Alomar Arnie Umbach	ATL	N	Dave Nicholson Bob Bruce
Aug. 17, 1967	DET	A	—	HOU	N	Fred Gladding Cash

Nelson Mathews

Date	Traded To		Traded With	Traded By		In Exchange For
Dec. 15, 1963	KC	A	—	CHI	N	Fred Norman

Christy Mathewson

Date	Traded To		Traded With	Traded By		In Exchange For
Dec. 15, 1900	NY	N	—	CIN	N	Amos Rusie
July 20, 1916	CIN	N	Edd Roush Bill McKechnie	NY	N	Buck Herzog Red Killefer

John Matias

Date	Traded To		Traded With	Traded By		In Exchange For
Nov. 29, 1967	CHI	A	*see Luis Aparicio*	BAL	A	—
Oct. 13, 1970	KC	A	Gail Hopkins	CHI	A	Pat Kelly Don O'Riley

Jon Matlack

Date	Traded To		Traded With	Traded By		In Exchange For
Dec. 8, 1977	TEX	A	John Milner	NY	N	Willie Montanez Tom Grieve Ken Henderson

(Part of four-team trade involving Texas, New York Mets, Pittsburgh, and Atlanta.)

Gary Matthews

Date	Traded To		Traded With	Traded By		In Exchange For
Nov. 17, 1976	ATL	N	—	SF	N	No compensation (free agent signing)
Mar. 25, 1981	PHI	N	—	ATL	N	Bob Walk
Mar. 26, 1984	CHI	N	Porfi Altamirano Bob Dernier	PHI	N	Bill Campbell Mike Diaz
July 12, 1987	SEA	A	—	CHI	N	Minor league P David Hartnett

Wid Matthews

Date	Traded To		Traded With	Traded By		In Exchange For
Jan. 1924	WAS	A	—	PHI	A	Cash

Bobby Mattick

Date	Traded To		Traded With	Traded By		In Exchange For
Dec. 4, 1940	CIN	N	Jim Gleeson	CHI	N	Billy Myers

Len Matuszek

Date	Traded To		Traded With	Traded By		In Exchange For
Apr. 1, 1985	TOR	A	—	PHI	N	Dave Shipanoff Minor league OF Ken Kinnard
July 9, 1985	LA	N	—	TOR	A	Al Oliver

Gene Mauch

Date	Traded To		Traded With	Traded By		In Exchange For
May 3, 1947	PIT	N	Kirby Higbe Hank Behrman Cal McLish Dixie Howell	BKN	N	Al Gionfriddo $100,000.
Dec. 8, 1947	BKN	N	Preacher Roe Billy Cox	PIT	N	Dixie Walker Hal Gregg Vic Lombardi
June 17, 1948	CHI	N	—	BKN	N	Waiver price
Dec. 14, 1949	BOS	N	Cash	CHI	N	Bill Voiselle
Mar. 26, 1952	STL	N	—	NY	A	Waiver price

Al Maul

Date	Traded To		Traded With	Traded By		In Exchange For
Feb. 1900	PHI	N	—	BKN	N	Cash

Carmen Mauro

Date	Traded To		Traded With	Traded By		In Exchange For
May 26, 1953	WAS	A	—	BKN	N	Waiver price
June 30, 1953	PHI	A	—	WAS	A	Waiver price
Dec. 16, 1953	NY	A	*see Harry Byrd*	PHI	A	—

Tim Mauser

Date	Traded To		Traded With	Traded By		In Exchange For
July 3, 1993	SD	N	—	PHI	N	Roger Mason

Dal Maxvill

Date	Traded To		Traded With	Traded By		In Exchange For
Aug. 30, 1972	OAK	A	—	STL	N	Minor leaguers IF Joe Lindsey and C Gene Dusan
July 7, 1973	PIT	N	—	OAK	A	Cash

Charlie Maxwell

Date	Traded To		Traded With	Traded By		In Exchange For
Nov. 24, 1954	BAL	A	—	BOS	A	Cash
May 11, 1955	DET	A	—	BAL	A	Cash
June 25, 1962	CHI	A	—	DET	A	Bob Farley

Carlos May

Date	Traded To		Traded With	Traded By		In Exchange For
May 18, 1976	NY	A	—	CHI	A	Ken Brett Rich Coggins
Sept. 16, 1977	CAL	A	—	NY	A	Cash

Dave May

Date	Traded To		Traded With	Traded By		In Exchange For
June 15, 1970	MIL	A	—	BAL	A	Dick Baney Buzz Stephen
Nov. 2, 1974	ATL	N	minor league P Roger Alexander	MIL	A	Hank Aaron
Dec. 9, 1976	TEX	A	Ken Henderson Carl Morton Roger Moret Adrian Devine $250,000.	ATL	N	Jeff Burroughs
May 17, 1978	MIL	A	—	TEX	A	Cash
Sept. 13, 1978	PIT	N	—	MIL	A	Cash

Derrick May

Date	Traded To		Traded With	Traded By		In Exchange For
June 21, 1995	HOU	N	—	MIL	A	Player to be named

(Milwaukee received IF Tommy Nevers on July 21, 1995.)

Jakie May

Date	Traded To		Traded With	Traded By		In Exchange For
Oct. 14, 1930	CHI	N	—	CIN	N	Cash

Jerry May

Date	Traded To		Traded With	Traded By		In Exchange For
Dec. 2, 1970	KC	A	*see Freddie Patek*	PIT	N	—
May 14, 1973	NY	N	—	KC	A	Cash

Lee May

Date	Traded To		Traded With	Traded By		In Exchange For
Nov. 29, 1971	HOU	N	Tommy Helms Jimmy Stewart	CIN	N	Joe Morgan Cesar Geronimo Denis Menke Jack Billingham Ed Armbrister
Dec. 3, 1974	BAL	A	Jay Schlueter	HOU	N	Enos Cabell Rob Andrews
Dec. 9, 1980	KC	A	—	BAL	A	No compensation (free agent signing)

Milt May

Date	Traded To	Traded With	Traded By	In Exchange For
Oct. 31, 1973	HOU N	—	PIT N	Jerry Reuss
Dec. 6, 1975	DET A	Dave Roberts Jim Crawford	HOU N	Leon Roberts Terry Humphrey Gene Pentz Mark Lemongello
May 27, 1979	CHI A	—	DET A	Cash
Nov. 1, 1979	SF N	—	CHI A	No compensation (free agent signing)
Aug. 19, 1983	PIT N	Cash	SF N	Steve Nicosia

Rudy May

Date	Traded To	Traded With	Traded By	In Exchange For
Oct. 15, 1964	PHI N	—	CHI A	Bill Heath minor league P Joel Gibson
Dec. 3, 1964	LA A	Costen Shockley	PHI N	Bo Belinsky
June 15, 1974	NY A	—	CAL A	Cash
June 15, 1976	BAL A	Rick Dempsey Tippy Martinez Dave Pagan Scott McGregor	NY A	Ken Holtzman Doyle Alexander Grant Jackson Ellie Hendricks Jimmy Freeman
Dec. 7, 1977	MON N	Randy Miller Bryn Smith	BAL A	Don Stanhouse Joe Kerrigan Gary Roenicke
Nov. 8, 1979	NY A	—	MON N	No compensation (free agent signing)

Scott May

Date	Traded To	Traded With	Traded By	In Exchange For
Dec. 23, 1987	TEX A	—	LA N	Javier Ortiz
June 29, 1989	MIL A	Minor league OF Mike Wilson	TEX A	LaVel Freeman Minor league P Todd Simmons

John Mayberry

Date	Traded To	Traded With	Traded By	In Exchange For
Dec. 2, 1971	KC A	minor league IF Dave Grangaard	HOU N	Jim York Lance Clemons
Apr. 4, 1978	TOR A	—	KC A	Cash
May 5, 1982	NY A	—	TOR A	Dave Revering minor league 3B Jeff Reynolds

Lee Maye

Date	Traded To	Traded With	Traded By	In Exchange For
May 13, 1965	HOU N	—	MIL N	Ken Johnson Jim Beauchamp
Jan. 4, 1967	CLE A	Ken Retzer	HOU N	Jim Landis Doc Edwards Jim Weaver
June 20, 1969	WAS A	—	CLE A	Bill Denehy Cash
Sept. 10, 1970	CHI A	—	WAS A	Cash

Ed Mayer

Date	Traded To	Traded With	Traded By	In Exchange For
Apr. 20, 1957	CHI N	Bobby Del Greco	STL N	Jim King

Erskine Mayer

Date	Traded To	Traded With	Traded By	In Exchange For
July 1, 1918	PIT N	—	PHI N	Elmer Jacobs
Aug. 1919	CHI A	—	PIT N	Waiver price

Wally Mayer

Date	Traded To	Traded With	Traded By	In Exchange For
Feb. 28, 1919	STL A	—	BOS A	$5000

Brent Mayne

Date	Traded To	Traded With	Traded By	In Exchange For
Dec. 19, 1995	NY N	—	KC A	Minor league OF Al Shirley

Eddie Mayo

Date	Traded To	Traded With	Traded By	In Exchange For
Dec. 4, 1936	BOS N	—	NY N	Mickey Haslin

Carl Mays

Date	Traded To	Traded With	Traded By	In Exchange For
July 29, 1919	NY A	—	BOS A	Allan Russell Bob McGraw $40,000.
Dec. 11, 1923	CIN N	—	NY A	Cash

Willie Mays

Date	Traded To	Traded With	Traded By	In Exchange For
May 11, 1972	NY N	—	SF N	Charlie Williams $50,000.

Lee Mazzilli

Date	Traded To	Traded With	Traded By	In Exchange For
Apr. 1, 1982	TEX A	—	NY N	Ron Darling Walt Terrell
Aug. 8, 1982	NY A	—	TEX A	Bucky Dent
Dec. 22, 1982	PIT N	—	NY A	Tim Burke Minor league P John Holland Minor league 1B Jose Rivera Minor league OF Don Aubin
Aug. 2, 1989	TOR A	—	NY N	Waiver price

Bill McAfee

Date	Traded To	Traded With	Traded By	In Exchange For
Oct. 14, 1930	BOS N	Wes Schulmerich	CHI N	Bob Smith Jimmy Welsh
Dec. 1933	STL A	—	WAS A	Cash

Sport McAllister

Date	Traded To	Traded With	Traded By	In Exchange For
Sept. 1902	BAL A	—	DET A	Cash

(Baltimore returned McAllister to Detroit later in September.)

Jim McAnany

Date	Traded To	Traded With	Traded By	In Exchange For
Apr. 1, 1961	CHI N	—	LA A	Lou Johnson

Jim McAndrew

Date	Traded To	Traded With	Traded By	In Exchange For
Dec. 20, 1973	SD N	—	NY N	Steve Simpson

Ike McAuley

Date	Traded To	Traded With	Traded By	In Exchange For
May 24, 1917	STL N	—	PIT N	Waiver price

Dick McAuliffe

Date	Traded To	Traded With	Traded By	In Exchange For
Oct. 23, 1973	BOS A	—	DET A	Ben Oglivie

Al McBean

Date	Traded To	Traded With	Traded By	In Exchange For
Apr. 17, 1969	LA N	—	SD N	Tommy Dean Leon Everitt

Algie McBride

Date	Traded To	Traded With	Traded By	In Exchange For
May 30, 1901	NY N	—	CIN N	Cash

Bake McBride

Date	Traded To	Traded With	Traded By	In Exchange For
June 15, 1977	PHI N	Steve Waterbury	STL N	Tom Underwood Rick Bosetti Dane Iorg
Feb. 16, 1982	CLE A	—	PHI N	Sid Monge

George McBride

Date	Traded To	Traded With	Traded By	In Exchange For
July 4, 1905	STL N	—	PIT N	Dave Brain

Tom McBride

Date	Traded To	Traded With	Traded By	In Exchange For
May 14, 1947	WAS A	—	BOS A	Cash

Bill McCabe

Date	Traded To	Traded With	Traded By	In Exchange For
May 1920	BKN N	—	CHI N	Cash

Joe McCabe

Date	Traded To	Traded With	Traded By	In Exchange For
Oct. 15, 1964	WAS A	—	MIN A	Ken Retzer

Larry McCall

Date	Traded To	Traded With	Traded By	In Exchange For
Sept. 16, 1974	CAL A	—	BAL A	Cash
Nov. 10, 1978	TEX A	—	NY A	*see Dave Righetti*

Larry McCall *continued*

Date	Traded To		Traded With	Traded By		In Exchange For
Jan. 4, 1980	CLE	A	Gary Gray minor league 3B-OF Mike Bucci	TEX	A	David Clyde Jim Norris

Roger McCardell

Date	Traded To		Traded With	Traded By		In Exchange For
Nov. 30, 1959	BAL	A	Jackie Brandt Gordon Jones	SF	N	Billy O'Dell Billy Loes

Alex McCarthy

Date	Traded To		Traded With	Traded By		In Exchange For
Sept. 5, 1915	CHI	N	—	PIT	N	Cash
July 1916	PIT	N	—	CHI	N	Cash

Jack McCarthy

Date	Traded To		Traded With	Traded By		In Exchange For
Feb. 10, 1900	CHI	N	—	PIT	N	$2,000.
Dec. 30, 1905	BKN	N	Billy Maloney Buttons Briggs Doc Casey $2,000.	CHI	N	Jimmy Sheckard

Johnny McCarthy

Date	Traded To		Traded With	Traded By		In Exchange For
Jan. 1936	NY	N	—	BKN	N	$40,000.
Dec. 11, 1941	STL	N	Ken O'Dea Bill Lohrman $50,000.	NY	N	Johnny Mize

Tom McCarthy

Date	Traded To		Traded With	Traded By		In Exchange For
Jan. 1908	PIT	N	—	CIN	N	Cash
June 18, 1908	BOS	N	Harley Young	PIT	N	Irv Young

Tom McCarthy

Date	Traded To		Traded With	Traded By		In Exchange For
Nov. 13, 1985	NY	N	*see Bob Ojeda*	BOS	A	—
Aug. 4, 1988	CHI	A	Steve Springer	NY	N	Mike Maksudian Minor league OF Vince Harris

David McCarty

Date	Traded To		Traded With	Traded By		In Exchange For
June 8, 1995	CIN	N	—	MIN	N	John Courtright
June 8, 1995	CIN	N	—	MIN	A	John Courtright
July 21, 1995	SF	N	*see Deion Sanders*	CIN	N	—

Lew McCarty

Date	Traded To		Traded With	Traded By		In Exchange For
Aug. 20, 1916	NY	N	—	BKN	N	Fred Merkle
July 4, 1920	STL	N	—	NY	N	Cash

Tim McCarver

Date	Traded To		Traded With	Traded By		In Exchange For
Oct. 7, 1969	PHI	N	Curt Flood Joe Hoerner Byron Browne	STL	N	Dick Allen Cookie Rojas Jerry Johnson

(Flood refused to report to the Philadelphia Phillies, and the Cardinals sent Willie Montanez and Bob Browning on April 8, 1970 to complete the trade.)

Date	Traded To		Traded With	Traded By		In Exchange For
June 14, 1972	MON	N	—	PHI	N	John Bateman
Nov. 6, 1972	STL	N	—	MON	N	Jorge Roque
Sept. 1, 1974	BOS	A	—	STL	N	Cash

Kirk McCaskill

Date	Traded To		Traded With	Traded By		In Exchange For
Dec. 28, 1991	CHI	A	—	CAL	A	No compensation (free agent signing)

Joe McClain

Date	Traded To		Traded With	Traded By		In Exchange For
June 14, 1958	NY	A	$25,000.	STL	N	Sal Maglie

Lloyd McClendon

Date	Traded To		Traded With	Traded By		In Exchange For
Dec. 16, 1982	CIN	N	Charlie Puleo Minor league OF Jason Felice	NY	N	Tom Seaver
Dec. 9, 1988	CHI	N	—	CIN	N	Rolando Roomes
Sept. 7, 1990	PIT	N	—	CHI	N	Player to be named

(Chicago received P Mike Pomeranz on September 28, 1990.)

Bob McClure

Date	Traded To		Traded With	Traded By		In Exchange For
Dec. 6, 1976	MIL	A	Jim Wohlford Jamie Quirk	KC	A	Jim Colborn Darrell Porter
June 8, 1986	MON	N	—	MIL	A	Cash

Amby McConnell

Date	Traded To		Traded With	Traded By		In Exchange For
Aug. 9, 1910	CHI	A	Harry Lord	BOS	A	Frank Smith Billy Purtell

George McConnell

Date	Traded To		Traded With	Traded By		In Exchange For
Sept. 23, 1913	CHI	N	—	NY	A	Cash
Feb. 10, 1916	CHI	N	*see Three Finger Brown*	CHI	F	—

Billy McCool

Date	Traded To		Traded With	Traded By		In Exchange For
Apr. 2, 1970	STL	N	—	SD	N	Steve Huntz

Barry McCormick

Date	Traded To		Traded With	Traded By		In Exchange For
July 1903	WAS	A	—	STL	A	Joe Martin

Frank McCormick

Date	Traded To		Traded With	Traded By		In Exchange For
Dec. 10, 1945	PHI	N	—	CIN	N	$30,000.

Mike McCormick

Date	Traded To		Traded With	Traded By		In Exchange For
June 3, 1946	BOS	N	—	CIN	N	Cash
Dec. 15, 1948	BKN	N	—	BOS	N	Pete Reiser
Dec. 11, 1950	WAS	A	—	CHI	A	Bud Stewart

Mike McCormick

Date	Traded To		Traded With	Traded By		In Exchange For
Dec. 15, 1962	BAL	A	Stu Miller John Orsino	SF	N	Jack Fisher Jimmie Coker Billy Hoeft
Apr. 4, 1965	WAS	A	—	BAL	A	Minor league P Steve Herman $20,000.
Dec. 13, 1966	SF	N	—	WAS	A	Cap Peterson Bob Priddy
July 20, 1970	NY	A	—	SF	N	John Cumberland

Moose McCormick

Date	Traded To		Traded With	Traded By		In Exchange For
July 1903	NY	N	—	PHI	N	Cash
July 3, 1904	CIN	N	—	NY	N	Mike Donlin
Aug. 9, 1904	PIT	N	—	NY	N	Cash
Aug. 11, 1904	PIT	N	—	CIN	N	Jimmy Sebring
Dec. 20, 1904	PHI	N	Kitty Bransfield Otto Krueger	PIT	N	Del Howard
May 1908	NY	N	—	PHI	N	Cash

Barney McCosky

Date	Traded To		Traded With	Traded By		In Exchange For
May 18, 1946	PHI	A	—	DET	A	George Kell
May 4, 1951	CIN	N	—	PHI	A	Cash
July 21, 1951	CLE	A	—	CIN	N	Waiver price

Willie McCovey

Date	Traded To		Traded With	Traded By		In Exchange For
Oct. 25, 1973	SD	N	Bernie Williams	SF	N	Mike Caldwell
Aug. 30, 1976	OAK	A	—	SD	N	Cash
Jan. 6, 1977	SF	N	—	OAK	A	No compensation (free agent signing)

Benny McCoy

Date	Traded To		Traded With	Traded By		In Exchange For
Dec. 9, 1939	PHI	A	Slick Coffman	DET	A	Wally Moses

(Commissioner Landis ruled that Detroit had kept McCoy covered up in the minors and declared him a free agent, cancelling the deal. McCoy then signed with Philadelphia for a $10,000 bonus.)

Tom McCraw

Date	Traded To		Traded With	Traded By		In Exchange For
Mar. 29, 1971	WAS	A	—	CHI	A	Ed Stroud
Apr. 3, 1972	CLE	A	Roy Foster	TEX	A	Ted Ford
Apr. 2, 1973	CAL	A	minor league 2B Bob Marcano	CLE	A	Leo Cardenas
July 17, 1974	CLE	A	—	CAL	A	Cash

Tom McCreery

Date	Traded To		Traded With	Traded By		In Exchange For
May 1901	BKN	N	—	PIT	N	Lefty Davis
June 1903	BOS	N	—	BKN	N	Cash

Lance McCullers

Date	Traded To		Traded With	Traded By		In Exchange For
Aug. 31, 1983	SD	N	Ed Wojna Marty Decker Minor league P Darren Burroughs	PHI	N	Sixto Lezcano Steve Fireovid
Oct. 24, 1988	NY	A	Jimmy Jones Stan Jefferson	SD	N	Jack Clark Pat Clements
June 4, 1990	DET	A	Clay Parker	NY	A	Matt Nokes

Clyde McCullough

Date	Traded To		Traded With	Traded By		In Exchange For
Dec. 8, 1948	PIT	N	Cliff Chambers	CHI	N	Cal McLish Frankie Gustine
Dec. 3, 1952	CHI	N	—	PIT	N	Dick Manville $25,000.

Harry McCurdy

Date	Traded To		Traded With	Traded By		In Exchange For
Dec. 11, 1929	PHI	N	Grover Alexander	STL	N	Homer Peel Bob McGraw
Nov. 1933	CIN	N	—	PHI	N	Cash

Jeff McCurry

Date	Traded To		Traded With	Traded By		In Exchange For
Nov. 20, 1995	PIT	N	—	DET	A	Waiver price

Lindy McDaniel

Date	Traded To		Traded With	Traded By		In Exchange For
Oct. 17, 1962	CHI	N	Larry Jackson Jimmie Schaffer	STL	N	George Altman Don Cardwell Moe Thacker
Dec. 2, 1965	SF	N	Don Landrum Jim Rittwage	CHI	N	Randy Hundley Bill Hands
July 12, 1968	NY	A	—	SF	N	Bill Monbouquette
Dec. 7, 1973	KC	A	—	NY	A	Lou Piniella Ken Wright

Terry McDaniel

Date	Traded To		Traded With	Traded By		In Exchange For
Nov. 19, 1991	PIT	N	—	NY	N	Waiver price

Ray McDavid

Date	Traded To		Traded With	Traded By		In Exchange For
Dec. 21, 1995	MON	N	—	SD	A	Waiver price

Mickey McDermott

Date	Traded To		Traded With	Traded By		In Exchange For
Dec. 9, 1953	WAS	A	Tommy Umphlett	BOS	A	Jackie Jensen
Feb. 8, 1956	NY	A	Bobby Kline	WAS	A	Lou Berberet Whitey Herzog Bob Wiesler Herb Plews Dick Tettelbach
Feb. 19, 1957	KC	A	*see Billy Hunter*	NY	A	—
Nov. 20, 1957	DET	A	*see Billy Martin*	KC	A	—
July 21, 1961	KC	A	—	STL	N	Cash

Danny McDevitt

Date	Traded To		Traded With	Traded By		In Exchange For
Dec. 16, 1960	NY	A	—	LA	N	Cash
June 14, 1961	MIN	A	—	NY	A	Billy Gardner
Apr. 10, 1962	KC	A	—	MIN	A	Cash

Dave McDonald

Date	Traded To		Traded With	Traded By		In Exchange For
May 15, 1970	MON	N	—	NY	A	Gary Waslewski
Dec. 30, 1970	SF	N	—	MON	N	Ron Hunt

Hank McDonald

Date	Traded To		Traded With	Traded By		In Exchange For
May 28, 1933	STL	A	—	PHI	A	Cash

Jim McDonald

Date	Traded To		Traded With	Traded By		In Exchange For
May 17, 1951	STL	A	Matt Batts Jim Suchecki $100,000.	BOS	A	Les Moss
Nov. 23, 1951	NY	A	—	STL	A	Clint Courtney
Nov. 18, 1954	BAL	A	—	NY	A	*see Bob Turley*
July 30, 1955	NY	A	—	BAL	A	Ed Lopat

Tex McDonald

Date	Traded To		Traded With	Traded By		In Exchange For
June 1913	BOS	N	—	CIN	N	Cash
Aug. 1914	BUF	F	—	PIT	F	Frank Delahanty

Jack McDowell

Date	Traded To		Traded With	Traded By		In Exchange For
Dec. 14, 1994	NY	A	—	CHI	A	Lyle Mouton Minor league P Keith Heberling

(Chicago received Mouton on April 22, 1995.)

Date	Traded To		Traded With	Traded By		In Exchange For
Dec. 14, 1995	CLE	A	—	NY	A	No compensation (free agent signing)

Oddibe McDowell

Date	Traded To		Traded With	Traded By		In Exchange For
Dec. 6, 1988	CLE	A	Pete O'Brien Jerry Browne	TEX	A	Julio Franco
July 2, 1989	ATL	N	—	CLE	A	Dion James

Roger McDowell

Date	Traded To		Traded With	Traded By		In Exchange For
June 18, 1989	PHI	N	Len Dykstra Tom Edens	NY	N	Juan Samuel

(Philadelphia received Edens on July 26, 1989.)

Date	Traded To		Traded With	Traded By		In Exchange For
July 31, 1991	LA	N	—	PHI	N	Mike Hartley Braulio Castillo
Dec. 18, 1995	BAL	A	—	TEX	A	No compensation (free agent signing)

Sam McDowell

Date	Traded To		Traded With	Traded By		In Exchange For
Nov. 29, 1971	SF	N	—	CLE	A	Gaylord Perry Frank Duffy
June 7, 1973	NY	A	—	SF	N	Cash

Chuck McElroy

Date	Traded To		Traded With	Traded By		In Exchange For
Apr. 7, 1991	CHI	N	Bob Scanlan	PHI	N	Mitch Williams
Dec. 10, 1993	CIN	N	—	CHI	N	Larry Luebbers Mike Anderson Minor league C Darron Cox

Will McEnaney

Date	Traded To		Traded With	Traded By		In Exchange For
Dec. 16, 1976	MON	N	Tony Perez	CIN	N	Woodie Fryman Dale Murray
Mar. 29, 1978	PIT	N	—	MON	N	Tim Jones

Leon McFadden

Date	Traded To		Traded With	Traded By		In Exchange For
June 13, 1970	STL	N	Jim Beauchamp	HOU	N	George Culver

Chappie McFarland

Date	Traded To		Traded With	Traded By		In Exchange For
June 3, 1906	PIT	N	—	STL	N	Cash
Aug. 1, 1906	BKN	N	—	PIT	N	Waiver price

Herm McFarland

Date	Traded To		Traded With	Traded By		In Exchange For
May 5, 1902	BAL	A	John Katoll	CHI	A	Cash

Orlando McFarlane

Date	Traded To		Traded With	Traded By		In Exchange For
Apr. 10, 1967	CAL	A	—	DET	A	Cash

Andy McGaffigan

Date	Traded To		Traded With	Traded By		In Exchange For
Mar. 30, 1982	SF	N	Ted Wilborn	NY	A	Doyle Alexander
Feb. 27, 1984	MON	N	Fred Breining Max Venable	SF	N	Al Oliver

(San Francisco sent McGaffigan to Montreal on April 1, 1984, after Breining reported to the Expos with a sore arm.)

Date	Traded To		Traded With	Traded By		In Exchange For
July 26, 1984	CIN	N	minor league P Jim Jefferson	MON	N	Dan Driessen
Dec. 19, 1985	MON	N	—	CIN	N	*see Bill Gullickson*
Apr. 7, 1990	SF	N	—	MON	N	Player to be named

(Montreal received IF Steve Hecht on June 26, 1990)

Dan McGann

Date	Traded To		Traded With	Traded By		In Exchange For
Jan. 17, 1900	STL	N	Gus Weyhing	WAS	N	Cash

Dan McGann *continued*

Date	Traded To	Traded With	Traded By	In Exchange For
Dec. 3, 1907	BOS N	Frank Bowerman Bill Dahlen George Browne George Ferguson	NY N	Fred Tenney Al Bridwell Tom Needham

Bill McGee

Date	Traded To	Traded With	Traded By	In Exchange For
May 14, 1941	NY N	—	STL N	Harry Gumbert Paul Dean Cash

Willie McGee

Date	Traded To	Traded With	Traded By	In Exchange For
Oct. 21, 1981	STL N	—	NY A	Bob Sykes
Aug. 29, 1990	OAK A	—	STL N	Felix Jose Stan Royer Minor league P Daryl Green
Dec. 3, 1990	SF N	—	OAK A	No compensation (free agent signing)

Kevin McGehee

Date	Traded To	Traded With	Traded By	In Exchange For
Apr. 29, 1993	BAL A	—	SF N	Luis Mercedes

Ed McGhee

Date	Traded To	Traded With	Traded By	In Exchange For
Jan. 27, 1953	PHI A	Joe De Maestri Eddie Robinson	CHI A	Ferris Fain minor league 2B Bob Wilson
June 11, 1954	CHI A	Morrie Martin	PHI A	Sonny Dixon Al Sima Bill Wilson $20,000.

Randy McGilberry

Date	Traded To	Traded With	Traded By	In Exchange For
June 17, 1980	NY N	—	KC A	Kevin Kobel

Dan McGinn

Date	Traded To	Traded With	Traded By	In Exchange For
Apr. 7, 1972	CHI N	—	MON N	Hector Torres Hal Breeden

Russ McGinnis

Date	Traded To	Traded With	Traded By	In Exchange For
June 29, 1987	OAK A	—	MIL A	Bill Mooneyham

Joe McGinnity

Date	Traded To	Traded With	Traded By	In Exchange For
Jan. 1900	BKN N	Harry Howell Jimmy Sheckard Jerry Nops Broadway Aleck Smith Frank Kitson	BAL N	Cash

Lynn McGlothen

Date	Traded To	Traded With	Traded By	In Exchange For
Dec. 7, 1973	STL N	John Curtis Mike Garman	BOS A	Reggie Cleveland Diego Segui Terry Hughes
Dec. 10, 1976	SF N	—	STL N	Ken Reitz
June 15, 1978	CHI N	—	SF N	Hector Cruz
Aug. 15, 1981	CHI A	—	CHI N	Bob Molinaro

(Cubs received Molinaro on March 29, 1982.)

Jim McGlothlin

Date	Traded To	Traded With	Traded By	In Exchange For
Nov. 25, 1969	CIN N	Pedro Borbon Vern Geishert	CAL A	Alex Johnson Chico Ruiz
Aug. 29, 1973	CHI A	—	CIN N	Steve Kealey

Bob McGraw

Date	Traded To	Traded With	Traded By	In Exchange For
July 29, 1919	BOS A	Allan Russell $40,000.	NY A	Carl Mays
May 1927	STL N	—	BKN N	Jake Flowers
Dec. 1927	PHI N	—	STL N	Cash
Dec. 11, 1929	STL N	Homer Peel	PHI N	Grover Alexander Harry McCurdy

John McGraw

Date	Traded To	Traded With	Traded By	In Exchange For
Feb. 11, 1900	STL N	Bill Keister Wilbert Robinson	BAL N	Cash

Tug McGraw

Date	Traded To	Traded With	Traded By	In Exchange For
Dec. 3, 1974	PHI N	Don Hahn Dave Schneck	NY N	Del Unser John Stearns Mac Scarce

Scott McGregor

Date	Traded To	Traded With	Traded By	In Exchange For
June 15, 1976	BAL A	Rudy May Rick Dempsey Tippy Martinez Dave Pagan	NY A	Ken Holtzman Doyle Alexander Grant Jackson Ellie Hendricks Jimmy Freeman

Fred McGriff

Date	Traded To	Traded With	Traded By	In Exchange For
Dec. 9, 1982	TOR A	Dave Collins Mike Morgan $400,000	NY A	Dale Murray Tom Dodd
Dec. 5, 1990	SD N	Tony Fernandez	TOR A	Joe Carter Roberto Alomar
July 18, 1993	ATL N	—	SD N	Melvin Nieves Donnie Elliott Minor league OF Vince Moore

Terry McGriff

Date	Traded To	Traded With	Traded By	In Exchange For
Aug. 31, 1990	HOU N	Butch Henry Minor league P Keith Kaiser	CIN N	Bill Doran

(McGriff, Henry, and Kaiser were assigned to Houston on September 7, 1990.)

Deacon McGuire

Date	Traded To	Traded With	Traded By	In Exchange For
Jan. 1904	NY A	—	DET A	Cash
June 29, 1907	BOS A	—	NY A	Waiver price

(McGuire was named Boston manager.)

Date	Traded To	Traded With	Traded By	In Exchange For
Aug. 1908	CLE A	—	BOS A	Cash

Marty McHale

Date	Traded To	Traded With	Traded By	In Exchange For
May 1916	CLE A	—	BOS A	Cash

Vance McHenry

Date	Traded To	Traded With	Traded By	In Exchange For
Jan. 27, 1983	TEX A	—	SEA A	Bob Babcock

Stuffy McInnis

Date	Traded To	Traded With	Traded By	In Exchange For
Jan. 10, 1918	BOS A	—	PHI A	Larry Gardner Hick Cady Tilly Walker
Dec. 24, 1921	CLE A	—	BOS A	George Burns Joe Harris Elmer Smith
Jan. 1923	BOS N	—	CLE A	Waiver price

Joe McIntosh

Date	Traded To	Traded With	Traded By	In Exchange For
Dec. 11, 1975	HOU N	Larry Hardy	SD N	Doug Rader

Tim McIntosh

Date	Traded To	Traded With	Traded By	In Exchange For
Apr. 14, 1993	MON N	—	MIL A	Waiver price

Matty McIntyre

Date	Traded To	Traded With	Traded By	In Exchange For
Jan. 1911	CHI A	—	DET A	Cash

Archie McKain

Date	Traded To	Traded With	Traded By	In Exchange For
Dec. 15, 1938	DET A	Pinky Higgins	BOS A	Eldon Auker Jake Wade Chet Morgan
Aug. 4, 1941	STL A	—	DET A	Cash
July 15, 1943	BKN N	Fritz Ostermueller	STL A	Bobo Newsom

Bill McKechnie

Date	Traded To	Traded With	Traded By	In Exchange For
Dec. 1912	BOS N	—	PIT N	Cash
Apr. 15, 1913	NY A	—	BOS N	Waiver price
Dec. 23, 1915	NY N	Bill Rariden	NWK F	Cash
July 20, 1916	CIN N	Christy Mathewson Edd Roush	NY N	Buck Herzog Red Killefer

Bill McKechnie *continued*

Date	Traded To	Traded With	Traded By	In Exchange For
Mar. 1918	PIT N	—	CIN N	$20,000.

Rich McKinney

Date	Traded To	Traded With	Traded By	In Exchange For
Dec. 2, 1971	NY A	—	CHI A	Stan Bahnsen
Nov. 24, 1972	OAK A	Rob Gardner	NY A	Matty Alou

Jim McKnight

Date	Traded To	Traded With	Traded By	In Exchange For
June 15, 1960	CHI N	—	STL N	Walt Moryn
Dec. 3, 1962	MIL N	—	CHI N	Ken Aspromonte

Denny McLain

Date	Traded To	Traded With	Traded By	In Exchange For
Oct. 9, 1970	WAS A	Don Wert Norm McRae Elliott Maddox	DET A	Joe Coleman Ed Brinkman Aurelio Rodriguez Jim Hannan
Mar. 4, 1972	OAK A	—	TEX A	Don Stanhouse Jim Panther
June 29, 1972	ATL N	—	OAK A	Orlando Cepeda

Bo McLaughlin

Date	Traded To	Traded With	Traded By	In Exchange For
May 25, 1979	ATL N	—	HOU N	Frank LaCorte

Byron McLaughlin

Date	Traded To	Traded With	Traded By	In Exchange For
Dec. 12, 1980	MIN A	—	SEA A	Willie Norwood

Joey McLaughlin

Date	Traded To	Traded With	Traded By	In Exchange For
Dec. 5, 1979	TOR A	Barry Bonnell Pat Rockett	ATL N	Chris Chambliss Luis Gomez

Warren McLaughlin

Date	Traded To	Traded With	Traded By	In Exchange For
Mar. 1903	PHI N	—	PIT N	Waiver price

Larry McLean

Date	Traded To	Traded With	Traded By	In Exchange For
Dec. 12, 1903	STL N	Jack Taylor	CHI N	Three Finger Brown Jack O'Neill
Aug. 6, 1913	NY N	—	STL N	Doc Crandall

Mark McLemore

Date	Traded To	Traded With	Traded By	In Exchange For
Sept. 6, 1989	CLE A	—	CAL A	Ron Tingley
	(Cleveland received McLemore on August 17, 1990.)			
Dec. 13, 1994	TEX A	—	BAL A	No compensation (free agent signing)

Cal McLish

Date	Traded To	Traded With	Traded By	In Exchange For
May 3, 1947	PIT N	Kirby Higbe Hank Behrman Gene Mauch Dixie Howell	BKN N	Al Gionfriddo $100,000.
Dec. 8, 1948	CHI N	Frankie Gustine	PIT N	Clyde McCullough Cliff Chambers
Dec. 15, 1959	CIN N	Gordy Coleman Billy Martin	CLE A	Johnny Temple
Dec. 15, 1960	CHI A	Juan Pizarro	CIN N	Gene Freese
Dec. 15, 1961	PHI N	Frank Barnes Andy Carey	CHI A	Bob Sadowski Taylor Phillips minor league IF Lou Vassie

(Carey refused to report, and the Phillies received McLish in exchange for Vassie to complete the trade on March 24, 1962.)

Jack McMahan

Date	Traded To	Traded With	Traded By	In Exchange For
June 23, 1956	KC A	—	PIT N	Spook Jacobs
Feb. 19, 1957	NY A	—	KC A	*see Billy Hunter*

Don McMahon

Date	Traded To	Traded With	Traded By	In Exchange For
May 9, 1962	HOU N	—	MIL N	Cash
Sept. 30, 1963	CLE A	—	HOU N	Cash
June 2, 1966	BOS A	Lee Stange	CLE A	Dick Radatz
June 3, 1967	CHI A	minor league P Bob Snow	BOS A	Jerry Adair
July 21, 1968	DET A	—	CHI A	Dennis Ribant

Don McMahon *continued*

Date	Traded To	Traded With	Traded By	In Exchange For
Aug. 9, 1969	SF N	—	DET A	Cash

Frank McManus

Date	Traded To	Traded With	Traded By	In Exchange For
July 25, 1904	NY A	—	DET A	Monte Beville

Jim McManus

Date	Traded To	Traded With	Traded By	In Exchange For
Nov. 20, 1957	KC A	—	DET A	*see Billy Martin*

Marty McManus

Date	Traded To	Traded With	Traded By	In Exchange For
Jan. 15, 1927	DET A	Pinky Hargrave Bobby LaMotte	STL A	Lefty Stewart Frank O'Rourke Billy Mullen Otto Miller
Aug. 31, 1931	BOS A	—	DET A	Muddy Ruel

Norm McMillan

Date	Traded To	Traded With	Traded By	In Exchange For
Jan. 30, 1923	BOS A	Camp Skinner George Murray $50,000.	NY A	Herb Pennock
Dec. 1923	STL A	—	BOS A	Homer Ezzell

Roy McMillan

Date	Traded To	Traded With	Traded By	In Exchange For
Dec. 15, 1960	MIL N	—	CIN N	Joey Jay Juan Pizarro
May 8, 1964	NY N	—	MIL N	Jay Hook Adrian Garrett

Tommy McMillan

Date	Traded To	Traded With	Traded By	In Exchange For
May 1910	CIN N	—	BKN N	Cash

Tommy McMillan

Date	Traded To	Traded With	Traded By	In Exchange For
Dec. 5, 1978	PIT N	—	SEA A	*see Mario Mendoza*

Ken McMullen

Date	Traded To	Traded With	Traded By	In Exchange For
Dec. 4, 1964	WAS A	Frank Howard Phil Ortega Pete Richert Dick Nen	LA N	Claude Osteen John Kennedy $100,000.
Apr. 27, 1970	CAL A	—	WAS A	Aurelio Rodriguez Rick Reichardt
Nov. 28, 1972	LA N	Andy Messersmith	CAL A	Frank Robinson Bill Singer Mike Strahler Billy Grabarkewitz Bobby Valentine
Feb. 25, 1977	MIL A	—	OAK A	Cash

Craig McMurtry

Date	Traded To	Traded With	Traded By	In Exchange For
Feb. 2, 1987	TOR A	—	ATL N	Damaso Garcia Luis Leal

Eric McNair

Date	Traded To	Traded With	Traded By	In Exchange For
Jan. 4, 1936	BOS A	Doc Cramer	PHI A	Hank Johnson Al Niemiec $75,000.
Dec. 21, 1938	CHI A	—	BOS A	Boze Berger
Dec. 18, 1940	DET A	—	CHI A	Waiver price
July 17, 1942	WAS A	—	DET A	Jack Wilson
	(McNair refused to report.)			
July 25, 1942	PHI A	—	DET A	Cash

Dave McNally

Date	Traded To	Traded With	Traded By	In Exchange For
Dec. 4, 1974	MON N	Rich Coggins minor league P Bill Kirkpatrick	BAL A	Ken Singleton Mike Torrez

Mike McNally

Date	Traded To	Traded With	Traded By	In Exchange For
Dec. 15, 1920	NY A	*see Waite Hoyt*	BOS A	—
Dec. 10, 1924	BOS A	—	NY A	Howard Shanks
Dec. 11, 1924	WAS A	—	BOS A	Doc Prothro

Date	Traded To		Traded With	Traded By		In Exchange For
Mike McNally *continued*						
Feb. 1925	WAS	A	—	NY	A	Cash
Tim McNamara						
Apr. 17, 1925	NY	N	—	BOS	N	Rosy Ryan
Rusty McNealy						
Dec. 9, 1981	OAK	A	minor league P Tim Hallgren	SEA	A	Roy Thomas
Dec. 7, 1983	MON	N	Cash	OAK	A	Ray Burris
Earl McNeely						
Oct. 19, 1927	STL	A	Dick Coffman	WAS	A	Milt Gaston
Jeff McNeely						
Dec. 7, 1994	STL	N	Nate Minchey	BOS	A	Luis Alicea
Jerry McNertney						
Oct. 20, 1970	STL	N	George Lauzerique minor league P Jesse Higgins	MIL	A	Carl Taylor Jim Ellis
May 4, 1973	PIT	N	—	OAK	A	Cash
Bill McNulty						
Aug. 31, 1971	CHI	N	Frank Fernandez	OAK	A	Adrian Garrett
Oct. 30, 1972	TEX	A	Brant Alyea	OAK	A	Paul Lindblad
Mar. 28, 1973	NY	N	—	TEX	A	Bill Sudakis
George McQuillan						
Feb. 1911	CIN	N	Johnny Bates Eddie Grant Lew Moren	PHI	N	Fred Beebe Jack Rowan Dode Paskert Hans Lobert
Feb. 14, 1915	PHI	N	—	PIT	N	Waiver price
Hugh McQuillan						
July 30, 1922	NY	N	—	BOS	N	Fred Toney Larry Benton $100,000.
(Toney refused to report and remained Giants' property.)						
June 12, 1927	BOS	N	Kent Greenfield Doc Farrell	NY	N	Zack Taylor Larry Benton Herb Thomas
George McQuinn						
Oct. 16, 1945	PHI	A	—	STL	A	Dick Siebert
Brian McRae						
Apr. 5, 1995	CHI	N	—	KC	A	Minor league Ps Derek Wallace and Geno Morones
Hal McRae						
Nov. 30, 1972	KC	A	Wayne Simpson	CIN	N	Roger Nelson Richie Scheinblum
Norm McRae						
Oct. 9, 1970	WAS	A	*see Denny McLain*	DET	A	—
May 30, 1972	DET	A	—	TEX	A	Dalton Jones
Nov. 30, 1972	PIT	N	Jim Foor	DET	A	Dick Sharon
Kevin McReynolds						
Dec. 11, 1986	NY	N	Gene Walter Minor league IF Adam Ging	SD	N	Kevin Mitchell Stan Jefferson Shawn Abner Minor league Ps Kevin Armstrong and Kevin Brown
Dec. 11, 1991	KC	A	Gregg Jefferies Keith Miller	NY	N	Bret Saberhagen Bill Pecota
Jan. 5, 1994	NY	N	—	KC	A	Vince Coleman

Date	Traded To		Traded With	Traded By		In Exchange For
Doug McWeeny						
Feb. 1930	CIN	N	—	BKN	N	Dolf Luque
Larry McWilliams						
June 30, 1982	PIT	N	—	ATL	N	Pascual Perez minor league SS Carlos Rios
Sept. 2, 1989	KC	A	—	PHI	N	Player to be named later
(Philadelphia received C Jeff Hulse on Oct. 20, 1989.)						
Bobby Meacham						
Dec. 14, 1982	NY	A	Stan Javier	STL	N	Minor league P Marty Mason Minor league P Steve Fincher Minor league OF Bob Helson
Dec. 5, 1988	TEX	A	—	NY	A	Bob Brower
Rusty Meacham						
Oct. 23, 1991	KC	A	—	DET	A	Waiver price
Lee Meadows						
July 14, 1919	PHI	N	Gene Paulette	STL	N	Elmer Jacobs Doug Baird Frank Woodward
May 22, 1923	PIT	N	Johnny Rawlings	PHI	N	Whitey Glazner Cotton Tierney $50,000.
Jim Mecir						
Dec. 6, 1995	NY	A	*see Tino Martinez*	SEA	A	—
Doc Medich						
Dec. 11, 1975	PIT	N	—	NY	A	Willie Randolph Ken Brett Dock Ellis
Mar. 15, 1977	OAK	A	Dave Giusti Tony Armas Doug Bair Rick Langford Mitchell Page	PIT	N	Phil Garner Tommy Helms Chris Batton
Sept. 13, 1977	SEA	A	—	OAK	A	Cash
Sept. 26, 1977	NY	N	—	SEA	A	Cash
Nov. 11, 1977	TEX	A	—	NY	N	No compensation (free agent signing)
Aug. 11, 1982	MIL	A	—	TEX	A	Cash
Scott Medvin						
Oct. 7, 1985	SF	N	—	DET	A	*see Dave LaPoint*
Aug. 12, 1987	PIT	N	Jeff Robinson	SF	N	Rick Reuschel
Joe Medwick						
June 12, 1940	BKN	N	Curt Davis	STL	N	Ernie Koy Carl Doyle Sam Nahem Bert Haas $125,000.
July 6, 1943	NY	N	—	BKN	N	Cash
June 16, 1945	BOS	N	Ewald Pyle	NY	N	Clyde Kluttz
Jouett Meekin						
Jan. 1900	PIT	N	—	BOS	N	Cash
Dave Meier						
Mar. 17, 1988	CHI	N	Greg Tabor	TEX	A	Ray Hayward
Roman Mejias						
Nov. 26, 1962	BOS	A	—	HOU	N	Pete Runnels
Sam Mejias						
June 7, 1976	STL	N	—	MIL	A	Danny Frisella

Sam Mejias *continued*

Date	Traded To	Traded With	Traded By	In Exchange For
Nov. 6, 1976	MON N	Bill Greif Angel Torres	STL N	Steve Dunning Pat Scanlon Tony Scott
Dec. 14, 1978	CHI N	—	MON N	Rodney Scott Jerry White
July 4, 1979	CIN N	—	CHI N	Cash

Sam Mele

Date	Traded To	Traded With	Traded By	In Exchange For
June 13, 1949	WAS A	Mickey Harris	BOS A	Walt Masterson
May 3, 1952	CHI A	—	WAS A	Jim Busby Mel Hoderlein
Feb. 5, 1954	BAL A	Neil Berry	CHI A	Johnny Groth Johnny Lipon
July 29, 1954	BOS A	—	BAL A	Waiver price
June 23, 1955	CIN N	—	BOS A	Cash

Francisco Melendez

Date	Traded To	Traded With	Traded By	In Exchange For
Mar. 22, 1987	SF N	—	PHI N	Cash
Mar. 24, 1989	BAL A	—	SF N	Ken Gerhart

Jose Melendez

Date	Traded To	Traded With	Traded By	In Exchange For
Mar. 26, 1991	SD N	—	SEA A	Waiver price
Dec. 9, 1992	BOS A	—	SD N	Phil Plantier

Luis Melendez

Date	Traded To	Traded With	Traded By	In Exchange For
May 19, 1976	SD N	—	STL N	Bill Greif

Oscar Melillo

Date	Traded To	Traded With	Traded By	In Exchange For
May 21, 1935	BOS A	—	STL A	Moose Solters Cash

Paul Meloan

Date	Traded To	Traded With	Traded By	In Exchange For
Apr. 1911	STL A	—	CHI A	Cash

Bill Melton

Date	Traded To	Traded With	Traded By	In Exchange For
Dec. 11, 1975	CAL A	Steve Dunning	CHI A	Jim Spencer Morris Nettles
Dec. 3, 1976	CLE A	—	CAL A	Stan Perzanowski Cash

Rube Melton

Date	Traded To	Traded With	Traded By	In Exchange For
Dec. 12, 1942	BKN N	—	PHI N	Johnny Allen $30,000.

Bob Melvin

Date	Traded To	Traded With	Traded By	In Exchange For
Oct. 7, 1985	SF N	Juan Berenguer Scott Medvin	DET A	Dave LaPoint Matt Nokes Eric King
		(San Francisco received Medvin on Dec. 11, 1985.)		
Jan. 24, 1989	BAL A	—	SF N	Terry Kennedy
Dec. 11, 1991	KC A	—	BAL A	Storm Davis
Dec. 14, 1992	BOS A	—	KC A	No compensation (free agent signing)
July 22, 1994	CAL A	—	NY A	Waiver price
July 22, 1994	CHI A	—	CAL A	Jeff Schwarz

Mario Mendoza

Date	Traded To	Traded With	Traded By	In Exchange For
Dec. 5, 1978	SEA A	Odell Jones Rafael Vasquez	PIT N	Enrique Romo Rick Jones Tommy McMillan
Dec. 12, 1980	TEX A	*see Rick Honeycutt*	SEA A	—

Paul Menhart

Date	Traded To	Traded With	Traded By	In Exchange For
Dec. 18, 1995	SEA A	Edwin Hurtado	TOR A	Bill Risley Minor league 2B Miguel Cairo

Denis Menke

Date	Traded To	Traded With	Traded By	In Exchange For
Oct. 8, 1967	HOU N	Denny Lemaster	ATL N	Sonny Jackson Chuck Harrison
Nov. 29, 1971	CIN N	*see Joe Morgan*	HOU N	—

Denis Menke *continued*

Date	Traded To	Traded With	Traded By	In Exchange For
Feb. 18, 1974	HOU N	—	CIN N	Pat Darcy Cash

Mike Menosky

Date	Traded To	Traded With	Traded By	In Exchange For
Feb. 10, 1916	WAS A	—	PIT F	Cash
Jan. 20, 1920	BOS A	Eddie Foster Harry Harper	WAS A	Braggo Roth Red Shannon

Mike Meola

Date	Traded To	Traded With	Traded By	In Exchange For
July 1936	BOS A	—	STL A	Cash

Rudi Meoli

Date	Traded To	Traded With	Traded By	In Exchange For
Sept. 17, 1975	SD N	Bobby Valentine	CAL A	Gary Ross
Apr. 5, 1976	CIN N	Cash	SD N	Merv Rettenmund

Orlando Mercado

Date	Traded To	Traded With	Traded By	In Exchange For
Apr. 4, 1985	TEX A	—	SEA A	Donnie Scott
Mar. 24, 1987	DET A	—	TEX A	Player to be named
		(Texas received OF Ruben Guzman on May 8, 1987.)		
May 5, 1987	DET A	—	LA N	Balvino Galvez
Aug. 30, 1990	MON N	—	NY N	Waiver price

Luis Mercedes

Date	Traded To	Traded With	Traded By	In Exchange For
Apr. 29, 1993	SF N	—	BAL A	Kevin McGehee

Win Mercer

Date	Traded To	Traded With	Traded By	In Exchange For
Feb. 9, 1900	NY N	—	WAS N	Cash

Kent Mercker

Date	Traded To	Traded With	Traded By	In Exchange For
Dec. 17, 1995	BAL A	—	ATL N	Joe Borowski Minor league P Rachaad Stewart

Spike Merena

Date	Traded To	Traded With	Traded By	In Exchange For
Sept. 24, 1934	DET A	—	BOS A	Cash

Ron Meridith

Date	Traded To	Traded With	Traded By	In Exchange For
Feb. 14, 1984	ATL N	—	HOU N	Jose Alvarez
Apr. 9, 1984	CHI N	—	ATL N	Terry Leach
July 26, 1986	TEX A	—	CHI N	Rich Surhoff Minor league P Bryan Dial

Fred Merkle

Date	Traded To	Traded With	Traded By	In Exchange For
Aug. 20, 1916	BKN N	—	NY N	Lew McCarty
Aug. 16, 1917	CHI N	—	BKN N	$3,500.

Brett Merriman

Date	Traded To	Traded With	Traded By	In Exchange For
Mar. 26, 1993	MIN A	—	CLR N	Gary Wayne Minor league P Rob Wassenaar

Lloyd Merriman

Date	Traded To	Traded With	Traded By	In Exchange For
Feb. 10, 1955	CHI A	—	CIN N	Cash
Apr. 16, 1955	CHI N	—	CHI A	Cash

Jim Merritt

Date	Traded To	Traded With	Traded By	In Exchange For
Nov. 21, 1968	CIN N	—	MIN A	Leo Cardenas
Dec. 1, 1972	TEX A	—	CIN N	Hal King Minor leaguer Jim Driscoll

Lloyd Merritt

Date	Traded To	Traded With	Traded By	In Exchange For
June 15, 1959	LA N	Chuck Essegian	STL N	Dick Gray

Sam Mertes

Date	Traded To	Traded With	Traded By	In Exchange For
July 13, 1906	STL N	Doc Marshall	NY N	Spike Shannon

Matt Merullo

Date	Traded To	Traded With	Traded By	In Exchange For
Mar. 30, 1994	CLE N	—	CHI A	Minor league OF Ken Ramos

Jose Mesa

Date	Traded To	Traded With	Traded By	In Exchange For
Aug. 31, 1987	BAL A	Oswald Peraza	TOR A	Mike Flanagan

(Baltimore received Mesa on September 4, 1987.)

Date	Traded To	Traded With	Traded By	In Exchange For
July 14, 1992	CLE A	—	BAL A	Minor league OF Kyle Washington

Steve Mesner

Date	Traded To	Traded With	Traded By	In Exchange For
Dec. 27, 1939	STL N	Gene Lillard Cash	CHI N	Ken Raffensberger
Feb. 1, 1943	BKN N	—	CIN N	Waiver price

(Landis voided the sale because Mesner had already been drafted at the time of the deal.)

Andy Messersmith

Date	Traded To	Traded With	Traded By	In Exchange For
Nov. 28, 1972	LA N	Ken McMullen	CAL A	Frank Robinson Bill Singer Mike Strahler Billy Grabarkewitz Bobby Valentine
Apr. 10, 1976	ATL N	—	LA N	No compensation (free agent signing)
Dec. 7, 1977	NY A	—	ATL N	Cash

Catfish Metkovich

Date	Traded To	Traded With	Traded By	In Exchange For
Apr. 2, 1947	CLE A	—	BOS A	Cash
Dec. 9, 1947	STL A	$50,000.	CLE A	Johnny Berardino

(Metkovich was returned to Cleveland because of a broken finger and the St. Louis Browns received another $15,000 to complete the trade.)

Date	Traded To	Traded With	Traded By	In Exchange For
June 4, 1953	CHI N	Joe Garagiola Ralph Kiner Howie Pollet	PIT N	Toby Atwell Bob Schultz Preston Ward George Freese Bob Addis Gene Hermanski $150,000.
Dec. 7, 1953	MIL N	—	CHI N	Cash

Charlie Metro

Date	Traded To	Traded With	Traded By	In Exchange For
Aug. 13, 1944	PHI A	—	DET A	Cash

Butch Metzger

Date	Traded To	Traded With	Traded By	In Exchange For
Dec. 6, 1974	SD N	Tito Fuentes	SF N	Derrel Thomas
May 17, 1977	STL N	—	SD N	John D'Acquisto Pat Scanlon
Apr. 5, 1978	NY N	—	STL N	Cash
July 4, 1978	PHI N	—	NY N	Cash

Roger Metzger

Date	Traded To	Traded With	Traded By	In Exchange For
Oct. 12, 1970	HOU N	—	CHI N	Hector Torres
June 15, 1978	SF N	—	HOU N	Cash

Alex Metzler

Date	Traded To	Traded With	Traded By	In Exchange For
July 21, 1930	STL A	—	CHI A	Cash

Bob Meusel

Date	Traded To	Traded With	Traded By	In Exchange For
Oct. 16, 1929	CIN N	—	NY A	Waiver price

Irish Meusel

Date	Traded To	Traded With	Traded By	In Exchange For
July 25, 1921	NY N	—	PHI N	Curt Walker Butch Henline Jesse Winters $30,000.

Benny Meyer

Date	Traded To	Traded With	Traded By	In Exchange For
May 1914	BUF F	—	PIT F	Cash

Bob Meyer

Date	Traded To	Traded With	Traded By	In Exchange For
June 12, 1964	LA A	—	NY A	Cash
July 29, 1964	KC A	—	LA A	Cash
Aug. 29, 1969	SEA A	Pete Koegel	OAK A	Fred Talbot

Dan Meyer

Date	Traded To	Traded With	Traded By	In Exchange For
Dec. 9, 1981	OAK A	—	SEA A	Rich Bordi

Dutch Meyer

Date	Traded To	Traded With	Traded By	In Exchange For
Apr. 27, 1945	CLE A	Don Ross	DET A	Roy Cullenbine

Joey Meyer

Date	Traded To	Traded With	Traded By	In Exchange For
Apr. 5, 1991	PIT N	—	MIN A	Minor league OF Greg Sims

Russ Meyer

Date	Traded To	Traded With	Traded By	In Exchange For
Oct. 11, 1948	PHI N	—	CHI N	Cash
Feb. 16, 1953	MIL N	Cash	PHI N	Earl Torgeson

(Part of four-team trade involving Milwaukee Braves, Philadelphia Phillies, Brooklyn, and Cincinnati.)

Date	Traded To	Traded With	Traded By	In Exchange For
Feb. 16, 1953	BKN N	—	MIL N	Rocky Bridges Jim Pendleton

(Part of four-team trade involving Milwaukee, Philadelphia Phillies, Brooklyn, and Cincinnati.)

Date	Traded To	Traded With	Traded By	In Exchange For
Dec. 9, 1955	CHI N	Don Hoak Walt Moryn	BKN N	Randy Jackson Don Elston
Sept. 1, 1956	CIN N	—	CHI N	Waiver price
Apr. 13, 1957	BOS A	—	CIN N	Waiver price

Scott Meyer

Date	Traded To	Traded With	Traded By	In Exchange For
Mar. 1, 1982	DET A	Jeff Cox	OAK A	Darrell Brown minor league Ps Mark Fellows Jack Smith

Chief Meyers

Date	Traded To	Traded With	Traded By	In Exchange For
Feb. 10, 1916	BKN N	—	NY N	Waiver price
Aug. 16, 1917	BOS N	—	BKN N	Waiver price

Dan Miceli

Date	Traded To	Traded With	Traded By	In Exchange For
July 31, 1993	PIT N	Jon Lieber	KC A	Stan Belinda

Gene Michael

Date	Traded To	Traded With	Traded By	In Exchange For
Dec. 1, 1966	LA N	Bob Bailey	PIT N	Maury Wills
Nov. 30, 1967	NY A	—	LA N	Cash

Cass Michaels

Date	Traded To	Traded With	Traded By	In Exchange For
May 31, 1950	WAS A	Bob Kuzava John Ostrowski	CHI A	Al Kozar Ray Scarborough Eddie Robinson
May 12, 1952	STL A	—	WAS A	Lou Sleater Freddie Marsh
Aug. 5, 1952	PHI A	—	STL A	Waiver price
Dec. 8, 1953	CHI A	—	PHI A	Cash

Ed Mickelson

Date	Traded To	Traded With	Traded By	In Exchange For
Oct. 1, 1952	STL A	—	STL N	Waiver price

Matt Mieske

Date	Traded To	Traded With	Traded By	In Exchange For
Mar. 27, 1992	MIL A	—	SD N	*see Gary Sheffield*

Pete Mikkelsen

Date	Traded To	Traded With	Traded By	In Exchange For
Dec. 10, 1965	PIT N	Cash	NY A	Bob Friend
Aug. 4, 1967	CHI N	—	PIT N	Waiver price
Apr. 22, 1968	STL N	Dave Dowling	CHI N	Jack Lamabe Ron Piche
Oct. 21, 1968	LA N	—	STL N	Cash

Eddie Miksis

Date	Traded To	Traded With	Traded By	In Exchange For
June 15, 1951	CHI N	Bruce Edwards Joe Hatten Gene Hermanski	BKN N	Johnny Schmitz Rube Walker Andy Pafko Wayne Terwilliger
Dec. 11, 1956	STL N	Hobie Landrith Sam Jones Jim Davis	CHI N	Tom Poholsky Jackie Collum Ray Katt minor league P Wally Lammers

Eddie Miksis *continued*

Date	Traded To		Traded With	Traded By		In Exchange For
Sept. 19, 1957	BAL	A	—	STL	N	Waiver price

Bob Milacki

Date	Traded To		Traded With	Traded By		In Exchange For
July 7, 1995	SEA	A	—	KC	A	Dave Fleming

Larry Milbourne

Date	Traded To		Traded With	Traded By		In Exchange For
Mar. 30, 1977	SEA	A	—	HOU	N	Roy Thomas
Nov. 18, 1980	NY	A	—	SEA	A	Brad Gulden $150,000.
May 12, 1982	MIN	A	John Pacella Pete Filson Cash	NY	A	Butch Wynegar Roger Erickson
July 3, 1982	CLE	A	—	MIN	A	Larry Littleton
Dec. 9, 1982	PHI	N	—	CLE	A	Cash
July 16, 1983	NY	A	—	PHI	N	Cash
Feb. 14, 1984	SEA	A	—	NY	A	Scott Nielsen Minor league P Eric Parent

Johnny Miljus

Date	Traded To		Traded With	Traded By		In Exchange For
July 10, 1928	CLE	A	—	PIT	N	Waiver price

Felix Millan

Date	Traded To		Traded With	Traded By		In Exchange For
Nov. 2, 1972	NY	N	George Stone	ATL	N	Gary Gentry Danny Frisella

Bill Miller

Date	Traded To		Traded With	Traded By		In Exchange For
Dec. 1, 1954	BAL	A	—	NY	A	*see Dick Kryhoski*

Bing Miller

Date	Traded To		Traded With	Traded By		In Exchange For
Jan. 10, 1922	PHI	A	Jose Acosta	WAS	A	Joe Dugan
(Part of three-team trade involving Boston, Philadelphia, and Washington.)						
June 15, 1926	STL	A	—	PHI	A	Baby Doll Jacobson
Dec. 13, 1927	PHI	A	—	STL	A	Sam Gray
Jan. 14, 1935	BOS	A	—	PHI	A	Cash

Bob Miller

Date	Traded To		Traded With	Traded By		In Exchange For
Nov. 30, 1962	LA	N	—	NY	N	Tim Harkness Larry Burright
Nov. 28, 1967	MIN	A	Johnny Roseboro Ron Perranoski	LA	N	Mudcat Grant Zoilo Versalles
Dec. 10, 1969	CLE	A	Dean Chance Graig Nettles Ted Uhlaender	MIN	A	Luis Tiant Stan Williams
June 15, 1970	CHI	A	Barry Moore	CLE	A	Buddy Bradford
Sept. 1, 1970	CHI	N	—	CHI	A	Cash
Aug. 10, 1971	PIT	N	—	SD	N	John Jeter Ed Acosta
June 22, 1973	SD	N	—	DET	A	Cash
Sept. 23, 1973	NY	N	—	SD	N	Cash

Bob Miller

Date	Traded To		Traded With	Traded By		In Exchange For
May 7, 1962	NY	N	Cliff Cook	CIN	N	Don Zimmer

Bruce Miller

Date	Traded To		Traded With	Traded By		In Exchange For
Aug. 17, 1972	CAL	A	Bruce Kimm	CHI	A	Eddie Fisher
Apr. 14, 1973	SF	N	—	CAL	A	Alan Gallagher

Doc Miller

Date	Traded To		Traded With	Traded By		In Exchange For
Apr. 1910	BOS	N	—	CHI	N	Lew Richie
July 1, 1912	PHI	N	—	BOS	N	John Titus
Dec. 1913	CIN	N	—	PHI	N	Cash

Dots Miller

Date	Traded To		Traded With	Traded By		In Exchange For
Dec. 12, 1913	STL	N	Art Butler Cozy Dolan Owen Wilson Hank Robinson	PIT	N	Ed Konetchy Bob Harmon Mike Mowrey

Dots Miller *continued*

Date	Traded To		Traded With	Traded By		In Exchange For
Jan. 1920	PHI	N	—	STL	N	Cash

Dusty Miller

Date	Traded To		Traded With	Traded By		In Exchange For
1900	STL	N	—	CIN	N	Cash

Dyar Miller

Date	Traded To		Traded With	Traded By		In Exchange For
June 13, 1977	CAL	A	—	BAL	A	Dick Drago
June 6, 1979	TOR	A	—	CAL	A	Cash
July 30, 1979	MON	N	—	TOR	A	Tony Solaita

Eddie Miller

Date	Traded To		Traded With	Traded By		In Exchange For
Aug. 10, 1938	BOS	N	—	CIN	N	Tommy Reis Johnny Babich Gil English Johnny Riddle Vince DiMaggio Cash
Dec. 4, 1942	CIN	N	—	BOS	N	Eddie Joost Nate Andrews $25,000.
Feb. 7, 1948	PHI	N	—	CIN	N	Johnny Wyrostek Cash
Apr. 3, 1950	STL	N	—	PHI	N	Waiver price

Eddie Miller

Date	Traded To		Traded With	Traded By		In Exchange For
Dec. 8, 1977	ATL	N	Adrian Devine Tommy Boggs	TEX	A	Willie Montanez
(Part of four-team trade involving Texas, Atlanta, Pittsburgh, and New York Mets.)						
Mar. 23, 1982	DET	A	—	ATL	N	Roger Weaver

Elmer Miller

Date	Traded To		Traded With	Traded By		In Exchange For
July 23, 1915	NY	A	—	STL	N	Cash
July 23, 1922	BOS	A	Chick Fewster Johnny Mitchell Lefty O'Doul $50,000.	NY	A	Joe Dugan Elmer Smith

Frank Miller

Date	Traded To		Traded With	Traded By		In Exchange For
Oct. 1919	WAS	A	—	PIT	N	Cash

John Miller

Date	Traded To		Traded With	Traded By		In Exchange For
Apr. 3, 1967	LA	N	Jack Cullen $25,000.	NY	A	John Kennedy

John Miller

Date	Traded To		Traded With	Traded By		In Exchange For
May 10, 1967	NY	N	—	BAL	A	Cash

Keith Miller

Date	Traded To		Traded With	Traded By		In Exchange For
Dec. 11, 1991	KC	A	—	NY	N	*see Bret Saberhagen*

Kurt Miller

Date	Traded To		Traded With	Traded By		In Exchange For
Aug. 30, 1991	TEX	A	Hector Fajardo	PIT	N	Steve Buechele
(Texas received Fajardo on September 6, 1991.)						

Larry Miller

Date	Traded To		Traded With	Traded By		In Exchange For
Oct. 15, 1964	NY	N	—	LA	N	Dick Smith

Norm Miller

Date	Traded To		Traded With	Traded By		In Exchange For
Apr. 22, 1973	ATL	N	—	HOU	N	Cecil Upshaw

Orlando Miller

Date	Traded To		Traded With	Traded By		In Exchange For
Mar. 13, 1990	HOU	N	—	NY	A	Dave Silvestri Player to be named
(New York received P Daven Bond on June 11, 1990.)						

Otto Miller

Date	Traded To		Traded With	Traded By		In Exchange For
Jan. 15, 1927	STL	A	—	DET	A	*see Marty McManus*

Ox Miller

Date	Traded To		Traded With	Traded By		In Exchange For
Aug. 18, 1943	STL	A	Ellis Clary Cash	WAS	A	Harlond Clift Johnny Niggeling

Randy Miller

Date	Traded To		Traded With	Traded By		In Exchange For
Dec. 7, 1977	MON	N	Rudy May Bryn Smith	BAL	A	Don Stanhouse Joe Kerrigan Gary Roenicke

Rick Miller

Date	Traded To		Traded With	Traded By		In Exchange For
Dec. 21, 1977	CAL	A	—	BOS	A	No compensation (free agent signing)
Dec. 10, 1980	BOS	A	Carney Lansford Mark Clear	CAL	A	Rick Burleson Butch Hobson

Roscoe Miller

Date	Traded To		Traded With	Traded By		In Exchange For
Feb. 1904	PIT	N	—	NY	N	Cash

Stu Miller

Date	Traded To		Traded With	Traded By		In Exchange For
May 11, 1956	PHI	N	Harvey Haddix Ben Flowers	STL	N	Murry Dickson Herm Wehmeier
Oct. 11, 1956	NY	N	—	PHI	N	Jim Hearn
Dec. 15, 1962	BAL	A	Mike McCormick John Orsino	SF	N	Jack Fisher Jimmie Coker Billy Hoeft
Apr. 1, 1968	ATL	N	—	BAL	A	Cash

Ward Miller

Date	Traded To		Traded With	Traded By		In Exchange For
May 28, 1909	CIN	N	Cash	PIT	N	Kid Durbin
Feb. 10, 1916	STL	A	*see Eddie Plank*	STL	F	—

Randy Milligan

Date	Traded To		Traded With	Traded By		In Exchange For
Mar. 26, 1988	PIT	N	Minor league P Scott Henion	NY	N	Mackey Sasser Tim Drummond
Nov. 9, 1988	BAL	A	—	PIT	N	player to be named
			(Pittsburgh received P Pete Blohm on December 7, 1988.)			
Aug. 17, 1993	CLE	A	—	CIN	N	Thomas Howard
			(Cincinnati received Howard on August 20, 1993.)			
Dec. 13, 1993	MON	N	—	CLE	A	Brian Barnes
			(Cleveland received Barnes on December 17.)			

Alan Mills

Date	Traded To		Traded With	Traded By		In Exchange For
Dec. 19, 1986	NY	A	Ron Romanick	CAL	A	Butch Wynegar
			(New York received Mills on June 22, 1987.)			
Feb. 29, 1992	BAL	A	—	NY	A	Francisco de la Rosa Minor league P Mark Carper
			(New York received de la Rosa on March 5, and Carper on June 8, 1992.)			

Buster Mills

Date	Traded To		Traded With	Traded By		In Exchange For
Dec. 2, 1937	STL	A	Bobo Newsom Red Kress	BOS	A	Joe Vosmik
Oct. 26, 1938	NY	A	Oral Hildebrand	STL	A	Joe Glenn Myril Hoag

Lefty Mills

Date	Traded To		Traded With	Traded By		In Exchange For
Feb. 5, 1941	BKN	N	—	STL	A	Cash

Al Milnar

Date	Traded To		Traded With	Traded By		In Exchange For
Aug. 27, 1943	STL	A	—	CLE	A	Cash

Eddie Milner

Date	Traded To		Traded With	Traded By		In Exchange For
Jan. 8, 1987	SF	N	—	CIN	N	Frank Williams Minor league P Timber Mead Minor league P Mike Villa
Feb. 10, 1988	CIN	N	—	SF	N	No compensation (free agent signing)

John Milner

Date	Traded To		Traded With	Traded By		In Exchange For
Dec. 8, 1977	TEX	A	Jon Matlack	NY	N	Willie Montanez Tom Grieve Ken Henderson
			(Part of four-team trade involving Texas, New York Mets, Pittsburgh, and Atlanta.)			
Dec. 8, 1977	PIT	N	Bert Blyleven	TEX	A	Al Oliver Nelson Norman
			(Part of four-team trade involving Texas, New York Mets, Pittsburgh, and Atlanta.)			
Aug. 20, 1981	MON	N	—	PIT	N	Willie Montanez

Don Mincher

Date	Traded To		Traded With	Traded By		In Exchange For
Apr. 4, 1960	WAS	A	Earl Battey $150,000.	CHI	A	Roy Sievers
Dec. 2, 1966	CAL	A	Jimmie Hall Pete Cimino	MIN	A	Dean Chance Jackie Hernandez
Jan. 15, 1970	OAK	A	Ron Clark	MIL	A	Mike Hershberger Lew Krausse Phil Roof Ken Sanders
May 8, 1971	WAS	A	Frank Fernandez Paul Lindblad Cash	OAK	A	Mike Epstein Darold Knowles
July 20, 1972	OAK	A	Ted Kubiak	TEX	A	Marty Martinez Vic Harris Steve Lawson

Nate Minchey

Date	Traded To		Traded With	Traded By		In Exchange For
July 2, 1989	ATL	N	Sergio Valdez Minor league OF Kevin Dean	MON	N	Zane Smith
Aug. 30, 1992	BOS	A	Minor league OF Sean Ross	ATL	N	Jeff Reardon
Dec. 7, 1994	STL	N	Jeff McNeely	BOS	A	Luis Alicea

Craig Minetto

Date	Traded To		Traded With	Traded By		In Exchange For
Feb. 24, 1982	BAL	A	—	OAK	A	Minor league P Allen Edwards
Dec. 21, 1983	HOU	N	—	BAL	A	Bobby Sprowl

Paul Minner

Date	Traded To		Traded With	Traded By		In Exchange For
Oct. 14, 1949	CHI	N	Preston Ward	BKN	N	$100,000.

Blas Minor

Date	Traded To		Traded With	Traded By		In Exchange For
Nov. 4, 1994	NY	N	—	PIT	N	Waiver price

Minnie Minoso

Date	Traded To		Traded With	Traded By		In Exchange For
Apr. 30, 1951	PHI	A	Sam Zoldak Ray Murray	CLE	A	Lou Brissie
			(Part of three-team trade involving Cleveland, Philadelphia A's, and Chicago White Sox.)			
Apr. 30, 1951	CHI	A	Paul Lehner	PHI	A	Gus Zernial Dave Philley
			(Part of three-team trade involving Chicago White Sox, Philadelphia A's, and Cleveland.)			
Dec. 4, 1957	CLE	A	Fred Hatfield	CHI	A	Early Wynn Al Smith
Dec. 6, 1959	CHI	A	Dick Brown Don Ferrarese Jake Striker	CLE	A	Johnny Romano Norm Cash Bubba Phillips
Nov. 27, 1961	STL	N	—	CHI	A	Joe Cunningham
Apr. 2, 1963	WAS	A	—	STL	N	Cash and minor league player to be named later

Jim Minshall

Date	Traded To		Traded With	Traded By		In Exchange For
Oct. 15, 1976	SEA	A	—	PIT	N	Cash

Greg Minton

Date	Traded To		Traded With	Traded By		In Exchange For
Apr. 2, 1973	SF	N	—	KC	A	Fran Healy

Paul Mirabella

Date	Traded To		Traded With	Traded By		In Exchange For
Nov. 10, 1978	NY	A	*see Dave Righetti*	TEX	A	—
Nov. 1, 1979	TOR	A	*see Chris Chambliss*	NY	A	—
Dec. 28, 1981	CHI	N	—	TOR	A	Dave Geisel
Mar. 26, 1982	TEX	A	minor league P Paul Semall Cash	CHI	N	Bump Wills

Willie Miranda

Date	Traded To		Traded With	Traded By		In Exchange For
Oct. 24, 1951	CHI	A	—	WAS	A	Floyd Baker
June 15, 1952	STL	A	Al Zarilla	CHI	A	Tom Wright Leo Thomas
June 28, 1952	CHI	A	—	STL	A	Waiver price
Oct. 16, 1952	STL	A	Hank Edwards	CHI	A	Joe De Maestri Tommy Byrne
June 12, 1953	NY	A	—	STL	A	Cash
Nov. 18, 1954	BAL	A	—	NY	A	*see Bob Turley*

Bobby Mitchell

Date	Traded To	Traded With	Traded By	In Exchange For
June 7, 1971	MIL A	Frank Tepedino	NY A	Danny Walton

Bobby Mitchell

Date	Traded To	Traded With	Traded By	In Exchange For
Apr. 5, 1981	PIT N	—	SD N	Dave Dravecky
Jan. 6, 1982	MIN A	*see Bobby Castillo*	LA N	—

Charlie Mitchell

Date	Traded To	Traded With	Traded By	In Exchange For
Dec. 12, 1985	MIN A	—	BOS A	Mike Stenhouse

Clarence Mitchell

Date	Traded To	Traded With	Traded By	In Exchange For
Oct. 16, 1917	BKN N	—	CIN N	Waiver price
Feb. 11, 1923	PHI N	—	BKN N	George Smith
May 15, 1930	NY N	—	STL N	Ralph Judd

Dale Mitchell

Date	Traded To	Traded With	Traded By	In Exchange For
July 29, 1956	BKN N	—	CLE A	Cash

Fred Mitchell

Date	Traded To	Traded With	Traded By	In Exchange For
Apr. 1902	PHI A	—	BOS A	Cash
Aug. 18, 1904	BKN N	—	PHI N	Cash
Dec. 14, 1916	CHI N	—	BOS N	Joe Kelly

John Mitchell

Date	Traded To	Traded With	Traded By	In Exchange For
Nov. 13, 1985	NY N	Bob Ojeda Tom McCarthy Minor league P Chris Bayer	BOS A	Calvin Schiraldi John Christensen Wes Gardner LaSchelle Tarver
Dec. 5, 1989	BAL A	Minor league OF Joaquin Contreras	NY N	Keith Hughes Minor league P Cesar Mejia

Johnny Mitchell

Date	Traded To	Traded With	Traded By	In Exchange For
July 23, 1922	BOS A	Chick Fewster Elmer Miller Lefty O'Doul $50,000.	NY A	Joe Dugan Elmer Smith
Nov. 1923	BKN N	—	BOS A	Cash

Kevin Mitchell

Date	Traded To	Traded With	Traded By	In Exchange For
Dec. 11, 1986	SD N	Stan Jefferson Shawn Abner Minor league Ps Kevin Armstrong and Kevin Brown	NY N	Kevin McReynolds Gene Walter Minor league IF Adam Ging
July 5, 1987	SF N	Craig Lefferts Dave Dravecky	SD N	Chris Brown Mark Davis Keith Comstock Mark Grant
Dec. 11, 1991	SEA A	Mike Remlinger	SF N	Bill Swift Mike Jackson Dave Burba
Nov. 17, 1992	CIN N	—	SEA A	Norm Charlton

Mike Mitchell

Date	Traded To	Traded With	Traded By	In Exchange For
Dec. 15, 1912	CHI N	Bert Humphries Red Corriden Pete Knisely Art Phelan	CIN N	Joe Tinker Grover Lowdermilk Harry Chapman
July 29, 1913	PIT N	—	CHI N	Waiver price
July 20, 1914	WAS A	—	PIT N	Waiver price

Paul Mitchell

Date	Traded To	Traded With	Traded By	In Exchange For
Apr. 2, 1976	OAK A	—	BAL A	*see Reggie Jackson*
Aug. 4, 1977	SEA A	—	OAK A	Cash
June 7, 1979	MIL A	—	SEA A	Randy Stein

Roy Mitchell

Date	Traded To	Traded With	Traded By	In Exchange For
Apr. 1918	CIN N	—	CHI A	Cash

Willie Mitchell

Date	Traded To	Traded With	Traded By	In Exchange For
June 20, 1916	DET A	—	CLE A	Waiver price

George Mitterwald

Date	Traded To	Traded With	Traded By	In Exchange For
Dec. 6, 1973	CHI N	—	MIN A	Randy Hundley

Johnny Mize

Date	Traded To	Traded With	Traded By	In Exchange For
Dec. 13, 1934	CIN N	—	STL N	Cash

(Mize was returned to St. Louis because of a bad knee.)

Date	Traded To	Traded With	Traded By	In Exchange For
Dec. 11, 1941	NY N	—	STL N	Ken O'Dea Bill Lohrman Johnny McCarthy $50,000.
Aug. 22, 1949	NY A	—	NY N	$40,000.

Vinegar Bend Mizell

Date	Traded To	Traded With	Traded By	In Exchange For
May 28, 1960	PIT N	Dick Gray	STL N	Julian Javier Ed Bauta
May 7, 1962	NY N	—	PIT N	Jim Marshall

Dave Mlicki

Date	Traded To	Traded With	Traded By	In Exchange For
Nov. 18, 1994	NY N	—	CLE A	*see Jeromy Burnitz*

Dave Moates

Date	Traded To	Traded With	Traded By	In Exchange For
May 23, 1977	NY A	—	TEX A	Cash

Danny Moeller

Date	Traded To	Traded With	Traded By	In Exchange For
Aug. 18, 1916	CLE A	Joe Boehling	WAS A	Elmer Smith Joe Leonard

Dennis Moeller

Date	Traded To	Traded With	Traded By	In Exchange For
Nov. 19, 1992	PIT N	Joel Johnston	KC A	Jose Lind

Randy Moffitt

Date	Traded To	Traded With	Traded By	In Exchange For
Feb. 15, 1983	TOR A	—	HOU N	No compensation (free agent signing)

Herb Moford

Date	Traded To	Traded With	Traded By	In Exchange For
Dec. 2, 1958	BOS A	—	DET A	Lou Berberet

George Mogridge

Date	Traded To	Traded With	Traded By	In Exchange For
Feb. 1915	NY A	—	CHI A	Cash
Jan. 20, 1921	WAS A	Duffy Lewis	NY A	Braggo Roth
June 8, 1925	STL A	Pinky Hargrave	WAS A	Hank Severeid
Mar. 1926	NY A	Cash	STL A	Wally Schang
June 1926	BOS N	—	NY A	Waiver price

Dale Mohorcic

Date	Traded To	Traded With	Traded By	In Exchange For
Aug. 30, 1988	NY A	—	TEX A	Cecilio Guante

Johnny Mokan

Date	Traded To	Traded With	Traded By	In Exchange For
July 14, 1922	PHI N	—	PIT N	Cash
Dec. 13, 1927	STL N	Jimmy Cooney Bubber Jonnard	PHI N	Johnny Schulte Jimmy Ring

Bob Molinaro

Date	Traded To	Traded With	Traded By	In Exchange For
Sept. 22, 1977	CHI A	—	DET A	Cash
Aug. 30, 1979	BAL A	—	CHI A	Cash
Oct. 3, 1979	CHI A	—	BAL A	Cash
Aug. 15, 1981	CHI N	—	CHI A	Lynn McGlothen

(Cubs received Molinaro on March 29, 1982.)

Date	Traded To	Traded With	Traded By	In Exchange For
Sept. 1, 1982	PHI N	—	CHI N	Cash

Paul Molitor

Date	Traded To	Traded With	Traded By	In Exchange For
Dec. 7, 1992	TOR A	—	MIL A	No compensation (free agent signing)
Dec. 5, 1995	MIN A	—	TOR A	No compensation (free agent signing)

Fritz Mollwitz

Date	Traded To	Traded With	Traded By	In Exchange For
July 20, 1914	CIN N	—	CHI N	Claud Derrick
July 22, 1916	CHI N	—	CIN N	Cash

Fritz Mollwitz *continued*

Date	Traded To	Traded With	Traded By	In Exchange For
Feb. 4, 1917	PIT N	—	CHI N	Cash
Aug. 1919	STL N	—	PIT N	Cash

Bill Monbouquette

Date	Traded To	Traded With	Traded By	In Exchange For
Oct. 4, 1965	DET A	—	BOS A	George Smith George Thomas
July 12, 1968	SF N	—	NY A	Lindy McDaniel
Dec. 21, 1968	HOU N	—	SF N	Cash

(Monbouquette was returned to San Francisco on April 5, 1969.)

Rick Monday

Date	Traded To	Traded With	Traded By	In Exchange For
Nov. 29, 1971	CHI N	—	OAK A	Ken Holtzman
Jan. 11, 1977	LA N	Mike Garman	CHI N	Bill Buckner Ivan DeJesus minor league P Jeff Albert

Don Money

Date	Traded To	Traded With	Traded By	In Exchange For
Dec. 15, 1967	PHI N	Woodie Fryman Bill Laxton minor league P Hal Clem	PIT N	Jim Bunning
Oct. 31, 1972	MIL A	John Vukovich Billy Champion	PHI N	Jim Lonborg Ken Sanders Ken Brett Earl Stephenson

Sid Monge

Date	Traded To	Traded With	Traded By	In Exchange For
May 11, 1977	CLE A	Bruce Bochte $250,000.	CAL A	Dave LaRoche Dave Schuler
Feb. 16, 1982	PHI N	—	CLE A	Bake McBride
May 22, 1983	SD N	—	PHI N	Joe Lefebvre
June 10, 1984	DET A	—	SD N	Cash

John Monroe

Date	Traded To	Traded With	Traded By	In Exchange For
June 1921	PHI N	—	NY N	Cash

John Montague

Date	Traded To	Traded With	Traded By	In Exchange For
Sept. 2, 1975	PHI N	—	MON N	Cash
Nov. 6, 1976	SEA A	—	PHI N	Cash
Aug. 29, 1979	CAL A	—	SEA A	Jim Anderson

Rafael Montalvo

Date	Traded To	Traded With	Traded By	In Exchange For
July 10, 1985	HOU N	German Rivera	LA N	Enos Cabell

Willie Montanez

Date	Traded To	Traded With	Traded By	In Exchange For
Apr. 8, 1970	PHI N	minor league P Bob Browning	STL N	Completion of Curt Flood trade of October 7, 1969
May 4, 1975	SF N	—	PHI N	Garry Maddox
June 13, 1976	ATL N	Craig Robinson Mike Eden Jake Brown	SF N	Darrell Evans Marty Perez
Dec. 8, 1977	TEX A	—	ATL N	Adrian Devine Tommy Boggs Eddie Miller

(Part of four-team trade involving Texas, Atlanta, Pittsburgh, and New York Mets.)

Date	Traded To	Traded With	Traded By	In Exchange For
Dec. 8, 1977	NY N	Tom Grieve Ken Henderson	TEX A	Jon Matlack John Milner

(Part of four-team trade involving Texas, New York Mets, Pittsburgh, and Atlanta.)

Date	Traded To	Traded With	Traded By	In Exchange For
Aug. 12, 1979	TEX A	—	NY N	Ed Lynch Mike Jorgensen
Feb. 15, 1980	SD N	—	TEX A	Gaylord Perry Tucker Ashford minor league P Joe Carroll
Aug. 31, 1980	MON N	—	SD N	Tony Phillips
Aug. 20, 1981	PIT N	—	MON N	John Milner

Aurelio Monteagudo

Date	Traded To	Traded With	Traded By	In Exchange For
May 17, 1966	HOU N	—	KC A	Cash
Sept. 27, 1966	CIN N	—	HOU N	Cash
Aug. 14, 1973	PHI N	Chris Coletta Billy Grabarkewitz	CAL A	Denny Doyle

John Montefusco

Date	Traded To	Traded With	Traded By	In Exchange For
Dec. 12, 1980	ATL N	minor league OF Craig Landis	SF N	Doyle Alexander
Mar. 6, 1982	SD N	—	ATL N	No compensation (free agent signing)
Aug. 26, 1983	NY A	—	SD N	Dennis Rasmussen Edwin Rodriguez $200,000.

Manny Montejo

Date	Traded To	Traded With	Traded By	In Exchange For
Dec. 1, 1961	HOU N	Bob Bruce	DET A	Sam Jones

Rich Monteleone

Date	Traded To	Traded With	Traded By	In Exchange For
Dec. 12, 1985	SEA A	—	DET A	Darnell Coles
Apr. 28, 1990	NY A	Claudell Washington	CAL A	Luis Polonia

Jeff Montgomery

Date	Traded To	Traded With	Traded By	In Exchange For
Feb. 15, 1988	KC A	—	CIN N	Van Snider

Charlie Montoyo

Date	Traded To	Traded With	Traded By	In Exchange For
Jan. 20, 1993	MON N	Oreste Marrero	MIL A	Minor league OF Todd Samples Minor league P Ron Gerstein

Wally Moon

Date	Traded To	Traded With	Traded By	In Exchange For
Dec. 4, 1958	LA N	Phil Paine	STL N	Gino Cimoli

Jim Mooney

Date	Traded To	Traded With	Traded By	In Exchange For
Oct. 10, 1932	STL N	Ethan Allen Bob O'Farrell Bill Walker	NY N	Gus Mancuso Ray Starr

Bill Mooneyham

Date	Traded To	Traded With	Traded By	In Exchange For
June 29, 1987	MIL A	—	OAK A	Russ McGinnis

Balor Moore

Date	Traded To	Traded With	Traded By	In Exchange For
Apr. 13, 1978	TOR A	—	CAL A	Cash

Barry Moore

Date	Traded To	Traded With	Traded By	In Exchange For
Dec. 5, 1969	CLE A	Dennis Higgins	WAS A	Dave Nelson Horacio Pina Ron Law
June 15, 1970	CHI A	Bob Miller	CLE A	Buddy Bradford
Dec. 3, 1970	NY A	—	CHI A	Bill Robinson

Charlie Moore

Date	Traded To	Traded With	Traded By	In Exchange For
June 5, 1987	TOR A	—	MIL A	No compensation (free agent signing)

Cy Moore

Date	Traded To	Traded With	Traded By	In Exchange For
Dec. 15, 1932	PHI N	Mickey Finn Jack Warner	BKN N	Ray Benge $15,000.

Donnie Moore

Date	Traded To	Traded With	Traded By	In Exchange For
Oct. 17, 1979	STL N	—	CHI N	Mike Tyson
Sept. 3, 1981	MIL A	—	STL N	Cash

(Moore was returned on November 5.)

Date	Traded To	Traded With	Traded By	In Exchange For
Feb. 1, 1982	ATL N	—	STL N	Dan Morogiello
Jan. 24, 1985	CAL A	—	ATL N	

(Claimed in compensation draft after California lost free agent Fred Lynn to Baltimore.)

Earl Moore

Date	Traded To	Traded With	Traded By	In Exchange For
May 16, 1907	NY A	—	CLE A	Walter Clarkson
Oct. 1907	PHI N	—	NY A	Waiver price
July 1913	CHI N	—	PHI N	Cash

Eddie Moore

Date	Traded To	Traded With	Traded By	In Exchange For
July 20, 1926	BOS N	—	PIT N	Cash

Euel Moore

Date	Traded To	Traded With	Traded By	In Exchange For
Aug. 2, 1935	NY N	—	PHI N	Cash

Gene Moore

Date	Traded To	Traded With	Traded By	In Exchange For
Feb. 6, 1936	BOS N	Johnny Babich	BKN N	Fred Frankhouse
Dec. 13, 1938	BKN N	Ira Hutchinson	BOS N	Jimmy Outlaw Buddy Hassett
May 29, 1940	BOS N	—	BKN N	Cash
Feb. 5, 1942	NY A	Buddy Hassett	BOS N	Tommy Holmes
Mar. 1, 1944	STL A	Tony Giuliani Cash	WAS A	Rick Ferrell

(Giuliani announced his retirement, and St. Louis received Moore to complete the trade.)

Jim Moore

Date	Traded To	Traded With	Traded By	In Exchange For
Apr. 24, 1932	CLE A	Bill Cissell	CHI A	Johnny Hodapp Bob Seeds

Johnny Moore

Date	Traded To	Traded With	Traded By	In Exchange For
Nov. 30, 1932	CIN N	Bob Smith Rollie Hemsley Lance Richbourg	CHI N	Babe Herman
May 16, 1934	PHI N	Syl Johnson	CIN N	Ted Kleinhans Wes Schulmerich Art Ruble

Kelvin Moore

Date	Traded To	Traded With	Traded By	In Exchange For
Feb. 19, 1984	MIL A	—	NY N	Minor league IF Billy Max

Marcus Moore

Date	Traded To	Traded With	Traded By	In Exchange For
Dec. 2, 1990	TOR A	*see Devon White*	CAL A	—
Apr. 10, 1995	CIN N	—	CLR N	Minor league IF Chris Sexton

Mike Moore

Date	Traded To	Traded With	Traded By	In Exchange For
Nov. 28, 1988	OAK A	—	SEA A	No compensation (free agent signing)
Dec. 9, 1992	DET A	—	OAK A	No compensation (free agent signing)

Randy Moore

Date	Traded To	Traded With	Traded By	In Exchange For
Dec. 12, 1935	BKN N	Ed Brandt	BOS N	Tony Cuccinello Ray Benge Al Lopez Bobby Reis
July 1937	STL N	—	BKN N	Cash

Ray Moore

Date	Traded To	Traded With	Traded By	In Exchange For
Dec. 3, 1957	CHI A	—	BAL A	*see Larry Doby*
June 13, 1960	WAS A	—	CHI A	Cash

Roy Moore

Date	Traded To	Traded With	Traded By	In Exchange For
July 13, 1922	DET A	—	PHI A	Cash

Tommy Moore

Date	Traded To	Traded With	Traded By	In Exchange For
Oct. 13, 1974	STL N	Ray Sadecki	NY N	Joe Torre
June 4, 1975	TEX A	Ed Brinkman	STL N	Willie Davis
Oct. 24, 1976	SEA A	—	TEX A	Cash
Dec. 7, 1977	BAL A	Carlos Lopez	SEA A	Mike Parrott

Wilcy Moore

Date	Traded To	Traded With	Traded By	In Exchange For
May 1, 1932	NY A	—	BOS A	Gordon Rhodes

Jerry Morales

Date	Traded To	Traded With	Traded By	In Exchange For
Nov. 7, 1973	CHI N	—	SD N	Glenn Beckert Bobby Fenwick
Dec. 8, 1977	STL N	Steve Swisher Cash	CHI N	Dave Rader Hector Cruz
Dec. 4, 1978	DET A	Aurelio Lopez	STL N	Bob Sykes minor league P Jack Murphy
Oct. 31, 1979	NY N	Phil Mankowski	DET A	Richie Hebner

Jose Morales

Date	Traded To	Traded With	Traded By	In Exchange For
Sept. 18, 1973	MON N	—	OAK A	Cash
Mar. 29, 1978	MIN A	—	MON N	Cash
Dec. 23, 1980	BAL A	—	MIN A	No compensation (free agent signing)
Apr. 28, 1982	LA N	—	BAL A	Leo Hernandez

Rich Morales

Date	Traded To	Traded With	Traded By	In Exchange For
May 26, 1973	SD N	—	CHI A	Cash

Al Moran

Date	Traded To	Traded With	Traded By	In Exchange For
Dec. 11, 1962	NY N	Tracy Stallard Pumpsie Green	BOS A	Felix Mantilla

Billy Moran

Date	Traded To	Traded With	Traded By	In Exchange For
June 11, 1964	CLE A	—	LA A	Jerry Kindall

(Part of three-team trade involving Los Angeles Angels, Cleveland, and Minnesota.)

Charlie Moran

Date	Traded To	Traded With	Traded By	In Exchange For
July 14, 1904	STL A	—	WAS A	Hunter Hill Frank Huelsman

(Huelsman went to Washington on loan.)

Herbie Moran

Date	Traded To	Traded With	Traded By	In Exchange For
Aug. 1908	BOS N	—	PHI A	Cash
Jan. 1914	BOS N	—	CIN N	Cash
Apr. 1914	CIN N	Earl Yingling	BKN N	Dick Egan

Pat Moran

Date	Traded To	Traded With	Traded By	In Exchange For
Feb. 1906	CHI N	—	BOS N	Cash

Ray Morehart

Date	Traded To	Traded With	Traded By	In Exchange For
Jan. 13, 1927	NY A	Johnny Grabowski	CHI A	Aaron Ward

Seth Morehead

Date	Traded To	Traded With	Traded By	In Exchange For
May 12, 1959	CHI N	—	PHI N	Taylor Phillips
Mar. 31, 1961	MIL N	Moe Drabowsky	CHI N	Andre Rodgers Daryl Robertson

Keith Moreland

Date	Traded To	Traded With	Traded By	In Exchange For
Dec. 8, 1981	CHI N	Dan Larson Dickie Noles	PHI N	Mike Krukow Cash
Feb. 12, 1988	SD N	Mike Brumley	CHI N	Goose Gossage Ray Hayward
Oct. 28, 1988	DET A	Chris Brown	SD N	Walt Terrell
July 28, 1989	BAL A	—	DET A	Brian Dubois

Lew Moren

Date	Traded To	Traded With	Traded By	In Exchange For
Feb. 1911	CIN N	—	PHI N	*see Dode Paskert*

Jose Moreno

Date	Traded To	Traded With	Traded By	In Exchange For
Mar. 27, 1979	NY N	Richie Hebner	PHI N	Nino Espinosa
Dec. 15, 1980	SD N	John Pacella	NY N	Randy Jones

Omar Moreno

Date	Traded To	Traded With	Traded By	In Exchange For
Dec. 10, 1982	HOU N	—	PIT N	No compensation (free agent signing)
Aug. 10, 1983	NY A	—	HOU N	Jerry Mumphrey

Roger Moret

Date	Traded To	Traded With	Traded By	In Exchange For
Dec. 12, 1975	ATL N	—	BOS A	Tom House
Dec. 9, 1976	TEX A	Ken Henderson Dave May Carl Morton Adrian Devine $250,000.	ATL N	Jeff Burroughs

Bobby Morgan

Date	Traded To	Traded With	Traded By	In Exchange For
Mar. 28, 1954	PHI N	—	BKN N	Dick Young $50,000.
May 14, 1956	STL N	—	PHI N	Solly Hemus
Nov. 19, 1956	PHI N	Rip Repulski	STL N	Del Ennis
May 13, 1957	CHI N	—	PHI N	Cash

Chet Morgan

Date	Traded To		Traded With	Traded By		In Exchange For
Dec. 15, 1938	BOS	A	Eldon Auker Jake Wade	DET	A	Pinky Higgins Archie McKain

Cy Morgan

Date	Traded To		Traded With	Traded By		In Exchange For
Aug. 1, 1907	BOS	A	—	STL	A	Cash

Eddie Morgan

Date	Traded To		Traded With	Traded By		In Exchange For
Mar. 6, 1938	PHI	N	$45,000.	BKN	N	Dolf Camilli

Joe Morgan

Date	Traded To		Traded With	Traded By		In Exchange For
June 23, 1960	PHI	N	—	MIL	N	Alvin Dark
Aug. 9, 1960	CLE	A	—	PHI	N	Cash
May 10, 1961	STL	N	Mike Lee Cash	CLE	A	Bob Nieman

(St. Louis received Lee on September 25.)

Joe Morgan

Date	Traded To		Traded With	Traded By		In Exchange For
Nov. 29, 1971	CIN	N	Cesar Geronimo Denis Menke Jack Billingham Ed Armbrister	HOU	N	Lee May Tommy Helms Jimmy Stewart
Jan. 31, 1980	HOU	N	—	CIN	N	No compensation (free agent signing)
Dec. 14, 1982	PHI	N	Al Holland	SF	N	Mike Krukow Mark Davis minor league OF Charles Penigar
Dec. 13, 1983	OAK	A	—	PHI	N	No compensation (free agent signing)

Mike Morgan

Date	Traded To		Traded With	Traded By		In Exchange For
Nov. 3, 1980	NY	A	—	OAK	A	Fred Stanley Brian Doyle
Dec. 9, 1982	TOR	A	*see Dave Collins*	NY	A	—
Dec. 9, 1987	BAL	A	—	SEA	A	Ken Dixon
Mar. 11, 1989	LA	N	—	BAL	A	Mike Devereaux
Dec. 3, 1991	CHI	N	—	LA	N	No compensation (free agent signing)
June 16, 1995	STL	N	Minor league IF-OF Paul Torres Minor league C Francisco Morales	CHI	N	Todd Zeile

Tom Morgan

Date	Traded To		Traded With	Traded By		In Exchange For
Feb. 19, 1957	KC	A	*see Billy Hunter*	NY	A	—
Nov. 20, 1957	DET	A	*see Billy Martin*	KC	A	—
July 22, 1960	WAS	A	—	DET	A	Bill Fischer
Jan. 31, 1961	LA	A	—	WAS	A	Cash

George Moriarty

Date	Traded To		Traded With	Traded By		In Exchange For
Jan. 1909	DET	A	—	NY	A	Cash

Dan Morogiello

Date	Traded To		Traded With	Traded By		In Exchange For
Feb. 1, 1982	STL	N	—	ATL	N	Donnie Moore

Jeff Moronko

Date	Traded To		Traded With	Traded By		In Exchange For
Apr. 4, 1985	TEX	A	—	CLE	A	Kevin Buckley

(Texas received Moronko on April 29, 1985.)

Hal Morris

Date	Traded To		Traded With	Traded By		In Exchange For
Dec. 12, 1989	CIN	N	Minor league P Rodney Imes	NY	A	Tim Leary Van Snider

Jack Morris

Date	Traded To		Traded With	Traded By		In Exchange For
Feb. 5, 1991	MIN	A	—	DET	A	No compensation (free agent signing)
Dec. 18, 1991	TOR	A	—	MIN	A	No compensation (free agent signing)

John Morris

Date	Traded To		Traded With	Traded By		In Exchange For
May 17, 1985	STL	N	—	KC	A	Lonnie Smith

John Morris *continued*

Date	Traded To		Traded With	Traded By		In Exchange For
Dec. 16, 1991	CAL	A	—	PHI	N	No compensation (free agent signing)

John Morris

Date	Traded To		Traded With	Traded By		In Exchange For
Dec. 15, 1966	BAL	A	—	PHI	N	Dick Hall

Jim Morrison

Date	Traded To		Traded With	Traded By		In Exchange For
Apr. 13, 1979	CHI	A	—	PHI	N	Jack Kucek
June 14, 1982	PIT	N	—	CHI	A	Eddie Solomon
Aug. 7, 1987	DET	A	—	PIT	N	Darnell Coles Morris Madden

(Pittsburgh received Madden on August 12, 1987.)

Bubba Morton

Date	Traded To		Traded With	Traded By		In Exchange For
May 4, 1963	MIL	N	—	DET	A	Cash
June 15, 1965	CAL	A	Cash	CLE	A	Phil Roof

(California received Morton on September 15, 1965.)

Carl Morton

Date	Traded To		Traded With	Traded By		In Exchange For
Feb. 28, 1973	ATL	N	—	MON	N	Pat Jarvis
Dec. 9, 1976	TEX	A	Ken Henderson Dave May Roger Moret Adrian Devine $250,000.	ATL	N	Jeff Burroughs

Kevin Morton

Date	Traded To		Traded With	Traded By		In Exchange For
Oct. 23, 1992	KC	A	—	BOS	A	Waiver price

Walt Moryn

Date	Traded To		Traded With	Traded By		In Exchange For
Dec. 9, 1955	CHI	N	Don Hoak Russ Meyer	BKN	N	Randy Jackson Don Elston
June 15, 1960	STL	N	—	CHI	N	Jim McKnight
June 15, 1961	PIT	N	—	STL	N	Cash

Lloyd Moseby

Date	Traded To		Traded With	Traded By		In Exchange For
Dec. 7, 1989	DET	A	—	TOR	A	No compensation (free agent signing)

Earl Moseley

Date	Traded To		Traded With	Traded By		In Exchange For
Dec. 23, 1915	CIN	N	—	NWK	F	$5,000.

Walter Moser

Date	Traded To		Traded With	Traded By		In Exchange For
June 1911	STL	A	—	BOS	A	Cash

Gerry Moses

Date	Traded To		Traded With	Traded By		In Exchange For
Oct. 11, 1970	CAL	A	*see Tony Conigliaro*	BOS	A	—
Oct. 5, 1971	CLE	A	*see Alex Johnson*	CAL	A	—
Nov. 27, 1972	NY	A	*see Graig Nettles*	CLE	A	—
Mar. 19, 1974	DET	A	—	NY	A	Rick Sawyer Ed Farmer Walt Williams

(Part of three-team trade involving Detroit, New York Yankees, and Cleveland.)

Date	Traded To		Traded With	Traded By		In Exchange For
Jan. 30, 1975	NY	N	—	DET	A	Cash
Apr. 28, 1975	SD	N	—	NY	N	Cash
July 18, 1975	CHI	A	—	SD	N	Cash

Wally Moses

Date	Traded To		Traded With	Traded By		In Exchange For
Dec. 9, 1939	DET	A	—	PHI	A	Benny McCoy Slick Coffman

(Commissioner Landis ruled that Detroit had kept McCoy covered up in the minors and declared him a free agent, cancelling the deal. McCoy then signed with Philadelphia for a $10,000 bonus.)

Date	Traded To		Traded With	Traded By		In Exchange For
Dec. 9, 1941	CHI	A	—	PHI	A	Mike Kreevich Jack Hallett
July 23, 1946	BOS	A	—	CHI	A	Cash

Paul Moskau

Date	Traded To		Traded With	Traded By		In Exchange For
Feb. 9, 1982	BAL	A	—	CIN	N	Wayne Krenchicki
Apr. 3, 1982	PIT	N	—	BAL	A	Cash

Les Moss

Date	Traded To		Traded With	Traded By		In Exchange For
May 17, 1951	BOS	A	—	STL	A	Matt Batts Jim Suchecki Jim McDonald $100,000.
Nov. 28, 1951	STL	A	Tom Wright	BOS	A	Ken Wood Gus Niarhos
June 6, 1955	CHI	A	—	BAL	A	Harry Dorish

Ray Moss

Date	Traded To		Traded With	Traded By		In Exchange For
May 28, 1931	BOS	N	—	BKN	N	Cash

Don Mossi

Date	Traded To		Traded With	Traded By		In Exchange For
Nov. 20, 1958	DET	A	Ossie Alvarez Ray Narleski	CLE	A	Billy Martin Al Cicotte
Mar. 18, 1964	CHI	A	—	DET	A	Cash

Jose Mota

Date	Traded To		Traded With	Traded By		In Exchange For
Nov. 25, 1985	TEX	A	*see Scott Fletcher*	CHI	A	—
June 25, 1987	LA	N	—	TEX	A	Larry See

Manny Mota

Date	Traded To		Traded With	Traded By		In Exchange For
Nov. 30, 1962	HOU	N	Dick LeMay	SF	N	Joey Amalfitano
Apr. 4, 1963	PIT	N	—	HOU	N	Howie Goss Cash
June 11, 1969	LA	N	Maury Wills	MON	N	Ron Fairly Paul Popovich

Darryl Motley

Date	Traded To		Traded With	Traded By		In Exchange For
Sept. 23, 1986	ATL	N	—	KC	A	Steve Shields

Curt Motton

Date	Traded To		Traded With	Traded By		In Exchange For
Dec. 9, 1971	MIL	A	—	BAL	A	Bob Reynolds Cash

Glen Moulder

Date	Traded To		Traded With	Traded By		In Exchange For
Apr. 6, 1948	CHI	A	—	STL	A	Cash

Lyle Mouton

Date	Traded To		Traded With	Traded By		In Exchange For
Dec. 14, 1994	CHI	A	Minor league P Keith Heberling	NY	A	Jack McDowell

(Chicago received Mouton on April 22, 1995.)

Mike Mowrey

Date	Traded To		Traded With	Traded By		In Exchange For
Oct. 1908	CIN	N	—	PHI	N	Cash
Aug. 22, 1909	STL	N	—	CIN	N	Chappy Charles
Dec. 12, 1913	PIT	N	Ed Konetchy Bob Harmon	STL	N	Art Butler Dots Miller Cozy Dolan Owen Wilson Hank Robinson
Feb. 10, 1916	BKN	N	—	PIT	F	Cash

Jamie Moyer

Date	Traded To		Traded With	Traded By		In Exchange For
Dec. 5, 1988	TEX	A	Rafael Palmeiro Drew Hall	CHI	N	Mitch Williams Paul Kilgus Steve Wilson Curtis Wilkerson Minor league IF Luis Benitez Minor league OF Pablo Delgado
Dec. 22, 1995	BOS	A	—	BAL	A	No compensation (free agent signing)

Don Mueller

Date	Traded To		Traded With	Traded By		In Exchange For
Mar. 21, 1958	CHI	A	—	SF	N	Cash

Heinie Mueller

Date	Traded To		Traded With	Traded By		In Exchange For
June 14, 1926	NY	N	—	STL	N	Billy Southworth

Ray Mueller

Date	Traded To		Traded With	Traded By		In Exchange For
Dec. 16, 1938	PIT	N	—	BOS	N	Al Todd Johnny Dickshot Cash
June 13, 1949	NY	N	—	CIN	N	Walker Cooper
May 17, 1950	PIT	N	—	NY	N	Cash

Billy Muffett

Date	Traded To		Traded With	Traded By		In Exchange For
Oct. 8, 1958	SF	N	Hobie Landrith Benny Valenzuela	STL	N	Ernie Broglio Marv Grissom

Hugh Mulcahy

Date	Traded To		Traded With	Traded By		In Exchange For
Jan. 1947	PIT	N	—	PHI	N	Cash

Terry Mulholland

Date	Traded To		Traded With	Traded By		In Exchange For
June 18, 1989	PHI	N	Dennis Cook Charlie Hayes	SF	N	Steve Bedrosian Rick Parker
Feb. 9, 1994	NY	A	Jeff Patterson	PHI	N	Bobby Munoz Ryan Karp Kevin Jordan

(New York received Patterson on November 8, 1994.)

Date	Traded To		Traded With	Traded By		In Exchange For
Apr. 8, 1995	SF	N	—	NY	A	No compensation (free agent signing)

Greg Mulleavy

Date	Traded To		Traded With	Traded By		In Exchange For
Dec. 15, 1932	BOS	A	Johnny Hodapp Bob Fothergill Bob Seeds	CHI	A	Ed Durham Hal Rhyne

Billy Mullen

Date	Traded To		Traded With	Traded By		In Exchange For
Jan. 15, 1927	STL	A	—	DET	A	*see Marty McManus*

Freddie Muller

Date	Traded To		Traded With	Traded By		In Exchange For
May 15, 1934	NY	A	$20,000.	BOS	A	Lyn Lary

George Mullin

Date	Traded To		Traded With	Traded By		In Exchange For
May 17, 1913	WAS	A	—	DET	A	Waiver price

Jim Mullin

Date	Traded To		Traded With	Traded By		In Exchange For
Aug. 31, 1904	WAS	A	—	PHI	A	Cash

Rance Mulliniks

Date	Traded To		Traded With	Traded By		In Exchange For
Dec. 6, 1979	KC	A	Willie Aikens	CAL	A	Al Cowens Todd Cruz Craig Eaton
Mar. 25, 1982	TOR	A	—	KC	A	Phil Huffman

Fran Mullins

Date	Traded To		Traded With	Traded By		In Exchange For
Nov. 21, 1983	CIN	N	—	CHI	A	Steve Christmas
Jan. 23, 1986	CLE	A	—	SF	N	Cash

Jerry Mumphrey

Date	Traded To		Traded With	Traded By		In Exchange For
Dec. 7, 1979	CLE	A	John Denny	STL	N	Bobby Bonds
Feb. 15, 1980	SD	N	—	CLE	A	Bob Owchinko Jim Wilhelm
Apr. 1, 1981	NY	A	John Pacella	SD	N	Ruppert Jones Joe Lefebvre Tim Lollar Chris Welsh
Aug. 10, 1983	HOU	N	—	NY	A	Omar Moreno
Dec. 16, 1985	CHI	N	—	HOU	N	Billy Hatcher Steve Engel

Bob Muncrief

Date	Traded To		Traded With	Traded By		In Exchange For
Nov. 20, 1947	CLE	A	Walt Judnich	STL	A	Dick Kokos Joe Frazier Bryan Stephens $25,000.
Nov. 20, 1948	PIT	N	—	CLE	A	$20,000.
June 6, 1949	CHI	N	—	PIT	N	Waiver price

George Munger

Date	Traded To		Traded With	Traded By		In Exchange For
May 3, 1952	PIT	N	—	STL	N	Bill Werle

Scott Munninghoff

Date	Traded To		Traded With	Traded By		In Exchange For
Nov. 20, 1981	CLE	A	Lonnie Smith	PHI	N	Bo Diaz

(Part of three-team trade involving Cleveland, Philadelphia, and St. Louis.)

Bobby Munoz

Date	Traded To		Traded With	Traded By		In Exchange For
Feb. 9, 1994	PHI	N	Ryan Karp Kevin Jordan	NY	A	Terry Mulholland Jeff Patterson

(New York received Patterson on November 8, 1994.)

Mike Munoz

Date	Traded To		Traded With	Traded By		In Exchange For
Sept. 30, 1990	DET	A	—	LA	N	Minor league P Mike Wilkins

Oscar Munoz

Date	Traded To		Traded With	Traded By		In Exchange For
Mar. 28, 1992	MIN	A	Curtis Leskanic	CLE	A	Paul Sorrento
Nov. 20, 1995	BAL	A	—	MIN	A	Waiver price

Pedro Munoz

Date	Traded To		Traded With	Traded By		In Exchange For
July 27, 1990	MIN	A	Nelson Liriano	TOR	A	John Candelaria

Steve Mura

Date	Traded To		Traded With	Traded By		In Exchange For
Dec. 10, 1981	STL	N	Ozzie Smith Al Olmsted	SD	N	Sixto Lezcano Luis DeLeon Garry Templeton

(Templeton and Smith were exchanged on February 11, 1982; Olmsted and DeLeon were exchanged on February 19.)

Date	Traded To		Traded With	Traded By		In Exchange For
Jan. 26, 1983	CHI	A	—	STL	N	

(Claimed in compensation draft after Chicago lost free agent OF Steve Kemp to Yankees.)

Bobby Murcer

Date	Traded To		Traded With	Traded By		In Exchange For
Oct. 22, 1974	SF	N	—	NY	A	Bobby Bonds
Feb. 11, 1977	CHI	N	Steve Ontiveros minor league P Andy Muhlstock	SF	N	Bill Madlock Rob Sperring
June 26, 1979	NY	A	—	CHI	N	Minor league P Paul Semall and cash

Dale Murphy

Date	Traded To		Traded With	Traded By		In Exchange For
Aug. 3, 1990	PHI	N	Tommy Greene	ATL	N	Jeff Parrett Jim Vatcher Victor Rosario

(Greene and Vatcher were exhanged on August 9, and Atlanta received Rosario on September 4, 1990.)

Danny Murphy

Date	Traded To		Traded With	Traded By		In Exchange For
Mar. 28, 1963	HOU	N	Dave Gerard	CHI	N	Merritt Ranew Hal Haydel Dick LeMay
Dec. 10, 1963	CHI	A	Jim Golden Cash	HOU	N	Nellie Fox
Mar. 31, 1971	BOS	A	Duane Josephson	CHI	A	Vicente Romo Tony Muser

Eddie Murphy

Date	Traded To		Traded With	Traded By		In Exchange For
July 15, 1915	CHI	A	—	PHI	A	$13,500.

Frank Murphy

Date	Traded To		Traded With	Traded By		In Exchange For
July 1901	NY	N	—	BOS	N	Cash

Rob Murphy

Date	Traded To		Traded With	Traded By		In Exchange For
Dec. 13, 1988	BOS	A	Nick Esasky	CIN	N	Todd Benzinger Jeff Sellers player to be named

(Cincinnati received P Luis Vasquez on January 12, 1989.)

Date	Traded To		Traded With	Traded By		In Exchange For
Apr. 1, 1991	SEA	A	—	BOS	A	Mike Gardiner
Jan. 7, 1993	STL	N	—	HOU	N	No compensation (free agent signing)
Aug. 3, 1994	NY	A	—	STL	N	Waiver price

Tom Murphy

Date	Traded To		Traded With	Traded By		In Exchange For
May 5, 1972	KC	A	—	CAL	A	Bob Oliver
May 8, 1973	STL	N	—	KC	A	Al Santorini
Dec. 8, 1973	MIL	A	—	STL	N	Bob Heise
June 3, 1976	BOS	A	Bobby Darwin	MIL	A	Bernie Carbo
July 27, 1977	TOR	A	—	BOS	A	Cash

Dale Murray

Date	Traded To		Traded With	Traded By		In Exchange For
Dec. 16, 1976	CIN	N	Woodie Fryman	MON	N	Tony Perez Will McEnaney
May 19, 1978	NY	N	—	CIN	N	Ken Henderson
Aug. 30, 1979	MON	N	—	NY	N	Cash
Dec. 9, 1982	NY	A	—	TOR	A	*see Dave Collins*

Eddie Murray

Date	Traded To		Traded With	Traded By		In Exchange For
Dec. 4, 1988	LA	N	—	BAL	A	Brian Holton Juan Bell Ken Howell
Nov. 27, 1991	NY	N	—	LA	N	No compensation (free agent signing)
Dec. 2, 1993	CLE	A	—	NY	N	No compensation (free agent signing)

George Murray

Date	Traded To		Traded With	Traded By		In Exchange For
Jan. 30, 1923	BOS	A	Camp Skinner Norm McMillan $50,000.	NY	A	Herb Pennock

Larry Murray

Date	Traded To		Traded With	Traded By		In Exchange For
Apr. 27, 1977	OAK	A	Dock Ellis Marty Perez	NY	A	Mike Torrez

Matt Murray

Date	Traded To		Traded With	Traded By		In Exchange For
July 31, 1995	BOS	A	Mike Stanton	ATL	N	Minor league OF Marc Lewis Minor league P Mike Jacobs

(Murray, Lewis, and Jacobs were exchanged on August 31, 1995.)

Ray Murray

Date	Traded To		Traded With	Traded By		In Exchange For
Apr. 30, 1951	PHI	A	Sam Zoldak Minnie Minoso	CLE	A	Lou Brissie

(Part of three-team trade involving Cleveland, Philadelphia A's, and Chicago White Sox.)

Date	Traded To		Traded With	Traded By		In Exchange For
Mar. 28, 1954	BAL	A	—	PHI	A	$25,000.

Red Murray

Date	Traded To		Traded With	Traded By		In Exchange For
Dec. 12, 1908	NY	N	Admiral Schlei Bugs Raymond	STL	N	Roger Bresnahan

Ivan Murrell

Date	Traded To		Traded With	Traded By		In Exchange For
Apr. 1, 1974	ATL	N	—	SD	N	Cash

Danny Murtaugh

Date	Traded To		Traded With	Traded By		In Exchange For
Nov. 18, 1947	PIT	N	Johnny Hopp	BOS	N	Jim Russell Bill Salkeld Al Lyons

Tony Muser

Date	Traded To		Traded With	Traded By		In Exchange For
Mar. 31, 1971	CHI	A	Vicente Romo	BOS	A	Duane Josephson Danny Murphy
June 15, 1975	BAL	A	—	CHI	A	Jesse Jefferson

Jeff Musselman

Date	Traded To		Traded With	Traded By		In Exchange For
July 31, 1989	NY	N	Minor league P Mike Brady	TOR	A	Mookie Wilson

Ron Musselman

Date	Traded To		Traded With	Traded By		In Exchange For
Dec. 21, 1982	TEX	A	—	SEA	A	Pat Putnam

Jeff Mutis

Date	Traded To		Traded With	Traded By		In Exchange For
Nov. 29, 1993	FLA	N	—	CLE	A	Waiver price

Buddy Myer

Date	Traded To		Traded With	Traded By		In Exchange For
May 2, 1927	BOS	A	—	WAS	A	Topper Rigney
Dec. 15, 1928	WAS	A	—	BOS	A	Milt Gaston Elliott Bigelow Hod Lisenbee Bobby Reeves Grant Gillis

Billy Myers

Date	Traded To	Traded With	Traded By	In Exchange For
Dec. 14, 1934	CIN N	Cash	NY N	Mark Koenig Allyn Stout
Dec. 4, 1940	CHI N	—	CIN N	Jim Gleeson Bobby Mattick

Elmer Myers

Date	Traded To	Traded With	Traded By	In Exchange For
Mar. 1, 1919	CLE A	Larry Gardner Charlie Jamieson	PHI A	Braggo Roth
June 1920	BOS A	—	CLE A	Waiver price

Greg Myers

Date	Traded To	Traded With	Traded By	In Exchange For
July 30, 1992	CAL A	Rob Ducey	TOR A	Mark Eichhorn
Dec. 8, 1995	MIN A	—	CAL A	No compensation (free agent signing)

Hap Myers

Date	Traded To	Traded With	Traded By	In Exchange For
May 1911	BOS A	—	STL A	Cash

Hy Myers

Date	Traded To	Traded With	Traded By	In Exchange For
Feb. 15, 1923	STL N	Ray Schmandt	BKN N	Jack Fournier
Apr. 22, 1925	CIN N	—	STL N	Cash
May 4, 1925	STL N	—	CIN N	Cash

Mike Myers

Date	Traded To	Traded With	Traded By	In Exchange For
Aug. 7, 1995	DET A	—	FLA N	Buddy Groom

Randy Myers

Date	Traded To	Traded With	Traded By	In Exchange For
Dec. 6, 1989	CIN N	Kip Gross	NY N	John Franco Minor league OF Don Brown
Dec. 8, 1991	SD N	—	CIN N	Bip Roberts Minor league OF Craig Pueschner
Dec. 9, 1992	CHI N	—	SD N	No compensation (free agent signing)
Dec. 14, 1995	BAL A	—	CHI N	No compensation (free agent signing)

Bob Myrick

Date	Traded To	Traded With	Traded By	In Exchange For
June 15, 1979	TEX A	Mike Bruhert	NY N	Dock Ellis

Chris Nabholz

Date	Traded To	Traded With	Traded By	In Exchange For
Feb. 14, 1994	CLE A	—	MON N	J. J. Thobe Minor league 1B Dave Duplessis
July 1, 1994	BOS A	Steve Farr	CLE A	Jeff Russell

Bill Nagel

Date	Traded To	Traded With	Traded By	In Exchange For
Mar. 21, 1941	PHI N	—	PHI A	Cash

Russ Nagelson

Date	Traded To	Traded With	Traded By	In Exchange For
May 22, 1970	DET A	Billy Rohr	CLE A	Fred Lasher

Judge Nagle

Date	Traded To	Traded With	Traded By	In Exchange For
June 21, 1911	BOS A	—	PIT N	Cash

Mike Nagy

Date	Traded To	Traded With	Traded By	In Exchange For
Jan. 24, 1973	STL N	—	BOS A	Lance Clemons
Feb. 1, 1973	TEX A	Charles Hudson	STL N	Mike Thompson
		(Thompson and Nagy were exchanged on March 31.)		
June 6, 1973	STL N	John Wockenfuss	TEX A	Jim Bibby

Sam Nahem

Date	Traded To	Traded With	Traded By	In Exchange For
June 12, 1940	STL N	Ernie Koy Carl Doyle Bert Haas $125,000.	BKN N	Joe Medwick Curt Davis

Bill Nahorodny

Date	Traded To	Traded With	Traded By	In Exchange For
Sept. 8, 1977	CHI A	—	PHI N	Cash
Dec. 3, 1979	ATL N	—	CHI A	Minor league P Rick Wieters

Danny Napoleon

Date	Traded To	Traded With	Traded By	In Exchange For
Apr. 1, 1967	STL N	Ed Bressoud Cash	NY N	Jerry Buchek Art Mahaffey Tony Martinez

Hal Naragon

Date	Traded To	Traded With	Traded By	In Exchange For
May 25, 1959	WAS A	Hal Woodeshick	CLE A	Ed Fitz Gerald

Ray Narleski

Date	Traded To	Traded With	Traded By	In Exchange For
Nov. 20, 1958	DET A	Don Mossi Ossie Alvarez	CLE A	Billy Martin Al Cicotte

Jerry Narron

Date	Traded To	Traded With	Traded By	In Exchange For
Nov. 1, 1979	SEA A	*see Jim Beattie*	NY A	—

Buster Narum

Date	Traded To	Traded With	Traded By	In Exchange For
Mar. 31, 1964	WAS A	—	BAL A	Lou Piniella
Feb. 13, 1968	CHI A	—	WAS A	*see Ron Hansen*

Cotton Nash

Date	Traded To	Traded With	Traded By	In Exchange For
May 6, 1967	CHI A	Cash	CAL A	Bill Skowron

Jim Nash

Date	Traded To	Traded With	Traded By	In Exchange For
Dec. 3, 1969	ATL N	—	OAK A	Felipe Alou
June 15, 1972	PHI N	Gary Neibauer	ATL N	Joe Hoerner Andre Thornton

Phil Nastu

Date	Traded To	Traded With	Traded By	In Exchange For
Dec. 12, 1980	CHI N	Joe Strain	SF N	Jerry Martin Jesus Figueroa minor league IF Mike Turgeon

Jaime Navarro

Date	Traded To	Traded With	Traded By	In Exchange For
Apr. 9, 1995	CHI N	—	MIL A	No compensation (free agent signing)

Julio Navarro

Date	Traded To	Traded With	Traded By	In Exchange For
Apr. 28, 1964	DET A	—	LA A	Willie Smith
June 14, 1966	BOS A	Don Demeter	DET A	Earl Wilson Joe Christopher

Earl Naylor

Date	Traded To	Traded With	Traded By	In Exchange For
June 1, 1943	STL N	Danny Litwhiler	PHI N	Buster Adams Coaker Triplett Dain Clay

Denny Neagle

Date	Traded To	Traded With	Traded By	In Exchange For
Mar. 17, 1992	PIT N	Midre Cummings	MIN A	John Smiley

Charlie Neal

Date	Traded To	Traded With	Traded By	In Exchange For
Dec. 15, 1961	NY N	—	LA N	Lee Walls $100,000.
July 1, 1963	CIN N	Sammy Taylor	NY N	Jesse Gonder

Greasy Neale

Date	Traded To	Traded With	Traded By	In Exchange For
Feb. 22, 1921	PHI N	Jimmy Ring	CIN N	Eppa Rixey
June 2, 1921	CIN N	—	PHI N	Waiver price

Tom Needham

Date	Traded To	Traded With	Traded By	In Exchange For
Dec. 3, 1907	NY N	*see Fred Tenney*	BOS N	—
Dec. 1908	CHI N	—	NY N	Cash

Troy Neel

Date	Traded To	Traded With	Traded By	In Exchange For
Jan. 16, 1991	OAK A	—	CLE A	Minor league IF Larry Arndt

Cal Neeman

Date	Traded To	Traded With	Traded By	In Exchange For
May 13, 1960	PHI N	Tony Taylor	CHI N	Ed Bouchee Don Cardwell

Ron Negray

Date	Traded To	Traded With	Traded By	In Exchange For
Apr. 5, 1957	BKN N	—	PHI N	*see Chico Fernandez*

Art Nehf

Date	Traded To	Traded With	Traded By	In Exchange For
Aug. 15, 1919	NY N	—	BOS N	Joe Oeschger Red Causey Johnny Jones Mickey O'Neil $55,000.
May 11, 1926	CIN N	—	NY N	Cash
Sept. 4, 1927	CHI N	—	CIN N	Cash

Gary Neibauer

Date	Traded To	Traded With	Traded By	In Exchange For
June 15, 1972	PHI N	Jim Nash	ATL N	Joe Hoerner Andre Thornton

Jim Neidlinger

Date	Traded To	Traded With	Traded By	In Exchange For
Oct. 3, 1988	LA N	—	PIT N	Bill Krueger

Bernie Neis

Date	Traded To	Traded With	Traded By	In Exchange For
Feb. 4, 1925	BOS N	—	BKN N	Cotton Tierney
June 15, 1927	CHI A	—	CLE A	Cash

Dave Nelson

Date	Traded To	Traded With	Traded By	In Exchange For
Dec. 5, 1969	WAS A	Horacio Pina Ron Law	CLE A	Dennis Higgins Barry Moore
Nov. 12, 1975	KC A	—	TEX A	Nellie Briles

Gene Nelson

Date	Traded To	Traded With	Traded By	In Exchange For
Aug. 1, 1979	NY A	Oscar Gamble Ray Fontenot minor league 3B Amos Lewis	TEX A	Mickey Rivers minor league Ps Bob Polinsky Neil Mersch and Mark Softy
Apr. 1, 1982	SEA A	Bill Caudill Bobby Brown	NY A	Shane Rawley
June 29, 1984	CHI A	Jerry Don Gleaton	SEA A	Salome Barojas
Dec. 11, 1986	OAK A	Bruce Tanner	CHI A	Donnie Hill

(Oakland received Tanner on Dec. 18, 1986.)

Jamie Nelson

Date	Traded To	Traded With	Traded By	In Exchange For
Dec. 7, 1984	CHI N	—	MIL A	Cash

(Nelson was returned to Milwaukee on March 22, 1985.)

Jeff Nelson

Date	Traded To	Traded With	Traded By	In Exchange For
Dec. 6, 1995	NY A	*see Tino Martinez*	SEA A	—

Lynn Nelson

Date	Traded To	Traded With	Traded By	In Exchange For
Feb. 23, 1940	DET A	—	PHI A	Waiver price

Red Nelson

Date	Traded To	Traded With	Traded By	In Exchange For
Aug. 1912	PHI N	—	STL A	Cash
June 5, 1913	CIN N	John Dodge	PHI N	Josh Devore Beals Becker

Ricky Nelson

Date	Traded To	Traded With	Traded By	In Exchange For
Dec. 17, 1986	NY N	—	SEA A	Doug Gwosdz
May 11, 1987	CLE A	—	NY N	Don Schulze

Rob Nelson

Date	Traded To	Traded With	Traded By	In Exchange For
Aug. 30, 1987	SD N	Dave Leiper	OAK A	Storm Davis

(San Diego received Nelson on September 8, 1987.)

Rocky Nelson

Date	Traded To	Traded With	Traded By	In Exchange For
May 17, 1951	PIT N	Erv Dusak	STL N	Stan Rojek
Sept. 20, 1951	CHI A	—	PIT N	Waiver price
July 30, 1956	STL N	—	BKN N	Waiver price

Roger Nelson

Date	Traded To	Traded With	Traded By	In Exchange For
Nov. 29, 1967	BAL A	—	CHI A	*see Luis Aparicio*
Nov. 30, 1972	CIN N	Richie Scheinblum	KC A	Hal McRae Wayne Simpson
Oct. 25, 1974	CHI A	—	CIN N	Cash

Dick Nen

Date	Traded To	Traded With	Traded By	In Exchange For
Dec. 4, 1964	WAS A	*see Frank Howard*	LA N	—
Apr. 3, 1968	CHI N	—	WAS A	Cash
Oct. 1, 1968	WAS A	—	CHI N	Cash

Robb Nen

Date	Traded To	Traded With	Traded By	In Exchange For
July 17, 1993	FLA N	Minor league P Kurt Miller	TEX A	Cris Carpenter

Graig Nettles

Date	Traded To	Traded With	Traded By	In Exchange For
Dec. 10, 1969	CLE A	Dean Chance Bob Miller Ted Uhlaender	MIN A	Luis Tiant Stan Williams
Nov. 27, 1972	NY A	Gerry Moses	CLE A	John Ellis Jerry Kenney Charlie Spikes Rusty Torres
Mar. 30, 1984	SD N	—	NY A	Dennis Rasmussen minor league P Darin Cloninger
Apr. 1, 1987	ATL N	—	SD N	No compensation (free agent signing)

Morris Nettles

Date	Traded To	Traded With	Traded By	In Exchange For
Dec. 11, 1975	CHI A	Jim Spencer	CAL A	Bill Melton Steve Dunning

Dan Neumeier

Date	Traded To	Traded With	Traded By	In Exchange For
Oct. 23, 1973	HOU N	—	CHI A	Hector Torres

Ernie Nevel

Date	Traded To	Traded With	Traded By	In Exchange For
Aug. 28, 1952	CIN N	—	NY A	*see Ewell Blackwell*
June 9, 1954	BKN N	Charlie Kress Johnny Bucha Cash	DET A	Wayne Belardi

Phil Nevin

Date	Traded To	Traded With	Traded By	In Exchange For
Aug. 8, 1995	DET A	—	HOU N	Mike Henneman

(Detroit received Nevin on August 15, 1995.)

Don Newcombe

Date	Traded To	Traded With	Traded By	In Exchange For
June 15, 1958	CIN N	—	LA N	Steve Bilko Johnny Klippstein
July 29, 1960	CLE A	—	CIN N	Cash

Marc Newfield

Date	Traded To	Traded With	Traded By	In Exchange For
July 31, 1995	SD N	Ron Villone	SEA A	Andy Benes Player to be named

(Seattle received P Greg Keagle on September 16, 1995.)

Al Newman

Date	Traded To	Traded With	Traded By	In Exchange For
July 21, 1984	MON N	—	SD N	Greg Harris
Feb. 20, 1987	MIN A	—	MON N	Minor league P Mike Shade

Jeff Newman

Date	Traded To	Traded With	Traded By	In Exchange For
Dec. 6, 1982	BOS A	Tony Armas	OAK A	Carney Lansford Garry Hancock minor league P Jerry King

Ray Newman

Date	Traded To	Traded With	Traded By	In Exchange For
Dec. 6, 1973	DET A	—	MIL A	Mike Strahler

Bobo Newsom

Date	Traded To	Traded With	Traded By	In Exchange For
May 21, 1935	WAS A	—	STL A	$40,000.

Bobo Newsom *continued*

Date	Traded To	Traded With	Traded By	In Exchange For
June 11, 1937	BOS A	Ben Chapman	WAS A	Wes Ferrell Mel Almada Rick Ferrell
Dec. 2, 1937	STL A	Red Kress Buster Mills	BOS A	Joe Vosmik
May 13, 1939	DET A	Beau Bell Red Kress Jim Walkup	STL A	Vern Kennedy Bob Harris George Gill Roxie Lawson Chet Laabs Mark Christman
Mar. 31, 1942	WAS A	—	DET A	$40,000.
Aug. 30, 1942	BKN N	—	WAS A	$25,000.
July 15, 1943	STL A	—	BKN N	Fritz Ostermueller Archie McKain
Aug. 31, 1943	WAS A	—	STL A	Cash
Dec. 13, 1943	PHI A	—	WAS A	Roger Wolff
July 11, 1947	NY A	—	WAS A	Waiver price

Skeeter Newsome

Date	Traded To	Traded With	Traded By	In Exchange For
Dec. 12, 1945	PHI N	—	BOS A	Cash

Warren Newson

Date	Traded To	Traded With	Traded By	In Exchange For
Mar. 31, 1991	CHI A	Joey Cora Minor league IF Kevin Garner	SD N	Adam Peterson Steve Rosenberg
July 18, 1995	SEA A	—	CHI A	Jeff Darwin

(Chicago received Darwin on October 9, 1995.)

Doc Newton

Date	Traded To	Traded With	Traded By	In Exchange For
July 1901	BKN N	—	CIN N	Cash

Gus Niarhos

Date	Traded To	Traded With	Traded By	In Exchange For
June 27, 1950	CHI A	—	NY A	$10,000.
Nov. 27, 1951	STL A	—	CHI A	*see Sherm Lollar*
Nov. 28, 1951	BOS A	Ken Wood	STL A	Les Moss Tom Wright

Carl Nichols

Date	Traded To	Traded With	Traded By	In Exchange For
Mar. 31, 1989	HOU N	—	BAL A	Dave Johnson Minor league OF Victor Hithe

Kid Nichols

Date	Traded To	Traded With	Traded By	In Exchange For
July 16, 1905	PHI N	—	STL N	Waiver price

Reid Nichols

Date	Traded To	Traded With	Traded By	In Exchange For
July 11, 1985	CHI A	—	BOS A	Tim Lollar

Bill Nicholson

Date	Traded To	Traded With	Traded By	In Exchange For
Oct. 4, 1948	PHI N	—	CHI N	Harry Walker

Dave Nicholson

Date	Traded To	Traded With	Traded By	In Exchange For
Jan. 14, 1963	CHI A	Hoyt Wilhelm Pete Ward Ron Hansen	BAL A	Luis Aparicio Al Smith
Dec. 1, 1965	HOU N	Bill Heath	CHI A	Jack Lamabe minor league P Ray Cordeiro Cash
Dec. 31, 1966	ATL N	Bob Bruce	HOU N	Sandy Alomar Eddie Mathews Arnie Umbach

Fred Nicholson

Date	Traded To	Traded With	Traded By	In Exchange For
June 30, 1919	PIT N	—	DET A	Waiver price
Feb. 23, 1921	BOS N	Billy Southworth Walter Barbare $15,000.	PIT N	Rabbit Maranville

Steve Nicosia

Date	Traded To	Traded With	Traded By	In Exchange For
Aug. 19, 1983	SF N	—	PIT N	Milt May Cash
Feb. 15, 1985	MON N	—	SF N	No compensation (free agent signing)

Tom Niedenfuer

Date	Traded To	Traded With	Traded By	In Exchange For
May 22, 1987	BAL A	—	LA N	John Shelby Brad Havens
Dec. 7, 1988	SEA A	—	BAL A	No compensation (free agent signing)

Al Niehaus

Date	Traded To	Traded With	Traded By	In Exchange For
Oct. 27, 1924	PIT N	Vic Aldridge George Grantham	CHI N	Charlie Grimm Rabbit Maranville Wilbur Cooper
May 20, 1925	CIN N	—	PIT N	Tom Sheehan

Bert Niehoff

Date	Traded To	Traded With	Traded By	In Exchange For
Nov. 1914	PHI N	—	CIN N	Red Dooin
Apr. 4, 1918	STL N	$500.	PHI N	Milt Watson
May 18, 1918	NY N	—	STL N	Waiver price

Joe Niekro

Date	Traded To	Traded With	Traded By	In Exchange For
Apr. 25, 1969	SD N	Francisco Libran Gary Ross	CHI N	Dick Selma
Dec. 4, 1969	DET A	—	SD N	Pat Dobson Dave Campbell
Aug. 7, 1973	ATL N	—	DET A	Cash
Apr. 6, 1975	HOU N	—	ATL N	$35,000.
Sept. 15, 1985	NY A	—	HOU N	Jim Deshaies Two players to be named

(Houston received IF Neder Horta and P Dody Rather on Jan. 11, 1986.)

Date	Traded To	Traded With	Traded By	In Exchange For
June 7, 1987	MIN A	Cash	NY A	Mark Salas

Phil Niekro

Date	Traded To	Traded With	Traded By	In Exchange For
Jan. 6, 1984	NY A	—	ATL N	No compensation (free agent signing)
Aug. 7, 1987	TOR A	—	CLE A	Don Gordon Minor league OF Darryl Landrum

Jerry Nielsen

Date	Traded To	Traded With	Traded By	In Exchange For
Dec. 6, 1992	CAL A	J. T. Snow Russ Springer	NY A	Jim Abbott

Scott Nielsen

Date	Traded To	Traded With	Traded By	In Exchange For
Feb. 14, 1984	NY A	Minor league P Eric Parent	SEA A	Larry Milbourne
Jan. 5, 1987	CHI A	Minor league IF Mike Soper	NY A	Pete Filson Randy Velarde
Nov. 12, 1987	NY A	*see Richard Dotson*	CHI A	—
July 10, 1989	NY N	—	NY A	Marcus Lawton

Bob Nieman

Date	Traded To	Traded With	Traded By	In Exchange For
Dec. 4, 1952	DET A	Owen Friend J. W. Porter	STL A	Virgil Trucks Johnny Groth Hal White
Dec. 6, 1954	CHI A	Walt Dropo Ted Gray	DET A	Leo Cristante Ferris Fain Jack Phillips
May 21, 1956	BAL A	Mike Fornieles Connie Johnson George Kell	CHI A	Jim Wilson Dave Philley
Dec. 2, 1959	STL N	—	BAL A	Gene Green minor league C Charles Staniland
May 10, 1961	CLE A	—	STL N	Joe Morgan Mike Lee Cash

(St. Louis received Lee on September 25.)

Date	Traded To	Traded With	Traded By	In Exchange For
Apr. 29, 1962	SF N	—	CLE A	Cash

Randy Niemann

Date	Traded To		Traded With	Traded By		In Exchange For
June 15, 1977	HOU	N	Dave Bergman Mike Fischlin	NY	A	Cliff Johnson
			(Houston received Bergman on November 23.)			
Aug. 31, 1981	PIT	N	Johnny Ray minor league OF Kevin Houston	HOU	N	Phil Garner
Sept. 7, 1983	CHI	A	—	PIT	N	Miguel Dilone minor league P Mike Maitland

Al Niemiec

Date	Traded To		Traded With	Traded By		In Exchange For
Jan. 4, 1936	PHI	A	Hank Johnson $75,000.	BOS	A	Doc Cramer Eric McNair

Tom Nieto

Date	Traded To		Traded With	Traded By		In Exchange For
Mar. 31, 1986	MON	N	—	STL	N	Fred Manrique
Feb. 3, 1987	MIN	A	*see Jeff Reardon*	MON	N	—
Oct. 24, 1988	PHI	N	Tommy Herr Eric Bullock	MIN	A	Shane Rawley Cash

Melvin Nieves

Date	Traded To		Traded With	Traded By		In Exchange For
July 18, 1993	SD	N	Donnie Elliott Minor league OF Vince Moore	ATL	N	Fred McGriff

Johnny Niggeling

Date	Traded To		Traded With	Traded By		In Exchange For
Jan. 4, 1940	STL	A	—	CIN	N	Waiver price
Aug. 18, 1943	WAS	A	Harlond Clift	STL	A	Ellis Clary Ox Miller Cash

Harry Niles

Date	Traded To		Traded With	Traded By		In Exchange For
Nov. 1907	NY	A	—	STL	A	Cash
Aug. 17, 1908	BOS	A	—	NY	A	Frank LaPorte
May 1910	CLE	A	—	BOS	A	Cash

Rabbit Nill

Date	Traded To		Traded With	Traded By		In Exchange For
Aug. 11, 1907	CLE	A	—	WAS	A	Pete O'Brien Howard Wakefield

Al Nipper

Date	Traded To		Traded With	Traded By		In Exchange For
Dec. 8, 1987	CHI	N	—	BOS	A	*see Lee Smith*

Ron Nischwitz

Date	Traded To		Traded With	Traded By		In Exchange For
Nov. 27, 1962	CLE	A	Gordon Seyfried	DET	A	Bubba Phillips

C. J. Nitkowski

Date	Traded To		Traded With	Traded By		In Exchange For
July 31, 1995	DET	A	Mark Lewis Minor league P Dave Tuttle	CIN	N	David Wells
			(Detroit received Lewis on November 16, 1995.)			

Donell Nixon

Date	Traded To		Traded With	Traded By		In Exchange For
Mar. 19, 1988	SF	N	—	SEA	A	Rod Scurry
			(San Francisco received Nixon on June 23, 1988.)			

Otis Nixon

Date	Traded To		Traded With	Traded By		In Exchange For
Feb. 5, 1984	CLE	A	—	NY	A	*see Toby Harrah*
Apr. 1, 1991	ATL	N	Minor league 3B Boi Rodriguez	MON	N	Jimmy Kremers Player to be named
			(Montreal received P Keith Morrison on June 3, 1991.)			
Dec. 7, 1993	BOS	A	—	ATL	N	No compensation (free agent signing)
Dec. 9, 1994	TEX	A	Luis Ortiz	BOS	A	Jose Canseco
Dec. 7, 1995	TOR	A	—	TEX	A	No compensation (free agent signing)

Russ Nixon

Date	Traded To		Traded With	Traded By		In Exchange For
Mar. 16, 1960	BOS	A	—	CLE	A	Sammy White Jim Marshall
			(Trade was cancelled when White decided to retire.)			
June 13, 1960	BOS	A	Carroll Hardy	CLE	A	Marty Keough Ted Bowsfield

Russ Nixon *continued*

Date	Traded To		Traded With	Traded By		In Exchange For
Apr. 6, 1966	MIN	A	Chuck Schilling	BOS	A	Dick Stigman minor league 1B Jose Calero

Junior Noboa

Date	Traded To		Traded With	Traded By		In Exchange For
Mar. 30, 1988	CAL	A	—	CLE	A	Minor league OF Ted Milner
Oct. 8, 1991	NY	N	—	MON	N	Waiver price

Paul Noce

Date	Traded To		Traded With	Traded By		In Exchange For
Apr. 2, 1989	SEA	A	Minor League IF Chuck Baldwin	CLE	A	Dave Hengel

Matt Nokes

Date	Traded To		Traded With	Traded By		In Exchange For
Oct. 7, 1985	DET	A	Dave LaPoint Eric King	SF	N	Juan Berenguer Bob Melvin Scott Medvin
			(San Francisco received Medvin on Dec. 11, 1985.)			
June 4, 1990	NY	A	—	DET	A	Lance McCullers Clay Parker
Dec. 9, 1994	BAL	A	—	NY	A	No compensation (free agent signing)

Gary Nolan

Date	Traded To		Traded With	Traded By		In Exchange For
June 15, 1977	CAL	A	—	CIN	N	Minor league IF Craig Henderson

Joe Nolan

Date	Traded To		Traded With	Traded By		In Exchange For
Mar. 26, 1982	BAL	A	—	CIN	N	Dallas Williams minor league P Brooks Carey

Dickie Noles

Date	Traded To		Traded With	Traded By		In Exchange For
Dec. 8, 1981	CHI	N	Keith Moreland Dan Larson	PHI	N	Mike Krukow Cash
July 1, 1984	TEX	A	—	CHI	N	Dwayne Henry minor league IF Jorge Gomez
			(Chicago received Henry and Gomez on December 22.)			
Sept. 22, 1987	DET	A	—	CHI	N	Player to be named
			(Noles was returned to Chicago on Oct. 23, 1987.)			

Pete Noonan

Date	Traded To		Traded With	Traded By		In Exchange For
July 1, 1906	STL	N	Fred Beebe Cash	CHI	N	Jack Taylor

Jerry Nops

Date	Traded To		Traded With	Traded By		In Exchange For
Jan. 1900	BKN	N	Harry Howell Jimmy Sheckard Broadway Aleck Smith Frank Kitson Joe McGinnity	BAL	N	Cash

Tim Nordbrook

Date	Traded To		Traded With	Traded By		In Exchange For
Sept. 9, 1976	CAL	A	—	BAL	A	Cash
Aug. 30, 1977	TOR	A	—	CHI	A	Cash
Apr. 29, 1978	MIL	A	—	TOR	A	Tim Johnson

Wayne Nordhagen

Date	Traded To		Traded With	Traded By		In Exchange For
June 7, 1973	ATL	N	Frank Tepedino Dave Cheadle Al Closter	NY	A	Pat Dobson
May 28, 1975	STL	N	Ron Reed	ATL	N	Elias Sosa Ray Sadecki
July 14, 1976	CHI	A	—	PHI	N	Rich Coggins
Apr. 2, 1982	TOR	A	—	CHI	A	Aurelio Rodriguez
June 15, 1982	PHI	N	—	TOR	A	Dick Davis
June 15, 1982	PIT	N	—	PHI	N	Bill Robinson
June 22, 1982	TOR	A	—	PIT	N	Dick Davis
Dec. 10, 1982	CHI	N	—	TOR	A	No compensation (free agent signing)

Irv Noren

Date	Traded To	Traded With	Traded By	In Exchange For
May 3, 1952	NY A	Tom Upton	WAS A	Jackie Jensen Spec Shea Jerry Snyder Archie Wilson
Feb. 19, 1957	KC A	*see Billy Hunter*	NY A	—
Aug. 31, 1957	STL N	—	KC A	Waiver price
May 19, 1959	CHI N	—	STL N	Charlie King

Dan Norman

Date	Traded To	Traded With	Traded By	In Exchange For
June 15, 1977	NY N	Pat Zachry Doug Flynn Steve Henderson	CIN N	Tom Seaver
May 29, 1981	MON N	Jeff Reardon	NY N	Ellis Valentine

Fred Norman

Date	Traded To	Traded With	Traded By	In Exchange For
Dec. 15, 1963	CHI N	—	KC A	Nelson Mathews
Sept. 28, 1970	STL N	—	LA N	Cash
June 11, 1971	SD N	Leron Lee	STL N	Al Santorini
June 12, 1973	CIN N	—	SD N	Gene Locklear Mike Johnson Cash

Nelson Norman

Date	Traded To	Traded With	Traded By	In Exchange For
Dec. 8, 1977	TEX A	Al Oliver	PIT N	Bert Blyleven John Milner

(Part of four-team trade involving Texas, New York Mets, Pittsburgh, and Atlanta.)

Jim Norris

Date	Traded To	Traded With	Traded By	In Exchange For
Jan. 4, 1980	TEX A	David Clyde	CLE A	Larry McCall Gary Gray minor league 3B-OF Mike Bucci

Billy North

Date	Traded To	Traded With	Traded By	In Exchange For
Nov. 21, 1972	OAK A	—	CHI N	Bob Locker
May 17, 1978	LA N	—	OAK A	Glenn Burke

Lou North

Date	Traded To	Traded With	Traded By	In Exchange For
June 17, 1924	BOS N	—	STL N	Cash

Hub Northen

Date	Traded To	Traded With	Traded By	In Exchange For
Apr. 1911	BKN N	—	CIN N	Cash

Ron Northey

Date	Traded To	Traded With	Traded By	In Exchange For
May 3, 1947	STL N	—	PHI N	Harry Walker Freddy Schmidt
Dec. 14, 1949	CIN N	Lou Klein	STL N	Harry Walker
June 7, 1950	CHI N	—	CIN N	Bob Scheffing

Jim Northrup

Date	Traded To	Traded With	Traded By	In Exchange For
Aug. 7, 1974	MON N	—	DET A	Cash
Sept. 16, 1974	BAL A	—	MON N	Cash

Willie Norwood

Date	Traded To	Traded With	Traded By	In Exchange For
Dec. 12, 1980	SEA A	—	MIN A	Byron McLaughlin

Joe Nossek

Date	Traded To	Traded With	Traded By	In Exchange For
May 11, 1966	KC A	—	MIN A	Cash
July 12, 1969	STL N	—	OAK A	Bob Johnson

Don Nottebart

Date	Traded To	Traded With	Traded By	In Exchange For
Nov. 30, 1962	HOU N	—	MIL N	Cash
Apr. 27, 1969	CHI N	—	CIN N	Minor league IF Jim Armstrong Cash

Rafael Novoa

Date	Traded To	Traded With	Traded By	In Exchange For
Dec. 19, 1993	CHI N	—	MIL A	Bob Scanlan Minor league OF Mike Carter

Wynn Noyes

Date	Traded To	Traded With	Traded By	In Exchange For
Aug. 1919	CHI A	—	PHI A	Cash

Les Nunamaker

Date	Traded To	Traded With	Traded By	In Exchange For
May 13, 1914	NY A	—	BOS A	Cash
Jan. 22, 1918	STL A	—	NY A	*see Eddie Plank*
Mar. 1919	CLE A	—	STL A	Josh Billings

Edwin Nunez

Date	Traded To	Traded With	Traded By	In Exchange For
July 11, 1988	NY N	—	SEA A	Gene Walter
Dec. 4, 1990	MIL A	—	DET A	No compensation (free agent signing)
May 25, 1992	TEX A	—	MIL A	Player to be named

(Milwaukee received P Mark Hampton on September 15, 1992.)

Jose Nunez

Date	Traded To	Traded With	Traded By	In Exchange For
Dec. 7, 1989	CHI N	—	TOR A	Paul Kilgus

Howie Nunn

Date	Traded To	Traded With	Traded By	In Exchange For
Dec. 21, 1961	NY N	—	CIN N	Cash

(Nunn was returned to Cincinnati on April 2, 1962.)

Joe Nuxhall

Date	Traded To	Traded With	Traded By	In Exchange For
Jan. 25, 1961	KC A	—	CIN N	John Tsitouris Johnny Briggs

Rich Nye

Date	Traded To	Traded With	Traded By	In Exchange For
Dec. 4, 1969	STL N	—	CHI N	Boots Day
May 15, 1970	MON N	—	STL N	Cash

Jerry Nyman

Date	Traded To	Traded With	Traded By	In Exchange For
Mar. 30, 1970	SD N	—	CHI A	Tommie Sisk

Nyls Nyman

Date	Traded To	Traded With	Traded By	In Exchange For
Aug. 31, 1977	STL N	Dave Hamilton Silvio Martinez	CHI A	Clay Carroll

Rebel Oakes

Date	Traded To	Traded With	Traded By	In Exchange For
Feb. 1910	STL N	Miller Huggins Frank Corridon	CIN N	Fred Beebe Alan Storke

Johnny Oates

Date	Traded To	Traded With	Traded By	In Exchange For
Nov. 30, 1972	ATL N	—	BAL A	*see Earl Williams*
May 7, 1975	PHI N	Dick Allen	ATL N	Jim Essian Barry Bonnell Cash
Dec. 20, 1976	LA N	minor league P Quincy Hill	PHI N	Ted Sizemore

Ken Oberkfell

Date	Traded To	Traded With	Traded By	In Exchange For
June 15, 1984	ATL N	—	STL N	Mike Jorgensen Ken Dayley
Aug. 28, 1988	PIT N	—	ATL N	Tommy Gregg
May 10, 1989	SF N	—	PIT N	Roger Samuels
Dec. 6, 1989	HOU N	—	SF N	No compensation (free agent signing)

(Atlanta received Gregg on September 1, 1988.)

Frank Oberlin

Date	Traded To	Traded With	Traded By	In Exchange For
Aug. 11, 1907	WAS A	—	BOS A	Cash

Mike O'Berry

Date	Traded To	Traded With	Traded By	In Exchange For
Aug. 17, 1979	CHI N	Cash	BOS A	Ted Sizemore
Oct. 17, 1980	CIN N	—	CHI N	Jay Howell
Jan. 10, 1983	CAL A	—	CIN N	John Harris
Dec. 8, 1983	NY A	—	CAL A	No compensation (free agent signing)

Bob O'Brien

Date	Traded To	Traded With	Traded By	In Exchange For
Dec. 2, 1971	BAL A	—	LA N	*see Frank Robinson*

Buck O'Brien

Date	Traded To	Traded With	Traded By	In Exchange For
July 1913	CHI A	—	BOS A	Cash

Charlie O'Brien

Date	Traded To	Traded With	Traded By	In Exchange For
Mar. 30, 1986	MIL A	—	OAK A	*see Moose Haas*
Aug. 31, 1990	NY N	Player to be named	MIL A	Julio Machado Kevin Brown

(Machado and Brown were assigned to Milwaukee on September 7 and New York received P Kevin Carmody on September 11, 1990.)

Date	Traded To	Traded With	Traded By	In Exchange For
Dec. 15, 1995	TOR A	—	ATL N	No compensation (free agent signing)

Dan O'Brien

Date	Traded To	Traded With	Traded By	In Exchange For
Nov. 9, 1979	SEA A	—	STL N	Cash

Jack O'Brien

Date	Traded To	Traded With	Traded By	In Exchange For
May 1901	CLE A	—	WAS A	Cash

John O'Brien

Date	Traded To	Traded With	Traded By	In Exchange For
Jan. 1900	LOU N	—	PIT N	*see Honus Wagner*

Johnny O'Brien

Date	Traded To	Traded With	Traded By	In Exchange For
June 15, 1958	STL N	Gene Freese	PIT N	Dick Schofield Cash
Mar. 31, 1959	MIL N	Stan Lopata Ted Kazanski	PHI N	Gene Conley Joe Koppe Harry Hanebrink

Pete O'Brien

Date	Traded To	Traded With	Traded By	In Exchange For
Dec. 6, 1988	CLE A	Oddibe McDowell Jerry Browne	TEX A	Julio Franco
Dec. 7, 1989	SEA A	—	CLE A	No compensation (free agent signing)

Pete O'Brien

Date	Traded To	Traded With	Traded By	In Exchange For
Dec. 1906	CLE A	—	STL A	Fritz Buelow
Aug. 11, 1907	WAS A	Howard Wakefield	CLE A	Rabbit Nill

Syd O'Brien

Date	Traded To	Traded With	Traded By	In Exchange For
Dec. 13, 1969	CHI A	Gerry Janeski minor league P Billy Farmer	BOS A	Don Pavletich Gary Peters

(Janeski replaced Farmer, who retired.)

Date	Traded To	Traded With	Traded By	In Exchange For
Nov. 30, 1970	CAL A	*see Ken Berry*	CHI A	—
July 28, 1972	MIL A	Joe Azcue	CAL A	Paul Ratliff Ron Clark

Tom O'Brien

Date	Traded To	Traded With	Traded By	In Exchange For
Feb. 1900	PIT N	—	NY N	Cash

Tommy O'Brien

Date	Traded To	Traded With	Traded By	In Exchange For
May 8, 1950	WAS A	Merrill Combs	BOS A	Clyde Vollmer

Alex Ochoa

Date	Traded To	Traded With	Traded By	In Exchange For
July 28, 1995	NY N	Damon Buford	BAL A	Bobby Bonilla Player to be named

(Baltimore received P Jimmy Williams on August 16, 1995.)

Danny O'Connell

Date	Traded To	Traded With	Traded By	In Exchange For
Dec. 26, 1953	MIL N	—	PIT N	Sid Gordon Max Surkont Sam Jethroe Curt Raydon Fred Walters minor league P Larry Lasalle and $100,000.
June 15, 1957	NY N	Ray Crone Bobby Thomson	MIL N	Red Schoendienst

Jack O'Connor

Date	Traded To	Traded With	Traded By	In Exchange For
May 10, 1900	PIT N	—	STL N	Cash

Jack O'Connor *continued*

Date	Traded To	Traded With	Traded By	In Exchange For
Oct. 26, 1903	STL A	—	NY A	John Anderson
Jan. 1904	STL A	Harry Howell	NY A	Jack Powell

Jack O'Connor

Date	Traded To	Traded With	Traded By	In Exchange For
Jan. 9, 1985	MON N	—	MIN A	Mike Stenhouse

Ken O'Dea

Date	Traded To	Traded With	Traded By	In Exchange For
Oct. 26, 1934	CHI N	—	STL N	Pat Malone
Dec. 6, 1938	NY N	Frank Demaree Bill Jurges	CHI N	Dick Bartell Hank Leiber Gus Mancuso
Dec. 11, 1941	STL N	Bill Lohrman Johnny McCarthy $50,000.	NY N	Johnny Mize
July 8, 1946	BOS N	—	STL N	Cash

Billy O'Dell

Date	Traded To	Traded With	Traded By	In Exchange For
Nov. 30, 1959	SF N	Billy Loes	BAL A	Jackie Brandt Gordon Jones Roger McCardell
Feb. 1, 1965	MIL N	—	SF N	Ed Bailey
June 15, 1966	PIT N	—	ATL N	Don Schwall

Blue Moon Odom

Date	Traded To	Traded With	Traded By	In Exchange For
May 20, 1975	CLE A	Cash	OAK A	Dick Bosman Jim Perry
June 7, 1975	ATL N	Rob Belloir	CLE A	Roric Harrison
June 15, 1976	CHI A	—	ATL N	Pete Varney

John O'Donoghue

Date	Traded To	Traded With	Traded By	In Exchange For
Apr. 6, 1966	CLE A	—	KC A	Ralph Terry Cash
Nov. 28, 1967	BAL A	Gordon Lund	CLE A	Eddie Fisher minor leaguers P Bob Scott and IF John Scruggs
Apr. 30, 1969	SEA A	Tom Fisher minor league P Lloyd Fourroux	BAL A	Gerry Schoen Mike Ferraro
June 15, 1970	MON N	—	MIL A	Cash

John O'Donoghue

Date	Traded To	Traded With	Traded By	In Exchange For
Dec. 19, 1994	LA N	—	BAL A	Minor league P John DeSilva

Lefty O'Doul

Date	Traded To	Traded With	Traded By	In Exchange For
July 23, 1922	BOS A	Chick Fewster Elmer Miller Johnny Mitchell $50,000.	NY A	Joe Dugan Elmer Smith
Oct. 29, 1928	PHI N	Cash	NY N	Freddy Leach
Oct. 14, 1930	BKN N	Fresco Thompson	PHI N	Clise Dudley Jumbo Elliott Hal Lee Cash
June 16, 1933	NY N	Watty Clark	BKN N	Sam Leslie

Bryan Oelkers

Date	Traded To	Traded With	Traded By	In Exchange For
Jan. 7, 1986	MIN A	—	CLE A	Ken Schrom

Joe Oeschger

Date	Traded To	Traded With	Traded By	In Exchange For
May 27, 1919	NY N	—	PHI N	George Smith
Aug. 15, 1919	BOS N	Red Causey Johnny Jones Mickey O'Neil $55,000.	NY N	Art Nehf
Nov. 12, 1923	NY N	Billy Southworth	BOS N	Casey Stengel Dave Bancroft Bill Cunningham

(Bancroft was named Boston manager.)

Date	Traded To	Traded With	Traded By	In Exchange For
July 1, 1924	PHI N	—	NY N	Waiver price
Apr. 20, 1925	BKN N	—	PHI N	Waiver price

Bob O'Farrell

Date	Traded To		Traded With	Traded By		In Exchange For
May 23, 1925	STL	N	—	CHI	N	Mike Gonzalez Howard Freigau
May 1, 1928	NY	N	—	STL	N	George Harper
Oct. 10, 1932	STL	N	Ethan Allen Bill Walker Jim Mooney	NY	N	Gus Mancuso Ray Starr
Jan. 11, 1934	CIN	N	Syl Johnson	STL	N	Glenn Spencer

(O'Farrell was named Cincinnati manager.)

Jose Offerman

Date	Traded To		Traded With	Traded By		In Exchange For
Dec. 17, 1995	KC	A	—	LA	N	Billy Brewer

Rowland Office

Date	Traded To		Traded With	Traded By		In Exchange For
Dec. 4, 1979	MON	N	—	ATL	N	No compensation (free agent signing)

Curly Ogden

Date	Traded To		Traded With	Traded By		In Exchange For
June 19, 1924	WAS	A	—	PHI	A	Cash

Jack Ogden

Date	Traded To		Traded With	Traded By		In Exchange For
May 7, 1933	STL	N	*see Leo Durocher*	CIN	N	—

Ben Oglivie

Date	Traded To		Traded With	Traded By		In Exchange For
Oct. 23, 1973	DET	A	—	BOS	A	Dick McAuliffe
Dec. 9, 1977	MIL	A	—	DET	A	Jim Slaton Rich Folkers

Hal O'Hagen

Date	Traded To		Traded With	Traded By		In Exchange For
July 1902	NY	N	—	CHI	N	Jack Hendricks

Greg O'Halloran

Date	Traded To		Traded With	Traded By		In Exchange For
Nov. 11, 1993	FLA	N	—	TOR	A	Cash

Bob Ojeda

Date	Traded To		Traded With	Traded By		In Exchange For
Nov. 13, 1985	NY	N	John Mitchell Tom McCarthy Minor league P Chris Bayer	BOS	A	Calvin Schiraldi John Christensen Wes Gardner LaSchelle Tarver
Dec. 15, 1990	LA	N	Greg Hansell	NY	N	Hubie Brooks
Dec. 8, 1992	CLE	A	—	LA	N	No compensation (free agent signing)
Jan. 28, 1994	NY	A	—	CLE	A	No compensation (free agent signing)

Bob Oldis

Date	Traded To		Traded With	Traded By		In Exchange For
Oct. 13, 1961	PHI	N	—	PIT	N	Cash

Rube Oldring

Date	Traded To		Traded With	Traded By		In Exchange For
Oct. 2, 1905	PHI	A	—	NY	A	Cash

Troy O'Leary

Date	Traded To		Traded With	Traded By		In Exchange For
Apr. 14, 1995	BOS	A	—	MIL	A	Waiver price

Jose Oliva

Date	Traded To		Traded With	Traded By		In Exchange For
Dec. 9, 1992	ATL	N	—	TEX	A	Charlie Leibrandt Pat Gomez
Aug. 25, 1995	STL	N	—	ATL	N	Minor league OF Anton French

Omar Olivares

Date	Traded To		Traded With	Traded By		In Exchange For
Feb. 27, 1990	STL	N	—	SD	N	Alex Cole Steve Peters
July 11, 1995	PHI	N	—	CLR	N	Waiver price

Al Oliver

Date	Traded To		Traded With	Traded By		In Exchange For
Dec. 8, 1977	TEX	A	Nelson Norman	PIT	N	Bert Blyleven John Milner

(Part of four-team trade involving Texas, New York Mets, Pittsburgh, and Atlanta.)

Date	Traded To		Traded With	Traded By		In Exchange For
Mar. 31, 1982	MON	N	—	TEX	A	Larry Parrish Dave Hostetler

Al Oliver *continued*

Date	Traded To		Traded With	Traded By		In Exchange For
Feb. 27, 1984	SF	N	—	MON	N	Fred Breining Max Venable Andy McGaffigan

(San Francisco sent McGaffigan to Montreal on April 1, 1984, after Breining reported to the Expos with a sore arm.)

Date	Traded To		Traded With	Traded By		In Exchange For
Aug. 20, 1984	PHI	N	Renie Martin	SF	N	Kelly Downs George Riley
Feb. 4, 1985	LA	N	—	PHI	N	Pat Zachry
July 9, 1985	TOR	A	—	LA	N	Len Matuszek

Bob Oliver

Date	Traded To		Traded With	Traded By		In Exchange For
Dec. 2, 1967	MIN	A	—	PIT	N	Ron Kline
May 5, 1972	CAL	A	—	KC	A	Tom Murphy
Sept. 11, 1974	BAL	A	—	CAL	A	Mickey Scott Cash
Dec. 1, 1974	NY	A	—	BAL	A	Cash

Dave Oliver

Date	Traded To		Traded With	Traded By		In Exchange For
July 11, 1980	MON	N	—	CLE	A	Ross Grimsley

Gene Oliver

Date	Traded To		Traded With	Traded By		In Exchange For
June 15, 1963	MIL	N	Bob Sadowski	STL	N	Lew Burdette
June 6, 1967	PHI	N	—	ATL	N	Bob Uecker
Dec. 15, 1967	BOS	A	Dick Ellsworth	PHI	N	Mike Ryan Cash
June 27, 1968	CHI	N	—	BOS	A	Cash

Nate Oliver

Date	Traded To		Traded With	Traded By		In Exchange For
Feb. 13, 1968	SF	N	Ron Hunt	LA	N	Tom Haller minor league P Frank Kasmeta
Dec. 6, 1968	NY	A	—	SF	N	Charley Smith
Apr. 19, 1969	CHI	N	—	NY	A	Lee Elia

Tom Oliver

Date	Traded To		Traded With	Traded By		In Exchange For
Jan. 29, 1930	BOS	A	—	PHI	A	Cash

Francisco Oliveras

Date	Traded To		Traded With	Traded By		In Exchange For
May 30, 1990	SF	N	—	MIN	A	Player to be named

(Minnesota received pitcher Ed Gustafson on September 26, 1990.)

Chi Chi Olivo

Date	Traded To		Traded With	Traded By		In Exchange For
Nov. 29, 1966	NY	A	Bill Robinson	ATL	N	Clete Boyer

Diomedes Olivo

Date	Traded To		Traded With	Traded By		In Exchange For
Nov. 19, 1962	STL	N	Dick Groat	PIT	N	Julio Gotay Don Cardwell

Luis Olmo

Date	Traded To		Traded With	Traded By		In Exchange For
Dec. 24, 1949	BOS	N	—	BKN	N	Jim Russell Ed Sauer Cash

Al Olmsted

Date	Traded To		Traded With	Traded By		In Exchange For
Dec. 8, 1980	SD	N	—	STL	N	*see Rollie Fingers*
Dec. 10, 1981	STL	N	Ozzie Smith Steve Mura	SD	N	Sixto Lezcano Luis DeLeon Garry Templeton

(Templeton and Smith were exchanged on February 11, 1982; Olmsted and DeLeon were exchanged on February 19.)

Ivy Olson

Date	Traded To		Traded With	Traded By		In Exchange For
Dec. 14, 1914	CIN	N	—	CLE	A	Cash
July 17, 1915	BKN	N	—	CIN	N	Waiver price

Karl Olson

Date	Traded To		Traded With	Traded By		In Exchange For
Nov. 8, 1955	WAS	A	—	BOS	A	*see Mickey Vernon*
Apr. 30, 1957	BOS	A	—	WAS	A	Cash
Apr. 30, 1957	DET	A	—	BOS	A	Jack Phillips

Ed Olwine

Date	Traded To		Traded With	Traded By		In Exchange For
Apr. 2, 1986	ATL	N	—	NY	N	Minor league P Mike Santiago

Tom O'Malley

Date	Traded To	Traded With	Traded By	In Exchange For
Aug. 31, 1984	CHI A	—	SF N	Mike Trujillo Minor league 1B Pat Adams
Sept. 1, 1988	MON N	—	TEX A	Jack Daugherty
(Texas received Daugherty on Sept. 13, 1988.)				
Mar. 28, 1989	NY N	Mark Bailey	MON N	Steve Frey

Randy O'Neal

Date	Traded To	Traded With	Traded By	In Exchange For
Jan. 27, 1987	ATL N	Chuck Cary	DET A	Terry Harper Minor league OF Freddie Tiburcio
July 23, 1987	STL N	—	ATL N	Joe Boever

Mickey O'Neil

Date	Traded To	Traded With	Traded By	In Exchange For
Aug. 15, 1919	BOS N	Joe Oeschger Red Causey Johnny Jones $55,000.	NY N	Art Nehf
Oct. 7, 1925	BKN N	Jesse Barnes Gus Felix	BOS N	Zack Taylor Jimmy Johnston Eddie Brown
Dec. 1926	WAS A	—	BKN N	Cash
May 25, 1927	NY N	—	WAS A	Cash

Bill O'Neill

Date	Traded To	Traded With	Traded By	In Exchange For
July 4, 1904	WAS A	—	BOS A	Kip Selbach

Jack O'Neill

Date	Traded To	Traded With	Traded By	In Exchange For
Dec. 12, 1903	CHI N	Three Finger Brown	STL N	Jack Taylor Larry McLean
Jan. 1906	BOS N	—	CHI N	Waiver price

Paul O'Neill

Date	Traded To	Traded With	Traded By	In Exchange For
Nov. 3, 1992	NY A	Minor league 1B Joe DeBerry	CIN N	Roberto Kelly

Steve O'Neill

Date	Traded To	Traded With	Traded By	In Exchange For
Aug. 20, 1911	CLE A	—	PHI A	Cash
Jan. 7, 1924	BOS A	Danny Boone Joe Connolly Bill Wambsganss	CLE A	George Burns Roxy Walters Chick Fewster
Dec. 12, 1924	NY A	—	BOS A	Waiver price

Steve Ontiveros

Date	Traded To	Traded With	Traded By	In Exchange For
Aug. 10, 1993	SEA A	—	MIN A	Minor league OF Greg Shockey

Steve Ontiveros

Date	Traded To	Traded With	Traded By	In Exchange For
Feb. 11, 1977	CHI N	Bobby Murcer minor league P Andy Muhlstock	SF N	Bill Madlock Rob Sperring

Jose Oquendo

Date	Traded To	Traded With	Traded By	In Exchange For
Apr. 2, 1985	STL N	Minor league P Mark J. Davis	NY N	Angel Salazar Minor league P John Young

Joe Orengo

Date	Traded To	Traded With	Traded By	In Exchange For
Nov. 25, 1940	NY N	—	STL N	Cash
July 31, 1943	BKN N	Bill Lohrman Bill Sayles	NY N	Dolf Camilli Johnny Allen
(Camilli refused to report to New York and retired.)				
Dec. 12, 1944	CHI A	—	DET A	Skeeter Webb

Don O'Riley

Date	Traded To	Traded With	Traded By	In Exchange For
Oct. 13, 1970	CHI A	Pat Kelly	KC A	Gail Hopkins John Matias

Jesse Orosco

Date	Traded To	Traded With	Traded By	In Exchange For
Dec. 8, 1978	NY N	minor league P Greg Field	MIN A	Jerry Koosman
Dec. 11, 1987	LA N	—	NY N	Jack Savage Wally Whitehurst Kevin Tapani
(Part of a three-team trade involving Los Angeles, Oakland, and New York Mets.)				

Jesse Orosco *continued*

Date	Traded To	Traded With	Traded By	In Exchange For
Dec. 3, 1988	CLE A	—	LA N	No compensation (free agent signing)
Dec. 6, 1991	MIL A	—	CLE A	Cash
Apr. 8, 1995	BAL A	—	MIL A	No compensation (free agent signing)

Frank O'Rourke

Date	Traded To	Traded With	Traded By	In Exchange For
Jan. 1920	WAS A	—	BKN N	Cash
Jan. 10, 1922	BOS A	Joe Dugan	WAS A	Roger Peckinpaugh
(Part of three-team trade involving Boston, Philadelphia, and Washington.)				
Oct. 24, 1922	DET A	—	BOS A	Waiver price
Jan. 15, 1927	STL A	Lefty Stewart Billy Mullen Otto Miller	DET A	Marty McManus Pinky Hargrave Bobby LaMotte

John Orsino

Date	Traded To	Traded With	Traded By	In Exchange For
Dec. 15, 1962	BAL A	Mike McCormick Stu Miller	SF N	Jack Fisher Jimmie Coker Billy Hoeft
Oct. 12, 1965	WAS A	—	BAL A	Woodie Held

Joe Orsulak

Date	Traded To	Traded With	Traded By	In Exchange For
Nov. 6, 1987	BAL A	—	PIT N	Rico Rossy Minor league IF Terry Crowley, Jr.
Dec. 18, 1992	NY N	—	BAL A	No compensation (free agent signing)
Dec. 5, 1995	FLA N	—	NY N	No compensation (free agent signing)

Jorge Orta

Date	Traded To	Traded With	Traded By	In Exchange For
Dec. 19, 1979	CLE A	—	CHI A	No compensation (free agent signing)
Dec. 9, 1981	LA N	Jack Fimple Larry White	CLE A	Rick Sutcliffe Jack Perconte
Dec. 28, 1982	NY N	—	LA N	Pat Zachry
Feb. 4, 1983	TOR A	—	NY N	Steve Senteney
Dec. 20, 1983	KC A	—	TOR A	Willie Aikens

Phil Ortega

Date	Traded To	Traded With	Traded By	In Exchange For
Dec. 4, 1964	WAS A	Frank Howard Pete Richert Dick Nen Ken McMullen	LA N	Claude Osteen John Kennedy $100,000.
Apr. 4, 1969	CAL A	—	WAS A	Cash

Frank Ortenzio

Date	Traded To	Traded With	Traded By	In Exchange For
Feb. 15, 1978	CHI A	—	MON N	Cash
(Ortenzio was returned to Montreal on April 4, 1978.)				

Al Orth

Date	Traded To	Traded With	Traded By	In Exchange For
July 13, 1904	NY A	—	WAS A	Long Tom Hughes Bill Wolfe

Javier Ortiz

Date	Traded To	Traded With	Traded By	In Exchange For
Dec. 23, 1987	LA N	—	TEX A	Scott May

Jose Ortiz

Date	Traded To	Traded With	Traded By	In Exchange For
Nov. 30, 1970	CHI N	Ossie Blanco	CHI A	Pat Jacquez Dave Lemonds Roe Skidmore

Junior Ortiz

Date	Traded To	Traded With	Traded By	In Exchange For
June 14, 1983	NY N	Minor league P Arthur Ray	PIT N	Marvell Wynne Steve Senteney
Apr. 4, 1990	MIN A	Minor league P Orlando Lind	PIT N	Minor league P Mike Pomeranz

Luis Ortiz

Date	Traded To	Traded With	Traded By	In Exchange For
Dec. 9, 1994	TEX A	Otis Nixon	BOS A	Jose Canseco

Date	Traded To		Traded With	Traded By		In Exchange For
Roberto Ortiz						
Mar. 8, 1943	BKN	N	—	PHI	N	Cash
Bob Osborn						
Jan. 1931	PIT	N	—	CHI	N	Cash
Danny Osborn						
Dec. 12, 1975	ATL	N	Ken Henderson Dick Ruthven	CHI	A	Ralph Garr Larvell Blanks
Bobo Osborne						
Mar. 23, 1963	WAS	A	—	DET	A	Wayne Comer
Tiny Osborne						
May 16, 1924	BKN	N	—	CHI	N	Cash
Pat Osburn						
Oct. 22, 1974	MIL	A	—	CIN	N	John Vukovich
Dan Osinski						
July 23, 1962	LA	A	—	KC	A	Gordie Windhorn Ted Bowsfield
			(Kansas City received Bowsfield on November 30.)			
Oct. 14, 1964	MIL	N	—	LA	A	Phil Roof Ron Piche
Dec. 15, 1965	BOS	A	Bob Sadowski	MIL	N	Lee Thomas Arnold Earley Jay Ritchie
Champ Osteen						
Jan. 1904	NY	A	—	WAS	A	Cash
Claude Osteen						
Sept. 16, 1961	WAS	A	—	CIN	N	Dave Sisler Cash
Dec. 4, 1964	LA	N	John Kennedy $100,000.	WAS	A	Frank Howard Phil Ortega Pete Richert Dick Nen Ken McMullen
Dec. 6, 1973	HOU	N	minor league P Dave Culpepper	LA	N	Jimmy Wynn
Aug. 15, 1974	STL	N	—	HOU	N	Dan Larson Minor league P Ron Selak
Darrell Osteen						
Oct. 20, 1967	KC	A	Floyd Robinson	CIN	N	Ron Tompkins
Fritz Ostermueller						
Dec. 3, 1940	STL	A	—	BOS	A	Cash
July 15, 1943	BKN	N	Archie McKain	STL	A	Bobo Newsom
Joe Ostrowski						
Nov. 17, 1947	STL	A	—	BOS	A	*see Vern Stephens*
June 15, 1950	NY	A	—	STL	A	*see Snuffy Stirnweiss*
John Ostrowski						
May 31, 1950	WAS	A	—	CHI	A	*see Eddie Robinson*
Al Osuna						
Mar. 28, 1994	LA	N	—	HOU	N	Minor league P James Daspit
Ricky Otero						
Dec. 14, 1995	PHI	N	—	NY	N	Minor league OF Phil Geisler
Amos Otis						
Dec. 3, 1969	KC	A	Bob Johnson	NY	N	Joe Foy
Amos Otis *continued*						
Dec. 19, 1983	PIT	N	—	KC	A	No compensation (free agent signing)
Denny O'Toole						
Oct. 26, 1973	STL	N	—	CHI	A	Jim Kremmel
Jim O'Toole						
Dec. 15, 1966	CHI	A	—	CIN	N	Floyd Robinson
Marty O'Toole						
Aug. 14, 1914	NY	N	—	PIT	N	Cash
Ed Ott						
Apr. 1, 1981	CAL	A	Mickey Mahler	PIT	N	Jason Thompson
Jimmy Outlaw						
Dec. 13, 1938	BKN	N	—	CIN	N	Lew Krausse Cash
Dec. 13, 1938	BOS	N	Buddy Hassett	BKN	N	Gene Moore Ira Hutchinson
Orval Overall						
June 2, 1906	CHI	N	—	CIN	N	Bob Wicker $2,000.
Stubby Overmire						
Dec. 1, 1949	STL	A	—	DET	A	Waiver price
June 15, 1951	NY	A	—	STL	A	Tommy Byrne $25,000.
May 13, 1952	STL	A	—	NY	A	Waiver price
Bob Owchinko						
Feb. 15, 1980	CLE	A	Jim Wilhelm	SD	N	Jerry Mumphrey
Dec. 9, 1980	PIT	N	—	CLE	A	*see Bert Blyleven*
Apr. 6, 1981	OAK	A	—	PIT	N	Ernie Camacho Cash
Nov. 12, 1983	CIN	N	—	PIT	N	Cash
Dave Owen						
Dec. 11, 1985	SF	N	—	CHI	N	Manny Trillo
Aug. 1, 1987	KC	A	—	TEX	A	Minor leeague P Rufus Ellis
Marv Owen						
Dec. 2, 1937	CHI	A	Mike Tresh Gee Walker	DET	A	Vern Kennedy Tony Piet Dixie Walker
Dec. 8, 1939	BOS	A	—	CHI	A	Cash
Mickey Owen						
Dec. 4, 1940	BKN	N	—	STL	N	Gus Mancuso Minor league P John Pintar $65,000.
Spike Owen						
Aug. 19, 1986	BOS	A	Dave Henderson	SEA	A	Rey Quinones Mike Trujillo John Christensen Mike Brown
			(Seattle received Trujillo and Brown on August 22 and Christensen on September 25, 1986.)			
Dec. 8, 1988	MON	N	Dan Gakeler	BOS	A	John Dopson Luis Rivera
Dec. 4, 1992	NY	A	—	MON	N	No compensation (free agent signing)
Dec. 9, 1993	CAL	A	Cash	NY	A	Minor league P Jose Musset
Jim Owens						
Nov. 27, 1962	CIN	N	—	PHI	N	Cookie Rojas

Rick Ownbey

Date	Traded To		Traded With	Traded By		In Exchange For
June 15, 1983	STL	N	Neil Allen	NY	N	Keith Hernandez

Ray Oyler

Date	Traded To		Traded With	Traded By		In Exchange For
Dec. 7, 1969	OAK	A	Diego Segui	SEA	A	Ted Kubiak George Lauzerique
Apr. 17, 1970	CAL	A	—	OAK	A	Cash

John Pacella

Date	Traded To		Traded With	Traded By		In Exchange For
Dec. 15, 1980	SD	N	Jose Moreno	NY	N	Randy Jones
Apr. 1, 1981	NY	A	Jerry Mumphrey	SD	N	Ruppert Jones Joe Lefebvre Tim Lollar Chris Welsh
May 12, 1982	MIN	A	Larry Milbourne Pete Filson Cash	NY	A	Butch Wynegar Roger Erickson
Nov. 1, 1982	TEX	A	—	MIN	A	Len Whitehouse

Pat Pacillo

Date	Traded To		Traded With	Traded By		In Exchange For
July 13, 1988	MON	N	*see Tracy Jones*	CIN	N	—
Feb. 27, 1990	SEA	A	—	MON	N	Jerry Goff

Tom Paciorek

Date	Traded To		Traded With	Traded By		In Exchange For
Nov. 17, 1975	ATL	N	Jimmy Wynn Lee Lacy Jerry Royster	LA	N	Dusty Baker Ed Goodson
Dec. 11, 1981	CHI	A	—	SEA	A	Todd Cruz Rod Allen Jim Essian
July 12, 1985	NY	N	—	CHI	A	Dave Cochrane

Gene Packard

Date	Traded To		Traded With	Traded By		In Exchange For
Feb. 10, 1916	CHI	N	Charlie Pechous	KC	F	Cash
Apr. 1917	STL	N	—	CHI	N	Cash
Jan. 21, 1919	PHI	N	Doug Baird Stuffy Stewart	STL	N	Milt Stock Pickles Dillhoefer Dixie Davis

Tom Padden

Date	Traded To		Traded With	Traded By		In Exchange For
Oct. 1937	STL	N	minor leaguer Bernie Cobb	PIT	N	Johnny Rizzo
Jan. 22, 1943	PHI	N	Al Gerheauser Ed Levy Al Gettel $10,000.	NY	A	Nick Etten

Del Paddock

Date	Traded To		Traded With	Traded By		In Exchange For
Jan. 1912	NY	A	—	CHI	A	Cash

Don Padgett

Date	Traded To		Traded With	Traded By		In Exchange For
Dec. 10, 1941	BKN	N	—	STL	N	$30,000.
June 12, 1946	BOS	N	—	BKN	N	Cash
Mar. 27, 1947	PHI	N	—	BOS	N	Andy Karl

Ernie Padgett

Date	Traded To		Traded With	Traded By		In Exchange For
Feb. 1926	CLE	A	—	BOS	N	Cash

Dennis Paepke

Date	Traded To		Traded With	Traded By		In Exchange For
Dec. 12, 1968	KC	A	Ed Kirkpatrick	CAL	A	Hoyt Wilhelm

Andy Pafko

Date	Traded To		Traded With	Traded By		In Exchange For
June 15, 1951	BKN	N	Johnny Schmitz Rube Walker Wayne Terwilliger	CHI	N	Bruce Edwards Joe Hatten Eddie Miksis Gene Hermanski
Jan. 17, 1953	MIL	N	—	BKN	N	Roy Hartsfield $50,000.

Dave Pagan

Date	Traded To		Traded With	Traded By		In Exchange For
June 15, 1976	BAL	A	*see Tippy Martinez*	NY	A	—
July 27, 1977	PIT	N	—	SEA	A	Rick Honeycutt

Jose Pagan

Date	Traded To		Traded With	Traded By		In Exchange For
May 22, 1965	PIT	N	—	SF	N	Dick Schofield

Mitchell Page

Date	Traded To		Traded With	Traded By		In Exchange For
Mar. 15, 1977	OAK	A	—	PIT	N	*see Phil Garner*

Karl Pagel

Date	Traded To		Traded With	Traded By		In Exchange For
June 23, 1980	CLE	A	Cash	CHI	N	Cliff Johnson

Jim Pagliaroni

Date	Traded To		Traded With	Traded By		In Exchange For
Nov. 20, 1962	PIT	N	Don Schwall	BOS	A	Jack Lamabe Dick Stuart
Dec. 3, 1967	OAK	A	—	PIT	N	Cash
May 27, 1969	SEA	A	—	OAK	A	Cash

Mike Pagliarulo

Date	Traded To		Traded With	Traded By		In Exchange For
July 22, 1989	SD	N	Don Schulze	NY	A	Walt Terrell Fred Toliver
Jan. 25, 1991	MIN	A	—	SD	N	No compensation (free agent signing)
Aug. 15, 1993	BAL	A	—	MIN	A	Erik Schullstrom

(New York received Toliver on Sept. 27, 1989.)

Phil Paine

Date	Traded To		Traded With	Traded By		In Exchange For
Apr. 19, 1958	STL	N	—	MIL	N	Waiver price
Dec. 4, 1958	LA	N	Wally Moon	STL	N	Gino Cimoli

Rey Palacios

Date	Traded To		Traded With	Traded By		In Exchange For
Aug. 31, 1988	KC	A	Mark Lee	DET	A	Ted Power

Erv Palica

Date	Traded To		Traded With	Traded By		In Exchange For
Mar. 17, 1955	BAL	A	—	BKN	N	Frank Kellert Cash

Donn Pall

Date	Traded To		Traded With	Traded By		In Exchange For
Sept. 1, 1993	PHI	N	—	CHI	A	Doug Lindsey

(Chicago received Lindsey on September 8, 1993.)

Rafael Palmeiro

Date	Traded To		Traded With	Traded By		In Exchange For
Dec. 5, 1988	TEX	A	Jamie Moyer Drew Hall	CHI	N	Mitch Williams Paul Kilgus Steve Wilson Curtis Wilkerson Minor league IF Luis Benitez Minor league OF Pablo Delgado
Dec. 12, 1993	BAL	A	—	TEX	A	No compensation (free agent signing)

David Palmer

Date	Traded To		Traded With	Traded By		In Exchange For
Dec. 18, 1987	PHI	N	—	ATL	N	No compensation (free agent signing)

Lowell Palmer

Date	Traded To		Traded With	Traded By		In Exchange For
Sept. 18, 1972	CLE	A	—	STL	N	Cash
June 12, 1973	NY	A	—	CLE	A	Mike Kekich
May 31, 1974	SD	N	—	NY	A	Cash

Stan Palys

Date	Traded To		Traded With	Traded By		In Exchange For
Apr. 30, 1955	CIN	N	—	PHI	N	*see Andy Seminick*
Apr. 3, 1958	DET	A	—	CIN	N	Waiver price

Jim Panther

Date	Traded To		Traded With	Traded By		In Exchange For
Mar. 4, 1972	TEX	A	Don Stanhouse	OAK	A	Denny McLain
Oct. 27, 1972	ATL	N	—	TEX	A	Rico Carty

Al Papai

Date	Traded To		Traded With	Traded By		In Exchange For
May 4, 1949	STL	A	—	STL	N	Waiver price
Dec. 1, 1949	BOS	A	—	STL	A	Waiver price

Stan Papi

Date	Traded To		Traded With	Traded By		In Exchange For
June 8, 1973	STL	N	—	HOU	N	Ray Busse

Stan Papi *continued*

Date	Traded To	Traded With	Traded By	In Exchange For
Dec. 7, 1978	BOS A	—	MON N	Bill Lee
Mar. 30, 1980	PHI N	Cash	BOS A	Dave Rader
May 29, 1980	DET A	—	PHI N	Cash

Frank Papish

Date	Traded To	Traded With	Traded By	In Exchange For
Dec. 2, 1948	CLE A	—	CHI A	Bob Kuzava Ernie Groth
Dec. 14, 1949	PIT N	—	CLE A	Cash

Milt Pappas

Date	Traded To	Traded With	Traded By	In Exchange For
Dec. 9, 1965	CIN N	Jack Baldschun Dick Simpson	BAL A	Frank Robinson
June 11, 1968	ATL N	Ted Davidson Bob Johnson	CIN N	Woody Woodward Clay Carroll Tony Cloninger
June 23, 1970	CHI N	—	ATL N	Cash

Freddy Parent

Date	Traded To	Traded With	Traded By	In Exchange For
Apr. 1908	CHI A	—	BOS A	Cash

Mark Parent

Date	Traded To	Traded With	Traded By	In Exchange For
Dec. 12, 1990	TEX A	—	SD N	Scott Coolbaugh
Oct. 11, 1994	PIT N	—	CHI N	Waiver price
Aug. 31, 1995	CHI N	Cash	PIT N	Player to be named
Dec. 13, 1995	DET A	—	CHI N	No compensation (free agent signing)

Kelly Paris

Date	Traded To	Traded With	Traded By	In Exchange For
Mar. 31, 1983	CIN N	—	STL N	Minor league P Jim Strichek
Nov. 28, 1983	CHI A	—	CIN N	Cash

Clay Parker

Date	Traded To	Traded With	Traded By	In Exchange For
Dec. 22, 1987	NY A	—	SEA A	*see Steve Trout*
June 4, 1990	DET A	Lance McCullers	NY A	Matt Nokes

Dave Parker

Date	Traded To	Traded With	Traded By	In Exchange For
Dec. 7, 1983	CIN N	—	PIT N	No compensation (free agent signing)
Dec. 8, 1987	OAK A	—	CIN N	Jose Rijo Tim Birtsas
Dec. 3, 1989	MIL A	—	OAK A	No compensation (free agent signing)
Mar. 14, 1991	CAL A	—	MIL A	Dante Bichette

Harry Parker

Date	Traded To	Traded With	Traded By	In Exchange For
Oct. 18, 1971	NY N	—	STL N	*see Jim Bibby*
Aug. 4, 1975	STL N	—	NY N	Cash
Apr. 7, 1976	CLE A	—	STL N	Roric Harrison

Rick Parker

Date	Traded To	Traded With	Traded By	In Exchange For
June 18, 1989	SF N	*see Steve Bedrosian*	PHI N	—

Roy Parmelee

Date	Traded To	Traded With	Traded By	In Exchange For
Dec. 9, 1935	STL N	Phil Weintraub Cash	NY N	Burgess Whitehead
Oct. 8, 1936	CHI N	Ripper Collins	STL N	Lon Warneke

Jose Parra

Date	Traded To	Traded With	Traded By	In Exchange For
July 31, 1995	MIN A	—	LA N	*see Kevin Tapani*

Jeff Parrett

Date	Traded To	Traded With	Traded By	In Exchange For
Dec. 6, 1988	PHI N	Floyd Youmans	MON N	Kevin Gross
Aug. 3, 1990	ATL N	Jim Vatcher Victor Rosario	PHI N	Dale Murphy Tommy Greene

(Greene and Vatcher were exhanged on August 9, and Atlanta received Rosario on September 4, 1990.)

Date	Traded To	Traded With	Traded By	In Exchange For
Jan. 21, 1993	CLR N	—	OAK A	No compensation (free agent signing)

Sam Parrilla

Date	Traded To	Traded With	Traded By	In Exchange For
Dec. 16, 1970	BAL A	Grant Jackson Jim Hutto	PHI N	Roger Freed

Lance Parrish

Date	Traded To	Traded With	Traded By	In Exchange For
Mar. 13, 1987	PHI N	—	DET A	No compensation (free agent signing)
Oct. 3, 1988	CAL A	—	PHI N	Minor league P David Holdridge
Jan. 8, 1993	LA N	—	SEA A	No compensation (free agent signing)

Larry Parrish

Date	Traded To	Traded With	Traded By	In Exchange For
Mar. 31, 1982	TEX A	Dave Hostetler	MON N	Al Oliver

Mike Parrott

Date	Traded To	Traded With	Traded By	In Exchange For
Dec. 7, 1977	SEA A	—	BAL A	Carlos Lopez Tommy Moore
Mar. 5, 1982	MIL A	—	SEA A	Thad Bosley

Bill Parsons

Date	Traded To	Traded With	Traded By	In Exchange For
June 24, 1974	OAK A	Cash	MIL A	Deron Johnson
Dec. 2, 1974	STL N	—	OAK A	Cash
June 30, 1975	CHI A	Cash	STL N	Buddy Bradford

Tom Parsons

Date	Traded To	Traded With	Traded By	In Exchange For
Oct. 19, 1965	HOU N	Cash	NY N	Jerry Grote

Roy Partee

Date	Traded To	Traded With	Traded By	In Exchange For
Nov. 17, 1947	STL A	—	BOS A	*see Vern Stephens*
Dec. 13, 1948	NY A	Fred Sanford	STL A	Sherm Lollar Red Embree Dick Starr $100,000.

Camilo Pascual

Date	Traded To	Traded With	Traded By	In Exchange For
Dec. 3, 1966	WAS A	Bernie Allen	MIN A	Ron Kline
July 7, 1969	CIN N	—	WAS A	Cash
May 22, 1971	SD N	—	CLE A	Cash

(Pascual was returned to Cleveland on May 26, 1971.)

Johnny Pasek

Date	Traded To	Traded With	Traded By	In Exchange For
Dec. 12, 1933	PHI A	$100,000.	DET A	Mickey Cochrane
Dec. 12, 1933	CHI A	George Earnshaw	PHI A	Charlie Berry $20,000.

Larry Pashnick

Date	Traded To	Traded With	Traded By	In Exchange For
Dec. 8, 1983	MIN A	—	DET A	Rusty Kuntz

Dode Paskert

Date	Traded To	Traded With	Traded By	In Exchange For
Feb. 1911	PHI N	Fred Beebe Jack Rowan Hans Lobert	CIN N	Johnny Bates Eddie Grant George McQuillan Lew Moren
Dec. 26, 1917	CHI N	—	PHI N	Cy Williams
Dec. 1920	CIN N	—	CHI N	Waiver price

Kevin Pasley

Date	Traded To	Traded With	Traded By	In Exchange For
Sept. 8, 1977	SEA A	—	LA N	Cash

Dan Pasqua

Date	Traded To	Traded With	Traded By	In Exchange For
Nov. 12, 1987	CHI A	Mark Salas Steve Rosenberg	NY A	Richard Dotson Scott Nielsen

Claude Passeau

Date	Traded To	Traded With	Traded By	In Exchange For
Nov. 21, 1935	PHI N	Earl Grace	PIT N	Al Todd
May 29, 1939	CHI N	—	PHI N	Joe Marty Ray Harrell Kirby Higbe

Freddie Patek

Date	Traded To	Traded With	Traded By	In Exchange For
Dec. 2, 1970	KC A	Bruce Dal Canton Jerry May	PIT N	Bob Johnson Jackie Hernandez Jim Campanis
Dec. 5, 1979	CAL A	—	KC A	No compensation (free agent signing)

Casey Patten

Date	Traded To	Traded With	Traded By	In Exchange For
July 1908	BOS A	—	WAS A	Jesse Tannehill Bob Unglaub

Bob Patterson

Date	Traded To	Traded With	Traded By	In Exchange For
Apr. 3, 1986	PIT N	—	SD N	Marvell Wynne
Jan. 18, 1994	CAL A	—	TEX A	No compensation (free agent signing)

Daryl Patterson

Date	Traded To	Traded With	Traded By	In Exchange For
May 22, 1971	OAK A	—	DET A	John Donaldson
June 25, 1971	STL N	—	OAK A	Cash

(Patterson was returned to Oakland on October 21, 1971.)

Jeff Patterson

Date	Traded To	Traded With	Traded By	In Exchange For
Feb. 9, 1994	NY A	Terry Mulholland	PHI N	Bobby Munoz Ryan Karp Kevin Jordan

(New York received Patterson on November 8, 1994.)

Ken Patterson

Date	Traded To	Traded With	Traded By	In Exchange For
Mar. 30, 1992	CHI N	Sammy Sosa	CHI A	George Bell
Dec. 8, 1993	CIN N	—	CAL A	No compensation (free agent signing)

Mike Patterson

Date	Traded To	Traded With	Traded By	In Exchange For
May 20, 1981	NY A	Dave Revering minor league P Chuck Dougherty	OAK A	Jim Spencer Tom Underwood

Reggie Patterson

Date	Traded To	Traded With	Traded By	In Exchange For
Dec. 10, 1982	CHI N	—	CHI A	Tye Waller

Marty Pattin

Date	Traded To	Traded With	Traded By	In Exchange For
Oct. 11, 1971	BOS A	Tommy Harper Lew Krausse Minor leaguer Pat Skrable	MIL A	George Scott Billy Conigliaro Joe Lahoud Jim Lonborg Ken Brett Don Pavletich
Oct. 24, 1973	KC A	—	BOS A	Dick Drago

Mike Paul

Date	Traded To	Traded With	Traded By	In Exchange For
Dec. 2, 1971	TEX A	—	CLE A	*see Del Unser*
Aug. 31, 1973	CHI N	—	TEX A	Larry Gura

Gene Paulette

Date	Traded To	Traded With	Traded By	In Exchange For
May 1917	STL N	—	STL A	Waiver price
July 14, 1919	PHI N	Lee Meadows	STL N	Elmer Jacobs Doug Baird Frank Woodward

Dave Pavlas

Date	Traded To	Traded With	Traded By	In Exchange For
May 16, 1987	TEX A	—	CHI N	Mike Mason

(Texas received Pavlas on June 6, 1987.)

Don Pavletich

Date	Traded To	Traded With	Traded By	In Exchange For
Dec. 5, 1968	CHI A	Don Secrist	CIN N	Jack Fisher
Dec. 13, 1969	BOS A	Gary Peters	CHI A	Syd O'Brien Gerry Janeski minor league P Billy Farmer

(Janeski replaced Farmer, who retired.)

Date	Traded To	Traded With	Traded By	In Exchange For
Oct. 11, 1971	MIL A	*see George Scott*	BOS A	—

Mike Paxton

Date	Traded To	Traded With	Traded By	In Exchange For
Mar. 30, 1978	CLE A	—	BOS A	*see Dennis Eckersley*

Mike Pazik

Date	Traded To	Traded With	Traded By	In Exchange For
May 4, 1974	MIN A	—	NY A	Dick Woodson

Johnny Peacock

Date	Traded To	Traded With	Traded By	In Exchange For
June 11, 1944	PHI N	—	BOS A	Cash
June 15, 1945	BKN N	—	PHI N	Ben Chapman

Albie Pearson

Date	Traded To	Traded With	Traded By	In Exchange For
Jan. 23, 1958	WAS A	Norm Zauchin	BOS A	Pete Runnels
May 26, 1959	BAL A	—	WAS A	Lenny Green

Monte Pearson

Date	Traded To	Traded With	Traded By	In Exchange For
Dec. 11, 1935	NY A	Steve Sundra	CLE A	Johnny Allen
Dec. 30, 1940	CIN N	—	NY A	Don Lang $20,000.

Charlie Pechous

Date	Traded To	Traded With	Traded By	In Exchange For
Feb. 10, 1916	CHI N	Gene Packard	KC F	Cash

Hal Peck

Date	Traded To	Traded With	Traded By	In Exchange For
May 15, 1943	CHI N	—	BKN N	Cash
June 20, 1946	NY A	—	PHI A	Cash
Dec. 20, 1946	CLE A	Gene Bearden Al Gettel	NY A	Sherm Lollar Ray Mack

Roger Peckinpaugh

Date	Traded To	Traded With	Traded By	In Exchange For
May 20, 1913	NY A	—	CLE A	Bill Stumpf Jack Lelivelt
Dec. 20, 1921	BOS A	Jack Quinn Rip Collins Bill Piercy	NY A	Everett Scott Joe Bush Sad Sam Jones
Jan. 10, 1922	WAS A	—	BOS A	Joe Dugan Frank O'Rourke

(Part of three-team trade involving Boston, Philadelphia, and Washington.)

Date	Traded To	Traded With	Traded By	In Exchange For
Jan. 15, 1927	CHI A	—	WAS A	Sloppy Thurston Leo Mangum

Bill Pecota

Date	Traded To	Traded With	Traded By	In Exchange For
Dec. 11, 1991	NY N	*see Bret Saberhagen*	KC A	—
Jan. 4, 1993	ATL N	—	NY N	No compensation (free agent signing)

Jorge Pedre

Date	Traded To	Traded With	Traded By	In Exchange For
Dec. 2, 1991	CHI N	—	KC A	Waiver price

Al Pedrique

Date	Traded To	Traded With	Traded By	In Exchange For
May 29, 1987	PIT N	Scott Little	NY N	Bill Almon

Homer Peel

Date	Traded To	Traded With	Traded By	In Exchange For
May 11, 1928	PHI N	Spud Davis	STL N	Jimmie Wilson
Dec. 11, 1929	STL N	Bob McGraw	PHI N	Grover Alexander Harry McCurdy

Julio Peguero

Date	Traded To	Traded With	Traded By	In Exchange For
Aug. 30, 1990	PHI N	Wes Chamberlain Tony Longmire	PIT N	Carmelo Martinez

(Philadelphia received Longmire on September 28, 1990.)

Date	Traded To	Traded With	Traded By	In Exchange For
July 2, 1992	LA N	Steve Searcy	PHI N	Stan Javier

(Los Angeles received Peguero on July 28, 1992.)

Steve Pegues

Date	Traded To	Traded With	Traded By	In Exchange For
July 28, 1994	PIT N	—	CIN N	Waiver price

Heinie Peitz

Date	Traded To	Traded With	Traded By	In Exchange For
Dec. 1905	PIT N	—	CIN N	Ed Phelps

Eddie Pellagrini

Date	Traded To		Traded With	Traded By		In Exchange For
Nov. 17, 1947	STL	A	—	BOS	A	*see Vern Stephens*
Dec. 10, 1951	CIN	N	—	PHI	N	*see Smoky Burgess*
Apr. 17, 1953	PIT	N	—	CIN	N	Waiver price

Barney Pelty

Date	Traded To		Traded With	Traded By		In Exchange For
June 1912	WAS	A	—	STL	A	Cash

Brock Pemberton

Date	Traded To		Traded With	Traded By		In Exchange For
Dec. 9, 1976	STL	N	Leon Brown	NY	N	Minor league 1B Ed Kurpiel

Alejandro Pena

Date	Traded To		Traded With	Traded By		In Exchange For
Dec. 20, 1989	NY	N	Mike Marshall	LA	N	Juan Samuel
Aug. 28, 1991	ATL	N	—	NY	N	Tony Castillo Joe Roa
Dec. 10, 1992	PIT	N	—	ATL	N	No compensation (free agent signing)
Aug. 31, 1995	ATL	N	—	FLA	N	Player to be named

(Florida received P Chris Seelbach on September 15, 1995.)

Hipolito Pena

Date	Traded To		Traded With	Traded By		In Exchange For
Mar. 30, 1988	NY	A	—	PIT	N	Orestes Destrade

Jim Pena

Date	Traded To		Traded With	Traded By		In Exchange For
Dec. 10, 1992	SD	N	—	SF	N	Paul Faries

Orlando Pena

Date	Traded To		Traded With	Traded By		In Exchange For
June 23, 1965	DET	A	—	KC	A	Cash
May 6, 1967	CLE	A	—	DET	A	Cash
June 15, 1973	STL	N	—	BAL	A	Cash
Sept. 5, 1974	CAL	A	—	STL	N	Rich Hand

(St. Louis received Hand on October 15, 1974.)

Roberto Pena

Date	Traded To		Traded With	Traded By		In Exchange For
Dec. 9, 1964	CHI	N	Cash	PIT	N	Andre Rodgers
Mar. 24, 1970	OAK	A	—	SD	N	Ramon Webster
May 18, 1970	MIL	A	—	OAK	A	John Donaldson

Tony Pena

Date	Traded To		Traded With	Traded By		In Exchange For
Apr. 1, 1987	STL	N	—	PIT	N	Andy Van Slyke Mike LaValliere Mike Dunne
Nov. 27, 1989	BOS	A	—	STL	N	No compensation (free agent signing)
Feb. 7, 1994	CLE	A	—	BOS	A	No compensation (free agent signing)

Jim Pendleton

Date	Traded To		Traded With	Traded By		In Exchange For
Feb. 16, 1953	MIL	N	Rocky Bridges	BKN	N	Russ Meyer

(Part of four-team trade involving Milwaukee, Philadelphia Phillies, Brooklyn, and Cincinnati.)

Date	Traded To		Traded With	Traded By		In Exchange For
Apr. 3, 1957	PIT	N	—	MIL	N	Dick Cole
Jan. 30, 1959	CIN	N	—	PIT	N	*see Harvey Haddix*

Terry Pendleton

Date	Traded To		Traded With	Traded By		In Exchange For
Dec. 3, 1990	ATL	N	—	STL	N	No compensation (free agent signing)
Apr. 7, 1995	FLA	N	—	ATL	N	No compensation (free agent signing)

Brad Pennington

Date	Traded To		Traded With	Traded By		In Exchange For
June 16, 1995	CIN	N	—	BAL	A	Minor league OF Danny Clyburn Minor league P Tony Nieto

Herb Pennock

Date	Traded To		Traded With	Traded By		In Exchange For
June 13, 1915	BOS	A	—	PHI	A	Waiver price
Jan. 30, 1923	NY	A	—	BOS	A	Camp Skinner Norm McMillan George Murray $50,000.

William Pennyfeather

Date	Traded To		Traded With	Traded By		In Exchange For
May 13, 1994	CIN	N	—	PIT	N	Waiver price

Gene Pentz

Date	Traded To		Traded With	Traded By		In Exchange For
Dec. 6, 1975	HOU	N	—	DET	A	*see Milt May*

Joe Pepitone

Date	Traded To		Traded With	Traded By		In Exchange For
Dec. 4, 1969	HOU	N	—	NY	A	Curt Blefary
July 29, 1970	CHI	N	—	HOU	N	Cash
May 19, 1973	ATL	N	—	CHI	N	Andre Thornton

Don Pepper

Date	Traded To		Traded With	Traded By		In Exchange For
Mar. 25, 1969	MON	N	—	DET	A	Cash

Oswald Peraza

Date	Traded To		Traded With	Traded By		In Exchange For
Aug. 31, 1987	BAL	A	Jose Mesa	TOR	A	Mike Flanagan

(Baltimore received Mesa on September 4, 1987.)

Jack Perconte

Date	Traded To		Traded With	Traded By		In Exchange For
Dec. 9, 1981	CLE	A	Rick Sutcliffe	LA	N	Jorge Orta Jack Fimple Larry White
Dec. 7, 1983	SEA	A	Gorman Thomas	CLE	A	Tony Bernazard

Hub Perdue

Date	Traded To		Traded With	Traded By		In Exchange For
June 1914	STL	N	—	BOS	N	Possum Whitted Ted Cather

Marty Perez

Date	Traded To		Traded With	Traded By		In Exchange For
Oct. 21, 1970	ATL	N	—	CAL	A	Minor league C John Burns
June 13, 1976	SF	N	*see Darrell Evans*	ATL	N	—
Mar. 14, 1977	NY	A	—	SF	N	Terry Whitfield
Apr. 27, 1977	OAK	A	Dock Ellis Larry Murray	NY	A	Mike Torrez

Melido Perez

Date	Traded To		Traded With	Traded By		In Exchange For
Dec. 10, 1987	CHI	A	John Davis Greg Hibbard Minor league P Chuck Mount	KC	A	Floyd Bannister Dave Cochrane
Jan. 10, 1992	NY	A	Bob Wickman Domingo Jean	CHI	A	Steve Sax

Pascual Perez

Date	Traded To		Traded With	Traded By		In Exchange For
June 30, 1982	ATL	N	minor league SS Carlos Rios	PIT	N	Larry McWilliams
Nov. 21, 1989	NY	A	—	MON	N	No compensation (free agent signing)

Tomas Perez

Date	Traded To		Traded With	Traded By		In Exchange For
Dec. 6, 1994	TOR	A	—	CAL	A	Cash

Tony Perez

Date	Traded To		Traded With	Traded By		In Exchange For
Dec. 16, 1976	MON	N	Will McEnaney	CIN	N	Woodie Fryman Dale Murray
Nov. 20, 1979	BOS	A	—	MON	N	No compensation (free agent signing)
Dec. 6, 1983	CIN	N	—	PHI	N	Cash

Yorkis Perez

Date	Traded To		Traded With	Traded By		In Exchange For
Feb. 3, 1987	MON	N	—	MIN	A	*see Jeff Reardon*
Sept. 29, 1991	CHI	N	Turk Wendell	ATL	N	Damon Berryhill Mike Bielecki
Sept. 29, 1991	CHI	N	—			

Tony Perezchica

Date	Traded To		Traded With	Traded By		In Exchange For
Aug. 6, 1991	CLE	A	—	SF	N	Waiver price

Broderick Perkins

Date	Traded To		Traded With	Traded By		In Exchange For
Nov. 18, 1982	CLE	A	Juan Eichelberger	SD	N	Ed Whitson

Cy Perkins

Date	Traded To		Traded With	Traded By		In Exchange For
Dec. 10, 1930	NY	A	—	PHI	A	Cash

Harry Perkowski

Date	Traded To		Traded With	Traded By		In Exchange For
Oct. 1, 1954	CHI	N	Ted Tappe Jim Bolger	CIN	N	Johnny Klippstein Jim Willis

Ron Perranoski

Date	Traded To		Traded With	Traded By		In Exchange For
Apr. 8, 1960	LA	N	John Goryl minor league OF Lee Handley $25,000.	CHI	N	Don Zimmer
Nov. 28, 1967	MIN	A	Johnny Roseboro Bob Miller	LA	N	Mudcat Grant Zoilo Versalles
July 30, 1971	DET	A	—	MIN	A	Cash

Pol Perritt

Date	Traded To		Traded With	Traded By		In Exchange For
Feb. 18, 1915	NY	N	—	STL	N	Cash
June 1921	DET	A	—	NY	N	Cash

Gaylord Perry

Date	Traded To		Traded With	Traded By		In Exchange For
Nov. 29, 1971	CLE	A	Frank Duffy	SF	N	Sam McDowell
June 13, 1975	TEX	A	—	CLE	A	Jim Bibby Jackie Brown Rick Waits $100,000.
Jan. 25, 1978	SD	N	—	TEX	A	Dave Tomlin $125,000.
Feb. 15, 1980	TEX	A	Tucker Ashford minor league P Joe Carroll	SD	N	Willie Montanez
Aug. 14, 1980	NY	A	—	TEX	A	Ken Clay minor league OF Marvin Thompson
Jan. 12, 1981	ATL	N	—	NY	A	No compensation (free agent signing)

Gerald Perry

Date	Traded To		Traded With	Traded By		In Exchange For
Dec. 15, 1989	KC	A	Minor league P Jim Lemasters	ATL	N	Charlie Leibrandt Rick Luecken
Dec. 13, 1990	STL	N	—	KC	A	No compensation (free agent signing)

Jim Perry

Date	Traded To		Traded With	Traded By		In Exchange For
May 2, 1963	MIN	A	—	CLE	A	Jack Kralick
Mar. 27, 1973	DET	A	—	MIN	A	Dan Fife Cash
Mar. 19, 1974	CLE	A	—	DET	A	Rick Sawyer Walt Williams
(Part of three-team trade involving Detroit, Cleveland, and New York Yankees.)						
May 20, 1975	OAK	A	Dick Bosman	CLE	A	Blue Moon Odom Cash

Pat Perry

Date	Traded To		Traded With	Traded By		In Exchange For
Aug. 31, 1987	CIN	N	—	STL	N	Scott Terry
(St. Louis received Terry on September 3, 1987.)						
May 19, 1988	CHI	N	Cash	CIN	N	Leon Durham

Scott Perry

Date	Traded To		Traded With	Traded By		In Exchange For
Apr. 26, 1917	CIN	N	—	CHI	N	Waiver price
May 28, 1917	BOS	N	—	CIN	N	Waiver price
Apr. 1918	PHI	A	—	BOS	N	Cash

Stan Perzanowski

Date	Traded To		Traded With	Traded By		In Exchange For
Feb. 25, 1975	TEX	A	—	CHI	A	Steve Dunning
May 28, 1976	CLE	A	Cash	TEX	A	Fritz Peterson
Dec. 3, 1976	CAL	A	Cash	CLE	A	Bill Melton

Johnny Pesky

Date	Traded To		Traded With	Traded By		In Exchange For
June 3, 1952	DET	A	Walt Dropo Bill Wight Fred Hatfield Don Lenhardt	BOS	A	Dizzy Trout George Kell Johnny Lipon Hoot Evers

Johnny Pesky *continued*

Date	Traded To		Traded With	Traded By		In Exchange For
June 14, 1954	WAS	A	—	DET	A	Mel Hoderlein

Roberto Petagine

Date	Traded To		Traded With	Traded By		In Exchange For
Dec. 28, 1994	SD	N	*see Ken Caminiti*	HOU	N	—

Gary Peters

Date	Traded To		Traded With	Traded By		In Exchange For
Dec. 13, 1969	BOS	A	Don Pavletich	CHI	A	Syd O'Brien Gerry Janeski minor league P Billy Farmer
(Janeski replaced Farmer, who retired.)						

Ray Peters

Date	Traded To		Traded With	Traded By		In Exchange For
Apr. 22, 1971	PHI	N	Pete Koegel	MIL	A	John Briggs

Rusty Peters

Date	Traded To		Traded With	Traded By		In Exchange For
Dec. 7, 1946	STL	A	—	CLE	A	Cash

Steve Peters

Date	Traded To		Traded With	Traded By		In Exchange For
Feb. 27, 1990	SD	N	Alex Cole	STL	N	Omar Olivares

Adam Peterson

Date	Traded To		Traded With	Traded By		In Exchange For
Mar. 31, 1991	SD	N	Steve Rosenberg	CHI	A	Joey Cora Warren Newson Minor league IF Kevin Garner

Cap Peterson

Date	Traded To		Traded With	Traded By		In Exchange For
Dec. 13, 1966	WAS	A	Bob Priddy	SF	N	Mike McCormick
Mar. 31, 1969	CLE	A	—	WAS	A	Minor league P George Woodson

Fritz Peterson

Date	Traded To		Traded With	Traded By		In Exchange For
Apr. 27, 1974	CLE	A	Steve Kline Fred Beene Tom Buskey	NY	A	Chris Chambliss Dick Tidrow Cecil Upshaw
May 28, 1976	TEX	A	—	CLE	A	Stan Perzanowski Cash

Kent Peterson

Date	Traded To		Traded With	Traded By		In Exchange For
May 23, 1952	PHI	N	Johnny Wyrostek	CIN	N	Bubba Church

Geno Petralli

Date	Traded To		Traded With	Traded By		In Exchange For
May 8, 1984	CLE	A	—	TOR	A	Cash

Dan Petry

Date	Traded To		Traded With	Traded By		In Exchange For
Nov. 13, 1987	CAL	A	—	DET	A	Gary Pettis
June 25, 1991	ATL	N	—	DET	A	Victor Rosario
Aug. 16, 1991	BOS	A	—	ATL	N	Player to be named
(Atlanta received OF Mickey Pina on November 13, 1991.)						

Joe Pettini

Date	Traded To		Traded With	Traded By		In Exchange For
June 13, 1979	SF	N	Cash	MON	N	John Tamargo

Gary Pettis

Date	Traded To		Traded With	Traded By		In Exchange For
Nov. 13, 1987	DET	A	—	CAL	A	Dan Petry
Nov. 24, 1989	TEX	A	—	DET	A	No compensation (free agent signing)

Jesse Petty

Date	Traded To		Traded With	Traded By		In Exchange For
Dec. 11, 1928	PIT	N	Harry Riconda	BKN	N	Glenn Wright
Aug. 24, 1930	CHI	N	—	PIT	N	Cash

Pretzels Pezzullo

Date	Traded To		Traded With	Traded By		In Exchange For
Nov. 1, 1934	PHI	N	Blondy Ryan Johnny Vergez George Watkins Cash	NY	N	Dick Bartell

Big Jeff Pfeffer

Date	Traded To		Traded With	Traded By		In Exchange For
Jan. 1906	BOS	N	—	CHI	N	Cash
Jan. 1911	BOS	N	Scotty Ingerton	CHI	N	Dave Shean

Jeff Pfeffer

Date	Traded To	Traded With	Traded By	In Exchange For
June 18, 1921	STL N	—	BKN N	Ferdie Schupp Hal Janvrin
May 1924	PIT N	—	STL N	Waiver price

Bobby Pfeil

Date	Traded To	Traded With	Traded By	In Exchange For
Apr. 10, 1965	STL N	minor league P Hal Gibson	CHI N	Bob Humphreys
Feb. 8, 1972	MIL A	—	PHI N	Minor league 3B Chico Vaughns
Mar. 20, 1972	BOS A	—	MIL A	Cash

Art Phelan

Date	Traded To	Traded With	Traded By	In Exchange For
Dec. 15, 1912	CHI N	—	CIN N	*see Joe Tinker*

Babe Phelps

Date	Traded To	Traded With	Traded By	In Exchange For
Dec. 31, 1934	BKN N	—	CHI N	Waiver price
Dec. 12, 1941	PIT N	Pete Coscarart Luke Hamlin Jimmy Wasdell	BKN N	Arky Vaughan
Dec. 30, 1943	PHI N	Cash	PIT N	Babe Dahlgren

Ed Phelps

Date	Traded To	Traded With	Traded By	In Exchange For
Dec. 1905	CIN N	—	PIT N	Heinie Peitz
May 20, 1906	PIT N	—	CIN N	Cash

Ken Phelps

Date	Traded To	Traded With	Traded By	In Exchange For
Jan. 19, 1982	MON N	—	KC A	Grant Jackson
Mar. 31, 1983	SEA A	—	MON N	Cash
July 21, 1988	NY A	—	SEA A	Jay Buhner Minor league P Rich Balabon player to be named

(Seattle received P Troy Evers on October 12, 1988.)

Date	Traded To	Traded With	Traded By	In Exchange For
Aug. 30, 1989	OAK A	—	NY A	Minor league P Scott Holcomb
June 17, 1990	CLE A	—	OAK A	Cash

Dave Philley

Date	Traded To	Traded With	Traded By	In Exchange For
Apr. 30, 1951	PHI A	Gus Zernial	CHI A	Paul Lehner Minnie Minoso

(Part of three-team trade involving Chicago White Sox, Philadelphia A's, and Cleveland.)

Date	Traded To	Traded With	Traded By	In Exchange For
Feb. 19, 1954	CLE A	—	PHI A	Bill Upton Lee Wheat
July 2, 1955	BAL A	—	CLE A	Waiver price
May 21, 1956	CHI A	Jim Wilson	BAL A	Bob Nieman Mike Fornieles Connie Johnson George Kell
June 14, 1957	DET A	—	CHI A	Earl Torgeson
Dec. 11, 1957	PHI N	—	DET A	Cash
May 12, 1960	SF N	—	PHI N	Cash
Sept. 1, 1960	BAL A	—	SF N	Cash
Mar. 24, 1962	BOS A	—	HOU N	Tom Borland

Deacon Phillippe

Date	Traded To	Traded With	Traded By	In Exchange For
Jan. 1900	PIT N	*see Honus Wagner*	LOU N	—

Adolfo Phillips

Date	Traded To	Traded With	Traded By	In Exchange For
Apr. 21, 1966	CHI N	John Herrnstein Ferguson Jenkins	PHI N	Larry Jackson Bob Buhl
June 11, 1969	MON N	Jack Lamabe	CHI N	Paul Popovich

Bubba Phillips

Date	Traded To	Traded With	Traded By	In Exchange For
Nov. 30, 1955	CHI A	—	DET A	Virgil Trucks
Dec. 6, 1959	CLE A	*see Norm Cash*	CHI A	—
Nov. 27, 1962	DET A	—	CLE A	Gordon Seyfried Ron Nischwitz

Eddie Phillips

Date	Traded To	Traded With	Traded By	In Exchange For
Jan. 1931	PIT N	—	PHI N	Cash

Eddie Phillips *continued*

Date	Traded To	Traded With	Traded By	In Exchange For
Dec. 1934	CLE A	—	WAS A	Cash

Jack Phillips

Date	Traded To	Traded With	Traded By	In Exchange For
Aug. 6, 1949	PIT N	—	NY A	Cash
Dec. 6, 1954	DET A	*see Ferris Fain*	CHI A	—
Apr. 30, 1957	BOS A	—	DET A	Karl Olson

Mike Phillips

Date	Traded To	Traded With	Traded By	In Exchange For
May 3, 1975	NY N	—	SF N	Cash
June 15, 1977	STL N	—	NY N	Joel Youngblood
Dec. 8, 1980	SD N	—	STL N	*see Rollie Fingers*
May 10, 1981	MON N	—	SD N	Cash

Taylor Phillips

Date	Traded To	Traded With	Traded By	In Exchange For
Dec. 5, 1957	CHI N	Sammy Taylor	MIL N	Eddie Haas Don Kaiser Bob Rush
May 12, 1959	PHI N	—	CHI N	Seth Morehead
Dec. 15, 1961	CHI A	Bob Sadowski minor league IF Lou Vassie	PHI N	Frank Barnes Andy Carey Cal McLish

(Carey refused to report, and the Phillies received McLish in exchange for Vassie to complete the trade on March 24, 1962.)

Tony Phillips

Date	Traded To	Traded With	Traded By	In Exchange For
Aug. 31, 1980	SD N	—	MON N	Willie Montanez
Mar. 27, 1981	OAK A	Kevin Bell minor league P Eric Mustard	SD N	Bob Lacey minor league P Ray Moretti
Dec. 5, 1989	DET A	—	OAK A	No compensation (free agent signing)
Apr. 13, 1995	CAL A	—	DET A	Chad Curtis

Tom Phoebus

Date	Traded To	Traded With	Traded By	In Exchange For
Dec. 1, 1970	SD N	Al Severinsen Fred Beene Enzo Hernandez	BAL A	Pat Dobson Tom Dukes
Apr. 20, 1972	CHI N	—	SD N	Cash
Oct. 20, 1972	ATL N	—	CHI N	Tony LaRussa

Doug Piatt

Date	Traded To	Traded With	Traded By	In Exchange For
Dec. 9, 1992	KC A	Mark Gardner	MON N	Tim Spehr Jeff Shaw

Wiley Piatt

Date	Traded To	Traded With	Traded By	In Exchange For
Aug. 27, 1901	CHI A	—	PHI A	Cash

Rob Picciolo

Date	Traded To	Traded With	Traded By	In Exchange For
May 14, 1982	MIL A	—	OAK A	Mike Warren minor league 1B John Evans
Feb. 6, 1984	CAL A	—	MIL A	No compensation (free agent signing)

Ron Piche

Date	Traded To	Traded With	Traded By	In Exchange For
Oct. 14, 1964	LA A	Phil Roof	MIL N	Dan Osinski
Apr. 22, 1968	CHI N	Jack Lamabe	STL N	Pete Mikkelsen Dave Dowling

Val Picinich

Date	Traded To	Traded With	Traded By	In Exchange For
Feb. 10, 1923	BOS A	Ed Goebel Howard Shanks	WAS A	Muddy Ruel Allan Russell
Feb. 10, 1926	CIN N	—	BOS A	$7,500.
Apr. 18, 1929	BKN N	—	CIN N	Johnny Gooch Rube Ehrhardt
June 23, 1933	PIT N	—	BKN N	Cash

Charlie Pick

Date	Traded To	Traded With	Traded By	In Exchange For
Aug. 1919	BOS N	Les Mann	CHI N	Buck Herzog

Ollie Pickering

Date	Traded To	Traded With	Traded By	In Exchange For
Feb. 1903	PHI A	—	CLE A	Cash

Ollie Pickering *continued*

Date	Traded To		Traded With	Traded By		In Exchange For
Oct. 5, 1907	WAS	A	—	STL	A	Charlie Jones

Billy Pierce

Date	Traded To		Traded With	Traded By		In Exchange For
Nov. 10, 1948	CHI	A	$10,000.	DET	A	Aaron Robinson
Nov. 30, 1961	SF	N	Don Larsen	CHI	A	Eddie Fisher Dom Zanni Verle Tiefenthaler Bob Farley

Jack Pierce

Date	Traded To		Traded With	Traded By		In Exchange For
Mar. 29, 1975	DET	A	—	ATL	N	Reggie Sanders

Jeff Pierce

Date	Traded To		Traded With	Traded By		In Exchange For
July 31, 1993	CIN	N	Johnny Ruffin	CHI	A	Tim Belcher

Bill Piercy

Date	Traded To		Traded With	Traded By		In Exchange For
Dec. 20, 1921	BOS	A	—	NY	A	*see Joe Bush*

Marino Pieretti

Date	Traded To		Traded With	Traded By		In Exchange For
June 9, 1948	CHI	A	—	WAS	A	Earl Harrist
Apr. 16, 1950	CLE	A	—	CHI	A	Waiver price

Jimmy Piersall

Date	Traded To		Traded With	Traded By		In Exchange For
Dec. 2, 1958	CLE	A	—	BOS	A	Vic Wertz Gary Geiger
Oct. 5, 1961	WAS	A	—	CLE	A	Dick Donovan Gene Green Jim Mahoney
May 23, 1963	NY	N	— (Hodges was named Washington manager.)	WAS	A	Gil Hodges

Tony Piet

Date	Traded To		Traded With	Traded By		In Exchange For
Nov. 17, 1933	CIN	N	Adam Comorosky	PIT	N	Red Lucas Wally Roettger
June 4, 1935	CHI	A	—	CIN	N	Cash
Dec. 2, 1937	DET	A	Vern Kennedy Dixie Walker	CHI	A	Marv Owen Mike Tresh Gee Walker

Joe Pignatano

Date	Traded To		Traded With	Traded By		In Exchange For
Jan. 31, 1961	KC	A	—	LA	N	Cash
Dec. 15, 1961	SF	N	—	KC	A	Jose Tartabull
July 13, 1962	NY	N	—	SF	N	Cash

Al Pilarcik

Date	Traded To		Traded With	Traded By		In Exchange For
Oct. 11, 1956	BAL	A	Art Ceccarelli	KC	A	Ryne Duren Jim Pisoni
Jan. 24, 1961	KC	A	—	BAL	A	*see Russ Snyder*
June 10, 1961	CHI	A	—	KC	A	*see Wes Covington*

Duane Pillette

Date	Traded To		Traded With	Traded By		In Exchange For
June 15, 1950	STL	A	Jim Delsing Don Johnson Snuffy Stirnweiss $50,000.	NY	A	Tom Ferrick Joe Ostrowski Leo Thomas Sid Schacht

Horacio Pina

Date	Traded To		Traded With	Traded By		In Exchange For
Dec. 5, 1969	WAS	A	Dave Nelson Ron Law	CLE	A	Dennis Higgins Barry Moore
Nov. 30, 1972	OAK	A	—	TEX	A	Mike Epstein
Dec. 3, 1973	CHI	N	—	OAK	A	Bob Locker
July 28, 1974	CAL	A	—	CHI	N	Rick Stelmaszek

Babe Pinelli

Date	Traded To		Traded With	Traded By		In Exchange For
Dec. 1919	DET	A	—	CHI	A	Cash

Lou Piniella

Date	Traded To		Traded With	Traded By		In Exchange For
Mar. 31, 1964	BAL	A	—	WAS	A	Buster Narum
Apr. 1, 1969	KC	A	—	SEA	A	Steve Whitaker John Gelnar
Dec. 7, 1973	NY	A	Ken Wright	KC	A	Lindy McDaniel

Vada Pinson

Date	Traded To		Traded With	Traded By		In Exchange For
Oct. 11, 1968	STL	N	—	CIN	N	Wayne Granger Bobby Tolan
Nov. 21, 1969	CLE	A	—	STL	N	Jose Cardenal
Oct. 5, 1971	CAL	A	Frank Baker Alan Foster	CLE	A	Alex Johnson Gerry Moses
Feb. 23, 1974	KC	A	—	CAL	A	Barry Raziano Cash

George Pipgras

Date	Traded To		Traded With	Traded By		In Exchange For
Jan. 3, 1923	NY	A	Harvey Hendrick	BOS	A	Al DeVormer Cash
May 12, 1933	BOS	A	Bill Werber	NY	A	$100,000.

Wally Pipp

Date	Traded To		Traded With	Traded By		In Exchange For
Jan. 7, 1915	NY	A	—	DET	A	Waiver price
Feb. 1, 1926	CIN	N	—	NY	A	$7,500.

Cotton Pippen

Date	Traded To		Traded With	Traded By		In Exchange For
Sept. 12, 1939	DET	A	—	PHI	A	Waiver price

Jim Pisoni

Date	Traded To		Traded With	Traded By		In Exchange For
Oct. 11, 1956	KC	A	Ryne Duren	BAL	A	Art Ceccarelli Al Pilarcik
June 15, 1957	NY	A	—	KC	A	*see Ralph Terry*

Skip Pitlock

Date	Traded To		Traded With	Traded By		In Exchange For
June 15, 1975	OAK	A	Stan Bahnsen	CHI	A	Dave Hamilton Chet Lemon

Chris Pittaro

Date	Traded To		Traded With	Traded By		In Exchange For
Jan. 18, 1986	MIN	A	Alejandro Sanchez	DET	A	Dave Engle

Togie Pittinger

Date	Traded To		Traded With	Traded By		In Exchange For
Dec. 20, 1904	PHI	N	—	BOS	N	Chick Fraser Harry Wolverton

Joe Pittman

Date	Traded To		Traded With	Traded By		In Exchange For
June 8, 1982	SD	N	—	HOU	N	Danny Boone
Dec. 6, 1983	SF	N	minor league OF Tommy Francis	SD	N	Champ Summers

Juan Pizarro

Date	Traded To		Traded With	Traded By		In Exchange For
Dec. 15, 1960	CIN	N	Joey Jay	MIL	N	Roy McMillan
Dec. 15, 1960	CHI	A	Cal McLish	CIN	N	Gene Freese
Oct. 12, 1966	PIT	N	—	CHI	A	Wilbur Wood
June 27, 1968	BOS	A	—	PIT	N	Cash
Apr. 19, 1969	CLE	A	*see Ken Harrelson*	BOS	A	—
Sept. 21, 1969	OAK	A	—	CLE	A	Cash
July 9, 1970	CHI	N	—	CAL	A	Archie Reynolds

Eddie Plank

Date	Traded To		Traded With	Traded By		In Exchange For
Feb. 10, 1916	STL	A	Babe Borton Harry Chapman Doc Crandall Charlie Deal Bob Groom Grover Hartley Armando Marsans Ward Miller Johnny Tobin Ernie Johnson	STL	F	Cash
Jan. 22, 1918	NY	A	Del Pratt $15,000.	STL	A	Les Nunamaker Joe Gedeon Fritz Maisel Nick Cullop Urban Shocker

Erik Plantenberg

Date	Traded To		Traded With	Traded By		In Exchange For
Nov. 17, 1994	SD	N	—	SEA	A	Waiver price

Phil Plantier

Date	Traded To		Traded With	Traded By		In Exchange For
Dec. 9, 1992	SD	N	—	BOS	A	Jose Melendez

Phil Plantier *continued*

Date	Traded To	Traded With	Traded By	In Exchange For
Dec. 28, 1994	HOU N	Derek Bell Pedro Martinez Doug Brocail Craig Shipley Ricky Gutierrez	SD N	Ken Caminiti Steve Finley Andujar Cedeno Brian Williams Roberto Petagine Player to be named

(San Diego received P Sean Fesh on May 1, 1995.)

Date	Traded To	Traded With	Traded By	In Exchange For
July 19, 1995	SD N	—	HOU N	Jeff Tabaka Minor league P Rich Loiselle

Whitey Platt

Date	Traded To	Traded With	Traded By	In Exchange For
Apr. 20, 1946	CHI A	—	CHI N	Waiver price

Dan Plesac

Date	Traded To	Traded With	Traded By	In Exchange For
Dec. 8, 1992	CHI N	—	MIL A	No compensation (free agent signing)
Nov. 9, 1994	PIT N	—	CHI N	No compensation (free agent signing)

Herb Plews

Date	Traded To	Traded With	Traded By	In Exchange For
Feb. 8, 1956	WAS A	*see Whitey Herzog*	NY A	—
June 11, 1959	BOS A	Dick Hyde	WAS A	Billy Consolo Murray Wall

(Hyde was returned to Washington and Wall was returned to Boston.)

Bill Plummer

Date	Traded To	Traded With	Traded By	In Exchange For
Jan. 9, 1969	CIN N	Clarence Jones minor league P Ken Myette	CHI N	Ted Abernathy

Eric Plunk

Date	Traded To	Traded With	Traded By	In Exchange For
Dec. 8, 1984	OAK A	—	NY A	*see Rickey Henderson*
June 21, 1989	NY A	Greg Cadaret Luis Polonia	OAK A	Rickey Henderson

Ray Poat

Date	Traded To	Traded With	Traded By	In Exchange For
June 6, 1949	PIT N	Bobby Rhawn	NY N	Kirby Higbe

Bud Podbielan

Date	Traded To	Traded With	Traded By	In Exchange For
June 15, 1952	CIN N	—	BKN N	Bud Byerly Cash

Johnny Podgajny

Date	Traded To	Traded With	Traded By	In Exchange For
June 15, 1943	PIT N	—	PHI N	Dutch Dietz

Johnny Podres

Date	Traded To	Traded With	Traded By	In Exchange For
May 10, 1966	DET A	—	LA N	Cash

John Poff

Date	Traded To	Traded With	Traded By	In Exchange For
Sept. 1, 1980	MIL A	—	PHI N	Cash
Apr. 1, 1981	CHI A	—	MIL A	Thad Bosley

Boots Poffenberger

Date	Traded To	Traded With	Traded By	In Exchange For
Jan. 1939	BKN N	—	DET A	Waiver price

Tom Poholsky

Date	Traded To	Traded With	Traded By	In Exchange For
Dec. 11, 1956	CHI N	Jackie Collum Ray Katt minor league P Wally Lammers	STL N	Hobie Landrith Sam Jones Jim Davis Eddie Miksis
Dec. 10, 1957	NY N	—	CHI N	Freddy Rodriguez

Aaron Pointer

Date	Traded To	Traded With	Traded By	In Exchange For
May 4, 1968	CHI N	—	HOU N	Byron Browne

Hugh Poland

Date	Traded To	Traded With	Traded By	In Exchange For
Apr. 27, 1943	BOS N	Connie Ryan	NY N	Ernie Lombardi
June 14, 1947	CIN N	Ken Raffensberger	PHI N	Al Lakeman

Gus Polidor

Date	Traded To	Traded With	Traded By	In Exchange For
Dec. 7, 1988	MIL A	—	CAL A	Bill Schroeder

Howie Pollet

Date	Traded To	Traded With	Traded By	In Exchange For
June 15, 1951	PIT N	Bill Howerton Joe Garagiola Ted Wilks Dick Cole	STL N	Cliff Chambers Wally Westlake
June 4, 1953	CHI N	Joe Garagiola Ralph Kiner Catfish Metkovich	PIT N	Toby Atwell Bob Schultz Preston Ward George Freese Bob Addis Gene Hermanski $150,000.
Apr. 16, 1956	PIT N	—	CHI A	Cash

John Poloni

Date	Traded To	Traded With	Traded By	In Exchange For
Dec. 14, 1977	BOS A	Cash	TEX A	Ferguson Jenkins

Luis Polonia

Date	Traded To	Traded With	Traded By	In Exchange For
June 21, 1989	NY A	Eric Plunk Greg Cadaret	OAK A	Rickey Henderson
Apr. 28, 1990	CAL A	—	NY A	Claudell Washington Rich Monteleone
Dec. 20, 1993	NY A	—	CAL A	No compensation (free agent signing)
Aug. 11, 1995	ATL N	—	NY A	Minor league OF Troy Hughes

Elmer Ponder

Date	Traded To	Traded With	Traded By	In Exchange For
July 1, 1921	CHI N	—	PIT N	Dave Robertson

Ed Poole

Date	Traded To	Traded With	Traded By	In Exchange For
Apr. 1902	CIN N	—	PIT N	Cash
Feb. 1904	BKN N	—	CIN N	Cash

Jim Poole

Date	Traded To	Traded With	Traded By	In Exchange For
Dec. 30, 1990	TEX A	Cash	LA N	Minor league Ps Steve Allen and David Lynch
May 31, 1991	BAL A	—	TEX A	Waiver price

Dave Pope

Date	Traded To	Traded With	Traded By	In Exchange For
June 15, 1955	BAL A	Wally Westlake	CLE A	Gene Woodling Billy Cox

(Cox refused to report and announced retirement. Cleveland received $15,000 to complete trade.)

Date	Traded To	Traded With	Traded By	In Exchange For
May 13, 1956	CLE A	—	BAL A	Hoot Evers

Paul Popovich

Date	Traded To	Traded With	Traded By	In Exchange For
Nov. 30, 1967	LA N	Jim Williams	CHI N	Lou Johnson
June 11, 1969	MON N	Ron Fairly	LA N	Maury Wills Manny Mota
June 11, 1969	CHI N	—	MON N	Adolfo Phillips Jack Lamabe
Apr. 1, 1974	PIT N	—	CHI N	Tom Dettore Cash

Tom Poquette

Date	Traded To	Traded With	Traded By	In Exchange For
June 13, 1979	BOS A	—	KC A	George Scott
Aug. 12, 1981	TEX A	—	BOS A	Cash
Jan. 15, 1982	KC A	—	TEX A	No compensation (free agent signing)

Darrell Porter

Date	Traded To	Traded With	Traded By	In Exchange For
Dec. 6, 1976	KC A	Jim Colborn	MIL A	Jim Wohlford Jamie Quirk Bob McClure
Dec. 13, 1980	STL N	—	KC A	No compensation (free agent signing)
Jan. 28, 1986	TEX A	—	STL N	No compensation (free agent signing)

Dick Porter

Date	Traded To	Traded With	Traded By	In Exchange For
May 25, 1934	BOS A	Wes Ferrell	CLE A	Bob Weiland Bob Seeds $25,000.

J. W. Porter

Date	Traded To	Traded With	Traded By	In Exchange For
July 28, 1952	STL A	Ray Coleman	CHI A	Jim Rivera Darrell Johnson
Dec. 4, 1952	DET A	—	STL A	*see Virgil Trucks*
Feb. 18, 1958	CLE A	Hal Woodeshick	DET A	Jim Hegan Hank Aguirre
Oct. 27, 1958	WAS A	—	CLE A	Ossie Alvarez
July 25, 1959	STL N	—	WAS A	Waiver price

Bob Porterfield

Date	Traded To	Traded With	Traded By	In Exchange For
June 15, 1951	WAS A	Fred Sanford Tom Ferrick	NY A	Bob Kuzava
Nov. 8, 1955	BOS A	Johnny Schmitz Mickey Vernon Tommy Umphlett	WAS A	Karl Olson Dick Brodowski Tex Clevenger Neil Chrisley minor league P Al Curtis
May 7, 1958	PIT N	—	BOS A	Cash
June 13, 1959	CHI N	—	PIT N	Waiver price

Arnie Portocarrero

Date	Traded To	Traded With	Traded By	In Exchange For
Apr. 17, 1958	BAL A	—	KC A	Bud Daley

Mark Portugal

Date	Traded To	Traded With	Traded By	In Exchange For
Dec. 4, 1988	HOU N	—	MIN A	Minor league P Todd McClure
Nov. 21, 1993	SF N	—	HOU N	No compensation (free agent signing)
July 21, 1995	CIN N	Dave Burba Darren Lewis	SF N	Deion Sanders John Roper Scott Service David McCarty Minor league P Ricky Pickett

Bill Posedel

Date	Traded To	Traded With	Traded By	In Exchange For
Mar. 31, 1939	BOS N	—	BKN N	Al Todd

Wally Post

Date	Traded To	Traded With	Traded By	In Exchange For
Dec. 16, 1957	PHI N	—	CIN N	Harvey Haddix
June 15, 1960	CIN N	Harry Anderson minor league 1B Fred Hopke	PHI N	Tony Gonzalez Lee Walls
May 16, 1963	MIN A	—	CIN N	Cash

Dykes Potter

Date	Traded To	Traded With	Traded By	In Exchange For
Feb. 10, 1916	CHI N	*see Three Finger Brown*	CHI F	—

Mike Potter

Date	Traded To	Traded With	Traded By	In Exchange For
June 26, 1978	SEA A	—	STL N	Jose Baez

Nels Potter

Date	Traded To	Traded With	Traded By	In Exchange For
June 30, 1941	BOS A	—	PHI A	Cash
May 15, 1948	PHI A	—	STL A	$17,500.

Alonzo Powell

Date	Traded To	Traded With	Traded By	In Exchange For
Oct. 24, 1985	MON N	George Riley	SF N	Bill Laskey
Aug. 28, 1989	MIN A	—	MON N	Jim Dwyer

(Minnesota received Powell on Sept. 15, 1989.)

Boog Powell

Date	Traded To	Traded With	Traded By	In Exchange For
Feb. 25, 1975	CLE A	Don Hood	BAL A	Dave Duncan minor league OF Al McGrew

Dennis Powell

Date	Traded To	Traded With	Traded By	In Exchange For
Dec. 10, 1986	SEA A	Minor league IF Mike Watters	LA N	Matt Young

Hosken Powell

Date	Traded To	Traded With	Traded By	In Exchange For
Dec. 28, 1981	TOR A	—	MIN A	Boomer Wells

Jack Powell

Date	Traded To	Traded With	Traded By	In Exchange For
Jan. 1904	NY A	—	STL A	Harry Howell Jack O'Connor
Feb. 1904	NY A	—	STL A	Cash
Sept. 1, 1905	STL A	—	NY A	Cash

Jake Powell

Date	Traded To	Traded With	Traded By	In Exchange For
June 14, 1936	NY A	—	WAS A	Ben Chapman

Jay Powell

Date	Traded To	Traded With	Traded By	In Exchange For
Dec. 6, 1994	FLA N	—	BAL A	Bret Barberie

Paul Ray Powell

Date	Traded To	Traded With	Traded By	In Exchange For
Oct. 22, 1971	LA N	—	MIN A	Bobby Darwin

Ray Powell

Date	Traded To	Traded With	Traded By	In Exchange For
Dec. 15, 1923	PHI N	Hod Ford	BOS N	Cotton Tierney

(Powell announced his intention to retire after the 1924 season. He remained with Boston, and Philadelphia received cash instead.)

Ross Powell

Date	Traded To	Traded With	Traded By	In Exchange For
Apr. 19, 1994	HOU N	Minor league P Marty Lister	CIN N	Eddie Taubensee

Ted Power

Date	Traded To	Traded With	Traded By	In Exchange For
Oct. 15, 1982	CIN N	—	LA N	Mike Ramsey Cash
Nov. 6, 1987	KC A	Kurt Stillwell	CIN N	Danny Jackson Angel Salazar
Aug. 31, 1988	DET A	—	KC A	Rey Palacios Mark Lee
Nov. 20, 1989	PIT N	—	STL N	No compensation (free agent signing)
Dec. 14, 1990	CIN N	—	PIT N	No compensation (free agent signing)

Vic Power

Date	Traded To	Traded With	Traded By	In Exchange For
Dec. 16, 1953	PHI A	Don Bollweg John Gray Jim Robertson Jim Finigan Bill Renna	NY A	Harry Byrd Eddie Robinson Tom Hamilton Carmen Mauro Loren Babe
June 15, 1958	CLE A	Woodie Held	KC A	Roger Maris Dick Tomanek Preston Ward
Apr. 2, 1962	MIN A	Dick Stigman	CLE A	Pedro Ramos
June 11, 1964	LA A	Lenny Green	MIN A	Jerry Kindall Frank Kostro

(Part of three-team trade involving Los Angeles Angels, Minnesota, and Cleveland.)

Date	Traded To	Traded With	Traded By	In Exchange For
Sept. 9, 1964	PHI N	—	LA A	Marcelino Lopez Cash
Nov. 30, 1964	LA A	—	PHI N	Cash

Johnny Powers

Date	Traded To	Traded With	Traded By	In Exchange For
Jan. 30, 1959	CIN N	—	PIT N	*see Harvey Haddix*
Dec. 15, 1959	BAL A	—	CIN N	Cash
May 12, 1960	CLE A	—	BAL A	Waiver price
June 2, 1960	PIT N	—	CLE A	Hank Foiles

Les Powers

Date	Traded To	Traded With	Traded By	In Exchange For
Dec. 7, 1938	PHI N	—	NY N	Cash

Mike Powers

Date	Traded To	Traded With	Traded By	In Exchange For
July 13, 1905	NY A	—	PHI A	Cash
Aug. 7, 1905	PHI A	—	NY A	Cash

Willie Prall

Date	Traded To	Traded With	Traded By	In Exchange For
Mar. 19, 1974	CHI N	—	SF N	Ken Rudolph

Johnny Pramesa

Date	Traded To	Traded With	Traded By	In Exchange For
Oct. 4, 1951	CHI N	Bob Usher	CIN N	Bob Borkowski Smoky Burgess

Del Pratt

Date	Traded To	Traded With	Traded By	In Exchange For
Jan. 22, 1918	NY A	Eddie Plank $15,000.	STL A	Les Nunamaker Joe Gedeon Fritz Maisel Nick Cullop Urban Shocker
Dec. 15, 1920	BOS A	Muddy Ruel Sammy Vick Hank Thormahlen	NY A	Waite Hoyt Harry Harper Wally Schang Mike McNally
Oct. 30, 1922	DET A	Rip Collins	BOS A	Carl Holling Danny Clark Howard Ehmke Babe Herman $25,000.

Larry Pratt

Date	Traded To	Traded With	Traded By	In Exchange For
Feb. 1915	NWK F	Hugh Bradley Tom Seaton	BKN F	Cy Falkenberg

Mike Prendergast

Date	Traded To	Traded With	Traded By	In Exchange For
Dec. 11, 1917	PHI N	Pickles Dillhoefer $55,000.	CHI N	Grover Alexander Bill Killefer

George Prentiss

Date	Traded To	Traded With	Traded By	In Exchange For
June 1902	BAL A	—	BOS A	Cash

Jim Presley

Date	Traded To	Traded With	Traded By	In Exchange For
Jan. 24, 1990	ATL N	—	SEA A	Gary Eave Minor league 3B Ken Pennington

Tot Pressnell

Date	Traded To	Traded With	Traded By	In Exchange For
Nov. 19, 1940	STL N	—	BKN N	Cash
Dec. 16, 1940	CIN N	—	STL N	Cash
Feb. 4, 1941	CHI N	—	CIN N	Cash

Jim Price

Date	Traded To	Traded With	Traded By	In Exchange For
Apr. 7, 1967	DET A	—	PIT N	Cash

Joe Price

Date	Traded To	Traded With	Traded By	In Exchange For
Feb. 5, 1987	SF N	—	CIN N	No compensation (free agent signing)
Jan. 12, 1990	BAL A	—	BOS A	No compensation (free agent signing)

Bob Priddy

Date	Traded To	Traded With	Traded By	In Exchange For
Feb. 11, 1965	SF N	Bob Burda	PIT N	Del Crandall
Dec. 13, 1966	WAS A	Cap Peterson	SF N	Mike McCormick
Feb. 13, 1968	CHI A	—	WAS A	*see Ron Hansen*
May 14, 1969	CAL A	Sandy Alomar	CHI A	Bobby Knoop
Sept. 9, 1969	ATL N	—	CAL A	Cash

Gerry Priddy

Date	Traded To	Traded With	Traded By	In Exchange For
Jan. 29, 1943	WAS A	Milo Candini	NY A	Bill Zuber Cash
Nov. 22, 1947	STL A	—	WAS A	Johnny Berardino

(Berardino announced his retirement to go into movies. Commissioner Chandler cancelled the trade. Berardino then unretired.)

Date	Traded To	Traded With	Traded By	In Exchange For
Dec. 8, 1947	STL A	—	WAS A	$25,000.
Dec. 14, 1949	DET A	—	STL A	Lou Kretlow $100,000.

Mike Proly

Date	Traded To	Traded With	Traded By	In Exchange For
Apr. 1, 1981	PHI N	—	CHI A	Jay Loviglio

Doc Prothro

Date	Traded To	Traded With	Traded By	In Exchange For
Dec. 11, 1924	BOS A	—	WAS A	Mike McNally

Ron Pruitt

Date	Traded To	Traded With	Traded By	In Exchange For
Dec. 9, 1975	CLE A	Stan Thomas	TEX A	John Ellis
June 13, 1980	CHI A	—	CLE A	Alan Bannister

Greg Pryor

Date	Traded To	Traded With	Traded By	In Exchange For
Feb. 17, 1977	NY A	Brian Doyle Cash	TEX A	Sandy Alomar
Nov. 28, 1977	CHI A	—	NY A	No compensation (free agent signing)
Mar. 24, 1982	KC A	—	CHI A	Jeff Schattinger

Terry Puhl

Date	Traded To	Traded With	Traded By	In Exchange For
Dec. 13, 1990	NY N	—	HOU N	No compensation (free agent signing)

Charlie Puleo

Date	Traded To	Traded With	Traded By	In Exchange For
Apr. 6, 1981	NY N	Cash	TOR A	Mark Bomback
Dec. 16, 1982	CIN N	Lloyd McClendon Minor league OF Jason Felice	NY N	Tom Seaver
June 5, 1985	ATL N	—	CIN N	Cash

Alfonso Pulido

Date	Traded To	Traded With	Traded By	In Exchange For
Dec. 20, 1984	NY A	—	PIT N	$400,000.

Bob Purkey

Date	Traded To	Traded With	Traded By	In Exchange For
Dec. 9, 1957	CIN N	—	PIT N	Don Gross
Dec. 14, 1964	STL N	—	CIN N	Charlie James Roger Craig
Apr. 7, 1966	PIT N	—	STL N	Cash

Billy Purtell

Date	Traded To	Traded With	Traded By	In Exchange For
Aug. 9, 1910	BOS A	Frank Smith	CHI A	Harry Lord Amby McConnell

Ed Putman

Date	Traded To	Traded With	Traded By	In Exchange For
Mar. 20, 1979	DET A	—	CHI N	Steve Dillard

Pat Putnam

Date	Traded To	Traded With	Traded By	In Exchange For
Dec. 21, 1982	SEA A	—	TEX A	Ron Musselman
Aug. 29, 1984	MIN A	—	SEA A	Cash
Feb. 7, 1985	KC A	—	MIN A	No compensation (free agent signing)

Ewald Pyle

Date	Traded To	Traded With	Traded By	In Exchange For
June 16, 1945	BOS N	Joe Medwick	NY N	Clyde Kluttz

Frankie Pytlak

Date	Traded To	Traded With	Traded By	In Exchange For
Dec. 12, 1940	BOS A	Odell Hale Joe Dobson	CLE A	Gene Desautels Jim Bagby Gee Walker

Tim Pyznarski

Date	Traded To	Traded With	Traded By	In Exchange For
June 12, 1986	MIL A	—	SD N	Randy Ready

(Milwaukee received Pyznarski on Oct. 29, 1986.)

Jimmy Qualls

Date	Traded To	Traded With	Traded By	In Exchange For
Apr. 22, 1970	MON N	—	CHI N	Cash

Tom Qualters

Date	Traded To	Traded With	Traded By	In Exchange For
Apr. 30, 1958	CHI A	—	PHI N	Cash

Paul Quantrill

Date	Traded To	Traded With	Traded By	In Exchange For
May 31, 1994	PHI N	Billy Hatcher	BOS A	Wes Chamberlain Minor league P Mike Sullivan
Dec. 6, 1995	TOR A	—	PHI N	Howard Battle Ricardo Jordan

Mel Queen

Date	Traded To	Traded With	Traded By	In Exchange For
Oct. 24, 1969	CAL A	—	CIN N	Cash

Mel Queen

Date	Traded To	Traded With	Traded By	In Exchange For
July 11, 1947	PIT N	—	NY A	Cash

Jack Quinn

Date	Traded To		Traded With	Traded By		In Exchange For
Dec. 20, 1921	BOS	A	Roger Peckinpaugh Rip Collins Bill Piercy	NY	A	Everett Scott Joe Bush Sad Sam Jones
July 10, 1925	PHI	A	—	BOS	A	Waiver price

Joe Quinn

Date	Traded To		Traded With	Traded By		In Exchange For
Jan. 1900	STL	N	Jack Harper Otto Krueger Jim Hughey	CLE	N	Cash
May 1900	CIN	N	—	STL	N	Cash

Luis Quinones

Date	Traded To		Traded With	Traded By		In Exchange For
Dec. 6, 1983	CLE	A	—	OAK	A	Jim Essian
May 7, 1985	SF	N	Mike Jeffcoat	CLE	A	Johnnie LeMaster
Jan. 30, 1987	CHI	N	—	OAK	A	Ron Cey
Apr. 1, 1988	CHI	N	—	CIN	N	Bill Landrum

Rey Quinones

Date	Traded To		Traded With	Traded By		In Exchange For
Aug. 19, 1986	SEA	A	Mike Trujillo John Christensen Mike Brown	BOS	A	Dave Henderson Spike Owen

(Seattle received Trujillo and Brown on August 22 and Christensen on September 25, 1986.)

Date	Traded To		Traded With	Traded By		In Exchange For
Apr. 21, 1989	PIT	N	Bill Wilkinson	SEA	A	Mike Dunne Mike Walker Minor league OF Mark Merchant

Jamie Quirk

Date	Traded To		Traded With	Traded By		In Exchange For
Dec. 6, 1976	MIL	A	Jim Wohlford Bob McClure	KC	A	Jim Colborn Darrell Porter
Aug. 3, 1978	KC	A	—	MIL	A	Minor league P Gerry Ako Cash
Feb. 16, 1983	STL	N	—	KC	A	No compensation (free agent signing)
Sept. 23, 1984	CLE	A	—	CHI	A	Cash
Dec. 19, 1988	NY	A	—	KC	A	No compensation (free agent signing)
Dec. 13, 1989	OAK	A	—	BAL	A	No compensation (free agent signing)

Johnny Rabb

Date	Traded To		Traded With	Traded By		In Exchange For
Apr. 17, 1985	ATL	N	—	SF	N	Alex Trevino

Marv Rackley

Date	Traded To		Traded With	Traded By		In Exchange For
May 18, 1949	PIT	N	—	BKN	N	Johnny Hopp $25,000.

(Trade was cancelled on June 7, 1949.)

Date	Traded To		Traded With	Traded By		In Exchange For
Oct. 14, 1949	CIN	N	—	BKN	N	$60,000.

Dick Radatz

Date	Traded To		Traded With	Traded By		In Exchange For
June 2, 1966	CLE	A	—	BOS	A	Don McMahon Lee Stange
Apr. 25, 1967	CHI	N	—	CLE	A	Bob Raudman Cash
June 15, 1969	MON	N	—	DET	A	Cash

Rip Radcliff

Date	Traded To		Traded With	Traded By		In Exchange For
Dec. 8, 1939	STL	A	—	CHI	A	Moose Solters
May 5, 1941	DET	A	—	STL	A	$25,000.
Oct. 11, 1943	PHI	A	—	DET	A	Don Heffner Bob Swift

Dave Rader

Date	Traded To		Traded With	Traded By		In Exchange For
Oct. 20, 1976	STL	N	*see Mike Caldwell*	SF	N	—
Dec. 8, 1977	CHI	N	Hector Cruz	STL	N	Jerry Morales Steve Swisher Cash
Feb. 23, 1979	PHI	N	*see Manny Trillo*	CHI	N	—
Mar. 30, 1980	BOS	A	—	PHI	N	Stan Papi Cash
Feb. 2, 1981	CAL	A	—	BOS	A	No compensation (free agent signing)

Doug Rader

Date	Traded To		Traded With	Traded By		In Exchange For
Dec. 11, 1975	SD	N	—	HOU	N	Joe McIntosh Larry Hardy
June 8, 1977	TOR	A	—	SD	N	Cash

Ken Raffensberger

Date	Traded To		Traded With	Traded By		In Exchange For
Dec. 27, 1939	CHI	N	—	STL	N	Steve Mesner Gene Lillard Cash
June 14, 1947	CIN	N	Hugh Poland	PHI	N	Al Lakeman

Pat Ragan

Date	Traded To		Traded With	Traded By		In Exchange For
May 20, 1909	CHI	N	—	CIN	N	Cash
Apr. 28, 1915	BOS	N	—	BKN	N	Cash
May 21, 1919	NY	N	—	BOS	N	Jim Thorpe
Sept. 1919	CHI	A	—	NY	N	Waiver price

Tom Ragland

Date	Traded To		Traded With	Traded By		In Exchange For
Nov. 30, 1972	CLE	A	—	TEX	A	Vince Colbert

Tim Raines

Date	Traded To		Traded With	Traded By		In Exchange For
Dec. 24, 1990	CHI	A	Minor league P Jeff Carter Player to be named	MON	N	Ivan Calderon Barry Jones

(Chicago received P Mario Brito on February 15, 1991.)

Date	Traded To		Traded With	Traded By		In Exchange For
Dec. 28, 1995	NY	A	—	CHI	A	Player to be named

(Chicago received P Blaise Kozeniewski on February 6, 1996.)

Chuck Rainey

Date	Traded To		Traded With	Traded By		In Exchange For
Dec. 10, 1982	CHI	N	—	BOS	A	Doug Bird
July 15, 1984	OAK	A	Minor league OF Damon Farmar	CHI	N	Davey Lopes

(Chicago received Lopes on August 31, 1984, and Oakland received Farmar on March 18, 1985.)

Dave Rajsich

Date	Traded To		Traded With	Traded By		In Exchange For
Nov. 10, 1978	TEX	A	—	NY	A	*see Dave Righetti*
Oct. 20, 1981	PHI	N	—	TEX	A	Ramon Aviles

Gary Rajsich

Date	Traded To		Traded With	Traded By		In Exchange For
Apr. 3, 1981	NY	N	—	HOU	N	Minor league OF John Csefalvay
Apr. 4, 1984	STL	N	—	NY	N	Cash
Feb. 1, 1985	SF	N	David Green Jose Uribe Dave LaPoint	STL	N	Jack Clark

Ed Rakow

Date	Traded To		Traded With	Traded By		In Exchange For
Mar. 30, 1961	KC	A	—	LA	N	Howie Reed Cash
Nov. 18, 1963	DET	A	—	KC	A	*see Rocky Colavito*

Bob Ramazzotti

Date	Traded To		Traded With	Traded By		In Exchange For
May 16, 1949	CHI	N	—	BKN	N	Hank Schenz

Milt Ramirez

Date	Traded To		Traded With	Traded By		In Exchange For
Nov. 28, 1972	HOU	N	Skip Jutze	STL	N	Ray Busse Bobby Fenwick

Rafael Ramirez

Date	Traded To		Traded With	Traded By		In Exchange For
Dec. 8, 1987	HOU	N	—	ATL	N	Ed Whited Minor league P Mike Stoker

Bobby Ramos

Date	Traded To		Traded With	Traded By		In Exchange For
Apr. 5, 1982	NY	A	—	MON	N	Brad Gulden
Nov. 3, 1982	MON	N	—	NY	A	Cash

Domingo Ramos

Date	Traded To		Traded With	Traded By		In Exchange For
Nov. 10, 1978	TEX	A	—	NY	A	*see Dave Righetti*
Nov. 5, 1979	TOR	A	—	TEX	A	Cash

Pedro Ramos

Date	Traded To	Traded With	Traded By	In Exchange For
Apr. 2, 1962	CLE A	—	MIN A	Dick Stigman Vic Power
Sept. 5, 1964	NY A	—	CLE A	Ralph Terry Bud Daley $75,000.
Dec. 14, 1966	PHI N	—	NY A	Joe Verbanic Cash

Willie Ramsdell

Date	Traded To	Traded With	Traded By	In Exchange For
May 10, 1950	CIN N	—	BKN N	Cash
Jan. 3, 1952	CHI N	—	CIN N	Frank Hiller

Mike Ramsey

Date	Traded To	Traded With	Traded By	In Exchange For
Oct. 15, 1982	LA N	Cash	CIN N	Ted Power

Mike Ramsey

Date	Traded To	Traded With	Traded By	In Exchange For
July 1, 1984	MON N	—	STL N	Chris Speier

Newt Randall

Date	Traded To	Traded With	Traded By	In Exchange For
June 24, 1907	BOS N	Bill Sweeney	CHI N	Del Howard

Lenny Randle

Date	Traded To	Traded With	Traded By	In Exchange For
Apr. 26, 1977	NY N	—	TEX A	Rick Auerbach Cash
June 28, 1979	PIT N	*see Bill Madlock*	SF N	—
Aug. 2, 1979	NY A	—	PIT N	Cash
Mar. 8, 1980	SEA A	—	NY N	No compensation (free agent signing)
Apr. 2, 1980	CHI N	—	SEA A	Cash
Apr. 6, 1981	SEA A	—	CHI N	No compensation (free agent signing)

Willie Randolph

Date	Traded To	Traded With	Traded By	In Exchange For
Dec. 11, 1975	NY A	Ken Brett Dock Ellis	PIT N	Doc Medich
Dec. 10, 1988	LA N	—	NY A	No compensation (free agent signing)
May 13, 1990	OAK A	—	LA N	Stan Javier
Dec. 20, 1991	NY N	—	MIL A	No compensation (free agent signing)

Merritt Ranew

Date	Traded To	Traded With	Traded By	In Exchange For
Mar. 28, 1963	CHI N	Hal Haydel Dick LeMay	HOU N	Dave Gerard Danny Murphy
June 3, 1964	MIL N	$40,000.	CHI N	Len Gabrielson

Earl Rapp

Date	Traded To	Traded With	Traded By	In Exchange For
Sept. 1, 1951	STL A	—	NY N	Waiver price
June 10, 1952	WAS A	—	STL A	Freddie Marsh

Goldie Rapp

Date	Traded To	Traded With	Traded By	In Exchange For
July 1, 1921	PHI N	Lee King Lance Richbourg	NY N	Casey Stengel Red Causey Johnny Rawlings

Vern Rapp

Date	Traded To	Traded With	Traded By	In Exchange For
May 7, 1949	CHI A	—	DET A	Don Kolloway

Bill Rariden

Date	Traded To	Traded With	Traded By	In Exchange For
Dec. 23, 1915	NY N	Bill McKechnie	NWK F	Cash
Feb. 2, 1919	CIN N	—	NY N	Hal Chase

Vic Raschi

Date	Traded To	Traded With	Traded By	In Exchange For
Feb. 23, 1954	STL N	—	NY A	$85,000.

Dennis Rasmussen

Date	Traded To	Traded With	Traded By	In Exchange For
Aug. 31, 1982	NY A	—	CAL A	Tommy John
Aug. 26, 1983	SD N	Edwin Rodriguez $200,000.	NY A	John Montefusco
Mar. 30, 1984	NY A	minor league P Darin Cloninger	SD N	Graig Nettles

Dennis Rasmussen *continued*

Date	Traded To	Traded With	Traded By	In Exchange For
Aug. 26, 1987	CIN N	—	NY A	Bill Gullickson
June 8, 1988	SD N	—	CIN N	Candy Sierra

Eric Rasmussen

Date	Traded To	Traded With	Traded By	In Exchange For
May 26, 1978	SD N	—	STL N	George Hendrick
Aug. 2, 1983	KC A	—	STL N	Cash

Morrie Rath

Date	Traded To	Traded With	Traded By	In Exchange For
July 23, 1910	CLE A	—	PHI A	Bris Lord

Gene Ratliff

Date	Traded To	Traded With	Traded By	In Exchange For
Oct. 13, 1966	ATL N	—	HOU N	*see Tom Dukes*

Paul Ratliff

Date	Traded To	Traded With	Traded By	In Exchange For
July 8, 1971	MIL A	—	MIN A	Phil Roof
July 28, 1972	CAL A	Ron Clark	MIL A	Syd O'Brien Joe Azcue

Steve Ratzer

Date	Traded To	Traded With	Traded By	In Exchange For
Dec. 11, 1981	NY N	Cash	MON N	Frank Taveras

Bob Rauch

Date	Traded To	Traded With	Traded By	In Exchange For
Nov. 27, 1972	CLE A	Brent Strom	NY N	Phil Hennigan

Bob Raudman

Date	Traded To	Traded With	Traded By	In Exchange For
Apr. 25, 1967	CLE A	Cash	CHI N	Dick Radatz
Nov. 21, 1967	CIN N	George Culver Fred Whitfield	CLE A	Tommy Harper

Lance Rautzhan

Date	Traded To	Traded With	Traded By	In Exchange For
May 11, 1979	MIL A	—	LA N	Cash
Oct. 24, 1979	KC A	—	MIL A	Minor league OF Kevin Gillen

Shane Rawley

Date	Traded To	Traded With	Traded By	In Exchange For
May 21, 1977	CIN N	Angel Torres	MON N	Santo Alcala
Dec. 9, 1977	SEA A	—	CIN N	Dave Collins
Apr. 1, 1982	NY A	—	SEA A	Bill Caudill Bobby Brown Gene Nelson
June 30, 1984	PHI N	—	NY A	Marty Bystrom Keith Hughes
Oct. 24, 1988	MIN A	Cash	PHI N	Tommy Herr Tom Nieto Eric Bullock
Jan. 9, 1990	BOS A	—	MIN A	No compensation (free agent signing)

Johnny Rawlings

Date	Traded To	Traded With	Traded By	In Exchange For
June 1920	PHI N	—	BOS N	Cash
July 1, 1921	NY N	Casey Stengel Red Causey	PHI N	Goldie Rapp Lee King Lance Richbourg
May 11, 1923	PHI N	—	NY N	Waiver price
May 22, 1923	PIT N	Lee Meadows	PHI N	Whitey Glazner Cotton Tierney $50,000.

Jim Ray

Date	Traded To	Traded With	Traded By	In Exchange For
Feb. 24, 1967	NY N	—	HOU N	Cash
		(Ray was returned to Houston on March 24.)		
Dec. 3, 1973	DET A	Gary Sutherland	HOU N	Fred Scherman Cash
Dec. 6, 1974	PIT N	—	DET A	Cash

Johnny Ray

Date	Traded To	Traded With	Traded By	In Exchange For
Aug. 31, 1981	PIT N	minor league OF Kevin Houston Randy Niemann	HOU N	Phil Garner
Aug. 29, 1987	CAL A	—	PIT N	Miguel Garcia Minor league IF Bill Merrifield

Curt Raydon

Date	Traded To		Traded With	Traded By		In Exchange For
Dec. 26, 1953	PIT	N	—	MIL	N	*see Danny O'Connell*

Floyd Rayford

Date	Traded To		Traded With	Traded By		In Exchange For
June 5, 1979	BAL	A	Cash	CAL	A	Larry Harlow
June 15, 1983	STL	N	—	BAL	A	Tito Landrum
Mar. 30, 1984	BAL	A	—	STL	N	Cash

Bugs Raymond

Date	Traded To		Traded With	Traded By		In Exchange For
Dec. 12, 1908	NY	N	Admiral Schlei Red Murray	STL	N	Roger Bresnahan

Claude Raymond

Date	Traded To		Traded With	Traded By		In Exchange For
Oct. 10, 1963	HOU	N	—	MIL	N	$30,000.
June 15, 1967	ATL	N	—	HOU	N	Wade Blasingame
Aug. 19, 1969	MON	N	—	ATL	N	Cash

Barry Raziano

Date	Traded To		Traded With	Traded By		In Exchange For
Feb. 23, 1974	CAL	A	Cash	KC	A	Vada Pinson

Randy Ready

Date	Traded To		Traded With	Traded By		In Exchange For
June 12, 1986	SD	N	—	MIL	A	Tim Pyznarski
			(Milwaukee received Pyznarski on Oct. 29, 1986.)			
June 2, 1989	PHI	N	John Kruk	SD	N	Chris James
Jan. 14, 1992	OAK	A	—	PHI	N	No compensation (free agent signing)

Jeff Reardon

Date	Traded To		Traded With	Traded By		In Exchange For
May 29, 1981	MON	N	Dan Norman	NY	N	Ellis Valentine
Feb. 3, 1987	MIN	A	Tom Nieto	MON	N	Neal Heaton Jeff Reed Yorkis Perez Minor league P Al Cardwood
Dec. 6, 1989	BOS	A	—	MIN	A	No compensation (free agent sighning)
Aug. 30, 1992	ATL	N	—	BOS	A	Nate Minchey Minor league OF Sean Ross
Jan. 19, 1993	CIN	N	—	ATL	N	No compensation (free agent signing)
Feb. 15, 1994	NY	A	—	CIN	N	No compensation (free agent signing)

Frank Reberger

Date	Traded To		Traded With	Traded By		In Exchange For
Dec. 5, 1969	SF	N	—	SD	N	Bob Barton Ron Herbel Bobby Etheridge

Gary Redus

Date	Traded To		Traded With	Traded By		In Exchange For
Dec. 11, 1985	PHI	N	Tom Hume	CIN	N	John Denny Jeff Gray
Mar. 26, 1987	CHI	A	—	PHI	N	Joe Cowley Cash
Aug. 19, 1988	PIT	N	—	CHI	A	Mike Diaz
Jan. 13, 1993	TEX	A	—	PIT	N	No compensation (free agent signing)

Darren Reed

Date	Traded To		Traded With	Traded By		In Exchange For
Dec. 11, 1987	NY	N	—	NY	A	*see Rafael Santana*
Apr. 2, 1991	MON	N	Alex Diaz	NY	N	Minor league OF-1B Terrell Hansen Minor league P David Sommer
Aug. 31, 1992	MIN	A	—	MON	N	Bill Krueger
Nov. 18, 1992	NY	N	—	MIN	A	Pat Howell

Howie Reed

Date	Traded To		Traded With	Traded By		In Exchange For
Mar. 30, 1961	LA	N	Cash	KC	A	Ed Rakow
May 27, 1966	CAL	A	—	LA	N	Dick Egan minor league IF John Butler
Apr. 3, 1969	MON	N	Leo Marentette	HOU	N	Cash

Jeff Reed

Date	Traded To		Traded With	Traded By		In Exchange For
Feb. 3, 1987	MON	N	—	MIN	A	*see Jeff Reardon*
July 13, 1988	CIN	N	Herm Winningham Randy St. Claire	MON	N	Tracy Jones Pat Pacillo
Dec. 18, 1995	CLR	N	—	SF	N	No compensation (free agent signing)

Jerry Reed

Date	Traded To		Traded With	Traded By		In Exchange For
Sept. 12, 1982	CLE	A	Wil Culmer Roy Smith	PHI	N	John Denny

Jody Reed

Date	Traded To		Traded With	Traded By		In Exchange For
Nov. 17, 1992	LA	N	—	CLR	N	Rudy Seanez
Apr. 19, 1995	SD	N	—	MIL	A	No compensation (free agent signing)

Rick Reed

Date	Traded To		Traded With	Traded By		In Exchange For
May 13, 1994	CIN	N	—	TEX	A	Waiver price

Ron Reed

Date	Traded To		Traded With	Traded By		In Exchange For
May 28, 1975	STL	N	Wayne Nordhagen	ATL	N	Elias Sosa Ray Sadecki
Dec. 9, 1975	PHI	N	—	STL	N	Mike Anderson
Dec. 5, 1983	CHI	A	—	PHI	N	Jerry Koosman

Jimmy Reese

Date	Traded To		Traded With	Traded By		In Exchange For
Jan. 1932	STL	N	—	NY	A	Waiver price

Rich Reese

Date	Traded To		Traded With	Traded By		In Exchange For
Nov. 30, 1972	DET	A	—	MIN	A	Cash

Bobby Reeves

Date	Traded To		Traded With	Traded By		In Exchange For
Dec. 15, 1928	BOS	A	Milt Gaston Elliott Bigelow Hod Lisenbee Grant Gillis	WAS	A	Buddy Myer

Bill Regan

Date	Traded To		Traded With	Traded By		In Exchange For
Jan. 1931	PIT	N	—	BOS	A	Waiver price

Phil Regan

Date	Traded To		Traded With	Traded By		In Exchange For
Dec. 15, 1965	LA	N	—	DET	A	Dick Tracewski
Apr. 23, 1968	CHI	N	Jim Hickman	LA	N	Ted Savage Jim Ellis
June 2, 1972	CHI	A	—	CHI	N	Cash

Wally Rehg

Date	Traded To		Traded With	Traded By		In Exchange For
Jan. 1913	BOS	A	—	PIT	N	Waiver price
Feb. 1919	CIN	N	—	BOS	N	Lena Blackburne

Herm Reich

Date	Traded To		Traded With	Traded By		In Exchange For
Apr. 30, 1949	WAS	A	—	CLE	A	Waiver price
			(Reich was returned to Cleveland on May 10.)			
May 18, 1949	CHI	N	—	CLE	A	Waiver price
Feb. 2, 1950	CHI	A	—	CHI	N	Cash

Rick Reichardt

Date	Traded To		Traded With	Traded By		In Exchange For
Apr. 27, 1970	WAS	A	Aurelio Rodriguez	CAL	A	Ken McMullen
Feb. 9, 1971	CHI	A	—	WAS	A	Gerry Janeski

Bill Reidy

Date	Traded To		Traded With	Traded By		In Exchange For
July 1903	BKN	N	—	STL	A	Clarence Wright

Kevin Reimer

Date	Traded To		Traded With	Traded By		In Exchange For
Nov. 17, 1992	MIL	A	—	CLR	N	Dante Bichette

Bobby Reis

Date	Traded To		Traded With	Traded By		In Exchange For
Dec. 12, 1935	BOS	N	Tony Cuccinello Ray Benge Al Lopez	BKN	N	Ed Brandt Randy Moore

Tommy Reis

Date	Traded To	Traded With	Traded By	In Exchange For
May 23, 1938	BOS N	—	PHI N	Cash
Aug. 10, 1938	CIN N	Johnny Babich Gil English Johnny Riddle Vince DiMaggio Cash	BOS N	Eddie Miller

Pete Reiser

Date	Traded To	Traded With	Traded By	In Exchange For
Dec. 15, 1948	BOS N	—	BKN N	Mike McCormick

Heinie Reitz

Date	Traded To	Traded With	Traded By	In Exchange For
Feb. 1900	PHI N	Tully Sparks	PIT N	Duff Cooley

Ken Reitz

Date	Traded To	Traded With	Traded By	In Exchange For
Dec. 8, 1975	SF N	—	STL N	Pete Falcone
Dec. 10, 1976	STL N	—	SF N	Lynn McGlothen
Dec. 9, 1980	CHI N	Leon Durham Tye Waller	STL N	Bruce Sutter

Mike Remlinger

Date	Traded To	Traded With	Traded By	In Exchange For
Dec. 11, 1991	SEA A	*see Kevin Mitchell*	SF N	—
May 11, 1995	CIN N	—	NY N	Minor league OF Cobi Cradle
Dec. 4, 1995	KC A	—	CIN N	Minor league OF Andre King

(Part of three way trade between Kansas City, Cincinnati, and St. Louis in which St. Louis received IF Luis Ordaz from Cincinnati and Miguel Mejia from Kansas City.)

Jerry Remy

Date	Traded To	Traded With	Traded By	In Exchange For
Dec. 8, 1977	BOS A	—	CAL A	Don Aase Cash

Hal Reniff

Date	Traded To	Traded With	Traded By	In Exchange For
June 29, 1967	NY N	—	NY A	Cash

Steve Renko

Date	Traded To	Traded With	Traded By	In Exchange For
June 15, 1969	MON N	Kevin Collins minor league Ps Bill Carden and Dave Colon	NY N	Donn Clendenon
May 17, 1976	CHI N	Larry Biittner	MON N	Andre Thornton
Aug. 18, 1977	CHI A	—	CHI N	Larry Anderson Cash
Mar. 30, 1978	OAK A	Jim Essian	CHI A	Pablo Torrealba
Jan. 20, 1979	BOS A	—	OAK A	No compensation (free agent signing)
Jan. 23, 1981	CAL A	Fred Lynn	BOS A	Frank Tanana Jim Dorsey Joe Rudi
Feb. 9, 1983	KC A	—	CAL A	No compensation (free agent signing)

Bill Renna

Date	Traded To	Traded With	Traded By	In Exchange For
Dec. 16, 1953	PHI A	—	NY A	*see Harry Byrd*
June 14, 1956	NY A	Moe Burtschy Cash	KC A	Lou Skizas Eddie Robinson

Tony Rensa

Date	Traded To	Traded With	Traded By	In Exchange For
June 1930	PHI N	—	DET A	Waiver price

Rick Renteria

Date	Traded To	Traded With	Traded By	In Exchange For
Dec. 5, 1986	SEA A	—	PIT N	player to be named

(Pittsburgh received P Bob Siegel on Dec. 10, 1986.)

Andy Replogle

Date	Traded To	Traded With	Traded By	In Exchange For
Apr. 4, 1978	MIL A	—	BAL A	Cash

Roger Repoz

Date	Traded To	Traded With	Traded By	In Exchange For
June 10, 1966	KC A	Gil Blanco Bill Stafford	NY A	Fred Talbot Billy Bryan
June 15, 1967	CAL A	—	KC A	Jack Sanford Jackie Warner

Roger Repoz *continued*

Date	Traded To	Traded With	Traded By	In Exchange For
June 10, 1972	BAL A	—	CAL A	Jerry DaVanon

Rip Repulski

Date	Traded To	Traded With	Traded By	In Exchange For
Nov. 19, 1956	PHI N	Bobby Morgan	STL N	Del Ennis
Dec. 23, 1958	LA N	Jim Golden Gene Snyder	PHI N	Sparky Anderson
May 6, 1960	BOS A	—	LA N	Nels Chittum

Dino Restelli

Date	Traded To	Traded With	Traded By	In Exchange For
Sept. 19, 1951	WAS A	—	PIT N	Waiver price
Dec. 17, 1951	CLE A	—	WAS A	Cash

Merv Rettenmund

Date	Traded To	Traded With	Traded By	In Exchange For
Dec. 4, 1973	CIN N	Junior Kennedy minor league C Bill Wood	BAL A	Ross Grimsley minor league C Wally Williams
Apr. 5, 1976	SD N	—	CIN N	Rudi Meoli Cash

Ken Retzer

Date	Traded To	Traded With	Traded By	In Exchange For
Oct. 15, 1964	MIN A	—	WAS A	Joe McCabe
Jan. 4, 1967	CLE A	Lee Maye	HOU N	Jim Landis Doc Edwards Jim Weaver

Ed Reulbach

Date	Traded To	Traded With	Traded By	In Exchange For
July 1913	BKN N	—	CHI N	Eddie Stack Cash
Apr. 12, 1916	BOS N	—	PIT N	Cash

Paul Reuschel

Date	Traded To	Traded With	Traded By	In Exchange For
June 26, 1978	CLE A	—	CHI N	Denny DeBarr

Rick Reuschel

Date	Traded To	Traded With	Traded By	In Exchange For
June 12, 1981	NY A	—	CHI N	Doug Bird Mike Griffin $400,000.
Feb. 28, 1985	PIT N	—	CHI N	No compensation (free agent signing)
Aug. 12, 1987	SF N	—	PIT N	Jeff Robinson Scott Medvin

Jerry Reuss

Date	Traded To	Traded With	Traded By	In Exchange For
Apr. 15, 1972	HOU N	—	STL N	Scipio Spinks Lance Clemons
Oct. 31, 1973	PIT N	—	HOU N	Milt May
Apr. 7, 1979	LA N	—	PIT N	Rick Rhoden
July 31, 1989	MIL A	—	CHI A	Minor league P Brian Drahman

Dave Revering

Date	Traded To	Traded With	Traded By	In Exchange For
Feb. 25, 1978	OAK A	Cash	CIN N	Doug Bair
May 20, 1981	NY A	Mike Patterson minor league P Chuck Dougherty	OAK A	Jim Spencer Tom Underwood
May 5, 1982	TOR A	minor league 3B Jeff Reynolds	NY A	John Mayberry
Aug. 6, 1982	SEA A	—	TOR A	No compensation (free agent signing)

Gilberto Reyes

Date	Traded To	Traded With	Traded By	In Exchange For
Mar. 27, 1989	MON N	—	LA N	Jeff Fischer

Allie Reynolds

Date	Traded To	Traded With	Traded By	In Exchange For
Oct. 19, 1946	NY A	—	CLE A	Joe Gordon Eddie Bockman

Archie Reynolds

Date	Traded To	Traded With	Traded By	In Exchange For
July 9, 1970	CAL A	—	CHI N	Juan Pizarro

Bob Reynolds

Date	Traded To	Traded With	Traded By	In Exchange For
June 15, 1971	STL N	—	MON N	Mike Torrez
July 29, 1971	MIL A	Jose Cardenal Dick Schofield	STL N	Ted Kubiak minor league P Charlie Loseth
Dec. 9, 1971	BAL A	Cash	MIL A	Curt Motton
May 29, 1975	DET A	—	BAL A	Fred Holdsworth
Aug. 26, 1975	CLE A	—	DET A	Cash

Carl Reynolds

Date	Traded To	Traded With	Traded By	In Exchange For
Dec. 4, 1931	WAS A	John Kerr	CHI A	Jackie Hayes Bump Hadley Sad Sam Jones
Dec. 14, 1932	STL A	Sammy West Lloyd Brown $20,000.	WAS A	Goose Goslin Fred Schulte Lefty Stewart
Dec. 14, 1933	BOS A	—	STL A	Ivy Andrews Smead Jolley Cash
Dec. 17, 1935	WAS A	Roy Johnson	BOS A	Heinie Manush

Craig Reynolds

Date	Traded To	Traded With	Traded By	In Exchange For
Dec. 7, 1976	SEA A	Jimmy Sexton	PIT N	Grant Jackson
Dec. 8, 1978	HOU N	—	SEA A	Floyd Bannister

Harold Reynolds

Date	Traded To	Traded With	Traded By	In Exchange For
Dec. 11, 1992	BAL A	—	SEA A	No compensation (free agent signing)
Jan. 28, 1994	SD N	—	BAL A	No compensation (free agent signing)
Mar. 29, 1994	CAL A	—	SD N	Hilly Hathaway

Ken Reynolds

Date	Traded To	Traded With	Traded By	In Exchange For
Nov. 30, 1972	MIN A	Ken Sanders Joe Lis	PHI N	Cesar Tovar
Mar. 27, 1973	MIL A	—	MIN A	Mike Ferraro
Apr. 8, 1976	SD N	minor leaguer Bob Stewart	STL N	Danny Frisella
Mar. 21, 1977	TOR A	—	SD N	Cash

R. J. Reynolds

Date	Traded To	Traded With	Traded By	In Exchange For
Aug. 31, 1985	PIT N	Sid Bream Cecil Espy	LA N	Bill Madlock

(Pittsburgh received Reynolds on Sept. 3 and Bream and Espy on September 9, 1985.)

Ronn Reynolds

Date	Traded To	Traded With	Traded By	In Exchange For
Jan. 16, 1986	PHI N	Jeff Bittiger	NY N	Minor league P Rodger Cole Minor league 1B Ronnie Gideon
Apr. 2, 1987	HOU N	—	PHI N	Jeff Calhoun

Tommie Reynolds

Date	Traded To	Traded With	Traded By	In Exchange For
May 16, 1970	CAL A	—	OAK A	Cash
Jan. 26, 1972	MIL A	—	CAL A	Andy Kosco

Bobby Rhawn

Date	Traded To	Traded With	Traded By	In Exchange For
June 6, 1949	PIT N	Ray Poat	NY N	Kirby Higbe

Flint Rhem

Date	Traded To	Traded With	Traded By	In Exchange For
May 30, 1932	PHI N	Eddie Delker	STL N	Cash
Feb. 11, 1934	STL N	—	PHI N	Cash
June 23, 1934	BOS N	—	STL N	Cash

Bob Rhoads

Date	Traded To	Traded With	Traded By	In Exchange For
Apr. 1903	STL N	—	CHI N	Bob Wicker

Rick Rhoden

Date	Traded To	Traded With	Traded By	In Exchange For
Apr. 7, 1979	PIT N	—	LA N	Jerry Reuss
Nov. 26, 1986	NY A	Cecilio Guante Pat Clements	PIT N	Doug Drabek Logan Easley Brian Fisher

Rick Rhoden *continued*

Date	Traded To	Traded With	Traded By	In Exchange For
Jan. 10, 1989	HOU N	—	NY A	John Fishel Minor league P Mike Hook Minor league P Pedro DeLeon

Charlie Rhodes

Date	Traded To	Traded With	Traded By	In Exchange For
May 1908	STL N	—	CIN N	Waiver price

Gordon Rhodes

Date	Traded To	Traded With	Traded By	In Exchange For
May 1, 1932	BOS A	—	NY A	Wilcy Moore
Dec. 10, 1935	PHI A	minor league C George Savino $150,000.	BOS A	Jimmie Foxx Johnny Marcum

Karl Rhodes

Date	Traded To	Traded With	Traded By	In Exchange For
July 30, 1993	NY A	—	KC A	John Habyan

(Part of three team trade involving New York Yankees, Chicago Cubs, and Kansas City Royals.)

Date	Traded To	Traded With	Traded By	In Exchange For
July 30, 1993	CHI N	—	NY A	Paul Assenmacher

(Part of three team trade involving New York Yankees, Chicago Cubs, and Kansas City Royals.)

Date	Traded To	Traded With	Traded By	In Exchange For
May 26, 1995	BOS A	—	CHI N	Waiver price

Hal Rhyne

Date	Traded To	Traded With	Traded By	In Exchange For
Dec. 15, 1932	CHI A	Ed Durham	BOS A	Johnny Hodapp Greg Mulleavy Bob Fothergill Bob Seeds

Dennis Ribant

Date	Traded To	Traded With	Traded By	In Exchange For
Aug. 8, 1964	NY N	Cash	MIL N	Frank Lary
Dec. 6, 1966	PIT N	Gary Kolb	NY N	Don Bosch Don Cardwell
Nov. 28, 1967	DET A	—	PIT N	Dave Wickersham
July 21, 1968	CHI A	—	DET A	Don McMahon
Dec. 15, 1968	KC A	—	DET A	Cash

Frank Riccelli

Date	Traded To	Traded With	Traded By	In Exchange For
Oct. 25, 1977	STL N	—	SF N	Jim Dwyer

(San Francisco received Dwyer on June 15, 1978.)

Date	Traded To	Traded With	Traded By	In Exchange For
June 8, 1978	HOU N	—	STL N	Bob Coluccio

Del Rice

Date	Traded To	Traded With	Traded By	In Exchange For
June 3, 1955	MIL N	—	STL N	Pete Whisenant

Hal Rice

Date	Traded To	Traded With	Traded By	In Exchange For
June 14, 1953	PIT N	Cash	STL N	Pete Castiglione
June 14, 1954	CHI N	—	PIT N	Luis Marquez

Harry Rice

Date	Traded To	Traded With	Traded By	In Exchange For
Dec. 2, 1927	DET A	Chick Galloway Elam Vangilder	STL A	Heinie Manush Lu Blue
May 30, 1930	NY A	Ownie Carroll Yats Wuestling	DET A	Waite Hoyt Mark Koenig
Jan. 13, 1931	WAS A	—	NY A	Waiver price

Lee Richard

Date	Traded To	Traded With	Traded By	In Exchange For
Dec. 12, 1975	STL N	—	CHI A	Buddy Bradford Greg Terlecky

Gene Richards

Date	Traded To	Traded With	Traded By	In Exchange For
Mar. 31, 1984	SF N	—	SD N	No compensation (free agent signing)

Paul Richards

Date	Traded To	Traded With	Traded By	In Exchange For
Dec. 1932	NY N	—	BKN N	Waiver price
May 25, 1935	PHI A	—	NY N	Cash

Gordie Richardson

Date	Traded To	Traded With	Traded By	In Exchange For
Dec. 7, 1964	NY N	Johnny Lewis	STL N	Tracy Stallard Elio Chacon

Jeff Richardson

Date	Traded To	Traded With	Traded By	In Exchange For
Sept. 15, 1987	CAL A	—	NY N	*see John Candelaria*

Jeff Richardson

Date	Traded To	Traded With	Traded By	In Exchange For
Apr. 3, 1990	PIT N	Mike Roesler	CIN N	Billy Hatcher
Apr. 2, 1993	BOS A	—	PIT N	Daryl Irvine

Mike Richardt

Date	Traded To	Traded With	Traded By	In Exchange For
May 25, 1984	HOU N	—	TEX A	Alan Bannister

Lance Richbourg

Date	Traded To	Traded With	Traded By	In Exchange For
July 1, 1921	PHI N	Goldie Rapp Lee King	NY N	Casey Stengel Red Causey Johnny Rawlings
Dec. 17, 1931	CHI N	—	BOS N	Waiver price
Nov. 30, 1932	CIN N	Bob Smith Rollie Hemsley Johnny Moore	CHI N	Babe Herman

Pete Richert

Date	Traded To	Traded With	Traded By	In Exchange For
Dec. 4, 1964	WAS A	Frank Howard Phil Ortega Dick Nen Ken McMullen	LA N	Claude Osteen John Kennedy $100,000.
May 29, 1967	BAL A	—	WAS A	Mike Epstein Frank Bertaina
Dec. 2, 1971	LA N	Frank Robinson	BAL A	Doyle Alexander Bob O'Brien Sergio Robles Royle Stillman
Dec. 5, 1973	STL N	—	LA N	Tommie Agee
June 21, 1974	PHI N	—	STL N	Cash

Lew Richie

Date	Traded To	Traded With	Traded By	In Exchange For
July 16, 1909	BOS N	Buster Brown Dave Shean	PHI N	Johnny Bates Charlie Starr
Apr. 1910	CHI N	—	BOS N	Doc Miller

Marv Rickert

Date	Traded To	Traded With	Traded By	In Exchange For
Oct. 8, 1947	CIN N	—	CHI N	Cash
May 11, 1948	BOS N	—	CIN N	Danny Litwhiler
Dec. 14, 1949	PIT N	—	BOS N	Cash
May 29, 1950	CHI A	—	PIT N	Cash

Dave Ricketts

Date	Traded To	Traded With	Traded By	In Exchange For
Oct. 21, 1969	PIT N	Dave Giusti	STL N	Carl Taylor minor league OF Frank Vanzin

Branch Rickey

Date	Traded To	Traded With	Traded By	In Exchange For
Feb. 1905	STL A	—	CHI A	Frank Roth
Dec. 1906	NY A	—	STL A	Cash

Fred Rico

Date	Traded To	Traded With	Traded By	In Exchange For
June 13, 1970	STL N	—	KC A	Cookie Rojas
Sept. 1, 1971	MIN A	minor league P Dan Ford	STL N	Stan Williams

Harry Riconda

Date	Traded To	Traded With	Traded By	In Exchange For
Dec. 11, 1928	PIT N	Jesse Petty	BKN N	Glenn Wright

Elmer Riddle

Date	Traded To	Traded With	Traded By	In Exchange For
Dec. 10, 1947	PIT N	—	CIN N	Cash

Johnny Riddle

Date	Traded To	Traded With	Traded By	In Exchange For
Aug. 10, 1938	CIN N	Tommy Reis Johnny Babich Gil English Vince DiMaggio Cash	BOS N	Eddie Miller

Denny Riddleberger

Date	Traded To	Traded With	Traded By	In Exchange For
Aug. 31, 1970	WAS A	Cash	PIT N	George Brunet
Dec. 2, 1971	CLE A	*see Del Unser*	TEX A	—

Steve Ridzik

Date	Traded To	Traded With	Traded By	In Exchange For
Apr. 30, 1955	CIN N	—	PHI N	*see Andy Seminick*
Apr. 13, 1966	PHI N	—	WAS A	Cash

Nikco Riesgo

Date	Traded To	Traded With	Traded By	In Exchange For
Aug. 31, 1990	PHI N	Minor league P Rocky Elli	NY N	Tommy Herr

Joe Riggert

Date	Traded To	Traded With	Traded By	In Exchange For
June 1914	STL N	—	BKN N	Casey Hageman

Lew Riggs

Date	Traded To	Traded With	Traded By	In Exchange For
Nov. 3, 1934	CIN N	—	STL N	$30,000.
Dec. 9, 1940	BKN N	—	CIN N	Pep Young

Dave Righetti

Date	Traded To	Traded With	Traded By	In Exchange For
Nov. 10, 1978	NY A	Juan Beniquez Mike Griffin Paul Mirabella minor league P Greg Jemison	TEX A	Domingo Ramos Sparky Lyle Mike Heath Larry McCall Dave Rajsich Cash
Dec. 4, 1990	SF N	—	NY A	No compensation (free agent signing)
Dec. 23, 1993	OAK A	—	SF N	No compensation (free agent signing)

Topper Rigney

Date	Traded To	Traded With	Traded By	In Exchange For
Apr. 7, 1926	BOS A	—	DET A	Cash
May 2, 1927	WAS A	—	BOS A	Buddy Myer

Jose Rijo

Date	Traded To	Traded With	Traded By	In Exchange For
Dec. 8, 1984	OAK A	Jay Howell Stan Javier Tim Birtsas Eric Plunk	NY A	Rickey Henderson Bert Bradley Cash
Dec. 8, 1987	CIN N	Tim Birtsas	OAK A	Dave Parker

Ernest Riles

Date	Traded To	Traded With	Traded By	In Exchange For
June 8, 1988	SF N	—	MIL A	Jeffrey Leonard
Dec. 4, 1990	OAK A	—	SF N	Darren Lewis Player to be named

(San Francisco received P Pedro Pena on December 17, 1990.)

George Riley

Date	Traded To	Traded With	Traded By	In Exchange For
Aug. 20, 1984	SF N	Kelly Downs	PHI N	Al Oliver Renie Martin
Oct. 24, 1985	MON N	—	SF N	*see Bill Laskey*

Jimmy Ring

Date	Traded To	Traded With	Traded By	In Exchange For
Feb. 22, 1921	PHI N	Greasy Neale	CIN N	Eppa Rixey
Dec. 30, 1925	NY N	—	PHI N	Jack Bentley Wayland Dean
Dec. 20, 1926	STL N	Frankie Frisch	NY N	Rogers Hornsby
Dec. 13, 1927	PHI N	Johnny Schulte	STL N	Johnny Mokan Jimmy Cooney Bubber Jonnard

Juan Rios

Date	Traded To	Traded With	Traded By	In Exchange For
Mar. 25, 1969	KC A	—	MON N	Cash
Sept. 15, 1970	MIL A	—	KC A	Cash

Allen Ripley

Date	Traded To	Traded With	Traded By	In Exchange For
Apr. 6, 1980	SF N	—	BOS A	Cash
Dec. 7, 1981	CHI N	—	SF N	Doug Capilla

Jimmy Ripple

Date	Traded To	Traded With	Traded By	In Exchange For
Aug. 23, 1939	BKN N	—	NY N	Ray Hayworth
Aug. 23, 1940	CIN N	—	BKN N	Waiver price

Bill Risley

Date	Traded To		Traded With	Traded By		In Exchange For
Dec. 11, 1991	MON	N	*see John Wetteland*	CIN	N	—
Mar. 17, 1994	SEA	A	—	MON	N	Waiver price
Dec. 18, 1995	TOR	A	Minor league 2B Miguel Cairo	SEA	A	Paul Menhart Edwin Hurtado

Claude Ritchey

Date	Traded To		Traded With	Traded By		In Exchange For
Jan. 1900	PIT	N	*see Honus Wagner*	LOU	N	—
Dec. 1906	BOS	N	Ginger Beaumont Patsy Flaherty	PIT	N	Ed Abbaticchio

Jay Ritchie

Date	Traded To		Traded With	Traded By		In Exchange For
Dec. 15, 1965	MIL	N	Lee Thomas Arnold Earley	BOS	A	Bob Sadowski Dan Osinski
Oct. 10, 1967	CIN	N	Jim Beauchamp Mack Jones	ATL	N	Deron Johnson

Jim Rittwage

Date	Traded To		Traded With	Traded By		In Exchange For
Dec. 1, 1965	CLE	A	Jim Landis	KC	A	Phil Roof Joe Rudi
Dec. 2, 1965	SF	N	—	CHI	N	*see Randy Hundley*

Ben Rivera

Date	Traded To		Traded With	Traded By		In Exchange For
May 28, 1992	PHI	N	—	ATL	N	Donnie Elliott

German Rivera

Date	Traded To		Traded With	Traded By		In Exchange For
July 10, 1985	HOU	N	—	LA	N	*see Enos Cabell*

Jim Rivera

Date	Traded To		Traded With	Traded By		In Exchange For
Nov. 27, 1951	STL	A	Joe De Maestri Dick Littlefield Gus Niarhos Gordon Goldsberry	CHI	A	Al Widmar Sherm Lollar Tom Upton
July 28, 1952	CHI	A	Darrell Johnson	STL	A	J. W. Porter Ray Coleman

Luis Rivera

Date	Traded To		Traded With	Traded By		In Exchange For
Dec. 8, 1988	BOS	A	—	MON	N	*see Spike Owen*

Mickey Rivers

Date	Traded To		Traded With	Traded By		In Exchange For
Dec. 11, 1975	NY	A	Ed Figueroa	CAL	A	Bobby Bonds
Aug. 1, 1979	TEX	A	minor league Ps Bob Polinsky Neil Mersch and Mark Softy	NY	A	Oscar Gamble Ray Fontenot Gene Nelson minor league 3B Amos Lewis

Eppa Rixey

Date	Traded To		Traded With	Traded By		In Exchange For
Feb. 22, 1921	CIN	N	—	PHI	N	Jimmy Ring Greasy Neale

Johnny Rizzo

Date	Traded To		Traded With	Traded By		In Exchange For
Oct. 1937	PIT	N	—	STL	N	Tom Padden minor leaguer Bernie Cobb
May 8, 1940	CIN	N	—	PIT	N	Vince DiMaggio
June 15, 1940	PHI	N	—	CIN	N	Morrie Arnovich
Dec. 10, 1941	BKN	N	—	PHI	N	Cash

Joe Roa

Date	Traded To		Traded With	Traded By		In Exchange For
Aug. 28, 1991	NY	N	Tony Castillo	ATL	N	Alejandro Pena
Nov. 18, 1994	CLE	A	*see Jeromy Burnitz*	NY	N	—

Mel Roach

Date	Traded To		Traded With	Traded By		In Exchange For
May 9, 1961	CHI	N	—	MIL	N	Frank Thomas
Mar. 20, 1962	PHI	N	—	CLE	A	Ken Lehman Tony Curry

Roxy Roach

Date	Traded To		Traded With	Traded By		In Exchange For
Dec. 1911	WAS	A	John Knight	NY	A	Gabby Street Jack Lelivelt

Mike Roarke

Date	Traded To		Traded With	Traded By		In Exchange For
Oct. 15, 1959	DET	A	Don Kaiser Casey Wise	MIL	N	Charlie Lau Don Lee

Bert Roberge

Date	Traded To		Traded With	Traded By		In Exchange For
Dec. 7, 1984	MON	N	Vance Law	CHI	A	Bob James Bryan Little

Kevin Roberson

Date	Traded To		Traded With	Traded By		In Exchange For
July 7, 1995	SEA	A	—	CHI	N	Waiver price

Bip Roberts

Date	Traded To		Traded With	Traded By		In Exchange For
Dec. 8, 1991	CIN	N	Minor league OF Craig Pueschner	SD	N	Randy Myers
Jan. 10, 1994	SD	N	—	CIN	N	No compensation (free agent signing)
Dec. 21, 1995	KC	A	Minor league P Bryan Wolff	SD	N	Wally Joyner Minor league P Aaron Dorlarque

Curt Roberts

Date	Traded To		Traded With	Traded By		In Exchange For
Feb. 19, 1957	NY	A	—	KC	A	*see Billy Hunter*

Dale Roberts

Date	Traded To		Traded With	Traded By		In Exchange For
Dec. 7, 1967	ATL	N	Bob Tillman	NY	A	Bobby Cox

Dave Roberts

Date	Traded To		Traded With	Traded By		In Exchange For
Nov. 22, 1976	TOR	A	Dave Hilton John Scott	SD	N	Cash
Feb. 16, 1977	SD	N	—	TOR	A	Jerry Johnson
Oct. 25, 1978	TEX	A	Oscar Gamble $300,000.	SD	N	Mike Hargrove Kurt Bevacqua Bill Fahey
Dec. 10, 1980	HOU	N	—	TEX	A	No compensation (free agent signing)
Mar. 28, 1982	PHI	N	—	HOU	N	Minor league P Steve Dunnegan

Dave Roberts

Date	Traded To		Traded With	Traded By		In Exchange For
Dec. 3, 1971	HOU	N	—	SD	N	Derrel Thomas Bill Greif Mark Schaeffer
Dec. 6, 1975	DET	A	Milt May Jim Crawford	HOU	N	Leon Roberts Terry Humphrey Gene Pentz Mark Lemongello
July 30, 1977	CHI	N	—	DET	A	Cash
June 28, 1979	PIT	N	*see Bill Madlock*	SF	N	—
Apr. 24, 1980	SEA	A	—	PIT	N	Cash
Dec. 23, 1980	NY	N	—	SEA	A	No compensation (free agent signing)

Dave Roberts

Date	Traded To		Traded With	Traded By		In Exchange For
Sept. 12, 1966	BAL	A	—	PIT	N	Cash

Leon Roberts

Date	Traded To		Traded With	Traded By		In Exchange For
Dec. 6, 1975	HOU	N	Terry Humphrey Gene Pentz Mark Lemongello	DET	A	Milt May Dave Roberts Jim Crawford
Dec. 5, 1977	SEA	A	—	HOU	N	Jimmy Sexton
Dec. 12, 1980	TEX	A	*see Rick Honeycutt*	SEA	A	—
July 15, 1982	TOR	A	—	TEX	A	Cash
Feb. 5, 1983	KC	A	—	TOR	A	Cecil Fielder

Robin Roberts

Date	Traded To		Traded With	Traded By		In Exchange For
Oct. 16, 1961	BAL	A	—	PHI	N	Cash

Andre Robertson

Date	Traded To	Traded With	Traded By	In Exchange For
June 29, 1986	ATL N	—	NY A	*see Claudell Washington*

Charlie Robertson

Date	Traded To	Traded With	Traded By	In Exchange For
Dec. 31, 1925	STL A	—	CHI A	Waiver price

Daryl Robertson

Date	Traded To	Traded With	Traded By	In Exchange For
Mar. 31, 1961	CHI N	Andre Rodgers	MIL N	Moe Drabowsky Seth Morehead
June 5, 1962	STL N	Bobby Gene Smith	CHI N	Don Landrum Alex Grammas

Dave Robertson

Date	Traded To	Traded With	Traded By	In Exchange For
July 25, 1919	CHI N	—	NY N	Phil Douglas
July 1, 1921	PIT N	—	CHI N	Elmer Ponder
Apr. 20, 1922	NY N	—	PIT N	Cash

Gene Robertson

Date	Traded To	Traded With	Traded By	In Exchange For
Sept. 17, 1929	BOS N	—	NY A	Cash

Jerry Robertson

Date	Traded To	Traded With	Traded By	In Exchange For
Dec. 3, 1969	DET A	—	MON N	Joe Sparma
Mar. 30, 1971	NY N	—	DET A	Dean Chance Bill Denehy

Jim Robertson

Date	Traded To	Traded With	Traded By	In Exchange For
Dec. 16, 1953	PHI A	—	NY A	*see Harry Byrd*

Rich Robertson

Date	Traded To	Traded With	Traded By	In Exchange For
Nov. 4, 1994	MIN A	—	PIT N	Waiver price

Rich Robertson

Date	Traded To	Traded With	Traded By	In Exchange For
Feb. 7, 1972	CHI A	—	SF N	Cash

(Robertson was returned to San Francisco on March 19.)

Sherry Robertson

Date	Traded To	Traded With	Traded By	In Exchange For
May 19, 1952	PHI A	—	WAS A	Waiver price

Aaron Robinson

Date	Traded To	Traded With	Traded By	In Exchange For
Feb. 24, 1948	CHI A	Fred Bradley Bill Wight	NY A	Ed Lopat
Nov. 10, 1948	DET A	—	CHI A	Billy Pierce $10,000.
Aug. 6, 1951	BOS A	—	DET A	Waiver price

Bill Robinson

Date	Traded To	Traded With	Traded By	In Exchange For
Nov. 29, 1966	NY A	Chi Chi Olivo	ATL N	Clete Boyer
Dec. 3, 1970	CHI A	—	NY A	Barry Moore
Dec. 3, 1971	PHI N	—	CHI A	Minor league C Jerry Rodriguez
Apr. 5, 1975	PIT N	—	PHI N	Wayne Simpson
June 15, 1982	PHI N	—	PIT N	Wayne Nordhagen

Bruce Robinson

Date	Traded To	Traded With	Traded By	In Exchange For
Feb. 3, 1979	NY A	—	OAK A	$400,000.

Craig Robinson

Date	Traded To	Traded With	Traded By	In Exchange For
Dec. 3, 1973	ATL N	Barry Lersch	PHI N	Ron Schueler
June 11, 1975	SF N	—	ATL N	Ed Goodson
June 13, 1976	ATL N	—	SF N	*see Darrell Evans*

Dewey Robinson

Date	Traded To	Traded With	Traded By	In Exchange For
Oct. 30, 1981	PHI N	Gary Holle	CHI A	Minor league IF Jose Castro

Don Robinson

Date	Traded To	Traded With	Traded By	In Exchange For
July 31, 1987	SF N	—	PIT N	Mackey Sasser Cash

Earl Robinson

Date	Traded To	Traded With	Traded By	In Exchange For
Dec. 15, 1960	BAL A	—	LA N	Cash

Eddie Robinson

Date	Traded To	Traded With	Traded By	In Exchange For
Dec. 14, 1948	WAS A	Joe Haynes Eddie Klieman	CLE A	Mickey Vernon Early Wynn
May 31, 1950	CHI A	Al Kozar Ray Scarborough	WAS A	Bob Kuzava Cass Michaels John Ostrowski
Jan. 27, 1953	PHI A	Joe De Maestri Ed McGhee	CHI A	Ferris Fain minor league 2B Bob Wilson
Dec. 16, 1953	NY A	Harry Byrd Tom Hamilton Carmen Mauro Loren Babe	PHI A	Don Bollweg John Gray Jim Robertson Jim Finigan Vic Power Bill Renna
June 14, 1956	KC A	Lou Skizas	NY A	Moe Burtschy Bill Renna Cash
Dec. 5, 1956	DET A	Jim Finigan Jack Crimian Bill Harrington	KC A	Ned Garver Gene Host Virgil Trucks Wayne Belardi $20,000.

Floyd Robinson

Date	Traded To	Traded With	Traded By	In Exchange For
Dec. 15, 1966	CIN N	—	CHI A	Jim O'Toole
Oct. 20, 1967	KC A	Darrell Osteen	CIN N	Ron Tompkins
July 31, 1968	BOS A	—	OAK A	Cash

Frank Robinson

Date	Traded To	Traded With	Traded By	In Exchange For
Dec. 9, 1965	BAL A	—	CIN N	Milt Pappas Jack Baldschun Dick Simpson
Dec. 2, 1971	LA N	Pete Richert	BAL A	Doyle Alexander Bob O'Brien Sergio Robles Royle Stillman
Nov. 28, 1972	CAL A	Bill Singer Mike Strahler Billy Grabarkewitz Bobby Valentine	LA N	Andy Messersmith Ken McMullen
Sept. 12, 1974	CLE A	—	CAL A	Ken Suarez Rusty Torres Cash

Hank Robinson

Date	Traded To	Traded With	Traded By	In Exchange For
Dec. 12, 1913	STL N	—	PIT N	*see Ed Konetchy*
June 20, 1918	NY A	—	STL N	Cash

Humberto Robinson

Date	Traded To	Traded With	Traded By	In Exchange For
Apr. 11, 1959	CLE A	—	MIL N	Mickey Vernon
May 16, 1959	PHI N	—	CLE A	Granny Hamner

Jackie Robinson

Date	Traded To	Traded With	Traded By	In Exchange For
Dec. 13, 1956	NY N	—	BKN N	Dick Littlefield $30,000.

(Trade was cancelled when Robinson retired.)

Jeff Robinson

Date	Traded To	Traded With	Traded By	In Exchange For
Jan. 11, 1991	BAL A	—	DET A	Mickey Tettleton
June 10, 1992	PIT N	—	TEX A	Waiver price

Jeff Robinson

Date	Traded To	Traded With	Traded By	In Exchange For
Aug. 12, 1987	PIT N	Scott Medvin	SF N	Rick Reuschel
Dec. 4, 1989	NY A	Willie Smith	PIT N	Don Slaught
Jan. 17, 1991	CAL A	—	NY A	No compensation (free agent signing)
Jan. 7, 1993	CHI N	—	CAL A	No compensation (free agent signing)

Ron Robinson

Date	Traded To	Traded With	Traded By	In Exchange For
June 9, 1990	MIL A	Bob Sebra	CIN N	Glenn Braggs Billy Bates

Date	Traded To	Traded With	Traded By	In Exchange For
Wilbert Robinson				
Feb. 11, 1900	STL N	Bill Keister John McGraw	BAL N	Cash
Rafael Robles				
June 20, 1972	STL N	—	SD N	Mike Fiore Bob Chlupsa
(Fiore was returned to St. Louis on July 3.)				
Sergio Robles				
Dec. 2, 1971	BAL A	—	LA N	*see Frank Robinson*
Mickey Rocco				
May 1946	CHI N	—	CLE A	Heinz Becker
Pat Rockett				
Dec. 5, 1979	TOR A	Barry Bonnell Joey McLaughlin	ATL N	Chris Chambliss Luis Gomez
Andre Rodgers				
Oct. 31, 1960	MIL N	—	SF N	Alvin Dark
Mar. 31, 1961	CHI N	Daryl Robertson	MIL N	Moe Drabowsky Seth Morehead
Dec. 9, 1964	PIT N	—	CHI N	Roberto Pena Cash
Bill Rodgers				
May 1915	BOS A	—	CLE A	Cash
June 1915	CIN N	—	BOS A	Cash
Aurelio Rodriguez				
Apr. 27, 1970	WAS A	Rick Reichardt	CAL A	Ken McMullen
Oct. 9, 1970	DET A	Joe Coleman Ed Brinkman Jim Hannan	WAS A	Denny McLain Don Wert Norm McRae Elliott Maddox
Dec. 7, 1979	SD N	—	DET A	$200,000.
Aug. 4, 1980	NY A	—	SD N	Cash
Nov. 17, 1981	TOR A	—	NY A	Minor league C Mike Lebo
Apr. 2, 1982	CHI A	—	TOR A	Wayne Nordhagen
Feb. 7, 1983	BAL A	—	CHI A	No compensation (free agent signing)
Ed Rodriguez				
Feb. 26, 1979	KC A	—	MIL A	Cash
Edwin Rodriguez				
Aug. 26, 1983	SD N	Dennis Rasmussen $200,000.	NY A	John Montefusco
Ellie Rodriguez				
Feb. 2, 1971	MIL A	—	KC A	Carl Taylor
Oct. 22, 1973	CAL A	—	MIL A	*see Clyde Wright*
Mar. 21, 1976	LA N	—	CAL A	Orlando Alvarez Cash
Frank Rodriguez				
July 6, 1995	MIN A	Player to be named	BOS A	Rick Aguilera
(Minnesota received OF J.J. Johnson on October 11, 1995.)				
Freddy Rodriguez				
Dec. 10, 1957	CHI N	—	NY N	Tom Poholsky
Henry Rodriguez				
May 23, 1995	MON N	Jeff Treadway	LA N	Roberto Kelly Joey Eischen
Rich Rodriguez				
June 24, 1993	FLA N	Gary Sheffield	SD N	Trevor Hoffman Jose Martinez Andres Berumen

Date	Traded To	Traded With	Traded By	In Exchange For
Roberto Rodriguez				
May 26, 1970	SD N	—	OAK A	Cash
June 23, 1970	CHI N	—	SD N	Cash
Rosario Rodriguez				
Dec. 20, 1990	PIT N	—	CIN N	Waiver price
Ruben Rodriguez				
Mar. 17, 1989	MIL A	—	PIT N	Lou Thornton
Steve Rodriguez				
Sept. 8, 1995	DET A	—	BOS A	Waiver price
Vic Rodriguez				
Feb. 7, 1985	SD N	—	BAL A	Fritz Connally
Preacher Roe				
Dec. 8, 1947	BKN N	Billy Cox Gene Mauch	PIT N	Dixie Walker Hal Gregg Vic Lombardi
Dec. 13, 1954	BAL A	Billy Cox	BKN N	Minor leaguers John Jancse and Harry Schwegeman $50,000.
(Roe retired; Erv Palica trade of March 17, 1955 was additional compensation.)				
Ed Roebuck				
July 20, 1963	WAS A	—	LA N	Marv Breeding
Apr. 21, 1964	PHI N	—	WAS A	Cash
Gary Roenicke				
Dec. 7, 1977	BAL A	Don Stanhouse Joe Kerrigan	MON N	Rudy May Randy Miller Bryn Smith
Dec. 12, 1985	NY A	Leo Hernandez	BAL A	Rich Bordi Rex Hudler
Jan. 23, 1987	ATL N	—	NY A	No compensation (free agent signing)
Mike Roesler				
Apr. 3, 1990	PIT N	Jeff Richardson	CIN N	Billy Hatcher
Wally Roettger				
Apr. 10, 1930	NY N	—	STL N	Showboat Fisher Doc Farrell
Oct. 29, 1930	CIN N	—	NY N	Cash
June 15, 1931	STL N	—	CIN N	Taylor Douthit
Dec. 1931	CIN N	—	STL N	Cash
Nov. 17, 1933	PIT N	Red Lucas	CIN N	Adam Comorosky Tony Piet
Billy Rogell				
Dec. 6, 1939	CHI N	—	DET A	Dick Bartell
Kenny Rogers				
Dec. 30, 1995	NY A	—	TEX A	No compensation (free agent signing)
Kevin Rogers				
Oct. 26, 1995	PIT N	—	SF N	Waiver price
Tom Rogers				
Apr. 1919	PHI A	—	STL A	Cash
Garry Roggenburk				
Sept. 7, 1966	BOS A	—	MIN A	Cash
June 23, 1969	SEA A	—	BOS A	Cash

Saul Rogovin

Date	Traded To	Traded With	Traded By	In Exchange For
May 15, 1951	CHI A	—	DET A	Bob Cain
Dec. 10, 1953	CIN N	Rocky Krsnich Connie Ryan	CHI A	Willard Marshall

Dave Rohde

Date	Traded To	Traded With	Traded By	In Exchange For
Dec. 10, 1991	CLE A	Kenny Lofton	HOU N	Eddie Taubensee Willie Blair

Dan Rohn

Date	Traded To	Traded With	Traded By	In Exchange For
Apr. 1, 1985	CLE A	—	CHI N	Jay Baller
Apr. 3, 1987	OAK A	*see Dennis Eckersley*	CHI N	—

Billy Rohr

Date	Traded To	Traded With	Traded By	In Exchange For
May 22, 1970	DET A	Russ Nagelson	CLE A	Fred Lasher

Cookie Rojas

Date	Traded To	Traded With	Traded By	In Exchange For
Nov. 27, 1962	PHI N	—	CIN N	Jim Owens
Oct. 7, 1969	STL N	—	PHI N	*see Curt Flood*
June 13, 1970	KC A	—	STL N	Fred Rico

Stan Rojek

Date	Traded To	Traded With	Traded By	In Exchange For
Nov. 14, 1947	PIT N	—	BKN N	Cash
May 17, 1951	STL N	—	PIT N	Erv Dusak Rocky Nelson
Jan. 24, 1952	STL A	—	STL N	Waiver price
Oct. 14, 1952	BKN N	Bob Mahoney Ray Coleman $90,000.	STL A	Billy Hunter

Jim Roland

Date	Traded To	Traded With	Traded By	In Exchange For
Feb. 24, 1969	OAK A	—	MIN A	Cash
Apr. 28, 1972	NY A	—	OAK A	Cash
Aug. 30, 1972	TEX A	—	NY A	Casey Cox

Jose Roman

Date	Traded To	Traded With	Traded By	In Exchange For
May 12, 1987	NY N	—	CLE A	Minor league OF Mike Westbrook

Ron Romanick

Date	Traded To	Traded With	Traded By	In Exchange For
Dec. 19, 1986	NY A	Alan Mills	CAL A	Butch Wynegar

(New York received Mills on June 22, 1987.)

Johnny Romano

Date	Traded To	Traded With	Traded By	In Exchange For
Dec. 6, 1959	CLE A	Norm Cash Bubba Phillips	CHI A	Dick Brown Don Ferrarese Jake Striker Minnie Minoso
Jan. 20, 1965	CHI A	Tommy John Tommie Agee	CLE A	Rocky Colavito Camilo Carreon

(Part of three-team trade involving Kansas City, Cleveland, and Chicago White Sox.)

Date	Traded To	Traded With	Traded By	In Exchange For
Dec. 14, 1966	STL N	minor league P Lee White	CHI A	Walt Williams Don Dennis

Ed Romero

Date	Traded To	Traded With	Traded By	In Exchange For
Dec. 11, 1985	BOS A	—	MIL A	Mark Clear
Aug. 23, 1989	MIL A	—	ATL N	Jay Aldrich
Jan. 15, 1990	DET A	—	MIL A	No compensation (free agent signing)

Enrique Romo

Date	Traded To	Traded With	Traded By	In Exchange For
Dec. 5, 1978	PIT N	Rick Jones Tommy McMillan	SEA A	Odell Jones Rafael Vasquez Mario Mendoza

Vicente Romo

Date	Traded To	Traded With	Traded By	In Exchange For
Apr. 19, 1969	BOS A	—	CLE A	*see Ken Harrelson*
Mar. 31, 1971	CHI A	Tony Muser	BOS A	Duane Josephson Danny Murphy
Oct. 28, 1972	SD N	—	CHI A	John Jeter

Gene Roof

Date	Traded To	Traded With	Traded By	In Exchange For
Sept. 16, 1983	MON N	—	STL N	Cash

Phil Roof

Date	Traded To	Traded With	Traded By	In Exchange For
Oct. 14, 1964	LA A	Ron Piche	MIL N	Dan Osinski
June 15, 1965	CLE A	—	CAL A	Bubba Morton Cash

(California received Morton on September 15, 1965.)

Date	Traded To	Traded With	Traded By	In Exchange For
Dec. 1, 1965	KC A	Joe Rudi	CLE A	Jim Landis Jim Rittwage
Jan. 15, 1970	MIL A	Mike Hershberger Lew Krausse Ken Sanders	OAK A	Don Mincher Ron Clark
July 8, 1971	MIN A	—	MIL A	Paul Ratliff
Oct. 21, 1976	TOR A	—	CHI A	Larry Anderson

(Chicago received Anderson on January 5, 1977.)

Jim Rooker

Date	Traded To	Traded With	Traded By	In Exchange For
Sept. 30, 1968	NY A	—	DET A	Cash
Oct. 25, 1972	PIT N	—	KC A	Gene Garber

Rolando Roomes

Date	Traded To	Traded With	Traded By	In Exchange For
Dec. 9, 1988	CIN N	—	CHI N	Lloyd McClendon
June 18, 1990	MON N	—	CIN N	Waiver price

Pat Rooney

Date	Traded To	Traded With	Traded By	In Exchange For
Dec. 20, 1983	NY A	—	MON N	Tim Burke

John Roper

Date	Traded To	Traded With	Traded By	In Exchange For
July 21, 1995	SF N	*see Deion Sanders*	CIN N	—

Jorge Roque

Date	Traded To	Traded With	Traded By	In Exchange For
Nov. 6, 1972	MON N	—	STL N	Tim McCarver

Buddy Rosar

Date	Traded To	Traded With	Traded By	In Exchange For
Dec. 17, 1942	CLE A	Roy Cullenbine	NY A	Roy Weatherly Oscar Grimes
May 29, 1945	PHI A	—	CLE A	Frankie Hayes
Oct. 8, 1949	BOS A	—	PHI A	Billy Hitchcock

Victor Rosario

Date	Traded To	Traded With	Traded By	In Exchange For
Aug. 3, 1990	ATL N	Jeff Parrett Jim Vatcher	PHI N	Dale Murphy Tommy Greene

(Greene and Vatcher were exhanged on August 9, and Atlanta received Rosario on September 4, 1990.)

Date	Traded To	Traded With	Traded By	In Exchange For
June 25, 1991	DET A	—	ATL N	Dan Petry

Don Rose

Date	Traded To	Traded With	Traded By	In Exchange For
Dec. 10, 1971	CAL A	Nolan Ryan Francisco Estrada Leroy Stanton	NY N	Jim Fregosi

Pete Rose

Date	Traded To	Traded With	Traded By	In Exchange For
Dec. 5, 1978	PHI N	—	CIN N	No compensation (free agent signing)
Jan. 20, 1984	MON N	—	PHI N	No compensation (free agent signing)
Aug. 16, 1984	CIN N	—	MON N	Tom Lawless

(Rose was named Cincinnati manager.)

Johnny Roseboro

Date	Traded To	Traded With	Traded By	In Exchange For
Nov. 28, 1967	MIN A	Ron Perranoski Bob Miller	LA N	Mudcat Grant Zoilo Versalles

Dave Rosello

Date	Traded To	Traded With	Traded By	In Exchange For
Dec. 5, 1977	CLE A	—	CHI N	Minor leaguers P Norm Churchill and OF Bruce Compton

Goody Rosen

Date	Traded To	Traded With	Traded By	In Exchange For
Apr. 27, 1946	NY N	—	BKN N	Cash

Steve Rosenberg

Date	Traded To	Traded With	Traded By	In Exchange For
Nov. 12, 1987	CHI A	—	NY A	*see Richard Dotson*

Steve Rosenberg *continued*

Date	Traded To	Traded With	Traded By	In Exchange For
Mar. 31, 1991	SD N	Adam Peterson	CHI A	Joey Cora Warren Newson Minor league IF Kevin Garner
Dec. 11, 1991	NY N	—	SD N	Jeff Gardner

Larry Rosenthal

Date	Traded To	Traded With	Traded By	In Exchange For
May 29, 1941	CLE A	—	CHI A	Cash
July 6, 1944	PHI A	—	NY A	Cash

Buck Ross

Date	Traded To	Traded With	Traded By	In Exchange For
Apr. 30, 1941	CHI A	—	PHI A	Cash

Don Ross

Date	Traded To	Traded With	Traded By	In Exchange For
Sept. 14, 1938	BKN N	—	DET A	Cash
Apr. 27, 1945	CLE A	Dutch Meyer	DET A	Roy Cullenbine

Gary Ross

Date	Traded To	Traded With	Traded By	In Exchange For
Apr. 25, 1969	SD N	Joe Niekro Francisco Libran	CHI N	Dick Selma
Sept. 17, 1975	CAL A	—	SD N	Bobby Valentine Rudi Meoli

Mark Ross

Date	Traded To	Traded With	Traded By	In Exchange For
Dec. 9, 1985	STL N	—	HOU N	Player to be named

(Ross was returned to Houston on March 31, 1986.)

Joe Rossi

Date	Traded To	Traded With	Traded By	In Exchange For
Oct. 14, 1952	PIT N	Cal Abrams Gail Henley	CIN N	Gus Bell

Claude Rossman

Date	Traded To	Traded With	Traded By	In Exchange For
Dec. 1906	DET A	—	CLE A	Cash
Aug. 20, 1909	STL A	—	DET A	Tom Jones

Rico Rossy

Date	Traded To	Traded With	Traded By	In Exchange For
Nov. 6, 1987	PIT N	Minor league IF Terry Crowley, Jr.	BAL A	Joe Orsulak
Dec. 10, 1991	KC A	—	ATL N	Minor league OF Bobby Moore

Braggo Roth

Date	Traded To	Traded With	Traded By	In Exchange For
Aug. 21, 1915	CLE A	Larry Chappell Ed Klepfer $31,500.	CHI A	Joe Jackson
Mar. 1, 1919	PHI A	—	CLE A	Larry Gardner Elmer Myers Charlie Jamieson
June 27, 1919	BOS A	Red Shannon	PHI A	Amos Strunk Jack Barry

(Barry refused to report, and retired.)

Date	Traded To	Traded With	Traded By	In Exchange For
Jan. 20, 1920	WAS A	Red Shannon	BOS A	Mike Menosky Eddie Foster Harry Harper
Jan. 20, 1921	NY A	—	WAS A	Duffy Lewis George Mogridge

Frank Roth

Date	Traded To	Traded With	Traded By	In Exchange For
Feb. 1905	CHI A	—	STL A	Branch Rickey

Jack Rothrock

Date	Traded To	Traded With	Traded By	In Exchange For
Apr. 30, 1932	CHI A	—	BOS A	Cash

Edd Roush

Date	Traded To	Traded With	Traded By	In Exchange For
Dec. 23, 1915	NY N	—	NWK F	$7,500.
July 20, 1916	CIN N	Christy Mathewson Bill McKechnie	NY N	Buck Herzog Red Killefer
Feb. 9, 1927	NY N	—	CIN N	George Kelly $100,000

Jack Rowan

Date	Traded To	Traded With	Traded By	In Exchange For
Feb. 1911	PHI N	*see Dode Paskert*	CIN N	—
Aug. 1911	CHI N	—	PHI N	Cliff Curtis

Wade Rowdon

Date	Traded To	Traded With	Traded By	In Exchange For
Aug. 23, 1982	CIN N	Leo Garcia	CHI A	Jim Kern
Feb. 17, 1987	CHI N	—	CIN N	Guy Hoffman

(Chicago received Rowdon on Feb. 23, 1987.)

Date	Traded To	Traded With	Traded By	In Exchange For
Mar. 29, 1988	BAL A	—	CHI N	Minor league SS Nick Ramirez Minor league P Tom Michno

Ken Rowe

Date	Traded To	Traded With	Traded By	In Exchange For
Sept. 10, 1964	BAL A	—	LA N	Cash

Schoolboy Rowe

Date	Traded To	Traded With	Traded By	In Exchange For
Apr. 30, 1942	BKN N	—	DET A	Cash
Mar. 24, 1943	PHI N	—	BKN N	Cash

Bama Rowell

Date	Traded To	Traded With	Traded By	In Exchange For
Mar. 6, 1948	BKN N	Ray Sanders $40,000.	BOS N	Eddie Stanky
Apr. 15, 1948	PHI N	—	BKN N	Waiver price

Rich Rowland

Date	Traded To	Traded With	Traded By	In Exchange For
Apr. 1, 1994	BOS A	—	DET A	John Flaherty

Luther Roy

Date	Traded To	Traded With	Traded By	In Exchange For
July 24, 1929	BKN N	—	PHI N	Lou Koupal

Stan Royer

Date	Traded To	Traded With	Traded By	In Exchange For
Aug. 29, 1990	STL N	Felix Jose Minor league P Daryl Green	OAK A	Willie McGee
July 15, 1994	BOS A	—	STL N	Waiver price

Jerry Royster

Date	Traded To	Traded With	Traded By	In Exchange For
Nov. 17, 1975	ATL N	Jimmy Wynn Tom Paciorek Lee Lacy	LA N	Dusty Baker Ed Goodson
Jan. 3, 1985	SD N	—	ATL N	No compenstion (free agent signing)
Jan. 21, 1987	CHI A	—	SD N	No compensation (free agent signing)
Aug. 26, 1987	NY A	Minor league IF Mike Soper	CHI A	Minor league P Ken Patterson player to be named

(Chicago received P Jeff Pries on Sept. 19, 1987.)

Dick Rozek

Date	Traded To	Traded With	Traded By	In Exchange For
Dec. 19, 1952	PHI A	minor league 2B Bob Wilson	CLE A	Bob Hooper

Dave Rozema

Date	Traded To	Traded With	Traded By	In Exchange For
Dec. 27, 1984	TEX A	—	DET A	No compensation (free agent signing)

Vic Roznovsky

Date	Traded To	Traded With	Traded By	In Exchange For
Mar. 30, 1966	BAL A	—	CHI N	Carl Warwick

Sonny Ruberto

Date	Traded To	Traded With	Traded By	In Exchange For
May 22, 1969	SD N	John Sipin	STL N	Bill Davis Jerry DaVanon

Jorge Rubio

Date	Traded To	Traded With	Traded By	In Exchange For
Nov. 29, 1967	CIN N	Bill Kelso	CAL A	Sammy Ellis

Art Ruble

Date	Traded To	Traded With	Traded By	In Exchange For
May 16, 1934	CIN N	Ted Kleinhans Wes Schulmerich	PHI N	Syl Johnson Johnny Moore

Dave Rucker

Date	Traded To	Traded With	Traded By	In Exchange For
June 22, 1983	STL N	—	DET A	Doug Bair

Dave Rucker *continued*

Date	Traded To	Traded With	Traded By	In Exchange For
Apr. 6, 1985	PHI N	—	STL N	Ivan DeJesus Bill Campbell

Joe Rudi

Date	Traded To	Traded With	Traded By	In Exchange For
Dec. 1, 1965	KC A	Phil Roof	CLE A	Jim Landis Jim Rittwage
Nov. 17, 1976	CAL A	—	OAK A	No compensation (free agent signing)
Jan. 23, 1981	BOS A	Frank Tanana Jim Dorsey	CAL A	Fred Lynn Steve Renko
Dec. 4, 1981	OAK A	—	BOS A	No compensation (free agent signing)

Don Rudolph

Date	Traded To	Traded With	Traded By	In Exchange For
May 1, 1959	CIN N	Lou Skizas	CHI A	Del Ennis
May 3, 1962	WAS A	Steve Hamilton	CLE A	Willie Tasby

Ken Rudolph

Date	Traded To	Traded With	Traded By	In Exchange For
Mar. 19, 1974	SF N	—	CHI N	Willie Prall
Oct. 14, 1974	STL N	Elias Sosa	SF N	Marc Hill
Mar. 31, 1977	SF N	—	STL N	Cash
July 27, 1977	BAL A	—	SF N	Cash

Muddy Ruel

Date	Traded To	Traded With	Traded By	In Exchange For
Aug. 21, 1917	NY A	—	STL A	Cash
Dec. 15, 1920	BOS A	Del Pratt Sammy Vick Hank Thormahlen	NY A	Waite Hoyt Harry Harper Wally Schang Mike McNally
Feb. 10, 1923	WAS A	Allan Russell	BOS A	Val Picinich Ed Goebel Howard Shanks
Dec. 15, 1930	BOS A	—	WAS A	Cash
Aug. 31, 1931	DET A	—	BOS A	Marty McManus
Dec. 1932	STL A	—	DET A	Waiver price

Dutch Ruether

Date	Traded To	Traded With	Traded By	In Exchange For
July 17, 1917	CIN N	—	CHI N	Waiver price
Dec. 15, 1920	BKN N	—	CIN N	Rube Marquard
Dec. 17, 1924	WAS A	—	BKN N	Cash
Aug. 27, 1926	NY A	—	WAS A	Garland Braxton Nick Cullop

(New York sent Braxton and Cullop to Washington on October 19, 1926.)

Rudy Rufer

Date	Traded To	Traded With	Traded By	In Exchange For
June 9, 1952	BKN N	Cash	CIN N	Cal Abrams

Bruce Ruffin

Date	Traded To	Traded With	Traded By	In Exchange For
Dec. 11, 1991	MIL A	—	PHI N	Dale Sveum

Johnny Ruffin

Date	Traded To	Traded With	Traded By	In Exchange For
July 31, 1993	CIN N	Jeff Pierce	CHI A	Tim Belcher

Red Ruffing

Date	Traded To	Traded With	Traded By	In Exchange For
May 6, 1930	NY A	—	BOS A	Cedric Durst $50,000.

Vern Ruhle

Date	Traded To	Traded With	Traded By	In Exchange For
Dec. 20, 1984	CLE A	—	HOU N	No compensation (free agent signing)

Chico Ruiz

Date	Traded To	Traded With	Traded By	In Exchange For
Nov. 25, 1969	CAL A	Alex Johnson	CIN N	Pedro Borbon Jim McGlothlin Vern Geishert

Pete Runnels

Date	Traded To	Traded With	Traded By	In Exchange For
Jan. 23, 1958	BOS A	—	WAS A	Albie Pearson Norm Zauchin
Nov. 26, 1962	HOU N	—	BOS A	Roman Mejias

Bob Rush

Date	Traded To	Traded With	Traded By	In Exchange For
Dec. 5, 1957	MIL N	Eddie Haas Don Kaiser	CHI N	Taylor Phillips Sammy Taylor
June 11, 1960	CHI A	—	MIL N	Cash

Amos Rusie

Date	Traded To	Traded With	Traded By	In Exchange For
Dec. 15, 1900	CIN N	—	NY N	Christy Mathewson

Scott Ruskin

Date	Traded To	Traded With	Traded By	In Exchange For
Aug. 8, 1990	MON N	Moises Alou Willie Greene	PIT N	Zane Smith

(Montreal received Alou on August 16, 1990.)

Date	Traded To	Traded With	Traded By	In Exchange For
Dec. 11, 1991	CIN N	Dave Martinez Willie Greene	MON N	John Wetteland Bill Risley

Allan Russell

Date	Traded To	Traded With	Traded By	In Exchange For
July 29, 1919	BOS A	Bob McGraw $40,000.	NY A	Carl Mays
Feb. 10, 1923	WAS A	Muddy Ruel	BOS A	Val Picinich Ed Goebel Howard Shanks

Jack Russell

Date	Traded To	Traded With	Traded By	In Exchange For
June 10, 1932	CLE A	—	BOS A	Pete Appleton
Dec. 15, 1932	WAS A	Bruce Connatser	CLE A	Harley Boss
June 13, 1936	BOS A	—	WAS A	Joe Cascarella

Jeff Russell

Date	Traded To	Traded With	Traded By	In Exchange For
July 19, 1985	TEX A	Duane Walker	CIN N	Buddy Bell
Aug. 31, 1992	OAK A	Ruben Sierra Bobby Witt Cash	TEX A	Jose Canseco
Mar. 1, 1993	BOS A	—	OAK A	No compensation (free agent signing)
July 1, 1994	CLE A	—	BOS A	Chris Nabholz Steve Farr
Apr. 11, 1995	TEX A	—	CLE A	No compensation (free agent signing)

Jim Russell

Date	Traded To	Traded With	Traded By	In Exchange For
Nov. 18, 1947	BOS N	Bill Salkeld Al Lyons	PIT N	Johnny Hopp Danny Murtaugh
Dec. 24, 1949	BKN N	Ed Sauer Cash	BOS N	Luis Olmo

John Russell

Date	Traded To	Traded With	Traded By	In Exchange For
Mar. 25, 1989	ATL N	—	PHI N	Cash

Babe Ruth

Date	Traded To	Traded With	Traded By	In Exchange For
Jan. 3, 1920	NY A	—	BOS A	$125,000 and a $300,000 loan to Boston owner Harry Frazee

Dick Ruthven

Date	Traded To	Traded With	Traded By	In Exchange For
Dec. 10, 1975	CHI A	Alan Bannister Roy Thomas	PHI N	Jim Kaat Mike Buskey
Dec. 12, 1975	ATL N	Ken Henderson Danny Osborn	CHI A	Ralph Garr Larvell Blanks
June 15, 1978	PHI N	—	ATL N	Gene Garber
May 22, 1983	CHI N	Bill Johnson	PHI N	Guillermo Hernandez

Blondy Ryan

Date	Traded To	Traded With	Traded By	In Exchange For
Nov. 1, 1934	PHI N	Pretzels Pezzullo Johnny Vergez George Watkins Cash	NY N	Dick Bartell
Aug. 6, 1935	NY A	—	PHI N	Cash

Connie Ryan

Date	Traded To	Traded With	Traded By	In Exchange For
Apr. 27, 1943	BOS N	Hugh Poland	NY N	Ernie Lombardi
May 10, 1950	CIN N	—	BOS N	Walker Cooper

Connie Ryan *continued*

Date	Traded To		Traded With	Traded By		In Exchange For
Dec. 10, 1951	PHI	N	Smoky Burgess Howie Fox	CIN	N	Andy Seminick Eddie Pellagrini Dick Sisler Niles Jordan
Aug. 25, 1953	CHI	A	—	PHI	N	Waiver price
Dec. 10, 1953	CIN	N	Saul Rogovin Rocky Krsnich	CHI	A	Willard Marshall

Jack Ryan

Date	Traded To		Traded With	Traded By		In Exchange For
Feb. 18, 1909	BOS	A	Charlie Chech $12,500.	CLE	A	Cy Young

Mike Ryan

Date	Traded To		Traded With	Traded By		In Exchange For
Dec. 15, 1967	PHI	N	Cash	BOS	A	Dick Ellsworth Gene Oliver
Jan. 31, 1974	PIT	N	—	PHI	N	Jackie Hernandez

Nolan Ryan

Date	Traded To		Traded With	Traded By		In Exchange For
Dec. 10, 1971	CAL	A	Francisco Estrada Don Rose Leroy Stanton	NY	N	Jim Fregosi
Nov. 19, 1979	HOU	N	—	CAL	A	No compensation (free agent signing)
Dec. 7, 1988	TEX	A	—	HOU	N	No compensation (free agent signing)

Rosy Ryan

Date	Traded To		Traded With	Traded By		In Exchange For
Apr. 17, 1925	BOS	N	—	NY	N	Tim McNamara

Gary Ryerson

Date	Traded To		Traded With	Traded By		In Exchange For
Oct. 22, 1973	CAL	A	—	MIL	A	*see Clyde Wright*

Bret Saberhagen

Date	Traded To		Traded With	Traded By		In Exchange For
Dec. 11, 1991	NY	N	Bill Pecota	KC	A	Kevin McReynolds Gregg Jefferies Keith Miller
July 31, 1995	CLR	N	Player to be named	NY	N	Juan Acevedo Minor league P Arnold Gooch

(Colorado received P David Swanson on August 4, 1995.)

Chris Sabo

Date	Traded To		Traded With	Traded By		In Exchange For
Jan. 14, 1994	BAL	A	—	CIN	N	No compensation (free agent signing)
Apr. 10, 1995	CHI	A	—	BAL	A	No compensation (free agent signing)

Ray Sadecki

Date	Traded To		Traded With	Traded By		In Exchange For
May 8, 1966	SF	N	—	STL	N	Orlando Cepeda
Dec. 12, 1969	NY	N	Dave Marshall	SF	N	Bob Heise Jim Gosger
Oct. 13, 1974	STL	N	Tommy Moore	NY	N	Joe Torre
May 28, 1975	ATL	N	Elias Sosa	STL	N	Ron Reed Wayne Nordhagen
June 30, 1975	KC	A	Cash	ATL	N	Bruce Dal Canton Norm Angelini Al Autry

(Atlanta received Angelini and Autry on September 4,1975.)

Bob Sadowski

Date	Traded To		Traded With	Traded By		In Exchange For
June 15, 1963	MIL	N	Gene Oliver	STL	N	Lew Burdette
Dec. 15, 1965	BOS	A	Dan Osinski	MIL	N	Lee Thomas Arnold Earley Jay Ritchie

Bob Sadowski

Date	Traded To		Traded With	Traded By		In Exchange For
Dec. 15, 1961	CHI	A	Taylor Phillips minor league IF Lou Vassie	PHI	N	Frank Barnes Andy Carey Cal McLish

(Carey refused to report, and the Phillies received McLish in exchange for Vassie to complete the trade on March 24, 1962.)

Jim Sadowski

Date	Traded To		Traded With	Traded By		In Exchange For
Nov. 6, 1976	CIN	N	—	PIT	N	Tom Carroll

Tom Saffell

Date	Traded To		Traded With	Traded By		In Exchange For
Sept. 14, 1955	KC	A	—	PIT	N	Waiver price
Apr. 16, 1956	BKN	N	Lee Wheat Cash	KC	A	Tim Thompson

Johnny Sain

Date	Traded To		Traded With	Traded By		In Exchange For
Aug. 30, 1951	NY	A	—	BOS	N	Lew Burdette $50,000.
May 11, 1955	KC	A	Enos Slaughter	NY	A	Sonny Dixon Cash

Lenn Sakata

Date	Traded To		Traded With	Traded By		In Exchange For
Dec. 6, 1979	BAL	A	—	MIL	A	John Flinn
Dec. 16, 1986	NY	A	—	OAK	A	No compensation (free agent signing)

Mark Salas

Date	Traded To		Traded With	Traded By		In Exchange For
June 7, 1987	NY	A	—	MIN	A	Joe Niekro Cash
Nov. 12, 1987	CHI	A	Dan Pasqua Steve Rosenberg	NY	A	Richard Dotson Scott Nielsen

Angel Salazar

Date	Traded To		Traded With	Traded By		In Exchange For
Jan. 24, 1985	STL	N	—	MON	N	

(Claimed in compensation draft after St. Louis lost free agent P Bruce Sutter to Atlanta.)

Date	Traded To		Traded With	Traded By		In Exchange For
Apr. 2, 1985	NY	N	Minor league P John Young	STL	N	Jose Oquendo Minor league P Mark J. Davis
Apr. 1, 1986	KC	A	—	NY	N	Tony Ferreira
Nov. 6, 1987	CIN	N	Danny Jackson	KC	A	Ted Power Kurt Stillwell

Luis Salazar

Date	Traded To		Traded With	Traded By		In Exchange For
Aug. 5, 1980	SD	N	Rick Lancellotti	PIT	N	Kurt Bevacqua Mark Lee
Dec. 6, 1984	CHI	A	—	SD	N	*see LaMarr Hoyt*
Mar. 23, 1989	SD	N	—	DET	A	Mike Brumley
Aug. 30, 1989	CHI	N	Marvell Wynne	SD	N	Calvin Schiraldi Darrin Jackson Phil Stephenson

(San Diego received Stephenson on Sept. 5, 1989.)

Bill Salkeld

Date	Traded To		Traded With	Traded By		In Exchange For
Nov. 18, 1947	BOS	N	Jim Russell Al Lyons	PIT	N	Johnny Hopp Danny Murtaugh
Sept. 26, 1949	CHI	A	—	BOS	N	Cash

Roger Salkeld

Date	Traded To		Traded With	Traded By		In Exchange For
May 15, 1995	CIN	N	—	SEA	A	Tim Belcher

Slim Sallee

Date	Traded To		Traded With	Traded By		In Exchange For
July 23, 1916	NY	N	—	STL	N	$10,000.
Mar. 8, 1919	CIN	N	—	NY	N	Waiver price
Sept. 5, 1920	NY	N	—	CIN	N	Waiver price

Chico Salmon

Date	Traded To		Traded With	Traded By		In Exchange For
Apr. 1, 1964	CLE	A	—	MIL	N	Mike de la Hoz
Mar. 31, 1969	BAL	A	—	SEA	A	Gene Brabender Gordon Lund

Jack Salveson

Date	Traded To		Traded With	Traded By		In Exchange For
Dec. 11, 1934	PIT	N	—	NY	N	Waiver price
June 16, 1935	CHI	A	—	PIT	N	Cash

Jack Salveson *continued*

Date	Traded To	Traded With	Traded By	In Exchange For
Dec. 10, 1936	CLE A	—	CHI A	Thornton Lee
	(Part of three-team trade involving Chicago, Cleveland, and Washington.)			
Dec. 10, 1936	WAS A	—	CLE A	Earl Whitehill
	(Part of three-team trade involving Chicago, Cleveland, and Washington.)			

Manny Salvo

Date	Traded To	Traded With	Traded By	In Exchange For
June 15, 1940	BOS N	Al Glossop	NY N	Tony Cuccinello
May 12, 1943	PHI N	—	BOS N	Cash

Ron Samford

Date	Traded To	Traded With	Traded By	In Exchange For
Apr. 8, 1955	DET A	—	NY N	Waiver price
Dec. 6, 1958	WAS A	—	DET A	*see Eddie Yost*
Apr. 3, 1960	BAL A	Clint Courtney	WAS A	Billy Gardner

Bill Sampen

Date	Traded To	Traded With	Traded By	In Exchange For
Aug. 29, 1992	KC A	Chris Haney	MON N	Sean Berry Archie Corbin

Billy Sample

Date	Traded To	Traded With	Traded By	In Exchange For
Feb. 27, 1985	NY A	player to be named	TEX A	Toby Harrah
	(New York received P Eric Dersin on July 14, 1985.)			
Dec. 6, 1985	ATL N	—	NY A	Minor league IF Miguel Sosa
Feb. 20, 1987	MIN A	—	ATL N	No compensation (free agent signing)

Amado Samuel

Date	Traded To	Traded With	Traded By	In Exchange For
Oct. 15, 1963	NY N	—	MIL N	Cash

Juan Samuel

Date	Traded To	Traded With	Traded By	In Exchange For
June 18, 1989	NY N	—	PHI N	Len Dykstra Roger McDowell Tom Edens
	(Philadelphia received Edens on July 26, 1989.)			
Dec. 20, 1989	LA N	—	NY N	Alejandro Pena Mike Marshall
Jan. 14, 1993	CIN N	—	KC A	No compensation (free agent signing)
Feb. 14, 1994	DET A	—	CIN N	No compensation (free agent signing)
Sept. 8, 1995	KC A	—	DET A	Phil Hiatt
	(Detroit received Hiatt on September 14, 1995.)			

Roger Samuels

Date	Traded To	Traded With	Traded By	In Exchange For
May 10, 1989	PIT N	—	SF N	Ken Oberkfell

Alejandro Sanchez

Date	Traded To	Traded With	Traded By	In Exchange For
Mar. 24, 1984	SF N	—	PHI N	Dave Bergman
Apr. 5, 1985	DET A	—	SF N	Roger Mason
Jan. 18, 1986	MIN A	—	DET A	*see Dave Engle*

Alex Sanchez

Date	Traded To	Traded With	Traded By	In Exchange For
Sept. 16, 1990	CLE A	—	TOR A	*see Bud Black*
Nov. 6, 1990	TOR A	—	CLE A	Willie Blair
Oct. 17, 1991	KC A	—	TOR A	Waiver price

Luis Sanchez

Date	Traded To	Traded With	Traded By	In Exchange For
Oct. 24, 1975	CIN N	minor league P Carlos Alfonso	HOU N	Joaquin Andujar
Dec. 27, 1985	CAL A	Minor league P Tim Arnold	MON N	Gary Lucas

Orlando Sanchez

Date	Traded To	Traded With	Traded By	In Exchange For
May 17, 1984	BAL A	—	KC A	Cash

Heinie Sand

Date	Traded To	Traded With	Traded By	In Exchange For
Dec. 13, 1928	STL N	$10,000.	PHI N	Tommy Thevenow

Ryne Sandberg

Date	Traded To	Traded With	Traded By	In Exchange For
Jan. 27, 1982	CHI N	Larry Bowa	PHI N	Ivan DeJesus

Deion Sanders

Date	Traded To	Traded With	Traded By	In Exchange For
May 29, 1994	CIN N	—	ATL N	Roberto Kelly Minor league P Roger Etheridge
July 21, 1995	SF N	John Roper Scott Service David McCarty Minor league P Ricky Pickett	CIN N	Mark Portugal Dave Burba Darren Lewis

Ken Sanders

Date	Traded To	Traded With	Traded By	In Exchange For
June 13, 1966	KC A	Jim Gosger Guido Grilli	BOS A	John Wyatt Rollie Sheldon Jose Tartabull
Jan. 15, 1970	MIL A	—	OAK A	*see Don Mincher*
Oct. 31, 1972	PHI N	—	MIL A	*see Don Money*
Nov. 30, 1972	MIN A	Joe Lis Ken Reynolds	PHI N	Cesar Tovar
Aug. 3, 1973	CLE A	—	MIN A	Cash
Mar. 22, 1975	NY N	—	CAL A	Ike Hampton
Sept. 17, 1976	KC A	—	NY N	Cash

Ray Sanders

Date	Traded To	Traded With	Traded By	In Exchange For
Apr. 15, 1946	BOS N	—	STL N	$25,000.
Mar. 6, 1948	BKN N	Bama Rowell $40,000.	BOS N	Eddie Stanky
Apr. 19, 1948	BOS N	—	BKN N	$60,000.

Reggie Sanders

Date	Traded To	Traded With	Traded By	In Exchange For
May 9, 1972	DET A	—	OAK A	Mike Kilkenny
Mar. 29, 1975	ATL N	—	DET A	Jack Pierce

Scott Sanderson

Date	Traded To	Traded With	Traded By	In Exchange For
Dec. 7, 1983	SD N	—	MON N	Gary Lucas
Dec. 7, 1983	CHI N	—	SD N	Carmelo Martinez Fritz Connally Craig Lefferts
	(Part of three-team trade involving Chicago Cubs, San Diego, and Montreal.)			
Dec. 13, 1989	OAK A	—	CHI N	No compensation (free agent signing)
Dec. 31, 1990	NY N	—	OAK A	Cash
Feb. 11, 1993	CAL A	—	NY A	No compensation (free agent signing)
Aug. 3, 1993	SF N	—	CAL A	Waiver price
Mar. 1, 1994	CHI A	—	SF N	No compensation (free agent signing)

Mike Sandlock

Date	Traded To	Traded With	Traded By	In Exchange For
Dec. 19, 1953	PHI N	—	PIT N	Cash

Charlie Sands

Date	Traded To	Traded With	Traded By	In Exchange For
Apr. 2, 1973	DET A	—	PIT N	Chris Zachary

Tom Sandt

Date	Traded To	Traded With	Traded By	In Exchange For
Mar. 25, 1977	STL N	—	OAK A	Cash

Fred Sanford

Date	Traded To	Traded With	Traded By	In Exchange For
Dec. 13, 1948	NY A	Roy Partee	STL A	Sherm Lollar Red Embree Dick Starr $100,000.
June 15, 1951	WAS A	Tom Ferrick Bob Porterfield	NY A	Bob Kuzava
July 30, 1951	STL A	—	WAS A	Dick Starr

Jack Sanford

Date	Traded To	Traded With	Traded By	In Exchange For
Dec. 3, 1958	SF N	—	PHI N	Valmy Thomas Ruben Gomez
Aug. 18, 1965	CAL A	—	SF N	Cash
June 15, 1967	KC A	Jackie Warner	CAL A	Roger Repoz

Manny Sanguillen

Date	Traded To	Traded With	Traded By	In Exchange For
Nov. 5, 1976	OAK A	$100,000.	PIT N	Chuck Tanner
	(Tanner was named Pittsburgh manager.)			

Manny Sanguillen *continued*

Date	Traded To		Traded With	Traded By		In Exchange For
Apr. 4, 1978	PIT	N	—	OAK	A	Miguel Dilone Elias Sosa Mike Edwards
Dec. 9, 1980	CLE	A	Bert Blyleven	PIT	N	Gary Alexander Victor Cruz Rafael Vasquez Bob Owchinko

Andres Santana

Date	Traded To		Traded With	Traded By		In Exchange For
Mar. 31, 1993	FLA	N	—	SF	N	Minor league P Brian Griffiths

Rafael Santana

Date	Traded To		Traded With	Traded By		In Exchange For
Feb. 16, 1981	STL	N	—	NY	A	Cash
Dec. 11, 1987	NY	A	Minor league P Victor Garcia	NY	N	Phil Lombardi Steve Frey Darren Reed

Benito Santiago

Date	Traded To		Traded With	Traded By		In Exchange For
Dec. 16, 1992	FLA	N	—	SD	N	No compensation (free agent signing)
Apr. 17, 1995	CIN	N	—	FLA	N	No compensation (free agent signing)

Jose Santiago

Date	Traded To		Traded With	Traded By		In Exchange For
May 16, 1956	KC	A	—	CLE	A	Cash

Ron Santo

Date	Traded To		Traded With	Traded By		In Exchange For
Dec. 11, 1973	CHI	A	—	CHI	N	Steve Stone Ken Frailing Steve Swisher Jim Kremmel

Al Santorini

Date	Traded To		Traded With	Traded By		In Exchange For
June 11, 1971	STL	N	—	SD	N	Leron Lee Fred Norman
May 8, 1973	KC	A	—	STL	N	Tom Murphy

Manny Sarmiento

Date	Traded To		Traded With	Traded By		In Exchange For
Apr. 8, 1981	BOS	A	—	SEA	A	Dick Drago
Oct. 23, 1981	PIT	N	—	BOS	A	Cash

Bill Sarni

Date	Traded To		Traded With	Traded By		In Exchange For
June 14, 1956	NY	N	*see Red Schoendienst*	STL	N	—

Mackey Sasser

Date	Traded To		Traded With	Traded By		In Exchange For
July 31, 1987	PIT	N	Cash	SF	N	Don Robinson
Mar. 26, 1988	NY	N	Tim Drummond	PIT	N	Randy Milligan Minor league P Scott Henion

Tom Satriano

Date	Traded To		Traded With	Traded By		In Exchange For
June 15, 1969	BOS	A	—	CAL	A	Joe Azcue

Kevin Saucier

Date	Traded To		Traded With	Traded By		In Exchange For
Sept. 13, 1980	TEX	A	—	PHI	N	Sparky Lyle
Dec. 10, 1980	DET	A	—	TEX	A	Mark Wagner

Ed Sauer

Date	Traded To		Traded With	Traded By		In Exchange For
June 15, 1949	PIT	N	—	STL	N	Cash
June 15, 1949	BOS	N	—	PIT	N	Phil Masi
Dec. 24, 1949	BKN	N	Jim Russell Cash	BOS	N	Luis Olmo

Hank Sauer

Date	Traded To		Traded With	Traded By		In Exchange For
June 15, 1949	CHI	N	Frankie Baumholtz	CIN	N	Harry Walker Peanuts Lowrey
Mar. 30, 1956	STL	N	—	CHI	N	Pete Whisenant

Bob Savage

Date	Traded To		Traded With	Traded By		In Exchange For
Dec. 16, 1948	STL	A	—	PHI	A	Waiver price

Jack Savage

Date	Traded To		Traded With	Traded By		In Exchange For
Dec. 11, 1987	NY	N	—	LA	N	*see Jesse Orosco*
July 31, 1989	MIN	A	—	NY	N	*see Frank Viola*

Ted Savage

Date	Traded To		Traded With	Traded By		In Exchange For
Nov. 28, 1962	PIT	N	Pancho Herrera	PHI	N	Don Hoak
May 14, 1967	CHI	N	—	STL	N	Cash
Apr. 23, 1968	LA	N	Jim Ellis	CHI	N	Jim Hickman Phil Regan
Mar. 30, 1969	CIN	N	—	LA	N	Jimmie Schaffer
Apr. 5, 1970	MIL	A	—	CIN	N	Cash
May 11, 1971	KC	A	—	MIL	A	Tom Matchick

Bob Saverine

Date	Traded To		Traded With	Traded By		In Exchange For
Apr. 24, 1965	HOU	N	Cash	BAL	A	Don Larsen

Carl Sawatski

Date	Traded To		Traded With	Traded By		In Exchange For
Nov. 30, 1953	CHI	A	—	CHI	N	Waiver price
June 13, 1958	PHI	N	—	MIL	N	Joe Lonnett
Dec. 4, 1959	STL	N	—	PHI	N	Bobby Gene Smith Bill Smith

Rick Sawyer

Date	Traded To		Traded With	Traded By		In Exchange For
Mar. 19, 1974	DET	A	Walt Williams	CLE	A	Jim Perry
(Part of three-team trade involving Detroit, Cleveland, and New York Yankees.)						
Mar. 19, 1974	NY	A	Ed Farmer Walt Williams	DET	A	Gerry Moses
(Part of three-team trade involving Detroit, New York Yankees, and Cleveland.)						
July 10, 1976	SD	N	—	NY	A	Gene Locklear
Sept. 29, 1977	MON	N	—	SD	N	Cash

Dave Sax

Date	Traded To		Traded With	Traded By		In Exchange For
Apr. 6, 1988	PIT	N	—	TEX	A	Minor league IF Bill Merrifield

Steve Sax

Date	Traded To		Traded With	Traded By		In Exchange For
Nov. 23, 1988	NY	A	—	LA	N	No compensation (free agent signing)
Jan. 10, 1992	CHI	A	—	NY	A	Melido Perez Bob Wickman Domingo Jean

Bill Sayles

Date	Traded To		Traded With	Traded By		In Exchange For
July 31, 1943	BKN	N	Bill Lohrman Joe Orengo	NY	N	Dolf Camilli Johnny Allen
(Camilli refused to report to New York and retired.)						

Bob Scanlan

Date	Traded To		Traded With	Traded By		In Exchange For
Apr. 7, 1991	CHI	N	Chuck McElroy	PHI	N	Mitch Williams
Dec. 19, 1993	MIL	A	Minor league OF Mike Carter	CHI	N	Rafael Novoa

Doc Scanlan

Date	Traded To		Traded With	Traded By		In Exchange For
Aug. 1, 1904	BKN	N	—	PIT	N	Cash

Pat Scanlon

Date	Traded To		Traded With	Traded By		In Exchange For
Nov. 6, 1976	STL	N	Steve Dunning Tony Scott	MON	N	Bill Greif Angel Torres Sam Mejias
May 17, 1977	SD	N	John D'Acquisto	STL	N	Butch Metzger

Randy Scarbery

Date	Traded To		Traded With	Traded By		In Exchange For
Aug. 12, 1977	STL	N	—	OAK	A	Steve Dunning
June 12, 1980	CAL	A	—	CHI	A	Todd Cruz

Ray Scarborough

Date	Traded To		Traded With	Traded By		In Exchange For
May 31, 1950	CHI	A	Al Kozar Eddie Robinson	WAS	A	Bob Kuzava Cass Michaels John Ostrowski
Dec. 10, 1950	BOS	A	Bill Wight	CHI	A	Joe Dobson Dick Littlefield Al Zarilla
Aug. 22, 1952	NY	A	—	BOS	A	Cash

Mac Scarce

Date	Traded To	Traded With	Traded By	In Exchange For
Dec. 3, 1974	NY N	Del Unser John Stearns	PHI N	Tug McGraw Don Hahn Dave Schneck
Apr. 15, 1975	CIN N	—	NY N	Tom Hall
Dec. 13, 1978	TEX A	—	MIN A	Mike Bacsik

Les Scarsella

Date	Traded To	Traded With	Traded By	In Exchange For
Dec. 6, 1939	BOS N	Cash	CIN N	Jim Turner

Steve Scarsone

Date	Traded To	Traded With	Traded By	In Exchange For
Aug. 11, 1992	BAL A	—	PHI N	Juan Bell
Mar. 20, 1993	SF N	—	BAL A	Mark Leonard

Paul Schaal

Date	Traded To	Traded With	Traded By	In Exchange For
Apr. 30, 1974	CAL A	—	KC A	Richie Scheinblum

Sid Schacht

Date	Traded To	Traded With	Traded By	In Exchange For
June 15, 1950	NY A	—	STL A	*see Snuffy Stirnweiss*
May 13, 1951	BOS N	—	STL A	Waiver price

Germany Schaefer

Date	Traded To	Traded With	Traded By	In Exchange For
Aug. 13, 1909	WAS A	Red Killefer	DET A	Jim Delahanty
Feb. 10, 1916	NY A	—	NWK F	Cash

Mark Schaeffer

Date	Traded To	Traded With	Traded By	In Exchange For
Dec. 3, 1971	SD N	Derrel Thomas Bill Greif	HOU N	Dave Roberts

Jimmie Schaffer

Date	Traded To	Traded With	Traded By	In Exchange For
Oct. 17, 1962	CHI N	*see Larry Jackson*	STL N	—
Dec. 1, 1964	CHI A	—	CHI N	Frank Baumann
July 8, 1965	NY N	—	CHI A	Frank Lary
Feb. 22, 1966	PHI N	Wayne Graham Bobby Klaus	NY N	Dick Stuart
Mar. 30, 1969	LA N	—	CIN N	Ted Savage

Joe Schaffernoth

Date	Traded To	Traded With	Traded By	In Exchange For
July 7, 1961	CLE A	—	CHI N	Cash
Oct. 14, 1961	WAS A	—	CLE A	Cash

Art Schallock

Date	Traded To	Traded With	Traded By	In Exchange For
May 11, 1955	BAL A	—	NY A	Waiver price

Bobby Schang

Date	Traded To	Traded With	Traded By	In Exchange For
June 1915	NY N	—	PIT N	Cash

Wally Schang

Date	Traded To	Traded With	Traded By	In Exchange For
Dec. 14, 1917	BOS A	Amos Strunk Joe Bush	PHI A	Vean Gregg Merlin Kopp Pinch Thomas $60,000.
Dec. 15, 1920	NY A	Waite Hoyt Harry Harper Mike McNally	BOS A	Muddy Ruel Del Pratt Sammy Vick Hank Thormahlen
Mar. 1926	STL A	—	NY A	George Mogridge Cash
Dec. 11, 1929	PHI A	—	STL A	Sammy Hale

George Scharein

Date	Traded To	Traded With	Traded By	In Exchange For
Dec. 8, 1936	PHI N	Cash	NY N	Lou Chiozza

Jeff Schattinger

Date	Traded To	Traded With	Traded By	In Exchange For
Mar. 24, 1982	CHI A	—	KC A	Greg Pryor

Dan Schatzeder

Date	Traded To	Traded With	Traded By	In Exchange For
Dec. 7, 1979	DET A	—	MON N	Ron LeFlore
Dec. 9, 1981	SF N	Mike Chris	DET A	Larry Herndon
June 15, 1982	MON N	—	SF N	Cash

Dan Schatzeder *continued*

Date	Traded To	Traded With	Traded By	In Exchange For
July 24, 1986	PHI N	Skeeter Barnes	MON N	Tom Foley Lary Sorensen
June 24, 1987	MIN A	Cash	PHI N	Minor league P Danny Clay Minor league 3B Tom Schwarz
Sept. 10, 1990	NY N	—	HOU N	Minor league P Steve LaRose Minor league IF Nicky Davis
Dec. 4, 1990	KC A	—	NY N	No compensation (free agent signing)

Rube Schauer

Date	Traded To	Traded With	Traded By	In Exchange For
Jan. 1917	PHI A	—	NY N	Waiver price

Bob Scheffing

Date	Traded To	Traded With	Traded By	In Exchange For
June 7, 1950	CIN N	—	CHI N	Ron Northey
Aug. 1, 1951	STL N	—	CIN N	Waiver price

Carl Scheib

Date	Traded To	Traded With	Traded By	In Exchange For
May 7, 1954	STL N	—	PHI A	Cash

(Scheib was returned to Philadelphia on June 1.)

Rich Scheid

Date	Traded To	Traded With	Traded By	In Exchange For
July 12, 1987	CHI N	—	NY A	*see Steve Trout*
July 4, 1992	HOU N	—	CHI A	Eric Yelding

Richie Scheinblum

Date	Traded To	Traded With	Traded By	In Exchange For
Oct. 23, 1970	WAS A	—	CLE A	Cash
Oct. 21, 1971	KC A	—	WAS A	Cash
Nov. 30, 1972	CIN N	Roger Nelson	KC A	Hal McRae Wayne Simpson
June 15, 1973	CAL A	—	CIN N	Terry Wilshusen minor league P Thor Skogan
Apr. 30, 1974	KC A	—	CAL A	Paul Schaal
Aug. 5, 1974	STL N	—	KC A	Cash

Hank Schenz

Date	Traded To	Traded With	Traded By	In Exchange For
May 16, 1949	BKN N	—	CHI N	Bob Ramazzotti
Nov. 4, 1949	PIT N	—	BKN N	Cash
July 10, 1951	NY N	—	PIT N	Waiver price

Fred Scherman

Date	Traded To	Traded With	Traded By	In Exchange For
Dec. 3, 1973	HOU N	Cash	DET A	Jim Ray Gary Sutherland
June 8, 1975	MON N	—	HOU N	Cash

Bill Scherrer

Date	Traded To	Traded With	Traded By	In Exchange For
Aug. 27, 1984	DET A	—	CIN N	Carl Willis Cash

Chuck Schilling

Date	Traded To	Traded With	Traded By	In Exchange For
Apr. 6, 1966	MIN A	Russ Nixon	BOS A	Dick Stigman minor league 1B Jose Calero

Curt Schilling

Date	Traded To	Traded With	Traded By	In Exchange For
July 29, 1988	BAL A	—	BOS A	*see Mike Boddicker*
Jan. 10, 1991	HOU N	Pete Harnisch Steve Finley	BAL A	Glenn Davis
Apr. 2, 1992	PHI N	—	HOU N	Jason Grimsley

Calvin Schiraldi

Date	Traded To	Traded With	Traded By	In Exchange For
Nov. 13, 1985	BOS A	John Christensen Wes Gardner LaSchelle Tarver	NY N	Bob Ojeda John Mitchell Tom McCarthy Minor league P Chris Bayer
Dec. 8, 1987	CHI N	Al Nipper	BOS A	Lee Smith
Aug. 30, 1989	SD N	Darrin Jackson Phil Stephenson	CHI N	Marvell Wynne Luis Salazar

(San Diego received Stephenson on Sept. 5, 1989.)

Calvin Schiraldi *continued*

Date	Traded To		Traded With	Traded By		In Exchange For
June 20, 1991	TEX	A	—	HOU	N	Cash

Admiral Schlei

Date	Traded To		Traded With	Traded By		In Exchange For
Dec. 12, 1908	STL	N	—	CIN	N	Ed Karger Art Fromme
Dec. 12, 1908	NY	N	Bugs Raymond Red Murray	STL	N	Roger Bresnahan

Rudy Schlesinger

Date	Traded To		Traded With	Traded By		In Exchange For
Nov. 30, 1967	CHI	N	Cash	BOS	A	Ray Culp
May 5, 1969	PHI	N	—	BOS	A	Don Lock

Dutch Schliebner

Date	Traded To		Traded With	Traded By		In Exchange For
May 1923	STL	A	—	BKN	N	Cash

Jay Schlueter

Date	Traded To		Traded With	Traded By		In Exchange For
Dec. 3, 1974	BAL	A	Lee May	HOU	N	Enos Cabell Rob Andrews

Norm Schlueter

Date	Traded To		Traded With	Traded By		In Exchange For
Dec. 29, 1939	STL	A	—	CHI	A	Cash

Ray Schmandt

Date	Traded To		Traded With	Traded By		In Exchange For
Feb. 15, 1923	STL	N	Hy Myers	BKN	N	Jack Fournier

George Schmees

Date	Traded To		Traded With	Traded By		In Exchange For
June 30, 1952	BOS	A	—	STL	A	Waiver price

Bob Schmidt

Date	Traded To		Traded With	Traded By		In Exchange For
Apr. 27, 1961	CIN	N	Don Blasingame Sherman Jones	SF	N	Ed Bailey
Dec. 15, 1961	WAS	A	Dave Stenhouse	CIN	N	Johnny Klippstein Marty Keough

Dave Schmidt

Date	Traded To		Traded With	Traded By		In Exchange For
Nov. 25, 1985	CHI	A	Wayne Tolleson	TEX	A	Ed Correa Scott Fletcher Jose Mota
			(Texas received Mota on December 12, 1985)			
Jan. 15, 1987	BAL	A	—	CHI	A	No compensation (free agent signing)
Dec. 13, 1989	MON	N	—	BAL	A	No compensation (free agent signing)

Freddy Schmidt

Date	Traded To		Traded With	Traded By		In Exchange For
May 3, 1947	PHI	N	Harry Walker	STL	N	Ron Northey

Willard Schmidt

Date	Traded To		Traded With	Traded By		In Exchange For
Dec. 5, 1957	CIN	N	Marty Kutyna Ted Wieand	STL	N	Curt Flood Joe Taylor

Johnny Schmitz

Date	Traded To		Traded With	Traded By		In Exchange For
June 15, 1951	BKN	N	Rube Walker Andy Pafko Wayne Terwilliger	CHI	N	Bruce Edwards Joe Hatten Eddie Miksis Gene Hermanski
Aug. 1, 1952	NY	A	—	BKN	N	Waiver price
Aug. 28, 1952	CIN	N	Jim Greengrass Ernie Nevel Bob Marquis $35,000.	NY	A	Ewell Blackwell
Feb. 17, 1953	NY	A	—	CIN	N	Cash
May 13, 1953	WAS	A	—	NY	A	Waiver price
Nov. 8, 1955	BOS	A	Bob Porterfield Mickey Vernon Tommy Umphlett	WAS	A	Karl Olson Dick Brodowski Tex Clevenger Neil Chrisley minor league P Al Curtis
May 14, 1956	BAL	A	—	BOS	A	Cash

Dave Schneck

Date	Traded To		Traded With	Traded By		In Exchange For
Dec. 3, 1974	PHI	N	*see Tug McGraw*	NY	N	—
Feb. 16, 1977	CHI	N	—	CIN	N	Champ Summers

Dan Schneider

Date	Traded To		Traded With	Traded By		In Exchange For
Oct. 13, 1966	HOU	N	*see Tom Dukes*	ATL	N	—

Jeff Schneider

Date	Traded To		Traded With	Traded By		In Exchange For
Jan. 28, 1982	CAL	A	Doug DeCinces	BAL	A	Dan Ford

Pete Schneider

Date	Traded To		Traded With	Traded By		In Exchange For
Dec. 9, 1918	NY	A	—	CIN	N	Cash

Gerry Schoen

Date	Traded To		Traded With	Traded By		In Exchange For
Apr. 30, 1969	BAL	A	Mike Ferraro	SEA	A	John O'Donoghue Tom Fisher minor league P Lloyd Fourroux

Red Schoendienst

Date	Traded To		Traded With	Traded By		In Exchange For
June 14, 1956	NY	N	Jackie Brandt Bobby Stephenson Dick Littlefield Bill Sarni	STL	N	Alvin Dark Ray Katt Don Liddle Whitey Lockman
June 15, 1957	MIL	N	—	NY	N	Danny O'Connell Ray Crone Bobby Thomson

Dick Schofield

Date	Traded To		Traded With	Traded By		In Exchange For
Apr. 12, 1992	NY	N	—	CAL	A	Julio Valera Player to be named
			(California received P Julian Vasquez on October 6, 1992.)			
Jan. 15, 1993	TOR	A	—	NY	N	No compensation (free agent signing)

Dick Schofield

Date	Traded To		Traded With	Traded By		In Exchange For
June 15, 1958	PIT	N	Cash	STL	N	Gene Freese Johnny O'Brien
May 22, 1965	SF	N	—	PIT	N	Jose Pagan
May 11, 1966	NY	A	—	SF	N	Cash
Sept. 10, 1966	LA	N	—	NY	A	Thad Tillotson Cash
Dec. 2, 1968	BOS	A	—	STL	N	Gary Waslewski
Oct. 21, 1970	STL	N	—	BOS	A	Jim Campbell
July 29, 1971	MIL	A	Jose Cardenal Bob Reynolds	STL	N	Ted Kubiak minor league P Charlie Loseth

Gene Schott

Date	Traded To		Traded With	Traded By		In Exchange For
May 5, 1939	BKN	N	—	CIN	N	Cash

Pete Schourek

Date	Traded To		Traded With	Traded By		In Exchange For
Apr. 7, 1994	CIN	N	—	NY	N	Waiver price

Ossee Schreckengost

Date	Traded To		Traded With	Traded By		In Exchange For
Oct. 1901	CLE	A	—	BOS	A	Cash
June 1902	PHI	A	Frank Bonner	CLE	A	Bill Bernhard
May 1908	CHI	A	—	PHI	A	Cash

Pop Schriver

Date	Traded To		Traded With	Traded By		In Exchange For
1901	STL	N	—	PIT	N	Cash

Bob Schroder

Date	Traded To		Traded With	Traded By		In Exchange For
Dec. 1, 1969	WAS	A	—	SF	N	Cash

Bill Schroeder

Date	Traded To		Traded With	Traded By		In Exchange For
Dec. 7, 1988	CAL	A	—	MIL	A	Gus Polidor

Al Schroll

Date	Traded To		Traded With	Traded By		In Exchange For
Dec. 1, 1959	CHI	N	—	BOS	A	Bobby Thomson

Ken Schrom

Date	Traded To		Traded With	Traded By		In Exchange For
June 3, 1980	TOR	A	—	CAL	A	Dave Lemanczyk

Ken Schrom *continued*

Date	Traded To		Traded With	Traded By		In Exchange For
Jan. 7, 1986	CLE	A	—	MIN	A	Bryan Oelkers

Rick Schu

Date	Traded To		Traded With	Traded By		In Exchange For
Mar. 21, 1988	BAL	A	Jeff Stone Keith Hughes	PHI	N	Mike Young player to be named
(Philadelphia received OF Frank Bellino on June 14, 1988.)						
May 19, 1989	DET	A	—	BAL	A	Cash

Ron Schueler

Date	Traded To		Traded With	Traded By		In Exchange For
Dec. 3, 1973	PHI	N	—	ATL	N	Barry Lersch Craig Robinson
Mar. 31, 1977	MIN	A	—	PHI	N	Cash

Dave Schuler

Date	Traded To		Traded With	Traded By		In Exchange For
May 11, 1977	CAL	A	Dave LaRoche	CLE	A	Bruce Bochte Sid Monge $250,000.

Erik Schullstrom

Date	Traded To		Traded With	Traded By		In Exchange For
Aug. 31, 1992	SD	N	Ricky Gutierrez	BAL	A	Craig Lefferts
(San Diego received Gutierrez on Sept. 4, 1992.)						
Apr. 1, 1993	BAL	A	—	SD	N	Waiver price
Aug. 15, 1993	MIN	A	—	BAL	A	Mike Pagliarulo

Wes Schulmerich

Date	Traded To		Traded With	Traded By		In Exchange For
Oct. 14, 1930	BOS	N	Bill McAfee	CHI	N	Bob Smith Jimmy Welsh
June 17, 1933	PHI	N	Fritz Knothe Cash	BOS	N	Hal Lee Pinky Whitney
May 16, 1934	CIN	N	Ted Kleinhans Art Ruble	PHI	N	Syl Johnson Johnny Moore

Art Schult

Date	Traded To		Traded With	Traded By		In Exchange For
June 12, 1957	WAS	A	—	CIN	N	Cash

Fred Schulte

Date	Traded To		Traded With	Traded By		In Exchange For
Dec. 14, 1932	WAS	A	Goose Goslin Lefty Stewart	STL	A	Sammy West Lloyd Brown Carl Reynolds $20,000.
Jan. 30, 1936	PIT	N	—	WAS	A	Waiver price

Johnny Schulte

Date	Traded To		Traded With	Traded By		In Exchange For
Dec. 13, 1927	PHI	N	Jimmy Ring	STL	N	Johnny Mokan Jimmy Cooney Bubber Jonnard
Apr. 1929	CHI	N	—	PHI	N	Cash

Wildfire Schulte

Date	Traded To		Traded With	Traded By		In Exchange For
July 29, 1916	PIT	N	Bill Fischer	CHI	N	Art Wilson Otto Knabe
June 14, 1917	PHI	N	—	PIT	N	Waiver price
Dec. 1917	WAS	A	—	PHI	N	Cash

Barney Schultz

Date	Traded To		Traded With	Traded By		In Exchange For
June 24, 1963	STL	N	—	CHI	N	Leo Burke

Bob Schultz

Date	Traded To		Traded With	Traded By		In Exchange For
June 4, 1953	PIT	N	—	CHI	N	*see Ralph Kiner*
Dec. 29, 1954	DET	A	—	PIT	N	Cash

Buddy Schultz

Date	Traded To		Traded With	Traded By		In Exchange For
Feb. 28, 1977	STL	N	—	CHI	N	Minor league P Mark Covert

Howie Schultz

Date	Traded To		Traded With	Traded By		In Exchange For
May 10, 1947	PHI	N	—	BKN	N	Cash

Joe Schultz

Date	Traded To		Traded With	Traded By		In Exchange For
Aug. 1915	CHI	N	$3,000.	BKN	N	Larry Cheney
Jan. 1916	PIT	N	—	CHI	N	Cash

Joe Schultz *continued*

Date	Traded To		Traded With	Traded By		In Exchange For
June 6, 1924	PHI	N	—	STL	N	Cash
June 23, 1925	CIN	N	—	PHI	N	Cash

Al Schulz

Date	Traded To		Traded With	Traded By		In Exchange For
Feb. 10, 1916	CIN	N	—	BUF	F	Cash

Don Schulze

Date	Traded To		Traded With	Traded By		In Exchange For
June 13, 1984	CLE	A	—	CHI	N	*see Rick Sutcliffe*
May 11, 1987	NY	N	—	CLE	A	Ricky Nelson
Mar. 28, 1988	DET	A	—	MIN	A	Karl Best
July 22, 1989	SD	N	Mike Pagliarulo	NY	A	Walt Terrell Fred Toliver
(New York received Toliver on Sept. 27, 1989.)						

Ferdie Schupp

Date	Traded To		Traded With	Traded By		In Exchange For
July 1919	STL	N	—	NY	N	Frank Snyder
June 18, 1921	BKN	N	Hal Janvrin	STL	N	Jeff Pfeffer
Dec. 1921	CHI	A	—	BKN	N	Cash

Bill Schuster

Date	Traded To		Traded With	Traded By		In Exchange For
June 15, 1939	BOS	N	Cash	PIT	N	Elbie Fletcher

Don Schwall

Date	Traded To		Traded With	Traded By		In Exchange For
Nov. 20, 1962	PIT	N	Jim Pagliaroni	BOS	A	Jack Lamabe Dick Stuart
June 15, 1966	ATL	N	—	PIT	N	Billy O'Dell

Jeff Schwarz

Date	Traded To		Traded With	Traded By		In Exchange For
July 22, 1994	CAL	A	—	CHI	A	Bob Melvin

Mike Scioscia

Date	Traded To		Traded With	Traded By		In Exchange For
Feb. 11, 1993	SD	N	—	LA	N	No compensation (free agent signing)

Herb Score

Date	Traded To		Traded With	Traded By		In Exchange For
Apr. 18, 1960	CHI	A	—	CLE	A	Barry Latman

Dick Scott

Date	Traded To		Traded With	Traded By		In Exchange For
Dec. 13, 1963	CHI	N	—	LA	N	Jim Brewer Cuno Barragan

Donnie Scott

Date	Traded To		Traded With	Traded By		In Exchange For
Apr. 4, 1985	SEA	A	—	TEX	A	Orlando Mercado

Everett Scott

Date	Traded To		Traded With	Traded By		In Exchange For
Dec. 20, 1921	NY	A	Joe Bush Sad Sam Jones	BOS	A	Roger Peckinpaugh Jack Quinn Rip Collins Bill Piercy
June 17, 1925	WAS	A	—	NY	A	Cash
Mar. 1926	CHI	A	—	WAS	A	Waiver price
July 6, 1926	CIN	N	—	CHI	A	Waiver price

Gary Scott

Date	Traded To		Traded With	Traded By		In Exchange For
Nov. 17, 1992	FLA	N	Alex Arias	CHI	N	Greg Hibbard
Mar. 27, 1993	CIN	N	Hector Carrasco	FLA	N	Chris Hammond
(Cincinnati received Carrasco on September 10, 1993.)						
June 30, 1993	MIN	A	—	CIN	N	Minor league P Alan Newman Minor league IF Tom Houk

George Scott

Date	Traded To		Traded With	Traded By		In Exchange For
Oct. 11, 1971	MIL	A	Billy Conigliaro Joe Lahoud Jim Lonborg Ken Brett Don Pavletich	BOS	A	Marty Pattin Tommy Harper Lew Krausse Minor leaguer Pat Skrable
Dec. 6, 1976	BOS	A	Bernie Carbo	MIL	A	Cecil Cooper

George Scott *continued*

Date	Traded To	Traded With	Traded By	In Exchange For
June 13, 1979	KC A	—	BOS A	Tom Poquette

Jack Scott

Date	Traded To	Traded With	Traded By	In Exchange For
Feb. 18, 1922	CIN N	Larry Kopf	BOS N	Rube Marquard
Jan. 9, 1927	PHI N	Fresco Thompson	NY N	George Harper Butch Henline

(Part of three-team trade involving Philadelphia, New York, and Brooklyn.)

John Scott

Date	Traded To	Traded With	Traded By	In Exchange For
Nov. 22, 1976	TOR A	Dave Hilton Dave Roberts	SD N	Cash
Dec. 6, 1977	STL N	Pete Vuckovich	TOR A	Tom Underwood Victor Cruz
Oct. 23, 1978	CHI A	—	STL N	Jim Willoughby

Mickey Scott

Date	Traded To	Traded With	Traded By	In Exchange For
Dec. 18, 1969	CHI A	Cash	NY A	Pete Ward
May 22, 1973	MON N	—	BAL A	Cash
Sept. 11, 1974	CAL A	Cash	BAL A	Bob Oliver

Mike Scott

Date	Traded To	Traded With	Traded By	In Exchange For
Dec. 10, 1982	HOU N	—	NY N	Danny Heep

Pete Scott

Date	Traded To	Traded With	Traded By	In Exchange For
Nov. 28, 1927	PIT N	Sparky Adams	CHI N	Kiki Cuyler

Rodney Scott

Date	Traded To	Traded With	Traded By	In Exchange For
Dec. 12, 1975	MON N	—	KC A	Cash
Mar. 15, 1977	TEX A	—	MON N	Jeff Terpko
Mar. 26, 1977	OAK A	Jim Umbarger Cash	TEX A	Claudell Washington
Mar. 29, 1978	CHI N	Cash	OAK A	Pete Broberg
Dec. 14, 1978	MON N	Jerry White	CHI N	Sam Mejias

Tim Scott

Date	Traded To	Traded With	Traded By	In Exchange For
June 23, 1993	MON N	—	SD N	Archi Cianfrocco

Tony Scott

Date	Traded To	Traded With	Traded By	In Exchange For
Nov. 6, 1976	STL N	Steve Dunning Pat Scanlon	MON N	Bill Greif Angel Torres Sam Mejias
June 7, 1981	HOU N	—	STL N	Joaquin Andujar

Scott Scudder

Date	Traded To	Traded With	Traded By	In Exchange For
Nov. 15, 1991	CLE A	Jack Armstrong Minor league P Joe Turek	CIN N	Greg Swindell

Rod Scurry

Date	Traded To	Traded With	Traded By	In Exchange For
Aug. 14, 1985	NY A	—	PIT N	Cash
Mar. 19, 1988	SEA A	—	SF N	Donell Nixon

(San Francisco received Nixon on June 23, 1988.)

Kim Seaman

Date	Traded To	Traded With	Traded By	In Exchange For
Dec. 5, 1978	STL N	Tom Grieve	NY N	Pete Falcone
Dec. 8, 1980	SD N	—	STL N	*see Rollie Fingers*
May 22, 1982	MON N	—	SD N	Jerry Manuel

Rudy Seanez

Date	Traded To	Traded With	Traded By	In Exchange For
Dec. 10, 1991	LA N	—	CLE A	Dennis Cook Mike Christopher
Nov. 17, 1992	CLR N	—	LA N	Jody Reed

Ray Searage

Date	Traded To	Traded With	Traded By	In Exchange For
Dec. 10, 1979	NY N	—	STL N	Jody Davis
Jan. 8, 1982	CLE A	—	NY N	Tom Veryzer
Dec. 15, 1982	SD N	—	CLE A	Cash

(Searage was returned to San Diego on March 28, 1983.)

Date	Traded To	Traded With	Traded By	In Exchange For
July 23, 1986	CHI A	—	MIL A	Al Jones Minor league OF Tom Hartley

Steve Searcy

Date	Traded To	Traded With	Traded By	In Exchange For
July 2, 1992	LA N	Julio Peguero	PHI N	Stan Javier

(Los Angeles received Peguero on July 28, 1992.)

Tom Seaton

Date	Traded To	Traded With	Traded By	In Exchange For
Feb. 1915	NWK F	Hugh Bradley Larry Pratt	BKN F	Cy Falkenberg
Feb. 10, 1916	CHI N	—	NWK F	Cash

Tom Seaver

Date	Traded To	Traded With	Traded By	In Exchange For
June 15, 1977	CIN N	—	NY N	Pat Zachry Doug Flynn Steve Henderson Dan Norman
Dec. 16, 1982	NY N	—	CIN N	Charlie Puleo Lloyd McClendon Minor league OF Jason Felice
Jan. 20, 1984	CHI A	—	NY N	

(Claimed in compensation draft after Chicago lost free agent P Dennis Lamp to Toronto.)

Date	Traded To	Traded With	Traded By	In Exchange For
June 29, 1986	BOS A	—	CHI A	Steve Lyons

Bob Sebra

Date	Traded To	Traded With	Traded By	In Exchange For
Nov. 2, 1985	MON N	Jim Anderson	TEX A	Pete Incaviglia
Sept. 1, 1988	PHI N	—	MON N	Minor league P Travis Chambers
July 13, 1989	CIN N	—	PHI N	Jeff Gray

(Philadelphia received Gray on Sept. 6, 1989.)

Date	Traded To	Traded With	Traded By	In Exchange For
June 9, 1990	MIL A	Ron Robinson	CIN N	Glenn Braggs Billy Bates

Jimmy Sebring

Date	Traded To	Traded With	Traded By	In Exchange For
Aug. 11, 1904	CIN N	—	PIT N	Moose McCormick
Sept. 1909	WAS A	—	BKN N	Cash

Don Secrist

Date	Traded To	Traded With	Traded By	In Exchange For
Dec. 5, 1968	CHI A	Don Pavletich	CIN N	Jack Fisher

Larry See

Date	Traded To	Traded With	Traded By	In Exchange For
June 25, 1987	TEX A	—	LA N	Jose Mota

Bob Seeds

Date	Traded To	Traded With	Traded By	In Exchange For
Apr. 24, 1932	CHI A	Johnny Hodapp	CLE A	Bill Cissell Jim Moore
Dec. 15, 1932	BOS A	Johnny Hodapp Greg Mulleavy Bob Fothergill	CHI A	Ed Durham Hal Rhyne
May 25, 1934	CLE A	Bob Weiland $25,000.	BOS A	Wes Ferrell Dick Porter
Jan. 11, 1935	DET A	—	CLE A	Cash

Pat Seerey

Date	Traded To	Traded With	Traded By	In Exchange For
June 2, 1948	CHI A	Al Gettel	CLE A	Bob Kennedy

Herman Segelke

Date	Traded To	Traded With	Traded By	In Exchange For
Oct. 15, 1982	SF N	—	CHI N	Alan Hargesheimer

Kal Segrist

Date	Traded To	Traded With	Traded By	In Exchange For
Dec. 1, 1954	BAL A	—	NY A	*see Dick Kryhoski*

David Segui

Date	Traded To	Traded With	Traded By	In Exchange For
Mar. 27, 1994	NY N	—	BAL A	Kevin Baez Minor league P Tom Wegmann
June 8, 1995	MON N	—	NY N	Reid Cornelius

Diego Segui

Date	Traded To	Traded With	Traded By	In Exchange For
Apr. 13, 1966	WAS A	—	KC A	Cash
July 30, 1966	KC A	—	WAS A	Jim Duckworth
Dec. 7, 1969	OAK A	Ray Oyler	SEA A	Ted Kubiak George Lauzerique
June 7, 1972	STL N	—	OAK A	Cash

Diego Segui *continued*

Date	Traded To		Traded With	Traded By		In Exchange For
Dec. 7, 1973	BOS	A	Reggie Cleveland Terry Hughes	STL	N	Lynn McGlothen John Curtis Mike Garman
Oct. 22, 1976	SEA	A	—	SD	N	Cash

Socks Seibold

Date	Traded To		Traded With	Traded By		In Exchange For
Nov. 7, 1928	BOS	N	Bruce Cunningham Percy Jones Lou Legett Freddie Maguire $200,000.	CHI	N	Rogers Hornsby

Kevin Seitzer

Date	Traded To		Traded With	Traded By		In Exchange For
Feb. 1, 1993	OAK	A	—	MIL	A	No compensation (free agent signing)

Kip Selbach

Date	Traded To		Traded With	Traded By		In Exchange For
Feb. 29, 1900	NY	N	—	CIN	N	Cash
July 4, 1904	BOS	A	—	WAS	A	Bill O'Neill

Jeff Sellers

Date	Traded To		Traded With	Traded By		In Exchange For
Dec. 13, 1988	CIN	N	—	BOS	A	*see Nick Esasky*

Dick Selma

Date	Traded To		Traded With	Traded By		In Exchange For
Apr. 25, 1969	CHI	N	—	SD	N	Joe Niekro Francisco Libran Gary Ross
Nov. 17, 1969	PHI	N	Oscar Gamble	CHI	N	Johnny Callison
July 29, 1974	MIL	A	—	CAL	A	Cash

(Selma was returned to California on August 12, 1974.)

Frank Seminara

Date	Traded To		Traded With	Traded By		In Exchange For
Dec. 10, 1993	NY	N	Minor league OF Tracy Sanders Minor league SS Pablo Martinez	SD	N	Marc Kroon Minor league OF Randy Curtis

(Martinez and Kroon were exchanged on December 13.)

Andy Seminick

Date	Traded To		Traded With	Traded By		In Exchange For
Dec. 10, 1951	CIN	N	Eddie Pellagrini Dick Sisler Niles Jordan	PHI	N	Smoky Burgess Howie Fox Connie Ryan
Apr. 30, 1955	PHI	N	Glen Gorbous Jim Greengrass	CIN	N	Smoky Burgess Steve Ridzik Stan Palys

Ray Semproch

Date	Traded To		Traded With	Traded By		In Exchange For
Dec. 5, 1959	DET	A	Chico Fernandez	PHI	N	Ken Walters Ted Lepcio minor league P Alex Cosmidis
June 15, 1960	LA	N	Cash	DET	A	Clem Labine
Apr. 7, 1961	LA	A	—	WAS	A	Cash

Sonny Senerchia

Date	Traded To		Traded With	Traded By		In Exchange For
Jan. 31, 1956	CIN	N	Brooks Lawrence	STL	N	Jackie Collum

Steve Senteney

Date	Traded To		Traded With	Traded By		In Exchange For
Feb. 4, 1983	NY	N	—	TOR	A	Jorge Orta
June 14, 1983	PIT	N	Marvell Wynne	NY	N	Junior Ortiz Minor league P Arthur Ray

Manny Seoane

Date	Traded To		Traded With	Traded By		In Exchange For
Oct. 25, 1977	CHI	N	—	PHI	N	Jose Cardenal

Bill Serena

Date	Traded To		Traded With	Traded By		In Exchange For
Sept. 30, 1954	CHI	A	—	CHI	N	Waiver price

Scott Servais

Date	Traded To		Traded With	Traded By		In Exchange For
June 28, 1995	CHI	N	Luis Gonzalez	HOU	N	Rick Wilkins

Scott Service

Date	Traded To		Traded With	Traded By		In Exchange For
June 28, 1993	CLR	N	—	CIN	N	Waiver price
July 7, 1993	CIN	N	—	CLR	N	Waiver price
July 21, 1995	SF	N	*see Deion Sanders*	CIN	N	—

Walter Sessi

Date	Traded To		Traded With	Traded By		In Exchange For
Jan. 30, 1947	BKN	N	—	STL	N	Cash

Hank Severeid

Date	Traded To		Traded With	Traded By		In Exchange For
June 8, 1925	WAS	A	—	STL	A	George Mogridge Pinky Hargrave
July 22, 1926	NY	A	—	WAS	A	Waiver price

Al Severinsen

Date	Traded To		Traded With	Traded By		In Exchange For
Dec. 1, 1970	SD	N	—	BAL	A	*see Pat Dobson*
Nov. 30, 1972	NY	N	—	SD	N	Dave Marshall

Luke Sewell

Date	Traded To		Traded With	Traded By		In Exchange For
Jan. 7, 1933	WAS	A	—	CLE	A	Roy Spencer
Jan. 22, 1935	STL	A	—	WAS	A	Bump Hadley
Jan. 22, 1935	CHI	A	—	STL	A	Cash
Dec. 19, 1938	BKN	N	—	CHI	A	Cash

Jimmy Sexton

Date	Traded To		Traded With	Traded By		In Exchange For
Dec. 7, 1976	SEA	A	Craig Reynolds	PIT	N	Grant Jackson
Dec. 5, 1977	HOU	N	—	SEA	A	Leon Roberts
Feb. 10, 1981	OAK	A	—	HOU	N	Rick Lysander

Gordon Seyfried

Date	Traded To		Traded With	Traded By		In Exchange For
Nov. 27, 1962	CLE	A	Ron Nischwitz	DET	A	Bubba Phillips

Cy Seymour

Date	Traded To		Traded With	Traded By		In Exchange For
July 14, 1906	NY	N	—	CIN	N	$12,000.

Art Shamsky

Date	Traded To		Traded With	Traded By		In Exchange For
Nov. 8, 1967	NY	N	—	CIN	N	Bob Johnson
Oct. 18, 1971	STL	N	Jim Bibby Rich Folkers Charles Hudson	NY	N	Jim Beauchamp Chuck Taylor Harry Parker Tom Coulter
June 28, 1972	OAK	A	—	CHI	N	Cash

Howard Shanks

Date	Traded To		Traded With	Traded By		In Exchange For
Feb. 10, 1923	BOS	A	Val Picinich Ed Goebel	WAS	A	Muddy Ruel Allan Russell
Dec. 10, 1924	NY	A	—	BOS	A	Mike McNally

Red Shannon

Date	Traded To		Traded With	Traded By		In Exchange For
June 27, 1919	BOS	A	Braggo Roth	PHI	A	Amos Strunk Jack Barry

(Barry refused to report, and retired.)

Date	Traded To		Traded With	Traded By		In Exchange For
Jan. 20, 1920	WAS	A	Braggo Roth	BOS	A	Mike Menosky Eddie Foster Harry Harper
July 1920	PHI	A	—	WAS	A	Fred Thomas

Spike Shannon

Date	Traded To		Traded With	Traded By		In Exchange For
July 13, 1906	NY	N	—	STL	N	Sam Mertes Doc Marshall
July 1908	PIT	N	—	NY	N	Cash

Bobby Shantz

Date	Traded To		Traded With	Traded By		In Exchange For
Feb. 19, 1957	NY	A	Art Ditmar Clete Boyer Jack McMahan Wayne Belardi Curt Roberts	KC	A	Billy Hunter Rip Coleman Tom Morgan Mickey McDermott Milt Graff Irv Noren

(New York received Roberts on April 4, and Boyer on June 4, 1957.)

Bobby Shantz *continued*

Date	Traded To	Traded With	Traded By	In Exchange For
Dec. 16, 1960	PIT N	—	WAS A	Bennie Daniels Harry Bright R C Stevens
May 7, 1962	STL N	—	HOU N	Carl Warwick John Anderson
June 15, 1964	CHI N	Ernie Broglio Doug Clemens	STL N	Lou Brock Jack Spring Paul Toth
Aug. 15, 1964	PHI N	—	CHI N	Cash

Dick Sharon

Date	Traded To	Traded With	Traded By	In Exchange For
Nov. 30, 1972	DET A	—	PIT N	Jim Foor Norm McRae
Nov. 18, 1974	SD N	Ed Brinkman Bob Strampe	DET A	Nate Colbert

(Part of three-team trade involving San Diego, Detroit, and St. Louis Cardinals.)

Date	Traded To	Traded With	Traded By	In Exchange For
Oct. 20, 1975	STL N	—	SD N	Willie Davis
Jan. 12, 1976	CAL A	—	STL N	Minor league P Bill Rothan
Mar. 3, 1976	BOS A	John Balaz Dave Machemer	CAL A	Dick Drago

Bill Sharp

Date	Traded To	Traded With	Traded By	In Exchange For
May 8, 1975	MIL A	—	CHI A	Bob Coluccio

Bud Sharpe

Date	Traded To	Traded With	Traded By	In Exchange For
Sept. 1910	PIT N	—	BOS N	Cash

Mike Sharperson

Date	Traded To	Traded With	Traded By	In Exchange For
Sept. 22, 1987	LA N	—	TOR A	Juan Guzman

Joe Shaute

Date	Traded To	Traded With	Traded By	In Exchange For
Dec. 1933	CIN N	—	BKN N	Cash

Al Shaw

Date	Traded To	Traded With	Traded By	In Exchange For
Jan. 1908	CHI A	—	BOS A	Cash

Bob Shaw

Date	Traded To	Traded With	Traded By	In Exchange For
June 15, 1958	CHI A	Ray Boone	DET A	Bill Fischer Tito Francona
June 10, 1961	KC A	Wes Covington Gerry Staley Stan Johnson	CHI A	Ray Herbert Don Larsen Andy Carey Al Pilarcik
Dec. 15, 1961	MIL N	Lou Klimchock	KC A	Joe Azcue Ed Charles Manny Jimenez
Dec. 3, 1963	SF N	—	MIL N	*see Felipe Alou*
June 10, 1966	NY N	—	SF N	Cash
July 24, 1967	CHI N	—	NY N	Cash

Don Shaw

Date	Traded To	Traded With	Traded By	In Exchange For
May 15, 1972	OAK A	—	STL N	Dwain Anderson

Jeff Shaw

Date	Traded To	Traded With	Traded By	In Exchange For
Dec. 9, 1992	MON N	Tim Spehr	KC A	Mark Gardner Doug Piatt
Aug. 28, 1995	CHI A	—	MON N	Jose DeLeon

Bob Shawkey

Date	Traded To	Traded With	Traded By	In Exchange For
July 7, 1915	NY A	—	PHI A	$18,000.

Merv Shea

Date	Traded To	Traded With	Traded By	In Exchange For
May 9, 1933	STL A	Cash	BOS A	Rick Ferrell Lloyd Brown
Dec. 11, 1933	CHI A	—	STL A	Cash

Spec Shea

Date	Traded To	Traded With	Traded By	In Exchange For
May 3, 1952	WAS A	Jackie Jensen Jerry Snyder Archie Wilson	NY A	Irv Noren Tom Upton

Steve Shea

Date	Traded To	Traded With	Traded By	In Exchange For
Apr. 3, 1969	MON N	—	HOU N	Cash

Dave Shean

Date	Traded To	Traded With	Traded By	In Exchange For
July 16, 1909	BOS N	Buster Brown Lew Richie	PHI N	Johnny Bates Charlie Starr
Jan. 1911	CHI N	—	BOS N	Scotty Ingerton Big Jeff Pfeffer
Oct. 1911	BOS N	—	CHI N	Cash
Apr. 1918	BOS A	—	CIN N	Rube Foster

(Foster refused to report to Cincinnati; Cincinnati received cash instead.)

Jimmy Sheckard

Date	Traded To	Traded With	Traded By	In Exchange For
Jan. 1900	BKN N	Harry Howell Jerry Nops Broadway Aleck Smith Frank Kitson Joe McGinnity	BAL N	Cash
Dec. 30, 1905	CHI N	—	BKN N	Billy Maloney Buttons Briggs Jack McCarthy Doc Casey $2,000.
Apr. 1913	STL N	—	CHI N	Cash
July 1913	CIN N	—	STL N	Waiver price

Tom Sheehan

Date	Traded To	Traded With	Traded By	In Exchange For
May 20, 1925	PIT N	—	CIN N	Al Niehaus

Tommy Sheehan

Date	Traded To	Traded With	Traded By	In Exchange For
Jan. 1908	BKN N	—	PIT N	Cash

Larry Sheets

Date	Traded To	Traded With	Traded By	In Exchange For
Jan. 10, 1990	DET A	—	BAL A	Mike Brumley
Sept. 2, 1993	SEA A	—	MIL A	Cash

Gary Sheffield

Date	Traded To	Traded With	Traded By	In Exchange For
Mar. 27, 1992	SD N	Minor league P Geoff Kellogg	MIL A	Ricky Bones Jose Valentin Matt Mieske
June 24, 1993	FLA N	Rich Rodriguez	SD N	Trevor Hoffman Jose Martinez Andres Berumen

John Shelby

Date	Traded To	Traded With	Traded By	In Exchange For
May 22, 1987	LA N	Brad Havens	BAL A	Tom Niedenfuer

Rollie Sheldon

Date	Traded To	Traded With	Traded By	In Exchange For
May 3, 1965	KC A	Johnny Blanchard	NY A	Doc Edwards
June 13, 1966	BOS A	*see John Wyatt*	KC A	—
Aug. 15, 1966	CIN N	Dick Stigman	BOS A	Hank Fischer

(Cincinnati received Stigman and Sheldon on December 15, 1966.)

Jim Shellenback

Date	Traded To	Traded With	Traded By	In Exchange For
May 17, 1969	WAS A	—	PIT N	Frank Kreutzer

Keith Shepherd

Date	Traded To	Traded With	Traded By	In Exchange For
Aug. 9, 1992	PHI N	—	CHI A	Dale Sveum
June 3, 1994	BOS A	—	CLR N	Minor league P Brian Conroy

Bill Sherdel

Date	Traded To	Traded With	Traded By	In Exchange For
June 16, 1930	BOS N	Fred Frankhouse	STL N	Burleigh Grimes
May 18, 1932	STL N	—	BOS N	Waiver price

Pat Sheridan

Date	Traded To	Traded With	Traded By	In Exchange For
June 16, 1989	SF N	—	DET A	Tracy Jones

Darrell Sherman

Date	Traded To	Traded With	Traded By	In Exchange For
Nov. 18, 1993	CLR N	—	SD N	Waiver price

Larry Sherry

Date	Traded To	Traded With	Traded By	In Exchange For
Apr. 9, 1964	DET A	—	LA N	Lou Johnson $10,000.
June 29, 1967	HOU N	—	DET A	Jim Landis

Norm Sherry

Date	Traded To		Traded With	Traded By		In Exchange For
Oct. 11, 1962	NY	N	—	LA	N	Cash

Barry Shetrone

Date	Traded To		Traded With	Traded By		In Exchange For
Dec. 5, 1962	WAS	A	Marv Breeding minor league P Art Quick	BAL	A	Bob Johnson Pete Burnside

Charlie Shields

Date	Traded To		Traded With	Traded By		In Exchange For
Sept. 1902	STL	A	—	BAL	A	Cash

Steve Shields

Date	Traded To		Traded With	Traded By		In Exchange For
Sept. 23, 1986	KC	A	—	ATL	N	Darryl Motley
Dec. 10, 1986	SEA	A	Scott Bankhead Mike Kingery	KC	A	Danny Tartabull Rick Luecken
Mar. 20, 1989	MIN	A	—	NY	A	Balvino Galvez

Zak Shinall

Date	Traded To		Traded With	Traded By		In Exchange For
Apr. 26, 1993	SEA	A	—	CLE	A	Waiver price

Dave Shipanoff

Date	Traded To		Traded With	Traded By		In Exchange For
Apr. 1, 1985	PHI	N	Minor league OF Ken Kinnard	TOR	A	Len Matuszek

Craig Shipley

Date	Traded To		Traded With	Traded By		In Exchange For
Apr. 1, 1988	NY	N	—	LA	N	John Gibbons
Dec. 28, 1994	HOU	N	—	SD	N	*see Ken Caminiti*

Art Shires

Date	Traded To		Traded With	Traded By		In Exchange For
June 16, 1930	WAS	A	—	CHI	A	Garland Braxton Bennie Tate

Bob Shirley

Date	Traded To		Traded With	Traded By		In Exchange For
Dec. 8, 1980	STL	N	*see Rollie Fingers*	SD	N	—
Apr. 1, 1982	CIN	N	—	STL	N	Jeff Lahti minor league P Jose Brito
Dec. 15, 1982	NY	A	—	CIN	N	No compensation (free agent signing)

Urban Shocker

Date	Traded To		Traded With	Traded By		In Exchange For
Jan. 22, 1918	STL	A	Les Nunamaker Joe Gedeon Fritz Maisel Nick Cullop	NY	A	Eddie Plank Del Pratt $15,000.
Dec. 17, 1924	NY	A	—	STL	A	Joe Bush Milt Gaston Joe Giard

Costen Shockley

Date	Traded To		Traded With	Traded By		In Exchange For
Dec. 3, 1964	LA	A	Rudy May	PHI	N	Bo Belinsky

Milt Shoffner

Date	Traded To		Traded With	Traded By		In Exchange For
Aug. 19, 1939	CIN	N	—	BOS	N	Waiver price

Ernie Shore

Date	Traded To		Traded With	Traded By		In Exchange For
Dec. 18, 1918	NY	A	Duffy Lewis Dutch Leonard	BOS	A	Frank Gilhooley Ray Caldwell Slim Love Roxy Walters $15,000.

Bill Short

Date	Traded To		Traded With	Traded By		In Exchange For
Aug. 15, 1966	BOS	A	—	BAL	A	Cash
Oct. 17, 1966	PIT	N	—	BOS	A	Cash
Nov. 29, 1967	NY	N	—	PIT	N	Cash

Chick Shorten

Date	Traded To		Traded With	Traded By		In Exchange For
Jan. 17, 1919	DET	A	Eddie Ainsmith Slim Love	BOS	A	Ossie Vitt
Dec. 14, 1921	STL	A	—	DET	A	Waiver price

Burt Shotton

Date	Traded To		Traded With	Traded By		In Exchange For
Dec. 15, 1917	WAS	A	Doc Lavan	STL	A	Bert Gallia $15,000.
Feb. 1, 1919	STL	N	—	WAS	A	Waiver price

Clyde Shoun

Date	Traded To		Traded With	Traded By		In Exchange For
Apr. 16, 1938	STL	N	Curt Davis Tuck Stainback $185,000.	CHI	N	Dizzy Dean
May 6, 1942	CIN	N	—	STL	N	Cash
June 7, 1947	BOS	N	—	CIN	N	Cash
May 11, 1949	CHI	A	—	BOS	N	Cash

Eric Show

Date	Traded To		Traded With	Traded By		In Exchange For
Dec. 10, 1990	OAK	A	—	SD	N	No compensation (free agent signing)

Harry Shuman

Date	Traded To		Traded With	Traded By		In Exchange For
July 27, 1944	PHI	N	—	PIT	N	Waiver price

Terry Shumpert

Date	Traded To		Traded With	Traded By		In Exchange For
Dec. 13, 1994	BOS	A	—	KC	A	Cash

Eddie Sicking

Date	Traded To		Traded With	Traded By		In Exchange For
May 14, 1919	PHI	N	—	NY	N	Cash
July 2, 1920	CIN	N	—	NY	N	Cash

Norm Siebern

Date	Traded To		Traded With	Traded By		In Exchange For
Dec. 11, 1959	KC	A	Hank Bauer Don Larsen Marv Throneberry	NY	A	Roger Maris Joe De Maestri Kent Hadley
Nov. 27, 1963	BAL	A	—	KC	A	Jim Gentile Cash
Dec. 2, 1965	CAL	A	—	BAL	A	Dick Simpson
Dec. 14, 1966	SF	N	—	CAL	A	Len Gabrielson
July 16, 1967	BOS	A	—	SF	N	Cash

Dick Siebert

Date	Traded To		Traded With	Traded By		In Exchange For
Oct. 16, 1945	STL	A	—	PHI	A	George McQuinn

Paul Siebert

Date	Traded To		Traded With	Traded By		In Exchange For
June 15, 1977	NY	N	Bobby Valentine	SD	N	Dave Kingman
Oct. 2, 1978	STL	N	—	NY	N	Bob Coluccio

Sonny Siebert

Date	Traded To		Traded With	Traded By		In Exchange For
Apr. 19, 1969	BOS	A	Joe Azcue Vicente Romo	CLE	A	Ken Harrelson Juan Pizarro Dick Ellsworth
May 4, 1973	TEX	A	—	BOS	A	Cash
Oct. 26, 1973	STL	N	—	TEX	A	Tommy Cruz Cash
Nov. 18, 1974	SD	N	Alan Foster Rich Folkers	STL	N	Ed Brinkman Danny Breeden
(Part of three-team trade involving San Diego, Detroit, and St. Louis Cardinals.)						
May 16, 1975	OAK	A	—	SD	N	Ted Kubiak

Candy Sierra

Date	Traded To		Traded With	Traded By		In Exchange For
June 8, 1988	CIN	N	—	SD	N	Dennis Rasmussen

Ruben Sierra

Date	Traded To		Traded With	Traded By		In Exchange For
Aug. 31, 1992	OAK	A	Bobby Witt Jeff Russell Cash	TEX	A	Jose Canseco
July 28, 1995	NY	A	Minor league P Jason Beverlin	OAK	A	Danny Tartabull

Ed Siever

Date	Traded To		Traded With	Traded By		In Exchange For
Dec. 1902	STL	A	—	DET	A	Cash

Roy Sievers

Date	Traded To		Traded With	Traded By		In Exchange For
Feb. 18, 1954	WAS	A	—	BAL	A	Gil Coan
Apr. 4, 1960	CHI	A	—	WAS	A	Earl Battey Don Mincher $150,000.
Nov. 28, 1961	PHI	N	—	CHI	A	John Buzhardt Charley Smith

Roy Sievers *continued*

Date	Traded To	Traded With	Traded By	In Exchange For
July 16, 1964	WAS A	—	PHI N	Cash

Frank Sigafoos

Date	Traded To	Traded With	Traded By	In Exchange For
June 22, 1929	CHI A	—	DET A	Cash

Charlie Silvera

Date	Traded To	Traded With	Traded By	In Exchange For
Dec. 11, 1956	CHI N	—	NY A	Cash

Dave Silvestri

Date	Traded To	Traded With	Traded By	In Exchange For
Mar. 13, 1990	NY A	Player to be named	HOU N	Orlando Miller
	(New York received P Daven Bond on June 11, 1990.)			
July 16, 1995	MON N	—	NY A	Minor league OF Tyrone Horne

Ken Silvestri

Date	Traded To	Traded With	Traded By	In Exchange For
Dec. 31, 1940	NY A	—	CHI A	Bill Knickerbocker

Al Sima

Date	Traded To	Traded With	Traded By	In Exchange For
June 11, 1954	PHI A	Sonny Dixon Bill Wilson $20,000.	CHI A	Ed McGhee Morrie Martin

Bill Simas

Date	Traded To	Traded With	Traded By	In Exchange For
July 27, 1995	CHI A	—	CAL A	*see Jim Abbott*

Al Simmons

Date	Traded To	Traded With	Traded By	In Exchange For
Sept. 28, 1932	CHI A	Jimmy Dykes Mule Haas	PHI A	$100,000.
Dec. 10, 1935	DET A	—	CHI A	$75,000.
Apr. 4, 1937	WAS A	—	DET A	$15,000.
Dec. 29, 1938	BOS N	—	WAS A	$3,000.
Aug. 31, 1939	CIN N	—	BOS N	Cash

Curt Simmons

Date	Traded To	Traded With	Traded By	In Exchange For
June 22, 1966	CHI N	—	STL N	Cash
Aug. 2, 1967	CAL A	—	CHI N	Cash

Nelson Simmons

Date	Traded To	Traded With	Traded By	In Exchange For
Aug. 11, 1987	SEA A	—	BAL A	Mike Brown
	(Baltimore received Brown on August 26, 1987.)			

Ted Simmons

Date	Traded To	Traded With	Traded By	In Exchange For
Dec. 12, 1980	MIL A	Pete Vuckovich Rollie Fingers	STL N	Sixto Lezcano David Green Lary Sorensen Dave LaPoint
Mar. 5, 1986	ATL N	—	MIL A	Rick Cerone Minor league SS Flavio Alfaro

Doug Simons

Date	Traded To	Traded With	Traded By	In Exchange For
Apr. 2, 1992	MON N	—	NY N	Minor league OF Rob Katzaroff

Dick Simpson

Date	Traded To	Traded With	Traded By	In Exchange For
Dec. 2, 1965	BAL A	—	CAL A	Norm Siebern
Dec. 9, 1965	CIN N	Milt Pappas Jack Baldschun	BAL A	Frank Robinson
Jan. 11, 1968	STL N	—	CIN N	Alex Johnson
June 15, 1968	HOU N	Hal Gilson	STL N	Ron Davis
Dec. 4, 1968	NY A	—	HOU N	Dooley Womack
May 19, 1969	SEA A	—	NY A	Jose Vidal
Dec. 12, 1969	SF N	Steve Whitaker	SEA A	Bobby Bolin

Harry Simpson

Date	Traded To	Traded With	Traded By	In Exchange For
May 11, 1955	KC A	—	CLE A	Cash
June 15, 1957	NY A	Ryne Duren Jim Pisoni Milt Graff	KC A	Billy Martin Woodie Held Ralph Terry Bob Martyn
June 15, 1958	KC A	Bob Grim	NY A	Duke Maas Virgil Trucks

Harry Simpson *continued*

Date	Traded To	Traded With	Traded By	In Exchange For
May 2, 1959	CHI A	—	KC A	Ray Boone
Aug. 25, 1959	PIT N	minor league IF Bob Sagers	CHI A	Ted Kluszewski
Oct. 13, 1959	CHI A	—	PIT N	Cash

Steve Simpson

Date	Traded To	Traded With	Traded By	In Exchange For
Dec. 20, 1973	NY N	—	SD N	Jim McAndrew

Wayne Simpson

Date	Traded To	Traded With	Traded By	In Exchange For
Nov. 30, 1972	KC A	Hal McRae	CIN N	Roger Nelson Richie Scheinblum
Mar. 28, 1974	PIT N	—	KC A	Jim Foor
Apr. 5, 1975	PHI N	—	PIT N	Bill Robinson
Apr. 8, 1976	CAL A	—	PHI N	Cash

Duke Sims

Date	Traded To	Traded With	Traded By	In Exchange For
Dec. 11, 1970	LA N	—	CLE A	Alan Foster Ray Lamb
Aug. 4, 1972	DET A	—	LA N	Cash
Sept. 24, 1973	NY A	—	DET A	Cash
May 8, 1974	TEX A	—	NY A	Larry Gura Cash

Matt Sinatro

Date	Traded To	Traded With	Traded By	In Exchange For
Apr. 6, 1989	HOU N	—	OAK A	Troy Afenir

Bill Singer

Date	Traded To	Traded With	Traded By	In Exchange For
Nov. 28, 1972	CAL A	Frank Robinson Mike Strahler Billy Grabarkewitz Bobby Valentine	LA N	Andy Messersmith Ken McMullen
Dec. 10, 1975	TEX A	—	CAL A	Jim Spencer $100,000.
June 1, 1976	MIN A	Roy Smalley Mike Cubbage Jim Gideon $250,000.	TEX A	Bert Blyleven Danny Thompson

Elmer Singleton

Date	Traded To	Traded With	Traded By	In Exchange For
Sept. 30, 1946	PIT N	Billy Herman Stan Wentzel Whitey Wietelmann	BOS N	Bob Elliott Hank Camelli
Nov. 13, 1956	CHI N	Ray Jablonski	CIN N	Don Hoak Warren Hacker Pete Whisenant

Ken Singleton

Date	Traded To	Traded With	Traded By	In Exchange For
Apr. 5, 1972	MON N	Tim Foli Mike Jorgensen	NY N	Rusty Staub
Dec. 4, 1974	BAL A	Mike Torrez	MON N	Dave McNally Rich Coggins minor league P Bill Kirkpatrick

John Sipin

Date	Traded To	Traded With	Traded By	In Exchange For
May 22, 1969	SD N	Sonny Ruberto	STL N	Bill Davis Jerry DaVanon

Doug Sisk

Date	Traded To	Traded With	Traded By	In Exchange For
Dec. 8, 1987	BAL A	—	NY N	Blaine Beatty Minor league P Greg Talamantez
July 22, 1990	ATL N	—	NY N	Minor league P Tony Valle

Tommie Sisk

Date	Traded To	Traded With	Traded By	In Exchange For
Mar. 28, 1969	SD N	Chris Cannizzaro	PIT N	Ron Davis Bobby Klaus
Mar. 30, 1970	CHI A	—	SD N	Jerry Nyman

Dave Sisler

Date	Traded To	Traded With	Traded By	In Exchange For
May 2, 1959	DET A	Ted Lepcio	BOS A	Billy Hoeft
Sept. 16, 1961	CIN N	Cash	WAS A	Claude Osteen

Dick Sisler

Date	Traded To	Traded With	Traded By	In Exchange For
Apr. 7, 1948	PHI N	—	STL N	Ralph LaPointe $30,000.
Dec. 10, 1951	CIN N	Andy Seminick Eddie Pellagrini Niles Jordan	PHI N	Smoky Burgess Howie Fox Connie Ryan
May 13, 1952	STL N	Virgil Stallcup	CIN N	Eddie Kazak Wally Westlake

George Sisler

Date	Traded To	Traded With	Traded By	In Exchange For
Dec. 14, 1927	WAS A	—	STL A	$25,000.
May 27, 1928	BOS N	—	WAS A	$7,500.

Jim Siwy

Date	Traded To	Traded With	Traded By	In Exchange For
June 21, 1984	CLE A	—	CHI A	Dan Spillner

Ted Sizemore

Date	Traded To	Traded With	Traded By	In Exchange For
Oct. 5, 1970	STL N	Bob Stinson	LA N	Dick Allen
Mar. 2, 1976	LA N	—	STL N	Willie Crawford
Dec. 20, 1976	PHI N	—	LA N	Johnny Oates minor league P Quincy Hill
Feb. 23, 1979	CHI N	—	PHI N	*see Manny Trillo*
Aug. 17, 1979	BOS A	—	CHI N	Mike O'Berry Cash

Dave Skaggs

Date	Traded To	Traded With	Traded By	In Exchange For
May 13, 1980	CAL A	—	BAL A	Cash

Roe Skidmore

Date	Traded To	Traded With	Traded By	In Exchange For
Nov. 30, 1970	CHI A	Pat Jacquez Dave Lemonds	CHI N	Jose Ortiz Ossie Blanco
July 27, 1973	STL N	Ed Sprague	CIN N	Ed Crosby minor league C Gene Dusan

Bob Skinner

Date	Traded To	Traded With	Traded By	In Exchange For
May 23, 1963	CIN N	—	PIT N	Jerry Lynch
June 13, 1964	STL N	—	CIN N	Minor league C Jim Saul Cash

Camp Skinner

Date	Traded To	Traded With	Traded By	In Exchange For
Jan. 30, 1923	BOS A	Norm McMillan George Murray $50,000.	NY A	Herb Pennock

Joel Skinner

Date	Traded To	Traded With	Traded By	In Exchange For
Feb. 2, 1982	CHI A	—	PIT N	
(Claimed in compensation draft after Chicago lost free agent P Ed Farmer to Philadelphia.)				
July 30, 1986	NY A	Ron Kittle Wayne Tolleson	CHI A	Ron Hassey Carlos Martinez Bill Lindsey
(Chicago received Lindsey on Dec. 24, 1986.)				
Mar. 19, 1989	CLE A	Turner Ward	NY A	Mel Hall

Lou Skizas

Date	Traded To	Traded With	Traded By	In Exchange For
June 14, 1956	KC A	Eddie Robinson	NY A	Moe Burtschy Bill Renna Cash
Nov. 20, 1957	DET A	*see Billy Martin*	KC A	—
May 1, 1959	CIN N	Don Rudolph	CHI A	Del Ennis

Craig Skok

Date	Traded To	Traded With	Traded By	In Exchange For
Nov. 17, 1975	TEX A	Juan Beniquez Steve Barr	BOS A	Ferguson Jenkins

Bill Skowron

Date	Traded To	Traded With	Traded By	In Exchange For
Nov. 26, 1962	LA N	—	NY A	Stan Williams

Bill Skowron *continued*

Date	Traded To	Traded With	Traded By	In Exchange For
Dec. 6, 1963	WAS A	—	LA N	Cash
July 13, 1964	CHI A	Carl Bouldin	WAS A	Joe Cunningham Frank Kreutzer
May 6, 1967	CAL A	—	CHI A	Cotton Nash Cash

Gordon Slade

Date	Traded To	Traded With	Traded By	In Exchange For
Feb. 1933	STL N	Dazzy Vance	BKN N	Jake Flowers Ownie Carroll
Dec. 1933	CIN N	—	STL N	Waiver price

Jimmy Slagle

Date	Traded To	Traded With	Traded By	In Exchange For
Jan. 1900	PHI N	—	WAS N	Cash
June 1901	BOS N	—	PHI N	Shad Barry

Jim Slaton

Date	Traded To	Traded With	Traded By	In Exchange For
Dec. 9, 1977	DET A	Rich Folkers	MIL A	Ben Oglivie
Nov. 29, 1978	MIL A	—	DET A	No compensation (free agent signing)
Dec. 20, 1983	CAL A	—	MIL A	Bobby Clark

Jack Slattery

Date	Traded To	Traded With	Traded By	In Exchange For
Apr. 1903	CHI A	—	CLE A	Cash

Don Slaught

Date	Traded To	Traded With	Traded By	In Exchange For
Jan. 18, 1985	MIL A	Frank Wills	KC A	Jim Sundberg
(Part of a four-team deal involving Texas, Milwaukee, Kansas City, and New York Mets.)				
Jan. 18, 1985	TEX A	—	MIL A	Danny Darwin Minor league C Bill Hance
(Part of a four-team trade involving Texas, Milwaukee, Kansas City, and New York Mets.)				
Nov. 2, 1987	NY A	—	TEX A	Brad Arnsberg
(Texas received Arnsberg on November 10, 1987.)				
Dec. 4, 1989	PIT N	—	NY A	Jeff Robinson Willie Smith

Enos Slaughter

Date	Traded To	Traded With	Traded By	In Exchange For
Apr. 11, 1954	NY A	—	STL N	Bill Virdon Mel Wright minor league OF Emil Tellinger
May 11, 1955	KC A	Johnny Sain	NY A	Sonny Dixon Cash
Aug. 25, 1956	NY A	—	KC A	Waiver price
Sept. 12, 1959	MIL N	—	NY A	Waiver price

Lou Sleater

Date	Traded To	Traded With	Traded By	In Exchange For
July 31, 1951	NY A	Bobby Hogue Kermit Wahl Tom Upton	STL A	Cliff Mapes
May 12, 1952	WAS A	Freddie Marsh	STL A	Cass Michaels
Apr. 28, 1955	KC A	—	NY A	Cash
June 2, 1958	BAL A	—	DET A	Waiver price

Heathcliff Slocumb

Date	Traded To	Traded With	Traded By	In Exchange For
June 1, 1993	CLE A	—	CHI N	Jose Hernandez
Nov. 2, 1993	PHI N	—	CLE A	Ruben Amaro

Craig Smajstrla

Date	Traded To	Traded With	Traded By	In Exchange For
Jan. 21, 1984	CLE A	—	CHI A	Tom Brennan
(Cleveland received Smajstrla on July 8, 1985.)				

Aaron Small

Date	Traded To	Traded With	Traded By	In Exchange For
Apr. 26, 1995	FLA N	—	TOR A	Player to be named
(Toronto received P Ernie Delgado on September 19, 1995.)				

Jim Small

Date	Traded To	Traded With	Traded By	In Exchange For
Nov. 20, 1957	KC A	—	DET A	*see Billy Martin*

Roy Smalley

Date	Traded To	Traded With	Traded By	In Exchange For
Mar. 20, 1954	MIL N	—	CHI N	Dave Cole Cash
Apr. 30, 1955	PHI N	—	MIL N	Cash

Roy Smalley

Date	Traded To	Traded With	Traded By	In Exchange For
June 1, 1976	MIN A	Bill Singer Mike Cubbage Jim Gideon $250,000.	TEX A	Bert Blyleven Danny Thompson
Apr. 10, 1982	NY A	—	MIN A	Ron Davis Paul Boris Greg Gagne
July 17, 1984	CHI A	—	NY A	Doug Drabek Kevin Hickey
Feb. 19, 1985	MIN A	—	CHI A	Randy Johnson Minor league OF Ron Scheer
Feb. 8, 1988	CHI A	—	MIN A	Cash

John Smiley

Date	Traded To	Traded With	Traded By	In Exchange For
Mar. 17, 1992	MIN A	—	PIT N	Denny Neagle Midre Cummings
Nov. 30, 1992	CIN N	—	MIN A	No compensation (free agent signing)

Al Smith

Date	Traded To	Traded With	Traded By	In Exchange For
Dec. 4, 1957	CHI A	Early Wynn	CLE A	Fred Hatfield Minnie Minoso
Jan. 14, 1963	BAL A	Luis Aparicio	CHI A	Hoyt Wilhelm Pete Ward Ron Hansen Dave Nicholson
Dec. 4, 1963	CLE A	$25,000.	BAL A	Willie Kirkland

Al Smith

Date	Traded To	Traded With	Traded By	In Exchange For
Dec. 20, 1937	STL N	—	NY N	Cash
Dec. 29, 1937	PHI N	—	STL N	Waiver price

Bill Smith

Date	Traded To	Traded With	Traded By	In Exchange For
Dec. 4, 1959	PHI N	Bobby Gene Smith	STL N	Carl Sawatski

Bob Smith

Date	Traded To	Traded With	Traded By	In Exchange For
Oct. 14, 1930	CHI N	Jimmy Welsh	BOS N	Bill McAfee Wes Schulmerich
Nov. 30, 1932	CIN N	Rollie Hemsley Johnny Moore Lance Richbourg	CHI N	Babe Herman
Aug. 2, 1933	BOS N	—	CIN N	Waiver price

Bob Smith

Date	Traded To	Traded With	Traded By	In Exchange For
May 14, 1957	PIT N	—	STL N	Cash
June 13, 1959	DET A	—	PIT N	Waiver price

Bobby Gene Smith

Date	Traded To	Traded With	Traded By	In Exchange For
Dec. 4, 1959	PHI N	Bill Smith	STL N	Carl Sawatski
Apr. 26, 1962	CHI N	—	NY N	Sammy Taylor
June 5, 1962	STL N	Daryl Robertson	CHI N	Don Landrum Alex Grammas

Broadway Aleck Smith

Date	Traded To	Traded With	Traded By	In Exchange For
Jan. 1900	BKN N	Harry Howell Jimmy Sheckard Jerry Nops Frank Kitson Joe McGinnity	BAL N	Cash

Bryn Smith

Date	Traded To	Traded With	Traded By	In Exchange For
Dec. 7, 1977	MON N	Rudy May Randy Miller	BAL A	Don Stanhouse Joe Kerrigan Gary Roenicke
Nov. 28, 1989	STL N	—	MON N	No compensation (free agent signing)

Carr Smith

Date	Traded To	Traded With	Traded By	In Exchange For
Dec. 12, 1924	CLE A	Byron Speece	WAS A	Stan Coveleski

Charley Smith

Date	Traded To	Traded With	Traded By	In Exchange For
May 4, 1961	PHI N	Don Demeter	LA N	Dick Farrell Joe Koppe
Nov. 28, 1961	CHI A	John Buzhardt	PHI N	Roy Sievers
Apr. 23, 1964	NY N	—	CHI A	Chico Fernandez minor league C Bobby Catton Cash
Oct. 20, 1965	STL N	Al Jackson	NY N	Ken Boyer
Dec. 8, 1966	NY A	—	STL N	Roger Maris
Dec. 6, 1968	SF N	—	NY A	Nate Oliver
Mar. 28, 1969	CHI N	—	SF N	Cash

Charlie Smith

Date	Traded To	Traded With	Traded By	In Exchange For
Sept. 1909	BOS A	—	WAS A	Doc Gessler
Apr. 1911	CHI N	—	BOS A	Cash

Chris Smith

Date	Traded To	Traded With	Traded By	In Exchange For
Mar. 31, 1980	MON N	LaRue Washington	TEX A	Rusty Staub
Feb. 2, 1983	SF N	—	MON N	Jim Wohlford

Dave Smith

Date	Traded To	Traded With	Traded By	In Exchange For
Dec. 17, 1990	CHI N	—	HOU N	No compensation (free agent signing)

Dick Smith

Date	Traded To	Traded With	Traded By	In Exchange For
Oct. 11, 1962	NY N	—	LA N	Cash
Oct. 15, 1964	LA N	—	NY N	Larry Miller

Dwight Smith

Date	Traded To	Traded With	Traded By	In Exchange For
Feb. 1, 1994	CAL A	—	CHI N	No compensation (free agent signing)
June 14, 1994	BAL A	—	CAL A	Player to be named

(California received OF Bo Ortiz on July 14, 1994.)

Earl Smith

Date	Traded To	Traded With	Traded By	In Exchange For
June 7, 1923	BOS N	Jesse Barnes	NY N	Hank Gowdy Mule Watson
July 6, 1924	PIT N	—	BOS N	Cash
July 10, 1928	STL N	—	PIT N	Cash

Earl Smith

Date	Traded To	Traded With	Traded By	In Exchange For
May 31, 1921	WAS A	—	STL A	Frank Ellerbe

Eddie Smith

Date	Traded To	Traded With	Traded By	In Exchange For
Apr. 27, 1939	CHI A	—	PHI A	Waiver price

Elmer Smith

Date	Traded To	Traded With	Traded By	In Exchange For
Aug. 18, 1916	WAS A	Joe Leonard	CLE A	Joe Boehling Danny Moeller
June 13, 1917	CLE A	—	WAS A	$4,000.
Dec. 24, 1921	BOS A	George Burns Joe Harris	CLE A	Stuffy McInnis
July 23, 1922	NY A	Joe Dugan	BOS A	Chick Fewster Elmer Miller Johnny Mitchell Lefty O'Doul $50,000.

Elmer Smith

Date	Traded To	Traded With	Traded By	In Exchange For
Aug. 8, 1900	NY N	—	CIN N	Cash
Jan. 1901	PIT N	—	NY N	Cash
May 1901	BOS N	—	PIT N	Cash

Frank Smith

Date	Traded To	Traded With	Traded By	In Exchange For
Dec. 8, 1954	STL N	—	CIN N	Ray Jablonski Gerry Staley
Apr. 10, 1956	CIN N	—	STL N	Waiver price

Frank Smith

Date	Traded To	Traded With	Traded By	In Exchange For
Aug. 9, 1910	BOS A	Billy Purtell	CHI A	Harry Lord Amby McConnell

Frank Smith *continued*

Date	Traded To	Traded With	Traded By	In Exchange For
May 11, 1911	CIN N	—	BOS A	$5,000.
June 1915	BKN F	—	BAL F	Steve Evans

Fred Smith

Date	Traded To	Traded With	Traded By	In Exchange For
July 1915	BKN F	—	BUF F	Ed Gagnier Ed Lafitte

George Smith

Date	Traded To	Traded With	Traded By	In Exchange For
Oct. 4, 1965	BOS A	George Thomas	DET A	Bill Monbouquette

George Smith

Date	Traded To	Traded With	Traded By	In Exchange For
June 20, 1918	NY N	—	CIN N	Cash
July 15, 1918	BKN N	—	NY N	Cash
Oct. 1918	NY N	—	BKN N	Cash
May 27, 1919	PHI N	—	NY N	Joe Oeschger
Feb. 11, 1923	BKN N	—	PHI N	Clarence Mitchell

Greg Smith

Date	Traded To	Traded With	Traded By	In Exchange For
Dec. 14, 1990	LA N	—	CHI N	Jose Vizcaino

Hal Smith

Date	Traded To	Traded With	Traded By	In Exchange For
Nov. 18, 1954	BAL A	—	NY A	*see Bob Turley*
Aug. 17, 1956	KC A	—	BAL A	Joe Ginsberg
Dec. 15, 1959	PIT N	—	KC A	Ken Hamlin Dick Hall

Harry Smith

Date	Traded To	Traded With	Traded By	In Exchange For
Jan. 1908	BOS N	—	PIT N	Cash

Heinie Smith

Date	Traded To	Traded With	Traded By	In Exchange For
June 1901	NY N	—	PIT N	Ed Doheny

Jack Smith

Date	Traded To	Traded With	Traded By	In Exchange For
Apr. 19, 1926	BOS N	—	STL N	Cash

Jimmy Smith

Date	Traded To	Traded With	Traded By	In Exchange For
Sept. 1915	BAL F	Adam Johnson	CHI F	Bill Bailey
Feb. 10, 1916	PIT N	Otto Knabe	BAL F	Cash
Jan. 1917	NY N	—	PIT N	Waiver price
Oct. 1918	BOS N	—	NY N	Cash
Feb. 1919	NY N	—	BOS N	Walter Holke
Feb. 1919	CIN N	—	NY N	Cash
June 28, 1921	PHI N	—	CIN N	Cash

Lee Smith

Date	Traded To	Traded With	Traded By	In Exchange For
Dec. 8, 1987	BOS A	—	CHI N	Calvin Schiraldi Al Nipper
May 4, 1990	STL N	—	BOS A	Tom Brunansky
Aug. 31, 1993	NY A	—	STL N	Richard Batchelor
Jan. 29, 1994	BAL A	—	NY A	No compensation (free agent signing)
Dec. 13, 1994	CAL A	—	BAL A	No compensation (free agent signing)

Lonnie Smith

Date	Traded To	Traded With	Traded By	In Exchange For
Nov. 20, 1981	CLE A	Scott Munninghoff	PHI N	Bo Diaz

(Part of three-team trade involving Cleveland, Philadelphia, and St. Louis.)

Date	Traded To	Traded With	Traded By	In Exchange For
Nov. 20, 1981	STL N	—	CLE A	Lary Sorensen Silvio Martinez

(Part of three-team trade involving Cleveland, Philadelphia, and St. Louis.)

Date	Traded To	Traded With	Traded By	In Exchange For
May 17, 1985	KC A	—	STL N	John Morris
Jan. 4, 1993	PIT N	—	ATL N	No compensation (free agent signing)
Sept. 8, 1993	BAL A	—	PIT N	Minor league OF Stanton Cameron Minor league P Terry Farrar

(Pittsburgh received Cameron and Farrar on September 14, 1993.)

Mike Smith

Date	Traded To	Traded With	Traded By	In Exchange For
Dec. 1, 1986	MON N	—	CIN N	Minor league P Bill Cutshall

Mike Smith *continued*

Date	Traded To	Traded With	Traded By	In Exchange For
Nov. 14, 1988	BAL A	—	MON N	player to be named

(Montreal received P Doug Cline on December 7, 1988.)

Milt Smith

Date	Traded To	Traded With	Traded By	In Exchange For
May 1, 1956	STL N	—	CIN N	Paul LaPalme

Nate Smith

Date	Traded To	Traded With	Traded By	In Exchange For
Sept. 10, 1962	BAL A	—	LA A	Cash

Ozzie Smith

Date	Traded To	Traded With	Traded By	In Exchange For
Dec. 10, 1981	STL N	Steve Mura Al Olmsted	SD N	Sixto Lezcano Luis DeLeon Garry Templeton

(Templeton and Smith were exchanged on February 11, 1982; Olmsted and DeLeon were exchanged on February 19.)

Paul Smith

Date	Traded To	Traded With	Traded By	In Exchange For
May 6, 1958	CHI N	—	PIT N	Cash

Pete Smith

Date	Traded To	Traded With	Traded By	In Exchange For
Dec. 10, 1985	ATL N	—	PHI N	*see Steve Bedrosian*
Nov. 24, 1993	NY N	—	ATL N	Dave Gallagher
Dec. 1, 1994	CIN N	—	NY N	No compensation (free agent signing)

Ray Smith

Date	Traded To	Traded With	Traded By	In Exchange For
Dec. 7, 1984	SD N	—	MIN A	Floyd Chiffer

Red Smith

Date	Traded To	Traded With	Traded By	In Exchange For
Aug. 10, 1914	BOS N	—	BKN N	Cash

Reggie Smith

Date	Traded To	Traded With	Traded By	In Exchange For
Oct. 26, 1973	STL N	Ken Tatum	BOS A	Rick Wise Bernie Carbo
June 15, 1976	LA N	—	STL N	Joe Ferguson Bob Detherage minor league IF Fred Tisdale
Feb. 27, 1982	SF N	—	LA N	No compensation (free agent signing)

Riverboat Smith

Date	Traded To	Traded With	Traded By	In Exchange For
Mar. 9, 1959	CHI N	—	BOS A	Chuck Tanner
May 4, 1959	CLE A	—	CHI N	Randy Jackson

Roy Smith

Date	Traded To	Traded With	Traded By	In Exchange For
Sept. 12, 1982	CLE A	Wil Culmer Jerry Reed	PHI N	John Denny

Sherry Smith

Date	Traded To	Traded With	Traded By	In Exchange For
Sept. 18, 1922	CLE A	—	BKN N	Waiver price

Syd Smith

Date	Traded To	Traded With	Traded By	In Exchange For
July 1908	STL A	—	PHI A	Bert Blue

Tommy Smith

Date	Traded To	Traded With	Traded By	In Exchange For
Dec. 16, 1968	KC A	Buck Martinez minor league IF Mickey Sinnerud	HOU N	Minor league C John Jones

Willie Smith

Date	Traded To	Traded With	Traded By	In Exchange For
Dec. 4, 1989	NY A	Jeff Robinson	PIT N	Don Slaught
Apr. 7, 1992	CLE A	—	NY A	Waiver price

Willie Smith

Date	Traded To	Traded With	Traded By	In Exchange For
Apr. 28, 1964	LA A	—	DET A	Julio Navarro
Oct. 13, 1966	CLE A	—	CAL A	Cash
June 28, 1968	CHI N	—	CLE A	Lou Johnson
Nov. 30, 1970	CIN N	—	CHI N	Danny Breeden

Zane Smith

Date	Traded To	Traded With	Traded By	In Exchange For
July 2, 1989	MON N	—	ATL N	Sergio Valdez Nate Minchey Minor league OF Kevin Dean
Aug. 8, 1990	PIT N	—	MON N	Scott Ruskin Moises Alou Willie Greene

(Montreal received Alou on August 16, 1990.)

Date	Traded To	Traded With	Traded By	In Exchange For
Apr. 18, 1995	BOS A	—	PIT N	No compensation (free agent signing)

Mike Smithson

Date	Traded To	Traded With	Traded By	In Exchange For
Apr. 9, 1982	TEX A	—	BOS A	John Henry Johnson
Dec. 7, 1983	MIN A	John Butcher minor league C Sam Sorce	TEX A	Gary Ward
Dec. 21, 1989	CAL A	—	BOS A	No compensation (free agent signing)

John Smoltz

Date	Traded To	Traded With	Traded By	In Exchange For
Aug. 12, 1987	ATL N	—	DET A	Doyle Alexander

Homer Smoot

Date	Traded To	Traded With	Traded By	In Exchange For
July 25, 1906	CIN N	—	STL N	Carl Druhot Shad Barry

Harry Smythe

Date	Traded To	Traded With	Traded By	In Exchange For
May 28, 1934	BKN N	—	NY A	Waiver price

Duke Snider

Date	Traded To	Traded With	Traded By	In Exchange For
Apr. 1, 1963	NY N	—	LA N	Cash
Apr. 14, 1964	SF N	—	NY N	Cash

Van Snider

Date	Traded To	Traded With	Traded By	In Exchange For
Feb. 15, 1988	CIN N	—	KC A	Jeff Montgomery
Dec. 12, 1989	NY A	Tim Leary	CIN N	Hal Morris Minor league P Rodney Imes

Fred Snodgrass

Date	Traded To	Traded With	Traded By	In Exchange For
Aug. 1915	BOS N	—	NY N	Cash

J. T. Snow

Date	Traded To	Traded With	Traded By	In Exchange For
Dec. 6, 1992	CAL A	Russ Springer Jerry Nielsen	NY A	Jim Abbott

Cory Snyder

Date	Traded To	Traded With	Traded By	In Exchange For
Dec. 4, 1990	CHI A	Minor league IF Lindsay Foster	CLE A	Eric King Shawn Hillegas
July 14, 1991	TOR A	—	CHI A	Steve Wapnick Shawn Jeter

(Chicago received Wapnick on September 4, 1991.)

Date	Traded To	Traded With	Traded By	In Exchange For
Dec. 5, 1992	LA N	—	SF N	No compensation (free agent signing)

Frank Snyder

Date	Traded To	Traded With	Traded By	In Exchange For
July 1919	NY N	—	STL N	Ferdie Schupp

Gene Snyder

Date	Traded To	Traded With	Traded By	In Exchange For
Dec. 23, 1958	LA N	Rip Repulski Jim Golden	PHI N	Sparky Anderson

Jerry Snyder

Date	Traded To	Traded With	Traded By	In Exchange For
May 3, 1952	WAS A	*see Jackie Jensen*	NY A	—

Russ Snyder

Date	Traded To	Traded With	Traded By	In Exchange For
Apr. 12, 1959	KC A	Tommy Carroll	NY A	Mike Baxes Bob Martyn
Jan. 24, 1961	BAL A	Whitey Herzog	KC A	Wayne Causey Jim Archer Bob Boyd Al Pilarcik

Russ Snyder *continued*

Date	Traded To	Traded With	Traded By	In Exchange For
Nov. 29, 1967	CHI A	Luis Aparicio John Matias	BAL A	Don Buford Bruce Howard Roger Nelson
June 13, 1968	CLE A	—	CHI A	Leon Wagner
Apr. 4, 1970	MIL A	Max Alvis	CLE A	Roy Foster Frank Coggins Cash

Eric Soderholm

Date	Traded To	Traded With	Traded By	In Exchange For
Nov. 26, 1976	CHI A	—	MIN A	No compensation (free agent signing)
June 15, 1979	TEX A	—	CHI A	Ed Farmer Gary Holle
Nov. 14, 1979	NY A	—	TEX A	Minor league 3B Amos Lewis minor league P Ricky Burdette Cash

Luis Sojo

Date	Traded To	Traded With	Traded By	In Exchange For
Dec. 2, 1990	CAL A	—	TOR A	*see Devon White*
Dec. 8, 1992	TOR A	cash	CAL A	Kelly Gruber
Jan. 10, 1994	SEA A	—	TOR A	No compensation (free agent signing)

Tony Solaita

Date	Traded To	Traded With	Traded By	In Exchange For
July 14, 1976	CAL A	—	KC A	Cash
Dec. 5, 1978	MON N	—	CAL A	Cash
July 30, 1979	TOR A	—	MON N	Dyar Miller

Julio Solano

Date	Traded To	Traded With	Traded By	In Exchange For
Sept. 30, 1987	SEA A	—	HOU A	Minor league P Doug Givler

Eddie Solomon

Date	Traded To	Traded With	Traded By	In Exchange For
May 2, 1975	CHI N	Geoff Zahn	LA N	Burt Hooton
Mar. 28, 1980	PIT N	—	ATL N	Minor league P Greg Field
June 14, 1982	CHI A	—	PIT N	Jim Morrison

Moose Solters

Date	Traded To	Traded With	Traded By	In Exchange For
May 21, 1935	STL A	Cash	BOS A	Oscar Melillo
Jan. 17, 1937	CLE A	Ivy Andrews Lyn Lary	STL A	Bill Knickerbocker Joe Vosmik Oral Hildebrand
Aug. 2, 1939	STL A	—	CLE A	Waiver price
Dec. 8, 1939	CHI A	—	STL A	Rip Radcliff

Bill Sommers

Date	Traded To	Traded With	Traded By	In Exchange For
Nov. 18, 1947	STL A	—	BOS A	*see Ellis Kinder*

Don Songer

Date	Traded To	Traded With	Traded By	In Exchange For
May 9, 1927	NY N	—	PIT N	Cash

Lary Sorensen

Date	Traded To	Traded With	Traded By	In Exchange For
Dec. 12, 1980	STL N	—	MIL A	*see Rollie Fingers*
Nov. 20, 1981	CLE A	Silvio Martinez	STL N	Lonnie Smith

(Part of three-team trade involving Cleveland, Philadelphia, and St. Louis.)

Date	Traded To	Traded With	Traded By	In Exchange For
Jan. 23, 1984	OAK A	—	CLE A	No compensation (free agent signing)
Dec. 18, 1984	CHI N	—	OAK A	No compensation (free agent signing)
July 24, 1986	MON N	Tom Foley	PHI N	Dan Schatzeder Skeeter Barnes

Paul Sorrento

Date	Traded To	Traded With	Traded By	In Exchange For
Nov. 3, 1988	MIN A	Mike Cook Minor league P Rob Wassenaar	CAL A	Bert Blyleven Minor league P Kevin Trudeau
Mar. 28, 1992	CLE A	—	MIN A	Curtis Leskanic Oscar Munoz

Elias Sosa

Date	Traded To	Traded With	Traded By	In Exchange For
Oct. 14, 1974	STL N	Ken Rudolph	SF N	Marc Hill
May 28, 1975	ATL N	Ray Sadecki	STL N	Ron Reed Wayne Nordhagen

Elias Sosa *continued*

Date	Traded To	Traded With	Traded By	In Exchange For
June 23, 1976	LA N	Lee Lacy	ATL N	Mike Marshall
Jan. 31, 1978	PIT N	—	LA N	Cash
Apr. 4, 1978	OAK A	Miguel Dilone Mike Edwards	PIT N	Manny Sanguillen
Jan. 9, 1979	MON N	—	OAK A	No compensation (free agent signing)
Mar. 30, 1982	DET A	—	MON N	Cash
Oct. 7, 1982	SD N	—	DET A	Cash

Sammy Sosa

Date	Traded To	Traded With	Traded By	In Exchange For
July 29, 1989	CHI A	Scott Fletcher Wilson Alvarez	TEX A	Harold Baines Fred Manrique
Mar. 30, 1992	CHI N	Ken Patterson	CHI A	George Bell

Denny Sothern

Date	Traded To	Traded With	Traded By	In Exchange For
Aug. 7, 1930	PIT N	—	PHI N	Fred Brickell

Allen Sothoron

Date	Traded To	Traded With	Traded By	In Exchange For
Jan. 1921	BOS A	—	STL A	Waiver price
Apr. 1921	CLE A	—	BOS A	Waiver price

Steve Souchock

Date	Traded To	Traded With	Traded By	In Exchange For
Dec. 14, 1948	CHI A	—	NY A	Jim Delsing

Bill Southworth

Date	Traded To	Traded With	Traded By	In Exchange For
July 22, 1967	NY N	J. C. Martin	CHI A	Ken Boyer

Billy Southworth

Date	Traded To	Traded With	Traded By	In Exchange For
Feb. 23, 1921	BOS N	Walter Barbare Fred Nicholson $15,000.	PIT N	Rabbit Maranville
Nov. 12, 1923	NY N	Joe Oeschger	BOS N	Casey Stengel Dave Bancroft Bill Cunningham
		(Bancroft was named Boston manager.)		
June 14, 1926	STL N	—	NY N	Heinie Mueller

Bob Spade

Date	Traded To	Traded With	Traded By	In Exchange For
Apr. 1910	STL A	—	CIN N	Cash

Warren Spahn

Date	Traded To	Traded With	Traded By	In Exchange For
Nov. 23, 1964	NY N	—	MIL N	Cash

Al Spangler

Date	Traded To	Traded With	Traded By	In Exchange For
June 1, 1965	CAL A	—	HOU N	Don Lee

Tully Sparks

Date	Traded To	Traded With	Traded By	In Exchange For
Feb. 1900	PHI N	Heinie Reitz	PIT N	Duff Cooley

Joe Sparma

Date	Traded To	Traded With	Traded By	In Exchange For
Dec. 3, 1969	MON N	—	DET A	Jerry Robertson

Bob Speake

Date	Traded To	Traded With	Traded By	In Exchange For
Apr. 3, 1958	SF N	Cash	CHI N	Bobby Thomson

Tris Speaker

Date	Traded To	Traded With	Traded By	In Exchange For
Apr. 12, 1916	CLE A	—	BOS A	Sad Sam Jones Fred Thomas $55,000.

Byron Speece

Date	Traded To	Traded With	Traded By	In Exchange For
Dec. 12, 1924	CLE A	Carr Smith	WAS A	Stan Coveleski

Tim Spehr

Date	Traded To	Traded With	Traded By	In Exchange For
Dec. 9, 1992	MON N	Jeff Shaw	KC A	Mark Gardner Doug Piatt

Chris Speier

Date	Traded To	Traded With	Traded By	In Exchange For
Apr. 27, 1977	MON N	—	SF N	Tim Foli
July 1, 1984	STL N	—	MON N	Mike Ramsey

Chris Speier *continued*

Date	Traded To	Traded With	Traded By	In Exchange For
Aug. 19, 1984	MIN A	—	STL N	Cash and player to be named
		(St. Louis received P Jay Pettibone on Oct. 2, 1984.)		
Apr. 8, 1985	CHI N	—	MIN A	No compensation (free agent signing)
Dec. 10, 1986	SF N	—	CHI N	No compensation (free agent signing)

Stan Spence

Date	Traded To	Traded With	Traded By	In Exchange For
Dec. 13, 1941	WAS A	Jack Wilson	BOS A	Ken Chase Johnny Welaj
Dec. 10, 1947	BOS A	—	WAS A	Leon Culberson Al Kozar
May 8, 1949	STL A	Cash	BOS A	Al Zarilla

Daryl Spencer

Date	Traded To	Traded With	Traded By	In Exchange For
Dec. 15, 1959	STL N	Leon Wagner	SF N	Don Blasingame
May 30, 1961	LA N	—	STL N	Bob Lillis Carl Warwick

Glenn Spencer

Date	Traded To	Traded With	Traded By	In Exchange For
Dec. 12, 1932	NY N	Gus Dugas	PIT N	Freddie Lindstrom
		(Part of three-team trade involving New York, Philadelphia, and Pittsburgh.)		
Nov. 15, 1933	CIN N	—	NY N	George Grantham
Jan. 11, 1934	STL N	—	CIN N	Bob O'Farrell Syl Johnson
		(O'Farrell was named Cincinnati manager.)		

Jim Spencer

Date	Traded To	Traded With	Traded By	In Exchange For
May 20, 1973	TEX A	Lloyd Allen	CAL A	Mike Epstein Rich Hand Rick Stelmaszek
Dec. 10, 1975	CAL A	$100,000.	TEX A	Bill Singer
Dec. 11, 1975	CHI A	Morris Nettles	CAL A	Bill Melton Steve Dunning
Dec. 12, 1977	NY A	Tommy Cruz minor league P Bob Polinsky	CHI A	Stan Thomas minor league P Ed Ricks and cash
May 20, 1981	OAK A	Tom Underwood	NY A	Dave Revering Mike Patterson minor league P Chuck Dougherty

Roy Spencer

Date	Traded To	Traded With	Traded By	In Exchange For
Jan. 7, 1933	CLE A	—	WAS A	Luke Sewell

Tom Spencer

Date	Traded To	Traded With	Traded By	In Exchange For
Nov. 6, 1976	CHI A	—	CIN N	Hugh Yancy

Tubby Spencer

Date	Traded To	Traded With	Traded By	In Exchange For
Dec. 12, 1908	BOS A	—	STL A	Lou Criger

Rob Sperring

Date	Traded To	Traded With	Traded By	In Exchange For
Feb. 11, 1977	SF N	Bill Madlock	CHI N	Bobby Murcer Steve Ontiveros minor league P Andy Muhlstock
Mar. 26, 1977	HOU N	Willie Crawford	SF N	Rob Andrews Cash

Bill Spiers

Date	Traded To	Traded With	Traded By	In Exchange For
Oct. 25, 1994	NY N	—	MIL A	Waiver price

Ed Spiezio

Date	Traded To	Traded With	Traded By	In Exchange For
Dec. 3, 1968	SD N	Danny Breeden Ron Davis minor league P Phil Knuckles	STL N	Dave Giusti
July 9, 1972	CHI A	—	SD N	Don Eddy Cash

Charlie Spikes

Date	Traded To	Traded With	Traded By	In Exchange For
Nov. 27, 1972	CLE A	—	NY A	*see Graig Nettles*
Dec. 9, 1977	DET A	—	CLE A	Tom Veryzer

Dan Spillner

Date	Traded To	Traded With	Traded By	In Exchange For
June 14, 1978	CLE A	—	SD N	Dennis Kinney
June 21, 1984	CHI A	—	CLE A	Jim Siwy

Harry Spilman

Date	Traded To	Traded With	Traded By	In Exchange For
June 8, 1981	HOU N	—	CIN N	Rafael Landestoy

Scipio Spinks

Date	Traded To	Traded With	Traded By	In Exchange For
Apr. 15, 1972	STL N	Lance Clemons	HOU N	Jerry Reuss
Mar. 23, 1974	CHI N	—	STL N	Jim Hickman

Al Spohrer

Date	Traded To	Traded With	Traded By	In Exchange For
June 15, 1928	BOS N	Ben Cantwell Virgil Barnes Bill Clarkson	NY N	Joe Genewich

Jerry Spradlin

Date	Traded To	Traded With	Traded By	In Exchange For
Aug. 4, 1994	FLA N	—	CIN N	Waiver price

Ed Sprague

Date	Traded To	Traded With	Traded By	In Exchange For
Oct. 20, 1970	CIN N	—	OAK A	Cash
July 27, 1973	STL N	Roe Skidmore	CIN N	Ed Crosby minor league C Gene Dusan
Sept. 4, 1973	MIL A	—	STL N	Cash

George Spriggs

Date	Traded To	Traded With	Traded By	In Exchange For
Mar. 15, 1971	NY N	—	KC A	Cash

Jack Spring

Date	Traded To	Traded With	Traded By	In Exchange For
June 24, 1958	WAS A	—	BOS A	Bud Byerly
May 15, 1964	CHI N	—	LA A	Cash
June 15, 1964	STL N	*see Lou Brock*	CHI N	—

Russ Springer

Date	Traded To	Traded With	Traded By	In Exchange For
Dec. 6, 1992	CAL A	J. T. Snow Jerry Nielsen	NY A	Jim Abbott
Aug. 8, 1995	PHI N	Kevin Flora	CAL A	Dave Gallagher

(Philadelphia received Springer on August 15, 1995.)

Steve Springer

Date	Traded To	Traded With	Traded By	In Exchange For
Aug. 4, 1988	CHI A	Tom McCarthy	NY N	Mike Maksudian Minor league OF Vince Harris

Bobby Sprowl

Date	Traded To	Traded With	Traded By	In Exchange For
June 13, 1979	HOU N	Pete Ladd Cash	BOS A	Bob Watson
Dec. 21, 1983	BAL A	—	HOU N	Craig Minetto

Ebba St. Claire

Date	Traded To	Traded With	Traded By	In Exchange For
Feb. 1, 1954	NY N	*see Johnny Antonelli*	MIL N	—

Randy St. Claire

Date	Traded To	Traded With	Traded By	In Exchange For
July 13, 1988	CIN N	—	MON N	*see Tracy Jones*

Eddie Stack

Date	Traded To	Traded With	Traded By	In Exchange For
Dec. 1911	BKN N	—	PHI N	Cash
July 1913	CHI N	Cash	BKN N	Ed Reulbach

Marv Staehle

Date	Traded To	Traded With	Traded By	In Exchange For
July 29, 1967	CLE A	Jim King	CHI A	Rocky Colavito
Sept. 13, 1969	MON N	—	SEA A	Cash

Bill Stafford

Date	Traded To	Traded With	Traded By	In Exchange For
June 10, 1966	KC A	Gil Blanco Roger Repoz	NY A	Fred Talbot Billy Bryan

Steve Staggs

Date	Traded To	Traded With	Traded By	In Exchange For
Mar. 25, 1978	OAK A	—	TOR A	Sheldon Mallory

Jake Stahl

Date	Traded To	Traded With	Traded By	In Exchange For
Jan. 16, 1904	WAS A	—	BOS A	Cash
Mar. 1907	CHI A	—	WAS A	Cash

(Stahl refused to report and was sold by Chicago to the New York Yankees.)

Date	Traded To	Traded With	Traded By	In Exchange For
Oct. 1907	NY A	—	CHI A	Cash
July 10, 1908	BOS A	—	NY A	Cash

Larry Stahl

Date	Traded To	Traded With	Traded By	In Exchange For
Oct. 14, 1966	NY N	—	KC A	Waiver price
Nov. 30, 1972	CIN N	—	SD N	Cash

Roy Staiger

Date	Traded To	Traded With	Traded By	In Exchange For
Dec. 9, 1977	NY A	—	NY N	Sergio Ferrer

Tuck Stainback

Date	Traded To	Traded With	Traded By	In Exchange For
Apr. 16, 1938	STL N	Curt Davis Clyde Shoun $185,000.	CHI N	Dizzy Dean
June 1938	PHI N	—	STL N	Waiver price
July 11, 1938	BKN N	—	PHI N	Gib Brack

Matt Stairs

Date	Traded To	Traded With	Traded By	In Exchange For
Feb. 18, 1994	BOS A	Minor league P Pete Young	MON N	Player to be named Cash

Gerry Staley

Date	Traded To	Traded With	Traded By	In Exchange For
Dec. 8, 1954	CIN N	Ray Jablonski	STL N	Frank Smith
Sept. 11, 1955	NY A	—	CIN N	Waiver price
May 28, 1956	CHI A	—	NY A	Waiver price
June 10, 1961	KC A	Wes Covington Bob Shaw Stan Johnson	CHI A	Ray Herbert Don Larsen Andy Carey Al Pilarcik
Aug. 2, 1961	DET A	Reno Bertoia	KC A	Ozzie Virgil Bill Fischer

Tracy Stallard

Date	Traded To	Traded With	Traded By	In Exchange For
Dec. 11, 1962	NY N	Pumpsie Green Al Moran	BOS A	Felix Mantilla
Dec. 7, 1964	STL N	Elio Chacon	NY N	Johnny Lewis Gordie Richardson

Virgil Stallcup

Date	Traded To	Traded With	Traded By	In Exchange For
May 13, 1952	STL N	Dick Sisler	CIN N	Eddie Kazak Wally Westlake

Oscar Stanage

Date	Traded To	Traded With	Traded By	In Exchange For
May 17, 1906	CIN N	—	STL N	Cash

Charley Stanceu

Date	Traded To	Traded With	Traded By	In Exchange For
May 1946	PHI N	—	NY A	Waiver price

Lee Stange

Date	Traded To	Traded With	Traded By	In Exchange For
June 15, 1964	CLE A	George Banks	MIN A	Mudcat Grant
June 2, 1966	BOS A	Don McMahon	CLE A	Dick Radatz
June 29, 1970	CHI A	—	BOS A	Cash

Don Stanhouse

Date	Traded To	Traded With	Traded By	In Exchange For
Mar. 4, 1972	TEX A	Jim Panther	OAK A	Denny McLain
Dec. 5, 1974	MON N	Pete Mackanin	TEX A	Willie Davis
Dec. 7, 1977	BAL A	Joe Kerrigan Gary Roenicke	MON N	Rudy May Randy Miller Bryn Smith
Nov. 17, 1979	LA N	—	BAL A	No compensation (free agent signing)

Andy Stankiewicz

Date	Traded To	Traded With	Traded By	In Exchange For
Nov. 27, 1993	HOU N	Domingo Jean	NY A	Xavier Hernandez

Eddie Stanky

Date	Traded To	Traded With	Traded By	In Exchange For
June 6, 1944	BKN N	—	CHI N	Bob Chipman
Mar. 6, 1948	BOS N	—	BKN N	Bama Rowell Ray Sanders $40,000.
Dec. 14, 1949	NY N	Alvin Dark	BOS N	Sid Gordon Buddy Kerr Willard Marshall Red Webb
Dec. 11, 1951	STL N	—	NY N	Chuck Diering Max Lanier

(Stanky was named St. Louis manager.)

Fred Stanley

Date	Traded To	Traded With	Traded By	In Exchange For
June 11, 1972	SD N	—	CLE A	Mike Kilkenny
Nov. 3, 1980	OAK A	Brian Doyle	NY A	Mike Morgan

Mike Stanley

Date	Traded To	Traded With	Traded By	In Exchange For
Dec. 14, 1995	BOS A	—	NY A	No compensation (free agent signing)

Leroy Stanton

Date	Traded To	Traded With	Traded By	In Exchange For
Dec. 10, 1971	CAL A	Nolan Ryan Francisco Estrada Don Rose	NY N	Jim Fregosi

Mike Stanton

Date	Traded To	Traded With	Traded By	In Exchange For
Mar. 29, 1978	TOR A	—	HOU N	Cash
Dec. 7, 1981	STL N	—	CLE A	Cash
Feb. 8, 1982	CLE A	—	STL N	Cash

Mike Stanton

Date	Traded To	Traded With	Traded By	In Exchange For
July 31, 1995	BOS A	Matt Murray	ATL N	Minor league OF Marc Lewis Minor league P Mike Jacobs

(Murray, Lewis, and Jacobs were exchanged on August 31, 1995.)

Dave Stapleton

Date	Traded To	Traded With	Traded By	In Exchange For
Dec. 23, 1986	SEA A	—	BOS A	No compensation (free agent signing)

Charlie Starr

Date	Traded To	Traded With	Traded By	In Exchange For
July 16, 1909	PHI N	Johnny Bates	BOS N	Buster Brown Lew Richie Dave Shean
Sept. 1909	BOS N	—	PIT N	Cash

Dick Starr

Date	Traded To	Traded With	Traded By	In Exchange For
Dec. 13, 1948	STL A	Sherm Lollar Red Embree $100,000.	NY A	Fred Sanford Roy Partee
July 30, 1951	WAS A	—	STL A	Fred Sanford

Ray Starr

Date	Traded To	Traded With	Traded By	In Exchange For
Oct. 10, 1932	NY N	Gus Mancuso	STL N	Ethan Allen Bob O'Farrell Bill Walker Jim Mooney
June 12, 1933	BOS N	—	NY N	Cash
May 27, 1944	PIT N	—	CIN N	Cash
June 23, 1945	CHI N	—	PIT N	Waiver price

Jigger Statz

Date	Traded To	Traded With	Traded By	In Exchange For
July 1920	BOS A	—	NY N	Cash

Rusty Staub

Date	Traded To	Traded With	Traded By	In Exchange For
Jan. 22, 1969	MON N	—	HOU N	Jesus Alou Donn Clendenon Jack Billingham Skip Guinn $100,000.

(Clendenon refused to report, and Houston sent Billingham, Guinn, and cash on April 8, 1969.)

Rusty Staub *continued*

Date	Traded To	Traded With	Traded By	In Exchange For
Apr. 5, 1972	NY N	—	MON N	Tim Foli Ken Singleton Mike Jorgensen
Dec. 12, 1975	DET A	Bill Laxton	NY N	Mickey Lolich Billy Baldwin
July 20, 1979	MON N	—	DET A	Minor league C Randy Schafer Cash
Mar. 31, 1980	TEX A	—	MON N	LaRue Washington Chris Smith
Dec. 16, 1980	NY N	—	TEX A	No compensation (free agent signing)

John Stearns

Date	Traded To	Traded With	Traded By	In Exchange For
Dec. 3, 1974	NY N	Del Unser Mac Scarce	PHI N	Tug McGraw Don Hahn Dave Schneck

Bill Steele

Date	Traded To	Traded With	Traded By	In Exchange For
July 1914	BKN N	—	STL N	Cash

Bob Steele

Date	Traded To	Traded With	Traded By	In Exchange For
June 14, 1917	PIT N	—	STL N	Doug Baird
June 1918	NY N	—	PIT N	Cash

Elmer Steele

Date	Traded To	Traded With	Traded By	In Exchange For
Feb. 1910	PIT N	—	BOS A	Waiver price
Sept. 16, 1911	BKN N	—	PIT N	Cash

Farmer Steelman

Date	Traded To	Traded With	Traded By	In Exchange For
Jan. 1900	BKN N	—	LOU N	Cash
Apr. 1901	PHI A	—	BKN N	Cash

James Steels

Date	Traded To	Traded With	Traded By	In Exchange For
Aug. 30, 1989	MON N	—	SF N	Player to be named

Bill Steen

Date	Traded To	Traded With	Traded By	In Exchange For
June 1915	DET A	—	CLE A	Cash

John Stefero

Date	Traded To	Traded With	Traded By	In Exchange For
Dec. 8, 1986	MON N	—	BAL A	Rene Gonzales

(Baltimore received Gonzales on Dec. 16, 1986, also completing Dennis Martinez deal.)

Dave Stegman

Date	Traded To	Traded With	Traded By	In Exchange For
Dec. 12, 1980	SD N	—	DET A	Dennis Kinney

Bill Stein

Date	Traded To	Traded With	Traded By	In Exchange For
Dec. 19, 1980	TEX A	—	SEA A	No compensation (free agent signing)

Justin Stein

Date	Traded To	Traded With	Traded By	In Exchange For
June 10, 1938	CIN N	—	PHI N	Buck Jordan

Randy Stein

Date	Traded To	Traded With	Traded By	In Exchange For
June 7, 1979	SEA A	—	MIL A	Paul Mitchell

Ray Steineder

Date	Traded To	Traded With	Traded By	In Exchange For
May 25, 1924	PHI N	—	PIT N	Cash

Harry Steinfeldt

Date	Traded To	Traded With	Traded By	In Exchange For
Mar. 1906	CHI N	—	CIN N	Hans Lobert Jake Weimer
Mar. 1911	BOS N	—	CHI N	Cash

Rick Stelmaszek

Date	Traded To	Traded With	Traded By	In Exchange For
May 20, 1973	CAL A	*see Mike Epstein*	TEX A	—
July 28, 1974	CHI N	—	CAL A	Horacio Pina

Casey Stengel

Date	Traded To		Traded With	Traded By		In Exchange For
Jan. 9, 1918	PIT	N	George Cutshaw	BKN	N	Chuck Ward Burleigh Grimes Al Mamaux
Aug. 1919	PHI	N	—	PIT	N	Possum Whitted
July 1, 1921	NY	N	Red Causey Johnny Rawlings	PHI	N	Goldie Rapp Lee King Lance Richbourg
Nov. 12, 1923	BOS	N	Dave Bancroft Bill Cunningham	NY	N	Billy Southworth Joe Oeschger

(Bancroft was named Boston manager.)

Dave Stenhouse

Date	Traded To		Traded With	Traded By		In Exchange For
Dec. 15, 1961	WAS	A	Bob Schmidt	CIN	N	Johnny Klippstein Marty Keough

Mike Stenhouse

Date	Traded To		Traded With	Traded By		In Exchange For
Jan. 9, 1985	MIN	A	—	MON	N	Jack O'Connor
Dec. 12, 1985	BOS	A	—	MIN	A	Charlie Mitchell

Rennie Stennett

Date	Traded To		Traded With	Traded By		In Exchange For
Nov. 29, 1979	SF	N	—	PIT	N	No compensation (free agent signing)

Buzz Stephen

Date	Traded To		Traded With	Traded By		In Exchange For
June 15, 1970	BAL	A	Dick Baney	MIL	A	Dave May

Bryan Stephens

Date	Traded To		Traded With	Traded By		In Exchange For
Nov. 20, 1947	STL	A	Dick Kokos Joe Frazier $25,000.	CLE	A	Bob Muncrief Walt Judnich

Gene Stephens

Date	Traded To		Traded With	Traded By		In Exchange For
June 9, 1960	BAL	A	—	BOS	A	Willie Tasby
June 8, 1961	KC	A	—	BAL	A	Marv Throneberry

Vern Stephens

Date	Traded To		Traded With	Traded By		In Exchange For
Nov. 17, 1947	BOS	A	Jack Kramer	STL	A	Roy Partee Jim Wilson Al Widmar Eddie Pellagrini Pete Layden Joe Ostrowski $310,000.
Feb. 9, 1953	CHI	A	—	BOS	A	Hal Brown Marv Grissom Bill Kennedy
July 20, 1953	STL	A	—	CHI	A	Waiver price

Bobby Stephenson

Date	Traded To		Traded With	Traded By		In Exchange For
June 14, 1956	NY	N	*see Red Schoendienst*	STL	N	—

Earl Stephenson

Date	Traded To		Traded With	Traded By		In Exchange For
Dec. 3, 1971	MIL	A	Brock Davis Jim Colborn	CHI	N	Jose Cardenal
Oct. 31, 1972	PHI	N	—	MIL	A	*see Don Money*

Johnny Stephenson

Date	Traded To		Traded With	Traded By		In Exchange For
June 12, 1967	CHI	N	Rob Gardner	NY	N	Bob Hendley

Phil Stephenson

Date	Traded To		Traded With	Traded By		In Exchange For
Jan. 17, 1986	CHI	N	Minor league IF Bob Bathe	OAK	A	Minor league P John Cox Minor league IF Gary Jones
Aug. 30, 1989	SD	N	Calvin Schiraldi Darrin Jackson	CHI	N	Marvell Wynne Luis Salazar

(San Diego received Stephenson on Sept. 5, 1989.)

Dave Stevens

Date	Traded To		Traded With	Traded By		In Exchange For
Nov. 24, 1993	MIN	A	Matt Walbeck	CHI	N	Willie Banks

Ed Stevens

Date	Traded To		Traded With	Traded By		In Exchange For
Nov. 14, 1947	PIT	N	—	BKN	N	Cash

Lee Stevens

Date	Traded To		Traded With	Traded By		In Exchange For
Jan. 15, 1993	MON	N	—	CAL	A	Minor league P Jeff Tuss

(Tuss retired and California acquired P Keith Morrison to complete deal on January 21.)

R C Stevens

Date	Traded To		Traded With	Traded By		In Exchange For
Dec. 16, 1960	WAS	A	Bennie Daniels Harry Bright	PIT	N	Bobby Shantz

Bud Stewart

Date	Traded To		Traded With	Traded By		In Exchange For
May 13, 1948	WAS	A	—	NY	A	Leon Culberson $15,000.
Dec. 11, 1950	CHI	A	—	WAS	A	Mike McCormick

Dave Stewart

Date	Traded To		Traded With	Traded By		In Exchange For
Aug. 19, 1983	TEX	A	Ricky Wright $200,000.	LA	N	Rick Honeycutt
Sept. 13, 1985	PHI	N	—	TEX	A	Rich Surhoff
Dec. 8, 1992	TOR	A	—	OAK	A	No compensation (free agent signing)
Apr. 8, 1995	OAK	A	—	TOR	A	No compensation (free agent signing)

Jimmy Stewart

Date	Traded To		Traded With	Traded By		In Exchange For
May 22, 1967	CHI	A	—	CHI	N	Cash
Nov. 29, 1971	HOU	N	—	CIN	N	*see Joe Morgan*

Lefty Stewart

Date	Traded To		Traded With	Traded By		In Exchange For
Jan. 15, 1927	STL	A	Frank O'Rourke Billy Mullen Otto Miller	DET	A	Marty McManus Pinky Hargrave Bobby LaMotte
Dec. 14, 1932	WAS	A	Goose Goslin Fred Schulte	STL	A	Sammy West Lloyd Brown Carl Reynolds $20,000.
May 14, 1935	CLE	A	—	WAS	A	Belve Bean

Sammy Stewart

Date	Traded To		Traded With	Traded By		In Exchange For
Dec. 17, 1985	BOS	A	—	BAL	A	Jackie Gutierrez

Stuffy Stewart

Date	Traded To		Traded With	Traded By		In Exchange For
Jan. 21, 1919	PHI	N	Doug Baird Gene Packard	STL	N	Milt Stock Pickles Dillhoefer Dixie Davis

Dave Stieb

Date	Traded To		Traded With	Traded By		In Exchange For
Dec. 8, 1992	CHI	A	—	TOR	A	No compensation (free agent signing)

Dick Stigman

Date	Traded To		Traded With	Traded By		In Exchange For
Apr. 2, 1962	MIN	A	Vic Power	CLE	A	Pedro Ramos
Apr. 6, 1966	BOS	A	minor league 1B Jose Calero	MIN	A	Russ Nixon Chuck Schilling
Aug. 15, 1966	CIN	N	Rollie Sheldon	BOS	A	Hank Fischer

(Cincinnati received Stigman and Sheldon on December 15, 1966.)

Royle Stillman

Date	Traded To		Traded With	Traded By		In Exchange For
Dec. 2, 1971	BAL	A	—	LA	N	*see Frank Robinson*

Kurt Stillwell

Date	Traded To		Traded With	Traded By		In Exchange For
Nov. 6, 1987	KC	A	Ted Power	CIN	N	Danny Jackson Angel Salazar
Feb. 21, 1992	SD	N	—	KC	A	No compensation (free agent signing)

Craig Stimac

Date	Traded To		Traded With	Traded By		In Exchange For
Jan. 27, 1982	CLE	A	—	SD	N	Cash

Bob Stinson

Date	Traded To	Traded With	Traded By	In Exchange For
Oct. 5, 1970	STL N	Ted Sizemore	LA N	Dick Allen
Nov. 3, 1971	HOU N	—	STL N	Marty Martinez
Mar. 28, 1973	MON N	—	HOU N	Cash
Mar. 31, 1975	KC A	—	MON N	Cash

Snuffy Stirnweiss

Date	Traded To	Traded With	Traded By	In Exchange For
June 15, 1950	STL A	Jim Delsing Don Johnson Duane Pillette $50,000.	NY A	Tom Ferrick Joe Ostrowski Leo Thomas Sid Schacht
Apr. 1, 1951	CLE A	Merrill Combs	STL A	Freddie Marsh $35,000.

Chuck Stobbs

Date	Traded To	Traded With	Traded By	In Exchange For
Nov. 13, 1951	CHI A	Mel Hoderlein	BOS A	Randy Gumpert Don Lenhardt
Dec. 10, 1952	WAS A	—	CHI A	Mike Fornieles
July 9, 1958	STL N	—	WAS A	Waiver price

Milt Stock

Date	Traded To	Traded With	Traded By	In Exchange For
Jan. 1915	PHI N	Al Demaree Bert Adams	NY N	Hans Lobert
Jan. 21, 1919	STL N	Pickles Dillhoefer Dixie Davis	PHI N	Doug Baird Stuffy Stewart Gene Packard
Apr. 27, 1924	BKN N	—	STL N	Mike Gonzalez

Wes Stock

Date	Traded To	Traded With	Traded By	In Exchange For
June 15, 1964	KC A	—	BAL A	Charlie Lau

Bob Stoddard

Date	Traded To	Traded With	Traded By	In Exchange For
Apr. 18, 1986	SD N	Minor league OF Kevin Russ	OAK A	Rusty Tillman

Tim Stoddard

Date	Traded To	Traded With	Traded By	In Exchange For
Dec. 8, 1983	OAK A	—	BAL A	Wayne Gross
Mar. 26, 1984	CHI N	—	OAK A	Minor leaguers P Stan Kyles and OF Stan Boderick
Jan. 8, 1985	SD N	—	CHI N	No compensation (free agent signing)
July 9, 1986	NY A	—	SD N	Ed Whitson

Dean Stone

Date	Traded To	Traded With	Traded By	In Exchange For
Apr. 29, 1957	BOS A	Bob Chakales	WAS A	Milt Bolling Russ Kemmerer Faye Throneberry
Mar. 15, 1959	STL N	—	BOS A	Nels Chittum
June 22, 1962	CHI A	—	HOU N	Russ Kemmerer

George Stone

Date	Traded To	Traded With	Traded By	In Exchange For
Jan. 16, 1904	WAS A	—	BOS A	Cash
Jan. 16, 1905	BOS A	—	WAS A	Cash
Jan. 16, 1905	STL A	—	BOS A	Jesse Burkett

George Stone

Date	Traded To	Traded With	Traded By	In Exchange For
Nov. 2, 1972	NY N	Felix Millan	ATL N	Gary Gentry Danny Frisella
Feb. 24, 1976	TEX A	—	NY N	Bill Hands

Jeff Stone

Date	Traded To	Traded With	Traded By	In Exchange For
Mar. 21, 1988	BAL A	Rick Schu Keith Hughes	PHI N	Mike Young player to be named

(Philadelphia received OF Frank Bellino on June 14, 1988.)

John Stone

Date	Traded To	Traded With	Traded By	In Exchange For
Dec. 20, 1933	WAS A	—	DET A	Goose Goslin

Ron Stone

Date	Traded To	Traded With	Traded By	In Exchange For
Jan. 20, 1969	PHI N	—	BAL A	Clay Dalrymple

Steve Stone

Date	Traded To	Traded With	Traded By	In Exchange For
Nov. 28, 1972	CHI A	Ken Henderson	SF N	Tom Bradley
Dec. 11, 1973	CHI N	Ken Frailing Steve Swisher Jim Kremmel	CHI A	Ron Santo
Nov. 24, 1976	CHI A	—	CHI N	No compensation (free agent signing)
Nov. 29, 1978	BAL A	—	CHI A	No compensation (free agent signing)

Bill Stoneman

Date	Traded To	Traded With	Traded By	In Exchange For
Apr. 4, 1974	CAL A	—	MON N	Cash

Alan Storke

Date	Traded To	Traded With	Traded By	In Exchange For
Aug. 19, 1909	STL N	Jap Barbeau	PIT N	Bobby Byrne
Feb. 1910	CIN N	Fred Beebe	STL N	Miller Huggins Rebel Oakes Frank Corridon

Mel Stottlemyre

Date	Traded To	Traded With	Traded By	In Exchange For
July 30, 1987	KC A	—	HOU N	Buddy Biancalana

Todd Stottlemyre

Date	Traded To	Traded With	Traded By	In Exchange For
Apr. 11, 1995	OAK A	—	TOR A	No compensation (free agent signing)

Allyn Stout

Date	Traded To	Traded With	Traded By	In Exchange For
May 7, 1933	CIN N	—	STL N	*see Leo Durocher*
Dec. 14, 1934	NY N	Mark Koenig	CIN N	Billy Myers Cash

George Stovall

Date	Traded To	Traded With	Traded By	In Exchange For
Jan. 1912	STL A	—	CLE A	Lefty George

Jesse Stovall

Date	Traded To	Traded With	Traded By	In Exchange For
Jan. 1904	DET A	Ed Killian	CLE A	Billy Lush

Mike Strahler

Date	Traded To	Traded With	Traded By	In Exchange For
Nov. 28, 1972	CAL A	—	LA N	*see Andy Messersmith*
Dec. 6, 1973	MIL A	—	DET A	Ray Newman

Joe Strain

Date	Traded To	Traded With	Traded By	In Exchange For
Dec. 12, 1980	CHI N	Phil Nastu	SF N	Jerry Martin Jesus Figueroa minor league IF Mike Turgeon

Bob Strampe

Date	Traded To	Traded With	Traded By	In Exchange For
Nov. 18, 1974	SD N	Ed Brinkman Dick Sharon	DET A	Nate Colbert

(Part of three-team trade involving San Diego, Detroit, and St. Louis Cardinals.)

Sammy Strang

Date	Traded To	Traded With	Traded By	In Exchange For
Feb. 1901	NY N	—	CHI N	Jack Doyle
Mar. 1903	BKN N	—	CHI N	Cash
Feb. 1905	NY N	—	BKN N	Cash

Alan Strange

Date	Traded To	Traded With	Traded By	In Exchange For
June 29, 1935	WAS A	—	STL A	Lyn Lary

Darryl Strawberry

Date	Traded To	Traded With	Traded By	In Exchange For
Nov. 8, 1990	LA N	—	NY N	No compensation (free agent signing)

Gabby Street

Date	Traded To	Traded With	Traded By	In Exchange For
June 6, 1905	BOS N	—	CIN N	Cash
July 30, 1905	CIN N	—	BOS N	Cash
Dec. 1911	NY A	Jack Lelivelt	WAS A	John Knight Roxy Roach

George Strickland

Date	Traded To	Traded With	Traded By	In Exchange For
Aug. 18, 1952	CLE A	Ted Wilks	PIT N	Johnny Berardino minor league P Charlie Sipple $50,000.

Jake Striker

Date	Traded To	Traded With	Traded By	In Exchange For
Dec. 6, 1959	CHI A	—	CLE A	*see Norm Cash*

Nick Strincevich

Date	Traded To	Traded With	Traded By	In Exchange For
May 7, 1941	PIT N	—	BOS N	Lloyd Waner
May 15, 1948	PHI N	—	PIT N	Cash

Joe Stripp

Date	Traded To	Traded With	Traded By	In Exchange For
Mar. 14, 1932	BKN N	Tony Cuccinello Clyde Sukeforth	CIN N	Babe Herman Wally Gilbert Ernie Lombardi
Oct. 4, 1937	STL N	Johnny Cooney Jim Bucher Roy Henshaw	BKN N	Leo Durocher
Aug. 1, 1938	BOS N	—	STL N	Cash
Dec. 13, 1938	BKN N	—	BOS N	Fred Frankhouse

John Strohmayer

Date	Traded To	Traded With	Traded By	In Exchange For
July 16, 1973	NY N	—	MON N	Cash

Brent Strom

Date	Traded To	Traded With	Traded By	In Exchange For
Nov. 27, 1972	CLE A	Bob Rauch	NY N	Phil Hennigan
June 15, 1974	SD N	minor league P Jerry Lee	CLE A	Steve Arlin

Ed Stroud

Date	Traded To	Traded With	Traded By	In Exchange For
June 15, 1967	WAS A	—	CHI A	Jim King
Mar. 29, 1971	CHI A	—	WAS A	Tom McCraw

Steve Stroughter

Date	Traded To	Traded With	Traded By	In Exchange For
Dec. 19, 1980	MIN A	—	SEA A	Mike Bacsik

Amos Strunk

Date	Traded To	Traded With	Traded By	In Exchange For
Dec. 14, 1917	BOS A	Joe Bush Wally Schang	PHI A	Vean Gregg Merlin Kopp Pinch Thomas $60,000.
June 27, 1919	PHI A	Jack Barry	BOS A	Braggo Roth Red Shannon
		(Barry refused to report, and retired.)		
July 23, 1920	CHI A	—	PHI A	Waiver price
Aug. 1924	PHI A	—	CHI A	Waiver price

Dick Stuart

Date	Traded To	Traded With	Traded By	In Exchange For
Nov. 20, 1962	BOS A	Jack Lamabe	PIT N	Jim Pagliaroni Don Schwall
Nov. 29, 1964	PHI N	—	BOS A	Dennis Bennett
Feb. 22, 1966	NY N	—	PHI N	Jimmie Schaffer Wayne Graham Bobby Klaus

Marlin Stuart

Date	Traded To	Traded With	Traded By	In Exchange For
Aug. 14, 1952	STL A	*see Vic Wertz*	DET A	—
July 4, 1954	NY A	—	BAL A	Waiver price

Franklin Stubbs

Date	Traded To	Traded With	Traded By	In Exchange For
Apr. 1, 1990	HOU N	—	LA N	Terry Wells
Dec. 5, 1990	MIL A	—	HOU N	No compensation (free agent signing)

Bill Stumpf

Date	Traded To	Traded With	Traded By	In Exchange For
May 20, 1913	CLE A	Jack Lelivelt	NY A	Roger Peckinpaugh

John Stuper

Date	Traded To	Traded With	Traded By	In Exchange For
Sept. 10, 1984	CIN N	—	STL N	Paul Householder
Dec. 19, 1985	MON N	—	CIN N	*see Bill Gullickson*

Tom Sturdivant

Date	Traded To	Traded With	Traded By	In Exchange For
May 26, 1959	KC A	Johnny Kucks Jerry Lumpe	NY A	Hector Lopez Ralph Terry
Dec. 3, 1959	BOS A	—	KC A	Pete Daley
June 29, 1961	PIT N	—	WAS A	Tom Cheney
May 4, 1963	DET A	—	PIT N	Cash
July 23, 1963	KC A	—	DET A	Cash

Bobby Sturgeon

Date	Traded To	Traded With	Traded By	In Exchange For
Mar. 1, 1948	BOS N	—	CHI N	Dick Culler

Chris Stynes

Date	Traded To	Traded With	Traded By	In Exchange For
Apr. 6, 1995	KC A	Minor league P David Sinnes Minor league SS Anthony Medrano	TOR A	David Cone

Ken Suarez

Date	Traded To	Traded With	Traded By	In Exchange For
Dec. 2, 1971	TEX A	—	CLE A	*see Del Unser*
Feb. 12, 1974	CLE A	—	TEX A	Leo Cardenas
Sept. 12, 1974	CAL A	Rusty Torres Cash	CLE A	Frank Robinson

Jim Suchecki

Date	Traded To	Traded With	Traded By	In Exchange For
May 17, 1951	STL A	Matt Batts Jim McDonald $100,000.	BOS A	Les Moss
Mar. 4, 1952	PIT N	—	STL A	Cash
May 5, 1952	CHI A	—	PIT N	Waiver price

Bill Sudakis

Date	Traded To	Traded With	Traded By	In Exchange For
Mar. 27, 1972	NY N	—	LA N	Cash
Mar. 28, 1973	TEX A	—	NY N	Bill McNulty
Dec. 7, 1973	NY A	—	TEX A	Cash
Dec. 3, 1974	CAL A	—	NY A	Skip Lockwood

Willie Sudhoff

Date	Traded To	Traded With	Traded By	In Exchange For
Dec. 1905	WAS A	—	STL A	Beany Jacobson

William Suero

Date	Traded To	Traded With	Traded By	In Exchange For
Aug. 9, 1991	MIL A	—	TOR A	*see Candy Maldonado*

Joe Sugden

Date	Traded To	Traded With	Traded By	In Exchange For
Feb. 1902	STL A	—	CHI A	Cash

Gus Suhr

Date	Traded To	Traded With	Traded By	In Exchange For
July 28, 1939	PHI N	—	PIT N	Max Butcher

Clyde Sukeforth

Date	Traded To	Traded With	Traded By	In Exchange For
Mar. 14, 1932	BKN N	Tony Cuccinello Joe Stripp	CIN N	Babe Herman Wally Gilbert Ernie Lombardi

Billy Sullivan

Date	Traded To	Traded With	Traded By	In Exchange For
Jan. 29, 1936	CLE A	—	CIN N	Cash
Feb. 10, 1938	STL A	Ed Cole Roy Hughes	CLE A	Rollie Hemsley
Jan. 30, 1940	DET A	—	STL A	Slick Coffman
Mar. 13, 1942	BKN N	—	DET A	Cash

Denny Sullivan

Date	Traded To	Traded With	Traded By	In Exchange For
Sept. 1908	CLE A	—	BOS A	Cash

Frank Sullivan

Date	Traded To	Traded With	Traded By	In Exchange For
Dec. 15, 1960	PHI N	—	BOS A	Gene Conley

Haywood Sullivan

Date	Traded To	Traded With	Traded By	In Exchange For
Dec. 29, 1960	KC A	—	WAS A	Marty Kutyna Cash

Joe Sullivan

Date	Traded To	Traded With	Traded By	In Exchange For
June 20, 1941	PIT N	—	BOS N	Cash

Date	Traded To	Traded With	Traded By	In Exchange For

John Sullivan

Date	Traded To	Traded With	Traded By	In Exchange For
Oct. 4, 1948	STL A	Tom Ferrick $25,000.	WAS A	Sam Dente

John Sullivan

Date	Traded To	Traded With	Traded By	In Exchange For
May 11, 1921	CHI N	—	BOS N	Cash

Marc Sullivan

Date	Traded To	Traded With	Traded By	In Exchange For
Dec. 14, 1987	HOU N	—	BOS A	player to be named

(Boston received SS Randy Randle on October 4, 1988.)

Homer Summa

Date	Traded To	Traded With	Traded By	In Exchange For
Jan. 5, 1929	PHI A	—	CLE A	Cash

Champ Summers

Date	Traded To	Traded With	Traded By	In Exchange For
Apr. 6, 1975	CHI N	Cash	OAK A	Jim Todd
Feb. 16, 1977	CIN N	—	CHI N	Dave Schneck
May 25, 1979	DET A	—	CIN N	Sheldon Burnside
Mar. 4, 1982	SF N	—	DET A	Enos Cabell Cash
Dec. 6, 1983	SD N	—	SF N	Joe Pittman minor league OF Tommy Francis

Jim Sundberg

Date	Traded To	Traded With	Traded By	In Exchange For
Dec. 8, 1983	MIL A	—	TEX A	Ned Yost minor league P Dan Scarpetta
Jan. 18, 1985	KC A	—	MIL A	Frank Wills Don Slaught

(Part of a four-team deal involving Texas, Milwaukee, Kansas City, and New York Mets.)

Date	Traded To	Traded With	Traded By	In Exchange For
Mar. 30, 1987	CHI N	—	KC A	Thad Bosley Dave Gumpert

Steve Sundra

Date	Traded To	Traded With	Traded By	In Exchange For
Dec. 11, 1935	NY A	Monte Pearson	CLE A	Johnny Allen
Mar. 27, 1941	WAS A	—	NY A	Cash
June 7, 1942	STL A	Mike Chartak	WAS A	Roy Cullenbine Bill Trotter

B. J. Surhoff

Date	Traded To	Traded With	Traded By	In Exchange For
Dec. 20, 1995	BAL A	—	MIL A	No compensation (free agent signing)

Rich Surhoff

Date	Traded To	Traded With	Traded By	In Exchange For
Sept. 13, 1985	TEX A	—	PHI N	Dave Stewart
July 26, 1986	CHI N	Minor league P Bryan Dial	TEX A	Ron Meridith

Max Surkont

Date	Traded To	Traded With	Traded By	In Exchange For
Dec. 26, 1953	PIT N	Sid Gordon Sam Jethroe Curt Raydon Fred Walters minor league P Larry Lasalle and $100,000.	MIL N	Danny O'Connell
May 5, 1956	STL N	—	PIT N	Luis Arroyo

George Susce

Date	Traded To	Traded With	Traded By	In Exchange For
May 12, 1958	DET A	—	BOS A	Waiver price

Rick Sutcliffe

Date	Traded To	Traded With	Traded By	In Exchange For
Dec. 9, 1981	CLE A	Jack Perconte	LA N	Jorge Orta Jack Fimple Larry White
June 13, 1984	CHI N	George Frazier Ron Hassey	CLE A	Mel Hall Joe Carter Don Schulze Minor league P Darryl Banks

Rick Sutcliffe *continued*

Date	Traded To	Traded With	Traded By	In Exchange For
Dec. 19, 1991	BAL A	—	CHI N	No compensation (free agent signing)
Jan. 31, 1994	STL N	—	BAL A	No compensation (free agent signing)

Gary Sutherland

Date	Traded To	Traded With	Traded By	In Exchange For
Dec. 3, 1973	DET A	Jim Ray	HOU N	Fred Scherman Cash
June 10, 1976	MIL A	—	DET A	Pedro Garcia

Bruce Sutter

Date	Traded To	Traded With	Traded By	In Exchange For
Dec. 9, 1980	STL N	—	CHI N	Leon Durham Ken Reitz Tye Waller
Dec. 7, 1984	ATL N	—	STL N	Free agent signing

(St. Louis claimed SS Argenis Salazar from Montreal in the compensation draft.)

Jack Sutthoff

Date	Traded To	Traded With	Traded By	In Exchange For
July 20, 1904	PHI N	Frank Corridon	CHI N	Shad Barry

Don Sutton

Date	Traded To	Traded With	Traded By	In Exchange For
Dec. 4, 1980	HOU N	—	LA N	No compensation (free agent signing)
Aug. 30, 1982	MIL A	—	HOU N	Kevin Bass Frank DiPino Mike Madden Cash
Dec. 7, 1984	OAK A	—	MIL A	Ray Burris minor league P Eric Barry Player to be named

(Milwaukee received P Ed Myers on March 25, 1985.)

Date	Traded To	Traded With	Traded By	In Exchange For
Sept. 10, 1985	CAL A	—	OAK A	Two players to be named

(Oakland received P Robert Sharpnack and OF Jerome Nelson on Sept. 25, 1985.)

Johnny Sutton

Date	Traded To	Traded With	Traded By	In Exchange For
Oct. 22, 1976	STL N	—	TEX A	Mike Wallace

Dale Sveum

Date	Traded To	Traded With	Traded By	In Exchange For
Dec. 11, 1991	PHI N	—	MIL A	Bruce Ruffin
Aug. 9, 1992	CHI A	—	PHI N	Keith Shepherd

Russ Swan

Date	Traded To	Traded With	Traded By	In Exchange For
May 24, 1990	SEA A	—	SF N	Gary Eave

Bill Sweeney

Date	Traded To	Traded With	Traded By	In Exchange For
June 24, 1907	BOS N	Newt Randall	CHI N	Del Howard
Feb. 1914	CHI N	Cash	BOS N	Johnny Evers

Mark Sweeney

Date	Traded To	Traded With	Traded By	In Exchange For
July 8, 1995	STL N	Player to be named	CAL A	John Habyan

Rick Sweet

Date	Traded To	Traded With	Traded By	In Exchange For
May 21, 1982	SEA A	—	NY N	Cash

Leo Sweetland

Date	Traded To	Traded With	Traded By	In Exchange For
Oct. 13, 1930	CHI N	—	PHI N	Cash

Steve Swetonic

Date	Traded To	Traded With	Traded By	In Exchange For
Feb. 23, 1934	BOS N	—	PIT N	Cash

Bill Swift

Date	Traded To	Traded With	Traded By	In Exchange For
Dec. 8, 1939	BOS N	Cash	PIT N	Danny MacFayden

Bill Swift

Date	Traded To	Traded With	Traded By	In Exchange For
Dec. 11, 1991	SF N	Mike Jackson Dave Burba	SEA A	Kevin Mitchell Mike Remlinger
Apr. 8, 1995	CLR N	—	SF N	No compensation (free agent signing)

Bob Swift

Date	Traded To	Traded With	Traded By	In Exchange For
June 1, 1942	PHI A	Bob Harris	STL A	Frankie Hayes
Oct. 11, 1943	DET A	Don Heffner	PHI A	Rip Radcliff

Greg Swindell

Date	Traded To	Traded With	Traded By	In Exchange For
Nov. 15, 1991	CIN N	—	CLE A	Jack Armstrong Scott Scudder Minor league P Joe Turek
Dec. 4, 1992	HOU N	—	CIN N	No compensation (free agent signing)

Steve Swisher

Date	Traded To	Traded With	Traded By	In Exchange For
Dec. 11, 1973	CHI N	Steve Stone Ken Frailing Jim Kremmel	CHI A	Ron Santo
Dec. 8, 1977	STL N	Jerry Morales Cash	CHI N	Dave Rader Hector Cruz
Dec. 8, 1980	SD N	—	STL N	*see Rollie Fingers*

Ron Swoboda

Date	Traded To	Traded With	Traded By	In Exchange For
Mar. 31, 1971	MON N	Rich Hacker	NY N	Don Hahn
June 25, 1971	NY A	—	MON N	Ron Woods

Bob Sykes

Date	Traded To	Traded With	Traded By	In Exchange For
Dec. 4, 1978	STL N	minor league P Jack Murphy	DET A	Jerry Morales Aurelio Lopez
Oct. 21, 1981	NY A	—	STL N	Willie McGee

Jeff Tabaka

Date	Traded To	Traded With	Traded By	In Exchange For
May 12, 1994	SD N	—	PIT N	Waiver price
July 19, 1995	HOU N	Minor league P Rich Loiselle	SD N	Phil Plantier

Jerry Tabb

Date	Traded To	Traded With	Traded By	In Exchange For
Mar. 15, 1977	OAK A	—	CHI N	Cash

Pat Tabler

Date	Traded To	Traded With	Traded By	In Exchange For
Aug. 19, 1981	CHI N	—	NY A	Bill Caudill Jay Howell
(New York received Caudill on April 1, 1982, and Howell on August 2, 1982.)				
Jan. 25, 1983	CHI A	Scott Fletcher Randy Martz Dick Tidrow	CHI N	Steve Trout Warren Brusstar
Apr. 1, 1983	CLE A	—	CHI A	Jerry Dybzinski
June 3, 1988	KC A	—	CLE A	Bud Black
Aug. 30, 1990	NY N	—	KC A	Archie Corbin
Dec. 5, 1990	TOR A	—	NY N	No compensation (free agent signing)

Greg Tabor

Date	Traded To	Traded With	Traded By	In Exchange For
Mar. 17, 1988	CHI N	Dave Meier	TEX A	Ray Hayward

Jim Tabor

Date	Traded To	Traded With	Traded By	In Exchange For
Jan. 22, 1946	PHI N	—	BOS A	Cash

Doug Taitt

Date	Traded To	Traded With	Traded By	In Exchange For
May 23, 1929	CHI A	—	BOS A	Bill Barrett

Fred Talbot

Date	Traded To	Traded With	Traded By	In Exchange For
Jan. 20, 1965	KC A	Jim Landis Mike Hershberger	CHI A	Rocky Colavito
(Part of three-team trade involving Kansas City, Cleveland, and the Chicago White Sox.)				
June 10, 1966	NY A	Billy Bryan	KC A	Gil Blanco Roger Repoz Bill Stafford
May 20, 1969	SEA A	—	NY A	Jack Aker
Aug. 29, 1969	OAK A	—	SEA A	Bob Meyer Pete Koegel

John Tamargo

Date	Traded To	Traded With	Traded By	In Exchange For
July 18, 1978	SF N	—	STL N	Rob Dressler
June 13, 1979	MON N	—	SF N	Joe Pettini Cash

Vito Tamulis

Date	Traded To	Traded With	Traded By	In Exchange For
May 20, 1938	BKN N	—	STL A	Waiver price
Nov. 11, 1940	PHI N	Bill Crouch Mickey Livingston $100,000.	BKN N	Kirby Higbe
May 6, 1941	BKN N	—	PHI N	Lee Grissom

Frank Tanana

Date	Traded To	Traded With	Traded By	In Exchange For
Jan. 23, 1981	BOS A	Jim Dorsey Joe Rudi	CAL A	Fred Lynn Steve Renko
Jan. 6, 1982	TEX A	—	BOS A	No compensation (free agent signing)
June 20, 1985	DET A	—	TEX A	Minor league P Duane James
Dec. 10, 1992	NY N	—	DET A	No compensation (free agent signing)
Sept. 17, 1993	NY A	—	NY N	Kenny Greer

Jesse Tannehill

Date	Traded To	Traded With	Traded By	In Exchange For
Dec. 1903	BOS A	—	NY A	Long Tom Hughes
July 1908	WAS A	Bob Unglaub	BOS A	Casey Patten

Bruce Tanner

Date	Traded To	Traded With	Traded By	In Exchange For
Dec. 11, 1986	OAK A	Gene Nelson	CHI A	Donnie Hill
(Oakland received Tanner on Dec. 18, 1986.)				

Chuck Tanner

Date	Traded To	Traded With	Traded By	In Exchange For
June 8, 1957	CHI N	—	MIL N	Waiver price
Mar. 9, 1959	BOS A	—	CHI N	Riverboat Smith
Nov. 5, 1976	PIT N	—	OAK A	Manny Sanguillen $100,000.
(Tanner was named Pittsburgh manager.)				

Kevin Tapani

Date	Traded To	Traded With	Traded By	In Exchange For
Dec. 11, 1987	NY N	Jack Savage Wally Whitehurst	LA N	Jesse Orosco
(Part of a three-team trade involving Los Angeles, Oakland, and New York Mets.)				
July 31, 1989	MIN A	—	NY N	*see Frank Viola*
July 31, 1995	LA N	Mark Guthrie	MIN A	Greg Hansell Jose Parra Ron Coomer Player to be named
(Minnesota received OF Chris Latham on October 30, 1995.)				

Ted Tappe

Date	Traded To	Traded With	Traded By	In Exchange For
Oct. 1, 1954	CHI N	Jim Bolger Harry Perkowski	CIN N	Johnny Klippstein Jim Willis

Tony Tarasco

Date	Traded To	Traded With	Traded By	In Exchange For
Apr. 6, 1995	MON N	Roberto Kelly Minor league P Esteban Yan	ATL N	Marquis Grissom

Danny Tartabull

Date	Traded To	Traded With	Traded By	In Exchange For
Dec. 10, 1986	KC A	Rick Luecken	SEA A	Scott Bankhead Mike Kingery Steve Shields
Jan. 6, 1992	NY A	—	KC A	No compensation (free agent signing)
July 28, 1995	OAK A	—	NY A	Ruben Sierra Minor league P Jason Beverlin

Jose Tartabull

Date	Traded To	Traded With	Traded By	In Exchange For
Dec. 15, 1961	KC A	—	SF N	Joe Pignatano
June 13, 1966	BOS A	John Wyatt Rollie Sheldon	KC A	Jim Gosger Ken Sanders Guido Grilli
May 7, 1969	OAK A	—	BOS A	Cash

LaSchelle Tarver

Date	Traded To	Traded With	Traded By	In Exchange For
Nov. 13, 1985	BOS A	—	NY N	*see Bob Ojeda*

Date	Traded To		Traded With	Traded By		In Exchange For

Willie Tasby

Date	Traded To		Traded With	Traded By		In Exchange For
June 9, 1960	BOS	A	—	BAL	A	Gene Stephens
May 3, 1962	CLE	A	—	WAS	A	Steve Hamilton Don Rudolph

Bennie Tate

Date	Traded To		Traded With	Traded By		In Exchange For
June 16, 1930	CHI	A	Garland Braxton	WAS	A	Art Shires
Apr. 29, 1932	BOS	A	Smead Jolley Cliff Watwood	CHI	A	Charlie Berry

Jarvis Tatum

Date	Traded To		Traded With	Traded By		In Exchange For
Oct. 11, 1970	BOS	A	—	CAL	A	*see Tony Conigliaro*

Ken Tatum

Date	Traded To		Traded With	Traded By		In Exchange For
Oct. 11, 1970	BOS	A	—	CAL	A	*see Tony Conigliaro*
Oct. 26, 1973	STL	N	Reggie Smith	BOS	A	Rick Wise Bernie Carbo
Apr. 27, 1974	CHI	A	—	STL	N	Luis Alvarado

Tommy Tatum

Date	Traded To		Traded With	Traded By		In Exchange For
May 13, 1947	CIN	N	—	BKN	N	Cash

Eddie Taubensee

Date	Traded To		Traded With	Traded By		In Exchange For
Apr. 4, 1991	CLE	A	—	OAK	A	Waiver price
Dec. 10, 1991	HOU	N	Willie Blair	CLE	A	Kenny Lofton Dave Rohde
Apr. 19, 1994	CIN	N	—	HOU	N	Ross Powell Minor league P Marty Lister

Jackie Tavener

Date	Traded To		Traded With	Traded By		In Exchange For
Dec. 11, 1928	CLE	A	Ken Holloway	DET	A	George Uhle

Frank Taveras

Date	Traded To		Traded With	Traded By		In Exchange For
Apr. 19, 1979	NY	N	—	PIT	N	Tim Foli minor league P Greg Field
Dec. 11, 1981	MON	N	—	NY	N	Steve Ratzer Cash

Ben Taylor

Date	Traded To		Traded With	Traded By		In Exchange For
Feb. 14, 1952	DET	A	—	STL	A	*see Gene Bearden*

Carl Taylor

Date	Traded To		Traded With	Traded By		In Exchange For
Oct. 21, 1969	STL	N	minor league OF Frank Vanzin	PIT	N	Dave Giusti Dave Ricketts
Oct. 20, 1970	MIL	A	Jim Ellis	STL	N	Jerry McNertney George Lauzerique minor league P Jesse Higgins
Feb. 2, 1971	KC	A	—	MIL	A	Ellie Rodriguez
Sept. 3, 1971	PIT	N	—	KC	A	Cash

Chuck Taylor

Date	Traded To		Traded With	Traded By		In Exchange For
Feb. 17, 1964	HOU	N	Jim Beauchamp	STL	N	Carl Warwick
June 15, 1965	STL	N	Hal Woodeshick	HOU	N	Mike Cuellar Ron Taylor
Oct. 18, 1971	NY	N	—	STL	N	*see Jim Bibby*
Sept. 13, 1972	MIL	A	—	NY	N	Cash

Danny Taylor

Date	Traded To		Traded With	Traded By		In Exchange For
May 7, 1932	BKN	N	—	CHI	N	Cash

Dorn Taylor

Date	Traded To		Traded With	Traded By		In Exchange For
June 25, 1990	BAL	A	—	PIT	N	Jay Tibbs

(Baltimore received Taylor on September 5, 1990.)

Hawk Taylor

Date	Traded To		Traded With	Traded By		In Exchange For
Dec. 2, 1963	NY	N	—	MIL	N	Cash
July 24, 1967	CAL	A	—	NY	N	Don Wallace Cash

Jack Taylor

Date	Traded To		Traded With	Traded By		In Exchange For
Dec. 12, 1903	STL	N	Larry McLean	CHI	N	Three Finger Brown Jack O'Neill
July 1, 1906	CHI	N	—	STL	N	Fred Beebe Pete Noonan Cash

Joe Taylor

Date	Traded To		Traded With	Traded By		In Exchange For
Dec. 5, 1957	STL	N	Curt Flood	CIN	N	Marty Kutyna Ted Wieand Willard Schmidt
July 25, 1958	BAL	A	—	STL	N	Waiver price

Ron Taylor

Date	Traded To		Traded With	Traded By		In Exchange For
Dec. 15, 1962	STL	N	Jack Kubiszyn	CLE	A	Fred Whitfield
June 15, 1965	HOU	N	Mike Cuellar	STL	N	Hal Woodeshick Chuck Taylor
Feb. 10, 1967	NY	N	—	HOU	N	Cash
Oct. 20, 1971	MON	N	—	NY	N	Cash

Sammy Taylor

Date	Traded To		Traded With	Traded By		In Exchange For
Dec. 5, 1957	CHI	N	Taylor Phillips	MIL	N	Eddie Haas Don Kaiser Bob Rush
Apr. 26, 1962	NY	N	—	CHI	N	Bobby Gene Smith
July 1, 1963	CIN	N	Charlie Neal	NY	N	Jesse Gonder
Aug. 1, 1963	CLE	A	—	CIN	N	Gene Green

Scott Taylor

Date	Traded To		Traded With	Traded By		In Exchange For
Apr. 14, 1995	TEX	A	—			
Apr. 14, 1995	TEX	A	—	MIL	A	David Hulse

Tony Taylor

Date	Traded To		Traded With	Traded By		In Exchange For
May 13, 1960	PHI	N	Cal Neeman	CHI	N	Ed Bouchee Don Cardwell
June 12, 1971	DET	A	—	PHI	N	Minor league Ps Mike Fremuth and Carl Cavanaugh

Wade Taylor

Date	Traded To		Traded With	Traded By		In Exchange For
Dec. 22, 1987	NY	A	—	SEA	A	*see Steve Trout*

Zack Taylor

Date	Traded To		Traded With	Traded By		In Exchange For
Oct. 7, 1925	BOS	N	Jimmy Johnston Eddie Brown	BKN	N	Jesse Barnes Mickey O'Neil Gus Felix
June 12, 1927	NY	N	Larry Benton Herb Thomas	BOS	N	Hugh McQuillan Kent Greenfield Doc Farrell
Feb. 1928	BOS	N	—	NY	N	Cash
July 6, 1929	CHI	N	—	BOS	N	Waiver price

Bud Teachout

Date	Traded To		Traded With	Traded By		In Exchange For
Dec. 1931	STL	N	Hack Wilson	CHI	N	Burleigh Grimes

Birdie Tebbetts

Date	Traded To		Traded With	Traded By		In Exchange For
May 20, 1947	BOS	A	—	DET	A	Hal Wagner
Dec. 13, 1950	CLE	A	—	BOS	A	Cash

Wil Tejada

Date	Traded To		Traded With	Traded By		In Exchange For
Nov. 20, 1988	SF	N	—	MON	N	Angel Escobar

Kent Tekulve

Date	Traded To		Traded With	Traded By		In Exchange For
Apr. 20, 1985	PHI	N	—	PIT	N	Al Holland Minor league P Frankie Griffin

Tom Tellmann

Date	Traded To		Traded With	Traded By		In Exchange For
Oct. 15, 1982	MIL	A	—	SD	N	Minor league Ps Weldon Swift Tim Cook

Johnny Temple

Date	Traded To	Traded With	Traded By	In Exchange For
Dec. 15, 1959	CLE A	—	CIN N	Cal McLish Gordy Coleman Billy Martin
Nov. 16, 1961	BAL A	—	CLE A	Ray Barker Harry Chiti minor leaguer Art Kay
Aug. 11, 1962	HOU N	—	BAL A	Cash

Garry Templeton

Date	Traded To	Traded With	Traded By	In Exchange For
Dec. 10, 1981	SD N	Sixto Lezcano Luis DeLeon	STL N	Ozzie Smith Steve Mura Al Olmsted

(Templeton and Smith were exchanged on February 11, 1982; Olmsted and DeLeon were exchanged on February 19.)

Date	Traded To	Traded With	Traded By	In Exchange For
May 31, 1991	NY N	—	SD N	Tim Teufel

Gene Tenace

Date	Traded To	Traded With	Traded By	In Exchange For
Dec. 14, 1976	SD N	—	OAK A	No compensation (free agent signing)
Dec. 8, 1980	STL N	Rollie Fingers Bob Shirley Bob Geren	SD N	Terry Kennedy Steve Swisher Mike Phillips John Littlefield John Urrea Kim Seaman Al Olmsted
Dec. 1, 1982	PIT N	—	STL N	No compensation (free agent signing)

Fred Tenney

Date	Traded To	Traded With	Traded By	In Exchange For
Dec. 3, 1907	NY N	Al Bridwell Tom Needham	BOS N	Dan McGann Frank Bowerman Bill Dahlen George Browne George Ferguson

Frank Tepedino

Date	Traded To	Traded With	Traded By	In Exchange For
June 7, 1971	MIL A	Bobby Mitchell	NY A	Danny Walton
June 7, 1973	ATL N	Dave Cheadle Wayne Nordhagen Al Closter	NY A	Pat Dobson

Greg Terlecky

Date	Traded To	Traded With	Traded By	In Exchange For
Dec. 12, 1975	CHI A	Buddy Bradford	STL N	Lee Richard

Jeff Terpko

Date	Traded To	Traded With	Traded By	In Exchange For
Nov. 3, 1970	PHI N	Greg Goossen Gene Martin	WAS A	Curt Flood
Mar. 15, 1977	MON N	—	TEX A	Rodney Scott

Walt Terrell

Date	Traded To	Traded With	Traded By	In Exchange For
Apr. 1, 1982	NY N	Ron Darling	TEX A	Lee Mazzilli
Dec. 7, 1984	DET A	—	NY N	Howard Johnson
Oct. 28, 1988	SD N	—	DET A	Keith Moreland Chris Brown
July 22, 1989	NY A	Fred Toliver	SD N	Mike Pagliarulo Don Schulze

(New York received Toliver on Sept. 27, 1989.)

Date	Traded To	Traded With	Traded By	In Exchange For
Nov. 29, 1989	PIT N	—	NY A	No compensation (free agent signing)

Ralph Terry

Date	Traded To	Traded With	Traded By	In Exchange For
June 15, 1957	KC A	Billy Martin Woodie Held Bob Martyn	NY A	Ryne Duren Jim Pisoni Milt Graff Harry Simpson
May 26, 1959	NY A	Hector Lopez	KC A	Johnny Kucks Tom Sturdivant Jerry Lumpe
Sept. 5, 1964	CLE A	Bud Daley $75,000.	NY A	Pedro Ramos

Ralph Terry *continued*

Date	Traded To	Traded With	Traded By	In Exchange For
Apr. 6, 1966	KC A	Cash	CLE A	John O'Donoghue
Aug. 6, 1966	NY N	—	KC A	Cash

Scott Terry

Date	Traded To	Traded With	Traded By	In Exchange For
Aug. 31, 1987	STL N	—	CIN N	Pat Perry

(St. Louis received Terry on September 3, 1987.)

Zeb Terry

Date	Traded To	Traded With	Traded By	In Exchange For
Jan. 1920	CHI N	—	PIT N	Cash

Wayne Terwilliger

Date	Traded To	Traded With	Traded By	In Exchange For
June 15, 1951	BKN N	*see Andy Pafko*	CHI N	—
Sept. 23, 1952	WAS A	—	BKN N	Waiver price

Dick Tettelbach

Date	Traded To	Traded With	Traded By	In Exchange For
Feb. 8, 1956	WAS A	*see Whitey Herzog*	NY A	—

Mickey Tettleton

Date	Traded To	Traded With	Traded By	In Exchange For
Jan. 11, 1991	DET A	—	BAL A	Jeff Robinson
Apr. 12, 1995	TEX A	—	DET A	No compensation (free agent signing)

Tim Teufel

Date	Traded To	Traded With	Traded By	In Exchange For
Jan. 16, 1986	NY N	Minor league OF Pat Crosby	MIN A	Billy Beane Bill Latham Joe Klink
May 31, 1991	SD N	—	NY N	Garry Templeton

Bob Tewksbury

Date	Traded To	Traded With	Traded By	In Exchange For
July 12, 1987	CHI N	Dean Wilkins Rich Scheid	NY A	Steve Trout Cash
Apr. 8, 1995	TEX A	—	STL N	No compensation (free agent signing)
Dec. 18, 1995	SD N	—	TEX A	No compensation (free agent signing)

Moe Thacker

Date	Traded To	Traded With	Traded By	In Exchange For
Oct. 17, 1962	STL N	—	CHI N	*see Larry Jackson*

Ron Theobald

Date	Traded To	Traded With	Traded By	In Exchange For
May 11, 1970	MIL A	Hank Allen	WAS A	Wayne Comer

Tommy Thevenow

Date	Traded To	Traded With	Traded By	In Exchange For
Dec. 13, 1928	PHI N	—	STL N	Heinie Sand $10,000.
Nov. 6, 1930	PIT N	Claude Willoughby	PHI N	Dick Bartell
Dec. 12, 1935	CIN N	—	PIT N	Cash
Jan. 6, 1937	BOS N	—	CIN N	Cash

Henry Thielman

Date	Traded To	Traded With	Traded By	In Exchange For
Jan. 1903	BKN N	—	CIN N	Cash

Jake Thielman

Date	Traded To	Traded With	Traded By	In Exchange For
Aug. 1908	BOS A	—	NY A	Cash

Bobby Thigpen

Date	Traded To	Traded With	Traded By	In Exchange For
Aug. 10, 1993	PHI N	—	CHI A	Jose DeLeon
Jan. 31, 1994	SEA A	—	PHI N	No compensation (free agent signing)

J. J. Thobe

Date	Traded To	Traded With	Traded By	In Exchange For
Feb. 14, 1994	MON N	Minor league 1B Dave Duplessis	CLE A	Chris Nabholz
Dec. 10, 1995	BOS A	—	MON N	Waiver price

Bud Thomas

Date	Traded To	Traded With	Traded By	In Exchange For
May 1, 1939	WAS A	—	PHI A	Waiver price
May 18, 1939	DET A	—	WAS A	Waiver price

Derrel Thomas

Date	Traded To	Traded With	Traded By	In Exchange For
Dec. 3, 1971	SD N	Bill Greif Mark Schaeffer	HOU N	Dave Roberts
Dec. 6, 1974	SF N	—	SD N	Tito Fuentes Butch Metzger
Feb. 28, 1978	SD N	—	SF N	Mike Ivie
Nov. 14, 1978	LA N	—	SD N	No compensation (free agent signing)
Feb. 7, 1984	MON N	—	LA N	No compensation (free agent signing)
Sept. 6, 1984	CAL A	—	MON N	Cash

Frank Thomas

Date	Traded To	Traded With	Traded By	In Exchange For
Jan. 30, 1959	CIN N	Whammy Douglas Jim Pendleton Johnny Powers	PIT N	Smoky Burgess Harvey Haddix Don Hoak
Dec. 6, 1959	CHI N	—	CIN N	Bill Henry Lou Jackson Lee Walls
May 9, 1961	MIL N	—	CHI N	Mel Roach
Nov. 28, 1961	NY N	—	MIL N	Gus Bell Cash
		(Milwaukee received Bell on May 21, 1962.)		
Aug. 7, 1964	PHI N	—	NY N	Gary Kroll Wayne Graham Cash
July 10, 1965	HOU N	—	PHI N	Cash
Sept. 1, 1965	MIL N	—	HOU N	Minor league IF Mickey Sinnerud

Fred Thomas

Date	Traded To	Traded With	Traded By	In Exchange For
Apr. 12, 1916	BOS A	Sad Sam Jones $55,000.	CLE A	Tris Speaker
Jan. 1919	PHI A	—	BOS A	Cash
July 1920	WAS A	—	PHI A	Red Shannon

George Thomas

Date	Traded To	Traded With	Traded By	In Exchange For
June 26, 1961	LA A	—	DET A	Cash
June 15, 1963	DET A	Cash	LA A	Frank Kostro Paul Foytack
Oct. 4, 1965	BOS A	George Smith	DET A	Bill Monbouquette

Gorman Thomas

Date	Traded To	Traded With	Traded By	In Exchange For
Aug. 20, 1977	TEX A	—	MIL A	Ed Kirkpatrick
Feb. 8, 1978	MIL A	—	TEX A	Cash
June 6, 1983	CLE A	Ernie Camacho Jamie Easterly	MIL A	Rick Manning Rick Waits
Dec. 7, 1983	SEA A	Jack Perconte	CLE A	Tony Bernazard

Herb Thomas

Date	Traded To	Traded With	Traded By	In Exchange For
June 12, 1927	NY N	Zack Taylor Larry Benton	BOS N	Hugh McQuillan Kent Greenfield Doc Farrell

Ira Thomas

Date	Traded To	Traded With	Traded By	In Exchange For
Dec. 12, 1907	DET A	—	NY A	Cash
Dec. 8, 1908	PHI A	—	DET A	Cash

Kite Thomas

Date	Traded To	Traded With	Traded By	In Exchange For
June 30, 1953	WAS A	—	PHI A	Waiver price
Mar. 27, 1954	CHI A	—	WAS A	Tom Wright

Lee Thomas

Date	Traded To	Traded With	Traded By	In Exchange For
May 8, 1961	LA A	Ryne Duren Johnny James	NY A	Tex Clevenger Bob Cerv
June 4, 1964	BOS A	—	LA A	Lu Clinton
Dec. 15, 1965	MIL N	Arnold Earley Jay Ritchie	BOS A	Bob Sadowski Dan Osinski
May 28, 1966	CHI N	—	ATL N	Ted Abernathy

Lee Thomas *continued*

Date	Traded To	Traded With	Traded By	In Exchange For
Feb. 9, 1968	HOU N	—	CHI N	Minor league OFs Tom Murray Levi Brown

Leo Thomas

Date	Traded To	Traded With	Traded By	In Exchange For
June 15, 1950	NY A	—	STL A	*see Snuffy Stirnweiss*
June 15, 1952	CHI A	Tom Wright	STL A	Willie Miranda Al Zarilla

Mike Thomas

Date	Traded To	Traded With	Traded By	In Exchange For
July 15, 1991	MON N	Ron Darling	NY N	Tim Burke

Myles Thomas

Date	Traded To	Traded With	Traded By	In Exchange For
June 18, 1929	WAS A	—	NY A	Cash

Pinch Thomas

Date	Traded To	Traded With	Traded By	In Exchange For
Dec. 14, 1917	PHI A	Vean Gregg Merlin Kopp $60,000.	BOS A	Amos Strunk Joe Bush Wally Schang
June 1, 1918	CLE A	—	BOS A	Cash

Roy Thomas

Date	Traded To	Traded With	Traded By	In Exchange For
Apr. 1908	PIT N	—	PHI N	Cash
Feb. 1909	BOS N	—	PIT N	Cash

Roy Thomas

Date	Traded To	Traded With	Traded By	In Exchange For
Dec. 10, 1975	CHI A	Dick Ruthven Alan Bannister	PHI N	Jim Kaat Mike Buskey
Mar. 30, 1977	HOU N	—	SEA A	Larry Milbourne
June 23, 1978	STL N	—	HOU N	Cash
Dec. 9, 1981	SEA A	—	OAK A	Rusty McNealy minor league P Tim Hallgren

Stan Thomas

Date	Traded To	Traded With	Traded By	In Exchange For
Dec. 9, 1975	CLE A	Ron Pruitt	TEX A	John Ellis
Aug. 2, 1977	NY A	—	SEA A	Cash
Dec. 12, 1977	CHI A	minor league P Ed Ricks and cash	NY A	Jim Spencer Tommy Cruz minor league P Bob Polinsky

Tommy Thomas

Date	Traded To	Traded With	Traded By	In Exchange For
June 11, 1932	WAS A	—	CHI A	Cash
May 20, 1935	PHI N	—	WAS A	Waiver price
Jan. 1936	STL A	—	PHI N	Cash

Valmy Thomas

Date	Traded To	Traded With	Traded By	In Exchange For
Dec. 3, 1958	PHI N	Ruben Gomez	SF N	Jack Sanford

Gary Thomasson

Date	Traded To	Traded With	Traded By	In Exchange For
Mar. 15, 1978	OAK A	—	SF N	*see Vida Blue*
June 15, 1978	NY A	—	OAK A	Dell Alston Mickey Klutts $50,000.
Feb. 15, 1979	LA N	—	NY A	Brad Gulden

Bobby Thompson

Date	Traded To	Traded With	Traded By	In Exchange For
Dec. 6, 1978	SEA A	—	TEX A	Cash

Danny Thompson

Date	Traded To	Traded With	Traded By	In Exchange For
June 1, 1976	TEX A	—	MIN A	*see Roy Smalley*

Fresco Thompson

Date	Traded To	Traded With	Traded By	In Exchange For
Jan. 9, 1927	PHI N	Jack Scott	NY N	George Harper Butch Henline

(Part of three-team trade involving Philadelphia, New York, and Brooklyn.)

Fresco Thompson *continued*

Date	Traded To	Traded With	Traded By	In Exchange For
Oct. 14, 1930	BKN N	Lefty O'Doul	PHI N	Clise Dudley Jumbo Elliott Hal Lee Cash

Jason Thompson

Date	Traded To	Traded With	Traded By	In Exchange For
May 27, 1980	CAL A	—	DET A	Al Cowens
Apr. 1, 1981	PIT N	—	CAL A	Ed Ott Mickey Mahler
Apr. 4, 1986	MON N	—	PIT N	two players to be named

(Pittsburgh received OF Ben Abner and IF Ronnie Giddens on April 7, 1985.)

Mike Thompson

Date	Traded To	Traded With	Traded By	In Exchange For
Feb. 1, 1973	STL N	—	TEX A	Charles Hudson Mike Nagy

(Thompson and Nagy were exchanged on March 31.)

Date	Traded To	Traded With	Traded By	In Exchange For
Sept. 10, 1974	ATL N	—	STL N	Cash
Apr. 7, 1976	CIN N	—	ATL N	Terry Crowley
Nov. 8, 1976	TEX A	—	CIN N	Minor league P Art DeFilippis

Milt Thompson

Date	Traded To	Traded With	Traded By	In Exchange For
Dec. 10, 1985	PHI N	Steve Bedrosian	ATL N	Ozzie Virgil Pete Smith
Dec. 16, 1988	STL N	—	PHI N	Curt Ford Steve Lake
Dec. 9, 1992	PHI N	—	STL N	No compensation (free agent signing)
July 31, 1994	HOU N	—	PHI N	Tom Edens

Rich Thompson

Date	Traded To	Traded With	Traded By	In Exchange For
Dec. 16, 1985	MIL A	—	CLE A	Minor league P Scott Roberts

Ryan Thompson

Date	Traded To	Traded With	Traded By	In Exchange For
Aug. 27, 1992	NY N	Jeff Kent	TOR A	David Cone

(New York received Thompson on September 1, 1992.)

Scot Thompson

Date	Traded To	Traded With	Traded By	In Exchange For
Aug. 1, 1985	MON N	player to be named	SF N	Dan Driessen

(Montreal returned Bill Laskey on Oct. 24 to complete deal.)

Tim Thompson

Date	Traded To	Traded With	Traded By	In Exchange For
Apr. 16, 1956	KC A	—	BKN N	Lee Wheat Tom Saffell Cash
Nov. 20, 1957	DET A	*see Billy Martin*	KC A	—

Tommy Thompson

Date	Traded To	Traded With	Traded By	In Exchange For
Apr. 27, 1939	STL A	—	CHI A	Cash

Bobby Thomson

Date	Traded To	Traded With	Traded By	In Exchange For
Feb. 1, 1954	MIL N	Sammy Calderone	NY N	Johnny Antonelli Don Liddle Ebba St. Claire Billy Klaus $50,000.
June 15, 1957	NY N	Danny O'Connell Ray Crone	MIL N	Red Schoendienst
Apr. 3, 1958	CHI N	—	SF N	Bob Speake Cash
Dec. 1, 1959	BOS A	—	CHI N	Al Schroll

Dickie Thon

Date	Traded To	Traded With	Traded By	In Exchange For
Apr. 1, 1981	HOU N	—	CAL A	Ken Forsch
Feb. 18, 1988	SD N	—	HOU N	No compensation (free agent signing)
Jan. 27, 1989	PHI N	—	SD N	Cash
Dec. 13, 1991	TEX A	—	PHI N	No compensation (free agent signing)

Jack Thoney

Date	Traded To	Traded With	Traded By	In Exchange For
Sept. 1902	BAL A	—	CLE A	
May 8, 1904	NY A	—	WAS A	Cash

Hank Thormahlen

Date	Traded To	Traded With	Traded By	In Exchange For
Dec. 15, 1920	BOS A	—	NY A	*see Waite Hoyt*

Paul Thormodsgard

Date	Traded To	Traded With	Traded By	In Exchange For
Dec. 7, 1979	PHI N	—	MIN A	Pete Mackanin

Andre Thornton

Date	Traded To	Traded With	Traded By	In Exchange For
June 15, 1972	ATL N	Joe Hoerner	PHI N	Jim Nash Gary Neibauer
May 19, 1973	CHI N	—	ATL N	Joe Pepitone
May 17, 1976	MON N	—	CHI N	Steve Renko Larry Biittner
Dec. 10, 1976	CLE A	—	MON N	Jackie Brown

Lou Thornton

Date	Traded To	Traded With	Traded By	In Exchange For
Mar. 17, 1989	PIT N	—	MIL A	Ruben Rodriguez

Jim Thorpe

Date	Traded To	Traded With	Traded By	In Exchange For
Apr. 24, 1917	CIN N	—	NY N	Cash

(Thorpe was returned to the Giants on August 1, 1917.)

Date	Traded To	Traded With	Traded By	In Exchange For
May 21, 1919	BOS N	—	NY N	Pat Ragan

Faye Throneberry

Date	Traded To	Traded With	Traded By	In Exchange For
Apr. 29, 1957	WAS A	Milt Bolling Russ Kemmerer	BOS A	Dean Stone Bob Chakales

Marv Throneberry

Date	Traded To	Traded With	Traded By	In Exchange For
Dec. 11, 1959	KC A	Hank Bauer Don Larsen Norm Siebern	NY A	Roger Maris Joe De Maestri Kent Hadley
June 8, 1961	BAL A	—	KC A	Gene Stephens
May 9, 1962	NY N	—	BAL A	Hobie Landrith Cash

George Throop

Date	Traded To	Traded With	Traded By	In Exchange For
Apr. 27, 1979	HOU N	—	KC A	Keith Drumright

Gary Thurman

Date	Traded To	Traded With	Traded By	In Exchange For
Mar. 26, 1993	DET A	—	KC A	Waiver price

Mark Thurmond

Date	Traded To	Traded With	Traded By	In Exchange For
July 9, 1986	DET A	—	SD N	Dave LaPoint
Feb. 27, 1988	BAL A	—	DET A	Ray Knight
May 1, 1990	SF N	—	HOU N	Cash

Sloppy Thurston

Date	Traded To	Traded With	Traded By	In Exchange For
May 12, 1923	CHI A	—	STL A	Cash
Jan. 15, 1927	WAS A	Leo Mangum	CHI A	Roger Peckinpaugh

Luis Tiant

Date	Traded To	Traded With	Traded By	In Exchange For
Dec. 10, 1969	MIN A	Stan Williams	CLE A	Dean Chance Bob Miller Graig Nettles Ted Uhlaender
Nov. 13, 1978	NY A	—	BOS A	No compensation (free agent signing)

Jay Tibbs

Date	Traded To	Traded With	Traded By	In Exchange For
June 15, 1984	CIN N	Eddie Williams Minor league P Matt Bullinger	NY N	Bruce Berenyi
Dec. 19, 1985	MON N	Andy McGaffigan Dann Bilardello John Stuper	CIN N	Bill Gullickson Sal Butera
Feb. 16, 1988	BAL A	Minor league P Al Cardwood	MON N	John Hoover Minor league Ps Doug Cinnella Rick Carriger
June 25, 1990	PIT N	—	BAL A	Dorn Taylor

(Baltimore received Taylor on September 5, 1990.)

Dick Tidrow

Date	Traded To	Traded With	Traded By	In Exchange For
Apr. 27, 1974	NY A	Chris Chambliss Cecil Upshaw	CLE A	Fritz Peterson Steve Kline Fred Beene Tom Buskey
May 23, 1979	CHI N	—	NY A	Ray Burris
Jan. 25, 1983	CHI A	Scott Fletcher Pat Tabler Randy Martz	CHI N	Steve Trout Warren Brusstar
Jan. 27, 1984	NY N	—	CHI A	No compensation (free agent signing)

Bobby Tiefenauer

Date	Traded To	Traded With	Traded By	In Exchange For
Sept. 8, 1955	DET A	—	STL N	Ben Flowers
Mar. 30, 1968	CHI N	—	CLE A	Rob Gardner

Verle Tiefenthaler

Date	Traded To	Traded With	Traded By	In Exchange For
Nov. 30, 1961	CHI A	—	SF N	*see Billy Pierce*

Cotton Tierney

Date	Traded To	Traded With	Traded By	In Exchange For
May 22, 1923	PHI N	Whitey Glazner $50,000.	PIT N	Lee Meadows Johnny Rawlings
Dec. 15, 1923	BOS N	—	PHI N	Hod Ford Ray Powell

(Powell announced his intention to retire after the 1924 season. He remained with Boston, and Philadelphia received cash instead.)

Date	Traded To	Traded With	Traded By	In Exchange For
Feb. 4, 1925	BKN N	—	BOS N	Bernie Neis

Les Tietje

Date	Traded To	Traded With	Traded By	In Exchange For
May 5, 1936	STL A	—	CHI A	Sugar Cain

Bob Tillman

Date	Traded To	Traded With	Traded By	In Exchange For
Aug. 8, 1967	NY A	—	BOS A	Cash
Dec. 7, 1967	ATL N	Dale Roberts	NY A	Bobby Cox
Dec. 2, 1970	MIL A	—	ATL N	Hank Allen minor leaguers P Paul Click and IF John Ryan

Rusty Tillman

Date	Traded To	Traded With	Traded By	In Exchange For
Mar. 31, 1985	SD N	—	NY N	Rick Lancellotti
Apr. 18, 1986	OAK A	—	SD N	Bob Stoddard Minor league OF Kevin Russ

Thad Tillotson

Date	Traded To	Traded With	Traded By	In Exchange For
Sept. 10, 1966	NY A	Cash	LA N	Dick Schofield

Tom Timmerman

Date	Traded To	Traded With	Traded By	In Exchange For
June 15, 1973	CLE A	Kevin Collins	DET A	Ed Farmer

Ron Tingley

Date	Traded To	Traded With	Traded By	In Exchange For
Sept. 6, 1989	CAL A	—	CLE A	Mark McLemore

(Cleveland received McLemore on August 17, 1990.)

Joe Tinker

Date	Traded To	Traded With	Traded By	In Exchange For
Dec. 15, 1912	CIN N	Grover Lowdermilk Harry Chapman	CHI N	Bert Humphries Red Corriden Pete Knisely Art Phelan Mike Mitchell
Dec. 1913	BKN N	—	CIN N	Dick Egan $6,500.

(Tinker demanded $2,000 of the purchase price; when this was refused, he jumped to the Federal League and the deal was cancelled.)

Date	Traded To	Traded With	Traded By	In Exchange For
Feb. 10, 1916	CHI N	*see Three Finger Brown*	CHI F	—

Bud Tinning

Date	Traded To	Traded With	Traded By	In Exchange For
Nov. 21, 1934	STL N	Dick Ward Cash	CHI N	Tex Carleton

Lee Tinsley

Date	Traded To	Traded With	Traded By	In Exchange For
July 26, 1991	CLE A	Minor league P Apolinar Garcia	OAK A	Brook Jacoby
Sept. 21, 1992	SEA A	—	CLE A	Waiver price

Lee Tinsley *continued*

Date	Traded To	Traded With	Traded By	In Exchange For
Mar. 22, 1994	BOS A	—	SEA A	Player to be named

(Seattle received P Jim Smith on September 15, 1994.)

Joe Tipton

Date	Traded To	Traded With	Traded By	In Exchange For
Nov. 22, 1948	CHI A	—	CLE A	Joe Haynes
Oct. 19, 1949	PHI A	—	CHI A	Nellie Fox
June 23, 1952	CLE A	—	PHI A	Waiver price
Jan. 20, 1954	WAS A	—	CLE A	Mickey Grasso

John Titus

Date	Traded To	Traded With	Traded By	In Exchange For
July 1, 1912	BOS N	—	PHI N	Doc Miller

Dave Tobik

Date	Traded To	Traded With	Traded By	In Exchange For
Mar. 24, 1983	TEX A	—	DET A	Johnny Grubb

Jack Tobin

Date	Traded To	Traded With	Traded By	In Exchange For
Feb. 1926	WAS A	Joe Bush	STL A	Tom Zachary Win Ballou
July 31, 1926	BOS A	—	WAS A	Cash

Jim Tobin

Date	Traded To	Traded With	Traded By	In Exchange For
Dec. 6, 1939	BOS N	Cash	PIT N	Johnny Lanning
Aug. 1945	DET A	—	BOS N	Cash

Johnny Tobin

Date	Traded To	Traded With	Traded By	In Exchange For
Feb. 10, 1916	STL A	*see Eddie Plank*	STL F	—

Al Todd

Date	Traded To	Traded With	Traded By	In Exchange For
Nov. 21, 1935	PIT N	—	PHI N	Claude Passeau Earl Grace
Dec. 16, 1938	BOS N	Johnny Dickshot Cash	PIT N	Ray Mueller
Mar. 31, 1939	BKN N	—	BOS N	Bill Posedel
Dec. 8, 1939	CHI N	—	BKN N	Gus Mancuso Newt Kimball

Jackson Todd

Date	Traded To	Traded With	Traded By	In Exchange For
Mar. 27, 1978	PHI N	—	NY N	Minor league C Ed Cuervo

Jim Todd

Date	Traded To	Traded With	Traded By	In Exchange For
Apr. 6, 1975	OAK A	—	CHI N	Champ Summers Cash
Mar. 15, 1977	CHI N	—	OAK A	Joe Coleman
Apr. 20, 1977	SEA A	—	CHI N	Pete Broberg

Phil Todt

Date	Traded To	Traded With	Traded By	In Exchange For
Feb. 3, 1931	PHI A	—	BOS A	Cash

Bobby Tolan

Date	Traded To	Traded With	Traded By	In Exchange For
Oct. 11, 1968	CIN N	Wayne Granger	STL N	Vada Pinson
Nov. 9, 1973	SD N	Dave Tomlin	CIN N	Clay Kirby

Fred Toliver

Date	Traded To	Traded With	Traded By	In Exchange For
Nov. 4, 1981	CIN N	minor league P Bryan Ryder	NY A	Ken Griffey
Aug. 8, 1985	PHI N	—	CIN N	*see Bo Diaz*
Feb. 5, 1988	MIN A	—	PHI N	Minor league C Chris Calvert
June 29, 1989	SD N	—	MIN A	Greg Booker
July 22, 1989	NY A	Walt Terrell	SD N	Mike Pagliarulo Don Schulze

(New York received Toliver on Sept. 27, 1989.)

Wayne Tolleson

Date	Traded To	Traded With	Traded By	In Exchange For
Nov. 25, 1985	CHI A	Dave Schmidt	TEX A	Ed Correa Scott Fletcher Jose Mota

(Texas received Mota on December 12, 1985)

Wayne Tolleson *continued*

Date	Traded To	Traded With	Traded By	In Exchange For
July 30, 1986	NY A	Ron Kittle Joel Skinner	CHI A	Ron Hassey Carlos Martinez Bill Lindsey

(Chicago received Lindsey on Dec. 24, 1986.)

Dick Tomanek

Date	Traded To	Traded With	Traded By	In Exchange For
June 15, 1958	KC A	Roger Maris Preston Ward	CLE A	Woodie Held Vic Power

Dave Tomlin

Date	Traded To	Traded With	Traded By	In Exchange For
Nov. 9, 1973	SD N	Bobby Tolan	CIN N	Clay Kirby
Jan. 25, 1978	TEX A	$125,000.	SD N	Gaylord Perry
Mar. 28, 1978	CIN N	—	TEX A	Cash
Sept. 8, 1982	MON N	—	CIN N	Cash
Aug. 2, 1983	PIT N	—	MON N	Cash

Ron Tompkins

Date	Traded To	Traded With	Traded By	In Exchange For
Oct. 20, 1967	CIN N	—	KC A	Floyd Robinson Darrell Osteen
Oct. 21, 1969	KC A	—	ATL N	Dave Wickersham

Fred Toney

Date	Traded To	Traded With	Traded By	In Exchange For
Feb. 22, 1915	CIN N	—	BKN N	Waiver price
July 25, 1918	NY N	—	CIN N	Cash
July 30, 1922	BOS N	Larry Benton $100,000.	NY N	Hugh McQuillan

(Toney refused to report and remained Giants' property.)

Date	Traded To	Traded With	Traded By	In Exchange For
Oct. 1922	STL N	—	NY N	Waiver price

Jeff Torborg

Date	Traded To	Traded With	Traded By	In Exchange For
Mar. 13, 1971	CAL A	—	LA N	Cash
Dec. 6, 1973	STL N	—	CAL A	John Andrews

Earl Torgeson

Date	Traded To	Traded With	Traded By	In Exchange For
Feb. 16, 1953	PHI N	—	MIL N	Russ Meyer Cash

(Part of four-team trade involving Milwaukee Braves, Philadelphia Phillies, Brooklyn, and Cincinnati.)

Date	Traded To	Traded With	Traded By	In Exchange For
June 15, 1955	DET A	—	PHI N	Cash
June 14, 1957	CHI A	—	DET A	Dave Philley

Joe Torre

Date	Traded To	Traded With	Traded By	In Exchange For
Mar. 17, 1969	STL N	—	ATL N	Orlando Cepeda
Oct. 13, 1974	NY N	—	STL N	Ray Sadecki Tommy Moore

Pablo Torrealba

Date	Traded To	Traded With	Traded By	In Exchange For
Mar. 29, 1977	OAK A	—	ATL N	Cash
Mar. 30, 1978	CHI A	—	OAK A	Steve Renko Jim Essian

Angel Torres

Date	Traded To	Traded With	Traded By	In Exchange For
Nov. 6, 1976	MON N	Bill Greif Sam Mejias	STL N	Steve Dunning Pat Scanlon Tony Scott
May 21, 1977	CIN N	Shane Rawley	MON N	Santo Alcala

Hector Torres

Date	Traded To	Traded With	Traded By	In Exchange For
Aug. 7, 1967	HOU N	—	CAL A	Jim Weaver
Oct. 12, 1970	CHI N	—	HOU N	Roger Metzger
Apr. 7, 1972	MON N	Hal Breeden	CHI N	Dan McGinn
Apr. 4, 1973	HOU N	—	MON N	Cash
Oct. 23, 1973	CHI A	—	HOU N	Dan Neumeier
Dec. 8, 1976	CLE A	Johnny Grubb Fred Kendall	SD N	George Hendrick
Mar. 29, 1977	TOR A	—	CLE A	John Lowenstein

Rusty Torres

Date	Traded To	Traded With	Traded By	In Exchange For
Nov. 27, 1972	CLE A	—	NY A	*see Graig Nettles*
Sept. 12, 1974	CAL A	Ken Suarez Cash	CLE A	Frank Robinson

Rusty Torres *continued*

Date	Traded To	Traded With	Traded By	In Exchange For
May 16, 1978	CHI A	Claudell Washington	TEX A	Bobby Bonds

Salomon Torres

Date	Traded To	Traded With	Traded By	In Exchange For
May 20, 1995	SEA A	—	SF N	Shawn Estes Minor league IF Wilson Delgado

Mike Torrez

Date	Traded To	Traded With	Traded By	In Exchange For
June 15, 1971	MON N	—	STL N	Bob Reynolds
Dec. 4, 1974	BAL A	Ken Singleton	MON N	Dave McNally Rich Coggins minor league P Bill Kirkpatrick
Apr. 2, 1976	OAK A	Don Baylor Paul Mitchell	BAL A	Reggie Jackson Ken Holtzman minor leaguer Bill Van Bommell
Apr. 27, 1977	NY A	—	OAK A	Dock Ellis Marty Perez Larry Murray
Nov. 23, 1977	BOS A	—	NY A	No compensation (free agent signing)
Jan. 14, 1983	NY N	—	BOS A	Minor league 3B Mike Davis

Lou Tost

Date	Traded To	Traded With	Traded By	In Exchange For
Mar. 25, 1947	PIT N	—	BOS N	Cash

Paul Toth

Date	Traded To	Traded With	Traded By	In Exchange For
Sept. 1, 1962	CHI N	—	STL N	Harvey Branch
June 15, 1964	STL N	*see Lou Brock*	CHI N	—

Cesar Tovar

Date	Traded To	Traded With	Traded By	In Exchange For
Dec. 4, 1964	MIN A	—	CIN N	Jerry Arrigo
Nov. 30, 1972	PHI N	—	MIN A	Ken Sanders Joe Lis Ken Reynolds
Dec. 7, 1973	TEX A	—	PHI N	Cash
Aug. 31, 1975	OAK A	—	TEX A	Cash

Jack Townsend

Date	Traded To	Traded With	Traded By	In Exchange For
Jan. 1906	CLE A	—	WAS A	Cash

Dick Tracewski

Date	Traded To	Traded With	Traded By	In Exchange For
Dec. 15, 1965	DET A	—	LA N	Phil Regan

Jim Tracy

Date	Traded To	Traded With	Traded By	In Exchange For
Dec. 9, 1981	HOU N	—	CHI N	Gary Woods

Walt Tragesser

Date	Traded To	Traded With	Traded By	In Exchange For
July 15, 1919	PHI N	—	BOS N	Cash

Bill Travers

Date	Traded To	Traded With	Traded By	In Exchange For
Jan. 26, 1981	CAL A	—	MIL A	No compensation (free agent signing)

Jeff Treadway

Date	Traded To	Traded With	Traded By	In Exchange For
Mar. 25, 1989	ATL N	—	CIN N	Cash
May 23, 1995	MON N	Henry Rodriguez	LA N	Roberto Kelly Joey Eischen

Mike Tresh

Date	Traded To	Traded With	Traded By	In Exchange For
Dec. 2, 1937	CHI A	Marv Owen Gee Walker	DET A	Vern Kennedy Tony Piet Dixie Walker
Jan. 12, 1949	CLE A	—	CHI A	Cash

Tom Tresh

Date	Traded To	Traded With	Traded By	In Exchange For
June 14, 1969	DET A	—	NY A	Ron Woods

Alex Trevino

Date	Traded To	Traded With	Traded By	In Exchange For
Feb. 10, 1982	CIN N	Jim Kern Greg Harris	NY N	George Foster
Apr. 24, 1984	ATL N	—	CIN N	Cash
Apr. 17, 1985	SF N	—	ATL N	Johnny Rabb
Dec. 11, 1985	LA N	—	SF N	Candy Maldonado
Sept. 7, 1990	CIN N	—	NY N	Waiver price
Jan. 2, 1991	STL N	—	CIN N	No compensation (free agent signing)

Gus Triandos

Date	Traded To	Traded With	Traded By	In Exchange For
Nov. 18, 1954	BAL A	—	NY A	*see Bob Turley*
Nov. 26, 1962	DET A	Whitey Herzog	BAL A	Dick Brown
Dec. 4, 1963	PHI N	Jim Bunning	DET A	Don Demeter Jack Hamilton
June 14, 1965	HOU N	—	PHI N	Cash

Manny Trillo

Date	Traded To	Traded With	Traded By	In Exchange For
Oct. 23, 1974	CHI N	Darold Knowles Bob Locker	OAK A	Billy Williams
Feb. 23, 1979	PHI N	Dave Rader Greg Gross	CHI N	Barry Foote Derek Botelho Ted Sizemore Jerry Martin minor league P Henry Mack
Dec. 9, 1982	CLE A	Jay Baller George Vukovich Julio Franco Jerry Willard	PHI N	Von Hayes
Aug. 17, 1983	MON N	—	CLE A	Minor league OF Don Carter $300,000.
Dec. 21, 1983	SF N	—	MON N	No compensation (free agent signing)
Dec. 11, 1985	CHI N	—	SF N	Dave Owen
Dec. 21, 1988	CIN N	—	CHI N	No compensation (free agent signing)

Ken Trinkle

Date	Traded To	Traded With	Traded By	In Exchange For
Dec. 14, 1948	PHI N	—	NY N	Cash

Coaker Triplett

Date	Traded To	Traded With	Traded By	In Exchange For
June 1, 1943	PHI N	Buster Adams Dain Clay	STL N	Danny Litwhiler Earl Naylor

Rick Trlicek

Date	Traded To	Traded With	Traded By	In Exchange For
Dec. 17, 1989	TOR A	—	ATL N	Kevin Batiste Ernie Whitt
Mar. 16, 1993	LA N	—	TOR A	Waiver price
Apr. 1, 1994	BOS A	—	LA N	Waiver price

Hal Trosky

Date	Traded To	Traded With	Traded By	In Exchange For
Nov. 6, 1943	CHI A	—	CLE A	Cash

Bill Trotter

Date	Traded To	Traded With	Traded By	In Exchange For
June 7, 1942	WAS A	Roy Cullenbine	STL A	Mike Chartak Steve Sundra

Dizzy Trout

Date	Traded To	Traded With	Traded By	In Exchange For
June 3, 1952	BOS A	George Kell Johnny Lipon Hoot Evers	DET A	Walt Dropo Bill Wight Fred Hatfield Johnny Pesky Don Lenhardt

Steve Trout

Date	Traded To	Traded With	Traded By	In Exchange For
Jan. 25, 1983	CHI N	Warren Brusstar	CHI A	Scott Fletcher Pat Tabler Randy Martz Dick Tidrow
July 12, 1987	NY A	Cash	CHI N	Bob Tewksbury Dean Wilkins Rich Scheid

Steve Trout *continued*

Date	Traded To	Traded With	Traded By	In Exchange For
Dec. 22, 1987	SEA A	Henry Cotto	NY A	Lee Guetterman Clay Parker Wade Taylor

Bob Trowbridge

Date	Traded To	Traded With	Traded By	In Exchange For
Oct. 12, 1959	KC A	—	MIL N	Cash

Virgil Trucks

Date	Traded To	Traded With	Traded By	In Exchange For
Dec. 4, 1952	STL A	Johnny Groth Hal White	DET A	Owen Friend Bob Nieman J. W. Porter
June 13, 1953	CHI A	Bob Elliott	STL A	Darrell Johnson Lou Kretlow $75,000.
Nov. 30, 1955	DET A	—	CHI A	Bubba Phillips
Dec. 5, 1956	KC A	Ned Garver Gene Host Wayne Belardi $20,000.	DET A	Jim Finigan Jack Crimian Bill Harrington Eddie Robinson
June 15, 1958	NY A	Duke Maas	KC A	Bob Grim Harry Simpson

Mike Trujillo

Date	Traded To	Traded With	Traded By	In Exchange For
Aug. 31, 1984	SF N	Minor league 1B Pat Adams	CHI A	Tom O'Malley
Aug. 19, 1986	SEA A	—	BOS A	*see Dave Henderson*

John Tsitouris

Date	Traded To	Traded With	Traded By	In Exchange For
Nov. 20, 1957	KC A	—	DET A	*see Billy Martin*
Jan. 25, 1961	CIN N	Johnny Briggs	KC A	Joe Nuxhall

Scooter Tucker

Date	Traded To	Traded With	Traded By	In Exchange For
Sept. 25, 1991	HOU N	—	SF N	Waiver price
May 15, 1995	CLE A	—	HOU N	Minor league P Matt Williams
June 29, 1995	ATL N	—	CLE A	Waiver price

Thurman Tucker

Date	Traded To	Traded With	Traded By	In Exchange For
Jan. 27, 1948	CLE A	—	CHI A	Ralph Weigel

John Tudor

Date	Traded To	Traded With	Traded By	In Exchange For
Dec. 6, 1983	PIT N	—	BOS A	Mike Easler
Dec. 12, 1984	STL N	Brian Harper	PIT N	George Hendrick minor league C Steve Barnard
Aug. 16, 1988	LA N	—	STL N	Pedro Guerrero
Dec. 14, 1989	STL N	—	LA N	No compensation (free agent signing)

Bob Tufts

Date	Traded To	Traded With	Traded By	In Exchange For
Mar. 30, 1982	KC A	*see Vida Blue*	SF N	—
June 7, 1983	CIN N	—	KC A	Charlie Leibrandt

Bob Turley

Date	Traded To	Traded With	Traded By	In Exchange For
Nov. 18, 1954	NY A	Don Larsen Billy Hunter	BAL A	Harry Byrd Jim McDonald Hal Smith Gus Triandos Gene Woodling Willie Miranda
(First part of 18-player trade completed on December 1, 1954; see Dick Kryhoski.)				
Oct. 29, 1962	LA A	—	NY A	Cash

Jerry Turner

Date	Traded To	Traded With	Traded By	In Exchange For
Sept. 9, 1981	CHI A	—	SD N	Cash
Feb. 12, 1982	DET A	—	CHI A	No compensation (free agent signing)

Jim Turner

Date	Traded To	Traded With	Traded By	In Exchange For
Dec. 6, 1939	CIN N	—	BOS N	Les Scarsella Cash

Jim Turner *continued*

Date	Traded To		Traded With	Traded By		In Exchange For
July 16, 1942	NY	A	—	CIN	N	Frankie Kelleher

Matt Turner

Date	Traded To		Traded With	Traded By		In Exchange For
July 31, 1991	HOU	N	Player to be named	ATL	N	Jim Clancy

(Houston received P Earl Sanders on November 15, 1991.)

Date	Traded To		Traded With	Traded By		In Exchange For
Apr. 3, 1994	CLE	A	—	FLA	N	Jeremy Hernandez

Shane Turner

Date	Traded To		Traded With	Traded By		In Exchange For
June 10, 1987	PHI	N	Keith Hughes	NY	A	Mike Easler
June 1, 1989	BAL	A	—	PHI	N	Minor league C John Posey

Terry Turner

Date	Traded To		Traded With	Traded By		In Exchange For
Jan. 1919	PHI	A	—	CLE	A	Waiver price

Tom Turner

Date	Traded To		Traded With	Traded By		In Exchange For
July 31, 1944	STL	A	—	CHI	A	Cash

Bill Tuttle

Date	Traded To		Traded With	Traded By		In Exchange For
Nov. 20, 1957	KC	A	—	DET	A	*see Billy Martin*
June 1, 1961	MIN	A	—	KC	A	Paul Giel Reno Bertoia

(Giel was returned to Minnesota for a cash payment.)

Wayne Twitchell

Date	Traded To		Traded With	Traded By		In Exchange For
Nov. 21, 1969	SEA	A	—	HOU	N	Cash
June 15, 1977	MON	N	Tim Blackwell	PHI	N	Barry Foote Dan Warthen
Aug. 19, 1979	SEA	A	—	NY	N	Cash

Lefty Tyler

Date	Traded To		Traded With	Traded By		In Exchange For
Jan. 4, 1918	CHI	N	—	BOS	N	Larry Doyle Art Wilson $15,000.

Dave Tyriver

Date	Traded To		Traded With	Traded By		In Exchange For
Oct. 14, 1961	WAS	A	—	CLE	A	Cash

Mike Tyson

Date	Traded To		Traded With	Traded By		In Exchange For
Oct. 17, 1979	CHI	N	—	STL	N	Donnie Moore

Bob Uecker

Date	Traded To		Traded With	Traded By		In Exchange For
Apr. 9, 1964	STL	N	—	MIL	N	Jimmie Coker Gary Kolb
Oct. 27, 1965	PHI	N	Bill White Dick Groat	STL	N	Pat Corrales Art Mahaffey Alex Johnson
June 6, 1967	ATL	N	—	PHI	N	Gene Oliver

Ted Uhlaender

Date	Traded To		Traded With	Traded By		In Exchange For
Dec. 10, 1969	CLE	A	*see Graig Nettles*	MIN	A	—
Dec. 6, 1971	CIN	N	—	CLE	A	Milt Wilcox

George Uhle

Date	Traded To		Traded With	Traded By		In Exchange For
Dec. 11, 1928	DET	A	—	CLE	A	Jackie Tavener Ken Holloway
Apr. 21, 1933	NY	N	—	DET	A	$20,000.

Arnie Umbach

Date	Traded To		Traded With	Traded By		In Exchange For
Dec. 31, 1966	HOU	N	Sandy Alomar Eddie Mathews	ATL	N	Dave Nicholson Bob Bruce

Jim Umbarger

Date	Traded To		Traded With	Traded By		In Exchange For
Mar. 26, 1977	OAK	A	Rodney Scott Cash	TEX	A	Claudell Washington
Aug. 25, 1977	TEX	A	—	OAK	A	Cash

Tommy Umphlett

Date	Traded To		Traded With	Traded By		In Exchange For
Dec. 9, 1953	WAS	A	Mickey McDermott	BOS	A	Jackie Jensen
Nov. 8, 1955	BOS	A	*see Mickey Vernon*	WAS	A	—

Tommy Umphlett *continued*

Date	Traded To		Traded With	Traded By		In Exchange For
June 12, 1962	NY	A	Cash	BOS	A	Billy Gardner

Pat Underwood

Date	Traded To		Traded With	Traded By		In Exchange For
June 30, 1983	CIN	N	—	DET	A	Wayne Krenchicki

Tom Underwood

Date	Traded To		Traded With	Traded By		In Exchange For
June 15, 1977	STL	N	Rick Bosetti Dane Iorg	PHI	N	Bake McBride Steve Waterbury
Dec. 6, 1977	TOR	A	Victor Cruz	STL	N	Pete Vuckovich John Scott
Nov. 1, 1979	NY	A	Rick Cerone Ted Wilborn	TOR	A	Chris Chambliss Damaso Garcia Paul Mirabella
May 20, 1981	OAK	A	Jim Spencer	NY	A	Dave Revering Mike Patterson minor league P Chuck Dougherty
Feb. 6, 1984	BAL	A	—	OAK	A	Free agent signing

(Oakland selected P Tim Belcher of New York Yankees from the compensation pool.)

Bob Unglaub

Date	Traded To		Traded With	Traded By		In Exchange For
June 18, 1904	BOS	A	—	NY	A	Patsy Dougherty
July 1908	WAS	A	Jesse Tannehill	BOS	A	Casey Patten

Del Unser

Date	Traded To		Traded With	Traded By		In Exchange For
Dec. 2, 1971	CLE	A	Denny Riddleberger Gary Jones minor league P Terry Ley	TEX	A	Roy Foster Rich Hand Ken Suarez Mike Paul
Nov. 30, 1972	PHI	N	minor league IF Terry Wedgewood	CLE	A	Oscar Gamble Roger Freed
Dec. 3, 1974	NY	N	John Stearns Mac Scarce	PHI	N	Tug McGraw Don Hahn Dave Schneck
July 21, 1976	MON	N	Wayne Garrett	NY	N	Jim Dwyer Pepe Mangual

Dixie Upright

Date	Traded To		Traded With	Traded By		In Exchange For
Jan. 20, 1953	STL	A	$25,000.	CHI	A	Freddie Marsh

Cecil Upshaw

Date	Traded To		Traded With	Traded By		In Exchange For
Apr. 22, 1973	HOU	N	—	ATL	N	Norm Miller
Dec. 3, 1973	CLE	A	—	HOU	N	Jerry Johnson
Apr. 27, 1974	NY	A	*see Chris Chambliss*	CLE	A	—
Dec. 5, 1974	CHI	A	—	NY	A	Eddie Leon

Willie Upshaw

Date	Traded To		Traded With	Traded By		In Exchange For
Mar. 25, 1988	CLE	A	—	TOR	A	Cash

Bill Upton

Date	Traded To		Traded With	Traded By		In Exchange For
Feb. 19, 1954	PHI	A	Lee Wheat	CLE	A	Dave Philley

Tom Upton

Date	Traded To		Traded With	Traded By		In Exchange For
July 31, 1951	NY	A	Bobby Hogue Kermit Wahl Lou Sleater	STL	A	Cliff Mapes
Nov. 27, 1951	CHI	A	*see Sherm Lollar*	STL	A	—
Nov. 27, 1951	WAS	A	—	CHI	A	Sam Dente
May 3, 1952	NY	A	—	WAS	A	*see Jackie Jensen*

Jack Urban

Date	Traded To		Traded With	Traded By		In Exchange For
Apr. 5, 1957	KC	A	—	NY	A	Continuation of Billy Hunter trade of February 19, 1957.
Apr. 8, 1959	NY	A	—	KC	A	Mark Freeman

(Freeman was returned to the Yankees on May 8, 1959.)

Jose Uribe

Date	Traded To	Traded With	Traded By	In Exchange For
Feb. 1, 1985	SF N	David Green Dave LaPoint Gary Rajsich	STL N	Jack Clark
Jan. 5, 1993	HOU N	—	SF N	No compensation (free agent signing)

John Urrea

Date	Traded To	Traded With	Traded By	In Exchange For
Dec. 8, 1980	SD N	—	STL N	*see Rollie Fingers*

Bob Usher

Date	Traded To	Traded With	Traded By	In Exchange For
Oct. 4, 1951	CHI N	Johnny Pramesa	CIN N	Bob Borkowski Smoky Burgess
May 15, 1957	WAS A	—	CLE A	Cash

Tex Vache

Date	Traded To	Traded With	Traded By	In Exchange For
Dec. 9, 1925	DET A	Homer Ezzell	BOS A	Fred Haney

Mike Vail

Date	Traded To	Traded With	Traded By	In Exchange For
Dec. 11, 1974	NY N	Jack Heidemann	STL N	Teddy Martinez
Mar. 26, 1978	CLE A	—	NY N	Cash
June 15, 1978	CHI N	—	CLE A	Joe Wallis
Dec. 12, 1980	CIN N	—	CHI N	Hector Cruz
Jan. 5, 1983	SF N	—	CIN N	Rich Gale
May 25, 1983	MON N	—	SF N	Wallace Johnson

Sandy Valdespino

Date	Traded To	Traded With	Traded By	In Exchange For
Aug. 30, 1969	SEA A	Danny Walton	HOU N	Tommy Davis

Efrain Valdez

Date	Traded To	Traded With	Traded By	In Exchange For
July 3, 1991	TOR A	—	CLE A	Waiver price

Sergio Valdez

Date	Traded To	Traded With	Traded By	In Exchange For
July 2, 1989	ATL N	Nate Minchey Minor league OF Kevin Dean	MON N	Zane Smith
Apr. 30, 1990	CLE A	—	ATL N	Waiver price

Jose Valentin

Date	Traded To	Traded With	Traded By	In Exchange For
Mar. 27, 1992	MIL A	—	SD N	*see Gary Sheffield*

Bobby Valentine

Date	Traded To	Traded With	Traded By	In Exchange For
Nov. 28, 1972	CAL A	—	LA N	*see Andy Messersmith*
Sept. 17, 1975	SD N	Rudi Meoli	CAL A	Gary Ross
June 15, 1977	NY N	Paul Siebert	SD N	Dave Kingman

Corky Valentine

Date	Traded To	Traded With	Traded By	In Exchange For
Apr. 9, 1956	MIL N	Bob Hazle	CIN N	George Crowe

Ellis Valentine

Date	Traded To	Traded With	Traded By	In Exchange For
May 29, 1981	NY N	—	MON N	Jeff Reardon Dan Norman
Jan. 24, 1983	CAL A	—	NY N	No compensation (free agent signing)

Fred Valentine

Date	Traded To	Traded With	Traded By	In Exchange For
Oct. 11, 1963	WAS A	—	BAL A	Cash
June 15, 1968	BAL A	—	WAS A	Bruce Howard

Vito Valentinetti

Date	Traded To	Traded With	Traded By	In Exchange For
May 23, 1957	CHI N	Jackie Collum	BKN N	Don Elston
Aug. 24, 1957	CLE A	—	CHI N	Cash
Mar. 27, 1958	DET A	Milt Bolling	CLE A	Pete Wojey $20,000.
June 23, 1958	WAS A	—	DET A	Al Cicotte
Apr. 1, 1959	BAL A	—	WAS A	Billy Loes

(Trade was cancelled on April 8, 1959, by Commissioner Frick due to Loes's sore arm.)

Benny Valenzuela

Date	Traded To	Traded With	Traded By	In Exchange For
Oct. 8, 1958	SF N	Hobie Landrith Billy Muffett	STL N	Ernie Broglio Marv Grissom

Julio Valera

Date	Traded To	Traded With	Traded By	In Exchange For
Apr. 12, 1992	CAL A	Player to be named	NY N	Dick Schofield

(California received P Julian Vasquez on October 6, 1992.)

Dave Valle

Date	Traded To	Traded With	Traded By	In Exchange For
Dec. 30, 1993	BOS A	—	SEA A	No compensation (free agent signing)
June 16, 1994	MIL A	—	BOS A	Tom Brunansky
Dec. 6, 1994	TEX A	—	MIL A	No compensation (free agent signing)

Elmer Valo

Date	Traded To	Traded With	Traded By	In Exchange For
Apr. 5, 1957	BKN N	Ron Negray Tim Harkness Ben Flowers minor league SS Mel Geho and $75,000.	PHI N	Chico Fernandez

Russ Van Atta

Date	Traded To	Traded With	Traded By	In Exchange For
May 15, 1935	STL A	—	NY A	Cash

Deacon Van Buren

Date	Traded To	Traded With	Traded By	In Exchange For
Apr. 30, 1904	PHI N	Jack Doyle	BKN N	Cash

Dazzy Vance

Date	Traded To	Traded With	Traded By	In Exchange For
Mar. 1915	NY A	—	PIT N	Cash
Feb. 1933	STL N	Gordon Slade	BKN N	Jake Flowers Ownie Carroll
June 25, 1934	CIN N	—	STL N	Waiver price

Ed Vande Berg

Date	Traded To	Traded With	Traded By	In Exchange For
Dec. 11, 1985	LA N	—	SEA A	Steve Yeager
Feb. 2, 1988	TEX A	—	CLE A	No compensation (free agent signing)

Hy Vandenburg

Date	Traded To	Traded With	Traded By	In Exchange For
Jan. 1941	STL N	—	NY N	Cash

Johnny Vander Meer

Date	Traded To	Traded With	Traded By	In Exchange For
Feb. 10, 1950	CHI N	—	CIN N	Cash

John Vander Wal

Date	Traded To	Traded With	Traded By	In Exchange For
Mar. 31, 1994	CLR N	—	MON N	Cash

Elam Vangilder

Date	Traded To	Traded With	Traded By	In Exchange For
Dec. 2, 1927	DET A	Chick Galloway Harry Rice	STL A	Heinie Manush Lu Blue

Andy Van Slyke

Date	Traded To	Traded With	Traded By	In Exchange For
Apr. 1, 1987	PIT N	Mike LaValliere Mike Dunne	STL N	Tony Pena
Apr. 21, 1995	BAL A	—	PIT N	No compensation (free agent signing)
June 18, 1995	PHI N	—	BAL A	Gene Harris

Pete Varney

Date	Traded To	Traded With	Traded By	In Exchange For
June 15, 1976	ATL N	—	CHI A	Blue Moon Odom

Gary Varsho

Date	Traded To	Traded With	Traded By	In Exchange For
Mar. 29, 1991	PIT N	—	CHI N	Steve Carter

Rafael Vasquez

Date	Traded To	Traded With	Traded By	In Exchange For
Dec. 5, 1978	SEA A	*see Mario Mendoza*	PIT N	—
Dec. 6, 1979	CLE A	Bud Anderson minor league P Bob Pietroburgo	SEA A	Ted Cox
Dec. 9, 1980	PIT N	—	CLE A	*see Bert Blyleven*

Jim Vatcher

Date	Traded To	Traded With	Traded By	In Exchange For
Aug. 3, 1990	ATL N	Jeff Parrett Victor Rosario	PHI N	Dale Murphy Tommy Greene
(Greene and Vatcher were exhanged on August 9, and Atlanta received Rosario on September 4, 1990.)				
Feb. 8, 1991	SD N	—	ATL N	Waiver price

Arky Vaughan

Date	Traded To	Traded With	Traded By	In Exchange For
Dec. 12, 1941	BKN N	—	PIT N	Pete Coscarart Luke Hamlin Babe Phelps Jimmy Wasdell

Fred Vaughn

Date	Traded To	Traded With	Traded By	In Exchange For
Jan. 2, 1946	CHI A	Alex Carrasquel	WAS A	Cash

Hippo Vaughn

Date	Traded To	Traded With	Traded By	In Exchange For
June 26, 1912	WAS A	—	NY A	Waiver price

Bobby Veach

Date	Traded To	Traded With	Traded By	In Exchange For
Mar. 12, 1924	BOS A	—	DET A	Cash
May 5, 1925	NY A	Alex Ferguson	BOS A	Ray Francis $9,000.
Aug. 17, 1925	WAS A	—	NY A	Waiver price

Coot Veal

Date	Traded To	Traded With	Traded By	In Exchange For
Nov. 21, 1961	PIT N	—	WAS A	Cash

Bob Veale

Date	Traded To	Traded With	Traded By	In Exchange For
Sept. 2, 1972	BOS A	—	PIT N	Cash

Randy Velarde

Date	Traded To	Traded With	Traded By	In Exchange For
Jan. 5, 1987	NY A	Pete Filson	CHI A	Scott Nielsen Minor league IF Mike Soper
Nov. 22, 1995	CAL A	—	NY A	No compensation (free agent signing)

Freddie Velazquez

Date	Traded To	Traded With	Traded By	In Exchange For
June 3, 1969	OAK A	—	SEA A	Cash

Max Venable

Date	Traded To	Traded With	Traded By	In Exchange For
Feb. 27, 1984	MON N	Fred Breining Andy McGaffigan	SF N	Al Oliver
(San Francisco sent McGaffigan to Montreal on April 1, 1984, after Breining reported to the Expos with a sore arm.)				
Apr. 26, 1985	CIN N	—	MON N	Skeeter Barnes

Quilvio Veras

Date	Traded To	Traded With	Traded By	In Exchange For
Nov. 29, 1994	FLA N	—	NY N	Carl Everett

Emil Verban

Date	Traded To	Traded With	Traded By	In Exchange For
May 2, 1946	PHI N	—	STL N	Clyde Kluttz
Aug. 3, 1948	CHI N	—	PHI N	Waiver price

Joe Verbanic

Date	Traded To	Traded With	Traded By	In Exchange For
Dec. 14, 1966	NY A	Cash	PHI N	Pedro Ramos

David Veres

Date	Traded To	Traded With	Traded By	In Exchange For
Jan. 15, 1991	LA N	—	OAK A	Kevin Campbell
Dec. 20, 1995	MON N	Minor league C Raul Chavez	HOU N	Sean Berry

Johnny Vergez

Date	Traded To	Traded With	Traded By	In Exchange For
Nov. 1, 1934	PHI N	Pretzels Pezzullo Blondy Ryan George Watkins Cash	NY N	Dick Bartell
July 1936	STL N	—	PHI N	Cash

John Verhoeven

Date	Traded To	Traded With	Traded By	In Exchange For
June 15, 1977	CHI A	Don Kirkwood John Flannery	CAL A	Ken Brett

John Verhoeven *continued*

Date	Traded To	Traded With	Traded By	In Exchange For
Jan. 26, 1982	BOS A	—	MIN A	Cash

Mickey Vernon

Date	Traded To	Traded With	Traded By	In Exchange For
Dec. 14, 1948	CLE A	Early Wynn	WAS A	Joe Haynes Eddie Klieman Eddie Robinson
June 14, 1950	WAS A	—	CLE A	Dick Weik
Nov. 8, 1955	BOS A	Bob Porterfield Johnny Schmitz Tommy Umphlett	WAS A	Karl Olson Dick Brodowski Tex Clevenger Neil Chrisley minor league P Al Curtis
Jan. 29, 1958	CLE A	—	BOS A	Waiver price
Apr. 11, 1959	MIL N	—	CLE A	Humberto Robinson

Zoilo Versalles

Date	Traded To	Traded With	Traded By	In Exchange For
Nov. 28, 1967	LA N	Mudcat Grant	MIN A	Johnny Roseboro Ron Perranoski Bob Miller
Oct. 21, 1968	CLE A	—	SD N	Bill Davis
July 26, 1969	WAS A	—	CLE A	Cash

Tom Veryzer

Date	Traded To	Traded With	Traded By	In Exchange For
Dec. 9, 1977	CLE A	—	DET A	Charlie Spikes
Jan. 8, 1982	NY N	—	CLE A	Ray Searage
Apr. 2, 1983	CHI N	—	NY N	Minor league Ps Craig Weissman Bob Schilling

Bob Veselic

Date	Traded To	Traded With	Traded By	In Exchange For
Jan. 12, 1983	HOU N	—	MIN A	Rick Lysander

Sammy Vick

Date	Traded To	Traded With	Traded By	In Exchange For
Dec. 15, 1920	BOS A	—	NY A	*see Waite Hoyt*

Jose Vidal

Date	Traded To	Traded With	Traded By	In Exchange For
May 19, 1969	NY A	—	SEA A	Dick Simpson

Ron Villone

Date	Traded To	Traded With	Traded By	In Exchange For
July 31, 1995	SD N	Marc Newfield	SEA A	Andy Benes Player to be named
(Seattle received P Greg Keagle on September 16, 1995.)				

Fernando Vina

Date	Traded To	Traded With	Traded By	In Exchange For
Nov. 30, 1994	MIL A	Minor league C Javier Gonzalez	NY N	Doug Henry
(Milwaukee received Gonzalez on December 6, and Vina on December 22, 1994.)				

Rube Vinson

Date	Traded To	Traded With	Traded By	In Exchange For
Feb. 1906	CHI A	—	CLE A	Cash

Frank Viola

Date	Traded To	Traded With	Traded By	In Exchange For
July 31, 1989	NY N	—	MIN A	Rick Aguilera David West Tim Drummond Kevin Tapani Jack Savage
(Minnesota received Savage on October 16, 1989.)				
Jan. 2, 1992	BOS A	—	NY N	No compensation (free agent signing)

Bill Virdon

Date	Traded To	Traded With	Traded By	In Exchange For
Apr. 11, 1954	STL N	Mel Wright minor league OF Emil Tellinger	NY A	Enos Slaughter
May 17, 1956	PIT N	—	STL N	Dick Littlefield Bobby Del Greco

Ozzie Virgil

Date	Traded To	Traded With	Traded By	In Exchange For
Jan. 28, 1958	DET A	Gail Harris	SF N	Jim Finigan $25,000.
Aug. 2, 1961	KC A	Bill Fischer	DET A	Gerry Staley Reno Bertoia

Ozzie Virgil *continued*

Date	Traded To	Traded With	Traded By	In Exchange For
Oct. 1, 1965	SF N	Joe Gibbon	PIT N	Matty Alou

Ozzie Virgil

Date	Traded To	Traded With	Traded By	In Exchange For
Dec. 10, 1985	ATL N	Pete Smith	PHI N	Steve Bedrosian Milt Thompson

Ossie Vitt

Date	Traded To	Traded With	Traded By	In Exchange For
Jan. 17, 1919	BOS A	—	DET A	Eddie Ainsmith Chick Shorten Slim Love

Jose Vizcaino

Date	Traded To	Traded With	Traded By	In Exchange For
Dec. 14, 1990	CHI N	—	LA N	Greg Smith
Mar. 30, 1994	NY N	—	CHI N	Anthony Young Minor league P Ottis Smith

Omar Vizquel

Date	Traded To	Traded With	Traded By	In Exchange For
Dec. 20, 1993	CLE A	—	SEA A	Felix Fermin Reggie Jefferson Cash

Jack Voigt

Date	Traded To	Traded With	Traded By	In Exchange For
May 16, 1995	TEX A	—	BAL A	John Dettmer
Aug. 31, 1995	BOS A	—	TEX A	Chris Howard

Bill Voiselle

Date	Traded To	Traded With	Traded By	In Exchange For
June 13, 1947	BOS N	Cash	NY N	Mort Cooper
Dec. 14, 1949	CHI N	—	BOS N	Gene Mauch Cash

Clyde Vollmer

Date	Traded To	Traded With	Traded By	In Exchange For
May 8, 1950	BOS A	—	WAS A	Tommy O'Brien Merrill Combs
Apr. 22, 1953	WAS A	—	BOS A	Cash

Ed Vosberg

Date	Traded To	Traded With	Traded By	In Exchange For
Dec. 13, 1988	HOU N	—	SD N	Minor league C Dan Walters

Joe Vosmik

Date	Traded To	Traded With	Traded By	In Exchange For
Jan. 17, 1937	STL A	Bill Knickerbocker Oral Hildebrand	CLE A	Ivy Andrews Lyn Lary Moose Solters
Dec. 2, 1937	BOS A	—	STL A	Bobo Newsom Red Kress Buster Mills
Feb. 12, 1940	BKN N	—	BOS A	$25,000.

Bill Voss

Date	Traded To	Traded With	Traded By	In Exchange For
Jan. 20, 1969	CAL A	minor league P Andy Rubicotta	CHI A	Sammy Ellis
Jan. 28, 1971	MIL A	—	CAL A	Gene Brabender
June 20, 1972	OAK A	—	MIL A	Ron Clark
Aug. 27, 1972	STL N	minor league P Steve Easton	OAK A	Matty Alou
Nov. 28, 1972	CIN N	—	STL N	Pat Jacquez

Pete Vuckovich

Date	Traded To	Traded With	Traded By	In Exchange For
Dec. 6, 1977	STL N	John Scott	TOR A	Tom Underwood Victor Cruz
Dec. 12, 1980	MIL A	Rollie Fingers Ted Simmons	STL N	Sixto Lezcano David Green Lary Sorensen Dave LaPoint

George Vukovich

Date	Traded To	Traded With	Traded By	In Exchange For
Dec. 9, 1982	CLE A	Manny Trillo Jay Baller Julio Franco Jerry Willard	PHI N	Von Hayes

John Vukovich

Date	Traded To	Traded With	Traded By	In Exchange For
Oct. 31, 1972	MIL A	*see Don Money*	PHI N	—
Oct. 22, 1974	CIN N	—	MIL A	Pat Osburn

Rube Waddell

Date	Traded To	Traded With	Traded By	In Exchange For
Jan. 1900	PIT N	*see Honus Wagner*	LOU N	—
May 1901	CHI N	—	PIT N	Cash
Feb. 7, 1908	STL A	—	PHI A	Cash

Ben Wade

Date	Traded To	Traded With	Traded By	In Exchange For
Aug. 8, 1954	STL N	—	BKN N	Waiver price
Jan. 11, 1955	PIT N	Cash	STL N	Paul LaPalme

Gale Wade

Date	Traded To	Traded With	Traded By	In Exchange For
Nov. 16, 1954	CHI N	Sam Jones $60,000.	CLE A	Ralph Kiner

Jake Wade

Date	Traded To	Traded With	Traded By	In Exchange For
Dec. 15, 1938	BOS A	Eldon Auker Chet Morgan	DET A	Pinky Higgins Archie McKain
Sept. 1939	STL A	—	BOS A	Cash
Dec. 15, 1944	NY A	—	CHI A	Johnny Johnson

Bill Wagner

Date	Traded To	Traded With	Traded By	In Exchange For
Oct. 1917	BOS N	—	PIT N	Cash

Gary Wagner

Date	Traded To	Traded With	Traded By	In Exchange For
Sept. 6, 1969	BOS A	—	PHI N	Mike Jackson

Hal Wagner

Date	Traded To	Traded With	Traded By	In Exchange For
May 7, 1944	BOS A	—	PHI A	Ford Garrison
May 20, 1947	DET A	—	BOS A	Birdie Tebbetts
Sept. 13, 1948	PHI N	—	DET A	Waiver price

Honus Wagner

Date	Traded To	Traded With	Traded By	In Exchange For
Jan. 1900	PIT N	Patsy Flaherty Deacon Phillippe Walt Woods Rube Waddell Icebox Chamberlain Chief Zimmer Tacks Latimer Claude Ritchey Fred Clarke Tommy Leach Mike Kelly Conny Doyle OF Tom Massitt	LOU N	Jack Chesbro Paddy Fox John O'Brien Art Madison $25,000.

(Sale of the chief assets of the Louisville franchise to Pittsburgh after Louisville was dropped by the National League.)

Leon Wagner

Date	Traded To	Traded With	Traded By	In Exchange For
Dec. 15, 1959	STL N	Daryl Spencer	SF N	Don Blasingame
Jan. 26, 1961	LA A	Cal Browning Ellis Burton Cash	STL N	Al Cicotte
Dec. 2, 1963	CLE A	—	LA A	Joe Adcock Barry Latman
June 13, 1968	CHI A	—	CLE A	Russ Snyder
Dec. 5, 1968	CIN N	—	CHI A	Cash

(Wagner was returned to Chicago on April 5, 1969.)

Mark Wagner

Date	Traded To	Traded With	Traded By	In Exchange For
Dec. 10, 1980	TEX A	—	DET A	Kevin Saucier

Kermit Wahl

Date	Traded To	Traded With	Traded By	In Exchange For
June 4, 1951	CHI A	—	PHI A	Hank Majeski
June 4, 1951	STL A	Paul Lehner Cash	CHI A	Don Lenhardt
July 31, 1951	NY A	Bobby Hogue Tom Upton Lou Sleater	STL A	Cliff Mapes

Dave Wainhouse

Date	Traded To	Traded With	Traded By	In Exchange For
Nov. 20, 1992	SEA A	Kevin Foster	MON N	Frank Bolick Player to be named

(Montreal received C Miah Bradbury on December 8, 1992.)

Eddie Waitkus

Date	Traded To	Traded With	Traded By	In Exchange For
Dec. 14, 1948	PHI N	Hank Borowy	CHI N	Monk Dubiel Dutch Leonard
Mar. 16, 1954	BAL A	—	PHI N	$40,000.

Rick Waits

Date	Traded To	Traded With	Traded By	In Exchange For
June 13, 1975	CLE A	Jim Bibby Jackie Brown $100,000.	TEX A	Gaylord Perry
June 6, 1983	MIL A	Rick Manning	CLE A	Gorman Thomas Ernie Camacho Jamie Easterly

Bill Wakefield

Date	Traded To	Traded With	Traded By	In Exchange For
Nov. 4, 1963	NY N	George Altman	STL N	Roger Craig

Dick Wakefield

Date	Traded To	Traded With	Traded By	In Exchange For
Dec. 17, 1949	NY A	—	DET A	Dick Kryhoski

Howard Wakefield

Date	Traded To	Traded With	Traded By	In Exchange For
Feb. 1906	WAS A	—	CLE A	Cash
Feb. 1907	CLE A	—	WAS A	Cash
Aug. 11, 1907	WAS A	Pete O'Brien	CLE A	Rabbit Nill

Matt Walbeck

Date	Traded To	Traded With	Traded By	In Exchange For
Nov. 24, 1993	MIN A	Dave Stevens	CHI N	Willie Banks

Rube Walberg

Date	Traded To	Traded With	Traded By	In Exchange For
Apr. 1923	PHI A	—	NY N	Waiver price
Dec. 12, 1933	BOS A	Lefty Grove Max Bishop	PHI A	Bob Kline Rabbit Warstler $125,000.

Bob Walk

Date	Traded To	Traded With	Traded By	In Exchange For
Mar. 25, 1981	ATL N	—	PHI N	Gary Matthews

Bill Walker

Date	Traded To	Traded With	Traded By	In Exchange For
Oct. 10, 1932	STL N	Ethan Allen Bob O'Farrell Jim Mooney	NY N	Gus Mancuso Ray Starr
Aug. 6, 1936	CIN N	—	STL N	Si Johnson

Chico Walker

Date	Traded To	Traded With	Traded By	In Exchange For
Oct. 16, 1987	CAL A	—	CHI N	Minor league P Todd Fischer
May 7, 1992	NY N	—	CHI N	Waiver price

Curt Walker

Date	Traded To	Traded With	Traded By	In Exchange For
July 25, 1921	PHI N	Butch Henline Jesse Winters $30,000.	NY N	Irish Meusel
May 30, 1924	CIN N	—	PHI N	George Harper

Dixie Walker

Date	Traded To	Traded With	Traded By	In Exchange For
May 4, 1936	CHI A	—	NY A	Waiver price
Dec. 2, 1937	DET A	Vern Kennedy Tony Piet	CHI A	Marv Owen Mike Tresh Gee Walker
July 24, 1939	BKN N	—	DET A	Waiver price
Dec. 8, 1947	PIT N	Hal Gregg Vic Lombardi	BKN N	Preacher Roe Billy Cox Gene Mauch

Duane Walker

Date	Traded To	Traded With	Traded By	In Exchange For
July 19, 1985	TEX A	Jeff Russell	CIN N	Buddy Bell

Gee Walker

Date	Traded To	Traded With	Traded By	In Exchange For
Dec. 2, 1937	CHI A	Marv Owen Mike Tresh	DET A	Vern Kennedy Tony Piet Dixie Walker

Gee Walker *continued*

Date	Traded To	Traded With	Traded By	In Exchange For
Dec. 8, 1939	WAS A	—	CHI A	Taffy Wright Pete Appleton
Dec. 12, 1940	BOS A	—	WAS A	Doc Cramer
Dec. 12, 1940	CLE A	Gene Desautels Jim Bagby	BOS A	Frankie Pytlak Odell Hale Joe Dobson
Mar. 26, 1942	CIN N	—	CLE A	Cash

Harry Walker

Date	Traded To	Traded With	Traded By	In Exchange For
May 3, 1947	PHI N	Freddy Schmidt	STL N	Ron Northey
Oct. 4, 1948	CHI N	—	PHI N	Bill Nicholson
June 15, 1949	CIN N	Peanuts Lowrey	CHI N	Frankie Baumholtz Hank Sauer
Dec. 14, 1949	STL N	—	CIN N	Lou Klein Ron Northey

Jerry Walker

Date	Traded To	Traded With	Traded By	In Exchange For
Apr. 12, 1961	KC A	Chuck Essegian	BAL A	Dick Hall Dick Williams
Feb. 27, 1963	CLE A	—	KC A	Chuck Essegian

Larry Walker

Date	Traded To	Traded With	Traded By	In Exchange For
Apr. 8, 1995	CLR N	—	MON N	No compensation (free agent signing)

Luke Walker

Date	Traded To	Traded With	Traded By	In Exchange For
Dec. 5, 1973	DET A	—	PIT N	Cash

Mike Walker

Date	Traded To	Traded With	Traded By	In Exchange For
Apr. 21, 1989	SEA A	—	PIT N	*see Rey Quinones*

Rube Walker

Date	Traded To	Traded With	Traded By	In Exchange For
June 15, 1951	BKN N	*see Andy Pafko*	CHI N	—

Tilly Walker

Date	Traded To	Traded With	Traded By	In Exchange For
Oct. 1912	STL A	—	WAS A	Cash
Apr. 8, 1916	BOS A	—	STL A	Cash
Jan. 10, 1918	PHI A	Larry Gardner Hick Cady	BOS A	Stuffy McInnis

Tom Walker

Date	Traded To	Traded With	Traded By	In Exchange For
Dec. 4, 1974	DET A	Terry Humphrey	MON N	Woodie Fryman
Feb. 3, 1976	STL N	—	DET A	Cash
July 13, 1977	CAL A	—	MON N	Cash

Tony Walker

Date	Traded To	Traded With	Traded By	In Exchange For
Mar. 31, 1983	HOU N	*see Bill Dawley*	CIN N	—

Jim Walkup

Date	Traded To	Traded With	Traded By	In Exchange For
May 13, 1939	DET A	*see Beau Bell*	STL A	—

Joe Wall

Date	Traded To	Traded With	Traded By	In Exchange For
July 1902	BKN N	Roy Evans	NY N	Cash

Murray Wall

Date	Traded To	Traded With	Traded By	In Exchange For
June 11, 1959	WAS A	Billy Consolo	BOS A	Dick Hyde Herb Plews

(Hyde was returned to Washington and Wall was returned to Boston.)

Don Wallace

Date	Traded To	Traded With	Traded By	In Exchange For
July 24, 1967	NY N	Cash	CAL A	Hawk Taylor

Mike Wallace

Date	Traded To	Traded With	Traded By	In Exchange For
May 3, 1974	NY A	—	PHI N	Ken Wright
June 13, 1975	STL N	—	NY A	Cash
Oct. 22, 1976	TEX A	—	STL N	Johnny Sutton

Tim Wallach

Date	Traded To	Traded With	Traded By	In Exchange For
Dec. 24, 1992	LA N	—	MON N	Minor league SS Tim Barker

Jack Wallaesa

Date	Traded To	Traded With	Traded By	In Exchange For
Dec. 13, 1946	CHI A	—	PHI A	Cash

Tye Waller

Date	Traded To	Traded With	Traded By	In Exchange For
Dec. 9, 1980	CHI N	Leon Durham Ken Reitz	STL N	Bruce Sutter
Dec. 10, 1982	CHI A	—	CHI N	Reggie Patterson

Denny Walling

Date	Traded To	Traded With	Traded By	In Exchange For
June 15, 1977	HOU N	Cash	OAK A	Willie Crawford
Aug. 31, 1988	STL N	—	HOU N	Bob Forsch

Joe Wallis

Date	Traded To	Traded With	Traded By	In Exchange For
June 15, 1978	CLE A	—	CHI N	Mike Vail
June 15, 1978	OAK A	—	CLE A	Gary Alexander

Lee Walls

Date	Traded To	Traded With	Traded By	In Exchange For
May 1, 1957	CHI N	Dale Long	PIT N	Gene Baker Dee Fondy
Dec. 6, 1959	CIN N	Bill Henry Lou Jackson	CHI N	Frank Thomas
June 15, 1960	PHI N	Tony Gonzalez	CIN N	Harry Anderson Wally Post minor league 1B Fred Hopke
Dec. 15, 1961	LA N	$100,000.	NY N	Charlie Neal

Jimmy Walsh

Date	Traded To	Traded With	Traded By	In Exchange For
Sept. 1915	STL F	—	BAL F	Cash

Jimmy Walsh

Date	Traded To	Traded With	Traded By	In Exchange For
June 10, 1914	PHI A	—	NY A	Tom Daley
Sept. 2, 1916	BOS A	—	PHI A	Ray Haley

Gene Walter

Date	Traded To	Traded With	Traded By	In Exchange For
Dec. 11, 1986	NY N	*see Kevin McReynolds*	SD N	—
July 11, 1988	SEA A	—	NY N	Edwin Nunez

Bucky Walters

Date	Traded To	Traded With	Traded By	In Exchange For
June 14, 1934	PHI N	—	BOS A	Cash
June 13, 1938	CIN N	—	PHI N	Spud Davis Al Hollingsworth $50,000.

Charley Walters

Date	Traded To	Traded With	Traded By	In Exchange For
Mar. 21, 1970	WAS A	Joe Grzenda	MIN A	Brant Alyea

Fred Walters

Date	Traded To	Traded With	Traded By	In Exchange For
Dec. 26, 1953	PIT N	—	MIL N	*see Danny O'Connell*

Ken Walters

Date	Traded To	Traded With	Traded By	In Exchange For
Dec. 5, 1959	PHI N	Ted Lepcio minor league P Alex Cosmidis	DET A	Chico Fernandez Ray Semproch

Mike Walters

Date	Traded To	Traded With	Traded By	In Exchange For
May 12, 1982	MIN A	Tom Brunansky $400,000.	CAL A	Doug Corbett Rob Wilfong

Roxy Walters

Date	Traded To	Traded With	Traded By	In Exchange For
Dec. 18, 1918	BOS A	—	NY A	*see Duffy Lewis*
Jan. 7, 1924	CLE A	—	BOS A	*see Bill Wambsganss*

Danny Walton

Date	Traded To	Traded With	Traded By	In Exchange For
Aug. 30, 1969	SEA A	Sandy Valdespino	HOU N	Tommy Davis
June 7, 1971	NY A	—	MIL A	Frank Tepedino Bobby Mitchell
Oct. 27, 1972	MIN A	—	NY A	Rick Dempsey

Danny Walton *continued*

Date	Traded To	Traded With	Traded By	In Exchange For
Dec. 15, 1980	CIN N	Greg Mahlberg	TEX A	Don Werner Minor leaguer Greg Hughes

Reggie Walton

Date	Traded To	Traded With	Traded By	In Exchange For
Apr. 9, 1982	PIT N	—	SEA A	Cash

Bill Wambsganss

Date	Traded To	Traded With	Traded By	In Exchange For
Jan. 7, 1924	BOS A	Danny Boone Steve O'Neill Joe Connolly	CLE A	George Burns Roxy Walters Chick Fewster
Dec. 12, 1925	PHI A	—	BOS A	$4,000.

Lloyd Waner

Date	Traded To	Traded With	Traded By	In Exchange For
May 7, 1941	BOS N	—	PIT N	Nick Strincevich
June 12, 1941	CIN N	—	BOS N	Johnny Hutchings
Mar. 9, 1943	BKN N	Al Glossop	PHI N	Babe Dahlgren

Steve Wapnick

Date	Traded To	Traded With	Traded By	In Exchange For
July 14, 1991	CHI A	Shawn Jeter	TOR A	Cory Snyder

(Chicago received Wapnick on September 4, 1991.)

Aaron Ward

Date	Traded To	Traded With	Traded By	In Exchange For
Jan. 13, 1927	CHI A	—	NY A	Johnny Grabowski Ray Morehart
Mar. 4, 1928	CLE A	—	CHI A	Waiver price

Chuck Ward

Date	Traded To	Traded With	Traded By	In Exchange For
Jan. 9, 1918	BKN N	Burleigh Grimes Al Mamaux	PIT N	Casey Stengel George Cutshaw

Colin Ward

Date	Traded To	Traded With	Traded By	In Exchange For
Nov. 11, 1985	SF N	—	CIN N	Bob Buchanan

Dick Ward

Date	Traded To	Traded With	Traded By	In Exchange For
Nov. 21, 1934	STL N	Bud Tinning Cash	CHI N	Tex Carleton

Duane Ward

Date	Traded To	Traded With	Traded By	In Exchange For
July 6, 1986	TOR A	—	ATL N	Doyle Alexander

Gary Ward

Date	Traded To	Traded With	Traded By	In Exchange For
Dec. 7, 1983	TEX A	—	MIN A	Mike Smithson John Butcher minor league C Sam Sorce
Dec. 24, 1986	NY A	—	TEX A	No compensation (free agent signing)

Joe Ward

Date	Traded To	Traded With	Traded By	In Exchange For
Mar. 1909	NY A	—	PHI N	Cash

(Ward was returned to Philadelphia on May 20.)

Pete Ward

Date	Traded To	Traded With	Traded By	In Exchange For
Jan. 14, 1963	CHI A	Hoyt Wilhelm Ron Hansen Dave Nicholson	BAL A	Luis Aparicio Al Smith
Dec. 18, 1969	NY A	—	CHI A	Mickey Scott Cash

Preston Ward

Date	Traded To	Traded With	Traded By	In Exchange For
Oct. 14, 1949	CHI N	Paul Minner	BKN N	$100,000.
June 4, 1953	PIT N	—	CHI N	*see Ralph Kiner*
May 15, 1956	CLE A	—	PIT N	Hank Foiles
June 15, 1958	KC A	Roger Maris Dick Tomanek	CLE A	Woodie Held Vic Power

Turner Ward

Date	Traded To	Traded With	Traded By	In Exchange For
Mar. 19, 1989	CLE A	—	NY A	*see Mel Hall*
June 27, 1991	TOR A	*see Tom Candiotti*	CLE A	—
Nov. 24, 1993	MIL A	—		

Curt Wardle

Date	Traded To	Traded With	Traded By	In Exchange For
Aug. 1, 1985	CLE A	—	MIN A	*see Bert Blyleven*
Feb. 23, 1987	OAK A	—	CLE A	Jeff Kaiser

Lon Warneke

Date	Traded To	Traded With	Traded By	In Exchange For
Oct. 8, 1936	STL N	—	CHI N	Ripper Collins Roy Parmelee
July 8, 1942	CHI N	—	STL N	$75,000.

Jack Warner

Date	Traded To	Traded With	Traded By	In Exchange For
Jan. 1905	STL N	—	NY N	Cash
Aug. 10, 1905	DET A	—	STL N	Cash
Aug. 13, 1906	WAS A	—	DET A	Cash

Jack Warner

Date	Traded To	Traded With	Traded By	In Exchange For
Dec. 19, 1928	WAS A	—	DET A	Bucky Harris
		(Harris was named Detroit manager.)		
Dec. 15, 1932	PHI N	Cy Moore Mickey Finn	BKN N	Ray Benge $15,000.

Jackie Warner

Date	Traded To	Traded With	Traded By	In Exchange For
June 15, 1967	KC A	Jack Sanford	CAL A	Roger Repoz

Bennie Warren

Date	Traded To	Traded With	Traded By	In Exchange For
Sept. 9, 1942	PIT N	—	PHI N	Waiver price
		(Deal was cancelled by Commissioner Landis.)		
Nov. 17, 1942	CHI N	—	PIT N	Cash
Apr. 4, 1946	NY N	—	CHI N	Waiver price

Mike Warren

Date	Traded To	Traded With	Traded By	In Exchange For
May 14, 1982	OAK A	minor league 1B John Evans	MIL A	Rob Picciolo

Rabbit Warstler

Date	Traded To	Traded With	Traded By	In Exchange For
Dec. 12, 1933	PHI A	Bob Kline $125,000.	BOS A	Lefty Grove Max Bishop Rube Walberg
July 6, 1936	BOS N	—	PHI A	Waiver price
July 24, 1940	CHI N	—	BOS N	Waiver price

Dan Warthen

Date	Traded To	Traded With	Traded By	In Exchange For
June 15, 1977	PHI N	Barry Foote	MON N	Wayne Twitchell Tim Blackwell

Carl Warwick

Date	Traded To	Traded With	Traded By	In Exchange For
May 30, 1961	STL N	Bob Lillis	LA N	Daryl Spencer
May 7, 1962	HOU N	John Anderson	STL N	Bobby Shantz
Feb. 17, 1964	STL N	—	HOU N	Jim Beauchamp Chuck Taylor
July 24, 1965	BAL A	—	STL N	Cash
Mar. 30, 1966	CHI N	—	BAL A	Vic Roznovsky

Jimmy Wasdell

Date	Traded To	Traded With	Traded By	In Exchange For
May 25, 1940	BKN N	—	WAS A	Cash
Dec. 12, 1941	PIT N	Pete Coscarart Luke Hamlin Babe Phelps	BKN N	Arky Vaughan
Apr. 30, 1943	PHI N	—	PIT N	Cash

George Washburn

Date	Traded To	Traded With	Traded By	In Exchange For
Apr. 16, 1943	PHI N	—	CHI N	Cash
Apr. 22, 1943	BKN N	Johnny Allen	PHI N	Cash

Ray Washburn

Date	Traded To	Traded With	Traded By	In Exchange For
Nov. 5, 1969	CIN N	—	STL N	George Culver

Claudell Washington

Date	Traded To	Traded With	Traded By	In Exchange For
Mar. 26, 1977	TEX A	—	OAK A	Jim Umbarger Rodney Scott Cash
May 16, 1978	CHI A	Rusty Torres	TEX A	Bobby Bonds

Claudell Washington *continued*

Date	Traded To	Traded With	Traded By	In Exchange For
June 7, 1980	NY N	—	CHI A	Minor league P Jesse Anderson
Nov. 17, 1980	ATL N	—	NY N	No compensation (free agent signing)
June 29, 1986	NY A	Paul Zuvella	ATL N	Ken Griffey Andre Robertson
		(Atlanta received Robertson on July 3, 1986.)		
Jan. 17, 1989	CAL A	—	NY A	No compensation (free agent signing)
Apr. 28, 1990	NY A	Rich Monteleone	CAL A	Luis Polonia

LaRue Washington

Date	Traded To	Traded With	Traded By	In Exchange For
Mar. 31, 1980	MON N	Chris Smith	TEX A	Rusty Staub

U. L. Washington

Date	Traded To	Traded With	Traded By	In Exchange For
Jan. 7, 1985	MON N	—	KC A	Mike Kinnunen Minor League OF Ken Baker
Apr. 24, 1986	PIT N	—	MON N	No compensation (free agent signing)

Mark Wasinger

Date	Traded To	Traded With	Traded By	In Exchange For
Apr. 25, 1987	SF N	Minor league P Tom Meagher	SD N	Minor league P Colin Ward Minor league IF Steve Miller

Gary Waslewski

Date	Traded To	Traded With	Traded By	In Exchange For
Dec. 2, 1968	STL N	—	BOS A	Dick Schofield
June 3, 1969	MON N	—	STL N	Mudcat Grant
May 15, 1970	NY A	—	MON N	Dave McDonald

Steve Waterbury

Date	Traded To	Traded With	Traded By	In Exchange For
June 15, 1977	PHI N	Bake McBride	STL N	Tom Underwood Rick Bosetti Dane Iorg

George Watkins

Date	Traded To	Traded With	Traded By	In Exchange For
Feb. 1934	NY N	—	STL N	Kiddo Davis
Nov. 1, 1934	PHI N	Pretzels Pezzullo Blondy Ryan Johnny Vergez Cash	NY N	Dick Bartell
May 1936	BKN N	—	PHI N	Cash

Allen Watson

Date	Traded To	Traded With	Traded By	In Exchange For
Dec. 14, 1995	SF N	Rich DeLucia Doug Creek	STL N	Royce Clayton

Bob Watson

Date	Traded To	Traded With	Traded By	In Exchange For
June 13, 1979	BOS A	—	HOU N	Pete Ladd Bobby Sprowl Cash
Nov. 8, 1979	NY A	—	BOS A	No compensation (free agent signing)
Apr. 23, 1982	ATL N	—	NY A	Minor league P Scott Patterson

Milt Watson

Date	Traded To	Traded With	Traded By	In Exchange For
Apr. 4, 1918	PHI N	—	STL N	Bert Niehoff $500.

Mule Watson

Date	Traded To	Traded With	Traded By	In Exchange For
May 28, 1920	PIT N	—	BOS N	Waiver price
June 30, 1920	BOS N	—	PIT N	Waiver price
June 7, 1923	NY N	Hank Gowdy	BOS N	Jesse Barnes Earl Smith

Eddie Watt

Date	Traded To	Traded With	Traded By	In Exchange For
Dec. 7, 1973	PHI N	—	BAL A	Cash

Cliff Watwood

Date	Traded To	Traded With	Traded By	In Exchange For
Apr. 29, 1932	BOS A	Bennie Tate Smead Jolley	CHI A	Charlie Berry

Gary Wayne

Date	Traded To	Traded With	Traded By	In Exchange For
Mar. 26, 1993	CLR N	Minor league P Rob Wassenaar	MIN A	Brett Merriman
Jan. 6, 1994	LA N	—	MIN A	No compensation (free agent signing)

Roy Weatherly

Date	Traded To	Traded With	Traded By	In Exchange For
Dec. 17, 1942	NY A	Oscar Grimes	CLE A	Roy Cullenbine Buddy Rosar

Art Weaver

Date	Traded To	Traded With	Traded By	In Exchange For
June 1903	PIT N	—	STL N	Cash

Floyd Weaver

Date	Traded To	Traded With	Traded By	In Exchange For
June 30, 1971	MIL A	—	CHI A	Cash

Jim Weaver

Date	Traded To	Traded With	Traded By	In Exchange For
May 15, 1934	CHI N	—	STL A	Waiver price
Nov. 22, 1934	PIT N	Guy Bush Babe Herman	CHI N	Larry French Freddie Lindstrom
Jan. 1938	STL A	—	PIT N	Cash
Apr. 25, 1938	CIN N	—	STL A	Cash

Jim Weaver

Date	Traded To	Traded With	Traded By	In Exchange For
Aug. 1, 1985	CLE A	—	MIN A	*see Bert Blyleven*

Jim Weaver

Date	Traded To	Traded With	Traded By	In Exchange For
Jan. 4, 1967	HOU N	Jim Landis Doc Edwards	CLE A	Lee Maye Ken Retzer
Aug. 7, 1967	CAL A	—	HOU N	Hector Torres

Monte Weaver

Date	Traded To	Traded With	Traded By	In Exchange For
Feb. 1939	BOS A	—	WAS A	Cash

Orlie Weaver

Date	Traded To	Traded With	Traded By	In Exchange For
June 10, 1911	BOS N	*see Johnny Kling*	CHI N	—

Roger Weaver

Date	Traded To	Traded With	Traded By	In Exchange For
Mar. 23, 1982	ATL N	—	DET A	Eddie Miller

Earl Webb

Date	Traded To	Traded With	Traded By	In Exchange For
Apr. 4, 1930	WAS A	—	CIN N	Waiver price
Apr. 30, 1930	BOS A	—	WAS A	Bill Barrett
Apr. 30, 1930	BOS A	—		
June 12, 1932	DET A	—	BOS A	Dale Alexander Roy Johnson
May 14, 1933	CHI A	—	DET A	Waiver price

Hank Webb

Date	Traded To	Traded With	Traded By	In Exchange For
Feb. 7, 1977	LA N	minor league P Dick Sander	NY N	Rick Auerbach

Red Webb

Date	Traded To	Traded With	Traded By	In Exchange For
Dec. 14, 1949	BOS N	Sid Gordon Buddy Kerr Willard Marshall	NY N	Eddie Stanky Alvin Dark

Skeeter Webb

Date	Traded To	Traded With	Traded By	In Exchange For
Dec. 12, 1944	DET A	—	CHI A	Joe Orengo

Lenny Webster

Date	Traded To	Traded With	Traded By	In Exchange For
Mar. 8, 1994	MON N	—	MIN A	Cash

Mitch Webster

Date	Traded To	Traded With	Traded By	In Exchange For
June 22, 1985	MON N	—	TOR A	Cliff Young

(Toronto received Young on Sep. 10, 1985.)

Date	Traded To	Traded With	Traded By	In Exchange For
July 14, 1988	CHI N	—	MON N	Dave Martinez
Nov. 20, 1989	CLE A	—	CHI N	Dave Clark

Mitch Webster *continued*

Date	Traded To	Traded With	Traded By	In Exchange For
May 16, 1991	PIT N	—	CLE A	Mike York
July 3, 1991	LA N	—	PIT N	Jose Gonzalez

Ramon Webster

Date	Traded To	Traded With	Traded By	In Exchange For
Mar. 24, 1970	SD N	—	OAK A	Roberto Pena
Oct. 19, 1970	OAK A	—	SD N	Cash
June 17, 1971	CHI N	—	OAK A	Cash

Ray Webster

Date	Traded To	Traded With	Traded By	In Exchange For
Jan. 8, 1960	BOS A	—	CLE A	Leo Kiely

Johnny Weekly

Date	Traded To	Traded With	Traded By	In Exchange For
June 15, 1964	BAL A	Cash	HOU N	Joe Gaines
Jan. 6, 1966	NY N	Cash	HOU N	Gary Kroll

Herm Wehmeier

Date	Traded To	Traded With	Traded By	In Exchange For
June 12, 1954	PHI N	—	CIN N	Cash
May 11, 1956	STL N	Murry Dickson	PHI N	Harvey Haddix Ben Flowers Stu Miller
May 13, 1958	DET A	—	STL N	Cash

Dave Wehrmeister

Date	Traded To	Traded With	Traded By	In Exchange For
June 15, 1979	NY A	—	SD N	Jay Johnstone

Ralph Weigel

Date	Traded To	Traded With	Traded By	In Exchange For
Jan. 27, 1948	CHI A	—	CLE A	Thurman Tucker
Apr. 15, 1949	WAS A	—	CHI A	Cash

Dick Weik

Date	Traded To	Traded With	Traded By	In Exchange For
June 14, 1950	CLE A	—	WAS A	Mickey Vernon
June 15, 1953	DET A	*see Ray Boone*	CLE A	—

Bob Weiland

Date	Traded To	Traded With	Traded By	In Exchange For
Dec. 2, 1931	BOS A	—	CHI A	Milt Gaston
May 25, 1934	CLE A	Bob Seeds $25,000.	BOS A	Wes Ferrell Dick Porter
Nov. 20, 1934	STL A	Johnny Burnett Cash	CLE A	Bruce Campbell

Jake Weimer

Date	Traded To	Traded With	Traded By	In Exchange For
Mar. 1906	CIN N	Hans Lobert	CHI N	Harry Steinfeldt

Phil Weintraub

Date	Traded To	Traded With	Traded By	In Exchange For
Dec. 9, 1935	STL N	Roy Parmelee Cash	NY N	Burgess Whitehead

Al Weis

Date	Traded To	Traded With	Traded By	In Exchange For
Dec. 15, 1967	NY N	Tommie Agee	CHI A	Tommy Davis Jack Fisher Billy Wynne Buddy Booker

Walt Weiss

Date	Traded To	Traded With	Traded By	In Exchange For
Nov. 17, 1992	FLA N	—	OAK A	Eric Helfand Scott Baker

(Oakland received Baker on November 20, 1992.)

Date	Traded To	Traded With	Traded By	In Exchange For
Jan. 7, 1994	CLR N	—	FLA N	No compensation (free agent signing)

Johnny Welaj

Date	Traded To	Traded With	Traded By	In Exchange For
Dec. 13, 1941	BOS A	Ken Chase	WAS A	Stan Spence Jack Wilson

Bob Welch

Date	Traded To	Traded With	Traded By	In Exchange For
Dec. 11, 1987	OAK A	Matt Young	LA N	Alfredo Griffin Jay Howell

(Part of three-team trade involving Oakland, Los Angeles and New York Mets.)

Frank Welch

Date	Traded To	Traded With	Traded By	In Exchange For
Nov. 1926	BOS A	—	PHI A	Cash

Date	Traded To		Traded With	Traded By		In Exchange For

Johnny Welch

July 1936	PIT	N	—	BOS	A	Waiver price

Brad Wellman

Mar. 30, 1982	SF	N	—	KC	A	*see Vida Blue*

Bob Wells

June 30, 1994	SEA	A	—	PHI	N	Waiver price

Boomer Wells

Dec. 28, 1981	MIN	A	—	TOR	A	Hosken Powell

David Wells

July 31, 1995	CIN	N	—	DET	A	C. J. Nitkowski Mark Lewis Minor league P Dave Tuttle

(Detroit received Lewis on November 16, 1995.)

Dec. 26, 1995	BAL	A	—	CIN	N	Curtis Goodwin Minor league OF Trovin Valdez

Ed Wells

Dec. 1932	STL	A	—	NY	A	Cash

Terry Wells

Apr. 1, 1990	LA	N	—	HOU	N	Franklin Stubbs

Chris Welsh

Apr. 1, 1981	SD	N	Ruppert Jones Joe Lefebvre Tim Lollar	NY	A	Jerry Mumphrey John Pacella
May 4, 1983	MON	N	—	SD	N	Cash
Nov. 8, 1984	TEX	A	—	MON	N	Dave Hostetler

Jimmy Welsh

Jan. 10, 1928	NY	N	Shanty Hogan	BOS	N	Rogers Hornsby
June 14, 1929	BOS	N	—	NY	N	Doc Farrell
Oct. 14, 1930	CHI	N	Bob Smith	BOS	N	Bill McAfee Wes Schulmerich

Turk Wendell

Sept. 29, 1991	CHI	N	Yorkis Perez	ATL	N	Damon Berryhill Mike Bielecki

Butch Wensloff

Apr. 12, 1948	CLE	A	—	NY	A	Cash

Stan Wentzel

Sept. 30, 1946	PIT	N	Billy Herman Elmer Singleton Whitey Wietelmann	BOS	N	Bob Elliott Hank Camelli

Fred Wenz

Nov. 25, 1969	PHI	N	—	BOS	A	Cash

Bill Werber

May 12, 1933	BOS	A	George Pipgras	NY	A	$100,000.
Dec. 9, 1936	PHI	A	—	BOS	A	Pinky Higgins
Mar. 16, 1939	CIN	N	—	PHI	A	Cash
Dec. 9, 1941	NY	N	—	CIN	N	Cash

Johnny Werhas

May 10, 1967	CAL	A	—	LA	N	Len Gabrielson

Bill Werle

May 3, 1952	STL	N	—	PIT	N	George Munger
Oct. 2, 1952	BOS	A	—	STL	N	Waiver price

Don Werner

Dec. 15, 1980	TEX	A	Minor leaguer Greg Hughes	CIN	N	Danny Walton Greg Mahlberg

Don Wert

Oct. 9, 1970	WAS	A	*see Denny McLain*	DET	A	—

Dennis Werth

Mar. 24, 1982	KC	A	—	NY	A	Minor league P Scott Behan

Bill Wertz

Nov. 18, 1994	BOS	A	—	CLE	A	Waiver price

Vic Wertz

Aug. 14, 1952	STL	A	Dick Littlefield Marlin Stuart Don Lenhardt	DET	A	Jim Delsing Ned Garver Dave Madison Bill Black
June 1, 1954	CLE	A	—	BAL	A	Bob Chakales
Dec. 2, 1958	BOS	A	Gary Geiger	CLE	A	Jimmy Piersall
Sept. 8, 1961	DET	A	—	BOS	A	Waiver price

David West

July 31, 1989	MIN	A	Rick Aguilera Tim Drummond Kevin Tapani Jack Savage	NY	N	Frank Viola

(Minnesota received Savage on October 16, 1989.)

Dec. 5, 1992	PHI	N	—	MIN	A	Mike Hartley

Max West

Apr. 18, 1946	CIN	N	—	BOS	N	Jim Konstanty Cash

Sammy West

Dec. 14, 1932	STL	A	Lloyd Brown Carl Reynolds $20,000.	WAS	A	Goose Goslin Fred Schulte Lefty Stewart
June 15, 1938	WAS	A	—	STL	A	Mel Almada

Wally Westlake

June 15, 1951	STL	N	Cliff Chambers	PIT	N	Bill Howerton Joe Garagiola Howie Pollet Ted Wilks Dick Cole
May 13, 1952	CIN	N	Eddie Kazak	STL	N	Dick Sisler Virgil Stallcup
Aug. 7, 1952	CLE	A	—	CIN	N	Cash
June 15, 1955	BAL	A	Dave Pope	CLE	A	Gene Woodling Billy Cox

(Cox refused to report and announced retirement. Cleveland received $15,000 to complete trade.)

Mickey Weston

Dec. 14, 1990	TOR	A	—	BAL	A	Paul Kilgus

Jeff Wetherby

Mar. 18, 1990	CLE	A	Minor league OF Miguel Sabino	ATL	N	Tommy Hinzo

John Wetteland

Nov. 27, 1991	CIN	N	Tim Belcher	LA	N	Eric Davis Kip Gross
Dec. 11, 1991	MON	N	Bill Risley	CIN	N	Dave Martinez Scott Ruskin Willie Greene
Apr. 5, 1995	NY	A	—	MON	N	Minor league OF Fernando Seguignol Player to be named Cash

Gus Weyhing

Jan. 17, 1900	STL	N	Dan McGann	WAS	N	Cash
July 1900	BKN	N	—	STL	N	Cash

Date	Traded To	Traded With	Traded By	In Exchange For

Lee Wheat

Date	Traded To	Traded With	Traded By	In Exchange For
Feb. 19, 1954	PHI A	Bill Upton	CLE A	Dave Philley
Apr. 16, 1956	BKN N	Tom Saffell Cash	KC A	Tim Thompson

Mack Wheat

Date	Traded To	Traded With	Traded By	In Exchange For
Jan. 12, 1920	PHI N	—	BKN N	Cash

Pete Whisenant

Date	Traded To	Traded With	Traded By	In Exchange For
June 3, 1955	STL N	—	MIL N	Del Rice
Mar. 30, 1956	CHI N	—	STL N	Hank Sauer
Nov. 13, 1956	CIN N	Don Hoak Warren Hacker	CHI N	Elmer Singleton Ray Jablonski
Apr. 29, 1960	CLE A	—	CIN N	Cash
May 15, 1960	WAS A	—	CLE A	Ken Aspromonte

Steve Whitaker

Date	Traded To	Traded With	Traded By	In Exchange For
Apr. 1, 1969	SEA A	John Gelnar	KC A	Lou Piniella
Dec. 12, 1969	SF N	Dick Simpson	SEA A	Bobby Bolin

Bill White

Date	Traded To	Traded With	Traded By	In Exchange For
Mar. 25, 1959	STL N	Ray Jablonski	SF N	Sam Jones Don Choate
Oct. 27, 1965	PHI N	Dick Groat Bob Uecker	STL N	Pat Corrales Art Mahaffey Alex Johnson
Apr. 3, 1969	STL N	—	PHI N	Jim Hutto Jerry Buchek

Charlie White

Date	Traded To	Traded With	Traded By	In Exchange For
Feb. 10, 1954	MIL N	$10,000.	BAL A	Vern Bickford

Devon White

Date	Traded To	Traded With	Traded By	In Exchange For
Dec. 2, 1990	TOR A	Willie Fraser Marcus Moore	CAL A	Junior Felix Luis Sojo Minor league C Ken Rivers
Nov. 21, 1995	FLA N	—	TOR A	No compensation (free agent signing)

Ernie White

Date	Traded To	Traded With	Traded By	In Exchange For
May 14, 1946	BOS N	—	STL N	Cash

Gabe White

Date	Traded To	Traded With	Traded By	In Exchange For
Dec. 15, 1995	CIN N	—	MON N	Minor league 2B Jhonny Carajal

Hal White

Date	Traded To	Traded With	Traded By	In Exchange For
Dec. 4, 1952	STL A	Virgil Trucks Johnny Groth	DET A	Owen Friend Bob Nieman J. W. Porter
June 2, 1953	STL N	—	STL A	Waiver price

Jerry White

Date	Traded To	Traded With	Traded By	In Exchange For
June 9, 1978	CHI N	—	MON N	Woodie Fryman
Dec. 14, 1978	MON N	Rodney Scott	CHI N	Sam Mejias

Jo-Jo White

Date	Traded To	Traded With	Traded By	In Exchange For
Aug. 19, 1944	CIN N	—	PHI A	Cash

Kirby White

Date	Traded To	Traded With	Traded By	In Exchange For
June 1, 1910	PIT N	—	BOS N	Sam Frock

Larry White

Date	Traded To	Traded With	Traded By	In Exchange For
Dec. 9, 1981	LA N	Jorge Orta Jack Fimple	CLE A	Rick Sutcliffe Jack Perconte

Sammy White

Date	Traded To	Traded With	Traded By	In Exchange For
Mar. 16, 1960	CLE A	Jim Marshall	BOS A	Russ Nixon
		(Trade was cancelled when White decided to retire.)		
June 15, 1961	MIL N	—	BOS A	Cash

Ed Whited

Date	Traded To	Traded With	Traded By	In Exchange For
Dec. 8, 1987	ATL N	Minor league P Mike Stoker	HOU N	Rafael Ramirez

Burgess Whitehead

Date	Traded To	Traded With	Traded By	In Exchange For
Dec. 9, 1935	NY N	—	STL N	Roy Parmelee Phil Weintraub Cash

John Whitehead

Date	Traded To	Traded With	Traded By	In Exchange For
June 2, 1939	STL A	—	CHI A	Johnny Marcum

Earl Whitehill

Date	Traded To	Traded With	Traded By	In Exchange For
Dec. 14, 1932	WAS A	—	DET A	Firpo Marberry Carl Fischer
Dec. 10, 1936	CLE A	—	WAS A	Jack Salveson
		(Part of three-team trade involving Chicago, Cleveland, and Washington.)		

Len Whitehouse

Date	Traded To	Traded With	Traded By	In Exchange For
Nov. 1, 1982	MIN A	—	TEX A	John Pacella

Wally Whitehurst

Date	Traded To	Traded With	Traded By	In Exchange For
Dec. 11, 1987	NY N	Jack Savage Kevin Tapani	LA N	Jesse Orosco
		(Part of a three-team trade involving Los Angeles, Oakland, and New York Mets.)		
Oct. 27, 1992	SD N	D. J. Dozier Player to be named	NY N	Tony Fernandez
		(San Diego received C Raul Casanova on December 7, 1992.)		

Mark Whiten

Date	Traded To	Traded With	Traded By	In Exchange For
June 27, 1991	CLE A	Glenallen Hill Denis Boucher Cash	TOR A	Tom Candiotti Turner Ward
Mar. 31, 1993	STL N	Minor league SS Juan Andujar	CLE A	Mark Clark
Apr. 8, 1995	BOS A	Rheal Cormier	STL N	Scott Cooper Cory Bailey Player to be named
July 24, 1995	PHI N	—	BOS A	Dave Hollins

Fred Whitfield

Date	Traded To	Traded With	Traded By	In Exchange For
Dec. 15, 1962	CLE A	—	STL N	Ron Taylor Jack Kubiszyn
Nov. 21, 1967	CIN N	George Culver Bob Raudman	CLE A	Tommy Harper

Terry Whitfield

Date	Traded To	Traded With	Traded By	In Exchange For
Mar. 14, 1977	SF N	—	NY A	Marty Perez

Dick Whitman

Date	Traded To	Traded With	Traded By	In Exchange For
Nov. 14, 1949	PHI N	—	BKN N	Cash
June 8, 1951	BKN N	Cash	PHI N	Tommy Brown

Pinky Whitney

Date	Traded To	Traded With	Traded By	In Exchange For
June 17, 1933	BOS N	Hal Lee	PHI N	Fritz Knothe Wes Schulmerich Cash
Apr. 30, 1936	PHI N	—	BOS N	Mickey Haslin

Ed Whitson

Date	Traded To	Traded With	Traded By	In Exchange For
June 28, 1979	SF N	Al Holland Fred Breining	PIT N	Bill Madlock Lenny Randle Dave Roberts
Nov. 14, 1981	CLE A	—	SF N	Duane Kuiper
Nov. 18, 1982	SD N	—	CLE A	Juan Eichelberger Broderick Perkins
Dec. 27, 1984	NY A	—	SD N	No compensation (free agent signing)

Ed Whitson *continued*

Date	Traded To		Traded With	Traded By		In Exchange For
July 9, 1986	SD	N	—	NY	A	Tim Stoddard

Ernie Whitt

Date	Traded To		Traded With	Traded By		In Exchange For
Dec. 17, 1989	ATL	N	Kevin Batiste	TOR	A	Rick Trlicek

Possum Whitted

Date	Traded To		Traded With	Traded By		In Exchange For
June 1914	BOS	N	Ted Cather	STL	N	Hub Perdue
Feb. 10, 1915	PHI	N	Oscar Dugey	BOS	N	Cash
Aug. 1919	PIT	N	—	PHI	N	Casey Stengel
Mar. 14, 1922	BKN	N	—	PIT	N	Cash

Kevin Wickander

Date	Traded To		Traded With	Traded By		In Exchange For
May 7, 1993	CIN	N	—	CLE	A	Player to be named

(Cleveland received P Todd Ruyak on June 4, 1993.)

Date	Traded To		Traded With	Traded By		In Exchange For
Aug. 29, 1995	MIL	A	—	DET	A	Player to be named

(Detroit received OF Derek Hacopian on September 12, 1995.)

Bob Wicker

Date	Traded To		Traded With	Traded By		In Exchange For
Apr. 1903	CHI	N	—	STL	N	Bob Rhoads
June 2, 1906	CIN	N	$2,000.	CHI	N	Orval Overall

Floyd Wicker

Date	Traded To		Traded With	Traded By		In Exchange For
June 1, 1971	SF	N	—	MIL	A	Bob Heise

Dave Wickersham

Date	Traded To		Traded With	Traded By		In Exchange For
Nov. 18, 1963	DET	A	—	KC	A	*see Rocky Colavito*
Nov. 28, 1967	PIT	N	—	DET	A	Dennis Ribant
Oct. 21, 1968	KC	A	—	PIT	N	Cash
Oct. 21, 1969	ATL	N	—	KC	A	Ron Tompkins

Al Wickland

Date	Traded To		Traded With	Traded By		In Exchange For
June 1, 1915	PIT	F	—	CHI	F	Cash
Jan. 1919	NY	A	—	BOS	N	Cash

Bob Wickman

Date	Traded To		Traded With	Traded By		In Exchange For
Jan. 10, 1992	NY	A	Melido Perez Domingo Jean	CHI	A	Steve Sax

Al Widmar

Date	Traded To		Traded With	Traded By		In Exchange For
Nov. 17, 1947	STL	A	—	BOS	A	*see Vern Stephens*
Nov. 27, 1951	CHI	A	*see Sherm Lollar*	STL	A	—

Ted Wieand

Date	Traded To		Traded With	Traded By		In Exchange For
Dec. 5, 1957	CIN	N	Marty Kutyna Willard Schmidt	STL	N	Curt Flood Joe Taylor

Tom Wieghaus

Date	Traded To		Traded With	Traded By		In Exchange For
Feb. 24, 1984	HOU	N	—	MON	N	George Bjorkman

(Montreal received Bjorkman on March 26, 1984.)

Bob Wiesler

Date	Traded To		Traded With	Traded By		In Exchange For
Feb. 8, 1956	WAS	A	*see Whitey Herzog*	NY	A	—

Whitey Wietelmann

Date	Traded To		Traded With	Traded By		In Exchange For
Sept. 30, 1946	PIT	N	Billy Herman Elmer Singleton Stan Wentzel	BOS	N	Bob Elliott Hank Camelli

Alan Wiggins

Date	Traded To		Traded With	Traded By		In Exchange For
June 27, 1985	BAL	A	—	SD	N	Roy Lee Jackson player to be named

(San Diego received P Rich Caldwell on Sept. 16, 1985.)

Bill Wight

Date	Traded To		Traded With	Traded By		In Exchange For
Feb. 24, 1948	CHI	A	Aaron Robinson Fred Bradley	NY	A	Ed Lopat
Dec. 10, 1950	BOS	A	Ray Scarborough	CHI	A	Joe Dobson Dick Littlefield Al Zarilla
June 3, 1952	DET	A	—	BOS	A	*see George Kell*

Bill Wight *continued*

Date	Traded To		Traded With	Traded By		In Exchange For
June 15, 1953	CLE	A	Art Houtteman Owen Friend Joe Ginsberg	DET	A	Ray Boone Al Aber Steve Gromek Dick Weik
July 13, 1955	BAL	A	—	CLE	A	Hoot Evers
Dec. 4, 1957	CIN	N	—	BAL	A	Waiver price

Del Wilber

Date	Traded To		Traded With	Traded By		In Exchange For
May 12, 1952	BOS	A	—	PHI	N	Cash
Dec. 14, 1954	NY	N	—	BOS	A	Billy Klaus

Ted Wilborn

Date	Traded To		Traded With	Traded By		In Exchange For
Nov. 1, 1979	NY	A	—	TOR	A	*see Chris Chambliss*
Mar. 30, 1982	SF	N	Andy McGaffigan	NY	A	Doyle Alexander

Milt Wilcox

Date	Traded To		Traded With	Traded By		In Exchange For
Dec. 6, 1971	CLE	A	—	CIN	N	Ted Uhlaender
Feb. 25, 1975	CHI	N	—	CLE	A	Dave LaRoche Brock Davis

Randy Wiles

Date	Traded To		Traded With	Traded By		In Exchange For
Aug. 23, 1977	STL	N	—	CHI	A	Cash
Dec. 9, 1977	HOU	N	—	STL	N	Minor league P Ron Selak

Mark Wiley

Date	Traded To		Traded With	Traded By		In Exchange For
Sept. 12, 1978	TOR	A	—	SD	N	Minor league OF Andy Dyes

Rob Wilfong

Date	Traded To		Traded With	Traded By		In Exchange For
May 12, 1982	CAL	A	Doug Corbett	MIN	A	Tom Brunansky Mike Walters $400,000.

Hoyt Wilhelm

Date	Traded To		Traded With	Traded By		In Exchange For
Feb. 26, 1957	STL	N	—	NY	N	Whitey Lockman
Sept. 21, 1957	CLE	A	—	STL	N	Cash
Aug. 23, 1958	BAL	A	—	CLE	A	Waiver price
Jan. 14, 1963	CHI	A	Pete Ward Ron Hansen Dave Nicholson	BAL	A	Luis Aparicio Al Smith
Dec. 12, 1968	CAL	A	—	KC	A	Ed Kirkpatrick Dennis Paepke
Sept. 8, 1969	ATL	N	—	CAL	A	Cash
Sept. 21, 1970	CHI	N	—	ATL	N	Cash
Nov. 30, 1970	ATL	N	—	CHI	N	Hal Breeden

Jim Wilhelm

Date	Traded To		Traded With	Traded By		In Exchange For
Feb. 15, 1980	CLE	A	Bob Owchinko	SD	N	Jerry Mumphrey

Kaiser Wilhelm

Date	Traded To		Traded With	Traded By		In Exchange For
Jan. 1904	BOS	N	—	PIT	N	Cash

Joe Wilhoit

Date	Traded To		Traded With	Traded By		In Exchange For
July 29, 1917	PIT	N	—	BOS	N	Waiver price
Aug. 5, 1917	NY	N	—	PIT	N	Waiver price

Curtis Wilkerson

Date	Traded To		Traded With	Traded By		In Exchange For
Dec. 5, 1988	CHI	N	—	TEX	A	*see Rafael Palmeiro*
Jan. 9, 1991	PIT	N	—	CHI	N	No compensation (free agent signing)

Dean Wilkins

Date	Traded To		Traded With	Traded By		In Exchange For
July 12, 1987	CHI	N	Bob Tewksbury Rich Scheid	NY	A	Steve Trout Cash

Rick Wilkins

Date	Traded To		Traded With	Traded By		In Exchange For
June 28, 1995	HOU	N	—	CHI	N	Luis Gonzalez Scott Servais

Bill Wilkinson

Date	Traded To		Traded With	Traded By		In Exchange For
Apr. 21, 1989	PIT	N	*see Rey Quinones*	SEA	A	—

Ted Wilks

Date	Traded To	Traded With	Traded By	In Exchange For
June 15, 1951	PIT N	Bill Howerton Joe Garagiola Howie Pollet Dick Cole	STL N	Cliff Chambers Wally Westlake
Aug. 18, 1952	CLE A	George Strickland	PIT N	Johnny Berardino minor league P Charlie Sipple $50,000.

Jerry Willard

Date	Traded To	Traded With	Traded By	In Exchange For
Dec. 9, 1982	CLE A	Manny Trillo Jay Baller George Vukovich Julio Franco	PHI N	Von Hayes

Carl Willey

Date	Traded To	Traded With	Traded By	In Exchange For
Mar. 23, 1963	NY N	—	MIL N	Cash

Nick Willhite

Date	Traded To	Traded With	Traded By	In Exchange For
Oct. 15, 1964	WAS A	—	LA N	Cash
May 11, 1965	LA N	—	WAS A	Cash
Dec. 15, 1966	CAL A	—	LA N	Bob Lee
June 10, 1967	NY N	—	CAL A	Jack Hamilton

Bernie Williams

Date	Traded To	Traded With	Traded By	In Exchange For
Oct. 25, 1973	SD N	Willie McCovey	SF N	Mike Caldwell

Billy Williams

Date	Traded To	Traded With	Traded By	In Exchange For
Oct. 23, 1974	OAK A	—	CHI N	Darold Knowles Bob Locker Manny Trillo

Brian Williams

Date	Traded To	Traded With	Traded By	In Exchange For
Dec. 28, 1994	SD N	*see Ken Caminiti*	HOU N	—

Buff Williams

Date	Traded To	Traded With	Traded By	In Exchange For
Jan. 1912	WAS A	—	BOS A	Waiver price

Charlie Williams

Date	Traded To	Traded With	Traded By	In Exchange For
May 11, 1972	SF N	$50,000.	NY N	Willie Mays

Cy Williams

Date	Traded To	Traded With	Traded By	In Exchange For
Dec. 26, 1917	PHI N	—	CHI N	Dode Paskert

Dallas Williams

Date	Traded To	Traded With	Traded By	In Exchange For
Mar. 26, 1982	CIN N	minor league P Brooks Carey	BAL A	Joe Nolan
Mar. 30, 1984	DET A	—	CIN N	Minor league P Charlie Nail

Dana Williams

Date	Traded To	Traded With	Traded By	In Exchange For
Aug. 2, 1989	CHI A	—	BOS A	Ray Chadwick

Dib Williams

Date	Traded To	Traded With	Traded By	In Exchange For
May 1, 1935	BOS A	—	PHI A	Cash

Dick Williams

Date	Traded To	Traded With	Traded By	In Exchange For
June 25, 1956	BAL A	—	BKN N	Waiver price
June 13, 1957	CLE A	—	BAL A	Jim Busby
Apr. 1, 1958	BAL A	Bud Daley Gene Woodling	CLE A	Larry Doby Don Ferrarese
Oct. 2, 1958	KC A	—	BAL A	Chico Carrasquel
Apr. 12, 1961	BAL A	Dick Hall	KC A	Jerry Walker Chuck Essegian
Oct. 12, 1962	HOU N	—	BAL A	Cash
Dec. 10, 1962	BOS A	—	HOU N	Carroll Hardy

Earl Williams

Date	Traded To	Traded With	Traded By	In Exchange For
Nov. 30, 1972	BAL A	Taylor Duncan	ATL N	Pat Dobson Roric Harrison Davey Johnson Johnny Oates

Earl Williams *continued*

Date	Traded To	Traded With	Traded By	In Exchange For
Apr. 17, 1975	ATL N	—	BAL A	Jimmy Freeman $75,000.
July 24, 1976	MON N	—	ATL N	Cash

Eddie Williams

Date	Traded To	Traded With	Traded By	In Exchange For
June 15, 1984	CIN N	—	NY N	*see Bruce Berenyi*
Jan. 23, 1989	CHI A	—	CLE A	Ed Wojna Joel Davis

Frank Williams

Date	Traded To	Traded With	Traded By	In Exchange For
Jan. 8, 1987	CIN N	Minor league P Timber Mead Minor league P Mike Villa	SF N	Eddie Milner
Jan. 16, 1989	DET A	—	CIN N	No compensation (free agent signing)

Jim Williams

Date	Traded To	Traded With	Traded By	In Exchange For
Nov. 30, 1967	LA N	Paul Popovich	CHI N	Lou Johnson

Jimmy Williams

Date	Traded To	Traded With	Traded By	In Exchange For
Feb. 1908	STL A	Hobe Ferris Danny Hoffman	NY A	Fred Glade Charlie Hemphill

Jimy Williams

Date	Traded To	Traded With	Traded By	In Exchange For
Feb. 8, 1968	CIN N	Pat Corrales	STL N	Johnny Edwards

Ken Williams

Date	Traded To	Traded With	Traded By	In Exchange For
Dec. 15, 1927	BOS A	—	STL A	$10,000.
Jan. 29, 1930	NY A	—	BOS A	Waiver price

Kenny Williams

Date	Traded To	Traded With	Traded By	In Exchange For
Mar. 23, 1989	DET A	—	CHI A	Eric King
June 18, 1990	TOR A	—	DET A	Waiver price
June 4, 1991	MON N	—	TOR A	Waiver price

Matt Williams

Date	Traded To	Traded With	Traded By	In Exchange For
Aug. 28, 1985	TEX A	—	TOR A	*see Cliff Johnson*

Mitch Williams

Date	Traded To	Traded With	Traded By	In Exchange For
Apr. 6, 1985	TEX A	—	SD N	Randy Asadoor
Dec. 5, 1988	CHI N	Paul Kilgus Steve Wilson Curtis Wilkerson Minor league IF Luis Benitez Minor league OF Pablo Delgado	TEX A	Rafael Palmeiro Jamie Moyer Drew Hall
Apr. 7, 1991	PHI N	—	CHI N	Chuck McElroy Bob Scanlan
Dec. 2, 1993	HOU N	—	PHI N	Doug Jones Jeff Juden

Otto Williams

Date	Traded To	Traded With	Traded By	In Exchange For
July 1903	CHI N	—	STL N	Cash

Pop Williams

Date	Traded To	Traded With	Traded By	In Exchange For
Apr. 1903	PHI N	—	CHI N	Cash
June 1903	BOS N	—	PHI N	Cash

Reggie Williams

Date	Traded To	Traded With	Traded By	In Exchange For
Apr. 5, 1988	CLE A	—	LA N	Minor league P Greg LaFever

Stan Williams

Date	Traded To	Traded With	Traded By	In Exchange For
Nov. 26, 1962	NY A	—	LA N	Bill Skowron
Mar. 30, 1965	CLE A	—	NY A	Cash
Dec. 10, 1969	MIN A	—	CLE A	*see Graig Nettles*
Sept. 1, 1971	STL N	—	MIN A	Fred Rico minor league P Dan Ford

Todd Williams

Date	Traded To		Traded With	Traded By		In Exchange For
Sept. 10, 1995	OAK	A	—	LA	N	Minor league P Matt McDonald

Walt Williams

Date	Traded To		Traded With	Traded By		In Exchange For
Dec. 14, 1966	CHI	A	Don Dennis	STL	N	Johnny Romano minor league P Lee White
Oct. 19, 1972	CLE	A	—	CHI	A	Eddie Leon
Mar. 19, 1974	DET	A	Rick Sawyer	CLE	A	Jim Perry
			(Part of three-team trade involving Detroit, Cleveland, and New York Yankees.)			
Mar. 19, 1974	NY	A	Rick Sawyer Ed Farmer	DET	A	Gerry Moses
			(Part of three-team trade involving Detroit, New York Yankees, and Cleveland.)			

Woody Williams

Date	Traded To		Traded With	Traded By		In Exchange For
Sept. 10, 1940	CIN	N	—	BKN	N	Waiver price

Mark Williamson

Date	Traded To		Traded With	Traded By		In Exchange For
Oct. 30, 1986	BAL	A	Terry Kennedy	SD	N	Storm Davis

Carl Willis

Date	Traded To		Traded With	Traded By		In Exchange For
Aug. 27, 1984	CIN	N	Cash	DET	A	Bill Scherrer
Jan. 19, 1988	CHI	A	—	CIN	N	Minor league OF Darrell Pruitt

Jim Willis

Date	Traded To		Traded With	Traded By		In Exchange For
Oct. 1, 1954	CIN	N	Johnny Klippstein	CHI	N	Ted Tappe Jim Bolger Harry Perkowski

Joe Willis

Date	Traded To		Traded With	Traded By		In Exchange For
Apr. 1911	STL	N	—	STL	A	Cash

Ron Willis

Date	Traded To		Traded With	Traded By		In Exchange For
Aug. 8, 1969	HOU	N	—	STL	N	Cash
			(Willis was returned to St. Louis on October 15.)			

Vic Willis

Date	Traded To		Traded With	Traded By		In Exchange For
Dec. 15, 1905	PIT	N	—	BOS	N	Dave Brain Del Howard Vive Lindaman
Jan. 1910	STL	N	—	PIT	N	Cash

Claude Willoughby

Date	Traded To		Traded With	Traded By		In Exchange For
Nov. 6, 1930	PIT	N	Tommy Thevenow	PHI	N	Dick Bartell

Jim Willoughby

Date	Traded To		Traded With	Traded By		In Exchange For
Oct. 14, 1974	STL	N	—	SF	N	Tom Heintzelman
Apr. 4, 1975	BOS	A	—	STL	N	Mario Guerrero
Apr. 5, 1978	CHI	A	—	BOS	A	Cash
Oct. 23, 1978	STL	N	—	CHI	A	John Scott

Bump Wills

Date	Traded To		Traded With	Traded By		In Exchange For
Mar. 26, 1982	CHI	N	—	TEX	A	Paul Mirabella minor league P Paul Semall Cash

Frank Wills

Date	Traded To		Traded With	Traded By		In Exchange For
Jan. 18, 1985	MIL	A	Don Slaught	KC	A	Jim Sundberg
			(Part of a four-team deal involving Texas, Milwaukee, Kansas City, and New York Mets.)			
Jan. 18, 1985	NY	N	—	MIL	A	Tim Leary
			(Part of a four-team trade involving Texas, Milwaukee, Kansas City, and New York Mets.)			
Mar. 29, 1985	SEA	A	—	NY	N	Minor league P Wray Bergendahl

Maury Wills

Date	Traded To		Traded With	Traded By		In Exchange For
Dec. 1, 1966	PIT	N	—	LA	N	Bob Bailey Gene Michael
June 11, 1969	LA	N	Manny Mota	MON	N	Ron Fairly Paul Popovich

Ted Wills

Date	Traded To		Traded With	Traded By		In Exchange For
May 8, 1962	CIN	N	—	BOS	A	Cash

Terry Wilshusen

Date	Traded To		Traded With	Traded By		In Exchange For
June 15, 1973	CIN	N	minor league P Thor Skogan	CAL	A	Richie Scheinblum

Archie Wilson

Date	Traded To		Traded With	Traded By		In Exchange For
May 3, 1952	WAS	A	*see Jackie Jensen*	NY	A	—
June 9, 1952	BOS	A	—	WAS	A	Ken Wood

Art Wilson

Date	Traded To		Traded With	Traded By		In Exchange For
Feb. 10, 1916	PIT	N	—	CHI	F	Cash
July 29, 1916	CHI	N	Otto Knabe	PIT	N	Wildfire Schulte Bill Fischer
Jan. 4, 1918	BOS	N	Larry Doyle $15,000.	CHI	N	Lefty Tyler

Bill Wilson

Date	Traded To		Traded With	Traded By		In Exchange For
June 11, 1954	PHI	A	Sonny Dixon Al Sima $20,000.	CHI	A	Ed McGhee Morrie Martin

Billy Wilson

Date	Traded To		Traded With	Traded By		In Exchange For
Nov. 7, 1973	MIL	A	—	PHI	N	Frank Linzy

Craig Wilson

Date	Traded To		Traded With	Traded By		In Exchange For
Feb. 22, 1993	KC	A	Felix Jose	STL	N	Gregg Jefferies Minor league OF Ed Gerald

Dan Wilson

Date	Traded To		Traded With	Traded By		In Exchange For
Nov. 2, 1993	SEA	A	Bobby Ayala	CIN	N	Erik Hanson Bret Boone

Earl Wilson

Date	Traded To		Traded With	Traded By		In Exchange For
June 14, 1966	DET	A	Joe Christopher	BOS	A	Julio Navarro Don Demeter
July 15, 1970	SD	N	—	DET	A	Cash

Frank Wilson

Date	Traded To		Traded With	Traded By		In Exchange For
May 10, 1928	STL	A	—	CLE	A	Cash

Glenn Wilson

Date	Traded To		Traded With	Traded By		In Exchange For
Mar. 24, 1984	PHI	N	John Wockenfuss	DET	A	Guillermo Hernandez Dave Bergman
Dec. 9, 1987	SEA	A	Mike Jackson Minor league OF Dave Brundage	PHI	N	Phil Bradley Tim Fortugno
July 22, 1988	PIT	N	—	SEA	A	Darnell Coles
Aug. 18, 1989	HOU	N	—	PIT	N	Billy Hatcher

Grady Wilson

Date	Traded To		Traded With	Traded By		In Exchange For
Apr. 5, 1948	PIT	N	—	PHI	N	Cash

Hack Wilson

Date	Traded To		Traded With	Traded By		In Exchange For
Dec. 1931	STL	N	Bud Teachout	CHI	N	Burleigh Grimes
Jan. 23, 1932	BKN	N	—	STL	N	Minor league P Bob Parham $45,000.

Jack Wilson

Date	Traded To		Traded With	Traded By		In Exchange For
Dec. 13, 1941	WAS	A	Stan Spence	BOS	A	Ken Chase Johnny Welaj
July 17, 1942	DET	A	—	WAS	A	Eric McNair
			(McNair refused to report.)			

Jim Wilson

Date	Traded To		Traded With	Traded By		In Exchange For
Nov. 17, 1947	STL	A	—	BOS	A	*see Vern Stephens*
Apr. 13, 1955	BAL	A	—	MIL	N	Cash

Jim Wilson *continued*

Date	Traded To	Traded With	Traded By	In Exchange For
May 21, 1956	CHI A	Dave Philley	BAL A	Bob Nieman Mike Fornieles Connie Johnson George Kell

Jimmie Wilson

Date	Traded To	Traded With	Traded By	In Exchange For
May 11, 1928	STL N	—	PHI N	Spud Davis Homer Peel
Nov. 15, 1933	PHI N	—	STL N	Spud Davis Eddie Delker

(Wilson was named manager of the Phillies.)

Mookie Wilson

Date	Traded To	Traded With	Traded By	In Exchange For
July 31, 1989	TOR A	—	NY N	Jeff Musselman Minor league P Mike Brady

Nigel Wilson

Date	Traded To	Traded With	Traded By	In Exchange For
Apr. 23, 1995	SF N	—	FLA N	Waiver price

Owen Wilson

Date	Traded To	Traded With	Traded By	In Exchange For
Dec. 12, 1913	STL N	Art Butler Dots Miller Cozy Dolan Hank Robinson	PIT N	Ed Konetchy Bob Harmon Mike Mowrey

Red Wilson

Date	Traded To	Traded With	Traded By	In Exchange For
May 29, 1954	DET A	—	CHI A	Matt Batts
July 26, 1960	CLE A	Rocky Bridges	DET A	Hank Foiles

Steve Wilson

Date	Traded To	Traded With	Traded By	In Exchange For
Dec. 5, 1988	CHI N	—	TEX A	*see Rafael Palmeiro*
Sept. 6, 1991	LA N	—	CHI N	Jeff Hartsock

Tack Wilson

Date	Traded To	Traded With	Traded By	In Exchange For
Mar. 28, 1983	MIN A	—	LA N	Minor league SS Ivan Mesa

Ted Wilson

Date	Traded To	Traded With	Traded By	In Exchange For
May 8, 1952	NY N	—	CHI A	$25,000.
Aug. 22, 1956	NY A	—	NY N	Waiver price

Willie Wilson

Date	Traded To	Traded With	Traded By	In Exchange For
Dec. 3, 1990	OAK A	—	KC A	No compensation (free agent signing)
Dec. 18, 1992	CHI N	—	OAK A	No compensation (free agent signing)

Hal Wiltse

Date	Traded To	Traded With	Traded By	In Exchange For
Apr. 25, 1928	STL A	—	BOS A	Wally Gerber

Snake Wiltse

Date	Traded To	Traded With	Traded By	In Exchange For
July 1901	PHI A	—	PIT N	Cash
July 1902	BAL A	—	PHI A	Cash

Gordie Windhorn

Date	Traded To	Traded With	Traded By	In Exchange For
Apr. 5, 1960	LA N	minor league 1B Dick Sanders	NY A	Fred Kipp
May 12, 1962	LA A	—	KC A	Marlan Coughtry
July 23, 1962	KC A	Ted Bowsfield	LA A	Dan Osinski

(Kansas City received Bowsfield on November 30.)

Robbie Wine

Date	Traded To	Traded With	Traded By	In Exchange For
Mar. 25, 1988	TEX A	—	HOU N	Mike Loynd
May 17, 1988	NY A	—	TEX A	Cash

Dave Winfield

Date	Traded To	Traded With	Traded By	In Exchange For
Dec. 15, 1980	NY A	—	SD N	No compensation (free agent signing)
May 11, 1990	CAL A	—	NY A	Mike Witt
Dec. 19, 1991	TOR A	—	CAL A	No compensation (free agent signing)

Dave Winfield *continued*

Date	Traded To	Traded With	Traded By	In Exchange For
Dec. 17, 1992	MIN A	—	TOR A	No compensation (free agent signing)
Aug. 31, 1994	CLE A	—	MIN A	Cash

Jim Winford

Date	Traded To	Traded With	Traded By	In Exchange For
Mar. 1939	BKN N	—	STL N	Waiver price

Ted Wingfield

Date	Traded To	Traded With	Traded By	In Exchange For
Sept. 10, 1924	BOS A	—	WAS A	Cash

Ivy Wingo

Date	Traded To	Traded With	Traded By	In Exchange For
Apr. 8, 1915	CIN N	—	STL N	Mike Gonzalez

Lave Winham

Date	Traded To	Traded With	Traded By	In Exchange For
Feb. 1903	PIT N	—	BKN N	Waiver price

Jim Winn

Date	Traded To	Traded With	Traded By	In Exchange For
Mar. 27, 1987	CHI A	—	PIT N	John Cangelosi

(Pittsburgh received Cangelosi on March 30, 1987.)

Herm Winningham

Date	Traded To	Traded With	Traded By	In Exchange For
Dec. 10, 1984	MON N	—	NY N	*see Gary Carter*
July 13, 1988	CIN N	Jeff Reed Randy St. Claire	MON N	Tracy Jones Pat Pacillo
Jan. 29, 1992	BOS A	—	CIN N	No compensation (free agent signing)

Tom Winsett

Date	Traded To	Traded With	Traded By	In Exchange For
Dec. 3, 1936	BKN N	—	STL N	Frenchy Bordagaray Dutch Leonard Jimmy Jordan

George Winter

Date	Traded To	Traded With	Traded By	In Exchange For
Jan. 1908	DET A	—	BOS A	Cash

Jesse Winters

Date	Traded To	Traded With	Traded By	In Exchange For
July 25, 1921	PHI N	Curt Walker Butch Henline $30,000.	NY N	Irish Meusel

Matt Winters

Date	Traded To	Traded With	Traded By	In Exchange For
Feb. 13, 1986	NY A	*see Ron Hassey*	CHI A	—

Alan Wirth

Date	Traded To	Traded With	Traded By	In Exchange For
Mar. 15, 1978	OAK A	—	SF N	*see Vida Blue*

Casey Wise

Date	Traded To	Traded With	Traded By	In Exchange For
Nov. 10, 1957	MIL N	—	CHI N	Ben Johnson Charlie King minor league OF Len Williams and cash
Oct. 15, 1959	DET A	Don Kaiser Mike Roarke	MIL N	Charlie Lau Don Lee

Rick Wise

Date	Traded To	Traded With	Traded By	In Exchange For
Feb. 25, 1972	STL N	—	PHI N	Steve Carlton
Oct. 26, 1973	BOS A	Bernie Carbo	STL N	Reggie Smith Ken Tatum
Mar. 30, 1978	CLE A	Bo Diaz Mike Paxton Ted Cox	BOS A	Dennis Eckersley Fred Kendall
Nov. 19, 1979	SD N	—	CLE A	No compensation (free agent signing)

Bobby Witt

Date	Traded To	Traded With	Traded By	In Exchange For
Aug. 31, 1992	OAK A	Ruben Sierra Jeff Russell Cash	TEX A	Jose Canseco
Apr. 8, 1995	FLA N	—	OAK A	No compensation (free agent signing)

Date	Traded To		Traded With	Traded By		In Exchange For

Bobby Witt *continued*

Aug. 8, 1995	TEX	A	—	FLA	N	Wilson Heredia Player to be named

(Florida received Heredia on August 11 and OF Scott Podsednik on October 2, 1995.)

George Witt

Oct. 10, 1961	LA	A	—	PIT	N	Cash

Mike Witt

May 11, 1990	NY	A	—	CAL	A	Dave Winfield

Whitey Witt

Apr. 17, 1922	NY	A	—	PHI	A	Cash

John Wockenfuss

June 6, 1973	STL	N	Mike Nagy	TEX	A	Jim Bibby
Mar. 24, 1984	PHI	N	Glenn Wilson	DET	A	Guillermo Hernandez Dave Bergman

Jim Wohlford

Dec. 6, 1976	MIL	A	Jamie Quirk Bob McClure	KC	A	Jim Colborn Darrell Porter
Nov. 29, 1979	SF	N	—	MIL	A	No compensation (free agent signing)
Feb. 2, 1983	MON	N	—	SF	N	Chris Smith

Pete Wojey

Mar. 27, 1958	CLE	A	$20,000.	DET	A	Milt Bolling Vito Valentinetti

Ed Wojna

Aug. 31, 1983	SD	N	—	PHI	N	*see Sixto Lezcano*
Oct. 5, 1987	CHI	A	—	SD	N	Player to be named
Jan. 23, 1989	CLE	A	Joel Davis	CHI	A	Eddie Williams

Wally Wolf

Jan. 20, 1964	CIN	N	Jim Dickson Cash	HOU	N	Eddie Kasko

Bill Wolfe

July 13, 1904	WAS	A	Long Tom Hughes	NY	A	Al Orth

Harry Wolfe

Aug. 1917	PIT	N	—	CHI	N	Cash

Larry Wolfe

Feb. 3, 1979	BOS	A	—	MIN	A	Dave Coleman

Roger Wolff

Dec. 13, 1943	WAS	A	—	PHI	A	Bobo Newsom
Mar. 4, 1947	CLE	A	—	WAS	A	George Case
June 14, 1947	PIT	N	—	CLE	A	Cash

Harry Wolter

June 17, 1907	PIT	N	—	CIN	N	Cash
July 4, 1907	STL	N	—	PIT	N	Cash
Jan. 1910	NY	A	—	BOS	A	Waiver price

Harry Wolverton

Apr. 28, 1900	PHI	N	—	CHI	N	Cash
Dec. 20, 1904	BOS	N	Chick Fraser	PHI	N	Togie Pittinger

Dooley Womack

Dec. 4, 1968	HOU	N	—	NY	A	Dick Simpson
Aug. 24, 1969	SEA	A	Roric Harrison	HOU	N	Jim Bouton

Jake Wood

June 23, 1967	CIN	N	—	DET	A	Cash

Ken Wood

Nov. 28, 1951	BOS	A	Gus Niarhos	STL	A	Les Moss Tom Wright
June 9, 1952	WAS	A	—	BOS	A	Archie Wilson

Roy Wood

Jan. 1914	CLE	A	—	PIT	N	Cash

Smoky Joe Wood

Feb. 24, 1917	CLE	A	—	BOS	A	$15,000.

Ted Wood

Mar. 23, 1993	MON	N	—	SF	N	Waiver price

Wilbur Wood

Oct. 12, 1966	CHI	A	—	PIT	N	Juan Pizarro

Hal Woodeshick

Feb. 18, 1958	CLE	A	J. W. Porter	DET	A	Jim Hegan Hank Aguirre
May 25, 1959	WAS	A	Hal Naragon	CLE	A	Ed Fitz Gerald
June 5, 1961	DET	A	—	WAS	A	Chuck Cottier
June 15, 1965	STL	N	Chuck Taylor	HOU	N	Mike Cuellar Ron Taylor

Gene Woodling

Dec. 7, 1946	PIT	N	—	CLE	A	Al Lopez
Nov. 18, 1954	BAL	A	—	NY	A	*see Bob Turley*
June 15, 1955	CLE	A	Billy Cox	BAL	A	Dave Pope Wally Westlake

(Cox refused to report and announced retirement. Cleveland received $15,000 to complete trade.)

Apr. 1, 1958	BAL	A	Bud Daley Dick Williams	CLE	A	Larry Doby Don Ferrarese
June 15, 1962	NY	N	—	WAS	A	Cash

Al Woods

Nov. 5, 1982	OAK	A	—	TOR	A	Cliff Johnson

Gary Woods

Dec. 4, 1978	HOU	N	—	TOR	A	Minor league OF Don Pisker
Dec. 9, 1981	CHI	N	—	HOU	N	Jim Tracy

Jim Woods

Jan. 11, 1960	PHI	N	—	CHI	N	*see Richie Ashburn*

Ron Woods

June 14, 1969	NY	A	—	DET	A	Tom Tresh
June 25, 1971	MON	N	—	NY	A	Ron Swoboda

Walt Woods

Jan. 1900	PIT	N	*see Honus Wagner*	LOU	N	—

Dick Woodson

May 4, 1974	NY	A	—	MIN	A	Mike Pazik

Tracy Woodson

Nov. 9, 1989	CHI	A	—	LA	N	Jeff Bittiger

Frank Woodward

July 14, 1919	STL	N	Elmer Jacobs Doug Baird	PHI	N	Lee Meadows Gene Paulette

Woody Woodward

June 11, 1968	CIN	N	Clay Carroll Tony Cloninger	ATL	N	Milt Pappas Ted Davidson Bob Johnson

Chuck Workman

June 12, 1946	PIT	N	—	BOS	N	Johnny Barrett

Ralph Works

Date	Traded To	Traded With	Traded By	In Exchange For
Aug. 1912	CIN N	—	DET A	Cash

Todd Worrell

Date	Traded To	Traded With	Traded By	In Exchange For
Dec. 9, 1992	LA N	—	STL N	No compensation (free agent signing)

Rich Wortham

Date	Traded To	Traded With	Traded By	In Exchange For
Dec. 12, 1980	MON N	—	CHI A	Tony Bernazard

Al Worthington

Date	Traded To	Traded With	Traded By	In Exchange For
Mar. 29, 1960	BOS A	—	SF N	Jim Marshall

Craig Worthington

Date	Traded To	Traded With	Traded By	In Exchange For
Feb. 17, 1992	SD N	Minor league P Tom Martin	BAL A	Jim Lewis Minor league OF Steve Martin
Aug. 16, 1995	TEX A	—	CIN N	Minor league OF Stephen Larkin Cash

Red Worthington

Date	Traded To	Traded With	Traded By	In Exchange For
Sept. 11, 1934	STL N	—	BOS N	Waiver price

Clarence Wright

Date	Traded To	Traded With	Traded By	In Exchange For
July 1903	STL A	—	BKN N	Bill Reidy

Clyde Wright

Date	Traded To	Traded With	Traded By	In Exchange For
Oct. 22, 1973	MIL A	Steve Barber Ken Berry Art Kusnyer Cash	CAL A	Ellie Rodriguez Skip Lockwood Gary Ryerson Ollie Brown Joe Lahoud
Dec. 5, 1974	TEX A	—	MIL A	Pete Broberg

George Wright

Date	Traded To	Traded With	Traded By	In Exchange For
June 18, 1986	MON N	—	TEX A	Cash

Glenn Wright

Date	Traded To	Traded With	Traded By	In Exchange For
Dec. 11, 1928	BKN N	—	PIT N	Jesse Petty Harry Riconda

Ken Wright

Date	Traded To	Traded With	Traded By	In Exchange For
Dec. 7, 1973	NY A	Lou Piniella	KC A	Lindy McDaniel
May 3, 1974	PHI N	—	NY A	Mike Wallace

Mel Wright

Date	Traded To	Traded With	Traded By	In Exchange For
Apr. 11, 1954	STL N	Bill Virdon minor league OF Emil Tellinger	NY A	Enos Slaughter

Ricky Wright

Date	Traded To	Traded With	Traded By	In Exchange For
Aug. 19, 1983	TEX A	Dave Stewart $200,000.	LA N	Rick Honeycutt

Taffy Wright

Date	Traded To	Traded With	Traded By	In Exchange For
Dec. 8, 1939	CHI A	Pete Appleton	WAS A	Gee Walker
Nov. 15, 1948	PHI A	—	CHI A	Cash

Tom Wright

Date	Traded To	Traded With	Traded By	In Exchange For
Nov. 28, 1951	STL A	Les Moss	BOS A	Ken Wood Gus Niarhos
June 15, 1952	CHI A	Leo Thomas	STL A	Willie Miranda Al Zarilla
Mar. 27, 1954	WAS A	—	CHI A	Kite Thomas

Russ Wrightstone

Date	Traded To	Traded With	Traded By	In Exchange For
May 29, 1928	NY N	—	PHI N	Art John

Yats Wuestling

Date	Traded To	Traded With	Traded By	In Exchange For
May 30, 1930	NY A	Ownie Carroll Harry Rice	DET A	Waite Hoyt Mark Koenig

John Wyatt

Date	Traded To	Traded With	Traded By	In Exchange For
June 13, 1966	BOS A	Rollie Sheldon Jose Tartabull	KC A	Jim Gosger Ken Sanders Guido Grilli
May 18, 1968	NY A	—	BOS A	Cash
June 15, 1968	DET A	—	NY A	Cash

Whit Wyatt

Date	Traded To	Traded With	Traded By	In Exchange For
June 2, 1933	CHI A	—	DET A	Vic Frasier
Mar. 28, 1945	PHI N	—	BKN N	$20,000.

Butch Wynegar

Date	Traded To	Traded With	Traded By	In Exchange For
May 12, 1982	NY A	Roger Erickson	MIN A	John Pacella Larry Milbourne Pete Filson Cash
Dec. 19, 1986	CAL A	—	NY A	Ron Romanick Alan Mills

(New York received Mills on June 22, 1987.)

Early Wynn

Date	Traded To	Traded With	Traded By	In Exchange For
Dec. 14, 1948	CLE A	Mickey Vernon	WAS A	Joe Haynes Eddie Klieman Eddie Robinson
Dec. 4, 1957	CHI A	Al Smith	CLE A	Fred Hatfield Minnie Minoso

Jimmy Wynn

Date	Traded To	Traded With	Traded By	In Exchange For
Dec. 6, 1973	LA N	—	HOU N	Claude Osteen minor league P Dave Culpepper
Nov. 17, 1975	ATL N	Tom Paciorek Lee Lacy Jerry Royster	LA N	Dusty Baker Ed Goodson
Nov. 29, 1976	NY A	—	ATL N	Cash

Billy Wynne

Date	Traded To	Traded With	Traded By	In Exchange For
Dec. 15, 1967	CHI A	—	NY N	*see Tommie Agee*
Nov. 30, 1970	CAL A	*see Ken Berry*	CHI A	—

Marvell Wynne

Date	Traded To	Traded With	Traded By	In Exchange For
Mar. 31, 1981	NY N	minor league P John Skinner	KC A	Juan Berenguer
June 14, 1983	PIT N	Steve Senteney	NY N	Junior Ortiz Minor league P Arthur Ray
Apr. 3, 1986	SD N	—	PIT N	Bob Patterson
Aug. 30, 1989	CHI N	Luis Salazar	SD N	Calvin Schiraldi Darrin Jackson Phil Stephenson

(San Diego received Stephenson on Sept. 5, 1989.)

Johnny Wyrostek

Date	Traded To	Traded With	Traded By	In Exchange For
Feb. 5, 1946	PHI N	—	STL N	Cash
Feb. 7, 1948	CIN N	Cash	PHI N	Eddie Miller
May 23, 1952	PHI N	Kent Peterson	CIN N	Bubba Church

Hugh Yancy

Date	Traded To	Traded With	Traded By	In Exchange For
Nov. 6, 1976	CIN N	—	CHI A	Tom Spencer

Al Yates

Date	Traded To	Traded With	Traded By	In Exchange For
June 24, 1967	BOS A	Cash	NY N	Dennis Bennett

Steve Yeager

Date	Traded To	Traded With	Traded By	In Exchange For
Dec. 11, 1985	SEA A	—	LA N	Ed Vande Berg

Eric Yelding

Date	Traded To	Traded With	Traded By	In Exchange For
July 4, 1992	CHI A	—	HOU N	Rich Scheid

Steve Yerkes

Date	Traded To	Traded With	Traded By	In Exchange For
Feb. 10, 1916	CHI N	—	PIT F	Cash

Rich Yett

Date	Traded To	Traded With	Traded By	In Exchange For
Aug. 1, 1985	CLE A	—	MIN A	*see Bert Blyleven*

Date	Traded To	Traded With	Traded By	In Exchange For

Rich Yett *continued*

Dec. 29, 1989	MIN A	—	CLE A	No compensation (free agent signing)

Earl Yingling

Apr. 1914	CIN N	Herbie Moran	BKN N	Dick Egan

Jim York

Dec. 2, 1971	HOU N	Lance Clemons	KC A	John Mayberry minor league IF Dave Grangaard
Jan. 8, 1976	NY A	—	HOU N	Cash

Mike York

May 16, 1991	CLE A	—	PIT N	Mitch Webster

Rudy York

Jan. 3, 1946	BOS A	—	DET A	Eddie Lake
June 14, 1947	CHI A	—	BOS A	Jake Jones

Eddie Yost

Dec. 6, 1958	DET A	Rocky Bridges Neil Chrisley	WAS A	Reno Bertoia Ron Samford Jim Delsing

Ned Yost

Dec. 8, 1983	TEX A	minor league P Dan Scarpetta	MIL A	Jim Sundberg

Floyd Youmans

Dec. 10, 1984	MON N	Hubie Brooks Mike Fitzgerald Herm Winningham	NY N	Gary Carter
Dec. 6, 1988	PHI N	Jeff Parrett	MON N	Kevin Gross

Anthony Young

Mar. 30, 1994	CHI N	Minor league P Ottis Smith	NY N	Jose Vizcaino

Babe Young

June 7, 1947	CIN N	—	NY N	Joe Beggs

Bobby Young

June 27, 1955	CLE A	—	BAL A	Hank Majeski

Cliff Young

June 22, 1985	TOR A	—	MON N	Mitch Webster
		(Toronto received Young on Sep. 10, 1985.)		
Mar. 9, 1989	CAL A	—	TOR A	DeWayne Buice

Cy Young

Feb. 18, 1909	CLE A	—	BOS A	Charlie Chech Jack Ryan $12,500.
July 1911	BOS N	—	CLE A	Waiver price

Dick Young

Mar. 28, 1954	BKN N	$50,000.	PHI N	Bobby Morgan

Don Young

May 14, 1967	STL N	—	CHI N	Cash
Aug. 1, 1967	CHI N	—	STL N	Cash

Gerald Young

Aug. 28, 1984	HOU N	Manny Lee Minor league P Mitch Cook	NY N	Ray Knight

Harley Young

June 18, 1908	BOS N	Tom McCarthy	PIT N	Irv Young

Irv Young

June 18, 1908	PIT N	—	BOS N	Tom McCarthy Harley Young

Matt Young

Dec. 10, 1986	LA N	—	SEA A	Dennis Powell Minor league IF Mike Watters
Dec. 11, 1987	OAK A	*see Bob Welch*	LA N	—
Dec. 15, 1989	SEA A	—	OAK A	No compensation (free agent signing)
Dec. 4, 1990	BOS A	—	SEA A	No compensation (free agent signing)

Mike Young

Mar. 21, 1988	PHI N	player to be named	BAL A	Rick Schu Jeff Stone Keith Hughes
		(Philadelphia received OF Frank Bellino on June 14, 1988.)		
Aug. 24, 1988	MIL A	—	PHI N	Alex Madrid

Pep Young

Dec. 9, 1940	CIN N	—	BKN N	Lew Riggs

Ralph Young

Apr. 3, 1922	PHI A	—	DET A	Waiver price

Joel Youngblood

Mar. 28, 1977	STL N	—	CIN N	Bill Caudill
June 15, 1977	NY N	—	STL N	Mike Phillips
Aug. 4, 1982	MON N	—	NY N	Tom Gorman
Feb. 7, 1983	SF N	—	MON N	No compensation (free agent signing)
Dec. 21, 1988	CIN N	—	SF N	No compensation (free agent signing)

Sal Yvars

June 15, 1953	STL N	—	NY N	$12,500.

Chris Zachary

July 1, 1970	STL N	—	KC A	Ted Abernathy
Apr. 2, 1973	PIT N	—	DET A	Charlie Sands

Tom Zachary

Feb. 1926	STL A	Win Ballou	WAS A	Joe Bush Jack Tobin
July 7, 1927	WAS A	—	STL A	General Crowder
Aug. 23, 1928	NY A	—	WAS A	Waiver price
May 12, 1930	BOS N	—	NY A	Waiver price

Elmer Zacher

May 8, 1910	STL N	—	NY N	Cash

Pat Zachry

June 15, 1977	NY N	Doug Flynn Steve Henderson Dan Norman	CIN N	Tom Seaver
Dec. 28, 1982	LA N	—	NY N	Jorge Orta
Feb. 4, 1985	PHI N	—	LA N	Al Oliver

Geoff Zahn

May 2, 1975	CHI N	Eddie Solomon	LA N	Burt Hooton
Dec. 2, 1980	CAL A	—	MIN A	No compensation (free agent signing)

Paul Zahniser

Apr. 26, 1925	BOS A	Roy Carlyle	WAS A	Joe Harris

Dom Zanni

Nov. 30, 1961	CHI A	—	SF N	*see Billy Pierce*
May 5, 1963	CIN N	—	CHI A	Jim Brosnan

Al Zarilla

Date	Traded To		Traded With	Traded By		In Exchange For
May 8, 1949	BOS	A	—	STL	A	Stan Spence Cash
Dec. 10, 1950	CHI	A	Joe Dobson Dick Littlefield	BOS	A	Ray Scarborough Bill Wight
June 15, 1952	STL	A	Willie Miranda	CHI	A	Tom Wright Leo Thomas
Aug. 31, 1952	BOS	A	—	STL	A	Cash

Jeff Zaske

Date	Traded To		Traded With	Traded By		In Exchange For
Sept. 30, 1986	TEX	A	—	PIT	N	Randy Kramer

Norm Zauchin

Date	Traded To		Traded With	Traded By		In Exchange For
Jan. 23, 1958	WAS	A	Albie Pearson	BOS	A	Pete Runnels

Joe Zdeb

Date	Traded To		Traded With	Traded By		In Exchange For
Jan. 15, 1980	CHI	A	—	KC	A	Eddie Bane

Rollie Zeider

Date	Traded To		Traded With	Traded By		In Exchange For
June 1, 1913	NY	A	Babe Borton	CHI	A	Hal Chase
Feb. 10, 1916	CHI	N	*see Three Finger Brown*	CHI	F	—

Todd Zeile

Date	Traded To		Traded With	Traded By		In Exchange For
June 16, 1995	CHI	N	—	STL	N	Mike Morgan Minor league IF-OF Paul Torres Minor league C Francisco Morales
Dec. 22, 1995	PHI	N	—	CHI	N	No compensation (free agent signing)

Bill Zepp

Date	Traded To		Traded With	Traded By		In Exchange For
Mar. 29, 1971	DET	A	—	MIN	A	Bob Adams Minor League P Art Clifford

Gus Zernial

Date	Traded To		Traded With	Traded By		In Exchange For
Apr. 30, 1951	PHI	A	Dave Philley	CHI	A	Paul Lehner Minnie Minoso
(Part of three-team trade involving Chicago White Sox, Philadelphia A's, and Cleveland.)						
Nov. 20, 1957	DET	A	Billy Martin Tom Morgan Lou Skizas Mickey McDermott Tim Thompson	KC	A	Bill Tuttle Jim Small Duke Maas John Tsitouris Frank House Kent Hadley Jim McManus

Chief Zimmer

Date	Traded To		Traded With	Traded By		In Exchange For
Jan. 1900	PIT	N	*see Honus Wagner*	LOU	N	—
Jan. 1903	PHI	N	—	PIT	N	Waiver price

Don Zimmer

Date	Traded To		Traded With	Traded By		In Exchange For
Apr. 8, 1960	CHI	N	—	LA	N	Ron Perranoski John Goryl minor league OF Lee Handley $25,000.
May 7, 1962	CIN	N	—	NY	N	Bob Miller Cliff Cook

Don Zimmer *continued*

Date	Traded To		Traded With	Traded By		In Exchange For
Jan. 24, 1963	LA	N	—	CIN	N	Minor league P Scott Breeden
June 24, 1963	WAS	A	—	LA	N	Cash

Heinie Zimmerman

Date	Traded To		Traded With	Traded By		In Exchange For
Aug. 28, 1916	NY	N	Mickey Doolan	CHI	N	Larry Doyle Herb Hunter Merwin Jacobson

Jerry Zimmerman

Date	Traded To		Traded With	Traded By		In Exchange For
Jan. 30, 1962	MIN	A	—	CIN	N	Dan Dobbek

Guy Zinn

Date	Traded To		Traded With	Traded By		In Exchange For
Dec. 1912	BOS	N	George Davis	NY	A	Cash

Richie Zisk

Date	Traded To		Traded With	Traded By		In Exchange For
Dec. 10, 1976	CHI	A	Silvio Martinez	PIT	N	Terry Forster Goose Gossage
Nov. 9, 1977	TEX	A	—	CHI	A	No compensation (free agent signing)
Dec. 12, 1980	SEA	A	Rick Auerbach Ken Clay Jerry Don Gleaton Brian Allard Minor league P Steve Finch	TEX	A	Rick Honeycutt Mario Mendoza Larry Cox Leon Roberts Willie Horton

Billy Zitzmann

Date	Traded To		Traded With	Traded By		In Exchange For
June 1919	CIN	N	—	PIT	N	Cash

Sam Zoldak

Date	Traded To		Traded With	Traded By		In Exchange For
Feb. 17, 1944	STL	A	minor league OF Barney Lutz	PHI	A	Frankie Hayes
June 15, 1948	CLE	A	—	STL	A	Bill Kennedy $100,000.
Apr. 30, 1951	PHI	A	Ray Murray Minnie Minoso	CLE	A	Lou Brissie
(Part of three-team trade involving Cleveland, Philadelphia A's, and Chicago White Sox.)						

Eddie Zosky

Date	Traded To		Traded With	Traded By		In Exchange For
Nov. 18, 1994	FLA	N	—	TOR	A	Player to be named
(Toronto received P Scott Pace on December 14, 1994.)						

Bill Zuber

Date	Traded To		Traded With	Traded By		In Exchange For
Apr. 21, 1941	WAS	A	—	CLE	A	Cash
Jan. 29, 1943	NY	A	Cash	WAS	A	Gerry Priddy Milo Candini
June 18, 1946	BOS	A	—	NY	A	Cash

Bob Zupcic

Date	Traded To		Traded With	Traded By		In Exchange For
May 5, 1994	CHI	A	—	BOS	A	Waiver price

Paul Zuvella

Date	Traded To		Traded With	Traded By		In Exchange For
June 29, 1986	NY	A	Claudell Washington	ATL	N	Ken Griffey Andre Robertson
(Atlanta received Robertson on July 3, 1986.)						

George Zuverink

Date	Traded To		Traded With	Traded By		In Exchange For
Apr. 26, 1954	DET	A	—	CIN	N	Cash
July 8, 1955	BAL	A	—	DET	A	Waiver price

PART ELEVEN

National Association Register

Alphabetical List of Every Man Who Ever
Played in the National Association
and His Record in That League

National Association Register

This section contains an alphabetical listing of every man who played in the National Association, baseball's first professional league, which lasted from 1871 through 1875. In addition to the facts about the players and their year-by-year batting and pitching records, there are team and managerial records for each year. Information about the National Association is not as complete as the other data that appear in this book. This is because many statistical items are not available as a result of poor newspaper coverage.

The records of men who played in the National Association and in the major leagues are not combined because the National Association is not considered a major league. The reasons for this, as defined by the Special Baseball Records Committee, were the erratic schedule and procedures of the National Association. For men who played in the National Association and went on to play or manage in the major leagues, their major league records can be found in the appropriate sections of this book. Appearing last, after the alphabetical player listing, are the yearly league standings and team data. All information and abbreviations that may appear unfamiliar are explained in the sample format presented below.

		Manager	W	L	Manager	W	L
1871	Philadelphia Athletics	Dick McBride	21	7			
	Chicago White Stockings	Jimmy Wood	19	9			
	Boston Red Stockings	Harry Wright	20	10			
	Washington Olympics	Nick Young	15	15			
	New York Mutuals	Bob Ferguson	16	17			
	Troy Haymakers	Lip Pike	1	3	Bill Craver	12	12
	Ft. Wayne Kekiongas	Bill Lennon	5	9	Harry Deanne	2	3
	Cleveland Forest Citys	Charlie Pabor	10	19			
	Rockford Forest Citys	Scott Hastings	4	21			

Team Column Headings and Statistical Information

	Manager	WL	Manager	W	L

W	Wins
L	Loses
PCT	Winning Percentage
GB	Games Behind the League Leader
R	Runs Scored
AB	At Bats
H	Hits
BA	Batting Average
Manager	The name and record of the man who managed the team. Teams with more than one manager have the managers listed in the order of when they managed.

The following is the record of John Doe, a fictitious player used as an example to illustrate the information about the players:

John Doe

DOE, JOHN LEE (Slim) BR TR 6'2" 165 lbs.
Played as John Cherry part of 1900.
Born John Lee Doughnut. Brother of Bill Doe.
B. Jan. 1, 1850, New York, N.Y. D. July 1, 1955, New York, N.Y.
Manager 1908–15.
Hall of Fame 1946.

		G	AB	H	R	BA	W	L	PCT	G by Pos
1871	Philadelphia Athletics	26	132	65	45	**.492**	2	2	.500	38-22, P-4
1872	Boston Red Stockings	26	169	43	25	.254	6	3	.600	38-20, P-15
1873		51	238	59	36	.248	7	4	.700	38-36, P-15
1874	2 teams New York Mutuals (25G. .314 W-2, L-2) Lord Baltimores (25G. .296 W-3, L-0)									
"	total	50	196	60	36	.305	5	2	.500	38-40, P-10
1875	Brooklyn Atlantics	1	0	0	0	—	0	0	—	P-1
	5 yrs.	163	735	227	142	.309	20	11	.645	38-118,P-45

Player Information

John Doe

This shortened version of the player's full name is the name most familiar to the fans. All players in this section are alphabetically arranged by the last name part of this name.

Doe, John Lee

Player's full name. The arrangement is last name first, then first and middle name(s).

(Slim)

Player's nickname. Any name appearing in parentheses is a nickname.

BR TR

The player's batting and throwing style. Doe, for instance, batted and threw right-handed. A "BB" would mean Doe was a switch hitter, a "BL" would mean that he batted left-handed, and a "TL" would mean that he threw left-handed.

6'2"

Player's height.

165 lbs.

Player's average playing weight.

Played as John Cherry part of 1871

The player at one time in his career played under another name and can be found in box scores or newspaper stories under that name. In the case of Doe, he was still an amateur athlete when he entered baseball in 1871, and in order to protect his amateur standing he adopted an alias.

Born John Lee Doughnut

The name the player was given at birth. (For the most part, the player never used this name while playing in the National Association, but if he did, it would be listed as "played as," which is explained above under the heading "Played as John Cherry part of 1871.")

Brother of Bill Doe

The player's brother. (Relatives indicated here are fathers, sons, and brothers who played or managed in the National Association and the major leagues.)

B. Jan. 1, 1850, New York, N.Y.

Date and place of birth.

D. July 1, 1955, New York, N.Y.

Date and place of death. (Since all men who played in the National Association are dead, the word "deceased" is shown if no information is now available.)

Hall of Fame 1946

Doe was elected to the Baseball Hall of Fame in 1946.

Manager 1872

Doe also served as a manager. All men who were managers, along with their managerial records, can also be found with the team information.

Player Column Headings Information

G	Games Played
AB	At Bats
H	Hits
R	Runs Scored
BA	Batting Average
W	Wins as a Pitcher
L	Losses as a Pitcher
PCT	Pitcher's Winning Percentage
G by POS	Games by Position (All fielding positions that a man played within the given year are shown. The position where the most games were played is listed first.)

Team Information

1871	Philadelphia Athletics									
1872	Boston Red Stockings									
1873										
1874	2 teams New York Mutuals (25G. .314 W-2, L-2) Lord Baltimores (25G. .296 W-3, L-0)									
	total	50	196	60	36	.305	5	2	.500	38-40, P-10
1875	Brooklyn Atlantics									
	5 yrs.									

Blank space appearing beneath a team indicates that the team is the same. Doe, for example, played for the Boston Red Stockings from 1872 through 1873.

2 Teams Total. Indicates a player played for more than one team in the same year. Doe played for two teams in 1874. The number of games he played, his batting average, and pitching decisions for each team are also shown. Directly beneath this line, following the word "total," is Doe's combined record for both teams in 1874.

Player Statistical Information

John Doe

DOE, JOHN LEE (Slim) TR 6′2″ 165 lbs.
Played as John Cherry part of 1900.
Born John Lee Doughnut. Brother of Bill Doe.
B. Jan. 1, 1850, New York, N.Y. D. July 1, 1955, New York, N.Y.
Manager 1908–15.
Hall of Fame 1946.

		G	AB	H	R	BA	W	L	PCT	G by Pos
1871	Philadelphia Athletics	26	132	65	45	**.492**	2	2	.500	38-22, P-4
1872	Boston Red Stockings	26	169	43	25	.254	6	3	.600	38-20, P-15
1873		51	238	59	36	.248	7	4	.700	38-36, P-15
1874	2 teams New York Mutuals (25G. .314 W-2, L-2) Lord Baltimores (25G. .296 W-3, L-0)									
	total	50	196	60	36	.305	5	2	.500	38-40, P-10
1875	Brooklyn Atlantics	1	0	0	0	—	0	0	—	P-1
	5 yrs.	163	735	227	142	.309	20	11	.645	38-118, P-45

Meaningless Averages. Indicated by the use of a dash (—). In the case of Doe, a dash is shown for his 1875 batting average. This means that although he played one game he had no official at bats. A batting average of .000 would mean he had at least one at bat with no hits. If a dash is shown in place of a pitcher's winning percentage, as it is in the case of Doe in 1875, it means that although he pitched in one game he never had a decision. A percentage of .000 would mean he had at least one loss.

League Leaders. Statistics that appear in boldfaced print indicate the player led the league that year in a particular statistical category. Doe, for example, led the National Association in batting in 1871. When there is a tie for league lead, the figures for all the men who tied are shown in boldface.

John Abadie

ABADIE, JOHN BR TR 6′ 192 lbs.
B. Nov. 4, 1854, Philadelphia, Pa. D. May 17, 1905, Pemberton, N. J.

		G	AB	H	R	BA	W	L	PCT	G by Pos
1875	**2 teams Brooklyn Atlantics** (1G .250) **Philadelphia Centennials** (11G .217)									
″	**total**	12	50	11	4	.220				1B-12

Dave Abercrombie

ABERCROMBIE, DAVID
B. May 6, 1840, Falkirk, Scotland D. Sept. 2, 1916, Baltimore, Md.

		G	AB	H	R	BA	W	L	PCT	G by Pos
1871	**Troy Haymakers**	1	4	0	0	.000				SS-1

Bob Addy

ADDY, ROBERT EDWARD (The Magnet) BL TL 5′ 8″ 160 lbs.
B. Feb. 1845, Rochester, N. Y. D. Apr. 9, 1910, Pocatello, Ida.
Manager 1877.

		G	AB	H	R	BA	W	L	PCT	G by Pos
1871	**Rockford Forest Citys**	25	122	31	29	.254				SS-3
1873	**2 teams Boston Red Stockings** (31G .340) **Philadelphias** (10G .286)									
″	**total**	41	218	71	49	.326				OF-31, 2B-10
1874	**Hartfords**	50	208	55	26	.264				2B-45, 3B-4, SS-1
1875	**Philadelphias**	69	308	81	60	.263				OF-66, 2B-3
	4 yrs.	185	856	238	164	.278				OF-97, 2B-58, 3B-4, SS-4

Ham Allen

ALLEN, HOMER S.
B. Aug. 1854, Hamden, Conn. D. Jan. 7, 1892, Hamden, Conn.

		G	AB	H	R	BA	W	L	PCT	G by Pos
1872	**Middletown Mansfields**	17	77	14	8	.182				OF-10, SS-7

Andy Allison

ALLISON, ANDREW K. 5′10″ 150 lbs.
B. 1848, New York, N. Y. Deceased.

		G	AB	H	R	BA	W	L	PCT	G by Pos
1872	**Brooklyn Eckfords**	25	107	15	11	.140				1B-23, OF-2

Art Allison

ALLISON, ARTHUR ALGERNON 5′ 8″ 150 lbs.
Brother of Doug Allison.
B. Jan. 29, 1849, Philadelphia, Pa. D. Feb. 25, 1916, Washington, D. C.

		G	AB	H	R	BA	W	L	PCT	G by Pos
1871	**Cleveland Forest Citys**	29	140	36	27	.257				OF-29
1872		18	88	23	13	.261				OF-18
1873	**Elizabeth Resolutes**	23	102	31	12	.304				OF-20, 1B-2, C-1
1875	**2 teams Hartfords** (35G .242) **Washington Nationals** (27G .169)									
″	**total**	62	279	59	42	.211				OF-36, 1B-24, C-1, 2B-1
	4 yrs.	132	609	149	94	.245				OF-103, 1B-26, C-2, 2B-1

Bill Allison

ALLISON, WILLIAM ANDREW
B. Sept. 17, 1848, Philadelphia, Pa. D. June 12, 1923

		G	AB	H	R	BA	W	L	PCT	G by Pos
1872	**Brooklyn Eckfords**	3	11	2	3	.182				OF-2, 2B-1

Doug Allison

ALLISON, DOUGLAS L. BR TR 5′10½″ 160 lbs.
Brother of Art Allison.
B. July 1845, Philadelphia, Pa. D. Dec. 19, 1916, Washington, D. C.

		G	AB	H	R	BA	W	L	PCT	G by Pos
1871	**Washington Olympics**	27	132	44	28	.333				C-27
1872	**2 teams Brooklyn Eckfords** (18G .299) **Troy Haymakers** (23G .319)									
″	**total**	41	206	64	41	.311				C-40, SS-1
1873	**2 teams New York Mutuals** (11G .245) **Elizabeth Resolutes** (18G .275)									
″	**total**	29	144	38	17	.264				C-26, OF-3
1874	**New York Mutuals**	65	326	88	65	.270				OF-41, C-24
1875	**Hartfords**	61	293	68	38	.232				C-59, 1B-3
	5 yrs.	223	1101	302	189	.274				C-176, OF-44, 1B-3, SS-1

Cap Anson

ANSON, ADRIAN CONSTANTINE (Pops, Old Anse) BR TR 6′ 227 lbs.
B. Apr. 11, 1852, Marshalltown, Iowa D. Apr. 14, 1922, Chicago, Ill.
Manager 1879–98.
Hall of Fame 1939.

		G	AB	H	R	BA	W	L	PCT	G by Pos
1871	**Rockford Forest Citys**	25	122	43	30	.352				3B-20, C-3, 2B-2, OF-1
1872	**Philadelphia Athletics**	45	231	88	60	.381				3B-45
1873		51	272	96	52	.353				1B-36, 3B-10, 2B-4, OF-1, C-1
1874		55	267	98	51	.367				1B-22, 3B-20, OF-8, SS-5
1875		69	330	105	84	.318				1B-32, OF-22, C-11, 3B-4
	5 yrs.	245	1222	430	277	.352				3B-99, 1B-90, OF-32, C-15, 2B-6, SS-5

Sam Armstrong

ARMSTRONG, SAMUEL 6′ 2″ 160 lbs.
B. 1850, Baltimore, Md. Deceased.

		G	AB	H	R	BA	W	L	PCT	G by Pos
1871	**Fort Wayne Kekiongas**	12	48	11	9	.229				OF-12

Billy Arnold

ARNOLD, WILLIS S.
B. Mar. 2, 1851, Middletown, Conn. D. Jan. 17, 1899, Albany, N. Y.

		G	AB	H	R	BA	W	L	PCT	G by Pos
1872	**Middletown Mansfields**	2	8	1	2	.125				OF-2

Harry Arundel

ARUNDEL, HARRY TR 5′ 6″ 145 lbs.
B. Feb. 1855, Philadelphia, Pa. D. Mar. 25, 1904, Cleveland, Ohio.

		G	AB	H	R	BA	W	L	PCT	G by Pos
1875	**Brooklyn Atlantics**	1	4	0	0	.000				OF-1

Ed Atkinson

ATKINSON, EDWARD
B. 1851, Baltimore, Md. Deceased.

Year	Team	G	AB	H	R	BA	W	L	PCT	G by Pos
1873	**Washington Nationals**	2	9	0	2	.000				OF-2

Henry Austin

AUSTIN, HENRY C.
B. 1844, Brooklyn, N. Y. D. Sept. 3, 1895, Amityville, N. Y.

Year	Team	G	AB	H	R	BA	W	L	PCT	G by Pos
1873	**Elizabeth Resolutes**	23	106	24	11	.226				OF-23

Stud Bancker

BANCKER, JOHN
B. Philadelphia, Pa. Deceased.

Year	Team	G	AB	H	R	BA	W	L	PCT	G by Pos
1875	**New Havens**	19	77	11	3	.143				C-12, 2B-3, 3B-3, SS-1

Al Barker

BARKER, ALFRED L
B. Jan. 18, 1839, Rockford, Ill. D. Sept. 15, 1912, Rockford, Ill.

Year	Team	G	AB	H	R	BA	W	L	PCT	G by Pos
1871	**Rockford Forest Citys**	1	5	1	0	.200				OF-1

Tom Barlow

BARLOW, THOMAS H.
Deceased.

Year	Team	G	AB	H	R	BA	W	L	PCT	G by Pos
1872	**Brooklyn Atlantics**	35	174	48	31	.276				C-34, SS-2
1873		55	283	71	48	.251				C-55
1874	**Hartfords**	32	157	49	37	.312				SS-32
1875	**2 teams** **Brooklyn Atlantics** (1G .000) **New Havens** (1G .200)									
″	**total**	2	9	1	1	.111				SS-1, 2B-1
4 yrs.		124	623	169	117	.271				C-89, SS-35, 2B-1

Ross Barnes

BARNES, ROSCOE CHARLES BR TR 5′ 8½″ 145 lbs.
B. May 8, 1850, Mount Morris, Ill. D. Feb. 5, 1915, Chicago, Ill.

Year	Team	G	AB	H	R	BA	W	L	PCT	G by Pos
1871	**Boston Red Stockings**	31	172	65	66	.378				2B-16, SS-15, 3B-1
1872		45	240	97	81	.404				2B-45
1873		60	338	136	126	.402				2B-47, 3B-13
1874		52	277	94	73	.339				2B-52
1875		78	398	148	116	.372				2B-78
5 yrs.		266	1425	540	462	.379				2B-238, SS-15, 3B-14

Billy Barnie

BARNIE, WILLIAM HARRISON (Bald Billy) 5′ 7″ 157 lbs.
B. Jan. 26, 1853, New York, N. Y. D. July 15, 1900, Hartford, Conn.
Manager 1883–94, 1897–98.

Year	Team	G	AB	H	R	BA	W	L	PCT	G by Pos
1874	**Hartfords**	45	184	36	19	.196				C-23, OF-21, SS-1
1875	**2 teams** **New York Mutuals** (10G .150) **Keokuk Westerns** (10G .108)									
″	**total**	20	77	10	4	.130				OF-10, C-10
2 yrs.		65	261	46	23	.176				C-33, OF-31, SS-1

Barrett

BARRETT
B. Brooklyn, N. Y.

Year	Team	G	AB	H	R	BA	W	L	PCT	G by Pos
1872	**Brooklyn Atlantics**	7	30	8	4	.267				OF-7

Bill Barrett

BARRETT, WILLIAM
B. Baltimore, Md. Deceased.

Year	Team	G	AB	H	R	BA	W	L	PCT	G by Pos
1871	**Fort Wayne Kekiongas**	1	5	1	1	.200				3B-1, C-1
1872	**Washington Olympics**	1	5	0	0	.000				C-1
1873	**Lord Baltimores**	1	4	1	0	.250				SS-1, OF-1
3 yrs.		3	14	2	1	.143				C-2, OF-1, SS-1, 3B-1

Frank Barrows

BARROWS, FRANKLIN L.
B. Oct. 22, 1846, Hudson, Ohio D. Feb. 6, 1922, Fitchburg, Mass.

Year	Team	G	AB	H	R	BA	W	L	PCT	G by Pos
1871	**Boston Red Stockings**	18	87	14	13	.161				OF-17, 2B-1

John Bass

BASS, JOHN E. 5′ 6″ 150 lbs.
B. 1850, Baltimore, Md. Deceased.

Year	Team	G	AB	H	R	BA	W	L	PCT	G by Pos
1871	**Cleveland Forest Citys**	22	91	25	18	.275				SS-22
1872	**Brooklyn Atlantics**	1	4	1	0	.250				OF-1
2 yrs.		23	95	26	18	.274				SS-22, OF-1

Joe Battin

BATTIN, JOSEPH V. BR TR
B. Nov. 11, 1851, Philadelphia, Pa. D. Dec. 10, 1937, Akron, Ohio.
Manager 1883–84.

Year	Team	G	AB	H	R	BA	W	L	PCT	G by Pos
1871	**Cleveland Forest Citys**	1	4	0	0	.000				OF-1
1873	**Philadelphia Athletics**	1	6	3	4	.500				OF-1
1874		51	228	62	41	.272				2B-40, OF-7, SS-4
1875	**St. Louis**	66	278	73	32	.263				2B-60, 3B-6
4 yrs.		119	516	138	77	.267				2B-100, OF-9, 3B-6, SS-4

		G	AB	H	R	BA	W	L	PCT	G by Pos

Tommy Beals

BEALS, THOMAS L. BR 5′ 5″ 144 lbs.
B. Aug. 1850, New York, N. Y. D. Oct. 2, 1915, San Francisco, Calif.

		G	AB	H	R	BA	W	L	PCT	G by Pos
1871	**Washington Olympics**	10	38	7	7	.184				OF-8, 2B-2
1872		9	39	11	8	.282				2B-5, SS-2, OF-2
1873	**Washington Nationals**	37	170	46	35	.271				2B-26, C-11, OF-1
1874	**Boston Red Stockings**	18	98	20	20	.204				2B-10, OF-8
1875		35	157	46	38	.293				OF-31, 2B-6
5 yrs.		109	502	130	108	.259				OF-50, 2B-49, C-11, SS-2

George Bechtel

BECHTEL, GEORGE A. 5′11″ 165 lbs.
B. Sept. 2, 1848, Philadelphia, Pa. Deceased.

		G	AB	H	R	BA	W	L	PCT	G by Pos
1871	**Philadelphia Athletics**	20	94	30	23	.319	1	2	.333	OF-15, P-3, 3B-2
1872	**New York Mutuals**	52	262	79	64	.302				OF-51, 1B-1
1873	**Philadelphias**	53	266	62	54	.233	0	3	.000	OF-50, P-3
1874		31	153	43	29	.281	1	3	.250	OF-27, P-4
1875	**2 teams Philadelphia Athletics** (34G .292 W-3 L-1) **Philadelphia Centennials** (14G .266 W-2 L-12)									
″	**total**	48	218	62	44	.284	5	13	.278	OF-30, P-18
5 yrs.		204	993	276	214	.278	7	21	.250	OF-173, P-28, 3B-2, 1B-1

Steve Bellan

BELLAN, ESTEBAN ENRIQUE 5′ 6″ 154 lbs.
B. 1850, Havana, Cuba D. Aug. 8, 1932, Havana, Cuba.

		G	AB	H	R	BA	W	L	PCT	G by Pos
1871	**Troy Haymakers**	29	136	29	25	.213				3B-28, SS-1
1872		23	115	32	22	.278				SS-9, 3B-8, OF-6
1873	**New York Mutuals**	7	37	7	4	.189				3B-7
3 yrs.		59	288	68	51	.236				3B-43, SS-10, OF-6

Cy Bentley

BENTLEY, CLYTUS G.
B. Nov. 23, 1850, East Haven, Conn. D. Feb. 26, 1873, Middletown, Conn.

		G	AB	H	R	BA	W	L	PCT	G by Pos
1872	**Middletown Mansfields**	23	113	27	26	.239	2	14	.125	P-16, OF-8

Nate Berkenstock

BERKENSTOCK, NATHAN
B. 1831, Pa. D. Feb. 23, 1900, Philadelphia, Pa.

		G	AB	H	R	BA	W	L	PCT	G by Pos
1871	**Philadelphia Athletics**	1	4	0	0	.000				OF-1

Tom Berry

BERRY, THOMAS HANEY 5′ 6″ 140 lbs.
B. Dec. 31, 1842, Chester, Pa. D. June 6, 1915, Chester, Pa.

		G	AB	H	R	BA	W	L	PCT	G by Pos
1871	**Philadelphia Athletics**	1	4	1	0	.250				OF-1

Harry Berthrong

BERTHRONG, HARRY W. 5′ 6½″ 140 lbs.
B. Dec. 31, 1843, Munford, N. Y. D. Apr. 24, 1928, Chelsea, Mass.

		G	AB	H	R	BA	W	L	PCT	G by Pos
1871	**Washington Olympics**	17	78	17	17	.218				OF-12, 2B-4, 3B-1

Bestick

BESTICK
B. New York, N. Y. Deceased.

		G	AB	H	R	BA	W	L	PCT	G by Pos
1872	**Brooklyn Eckfords**	4	14	3	0	.214				C-4

E. P. Bevans

BEVANS, E. P. 5′ 8″ 138 lbs.
B. 1848, N. Y. Deceased.

		G	AB	H	R	BA	W	L	PCT	G by Pos
1871	**Troy Haymakers**	3	15	5	7	.333				2B-3
1872	**Brooklyn Atlantics**	10	44	9	7	.205				2B-8, SS-1, OF-1
2 yrs.		13	59	14	14	.237				2B-11, SS-1, OF-1

Oscar Bielaski

BIELASKI, OSCAR BR TR 5′10½″ 170 lbs.
B. Mar. 21, 1847, Washington, D. C. D. Nov. 8, 1911, Washington, D. C.

		G	AB	H	R	BA	W	L	PCT	G by Pos
1872	**Washington Nationals**	10	47	8	12	.170				OF-10
1873		38	187	49	35	.262				OF-38
1874	**Lord Baltimores**	44	202	48	24	.238				OF-42, 2B-1, 1B-1
1875	**Chicago White Stockings**	52	211	49	21	.232				OF-52
4 yrs.		144	647	154	92	.238				OF-142, 2B-1, 1B-1

Charlie Bierman

BIERMAN, CHARLES S. 6′ 180 lbs.
B. 1845, Hoboken, N. J. D. Aug. 4, 1879, Hoboken, N. J.

		G	AB	H	R	BA	W	L	PCT	G by Pos
1871	**Fort Wayne Kekiongas**	1	3	0	0	.000				1B-1

George Bird

BIRD, GEORGE RAYMOND BR TR 5′ 9″ 150 lbs.
B. June 23, 1850, Stillman Valley, Ill. D. Nov. 9, 1940, Rockford, Ill.

		G	AB	H	R	BA	W	L	PCT	G by Pos
1871	**Rockford Forest Citys**	25	112	24	18	.214				OF-25

Dave Birdsall

BIRDSALL, DAVID SOLOMON 5′ 9″ 126 lbs.
B. July 16, 1838, New York, N. Y. D. Dec. 30, 1896, Boston, Mass.

		G	AB	H	R	BA	W	L	PCT	G by Pos
1871	**Boston Red Stockings**	29	155	43	51	.277				OF-26, C-3
1872		14	78	14	10	.179				C-11, OF-5
1873		3	12	1	4	.083				OF-3
3 yrs.		46	245	58	65	.237				OF-34, C-14

Joe Blong

BLONG, JOSEPH MYLES BR TR
B. Sept. 17, 1853, St. Louis, Mo. D. Sept. 16, 1892, St. Louis, Mo.

Year	Team	G	AB	H	R	BA	W	L	PCT	G by Pos
1875	**St. Louis Reds**	16	70	10	3	.143	3	11	.214	P-14, OF-3

Fred Boardman

BOARDMAN, FREDERICK
B. Chicago, Ill. Deceased.

Year	Team	G	AB	H	R	BA	W	L	PCT	G by Pos
1874	**Lord Baltimores**	1	3	1	0	.333				OF-1

Boland

BOLAND
Deceased.

Year	Team	G	AB	H	R	BA	W	L	PCT	G by Pos
1875	**Brooklyn Atlantics**	1	4	0	0	.000				OF-1

Tommy Bond

BOND, THOMAS HENRY BR TR 5′ 7½″ 160 lbs.
B. Apr. 2, 1856, Granard, Ireland D. Jan. 24, 1941, Boston, Mass.
Manager 1882.

Year	Team	G	AB	H	R	BA	W	L	PCT	G by Pos
1874	**Brooklyn Atlantics**	55	249	54	25	.217	22	32	.407	P-55
1875	**Hartfords**	71	297	78	30	.263	19	16	.543	P-39, OF-29, 2B-2, 1B-2
2 yrs.		126	546	132	55	.242	41	48	.461	P-94, OF-29, 2B-2, 1B-2

Booth

BOOTH

Year	Team	G	AB	H	R	BA	W	L	PCT	G by Pos
1875	**New Havens**	1	2	0	0	.000				SS-1

Eddie Booth

BOOTH, EDWARD H.
B. Brooklyn, N. Y. Deceased.

Year	Team	G	AB	H	R	BA	W	L	PCT	G by Pos
1872	**2 teams Brooklyn Atlantics** (14G .250) **Middletown Mansfields** (24G .336)									
″	**total**	38	180	55	36	.306				2B-21, OF-17
1873	**2 teams Brooklyn Atlantics** (15G .171) **Elizabeth Resolutes** (18G .299)									
″	**total**	33	147	35	17	.238				OF-31, 2B-2
1874	**Brooklyn Atlantics**	44	194	46	24	.237				OF-44
1875	**New York Mutuals**	68	286	57	33	.199				OF-62, 2B-6
4 yrs.		183	807	193	110	.239				OF-154, 2B-29

Joe Borden

BORDEN, JOSEPH EMLEY BR TR 5′ 9″ 140 lbs.
Also appeared in box score as Josephs.
B. May 9, 1854, Jacobstown, N. J. D. Oct. 14, 1929, Yeadon, Pa.

Year	Team	G	AB	H	R	BA	W	L	PCT	G by Pos
1875	**Philadelphias**	7	29	3	3	.103	2	4	.333	P-7

Bill Boyd

BOYD, WILLIAM J. 250 lbs.
B. Dec. 22, 1852, New York D. Sept. 30, 1912, Queens, N. Y.

Year	Team	G	AB	H	R	BA	W	L	PCT	G by Pos
1872	**New York Mutuals**	35	169	43	25	.254				3B-33, SS-1, OF-1
1873	**Brooklyn Atlantics**	48	233	63	31	.270				OF-43, 3B-5
1874	**Hartfords**	26	123	47	22	.382				3B-25, OF-21
1875	**Brooklyn Atlantics**	36	154	45	14	.292				2B-15, OF-11, 3B-9, 1B-1
4 yrs.		145	679	198	92	.292				OF-76, 3B-72, 2B-15, 1B-1, SS-1

George Bradley

BRADLEY, GEORGE WASHINGTON (Grin) BR TR 5′10½″ 175 lbs.
B. July 13, 1852, Reading, Pa. D. Oct. 2, 1931, Philadelphia, Pa.

Year	Team	G	AB	H	R	BA	W	L	PCT	G by Pos
1875	**St. Louis**	61	250	67	28	.268	33	26	.559	P-60, OF-1, 3B-1

Brady

BRADY
Deceased.

Year	Team	G	AB	H	R	BA	W	L	PCT	G by Pos
1875	**Chicago White Stockings**	1	4	1	1	.250				OF-1

Steve Brady

BRADY, STEPHEN A. 5′ 9½″ 165 lbs.
B. July 14, 1851, Worcester, Mass. D. Nov. 1, 1917, Hartford, Conn.

Year	Team	G	AB	H	R	BA	W	L	PCT	G by Pos
1874	**Hartfords**	25	110	37	18	.336				3B-17, OF-8
1875	**2 teams Hartfords** (1G .000) **Washington Nationals** (19G .133)									
″	**total**	20	87	11	4	.126				2B-16, OF-3, 1B-1
2 yrs.		45	197	48	22	.244				3B-17, 2B-16, OF-11, 1B-1

Asa Brainard

BRAINARD, ASA (Count) TR 5′ 8½″ 150 lbs.
B. 1841, Albany, N. Y. D. Dec. 29, 1888, Denver, Colo.

Year	Team	G	AB	H	R	BA	W	L	PCT	G by Pos
1871	**Washington Olympics**	30	140	28	24	.200	13	15	.464	P-30
1872	**2 teams Middletown Mansfields** (7G .161 W-0 L-3) **Washington Olympics** (9G .405 W-2 L-7)									
″	**total**	16	73	22	10	.301	2	10	.167	P-12, 2B-4
1873	**Lord Baltimores**	15	64	16	16	.250	4	7	.364	P-13, OF-2
1874		47	209	50	19	.239	5	24	.172	P-29, 2B-17, OF-2
4 yrs.		108	486	116	69	.239	24	56	.300	P-84, 2B-21, OF-4

Mike Brannock

BRANNOCK, MICHAEL J. 5′ 8″ 162 lbs.
B. 1853, Guelph, Ont., Canada. Deceased.

Year	Team	G	AB	H	R	BA	W	L	PCT	G by Pos
1871	**Chicago White Stockings**	3	13	1	2	.077				3B-3
1875		2	9	1	2	.111				3B-2
2 yrs.		5	22	2	4	.091				3B-5

Jim Britt

BRITT, JAMES EDWARD
B. Feb. 25, 1856, Brooklyn, N. Y. D. Feb. 28, 1923, San Francisco, Calif.

Year	Team	G	AB	H	R	BA	W	L	PCT	G by Pos
1872	**Brooklyn Atlantics**	35	155	34	24	.219	8	27	.229	P-35
1873		54	246	47	29	.191	17	36	.321	P-54
2 yrs.		89	401	81	53	.202	25	63	.284	P-89

Brown

BROWN
Deceased.

Year	Team	G	AB	H	R	BA	W	L	PCT	G by Pos
1874	**Lord Baltimores**	1	5	0	0	.000				SS-2

Oliver Brown

BROWN, OLIVER EDWARD BR TR 6′ 150 lbs.
B. May 3, 1849, Brooklyn, N. Y. D. Sept. 23, 1932, Brooklyn, N. Y.

Year	Team	G	AB	H	R	BA	W	L	PCT	G by Pos
1872	**Brooklyn Atlantics**	4	17	1	0	.059				OF-4
1875		3	14	1	0	.071				1B-3
2 yrs.		7	31	2	0	.065				OF-4, 1B-3

Jack Burdock

BURDOCK, JOHN JOSEPH (Black Jack) BR TR 5′ 9½″ 158 lbs.
B. Apr. 1852, Brooklyn, N. Y. D. Nov. 27, 1931, Brooklyn, N. Y.
Manager 1883.

Year	Team	G	AB	H	R	BA	W	L	PCT	G by Pos
1872	**Brooklyn Atlantics**	35	176	44	27	.250				SS-33, C-2, 2B-1
1873		55	261	62	56	.238				2B-55
1874	**New York Mutuals**	61	284	78	46	.275				3B-61
1875	**Hartfords**	73	360	102	72	.283				2B-72, 3B-1
4 yrs.		224	1081	286	201	.265				2B-128, 3B-62, SS-33, C-2

Henry Burroughs

BURROUGHS, HENRY F. 5′ 8″ 147 lbs.
B. 1845, Detroit, Mich. Deceased.

Year	Team	G	AB	H	R	BA	W	L	PCT	G by Pos
1871	**Washington Olympics**	12	63	14	11	.222				OF-8, 3B-5
1872		2	8	1	1	.125				OF-2
2 yrs.		14	71	15	12	.211				OF-10, 3B-5

Doc Bushong

BUSHONG, ALBERT JOHN BR TR 5′11″ 165 lbs.
B. Sept. 15, 1856, Philadelphia, Pa. D. Aug. 19, 1908, Brooklyn, N. Y.

Year	Team	G	AB	H	R	BA	W	L	PCT	G by Pos
1875	**Brooklyn Atlantics**	1	5	3	0	.600				C-1

Frank Buttery

BUTTERY, FRANK
B. May 13, 1851, Silver Mine, Conn. D. Dec. 16, 1902, Silver Mine, Conn.

Year	Team	G	AB	H	R	BA	W	L	PCT	G by Pos
1872	**Middletown Mansfields**	17	88	26	18	.295	3	2	.600	3B-6, OF-6, P-6

Hugh Campbell

CAMPBELL, HUGH F.
B. 16, 1846, Ireland D. Mar. 1, 1881, Elizabeth, N. J.

Year	Team	G	AB	H	R	BA	W	L	PCT	G by Pos
1873	**Elizabeth Resolutes**	20	93	12	9	.129	2	16	.111	P-18, OF-1, 2B-1

Mike Campbell

CAMPBELL, MICHAEL
B. 1850, Ireland Deceased.

Year	Team	G	AB	H	R	BA	W	L	PCT	G by Pos
1873	**Elizabeth Resolutes**	21	89	13	9	.146				1B-17, SS-3, OF-1

Jack Carbine

CARBINE, JOHN C. 6′ 187 lbs.
B. Oct. 12, 1855, Syracuse, N. Y. D. Sept. 11, 1915, Forest Park, Ill.

Year	Team	G	AB	H	R	BA	W	L	PCT	G by Pos
1875	**Keokuk Westerns**	10	39	2	1	.051				1B-10

Tom Carey

CAREY, THOMAS JOHN BR TR 5′ 8″ 145 lbs.
Born J. J. Norton.
B. 1849, Brooklyn, N. Y. D. Feb. 13, 1899, Los Angeles, Calif.

Year	Team	G	AB	H	R	BA	W	L	PCT	G by Pos
1871	**Fort Wayne Kekiongas**	19	85	20	15	.235				2B-18, SS-1
1872	**Lord Baltimores**	41	196	58	39	.296				2B-26, SS-8, OF-3, 3B-3, 1B-1
1873		55	292	95	72	.325				2B-51, SS-3, 3B-3
1874	**New York Mutuals**	64	292	83	55	.284				SS-51, 2B-13
1875	**Hartfords**	85	390	99	63	.254				SS-85
5 yrs.		264	1255	355	244	.283				SS-148, 2B-108, 3B-6, OF-3, 1B-1

Lew Carl

CARL, LEWIS
B. Baltimore, Md. Deceased.

Year	Team	G	AB	H	R	BA	W	L	PCT	G by Pos
1874	**Lord Baltimores**	1	4	0	0	.000				C-1

Jim Carlton

CARLTON, JAMES 5′ 8″ 155 lbs.
B. 1849, N. Y. Deceased.

Year	Team	G	AB	H	R	BA	W	L	PCT	G by Pos
1871	**Cleveland Forest Citys**	29	136	32	31	.235				1B-29
1872		7	38	12	8	.316				1B-7
2 yrs.		36	174	44	39	.253				1B-36

John Cassidy

CASSIDY, JOHN P. BR TL 5′ 8″ 168 lbs.
B. 1855, Brooklyn, N. Y. D. July 3, 1891, Brooklyn, N. Y.

Year	Team	G	AB	H	R	BA	W	L	PCT	G by Pos
1875	**2 teams New Havens** (6G .125) **Brooklyn Atlantics** (40G .168 W-1 L-25)									
″	**total**	46	191	31	16	.162	1	25	.038	P-27, 1B-13, OF-10

Jack Chapman

CHAPMAN, JOHN CURTIS TR 5′11″ 170 lbs.
B. May 8, 1843, Brooklyn, N. Y. D. June 10, 1916, Brooklyn, N. Y.
Manager 1876–78, 1882–85, 1889–92.

		G	AB	H	R	BA	W	L	PCT	G by Pos
1874	**Brooklyn Atlantics**	53	248	64	32	.258				OF-52, 1B-1
1875	**St. Louis**	43	187	46	27	.246				OF-43
2 yrs.		96	435	110	59	.253				OF-95, 1B-1

Bobby Clack

CLACK, ROBERT S. (Gentlemanly Bobby) BR TR 5′ 9″ 153 lbs.
Born Robert S. Clark.
B. June 1850, England D. Oct. 22, 1933, Danvers, Mass.

		G	AB	H	R	BA	W	L	PCT	G by Pos
1874	**Brooklyn Atlantics**	33	138	21	22	.152				OF-31, 1B-2
1875		17	60	6	1	.100				OF-17
2 yrs.		50	198	27	23	.136				OF-48, 1B-2

John Clapp

CLAPP, JOHN EDGAR BR TR 5′ 7″ 194 lbs.
Brother of Aaron Clapp.
B. July 17, 1851, Ithaca, N. Y. D. Dec. 18, 1904, Ithaca, N. Y.
Manager 1878–81, 1883.

		G	AB	H	R	BA	W	L	PCT	G by Pos
1872	**Middletown Mansfields**	19	98	30	30	.306				C-19
1873	**Philadelphia Athletics**	45	219	63	35	.288				C-42, SS-2, 2B-1
1874		39	169	56	46	.331				C-26, OF-13, SS-1
1875		60	298	74	65	.248				C-60
4 yrs.		163	784	223	176	.284				C-147, OF-13, SS-3, 2B-1

Denny Clare

CLARE, DENNIS J.
B. Jan. 1853, Brooklyn, N. Y. D. Nov. 26, 1928, Brooklyn, N. Y.

		G	AB	H	R	BA	W	L	PCT	G by Pos
1872	**Brooklyn Atlantics**	2	7	1	1	.143				2B-2

Jim Clinton

CLINTON, JAMES LAWRENCE (Big Jim) BR TR 5′ 8½″ 174 lbs.
B. Aug. 10, 1850, New York, N. Y. D. Sept. 3, 1921, Brooklyn, N. Y.

		G	AB	H	R	BA	W	L	PCT	G by Pos
1872	**Brooklyn Eckfords**	24	101	19	11	.188				3B-9, OF-8, SS-4, 2B-3
1873	**Elizabeth Resolutes**	9	40	9	5	.225				3B-8, OF-1
1874	**Brooklyn Atlantics**	2	11	2	3	.182				OF-1, 2B-1
1875		22	83	10	3	.120	1	12	.077	P-14, OF-5, 1B-4, 2B-1
4 yrs.		57	235	40	22	.170	1	12	.077	3B-17, OF-15, P-14, 2B-5, 1B-4, SS-4

Dan Collins

COLLINS, DANIEL THOMAS
B. July 12, 1854, St. Louis, Mo. D. Sept. 21, 1883, New Orleans, La.

		G	AB	H	R	BA	W	L	PCT	G by Pos
1874	**Chicago White Stockings**	3	12	1	1	.083	1	1	.500	OF-2, P-2, SS-1

Fred Cone

CONE, JOSEPH FREDERICK 5′ 9½″ 171 lbs.
B. May 1848, Rockford, Ill. D. Apr. 13, 1909, Chicago, Ill.

		G	AB	H	R	BA	W	L	PCT	G by Pos
1871	**Boston Red Stockings**	18	85	20	17	.235				OF-18

Terry Connell

CONNELL, TERENCE G.
B. June 17, 1855, Philadelphia, Pa. D. Mar. 25, 1924, Philadelphia, Pa.

		G	AB	H	R	BA	W	L	PCT	G by Pos
1874	**Chicago White Stockings**	1	4	0	0	.000	0	0	—	C-1

Ned Connors

CONNORS, JOSEPH P. 5′ 9″ 156 lbs.
B. 1850, N. Y. Deceased.

		G	AB	H	R	BA	W	L	PCT	G by Pos
1871	**Troy Haymakers**	7	33	6	7	.182				1B-4, OF-2, 2B-1

William Coon

COON, WILLIAM K.
B. Mar. 21, 1855, Philadelphia, Pa. D. Aug. 30, 1915, Burlington, N. J.

		G	AB	H	R	BA	W	L	PCT	G by Pos
1875	**Philadelphia Athletics**	4	14	2	1	.143				C-4

Dennis Coughlin

COUGHLIN, DENNIS F.
Deceased.

		G	AB	H	R	BA	W	L	PCT	G by Pos
1872	**Washington Nationals**	8	37	12	5	.324				OF-5, SS-2, 2B-1

Fred Crane

CRANE, FREDERICK WILLIAM HOTCHKISS
B. Nov. 4, 1840, Saybrook, Conn. D. Apr. 27, 1925, Brooklyn, N. Y.

		G	AB	H	R	BA	W	L	PCT	G by Pos
1873	**Elizabeth Resolutes**	1	4	1	0	.250				2B-1
1875	**Brooklyn Atlantics**	21	81	17	7	.210				1B-20, OF-1
2 yrs.		22	85	18	7	.212				1B-20, OF-1, 2B-1

Bill Craver

CRAVER, WILLIAM H. BR TR 5′ 9″ 160 lbs.
B. June 1844, Troy, N. Y. D. June 17, 1901, Troy, N. Y.
Manager 1876.

		G	AB	H	R	BA	W	L	PCT	G by Pos
1871	**Troy Haymakers**	27	122	37	26	.303				2B-18, SS-4, C-3, 1B-2
1872	**Lord Baltimores**	33	180	50	52	.278				C-25, OF-5, 3B-2, 2B-2
1873		36	185	52	38	.281				C-20, SS-12, OF-3, 1B-1

Bill Craver *continued*

Year	Team	G	AB	H	R	BA	W	L	PCT	G by Pos
1874	**Philadelphias**	55	275	95	71	.345				2B-53, C-3
1875	**2 teams Philadelphia Athletics** (54G .314) **Philadelphia Centennials** (14G .265)									
"	**total**	68	332	101	79	.304				2B-53, SS-9, 3B-4, 1B-1, C-1
	5 yrs.	219	1094	335	266	.306				2B-126, C-52, SS-25, OF-8, 3B-6, 1B-4

Art Croft

CROFT, ARTHUR F.
B. Jan. 23, 1855, St. Louis, Mo. D. Mar. 16, 1884, St. Louis, Mo.

Year	Team	G	AB	H	R	BA	W	L	PCT	G by Pos
1875	**St. Louis Reds**	18	72	11	4	.153				OF-18

Bill Crowley

CROWLEY, WILLIAM MICHAEL BR TR 5′ 7½″ 159 lbs.
B. Apr. 8, 1857, Philadelphia, Pa. D. July 14, 1891, Gloucester, N. J.

Year	Team	G	AB	H	R	BA	W	L	PCT	G by Pos
1875	**Philadelphias**	9	37	4	4	.108				OF-4, 3B-3, 2B-1, 1B-1

Candy Cummings

CUMMINGS, WILLIAM ARTHUR BR TR 5′ 9″ 120 lbs.
B. Oct. 18, 1848, Ware, Mass. D. May 16, 1924, Toledo, Ohio.
Hall of Fame 1939.

Year	Team	G	AB	H	R	BA	W	L	PCT	G by Pos
1872	**New York Mutuals**	55	260	51	36	.196	33	20	.623	P-55, OF-1
1873	**Lord Baltimores**	42	200	50	31	.250	28	14	.667	P-42
1874	**Philadelphias**	54	240	50	30	.208	28	26	.519	P-54
1875	**Hartfords**	52	235	43	32	.183	35	12	.745	P-47, OF-6
	4 yrs.	203	935	194	129	.207	124	72	.633	P-198, OF-7

Ned Cuthbert

CUTHBERT, EDGAR EDWARD BR TR 5′ 6″ 140 lbs.
B. June 20, 1845, Philadelphia, Pa. D. Feb. 6, 1905, St. Louis, Mo.
Manager 1882.

Year	Team	G	AB	H	R	BA	W	L	PCT	G by Pos
1871	**Philadelphia Athletics**	28	162	39	47	.241				OF-27, C-1
1872		46	265	87	80	.328				OF-46
1873	**Philadelphias**	51	284	75	79	.264				OF-51
1874	**Chicago White Stockings**	58	306	79	64	.258				OF-55, C-3
1875	**St. Louis**	68	308	82	69	.266				OF-67, C-2
	5 yrs.	251	1325	362	339	.273				OF-246, C-6

John Dailey

DAILEY, JOHN J.
B. Brooklyn, N. Y. D. Jan. 8, 1898, Brooklyn, N. Y.

Year	Team	G	AB	H	R	BA	W	L	PCT	G by Pos
1875	**2 teams Brooklyn Atlantics** (2G .125) **Washington Nationals** (26G .208)									
"	**total**	28	114	23	18	.202				SS-17, 3B-7, 2B-2, OF-1, 1B-1

Harry Deane

DEANE, JOHN HENRY 5′ 7″ 150 lbs.
B. May 6, 1846, Trenton, N. J. D. May 31, 1925, Indianapolis, Ind.

Year	Team	G	AB	H	R	BA	W	L	PCT	G by Pos
1871	**Fort Wayne Kekiongas**	5	24	4	3	.167				OF-5
1874	**Lord Baltimores**	47	212	49	29	.231				OF-45, 2B-2
	2 yrs.	52	236	53	32	.225				OF-50, 2B-2

Dutch Dehlman

DEHLMAN, HERMAN J.
B. 1850, Catasauqua, Pa. D. Mar. 13, 1885, Wilkes-Barre, Pa.

Year	Team	G	AB	H	R	BA	W	L	PCT	G by Pos
1872	**Brooklyn Atlantics**	35	164	33	26	.201				1B-35
1873		54	236	50	50	.212				1B-54
1874		53	232	51	40	.220				1B-53
1875	**St. Louis**	67	284	61	43	.215				1B-67
	4 yrs.	209	916	195	159	.213				1B-209

Jim Devlin

DEVLIN, JAMES ALEXANDER BR TR 5′11″ 175 lbs.
B. 1849, Philadelphia, Pa. D. Oct. 10, 1883, Philadelphia, Pa.

Year	Team	G	AB	H	R	BA	W	L	PCT	G by Pos
1873	**Philadelphias**	22	104	26	18	.250				1B-12, 3B-5, SS-3, OF-2
1874	**Chicago White Stockings**	44	215	59	28	.274				1B-22, OF-16, 3B-6
1875		70	336	95	60	.283	6	16	.273	1B-43, P-26, OF-3
	3 yrs.	136	655	180	106	.275	6	16	.273	1B-77, P-26, OF-21, 3B-11, SS-3

John Dillon

DILLON, JOHN
Brother of Packy Dillon.
B. St. Louis, Mo. Deceased.

Year	Team	G	AB	H	R	BA	W	L	PCT	G by Pos
1875	**St. Louis Reds**	1	1	0	0	.000				SS-1

Packy Dillon

DILLON, PACKARD ANDREW
Brother of John Dillon.
B. St. Louis, Mo. D. Jan. 9, 1890, Guelph, Ont., Canada.

Year	Team	G	AB	H	R	BA	W	L	PCT	G by Pos
1875	**St. Louis Reds**	3	15	3	1	.200				C-3

Lester Dole

DOLE, LESTER CARRINGTON 5′11″
B. July 8, 1855, Meriden, Conn. D. Dec. 10, 1918, Concord, N. H.

Year	Team	G	AB	H	R	BA	W	L	PCT	G by Pos
1875	**New Havens**	1	4	2	1	.500				OF-1

Pete Donnelly

DONNELLY, PETER J.
B. Oct. 8, 1849, Philadelphia, Pa. D. Oct. 1, 1890, Jersey City, N. J.

Year	Team	G	AB	H	R	BA	W	L	PCT	G by Pos
1871	**Fort Wayne Kekiongas**	9	35	7	8	.200				OF-9, 3B-1
1873	**Washington Nationals**	30	141	35	15	.248				SS-13, 2B-11, OF-6
1874	**Philadelphias**	5	21	5	2	.238				OF-2, SS-2, 2B-1
3 yrs.		44	197	47	25	.239				OF-17, SS-15, 2B-12, 3B-1

Herm Doscher

DOSCHER, JOHN HENRY, SR. BR TR 5′10″ 182 lbs.
Father of Jack Doscher.
B. Dec. 20, 1852, New York, N. Y. D. Mar. 20, 1934, Buffalo, N. Y.

Year	Team	G	AB	H	R	BA	W	L	PCT	G by Pos
1872	**Brooklyn Atlantics**	6	26	9	4	.346				OF-6
1873		1	6	1	1	.167				OF-1
1875	**Washington Nationals**	21	75	12	3	.160				3B-19, SS-2
3 yrs.		28	107	22	8	.206				3B-19, OF-7, SS-2

Joe Doyle

DOYLE, JOSEPH K.
B. Cincinnati, Ohio Deceased.

Year	Team	G	AB	H	R	BA	W	L	PCT	G by Pos
1872	**Washington Nationals**	8	36	8	4	.222				SS-6, 3B-1, 2B-1

Ed Duffy

DUFFY, EDWARD CHARLES TR 5′ 7½″ 152 lbs.
B. 1844, Ireland D. June 1889, Brooklyn, N. Y.

Year	Team	G	AB	H	R	BA	W	L	PCT	G by Pos
1871	**Chicago White Stockings**	25	121	28	31	.231				SS-24, 3B-1

Edwards

EDWARDS
Deceased.

Year	Team	G	AB	H	R	BA	W	L	PCT	G by Pos
1875	**Brooklyn Atlantics**	1	5	1	1	.200	0	0	—	OF-1, P-1

Dave Eggler

EGGLER, DAVID DANIEL BR TR 5′ 9″ 165 lbs.
B. Apr. 30, 1851, Brooklyn, N. Y. D. Apr. 5, 1902, Buffalo, N. Y.

Year	Team	G	AB	H	R	BA	W	L	PCT	G by Pos
1871	**New York Mutuals**	33	150	47	37	.313				OF-33
1872		56	295	102	95	.346				OF-56
1873		53	281	92	83	.327				OF-53
1874	**Philadelphias**	58	306	96	70	.314				OF-56, 2B-2
1875	**Philadelphia Athletics**	66	302	87	65	.288				OF-66
5 yrs.		266	1334	424	350	.318				OF-264, 2B-2

Eland

ELAND
Deceased.

Year	Team	G	AB	H	R	BA	W	L	PCT	G by Pos
1873	**Marylands**	1	4	0	0	.000				OF-1

Joe Ellick

ELLICK, JOSEPH J. 5′10″ 162 lbs.
B. Apr. 3, 1854, Cincinnati, Ohio D. Apr. 21, 1923, Kansas City, Mo.
Manager 1884.

Year	Team	G	AB	H	R	BA	W	L	PCT	G by Pos
1875	**St. Louis Reds**	6	24	5	1	.208				3B-3, OF-2, SS-1

Evans

EVANS
Deceased.

Year	Team	G	AB	H	R	BA	W	L	PCT	G by Pos
1875	**New Havens**	1	4	2	1	.500				OF-1

G. Ewell

EWELL, G.
Deceased.

Year	Team	G	AB	H	R	BA	W	L	PCT	G by Pos
1871	**Cleveland Forest Citys**	1	4	0	0	.000				OF-1

Jack Farrell

FARRELL, JOHN (Hartford Jack)
B. Jan. 2, 1856, Hartford, Conn. D. Nov. 15, 1916, Hartford, Conn.

Year	Team	G	AB	H	R	BA	W	L	PCT	G by Pos
1874	**Hartfords**	3	15	5	3	.333				OF-3

John Farrow

FARROW, JOHN JACOB BL TR
B. Nov. 8, 1853, Verplanc Point, N. Y. D. Dec. 31, 1914, Perth Amboy, N. J.

Year	Team	G	AB	H	R	BA	W	L	PCT	G by Pos
1873	**Elizabeth Resolutes**	12	51	8	2	.157				C-7, OF-2, SS-2, 1B-1
1874	**Brooklyn Atlantics**	27	125	26	16	.208				C-15, 2B-12
2 yrs.		39	176	34	18	.193				C-22, 2B-12, SS-2, OF-2, 1B-1

Bob Ferguson

FERGUSON, ROBERT VAVASOUR (Death to Flying Things) BB TR 5′ 9½″ 149 lbs.
B. Jan. 31, 1845, Brooklyn, N. Y. D. May 3, 1894, Brooklyn, N. Y.
Manager 1876–84, 1886–87.

Year	Team	G	AB	H	R	BA	W	L	PCT	G by Pos
1871	**New York Mutuals**	33	156	34	30	.218				3B-19, 2B-10, C-4
1872	**Brooklyn Atlantics**	35	164	43	34	.262				3B-35
1873		51	238	59	36	.248	0	1	.000	3B-50, P-1
1874		56	249	64	34	.257	0	1	.000	3B-55, C-2, P-1
1875	**Hartfords**	84	373	87	65	.233				3B-84
5 yrs.		259	1180	287	199	.243	0	2	.000	3B-243, 2B-10, C-6, P-2

Sam Field

FIELD, SAMUEL JAY BR TR 5′ 9½″ 182 lbs.
B. Oct. 12, 1848, Philadelphia, Pa. D. Oct. 28, 1904, Sinking Spring, Pa.

		G	AB	H	R	BA	W	L	PCT	G by Pos
1875	**2 teams Washington Nationals** (5G .235) **Philadelphia Centennials** (3G .091)									
″	**total**	8	28	5	2	.179				C-6, OF-2

George Fields

FIELDS, GEORGE W.
B. July 1853, Waterbury, Conn. D. Sept. 22, 1933, Waterbury, Conn.

		G	AB	H	R	BA	W	L	PCT	G by Pos
1872	**Middletown Mansfields**	17	71	20	18	.282				3B-10, OF-6, SS-1

Cherokee Fisher

FISHER, WILLIAM CHARLES BR TR 5′ 9″ 164 lbs.
B. Dec. 1845, Philadelphia, Pa. D. Sept. 26, 1912, New York, N. Y.

		G	AB	H	R	BA	W	L	PCT	G by Pos
1871	**Rockford Forest Citys**	25	124	28	24	.226	4	20	.167	P-24, SS-1
1872	**Lord Baltimores**	44	234	48	39	.205	9	3	.750	3B-17, OF-16, P-13
1873	**Philadelphia Athletics**	51	259	66	51	.255	2	2	.500	OF-45, P-7, 1B-1
1874	**Hartfords**	52	231	53	29	.229	14	21	.400	P-35, OF-10, 3B-6, SS-1
1875	**Philadelphias**	41	169	39	26	.231	22	18	.550	P-40, OF-1
	5 yrs.	213	1017	234	169	.230	51	64	.443	P-119, OF-72, 3B-23, SS-2, 1B-1

Wes Fisler

FISLER, WESTON DICKSON BR 5′ 6″ 137 lbs.
B. July 5, 1841, Camden, N. J. D. Dec. 25, 1922, Philadelphia, Pa.

		G	AB	H	R	BA	W	L	PCT	G by Pos
1871	**Philadelphia Athletics**	28	150	44	43	.293				1B-26, 2B-2
1872		46	248	81	50	.327				2B-46
1873		43	227	71	42	.313				2B-35, 1B-8
1874		37	175	67	27	.383				1B-28, 2B-9
1875		57	272	75	54	.276				1B-44, OF-9, 2B-4
	5 yrs.	211	1072	338	216	.315				1B-106, 2B-96, OF-9

Frank Fleet

FLEET, FRANK H.
B. 1848, New York, N. Y. D. June 13, 1900, New York, N. Y.

		G	AB	H	R	BA	W	L	PCT	G by Pos
1871	**New York Mutuals**	1	5	2	1	.400	0	1	.000	P-1
1872	**Brooklyn Eckfords**	13	58	11	10	.190				3B-10, 2B-2, OF-1
1873	**Elizabeth Resolutes**	22	96	22	11	.229	0	3	.000	2B-8, SS-7, 3B-3, P-3, 1B-1
1874	**Brooklyn Atlantics**	20	94	22	18	.234				C-12, 2B-7, OF-1
1875	**2 teams Brooklyn Atlantics** (26G .216 W-0 L-1) **St. Louis** (3G .083 W-2 L-1)									
″	**total**	29	128	26	14	.203	2	2	.500	2B-11, C-10, SS-6, P-4
	5 yrs.	85	381	83	54	.218	2	6	.250	2B-28, C-22, 3B-13, SS-13, P-8, OF-2, 1B-1

George Fletcher

FLETCHER, GEORGE HORACE ELLIOT
B. Apr. 21, 1845, Brooklyn, N. Y. Deceased.

		G	AB	H	R	BA	W	L	PCT	G by Pos
1872	**Brooklyn Eckfords**	2	8	2	1	.250				OF-2

Silver Flint

FLINT, FRANK SYLVESTER BR TR 6′ 180 lbs.
B. Aug. 3, 1855, Philadelphia, Pa. D. Jan. 14, 1892, Chicago, Ill.
Manager 1879.

		G	AB	H	R	BA	W	L	PCT	G by Pos
1875	**St. Louis Reds**	16	58	5	3	.086				C-15, 3B-1

Dickie Flowers

FLOWERS, CHARLES RICHARD
B. 1850, Philadelphia, Pa. D. Oct. 5, 1892, Philadelphia, Pa.

		G	AB	H	R	BA	W	L	PCT	G by Pos
1871	**Troy Haymakers**	21	109	33	40	.303				SS-20, 2B-1
1872	**Philadelphia Athletics**	3	17	4	1	.235				SS-3
	2 yrs.	24	126	37	41	.294				SS-23, 2B-1

Clipper Flynn

FLYNN, WILLIAM TR 5′ 7″ 140 lbs.
B. Apr. 29, 1849, Lansingburg, N. Y. D. Nov. 2, 1881, Troy, N. Y.

		G	AB	H	R	BA	W	L	PCT	G by Pos
1871	**Troy Haymakers**	29	148	46	44	.311				1B-19, OF-9, 3B-1
1872	**Washington Olympics**	9	41	9	4	.220				1B-9
	2 yrs.	38	189	55	48	.291				1B-28, OF-9, 3B-1

Tom Foley

FOLEY, THOMAS J. 5′ 9½″ 157 lbs.
B. 1847, Chicago, Ill. D. Jan. 4, 1896, LaGrange, Ill.

		G	AB	H	R	BA	W	L	PCT	G by Pos
1871	**Chicago White Stockings**	18	84	21	18	.250				OF-14, C-3, 3B-1

Will Foley

FOLEY, WILLIAM BROWN BR TR 5′ 9½″ 150 lbs.
B. Nov. 15, 1855, Chicago, Ill. D. Nov. 12, 1916, Chicago, Ill.

		G	AB	H	R	BA	W	L	PCT	G by Pos
1875	**Chicago White Stockings**	3	14	3	0	.214				3B-3

Jim Foran

FORAN, JAMES H. 5′ 6½″ 159 lbs.
B. 1848, N. Y. Deceased.

		G	AB	H	R	BA	W	L	PCT	G by Pos
1871	**Fort Wayne Kekiongas**	19	90	31	20	.344				1B-15, OF-4

Davy Force

FORCE, DAVID W. (Tom Thumb) BR TR 5′ 4″ 130 lbs.
B. July 27, 1849, New York, N. Y. D. June 21, 1918, Englewood, N. J.

Year	Team	G	AB	H	R	BA	W	L	PCT	G by Pos
1871	**Washington Olympics**	32	166	44	45	.265				SS-31, 3B-1
1872	**2 teams Lord Baltimores** (18G .409) **Troy Haymakers** (25G .414)									
″	**total**	43	226	93	69	.412				3B-34, SS-9
1873	**Lord Baltimores**	48	250	85	75	.340	1	1	.500	3B-32, SS-15, P-2
1874	**Chicago White Stockings**	59	305	92	61	.302				3B-38, SS-20, P-1, OF-1
1875	**Philadelphia Athletics**	77	391	122	77	.312				SS-77
	5 yrs.	259	1338	436	327	.326	1	1	.500	SS-152, 3B-105, P-3, OF-1

Bill French

FRENCH, WILLIAM
B. Baltimore, Md. Deceased.

Year	Team	G	AB	H	R	BA	W	L	PCT	G by Pos
1873	**Marylands**	5	19	4	3	.211	0	1	.000	1B-2, OF-2, P-1

Chick Fulmer

FULMER, CHARLES JOHN BR TR 6′ 158 lbs.
Brother of Washington Fulmer.
B. Feb. 12, 1851, Philadelphia, Pa. D. Feb. 15, 1940, Philadelphia, Pa.

Year	Team	G	AB	H	R	BA	W	L	PCT	G by Pos
1871	**Rockford Forest Citys**	16	70	17	12	.243				SS-15, 1B-1
1872	**New York Mutuals**	36	169	51	29	.302				3B-23, SS-13
1873	**Philadelphias**	49	244	64	41	.262				SS-48, C-1
1874		57	265	70	49	.264				SS-31, 3B-26
1875		68	288	64	49	.222				SS-54, 3B-14
	5 yrs.	226	1036	266	180	.257				SS-161, 3B-63, C-1, 1B-1

Washington Fulmer

FULMER, WASHINGTON FAYETTE
Brother of Chick Fulmer.
B. June 15, 1840, Philadelphia, Pa. D. Dec. 8, 1907, Philadelphia, Pa.

Year	Team	G	AB	H	R	BA	W	L	PCT	G by Pos
1875	**Brooklyn Atlantics**	1	4	2	1	.500				3B-1

John Galvin

GALVIN, JOHN S.
B. 1851 D. Apr. 20, 1904, Brooklyn, N. Y.

Year	Team	G	AB	H	R	BA	W	L	PCT	G by Pos
1872	**Brooklyn Atlantics**	1	4	0	0	.000				2B-1
1874		1	4	0	1	.000				2B-1
	2 yrs.	2	8	0	1	.000				2B-2

Pud Galvin

GALVIN, JAMES FRANCIS (Gentle Jeems, The Little Steam Engine) BR TR 5′ 8″ 190 lbs.
B. Dec. 25, 1856, St. Louis, Mo. D. Mar. 7, 1902, Pittsburgh, Pa.
Manager 1885.
Hall of Fame 1965.

Year	Team	G	AB	H	R	BA	W	L	PCT	G by Pos
1875	**St. Louis**	12	37	8	8	.216	4	2	.667	P-8, OF-5

Count Gedney

GEDNEY, ALFRED W. 5′ 9″ 140 lbs.
B. May 10, 1849, Brooklyn, N. Y. D. Mar. 26, 1922, Hackensack, N. J.

Year	Team	G	AB	H	R	BA	W	L	PCT	G by Pos
1872	**2 teams Brooklyn Eckfords** (18G .158) **Troy Haymakers** (9G .413)									
″	**total**	27	122	31	23	.254				OF-27
1873	**New York Mutuals**	53	236	60	41	.254				OF-53
1874	**Philadelphia Athletics**	54	235	76	48	.323				OF-50, 1B-4
1875	**New York Mutuals**	67	263	52	29	.198	1	0	1.000	OF-66, P-1
	4 yrs.	201	856	219	141	.256	1	0	1.000	OF-196, 1B-4, P-1

Billy Geer

GEER, WILLIAM HENRY HARRISON TR 5′ 8″ 160 lbs.
Born George Harrison Geer.
B. Aug. 13, 1849, Syracuse, N. Y. D. Jan. 5, 1922, Syracuse, N. Y.

Year	Team	G	AB	H	R	BA	W	L	PCT	G by Pos
1874	**New York Mutuals**	2	8	2	0	.250				OF-2
1875	**New Havens**	37	173	39	20	.225				OF-17, 2B-13, SS-5, 3B-1, 1B-1
	2 yrs.	39	181	41	20	.227				OF-19, 2B-13, SS-5, 3B-1, 1B-1

Joe Gerhardt

GERHARDT, JOHN JOSEPH (Move Up Joe) BR TR 6′ 160 lbs.
B. Feb. 14, 1855, Washington, D. C. D. Mar. 11, 1922, Middletown, N. Y.
Manager 1883, 1890.

Year	Team	G	AB	H	R	BA	W	L	PCT	G by Pos
1873	**Washington Nationals**	13	56	11	6	.196				SS-13
1874	**Lord Baltimores**	14	65	20	10	.308				SS-14
1875	**New York Mutuals**	57	254	54	29	.213				3B-44, 2B-12, SS-1
	3 yrs.	84	375	85	45	.227				3B-44, SS-28, 2B-12

Barney Gilligan

GILLIGAN, ANDREW BERNARD BR TR 5′ 6½″ 130 lbs.
B. Jan. 3, 1856, Cambridge, Mass. D. Apr. 1, 1934, Lynn, Mass.

Year	Team	G	AB	H	R	BA	W	L	PCT	G by Pos
1875	**Brooklyn Atlantics**	2	8	2	2	.250				OF-1, C-1

Jim Gilmore

GILMORE, JAMES
B. May 1853, Baltimore, Md. D. Nov. 18, 1928, Baltimore, Md.

Year	Team	G	AB	H	R	BA	W	L	PCT	G by Pos
1875	**Washington Nationals**	4	15	5	4	.333				C-2, 3B-1, 2B-1

Gilroy

GILROY
Deceased.

Year	Team	G	AB	H	R	BA	W	L	PCT	G by Pos
1874	**Chicago White Stockings**	8	39	8	4	.205				C-8
1875	**Philadelphia Athletics**	2	8	2	0	.250				OF-1, C-1
2 yrs.		10	47	10	4	.213				C-9, OF-1

John Glenn

GLENN, JOHN W. BR TR 5′ 8½″ 169 lbs.
B. 1849, Rochester, N. Y. D. Nov. 10, 1888, Sandy Hill, N. Y.

Year	Team	G	AB	H	R	BA	W	L	PCT	G by Pos
1871	**Washington Olympics**	26	123	37	24	.301				OF-26
1872	**2 teams Washington Nationals** (1G .500) **Washington Olympics** (9G .150)									
″	**total**	10	44	8	5	.182				OF-10
1873	**Washington Nationals**	39	194	49	39	.253				1B-39
1874	**Chicago White Stockings**	55	245	64	34	.261				1B-38, OF-17
1875		70	325	76	48	.234				OF-44, 1B-26
5 yrs.		200	931	234	150	.251				1B-103, OF-97

Mike Golden

GOLDEN, MICHAEL HENRY BR TR 5′ 7″ 166 lbs.
B. Sept. 11, 1851, Shirley, Mass. D. Jan. 11, 1929, Rockford, Ill.

Year	Team	G	AB	H	R	BA	W	L	PCT	G by Pos
1875	**2 teams Chicago White Stockings** (39G .242 W-7 L-7) **Keokuk Westerns** (13G .140 W-1 L-12)									
″	**total**	52	211	46	21	.218	8	19	.296	P-28, OF-24, 1B-1

Fred Goldsmith

GOLDSMITH, FRED ERNEST BR TR 6′ 1″ 195 lbs.
B. May 15, 1852, New Haven, Conn. D. Mar. 28, 1939, Berkley, Mich.

Year	Team	G	AB	H	R	BA	W	L	PCT	G by Pos
1875	**New Havens**	1	4	2	0	.500				2B-1

Wally Goldsmith

GOLDSMITH, WALLACE 5′ 7″ 146 lbs.
B. 1849, Baltimore, Md. Deceased.

Year	Team	G	AB	H	R	BA	W	L	PCT	G by Pos
1871	**Fort Wayne Kekiongas**	19	91	19	9	.209				SS-12, 3B-5, 2B-1, C-1
1872	**Washington Olympics**	9	40	9	4	.225				SS-5, 2B-4
1873	**Marylands**	1	4	0	0	.000				2B-1
1875	**Keokuk Westerns**	13	53	6	3	.113				3B-13
4 yrs.		42	188	34	16	.181				3B-18, SS-17, 2B-6, C-1

Charlie Gould

GOULD, CHARLES HARVEY BR TR 6′ 172 lbs.
B. Aug. 21, 1847, Cincinnati, Ohio D. Apr. 10, 1917, Flushing, N. Y.
Manager 1876.

Year	Team	G	AB	H	R	BA	W	L	PCT	G by Pos
1871	**Boston Red Stockings**	31	156	42	38	.269				1B-30, OF-1
1872		45	223	57	41	.256				1B-44, OF-2
1874	**Lord Baltimores**	33	151	34	20	.225				1B-32, C-1
1875	**New Havens**	27	115	29	9	.252				1B-26, OF-1
4 yrs.		136	645	162	108	.251				1B-132, OF-4, C-1

Greyson

GREYSON TL
Deceased.

Year	Team	G	AB	H	R	BA	W	L	PCT	G by Pos
1873	**Washington Nationals**	8	35	5	4	.143	1	7	.125	P-8

Bill Hague

HAGUE, WILLIAM L. BR TR 5′ 9″ 164 lbs.
Born William L. Haug.
B. 1852, Philadelphia, Pa. Deceased.

Year	Team	G	AB	H	R	BA	W	L	PCT	G by Pos
1875	**St. Louis**	62	261	59	24	.226				3B-61, 1B-1

George Hall

HALL, GEORGE WILLIAM BL 5′ 7″ 142 lbs.
B. Mar. 29, 1849, Stepney, England D. June 11, 1923, Ridgewood, N. Y.

Year	Team	G	AB	H	R	BA	W	L	PCT	G by Pos
1871	**Washington Olympics**	32	146	38	31	.260				OF-32
1872	**Lord Baltimores**	54	263	79	69	.300				OF-53, 1B-1
1873		34	169	54	43	.320				OF-34
1874	**Boston Red Stockings**	47	209	67	58	.321				OF-47
1875	**Philadelphia Athletics**	77	362	108	70	.298				OF-77
5 yrs.		244	1149	346	271	.301				OF-243, 1B-1

Jim Hall

HALL, JAMES
Deceased.

Year	Team	G	AB	H	R	BA	W	L	PCT	G by Pos
1872	**Brooklyn Atlantics**	13	57	14	8	.246				2B-12, OF-1
1874		2	8	1	0	.125				2B-2
1875	**Keokuk Westerns**	1	4	1	0	.250				OF-1
3 yrs.		16	69	16	8	.232				2B-14, OF-2

Jimmy Hallinan

HALLINAN, JAMES H. BL TL 5′ 9″ 172 lbs.
B. May 27, 1849, Ireland D. Oct. 28, 1879, Chicago, Ill.

Year	Team	G	AB	H	R	BA	W	L	PCT	G by Pos
1871	**Fort Wayne Kekiongas**	5	25	5	7	.200				SS-5
1875	**2 teams New York Mutuals** (44G .299) **Keokuk Westerns** (13G .241)									
″	**total**	57	262	75	42	.286				SS-56, 3B-1
2 yrs.		62	287	80	49	.279				SS-61, 3B-1

Ralph Ham

HAM, RALPH A. 5′ 8″ 158 lbs.
B. Mar. 1849, Troy, N. Y. D. Feb. 13, 1905, Troy, N. Y.

Year	Team	G	AB	H	R	BA	W	L	PCT	G by Pos
1871	**Rockford Forest Citys**	25	118	26	25	.220				OF-18, 3B-7, SS-2

Bill Harbidge

HARBIDGE, WILLIAM ARTHUR BL TL 162 lbs.
B. Mar. 29, 1855, Philadelphia, Pa. D. Mar. 17, 1924, Philadelphia, Pa.

Year	Team	G	AB	H	R	BA	W	L	PCT	G by Pos
1875	**Hartfords**	51	227	49	32	.216				C-25, OF-13, 2B-10, 1B-3

Rit Harrison

HARRISON, WASHINGTON RITTER
B. Sept. 16, 1849, Haverstraw, N. Y. D. Nov. 7, 1888, Bridgeport, Conn.

Year	Team	G	AB	H	R	BA	W	L	PCT	G by Pos
1875	**New Havens**	1	4	2	0	.500				C-1

Scott Hastings

HASTINGS, WINFIELD SCOTT BR TR 5′ 8″ 161 lbs.
B. Aug. 10, 1846, Hillsboro, Ohio D. Aug. 14, 1907, Sawtelle, Calif.

Year	Team	G	AB	H	R	BA	W	L	PCT	G by Pos
1871	**Rockford Forest Citys**	25	120	28	27	.233				C-23, 2B-2, OF-1
1872	**2 teams Lord Baltimores** (11G .196) **Cleveland Forest Citys** (21G .422)									
″	**total**	32	172	60	52	.349				C-20, OF-7, 2B-6
1873	**Lord Baltimores**	30	160	41	42	.256				C-19, OF-10, 2B-1
1874	**Hartfords**	52	237	88	60	.371				C-31, OF-20, 2B-1
1875	**Chicago White Stockings**	66	298	74	43	.248				C-39, OF-25, 2B-2
5 yrs.		205	987	291	224	.295				C-132, OF-63, 2B-12

John Hatfield

HATFIELD, JOHN VAN BUSKIRK 5′10″ 165 lbs.
Brother of Gil Hatfield.
B. July 20, 1847, N. J. D. Feb. 20, 1909, Long Island City, N. Y.

Year	Team	G	AB	H	R	BA	W	L	PCT	G by Pos
1871	**New York Mutuals**	33	168	44	41	.262				OF-24, 2B-7, 3B-2
1872		56	297	90	75	.303				2B-56
1873		52	260	76	54	.292				3B-42, 2B-10
1874		63	299	67	47	.224	0	0	—	OF-59, 3B-4, P-1, 1B-1
1875		2	9	4	2	.444				OF-2
5 yrs.		206	1033	281	219	.272	0	0		OF-85, 2B-73, 3B-48, P-1, 1B-1

Charlie Hautz

HAUTZ, CHARLES A. BR 5′ 7″ 150 lbs.
B. Feb. 5, 1852, St. Louis, Mo. D. Jan. 24, 1929, St. Louis, Mo.

Year	Team	G	AB	H	R	BA	W	L	PCT	G by Pos
1875	**St. Louis Reds**	18	75	23	5	.307				1B-18

Hearn

HEARN
Deceased.

Year	Team	G	AB	H	R	BA	W	L	PCT	G by Pos
1872	**Washington Olympics**	1	3	1	0	.333				SS-1

Frank Heifer

HEIFER, FRANKLIN (Heck) 5′10½″ 175 lbs.
B. Jan. 18, 1854, Reading, Pa. D. Aug. 29, 1893, Reading, Pa.

Year	Team	G	AB	H	R	BA	W	L	PCT	G by Pos
1875	**Boston Red Stockings**	11	48	16	11	.333	0	0	—	1B-7, OF-5, P-1

Hellings

HELLINGS
B. Philadelphia, Pa. Deceased.

Year	Team	G	AB	H	R	BA	W	L	PCT	G by Pos
1875	**Brooklyn Atlantics**	1	4	1	0	.250				2B-1

George Heubel

HEUBEL, GEORGE A. 5′11½″ 178 lbs.
B. 1849, Paterson, N. J. D. Jan. 22, 1896, Philadelphia, Pa.

Year	Team	G	AB	H	R	BA	W	L	PCT	G by Pos
1871	**Philadelphia Athletics**	17	78	25	10	.321				OF-16, 1B-1
1872	**Washington Olympics**	5	24	3	2	.125				OF-5
2 yrs.		22	102	28	12	.275				OF-21, 1B-1

Nat Hicks

HICKS, NATHANIEL WOODHULL BR TR 6′ 1″ 186 lbs.
B. Apr. 19, 1845, Hempstead, N. Y. D. Apr. 21, 1907, Hoboken, N. J.

Year	Team	G	AB	H	R	BA	W	L	PCT	G by Pos
1872	**New York Mutuals**	56	276	85	54	.308				C-55, OF-2
1873		28	132	28	12	.212				C-28
1874	**Philadelphias**	58	284	73	51	.257				C-56, OF-2
1875	**New York Mutuals**	62	270	63	32	.233				C-59, OF-3
4 yrs.		204	962	249	149	.259				C-198, OF-7

Higby

HIGBY
Deceased.

Year	Team	G	AB	H	R	BA	W	L	PCT	G by Pos
1872	**Brooklyn Atlantics**	1	4	0	0	.000				OF-1

Dick Higham

HIGHAM, RICHARD BL TR
B. July 1851, England D. Mar. 18, 1905, Chicago, Ill.

Year	Team	G	AB	H	R	BA	W	L	PCT	G by Pos
1871	**New York Mutuals**	21	97	32	21	.330				2B-11, OF-8, C-1, 3B-1
1872	**Lord Baltimores**	46	242	82	67	.339				C-21, OF-18, 2B-6, 1B-1
1873	**New York Mutuals**	49	247	75	57	.304				OF-18, 2B-16, C-14, 3B-1
1874		65	342	87	58	.254				C-41, OF-23, 2B-1
1875	**2 teams New York Mutuals** (15G .333) **Chicago White Stockings** (43G .234)									
″	**total**	58	280	72	55	.257				C-30, 2B-19, OF-7, 1B-2
5 yrs.		239	1208	348	258	.288				C-107, OF-74, 2B-53, 1B-3, 3B-2

Paul Hines

HINES, PAUL A. BR TR 5′ 9½″ 173 lbs.
B. Mar. 1, 1852, Washington, D. C. D. July 10, 1935, Hyattsville, Md.

Year	Team	G	AB	H	R	BA	W	L	PCT	G by Pos
1872	**Washington Nationals**	11	49	14	10	.286				1B-10, 3B-1
1873		39	186	61	33	.328				OF-36, 2B-2, C-1
1874	**Chicago White Stockings**	59	283	78	47	.276				OF-46, 2B-12, SS-2
1875		69	322	101	42	.314				OF-41, 2B-28
4 yrs.		178	840	254	132	.302				OF-123, 2B-42, 1B-10, SS-2, C-1, 3B-1

Charlie Hodes

HODES, CHARLES TR 5′11½″ 175 lbs.
B. 1848, New York, N. Y. D. Feb. 14, 1875, Brooklyn, N. Y.

Year	Team	G	AB	H	R	BA	W	L	PCT	G by Pos
1871	**Chicago White Stockings**	28	138	34	32	.246				C-18, 3B-7, OF-2, SS-1
1872	**Troy Haymakers**	13	65	15	17	.231				SS-5, OF-4, C-3, 3B-1
1874	**Brooklyn Atlantics**	21	84	12	8	.143				OF-19, 2B-2
3 yrs.		62	287	61	57	.213				OF-25, C-21, 3B-8, SS-6, 2B-2

Jim Holdsworth

HOLDSWORTH, JAMES (Long Jim) BR TR
B. July 14, 1850, New York, N. Y. D. Mar. 22, 1918, New York, N. Y.

Year	Team	G	AB	H	R	BA	W	L	PCT	G by Pos
1872	**2 teams Brooklyn Eckfords** (2G .250) **Cleveland Forest Citys** (21G .321)									
″	**total**	23	117	37	19	.316				SS-23
1873	**New York Mutuals**	53	232	71	45	.306				SS-53
1874	**Philadelphias**	58	302	99	59	.328				3B-31, SS-23, OF-4
1875	**New York Mutuals**	71	339	92	47	.271				OF-45, SS-26
4 yrs.		205	990	299	170	.302				SS-125, OF-49, 3B-31

Holly Hollingshead

HOLLINGSHEAD, JOHN SAMUEL
Also appeared in box score as Holly.
B. Jan. 17, 1853, Washington, D. C. D. Oct. 6, 1926, Washington, D. C.
Manager 1884.

Year	Team	G	AB	H	R	BA	W	L	PCT	G by Pos
1872	**Washington Nationals**	9	45	14	12	.311				2B-9
1873		30	137	35	25	.255				OF-30, 2B-1
1875		19	88	20	8	.227				OF-19
3 yrs.		58	270	69	45	.256				OF-49, 2B-10

Mike Hooper

HOOPER, MICHAEL H. 5′ 6″ 165 lbs.
B. Feb. 20, 1850, Baltimore, Md. D. Dec. 1, 1927, Baltimore, Md.

Year	Team	G	AB	H	R	BA	W	L	PCT	G by Pos
1873	**Marylands**	2	9	0	0	.000				OF-1, C-1

Dick Hunt

HUNT, RICHARD M. 5′ 9″ 145 lbs.
B. 1847, N. Y. D. Nov. 20, 1895, Brooklyn, N. Y.

Year	Team	G	AB	H	R	BA	W	L	PCT	G by Pos
1872	**Brooklyn Eckfords**	11	52	15	11	.288				OF-8, 2B-3

Dick Hurley

HURLEY, WILLIAM F. BL 5′ 7″ 160 lbs.
B. 1847, Honesdale, Pa. Deceased.

Year	Team	G	AB	H	R	BA	W	L	PCT	G by Pos
1872	**Washington Olympics**	2	8	0	0	.000				OF-2

Sam Jackson

JACKSON, SAMUEL BR TR 5′ 5½″ 160 lbs.
B. Mar. 24, 1849, Ripon, England D. Aug. 4, 1893, Clifton Springs, N. Y.

Year	Team	G	AB	H	R	BA	W	L	PCT	G by Pos
1871	**Boston Red Stockings**	15	77	15	15	.195				2B-14, OF-1
1872	**Brooklyn Atlantics**	3	13	2	0	.154				OF-3
2 yrs.		18	90	17	15	.189				2B-14, OF-4

Nat Jewett

JEWETT, NATHAN W. 5′ 6″ 137 lbs.
B. Dec. 25, 1842, New York D. Feb. 23, 1914, Bronx, N. Y.

Year	Team	G	AB	H	R	BA	W	L	PCT	G by Pos
1872	**Brooklyn Eckfords**	2	8	1	1	.125				C-2

Tom Johns

JOHNS, THOMAS PEARCE 5′11″ 170 lbs.
B. Sept. 7, 1851, Baltimore, Md. D. Apr. 13, 1927, Baltimore, Md.

Year	Team	G	AB	H	R	BA	W	L	PCT	G by Pos
1873	**Marylands**	1	5	0	0	.000				OF-1

Caleb Johnson

JOHNSON, CALEB CLARK
B. May 23, 1844, Fulton, Ill. D. Mar. 7, 1925, Sterling, Ill.

Year	Team	G	AB	H	R	BA	W	L	PCT	G by Pos
1871	**Cleveland Forest Citys**	16	65	16	10	.246				2B-8, OF-7, SS-1

Charley Jones

JONES, CHARLES WESLEY (Long Charley) BR TR 5′11½″ 202 lbs.
Born Benjamin Wesley Rippay.
B. Apr. 3, 1850, Alamance County, N. C. Deceased.

Year	Team	G	AB	H	R	BA	W	L	PCT	G by Pos
1875	**Keokuk Westerns**	12	52	13	4	.250				OF-12

Kavanaugh

KAVANAUGH
Deceased.

Year	Team	G	AB	H	R	BA	W	L	PCT	G by Pos
1872	**Brooklyn Eckfords**	5	22	4	5	.182				1B-4, OF-1

Jim Keenan

KEENAN, JAMES WILLIAM BR TR 5′10″ 186 lbs.
B. Feb. 10, 1858, New Haven, Conn. D. Sept. 21, 1926, Cincinnati, Ohio.

		G	AB	H	R	BA	W	L	PCT	G by Pos
1875	**New Havens**	3	12	1	1	.083				3B-2, C-1

George Keerl

KEERL, GEORGE HENRY (Cap) BR TR 5′ 7″ 145 lbs.
B. Apr. 10, 1847, Baltimore, Md. D. Sept. 13, 1923, Menominee, Mich.

		G	AB	H	R	BA	W	L	PCT	G by Pos
1875	**Chicago White Stockings**	6	26	3	2	.115				2B-6

Bill Kelley

KELLEY, WILLIAM J.
B. New York, N. Y. Deceased.

		G	AB	H	R	BA	W	L	PCT	G by Pos
1871	**Fort Wayne Kekiongas**	18	71	15	17	.211				OF-17, 1B-1

John Kenney

KENNEY, JOHN
Deceased.

		G	AB	H	R	BA	W	L	PCT	G by Pos
1872	**Brooklyn Atlantics**	5	21	0	0	.000				2B-3, OF-2

Joe Kernan

KERNAN, JOSEPH
B. Baltimore, Md. Deceased.

		G	AB	H	R	BA	W	L	PCT	G by Pos
1873	**Marylands**	2	8	3	1	.375				OF-1, 2B-1

Henry Kessler

KESSLER, HENRY (Lucky) BR TR 5′10″ 144 lbs.
B. 1847, Brooklyn, N. Y. D. Jan. 9, 1900, Franklin, Pa.

		G	AB	H	R	BA	W	L	PCT	G by Pos
1873	**Brooklyn Atlantics**	1	6	1	0	.167				1B-1
1874		14	57	16	8	.281				C-8, 2B-4, OF-2, 3B-1
1875		25	108	26	17	.241				SS-18, OF-6, C-1, 2B-1
3 yrs.		40	171	43	25	.251				SS-18, C-9, OF-8, 2B-5, 3B-1, 1B-1

Gene Kimball

KIMBALL, EUGENE BOYNTON 5′10″ 160 lbs.
B. Aug. 31, 1850, Rochester, N. Y. D. Aug. 2, 1882, Rochester, N. Y.

		G	AB	H	R	BA	W	L	PCT	G by Pos
1871	**Cleveland Forest Citys**	29	136	25	18	.184				2B-17, SS-6, OF-6

Mart King

KING, MARSHALL NEY TR 5′ 9½″ 176 lbs.
B. Dec. 1848, Troy, N. Y. D. Oct. 19, 1911, Troy, N. Y.

		G	AB	H	R	BA	W	L	PCT	G by Pos
1871	**Chicago White Stockings**	20	109	16	23	.147				OF-10, C-7, SS-3
1872	**Troy Haymakers**	3	12	0	0	.000				OF-3
2 yrs.		23	121	16	23	.132				OF-13, C-7, SS-3

Steve King

KING, STEPHEN F. 5′ 9″ 175 lbs.
B. 1842, Troy, N. Y. D. July 8, 1895, Troy, N. Y.

		G	AB	H	R	BA	W	L	PCT	G by Pos
1871	**Troy Haymakers**	29	144	57	45	.396				OF-29
1872		25	128	38	31	.297				OF-25
2 yrs.		54	272	95	76	.349				OF-54

George Knight

KNIGHT, GEORGE HENRY
B. Nov. 24, 1855, Lakeville, Conn. D. Oct. 4, 1912, Lakeville, Conn.

		G	AB	H	R	BA	W	L	PCT	G by Pos
1875	**New Havens**	1	4	0	0	.000	1	0	1.000	P-1

Lon Knight

KNIGHT, ALONZO P. BR TR 5′11½″ 165 lbs.
B. June 16, 1853, Philadelphia, Pa. D. Apr. 23, 1932, Philadelphia, Pa.
Manager 1883–84.

		G	AB	H	R	BA	W	L	PCT	G by Pos
1875	**Philadelphia Athletics**	13	51	6	5	.118	6	5	.545	P-13

Jake Knowdell

KNOWDELL, JACOB AUGUSTUS 5′ 7½″ 148 lbs.
B. July 27, 1840, Brooklyn, N. Y. Deceased.

		G	AB	H	R	BA	W	L	PCT	G by Pos
1874	**Brooklyn Atlantics**	23	90	12	8	.133				C-20, OF-3
1875		43	165	32	17	.194				C-33, SS-8, OF-3
2 yrs.		66	255	44	25	.173				C-53, SS-8, OF-6

Henry Kohler

KOHLER, HENRY C.
B. May 5, 1852, Baltimore, Md. D. Aug. 27, 1934, Baltimore, Md.

		G	AB	H	R	BA	W	L	PCT	G by Pos
1871	**Fort Wayne Kekiongas**	3	12	2	0	.167				1B-2, 3B-1
1873	**Marylands**	5	22	3	2	.136				3B-5, C-1
1874	**Lord Baltimores**	1	4	0	0	.000				1B-1
3 yrs.		9	38	5	2	.132				3B-6, 1B-3, C-1

Juice Latham

LATHAM, GEORGE WARREN (Jumbo) BR TR 5′ 8″ 164 lbs.
B. Sept. 6, 1852, Utica, N. Y. D. May 26, 1914, Utica, N. Y.
Manager 1882.

		G	AB	H	R	BA	W	L	PCT	G by Pos
1875	**2 teams New Havens** (20G .183) **Boston Red Stockings** (16G .321)									
″	**total**	36	160	40	28	.250				1B-29, SS-4, 3B-3

Ben Laughlin

LAUGHLIN, BENJAMIN
Deceased.

		G	AB	H	R	BA	W	L	PCT	G by Pos
1873	**Elizabeth Resolutes**	12	54	12	3	.222				2B-10, 3B-1, 1B-1

Mike Ledwith

LEDWITH, MICHAEL
B. Brooklyn, N. Y. D. Jan. 2, 1929, Bronx, N. Y.

Year	Team	G	AB	H	R	BA	W	L	PCT	G by Pos
1874	**Brooklyn Atlantics**	1	4	1	0	.250				C-1

Billy Lennon

LENNON, WILLIAM F. 5′ 7″ 145 lbs.
B. 1848, Brooklyn, N. Y. Deceased.

Year	Team	G	AB	H	R	BA	W	L	PCT	G by Pos
1871	**Fort Wayne Kekiongas**	12	48	11	4	.229				C-12
1872	**Washington Nationals**	11	52	12	11	.231				C-11
1873	**Marylands**	4	15	3	1	.200				1B-3, 3B-1, C-1
3 yrs.		27	115	26	16	.226				C-24, 1B-3, 3B-1

Andy Leonard

LEONARD, ANDREW JACKSON BR TR 5′ 7″ 168 lbs.
B. June 1, 1846, County Cavan, Ireland D. Aug. 21, 1903, Boston, Mass.

Year	Team	G	AB	H	R	BA	W	L	PCT	G by Pos
1871	**Washington Olympics**	31	151	43	34	.285				2B-20, OF-10, SS-1
1872	**Boston Red Stockings**	46	252	86	60	.341				OF-37, 3B-6, 2B-3
1873		58	319	95	83	.298				OF-45, 2B-12, SS-1
1874		71	350	119	71	.340				OF-51, SS-11, 2B-9
1875		80	396	128	87	.323				OF-73, SS-3, 3B-3, 2B-1
5 yrs.		286	1468	471	335	.321				OF-216, 2B-45, SS-16, 3B-9

Leutz

LEUTZ
Deceased.

Year	Team	G	AB	H	R	BA	W	L	PCT	G by Pos
1872	**Brooklyn Eckfords**	4	15	2	3	.133				C-4

Len Lovett

LOVETT, LEONARD WALKER BR TR
B. July 17, 1852, Lancaster County, Pa. D. Nov. 18, 1922, Lancaster County, Pa.

Year	Team	G	AB	H	R	BA	W	L	PCT	G by Pos
1873	**Elizabeth Resolutes**	1	5	2	1	.400	0	1	.000	P-1
1875	**Philadelphia Centennials**	5	22	4	2	.182				OF-5
2 yrs.		6	27	6	3	.222	0	1	.000	OF-5, P-1

Charlie Lowe

LOWE, CHARLES
B. Baltimore, Md. Deceased.

Year	Team	G	AB	H	R	BA	W	L	PCT	G by Pos
1872	**Brooklyn Atlantics**	6	27	4	1	.148				2B-6

John Lowry

LOWRY, JOHN D.
B. Baltimore, Md. Deceased.

Year	Team	G	AB	H	R	BA	W	L	PCT	G by Pos
1875	**Washington Nationals**	5	17	3	1	.176				OF-5

Henry Luff

LUFF, HENRY T. 5′11″ 175 lbs.
B. Sept. 14, 1856, Philadelphia, Pa. D. Oct. 11, 1916, Philadelphia, Pa.

Year	Team	G	AB	H	R	BA	W	L	PCT	G by Pos
1875	**New Havens**	38	172	45	15	.262	1	7	.125	3B-26, P-8, OF-4

Denny Mack

MACK, DENNIS JOSEPH BR TR 5′ 7″ 164 lbs.
Born Dennis Joseph McGee.
B. 1851, Easton, Pa. D. Apr. 10, 1888, Wilkes-Barre, Pa.
Manager 1882.

Year	Team	G	AB	H	R	BA	W	L	PCT	G by Pos
1871	**Rockford Forest Citys**	25	130	31	34	.238	0	1	.000	1B-24, SS-1, P-1
1872	**Philadelphia Athletics**	46	227	56	66	.247				1B-24, SS-22
1873	**Philadelphias**	46	218	61	54	.280				1B-40, OF-4, 2B-1, SS-1
1874		56	261	53	47	.203				1B-56
4 yrs.		173	836	201	201	.240	0	1	.000	1B-144, SS-24, OF-4, 2B-1, P-1

Fergy Malone

MALONE, FERGUSON G. BR TL 5′ 8″ 156 lbs.
B. 1842, Ireland D. Jan. 1, 1905, Seattle, Wash.
Manager 1884.

Year	Team	G	AB	H	R	BA	W	L	PCT	G by Pos
1871	**Philadelphia Athletics**	27	145	46	33	.317				C-27
1872		39	216	58	46	.269				C-21, 1B-18
1873	**Philadelphias**	53	284	76	59	.268				C-52, SS-1
1874	**Chicago White Stockings**	47	238	53	33	.223				C-47
1875	**Philadelphias**	27	114	26	15	.228				1B-21, C-4, OF-2
5 yrs.		193	997	259	186	.260				C-151, 1B-39, OF-2, SS-1

Martin Malone

MALONE, MARTIN
Deceased.

Year	Team	G	AB	H	R	BA	W	L	PCT	G by Pos
1872	**Brooklyn Eckfords**	4	16	4	1	.250	0	3	.000	P-3, OF-1

Jack Manning

MANNING, JOHN E. BR TR 5′ 8½″ 158 lbs.
B. Dec. 20, 1853, Braintree, Mass. D. Aug. 15, 1929, Boston, Mass.
Manager 1877.

Year	Team	G	AB	H	R	BA	W	L	PCT	G by Pos
1873	**Boston Red Stockings**	33	169	44	30	.260				1B-28, OF-5
1874	**2 teams Hartfords** (1G .250) **Lord Baltimores** (42G .299 W-4 L-14)									
″	**total**	43	188	56	36	.298	4	14	.222	2B-20, P-19, SS-5, 3B-1
1875	**Boston Red Stockings**	77	351	100	71	.285	13	3	.813	OF-58, P-17, 1B-2, 3B-2
3 yrs.		153	708	200	137	.282	17	17	.500	OF-63, P-36, 1B-30, 2B-20, SS-5, 3B-3

Al Martin

MARTIN, ALBERT
Deceased.

Year	Team	G	AB	H	R	BA	W	L	PCT	G by Pos
1872	**Brooklyn Eckfords**	4	19	5	2	.263				2B-4
1874	**Brooklyn Atlantics**	7	35	4	1	.114				2B-6, OF-1
1875		6	26	3	1	.115				OF-6
3 yrs.		17	80	12	4	.150				2B-10, OF-7

Phoney Martin

MARTIN, ALPHONSE CASE 5′ 7″ 148 lbs.
B. Aug. 4, 1845, New York, N. Y. D. May 24, 1933, Hollis, N. Y.

Year	Team	G	AB	H	R	BA	W	L	PCT	G by Pos
1872	**2 teams** **Brooklyn Eckfords** (18G .183 W-2 L-8) **Troy Haymakers** (25G .287 W-1 L-2)									
″	**total**	43	204	50	37	.245	3	10	.231	OF-31, P-13
1873	**New York Mutuals**	29	139	29	12	.209	0	2	.000	OF-27, P-2
2 yrs.		72	343	79	49	.230	3	12	.200	OF-58, P-15

Charlie Mason

MASON, CHARLES E. BR TR
B. June 25, 1853, New Orleans, La. D. Oct. 21, 1936, Philadelphia, Pa.
Manager 1887.

Year	Team	G	AB	H	R	BA	W	L	PCT	G by Pos
1875	**2 teams** **Washington Nationals** (7G .100) **Philadelphia Centennials** (12G .229)									
″	**total**	19	78	14	6	.179				OF-17, 1B-2

Bobby Mathews

MATHEWS, ROBERT T. BR TR 5′ 5½″ 140 lbs.
B. Nov. 21, 1851, Baltimore, Md. D. Apr. 17, 1898, Baltimore, Md.

Year	Team	G	AB	H	R	BA	W	L	PCT	G by Pos
1871	**Fort Wayne Kekiongas**	19	89	25	17	.281	7	12	.368	P-19
1872	**Lord Baltimores**	47	218	50	30	.229	25	16	.610	P-45, OF-3, 3B-2
1873	**New York Mutuals**	52	235	43	39	.183	29	22	.569	P-51, OF-1
1874		65	303	71	46	.234	42	23	.646	P-65
1875		70	278	49	23	.176	29	38	.433	P-70
5 yrs.		253	1123	238	155	.212	132	111	.543	P-250, OF-4, 3B-2

Bub McAtee

McATEE, MICHAEL JAMES (Butch, Butcher) TR 6′ 1″ 160 lbs.
B. Mar. 1845, Troy, N. Y. D. Oct. 18, 1876, Troy, N. Y.

Year	Team	G	AB	H	R	BA	W	L	PCT	G by Pos
1871	**Chicago White Stockings**	26	141	39	34	.277				1B-26
1872	**Troy Haymakers**	25	129	27	31	.209				1B-25
2 yrs.		51	270	66	65	.244				1B-51

Dick McBride

McBRIDE, JAMES DICKSON TR 5′ 9″ 150 lbs.
B. 1845, Philadelphia, Pa. D. Oct. 10, 1916, Philadelphia, Pa.

Year	Team	G	AB	H	R	BA	W	L	PCT	G by Pos
1871	**Philadelphia Athletics**	25	141	30	36	.213	20	5	.800	P-25
1872		46	262	72	58	.275	30	14	.682	P-46
1873		49	267	68	42	.255	25	21	.543	P-46, OF-5
1874		55	268	72	31	.269	33	22	.600	P-55
1875		60	275	73	43	.265	44	14	.759	P-60
5 yrs.		235	1213	315	210	.260	152	76	.667	P-232, OF-5

Frank McCarton

McCARTON, FRANCIS
B. Oct. 6, 1857, N. Y. D. June 17, 1907, New York, N. Y.

Year	Team	G	AB	H	R	BA	W	L	PCT	G by Pos
1872	**Middletown Mansfields**	19	85	23	17	.271				OF-19

McCloskey

McCLOSKEY
B. Brooklyn, N. Y. Deceased.

Year	Team	G	AB	H	R	BA	W	L	PCT	G by Pos
1875	**Washington Nationals**	10	38	5	1	.132				C-10

Joe McDermott

McDERMOTT, JOSEPH
Deceased.

Year	Team	G	AB	H	R	BA	W	L	PCT	G by Pos
1871	**Fort Wayne Kekiongas**	2	9	1	3	.111				OF-2
1872	**Brooklyn Eckfords**	7	33	9	3	.273	0	7	.000	P-7
2 yrs.		9	42	10	6	.238	0	7	.000	P-7, OF-2

Jack McDonald

McDONALD, DANIEL 5′11″ 154 lbs.
B. 1847, Brooklyn, N. Y. D. Nov. 23, 1880, Brooklyn, N. Y.

Year	Team	G	AB	H	R	BA	W	L	PCT	G by Pos
1872	**2 teams** **Brooklyn Eckfords** (1G .000) **Brooklyn Atlantics** (14G .214)									
″	**total**	15	61	12	8	.197				OF-14, SS-1

McDoolan

McDOOLAN
Deceased.

Year	Team	G	AB	H	R	BA	W	L	PCT	G by Pos
1873	**Marylands**	1	4	0	1	.000	0	1	.000	P-1

Mike McGeary

McGEARY, MICHAEL HENRY BR TR 5′ 7″ 138 lbs.
B. 1851, Philadelphia, Pa. Deceased.
Manager 1880–81.

Year	Team	G	AB	H	R	BA	W	L	PCT	G by Pos
1871	**Troy Haymakers**	29	156	38	42	.244				C-26, SS-3
1872	**Philadelphia Athletics**	46	227	78	67	.344				C-25, SS-20, OF-1
1873		52	286	81	63	.283				SS-43, C-10

Mike McGeary *continued*

Year	Team	G	AB	H	R	BA	W	L	PCT	G by Pos
1874		54	276	100	61	.362				SS-26, C-24, OF-4
1875	**Philadelphias**	69	313	92	71	.294				3B-24, 2B-23, SS-18, OF-3, C-1
5 yrs.		250	1258	389	304	.309				SS-110, C-86, 3B-24, 2B-23, OF-8

Pat McGee

McGEE, PATRICK
B. Philadelphia, Pa. D. June 21, 1889, New York, N. Y.

Year	Team	G	AB	H	R	BA	W	L	PCT	G by Pos
1874	**Brooklyn Atlantics**	16	66	10	4	.152				OF-15, SS-2, 2B-1
1875	**2 teams Brooklyn Atlantics** (18G .134) **New York Mutuals** (25G .158)									
"	**total**	43	168	25	7	.149				OF-38, 2B-5
2 yrs.		59	234	35	11	.150				OF-53, 2B-6, SS-2

Tim McGinley

McGINLEY, TIMOTHY S. 5′ 9½″ 155 lbs.
B. Philadelphia, Pa. D. Nov. 2, 1899, Oakland, Calif.

Year	Team	G	AB	H	R	BA	W	L	PCT	G by Pos
1875	**2 teams New Havens** (33G .255) **Philadelphia Centennials** (13G .226)									
"	**total**	46	194	48	19	.247				C-45, OF-1

John McKelvey

McKELVEY, JOHN WELLINGTON BR TR 5′ 7½″ 175 lbs.
B. Aug. 27, 1847, Rochester, N. Y. D. May 31, 1944, Rochester, N. Y.

Year	Team	G	AB	H	R	BA	W	L	PCT	G by Pos
1875	**New Havens**	43	202	42	26	.208				OF-39, 3B-4

Ed McKenna

McKENNA, EDWARD J.
B. St. Louis, Mo. Deceased.

Year	Team	G	AB	H	R	BA	W	L	PCT	G by Pos
1874	**Philadelphias**	1	4	0	0	.000				1B-1

John McMullin

McMULLIN, JOHN F. (Lefty) BR TL 5′ 9″ 160 lbs.
B. 1849, Philadelphia, Pa. D. Apr. 11, 1881, Philadelphia, Pa.

Year	Team	G	AB	H	R	BA	W	L	PCT	G by Pos
1871	**Troy Haymakers**	29	145	38	38	.262	13	15	.464	P-29
1872	**New York Mutuals**	54	256	60	49	.234	1	0	1.000	OF-53, P-2
1873	**Philadelphia Athletics**	52	240	61	54	.254	1	0	1.000	OF-51, P-1
1874		55	271	105	61	.387				OF-54, C-1
1875	**Philadelphias**	54	225	56	34	.249	0	1	.000	OF-53, P-1
5 yrs.		244	1137	320	236	.281	15	16	.484	OF-211, P-33, C-1

Trick McSorley

McSORLEY, JOHN BERNARD BR TR 5′ 4″ 142 lbs.
B. Dec. 16, 1852, St. Louis, Mo. D. Feb. 9, 1936, St. Louis, Mo.

Year	Team	G	AB	H	R	BA	W	L	PCT	G by Pos
1875	**St. Louis Reds**	14	51	9	4	.176				3B-8, OF-6

Cal McVey

McVEY, CALVIN ALEXANDER BR TR 5′ 9″ 170 lbs.
B. Aug. 30, 1850, Montrose, Iowa D. Aug. 20, 1926, San Francisco, Calif.
Manager 1878–79.

Year	Team	G	AB	H	R	BA	W	L	PCT	G by Pos
1871	**Boston Red Stockings**	29	155	65	43	.419				C-28, OF-1
1872		46	242	74	56	.306				C-40, OF-9
1873	**Lord Baltimores**	35	187	69	47	.369				C-17, OF-6, SS-5, 2B-3, 1B-3, 3B-1
1874	**Boston Red Stockings**	70	343	131	90	.382				OF-55, C-15
1875		82	392	138	90	.352	1	0	1.000	1B-54, OF-17, C-11, P-2
5 yrs.		262	1319	477	326	.362	1	0	1.000	C-111, OF-88, 1B-57, SS-5, 2B-3, P-2, 3B-1

Bob Metcalf

METCALF, ROBERT
B. Brooklyn, N. Y. Deceased.

Year	Team	G	AB	H	R	BA	W	L	PCT	G by Pos
1875	**New York Mutuals**	7	31	6	1	.194				3B-4, OF-2, SS-1

Levi Meyerle

MEYERLE, LEVI SAMUEL (Long Levi) BR TR 6′ 1″ 177 lbs.
B. July 1845, Philadelphia, Pa. D. Nov. 4, 1921, Philadelphia, Pa.

Year	Team	G	AB	H	R	BA	W	L	PCT	G by Pos
1871	**Philadelphia Athletics**	26	132	65	45	.492				3B-26
1872		27	154	49	30	.318				OF-25, SS-1, 3B-1
1873	**Philadelphias**	48	248	82	52	.331				3B-48
1874	**Chicago White Stockings**	52	263	97	63	.369				2B-26, 3B-14, OF-7, SS-5
1875	**Philadelphias**	68	296	93	55	.314				2B-32, 3B-21, 1B-15
5 yrs.		221	1093	386	245	.353				3B-110, 2B-58, OF-32, 1B-15, SS-6

Joe Miller

MILLER, JOSEPH WICK 5′10½″ 169 lbs.
B. July 24, 1850, Germany D. Aug. 30, 1891, White Bear Lake, Minn.

Year	Team	G	AB	H	R	BA	W	L	PCT	G by Pos
1872	**Washington Nationals**	1	4	1	0	.250				1B-1
1875	**2 teams Chicago White Stockings** (16G .138) **Keokuk Westerns** (13G .111)									
"	**total**	29	119	15	6	.126				2B-27, OF-2
2 yrs.		30	123	16	6	.130				2B-27, OF-2, 1B-1

		G	AB	H	R	BA	W	L	PCT	G by Pos

Reddy Miller

MILLER, THOMAS P. 5′10½″ 160 lbs.
B. Philadelphia, Pa. D. May 29, 1876, Philadelphia, Pa.

		G	AB	H	R	BA	W	L	PCT	G by Pos
1874	**Philadelphia Athletics**	4	16	8	1	.500				C-4
1875	**St. Louis**	54	211	35	17	.166				C-52, 3B-3
2 yrs.		58	227	43	18	.189				C-56, 3B-3

Charlie Mills

MILLS, CHARLES 6′
B. Brooklyn, N. Y. D. Apr. 10, 1874, Brooklyn, N. Y.

		G	AB	H	R	BA	W	L	PCT	G by Pos
1871	**New York Mutuals**	32	149	37	27	.248				C-28, OF-3, 2B-1
1872		6	30	4	6	.133				OF-5, C-2
2 yrs.		38	179	41	33	.229				C-30, OF-8, 2B-1

Everett Mills

MILLS, EVERETT 6′ 1″ 174 lbs.
B. Jan. 20, 1845, Newark, N. J. D. June 22, 1908, Newark, N. J.

		G	AB	H	R	BA	W	L	PCT	G by Pos
1871	**Washington Olympics**	32	161	44	38	.273				1B-32
1872	**Lord Baltimores**	53	259	71	52	.274				1B-53
1873		53	262	83	62	.317				1B-52, OF-1
1874	**Hartfords**	53	242	69	40	.285				1B-53
1875		78	353	92	58	.261				1B-78
5 yrs.		269	1277	359	250	.281				1B-268, OF-1

Ed Mincher

MINCHER, EDWARD JOHN
B. Baltimore, Md. Deceased.

		G	AB	H	R	BA	W	L	PCT	G by Pos
1871	**Fort Wayne Kekiongas**	9	36	8	4	.222				OF-9
1872	**Washington Nationals**	11	51	6	5	.118				OF-11
2 yrs.		20	87	14	9	.161				OF-20

Maury Moore

MOORE, MAURICE
D. Feb. 24, 1881, New York, N. Y.

		G	AB	H	R	BA	W	L	PCT	G by Pos
1875	**Brooklyn Atlantics**	23	90	20	6	.222				SS-14, 1B-6, 3B-3

Bill Morgan

MORGAN, HENRY WILLIAM
B. Brooklyn, N. Y. Deceased.

		G	AB	H	R	BA	W	L	PCT	G by Pos
1875	**St. Louis Reds**	18	73	15	11	.205	1	3	.250	OF-8, 3B-6, P-5

Mullen

MULLEN
Deceased.

		G	AB	H	R	BA	W	L	PCT	G by Pos
1872	**Cleveland Forest Citys**	1	6	4	1	.667				OF-1

Horatio Munn

MUNN, HORATIO B.
Deceased.

		G	AB	H	R	BA	W	L	PCT	G by Pos
1875	**Brooklyn Atlantics**	1	4	0	0	.000				2B-1

Tim Murnane

MURNANE, TIMOTHY HAYES BL TR 5′ 9½″ 172 lbs.
B. June 4, 1852, Naugatuck, Conn. D. Feb. 7, 1917, Boston, Mass.
Manager 1884.

		G	AB	H	R	BA	W	L	PCT	G by Pos
1872	**Middletown Mansfields**	24	115	34	29	.296				1B-24
1873	**Philadelphia Athletics**	42	201	43	54	.214				OF-29, 1B-8, 2B-6
1874		19	84	21	9	.250				OF-12, 2B-6, 1B-1
1875	**Philadelphias**	69	316	90	71	.285				1B-31, OF-26, 2B-12
4 yrs.		154	716	188	163	.263				OF-67, 1B-64, 2B-24

Candy Nelson

NELSON, JOHN W. BL TR 5′ 6″ 145 lbs.
B. Mar. 12, 1854, Portland, Me. D. Sept. 4, 1910, Brooklyn, N. Y.

		G	AB	H	R	BA	W	L	PCT	G by Pos
1872	**2 teams Brooklyn Eckfords** (18G .235) **Troy Haymakers** (4G .368)									
″	**total**	22	100	26	14	.260				OF-11, 2B-8, 3B-2, SS-1
1873	**New York Mutuals**	36	177	54	27	.305				2B-27, OF-6, 3B-3
1874		65	313	69	57	.220				2B-51, SS-14
1875		70	300	56	28	.187				2B-47, 3B-22, OF-1
4 yrs.		193	890	205	126	.230				2B-133, 3B-27, OF-18, SS-15

Al Nevin

NEVIN, ALEXANDER BROWN
B. Oct. 3, 1850, Allegheny City, Pa. D. Oct. 10, 1921, Pensacola, Fla.

		G	AB	H	R	BA	W	L	PCT	G by Pos
1873	**Elizabeth Resolutes**	13	56	11	7	.196				3B-11, OF-1, 2B-1

Al Nichols

NICHOLS, ALBERT H. 5′11″ 180 lbs.
B. Brooklyn, N. Y. Deceased.

		G	AB	H	R	BA	W	L	PCT	G by Pos
1875	**Brooklyn Atlantics**	32	132	21	4	.159				3B-32

Tricky Nichols

NICHOLS, FREDERICK C. BR TR 5′ 7½″ 150 lbs.
B. July 26, 1850, Bridgeport, Conn. D. Aug. 22, 1897, Bridgeport, Conn.

		G	AB	H	R	BA	W	L	PCT	G by Pos
1875	**New Havens**	33	126	22	12	.175	4	28	.125	P-32, OF-1

Pete Norton

NORTON, PETER J.
B. June 19, 1850, Watertown, Wis. D. Feb. 8, 1923, Oak Park, Ill.

Year	Team	G	AB	H	R	BA	W	L	PCT	G by Pos
1871	**Washington Olympics**	1	0	0	0	—				OF-1

Fancy O'Neal

O'NEAL
B. Hartford, Conn. Deceased.

Year	Team	G	AB	H	R	BA	W	L	PCT	G by Pos
1874	**Hartfords**	1	3	0	0	.000				OF-1

O'Neill

O'NEILL
B. Brooklyn, N. Y. Deceased.

Year	Team	G	AB	H	R	BA	W	L	PCT	G by Pos
1875	**Brooklyn Atlantics**	7	26	3	3	.115	0	4	.000	P-4, OF-3

Tom Oran

ORAN, THOMAS
D. Sept. 22, 1886, St. Louis, Mo.

Year	Team	G	AB	H	R	BA	W	L	PCT	G by Pos
1875	**St. Louis Reds**	18	79	14	8	.177				OF-18

O'Rourke

O'ROURKE
Deceased.

Year	Team	G	AB	H	R	BA	W	L	PCT	G by Pos
1872	**Brooklyn Eckfords**	1	4	2	0	.500	0	1	.000	P-1

Jim O'Rourke

O'ROURKE, JAMES HENRY (Orator Jim) BR TR 5′ 8″ 185 lbs.
Brother of John O'Rourke. Father of Queenie O'Rourke.
B. Sept. 1, 1850, Bridgeport, Conn. D. Jan. 8, 1919, Bridgeport, Conn.
Manager 1881–84, 1893.
Hall of Fame 1945.

Year	Team	G	AB	H	R	BA	W	L	PCT	G by Pos
1872	**Middletown Mansfields**	23	101	29	23	.287				SS-16, C-5, 3B-2
1873	**Boston Red Stockings**	57	300	99	79	.330				1B-32, OF-20, C-5
1874		70	334	115	80	.344				1B-70
1875		75	374	108	96	.289				OF-45, 3B-27, 1B-3
4 yrs.		225	1109	351	278	.317				1B-105, OF-65, 3B-29, SS-16, C-10

Charlie Pabor

PABOR, CHARLES HENRY (The Old Woman In The Red Cap) BL TL 5′ 8″ 155 lbs.
B. Sept. 24, 1846, Brooklyn, N. Y. D. Apr. 23, 1913, New Haven, Conn.

Year	Team	G	AB	H	R	BA	W	L	PCT	G by Pos
1871	**Cleveland Forest Citys**	29	142	44	24	.310	0	1	.000	OF-28, P-1
1872		20	93	25	12	.269	1	0	1.000	OF-19, P-1
1873	**Brooklyn Atlantics**	55	237	82	36	.346				OF-55
1874	**Philadelphias**	17	83	18	11	.217				OF-17
1875	**2 teams** **New Havens** (6G .320) **Brooklyn Atlantics** (42G .229 W-0 L-0)									
″	**total**	48	182	44	19	.242	0	0	—	OF-47, P-2
5 yrs.		169	737	213	102	.289	1	1	.500	OF-166, P-4

Bill Parks

PARKS, WILLIAM ROBERT BR TR 5′ 8″ 150 lbs.
B. June 4, 1849, Easton, Pa. D. Oct. 10, 1911, Easton, Pa.

Year	Team	G	AB	H	R	BA	W	L	PCT	G by Pos
1875	**2 teams** **Philadelphias** (2G .125) **Washington Nationals** (26G .183 W-3 L-9)									
″	**total**	28	123	22	12	.179	3	9	.250	OF-17, P-12

Dan Patterson

PATTERSON, DANIEL THOMAS TL 5′ 9″ 143 lbs.
B. 1846, New York, N. Y. Deceased.

Year	Team	G	AB	H	R	BA	W	L	PCT	G by Pos
1871	**New York Mutuals**	32	151	31	31	.205				OF-31, 2B-1
1872	**Brooklyn Eckfords**	12	50	8	5	.160				OF-11, 1B-1
1874	**New York Mutuals**	1	5	2	1	.400				OF-1, 1B-1
1875	**Brooklyn Atlantics**	10	38	8	3	.211				OF-5, 2B-5
4 yrs.		55	244	49	40	.201				OF-48, 2B-6, 1B-2

Dickey Pearce

PEARCE, RICHARD J. BR TR 5′ 3½″ 161 lbs.
B. Feb. 29, 1836, Brooklyn, N. Y. D. Oct. 12, 1908, Onset, Mass.

Year	Team	G	AB	H	R	BA	W	L	PCT	G by Pos
1871	**New York Mutuals**	33	165	44	31	.267				SS-33
1872		43	208	39	28	.188				SS-42, OF-1
1873	**Brooklyn Atlantics**	55	279	72	42	.258				SS-55
1874		56	262	76	49	.290				SS-56, 3B-2
1875	**St. Louis**	70	293	75	49	.256				SS-70
5 yrs.		257	1207	306	199	.254				SS-256, 3B-2, OF-1

Johnny Peters

PETERS, JOHN PAUL BR TR 180 lbs.
B. Apr. 8, 1850, Louisiana, Mo. D. Jan. 4, 1924, St. Louis, Mo.

Year	Team	G	AB	H	R	BA	W	L	PCT	G by Pos
1874	**Chicago White Stockings**	54	248	69	39	.278				SS-32, 2B-21, 3B-1
1875		70	314	87	40	.277				SS-66, 2B-4
2 yrs.		124	562	156	79	.278				SS-98, 2B-25, 3B-1

Neal Phelps

PHELPS, CORNELIUS CARMAN
B. Nov. 19, 1840, New York, N. Y. D. Feb. 12, 1885, New York, N. Y.

Year	Team	G	AB	H	R	BA	W	L	PCT	G by Pos
1871	**Fort Wayne Kekiongas**	1	4	0	0	.000				1B-1
1873	**New York Mutuals**	1	6	0	0	.000				OF-1

Neal Phelps *continued*

Year	Team	G	AB	H	R	BA	W	L	PCT	G by Pos
1874		6	23	3	5	.130				OF-6
1875		2	6	2	1	.333				OF-2
4 yrs.		10	39	5	6	.128				OF-9, 1B-1

Lip Pike

PIKE, LIPMAN EMANUEL (The Iron Batter) BL TL 5′ 8″ 158 lbs.
Brother of Jay Pike.
B. May 25, 1845, New York, N. Y. D. Oct. 10, 1893, Brooklyn, N. Y.
Manager 1877.

Year	Team	G	AB	H	R	BA	W	L	PCT	G by Pos
1871	**Troy Haymakers**	28	134	47	42	.351				OF-18, 2B-6, 1B-4
1872	**Lord Baltimores**	54	278	80	69	.288				OF-24, 2B-21, 3B-9
1873		56	301	89	73	.296				OF-56, 2B-1
1874	**Hartfords**	52	228	79	58	.346				OF-27, SS-18, 2B-7
1875	**St. Louis**	70	313	107	61	.342				OF-62, 2B-8
5 yrs.		260	1254	402	303	.321				OF-187, 2B-43, SS-18, 3B-9, 1B-4

Ed Pinkham

PINKHAM, EDWARD TL 5′ 7″ 142 lbs.
B. 1849, Brooklyn, N. Y. Deceased.

Year	Team	G	AB	H	R	BA	W	L	PCT	G by Pos
1871	**Chicago White Stockings**	24	110	25	27	.227	1	0	1.000	3B-16, OF-7, P-1

George Popplein

POPPLEIN, GEORGE J.
B. Aug. 1840, Baltimore, Md. D. Mar. 31, 1901, Baltimore, Md.

Year	Team	G	AB	H	R	BA	W	L	PCT	G by Pos
1873	**Marylands**	1	4	0	0	.000				OF-1, 3B-1

Al Pratt

PRATT, ALBERT G. (Uncle Al) TR 5′ 7″ 140 lbs.
B. Nov. 19, 1847, Pittsburgh, Pa. D. Nov. 21, 1937, Pittsburgh, Pa.
Manager 1882–83.

Year	Team	G	AB	H	R	BA	W	L	PCT	G by Pos
1871	**Cleveland Forest Citys**	29	130	33	32	.254	10	18	.357	P-28, OF-1
1872		15	69	18	10	.261	3	9	.250	P-13, OF-3
2 yrs.		44	199	51	42	.256	13	27	.325	P-41, OF-4

Tom Pratt

PRATT, THOMAS J. 5′ 7½″ 150 lbs.
B. Jan. 26, 1844, Chelsea, Mass. D. Sept. 28, 1908, Philadelphia, Pa.

Year	Team	G	AB	H	R	BA	W	L	PCT	G by Pos
1871	**Philadelphia Athletics**	1	6	2	2	.333				1B-1

Joe Quest

QUEST, JOSEPH L. BR TR 5′ 6″ 150 lbs.
B. Nov. 16, 1852, New Castle, Pa. D. Nov. 14, 1924, San Diego, Calif.

Year	Team	G	AB	H	R	BA	W	L	PCT	G by Pos
1871	**Cleveland Forest Citys**	3	16	3	1	.188				2B-2, SS-1

Quinlan

QUINLAN
Deceased.

Year	Team	G	AB	H	R	BA	W	L	PCT	G by Pos
1874	**Philadelphias**	1	3	0	0	.000				SS-1

Joe Quinn

QUINN, JOSEPH C. 5′ 8½″ 148 lbs.
B. 1849, Chicago, Ill. D. Jan. 2, 1909, Chicago, Ill.

Year	Team	G	AB	H	R	BA	W	L	PCT	G by Pos
1871	**Fort Wayne Kekiongas**	5	21	4	8	.190				C-5

Paddy Quinn

QUINN, PADDY
Deceased.

Year	Team	G	AB	H	R	BA	W	L	PCT	G by Pos
1875	**3 teams** **Chicago White Stockings** (17G .194) **Hartfords** (3G .100) **Keokuk Westerns** (11G .298)									
″	**total**	31	124	28	16	.226				C-19, OF-13

Paddy Quinn

QUINN, PATRICK 5′ 8″ 162 lbs.
B. Boston, Mass. D. Mar. 1893

Year	Team	G	AB	H	R	BA	W	L	PCT	G by Pos
1875	**Brooklyn Atlantics**	2	8	1	2	.125				OF-2

John Radcliffe

RADCLIFFE, JOHN Y. 5′ 6″ 140 lbs.
B. June 28, 1848, Philadelphia, Pa. D. July 26, 1911, Ocean City, N. J.

Year	Team	G	AB	H	R	BA	W	L	PCT	G by Pos
1871	**Philadelphia Athletics**	28	153	40	47	.261				SS-28
1872	**Lord Baltimores**	54	293	83	71	.283				SS-48, 3B-5, 2B-1
1873		44	246	69	57	.280				SS-22, 3B-22
1874	**Philadelphias**	23	102	21	19	.206				OF-16, 2B-3, SS-2, 3B-1, 1B-1
1875	**Philadelphia Centennials**	5	25	4	2	.160				SS-5
5 yrs.		154	819	217	196	.265				SS-105, 3B-28, OF-16, 2B-4, 1B-1

Al Reach

REACH, ALFRED JAMES BL TL 5′ 6″ 155 lbs.
Brother of Bob Reach.
B. May 25, 1840, London, England D. Jan. 14, 1928, Atlantic City, N. J.
Manager 1890.

Year	Team	G	AB	H	R	BA	W	L	PCT	G by Pos
1871	**Philadelphia Athletics**	26	135	47	43	.348				2B-26
1872		23	115	22	21	.191				OF-19, 1B-4
1873		13	64	15	13	.234				OF-8, 2B-5

	G	AB	H	R	BA	W	L	PCT	G by Pos

Al Reach *continued*

	G	AB	H	R	BA	W	L	PCT	G by Pos
1874	14	53	9	8	.170				OF-14
1875	5	22	5	4	.227				OF-3, 2B-2
5 yrs.	81	389	98	89	.252				OF-44, 2B-33, 1B-4

Bob Reach

REACH, ROBERT 5′ 5″ 155 lbs.
Brother of Al Reach.
B. Aug. 28, 1843, Brooklyn, N. Y. D. May 19, 1922, Springfield, Mass.

	G	AB	H	R	BA	W	L	PCT	G by Pos
1872 **Washington Olympics**	1	5	1	1	.200				SS-1
1873 **Washington Nationals**	1	5	1	1	.200				SS-1
2 yrs.	2	10	2	2	.200				SS-2

Billy Redmond

REDMOND, WILLIAM T. BL TL
B. Brooklyn, N. Y. Deceased.

	G	AB	H	R	BA	W	L	PCT	G by Pos
1875 **St. Louis Reds**	18	80	14	10	.175				SS-17, 3B-1, C-1

Hugh Reed

REED, HUGH
B. 1837, Chicago, Ill. D. Nov. 3, 1883, Chicago, Ill.

	G	AB	H	R	BA	W	L	PCT	G by Pos
1874 **Lord Baltimores**	1	4	0	0	.000				OF-1

Jack Remsen

REMSEN, JOHN JAY BR TR 5′11″ 170 lbs.
B. Apr. 1851, Brooklyn, N. Y. Deceased.

	G	AB	H	R	BA	W	L	PCT	G by Pos
1872 **Brooklyn Atlantics**	35	166	34	22	.205				OF-35
1873	51	215	63	29	.293				OF-51
1874 **New York Mutuals**	64	286	64	51	.224				OF-63, 1B-1
1875 **Hartfords**	85	371	95	71	.256				OF-85
4 yrs.	235	1038	256	173	.247				OF-234, 1B-1

Larry Ressler

RESSLER, LAWRENCE P.
B. Aug. 10, 1848, France D. June 12, 1918, Reading, Pa.

	G	AB	H	R	BA	W	L	PCT	G by Pos
1875 **Washington Nationals**	26	106	20	15	.189				OF-19, 2B-7

Henry Reville

REVILLE, HENRY
B. Baltimore, Md. Deceased.

	G	AB	H	R	BA	W	L	PCT	G by Pos
1874 **Lord Baltimores**	1	4	0	0	.000				OF-1

Bill Rexter

REXTER, WILLIAM H.
B. Brooklyn, N. Y. Deceased.

	G	AB	H	R	BA	W	L	PCT	G by Pos
1875 **Brooklyn Atlantics**	1	5	0	0	.000				OF-1

John Richmond

RICHMOND, JOHN H. TR 5′ 9″ 170 lbs.
B. 1854, Pennsylvania Deceased.

	G	AB	H	R	BA	W	L	PCT	G by Pos
1875 **Philadelphia Athletics**	29	122	26	30	.213				2B-16, OF-11, C-2

Billy Riley

RILEY, WILLIAM JAMES (Pigtail Billy) BR TR 5′10″ 160 lbs.
B. 1855, Cincinnati, Ohio D. Nov. 9, 1887, Cincinnati, Ohio.

	G	AB	H	R	BA	W	L	PCT	G by Pos
1875 **Keokuk Westerns**	8	34	5	4	.147				OF-8

Al Robinson

ROBINSON, ALFRED N.
Deceased.

	G	AB	H	R	BA	W	L	PCT	G by Pos
1872 **Washington Olympics**	7	32	6	6	.188				OF-7

Adam Rocap

ROCAP, ADAM 5′ 9″ 170 lbs.
B. 1854, Philadelphia, Pa. D. Mar. 29, 1892, Philadelphia, Pa.

	G	AB	H	R	BA	W	L	PCT	G by Pos
1875 **Philadelphia Athletics**	14	70	12	13	.171				OF-11, 2B-3

Fraley Rogers

ROGERS, FRALEY W. 5′ 8″ 184 lbs.
B. 1850, Brooklyn, N. Y. D. May 10, 1881, New York, N. Y.

	G	AB	H	R	BA	W	L	PCT	G by Pos
1872 **Boston Red Stockings**	46	201	59	40	.294				OF-42, 1B-6

Johnny Ryan

RYAN, JOHN JOSEPH 5′ 7½″ 150 lbs.
B. Oct. 1853, Philadelphia, Pa. D. Mar. 22, 1902, Philadelphia, Pa.

	G	AB	H	R	BA	W	L	PCT	G by Pos
1873 **Philadelphias**	2	9	2	1	.222				OF-1, 1B-1
1874 **Lord Baltimores**	47	196	35	28	.179				OF-47
1875 **New Havens**	37	153	23	17	.150	1	5	.167	OF-29, P-6, 3B-1, SS-1
3 yrs.	86	358	60	46	.168	1	5	.167	OF-77, P-6, SS-1, 3B-1, 1B-1

Pony Sager

SAGER, SAMUEL B. 140 lbs.
B. 1847, Marshalltown, Iowa Deceased.

	G	AB	H	R	BA	W	L	PCT	G by Pos
1871 **Rockford Forest Citys**	8	40	12	9	.300				SS-4, OF-4

Lew Say

SAY, LOUIS I. BR TR 5′ 7″ 145 lbs.
Brother of Jimmy Say.
B. Feb. 4, 1854, Baltimore, Md. D. June 5, 1930, Fallston, Md.

	G	AB	H	R	BA	W	L	PCT	G by Pos
1873 **Marylands**	3	12	2	1	.167				SS-2, OF-1
1874 **Lord Baltimores**	18	71	12	3	.169				SS-18
1875 **Washington Nationals**	10	38	9	4	.237				SS-8, OF-1, 2B-1
3 yrs.	31	121	23	8	.190				SS-28, OF-2, 2B-1

Harry Schafer

SCHAFER, HARRY C. (Silk Stocking) BR TR 5′ 9½″ 143 lbs.
B. Aug. 14, 1846, Philadelphia, Pa. D. Feb. 28, 1935, Philadelphia, Pa.

	G	AB	H	R	BA	W	L	PCT	G by Pos
1871 **Boston Red Stockings**	31	151	41	38	.272				3B-31, 2B-1
1872	48	225	59	50	.262				3B-43, OF-5
1873	60	301	79	64	.262				3B-47, OF-13
1874	71	324	86	71	.265				3B-71
1875	51	224	66	50	.295				3B-50, OF-1
5 yrs.	261	1225	331	273	.270				3B-242, OF-19, 2B-1

Frank Selman

SELMAN, FRANK C.
Played as Frank Williams From 1871-73.
Born Frank C. Williams.
B. Baltimore, Md. Deceased.

	G	AB	H	R	BA	W	L	PCT	G by Pos
1871 **Fort Wayne Kekiongas**	14	69	15	12	.217				3B-13, C-2, SS-1
1872 **Washington Olympics**	8	40	11	3	.275				C-6, 3B-2
1873 **Marylands**	1	5	1	1	.200	0	1	.000	P-1
1874 **Lord Baltimores**	12	58	16	9	.276				SS-7, C-6, OF-1
4 yrs.	35	172	43	25	.250	0	1	.000	3B-15, C-14, SS-8, OF-1, P-1

Count Sensenderfer

SENSENDERFER, JOHN PHILLIPS JENKINS (Sen-Sen) 5′ 9″ 170 lbs.
B. Dec. 28, 1847, Philadelphia, Pa. D. May 3, 1903, Philadelphia, Pa.

	G	AB	H	R	BA	W	L	PCT	G by Pos
1871 **Philadelphia Athletics**	25	127	43	38	.339				OF-25
1872	1	5	2	2	.400				OF-1
1873	19	88	22	12	.250				OF-19
1874	4	16	4	3	.250				OF-4
4 yrs.	49	236	71	55	.301				OF-49

George Seward

SEWARD, GEORGE E. 5′ 7½″ 145 lbs.
B. St. Louis, Mo. Deceased.

	G	AB	H	R	BA	W	L	PCT	G by Pos
1875 **St. Louis**	24	95	20	12	.211				C-17, OF-5, 2B-2

Shaffer

SHAFFER
Deceased.

	G	AB	H	R	BA	W	L	PCT	G by Pos
1875 **Brooklyn Atlantics**	1	4	0	0	.000				OF-1

Orator Shaffer

SHAFFER, GEORGE BL TR 5′ 9″ 165 lbs.
Brother of Taylor Shaffer.
B. 1852, Philadelphia, Pa. Deceased.

	G	AB	H	R	BA	W	L	PCT	G by Pos
1874 **2 teams New York Mutuals** (1G .167) **Hartfords** (9G .200)									
″ **total**	10	41	8	7	.195				OF-10
1875 **Philadelphias**	18	79	19	11	.241				OF-10, 3B-6, 1B-2
2 yrs.	28	120	27	18	.225				OF-20, 3B-6, 1B-2

John Sheppard

SHEPPARD, JOHN
B. Baltimore, Md. Deceased.

	G	AB	H	R	BA	W	L	PCT	G by Pos
1873 **Marylands**	2	7	0	0	.000				OF-1, C-1

Sheridan

SHERIDAN
Deceased.

	G	AB	H	R	BA	W	L	PCT	G by Pos
1875 **Brooklyn Atlantics**	1	4	0	0	.000				OF-1

Joe Simmons

SIMMONS, JOSEPH S. 5′ 9½″ 166 lbs.
B. June 13, 1845, New York, N. Y. Deceased.
Manager 1884.

	G	AB	H	R	BA	W	L	PCT	G by Pos
1871 **Chicago White Stockings**	27	134	27	29	.201				OF-25, 1B-2
1872 **Cleveland Forest Citys**	17	87	20	11	.230				1B-14, OF-3
1875 **Keokuk Westerns**	13	56	9	5	.161				OF-10, 1B-3
3 yrs.	57	277	56	45	.202				OF-38, 1B-19

Marty Simpson

SIMPSON, MARTIN
B. Baltimore, Md. Deceased.

	G	AB	H	R	BA	W	L	PCT	G by Pos
1873 **Marylands**	3	11	0	2	.000				2B-2, C-1

Bill Smiley

SMILEY, WILLIAM B.
B. 1856, Baltimore, Md. D. July 11, 1884, Baltimore, Md.

	G	AB	H	R	BA	W	L	PCT	G by Pos
1874 **Lord Baltimores**	2	7	0	0	.000				3B-2

		G	AB	H	R	BA	W	L	PCT	G by Pos

Bill Smith

SMITH, WILLIAM J.
B. Baltimore, Md. D. Aug. 9, 1886, Baltimore, Md.

		G	AB	H	R	BA	W	L	PCT	G by Pos
1873	**Marylands**	4	16	1	1	.063				OF-3, C-1

Charlie Smith

SMITH, CHARLES J. 5′10½″ 150 lbs.
B. Dec. 11, 1840, Brooklyn, N. Y. D. Nov. 15, 1897, Great Neck, N. Y.

		G	AB	H	R	BA	W	L	PCT	G by Pos
1871	**New York Mutuals**	14	72	17	15	.236				3B-11, 2B-3

John Smith

SMITH, JOHN
B. Baltimore, Md. Deceased.

		G	AB	H	R	BA	W	L	PCT	G by Pos
1873	**Marylands**	5	21	4	1	.190				OF-2, SS-2, 2B-1
1874	**Lord Baltimores**	5	19	3	1	.158				SS-5, OF-1
1875	**New Havens**	1	4	0	0	.000				SS-1
3 yrs.		11	44	7	2	.159				SS-8, OF-3, 2B-1

Tom Smith

SMITH, THOMAS N.
B. 1851, Guelph, Ont., Canada. D. Mar. 28, 1889, Detroit, Mich.

		G	AB	H	R	BA	W	L	PCT	G by Pos
1875	**Brooklyn Atlantics**	3	14	1	0	.071				2B-3

Charlie Snow

SNOW, CHARLES M.
B. Aug. 3, 1849, Lowell, Mass. Deceased.

		G	AB	H	R	BA	W	L	PCT	G by Pos
1874	**Brooklyn Atlantics**	1	1	0	0	.000				OF-1

Jim Snyder

SNYDER, JAMES 5′ 7″ 130 lbs.
B. Sept. 15, 1847, Brooklyn, N. Y. D. Dec. 1, 1922, Rockaway Beach, N. Y.

		G	AB	H	R	BA	W	L	PCT	G by Pos
1872	**Brooklyn Eckfords**	26	109	30	15	.275				SS-22, OF-3, C-1

Josh Snyder

SNYDER, JOSHUA M.
B. Mar. 1844, Brooklyn, N. Y. D. Apr. 21, 1881, Brooklyn, N. Y.

		G	AB	H	R	BA	W	L	PCT	G by Pos
1872	**Brooklyn Eckfords**	9	41	7	3	.171				OF-9

Pop Snyder

SNYDER, CHARLES N. BR TR 5′11½″ 184 lbs.
B. Oct. 6, 1854, Washington, D. C. D. Oct. 29, 1924, Washington, D. C.
Manager 1882–84, 1891.

		G	AB	H	R	BA	W	L	PCT	G by Pos
1873	**Washington Nationals**	28	118	18	16	.153				C-28, OF-1
1874	**Lord Baltimores**	39	168	32	23	.190				C-39
1875	**Philadelphias**	66	206	62	39	.301				C-65, OF-1
3 yrs.		133	492	112	78	.228				C-132, OF-2

Ed Somerville

SOMERVILLE, EDWARD G. BR TR
B. Mar. 1, 1853, Philadelphia, Pa. D. Oct. 1, 1877, London, Ont., Canada.

		G	AB	H	R	BA	W	L	PCT	G by Pos
1875	**2 teams** **New Havens** (33G .207) **Philadelphia Centennials** (14G .220)									
"	**total**	47	204	43	21	.211				2B-44, SS-1, 3B-1, 1B-1

Al Spalding

SPALDING, ALBERT GOODWILL BR TR 6′ 1″ 170 lbs.
B. Sept. 2, 1850, Byron, Ill. D. Sept. 9, 1915, San Diego, Calif.
Manager 1876–77.
Hall of Fame 1939.

		G	AB	H	R	BA	W	L	PCT	G by Pos
1871	**Boston Red Stockings**	31	151	40	43	.265	20	10	.667	P-31, OF-2
1872		48	248	84	59	.339	37	8	.822	P-48, OF-2
1873		60	331	105	85	.317	41	15	.732	P-57, OF-3
1874		71	363	121	80	.333	52	18	.743	P-71
1875		74	352	112	67	.318	57	5	.919	P-66, OF-10, 1B-2
5 yrs.		284	1445	462	334	.320	207	56	.787	P-273, OF-17, 1B-2

Spencer

SPENCER
Deceased.

		G	AB	H	R	BA	W	L	PCT	G by Pos
1872	**Washington Nationals**	2	10	2	3	.200				SS-2

Joe Start

START, JOSEPH (Old Reliable) BL TL 5′ 9″ 165 lbs.
B. Oct. 14, 1842, New York, N. Y. D. Mar. 27, 1927, Providence, R. I.

		G	AB	H	R	BA	W	L	PCT	G by Pos
1871	**New York Mutuals**	33	165	56	35	.339				1B-33
1872		55	281	77	62	.274				1B-55
1873		53	262	66	44	.252				1B-53
1874		63	321	93	68	.290				1B-63
1875		69	324	90	57	.278				1B-69
5 yrs.		273	1353	382	266	.282				1B-273

Bill Stearns

STEARNS, WILLIAM E. TR
B. Mar. 20, 1853, Washington, D. C. D. Dec. 30, 1898, Washington, D. C.

		G	AB	H	R	BA	W	L	PCT	G by Pos
1871	**Washington Olympics**	2	11	0	1	.000	2	0	1.000	P-2
1872	**Washington Nationals**	11	47	12	7	.255	0	11	.000	P-11
1873		31	140	24	22	.171	7	24	.226	P-31

Bill Stearns *continued*

		G	AB	H	R	BA	W	L	PCT	G by Pos
1874	**Hartfords**	32	130	25	16	.192	2	16	.111	P-18, OF-14
1875	**Washington Nationals**	21	78	20	9	.256	1	14	.067	P-16, OF-6
5 yrs.		97	406	81	55	.200	12	65	.156	P-78, OF-20

Bob Stevens

STEVENS, ROBERT
Deceased.

		G	AB	H	R	BA	W	L	PCT	G by Pos
1875	**Washington Nationals**	1	4	1	0	.250				OF-1

Gat Stires

STIRES, GARRETT BL TR 5′ 8″ 180 lbs.
B. Oct. 13, 1849, Hunterdon County, N. J. D. June 13, 1933, Byron, Ill.

		G	AB	H	R	BA	W	L	PCT	G by Pos
1871	**Rockford Forest Citys**	25	118	32	23	.271				OF-25

Stoddard

STODDARD
Deceased.

		G	AB	H	R	BA	W	L	PCT	G by Pos
1875	**Brooklyn Atlantics**	2	9	1	1	.111				OF-2

Ed Stratton

STRATTON, WILLIAM EDWARD
B. Baltimore, Md. Deceased.

		G	AB	H	R	BA	W	L	PCT	G by Pos
1873	**Marylands**	3	12	2	1	.167	0	2	.000	P-2, OF-1

Sy Studley

STUDLEY, SEYMOUR L. (Warhorse)
B. Washington, D. C. D. 1874, Washington, D. C.

		G	AB	H	R	BA	W	L	PCT	G by Pos
1872	**Washington Nationals**	5	22	3	3	.136				OF-5

Sullivan

SULLIVAN
B. Bristol, R. I. Deceased.

		G	AB	H	R	BA	W	L	PCT	G by Pos
1875	**New Havens**	2	10	3	3	.300				OF-2

Ezra Sutton

SUTTON, EZRA BALLOU BR TR 5′ 8½″ 153 lbs.
B. Sept. 17, 1850, Palmyra, N. Y. D. June 20, 1907, Braintree, Mass.

		G	AB	H	R	BA	W	L	PCT	G by Pos
1871	**Cleveland Forest Citys**	29	130	45	35	.346				3B-29
1872		21	110	31	30	.282				3B-21
1873	**Philadelphia Athletics**	51	258	82	52	.318				3B-44, SS-7, 2B-1
1874		55	246	85	54	.346				3B-36, SS-20
1875		75	357	117	85	.328				3B-73, OF-1, 1B-1
5 yrs.		231	1101	360	256	.327				3B-203, SS-27, 1B-1, OF-1, 2B-1

Marty Swandell

SWANDELL, JOHN MARTIN TL 5′10½″ 146 lbs.
Born Martin Schwendel.
B. 1845, Brooklyn, N. Y. D. Oct. 25, 06 , Brooklyn, N. Y.

		G	AB	H	R	BA	W	L	PCT	G by Pos
1872	**Brooklyn Eckfords**	14	58	12	6	.207				3B-8, OF-4, 2B-1, 1B-1
1873	**Elizabeth Resolutes**	2	10	1	1	.100				OF-1, 1B-1
2 yrs.		16	68	13	7	.191				3B-8, OF-5, 1B-2, 2B-1

Charlie Sweasy

SWEASY, CHARLES JAMES BR TR 5′ 9″ 172 lbs.
Born Charles James Swasey.
B. Nov. 2, 1847, Newark, N. J. D. Mar. 30, 1908, Newark, N. J.

		G	AB	H	R	BA	W	L	PCT	G by Pos
1871	**Washington Olympics**	5	20	4	4	.200				2B-5
1872	**Cleveland Forest Citys**	11	54	12	8	.222				2B-10, OF-1
1873	**Boston Red Stockings**	1	5	1	0	.200				2B-1
1874	**2 teams Brooklyn Atlantics** (10G .128) **Lord Baltimores** (8G .235)									
″	**total**	18	73	13	6	.178				2B-17, OF-1
1875	**St. Louis Reds**	18	72	12	5	.167				2B-18
5 yrs.		53	224	42	23	.188				2B-51, OF-2

Zachary Taylor

TAYLOR, ZACHARY H.
Deceased.

		G	AB	H	R	BA	W	L	PCT	G by Pos
1874	**Lord Baltimores**	13	51	10	3	.196				1B-13

Terry

TERRY
B. Attleboro, Pa. Deceased.

		G	AB	H	R	BA	W	L	PCT	G by Pos
1875	**Washington Nationals**	6	24	2	0	.083				OF-4, 1B-2

Al Thake

THAKE, ALBERT 6′
B. Sept. 21, 1849, Wymondham, England D. Sept. 1, 1872, Ft. Hamilton, N. Y.

		G	AB	H	R	BA	W	L	PCT	G by Pos
1872	**Brooklyn Atlantics**	17	73	20	12	.274				OF-16, 2B-1

Thompson

THOMPSON
Deceased.

		G	AB	H	R	BA	W	L	PCT	G by Pos
1875	**Brooklyn Atlantics**	1	5	2	1	.400				OF-1

Andrew Thompson

THOMPSON, ANDREW M.
B. 1846, Ill. Deceased.
Manager 1884.

Year	Team	G	AB	H	R	BA	W	L	PCT	G by Pos
1875	**Washington Nationals**	11	42	4	3	.095				C-10, OF-1

Jim Tipper

TIPPER, JAMES 5′ 5½″ 148 lbs.
B. June 18, 1849, Middletown, Conn. D. Apr. 19, 1895, New Haven, Conn.

Year	Team	G	AB	H	R	BA	W	L	PCT	G by Pos
1872	**Middletown Mansfields**	24	110	29	23	.264				OF-18, 3B-6
1874	**Hartfords**	45	196	60	36	.306				OF-45
1875	**New Havens**	41	170	25	9	.147				OF-41
3 yrs.		110	476	114	68	.239				OF-104, 3B-6

Fred Treacey

TREACEY, FREDERICK S. TR 5′ 9½″ 145 lbs.
Brother of Pete Treacey.
B. 1847, Brooklyn, N. Y. Deceased.

Year	Team	G	AB	H	R	BA	W	L	PCT	G by Pos
1871	**Chicago White Stockings**	25	125	43	39	.344				OF-25
1872	**Philadelphia Athletics**	46	242	62	53	.256				OF-46
1873	**Philadelphias**	51	246	62	49	.252				OF-51
1874	**Chicago White Stockings**	35	160	28	18	.175				OF-35
1875	**2 teams Philadelphias** (42G .207) **Philadelphia Centennials** (11G .271)									
″	**total**	53	227	50	28	.220				OF-53
5 yrs.		210	1000	245	187	.245				OF-210

George Trenwith

TRENWITH, GEORGE
B. Ireland D. Feb. 1, 1890, Philadelphia, Pa.

Year	Team	G	AB	H	R	BA	W	L	PCT	G by Pos
1875	**2 teams New Havens** (6G .200) **Philadelphia Centennials** (10G .174)									
″	**total**	16	71	13	6	.183				3B-16

Charlie Waitt

WAITT, CHARLES C. 5′11″ 165 lbs.
B. Oct. 14, 1853, Hallowell, Me. D. Oct. 21, 1912, San Francisco, Calif.

Year	Team	G	AB	H	R	BA	W	L	PCT	G by Pos
1875	**St. Louis**	31	122	26	14	.213				OF-29, 1B-2

Oscar Walker

WALKER, OSCAR BL TL 5′10″ 166 lbs.
B. Mar. 18, 1854, Brooklyn, N. Y. D. May 20, 1889, Brooklyn, N. Y.

Year	Team	G	AB	H	R	BA	W	L	PCT	G by Pos
1875	**Brooklyn Atlantics**	1	3	0	0	.000				OF-1

Wall

WALL
Deceased.

Year	Team	G	AB	H	R	BA	W	L	PCT	G by Pos
1873	**Washington Nationals**	1	4	1	1	.250				SS-1

Fred Warner

WARNER, FREDERICK JOHN RODNEY 5′ 7″ 155 lbs.
B. 1855, Philadelphia, Pa. D. Feb. 13, 1886, Philadelphia, Pa.

Year	Team	G	AB	H	R	BA	W	L	PCT	G by Pos
1875	**Philadelphia Centennials**	14	59	14	11	.237				OF-14

Fred Waterman

WATERMAN, FREDERICK A. 5′ 7½″ 148 lbs.
B. 1845, New York, N. Y. D. Dec. 16, 1899, Cincinnati, Ohio.

Year	Team	G	AB	H	R	BA	W	L	PCT	G by Pos
1871	**Washington Olympics**	32	167	51	46	.305				3B-27, C-6
1872		9	45	18	13	.400				3B-7, C-2
1873	**Washington Nationals**	15	81	27	20	.333				SS-9, OF-4, 3B-2
1875	**Chicago White Stockings**	5	23	6	2	.261				3B-4, 2B-1
4 yrs.		61	316	102	81	.323				3B-40, SS-9, C-8, OF-4, 2B-1

Sam Weaver

WEAVER, SAMUEL H. BR TR 5′10″ 185 lbs.
B. July 10, 1855, Philadelphia, Pa. D. Feb. 1, 1914, Philadelphia, Pa.

Year	Team	G	AB	H	R	BA	W	L	PCT	G by Pos
1875	**Philadelphias**	1	4	1	1	.250	1	0	1.000	P-1

Billy West

WEST, WILLIAM NELSON
B. Aug. 21, 1840, Philadelphia, Pa. D. Aug. 18, 1891, Radnor, Pa.

Year	Team	G	AB	H	R	BA	W	L	PCT	G by Pos
1874	**Brooklyn Atlantics**	10	43	8	4	.186				2B-10

Deacon White

WHITE, JAMES LAURIE BL TR 5′11″ 175 lbs.
Brother of Will White.
B. Dec. 7, 1847, Caton, N. Y. D. July 7, 1939, Aurora, Ill.
Manager 1879.

Year	Team	G	AB	H	R	BA	W	L	PCT	G by Pos
1871	**Cleveland Forest Citys**	29	149	47	40	.315				C-27, 2B-2
1872		21	110	37	21	.336				C-13, 2B-6, OF-3
1873	**Boston Red Stockings**	60	325	124	76	.382				C-55, OF-5
1874		69	349	112	73	.321				C-55, OF-12, 2B-1, 1B-1
1875		80	383	136	77	.355				C-72, OF-7, 1B-1
5 yrs.		259	1316	456	287	.347				C-222, OF-27, 2B-9, 1B-2

Elmer White

WHITE, ELMER
B. Dec. 7, 1850, Caton, N. Y. D. Mar. 17, 1872, Caton, N. Y.

Year	Team	G	AB	H	R	BA	W	L	PCT	G by Pos
1871	**Cleveland Forest Citys**	15	71	20	13	.282				OF-13, C-2

			G	AB	H	R	BA	W	L	PCT	G by Pos
Warren White		**WHITE, WILLIAM WARREN**									
		Deceased.									
	1871	**Washington Olympics**	1	4	0	0	.000				2B-1
	1872	**Washington Nationals**	10	44	14	8	.318				3B-9, SS-1
	1873		39	166	44	29	.265				3B-37, SS-2
	1874	**Lord Baltimores**	45	224	57	21	.254				3B-45
	1875	**Chicago White Stockings**	70	304	72	37	.237				3B-61, SS-4, OF-3, 2B-2
	5 yrs.		165	742	187	95	.252				3B-152, SS-7, OF-3, 2B-3
Witherow		**WITHEROW**									
		Deceased.									
	1875	**Washington Nationals**	1	1	0	0	.000	0	1	.000	P-1
Rynie Wolters		**WOLTERS, REINDER ALBERTUS** TR 6′ 165 lbs.									
		B. Mar. 17, 1842, Schantz, Netherlands D. Jan. 3, 1917, Newark, N. J.									
	1871	**New York Mutuals**	32	150	48	33	.320	16	16	.500	P-32
	1872	**Cleveland Forest Citys**	15	77	17	7	.221	2	6	.250	OF-8, P-8
	1873	**Elizabeth Resolutes**	1	4	0	1	.000	0	1	.000	P-1
	3 yrs.		48	231	65	41	.281	18	23	.439	P-41, OF-8
Wood		**WOOD**									
		Deceased.									
	1874	**Lord Baltimores**	1	6	0	0	.000				2B-1
Jimmy Wood		**WOOD, JAMES LEON** TR 5′ 8½″ 150 lbs.									
		B. Dec. 1, 1844, Brooklyn, N. Y. Deceased.									
	1871	**Chicago White Stockings**	28	145	51	44	.352				2B-28
	1872	**2 teams Brooklyn Eckfords** (7G .176) **Troy Haymakers** (25G .322)									
	″	**total**	32	152	44	49	.289				2B-32
	1873	**Philadelphias**	42	224	66	67	.295				2B-42
	3 yrs.		102	521	161	160	.309				2B-102
Red Woodhead		**WOODHEAD, JAMES** 5′ 6″ 160 lbs.									
		B. July 9, 1851, Chelsea, Mass. D. Sept. 7, 1881, Boston, Mass.									
	1873	**Marylands**	1	5	0	1	.000				SS-1
Favel Wordsworth		**WORDSWORTH, FAVEL PERRY (Red)**									
		B. Dec. 22, 1850, New York, N. Y. D. Aug. 12, 1888, New York, N. Y.									
	1873	**Elizabeth Resolutes**	11	45	10	6	.222				SS-11
Herb Worth		**WORTH, HERBERT**									
		B. May 2, 1847 D. Apr. 27, 1914, Brooklyn, N. Y.									
	1872	**Brooklyn Atlantics**	1	6	1	1	.167				OF-1
George Wright		**WRIGHT, GEORGE** BR TR 5′ 9½″ 150 lbs.									
		Brother of Harry Wright. Brother of Sam Wright.									
		B. Jan. 28, 1847, Yonkers, N. Y. D. Aug. 21, 1937, Boston, Mass.									
		Manager 1879.									
		Hall of Fame 1937.									
	1871	**Boston Red Stockings**	16	88	36	35	.409				SS-15, 1B-1
	1872		48	253	85	86	.336				SS-48
	1873		59	333	126	98	.378				SS-59
	1874		60	319	110	75	.345				SS-60
	1875		79	407	137	105	.337				SS-79
	5 yrs.		262	1400	494	399	.353				SS-261, 1B-1
Harry Wright		**WRIGHT, WILLIAM HENRY** BR TR 5′ 9½″ 157 lbs.									
		Brother of Sam Wright. Brother of George Wright.									
		B. Jan. 10, 1835, Sheffield, England D. Oct. 3, 1895, Atlantic City, N. J.									
		Manager 1876–93.									
		Hall of Fame 1953.									
	1871	**Boston Red Stockings**	31	161	43	42	.267	0	0	—	OF-30, P-2, SS-1
	1872		48	214	56	38	.262	2	0	1.000	OF-48, P-2
	1873		58	283	66	57	.233	2	1	.667	OF-55, P-3
	1874		41	189	58	44	.307				OF-40, C-1
	1875		1	4	1	1	.250				OF-1
	5 yrs.		179	851	224	182	.263	4	1	.800	OF-174, P-7, C-1, SS-1
Sam Wright		**WRIGHT, SAMUEL** BR TR 5′ 7½″ 146 lbs.									
		Brother of Harry Wright. Brother of George Wright.									
		B. Nov. 25, 1848, New York, N. Y. D. May 6, 1928, Boston, Mass.									
	1875	**New Havens**	33	137	24	11	.175				SS-33

		G	AB	H	R	BA	W	L	PCT	G by Pos

Bill Yeatman

YEATMAN, WILLIAM SUTER
B. Mar. 1839, Alexandria, Va. D. Apr. 20, 1901, York, Pa.

		G	AB	H	R	BA	W	L	PCT	G by Pos
1872	**Washington Nationals**	1	3	0	0	.000				OF-2

Tom York

YORK, THOMAS JEFFERSON BL 5′ 9″ 165 lbs.
B. July 13, 1851, Brooklyn, N. Y. D. Feb. 17, 1936, New York, N. Y.
Manager 1878, 1881.

		G	AB	H	R	BA	W	L	PCT	G by Pos
1871	**Troy Haymakers**	29	156	34	37	.218				OF-29
1872	**Lord Baltimores**	49	249	67	60	.269				OF-49
1873		56	279	79	68	.283				OF-56
1874	**Philadelphias**	50	241	60	37	.249				OF-50
1875	**Hartfords**	85	387	110	66	.284				OF-85
5 yrs.		269	1312	350	268	.267				OF-269

George Zettlein

ZETTLEIN, GEORGE (The Charmer) BR TR 5′ 9″ 162 lbs.
B. July 18, 1844, Brooklyn, N. Y. D. May 23, 1905, Patchogue, N. Y.

		G	AB	H	R	BA	W	L	PCT	G by Pos
1871	**Chicago White Stockings**	28	130	31	23	.238	18	9	.667	P-27, OF-1
1872	**2 teams Brooklyn Eckfords** (9G .059 W-1 L-7) **Troy Haymakers** (25G .248 W-14 L-8)									
″	**total**	34	151	31	26	.205	15	15	.500	P-31, OF-4
1873	**Philadelphias**	50	235	49	40	.209	36	14	.720	P-50
1874	**Chicago White Stockings**	57	247	46	26	.186	27	30	.474	P-57
1875	**2 teams Philadelphias** (21G .203) **Chicago White Stockings** (32G .216 W-17 L-14)									
″	**total**	53	213	45	19	.211	29	22	.569	P-52, 1B-2
5 yrs.		222	976	202	134	.207	125	90	.581	P-217, OF-5, 1B-2

FINAL NATIONAL ASSOCIATION STANDINGS

		W	L	PCT	GB	R	AB	H	BA	Manager	W	L	Manager	W	L
1871	Philadelphia Athletics	21	7	.750		367	1331	412	**.310**	Dick McBride	21	7			
	Chicago White Stockings	19	9	.679	2	302	1250	316	.253	Jimmy Wood	19	9			
	Boston Red Stockings	20	10	.667	2	**401**	**1438**	**424**	.295	Harry Wright	20	10			
	Washington Olympics	15	15	.500	7	310	1400	371	.265	Nick Young	15	15			
	New York Mutuals	16	17	.485	7.5	302	1428	392	.275	Bob Ferguson	16	17			
	Troy Haymakers	13	15	.464	8	353	1302	370	.284	Lip Pike	1	3	Bill Craver	12	12
	Fort Wayne Kekiongas	7	12	.368	9.5	137	765	179	.234	Billy Lennon	5	9	Harry Deane	2	3
	Cleveland Forest Citys	10	19	.345	11.5	249	1214	326	.269	Charlie Pabor	10	19			
	Rockford Forest Citys	4	21	.160	15.5	231	1081	273	.253	Scott Hastings	4	21			
1872	Boston Red Stockings	39	8	.830		521	2176	671	**.308**	Harry Wright	39	8			
	Philadelphia Athletics	30	14	.682	7.5	534	2209	659	.298	Dick McBride	30	14			
	Lord Baltimores	35	19	.648	7.5	**597**	**2561**	**717**	.280	Bill Craver	27	13	Everett Mills	8	6
	New York Mutuals	34	20	.630	8.5	523	2503	681	.272	Dickey Pearce	34	20			
	Troy Haymakers	15	10	.600	13	272	1123	333	.297	Jimmy Wood	15	10			
	Cleveland Forest	6	16	.273	20.5	171	957	283	.296	Scott Hastings	6	14	Deacon White	0	2
	Brooklyn Atlantics	9	28	.243	25	220	1452	334	.230	Bob Ferguson	9	28			
	Wahington Olympics	2	7	.222	18	54	372	93	.250	Nick Young	2	7			
	Middletown Mansfields	5	19	.208	22.5	223	1013	277	.273	John Clapp	5	19			
	Brooklyn Eckfords	3	26	.103	27	151	1133	233	.206	Jim Clinton	0	11	Jimmy Wood	3	15
	Washington Nationals	0	11	.000	21	80	451	108	.239	Joe Miller	0	11			
1873	Boston Red Stockings	43	16	.729		**739**	**2878**	**931**	**.323**	Harry Wright	43	16			
	Philadelphias (White Stockings)	36	17	.679	4	526	2418	641	.265	Fergy Malone	8	2	Jimmy Wood	28	15
	Lord Baltimores	33	22	.600	8	624	2599	783	.301	Cal McVey	19	13	Tom Carey	14	9
	Philadelphia Athletics	28	23	.549	11	474	2387	671	.281	Dick McBride	28	23			
	New York Mutuals	29	24	.547	11	424	2297	614	.267	John Hatfield	11	17	Joe Start	18	7
	Brooklyn Atlantics	17	37	.315	23.5	366	2310	583	.252	Bob Ferguson	17	37			
	Washington Nationals	8	31	.205	25	283	1629	406	.249	Nick Young	8	31			
	Elizabeth Resolutes	2	21	.087	23	98	923	204	.221	John Benjamin	2	21			
	Marylands	0	5	.000	16	16	184	26	.141	Bill Smith	0	5			
1874	Boston Red Stockings	52	18	.743		**735**	**3155**	**1033**	.327	Harry Wright	52	18			
	New York Mutuals	42	23	.646	7.5	500	2808	708	.252	Tom Carey	13	12	Dick Higham	29	11
	Philadelphia Athletics	33	23	.589	12	441	2304	763	**.331**	Dick McBride	33	23			
	Philadelphias (White Stockings)	29	29	.500	17	475	2537	683	.269	Bill Craver	29	29			
	Chicago White Stockings	28	31	.475	18.5	418	2565	674	.263	Fergy Malone	18	18	Jimmy Wood	10	13
	Brooklyn Atlantics	22	33	.400	22.5	301	2233	495	.222	Bob Ferguson	22	33			
	Hartfords (Dark Blues)	17	37	.315	27	371	2103	611	.291	Lip Pike	17	37			
	Lord Baltimores	9	38	.191	31.5	227	1890	430	.228	Warren White	9	38			
1875	Boston Red Stockings	71	8	.899		**832**	**3564**	**1161**	**.326**	Harry Wright	71	8			
	Philadelphia Athletics	53	20	.726	15	699	3292	942	.286	Dick McBride	49	18	Cap Anson	4	2
	Hartfords (Dark Blues)	54	28	.659	18.5	554	3466	863	.249	Bob Ferguson	54	28			
	St. Louis (Brown Stockings)	39	29	.574	27	385	2651	660	.249	Dickey Pearce	39	29			
	Philadelphias (White Stockings)	37	31	.544	28.5	469	2645	683	.258	Mike McGeary	34	27	Bob Addy	3	4
	Chicago White Stockings	30	37	.448	35	380	2832	709	.250	Jimmy Wood	30	37			
	New York Mutuals	30	38	.441	35.5	328	2771	630	.227	Nat Hicks	30	38			
	St. Louis Reds	4	14	.222	36.5	55	670	121	.181	Charlie Sweasy	4	14			
	New Havens (Elm Citys)	7	40	.149	48	170	1814	368	.203	Charlie Gould	2	21	Juice Latham	4	14
										Charlie Pabor	1	5			
	Washington Nationals	4	23	.148	41	96	990	181	.183	Holly Hollingshead	4	16	Bill Parks	0	7
	Philadelphia Centennials	2	12	.143	36.5	70	549	125	.228	Bill Craver	2	12			
	Keokuk Westerns	1	12	.077	37	45	484	81	.167	Joe Simmon	1	12			
	Brooklyn Atlantics	2	42	.045	51.5	132	1590	306	.192	Charlie Pabor	2	40	Bill Boyd	0	2

PART TWELVE

Negro Leagues Register

Player Register
Pitcher Register

Negro Leagues Register

As most baseball fans know, long before the major leagues became integrated in 1947, hundreds of the most talented ballplayers in this nation were denied an opportunity to play in the majors because of the color of their skin. That injustice, of course, can never be corrected, but it continues to be the collective editorial opinion of *The Baseball Encyclopedia* staff that we should at least recognize the accomplishments of those talented men. To that end, we introduced the Negro Leagues Register in the eighth edition of the *Encyclopedia*, and with this tenth edition we continue to include updated and more accurate statistics for those players and pitchers.

As with the rest of the book, the Negro Leagues Register is constantly being searched and researched to improve its overall quality. We have tapped the resources of the best-known Negro league historians as well as some of the players themselves to help us compile this section. However, as you will notice in scanning these pages, some of the data here are still incomplete, despite the very diligent efforts of a most capable research staff headed by John Holway, Dick Clark, and Jim Riley, all baseball historians and members of the Society for American Baseball Research (SABR). Their research here represents literally years of painstaking detailed effort, but even they are the first to admit that they are eager to fill in the gaps in their research.

As we did in the last two editions of the *Encyclopedia*, we continue here our open invitation to those baseball fans worldwide who can help us in our continuing research. Certainly the last three years have brought dozens of letters, calls, and statistics, and we are proud that this edition of the Negro Leagues Register is greatly improved from the last book. However, we strive to be as accurate as possible in our research.

This section is not meant to be a full compilation of every man who played in the Negro leagues, but rather a listing of more than 130 of the best, as selected by our research staff. Unfortunately, some of the statistics usually found in baseball records just do not exist for these players, at least not where our historians could locate them. For example, pitchers' earned run averages do not exist nor were runs batted in kept. Sadly, these statistics are not reflected in our research, but we certainly hope to fill in the missing data in the years to come.

One other important fact to bear in mind is that many of these legendary ballplayers played in barnstorming tours and exhibition games all over the country. While many of these players gained substantial reputations through these exhibition games, they were not considered part of the actual Negro leagues and thus, statistics from those games are not included here.

The Negro leagues statistics were edited by Dick Clark, Jim Riley, and John Holway. The following persons contributed to the original eigth-edition research: Russ Adams, Joe Adler, Shaikh Aizaz, Chris Allen, Terry Baxter, Gary Brinkmeyer, Daniel Coffeen, Craig Cohen, Karen Constantino, Harry Conwell, Dick Cramer, Debbie Crawford, Tracy Curtis, Michael Deault, Rod Drew, Greg Ficery, Garret Finney, Dan Friedman, Jared Gardner, Bob Gill, Troy Greene, Richard Hall, Pete Hegarty, David Heller, Jim Holway, John Holway, Jr., Joel Hurwitz, Carolyn Jones, Tim Joyce, Merl Kleinknecht, Jeff Krosse, Paul Kubicek, Catherine Kuchar, Neil Lanctot, Rob Langenderfer, Jeff Lapin, Kevin Lemmer, Larry Lester, Adam Levine, Peter Levitt, Raymond Marks, Willa Martin, Michael Mazur, Joe McGillen, Jeremy Myers, Steve Neumann, Erick Norlin, Jim O'Connor, Denise Oliver, Josh Orenstein, Joe Overfield, Mona Peach, Frank Perretti, Edward Pettit, Walt Peycha, Jonathan Pine, Katrina Powers, Mark Presswood, Jeff Rhodes, Cynthia Rigg, Greg Rosenstein, Paul Rubin, Rob Ruck, Warren Rush, Robin Rutledge, Mike Sampson, Susan Scheller, Bill Schopmeyer, Arthur Schott, Norm Schrager, Dawn Schurek, Jonathan Seamon, Andrew Shields, Jonathan Shiffman, Mathew Shine, Prashant Shukla, Andy Siegel, Amanda Siegfried, Tania Sims, Justin Sloss, David Stark, Roger Still, A. D. Suehsdorf, Diane Walker, Lance Wallace, Dan Wilkison, Edie Williams, Bill Wold, Wendell Wolff, and Charles Zarelli.

The editors wish to thank the following persons who helped with the tenth edition: Susan Baldwin, Todd Bolton, Harry Brunt, Michael Campion, Richard Cramer, Paul Doherty, Larry Hogan, Matthew Hogan, John Holway, Jr., Joshua Hojvat-Gallin, Tim Joyce, Merl Kleinknecht, Larry Lester, Mary Lockhard, Jerry Malloy, Bill Plott, Dave Renfrow, and Mike Stahl.

About the Negro Leagues

As you might imagine, not all black games were reported in the press. Some cities covered their home teams very well, in both the black and white press, while other localities ignored the black games. Games in neutral third cities were often unreported. The black press had good coverage of games in the 1920s, but the hard times of the Depression caused cutbacks in coverage. Black papers relied on teams sending in their own box scores, which not every team did. And deadlines meant that the last two days before weekly publication went uncovered.

Occasionally two or more papers covered the same game-with slightly different box scores. At other times box score figures did not add up correctly, or the game account and the box score differed.

Some black papers did not have an at bats column. This forced us to estimate at-bats, based on the score, total hits, walks, and sacrifices (if known), errors, position in the batting order, and so forth.

Some box scores did not carry extra-base hits, stolen bases, or the pitching breakdown of strikeouts, walks, innings pitched, and the like. Sometimes some or all of this could be found in the game accounts. However, this information is certainly underrepresented in the statistical profiles. Thus home runs do not relate to at bats, nor strikeouts to innings pitched.

Sometimes all we had was a brief game account without a box score, giving only the winning pitcher and any home runs hit. So, just as we sometimes had at bats without knowing the home runs, occasionally we had information on a home run without knowing the at bats. Stolen bases were especially neglected in the box scores. Most probably, the box score compilers simply forgot to report steals.

Some pitching data had to be derived from line scores only, which gave the hits and runs for complete-game pitchers, but did not break them down if two or more pitchers were involved. In almost no cases did the box score give offensive strikeouts or walks, or runs batted in. When this project was first undertaken, about twenty years ago, we arbitrarily (and mistakenly) decided not to count runs either.

The seasons usually ran from early May to early September. In the 1920s, especially in the West, teams played six games a week, or about one hundred games a season. In the 1930s, the hard-pressed teams in both sections cut way back on league games, doing more barnstorming against white semipro clubs. Thus players whose careers were primarily in the 20s will have larger totals than those such as Josh Gibson, who played mostly in the 30s and 40s.

Games were arbitrarily designated "league" games or "exhibition" games. The former counted towards the pennant race. However, the distinction was often blurry, even though the competition was equally fierce in boths types of contest. We have decided to count all games between major black teams, including interleague games between clubs of the Eastern and Western leagues.

Rosters varied from fourteen to eighteen players. Pitching staffs were small. Rarely did a starter see a reliever in the bullpen behind him. Thus saves were rare. And starters paced themselves. Back then pitchers threw only as hard as necessary to win. (Christy Mathewson, Walter Johnson, et al., said they did the same thing in the white leagues.) A pitcher might win 12–9 or 2–1, depending on how much run support he received.

Negro league scores tended to be higher than major league scores of that era. Shutouts and no-hitters were rare. Balls favored the pitchers. They were cheaper than those used by the white majors, and black veterans say they didn't have the bounce that the Reach and Spalding balls had. There were also tobacco juice and manifold trick pitches to contend with.

Parks varied widely. The Chicago American Giants played in huge Southside Park, home of the famous "Hitless Wonders" White Sox of the 1906 era. The St. Louis Stars played in a bandbox with a left-field foul line estimated at between 250 and 260 feet. The teams also used white big league stadia, which also varied widely, from the cozy Polo Grounds to wide-open Griffith Stadium and Forbes Field. This wide difference affected both the pitching and batting stats. A good example is home-run king Mule Suttles, who went from spacious Rickwood Park in Birmingham to the little St. Louis field, to the open spaces of Chicago, and finally to friendly Ruppert Stadium, Newark. His home run totals reflected his travels. Josh Gibson was generally handicapped by his home fields in Pittsburgh and Washington.

There were many variables within the black leagues and between the black leagues and the white. But in the many post-season exhibitions against white big leaguers, Negro league pitchers and hitters performed generally as they had against black competition. A .350 hitter in the black leagues hit about as well against white league hurlers as against black.

The first black league, the Negro National League, was founded in 1920 and included six midwestern cities. It lasted through 1930. In 1923 six eastern clubs formed the Eastern Colored League and raided the West for its stars. It survived, with a change of name, through 1929. For four years, 1924–1927, the two winners met in a World Series.

The stock market crash wiped out the leagues and many teams. From 1931 to 1932 teams were born and folded in rapid succession. In 1933 one league of six to eight teams was formed, the Negro National League. It split into two half-seasons, and the two winners met in a championship series. The league endured for four years.

In 1937 the two regional leagues reappearedthe Negro National League, now in the East, and the Negro American League in the West. Each had six teams. Again the champions faced each other in a black world series each September or October. Raids by the Dominican Republic and Mexico, however, took much of the black talent away from these leagues.

Jackie Robinson's signing a contract with the Brooklyn Dodgers organization in 1945 was the death knell for the Negro leagues. As they lost more of their stars to the white raiders, the black teams began to die off. By 1949 the league remained in name only.

John B. Holway

The Negro Leagues Player and Pitcher registers are alphabetical listings of more than 130 of the best Negro league players. The registers follow the format of the registers of major league players and pitchers in Parts Eight and Nine, but because of the difficulty of compiling statistics, the register formats have been modified.

Player Information

John Doe

DOE, JOHN LEE (Slim) BR TR 6′2″ 165 lbs.
Played as John Cherry part of 1900.
Born John Lee Doughnut. Brother of Bill Doe.
B. Jan. 1, 1850, New York, N.Y. D. July 1, 1955, New York, N.Y.
Manager 1908–15.
Hall of Fame 1946.

		G	AB	H	2B	3B	HR	SB	BA	Pos
1941	PHI Stars	73	274	61	1	1	1	4	.223	3B
1942		68	284	66	4	1	1	1	.232	3B
1943		39	154	45	2	0	3	0	.292	3B
1944		17	58	13	0	0		0	.224	3B
1945		9	27	1	0	0	0	0	.037	3B
5 yrs.		208	797	186	7	2	(5)	5	.233	38-118, P-45

John Doe

This shortened version of the player's full name is the name most familiar to the fans.

Doe, John Lee

Player's full name. The arrangement is last name first, then first and middle name(s).

(Slim)

Player's nickname. Any name appearing in parentheses is a nickname.

BR TR

The player's main batting and throwing style. Doe, for instance, batted and threw right-handed.

6'2"

Player's height.

165 lbs.

Player's average playing weight.

Brother of Bill Doe

The player's brother.

B. Jan. 1, 1910, Bronx, N.Y.

Date and place of birth.

D. July 1, 1985, Bronx, N.Y.

Date and place of death. (Players are listed simply as "deceased" if no certification of death or other information is available, but it is reasonably certain they are dead.)

Manager 1945

Doe also served as a Negro league manager.

Major Leagues 1947–49

Doe played in the major leagues from 1947 to 1949. See the major league registers.

Hall of Fame 1976

Doe was elected to the Baseball Hall of Fame in 1976.

Column Headings Information

G AB H 2B 3B HR SB BA Pos

G	Games
AB	At Bats
H	Hits
2B	Doubles
3B	Triples
HR	Home Runs
SB	Stolen Bases
BA	Batting Average
POS	Position

Negro Leagues Ballclubs

	All Nations	All Nations
	Almendares	Almendares
ATL	Black Crackers	Atlanta Black Crackers
AC	Bacharach Giants	Atlantic City Bacharach Giants
BAL	Black Sox	Baltimore Black Sox
BAL	Giants	Baltimore Giants
BIR	Black Barons	Birmingham Black Barons
BIR	Giants	Birmingham Giants
BKN	Eagles	Brooklyn Eagles
BKN	Royal Giants	Brooklyn Royal Giants
CHI	Am. Giants	Chicago American Giants
CHI	Columbia Giants	Chicago Columbia Giants
CHI	Giants	Chicago Giants
CHI	Leland Giants	Chicago Leland Giants
CHI	Union Giants	Chicago Union Giants
CIN	Buckeyes	Cincinnati Buckeyes
CIN	Clowns	Cincinnati Clowns
CIN	Cubans	Cincinnati Cubans
CIN	Tigers	Cincinnati Tigers
CLA	Tigers	Claybrook (Ark.) Tigers
CLE	Bears	Cleveland Bears
CLE	Browns	Cleveland Browns
CLE	Buckeyes	Cleveland Buckeyes
CLE	Cubs	Cleveland Cubs
CLE	Elite Giants	Cleveland Elite Giants
CLE	Hornets	Cleveland Hornets
CLE	Red Sox	Cleveland Red Sox
CLE	Tate Stars	Cleveland Tate Stars
COL	Blue Birds	Columbus Blue Birds
COL	Buckeyes	Columbus Buckeyes
COL	Elite Giants	Columbus Elite Giants
	Cubans	Cubans
	Cuban Giants	Cuban Giants
	Cuban Stars	Cuban Stars
	Cuban X-Giants	Cuban X-Giants
DAY	Marcos	Dayton Marcos
DET	Stars	Detroit Stars
DET	Wolves	Detroit Wolves
	Elite Giants	Elite Giants
HBG	Giants	Harrisburg Giants
	Homestead Grays	Homestead Grays
HOU	Eagles	Houston Eagles
IND	ABCs	Indianapolis ABCs
IND	Clowns	Indianapolis Clowns
IND	Jewel's ABCs	Indianapolis Jewel's ABCs
JAC	Red Caps	Jacksonville Red Caps
KC	Giants	Kansas City Giants
KC	Monarchs	Kansas City Monarchs
LOU	Black Caps	Louisville Black Caps
LOU	White Sox	Louisville White Sox
MAD	Stars	Madison Stars (farm team)
MEM	Red Sox	Memphis Red Sox
MIL	Bears	Milwaukee Bears
MRO	Monarchs	Monroe Monarchs
NASE	lite Giants	Nashville Elite Giants
NOR		New Orleans
NWK	Browns	Newark Browns
NWK	Dodgers	Newark Dodgers
NWK	Eagles	Newark Eagles
NWK	Stars	Newark Stars
NY	Black Yankees	New York Black Yankees
NY	Cubans	New York Cubans
NY	Cuban Stars	New York Cuban Stars
NY	Harlem Stars	New York Harlem Stars
NY	Lincoln Giants	New York Lincoln Giants
NY	Lincoln Stars	New York Lincoln Stars
OK	Giants	Oklahoma Giants
PHI	Hilldales	Philadelphia Hilldales
PHI	Stars	Philadelphia Stars
PIT	Crawfords	Pittsburgh Crawfords
PIT	Keystones	Pittsburgh Keystones
SCN	Mohawk Giants	Schenectady Mohawk Giants
	Stars of Cuba	Stars of Cuba
STL	Giants	St. Louis Giants
STL	Stars	St. Louis Stars
TOL	Crawfords	Toledo Crawfords
TOL	Tigers	Toledo Tigers
WAS	Black Senators	Washington Black Senators
WAS	Elite Giants	Washington Elite Giants
WAS	Homestead Grays	Washington Homestead Grays
WAS	Pilots	Washington Pilots
WAS	Potomacs	Washington Potomacs
WB	Sprudels	West Baden (Ind.) Sprudels

WIL	Hornets	Wilmington Hornets
WIL	Potomacs	Wilmington Potomacs
WL	Plutos	West Lick (Ind.) Plutos

The following teams were not in the Negro leagues, but played against league teams:

	Cuban HoD Cuban	House of David
	Ethiopian Clowns	Ethiopian Clowns
MAD	Stars	Madison Stars

Statistical Information

Unavailable Information. Any time a blank space is shown in a particular statistical column, such as in Doe's 1944 home run total, it indicates the information was unavailable or incomplete.

Partial Career Totals. Indicated by parentheses. Doe's career home run total of (5) is based on incomplete information. Whenever a player's statistics in a particular category are incomplete, his lifetime total appears in parentheses.

Pitcher Register Column Headings Information

W	L	PCT	G	GS	CG	IP	H	BB	SO	ShO	SV

Total Pitching (including all starting and relief appearances)

W	Wins
L	Losses
PCT	Winning Percentage
G	Games Pitched In
G S	Games Started
CG	Complete Games
IP	Innings Pitched
H	Hits Allowed
BB	Bases on Balls Allowed
SO	Strikeouts
ShO	Shutouts

Relief Pitching

SV	Saves

Negro Leagues Player Register

Newt Allen

ALLEN, NEWTON HENRY (Colt) BB TR 5′8″ 158 lbs.
B. May 19, 1901, Austin, Tex. D. June 11, 1988, Cincinnati, Ohio.
Manager 1941

Year	Team	G	AB	H	2B	3B	HR	SB	BA	POS
1922	KC Monarchs	1	4	3	0	0	0	0	.750	2B
1923		14	53	13	0	1	0	0	.245	SS, 3B
1924		88	364	101	11	3	2	0	.277	2B
1925		82	334	103	6	9	4	15	.308	2B
1926		71	278	72	14	3	1	10	.259	2B
1927		77	293	98	16	3	2	7	.334	SS
1928		70	282	79	13	4	2	12	.280	SS, 2B
1929		77	303	100	24	6	3	23	.330	2B
1930		58	239	84	12	6	3	9	.351	2B
1931	2 teams KC Monarchs STL Stars									
″	total	29	87	25	4	1	1	1	.287	2B
1932	2 teams DET Wolves KC Monarchs									
″	total	25	95	31	2	0	0	4	.326	2B
1935	KC Monarchs	2	8	4	1	0	0	0	.500	2B
1936		7	26	10	3	1	0	1	.385	2B
1937		33	146	53	4	2	0	6	.363	2B
1938		22	77	21	2	0	0	2	.273	2B
1939		31	102	26	2	1	0	0	.255	2B
1940		22	96	31	4	1	1	1	.323	OF, SS, 2B
1941		24	89	26	2	1	0	1	.292	3B, 2B
1942		21	75	23	0	0	1	0	.307	3B
1943			102	23	4	1	0	0	.225	2B
1944		50	177	36	7	1	0	4	.203	3B
	21 years	(804)	3230	962	131	44	20	96	.298	
PLAYOFFS										
1925	KC Monarchs	6	24	9	0	0	1	0	.375	2B
1926		7	26	4	0	0	0	0	.154	2B
1929		2	6	4	0	1	0	0	.667	2B
1937		3	13	4	0	0	0	0	.308	2B
	4 years	18	69	21	0	1	1	0	.304	
WORLD SERIES										
1924	KC Monarchs	10	39	11	7	0	0	1	.282	2B
1925		6	27	7	1	0	0	1	.259	2B
1937		2	8	2	0	0	1	0	.250	2B
1942		3	15	4	1	0	0	0	.267	3B
	4 years	21	89	24	9	0	1	2	.270	
ALL STAR (1936–41)		4	15	0	0	0	0	0	.000	SS, 2B

Sam Bankhead

BANKHEAD, SAM BR TR 5′8″ 175 lbs.
B. Sept. 18, 1905, Empire, Ala. D. July 24, 1976, Pittsburgh, PA.
Brother of Dan Bankhead.

Year	Team	G	AB	H	2B	3B	HR	SB	BA	POS
1931	BIR Black Barons	1	4	2	1	1	0	0	.500	2B
1932	3 teams LOU Black Caps BIR Black Barons NAS Elite Giants									
″	total	5	10	4	1	0	0	0	.400	P
1933	NAS Elite Giants	22	86	27	3	1	1	3	.314	OF, C
1934		19	80	27	0	1	0	4	.338	SS
1935	PIT Crawfords	42	171	56	8	4	1	7	.327	SS, OF
1936		30	129	28	5	0	0	2	.217	OF, 2B
1937	Dominican Republic									
1938	PIT Crawfords	15	54	10	3	0	1	3	.185	OF
1939	WAS Homestead Grays	24	96	28	3	1	3	1	.292	2B
1940	Mexico									
1941										
1942	WAS Homestead Grays	43	145	40	3	3	3	0	.276	SS
1943		49	175	50	2	1	1	4	.286	SS
1944		32	115	32	4	4	0	0	.278	SS
1945		20	71	33	4	2	0	0	.465	SS, 3B
1946		40	151	40	1	0	3	1	.265	SS
1947			244	60	12		3	8	.246	SS
	(14 years)	(342)	1531	437	50	(18)	16	33	.285	
PLAYOFFS										
1935	PIT Crawfords	5	19	6	0	0	0	0	.316	SS
1939	WAS Homestead Grays	5	16	1	1	0	0	0	.063	2B
	2 years	10	35	7	1	0	0	0	.200	
WORLD SERIES										
1938	Homestead Grays	1	3	0	0	0	0	0	.000	OF
1942		2	8	2	0	0	0	0	.250	SS
1943		4	13	3	0	0	0	0	.231	SS

Sam Bankhead *continued*

Year	Team	G	AB	H	2B	3B	HR	SB	BA	POS
1944		5	20	7	0	0	0	0	.350	SS
1945		4	16	1	0	0	0	1	.063	SS
	5 years	16	60	13	0	0	0	1	.217	
ALL STAR (1933–46)		11	40	11	3	0	0	0	.275	IF, OF,

Ernie Banks

BANKS, ERNEST (Mr. Cub) BR TR 6′ 1″ 180 lbs.
B. Jan. 31, 1931, Dallas, Tex.
Major Leagues 1953-71.
Hall of Fame 1977.

Year	Team	G	AB	H	2B	3B	HR	SB	BA	POS
1950	KC Monarchs	53	196	50	11	1	1	3	.255	SS

Bernardo Baro

BARO, BERNARDO BR TR 5′8″ 160 lbs.
B. Cuba D. June 1930, Cuba.

Year	Team	G	AB	H	2B	3B	HR	SB	BA	POS
1915	Almendares	1	4	2	0	0	0	0	.500	P
1916	Cubans	2	7	2	1	0	0	0	.286	OF, P
1917		12	43	9	0	2	0	1	.209	OF, P
1918		4	15	3	0	0	0	0	.200	OF, P
1919		7	29	10	1	2	0	0	.345	OF, P
1920	Cuban Stars	5								
1921		43	160	53	7	4	5	13	.331	OF
1923		16	63	24	0	0	0	6	.381	OF
1924		10	33	12	3	3	2	4	.364	1B
1925		39	159	46	1	2	0	4	.289	1B, P
1926		19	79	15	2	0	1	1	.190	OF, P
1927		39	150	45	4	2	0	2	.300	OF, P
1928		17	72	21	4	0	0	4	.292	OF
1929		36	131	36	5	0	0	0	.275	OF
	14 years	250	(945)	(278)	(28)	(15)	(8)	(35)	(.294)	

John Beckwith

BECKWITH, JOHN BR TR 6′3″ 230 lbs.
D. 1956, New York, N.Y.

Year	Team	G	AB	H	2B	3B	HR	SB	BA	POS
1916	MON Giants	2	6	0	0	0	0	0	.000	
1917	CHI Am. Giants	1	4	0	0	0	0	0	.000	SS
1918		1	4	1	0	0	0	0	.250	C
1920	CHI Giants	15	46	10	1	1	0	1	.217	P, SS, C
1921		36	123	50	5	4	4	0	.407	
1922	CHI Am. Giants	48	159	48	11	2	3	3	.302	UT
1923		60	232	75	19	9	13	5	.323	3B, 1B
1924	2 teams Homestead Grays BAL Black Sox									
″	total	33	119	48	8	1	7	7	.403	SS
1925	BAL Black Sox	47	174	70	14	1	14	2	.402	SS
1926	2 teams BAL Black Sox HBG Giants									
″	total	34	119	43	7	1	9	1	.361	UT, SS
1927	HBG Giants	46	188	63	13	2	7	1	.335	UT, 3B
1929	2 teams Homestead Grays NY Lincoln Giants									
″	total	40	163	62	10	2	11	6	.380	3B, OF, SS, 1B
1930	NY Lincoln Giants	19	67	33	4	2	6	0	.493	3B, 1B
1931	2 teams BAL Black Sox NWK Browns									
″	total	53	198	69	4	0	16	0	.348	3B
1932	NWK Browns	3	12	4	1	0	1	0	.333	3B
1933	NY Black Yankees	2	9	4	0	0	0	0	.444	3B
1934	2 teams NY Black Yankees NWK Browns									
″	total	12	11	3	1	0	0	0	.273	PH
1935	Homestead Grays	1	4	0	0	0	0	0	.000	C
	18 years	453	1638	583	98	25	91	26	.356	
PLAYOFFS										
1930	NY Lincoln Giants	4	8	1	0	0	0	0	.125	PH, 1B

Cool Papa Bell

BELL, JAMES THOMAS BB TL 6′ 165 lbs.
B. May 17, 1903, Starkville, Miss. D. Mar. 7, 1991, St. Louis, Mo.
Hall of Fame 1974.

Year	Team	G	AB	H	2B	3B	HR	SB	BA	POS
1922	STL Stars	22	60	25	3	1	3	0	.417	OF, P
1923		34	74	22	5	1	1	0	.297	1B, OF, P
1924		59	216	67	15	1	0	9	.310	OF, P
1925		89	362	128	29	7	11	24	.354	OF
1926		85	370	134	24	7	15	23	.362	OF
1927		93	401	128	18	3	5	13	.319	OF
1928		72	310	103	16	6	4	7	.332	OF
1929		89	359	112	25	6	4	28	.312	OF
1930		62	264	93	17	6	7	15	.352	OF
1931		19	68	20	0	1	0	0	.294	OF

Cool Papa Bell *continued*

Year	Team	G	AB	H	2B	3B	HR	SB	BA	POS
1932	2 teams DET Wolves KC Monarchs									
″	total	37	138	53	7	3	2	3	.384	OF
1933	PIT Crawfords	37	137	41	6	6	1	6	.299	OF
1934		40	153	49	0	0	0	5	.320	OF
1935		40	157	52	7	7	1	7	.331	OF
1936		22	86	23	1	1	0	1	.267	OF
1937	Dominican Republic									
1938	Mexico									
1939										
1940										
1941										
1942	CHI Am. Giants	17	71	26	3	0	0	0	.366	OF
1943	WAS Homestead Grays	44	178	70	6	5	6	2	.393	1B
1944		30	114	40	5	2	2	0	.351	OF
1945		27	103	25	6	0	1	0	.243	OF
1946		25	86	37	1	1	0	0	.430	OF
	(20 years)	943	3707	1248	194	64	63	143	.337	
PLAYOFFS										
1925	STL Stars	6	25	8	1	0	0	2	.320	OF
1928		7	27	11	0	1	0	1	.407	OF
1930		6	25	7	3	0	1	2	.280	OF
1935	PIT Crawfords	5	14	1	0	0	0	1	.071	OF
	4 years	24	91	27	4	1	1	6	.297	
WORLD SERIES										
1943	WAS Homestead Grays	6	26	8	1	1	0	0	.308	OF
1944		5	23	6	0	1	0	2	.261	OF
1945		4	14	4	1	0	0	0	.286	OF
	3 years	15	63	18	2	2	0	2	.286	
ALL STAR (1933–44)		9	35	7	1	0	0	0	.200	OF

Jerry Benjamin

BENJAMIN, JERRY

Year	Team	G	AB	H	2B	3B	HR	SB	BA	POS
1933	DET Stars	27	91	29	4	2	0	11	.319	OF
1934	BIR Black Barons	2	7	2	1	0	0	1	.286	OF
1935	Homestead Grays	46	167	50	7	1	1	2	.299	OF
1936		6	27	5	0	0	0	1	.185	OF
1937		18	73	19	4	0	0	0	.260	OF
1938		18	71	18	0	0	2	0	.254	OF
1939	WAS Homestead Grays	1	4	0	0	0	0	0	.000	OF
1940	2 teams WAS Homestead WAS Homestead Grays									
″	total	40	157	48	3	1	1	2	.306	OF
1941	2 teams WAS Homestead WAS Homestead Grays									
″	total	26	103	27	1	0	0	0	.262	OF
1942	WAS Homestead Grays	47	181	44	7	0	2	1	.243	OF
1943		45	190	71	6	5	2	4	.374	OF
1944		33	138	51	7	1	1	0	.370	OF
1945		28	113	35	3	0	0	0	.310	OF
1946		31	129	31	1	4	1	1	.240	OF, 3B
	14 years	368	1451	430	44	14	10	23	.296	
PLAYOFFS										
1941	WAS Homestead Grays	2	9	1	0	0	0	0	.111	OF
WORLD SERIES										
1937	Homestead Grays	2	7	1	0	0	0	0	.143	OF
1942	WAS Homestead Grays	4	18	4	0	0	0	0	.222	OF
1943		6	25	5	0	0	0	3	.200	OF
1944		5	19	5	1	0	0	0	.263	OF
1945		4	13	2	0	0	0	0	.154	OF
	5 years	21	82	17	1	0	0	3	.207	
ALL STAR (1937–45)		4	16	3	0	0	0	0	.188	OF

Gene Benson

BENSON, GENE BL TL 5′8″ 190 lbs.
B. Oct. 4, 1913, Pittsburgh, Pa.

Year	Team	G	AB	H	2B	3B	HR	SB	BA	POS
1934	AC Bacharach Giants	7	27	11	0	0	0	0	.407	OF
1936		2	8	2	0	0	0	0	.250	OF
1937	PHI Stars	35	143	40	4	0	3	2	.280	OF
1938	2 teams PHI Stars PIT Crawfords									
″	total	25	100	24	1	0	0	0	.240	OF
1939	PHI Stars	51	169	62	7	0	1	1	.367	OF
1940		49	185	44	4	3	7	0	.238	OF

Gene Benson *continued*

Year	Team	G	AB	H	2B	3B	HR	SB	BA	POS
1941		37	133	34	8	1	1	2	.256	OF
1942		53	189	42	4	0	0	0	.222	OF
1943			227	77	9	9	0	2	.339	OF
1944		39	162	55	7	3	0	0	.340	OF
1945		36	144	42	1	2	1	0	.292	OF
1946		38	159	52	1	1	0	0	.327	OF
1947		87	217	62	12	0	1	4	.286	OF
13 years		(459)	1863	547	58	19	14	11	.294	
PLAYOFFS										
1939	PHI Stars	3	10	4	0	1	0	0	.400	OF
ALL STAR (1940–46)		7	25	8	1	0	0	0	.320	OF

Charles Blackwell

BLACKWELL, CHARLES BL
D. May 12, 1935, Chicago, Ill.

Year	Team	G	AB	H	2B	3B	HR	SB	BA	POS
1915	WB Sprudels	7	24	4	1	0	1	0	.167	OF
1916	STL Giants	8	31	9	2	0	0	1	.290	OF
1917	IND ABCs	16	58	15	1	1	0	0	.259	OF
1920	STL Giants	52	183	59	7		4	9	.322	OF
1921		62	221	99	16	8	10	27	.448	OF
1922		73	275	105	21	10	7	17	.382	OF
1923		52	180	56	10	6	3	8	.311	OF
1924	STL Stars	57	194	50	5	3	6	1	.258	OF
1925	BIR Black Barons	75	296	91	11	4	15	9	.307	OF
1926	DET Stars	73	246	68	11	5	4	11	.276	OF
1928	STL Giants	5	19	9	0	0	1	0	.474	OF
1929	NAS Elite Giants	20	70	18	3	1	2	0	.257	OF
12 years		500	1797	583	88	(38)	53	83	.324	

Lyman Bostock

BOSTOCK, LYMAN SR. BL TR 6′ 1″ 215 lbs.
Father of Lyman Bostock.
B. Mar. 11, 1918, Birmingham, Ala.

Year	Team	G	AB	H	2B	3B	HR	SB	BA	POS
1940	BIR Black Barons	19	74	22	0	0	0	0	.297	
1941			41	18	1	0	0	0	.439	1B
1942		9	30	10	2	1	0	0	.333	1B
1943			17	7	0	0	0	0	.412	
4 years		(28)	162	57	3	1	0	0	.352	
ALL STAR (1941)		1	2	1	1	0	0	0	.500	1B

Bob Boyd

BOYD, ROBERT RICHARD (The Rope) BL TL 5′10″ 170 lbs.
B. Oct. 1, 1925, Potts Camp, Miss.
Major leagues 1951-61.

Year	Team	G	AB	H	2B	3B	HR	SB	BA	POS
1947	MEM Red Sox	73	283	96	0	0	4	0	.339	1B
1948		77	303	114		9			.376	1B
1949		76	293	110					.375	1B
1950		63	250	89	27	8	7	9	.356	1B
4 years		289	1129	409	(27)	(17)	(11)	(9)	.362	
ALL STAR (1948)		1	4	2	0	0	0	0	.500	1B

Jim Brown

BROWN, JIM BB TR
D. Jan. 21, 1943, San Antonio, Tex.

Year	Team	G	AB	H	2B	3B	HR	SB	BA	POS
1920	CHI Am. Giants	24	93	23	1	0	0	8	.247	C
1921		36	106	30	3	1	1	5	.283	C
1922			145	39	8	2	0	6	.269	C
1923		46	167	43	6	2	2	3	.257	C
1924		66	201	55	11	1	0	5	.274	C
1925		82	230	53	6	4	0	7	.230	C
1926		63	221	74	14	5	4	6	.335	C
1927		67	236	70	12	5	0	9	.297	C
1928		24	76	13	1	0	0	0	.171	C
1929		45	137	32	8	1	1	1	.234	C
1930		43	137	42	11	5	2	3	.307	UT
1931		1	5	4					.800	1B, C
1933		26	84	22	1	2	0	1	.262	
1935		8	19	9	0	0	0	0	.474	1B
14 years		(531)	1857	509	(82)	(28)	(10)	(54)	.274	
WORLD SERIES										
1926	CHI Am. Giants	11	38	6	1	1	0	0	.158	C
1927		9	35	11	1	0	2	0	.314	C
2 years		20	73	17	2	1	2	0	.233	

Larry Brown

BROWN, LARRY BR TR 5′ 7″ 160 lbs.
B. Sept. 5, 1905, Pratt, City D. Apr. 7, 1972, Memphis, Tenn.
Manager 1935, 1939-48.

		G	AB	H	2B	3B	HR	SB	BA	POS
1923	2 teams IND ABCs MEM Red Sox									
″	total	10	28	4	0	0	0	1		C
1924	MEM Red Sox	57	172	35	5	6	1	3		C
1925		50	151	30	6	3	1	0		C
1926	DET Stars	47	135	33	3	4	2	1		C
1927	2 teams MEM Red Sox CHI Am. Giants									
″	total	79	198	50	10	3	0	4		C
1928	MEM Red Sox	76	257	75	15	2	1	1		C
1929	2 teams MEM Red Sox CHI Am. Giants									
″	total	71	235	68	9	2	5	0		C
1930	NY Lincoln Giants	21	70	19	4	0	1	0		C
1931	2 teams NY Lincoln Giants MEM Red Sox									
″	total	7	12	5	0	0	1	0		C
1932	CHI Am. Giants	22	72	31	4	0	0	0		C
1933		26	84	22	1	2	0	1		C
1934		22	72	31	4	0	0	0		C
1935		31	94	23	1	5	0	0		C
1936	PHI Stars	26	82	16	1	1	0	0		C
1937		19	65	7	0	0	0	0		C
1938	MEM Red Sox	12	34	5	0	0	0	0		C
1939		18	61	16	1	0	0	1		C
1940		20	70	18	2	1	0	1		C
1941		6	23	5	2	0	0	0		C
1942		14	43	10	3	0	0	0		C
1943		9	29	7	2	0	0	0		C
1944		36	82	16	2	1	0	2		C
1945		16	28	8	2	0	0	0		C
1946		1	1	0	0	0	0	0		
1947		50	211	71	4	2	1	1		C
1948		14	18	0	0	0	0	0		C
	26 years	760	2327	605	81	32	13	16	(.260)	
PLAYOFFS										
1927	CHI Am. Giants	4	16	4	0	1	0	0		C
1930	NY Lincoln Giants	8	32	12	0	2	0	0		C
1934	PHI Stars	1	3	1	0	0	0	0		C
1937	CHI Am. Giants	3	11	4	0	0	0	1		C
	4 years	16	62	21	0	3	0	1	(.339)	
WORLD SERIES										
1927	CHI Am. Giants	8	21	4	1	0	1	0		C
1937	CHI-KC	1	2	1	1	0	0	0		C
1938		1	3	0	0	0	0	0		C
	3 years	10	26	5	2	0	1	0	(.192)	
ALL STAR (1933–41)		7	14	4	0	1	0	0	(.286)	C

Ray Brown

BROWN, RAYMOND BB TR 6′ 1″ 195 lbs.
B. Feb. 23, 1908, Ashland Grove, Ohio D. 1968, Dayton, Ohio.

		G	AB	H	2B	3B	HR	SB	BA	POS
1933	Homestead Grays	13	54	18	3	4	1	1	.333	OF, P
1934		4	17	3	0	0	0	0	.176	P
1935		43	133	34	4	2	5	1	.256	OF, P
1936		1	3	1	0	0	0	0	.333	P
1937	No Data Available									
1938		12	33	7	0	0	5	0	.212	OF, P
1939	WAS Homestead Grays	18	58	15	3	0	1	1	.259	P
1941		7	17	3	1	0	3	2	.176	P
1942		26	74	15	5	0	0	0	.203	OF, PH, P
1943		17	44	13	0	3	2	0	.295	OF, P
1944		12	31	10	3	2	0	0	.323	OF, PH, P
1945		8	23	3	0	0	0	0	.130	3B, OF, P
	(11 years)	161	487	122	19	11	17	5	.251	
PLAYOFFS										
1939	WAS Homestead Grays	3	7	0	0	0	0	0	.000	1B, PH, P
1941		1	5	3	0	0	1	0	.600	P
	2 years	4	12	3	0	0	1	0	.250	
WORLD SERIES										
1937	Homestead Grays	1	1	1	0	0	0	1	1.000	P
1942	WAS Homestead Grays	3	10	4	2	0	0	0	.400	OF, P
1943		3	7	1	0	0	0	0	.143	PH, P

Ray Brown *continued*

Year	Team	G	AB	H	2B	3B	HR	SB	BA	POS
1944		1	5	2	0	0	0	0	.400	P
1945		1	2	0	0	0	0	0	.000	P
	5 years	9	25	8	2	0	0	1	.320	
ALL STAR (1935–40)		2	3	0	0	0	0	0	.000	P

Willard Brown

BROWN, WILLARD JESSIE BR TR 5′11½″ 200 lbs.
B. June 26, 1913, Shreveport, La.
Major leagues 1947.

Year	Team	G	AB	H	2B	3B	HR	SB	BA	POS
1935	KC Monarchs	4	14	7	0	0	1	1	.500	SS
1936		6	30	11	0	0	1	2	.367	SS
1937		32	143	53	10	3	8	4	.371	SS
1938		29	104	37	3	3	6	10	.356	OF
1939		31	119	40	9	1	1	4	.336	OF
1940		2	7	0	0	0	0	0	.000	OF
1941		25	96	32	5	4	2	2	.333	OF
1942		38	150	47	4	2	9	3	.313	OF
1943			116	40	5	0	6	0	.345	OF
1944	US Army									
1945	US Army									
1946	KC Monarchs	58	230	80		4		3	.348	OF
1947		50	211	71					.336	OF
1948		66	262	98	20	5		13	.374	OF
1949		83	291	108					.371	OF
	(13 years)	(424)	1773	624	(56)	(22)	(34)	(42)	.352	
WORLD SERIES										
1937	KC Monarchs	1	2	1	1	0	0	0	.500	OF
1942		4	17	7	1	1	1	1	.412	OF
1946		7	29	7	1	0	2	3	.241	OF
	3 years	12	48	15	3	1	3	4	.313	
ALL STAR (1936–48)		5	14	4	1	0	0	1	.286	OF, SS, 3B

Pee Wee Butts

BUTTS, TOM BR TR 5′9″ 145 lbs.
B. Aug. 27, 1919, Sparta, Ga. D. Jan. 1973, Atlanta, Ga.

Year	Team	G	AB	H	2B	3B	HR	SB	BA	POS
1938	ATL Black Crackers	6	21	8	0	0	0	0	.381	SS
1939	2 teams IND ABCs BAL Elite Giants									
″	total	23	73	35	2	0	0	1	.479	SS
1940	BAL Elite Giants	57	216	71	13	0	1	1	.329	SS
1941		37	131	23	1	0	0	1	.176	SS
1942		42	162	36	0	2	0	4	.222	SS
1943	No Data Available									
1944	BAL Elite Giants	23	86	20	3	0	0	0	.233	SS
1945		25	93	22	2	2	0	0	.237	SS
1946		46	165	56	4	2	2	1	.339	SS
1947		74	296	97	7	0	1	6	.328	SS
1948										
1949		86	333	87					.261	SS
1950	2 teams BAL Elite Giants IND ABCs									
″	total	65	208	45	5	1	0	4	.216	SS, P
	(12 years)	(484)	(1784)	(500)	(37)	(7)	(4)	(18)	(.280)	
PLAYOFFS										
1939	BAL Elite Giants	7	20	6	0	0	0	0	.300	SS
ALL STAR (1944–48)		4	6	0	0	0	0	0	.000	SS

Bill Byrd

BYRD, BILL BB TR 6′ 1″ 200 lbs.
B. July 15, 1907, Canton, Ga. D. Jan. 4, 1991, Philadelphia, Pa.

Year	Team	G	AB	H	2B	3B	HR	SB	BA	POS
1934	CLE Browns	9	24	8	0	0	0	0	.333	OF, P
1935	COL Elite Giants	13	33	12	0	0	2	0	.364	3B, OF, P
1936	WAS Elite Giants									
1937										
1938	BAL Elite Giants									
1939		22	63	17	3	2	3	0	.270	OF, PH, P
1940	No Data Available									
1941	BAL Elite Giants	5	11	1	0	0	0	0	.091	OF, P
1942		15	32	14	1	2	0	0	.438	1B, PH, P
1943			64	22	3	0	2	0	.344	OF, P
1944		4	12	3	2	0	0	0	.250	P
1945										
1946		6	13	2	0	0	0	0	.154	P
1947										
1948										

Bill Byrd *continued*

		G	AB	H	2B	3B	HR	SB	BA	POS
1949										
1950										
	(8 years)	(74)	(252)	(79)	(9)	(4)	(7)	(0)	(.313)	
PLAYOFFS										
1939	BAL Elite Giants	3	7	3	1	0	1	0	.429	P
ALL STAR (1938–46)		9	10	0	0	0	0	0	.000	P

Roy Campanella

CAMPANELLA, ROY (Campy) BR TR 5′ 9½″ 190 lbs.
B. Nov. 19, 1921, Philadelphia, Pa. D. June 26, 1993, Woodland Hills, Calif.
Major leagues 1948-57.
Hall of Fame 1969.

		G	AB	H	2B	3B	HR	SB	BA	POS
1938	BAL Elite Giants	2	3	0	0	0	0	0	.000	C
1939		19	56	13	1	0	1	0	.232	C
1940		26	74	23	1	0	6	0	.311	C
1941		17	56	18	3	0	3	1	.321	C
1942		35	127	39	7	4	1	1	.307	C
1943	Mexico	24	96	34	9	0	0	1	.354	
1944	BAL Elite Giants	23	93	32	7	0	0	1	.344	C
1945		35	113	38	7	0	4	0	.336	P, C
	(7 years)	157	522	163	26	4	15	3	.312	
PLAYOFFS										
1939	BAL Elite Giants	8	26	7	2	0	1	0	.269	C
ALL STAR (1941–45)		3	11	4	0	0	0	0	.364	C

Rev Cannady

CANNADY, WALTER BR
Manager 1938

		G	AB	H	2B	3B	HR	SB	BA	POS
1922	CLE Tate Stars	14	38	12	3	2	0	3	.316	OF, SS, P
1923	Homestead Grays									
1924										
1925	HBG Giants	69	262	104	14	1	12	10	.397	SS
1926		26	101	24	3	0	0	2	.238	SS
1927		50	189	61	12	7	2	7	.323	SS, 3B
1928	NY Lincoln Giants	52	205	61	4	3	2	5	.298	SS
1929	Homestead Grays	30	107	36	5	2	2	3	.336	2B, SS, 1B
1930	NY Lincoln Giants	34	130	35	6	2	6	0	.269	2B
1932	2 teams Homestead Grays PIT Crawfords									
″	total	26	88	20	3	1	1	0	.227	
1933	NY Black Yankees	2	8	1	0	0	0	0	.125	2B
1934		13	45	7	0	0	0	0	.156	2B
1936		17	69	19	2	1	0	3	.275	2B
1937		13	45	14	2	0	0	0	.311	3B
1938		13	45	5	0	1	0	1	.111	3B
1939		14	55	17	0	0	2	0	.309	SS, 3B
1942	CHI Am. Giants	15	55	21	1	0	1	0	.382	2B
1943										
1944	WAS Homestead Grays	14	47	19	4	0	0	1	.404	2B
1945	NY Cubans	2	7	0	0	0	0	0	.000	2B
	(17 years)	(404)	(1496)	(456)	(59)	(20)	(28)	(35)	(.305)	
PLAYOFFS										
1930	NY Lincoln Giants	9	31	10	1	0	1	0	.323	2B
WORLD SERIES										
1944	WAS Homestead Grays	5	18	3	1	0	0	1	.167	2B
ALL STAR (1938)		1	3	1	1	0	0	0	.333	3B

Lick Carlisle

CARLISLE, MATHEW

		G	AB	H	2B	3B	HR	SB	BA	POS
1931	BIR Black Barons	2	7	4	0	0	0	0	.571	2B
1932		2	7	2	0	0	0	0	.286	2B
1933										
1934		3	11	2	0	0	0	0	.182	2B
1935	Homestead Grays	41	157	69	5	4	1	3	.439	2B
1936		6	21	4	1	0	0	0	.190	2B
1937										
1938		17	64	20	0	0	0	0	.313	2B
1939										
1940	WAS Homestead Grays	20	71	21	0	3	0	1	.296	2B
1941		31	98	21	0	0	1	1	.214	2B
1942		21	75	22	0	4	0	1	.293	2B
1943		7	23	10	0	0	0	0	.435	2B

Lick Carlisle *continued*

Year	Team	G	AB	H	2B	3B	HR	SB	BA	POS
1944										
1945										
1946		3	8	2	0	0	0	1	.250	2B
	(11 years)	(153)	(542)	(177)	(6)	(11)	(2)	(7)	(.327)	
PLAYOFFS										
1941	WAS Homestead Grays	2	9	4	0	0	0	0	.444	2B
WORLD SERIES										
1937	Homestead Grays	2	9	1	0	0	1	0	.111	2B
1942	WAS Homestead Grays	3	9	0	0	0	0	0	.000	2B
	2 years	5	18	1	0	0	1	0	.056	
ALL STAR (1943)		2	7	1	0	0	0	0	.143	2B

Tank Carr

CARR, GEORGE BB TR 6′2″ 230 lbs.
B. 1895, Calif.

Year	Team	G	AB	H	2B	3B	HR	SB	BA	POS
1920	KC Monarchs	28	115	34	4	2	2	8	.296	1B
1921		55	196	61	9	8	5	5	.311	UT
1922		69	252	69	6	2	8	6	.274	UT
1923	PHI Hilldales	18	69	14	1	1	1	3	.203	1B
1924		52	161	49	12	4	1	9	.304	1B
1925		67	259	94	19	9	10	24	.363	1B
1926		80	282	89	21	4	2	19	.316	1B
1927		58	198	67	1	1	1	6	.338	1B
1928	3 teams PHI Hilldales NY Lincoln Giants AC Bacharach Giants									
″	total	74	270	83	10	2	7	7	.307	1B
1929	AC Bacharach Giants	5	34	14	1	0	0	3	.412	1B
1933		2	8	1	0	0	0	0	.125	1B
1934	PHI Stars	4	14	6	1	0	0	0	.429	
	12 years	512	1858	581	85	33	37	90	.313	
WORLD SERIES										
1924	PHI Hilldales	8	18	6	0	0	0	2	.333	1B
1925		6	25	8	0	0	1	1	.320	1B
	2 years	14	43	14	0	0	1	3	.326	

Pelayo Chacon

CHACON, PELAYO BR TR
B. Sept. 22, 1888, Havana, Cuba D. June 1930, Venezuela.
Father of Elio Chacon.

Year	Team	G	AB	H	2B	3B	HR	SB	BA	POS
1910	Stars of Cuba	10	36	8	2	0	1	0	.222	SS
1911	Cubans	2	7	1	1	0	0	0	.143	SS, OF
1912		2	8	2	0	0	0	0	.250	SS
1913		10	31	8	6	0	0	0	.258	SS
1914		16	63	16	1	0	0	1	.254	SS
1915	Stars of Cuba	30	117	25	1	1	1	0	.214	SS
1916	Cuban Stars	26	107	32	9	1	0	3	.299	SS
1917		13	52	26	0	1	0	0	.500	SS
1918		7	24	13	0	0	1	0	.542	SS
1919		7	28	10	0	0	0	0	.357	SS
1920		3	14	1	0	0	0	0	.071	SS
1921	No Data Available									
1922	No Data Available									
1923	No Data Available									
1924	Cubans	37	126	32	3	2	0	3	.254	SS
1925		43	159	43	5	6	0	2	.270	SS
1926		5	21	6	1	0	0	0	.286	SS
1927	No Data Available									
1928	No Data Available									
1929	No Data Available									
1930	Stars of Cuba	8	26	8	2	0	0	0	.308	SS
	(15 years)	(219)	(819)	(231)	(31)	(11)	(3)	(9)	(.282)	

Oscar Charleston

CHARLESTON, OSCAR MCKINLEY BL TL 6′1″ 185 lbs.
B. Oct. 14, 1896, Indianapolis, Ind. D. Oct. 6, 1954, Philadelphia, Pa.
Manager 1932-38, 1940-41.
Hall of Fame 1976.

Year	Team	G	AB	H	2B	3B	HR	SB	BA	POS
1915	IND ABCs	33	139	32	3	5	1	12	.230	OF, P
1916	2 teams IND ABCs NY Lincoln Giants									
″	total	12	46	8	0	1	0	2	.174	OF
1917	IND ABCs	19	69	21	0	4	1	1	.304	OF, P
1918	2 teams IND ABCs CHI Am. Giants									
″	total	10	39	14	3	0	1	0	.359	OF, P

Oscar Charleston *continued*

Year	Team	G	AB	H	2B	3B	HR	SB	BA	POS
1919	2 teams DET Stars CHI Am. Giants									
"	total	15	56	19	1	1	1	0	.339	OF
1920	IND ABCs	44	167	56	8	5	6	6	.335	OF
1921	STL Giants	60	212	92	14	11	15	34	.434	OF
1922	IND ABCs	66	281	104	23	8	16	23	.370	OF
1923		66	238	74	15	8	9	18	.311	OF
1924	HBG Giants	56	175	72	13	1	14	3	.411	OF
1925		68	238	106	21	4	20	15	.445	OF
1926		27	93	32	7	0	7	11	.344	OF, P
1927		49	185	71	14	1	11	7	.384	OF
1928	PHI Hilldales	52	204	74	8	2	8	9	.363	OF
1929		58	204	76	5	4	6	10	.373	OF
1930	Homestead Grays	18	73	25	4	4	6	1	.342	1B
1931		34	137	53	12	4	4	0	.387	1B
1932	PIT Crawfords	43	171	49	7	2	5	2	.287	1B
1933		40	129	48	9	4	10	3	.372	1B, PH, P
1934		37	133	35	6	1	4	1	.263	1B
1935		38	129	35	4	1	4	5	.271	1B
1936		15	46	12	5	0	1	0	.261	1B
1937		8	26	5	2	0	0	0	.192	1B
1938		1	1	0	0	0	0	0	.000	PH
1939	No Data Available									
1940	TOL Crawfords	2	4	2	0	0	0	0	.500	1B
1941		1	3	0	0	0	0	0	.000	1B
1942	No Data Available									
1943	No Data Available									
1944	PHI Cuban Yankees									
	(26 years)	(872)	(3198)	(1115)	(184)	(71)	(150)	(163)	(.349)	
PLAYOFFS										
1916	IND ABCs	3	11	3	0	1	0	0	.273	OF
1930	Homestead Grays	7	29	5	1	0	0	0	.172	1B
1935	PIT Crawfords	5	18	5	0	0	2	0	.278	1B
	3 years	15	58	13	1	1	2	0	.224	
WORLD SERIES										
1917	IND ABCs	3	12	3	0	1	0	0	.250	
ALL STAR (1933–35)		3	9	0	0	0	0	1	.000	1B

Morty Clark

CLARK, MORTY

BR

Year	Team	G	AB	H	2B	3B	HR	SB	BA	POS
1910	WB Sprudels	4	18	4	2	1	0	0	.222	SS
1911	No Data Available									
1912	No Data Available									
1913	WB Sprudels	5	14	2	2	1	0	0	.143	SS
1914	BKN Royal Giants	11	50	15	3	0	0	2	.300	SS
1915	2 teams CHI Am. Giants IND ABCs									
"	total	31	120	19	1	0	0	14	.158	SS, OF
1916	IND ABCs	30	110	37	3	1	0	6	.336	SS
1917		21	72	10	3	0	0	1	.139	SS
1918		5	18	4	0	0	0	0	.222	SS
1919		4	17	6	1	0	0	1	.353	SS
1920		50	147	37	5	1	1	10	.252	SS
1921		58	212	47	5	7	1	12	.222	SS
1922		60	260	44	7	3	0	9	.169	SS
	(11 years)	(279)	(1038)	(225)	(32)	(14)	(2)	(55)	(.217)	
PLAYOFFS										
1916	IND ABCs	3	10	4	0	0	0	0	.400	SS
WORLD SERIES										
1914	BKN Royal Giants	2	8	3	0	0	0	0	.375	SS

Francisco Coimbre

COIMBRE, FRANCISCO (Pancho)

B. Jan. 29, 1909, Coamo, Puerto Rico D. Nov. 8, 1989, Ponce, Puerto Rico.

BR TR

Year	Team	G	AB	H	2B	3B	HR	SB	BA	POS
1940	NY Cuban Stars	28	124	41	2	0	2	0	.331	OF, 2B
1941		30	111	40	5	2	4	0	.360	OF
1943			137	60	11	0	1	0	.438	OF, P
1944		22	80	22	3	0	2	0	.275	OF, P
	4 years	(80)	452	163	21	2	9	0	.361	
ALL STAR (1941–44)		3	14	1	0	0	0	0	.071	OF

Dewey Creacy

CREACY, DEWEY BR TR 5′9″ 160 lbs.

Year	Team	G	AB	H	2B	3B	HR	SB	BA	POS
1924	STL Stars	56	182	56	7	9	0	3	.308	3B
1925		78	313	102	19	4	12	16	.326	3B
1926		89	369	126	24	7	23	2	.341	3B
1927		90	324	103	12	9	10	1	.318	3B
1928		72	272	89	17	4	7	2	.327	3B
1929		86	320	82	5	2	6	1	.256	3B
1930		74	274	77	4	5	5	7	.281	
1931		20	65	13	0	0	0	0	.200	3B
1932	2 teams DET Wolves WAS Pilots									
″	total	25	90	23	4	2	1	0	.256	3B
1933	COL Blue Birds	21	69	22	6	2	0	1	.319	3B
1934	PHI Stars	33	120	25	1	1	0	1	.208	OF, 3B
1935		37	216	54	0	2	2	0	.250	OF, 3B
1936		41	160	46	3	0	2	0	.287	3B
1937		17	58	13	0	0	0	0	.224	3B
1938		9	27	1	0	0	0	0	.037	3B
	15 years	748	2859	832	102	47	68	34	.291	
PLAYOFFS										
1925	STL Stars	6	19	4	0	0	1	0	.211	
1928		7	27	8	1	0	1	0	.296	
1939		6	23	8	0	1	0	1	.348	
	3 years	19	69	20	1	1	2	1	.290	

Jimmy Crutchfield

CRUTCHFIELD, JIMMY BL TR 5′7″ 150 lbs.
B. Mar. 25, 1910, Ardmore, Mo. D. Mar. 31, 1993, Chicago, Ill.

Year	Team	G	AB	H	2B	3B	HR	SB	BA	POS
1930	BIR Black Barons	67	248	71	5	9	2	3	.286	OF
1931	2 teams PIT Crawfords IND ABCs									
″	total	32	117	33	6	6	0	0	.282	OF
1933	PIT Crawfords	27	85	18	2	1	0	1	.212	OF
1934		26	85	23	1	0	0	1	.271	OF
1935		35	129	42	6	2	1	3	.326	OF
1936		25	89	21	3	2	0	1	.236	OF
1937	NWK Eagles	10	61	17	2	0	0	4	.279	OF
1938		16	65	15	0	1	0	0	.231	OF
1939	TOL Crawfords	5	19	3	1	0	0	1	.158	OF
1940										
1941	CHI Am. Giants	8	33	10	0	1	0	2	.303	OF
1942		19	61	15	0	1	0	0	.246	PH, OF
	(11 years)	(270)	(992)	(268)	(26)	(23)	(3)	(16)	(.270)	
PLAYOFFS										
1935	PIT Crawfords	3	10	2	0	0	0	0	.200	OF
ALL STAR (1934–41)		4	10	1	0	0	0	0	.100	OF

Ray Dandridge

DANDRIDGE, RAYMOND EMMETT BR TR 5′7″ 175 lbs.
B. Aug. 31, 1913, Richmond, Va.
Hall of Fame 1987.

Year	Team	G	AB	H	2B	3B	HR	SB	BA	POS
1933	2 teams DET Stars NAS Elite Giants									
″	total	14	38	8	1	2	0	0	.211	SS
1934	NWK Dodgers	29	110	48	5	2	0	0	.436	3B
1935		53	198	71	7	6	0	0	.359	3B
1936	NWK Eagles	31	103	31	4	0	1	1	.301	3B
1937		25	96	34	3	1	1	0	.354	3B
1938		1	3	0	0	0	0	0	.000	3B
1939	Mexico									
1940										
1941										
1942	NWK Eagles	27	93	16	1	1	1	0	.172	3B
1943	Mexico									
1944	NWK Eagles	28	122	39	1	0	1	0	.320	SS
1945		26	115	36	4	1	1	0	.313	SS
	(9 years)	234	878	283	26	13	5	1	.322	
ALL STAR (1935–44)		3	11	6	1	0	0	1	.545	3B, 2B

Cherokee Davis

DAVIS, JOHN BR TR 6′3″ 215 lbs.
B. Feb. 6, 1918, Newark, N.J. D. Nov. 17, 1982, Ft. Lauderdale, Fla.

Year	Team	G	AB	H	2B	3B	HR	SB	BA	POS
1941	NWK Eagles	17	63	14	1	1	2	1	.222	OF
1942		16	56	18	1	2	2	1	.321	IF
1943			144	42	5	2	4	0	.292	OF, P
1944		25	86	30	4	2	2	0	.349	OF, P
1945		22	82	29	3	0	2	0	.354	OF
1946		35	131	44	4	0	6	0	.336	OF, P

Cherokee Davis *continued*

Year	Team	G	AB	H	2B	3B	HR	SB	BA	POS
1947		80	262	69	13	0	13	3	.263	OF, P
1948		82	299	113					.378	OF
1949		66	262	60					.229	OF
9 years		(343)	1385	419	(31)	(7)	(31)	(5)	.303	
WORLD SERIES										
1937	NWK Eagles	3	8	3	0	0	1	0	.375	3B
1938		1	4	0	0	0	0	0	.000	3B
1946		7	24	7	3	0	0	1	.292	3B
3 years		11	36	10	3	0	1	1	.278	
ALL STAR (1943–45)		3	9	3	0	1	0	0	.333	OF

Piper Davis

DAVIS, LORENZO BR TR 6'3" 187 lbs.
B. July 3, 1917, Piper, Ala.
Manager 1948-50.

Year	Team	G	AB	H	2B	3B	HR	SB	BA	POS
1942	BIR Black Barons	2	4	0	0	0	0	0	.000	IF
1943			57	22	9	1	1	1	.386	
1944		64	253	38	3	3	2	7	.150	IF
1945		58	211	66	10	7	3	7	.313	IF
1946		4	11	3	0	1	0	0	.273	2B
1947		56	228	62	1	0	2	0	.272	IF
1948		76	295	104	19	8	7	6	.353	IF
1949		82	299	113					.378	IF
1950		42	149	57	10	2	3	4	.383	SS, 2B
9 years		(384)	1507	465	(52)	(22)	(18)	(25)	.309	
WORLD SERIES										
1943	BIR Black Barons	6	24	4	0	0	0	0	.167	SS
1944		5	22	4	0	0	0	1	.182	SS
2 years		11	46	8	0	0	0	1	.174	
ALL STAR (1946–48)		4	13	6	2	0	0	2	.462	2B

Walter Davis

DAVIS, WALTER (Steel Arm) BL TL 6'1" 175 lbs.
B. 1902, Madison, Wis. D. 1935, Chicago, Il.

Year	Team	G	AB	H	2B	3B	HR	SB	BA	POS
1924	CHI Am. Giants	17	62	17	1	0	0	0	.274	OF
1925	No Data Available									
1926										
1927	CHI Am. Giants	72	275	106	18	7	3	10	.385	OF
1928		64	205	71	12	4	2	6	.346	
1929		67	247	66	12	7	6	3	.267	
1930		71	214	72	15	7	2	5	.336	OF, 1B
1931	No Data Available									
1932	CHI Am. Giants	39	146	43	7	3	4	1	.295	
1933		22	87	24	7	4	2	0	.276	
(7 years)		(352)	(1236)	(399)	(72)	(32)	(19)	(25)	(.323)	
WORLD SERIES										
1927	CHI Am. Giants	9	36	13	1	2	1	2	.361	OF

Leon Day

DAY, LEON BR TR 5'8" 175 lbs.
B. Oct. 30, 1916, Alexandria, Va. D. Mar. 13, 1995, Baltimore, Md.
Hall of Fame 1995.

Year	Team	G	AB	H	2B	3B	HR	SB	BA	POS
1934	No Data Available									
1935	BKN Eagles	12	31	7	2	0	0	0	.226	P
1936	NWK Eagles	6	11	3	0	0	0	0	.273	P
1937		3	9	1	0	0	0	0	.111	P
1938	No Data Available									
1939	NWK Eagles	10	28	8	0	2	0	0	.286	P
1940	No Data Available									
1941	NWK Eagles	32	118	39	5	6	4	1	.331	2B, OF, P
1942		32	105	29	5	1	0	1	.276	OF, P
1943			69	19	4	0	1	1	.275	2B, P
1944	Military Service									
1945	Military Service									
1946	NWK Eagles	22	39	15	0	0	1	0	.385	PH, P
1947	Mexico									
1948	Mexico									
1949	BAL Elite Giants	57	181	49					.271	P
(9 years)		(174)	(591)	(170)	(16)	(9)	(6)	(3)	(.288)	
PLAYOFFS										
1939	NWK Eagles	1	2	0	0	0	0	0	.000	P

Leon Day *continued*

Year	Team	G	AB	H	2B	3B	HR	SB	BA	POS
WORLD SERIES										
1937	NWK Eagles	1	2	0	0	0	0	0	.000	P
1946		2	4	0	0	0	0	0	.000	OF, P
	2 years	3	6	0	0	0	0	0	.000	
ALL STAR (1937–46)		9	15	6	1	0	0	0	.400	P

Bingo DeMoss

DeMOSS, ELWOOD BR TR 6′2″ 175 lbs.
B. Sept. 5, 1889, Topeka, Kans. D. Jan. 26, 1965, Chicago, Ill.
Manager 1926-29.

Year	Team	G	AB	H	2B	3B	HR	SB	BA	POS
1910	2 teams OKLA Giants KC Giants									
″	total	2	8	0	0	0	0	0	.000	2B
1911	No Data Available									
1912	No Data Available									
1913	3 teams WL Plutos CHI Am. Giants STL Giants									
″	total	5	19	4	0	0	0	0	.211	2B
1914	3 teams WB Sprudels WL Plutos CHI Am. Giants									
″	total	7	33	6	1	0	0	2	.182	2B
1915	IND ABCs	14	31	8	3	0	0	8	.258	2B
1916	3 teams IND ABCs IND Jewell's ABCs STL Giants									
″	total	13	45	11	1	2	0	3	.244	2B
1917	2 teams CHI Am. Giants IND Jewell's ABCs									
″	total	20	78	15	0	0	0	2	.192	2B
1918	CHI Am. Giants	9	35	6	1	0	0	0	.171	2B
1919		12	45	10	3	0	0	0	.222	2B
1920		35	133	38	6	1	0	9	.286	2B
1921		60	222	58	9	2	1	14	.261	2B
1923		65	236	60	6	1	2	10	.254	2B
1924		62	210	47	4	1	0	6	.224	2B
1925		58	185	42	6	0	0	4	.227	2B
1926	IND ABCs	67	306	80	9	3	0	26	.261	2B
1927	DET Stars	38	133	28	3	2	1	0	.211	2B, 1B
1928		43	129	20	5	1	0	0	.155	2B
1929		13	51	16	1	0	0	4	.314	2B
	(17 years)	(523)	(1899)	(449)	(58)	(13)	(4)	(88)	(.236)	
PLAYOFFS										
1916	IND ABCs	3	11	1	0	1	0	1	.091	2B
1925	CHI Am. Giants	3	10	3	1	0	0	0	.300	2B
1930	DET	1	5	1	0	0	0	0	.200	2B
	3 years	7	26	5	1	1	0	1	.192	

Martin Dihigo

DIHIGO, MARTIN BR TR 6′1″ 190 lbs.
B. May 25, 1905, Matanzas, Cuba D. May 20, 1971, Cienfuegos, Cuba.
Hall of Fame 1977.

Year	Team	G	AB	H	2B	3B	HR	SB	BA	POS
1923	Cuban Stars	17	63	17	1	1	0	1	.270	1B, P
1924		52	190	47	8	3	3	4	.247	2B, OF, P
1925		41	149	45	7	1	2	3	.302	UT, P
1926		21	76	32	5	0	8	3	.421	UT, P
1927		40	154	57	3	2	10	9	.370	SS, UT, P
1928	Grays									
1929	PHI Hilldales	68	207	77	8	1	13	7	.372	1B, 2B, 3B, SS, P
1930	Stars of Cuba	24	98	40	5	3	7	0	.408	3B, P
1931	2 teams BAL Black Sox PHI Hilldales									
″	total	50	193	51	1	3	2	0	.264	3B, OF, P
1932	Did not play									
1933	Venezuela									
1934	Did not play									
1935	NY Cubans	38	120	37	8	4	7	5	.308	2B, 3B, OF, SS, P
1936		33	93	31	6	1	10	2	.333	2B, 3B, OF, SS, P
1937	Latin America									
1938										
1939										
1940										
1944										
1945	NY Cubans	7	20	1	0	0	0	0	.050	1B, P
	(11 years)	(391)	(1363)	(435)	(52)	(19)	(62)	(34)	(.319)	
PLAYOFFS										
1935	NY Cubans	6	23	7	0	0	0	0	.304	3B, P
ALL STAR (1935–45)		2	6	1	0	0	0	1	.167	OF, P

		G	AB	H	2B	3B	HR	SB	BA	POS

Rap Dixon

DIXON, HERBERT ALBERT BR TR 6′2″ 185 lbs.
B. Sept. 2, 1902, Kingston, Ga. D. July 20, 1945, Detroit, Mich.

		G	AB	H	2B	3B	HR	SB	BA	POS
1924	HBG Giants	40	132	29	0	0	3	1	.220	OF
1925		70	266	95	10	5	7	15	.357	OF
1926		26	109	39	6	3	3	4	.358	OF
1927		14	48	11	0	1	0	2	.229	OF
1928	2 teams HBG Giants BAL Black Sox									
″	total	35	131	46	10	3	8	7	.351	OF
1929	BAL Black Sox	52	217	83	12	7	9	18	.382	OF
1930		60	264	63	9	4	3	7	.239	OF
1931	2 teams BAL Black Sox PHI Hilldales									
″	total	52	201	46	5	3	0	2	.229	OF
1932	2 teams WAS Pilots PIT Crawfords									
″	total	33	126	39	6	2	2	0	.310	OF
1933	PHI Stars	11	38	14	2	1	0	0	.368	OF
1934	2 teams BAL Black Sox PIT Crawfords									
″	total	2	10	4	0	0	0	0	.400	OF
1935	2 teams BKN Eagles NY Cubans									
″	total	29	78	24	7	0	2	2	.308	OF
1937	PIT Crawfords	1	1	0	0	0	0	0	.000	
	13 years	425	1621	493	67	29	37	58	.304	
PLAYOFFS										
1935	NY Cubans	3	8	2	0	0	1	0	.250	OF
ALL STAR (1933)		1	3	1	0	0	0	1	.333	OF

Larry Doby

DOBY, LAWRENCE EUGENE BL TR 6′ 1″ 180 lbs.
B. Dec. 13, 1924, Camden, S. C.
Also played as Larry Walker

		G	AB	H	2B	3B	HR	SB	BA	POS
1942	NWK Eagles	41	162	67	16		14		.414	2B
1943		29	108	31	1	3	5	0	.287	2B
1944	Military Service									
1945	Military Service									
1946	NWK Eagles	38	141	56	4	6	5	0	.397	2B
1947		41	162	67	16		14		.414	2B
	4 years	139	513	194	25	(14)	25	(1)	.378	
WORLD SERIES										
1946	NWK Eagles	7	22	5	1	1	1	3	.227	2B
ALL STAR (1946)		2	7	3	0	0	0	1	.429	2B

Valentin Dreke

DREKE, VALENTIN BR TR 5′8″ 160 lbs.
B. June 21, 1898, Union de Reyes, Cuba D. Sept. 25, 1929

		G	AB	H	2B	3B	HR	SB	BA	POS
1919	Cuban Stars	5	20	5	0	0	0	0	.250	OF
1920		20	85	30	2	1	0	2	.353	OF
1921		44	174	48	6	0	1	3	.276	OF
1922		65	254	74	13	4	2	13	.291	OF
1923		46	188	71	7	4	2	1	.378	OF
1924		51	212	91	15	1	2	6	.429	OF
1925		48	207	66	11	4	2	6	.319	OF
1926		45	177	56	6	1	1	0	.316	OF
1927		56	208	68	7	4	1	6	.327	OF
	9 years	380	1525	509	67	19	11	37	.334	

Frank Duncan

DUNCAN, FRANK BR TR 6′ 170 lbs.
B. Feb. 14, 1901, Kansas City, Mo. D. Dec. 4, 1973, Kansas City, Mo.
Manager 1942-45.
Father of Frank Duncan III.

		G	AB	H	2B	3B	HR	SB	BA	POS
1921	2 teams CHI Am. Giants KC Monarchs									
″	total	39	115	26	1	0	0	4	.226	C
1922	KC Monarchs	77	281	62	11	3	3	5	.221	C
1923		40	165	35	6	0	0	5	.212	C
1924		80	283	70	12	2	0	0	.247	C
1925		49	141	33	4	0	1	2	.234	C
1926		53	155	44	9	1	4	2	.284	C
1927		15	43	17	2	3	0	1	.395	C
1928		44	140	40	7	1	2	2	.286	C
1929		44	136	47	4	4	1	7	.346	1B, OF, C
1930		52	156	56	9	5	1	4	.359	1B, OF, C
1931	2 teams KC Monarchs NY Harlem Stars									
″	total	14	46	9	2	0	0	0	.196	C
1932	2 teams Homestead Grays PIT Crawfords									
″	total	16	50	11	0	1	0	0	.220	C
1935	NY Cubans	31	99	17	3	0	0	0	.172	C
1936		28	94	22	1	0	1	0	.234	C
1937	KC Monarchs	23	78	16	3	0	0	1	.205	C

Frank Duncan *continued*

		G	AB	H	2B	3B	HR	SB	BA	POS
1938	2 teams KC Monarchs CHI Am. Giants									
"	total	27	77	20	2	2	0	2	.260	C
1939	No Data Available									
1940	No Data Available									
1941	KC Monarchs	8	23	3	1	0	0	0	.130	C
1942		10	17	1	1	0	0	0	.059	C
1943			24	0	0	0	0	0	.000	C
1944		23	44	6	2	0	0	0	.136	C
1945		12	29	5	3	0	0	0	.172	C
	(21 years)	(685)	(2196)	(540)	(83)	(22)	(13)	(35)	(.246)	
PLAYOFFS										
1925	KC Monarchs	5	16	3	0	0	1	0	.188	C
1926		7	15	3	0	0	0	0	.200	C
1935	NY Cubans	6	23	7	0	0	0	0	.304	C
1937	KC Monarchs	3	5	1	0	0	0	0	.200	C
	4 years	21	59	14	0	0	1	0	.237	
WORLD SERIES										
1924	KC Monarchs	10	36	5	1	0	0	2	.139	C
1925		6	21	4	2	0	0	0	.190	C
1937		2	4	1	0	0	0	0	.250	C
	3 years	18	61	10	3	0	0	2	.164	
ALL STAR (1938)		1	1	0	0	0	0	0	.000	C

Luke Easter

EASTER, LUSCIOUS LUKE BL TR 6′ 4½″ 240 lbs.
B. Aug. 4, 1915, Jonestown, Miss. D. Mar. 29, 1979, Euclid, Ohio.
Major leagues 1949-54.

		G	AB	H	2B	3B	HR	SB	BA	POS
1947	WAS Homestead Grays		219	68	11	0	10	1	.311	OF
1948		58	215	78	22	8	13		.363	OF
	2 years	(58)	434	146	33	8	23	(1)	.336	
WORLD SERIES										
1948	WAS Homestead Grays	4	4	1	2	0	1	0	.250	OF
ALL STAR (1948)		1	1	0	0	0	0	0	.000	OF

Howard Easterling

EASTERLING, HOWARD BR TR 6′ 180 lbs.
B. Nov. 26, 1911, Mount Olive, Miss.

		G	AB	H	2B	3B	HR	SB	BA	POS
1937	CIN Tigers	18	70	27	4	2	0	0	.386	SS
1938	No Data Available									
1939	No Data Available									
1940	WAS Homestead Grays	46	167	56	8	4	1	0	.335	OF, 3B
1941		31	122	34	4	2	2	0	.279	3B, 2B
1942		42	148	34	6	1	1	2	.230	OF, 3B
1943		47	173	69	9	7	1	2	.399	OF, 2B
1944	Military Service									
1945	No Data Available									
1946	WAS Homestead Grays	16	56	19	4	3	1	0	.339	3B
1947	No Data Available									
1948	No Data Available									
1949	NY Cubans	45	189	57					.302	
	(7 years)	(245)	(925)	(296)	(35)	(19)	(6)	(4)	(.320)	
PLAYOFFS										
1941	WAS Homestead Grays	2	10	6	0	1	0	0	.600	
WORLD SERIES										
1942	WAS Homestead Grays	4	15	5	0	0	1	0	.333	OF, IF
1943		6	25	7	1	0	0	2	.280	SS, 2B
	2 years	10	40	12	1	0	1	2	.300	
ALL STAR (1937–46)		8	31	10	1	0	0	0	.323	IF

Red Farrell

FARRELL, LUTHER BL TL 6′ 1″ 190 lbs.

		G	AB	H	2B	3B	HR	SB	BA	POS
1928	AC Bacharach Giants	43	106	39	2	0	13	0	.368	OF, P
1930	NY Lincoln Giants	16	46	25	3	2	4	0	.543	OF, P
	2 years	59	152	64	5	2	17	0	.421	

Red Farrell *continued*

		G	AB	H	2B	3B	HR	SB	BA	POS
PLAYOFFS										
1930	NY Lincoln Giants	5	11	1	0	0	0	0	.091	OF, P
1935	AC Bacharach Giants	7	25	8	0	0	0	0	.320	
	2 years	12	36	9	0	0	0	0	.250	
WORLD SERIES										
1926	AC Bacharach Giants	11	34	7	0	0	1	2	.206	OF
1927		8	21	4	1	1	0	0	.190	OF, P
	2 years	19	55	11	1	1	1	2	.200	

Rube Foster

FOSTER, ANDREW BR TR

B. Sept. 17, 1878, Calvert, Tex. D. Dec. 9, 1930, Kankakee, Ill.
Manager 1910-1926.
Brother of Bill Foster.
Hall of Fame 1981.

		G	AB	H	2B	3B	HR	SB	BA	POS
1904	PHI Giants	2	8	4	2	0	0	0	.500	OF
1905		2	8	3	0	0	0	0	.375	OF, P
1906		4	16	5	1	0	0	0	.313	OF, P
1907	No Data Available									
1908	CHI Leland Giants									
1909	No Data Available									
1910	CHI Leland Giants	2	7	1	0	0	0	0	.143	P
1911	CHI Am. Giants									
1912	No Data Available									
1913	CHI Am. Giants	1	4	1	0	0	0	0	.250	P
1914		6	28	13	1	0	3	0	.464	P
1915		3	9	3	0	0	0	0	.333	P
1916	No Data Available									
1917	CHI Am. Giants	2	7	0	0	0	0	0	.000	1B, P
1918		1			1					P
	(9 years)	(23)	(87)	(30)	(5)	(0)	(3)	(0)	(.345)	
PLAYOFFS										
1903	Cuban X-Giants	1	4	2	0	1	0	0	.500	P
1904	PHI Giants	2	8	4	0	0	0	0	.500	PH, P
1908	CHI Leland Giants	1	4	0	0	0	0	0	.000	P
1915	CHI Am. Giants	1	4	0	0	0	0	0	.000	P
	4 years	5	20	6	0	1	0	0	.300	

Jelly Gardner

GARDNER, FLOYD BL TR 5′7″ 160 lbs.

B. Sept. 26, 1890, Russellville, Ark. D. 1976, Chicago, Ill.

		G	AB	H	2B	3B	HR	SB	BA	POS
1919	DET Stars	1	3	2	0	0	0	0	.667	OF
1920	CHI Am. Giants	14	55	10	3	1	0	3	.182	OF
1921		53	169	37	3	0	0	11	.219	OF
1922		57	178	42	1	1	0	6	.236	OF
1923		69	258	78	9	0	0	15	.302	OF
1924		74	269	96	11	1	0	6	.357	OF
1925		92	348	100	12	3	1	5	.287	OF
1926		59	216	72	11	4	0	5	.333	OF
1927	No Data Available									
1928	2 teams CHI Am. Giants Homestead Grays									
″	total	49	173	50	7	2	0	8	.289	OF
1929	CHI Am. Giants	68	241	73	8	4	0	6	.303	OF
1930		30	86	20	3	0	0	1	.233	OF
1931	DET Wolves	27	88	17	2	0	0	6	.193	OF
	(12 years)	(593)	(2084)	(597)	(70)	(16)	(1)	(72)	(.286)	
PLAYOFFS										
1926	CHI Am. Giants	7	20	6	0	0	0	1	.300	
WORLD SERIES										
1925	CHI Am. Giants	4	11	4	0	0	0	0	.364	OF
1926		11	36	8	2	0	0	3	.222	OF
	2 years	15	47	12	2	0	0	3	.255	

Josh Gibson

GIBSON, JOSHUA BR TR 6′2″ 217 lbs.

B. Dec. 21, 1911, Buena Vista, Ga. D. Jan. 20, 1947, Pittsburgh, Pa.
Hall of Fame 1972.

		G	AB	H	2B	3B	HR	SB	BA	POS
1930	Homestead Grays	10	33	8	1	0	1	1	.242	C
1931		32	129	48	8	0	6	0	.372	C
1932	PIT Crawfords	46	147	42	3	5	7	1	.286	OF, C
1933	Homestead Grays	34	116	42	8	1	6	1	.362	P, 3B, PH, C
1934	PIT Crawfords	41	146	46	8	3	11	1	.315	C
1935		37	129	43	7	1	11	3	.333	OF, C

Josh Gibson *continued*

Year	Team	G	AB	H	2B	3B	HR	SB	BA	POS
1936		23	75	27	3	0	11	0	.360	C
1937	Homestead Grays	12	42	21	0	4	7	0	.500	C
1938		19	74	23	1	0	4	1	.311	C
1939	WAS Homestead	29	88	29	2	2	17	0	.330	C
1940	Homestead Grays	2	6	1	0	0	1	0	.167	C
1941	Mexico									
1942	WAS Homestead	51	158	53	8	1	15	3	.335	C
1943	Homestead Grays	57	209	108	23	8	16	0	.517	C
1944		28	97	35	3	3	6	0	.361	C
1945		31	98	31	3	3	11	0	.316	C
1946		49	132	50	11	4	16	0	.379	C
	(16 years)	501	1679	607	89	35	146	11	.362	
PLAYOFFS										
1930	Homestead Grays	9	38	14	0	1	3	0	.368	C
1935	PIT Crawfords	5	20	7	0	1	1	0	.350	C
1938	Homestead Grays					1				
1939	WAS Homestead Grays	7	22	7	0	0	3	0	.318	C
	4 years	(21)	(80)	(28)	(0)	3	(7)	(0)	(.350)	
WORLD SERIES										
1937	Homestead Grays	2	8	2	0	1	1	0	.250	C
1938		1	1	0	0	0	0	0	.000	C
1942	WAS Homestead	4	13	2	0	0	0	1	.154	C
1943	Homestead Grays	6	20	5	1	0	0	1	.250	C
1944		5	15	6	0	0	1	0	.400	C
1945		4	15	2	0	0	0	0	.133	C
	6 years	22	72	17	1	1	2	2	.236	
ALL STAR (1933–46)		15	49	20	4	1	0	0	.408	OF, C

George Giles

GILES, GEORGE FRANKLIN BL TR 6′1″ 175 lbs.
B. May 2, 1909, Junction City, Kans. D. Mar. 3, 1992, Manhattan, Kans.

Year	Team	G	AB	H	2B	3B	HR	SB	BA	POS
1927	KC Monarchs	51	171	50	8	5	0	1	.292	1B
1928		67	252	76	11	7	1	4	.302	1B
1929	Semipro									
1930	STL Stars	66	272	87	15	4	3	7	.320	1B
1931		20	78	20	0	1	0	0	.256	1B
1932	3 teams KC Monarchs DET Wolves Homestead Grays									
″	total	29	117	36	3	0	0	6	.308	1B
1933	BAL Black Sox	2	6	2	1	0	0	0	.333	1B
1935	BKN Eagles	47	189	69	9	3	4	3	.365	1B
1936	NY Black Yankees	12	46	17	1	0	0	0	.370	1B
1937		12	43	16	1	0	0	0	.372	1B
1938	2 teams PIT Crawfords PHI Stars									
″	total	29	116	31	0	1	0	1	.267	1B
	(10 years)	335	1290	404	49	21	8	22	.313	
PLAYOFFS										
1930	STL Stars	7	26	9	3	0	0	2	.346	
ALL STAR (1935)		1	5	0	0	0	0	1	.000	1B

Jim Gilliam

GILLIAM, JAMES WILLIAM (Junior) BB TR 5′10½″ 175 lbs.
B. Oct. 17, 1928, Nashville, Tenn. D. Oct. 8, 1978, Inglewood, Calif.
Major leagues 1953-66.

Year	Team	G	AB	H	2B	3B	HR	SB	BA	POS
1946	BAL Elite Giants	7	13	6	1	0	0	0	.462	2B
1947		71	257	65	1		0	9	.253	2B
1948	No Data Available									
1949	No Data Available									
1950	BAL Elite Giants	42	162	43	10	5	2	13	.265	2B
	(3 years)	(120)	(432)	(114)	(12)	(5)	(2)	(22)	(.264)	
ALL STAR (1948)		1	3	1	0	0	0	0	.333	2B

Vic Harris

HARRIS, ELANDER VICTOR BL TR 5′10″ 164 lbs.
B. June 10, 1905, Pensacola, Fla. D. Feb. 23, 1978, San Fernando, Calif.
Manager 1935-43, 1945.

Year	Team	G	AB	H	2B	3B	HR	SB	BA	POS
1923	2 teams TOL Tigers CLE Tate Stars									
″	total	20	69	21	1	0	0	0	.304	IF, 3B
1924	2 teams CLE Browns CHI Am. Giants									
″	total	39	137	38	5	2	2	1	.277	OF
1925	Homestead Grays									
1926										
1927										

Vic Harris *continued*

		G	AB	H	2B	3B	HR	SB	BA	POS
1928		8	30	7	1	0	0	0	.233	OF
1929		41	159	59	12	5	5	2	.371	OF
1930		18	78	26	4	3	0	1	.333	OF
1931		23	79	19	3	1	0	0	.241	OF
1932	2 teams DET Wolves Homestead Grays									
"	total	37	132	46	9	2	3	3	.348	OF
1933	Homestead Grays	16	74	26	3	0	2	1	.351	OF
1934	PIT Crawfords	39	132	57	5	1	2	2	.432	OF
1935	Homestead Grays	48	184	63	11	0	7	5	.342	OF
1936		5	19	2	2	0	0	0	.105	OF
1937	WAS Homestead Grays	18	79	18	1	0	1	0	.228	OF
1938		14	55	14	1	0	0	0	.255	OF
1939		20	73	12	3	0	0	0	.164	OF
1940		40	164	41	4	4	1	0	.250	OF
1941		28	111	26	4	0	0	0	.234	OF
1942		35	110	25	4	2	0	0	.227	OF
1943		16	60	19	3	0	0	0	.317	OF
1944		8	13	10	0	0	0	0	.769	PH, OF
1945		7	16	5	0	0	0	0	.313	OF
	(20 years)	(480)	(1774)	(534)	(76)	(20)	(23)	(15)	(.301)	
PLAYOFFS										
1930	Homestead Grays	9	39	17	1	0	0	0	.436	OF
1939	WAS Homestead Grays	4	13	1	1	0	0	0	.077	OF
1941		2	9	6	2	1	0	0	.667	OF
	3 years	15	61	24	4	1	0	0	.393	
WORLD SERIES										
1937	WAS Homestead Grays	2	9	5	0	0	0	0	.556	OF
1942		4	16	2	0	0	0	0	.125	OF
1943		6	21	4	0	1	0	2	.190	OF
1945		3	3	0	0	0	0	0	.000	PH
	4 years	15	49	11	0	1	0	2	.224	
ALL STAR (1933–47)		4	20	5	0	0	0	0	.250	OF

Pete Hill

HILL, PRESTON BL TR

B. Oct. 12, 1880, Pittsburgh, Pa. D. 1951, Buffalo, N.Y.
Manager 1920, 1921, 1924, 1925.

		G	AB	H	2B	3B	HR	SB	BA	POS
1904	PHI Giants	2	8	1	0	0	0	0	.125	OF
1905		3	12	7	0	0	1	0	.583	OF
1906		6	24	12	1	0	0	0	.500	OF
1907	No Data Available									
1908	CHI Leland Giants									
1909	No Data Available									
1910	CHI Am. Giants	11	46	24	3	3	1	1	.522	OF
1911		3	12	3	1	0	0	0	.250	OF
1912		1	4	3	1	1	0	0	.750	OF
1913		17	72	26	4	0	0	0	.361	OF
1914		26	108	25	5	0	1	0	.231	OF
1915		36	141	31	8	2	2	0	.220	OF
1916		25	97	27	5	1	1	1	.278	OF
1917		24	82	17	4	1	0	1	.207	OF
1918	2 teams CHI Am. Giants CHI Columbia Giants									
"	total	8	31	10	2	0	0	0	.323	OF
1919	DET Stars	8	26	8	0	1	1	0	.308	OF
1920		44	113	35	8	1	5	4	.310	OF
1921		41	138	54	5	5	3	3	.391	OF, 1B
1923	MIL Bears	13	46	15	2	0	0	1	.326	OF
1924	BAL Black Sox	16	52	14	2	0	0	1	.269	PH, OF
1925		6	13	4	0	0	1	0	.308	OF, PH, 1B
	(18 years)	(290)	(1025)	(316)	(51)	(15)	(16)	(12)	(.308)	
PLAYOFFS										
1904	PHI Giants	3	12	1	0	0	0	0	.083	OF
1908	CHI Leland Giants	1	4	0	0	0	0	0	.000	OF
1916		4	14	2	0	0	0	2	.143	OF
	3 years	8	30	3	0	0	0	2	.100	
WORLD SERIES										
1909	CHI Leland Giants	3	11	2	0	0	0	0	.182	OF
1914	CHI Am. Giants	2	8	1	0	0	0	0	.125	OF
1915		10	39	6	2	1	0		.154	OF
1916		3	12	1	0	0	0	1	.083	OF
	4 years	18	70	10	2	1	0	(1)	.143	

Crush Holloway

HOLLOWAY, CHRISTOPHER COLUMBUS BB TR 5′11″
B. Sept. 6, 1896, Hillsboro, Tex. D. June 24, 1972, Baltimore, Md.

Year	Team	G	AB	H	2B	3B	HR	SB	BA	POS
1921	IND ABCs	70	251	73	4	4	4	5	.291	
1922		49	181	42	11	4	0	8	.232	
1923		63	254	81	7	7	1	9	.319	OF
1924	BAL Black Sox	97	368	111	14	8	9	18	.302	OF
1925		86	329	94	8	0	0	10	.286	OF
1926		73	293	82	9	3	1	12	.280	OF
1927		67	262	65	4	4	4	8	.248	OF
1928		37	156	57	7	3	2	5	.365	OF
1929	PHI Hilldales	23	90	21	6	0	0	3	.233	OF
1930	DET Stars	63	256	64	9	8	0	10	.250	OF
1931	BAL Black Sox	63	243	75	6	4	0	3	.309	OF
1932	3 teams BAL Black Sox NY Black Yankees PHI Hilldales									
″	total	8	32	14	1	0	1	0	.438	OF
1933	BAL Black Sox	20	73	21	3	2	2	4	.288	OF
1934	AC Bacharach Giants	16	61	10	0	0	1	0	.164	OF
1935	BAL Elite Giants									
	(14 years)	(735)	(2849)	(810)	(89)	(47)	(25)	(95)	(.284)	
PLAYOFFS										
1930	DET Stars	7	29	11	0	0	0	1	.379	

Elston Howard

HOWARD, ELSTON GENE (Ellie) BR TR 6′ 2″ 196 lbs.
B. Feb. 23, 1929, St. Louis, Mo. D. Dec. 14, 1980, New York, N. Y.
Major leagues 1955-67.

Year	Team	G	AB	H	2B	3B	HR	SB	BA	POS
1949	KC Monarchs	85	307	83					.270	
1950		49	188	60	13	5	3	0	.319	OF
	2 years	134	495	143	(13)	(5)	(3)	(0)	.289	

Robert Hudspeth

HUDSPETH, ROBERT (High Pockets)

Year	Team	G	AB	H	2B	3B	HR	SB	BA	POS
1920	IND ABCs	5	11	2	0	0	0	0	.182	1B
1921	COL Buckeyes	56	224	62	13	2	4	2	.277	1B
1922	AC Bacharach Giants	24	86	26	6	3	3	1	.302	1B
1923	NY Lincoln Giants	23	87	32	1	4	2	1	.368	1B
1924		62	221	80	17	2	7	2	.362	1B
1925		49	183	49	8	0	7	1	.268	1B
1926		40	156	57	7	3	7	0	.365	1B
1927	BKN Royal Giants	21	87	23	0	0	3	0	.264	1B
1928		10	36	7	0	0	0	0	.194	1B
1929	2 teams BKN Royal Giants PHI Hilldales									
″	total	44	158	43	9	1	0	2	.272	1B
1930	BKN Royal Giants	6	25	5	0	0	1	0	.200	1B
1932	NY Black Yankees	6	24	6	0	0	0	0	.250	1B
	12 years	346	1298	392	61	15	34	9	.302	

Sammy T. Hughes

HUGHES, SAMUEL THOMAS BR TR 6′3″ 190 lbs.
B. Oct. 20, 1910, Louisville, Ky. D. 1973, Los Angeles, Calif.

Year	Team	G	AB	H	2B	3B	HR	SB	BA	POS
1930	LOU Black Caps	16	54	14	0	2	1	1	.259	2B
1931	2 teams LOU Black Caps PIT Crawfords									
″	total	5	16	4	0	0	0	0	.250	2B, P
1932	WAS Pilots	11	36	12	0	0	1	0	.333	2B
1933	NAS Elite Giants	13	51	18	3	2	0	0	.353	2B
1934	CLE Elite Giants	1	3	1	0	0	0	0	.333	2B
1935		30	133	47	5	1	0	0	.353	2B, 1B
1936	WAS Elite Giants	31	102	36	0	1	3	0	.353	2B
1937		24	91	29	5	0	2	0	.319	2B
1938	BAL Elite Giants	17	63	19	4	1	1	3	.302	2B
1939		26	101	33	6	2	0	1	.327	2B
1940		56	230	57	13	3	7	0	.248	2B
1941	Mexico									
1942	BAL Elite Giants	41	160	49	11	1	1	0	.306	2B
1943	Military Service									
1944										
1945										
1946	BAL Elite Giants	22	65	13	2	0	1	0	.200	3B
	(13 years)	293	1105	332	49	13	17	5	.300	
PLAYOFFS										
1939	BAL Elite Giants	6	19	8	4	0	1	1	.421	2B
ALL STAR (1934–39)		7	26	6	2	0	0	0	.231	2B

Monte Irvin

IRVIN, MONFORD MERRILL BR TR 6′ 1″ 195 lbs.
B. Feb. 25, 1919, Columbus, Ala.
Major leagues 1949-56.
Also played under the name Jimmy Nelson.
Hall of Fame 1973.

Year	Team	G	AB	H	2B	3B	HR	SB	BA	POS
1939	NWK Eagles	5	16	4	0	0	0	0	.250	OF, 3B
1940		45	158	60	10	2	6	1	.380	SS, OF
1941		31	110	42	5	1	6	1	.382	SS, OF
1942		8	32	17	6	4	2	1	.531	OF
1943	Mexico									
1944	Military Service									
1945										
1946	NWK Eagles	33	112	36	5	0	5	0	.321	SS
1947		81	287	91	18	0	14	19	.317	OF
1948		42	135	43					.319	OF
	(7 years)	245	850	293	(44)	(7)	(33)	(22)	.345	
PLAYOFFS										
1939	NWK Eagles	3	10	3	0	0	0	0	.300	SS
WORLD SERIES										
1946	NWK Eagles	7	26	12	2	0	3	1	.462	SS
ALL STAR (1941–48)		5	17	3	1	0	0	2	.176	OF, 3B

Fats Jenkins

JENKINS, CLARENCE R. BL TL 5′7″
B. Jan. 10, 1898, New York, N. Y. D. Dec. 6, 1968, Philadelphia, Pa.

Year	Team	G	AB	H	2B	3B	HR	SB	BA	POS
1920	NY Lincoln Giants	1	4	2	0	0	0	0	.500	OF
1921	No Data Available									
1922	AC Bacharach Giants	2	6	3	0	0	0	0	.500	OF
1923	HBG Giants									
1924		56	183	58	4	0	0	4	.317	OF
1925		69	289	91	9	2	2	15	.315	OF
1926		27	106	30	1	1	0	5	.283	OF
1927		50	216	86	8	4	4	10	.398	OF
1928	2 teams NY Lincoln Giants AC Bacharach Giants									
″	total	63	248	94	4	3	0	2	.379	OF
1929	AC Bacharach Giants	44	179	68	5	0	2	4	.380	OF
1930	NY Lincoln Giants	20	78	30	6	2	0	1	.385	OF
1931		17	66	17	2	0	1	0	.258	OF
1932	2 teams PIT Crawfords NY Black Yankees									
″	total	15	66	19	2	0	0	1	.288	OF
1934	NY Lincoln Giants	15	49	16	1	0	0	1	.327	OF
1935	2 teams BKN Eagles NWK Dodgers									
″	total	52	205	65	8	1	3	0	.317	OF
1936	NY Black Yankees	16	65	12	3	0	0	2	.185	OF
1937		14	40	12	2	0	2	0	.300	OF
1938	2 teams PIT Crawfords NY Black Yankees									
″	total	10	37	13	0	0	0	2	.351	OF
	(16 years)	(471)	(1837)	(616)	(55)	(13)	(14)	(47)	(.335)	
PLAYOFFS										
1930	NY	9	42	15	0	0	1	0	.357	OF

Sam Jethroe

JETHROE, SAMUEL (Jet) BB TR 6′ 1″ 178 lbs.
B. Jan. 20, 1918, East St. Louis, Ill.
Major Leagues 1950-54.

Year	Team	G	AB	H	2B	3B	HR	SB	BA	POS
1942	CLE Buckeyes		39	19	5	1	0	1	.487	OF
1943			103	30	8	4	2	0	.291	OF
1944		68	275	97	14	2	2	18	.353	OF
1945		56	214	84	10	10	3	21	.393	OF
1946		62	226	70			6	20	.310	OF
1947		70	288	98	5	0	2	3	.340	OF
1948		47	186	55	13	4	5	29	.296	OF
	7 years	(303)	1331	453	(55)	(21)	20	92	.340	
WORLD SERIES										
1945	CLE Buckeyes	4	15	5	0	1	0	0	.333	OF
1947		5	19	6	2	0	0	0	.316	OF
	2 years	9	34	11	2	1	0	0	.324	
ALL STAR (1942–47)		5	14	1	0	1	0	2	.071	OF

Heavy Johnson

JOHNSON, OSCAR
B. 1896, Atchison, Kans. D. 1966, Cleveland, Ohio.

Year	Team	G	AB	H	2B	3B	HR	SB	BA	POS
1922	KC Monarchs	55	208	81	17	10	7	6	.389	OF
1923		46	179	68	19	9	18	6	.380	OF
1924		81	299	123	18	11	7	1	.411	OF

Heavy Johnson *continued*

Year	Team	G	AB	H	2B	3B	HR	SB	BA	POS
1925	BAL Black Sox	55	200	69	13	3	7	4	.345	OF
1926		28	95	32	3	2	6	12	.337	OF
1927	HBG Giants	40	152	48	8	3	3	0	.316	OF
1928	2 teams CLE Hornets MEM Red Sox									
"	total	56	197	62	13	3	1	1	.315	OF
1929	No Data Available									
1930	MEM Red Sox	7	17	6	0	1	0	1	.353	PH, OF
	(8 years)	(368)	(1347)	(489)	(91)	(42)	(49)	(31)	(.363)	
WORLD SERIES										
1924	KC Monarchs	9	27	8	3	0	0	0	.296	OF

Judy Johnson

JOHNSON, WILLIAM JULIUS BR TR 5′11″ 150 lbs.
B. Oct. 26, 1899, Snow Hill, Md. D. June 15, 1989, Wilmington, Del.
Hall of Fame 1975.

Year	Team	G	AB	H	2B	3B	HR	SB	BA	POS
1919	MAD Stars	1	4	0	0	0	0	0	.000	3B
1920	No Data Available									
1921	PHI Hilldales	22	88	20	3	2	2	1	.227	SS, 3B
1922		7	25	2	0	0	0	0	.080	SS
1923		27	86	31	12	1	1	2	.360	3B
1924		71	245	84	19	6	2	4	.343	3B
1925		66	249	97	12	8	4	7	.390	3B
1926		87	339	111	21	6	2	14	.327	3B
1927		51	183	49	5	2	1	2	.268	3B
1928		52	205	46	3	3	1	0	.224	3B
1929		74	256	104	13	1	3	12	.406	SS, 3B
1930	Homestead Grays	17	73	21	0	1	0	0	.288	3B
1931	PHI Hilldales	56	205	56	3	3	0	2	.273	3B
1932	2 teams PHI Hilldales PIT Crawfords									
"	total	32	115	31	2	4	1	2	.270	3B
1933	PIT Crawfords	36	121	27	8	0	0	0	.223	3B
1934		41	154	36	8	2	0	1	.234	3B
1935		44	179	51	8	3	2	3	.285	3B
1936		26	90	23	4	1	0	1	.256	3B
	(17 years)	(710)	(2617)	(789)	(121)	(43)	(19)	(51)	(.301)	
PLAYOFFS										
1930	Homestead Grays	9	43	12	1	0	0	0	.279	3B
1935	PIT Crawfords	2	6	1	0	0	0	0	.167	3B
	2 years	11	49	13	1	0	0	0	.265	
WORLD SERIES										
1924	PHI Hilldales	10	44	16	5	1	1	0	.364	SS, 3B
1925		6	24	6	1	0	0	1	.250	3B
	2 years	16	68	22	6	1	1	1	.324	
ALL STAR (1933–36)		2	2	1	0	0	0	0	.500	3B

Newt Joseph

JOSEPH, NEWTON BL TR
B. Oct. 27, 1899, Montgomery, Ala. D. Jan. 18, 1953, Kansas City, Mo.

Year	Team	G	AB	H	2B	3B	HR	SB	BA	POS
1922	KC Monarchs	70	261	61	10	1	2	8	.234	3B
1923		32	121	22	6	2	8	1	.182	3B
1924		84	338	113	24	7	8	2	.334	3B
1925		50	193	63	12	0	1	9	.326	3B
1926		59	203	60	10	4	4	3	.296	3B
1927		69	238	69	15	5	5	7	.290	3B
1928		72	261	69	12	2	1	16	.264	3B
1929		72	233	66	7	3	5	6	.283	3B
1930		53	179	48	10	3	3	14	.268	3B
1931		8	27	10	3	0	0	0	.370	3B
1932		3	8	0	0	0	0	1	.000	3B
1933	Team not in the league									
1934	Team not in the league									
1935	KC Monarchs	2	6	1	0	0	0	0	.167	3B
	(12 years)	574	2068	582	109	27	37	67	.281	
PLAYOFFS										
1925	KC Monarchs	6	18	1	0	1	0	0	.056	3B
1926		7	27	8	2	0	0	2	.296	3B
1929		2	9	1	0	0	0	0	.111	3B
	3 years	15	54	10	2	1	0	2	.185	

		G	AB	H	2B	3B	HR	SB	BA	POS

Newt Joseph *continued*

WORLD SERIES

		G	AB	H	2B	3B	HR	SB	BA	POS
1924	KC Monarchs	10	38	5	1	0	1	3	.132	3B
1925		6	22	4	0	1	0	0	.182	3B
	2 years	16	60	9	1	1	1	3	.150	

Jumbo Kimbro

KIMBRO, HENRY ALLEN BL TL 5′8″ 175 lbs.
B. Feb. 10, 1912, Nashville, Tenn.

		G	AB	H	2B	3B	HR	SB	BA	POS
1937	WAS Elite Giants	25	98	27	3	1	5	0	.276	OF
1938		21	85	27	1	1	0	0	.318	OF
1939	BAL Elite Giants	33	131	36	3	0	1	0	.275	OF
1940		56	223	58	5	0	3	2	.260	OF
1941	NY Black Giants	20	72	23	2	0	0	1	.319	OF
1942	BAL Elite Giants	46	187	52	4	2	2	3	.278	OF
1943		35	144	41	5	3	0	3	.285	OF
1944		23	94	35	7	1	0	0	.372	OF
1945		23	135	35	9	6	2	1	.259	OF
1946		47	173	68	6	2	3	0	.393	OF
1947		77	284	103					.363	OF
1948		71	239	75					.314	OF
1949		83	307	108					.352	OF
1950		45	165	61	11	4	2	9	.370	OF
	14 years	605	2337	749	(56)	(20)	(18)	(19)	.320	

PLAYOFFS

		G	AB	H	2B	3B	HR	SB	BA	POS
1939	BAL Elite Giants	7	27	5	1	0	0	0	.185	OF
ALL STAR (1941–47)		7	20	6	1	0	0	2	.300	OF

Buck Leonard

LEONARD, WALTER FENNER BL TL 5′10″ 185 lbs.
B. Sept. 8, 1907, Rocky Mount, N. C.
Hall of Fame 1972.

		G	AB	H	2B	3B	HR	SB	BA	POS
1934	WAS Homestead Grays	11	42	17	2	0	3	0	.405	1B
1935		52	200	59	8	1	2	2	.295	1B
1936		5	21	5	1	0	3	0	.238	1B
1937		14	54	18	1	0	2	0	.333	1B
1938		19	68	25	0	0	4	0	.368	1B
1939		21	77	31	3	1	8	0	.403	1B
1940		49	175	61	16	3	9	0	.349	1B
1941		37	111	31	4	5	5	0	.279	1B
1942		23	85	14	4	0	0	2	.165	1B
1943		52	196	62	12	7	3	0	.316	1B
1944		32	112	37	7	3	4	0	.330	1B
1945		23	86	30	4	0	2	0	.349	1B
1946		46	112	30	1	3	4	0	.268	1B
1947		31	105	43	11	0	7	1	.410	1B
1948		47	157	62			13		.395	1B
	15 years	462	1601	525	(74)	(23)	69	(5)	.328	

PLAYOFFS

		G	AB	H	2B	3B	HR	SB	BA	POS
1939	WAS Homestead Grays	7	23	10	1	0	3	0	.435	1B
1941		2	7	3	0	0	1	0	.429	1B
	2 years	9	30	13	1	0	4	0	.433	

WORLD SERIES

		G	AB	H	2B	3B	HR	SB	BA	POS
1937	WAS Homestead Grays	2	7	4	2	0	0	0	.571	1B
1942		4	16	3	0	0	0	0	.188	1B
1943		6	21	6	1	1	0	1	.286	1B
1944		5	16	8	1	0	1	1	.500	1B
1945		4	15	3	0	0	0	0	.200	1B
	5 years	21	75	24	4	1	1	2	.320	
ALL STAR (1935–48)		14	51	15	1	1	3	2	.294	1B

Pop Lloyd

LLOYD, JOHN HENRY BL TR 6′ ″
B. Apr. 25, 1884, Palatka, Fla. D. Mar. 19, 1965, Atlantic City, N. J.
Manager 1921-31.
Hall of Fame 1977.

		G	AB	H	2B	3B	HR	SB	BA	POS
1906	Cuban X-Giants	3	12	0	0	0	0	0	.000	2B
1909	PHI Giants	2	8	6	1	0	0	0	.750	SS
1910	CHI Leland Giants	11	42	15	2	0	0	2	.357	SS
1911	NY Lincoln Giants	1	4	3	0	0	1	0	.750	SS
1912		6	24	4	0	0	1	0	.167	SS
1913		1	4	3	0	0	0	0	.750	SS
1914	CHI Am. Giants	30	124	36	6	3	0	6	.290	SS

Pop Lloyd *continued*

Year	Team	G	AB	H	2B	3B	HR	SB	BA	POS
1915	3 teams NY Lincoln Stars CHI Am. Giants CHI Black Sox									
"	total	30	125	39	2	1	0	1	.312	SS
1916	2 teams NY Lincoln Stars CHI Am. Giants									
"	total	19	72	23	4	1	0	0	.319	SS
1917	CHI Am. Giants	22	87	20	1	1	0	1	.230	SS
1918	BKN Royal Giants	4	16	4	0	0	0	0	.250	SS
1919		2	8	3	0	0	0	0	.375	SS
1920		11	45	14	0	0	0	1	.311	SS
1921	COL Buckeyes	63	247	83	17	3	1	17	.336	SS
1922	AC Bacharach Giants	24	75	29	6	0	1	3	.387	SS, 2B
1923	PHI Hilldales	19	70	27	10	1	2	4	.386	SS
1924	AC Bacharach Giants	59	194	84	10	2	1	3	.433	2B
1925		61	221	73	5	5	2	9	.330	2B
1926	NY Lincoln Giants	40	146	51	6	3	1	4	.349	2B
1927		20	80	30	9	0	2	1	.375	2B
1928		37	149	84	4	1	11	10	.564	1B
1929		55	206	80	15	3	2	1	.388	1B
1930		52	199	62	6	0	2	0	.312	1B
1931	2 teams NY Harlem Stars AC Bacharach Giants									
"	total	18	62	12	1	0	0	1	.194	1B
1932	AC Bacharach Giants	3	11	3	0	0	0	0	.273	1B
	25 years	593	2231	788	105	24	27	64	.353	
PLAYOFFS										
1908	PHI Giants	1	4	4	1	0	0	0	1.000	SS
1916		2	12	2	0	0	0	0	.167	SS
1930	NY Lincoln Giants	8	32	12	0	2	0	0	.375	SS
	3 years	11	48	18	1	2	0	0	.375	
WORLD SERIES										
1909	CHI Leland Giants	3	14	5	2	0	0	0	.357	SS
1914		2	8	1	0	0	0	0	.125	SS
1916		3	11	1	0	0	0	0	.091	SS
	3 years	8	33	7	2	0	0	0	.212	

Lester Lockett

LOCKETT, LESTER BR TR 6′ ″ 195 lbs.
B. Mar. 25, 1912, Princeton, Ind.

Year	Team	G	AB	H	2B	3B	HR	SB	BA	POS
1938	BIR Black Barons	2	5	0	0	0	0	0	.000	SS
1939	No Data Available									
1940	BIR Black Barons	2	7	1	0	0	0	0	.143	
1941	2 teams BIR Black Barons PHI Stars									
"	total		56	20	1	0	0	0	.357	SS
1942	2 teams BIR Black Barons CHI Am. Giants									
"	total	23	54	32	4	0	0	0	.593	SS, 3B
1943	BIR Black Barons		73	30	5	4	2	0	.411	OF, 3B
1944		57	191	49	8	4	0	3	.257	
1945		61	229	70	11	2	3	8	.306	
1946		3	14	2	1	1	0	0	.143	OF, 3B
1947	BAL Elite Giants	76	278	87	11	0	1	4	.313	
1948		71	277	107					.386	
1949	No Data Available									
1950	CHI Am. Giants	31	103	31	7	0	2	9	.301	OF
	(11 years)	(326)	(1287)	(429)	(48)	(11)	(8)	(24)	(.333)	
PLAYOFFS										
1943	BIR Black Barons	1	3	0	0	0	0	0	.000	OF
WORLD SERIES										
1943	BIR Black Barons	6	24	3	1	0	0	0	.125	OF, 3B
1944		5	19	6	1	0	0	0	.316	OF, 3B
	2 years	11	43	9	2	0	0	0	.209	
ALL STAR (1943–48)		3	6	0	0	0	0	0	.000	OF

Dick Lundy

LUNDY, RICHARD (King Richard) BB TR
B. July 10, 1898, Jacksonville, Fla. D. 1965, Jacksonville, Fla.
Manager 1926-34, 1937.

Year	Team	G	AB	H	2B	3B	HR	SB	BA	POS
1918	AC Bacharach Giants	2	8	1	0	0	0	0	.125	SS
1919	2 teams AC Bacharach Giants PHI Hilldales									
"	total	11	41	15	0	0	1	0	.366	SS
1920	AC Bacharach Giants	9	32	11	3	0	2	1	.344	SS
1921		25	91	33	5	4	3	5	.363	SS
1922		8	30	10	1	0	1	0	.333	SS
1923		19	71	22	6	3	4	2	.310	SS

Dick Lundy *continued*

		G	AB	H	2B	3B	HR	SB	BA	POS
1924		60	228	84	9	3	14	11	.368	SS
1925		62	236	64	10	1	5	5	.271	SS
1926		33	121	42	5	1	1	1	.347	SS
1927		55	202	62	5	0	2	1	.307	SS
1928		57	208	85	11	3	7	6	.409	SS
1929	BAL Black Sox	57	213	67	11	0	4	8	.315	SS
1930		32	134	43	6	1	2	1	.321	SS
1931		27	93	32	0	0	0	1	.344	SS
1932		25	85	29	0	0	0	1	.341	SS, PH
1933	PHI Stars	12	39	6	0	0	0	0	.154	
1934	BKN Eagles	17	55	13	0	0	0	0	.236	SS
1935	2 teams NY Cubans NWK Dodgers									
″	total	26	87	27	5	0	1	0	.310	SS, 2B
1936	No Data Available									
1937	NWK Eagles	12	43	8	1	2	0	0	.186	SS
	(19 years)	(549)	(2017)	(654)	(78)	(18)	(47)	(43)	(.324)	
WORLD SERIES										
1926	AC Bacharach Giants	11	40	13	2	1	0	6	.325	SS
1927		9	36	9	1	0	0	0	.250	SS
	2 years	20	76	22	3	1	0	6	.289	
ALL STAR (1933–34)		2	7	0	0	0	0	0	.000	SS

Jimmy Lyons

LYONS, JIMMY BL TR 5′8″ 175 lbs.
B. Chicago, Ill.

		G	AB	H	2B	3B	HR	SB	BA	POS
1910	STL Giants									
1911	No Data Available									
1912	No Data Available									
1913	No Data Available									
1914	BKN Royal Giants	10	49	14	1	0	1	5	.286	OF
1915	STL Giants	5	19	6	0	1	0	0	.316	OF
1916		11	50	17	4	1	1	6	.340	OF, P
1917	2 teams IND Jewell's ABCs All Nations									
″	total	5	20	3	0	0	0	0	.150	1B, OF, P
1918	IND ABCs	8	27	6	1	1	0	0	.222	OF
1920	CHI Am. Giants	56	212	86	15	5	8	22	.406	1B, OF, P
1921		58	194	56	2	3	4	28	.289	OF
1922		53	201	50	4	3	2	8	.249	OF
1923		56	183	46	12	1	0	13	.251	OF
1924		2	0	0	0	0	0	0	—	
	(10 years)	(264)	(955)	(284)	(39)	(15)	(16)	(82)	(.297)	
WORLD SERIES										
1914	BKN Royal Giants	2	8	1	0	0	0	0	.125	OF

Biz Mackey

MACKEY, RALEIGH BB TR 6′2″ 210 lbs.
B. July 27, 1897, Eagle Pass, Tex. D. 1959, Los Angeles, Calif.
Manager.

		G	AB	H	2B	3B	HR	SB	BA	POS
1920	IND ABCs	17	49	15	3	1	1	0	.306	UT
1921		66	226	67	8	9	11	4	.296	SS, C
1922		62	219	79	15	13	6	5	.361	OF, C
1923	PHI Hilldales	24	90	39	4	2	4	1	.433	SS, C
1924		71	255	86	16	3	4	6	.337	SS, C
1925		60	206	72	14	3	6	12	.350	SS, C
1926		85	315	103	19	3	10	14	.327	C
1927		16	56	21	1	1	0	1	.375	C
1928		53	205	67	3	2	2	3	.327	C
1929		29	135	45	2	0	1	2	.333	SS, C
1930		29	105	42	6	4	4	2	.400	3B, SS, C
1931		51	173	65	2	1	2	0	.376	C
1932	No Data Available									
1933	PHI Stars	13	47	14	2	0	0	0	.298	C
1934		19	60	21	3	0	2	0	.350	C
1935		45	156	38	5	0	0	1	.244	C
1936	BAL Elite Giants	23	87	21	3	1	0	0	.241	C
1937		16	50	16	2	0	0	0	.320	C
1938		20	70	18	0	0	0	0	.257	C
1939	2 teams BAL Elite Giants NWK Eagles									
″	total	21	78	20	1	0	4	0	.256	C
1940	NWK Eagles	44	142	41	3	0	1	0	.289	C
1941		18	47	14	1	0	0	0	.298	1B, C
1942	No Data Available									
1943	No Data Available									
1944	NWK Eagles	1	2	2	0	0	0	0	1.000	C
1945		16	57	15	0	0	1	0	.263	C

Biz Mackey *continued*

		G	AB	H	2B	3B	HR	SB	BA	POS
1946		3	3	0	0	0	0	0	.000	
1947			92	21	4	0	1	0	.228	C
	(25 years)	(802)	(2925)	(942)	(117)	(43)	(60)	(51)	(.322)	
PLAYOFFS										
1934	PHI Stars	1	4	0	0	0	0	0	.000	C
1939	NWK Eagles	2	8	4	0	0	0	0	.500	C
	2 years	3	12	4	0	0	0	0	.333	
WORLD SERIES										
1924	PHI Hilldales	10	41	10	0	1	0	1	.244	3B, C
1925		6	25	9	3	1	1	0	.360	C
1946	NWK Eagles	1	1	1	0	0	0	0	1.000	PH
	3 years	17	67	20	3	2	1	1	.299	
ALL STAR (1933–47)		6	15	3	0	0	0	0	.200	C

Dave Malarcher

MALARCHER, DAVID JULIUS (Gentleman Dave) BB TR 5′7″ 147 lbs.
B. Oct. 18, 1894, Whitehall, La. D. May 11, 1982, Chicago, Ill.
Manager 1925-28, 1931, 1933-34.

		G	AB	H	2B	3B	HR	SB	BA	POS
1916	IND ABCs	10	32	8	0	0	0	1	.250	SS, 2B
1917		21	75	15	0	0	0	0	.200	OF, 3B
1918		8	25	6	1	0	0	0	.240	3B
1920	CHI Am. Giants	29	114	31	3	1	0	4	.272	3B
1921		58	208	46	5	1	0	11	.221	3B
1922		25	81	13	0	0	0	2	.160	3B
1923		65	234	69	15	3	1	12	.295	3B
1924		72	287	84	9	1	0	14	.293	3B
1925		84	321	106	9	0	2	12	.330	3B, 2B
1926		70	250	64	8	0	1	8	.256	3B, 2B
1927		77	276	69	7	3	1	16	.250	3B
1928		17	57	14	0	0	0	2	.246	3B
1929	No Data Available									
1930	No Data Available									
1931	CHI Am. Giants	14	44	12	0	0	0	0	.273	3B
1932	No Data Available									
1933	CHI Am. Giants	2	7	0	0	0	0	0	.000	3B
1934		1	1	0	0	0	0	0	.000	PH
	(15 years)	(553)	(2012)	(537)	(57)	(9)	(5)	(82)	(.267)	
PLAYOFFS										
1916	IND ABCs	1	1	0	0	0	0	0	.000	
1926	CHI Am. Giants	7	25	8	0	1	0	2	.320	
1927		4	14	5	0	0	0	1	.357	
	3 years	12	40	13	0	1	0	3	.325	
WORLD SERIES										
1916	IND ABCs	5	18	5	0	0	0	1	.278	
1926	CHI Am. Giants	11	35	9	0	0	0	4	.257	3B
1927		9	28	6	1	0	0	3	.214	3B
	3 years	25	81	20	1	0	0	8	.247	

Oliver Marcelle

MARCELLE, OLIVER (Ghost) BR TR 5′9″ 160 lbs.
B. June 24, 1897, Thibedeaux, La. D. June 12, 1949, Denver, Colo.

		G	AB	H	2B	3B	HR	SB	BA	POS
1918	BKN Royal Giants	4	15	2	0	0	0	0	.133	3B
1919		7	30	14	0	1	0	0	.467	3B
1920	AC Bacharach Giants	9	29	6	0	2	0	1	.207	3B
1921		43	164	50	7	3	1	7	.305	3B
1922		27	99	36	5	1	0	2	.364	3B
1923		15	61	18	0	0	2	6	.295	3B
1924	NY Lincoln Giants	45	175	60	13	3	1	12	.343	3B
1925	2 teams NY Lincoln Giants AC Bacharach Giants									
″	total	58	195	60	5	3	2	3	.308	3B
1926	AC Bacharach Giants	31	106	27	1	1	1	1	.255	3B
1927		48	180	55	4	3	2	2	.306	3B
1928			169	50	2	3	3	0	.296	3B
1929	BAL Black Sox	58	207	57	4	2	0	7	.275	3B
1930	BKN Royal Giants	5	25	8	1	0	0	0	.320	3B
	13 years	(350)	1455	443	42	22	12	41	.304	
WORLD SERIES										
1926	AC Bacharach Giants	11	41	12	2	0	0	2	.293	3B
1927		9	34	8	1	0	0	0	.235	3B
	2 years	20	75	20	3	0	0	2	.267	

Willie Mays

MAYS, WILLIE HOWARD (Say Hey) BR TR 5′10½″ 170 lbs.
B. May 6, 1931, Westfield, Ala.
Major leagues 1951-73.
Hall of Fame 1979.

		G	AB	H	2B	3B	HR	SB	BA	POS
1948	BIR Black Barons	25	84	22	3	0	1	1	.262	OF
1949		75	270	84					.311	OF
1950		27	106	35	7	2	4	2	.330	OF
	3 years	127	460	141	(10)	(2)	(5)	(3)	.307	
WORLD SERIES										
1948	BIR Black Barons	2	3	0	0	0	0	0	.000	OF

Terris McDuffie

McDUFFIE, TERRIS (The Great) BR TR 6′2″ 200 lbs.
B. July 22, 1910, Mobile, Ala. D. New York, N.Y.

		G	AB	H	2B	3B	HR	SB	BA	POS
1930	BIR Black Barons	64	195	58	11	2	3	18	.297	OF
1932	BAL Black Sox	11	33	11	0	0	0	0	.333	OF, P
1935	BKN Eagles	16	42	11	2	0	0	0	.262	OF, P
1938	NY Black Yankees	1	1	1	0	0	0	0	1.000	P
1941	WAS Homestead Grays	7	14	3	1	0	0	0	.214	P
1942	PHI Stars	1	4	0	0	0	0	0	.000	P
1943	No Data Available									
1944	NWK Eagles	4	7	1	0	0	0	0	.143	P
	(7 years)	(104)	(296)	(85)	(14)	(2)	(3)	(18)	(.287)	
WORLD SERIES										
1937	NWK Eagles	2	4	0	0	0	0	0	.000	P
ALL STAR (1941–44)		2	1	1	0	1	0	0	1.000	P

Hurley McNair

McNAIR, HURLEY ALLEN BB TR 5′6″ 155 lbs.
B. Oct. 28, 1888, Marshall, Tex. D. Dec. 2, 1948, Kansas City, Mo.

		G	AB	H	2B	3B	HR	SB	BA	POS
1913	CHI Leland Giants									
1914	CHI Union Giants	3	13	4	0	1	0	0	.308	OF, P
1915	CHI Am. Giants	35	135	39	8	3	0	0	.289	OF, P
1920	KC Monarchs	28	125	39	9	2	2	3	.312	OF
1921		53	196	60	9	8	5	5	.306	OF, P
1922		86	331	124	19	4	11	10	.375	OF, P
1923		43	181	64	6	3	11	5	.354	OF
1924		80	331	103	18	7	5	4	.311	OF
1925		74	289	104	11	9	3	10	.360	OF
1926		59	211	59	11	2	0	10	.280	OF
1927		77	277	77	15	5	6	7	.278	OF
1928	DET Stars	68	241	66	8	6	3	6	.274	OF
	(11 years)	(606)	(2330)	(739)	(114)	(50)	(46)	(60)	(.317)	
PLAYOFFS										
1925	KC Monarchs	6	16	4	0	0	0	0	.250	OF
1926		7	25	4	1	0	0	0	.160	OF
	2 years	13	41	8	1	0	0	0	.195	
WORLD SERIES										
1924	KC Monarchs	10	35	5	0	0	0	0	.143	OF
1925		6	22	6	2	0	0	1	.273	OF
	2 years	16	57	11	2	0	0	1	.193	

Pablo Mesa

MESA, PABLO B.

		G	AB	H	2B	3B	HR	SB	BA	POS
1922	Cuban Stars	2	9	2	1	0	0	0	.222	OF
1923		17	66	17	3	2	1	1	.258	OF
1924		47	196	58	13	2	1	14	.296	OF
1925		41	161	50	4	1	2	2	.311	OF
1926		17	65	18	3	0	0	0	.277	OF
1927		19	69	15	0	0	0	1	.217	OF
	6 years	143	566	160	24	5	4	18	.283	

Minnie Minoso

MINOSO, SATURNINO ORESTES ARMAS BR TR 5′10″ 175 lbs.
Born Saturnino Orestes Armas Minoso (Arrieta).
B. Nov. 29, 1922, Havana, Cuba.
Major leagues 1949-80.

		G	AB	H	2B	3B	HR	SB	BA	POS
1946	NY Cubans	16	59	17	3	1	1	0	.288	3B
1947		55	228	67	14	0	3	7	.294	3B
	2 years	71	287	84	17	1	4	7	.293	
WORLD SERIES										
1947	NY Cubans	6	26	11	2	0	0	0	.423	3B
ALL STAR (1947–48)		2	7	1	0	0	0	0	.143	3B

Dobie Moore

MOORE, DOBIE BR TR 5′11″ 230 lbs.
B. 1893, Ga.. D. Detroit, Mich.

		G	AB	H	2B	3B	HR	SB	BA	POS
1920	KC Monarchs	21	84	23	3	0	2	2	.274	SS
1921		36	125	33	7	4	6	4	.264	SS
1922		77	312	120	22	3	8	11	.385	SS
1923		43	170	62	7	8	8	2	.365	SS
1924		79	307	139	26	9	10	1	.453	SS
1925		83	332	108	20	12	7	9	.325	SS
1926		18	63	24	3	3	0	2	.381	SS
	7 years	357	1393	509	88	39	41	31	.365	
PLAYOFFS										
1925	KC Monarchs	6	23	4	0	2	0	0	.174	SS
WORLD SERIES										
1924	KC Monarchs	10	40	12	0	0	0	2	.300	SS
1925		6	22	8	3	1	0	1	.364	SS
	2 years	16	62	20	3	1	0	3	.323	

Leroy Morney

MORNEY, LEROY

		G	AB	H	2B	3B	HR	SB	BA	POS
1933	2 teams Homestead Grays Elite Giants									
″	total	16	71	28	9	3	0	2	.394	SS
1934	PIT Crawfords	36	120	26	1	0	1	0	.217	SS
1935	WAS Elite Giants	20	102	43	1	0	0	1	.422	SS
1936		12	33	4	1	0	0	0	.121	SS
1937	No Data Available									
1938	NY Black Yankees	12	39	3	0	0	0	0	.077	SS
1939	2 teams PHI Stars TOL Crawfords									
″	total	9	27	11	2	0	1	0	.407	
1940	CHI Am. Giants	8	29	8	1	0	0	0	.276	SS
1941										
1942	BIR Black Barons	22	73	21	3	0	2	1	.288	PH, SS, OF
1943			75	18	2	0	2	0	.240	OF
	(9 years)	(135)	(569)	(162)	(20)	(3)	(6)	(4)	(.285)	
ALL STAR (1933–40)		3	7	1	0	0	0	0	.143	SS, 2B

Don Newcombe

NEWCOMBE, DONALD (Newk) BL TR 6′ 4″ 220 lbs.
B. June 14, 1926, Madison, N. J.
Major leagues 1949-1960

		G	AB	H	2B	3B	HR	SB	BA	POS
1944	NWK Eagles	1	4	2	1	0	0	0	.500	P

Ray Noble

NOBLE, RAFAEL MIGUEL BR TR 5′11″ 210 lbs.
Born Rafael Miguel Noble (Magee).
B. Mar. 15, 1919, Central Hatillo, Cuba.
Major leagues 1951-53

		G	AB	H	2B	3B	HR	SB	BA	POS
1945	PHI Stars	5	10	1	0	0	0	0	.100	C
1946	NY Cubans	3	10	1	1	0	0	0	.100	C
	2 years	8	20	2	1	0	0	0	.100	

Alejandro Oms

OMS, ALEJANDRO BL TL 5′8″ 190 lbs.
B. Mar. 13, 1895, Santa Clara, Cuba D. Nov. 9, 1946

		G	AB	H	2B	3B	HR	SB	BA	POS
1921	Cuban Stars	1					3			OF
1922		2	9	3	1	0	0	0	.333	OF
1923		16	65	26	2	2	1	2	.400	OF
1924		39	129	42	9	4	4	3	.326	OF
1925		43	157	50	13	1	6	4	.318	OF
1926		20	73	25	5	2	2	1	.342	OF
1927		39	132	46	10	2	3	5	.348	OF
1928		29	117	36	11	0	6	1	.308	OF
1929	No Data Available									
1930	Stars of Cuba	19	75	24	7	2	1	1	.320	OF, P
1931		8	33	2	0	0	1	0	.061	OF
1933	No Data Available									
1934	Team not in the league									
1935	NY Cubans	31	123	25	8	2	2	1	.203	OF
	(11 years)	(247)	(913)	(279)	(66)	(15)	(29)	(18)	(.306)	
PLAYOFFS										
1935	NY Cubans	2	8	0	0	0	0	0	.000	OF
ALL STAR (1935)		1	4	2	0	0	0	0	.500	OF

Buck O'Neil

O'NEIL, JOHN JORDAN BR TR 6′ 2″ 190 lbs.
B. Nov. 13, 1911, Carrabelle, Fla.
Manager 1948-50.

Year	Team	G	AB	H	2B	3B	HR	SB	BA	POS
1937	MEM Red Sox	3	11	1	0	0	0	0		OF, 2B
1938	KC Monarchs	27	89	23	5	2	1	7		1B
1939		30	101	26	7	2	2	3		1B
1940		30	113	39	5	3	1	6		1B
1941		25	95	25	4	3	0	3		1B
1942		39	137	36	3	1	2	1		1B
1943			99	22	0	2	2	1		1B
1944	US Navy									
1945										
1946	KC Monarchs	58	197	69	1	1	2	1		1B
1947		46	162	58						1B
1948		42	162	41	6	1	1	3		1B
1949		45	109	36						1B
1950		31	83	21	5	2	1	5		1B
	(12 years)	(376)	1358	397	(36)	(17)	(12)	(30)	(.292)	
WORLD SERIES										
1942	KC Monarchs	4	17	6	0	2	0	1		1B
1946		7	27	9	0	1	2	2		1B
	2 years	11	44	15	0	3	2	3	(.341)	
ALL STAR (1942–43)		2	6	0	0	0	0	0	(.000)	1B

Ted Page

PAGE, TED BL
B. Apr. 22, 1903, Bowling Green, Ky. D. Dec. 1, 1984, Pittsburgh, Pa.

Year	Team	G	AB	H	2B	3B	HR	SB	BA	POS
1926	NWK Stars	2	5	1	0	0	0	0	.200	OF
1931	Homestead Grays	33	143	42	2	5	0	0	.294	OF
1934	PIT Crawfords	15	44	5	2	0	0	0	.114	OF
1935	PHI Stars	34	138	42	3	1	1	1	.304	OF
	4 years	84	330	90	7	6	1	1	.273	

Spoony Palm

PALM, CLARENCE TR

Year	Team	G	AB	H	2B	3B	HR	SB	BA	POS
1927	BIR Black Barons	47	133	41	5	3	10	2	.308	C
1928	STL Stars	33	93	28	3	0	7	0	.301	C
1929		60	192	67	16	4	19	1	.349	
1930	DET Stars	41	127	40	8	3	5	3	.315	C
1931		34	120	36	6	1	2	3	.300	C
1932										
1933	DET Wolves	8	26	8	3	1	0	0	.308	C
1934	2 teams Homestead Grays PIT Crawfords									
″	total	11	23	4	0	0	0	0	.174	C
1935	NY Black Yankees	9	20	6	1	0	0	0	.300	C
1936		5	10	3	0	0	0	0	.300	PH, C
1939	PHI Stars	15	48	13	0	0	0	0	.271	C
1940		9	28	8	0	0	0	0	.286	PH, C
1941	2 teams PHI Stars WAS Homestead Grays									
″	total	9	29	12	1	0	0	0	.414	C
1942	PHI Stars	2	4	2	0	0	1	0	.500	C
1943	NY Black Yankees	9	23	4	0	0	0	0	.174	C
1944	2 teams PHI Stars NY Black Yankees									
″	total	7	15	3	0	0	0	0	.200	C
1945	2 teams NY Black Yankees PHI Stars									
″	total	3	10	3	0	0	0	0	.300	C
1946	NY Black Yankees	4	5	2	0	0	0	0	.400	
	(17 years)	(306)	(906)	(280)	(43)	(12)	(44)	(9)	(.309)	
PLAYOFFS										
1930	DET	6	25	8	1	0	0	0	.320	C

Red Parnell

PARNELL, ROY

Year	Team	G	AB	H	2B	3B	HR	SB	BA	POS
1927	BIR Black Barons	78	305	130	19	6	10	18	.426	OF
1928		64	224	73	18	7	7	3	.326	OF
1929	No Data Available									
1930	No Data Available									
1934	WAS Elite Giants	2	9	2	1	0	0	0	.222	OF
1935		33	133	34	4	0	1	3	.256	OF
1936	PHI Stars	36	153	48	4	0	0	2	.314	OF
1937	NY Black Yankees	6	23	11	0	0	0	2	.478	OF
1938	PHI Stars	30	148	30	2	0	6	0	.203	OF
1939		42	147	40	4	2	2	0	.272	OF
1940		42	157	39	4	0	3	0	.248	OF
1941		65	248	80	8	0	0	1	.323	OF

Red Parnell *continued*

		G	AB	H	2B	3B	HR	SB	BA	POS
1942		54	205	59	9	0	1	0	.288	OF
1943			173	48	2	4	0	0	.277	OF
	(12 years)	(452)	(1925)	(594)	(75)	(19)	(30)	(29)	(.309)	
PLAYOFFS										
1927	BIR Black Barons	4	16	2	0	0	0	2	.125	
1938	PHI Stars					1				
	2 years	(4)	(16)	(2)	(0)	1	(0)	(2)	(.125)	
ALL STAR (1934–39)		2	6	0	0	0	0	0	.000	OF

Lenny Pearson

PEARSON, LEONARD CURTIS (Horse) BR TR 6′ 2″ 200 lbs.
B. May 23, 1918, Akron, Ohio D. 1984, Newark, N.J.

		G	AB	H	2B	3B	HR	SB	BA	POS
1938	NWK Eagles	9	19	11	0	0	1	1	.579	OF
1939		19	71	18	0	0	2	0	.254	2B, OF, 1B
1940		46	167	65	0	3	1	1	.389	3B
1941		28	99	30	1	0	5	1	.303	3B
1942		35	128	39	8	0	9	1	.305	OF, 1B
1943		33	117	40	5	5	8	2	.342	1B
1944		29	116	34	4	2	2	0	.293	OF, 1B
1945		19	75	21	1	0	1	0	.280	1B
1946		37	126	32	4	2	5	0	.254	1B
1947		80	313	91	19		10	10	.291	OF
1948			6	4	3	0	1	0	.667	OF
1949	BAL Elite Giants	90	331	110					.332	
	12 years	(425)	1568	495	(45)	(12)	(45)	(16)	.316	
WORLD SERIES										
1946	NWK Eagles	7	28	11	1	0	1	1	.393	1B
ALL STAR (1941–46)		8	23	3	1	0	0	0	.130	OF

Cy Perkins

PERKINS, WILLIAM GEORGE (Bill) BR TR 6′ ″
Manager 1945

		G	AB	H	2B	3B	HR	SB	BA	POS
1928	BIR Black Barons	53	201	49	7	4	5	2	.244	C
1929	No Data Available									
1930	BIR Black Barons	62	205	63	7	3	5	6	.307	C
1931	CLE Cubs	1	4	2	2	0	0	0	.500	C
1932	PIT Crawfords	22	81	33	3	3	4	0	.407	C
1933										
1934		3	11	2	0	0	0	0	.182	
1935		37	146	44	7	3	1	2	.301	OF, C
1936		22	69	17	1	0	0	0	.246	OF, C
1937	Dominican Republic									
1938	PHI Stars	21	115	36	0	0	4	0	.313	C
1939		20	55	14	1	0	0	0	.255	C
1940	BAL Elite Giants	47	153	43	4	0	0	1	.281	C
1941	No Data Available									
1942	No Data Available									
1943	No Data Available									
1944	No Data Available									
1945		2	5	2	0	0	0	0	.400	
1946	2 teams NY Black Yankees PHI Stars									
″	total	5	17	5	1	0	0	0	.294	OF
1947	PHI Stars		36	5	0	0	0	0	.139	OF, C
	(12 years)	(295)	(1098)	(315)	(33)	(13)	(19)	(11)	(.287)	
PLAYOFFS										
1935	PIT Crawfords	4	12	3	0	0	0	0	.250	
ALL STAR (1934–40)		2	6	2	0	0	0	0	.333	C

Bruce Petway

PETWAY, BRUCE (Buddy) BL TR 170 lbs.
B. 1883, Nashville, Tenn. D. July 4, 1941, Chicago, Ill.
Manager 1922-25.

		G	AB	H	2B	3B	HR	SB	BA	POS
1906	Cuban X-Giants	1	4	0	0	0	0	0	.000	C
1907	PHI Giants									
1908	No Data Available									
1909	PHI Giants	2	8	0	0	0	0	0	.000	C
1910	CHI Leland Giants	8	33	11	1	0	0	0	.333	C
1911		1	5	1	1	0	0	0	.200	C
1912										
1913	CHI Am. Giants	19	72	20	3	0	0	2	.278	C
1914		5	19	5	0	0	0	0	.263	C
1915		4	18	4	2	0	0	0	.222	C

Bruce Petway *continued*

		G	AB	H	2B	3B	HR	SB	BA	POS
1916		14	46	8	0	1	1	0	.174	C
1917		16	67	10	1	0	0	1	.149	1B, OF, C
1918		5	19	3	1	0	0	0	.158	C
1919	DET Stars	6	18	1	0	0	0	0	.056	OF
1920		41	126	26	2	0	0	6	.206	C
1921		43	143	44	6	2	2	9	.308	C
1922		30	82	22	2	0	2	3	.268	C
1923		49	89	30	2	1	0	0	.337	C
1924		32	86	29	3	3	1	1	.337	1B, OF, C
1925		18	36	7	1	0	0	1	.194	PH, C
	(17 years)	(294)	(871)	(221)	(25)	(7)	(6)	(23)	(.254)	
PLAYOFFS										
1908	PHI Giants	1	4	2	0	0	0	0	.500	C
1916	CHI Am. Giants	3	10	0	0	0	0	0	.000	
1925	DET Stars	1	4	1	0	0	0	0	.250	
	3 years	5	18	3	0	0	0	0	.167	
WORLD SERIES										
1909	PHI Giants	3	10	2	2	0	0	0	.200	C
1914	CHI Am. Giants	1	4	2	0	0	0	0	.500	C
	2 years	4	14	4	2	0	0	0	.286	

Spot Poles

POLES, SPOTTSWOOD BB TR

B. Nov. 7, 1886, Winchester, Va. D. Sept. 12, 1962, Harrisburg, Pa.

		G	AB	H	2B	3B	HR	SB	BA	POS
1909	PHI Giants	2	8	2	0	0	0	0	.250	OF
1910		8	33	10	0	0	1	0	.303	
1911	NY Lincoln Giants	1	5	2	0	0	0	0	.400	OF
1912	2 teams NY Lincoln Giants BKN Royal Giants									
"	total	6	24	7	0	0	0	0	.292	OF
1913	NY Lincoln Giants	7	25	9	2	0	0	0	.360	OF
1914		6	26	15	3	0	0	0	.577	OF
1915	NY Lincoln Stars	19	83	20	3	0	0	6	.241	OF
1916	NY Lincoln Giants	5	22	5	0	0	1	0	.227	OF
1917		10	39	9	0	0	0	0	.231	OF
1918	Military Service									
1919	NY Lincoln Giants	2	6	0	0	0	0	0	.000	OF
	(10 years)	66	271	79	8	0	2	6	.292	
WORLD SERIES										
1909	PHI Giants	3	12	1	0	0	0	0	.083	OF

Alec Radcliff

RADCLIFF, ALEXANDER BR TR 6′ 190 lbs.

B. July 26, 1905, Mobile, Ala. D. July 18, 1983, Chicago, Ill.
Brother of Double Duty Radcliffe.

		G	AB	H	2B	3B	HR	SB	BA	POS
1926	DAY Marcos	1	3	0	0	0	0	0	.000	SS
1932	CHI Am. Giants	42	142	39	9	0	5	2	.275	3B
1933		25	101	33	10	3	0	3	.327	3B
1934		25	94	29	5	0	1	1	.309	3B
1935		42	184	60	9	2	1	1	.326	3B
1936	2 teams NY Cubans CHI Am. Giants									
"	total	17	68	24	6	0	1	0	.353	3B
1937	CHI Am. Giants	29	104	24	1	5	1	1	.231	SS, 3B
1938		24	64	14	5	3	0	5	.219	SS, 3B
1939		18	65	19	3	3	1	0	.292	3B
1940	No Data Available									
1941	CHI Am. Giants	3	9	3	1	0	0	0	.333	3B
1942	2 teams CHI Am. Giants BIR Black Barons									
"	total	22	83	19	1	1	0	0	.229	3B
1943	CHI Am. Giants		96	34	1	0	2	1	.354	3B, P
1944		48	174	50	11	0	5	3	.287	3B
1945		50	175	58	7	1	7	3	.331	3B
1946	MEM Red Sox	2	7	1	0	0	0	0	.143	SS, 3B
1947	No Data Available									
1948										
1949	CHI Am. Giants	57	180	43					.239	3B
	(16 years)	(405)	(1549)	(450)	(69)	(18)	(24)	(20)	(.291)	
PLAYOFFS										
1934	CHI Am. Giants	1	4	1	0	0	0	0	.250	3B
1937		2	9	2	0	0	0	2	.222	3B
1943		1	3	0	0	0	0	0	.000	3B
	3 years	4	16	3	0	0	0	2	.188	

Alec Radcliff *continued*

		G	AB	H	2B	3B	HR	SB	BA	POS
WORLD SERIES										
1937	CHI Am. Giants	1	2	0	0	0	0	0	.000	SS
ALL STAR (1933–46)		12	47	15	2	1	0	0	.319	SS, 3B

Double Duty Radcliffe

RADCLIFFE, TED BR TR 5′10″ 212 lbs.
B. July 7, 1902, Mobile, Ala.
Manager 1937-38, 1943.
Brother of Alec Radcliff.

		G	AB	H	2B	3B	HR	SB	BA	POS
1928	DET Stars	67	256	68	13	4	8	1	.266	C
1929		32	126	39	7	2	3	4	.310	C
1930	STL Stars	55	180	51	11	2	6	4	.283	P, C
1931	2 teams DET Wolves Homestead Grays									
″	total	17	47	14	3	1	1	0	.298	P, C
1932	PIT Crawfords	15	47	11	3	0	2	0	.234	P, C
1933	3 teams Homestead Grays CLE Browns COL Blue Birds									
″	total	12	47	15	1	1	0	1	.319	P, C
1934	CHI Am. Giants	1	2	2	0	0	0	0	1.000	P, C
1935	BKN Eagles	16	42	11	2	0	0	0	.262	P, C
1936	Semipro									
1937	CLA Tigers	24	87	31	3	2	0	0	.356	P, C
1938	MEM Red Sox	11	31	7	0	0	0	2	.226	C, P, PH,
1939		13	26	8	0	0	0	0	.308	P, PH, C
1940	Mexico									
1941	CLE Red Sox	6	6	2	1	0	0	0	.333	P
1942	2 teams BIR Black Barons CHI Am. Giants									
″	total	13	39	11	1	0	0	0	.282	C, P
1943	CHI Am. Giants		52	13	1	0	0	0	.250	C, P
1944	BIR Black Barons	26	93	20	4	0	0	1	.215	C, P
1945	No Data Available									
	(15 years)	(308)	(1081)	(303)	(50)	(12)	(20)	(13)	(.280)	
PLAYOFFS										
1930	STL Stars	6	15	4	1	0	0	0	.267	P
WORLD SERIES										
1943	BIR Black Barons	6	25	8	0	0	0	0	.320	C
1944		5	20	3	0	0	0	0	.150	C
	2 years	11	45	11	0	0	0	0	.244	
ALL STAR (1937–44)		6	13	4	0	0	1	0	.308	C, P

Frog Redus

REDUS, WILSON BR TR 5′5″ 155 lbs.
B. Jan. 29, 1905, Muskogee, Okla. D. 1986, Okla.

		G	AB	H	2B	3B	HR	SB	BA	POS
1924	3 teams IND ABCs CLE Browns STL Stars									
″	total	19	70	25	2	2	2	0	.357	OF
1925	STL Stars	70	244	96	15	7	11	0	.393	OF
1926		61	215	71	9	6	6	4	.330	OF
1927		97	367	131	18	7	15	1	.357	OF
1928		73	278	96	12	6	21	1	.345	OF
1929		85	324	104	24	2	11	6	.321	OF
1930		34	110	33	9	3	5	3	.300	OF
1931		13	37	7	1	0	0	0	.189	OF
1932	No Data Available									
1933	2 teams COL Blue Birds CLE Red Sox									
″	total	21	81	26	6	1	9	1	.321	OF
1934	CLE Red Sox	8	30	11	0	0	0	0	.367	OF
1935	CHI Am. Giants	42	146	26	1	2	1	0	.178	OF
1936		11	50	7	0	0	0	0	.140	OF
1937		27	93	22	2	0	0	2	.237	OF
1938		29	77	22	6	0	1	4	.286	OF
1939	No Data Available									
1940	CHI Am. Giants	5	8	3	0	0	0	0	.375	OF
	(15 years)	(595)	(2130)	(680)	(105)	(36)	(82)	(22)	(.319)	
PLAYOFFS										
1925	STL Stars	6	21	6	0	1	0	0	.286	OF
1928		7	26	4	2	0	0	0	.154	OF
1930		5	12	4	1	0	0	0	.333	OF
	3 years	18	59	14	3	1	0	0	.237	
ALL STAR (1936–37)		2	2	0	0	0	0	0	.000	OF

Orville Riggins

RIGGINS, ORVILLE BR TR

Year	Team	G	AB	H	2B	3B	HR	SB	BA	POS
1920	DET Stars	52	187	53	17	3	1	1	.283	SS
1921		52	206	67	17	2	1	4	.325	SS
1922		61	218	75	10	5	12	6	.344	SS
1923		60	223	64	9	3	5	1	.287	SS
1924		60	255	76	7	6	1	5	.298	SS
1925		86	332	92	16	9	8	18	.277	SS
1926		80	295	89	16	7	7	16	.302	SS
1927	CLE Hornets	34	125	42	5	3	3	2	.336	SS
1928	No Data Available									
1929	NY Lincoln Giants	60	228	70	13	3	4	6	.307	3B, 2B
1930		30	117	39	1	0	4	0	.333	SS
1931	NY Harlem Stars	21	75	18	14	2	0	2	.240	SS
	(11 years)	(596)	(2261)	(685)	(125)	(43)	(46)	(61)	(.303)	
PLAYOFFS										
1925	DET Stars	6	25	3	0	1	0	0	.120	
1930	NY Lincoln Giants	9	36	8	0	0	0	1	.222	
	2 years	15	61	11	0	1	0	1	.180	

Ed Rile

RILE, ED (Huck) BR TR 6′ 4″ 230 lbs.

Year	Team	G	AB	H	2B	3B	HR	SB	BA	POS
1920	2 teams IND ABCs NY Lincoln Giants									
″	total	2	8	3	1	0	0	0	.375	P
1921	2 teams NY Lincoln Giants COL Buckeyes									
″	total	2	8	4	0	1	0	0	.500	1B, P
1922	CHI Am. Giants									
1923	No Data Available									
1924										
1925	IND ABCs									
1926		59	215	70	16	5	2	2	.326	1B, P
1927	DET Stars	70	242	96	23	6	10	3	.397	1B, P
1928		84	302	111	27	2	8	7	.368	1B, P
1929		68	251	75	12	2	10	2	.299	1B, P
1930		61	226	73	17	9	8	7	.323	1B, P
1931	BKN Royal Giants	2	5	0	0	0	0	0	.000	1B
	(8 years)	(348)	(1257)	(432)	(96)	(25)	(38)	(21)	(.344)	
PLAYOFFS										
1930	DET Stars	6	23	8	1	0	0	1	.348	2B, 1B

Jackie Robinson

ROBINSON, JOHN ROOSEVELT BR TR 5′11½″ 195 lbs.
B. Jan. 31, 1919, Cairo, Ga. D. Oct. 24, 1972, Stamford, Conn.
Major leagues 1947-56.
Hall of Fame 1962.

Year	Team	G	AB	H	2B	3B	HR	SB	BA	POS
1945	KC Monarchs	47	163	63	14	4	5	13	.387	SS
ALL STAR (1945)		1	5	0	0	0	0	0	.000	2B

Neil Robinson

ROBINSON, NEIL BR TR 5′11″ 182 lbs.
B. July 7, 1908, Grand Rapids, Mich.

Year	Team	G	AB	H	2B	3B	HR	SB	BA	POS
1936	CIN Tigers	3	13	5	1	1	0	0	.385	OF
1937		25	84	33	4	3	2	0	.393	OF
1938	MEM Red Sox	17	58	19	4	1	4	0	.328	SS
1939		30	70	19	5	1	1	2	.271	OF
1940			49	10	2	0	1	0	.204	OF
1941		9	29	10	1	1	1	0	.345	OF
1942		23	80	25	7	1	3	1	.313	OF
1943		15	46	11	1	2	1	0	.239	OF
1944		64	232	74	12	5	4	17	.319	OF
1945		60	198	60	7	1	3	3	.303	OF
1946		1	3	0	0	0	0	0	.000	OF
1947							2			
1948		74	258	86	23	4	7	4	.333	OF
1949		71	232	63					.272	OF
1950		66	251	71	14	3	10	7	.283	OF
	15 years	(458)	(1603)	(486)	(81)	(23)	(39)	(34)	(.303)	
WORLD SERIES										
1938	MEM Red Sox	1	4	1	0	0	0	0	.250	SS
ALL STAR (1938–48)		8	21	10	1	0	2	0	.476	OF

Bullet Joe Rogan

ROGAN, WILBER JOE BR TR 5′ 9″ 160 lbs.
B. July 28, 1889, Oklahoma City, Okla. D. Mar. 4, 1967, Kansas City, Mo.

Year	Team	G	AB	H	2B	3B	HR	SB	BA	POS
1920	KC Monarchs	19	76	21	4	3	0	6	.276	UT, P
1921		45	137	36	7	2	3	13	.263	2B, OF, P

Bullet Joe Rogan *continued*

Year	Team	G	AB	H	2B	3B	HR	SB	BA	POS
1922		74	251	88	9	8	16	17	.351	OF, P
1923		27	89	37	3	1	7	6	.416	OF, P
1924		52	153	63	11	7	5	0	.412	OF, P
1925		58	161	59	12	8	3	6	.366	OF, P
1926		46	118	37	6	3	2	3	.314	OF, P
1927		50	103	34	3	2	2	1	.330	OF, P
1928		62	201	71	15	4	6	5	.353	2B, OF, P
1929		76	270	92	18	8	7	23	.341	OF, P
1930		28	103	32	5	0	1	6	.311	OF, P
1931		7	24	7	1	0	0	2	.292	OF, P
1932	Team not in the league									
1933	Team not in the league									
1934	Team not in the league									
1935	Team not in the league									
1936	KC Monarchs	3	5	3	0	0	0	0	.600	1B, P
1937		13	22	11	1	1	0	1	.500	1B, OF, PH, P
1938		10	33	8	0	0	0	1	.242	OF, PH, P
	(15 years)	570	1746	599	95	47	52	90	.343	
PLAYOFFS										
1925	KC Monarchs	6	15	7	0	0	0	0	.467	P
1926		5	8	3	1	0	0	0	.375	P
1929		2	8	2	1	0	0	0	.250	P
1937		1	6	0	0	0	0	0	.000	OF
	4 years	14	37	12	2	0	0	0	.324	
WORLD SERIES										
1924	KC Monarchs	10	40	13	1	0	0	3	.325	OF, P

Nat Rogers

ROGERS, WILLIAM BL TR 5′11″ 160 lbs.
B. June 7, 1893, Spartanburg, S.C.

Year	Team	G	AB	H	2B	3B	HR	SB	BA	POS
1927	2 teams MEM Red Sox CHI Am. Giants									
″	total	66	243	72	12	7	3	5	.296	OF
1928	2 teams CHI Am. Giants MEM Red Sox									
″	total	36	132	44	6	4	2	2	.333	OF
1929	MEM Red Sox	52	197	56	7	1	3	0	.284	OF
1930	2 teams MEM Red Sox BIR Black Barons									
″	total	69	251	85	21	7	5	5	.339	OF
1931	CHI Am. Giants	19	70	30	6	1	0	1	.429	OF
1932		39	134	42	8	1	0	4	.313	OF
1937	MEM Red Sox	6	24	9	0	0	0	0	.375	OF
1938		16	51	16	2	1	1	1	.314	OF
1939		11	25	2	0	0	0	0	.080	PH, OF
1940			28	6	0	0	0	0	.214	
1941		2	6	3	2	0	0	0	.500	
1942		2	2	0	0	0	0	0	.000	
1943		9	22	5	0	0	0	0	.227	PH, OF
1944	2 teams MEM Red Sox CHI Am. Giants									
″	total	26	46	8	2	1	0	0	.174	OF
1945	MEM Red Sox	22	35	8	1	0	0	0	.229	PH, OF
	15 years	(375)	1266	386	67	23	14	18	.305	
PLAYOFFS										
1927	CHI Am. Giants	3	12	6	0	2	0	1	.500	
WORLD SERIES										
1927	CHI Am. Giants	5	15	6	2	0	0	1	.400	OF
ALL STAR (1938)		1	4	2	0	0	0	0	.500	OF

Julio Rojo

ROJO, JULIO BR TR

Year	Team	G	AB	H	2B	3B	HR	SB	BA	POS
1916	Cubans	2	9	1	0	1	0	0	.111	C
1917		10	40	12	0	0	0	0	.300	P, OF, C
1918		4	16	5	0	0	0	0	.313	C
1919		5	24	4	0	0	0	0	.167	P, C
1920	No Data Available									
1921	AC Bacharach Giants	13	45	13	0	0	0	2	.289	C
1922		27	96	26	3	2	0	2	.271	C
1923	BAL Black Sox	18	67	18	3	2	0	5	.269	C
1924		39	123	38	5	1	1	9	.309	C
1925		45	143	38	7	0	0	8	.266	C
1926		13	44	7	0	0	0	3	.159	C
1927	NY Lincoln Giants	13	45	14	3	1	1	2	.311	C
1928		27	94	32	11	0	1	2	.340	C

Julio Rojo *continued*

Year	Team	G	AB	H	2B	3B	HR	SB	BA	POS
1929		15	45	16	2	0	1	6	.356	C
1930		16	68	20	4	2	0	0	.294	C
	(14 years)	(247)	(859)	(244)	(38)	(9)	(4)	(39)	(.284)	
PLAYOFFS										
1930	NY Lincoln Giants	4	8	4	0	1	0	0	.500	C

Pythias Russ

RUSS, PYTHIAS
D. Aug. 1930, Chicago, Ill.

Year	Team	G	AB	H	2B	3B	HR	SB	BA	POS
1925	MEM Red Sox	43	147	48	3	2	2	1	.327	C
1926	CHI Am. Giants	41	148	41	7	2	4	4	.277	C
1927		74	275	91		2	4		.331	C
1928		57	173	70	15	5	0	1	.405	C
1929		46	169	66	5	12	3	10	.391	C
	5 years	261	912	316	(30)	23	13	(16)	.346	
WORLD SERIES										
1927	CHI Am. Giants	9	35	8	1	0	0	1	.229	

Branch Russell

RUSSELL, BRANCH BL TR 5′10″ 170 lbs.
Brother of Johnny Russell.
B. Oct. 9, 1895, South Boston, Va. D. May 1, 1959, St. Louis, Mo.
Brother of Johnny Russell.

Year	Team	G	AB	H	2B	3B	HR	SB	BA	POS
1923	STL Stars	59	212	65	8	8	5	5	.307	OF
1924		66	264	84	17	7	7	8	.318	OF
1925		87	289	88	11	12	9	9	.304	OF
1926		79	268	78	13	7	8	9	.291	OF
1927		92	368	116	16	7	9	4	.315	OF
1928		73	287	82	15	6	3	0	.286	OF
1929		81	290	97	21	10	3	3	.334	OF
1930		72	278	92	11	3	8	7	.331	OF
1931		17	44	16	0	0	1	0	.364	OF
1932		3	11	4	0	0	0	0	.364	OF
	10 years	629	2311	722	112	60	53	45	.312	
PLAYOFFS										
1930	STL Stars	7	24	7	1	1	0	1	.292	OF

Johnny Russell

RUSSELL, JOHN HENRY (Pistol) BR TR
Brother of Branch Russell.

Year	Team	G	AB	H	2B	3B	HR	SB	BA	POS
1922	STL Giants	64	252	77	8	5	3	10	.306	2B
1923	MEM Red Sox	18	66	22	2	3	0	2	.333	2B
1924		53	203	58	8	4	0	6	.286	2B
1925		72	277	78	10	4	0	2	.282	2B
1926	STL Stars	82	313	97	14	6	5	15	.310	2B
1927		83	273	78	10	5	10	2	.286	2B
1928		73	269	68	6	2	2	0	.253	2B
1929		59	199	53	1	2	1	0	.266	2B
1930		73	264	81	11	6	5	2	.307	2B
1931	2 teams IND ABCs PIT Crawfords									
″	total	8	21	6	0	0	0	0	.286	2B
1932	2 teams DET Wolves PIT Crawfords									
″	total	41	149	41	4	1	0	0	.275	2B
1933	PIT Crawfords	30	109	23	8	0	0	0	.211	2B
	12 years	656	2395	682	82	38	26	39	.285	
PLAYOFFS										
1928	STL Stars	7	21	6	1	0	1	1	.286	2B
1930		7	30	9	2	1	1	0	.300	2B
	2 years	14	51	15	3	1	2	1	.294	

Lazaro Salazar

SALAZAR, LAZARO BL TL 5′9″ 177 lbs.
B. Feb. 4, 1912, Havana, Cuba D. Apr. 25, 1957

Year	Team	G	AB	H	2B	3B	HR	SB	BA	POS
1930	NY Cubans	39	138	31	3	2	1	1	.225	OF, P
1932		14	45	16	0	0	0	3	.356	OF, P
1933		3	11	7	0	0	0	0	.636	OF
1934	Team not in the league									
1935	NY Cubans	38	131	46	11	1	4	3	.351	OF, 1B
1936		28	98	36	6	0	4	4	.367	PH, OF
1937	Team not in the league									

Lazaro Salazar *continued*

		G	AB	H	2B	3B	HR	SB	BA	POS
1938	Team not in the league									
1939	No Data Available									
	(5 years)	(122)	(423)	(136)	(20)	(3)	(9)	(11)	(.322)	
PLAYOFFS										
1935	NY Cubans	6	19	6	1	0	0	0	.316	1B

Louis Santop

SANTOP, LOUIS LOFTIN (Top) BL TR 6′4″ 242 lbs.
B. Jan. 17, 1890, Tyler, Tex. D. Jan. 6, 1942, Philadelphia, Pa.

		G	AB	H	2B	3B	HR	SB	BA	POS
1911	NY Lincoln Giants	1	5	1	0	0	0	0	.200	C
1912		4	16	5	1	2	0	0	.313	OF
1913		5	19	6	2	0	0	0	.316	OF, C
1914		6	26	10	1	0	0	0	.385	C
1915	NY Lincoln Stars	19	80	18	2	1	1	0	.225	C
1916	2 teams NY Lincoln Stars BKN Royal Giants									
″	total	16	59	16	2	2	0	4	.271	C
1917	2 teams NY Lincoln Giants BKN Royal Giants									
″	total	5	20	10	0	0	0	0	.500	OF, C
1918	2 teams PHI Hilldales BKN Royal Giants									
″	total	6	20	10	0	2	2	0	.500	C
1919	2 teams PHI Hilldales BKN Royal Giants									
″	total	6	24	5	0	0	0	1	.208	C
1920	PHI Hilldales	16	59	16	1	0	0	0	.271	C
1921		30	107	33	6	1	6	6	.308	OF, C
1922		7	22	12	2	0	0	0	.545	1B, C
1923		15	55	14	3	2	1	4	.255	C
1924		48	167	65	7	1	4	2	.389	C
1925		21	30	5	1	0	0	1	.167	PH, C
1926		12	26	10	0	0	0	1	.385	C
	16 years	217	735	236	28	11	14	19	.321	
WORLD SERIES										
1916	NY Lincoln Stars	5	18	3	0	0	0	2	.167	C
1924	PHI Stars	9	24	8	0	0	0	0	.333	C
1925		2	2	0	0	0	0	0	.000	P
	3 years	16	44	11	0	0	0	2	.250	

George Scales

SCALES, GEORGE (Tubby) BR TR 5′11″ 195 lbs.
B. Aug. 16, 1900, Talladega, Ala. D. Apr. 15, 1976, Los Angeles, Calif.

		G	AB	H	2B	3B	HR	SB	BA	POS
1921	STL Giants	10	35	7	2	0	0	1	.200	
1922		24	72	15	7	0	1	1	.208	3B
1923	2 teams STL Stars NY Lincoln Giants									
″	total	50	154	66	10	7	11	6	.429	3B, 2B
1924	NY Lincoln Giants	54	180	66	14	1	5	4	.367	2B
1925	2 teams NY Lincoln Giants Homestead Grays									
″	total	31	108	39	8	0	5	2	.361	SS, 3B
1926	2 teams NY Lincoln Giants Homestead Grays									
″	total	13	45	10	1	1	0	0	.222	SS
1927	NY Lincoln Giants	19	65	29	8	1	3	1	.446	3B
1928		36	130	44	17	2	8	10	.338	IF
1929		48	181	73	12	0	9	6	.403	2B
1930	Homestead Grays	18	68	20	2	2	2	2	.294	2B
1931		31	113	44	9	5	3	0	.389	
1932	NY Black Yankees	13	46	10	3	0	1	0	.217	2B
1933		2	8	2	0	0	0	0	.250	OF
1934		14	48	7	2	0	0	2	.146	2B
1935	Homestead Grays	41	137	34	5	1	3	1	.248	2B
1936	NY Black Yankees	16	60	13	0	1	4	1	.217	3B
1937	Dominican Republic									
1938	BAL Elite Giants	9	16	3	0	0	0	0	.188	3B
1939	NY Black Yankees	14	47	10	0	1	2	0	.213	3B
1940	BAL Elite Giants	43	133	35	9	2	3	0	.263	PH, OF
1941		21	54	15	1	0	2	0	.278	
1942		55	170	42	10	1	3	0	.247	1B
1943			112	30	7	2	1	0	.268	OF, 1B
1944		6	19	4	0	0	0	1	.211	OF
1945	NY Black Yankees	3	9	2	1	0	0	0	.222	1B
1946	BAL Elite Giants	9	22	7	1	0	0	0	.318	1B
	(25 years)	(580)	2032	627	129	27	66	38	.309	
PLAYOFFS										
1930	BAL Elite Giants	9	40	16	2	0	0	0	.400	
ALL STAR (1943)		1	0	0	0	0	0	0		PH

Dick Seay

SEAY, RICHARD WILLIAM BR TR 5′8″ 160 lbs.
B. Nov. 30, 1904, West New York, N. J. D. Apr. 6, 1981, Jersey City, N. J.

Year	Team	G	AB	H	2B	3B	HR	SB	BA	POS
1926	BAL Black Sox	11	33	4	0	0	0	0	.121	SS
1927	BKN Royal Giants	13	49	9	1	0	0	0	.184	SS
1928	Team not in the league									
1929										
1930	BKN Royal Giants	6	20	4	0	0	0	0	.200	2B
1931		4	14	0	0	0	0	0	.000	2B
1932	BAL Black Sox	29	104	32	0	0	0	0	.308	2B
1933		20	73	22	0	0	0	3	.301	2B
1934	PHI Stars	33	122	19	0	0	0	3	.156	2B
1935		53	201	44	1	3	2	1	.219	1B, 2B, P
1936	NY Black Yankees	1	6	3	0	0	0	0	.500	2B
1937	NWK Eagles	19	78	9	1	0	1	2	.115	2B
1938		16	61	16	0	0	0	0	.262	2B
1939		31	119	22	0	0	2	0	.185	2B
1940		28	104	29	2	2	5	1	.279	2B
1941	2 teams NY Black Yankees NWK Eagles									
″	total	25	96	11	1	0	1	0	.115	SS
1942	2 teams NY Black Yankees NWK Eagles									
″	total									
1943	US Army									
1944										
1945	NY Black Yankees	1	4	2	0	0	0	0	.500	2B
1946		6	22	4	0	0	0	0	.182	2B
1947			78	15	1	0	0	1	.192	2B
	(17 years)	(296)	(1184)	(245)	(7)	(5)	(11)	(11)	(.207)	
PLAYOFFS										
1939	NWK Eagles	3	9	2	1	0	0	0	.222	2B
ALL STAR (1935–41)		3	11	1	0	0	0	0	.091	2B

Barney Serrell

SERRELL, WILLIAM C. BL TR 5′11″ 160 lbs.

Year	Team	G	AB	H	2B	3B	HR	SB	BA	POS
1942	KC Monarchs	34	119	50	6	4	4	1	.420	2B
1943			127	34	6	1	0	1	.268	2B
1944		19	77	32	1	3	2	4	.416	
1945		1	4	1	0	0	0	0	.250	
1946	Mexico									
	(4 years)	(54)	327	117	13	8	6	6	.358	
WORLD SERIES										
1942	KC Monarchs	4	18	10	1	1	0	0	.556	
ALL STAR (1944)		1	3	2	0	0	0	0	.667	2B

George Shively

SHIVELY, GEORGE

Year	Team	G	AB	H	2B	3B	HR	SB	BA	POS
1913	WB Sprudels	4	14	4	0	0	0	0	.286	OF
1914	IND ABCs	25	99	32	5	0	3	4	.323	OF
1915		37	151	46	2	1	2	18	.305	OF
1916		29	110	35	7	1	0	9	.318	OF
1917		5	21	10	0	0	0	0	.476	OF
1918		9	28	10	0	0	0	0	.357	OF
1919	3 teams AC Bacharach Giants IND ABCs DAY Marcos									
″	total	7	29	8	0	0	0	0	.276	OF
1920	IND ABCs	23	65	20	1	1	0	3	.308	OF
1921	AC Bacharach Giants	29	83	24	2	1	0	7	.289	OF
1922		24	91	22	2	1	0	1	.242	OF
1923	IND ABCs	55	214	68	8	5	0	4	.318	OF
1924	2 teams No Data Available WAS Potomacs									
″	total	56	216	67	0	0	1	5	.310	
	(11 years)	303	1121	346	27	10	6	51	.309	
PLAYOFFS										
1916	IND ABCs	3	11	4	1	0	0	0	.364	OF

Harry Simpson

SIMPSON, HARRY LEON (Suitcase) BL TR 6′ 1″ 180 lbs.
B. Dec. 3, 1925, Atlanta, Ga. D. Apr. 3, 1979, Akron, Ohio.
Major Leagues 1951-59.

Year	Team	G	AB	H	2B	3B	HR	SB	BA	POS
1946	PHI Stars	24	65	14	0	1	1	0	.215	OF
1947			135	33	5		1	0	.244	OF
	2 years	(24)	200	47	5	(1)	2	0	.235	

Chino Smith

SMITH, CHARLIE BL TR 5′6″
B. 1903, Greenwood, S. C. D. Jan. 16, 1932

Year	Team	G	AB	H	2B	3B	HR	SB	BA	POS
1925	BKN Royal Giants	35	131	43	7	0	5	2	.328	OF, 2B
1927		24	85	41	8	2	5	2	.482	UT, OF
1928		9	37	10	2	1	0	0	.270	OF
1929	NY Lincoln Giants	60	229	104	22	1	20	4	.454	OF
1930		35	128	63	17	5	7	0	.492	OF
	5 years	163	610	261	56	9	37	8	.428	
PLAYOFFS										
1930	NY Lincoln Giants	9	28	6	0	0	0	1	.214	OF

Hilton Smith

SMITH, HILTON BR TR
B. Feb. 27, 1912, Giddings, Tex. D. Nov. 18, 1983, Kansas City, Mo.

Year	Team	G	AB	H	2B	3B	HR	SB	BA	POS
1942	KC Monarchs		24	9	3	0	0	1	.375	P
PLAYOFFS										
1937	KC Monarchs	1	1	1	0	0	0	0	1.000	P
WORLD SERIES										
1937	KC Monarchs	2	2	0	0	0	0	0	.000	P
ALL STAR (1937–42)		6	6	1	0	0	0	0	.167	P

Turkey Stearnes

STEARNES, NORMAN THOMAS BL TL 6′ 170 lbs.
B. May 8, 1901, Nashville, Tenn. D. Sept. 4, 1979, Detroit, Mich.
Name also spelled Turkey Stearns.

Year	Team	G	AB	H	2B	3B	HR	SB	BA	POS
1923	DET Stars	60	244	89	16	15	17	1	.365	OF
1924		60	240	86	7	12	10	3	.358	OF
1925		88	336	124	22	11	18	11	.369	OF
1926		82	301	113	24	10	20	13	.375	OF
1927		85	312	108	24	12	20	13	.346	OF
1928		82	313	102	18	7	24	5	.326	OF
1929		69	259	98	15	5	19	12	.378	OF
1930	2 teams NY Lincoln Giants DET Stars									
″	total	53	196	71	17	14	3	6	.362	OF
1931	2 teams DET Stars KC Monarchs									
″	total	41	139	48	9	3	8	5	.345	OF, 1B
1932	CHI Am. Giants	43	141	42	10	4	5	13	.298	OF
1933		30	120	41	11	1	7	2	.342	OF
1934		27	107	40	2	4	6	1	.374	OF
1935		42	145	63	8	3	6	1	.434	OF
1936	PHI Stars	41	185	53	1	0	7	1	.286	OF
1937	2 teams DET Stars CHI Am. Giants									
″	total	18	47	18	2	2	2	0	.383	OF
1938	2 teams CHI Am. Giants KC Monarchs									
″	total	17	48	14	4	2	2	1	.292	OF
1939	KC Monarchs	35	120	42	8	0	2	4	.350	OF
1940		30	105	31	3	2	5	1	.295	
	18 years	903	3358	1183	201	107	181	93	.352	
PLAYOFFS										
1925	DET Stars	6	23	8	2	1	1	0	.348	OF
1930		7	30	14	4	1	3	1	.467	OF
1934	CHI Am. Giants	1	4	2	0	1	0	1	.500	OF
1937		3	16	5	1	0	1	0	.313	OF
	4 years	17	73	29	7	3	5	2	.397	
WORLD SERIES										
1937	CHI Am. Giants	2	8	4	0	0	1	0	.500	OF
ALL STAR (1933–39)		5	19	4	1	0	0	0	.211	OF

Jake Stephens

STEPHENS, PAUL EUGENE BR TR 5′6″ 158 lbs.
B. Feb. 10, 1900, Pleasureville, Pa. D. Feb. 5, 1981, York, Pa.

Year	Team	G	AB	H	2B	3B	HR	SB	BA	POS
1921	PHI Hilldales	7	26	4	2	0	0	0	.154	SS
1922		1	4	1	0	0	0	0	.250	SS
1923		6	11	0	0	0	0	0	.000	SS
1924		28	105	22	4	1	0	3	.210	SS
1925		51	172	37	9	2	0	9	.215	SS
1926		65	205	51	5	1	0	13	.249	SS
1927		60	212	45	2	2	0	8	.212	SS
1928		47	194	31	2	0	0	0	.160	SS
1929		5	20	9	1	0	0	1	.450	SS
1930	Homestead Grays	18	77	24	2	2	1	1	.312	SS
1931		10	40	8	4	0	0	0	.200	SS
1932	2 teams Homestead Grays PIT Crawfords									
″	total	29	114	23	2	0	0	2	.202	SS

Jake Stephens *continued*

Year	Team	G	AB	H	2B	3B	HR	SB	BA	POS
1933	PHI Stars	12	47	15	0	0	1	0	.319	SS
1934		30	113	32	1	0	1	0	.283	SS
1935		38	150	36	0	0	0	0	.240	SS
1936	NY Black Yankees	15	55	9	0	0	0	0	.164	SS
1937		9	26	7	0	0	0	0	.269	SS, 2B
	17 years	431	1571	354	34	8	3	37	.225	
PLAYOFFS										
1930	Homestead Grays	9	37	10	0	0	0	2	.270	SS
1934	PHI Stars	1	3	0	0	0	0	0	.000	SS
	2 years	10	40	10	0	0	0	2	.250	
WORLD SERIES										
1924	PHI Stars	1	2	0	0	0	0	0	.000	SS
1925		6	20	5	2	0	0	1	.250	SS
	2 years	7	22	5	2	0	0	1	.227	
ALL STAR (1935)		1	6	2	0	0	0	0	.333	SS

Ed Stone

STONE, ED BL TR 6′2″ 190 lbs.
B. 1909, Black Cat, Del. D. Mar. 20, 1983, New York, N. Y.

Year	Team	G	AB	H	2B	3B	HR	SB	BA	POS
1931	AC Bacharach Giants	4	16	5	0	0	0	0	.313	OF
1932	WIL Hornets	1	3	0	0	0	0	0	.000	OF
1933	AC Bacharach Giants	2	8	2	0	0	0	0	.250	OF
1935	BKN Eagles	45	167	54	4	2	3	2	.323	OF
1936	NWK Eagles	13	41	13	2	2	1	0	.317	OF
1937		22	82	15	1	3	4	0	.183	OF
1938		10	45	10	0	0	3	0	.222	OF
1939		29	107	47	2	1	4	1	.439	OF
1940			141	35	3	5	2	1	.248	OF
1941		2	8	1	0	0	0	0	.125	OF
1942		31	118	27	4	1	3	0	.229	OF
1943		12	36	9	1	1	1	2	.250	
1944	PHI Stars	32	125	39	6	0	0	0	.312	OF
1945		35	131	39	9	0	1	3	.298	OF
1946		16	62	24	3	0	0	0	.387	OF
	15 years	(254)	1090	320	35	15	22	9	.294	

Mule Suttles

SUTTLES, GEORGE BR TR 6′1″ 212 lbs.
B. Mar. 2, 1901, Brockton, Ala. D. 1968, Newark, N.J.
Manager 1944.

Year	Team	G	AB	H	2B	3B	HR	SB	BA	POS
1923	BIR Black Barons	35	132	34	4	3	1	3	.258	OF
1924		85	296	93	23	3	2	1	.314	OF
1925		74	266	88	5	5	13	6	.331	OF
1926	STL Stars	87	342	143	25	19	27	11	.418	OF, 1B
1927		30	79	36	8	3	8	1	.456	1B
1928		72	274	102	12	9	19	1	.372	1B
1929		82	304	108	29	7	20	3	.355	1B
1930	2 teams STL Stars BAL Black Sox									
″	total	51	196	75	14	9	17	8	.383	OF, 1B
1931	STL Stars	21	63	21	4	1	1	1	.333	OF
1932	2 teams DET Wolves WAS Pilots									
″	total	28	96	33	11	0	5	1	.344	1B
1933	CHI Am. Giants	30	94	25	4	1	7	4	.266	1B
1934		26	104	29	2	1	6	1	.279	1B
1935		39	127	31	7	0	8	1	.244	1B
1936	NWK Eagles	30	118	41	3	1	10	0	.347	1B
1937		27	91	29	2	0	12	0	.319	OF, 1B
1938		25	56	13	0	0	12	0	.232	1B
1939	2 teams NWK Eagles IND ABCs									
″	total	42	145	44	5	2	13	0	.303	OF, 1B
1940	NWK Eagles	44	144	37	8	0	7	3	.257	OF, 1B
1941	2 teams NY Black Yankees NWK Eagles									
″	total	22	107	16	4	0	1	0	.150	OF
1942	NWK Eagles	8	13	5	1	0	0	1	.385	
1943		2	2	0	0	0	0	0	.000	PH
1944		10	28	8	0	1	1	0	.286	1B
	22 years	870	3077	1011	171	65	190	46	.329	
PLAYOFFS										
1928	STL Stars	7	27	9	2	1	0	0	.333	1B
1930		7	23	8	0	1	1	0	.348	1B

Mule Suttles *continued*

Year	Team	G	AB	H	2B	3B	HR	SB	BA	POS
1934	CHI Am. Giants	1	3	0	0	0	0	0	.000	1B
1939	NWK Eagles	3	11	1	0	0	1	0	.091	1B
	4 years	18	64	18	2	2	2	0	.281	
WORLD SERIES										
1938	NWK Eagles	1	4	0	0	0	0	0	.000	
ALL STAR (1933–41)		6	21	8	0	1	2	1	.381	OF, 1B

Ben Taylor

TAYLOR, BEN BL TL 6′ 190 lbs.

B. July 1, 1888, Anderson, S.C. D. Jan. 24, 1953, Baltimore, Md.
Manager 1924, 1926-29.
Brother of Candy Jim Taylor.
Brother of C.I. Taylor.
Brother of John Taylor.

Year	Team	G	AB	H	2B	3B	HR	SB	BA	POS
1909	BIR Giants									
1910	WB Sprudels	4	16	2	0	0	0	0	.125	1B, P
1913		13	51	16	4	0	1	1	.314	1B, 2
1914	IND ABCs	29	100	31	11	3	4	11	.310	1B, P
1915		37	154	44	11	4	1	21	.286	1B, P
1916		30	111	38	2	0	0	4	.342	1B
1917		21	79	22	2	0	0	1	.278	1B, P
1918		8	30	5	1	0	1	0	.167	1B
1919	IND Jewell's ABCs	2	8	2	1	0	0	1	.250	1B
1920	IND ABCs	44	146	46	10	1	3	8	.315	1B, P
1921		77	268	109	21	6	4	14	.407	1B
1922		64	257	92	24	4	2	1	.358	1B
1923	WAS Potomacs									
1924		59	207	65	4	1	2	4	.314	1B
1925	HBG Giants	67	251	82	12	5	3	0	.327	1B
1926	BAL Black Sox	30	99	24	2	1	0	2	.242	1B
1927		52	189	58	12	6	1	0	.307	1B
1928		31	119	40	5	1	2	0	.336	1B
1929		18	59	19	1	0	1	1	.322	1B
	(17 years)	(586)	(2144)	(695)	(123)	(32)	(25)	(69)	(.324)	
PLAYOFFS										
1916	IND ABCs	3	13	6	0	0	0	0	.462	1B, P
WORLD SERIES										
1916	IND ABCs	5	18	11	0	0	0	3	.611	

Candy Jim Taylor

TAYLOR, JAMES BR

B. Feb. 1, 1884, Anderson, S. C. D. Apr. 3, 1948, Chicago, Ill.
Manager 1945.
Brother of Ben Taylor.
Brother of C.I. Taylor.
Brother of John Taylor.

Year	Team	G	AB	H	2B	3B	HR	SB	BA	POS
1910	WB Sprudels	1	4	0	0	0	0	0	.000	3B
1911										
1913	CHI Am. Giants	19	75	21	6	0	0	0	.280	3B, 2B
1914	IND ABCs	28	104	28	2	2	2	6	.269	3B
1915	2 teams WB Sprudels CHI Am. Giants									
″	total	5	23	5	1	0	0	1	.217	3B, 2B
1916	IND ABCs	30	113	34	8	2	1	10	.301	3B
1917		22	76	20	3	2	0	3	.263	3B
1918		5	19	4	0	0	0	0	.211	3B
1919	2 teams DAY Marcos CHI Giants									
″	total	3	13	1	0	0	0	1	.077	SS, 3B
1920	2 teams DAY Marcos CHI Giants									
″	total	7	15	2	1	0	0	2	.133	3B, P
1921	No Data Available									
1922	CLE Tate Stars	32	89	20	5	1	1	3	.225	3B
1923	2 teams STL Stars TOL Tigers									
″	total	21	80	23	1	2	10	1	.287	3B
1924	STL Stars	39	111	38	5	1	1	1	.342	3B
1925		37	43	8	0	0	2	3	.186	3B
1926	2 teams DET Stars CLE Browns									
″	total	37	69	21	1	1	1	0	.304	3B
1927	STL Stars	25	38	15	4	0	0	1	.395	3B
1928		14	14	4	0	0	0	0	.286	
	(16 years)	(325)	(886)	(244)	(37)	(11)	(18)	(32)	(.275)	
PLAYOFFS										
1916	IND ABCs	3	11	8	0	0	0	0	.727	3B

Clint Thomas

THOMAS, CLINTON C. (Buckeye) BR TR 5′8″ 185 lbs.
B. Nov. 25, 1896, Greenup, Ky. D. Dec. 12, 1990, Charleston, W. Va.

Year	Team	G	AB	H	2B	3B	HR	SB	BA	POS
1921	COL Buckeyes	56	221	62	7	9	5	7	.281	2B
1922	DET Stars	60	231	79	15	7	7	7	.342	OF, 2B
1923	PHI Hilldales	25	105	23	2	1	1	5	.219	OF
1924		70	233	83	7	6	5	11	.356	OF
1925		67	241	86	21	3	6	16	.357	OF
1926		88	326	102	16	9	8	23	.313	OF
1927		57	202	53	9	3	1	5	.262	OF
1928	3 teams PHI Hilldales AC Bacharach Giants NY Lincoln Giants									
″	total	47	186	44	6	5	2	2	.237	OF
1929	AC Bacharach Giants	31	119	41	6	0	7	5	.345	OF
1930	NY Lincoln Giants	35	135	59	13	2	2	0	.437	OF
1931	NY Harlem Stars	22	78	13	1	1	0	1	.167	OF
1932	2 teams IND ABCs NY Black Yankees									
″	total	46	164	48	12	0	2	8	.293	OF
1933	NY Black Yankees	2	9	2	0	0	0	0	.222	OF
1934		16	48	11	0	0	2	0	.229	OF
1936	2 teams NY Cubans NWK Eagles									
″	total	17	41	9	0	0	0	8	.220	OF
1937	NY Black Yankees	14	43	12	1	1	3	0	.279	OF
1938		3	10	2	1	0	0	0	.200	OF
	17 years	656	2392	729	117	47	51	98	.305	
PLAYOFFS										
1930	NY Lincoln Giants	8	36	9	0	0	1	1	.250	OF
1935	NY Cubans	7	28	8	0	0	0	0	.286	OF
	2 years	15	64	17	0	0	1	1	.266	
WORLD SERIES										
1924	PHI Hilldales	10	39	8	1	0	0	1	.205	OF
1925		6	22	6	2	0	0	2	.273	OF
	2 years	16	61	14	3	0	0	3	.230	

Showboat Thomas

THOMAS, DAVID BL TL 6′ 180 lbs.
B. 1904, Mobile, Ala.

Year	Team	G	AB	H	2B	3B	HR	SB	BA	POS
1930	BAL Black Sox	8	26	8	1	0	0	0	.308	1B
1931		63	228	43	8	1	3	0	.189	1B
1932	2 teams BAL Black Sox NY Black Yankees									
″	total	24	90	21	1	0	1	0	.233	1B
1933	NY Black Yankees	3	9	3	0	0	1	0	.333	1B
1934		15	52	10	0	0	0	0	.192	1B
1935	NY Cubans	8	34	9	0	1	1	0	.265	1B
1936		31	129	32	6	0	0	0	.248	1B
1937	No Data Available									
1938	WAS Black Senators	11	43	15	2	1	0	0	.349	1B
1940	NY Cubans	2	7	0	0	0	0	0	.000	1B
1941		2	6	2	0	1	0	0	.333	1B
1942		19	73	18	3	3	0	0	.247	1B
1943			143	46	10	0	2	0	.322	1B
1944		13	54	14	1	0	1	0	.259	
1945		6	22	7	1	0	0	0	.318	1B
1946		27	110	37	3	0	1	0	.336	1B
	(15 years)	(232)	(1026)	(265)	(36)	(7)	(10)	(0)	(.258)	

Hank Thompson

THOMPSON, HENRY CURTIS BL TR 5′ 9″ 174 lbs.
B. Dec. 8, 1925, Oklahoma City, Okla. D. Sept. 30, 1969, Fresno, Calif.
Major leagues 1947-1956.

Year	Team	G	AB	H	2B	3B	HR	SB	BA	POS
1942	KC Monarchs		82	26	6	3	2	1	.317	
1943			70	22	6	1	2	1	.314	2B
1944	Military Service									
1945	KC Monarchs	5	6	1	0	0	0	0	.167	2B
1946		8	27	6	0	0	4	2	.222	2B
1947		48	189	65	3	2	2	0	.344	IF
1948		70	267	100	20	8	11	20	.375	IF
	(6 years)	(131)	641	220	35	14	21	24	.343	
WORLD SERIES										
1946	KC Monarchs	7	27	8	1	0	0	1	.296	2B

Cristobal Torriente

TORRIENTE, CRISTOBAL BL TL 5′10″ 190 lbs.
B. 1895, Cuba D. 1938, New York, N.Y.

Year	Team	G	AB	H	2B	3B	HR	SB	BA	POS
1913	NY Cubans	10	35	15	7	2	2	1	.429	OF
1914	CHI Am. Giants	21	64	26	8	0	3	2	.406	OF, P
1915	NY Cubans	31	127	43	6	5	1	5	.339	OF, P

Cristobal Torriente *continued*

Year	Team		G	AB	H	2B	3B	HR	SB	BA	POS
1916	2 teams	NY Cubans / All Nations									
"	total		33	112	40	8	1	3	7	.357	OF, P
1917	All Nations		1	4	1	0	0	0	0	.250	OF
1918	2 teams	NY Cubans / CHI Am. Giants									
"	total		6	23	9	3	0	0	0	.391	OF
1919	CHI Am. Giants		12	47	7	2	0	0	0	.149	OF
1920			35	129	53	11	4	2	5	.411	OF, P
1921			64	201	68	5	10	7	18	.338	OF, P
1922			36	117	40	1	2	3	3	.342	OF, P
1923			63	233	96	18	3	7	1	.412	OF, P
1924			72	253	85	22	4	9	11	.336	OF
1925			86	292	70	8	6	6	2	.240	OF
1926	KC Monarchs		70	254	86	17	5	4	5	.339	OF
1927	DET Stars		83	297	95	17	2	4	6	.320	OF, P
1928			40	119	39	5	3	2	3	.328	OF, P
1932	CLE Cubs		1	4	1	0	0	0	0	.250	1B
	17 years		664	2311	774	138	47	53	69	.335	
PLAYOFFS											
1925	CHI Am. Giants		6	20	3	0	0	0	0	.150	OF
1926	KC Monarchs		7	27	11	2	0	0	0	.407	OF
	2 years		13	47	14	2	0	0	0	.298	

Quincy Troupe

TROUPPE, QUINCY THOMAS
B. Dec. 25, 1912, Dublin, Ga. D. Aug. 12, 1993, Creve Coeur, Mo. BB TR 6′ 2½″ 225 lbs.
Manager 1945.

Year	Team		G	AB	H	2B	3B	HR	SB	BA	POS
1930	STL Stars		0								P
1931			7	19	6	1	0	0	0	.316	C,
1932	3 teams	DET Stars / Homestead Grays / KC Monarchs									
"	total		40	143	54	11	0	1	4	.378	P, C
1933	Latin America										
1934											
1935											
1936											
1937											
1938											
1939	2 teams	STL Stars / IND ABCs									
"	total		2	3	0	0	0	0	0	.000	C
	(4 years)		49	(165)	(60)	(12)	(0)	(1)	(4)	(.364)	
WORLD SERIES											
1945	CLE Browns		4	15	6	1	1	0	0	.400	
ALL STAR (1938–48)			6	12	2	0	1	0	0	.167	C

Tetelo Vargas

VARGAS, JUAN ESTEBAN VARGAS MARCANO
B. Apr. 11, 1906, Santo Domingo de Guzman, Dominican Republic BR TR
D. 1971, Guayama, Puerto Rico.

Year	Team	G	AB	H	2B	3B	HR	SB	BA	POS
1931	NY Cubans	5	20	6	1	0	0	0	.300	OF
1938		1	4	2	0	0	0	0	.500	OF
1939		17	62	19	1	0	1	0	.306	OF
1940	No Data Available									
1941	NY Cuban Stars	23	80	26	0	1	0	0	.325	OF
1942		18	60	19	3	3	0	1	.317	OF
1943			140	67	10	3	0	1	.479	OF
1944		22	81	14	1	0	0	0	.173	OF
	(7 years)	(86)	(447)	(153)	(16)	(7)	(1)	(2)	(.342)	
ALL STAR (1942–43)		2	5	1	0	0	0	1	.200	OF

Frank Warfield

WARFIELD, FRANCIS XAVIER
B. 1895, Indianapolis, Ind. D. July 24, 1932, Pittsburgh, Pa. BR TR 5′7″ 170 lbs.
Manager 1925-28, 1932.

Year	Team	G	AB	H	2B	3B	HR	SB	BA	POS
1916	STL Giants	10	40	16	2	2	0	7	.400	SS
1917	IND ABCs	20	75	17	2	1	0	3	.227	2B
1918		7	28	11	3	0	0	1	.393	SS, 2B
1919	DET Stars	7	25	5	0	0	0	0	.200	SS
1920		60	268	73	15	5	1	3	.272	3B, 2B
1921		54	197	53	8	5	2	9	.269	2B
1922		58	228	78	10	3	0	10	.342	3B, 2B
1923	PHI Hilldales	26	100	30	9	2	0	5	.300	2B
1924		71	240	82	16	1	2	20	.342	2B
1925		66	230	71	11	5	3	14	.309	2B
1926		88	331	83	10	3	3	12	.251	2B
1927		64	225	49	7	5	0	10	.218	2B

Frank Warfield *continued*

Year	Team	G	AB	H	2B	3B	HR	SB	BA	POS
1928		53	210	41	1	1	2	0	.195	2B
1929	BAL Black Sox	59	232	61	4	1	0	8	.263	2B
1930		28	112	24	2	0	0	0	.214	2B
1931	2 teams BAL Black Sox WAS Pilots									
"	total	58	201	31	2	0	0	1	.154	3B, 2B
1932	WAS Pilots	12	43	10	0	0	0	1	.233	2B
	17 years	741	2785	735	102	34	13	104	.264	
WORLD SERIES										
1924	PHI Hilldales	10	37	9	2	0	0	2	.243	2B
1925		6	23	6	0	1	0	1	.261	2B
	2 years	16	60	15	2	1	0	3	.250	

Willie Wells

WELLS, WILLIE JAMES (Devil) BR TR 5′9″ 166 lbs.
B. Aug. 10, 1908, Austin, Tex. D. Jan. 22, 1989, Austin, Tex.
Manager 1946.
Father of Willie Wells, Jr.

Year	Team	G	AB	H	2B	3B	HR	SB	BA	POS
1924	STL Stars	54	208	55	16	3	1	2	.264	SS
1925		89	325	96	13	6	6	15	.295	SS
1926		78	254	96	13	3	12	8	.378	SS
1927		96	351	134	18	5	23	5	.382	SS
1928		72	289	102	22	4	17	2	.353	SS
1929		88	334	123	21	6	27	21	.368	SS
1930		73	273	110	31	3	14	16	.403	SS
1931		22	76	23	3	0	5	1	.303	SS
1932	3 teams KC Monarchs DET Wolves Homestead Grays									
"	total	36	130	34	14	3	1	6	.262	SS
1933	CHI Am. Giants	26	109	31	3	3	0	6	.284	SS
1934		26	104	25	7	5	0	2	.240	SS
1935		42	146	40	9	3	2	13	.274	SS
1936	NWK Eagles	27	101	27	5	0	3	0	.267	SS
1937		21	85	25	4	0	1	1	.294	SS
1938		16	57	23	1	0	3	1	.404	SS
1939		33	124	44	2	1	2	3	.355	SS
1940	Mexico									
1941										
1942	NWK Eagles	39	149	51	7	0	6	5	.342	SS
1943	No Data Available									
1944	NY Black Yankees	2	8	3	0	0	0	0	.375	
1945	2 teams NY Black Yankees NWK Eagles									
"	total	19	62	16	4	0	0	0	.258	SS
1946	2 teams NY Black Yankees BAL Elite Giants									
"	total	37	133	30	7	2	1	0	.226	3B, 2B
1947	No Data Available									
1948	MEM Red Sox	49	137	45	9	1	2	0	.328	SS
	(21 years)	(945)	(3455)	(1133)	(209)	(48)	(126)	(107)	(.328)	
PLAYOFFS										
1925	STL Stars	6	20	4	1	0	1	0	.200	SS
1928		7	25	8	1	1	3	0	.320	SS
1930		7	30	13	2	0	2	3	.433	SS
1934	CHI Am. Giants	1	3	0	0	0	0	0	.000	SS
1939	NWK Eagles	3	9	1	0	0	0	0	.111	SS
	5 years	24	87	26	4	1	6	3	.299	
WORLD SERIES										
1937	Homestead Grays	2	10	0	0	0	0	0	.000	SS
1938		1	3	1	0	0	0	0	.333	SS
	2 years	3	13	1	0	0	0	0	.077	
ALL STAR (1933–45)		9	36	10	3	1	0	1	.278	SS, 2B

Edgar Wesley

WESLEY, EDGAR BL

Year	Team	G	AB	H	2B	3B	HR	SB	BA	POS
1919	DET Stars	7	25	4	0	0	0	0	.160	1B
1920		50	235	65	19	3	13	3	.277	1B
1921	2 teams DET Stars COL Buckeyes									
"	total	40	145	42	8	0	7	3	.290	1B
1922	DET Stars	61	218	75	10	5	12	6	.344	1B
1923		61	225	76	13	0	17	0	.338	1B
1924	HBG Giants	55	177	47	7	5	2	2	.266	1B
1925	DET Stars	57	214	89	13	6	18	9	.416	1B
1926		74	257	77	6	1	15	5	.300	1B

Edgar Wesley *continued*

Year	Team	G	AB	H	2B	3B	HR	SB	BA	POS
1927	2 teams DET Stars CLE Hornets									
"	total	37	140	59	8	2	0	2	.421	1B
1931	AC Bacharach Giants	4	13	1	0	0	0	0	.077	1B
	10 years	446	1649	535	84	22	84	30	.324	
PLAYOFFS										
1924	DET Stars	3	10	2	0	0	0	0	.200	

Jim West

WEST, JIM (Shifty)
B. 1912, Mobile, Ala. D. 1970, Philadelphia, Pa. BB TR 6′2″ 216 lbs.

Year	Team	G	AB	H	2B	3B	HR	SB	BA	POS
1930	2 teams BIR Black Barons MEM Red Sox									
"	total	44	149	39	8	2	1	3	.262	1B
1931	CLE Cubs	16	57	12	2	1	1	0	.211	1B
1932	2 teams BIR Black Barons MEM Red Sox									
"	total	9	30	10	0	1	0	2	.333	1B
1933	NAS Elite Giants	22	79	17	1	0	0	0	.215	1B
1934	BAL Elite Giants	20	83	35	4	1	0	1	.422	OF, C
1935	COL Elite Giants	24	86	26	1	3	5	0	.302	1B
1936	WAS Elite Giants	20	67	25	3	1	0	0	.373	1B
1937		29	107	40	1	0	6	0	.374	1B
1938	BAL Elite Giants	21	77	31	5	0	2	0	.403	1B
1939	PHI Stars	26	88	23	4	2	1	0	.261	1B
1940		49	182	53	7	6	0	0	.291	1B
1941		64	236	51	3	1	2	0	.216	1B
1942		57	196	52	7	7	5	1	.265	1B
1943			212	68	8	4	0	2	.321	1B
1944		36	146	51	4	2	0	1	.349	1B
1945		38	148	37	0	0	0	0	.250	1B
1946	No Data Available									
1947	PHI Stars		33	8	1	0	1	0	.242	1B
	(17 years)	(475)	(1976)	(578)	(59)	(31)	(24)	(10)	(.293)	
ALL STAR (1936–43)		4	14	2	0	0	0	0	.143	1B

Chaney White

WHITE, CHANEY
B. Dallas, Tex. D. 1966 BR TL 5′10″ 195 lbs.

Year	Team	G	AB	H	2B	3B	HR	SB	BA	POS
1919	PHI Hilldales	8	34	6	0	0	0	0	.176	OF
1920		10	40	6	0	0	0	0	.150	OF
1921		37	144	40	10	2	1	11	.278	OF
1922		7	32	10	2	0	0	3	.313	OF
1923	AC Bacharach Giants	14	52	20	3	1	0	1	.385	OF
1924	2 teams AC Bacharach Giants WAS Potomacs									
"	total	43	165	58	4	2	2	4	.352	OF
1925	2 teams WIL Hornets AC Bacharach Giants									
"	total	54	207	74	10	3	6	9	.357	OF
1926	AC Bacharach Giants	35	122	36	6	2	1	2	.295	OF
1927		56	208	57	7	0	2	4	.274	OF
1928			237	80	1	4	5	2	.338	OF
1929		47	183	66	7	3	4	1	.361	OF
1930	Homestead Grays	16	67	23	2	0	1	2	.343	OF
1931	PHI Hilldales	54	214	59	4	2	1	1	.276	OF
1932	No Data Available									
1933	PHI Stars	11	44	12	1	0	0	0	.273	OF
1934		32	118	39	3	1	4	1	.331	OF
1935		56	205	53	2	0	2	1	.259	OF
	(16 years)	(480)	(2072)	(639)	(62)	(20)	(29)	(42)	(.308)	
PLAYOFFS										
1934	PHI Stars	1	3	0	0	0	0	0	.000	OF
WORLD SERIES										
1926	AC Bacharach Giants	10	37	9	0	1	0	5	.243	OF
1927		9	33	5	1	1	1	0	.152	OF
	2 years	19	70	14	1	2	1	5	.200	

Sol White

WHITE, SOL
B. June 12, 1868, Bellaire, Ohio D. 1948, New York, N. Y.
Manager 1904-11.

Year	Team	G	AB	H	2B	3B	HR	SB	BA	POS
1904	PHI Giants	2	8	2	0	0	0	0	.250	1B
1905		2	8	1	1	0	0	0	.125	1B
	2 years	4	16	3	1	0	0	0	.188	

Negro Leagues Pitcher Register

Dan Bankhead

BANKHEAD, DANIEL ROBERT BR TR 6′ 1″ 184 lbs.
B. May 3, 1920, Empire, Ala. D. May 2, 1976, Houston, Tex.
Major leagues 1947-51.
Brother of Sam Bankhead.

Year	Team	W	L	PCT	G	GS	CG	IP	H	BB	SO	ShO	SV
1941	BIR Black Barons	6	1	.857	No further data available								
1942	**2 teams** CLE Buckeyes BIR Black Barons												
″	total	1	0	1.000	2	1	0	7	4			1	
1943	No Record												
1944													
1945													
1946	MEM Red Sox	5	2	.714	8	7	6	63	24	8	36	1	
1947		4	4	.500	9	9	6	54	41	7	24	0	
	(4 years)	16	7	.696	(19)	(17)	(12)	(124)	(69)	(15)	(60)	(2)	

Sam Bankhead

BANKHEAD, SAM BR TR 5′8″ 175 lbs.
B. Sept. 18, 1905, Empire, Ala. D. July 24, 1976, Pittsburgh, PA.
Brother of Dan Bankhead.

Year	Team	W	L	PCT	G	GS	CG	IP	H	BB	SO	ShO	SV
1932	**3 teams** LOU Black Caps BIR Black Barons NAS Elite Giants												
″	total	2	6	.250	No further data available								

Dave Barnhill

BARNHILL, DAVID (Impo, Skinny) 5′ 7″ 155 lbs.
B. Oct. 30, 1914, Greenville, N.C. D. Jan. 8, 1983, Miami, Fla.

Year	Team	W	L	PCT	G	GS	CG	IP	H	BB	SO	ShO	SV
1938	**2 teams** JAC Red Caps IND Clowns												
″	total	1	0	1.000	2		0	9	8			0	0
1939	No Data Available												
1940	Ethio. Clowns	2	0	1.000	3	3	1	13	5	0	20	0	0
1941	NY Cuban Stars	10	5	.667	17	14	13	132	81	9	55	0	0
1942	NY Cubans	4	7	.364	11	10	10	89	77	18	43	1	0
1943		12	3	.800	18	16	13	138	93	25	55	5	0
1944		4	1	.800	6		2	46	33	13	12		
1945		1	3	.250	5		2	23	29	9	21	0	
1946		8	3	.727	10	8	7	72	47	13	19	0	0
1947		4	0	1.000	7			47	39		35	2	
1948		2	0	1.000	2	2	2	18	9		9		0
	(10 years)	(48)	(22)	(.686)	(81)	(53)	(50)	(587)	(421)	(87)	(269)	(8)	(0)
WORLD SERIES													
1947	NY Cubans	1	0	1.000	2	2	1	10	12	3	4	0	0
ALL STAR (1941–43)		1	0	1.000	4	1	0	6	4	4	5	0	0

Bernardo Baro

BARO, BERNARDO BR TR 5′8″ 160 lbs.
B. Cuba D. June 1930, Cuba.

Year	Team	W	L	PCT	G	GS	CG	IP	H	BB	SO	ShO	SV
1915	Almendares	1	0	1.000	1	1	1	7	7	1	1	0	0
1916		0	1	.000	1	1						0	0
1917	Cubans	1	0	1.000	1	1	1	9	5	9	3	0	0
1918		1	0	1.000	1	1	1	9	0			1	0
1919		0	0	—	2	2	0			3	6	0	0
1925	Cuban Stars	0	2	.000	No further data available								
1926		1	1	.500	No further data available								
1927		0	1	.000	No further data available								
	8 years	4	5	.444	(6)	(6)	(3)	(25)	(12)	(13)	(10)	(1)	(0)

Cool Papa Bell

BELL, JAMES THOMAS BB TL 6′ 165 lbs.
B. May 17, 1903, Starkville, Miss. D. Mar. 7, 1991, St. Louis, Mo.
Hall of Fame 1974.

Year	Team	W	L	PCT	G	GS	CG	IP	H	BB	SO	ShO	SV
1922	STL Stars	7	6	.538	No further data available								
1923	No Data Available												
1924		3	1	.750	No further data available								

William Bell

BELL, WILLIAM BR TR 6′ 1″ 205 lbs.
B. Aug. 31, 1897, Lazaca County, Tex. D. Mar. 1969, El Campo, Tex.

Year	Team	W	L	PCT	G	GS	CG	IP	H	BB	SO	ShO	SV
1923	KC Monarchs	0	1	.000	3	2	1	19	12	2	3	0	0
1924		10	2	.833	16	13	8	114	110	26	36	0	0
1925		9	3	.750	17	12	7	95	45	26	40	1	1
1926		16	3	.842	23	18	15	156	100	22	49	1	2
1927		13	6	.684	26	19	14	166	142	31	47	2	0
1928		10	7	.588	25	16	13	164	153	22	71	1	0
1929		17	4	.810	29	19	13	166	146	29	91	0	3
1930		9	3	.750	13	11	11	100	90	13	65	2	1
1931	No Data Available												
1932	**2 teams** DET Wolves Homestead Grays												
″	total	5	1	.833	7	6	4	42	31	4	9	0	0
	(9 years)	(89)	(30)	(.748)	(159)	(116)	(86)	(1022)	(829)	(175)	(411)	(7)	(7)

William Bell *continued*

Year	Team	W	L	PCT	G	GS	CG	IP	H	BB	SO	ShO	SV
PLAYOFFS													
1925	KC Monarchs	1	1	.500	2	2	2	17	11	3	5	0	0
1926		2	1	.667	2	2	1	13	13	6	7	0	0
1929		2	0	1.000	2	2	1	15	15	1	6	0	0
	3 years	5	2	.714	6	6	4	45	39	10	18	0	0
WORLD SERIES													
1924	KC Monarchs	1	0	1.000	3	3	0	26	29	13	5	0	0
1925		0	1	.000	3	2	1	16	19	10	4	0	0
	2 years	1	1	.500	6	5	1	42	48	23	9	0	0

Joe Black

BLACK, JOSEPH BR TR 6′ 2″ 220 lbs.
B. Feb. 8, 1924, Plainfield, N. J.
Major leagues 1952-57.

Year	Team	W	L	PCT	G	GS	CG	IP	H	BB	SO	ShO	SV
1942	BAL Elite Giants	0	1	.000	1	1	0	3	4	2	5	0	0
1944		3	3	.500	9	4		59	58	19	27		
1945		0	1	.000	1	1	0	7	5			0	0
1946		1	3	.250	6	3	2	38	36	3	18	0	0
1947		9	9	.500	26		12	148	174		78	0	
1948		10	5	.667	21				117	36	90		
1949		11	7	.611	23		13	153	164	44	64	1	
1950		8	3	.727	13		8	94	87			1	
	8 years	42	32	.568	100	(9)	(35)	(502)	645	(104)	(282)	(2)	(0)
ALL STAR (1950)		0	0		1	1	0			1	0	0	0

Eugene Bremer

BREMER, EUGENE BR TR 5′8″ 160 lbs.
B. June 16, 1915, New Orleans, La.

Year	Team	W	L	PCT	G	GS	CG	IP	H	BB	SO	ShO	SV
1937	CIN Tigers	4	0	1.000	4			36	25		13	0	0
1938	MEM Red Sox	1	1	.500	4	3	2	21	19	0	4	0	0
1939		0	5	.000	6	6	3	42	37	17	9	0	0
1940		5	2	.714	7	6	6	53	20	16	10	2	0
1941	No Data Available												
1942	CLE Buckeyes	6	1	.857	7	7	7	63	27	0	5	1	0
1943		8	2	.800	11	11	10	84	55	6	11	3	0
1944		10	6	.625	20			113	109	34	44	2	
1945		8	4	.667	15		10	96	78	17	30		
1946		1	0	1.000	2	2	0	8	7	1	2	0	0
1947		1	0	1.000								0	
1948		0	1	.000								0	
	(11 years)	(44)	(22)	(.667)	(76)	(35)	(38)	(516)	(377)	(91)	(128)	(8)	(0)
WORLD SERIES													
1945	CLE Buckeyes	1	0	1.000	1	1	1	9	7	2	1	0	0
1947		0	1	.000	1	1	1	8	12	4	1	0	0
	2 years	1	1	.500	2	2	2	17	19	6	2	0	0
ALL STAR (1940–45)		0	1	.000	4	1	0	3	1	2	8	0	2

Chet Brewer

BREWER, CHESTER ARTHUR BL TR 6′4″ 176 lbs.
B. Jan. 14, 1907, Leavenworth, Kans. D. Mar. 26, 1990, Whittier, Calif.

Year	Team	W	L	PCT	G	GS	CG	IP	H	BB	SO	ShO	SV
1925	KC Monarchs	1	0	1.000	9	5	0	20	21	16	11	0	0
1926		12	1	.923	16	12	8	110	72	40	63	2	0
1927		8	7	.533	20	14	7	103	98	38	46	1	0
1928		7	9	.438	19	15	10	135	130	27	51	0	1
1929		17	3	.850	24	17	16	167	124	35	83	2	1
1930		8	9	.471	18	16	16	154	163	34	78	2	0
1931		2	2	.500	4	4	3	31	14	3	4	2	0
1932	**2 teams** KC Monarchs WAS Pilots												
″	total	5	1	.833	7	5	5	45	32	7	13	3	0
1933	Semipro												
1934	No Data Available												
1935	KC Monarchs	0	1	.000	1	1	0	25	16			0	0
1936	NY Cubans	4	6	.400	12	10	8	86	64	25	40	0	0
1937	KC Monarchs	1	1	.500	1	1	1	9	1			0	0
1938	Latin America												
1939													
1940													
1941	PHI Stars	2	4	.333	8	5	5	58	47	6	6	0	0
1942	Latin America												
1943													
1944													
1945													

Chet Brewer *continued*

Year	Team	W	L	PCT	G	GS	CG	IP	H	BB	SO	ShO	SV
1946	**2 teams** CHI Am. Giants CLE Buckeyes												
″	total	4	6	.400	8	8	6	51	31	0	4	1	0
1947	CLE Buckeyes	12	6	.667					137	29	81	2	0
1948		5	5	.500	15		10	96	118	19	55		
	(15 years)	(88)	(61)	(.591)	(162)	(113)	(95)	(1090)	(1068)	(279)	(535)	(15)	(2)
PLAYOFFS													
1926	KC Monarchs	1	1	.500	4	3	2	22	15	8	12	1	0
1929		1	0	1.000	1	1	1	9	8			0	0
	2 years	2	1	.667	5	4	3	31	23	(8)	(12)	1	0
WORLD SERIES													
1947	CLE Buckeyes	0	1	.000	2	2	1					0	0
ALL STAR (1934–47)		0	0		2	0	0	3	2	2	2	0	1

Dave Brown

BROWN, DAVE BL 0'10″

B. 1896, Tex.

Year	Team	W	L	PCT	G	GS	CG	IP	H	BB	SO	ShO	SV
1920	CHI Am. Giants	10	2	.833	14	13	10	107	51	33	62	1	0
1921		11	3	.786	22	16	13	148	98	26	88	5	2
1922		8	3	.727	18	9	5	75	57	30	61	2	0
1923	NY Lincoln Giants	4	7	.364	12	12	6	62	65	6	25	1	0
1924		12	7	.632	27	18	17	175	155	28	88	1	2
1925		1	0	1.000	1	1	1	9	7	6	8	0	0
	6 years	46	22	.676	94	69	52	576	433	129	332	10	4

Ray Brown

BROWN, RAYMOND BB TR 6′1″ 195 lbs.

B. Feb. 23, 1908, Ashland Grove, Ohio D. 1968, Dayton, Ohio.

Year	Team	W	L	PCT	G	GS	CG	IP	H	BB	SO	ShO	SV
1932	**2 teams** DET Wolves Homestead Grays												
″	total	7	5	.583	15	11	10	91	63	7	7	1	0
1933	Homestead Grays	6	1	.857	8	6	6	47	41	5	18	0	0
1934		3	1	.750	4	4	4	19	8	2	12	0	0
1935		12	3	.800	18	13	12	120	82	34	45	2	0
1936		0	1	.000	2	1	1	9	9	0	4	0	0
1937	WAS Homestead Grays	3	2	.600	6	4	4	41	31	2	13	0	0
1938		7	0	1.000	9	7	6	36	28			3	0
1939		4	1	.800	6	5	5	48	34	4	3	0	0
1940		19	2	.905	23	17	17	168	115	20	29	4	0
1941		6	5	.545	18	13	10	108	105	21	21	0	3
1942		13	4	.765	18	13	11	123	88	32	46	2	0
1943		6	1	.857	12	9	6	70	57	21	25	1	0
1944		12	3	.800	21		13	134	128	23	42	3	
1945		3	1	.750	4	3	0	20		1	6	0	0
	14 years	101	30	.771	164	(106)	105	1034	(789)	(172)	(271)	16	(3)
PLAYOFFS													
1939	WAS Homestead Grays	1	0	1.000	1	1	1	9	7	2	6	1	0
1941		1	0	1.000	1	1	1	9	2				
	2 years	2	0	1.000	2	2	2	18	9	(2)	(6)	(1)	(0)
WORLD SERIES													
1937	WAS Homestead Grays	0	0	—	1	0	0	4	5	2	2	0	1
1942		0	1	.000	1	1	1	9	16	2	7	0	0
1943		2	0	1.000	4	1	0	12	5	5	6	0	0
1944		1	0	1.000	1	1	1	13	18	1	13	1	0
1945		0	1	.000	1	1	1	9	10	1	1	0	0
	5 years	3	2	.600	8	4	3	47	54	11	29	1	1
ALL STAR (1935–40)		0	0		2	1	0	5	2	0	1	0	0

Bill Byrd

BYRD, BILL BB TR 6′1″ 200 lbs.

B. July 15, 1907, Canton, Ga. D. Jan. 4, 1991, Philadelphia, Pa.

Year	Team	W	L	PCT	G	GS	CG	IP	H	BB	SO	ShO	SV
1933	NAS Elite Giants	3	6	.333	13	9	7	70	60	4	13	0	3
1934	CLE Red Sox	1	6	.143	7	6	3	40	43	4	9	0	0
1935	COL Elite Giants	2	3	.400	8	4	2	25	14	3	11	0	0
1936	WAS Elite Giants	8	4	.667	11	8	6	79	54	4	14	2	0
1937		5	5	.500	13	10	6	65	44	8	5	0	0
1938	BAL Elite Giants	6	3	.667	7	6	3	46	45	1	7	0	0
1939		9	4	.692	14	13	13	98	103	11	25	0	0
1940	No Data Available												
1941	BAL Elite Giants	7	6	.538	16	11	7	82	53	12	36	1	2
1942		15	4	.789	22	17	13	147	117	31	75	2	1
1943	**2 teams** BAL Elite Giants PHI Stars												
″	total	9	5	.643	16	12	10	119	104	29	57	1	0

Bill Byrd *continued*

Year	Team	W	L	PCT	G	GS	CG	IP	H	BB	SO	ShO	SV
1944	BAL Elite Giants	10	7	.588	19		13	124	103	20	75	2	
1945		6	3	.667	11	9	8	83	59	9	8	0	1
1946		3	7	.300	14	7	7	74	50	21	7	0	1
1947		9	6	.600	18		13	134	124		68	0	
1948		11	6	.647	20				124	23	82		
1949		12	3	.800	25		11	144	145	30	57	0	
1950		0	0	—	1		0	2				0	0
	(17 years)	(116)	(78)	(.598)	(235)	(112)	(122)	(1332)	(1242)	(210)	(549)	(8)	(8)
PLAYOFFS													
1939	BAL Elite Giants	2	1	.667	3	3	3	27	23	0	6	0	0
ALL STAR (1936–46)		1	1	.500	8	2	0	10	12	6	9	0	0

Roy Campanella

CAMPANELLA, ROY (Campy) BR TR 5′ 9½″ 190 lbs.
B. Nov. 19, 1921, Philadelphia, Pa. D. June 26, 1993, Woodland Hills, Calif.
Major leagues 1948-57.
Hall of Fame 1969.

Year	Team	W	L	PCT	G	GS	CG	IP	H	BB	SO	ShO	SV
1945	BAL Elite Giants	1	0	1.000	1	1	1	9	5		13	0	0

Rev Cannady

CANNADY, WALTER BR

Manager 1938

Year	Team	W	L	PCT	G	GS	CG	IP	H	BB	SO	ShO	SV
1922	CLE Tate Stars	3	3	.500	No further data available								

Oscar Charleston

CHARLESTON, OSCAR MCKINLEY BL TL 6′1″ 185 lbs.
B. Oct. 14, 1896, Indianapolis, Ind. D. Oct. 6, 1954, Philadelphia, Pa.
Manager 1932-38, 1940-41.
Hall of Fame 1976.

Year	Team	W	L	PCT	G	GS	CG	IP	H	BB	SO	ShO	SV
1915	IND ABCs	0	1	.000	2	2	0	5	4				
1917		0	0	—	3	1	0	7	2	12	9	0	0
1918		0	0	—	1	0	0	2				0	0
1926	HBG Giants	0	1	.000	No further data available								
1933	PIT Crawfords	0	0	—									0
	5 years	0	2	.000	(6)	(3)	(0)	(14)	(6)	(12)	(9)	(0)	(0)

Phil Cockrell

COCKRELL, PHIL BR TR
B. 1898, Augusta, Ga. D. Apr. 7, 1951, Philadelphia, Pa.
Manager 1930.

Year	Team	W	L	PCT	G	GS	CG	IP	H	BB	SO	ShO	SV
1918	PHI Hilldales	3	1	.750	5	2	1			1	3	0	0
1919		5	2	.714	7	7	7	46	20			0	0
1920		2	2	.500	6	5	5	47	39			0	0
1921		9	6	.600	17	12	10	87	63	12	34	1	0
1922		3	0	1.000	4	4	3					2	0
1923		2	4	.333	6	4	4	39	51	0	2	0	0
1924		10	1	.909	16	15	8	104	76	23	33	0	0
1925		13	3	.813	20	15	13	141	116	36	47	1	0
1926		10	3	.769	16	16	12	119	102	35	52	1	0
1927		11	13	.458	26	24	15	61	71	15	31	1	0
1928		8	12	.400	24	17	4	138	117	16	18	0	0
1929		2	3	.400	8	5	3	31	18	8	9	0	0
1930		1	5	.167	9	6	6	54	71	20	21	0	0
1931		5	0	1.000	6	2	2	48	17	2	2	1	0
1932	**2 teams** PHI Hilldales AC Bacharach Giants												
″	total	2	7	.222	10	7	5	62	50			0	0
1933	AC Bacharach Giants	0	0	—	1	0	0	9	11			0	0
1934	PHI Stars	1	4	.200	8	5	2	34	35			0	0
	17 years	87	66	.569	189	146	100	(1020)	(857)	(168)	(252)	7	0
WORLD SERIES													
1924	PHI Hilldales	0	1	.000	2	2	1	10	11	4	6	0	0
1925		1	1	.500	2	2	2	17	18	8	10	0	0
	2 years	1	2	.333	4	4	3	27	29	12	16	0	0

Francisco Coimbre

COIMBRE, FRANCISCO (Pancho) BR TR
B. Jan. 29, 1909, Coamo, Puerto Rico D. Nov. 8, 1989, Ponce, Puerto Rico.

Year	Team	W	L	PCT	G	GS	CG	IP	H	BB	SO	ShO	SV
1943	NY Cubans	0	1	.000	1	1	1	9	8	1	2	0	0

Andy Cooper

COOPER, ANDY (Lefty) TL 6′ 1″ 210 lbs.
B. Mar. 4, 1896, Waco, Tex. D. June 10, 1941, Waco, Tex.
Manager 1934-41.

Year	Team	W	L	PCT	G	GS	CG	IP	H	BB	SO	ShO	SV
1920	DET Stars	0	2	.000	8	3	1	37	31	19	10	0	1
1921		5	9	.357	24	17	9	117	125	13	29	1	0
1922		14	5	.737	25	22	16	153	132	21	43	4	0

Andy Cooper *continued*

Year	Team	W	L	PCT	G	GS	CG	IP	H	BB	SO	ShO	SV
1923		15	8	.652	37	20	14	173	147	43	60	1	5
1924		12	5	.706	31	13	7	128	124	33	76	1	6
1925		12	1	.923	31	12	6	137	51	25	47	1	6
1926		12	8	.600	36	22	12	178	178	21	48	1	4
1927		7	3	.700	13	11	6	80	89	3	34	0	1
1928	KC Monarchs	13	7	.650	27	19	11	144	146	53	18	2	1
1929		13	3	.813	24	15	11	147	146	22	61	2	4
1930	DET Stars	15	6	.714	27	20	16	161	161	10	50	2	2
	11 years	118	57	.674	283	174	109	1455	1330	263	476	15	30
PLAYOFFS													
1929	KC Monarchs	1	0	1.000	1	1	1	9	4	2	7	0	0
1930	DET Stars	0	0	—	2	0	0	2	7	1	1	0	1
1937	KC Monarchs	1	0	1.000	1	1	1	17				0	0
	3 years	2	0	1.000	4	2	2	28	(11)	(3)	(8)	0	1
ALL STAR (1936)		0	0		1	0	0			0	0	0	

Sug Cornelius

CORNELIUS, WILLIAM McKINLEY 5′ 7″ 175 lbs.
B. Sept. 4, 1908, Atlanta, Ga. D. Oct. 30, 1989, Chicago, Ill.

Year	Team	W	L	PCT	G	GS	CG	IP	H	BB	SO	ShO	SV
1928	NAS Elite Giants												
1929	**2 teams** NAS Elite Giants MEM Red Sox												
″	total	4	7	.364	14	8	6	65	69	16	35	0	
1930	**2 teams** MEM Red Sox BIR Black Barons												
″	total	7	11	.389	29	18	9	133	124	55	60		
1931	MEM Red Sox	2	1	.667	3	3	1	23	6	2	1		
1932	BIR Black Barons												
1933	CHI Am. Giants	5	4	.556	11	12	6	53	59				
1934	No Data Available												
1935		4	4	.500	8	4	3	39	20	9	13		
1936		2	3	.400		6	4	43	48	14	33		
1937		7	4	.636	15	10	8	94	48	15	49		
1938		7	4	.636	19	10	8	87	58	15	55		
1939		5	5	.500	15	10	2	70	44	14	40		
1940	Mexico												
1941	CHI Am. Giants	3	6	.333	9	4	3	28	15	3	7		
1942	**2 teams** CHI Am. Giants CLE Buckeyes												
″	total	0	5	.000	No further data available								
1943	CHI Am. Giants	0	5	.000				91	107	19	36		
1944	Mexico												
1945	CHI Am. Giants	5	4	.556	No further data available								
1946	No Data Available												
	(8 years)	(51)	(63)	(.447)	(123)	(85)	(50)	(726)	(598)	(162)	(329)	(0)	
PLAYOFFS													
1937	CHI Am. Giants	0	1	.000	1	1	1						
WORLD SERIES													
1937	CHI Am. Giants	0	0	—	1	1	0	4	10	2	1	0	0
ALL STAR (1935–38)		1	1	.500	3	2	0	3	5	1	3	0	

Rube Currie

CURRIE, REUBEN BR TR 6′4″ 195 lbs.
B. 1898, Kansas City, Mo. D. 1969, Chicago, Ill.

Year	Team	W	L	PCT	G	GS	CG	IP	H	BB	SO	ShO	SV
1920	KC Monarchs	10	12	.455	27	19	13	188	166	31	89	1	2
1921		12	10	.545	24	16	14	140	118	24	57	0	0
1922		12	7	.632	22	20	16	179	190	40	92	1	0
1923		14	7	.667	26	18	16	187	160	30	66	1	0
1924	PHI Hilldales	1	5	.167	10	6	2	34	28	7	9	0	0
1925		13	1	.929	22	17	11	139	128	14	44	0	2
1926	CHI Am. Giants	8	3	.727	17	13	7	108	114	22	42	2	1
1927		4	5	.444	13	13	8	96	94	13	22	2	0
1928	KC Monarchs	6	6	.500	20	13	7	95	99	17	21	1	0
	9 years	80	56	.588	181	135	94	1166	1097	198	442	8	5
PLAYOFFS													
1926	CHI Am. Giants	2	0	1.000	3	2	1	19	12	5	4	0	0
1935	NY Cubans	1	1	.500	No further data available								
	2 years	3	1	.750	(3)	(2)	(1)	(19)	(12)	(5)	(4)	(0)	(0)
WORLD SERIES													
1924	PHI Hilldales	1	1	.500	3	1	1	16	12	2	3	0	0
1925		2	0	1.000	2	2	2	21	16	2	10	0	0

Rube Currie *continued*

Year	Team	W	L	PCT	G	GS	CG	IP	H	BB	SO	ShO	SV
1926	CHI Am. Giants	1	1	.500	3	3	1	21	27	1	11	0	0
1927		0	0	—	1	0	0	2	0	0	0	0	0
	4 years	4	2	.667	9	6	4	60	55	5	24	0	0

Cherokee Davis

DAVIS, JOHN
B. Feb. 6, 1918, Newark, N.J. D. Nov. 17, 1982, Ft. Lauderdale, Fla. BR TR 6′3″ 215 lbs.

Year	Team	W	L	PCT	G	GS	CG	IP	H	BB	SO	ShO	SV
1944	NWK Eagles	3	0	1.000									2
1946		1	1	.500	No further data available								
1947		1	0	1.000	No further data available								
1950	HOU Eagles	1	0	1.000	No further data available								
	4 years	6	1	.857									(2)

Roosevelt Davis

DAVIS, ROOSEVELT

Year	Team	W	L	PCT	G	GS	CG	IP	H	BB	SO	ShO	SV
1924	STL Stars	11	3	.786	29	14	9	122	130	22	36	0	1
1925		11	5	.688	26	18	11	139	99	22	49	2	0
1926		6	5	.545	26	12	1	57	70	13	14	0	4
1927		10	10	.500	35	18	9	181	79	34	69	0	2
1928		11	1	.917	26	11	6	94	94	11	25	0	0
1929		6	11	.353	34	16	9	140	143	24	45	1	0
1930		8	3	.727	18	12	7	95	92	24	47	1	1
1931	No Data Available												
1932													
1933	COL Elite Giants	3	3	.500	9	6	4	40	50	6	12	0	0
1935	PIT Crawfords												
1940	BAL Elite Giants	1	0	1.000	2	1	0	8	6			0	
1941	No Data Available												
1942													
1943	CIN Clowns	1	0	1.000	1	1	1	9	3		14	1	0
	(10 years)	(68)	(41)	(.624)	(206)	(109)	(57)	(885)	(766)	(156)	(311)	(5)	(8)

Leon Day

DAY, LEON
B. Oct. 30, 1916, Alexandria, Va. D. Mar. 13, 1995, Baltimore, Md. BR TR 5′8″ 175 lbs.
Hall of Fame 1995.

Year	Team	W	L	PCT	G	GS	CG	IP	H	BB	SO	ShO	SV
1934	BAL Black Sox	0	1	.000	2					1	1	0	0
1935	BKN Eagles	9	2	.818	12	10	8	79	60	7	38	0	1
1936	NWK Eagles	3	4	.429	7	4	4	34	28	4	24	0	0
1937		6	0	1.000	8	6	6	55	36	0	16	0	0
1938		2	1	.667	4	4	2	9	3	1	4	1	0
1939		14	7	.667	25	20	14	130	110	16	54	3	0
1940	No Data Available												
1941	NWK Eagles	3	0	1.000	3	1	0	16	8				
1942		6	2	.750	9	9	8	81	39	18	42	1	0
1943		4	3	.571	10	8	3	46	45	10	27	0	0
1944	US Army												
1945													
1946	NWK Eagles	13	4	.765	19	18	16	141	97	34	65	3	0
1947	Mexico												
1948													
1949	BAL Elite Giants	7	5	.583	14	9	5	110	25	51	0	0	
	(11 years)	(67)	(29)	(.698)	(113)	(89)	(66)	(701)	(451)	(142)	(271)	(8)	(1)
PLAYOFFS													
1939	NWK Eagles	0	1	.000	1	1	0	5					
WORLD SERIES													
1937	NWK Eagles	1	0	1.000	2	2	0					0	0
ALL STAR (1933–46)		1	1	.500	2	1	0	20	9	6	15	0	2

Martin Dihigo

DIHIGO, MARTIN
B. May 25, 1905, Matanzas, Cuba D. May 20, 1971, Cienfuegos, Cuba. BR TR 6′1″ 190 lbs.
Hall of Fame 1977.

Year	Team	W	L	PCT	G	GS	CG	IP	H	BB	SO	ShO	SV
1923	Cuban Stars	1	0	1.000	No further data available								
1924		2	2	.500	5	3	3	28	9	0	8	0	0
1925		3	3	.500	8	6	6	53	52	16	12	0	1
1926		2	0	1.000	2	1	1	9	3	1	6	0	0
1927		1	0	1.000	No further data available								
1928	Homestead Grays	1	1	.500	2	1	1	9	9	0	10	0	0
1929	PHI Hilldales	4	2	.667	2	2	2	16	11	2	5	0	0
1930	NY Cubans	0	3	.000	3							0	0
1931	PHI Hilldales	1	2	.333	4	3	3	27	19	2	6	0	0
1935	NY Cubans	7	3	.700	14	9	9	94	72	25	33	0	0

Martin Dihigo *continued*

Year	Team	W	L	PCT	G	GS	CG	IP	H	BB	SO	ShO	SV
1936		5	4	.556	9	8	7	67	54	12	39	0	0
1945	Cuban Stars	0	1	.000	1	1	0					0	0
	12 years	27	21	.563	(50)	(34)	(32)	(303)	(229)	(58)	(119)	(0)	(1)
ALL STAR (1935–45)		0	1	.000	2	0	0			1	2	0	0

Dizzy Dismukes

DISMUKES, WILLIAM BR TR
B. Mar. 15, 1890, Birmingham, Ala. D. June 30, 1961, Campbell, Ohio.

Year	Team	W	L	PCT	G	GS	CG	IP	H	BB	SO	ShO	SV
1910	WB Sprudels												
1911	No Data Available												
1912	STL Giants	1	0	1.000	1	1	1	9	4	1	3		
1913	BKN Royal Giants	1	0	1.000	1	1	1	9	6				
1914		2	4	.333	6	6	4	40	52	12	19	1	0
1915	IND ABCs	16	6	.727	23	23	20	205	125	49	52	4	0
1916		6	6	.500	13	10	9	99	65	24	29	1	0
1917		0	1	.000	1	1	0			2	4	0	0
1918		0	1	.000	1	1	1	9	7			0	0
1919	No Data Available												
1920	IND ABCs	12	6	.667	29	23	12	138	72	35	37	0	0
1921		1	2	.333	6	4	3	39	23	4	4	0	0
1922	PIT Keystones	0	1	.000	2	1	0	4	8	4	5	0	0
1923	IND ABCs	6	4	.600	12	12	8	92	71	19	8	0	0
1924	**2 teams** IND ABCs BIR Black Barons												
″	total	3	8	.273	13	10	5	72	79	16	20	1	0
1925	**2 teams** IND ABCs MEM Red Sox												
″	total	6	4	.600	16	7	4	83	76	16	24	2	0
1926	STL Stars	1	0	1.000	3	3	0	16	23	1	7	0	0
1927	No Data Available												
1928													
1929													
1930													
1931	CIN Buckeyes	0	1	.000	1	1	0					0	0
	(15 years)	(55)	(44)	(.556)	(128)	(104)	(68)	(815)	(611)	(183)	(212)	(9)	(0)
PLAYOFFS													
1916	IND	1	0	1.000	1	1	0	7	11	3	0	0	0
WORLD SERIES													
1914	BKN Royal Giants	0	1	.000	1	1	1	8	13	4	2	0	0

Bill Drake

DRAKE, WILLIAM P (Plunk) BR TR 6′ 209 lbs.
B. June 8, 1895, Sedalia, Mo. D. Oct. 30, 1977, St. Louis, Mo.

Year	Team	W	L	PCT	G	GS	CG	IP	H	BB	SO	ShO	SV
1916	STL Giants	0	0	—	1								
1920		9	12	.429	24	22	18	181	196	50	72	1	1
1921		20	10	.667	33	26	22	231	204	66	123	3	4
1922	KC Monarchs	8	8	.500	20	14	5	96	108	32	46	0	0
1923		9	7	.563	19	16	11	128	92	31	24	0	0
1924		10	8	.556	25	19	11	140	135	57	60	0	1
1925		9	5	.643	22	13	8	113	96	33	62	3	0
1926	DAY Marcos	6	6	.500	17	9	9	86	55	20	20	0	0
1927	DET Stars	8	6	.571	16	14	8	115	110	44	35	0	0
1928	No Data Available												
1929													
1930	STL Stars	1	0	1.000	1	1		8	12	3	2	0	0
	(10 years)	(80)	(62)	(.563)	(178)	(134)	(92)	(1098)	(1008)	(336)	(444)	(7)	(6)
PLAYOFFS													
1925	KC Monarchs	0	1	.000	2	1	1	9	4	6	7	0	0
WORLD SERIES													
1924	KC Monarchs	0	1	.000	4	0	0	14	14	5	5	0	0
1925		0	2	.000	2	1	1	11	16	3	6	0	0
	2 years	0	3	.000	6	1	1	25	30	8	11	0	0

Red Farrell

FARRELL, LUTHER BL TL 6′ 1″ 190 lbs.

Year	Team	W	L	PCT	G	GS	CG	IP	H	BB	SO	ShO	SV
1920	**3 teams** NY Lincoln Giants STL Giants CHI Giants												
″	total	3	8	.273	12	10	7	68	45	16	26	0	
1921	CHI Giants	3	6	.333	14	10	6	73	86	22	18	0	
1923	CHI Am. Giants	1	0	1.000	2	1	1	9	11	2	2	0	
1924	Semipro												
1925	**2 teams** NY Lincoln Giants AC Bacharach Giants												
″	total	3	7	.300	13	9	7	74	72	12	34	0	
1926	AC Bacharach Giants	1	2	.333	4	3	2	18	17				
1927		17	13	.567	33	22	14					2	

Red Farrell *continued*

		W	L	PCT	G	GS	CG	IP	H	BB	SO	ShO	SV
1928		9	10	.474	26	20	16	155	140	15	37		2
1929		0	2	.000	3	3	2	16	24	2	7	0	
1930	NY Lincoln Giants	9	1	.900	13	11	9	94	98	24	39		
1931	No Data Available												
1932	NY Black Yankees	0	3	.000	5	1						0	
1933	No Data Available												
1934	AC Bacharach Giants	1	3	.250	6	2	1	14	12	3	2	0	
	(11 years)	(47)	(55)	(.461)	(131)	(92)	(65)	(521)	(505)	(96)	(165)	(2)	(2)
PLAYOFFS													
1930	NY Lincoln Giants	0	1	.000	3	3	1	10	8	3	2	0	0
WORLD SERIES													
1927	AC Bacharach Giants	2	2	.500	5	4	4	38	36	19	23	0	0

Bill Foster

FOSTER, WILLIAM HENDRICK BB TL 6′1″ 196 lbs.
B. June 12, 1904, Calvert, Tex. D. Sept. 16, 1978, Lorman, Miss.
Brother of Rube Foster.
Hall of Fame 1996.

		W	L	PCT	G	GS	CG	IP	H	BB	SO	ShO	SV
1923	**2 teams** MEM Red Sox CHI Am. Giants												
″	total	5	2	.714	11	8	6	64	34	14	38	1	0
1924	**2 teams** MEM Red Sox CHI Am. Giants												
″	total	6	1	.857	11	8	5	59	34	19	38	3	0
1925	**2 teams** CHI Am. Giants BIR Black Barons												
″	total	7	1	.875	14	10	7	87	24	20	40	2	0
1926	CHI Am. Giants	11	4	.733	20	14	10	137	86	37	72	4	1
1927		21	3	.875	29	21	18	199	164	21	50	5	0
1928		14	10	.583	30	21	20	208	85	55	118	2	0
1929		11	7	.611	26	18	15	152	60	39	75	3	3
1930		16	10	.615	34	20	18	199	173	51	134	3	3
1931	**2 teams** Homestead Grays KC Monarchs												
″	total	9	2	.818	14	11	11	103	35	10	40	3	0
1932	CHI Am. Giants	15	8	.652	28	23	23	198	100	61	49	4	3
1933		8	4	.667	17	12	10	96	55	8	52	1	2
1934		3	2	.600	7	4	4	36	29	10	6	1	0
1935		4	2	.667	7	4	3	36	28	11	10	1	0
1936	PIT Crawfords	2	2	.500	4	4	3	24	18	9	4	0	0
1937	CHI Am. Giants	5	4	.556	13	14	8	61	47	5	8	1	0
	15 years	137	62	.688	265	192	161	1659	972	370	734	34	12
PLAYOFFS													
1926	CHI Am. Giants	2	2	.500	5	4	3	32	13	8	7	2	0
1927		2	0	1.000	3	2	2	18	11	3	11	0	0
1932		2	0	1.000	2								0
1934		0	1	.000	1	1	1						0
	4 years	6	3	.667	11	(7)	(6)	(50)	(24)	(11)	(18)	(2)	0
WORLD SERIES													
1926	CHI Am. Giants	2	0	1.000	4	3	3	28	26	13	19	1	0
1927		2	2	.500	4	2	2	24	28	10	13	0	0
1937	KC Monarchs	1	0	1.000	1	0	0	3	2	0	2	0	0
	3 years	5	2	.714	9	5	5	55	56	23	34	1	0
ALL STAR (1933–34)		1	1	.500	3	3	1			4	6	0	0

Rube Foster

FOSTER, ANDREW BR TR
B. Sept. 17, 1878, Calvert, Tex. D. Dec. 9, 1930, Kankakee, Ill.
Manager 1910-1926.
Brother of Bill Foster.
Hall of Fame 1981.

		W	L	PCT	G	GS	CG	IP	H	BB	SO	ShO	SV
1905	PHI Giants	0	0	—	1	1	1	13	3	0	8	0	0
1906		2	0	1.000	3	3	3	28	28	7	13	1	0
1908	No Data Available												
1910	CHI Leland Giants	2	0	1.000	3	3	3	30	25	4	13	0	0
1911	CHI Am. Giants	1	0	1.000	1	0	0	8	10	0	4	0	0
1912		1	0	1.000	2	2	2	21		6	12	0	0
1913		2	2	.500	4	4	4	38	39	9	18		0
1914		5	8	.385	14							2	0
1915		1	3	.250	5	4	4	36	23	9	14	0	0
1916	No Data Available												
1917	CHI Am. Giants	0	1	.000	1	1	1		7	7	0	0	0
	(9 years)	(14)	(14)	(.500)	(34)	(18)	(18)	(174)	(135)	(42)	(82)	(3)	(0)

Rube Foster *continued*

PLAYOFFS

Year	Team	W	L	PCT	G	GS	CG	IP	H	BB	SO	ShO	SV
1903	Cuban X-Giants	1	0	1.000	1	1	1	9	6	3	0	0	0
1904	PHI Giants	2	0	1.000	2	2	2	18	10	4	24	0	0
1908	CHI Leland Giants	0	1	.000	1	1	1	9	12	3	2	0	0
	3 years	3	1	.750	4	4	4	36	28	10	26	0	0

Josh Gibson

GIBSON, JOSHUA BR TR 6′2″ 217 lbs.
B. Dec. 21, 1911, Buena Vista, Ga. D. Jan. 20, 1947, Pittsburgh, Pa.
Hall of Fame 1972.

Year	Team	W	L	PCT	G	GS	CG	IP	H	BB	SO	ShO	SV
1933	Homestead Grays	0	0	—									1

Rats Henderson

HENDERSON, ARTHUR CHAUNCEY BR TR 5′7″ 180 lbs.
B. Aug. 29, 1897, Richmond, Va. D. Wilmington, Del.

Year	Team	W	L	PCT	G	GS	CG	IP	H	BB	SO	ShO	SV
1923	AC Bacharach Giants	8	6	.571	16	12	10	96	75	2	7	0	2
1924		8	1	.889	11	10	8	78	55	5	23	1	0
1925		14	10	.583	29	23	20	206	104	38	80	2	1
1926		7	3	.700	11	10	9	88	70	9	10	1	0
1927		19	7	.731	30	20	13	18	12	0	6	2	1
1928		8	4	.667	15	11	7	82	59	6	16	0	0
1929		5	6	.455	16	9	8	70	84	19	19	1	0
	7 years	69	37	.651	128	95	75	638	459	79	161	7	4

WORLD SERIES

Year	Team	W	L	PCT	G	GS	CG	IP	H	BB	SO	ShO	SV
1926	AC Bacharach Giants	1	1	.500	5	3	3	31	30	10	19	1	0

Logan Hensley

HENSLEY, LOGAN (Eggie, Slap)

Year	Team	W	L	PCT	G	GS	CG	IP	H	BB	SO	ShO	SV
1922	STL Stars	0	1	.000	2	1	0	19	20	9	11	0	0
1923		0	3	.000	6	3	0	10	26	6	2	0	0
1924	**2 teams** STL Stars CLE Browns												
″	total	5	5	.500	13	7	5	61	83	19	30	0	0
1925	STL Stars	6	3	.667	18	10	4	82	70	40	41	0	0
1926		12	6	.667	27	17	9	146	132	36	52	0	0
1927		0	3	.000	5	4	1	15	10	3	4	0	0
1928		13	5	.722	30	17	8	145	133	53	75	2	2
1929		14	6	.700	31	19	10	148	148	53	56	2	2
1930		17	6	.739	27	22	15	179	177	47	61	0	1
1931		3	1	.750	6	3	2	21	11	3	8	0	0
	10 years	70	39	.642	165	103	54	826	810	269	340	4	5

PLAYOFFS

Year	Team	W	L	PCT	G	GS	CG	IP	H	BB	SO	ShO	SV
1930	STL Stars	1	1	.500	2	2	1	17	13	5	10	0	0

Bill Holland

HOLLAND, ELVIS WILLIAM BB TR 5′ 8″ 175 lbs.
B. Feb. 28, 1901, Indianapolis, Ind. D. Dec. 1973, New York, N. Y.

Year	Team	W	L	PCT	G	GS	CG	IP	H	BB	SO	ShO	SV
1917	IND ABCs	0	1	.000	1								
1920	DET Stars	12	7	.632	27	20	14	175	146	43	84	1	2
1921	**2 teams** DET Stars CHI Am. Giants												
″	total	13	12	.520	32	22	20	190	169	38	104	1	0
1922	DET Stars	16	13	.552	35	23	18	204	182	25	95	2	1
1923	NY Lincoln Giants	2	5	.286	10	6	3	31	35	3	13	0	1
1924		8	5	.615	16	12	10	109	100	14	26	0	0
1925	BKN Royal Giants	3	5	.375	10	7	5	51	74	14	33	0	0
1926		0	3	.000	3	3	2	16	12	3	8	0	0
1927		3	4	.429	7	5	4	35	44	1	5	0	0
1928		1	1	.500	2	1	1	17	22	1	12	0	0
1929	NY Lincoln Giants	13	7	.650	18	16	15	124	122	19	53	1	0
1930	NY Black Yankees	12	1	.923	14	10	10	86	91	31	59	0	0
1931		2	4	.333	7	6	6	47	7	2	6	0	0
1932		6	1	.857	9	9	9	83	39	10	19	2	0
1933	No Data Available												
1934	NY Black Yankees	0	3	.000	3	3	2	16	9	1	7	0	0
1936		4	2	.667	5	5	5	45	43	10	22	0	0
1937		1	1	.500	3	3	2	23	23	3	2	0	0
1938		2	3	.400	10	6	5	59	52	2	15	0	1
1939	No Data Available												
1940	NY Black Yankees	1	3	.250	4	4	2	25	33	9	12	0	0
1941		0	0	—	2	1	0		5	5	1	0	0
	(20 years)	(99)	(81)	(.550)	(218)	(162)	(133)	(1336)	(1208)	(234)	(576)	(7)	(5)

PLAYOFFS

Year	Team	W	L	PCT	G	GS	CG	IP	H	BB	SO	ShO	SV
1930	NY Black Yankees	2	2	.500	4	4	3	26	21			0	0
ALL STAR (1939)		0	0		1	0	0			1	0	0	0

Sammy T. Hughes

HUGHES, SAMUEL THOMAS BR TR 6′3″ 190 lbs.
B. Oct. 20, 1910, Louisville, Ky. D. 1973, Los Angeles, Calif.

Year	Team	W	L	PCT	G	GS	CG	IP	H	BB	SO	ShO	SV
1931	LOU Black Caps	0	1	.000	No further data available								

Connie Johnson

JOHNSON, CLIFFORD BR TR 6′ 4″ 200 lbs.
B. Dec. 27, 1922, Stone Mountain, Ga.
Major leagues 1953-1958.

Year	Team	W	L	PCT	G	GS	CG	IP	H	BB	SO	ShO	SV
1941	KC Monarchs	2	2	.500	2	0	0	8	3	0	4	0	
1942		3	0	1.000	No further data available								
1943	Military Service												
1944													
1945													
1946	KC Monarchs	9	3	.750	13	7	6	85	33	9	18	1	
1947		1	1	.500	3	1	1	10	5			0	
	(4 years)	15	6	.714	(18)	(8)	(7)	(103)	(41)	(9)	(22)	(1)	

Stuart Jones

JONES, STUART (Slim) BL TL 6′6″ 185 lbs.
B. May 6, 1913, Baltimore, Md. D. Dec. 1938, Baltimore, Md.

Year	Team	W	L	PCT	G	GS	CG	IP	H	BB	SO	ShO	SV
1933	BAL Black Sox	4	2	.667	8	4	2	31	16	10	31	0	0
1934	PHI Stars	22	3	.880	29	20	19	180	109	14	83	4	0
1935		4	10	.286	19	10	7	86	34	13	13	0	0
1936		3	3	.500	11	5	2	18	11	11	11	0	0
1937		1	0	1.000	1	1	0	5				0	0
1938		2	1	.667	4	1	1				0	0	0
	6 years	36	19	.655	72	41	31	(320)	(170)	(48)	(138)	4	0

Jimmy Lyons

LYONS, JIMMY BL TR 5′8″ 175 lbs.
B. Chicago, Ill.

Year	Team	W	L	PCT	G	GS	CG	IP	H	BB	SO	ShO	SV
1917	IND Jewell's ABCs	0	0	—	1	0	0			4	1	0	0
1920	CHI Am. Giants	1	1	.500	No further data available								
	2 years	1	1	.500	(1)	(0)	(0)			(4)	(1)	(0)	(0)

Max Manning

MANNING, MAX BL TR 6′4″ 180 lbs.
B. Nov. 18, 1918, Rome, Ga.

Year	Team	W	L	PCT	G	GS	CG	IP	H	BB	SO	ShO	SV
1939	NWK Eagles	4	3	.571	9	5	3	35	19	3	20	1	1
1940		9	3	.750	15	11	6	81	36	4	14	0	1
1941		5	5	.500	16	11	5	82	58	14	21	1	0
1942		7	7	.500	16	11	10	91	55	15	24	1	0
1943	Military Service												
1944													
1945													
1946	NWK Eagles	10	0	1.000	13	9	9	86	39	0	10	0	0
1947		15	6	.714	23		18	169	153		104	0	
1948		10	4	.714	16				95	35	73		
1949		8	4	.667	16		8	94	87	16	28	1	
	(8 years)	68	32	.680	124	(47)	(59)	(638)	542	(87)	294	(4)	(2)
PLAYOFFS													
1939	NWK Eagles	0	1	.000							5		
WORLD SERIES													
1946	NWK Eagles	1	1	.500	3	2	2	17	16	6	15	0	0
ALL STAR (1947)		0	1	.000	1	1	0	2	5	2	3	0	0

Verdell Mathis

MATHIS, VERDELL (Lefty) BL TL 5′11″ 150 lbs.
B. Nov. 18, 1921, Crawfordville, Ark.

Year	Team	W	L	PCT	G	GS	CG	IP	H	BB	SO	ShO	SV
1940	MEM Red Sox	2	2	.500	4	3	2	24	15	2	16	0	0
1941		1	2	.333	5	3	2	19	22	4	12	0	0
1942		7	5	.583	14	8	6	74	37	8	20	2	0
1943		7	5	.583	18	15	10	102	88	12	31	1	0
1944		9	9	.500	21			130	130	35	86	1	
1945		10	11	.476	25		18	168	162	32	85		
1946		2	6	.250				35	22	2	6	1	1
1947		5	5	.500	15			75	77		38	1	1
1948		9	12	.429	31		10	153	196	48	82		
1949		9	11	.450	23		12	155	166		70	0	
	10 years	61	68	.473	(156)	(29)	(60)	935	915	(143)	446	(6)	(2)
ALL STAR (1944–45)		2	0	1.000	2	2	0	3	3	1	4	0	0

Leroy Matlock

MATLOCK, LEROY BL TL 5′10″ 180 lbs.
B. Mar. 12, 1907, Moberly, Mo. D. Feb. 6, 1968, St. Paul, Minn.

Year	Team	W	L	PCT	G	GS	CG	IP	H	BB	SO	ShO	SV
1929	STL Stars	5	2	.714	13	8	4	65	75	42	73	1	0
1930		11	3	.786	17	14	8	89	92	34	56	1	0
1931		1	1	.500	2	1	1	8	5		8		

Leroy Matlock *continued*

		W	L	PCT	G	GS	CG	IP	H	BB	SO	ShO	SV
1932	**2 teams** WAS Pilots Homestead Grays												
"	total	2	4	.333	10	6	2	46	19	14	23	0	0
1933	PIT Crawfords	7	3	.700	12	8	6	85	75	14	38	1	0
1934		5	3	.625	14	7	7	66	31	3	17	1	0
1935		18	0	1.000	18	16	16	159	77	7	29	2	0
1936		3	2	.600	5	4	2	20	19	2	3	0	0
1937	Dominican Republic												
1938	PIT Crawfords	2	5	.286	7	5	5	43	37	1	3		0
	(9 years)	54	23	.701	98	69	51	581	430	(117)	250	(6)	(0)
PLAYOFFS													
1930	STL Stars	0	0	—	1			3	3	2	2	0	0
1935	PIT Crawfords	2	0	1.000	2	1	1	5	2	9		1	0
	2 years	2	0	1.000	3	(1)	(1)	8	5	11	(2)	1	0
ALL STAR (1935–36)		1	0	1.000	2	1	0	3	2	1	1	0	0

Webster McDonald

McDONALD, WEBSTER BL TR 6′ 180 lbs.
B. Jan. 1, 1900, Wilmington, Del. D. June 12, 1982, Philadelphia, Pa.
Manager 1934-40.

		W	L	PCT	G	GS	CG	IP	H	BB	SO	ShO	SV
1925	CHI Am. Giants	6	2	.750	11	8	6	76	22	19	47	2	0
1926		14	9	.609	20	14	9	112	100	27	70	0	1
1927		10	5	.667	18	14	11	136	111	26	64	1	0
1928	Homestead Grays	2	0	1.000	2	2	2	14	8	1	7	2	0
1929	CHI Am. Giants	2	2	.500	4	4	3	33	34	5	10	0	0
1930	**3 teams** CHI Am. Giants BAL Black Sox PHI Hilldales												
"	total	12	13	.480	35	25	13	172	186	28	42	2	1
1931	**2 teams** PHI Hilldales CHI Am. Giants												
"	total	8	2	.800	11	10	10	93	58	9	21	5	0
1932	Semipro												
1933	PHI Stars	3	2	.600	6	6	5	46	57			0	0
1934		8	2	.800	17	13	8	103	66	3	17	0	0
1935		10	6	.625	25	14	8	129	98	14	9	0	0
1936		7	2	.778	17	2	0	28		5		0	0
1937		4	4	.500	13	9	5	60	23		9	0	0
1938		4	5	.444	13	3	7	38	29	5	0	1	0
1939		2	5	.286	14	4	4	47	40	0	3	0	0
1940		1	1	.500	No further data available								
	15 years	93	60	.608	(206)	(128)	(91)	(1087)	(832)	(142)	(299)	(13)	(2)
PLAYOFFS													
1925	CHI Am. Giants	2	0	1.000	2	2	2	18	12	3	12	0	0
1926		0	1	.000	1	1	1	8	9	1	5	0	0
1934	PHI Stars	2	0	1.000	2	2	2						
	3 years	4	1	.800	5	5	5	(26)	(21)	(4)	(17)	(0)	(0)
WORLD SERIES													
1926	CHI Am. Giants	0	1	.000	2	1	0	11	15	5	2	0	0
1927		1	0	1.000	2	2	1	13	14	2	8	0	0
	2 years	1	1	.500	4	3	1	24	29	7	10	0	0
ALL STAR (1941–44)		1	0	1.000	2	2	0					0	0

Terris McDuffie

McDUFFIE, TERRIS (The Great) BR TR 6′2″ 200 lbs.
B. July 22, 1910, Mobile, Ala. D. New York, N.Y.

		W	L	PCT	G	GS	CG	IP	H	BB	SO	ShO	SV
1932	BAL Black Sox	4	0	1.000	5	2	2	37	31	5	5	0	0
1933	No Data Available												
1934													
1935	BKN Eagles	0	1	.000	1	1	1	5	10	1	1	0	0
1936		2	2	.500	5	2	2	16	10	6	6	0	0
1937		7	3	.700	11	10	10	79	54	5	9	1	0
1938	**2 teams** NWK Eagles NY Black Yankees												
"	total	12	5	.706	20	15	11	122	98	5	21		
1939	NY Black Yankees	5	3	.625	9	7	0	54	44	6	9	1	0
1940	PHI Stars	5	3	.625	9	7	5	47	34	5	7	1	0
1941	WAS Homestead Grays	5	6	.455	13	11	7	79	59	10	21	1	0
1942	PHI Stars	5	3	.625	10	7	2	49	37	2	6	1	0
1943	No Data Available												
1944	**2 teams** NWK Eagles NY Black Yankees												
"	total	2	6	.250	9	7	5	59	63	9	11	0	0
1945	NWK Eagles	2	1	.667	4	3	2	25	21	3	0	0	0
	(11 years)	(49)	(33)	(.598)	(96)	(72)	(47)	(572)	(461)	(57)	(96)	(5)	(0)

Terris McDuffie *continued*

		W	L	PCT	G	GS	CG	IP	H	BB	SO	ShO	SV
PLAYOFFS													
1941	WAS Homestead Grays	1	0	1.000	1	1	1	9	3	0	4	1	0
WORLD SERIES													
1937	BKN Eagles	2	0	1.000	3	2	0	11	11	5	8	0	
1941	WAS Homestead Grays	1	0	1.000	1	1	1	9	3	0	4	1	0
	2 years	3	0	1.000	4	3	1	20	14	5	12	1	(0)
ALL STAR (1939–44)		1	0	1.000	3	2	0	8	5	3	5	0	0

Hurley McNair

McNAIR, HURLEY ALLEN BB TR 5′6″ 155 lbs.
B. Oct. 28, 1888, Marshall, Tex. D. Dec. 2, 1948, Kansas City, Mo.

		W	L	PCT									
1915	CHI Am. Giants	0	1	.000	No further data available								
1921	KC Monarchs	1	1	.500	No further data available								
1922		2	0	1.000	No further data available								
	3 years	3	2	.600									

Don Newcombe

NEWCOMBE, DONALD (Newk) BL TR 6′ 4″ 220 lbs.
B. June 14, 1926, Madison, N. J.
Major leagues 1949-1960

		W	L	PCT	G	GS	CG	IP	H	BB	SO	ShO	SV
1944	NWK Eagles	1	2	.333	4	3	2	18	29	8	8	0	0
1945		6	2	.750	9	7	6	70	48	3	23	0	0
	2 years	7	4	.636	13	10	8	88	77	11	31	0	0

Alejandro Oms

OMS, ALEJANDRO BL TL 5′8″ 190 lbs.
B. Mar. 13, 1895, Santa Clara, Cuba D. Nov. 9, 1946

		W	L	PCT									
1930	Cuban Stars	2	0	1.000	No further data available								

Satchel Paige

PAIGE, LEROY ROBERT BR TR 6′ 3∫″ 180 lbs.
B. July 7, 1906, Mobile, Ala. D. June 8, 1982, Kansas City, Mo.
Major leagues, 1948-49, 1951-53, 1965.
Hall of Fame 1971.

		W	L	PCT	G	GS	CG	IP	H	BB	SO	ShO	SV
1927	BIR Black Barons	8	3	.727	20	9	6	93	63	19	80	3	1
1928		12	4	.750	26	16	10	120	107	19	112	3	0
1929		11	11	.500	31	20	15	196	191	39	184	0	3
1930	**2 teams** BAL Black Sox BIR Black Barons												
″	total	12	4	.750	20	15	13	129	97	16	95	3	1
1931	**2 teams** CLE Cubs PIT Crawfords												
″	total	5	6	.455	14	12	8	73	73	9	24	2	0
1932	PIT Crawfords	14	8	.636	29	23	19	181	92	13	109	3	2
1933		5	7	.417	13	12	10	95	39	10	57	0	0
1934		13	3	.813	20	17	15	154	85	21	97	6	0
1935	KC Monarchs	0	0	—	2	2	0	7	0	0	10	0	0
1936	PIT Crawfords	7	2	.778	9	9	9	70	54	11	59	3	0
1937	STL Stars	1	2	.333	3	3	2	26	22	6	11	0	0
1938	Mexico												
1939	Monarchs' B team												
1940	KC Monarchs	2	0	1.000	2	2	1	16	9		18	0	0
1941		8	1	.889	14	13	3	62	46	6	61	0	0
1942		6	6	.500	17	13	3	72	62	9	42	0	0
1943		9	13	.409	29	23	5	108	52	24	72	2	1
1944	No Data Available												
1945	KC Monarchs	4	6	.400	20		2	82	49	16	30	0	0
1946		5	1	.833	9	9	1	38	22	2	23	0	0
1947		1	1	.500	2	2	2	11	5			0	0
1950	**2 teams** KC Monarchs PHI Stars												
″	total	1	2	.333		8			26	28			0
	(17 years)	(124)	(80)	(.608)	(280)	(208)	(124)	(1533)	(1094)	(248)	(1084)	(25)	(8)
PLAYOFFS													
1927	BIR Black Barons	0	0	—	2	1	0	7	4	0	5	0	0
ALL STAR (1934–43)		2	1	.667	5	1	0	8	8	3	13	0	0

Red Parnell

PARNELL, ROY

		W	L	PCT	G	GS	CG	IP	H	BB	SO	ShO	SV
1932	MON Monarchs	5	1	.833	6	6	5	45	8	6	8	1	0

Willie Powell

POWELL, ERNEST (Piggie) BL TR 5′9″ 154 lbs.
B. Oct. 30, 1903, Eutah, Ala. D. May 16, 1987, Three Rivers, Mich.

		W	L	PCT	G	GS	CG	IP	H	BB	SO	ShO	SV
1925	CHI Am. Giants	3	2	.600	5	4	4	33	15	7	20	0	0
1926		2	2	.500	5	4	0	18	17	11	13	0	0
1927		9	4	.692	15	14	7	114	119	31	57	2	0

Willie Powell *continued*

		W	L	PCT	G	GS	CG	IP	H	BB	SO	ShO	SV
1928		9	9	.500	22	21	15	156	135	20	82	4	1
1929		3	1	.750	9	4	3	53	60	26	20	0	0
1930	DET Stars	9	10	.474	25	19	12	143	146	27	60	1	1
1931	DET Wolves	4	7	.364	14	11	9	80	71	20	30	2	0
1932	CHI Am. Giants	13	7	.650	22	18	13	147	87	20	20	5	0
1933		6	3	.667	10	6	3	31	14	0	3	1	0
	9 years	58	45	.563	127	101	66	775	664	162	305	15	2
PLAYOFFS													
1925	CHI Am. Giants	2	0	1.000	2	1	1	12	4	7	12	0	0
1926		0	0	—	1	0	0	4	3	3	4	0	0
1927		2	0	1.000	2	2	1	16	13	3	1	0	0
1930	DET Stars	2	0	1.000	2	1	0	10	10	8	13	0	0
1932	LOU White Sox	1	1	.500	2								
	5 years	7	1	.875	9	(4)	(2)	(42)	(30)	(21)	(30)	(0)	(0)
WORLD SERIES													
1926	CHI Am. Giants	1	1	.500	3	2	2	20	9	4	4	1	0
1927		1	0	1.000	3	3	1	16	0	7	10	0	0
	2 years	2	1	.667	6	5	3	36	9	11	14	1	0

Double Duty Radcliffe

RADCLIFFE, TED BR TR 5′10″ 212 lbs.

B. July 7, 1902, Mobile, Ala.
Manager 1937-38, 1943.
Brother of Alec Radcliff.

		W	L	PCT	G	GS	CG	IP	H	BB	SO	ShO	SV
1930	STL Stars	9	3	.750	20	11	9	94	89	24	40	1	3
1931	**2 teams** DET Wolves Homestead Grays												
″	total	9	5	.643	17	13	12	106	22	15	39	0	0
1932	PIT Crawfords	13	5	.722	24	21	14	156	60	14	17	0	1
1933	**3 teams** Homestead Grays NY Black Yankees COL Blue Birds												
″	total	0	1	.000	1		0					0	1
1934	CHI Am. Giants	0	1	.000	2		0	6	3			0	0
1935	BKN Eagles	4	6	.400	13	8	6	58	59	9	19	0	0
1936	Semipro												
1937	CLA Tigers	0	1	.000	1	0	0				4	0	0
1938	MEM Red Sox	3	2	.600	8	4	4	38	20	0	3	0	0
1939		4	3	.571	10	6	5	49	45	26	9	0	0
1940	Mexico												
1941	MEM Red Sox	1	2	.333	7	2	1	35	38	1	7	0	1
1942	No Data Available												
1943													
1944													
1945	KC Monarchs	3	0	1.000	No further data available								
1946	**2 teams** BIR Black Barons WAS Homestead Grays												
″	total	3	2	.600	14	3	2	32	45	3	12	0	3
	(12 years)	(49)	(31)	(.613)	(117)	(68)	(53)	(574)	(381)	(92)	(150)	(1)	(9)
PLAYOFFS													
1930	STL Stars	0	1	.000	3	1	0	7	12	2	4	0	0
ALL STAR (1938–41)		1	0	1.000	3	0	0	1	4	3	2	0	0

Connie Rector

RECTOR, CONNIE (Broadway) BR TR 5′8″ 170 lbs.

		W	L	PCT	G	GS	CG	IP	H	BB	SO	ShO	SV
1920	PHI Hilldales	1	1	.500	3	3	3	20	12	4	12	0	0
1921		5	1	.833	10	6	5	69	38	24	19	0	0
1922	No Data Available												
1923	PHI Hilldales	3	1	.750	5	4	3	27	32	2	5	0	0
1924	BKN Royal Giants	1	1	.500	4	3	2	25	17	2	6	0	0
1925		3	2	.600	9	7	4	47	48	8	10	0	0
1926		1	2	.333	4	4	3	35	44	10	6	0	0
1927	NY Lincoln Giants	6	6	.500	12	9	8	78	65	24	14	0	1
1928		6	9	.400	20	14	14	132	151	12	16	0	2
1929		20	2	.909	25	15	13	161	122	24	25	1	0
1930	NY Black Yankees	3	1	.750	6	5	3	41	25	14	7	1	0
1931		2	6	.250	8	8	6	50	14	0	3	0	0
1932		4	1	.800	5	4	1	18	9			0	0
1933	Team not in the league												
1934													
1935													
1936	NY Black Yankees	1	0	1.000	1	1	0	6	7	1	2	0	0
1937	No Data Available												
1938	NY Black Yankees	0	0	—	1	0	0					0	0
1939	NY Cubans	0	1	.000	6	0	0					0	0
1940	No Data Available												

Connie Rector *continued*

Year	Team	W	L	PCT	G	GS	CG	IP	H	BB	SO	ShO	SV
1941	NY Black Yankees	2	5	.286	10	5	2	48	49	11	8	0	0
1944		0	0	—	1								
1945	No Data Available												
1946	NY Black Yankees	0	0	—	1								
	(18 years)	(58)	(39)	(.598)	(131)	(88)	(67)	(757)	(633)	(136)	(133)	(2)	(3)
PLAYOFFS													
1930	NY Black Yankees	1	1	.500	3								

Dick Redding

REDDING, DICK (Cannonball) BR TR 6′ 4″ 210 lbs.
B. 1891, Atlanta, Ga. D. 1940, Islip, N. Y.
Manager 1923-31.

Year	Team	W	L	PCT	G	GS	CG	IP	H	BB	SO	ShO	SV
1911	NY Lincoln Giants	0	1	.000	1	1	0	2	6	3	0	0	0
1912		2	2	.500	4	4	4	37	31	5	18	0	0
1913		1	0	1.000	3	3						0	0
1914		2	2	.500	6	5	4	25	35	19	19	1	0
1915	NY Lincoln Stars	6	3	.667	10	7	7	73	51	17	42	1	1
1916	NY Lincoln Giants	4	1	.800	6	4	3	29	30	5	18	1	1
1917	CHI Am. Giants	7	1	.875	10	7	6	59	30	17	32	2	1
1918	BKN Royal Giants	2	0	1.000	2	0	0					0	0
1919		3	3	.500	6	6	6	45	9			0	0
1920		6	3	.667	10	9	8	78	42	8	17	3	1
1921	AC Bacharach Giants	17	12	.586	30	23	21	213	189	38	81	3	1
1922		8	8	.500	14	13	12	113	59	10	14	2	0
1923	BKN Royal Giants	3	1	.750	5	4	2	21	17	2	2	0	0
1924		1	4	.200	6	6	5	42	56	2	13	0	0
1925		3	3	.500	6	6	4	55	24	4	12	0	0
1926		0	1	.000	2							0	0
1927		3	6	.333	11	9	5					0	0
1928		1	0	1.000	1	1	1	9	10			0	0
1929	Team not in the league												
1930	BKN Royal Giants	0	2	.000	2	1	1	18	24	1	3	0	0
1931		0	1	.000	1	1	0	4	7	1	0	0	0
	(20 years)	69	54	.561	136	(110)	(89)	(823)	(620)	(132)	(271)	13	5

Ed Rile

RILE, ED (Huck) BR TR 6′ 4″ 230 lbs.

Year	Team	W	L	PCT	G	GS	CG	IP	H	BB	SO	ShO	SV
1920	IND ABCs	2	1	.667	7	6	3	27	14	24	17	1	0
1921	**2 teams** COL Buckeyes NY Lincoln Giants												
″	total	4	1	.800	3	3	3	29	15	7	11	2	0
1922	CHI Am. Giants	4	5	.444	16	10	6	77	45	18	22	0	0
1923		14	8	.636	26	15	13	159	120	34	64	2	0
1924		5	1	.833	12	7	2	59	70	32	18	0	0
1925	IND ABCs	2	8	.200	13	10	9	83	107	19	46	0	0
1926		4	1	.800	10	6	4	40	35	7	13	2	1
1927	DET Stars	14	6	.700	21	19	12	163	139	19	47	2	0
1928		2	2	.500	4	4	3	106	63	2	3	1	0
1929		0	2	.000	3	2	0	7	19	1	1	0	0
1930		2	0	1.000	3	2	1	7	8			0	0
	11 years	53	35	.602	118	84	56	757	635	(163)	(242)	10	1

Bullet Joe Rogan

ROGAN, WILBER JOE BR TR 5′ 9″ 160 lbs.
B. July 28, 1889, Oklahoma City, Okla. D. Mar. 4, 1967, Kansas City, Mo.

Year	Team	W	L	PCT	G	GS	CG	IP	H	BB	SO	ShO	SV
1920	KC Monarchs	7	5	.583	14	12	12	114	97	44	77	0	1
1921		14	7	.667	21	20	20	172	123	46	68	3	2
1922		13	6	.684	23	18	18	172	146	36	96	2	1
1923		11	7	.611	20	18	15	178	124	38	71	4	1
1924		16	5	.762	23	22	17	176	154	50	101	1	0
1925		15	2	.882	22	16	15	154	122	28	69	4	2
1926		12	4	.750	19	11	9	105	87	21	46	0	1
1927		15	6	.714	30	16	15	152	121	30	89	4	6
1928		9	3	.750	16	11	9	102	117	14	52	0	0
1929		0	0	—	2	0	0	6	7	1	5	0	1
1930	No Data Available												
1931													
1932	Team not in the league												
1933													
1934													
1935													
1936	KC Monarchs	1	0	1.000	1	1	1	6	3	0	3	0	0
1937		0	0	—	1		0					0	
1938	No Data Available												
	(12 years)	(113)	(45)	(.715)	(192)	(145)	(131)	(1337)	(1101)	(308)	(677)	(18)	(15)

Bullet Joe Rogan *continued*

		W	L	PCT	G	GS	CG	IP	H	BB	SO	ShO	SV
PLAYOFFS													
1925	KC Monarchs	3	0	1.000	3	3	3	26	20	2	16	1	0
1926		3	2	.600	5	3	3	40	14	6	7	0	0
1929		0	0	—	1	0	0	3	5	1	2	0	0
	3 years	6	2	.750	9	6	6	69	39	9	25	1	0
WORLD SERIES													
1924	KC Monarchs	2	1	.667	4	3	3	28	27	9	13	0	0

Lazaro Salazar

SALAZAR, LAZARO BL TL 5′9″ 177 lbs.
B. Feb. 4, 1912, Havana, Cuba D. Apr. 25, 1957

		W	L	PCT	
1930	NY Cubans	1	2	.333	No further data available
1932		2	1	.667	No further data available
	2 years	3	3	.500	

Harry Salmon

SALMON, HARRY BR TR 5′10″ 180 lbs.
B. May 30, 1895, Warrior, Ala. D. July 1983, Pittsburgh, Pa.

		W	L	PCT	G	GS	CG	IP	H	BB	SO	ShO	SV
1923	BIR Black Barons	7	3	.700	14	10	9	92	82	11	45	3	0
1924	**2 teams** MEM Red Sox BIR Black Barons												
″	total	8	3	.727	13	10	8	88	88	20	42	1	0
1925	BIR Black Barons	7	6	.538	20	13	11	127	139	28	56	0	0
1926	Team not in the league												
1927	BIR Black Barons	14	6	.700	27	18	13	199	164	27	74	1	0
1928		11	10	.524	24	20	11	164	170	16	84	3	0
1929		10	15	.400	34	22	18	177	144	19	92	3	3
1930	**2 teams** BIR Black Barons MEM Red Sox												
″	total	11	11	.500	28	18	15	176	200	34	101	0	2
1931	BIR Black Barons	1	0	1.000	1	1	1	9	6			0	0
1932		1	0	1.000	1	1	1	9				0	0
	(9 years)	70	54	.565	162	113	87	1041	(993)	(155)	(494)	11	5
PLAYOFFS													
1927	BIR Black Barons	0	1	.000	2		0	1	2	0	1	0	0
1933	Homestead Grays	1	1	.500	2	1	1	9	5				0
	2 years	1	2	.333	4	(1)	1	10	7	(0)	(1)	(0)	0

Hilton Smith

SMITH, HILTON BR TR
B. Feb. 27, 1912, Giddings, Tex. D. Nov. 18, 1983, Kansas City, Mo.

		W	L	PCT	G	GS	CG	IP	H	BB	SO	ShO	SV
1933	NOR	1	0	1.000	2	0	0	3	6			0	0
1934	Team not in the league												
1935													
1936													
1937	KC Monarchs	6	4	.600	11	9	6	54	28	7	28	1	0
1938		8	1	.889	14	9	4	84	28	6	54	1	0
1939		8	2	.800	7	3	3	70	49	12	60	1	6
1940		5	3	.625	10	5	4	37	20	36	11	0	1
1941		10	0	1.000	15	13	3	62	26	2	21	0	3
1942		4	4	.500	10	5	5	34	61	13	22	1	1
1943		4	4	.500	11	8	7	76	42	2	17	0	0
1944		2	5	.286	11	0	0	53	55	12	10	0	0
1945		5	3	.625	13		6	76	67	11	43		
1946		8	2	.800	13	10	5	46	26	7	15	1	3
1947		7	3	.700	11			88	90		30		
1948		1	2	.333	11	0	2	46	68	23	27		
	(13 years)	69	33	.676	139	(62)	(45)	729	566	(131)	(338)	(5)	(14)
PLAYOFFS													
1937	KC Monarchs	1	0	1.000	1								0
WORLD SERIES													
1937	KC Monarchs	0	0	—	1	0	0	2	1	0	2	0	1
1942		1	0	1.000	1	1	0	5	7	1	1	0	0
1946		1	0	1.000	2	2	1	14	15	3	12	0	
	3 years	2	0	1.000	4	3	1	21	23	4	15	0	(1)
ALL STAR (1937–42)		1	2	.333	6	2	0	6	10	6	13	0	1

Sam Streeter

STREETER, SAMUEL BR TL 5′7″ 170 lbs.
B. Sept. 17, 1900, New Market, Ala. D. Aug. 9, 1985, Pittsburgh, Pa.

		W	L	PCT	G	GS	CG	IP	H	BB	SO	ShO	SV
1921	CHI Am. Giants	0	1	.000	4	2	1	16	13	4	6	0	0
1922	AC Bacharach Giants	1	0	1.000	4	4	3					0	0
1923	NY Lincoln Giants	2	2	.500	11	10	0	61	38	0	0	1	0
1924	BIR Black Barons	14	7	.667	27	24	21	208	201	20	127	2	1

Sam Streeter *continued*

Year	Team	W	L	PCT	G	GS	CG	IP	H	BB	SO	ShO	SV
1925		0	1	.000	3	0	0	8	18	1	4	0	0
1926	Team not in the league												
1927	BIR Black Barons	14	12	.538	29	21	18	204	160	28	89	2	0
1928	**2 teams** BIR Black Barons Homestead Grays												
"	total	4	3	.571	9	7	7	73	69	14	30	1	0
1929	Homestead Grays	9	5	.643	18	10	4	69	71	16	22	0	1
1930	**2 teams** BIR Black Barons BAL Black Sox												
"	total	12	11	.522	30	24	20	186	195	30	61	0	0
1931	**2 teams** CLE Cubs PIT Crawfords												
"	total	3	2	.600	5	3	3	26	11	0	7	0	0
1932	PIT Crawfords	4	5	.444	12	7	6	66	47	10	23	0	0
1933		2	3	.400	5	5	5	44	35	0	3	0	0
1934		3	0	1.000	10	5	2	36	39	10	9	2	0
1935		2	0	1.000	5	2	2	18	21	3	2	0	0
1936		3	1	.750	5	5	3	32	26	3	5	0	0
	(15 years)	73	53	.579	177	129	95	(1047)	(944)	(139)	(388)	8	2
PLAYOFFS													
1927	BIR Black Barons	0	2	.000	2	2	0	3	11	0	3	0	0
1935	PIT Crawfords	0	1	.000	1	1	1	9	11		6	0	0
	2 years	0	3	.000	3	3	1	12	22	(0)	9	0	0
ALL STAR (1933)		0	1	.000	1	1	0			0	4	0	

Ben Taylor

TAYLOR, BEN BL TL 6′ 190 lbs.
B. July 1, 1888, Anderson, S.C. D. Jan. 24, 1953, Baltimore, Md.
Manager 1924, 1926-29.
Brother of Candy Jim Taylor.
Brother of C.I. Taylor.
Brother of John Taylor.

Year	Team	W	L	PCT	G	GS	CG	IP	H	BB	SO	ShO	SV
1910	WB Sprudels	0	3	.000	3	3	3	27		5	2	0	0
1914	IND ABCs	1	0	1.000	1	1	1	9	10	3	3	0	0
1917		0	1	.000	1	1	1	9	7	4	2	0	0
1920		1	1	.500	No further data available								
	4 years	2	5	.286	(5)	(5)	(5)	(45)	(17)	(12)	(7)	(0)	(0)
PLAYOFFS													
1916	IND ABCs	0	0	—	1	0	0	2	3	0	0	0	0

Luis Tiant

TIANT, LUIS, SR. BL TL 5′10″ 165 lbs.
B. Aug. 27, 1906, Havana, Cuba D. Dec. 12, 1971
Father of Luis Tiant.

Year	Team	W	L	PCT	G	GS	CG	IP	H	BB	SO	ShO	SV
1930	NY Cubans	4	14	.222	23	18	11	121	126	33	67	1	0
1931	Cuban HoD	1	4	.200	5	4	2	24	36	2	10	0	0
1932	NY Cubans	4	1	.800	7	4	2	50	16	6	12	1	0
1933	Team not in the league												
1934													
1935	NY Cubans	7	4	.636	15	8	5	70	31	26	51	3	0
1936		1	0	1.000	4	1	1	14		3	4	0	0
1937	Team not in the league												
1938													
1939	NY Cubans	1	3	.250	6	4	3	37	41	3	4	0	0
1940	No Data Available												
1941													
1942													
1943	NY Cubans	0	0	—	2	0	0					0	0
1944		3	2	.600	5		2	28	29	8	31	0	
1945		3	2	.600	5	5	3	27	14	10	16	1	0
1946		1	1	.500	5	2	2	72	47	6	13	0	0
1947		10	0	1.000	17		8	90	80		46	3	0
	(11 years)	(35)	(31)	(.530)	(94)	(46)	(39)	(533)	(420)	(97)	(254)	(9)	(0)
PLAYOFFS													
1935	NY Cubans	0	1	.000	No further data available								
WORLD SERIES													
1947	NY Cubans	0	0	—	2	2	0	2		0	1	0	
ALL STAR (1935–47)		0	0		2	0	0	3	2	0	0	0	0

Cristobal Torriente

TORRIENTE, CRISTOBAL BL TL 5′10″ 190 lbs.
B. 1895, Cuba D. 1938, New York, N.Y.

Year	Team	W	L	PCT	G	GS	CG	IP	H	BB	SO	ShO	SV
1914	CHI Am. Giants	1	3	.250	4	2	2	18	38	3	10	0	0
1915	Cuban Stars	0	0	—	3	0	0						
1916		3	2	.600	5	5	4	35	52	7	16	0	0

Cristobal Torriente *continued*

Year	Team	W	L	PCT	G	GS	CG	IP	H	BB	SO	ShO	SV
1920		0	1	.000									0
1921		4	1	.800									0
1922		1	0	1.000									0
1923		1	0	1.000									0
1927	DET Stars	2	1	.667									0
1928		7	3	.700									2
9 years		19	11	.633	(12)	(7)	(6)	(53)	(90)	(10)	(26)	(0)	(2)
PLAYOFFS													
1932	CLE Cubs	0	1	.000	2			8	10	2	1	0	

Ted Trent

TRENT, THEODORE (Ted, Big Florida) BR TR 6′ 3″ 185 lbs.
B. Dec. 17, 1903, Jacksonville, Fla. D. Jan. 10, 1944, Chicago, Ill.

Year	Team	W	L	PCT	G	GS	CG	IP	H	BB	SO	ShO	SV
1927	STL Stars	15	11	.577	35	25	16	204	155	71	127	2	0
1928		21	2	.913	28	22	16	185	162	36	86	2	0
1929		12	8	.600	29	22	14	174	167	42	73	3	1
1930		11	2	.846	20	11	7	104	103	34	56	1	1
1931		3	1	.750	5	3	2	21	11	3	8	1	0
1932	**2 teams** DET Wolves WAS Pilots												
″	total	5	4	.556	14	10	5	77	77	17	20	1	0
1933	NY Black Yankees	0	0	—	1	0	0					0	0
1934	**2 teams** NY Black Yankees CHI Am. Giants												
″	total	4	4	.500	9	7	7	73	61	8	22	0	0
1935	CHI Am. Giants	4	7	.364	13	8	7	78	62	19	32	0	0
1936		2	1	.667	5	1	0	24	24	2	5	0	0
1937		8	2	.800	14	9	9	91	41	13	37	5	1
1938		6	4	.600	18	11	7	83	57	3	26	1	0
1939		2	3	.400	12	2	1	26	21	4	13	0	0
13 years		93	49	.655	203	131	91	(1140)	(941)	(252)	(505)	16	3
PLAYOFFS													
1928	STL Stars	2	1	.667	4	3	2	27	30	4	16	0	0
1930		2	0	1.000	3	2	1	20	19	8	20	0	0
1934	CHI Am. Giants	1	0	1.000	No further data available								
3 years		5	1	.833	(7)	(5)	(3)	(47)	(49)	(12)	(36)	(0)	(0)
ALL STAR (1934–37)		0	0		4	2	0			4	6	0	

Quincy Trouppe

TROUPPE, QUINCY THOMAS BB TR 6′ 2½″ 225 lbs.
B. Dec. 25, 1912, Dublin, Ga. D. Aug. 12, 1993, Creve Coeur, Mo.
Manager 1945.

Year	Team	W	L	PCT	G	GS	CG	IP	H	BB	SO	ShO	SV
1932	KC Monarchs	0	1	.000	1	1	1	8	11	2	6	0	

Frank Wickware

WICKWARE, FRANK (The Red Ant) TR
B. 1888, Coffeyville, Kans. D. Nov. 2, 1967, Schenectady, N. Y.

Year	Team	W	L	PCT	G	GS	CG	IP	H	BB	SO	ShO	SV
1910	CHI Leland Giants	6	0	1.000	6	6	6	54		6	33	1	0
1911		1	1	.500	3	3	2	12	11	7	5	0	0
1912	BKN Royal Giants	2	0	1.000	2	2	2	18	16	2	5	1	0
1913	Schenectady Mohawk Giants												
1914	**2 teams** Schenectady Mohawk Giants CHI Am. Giants												
″	total												
1915	CHI Am. Giants	6	6	.500	15	12	8	81	63	22	35	0	0
1916	CHI	5	2	.714	10	7	4	46	27	25	47	1	0
1917	**2 teams** IND Jewell's ABCs CHI Giants												
″	total	1	1	.500	2	2	2	18	12	9	3	0	0
1918	CHI Am. Giants	1	0	1.000	2	1	1	11	2			0	0
1919	**2 teams** CHI Am. Giants DET Stars												
″	total	0	0	—	2	1	0	6					
1920	CHI Am. Giants	2	2	.500	5	3	3	31	19	3	19	0	0
1921		0	2	.000	3	3	0	9	18	7	3	0	0
(10 years)		(24)	(14)	(.632)	(50)	(40)	(28)	(286)	(168)	(81)	(150)	(3)	(0)
WORLD SERIES													
1914	CHI Am. Giants	1	0	1.000	1	1	1	9	3	2	12	1	0
1915		2	2	.500	4	4	3	30	23	4	16	0	0
2 years		3	2	.600	5	5	4	39	26	6	28	1	0

Joe Williams

WILLIAMS, JOE (Smokey, Cyclone) BR TR 6′4″ 200 lbs.
B. Apr. 6, 1885, Seguin, Tex. D. Mar. 12, 1946, New York, N. Y.

Year	Team	W	L	PCT	G	GS	CG	IP	H	BB	SO	ShO	SV
1910	CHI Leland Giants	3	1	.750	4					1	10		
1911		0	0	—	2	1				5	6		
1912	NY Lincoln Giants	3	2	.600	5	5	5	45	41	4	37	0	0
1913		10	4	.714	13	13	10	127	52	23	41	2	1
1914		2	1	.667	4	3	2	17	18	3	10	1	0

Joe Williams *continued*

		W	L	PCT	G	GS	CG	IP	H	BB	SO	ShO	SV
1915	**2 teams** NY Lincoln Giants CHI Am. Giants												
″	total	1	0	1.000	2	2	1	11	16	2	6		
1916	**2 teams** NY Lincoln Giants BKN Royal Giants												
″	total	5	4	.556	9	8	5	53	54	5	21	0	0
1917	NY Lincoln Giants	3	1	.750	3	3	3	18	19			1	0
1918		7	2	.778	9	9	9	86	92	3	21	1	0
1919		8	2	.800	11	10	10	101	53	29	53	2	0
1920		0	2	.000	2	2	2	18		0	11	0	0
1921	**2 teams** NY Lincoln Giants AC Bacharach Giants												
″	total	5	1	.833	8	6	6	52	19	1	8	0	0
1922	No Data Available												
1923	NY Lincoln Giants	3	6	.333	10	9	4	44	57	1	16	0	0
1924	BKN Royal Giants	3	6	.333	13	10	7	89	90	10	28	1	0
1925	Team not in the league												
1926													
1927	Homestead Grays	1	0	1.000	1	1	1	9	9	0	8	1	0
1928		2	1	.667	4	2	2	21	3	8	6	0	0
1929		12	7	.632	23	12	7	77	24	8	10	0	1
1930		7	2	.778	9	9	9			8	46	1	0
1931		5	6	.455	13	13	9	85	28	3	3	0	0
1932	DET Wolves	0	0	—	2	1	0	7	10			0	
	(20 years)	(80)	(48)	(.625)	(147)	(119)	(92)	(860)	(585)	(114)	(341)	(10)	(2)
PLAYOFFS													
1930	Homestead Grays	1	3	.250	4	4	1	17	13			0	0

Nip Winters

WINTERS, JESSE BL TL 6′ 5″ 235 lbs.
B. 1899, Washington, D.C. D. Dec. 1971, Hokessin, Del.

		W	L	PCT	G	GS	CG	IP	H	BB	SO	ShO	SV
1921	AC Bacharach Giants	3	2	.600	6	6	5	40	22	16	10	3	0
1922		4	3	.571	7	6	5	38	22	22	32	0	0
1923		6	3	.667	11	10	9	81	51	6	16	0	0
1924	PHI Hilldales	19	5	.792	27	22	20	190	131	24	72	2	2
1925		21	10	.677	32	27	22	254	213	39	86	1	0
1926		15	5	.750	23	17	14	149	116	46	62	2	1
1927		14	8	.636	22	22	12	81	72	34	32	1	0
1928	NY Lincoln Giants	8	7	.533	16	15	10	120	122	19	28	0	0
1929		3	5	.375	12	8	6	52	44	10	7	0	0
1930	No Data Available												
1931	**3 teams** PHI Hilldales NWK Browns AC Bacharach Giants												
″	total	1	5	.167	9	6	5	2	39	10			0
1932	AC Bacharach Giants	1	1	.500	1	1	1	9	5			0	0
	(11 years)	(95)	(54)	(.638)	(166)	(140)	(190)	(1016)	(837)	(226)	(345)	(9)	(3)
WORLD SERIES													
1924	PHI Hilldales	3	1	.750	4	4	4	39	28	8	21	1	0
1925		1	0	1.000	1	1	1	9	8	3	8	0	0
	2 years	4	1	.800	5	5	5	48	36	11	29	1	0

PART THIRTEEN

The World Series and Championship Playoffs

Results and Highlights of Each Playoff
And Series and Composite Box Scores

The World Series

Before the World Series started in 1903 there were other postseason championships, which took place as early as 1884. Although they are not officially recognized as part of World Series history, they provided a basis for the establishment of the World Series. The first of these was between the 1884 pennant winners. The National League's Providence team swept the three-game series from the American Association's New York Metropolitans. Postseason series between the two league champions continued until 1891 when renewed fighting between the leagues prevented the games.

The twelve-team National League played a split season in 1892 to create a postseason playoff. Boston, first-half winners, met Cleveland, the second-half champions. Boston won five of the six games, Cleveland managing only one tie. In 1893 the split season was dropped and no playoffs were held. Then, in 1894, William C. Temple, a Pittsburgh sportsman, donated an expensive trophy in his name to be awarded to the winner of a playoff series between the teams that finished first and second in the pennant race. These best four-out-of-seven-game series lasted for four years, but the games were often ragged and one-sided and public interest was never very great.

Then, in 1903, with the National League sharing the spotlight with its junior competitor, the American League, the first World Series was held. The American League won the Series and caused an embarrassment that prevented the games from being held in 1904. Both leagues made peace in 1905 and signed an agreement governing the rules of postseason championship play, and the World Series was resumed, becoming an annual feature and attracting millions of people.

This section provides information on all World Series through today. Included are facts about the individual games and series and lifetime leaders. Most of the information is self-explanatory. That which may appear unfamiliar is listed below. Appearing first, before the individual series information, is a table showing the number of World Series games each franchise has played along with their wins, losses, and winning percentage.

When teams in this section are listed by an abbreviation of the city in which the team played, they appear as follows:

ATL	Atlanta	CLE	Cleveland
BAL	Baltimore	DET	Detroit
BKN	Brooklyn	KC	Kansas City
BOS	Boston	LA	Los Angeles
CHI	Chicago	MIL	Milwaukee
CIN	Cincinnati	MIN	Minnesota
NY	New York	SF	San Francisco
OAK	Oakland	STL	St. Louis
PHI	Philadelphia	TOR	Toronto
PIT	Pittsburgh	WAS	Washington
SD	San Diego		

Franchise Summary

TEAM	LEAGUE	SERIES WON	SERIES LOST	SERIES PCT.	GAMES WON	GAMES LOST	GAMES PCT.
Toronto	AL	2	0	1.000	8	4	.667
Pittsburgh	NL	5	2	.714	23	14	.609
New York	AL	22	11	.667	109	77	.586
Oakland	AL	4	2	.667	17	15	.531
New York Mets	NL	2	1	.667	11	8	.579
Minnesota	AL	2	1	.667	11	10	.524
Philadelphia	AL	5	3	.625	24	19	.558
St. Louis	NL	9	6	.600	48	48	.500
Boston	AL	5	4	.556	33	26	.559
Cincinnati	NL	5	4	.556	26	25	.510
Los Angeles	NL	5	4	.556	25	24	.510
Baltimore	AL	3	3	.500	19	14	.576
Chicago	AL	2	2	.500	13	13	.500
Cleveland	AL	2	2	.500	11	12	.478
Boston	NL	1	1	.500	6	4	.600
Milwaukee	NL	1	1	.500	7	7	.500
Kansas City Royals	AL	1	1	.500	6	7	.462
Detroit	AL	4	5	.444	26	29	.473
New York Giants	NL	5	9	.367	39	41	.488
Washington	AL	1	2	.333	8	11	.421
Atlanta	NL	1	2	.333	9	10	.444
Philadelphia	NL	1	4	.200	8	18	.333
Chicago	NL	2	8	.200	19	33	.365
Brooklyn	NL	1	8	.111	20	36	.357
Milwaukee	AL	0	1	.000	3	4	.429
St. Louis	AL	0	1	.000	2	4	.333
San Diego	NL	0	1	.000	1	4	.200
San Francisco	NL	0	2	.000	3	8	.273

Individual Game Information

Innings Pitched. Pitchers are listed in the order of appearance. In parentheses, following each pitcher's name, are the number of innings he pitched in the game. For example: Doe (2.1) would mean that he pitched $2\frac{1}{3}$ innings. (2.0 would mean he started a third inning but failed to retire a batter.)

Winning and Losing Pitchers. Indicated by boldfaced print.

Save. The pitcher who is credited with a Save is indicated by the abbreviation SV, which appears in boldfaced print after his innings pitched.

Home Runs. Players are listed in the order their home runs were hit.

Composite Box Score Information

The following is an explanation of the column headings:

Batting and Fielding

(Pitchers who would appear with all zeros in their information are not included.)

AB	At Bats
H	Hits
2B	Doubles
3B	Triples
HR	Home Runs
R	Runs Scored
RBI	Runs Batted In
BA	Batting Average

(Errors and Stolen Bases appear beneath this information.)

Pitching

W	Wins
L	Losses
ERA	Earned Run Average
IP	Innings Pitched
H	Hits Allowed
BB	Bases on Balls Allowed
SO	Strikeouts
SV	Saves

The League Championship Series started in 1969 as a best-of five game series between the East and West division champions in each league. The format was expanded to best-of-seven in 1985. The Divisional Playoff Series, or Division Series, was played for the first time in 1995. There were two best-of-five series in each league, with the champions of the East, Central, and West divisions along with the second-place team with the best record (wild card) facing off. The winners of those series then advanced to the League Championship Series.

1903 WORLD SERIES

Boston (A.L.) defeats Pittsburgh (N.L.) 5 games to 3

LINE SCORES			R	H	E	PITCHERS (innings pitched)	HOME RUNS (men on)	HIGHLIGHTS
GAME 1 - OCTOBER 1								Four runs in the first, three of them unearned, were enough to stake Phillippe to a win over the Red Sox. Phillippe struck out ten, Sebring had four RBIs, and Leach contributed four hits.
PIT	**N**	401 100 100	7	12	2	**Phillippe** (9)	Sebring	
BOS	**A**	000 000 201	3	6	4	**Young** (9)		
GAME 2 - OCTOBER 2								The Red Sox evened the Series behind Dinneen's 11-strikeout pitching performance and Dougherty's two home runs.
PIT	**N**	000 000 000	0	3	2	**Leever** (1), Veil (7)		
BOS	**A**	200 001 00x	3	9	0	**Dinneen** (9)	Dougherty, Dougherty	
GAME 3 - OCTOBER 3								The Pirates built an early 3-0 lead and scored an insurance run on Young's error in the eighth to give Phillippe his second victory.
PIT	**N**	012 000 010	4	7	0	**Phillippe** (9)		
BOS	**A**	000 100 010	2	4	2	**Hughes** (2), Young (7)		
GAME 4 - OCTOBER 6								After a one-day rain delay, Phillippe returned with his third complete-game win of the Series. Boston had the tying run on second with one out in the ninth but could not bring it across.
BOS	**A**	000 010 003	4	9	1	**Dinneen** (8)		
PIT	**N**	100 010 30x	5	12	1	**Phillippe** (9)		
GAME 5 - OCTOBER 7								The Red Sox sent ten men to the plate in the sixth, breaking open a scoreless game. Dougherty had three hits, including two of Boston's five triples.
BOS	**A**	000 006 410	11	14	2	**Young** (9)		
PIT	**N**	000 000 020	2	6	4	**Kennedy** (7), Thompson (2)		
GAME 6 - OCTOBER 8								Three singles, a walk, a steal, and an error added up to three runs in the Boston third. Beaumont had four hits and two stolen bases in a losing effort.
BOS	**A**	003 020 100	6	10	1	**Dinneen** (9)		
PIT	**N**	000 000 300	3	10	3	**Leever** (9)		
GAME 7 - OCTOBER 10								The Pirates put men on base in every inning but stranded nine as Young scattered ten hits to pin the first loss on Deacon Phillippe.
BOS	**A**	200 202 010	7	11	4	**Young** (9)		
PIT	**N**	000 101 001	3	10	3	**Phillippe** (9)		
GAME 8 - OCTOBER 13								Phillippe threw his fifth complete game of the Series, but was outdone by Dinneen's four-hitter. Boston bunched six of their eight hits into their two scoring frames to take the Series.
PIT	**N**	000 000 000	0	4	3	**Phillippe** (8)		
BOS	**A**	000 201 00x	3	8	0	**Dinneen** (9)		

Team totals

		W	AB	H	2B	3B	HR	R	RBI	BA	BB	SO	ERA
BOS	**A**	5	282	71	4	16	2	39	35	.252	13	27	2.03
PIT	**N**	3	271	64	7	9	1	24	23	.236	14	45	3.73

Individual Batting

BOSTON (A.L.)

	AB	H	2B	3B	HR	R	RBI	BA
J. Collins, 3b	36	9	1	2	0	5	1	.250
P. Dougherty, of	34	8	0	2	2	3	5	.235
C. Stahl, of	33	10	1	3	0	6	3	.303
B. Freeman, of	32	9	0	3	0	6	4	.281
F. Parent, ss	32	9	0	3	0	8	3	.281
H. Ferris, 2b	31	9	0	1	0	3	7	.290
C. LaChance, 1b	27	6	2	1	0	5	4	.222
L. Criger, c	26	6	0	0	0	1	4	.231
C. Young, p	15	2	0	1	0	1	3	.133
B. Dinneen, p	12	3	0	0	0	1	0	.250
D. Farrell	2	0	0	0	0	0	1	.000
J. O'Brien	2	0	0	0	0	0	0	.000

Errors: L. Criger (3), C. LaChance (3), J. Collins (2), H. Ferris (2), F. Parent (2), P. Dougherty, C. Young

Stolen Bases: J. Collins (3), C. Stahl (2)

PITTSBURGH (N.L.)

	AB	H	2B	3B	HR	R	RBI	BA
G. Beaumont, of	34	9	0	1	0	6	0	.265
F. Clarke, of	34	9	2	1	0	3	2	.265
T. Leach, 3b	33	9	0	4	0	3	7	.273
J. Sebring, of	30	11	0	1	1	3	5	.367
K. Bransfield, 1b	30	6	0	2	0	3	1	.200
H. Wagner, ss	27	6	1	0	0	2	3	.222
C. Ritchey, 2b	27	3	1	0	0	2	2	.111
E. Phelps, c	26	6	2	0	0	1	2	.231
D. Phillippe, p	18	4	0	0	0	1	1	.222
S. Leever, p	4	0	0	0	0	0	0	.000
H. Smith, c	3	0	0	0	0	0	0	.000
B. Kennedy, p	2	1	1	0	0	0	0	.500
B. Veil, p	2	0	0	0	0	0	0	.000
G. Thompson, p	1	0	0	0	0	0	0	.000

Errors: H. Wagner (6), T. Leach (4), K. Bransfield (2), E. Phelps (2), F. Clarke, D. Phillippe, H. Smith, B. Veil

Stolen Bases: H. Wagner (3), G. Beaumont (2), T. Leach (2), K. Bransfield, F. Clarke, C. Ritchey

Individual Pitching

BOSTON (A.L.)

	W	L	ERA	IP	H	BB	SO	SV
B. Dinneen	3	1	2.06	35	29	8	28	0
C. Young	2	1	1.59	34	31	4	17	0
L. Hughes	0	1	9.00	2	4	2	0	0

PITTSBURGH (N.L.)

	W	L	ERA	IP	H	BB	SO	SV
D. Phillippe	3	2	3.27	44	38	3	20	0
S. Leever	0	2	6.30	10	13	3	2	0
B. Kennedy	0	1	5.14	7	11	3	3	0
B. Veil	0	0	1.29	7	6	4	1	0
G. Thompson	0	0	4.50	2	3	0	1	0

1905 WORLD SERIES

LINE SCORES						PITCHERS (innings pitched)	HOME RUNS (men on)	HIGHLIGHTS

New York (N.L.) defeats Philadelphia (A.L.) 4 games to 1

GAME 1 - OCTOBER 9								The Giants refused to play the Series in 1904, but acceded to public demand a year later. Mathewson opened the Series masterfully, allowing just four hits and walking none.
NY	N	000 020 001	3	10	1	**Mathewson** (9)		
PHI	A	000 000 000	0	4	0	**Plank** (9)		
GAME 2 - OCTOBER 10								Bender, Philadelphia's tall Indian, evened the Series with his shutout, aided by Bris Lord's two RBIs.
PHI	A	001 000 020	3	6	2	**Bender** (9)		
NY	N	000 000 000	0	4	2	**McGinnity** (8), Ames (1)		
GAME 3 - OCTOBER 12								A day of rain allowed Mathewson to return to post his second shutout, once again holding the Athletics to four hits. McGann drove in four runs on three hits.
NY	N	200 050 002	9	9	1	**Mathewson** (9)		
PHI	A	000 000 000	0	4	5	**Coakley** (9)		
GAME 4 - OCTOBER 13								Plank allowed just four hits, but was beaten by McGinnity's shutout. An unearned run in the fourth accounted for all the scoring.
PHI	A	000 000 000	0	5	2	**Plank** (8)		
NY	N	000 100 00x	1	4	1	**McGinnity** (9)		
GAME 5 - OCTOBER 14								Mathewson gained his third shutout to clinch a Series in which every game was a shutout. In his three victories, Matty allowed just fourteen hits, struck out eighteen, and walked but one.
PHI	A	000 000 000	0	6	0	**Bender** (8)		
NY	N	000 010 01x	2	5	1	**Mathewson** (9)		

Team totals

		W	AB	H	2B	3B	HR	R	RBI	BA	BB	SO	ERA
NY	N	4	153	32	7	0	0	15	13	.209	15	26	0.00
PHI	A	1	155	25	5	0	0	3	2	.161	5	25	1.47

Individual Batting

NEW YORK (N.L.)

	AB	H	2B	3B	HR	R	RBI	BA
G. Browne, of	22	4	0	0	0	2	1	.182
M. Donlin, of	19	6	1	0	0	4	1	.316
B. Gilbert, 2b	17	4	0	0	0	1	1	.235
D. McGann, 1b	17	4	2	0	0	1	4	.235
S. Mertes, of	17	3	1	0	0	2	3	.176
R. Bresnahan, c	16	5	2	0	0	3	1	.313
A. Devlin, 3b	16	4	1	0	0	0	1	.250
B. Dahlen, ss	15	0	0	0	0	1	1	.000
C. Mathewson, p	8	2	0	0	0	1	0	.250
J. McGinnity, p	5	0	0	0	0	0	0	.000
S. Strang	1	0	0	0	0	0	0	.000

Errors: A. Devlin (2), M. Donlin (2), C. Mathewson, D. McGann
Stolen Bases: A. Devlin (3), G. Browne (2), B. Dahlen (2), M. Donlin (2), R. Bresnahan, B. Gilbert

PHILADELPHIA (A.L.)

	AB	H	2B	3B	HR	R	RBI	BA
H. Davis, 1b	20	4	1	0	0	0	0	.200
B. Lord, of	20	2	0	0	0	0	2	.100
L. Cross, 3b	19	2	0	0	0	0	0	.105
T. Hartsel, of	17	5	1	0	0	1	0	.294
M. Cross, ss	17	3	0	0	0	0	0	.176
D. Murphy, 2b	16	3	1	0	0	0	0	.188
S. Seybold, of	16	2	0	0	0	0	0	.125
O. Schreckengost, c	9	2	1	0	0	2	0	.222
M. Powers, c	7	1	1	0	0	0	0	.143
E. Plank, p	6	1	0	0	0	0	0	.167
C. Bender, p	5	0	0	0	0	0	0	.000
A. Coakley, p	2	0	0	0	0	0	0	.000
D. Hoffman	1	0	0	0	0	0	0	.000

Errors: D. Murphy (4), L. Cross (2), M. Cross (2), T. Hartsel
Stolen Bases: T. Hartsel (2)

Individual Pitching

NEW YORK (N.L.)

	W	L	ERA	IP	H	BB	SO	SV
C. Mathewson	3	0	0.00	27	14	1	18	0
J. McGinnity	1	1	0.00	17	10	3	6	0
R. Ames	0	0	0.00	1	1	1	1	0

PHILADELPHIA (A.L.)

	W	L	ERA	IP	H	BB	SO	SV
C. Bender	1	1	1.06	17	9	6	13	0
E. Plank	0	2	1.59	17	14	4	11	0
A. Coakley	0	1	2.00	9	9	5	2	0

1906 WORLD SERIES

Chicago (A.L.) defeats Chicago (N.L.) 4 games to 2

LINE SCORES					PITCHERS (innings pitched)	HOME RUNS (men on)	HIGHLIGHTS
GAME 1 - OCTOBER 9							Isbell scored Jones with the tie-breaking run on a single in the sixth in a game played in bitterly cold weather and snow flurries.
CHI A	000 011 000	2	4	1	**Altrock** (9)		
CHI N	000 001 000	1	4	2	**Brown** (9)		
GAME 2 - OCTOBER 10							Reulbach pitched six no-hit innings before yielding a single to Donahue. He finished with a one-hitter, but walked six and hit one batter.
CHI N	031 001 020	7	10	2	**Reulbach** (9)		
CHI A	000 010 000	1	1	2	**White** (3), Owen (6)		
GAME 3 - OCTOBER 11							Rohe's three-run triple in the sixth broke open the game and aided Walsh's record 12-strikeout pitching performance.
CHI A	000 003 000	3	4	1	**Walsh** (9)		
CHI N	000 000 000	0	2	2	**Pfiester** (9)		
GAME 4 - OCTOBER 12							Evers singled in Chance in the seventh to back up Brown's two-hitter.
CHI N	000 000 100	1	7	1	**Brown** (9)		
CHI A	000 000 000	0	2	1	**Altrock** (9)		
GAME 5 - OCTOBER 13							Isbell hit four doubles, scored three runs and drove in two to pace the White Sox' twelve-hit attack.
CHI A	102 401 000	8	12	6	**Walsh** (6.1), White (2.2) **SV**		
CHI N	300 102 000	6	6	0	Reulbach (2), **Pfiester** (1.1), Overall (5.2)		
GAME 6 - OCTOBER 14							The White Sox jumped to a 7-1 lead after two innings and won the Series as Hahn contributed four hits and Donahue and Davis each drove in three runs.
CHI N	100 010 001	3	7	0	**Brown** (1.2), Overall (6.1)		
CHI A	340 000 01x	8	14	3	**White** (9)		

Team totals

	W	AB	H	2B	3B	HR	R	RBI	BA	BB	SO	ERA
CHI A	4	187	37	10	3	0	22	19	.198	18	35	1.67
CHI N	2	184	36	9	0	0	18	11	.196	18	27	3.40

Individual Batting

CHICAGO (A.L.)

	AB	H	2B	3B	HR	R	RBI	BA
F. Isbell, 2b	26	8	4	0	0	4	4	.308
E. Hahn, of	22	6	0	0	0	4	0	.273
G. Rohe, 3b	21	7	1	2	0	2	4	.333
F. Jones, of	21	2	0	0	0	4	0	.095
B. Sullivan, c	21	0	0	0	0	0	0	.000
P. Dougherty, of	20	2	0	0	0	1	1	.100
J. Donahue, 1b	18	6	2	1	0	0	4	.333
G. Davis, ss	13	4	3	0	0	4	6	.308
L. Tannehill, ss	9	1	0	0	0	1	0	.111
N. Altrock, p	4	1	0	0	0	0	0	.250
E. Walsh, p	4	0	0	0	0	1	0	.000
D. White, p	3	0	0	0	0	0	0	.000
F. Owen, p	2	0	0	0	0	0	0	.000
E. McFarland	1	0	0	0	0	0	0	.000
B. O'Neill, of	1	0	0	0	0	1	0	.000
B. Towne	1	0	0	0	0	0	0	.000

Errors: F. Isbell (5), G. Rohe (3), G. Davis (2), J. Donahue, P. Dougherty, B. Sullivan, E. Walsh

Stolen Bases: P. Dougherty (2), G. Rohe (2), G. Davis, F. Isbell

CHICAGO (N.L.)

	AB	H	2B	3B	HR	R	RBI	BA
W. Schulte, of	26	7	3	0	0	1	3	.269
S. Hofman, of	23	7	1	0	0	3	2	.304
F. Chance, 1b	21	5	1	0	0	3	0	.238
J. Sheckard, of	21	0	0	0	0	0	1	.000
H. Steinfeldt, 3b	20	5	1	0	0	2	2	.250
J. Evers, 2b	20	3	1	0	0	2	1	.150
J. Tinker, ss	18	3	0	0	0	4	1	.167
J. Kling, c	17	3	1	0	0	2	0	.176
T. Brown, p	6	2	0	0	0	0	0	.333
O. Overall, p	4	1	1	0	0	1	0	.250
E. Reulbach, p	3	0	0	0	0	0	1	.000
P. Moran	2	0	0	0	0	0	0	.000
J. Pfiester, p	2	0	0	0	0	0	0	.000
D. Gessler	1	0	0	0	0	0	0	.000

Errors: J. Tinker (2), T. Brown, J. Evers, J. Kling, J. Pfiester, H. Steinfeldt

Stolen Bases: F. Chance (2), J. Evers (2), J. Tinker (2), S. Hofman, J. Sheckard

Individual Pitching

CHICAGO (A.L.)

	W	L	ERA	IP	H	BB	SO	SV
N. Altrock	1	1	1.00	18	11	2	5	0
E. Walsh	2	0	1.80	15	7	6	17	0
D. White	1	1	1.80	15	12	7	4	1
F. Owen	0	0	3.00	6	6	3	2	0

CHICAGO (N.L.)

	W	L	ERA	IP	H	BB	SO	SV
T. Brown	1	2	3.66	19.2	14	4	12	0
O. Overall	0	0	1.50	12	10	3	8	0
E. Reulbach	1	0	2.45	11	6	8	4	0
J. Pfiester	0	2	6.10	10.1	7	3	11	0

1907 WORLD SERIES

LINE SCORES						PITCHERS (innings pitched)	HOME RUNS (men on)	HIGHLIGHTS

Chicago (N.L.) defeats Detroit (A.L.) 4 games to 0

			R	H	E	PITCHERS (innings pitched)	HOME RUNS (men on)	HIGHLIGHTS
GAME 1 - OCTOBER 8								Schmidt's third-strike passed ball with two out in the ninth allowed the Cubs to even the game, which ended after 12 in a 3-3 tie. Donovan struck out 12 and the Cubs stole seven bases.
DET	**A**	000 000 030 000	3	9	3	Donovan (12)		
CHI	**N**	000 100 002 000	3	10	5	Overall (9), Reulbach (3)		
GAME 2 - OCTOBER 9								Slagle drove in the go-ahead run with a single in the fourth, then scored an insurance run on Sheckard's double.
DET	**A**	010 000 000	1	9	1	**Mullin** (8)		
CHI	**N**	010 200 00x	3	9	1	**Pfiester** (9)		
GAME 3 - OCTOBER 10								Evers's three hits led the Cubs' attack as Reulbach subdued the Tigers on six scattered hits.
DET	**A**	000 001 000	1	6	1	**Siever** (4), Killian (4)		
CHI	**N**	010 310 00x	5	10	1	**Reulbach** (9)		
GAME 4 - OCTOBER 11								Overall aided his own cause with a go-ahead two-run single in the fifth as he held the Tigers to five hits.
CHI	**N**	000 020 301	6	7	2	**Overall** (9)		
DET	**A**	000 100 000	1	5	2	**Donovan** (9)		
GAME 5 - OCTOBER 12								The Cubs swept the Series behind Brown's shutout. The Cubs swiped 18 bases in the five games, and held batting champ Ty Cobb to a .200 average.
CHI	**N**	110 000 000	2	7	1	**Brown** (9)		
DET	**A**	000 000 000	0	7	2	**Mullin** (9)		

Team totals

		W	AB	H	2B	3B	HR	R	RBI	BA	BB	SO	ERA
CHI	**N**	4	167	43	6	1	0	19	16	.257	12	25	0.75
DET	**A**	0	172	36	1	2	0	6	6	.209	9	22	1.96

Individual Batting

CHICAGO (N.L.)

	AB	H	2B	3B	HR	R	RBI	BA
J. Slagle, of	22	6	0	0	0	3	4	.273
J. Sheckard, of	21	5	2	0	0	0	2	.238
J. Evers, 2b, ss	20	7	2	0	0	2	1	.350
W. Schulte, of	20	5	0	0	0	3	2	.250
J. Kling, c	19	4	0	0	0	2	1	.211
H. Steinfeldt, 3b	17	8	1	1	0	2	2	.471
F. Chance, 1b	14	3	1	0	0	3	0	.214
J. Tinker, ss	13	2	0	0	0	4	1	.154
D. Howard, 1b	5	1	0	0	0	0	0	.200
O. Overall, p	5	1	0	0	0	0	2	.200
E. Reulbach, p	5	1	0	0	0	0	1	.200
T. Brown, p	3	0	0	0	0	0	0	.000
J. Pfiester, p	2	0	0	0	0	0	0	.000
H. Zimmerman, 2b	1	0	0	0	0	0	0	.000
P. Moran	0	0	0	0	0	0	0	—

Errors: J. Evers (3), J. Tinker (3), W. Schulte (2), J. Kling, J. Slagle

Stolen Bases: J. Slagle (6), F. Chance (3), J. Evers (3), J. Tinker (2), D. Howard, W. Schulte, J. Sheckard, H. Steinfeldt

DETROIT (A.L.)

	AB	H	2B	3B	HR	R	RBI	BA
S. Crawford, of	21	5	1	0	0	1	2	.238
G. Schaefer, 2b	21	3	0	0	0	1	0	.143
C. Rossman, 1b	20	8	0	1	0	1	2	.400
B. Coughlin, 3b	20	5	0	0	0	0	0	.250
T. Cobb, of	20	4	0	1	0	1	1	.200
D. Jones, of	17	6	0	0	0	1	0	.353
C. O'Leary, ss	17	1	0	0	0	0	0	.059
B. Schmidt, c	12	2	0	0	0	0	0	.167
W. Donovan, p	8	0	0	0	0	0	0	.000
G. Mullin, p	6	0	0	0	0	0	0	.000
F. Payne, c	4	1	0	0	0	0	1	.250
J. Archer, c	3	0	0	0	0	0	0	.000
E. Killian, p	2	1	0	0	0	1	0	.500
E. Siever, p	1	0	0	0	0	0	0	.000

Errors: B. Coughlin (2), C. O'Leary (2), B. Schmidt (2), D. Jones, F. Payne, C. Rossman

Stolen Bases: D. Jones (3), C. Rossman (2), B. Coughlin, G. Schaefer

Individual Pitching

CHICAGO (N.L.)

	W	L	ERA	IP	H	BB	SO	SV
O. Overall	1	0	1.00	18	14	4	11	0
E. Reulbach	1	0	0.75	12	6	3	4	0
T. Brown	1	0	0.00	9	7	1	4	0
J. Pfiester	1	0	1.00	9	9	1	3	0

DETROIT (A.L.)

	W	L	ERA	IP	H	BB	SO	SV
W. Donovan	0	1	1.29	21	17	5	16	0
G. Mullin	0	2	2.12	17	16	6	7	0
E. Killian	0	0	2.25	4	3	1	1	0
E. Siever	0	1	4.50	4	7	0	1	0

1908 WORLD SERIES

Chicago (N.L.) defeats Detroit (A.L.) 4 games to 1

LINE SCORES			R	H	E	PITCHERS (innings pitched)	HOME RUNS (men on)	HIGHLIGHTS
GAME 1 - OCTOBER 10								Five Cub runs in the ninth, four scoring on two-run singles by Hofman and Kling, broke open a game played in heavy rain.
CHI	**N**	004 000 105	10	14	2	Reulbach (6.2), Overall (0.1), **Brown** (2)		
DET	**A**	100 000 320	6	10	4	Killian (2.1), **Summers** (6.2)		
GAME 2 - OCTOBER 11								Donovan held the Cubs to one hit in seven innings, but Tinker's homer sparked a six-run rally that broke up a scoreless deadlock.
DET	**A**	000 000 001	1	4	1	**Donovan** (8)		
CHI	**N**	000 000 06x	6	7	1	**Overall** (9)	Tinker (1 on)	
GAME 3 - OCTOBER 12								Cobb's four hits led the Detroit attack to a come-from-behind victory.
DET	**A**	100 005 020	8	11	4	**Mullin** (9)		
CHI	**N**	000 300 000	3	7	2	**Pfiester** (8), Reulbach (1)		
GAME 4 - OCTOBER 13								Back-to-back scoring singles by Steinfeldt and Hofman in the third gave Brown all the runs he needed to subdue the Tigers.
DET	**A**	002 000 001	3	10	0	**Brown** (9)		
DET	**A**	000 000 000	0	4	1	**Summers** (8), Winter (1)		
GAME 5 - OCTOBER 14								Three hits and one RBI each by Evers and Chance aided Overall's 10-strikeout pitching in the Series clincher.
CHI	**N**	100 010 000	2	10	0	**Overall** (9)		
DET	**A**	000 000 000	0	3	0	**Donovan** (9)		

Team totals

		W	AB	H	2B	3B	HR	R	RBI	BA	BB	SO	ERA
CHI	**N**	4	164	48	4	2	1	24	20	.293	13	26	2.60
DET	**A**	1	158	32	5	0	0	15	14	.203	12	26	3.48

Individual Batting

CHICAGO (N.L.)

	AB	H	2B	3B	HR	R	RBI	BA
J. Sheckard, of	21	5	2	0	0	2	1	.238
J. Evers, 2b	20	7	1	0	0	5	2	.350
F. Chance, 1b	19	8	0	0	0	4	2	.421
S. Hofman, of	19	6	0	1	0	2	4	.316
J. Tinker, ss	19	5	0	0	1	2	5	.263
W. Schulte, of	18	7	0	1	0	4	2	.389
J. Kling, c	16	4	1	0	0	2	1	.250
H. Steinfeldt, 3b	16	4	0	0	0	3	3	.250
O. Overall, p	6	2	0	0	0	0	0	.333
T. Brown, p	4	0	0	0	0	0	0	.000
E. Reulbach, p	3	0	0	0	0	0	0	.000
J. Pfiester, p	2	0	0	0	0	0	0	.000
D. Howard	1	0	0	0	0	0	0	.000

Errors: F. Chance (3), J. Evers, H. Steinfeldt

Stolen Bases: F. Chance (5), J. Evers (2), S. Hofman (2), W. Schulte (2), J. Sheckard, H. Steinfeldt, J. Tinker

DETROIT (A.L.)

	AB	H	2B	3B	HR	R	RBI	BA
S. Crawford, of	21	5	1	0	0	2	1	.238
T. Cobb, of	19	7	1	0	0	3	4	.368
C. Rossman, 1b	19	4	0	0	0	3	3	.211
C. O'Leary, ss	19	3	0	0	0	2	0	.158
M. McIntyre, of	18	4	1	0	0	2	0	.222
G. Schaefer, 2b, 3b	16	2	0	0	0	0	0	.125
B. Schmidt, c	14	1	0	0	0	0	1	.071
B. Coughlin, 3b	8	1	0	0	0	0	1	.125
R. Downs, 2b	6	1	1	0	0	1	1	.167
E. Summers, p	5	1	0	0	0	0	1	.200
I. Thomas, c	4	2	1	0	0	0	1	.500
W. Donovan, p	4	0	0	0	0	0	0	.000
G. Mullin, p	3	1	0	0	0	1	1	.333
D. Jones	2	0	0	0	0	1	0	.000

Errors: T. Cobb (2), C. Rossman (2), B. Coughlin, W. Donovan, R. Downs, M. McIntyre, C. O'Leary, G. Schaefer

Stolen Bases: T. Cobb (2), W. Donovan, M. McIntyre

Individual Pitching

CHICAGO (N.L.)

	W	L	ERA	IP	H	BB	SO	SV
O. Overall	2	0	0.98	18.1	7	7	15	0
T. Brown	2	0	0.00	11	6	1	5	0
J. Pfiester	0	1	7.88	8	10	3	1	0
E. Reulbach	0	0	4.70	7.2	9	1	5	0

DETROIT (A.L.)

	W	L	ERA	IP	H	BB	SO	SV
W. Donovan	0	2	4.24	17	17	4	10	0
E. Summers	0	2	4.30	14.2	18	4	7	0
G. Mullin	1	0	1.00	9	7	1	8	0
E. Killian	0	0	7.71	2.1	5	3	1	0
G. Winter	0	0	0.00	1	1	1	0	0

1909 WORLD SERIES

LINE SCORES						PITCHERS (innings pitched)	HOME RUNS (men on)	HIGHLIGHTS

Pittsburgh (N.L.) defeats Detroit (A.L.) 4 games to 3

GAME 1 - OCTOBER 8

DET	A	100 000 000	1	6	4	**Mullin** (8)	
PIT	N	000 121 00x	4	5	0	**Adams** (9)	Clarke

Leach made a running catch of Cobb's fly in the seventh with two on and two out to preserve the 4-1 lead.

GAME 2 - OCTOBER 9

DET	A	023 020 000	7	9	3	**Donovan** (9)	
PIT	N	200 000 000	2	5	1	**Camnitz** (2.2), Willis (6.1)	

Three in the third, capped by Cobb's steal of home, broke open the game. Every Tiger hitter except Donovan had at least one hit.

GAME 3 - OCTOBER 11

PIT	N	510 000 002	8	10	3	**Maddox** (9)	
DET	A	000 000 402	6	10	5	**Summers** (0.1), Willett (6.2), Works (2)	

The Pirates held off a late Tiger rally for the win. Wagner was the hitting star, with three singles, three RBIs, three stolen bases.

GAME 4 - OCTOBER 12

PIT	N	000 000 000	0	5	6	**Leifield** (4), Phillippe (4)	
DET	A	020 300 00x	5	8	0	**Mullin** (9)	

Cobb and Stanage contributed two RBIs each as the Tigers evened the Series, Mullin striking out ten Pirates.

GAME 5 - OCTOBER 13

DET	A	100 002 010	4	6	1	**Summers** (7), Willett (1)	D. Jones, Crawford
PIT	N	111 000 41x	8	10	2	**Adams** (9)	Clarke (2 on)

Clarke's two-run homer in the seventh broke open the 3-3 deadlock, off-setting Crawford's 3-for-4 performance that included a double and homer of his own.

GAME 6 - OCTOBER 14

PIT	N	300 000 001	4	7	3	**Willis** (5), Camnitz (1), Phillippe (2)	
DET	A	100 211 00x	5	10	3	**Mullin** (9)	

The Tigers suffered four injuries in the ninth but hung on to win. Tom Jones ran over Wilson to let in one run, but Schmidt and Moriarty ended the game by recording putouts while being spiked on close plays at the plate and at third.

GAME 7 - OCTOBER 16

PIT	N	020 203 010	8	7	0	**Adams** (9)	
DET	A	000 000 000	0	6	3	**Donovan** (3), Mullin (6)	

Clarke is walked four times and Wagner and Miller each had two RBIs to pace the Pirates' Series victory. Eighteen Buc stolen bases tied the Series record set by the Cubs in 1906.

Team totals

		W	AB	H	2B	3B	HR	R	RBI	BA	BB	SO	ERA
PIT	N	4	223	49	13	1	2	34	25	.220	20	34	3.10
DET	A	3	233	55	16	0	2	28	26	.236	20	22	3.10

Individual Batting

PITTSBURGH (N.L.)

	AB	H	2B	3B	HR	R	RBI	BA
D. Miller, 2b	28	7	1	0	0	2	4	.250
B. Abstein, 1b	26	6	2	0	0	3	2	.231
O. Wilson, of	26	4	1	0	0	2	1	.154
T. Leach, 3b, of	25	8	4	0	0	8	2	.320
G. Gibson, c	25	6	2	0	0	2	2	.240
H. Wagner, ss	24	8	2	1	0	4	6	.333
B. Byrne, 3b	24	6	1	0	0	5	0	.250
F. Clarke, of	19	4	0	0	2	7	7	.211
B. Adams, p	9	0	0	0	0	0	0	.000
H. Hyatt, of	4	0	0	0	0	1	1	.000
N. Maddox, p	4	0	0	0	0	0	0	.000
V. Willis, p	4	0	0	0	0	0	0	.000
E. Abbaticchio	1	0	0	0	0	0	0	.000
H. Camnitz, p	1	0	0	0	0	0	0	.000
L. Leifield, p	1	0	0	0	0	0	0	.000
P. O'Connor	1	0	0	0	0	0	0	.000
D. Phillippe, p	1	0	0	0	0	0	0	.000

Errors: B. Abstein (5), D. Miller (3), D. Phillippe (2), H. Wagner (2), B. Byrne, F. Clarke, O. Wilson

Stolen Bases: H. Wagner (6), F. Clarke (3), D. Miller (3), G. Gibson (2), B. Abstein, B. Byrne, T. Leach, O. Wilson

DETROIT (A.L.)

	AB	H	2B	3B	HR	R	RBI	BA
D. Jones, of	30	7	0	0	1	6	2	.233
S. Crawford, 1b, of	28	7	3	0	1	4	3	.250
J. Delahanty, 2b	26	9	4	0	0	2	4	.346
T. Cobb, of	26	6	3	0	0	3	6	.231
T. Jones, 1b	24	6	1	0	0	3	2	.250
D. Bush, ss	23	6	1	0	0	5	2	.261
G. Moriarty, 3b	22	6	1	0	0	4	1	.273
B. Schmidt, c	18	4	2	0	0	0	4	.222
G. Mullin, p	16	3	1	0	0	1	0	.188
O. Stanage, c	5	1	0	0	0	0	2	.200
W. Donovan, p	4	0	0	0	0	0	0	.000
M. McIntyre, of	3	0	0	0	0	0	0	.000
C. O'Leary, 3b	3	0	0	0	0	0	0	.000
E. Summers, p	3	0	0	0	0	0	0	.000
E. Willett, p	2	0	0	0	0	0	0	.000

Errors: D. Bush (5), B. Schmidt (5), S. Crawford (2), J. Delahanty (2), T. Cobb, W. Donovan, D. Jones, T. Jones, E. Willett

Stolen Bases: T. Cobb (2), D. Bush, S. Crawford, D. Jones, T. Jones

Individual Pitching

PITTSBURGH (N.L.)

	W	L	ERA	IP	H	BB	SO	SV
B. Adams	3	0	1.33	27	18	6	11	0
V. Willis	0	1	4.76	11.1	10	8	3	0
N. Maddox	1	0	1.00	9	10	2	4	0
D. Phillippe	0	0	0.00	6	2	1	2	0
L. Leifield	0	1	11.25	4	7	1	0	0
H. Camnitz	0	1	12.27	3.2	8	2	2	0

DETROIT (A.L.)

	W	L	ERA	IP	H	BB	SO	SV
G. Mullin	2	1	2.25	32	22	8	20	0
W. Donovan	1	1	3.00	12	7	8	7	0
E. Willett	0	0	0.00	7.2	3	0	1	0
E. Summers	0	2	8.59	7.1	13	4	4	0
R. Works	0	0	9.00	2	4	0	2	0

1910 WORLD SERIES

LINE SCORES						PITCHERS (innings pitched)	HOME RUNS (men on)	HIGHLIGHTS

Philadelphia (A.L.) defeats Chicago (N.L.) 4 games to 1

GAME 1 - OCTOBER 17								Baker's single, two doubles, and two RBIs paced the Athletics' attack. Bender lost his shutout in the ninth thanks to errors by Thomas and Strunk.
CHI	N	000 000 001	1	3	1	**Overall** (3), McIntire (5)		
PHI	A	021 000 01x	4	7	2	**Bender** (9)		
GAME 2 - OCTOBER 18								The Athletics broke open the game with a six-run seventh featuring four Athletics doubles. Everyone in the Philadelphia lineup contributed at least one hit.
CHI	N	100 000 101	3	8	3	**Brown** (7), Richie (1)		
PHI	A	002 010 60x	9	14	4	**Coombs** (9)		
GAME 3 - OCTOBER 20								Murphy's three-run homer sparked a five-run third inning to put the game out of reach of the Cubs. Coombs aided his own cause with three hits and three RBIs.
PHI	A	125 000 400	12	15	1	**Coombs** (9)	Murphy (2 on)	
CHI	N	120 000 020	5	6	5	Reulbach (2), **McIntire** (0.1) Pfiester (6.2)		
GAME 4 - OCTOBER 22								Chance's triple with one out in the ninth tied the game and Sheckard's game-winning single in the bottom of the tenth prevented a Series sweep.
PHI	A	001 200 000 0	3	11	3	**Bender** (9.2)		
CHI	N	100 100 001 1	4	9	1	Cole (8), **Brown** (2)		
GAME 5 - OCTOBER 23								Athletics scored five times in the eighth to break open a tight game and wrap up the Series in five games. Coombs posted his third victory and Collins led the offense with three hits and two RBIs.
PHI	A	100 010 050	7	9	1	**Coombs** (9)		
CHI	N	010 000 010	2	9	2	**Brown** (9)		

Team totals

		W	AB	H	2B	3B	HR	R	RBI	BA	BB	SO	ERA
PHI	A	4	177	56	19	1	1	35	29	.316	17	24	2.76
CHI	N	1	158	35	11	1	0	15	13	.222	18	31	4.70

Individual Batting

PHILADELPHIA (A.L.)

	AB	H	2B	3B	HR	R	RBI	BA
F. Baker, 3b	22	9	3	0	0	6	4	.409
B. Lord, of	22	4	2	0	0	3	1	.182
E. Collins, 2b	21	9	4	0	0	5	3	.429
D. Murphy, of	20	7	3	0	1	6	8	.350
A. Strunk, of	18	5	1	1	0	2	2	.278
H. Davis, 1b	17	6	3	0	0	5	2	.353
J. Barry, ss	17	4	2	0	0	3	3	.235
J. Coombs, p	13	5	1	0	0	0	3	.385
I. Thomas, c	12	3	0	0	0	2	1	.250
C. Bender, p	6	2	0	0	0	1	1	.333
T. Hartsel, of	5	1	0	0	0	2	0	.200
J. Lapp, c	4	1	0	0	0	0	1	.250

Errors: F. Baker (3), H. Davis (3), J. Coombs (2), E. Collins, A. Strunk, I. Thomas

Stolen Bases: E. Collins (4), T. Hartsel (2), D. Murphy

CHICAGO (N.L.)

	AB	H	2B	3B	HR	R	RBI	BA
H. Steinfeldt, 3b	20	2	1	0	0	0	1	.100
J. Tinker, ss	18	6	2	0	0	2	0	.333
F. Chance, 1b	17	6	1	1	0	1	4	.353
W. Schulte, of	17	6	3	0	0	3	2	.353
H. Zimmerman, 2b	17	4	1	0	0	0	2	.235
S. Hofman, of	15	4	0	0	0	2	2	.267
J. Sheckard, of	14	4	2	0	0	5	1	.286
J. Kling, c	13	1	0	0	0	0	1	.077
J. Archer, 1b, c	11	2	1	0	0	1	0	.182
T. Brown, p	7	0	0	0	0	0	0	.000
G. Beaumont	2	0	0	0	0	1	0	.000
K. Cole, p	2	0	0	0	0	0	0	.000
J. Pfiester, p	2	0	0	0	0	0	0	.000
H. McIntire, p	1	0	0	0	0	0	0	.000
T. Needham	1	0	0	0	0	0	0	.000
O. Overall, p	1	0	0	0	0	0	0	.000
J. Kane	0	0	0	0	0	0	0	—

Errors: H. Steinfeldt (4), J. Tinker (2), T. Brown, S. Hofman, H. McIntire, W. Schulte, J. Sheckard, H. Zimmerman

Stolen Bases: J. Sheckard, J. Tinker, H. Zimmerman

Individual Pitching

PHILADELPHIA (A.L.)

	W	L	ERA	IP	H	BB	SO	SV
J. Coombs	3	0	3.33	27	23	14	17	0
C. Bender	1	1	1.93	18.2	12	4	14	0

CHICAGO (N.L.)

	W	L	ERA	IP	H	BB	SO	SV
T. Brown	1	2	5.00	18	23	7	14	0
K. Cole	0	0	3.38	8	10	3	5	0
J. Pfiester	0	0	0.00	6.2	9	1	1	0
H. McIntire	0	1	6.75	5.1	4	3	3	0
O. Overall	0	1	9.00	3	6	1	1	0
E. Reulbach	0	0	13.50	2	3	2	0	0
L. Richie	0	0	0.00	1	1	0	0	0

1911 WORLD SERIES

Philadelphia (A.L.) defeats New York (N.L.) 4 games to 2

LINE SCORES			R	H	E	PITCHERS (innings pitched)	HOME RUNS (men on)	HIGHLIGHTS
GAME 1 - OCTOBER 14								Devore's go-ahead single in the seventh gave Mathewson and the Giants a 2-1 victory over Bender, who struck out 11 in a losing cause.
PHI	**A**	010 000 000	1	6	2	**Bender** (8)		
NY	**N**	000 100 10x	2	5	0	**Mathewson** (9)		
GAME 2 - OCTOBER 16								Baker's two-run homer in the sixth broke a 1-1 deadlock and evened the Series.
NY	**N**	010 000 000	1	5	3	**Marquard** (7), Crandall (1)		
PHI	**A**	100 002 00x	3	4	0	**Plank** (9)	Baker (1 on)	
GAME 3 - OCTOBER 17								Baker's homer in the top of the ninth sent the game into extra innings. The Athletics scored twice in the 11th; Davis's RBI single proved the deciding run as the Giants countered with a run in their half of the inning.
PHI	**A**	000 000 001 02	3	9	2	**Coombs** (11)	Baker	
NY	**N**	001 000 000 01	2	3	5	**Mathewson** (11)		
GAME 4 - OCTOBER 24								The Giants' two-run lead was overcome in the fourth as the Athletics scored three times. Baker, Murphy, and Barry led the attack with two doubles each.
NY	**N**	200 000 000	2	7	3	**Mathewson** (7), Wiltse (1)		
PHI	**A**	000 310 00x	4	11	1	**Bender** (9)		
GAME 5 - OCTOBER 25								The Giants scored two runs in the ninth, tying the game and offsetting Oldring's third inning three-run shot. Merkle's sacrifice fly in the bottom of the tenth drove in the winning run.
PHI	**A**	003 000 000 0	3	7	1	Coombs (9), **Plank** (0.2)	Oldring (2 on)	
NY	**N**	000 000 102 1	4	9	2	Marquard (3), Ames (4), **Crandall** (3)		
GAME 6 - OCTOBER 26								Six singles, a double, an error, and a wild pitch led to seven Philadelphia runs and a World Series crown.
NY	**N**	100 000 001	2	4	3	**Ames** (4), Wiltse (2.1), Marquard (1.2)		
PHI	**A**	001 401 70x	13	13	5	**Bender** (9)		

Team totals

		W	AB	H	2B	3B	HR	R	RBI	BA	BB	SO	ERA
PHI	**A**	4	205	50	15	0	3	27	20	.244	4	31	1.29
NY	**N**	2	189	33	11	1	0	13	10	.175	14	44	2.83

Individual Batting

PHILADELPHIA (A.L.)

	AB	H	2B	3B	HR	R	RBI	BA
B. Lord, of	27	5	2	0	0	2	1	.185
R. Oldring, of	25	5	2	0	1	2	3	.200
F. Baker, 3b	24	9	2	0	2	7	5	.375
H. Davis, 1b	24	5	1	0	0	3	5	.208
D. Murphy, of	23	7	3	0	0	4	2	.304
E. Collins, 2b	21	6	1	0	0	4	1	.286
J. Barry, ss	19	7	4	0	0	2	2	.368
I. Thomas, c	12	1	0	0	0	1	1	.083
C. Bender, p	11	1	0	0	0	0	0	.091
J. Coombs, p	8	2	0	0	0	1	0	.250
J. Lapp, c	8	2	0	0	0	1	0	.250
E. Plank, p	3	0	0	0	0	0	0	.000
S. McInnis, 1b	0	0	0	0	0	0	0	—
A. Strunk	0	0	0	0	0	0	0	—

Errors: E. Collins (4), J. Barry (3), F. Baker (2), D. Murphy, R. Oldring

Stolen Bases: J. Barry (2), E. Collins (2)

NEW YORK (N.L.)

	AB	H	2B	3B	HR	R	RBI	BA
J. Devore, of	24	4	1	0	0	1	3	.167
L. Doyle, 2b	23	7	3	1	0	3	1	.304
A. Fletcher, ss	23	3	1	0	0	1	1	.130
B. Herzog, 3b	21	4	2	0	0	3	0	.190
R. Murray, of	21	0	0	0	0	0	0	.000
C. Meyers, c	20	6	2	0	0	2	2	.300
F. Merkle, 1b	20	3	1	0	0	1	1	.150
F. Snodgrass, of	19	2	0	0	0	1	1	.105
C. Mathewson, p	7	2	0	0	0	0	0	.286
B. Becker	3	0	0	0	0	0	0	.000
R. Ames, p	2	1	0	0	0	0	0	.500
D. Crandall, p	2	1	1	0	0	1	1	.500
R. Marquard, p	2	0	0	0	0	0	0	.000
A. Wilson, c	1	0	0	0	0	0	0	.000
H. Wiltse, p	1	0	0	0	0	0	0	.000

Errors: A. Fletcher (4), B. Herzog (3), R. Murray (3), F. Merkle (2), R. Ames, J. Devore, L. Doyle, C. Mathewson

Stolen Bases: L. Doyle (2), B. Herzog (2)

Individual Pitching

PHILADELPHIA (A.L.)

	W	L	ERA	IP	H	BB	SO	SV
C. Bender	2	1	1.04	26	16	8	20	0
J. Coombs	1	0	1.35	20	11	6	16	0
E. Plank	1	1	1.86	9.2	6	0	8	0

NEW YORK (N.L.)

	W	L	ERA	IP	H	BB	SO	SV
C. Mathewson	1	2	2.00	27	25	2	13	0
R. Marquard	0	1	1.54	11.2	9	1	8	0
R. Ames	0	1	2.25	8	6	1	6	0
D. Crandall	1	0	0.00	4	2	0	2	0
H. Wiltse	0	0	18.90	3.1	8	0	2	0

1912 WORLD SERIES

LINE SCORES					PITCHERS (innings pitched)	HOME RUNS (men on)	HIGHLIGHTS

Boston (A.L.) defeats New York (N.L.) 4 games to 3

LINE SCORES			R	H	E	PITCHERS (innings pitched)	HOME RUNS (men on)	HIGHLIGHTS
GAME 1 - OCTOBER 8								Yerkes's single in the seventh drove in the go-ahead and deciding runs and Wood held off the Giants' ninth-inning rally. Wood had 11 strikeouts in the game.
BOS	**A**	000 001 300	4	6	1	**Wood** (9)		
NY	**N**	002 000 001	3	8	1	**Tesreau** (7), Crandall (2)		
GAME 2 - OCTOBER 9								Five Giant errors, three by Fletcher, led to four unearned Boston runs in a game called on account of darkness after eleven innings.
NY	**N**	010 100 030 10	6	11	5	Mathewson (11)		
BOS	**A**	300 010 010 10	6	10	1	Collins (7.1), Hall (2.2), Bedient (1)		
GAME 3 - OCTOBER 10								Devore's running catch in the bottom of the ninth with two on and two out saved the game for the Giants.
NY	**N**	010 010 000	2	7	1	**Marquard** (9)		
BOS	**A**	000 000 001	1	7	0	**O'Brien** (8), Bedient (1)		
GAME 4 - OCTOBER 11								Wood scattered nine hits, struck out eight, and drove in one man with a single to aid his own cause.
BOS	**A**	010 100 001	3	8	1	**Wood** (9)		
NY	**N**	000 000 100	1	9	1	**Tesreau** (7), Ames (2)		
GAME 5 - OCTOBER 12								Back-to-back triples by Hooper and Yerkes and Doyle's error in the third gave the Red Sox their two runs. Mathewson settled down to retire the last 17 batters in a row, but the Giants managed just three hits against Bedient.
NY	**N**	000 000 100	1	3	1	**Mathewson** (8)		
BOS	**A**	002 000 00x	2	5	1	**Bedient** (9)		
GAME 6 - OCTOBER 14								The Giants took charge with five runs in the first, including back-to-back RBI doubles by Merkle and Herzog.
BOS	**A**	020 000 000	2	7	2	**O'Brien** (1), Collins (7)		
NY	**N**	500 000 00x	5	11	2	**Marquard** (9)		
GAME 7 - OCTOBER 15								The Giants again jumped to an early lead and held to to even the Series.
NY	**N**	610 002 101	11	16	4	**Tesreau** (9)	Doyle (1 on)	
BOS	**A**	010 000 210	4	9	3	**Wood** (1), Hall (8)	Gardner	
GAME 8 - OCTOBER 16								New York scored in the top of the tenth, but Snodgrass dropped a fly ball and Merkle let Speaker's foul pop get away, allowing the Red Sox to tie the game before winning on a sacrifice fly by Gardner.
NY	**N**	001 000 000 1	2	9	2	**Mathewson** (9.2)		
BOS	**A**	000 000 100 2	3	8	5	Bedient (7), **Wood** (3)		

Team totals

		W	AB	H	2B	3B	HR	R	RBI	BA	BB	SO	ERA
BOS	**A**	4	273	60	14	6	1	25	21	.220	19	36	2.92
NY	**N**	3	274	74	14	4	1	31	25	.270	22	39	1.83

Individual Batting

BOSTON (A.L.)

	AB	H	2B	3B	HR	R	RBI	BA
J. Stahl, 1b	32	9	2	0	0	3	2	.281
S. Yerkes, 2b	32	8	0	2	0	3	4	.250
D. Lewis, of	32	5	3	0	0	4	2	.156
H. Hooper, of	31	9	2	1	0	3	2	.290
T. Speaker, of	30	9	1	2	0	4	2	.300
H. Wagner, ss	30	5	1	0	0	1	0	.167
L. Gardner, 3b	28	5	2	1	1	4	4	.179
H. Cady, c	22	3	0	0	0	1	1	.136
S. Wood, p	7	2	0	0	0	1	1	.286
B. Carrigan, c	7	0	0	0	0	0	0	.000
H. Bedient, p	6	0	0	0	0	0	0	.000
R. Collins, p	5	0	0	0	0	0	0	.000
C. Hall, p	4	3	1	0	0	0	0	.750
C. Engle	3	1	1	0	0	1	2	.333
B. O'Brien, p	2	0	0	0	0	0	0	.000
O. Henriksen	1	1	1	0	0	0	1	1.000
N. Ball	1	0	0	0	0	0	0	.000

Errors: L. Gardner (4), H. Wagner (3), T. Speaker (2), H. Cady, C. Hall, D. Lewis, J. Stahl, S. Yerkes

Stolen Bases: H. Hooper (2), J. Stahl (2), T. Speaker, H. Wagner

NEW YORK (N.L.)

	AB	H	2B	3B	HR	R	RBI	BA
F. Merkle, 1b	33	9	2	1	0	5	3	.273
L. Doyle, 2b	33	8	1	0	1	5	2	.242
F. Snodgrass, of	33	7	2	0	0	2	2	.212
R. Murray, of	31	10	4	1	0	5	5	.323
B. Herzog, 3b	30	12	4	1	0	6	4	.400
C. Meyers, c	28	10	0	1	0	2	3	.357
A. Fletcher, ss	28	5	1	0	0	1	3	.179
J. Devore, of	24	6	0	0	0	4	0	.250
C. Mathewson, p	12	2	0	0	0	0	0	.167
J. Tesreau, p	8	3	0	0	0	0	2	.375
M. McCormick	4	1	0	0	0	0	1	.250
B. Becker, of	4	0	0	0	0	1	0	.000
R. Marquard, p	4	0	0	0	0	0	0	.000
A. Wilson, c	1	1	0	0	0	0	0	1.000
D. Crandall, p	1	0	0	0	0	0	0	.000
T. Shafer, ss	0	0	0	0	0	0	0	—

Errors: L. Doyle (4), A. Fletcher (4), F. Merkle (3), J. Devore (2), R. Marquard, C. Meyers, F. Snodgrass, A. Wilson

Stolen Bases: J. Devore (4), L. Doyle (2), B. Herzog (2), A. Fletcher, F. Merkle, C. Meyers, F. Snodgrass

Individual Pitching

BOSTON (A.L.)

	W	L	ERA	IP	H	BB	SO	SV
S. Wood	3	1	3.68	22	27	3	21	0
H. Bedient	1	0	0.50	18	10	7	7	0
R. Collins	0	0	1.88	14.1	14	0	6	0
C. Hall	0	0	3.38	10.2	11	9	1	0
B. O'Brien	0	2	7.00	9	12	3	4	0

NEW YORK (N.L.)

	W	L	ERA	IP	H	BB	SO	SV
C. Mathewson	0	2	1.57	28.2	23	5	10	0
J. Tesreau	1	2	3.13	23	19	11	15	0
R. Marquard	2	0	0.50	18	14	2	9	0
R. Ames	0	0	4.50	2	3	1	0	0
D. Crandall	0	0	0.00	2	1	0	2	0

1913 WORLD SERIES

Philadelphia (A.L.) defeats New York (N.L.) 4 games to 1

LINE SCORES						PITCHERS (innings pitched)	HOME RUNS (men on)	HIGHLIGHTS
GAME 1 - OCTOBER 7								Baker had three RBIs and three hits including a home run in the fifth for the A's.
PHI	A	000 320 010	6	11	1	Bender (9)	Baker (1 on)	
NY	N	001 030 000	4	11	0	Marquard (5), Crandall (2), Tesreau (2)		
GAME 2 - OCTOBER 8								The Giants scored three times in the tenth as Mathewson drove in the game-winning run with a single.
NY	N	000 000 000 3	3	7	2	Mathewson (10)		
PHI	A	000 000 000 0	0	8	2	Plank (10)		
GAME 3 - OCTOBER 9								The Athletics jumped to an early 5-0 lead and coasted on to the victory, paced by Collins's second three-hit game of the Series.
PHI	A	320 000 210	8	12	1	Bush (9)	Schang	
NY	N	000 010 100	2	5	1	Tesreau (6.1), Crandall (2.2)		
GAME 4 - OCTOBER 10								Bender posted his second victory, aided by Schang's three RBIs. He wavered in the late innings, giving up Merkle's three-run homer in the seventh and three more hits in the eighth, but held on for the win.
NY	N	000 000 320	5	8	2	Demaree (4), Marquard (4)	Merkle (2 on)	
PHI	A	010 320 00x	6	9	0	Bender (9)		
GAME 5 - OCTOBER 11								Plank allowed just two hits, singles by Mathewson and McLean, and faced only 29 men in leading the Athletics to their third Series triumph in four years.
PHI	A	102 000 000	3	6	1	Plank (9)		
NY	N	000 010 000	1	2	2	Mathewson (9)		

Team totals

		W	AB	H	2B	3B	HR	R	RBI	BA	BB	SO	ERA
PHI	A	4	174	46	4	4	2	23	21	.264	7	16	2.15
NY	N	1	164	33	3	1	1	15	15	.201	8	19	3.60

Individual Batting

PHILADELPHIA (A.L.)

	AB	H	2B	3B	HR	R	RBI	BA
R. Oldring, of	22	6	0	1	0	5	0	.273
E. Murphy, of	22	5	0	0	0	2	0	.227
F. Baker, 3b	20	9	0	0	1	2	7	.450
J. Barry, ss	20	6	3	0	0	3	2	.300
E. Collins, 2b	19	8	0	2	0	5	3	.421
S. McInnis, 1b	17	2	1	0	0	1	2	.118
A. Strunk, of	17	2	0	0	0	3	0	.118
W. Schang, c	14	5	0	1	1	2	6	.357
C. Bender, p	8	0	0	0	0	0	1	.000
E. Plank, p	7	1	0	0	0	0	0	.143
J. Bush, p	4	1	0	0	0	0	0	.250
J. Lapp, c	4	1	0	0	0	0	0	.250

Errors: F. Baker, J. Barry, E. Collins, E. Plank, W. Schang

Stolen Bases: E. Collins (3), F. Baker, R. Oldring

NEW YORK (N.L.)

	AB	H	2B	3B	HR	R	RBI	BA
L. Doyle, 2b	20	3	0	0	0	1	2	.150
G. Burns, of	19	3	2	0	0	2	1	.158
T. Shafer, 3b, of	19	3	1	1	0	2	1	.158
B. Herzog, 3b	19	1	0	0	0	1	0	.053
A. Fletcher, ss	18	5	0	0	0	1	4	.278
R. Murray, of	16	4	0	0	0	2	1	.250
F. Merkle, 1b	13	3	0	0	1	3	3	.231
L. McLean, c	12	6	0	0	0	0	2	.500
C. Mathewson, p	5	3	0	0	0	1	1	.600
D. Crandall, p	4	0	0	0	0	0	0	.000
C. Meyers, c	4	0	0	0	0	0	0	.000
F. Snodgrass, 1b, of	3	1	0	0	0	0	0	.333
A. Wilson, c	3	0	0	0	0	0	0	.000
M. McCormick	2	1	0	0	0	1	0	.500
J. Tesreau, p	2	0	0	0	0	0	0	.000
H. Wiltse, 1b	2	0	0	0	0	0	0	.000
A. Demaree, p	1	0	0	0	0	0	0	.000
E. Grant	1	0	0	0	0	1	0	.000
R. Marquard, p	1	0	0	0	0	0	0	.000
C. Cooper	0	0	0	0	0	0	0	—

Errors: L. Doyle (3), F. Merkle (2), G. Burns, A. Fletcher

Stolen Bases: R. Murray (2), G. Burns, C. Cooper, A. Fletcher

Individual Pitching

PHILADELPHIA (A.L.)

	W	L	ERA	IP	H	BB	SO	SV
E. Plank	1	1	0.95	19	9	3	7	0
C. Bender	2	0	4.00	18	19	1	9	0
J. Bush	1	0	1.00	9	5	4	3	0

NEW YORK (N.L.)

	W	L	ERA	IP	H	BB	SO	SV
C. Mathewson	1	1	0.95	19	14	2	7	0
R. Marquard	0	1	7.00	9	10	3	3	0
J. Tesreau	0	1	5.40	8.1	11	1	4	0
D. Crandall	0	0	3.86	4.2	4	0	2	0
A. Demaree	0	1	4.50	4	7	1	0	0

1914 WORLD SERIES

LINE SCORES					PITCHERS (innings pitched)	HOME RUNS (men on)	HIGHLIGHTS

Boston (N.L.) defeats Philadelphia (A.L.) 4 games to 0

GAME 1 - OCTOBER 9

						PITCHERS	HOME RUNS
BOS	**N**	020 013 010	7	11	2	**Rudolph** (9)	
PHI	**A**	010 000 000	1	5	0	**Bender** (5.1), cyckoff (3.2)	

Gowdy's single, double, and triple paced the attack as the Braves knocked Bender out of the box for the first time in his ten World Series starts.

GAME 2 - OCTOBER 10

						PITCHERS	HOME RUNS
BOS	**N**	000 000 001	1	7	1	**James** (9)	
PHI	**A**	000 000 000	0	2	1	**Plank** (9)	

Deal reached second with one out in the top of the ninth when Strunk misplayed his fly ball, and scored on Mann's two-out single for the game's only run.

GAME 3 - OCTOBER 12

						PITCHERS	HOME RUNS
PHI	**A**	100 100 000 200	4	8	2	**Bush** (11)	
BOS	**N**	010 100 000 201	5	9	1	Tyler (10), **James** (2)	Gowdy

Bush's wild throw in the bottom of the 12th allowed the winning run to score. The Braves nearly gave the Athletics the game in the tenth when Evers muffed a grounder with the bases loaded to allow a run, and then continued to hold the ball, letting Murphy score. But Gowdy's homer and Connolly's sac fly to score Moran evened the game in the Braves' half of the 10th.

GAME 4 - OCTOBER 13

						PITCHERS	HOME RUNS
PHI	**A**	000 010 000	1	7	0	**Shawkey** (5), Pennock (3)	
BOS	**N**	000 120 00x	3	6	0	**Rudolph** (9)	

The Braves swept the Series on Evers's go-ahead two-run single in the fifth. The hitting star of the Series for the Braves was Gowdy, who batted .545 with five extra-base hits in eleven at bats.

Team totals

		W	AB	H	2B	3B	HR	R	RBI	BA	BB	SO	ERA
BOS	**N**	4	135	33	6	2	1	16	14	.244	15	18	1.15
PHI	**A**	0	128	22	9	0	0	6	5	.172	13	28	3.65

Individual Batting

BOSTON (N.L.)

	AB	H	2B	3B	HR	R	RBI	BA
B. Schmidt, 1b	17	5	0	0	0	2	2	.294
J. Evers, 2b	16	7	0	0	0	2	2	.438
C. Deal, 3b	16	2	2	0	0	1	0	.125
P. Whitted, of	14	3	0	1	0	2	2	.214
R. Maranville, ss	13	4	0	0	0	1	3	.308
H. Moran, of	13	1	1	0	0	2	0	.077
H. Gowdy, c	11	6	3	1	1	3	3	.545
J. Connolly, of	9	1	0	0	0	1	1	.111
L. Mann, of	7	2	0	0	0	1	1	.286
D. Rudolph, p	6	2	0	0	0	1	0	.333
T. Cather, of	5	0	0	0	0	0	0	.000
B. James, p	4	0	0	0	0	0	0	.000
L. Tyler, p	3	0	0	0	0	0	0	.000
J. Devore	1	0	0	0	0	0	0	.000
L. Gilbert	0	0	0	0	0	0	0	—

Errors: J. Connolly, J. Evers, R. Maranville, H. Moran

Stolen Bases: C. Deal (2), R. Maranville (2), J. Evers, H. Gowdy, H. Moran, B. Schmidt, P. Whitted

PHILADELPHIA (A.L.)

	AB	H	2B	3B	HR	R	RBI	BA
F. Baker, 3b	16	4	2	0	0	0	2	.250
E. Murphy, of	16	3	2	0	0	2	0	.188
R. Oldring, of	15	1	0	0	0	0	0	.067
E. Collins, 2b	14	3	0	0	0	0	1	.214
S. McInnis, 1b	14	2	1	0	0	2	0	.143
J. Barry, ss	14	1	0	0	0	1	0	.071
W. Schang, c	12	2	1	0	0	1	0	.167
A. Strunk, of	7	2	0	0	0	0	0	.286
J. Walsh, of	6	2	1	0	0	0	1	.333
J. Bush, p	5	0	0	0	0	0	0	.000
B. Shawkey, p	2	1	1	0	0	0	1	.500
C. Bender, p	2	0	0	0	0	0	0	.000
E. Plank, p	2	0	0	0	0	0	0	.000
J. Wyckoff, p	1	1	1	0	0	0	0	1.000
J. Lapp, c	1	0	0	0	0	0	0	.000
H. Pennock, p	1	0	0	0	0	0	0	.000

Errors: J. Bush, S. McInnis, W. Schang

Stolen Bases: J. Barry, E. Collins

Individual Pitching

BOSTON (N.L.)

	W	L	ERA	IP	H	BB	SO	SV
D. Rudolph	2	0	0.50	18	12	4	15	0
B. James	2	0	0.00	11	2	6	9	0
L. Tyler	0	0	3.60	10	8	3	4	0

PHILADELPHIA (A.L.)

	W	L	ERA	IP	H	BB	SO	SV
J. Bush	0	1	3.27	11	9	4	4	0
E. Plank	0	1	1.00	9	7	4	6	0
C. Bender	0	1	10.13	5.1	8	2	3	0
B. Shawkey	0	1	5.40	5	4	2	0	0
J. Wyckoff	0	0	2.45	3.2	3	1	2	0
H. Pennock	0	0	0.00	3	2	2	3	0

1915 WORLD SERIES

LINE SCORES					PITCHERS (innings pitched)	HOME RUNS (men on)	HIGHLIGHTS

Boston (A.L.) defeats Philadelphia (N.L.) 4 games to 1

LINE SCORES					PITCHERS (innings pitched)	HOME RUNS (men on)	HIGHLIGHTS
GAME 1 - OCTOBER 8							Cravath drove in the deciding run in the eighth on a groundout as Alexander scattered eight singles.
BOS A	000 000 010	1	8	1	**Shore** (8)		
PHI N	000 100 02x	3	5	1	**Alexander** (9)		
GAME 2 - OCTOBER 9							Foster faced only 30 men and drove in the game-winning run with his single in the top of the ninth.
BOS A	100 000 001	2	10	0	**Foster** (9)		
PHI N	000 010 000	1	3	1	**Mayer** (9)		
GAME 3 - OCTOBER 11							Lewis singled home Hooper in the bottom of the ninth to support Leonard's three-hitter. Leonard retired the last twenty batters to face him.
PHI N	001 000 000	1	3	0	**Alexander** (8.2)		
BOS A	000 100 001	2	6	1	**Leonard** (9)		
GAME 4 - OCTOBER 12							Lewis doubled in Hoblitzell with what proved to be the deciding run in the sixth. Shore lost his shutout when Cravath's hit bounced over Speaker's head for a triple and Luderus singled him home.
PHI N	000 000 010	1	7	0	**Chalmers** (8)		
BOS A	001 001 00x	2	8	1	**Shore** (9)		
GAME 5 - OCTOBER 13							Hooper hit his second home run of the game in the top of the ninth to give Boston the Series. Lewis's two-run homer in the eighth tied the score and cancelled out Luderus's three RBIs.
BOS A	011 000 021	5	10	1	**Foster** (9)	Hooper, Lewis (1 on), Hooper	
PHI N	200 200 000	4	9	1	Mayer (2.1), **Rixey** (6.2)	Luderus	

Team totals

		W	AB	H	2B	3B	HR	R	RBI	BA	BB	SO	ERA
BOS	**A**	4	159	42	2	2	3	12	11	.264	11	25	1.84
PHI	**N**	1	148	27	4	1	1	10	9	.182	10	25	2.27

Individual Batting

BOSTON (A.L.)

	AB	H	2B	3B	HR	R	RBI	BA
H. Hooper, of	20	7	0	0	2	4	3	.350
D. Lewis, of	18	8	1	0	1	1	5	.444
E. Scott, ss	18	1	0	0	0	0	0	.056
T. Speaker, of	17	5	0	1	0	2	0	.294
L. Gardner, 3b	17	4	0	1	0	2	0	.235
J. Barry, 2b	17	3	0	0	0	1	1	.176
D. Hoblitzell, 1b	16	5	0	0	0	1	1	.313
R. Foster, p	8	4	1	0	0	0	1	.500
H. Cady, c	6	2	0	0	0	0	0	.333
E. Shore, p	5	1	0	0	0	0	0	.200
P. Thomas, c	5	1	0	0	0	0	0	.200
D. Gainer, 1b	3	1	0	0	0	1	0	.333
D. Leonard, p	3	0	0	0	0	0	0	.000
B. Carrigan, c	2	0	0	0	0	0	0	.000
O. Henriksen	2	0	0	0	0	0	0	.000
H. Janvrin, ss	1	0	0	0	0	0	0	.000
B. Ruth	1	0	0	0	0	0	0	.000

Errors: J. Barry, D. Hoblitzell, H. Hooper, E. Shore
Stolen Bases: D. Hoblitzell

PHILADELPHIA (N.L.)

	AB	H	2B	3B	HR	R	RBI	BA
D. Paskert, of	19	3	0	0	0	2	0	.158
D. Bancroft, ss	17	5	0	0	0	2	1	.294
M. Stock, 3b	17	2	1	0	0	1	0	.118
F. Luderus, 1b	16	7	2	0	1	1	6	.438
E. Burns, c	16	3	0	0	0	1	0	.188
G. Cravath, of	16	2	1	1	0	2	1	.125
B. Niehoff, 2b	16	1	0	0	0	1	0	.063
P. Whitted, 1b, of	15	1	0	0	0	0	1	.067
G. Alexander, p	5	1	0	0	0	0	0	.200
E. Mayer, p	4	0	0	0	0	0	0	.000
G. Chalmers, p	3	1	0	0	0	0	0	.333
E. Rixey, p	2	1	0	0	0	0	0	.500
B. Byrne	1	0	0	0	0	0	0	.000
B. Killefer	1	0	0	0	0	0	0	.000
B. Becker, of	0	0	0	0	0	0	0	—
O. Dugey	0	0	0	0	0	0	0	—

Errors: D. Bancroft, E. Burns, F. Luderus
Stolen Bases: O. Dugey, P. Whitted

Individual Pitching

BOSTON (A.L.)

	W	L	ERA	IP	H	BB	SO	SV
R. Foster	2	0	2.00	18	12	2	13	0
E. Shore	1	1	2.12	17	12	8	6	0
D. Leonard	1	0	1.00	9	3	0	6	0

PHILADELPHIA (N.L.)

	W	L	ERA	IP	H	BB	SO	SV
G. Alexander	1	1	1.53	17.2	14	4	10	0
E. Mayer	0	1	2.38	11.1	16	2	7	0
G. Chalmers	0	1	2.25	8	8	3	6	0
E. Rixey	0	1	4.05	6.2	4	2	2	0

1916 WORLD SERIES

Boston (A.L.) defeats Brooklyn (N.L.) 4 games to 1

LINE SCORES			R	H	E	PITCHERS (innings pitched)	HOME RUNS (men on)	HIGHLIGHTS
GAME 1 - OCTOBER 7								The Dodgers' ninth-inning rally fell short when Scott made a great stop of Daubert's hard grounder with two out and the bases filled.
BKN	**N**	000 100 004	5	10	4	**Marquard** (7), Pfeffer (1)		
BOS	**A**	001 010 31x	6	8	1	**Shore** (8.2), Mays (0.1) **SV**		
GAME 2 - OCTOBER 9								Gainer's pinch single in the 14th scored pinch-runner McNally to break the 1-1 deadlock. The only Dodger run off Ruth came on Myers's inside-the-park homer in the first.
BKN	**N**	100 000 000 000 00	1	6	2	**Smith** (13.1)	Myers	
BOS	**A**	001 000 000 000 01	2	7	1	**Ruth** (14)		
GAME 3 - OCTOBER 10								Pfeffer retired all eight men he faced after relieving Coombs in the seventh to preserve Brooklyn's one-run lead.
BOS	**A**	000 002 100	3	7	1	**Mays** (5), Foster (3)	Gardner	
BKN	**N**	001 120 00x	4	10	0	**Coombs** (6.1), Pfeffer (2.2) **SV**		
GAME 4 - OCTOBER 11								Gardner's three-run homer in the second paced Boston's attack. Leonard held the Dodgers to three hits and no runs after their two-run first.
BOS	**A**	030 110 100	6	10	1	**Leonard** (9)	Gardner (2 on)	
BKN	**N**	200 000 000	2	5	4	**Marquard** (4), Cheney (3), Rucker (2)		
GAME 5 - OCTOBER 12								Shore held Brooklyn hitless for four and a third innings and then scattered three singles in locking up the Series for Boston.
BKN	**N**	010 000 000	1	3	3	**Pfeffer** (7), Dell (1)		
BOS	**A**	012 010 00x	4	7	2	**Shore** (9)		

Team totals

		W	AB	H	2B	3B	HR	R	RBI	BA	BB	SO	ERA
BOS	**A**	4	164	39	7	6	2	21	18	.238	18	25	1.47
BKN	**N**	1	170	34	2	5	1	13	11	.200	14	19	2.85

Individual Batting

BOSTON (A.L.)

	AB	H	2B	3B	HR	R	RBI	BA
H. Janvrin, 2b	23	5	3	0	0	2	1	.217
H. Hooper, of	21	7	1	1	0	6	1	.333
D. Lewis, of	17	6	2	1	0	3	1	.353
D. Hoblitzell, 1b	17	4	1	1	0	3	2	.235
L. Gardner, 3b	17	3	0	0	2	2	6	.176
E. Scott, ss	16	2	0	1	0	1	1	.125
T. Walker, of	11	3	0	1	0	1	1	.273
C. Shorten, of	7	4	0	0	0	0	2	.571
P. Thomas, c	7	1	0	1	0	0	0	.143
E. Shore, p	7	0	0	0	0	0	0	.000
B. Ruth, p	5	0	0	0	0	0	1	.000
H. Cady, c	4	1	0	0	0	1	0	.250
B. Carrigan, c	3	2	0	0	0	0	1	.667
D. Leonard, p	3	0	0	0	0	0	0	.000
J. Walsh, of	3	0	0	0	0	0	0	.000
D. Gainer	1	1	0	0	0	0	1	1.000
R. Foster, p	1	0	0	0	0	0	0	.000
C. Mays, p	1	0	0	0	0	0	0	.000
O. Henriksen	0	0	0	0	0	1	0	—
M. McNally	0	0	0	0	0	1	0	—

Errors: L. Gardner (2), H. Janvrin (2), E. Scott (2)

Stolen Bases: H. Hooper

BROOKLYN (N.L.)

	AB	H	2B	3B	HR	R	RBI	BA
H. Myers, of	22	4	0	0	1	2	3	.182
Z. Wheat, of	19	4	0	1	0	2	1	.211
G. Cutshaw, 2b	19	2	1	0	0	2	2	.105
J. Daubert, 1b	17	3	0	1	0	1	0	.176
M. Mowrey, 3b	17	3	0	0	0	2	1	.176
I. Olson, ss	16	4	0	1	0	1	2	.250
C. Stengel, of	11	4	0	0	0	2	0	.364
J. Johnston, of	10	3	0	1	0	1	0	.300
C. Meyers, c	10	2	0	1	0	0	1	.200
O. Miller, c	8	1	0	0	0	0	0	.125
S. Smith, p	5	1	1	0	0	0	0	.200
F. Merkle, 1b	4	1	0	0	0	0	0	.250
J. Pfeffer, p	4	1	0	0	0	0	0	.250
J. Coombs, p	3	1	0	0	0	0	1	.333
R. Marquard, p	3	0	0	0	0	0	0	.000
G. Getz	1	0	0	0	0	0	0	.000
O. O'Mara	1	0	0	0	0	0	0	.000

Errors: I. Olson (4), G. Cutshaw (2), M. Mowrey (2), L. Cheney, J. Johnston, F. Merkle, C. Stengel, Z. Wheat

Stolen Bases: Z. Wheat

Individual Pitching

BOSTON (A.L.)

	W	L	ERA	IP	H	BB	SO	SV
E. Shore	2	0	1.53	17.2	12	4	9	0
B. Ruth	1	0	0.64	14	6	3	4	0
D. Leonard	1	0	1.00	9	5	4	3	0
C. Mays	0	1	5.06	5.1	8	3	2	1
R. Foster	0	0	0.00	3	3	0	1	0

BROOKLYN (N.L.)

	W	L	ERA	IP	H	BB	SO	SV
S. Smith	0	1	1.35	13.1	7	6	2	0
R. Marquard	0	2	4.91	11	12	6	9	0
J. Pfeffer	0	1	2.53	10.2	7	4	5	1
J. Coombs	1	0	4.26	6.1	7	1	1	0
L. Cheney	0	0	3.00	3	4	1	5	0
N. Rucker	0	0	0.00	2	1	0	3	0
W. Dell	0	0	0.00	1	1	0	0	0

1917 WORLD SERIES

Chicago (A.L.) defeats New York (N.L.) 4 games to 2

LINE SCORES						PITCHERS (innings pitched)	HOME RUNS (men on)	HIGHLIGHTS
GAME 1 - OCTOBER 6								Felsch's homer in the fourth and Shano Collins's three hits backed up Cicotte's seven-hit pitching.
NY	**N**	000 010 000	1	7	1	**Sallee** (8)		
CHI	**A**	001 100 00x	2	7	1	**Cicotte** (9)	Felsch	
GAME 2 - OCTOBER 7								Six singles led to five fourth-inning runs for Chicago, allowing Faber to coast on in for the victory.
NY	**N**	020 000 000	2	8	1	Schupp (1.1), **Anderson** (2), Perritt (3.2), Tesreau (1)		
CHI	**A**	020 500 00x	7	14	1	**Faber** (9)		
GAME 3 - OCTOBER 10								Robertson's triple and Holke's double in the fourth gave the Giants the lead and the game. Benton walked none in his five-hit shutout.
CHI	**A**	000 000 000	0	5	3	**Cicotte** (8)		
NY	**N**	000 200 00x	2	8	2	**Benton** (9)		
GAME 4 - OCTOBER 11								Kauff's two homers paced the Giants attack as Schupp allowed seven hits in posting a 5-0 shutout.
CHI	**A**	000 000 000	0	7	0	**Faber** (7), Danforth (1)		
NY	**N**	000 110 12x	5	10	1	**Schupp** (9)	Kauff, Kauff (1 on)	
GAME 5 - OCTOBER 13								Eddie Collins singled in the go-ahead run in a three-run eighth to break open a 5-5 deadlock as the teams combined for 26 hits.
NY	**N**	200 200 100	5	12	3	**Sallee** (7.1), Perritt (0.2)		
CHI	**A**	001 001 33x	8	14	6	Russell (0), Cicotte (6), Williams (1), **Faber** (2)		
GAME 6 - OCTOBER 15								The White Sox scored all of their runs on Giant miscues as Faber scattered six hits for his third win of the Series.
CHI	**A**	000 300 001	4	7	1	**Faber** (9)		
NY	**N**	000 020 000	2	6	3	**Benton** (5), Perritt (4)		

Team totals

		W	AB	H	2B	3B	HR	R	RBI	BA	BB	SO	ERA
CHI	**A**	4	197	54	6	0	1	21	18	.274	11	28	2.77
NY	**N**	2	199	51	5	4	2	17	16	.256	6	27	2.82

Individual Batting

CHICAGO (A.L.)

	AB	H	2B	3B	HR	R	RBI	BA
F. McMullin, 3b	24	3	1	0	0	1	2	.125
J. Jackson, of	23	7	0	0	0	4	2	.304
C. Gandil, 1b	23	6	1	0	0	1	5	.261
E. Collins, 2b	22	9	1	0	0	4	2	.409
H. Felsch, of	22	6	1	0	1	4	3	.273
B. Weaver, ss	21	7	1	0	0	3	1	.333
S. Collins, of	21	6	1	0	0	2	0	.286
R. Schalk, c	19	5	0	0	0	1	0	.263
E. Cicotte, p	7	1	0	0	0	0	0	.143
R. Faber, p	7	1	0	0	0	0	0	.143
N. Leibold, of	5	2	0	0	0	1	2	.400
S. Risberg	2	1	0	0	0	0	1	.500
B. Lynn	1	0	0	0	0	0	0	.000

Errors: B. Weaver (4), S. Collins (3), R. Schalk (2), E. Cicotte, C. Gandil, L. Williams

Stolen Bases: E. Collins (3), C. Gandil, J. Jackson, R. Schalk

NEW YORK (N.L.)

	AB	H	2B	3B	HR	R	RBI	BA
A. Fletcher, ss	25	5	1	0	0	2	0	.200
B. Kauff, of	25	4	1	0	2	2	5	.160
H. Zimmerman, 3b	25	3	0	1	0	1	0	.120
B. Herzog, 2b	24	6	0	1	0	1	2	.250
D. Robertson, of	22	11	1	1	0	3	1	.500
G. Burns, of	22	5	0	0	0	3	2	.227
W. Holke, 1b	21	6	2	0	0	2	1	.286
B. Rariden, c	13	5	0	0	0	2	2	.385
S. Sallee, p	6	1	0	0	0	0	1	.167
L. McCarty, c	5	2	0	1	0	1	1	.400
F. Schupp, p	4	1	0	0	0	0	1	.250
R. Benton, p	4	0	0	0	0	0	0	.000
P. Perritt, p	2	2	0	0	0	0	0	1.000
J. Wilhoit	1	0	0	0	0	0	0	.000
J. Thorpe, of	0	0	0	0	0	0	0	—

Errors: A. Fletcher (3), B. Herzog (2), H. Zimmerman (2), W. Holke, B. Kauff, L. McCarty, D. Robertson

Stolen Bases: D. Robertson (2), G. Burns, B. Kauff

Individual Pitching

CHICAGO (A.L.)

	W	L	ERA	IP	H	BB	SO	SV
R. Faber	3	1	2.33	27	21	3	9	0
E. Cicotte	1	1	1.96	23	23	2	13	0
D. Danforth	0	0	18.00	1	3	0	2	0
L. Williams	0	0	9.00	1	2	0	3	0
R. Russell	0	0	∞	0.0	2	1	0	0

NEW YORK (N.L.)

	W	L	ERA	IP	H	BB	SO	SV
S. Sallee	0	2	4.70	15.1	20	4	4	0
R. Benton	1	1	0.00	14	9	1	8	0
F. Schupp	1	0	1.74	10.1	11	2	9	0
P. Perritt	0	0	2.16	8.1	9	3	3	0
F. Anderson	0	1	18.00	2	5	0	3	0
J. Tesreau	0	0	0.00	1	0	1	1	0

1918 WORLD SERIES

Boston (A.L.) defeats Chicago (N.L.) 4 games to 2

LINE SCORES			R	H	E	PITCHERS (innings pitched)	HOME RUNS (men on)	HIGHLIGHTS
GAME 1 - SEPTEMBER 5								Ruth and Vaughn allowed just eleven singles between them, but Boston packaged two of them with a walk in the fourth for the game's only run.
BOS	**A**	000 100 000	1	5	0	**Ruth** (9)		
CHI	**N**	000 000 000	0	6	0	**Vaughn** (9)		
GAME 2 - SEPTEMBER 6								Tyler went the distance and singled in two runs in the second. The shutout was spoiled when Strunk and Whiteman tripled in the ninth.
BOS	**A**	000 000 001	1	6	1	**Bush** (8)		
CHI	**N**	030 000 00x	3	7	1	**Tyler** (9)		
GAME 3 - SEPTEMBER 7								Scott singled home McInnis with the deciding run in the fourth. Pick tried to score from second on a passed ball with two out in the bottom of the ninth, but got caught in a rundown and retired.
BOS	**A**	000 200 000	2	7	0	**Mays** (9)		
CHI	**N**	000 010 000	1	7	1	**Vaughn** (9)		
GAME 4 - SEPTEMBER 9								Schang scored the go-ahead run in the eighth on Killefer's passed ball and Douglas's wild throw. Ruth's record scoreless inning streak dating back to the 1916 Series was stopped in the eighth after 29.2 innings.
CHI	**N**	000 000 020	2	7	1	Tyler (7), **Douglas** (1)		
BOS	**A**	000 200 01x	3	4	0	**Ruth** (8), Bush (1) **SV**		
GAME 5 - SEPTEMBER 10								Vaughn stopped Boston on five hits after two hard-luck losses.
CHI	**N**	001 000 020	3	7	0	**Vaughn** (9)		
BOS	**A**	000 000 000	0	5	0	**Jones** (9)		
GAME 6 - SEPTEMBER 11								Flack's error in the third let in two runs as Mays subdued Chicago on three hits.
CHI	**N**	000 100 000	1	3	2	**Tyler** (7), Hendrix (1)		
BOS	**A**	002 000 00x	2	5	0	**Mays** (9)		

Team totals

		W	AB	H	2B	3B	HR	R	RBI	BA	BB	SO	ERA
BOS	**A**	4	172	32	2	3	0	9	6	.186	16	21	1.70
CHI	**N**	2	176	37	5	1	0	10	10	.210	18	14	1.04

Individual Batting

BOSTON (A.L.)

	AB	H	2B	3B	HR	R	RBI	BA
A. Strunk, of	23	4	1	1	0	1	0	.174
S. McInnis, 1b	20	5	0	0	0	2	1	.250
G. Whiteman, of	20	5	0	1	0	2	1	.250
H. Hooper, of	20	4	0	0	0	0	0	.200
E. Scott, ss	20	2	0	0	0	0	0	.100
D. Shean, 2b	19	4	1	0	0	2	0	.211
F. Thomas, 3b	17	2	0	0	0	0	1	.118
W. Schang, c	9	4	0	0	0	1	1	.444
S. Agnew, c	9	0	0	0	0	0	0	.000
C. Mays, p	5	1	0	0	0	1	0	.200
B. Ruth, of, p	5	1	0	1	0	0	2	.200
J. Bush, p	2	0	0	0	0	0	0	.000
J. Dubuc	1	0	0	0	0	0	0	.000
S. Jones, p	1	0	0	0	0	0	0	.000
H. Miller	1	0	0	0	0	0	0	.000

Errors: G. Whiteman
Stolen Bases: W. Schang, D. Shean, G. Whiteman

CHICAGO (N.L.)

	AB	H	2B	3B	HR	R	RBI	BA
L. Mann, of	22	5	2	0	0	0	2	.227
C. Hollocher, ss	21	4	0	1	0	2	0	.190
D. Paskert, of	21	4	1	0	0	0	2	.190
M. Flack, of	19	5	0	0	0	2	1	.263
C. Pick, 2b	18	7	1	0	0	2	0	.389
F. Merkle, 1b	18	5	0	0	0	1	1	.278
C. Deal, 3b	17	3	0	0	0	0	0	.176
B. Killefer, c	17	2	1	0	0	2	2	.118
H. Vaughn, p	10	0	0	0	0	0	0	.000
L. Tyler, p	5	1	0	0	0	0	2	.200
B. O'Farrell, c	3	0	0	0	0	0	0	.000
T. Barber	2	0	0	0	0	0	0	.000
C. Hendrix, p	1	1	0	0	0	0	0	1.000
B. McCabe	1	0	0	0	0	1	0	.000
C. Wortman, 2b	1	0	0	0	0	0	0	.000
R. Zeider, 3b	0	0	0	0	0	0	0	—

Errors: C. Deal, P. Douglas, M. Flack, C. Hollocher, L. Tyler
Stolen Bases: C. Hollocher (2), M. Flack

Individual Pitching

BOSTON (A.L.)

	W	L	ERA	IP	H	BB	SO	SV
C. Mays	2	0	1.00	18	10	3	5	0
B. Ruth	2	0	1.06	17	13	7	4	0
J. Bush	0	1	3.00	9	7	3	0	1
S. Jones	0	1	3.00	9	7	5	5	0

CHICAGO (N.L.)

	W	L	ERA	IP	H	BB	SO	SV
H. Vaughn	1	2	1.00	27	17	5	17	0
L. Tyler	1	1	1.17	23	14	11	4	0
P. Douglas	0	1	0.00	1	1	0	0	0
C. Hendrix	0	0	0.00	1	0	0	0	0

1919 WORLD SERIES

Cincinnati (N.L.) defeats Chicago (A.L.) 5 games to 3

LINE SCORES			R	H	E	PITCHERS (innings pitched)	HOME RUNS (men on)	HIGHLIGHTS
GAME 1 - OCTOBER 1								The Reds' five runs off Cicotte in the fourth broke a 1-1 deadlock. Ruether held Chicago to six hits and had three of his own.
CHI	**A**	010 000 000	1	6	1	**Cicotte** (3.2), Wilkinson (3.1), Lowdermilk (1)		
CIN	**N**	100 500 21x	9	14	1	**Ruether** (9)		
GAME 2 - OCTOBER 2								Kopf's two-run triple in the fourth capped a three-run inning after Williams walked three.
CHI	**A**	000 000 200	2	10	1	**Williams** (8)		
CIN	**N**	000 301 00x	4	4	2	**Sallee** (9)		
GAME 3 - OCTOBER 3								Kerr allowed three hits in shutting out the Reds. Gandil's double drove in Jackson and Felsch in the second.
CIN	**N**	000 000 000	0	3	1	**Fisher** (7), Luque (1)		
CHI	**A**	020 100 00x	3	7	0	**Kerr** (9)		
GAME 4 - OCTOBER 4								Ring allowed three hits and posted a shutout as the Reds scored twice in the fifth on Cicotte's two errors.
CIN	**N**	000 020 000	2	5	2	**Ring** (9)		
CHI	**A**	000 000 000	0	3	2	**Cicotte** (9)		
GAME 5 - OCTOBER 6								Four runs in the sixth capped by Roush's triple broke open a tie game. Eller fanned nine, six in succession. (There is no taint on the streak; among those fanned were Schalk, Leibold, and Eddie Collins.)
CIN	**N**	000 004 001	5	4	0	**Eller** (9)		
CHI	**A**	000 000 000	0	3	3	**Williams** (8), Mayer (1)		
GAME 6 - OCTOBER 7								Gandil singled home Weaver in the tenth with the deciding run.
CHI	**A**	000 013 000 1	5	10	3	**Kerr** (10)		
CIN	**N**	002 200 000 0	4	11	0	Ruether (5), **Ring** (5)		
GAME 7 - OCTOBER 8								Shano Collins scored the deciding run on Jackson's single as Cicotte scattered seven hits.
CHI	**A**	101 020 000	4	10	1	**Cicotte** (9)		
CIN	**N**	000 001 000	1	7	4	**Sallee** (4.1), Fisher (0.2), Luque (4)		
GAME 8 - OCTOBER 9								The Reds scored four times in the first to wrap up the series on Williams's third loss of the Series. (Williams, Cicotte, Gandil, Felsch, Jackson, McMullin, Risberg and Weaver were later barred for life for their part in fixing the Series.)
CIN	**N**	410 013 010	10	16	2	**Eller** (9)		
CHI	**A**	001 000 040	5	10	1	**Williams** (0.1), James (4.2), Wilkinson (4)	Jackson	

Team totals

		W	AB	H	2B	3B	HR	R	RBI	BA	BB	SO	ERA
CIN	**N**	5	251	64	10	7	0	35	33	.255	25	22	1.63
CHI	**A**	3	263	59	10	3	1	20	17	.224	15	30	3.68

Individual Batting

CINCINNATI (N.L.)

	AB	H	2B	3B	HR	R	RBI	BA
M. Rath, 2b	31	7	1	0	0	5	2	.226
J. Daubert, 1b	29	7	0	1	0	4	1	.241
H. Groh, 3b	29	5	2	0	0	6	2	.172
G. Neale, of	28	10	1	1	0	3	4	.357
E. Roush, of	28	6	2	1	0	6	7	.214
L. Kopf, ss	27	6	0	2	0	3	3	.222
P. Duncan, of	26	7	2	0	0	3	8	.269
B. Rariden, c	19	4	0	0	0	0	2	.211
I. Wingo, c	7	4	0	0	0	1	1	.571
H. Eller, p	7	2	1	0	0	2	0	.286
D. Ruether, p	6	4	1	2	0	2	4	.667
J. Ring, p	5	0	0	0	0	0	0	.000
S. Sallee, p	4	0	0	0	0	0	0	.000
R. Fisher, p	2	1	0	0	0	0	0	.500
S. Magee	2	1	0	0	0	0	0	.500
D. Luque, p	1	0	0	0	0	0	0	.000
J. Smith	0	0	0	0	0	0	0	—

Errors: J. Daubert (2), H. Groh (2), M. Rath (2), E. Roush (2), R. Fisher, L. Kopf, G. Neale, B. Rariden

Stolen Bases: M. Rath (2), E. Roush (2), J. Daubert, G. Neale, B. Rariden

CHICAGO (A.L.)

	AB	H	2B	3B	HR	R	RBI	BA
B. Weaver, 3b	34	11	4	1	0	4	0	.324
J. Jackson, of	32	12	3	0	1	5	6	.375
E. Collins, 2b	31	7	1	0	0	2	1	.226
C. Gandil, 1b	30	7	0	1	0	1	5	.233
H. Felsch, of	26	5	1	0	0	2	3	.192
S. Risberg, ss	25	2	0	1	0	3	0	.080
R. Schalk, c	23	7	0	0	0	1	2	.304
N. Leibold, of	18	1	0	0	0	0	0	.056
S. Collins, of	16	4	1	0	0	2	0	.250
E. Cicotte, p	8	0	0	0	0	0	0	.000
D. Kerr, p	6	1	0	0	0	0	0	.167
L. Williams, p	5	1	0	0	0	0	0	.200
F. McMullin	2	1	0	0	0	0	0	.500
B. James, p	2	0	0	0	0	0	0	.000
E. Murphy	2	0	0	0	0	0	0	.000
R. Wilkinson, p	2	0	0	0	0	0	0	.000
B. Lynn, c	1	0	0	0	0	0	0	.000

Errors: S. Risberg (4), E. Cicotte (2), E. Collins (2), H. Felsch (2), C. Gandil, R. Schalk

Stolen Bases: E. Collins, C. Gandil, N. Leibold, S. Risberg, R. Schalk

Individual Pitching

CINCINNATI (N.L.)

	W	L	ERA	IP	H	BB	SO	SV
H. Eller	2	0	2.00	18	13	2	15	0
J. Ring	1	1	0.64	14	7	6	4	0
D. Ruether	1	0	2.57	14	12	4	1	0
S. Sallee	1	1	1.35	13.1	19	1	2	0
R. Fisher	0	1	2.35	7.2	7	2	2	0
D. Luque	0	0	0.00	5	1	0	6	0

CHICAGO (A.L.)

	W	L	ERA	IP	H	BB	SO	SV
E. Cicotte	1	2	2.91	21.2	19	5	7	0
D. Kerr	2	0	1.42	19	14	3	6	0
L. Williams	0	3	6.61	16.1	12	8	4	0
R. Wilkinson	0	0	3.68	7.1	9	4	3	0
B. James	0	0	5.79	4.2	8	3	2	0
G. Lowdermilk	0	0	9.00	1	2	1	0	0
E. Mayer	0	0	0.00	1	0	1	0	0

1920 WORLD SERIES

Cleveland (A.L.) defeats Brooklyn (N.L.) 5 games to 2

LINE SCORES			R	H	E	PITCHERS (innings pitched)	HOME RUNS (men on)	HIGHLIGHTS
GAME 1 - OCTOBER 5								O'Neill drove in two runs and Wood scored two to back up Coveleski's five-hitter.
CLE	**A**	020 100 000	3	5	0	**Coveleski** (9)		
BKN	**N**	000 000 100	1	5	1	**Marquard** (6), Mamaux (2), Cadore (1)		
GAME 2 - OCTOBER 6								Brooklyn bounced back as Grimes, like Coveleski a spitballer, blanked the Tribe on seven hits.
CLE	**A**	000 000 000	0	7	1	**Bagby** (6), Uhle (2)		
BKN	**N**	101 010 00x	3	7	0	**Grimes** (9)		
GAME 3 - OCTOBER 7								The Dodgers made quick work of Caldwell, batting him out in the first, and Sherry Smith allowed just three hits while inducing twenty ground-ball outs.
CLE	**A**	000 100 000	1	3	1	**Caldwell** (0.1), Mails (6.2), Uhle (1)		
BKN	**N**	200 000 00x	2	6	1	**S. Smith** (9)		
GAME 4 - OCTOBER 9								Coveleski again baffled Brooklyn as Wambsganss and Speaker each had two hits and scored two runs.
BKN	**N**	000 100 000	1	5	1	**Cadore** (1), Mamaux (1), Marquard (3), Pfeffer (3)		
CLE	**A**	202 001 00x	5	12	2	**Coveleski** (9)		
GAME 5 - OCTOBER 10								In a strange and memorable game, Elmer Smith hit the first World Series grand slam and Bagby hit the first home run by a pitcher. But they were overshadowed by Wambsganss's unassisted triple play in the fifth, as he caught Mitchell's line drive, stepped on second before Kilduff could duck back, and tagged Miller, running from first on the pitch.
BKN	**N**	000 000 001	1	13	1	**Grimes** (3.1), Mitchell (4.2)		
CLE	**A**	400 310 00x	8	12	2	**Bagby** (9)	E. Smith (3 on), Bagby (2 on)	
GAME 6 - OCTOBER 11								The Indians scored the only run in the sixth when Speaker singled with two out and tallied on a double by Burns to the centerfield fence.
BKN	**N**	000 000 000	0	3	0	**S. Smith** (8)		
CLE	**A**	000 001 00x	1	7	3	**Mails** (9)		
GAME 7 - OCTOBER 12								Coveleski won for the third time with a superb shutout, yielding five harmless singles: three starts, three wins, three five-hitters.
BKN	**N**	000 000 000	0	5	2	**Grimes** (7), Mamaux (1)		
CLE	**A**	000 110 10x	3	7	3	**Coveleski** (9)		

Team totals

		W	AB	H	2B	3B	HR	R	RBI	BA	BB	SO	ERA
CLE	**A**	5	217	53	9	2	2	21	18	.244	21	21	0.89
BKN	**N**	2	215	44	5	1	0	8	8	.205	10	20	2.59

Individual Batting

CLEVELAND (A.L.)

	AB	H	2B	3B	HR	R	RBI	BA
B. Wambsganss, 2b	26	4	0	0	0	3	1	.154
T. Speaker, of	25	8	2	1	0	6	1	.320
L. Gardner, 3b	24	5	1	0	0	1	1	.208
J. Sewell, ss	23	4	0	0	0	0	0	.174
S. O'Neill, c	21	7	3	0	0	1	2	.333
C. Jamieson, of	15	5	1	0	0	2	1	.333
J. Evans, of	13	4	0	0	0	0	0	.308
E. Smith, of	13	4	0	1	1	1	6	.308
D. Johnston, 1b	11	3	0	0	0	1	0	.273
G. Burns, 1b	10	3	1	0	0	1	3	.300
S. Wood, of	10	2	1	0	0	2	0	.200
S. Coveleski, p	10	1	0	0	0	2	0	.100
J. Bagby, p	6	2	0	0	1	1	3	.333
D. Mails, p	5	0	0	0	0	0	0	.000
J. Graney, of	3	0	0	0	0	0	0	.000
L. Nunamaker, c	2	1	0	0	0	0	0	.500
H. Lunte, ss	0	0	0	0	0	0	0	—
P. Thomas, c	0	0	0	0	0	0	0	—

Errors: J. Sewell (6), L. Gardner (2), J. Bagby, G. Burns, S. Coveleski, S. O'Neill

Stolen Bases: C. Jamieson, D. Johnston

BROOKLYN (N.L.)

	AB	H	2B	3B	HR	R	RBI	BA
Z. Wheat, of	27	9	2	0	0	2	2	.333
H. Myers, of	26	6	0	0	0	0	1	.231
I. Olson, ss	25	8	1	0	0	2	0	.320
E. Konetchy, 1b	23	4	0	1	0	0	2	.174
T. Griffith, of	21	4	2	0	0	1	3	.190
P. Kilduff, 2b	21	2	0	0	0	0	0	.095
J. Johnston, 3b	14	3	0	0	0	2	0	.214
O. Miller, c	14	2	0	0	0	0	0	.143
J. Sheehan, 3b	11	2	0	0	0	0	0	.182
B. Grimes, p	6	2	0	0	0	1	0	.333
E. Krueger, c	6	1	0	0	0	0	0	.167
S. Smith, p	6	0	0	0	0	0	0	.000
B. Neis, of	5	0	0	0	0	0	0	.000
C. Mitchell, p	3	1	0	0	0	0	0	.333
B. Lamar	3	0	0	0	0	0	0	.000
A. Mamaux, p	1	0	0	0	0	0	0	.000
R. Marquard, p	1	0	0	0	0	0	0	.000
J. Pfeffer, p	1	0	0	0	0	0	0	.000
R. Schmandt	1	0	0	0	0	0	0	.000
B. McCabe	0	0	0	0	0	0	0	—

Errors: J. Sheehan (2), Z. Wheat (2), B. Grimes, E. Konetchy

Stolen Bases: J. Johnston

Individual Pitching

CLEVELAND (A.L.)

	W	L	ERA	IP	H	BB	SO	SV
S. Coveleski	3	0	0.67	27	15	2	8	0
D. Mails	1	0	0.00	15.2	6	6	6	0
J. Bagby	1	1	1.80	15	20	1	3	0
G. Uhle	0	0	0.00	3	1	0	3	0
R. Caldwell	0	1	27.00	0.1	2	1	0	0

BROOKLYN (N.L.)

	W	L	ERA	IP	H	BB	SO	SV
B. Grimes	1	2	4.19	19.1	23	9	4	0
S. Smith	1	1	0.53	17	10	3	3	0
R. Marquard	0	1	2.00	9	7	3	6	0
C. Mitchell	0	0	0.00	4.2	3	3	1	0
A. Mamaux	0	0	4.50	4	2	0	5	0
J. Pfeffer	0	0	3.00	3	4	2	1	0
L. Cadore	0	1	9.00	2	4	1	1	0

1921 WORLD SERIES

New York (N.L.) defeats New York (A.L.) 5 games to 3

LINE SCORES			R	H	E	PITCHERS (innings pitched)	HOME RUNS (men on)	HIGHLIGHTS
		GAME 1 - OCTOBER 5						Mays's underhand delivery baffled all the Giants but Frisch, who collected four of their five hits in the losing cause.
NY	A	100 011 000	3	7	0	**Mays** (9)		
NY	N	000 000 000	0	5	0	**Douglas** (8), Barnes (1)		
		GAME 2 - OCTOBER 6						The Giants are shut out for the second day in a row, Hoyt allowing only singles by Frisch and Rawlings.
NY	N	000 000 000	0	2	3	**Nehf** (8)		
NY	A	000 100 02x	3	3	0	**Hoyt** (9)		
		GAME 3 - OCTOBER 7						An eight-run explosion in the seventh made a rout of the contest with the Giants pounding out 20 hits, including four each by Burns and Snyder.
NY	A	004 000 010	5	8	0	Shawkey (2.1), **Quinn** (3.2), Collins (1.2), Rogers (1.1)		
NY	N	004 000 81x	13	20	0	Toney (2), **Barnes** (7)		
		GAME 4 - OCTOBER 9						Douglas squared the Series in his second meeting with Mays on a two-run double by Burns that provided the winning margin.
NY	N	000 000 031	4	9	1	**Douglas** (9)		
NY	A	000 010 001	2	7	1	**Mays** (9)	Ruth	
		GAME 5 - OCTOBER 10						A surprise bunt single by Ruth started off the winning rally as Hoyt allowed only one run, that one unearned.
NY	A	001 200 000	3	6	1	**Hoyt** (9)		
NY	N	100 000 000	1	10	1	**Nehf** (9)		
		GAME 6 - OCTOBER 11						Barnes picked up his second win in relief of Toney, striking out ten. Injuries kept Ruth out of the Yankee lineup.
NY	N	030 401 000	8	13	0	Toney (0.2), **Barnes** (8.1)	I. Meusel (1 on), Snyder	
NY	A	320 000 000	5	7	2	Harper (1.1), **Shawkey** (6.2), Piercy (1)	Fewster (1 on)	
		GAME 7 - OCTOBER 12						A double by Snyder drove in the winning run as Douglas edged Mays for the second time in their three meetings.
NY	A	010 000 000	1	8	1	**Mays** (8)		
NY	N	000 100 10x	2	6	0	**Douglas** (9)		
		GAME 8 - OCTOBER 13						The only run off Hoyt was unearned, scoring on a bobble by Peckinpaugh, but it was enough as Nehf held the Yankees scoreless to win the Series.
NY	N	100 000 000	1	6	0	**Nehf** (9)		
NY	A	000 000 000	0	4	1	**Hoyt** (9)		

Team totals

		W	AB	H	2B	3B	HR	R	RBI	BA	BB	SO	ERA
NY	N	5	264	71	13	4	2	29	26	.269	22	38	2.54
NY	A	3	241	50	7	1	2	22	20	.207	27	44	3.09

Individual Batting

NEW YORK (N.L.)

	AB	H	2B	3B	HR	R	RBI	BA
G. Burns, of	33	11	4	1	0	2	2	.333
D. Bancroft, ss	33	5	1	0	0	3	3	.152
J. Rawlings, 2b	30	10	3	0	0	2	4	.333
F. Frisch, 3b	30	9	0	1	0	5	1	.300
G. Kelly, 1b	30	7	1	0	0	3	3	.233
I. Meusel, of	29	10	2	1	1	4	7	.345
R. Youngs, of	25	7	1	1	0	3	3	.280
F. Snyder, c	22	8	1	0	1	4	3	.364
J. Barnes, p	9	4	0	0	0	3	0	.444
A. Nehf, p	9	0	0	0	0	0	0	.000
P. Douglas, p	7	0	0	0	0	0	0	.000
E. Smith, c	7	0	0	0	0	0	0	.000

Errors: F. Frisch (2), D. Bancroft, A. Nehf, E. Smith

Stolen Bases: F. Frisch (3), R. Youngs (2), G. Burns, I. Meusel

NEW YORK (A.L.)

	AB	H	2B	3B	HR	R	RBI	BA
E. Miller, of	31	5	1	0	0	3	2	.161
B. Meusel, of	30	6	2	0	0	3	3	.200
R. Peckinpaugh, ss	28	5	1	0	0	2	0	.179
A. Ward, 2b	26	6	0	0	0	1	4	.231
W. Pipp, 1b	26	4	1	0	0	1	2	.154
W. Schang, c	21	6	1	1	0	1	1	.286
M. McNally, 3b	20	4	1	0	0	3	1	.200
B. Ruth, of	16	5	0	0	1	3	4	.313
C. Fewster, of	10	2	0	0	1	3	2	.200
W. Hoyt, p	9	2	0	0	0	0	1	.222
C. Mays, p	9	1	0	0	0	0	0	.111
F. Baker, 3b	8	2	0	0	0	0	0	.250
B. Shawkey, p	4	2	0	0	0	2	0	.500
J. Quinn, p	2	0	0	0	0	0	0	.000
A. DeVormer, c	1	0	0	0	0	0	0	.000

Errors: M. McNally (3), A. Ward (2), R. Peckinpaugh

Stolen Bases: M. McNally (2), B. Ruth (2), B. Meusel, W. Pipp

Individual Pitching

NEW YORK (N.L.)

	W	L	ERA	IP	H	BB	SO	SV
P. Douglas	2	1	2.08	26	24	5	17	0
A. Nehf	1	2	1.38	26	13	13	8	0
J. Barnes	2	0	1.65	16.1	6	6	18	0
F. Toney	0	0	23.63	2.2	7	3	1	0

NEW YORK (A.L.)

	W	L	ERA	IP	H	BB	SO	SV
W. Hoyt	2	1	0.00	27	18	11	18	0
C. Mays	1	2	1.73	26	20	0	9	0
B. Shawkey	0	1	7.00	9	13	6	5	0
J. Quinn	0	1	9.82	3.2	8	2	2	0
H. Harper	0	0	20.25	1.1	3	2	1	0
T. Rogers	0	0	6.75	1.1	3	0	1	0
B. Piercy	0	0	0.00	1	2	0	2	0
R. Collins	0	0	54.00	0.2	4	1	0	0

1922 WORLD SERIES

New York (N.L.) defeats New York (A.L.) 4 games to 0

LINE SCORES			R	H	E	PITCHERS (innings pitched)	HOME RUNS (men on)	HIGHLIGHTS
GAME 1 - OCTOBER 4								Irish Meusel's two-run single and sacrifice fly by Youngs gave the Giants three in the eighth for the win. Groh went three-for-three for the victors.
NY	**A**	000 001 100	2	7	0	**Bush** (7), Hoyt (1)		
NY	**N**	000 000 03x	3	11	3	Nehf (7), **Ryan** (2)		
GAME 2 - OCTOBER 5								The sun was high in the sky when the game was called ``on account of darkness''. Judge Landis was so irate at the decision that he donated the receipts to charity.
NY	**N**	300 000 000 0	3	8	1	Barnes (10)	I. Meusel (2 on)	
NY	**A**	100 100 010 0	3	8	0	Shawkey (10)	Ward	
GAME 3 - OCTOBER 6								Jack Scott, rescued from the sore arm junkheap by McGraw, whitewashed the Yankees, holding the powerful Yankee lineup to a double and three singles.
NY	**A**	000 000 000	0	4	1	**Hoyt** (7), Jones (1)		
NY	**N**	002 000 10x	3	12	1	**Scott** (9)		
GAME 4 - OCTOBER 7								The Giants scored all their runs in the fifth, Bancroft's bad-hop single over Ward's head driving in the first two.
NY	**N**	000 040 000	4	9	1	**McQuillan** (9)		
NY	**A**	200 000 100	3	8	0	**Mays** (8), Jones (1)	Ward	
GAME 5 - OCTOBER 8								Kelly's clean single in the eighth gave the Giants the winning margin as Nehf won the decisive game for the second year in a row. Ruth ended a poor Series with his third consecutive hitless game.
NY	**A**	100 010 100	3	5	0	**Bush** (8)		
NY	**N**	020 000 03x	5	10	0	**Nehf** (9)		

Team totals

		W	AB	H	2B	3B	HR	R	RBI	BA	BB	SO	ERA
NY	**N**	4	162	50	2	1	1	18	18	.309	12	15	1.76
NY	**A**	0	158	32	6	1	2	11	11	.203	8	20	3.35

Individual Batting

NEW YORK (N.L.)

	AB	H	2B	3B	HR	R	RBI	BA
I. Meusel, of	20	5	0	0	1	3	7	.250
H. Groh, 3b	19	9	0	1	0	4	0	.474
D. Bancroft, ss	19	4	0	0	0	4	2	.211
G. Kelly, 1b	18	5	0	0	0	0	2	.278
F. Frisch, 2b	17	8	1	0	0	3	2	.471
R. Youngs, of	16	6	0	0	0	2	2	.375
F. Snyder, c	15	5	0	0	0	1	0	.333
B. Cunningham, of	10	2	0	0	0	0	2	.200
E. Smith, c	7	1	0	0	0	0	0	.143
C. Stengel, of	5	2	0	0	0	0	0	.400
H. McQuillan, p	4	1	1	0	0	1	0	.250
J. Scott, p	4	1	0	0	0	0	0	.250
J. Barnes, p	4	0	0	0	0	0	0	.000
A. Nehf, p	3	0	0	0	0	0	0	.000
L. King, of	1	1	0	0	0	0	1	1.000

Errors: R. Youngs (2), D. Bancroft, F. Frisch, A. Nehf, F. Snyder
Stolen Bases: F. Frisch

NEW YORK (A.L.)

	AB	H	2B	3B	HR	R'	RBI	BA
W. Pipp, 1b	21	6	1	0	0	0	3	.286
B. Meusel, of	20	6	1	0	0	2	2	.300
J. Dugan, 3b	20	5	1	0	0	4	0	.250
W. Witt, of	18	4	1	1	0	1	0	.222
B. Ruth, of	17	2	1	0	0	1	1	.118
W. Schang, c	16	3	1	0	0	0	0	.188
E. Scott, ss	14	2	0	0	0	0	1	.143
A. Ward, 2b	13	2	0	0	2	3	3	.154
J. Bush, p	6	1	0	0	0	0	1	.167
B. Shawkey, p	4	0	0	0	0	0	0	.000
W. Hoyt, p	2	1	0	0	0	0	0	.500
C. Mays, p	2	0	0	0	0	0	0	.000
N. McMillan, of	2	0	0	0	0	0	0	.000
E. Smith	2	0	0	0	0	0	0	.000
F. Baker	1	0	0	0	0	0	0	.000
M. McNally, 2b	0	0	0	0	0	0	0	—

Errors: A. Ward
Stolen Bases: B. Meusel, W. Pipp

Individual Pitching

NEW YORK (N.L.)

	W	L	ERA	IP	H	BB	SO	SV
A. Nehf	1	0	2.25	16	11	3	6	0
J. Barnes	0	0	1.80	10	8	2	6	0
H. McQuillan	1	0	3.00	9	8	2	4	0
J. Scott	1	0	0.00	9	4	1	2	0
R. Ryan	1	0	0.00	2	1	0	2	0

NEW YORK (A.L.)

	W	L	ERA	IP	H	BB	SO	SV
J. Bush	0	2	4.80	15	21	5	6	0
B. Shawkey	0	0	2.70	10	8	2	4	0
W. Hoyt	0	1	1.13	8	11	2	4	0
C. Mays	0	1	4.50	8	9	2	1	0
S. Jones	0	0	0.00	2	1	1	0	0

1923 WORLD SERIES

New York (A.L.) defeats New York (N.L.) 4 games to 2

LINE SCORES			R	H	E	PITCHERS (innings pitched)	HOME RUNS (men on)	HIGHLIGHTS
GAME 1 - OCTOBER 10								Stengel's inside-the-park home run with two out in the ninth won the game for the Giants.
NY	**N**	004 000 001	5	8	0	Watson (2), **Ryan** (7)	Stengel	
NY	**A**	120 000 100	4	12	1	Hoyt (2.1), **Bush** (6.2)		
GAME 2 - OCTOBER 11								Two long home runs by Ruth enabled Pennock to win. Ruth's longest blow was a drive to deepest center field caught by Stengel in the ninth.
NY	**A**	010 210 000	4	10	0	**Pennock** (9)	Ward, Ruth, Ruth	
NY	**N**	010 001 000	2	9	2	**McQuillan** (3.2), Bentley (5.1)	I. Meusel	
GAME 3 - OCTOBER 12								Stengel again provided the winning margin with his seventh-inning drive into the bleachers in right field.
NY	**N**	000 000 100	1	4	0	**Nehf** (9)	Stengel	
NY	**A**	000 000 000	0	6	1	**Jones** (8), Bush (1)		
GAME 4 - OCTOBER 13								The Yankees evened the Series thanks to a six-run outburst in the second. Shawkey allowed twelve hits and had to yield to Pennock in the eighth.
NY	**A**	061 100 000	8	13	1	**Shawkey** (7.2), Pennock (1.1) **SV**		
NY	**N**	000 000 031	4	13	1	**J. Scott** (1), Ryan (0.2) McQuillan (5.1), Jonnard (1), Barnes (1)	Youngs	
GAME 5 - OCTOBER 14								Dugan's four hits paced the Yankees' 14-hit attack as Irish Meusel had all three of the Giants' hits.
NY	**N**	010 000 000	1	3	2	**Bentley** (1.1), J. Scott (2), Barnes (3.2), Jonnard (1)		
NY	**A**	340 100 00x	8	14	0	**Bush** (9)	Dugan (2 on)	
GAME 6 - OCTOBER 15								Nehf allowed two hits in the first seven innings, but after allowing two more in the eighth walked the eventual tying and winning runs on eight straight balls.
NY	**A**	100 000 050	6	5	0	**Pennock** (7), Jones (2) **SV**	Ruth	
NY	**N**	100 111 000	4	10	1	**Nehf** (7.1), Ryan (1.2)	Snyder	

Team totals

		W	AB	H	2B	3B	HR	R	RBI	BA	BB	SO	ERA
NY	**A**	4	205	60	8	4	5	30	29	.293	20	22	2.83
NY	**N**	2	201	47	2	3	5	17	17	.234	12	18	4.25

Individual Batting

NEW YORK (A.L.)

	AB	H	2B	3B	HR	R	RBI	BA
B. Meusel, of	26	7	1	2	0	1	8	.269
J. Dugan, 3b	25	7	2	1	1	5	5	.280
W. Witt, of	25	6	2	0	0	1	4	.240
A. Ward, 2b	24	10	0	0	1	4	2	.417
W. Schang, c	22	7	1	0	0	3	0	.318
E. Scott, ss	22	7	0	0	0	2	3	.318
W. Pipp, 1b	20	5	0	0	0	2	2	.250
B. Ruth, 1b, of	19	7	1	1	3	8	3	.368
J. Bush, p	7	3	1	0	0	2	1	.429
H. Pennock, p	6	0	0	0	0	0	0	.000
B. Shawkey, p	3	1	0	0	0	0	1	.333
S. Jones, p	2	0	0	0	0	0	0	.000
H. Haines, of	1	0	0	0	0	1	0	.000
H. Hendrick	1	0	0	0	0	0	0	.000
F. Hofmann	1	0	0	0	0	0	0	.000
W. Hoyt, p	1	0	0	0	0	0	0	.000
E. Johnson, ss	0	0	0	0	0	1	0	—

Errors: B. Ruth, W. Schang, E. Scott
Stolen Bases: A. Ward

NEW YORK (N.L.)

	AB	H	2B	3B	HR	R	RBI	BA
F. Frisch, 2b	25	10	0	1	0	2	1	.400
I. Meusel, of	25	7	1	1	1	3	2	.280
D. Bancroft, ss	24	2	0	0	0	1	1	.083
R. Youngs, of	23	8	0	0	1	2	3	.348
H. Groh, 3b	22	4	0	1	0	3	2	.182
G. Kelly, 1b	22	4	0	0	0	1	1	.182
F. Snyder, c	17	2	0	0	1	1	2	.118
C. Stengel, of	12	5	0	0	2	3	4	.417
B. Cunningham, of	7	1	0	0	0	0	1	.143
A. Nehf, p	6	1	0	0	0	0	0	.167
J. Bentley, p	5	3	1	0	0	0	0	.600
H. Gowdy, c	4	0	0	0	0	0	0	.000
H. McQuillan, p	3	0	0	0	0	0	0	.000
R. Ryan, p	2	0	0	0	0	0	0	.000
V. Barnes, p	1	0	0	0	0	0	0	.000
T. Jackson	1	0	0	0	0	0	0	.000
J. O'Connell	1	0	0	0	0	0	0	.000
J. Scott, p	1	0	0	0	0	0	0	.000
D. Gearin	0	0	0	0	0	0	0	—
F. Maguire	0	0	0	0	0	1	0	—

Errors: R. Youngs (2), B. Cunningham, F. Frisch, G. Kelly, M. Watson
Stolen Bases: D. Bancroft

Individual Pitching

NEW YORK (A.L.)

	W	L	ERA	IP	H	BB	SO	SV
H. Pennock	2	0	3.63	17.1	19	1	8	1
J. Bush	1	1	1.08	16.2	7	4	5	0
S. Jones	0	1	0.90	10	5	2	3	1
B. Shawkey	1	0	3.52	7.2	12	4	2	0
W. Hoyt	0	0	15.43	2.1	4	1	0	0

NEW YORK (N.L.)

	W	L	ERA	IP	H	BB	SO	SV
A. Nehf	1	1	2.76	16.1	10	6	7	0
R. Ryan	1	0	0.96	9.1	11	3	3	0
H. McQuillan	0	1	5.00	9	11	4	3	0
J. Bentley	0	1	9.45	6.2	10	4	1	0
V. Barnes	0	0	0.00	4.2	4	0	4	0
J. Scott	0	1	12.00	3	9	1	2	0
C. Jonnard	0	0	0.00	2	1	1	1	0
M. Watson	0	0	13.50	2	4	1	1	0

1924 WORLD SERIES

Washington (A.L.) defeats New York (N.L.) 4 games to 3

LINE SCORES					PITCHERS (innings pitched)	HOME RUNS (men on)	HIGHLIGHTS
GAME 1 - OCTOBER 4							Johnson, in his first World Series after 18 years in the majors, fanned 12 but lost on Youngs's bases-loaded single in the twelfth.
NY N	010 100 000 002	4	14	1	**Nehf** (12)	Kelly, Terry	
WAS A	000 001 001 001	3	10	1	**Johnson** (12)		
GAME 2 - OCTOBER 5							Peckinpaugh's double in the ninth drove in the winning run after the Senators blew an early lead built on homers by Goslin and Harris.
NY N	000 000 102	3	6	0	**Bentley** (8.1)		
WAS A	200 010 001	4	6	1	**Zachary** (8.2), Marberry (0.1) **SV**	Goslin (1 on), Harris	
GAME 3 - OCTOBER 6							Harris's error on an attempted double play in the second set up two runs for the Giants and gave them a lead they never relinquished.
WAS A	000 200 011	4	9	2	**Marberry** (3), Russell (3), Martina (1), Speece (1)		
NY N	021 101 01x	6	12	0	McQuillan (3.2), **Ryan** (4.2), Jonnard (0), Watson (0.2) **SV**	Ryan	
GAME 4 - OCTOBER 7							Goslin's four hits, including a home run, sparked the Senators to an easy triumph.
WAS A	003 020 020	7	13	3	**Mogridge** (7.1), Marberry (1.2) **SV**	Goslin (2 on)	
NY N	100 001 011	4	6	1	**Barnes** (5), Baldwin (2), Dean (2)		
GAME 5 - OCTOBER 8							Johnson again lost as Lindstrom had four hits and Bentley added a two-run homer.
WAS A	000 100 010	2	9	1	**Johnson** (8)	Goslin	
NY N	001 020 03x	6	13	0	**Bentley** (7.1), McQuillan (1.2) **SV**	Bentley (1 on)	
GAME 6 - OCTOBER 9							The duel of southpaws went to Zachary when Harris's single scored two runs in the fifth.
NY N	100 000 000	1	7	1	**Nehf** (7), Ryan (1)		
WAS A	000 020 00x	2	4	0	**Zachary** (9)		
GAME 7 - OCTOBER 10							The Series closed as it opened: with a 12-inning encounter, but this time Johnson was the winner when McNeely's roller hopped over Lindstrom's head at third base.
NY N	000 003 000 000	3	8	3	Barnes (7.2), Nehf (0.2), McQuillan (1.2), **Bentley** (1.1)		
WAS A	000 100 020 001	4	10	4	Ogden (0.1), Mogridge (4.2), Marberry (3), **Johnson** (4)	Harris	

Team totals

	W	AB	H	2B	3B	HR	R	RBI	BA	BB	SO	ERA
WAS A	4	248	61	9	0	5	26	25	.246	29	34	2.28
NY N	3	253	66	9	2	4	27	21	.261	25	40	3.11

Individual Batting

WASHINGTON (A.L.)

	AB	H	2B	3B	HR	R	RBI	BA
B. Harris, 2b	33	11	0	0	2	5	7	.333
G. Goslin, of	32	11	1	0	3	4	7	.344
S. Rice, of	29	6	0	0	0	2	1	.207
E. McNeely, of	27	6	3	0	0	4	1	.222
J. Judge, 1b	26	10	1	0	0	4	0	.385
O. Bluege, 3b, ss	26	5	0	0	0	2	3	.192
M. Ruel, c	21	2	1	0	0	2	0	.095
R. Peckinpaugh, ss	12	5	2	0	0	1	2	.417
R. Miller, 3b	11	2	0	0	0	0	2	.182
W. Johnson, p	9	1	0	0	0	0	0	.111
N. Leibold, of	6	1	1	0	0	1	0	.167
G. Mogridge, p	5	0	0	0	0	0	0	.000
T. Zachary, p	5	0	0	0	0	0	0	.000
M. Shirley	2	1	0	0	0	1	1	.500
F. Marberry, p	2	0	0	0	0	0	0	.000
T. Taylor, 3b	2	0	0	0	0	0	0	.000
B. Tate	0	0	0	0	0	0	1	—

Errors: O. Bluege (3), B. Harris (2), R. Miller (2), W. Johnson, J. Judge, E. McNeely, S. Rice, T. Taylor

Stolen Bases: S. Rice (2), O. Bluege, E. McNeely, R. Peckinpaugh

NEW YORK (N.L.)

	AB	H	2B	3B	HR	R	RBI	BA
G. Kelly, 1b, 2b, of	31	9	1	0	1	7	4	.290
F. Frisch, 2b, 3b	30	10	4	1	0	1	0	.333
F. Lindstrom, 3b	30	10	2	0	0	1	4	.333
H. Wilson, of	30	7	1	0	0	1	3	.233
H. Gowdy, c	27	7	0	0	0	4	1	.259
R. Youngs, of	27	5	1	0	0	3	1	.185
T. Jackson, ss	27	2	0	0	0	3	1	.074
B. Terry, 1b	14	6	0	1	1	3	1	.429
I. Meusel, of	13	2	0	0	0	0	1	.154
A. Nehf, p	7	3	0	0	0	1	0	.429
J. Bentley, p	7	2	0	0	1	1	2	.286
V. Barnes, p	4	0	0	0	0	0	0	.000
R. Ryan, p	2	1	0	0	1	1	2	.500
H. Groh	1	1	0	0	0	0	0	1.000
H. McQuillan, p	1	1	0	0	0	0	1	1.000
F. Snyder	1	0	0	0	0	0	0	.000
B. Southworth, of	1	0	0	0	0	1	0	.000

Errors: T. Jackson (3), H. Gowdy, G. Kelly, I. Meusel

Stolen Bases: F. Frisch, T. Jackson, R. Youngs

Individual Pitching

WASHINGTON (A.L.)

	W	L	ERA	IP	H	BB	SO	SV
W. Johnson	1	2	2.63	24	30	11	20	0
T. Zachary	2	0	2.04	17.2	13	3	3	0
G. Mogridge	1	0	2.25	12	7	6	5	0
F. Marberry	0	1	1.13	8	9	4	10	2
A. Russell	0	0	3.00	3	4	0	0	0
J. Martina	0	0	0.00	1	0	0	1	0
B. Speece	0	0	9.00	1	3	0	0	0
C. Ogden	0	0	0.00	0.1	0	1	1	0

NEW YORK (N.L.)

	W	L	ERA	IP	H	BB	SO	SV
A. Nehf	1	1	1.83	19.2	15	9	7	0
J. Bentley	1	2	3.18	17	18	8	10	0
V. Barnes	0	1	5.68	12.2	15	1	9	0
H. McQuillan	0	0	2.57	7	2	6	2	1
R. Ryan	1	0	3.18	5.2	7	4	3	0
H. Baldwin	0	0	0.00	2	1	0	1	0
W. Dean	0	0	4.50	2	3	0	2	0
M. Watson	0	0	0.00	0.2	0	0	0	1
C. Jonnard	0	0	—	0.0	0	1	0	0

1925 WORLD SERIES

Pittsburgh (N.L.) defeats Washington (A.L.) 4 games to 3

LINE SCORES			R	H	E	PITCHERS (innings pitched)	HOME RUNS (men on)	HIGHLIGHTS
GAME 1 - OCTOBER 7								Johnson checked the Pirates and struck out ten as Rice delivered the key blow with a single in the fifth driving in two runs to decide the game.
WAS	**A**	010 020 001	4	8	1	**Johnson** (9)	J. Harris	
PIT	**N**	000 010 000	1	5	0	**Meadows** (8), Morrison (1)	Traynor	
GAME 2 - OCTOBER 8								Peckinpaugh's two errors in the eighth, one of which allowed the tying run to get on base before Cuyler's homer, helped the Pirates to their victory.
WAS	**A**	010 000 001	2	8	2	**Coveleski** (8)	Judge	
PIT	**N**	000 100 02x	3	7	0	**Aldridge** (9)	Wright, Cuyler (1 on)	
GAME 3 - OCTOBER 10								With the Senators leading 4-3 in the bottom of the eighth, Earl Smith hit a ball to the center field bleachers. Rice, attempting to catch it, fell over the bleacher railing and disappeared. He then reappeared with the ball for the most controversial ``out'' in Series play.
PIT	**N**	010 101 000	3	8	3	**Kremer** (8)		
WAS	**A**	001 001 02x	4	10	1	**Ferguson** (7), Marberry (2) **SV**	Goslin	
GAME 4 - OCTOBER 11								Back-to-back homers by Goslin and Joe Harris staked Johnson to a four-run third inning lead as he posted his only post-season shutout.
PIT	**N**	000 000 000	0	6	1	**Yde** (2.1), Morrison (4.2), B. Adams (1)		
WAS	**A**	004 000 00x	4	12	0	**Johnson** (9)	Goslin (2 on), J. Harris	
GAME 5 - OCTOBER 12								Back-to-back RBI singles by Cuyler and Barnhart broke a 2-2 tie as Pittsburgh staved off elimination.
PIT	**N**	002 000 211	6	13	0	**Aldridge** (9)		
WAS	**A**	100 100 100	3	8	1	**Coveleski** (6.1), Ballou (0.2), Zachary (1.2), Marberry (0.1)	J. Harris	
GAME 6 - OCTOBER 13								Moore's solo homer in the fifth gave the Pirates a tie in the Series. The temporary screen in center field turned Joe Harris's bid for a game-tying homer in the ninth into a double.
WAS	**A**	110 000 000	2	6	2	**Ferguson** (7), Ballou (1)	Goslin	
PIT	**N**	002 010 00x	3	7	1	**Kremer** (9)	Moore	
GAME 7 - OCTOBER 15								The Pirates battered Johnson for 15 hits in their come-from-behind win. The Pirates were the first team to come back from 3-1 down in a seven-game Series.
WAS	**A**	400 200 010	7	7	2	**Johnson** (8)	Peckinpaugh	
PIT	**N**	003 010 23x	9	15	2	Aldridge (0.1), Morrison (3.2), **Kremer** (4), Oldham (1) **SV**		

Team totals

		W	AB	H	2B	3B	HR	R	RBI	BA	BB	SO	ERA
PIT	**N**	4	230	61	12	2	4	25	25	.265	17	32	3.54
WAS	**A**	3	225	59	8	0	8	26	24	.262	17	31	2.85

Individual Batting

PITTSBURGH (N.L.)

	AB	H	2B	3B	HR	R	RBI	BA
C. Barnhart, of	28	7	1	0	0	1	5	.250
G. Wright, ss	27	5	1	0	1	3	3	.185
P. Traynor, 3b	26	9	0	2	1	2	4	.346
K. Cuyler, of	26	7	3	0	1	3	6	.269
E. Moore, 2b	26	6	1	0	1	7	2	.231
M. Carey, of	24	11	4	0	0	6	2	.458
E. Smith, c	20	7	1	0	0	0	0	.350
G. Grantham, 1b	15	2	0	0	0	0	0	.133
S. McInnis, 1b	14	4	0	0	0	0	1	.286
R. Kremer, p	7	1	0	0	0	0	1	.143
V. Aldridge, p	7	0	0	0	0	0	0	.000
C. Bigbee, of	3	1	1	0	0	1	1	.333
J. Gooch, c	3	0	0	0	0	0	0	.000
J. Morrison, p	2	1	0	0	0	1	0	.500
L. Meadows, p	1	0	0	0	0	0	0	.000
E. Yde, p	1	0	0	0	0	1	0	.000

Errors: G. Wright (2), M. Carey, K. Cuyler, R. Kremer, E. Moore, E. Smith

Stolen Bases: M. Carey (3), C. Barnhart, C. Bigbee, G. Grantham, P. Traynor

WASHINGTON (A.L.)

	AB	H	2B	3B	HR	R	RBI	BA
S. Rice, of	33	12	0	0	0	5	3	.364
G. Goslin, of	26	8	1	0	3	6	5	.308
J. Harris, of	25	11	2	0	3	5	6	.440
R. Peckinpaugh, ss	24	6	1	0	1	1	2	.250
J. Judge, 1b	23	4	1	0	1	2	4	.174
B. Harris, 2b	23	2	0	0	0	2	0	.087
M. Ruel, c	19	6	1	0	0	0	1	.316
O. Bluege, 3b	18	5	1	0	0	2	2	.278
W. Johnson, p	11	1	0	0	0	0	0	.091
B. Myer, 3b	8	2	0	0	0	0	0	.250
A. Ferguson, p	4	0	0	0	0	0	0	.000
H. Severeid, c	3	1	0	0	0	0	0	.333
S. Coveleski, p	3	0	0	0	0	0	0	.000
N. Leibold	2	1	1	0	0	1	0	.500
S. Adams, 2b	1	0	0	0	0	0	0	.000
D. Ruether	1	0	0	0	0	0	0	.000
B. Veach	1	0	0	0	0	0	1	.000
E. McNeely, of	0	0	0	0	0	2	0	—

Errors: R. Peckinpaugh (8), H. Severeid

Stolen Bases: G. Goslin, E. McNeely, R. Peckinpaugh

Individual Pitching

PITTSBURGH (N.L.)

	W	L	ERA	IP	H	BB	SO	SV
R. Kremer	2	1	3.00	21	17	4	9	0
V. Aldridge	2	0	3.93	18.1	18	9	9	0
J. Morrison	0	0	2.89	9.1	11	1	7	0
L. Meadows	0	1	3.38	8	6	0	4	0
E. Yde	0	1	11.57	2.1	5	3	1	0
B. Adams	0	0	0.00	1	2	0	0	0
R. Oldham	0	0	0.00	1	0	0	2	1

WASHINGTON (A.L.)

	W	L	ERA	IP	H	BB	SO	SV
W. Johnson	2	1	2.08	26	26	4	15	0
S. Coveleski	0	2	3.77	14.1	16	5	3	0
A. Ferguson	1	1	3.21	14	13	6	11	0
F. Marberry	0	0	0.00	2.1	3	0	2	1
W. Ballou	0	0	0.00	1.2	0	1	1	0
T. Zachary	0	0	10.80	1.2	3	1	0	0

1926 WORLD SERIES

St. Louis (N.L.) defeats New York (A.L.) 4 games to 3

LINE SCORES			R	H	E	PITCHERS (innings pitched)	HOME RUNS (men on)	HIGHLIGHTS
GAME 1 - OCTOBER 2								Gehrig's single in the sixth sent Ruth home to break a 1-1 tie. Bottomley collected two of the Cardinals' three hits in the loss.
STL	**N**	100 000 000	1	3	1	**Sherdel** (7), Haines (1)		
NY	**A**	100 001 00x	2	6	0	**Pennock** (9)		
GAME 2 - OCTOBER 3								Alexander struck out ten Yankees and retired the last 21 men in succession as Southworth's three-run homer in the seventh won the game.
STL	**N**	002 000 301	6	12	1	**Alexander** (9)	Southworth (2 on), Thevenow	
NY	**A**	020 000 000	2	4	0	**Shocker** (7), Shawkey (1), Jones (1)		
GAME 3 - OCTOBER 5								The Cardinals put together three runs in the fourth to break open the game. Haines aided his own cause with two hits, one a two-run homer.
NY	**A**	000 000 000	0	5	1	**Ruether** (4.1), Shawkey (2.2), Thomas (1)		
STL	**N**	000 310 00x	4	8	0	**Haines** (9)	Haines (1 on)	
GAME 4 - OCTOBER 6								Ruth unloaded a record three home runs in leading the Yankee bombardment which knotted the Series.
NY	**A**	101 142 100	10	14	1	**Hoyt** (9)	Ruth, Ruth, Ruth (1 on)	
STL	**N**	100 300 001	5	14	0	Rhem (4), **Reinhart** (0), H. Bell (2), Hallahan (2), Keen (1)		
GAME 5 - OCTOBER 7								Lazzeri's sacrifice fly in the tenth scored Koenig with the winning tally of the game after Sherdel's wild pitch set up the run. O'Farrell had three hits in the losing cause.
NY	**A**	000 001 001 1	3	9	1	**Pennock** (10)		
STL	**N**	000 100 100 0	2	7	1	**Sherdel** (10)		
GAME 6 - OCTOBER 9								Les Bell had three hits and four RBIs that capped Cardinal rallies in the first and seventh. Alexander won his second complete game of the Series.
STL	**N**	300 010 501	10	13	2	**Alexander** (9)	L. Bell (1 on)	
NY	**A**	000 100 100	2	8	1	**Shawkey** (6.1), Shocker (0.2), Thomas (2)		
GAME 7 - OCTOBER 10								The Cardinals scored three unearned runs in the fourth and Alexander saved the victory in the seventh when, with two out and the bases loaded, he struck out Lazzeri.
STL	**N**	000 300 000	3	8	0	**Haines** (6.2), Alexander (2.1) **SV**		
NY	**A**	001 001 000	2	8	3	**Hoyt** (6), Pennock (3)	Ruth	

Team totals

		W	AB	H	2B	3B	HR	R	RBI	BA	BB	SO	ERA
STL	**N**	4	239	65	12	1	4	31	30	.272	11	30	2.57
NY	**A**	3	223	54	10	1	4	21	19	.242	31	31	3.14

Individual Batting

ST. LOUIS (N.L.)

	AB	H	2B	3B	HR	R	RBI	BA
J. Bottomley, 1b	29	10	3	0	0	4	5	.345
B. Southworth, of	29	10	1	1	1	6	4	.345
R. Hornsby, 2b	28	7	1	0	0	2	4	.250
L. Bell, 3b	27	7	1	0	1	4	6	.259
C. Hafey, of	27	5	2	0	0	2	0	.185
T. Thevenow, ss	24	10	1	0	1	5	4	.417
B. O'Farrell, c	23	7	1	0	0	2	2	.304
W. Holm, of	16	2	0	0	0	1	1	.125
T. Douthit, of	15	4	2	0	0	3	1	.267
G. Alexander, p	7	0	0	0	0	1	0	.000
J. Haines, p	5	3	0	0	1	1	2	.600
B. Sherdel, p	5	0	0	0	0	0	0	.000
J. Flowers	3	0	0	0	0	0	0	.000
F. Rhem, p	1	0	0	0	0	0	0	.000
S. Toporcer	0	0	0	0	0	0	1	—

Errors: L. Bell (2), T. Thevenow (2), G. Alexander

Stolen Bases: R. Hornsby, B. Southworth

NEW YORK (A.L.)

	AB	H	2B	3B	HR	R	RBI	BA
M. Koenig, ss	32	4	1	0	0	2	2	.125
E. Combs, of	28	10	2	0	0	3	2	.357
T. Lazzeri, 2b	26	5	1	0	0	2	3	.192
J. Dugan, 3b	24	8	1	0	0	2	2	.333
L. Gehrig, 1b	23	8	2	0	0	1	3	.348
H. Severeid, c	22	6	1	0	0	1	1	.273
B. Meusel, of	21	5	1	1	0	3	0	.238
B. Ruth, of	20	6	0	0	4	6	5	.300
H. Pennock, p	7	1	1	0	0	1	0	.143
W. Hoyt, p	6	0	0	0	0	0	0	.000
B. Paschal	4	1	0	0	0	0	1	.250
D. Ruether, p	4	0	0	0	0	0	0	.000
P. Collins, c	2	0	0	0	0	0	0	.000
B. Shawkey, p	2	0	0	0	0	0	0	.000
U. Shocker, p	2	0	0	0	0	0	0	.000
S. Adams	0	0	0	0	0	0	0	—
M. Gazella, 3b	0	0	0	0	0	0	0	—

Errors: M. Koenig (4), J. Dugan, T. Lazzeri, B. Meusel

Stolen Bases: B. Ruth

Individual Pitching

ST. LOUIS (N.L.)

	W	L	ERA	IP	H	BB	SO	SV
G. Alexander	2	0	0.89	20.1	12	4	17	1
B. Sherdel	0	2	2.12	17	15	8	3	0
J. Haines	2	0	1.08	16.2	13	9	5	0
F. Rhem	0	0	6.75	4	7	2	4	0
H. Bell	0	0	9.00	2	4	1	1	0
B. Hallahan	0	0	4.50	2	2	3	1	0
V. Keen	0	0	0.00	1	0	0	0	0
A. Reinhart	0	1	∞	0.0	1	4	0	0

NEW YORK (A.L.)

	W	L	ERA	IP	H	BB	SO	SV
H. Pennock	2	0	1.23	22	13	4	8	0
W. Hoyt	1	1	1.20	15	19	1	10	0
B. Shawkey	0	1	5.40	10	8	2	7	0
U. Shocker	0	1	5.87	7.2	13	0	3	0
D. Ruether	0	1	8.31	4.1	7	2	1	0
M. Thomas	0	0	3.00	3	3	0	0	0
S. Jones	0	0	9.00	1	2	2	1	0

1927 WORLD SERIES

New York (A.L.) defeats Pittsburgh (N.L.) 4 games to 0

LINE SCORES			R	H	E	PITCHERS (innings pitched)	HOME RUNS (men on)	HIGHLIGHTS
GAME 1 - OCTOBER 5								Three hits by Ruth and two RBIs by Gehrig gave the Yankees the win. Paul Waner had three hits of his own for the losers.
NY	**A**	103 010 000	5	6	1	**Hoyt** (7.1), Moore (1.2) **SV**		
PIT	**N**	101 010 010	4	9	2	**Kremer** (5), Miljus (4)		
GAME 2 - OCTOBER 6								The Yankees again scored three in the third with Gehrig's double highlighting the frame, enabling Pipgras to breeze. Koenig had three hits for New York.
NY	**A**	003 000 030	6	11	0	**Pipgras** (9)		
PIT	**N**	100 000 010	2	7	2	**Aldrich** (7.1), Cvengros (0.2), Dawson (1)		
GAME 3 - OCTOBER 7								Pennock retired the first 22 men in succession before Traynor broke the spell with a single in the eighth. Gehrig's two-run triple settled the issue in the first and Ruth's three-run homer added icing in the seventh.
PIT	**N**	000 000 010	1	3	1	**Meadows** (6.1), Cvengros (1.2)		
NY	**A**	200 000 60x	8	9	0	**Pennock** (9)	Ruth (2 on)	
GAME 4 - OCTOBER 8								A walk, a bunt, a wild pitch, and an intentional walk loaded the bases for Yanks in the bottom of the ninth. Miljus then struck out Gehrig and Meusel, but then threw a wild pitch to bring home the Series-ending run.
PIT	**N**	100 000 200	3	10	1	Hill (6), **Miljus** (2.2)		
NY	**A**	100 020 001	4	12	2	**Moore** (9)	Ruth (1 on)	

Team totals

		W	AB	H	2B	3B	HR	R	RBI	BA	BB	SO	ERA
NY	**A**	4	136	38	6	2	2	23	20	.279	13	25	2.00
PIT	**N**	0	130	29	6	1	0	10	10	.223	4	7	5.19

Individual Batting

NEW YORK (A.L.)

	AB	H	2B	3B	HR	R	RBI	BA
M. Koenig, ss	18	9	2	0	0	5	2	.500
B. Meusel, of	17	2	0	0	0	1	1	.118
E. Combs, of	16	5	0	0	0	6	2	.313
B. Ruth, of	15	6	0	0	2	4	7	.400
T. Lazzeri, 2b	15	4	1	0	0	1	2	.267
J. Dugan, 3b	15	3	0	0	0	2	0	.200
L. Gehrig, 1b	13	4	2	2	0	2	5	.308
P. Collins, c	5	3	1	0	0	0	0	.600
W. Moore, p	5	1	0	0	0	0	0	.200
B. Bengough, c	4	0	0	0	0	1	0	.000
H. Pennock, p	4	0	0	0	0	1	1	.000
G. Pipgras, p	3	1	0	0	0	0	0	.333
W. Hoyt, p	3	0	0	0	0	0	0	.000
J. Grabowski, c	2	0	0	0	0	0	0	.000
C. Durst	1	0	0	0	0	0	0	.000

Errors: T. Lazzeri, B. Meusel, W. Moore
Stolen Bases: B. Meusel, B. Ruth

PITTSBURGH (N.L.)

	AB	H	2B	3B	HR	R	RBI	BA
C. Barnhart, of	16	5	1	0	0	0	4	.313
L. Waner, of	15	6	1	1	0	5	0	.400
P. Waner, of	15	5	1	0	0	0	3	.333
J. Harris, 1b	15	3	0	0	0	0	1	.200
P. Traynor, 3b	15	3	1	0	0	1	0	.200
G. Wright, ss	13	2	0	0	0	1	2	.154
G. Grantham, 2b	11	4	1	0	0	0	0	.364
E. Smith, c	8	0	0	0	0	0	0	.000
J. Gooch, c	5	0	0	0	0	0	0	.000
H. Rhyne, 2b	4	0	0	0	0	0	0	.000
R. Kremer, p	2	1	1	0	0	1	0	.500
V. Aldridge, p	2	0	0	0	0	0	0	.000
F. Brickell	2	0	0	0	0	1	0	.000
L. Meadows, p	2	0	0	0	0	0	0	.000
J. Miljus, p	2	0	0	0	0	0	0	.000
H. Groh	1	0	0	0	0	0	0	.000
C. Hill, p	1	0	0	0	0	0	0	.000
R. Spencer, c	1	0	0	0	0	0	0	.000
E. Yde	0	0	0	0	0	1	0	—

Errors: L. Waner (2), G. Grantham, E. Smith, P. Traynor, G. Wright

Individual Pitching

NEW YORK (A.L.)

	W	L	ERA	IP	H	BB	SO	SV
W. Moore	1	0	0.84	10.2	11	2	2	1
H. Pennock	1	0	1.00	9	3	0	1	0
G. Pipgras	1	0	2.00	9	7	1	2	0
W. Hoyt	1	0	4.91	7.1	8	1	2	0

PITTSBURGH (N.L.)

	W	L	ERA	IP	H	BB	SO	SV
V. Aldridge	0	1	7.36	7.1	10	4	4	0
J. Miljus	0	1	1.35	6.2	4	4	6	0
L. Meadows	0	1	9.95	6.1	7	1	6	0
C. Hill	0	0	4.50	6	9	1	6	0
R. Kremer	0	1	3.60	5	5	3	1	0
M. Cvengros	0	0	3.86	2.1	3	0	2	0
J. Dawson	0	0	0.00	1	0	0	0	0

1928 WORLD SERIES

New York (A.L.) defeats St. Louis (N.L.) 4 games to 0

LINE SCORES			R	H	E	PITCHERS (innings pitched)	HOME RUNS (men on)	HIGHLIGHTS
GAME 1 - OCTOBER 4								Hoyt opened with a win for the second year in a row, notching a three-hitter. Meusel's homer in the fourth scored two; Bottomley's blast spoiled the shutout.
STL	**N**	000 000 100	1	3	1	**Sherdel** (7), Johnson (1)	Bottomley	
NY	**A**	100 200 01x	4	7	0	**Hoyt** (9)	Meusel (1 on)	
GAME 2 - OCTOBER 5								Gehrig's homer in the first led the Yankees to a revenge win over Alexander, the hero of the 1926 classic. Pipgras, relying on curve balls, went the distance despite a shaky start.
STL	**N**	030 000 000	3	4	1	**Alexander** (2.1), Mitchell (5.2)		
NY	**A**	314 000 10x	9	8	2	**Pipgras** (9)	Gehrig (2 on)	
GAME 3 - OCTOBER 7								Zachary, a surprise southpaw starter, had an easy task when Gehrig connected twice for homers, batting in three as the Yankees dispose of Haines in six.
NY	**A**	010 203 100	7	7	2	**Zachary** (9)	Gehrig, Gehrig (1 on)	
STL	**N**	200 010 000	3	9	3	**Haines** (6), Johnson (1), Rhem (2)		
GAME 4 - OCTOBER 9								Ruth rose to heights with three homers, aided by the umpire's ruling depriving Sherdel of a strikeout on a ``quick-pitch''.
NY	**A**	000 100 420	7	15	2	**Hoyt** (9)	Ruth, Ruth, Gehrig, Durst, Ruth	
STL	**N**	001 100 001	3	11	0	**Sherdel** (6.1), Alexander (2.2)		

Team totals

		W	AB	H	2B	3B	HR	R	RBI	BA	BB	SO	ERA
NY	**A**	4	134	37	7	0	9	27	25	.276	13	12	2.00
STL	**N**	0	131	27	5	1	1	10	8	.206	11	29	6.09

Individual Batting

NEW YORK (A.L.)

	AB	H	2B	3B	HR	R	RBI	BA
M. Koenig, ss	19	3	0	0	0	1	0	.158
B. Ruth, of	16	10	3	0	3	9	4	.625
B. Meusel, of	15	3	1	0	1	5	3	.200
B. Bengough, c	13	3	0	0	0	1	1	.231
T. Lazzeri, 2b	12	3	1	0	0	2	0	.250
L. Gehrig, 1b	11	6	1	0	4	5	9	.545
B. Paschal, of	10	2	0	0	0	0	1	.200
C. Durst, of	8	3	0	0	1	3	2	.375
G. Robertson, 3b	8	1	0	0	0	1	2	.125
W. Hoyt, p	7	1	0	0	0	0	0	.143
J. Dugan, 3b	6	1	0	0	0	0	1	.167
T. Zachary, p	4	0	0	0	0	0	0	.000
L. Durocher, 2b	2	0	0	0	0	0	0	.000
G. Pipgras, p	2	0	0	0	0	0	1	.000
P. Collins, c	1	1	1	0	0	0	0	1.000
E. Combs	0	0	0	0	0	0	1	—

Errors: M. Koenig (2), T. Lazzeri (2), W. Hoyt, G. Robertson
Stolen Bases: T. Lazzeri (2), B. Meusel (2)

ST. LOUIS (N.L.)

	AB	H	2B	3B	HR	R	RBI	BA
A. High, 3b	17	5	2	0	0	1	1	.294
C. Hafey, of	15	3	0	0	0	0	0	.200
J. Bottomley, 1b	14	3	0	1	1	1	3	.214
R. Maranville, ss	13	4	1	0	0	2	0	.308
F. Frisch, 2b	13	3	0	0	0	1	1	.231
T. Douthit, of	11	1	0	0	0	1	0	.091
J. Wilson, c	11	1	1	0	0	1	1	.091
G. Harper, of	9	1	0	0	0	1	0	.111
E. Orsatti, of	7	2	1	0	0	1	0	.286
W. Holm, of	6	1	0	0	0	0	1	.167
B. Sherdel, p	5	0	0	0	0	0	0	.000
E. Smith, c	4	3	0	0	0	0	0	.750
J. Haines, p	2	0	0	0	0	0	0	.000
C. Mitchell, p	2	0	0	0	0	0	0	.000
G. Alexander, p	1	0	0	0	0	0	1	.000
R. Blades	1	0	0	0	0	0	0	.000
P. Martin	0	0	0	0	0	1	0	—
T. Thevenow, ss	0	0	0	0	0	0	0	—

Errors: J. Wilson (2), C. Hafey, R. Maranville, C. Mitchell
Stolen Bases: F. Frisch (2), R. Maranville

Individual Pitching

NEW YORK (A.L.)

	W	L	ERA	IP	H	BB	SO	SV
W. Hoyt	2	0	1.50	18	14	6	14	0
G. Pipgras	1	0	2.00	9	4	4	8	0
T. Zachary	1	0	3.00	9	9	1	7	0

ST. LOUIS (N.L.)

	W	L	ERA	IP	H	BB	SO	SV
B. Sherdel	0	2	4.72	13.1	15	3	3	0
J. Haines	0	1	4.50	6	6	3	3	0
C. Mitchell	0	0	1.59	5.2	2	2	2	0
G. Alexander	0	1	19.80	5	10	4	2	0
S. Johnson	0	0	4.50	2	4	1	1	0
F. Rhem	0	0	0.00	2	0	0	1	0

1929 WORLD SERIES

Philadelphia (A.L.) defeats Chicago (N.L.) 4 games to 1

LINE SCORES						PITCHERS (innings pitched)	HOME RUNS (men on)	HIGHLIGHTS
GAME 1 - OCTOBER 8								
PHI	A	000 000 102	3	6	1	**Ehmke** (9)	Foxx	Ehmke struck out 13, surpassing the Series record of 12 set by Walsh in 1906. Foxx's home run in the seventh broke a scoreless deadlock, and Miller's two-run single in the ninth applied the crusher.
CHI	N	000 000 001	1	8	2	**Root** (7), Bush (2)		
GAME 2 - OCTOBER 9								
PHI	A	003 300 120	9	12	0	**Earnshaw** (4.2), Grove (4.1) **SV**	Foxx (2 on), Simmons (1 on)	Foxx again took charge, his three-run homer in the third launching the scoring. Earnshaw got credit for the win despite being relieved by Grove in the fifth.
CHI	N	000 030 000	3	10	1	**Malone** (3.2), Blake (1.1), Carlson (3), Nehf (1)		
GAME 3 - OCTOBER 11								
CHI	N	000 003 000	3	6	1	**Bush** (9)		A two-run single in the sixth by Cuyler gives the National League its first Series victory after ten straight setbacks. Earnshaw, on one day's rest, struck out ten, but lost on two unearned runs.
PHI	A	000 010 000	1	9	1	**Earnshaw** (9)		
GAME 4 - OCTOBER 12								
CHI	N	000 205 100	8	10	2	Root (6.1), Nehf (0), **Blake** (0), Malone (0.2), Carlson (1)	Grimm (1 on)	A fabulous ten-run seventh overcame an 8-0 deficit and lifted the A's to an incredible triumph. Wilson contributed to the scoring binge by losing two balls in the sun.
PHI	A	000 000 (10)0x	10	15	2	Quinn (5), Walberg (1), **Rommel** (1), Grove (2) **SV**	Simmons, Haas (2 on)	
GAME 5 - OCTOBER 14								
CHI	N	000 200 000	2	8	1	**Malone** (8.2)		Three runs in the last of the ninth brought a dramatic end to the Series. A two-run homer by Haas tied the score before Simmons and Miller doubled to score the winning run.
PHI	A	000 000 003	3	6	0	Ehmke (3.2), **Walberg** (5.1)	Haas (1 on)	

Team totals

		W	AB	H	2B	3B	HR	R	RBI	BA	BB	SO	ERA
PHI	A	4	171	48	5	0	6	26	26	.281	13	27	2.40
CHI	N	1	173	43	6	2	1	17	15	.249	13	50	4.33

Individual Batting

PHILADELPHIA (A.L.)

	AB	H	2B	3B	HR	R	RBI	BA
M. Haas, of	21	5	0	0	2	3	6	.238
M. Bishop, 2b	21	4	0	0	0	2	1	.190
J. Foxx, 1b	20	7	1	0	2	5	5	.350
A. Simmons, of	20	6	1	0	2	6	5	.300
J. Dykes, 3b	19	8	1	0	0	2	4	.421
B. Miller, of	19	7	1	0	0	1	4	.368
J. Boley, ss	17	4	0	0	0	1	1	.235
M. Cochrane, c	15	6	1	0	0	5	0	.400
H. Ehmke, p	5	1	0	0	0	0	0	.200
G. Earnshaw, p	5	0	0	0	0	1	0	.000
G. Burns	2	0	0	0	0	0	0	.000
L. Grove, p	2	0	0	0	0	0	0	.000
J. Quinn, p	2	0	0	0	0	0	0	.000
W. French	1	0	0	0	0	0	0	.000
H. Summa	1	0	0	0	0	0	0	.000
R. Walberg, p	1	0	0	0	0	0	0	.000

Errors: J. Dykes (2), B. Miller, R. Walberg

CHICAGO (N.L.)

	AB	H	2B	3B	HR	R	RBI	BA
R. Hornsby, 2b	21	5	1	1	0	4	1	.238
W. English, ss	21	4	2	0	0	1	0	.190
K. Cuyler, of	20	6	1	0	0	4	4	.300
N. McMillan, 3b	20	2	0	0	0	0	0	.100
R. Stephenson, of	19	6	1	0	0	3	3	.316
C. Grimm, 1b	18	7	0	0	1	2	4	.389
H. Wilson, of	17	8	0	1	0	2	0	.471
Z. Taylor, c	17	3	0	0	0	0	3	.176
C. Root, p	5	0	0	0	0	0	0	.000
P. Malone, p	4	1	1	0	0	0	0	.250
G. Bush, p	3	0	0	0	0	1	0	.000
G. Hartnett	3	0	0	0	0	0	0	.000
S. Blake, p	1	1	0	0	0	0	0	1.000
F. Blair	1	0	0	0	0	0	0	.000
M. Gonzalez, c	1	0	0	0	0	0	0	.000
C. Heathcote	1	0	0	0	0	0	0	.000
C. Tolson	1	0	0	0	0	0	0	.000

Errors: W. English (4), K. Cuyler, R. Hornsby, H. Wilson
Stolen Bases: N. McMillan

Individual Pitching

PHILADELPHIA (A.L.)

	W	L	ERA	IP	H	BB	SO	SV
G. Earnshaw	1	1	2.63	13.2	14	6	17	0
H. Ehmke	1	0	1.42	12.2	14	3	13	0
L. Grove	0	0	0.00	6.1	3	1	10	2
R. Walberg	1	0	0.00	6.1	3	0	8	0
J. Quinn	0	0	9.00	5	7	2	2	0
E. Rommel	1	0	9.00	1	2	1	0	0

CHICAGO (N.L.)

	W	L	ERA	IP	H	BB	SO	SV
C. Root	0	1	4.72	13.1	12	2	8	0
P. Malone	0	2	4.15	13	12	7	11	0
G. Bush	1	0	0.82	11	12	2	4	0
H. Carlson	0	0	6.75	4	7	1	3	0
S. Blake	0	1	13.50	1.1	4	0	1	0
A. Nehf	0	0	18.00	1	1	1	0	0

1930 WORLD SERIES

Philadelphia (A.L.) defeats St. Louis (N.L.) 4 games to 2

LINE SCORES			R	H	E	PITCHERS (innings pitched)	HOME RUNS (men on)	HIGHLIGHTS
GAME 1 - OCTOBER 1								The Athletics got only five hits in five different innings off Grimes but all were for extra bases and each produced a run.
STL	**N**	002 000 000	2	9	0	**Grimes** (8)		
PHI	**A**	010 101 11x	5	5	0	**Grove** (9)	Simmons, Cochrane	
GAME 2 - OCTOBER 2								The Athletics scored six runs off Rhem in the first four innings to win easily. Earnshaw walked one and struck out eight.
STL	**N**	010 000 000	1	6	2	**Rhem** (3.1), Lindsey (2.2), Johnson (2)	Watkins	
PHI	**A**	202 200 00x	6	7	2	**Earnshaw** (9)	Cochrane	
GAME 3 - OCTOBER 4								Hallahan had an easy shutout after escaping from a first inning jam.
PHI	**A**	000 000 000	0	7	0	**Walberg** (4.2), Shores (1.1), Quinn (2)		
STL	**N**	000 110 21x	5	10	0	**Hallahan** (9)	Douthit	
GAME 4 - OCTOBER 5								Dykes's error allowed the Cardinals to score twice in the fourth. Haines did not allow a hit after the third inning.
PHI	**A**	100 000 000	1	4	1	**Grove** (8)		
STL	**N**	001 200 00x	3	5	1	**Haines** (9)		
GAME 5 - OCTOBER 6								Foxx's homer won for the Athletics in the ninth as Earnshaw and Grove kept the Cardinals from reaching third.
PHI	**A**	000 000 002	2	5	0	Earnshaw (7), **Grove** (2)	Foxx (1 on)	
STL	**N**	000 000 000	0	3	1	**Grimes** (9)		
GAME 6 - OCTOBER 8								Once again the Athletics got only extra base hits and turned each into a run as Earnshaw, with only one day's rest, pitched a strong five-hitter.
STL	**N**	000 000 001	1	5	1	**Hallahan** (2), Johnson (3), Lindsey (2), Bell (1)		
PHI	**A**	201 211 00x	7	7	0	**Earnshaw** (9)	Simmons, Dykes (1 on)	

Team totals

		W	AB	H	2B	3B	HR	R	RBI	BA	BB	SO	ERA
PHI	**A**	4	178	35	10	2	6	21	20	.197	24	32	1.73
STL	**N**	2	190	38	10	1	2	12	11	.200	11	33	3.35

Individual Batting

PHILADELPHIA (A.L.)

	AB	H	2B	3B	HR	R	RBI	BA
A. Simmons, of	22	8	2	0	2	4	4	.364
J. Foxx, 1b	21	7	2	1	1	3	3	.333
B. Miller, of	21	3	2	0	0	0	3	.143
J. Boley, ss	21	2	0	0	0	1	1	.095
M. Bishop, 2b	18	4	0	0	0	5	0	.222
M. Cochrane, c	18	4	1	0	2	5	3	.222
J. Dykes, 3b	18	4	3	0	1	2	5	.222
M. Haas, of	18	2	0	1	0	1	1	.111
G. Earnshaw, p	9	0	0	0	0	0	0	.000
L. Grove, p	6	0	0	0	0	0	0	.000
J. Moore, of	3	1	0	0	0	0	0	.333
R. Walberg, p	2	0	0	0	0	0	0	.000
E. McNair	1	0	0	0	0	0	0	.000

Errors: J. Boley, M. Cochrane, J. Dykes

ST. LOUIS (N.L.)

	AB	H	2B	3B	HR	R	RBI	BA
F. Frisch, 2b	24	5	2	0	0	0	0	.208
T. Douthit, of	24	2	0	0	1	1	2	.083
C. Hafey, of	22	6	5	0	0	2	2	.273
J. Bottomley, 1b	22	1	1	0	0	1	0	.045
S. Adams, 3b	21	3	0	0	0	0	1	.143
C. Gelbert, ss	17	6	0	1	0	2	2	.353
J. Wilson, c	15	4	1	0	0	0	2	.267
G. Watkins, of	12	2	0	0	1	2	1	.167
R. Blades, of	9	1	0	0	0	2	0	.111
G. Mancuso, c	7	2	0	0	0	1	0	.286
B. Grimes, p	5	2	0	0	0	0	0	.400
S. Fisher	2	1	1	0	0	0	0	.500
J. Haines, p	2	1	0	0	0	0	1	.500
A. High, 3b	2	1	0	0	0	1	0	.500
B. Hallahan, p	2	0	0	0	0	0	0	.000
J. Lindsey, p	1	1	0	0	0	0	0	1.000
E. Orsatti	1	0	0	0	0	0	0	.000
G. Puccinelli	1	0	0	0	0	0	0	.000
F. Rhem, p	1	0	0	0	0	0	0	.000

Errors: F. Frisch (3), F. Rhem, G. Watkins

Stolen Bases: F. Frisch

Individual Pitching

PHILADELPHIA (A.L.)

	W	L	ERA	IP	H	BB	SO	SV
G. Earnshaw	2	0	0.72	25	13	7	19	0
L. Grove	2	1	1.42	19	15	3	10	0
R. Walberg	0	1	3.86	4.2	4	1	3	0
J. Quinn	0	0	4.50	2	3	0	1	0
B. Shores	0	0	13.50	1.1	3	0	0	0

ST. LOUIS (N.L.)

	W	L	ERA	IP	H	BB	SO	SV
B. Grimes	0	2	3.71	17	10	6	13	0
B. Hallahan	1	1	1.64	11	9	8	8	0
J. Haines	1	0	1.00	9	4	4	2	0
S. Johnson	0	0	7.20	5	4	3	4	0
J. Lindsey	0	0	1.93	4.2	1	1	2	0
F. Rhem	0	1	10.80	3.1	7	2	3	0
H. Bell	0	0	0.00	1	0	0	0	0

1931 WORLD SERIES

St. Louis (N.L.) defeats Philadelphia (A.L.) 4 games to 3

LINE SCORES			R	H	E	PITCHERS (innings pitched)	HOME RUNS (men on)	HIGHLIGHTS
GAME 1 - OCTOBER 1								The A's gave Grove four third-inning runs, and he coasted from there. He scattered twelve hits, three by Pepper Martin.
PHI	**A**	004 000 200	6	11	0	**Grove** (9)	Simmons (1 on)	
STL	**N**	200 000 000	2	12	0	**Derringer** (7), Johnson (2)		
GAME 2 - OCTOBER 2								Pepper Martin, with two hits and two stolen bases, scored both Cardinal runs to support Hallahan's shutout pitching.
PHI	**A**	000 000 000	0	3	0	**Earnshaw** (8)		
STL	**N**	010 000 01x	2	6	1	**Hallahan** (9)		
GAME 3 - OCTOBER 5								Grimes supported his two-hitter with a two-run single in the fourth.
STL	**N**	020 200 001	5	12	0	**Grimes** (9)		
PHI	**A**	000 000 002	2	2	0	**Grove** (8), Mahaffey (1)	Simmons (1 on)	
GAME 4 - OCTOBER 6								Simmons doubled home Bishop in the first to give Earnshaw the only run he needed. Martin had both Cardinal hits.
STL	**N**	000 000 000	0	2	1	**Johnson** (5.2), Lindsey (1.1), Derringer (1)		
PHI	**A**	100 002 00x	3	10	0	**Earnshaw** (9)	Foxx	
GAME 5 - OCTOBER 7								Martin, with three hits and a long fly, drove in four runs to lead the Cardinal attack.
STL	**N**	100 002 011	5	12	0	**Hallahan** (9)	Martin (1 on)	
PHI	**A**	000 000 100	1	9	0	**Hoyt** (6), Walberg (2), Rommel (1)		
GAME 6 - OCTOBER 9								The Athletics broke a scoreless tie with four runs in the fifth on two singles, four walks and an error.
PHI	**A**	000 040 400	8	8	1	**Grove** (9)		
STL	**N**	000 001 000	1	5	2	**Derringer** (4.2), Johnson (1.1), Lindsey (2), Rhem (1)		
GAME 7 - OCTOBER 10								Watkins's two-run homer in the third gave the Cardinals a 4-0 lead and enabled them to withstand a late Athletics rally, Hallahan nailing down the final out for a tiring Grimes.
PHI	**A**	000 000 002	2	7	1	**Earnshaw** (7), Walberg (1)		
STL	**N**	202 000 00x	4	5	0	**Grimes** (8.2), Hallahan (0.1) **SV**	Watkins (1 on)	

Team totals

		W	AB	H	2B	3B	HR	R	RBI	BA	BB	SO	ERA
STL	**N**	4	229	54	11	0	2	19	17	.236	9	41	2.32
PHI	**A**	3	227	50	5	0	3	22	20	.220	28	46	2.66

Individual Batting

ST. LOUIS (N.L.)

	AB	H	2B	3B	HR	R	RBI	BA
F. Frisch, 2b	27	7	2	0	0	2	1	.259
J. Bottomley, 1b	25	4	1	0	0	2	2	.160
P. Martin, of	24	12	4	0	1	5	5	.500
C. Hafey, of	24	4	0	0	0	1	0	.167
C. Gelbert, ss	23	6	1	0	0	0	3	.261
J. Wilson, c	23	5	0	0	0	0	2	.217
A. High, 3b	15	4	0	0	0	3	0	.267
W. Roettger, of	14	4	1	0	0	1	0	.286
G. Watkins, of	14	4	1	0	1	4	2	.286
J. Flowers, 3b	11	1	1	0	0	1	0	.091
B. Grimes, p	7	2	0	0	0	0	2	.286
B. Hallahan, p	6	0	0	0	0	0	0	.000
S. Adams, 3b	4	1	0	0	0	0	0	.250
E. Orsatti, of	3	0	0	0	0	0	0	.000
R. Blades	2	0	0	0	0	0	0	.000
R. Collins	2	0	0	0	0	0	0	.000
P. Derringer, p	2	0	0	0	0	0	0	.000
S. Johnson, p	2	0	0	0	0	0	0	.000
G. Mancuso, c	1	0	0	0	0	0	0	.000

Errors: J. Bottomley, J. Flowers, C. Hafey, J. Wilson
Stolen Bases: P. Martin (5), F. Frisch, C. Hafey, G. Watkins

PHILADELPHIA (A.L.)

	AB	H	2B	3B	HR	R	RBI	BA
A. Simmons, of	27	9	2	0	2	4	8	.333
M. Bishop, 2b	27	4	0	0	0	4	0	.148
B. Miller, of	26	7	1	0	0	3	1	.269
D. Williams, ss	25	8	1	0	0	2	1	.320
M. Cochrane, c	25	4	0	0	0	2	1	.160
J. Foxx, 1b	23	8	0	0	1	3	3	.348
M. Haas, of	23	3	1	0	0	1	2	.130
J. Dykes, 3b	22	5	0	0	0	2	2	.227
L. Grove, p	10	0	0	0	0	0	0	.000
G. Earnshaw, p	8	0	0	0	0	0	0	.000
J. Moore, of	3	1	0	0	0	0	0	.333
D. Cramer	2	1	0	0	0	0	2	.500
W. Hoyt, p	2	0	0	0	0	0	0	.000
E. McNair, 2b	2	0	0	0	0	1	0	.000
J. Boley	1	0	0	0	0	0	0	.000
J. Heving	1	0	0	0	0	0	0	.000
P. Todt	0	0	0	0	0	0	0	—

Errors: M. Cochrane, J. Foxx

Individual Pitching

ST. LOUIS (N.L.)

	W	L	ERA	IP	H	BB	SO	SV
B. Hallahan	2	0	0.49	18.1	12	8	12	1
B. Grimes	2	0	2.04	17.2	9	9	11	0
P. Derringer	0	2	4.26	12.2	14	7	14	0
S. Johnson	0	1	3.00	9	10	1	6	0
J. Lindsey	0	0	5.40	3.1	4	3	2	0
F. Rhem	0	0	0.00	1	1	0	1	0

PHILADELPHIA (A.L.)

	W	L	ERA	IP	H	BB	SO	SV
L. Grove	2	1	2.42	26	28	2	16	0
G. Earnshaw	1	2	1.88	24	12	4	20	0
W. Hoyt	0	1	4.50	6	7	0	1	0
R. Walberg	0	0	3.00	3	3	2	4	0
R. Mahaffey	0	0	9.00	1	1	1	0	0
E. Rommel	0	0	9.00	1	3	0	0	0

1932 WORLD SERIES

New York (A.L.) defeats Chicago (N.L.) 4 games to 0

LINE SCORES					PITCHERS (innings pitched)	HOME RUNS (men on)	HIGHLIGHTS
GAME 1 - SEPTEMBER 28							Bush retired the first nine batters, but the Yanks exploded, thanks to Gehrig's two-run homer in the fourth, and two-run singles by Dickey and Combs. Ruffing struck out ten in going the distance.
CHI N	200 000 220	6	10	1	**Bush** (5.1), Grimes (1.2), Smith (1)		
NY A	000 305 31x	12	8	2	**Ruffing** (9)	Gehrig (1 on)	
GAME 2 - SEPTEMBER 29							Chapman's single in the third gave the Yankees the lead, and Gomez shut the Cubs down. Gehrig had three hits and scored two runs.
CHI N	101 000 000	2	9	0	**Warneke** (8)		
NY A	202 010 00x	5	10	1	**Gomez** (9)		
GAME 3 - OCTOBER 1							In a home run carnival which featured two homers each by Ruth and Gehrig, the Yankees took a commanding three-game lead in the Series. Back-to-back home runs in the fifth by the two sluggers decided the game.
NY A	301 020 001	7	8	1	**Pipgras** (8), Pennock (1) **SV**	Ruth (2 on), Gehrig, Ruth, Gehrig	
CHI N	102 100 001	5	9	4	**Root** (4.1), Malone (2.2), May (1.1), Tinning (0.2)	Cuyler, Hartnett	
GAME 4 - OCTOBER 2							The Yankees came back from a 4-1 first inning deficit to sweep the Series. The Cubs held Ruth to just one single, but six other Yankees had two or more hits on the day.
NY A	102 002 404	13	19	4	Allen (0.2.), **W. Moore** (5.1), Pennock (3) **SV**	Lazzeri (1 on), Combs, Lazzeri (1 on)	
CHI N	400 001 001	6	9	1	Bush (0.1), Warneke (2.2), **May** (3.1), Tinning (1.2), Grimes (1)	Demaree (2 on)	

Team totals

		W	AB	H	2B	3B	HR	R	RBI	BA	BB	SO	ERA
NY	**A**	4	144	45	6	0	8	37	36	.313	23	26	3.25
CHI	**N**	0	146	37	8	2	3	19	16	.253	11	25	9.26

Individual Batting

NEW YORK (A.L.)

	AB	H	2B	3B	HR	R	RBI	BA
L. Gehrig, 1b	17	9	1	0	3	9	8	.529
B. Chapman, of	17	5	1	0	0	1	6	.294
T. Lazzeri, 2b	17	5	0	0	2	4	5	.294
B. Dickey, c	16	7	0	0	0	2	4	.438
E. Combs, of	16	6	1	0	1	8	4	.375
B. Ruth, of	15	5	0	0	2	6	6	.333
J. Sewell, 3b	15	5	1	0	0	4	3	.333
F. Crosetti, ss	15	2	1	0	0	2	0	.133
G. Pipgras, p	5	0	0	0	0	0	0	.000
R. Ruffing, p	4	0	0	0	0	0	0	.000
W. Moore, p	3	1	0	0	0	0	0	.333
L. Gomez, p	3	0	0	0	0	0	0	.000
H. Pennock, p	1	0	0	0	0	0	0	.000
S. Byrd, of	0	0	0	0	0	0	0	—
M. Hoag	0	0	0	0	0	1	0	—

Errors: F. Crosetti (4), L. Gehrig, T. Lazzeri, B. Ruth, J. Sewell

CHICAGO (N.L.)

	AB	H	2B	3B	HR	R	RBI	BA
R. Stephenson, of	18	8	1	0	0	2	4	.444
K. Cuyler, of	18	5	1	1	1	2	2	.278
B. Herman, 2b	18	4	1	0	0	5	1	.222
W. English, 3b	17	3	0	0	0	2	1	.176
G. Hartnett, c	16	5	2	0	1	2	1	.313
C. Grimm, 1b	15	5	2	0	0	2	1	.333
B. Jurges, ss	11	4	1	0	0	1	1	.364
F. Demaree, of	7	2	0	0	1	1	4	.286
J. Moore, of	7	0	0	0	0	1	0	.000
M. Koenig, ss	4	1	0	1	0	1	1	.250
L. Warneke, p	4	0	0	0	0	0	0	.000
R. Hemsley, c	3	0	0	0	0	0	0	.000
M. Gudat	2	0	0	0	0	0	0	.000
J. May, p	2	0	0	0	0	0	0	.000
C. Root, p	2	0	0	0	0	0	0	.000
G. Bush, p	1	0	0	0	0	0	0	.000
B. Grimes, p	1	0	0	0	0	0	0	.000
S. Hack	0	0	0	0	0	0	0	—

Errors: B. Jurges (2), F. Demaree, W. English, G. Hartnett, B. Herman

Stolen Bases: K. Cuyler, B. Jurges

Individual Pitching

NEW YORK (A.L.)

	W	L	ERA	IP	H	BB	SO	SV
L. Gomez	1	0	1.00	9	9	1	8	0
R. Ruffing	1	0	4.00	9	10	6	10	0
G. Pipgras	1	0	4.50	8	9	3	1	0
W. Moore	1	0	0.00	5.1	2	0	1	0
H. Pennock	0	0	2.25	4	2	1	4	2
J. Allen	0	0	40.50	0.2	5	0	0	0

CHICAGO (N.L.)

	W	L	ERA	IP	H	BB	SO	SV
L. Warneke	0	1	5.91	10.2	15	5	8	0
G. Bush	0	1	14.29	5.2	5	6	2	0
J. May	0	1	11.57	4.2	9	3	4	0
C. Root	0	1	10.38	4.1	6	3	4	0
B. Grimes	0	0	23.63	2.2	7	2	0	0
P. Malone	0	0	0.00	2.2	1	4	4	0
B. Tinning	0	0	0.00	2.1	0	0	3	0
B. Smith	0	0	9.00	1	2	0	1	0

1933 WORLD SERIES

LINE SCORES					PITCHERS (innings pitched)	HOME RUNS (men on)	HIGHLIGHTS

New York (N.L.) defeats Washington (A.L.) 4 games to 1

LINE SCORES		R	H	E	PITCHERS (innings pitched)	HOME RUNS (men on)	HIGHLIGHTS
GAME 1 - OCTOBER 3							Ott had four hits and three RBIs and Hubbell struck out ten and allowed two unearned runs.
WAS A	000 100 001	2	5	3	**Stewart** (2), Russell (5), Thomas (1)		
NY N	202 000 00x	4	10	2	**Hubbell** (9)	Ott (1 on)	
GAME 2 - OCTOBER 4							The Giants overcame a 1-0 deficit with six in the sixth. O'Doul drove in two with a pinch single and Mancuso drove in another with a bunt single.
WAS A	001 000 000	1	5	0	**Crowder** (5.2), Thomas (0.1), McCool (2)	Goslin	
NY N	000 006 00x	6	10	0	**Schumacher** (9)		
GAME 3 - OCTOBER 5							The Senators scored two in the first on Myer's single and doubles by Goslin and Schulte to support Whitehill's six-hit shutout.
NY N	000 000 000	0	5	0	**Fitzsimmons** (7), Bell (1)		
WAS A	210 000 10x	4	9	1	**Whitehill** (9)		
GAME 4 - OCTOBER 6							Jackson, although suffering from a severe leg injury, led off the eleventh by beating out a bunt, moved to second on a a sacrifice, and scored on Ryan's single. Hubbell secured the victory by getting pinch-hitter Bolton to ground into a double play with the bases loaded and one out in the bottom of the eleventh.
NY N	000 100 000 01	2	11	1	**Hubbell** (11)	Terry	
WAS A	000 000 100 00	1	8	0	**Weaver** (10.1), Russell (0.2)		
GAME 5 - OCTOBER 7							Ott's homer in the tenth won the Series after Schulte tied the game with a two-out three-run homer in the sixth.
NY N	020 001 000 1	4	11	1	Schumacher (5.2), **Luque** (4.1)	Ott	
WAS A	000 003 000 0	3	10	0	Crowder (5.1), **Russell** (4.2)	Schulte (2 on)	

Team totals

	W	AB	H	2B	3B	HR	R	RBI	BA	BB	SO	ERA
NY N	4	176	47	5	0	3	16	16	.267	11	21	1.53
WAS A	1	173	37	4	0	2	11	11	.214	13	25	2.74

Individual Batting

NEW YORK (N.L.)

	AB	H	2B	3B	HR	R	RBI	BA
B. Terry, 1b	22	6	1	0	1	3	1	.273
J. Moore, of	22	5	1	0	0	1	1	.227
H. Critz, 2b	22	3	0	0	0	2	0	.136
K. Davis, of	19	7	1	0	0	1	0	.368
M. Ott, of	18	7	0	0	2	3	4	.389
B. Ryan, ss	18	5	0	0	0	0	1	.278
T. Jackson, 3b	18	4	1	0	0	3	2	.222
G. Mancuso, c	17	2	1	0	0	2	2	.118
C. Hubbell, p	7	2	0	0	0	0	0	.286
H. Schumacher, p	7	2	0	0	0	0	3	.286
F. Fitzsimmons, p	2	1	0	0	0	0	0	.500
H. Peel, of	2	1	0	0	0	0	0	.500
D. Luque, p	1	1	0	0	0	0	0	1.000
L. O'Doul	1	1	0	0	0	1	2	1.000

Errors: H. Critz, C. Hubbell, T. Jackson, B. Ryan

WASHINGTON (A.L.)

	AB	H	2B	3B	HR	R	RBI	BA
J. Cronin, ss	22	7	0	0	0	1	2	.318
F. Schulte, of	21	7	1	0	1	1	4	.333
B. Myer, 2b	20	6	1	0	0	2	2	.300
G. Goslin, of	20	5	1	0	1	2	1	.250
J. Kuhel, 1b	20	3	0	0	0	1	1	.150
H. Manush, of	18	2	0	0	0	2	0	.111
L. Sewell, c	17	3	0	0	0	1	1	.176
O. Bluege, 3b	16	2	1	0	0	1	0	.125
G. Crowder, p	4	1	0	0	0	0	0	.250
M. Weaver, p	4	0	0	0	0	0	0	.000
E. Whitehill, p	3	0	0	0	0	0	0	.000
C. Bolton	2	0	0	0	0	0	0	.000
D. Harris, of	2	0	0	0	0	0	0	.000
J. Russell, p	2	0	0	0	0	0	0	.000
S. Rice	1	1	0	0	0	0	0	1.000
L. Stewart, p	1	0	0	0	0	0	0	.000
J. Kerr	0	0	0	0	0	0	0	—

Errors: B. Myer (3), J. Cronin

Stolen Bases: L. Sewell

Individual Pitching

NEW YORK (N.L.)

	W	L	ERA	IP	H	BB	SO	SV
C. Hubbell	2	0	0.00	20	13	6	15	0
H. Schumacher	1	0	2.45	14.2	13	5	3	0
F. Fitzsimmons	0	1	5.14	7	9	0	2	0
D. Luque	1	0	0.00	4.1	2	2	5	0
H. Bell	0	0	0.00	1	0	0	0	0

WASHINGTON (A.L.)

	W	L	ERA	IP	H	BB	SO	SV
G. Crowder	0	1	7.36	11	16	5	7	0
J. Russell	0	1	0.87	10.1	8	0	7	0
M. Weaver	0	1	1.74	10.1	11	4	3	0
E. Whitehill	1	0	0.00	9	5	2	2	0
A. McColl	0	0	0.00	2	0	0	0	0
L. Stewart	0	1	9.00	2	6	0	0	0
T. Thomas	0	0	0.00	1.1	1	0	2	0

1934 WORLD SERIES

St. Louis (N.L.) defeats Detroit (A.L.) 4 games to 3

LINE SCORES						PITCHERS (innings pitched)	HOME RUNS (men on)	HIGHLIGHTS
GAME 1 - OCTOBER 3								The Cardinals capitalized on five errors by the Tiger infield. Medwick leads the attack with four hits.
STL	**N**	021 014 000	8	13	2	**D. Dean** (9)	Medwick	
DET	**A**	001 001 010	3	8	5	**Crowder** (5), Marberry (0.2), Hogsett (3.1)	Greenberg	
GAME 2 - OCTOBER 4								Gee Walker, given a chance when Collins and DeLancey failed to catch his pop foul, singled in the tying run for the Tigers in the ninth. They went on to win in the twelfth when Goslin singled following walks to Gehringer and Greenberg.
STL	**N**	011 000 000 000	2	7	3	Hallahan (8.1), **B. Walker** (3)		
DET	**A**	000 100 001 001	3	7	0	**Rowe** (12)		
GAME 3 - OCTOBER 5								The Tigers left 13 men on base as Martin's double, triple, and two runs scored led the Cardinals.
DET	**A**	000 000 001	1	8	2	**Bridges** (4), Hogsett (4)		
STL	**N**	110 020 00x	4	9	1	**P. Dean** (9)		
GAME 4 - OCTOBER 6								The Tigers evened the Series thanks to Greenberg's three hits and three RBIs and Rogell's four RBIs.
DET	**A**	003 100 150	10	13	1	**Auker** (9)		
STL	**N**	011 200 000	4	10	5	Carleton (2.2), Vance (1.1), **B. Walker** (3.1), Haines (0.2), Mooney (1)		
GAME 5 - OCTOBER 7								Bridges returned after a day's rest to subdue the Cardinals. Gehringer's home run in the sixth was the game-winner.
DET	**A**	010 002 000	3	7	0	**Bridges** (9)	Gehringer	
STL	**N**	000 000 100	1	7	1	**D. Dean** (8), Carleton (1)	DeLancey	
GAME 6 - OCTOBER 8								Paul Dean aided his own cause with a single in the seventh that sent in the deciding run.
STL	**N**	100 020 100	4	10	2	**P. Dean** (9)		
DET	**A**	001 002 000	3	7	1	**Rowe** (9)		
GAME 7 - OCTOBER 9								The Cardinals easily romped to the Series crown. Medwick was replaced for his own protection in the sixth after the crowd pelted him with fruit and bottles.
STL	**N**	007 002 200	11	17	1	**D. Dean** (9)		
DET	**A**	000 000 000	0	6	3	**Auker** (2.1), Rowe (0.1), Hogsett (0), Bridges (4.1), Marberry (1), Crowder (1)		

Team totals

		W	AB	H	2B	3B	HR	R	RBI	BA	BB	SO	ERA
STL	**N**	4	262	73	14	5	2	34	32	.279	11	31	2.34
DET	**A**	3	250	56	12	1	2	23	20	.224	25	43	3.74

Individual Batting

ST. LOUIS (N.L.)

	AB	H	2B	3B	HR	R	RBI	BA
P. Martin, 3b	31	11	3	1	0	8	3	.355
F. Frisch, 2b	31	6	1	0	0	2	4	.194
R. Collins, 1b	30	11	1	0	0	4	4	.367
J. Rothrock, of	30	7	3	1	0	3	6	.233
J. Medwick, of	29	11	0	1	1	4	5	.379
B. DeLancey, c	29	5	3	0	1	3	4	.172
L. Durocher, ss	27	7	1	1	0	4	0	.259
E. Orsatti, of	22	7	0	1	0	3	2	.318
D. Dean, p	12	3	2	0	0	3	1	.250
P. Dean, p	6	1	0	0	0	0	2	.167
C. Fullis, of	5	2	0	0	0	0	0	.400
B. Hallahan, p	3	0	0	0	0	0	0	.000
S. Davis	2	2	0	0	0	0	1	1.000
P. Crawford	2	0	0	0	0	0	0	.000
B. Walker, p	2	0	0	0	0	0	0	.000
T. Carleton, p	1	0	0	0	0	0	0	.000
B. Whitehead, ss	0	0	0	0	0	0	0	—

Errors: P. Martin (4), F. Frisch (2), E. Orsatti (2), R. Collins, B. DeLancey, P. Dean, C. Fullis, B. Hallahan, J. Rothrock, B. Walker

Stolen Bases: P. Martin (2)

DETROIT (A.L.)

	AB	H	2B	3B	HR	R	RBI	BA
C. Gehringer, 2b	29	11	1	0	1	5	2	.379
B. Rogell, ss	29	8	1	0	0	3	4	.276
G. Goslin, of	29	7	1	0	0	2	2	.241
M. Owen, 3b	29	2	0	0	0	0	1	.069
H. Greenberg, 1b	28	9	2	1	1	4	7	.321
P. Fox, of	28	8	6	0	0	1	2	.286
M. Cochrane, c	28	6	1	0	0	2	1	.214
J. White, of	23	3	0	0	0	6	0	.130
T. Bridges, p	7	1	0	0	0	0	0	.143
S. Rowe, p	7	0	0	0	0	0	0	.000
E. Auker, p	4	0	0	0	0	0	0	.000
G. Walker	3	1	0	0	0	0	1	.333
C. Hogsett, p	3	0	0	0	0	0	0	.000
F. Doljack, of	2	0	0	0	0	0	0	.000
G. Crowder, p	1	0	0	0	0	0	0	.000
R. Hayworth, c	0	0	0	0	0	0	0	—

Errors: C. Gehringer (3), B. Rogell (3), G. Goslin (2), M. Owen (2), H. Greenberg, J. White

Stolen Bases: C. Gehringer, H. Greenberg, M. Owen, J. White

Individual Pitching

ST. LOUIS (N.L.)

	W	L	ERA	IP	H	BB	SO	SV
D. Dean	2	1	1.73	26	20	5	17	0
P. Dean	2	0	1.00	18	15	7	11	0
B. Hallahan	0	0	2.16	8.1	6	4	6	0
B. Walker	0	2	7.11	6.1	6	6	2	0
T. Carleton	0	0	7.36	3.2	5	2	2	0
D. Vance	0	0	0.00	1.1	2	1	3	0
J. Mooney	0	0	0.00	1	1	0	0	0
J. Haines	0	0	0.00	0.2	1	0	2	0

DETROIT (A.L.)

	W	L	ERA	IP	H	BB	SO	SV
S. Rowe	1	1	2.95	21.1	19	0	12	0
T. Bridges	1	1	3.63	17.1	21	1	12	0
E. Auker	1	1	5.56	11.1	16	5	2	0
C. Hogsett	0	0	1.23	7.1	6	3	3	0
G. Crowder	0	1	1.50	6	6	1	2	0
F. Marberry	0	0	21.60	1.2	5	1	0	0

1935 WORLD SERIES

Detroit (A.L.) defeats Chicago (N.L.) 4 games to 2

LINE SCORES			R	H	E	PITCHERS (innings pitched)	HOME RUNS (men on)	HIGHLIGHTS
GAME 1 - OCTOBER 2								Chicago scored twice in the first on hits by Galan and Hartnett and Rowe's error as Warneke pitched a four-hit shutout.
CHI	**N**	200 000 001	3	7	0	**Warneke** (9)	Demaree	
DET	**A**	000 000 000	0	4	3	**Rowe** (9)		
GAME 2 - OCTOBER 3								Hits by the first four batters in the Tiger first, capped by Greenberg's homer, chased Root and ensured the victory.
CHI	**N**	000 010 200	3	6	1	**Root** (0), Henshaw (3.2), Kowalik (4.1)		
DET	**A**	400 300 10x	8	9	2	**Bridges** (9)	Greenberg (1 on)	
GAME 3 - OCTOBER 4								White's single scored Owen with the winning run in the eleventh after the Cubs tied the game in the ninth on singles by Hack, Klein, and O'Dea and a long fly by Galan.
DET	**A**	000 001 040 01	6	12	2	Auker (6), Hogsett (1), **Rowe** (4)		
CHI	**N**	020 010 002 00	5	10	3	Lee (7.1), Warneke (1.2), **French** (2)	Demaree	
GAME 4 - OCTOBER 5								The Tigers scored the winning run in the sixth on errors by Galan and Jurges.
DET	**A**	001 001 000	2	7	0	**Crowder** (9)		
CHI	**N**	010 000 000	1	5	2	**Carleton** (7), Root (2)	Hartnett	
GAME 5 - OCTOBER 6								The Cubs scored twice in the third on Herman's triple and Klein's homer. Warneke left after six shutout innings because of a sore shoulder. Lee had to retire Clifton with two out and runners on second and third in the ninth to preserve the victory.
DET	**A**	000 000 001	1	7	1	**Rowe** (8)		
CHI	**N**	002 000 10x	3	8	0	**Warneke** (6), Lee (3) **SV**	Klein (1 on)	
GAME 6 - OCTOBER 7								The Tigers won in the ninth inning when Cochrane singled, Gehringer's grounder moved him to second, and Goslin's single brought him in for the Series-ending run.
CHI	**N**	001 020 000	3	12	0	**French** (8.2)	Herman (1 on)	
DET	**A**	100 101 001	4	12	1	**Bridges** (9)		

Team totals

		W	AB	H	2B	3B	HR	R	RBI	BA	BB	SO	ERA
DET	**A**	4	206	51	11	1	1	21	18	.248	25	27	2.29
CHI	**N**	2	202	48	6	2	5	18	17	.238	11	29	2.81

Individual Batting

DETROIT (A.L.)

	AB	H	2B	3B	HR	R	RBI	BA
P. Fox, of	26	10	3	1	0	1	4	.385
C. Gehringer, 2b	24	9	3	0	0	4	4	.375
M. Cochrane, c	24	7	1	0	0	3	1	.292
B. Rogell, ss	24	7	2	0	0	1	1	.292
G. Goslin, of	22	6	1	0	0	2	3	.273
M. Owen, 1b, 3b	20	1	0	0	0	2	1	.050
J. White, of	19	5	0	0	0	3	1	.263
F. Clifton, 3b	16	0	0	0	0	1	0	.000
S. Rowe, p	8	2	1	0	0	0	0	.250
T. Bridges, p	8	1	0	0	0	1	1	.125
H. Greenberg, 1b	6	1	0	0	1	1	2	.167
G. Walker, of	4	1	0	0	0	1	0	.250
G. Crowder, p	3	1	0	0	0	1	0	.333
E. Auker, p	2	0	0	0	0	0	0	.000

Errors: H. Greenberg (3), F. Clifton, M. Cochrane, P. Fox, G. Goslin, M. Owen, S. Rowe

Stolen Bases: C. Gehringer

CHICAGO (N.L.)

	AB	H	2B	3B	HR	R	RBI	BA
A. Galan, of	25	4	1	0	0	2	2	.160
B. Herman, 2b	24	8	2	1	1	3	6	.333
G. Hartnett, c	24	7	0	0	1	1	2	.292
F. Demaree, of	24	6	1	0	2	2	2	.250
P. Cavarretta, 1b	24	3	0	0	0	1	0	.125
S. Hack, 3b, ss	22	5	1	1	0	2	0	.227
B. Jurges, ss	16	4	0	0	0	3	1	.250
F. Lindstrom, 3b, of	15	3	1	0	0	0	0	.200
C. Klein, of	12	4	0	0	1	2	2	.333
L. Warneke, p	5	1	0	0	0	0	0	.200
L. French, p	4	1	0	0	0	1	0	.250
F. Kowalik, p	2	1	0	0	0	1	0	.500
K. O'Dea	1	1	0	0	0	0	1	1.000
T. Carleton, p	1	0	0	0	0	0	0	.000
R. Henshaw, p	1	0	0	0	0	0	0	.000
B. Lee, p	1	0	0	0	0	0	1	.000
W. Stephenson	1	0	0	0	0	0	0	.000

Errors: P. Cavarretta, A. Galan, B. Herman, B. Jurges, F. Kowalik, F. Lindstrom

Stolen Bases: S. Hack

Individual Pitching

DETROIT (A.L.)

	W	L	ERA	IP	H	BB	SO	SV
S. Rowe	1	2	2.57	21	19	1	14	0
T. Bridges	2	0	2.50	18	18	4	9	0
G. Crowder	1	0	1.00	9	5	3	5	0
E. Auker	0	0	3.00	6	6	2	1	0
C. Hogsett	0	0	0.00	1	0	1	0	0

CHICAGO (N.L.)

	W	L	ERA	IP	H	BB	SO	SV
L. Warneke	2	0	0.54	16.2	9	4	5	0
L. French	0	2	3.38	10.2	15	2	8	0
B. Lee	0	0	3.48	10.1	11	5	5	1
T. Carleton	0	1	1.29	7	6	7	4	0
F. Kowalik	0	0	2.08	4.1	3	1	1	0
R. Henshaw	0	0	7.36	3.2	2	5	2	0
C. Root	0	1	18.00	2	5	1	2	0

1936 WORLD SERIES

New York (A.L.) defeats New York (N.L.) 4 games to 2

LINE SCORES		R	H	E	PITCHERS (innings pitched)	HOME RUNS (men on)	HIGHLIGHTS
GAME 1 - SEPTEMBER 30							Hubbell's masterful pitching ended a Yankee streak of 12 consecutive Series victories. Giant outfielders had no fielding chances.
NY A	001 000 000	1	7	2	**Ruffing** (8)	Selkirk	
NY N	000 011 04x	6	9	1	**Hubbell** (9)	Bartell	
GAME 2 - OCTOBER 2							The Yankees set a Series record by scoring 18 runs as every man in their line-up had at least one hit and scored at least one run. Lazzeri and Dickey paced the onslaught with five RBIs each.
NY A	207 001 206	18	17	0	**Gomez** (9)	Lazzeri (3 on), Dickey (2 on)	
NY N	010 300 000	4	6	1	**Schumacher** (2.0), Smith (0.1), Coffman (1.2), Gabler (4), Gumbert (1)		
GAME 3 - OCTOBER 3							Crosetti's single scored Powell with the winning run in the eighth after Ripple's homer tied the game for the Giants in the fifth.
NY N	000 010 000	1	11	0	**Fitzsimmons** (8)	Ripple	
NY A	010 000 01x	2	4	0	**Hadley** (8), Malone (1) **SV**	Gehrig	
GAME 4 - OCTOBER 4							Three in the third on Crosetti's double, Rolfe's single, and Gehrig's homer provided the cushion for Pearson.
NY N	000 100 010	2	7	1	**Hubbell** (7), Gabler (1)		
NY A	013 000 01x	5	10	1	**Pearson** (9)	Gehrig (1 on)	
GAME 5 - OCTOBER 5							Jackson's error enabled the Yankees to tie the game with two in the sixth, but the Giants won in the tenth on Moore's double, Bartell's sacrifice, and Terry's long fly.
NY N	300 001 000 1	5	8	3	**Schumacher** (10)		
NY A	011 002 000 0	4	10	1	Ruffing (6), **Malone** (4)	Selkirk	
GAME 6 - OCTOBER 6							The Yankees broke open a 6-5 game with seven runs in the ninth on five hits and four walks.
NY A	021 200 017	13	17	2	**Gomez** (6.1), Murphy (2.2) **SV**	Powell (1 on)	
NY N	200 010 110	5	9	1	**Fitzsimmons** (3.2), Castleman (4.1), Coffman (0), Gumbert (1)	Moore, Ott	

Team totals

	W	AB	H	2B	3B	HR	R	RBI	BA	BB	SO	ERA
NY A	4	215	65	8	1	7	43	41	.302	26	35	3.33
NY N	2	203	50	9	0	4	23	20	.246	21	33	6.79

Individual Batting

NEW YORK (A.L.)

	AB	H	2B	3B	HR	R	RBI	BA
J. DiMaggio, of	26	9	3	0	0	3	3	.346
F. Crosetti, ss	26	7	2	0	0	5	3	.269
R. Rolfe, 3b	25	10	0	0	0	5	4	.400
B. Dickey, c	25	3	0	0	1	5	5	.120
G. Selkirk, of	24	8	0	1	2	6	3	.333
L. Gehrig, 1b	24	7	1	0	2	5	7	.292
J. Powell, of	22	10	1	0	1	8	5	.455
T. Lazzeri, 2b	20	5	0	0	1	4	7	.250
L. Gomez, p	8	2	0	0	0	1	3	.250
R. Ruffing, p	5	0	0	0	0	0	0	.000
M. Pearson, p	4	2	1	0	0	0	0	.500
J. Murphy, p	2	1	0	0	0	1	1	.500
B. Hadley, p	2	0	0	0	0	0	0	.000
P. Malone, p	1	1	0	0	0	0	0	1.000
R. Johnson	1	0	0	0	0	0	0	.000
B. Seeds	0	0	0	0	0	0	0	—

Errors: F. Crosetti (2), J. DiMaggio, B. Dickey, R. Rolfe, G. Selkirk
Stolen Bases: J. Powell

NEW YORK (N.L.)

	AB	H	2B	3B	HR	R	RBI	BA
J. Moore, of	28	6	2	0	1	4	1	.214
B. Terry, 1b	25	6	0	0	0	1	5	.240
M. Ott, of	23	7	2	0	1	4	3	.304
D. Bartell, ss	21	8	3	0	1	5	3	.381
T. Jackson, 3b	21	4	0	0	0	1	1	.190
B. Whitehead, 2b	21	1	0	0	0	1	2	.048
G. Mancuso, c	19	5	2	0	0	3	1	.263
J. Ripple, of	12	4	0	0	1	2	3	.333
C. Hubbell, p	6	2	0	0	0	0	1	.333
H. Leiber, of	6	0	0	0	0	0	0	.000
F. Fitzsimmons, p	4	2	0	0	0	0	0	.500
H. Schumacher, p	4	0	0	0	0	0	0	.000
S. Leslie	3	2	0	0	0	0	0	.667
M. Koenig, 2b	3	1	0	0	0	0	0	.333
S. Castleman, p	2	1	0	0	0	0	0	.500
K. Davis	2	1	0	0	0	2	0	.500
H. Danning, c	2	0	0	0	0	0	0	.000
E. Mayo, 3b	1	0	0	0	0	0	0	.000

Errors: T. Jackson (3), D. Bartell, H. Danning, C. Hubbell, M. Ott

Individual Pitching

NEW YORK (A.L.)

	W	L	ERA	IP	H	BB	SO	SV
L. Gomez	2	0	4.70	15.1	14	11	9	0
R. Ruffing	0	1	4.50	14	16	5	12	0
M. Pearson	1	0	2.00	9	7	2	7	0
B. Hadley	1	0	1.13	8	10	1	2	0
P. Malone	0	1	1.80	5	2	1	2	1
J. Murphy	0	0	3.38	2.2	1	1	1	1

NEW YORK (N.L.)

	W	L	ERA	IP	H	BB	SO	SV
C. Hubbell	1	1	2.25	16	15	2	10	0
H. Schumacher	1	1	5.25	12	13	10	11	0
F. Fitzsimmons	0	2	5.40	11.2	13	2	6	0
F. Gabler	0	0	7.20	5	7	4	0	0
S. Castleman	0	0	2.08	4.1	3	2	5	0
H. Gumbert	0	0	36.00	2	7	4	2	0
D. Coffman	0	0	32.40	1.2	5	1	1	0
A. Smith	0	0	81.00	0.1	2	1	0	0

1937 WORLD SERIES

New York (A.L.) defeats New York (N.L.) 4 games to 1

LINE SCORES						PITCHERS (innings pitched)	HOME RUNS (men on)	HIGHLIGHTS
GAME 1 - OCTOBER 6								The Yankees, losing 1-0, racked Hubbell, Gumbert, and Coffman for seven in the sixth. DiMaggio and Selkirk each drove in two runs with bases-loaded singles.
NY	**N**	000 010 000	1	6	2	**Hubbell** (5.1), Gumbert (0), Coffman (1.2), Smith (1)		
NY	**A**	000 007 01x	8	7	0	**Gomez** (9)	Lazzeri	
GAME 2 - OCTOBER 7								The Yankees again overcame a 1-0 Giant lead and romped to an easy win. Ruffing supported his pitching with two hits and three RBIs.
NY	**N**	100 000 000	1	7	0	**Melton** (4), Gumbert (1.1), Coffman (2.2)		
NY	**A**	000 024 20x	8	12	0	**Ruffing** (9)		
GAME 3 - OCTOBER 8								The Yankees scored early and often, with Dickey's triple in the third the big hit. Pearson loaded the bases in the ninth, but Murphy retired Danning to preserve the victory.
NY	**A**	012 110 000	5	9	0	**Pearson** (8.2), Murphy (0.1) **SV**		
NY	**N**	000 000 100	1	5	4	**Schumacher** (6), Melton (2), Brennan (1)		
GAME 4 - OCTOBER 9								Leiber had two hits in the six-run second inning as Hubbell pitched the Giants to their only win of the Series.
NY	**A**	101 000 010	3	6	0	**Hadley** (1.1), Andrews (5.2), Wicker (1)	Gehrig	
NY	**N**	060 000 10x	7	12	3	**Hubbell** (9)		
GAME 5 - OCTOBER 10								With the score tied 2-2, Lazzeri led off the Yankee fifth with a triple and Gomez, a career .147 hitter, drove in the winning run with a single off Whitehead's glove.
NY	**A**	011 020 000	4	8	0	**Gomez** (9)	DiMaggio, Hoag	
NY	**N**	002 000 000	2	10	0	**Melton** (5), Smith (2), Brennan (2)	Ott (1 on)	

Team totals

		W	AB	H	2B	3B	HR	R	RBI	BA	BB	SO	ERA
NY	**A**	4	169	42	6	4	4	28	25	.249	21	21	2.45
NY	**N**	1	169	40	6	0	1	12	12	.237	11	21	4.81

Individual Batting

NEW YORK (A.L.)

	AB	H	2B	3B	HR	R	RBI	BA
J. DiMaggio, of	22	6	0	0	1	2	4	.273
F. Crosetti, ss	21	1	0	0	0	2	0	.048
M. Hoag, of	20	6	1	0	1	4	2	.300
R. Rolfe, 3b	20	6	2	1	0	3	1	.300
G. Selkirk, of	19	5	1	0	0	5	6	.263
B. Dickey, c	19	4	0	1	0	3	3	.211
L. Gehrig, 1b	17	5	1	1	1	4	3	.294
T. Lazzeri, 2b	15	6	0	1	1	3	2	.400
L. Gomez, p	6	1	0	0	0	2	1	.167
R. Ruffing, p	4	2	1	0	0	0	3	.500
M. Pearson, p	3	0	0	0	0	0	0	.000
I. Andrews, p	2	0	0	0	0	0	0	.000
J. Powell	1	0	0	0	0	0	0	.000

NEW YORK (N.L.)

	AB	H	2B	3B	HR	R	RBI	BA
J. Moore, of	23	9	1	0	0	1	1	.391
D. Bartell, ss	21	5	1	0	0	3	1	.238
M. Ott, 3b	20	4	0	0	1	1	3	.200
J. McCarthy, 1b	19	4	1	0	0	1	1	.211
J. Ripple, of	17	5	0	0	0	2	0	.294
B. Whitehead, 2b	16	4	2	0	0	1	0	.250
H. Danning, c	12	3	1	0	0	0	2	.250
H. Leiber, of	11	4	0	0	0	2	2	.364
G. Mancuso, c	8	0	0	0	0	0	1	.000
L. Chiozza, of	7	2	0	0	0	0	0	.286
C. Hubbell, p	6	0	0	0	0	1	1	.000
W. Berger	3	0	0	0	0	0	0	.000
C. Melton, p	2	0	0	0	0	0	0	.000
D. Coffman, p	1	0	0	0	0	0	0	.000
S. Leslie	1	0	0	0	0	0	0	.000
B. Ryan	1	0	0	0	0	0	0	.000
H. Schumacher, p	1	0	0	0	0	0	0	.000

Errors: D. Bartell (3), J. McCarthy (2), L. Chiozza, C. Melton, M. Ott, B. Whitehead

Stolen Bases: B. Whitehead

Individual Pitching

NEW YORK (A.L.)

	W	L	ERA	IP	H	BB	SO	SV
L. Gomez	2	0	1.50	18	16	2	8	0
R. Ruffing	1	0	1.00	9	7	3	8	0
M. Pearson	1	0	1.04	8.2	5	2	4	0
I. Andrews	0	0	3.18	5.2	6	4	1	0
B. Hadley	0	1	33.75	1.1	6	0	0	0
K. Wicker	0	0	0.00	1	0	0	0	0
J. Murphy	0	0	0.00	0.1	0	0	0	1

NEW YORK (N.L.)

	W	L	ERA	IP	H	BB	SO	SV
C. Hubbell	1	1	3.77	14.1	12	4	7	0
C. Melton	0	2	4.91	11	12	6	7	0
H. Schumacher	0	1	6.00	6	9	4	3	0
D. Coffman	0	0	4.15	4.1	2	5	1	0
D. Brennan	0	0	0.00	3	1	1	1	0
A. Smith	0	0	3.00	3	2	0	1	0
H. Gumbert	0	0	27.00	1.1	4	1	1	0

1938 WORLD SERIES

New York (A.L.) defeats Chicago (N.L.) 4 games to 0

LINE SCORES			R	H	E	PITCHERS (innings pitched)	HOME RUNS (men on)	HIGHLIGHTS
GAME 1 - OCTOBER 5								Dickey's four singles led the New York attack in support of Ruffing's nine-hit effort.
NY	**A**	020 000 100	3	12	1	**Ruffing** (9)		
CHI	**N**	001 000 000	1	9	1	**Lee** (8), Russell (1)		
GAME 2 - OCTOBER 6								Crosetti batted in the tying and winning runs with an eighth-inning homer after Dizzy Dean, with no fastball left due to a sore arm, had held the Yankees to five hits in the first seven innings.
NY	**A**	020 000 022	6	7	2	**Gomez** (7), Murphy (2) **SV**	Crosetti (1 on), DiMaggio (1 on)	
CHI	**N**	102 000 000	3	11	0	**Dean** (8), French (1)		
GAME 3 - OCTOBER 8								Gordon's homer in the fifth was the first Yankee hit off Bryant, and his two-run single in the sixth gave the Yankees a three-run cushion.
CHI	**N**	000 010 010	2	5	1	**Bryant** (5.1), Russell (0.2), French (2)	Marty	
NY	**A**	000 022 01x	5	7	2	**Pearson** (9)	Gordon, Dickey	
GAME 4 - OCTOBER 9								New York scored three runs in the second on a two-out error by Jurges, two singles, and Crosetti's triple. Four more in the eighth ensured the clincher after O'Dea's homer in the top of the eighth narrowed the lead to one run.
CHI	**N**	000 100 020	3	8	1	**Lee** (3), Root (3), Page (1.1), French (0.1), Carleton (0), Dean (0.1)	O'Dea (1 on)	
NY	**A**	030 001 04x	8	11	1	**Ruffing** (9)	Henrich	

Team totals

		W	AB	H	2B	3B	HR	R	RBI	BA	BB	SO	ERA
NY	**A**	4	135	37	6	1	5	22	21	.274	11	16	1.75
CHI	**N**	0	136	33	4	1	2	9	8	.243	6	26	5.03

Individual Batting

NEW YORK (A.L.)

	AB	H	2B	3B	HR	R	RBI	BA
R. Rolfe, 3b	18	3	0	0	0	0	1	.167
F. Crosetti, ss	16	4	2	1	1	1	6	.250
T. Henrich, of	16	4	1	0	1	3	1	.250
B. Dickey, c	15	6	0	0	1	2	2	.400
J. Gordon, 2b	15	6	2	0	1	3	6	.400
J. DiMaggio, of	15	4	0	0	1	4	2	.267
L. Gehrig, 1b	14	4	0	0	0	4	0	.286
G. Selkirk, of	10	2	0	0	0	0	1	.200
R. Ruffing, p	6	1	0	0	0	1	1	.167
M. Hoag, of	5	2	1	0	0	3	1	.400
M. Pearson, p	3	1	0	0	0	1	0	.333
L. Gomez, p	2	0	0	0	0	0	0	.000
J. Powell, of	0	0	0	0	0	0	0	—

Errors: J. Gordon (2), R. Rolfe (2), F. Crosetti, T. Henrich
Stolen Bases: B. Dickey, J. Gordon, R. Rolfe

CHICAGO (N.L.)

	AB	H	2B	3B	HR	R	RBI	BA
S. Hack, 3b	17	8	1	0	0	3	1	.471
B. Herman, 2b	16	3	0	0	0	1	0	.188
R. Collins, 1b	15	2	0	0	0	1	0	.133
P. Cavarretta, of	13	6	1	0	0	1	0	.462
B. Jurges, ss	13	3	1	0	0	0	0	.231
J. Marty, of	12	6	1	0	1	1	5	.500
C. Reynolds, of	12	0	0	0	0	0	0	.000
G. Hartnett, c	11	1	0	1	0	0	0	.091
F. Demaree, of	10	1	0	0	0	1	0	.100
K. O'Dea, c	5	1	0	0	1	1	2	.200
D. Dean, p	3	2	0	0	0	0	0	.667
B. Lee, p	3	0	0	0	0	0	0	.000
C. Bryant, p	2	0	0	0	0	0	0	.000
A. Galan	2	0	0	0	0	0	0	.000
T. Lazzeri	2	0	0	0	0	0	0	.000

Errors: B. Herman (2), B. Jurges

Individual Pitching

NEW YORK (A.L.)

	W	L	ERA	IP	H	BB	SO	SV
R. Ruffing	2	0	1.50	18	17	2	11	0
M. Pearson	1	0	1.00	9	5	2	9	0
L. Gomez	1	0	3.86	7	9	1	5	0
J. Murphy	0	0	0.00	2	2	1	1	1

CHICAGO (N.L.)

	W	L	ERA	IP	H	BB	SO	SV
B. Lee	0	2	2.45	11	15	1	8	0
D. Dean	0	1	6.48	8.1	8	1	2	0
C. Bryant	0	1	6.75	5.1	6	5	3	0
L. French	0	0	2.70	3.1	1	1	2	0
C. Root	0	0	3.00	3	3	0	1	0
J. Russell	0	0	0.00	1.2	1	1	0	0
V. Page	0	0	13.50	1.1	2	0	0	0
T. Carleton	0	0	∞	0.0	1	2	0	0

1939 WORLD SERIES

New York (A.L.) defeats Cincinnati (N.L.) 4 games to 0

LINE SCORES			R	H	E	PITCHERS (innings pitched)	HOME RUNS (men on)	HIGHLIGHTS
GAME 1 - OCTOBER 4								Keller led off the Yankee ninth with a triple just past Goodman's lunge. After an intentional walk to DiMaggio, Dickey singled home the winning run.
CIN	**N**	000 100 000	1	4	0	**Derringer** (8.1)		
NY	**A**	000 010 001	2	6	0	**Ruffing** (9)		
GAME 2 - OCTOBER 5								Pearson had a no-hiter for seven and a third innings before Lombardi singled to break it up. Dahlgren's double and homer gave Pearson all the help he needed.
CIN	**N**	000 000 000	0	2	0	**Walters** (8)		
NY	**A**	003 100 00x	4	9	0	**Pearson** (9)	Dahlgren	
GAME 3 - OCTOBER 7								Keller spearheaded the Yankee attack with two homers, four RBIs, and three runs scored. Gomez and Hadley allowed ten Cincinnati hits, but all ten were singles and only three came after the second inning.
NY	**A**	202 030 000	7	5	1	Gomez (1), **Hadley** (8)	Keller (1 on), DiMaggio (1 on), Keller (1 on), Dickey	
CIN	**N**	120 000 000	3	10	0	**Thompson** (4.2), Grissom (1.1), Moore (3)		
GAME 4 - OCTOBER 8								Myers's error on a potential double-play ball in the ninth allowed one run to score and set up the tying run. Three more Red errors in the tenth helped the Yankees score three runs and sweep the Series.
NY	**A**	000 000 202 3	7	7	1	Hildebrand (4), Sundra (2.2), **Murphy** (3.1)	Keller, Dickey	
CIN	**N**	000 000 310 0	4	11	4	Derringer (7), **Walters** (3)		

Team totals

		W	AB	H	2B	3B	HR	R	RBI	BA	BB	SO	ERA
NY	**A**	4	131	27	4	1	7	20	18	.206	9	20	1.22
CIN	**N**	0	133	27	3	1	0	8	8	.203	6	22	4.33

Individual Batting

NEW YORK (A.L.)

	AB	H	2B	3B	HR	R	RBI	BA
C. Keller, of	16	7	1	1	3	8	6	.438
J. DiMaggio, of	16	5	0	0	1	3	3	.313
R. Rolfe, 3b	16	2	0	0	0	2	0	.125
F. Crosetti, ss	16	1	0	0	0	2	1	.063
B. Dickey, c	15	4	0	0	2	2	5	.267
B. Dahlgren, 1b	14	3	2	0	1	2	2	.214
J. Gordon, 2b	14	2	0	0	0	1	1	.143
G. Selkirk, of	12	2	1	0	0	0	0	.167
R. Ruffing, p	3	1	0	0	0	0	0	.333
B. Hadley, p	3	0	0	0	0	0	0	.000
J. Murphy, p	2	0	0	0	0	0	0	.000
M. Pearson, p	2	0	0	0	0	0	0	.000
L. Gomez, p	1	0	0	0	0	0	0	.000
O. Hildebrand, p	1	0	0	0	0	0	0	.000

Errors: B. Hadley, R. Rolfe

CINCINNATI (N.L.)

	AB	H	2B	3B	HR	R	RBI	BA
L. Frey, 2b	17	0	0	0	0	0	0	.000
B. Werber, 3b	16	4	0	0	0	1	2	.250
F. McCormick, 1b	15	6	1	0	0	1	1	.400
I. Goodman, of	15	5	1	0	0	3	1	.333
W. Berger, of	15	0	0	0	0	0	1	.000
E. Lombardi, c	14	3	0	0	0	0	2	.214
B. Myers, ss	12	4	0	1	0	2	0	.333
H. Craft, of	11	1	0	0	0	0	0	.091
P. Derringer, p	5	1	0	0	0	0	0	.200
A. Simmons, of	4	1	1	0	0	1	0	.250
B. Walters, p	3	0	0	0	0	0	0	.000
W. Hershberger, c	2	1	0	0	0	0	1	.500
J. Thompson, p	1	1	0	0	0	0	0	1.000
N. Bongiovanni	1	0	0	0	0	0	0	.000
L. Gamble	1	0	0	0	0	0	0	.000
W. Moore, p	1	0	0	0	0	0	0	.000
F. Bordagaray	0	0	0	0	0	0	0	—

Errors: B. Myers (2), I. Goodman, E. Lombardi

Stolen Bases: I. Goodman

Individual Pitching

NEW YORK (A.L.)

	W	L	ERA	IP	H	BB	SO	SV
M. Pearson	1	0	0.00	9	2	1	8	0
R. Ruffing	1	0	1.00	9	4	1	4	0
B. Hadley	1	0	2.25	8	7	3	2	0
O. Hildebrand	0	0	0.00	4	2	0	3	0
J. Murphy	1	0	2.70	3.1	5	0	2	0
S. Sundra	0	0	0.00	2.2	4	1	2	0
L. Gomez	0	0	9.00	1	3	0	1	0

CINCINNATI (N.L.)

	W	L	ERA	IP	H	BB	SO	SV
P. Derringer	0	1	2.35	15.1	9	3	9	0
B. Walters	0	2	4.91	11	13	1	6	0
J. Thompson	0	1	13.50	4.2	5	4	3	0
W. Moore	0	0	0.00	3	0	0	2	0
L. Grissom	0	0	0.00	1.1	0	1	0	0

1940 WORLD SERIES

Cincinnati (N.L.) defeats Detroit (A.L.) 4 games to 3

LINE SCORES						PITCHERS (innings pitched)	HOME RUNS (men on)	HIGHLIGHTS
GAME 1 - OCTOBER 2								Derringer was knocked out in the second as Newsom breezed to the American League's tenth successive World Series triumph.
DET	**A**	050 020 000	7	10	1	**Newsom** (9)	Campbell (1 on)	
CIN	**N**	000 100 010	2	8	3	**Derringer** (1.1), Moore (6.2), Riddle (1)		
GAME 2 - OCTOBER 3								Walters pitched a three-hitter with Ripple's third-inning home run providing the winning run.
DET	**A**	200 001 000	3	3	1	**Rowe** (3.1), Gorsica (4.2)		
CIN	**N**	022 100 00x	5	9	0	**Walters** (9)	Ripple (1 on)	
GAME 3 - OCTOBER 4								Two-run homers by York and Higgins in the seventh decided the outcome.
CIN	**N**	100 000 012	4	10	1	**Turner** (6), Moore (1), Beggs (1)		
DET	**A**	000 100 42x	7	13	1	**Bridges** (9)	York (1 on), Higgins (1 on)	
GAME 4 - OCTOBER 5								Derringer coasted to victory. Werber, Frank McCormick, Goodman, and Mike McCormick, the first four Cincinnati hitters, each had two hits.
CIN	**N**	201 100 010	5	11	1	**Derringer** (9)		
DET	**A**	001 001 000	2	5	1	**Trout** (2), Smith (4), McKain (3)		
GAME 5 - OCTOBER 6								Newsom held the Reds to three singles for the shutout win, backed by 13 hits including Greenberg's three-run homer.
CIN	**N**	000 000 000	0	3	0	**Thompson** (3.1), Moore (0.2) Vander Meer (3), Hutchings (1)		
DET	**A**	003 400 01x	8	13	0	**Newsom** (9)	Greenberg (2 on)	
GAME 6 - OCTOBER 7								Walters drew the Reds even with a shutout and contributed a homer to his cause. The Reds chased Rowe with four hits and two runs in a third of an inning.
DET	**A**	000 000 000	0	5	0	**Rowe** (0.1), Gorsica (6.2), Hutchinson (1)		
CIN	**N**	200 001 01x	4	10	2	**Walters** (9)	Walters	
GAME 7 - OCTOBER 8								Doubles by Frank McCormick and Ripple and a long fly by Myers brought Cincinnati its first World Championship since the tainted Series of 1919.
DET	**A**	001 000 000	1	7	0	**Newsom** (8)		
CIN	**N**	000 000 20x	2	7	1	**Derringer** (9)		

Team totals

		W	AB	H	2B	3B	HR	R	RBI	BA	BB	SO	ERA
CIN	**N**	4	232	58	14	0	2	22	21	.250	15	30	3.69
DET	**A**	3	228	56	9	3	4	28	24	.246	30	30	3.00

Individual Batting

CINCINNATI (N.L.)

	AB	H	2B	3B	HR	R	RBI	BA
M. McCormick, of	29	9	3	0	0	1	2	.310
I. Goodman, of	29	8	2	0	0	5	5	.276
F. McCormick, 1b	28	6	1	0	0	2	0	.214
B. Werber, 3b	27	10	4	0	0	5	2	.370
E. Joost, 2b	25	5	0	0	0	0	2	.200
B. Myers, ss	23	3	0	0	0	0	2	.130
J. Ripple, of	21	7	2	0	1	3	6	.333
J. Wilson, c	17	6	0	0	0	2	0	.353
B. Walters, p	7	2	1	0	1	2	2	.286
P. Derringer, p	7	0	0	0	0	0	0	.000
B. Baker, c	4	1	0	0	0	1	0	.250
E. Lombardi, c	3	1	1	0	0	0	0	.333
L. Riggs	3	0	0	0	0	1	0	.000
L. Frey	2	0	0	0	0	0	0	.000
W. Moore, p	2	0	0	0	0	0	0	.000
J. Turner, p	2	0	0	0	0	0	0	.000
M. Arnovich, of	1	0	0	0	0	0	0	.000
H. Craft	1	0	0	0	0	0	0	.000
J. Thompson, p	1	0	0	0	0	0	0	.000

Errors: F. McCormick (2), B. Myers (2), B. Werber (2), B. Baker, M. McCormick

Stolen Bases: J. Wilson

DETROIT (A.L.)

	AB	H	2B	3B	HR	R	RBI	BA
H. Greenberg, of	28	10	2	1	1	5	6	.357
C. Gehringer, 2b	28	6	0	0	0	3	1	.214
D. Bartell, ss	26	7	2	0	0	2	3	.269
R. York, 1b	26	6	0	1	1	3	2	.231
B. Campbell, of	25	9	1	0	1	4	5	.360
P. Higgins, 3b	24	8	3	1	1	2	6	.333
B. McCosky, of	23	7	1	0	0	5	1	.304
B. Sullivan, c	13	2	0	0	0	3	0	.154
B. Tebbetts, c	11	0	0	0	0	0	0	.000
B. Newsom, p	10	1	0	0	0	1	0	.100
J. Gorsica, p	4	0	0	0	0	0	0	.000
E. Averill	3	0	0	0	0	0	0	.000
T. Bridges, p	3	0	0	0	0	0	0	.000
P. Fox	1	0	0	0	0	0	0	.000
S. Rowe, p	1	0	0	0	0	0	0	.000
C. Smith, p	1	0	0	0	0	0	0	.000
D. Trout, p	1	0	0	0	0	0	0	.000
F. Croucher, ss	0	0	0	0	0	0	0	—

Errors: P. Higgins (2), D. Bartell, B. Tebbetts

Individual Pitching

CINCINNATI (N.L.)

	W	L	ERA	IP	H	BB	SO	SV
P. Derringer	2	1	2.79	19.1	17	10	6	0
B. Walters	2	0	1.50	18	8	6	6	0
W. Moore	0	0	3.24	8.1	8	6	7	0
J. Turner	0	1	7.50	6	8	0	4	0
J. Thompson	0	1	16.20	3.1	8	4	2	0
J. Vander Meer	0	0	0.00	3	2	3	2	0
J. Beggs	0	0	9.00	1	3	0	1	0
J. Hutchings	0	0	9.00	1	2	1	0	0
E. Riddle	0	0	0.00	1	0	0	2	0

DETROIT (A.L.)

	W	L	ERA	IP	H	BB	SO	SV
B. Newsom	2	1	1.38	26	18	4	17	0
J. Gorsica	0	0	0.79	11.1	6	4	4	0
T. Bridges	1	0	3.00	9	10	1	5	0
C. Smith	0	0	2.25	4	1	3	1	0
S. Rowe	0	2	17.18	3.2	12	1	1	0
A. McKain	0	0	3.00	3	4	0	0	0
D. Trout	0	1	9.00	2	6	1	1	0
F. Hutchinson	0	0	9.00	1	1	1	1	0

1941 WORLD SERIES

LINE SCORES						PITCHERS (innings pitched)	HOME RUNS (men on)	HIGHLIGHTS

New York (A.L.) defeats Brooklyn (N.L.) 4 games to 1

GAME 1 - OCTOBER 1								The Brooklyn rally in the seventh fell short when Reese was thrown out trying to go from second to third with one out on Wasdell's foul pop to Rolfe.
BKN	**N**	000 010 100	2	6	0	**Davis** (5.1), Casey (0.2), Allen (2)		
NY	**A**	010 101 00x	3	6	1	**Ruffing** (9)	Gordon	
GAME 2 - OCTOBER 2								Camilli's single in the sixth brought home Walker with the deciding run of the game, stopping the Yankees' Series winning streak at ten games.
BKN	**N**	000 021 000	3	6	2	**Wyatt** (9)		
NY	**A**	011 000 000	2	9	1	**Chandler** (5), Murphy (4)		
GAME 3 - OCTOBER 4								The Dodgers' Series hopes were shaken when Russo's savage drive caromed off Fitzsimmons's leg in the seventh, forcing him out of the game. The Yankees, who had just four hits to that point, reached Casey for four more and two runs.
NY	**A**	000 000 020	2	8	0	**Russo** (9)		
BKN	**N**	000 000 010	1	4	0	Fitzsimmons (7), **Casey** (0.1), French (0.2), Allen (1)		
GAME 4 - OCTOBER 5								The Dodgers led 4-3 in the top of of the ninth with two outs. Casey threw strike three past Henrich, but it also got past catcher Owen, allowing Henrich to reach first. The Yankees then pounced for four runs to take a commanding 3-1 Series lead. Keller's double, scoring two runs, keyed the big inning.
NY	**A**	100 200 004	7	12	0	Donald (4), Breuer (3), **Murphy** (2)		
BKN	**N**	000 220 000	4	9	1	Higbe (3.2), French (0.1), Allen (0.2), **Casey** (4.1)	Reiser (1 on)	
GAME 5 - OCTOBER 6								Bonham allows only one hit after the third to check the Dodgers and bring the Yankees another Series victory. Gordon's single in the second sent home Keller with the deciding run.
NY	**A**	020 010 000	3	6	0	**Bonham** (9)	Henrich	
BKN	**N**	001 000 000	1	4	1	**Wyatt** (9)		

Team totals

		W	AB	H	2B	3B	HR	R	RBI	BA	BB	SO	ERA
NY	**A**	4	166	41	5	1	2	17	16	.247	23	18	1.80
BKN	**N**	1	159	29	7	2	1	11	11	.182	14	21	2.66

Individual Batting

NEW YORK (A.L.)

	AB	H	2B	3B	HR	R	RBI	BA
J. Sturm, 1b	21	6	0	0	0	0	2	.286
R. Rolfe, 3b	20	6	0	0	0	2	0	.300
J. DiMaggio, of	19	5	0	0	0	1	1	.263
C. Keller, of	18	7	2	0	0	5	5	.389
B. Dickey, c	18	3	1	0	0	3	1	.167
T. Henrich, of	18	3	1	0	1	4	1	.167
P. Rizzuto, ss	18	2	0	0	0	0	0	.111
J. Gordon, 2b	14	7	1	1	1	2	5	.500
E. Bonham, p	4	0	0	0	0	0	0	.000
M. Russo, p	4	0	0	0	0	0	0	.000
R. Ruffing, p	3	0	0	0	0	0	0	.000
S. Chandler, p	2	1	0	0	0	0	1	.500
G. Selkirk	2	1	0	0	0	0	0	.500
A. Donald, p	2	0	0	0	0	0	0	.000
J. Murphy, p	2	0	0	0	0	0	0	.000
M. Breuer, p	1	0	0	0	0	0	0	.000
F. Bordagaray	0	0	0	0	0	0	0	—
B. Rosar, c	0	0	0	0	0	0	0	—

Errors: J. Gordon, P. Rizzuto
Stolen Bases: P. Rizzuto, J. Sturm

BROOKLYN (N.L.)

	AB	H	2B	3B	HR	R	RBI	BA
P. Reese, ss	20	4	0	0	0	1	2	.200
P. Reiser, of	20	4	1	1	1	1	3	.200
D. Walker, of	18	4	2	0	0	3	0	.222
D. Camilli, 1b	18	3	1	0	0	1	1	.167
J. Medwick, of	17	4	1	0	0	1	0	.235
M. Owen, c	12	2	0	1	0	1	2	.167
C. Lavagetto, 3b	10	1	0	0	0	1	0	.100
L. Riggs, 3b	8	2	0	0	0	0	1	.250
B. Herman, 2b	8	1	0	0	0	0	0	.125
P. Coscarart, 2b	7	0	0	0	0	1	0	.000
W. Wyatt, p	6	1	1	0	0	1	0	.167
J. Wasdell, of	5	1	1	0	0	0	2	.200
H. Casey, p	2	1	0	0	0	0	0	.500
C. Davis, p	2	0	0	0	0	0	0	.000
F. Fitzsimmons, p	2	0	0	0	0	0	0	.000
A. Galan	2	0	0	0	0	0	0	.000
K. Higbe, p	1	1	0	0	0	0	0	1.000
H. Franks, c	1	0	0	0	0	0	0	.000

Errors: P. Reese (3), M. Owen

Individual Pitching

NEW YORK (A.L.)

	W	L	ERA	IP	H	BB	SO	SV
E. Bonham	1	0	1.00	9	4	2	2	0
R. Ruffing	1	0	1.00	9	6	3	5	0
M. Russo	1	0	1.00	9	4	2	5	0
J. Murphy	1	0	0.00	6	2	1	3	0
S. Chandler	0	1	3.60	5	4	2	2	0
A. Donald	0	0	9.00	4	6	3	2	0
M. Breuer	0	0	0.00	3	3	1	2	0

BROOKLYN (N.L.)

	W	L	ERA	IP	H	BB	SO	SV
W. Wyatt	1	1	2.50	18	15	10	14	0
F. Fitzsimmons	0	0	0.00	7	4	3	1	0
H. Casey	0	2	3.38	5.1	9	2	1	0
C. Davis	0	1	5.06	5.1	6	3	1	0
J. Allen	0	0	0.00	3.2	1	3	0	0
K. Higbe	0	0	7.36	3.2	6	2	1	0
L. French	0	0	0.00	1	0	0	0	0

1942 WORLD SERIES

St. Louis (N.L.) defeats New York (A.L.) 4 games to 1

LINE SCORES			R	H	E	PITCHERS (innings pitched)	HOME RUNS (men on)	HIGHLIGHTS
GAME 1 - SEPTEMBER 30								The Yankees made an early lead stand up, but four in the ninth by the Cardinals gave an omen of things to come. Ruffing did not allow a hit until there were two out in the eighth to become the first pitcher to win seven World Series games.
NY	A	000 110 032	7	11	0	**Ruffing** (8.2), Chandler (0.1) **SV**		
STL	N	000 000 004	4	7	4	**M. Cooper** (7.2), Gumbert (0.1), Lanier (1)		
GAME 2 - OCTOBER 1								A two-run homer by Keller tied the score in the eighth, but the Cardinals eked out a win in the home half when Slaughter doubled and Musial singled. Slaughter then saved the day by throwing out Stainback going from first to third on a single with none out in the ninth.
NY	A	000 000 030	3	10	2	**Bonham** (8)	Keller (1 on)	
STL	N	200 000 11x	4	6	0	**Beazley** (9)		
GAME 3 - OCTOBER 3								White's six-hit gem is the first Series whitewash of the Yankees since Haines did the trick in 1926. The Cardinals got their runs on Brown's infield out in the third and Slaughter's single in the ninth.
STL	N	001 000 001	2	5	1	**White** (9)		
NY	A	000 000 000	0	6	1	**Chandler** (8), Breuer (0), Turner (1)		
GAME 4 - OCTOBER 4								The teams traded big innings before the Cardinals took charge in the seventh. Walker Cooper's single scored Slaughter, and Marion hit a long fly, scoring Musial for the decisive two runs.
STL	N	000 600 201	9	12	1	M. Cooper (5.1), Gumbert (0.1), Pollet (0.1), **Lanier** (3)		
NY	A	100 005 000	6	10	1	Borowy (3), **Donald** (3), Bonham (3)	Keller (2 on)	
GAME 5 - OCTOBER 5								Kurowski's two-run homer in the ninth gave the Cardinals the Series. It was the Yankees' first Series defeat in their last nine appearances, dating back to St. Louis's victory over them in 1926.
STL	N	000 101 002	4	9	4	**Beazley** (9)	Slaughter, Kurowski (1 on)	
NY	A	100 100 000	2	7	1	**Ruffing** (9)	Rizzuto	

Team totals

		W	AB	H	2B	3B	HR	R	RBI	BA	BB	SO	ERA
STL	N	4	163	39	4	2	2	23	23	.239	17	19	2.60
NY	A	1	178	44	6	0	3	18	14	.247	8	22	4.50

Individual Batting

ST. LOUIS (N.L.)

	AB	H	2B	3B	HR	R	RBI	BA
W. Cooper, c	21	6	1	0	0	3	4	.286
J. Brown, 2b	20	6	0	0	0	2	1	.300
E. Slaughter, of	19	5	1	0	1	3	2	.263
S. Musial, of	18	4	1	0	0	2	2	.222
M. Marion, ss	18	2	0	1	0	2	3	.111
T. Moore, of	17	5	1	0	0	2	2	.294
J. Hopp, 1b	17	3	0	0	0	3	0	.176
W. Kurowski, 3b	15	4	0	1	1	3	5	.267
J. Beazley, p	7	1	0	0	0	0	0	.143
M. Cooper, p	5	1	0	0	0	1	2	.200
E. White, p	2	0	0	0	0	0	0	.000
M. Lanier, p	1	1	0	0	0	0	1	1.000
K. O'Dea	1	1	0	0	0	0	1	1.000
R. Sanders	1	0	0	0	0	1	0	.000
H. Walker	1	0	0	0	0	0	0	.000
C. Crespi	0	0	0	0	0	1	0	—

Errors: J. Brown (3), M. Lanier (2), J. Beazley, W. Cooper, J. Hopp, W. Kurowski, E. Slaughter

NEW YORK (A.L.)

	AB	H	2B	3B	HR	R	RBI	BA
P. Rizzuto, ss	21	8	0	0	1	2	1	.381
J. DiMaggio, of	21	7	0	0	0	3	3	.333
J. Gordon, 2b	21	2	1	0	0	1	0	.095
C. Keller, of	20	4	0	0	2	2	5	.200
R. Cullenbine, of	19	5	1	0	0	3	2	.263
B. Dickey, c	19	5	0	0	0	1	0	.263
R. Rolfe, 3b	17	6	2	0	0	5	0	.353
G. Priddy, 1b, 3b	10	1	1	0	0	0	1	.100
B. Hassett, 1b	9	3	1	0	0	1	2	.333
R. Ruffing, p	9	2	0	0	0	0	0	.222
F. Crosetti, 3b	3	0	0	0	0	0	0	.000
E. Bonham, p	2	0	0	0	0	0	0	.000
S. Chandler, p	2	0	0	0	0	0	0	.000
A. Donald, p	2	0	0	0	0	0	0	.000
B. Rosar	1	1	0	0	0	0	0	1.000
H. Borowy, p	1	0	0	0	0	0	0	.000
G. Selkirk	1	0	0	0	0	0	0	.000
T. Stainback	0	0	0	0	0	0	0	—

Errors: M. Breuer, B. Dickey, B. Hassett, G. Priddy, P. Rizzuto

Stolen Bases: P. Rizzuto (2), R. Cullenbine

Individual Pitching

ST. LOUIS (N.L.)

	W	L	ERA	IP	H	BB	SO	SV
J. Beazley	2	0	2.50	18	17	3	6	0
M. Cooper	0	1	5.54	13	17	4	9	0
E. White	1	0	0.00	9	6	0	6	0
M. Lanier	1	0	0.00	4	3	1	1	0
H. Gumbert	0	0	0.00	0.2	1	0	0	0
H. Pollet	0	0	0.00	0.1	0	0	0	0

NEW YORK (A.L.)

	W	L	ERA	IP	H	BB	SO	SV
R. Ruffing	1	1	4.08	17.2	14	7	11	0
E. Bonham	0	1	4.09	11	9	3	3	0
S. Chandler	0	1	1.08	8.1	5	1	3	1
H. Borowy	0	0	18.00	3	6	3	1	0
A. Donald	0	1	6.00	3	3	2	1	0
J. Turner	0	0	0.00	1	0	1	0	0
M. Breuer	0	0	—	0.0	2	0	0	0

1943 WORLD SERIES

LINE SCORES						PITCHERS (innings pitched)	HOME RUNS (men on)	HIGHLIGHTS

New York (A.L.) defeats St. Louis (N.L.) 4 games to 1

GAME 1 - OCTOBER 5

			R	H	E	Pitchers	Home Runs	Highlights
STL	N	010 010 000	2	7	2	**Lanier** (7), Brecheen (1)		The Yankees broke a 2-2 tie in the sixth with two runs on singles by Crosetti, Johnson and Dickey and a wild pitch by Lanier.
NY	A	000 202 00x	4	8	2	**Chandler** (9)	Gordon	

GAME 2 - OCTOBER 6

			R	H	E	Pitchers	Home Runs	Highlights
STL	N	001 300 000	4	7	2	**M. Cooper** (9)	Marion, Sanders (1 on)	Three in the fourth for the Cards on singles by Musial and Kurowski and a homer by Sanders stood up for the win, as New York's ninth inning rally fell short.
NY	A	000 100 002	3	6	0	**Bonham** (8), Murphy (1)		

GAME 3 - OCTOBER 7

			R	H	E	Pitchers	Home Runs	Highlights
STL	N	000 200 000	2	6	4	**Brazle** (7.1), Krist (0), Brecheen (0.2)		The Yankees erased a 2-1 deficit with five in the eighth as Johnson drove in three with a bases-loaded triple.
NY	A	000 001 05x	6	8	0	**Borowy** (8), Murphy (1) **SV**		

GAME 4 - OCTOBER 10

			R	H	E	Pitchers	Home Runs	Highlights
NY	A	000 100 010	2	6	2	**Russo** (9)		Russo allowed one unearned run and scored the winning run in the eighth on his double and a long fly by Crosetti.
STL	N	000 000 100	1	7	1	Lanier (7), **Brecheen** (2)		

GAME 5 - OCTOBER 11

			R	H	E	Pitchers	Home Runs	Highlights
NY	A	000 002 000	2	7	1	**Chandler** (9)	Dickey (1 on)	Dickey's homer followed Keller's single in the sixth for the only runs as the Cardinals stranded eleven runners.
STL	N	000 000 000	0	10	1	**M. Cooper** (7), Lanier (1.1), Dickson (0.2)		

Team totals

		W	AB	H	2B	3B	HR	R	RBI	BA	BB	SO	ERA
NY	A	4	159	35	5	2	2	17	14	.220	12	30	1.40
STL	N	1	165	37	5	0	2	9	8	.224	11	26	2.51

Individual Batting

NEW YORK (A.L.)

	AB	H	2B	3B	HR	R	RBI	BA
B. Johnson, 3b	20	6	1	1	0	3	3	.300
N. Etten, 1b	19	2	0	0	0	0	2	.105
F. Crosetti, ss	18	5	0	0	0	4	1	.278
B. Dickey, c	18	5	0	0	1	1	4	.278
C. Keller, of	18	4	0	1	0	3	2	.222
J. Gordon, 2b	17	4	1	0	1	2	2	.235
T. Stainback, of	17	3	0	0	0	0	0	.176
J. Lindell, of	9	1	0	0	0	1	0	.111
B. Metheny, of	8	1	0	0	0	0	0	.125
S. Chandler, p	6	1	0	0	0	0	0	.167
M. Russo, p	3	2	2	0	0	1	0	.667
H. Borowy, p	2	1	1	0	0	1	0	.500
E. Bonham, p	2	0	0	0	0	0	0	.000
S. Stirnweiss	1	0	0	0	0	1	0	.000
R. Weatherly	1	0	0	0	0	0	0	.000

Errors: F. Crosetti (3), N. Etten, B. Johnson
Stolen Bases: F. Crosetti, C. Keller

ST. LOUIS (N.L.)

	AB	H	2B	3B	HR	R	RBI	BA
L. Klein, 2b	22	3	0	0	0	0	0	.136
S. Musial, of	18	5	0	0	0	2	0	.278
W. Kurowski, 3b	18	4	1	0	0	2	1	.222
H. Walker, of	18	3	1	0	0	0	0	.167
W. Cooper, c	17	5	0	0	0	1	0	.294
R. Sanders, 1b	17	5	0	0	1	3	2	.294
D. Litwhiler, of	15	4	1	0	0	0	2	.267
M. Marion, ss	14	5	2	0	1	1	2	.357
M. Cooper, p	5	0	0	0	0	0	0	.000
D. Garms, of	5	0	0	0	0	0	0	.000
M. Lanier, p	4	1	0	0	0	0	1	.250
J. Hopp, of	4	0	0	0	0	0	0	.000
K. O'Dea, c	3	2	0	0	0	0	0	.667
A. Brazle, p	3	0	0	0	0	0	0	.000
F. Demaree	1	0	0	0	0	0	0	.000
S. Narron	1	0	0	0	0	0	0	.000
E. White	0	0	0	0	0	0	0	—

Errors: W. Cooper (2), L. Klein (2), W. Kurowski (2), H. Walker (2), M. Lanier, M. Marion
Stolen Bases: M. Marion

Individual Pitching

NEW YORK (A.L.)

	W	L	ERA	IP	H	BB	SO	SV
S. Chandler	2	0	0.50	18	17	3	10	0
M. Russo	1	0	0.00	9	7	1	2	0
E. Bonham	0	1	4.50	8	6	3	9	0
H. Borowy	1	0	2.25	8	6	3	4	0
J. Murphy	0	0	0.00	2	1	1	1	1

ST. LOUIS (N.L.)

	W	L	ERA	IP	H	BB	SO	SV
M. Cooper	1	1	2.81	16	11	3	10	0
M. Lanier	0	1	1.76	15.1	13	3	13	0
A. Brazle	0	1	3.68	7.1	5	2	4	0
H. Brecheen	0	1	2.45	3.2	5	3	3	0
M. Dickson	0	0	0.00	0.2	0	1	0	0
H. Krist	0	0	—	0.0	1	0	0	0

1944 WORLD SERIES

St. Louis (N.L.) defeats St. Louis (A.L.) 4 games to 2

LINE SCORES			R	H	E	PITCHERS (innings pitched)	HOME RUNS (men on)	HIGHLIGHTS
GAME 1 - OCTOBER 4								Cooper allowed just two hits, but one was McQuinn's homer in the fourth, which gave Galehouse enough for the win.
STL	**A**	000 200 000	2	2	0	**Galehouse** (9)	McQuinn (1 on)	
STL	**N**	000 000 001	1	7	0	**M. Cooper** (7), Donnelly (2)		
GAME 2 - OCTOBER 5								Donnelly struck out seven and allowed only three balls to be hit out of the infield in four innings of relief. The Cardinals won in the eleventh on O'Dea's pinch-hit single with two on.
STL	**A**	000 000 200 00	2	7	4	Potter (6), **Muncrief** (4.1)		
STL	**N**	001 100 000 01	3	7	0	Lanier (7), **Donnelly** (4)		
GAME 3 - OCTOBER 6								Five straight singles, a walk, and a wild pitch, all after two out, gave the Browns four runs and a 2-1 lead in the Series.
STL	**N**	100 000 100	2	7	0	**Wilks** (2.2), Schmidt (3.1), Jurisich (0.2), Byerly (1.1)		
STL	**A**	004 000 20x	6	8	2	**Kramer** (9)		
GAME 4 - OCTOBER 7								Musial's three hits paced the Cardinals to a 5-0 lead. The Browns' only threat was cutoff in the eighth by a spectacular double play started by Marion.
STL	**N**	202 001 000	5	12	0	**Brecheen** (9)	Musial (1 on)	
STL	**A**	000 000 010	1	9	1	**Jakucki** (3), Hollingsworth (4), Shirley (2)		
GAME 5 - OCTOBER 8								Homers by Sanders and Litwhiler decided the duel as Cooper struck out 12 and Galehouse 10.
STL	**N**	000 001 010	2	6	1	**M. Cooper** (9)	Sanders, Litwhiler	
STL	**A**	000 000 000	0	7	1	**Galehouse** (9)		
GAME 6 - OCTOBER 9								Wilks entered the game in the sixth with one out and men on second and third, and retired the last 11 batters in a row to preserve the 3-1 margin.
STL	**A**	010 000 000	1	3	2	**Potter** (3.2), Muncrief (2.1), Kramer (2)		
STL	**N**	000 300 00x	3	10	0	**Lanier** (5.1), Wilks (3.2) **SV**		

Team totals

		W	AB	H	2B	3B	HR	R	RBI	BA	BB	SO	ERA
STL	**N**	4	204	49	9	1	3	16	15	.240	19	43	1.96
STL	**A**	2	197	36	9	1	1	12	9	.183	23	49	1.49

Individual Batting

ST. LOUIS (N.L.)

	AB	H	2B	3B	HR	R	RBI	BA
J. Hopp, of	27	5	0	0	0	2	0	.185
S. Musial, of	23	7	2	0	1	2	2	.304
W. Kurowski, 3b	23	5	1	0	0	2	1	.217
W. Cooper, c	22	7	2	1	0	1	2	.318
M. Marion, ss	22	5	3	0	0	1	2	.227
R. Sanders, 1b	21	6	0	0	1	5	1	.286
D. Litwhiler, of	20	4	1	0	1	2	1	.200
E. Verban, 2b	17	7	0	0	0	1	2	.412
A. Bergamo, of	6	0	0	0	0	0	1	.000
M. Lanier, p	4	2	0	0	0	0	1	.500
H. Brecheen, p	4	0	0	0	0	0	0	.000
M. Cooper, p	4	0	0	0	0	0	0	.000
K. O'Dea	3	1	0	0	0	0	2	.333
G. Fallon, 2b	2	0	0	0	0	0	0	.000
D. Garms	2	0	0	0	0	0	0	.000
T. Wilks, p	2	0	0	0	0	0	0	.000
B. Donnelly, p	1	0	0	0	0	0	0	.000
F. Schmidt, p	1	0	0	0	0	0	0	.000

Errors: S. Musial

ST. LOUIS (A.L.)

	AB	H	2B	3B	HR	R	RBI	BA
M. Kreevich, of	26	6	3	0	0	0	0	.231
V. Stephens, ss	22	5	1	0	0	2	0	.227
G. Moore, of	22	4	0	0	0	4	0	.182
M. Christman, 3b	22	2	0	0	0	0	1	.091
D. Gutteridge, 2b	21	3	1	0	0	1	0	.143
R. Hayworth, c	17	2	1	0	0	1	1	.118
G. McQuinn, 1b	16	7	2	0	1	2	5	.438
C. Laabs, of	15	3	1	1	0	1	0	.200
A. Zarilla, of	10	1	0	0	0	1	1	.100
D. Galehouse, p	5	1	0	0	0	0	0	.200
J. Kramer, p	4	0	0	0	0	0	0	.000
N. Potter, p	4	0	0	0	0	0	0	.000
F. Mancuso, c	3	2	0	0	0	0	1	.667
F. Baker, 2b	2	0	0	0	0	0	0	.000
M. Byrnes	2	0	0	0	0	0	0	.000
M. Chartak	2	0	0	0	0	0	0	.000
E. Clary	1	0	0	0	0	0	0	.000
A. Hollingsworth, p	1	0	0	0	0	0	0	.000
B. Muncrief, p	1	0	0	0	0	0	0	.000
T. Turner	1	0	0	0	0	0	0	.000

Errors: D. Gutteridge (3), V. Stephens (3), N. Potter (2), M. Christman, R. Hayworth

Individual Pitching

ST. LOUIS (N.L.)

	W	L	ERA	IP	H	BB	SO	SV
M. Cooper	1	1	1.13	16	9	5	16	0
M. Lanier	1	0	2.19	12.1	8	8	11	0
H. Brecheen	1	0	1.00	9	9	4	4	0
T. Wilks	0	1	5.68	6.1	5	3	7	1
B. Donnelly	1	0	0.00	6	2	1	9	0
F. Schmidt	0	0	0.00	3.1	1	1	1	0
B. Byerly	0	0	0.00	1.1	0	0	1	0
A. Jurisich	0	0	27.00	0.2	2	1	0	0

ST. LOUIS (A.L.)

	W	L	ERA	IP	H	BB	SO	SV
D. Galehouse	1	1	1.50	18	13	5	15	0
J. Kramer	1	0	0.00	11	9	4	12	0
N. Potter	0	1	0.93	9.2	10	3	6	0
B. Muncrief	0	1	1.35	6.2	5	4	4	0
A. Hollingsworth	0	0	2.25	4	5	2	1	0
S. Jakucki	0	1	9.00	3	5	0	4	0
T. Shirley	0	0	0.00	2	2	1	1	0

1945 WORLD SERIES

Detroit (A.L.) defeats Chicago (N.L.) 4 games to 3

LINE SCORES						PITCHERS (innings pitched)	HOME RUNS (men on)	HIGHLIGHTS
GAME 1 - OCTOBER 3								Newhouser gave up seven hits and eight runs in the first three innings as Cavarretta and Pafko scored three runs each and Nicholson had three RBIs.
CHI	**N**	403 000 200	9	13	0	**Borowy** (9)	Cavarretta	
DET	**A**	000 000 000	0	6	0	**Newhouser** (2.2), Benton (1.1), Tobin (3), Mueller (2)		
GAME 2 - OCTOBER 4								Greenberg's homer with two on in the fifth broke open the game.
CHI	**N**	000 100 000	1	7	0	**Wyse** (6), Erickson (2)		
DET	**A**	000 040 00x	4	7	0	**Trucks** (9)	Greenberg (2 on)	
GAME 3 - OCTOBER 5								Passeau allowed only a single to York in the third and a walk to Swift in the sixth.
CHI	**N**	000 200 100	3	8	0	**Passeau** (9)		
DET	**A**	000 000 000	0	1	2	**Overmire** (6), Benton (3)		
GAME 4 - OCTOBER 6								Prim retired the first ten batters in the game, but the Tigers knocked him out with four in the fourth.
DET	**A**	000 400 000	4	7	1	**Trout** (9)		
CHI	**N**	000 001 000	1	5	1	**Prim** (3.1), Derringer (1.2), Vandenburg (2), Erickson (2)		
GAME 5 - OCTOBER 7								Newhouser benefitted from another four-run Tiger rally and struck out nine Cubs in the victory. Greenberg's three doubles keyed the attack.
DET	**A**	001 004 102	8	11	0	**Newhouser** (9)		
CHI	**N**	001 000 201	4	7	2	**Borowy** (5), Vandenburg (0.2), Chipman (0.1), Derringer (2), Erickson (1)		
GAME 6 - OCTOBER 8								Hack's drive bounced past Greenberg for a double and brought home the winning run in the twelfth after Greenberg tied the game with a homer in the eighth. Borowy held the Tigers scoreless over the last four innings.
DET	**A**	010 000 240 000	7	13	1	Trucks (4.1), Caster (0.2), Bridges (1.2), Benton (0.1), **Trout** (4.2)	Greenberg	
CHI	**N**	000 041 200 001	8	15	3	Passeau (6.2), Wyse (0.2), Prim (0.2), **Borowy** (4)		
GAME 7 - OCTOBER 10								The Cubs gambled and sent in Borowy with only a day's rest. The Tigers hit three successive singles to knock him out in the first, and went on to score five in the frame to sew up the Series.
DET	**A**	510 000 120	9	9	1	**Newhouser** (9)		
CHI	**N**	100 100 010	3	10	0	**Borowy** (0), Derringer (1.2), Vandenberg (3.1), Erickson (2), Passeau (1), Wyse (1)		

Team totals

		W	AB	H	2B	3B	HR	R	RBI	BA	BB	SO	ERA
DET	**A**	4	242	54	10	0	2	32	32	.223	33	22	3.84
CHI	**N**	3	246	65	16	3	1	29	27	.264	19	48	4.15

Individual Batting

DETROIT (A.L.)

	AB	H	2B	3B	HR	R	RBI	BA
D. Cramer, of	29	11	0	0	0	7	4	.379
E. Mayo, 2b	28	7	1	0	0	4	2	.250
J. Outlaw, 3b	28	5	0	0	0	1	3	.179
R. York, 1b	28	5	1	0	0	1	3	.179
S. Webb, ss	27	5	0	0	0	4	1	.185
H. Greenberg, of	23	7	3	0	2	7	7	.304
R. Cullenbine, of	22	5	2	0	0	5	4	.227
P. Richards, c	19	4	2	0	0	0	6	.211
H. Newhouser, p	8	0	0	0	0	0	1	.000
D. Trout, p	6	1	0	0	0	0	0	.167
B. Swift, c	4	1	0	0	0	1	0	.250
V. Trucks, p	4	0	0	0	0	0	0	.000
J. Hoover, ss	3	1	0	0	0	1	1	.333
C. Hostetler	3	0	0	0	0	0	0	.000
J. McHale	3	0	0	0	0	0	0	.000
H. Walker	2	1	1	0	0	1	0	.500
B. Maier	1	1	0	0	0	0	0	1.000
R. Borom	1	0	0	0	0	0	0	.000
Z. Eaton	1	0	0	0	0	0	0	.000
S. Overmire, p	1	0	0	0	0	0	0	.000
J. Tobin, p	1	0	0	0	0	0	0	.000
E. Mierkowicz, of	0	0	0	0	0	0	0	—

Errors: E. Mayo, H. Newhouser, P. Richards, S. Webb, R. York
Stolen Bases: D. Cramer, R. Cullenbine, J. Outlaw

CHICAGO (N.L.)

	AB	H	2B	3B	HR	R	RBI	BA
S. Hack, 3b	30	11	3	0	0	1	4	.367
P. Lowrey, of	29	9	1	0	0	4	0	.310
D. Johnson, 2b	29	5	2	1	0	4	0	.172
B. Nicholson, of	28	6	1	1	0	1	8	.214
A. Pafko, of	28	6	2	1	0	5	2	.214
P. Cavarretta, 1b	26	11	2	0	1	7	5	.423
M. Livingston, c	22	8	3	0	0	3	4	.364
R. Hughes, ss	17	5	1	0	0	1	3	.294
C. Passeau, p	7	0	0	0	0	1	1	.000
P. Gillespie, c	6	0	0	0	0	0	0	.000
F. Secory	5	2	0	0	0	0	0	.400
H. Borowy, p	5	1	1	0	0	1	0	.200
H. Wyse, p	3	0	0	0	0	0	0	.000
H. Becker	2	1	0	0	0	0	0	.500
L. Merullo, ss	2	0	0	0	0	0	0	.000
E. Sauer	2	0	0	0	0	0	0	.000
D. Williams, c	2	0	0	0	0	0	0	.000
C. McCullough	1	0	0	0	0	0	0	.000
B. Schuster, ss	1	0	0	0	0	1	0	.000
H. Vandenburg, p	1	0	0	0	0	0	0	.000
C. Block	0	0	0	0	0	0	0	—

Errors: S. Hack (3), D. Johnson, B. Nicholson, A. Pafko
Stolen Bases: P. Lowrey

Individual Pitching

DETROIT (A.L.)

	W	L	ERA	IP	H	BB	SO	SV
H. Newhouser	2	1	6.10	20.2	25	4	22	0
D. Trout	1	1	0.66	13.2	9	3	9	0
V. Trucks	1	0	3.38	13.1	14	5	7	0
S. Overmire	0	1	3.00	6	4	2	2	0
A. Benton	0	0	1.93	4.2	6	0	5	0
J. Tobin	0	0	6.00	3	4	1	0	0
L. Mueller	0	0	0.00	2	0	1	1	0
T. Bridges	0	0	16.20	1.2	3	3	1	0
G. Caster	0	0	0.00	0.2	0	0	1	0

CHICAGO (N.L.)

	W	L	ERA	IP	H	BB	SO	SV
H. Borowy	2	2	4.00	18	21	6	8	0
C. Passeau	1	0	2.70	16.2	7	8	3	0
H. Wyse	0	1	7.04	7.2	8	4	1	0
P. Erickson	0	0	3.86	7	8	3	5	0
H. Vandenburg	0	0	0.00	6	1	3	3	0
P. Derringer	0	0	6.75	5.1	5	7	1	0
R. Prim	0	1	9.00	4	4	1	1	0
B. Chipman	0	0	0.00	0.1	0	1	0	0

1946 WORLD SERIES

LINE SCORES						PITCHERS (innings pitched)	HOME RUNS (men on)	HIGHLIGHTS

St. Louis (N.L.) defeats Boston (A.L.) 4 games to 3

			R	H	E	PITCHERS (innings pitched)	HOME RUNS (men on)	HIGHLIGHTS
GAME 1 - OCTOBER 6								The Red Sox tied the game in the ninth when a ground ball took a freak bounce through Marion's legs, setting the stage for York, who homered in the tenth.
BOS	**A**	010 000 001 1	3	9	2	Hughson (8), **Johnson** (2)	York	
STL	**N**	000 001 010 0	2	7	0	**Pollet** (10)		
GAME 2 - OCTOBER 7								Brecheen drove in the first run of the game and allowed only four singles.
BOS	**A**	000 000 000	0	4	1	**Harris** (7), Dobson (1)		
STL	**N**	001 020 00x	3	6	0	**Brecheen** (9)		
GAME 3 - OCTOBER 9								The Red Sox broke the game open in the first on York's three-run homer. Ferriss's shutout is the 50th in Series history.
STL	**N**	000 000 000	0	6	1	**Dickson** (7), Wilks (1)		
BOS	**A**	300 000 01x	4	8	0	**Ferriss** (9)	York (2 on)	
GAME 4 - OCTOBER 10								Slaughter, Kurowski, and Garagiola each had four hits as the Cardinals tied a Series record with their 20 hits.
STL	**N**	033 010 104	12	20	1	**Munger** (9)	Slaughter	
BOS	**A**	000 100 020	3	9	4	**Hughson** (2), Bagby (3), Zuber (2), Brown (1), Ryba (0.2), Dreisewerd (0.1)	Doerr (1 on)	
GAME 5 - OCTOBER 11								Higgins's double in the seventh scored DiMaggio for the deciding run of the game. All three St. Louis runs off Dobson were unearned.
STL	**N**	010 000 020	3	4	1	Pollet (0.1), **Brazle** (6.2), Beazley (1)		
BOS	**A**	110 001 30x	6	11	3	**Dobson** (9)	Culberson	
GAME 6 - OCTOBER 13								Brecheen shut down the Red Sox on seven hits as the Cardinals evened the Series.
BOS	**A**	000 000 100	1	7	0	**Harris** (2.2), Hughson (4.1), Johnson (1)		
STL	**N**	003 000 01x	4	8	0	**Brecheen** (9)		
GAME 7 - OCTOBER 15								Pesky hesitated throwing the ball in after Walker's double in the eighth and Slaughter raced home from first with the deciding run. Brecheen recorded his third victory of the Series.
BOS	**A**	100 000 020	3	8	0	Ferriss (4.1), Dobson (2.2), **Klinger** (0.2), Johnson (0.1)		
STL	**N**	010 020 01x	4	9	1	Dickson (7), **Brecheen** (2)		

Team totals

		W	AB	H	2B	3B	HR	R	RBI	BA	BB	SO	ERA
STL	**N**	4	232	60	19	2	1	28	27	.259	19	30	2.32
BOS	**A**	3	233	56	7	1	4	20	18	.240	22	28	2.95

Individual Batting

ST. LOUIS (N.L.)

	AB	H	2B	3B	HR	R	RBI	BA
R. Schoendienst, 2b	30	7	1	0	0	3	1	.233
W. Kurowski, 3b	27	8	3	0	0	5	2	.296
S. Musial, 1b	27	6	4	1	0	3	4	.222
T. Moore, of	27	4	0	0	0	1	2	.148
E. Slaughter, of	25	8	1	1	1	5	2	.320
M. Marion, ss	24	6	2	0	0	1	4	.250
J. Garagiola, c	19	6	2	0	0	2	4	.316
H. Walker, of	17	7	2	0	0	3	6	.412
H. Brecheen, p	8	1	0	0	0	2	1	.125
D. Rice, c	6	3	1	0	0	2	0	.500
M. Dickson, p	5	2	2	0	0	1	1	.400
E. Dusak, of	4	1	1	0	0	0	0	.250
G. Munger, p	4	1	0	0	0	0	0	.250
H. Pollet, p	4	0	0	0	0	0	0	.000
A. Brazle, p	2	0	0	0	0	0	0	.000
D. Sisler	2	0	0	0	0	0	0	.000
N. Jones	1	0	0	0	0	0	0	.000

Errors: M. Marion (2), W. Kurowski, R. Schoendienst
Stolen Bases: S. Musial, R. Schoendienst, E. Slaughter

BOSTON (A.L.)

	AB	H	2B	3B	HR	R	RBI	BA
J. Pesky, ss	30	7	0	0	0	2	0	.233
D. DiMaggio, of	27	7	3	0	0	2	3	.259
T. Williams, of	25	5	0	0	0	2	1	.200
P. Higgins, 3b	24	5	1	0	0	1	2	.208
R. York, 1b	23	6	1	1	2	6	5	.261
B. Doerr, 2b	22	9	1	0	1	1	3	.409
H. Wagner, c	13	0	0	0	0	0	0	.000
W. Moses, of	12	5	0	0	0	1	0	.417
T. McBride, of	12	2	0	0	0	0	1	.167
R. Partee, c	10	1	0	0	0	1	1	.100
L. Culberson, of	9	2	0	0	1	1	1	.222
B. Ferriss, p	6	0	0	0	0	0	0	.000
D. Gutteridge, 2b	5	2	0	0	0	1	1	.400
M. Harris, p	3	1	0	0	0	0	0	.333
T. Hughson, p	3	1	0	0	0	0	0	.333
J. Dobson, p	3	0	0	0	0	0	0	.000
R. Russell, 3b	2	2	0	0	0	1	0	1.000
C. Metkovich	2	1	1	0	0	1	0	.500
J. Bagby, p	1	0	0	0	0	0	0	.000
E. Johnson, p	1	0	0	0	0	0	0	.000
P. Campbell	0	0	0	0	0	0	0	—

Errors: J. Pesky (4), P. Higgins (2), T. Hughson, T. McBride, M. Ryba, R. York
Stolen Bases: L. Culberson, J. Pesky

Individual Pitching

ST. LOUIS (N.L.)

	W	L	ERA	IP	H	BB	SO	SV
H. Brecheen	3	0	0.45	20	14	5	11	0
M. Dickson	0	1	3.86	14	11	4	7	0
H. Pollet	0	1	3.48	10.1	12	4	3	0
G. Munger	1	0	1.00	9	9	3	2	0
A. Brazle	0	1	5.40	6.2	7	6	4	0
J. Beazley	0	0	0.00	1	1	0	1	0
T. Wilks	0	0	0.00	1	2	0	0	0

BOSTON (A.L.)

	W	L	ERA	IP	H	BB	SO	SV
T. Hughson	0	1	3.14	14.1	14	3	8	0
B. Ferriss	1	0	2.02	13.1	13	2	4	0
J. Dobson	1	0	0.00	12.2	4	3	10	0
M. Harris	0	2	3.72	9.2	11	4	5	0
E. Johnson	1	0	2.70	3.1	1	2	1	0
J. Bagby	0	0	3.00	3	6	1	1	0
B. Zuber	0	0	4.50	2	3	1	1	0
M. Brown	0	0	27.00	1	4	1	0	0
B. Klinger	0	1	13.50	0.2	2	1	0	0
M. Ryba	0	0	13.50	0.2	2	1	0	0
C. Dreisewerd	0	0	0.00	0.1	0	0	0	0

1947 WORLD SERIES

New York (A.L.) defeats Brooklyn (N.L.) 4 games to 3

LINE SCORES			R	H	E	PITCHERS (innings pitched)	HOME RUNS (men on)	HIGHLIGHTS
GAME 1 - SEPTEMBER 30								Branca retired the first twelve batters but was knocked out as the Yankees got five in the fifth on three hits, three walks, and a hit batsman.
BKN	**N**	100 001 100	3	6	0	**Branca** (4), Behrman (2), Casey (2)		
NY	**A**	000 050 00x	5	4	0	**Shea** (5), Page (4) **SV**		
GAME 2 - OCTOBER 1								Reynolds spaced nine Dodger hits and fanned 12 as he breezed to an easy win.
BKN	**N**	001 100 001	3	9	2	**Lombardi** (4), Gregg (2), Behrman (0.1), Barney (1.2)	Walker	
NY	**A**	101 121 40x	10	15	1	**Reynolds** (9)	Henrich	
GAME 3 - OCTOBER 2								The Dodgers jumped on Newsom and Raschi for six runs in the second to outlast the Yankees in the slugfest. Berra's pinch homer was the first in Series history.
NY	**A**	002 221 100	8	13	0	**Newsom** (1.2), Raschi (0.1), Drew (1), Chandler (2), Page (3)	DiMaggio (1 on), Berra	
BKN	**N**	061 200 00x	9	13	1	Hatten (4.1), Branca (2), **Casey** (2.2)		
GAME 4 - OCTOBER 3								Bevens was one out from the first Series no-hitter when Lavagetto doubled home two men to win the game for the Dodgers.
NY	**A**	100 100 000	2	8	1	**Bevens** (8.2)		
BKN	**N**	000 010 002	3	1	3	Taylor (0), Gregg (7), Behrman (1.1), **Casey** (0.2)		
GAME 5 - OCTOBER 4								A fifth-inning homer by DiMaggio proved the deciding run. Shea aided his own cause with two hits and an RBI.
NY	**A**	000 110 000	2	5	0	**Shea** (9)	DiMaggio	
BKN	**N**	000 001 000	1	4	1	**Barney** (4.2), Hatten (1.1), Behrman (1), Casey (2)		
GAME 6 - OCTOBER 5								A record 38 players were used as the Dodgers knotted the Series. Gionfriddo's great catch of DiMaggio's 415-foot drive in the sixth with two aboard helped to subdue the Yankees.
BKN	**N**	202 004 000	8	12	1	Lombardi (2.2), **Branca** (2.1), Hatten (3), Casey (1) **SV**		
NY	**A**	004 100 001	6	15	2	Reynolds (2.1), Drews (2), **Page** (1), Newsom (0.2), Raschi (1), Wensloff (2)		
GAME 7 - OCTOBER 6								Page, the Yankees' relief ace, checked the Dodgers on one hit for the last five innings to give the Yankees the Series victory. Henrich's go-ahead RBI single in the fourth marked the third time in the Series that he delivered the clutch run.
BKN	**N**	020 000 000	2	7	0	**Gregg** (3.2), Behrman (1.2), Hatten (0.1), Barney (0.1), Casey (2)		
NY	**A**	010 201 10x	5	7	0	Shea (1.1), Bevens (2.2), **Page** (5)		

Team totals

		W	AB	H	2B	3B	HR	R	RBI	BA	BB	SO	ERA
NY	**A**	4	238	67	11	5	4	38	36	.282	38	35	4.09
BKN	**N**	3	226	52	13	1	1	29	26	.230	30	32	5.55

Individual Batting

NEW YORK (A.L.)

	AB	H	2B	3B	HR	R	RBI	BA
T. Henrich, of	31	10	2	0	1	2	5	.323
S. Stirnweiss, 2b	27	7	0	1	0	3	3	.259
P. Rizzuto, ss	26	8	1	0	0	3	2	.308
B. Johnson, 3b	26	7	0	3	0	8	2	.269
J. DiMaggio, of	26	6	0	0	2	4	5	.231
G. McQuinn, 1b	23	3	0	0	0	3	1	.130
Y. Berra, c, of	19	3	0	0	1	2	2	.158
J. Lindell, of	18	9	3	1	0	3	7	.500
A. Robinson, c	10	2	0	0	0	2	1	.200
S. Shea, p	5	2	1	0	0	0	1	.400
S. Lollar, c	4	3	2	0	0	3	1	.750
A. Reynolds, p	4	2	0	0	0	2	1	.500
B. Bevens, p	4	0	0	0	0	0	0	.000
J. Page, p	4	0	0	0	0	0	0	.000
B. Brown	3	3	2	0	0	2	3	1.000
A. Clark, of	2	1	0	0	0	1	1	.500
K. Drews, p	2	0	0	0	0	0	0	.000
J. Phillips, 1b	2	0	0	0	0	0	0	.000
R. Houk	1	1	0	0	0	0	0	1.000
L. Frey	1	0	0	0	0	0	1	.000

Errors: Y. Berra (2), G. McQuinn, A. Robinson
Stolen Bases: P. Rizzuto (2)

BROOKLYN (N.L.)

	AB	H	2B	3B	HR	R	RBI	BA
J. Robinson, 1b	27	7	2	0	0	3	3	.259
B. Edwards, c	27	6	1	0	0	3	2	.222
D. Walker, of	27	6	1	0	1	1	4	.222
E. Stanky, 2b	25	6	1	0	0	4	2	.240
P. Reese, ss	23	7	1	0	0	5	4	.304
S. Jorgensen, 3b	20	4	2	0	0	1	3	.200
G. Hermanski, of	19	3	0	1	0	4	1	.158
C. Furillo, of	17	6	2	0	0	2	3	.353
P. Reiser, of	8	2	0	0	0	1	0	.250
C. Lavagetto, 3b	7	1	1	0	0	0	3	.143
E. Miksis, 2b, of	4	1	0	0	0	1	0	.250
R. Branca, p	4	0	0	0	0	0	0	.000
J. Hatten, p	3	1	0	0	0	1	0	.333
A. Gionfriddo, of	3	0	0	0	0	2	0	.000
H. Gregg, p	3	0	0	0	0	0	0	.000
V. Lombardi, p	3	0	0	0	0	0	0	.000
A. Vaughan	2	1	1	0	0	0	0	.500
B. Bragan	1	1	1	0	0	0	1	1.000
R. Barney, p	1	0	0	0	0	0	0	.000
H. Casey, p	1	0	0	0	0	0	0	.000
G. Hodges	1	0	0	0	0	0	0	.000
D. Bankhead	0	0	0	0	0	1	0	—

Errors: S. Jorgensen (2), B. Edwards, C. Furillo, E. Miksis, P. Reese, P. Reiser, E. Stanky
Stolen Bases: P. Reese (3), J. Robinson (2), A. Gionfriddo, D. Walker

Individual Pitching

NEW YORK (A.L.)

	W	L	ERA	IP	H	BB	SO	SV
S. Shea	2	0	2.35	15.1	10	8	10	0
J. Page	1	1	4.15	13	12	2	7	1
B. Bevens	0	1	2.38	11.1	3	11	7	0
A. Reynolds	1	0	4.76	11.1	15	3	6	0
K. Drews	0	0	3.00	3	2	1	0	0
B. Newsom	0	1	19.29	2.1	6	2	0	0
S. Chandler	0	0	9.00	2	2	3	1	0
B. Wensloff	0	0	0.00	2	0	0	0	0
V. Raschi	0	0	6.75	1.1	2	0	1	0

BROOKLYN (N.L.)

	W	L	ERA	IP	H	BB	SO	SV
H. Gregg	0	1	3.55	12.2	9	8	10	0
H. Casey	2	0	0.87	10.1	5	1	3	1
J. Hatten	0	0	7.00	9	12	7	5	0
R. Branca	1	1	8.64	8.1	12	5	8	0
R. Barney	0	1	2.70	6.2	4	10	3	0
V. Lombardi	0	1	12.15	6.2	14	1	5	0
H. Behrman	0	0	7.11	6.1	9	5	3	0
H. Taylor	0	0	—	0.0	2	1	0	0

1948 WORLD SERIES

Cleveland (A.L.) defeats Boston (N.L.) 4 games to 2

LINE SCORES			R	H	E	PITCHERS (innings pitched)	HOME RUNS (men on)	HIGHLIGHTS
GAME 1 - OCTOBER 6								Holmes singled Masi home in the eighth after Masi was almost picked off second by Feller.
CLE	**A**	000 000 000	0	4	0	**Feller** (8)		
BOS	**N**	000 000 01x	1	2	2	**Sain** (9)		
GAME 2 - OCTOBER 7								The Indians went ahead with two runs in the fourth on hits by Boudreau, Gordon, and Doby.
CLE	**A**	000 210 001	4	8	1	**Lemon** (9)		
BOS	**N**	100 000 000	1	8	3	**Spahn** (4.1), Barrett (2.2), Potter (2)		
GAME 3 - OCTOBER 8								Bearden faced only 30 batters and doubled in the third, scoring the go-ahead run on Dark's error. Hegan singled in an insurance run in the fourth.
BOS	**N**	000 000 000	0	5	1	**Bickford** (3.1), Voiselle (3.2), Barrett (1)		
CLE	**A**	001 100 00x	2	5	0	**Bearden** (9)		
GAME 4 - OCTOBER 9								Doby's homer in the third became decisive when Rickert homered to spoil Gromek's shutout attempt in the seventh.
BOS	**N**	000 000 100	1	7	0	**Sain** (8)	Rickert	
CLE	**A**	101 000 00x	2	5	0	**Gromek** (9)	Doby	
GAME 5 - OCTOBER 10								Elliott's two home runs drove in four runs in the first and third. The Braves broke a 5-5 tie with six runs in the seventh on five singles off four Indian pitchers.
BOS	**N**	301 001 600	11	12	0	Potter (3.1), **Spahn** (5.2)	Elliott (2 on), Elliott, Salkeld	
CLE	**A**	100 400 000	5	6	2	**Feller** (6.1), Klieman (0), Christopher (0), Paige (0.2), Muncrief (2)	Mitchell, Hegan (2 on)	
GAME 6 - OCTOBER 11								Masi's pinch-hit double off Bearden in the eighth brought the Braves within one run of the Indians, but Bearden retired the next four men to nail down the win.
CLE	**A**	001 002 010	4	10	0	**Lemon** (7.1), Bearden (1.2) **SV**	Gordon	
BOS	**N**	000 100 020	3	9	0	**Voiselle** (7), Spahn (2)		

Team totals

		W	AB	H	2B	3B	HR	R	RBI	BA	BB	SO	ERA
CLE	**A**	4	191	38	7	0	4	17	16	.199	12	26	2.72
BOS	**N**	2	187	43	6	0	4	17	16	.230	16	19	2.60

Individual Batting

CLEVELAND (A.L.)

	AB	H	2B	3B	HR	R	RBI	BA
D. Mitchell, of	23	4	1	0	1	4	1	.174
L. Doby, of	22	7	1	0	1	1	2	.318
L. Boudreau, ss	22	6	4	0	0	1	3	.273
J. Gordon, 2b	22	4	0	0	1	3	2	.182
K. Keltner, 3b	21	2	0	0	0	3	0	.095
E. Robinson, 1b	20	6	0	0	0	0	1	.300
J. Hegan, c	19	4	0	0	1	2	5	.211
W. Judnich, of	13	1	0	0	0	1	1	.077
B. Lemon, p	7	0	0	0	0	0	0	.000
G. Bearden, p	4	2	1	0	0	1	0	.500
B. Feller, p	4	0	0	0	0	0	0	.000
T. Tucker, of	3	1	0	0	0	1	0	.333
A. Clark, of	3	0	0	0	0	0	0	.000
S. Gromek, p	3	0	0	0	0	0	0	.000
B. Kennedy, of	2	1	0	0	0	0	1	.500
R. Boone	1	0	0	0	0	0	0	.000
A. Rosen	1	0	0	0	0	0	0	.000
J. Tipton	1	0	0	0	0	0	0	.000
H. Peck, of	0	0	0	0	0	0	0	—

Errors: L. Doby, J. Gordon, K. Keltner
Stolen Bases: J. Gordon, J. Hegan

BOSTON (N.L.)

	AB	H	2B	3B	HR	R	RBI	BA
T. Holmes, of	26	5	0	0	0	3	1	.192
A. Dark, ss	24	4	1	0	0	2	0	.167
M. McCormick, of	23	6	0	0	0	1	2	.261
B. Elliott, 3b	21	7	0	0	2	4	5	.333
M. Rickert, of	19	4	0	0	1	2	2	.211
E. Torgeson, 1b	18	7	3	0	0	2	1	.389
E. Stanky, 2b	14	4	1	0	0	0	1	.286
B. Salkeld, c	9	2	0	0	1	2	1	.222
P. Masi, c	8	1	1	0	0	1	1	.125
F. McCormick, 1b	5	1	0	0	0	0	0	.200
J. Sain, p	5	1	0	0	0	0	0	.200
C. Conatser, of	4	0	0	0	0	0	1	.000
W. Spahn, p	4	0	0	0	0	0	1	.000
N. Potter, p	2	1	0	0	0	0	0	.500
B. Voiselle, p	2	0	0	0	0	0	0	.000
C. Ryan	1	0	0	0	0	0	0	.000
R. Sanders	1	0	0	0	0	0	0	.000
S. Sisti, 2b	1	0	0	0	0	0	0	.000

Errors: A. Dark (3), B. Elliott (3)
Stolen Bases: E. Torgeson

Individual Pitching

CLEVELAND (A.L.)

	W	L	ERA	IP	H	BB	SO	SV
B. Lemon	2	0	1.65	16.1	16	7	6	0
B. Feller	0	2	5.02	14.1	10	5	7	0
G. Bearden	1	0	0.00	10.2	6	1	4	1
S. Gromek	1	0	1.00	9	7	1	2	0
B. Muncrief	0	0	0.00	2	1	0	0	0
S. Paige	0	0	0.00	0.2	0	0	0	0
R. Christopher	0	0	∞	0.0	2	0	0	0
E. Klieman	0	0	∞	0.0	1	2	0	0

BOSTON (N.L.)

	W	L	ERA	IP	H	BB	SO	SV
J. Sain	1	1	1.06	17	9	0	9	0
W. Spahn	1	1	3.00	12	10	3	12	0
B. Voiselle	0	1	2.53	10.2	8	2	2	0
N. Potter	0	0	8.44	5.1	6	2	1	0
R. Barrett	0	0	0.00	3.2	1	0	1	0
V. Bickford	0	1	2.70	3.1	4	5	1	0

1949 WORLD SERIES

LINE SCORES | **PITCHERS (innings pitched)** | **HOME RUNS (men on)** | **HIGHLIGHTS**

New York (A.L.) defeats Brooklyn (N.L.) 4 games to 1

LINE SCORES			R	H	E	PITCHERS (innings pitched)	HOME RUNS (men on)	HIGHLIGHTS
GAME 1 - OCTOBER 5								A stirring pitching duel was resolved in the ninth when Henrich hit a leadoff homer for the game's only run.
BKN	**N**	000 000 000	0	2	0	**Newcombe** (8)		
NY	**A**	000 000 001	1	5	1	**Reynolds** (9)	Henrich	
GAME 2 - OCTOBER 6								The Dodgers reversed the score and squared accounts when Roe blanked the Yankees on six hits. Robinson scored the only Dodger run on Hodges's single.
BKN	**N**	010 000 000	1	7	2	**Roe** (9)		
NY	**A**	000 000 000	0	6	1	**Raschi** (8), Page (1)		
GAME 3 - OCTOBER 7								With the score tied 1-1 in the ninth, the Yankees scored three times, and the Dodgers came back with two. A two-run pinch single by Mize is the big blow for the Bombers, while homers by Olmo and Campanella left Brooklyn one run short.
NY	**A**	001 000 003	4	5	0	Byrne (3.1), **Page** (5.2)		
BKN	**N**	000 100 002	3	5	0	**Branca** (8.2), Banta (0.1)	Reese, Olmo, Campanella	
GAME 4 - OCTOBER 8								Reynolds came into the game with runners on first and third and two out in the sixth. He retired all ten batters who faced him to save Lopat's win.
NY	**A**	000 330 000	6	10	0	**Lopat** (5.2), Reynolds (3.1) **SV**		
BKN	**N**	000 004 000	4	9	1	**Newcombe** (3.2), Hatten (1.1), Erskine (1), Banta (3)		
GAME 5 - OCTOBER 9								Barney's wildness enabled the Yankees to take an early lead and Page relieved Raschi to choke off the Dodger comeback effort.
NY	**A**	203 113 000	10	11	1	**Raschi** (6.2), Page (2.1) **SV**	DiMaggio	
BKN	**N**	001 001 400	6	11	2	**Barney** (2.2), Banta (2.1), Erskine (0.2), Hatten (0.1), Palica (2), Minner (1)	Hodges (2 on)	

Team totals

		W	AB	H	2B	3B	HR	R	RBI	BA	BB	SO	ERA
NY	**A**	4	164	37	10	2	2	21	20	.226	18	27	2.80
BKN	**N**	1	162	34	7	1	4	14	14	.210	15	38	4.30

Individual Batting

NEW YORK (A.L.)

	AB	H	2B	3B	HR	R	RBI	BA
J. Coleman, 2b	20	5	3	0	0	0	4	.250
T. Henrich, 1b	19	5	0	0	1	4	1	.263
P. Rizzuto, ss	18	3	0	0	0	2	1	.167
J. DiMaggio, of	18	2	0	0	1	2	2	.111
Y. Berra, c	16	1	0	0	0	2	1	.063
B. Brown, 3b	12	6	1	2	0	4	5	.500
G. Woodling, of	10	4	3	0	0	4	0	.400
C. Mapes, of	10	1	1	0	0	3	2	.100
B. Johnson, 3b	7	1	0	0	0	0	0	.143
J. Lindell, of	7	1	0	0	0	0	0	.143
H. Bauer, of	6	1	0	0	0	0	0	.167
V. Raschi, p	5	1	0	0	0	0	1	.200
A. Reynolds, p	4	2	1	0	0	0	0	.500
J. Page, p	4	0	0	0	0	0	0	.000
E. Lopat, p	3	1	1	0	0	0	1	.333
J. Mize	2	2	0	0	0	0	2	1.000
C. Silvera, c	2	0	0	0	0	0	0	.000
T. Byrne, p	1	1	0	0	0	0	0	1.000
G. Niarhos, c	0	0	0	0	0	0	0	—
S. Stirnweiss	0	0	0	0	0	0	0	—

Errors: J. Coleman, J. Lindell, C. Mapes

Stolen Bases: B. Johnson, P. Rizzuto

BROOKLYN (N.L.)

	AB	H	2B	3B	HR	R	RBI	BA
D. Snider, of	21	3	1	0	0	2	0	.143
P. Reese, ss	19	6	1	0	1	2	2	.316
G. Hodges, 1b	17	4	0	0	1	2	4	.235
J. Robinson, 2b	16	3	1	0	0	2	2	.188
R. Campanella, c	15	4	1	0	1	2	2	.267
G. Hermanski, of	13	4	0	1	0	1	2	.308
L. Olmo, of	11	3	0	0	1	2	2	.273
S. Jorgensen, 3b	11	2	2	0	0	1	0	.182
C. Furillo, of	8	1	0	0	0	0	0	.125
E. Miksis, 3b	7	2	1	0	0	0	0	.286
M. Rackley, of	5	0	0	0	0	0	0	.000
D. Newcombe, p	4	0	0	0	0	0	0	.000
B. Cox, 3b	3	1	0	0	0	0	0	.333
R. Branca, p	3	0	0	0	0	0	0	.000
P. Roe, p	3	0	0	0	0	0	0	.000
B. Edwards	2	1	0	0	0	0	0	.500
T. Brown	2	0	0	0	0	0	0	.000
J. Banta, p	1	0	0	0	0	0	0	.000
D. Whitman	1	0	0	0	0	0	0	.000
M. McCormick, of	0	0	0	0	0	0	0	—

Errors: R. Barney, E. Miksis, P. Reese, J. Robinson, P. Roe

Stolen Bases: P. Reese

Individual Pitching

NEW YORK (A.L.)

	W	L	ERA	IP	H	BB	SO	SV
V. Raschi	1	1	4.30	14.2	15	5	11	0
A. Reynolds	1	0	0.00	12.1	2	4	14	1
J. Page	1	0	2.00	9	6	3	8	1
E. Lopat	1	0	6.35	5.2	9	1	4	0
T. Byrne	0	0	2.70	3.1	2	2	1	0

BROOKLYN (N.L.)

	W	L	ERA	IP	H	BB	SO	SV
D. Newcombe	0	2	3.09	11.2	10	3	11	0
P. Roe	1	0	0.00	9	6	0	3	0
R. Branca	0	1	4.15	8.2	4	4	6	0
J. Banta	0	0	3.18	5.2	5	1	4	0
R. Barney	0	1	16.88	2.2	3	6	2	0
E. Palica	0	0	0.00	2	1	1	1	0
C. Erskine	0	0	16.20	1.2	3	1	0	0
J. Hatten	0	0	16.20	1.2	4	2	0	0
P. Minner	0	0	0.00	1	1	0	0	0

1950 WORLD SERIES

LINE SCORES						PITCHERS (innings pitched)	HOME RUNS (men on)	HIGHLIGHTS

New York (A.L.) defeats Philadelphia (N.L.) 4 games to 0

		GAME 1 - OCTOBER 4						
NY	A	000 100 000	1	5	0	**Raschi** (9)		Raschi allowed only two singles. The Yankees scored in the fourth on a double by Brown and long flies by Bauer and Coleman.
PHI	N	000 000 000	0	2	1	**Konstanty** (8), Meyer (1)		
		GAME 2 - OCTOBER 5						
NY	A	010 000 000 1	2	10	0	**Reynolds** (10)	DiMaggio	DiMaggio homered in the tenth to decide pitcher's duel between Reynolds and Roberts.
PHI	N	000 010 000 0	1	7	0	**Roberts** (10)		
		GAME 3 - OCTOBER 6						
PHI	N	000 001 100	2	10	2	Heintzelman (7.2), Konstanty (0.1), **Meyer** (0.2)		Coleman's single in the ninth drove in Woodling with the winning run after the Yankees tied the game in the eighth on Hamner's bases-loaded error.
NY	A	001 000 011	3	7	0	Lopat (8), **Ferrick** (1)		
		GAME 4 - OCTOBER 7						
PHI	N	000 000 002	2	7	1	**Miller** (0.1), Konstanty (6.2), Roberts (1)		Berra's homer and Brown's triple highlighted the Yankees' three-run fifth. Ford held the Phillies to seven hits, but needed ninth inning help from Reynolds, who struck out Lopata with two men on.
NY	A	200 003 00x	5	8	2	**Ford** (8.2), Reynolds (0.1) **SV**	Berra	

Team totals

		W	AB	H	2B	3B	HR	R	RBI	BA	BB	SO	ERA
NY	A	4	135	30	3	1	2	11	10	.222	13	12	0.73
PHI	N	0	128	26	6	1	0	5	3	.203	7	24	2.27

Individual Batting

NEW YORK (A.L.)

	AB	H	2B	3B	HR	R	RBI	BA
Y. Berra, c	15	3	0	0	1	2	2	.200
H. Bauer, of	15	2	0	0	0	0	1	.133
J. Mize, 1b	15	2	0	0	0	0	0	.133
G. Woodling, of	14	6	0	0	0	2	1	.429
J. Coleman, 2b	14	4	1	0	0	2	3	.286
P. Rizzuto, ss	14	2	0	0	0	1	0	.143
J. DiMaggio, of	13	4	1	0	1	2	2	.308
B. Brown, 3b	12	4	1	1	0	2	1	.333
B. Johnson, 3b	6	0	0	0	0	0	0	.000
C. Mapes, of	4	0	0	0	0	0	0	.000
V. Raschi, p	3	1	0	0	0	0	0	.333
A. Reynolds, p	3	1	0	0	0	0	0	.333
W. Ford, p	3	0	0	0	0	0	0	.000
E. Lopat, p	2	1	0	0	0	0	0	.500
J. Hopp, 1b	2	0	0	0	0	0	0	.000
J. Collins, 1b	0	0	0	0	0	0	0	—
J. Jensen	0	0	0	0	0	0	0	—

Errors: B. Brown, G. Woodling
Stolen Bases: P. Rizzuto

PHILADELPHIA (N.L.)

	AB	H	2B	3B	HR	R	RBI	BA
R. Ashburn, of	17	3	1	0	0	0	1	.176
D. Sisler, of	17	1	0	0	0	0	1	.059
E. Waitkus, 1b	15	4	1	0	0	0	0	.267
G. Hamner, ss	14	6	2	1	0	1	0	.429
W. Jones, 3b	14	4	1	0	0	1	0	.286
M. Goliat, 2b	14	3	0	0	0	1	1	.214
D. Ennis, of	14	2	1	0	0	1	0	.143
A. Seminick, c	11	2	0	0	0	0	0	.182
J. Konstanty, p	4	1	0	0	0	0	0	.250
K. Heintzelman, p	2	0	0	0	0	0	0	.000
R. Roberts, p	2	0	0	0	0	0	0	.000
D. Whitman	2	0	0	0	0	0	0	.000
P. Caballero	1	0	0	0	0	0	0	.000
S. Lopata, c	1	0	0	0	0	0	0	.000
J. Bloodworth, 2b	0	0	0	0	0	0	0	—
K. Johnson	0	0	0	0	0	1	0	—
J. Mayo, of	0	0	0	0	0	0	0	—
K. Silvestri, c	0	0	0	0	0	0	0	—

Errors: M. Goliat, G. Hamner, W. Jones, A. Seminick
Stolen Bases: G. Hamner

Individual Pitching

NEW YORK (A.L.)

	W	L	ERA	IP	H	BB	SO	SV
A. Reynolds	1	0	0.87	10.1	7	4	7	1
V. Raschi	1	0	0.00	9	2	1	5	0
W. Ford	1	0	0.00	8.2	7	1	7	0
E. Lopat	0	0	2.25	8	9	0	5	0
T. Ferrick	1	0	0.00	1	1	1	0	0

PHILADELPHIA (N.L.)

	W	L	ERA	IP	H	BB	SO	SV
J. Konstanty	0	1	2.40	15	9	4	3	0
R. Roberts	0	1	1.64	11	11	3	5	0
K. Heintzelman	0	0	1.17	7.2	4	6	3	0
R. Meyer	0	1	5.40	1.2	4	0	1	0
B. Miller	0	1	27.00	0.1	2	0	0	0

1951 WORLD SERIES

LINE SCORES			R	H	E	PITCHERS (innings pitched)	HOME RUNS (men on)	HIGHLIGHTS

New York (A.L.) defeats New York (N.L.) 4 games to 2

LINE SCORES			R	H	E	PITCHERS (innings pitched)	HOME RUNS (men on)	HIGHLIGHTS
GAME 1 - OCTOBER 4								Irvin's four hits and steal of home paced the Giant attack as surprise starter Koslo went the distance.
NY	**N**	200 003 000	5	10	1	**Koslo** (9)	Dark (2 on)	
NY	**A**	010 000 000	1	7	1	**Reynolds** (6), Hogue (1), Morgan (2)		
GAME 2 - OCTOBER 5								Irvin hit safely three times but the Giants had only two more hits off Lopat. Collins contributed a home run to the Yankee cause.
NY	**N**	000 000 100	1	5	1	**Jansen** (6), Spencer (2)		
NY	**A**	110 000 01x	3	6	0	**Lopat** (9)	Collins	
GAME 3 - OCTOBER 6								Stanky kicked the ball out of Rizzuto's glove on a steal attempt, setting up the Giants' explosion in the fifth, capped by Lockman's three-run homer.
NY	**A**	000 000 011	2	5	2	**Raschi** (4.1), Hogue (1.2), Ostrowski (2)	Woodling	
NY	**N**	010 050 00x	6	7	2	**Hearn** (7.2), Jones (1.1) **SV**	Lockman (2 on)	
GAME 4 - OCTOBER 8								DiMaggio, hitless in the first three games, paced the Yankee attack with a single and a two-run homer.
NY	**A**	010 120 200	6	12	0	**Reynolds** (9)	DiMaggio (1 on)	
NY	**N**	100 000 001	2	8	2	**Maglie** (5), Jones (3), Kennedy (1)		
GAME 5 - OCTOBER 9								The Yankees took the lead in the Series for the first time as McDougald's grand slam in the third started a rout.
NY	**A**	005 202 400	13	12	1	**Lopat** (9)	McDougald (3 on), Rizzuto (1 on)	
NY	**N**	100 000 000	1	5	3	**Jansen** (3), Kennedy (2), Spencer (1.1), Corwin (1.2), Konikowski (1)		
GAME 6 - OCTOBER 10								Bauer's three-run triple in the sixth led the Yankees to victory.
NY	**N**	000 010 002	3	11	1	**Koslo** (6), Hearn (1), Jansen (1)		
NY	**A**	100 003 00x	4	7	0	**Raschi** (6), Sain (2), Kuzava (1) **SV**		

Team totals

		W	AB	H	2B	3B	HR	R	RBI	BA	BB	SO	ERA
NY	**A**	4	199	49	7	2	5	29	25	.246	26	23	1.87
NY	**N**	2	194	46	7	1	2	18	15	.237	25	22	4.67

Individual Batting

NEW YORK (A.L.)

	AB	H	2B	3B	HR	R	RBI	BA
P. Rizzuto, ss	25	8	0	0	1	5	3	.320
Y. Berra, c	23	6	1	0	0	4	0	.261
J. DiMaggio, of	23	6	2	0	1	3	5	.261
G. McDougald, 2b, 3b	23	6	1	0	1	2	7	.261
J. Collins, 1b, of	18	4	0	0	1	2	3	.222
H. Bauer, of	18	3	0	1	0	0	3	.167
G. Woodling, of	18	3	1	1	1	6	1	.167
B. Brown, 3b	14	5	1	0	0	1	0	.357
J. Coleman, 2b	8	2	0	0	0	2	0	.250
E. Lopat, p	8	1	0	0	0	0	1	.125
J. Mize, 1b	7	2	1	0	0	2	1	.286
A. Reynolds, p	6	2	0	0	0	0	1	.333
M. Mantle, of	5	1	0	0	0	1	0	.200
V. Raschi, p	2	0	0	0	0	0	0	.000
J. Sain, p	1	0	0	0	0	0	0	.000
J. Hopp	0	0	0	0	0	0	0	—
B. Martin	0	0	0	0	0	1	0	—

Errors: Y. Berra, G. McDougald, P. Rizzuto, G. Woodling

NEW YORK (N.L.)

	AB	H	2B	3B	HR	R	RBI	BA
W. Lockman, 1b	25	6	2	0	1	1	4	.240
M. Irvin, of	24	11	0	1	0	4	2	.458
A. Dark, ss	24	10	3	0	1	5	4	.417
W. Mays, of	22	4	0	0	0	1	1	.182
E. Stanky, 2b	22	3	0	0	0	3	1	.136
B. Thomson, 3b	21	5	1	0	0	1	2	.238
W. Westrum, c	17	4	1	0	0	1	0	.235
H. Thompson, of	14	2	0	0	0	2	0	.143
D. Koslo, p	5	0	0	0	0	0	0	.000
B. Rigney	4	1	0	0	0	0	1	.250
C. Hartung, of	4	0	0	0	0	0	0	.000
J. Hearn, p	3	0	0	0	0	0	0	.000
L. Jansen, p	2	0	0	0	0	0	0	.000
L. Lohrke	2	0	0	0	0	0	0	.000
R. Noble, c	2	0	0	0	0	0	0	.000
S. Maglie, p	1	0	0	0	0	0	0	.000
D. Williams	1	0	0	0	0	0	0	.000
S. Yvars	1	0	0	0	0	0	0	.000
H. Schenz	0	0	0	0	0	0	0	—

Errors: W. Lockman (2), H. Thompson (2), B. Thomson (2), C. Hartung, M. Irvin, E. Stanky, W. Westrum

Stolen Bases: M. Irvin (2)

Individual Pitching

NEW YORK (A.L.)

	W	L	ERA	IP	H	BB	SO	SV
E. Lopat	2	0	0.50	18	10	3	4	0
A. Reynolds	1	1	4.20	15	16	11	8	0
V. Raschi	1	1	0.87	10.1	12	8	4	0
B. Hogue	0	0	0.00	2.2	1	0	0	0
T. Morgan	0	0	0.00	2	2	1	3	0
J. Ostrowski	0	0	0.00	2	1	0	1	0
J. Sain	0	0	9.00	2	4	2	2	0
B. Kuzava	0	0	0.00	1	0	0	0	1

NEW YORK (N.L.)

	W	L	ERA	IP	H	BB	SO	SV
D. Koslo	1	1	3.00	15	12	7	6	0
L. Jansen	0	2	6.30	10	8	4	6	0
J. Hearn	1	0	1.04	8.2	5	8	1	0
S. Maglie	0	1	7.20	5	8	2	3	0
S. Jones	0	0	2.08	4.1	5	1	2	1
G. Spencer	0	0	18.90	3.1	6	3	0	0
M. Kennedy	0	0	6.00	3	3	1	4	0
A. Corwin	0	0	0.00	1.2	1	0	1	0
A. Konikowski	0	0	0.00	1	1	0	0	0

1952 WORLD SERIES

New York (A.L.) defeats Brooklyn (N.L.) 4 games to 3

LINE SCORES			R	H	E	PITCHERS (innings pitched)	HOME RUNS (men on)	HIGHLIGHTS
GAME 1 - OCTOBER 1								Snider's two-run homer in the sixth gave the Dodgers a lead they never relinquished.
NY	**A**	001 000 010	2	6	2	**Reynolds** (7), Scarborough (1)	McDougald	
BKN	**N**	010 002 01x	4	6	0	**Black** (9)	Robinson, Snider (1 on), Reese	
GAME 2 - OCTOBER 2								Martin's double, homer, and four RBIs led the Yankee attack. Brooklyn got all three of their hits in the third.
NY	**A**	000 115 000	7	10	0	**Raschi** (9)	Martin (2 on)	
BKN	**N**	001 000 000	1	3	1	**Erskine** (5), Loes (2), Lehman (2)		
GAME 3 - OCTOBER 3								A passed ball by Berra let in two runs in the ninth. Mize's pinch-hit homer in the bottom of the frame went for naught.
BKN	**N**	001 010 012	5	11	0	**Roe** (9)		
NY	**A**	010 000 011	3	6	2	**Lopat** (8.1), Gorman (0.2)	Berra, Mize	
GAME 4 - OCTOBER 4								Reynolds allowed four singles and struck out ten as the Yankees scored on Mize's homer in the fourth, and Mantle's triple and Reese's error in the eighth.
BKN	**N**	000 000 000	0	4	1	**Black** (7), Rutherford (1)		
NY	**A**	000 100 01x	2	4	1	**Reynolds** (9)	Mize	
GAME 5 - OCTOBER 5								Erskine retired the last 19 batters after the Yankees scored five runs in the fifth. Snider's single drove in the winning run in the eleventh.
BKN	**N**	010 030 100 01	6	10	0	**Erskine** (11)	Snider (1 on)	
NY	**A**	000 050 000 00	5	5	1	Blackwell (5), **Sain** (6)	Mize (2 on)	
GAME 6 - OCTOBER 6								Berra's homer, Woodling's single, a balk by Loes, and Raschi's ground single off Loes's knee gave the Yanks the lead in the seventh, and Mantle's homer in the eighth insured the victory.
NY	**A**	000 000 210	3	9	0	**Raschi** (7.2), Reynolds (1.1) **SV**	Berra, Mantle	
BKN	**N**	000 001 010	2	8	1	**Loes** (8.1), Roe (0.2)	Snider, Snider	
GAME 7 - OCTOBER 7								The Yankees went ahead on Mantle's homer in the sixth and Kuzava saved the victory by retiring the last eight batters.
NY	**A**	000 111 100	4	10	4	Lopat (3), **Reynolds** (3), Raschi (0.1), Kuzava (2.2) **SV**	Woodling, Mantle	
BKN	**N**	000 110 000	2	8	1	**Black** (5.1), Roe (1.2), Erskine (2)		

Team totals

		W	AB	H	2B	3B	HR	R	RBI	BA	BB	SO	ERA
NY	**A**	4	232	50	5	2	10	26	24	.216	31	32	2.81
BKN	**N**	3	233	50	7	0	6	20	18	.215	24	49	3.52

Individual Batting

NEW YORK (A.L.)

	AB	H	2B	3B	HR	R	RBI	BA
M. Mantle, of	29	10	1	1	2	5	3	.345
Y. Berra, c	28	6	1	0	2	2	3	.214
P. Rizzuto, ss	27	4	1	0	0	2	0	.148
G. McDougald, 3b	25	5	0	0	1	5	3	.200
G. Woodling, of	23	8	1	1	1	4	1	.348
B. Martin, 2b	23	5	0	0	1	2	4	.217
H. Bauer, of	18	1	0	0	0	2	1	.056
J. Mize, 1b	15	6	1	0	3	3	6	.400
J. Collins, 1b	12	0	0	0	0	1	0	.000
I. Noren, of	10	3	0	0	0	0	1	.300
A. Reynolds, p	7	0	0	0	0	0	0	.000
V. Raschi, p	6	1	0	0	0	0	1	.167
E. Lopat, p	3	1	0	0	0	0	1	.333
J. Sain, p	3	0	0	0	0	0	0	.000
E. Blackwell, p	1	0	0	0	0	0	0	.000
R. Houk	1	0	0	0	0	0	0	.000
B. Kuzava, p	1	0	0	0	0	0	0	.000

Errors: G. McDougald (4), A. Reynolds (2), Y. Berra, B. Martin, P. Rizzuto, G. Woodling
Stolen Bases: G. McDougald

BROOKLYN (N.L.)

	AB	H	2B	3B	HR	R	RBI	BA
P. Reese, ss	29	10	0	0	1	4	4	.345
D. Snider, of	29	10	2	0	4	5	8	.345
R. Campanella, c	28	6	0	0	0	0	1	.214
B. Cox, 3b	27	8	2	0	0	4	0	.296
C. Furillo, of	23	4	2	0	0	1	0	.174
J. Robinson, 2b	23	4	0	0	1	4	2	.174
A. Pafko, of	21	4	0	0	0	0	2	.190
G. Hodges, 1b	21	0	0	0	0	1	1	.000
G. Shuba, of	10	3	1	0	0	0	0	.300
J. Black, p	6	0	0	0	0	0	0	.000
C. Erskine, p	6	0	0	0	0	1	0	.000
B. Loes, p	3	1	0	0	0	0	0	.333
R. Nelson	3	0	0	0	0	0	0	.000
P. Roe, p	2	0	0	0	0	0	0	.000
T. Holmes, of	1	0	0	0	0	0	0	.000
B. Morgan, 3b	1	0	0	0	0	0	0	.000
S. Amoros	0	0	0	0	0	0	0	—

Errors: P. Reese (2), B. Cox, G. Hodges
Stolen Bases: J. Robinson (2), B. Loes, P. Reese, D. Snider

Individual Pitching

NEW YORK (A.L.)

	W	L	ERA	IP	H	BB	SO	SV
A. Reynolds	2	1	1.77	20.1	12	6	18	1
V. Raschi	2	0	1.59	17	12	8	18	0
E. Lopat	0	1	4.76	11.1	14	4	3	0
J. Sain	0	1	3.00	6	6	3	3	0
E. Blackwell	0	0	7.20	5	4	3	4	0
B. Kuzava	0	0	0.00	2.2	0	0	2	1
R. Scarborough	0	0	9.00	1	1	0	1	0
T. Gorman	0	0	0.00	0.2	1	0	0	0

BROOKLYN (N.L.)

	W	L	ERA	IP	H	BB	SO	SV
J. Black	1	2	2.53	21.1	15	8	9	0
C. Erskine	1	1	4.50	18	12	10	10	0
P. Roe	1	0	3.18	11.1	9	6	7	0
B. Loes	0	1	4.35	10.1	11	5	5	0
K. Lehman	0	0	0.00	2	2	1	0	0
J. Rutherford	0	0	9.00	1	1	1	1	0

1953 WORLD SERIES

New York (A.L.) defeats Brooklyn (N.L.) 4 games to 2

LINE SCORES			R	H	E	PITCHERS (innings pitched)	HOME RUNS (men on)	HIGHLIGHTS
GAME 1 - SEPTEMBER 30								Martin's triple with the bases loaded in the first gave the Yankees the lead, and after the Dodgers tied the score in the sixth, Collins's homer in the seventh provided the go-ahead run.
BKN	**N**	000 013 100	5	12	2	Erskine (1), Hughes (4), **Labine** (1.2), Wade (1.1)	Gilliam, Hodges, Shuba (1 on)	
NY	**A**	400 010 13x	9	12	0	Reynolds (5.1), **Sain** (3.2)	Berra, Collins	
GAME 2 - OCTOBER 1								Mantle homered in the eighth to break the deadlock.
BKN	**N**	000 200 000	2	9	1	**Roe** (8)		
NY	**A**	100 000 12x	4	5	0	**Lopat** (9)	Martin, Mantle (1 on)	
GAME 3 - OCTOBER 2								Erskine struck out 14, including Mantle four times in four appearances, to set a new Series record.
NY	**A**	000 010 010	2	6	0	**Raschi** (8)		
BKN	**N**	000 011 01x	3	9	0	**Erskine** (9)	Campanella	
GAME 4 - OCTOBER 3								Snider drove in four runs with two doubles and a homer.
NY	**A**	000 020 001	3	9	0	**Ford** (1), Gorman (3), Sain (2), Schallock (2)	McDougald (1 on)	
BKN	**N**	300 102 10x	7	12	0	**Loes** (8), Labine (1) **SV**	Snider	
GAME 5 - OCTOBER 4								Mantle homered with the bases full after a two-out error by Hodges in the third. A Series record was set as both teams combined for 47 total bases.
NY	**A**	105 000 311	11	11	1	**McDonald** (7.2), Kuzava (0.2), Reynolds (0.2) **SV**	Woodling, Mantle (3 on), Martin (1 on), McDougald	
BKN	**N**	010 010 041	7	14	1	**Podres** (2.2), Meyer (4.1), Wade (1), Black (1)	Cox (2 on), Gilliam	
GAME 6 - OCTOBER 5								Martin's twelfth hit of the Series in the bottom of the ninth scored Bauer for the winning run. The win gave the Yankees their fifth consecutive World Series crown, an all-time record.
BKN	**N**	000 001 002	3	8	3	Erskine (4), Milliken (2), **Labine** (2.1)	Furillo (1 on)	
NY	**A**	210 000 001	4	13	0	Ford (7), **Reynolds** (2)		

Team totals

		W	AB	H	2B	3B	HR	R	RBI	BA	BB	SO	ERA
NY	**A**	4	201	56	6	4	9	33	32	.279	25	43	4.50
BKN	**N**	2	213	64	13	1	8	27	26	.300	15	30	4.91

Individual Batting

NEW YORK (A.L.)

	AB	H	2B	3B	HR	R	RBI	BA
B. Martin, 2b	24	12	1	2	2	5	8	.500
M. Mantle, of	24	5	0	0	2	3	7	.208
J. Collins, 1b	24	4	1	0	1	4	2	.167
G. McDougald, 3b	24	4	0	1	2	2	4	.167
H. Bauer, of	23	6	0	1	0	6	1	.261
Y. Berra, c	21	9	1	0	1	3	4	.429
G. Woodling, of	20	6	0	0	1	5	3	.300
P. Rizzuto, ss	19	6	1	0	0	4	0	.316
W. Ford, p	3	1	0	0	0	0	0	.333
E. Lopat, p	3	0	0	0	0	0	0	.000
J. Mize	3	0	0	0	0	0	0	.000
J. McDonald, p	2	1	1	0	0	0	1	.500
A. Reynolds, p	2	1	0	0	0	0	0	.500
J. Sain, p	2	1	1	0	0	1	2	.500
D. Bollweg, 1b	2	0	0	0	0	0	0	.000
V. Raschi, p	2	0	0	0	0	0	0	.000
T. Gorman, p	1	0	0	0	0	0	0	.000
B. Kuzava, p	1	0	0	0	0	0	0	.000
I. Noren	1	0	0	0	0	0	0	.000

Errors: P. Rizzuto

Stolen Bases: B. Martin, P. Rizzuto

BROOKLYN (N.L.)

	AB	H	2B	3B	HR	R	RBI	BA
J. Gilliam, 2b	27	8	3	0	2	4	4	.296
J. Robinson, of	25	8	2	0	0	3	2	.320
D. Snider, of	25	8	3	0	1	3	5	.320
C. Furillo, of	24	8	2	0	1	4	4	.333
P. Reese, ss	24	5	0	1	0	0	0	.208
B. Cox, 3b	23	7	3	0	1	3	6	.304
G. Hodges, 1b	22	8	0	0	1	3	1	.364
R. Campanella, c	22	6	0	0	1	6	2	.273
C. Erskine, p	4	1	0	0	0	0	0	.250
B. Loes, p	3	2	0	0	0	0	0	.667
P. Roe, p	3	0	0	0	0	0	0	.000
D. Williams	2	1	0	0	0	0	0	.500
W. Belardi	2	0	0	0	0	0	0	.000
C. Labine, p	2	0	0	0	0	0	0	.000
J. Podres, p	1	1	0	0	0	0	0	1.000
G. Shuba	1	1	0	0	1	1	2	1.000
J. Hughes, p	1	0	0	0	0	0	0	.000
R. Meyer, p	1	0	0	0	0	0	0	.000
B. Morgan	1	0	0	0	0	0	0	.000
D. Thompson, of	0	0	0	0	0	0	0	—

Errors: C. Furillo (2), B. Cox, C. Erskine, J. Gilliam, G. Hodges, J. Hughes

Stolen Bases: G. Hodges, J. Robinson

Individual Pitching

NEW YORK (A.L.)

	W	L	ERA	IP	H	BB	SO	SV
E. Lopat	1	0	2.00	9	9	4	3	0
W. Ford	0	1	4.50	8	9	2	7	0
V. Raschi	0	1	3.38	8	9	3	4	0
A. Reynolds	1	0	6.75	8	9	4	9	1
J. McDonald	1	0	5.87	7.2	12	0	3	0
J. Sain	1	0	4.76	5.2	8	1	1	0
T. Gorman	0	0	3.00	3	4	0	1	0
A. Schallock	0	0	4.50	2	2	1	1	0
B. Kuzava	0	0	13.50	0.2	2	0	1	0

BROOKLYN (N.L.)

	W	L	ERA	IP	H	BB	SO	SV
C. Erskine	1	0	5.79	14	14	9	16	0
B. Loes	1	0	3.38	8	8	2	8	0
P. Roe	0	1	4.50	8	5	4	4	0
C. Labine	0	2	3.60	5	10	1	3	1
R. Meyer	0	0	6.23	4.1	8	4	5	0
J. Hughes	0	0	2.25	4	3	1	3	0
J. Podres	0	1	3.38	2.2	1	2	0	0
B. Wade	0	0	15.43	2.1	4	1	2	0
B. Milliken	0	0	0.00	2	2	1	0	0
J. Black	0	0	9.00	1	1	0	2	0

1954 WORLD SERIES

LINE SCORES						PITCHERS (innings pitched)	HOME RUNS (men on)	HIGHLIGHTS

New York (N.L.) defeats Cleveland (A.L.) 4 games to 0

						PITCHERS (innings pitched)	HOME RUNS (men on)	HIGHLIGHTS
GAME 1 - SEPTEMBER 29								With the score tied 2-2, Mays made a back-to-the-plate catch of Wertz's 440-foot fly with two men on in the eighth to preserve the tie until the tenth, when Rhodes delivered a pinch homer with two on to win the game.
CLE	**A**	200 000 000 0	2	8	0	**Lemon** (9.1)		
NY	**N**	002 000 000 3	5	9	3	Maglie (7), Liddle (0.1), **Grissom** (2.2)	Rhodes (2 on)	
GAME 2 - SEPTEMBER 30								Rhodes again proved the big gun with a pinch-hit single in the fifth that tied the game and a home run in the seventh that provided an insurance run. The Indians' early lead came on Smith's home run off Antonelli's first pitch.
CLE	**A**	100 000 000	1	8	0	**Wynn** (7), Mossi (1)	Smith	
NY	**N**	000 020 10x	3	4	0	**Antonelli** (9)	Rhodes	
GAME 3 - OCTOBER 1								Rhodes pinch-hit for Irvin in the third with the bases loaded and singled to drive in two runs, giving the Giants a 3-0 lead. The Indians broke through in the seventh and knocked Gomez out in the eighth as he faltered behind uneven fielding. Wilhelm relieved and checked the Indians, retiring the last five batters in a row.
NY	**N**	103 011 000	6	10	1	**Gomez** (7.1), Wilhelm (1.2) **SV**		
CLE	**A**	000 000 110	2	4	2	**Garcia** (3), Houtteman (2), Narleski (3), Mossi (1)	Wertz	
GAME 4 - OCTOBER 2								Rhodes rested as the Giants jumped out to a 7-0 lead to nail down the first National League Series victory since 1946. The Indian pitching staff was the disappointment of the Series as they allowed 21 runs in four games after going through the regular season with a 2.78 ERA.
NY	**N**	021 040 000	7	10	3	**Liddle** (6.2), Wilhelm (0.2), Antonelli (1.2) **SV**		
CLE	**A**	000 030 100	4	6	2	**Lemon** (4), Newhouser (0), Narleski (1), Mossi (2), Garcia (2)	Majeski (2 on)	

Team totals

		W	AB	H	2B	3B	HR	R	RBI	BA	BB	SO	ERA
NY	**N**	4	130	33	3	0	2	21	20	.254	17	24	1.46
CLE	**A**	0	137	26	5	1	3	9	9	.190	16	23	4.84

Individual Batting

NEW YORK (N.L.)

	AB	H	2B	3B	HR	R	RBI	BA
D. Mueller, of	18	7	0	0	0	4	1	.389
W. Lockman, 1b	18	2	0	0	0	2	0	.111
A. Dark, ss	17	7	0	0	0	2	0	.412
W. Mays, of	14	4	1	0	0	4	3	.286
H. Thompson, 3b	11	4	1	0	0	6	2	.364
W. Westrum, c	11	3	0	0	0	0	3	.273
D. Williams, 2b	11	0	0	0	0	0	1	.000
M. Irvin, of	9	2	1	0	0	1	2	.222
D. Rhodes, of	6	4	0	0	2	2	7	.667
R. Gomez, p	4	0	0	0	0	0	0	.000
J. Antonelli, p	3	0	0	0	0	0	1	.000
D. Liddle, p	3	0	0	0	0	0	0	.000
S. Maglie, p	3	0	0	0	0	0	0	.000
M. Grissom, p	1	0	0	0	0	0	0	.000
H. Wilhelm, p	1	0	0	0	0	0	0	.000

Errors: D. Mueller (2), A. Dark, M. Irvin, D. Liddle, H. Wilhelm, D. Williams

Stolen Bases: W. Mays

CLEVELAND (A.L.)

	AB	H	2B	3B	HR	R	RBI	BA
V. Wertz, 1b	16	8	2	1	1	2	3	.500
L. Doby, of	16	2	0	0	0	0	0	.125
B. Avila, 2b	15	2	0	0	0	1	0	.133
A. Smith, of	14	3	0	0	1	2	2	.214
J. Hegan, c	13	2	1	0	0	1	0	.154
A. Rosen, 3b	12	3	0	0	0	0	0	.250
G. Strickland, ss	9	0	0	0	0	0	0	.000
D. Philley, of	8	1	0	0	0	0	0	.125
W. Westlake, of	7	1	0	0	0	0	0	.143
H. Majeski, 3b	6	1	0	0	1	1	3	.167
B. Lemon, p	6	0	0	0	0	0	0	.000
R. Regalado, 3b	3	1	0	0	0	0	1	.333
S. Dente, ss	3	0	0	0	0	1	0	.000
D. Pope, of	3	0	0	0	0	0	0	.000
B. Glynn, 1b	2	1	1	0	0	1	0	.500
E. Wynn, p	2	1	1	0	0	0	0	.500
D. Mitchell	2	0	0	0	0	0	0	.000
M. Grasso, c	0	0	0	0	0	0	0	—
H. Naragon, c	0	0	0	0	0	0	0	—

Errors: M. Garcia, G. Strickland, V. Wertz, W. Westlake

Individual Pitching

NEW YORK (N.L.)

	W	L	ERA	IP	H	BB	SO	SV
J. Antonelli	1	0	0.84	10.2	8	7	12	1
R. Gomez	1	0	2.45	7.1	4	3	2	0
D. Liddle	1	0	1.29	7	5	1	2	0
S. Maglie	0	0	2.57	7	7	2	2	0
M. Grissom	1	0	0.00	2.2	1	3	2	0
H. Wilhelm	0	0	0.00	2.1	1	0	3	1

CLEVELAND (A.L.)

	W	L	ERA	IP	H	BB	SO	SV
B. Lemon	0	2	6.75	13.1	16	8	11	0
E. Wynn	0	1	3.86	7	4	2	5	0
M. Garcia	0	1	5.40	5	6	4	4	0
D. Mossi	0	0	0.00	4	3	0	1	0
R. Narleski	0	0	2.25	4	1	1	2	0
A. Houtteman	0	0	4.50	2	2	1	1	0
H. Newhouser	0	0	∞	0.0	1	1	0	0

1955 WORLD SERIES

LINE SCORES			R	H	E	PITCHERS (innings pitched)	HOME RUNS (men on)	HIGHLIGHTS

Brooklyn (N.L.) defeats New York (A.L.) 4 games to 3

LINE SCORES			R	H	E	PITCHERS (innings pitched)	HOME RUNS (men on)	HIGHLIGHTS
GAME 1 - SEPTEMBER 28								Collins's two-run homer in the sixth put the Yankees ahead 6-3. Robinson stole home in the eighth to bring the Dodgers within one run of a tie.
BKN	**N**	021 000 020	5	10	0	**Newcombe** (5.2), Bessent (1.1), Labine (1)	Furillo, Snider	
NY	**A**	021 102 00x	6	9	1	**Ford** (8), Grim (1) **SV**	Howard (1 on), Collins, Collins (1 on)	
GAME 2 - SEPTEMBER 29								Byrne capped a four-run fourth-inning with a two-run single and became the first lefty to pitch a complete game victory over the Dodgers in 1955.
BKN	**N**	000 110 000	2	5	2	**Loes** (3.2), Bessent (0.1), Spooner (3), Labine (1)		
NY	**A**	000 400 00x	4	8	0	**Byrne** (9)		
GAME 3 - SEPTEMBER 30								Campanella led the Dodger attack with three hits and three RBIs.
NY	**A**	020 000 100	3	7	0	**Turley** (1.1), Morgan (2.2), Kucks (2), Sturdivant (2)	Mantle	
BKN	**N**	220 200 20x	8	11	1	**Podres** (9)	Campanella (1 on)	
GAME 4 - OCTOBER 1								Homers by Campanella and Hodges gave the Dodgers a 4-3 lead in the fourth and Snider's three-run homer in the fifth insured the victory.
NY	**A**	110 102 000	5	9	0	**Larsen** (4), Kucks (1), Coleman (1), Morgan (1), Sturdivant (1)	McDougald	
BKN	**N**	001 330 10x	8	14	0	Erskine (3), Bessent (1.2), **Labine** (4.1)	Campanella, Hodges (1 on), Snider (2 on)	
GAME 5 - OCTOBER 2								Three homers off Grim in the first five innings (two by Snider) paced the Dodger victory.
NY	**A**	000 100 110	3	6	0	**Grim** (6), Turley (2)	Cerv, Berra	
BKN	**N**	021 010 01x	5	9	2	**Craig** (6), Labine (3) **SV**	Amoros (1 on), Snider, Snider	
GAME 6 - OCTOBER 3								The Yankees knocked out Spooner with five runs in the first on two walks, singles by Berra and Bauer, and Skowron's homer.
BKN	**N**	000 100 000	1	4	1	**Spooner** (0.1), Meyer (5.2), Roebuck (2)		
NY	**A**	500 000 00x	5	8	0	**Ford** (9)	Skowron (2 on)	
GAME 7 - OCTOBER 4								The Dodgers won their first Series on Podres's shutout and two RBIs by Hodges. Amoros saved the game in the sixth with a spectacular running catch of Berra's fly down the left field line.
BKN	**N**	000 101 000	2	5	0	**Podres** (9)		
NY	**A**	000 000 000	0	8	1	**Byrne** (5.1), Grim (1.2), Turley (2)		

Team totals

		W	AB	H	2B	3B	HR	R	RBI	BA	BB	SO	ERA
BKN	**N**	4	223	58	8	1	9	31	30	.260	33	38	3.75
NY	**A**	3	222	55	4	2	8	26	25	.248	22	39	4.20

Individual Batting

BROOKLYN (N.L.)

	AB	H	2B	3B	HR	R	RBI	BA
C. Furillo, of	27	8	1	0	1	4	3	.296
P. Reese, ss	27	8	1	0	0	5	2	.296
R. Campanella, c	27	7	3	0	2	4	4	.259
D. Snider, of	25	8	1	0	4	5	7	.320
J. Gilliam, 2b, of	24	7	1	0	0	2	3	.292
G. Hodges, 1b	24	7	0	0	1	2	5	.292
J. Robinson, 3b	22	4	1	1	0	5	1	.182
S. Amoros, of	12	4	0	0	1	3	3	.333
D. Zimmer, 2b	9	2	0	0	0	0	2	.222
J. Podres, p	7	1	0	0	0	1	0	.143
C. Labine, p	4	0	0	0	0	0	0	.000
D. Hoak, 3b	3	1	0	0	0	0	0	.333
F. Kellert	3	1	0	0	0	0	0	.333
D. Newcombe, p	3	0	0	0	0	0	0	.000
R. Meyer, p	2	0	0	0	0	0	0	.000
D. Bessent, p	1	0	0	0	0	0	0	.000
C. Erskine, p	1	0	0	0	0	0	0	.000
B. Loes, p	1	0	0	0	0	0	0	.000
G. Shuba	1	0	0	0	0	0	0	.000

Errors: J. Robinson (2), D. Zimmer (2), R. Campanella, P. Reese
Stolen Bases: J. Gilliam, J. Robinson

NEW YORK (A.L.)

	AB	H	2B	3B	HR	R	RBI	BA
G. McDougald, 3b	27	7	0	0	1	2	1	.259
E. Howard, of	26	5	0	0	1	3	3	.192
B. Martin, 2b	25	8	1	1	0	2	4	.320
Y. Berra, c	24	10	1	0	1	5	2	.417
B. Cerv, of	16	2	0	0	1	1	1	.125
I. Noren, of	16	1	0	0	0	0	1	.063
P. Rizzuto, ss	15	4	0	0	0	2	1	.267
H. Bauer, of	14	6	0	0	0	1	1	.429
B. Skowron, 1b	12	4	2	0	1	2	3	.333
J. Collins, 1b, of	12	2	0	0	2	6	3	.167
M. Mantle, of	10	2	0	0	1	1	1	.200
T. Byrne, p	6	1	0	0	0	0	2	.167
W. Ford, p	6	0	0	0	0	1	0	.000
E. Robinson, 1b	3	2	0	0	0	0	1	.667
J. Coleman, ss	3	0	0	0	0	0	0	.000
A. Carey	2	1	0	1	0	0	1	.500
B. Grim, p	2	0	0	0	0	0	0	.000
D. Larsen, p	2	0	0	0	0	0	0	.000
B. Turley, p	1	0	0	0	0	0	0	.000
T. Carroll	0	0	0	0	0	0	0	—

Errors: G. McDougald, B. Skowron
Stolen Bases: P. Rizzuto (2), J. Collins

Individual Pitching

BROOKLYN (N.L.)

	W	L	ERA	IP	H	BB	SO	SV
J. Podres	2	0	1.00	18	15	4	10	0
C. Labine	1	0	2.89	9.1	6	2	2	1
R. Craig	1	0	3.00	6	4	5	4	0
R. Meyer	0	0	0.00	5.2	4	2	4	0
D. Newcombe	0	1	9.53	5.2	8	2	4	0
B. Loes	0	1	9.82	3.2	7	1	5	0
D. Bessent	0	0	0.00	3.1	3	1	1	0
K. Spooner	0	1	13.50	3.1	4	3	6	0
C. Erskine	0	0	9.00	3	3	2	3	0
E. Roebuck	0	0	0.00	2	1	0	0	0

NEW YORK (A.L.)

	W	L	ERA	IP	H	BB	SO	SV
W. Ford	2	0	2.12	17	13	8	10	0
T. Byrne	1	1	1.88	14.1	8	8	8	0
B. Grim	0	1	4.15	8.2	8	5	8	1
B. Turley	0	1	8.44	5.1	7	4	7	0
D. Larsen	0	1	11.25	4	5	2	2	0
T. Morgan	0	0	4.91	3.2	3	3	1	0
J. Kucks	0	0	6.00	3	4	1	1	0
T. Sturdivant	0	0	6.00	3	5	2	0	0
R. Coleman	0	0	9.00	1	5	0	1	0

1956 WORLD SERIES

New York (A.L.) defeats Brooklyn (N.L.) 4 games to 3

LINE SCORES						PITCHERS (innings pitched)	HOME RUNS (men on)	HIGHLIGHTS
GAME 1 - OCTOBER 3								Hodges' three-run homer in the third broke a 2-2 deadlock.
NY	**A**	200 100 000	3	9	1	**Ford** (3), Kucks (2), Morgan (2), Turley (1)	Mantle (1 on), Martin	
BKN	**N**	023 100 00x	6	9	0	**Maglie** (9)	Robinson, Hodges (2 on)	
GAME 2 - OCTOBER 5								The Yankees used seven pitchers to set a Series record as the Dodgers won the slugfest in the longest nine-inning game in Series history (3 hours, 26 minutes).
NY	**A**	150 100 001	8	12	2	Larsen (1.2), Kucks (0), Byrne (0.1), Sturdivant (0.2), **Morgan** (2), Turley (0.1), McDermott (3)	Berra (3 on)	
BKN	**N**	061 220 02x	13	12	0	Newcombe (1.2), Roebuck (0.1), **Bessent** (7)	Snider (2 on)	
GAME 3 - OCTOBER 6								Slaughter's three-run homer in the sixth put the Yankees ahead to stay.
BKN	**N**	010 001 100	3	8	1	**Craig** (6), Labine (2)		
NY	**A**	010 003 01x	5	8	1	**Ford** (9)	Martin, Slaughter (2 on)	
GAME 4 - OCTOBER 7								Martin's single in the fourth scored the go-ahead run, and homers by Mantle in the sixth and Bauer in the seventh iced the game.
BKN	**N**	000 100 001	2	6	0	**Erskine** (4), Roebuck (2), Drysdale (2)		
NY	**A**	100 201 20x	6	7	2	**Sturdivant** (9)	Mantle, Bauer (1 on)	
GAME 5 - OCTOBER 8								Larsen threw 97 pitches in hurling a perfect game for the first World Series no-hitter.
BKN	**N**	000 000 000	0	0	0	**Maglie** (8)		
NY	**A**	000 101 00x	2	5	0	**Larsen** (9)	Mantle	
GAME 6 - OCTOBER 9								Robinson singled in the winning run in the tenth on a fly ball misjudged by Slaughter.
NY	**A**	000 000 000 0	0	7	0	**Turley** (9.2)		
BKN	**N**	000 000 000 1	1	4	0	**Labine** (10)		
GAME 7 - OCTOBER 10								Kucks allowed three hits and Skowron hit a grand-slam homer to give the Yankees the Series victory.
NY	**A**	202 100 400	9	10	0	**Kucks** (9)	Berra (1 on), Berra (1 on), Howard, Skowron (3 on)	
BKN	**N**	000 000 000	0	3	1	**Newcombe** (3), Bessent (3), Craig (0), Roebuck (2), Erskine (1)		

Team totals

		W	AB	H	2B	3B	HR	R	RBI	BA	BB	SO	ERA
NY	**A**	4	229	58	6	0	12	33	33	.253	21	43	2.48
BKN	**N**	3	215	42	8	1	3	25	24	.195	32	47	4.72

Individual Batting

NEW YORK (A.L.)

	AB	H	2B	3B	HR	R	RBI	BA
H. Bauer, of	32	9	0	0	1	3	3	.281
B. Martin, 2b, 3b	27	8	0	0	2	5	3	.296
Y. Berra, c	25	9	2	0	3	5	10	.360
M. Mantle, of	24	6	1	0	3	6	4	.250
J. Collins, 1b	21	5	2	0	0	2	2	.238
G. McDougald, ss	21	3	0	0	0	0	1	.143
E. Slaughter, of	20	7	0	0	1	6	4	.350
A. Carey, 3b	19	3	0	0	0	2	0	.158
B. Skowron, 1b	10	1	0	0	1	1	4	.100
E. Howard, of	5	2	1	0	1	1	1	.400
W. Ford, p	4	0	0	0	0	0	0	.000
B. Turley, p	4	0	0	0	0	0	0	.000
D. Larsen, p	3	1	0	0	0	1	1	.333
T. Sturdivant, p	3	1	0	0	0	0	0	.333
J. Kucks, p	3	0	0	0	0	0	0	.000
J. Coleman, 2b	2	0	0	0	0	0	0	.000
B. Cerv	1	1	0	0	0	0	0	1.000
M. McDermott, p	1	1	0	0	0	0	0	1.000
T. Morgan, p	1	1	0	0	0	1	0	1.000
T. Byrne, p	1	0	0	0	0	0	0	.000
N. Siebern	1	0	0	0	0	0	0	.000
T. Wilson	1	0	0	0	0	0	0	.000

Errors: A. Carey (2), J. Collins (2), H. Bauer, B. Skowron

Stolen Bases: H. Bauer, M. Mantle

BROOKLYN (N.L.)

	AB	H	2B	3B	HR	R	RBI	BA
P. Reese, ss	27	6	0	1	0	3	2	.222
C. Furillo, of	25	6	2	0	0	2	1	.240
J. Robinson, 3b	24	6	1	0	1	5	2	.250
J. Gilliam, 2b, of	24	2	0	0	0	2	2	.083
G. Hodges, 1b	23	7	2	0	1	5	8	.304
D. Snider, of	23	7	1	0	1	5	4	.304
R. Campanella, c	22	4	1	0	0	2	3	.182
S. Amoros, of	19	1	0	0	0	1	1	.053
S. Maglie, p	5	0	0	0	0	0	0	.000
C. Labine, p	4	1	1	0	0	0	0	.250
D. Mitchell	4	0	0	0	0	0	0	.000
C.'Neal, 2b	4	0	0	0	0	0	0	.000
R. Jackson	3	0	0	0	0	0	0	.000
D. Bessent, p	2	1	0	0	0	0	1	.500
R. Craig, p	2	1	0	0	0	0	0	.500
R. Walker	2	0	0	0	0	0	0	.000
C. Erskine, p	1	0	0	0	0	0	0	.000
D. Newcombe, p	1	0	0	0	0	0	0	.000
G. Cimoli, of	0	0	0	0	0	0	0	—

Errors: C. Neal, P. Reese

Stolen Bases: J. Gilliam

Individual Pitching

NEW YORK (A.L.)

	W	L	ERA	IP	H	BB	SO	SV
W. Ford	1	1	5.25	12	14	2	8	0
J. Kucks	1	0	0.82	11	6	3	2	0
B. Turley	0	1	0.82	11	4	8	14	0
D. Larsen	1	0	0.00	10.2	1	4	7	0
T. Sturdivant	1	0	2.79	9.2	8	8	9	0
T. Morgan	0	1	9.00	4	6	4	3	0
M. McDermott	0	0	3.00	3	2	3	3	0
T. Byrne	0	0	0.00	0.1	1	0	1	0

BROOKLYN (N.L.)

	W	L	ERA	IP	H	BB	SO	SV
S. Maglie	1	1	2.65	17	14	6	15	0
C. Labine	1	0	0.00	12	8	3	7	0
D. Bessent	1	0	1.80	10	8	3	5	0
R. Craig	0	1	12.00	6	10	3	4	0
C. Erskine	0	1	5.40	5	4	2	2	0
D. Newcombe	0	1	21.21	4.2	11	3	4	0
E. Roebuck	0	0	2.08	4.1	1	0	5	0
D. Drysdale	0	0	9.00	2	2	1	1	0

1957 WORLD SERIES

Milwaukee (N.L.) defeats New York (A.L.) 4 games to 3

LINE SCORES						PITCHERS (innings pitched)	HOME RUNS (men on)	HIGHLIGHTS
GAME 1 - OCTOBER 2								Carey knocked out Spahn with a run-scoring single in the sixth and Coleman then squeezed across an insurance run.
MIL	**N**	000 000 100	1	5	0	**Spahn** (5.1), Johnson (0.2), McMahon (2)		
NY	**A**	000 012 00x	3	9	1	**Ford** (9)		
GAME 2 - OCTOBER 3								The Braves broke a 2-2 tie in the fourth on three singles and an error by Kubek. Covington's spectacular catch snuffed out a Yankee rally in the second.
MIL	**N**	011 200 000	4	8	0	**Burdette** (9)	Logan	
NY	**A**	011 000 000	2	7	2	**Shantz** (3), Ditmar (4), Grim (2)	Bauer	
GAME 3 - OCTOBER 5								The Yankees capitalized on 11 walks allowed by six Brave pitchers with Kubek leading the attack with two homers and four RBIs.
NY	**A**	302 200 500	12	9	0	Turley (1.2), **Larsen** (7.1)	Kubek, Mantle (1 on), Kubek (2 on)	
MIL	**N**	010 020 000	3	8	1	**Buhl** (0.2), Pizarro (1.2), Conley (1.2), Johnson (2), Trowbridge (1), McMahon (2)	Aaron (1 on)	
GAME 4 - OCTOBER 6								The Yankees, down 4-1 with two out in the ninth, tied the game on Howard's homer and went ahead in the tenth on Kubek's single and Bauer's triple. In the bottom of the tenth, Jones was ruled hit by a pitch after a long argument, Logan doubled to tie, and Mathews homered to win.
NY	**A**	100 000 003 1	5	11	0	Sturdivant (4), Shantz (3), Kucks (0.2), Byrne (1.1), **Grim** (0.1),	Howard (2 on)	
MIL	**N**	000 400 000 3	7	7	0	**Spahn** (10)	Aaron (2 on), Torre, Mathews (1 on)	
GAME 5 - OCTOBER 7								Adcock's single in the sixth drove in the only run after Covington's catch robbed McDougald of a possible home run in the fourth.
NY	**A**	000 000 000	0	7	0	**Ford** (7), Turley (1)		
MIL	**N**	000 001 00x	1	6	1	**Burdette** (9)		
GAME 6 - OCTOBER 9								Aaron's homer in the top of the seventh tied the score at 2-2, but Bauer homered in the bottom of the inning for the decisive run.
MIL	**N**	000 010 100	2	4	0	Buhl (2.2), **Johnson** (4.1), McMahon (1)	Torre, Aaron	
NY	**A**	002 000 10x	3	7	0	**Turley** (9)	Berra (1 on), Bauer	
GAME 7 - OCTOBER 10								Burdette won his third complete game of the Series and posted his second successive shutout as Kubek's error paved the way for four runs in the third.
MIL	**N**	004 000 010	5	9	1	**Burdette** (9)	Crandall	
NY	**A**	000 000 000	0	7	3	**Larsen** (2.1), Shantz (0.2), Ditmar (2), Sturdivant (2), Byrne (2)		

Team totals

		W	AB	H	2B	3B	HR	R	RBI	BA	BB	SO	ERA
MIL	**N**	4	225	47	6	1	8	23	22	.209	22	40	3.48
NY	**A**	3	230	57	7	1	7	25	25	.248	22	34	2.89

Individual Batting

MILWAUKEE (N.L.)

	AB	H	2B	3B	HR	R	RBI	BA
H. Aaron, of	28	11	0	1	3	5	7	.393
J. Logan, ss	27	5	1	0	1	5	2	.185
W. Covington, of	24	5	1	0	0	1	1	.208
E. Mathews, 3b	22	5	3	0	1	4	4	.227
D. Crandall, c	19	4	0	0	1	1	1	.211
R. Schoendienst, 2b	18	5	1	0	0	0	2	.278
J. Adcock, 1b	15	3	0	0	0	1	2	.200
A. Pafko, of	14	3	0	0	0	1	0	.214
B. Hazle, of	13	2	0	0	0	2	0	.154
F. Torre, 1b	10	3	0	0	2	2	3	.300
F. Mantilla, 2b	10	0	0	0	0	1	0	.000
L. Burdette, p	8	0	0	0	0	0	0	.000
D. Rice, c	6	1	0	0	0	0	0	.167
W. Spahn, p	4	0	0	0	0	0	0	.000
N. Jones	2	0	0	0	0	0	0	.000
C. Sawatski	2	0	0	0	0	0	0	.000
B. Buhl, p	1	0	0	0	0	0	0	.000
E. Johnson, p	1	0	0	0	0	0	0	.000
J. Pizarro, p	1	0	0	0	0	0	0	.000
J. DeMerit	0	0	0	0	0	0	0	—

Errors: J. Adcock, B. Buhl, E. Mathews
Stolen Bases: W. Covington

NEW YORK (A.L.)

	AB	H	2B	3B	HR	R	RBI	BA
H. Bauer, of	31	8	2	1	2	3	6	.258
T. Kubek, 3b, of	28	8	0	0	2	4	4	.286
Y. Berra, c	25	8	1	0	1	5	2	.320
G. McDougald, ss	24	6	0	0	0	3	2	.250
J. Coleman, 2b	22	8	2	0	0	2	2	.364
M. Mantle, of	19	5	0	0	1	3	2	.263
J. Lumpe, 3b	14	4	0	0	0	0	2	.286
E. Slaughter, of	12	3	1	0	0	2	0	.250
H. Simpson, 1b	12	1	0	0	0	0	1	.083
E. Howard, 1b	11	3	0	0	1	2	3	.273
A. Carey, 3b	7	2	1	0	0	0	1	.286
J. Collins, 1b	5	0	0	0	0	0	0	.000
W. Ford, p	5	0	0	0	0	0	0	.000
B. Skowron, 1b	4	0	0	0	0	0	0	.000
B. Turley, p	4	0	0	0	0	0	0	.000
T. Byrne, p	2	1	0	0	0	0	0	.500
D. Larsen, p	2	0	0	0	0	1	0	.000
A. Ditmar, p	1	0	0	0	0	0	0	.000
B. Shantz, p	1	0	0	0	0	0	0	.000
T. Sturdivant, p	1	0	0	0	0	0	0	.000
B. Richardson, 2b	0	0	0	0	0	0	0	—

Errors: T. Kubek (2), Y. Berra, E. Howard, M. Mantle, G. McDougald
Stolen Bases: G. McDougald

Individual Pitching

MILWAUKEE (N.L.)

	W	L	ERA	IP	H	BB	SO	SV
L. Burdette	3	0	0.67	27	21	4	13	0
W. Spahn	1	1	4.70	15.1	18	2	2	0
E. Johnson	0	1	1.29	7	2	1	8	0
D. McMahon	0	0	0.00	5	3	3	5	0
B. Buhl	0	1	10.80	3.1	6	6	4	0
G. Conley	0	0	10.80	1.2	2	1	0	0
J. Pizarro	0	0	10.80	1.2	3	2	1	0
B. Trowbridge	0	0	45.00	1	2	3	1	0

NEW YORK (A.L.)

	W	L	ERA	IP	H	BB	SO	SV
W. Ford	1	1	1.13	16	11	5	7	0
B. Turley	1	0	2.31	11.2	7	6	12	0
D. Larsen	1	1	3.72	9.2	8	5	6	0
B. Shantz	0	1	4.05	6.2	8	2	7	0
A. Ditmar	0	0	0.00	6	2	0	2	0
T. Sturdivant	0	0	6.00	6	6	1	2	0
T. Byrne	0	0	5.40	3.1	1	2	1	0
B. Grim	0	1	7.71	2.1	3	0	2	0
J. Kucks	0	0	0.00	0.2	1	1	1	0

1958 WORLD SERIES

New York (A.L.) defeats Milwaukee (N.L.) 4 games to 3

LINE SCORES				R	H	E	PITCHERS (innings pitched)	HOME RUNS (men on)	HIGHLIGHTS
GAME 1 - OCTOBER 1									The Braves won in the tenth on singles by Adcock, Crandall, and Bruton.
	NY	**A**	000 120 000 0	3	8	1	Ford (7), **Duren** (2.2)	Skowron, Bauer (1 on)	
	MIL	**N**	000 200 010 1	4	10	0	**Spahn** (10)		
GAME 2 - OCTOBER 2									The Braves battered Turley and Maas for seven runs in the first inning capped by Burdette's homer.
	NY	**A**	100 100 003	5	7	0	**Turley** (0.1), Maas (0.1), Kucks (3.1), Dickson (3), Monroe (1)	Mantle, Bauer, Mantle (1 on)	
	MIL	**N**	710 000 23x	13	15	1	**Burdette** (9)	Bruton, Burdette (2 on)	
GAME 3 - OCTOBER 4									Bauer drove in all the runs on a single following three walks in the fifth, and a two-run homer off McMahon in the seventh.
	MIL	**N**	000 000 000	0	6	0	**Rush** (6), McMahon (2)		
	NY	**A**	000 020 20x	4	4	0	**Larsen** (7), Duren (2) **SV**	Bauer (1 on)	
GAME 4 - OCTOBER 5									Spahn pitched a two-hitter and stopped Bauer's 17-game Series hitting streak. Siebern lost two fly balls in the sun to set up runs for the Braves.
	MIL	**N**	000 001 110	3	9	0	**Spahn** (9)		
	NY	**A**	000 000 000	0	2	1	**Ford** (7), Kucks (1), Dickson (1)		
GAME 5 - OCTOBER 6									The Yankees broke open the game with a six-run seventh after McDougald's homer gave them a 1-0 lead in the third inning.
	MIL	**N**	000 000 000	0	5	0	**Burdette** (5.1), Pizarro (1.2), Willey (1)		
	NY	**A**	001 006 00x	7	10	0	**Turley** (9)	McDougald	
GAME 6 - OCTOBER 8									The Yankees scored twice in the tenth on a homer by McDougald and singles by Howard, Berra, and Skowron. Turley retired Torre with the tying run at third and two out to pick up the save.
	NY	**A**	100 001 000 2	4	10	1	Ford (1), Ditmar (3.2), **Duren** (4.2), Turley (0.1) **SV**	Bauer, McDougald	
	MIL	**N**	110 000 000 1	3	10	4	**Spahn** (9.2), McMahon (0.1)		
GAME 7 - OCTOBER 9									The Yankees became the first team since 1925 to win the Series after being down three games to one as they scored four runs in the eighth after two out on Howard's tie-breaking single and Skowron's homer.
	NY	**A**	020 000 040	6	8	0	Larsen (2.1), **Turley** (6.2)	Skowron (2 on)	
	MIL	**N**	100 001 000	2	5	2	**Burdette** (8), McMahon (1)	Crandall	

Team totals

		W	AB	H	2B	3B	HR	R	RBI	BA	BB	SO	ERA
NY	**A**	4	233	49	5	1	10	29	29	.210	21	42	3.39
MIL	**N**	3	240	60	10	1	3	25	24	.250	27	56	3.71

Individual Batting

NEW YORK (A.L.)

	AB	H	2B	3B	HR	R	RBI	BA
H. Bauer, of	31	10	0	0	4	6	8	.323
G. McDougald, 2b	28	9	2	0	2	5	4	.321
B. Skowron, 1b	27	7	0	0	2	3	7	.259
Y. Berra, c	27	6	3	0	0	3	2	.222
M. Mantle, of	24	6	0	1	2	4	3	.250
T. Kubek, ss	21	1	0	0	0	0	1	.048
E. Howard, of	18	4	0	0	0	4	2	.222
J. Lumpe, 3b, ss	12	2	0	0	0	0	0	.167
A. Carey, 3b	12	1	0	0	0	1	0	.083
N. Siebern, of	8	1	0	0	0	1	0	.125
B. Turley, p	5	1	0	0	0	0	2	.200
B. Richardson, 3b	5	0	0	0	0	0	0	.000
W. Ford, p	4	0	0	0	0	1	0	.000
R. Duren, p	3	0	0	0	0	0	0	.000
E. Slaughter	3	0	0	0	0	1	0	.000
D. Larsen, p	2	0	0	0	0	0	0	.000
J. Kucks, p	1	1	0	0	0	0	0	1.000
A. Ditmar, p	1	0	0	0	0	0	0	.000
M. Throneberry	1	0	0	0	0	0	0	.000

Errors: T. Kubek (2), A. Ditmar

Stolen Bases: E. Howard

MILWAUKEE (N.L.)

	AB	H	2B	3B	HR	R	RBI	BA
R. Schoendienst, 2b	30	9	3	1	0	5	0	.300
H. Aaron, of	27	9	2	0	0	3	2	.333
W. Covington, of	26	7	0	0	0	2	4	.269
D. Crandall, c	25	6	0	0	1	4	3	.240
E. Mathews, 3b	25	4	2	0	0	3	3	.160
J. Logan, ss	25	3	2	0	0	3	2	.120
B. Bruton, of	17	7	0	0	1	2	2	.412
F. Torre, 1b	17	3	0	0	0	0	1	.176
J. Adcock, 1b	13	4	0	0	0	1	0	.308
W. Spahn, p	12	4	0	0	0	0	3	.333
A. Pafko, of	9	3	1	0	0	0	1	.333
L. Burdette, p	9	1	0	0	1	1	3	.111
H. Hanebrink	2	0	0	0	0	0	0	.000
B. Rush, p	2	0	0	0	0	0	0	.000
C. Wise	1	0	0	0	0	0	0	.000
F. Mantilla, ss	0	0	0	0	0	1	0	—

Errors: J. Logan (2), F. Torre (2), B. Bruton, E. Mathews, R. Schoendienst

Stolen Bases: E. Mathews

Individual Pitching

NEW YORK (A.L.)

	W	L	ERA	IP	H	BB	SO	SV
B. Turley	2	1	2.76	16.1	10	7	13	1
W. Ford	0	1	4.11	15.1	19	5	16	0
R. Duren	1	1	1.93	9.1	7	6	14	1
D. Larsen	1	0	0.96	9.1	9	6	9	0
J. Kucks	0	0	2.08	4.1	4	1	0	0
M. Dickson	0	0	4.50	4	4	0	1	0
A. Ditmar	0	0	0.00	3.2	2	0	2	0
Z. Monroe	0	0	27.00	1	3	1	1	0
D. Maas	0	0	81.00	0.1	2	1	0	0

MILWAUKEE (N.L.)

	W	L	ERA	IP	H	BB	SO	SV
W. Spahn	2	1	2.20	28.2	19	8	18	0
L. Burdette	1	2	5.64	22.1	22	4	12	0
B. Rush	0	1	3.00	6	3	5	2	0
D. McMahon	0	0	5.40	3.1	3	3	5	0
J. Pizarro	0	0	5.40	1.2	2	1	3	0
C. Willey	0	0	0.00	1	0	0	2	0

1959 WORLD SERIES

Los Angeles (N.L.) defeats Chicago (A.L.) 4 games to 2

LINE SCORES			R	H	E	PITCHERS (innings pitched)	HOME RUNS (men on)	HIGHLIGHTS
GAME 1 - OCTOBER 1								
LA	N	000 000 000	0	8	3	**Craig** (2.1), Churn (0.2), Labine (1), Koufax (2), Klippstein (2)		Wynn and Staley subdued the Dodgers as Kluszewski's five RBIs pace the 11-run attack.
CHI	A	207 200 00x	11	11	0	**Wynn** (7), Staley (2) **SV**	Kluszewski (1 on), Kluszewski (1 on)	
GAME 2 - OCTOBER 2								
LA	N	000 010 300	4	9	1	**Podres** (6), Sherry (3) **SV**	Neal, Essegian, Neal (1 on)	Two home runs by Neal and Essegian's two-out pinch homer in the seventh gave the Dodgers the win.
CHI	A	200 000 010	3	8	0	**Shaw** (6.2), Lown (2.1)		
GAME 3 - OCTOBER 4								
CHI	A	000 000 010	1	12	0	**Donovan** (6.2), Staley (1.1)		Furillo's pinch-hit single in the seventh with the bases full broke a scoreless tie and provided the winning margin.
LA	N	000 000 21x	3	5	0	**Drysdale** (7), Sherry (2) **SV**		
GAME 4 - OCTOBER 5								
CHI	A	000 000 400	4	10	3	Wynn (2.2), Lown (0.1), Pierce (3), **Staley** (2)	Lollar (2 on)	Hodges's homer in the eighth broke the deadlock after Lollar's three-run shot in the seventh pulled the White Sox even.
LA	N	004 000 01x	5	9	0	Craig (7), **Sherry** (2)	Hodges	
GAME 5 - OCTOBER 6								
CHI	A	000 100 000	1	5	0	**Shaw** (7.1), Pierce (0), Donovan (1.2) **SV**		Rivera's back-to-the-plate catch of Neal's fly with two men on and two out in the seventh choked off a Dodger rally. The White Sox set a Series record by using three pitchers in posting a 1-0 shutout. The game was witnessed by a record crowd of 92,706.
LA	N	000 000 000	0	9	0	**Koufax** (7), Williams (2)		
GAME 6 - OCTOBER 8								
LA	N	002 600 001	9	13	0	Podres (3.1), **Sherry** (5.2)	Snider (1 on), Moon (1 on), Essegian	The Dodgers jumped to an early 8-0 lead. Kluszewski homered for three runs in the fourth before Sherry came on to check the White Sox. It was Sherry's second win to go along with his two saves.
CHI	A	000 300 000	3	6	1	**Wynn** (3.1), Donovan (0), Lown (0.2), Staley (3), Pierce (1), Moore (1)	Kluszewski (2 on)	

Team totals

		W	AB	H	2B	3B	HR	R	RBI	BA	BB	SO	ERA
LA	N	4	203	53	3	1	7	21	19	.261	12	27	3.23
CHI	A	2	199	52	10	0	4	23	19	.261	20	33	3.46

Individual Batting

LOS ANGELES (N.L.)

	AB	H	2B	3B	HR	R	RBI	BA
C. Neal, 2b	27	10	2	0	2	4	6	.370
J. Gilliam, 3b	25	6	0	0	0	2	0	.240
G. Hodges, 1b	23	9	0	1	1	2	2	.391
W. Moon, of	23	6	0	0	1	3	2	.261
J. Roseboro, c	21	2	0	0	0	0	1	.095
M. Wills, ss	20	5	0	0	0	2	1	.250
N. Larker, of	16	3	0	0	0	2	0	.188
D. Demeter, of	12	3	0	0	0	2	0	.250
D. Snider, of	10	2	0	0	1	1	2	.200
J. Podres, p	4	2	1	0	0	1	1	.500
L. Sherry, p	4	2	0	0	0	0	0	.500
C. Furillo, of	4	1	0	0	0	0	2	.250
C. Essegian	3	2	0	0	2	2	2	.667
R. Craig, p	3	0	0	0	0	0	0	.000
R. Fairly, of	3	0	0	0	0	0	0	.000
D. Drysdale, p	2	0	0	0	0	0	0	.000
S. Koufax, p	2	0	0	0	0	0	0	.000
D. Zimmer, ss	1	0	0	0	0	0	0	.000
J. Pignatano, c	0	0	0	0	0	0	0	—
R. Repulski, of	0	0	0	0	0	0	0	—

Errors: D. Snider (2), C. Neal, M. Wills
Stolen Bases: J. Gilliam (2), W. Moon, C. Neal, M. Wills

CHICAGO (A.L.)

	AB	H	2B	3B	HR	R	RBI	BA
L. Aparicio, ss	26	8	1	0	0	1	0	.308
N. Fox, 2b	24	9	3	0	0	4	0	.375
J. Landis, of	24	7	0	0	0	6	1	.292
T. Kluszewski, 1b	23	9	1	0	3	5	10	.391
S. Lollar, c	22	5	0	0	1	3	5	.227
A. Smith, of	20	5	3	0	0	1	1	.250
B. Goodman, 3b	13	3	0	0	0	1	1	.231
J. Rivera, of	11	0	0	0	0	1	0	.000
B. Phillips, 3b, of	10	3	1	0	0	0	0	.300
E. Wynn, p	5	1	1	0	0	0	1	.200
J. McAnany, of	5	0	0	0	0	0	0	.000
B. Shaw, p	4	1	0	0	0	0	0	.250
N. Cash	4	0	0	0	0	0	0	.000
D. Donovan, p	3	1	0	0	0	0	0	.333
S. Esposito, 3b	2	0	0	0	0	0	0	.000
J. Romano	1	0	0	0	0	0	0	.000
G. Staley, p	1	0	0	0	0	0	0	.000
E. Torgeson, 1b	1	0	0	0	0	1	0	.000

Errors: L. Aparicio (2), J. Landis, B. Pierce
Stolen Bases: L. Aparicio, J. Landis

Individual Pitching

LOS ANGELES (N.L.)

	W	L	ERA	IP	H	BB	SO	SV
L. Sherry	2	0	0.71	12.2	8	2	5	2
R. Craig	0	1	8.68	9.1	15	5	8	0
J. Podres	1	0	4.82	9.1	7	6	4	0
S. Koufax	0	1	1.00	9	5	1	7	0
D. Drysdale	1	0	1.29	7	11	4	5	0
J. Klippstein	0	0	0.00	2	1	0	2	0
S. Williams	0	0	0.00	2	0	2	1	0
C. Labine	0	0	0.00	1	0	0	1	0
C. Churn	0	0	27.00	0.2	5	0	0	0

CHICAGO (A.L.)

	W	L	ERA	IP	H	BB	SO	SV
B. Shaw	1	1	2.57	14	17	2	2	0
E. Wynn	1	1	5.54	13	19	4	10	0
D. Donovan	0	1	5.40	8.1	4	3	5	1
G. Staley	0	1	2.16	8.1	8	0	3	1
B. Pierce	0	0	0.00	4	2	2	3	0
T. Lown	0	0	0.00	3.1	2	1	3	0
R. Moore	0	0	9.00	1	1	0	1	0

1960 WORLD SERIES

Pittsburgh (N.L.) defeats New York (A.L.) 4 games to 3

LINE SCORES							PITCHERS (innings pitched)	HOME RUNS (men on)	HIGHLIGHTS
GAME 1 - OCTOBER 5									Mazeroski's two-run homer in the fourth gave the Pirates enough of a lead to withstand Howard's homer in the ninth.
NY	**A**	100 100 002	4	13	2		**Ditmar** (0.1), Coates (3.2), Maas (2), Duren (2)	Maris, Howard (1 on)	
PIT	**N**	300 201 00x	6	8	0		**Law** (7), Face (2) **SV**	Mazeroski (1 on)	
GAME 2 - OCTOBER 6									The two teams combined for a Series record of 32 hits as Mantle led the assault with two homers and five RBIs. Kubek and Richardson scored three runs apiece.
NY	**A**	002 127 301	16	19	1		**Turley** (8.1), Shantz (0.2) **SV**	Mantle (1 on), Mantle (2 on)	
PIT	**N**	000 100 002	3	13	1		**Friend** (4), Green (1), Labine (0.2), Witt (0.1), Gibbon (2), Cheney (1)		
GAME 3 - OCTOBER 8									Richardson set a Series record with 6 RBIs as the Yankees romped behind Ford.
PIT	**N**	000 000 000	0	4	0		**Mizell** (0.1), Labine (0.1), Green (3), Witt (1.1), Cheney (2), Gibbon (1)		
NY	**A**	600 400 00x	10	16	1		**Ford** (9)	Richardson (3 on), Mantle (1 on)	
GAME 4 - OCTOBER 9									Law's double and Virdon's single capped the Pirates' three-run fifth and gave them the lead. Face retired all eight men he faced in relief of Law.
PIT	**N**	000 030 000	3	7	0		**Law** (6.1), Face (2.2) **SV**		
NY	**A**	000 100 100	2	8	0		**Terry** (6.1), Shantz (0.2), Coates (2)	Skowron	
GAME 5 - OCTOBER 10									Face again pitched 2 2/3 innings of hitless relief to save a Pirate victory.
PIT	**N**	031 000 001	5	10	2		**Haddix** (6.1), Face (2.2) **SV**		
NY	**A**	011 000 000	2	5	2		**Ditmar** (1.1), Arroyo (0.2), Stafford (5), Duren (2)	Maris	
GAME 6 - OCTOBER 12									Ford got his second shutout in another laugher. Richardson hit two triples and established a Series record with 12 RBIs.
NY	**A**	015 002 220	12	17	1		**Ford** (9)		
PIT	**N**	000 000 000	0	7	1		**Friend** (2), Cheney (1), Mizell (2), Green (0), Labine (3), Witt (1)		
GAME 7 - OCTOBER 13									Capitalizing on a break when a ground ball took a bad hop and struck Kubek in the neck, the Pirates scored five in the eighth, capped by Smith's three-run homer. New York tied the score but Mazeroski's homer in the bottom of the ninth won it.
NY	**A**	000 014 022	9	13	1		Turley (1), Stafford (1), Shantz (5), Coates (0.2), **Terry** (0.1)	Skowron, Berra (2 on)	
PIT	**N**	220 000 051	10	11	0		Law (5), Face (3), Friend (0), **Haddix** (1)	Nelson (1 on), Smith (2 on), Mazeroski	

Team totals

		W	AB	H	2B	3B	HR	R	RBI	BA	BB	SO	ERA
PIT	**N**	4	234	60	11	0	4	27	26	.256	12	26	7.11
NY	**A**	3	269	91	13	4	10	55	54	.338	18	40	3.54

Individual Batting

PITTSBURGH (N.L.)

	AB	H	2B	3B	HR	R	RBI	BA
R. Clemente, of	29	9	0	0	0	1	3	.310
B. Virdon, of	29	7	3	0	0	2	5	.241
D. Groat, ss	28	6	2	0	0	3	2	.214
B. Mazeroski, 2b	25	8	2	0	2	4	5	.320
D. Hoak, 3b	23	5	2	0	0	3	3	.217
G. Cimoli, of	20	5	0	0	0	4	1	.250
D. Stuart, 1b	20	3	0	0	0	0	0	.150
S. Burgess, c	18	6	1	0	0	2	0	.333
R. Nelson, 1b	9	3	0	0	1	2	2	.333
H. Smith, c	8	3	0	0	1	1	3	.375
V. Law, p	6	2	1	0	0	1	1	.333
B. Skinner, of	5	1	0	0	0	2	1	.200
H. Haddix, p	3	1	0	0	0	0	0	.333
D. Schofield, ss	3	1	0	0	0	0	0	.333
G. Baker	3	0	0	0	0	0	0	.000
R. Face, p	3	0	0	0	0	0	0	.000
B. Friend, p	1	0	0	0	0	0	0	.000
F. Green, p	1	0	0	0	0	0	0	.000
J. Christopher	0	0	0	0	0	2	0	—
B. Oldis, c	0	0	0	0	0	0	0	—

Errors: D. Groat (2), D. Hoak, B. Virdon
Stolen Bases: B. Skinner, B. Virdon

NEW YORK (A.L.)

	AB	H	2B	3B	HR	R	RBI	BA
B. Skowron, 1b	32	12	2	0	2	7	6	.375
B. Richardson, 2b	30	11	2	2	1	8	12	.367
T. Kubek, of, ss	30	10	1	0	0	6	3	.333
R. Maris, of	30	8	1	0	2	6	2	.267
M. Mantle, of	25	10	1	0	3	8	11	.400
Y. Berra, c, of	22	7	0	0	1	6	8	.318
G. McDougald, 3b	18	5	1	0	0	4	2	.278
B. Cerv, of	14	5	0	0	0	1	0	.357
E. Howard, c	13	6	1	1	1	4	4	.462
C. Boyer, 3b, ss	12	3	2	1	0	1	1	.250
J. Blanchard, c	11	5	2	0	0	2	2	.455
W. Ford, p	8	2	0	0	0	1	2	.250
H. Lopez, of	7	3	0	0	0	0	0	.429
B. Turley, p	4	1	0	0	0	0	1	.250
D. Long	3	1	0	0	0	0	0	.333
B. Shantz, p	3	1	0	0	0	0	0	.333
J. De Maestri, ss	2	1	0	0	0	1	0	.500
R. Terry, p	2	0	0	0	0	0	0	.000
L. Arroyo, p	1	0	0	0	0	0	0	.000
J. Coates, p	1	0	0	0	0	0	0	.000
B. Stafford, p	1	0	0	0	0	0	0	.000
E. Grba	0	0	0	0	0	0	0	—

Errors: T. Kubek (3), B. Richardson (2), B. Cerv, R. Maris, G. McDougald

Individual Pitching

PITTSBURGH (N.L.)

	W	L	ERA	IP	H	BB	SO	SV
V. Law	2	0	3.44	18.1	22	3	8	0
R. Face	0	0	5.23	10.1	9	2	4	3
H. Haddix	2	0	2.45	7.1	6	2	6	0
B. Friend	0	2	13.50	6	13	3	7	0
T. Cheney	0	0	4.50	4	4	1	6	0
F. Green	0	0	22.50	4	11	1	3	0
C. Labine	0	0	13.50	4	13	1	2	0
J. Gibbon	0	0	9.00	3	4	1	2	0
G. Witt	0	0	0.00	2.2	5	2	1	0
V. Mizell	0	1	15.43	2.1	4	2	1	0

NEW YORK (A.L.)

	W	L	ERA	IP	H	BB	SO	SV
W. Ford	2	0	0.00	18	11	2	8	0
B. Turley	1	0	4.82	9.1	15	4	0	0
R. Terry	0	2	5.40	6.2	7	1	5	0
J. Coates	0	0	5.68	6.1	6	1	3	0
B. Shantz	0	0	4.26	6.1	4	1	1	1
B. Stafford	0	0	1.50	6	5	1	2	0
R. Duren	0	0	2.25	4	2	1	5	0
D. Maas	0	0	4.50	2	2	0	1	0
A. Ditmar	0	2	21.60	1.2	6	1	0	0
L. Arroyo	0	0	13.50	0.2	2	0	1	0

1961 WORLD SERIES

New York (A.L.) defeats Cincinnati (N.L.) 4 games to 1

LINE SCORES			R	H	E	PITCHERS (innings pitched)	HOME RUNS (men on)	HIGHLIGHTS
GAME 1 - OCTOBER 4								Howard and Skowron powered Ford to his record eighth World Series victory. Richardson had three of the Yankees' six hits.
CIN	**N**	000 000 000	0	2	0	**O'Toole** (7), Brosnan (1)		
NY	**A**	000 101 00x	2	6	0	**Ford** (9)	Howard, Skowron	
GAME 2 - OCTOBER 5								Chacon's alert base-running gave the Reds the go-ahead run. The game was then iced when the Yankees twice intentionally walked batters to face Edwards, and he upset their strategy by batting in runs each time.
CIN	**N**	000 211 020	6	9	0	**Jay** (9)	Coleman (1 on)	
NY	**A**	000 200 000	2	4	3	**Terry** (7), Arroyo (2)	Berra (1 on)	
GAME 3 - OCTOBER 7								Blanchard delivered a clutch pinch-hit homer in the top of the eighth to tie the score before Maris won the game with a homer in the ninth. The Yankees' first run came on a two-out blooper by Berra that scored Kubek when Chacon and Robinson collided on the play.
NY	**A**	000 000 111	3	6	1	Stafford (6.2), Daley (0.1), **Arroyo** (2)	Blanchard, Maris	
CIN	**N**	001 000 100	2	8	0	**Purkey** (9)		
GAME 4 - OCTOBER 8								An ankle injury forced Ford to retire in the sixth after he extended his Series scoreless inning streak to 32 and eclipsed Ruth's record of 29.2 innings.
NY	**A**	000 112 300	7	11	0	**Ford** (5), Coates (4) **SV**		
CIN	**N**	000 000 000	0	5	1	**O'Toole** (5), Brosnan (3), Henry (1)		
GAME 5 - OCTOBER 9								With Mantle and Berra out of the lineup with injuries and with Maris finishing the Series with a .105 batting average, the Yankees resorted to their bench and erupted for five runs in the first and five more in the fourth. Lopez drove in five runs, and Blanchard added two more.
NY	**A**	510 502 000	13	15	1	Terry (2.1), **Daley** (6.2)	Blanchard (1 on), Lopez (2 on)	
CIN	**N**	003 020 000	5	11	3	**Jay** (0.2), Maloney (0.2), K. Johnson (0.2), Henry (1.1), Jones (0.2), Purkey (2), Brosnan (2), Hunt (1)	Robinson (2 on), Post (1 on)	

Team totals

		W	AB	H	2B	3B	HR	R	RBI	BA	BB	SO	ERA
NY	**A**	4	165	42	8	1	7	27	26	.255	24	25	1.60
CIN	**N**	1	170	35	8	0	3	13	11	.206	8	27	4.91

Individual Batting

NEW YORK (A.L.)

	AB	H	2B	3B	HR	R	RBI	BA
B. Richardson, 2b	23	9	1	0	0	2	0	.391
T. Kubek, ss	22	5	0	0	0	3	1	.227
E. Howard, c	20	5	3	0	1	5	1	.250
R. Maris, of	19	2	1	0	1	4	2	.105
B. Skowron, 1b	17	6	0	0	1	3	5	.353
C. Boyer, 3b	15	4	2	0	0	0	3	.267
Y. Berra, of	11	3	0	0	1	2	3	.273
J. Blanchard, of	10	4	1	0	2	4	3	.400
H. Lopez, of	9	3	0	1	1	3	7	.333
M. Mantle, of	6	1	0	0	0	0	0	.167
W. Ford, p	5	0	0	0	0	1	0	.000
R. Terry, p	3	0	0	0	0	0	0	.000
B. Stafford, p	2	0	0	0	0	0	0	.000
J. Coates, p	1	0	0	0	0	0	0	.000
B. Daley, p	1	0	0	0	0	0	1	.000
B. Gardner	1	0	0	0	0	0	0	.000
J. Reed, of	0	0	0	0	0	0	0	—

Errors: L. Arroyo, Y. Berra, C. Boyer, B. Daley, B. Stafford
Stolen Bases: B. Richardson

CINCINNATI (N.L.)

	AB	H	2B	3B	HR	R	RBI	BA
E. Kasko, ss	22	7	0	0	0	1	1	.318
V. Pinson, of	22	2	1	0	0	0	0	.091
G. Coleman, 1b	20	5	0	0	1	2	2	.250
W. Post, of	18	6	1	0	1	3	2	.333
G. Freese, 3b	16	1	1	0	0	0	0	.063
F. Robinson, of	15	3	2	0	1	3	4	.200
E. Chacon, 2b	12	3	0	0	0	2	0	.250
J. Edwards, c	11	4	2	0	0	1	2	.364
D. Blasingame, 2b	7	1	0	0	0	1	0	.143
D. Johnson, c	4	2	0	0	0	0	0	.500
D. Gernert	4	0	0	0	0	0	0	.000
J. Jay, p	4	0	0	0	0	0	0	.000
L. Cardenas	3	1	1	0	0	0	0	.333
G. Bell	3	0	0	0	0	0	0	.000
J. Lynch	3	0	0	0	0	0	0	.000
J. O'Toole, p	3	0	0	0	0	0	0	.000
B. Purkey, p	3	0	0	0	0	0	0	.000
J. Zimmerman, c	0	0	0	0	0	0	0	—

Errors: G. Coleman, E. Kasko, V. Pinson, B. Purkey

Individual Pitching

NEW YORK (A.L.)

	W	L	ERA	IP	H	BB	SO	SV
W. Ford	2	0	0.00	14	6	1	7	0
R. Terry	0	1	4.82	9.1	12	2	7	0
B. Daley	1	0	0.00	7	5	0	3	0
B. Stafford	0	0	2.70	6.2	7	2	5	0
L. Arroyo	1	0	2.25	4	4	2	3	0
J. Coates	0	0	0.00	4	1	1	2	1

CINCINNATI (N.L.)

	W	L	ERA	IP	H	BB	SO	SV
J. O'Toole	0	2	3.00	12	11	7	4	0
B. Purkey	0	1	1.64	11	6	3	5	0
J. Jay	1	1	5.59	9.2	8	6	6	0
J. Brosnan	0	0	7.50	6	9	4	5	0
B. Henry	0	0	19.29	2.1	4	2	3	0
K. Hunt	0	0	0.00	1	0	1	1	0
K. Johnson	0	0	0.00	0.2	0	0	0	0
S. Jones	0	0	0.00	0.2	0	0	0	0
J. Maloney	0	0	27.00	0.2	4	1	1	0

1962 WORLD SERIES

New York (A.L.) defeats San Francisco (N.L.) 4 games to 3

LINE SCORES			R	H	E	PITCHERS (innings pitched)	HOME RUNS (men on)	HIGHLIGHTS
GAME 1 - OCTOBER 4								Ford's tenth Series triumph came when Clete Boyer broke a 2-2 tie with his seventh-inning homer.
NY	**A**	200 000 121	6	11	0	**Ford** (9)	Boyer	
SF	**N**	011 000 000	2	10	0	**O'Dell** (7.1), Larsen (1), Miller (0.2)		
GAME 2 - OCTOBER 5								Sanford held the Yankees to three hits; the lead run scored when Hiller doubled and scored on an infield out. The insurance tally came on McCovey's seventh-inning homer.
NY	**A**	000 000 000	0	3	1	**Terry** (7), Daley (1)		
SF	**N**	100 000 10x	2	6	0	**Sanford** (9)	McCovey	
GAME 3 - OCTOBER 7								Maris singled off Pierce to drive in the first two Yankee runs. The Giants rallied on Bailey's homer but fell short.
SF	**N**	000 000 002	2	4	3	**Pierce** (6), Larsen (1), Bolin (1)	Bailey (1 on)	
NY	**A**	000 000 30x	3	5	1	**Stafford** (9)		
GAME 4 - OCTOBER 8								Hiller connected off Bridges for the first National League grand slam in Series competition, breaking a tie in the seventh.
SF	**N**	020 000 401	7	9	1	Marichal (4), Bolin (1.2), **Larsen** (0.1), O'Dell (3) **SV**	Haller (1 on), Hiller (3 on)	
NY	**A**	000 002 001	3	9	1	Ford (6), **Coates** (0.1), Bridges (2.2)		
GAME 5 - OCTOBER 10								Sanford struck out ten, but a three- run homer by Tresh won the game for Terry.
SF	**N**	001 010 001	3	8	2	**Sanford** (7.1), Miller (0.2)	Pagan	
NY	**A**	000 101 03x	5	6	0	**Terry** (9)	Tresh (2 on)	
GAME 6 - OCTOBER 15								After a three-day rain delay, Pierce was masterful as Cepeda ignited the Giant attack with three hits.
NY	**A**	000 010 010	2	3	2	**Ford** (4.2), Coates (2.1), Bridges (1)	Maris	
SF	**N**	000 320 00x	5	10	1	**Pierce** (9)		
GAME 7 - OCTOBER 16								McCovey's line drive with two out and two on in the ninth was caught by Richardson, providing a dramatic end to the Series.
NY	**A**	000 010 000	1	7	0	**Terry** (9)		
SF	**N**	000 000 000	0	4	1	**Sanford** (7), O'Dell (2)		

Team totals

		W	AB	H	2B	3B	HR	R	RBI	BA	BB	SO	ERA
NY	**A**	4	221	44	6	1	3	20	17	.199	21	39	2.95
SF	**N**	3	226	51	10	2	5	21	19	.226	12	39	2.66

Individual Batting

NEW YORK (A.L.)

	AB	H	2B	3B	HR	R	RBI	BA
T. Kubek, ss	29	8	1	0	0	2	1	.276
T. Tresh, of	28	9	1	0	1	5	4	.321
B. Richardson, 2b	27	4	0	0	0	3	0	.148
M. Mantle, of	25	3	1	0	0	2	0	.120
R. Maris, of	23	4	1	0	1	4	5	.174
C. Boyer, 3b	22	7	1	0	1	2	4	.318
E. Howard, c	21	3	1	0	0	1	1	.143
B. Skowron, 1b	18	4	0	1	0	1	1	.222
R. Terry, p	8	1	0	0	0	0	0	.125
W. Ford, p	7	0	0	0	0	0	0	.000
D. Long, 1b	5	1	0	0	0	0	1	.200
B. Stafford, p	3	0	0	0	0	0	0	.000
Y. Berra, c	2	0	0	0	0	0	0	.000
H. Lopez	2	0	0	0	0	0	0	.000
J. Blanchard	1	0	0	0	0	0	0	.000

Errors: C. Boyer (2), W. Ford, T. Kubek, B. Richardson

Stolen Bases: M. Mantle (2), T. Tresh (2)

SAN FRANCISCO (N.L.)

	AB	H	2B	3B	HR	R	RBI	BA
W. Mays, of	28	7	2	0	0	3	1	.250
F. Alou, of	26	7	1	1	0	2	1	.269
C. Hiller, 2b	26	7	3	0	1	4	5	.269
J. Davenport, 3b	22	3	1	0	0	1	1	.136
J. Pagan, ss	19	7	0	0	1	2	2	.368
O. Cepeda, 1b	19	3	1	0	0	1	2	.158
W. McCovey, 1b, of	15	3	0	1	1	2	1	.200
T. Haller, c	14	4	1	0	1	1	3	.286
E. Bailey, c	14	1	0	0	1	1	2	.071
M. Alou, of	12	4	1	0	0	2	1	.333
H. Kuenn, of	12	1	0	0	0	1	0	.083
J. Sanford, p	7	3	0	0	0	0	0	.429
B. Pierce, p	5	0	0	0	0	0	0	.000
B. O'Dell, p	3	1	0	0	0	0	0	.333
J. Marichal, p	2	0	0	0	0	0	0	.000
E. Bowman, ss	1	0	0	0	0	1	0	.000
J. Orsino, c	1	0	0	0	0	0	0	.000
B. Nieman	0	0	0	0	0	0	0	—

Errors: J. Davenport (3), W. McCovey (2), F. Alou, C. Hiller, J. Pagan

Stolen Bases: W. Mays

Individual Pitching

NEW YORK (A.L.)

	W	L	ERA	IP	H	BB	SO	SV
R. Terry	2	1	1.80	25	17	2	16	0
W. Ford	1	1	4.12	19.2	24	4	12	0
B. Stafford	1	0	2.00	9	4	2	5	0
M. Bridges	0	0	4.91	3.2	4	2	3	0
J. Coates	0	1	6.75	2.2	1	1	3	0
B. Daley	0	0	0.00	1	1	1	0	0

SAN FRANCISCO (N.L.)

	W	L	ERA	IP	H	BB	SO	SV
J. Sanford	1	2	1.93	23.1	16	8	19	0
B. Pierce	1	1	2.40	15	8	2	5	0
B. O'Dell	0	1	4.38	12.1	12	3	9	1
J. Marichal	0	0	0.00	4	2	2	4	0
B. Bolin	0	0	6.75	2.2	4	2	2	0
D. Larsen	1	0	3.86	2.1	1	2	0	0
S. Miller	0	0	0.00	1.1	1	2	0	0

1963 WORLD SERIES

Los Angeles (N.L.) defeats New York (A.L.) 4 games to 0

LINE SCORES			R	H	E	PITCHERS (innings pitched)	HOME RUNS (men on)	HIGHLIGHTS
GAME 1 - OCTOBER 2								
LA	**N**	041 000 000	5	9	0	**Koufax** (9)	Roseboro (2 on)	Koufax struck out 15 to set a new Series record and Roseboro hit a three-run homer in the second. Yankee pitchers struck out ten Dodgers, bringing the two-team total to 25 strikeouts, also a record.
NY	**A**	000 000 020	2	6	0	**Ford** (5), Williams (3), Hamilton (1)	Tresh (1 on)	
GAME 2 - OCTOBER 3								
LA	**N**	200 100 010	4	10	1	**Podres** (8.1), Perranoski (0.2) **SV**	Skowron	Willie Davis drove in two runs in the first on a ball that went for a double after Maris slipped chasing the hit.
NY	**A**	000 000 001	1	7	0	**Downing** (5), Terry (3), Reniff (1)		
GAME 3 - OCTOBER 5								
NY	**A**	000 000 000	0	3	0	**Bouton** (7), Reniff (1)		Drysdale allowed three hits in pitching a shutout, walking only one batter while striking out nine. The Dodgers' run came in the first when Gilliam scored on Tommy Davis's single.
LA	**N**	100 000 00x	1	4	1	**Drysdale** (9)		
GAME 4 - OCTOBER 6								
NY	**A**	000 000 100	1	6	1	**Ford** (7), Reniff (1)	Mantle	Pepitone lost Boyer's throw in the shirts in the crowd, and Gilliam sped around to third to lead off the seventh. Willie Davis's sacrifice fly then scored him with the winning run.
LA	**N**	000 010 10x	2	2	1	**Koufax** (9)	F. Howard	

Team totals

		W	AB	H	2B	3B	HR	R	RBI	BA	BB	SO	ERA
LA	**N**	4	117	25	3	2	3	12	12	.214	11	25	1.00
NY	**A**	0	129	22	3	0	2	4	4	.171	5	37	2.91

Individual Batting

LOS ANGELES (N.L.)

	AB	H	2B	3B	HR	R	RBI	BA
T. Davis, of	15	6	0	2	0	0	2	.400
M. Wills, ss	15	2	0	0	0	1	0	.133
J. Roseboro, c	14	2	0	0	1	1	3	.143
B. Skowron, 1b	13	5	0	0	1	2	3	.385
J. Gilliam, 3b	13	2	0	0	0	3	0	.154
D. Tracewski, 2b	13	2	0	0	0	1	0	.154
W. Davis, of	12	2	2	0	0	2	3	.167
F. Howard, of	10	3	1	0	1	2	1	.300
S. Koufax, p	6	0	0	0	0	0	0	.000
J. Podres, p	4	1	0	0	0	0	0	.250
D. Drysdale, p	1	0	0	0	0	0	0	.000
R. Fairly, of	1	0	0	0	0	0	0	.000

Errors: J. Podres, D. Tracewski, M. Wills
Stolen Bases: T. Davis, M. Wills

NEW YORK (A.L.)

	AB	H	2B	3B	HR	R	RBI	BA
T. Kubek, ss	16	3	0	0	0	1	0	.188
E. Howard, c	15	5	0	0	0	0	1	.333
T. Tresh, of	15	3	0	0	1	1	2	.200
M. Mantle, of	15	2	0	0	1	1	1	.133
B. Richardson, 2b	14	3	1	0	0	0	0	.214
J. Pepitone, 1b	13	2	0	0	0	0	0	.154
C. Boyer, 3b	13	1	0	0	0	0	0	.077
H. Lopez, of	8	2	2	0	0	1	0	.250
R. Maris, of	5	0	0	0	0	0	0	.000
P. Linz	3	1	0	0	0	0	0	.333
J. Blanchard, of	3	0	0	0	0	0	0	.000
W. Ford, p	3	0	0	0	0	0	0	.000
J. Bouton, p	2	0	0	0	0	0	0	.000
H. Bright	2	0	0	0	0	0	0	.000
Y. Berra	1	0	0	0	0	0	0	.000
A. Downing, p	1	0	0	0	0	0	0	.000

Errors: J. Pepitone

Individual Pitching

LOS ANGELES (N.L.)

	W	L	ERA	IP	H	BB	SO	SV
S. Koufax	2	0	1.50	18	12	3	23	0
D. Drysdale	1	0	0.00	9	3	1	9	0
J. Podres	1	0	1.08	8.1	6	1	4	0
R. Perranoski	0	0	0.00	0.2	1	0	1	1

NEW YORK (A.L.)

	W	L	ERA	IP	H	BB	SO	SV
W. Ford	0	2	4.50	12	10	3	8	0
J. Bouton	0	1	1.29	7	4	5	4	0
A. Downing	0	1	5.40	5	7	1	6	0
H. Reniff	0	0	0.00	3	0	1	1	0
R. Terry	0	0	3.00	3	3	1	0	0
S. Williams	0	0	0.00	3	1	0	5	0
S. Hamilton	0	0	0.00	1	0	0	1	0

1964 WORLD SERIES

St. Louis (N.L.) defeats New York (A.L.) 4 games to 3

LINE SCORES			R	H	E	PITCHERS (innings pitched)	HOME RUNS (men on)	HIGHLIGHTS
GAME 1 - OCTOBER 7								The Cardinals erased a 4-2 deficit with four runs in the sixth as Shannon's homer tied the game, and Warwick's pinch single and Flood's triple drove in the go-ahead runs.
NY	A	030 010 010	5	12	2	**Ford** (5.1), Downing (1.2), Sheldon (0.2), Mikkelsen (0.1)	Tresh (1 on)	
STL	N	110 004 03x	9	12	0	**Sadecki** (6), Schultz (3) **SV**	Shannon (1 on)	
GAME 2 - OCTOBER 8								The Yankees broke the game open with four runs in the ninth after Gibson was removed for a pinch-hitter.
NY	A	000 101 204	8	12	0	**Stottlemyre** (9)	Linz	
STL	N	001 000 011	3	7	0	**Gibson** (8), Schultz (0.1), G. Richardson (0.1), Craig (0.1)		
GAME 3 - OCTOBER 10								Mantle led off the bottom of the ninth with a home run off Schultz's first pitch after Simmons was removed for a pinch- hitter.
STL	N	000 010 000	1	6	0	Simmons (8), **Schultz** (0)		
NY	A	010 000 001	2	5	2	**Bouton** (9)	Mantle	
GAME 4 - OCTOBER 11								A grand-slam homer by Ken Boyer in the fifth wiped out a 3-0 Yankee lead. Craig and Taylor allowed only two hits in eight and two-thirds innings of relief pitching.
STL	N	000 040 000	4	6	1	Sadecki (0.1) **Craig** (4.2) Taylor (4) **S V**	K. Boyer (3 on)	
NY	A	300 000 000	3	6	1	**Downing** (6), Mikkelsen (1), Terry (2)		
GAME 5 - OCTOBER 12								McCarver's three-run homer in the tenth won after Tresh's two-run homer tied the game with two out in the ninth. Gibson struck out 13.
STL	N	000 020 000 3	5	10	1	**Gibson** (10)	McCarver (2 on)	
NY	A	000 000 002 0	2	6	2	Stottlemyre (7), Reniff (0.1), **Mikkelsen** (2.2)	Tresh (1 on)	
GAME 6 - OCTOBER 14								Consecutive homers by Maris and Mantle gave the Yankees a 3-1 lead in the sixth. Pepitone's grand slam in the eighth insured the victory.
NY	A	000 012 050	8	10	0	**Bouton** (8.1), Hamilton (0.2) **SV**	Maris, Mantle, Pepitone (3 on)	
STL	N	100 000 011	3	10	1	**Simmons** (6.1), Taylor (0.2), Schultz (0.2), G. Richardson (0.1), Humphreys (1)		
GAME 7 - OCTOBER 15								Gibson pitched his second complete game of the Series and struck out nine for a Series total of 31. Richardson set an all-time Series record with 13 hits.
NY	A	000 003 002	5	9	2	**Stottlemyre** (4), Downing (0), Sheldon (2), Hamilton (1.1), Mikkelsen (0.2)	Mantle (2 on), C. Boyer, Linz	
STL	N	000 330 10x	7	10	1	**Gibson** (9)	Brock, K. Boyer	

Team totals

		W	AB	H	2B	3B	HR	R	RBI	BA	BB	SO	ERA
STL	N	4	240	61	8	3	5	32	29	.254	18	39	4.29
NY	A	3	239	60	11	0	10	33	33	.251	25	54	3.77

Individual Batting

ST. LOUIS (N.L.)

	AB	H	2B	3B	HR	R	RBI	BA
L. Brock, of	30	9	2	0	1	2	5	.300
C. Flood, of	30	6	0	1	0	5	3	.200
M. Shannon, of	28	6	0	0	1	6	2	.214
K. Boyer, 3b	27	6	1	0	2	5	6	.222
B. White, 1b	27	3	1	0	0	2	2	.111
D. Groat, ss	26	5	1	1	0	3	1	.192
T. McCarver, c	23	11	1	1	1	4	5	.478
D. Maxvill, 2b	20	4	1	0	0	0	1	.200
B. Gibson, p	9	2	0	0	0	1	0	.222
C. Warwick	4	3	0	0	0	2	1	.750
C. Simmons, p	4	2	0	0	0	0	1	.500
B. Skinner	3	2	1	0	0	0	1	.667
C. James	3	0	0	0	0	0	0	.000
R. Sadecki, p	2	1	0	0	0	0	1	.500
J. Buchek, 2b	1	1	0	0	0	1	0	1.000
R. Craig, p	1	0	0	0	0	0	0	.000
B. Schultz, p	1	0	0	0	0	0	0	.000
R. Taylor, p	1	0	0	0	0	0	0	.000
J. Javier, 2b	0	0	0	0	0	1	0	—

Errors: D. Groat (2), K. Boyer, L. Brock
Stolen Bases: T. McCarver, M. Shannon, B. White

NEW YORK (A.L.)

	AB	H	2B	3B	HR	R	RBI	BA
B. Richardson, 2b	32	13	2	0	0	3	3	.406
P. Linz, ss	31	7	1	0	2	5	2	.226
R. Maris, of	30	6	0	0	1	4	1	.200
J. Pepitone, 1b	26	4	1	0	1	1	5	.154
M. Mantle, of	24	8	2	0	3	8	8	.333
E. Howard, c	24	7	1	0	0	5	2	.292
C. Boyer, 3b	24	5	1	0	1	2	3	.208
T. Tresh, of	22	6	2	0	2	4	7	.273
M. Stottlemyre, p	8	1	0	0	0	0	0	.125
J. Bouton, p	7	1	0	0	0	0	1	.143
J. Blanchard	4	1	1	0	0	0	0	.250
A. Downing, p	2	0	0	0	0	0	0	.000
H. Lopez, of	2	0	0	0	0	0	0	.000
W. Ford, p	1	1	0	0	0	0	1	1.000
P. Gonzalez, 3b	1	0	0	0	0	0	0	.000
M. Hegan	1	0	0	0	0	1	0	.000

Errors: C. Boyer (2), P. Linz (2), M. Mantle (2), B. Richardson (2), E. Howard
Stolen Bases: C. Boyer, B. Richardson

Individual Pitching

ST. LOUIS (N.L.)

	W	L	ERA	IP	H	BB	SO	SV
B. Gibson	2	1	3.00	27	23	8	31	0
C. Simmons	0	1	2.51	14.1	11	3	8	0
R. Sadecki	1	0	8.53	6.1	12	5	2	0
R. Craig	1	0	0.00	5	2	3	9	0
R. Taylor	0	0	0.00	4.2	0	1	2	1
B. Schultz	0	1	18.00	4	9	3	1	1
B. Humphreys	0	0	0.00	1	0	0	1	0
G. Richardson	0	0	40.50	0.2	3	2	0	0

NEW YORK (A.L.)

	W	L	ERA	IP	H	BB	SO	SV
M. Stottlemyre	1	1	3.15	20	18	6	12	0
J. Bouton	2	0	1.56	17.1	15	5	7	0
A. Downing	0	1	8.22	7.2	9	2	5	0
W. Ford	0	1	8.44	5.1	8	1	4	0
P. Mikkelsen	0	1	5.79	4.2	4	2	4	0
R. Sheldon	0	0	0.00	2.2	0	2	2	0
S. Hamilton	0	0	4.50	2	3	0	2	1
R. Terry	0	0	0.00	2	2	0	3	0
H. Reniff	0	0	0.00	0.1	2	0	0	0

1965 WORLD SERIES

Los Angeles (N.L.) defeats Minnesota (A.L.) 4 games to 3

LINE SCORES						PITCHERS (innings pitched)	HOME RUNS (men on)	HIGHLIGHTS
GAME 1 - OCTOBER 6								The Twins broke away on a six-run third- inning barrage featuring Versalles's three-run homer and Quilici's two singles.
LA	**N**	010 000 001	2	10	1	**Drysdale** (2.2), Reed (1.1), Brewer (2), Perranoski (2)	Fairly	
MIN	**A**	016 001 00x	8	10	0	**Grant** (9)	Mincher, Versalles (2 on)	
GAME 2 - OCTOBER 7								The Twins rolled behind Kaat as Oliva and Killebrew supplied the hitting. Allison made a diving catch of Lefebvre's drive to spark the defense.
LA	**N**	000 000 100	1	7	3	**Koufax** (6), Perranoski (1.2), Miller (0.1)		
MIN	**A**	000 002 12x	5	9	0	**Kaat** (9)		
GAME 3 - OCTOBER 9								Roseboro opened the scoring with a single driving in two runs as Osteen checked the Twins on five hits.
MIN	**A**	000 000 000	0	5	0	**Pascual** (5), Merritt (2), Klippstein (1)		
LA	**N**	000 211 00x	4	10	1	**Osteen** (9)		
GAME 4 - OCTOBER 10								Drysdale returned with an 11-strikeout performance as Fairly drove in three runs.
MIN	**A**	000 101 000	2	5	2	**Grant** (5), Worthington (2), Pleis (1)	Killebrew, Oliva	
LA	**N**	110 103 01x	7	10	0	**Drysdale** (9)	Parker, Johnson	
GAME 5 - OCTOBER 11								Koufax regained his form, striking out ten and scattering four singles. Wills had two singles and two doubles, while Willie Davis stole three bases.
MIN	**A**	000 000 000	0	4	1	**Kaat** (2.1), Boswell (2.2), Perry (3)		
LA	**N**	202 100 20x	7	14	0	**Koufax** (9)		
GAME 6 - OCTOBER 13								The Twins tied the Series behind Grant's six-hit pitching and his three-run homer.
LA	**N**	000 000 100	1	6	1	**Osteen** (5), Reed (2), Miller (1)	Fairly	
MIN	**A**	000 203 00x	5	6	1	**Grant** (9)	Allison (1 on), Grant (2 on)	
GAME 7 - OCTOBER 14								Koufax ended the Series with a flourish, earning his second shutout and again fanning ten. Lou Johnson's homer provided the winning margin.
LA	**N**	000 200 000	2	7	0	**Koufax** (9)	Johnson	
MIN	**A**	000 000 000	0	3	1	**Kaat** (3), Worthington (2), Klippstein (1.2), Merritt (1.1) Perry (1)		

Team totals

		W	AB	H	2B	3B	HR	R	RBI	BA	BB	SO	ERA
LA	**N**	4	234	64	10	1	5	24	21	.274	13	31	2.10
MIN	**A**	3	215	42	7	2	6	20	19	.195	19	54	3.15

Individual Batting

LOS ANGELES (N.L.)

	AB	H	2B	3B	HR	R	RBI	BA
M. Wills, ss	30	11	3	0	0	3	3	.367
R. Fairly, of	29	11	3	0	2	7	6	.379
J. Gilliam, 3b	28	6	1	0	0	2	2	.214
L. Johnson, of	27	8	2	0	2	3	4	.296
W. Davis, of	26	6	0	0	0	3	0	.231
W. Parker, 1b	23	7	0	1	1	3	2	.304
J. Roseboro, c	21	6	1	0	0	1	3	.286
D. Tracewski, 2b	17	2	0	0	0	0	0	.118
J. Lefebvre, 2b	10	4	0	0	0	2	0	.400
S. Koufax, p	9	1	0	0	0	0	1	.111
D. Drysdale, p	5	0	0	0	0	0	0	.000
C. Osteen, p	3	1	0	0	0	0	0	.333
W. Crawford	2	1	0	0	0	0	0	.500
W. Moon	2	0	0	0	0	0	0	.000
J. Kennedy, 3b	1	0	0	0	0	0	0	.000
D. LeJohn	1	0	0	0	0	0	0	.000

Errors: J. Gilliam (2), L. Johnson, J. Kennedy, J. Lefebvre, D. Tracewski

Stolen Bases: W. Davis (3), M. Wills (3), W. Parker (2), J. Roseboro

MINNESOTA (A.L.)

	AB	H	2B	3B	HR	R	RBI	BA
Z. Versalles, ss	28	8	1	1	1	3	4	.286
T. Oliva, of	26	5	1	0	1	2	2	.192
E. Battey, c	25	3	0	1	0	1	2	.120
D. Mincher, 1b	23	3	0	0	1	3	1	.130
H. Killebrew, 3b	21	6	0	0	1	2	2	.286
J. Nossek, of	20	4	0	0	0	0	0	.200
F. Quilici, 2b	20	4	2	0	0	2	1	.200
B. Allison, of	16	2	1	0	1	3	2	.125
S. Valdespino, of	11	3	1	0	0	1	0	.273
M. Grant, p	8	2	1	0	1	3	3	.250
J. Hall, of	7	1	0	0	0	0	0	.143
J. Kaat, p	6	1	0	0	0	0	2	.167
R. Rollins	2	0	0	0	0	0	0	.000
C. Pascual, p	1	0	0	0	0	0	0	.000
J. Zimmerman, c	1	0	0	0	0	0	0	.000

Errors: F. Quilici (2), H. Killebrew, T. Oliva, A. Worthington

Stolen Bases: B. Allison, Z. Versalles

Individual Pitching

LOS ANGELES (N.L.)

	W	L	ERA	IP	H	BB	SO	SV
S. Koufax	2	1	0.38	24	13	5	29	0
C. Osteen	1	1	0.64	14	9	5	4	0
D. Drysdale	1	1	3.86	11.2	12	3	15	0
R. Perranoski	0	0	7.36	3.2	3	4	1	0
H. Reed	0	0	8.10	3.1	2	2	4	0
J. Brewer	0	0	4.50	2	3	0	1	0
B. Miller	0	0	0.00	1.1	0	0	0	0

MINNESOTA (A.L.)

	W	L	ERA	IP	H	BB	SO	SV
M. Grant	2	1	2.74	23	22	2	12	0
J. Kaat	1	2	3.77	14.1	18	2	6	0
C. Pascual	0	1	5.40	5	8	1	0	0
J. Perry	0	0	4.50	4	5	2	4	0
A. Worthington	0	0	0.00	4	2	2	2	0
J. Merritt	0	0	2.70	3.1	2	0	1	0
D. Boswell	0	0	3.38	2.2	3	2	3	0
J. Klippstein	0	0	0.00	2.2	2	2	3	0
B. Pleis	0	0	9.00	1	2	0	0	0

1966 WORLD SERIES

Baltimore (A.L.) defeats Los Angeles (N.L.) 4 games to 0

LINE SCORES			R	H	E	PITCHERS (innings pitched)	HOME RUNS (men on)	HIGHLIGHTS
GAME 1 - OCTOBER 5								Superb relief work by Drabowsky, who fanned 11 (including six in a row) after rushing to the aid of McNally in the third, preserved the victory for the Orioles. Baltimore took the early lead on back-to-back homers in the first by Frank and Brooks Robinson.
BAL	**A**	310 100 000	5	9	0	McNally (2.1), **Drabowsky** (6.2)	F. Robinson (1 on), B. Robinson	
LA	**N**	011 000 000	2	3	0	**Drysdale** (2), Moeller (2), Miller (3), Perranoski (2)	Lefebvre	
GAME 2 - OCTOBER 6								Palmer blanked the Dodgers as Koufax was victimized by Willie Davis's three successive errors in the fifth.
BAL	**A**	000 031 020	6	8	0	**Palmer** (9)		
LA	**N**	000 000 000	0	4	6	**Koufax** (6), Perranoski (1.1), Regan (0.2), Brewer (1)		
GAME 3 - OCTOBER 8								Blair's 430-foot homer in the fifth gave Bunker all the edge he needed. The Dodgers doubled the Orioles' hit total, but were unable to score as only one of their six hits went for extra bases.
LA	**N**	000 000 000	0	6	0	**Osteen** (7), Regan (1)		
BAL	**A**	000 010 00x	1	3	0	**Bunker** (9)	Blair	
GAME 4 - OCTOBER 9								The Orioles swept the Series on a fourth- inning homer by Frank Robinson as the Dodgers went scoreless again, completing a streak of 33 consecutive innings without a run.
LA	**N**	000 000 000	0	4	0	**Drysdale** (8)		
BAL	**A**	000 100 00x	1	4	0	**McNally** (9)	F. Robinson	

Team totals

		W	AB	H	2B	3B	HR	R	RBI	BA	BB	SO	ERA
BAL	**A**	4	120	24	3	1	4	13	10	.200	11	17	0.50
LA	**N**	0	120	17	3	0	1	2	2	.142	13	28	2.65

Individual Batting

BALTIMORE (A.L.)

	AB	H	2B	3B	HR	R	RBI	BA
L. Aparicio, ss	16	4	1	0	0	0	2	.250
B. Powell, 1b	14	5	1	0	0	1	1	.357
D. Johnson, 2b	14	4	1	0	0	1	1	.286
F. Robinson, of	14	4	0	1	2	4	3	.286
B. Robinson, 3b	14	3	0	0	1	2	1	.214
C. Blefary, of	13	1	0	0	0	0	0	.077
A. Etchebarren, c	12	1	0	0	0	2	0	.083
P. Blair, of	6	1	0	0	1	2	1	.167
R. Snyder, of	6	1	0	0	0	1	1	.167
J. Palmer, p	4	0	0	0	0	0	0	.000
D. McNally, p	3	0	0	0	0	0	0	.000
W. Bunker, p	2	0	0	0	0	0	0	.000
M. Drabowsky, p	2	0	0	0	0	0	0	.000

LOS ANGELES (N.L.)

	AB	H	2B	3B	HR	R	RBI	BA
W. Davis, of	16	1	0	0	0	0	0	.063
L. Johnson, of	15	4	1	0	0	1	0	.267
J. Roseboro, c	14	1	0	0	0	0	0	.071
W. Parker, 1b	13	3	2	0	0	0	0	.231
M. Wills, ss	13	1	0	0	0	0	0	.077
J. Lefebvre, 2b	12	2	0	0	1	1	1	.167
T. Davis, of	8	2	0	0	0	0	0	.250
R. Fairly, 1b, of	7	1	0	0	0	0	0	.143
J. Gilliam, 3b	6	0	0	0	0	0	1	.000
J. Kennedy, 3b	5	1	0	0	0	0	0	.200
D. Drysdale, p	2	0	0	0	0	0	0	.000
S. Koufax, p	2	0	0	0	0	0	0	.000
C. Osteen, p	2	0	0	0	0	0	0	.000
D. Stuart	2	0	0	0	0	0	0	.000
A. Ferrara	1	1	0	0	0	0	0	1.000
J. Barbieri	1	0	0	0	0	0	0	.000
W. Covington	1	0	0	0	0	0	0	.000
N. Oliver	0	0	0	0	0	0	0	—

Errors: W. Davis (3), R. Fairly, J. Gilliam, R. Perranoski

Stolen Bases: M. Wills

Individual Pitching

BALTIMORE (A.L.)

	W	L	ERA	IP	H	BB	SO	SV
D. McNally	1	0	1.59	11.1	6	7	5	0
W. Bunker	1	0	0.00	9	6	1	6	0
J. Palmer	1	0	0.00	9	4	3	6	0
M. Drabowsky	1	0	0.00	6.2	1	2	11	0

LOS ANGELES (N.L.)

	W	L	ERA	IP	H	BB	SO	SV
D. Drysdale	0	2	4.50	10	8	3	6	0
C. Osteen	0	1	1.29	7	3	1	3	0
S. Koufax	0	1	1.50	6	6	2	2	0
R. Perranoski	0	0	5.40	3.1	4	1	2	0
B. Miller	0	0	0.00	3	2	2	1	0
J. Moeller	0	0	4.50	2	1	1	0	0
P. Regan	0	0	0.00	1.2	0	1	2	0
J. Brewer	0	0	0.00	1	0	0	1	0

1967 WORLD SERIES

St. Louis (N.L.) defeats Boston (A.L.) 4 games to 3

LINE SCORES			R	H	E	PITCHERS (innings pitched)	HOME RUNS (men on)	HIGHLIGHTS
GAME 1 - OCTOBER 4								Gibson scattered six hits and struck out ten as Brock collected four singles and two stolen bases to pace the Cardinal attack.
STL	**N**	001 000 100	2	10	0	**B. Gibson** (9)		
BOS	**A**	001 000 000	1	6	0	**Santiago** (7), Wyatt (2)	Santiago	
GAME 2 - OCTOBER 5								Lonborg retired the first 20 batters until Javier doubled for the only Cardinal hit of the game. Yastrzemski homered twice for Red Sox.
STL	**N**	000 000 000	0	1	1	**Hughes** (5.1), Willis (0.2), Hoerner (0.2), Lamabe (1.1)		
BOS	**A**	000 101 30x	5	9	0	**Lonborg** (9)	Yastrzemski, Yastrzemski (2 on)	
GAME 3 - OCTOBER 7								Shannon homered with Maxvill on base in the second for the deciding runs. Briles held Boston to seven hits.
BOS	**A**	000 001 100	2	7	1	**Bell** (2), Waslewski (3), Stange (2), Osinski (1)	Smith	
STL	**N**	120 001 01x	5	10	0	**Briles** (9)	Shannon (1 on)	
GAME 4 - OCTOBER 8								Gibson allowed five hits and coasted to a 6-0 shutout win.
BOS	**A**	000 000 000	0	5	0	**Santiago** (0.2), Bell (1.1), Stephenson (2), Morehead (3), Brett (1)		
STL	**N**	402 000 00x	6	9	0	**B. Gibson** (9)		
GAME 5 - OCTOBER 9								Howard's single in the ninth inning with the bases filled scored the deciding run. Maris homered in the bottom of the inning for the Cardinals' only run.
BOS	**A**	001 000 002	3	6	1	**Lonborg** (9)		
STL	**N**	000 000 001	1	3	2	**Carlton** (6), Washburn (2), Willis (0), Lamabe (1)	Maris	
GAME 6 - OCTOBER 11								Fourth-inning home runs by Yastrzemski, Smith, and Petrocelli set a Series record, and St. Louis tied another record by using eight pitchers.
STL	**N**	002 000 200	4	8	0	Hughes (3.2), Willis (0.1), Briles (2), **Lamabe** (0.1), Hoerner (0), Jaster (0.1), Washburn (0.1), Woodeshick (1)	Brock (1 on)	
BOS	**A**	010 300 40x	8	12	1	Waslewski (5.1), **Wyatt** (1.2), Bell (2) **SV**	Petrocelli, Yastrzemski, Smith, Petrocelli	
GAME 7 - OCTOBER 12								Gibson allowed three hits and struck out ten as St. Louis routed Lonborg for the Series victory.
STL	**N**	002 023 000	7	10	1	**B. Gibson** (9)	B. Gibson, Javier (2 on)	
BOS	**A**	000 010 010	2	3	1	**Lonborg** (6), Santiago (2), Morehead (0.1), Osinski (0.1), Brett (0.1)		

Team totals

		W	AB	H	2B	3B	HR	R	RBI	BA	BB	SO	ERA
STL	**N**	4	229	51	11	2	5	25	24	.223	17	30	2.66
BOS	**A**	3	222	48	6	1	8	21	19	.216	17	49	3.39

Individual Batting

ST. LOUIS (N.L.)

	AB	H	2B	3B	HR	R	RBI	BA
L. Brock, of	29	12	2	1	1	8	3	.414
O. Cepeda, 1b	29	3	2	0	0	1	1	.103
C. Flood, of	28	5	1	0	0	2	3	.179
R. Maris, of	26	10	1	0	1	3	7	.385
J. Javier, 2b	25	9	3	0	1	2	4	.360
M. Shannon, 3b	24	5	1	0	1	3	2	.208
T. McCarver, c	24	3	1	0	0	3	2	.125
D. Maxvill, ss	19	3	0	1	0	1	1	.158
B. Gibson, p	11	1	0	0	1	1	1	.091
N. Briles, p	3	0	0	0	0	0	0	.000
D. Hughes, p	3	0	0	0	0	0	0	.000
D. Ricketts	3	0	0	0	0	0	0	.000
B. Tolan	2	0	0	0	0	1	0	.000
S. Carlton, p	1	0	0	0	0	0	0	.000
P. Gagliano	1	0	0	0	0	0	0	.000
E. Spiezio	1	0	0	0	0	0	0	.000
E. Bressoud, ss	0	0	0	0	0	0	0	—

Errors: M. Shannon (2), J. Javier, R. Maris
Stolen Bases: L. Brock (7)

BOSTON (A.L.)

	AB	H	2B	3B	HR	R	RBI	BA
G. Scott, 1b	26	6	1	1	0	3	0	.231
C. Yastrzemski, of	25	10	2	0	3	4	5	.400
R. Smith, of	24	6	1	0	2	3	3	.250
R. Petrocelli, ss	20	4	1	0	2	3	3	.200
D. Jones, 3b	18	7	0	0	0	2	1	.389
E. Howard, c	18	2	0	0	0	0	1	.111
J. Adair, 2b	16	2	0	0	0	0	1	.125
J. Foy, 3b	15	2	1	0	0	2	1	.133
M. Andrews, 2b	13	4	0	0	0	2	1	.308
J. Tartabull, of	13	2	0	0	0	1	0	.154
K. Harrelson, of	13	1	0	0	0	0	1	.077
J. Lonborg, p	9	0	0	0	0	0	0	.000
N. Siebern, of	3	1	0	0	0	0	1	.333
J. Santiago, p	2	1	0	0	1	1	1	.500
R. Gibson, c	2	0	0	0	0	0	0	.000
M. Ryan, c	2	0	0	0	0	0	0	.000
G. Thomas, of	2	0	0	0	0	0	0	.000
G. Waslewski, p	1	0	0	0	0	0	0	.000

Errors: R. Petrocelli (2), J. Foy, L. Stange
Stolen Bases: J. Adair

Individual Pitching

ST. LOUIS (N.L.)

	W	L	ERA	IP	H	BB	SO	SV
B. Gibson	3	0	1.00	27	14	5	26	0
N. Briles	1	0	1.64	11	7	1	4	0
D. Hughes	0	1	5.00	9	9	3	7	0
S. Carlton	0	1	0.00	6	3	2	5	0
J. Lamabe	0	1	6.75	2.2	5	0	4	0
R. Washburn	0	0	0.00	2.1	1	1	2	0
R. Willis	0	0	27.00	1	2	4	1	0
H. Woodeshick	0	0	0.00	1	1	0	0	0
J. Hoerner	0	0	40.50	0.2	4	1	0	0
L. Jaster	0	0	0.00	0.1	2	0	0	0

BOSTON (A.L.)

	W	L	ERA	IP	H	BB	SO	SV
J. Lonborg	2	1	2.63	24	14	2	11	0
J. Santiago	0	2	5.59	9.2	16	3	6	0
G. Waslewski	0	0	2.16	8.1	4	2	7	0
G. Bell	0	1	5.06	5.1	8	1	1	1
J. Wyatt	1	0	4.91	3.2	1	3	1	0
D. Morehead	0	0	0.00	3.1	0	4	3	0
L. Stange	0	0	0.00	2	3	0	0	0
J. Stephenson	0	0	9.00	2	3	1	0	0
K. Brett	0	0	0.00	1.1	0	1	1	0
D. Osinski	0	0	6.75	1.1	2	0	0	0

1968 WORLD SERIES

Detroit (A.L.) defeats St. Louis (N.L.) 4 games to 3

LINE SCORES			R	H	E	PITCHERS (innings pitched)	HOME RUNS (men on)	HIGHLIGHTS
GAME 1 - OCTOBER 2								Gibson subdued the Tigers on a Series record 17-strikeout performance as McLain, the first 30-game winner since 1934, lasted only until the sixth.
DET	**A**	000 000 000	0	5	3	**McLain** (5), Dobson (2), McMahon (1)		
STL	**N**	000 300 10x	4	6	0	**Gibson** (9)	Brock	
GAME 2 - OCTOBER 3								Lolich hit his first homer in the majors, aiding his own cause as he allowed the Cardinals six singles.
DET	**A**	011 003 102	8	13	1	**Lolich** (9)	Horton, Lolich, Cash	
STL	**N**	000 001 000	1	6	1	**Briles** (5), Carlton (1), Willis (2), Hoerner (1)		
GAME 3 - OCTOBER 5								McCarver's go-ahead three-run homer in the fifth and Cepeda's three-run homer in the seventh upended the Tigers.
STL	**N**	000 040 300	7	13	0	**Washburn** (5.1), Hoerner (3.2) **SV**	McCarver (2 on), Cepeda (2 on)	
DET	**A**	002 010 000	3	4	0	**Wilson** (4.1), Dobson (0.2), McMahon (1), Patterson (1), Hiller (2)	Kaline (1 on), McAuliffe	
GAME 4 - OCTOBER 6								Gibson coasted to his seventh straight victory, a Series record, striking out ten as Brock collected four RBIs.
STL	**N**	202 200 040	10	13	0	**Gibson** (9)	Brock, Gibson	
DET	**A**	000 100 000	1	5	4	**McLain** (2.2), Sparma (0.1), Patterson (2), Lasher (2), Hiller (0), Dobson (2)	Northrup	
GAME 5 - OCTOBER 7								Brock failed to slide on a play at the plate in the fifth and was tagged out after colliding with Freehan. Detroit went on to win the game on Kaline's bases-loaded single in the seventh.
STL	**N**	300 000 000	3	9	0	Briles (6.1), **Hoerner** (0), Willis (1.2)	Cepeda (2 on)	
DET	**A**	000 200 30x	5	9	1	**Lolich** (9)		
GAME 6 - OCTOBER 9								Northrup's grand slam highlighted the Tigers' ten-run third-inning barrage.
DET	**A**	02(10) 010 000	13	12	1	**McLain** (9)	Northrup (3 on), Kaline	
STL	**N**	000 000 001	1	9	1	**Washburn** (2), Jaster (0), Willis (0.2), Hughes (0.1), Carlton (3), Granger (2), Nelson (1)		
GAME 7 - OCTOBER 10								The Tigers won the Series behind Northrup's go-ahead, two-run triple in the seventh. Gibson's eight strikeouts gave him a single-Series record of 35. Key plays came in the sixth when Lolich picked Brock and Flood off first.
DET	**A**	000 000 301	4	8	1	**Lolich** (9)		
STL	**N**	000 000 001	1	5	0	**Gibson** (9)	Shannon	

Team totals

		W	AB	H	2B	3B	HR	R	RBI	BA	BB	SO	ERA
DET	**A**	4	231	56	4	3	8	34	33	.242	27	59	3.48
STL	**N**	3	239	61	7	3	7	27	27	.255	21	40	4.65

Individual Batting

DETROIT (A.L.)

	AB	H	2B	3B	HR	R	RBI	BA
A. Kaline, of	29	11	2	0	2	6	8	.379
J. Northrup, of	28	7	0	1	2	4	8	.250
M. Stanley, of, ss	28	6	0	1	0	4	0	.214
D. McAuliffe, 2b	27	6	0	0	1	5	3	.222
N. Cash, 1b	26	10	0	0	1	5	5	.385
B. Freehan, c	24	2	1	0	0	0	2	.083
W. Horton, of	23	7	1	1	1	6	3	.304
D. Wert, 3b	17	2	0	0	0	1	2	.118
M. Lolich, p	12	3	0	0	1	2	2	.250
D. McLain, p	6	0	0	0	0	0	0	.000
E. Mathews, 3b	3	1	0	0	0	0	0	.333
T. Matchick	3	0	0	0	0	0	0	.000
J. Price	2	0	0	0	0	0	0	.000
W. Comer	1	1	0	0	0	0	0	1.000
G. Brown	1	0	0	0	0	0	0	.000
E. Wilson, p	1	0	0	0	0	0	0	.000
R. Oyler, ss	0	0	0	0	0	0	0	—
D. Tracewski, 3b	0	0	0	0	0	1	0	—

Errors: N. Cash (2), B. Freehan (2), J. Northrup (2), M. Stanley (2), W. Horton, E. Mathews, D. McLain

ST. LOUIS (N.L.)

	AB	H	2B	3B	HR	R	RBI	BA
M. Shannon, 3b	29	8	1	0	1	3	4	.276
L. Brock, of	28	13	3	1	2	6	5	.464
C. Flood, of	28	8	1	0	0	4	2	.286
O. Cepeda, 1b	28	7	0	0	2	2	6	.250
J. Javier, 2b	27	9	1	0	0	1	3	.333
T. McCarver, c	27	9	0	2	1	3	4	.333
D. Maxvill, ss	22	0	0	0	0	1	0	.000
R. Maris, of	19	3	1	0	0	5	1	.158
B. Gibson, p	8	1	0	0	1	2	2	.125
R. Davis, of	7	0	0	0	0	0	0	.000
N. Briles, p	4	0	0	0	0	0	0	.000
P. Gagliano	3	0	0	0	0	0	0	.000
R. Washburn, p	3	0	0	0	0	0	0	.000
J. Hoerner, p	2	1	0	0	0	0	0	.500
D. Ricketts	1	1	0	0	0	0	0	1.000
E. Spiezio	1	1	0	0	0	0	0	1.000
J. Edwards	1	0	0	0	0	0	0	.000
B. Tolan	1	0	0	0	0	0	0	.000
D. Schofield	0	0	0	0	0	0	0	—

Errors: L. Brock, M. Shannon

Stolen Bases: L. Brock (7), C. Flood (3), J. Javier

Individual Pitching

DETROIT (A.L.)

	W	L	ERA	IP	H	BB	SO	SV
M. Lolich	3	0	1.67	27	20	6	21	0
D. McLain	1	2	3.24	16.2	18	4	13	0
P. Dobson	0	0	3.86	4.2	5	1	0	0
E. Wilson	0	1	6.23	4.1	4	6	3	0
D. Patterson	0	0	0.00	3	1	1	0	0
J. Hiller	0	0	13.50	2	6	3	1	0
F. Lasher	0	0	0.00	2	1	0	1	0
D. McMahon	0	0	13.50	2	4	0	1	0
J. Sparma	0	0	54.00	0.1	2	0	0	0

ST. LOUIS (N.L.)

	W	L	ERA	IP	H	BB	SO	SV
B. Gibson	2	1	1.67	27	18	4	35	0
N. Briles	0	1	5.56	11.1	13	4	7	0
R. Washburn	1	1	9.82	7.1	7	7	6	0
J. Hoerner	0	1	3.86	4.2	5	5	3	1
R. Willis	0	0	8.31	4.1	2	4	3	0
S. Carlton	0	0	6.75	4	7	1	3	0
W. Granger	0	0	0.00	2	0	1	1	0
M. Nelson	0	0	0.00	1	0	0	1	0
D. Hughes	0	0	0.00	0.1	2	0	0	0
L. Jaster	0	0	∞	0.0	2	1	0	0

1969 NATIONAL LEAGUE CHAMPIONSHIP SERIES

LINE SCORES						PITCHERS (innings pitched)	HOME RUNS (men on)	HIGHLIGHTS

New York (East) defeats Atlanta (West) 3 games to 0

LINE SCORES			R	H	E	PITCHERS (innings pitched)	HOME RUNS (men on)	HIGHLIGHTS
GAME 1 - OCTOBER 4								Aaron's home run off Seaver gave Atlanta a 5-4 lead in the seventh. But the Mets scored five in the eighth off Niekro as Garrett doubled past Boyer, Jones looped a single to left, Shamsky singled, Jones stole third when caught off second, Cepeda made a wild throw home on Kranepool's grounder and Martin pinch hit a two-run single after an intentional pass to Harrelson. The fifth run scored as Gonzalez let Martin's hit bounce past in center.
NY	**E**	020 200 050	9	10	1	**Seaver** (7), Taylor (2) **SV**		
ATL	**W**	012 010 100	5	10	2	**Niekro** (8), Upshaw (1)	Gonzalez, H. Aaron	
GAME 2 - OCTOBER 5								The Mets piled up an 8-0 lead in four innings, scoring on a double steal and an infield hit in the first, on Agee's homer and a scoring single by Shamsky in the second, on two unearned runs in the third, and Boswell's homer in the fourth. Koosman was knocked out in the fifth by Aaron's homer, a walk, Cepeda's double and Boyer's two-run single, all with two out. But with the score 9-6, Taylor and McGraw stifled the Braves while Jones's homer gives New York an extra safety margin in the seventh.
NY	**E**	132 210 200	11	13	1	Koosman (4.2), **Taylor** (1.1), McGraw (3) **SV**	Agee (1 on), Boswell (1 on), Jones (1 on)	
ATL	**W**	000 150 000	6	9	3	**Reed** (1.2), Doyle (1), Pappas (2.1), Britton (0.1), Upshaw (2.2), Neibauer (1)	H. Aaron (2 on)	
GAME 3 - OCTOBER 6								After Aaron's homer in the first, Ryan relieved Gentry with two on, none out in the third and a one-ball, two-strike count on Carty. He struck out Carty, and got out of the inning. Agee's homer in the third and Boswell's homer in the fourth put the Mets ahead, 3-2, but Cepeda's homer in the fifth made the score 4-3. But in the Met fifth, Garrett greeted reliever Stone with a homer and Jones followed with a double. Boswell's single off Upshaw made it 6-4 and Ryan coasted home.
ATL	**W**	200 020 000	4	8	1	**Jarvis** (4.1), Stone (1), Upshaw (2.2)	H. Aaron (1 on), Cepeda (1 on)	
NY	**E**	001 231 00x	7	14	0	Gentry (2), **Ryan** (7)	Agee, Boswell (1 on), Garrett (1 on)	

Team totals

		W	AB	H	2B	3B	HR	R	RBI	BA	BB	SO	ERA
NY	**E**	3	113	37	8	1	6	27	24	.327	10	25	5.00
ATL	**W**	0	106	27	9	0	5	15	15	.255	11	20	6.92

Individual Batting

NEW YORK (EAST)

	AB	H	2B	3B	HR	R	RBI	BA
C. Jones, of	14	6	2	0	1	4	4	.429
T. Agee, of	14	5	1	0	2	4	4	.357
A. Shamsky, of	13	7	0	0	0	3	1	.538
W. Garrett, 3b	13	5	2	0	1	3	3	.385
K. Boswell, 2b	12	4	0	0	2	4	5	.333
E. Kranepool, 1b	12	3	1	0	0	2	1	.250
J. Grote, c	12	2	1	0	0	3	1	.167
B. Harrelson, ss	11	2	1	1	0	2	3	.182
N. Ryan, p	4	2	0	0	0	1	0	.500
T. Seaver, p	3	0	0	0	0	0	0	.000
J. Martin	2	1	0	0	0	0	2	.500
J. Koosman, p	2	0	0	0	0	1	0	.000
A. Weis, 2b	1	0	0	0	0	0	0	.000
R. Gaspar, of	0	0	0	0	0	0	0	—

Errors: K. Boswell, B. Harrelson

Stolen Bases: T. Agee (2), C. Jones (2), W. Garrett

ATLANTA (WEST)

	AB	H	2B	3B	HR	R	RBI	BA
H. Aaron, of	14	5	2	0	3	3	7	.357
T. Gonzalez, of	14	5	1	0	1	4	2	.357
F. Millan, 2b	12	4	1	0	0	2	0	.333
O. Cepeda, 1b	11	5	2	0	1	2	3	.455
B. Didier, c	11	0	0	0	0	0	0	.000
R. Carty, of	10	3	2	0	0	4	0	.300
G. Garrido, ss	10	2	0	0	0	0	0	.200
C. Boyer, 3b	9	1	0	0	0	0	3	.111
B. Aspromonte	3	0	0	0	0	0	0	.000
P. Niekro, p	3	0	0	0	0	0	0	.000
M. Lum, of	2	2	1	0	0	0	0	1.000
P. Jarvis, p	2	0	0	0	0	0	0	.000
T. Aaron	1	0	0	0	0	0	0	.000
F. Alou	1	0	0	0	0	0	0	.000
M. Pappas, p	1	0	0	0	0	0	0	.000
G. Stone, p	1	0	0	0	0	0	0	.000
C. Upshaw, p	1	0	0	0	0	0	0	.000
S. Jackson, ss	0	0	0	0	0	0	0	—
B. Tillman, c	0	0	0	0	0	0	0	—

Errors: O. Cepeda (2), H. Aaron, C. Boyer, T. Gonzalez, F. Millan

Stolen Bases: O. Cepeda

Individual Pitching

NEW YORK (EAST)

	W	L	ERA	IP	H	BB	SO	SV
N. Ryan	1	0	2.57	7	3	2	7	0
T. Seaver	1	0	6.43	7	8	3	2	0
J. Koosman	0	0	11.57	4.2	7	4	5	0
R. Taylor	1	0	0.00	3.1	3	0	4	1
T. McGraw	0	0	0.00	3	1	1	1	1
G. Gentry	0	0	9.00	2	5	1	1	0

ATLANTA (WEST)

	W	L	ERA	IP	H	BB	SO	SV
P. Niekro	0	1	4.50	8	9	4	4	0
C. Upshaw	0	0	2.84	6.1	5	1	4	0
P. Jarvis	0	1	12.46	4.1	10	0	6	0
M. Pappas	0	0	11.57	2.1	4	0	4	0
R. Reed	0	1	21.60	1.2	5	3	3	0
P. Doyle	0	0	0.00	1	2	1	3	0
G. Neibauer	0	0	0.00	1	0	0	1	0
G. Stone	0	0	9.00	1	2	0	0	0
J. Britton	0	0	0.00	0.1	0	1	0	0

1969 AMERICAN LEAGUE CHAMPIONSHIP SERIES

Baltimore (East) defeats Minnesota (West) 3 games to 0

LINE SCORES			R	H	E	PITCHERS (innings pitched)	HOME RUNS (men on)	HIGHLIGHTS
GAME 1 - OCTOBER 4								
MIN	**W**	000 010 200 000	3	4	2	Perry (8), **Perranoski** (3.2)	Oliva (1 on)	Belanger raced home with the winning run in the 12th-inning on Blair's two-out suicide squeeze bunt to give Baltimore the edge over Minnesota in the opening of the first Championship Playoff Series since 1897. The American League's Eastern Division winners were boosted by three solo home runs: Frank Robinson's in fourth-inning, Belanger's in the fifth, Powell's in the ninth, which tied the game and erased Minnesota's 3-2 lead which came in the seventh on Oliva's home run with Carew aboard.
BAL	**E**	000 110 001 001	4	10	1	Cuellar (8), Richert (1), Watt (2), Lopez (0.1), **Hall** (0.2)	F. Robinson, Belanger, Powell	
GAME 2 - OCTOBER 5								
MIN	**W**	000 000 000 00	0	3	1	**Boswell** (10.2), Perranoski (0)		McNally struck out ten batters in going the extra distance to shut out Minnesota. The duel ended in the 11th-inning when, with two outs, Motton pinch hit for Hendricks and drove in Powell with a liner over second baseman Carew's out-stretched glove. Baltimore again pitched around Killebrew, walking him for the fifth time in two games.
BAL	**E**	000 000 000 01	1	8	0	**McNally** (11)		
GAME 3 - OCTOBER 6								
BAL	**E**	030 201 023	11	18	0	**Palmer** (9)	Blair (1 on)	Baltimore wrapped up the American League pennant by routing Minnesota 11-2, as Blair led the attack with a home run and two doubles in a 5-for-6 day with five RBIs. Buford chipped in with four hits of his own, and Hendricks drove in 3 runs. Baltimore's three-game sweep was aided by their holding Carew, the AL batting champ, to one hit in 14 trips, as well as avoiding Killebrew's power.
MIN	**W**	100 010 000	2	10	2	**Miller** (1.2), Woodson (1.2), Hall (0.2), Worthington (1.1), Grzenda (0.2), Chance (2), Perranoski (1)		

Team totals

		W	AB	H	2B	3B	HR	R	RBI	BA	BB	SO	ERA
BAL	**E**	3	123	36	8	1	4	16	15	.293	13	14	1.13
MIN	**W**	0	110	17	3	1	1	5	5	.155	12	27	4.02

Individual Batting

BALTIMORE (EAST)

	AB	H	2B	3B	HR	R	RBI	BA
P. Blair, of	15	6	2	0	1	1	6	.400
M. Belanger, ss	15	4	0	1	1	4	1	.267
B. Robinson, 3b	14	7	1	0	0	1	0	.500
D. Buford, of	14	4	1	0	0	3	1	.286
B. Powell, 1b	13	5	0	0	1	2	1	.385
D. Johnson, 2b	13	3	0	0	0	2	0	.231
F. Robinson, of	12	4	2	0	1	1	2	.333
E. Hendricks, c	8	2	2	0	0	2	3	.250
J. Palmer, p	5	0	0	0	0	0	0	.000
A. Etchebarren, c	4	0	0	0	0	0	0	.000
D. McNally, p	4	0	0	0	0	0	0	.000
C. Motton	2	1	0	0	0	0	1	.500
M. Cuellar, p	2	0	0	0	0	0	0	.000
D. May	1	0	0	0	0	0	0	.000
C. Salmon	1	0	0	0	0	0	0	.000
M. Rettenmund	0	0	0	0	0	0	0	—

Errors: F. Robinson

MINNESOTA (WEST)

	AB	H	2B	3B	HR	R	RBI	BA
R. Carew, 2b	14	1	0	0	0	0	0	.071
T. Oliva, of	13	5	2	0	1	3	2	.385
L. Cardenas, ss	13	2	0	1	0	0	0	.154
C. Tovar, of	13	1	0	0	0	0	0	.077
R. Reese, 1b	12	2	0	0	0	0	2	.167
H. Killebrew, 3b	8	1	1	0	0	2	0	.125
B. Allison, of	8	0	0	0	0	0	1	.000
G. Mitterwald, c	7	1	0	0	0	0	0	.143
T. Uhlaender, of	6	1	0	0	0	0	0	.167
J. Roseboro, c	5	1	0	0	0	0	0	.200
D. Boswell, p	4	0	0	0	0	0	0	.000
J. Perry, p	3	0	0	0	0	0	0	.000
G. Nettles	1	1	0	0	0	0	0	1.000
D. Woodson, p	1	1	0	0	0	0	0	1.000
R. Perranoski, p	1	0	0	0	0	0	0	.000
R. Renick	1	0	0	0	0	0	0	.000
C. Manuel	0	0	0	0	0	0	0	—

Errors: T. Oliva (2), L. Cardenas, R. Carew, T. Uhlaender

Stolen Bases: T. Oliva

Individual Pitching

BALTIMORE (EAST)

	W	L	ERA	IP	H	BB	SO	SV
D. McNally	1	0	0.00	11	3	5	11	0
J. Palmer	1	0	2.00	9	10	2	4	0
M. Cuellar	0	0	2.25	8	3	1	7	0
E. Watt	0	0	0.00	2	0	0	2	0
P. Richert	0	0	0.00	1	0	2	2	0
D. Hall	1	0	0.00	0.2	0	0	1	0
M. Lopez	0	0	0.00	0.1	1	2	0	0

MINNESOTA (WEST)

	W	L	ERA	IP	H	BB	SO	SV
D. Boswell	0	1	0.84	10.2	7	7	4	0
J. Perry	0	0	3.38	8	6	3	3	0
R. Perranoski	0	1	5.79	4.2	8	0	2	0
D. Chance	0	0	13.50	2	4	0	2	0
B. Miller	0	1	5.40	1.2	5	0	0	0
D. Woodson	0	0	10.80	1.2	3	3	2	0
A. Worthington	0	0	6.75	1.1	3	0	1	0
J. Grzenda	0	0	0.00	0.2	0	0	0	0
T. Hall	0	0	0.00	0.2	0	0	0	0

1969 WORLD SERIES

New York (N.L.) defeats Baltimore (A.L.) 4 games to 1

LINE SCORES						PITCHERS (innings pitched)	HOME RUNS (men on)	HIGHLIGHTS
GAME 1 - OCTOBER 11								Buford greeted Seaver with a home run on his second pitch. The Orioles added three in the fourth, and Cuellar scattered six hits for the win.
NY	**N**	000 000 100	1	6	1	**Seaver** (5), Cardwell (1), Taylor (2)		
BAL	**A**	100 300 00x	4	6	0	**Cuellar** (9)	Buford	
GAME 2 - OCTOBER 12								Koosman pitched six no-hit innings until singles by Blair and Brooks Robinson broke the spell and tied the score. The Mets won the game on two-out singles by Charles, Grote, and Weis in the ninth.
NY	**N**	000 100 001	2	6	0	**Koosman** (8.2), Taylor (0.1) **SV**	Clendenon	
BAL	**A**	000 000 100	1	2	0	**McNally** (9)		
GAME 3 - OCTOBER 14								Agee homered in first and made two spectacular catches (one in left center and one in right center) that saved five runs for Gentry and Ryan.
BAL	**A**	000 000 000	0	4	1	**Palmer** (6), Leonhard (2)		
NY	**N**	120 001 01x	5	6	0	**Gentry** (6.2), Ryan (2.1) **SV**	Agee, Kranepool	
GAME 4 - OCTOBER 15								Seaver took a 1-0 lead into ninth, thanks to Clendenon's homer in second. But Frank Robinson and Powell singled with one out, and Swoboda's diving catch robbed Brooks Robinson of a triple but the tying run scored. Grote led off the 10th with a double, and pinch-runner Gaspar scored when Richert's throw on Martin's bunt hit his wrist and went wide of first.
BAL	**A**	000 000 001 0	1	6	1	Cuellar (7), Watt (2), **Hall** (0), Richert (0)		
NY	**N**	010 000 000 1	2	10	1	**Seaver** (10)	Clendenon	
GAME 5 - OCTOBER 16								Third-inning homers by McNally and Frank Robinson gave Baltimore a 3-0 lead. But Clendenon's homer in sixth after a pitch nicked Jones's shoe, and Weis's homer in seventh tied it. Doubles by Jones and Swoboda off Watt scored the winning run in eighth.
BAL	**A**	003 000 000	3	5	2	McNally (7), **Watt** (1)	McNally (1 on), F. Robinson	
NY	**N**	000 002 12x	5	7	0	**Koosman** (9)	Clendenon (1 on), Weis	

Team totals

		W	AB	H	2B	3B	HR	R	RBI	BA	BB	SO	ERA
NY	**N**	4	159	35	8	0	6	15	13	.220	15	35	1.80
BAL	**A**	1	157	23	1	0	3	9	9	.146	15	28	2.72

Individual Batting

NEW YORK (N.L.)

	AB	H	2B	3B	HR	R	RBI	BA
J. Grote, c	19	4	2	0	0	1	1	.211
C. Jones, of	19	3	1	0	0	2	0	.158
T. Agee, of	18	3	0	0	1	1	1	.167
B. Harrelson, ss	17	3	0	0	0	1	0	.176
R. Swoboda, of	15	6	1	0	0	1	1	.400
E. Charles, 3b	15	2	1	0	0	1	0	.133
D. Clendenon, 1b	14	5	1	0	3	4	4	.357
A. Weis, 2b	11	5	0	0	1	1	3	.455
J. Koosman, p	7	1	1	0	0	0	0	.143
A. Shamsky, of	6	0	0	0	0	0	0	.000
E. Kranepool, 1b	4	1	0	0	1	1	1	.250
T. Seaver, p	4	0	0	0	0	0	0	.000
K. Boswell, 2b	3	1	0	0	0	1	0	.333
G. Gentry, p	3	1	1	0	0	0	2	.333
R. Gaspar, of	2	0	0	0	0	1	0	.000
D. Dyer	1	0	0	0	0	0	0	.000
W. Garrett, 3b	1	0	0	0	0	0	0	.000
J. Martin	0	0	0	0	0	0	0	—

Errors: W. Garrett, A. Weis
Stolen Bases: T. Agee

BALTIMORE (A.L.)

	AB	H	2B	3B	HR	R	RBI	BA
P. Blair, of	20	2	0	0	0	1	0	.100
D. Buford, of	20	2	1	0	1	1	2	.100
B. Powell, 1b	19	5	0	0	0	0	0	.263
B. Robinson, 3b	19	1	0	0	0	0	2	.053
F. Robinson, of	16	3	0	0	1	2	1	.188
D. Johnson, 2b	16	1	0	0	0	1	0	.063
M. Belanger, ss	15	3	0	0	0	2	1	.200
E. Hendricks, c	10	1	0	0	0	1	0	.100
A. Etchebarren, c	6	0	0	0	0	0	0	.000
M. Cuellar, p	5	2	0	0	0	0	1	.400
D. McNally, p	5	1	0	0	1	1	2	.200
C. Dalrymple	2	2	0	0	0	0	0	1.000
J. Palmer, p	2	0	0	0	0	0	0	.000
D. May	1	0	0	0	0	0	0	.000
C. Motton	1	0	0	0	0	0	0	.000
M. Rettenmund	0	0	0	0	0	0	0	—
C. Salmon	0	0	0	0	0	0	0	—

Errors: J. Palmer, B. Powell, P. Richert, E. Watt
Stolen Bases: P. Blair

Individual Pitching

NEW YORK (N.L.)

	W	L	ERA	IP	H	BB	SO	SV
J. Koosman	2	0	2.04	17.2	7	4	9	0
T. Seaver	1	1	3.00	15	12	3	9	0
G. Gentry	1	0	0.00	6.2	3	5	4	0
N. Ryan	0	0	0.00	2.1	1	2	3	1
R. Taylor	0	0	0.00	2.1	0	1	3	1
D. Cardwell	0	0	0.00	1	0	0	0	0

BALTIMORE (A.L.)

	W	L	ERA	IP	H	BB	SO	SV
M. Cuellar	1	0	1.13	16	13	4	13	0
D. McNally	0	1	2.81	16	11	5	13	0
J. Palmer	0	1	6.00	6	5	4	5	0
E. Watt	0	1	3.00	3	4	0	3	0
D. Leonhard	0	0	4.50	2	1	1	1	0
D. Hall	0	1	—	0.0	1	1	0	0
P. Richert	0	0	—	0.0	0	0	0	0

1970 NATIONAL LEAGUE CHAMPIONSHIP SERIES

Cincinnati (West) defeats Pittsburgh (East) 3 games to 0

LINE SCORES			R	H	E	PITCHERS (innings pitched)	HOME RUNS (men on)	HIGHLIGHTS
GAME 1 - OCTOBER 3								Pete Rose's run-scoring single in the 10th inning followed by Lee May's two-run double broke up a scoreless pitching duel between Gary Nolan and Dock Ellis.
CIN	**W**	000 000 000 3	3	9	0	**Nolan** (9), Carroll (1), **SV**		
PIT	**E**	000 000 000 0	0	8	0	**Ellis** (9.2), Gibbon (0.1)		
GAME 2 - OCTOBER 4								Tolan cracked three hits including a home run, and scored all three Cincinnati runs as starter Jim Merritt earned his seventh straight victory over the Pirates.
CIN	**W**	001 010 010	3	8	1	**Merritt** (5.1), Carroll (0.1), Gullett (3.1), **SV**	Tolan	
PIT	**E**	000 001 000	1	5	2	**Walker** (7), Giusti (2)		
GAME 3 - OCTOBER 5								Pinch hitter Ty Cline walked in the eighth and came home on successive singles by Rose and Tolan, enabling the Reds to snap a 2-2 tie for a sweep.
PIT	**E**	100 010 000	2	10	0	**Moose** (7.2), Gibbon (0), Giusti (0.1)		
CIN	**W**	200 000 01x	3	5	0	Cloninger (5), **Wilcox** (3), Granger (0.2), Gullett (0.1), **SV**	Perez, Bench	

Team totals

		W	AB	H	2B	3B	HR	R	RBI	BA	BB	SO	ERA
CIN	**W**	3	100	22	3	1	3	9	8	.220	8	12	0.96
PIT	**E**	0	102	23	6	0	0	3	3	.225	12	19	2.67

Individual Batting

CINCINNATI (WEST)

	AB	H	2B	3B	HR	R	RBI	BA
P. Rose, of	13	3	0	0	0	1	1	.231
B. Tolan, of	12	5	0	0	1	3	2	.417
T. Perez, 1b, 3b	12	4	2	0	1	1	2	.333
L. May, 1b	12	2	1	0	0	0	2	.167
T. Helms, 2b	11	3	0	0	0	0	0	.273
W. Woodward, 3b, ss	10	1	0	0	0	0	0	.100
J. Bench, c	9	2	0	0	1	2	1	.222
B. Carbo, of	6	0	0	0	0	0	0	.000
H. McRae, of	4	0	0	0	0	0	0	.000
G. Nolan, p	3	1	0	0	0	0	0	.333
J. Merritt, p	2	0	0	0	0	0	0	.000
J. Stewart, of	2	0	0	0	0	0	0	.000
T. Cline, of	1	1	0	1	0	2	0	1.000
A. Bravo	1	0	0	0	0	0	0	.000
T. Cloninger, p	1	0	0	0	0	0	0	.000
D. Gullett, p	1	0	0	0	0	0	0	.000
D. Concepcion, ss	0	0	0	0	0	0	0	—

Stolen Bases: B. Tolan

PITTSBURGH (EAST)

	AB	H	2B	3B	HR	R	RBI	BA
R. Clemente, of	14	3	0	0	0	1	1	.214
W. Stargell, of	12	6	1	0	0	0	1	.500
M. Alou, of	12	3	1	0	0	1	0	.250
M. Sanguillen, c	12	2	0	0	0	0	0	.167
A. Oliver, 1b	8	2	0	0	0	0	1	.250
D. Cash, 2b	8	1	1	0	0	1	0	.125
G. Alley, ss	7	0	0	0	0	0	0	.000
R. Hebner, 3b	6	4	2	0	0	0	0	.667
B. Robertson, 1b	5	1	1	0	0	0	0	.200
B. Moose, p	4	0	0	0	0	0	0	.000
J. Pagan, 3b	3	1	0	0	0	0	0	.333
F. Patek, ss	3	0	0	0	0	0	0	.000
D. Ellis, p	2	0	0	0	0	0	0	.000
J. Jeter, of	2	0	0	0	0	0	0	.000
B. Mazeroski, 2b	2	0	0	0	0	0	0	.000
L. Walker, p	2	0	0	0	0	0	0	.000

Errors: M. Sanguillen, L. Walker

Individual Pitching

CINCINNATI (WEST)

	W	L	ERA	IP	H	BB	SO	SV
G. Nolan	1	0	0.00	9	8	4	6	0
J. Merritt	1	0	1.69	5.1	3	0	2	0
T. Cloninger	0	0	3.60	5	7	4	1	0
D. Gullett	0	0	0.00	3.2	1	2	3	2
M. Wilcox	1	0	0.00	3	1	2	5	0
C. Carroll	0	0	0.00	1.1	2	0	2	1
W. Granger	0	0	0.00	0.2	1	0	0	0

PITTSBURGH (EAST)

	W	L	ERA	IP	H	BB	SO	SV
D. Ellis	0	1	2.79	9.2	9	4	1	0
B. Moose	0	1	3.52	7.2	4	2	4	0
L. Walker	0	1	1.29	7	5	1	5	0
D. Giusti	0	0	3.86	2.1	3	1	1	0
J. Gibbon	0	0	0.00	0.1	1	0	1	0

1970 AMERICAN LEAGUE CHAMPIONSHIP SERIES

Baltimore (East) defeats Minnesota (West) 3 games to 0

LINE SCORES			R	H	E	PITCHERS (innings pitched)	HOME RUNS (men on)	HIGHLIGHTS
GAME 1 - OCTOBER 3								With the score tied at 2-2 in the fourth inning, the Orioles erupted for seven runs to hang the defeat on Twins starter Jim Perry. Pitcher Mike Cuellar's grand slam homer led the attack.
BAL	**E**	020 701 000	10	13	0	Cuellar (4.1), **R. Hall** (4.2)	Buford, Cuellar (3 on), Powell (1 on)	
MIN	**W**	110 130 000	6	11	2	**Perry** (3.1), Zepp (0.2), Woodson (1), Williams (3), Perranoski (1)	Killebrew (1 on)	
GAME 2 - OCTOBER 4								Dave McNally went the distance, permitting six hits, the Minnesota runs coming on home runs by Harmon Killebrew and Tony Oliva.
BAL	**E**	102 100 007	11	13	0	**McNally** (9)	F. Robinson (1 on), Johnson (2 on)	
MIN	**W**	000 300 000	3	6	2	**T. Hall** (3.1), Zepp (0.2), Williams (3), Perranoski (1), Tiant (0.2)	Killebrew (1 on), Oliva	
GAME 3 - OCTOBER 5								Brooks Robinson enjoyed another 3-hit game and Davey Johnson hit another homer as the Orioles wrapped up the pennant early, scoring five runs in the first three innings.
MIN	**W**	000 010 000	1	7	2	**Kaat** (2), Blyleven (2), Hall (2), Perry (2)		
BAL	**E**	113 000 10x	6	10	0	**Palmer** (9)	Johnson	

Team totals

		W	AB	H	2B	3B	HR	R	RBI	BA	BB	SO	ERA
BAL	**E**	3	109	36	7	0	6	27	24	.330	12	19	3.33
MIN	**W**	0	101	24	4	1	3	10	10	.238	9	22	7.62

Individual Batting

BALTIMORE (EAST)

	AB	H	2B	3B	HR	R	RBI	BA
B. Powell, 1b	14	6	2	0	1	2	6	.429
P. Blair, of	13	1	0	0	0	0	0	.077
B. Robinson, 3b	12	7	2	0	0	4	1	.583
M. Belanger, ss	12	4	0	0	0	5	1	.333
D. Johnson, 2b	11	4	0	0	2	4	4	.364
F. Robinson, of	10	2	0	0	1	3	2	.200
A. Etchebarren, c	9	1	0	0	0	1	0	.111
D. Buford, of	7	3	1	0	1	2	3	.429
E. Hendricks, c	5	2	0	0	0	2	0	.400
D. McNally, p	5	2	1	0	0	1	1	.400
J. Palmer, p	4	1	1	0	0	1	1	.250
M. Rettenmund, of	3	1	0	0	0	1	1	.333
M. Cuellar, p	2	1	0	0	1	1	4	.500
D. Hall, p	2	1	0	0	0	0	0	.500

Stolen Bases: D. McNally, M. Rettenmund

MINNESOTA (WEST)

	AB	H	2B	3B	HR	R	RBI	BA
C. Tovar, 2b, of	13	5	0	1	0	2	1	.385
T. Oliva, of	12	6	2	0	1	2	1	.500
H. Killebrew, 1b, 3b	11	3	0	0	2	2	4	.273
L. Cardenas, ss	11	2	0	0	0	1	1	.182
G. Mitterwald, c	8	4	1	0	0	2	2	.500
D. Thompson, 2b	8	1	1	0	0	0	0	.125
R. Reese, 1b	7	1	0	0	0	0	0	.143
B. Alyea, of	7	0	0	0	0	1	0	.000
R. Renick, 3b	5	1	0	0	0	0	0	.200
J. Holt, of	5	0	0	0	0	0	0	.000
P. Ratliff, c	4	1	0	0	0	0	0	.250
B. Allison	2	0	0	0	0	0	0	.000
R. Carew	2	0	0	0	0	0	0	.000
F. Quilici, 2b	2	0	0	0	0	0	0	.000
T. Hall, p	1	0	0	0	0	0	0	.000
J. Kaat, p	1	0	0	0	0	0	0	.000
C. Manuel	1	0	0	0	0	0	0	.000
J. Perry, p	1	0	0	0	0	0	0	.000

Errors: L. Cardenas (2), J. Holt, H. Killebrew, P. Ratliff, D. Thompson

Individual Pitching

BALTIMORE (EAST)

	W	L	ERA	IP	H	BB	SO	SV
D. McNally	1	0	3.00	9	6	5	5	0
J. Palmer	1	0	1.00	9	7	3	12	0
D. Hall	1	0	0.00	4.2	1	0	3	0
M. Cuellar	0	0	12.46	4.1	10	1	2	0

MINNESOTA (WEST)

	W	L	ERA	IP	H	BB	SO	SV
S. Williams	0	0	0.00	6	2	1	2	0
T. Hall	0	1	6.75	5.1	6	4	6	0
J. Perry	0	1	13.50	5.1	10	1	3	0
R. Perranoski	0	0	19.29	2.1	5	1	3	0
B. Blyleven	0	0	0.00	2	2	0	2	0
J. Kaat	0	1	9.00	2	6	2	1	0
B. Zepp	0	0	6.75	1.1	2	2	2	0
D. Woodson	0	0	9.00	1	2	1	0	0
L. Tiant	0	0	13.50	0.2	1	0	0	0

1970 WORLD SERIES

Baltimore (A.L.) defeats Cincinnati (N.L.) 4 games to 1

LINE SCORES			R	H	E	PITCHERS (innings pitched)	HOME RUNS (men on)	HIGHLIGHTS
GAME 1 - OCTOBER 10								Powell hit a two-run homer, and Hendricks and B. Robinson added solo shots, enabling the Orioles to overcome a 3-0 deficit and spoil the Reds' first Series game in Riverfront Stadium.
BAL	**A**	000 210 100	4	7	2	**Palmer** (8.2), Richert (0.1), **SV**	Powell (1 on), Hendricks, B. Robinson	
CIN	**N**	102 000 000	3	5	0	**Nolan** (6.2), Carroll (2.1)	May (1 on)	
GAME 2 - OCTOBER 11								Reds again took an early 3-0 lead, and again lost by one run, as Powell smashed his second homer of Series and Hendricks capped a five-run rally in the fifth with a two-run double.
BAL	**A**	000 150 000	6	10	2	Cuellar (2.1), **Phoebus** (1.2), Drabowsky (2.1), Lopez (0.1), Hall (2.1), **SV**	Powell	
CIN	**N**	301 001 000	5	7	0	McGlothlin (4.1), **Wilcox** (0.1), Carroll (2.1), Gullett (2)	Bench, Tolan	
GAME 3 - OCTOBER 13								McNally helped his own cause with a grand slam homer, while Frank Robinson and Buford also homered, and Brooks Robinson contributed a two-run double and two fielding gems.
CIN	**N**	010 000 200	3	9	0	**Cloninger** (5.1), Granger (0.2), Gullett (2)		
BAL	**A**	201 014 10x	9	10	1	**McNally** (9)	F. Robinson, Buford, McNally (3 on)	
GAME 4 - OCTOBER 14								May's clutch three-run homer in eighth gave the Reds their first victory and ended Baltimore's 17-game winning streak, including the last 11 games of the regular season and three in the A.L. playoffs.
CIN	**N**	011 010 030	6	8	3	Nolan (2.2), Gullett (2.2), **Carroll** (3.2)	Rose, May (2 on)	
BAL	**A**	013 001 000	5	8	0	Palmer (7), **Watt** (1), Drabowsky (1)	B. Robinson	
GAME 5 - OCTOBER 15								The Orioles again overcome a three-run deficit, as Frank Robinson and Rettenmund each homered and drove in two runs. Cuellar allowed only two hits after first inning.
CIN	**N**	300 000 000	3	6	0	**Merritt** (1.2), Granger (0.2), Wilcox (1.2), Cloninger (2), Washburn (1.1), Carroll (0.2)		
BAL	**A**	222 010 02x	9	15	0	**Cuellar** (9)	F. Robinson (1 on), Rettenmund	

Team totals

		W	AB	H	2B	3B	HR	R	RBI	BA	BB	SO	ERA
BAL	**A**	4	171	50	7	0	10	33	32	.292	20	33	3.40
CIN	**N**	1	164	35	6	1	5	20	20	.213	15	23	6.70

Individual Batting

BALTIMORE (A.L.)

	AB	H	2B	3B	HR	R	RBI	BA
F. Robinson, of	22	6	0	0	2	5	4	.273
B. Robinson, 3b	21	9	2	0	2	5	6	.429
P. Blair, of	19	9	1	0	0	5	3	.474
M. Belanger, ss	19	2	0	0	0	0	1	.105
B. Powell, 1b	17	5	1	0	2	6	5	.294
D. Johnson, 2b	16	5	2	0	0	2	2	.313
D. Buford, of	15	4	0	0	1	3	1	.267
E. Hendricks, c	11	4	1	0	1	1	4	.364
A. Etchebarren, c	7	1	0	0	0	1	0	.143
J. Palmer, p	7	1	0	0	0	1	0	.143
M. Rettenmund, of	5	2	0	0	1	2	2	.400
D. McNally, p	4	1	0	0	1	1	4	.250
M. Cuellar, p	4	0	0	0	0	0	0	.000
C. Salmon	1	1	0	0	0	1	0	1.000
T. Crowley	1	0	0	0	0	0	0	.000
M. Drabowsky, p	1	0	0	0	0	0	0	.000
D. Hall, p	1	0	0	0	0	0	0	.000

Errors: M. Belanger, P. Blair, A. Etchebarren, E. Hendricks, B. Robinson

CINCINNATI (N.L.)

	AB	H	2B	3B	HR	R	RBI	BA
P. Rose, of	20	5	1	0	1	2	2	.250
J. Bench, c	19	4	0	0	1	3	3	.211
B. Tolan, of	19	4	1	0	1	5	1	.211
L. May, 1b	18	7	2	0	2	6	8	.389
T. Helms, 2b	18	4	0	0	0	1	0	.222
T. Perez, 3b	18	1	0	0	0	2	0	.056
H. McRae, of	11	5	2	0	0	1	3	.455
D. Concepcion, ss	9	3	0	1	0	0	3	.333
B. Carbo, of	8	0	0	0	0	0	0	.000
W. Woodward, ss	5	1	0	0	0	0	0	.200
T. Cline	3	1	0	0	0	0	0	.333
G. Nolan, p	3	0	0	0	0	0	0	.000
A. Bravo	2	0	0	0	0	0	0	.000
T. Cloninger, p	2	0	0	0	0	0	0	.000
J. McGlothlin, p	2	0	0	0	0	0	0	.000
J. Stewart	2	0	0	0	0	0	0	.000
C. Carroll, p	1	0	0	0	0	0	0	.000
D. Chaney, ss	1	0	0	0	0	0	0	.000
P. Corrales	1	0	0	0	0	0	0	.000
D. Gullett, p	1	0	0	0	0	0	0	.000
J. Merritt, p	1	0	0	0	0	0	0	.000

Errors: T. Perez, P. Rose, B. Tolan

Stolen Bases: B. Tolan

Individual Pitching

BALTIMORE (A.L.)

	W	L	ERA	IP	H	BB	SO	SV
J. Palmer	1	0	4.60	15.2	11	9	9	0
M. Cuellar	1	0	3.18	11.1	10	2	5	0
D. McNally	1	0	3.00	9	9	2	5	0
M. Drabowsky	0	0	2.70	3.1	2	1	1	0
D. Hall	0	0	0.00	2.1	0	0	0	1
T. Phoebus	1	0	0.00	1.2	1	0	0	0
E. Watt	0	1	9.00	1	2	1	3	0
M. Lopez	0	0	0.00	0.1	0	0	0	0
P. Richert	0	0	0.00	0.1	0	0	0	1

CINCINNATI (N.L.)

	W	L	ERA	IP	H	BB	SO	SV
G. Nolan	0	1	7.71	9.1	9	3	9	0
C. Carroll	1	0	0.00	9	5	2	11	0
T. Cloninger	0	1	7.36	7.1	10	5	4	0
D. Gullett	0	0	1.35	6.2	5	4	4	0
J. McGlothlin	0	0	8.31	4.1	6	2	2	0
M. Wilcox	0	1	9.00	2	3	0	2	0
J. Merritt	0	1	21.60	1.2	3	1	0	0
W. Granger	0	0	33.75	1.1	7	1	1	0
R. Washburn	0	0	13.50	1.1	2	2	0	0

1971 NATIONAL LEAGUE CHAMPIONSHIP SERIES

Pittsburgh (East) defeats San Francisco (West) 3 games to 1

LINE SCORES			R	H	E	PITCHERS (innings pitched)	HOME RUNS (men on)	HIGHLIGHTS
GAME 1 - OCTOBER 2								Tito Fuentes and Willie McCovey poled two-run home runs in the fifth inning as the Giants overcame a 2-1 deficit.
PIT	**E**	002 000 200	4	9	0	**Blass** (5), Moose (2), Giusti (1)		
SF	**W**	001 040 00x	5	7	2	**Perry** (9)	McCovey (1 on), Fuentes (1 on)	
GAME 2 - OCTOBER 3								Bob Robertson, in a one-man display of power, hammered three home runs and a double to drive in five runs as the Pirates evened the series.
PIT	**E**	010 210 401	9	15	0	**Ellis** (5), Miller (3), Giusti (1), **SV**	Robertson, Robertson (2 on), Robertson, Clines	
SF	**W**	110 000 002	4	9	0	**Cumberland** (3), Barr (1), McMahon (2), Carrithers (0), Bryant (2), Hamilton (1)	Mays	
GAME 3 - OCTOBER 5								Richie Hebner's homer off Juan Marichal in the eighth inning snapped a 1-1 tie and gave Bob Johnson a 2-1 victory.
SF	**W**	000 001 000	1	5	2	**Marichal** (8)		
PIT	**E**	010 000 01x	2	4	1	**Johnson** (8), Giusti (1), **SV**	Robertson, Hebner	
GAME 4 - OCTOBER 6								Richie Hebner drove in three runs with three hits including a home run, and rookie right-hander Bruce Kison pitched two-hit scoreless ball in 4.2 innings.
SF	**W**	140 000 000	5	10	0	**Perry** (5.2), Johnson (1.1), McMahon (1)	Speier, McCovey (2 on)	
PIT	**E**	230 004 00x	9	11	2	Blass (2), **Kison** (4.2), Giusti (2.1) **SV**	Hebner (2 on), Oliver (2 on)	

Team totals

		W	AB	H	2B	3B	HR	R	RBI	BA	BB	SO	ERA
PIT	**E**	3	144	39	4	0	8	24	23	.271	5	33	3.34
SF	**W**	1	132	31	5	0	5	15	14	.235	16	28	6.09

Individual Batting

PITTSBURGH (EAST)

	AB	H	2B	3B	HR	R	RBI	BA
D. Cash, 2b	19	8	2	0	0	5	1	.421
R. Clemente, of	18	6	0	0	0	2	4	.333
R. Hebner, 3b	17	5	1	0	2	3	4	.294
B. Robertson, 1b	16	7	1	0	4	5	6	.438
M. Sanguillen, c	15	4	0	0	0	1	1	.267
W. Stargell, of	14	0	0	0	0	1	0	.000
J. Hernandez, ss	13	3	0	0	0	2	1	.231
A. Oliver, of	12	3	0	0	1	2	5	.250
G. Clines, of	3	1	0	0	1	1	1	.333
D. Ellis, p	3	0	0	0	0	0	0	.000
G. Alley, ss	2	1	0	0	0	1	0	.500
V. Davalillo	2	0	0	0	0	0	0	.000
B. Johnson, p	2	0	0	0	0	0	0	.000
B. Kison, p	2	0	0	0	0	0	0	.000
B. Mazeroski	1	1	0	0	0	1	0	1.000
S. Blass, p	1	0	0	0	0	0	0	.000
D. Giusti, p	1	0	0	0	0	0	0	.000
M. May	1	0	0	0	0	0	0	.000
B. Miller, p	1	0	0	0	0	0	0	.000
J. Pagan, 3b	1	0	0	0	0	0	0	.000

Errors: D. Cash, R. Hebner, J. Hernandez
Stolen Bases: D. Cash, M. Sanguillen

SAN FRANCISCO (WEST)

	AB	H	2B	3B	HR	R	RBI	BA
T. Fuentes, 2b	16	5	1	0	1	4	2	.313
K. Henderson, of	16	5	1	0	0	3	2	.313
W. Mays, of	15	4	2	0	1	2	3	.267
D. Dietz, c	15	1	0	0	0	0	0	.067
W. McCovey, 1b	14	6	0	0	2	2	6	.429
C. Speier, ss	14	5	1	0	1	4	1	.357
A. Gallagher, 3b	10	1	0	0	0	0	0	.100
D. Kingman, of	9	1	0	0	0	0	0	.111
B. Bonds, of	8	2	0	0	0	0	0	.250
J. Hart, 3b	5	0	0	0	0	0	0	.000
G. Perry, p	4	1	0	0	0	0	0	.250
J. Marichal, p	3	0	0	0	0	0	0	.000
J. Barr, p	1	0	0	0	0	0	0	.000
F. Duffy	1	0	0	0	0	0	0	.000
H. Lanier, 3b	1	0	0	0	0	0	0	.000
J. Rosario	0	0	0	0	0	0	0	—

Errors: B. Bonds, T. Fuentes, W. McCovey, C. Speier
Stolen Bases: K. Henderson, W. Mays

Individual Pitching

PITTSBURGH (EAST)

	W	L	ERA	IP	H	BB	SO	SV
B. Johnson	1	0	0.00	8	5	3	7	0
S. Blass	0	1	11.57	7	14	2	11	0
D. Giusti	0	0	0.00	5.1	1	2	3	3
D. Ellis	1	0	3.60	5	6	4	1	0
B. Kison	1	0	0.00	4.2	2	2	3	0
B. Miller	0	0	6.00	3	3	3	3	0
B. Moose	0	0	0.00	2	0	0	0	0

SAN FRANCISCO (WEST)

	W	L	ERA	IP	H	BB	SO	SV
G. Perry	1	1	6.14	14.2	19	3	11	0
J. Marichal	0	1	2.25	8	4	0	6	0
J. Cumberland	0	1	9.00	3	7	0	4	0
D. McMahon	0	0	0.00	3	0	0	3	0
R. Bryant	0	0	4.50	2	1	1	2	0
J. Johnson	0	0	13.50	1.1	1	1	2	0
J. Barr	0	0	9.00	1	3	0	2	0
S. Hamilton	0	0	9.00	1	1	0	3	0
D. Carrithers	0	0	∞	0.0	3	0	0	0

1971 AMERICAN LEAGUE CHAMPIONSHIP SERIES

Baltimore (East) defeats Oakland (West) 3 games to 0

LINE SCORES		R	H	E	PITCHERS (innings pitched)	HOME RUNS (men on)	HIGHLIGHTS
GAME 1 - OCTOBER 3							Paul Blair's two-run double climaxed a four-run uprising against Vida Blue in the seventh to give the Orioles a 5-3 victory.
OAK W	020 100 000	3	9	0	**Blue** (7), Fingers (1)		
BAL E	000 100 40x	5	7	1	**McNally** (7), Watt (2), **SV**		
GAME 2 - OCTOBER 4							The Orioles managed only seven hits off Catfish Hunter but four of them were home runs. Boog Powell hit two and drove in three runs.
OAK W	000 100 000	1	6	0	**Hunter** (8)		
BAL E	011 000 12x	5	7	0	**Cuellar** (9)	Powell (1 on), Powell, Hendricks, B. Robinson	
GAME 3 - OCTOBER 5							Brooks Robinson singled home two runs after A's manager Dick Williams had ordered an intentional pass to Ellie Hendricks, loading the bases. Jim Palmer yielded three home runs, two to Reggie Jackson, but all came with the bases empty.
BAL E	100 020 200	5	12	0	**Palmer** (9)		
OAK W	001 001 010	3	7	0	**Segui** (4.2), Fingers (1.1), Knowles (0.1), Locker (0.2), Grant (0.2)	Jackson, Jackson, Bando	

Team totals

	W	AB	H	2B	3B	HR	R	RBI	BA	BB	SO	ERA
BAL E	3	95	26	7	1	4	15	14	.274	13	22	2.33
OAK W	0	96	22	8	1	3	7	7	.229	5	16	5.40

Individual Batting

BALTIMORE (EAST)

	AB	H	2B	3B	HR	R	RBI	BA
F. Robinson, of	12	1	1	0	0	2	1	.083
B. Robinson, 3b	11	4	1	0	1	2	3	.364
D. Johnson, 2b	10	3	2	0	0	2	0	.300
B. Powell, 1b	10	3	0	0	2	4	3	.300
P. Blair, of	9	3	1	0	0	1	2	.333
M. Belanger, ss	8	2	0	0	0	1	1	.250
M. Rettenmund, of	8	2	1	0	0	0	1	.250
D. Buford, of	7	3	0	1	0	1	0	.429
J. Palmer, p	5	1	0	0	0	1	0	.200
A. Etchebarren, c	5	0	0	0	0	0	0	.000
E. Hendricks, c	4	2	0	0	1	1	2	.500
M. Cuellar, p	3	1	0	0	0	0	0	.333
D. McNally, p	2	0	0	0	0	0	0	.000
C. Motton	1	1	1	0	0	0	1	1.000

Errors: D. Johnson

OAKLAND (WEST)

	AB	H	2B	3B	HR	R	RBI	BA
R. Jackson, of	12	4	1	0	2	2	2	.333
B. Campaneris, ss	12	2	1	0	0	0	0	.167
A. Mangual, of	12	2	1	1	0	1	2	.167
S. Bando, 3b	11	4	2	0	1	3	1	.364
T. Davis, 1b	8	3	1	0	0	1	0	.375
D. Green, 2b	7	2	0	0	0	0	0	.286
J. Rudi, of	7	1	1	0	0	0	0	.143
D. Duncan, c	6	3	1	0	0	0	2	.500
M. Epstein, 1b	5	1	0	0	0	0	0	.200
V. Blue, p	3	0	0	0	0	0	0	.000
C. Hunter, p	3	0	0	0	0	0	0	.000
R. Monday, of	3	0	0	0	0	0	0	.000
G. Tenace, c	3	0	0	0	0	0	0	.000
D. Segui, p	2	0	0	0	0	0	0	.000
C. Blefary	1	0	0	0	0	0	0	.000
M. Hegan	1	0	0	0	0	0	0	.000

Individual Pitching

BALTIMORE (EAST)

	W	L	ERA	IP	H	BB	SO	SV
M. Cuellar	1	0	1.00	9	6	1	2	0
J. Palmer	1	0	3.00	9	7	3	8	0
D. McNally	1	0	3.86	7	7	1	5	0
E. Watt	0	0	0.00	2	2	0	1	1

OAKLAND (WEST)

	W	L	ERA	IP	H	BB	SO	SV
C. Hunter	0	1	5.63	8	7	2	6	0
V. Blue	0	1	6.43	7	7	2	8	0
D. Segui	0	1	5.79	4.2	6	6	4	0
R. Fingers	0	0	7.71	2.1	2	1	2	0
M. Grant	0	0	0.00	2	3	0	2	0
B. Locker	0	0	0.00	0.2	0	2	0	0
D. Knowles	0	0	0.00	0.1	1	0	0	0

1971 WORLD SERIES

Pittsburgh (N.L.) defeats Baltimore (A.L.) 4 games to 3

LINE SCORES			R	H	E	PITCHERS (innings pitched)	HOME RUNS (men on)	HIGHLIGHTS
GAME 1 - OCTOBER 9								
PIT	N	030 000 000	3	3	0	**Ellis** (2.1), Moose (3.2), Miller (2)		Rettenmund's three-run homer and solo blasts by Frank Robinson and Buford backed McNally, who allowed three hits, none after the third inning.
BAL	A	013 010 00x	5	10	3	**McNally** (9)	F. Robinson, Rettenmund (2 on), Buford	
GAME 2 - OCTOBER 11								
PIT	N	000 000 030	3	8	1	**R. Johnson** (3.1), Kison (0), Moose (1), Veale (0.2), Miller (2), Giusti (1)	Hebner (2 on)	The Orioles rapped out 14 singles and Brooks Robinson tied a Series record by reaching base five straight times on three hits and two walks.
BAL	A	010 361 00x	11	14	1	**Palmer** (8), Hall (1), **SV**		
GAME 3 - OCTOBER 12								
BAL	A	000 000 100	1	3	3	**Cuellar** (6), Dobson (1), Watt (1)	F. Robinson	Blass silenced the Orioles' bats on three hits and eight strikeouts before a record Pittsburgh crowd of 50,403.
PIT	N	100 001 30x	5	7	0	**Blass** (9)	Robertson (2 on)	
GAME 4 - OCTOBER 13								
BAL	A	300 000 000	3	4	1	**Dobson** (5.1), Jackson (0.2), Watt (1.1), Richert (0.2)		Rookie Kison pitched one-hit relief for 6.1 innings and May delivered a tie- breaking, run-scoring pinch single as Pittsburgh rallied from a 3-0 deficit to win the first night game in World Series history.
PIT	N	201 000 01x	4	14	0	Walker (0.2), **Kison** (6.1), Giusti (2) **SV**		
GAME 5 - OCTOBER 14								
BAL	A	000 000 000	0	2	1	**McNally** (4), Leonhard (1), Dukes (3)		Briles, with only four complete games during regular season, permitted only two singles and helped himself with a run- scoring single, while Clemente hit safely in his 12th straight Series game.
PIT	N	021 010 00x	4	9	0	**Briles** (9)	Robertson	
GAME 6 - OCTOBER 16								
PIT	N	011 000 000 0	2	9	1	Moose (5), R. Johnson (1.2), Giusti (2.1), **Miller** (0.2)	Clemente	Brooks Robinson's sacrifice fly, following singles by Frank Robinson and Rettenmund in the 10th inning gave the Orioles a dramatic victory, after McNally escaped a bases-loaded jam in the top of inning.
BAL	A	000 001 100 1	3	8	0	Palmer (9), Dobson (0.2), **McNally** (0.1)	Buford	
GAME 7 - OCTOBER 17								
PIT	N	000 100 010	2	6	1	**Blass** (9)	Clemente	The Pirates became only the sixth club in Series history to take the title after losing the first two games, thanks to Blass's sparkling four-hitter.
BAL	A	000 000 010	1	4	0	**Cuellar** (8), Dobson (0.2), McNally (0.1)		

Team totals

		W	AB	H	2B	3B	HR	R	RBI	BA	BB	SO	ERA
PIT	N	4	238	56	9	2	5	23	21	.235	26	47	3.50
BAL	A	3	219	45	3	1	5	24	22	.205	20	35	2.66

Individual Batting

PITTSBURGH (N.L.)

	AB	H	2B	3B	HR	R	RBI	BA
D. Cash, 2b	30	4	1	0	0	2	1	.133
R. Clemente, of	29	12	2	1	2	3	4	.414
M. Sanguillen, c	29	11	1	0	0	3	0	.379
B. Robertson, 1b	25	6	0	0	2	4	5	.240
W. Stargell, of	24	5	1	0	0	3	1	.208
A. Oliver, of	19	4	2	0	0	1	2	.211
J. Hernandez, ss	18	4	0	0	0	2	1	.222
J. Pagan, 3b	15	4	2	0	0	0	2	.267
R. Hebner, 3b	12	2	0	0	1	2	3	.167
G. Clines, of	11	1	0	1	0	2	0	.091
S. Blass, p	7	0	0	0	0	0	0	.000
V. Davalillo, of	3	1	0	0	0	1	0	.333
B. Johnson, p	3	0	0	0	0	0	0	.000
N. Briles, p	2	1	0	0	0	0	1	.500
M. May	2	1	0	0	0	0	1	.500
G. Alley, ss	2	0	0	0	0	0	0	.000
B. Kison, p	2	0	0	0	0	0	0	.000
B. Moose, p	2	0	0	0	0	0	0	.000
D. Ellis, p	1	0	0	0	0	0	0	.000
B. Mazeroski	1	0	0	0	0	0	0	.000
C. Sands	1	0	0	0	0	0	0	.000

Errors: R. Hebner, A. Oliver, B. Robertson

Stolen Bases: M. Sanguillen (2), D. Cash, G. Clines, J. Hernandez

BALTIMORE (A.L.)

	AB	H	2B	3B	HR	R	RBI	BA
M. Rettenmund, of	27	5	0	0	1	3	4	.185
D. Johnson, 2b	27	4	0	0	0	1	3	.148
B. Powell, 1b	27	3	0	0	0	1	1	.111
F. Robinson, of	25	7	0	0	2	5	2	.280
D. Buford, of	23	6	1	0	2	3	4	.261
B. Robinson, 3b	22	7	0	0	0	2	5	.318
M. Belanger, ss	21	5	0	1	0	4	0	.238
E. Hendricks, c	19	5	1	0	0	3	1	.263
P. Blair, of	9	3	1	0	0	2	0	.333
D. McNally, p	4	0	0	0	0	0	0	.000
J. Palmer, p	4	0	0	0	0	0	2	.000
T. Shopay	4	0	0	0	0	0	0	.000
M. Cuellar, p	3	0	0	0	0	0	0	.000
P. Dobson, p	2	0	0	0	0	0	0	.000
A. Etchebarren, c	2	0	0	0	0	0	0	.000

Errors: M. Belanger (3), B. Robinson (2), P. Blair, M. Cuellar, E. Hendricks, B. Powell

Stolen Bases: M. Belanger

Individual Pitching

PITTSBURGH (N.L.)

	W	L	ERA	IP	H	BB	SO	SV
S. Blass	2	0	1.00	18	7	4	13	0
B. Moose	0	0	6.52	9.2	12	2	7	0
N. Briles	1	0	0.00	9	2	2	2	0
B. Kison	1	0	0.00	6.1	1	2	3	0
D. Giusti	0	0	0.00	5.1	3	2	4	1
B. Johnson	0	1	9.00	5	5	3	3	0
B. Miller	0	1	3.86	4.2	7	1	2	0
D. Ellis	0	1	15.43	2.1	4	1	1	0
B. Veale	0	0	13.50	0.2	1	2	0	0
L. Walker	0	0	40.50	0.2	3	1	0	0

BALTIMORE (A.L.)

	W	L	ERA	IP	H	BB	SO	SV
J. Palmer	1	0	2.65	17	15	9	15	0
M. Cuellar	0	2	3.86	14	11	6	10	0
D. McNally	2	1	1.98	13.2	10	5	12	0
P. Dobson	0	0	4.05	6.2	13	4	6	0
T. Dukes	0	0	0.00	4	2	0	1	0
E. Watt	0	1	3.86	2.1	4	0	2	0
D. Hall	0	0	0.00	1	1	0	0	1
D. Leonhard	0	0	0.00	1	0	1	0	0
G. Jackson	0	0	0.00	0.2	0	1	0	0
P. Richert	0	0	0.00	0.2	0	0	1	0

1972 NATIONAL LEAGUE CHAMPIONSHIP SERIES

Cincinnati (West) defeats Pittsburgh (East) 3 games to 2

LINE SCORES			R	H	E	PITCHERS (innings pitched)	HOME RUNS (men on)	HIGHLIGHTS
GAME 1 - OCTOBER 7								Joe Morgan, second batter to face Steve Blass, hit a home run, but the Pirates came up with three runs in their half of the first inning, more than enough to win the opener, 5-1.
CIN	**W**	100 000 000	1	8	0	**Gullett** (6), Borbon (2)	Morgan	
PIT	**E**	300 020 00x	5	6	0	**Blass** (8.1), Hernandez (0.2) **SV**	Oliver (1 on)	
GAME 2 - OCTOBER 8								Pirate starter Bob Moose failed to retire a batter as the Reds raked him for five straight hits in the first inning.
CIN	**W**	400 000 010	5	8	1	Billingham (4.2), **Hall** (4.1)	Morgan	
PIT	**E**	000 111 000	3	7	1	**Moose** (0), Johnson (5), Kison (1), Hernandez (2), Giusti (1)		
GAME 3 - OCTOBER 9								Manny Sanguillen homered for the first Pittsburgh run and drove in the tie-breaking run in the eighth inning to give the Pirates a 3-2 victory.
PIT	**E**	000 010 110	3	7	0	Briles (6), **Kison** (1.1), Giusti (1.2) **SV**	Sanguillen	
CIN	**W**	002 000 000	2	8	1	Nolan (6), Borbon (0.1), **Carroll** (1.2), McGlothlin (1)		
GAME 4 - OCTOBER 10								Ross Grimsley handcuffed the hard-hitting Pirates, limiting them to two hits, including Roberto Clemente's solo homer.
PIT	**E**	000 000 100	1	2	3	**Ellis** (5), Johnson (1), Walker (1), Miller (1)	Clemente	
CIN	**W**	100 202 20x	7	11	1	**Grimsley** (9)		
GAME 5 - OCTOBER 11								Pittsburgh was leading 3-2 as the Reds came to bat in the ninth. Bench, the first batter to face Giusti, hit a home run to tie the game. When Perez and Menke followed with singles, manager Bill Virdon brought in Bob Moose. With pinch hitter Hal McRae at the plate, Moose uncorked a wild pitch and Foster raced home with the winning run.
PIT	**E**	020 100 000	3	8	0	Blass (7.1), Hernandez (0.2), **Giusti** (0), Moose (0.2)		
CIN	**W**	001 010 002	4	7	1	Gullett (3), Borbon (2), Hall (3), **Carroll** (1)	Geronimo, Bench	

Team totals

		W	AB	H	2B	3B	HR	R	RBI	BA	BB	SO	ERA
CIN	**W**	3	166	42	9	2	4	19	16	.253	10	28	3.07
PIT	**E**	2	158	30	6	1	3	15	14	.190	9	27	3.30

Individual Batting

CINCINNATI (WEST)

	AB	H	2B	3B	HR	R	RBI	BA
B. Tolan, of	21	5	1	1	0	3	4	.238
P. Rose, of	20	9	4	0	0	1	2	.450
T. Perez, 1b	20	4	1	0	0	0	2	.200
C. Geronimo, of	20	2	0	0	1	2	1	.100
J. Morgan, 2b	19	5	0	0	2	5	3	.263
J. Bench, c	18	6	1	1	1	3	2	.333
D. Menke, 3b	16	4	1	0	0	1	0	.250
D. Chaney, ss	16	3	0	0	0	3	1	.188
R. Grimsley, p	4	2	1	0	0	0	1	.500
D. Gullett, p	2	1	0	0	0	0	0	.500
T. Uhlaender	2	1	0	0	0	0	0	.500
J. Billingham, p	2	0	0	0	0	0	0	.000
D. Concepcion, ss	2	0	0	0	0	0	0	.000
G. Nolan, p	2	0	0	0	0	0	0	.000
J. Hague	1	0	0	0	0	0	0	.000
T. Hall, p	1	0	0	0	0	0	0	.000
G. Foster	0	0	0	0	0	1	0	—
H. McRae	0	0	0	0	0	0	0	—

Errors: D. Chaney (3), J. Bench
Stolen Bases: J. Bench (2), D. Chaney, J. Morgan

PITTSBURGH (EAST)

	AB	H	2B	3B	HR	R	RBI	BA
R. Stennett, 2b, of	21	6	0	0	0	2	1	.286
A. Oliver, of	20	5	2	1	1	3	3	.250
D. Cash, 2b	19	4	0	0	0	0	3	.211
R. Clemente, of	17	4	1	0	1	1	2	.235
M. Sanguillen, c	16	5	1	0	1	4	2	.313
R. Hebner, 3b	16	3	1	0	0	2	1	.188
W. Stargell, 1b, of	16	1	1	0	0	1	1	.063
G. Alley, ss	16	0	0	0	0	1	0	.000
S. Blass, p	6	0	0	0	0	0	0	.000
M. May, c	2	1	0	0	0	0	1	.500
B. Mazeroski	2	1	0	0	0	0	0	.500
N. Briles, p	2	0	0	0	0	0	0	.000
G. Clines	2	0	0	0	0	1	0	.000
D. Ellis, p	1	0	0	0	0	0	0	.000
D. Giusti, p	1	0	0	0	0	0	0	.000
B. Johnson, p	1	0	0	0	0	0	0	.000
V. Davalillo	0	0	0	0	0	0	0	—
B. Robertson, 1b	0	0	0	0	0	0	0	—

Errors: G. Alley (2), D. Cash, M. Sanguillen

Individual Pitching

CINCINNATI (WEST)

	W	L	ERA	IP	H	BB	SO	SV
R. Grimsley	1	0	1.00	9	2	0	5	0
D. Gullett	0	1	8.00	9	12	0	5	0
T. Hall	1	0	1.23	7.1	3	3	8	0
G. Nolan	0	0	1.50	6	4	1	4	0
J. Billingham	0	0	3.86	4.2	5	2	4	0
P. Borbon	0	0	2.08	4.1	2	0	1	0
C. Carroll	1	1	3.38	2.2	2	3	0	0
J. McGlothlin	0	0	0.00	1	0	0	0	0

PITTSBURGH (EAST)

	W	L	ERA	IP	H	BB	SO	SV
S. Blass	1	0	1.72	15.2	12	6	5	0
N. Briles	0	0	3.00	6	6	1	3	0
B. Johnson	0	0	3.00	6	4	2	7	0
D. Ellis	0	1	0.00	5	5	1	3	0
R. Hernandez	0	0	2.70	3.1	1	0	3	1
D. Giusti	0	1	6.75	2.2	5	0	3	1
B. Kison	1	0	0.00	2.1	1	0	3	0
B. Miller	0	0	0.00	1	0	0	1	0
L. Walker	0	0	18.00	1	3	0	0	0
B. Moose	0	1	54.00	0.2	5	0	0	0

1972 AMERICAN LEAGUE CHAMPIONSHIP SERIES

Oakland (West) defeats Detroit (East) 3 games to 2

LINE SCORES			R	H	E	PITCHERS (innings pitched)	HOME RUNS (men on)	HIGHLIGHTS
GAME 1 - OCTOBER 7								
DET	E	010 000 000 01	2	6	2	**Lolich** (10), Seelbach (0.1)	Cash, Kaline	Mickey Lolich carried a 2-1 lead into the last of the 11th, but the A's scored twice to beat the Tiger ace, 3-2. Gonzalo Marquez drove in the tying run, and the winning run scored on Kaline's throwing error.
OAK	W	001 000 000 02	3	10	1	Hunter (8), Blue (0), **Fingers** (3)		
GAME 2 - OCTOBER 8								
DET	E	000 000 000	0	3	1	**Fryman** (4.1), Zachary (0), Scherman (2.2), LaGrow (1), Hiller (2)		Blue Moon Odom pitched a magnificent three-hitter and did not walk a batter as the A's made it two straight, 5-0.
OAK	W	100 040 00x	5	8	0	**Odom** (9)		
GAME 3 - OCTOBER 10								
OAK	W	000 000 000	0	7	0	**Holtzman** (4), Fingers (1.2), Blue (0.1), Locker (2)		Joe Coleman struck out 14, setting a playoff record, as the Tigers bounced back to win the third game, 3-0.
DET	E	000 200 01x	3	8	1	**Coleman** (6)	Freehan	
GAME 4 - OCTOBER 11								
OAK	W	000 000 100 2	3	9	2	Hunter (7.1), Fingers (0.2), Blue (1), Locker (3), **Horlen** (0), Hamilton (0)	Epstein	The Tigers appeared hopelessly lost coming to bat in the 10th after the A's scored twice in the top of the inning to take a 3-1 lead. Detroit's comeback began with singles by Dick McAuliffe and Al Kaline. A wild pitch, a walk, and an error produced one run before Hamilton walked home the tying run and Jim Northrup knocked in the game- winner.
DET	E	001 000 000 3	4	10	1	Lolich (9), Seelbach (0.2), **Hiller** (0.1)	McAuliffe	
GAME 5 - OCTOBER 12								
OAK	W	010 100 000	2	4	0	**Odom** (5), Blue (4), **SV**		Gene Tenace's only hit of the series, a single with two out in the fourth, drove home George Hendrick from second with the winning run.
DET	E	100 000 000	1	5	2	**Fryman** (8), Hiller (1)		

Team totals

		W	AB	H	2B	3B	HR	R	RBI	BA	BB	SO	ERA
OAK	W	3	170	38	8	0	1	13	10	.224	12	35	1.76
DET	E	2	162	32	6	1	4	10	10	.198	13	25	2.14

Individual Batting

OAKLAND (WEST)

	AB	H	2B	3B	HR	R	RBI	BA
M. Alou, of	21	8	4	0	0	2	2	.381
J. Rudi, of	20	5	1	0	0	1	2	.250
S. Bando, 3b	20	4	0	0	0	0	0	.200
R. Jackson, of	18	5	1	0	0	1	2	.278
G. Tenace, 2b, c	17	1	0	0	0	1	1	.059
M. Epstein, 1b	16	3	0	0	1	1	1	.188
D. Green, 2b	8	1	1	0	0	0	0	.125
D. Maxvill, 2b, ss	8	1	0	0	0	0	0	.125
B. Campaneris, ss	7	3	0	0	0	3	0	.429
G. Hendrick, of	7	1	0	0	0	2	0	.143
C. Hunter, p	6	1	0	0	0	0	0	.167
T. Kubiak, 2b, ss	4	2	0	0	0	0	1	.500
B. Odom, p	4	1	1	0	0	0	0	.250
G. Marquez	3	2	0	0	0	1	1	.667
A. Mangual	3	0	0	0	0	0	0	.000
D. Duncan, c	2	0	0	0	0	0	0	.000
V. Blue, p	1	0	0	0	0	0	0	.000
T. Cullen, ss	1	0	0	0	0	0	0	.000
R. Fingers, p	1	0	0	0	0	0	0	.000
M. Hegan, 1b	1	0	0	0	0	1	0	.000
K. Holtzman, p	1	0	0	0	0	0	0	.000
D. Mincher	1	0	0	0	0	0	0	.000

Errors: R. Jackson, T. Kubiak, G. Tenace

Stolen Bases: B. Campaneris (2), R. Jackson (2), M. Alou, D. Maxvill

DETROIT (EAST)

	AB	H	2B	3B	HR	R	RBI	BA
D. McAuliffe, 2b, ss	20	4	0	0	1	3	1	.200
A. Kaline, of	19	5	0	0	1	3	1	.263
A. Rodriguez, 3b	16	0	0	0	0	0	0	.000
N. Cash, 1b	15	4	0	0	1	1	2	.267
T. Taylor, 2b	15	2	2	0	0	0	0	.133
J. Northrup, of	14	5	0	0	0	0	1	.357
D. Sims, c, of	14	3	2	1	0	0	0	.214
B. Freehan, c	12	3	1	0	1	2	3	.250
W. Horton, of	10	1	0	0	0	0	0	.100
M. Lolich, p	7	0	0	0	0	0	0	.000
M. Stanley, of	6	2	0	0	0	0	0	.333
E. Brinkman, ss	4	1	1	0	0	0	0	.250
W. Fryman, p	3	0	0	0	0	0	0	.000
I. Brown, 1b	2	1	0	0	0	0	2	.500
J. Coleman, p	2	1	0	0	0	0	0	.500
G. Brown	2	0	0	0	0	1	0	.000
T. Haller	1	0	0	0	0	0	0	.000
J. Knox	0	0	0	0	0	0	0	—
J. Niekro	0	0	0	0	0	0	0	—

Errors: D. McAuliffe (4), A. Kaline, A. Rodriguez, D. Sims

Individual Pitching

OAKLAND (WEST)

	W	L	ERA	IP	H	BB	SO	SV
C. Hunter	0	0	1.17	15.1	10	5	9	0
B. Odom	2	0	0.00	14	5	2	5	0
V. Blue	0	0	0.00	5.1	4	1	5	1
R. Fingers	1	0	1.69	5.1	4	1	3	0
K. Holtzman	0	1	4.50	4	4	2	2	0
B. Locker	0	0	13.50	2	4	0	1	0
D. Hamilton	0	0	—	0.0	1	1	0	0
J. Horlen	0	1	∞	0.0	0	1	0	0

DETROIT (EAST)

	W	L	ERA	IP	H	BB	SO	SV
M. Lolich	0	1	1.42	19	14	5	10	0
W. Fryman	0	2	3.65	12.1	11	2	8	0
J. Coleman	1	0	0.00	9	7	3	14	0
J. Hiller	1	0	0.00	3.1	1	1	1	0
L. LaGrow	0	0	0.00	1	0	0	1	0
C. Seelbach	0	0	18.00	1	4	0	0	0
F. Scherman	0	0	0.00	0.2	1	0	1	0
C. Zachary	0	0	∞	0.0	0	1	0	0

1972 WORLD SERIES

Oakland (A.L.) defeats Cincinnati (N.L.) 4 games to 3

LINE SCORES			R	H	E	PITCHERS (innings pitched)	HOME RUNS (men on)	HIGHLIGHTS
GAME 1 - OCTOBER 14								Tenace made Series history, becoming the first player to hit home runs in his first two Series at bats. He knocked in all three Oakland runs before a record Cincinnati crowd of 52,918.
OAK	**A**	020 010 000	3	4	0	**Holtzman** (5), Fingers (1.2), Blue (2.1) **SV**	Tenace (1 on), Tenace	
CIN	**N**	010 100 000	2	7	0	**Nolan** (6), Borbon (1), Carroll (2)		
GAME 2 - OCTOBER 15								Rudi excelled at bat and in the field, with a home run and game-saving catch in the ninth before another Cincinnati record crowd of 53,224.
OAK	**A**	011 000 000	2	9	2	**Hunter** (8.2), Fingers (0.1), **SV**	Rudi	
CIN	**N**	000 000 001	1	6	0	**Grimsley** (5), Borbon (2), Hall (2)		
GAME 3 - OCTOBER 18								The Reds got the game's only run in the seventh on Perez's single, Menke's bunt and Geronimo's single. Odom struck out eleven and allowed just three hits in a losing cause.
CIN	**N**	000 000 100	1	4	2	**Billingham** (8), Carroll (1), **SV**		
OAK	**A**	000 000 000	0	3	2	**Odom** (7), Blue (0.1), Fingers (1.2)		
GAME 4 - OCTOBER 19								The A's scored two in the ninth on four straight singles (three by pinch-hitters) in posting their third one-run victory of the Series. Hits by Marquez, Tenace, Mincher and Mangual won it.
CIN	**N**	000 000 020	2	7	1	Gullett (7), Borbon (1.1), **Carroll** (0)		
OAK	**A**	000 010 002	3	10	1	Holtzman (7.2), Blue (0.1), **Fingers** (1)	Tenace	
GAME 5 - OCTOBER 20								Rose began the scoring with a first-pitch homer and ended it with a run-scoring single in ninth. The Reds threw out the tying run at home in the bottom of ninth.
CIN	**N**	100 110 011	5	8	0	McGlothlin (3), Borbon (1), Hall (2), Carroll (1.2), **Grimsley** (0.2), Billingham (0.2), **SV**	Rose, Menke	
OAK	**A**	030 100 000	4	7	2	Hunter (4.2), **Fingers** (3.2), Hamilton (0.2)	Tenace (2 on)	
GAME 6 - OCTOBER 21								The Reds ended their seven-game Series home losing streak, with Tolan and Geronimo each knocking in two runs.
OAK	**A**	000 010 000	1	7	1	**Blue** (5.2), Locker (0.1), Hamilton (0.2), Horlen (1.1)		
CIN	**N**	000 111 50x	8	10	0	Nolan (4.2), **Grimsley** (1) Borbon (1), Hall (2.1), **SV**	Bench	
GAME 7 - OCTOBER 22								The A's won their first World Series title since 1930, with Tenace the unlikely hero on two hits and two RBIs.
OAK	**A**	100 002 000	3	6	1	Odom (4.1), **Hunter** (2.2), Holtzman (0), Fingers (2), **SV**		
CIN	**N**	000 010 010	2	4	2	Billingham (5), **Borbon** (0.2), Carroll (1), Granger (0.1), Hall (2)		

Team totals

		W	AB	H	2B	3B	HR	R	RBI	BA	BB	SO	ERA
OAK	**A**	4	220	46	4	0	5	16	16	.209	21	37	3.05
CIN	**N**	3	220	46	8	1	3	21	21	.209	27	46	2.17

Individual Batting

OAKLAND (A.L.)

	AB	H	2B	3B	HR	R	RBI	BA
B. Campaneris, ss	28	5	0	0	0	1	0	.179
S. Bando, 3b	26	7	1	0	0	2	1	.269
J. Rudi, of	25	6	0	0	1	1	1	.240
M. Alou, of	24	1	0	0	0	0	0	.042
G. Tenace, 1b, c	23	8	1	0	4	5	9	.348
D. Green, 2b	18	6	2	0	0	0	1	.333
M. Epstein, 1b	16	0	0	0	0	1	0	.000
G. Hendrick, of	15	2	0	0	0	3	0	.133
A. Mangual, of	10	3	0	0	0	1	1	.300
G. Marquez	5	3	0	0	0	0	1	.600
D. Duncan, c	5	1	0	0	0	0	0	.200
M. Hegan, 1b	5	1	0	0	0	0	0	.200
C. Hunter, p	5	1	0	0	0	0	1	.200
K. Holtzman, p	5	0	0	0	0	0	0	.000
B. Odom, p	4	0	0	0	0	0	0	.000
T. Kubiak, 2b	3	1	0	0	0	0	0	.333
D. Mincher	1	1	0	0	0	0	1	1.000
V. Blue, p	1	0	0	0	0	0	0	.000
R. Fingers, p	1	0	0	0	0	0	0	.000
A. Lewis	0	0	0	0	0	2	0	—

Errors: M. Epstein (2), M. Alou, S. Bando, B. Campaneris, K. Holtzman, C. Hunter, A. Mangual, G. Tenace
Stolen Bases: M. Alou

CINCINNATI (N.L.)

	AB	H	2B	3B	HR	R	RBI	BA
P. Rose, of	28	6	0	0	1	3	2	.214
B. Tolan, of	26	7	1	0	0	2	6	.269
J. Morgan, 2b	24	3	2	0	0	4	1	.125
D. Menke, 3b	24	2	0	0	1	1	2	.083
T. Perez, 1b	23	10	2	0	0	3	2	.435
J. Bench, c	23	6	1	0	1	4	1	.261
C. Geronimo, of	19	3	0	0	0	1	3	.158
D. Concepcion, ss	13	4	0	1	0	2	2	.308
H. McRae, of	9	4	1	0	0	1	2	.444
D. Chaney, ss	7	0	0	0	0	0	0	.000
J. Billingham, p	5	0	0	0	0	0	0	.000
T. Uhlaender	4	1	1	0	0	0	0	.250
J. Hague, of	3	0	0	0	0	0	0	.000
G. Nolan, p	3	0	0	0	0	0	0	.000
R. Grimsley, p	2	0	0	0	0	0	0	.000
D. Gullett, p	2	0	0	0	0	0	0	.000
T. Hall, p	2	0	0	0	0	0	0	.000
J. Javier	2	0	0	0	0	0	0	.000
J. McGlothlin, p	1	0	0	0	0	0	0	.000
G. Foster, of	0	0	0	0	0	0	0	—

Errors: J. Bench, D. Concepcion, J. Morgan, T. Perez, B. Tolan
Stolen Bases: B. Tolan (5), J. Bench (2), J. Morgan (2), D. Concepcion, C. Geronimo, P. Rose

Individual Pitching

OAKLAND (A.L.)

	W	L	ERA	IP	H	BB	SO	SV
C. Hunter	2	0	2.81	16	12	6	11	0
K. Holtzman	1	0	2.13	12.2	11	3	4	0
B. Odom	0	1	1.59	11.1	5	6	13	0
R. Fingers	1	1	1.74	10.1	4	4	11	2
V. Blue	0	1	4.15	8.2	8	5	5	1
D. Hamilton	0	0	27.00	1.1	3	1	1	0
J. Horlen	0	0	6.75	1.1	2	2	1	0
B. Locker	0	0	0.00	0.1	1	0	0	0

CINCINNATI (N.L.)

	W	L	ERA	IP	H	BB	SO	SV
J. Billingham	1	0	0.00	13.2	6	4	11	1
G. Nolan	0	1	3.38	10.2	7	2	3	0
T. Hall	0	0	0.00	8.1	6	2	7	1
P. Borbon	0	1	3.86	7	7	2	4	0
R. Grimsley	2	1	2.57	7	7	3	2	0
D. Gullett	0	0	1.29	7	5	2	4	0
C. Carroll	0	1	1.59	5.2	6	4	3	1
J. McGlothlin	0	0	12.00	3	2	2	3	0

1973 NATIONAL LEAGUE CHAMPIONSHIP SERIES

New York (East) defeats Cincinnati (West) 3 games to 2

LINE SCORES			R	H	E	PITCHERS (innings pitched)	HOME RUNS (men on)	HIGHLIGHTS
GAME 1 - OCTOBER 6								Tom Seaver set a league playoff record by striking out 13 Reds, but after seven superb scoreless innings, Pete Rose homered in the eighth and Johnny Bench in the ninth as the Reds won.
NY	**E**	010 000 000	1	3	0	**Seaver** (9)		
CIN	**W**	000 000 011	2	6	0	Billingham (8), Hall (0), **Borbon** (1)	Rose, Bench	
GAME 2 - OCTOBER 7								Jon Matlack pitched a two-hitter and struck out nine pitching the Mets to a 5-0 triumph that evened the Series.
NY	**E**	000 100 004	5	7	0	**Matlack** (9)	Staub	
CIN	**W**	000 000 000	0	2	0	**Gullett** (5), Carroll (3), Hall (0.1), Borbon (0.2)		
GAME 3 - OCTOBER 8								Rusty Staub homered in his first two times at bat to lead Jerry Koosman to an easy win in a game marred by a brawl triggered by Rose's hard slide into Bud Harrelson in the fifth.
CIN	**W**	002 000 000	2	8	1	**Grimsley** (1.2), Hall (0.1), Tomlin (1.2), Nelson (2.1), Borbon (2)	Menke	
NY	**E**	151 200 00x	9	11	1	**Koosman** (9)	Staub, Staub (2 on)	
GAME 4 - OCTOBER 9								Pete Rose hit a home run off Harry Parker in the 12th inning to give the Reds a 2-1 victory that evened the series at two games apiece.
CIN	**W**	000 000 100 001	2	8	0	Norman (5), Gullett (4), **Carroll** (2), Borbon (1) **SV**	Perez, Rose	
NY	**E**	001 000 000 000	1	3	2	Stone (6.2), McGraw (4.1), **Parker** (1)		
GAME 5 - OCTOBER 10								Tom Seaver, a victim of non-support most of the regular season, was backed by a 13-hit attack and easily outpitched Cincinnati ace Jack Billingham to give the Mets a 7-2 victory and the pennant.
CIN	**W**	001 010 000	2	7	1	**Billingham** (4), Gullett (0), Carroll (2), Grimsley (2)		
NY	**E**	200 041 00x	7	13	1	**Seaver** (8.1), McGraw (0.2) **SV**		

Team totals

		W	AB	H	2B	3B	HR	R	RBI	BA	BB	SO	ERA
NY	**E**	3	168	37	5	0	3	23	22	.220	19	28	1.33
CIN	**W**	2	167	31	6	0	5	8	8	.186	13	42	4.50

Individual Batting

NEW YORK (EAST)

	AB	H	2B	3B	HR	R	RBI	BA
W. Garrett, 3b	23	2	1	0	0	1	1	.087
C. Jones, of	20	6	2	0	0	3	3	.300
F. Millan, 2b	19	6	0	0	0	5	2	.316
J. Grote, c	19	4	0	0	0	2	2	.211
B. Harrelson, ss	18	3	0	0	0	1	2	.167
D. Hahn, of	17	4	0	0	0	2	1	.235
J. Milner, 1b	17	3	0	0	0	2	1	.176
R. Staub, of	15	3	0	0	3	4	5	.200
T. Seaver, p	6	2	2	0	0	1	1	.333
J. Koosman, p	4	2	0	0	0	1	1	.500
W. Mays, of	3	1	0	0	0	1	1	.333
E. Kranepool, of	2	1	0	0	0	0	2	.500
J. Matlack, p	2	0	0	0	0	0	0	.000
K. Boswell	1	0	0	0	0	0	0	.000
T. McGraw, p	1	0	0	0	0	0	0	.000
G. Stone, p	1	0	0	0	0	0	0	.000

Errors: W. Garrett, J. Grote, C. Jones, T. McGraw

CINCINNATI (WEST)

	AB	H	2B	3B	HR	R	RBI	BA
T. Perez, 1b	22	2	0	0	1	1	2	.091
P. Rose, of	21	8	1	0	2	3	2	.381
J. Morgan, 2b	20	2	1	0	0	1	1	.100
J. Bench, c	19	5	2	0	1	1	1	.263
C. Geronimo, of	15	1	0	0	0	0	0	.067
D. Driessen, 3b	12	2	1	0	0	0	1	.167
A. Kosco, of	10	3	0	0	0	0	0	.300
D. Menke, 3b, ss	9	2	0	0	1	1	1	.222
D. Chaney, ss	9	0	0	0	0	0	0	.000
K. Griffey, of	7	1	1	0	0	0	0	.143
E. Armbrister, of	6	1	0	0	0	0	0	.167
L. Stahl	4	2	0	0	0	1	0	.500
J. Billingham, p	3	0	0	0	0	0	0	.000
P. Gagliano	3	0	0	0	0	0	0	.000
E. Crosby, ss	2	1	0	0	0	0	0	.500
H. King	2	1	0	0	0	0	0	.500
D. Gullett, p	1	0	0	0	0	0	0	.000
R. Nelson, p	1	0	0	0	0	0	0	.000
F. Norman, p	1	0	0	0	0	0	0	.000

Errors: D. Driessen, A. Kosco

Individual Pitching

NEW YORK (EAST)

	W	L	ERA	IP	H	BB	SO	SV
T. Seaver	1	1	1.62	16.2	13	5	17	0
J. Koosman	1	0	2.00	9	8	0	9	0
J. Matlack	1	0	0.00	9	2	3	9	0
G. Stone	0	0	1.35	6.2	3	2	4	0
T. McGraw	0	0	0.00	5	4	3	3	1
H. Parker	0	1	9.00	1	1	0	0	0

CINCINNATI (WEST)

	W	L	ERA	IP	H	BB	SO	SV
J. Billingham	0	1	4.50	12	9	4	9	0
D. Gullett	0	1	2.00	9	4	3	6	0
C. Carroll	1	0	1.29	7	5	1	2	0
F. Norman	0	0	1.80	5	1	3	3	0
P. Borbon	1	0	0.00	4.2	3	0	3	1
R. Grimsley	0	1	12.27	3.2	7	2	3	0
R. Nelson	0	0	0.00	2.1	0	1	0	0
D. Tomlin	0	0	16.20	1.2	5	1	1	0
T. Hall	0	0	67.50	0.2	3	4	1	0

1973 AMERICAN LEAGUE CHAMPIONSHIP SERIES

Oakland (West) defeats Baltimore (East) 3 games to 2

LINE SCORES		R	H	E	PITCHERS (innings pitched)	HOME RUNS (men on)	HIGHLIGHTS
GAME 1 - OCTOBER 6							Baltimore pounced upon Vida Blue, knocking him out of the box in the first with a four-run barrage.
OAK W	000 000 000	0	5	1	**Blue** (0.2), Pina (2), Odom (5), Fingers (0.1)		
BAL E	400 000 11x	6	12	0	**Palmer** (9)		
GAME 2 - OCTOBER 7							Sal Bando, robbed of a home run when Al Bumbry made a spectacular leaping catch of his drive in the third inning, followed with two four-baggers, one with a runner aboard, to lead the A's to a 6-3 triumph.
OAK W	100 002 021	6	9	0	**Hunter** (7.1), Fingers (1.2), **SV**	Bando (1 on), Bando, Rudi, Campaneris	
BAL E	100 001 010	3	8	0	**McNally** (7.2), Reynolds (1), Jackson (0.1)		
GAME 3 - OCTOBER 9							Bert Campaneris, not known for his batting power, hammered a home run off Mike Cuellar leading off the bottom of the 11th inning to give the A's a thrilling 2-1 triumph over the Orioles.
BAL E	010 000 000 00	1	3	0	**Cuellar** (10)	Williams	
OAK W	000 000 010 01	2	4	3	**Holtzman** (11)	Campaneris	
GAME 4 - OCTOBER 10							Bobby Grich hit a home run in the eighth inning to break a 4-4 tie and give the Orioles a 5-4 comeback victory.
BAL E	000 000 410	5	8	0	Palmer (1.1), Reynolds (4.2), Watt (0.1), **Jackson** (2.2)	Etchebarren (2 on), Grich	
OAK W	030 001 000	4	7	0	Blue (6.1), **Fingers** (2.2)		
GAME 5 - OCTOBER 11							Catfish Hunter overpowered the Orioles in the final game, shutting them out 3-0 on a five-hitter. Not a single Oriole reached third base and no more than one runner was on base in any one inning.
BAL E	000 000 000	0	5	2	**Alexander** (3.2), Palmer (4.1)		
OAK W	001 200 00x	3	7	0	**Hunter** (9)		

Team totals

		W	AB	H	2B	3B	HR	R	RBI	BA	BB	SO	ERA
OAK	**W**	3	160	32	5	1	5	15	15	.200	17	39	2.74
BAL	**E**	2	171	36	7	0	3	15	15	.211	16	25	2.80

Individual Batting

OAKLAND (WEST)

	AB	H	2B	3B	HR	R	RBI	BA
B. Campaneris, ss	21	7	1	0	2	3	3	.333
R. Jackson, of	21	3	0	0	0	0	0	.143
J. Rudi, of	18	4	0	0	1	1	3	.222
S. Bando, 3b	18	3	0	0	2	2	3	.167
G. Tenace, 1b, c	17	4	1	0	0	3	0	.235
D. Green, 2b	13	1	1	0	0	0	1	.077
R. Fosse, c	11	1	1	0	0	2	3	.091
D. Johnson, dh	10	1	0	0	0	0	0	.100
A. Mangual, of	9	1	0	0	0	1	0	.111
V. Davalillo, 1b, of	8	5	1	1	0	2	1	.625
J. Alou, dh	6	2	0	0	0	0	1	.333
B. Conigliaro, of	4	0	0	0	0	0	0	.000
T. Kubiak, 2b	2	0	0	0	0	0	0	.000
M. Andrews, 1b, dh	1	0	0	0	0	0	0	.000
P. Bourque, dh	1	0	0	0	0	0	0	.000
A. Lewis	0	0	0	0	0	1	0	—

Errors: D. Green (2), B. Campaneris, V. Davalillo
Stolen Bases: B. Campaneris (3), G. Tenace

BALTIMORE (EAST)

	AB	H	2B	3B	HR	R	RBI	BA
T. Davis, dh	21	6	1	0	0	1	2	.286
B. Robinson, 3b	20	5	2	0	0	1	2	.250
B. Grich, 2b	20	2	0	0	1	1	1	.100
E. Williams, 1b, c	18	5	2	0	1	2	4	.278
P. Blair, of	18	3	0	0	0	2	0	.167
M. Belanger, ss	16	2	0	0	0	0	1	.125
A. Etchebarren, c	14	5	1	0	1	1	4	.357
D. Baylor, of	11	3	0	0	0	3	1	.273
M. Rettenmund, of	11	1	0	0	0	1	0	.091
R. Coggins, of	9	4	1	0	0	1	0	.444
A. Bumbry, of	7	0	0	0	0	1	0	.000
B. Powell, 1b	4	0	0	0	0	1	0	.000
T. Crowley, of	2	0	0	0	0	0	0	.000
F. Baker, ss	0	0	0	0	0	0	0	—
L. Brown, 3b	0	0	0	0	0	0	0	—
D. Hood	0	0	0	0	0	0	0	—

Errors: A. Bumbry, B. Robinson

Individual Pitching

OAKLAND (WEST)

	W	L	ERA	IP	H	BB	SO	SV
C. Hunter	2	0	1.65	16.1	12	5	6	0
K. Holtzman	1	0	0.82	11	3	1	7	0
V. Blue	0	1	10.29	7	8	5	3	0
B. Odom	0	0	1.80	5	6	2	4	0
R. Fingers	0	1	1.93	4.2	4	2	4	1
H. Pina	0	0	0.00	2	3	1	1	0

BALTIMORE (EAST)

	W	L	ERA	IP	H	BB	SO	SV
J. Palmer	1	0	1.84	14.2	11	8	15	0
M. Cuellar	0	1	1.80	10	4	3	11	0
D. McNally	0	1	5.87	7.2	7	2	7	0
B. Reynolds	0	0	3.18	5.2	5	3	5	0
D. Alexander	0	1	4.91	3.2	5	0	1	0
G. Jackson	1	0	0.00	3	0	1	0	0
E. Watt	0	0	0.00	0.1	0	0	0	0

1973 WORLD SERIES

Oakland (A.L.) defeats New York (N.L.) 4 games to 3

LINE SCORES						PITCHERS (innings pitched)	HOME RUNS (men on)	HIGHLIGHTS
GAME 1 - OCTOBER 13								Oakland scored two unearned runs in the third, with help from errors by Millan and Mays, and hung on for the victory.
NY	**N**	000 100 000	1	7	2	**Matlack** (6), McGraw (2)		
OAK	**A**	002 000 00x	2	4	0	**Holtzman** (5), Fingers (3.1), Knowles (0.2) **SV**		
GAME 2 - OCTOBER 14								In the longest (4:13) and perhaps the loosest Series game in history, the Mets prevailed by virtue of two costly errors by Andrews in the 12th, when New York pushed across four runs. The two teams tied a record by using 11 pitchers.
NY	**N**	011 004 000 004	10	15	1	Koosman (2.1), Sadecki (1.2), Parker (1), **McGraw** (6), Stone (1), **SV**	Jones, Garrett	
OAK	**A**	210 000 102 001	7	13	5	Blue (5.1), Pina (0), Knowles (1.2), Odom (2), **Fingers** (2.2), Lindblad (0.1)		
GAME 3 - OCTOBER 16								Campaneris got the decisive hit, rapping a single following a walk and passed ball on a third strike in the 11th. Seaver fanned 12 in eight innings.
OAK	**A**	000 001 010 01	3	10	1	Hunter (6), Knowles (2), **Lindblad** (2), Fingers (1), **SV**		
NY	**N**	200 000 000 00	2	10	2	Seaver (8), Sadecki (0), McGraw (2), **Parker** (1)	Garrett	
GAME 4 - OCTOBER 17								Staub had a perfect night with three singles and a three-run homer for five RBIs, while Matlack throttled the A's on three hits in eight innings.
OAK	**A**	000 100 000	1	5	1	**Holtzman** (0.1), Odom (2.2), Knowles (1), Pina (3), Lindblad (1)		
NY	**N**	300 300 00x	6	13	1	**Matlack** (8), Sadecki (1), **SV**	Staub (2 on)	
GAME 5 - OCTOBER 18								Jones doubled in a run in the second and Hahn tripled home the other in the sixth. Koosman and McGraw allowed just two singles and a double.
OAK	**A**	000 000 000	0	3	1	**Blue** (5.2), Knowles (0.1), Fingers (2)		
NY	**N**	010 001 00x	2	7	1	**Koosman** (6.1), McGraw (2.2), **SV**		
GAME 6 - OCTOBER 20								Jackson ripped two RBI doubles, then singled and scored the A's other run.
NY	**N**	000 000 010	1	6	2	**Seaver** (7), McGraw (1)		
OAK	**A**	101 000 01x	3	7	0	**Hunter** (7.1), Knowles (0.1), Fingers (1.1) **SV**		
GAME 7 - OCTOBER 21								Campaneris and Jackson bashed two-run homers in third inning for the A's first two homers of Series as Oakland captured their second World Series title in a row. After the game, A's manager Dick Williams quit.
NY	**N**	000 001 001	2	8	1	**Matlack** (2.2), Parker (1.1), Sadecki (2), Stone (2)		
OAK	**A**	004 010 00x	5	9	1	**Holtzman** (5.1), Fingers (3.1), Knowles (0.1), **SV**	Campaneris (1 on), Jackson (1 on)	

Team totals

		W	AB	H	2B	3B	HR	R	RBI	BA	BB	SO	ERA
OAK	**A**	4	241	51	12	3	2	21	20	.212	28	62	2.32
NY	**N**	3	261	66	7	2	4	24	16	.253	26	36	2.22

Individual Batting

OAKLAND (A.L.)

	AB	H	2B	3B	HR	R	RBI	BA
B. Campaneris, ss	31	9	0	1	1	6	3	.290
R. Jackson, of	29	9	3	1	1	3	6	.310
J. Rudi, of	27	9	2	0	0	3	4	.333
S. Bando, 3b	26	6	1	1	0	5	1	.231
J. Alou, of	19	3	1	0	0	0	3	.158
R. Fosse, c	19	3	1	0	0	0	0	.158
G. Tenace, 1b, c	19	3	1	0	0	0	3	.158
D. Green, 2b	16	1	0	0	0	0	0	.063
V. Davalillo, 1b, of	11	1	0	0	0	0	0	.091
D. Johnson, 1b	10	3	1	0	0	0	0	.300
A. Mangual, of	6	0	0	0	0	0	0	.000
C. Hunter, p	5	0	0	0	0	0	0	.000
V. Blue, p	4	0	0	0	0	0	0	.000
K. Holtzman, p	3	2	2	0	0	2	0	.667
R. Fingers, p	3	1	0	0	0	0	0	.333
M. Andrews, 2b	3	0	0	0	0	0	0	.000
B. Conigliaro	3	0	0	0	0	0	0	.000
T. Kubiak, 2b	3	0	0	0	0	1	0	.000
P. Bourque, 1b	2	1	0	0	0	0	0	.500
P. Lindblad, p	1	0	0	0	0	0	0	.000
B. Odom, p	1	0	0	0	0	0	0	.000
A. Lewis	0	0	0	0	0	1	0	—

Errors: M. Andrews (2), G. Tenace (2), S. Bando, B. Campaneris, D. Green, C. Hunter, D. Knowles

Stolen Bases: B. Campaneris (3)

NEW YORK (N.L.)

	AB	H	2B	3B	HR	R	RBI	BA
F. Millan, 2b	32	6	1	1	0	3	1	.188
J. Grote, c	30	8	0	0	0	2	0	.267
W. Garrett, 3b	30	5	0	0	2	4	2	.167
D. Hahn, of	29	7	1	1	0	2	2	.241
C. Jones, of	28	8	2	0	1	5	1	.286
J. Milner, 1b	27	8	0	0	0	2	2	.296
R. Staub, of	26	11	2	0	1	1	6	.423
B. Harrelson, ss	24	6	1	0	0	2	1	.250
W. Mays, of	7	2	0	0	0	1	1	.286
T. Seaver, p	5	0	0	0	0	0	0	.000
J. Matlack, p	4	1	0	0	0	0	0	.250
J. Beauchamp	4	0	0	0	0	0	0	.000
J. Koosman, p	4	0	0	0	0	0	0	.000
K. Boswell	3	3	0	0	0	1	0	1.000
T. McGraw, p	3	1	0	0	0	1	0	.333
E. Kranepool	3	0	0	0	0	0	0	.000
G. Theodore, of	2	0	0	0	0	0	0	.000
R. Hodges	0	0	0	0	0	0	0	—
T. Martinez	0	0	0	0	0	0	0	—

Errors: W. Garrett (3), F. Millan (3), D. Hahn, C. Jones, J. Koosman, W. Mays

Individual Pitching

OAKLAND (A.L.)

	W	L	ERA	IP	H	BB	SO	SV
R. Fingers	0	1	0.66	13.2	13	4	8	2
C. Hunter	1	0	2.02	13.1	11	4	6	0
V. Blue	0	1	4.91	11	10	3	8	0
K. Holtzman	2	1	4.22	10.2	13	5	6	0
D. Knowles	0	0	0.00	6.1	4	5	5	2
B. Odom	0	0	3.86	4.2	5	2	2	0
P. Lindblad	1	0	0.00	3.1	4	1	1	0
H. Pina	0	0	0.00	3	6	2	0	0

NEW YORK (N.L.)

	W	L	ERA	IP	H	BB	SO	SV
J. Matlack	1	2	2.16	16.2	10	5	11	0
T. Seaver	0	1	2.40	15	13	3	18	0
T. McGraw	1	0	2.63	13.2	8	9	14	1
J. Koosman	1	0	3.12	8.2	9	7	8	0
R. Sadecki	0	0	1.93	4.2	5	1	6	1
H. Parker	0	1	0.00	3.1	2	2	2	0
G. Stone	0	0	0.00	3	4	1	3	1

1974 NATIONAL LEAGUE CHAMPIONSHIP SERIES

Los Angeles (West) defeats Pittsburgh (East) 3 games to 1

LINE SCORES			R	H	E	PITCHERS (innings pitched)	HOME RUNS (men on)	HIGHLIGHTS
GAME 1 - OCTOBER 5								Don Sutton pitched a 4-hitter for his 10th straight victory while Jimmy Wynn, Joe Ferguson and Dave Lopes drove in a run each off loser Jerry Reuss in the Dodgers' opening win.
LA	**W**	010 000 002	3	9	2	**Sutton** (9)		
PIT	**E**	000 000 000	0	4	0	**Reuss** (7), Giusti (2)		
GAME 2 - OCTOBER 6								Ron Cey slammed a homer, two doubles and a single as the Dodgers racked four Pittsburgh pitchers for 12 hits and gained a 2-0 lead in the series. Andy Messersmith was the winner.
LA	**W**	100 100 030	5	12	0	**Messersmith** (7), Marshall (2)	Cey	
PIT	**E**	000 000 200	2	8	3	Rooker (7), **Giusti** (0), Demery (0), Hernandez (2)		
GAME 3 - OCTOBER 8								Willie Stargell and Richie Hebner each hammered two hits, including home runs, and drove in six runs between them as the Pirates broke through for their only victory. Bruce Kison and Ramon Hernandez combined on the shutout.
PIT	**E**	502 000 000	7	10	0	**Kison** (6.2), Hernandez (2.1)	Hebner (1 on), Stargell (2 on)	
LA	**W**	000 000 000	0	4	5	**Rau** (0.2), Hough (2.1), Downing (4), Solomon (2)		
GAME 4 - OCTOBER 9								Steve Garvey slammed two home runs and two singles, driving in four runs as the Dodgers clobbered 5 Pittsburgh pitchers for 12 hits to clinch the series. Don Sutton hurled his 2nd series win and 11th consecutive victory of the year.
PIT	**E**	000 000 100	1	3	1	**Reuss** (2.2), Brett (2.1), Demery (1), Giusti (1.1), Pizarro (0.2)	Stargell	
LA	**W**	102 022 23x	12	12	0	**Sutton** (8), Marshall (1)	Garvey (1 on), Garvey	

Team totals

		W	AB	H	2B	3B	HR	R	RBI	BA	BB	SO	ERA
LA	**W**	3	138	37	8	1	3	20	19	.268	30	16	2.00
PIT	**E**	1	129	25	1	1	3	10	10	.194	8	17	4.89

Individual Batting

LOS ANGELES (WEST)

	AB	H	2B	3B	HR	R	RBI	BA
S. Garvey, 1b	18	7	1	0	2	4	5	.389
B. Russell, ss	18	7	0	0	0	1	3	.389
B. Buckner, of	18	3	1	0	0	0	0	.167
R. Cey, 3b	16	5	3	0	1	2	1	.313
D. Lopes, 2b	15	4	0	1	0	4	3	.267
J. Ferguson, c, of	13	3	0	0	0	3	2	.231
J. Wynn, of	10	2	2	0	0	4	2	.200
S. Yeager, c	9	0	0	0	0	1	0	.000
D. Sutton, p	7	2	0	0	0	0	1	.286
W. Crawford, of	4	1	0	0	0	1	1	.250
M. Mota, of	3	1	0	0	0	0	1	.333
A. Messersmith, p	3	0	0	0	0	0	0	.000
R. Auerbach	1	1	1	0	0	0	0	1.000
T. Paciorek, of	1	1	0	0	0	0	0	1.000
A. Downing, p	1	0	0	0	0	0	0	.000
K. McMullen	1	0	0	0	0	0	0	.000
V. Joshua	0	0	0	0	0	0	0	—
L. Lacy	0	0	0	0	0	0	0	—

Errors: R. Cey (2), A. Downing, J. Ferguson, S. Garvey, C. Hough, D. Lopes

Stolen Bases: D. Lopes (3), J. Wynn, S. Yeager

PITTSBURGH (EAST)

	AB	H	2B	3B	HR	R	RBI	BA
M. Sanguillen, c	16	4	1	0	0	0	0	.250
R. Stennett, 2b	16	1	0	0	0	1	0	.063
W. Stargell, of	15	6	0	0	2	3	4	.400
A. Oliver, of	14	2	0	0	0	1	1	.143
R. Hebner, 3b	13	3	0	0	1	1	4	.231
R. Zisk, of	10	3	0	0	0	1	0	.300
E. Kirkpatrick, 1b	9	0	0	0	0	0	0	.000
D. Parker, of	8	1	0	0	0	0	0	.125
P. Popovich, ss	5	3	0	0	0	1	0	.600
M. Mendoza, ss	5	1	0	0	0	0	1	.200
B. Robertson, 1b	5	0	0	0	0	1	0	.000
B. Kison, p	3	0	0	0	0	0	0	.000
J. Rooker, p	2	1	0	0	0	0	0	.500
J. Reuss, p	2	0	0	0	0	0	0	.000
F. Taveras, ss	2	0	0	0	0	0	0	.000
K. Brett, p	1	0	0	0	0	0	0	.000
G. Clines, of	1	0	0	0	0	1	0	.000
R. Hernandez, p	1	0	0	0	0	0	0	.000
A. Howe	1	0	0	0	0	0	0	.000

Errors: M. Sanguillen (2), J. Rooker, R. Stennett

Stolen Bases: F. Taveras

Individual Pitching

LOS ANGELES (WEST)

	W	L	ERA	IP	H	BB	SO	SV
D. Sutton	2	0	0.53	17	7	2	13	0
A. Messersmith	1	0	2.57	7	8	3	0	0
A. Downing	0	0	0.00	4	1	1	0	0
M. Marshall	0	0	0.00	3	0	0	1	0
C. Hough	0	0	7.71	2.1	4	0	2	0
E. Solomon	0	0	0.00	2	2	1	1	0
D. Rau	0	1	40.50	0.2	3	1	0	0

PITTSBURGH (EAST)

	W	L	ERA	IP	H	BB	SO	SV
J. Reuss	0	2	3.72	9.2	7	8	3	0
J. Rooker	0	0	2.57	7	6	5	4	0
B. Kison	1	0	0.00	6.2	2	6	5	0
R. Hernandez	0	0	0.00	4.1	3	1	2	0
D. Giusti	0	1	21.60	3.1	13	5	1	0
K. Brett	0	0	7.71	2.1	3	2	1	0
L. Demery	0	0	27.00	1	3	2	0	0
J. Pizarro	0	0	0.00	0.2	0	1	0	0

1974 AMERICAN LEAGUE CHAMPIONSHIP SERIES

Oakland (West) defeats Baltimore (East) 3 games to 1

LINE SCORES			R	H	E	PITCHERS (innings pitched)	HOME RUNS (men on)	HIGHLIGHTS
GAME 1 - OCTOBER 5								A 2-run homer by Bobby Grich and solo homers by Paul Blair and Brooks Robinson supported Mike Cuellar's 9-hit pitching as Baltimore drew first blood at the expense of Catfish Hunter.
BAL	**E**	100 140 000	6	10	0	**Cuellar** (8), Grimsley (1)	Blair, Robinson (1 on), Grich (1 on)	
OAK	**W**	001 010 001	3	9	0	**Hunter** (4.2), Odom (3.1), Fingers (1)		
GAME 2 - OCTOBER 6								Ray Fosse hit a 3-run homer, Sal Bando hit his first homer of the year off Baltimore pitching, and Ken Holtzman hurled a 5-hit shutout as the A's evened the series.
BAL	**E**	000 000 000	0	5	2	**McNally** (5.2), Garland (0.2), Reynolds (1.1), Jackson (0.1)	Fosse (2 on), Bando	
OAK	**W**	000 101 03x	5	8	0	**Holtzman** (9)		
GAME 3 - OCTOBER 8								Vida Blue pitched a masterful two-hitter, striking out seven and walking none, and Bando added another homer to provide the game's only run.
OAK	**W**	000 100 000	1	4	2	**Blue** (9)	Bando	
BAL	**E**	000 000 000	0	2	1	**Palmer** (9)		
GAME 4 - OCTOBER 9								One hit was all the A's needed to win the final game. They drew 11 walks, nine off loser Cuellar, who walked Gene Tenace in the 5th to force in a run. Reggie Jackson doubled in Bando with what proved to be the winning run in the seventh.
OAK	**W**	000 010 100	2	1	0	**Hunter** (7), Fingers (2), **SV**		
BAL	**E**	000 000 001	1	5	1	**Cuellar** (4.2), Grimsley (4.1)		

Team totals

		W	AB	H	2B	3B	HR	R	RBI	BA	BB	SO	ERA
OAK	**W**	3	120	22	4	1	3	11	11	.183	22	16	1.75
BAL	**E**	1	124	22	1	0	3	7	7	.177	5	20	1.80

Individual Batting

OAKLAND (WEST)

	AB	H	2B	3B	HR	R	RBI	BA
B. Campaneris, ss	17	3	0	0	0	0	3	.176
B. North, of	16	1	1	0	0	3	0	.063
S. Bando, 3b	13	3	0	0	2	4	2	.231
J. Rudi, of	13	2	0	1	0	0	1	.154
R. Fosse, c	12	4	1	0	1	1	3	.333
R. Jackson, dh, of	12	2	1	0	0	0	1	.167
C. Washington, of	11	3	1	0	0	1	0	.273
G. Tenace, 1b	11	0	0	0	0	1	1	.000
D. Green, 2b	9	2	0	0	0	0	0	.222
A. Mangual, dh	4	1	0	0	0	0	0	.250
J. Alou	1	1	0	0	0	0	0	1.000
D. Maxvill, 2b	1	0	0	0	0	0	0	.000
J. Holt, 1b	0	0	0	0	0	0	0	—
M. Trillo	0	0	0	0	0	1	0	—
H. Washington	0	0	0	0	0	0	0	—

Errors: D. Green (2)
Stolen Bases: B. Campaneris, B. North, G. Tenace

BALTIMORE (EAST)

	AB	H	2B	3B	HR	R	RBI	BA
B. Grich, 2b	16	4	1	0	1	2	2	.250
D. Baylor, of	15	4	0	0	0	0	0	.267
T. Davis, dh	15	4	0	0	0	0	1	.267
P. Blair, of	14	4	0	0	1	3	2	.286
B. Robinson, 3b	12	1	0	0	1	1	1	.083
R. Coggins, of	11	0	0	0	0	0	0	.000
M. Belanger, ss	9	0	0	0	0	0	0	.000
B. Powell, 1b	8	1	0	0	0	0	1	.125
A. Etchebarren, c	6	2	0	0	0	0	0	.333
E. Hendricks, c	6	1	0	0	0	1	0	.167
E. Williams, 1b	6	0	0	0	0	0	0	.000
E. Cabell, of	4	1	0	0	0	0	0	.250
A. Bumbry	1	0	0	0	0	0	0	.000
C. Motton	1	0	0	0	0	0	0	.000
F. Baker, ss	0	0	0	0	0	0	0	—

Errors: F. Baker, M. Belanger, B. Grich, E. Williams

Individual Pitching

OAKLAND (WEST)

	W	L	ERA	IP	H	BB	SO	SV
C. Hunter	1	1	4.63	11.2	11	2	6	0
V. Blue	1	0	0.00	9	2	0	7	0
K. Holtzman	1	0	0.00	9	5	2	3	0
B. Odom	0	0	0.00	3.1	1	0	1	0
R. Fingers	0	0	3.00	3	3	1	3	1

BALTIMORE (EAST)

	W	L	ERA	IP	H	BB	SO	SV
M. Cuellar	1	1	2.84	12.2	9	13	6	0
J. Palmer	0	1	1.00	9	4	1	4	0
D. McNally	0	1	1.59	5.2	6	2	2	0
R. Grimsley	0	0	1.69	5.1	1	2	2	0
B. Reynolds	0	0	0.00	1.1	0	3	1	0
W. Garland	0	0	0.00	0.2	1	1	0	0
G. Jackson	0	0	0.00	0.1	1	0	1	0

1974 WORLD SERIES

Oakland (A.L.) defeats Los Angeles (N.L.) 4 games to 1

LINE SCORES						PITCHERS (innings pitched)	HOME RUNS (men on)	HIGHLIGHTS
GAME 1 - OCTOBER 12								A second-inning home run by Jackson proved to be the difference. Starting pitcher Holtzman doubled in the fifth and scored on a squeeze bunt by Campaneris. Fingers, in relief, was credited with the victory.
OAK	**A**	010 010 010	3	6	2	Holtzman (4.1), **Fingers** (4.1), Hunter (0.1), **SV**	Jackson	
LA	**N**	000 010 001	2	11	1	**Messersmith** (8), Marshall (1)	Wynn	
GAME 2 - OCTOBER 13								Ferguson's home run with a runner on base in the sixth off Blue gave Sutton the victory with help from Marshall, who picked off designated pinch runner Herb Washington in the ninth.
OAK	**A**	000 000 002	2	6	0	**Blue** (7), Odom (1)		
LA	**N**	010 002 00x	3	6	1	**Sutton** (8), Marshall (1), **SV**	Ferguson (1 on)	
GAME 3 - OCTOBER 15								Two unearned runs in the third brought about the downfall of Al Downing and gave the A's their second victory in three 3-2 decisions. Oakland scored their firstrun when Dodger catcher Ferguson couldn't handle Jackson's bouncer in front of the plate as North scored. Rudi followed with a run scoring single for a 2-0 lead.
LA	**N**	000 000 011	2	7	2	**Downing** (3.2), Brewer (0.1), Hough (2), Marshall (2)	Buckner, Crawford	
OAK	**A**	002 100 00x	3	5	2	**Hunter** (7.1), Fingers (1.2)		
GAME 4 - OCTOBER 16								Holtzman helped his cause with a home run after the Dodgers had taken a 2-1 lead on Russell's two-run triple. The A's erupted for 4 runs in the sixth. Pinch hitter Holt drove in two runs with a single.
LA	**N**	000 200 000	2	7	1	**Messersmith** (8), Marshall		
OAK	**A**	001 004 00x	5	7	0	**Holtzman** (7.2), Fingers (1.1), **SV**	Holtzman	
GAME 5 - OCTOBER 17								Rudi's home run off ace reliever Marshall broke a 2-2 tie in the 7th, giving the A's their third 3-2 victory and their third straight Series title.
LA	**N**	000 002 000	2	5	1	Sutton (5), **Marshall** (3)		
OAK	**A**	110 000 10x	3	6	1	Blue (6.2), **Odom** (0.1), Fingers (2), **SV**	Fosse, Rudi	

Team totals

		W	AB	H	2B	3B	HR	R	RBI	BA	BB	SO	ERA
OAK	**A**	4	142	30	4	0	4	16	14	.211	16	42	2.05
LA	**N**	1	158	36	4	1	4	11	10	.228	16	32	2.79

Individual Batting

OAKLAND (A.L.)

	AB	H	2B	3B	HR	R	RBI	BA
J. Rudi, 1b, of	18	6	0	0	1	1	4	.333
B. Campaneris, ss	17	6	2	0	0	1	2	.353
B. North, of	17	1	0	0	0	3	0	.059
S. Bando, 3b	16	1	0	0	0	3	2	.063
R. Jackson, of	14	4	1	0	1	3	1	.286
R. Fosse, c	14	2	0	0	1	1	1	.143
D. Green, 2b	13	0	0	0	0	1	1	.000
G. Tenace, 1b	9	2	0	0	0	0	0	.222
C. Washington, of	7	4	0	0	0	1	0	.571
K. Holtzman, p	4	2	1	0	1	2	1	.500
V. Blue, p	4	0	0	0	0	0	0	.000
J. Holt, 1b	3	2	0	0	0	0	2	.667
R. Fingers, p	2	0	0	0	0	0	0	.000
C. Hunter, p	2	0	0	0	0	0	0	.000
J. Alou	1	0	0	0	0	0	0	.000
A. Mangual	1	0	0	0	0	0	0	.000
L. Haney, c	0	0	0	0	0	0	0	—
D. Maxvill, 2b	0	0	0	0	0	0	0	—
H. Washington	0	0	0	0	0	0	0	—

Errors: B. Campaneris (2), D. Green, R. Jackson, B. North

Stolen Bases: B. Campaneris, R. Jackson, B. North

LOS ANGELES (N.L.)

	AB	H	2B	3B	HR	R	RBI	BA
S. Garvey, 1b	21	8	0	0	0	2	1	.381
B. Buckner, of	20	5	1	0	1	1	1	.250
B. Russell, ss	18	4	0	1	0	0	2	.222
D. Lopes, 2b	18	2	0	0	0	2	0	.111
R. Cey, 3b	17	3	0	0	0	1	0	.176
J. Wynn, of	16	3	1	0	1	1	2	.188
J. Ferguson, c, of	16	2	0	0	1	2	2	.125
S. Yeager, c	11	4	1	0	0	0	1	.364
W. Crawford, of	6	2	0	0	1	1	0	.333
A. Messersmith, p	4	2	0	0	0	0	0	.500
V. Joshua	4	0	0	0	0	0	0	.000
D. Sutton, p	3	0	0	0	0	0	0	.000
T. Paciorek	2	1	1	0	0	1	0	.500
A. Downing, p	1	0	0	0	0	0	0	.000
L. Lacy	1	0	0	0	0	0	0	.000
R. Auerbach	0	0	0	0	0	0	0	—
M. Marshall, p	0	0	0	0	0	0	1	—

Errors: J. Ferguson (2), R. Cey, A. Messersmith, B. Russell, S. Yeager

Stolen Bases: D. Lopes (2), J. Ferguson

Individual Pitching

OAKLAND (A.L.)

	W	L	ERA	IP	H	BB	SO	SV
V. Blue	0	1	3.29	13.2	10	7	9	0
K. Holtzman	1	0	1.50	12	13	4	10	0
R. Fingers	1	0	1.93	9.1	8	2	6	2
C. Hunter	1	0	1.17	7.2	5	2	5	1
B. Odom	1	0	0.00	1.1	0	1	2	0

LOS ANGELES (N.L.)

	W	L	ERA	IP	H	BB	SO	SV
A. Messersmith	0	2	4.50	14	11	7	12	0
D. Sutton	1	0	2.77	13	9	3	12	0
M. Marshall	0	1	1.00	9	6	1	10	1
A. Downing	0	1	2.45	3.2	4	4	3	0
C. Hough	0	0	0.00	2	0	1	4	0
J. Brewer	0	0	0.00	0.1	0	0	1	0

1975 NATIONAL LEAGUE CHAMPIONSHIP SERIES

Cincinnati (West) defeats Pittsburgh (East) 3 games to 0

LINE SCORES			R	H	E	PITCHERS (innings pitched)	HOME RUNS (men on)	HIGHLIGHTS
GAME 1 - OCTOBER 4								Gullett pitched an 8-hitter and had 3 RBIs with a homer and single.
PIT	**E**	020 000 001	3	8	0	**Reuss** (2.2), Brett (1.2), Demery (2), Ellis (2)		
CIN	**W**	013 040 00x	8	11	0	**Gullett** (9)	Gullett	
GAME 2 - OCTOBER 5								Perez drove in 3 runs with a home run and single, and Eastwick saved Norman's victory.
PIT	**E**	000 100 000	1	5	0	**Rooker** (4), Tekulve (1), Brett (1), Kison (2)		
CIN	**W**	200 201 10x	6	12	1	**Norman** (6), Eastwick (3) **SV**	Perez (1 on)	
GAME 3 - OCTOBER 7								Rose's 2-run home run and Armbrister's tie-breaking sacrifice fly ruined rookie Candelaria's 14-strikeout performance.
CIN	**W**	010 000 020 2	5	6	0	Nolan (6), C. Carroll (1), McEnaney (1.1), **Eastwick** (0.2), Borbon (1) **SV**	Rose (1 on), Concepcion	
PIT	**E**	000 002 001 0	3	7	2	Candelaria (7.2), Giusti (1.2), **Hernandez** (0.2), Tekulve (0.1)	Oliver (1 on)	

Team totals

		W	AB	H	2B	3B	HR	R	RBI	BA	BB	SO	ERA
CIN	**W**	3	102	29	4	0	4	19	18	.284	9	28	2.25
PIT	**E**	0	101	20	3	0	1	7	7	.198	10	18	6.58

Individual Batting

CINCINNATI (WEST)

	AB	H	2B	3B	HR	R	RBI	BA
P. Rose, 3b	14	5	0	0	1	3	2	.357
J. Bench, c	13	1	0	0	0	1	0	.077
T. Perez, 1b	12	5	0	0	1	3	4	.417
K. Griffey, of	12	4	1	0	0	4	4	.333
D. Concepcion, ss	11	5	0	0	1	2	1	.455
G. Foster, of	11	4	0	0	0	3	0	.364
J. Morgan, 2b	11	3	3	0	0	2	1	.273
C. Geronimo, of	10	0	0	0	0	0	1	.000
D. Gullett, p	4	2	0	0	1	1	3	.500
G. Nolan, p	2	0	0	0	0	0	0	.000
F. Norman, p	1	0	0	0	0	0	1	.000
M. Rettenmund	1	0	0	0	0	0	0	.000
E. Armbrister	0	0	0	0	0	0	1	—
T. Crowley	0	0	0	0	0	0	0	—

Errors: D. Concepcion
Stolen Bases: J. Morgan (4), K. Griffey (3), D. Concepcion (2), J. Bench, G. Foster

PITTSBURGH (EAST)

	AB	H	2B	3B	HR	R	RBI	BA
R. Stennett, 2b, ss	14	3	0	0	0	0	0	.214
R. Hebner, 3b	12	4	1	0	0	2	2	.333
M. Sanguillen, c	12	2	0	0	0	0	0	.167
A. Oliver, of	11	2	0	0	1	1	2	.182
W. Stargell, 1b	11	2	1	0	0	1	0	.182
R. Zisk, of	10	5	1	0	0	0	0	.500
D. Parker, of	10	0	0	0	0	2	0	.000
F. Taveras, ss	7	1	0	0	0	0	1	.143
J. Candelaria, p	3	0	0	0	0	0	0	.000
B. Robertson, 1b	2	1	0	0	0	0	1	.500
E. Kirkpatrick	2	0	0	0	0	0	0	.000
W. Randolph, 2b	2	0	0	0	0	1	0	.000
B. Robinson	2	0	0	0	0	0	0	.000
J. Reuss, p	1	0	0	0	0	0	0	.000
C. Reynolds, ss	1	0	0	0	0	0	0	.000
J. Rooker, p	1	0	0	0	0	0	0	.000
D. Dyer	0	0	0	0	0	0	1	—

Errors: C. Reynolds, M. Sanguillen

Individual Pitching

CINCINNATI (WEST)

	W	L	ERA	IP	H	BB	SO	SV
D. Gullett	1	0	3.00	9	8	2	5	0
G. Nolan	0	0	3.00	6	5	0	5	0
F. Norman	1	0	1.50	6	4	5	4	0
R. Eastwick	1	0	0.00	3.2	2	2	1	1
W. McEnaney	0	0	6.75	1.1	1	0	1	0
P. Borbon	0	0	0.00	1	0	0	1	0
C. Carroll	0	0	0.00	1	0	1	1	0

PITTSBURGH (EAST)

	W	L	ERA	IP	H	BB	SO	SV
J. Candelaria	0	0	3.52	7.2	3	2	14	0
J. Rooker	0	1	9.00	4	7	0	5	0
J. Reuss	0	1	13.50	2.2	4	4	1	0
K. Brett	0	0	0.00	2.1	1	0	1	0
L. Demery	0	0	18.00	2	4	1	1	0
D. Ellis	0	0	0.00	2	2	0	2	0
B. Kison	0	0	4.50	2	2	1	1	0
D. Giusti	0	0	0.00	1.1	0	0	1	0
K. Tekulve	0	0	6.75	1.1	3	1	2	0
R. Hernandez	0	1	27.00	0.2	3	0	0	0

1975 AMERICAN LEAGUE CHAMPIONSHIP SERIES

Boston (East) defeats Oakland (West) 3 games to 0

LINE SCORES					PITCHERS (innings pitched)	HOME RUNS (men on)	HIGHLIGHTS
GAME 1 - OCTOBER 4							Tiant pitched a three-hitter and Lynn doubled home two runs in Boston's five-run seventh to put the game away.
OAK W	000 000 010	1	3	4	**Holtzman** (6.1), Todd (0), Lindblad (0.1) Bosman (0.1), Abbott (1)		
BOS E	200 000 50x	7	8	3	**Tiant** (9)		
GAME 2 - OCTOBER 5							Boston's win featured Yastrzemski's homer and Drago's scoreless relief pitching.
OAK W	200 100 000	3	10	0	Blue (3), Todd (1), **Fingers** (4)	Jackson (1 on)	
BOS E	000 301 11x	6	12	0	Cleveland (5), **Moret** (1), Drago (3) **SV**	Petrocelli, Yastrzemski (1 on)	
GAME 3 - OCTOBER 7							Yastrzemski cracked two hits and made two defensive gems to spark the Red Sox to a three-game sweep.
BOS E	000 130 010	5	11	1	**Wise** (7.1), Drago (2.1) **SV**		
OAK W	000 001 020	3	6	2	**Holtzman** (4.2), Todd (0), Lindblad (4.1)		

Team totals

		W	AB	H	2B	3B	HR	R	RBI	BA	BB	SO	ERA
BOS	**E**	3	98	31	8	0	2	18	14	.316	3	12	1.67
OAK	**W**	0	98	19	6	0	1	7	7	.194	9	14	4.32

Individual Batting

BOSTON (EAST)

	AB	H	2B	3B	HR	R	RBI	BA
C. Fisk, c	12	5	1	0	0	4	2	.417
J. Beniquez, dh	12	3	0	0	0	2	1	.250
R. Petrocelli, 3b	12	2	0	0	1	1	2	.167
C. Yastrzemski, of	11	5	1	0	1	4	2	.455
F. Lynn, of	11	4	1	0	0	1	3	.364
D. Doyle, 2b	11	3	0	0	0	3	1	.273
C. Cooper, 1b	10	4	2	0	0	0	1	.400
D. Evans, of	10	1	1	0	0	1	1	.100
R. Burleson, ss	9	4	2	0	0	2	1	.444

Errors: R. Burleson, C. Cooper, D. Doyle, F. Lynn

Stolen Bases: J. Beniquez (2), C. Fisk

OAKLAND (WEST)

	AB	H	2B	3B	HR	R	RBI	BA
S. Bando, 3b	12	6	2	0	0	1	2	.500
R. Jackson, of	12	5	0	0	1	1	3	.417
J. Rudi, 1b, of	12	3	2	0	0	1	0	.250
C. Washington, dh, of	12	3	1	0	0	1	1	.250
B. Campaneris, ss	11	0	0	0	0	1	0	.000
B. North, of	10	0	0	0	0	0	1	.000
G. Tenace, 1b, c	9	0	0	0	0	0	0	.000
B. Williams, dh	8	0	0	0	0	0	0	.000
P. Garner, 2b	5	0	0	0	0	0	0	.000
J. Holt, 1b	3	1	1	0	0	0	0	.333
C. Tovar, 2b	2	1	0	0	0	2	0	.500
R. Fosse, c	2	0	0	0	0	0	0	.000
T. Harper	0	0	0	0	0	0	0	—
D. Hopkins, dh	0	0	0	0	0	0	0	—
T. Martinez, 2b	0	0	0	0	0	0	0	—

Errors: C. Washington (2), S. Bando, P. Garner, B. North, C. Tovar

Individual Pitching

BOSTON (EAST)

	W	L	ERA	IP	H	BB	SO	SV
L. Tiant	1	0	0.00	9	3	3	8	0
R. Wise	1	0	2.45	7.1	6	3	2	0
R. Cleveland	0	0	5.40	5	7	1	2	0
D. Drago	0	0	0.00	4.2	2	1	2	2
R. Moret	1	0	0.00	1	1	1	0	0

OAKLAND (WEST)

	W	L	ERA	IP	H	BB	SO	SV
K. Holtzman	0	2	4.09	11	12	1	7	0
P. Lindblad	0	0	0.00	4.2	5	1	0	0
R. Fingers	0	1	6.75	4	5	1	3	0
V. Blue	0	0	9.00	3	6	0	2	0
G. Abbott	0	0	0.00	1	0	0	0	0
J. Todd	0	0	9.00	1	3	0	0	0
D. Bosman	0	0	0.00	0.1	0	0	0	0

1975 WORLD SERIES

Cincinnati (N.L.) defeats Boston (A.L.) 4 games to 3

LINE SCORES			R	H	E	PITCHERS (innings pitched)	HOME RUNS (men on)	HIGHLIGHTS
GAME 1 - OCTOBER 11								Tiant pitched a five-hitter, singled and scored the first run to lead Boston to a 6-0 victory over Cincinnati.
CIN	**N**	000 000 000	0	5	0	**Gullett** (6), Carroll (0), McEnaney (1)		
BOS	**A**	000 000 60x	6	12	0	**Tiant** (9)		
GAME 2 - OCTOBER 12								Trailing 2-1 in the ninth, Bench doubled against Boston starter Lee. Drago retired two batters, but Concepcion singled home Bench, stole second, and scored on Griffey's double.
CIN	**N**	000 100 002	3	7	1	Billingham (5.2), Borbon (0.1), McEnaney (1), **Eastwick** (2)		
BOS	**A**	100 001 000	2	7	0	Lee (8), **Drago** (1)		
GAME 3 - OCTOBER 14								A record six home runs were hit but a 10th inning bunt was decisive as the Reds scored in the extra inning for a 6-5 victory. Trailing 5-1, the Red Sox had rallied to score the tying run on Evans's ninth-inning homer.
BOS	**A**	010 001 102 0	5	10	2	Wise (4.1), Burton (0.1), Cleveland (1.1), **Willoughby** (3), Moret (0.1)	Fisk, Carbo, Evans (1 on)	
CIN	**N**	000 230 000 1	6	7	0	Nolan (4), Darcy (2), Carroll (0.2), McEnaney (1.2), **Eastwick** (1.2)	Bench, Concepcion, Geronimo	
GAME 4 - OCTOBER 15								Although he needed 163 pitches to do it, Tiant went the distance defeating the Reds 5-4 to even the Series at two apiece.
BOS	**A**	000 500 000	5	11	1	**Tiant** (9)		
CIN	**N**	200 200 000	4	9	1	**Norman** (3.1), Borbon (0.2), Carroll (2), Eastwick (3)		
GAME 5 - OCTOBER 16								After going 0-for-15, Perez broke loose, driving in four runs with two home runs to lead the Reds to a 6-2 victory and a 3 games to 2 edge.
BOS	**A**	100 000 001	2	5	0	**Cleveland** (5), Willoughby (2), Pole (0), Segui (1)		
CIN	**N**	000 113 01x	6	8	0	**Gullett** (8.2), Eastwick (0.1) **SV**	Perez (2 on), Perez	
GAME 6 - OCTOBER 21								After tying the score in the 8th on pinch hitter Carbo's 3-run homer, the Red Sox filled the bases with nobody out in the 9th but failed to score. Fisk's home run off the foul pole in the 12th ended one of the most thrilling games in Series history.
CIN	**N**	000 030 210 000	6	14	0	Nolan (2), Norman (0.2), Billingham (1.1), Carroll (1), Eastwick (1.0), McEnaney (1) Borbon (2.0), **Darcy** (2.0)	Geronimo	
BOS	**A**	300 000 030 001	7	10	1	Tiant (7.0), Moret (1), Drago (3), **Wise** (1)	Lynn (2 on), Carbo (2 on), Fisk	
GAME 7 - OCTOBER 22								The Reds overcame a 3-0 deficit, defeating the Red Sox 4-3 on Morgan's single with two out in the 9th. It was the Reds' first world championship since 1940.
CIN	**N**	000 002 101	4	9	0	Gullett (4), Billingham (2), **Carroll** (2), McEnaney (1), **SV**	Perez (1 on)	
BOS	**A**	003 000 000	3	5	2	Lee (6.1), Moret (0.1), Willoughby (1.1), **Burton** (0.2), Cleveland (0.1)		

Team totals

		W	AB	H	2B	3B	HR	R	RBI	BA	BB	SO	ERA
CIN	**N**	4	244	59	9	3	7	29	29	.242	25	30	3.88
BOS	**A**	3	239	60	7	2	6	30	30	.251	30	40	3.88

Individual Batting

CINCINNATI (N.L.)

	AB	H	2B	3B	HR	R	RBI	BA
G. Foster, lf	29	8	1	0	0	1	2	.276
J. Bench, c	29	6	2	0	1	5	4	.207
D. Concepcion, ss	28	5	1	0	1	3	4	.179
T. Perez, 1b	28	5	0	0	3	4	7	.179
P. Rose, 3b	27	10	1	1	0	3	2	.370
J. Morgan, 2b	27	7	1	0	0	4	3	.259
K. Griffey, rf	26	7	3	1	0	4	4	.269
C. Geronimo, cf	25	7	0	1	2	3	3	.280
D. Gullett, p	7	2	0	0	0	1	0	.286
M. Rettenmund	3	0	0	0	0	0	0	.000
T. Crowley	2	1	0	0	0	0	0	.500
J. Billingham, p	2	0	0	0	0	0	0	.000
D. Chaney	2	0	0	0	0	0	0	.000
D. Driessen	2	0	0	0	0	0	0	.000
W. McEnaney, p	1	1	0	0	0	0	0	1.000
E. Armbrister	1	0	0	0	0	1	0	.000
P. Borbon, p	1	0	0	0	0	0	0	.000
P. Darcy, p	1	0	0	0	0	0	0	.000
R. Eastwick, p	1	0	0	0	0	0	0	.000
G. Nolan, p	1	0	0	0	0	0	0	.000
F. Norman, p	1	0	0	0	0	0	0	.000

Errors: D. Concepcion, T. Perez

Stolen Bases: D. Concepcion (3), K. Griffey (2), J. Morgan (2), G. Foster, T. Perez

BOSTON (A.L.)

	AB	H	2B	3B	HR	R	RBI	BA
D. Doyle, 2b	30	8	1	1	0	3	0	.267
C. Yastrzemski, 1b, of	29	9	0	0	0	7	4	.310
R. Petrocelli, 3b	26	8	1	0	0	3	4	.308
F. Lynn, cf	25	7	1	0	1	3	5	.280
C. Fisk, c	25	6	0	0	2	5	4	.240
R. Burleson, ss	24	7	1	0	0	1	2	.292
D. Evans, rf	24	7	1	1	1	3	5	.292
C. Cooper, 1b	19	1	1	0	0	0	1	.053
L. Tiant, p	8	2	0	0	0	2	0	.250
J. Beniquez, of	8	1	0	0	0	0	1	.125
B. Carbo, lf	7	3	1	0	2	3	4	.429
B. Lee, p	6	1	0	0	0	0	0	.167
R. Cleveland, p	2	0	0	0	0	0	0	.000
R. Miller, of	2	0	0	0	0	0	0	.000
R. Wise, p	2	0	0	0	0	0	0	.000
D. Griffin	1	0	0	0	0	0	0	.000
B. Montgomery	1	0	0	0	0	0	0	.000

Errors: D. Doyle (3), C. Fisk (2), R. Burleson

Individual Pitching

CINCINNATI (N.L.)

	W	L	ERA	IP	H	BB	SO	SV
D. Gullett	1	1	4.34	18.2	19	10	15	0
J. Billingham	0	0	1.00	9	8	5	7	0
R. Eastwick	2	0	2.25	8	6	3	4	1
W. McEnaney	0	0	2.70	6.2	3	2	5	1
G. Nolan	0	0	6.00	6	6	1	2	0
C. Carroll	1	0	3.18	5.2	4	2	3	0
P. Darcy	0	1	4.50	4	3	2	1	0
F. Norman	0	1	9.00	4	8	3	2	0
P. Borbon	0	0	6.00	3	3	2	1	0

BOSTON (A.L.)

	W	L	ERA	IP	H	BB	SO	SV
L. Tiant	2	0	3.60	25	25	8	12	0
B. Lee	0	0	3.14	14.1	12	3	7	0
R. Cleveland	0	1	6.75	6.2	7	3	5	0
J. Willoughby	0	1	0.00	6.1	3	0	2	0
R. Wise	1	0	8.44	5.1	6	2	2	0
D. Drago	0	1	2.25	4	3	1	1	0
R. Moret	0	0	0.00	1.2	2	3	1	0
J. Burton	0	1	9.00	1	1	3	0	0
D. Segui	0	0	0.00	1	0	0	0	0
D. Pole	0	0	∞	0.0	0	2	0	0

1976 NATIONAL LEAGUE CHAMPIONSHIP SERIES

Cincinnati (West) defeats Philadelphia (East) 3 games to 0

LINE SCORES						PITCHERS (innings pitched)	HOME RUNS (men on)	HIGHLIGHTS
GAME 1 - OCTOBER 9								George Foster homered, Pete Rose got 3 hits and Don Gullett allowed 2 hits in 8 innings.
CIN	**W**	001 002 030	6	10	0	**Gullett** (8), Eastwick (1)	Foster	
PHI	**E**	100 000 002	3	6	1	**Carlton** (7), McGraw (2)		
GAME 2 - OCTOBER 10								Pete Rose and Ken Griffey had 2 hits each, and Pedro Borbon saved Pat Zachry's victory with 4 scoreless innings in relief.
CIN	**W**	000 004 200	6	6	0	**Zachry** (5.1), Borbon (4), **SV**		
PHI	**E**	010 010 000	2	10	1	**Lonborg** (5.1), Garber (0.2), McGraw (0.1), Reed (2.2)	Luzinski	
GAME 3 - OCTOBER 12								Trailing 6-4, the Reds rallied for 3 runs in the 9th. Foster and Bench hit successive homers to ignite the pennant-clinching rally.
PHI	**E**	000 100 221	6	11	0	Kaat (6), Reed (2), **Garber** (0), Underwood (0.1)		
CIN	**W**	000 000 403	7	9	2	Nolan (5.2), Sarmiento (1), Borbon, **Eastwick** (2)	Foster, Bench	

Team totals

		W	AB	H	2B	3B	HR	R	RBI	BA	BB	SO	ERA
CIN	**W**	3	99	25	5	3	3	19	17	.253	15	16	3.33
PHI	**E**	0	100	27	8	1	1	11	11	.270	12	9	5.13

Individual Batting

CINCINNATI (WEST)

	AB	H	2B	3B	HR	R	RBI	BA
P. Rose, 3b	14	6	2	1	0	3	2	.429
K. Griffey, of	13	5	0	1	0	2	2	.385
J. Bench, c	12	4	1	0	1	3	1	.333
G. Foster, of	12	2	0	0	2	2	4	.167
C. Geronimo, of	11	2	0	1	0	0	2	.182
D. Concepcion, ss	10	2	1	0	0	4	0	.200
T. Perez, 1b	10	2	0	0	0	1	3	.200
J. Morgan, 2b	7	0	0	0	0	2	0	.000
D. Gullett, p	4	2	1	0	0	1	3	.500
P. Borbon, p	2	0	0	0	0	1	0	.000
D. Driessen	1	0	0	0	0	0	0	.000
M. Lum	1	0	0	0	0	0	0	.000
M. Sarmiento, p	1	0	0	0	0	0	0	.000
P. Zachry, p	1	0	0	0	0	0	0	.000
E. Armbrister	0	0	0	0	0	0	0	—
D. Flynn, 2b	0	0	0	0	0	0	0	—

Errors: T. Perez, P. Rose
Stolen Bases: K. Griffey (2), J. Morgan (2), J. Bench

PHILADELPHIA (EAST)

	AB	H	2B	3B	HR	R	RBI	BA
D. Cash, 2b	13	4	1	0	0	1	1	.308
M. Schmidt, 3b	13	4	2	0	0	1	2	.308
G. Maddox, of	13	3	1	0	0	2	1	.231
G. Luzinski, of	11	3	2	0	1	2	3	.273
J. Johnstone, of	9	7	1	1	0	1	2	.778
D. Allen, 1b	9	2	0	0	0	1	0	.222
L. Bowa, ss	8	1	1	0	0	1	1	.125
B. Boone, c	7	2	0	0	0	0	1	.286
T. McCarver, c	4	0	0	0	0	0	0	.000
J. Kaat, p	2	1	0	0	0	0	0	.500
O. Brown, of	2	0	0	0	0	0	0	.000
S. Carlton, p	2	0	0	0	0	0	0	.000
B. Tolan, 1b, of	2	0	0	0	0	0	0	.000
T. Hutton	1	0	0	0	0	0	0	.000
J. Lonborg, p	1	0	0	0	0	0	0	.000
J. Martin, of	1	0	0	0	0	1	0	.000
J. Oates, c	1	0	0	0	0	0	0	.000
R. Reed, p	1	0	0	0	0	0	0	.000
T. Harmon	0	0	0	0	0	1	0	—

Errors: D. Allen, M. Schmidt

Individual Pitching

CINCINNATI (WEST)

	W	L	ERA	IP	H	BB	SO	SV
D. Gullett	1	0	1.13	8	2	3	4	0
G. Nolan	0	0	1.59	5.2	6	2	1	0
P. Zachry	1	0	3.60	5	6	3	3	0
P. Borbon	0	0	0.00	4.1	4	1	0	1
R. Eastwick	1	0	12.00	3	7	2	1	0
M. Sarmiento	0	0	18.00	1	2	1	0	0

PHILADELPHIA (EAST)

	W	L	ERA	IP	H	BB	SO	SV
S. Carlton	0	1	5.14	7	8	5	6	0
J. Kaat	0	0	3.00	6	2	2	1	0
J. Lonborg	0	1	1.69	5.1	2	2	2	0
R. Reed	0	0	7.71	4.2	6	2	2	0
T. McGraw	0	0	11.57	2.1	4	1	5	0
G. Garber	0	1	13.50	0.2	2	1	0	0
T. Underwood	0	0	0.00	0.1	1	2	0	0

1976 AMERICAN LEAGUE CHAMPIONSHIP SERIES

New York (East) defeats Kansas City (West) 3 games to 2

LINE SCORES			R	H	E	PITCHERS (innings pitched)	HOME RUNS (men on)	HIGHLIGHTS
GAME 1 - OCTOBER 9								A pair of misplays by George Brett gave the Yankees two unearned runs in the first inning, and Hunter made them stand up as he held Royals to 5 hits.
NY	**E**	200 000 002	4	12	0	**Hunter** (9)		
KC	**W**	000 000 010	1	5	2	**Gura** (8.2), Littell (0.1)		
GAME 2 - OCTOBER 10								Paul Splittorff pitched 5.2 innings of scoreless relief, and Tom Poquette and Buck Martinez each had two RBIs.
NY	**E**	012 000 000	3	12	5	**Figueroa** (5.1), Tidrow (2.2)		
KC	**W**	200 002 03x	7	9	0	Leonard (2.1), **Splittorff** (5.2), Mingori (1)		
GAME 3 - OCTOBER 12								Chambliss got two hits, one a homer, and drove in three runs as Yanks overcame early 3-0 deficit.
KC	**W**	300 000 000	3	6	0	**Hassler** (5), Pattin (0), Hall (0.1), Mingori (0), Littell (2.2)		
NY	**E**	000 203 00x	5	9	0	**Ellis** (8), Lyle (1) **SV**	Chambliss (1 on)	
GAME 4 - OCTOBER 13								Freddie Patek drove in three runs with three hits, and Doug Bird pitched strong relief to even the series.
KC	**W**	030 201 010	7	9	1	Gura (2), **Bird** (4.2), Mingori (2.1) **SV**		
NY	**E**	020 000 101	4	11	0	**Hunter** (3), Tidrow (3.2), Jackson (2.1)	Nettles (1 on), Nettles	
GAME 5 - OCTOBER 14								Chambliss's homer off Mark Littell in the bottom of the 9th snapped a 6-6 tie, giving Yanks their first A.L. pennant in 12 years. Royals had tied game on Brett's three run homer in the eighth.
KC	**W**	210 000 030	6	11	1	Leonard (0), Splittorff (3.2), Pattin (0.1), Hassler (2.1), **Littell** (1.2)	Mayberry (1 on), Brett (2 on)	
NY	**E**	202 002 001	7	11	1	Figueroa (7), Jackson (1), **Tidrow** (1)	Chambliss	

Team totals

		W	AB	H	2B	3B	HR	R	RBI	BA	BB	SO	ERA
NY	**E**	3	174	55	13	2	4	23	21	.316	16	15	4.70
KC	**W**	2	162	40	6	4	2	24	24	.247	11	18	4.40

Individual Batting

NEW YORK (EAST)

	AB	H	2B	3B	HR	R	RBI	BA
T. Munson, c	23	10	2	0	0	3	3	.435
M. Rivers, of	23	8	0	1	0	5	0	.348
C. Chambliss, 1b	21	11	1	1	2	5	8	.524
R. White, of	17	5	3	0	0	4	3	.294
G. Nettles, 3b	17	4	1	0	2	2	4	.235
W. Randolph, 2b	17	2	0	0	0	0	1	.118
F. Stanley, ss	15	5	2	0	0	1	0	.333
L. Piniella, dh	11	3	1	0	0	1	0	.273
C. May, dh	10	2	1	0	0	1	0	.200
E. Maddox, of	9	2	1	0	0	0	1	.222
O. Gamble, of	8	2	1	0	0	1	1	.250
E. Hendricks	1	1	0	0	0	0	0	1.000
S. Alomar, dh	1	0	0	0	0	0	0	.000
O. Velez	1	0	0	0	0	0	0	.000
J. Mason, ss	0	0	0	0	0	0	0	—

Errors: O. Gamble (2), T. Munson (2), C. Chambliss, F. Stanley
Stolen Bases: C. Chambliss (2), W. Randolph, R. White

KANSAS CITY (WEST)

	AB	H	2B	3B	HR	R	RBI	BA
A. Cowens, of	21	4	0	1	0	3	0	.190
G. Brett, 3b	18	8	1	1	1	4	5	.444
F. Patek, ss	18	7	2	0	0	2	4	.389
J. Mayberry, 1b	18	4	0	0	1	4	3	.222
H. McRae, dh, of	17	2	1	1	0	2	1	.118
T. Poquette, of	16	3	2	0	0	1	4	.188
B. Martinez, c	15	5	0	0	0	0	4	.333
J. Wohlford, of	11	2	0	0	0	3	0	.182
C. Rojas, 2b	9	3	0	0	0	2	1	.333
F. White, 2b	8	1	0	0	0	2	0	.125
J. Quirk, dh	7	1	0	1	0	1	2	.143
D. Nelson	2	0	0	0	0	0	0	.000
A. Otis, of	1	0	0	0	0	0	0	.000
B. Stinson, c	1	0	0	0	0	0	0	.000
J. Wathan, c	0	0	0	0	0	0	0	—

Errors: G. Brett (3), D. Bird
Stolen Bases: A. Cowens (2), J. Wohlford (2), C. Rojas

Individual Pitching

NEW YORK (EAST)

	W	L	ERA	IP	H	BB	SO	SV
E. Figueroa	0	1	5.84	12.1	14	2	5	0
C. Hunter	1	1	4.50	12	10	1	5	0
D. Ellis	1	0	3.38	8	6	2	5	0
D. Tidrow	1	0	3.68	7.1	6	4	0	0
G. Jackson	0	0	8.10	3.1	4	1	3	0
S. Lyle	0	0	0.00	1	0	1	0	1

KANSAS CITY (WEST)

	W	L	ERA	IP	H	BB	SO	SV
L. Gura	0	1	4.22	10.2	18	1	4	0
P. Splittorff	1	0	1.93	9.1	7	5	2	0
A. Hassler	0	1	6.14	7.1	8	6	4	0
D. Bird	1	0	1.93	4.2	4	0	1	0
M. Littell	0	1	1.93	4.2	4	1	3	0
S. Mingori	0	0	2.70	3.1	4	0	1	1
D. Leonard	0	0	19.29	2.1	9	2	0	0
T. Hall	0	0	0.00	0.1	1	0	0	0
M. Pattin	0	0	27.00	0.1	0	1	0	0

1976 WORLD SERIES

LINE SCORES						PITCHERS (innings pitched)	HOME RUNS (men on)	HIGHLIGHTS

Cincinnati (N.L.) defeats New York (A.L.) 4 games to 0

			R	H	E	PITCHERS (innings pitched)	HOME RUNS (men on)	HIGHLIGHTS
GAME 1 - OCTOBER 16								The Yankees returned to World Series play after a 12-year absence, but ran into an inspired Reds club. Three hits by Perez and Gullett's five-hit pitching gave Cincinnati the opener.
NY	A	010 000 000	1	5	1	**Alexander** (6), Lyle (2)		
CIN	N	101 001 20x	5	10	1	**Gullett** (7.1), Borbon (1.2)	Morgan	
GAME 2 - OCTOBER 17								The Reds broke a 3-3 tie with two out in the 9th when Stanley threw Griffey's grounder into the dugout for two bases. Griffey then scored on Perez's single.
NY	A	000 100 200	3	9	1	**Hunter** (8.2)		
CIN	N	030 000 001	4	10	0	Norman (6.1), **Billingham** (2.2)		
GAME 3 - OCTOBER 19								Driessen cracked three hits, including a home run, and Zachry and McEnaney scattered eight hits for the win.
CIN	N	030 100 020	6	13	2	**Zachry** (6.2), McEnaney (2.1), **SV**	Driessen	
NY	A	000 100 100	2	8	0	**Ellis** (3.1), Jackson (3.2), Tidrow (2)	Mason	
GAME 4 - OCTOBER 21								Bench drove in five runs with a pair of homers as the Reds won in four straight. Bench ended the Series with a .533 average, overshadowing Munson's fine .529 perfomance.
CIN	N	000 300 004	7	9	2	**Nolan** (6.2), McEnaney (2.1), **SV**	Bench (1 on), Bench (2 on)	
NY	A	100 010 000	2	8	0	**Figueroa** (8), Tidrow (0.1), Lyle (0.2)		

Team totals

		W	AB	H	2B	3B	HR	R	RBI	BA	BB	SO	ERA
CIN	N	4	134	42	10	3	4	22	21	.313	12	16	2.00
NY	A	0	135	30	3	1	1	8	8	.222	12	16	5.45

Individual Batting

CINCINNATI (N.L.)

	AB	H	2B	3B	HR	R	RBI	BA
K. Griffey, of	17	1	0	0	0	2	1	.059
T. Perez, 1b	16	5	1	0	0	1	2	.313
P. Rose, 3b	16	3	1	0	0	1	1	.188
J. Bench, c	15	8	1	1	2	4	6	.533
J. Morgan, 2b	15	5	1	1	1	3	2	.333
G. Foster, of	14	6	1	0	0	3	4	.429
D. Concepcion, ss	14	5	1	1	0	1	3	.357
D. Driessen, dh	14	5	2	0	1	4	1	.357
C. Geronimo, of	13	4	2	0	0	3	1	.308

Errors: J. Morgan (2), D. Concepcion, C. Geronimo, P. Zachry
Stolen Bases: C. Geronimo (2), J. Morgan (2), D. Concepcion, D. Driessen, K. Griffey

NEW YORK (A.L.)

	AB	H	2B	3B	HR	R	RBI	BA
M. Rivers, of	18	3	0	0	0	1	0	.167
T. Munson, c	17	9	0	0	0	2	2	.529
C. Chambliss, 1b	16	5	1	0	0	1	1	.313
R. White, of	15	2	0	0	0	0	0	.133
W. Randolph, 2b	14	1	0	0	0	1	0	.071
G. Nettles, 3b	12	3	0	0	0	0	2	.250
L. Piniella, dh, of	9	3	1	0	0	1	0	.333
C. May, dh	9	0	0	0	0	0	0	.000
O. Gamble, of	8	1	0	0	0	0	1	.125
F. Stanley, ss	6	1	1	0	0	1	1	.167
E. Maddox, dh, of	5	1	0	1	0	0	0	.200
O. Velez	3	0	0	0	0	0	0	.000
E. Hendricks	2	0	0	0	0	0	0	.000
J. Mason, ss	1	1	0	0	1	1	1	1.000

Errors: C. Chambliss, F. Stanley
Stolen Bases: M. Rivers

Individual Pitching

CINCINNATI (N.L.)

	W	L	ERA	IP	H	BB	SO	SV
D. Gullett	1	0	1.23	7.1	5	3	4	0
G. Nolan	1	0	2.70	6.2	8	1	1	0
P. Zachry	1	0	2.70	6.2	6	5	6	0
F. Norman	0	0	4.26	6.1	9	2	2	0
W. McEnaney	0	0	0.00	4.2	2	1	2	2
J. Billingham	1	0	0.00	2.2	0	0	1	0
P. Borbon	0	0	0.00	1.2	0	0	0	0

NEW YORK (A.L.)

	W	L	ERA	IP	H	BB	SO	SV
C. Hunter	0	1	3.12	8.2	10	4	5	0
E. Figueroa	0	1	5.63	8	6	5	2	0
D. Alexander	0	1	7.50	6	9	2	1	0
G. Jackson	0	0	4.91	3.2	4	0	3	0
D. Ellis	0	1	10.80	3.1	7	0	1	0
S. Lyle	0	0	0.00	2.2	1	0	3	0
D. Tidrow	0	0	7.71	2.1	5	1	1	0

1977 NATIONAL LEAGUE CHAMPIONSHIP SERIES

Los Angeles (West) defeats Philadelphia (East) 3 games to 1

LINE SCORES						PITCHERS (innings pitched)	HOME RUNS (men on)	HIGHLIGHTS
GAME 1 - OCTOBER 4								The Phillies broke a 5-5 tie in the ninth on singles by Bake McBride, Larry Bowa and Mike Schmidt, good for two runs.
PHI	**E**	200 021 002	7	9	0	Carlton (6.2), **Garber** (1.1), McGraw (1) **SV**	Luzinski (1 on)	
LA	**W**	000 010 400	5	9	2	John (4.2), Garman (0.1), Hough (2), **Sosa** (2)	Cey (3 on)	
GAME 2 - OCTOBER 5								Dusty Baker's grand slam snapped a 1-1 tie, and Don Sutton spaced 9 hits.
PHI	**E**	001 000 000	1	9	1	**Lonborg** (4), Reed (2), Brusstar (2)	McBride	
LA	**W**	001 401 10x	7	9	1	**Sutton** (9)	Baker (3 on)	
GAME 3 - OCTOBER 7								The Dodgers rallied for three runs with two outs in the 9th. Pinch hitter Manny Mota doubled after Vic Davalillo singled. Davey Lopes singled in the tying run and scored the winning run on a single by Bill Russell.
LA	**W**	020 100 003	6	12	2	Hooton (1.2), Rhoden (4.1), Rau (1), Sosa (0.2), **Rautzhan** (0.1), Garman (1) **SV**		
PHI	**E**	030 000 020	5	6	2	Christenson (3.1), Brusstar (0.2), Reed (2), **Garber** (3)		
GAME 4 - OCTOBER 8								Dusty Baker drove in 2 runs with his second homer, scored twice, and Tommy John permitted only 7 hits as the Dodgers clinched the series.
LA	**W**	020 020 000	4	5	0	**John** (9)	Baker (1 on)	
PHI	**E**	000 100 000	1	7	0	**Carlton** (5), Reed (1), McGraw (2), Garber (1)		

Team totals

		W	AB	H	2B	3B	HR	R	RBI	BA	BB	SO	ERA
LA	**W**	3	133	35	6	1	3	22	20	.263	14	22	2.25
PHI	**E**	1	138	31	3	0	2	14	12	.225	11	21	5.40

Individual Batting

LOS ANGELES (WEST)

	AB	H	2B	3B	HR	R	RBI	BA
B. Russell, ss	18	5	1	0	0	3	2	.278
D. Lopes, 2b	17	4	0	0	0	2	3	.235
R. Smith, of	16	3	0	1	0	2	1	.188
D. Baker, of	14	5	1	0	2	4	8	.357
R. Cey, 3b	13	4	1	0	1	4	4	.308
S. Garvey, 1b	13	4	0	0	0	2	0	.308
S. Yeager, c	13	3	0	0	0	1	2	.231
R. Monday, of	7	2	1	0	0	1	0	.286
G. Burke, of	7	0	0	0	0	0	0	.000
T. John, p	5	1	0	0	0	0	0	.200
D. Sutton, p	3	0	0	0	0	0	0	.000
V. Davalillo	1	1	0	0	0	1	0	1.000
B. Hooton, p	1	1	1	0	0	0	0	1.000
L. Lacy	1	1	0	0	0	1	0	1.000
M. Mota	1	1	1	0	0	1	0	1.000
E. Goodson	1	0	0	0	0	0	0	.000
R. Rhoden, p	1	0	0	0	0	0	0	.000
E. Sosa, p	1	0	0	0	0	0	0	.000
J. Grote, c	0	0	0	0	0	0	0	—

Errors: B. Russell (2), R. Cey, D. Lopes, R. Smith

Stolen Bases: R. Cey, S. Garvey, R. Smith

PHILADELPHIA (EAST)

	AB	H	2B	3B	HR	R	RBI	BA
B. McBride, of	18	4	0	0	1	2	2	.222
L. Bowa, ss	17	2	0	0	0	2	1	.118
M. Schmidt, 3b	16	1	0	0	0	2	1	.063
R. Hebner, 1b	14	5	2	0	0	2	0	.357
G. Luzinski, of	14	4	1	0	1	2	2	.286
T. Sizemore, 2b	13	3	0	0	0	1	0	.231
B. Boone, c	10	4	0	0	0	1	0	.400
G. Maddox, of	7	3	0	0	0	1	2	.429
T. McCarver, c	6	1	0	0	0	1	0	.167
J. Johnstone, of	5	1	0	0	0	0	0	.200
S. Carlton, p	4	2	0	0	0	0	1	.500
D. Johnson, 1b	4	1	0	0	0	0	2	.250
J. Martin, of	4	0	0	0	0	0	0	.000
T. Hutton, 1b	3	0	0	0	0	0	0	.000
O. Brown	2	0	0	0	0	0	0	.000
J. Lonborg, p	1	0	0	0	0	0	0	.000
L. Christenson, p	0	0	0	0	0	0	1	—

Errors: T. Sizemore (2), G. Garber

Stolen Bases: G. Luzinski

Individual Pitching

LOS ANGELES (WEST)

	W	L	ERA	IP	H	BB	SO	SV
T. John	1	0	0.66	13.2	11	5	11	0
D. Sutton	1	0	1.00	9	9	0	4	0
R. Rhoden	0	0	0.00	4.1	2	2	0	0
E. Sosa	0	1	10.13	2.2	5	0	0	0
C. Hough	0	0	4.50	2	2	0	3	0
B. Hooton	0	0	16.20	1.2	2	4	1	0
M. Garman	0	0	0.00	1.1	0	0	1	1
D. Rau	0	0	0.00	1	0	0	1	0
L. Rautzhan	1	0	0.00	0.1	0	0	0	0

PHILADELPHIA (EAST)

	W	L	ERA	IP	H	BB	SO	SV
S. Carlton	0	1	6.94	11.2	13	8	6	0
G. Garber	1	1	3.38	5.1	4	0	3	0
R. Reed	0	0	1.80	5	3	2	5	0
J. Lonborg	0	1	11.25	4	5	1	1	0
L. Christenson	0	0	8.10	3.1	7	0	2	0
T. McGraw	0	0	0.00	3	1	2	3	1
W. Brusstar	0	0	3.38	2.2	2	1	2	0

1977 AMERICAN LEAGUE CHAMPIONSHIP SERIES

New York (East) defeats Kansas City (West) 3 games to 2

LINE SCORES			R	H	E	PITCHERS (innings pitched)	HOME RUNS (men on)	HIGHLIGHTS
GAME 1 - OCTOBER 5								Hal McRae, John Mayberry and Al Cowens homered to account for five Royals' runs.
KC	**W**	222 000 010	7	9	0	**Splittorff** (8), Bird (1)	McRae (1 on), Mayberry (1 on), Cowens	
NY	**E**	002 000 000	2	9	0	**Gullett** (2), Tidrow (6.2), Lyle (0.1)	Munson (1 on)	
GAME 2 - OCTOBER 6								Ron Guidry pitched a 3-hitter, and Cliff Johnson homered as Yanks tied series.
KC	**W**	001 001 000	2	3	1	**Hassler** (5.2), Littell (2), Mingori (0.1)		
NY	**E**	000 023 01x	6	10	1	**Guidry** (9)	Johnson	
GAME 3 - OCTOBER 7								Hal McRae doubled twice and scored twice, and Amos Otis hit a pinch double in support of Dennis Leonard's 4-hitter.
NY	**E**	000 010 001	2	4	1	**Torrez** (5.2), Lyle (2.1)		
KC	**W**	011 012 10x	6	12	1	**Leonard** (9)		
GAME 4 - OCTOBER 8								Mickey Rivers banged four hits and Sparky Lyle hurled scoreless ball through 5.2 relief innings as the Yankees evened the series.
NY	**E**	121 100 001	6	13	0	Figueroa (3.1), Tidrow (0.1), **Lyle** (5.1)		
KC	**W**	002 200 000	4	8	2	**Gura** (2), Pattin (6), Mingori (0.1), Bird (0.1)		
GAME 5 - OCTOBER 9								Trailing 3-1, the Yanks scored one run in the 8th and three in the 9th to win the pennant. Rivers delivered the game-winning hit, and Lyle gained his second straight victory in relief.
NY	**E**	001 000 013	5	10	0	Guidry (2.1), Torrez (5.1), **Lyle** (1.1)		
KC	**W**	201 000 000	3	10	1	Splittorff (7), Bird (0.1), Mingori (0.2), Gura (0), **Leonard** (0), Littell (1)		

Team totals

		W	AB	H	2B	3B	HR	R	RBI	BA	BB	SO	ERA
NY	**E**	3	175	46	12	0	2	21	17	.263	9	16	4.50
KC	**W**	2	163	42	9	3	3	22	21	.258	15	22	3.27

Individual Batting

NEW YORK (EAST)

	AB	H	2B	3B	HR	R	RBI	BA
M. Rivers, of	23	9	2	0	0	5	2	.391
L. Piniella, dh, of	21	7	3	0	0	1	2	.333
T. Munson, c	21	6	1	0	1	3	5	.286
G. Nettles, 3b	20	3	0	0	0	1	1	.150
W. Randolph, 2b	18	5	1	0	0	4	2	.278
C. Chambliss, 1b	17	1	0	0	0	0	0	.059
R. Jackson, dh, of	16	2	0	0	0	1	1	.125
C. Johnson, dh	15	6	2	0	1	2	2	.400
B. Dent, ss	14	3	1	0	0	1	2	.214
P. Blair, of	5	2	0	0	0	1	0	.400
R. White, dh, of	5	2	2	0	0	2	0	.400
F. Stanley, ss	0	0	0	0	0	0	0	—

Errors: B. Dent, R. White
Stolen Bases: R. Jackson, M. Rivers

KANSAS CITY (WEST)

	AB	H	2B	3B	HR	R	RBI	BA
G. Brett, 3b	20	6	0	2	0	2	2	.300
A. Cowens, of	19	5	0	0	1	2	5	.263
H. McRae, dh, of	18	8	3	0	1	6	2	.444
F. Patek, ss	18	7	3	1	0	4	5	.389
F. White, 2b	18	5	1	0	0	1	2	.278
A. Otis, of	16	2	1	0	0	1	2	.125
D. Porter, c	15	5	0	0	0	3	0	.333
J. Mayberry, 1b	12	2	1	0	1	1	3	.167
J. Zdeb, of	9	0	0	0	0	0	0	.000
T. Poquette, of	6	1	0	0	0	0	0	.167
J. Wathan, 1b, c, dh	6	0	0	0	0	0	0	.000
C. Rojas, dh	4	1	0	0	0	0	0	.250
P. LaCock, 1b	1	0	0	0	0	0	0	.000
J. Lahoud, dh	1	0	0	0	0	2	0	.000

Errors: G. Brett (2), J. Mayberry (2), F. Patek
Stolen Bases: A. Otis (2), C. Rojas, F. White, J. Zdeb

Individual Pitching

NEW YORK (EAST)

	W	L	ERA	IP	H	BB	SO	SV
R. Guidry	1	0	3.97	11.1	9	3	8	0
M. Torrez	0	1	4.09	11	11	5	5	0
S. Lyle	2	0	0.96	9.1	7	0	3	0
D. Tidrow	0	0	3.86	7	6	3	3	0
E. Figueroa	0	0	10.80	3.1	5	2	3	0
D. Gullett	0	1	18.00	2	4	2	0	0

KANSAS CITY (WEST)

	W	L	ERA	IP	H	BB	SO	SV
P. Splittorff	1	0	2.40	15	14	3	4	0
D. Leonard	1	1	3.00	9	5	2	4	0
M. Pattin	0	0	1.50	6	6	0	0	0
A. Hassler	0	1	4.76	5.2	5	0	3	0
M. Littell	0	0	3.00	3	5	3	1	0
D. Bird	0	0	0.00	2	4	0	1	0
L. Gura	0	1	18.00	2	7	1	2	0
S. Mingori	0	0	0.00	1.1	0	0	1	0

1977 WORLD SERIES

New York (A.L.) defeats Los Angeles (N.L.) 4 games to 2

LINE SCORES			R	H	E	PITCHERS (innings pitched)	HOME RUNS (men on)	HIGHLIGHTS
GAME 1 - OCTOBER 11								Randolph doubled in the twelfth and scored on a single by Blair against loser Rhoden.
LA	N	200 000 001 000	3	6	0	Sutton (7), Rautzhan (0.1), Sosa (0.2), Garman (3), **Rhoden** (0)		
NY	A	100 001 010 001	4	11	0	Gullett (8.1), **Lyle** (3.2)	Randolph	
GAME 2 - OCTOBER 12								The Dodgers exploded for four homers to rout Hunter. Hooton allowed just five singles.
LA	N	212 000 001	6	9	0	**Hooton** (9)	Cey (1 on), Yeager, Smith (1 on), Garvey	
NY	A	000 100 000	1	5	0	**Hunter** (2.1), Tidrow (2.2), Clay (3), Lyle (1)		
GAME 3 - OCTOBER 14								Rivers cracked three hits, including two doubles, to lead the Yankees' attack against loser John.
NY	A	300 110 000	5	10	0	**Torrez** (9)		
LA	N	003 000 000	3	7	1	**John** (6), Hough (3)	Baker (2 on)	
GAME 4 - OCTOBER 15								Jackson homered and doubled in support of Ron Guidry's four-hitter. Guidry fanned seven.
NY	A	030 001 000	4	7	0	**Guidry** (9)	Jackson	
LA	N	002 000 000	2	4	0	**Rau** (1), Rhoden (7), Garman (1)	Lopes (1 on)	
GAME 5 - OCTOBER 16								Yeager homered and drove in four runs, Baker had three hits, and Sutton breezed to an easy victory.
NY	A	000 000 220	4	9	2	**Gullett** (4.1), Clay (0.2), Tidrow (1), Hunter (2)	Munson, Jackson	
LA	N	100 432 00x	10	13	0	**Sutton** (9)	Yeager (2 on), Smith (1 on)	
GAME 6 - OCTOBER 18								Jackson hit three successive homers, each on the first pitch, each off a different pitcher, amounting to five RBIs to give the Yankees their first World Series title since 1962.
LA	N	201 000 001	4	9	0	**Hooton** (3), Sosa (1.2), Rau (1.1), Hough (2)	Smith	
NY	A	020 320 01x	8	8	1	**Torrez** (9)	Chambliss (1 on), Jackson (1 on), Jackson (1 on), Jackson	

Team totals

		W	AB	H	2B	3B	HR	R	RBI	BA	BB	SO	ERA
NY	A	4	205	50	10	0	8	26	25	.244	11	37	4.02
LA	N	2	208	48	5	3	9	28	28	.231	16	36	4.09

Individual Batting

NEW YORK (A.L.)

	AB	H	2B	3B	HR	R	RBI	BA
M. Rivers, of	27	6	2	0	0	1	1	.222
T. Munson, c	25	8	2	0	1	4	3	.320
W. Randolph, 2b	25	4	2	0	1	5	1	.160
C. Chambliss, 1b	24	7	2	0	1	4	4	.292
L. Piniella, of	22	6	0	0	0	1	3	.273
G. Nettles, 3b	21	4	1	0	0	1	2	.190
R. Jackson, of	20	9	1	0	5	10	8	.450
B. Dent, ss	19	5	0	0	0	0	2	.263
M. Torrez, p	6	0	0	0	0	0	0	.000
P. Blair, of	4	1	0	0	0	0	1	.250
R. Guidry, p	2	0	0	0	0	0	0	.000
D. Gullett, p	2	0	0	0	0	0	0	.000
S. Lyle, p	2	0	0	0	0	0	0	.000
R. White	2	0	0	0	0	0	0	.000
G. Zeber	2	0	0	0	0	0	0	.000
C. Johnson, c	1	0	0	0	0	0	0	.000
D. Tidrow, p	1	0	0	0	0	0	0	.000
F. Stanley, ss	0	0	0	0	0	0	0	—

Errors: B. Dent, G. Nettles, L. Piniella
Stolen Bases: M. Rivers

LOS ANGELES (N.L.)

	AB	H	2B	3B	HR	R	RBI	BA
B. Russell, ss	26	4	0	1	0	3	2	.154
S. Garvey, 1b	24	9	1	1	1	5	3	.375
D. Baker, of	24	7	0	0	1	4	5	.292
D. Lopes, 2b	24	4	0	1	1	3	2	.167
R. Smith, of	22	6	1	0	3	7	5	.273
R. Cey, 3b	21	4	1	0	1	2	3	.190
S. Yeager, c	19	6	1	0	2	2	5	.316
R. Monday, of	12	2	0	0	0	0	0	.167
L. Lacy, of	7	3	0	0	0	1	2	.429
D. Sutton, p	6	0	0	0	0	0	0	.000
G. Burke, of	5	1	0	0	0	0	0	.200
B. Hooton, p	5	0	0	0	0	0	0	.000
V. Davalillo	3	1	0	0	0	0	1	.333
M. Mota	3	0	0	0	0	0	0	.000
R. Rhoden, p	2	1	1	0	0	1	0	.500
T. John, p	2	0	0	0	0	0	0	.000
E. Goodson	1	0	0	0	0	0	0	.000
J. Grote, c	1	0	0	0	0	0	0	.000
J. Oates, c	1	0	0	0	0	0	0	.000
R. Landestoy	0	0	0	0	0	0	0	—

Errors: D. Baker
Stolen Bases: D. Lopes (2)

Individual Pitching

NEW YORK (A.L.)

	W	L	ERA	IP	H	BB	SO	SV
M. Torrez	2	0	2.50	18	16	5	15	0
D. Gullett	0	1	6.39	12.2	13	7	10	0
R. Guidry	1	0	2.00	9	4	3	7	0
S. Lyle	1	0	1.93	4.2	2	0	2	0
C. Hunter	0	1	10.38	4.1	6	0	1	0
K. Clay	0	0	2.45	3.2	2	1	0	0
D. Tidrow	0	0	4.91	3.2	5	0	1	0

LOS ANGELES (N.L.)

	W	L	ERA	IP	H	BB	SO	SV
D. Sutton	1	0	3.94	16	17	1	6	0
B. Hooton	1	1	3.75	12	8	2	9	0
R. Rhoden	0	1	2.57	7	4	1	5	0
T. John	0	1	6.00	6	9	3	7	0
C. Hough	0	0	1.80	5	3	0	5	0
M. Garman	0	0	0.00	4	2	1	3	0
D. Rau	0	1	11.57	2.1	4	0	1	0
E. Sosa	0	0	11.57	2.1	3	1	1	0
L. Rautzhan	0	0	0.00	0.1	0	2	0	0

1978 NATIONAL LEAGUE CHAMPIONSHIP SERIES

LINE SCORES						PITCHERS (innings pitched)	HOME RUNS (men on)	HIGHLIGHTS

Los Angeles (West) defeats Philadelphia (East) 3 games to 1

			R	H	E	PITCHERS (innings pitched)	HOME RUNS (men on)	HIGHLIGHTS
GAME 1 - OCTOBER 4								Garvey drove in four runs with 2 home runs and a triple, and Welch pitched two-hit ball for 4.1 innings in relief.
LA	**W**	004 211 001	9	13	1	Hooton (4.2), **Welch** (4.1)	Lopes, Yeager, Garvey, Garvey (1 on)	
PHI	**E**	010 030 001	5	12	1	**Christensen** (4.1), Brusstar (0.2), Eastwick (1), McGraw (3)	Martin	
GAME 2 - OCTOBER 5								Tommy John pitched a 4-hit shutout, and Davey Lopes drove in 3 runs with a homer, triple and single.
LA	**W**	000 120 100	4	8	0	**John** (9)	Lopes (1 on)	
PHI	**E**	000 000 000	0	4	0	**Ruthven** (4.2), Brusstar (1.1), Reed (2), McGraw (1)		
GAME 3 - OCTOBER 6								Carlton helped his cause at bat, driving in 4 runs with a home run and sacrifice fly as he went the route on an 8-hitter.
PHI	**E**	040 003 101	9	11	1	**Carlton** (9)	Carlton (2 on), Luzinski	
LA	**W**	012 000 010	4	8	2	**Sutton** (5.2), Rautzhan (1.1), Hough (2)	Garvey	
GAME 4 - OCTOBER 7								Bill Russell's 10th inning single, after a muff of a fly ball by Garry Maddox, scored Ron Cey with the winning run giving the Dodgers the NL championship.
PHI	**E**	002 000 100 0	3	8	2	Lerch (5.1), Brusstar (0.2), Reed (2), **McGraw** (1.2)	Luzinski (1 on), McBride	
LA	**W**	010 101 000 1	4	13	0	Rau (5), Rhoden (4), **Forster** (1)	Cey, Garvey	

Team totals

		W	AB	H	2B	3B	HR	R	RBI	BA	BB	SO	ERA
LA	**W**	3	147	42	8	3	8	21	21	.286	9	22	3.41
PHI	**E**	1	140	35	3	2	5	17	16	.250	9	21	4.66

Individual Batting

LOS ANGELES (WEST)

	AB	H	2B	3B	HR	R	RBI	BA
S. Garvey, 1b	18	7	1	1	4	6	7	.389
D. Lopes, 2b	18	7	1	1	2	3	5	.389
B. Russell, ss	17	7	1	0	0	1	2	.412
R. Cey, 3b	16	5	1	0	1	4	3	.313
R. Smith, of	16	3	1	0	0	2	1	.188
D. Baker, of	15	7	2	0	0	1	1	.467
S. Yeager, c	13	3	0	0	1	2	2	.231
R. Monday, of	10	2	0	1	0	2	0	.200
B. North, of	8	0	0	0	0	0	0	.000
T. John, p	3	0	0	0	0	0	0	.000
J. Ferguson	2	0	0	0	0	0	0	.000
B. Hooton, p	2	0	0	0	0	0	0	.000
L. Lacy	2	0	0	0	0	0	0	.000
D. Sutton, p	2	0	0	0	0	0	0	.000
B. Welch, p	2	0	0	0	0	0	0	.000
M. Mota	1	1	1	0	0	0	0	1.000
D. Rau, p	1	0	0	0	0	0	0	.000
R. Rhoden, p	1	0	0	0	0	0	0	.000
J. Grote, c	0	0	0	0	0	0	0	—

Errors: D. Lopes (2), R. Smith
Stolen Bases: D. Lopes, S. Yeager

PHILADELPHIA (EAST)

	AB	H	2B	3B	HR	R	RBI	BA
G. Maddox, of	19	5	0	0	0	1	2	.263
L. Bowa, ss	18	6	0	0	0	2	0	.333
G. Luzinski, of	16	6	0	1	2	3	3	.375
M. Schmidt, 3b	15	3	2	0	0	1	1	.200
T. Sizemore, 2b	13	5	0	1	0	3	1	.385
B. Boone, c	11	2	0	0	0	0	0	.182
J. Martin, of	9	2	1	0	1	1	2	.222
B. McBride, of	9	2	0	0	1	2	1	.222
R. Hebner, 1b	9	1	0	0	0	0	1	.111
J. Cardenal, 1b	6	1	0	0	0	0	0	.167
S. Carlton, p	4	2	0	0	1	2	4	.500
T. McCarver, c	4	0	0	0	0	2	1	.000
R. Lerch, p	2	0	0	0	0	0	0	.000
L. Christenson, p	1	0	0	0	0	0	0	.000
B. Foote	1	0	0	0	0	0	0	.000
O. Gonzalez	1	0	0	0	0	0	0	.000
J. Morrison	1	0	0	0	0	0	0	.000
D. Ruthven, p	1	0	0	0	0	0	0	.000

Errors: M. Schmidt (2), B. Boone, G. Maddox

Individual Pitching

LOS ANGELES (WEST)

	W	L	ERA	IP	H	BB	SO	SV
T. John	1	0	0.00	9	4	2	4	0
D. Sutton	0	1	6.35	5.2	7	2	0	0
D. Rau	0	0	3.60	5	5	2	1	0
B. Hooton	0	0	7.71	4.2	10	0	5	0
B. Welch	1	0	2.08	4.1	2	0	5	0
R. Rhoden	0	0	2.25	4	2	1	3	0
C. Hough	0	0	4.50	2	1	0	1	0
L. Rautzhan	0	0	6.75	1.1	3	2	0	0
T. Forster	1	0	0.00	1	1	0	2	0

PHILADELPHIA (EAST)

	W	L	ERA	IP	H	BB	SO	SV
S. Carlton	1	0	4.00	9	8	2	8	0
T. McGraw	0	1	1.59	5.2	3	5	5	0
R. Lerch	0	0	5.06	5.1	7	0	0	0
D. Ruthven	0	1	5.79	4.2	6	0	3	0
L. Christenson	0	1	12.46	4.1	7	1	3	0
R. Reed	0	0	2.25	4	6	0	2	0
W. Brusstar	0	0	0.00	2.2	2	1	0	0
R. Eastwick	0	0	9.00	1	3	0	1	0

1978 AMERICAN LEAGUE CHAMPIONSHIP SERIES

New York (East) defeats Kansas City (West) 3 games to 1

LINE SCORES			R	H	E	PITCHERS (innings pitched)	HOME RUNS (men on)	HIGHLIGHTS
GAME 1 - OCTOBER 3								Jackson accounted for 5 runs, scoring two and driving in three with 3 hits, including a double and a homer.
NY	E	011 020 030	7	16	0	**Beattie** (5.1), Clay (3.2), **SV**	Jackson (2 on)	
KC	W	000 001 000	1	2	2	**Leonard** (4), Mingori (3.2), Hrabosky (0.1), Bird (1)		
GAME 2 - OCTOBER 4								Kansas City raked three Yankee pitchers for sixteen hits and an easy win.
NY	E	000 000 220	4	12	1	**Figueroa** (1), Tidrow (5.2), Lyle (1.1)		
KC	W	140 000 32x	10	16	1	**Gura** (6.1), Pattin (0.2), Hrabosky (2)	Patek (1 on)	
GAME 3 - OCTOBER 6								Munson's 8th inning homer with White on base gave the Yankees an uphill victory and a 2-1 lead in games, offsetting Brett's 3 home runs.
KC	W	101 010 020	5	10	1	Splittorff (7.1), **Bird** (0), Hrabosky (0.2)	Brett, Brett, Brett	
NY	E	010 201 02x	6	10	0	Hunter (6), **Gossage** (3)	Jackson (1 on), Munson (1 on)	
GAME 4 - OCTOBER 7								White broke a 1-1 tie with a homer in the 6th, giving the Yankees their third straight championship series win over the Royals.
KC	W	100 000 000	1	7	0	**Leonard** (8)		
NY	E	010 001 00x	2	4	0	**Guidry** (8), Gossage (1), **SV**	Nettles, White	

Team totals

		W	AB	H	2B	3B	HR	R	RBI	BA	BB	SO	ERA
NY	E	3	140	42	3	1	5	19	18	.300	7	18	3.86
KC	W	1	133	35	6	3	4	17	16	.263	14	21	4.76

Individual Batting

NEW YORK (EAST)

	AB	H	2B	3B	HR	R	RBI	BA
T. Munson, c	18	5	1	0	1	2	2	.278
L. Piniella, of	17	4	0	0	0	2	0	.235
R. White, dh, of	16	5	1	0	1	5	1	.313
C. Chambliss, 1b	15	6	0	0	0	1	2	.400
G. Nettles, 3b	15	5	0	1	1	3	2	.333
B. Dent, ss	15	3	0	0	0	0	4	.200
R. Jackson, dh, of	13	6	1	0	2	5	6	.462
M. Rivers, of	11	5	0	0	0	0	0	.455
B. Doyle, 2b	7	2	0	0	0	0	1	.286
P. Blair, 2b, of	6	0	0	0	0	1	0	.000
F. Stanley, 2b	5	1	0	0	0	0	0	.200
C. Johnson	1	0	0	0	0	0	0	.000
G. Thomasson, of	1	0	0	0	0	0	0	.000

Errors: B. Dent

KANSAS CITY (WEST)

	AB	H	2B	3B	HR	R	RBI	BA
G. Brett, 3b	18	7	1	1	3	7	3	.389
A. Cowens, of	15	2	0	0	0	2	1	.133
A. Otis, of	14	6	2	0	0	2	1	.429
D. Porter, c	14	5	1	0	0	1	3	.357
H. McRae, dh	14	3	0	0	0	0	2	.214
F. White, 2b	13	3	0	0	0	1	2	.231
F. Patek, ss	13	1	0	0	1	2	2	.077
P. LaCock, 1b	11	4	2	1	0	1	1	.364
C. Hurdle, of	8	3	0	1	0	1	1	.375
S. Braun, of	5	0	0	0	0	0	0	.000
W. Wilson, of	4	1	0	0	0	0	0	.250
J. Wathan, 1b	3	0	0	0	0	0	0	.000
T. Poquette	1	0	0	0	0	0	0	.000

Errors: F. Patek (2), G. Brett, A. Otis

Stolen Bases: A. Otis (4), P. LaCock, H. McRae

Individual Pitching

NEW YORK (EAST)

	W	L	ERA	IP	H	BB	SO	SV
R. Guidry	1	0	1.13	8	7	1	7	0
C. Hunter	0	0	4.50	6	7	3	5	0
D. Tidrow	0	0	4.76	5.2	8	2	1	0
J. Beattie	1	0	1.69	5.1	2	5	3	0
G. Gossage	1	0	4.50	4	3	0	3	1
K. Clay	0	0	0.00	3.2	0	3	2	1
S. Lyle	0	0	13.50	1.1	3	0	0	0
E. Figueroa	0	1	27.00	1	5	0	0	0

KANSAS CITY (WEST)

	W	L	ERA	IP	H	BB	SO	SV
D. Leonard	0	2	3.75	12	13	2	11	0
P. Splittorff	0	0	4.91	7.1	9	0	2	0
L. Gura	1	0	2.84	6.1	8	2	2	0
S. Mingori	0	0	7.36	3.2	5	3	0	0
A. Hrabosky	0	0	3.00	3	3	0	2	0
D. Bird	0	1	9.00	1	2	0	1	0
M. Pattin	0	0	27.00	0.2	2	0	0	0

1978 WORLD SERIES

New York (A.L.) defeats Los Angeles (N.L.) 4 games to 2

LINE SCORES			R	H	E	PITCHERS (innings pitched)	HOME RUNS (men on)	HIGHLIGHTS
GAME 1 - OCTOBER 10								Lopes hammered two homers for five RBIs while Russell and Baker had three hits each as the Dodgers rapped four Yankee pitchers for 15 hits.
NY	**A**	000 000 320	5	9	1	**Figueroa** (1.2), Clay (2.1), Lindblad (2.1), Tidrow (1.2)	Jackson	
LA	**N**	030 310 31x	11	15	2	**John** (7.2), Foster (1.1)	Lopes (1 on), Lopes (2 on), Baker	
GAME 2 - OCTOBER 11								Cey drove in all four runs with a single and three-run homer off Hunter. Welch saved Hooton's victory by striking out Jackson in the ninth.
NY	**A**	002 000 100	3	11	0	**Hunter** (6), Gossage (2)		
LA	**N**	000 103 00x	4	7	0	**Hooton** (6), Forster (2.1), Welch (0.2), **SV**	Cey (2 on)	
GAME 3 - OCTOBER 13								Aided by the spectacular fielding of third baseman Nettles, who made four dazzling stops, Guidry went the distance despite allowing 8 hits and 7 walks.
LA	**N**	001 000 000	1	8	0	**Sutton** (6.1), Rautzhan (0.2), Hough (1)		
NY	**A**	110 000 30x	5	10	1	**Guidry** (9)	White	
GAME 4 - OCTOBER 14								Piniella's single off Welch with two out in the tenth enabled the Yankees to square the Series. The hit scored White, who had walked and was singled to second by Reggie Jackson.
LA	**N**	000 030 000 0	3	6	1	John (7), Forster (0.1), **Welch** (2.1)	Smith (2 on)	
NY	**A**	000 002 010 1	4	9	0	Figueroa (5), Tidrow (3), **Gossage** (2)		
GAME 5 - OCTOBER 15								The Yankees routed three Dodger pitchers with an 18-hit attack that included 3 each by Rivers, Doyle and Dent. Jim Beattie went the route for the first time in his major league career.
LA	**N**	101 000 000	2	9	3	**Hooton** (2.1), Rautzhan (1.1), Hough (4.1)		
NY	**A**	004 300 41x	12	18	0	**Beattie** (9)		
GAME 6 - OCTOBER 17								Hunter scattered 6 hits in 7 innings, and Doyle and Dent had 3 hits apiece as the Yankees wrapped up their 22nd world championship. Dent was named the Series MVP.
NY	**A**	030 002 200	7	11	0	**Hunter** (7), Gossage (2)	Jackson	
LA	**N**	101 000 000	2	7	1	**Sutton** (5.2), Welch (1.1), Rau (2)	Lopes	

Team totals

		W	AB	H	2B	3B	HR	R	RBI	BA	BB	SO	ERA
NY	**A**	4	222	68	8	0	3	36	34	.306	16	40	3.74
LA	**N**	2	199	52	8	0	6	23	22	.261	20	31	5.46

Individual Batting

NEW YORK (A.L.)

	AB	H	2B	3B	HR	R	RBI	BA
T. Munson, c	25	8	3	0	0	5	7	.320
L. Piniella, of	25	7	0	0	0	3	4	.280
G. Nettles, 3b	25	4	0	0	0	2	1	.160
B. Dent, ss	24	10	1	0	0	3	7	.417
R. White, of	24	8	0	0	1	9	4	.333
R. Jackson, dh	23	9	1	0	2	2	8	.391
M. Rivers, of	18	6	0	0	0	2	1	.333
B. Doyle, 2b	16	7	1	0	0	4	2	.438
J. Spencer, 1b	12	2	0	0	0	3	0	.167
C. Chambliss, 1b	11	2	0	0	0	1	0	.182
P. Blair, of	8	3	1	0	0	2	0	.375
F. Stanley, 2b	5	1	1	0	0	0	0	.200
G. Thomasson, of	4	1	0	0	0	0	0	.250
C. Johnson	2	0	0	0	0	0	0	.000
M. Heath, c	0	0	0	0	0	0	0	—
J. Johnstone, of	0	0	0	0	0	0	0	—

Errors: B. Dent (2)
Stolen Bases: R. White (2), T. Munson, L. Piniella, M. Rivers

LOS ANGELES (N.L.)

	AB	H	2B	3B	HR	R	RBI	BA
B. Russell, ss	26	11	2	0	0	1	2	.423
D. Lopes, 2b	26	8	0	0	3	7	7	.308
R. Smith, of	25	5	0	0	1	3	5	.200
S. Garvey, 1b	24	5	1	0	0	1	0	.208
R. Cey, 3b	21	6	0	0	1	2	4	.286
D. Baker, of	21	5	0	0	1	2	1	.238
L. Lacy, dh	14	2	0	0	0	0	1	.143
S. Yeager, c	13	3	1	0	0	2	0	.231
R. Monday, dh, of	13	2	1	0	0	2	0	.154
B. North, of	8	1	1	0	0	2	2	.125
J. Ferguson, c	4	2	2	0	0	1	0	.500
V. Davalillo, dh	3	1	0	0	0	0	0	.333
J. Oates, c	1	1	0	0	0	0	0	1.000
J. Grote, c	0	0	0	0	0	0	0	—
M. Mota	0	0	0	0	0	0	0	—

Errors: B. Russell (3), J. Ferguson, S. Garvey, D. Lopes, R. Smith
Stolen Bases: D. Lopes (2), S. Garvey, B. North, B. Russell

Individual Pitching

NEW YORK (A.L.)

	W	L	ERA	IP	H	BB	SO	SV
C. Hunter	1	1	4.15	13	13	1	5	0
J. Beattie	1	0	2.00	9	9	4	8	0
R. Guidry	1	0	1.00	9	8	7	4	0
E. Figueroa	0	1	8.10	6.2	9	5	2	0
G. Gossage	1	0	0.00	6	1	1	4	0
D. Tidrow	0	0	1.93	4.2	4	0	5	0
K. Clay	0	0	11.57	2.1	4	2	2	0
P. Lindblad	0	0	11.57	2.1	4	0	1	0

LOS ANGELES (N.L.)

	W	L	ERA	IP	H	BB	SO	SV
T. John	1	0	3.07	14.2	14	4	6	0
D. Sutton	0	2	7.50	12	17	4	8	0
B. Hooton	1	1	6.48	8.1	13	3	6	0
C. Hough	0	0	8.44	5.1	10	2	5	0
B. Welch	0	1	6.23	4.1	4	2	6	1
T. Forster	0	0	0.00	4	5	1	6	0
D. Rau	0	0	0.00	2	1	0	3	0
L. Rautzhan	0	0	13.50	2	4	0	0	0

1979 NATIONAL LEAGUE CHAMPIONSHIP SERIES

Pittsburgh (East) defeats Cincinnati (West) 3 games to 0

LINE SCORES			R	H	E	PITCHERS (innings pitched)	HOME RUNS (men on)	HIGHLIGHTS
GAME 1 - OCTOBER 2								Stargell's 3-run homer in the 11th broke a 2-2 tie.
PIT	**E**	002 000 000 03	5	10	0	Candelaria (7), Romo (0.1), Tekulve (1.2), **Jackson** (0.1), Robinson (1.2) **SV**	Garner, Stargell (2 on)	
CIN	**W**	000 200 000 00	2	7	0	Seaver (8), **Hume** (2.1), Tomlin (0.2)	Foster (1 on)	
GAME 2 - OCTOBER 3								Singles by Moreno and Parker sandwiched around Foli's sacrifice broke a 2-2 tie in the 10th inning.
PIT	**E**	000 110 000 1	3	11	0	Bibby (7), Jackson (0.1), Romo (0), Tekulve (1), Roberts (0), **Robinson** (1.2)		
CIN	**W**	010 000 001 0	2	8	0	Pastore (7), Tomlin (0.2), **Hume** (1.1),		
GAME 3 - OCTOBER 5								Blyleven went the route, scattering 8 hits and fanning 9, while Stargell socked his second homer as Bucs completed series sweep.
CIN	**W**	000 001 000	1	8	1	**LaCoss** (1.2), Norman (2), Leibrandt (0.1), Soto (2), Tomlin (1.2), Hume (0.1)	Bench	
PIT	**E**	112 200 01x	7	7	0	**Blyleven** (9)	Madlock, Stargell	

Team totals

		W	AB	H	2B	3B	HR	R	RBI	BA	BB	SO	ERA
PIT	**E**	3	105	28	3	2	4	15	14	.267	13	13	1.50
CIN	**W**	0	107	23	4	1	2	5	5	.215	11	26	4.34

Individual Batting

PITTSBURGH (EAST)

	AB	H	2B	3B	HR	R	RBI	BA
E. Ott, c	13	3	0	0	0	0	0	.231
P. Garner, 2b, ss	12	5	0	1	1	4	1	.417
T. Foli, ss	12	4	1	0	0	1	3	.333
D. Parker, of	12	4	0	0	0	2	2	.333
B. Madlock, 3b	12	3	0	0	1	1	2	.250
O. Moreno, of	12	3	0	1	0	3	0	.250
W. Stargell, 1b	11	5	2	0	2	2	6	.455
J. Milner, of	9	0	0	0	0	0	0	.000
B. Blyleven, p	3	1	0	0	0	1	0	.333
J. Candelaria, p	3	0	0	0	0	0	0	.000
B. Robinson, of	3	0	0	0	0	0	0	.000
M. Easler	1	0	0	0	0	0	0	.000
G. Jackson, p	1	0	0	0	0	0	0	.000
K. Tekulve, p	1	0	0	0	0	0	0	.000
M. Alexander	0	0	0	0	0	1	0	—
R. Stennett, 2b	0	0	0	0	0	0	0	—

Stolen Bases: B. Madlock (2), O. Moreno, D. Parker

CINCINNATI (WEST)

	AB	H	2B	3B	HR	R	RBI	BA
D. Concepcion, ss	14	6	1	0	0	1	0	.429
D. Collins, of	14	5	1	0	0	0	1	.357
R. Knight, 3b	14	4	1	0	0	0	0	.286
J. Bench, c	12	3	0	1	1	1	1	.250
D. Driessen, 1b	12	1	0	0	0	1	0	.083
J. Morgan, 2b	11	0	0	0	0	0	0	.000
G. Foster, of	10	2	0	0	1	1	2	.200
C. Geronimo, of	7	1	0	0	0	0	0	.143
H. Cruz, of	5	1	1	0	0	1	0	.200
R. Auerbach	2	0	0	0	0	0	0	.000
T. Seaver, p	2	0	0	0	0	0	0	.000
H. Spilman	2	0	0	0	0	0	0	.000
T. Hume, p	1	0	0	0	0	0	0	.000
F. Norman, p	1	0	0	0	0	0	0	.000
F. Pastore, p	0	0	0	0	0	0	1	—

Errors: C. Geronimo

Stolen Bases: D. Collins (2), R. Knight, J. Morgan

Individual Pitching

PITTSBURGH (EAST)

	W	L	ERA	IP	H	BB	SO	SV
B. Blyleven	1	0	1.00	9	8	0	9	0
J. Bibby	0	0	1.29	7	4	4	5	0
J. Candelaria	0	0	2.57	7	5	1	4	0
K. Tekulve	0	0	3.00	3	2	2	2	0
G. Jackson	1	0	0.00	2	1	1	2	0
D. Robinson	1	0	0.00	2	0	1	3	1
E. Romo	0	0	0.00	0.1	3	1	1	0
D. Roberts	0	0	—	0.0	0	1	0	0

CINCINNATI (WEST)

	W	L	ERA	IP	H	BB	SO	SV
T. Seaver	0	0	2.25	8	5	2	5	0
F. Pastore	0	0	2.57	7	7	3	1	0
T. Hume	0	1	6.75	4	6	0	2	0
D. Tomlin	0	0	0.00	3	3	2	3	0
F. Norman	0	0	18.00	2	4	1	1	0
M. Soto	0	0	0.00	2	0	0	1	0
M. LaCoss	0	1	10.80	1.2	1	4	0	0
D. Bair	0	1	9.00	1	2	1	0	0
C. Leibrandt	0	0	0.00	0.1	0	0	0	0

1979 AMERICAN LEAGUE CHAMPIONSHIP SERIES

Baltimore (East) defeats California (West) 3 games to 1

LINE SCORES			R	H	E	PITCHERS (innings pitched)	HOME RUNS (men on)	HIGHLIGHTS
GAME 1 - OCTOBER 3								John Lowenstein, a pinch hitter, stroked a 10th-inning homer with two on to snap a 3-3 tie.
CAL	**W**	101 001 000 0	3	7	1	Ryan (7), **Montague** (2.2)	Ford	
BAL	**E**	002 100 000 3	6	6	0	Palmer (9), **Stanhouse** (1)	Lowenstein (2 on)	
GAME 2 - OCTOBER 4								Eddie Murray drove in 4 runs with a single and a homer to give the Orioles an early 9-1 lead. California scored 7 runs in the last 4 innings to fall short by one run.
CAL	**W**	100 001 132	8	10	1	**Frost** (1.1), Clear (5.2), Aase (1)	Ford	
BAL	**E**	441 000 00x	9	11	1	**Flanagan** (7), Stanhouse (2)	Murray (2 on)	
GAME 3 - OCTOBER 5								California rallied for 2 runs in the 9th to pull the game out the fire. Larry Harlow's looping double off relief ace Stanhouse drove in the winning run.
BAL	**E**	000 101 100	3	8	3	D. Martinez (8.2), **Stanhouse** (0.1)		
CAL	**W**	100 100 002	4	9	0	Tanana (5), **Aase** (4)	Baylor	
GAME 4 - OCTOBER 6								McGregor hurled a 6-hitter and Pat Kelly knocked in 3 runs with a homer and single to help the Orioles win the championship in four games.
BAL	**E**	002 100 500	8	12	1	**McGregor** (9)	Kelly (2 on)	
CAL	**W**	000 000 000	0	6	0	**Knapp** (2.1), LaRoche (1.1), Frost (3), Montague (1.1), Barlow (1)		

Team totals

		W	AB	H	2B	3B	HR	R	RBI	BA	BB	SO	ERA
BAL	**E**	3	133	37	5	1	3	26	25	.278	18	24	2.97
CAL	**W**	1	137	32	7	0	3	15	14	.234	7	13	5.80

Individual Batting

BALTIMORE (EAST)

	AB	H	2B	3B	HR	R	RBI	BA
K. Singleton, of	16	6	2	0	0	4	2	.375
A. Bumbry, of	16	4	0	1	0	5	0	.250
D. DeCinces, 3b	13	4	1	0	0	4	3	.308
E. Murray, 1b	12	5	0	0	1	3	5	.417
P. Kelly, dh, of	11	4	0	0	1	3	4	.364
K. Garcia, ss	11	3	0	0	0	1	2	.273
R. Dauer, 2b	11	2	0	0	0	0	0	.182
R. Dempsey, c	10	4	2	0	0	3	2	.400
L. May, dh	7	1	0	0	0	0	1	.143
J. Lowenstein, of	6	1	0	0	1	2	3	.167
M. Belanger, ss	5	1	0	0	0	0	1	.200
G. Roenicke, of	5	1	0	0	0	1	1	.200
D. Skaggs, c	4	0	0	0	0	0	0	.000
B. Smith, 2b	4	0	0	0	0	0	0	.000
T. Crowley	2	1	0	0	0	0	1	.500

Errors: K. Garcia (2), E. Murray (2), A. Bumbry

Stolen Bases: A. Bumbry (2), P. Kelly (2), R. Dempsey

CALIFORNIA (WEST)

	AB	H	2B	3B	HR	R	RBI	BA
R. Carew, 1b	17	7	3	0	0	4	1	.412
D. Ford, of	17	5	1	0	2	2	4	.294
C. Lansford, 3b	17	5	0	0	0	2	3	.294
R. Miller, of	16	4	0	0	0	2	0	.250
D. Baylor, dh, of	16	3	0	0	1	2	2	.188
B. Downing, c	15	3	0	0	0	1	1	.200
B. Grich, 2b	13	2	1	0	0	0	2	.154
J. Anderson, ss	11	1	0	0	0	0	0	.091
L. Harlow, of	8	1	1	0	0	0	1	.125
B. Clark, of	3	0	0	0	0	0	0	.000
W. Davis	2	1	1	0	0	1	0	.500
M. Rettenmund, dh	2	0	0	0	0	0	0	.000
B. Campaneris, ss	0	0	0	0	0	0	0	—
D. Thon, ss	0	0	0	0	0	1	0	—

Errors: D. Ford, B. Grich

Stolen Bases: R. Carew, C. Lansford

Individual Pitching

BALTIMORE (EAST)

	W	L	ERA	IP	H	BB	SO	SV
S. McGregor	1	0	0.00	9	6	1	4	0
J. Palmer	0	0	3.00	9	7	2	3	0
D. Martinez	0	0	3.24	8.1	8	0	4	0
M. Flanagan	1	0	5.14	7	6	1	2	0
D. Stanhouse	1	1	6.00	3	5	3	0	0

CALIFORNIA (WEST)

	W	L	ERA	IP	H	BB	SO	SV
N. Ryan	0	0	1.29	7	4	3	8	0
M. Clear	0	0	4.76	5.2	4	2	3	0
D. Aase	1	0	1.80	5	4	2	6	0
F. Tanana	0	0	3.60	5	6	2	3	0
D. Frost	0	1	18.69	4.1	8	5	1	0
J. Montague	0	1	9.00	4	4	2	2	0
C. Knapp	0	1	7.71	2.1	5	1	0	0
D. LaRoche	0	0	6.75	1.1	2	1	1	0
M. Barlow	0	0	0.00	1	0	0	0	0

1979 WORLD SERIES

Pittsburgh (N.L.) defeats Baltimore (A.L.) 4 games to 3

LINE SCORES			R	H	E	PITCHERS (innings pitched)	HOME RUNS (men on)	HIGHLIGHTS
GAME 1 - OCTOBER 10								Baltimore erupted for 5 runs in the first inning and Flanagan withstood a late Pittsburgh rally, going the route despite giving up 11 hits.
PIT	**N**	000 102 010	4	11	3	**Kison** (0.1), Rooker (3.2), Romo (1), D. Robinson (2), Jackson (1)	Stargell	
BAL	**A**	500 000 00x	5	6	3	**Flanagan** (9)	DeCinces (1 on)	
GAME 2 - OCTOBER 11								Sanguillen, a pinch hitter, singled with two out in the 9th to score Ed Ott with the tie-breaking run off Oriole relief ace Stanhouse.
PIT	**N**	020 000 001	3	11	2	Blyleven (6), **D. Robinson** (2), Tekulve (1) **SV**		
BAL	**A**	010 001 000	2	6	1	Palmer (7), T. Martinez (1), **Stanhouse** (1)	Murray	
GAME 3 - OCTOBER 12								Kiko Garcia enjoyed a 4-for-4 day, including a double and a triple, and drove in 4 runs as McGregor went the distance spacing 9 hits.
BAL	**A**	002 500 100	8	13	0	**Mc Gregor** (9)	Ayala (1 on)	
PIT	**N**	120 001 000	4	9	2	**Candelaria** (3), Romo (3.2), Jackson (0.1), Tekulve (2)		
GAME 4 - OCTOBER 13								Baltimore exploded for 6 runs in the 8th to overcome a 6-3 deficit. Doubles by pinch hitters Lowenstein and Crowley accounted for 4 of the runs.
BAL	**A**	003 000 060	9	12	0	D. Martinez (1.1), Stewart (2.2), Stone (2), **Stoddard** (3)		
PIT	**N**	040 011 000	6	17	1	Bibby (6.1), Jackson (0.2), D. Robinson (0.1), **Tekulve** (1.2)	Stargell	
GAME 5 - OCTOBER 14								Bill Madlock had 4 hits and Tim Foli drove in 3 runs as Pittsburgh staved off elimination. Blyleven pitched four shutout innings in relief to gain the victory.
BAL	**A**	000 010 000	1	6	2	**Flanagan** (6), Stoddard (0.2), T. Martinez (0.1), Stanhouse (1)		
PIT	**N**	000 002 23x	7	13	1	Rooker (5), **Blyleven** (4)		
GAME 6 - OCTOBER 16								Candelaria and Tekulve combined to blank the Orioles on 7 hits to square the Series. Moreno led the 10-hit attack on Palmer with 3 singles.
PIT	**N**	000 000 220	4	10	0	**Candelaria** (6), Tekulve (3) **SV**		
BAL	**A**	000 000 000	0	7	1	**Palmer** (8), Stoddard (1)		
GAME 7 - OCTOBER 17								Stargell homered with one on in the 6th as Pittsburgh overcame a 1-0 deficit and went on to defeat McGregor and the Orioles to win the World Series, after trailing three games to one.
PIT	**N**	000 002 002	4	10	0	Bibby (4), D. Robinson (0.2) **Jackson** (2.2), Tekulve (1.2) **SV**	Stargell (1 on)	
BAL	**A**	001 000 000	1	4	2	**McGregor** (8), Stoddard (0.1), Flanagan (0), Stanhouse (0), T. Martinez (0), D. Martinez (0.2)	Dauer	

Team totals

		W	AB	H	2B	3B	HR	R	RBI	BA	BB	SO	ERA
PIT	**N**	4	251	81	18	1	3	32	32	.323	16	35	3.19
BAL	**A**	3	233	54	10	1	4	26	23	.232	26	41	4.35

Individual Batting

PITTSBURGH (N.L.)

	AB	H	2B	3B	HR	R	RBI	BA
O. Moreno, of	33	11	2	0	0	4	3	.333
W. Stargell, 1b	30	12	4	0	3	7	7	.400
T. Foli, ss	30	10	1	1	0	6	3	.333
D. Parker, of	29	10	3	0	0	2	4	.345
P. Garner, 2b	24	12	4	0	0	4	5	.500
B. Madlock, 3b	24	9	1	0	0	2	3	.375
B. Robinson, of	19	5	1	0	0	2	2	.263
S. Nicosia, c	16	1	0	0	0	1	0	.063
E. Ott, c	12	4	1	0	0	2	3	.333
J. Milner, of	9	3	1	0	0	2	1	.333
L. Lacy	4	1	0	0	0	0	0	.250
J. Bibby, p	4	0	0	0	0	0	0	.000
J. Candelaria, p	3	1	0	0	0	0	0	.333
M. Sanguillen	3	1	0	0	0	0	1	.333
B. Blyleven, p	3	0	0	0	0	0	0	.000
J. Rooker, p	2	0	0	0	0	0	0	.000
K. Tekulve, p	2	0	0	0	0	0	0	.000
R. Stennett	1	1	0	0	0	0	0	1.000
M. Easler	1	0	0	0	0	0	0	.000
G. Jackson, p	1	0	0	0	0	0	0	.000
E. Romo, p	1	0	0	0	0	0	0	.000
M. Alexander, of	0	0	0	0	0	0	0	—

Errors: T. Foli (3), P. Garner (2), W. Stargell (2), B. Madlock, D. Parker

BALTIMORE (A.L.)

	AB	H	2B	3B	HR	R	RBI	BA
K. Singleton, of	28	10	1	0	0	1	2	.357
E. Murray, 1b	26	4	1	0	1	3	2	.154
D. DeCinces, 3b	25	5	0	0	1	2	3	.200
R. Dempsey, c	21	6	2	0	0	3	0	.286
A. Bumbry, of	21	3	0	0	0	3	1	.143
K. Garcia, ss	20	8	2	1	0	4	6	.400
R. Dauer, 2b	17	5	1	0	1	2	1	.294
G. Roenicke, of	16	2	1	0	0	1	0	.125
J. Lowenstein, of	13	3	1	0	0	2	3	.231
B. Smith, 2b	7	2	0	0	0	1	0	.286
B. Ayala, of	6	2	0	0	1	1	2	.333
M. Belanger, ss	6	0	0	0	0	1	0	.000
M. Flanagan, p	5	0	0	0	0	0	0	.000
T. Crowley	4	1	1	0	0	0	2	.250
P. Kelly	4	1	0	0	0	0	0	.250
S. McGregor, p	4	0	0	0	0	1	0	.000
J. Palmer, p	4	0	0	0	0	0	0	.000
D. Skaggs, c	3	1	0	0	0	1	0	.333
T. Stoddard, p	1	1	0	0	0	0	1	1.000
L. May	1	0	0	0	0	0	0	.000
S. Stewart, p	1	0	0	0	0	0	0	.000

Errors: D. DeCinces (3), M. Belanger, A. Bumbry, K. Garcia, J. Lowenstein, D. Stanhouse, T. Stoddard

Stolen Bases: D. DeCinces, E. Murray

Individual Pitching

PITTSBURGH (N.L.)

	W	L	ERA	IP	H	BB	SO	SV
J. Bibby	0	0	2.61	10.1	10	2	10	0
B. Blyleven	1	0	1.80	10	8	3	4	0
K. Tekulve	0	1	2.89	9.1	4	3	10	3
J. Candelaria	1	1	5.00	9	14	2	4	0
J. Rooker	0	0	1.04	8.2	5	3	4	0
D. Robinson	1	0	5.40	5	4	6	3	0
G. Jackson	1	0	0.00	4.2	1	2	2	0
E. Romo	0	0	3.86	4.2	5	3	4	0
B. Kison	0	1	108.00	0.1	3	2	0	0

BALTIMORE (A.L.)

	W	L	ERA	IP	H	BB	SO	SV
S. McGregor	1	1	3.18	17	16	2	8	0
M. Flanagan	1	1	3.00	15	18	2	13	0
J. Palmer	0	1	3.60	15	18	5	8	0
T. Stoddard	1	0	5.40	5	6	1	3	0
S. Stewart	0	0	0.00	2.2	4	1	0	0
D. Martinez	0	0	18.00	2	6	0	0	0
D. Stanhouse	0	1	13.50	2	6	3	0	0
S. Stone	0	0	9.00	2	4	2	2	0
T. Martinez	0	0	6.75	1.1	3	0	1	0

1980 NATIONAL LEAGUE CHAMPIONSHIP SERIES

Philadelphia (East) defeats Houston (West) 3 games to 2

LINE SCORES			R	H	E	PITCHERS (innings pitched)	HOME RUNS (men on)	HIGHLIGHTS
GAME 1 - OCTOBER 7								A two-run homer by Luzinski lifted the Phillies to a 3-1 victory. Carlton got the victory and McGraw the save.
HOU	**W**	001 000 000	1	7	0	**K. Forsch** (8)		
PHI	**E**	000 002 10x	3	8	1	**Carlton** (7), McGraw (2) **SV**	Luzinski (1 on)	
GAME 2 - OCTOBER 8								Jose Cruz singled in one run and Bergman tripled in two to highlight a 4-run outburst in the 10th, snapping a 3-3 deadlock and evening the series.
HOU	**W**	001 000 110 4	7	8	1	Ryan (6.2), Sambito (0.1), D. Smith (1.2), **LaCorte** (1), Andujar (1) **SV**		
PHI	**E**	000 200 010 1	4	14	2	Ruthven (7), McGraw (1), **Reed** (1.1), Saucier (0.2)		
GAME 3 - OCTOBER 10								Joe Morgan's leadoff triple in the 11th and Walling's sacrifice fly off loser Tug McGraw accounted for the game's only run. Joe Niekro pitched 10 scoreless innings for the Astros, but Smith got the win.
PHI	**E**	000 000 000 00	0	7	1	Christenson (6), Noles (1.1), **McGraw** (3)		
HOU	**W**	000 000 000 01	1	6	1	J. Niekro (10), **D. Smith** (1)		
GAME 4 - OCTOBER 11								Luzinski and Trillo followed Rose's single with doubles for a 2-run rally in the 10th to give the Phillies the winning runs in a controversial see-saw game.
PHI	**E**	000 000 030 2	5	13	0	Carlton (5.1), Noles (1.1), Saucier (0), Reed (0.1), **Brusstar** (2), McGraw (1) **SV**		
HOU	**W**	000 110 001 0	3	5	1	Ruhle (7), D. Smith (0), **Sambito** (3)		
GAME 5 - OCTOBER 12								A double by Maddox in the 10th inning drove Unser home with the decisive run as the Phillies outlasted the Astros to win the 5th game and capture their first pennant since 1950. The Phillies rallied for 5 runs in the 8th to take a 7-5 lead but the Astros tallied twice in their half to force the fourth straight overtime game.
PHI	**E**	020 000 050 1	8	13	2	Bystrom (5.1), Brusstar (0.2), Christenson (0.2), Reed (0.1), McGraw (1), **Ruthven** (2)		
HOU	**W**	100 001 320 0	7	14	0	Ryan (7), Sambito (0.1), K. Forsch (0.2), **LaCorte** (2)		

Team totals

		W	AB	H	2B	3B	HR	R	RBI	BA	BB	SO	ERA
PHI	**E**	3	190	55	8	1	1	20	19	.289	13	37	3.28
HOU	**W**	2	172	40	7	5	0	19	18	.233	31	19	3.49

Individual Batting

PHILADELPHIA (EAST)

	AB	H	2B	3B	HR	R	RBI	BA
M. Schmidt, 3b	24	5	1	0	0	1	1	.208
M. Trillo, 2b	21	8	2	1	0	1	4	.381
B. McBride, of	21	5	0	0	0	0	0	.238
P. Rose, 1b	20	8	0	0	0	3	2	.400
G. Maddox, of	20	6	2	0	0	2	3	.300
L. Bowa, ss	19	6	0	0	0	2	0	.316
B. Boone, c	18	4	0	0	0	1	2	.222
G. Luzinski, of	17	5	2	0	1	3	4	.294
L. Smith, of	5	3	0	0	0	2	0	.600
D. Unser, of	5	2	1	0	0	2	1	.400
G. Gross, of	4	3	0	0	0	2	1	.750
S. Carlton, p	4	0	0	0	0	0	0	.000
G. Vukovich, of	3	0	0	0	0	0	0	.000
M. Bystrom, p	2	0	0	0	0	0	0	.000
L. Christenson, p	2	0	0	0	0	0	0	.000
D. Ruthven, p	2	0	0	0	0	0	0	.000
W. Brusstar, p	1	0	0	0	0	0	0	.000
T. McGraw, p	1	0	0	0	0	0	0	.000
K. Moreland, c	1	0	0	0	0	0	1	.000
R. Aviles	0	0	0	0	0	1	0	—

Errors: L. Bowa, L. Christenson, G. Luzinski, B. McBride, M. Schmidt, M. Trillo

Stolen Bases: G. Maddox (2), B. McBride (2), L. Bowa, M. Schmidt, L. Smith

HOUSTON (WEST)

	AB	H	2B	3B	HR	R	RBI	BA
E. Cabell, 3b	21	5	1	0	0	1	0	.238
T. Puhl, of	19	10	2	0	0	4	3	.526
J. Cruz, of	15	6	1	1	0	3	4	.400
A. Howe, 1b	15	3	1	1	0	0	2	.200
J. Morgan, 2b	13	2	1	1	0	1	0	.154
C. Reynolds, ss	13	2	1	0	0	2	0	.154
C. Cedeno, of	11	2	0	0	0	1	1	.182
L. Pujols, c	10	1	0	1	0	1	0	.100
R. Landestoy, 2b, ss	9	2	0	0	0	3	2	.222
D. Walling, 1b, of	9	1	0	0	0	2	2	.111
G. Woods, of	8	2	0	0	0	0	1	.250
A. Ashby, c	8	1	0	0	0	0	1	.125
N. Ryan, p	4	0	0	0	0	1	0	.000
D. Bergman, 1b	3	1	0	1	0	0	2	.333
J. Leonard, of	3	0	0	0	0	0	0	.000
J. Niekro, p	3	0	0	0	0	0	0	.000
V. Ruhle, p	3	0	0	0	0	0	0	.000
K. Forsch, p	2	2	0	0	0	0	0	1.000
B. Bochy, c	1	0	0	0	0	0	0	.000
D. Heep	1	0	0	0	0	0	0	.000
F. LaCorte, p	1	0	0	0	0	0	0	.000

Errors: D. Bergman, R. Landestoy, C. Reynolds

Stolen Bases: T. Puhl (2), R. Landestoy, G. Woods

Individual Pitching

PHILADELPHIA (EAST)

	W	L	ERA	IP	H	BB	SO	SV
S. Carlton	1	0	2.19	12.1	11	8	6	0
D. Ruthven	1	0	2.00	9	3	5	4	0
T. McGraw	0	1	4.50	8	8	4	5	2
L. Christenson	0	0	4.05	6.2	5	5	2	0
M. Bystrom	0	0	1.69	5.1	7	2	1	0
W. Brusstar	1	0	3.38	2.2	1	1	0	0
D. Noles	0	0	0.00	2.2	1	3	0	0
R. Reed	0	1	18.00	2	3	1	1	0
K. Saucier	0	0	0.00	0.2	1	2	0	0

HOUSTON (WEST)

	W	L	ERA	IP	H	BB	SO	SV
N. Ryan	0	0	5.40	13.1	16	3	14	0
J. Niekro	0	0	0.00	10	6	1	2	0
K. Forsch	0	1	4.15	8.2	10	1	6	0
V. Ruhle	0	0	3.86	7	8	1	3	0
J. Sambito	0	1	4.91	3.2	4	2	6	0
F. LaCorte	1	1	3.00	3	7	2	2	0
D. Smith	1	0	3.86	2.1	4	2	4	0
J. Andujar	0	0	0.00	1	0	1	0	1

1980 AMERICAN LEAGUE CHAMPIONSHIP SERIES

Kansas City (West) defeats New York (East) 3 games to 0

LINE SCORES			R	H	E	PITCHERS (innings pitched)	HOME RUNS (men on)	HIGHLIGHTS
GAME 1 - OCTOBER 8								Gura spaced ten hits and White drove in two runs with three hits.
NY	**E**	020 000 000	2	10	1	**Guidry** (3), Davis (4), Underwood (1)	Cerone, Piniella	
KC	**W**	022 000 12x	7	10	0	**Gura** (9)	G. Brett	
GAME 2 - OCTOBER 9								Four straight hits accounted for all of KC's runs in the 3rd inning. Wilson drove in two with a triple and Washington doubled in the other run. Game ended with Randolph tagged out at plate trying to score tying run.
NY	**E**	000 020 000	2	8	0	**May** (8)	Nettles	
KC	**W**	003 000 00x	3	6	0	**Leonard** (8), Quisenberry (1) **SV**		
GAME 3 - OCTOBER 10								Powered by George Brett's three-run blast in the 7th off Goose Gossage, the Royals swept the Yanks for their first American League pennant.
KC	**W**	000 010 300	4	12	1	Splittorff (5.1), **Quisenberry** (3.2)	G. Brett (2 on), White	
NY	**E**	000 002 000	2	8	0	John (6.2), **Gossage** (0.1), Underwood (2)		

Team totals

		W	AB	H	2B	3B	HR	R	RBI	BA	BB	SO	ERA
KC	**W**	3	97	28	6	1	3	14	14	.289	9	15	1.67
NY	**E**	0	102	26	7	1	3	6	5	.255	6	16	4.32

Individual Batting

KANSAS CITY (WEST)

	AB	H	2B	3B	HR	R	RBI	BA
W. Wilson, of	13	4	2	1	0	2	4	.308
A. Otis, of	12	4	1	0	0	2	0	.333
F. White, 2b	11	6	1	0	1	3	3	.545
W. Aikens, 1b	11	4	0	0	0	0	2	.364
U. Washington, ss	11	4	1	0	0	1	1	.364
G. Brett, 3b	11	3	1	0	2	3	4	.273
H. McRae, dh	10	2	0	0	0	0	0	.200
D. Porter, c	10	1	0	0	0	2	0	.100
J. Wathan, of	6	0	0	0	0	1	0	.000
C. Hurdle, of	2	0	0	0	0	0	0	.000
P. LaCock, 1b	0	0	0	0	0	0	0	—

Errors: F. White
Stolen Bases: A. Otis (2), F. White

NEW YORK (EAST)

	AB	H	2B	3B	HR	R	RBI	BA
W. Randolph, 2b	13	5	2	0	0	0	1	.385
B. Watson, 1b	12	6	3	1	0	0	0	.500
R. Cerone, c	12	4	0	0	1	1	2	.333
R. Jackson, of	11	3	1	0	0	1	0	.273
B. Dent, ss	11	2	0	0	0	0	0	.182
B. Brown, of	10	0	0	0	0	1	0	.000
A. Rodriguez, 3b	6	2	1	0	0	0	0	.333
G. Nettles, 3b	6	1	0	0	1	1	1	.167
E. Soderholm, dh	6	1	0	0	0	0	0	.167
O. Gamble, dh, of	5	1	0	0	0	1	0	.200
L. Piniella, of	5	1	0	0	1	1	1	.200
B. Murcer, dh	4	0	0	0	0	0	0	.000
J. Spencer	1	0	0	0	0	0	0	.000
J. Lefebvre, of	0	0	0	0	0	0	0	—

Errors: B. Watson

Individual Pitching

KANSAS CITY (WEST)

	W	L	ERA	IP	H	BB	SO	SV
L. Gura	1	0	2.00	9	10	1	4	0
D. Leonard	1	0	2.25	8	7	1	8	0
P. Splittorff	0	0	1.69	5.1	5	2	3	0
D. Quisenberry	1	0	0.00	4.2	4	2	1	1

NEW YORK (EAST)

	W	L	ERA	IP	H	BB	SO	SV
R. May	0	1	3.38	8	6	3	4	0
T. John	0	0	2.70	6.2	8	1	3	0
R. Davis	0	0	2.25	4	3	1	3	0
R. Guidry	0	1	12.00	3	5	4	2	0
T. Underwood	0	0	0.00	3	3	0	3	0
G. Gossage	0	1	54.00	0.1	3	0	0	0

1980 WORLD SERIES

Philadelphia (N.L.) defeats Kansas City (A.L.) 4 games to 2

LINE SCORES			R	H	E	PITCHERS (innings pitched)	HOME RUNS (men on)	HIGHLIGHTS
GAME 1 - OCTOBER 14								The Phillies erupted for 5 runs in the 3rd inning to offset an early 4-0 Kansas City lead. McBride's 3-run homer was the big blow. Aikens slammed a pair of 2-run homers for the Royals.
KC	**A**	022 000 020	6	9	1	**Leonard** (3.2), Martin (4), Quisenberry (0.1)	Aikens (1 on), Aikens (1 on), Otis (1 on)	
PHI	**N**	005 110 00x	7	11	0	**Walk** (7), McGraw (2) **SV**	McBride (2 on)	
GAME 2 - OCTOBER 15								Philadelphia came from behind, pummeling relief ace Quisenberry for 4 runs in the 8th to overcome a 4-2 deficit. Doubles by pinch hitter Unser and Mike Schmidt were the key blows.
KC	**A**	000 001 300	4	11	0	Gura (6), **Quisenberry** (2)		
PHI	**N**	000 020 04x	6	8	1	**Carlton** (8), Reed (1) **SV**		
GAME 3 - OCTOBER 17								Aikens's first major league triple scored Willie Wilson with the winning run in the 10th inning. Quisenberry, in relief, was the winner, McGraw the loser.
PHI	**N**	010 010 010 0	3	14	0	Ruthven (9), **McGraw** (0.2)	Schmidt	
KC	**A**	100 100 100 1	4	11	0	Gale (4.1), Martin (3.1) **Quisenberry** (2.1)	Brett, Otis	
GAME 4 - OCTOBER 18								Aikens drove in 3 runs with 2 home runs, becoming the first player to have two multiple-homer games in the same Series.
PHI	**N**	010 000 110	3	10	1	**Christenson** (0.1), Noles (4.2), Saucier (0.2), Brusstar (2.1)		
KC	**A**	410 000 00x	5	10	2	**Leonard** (7), Quisenberry (2) **SV**	Aikens, Aikens (1 on)	
GAME 5 - OCTOBER 19								Pinch-hitter Unser doubled home Schmidt with the tying run in the 9th and Trillo followed with a game-winning single as the Phillies defeated Quisenberry for the second time. McGraw fanned Cardenal with the bases full in the bottom of the 9th inning.
PHI	**N**	000 200 002	4	7	0	Bystrom (5), Reed (1), **McGraw** (3)	Schmidt (1 on)	
KC	**A**	000 012 000	3	12	2	Gura (6.1), **Quisenberry** (2.2)	Otis	
GAME 6 - OCTOBER 21								Schmidt knocked in 2 runs and relief ace McGraw twice stopped the Royals with the bases full as the Phillies won the first World Series in their history.
KC	**A**	000 000 010	1	7	2	**Gale** (2), Martin (2.1), Splittorff (1.2), Pattin (1), Quisenberry (1)		
PHI	**N**	002 011 00x	4	9	0	**Carlton** (7), McGraw (2) **SV**		

Team totals

		W	AB	H	2B	3B	HR	R	RBI	BA	BB	SO	ERA
PHI	**N**	4	201	59	13	0	3	27	26	.294	15	17	3.69
KC	**A**	2	207	60	9	2	8	23	22	.290	26	49	4.15

Individual Batting

PHILADELPHIA (N.L.)

	AB	H	2B	3B	HR	R	RBI	BA
L. Bowa, ss	24	9	1	0	0	3	2	.375
B. McBride, of	23	7	1	0	1	3	5	.304
P. Rose, 1b	23	6	1	0	0	2	1	.261
M. Trillo, 2b	23	5	2	0	0	4	2	.217
G. Maddox, of	22	5	2	0	0	1	1	.227
M. Schmidt, 3b	21	8	1	0	2	6	7	.381
L. Smith, dh, of	19	5	1	0	0	2	1	.263
B. Boone, c	17	7	2	0	0	3	4	.412
K. Moreland, dh	12	4	0	0	0	1	1	.333
G. Luzinski, dh, of	9	0	0	0	0	0	0	.000
D. Unser, of	6	3	2	0	0	2	2	.500
G. Gross, of	2	0	0	0	0	0	0	.000

Errors: L. Christenson, M. Trillo
Stolen Bases: L. Bowa (3)

KANSAS CITY (A.L.)

	AB	H	2B	3B	HR	R	RBI	BA
W. Wilson, of	26	4	1	0	0	3	0	.154
F. White, 2b	25	2	0	0	0	0	0	.080
G. Brett, 3b	24	9	2	1	1	3	3	.375
H. McRae, dh	24	9	3	0	0	3	1	.375
A. Otis, of	23	11	2	0	3	4	7	.478
U. Washington, ss	22	6	0	0	0	1	2	.273
W. Aikens, 1b	20	8	0	1	4	5	8	.400
D. Porter, c	14	2	0	0	0	1	0	.143
C. Hurdle, of	12	5	1	0	0	1	0	.417
J. Cardenal, of	10	2	0	0	0	0	0	.200
J. Wathan, c, of	7	2	0	0	0	1	1	.286
D. Chalk, 3b	0	0	0	0	0	1	0	—
O. Concepcion	0	0	0	0	0	0	0	—
P. LaCock, 1b	0	0	0	0	0	0	0	—

Errors: W. Aikens (2), F. White (2), G. Brett, D. Leonard, U. Washington
Stolen Bases: W. Wilson (2), G. Brett, D. Chalk, C. Hurdle, F. White

Individual Pitching

PHILADELPHIA (N.L.)

	W	L	ERA	IP	H	BB	SO	SV
S. Carlton	2	0	2.40	15	14	9	17	0
D. Ruthven	0	0	3.00	9	9	0	7	0
T. McGraw	1	1	1.17	7.2	7	8	10	2
B. Walk	1	0	7.71	7	8	3	3	0
M. Bystrom	0	0	5.40	5	10	1	4	0
D. Noles	0	0	1.93	4.2	5	2	6	0
W. Brusstar	0	0	0.00	2.1	0	1	0	0
R. Reed	0	0	0.00	2	2	0	2	1
K. Saucier	0	0	0.00	0.2	0	2	0	0
L. Christenson	0	1	108.00	0.1	5	0	0	0

KANSAS CITY (A.L.)

	W	L	ERA	IP	H	BB	SO	SV
L. Gura	0	0	2.19	12.1	8	3	4	0
D. Leonard	1	1	6.75	10.2	15	2	5	0
D. Quisenberry	1	2	5.23	10.1	10	3	0	1
R. Martin	0	0	2.79	9.2	11	3	2	0
R. Gale	0	1	4.26	6.1	11	4	4	0
P. Splittorff	0	0	5.40	1.2	4	0	0	0
M. Pattin	0	0	0.00	1	0	0	2	0

1981 NATIONAL LEAGUE DIVISIONAL PLAYOFFS

Montreal (East) defeats Philadelphia (East) 3 games to 2

LINE SCORES			R	H	E	PITCHERS (innings pitched)	HOME RUNS (men on)	HIGHLIGHTS
GAME 1 - OCTOBER 7								Speier drove in a run and scored another to lead the Expos to a 3-1 win over the Phillies.
PHI	**E**	010 000 000	1	10	1	**Carlton** (6), R. Reed (2)	Moreland	
MON	**E**	110 100 00x	3	8	0	**Rogers** (8.1), Reardon (0.2) **SV**		
GAME 2 - OCTOBER 8								Speier's run-scoring single and Carter's two-run homer carried the Expos to a second 3-1 triumph over the Phillies.
PHI	**E**	000 000 010	1	6	2	**Ruthven** (4), Brusstar (2), Lyle (1), McGraw (1)		
MON	**E**	012 000 00x	3	7	0	**Gullickson** (7.2), Reardon (1.1) **SV**	Carter (1 on)	
GAME 3 - OCTOBER 9								The Phillies pounded four pitchers for 13 hits, including 3 by Matthews, to stave off elimination. Christenson allowed 4 hits in 6 innings.
MON	**E**	010 000 010	2	8	4	**Burris** (5.1), Lee (0.2), Sosa (2)		
PHI	**E**	020 002 20x	6	13	0	**Christenson** (6), Lyle (1), R. Reed (2)		
GAME 4 - OCTOBER 10								A pinch homer by Vukovich in the bottom of the 10th enabled the Phillies to edge out the Expos, 6-5. McGraw pitched 1-hit relief for 3 innings to gain credit for the win.
MON	**E**	000 112 100 0	5	10	1	Sanderson (2.2), Bahnsen (1.1), Sosa (1), Fryman (1.1), **Reardon** (2.2)	Carter	
PHI	**E**	202 001 000 1	6	9	0	Noles (4), Brusstar (1.2), Lyle (0.1), R. Reed (1), **McGraw** (3)	Schmidt (1 on), Matthews, Vukovich	
GAME 5 - OCTOBER 11								Rogers pitched a 6-hit shutout and knocked in 2 runs with a pair of hits as the Expos defeated Carlton for the second time, 3-0, to capture the NL East Division Series.
MON	**E**	000 021 000	3	8	1	**Rogers** (9)		
PHI	**E**	000 000 000	0	6	0	**Carlton** (8), R. Reed (1)		

Team totals

		W	AB	H	2B	3B	HR	R	RBI	BA	BB	SO	ERA
MON	**E**	3	161	41	10	1	2	16	16	.255	18	36	2.05
PHI	**E**	2	166	44	6	1	4	14	12	.265	13	19	3.07

Individual Batting

MONTREAL (EAST)

	AB	H	2B	3B	HR	R	RBI	BA
W. Cromartie, 1b	22	5	2	0	0	1	1	.227
A. Dawson, of	20	6	0	1	0	1	0	.300
L. Parrish, 3b	20	3	1	0	0	3	1	.150
G. Carter, c	19	8	3	0	2	3	6	.421
J. White, of	18	3	1	0	0	3	1	.167
C. Speier, ss	15	6	2	0	0	4	3	.400
J. Manuel, 2b	14	1	0	0	0	0	0	.071
T. Francona, of	12	4	0	0	0	0	0	.333
S. Rogers, p	5	2	0	0	0	0	2	.400
T. Wallach, of	4	1	1	0	0	1	0	.250
B. Gullickson, p	3	0	0	0	0	0	0	.000
W. Johnson	2	1	0	0	0	0	1	.500
J. Milner	2	1	0	0	0	0	1	.500
R. Burris, p	2	0	0	0	0	0	0	.000
M. Phillips, 2b	1	0	0	0	0	0	0	.000
J. Reardon, p	1	0	0	0	0	0	0	.000
S. Sanderson, p	1	0	0	0	0	0	0	.000
B. Mills	0	0	0	0	0	0	0	—

Errors: J. Manuel (3), W. Cromartie, A. Dawson, E. Sosa
Stolen Bases: J. White (3), A. Dawson (2), T. Francona (2)

PHILADELPHIA (EAST)

	AB	H	2B	3B	HR	R	RBI	BA
G. Matthews, of	20	8	0	1	1	3	1	.400
P. Rose, 1b	20	6	1	0	0	1	2	.300
L. Smith, of	19	5	1	0	0	1	0	.263
L. Bowa, ss	17	3	1	0	0	0	1	.176
M. Schmidt, 3b	16	4	1	0	1	3	2	.250
M. Trillo, 2b	16	3	0	0	0	1	1	.188
B. McBride, of	15	3	1	0	0	1	0	.200
K. Moreland, c	13	6	0	0	1	2	3	.462
G. Vukovich, of	9	4	0	0	1	1	2	.444
B. Boone, c	5	0	0	0	0	0	0	.000
S. Carlton, p	4	1	0	0	0	0	0	.250
G. Gross, of	4	0	0	0	0	0	0	.000
G. Maddox, of	3	1	1	0	0	0	0	.333
L. Christenson, p	2	0	0	0	0	0	0	.000
D. Davis, of	2	0	0	0	0	0	0	.000
D. Ruthven, p	1	0	0	0	0	0	0	.000
L. Aguayo	0	0	0	0	0	1	0	—
R. Aviles	0	0	0	0	0	0	0	—

Errors: L. Bowa, K. Moreland, M. Schmidt

Individual Pitching

MONTREAL (EAST)

	W	L	ERA	IP	H	BB	SO	SV
S. Rogers	2	0	0.51	17.2	16	3	5	0
B. Gullickson	1	0	1.17	7.2	6	1	3	0
R. Burris	0	1	5.06	5.1	7	4	4	0
J. Reardon	0	1	2.08	4.1	1	1	2	2
E. Sosa	0	0	3.00	3	4	0	1	0
S. Sanderson	0	0	6.75	2.2	4	2	2	0
S. Bahnsen	0	0	0.00	1.1	1	1	1	0
W. Fryman	0	0	6.75	1.1	3	1	0	0
B. Lee	0	0	0.00	0.2	2	0	1	0

PHILADELPHIA (EAST)

	W	L	ERA	IP	H	BB	SO	SV
S. Carlton	0	2	3.86	14	14	8	13	0
L. Christenson	1	0	1.50	6	4	1	8	0
R. Reed	0	0	3.00	6	5	3	4	0
T. McGraw	1	0	0.00	4	2	0	2	0
D. Noles	0	0	4.50	4	4	2	5	0
D. Ruthven	0	1	4.50	4	3	1	0	0
W. Brusstar	0	0	4.91	3.2	5	1	3	0
S. Lyle	0	0	0.00	2.1	4	2	1	0

1981 NATIONAL LEAGUE DIVISIONAL PLAYOFFS

Los Angeles (West) defeats Houston (West) 3 games to 2

LINE SCORES			R	H	E	PITCHERS (innings pitched)	HOME RUNS (men on)	HIGHLIGHTS
GAME 1 - OCTOBER 6								Ashby's 2-run homer in the 9th lifted Ryan and the Astros to a 3-1 win.
LA	**W**	000 000 100	1	2	0	Valenzuela (8), **Stewart** (0.2)	Garvey	
HOU	**W**	000 001 002	3	8	0	**Ryan** (9)	Ashby (1 on)	
GAME 2 - OCTOBER 7								Pinch hitter Denny Walling singled with 2 out and the bases full in the 11th inning to drive in the run that gave the Astros a 1-0 victory and a 2-0 lead in the series.
LA	**W**	000 000 000 00	0	9	1	Reuss (9), S. Howe (1), **Stewart** (0), Forster (0.1), Niedenfuer (0.1)		
HOU	**W**	000 000 000 01	1	9	0	J. Niekro (8), D. Smith (2) **Sambito** (1)		
GAME 3 - OCTOBER 9								A 2-run homer by Garvey capped a 3-run first inning that sent the Dodgers to a 6-1 win. Hooton allowed 3 hits in 7 innings for the victory.
HOU	**W**	001 000 000	1	3	2	**Knepper** (5), LaCorte (2), Sambito (0.2), B. Smith (0.1)	A. Howe	
LA	**W**	300 000 03x	6	10	0	**Hooton** (7), S. Howe (1), Welch (1)	Garvey (1 on)	
GAME 4 - OCTOBER 10								A home run by Guerrero and a run-producing single by Russell gave the Dodgers a 2-1 win and tied the series.
HOU	**W**	000 000 001	1	4	0	**Ruhle** (8)		
LA	**W**	000 010 10x	2	4	0	**Valenzuela** (9)	Guerrero	
GAME 5 - OCTOBER 11								A 3-run outburst in the 6th broke up a scoreless duel between Reuss and Ryan and enabled the Dodgers to win three straight after losing the first two games. Garvey led the attack with a single and triple as the Dodgers won the NL West Division Series.
HOU	**W**	000 000 000	0	5	3	**Ryan** (6), D. Smith (0.1), LaCorte (1.2)		
LA	**W**	000 003 10x	4	7	2	**Reuss** (9)		

Team totals

		W	AB	H	2B	3B	HR	R	RBI	BA	BB	SO	ERA
LA	**W**	3	162	32	6	1	3	13	12	.198	13	34	1.17
HOU	**W**	2	162	29	3	0	2	6	6	.179	13	24	2.45

Individual Batting

LOS ANGELES (WEST)

	AB	H	2B	3B	HR	R	RBI	BA
K. Landreaux, of	20	4	1	0	0	1	1	.200
D. Lopes, 2b	20	4	1	0	0	1	0	.200
S. Garvey, 1b	19	7	0	1	2	4	4	.368
D. Baker, of	18	3	1	0	0	2	1	.167
P. Guerrero, 3b	17	3	1	0	1	1	1	.176
B. Russell, ss	16	4	1	0	0	1	2	.250
R. Monday, of	14	3	0	0	0	1	1	.214
M. Scioscia, c	13	2	0	0	0	0	1	.154
J. Reuss, p	8	0	0	0	0	0	0	.000
S. Yeager, c	5	2	1	0	0	1	0	.400
F. Valenzuela, p	4	0	0	0	0	0	0	.000
B. Hooton, p	3	0	0	0	0	0	0	.000
D. Thomas, of	2	0	0	0	0	1	0	.000
J. Johnstone	1	0	0	0	0	0	0	.000
M. Marshall	1	0	0	0	0	0	0	.000
R. Smith	1	0	0	0	0	0	1	.000
S. Sax, 2b	0	0	0	0	0	0	0	—

Errors: B. Russell (2), P. Guerrero
Stolen Bases: P. Guerrero, D. Lopes

HOUSTON (WEST)

	AB	H	2B	3B	HR	R	RBI	BA
T. Puhl, of	21	4	1	0	0	2	0	.190
J. Cruz, of	20	6	1	0	0	0	0	.300
T. Scott, of	20	3	0	0	0	0	2	.150
P. Garner, 2b	18	2	0	0	0	1	0	.111
A. Howe, 3b	17	4	0	0	1	1	1	.235
C. Cedeno, 1b	13	3	1	0	0	0	0	.231
D. Thon, ss	11	2	0	0	0	0	0	.182
A. Ashby, c	9	1	0	0	1	1	2	.111
D. Walling, 1b, of	6	2	0	0	0	0	1	.333
L. Pujols, c	6	0	0	0	0	0	0	.000
N. Ryan, p	4	1	0	0	0	0	0	.250
K. Garcia, ss	4	0	0	0	0	0	0	.000
C. Reynolds, ss	3	1	0	0	0	1	0	.333
J. Niekro, p	2	0	0	0	0	0	0	.000
J. Pittman	2	0	0	0	0	0	0	.000
G. Woods	2	0	0	0	0	0	0	.000
B. Knepper, p	1	0	0	0	0	0	0	.000
D. Roberts	1	0	0	0	0	0	0	.000
V. Ruhle, p	1	0	0	0	0	0	0	.000
H. Spilman	1	0	0	0	0	0	0	.000

Errors: C. Cedeno, J. Cruz, P. Garner, D. Thon, D. Walling
Stolen Bases: C. Cedeno (2), J. Cruz, T. Puhl

Individual Pitching

LOS ANGELES (WEST)

	W	L	ERA	IP	H	BB	SO	SV
J. Reuss	1	0	0.00	18	10	5	7	0
F. Valenzuela	1	0	1.06	17	10	3	10	0
B. Hooton	1	0	1.29	7	3	3	2	0
S. Howe	0	0	0.00	2	1	0	2	0
B. Welch	0	0	0.00	1	0	1	1	0
D. Stewart	0	2	40.50	0.2	4	0	1	0
T. Forster	0	0	0.00	0.1	0	0	0	0
T. Niedenfuer	0	0	0.00	0.1	1	1	1	0

HOUSTON (WEST)

	W	L	ERA	IP	H	BB	SO	SV
N. Ryan	1	1	1.80	15	6	3	14	0
J. Niekro	0	0	0.00	8	7	3	4	0
V. Ruhle	0	1	2.25	8	4	2	1	0
B. Knepper	0	1	5.40	5	6	2	4	0
F. LaCorte	0	0	0.00	3.2	2	1	5	0
D. Smith	0	0	3.86	2.1	2	0	4	0
J. Sambito	1	0	16.20	1.2	5	2	2	0
B. Smith	0	0	0.00	0.1	0	0	0	0

1981 NATIONAL LEAGUE CHAMPIONSHIP SERIES

Los Angeles (West) defeats Montreal (East) 3 games to 2

LINE SCORES			R	H	E	PITCHERS (innings pitched)	HOME RUNS (men on)	HIGHLIGHTS
GAME 1 - OCTOBER 13								Cey, activated prior to the start of the series, doubled home the first run and scored another to lead the Dodgers to an opening win over the Expos. Homers by Guerrero and Scioscia ensured victory.
MON	**E**	000 000 001	1	9	0	**Gullickson** (7), Reardon (1)		
LA	**W**	020 000 03x	5	8	0	**Hooton** (7.1), Welch (0.2), Howe (1)	Guerrero (2 on), Scioscia	
GAME 2 - OCTOBER 14								Burris pitched a 5-hitter and Raines rapped 3 hits to enable the Expos to deadlock the series with a 3-0 victory.
MON	**E**	020 001 000	3	10	1	**Burris** (9)		
LA	**W**	000 000 000	0	5	1	**Valenzuela** (6), Niedenfuer (0.1), Forster (0.1), Pena (1.1), Castillo (1)		
GAME 3 - OCTOBER 16								A 3-run homer by White highlighted a 4-run outburst in the 6th that carried the Expos to a 4-1 triumph behind Rogers's seven-hit pitching.
LA	**W**	000 100 000	1	7	0	**Reuss** (7), Pena (1)		
MON	**E**	000 004 00x	4	7	1	**Rogers** (9)	White (2 on)	
GAME 4 - OCTOBER 17								Garvey's 2-run homer in the 8th broke a 1-1 tie and led the Dodgers to a 7-1 win that evened the series at 2 games apiece.
LA	**W**	001 000 024	7	12	1	**Hooton** (7.1), Welch (0.2), Howe (1)	Garvey (1 on)	
MON	**E**	000 100 000	1	5	1	**Gullickson** (7.1), Fryman (1), Sosa (0.1), Lee (0.1)		
GAME 5 - OCTOBER 19								Monday walloped a 2-out homer in the 9th inning, giving the Dodgers a 2-1 victory over the Expos and the NL pennant. Valenzuela allowed 3 hits but needed help from Welch to get the last out.
LA	**W**	000 010 001	2	6	0	**Valenzuela** (8.2), Welch (0.1) **SV**	Monday	
MON	**E**	100 000 000	1	3	1	Burris (8), **Rogers** (1)		

Team totals

		W	AB	H	2B	3B	HR	R	RBI	BA	BB	SO	ERA
LA	**W**	3	163	38	3	1	4	15	15	.233	12	23	1.84
MON	**E**	2	158	34	7	0	1	10	8	.215	12	25	2.86

Individual Batting

LOS ANGELES (WEST)

	AB	H	2B	3B	HR	R	RBI	BA
S. Garvey, 1b	21	6	0	0	1	2	2	.286
D. Baker, of	19	6	1	0	0	3	3	.316
P. Guerrero, of	19	2	0	0	1	1	2	.105
R. Cey, 3b	18	5	1	0	0	1	3	.278
D. Lopes, 2b	18	5	0	0	0	0	0	.278
B. Russell, ss	16	5	0	1	0	2	1	.313
M. Scioscia, c	15	2	0	0	1	1	1	.133
K. Landreaux, of	10	1	1	0	0	0	0	.100
R. Monday, of	9	3	0	0	1	2	1	.333
B. Hooton, p	5	0	0	0	0	0	0	.000
F. Valenzuela, p	5	0	0	0	0	0	1	.000
S. Yeager, c	2	1	0	0	0	1	0	.500
J. Johnstone	2	0	0	0	0	0	0	.000
J. Reuss, p	2	0	0	0	0	0	0	.000
R. Smith	1	1	0	0	0	0	1	1.000
D. Thomas, 3b, of	1	1	0	0	0	2	0	1.000
S. Sax, 2b	0	0	0	0	0	0	0	—

Errors: D. Baker, R. Cey
Stolen Bases: D. Lopes (5)

MONTREAL (EAST)

	AB	H	2B	3B	HR	R	RBI	BA
T. Raines, of	21	5	2	0	0	1	1	.238
A. Dawson, of	20	3	0	0	0	2	0	.150
L. Parrish, 3b	19	5	2	0	0	2	2	.263
W. Cromartie, 1b	18	3	1	0	0	0	2	.167
R. Scott, 2b	18	3	0	0	0	0	0	.167
G. Carter, c	16	7	1	0	0	3	0	.438
J. White, of	16	5	1	0	1	2	3	.313
C. Speier, ss	16	3	0	0	0	0	0	.188
R. Burris, p	6	0	0	0	0	0	0	.000
B. Gullickson, p	3	0	0	0	0	0	0	.000
S. Rogers, p	2	0	0	0	0	0	0	.000
T. Francona, of	1	0	0	0	0	0	0	.000
J. Milner	1	0	0	0	0	0	0	.000
T. Wallach	1	0	0	0	0	0	0	.000
J. Manuel	0	0	0	0	0	0	0	—

Errors: C. Speier (2), L. Parrish, R. Scott
Stolen Bases: R. Scott, J. White

Individual Pitching

LOS ANGELES (WEST)

	W	L	ERA	IP	H	BB	SO	SV
B. Hooton	2	0	0.00	14.2	11	6	7	0
F. Valenzuela	1	1	2.45	14.2	10	5	10	0
J. Reuss	0	1	5.14	7	7	1	2	0
A. Pena	0	0	0.00	2.1	1	0	0	0
S. Howe	0	0	0.00	2	1	0	2	0
B. Welch	0	0	5.40	1.2	2	0	2	1
B. Castillo	0	0	0.00	1	0	0	1	0
T. Forster	0	0	0.00	0.1	0	0	1	0
T. Niedenfuer	0	0	0.00	0.1	2	0	0	0

MONTREAL (EAST)

	W	L	ERA	IP	H	BB	SO	SV
R. Burris	1	0	0.53	17	10	3	4	0
B. Gullickson	0	2	2.51	14.1	12	6	12	0
S. Rogers	1	1	1.80	10	8	1	6	0
W. Fryman	0	0	36.00	1	3	1	1	0
J. Reardon	0	0	27.00	1	3	0	0	0
B. Lee	0	0	0.00	0.1	1	0	0	0
E. Sosa	0	0	0.00	0.1	1	1	0	0

1981 AMERICAN LEAGUE DIVISIONAL PLAYOFFS

New York (East) defeats Milwaukee (East) 3 games to 2

LINE SCORES						PITCHERS (innings pitched)	HOME RUNS (men on)	HIGHLIGHTS
GAME 1 - OCTOBER 7								Gamble's 2-run homer highlighted a 4-run 4th inning, giving the Yankees a 5-3 win. Davis and Gossage were superb in relief.
NY	**E**	000 400 001	5	13	1	Guidry (4.1), **Davis** (2.2), Gossage (2) **SV**	Gamble (1 on)	
MIL	**E**	011 010 000	3	8	3	**Haas** (3.1), Bernard (0.2), McClure (1.1), Slaton (2.1), Fingers (1.1)		
GAME 2 - OCTOBER 8								Homers by Piniella and Jackson accounted for all Yankee runs. Righetti, Davis, and Gossage fanned 14 Brewers.
NY	**E**	000 100 002	3	7	0	**Righetti** (6), Davis (0.1), Gossage (2.2) **SV**	Piniella, Jackson (1 on)	
MIL	**E**	000 000 000	0	7	0	**Caldwell** (8.1), Slaton (0.2)		
GAME 3 - OCTOBER 9								Molitor's homer in the 8th inning broke a 3-3 tie enabling the Brewers to stave off elimination. Simmons hit a 2-run homer for the Brewers in the 7th.
MIL	**E**	000 000 320	5	9	0	Lerch (6), **Fingers** (3)	Simmons (1 on), Molitor	
NY	**E**	000 100 200	3	8	2	**John** (7), May (2)		
GAME 4 - OCTOBER 10								Oglivie's 2-out double drove in what proved to be the winning run as the Brewers evened the series at two wins apiece. Vuckovich, despite a heavy cold, pitched 5 innings for the victory with Fingers getting the save.
MIL	**E**	000 200 000	2	4	2	**Vuckovich** (5), Easterly (1), Slaton (1.2), McClure (1), Fingers (0.1) **SV**		
NY	**E**	000 001 000	1	5	0	**Reuschel** (6), Davis (3)		
GAME 5 - OCTOBER 11								Pounding Milwaukee pitching for 13 hits, including 3 homers, the Yankees downed the Brewers 7-3 to capture the AL Divisional crown in the East. Gossage earned his third save.
MIL	**E**	011 000 100	3	8	0	**Haas** (3.1), Caldwell (0), Bernard (1.2), McClure (1), Slaton (1.1), Easterly (0.1), Vuckovich (0.1)	Thomas	
NY	**E**	000 400 12x	7	13	0	Guidry (4), **Righetti** (3), Gossage (2) **SV**	Jackson (1 on), Gamble, Cerone	

Team totals

		W	AB	H	2B	3B	HR	R	RBI	BA	BB	SO	ERA
NY	**E**	3	171	46	8	0	6	19	18	.269	9	22	2.60
MIL	**E**	2	162	36	6	1	3	13	13	.222	13	39	3.48

Individual Batting

NEW YORK (EAST)

	AB	H	2B	3B	HR	R	RBI	BA
J. Mumphrey, of	21	2	0	0	0	2	0	.095
D. Winfield, of	20	7	3	0	0	2	0	.350
R. Jackson, of	20	6	0	0	2	4	4	.300
W. Randolph, 2b	20	4	0	0	0	0	1	.200
L. Milbourne, ss	19	6	1	0	0	4	0	.316
R. Cerone, c	18	6	2	0	1	1	5	.333
G. Nettles, 3b	17	1	0	0	0	1	1	.059
B. Watson, 1b	16	7	0	0	0	2	1	.438
L. Piniella, dh	10	2	1	0	1	1	3	.200
O. Gamble, dh	9	5	1	0	2	2	3	.556
B. Murcer	1	0	0	0	0	0	0	.000
B. Brown	0	0	0	0	0	0	0	—
B. Foote	0	0	0	0	0	0	0	—
D. Revering, 1b	0	0	0	0	0	0	0	—

Errors: R. Cerone, R. May, B. Watson
Stolen Bases: J. Mumphrey

MILWAUKEE (EAST)

	AB	H	2B	3B	HR	R	RBI	BA
P. Molitor, of	20	5	0	0	1	2	1	.250
R. Yount, ss	19	6	0	1	0	4	1	.316
T. Simmons, c	19	4	1	0	1	1	4	.211
C. Cooper, 1b	18	4	0	0	0	1	3	.222
B. Oglivie, of	18	3	1	0	0	0	1	.167
S. Bando, 3b	17	5	3	0	0	1	1	.294
G. Thomas, dh, of	17	2	0	0	1	2	1	.118
J. Gantner, 2b	14	2	1	0	0	1	0	.143
C. Moore, dh, of	9	2	0	0	0	0	1	.222
R. Howell, dh	5	2	0	0	0	0	0	.400
D. Money, 2b, dh	3	0	0	0	0	0	0	.000
E. Romero, 2b	2	1	0	0	0	1	0	.500
M. Edwards, of	1	0	0	0	0	0	0	.000
T. Bosley, dh	0	0	0	0	0	0	0	—

Errors: J. Gantner (2), C. Cooper, T. Simmons, R. Yount
Stolen Bases: R. Yount

Individual Pitching

NEW YORK (EAST)

	W	L	ERA	IP	H	BB	SO	SV
D. Righetti	2	0	1.00	9	8	3	13	0
R. Guidry	0	0	5.40	8.1	11	3	8	0
T. John	0	1	6.43	7	8	2	0	0
G. Gossage	0	0	0.00	6.2	3	2	8	3
R. Davis	1	0	0.00	6	1	2	6	0
R. Reuschel	0	1	3.00	6	4	1	3	0
R. May	0	0	0.00	2	1	0	1	0

MILWAUKEE (EAST)

	W	L	ERA	IP	H	BB	SO	SV
M. Caldwell	0	1	4.32	8.1	9	0	4	0
M. Haas	0	2	9.45	6.2	13	1	1	0
R. Lerch	0	0	1.50	6	3	4	3	0
J. Slaton	0	0	3.00	6	6	0	2	0
P. Vuckovich	1	0	0.00	5.1	2	3	4	0
R. Fingers	1	0	3.86	4.2	7	1	5	1
B. McClure	0	0	0.00	3.1	4	0	2	0
D. Bernard	0	0	0.00	2.1	0	0	0	0
J. Easterly	0	0	6.75	1.1	2	0	1	0

1981 AMERICAN LEAGUE DIVISIONAL PLAYOFFS

LINE SCORES					PITCHERS (innings pitched)	HOME RUNS (men on)	HIGHLIGHTS

Oakland (West) defeats Kansas City (West) 3 games to 0

GAME 1 - OCTOBER 6							Homers by Gross and Murphy, backed by the 4-hit pitching of Norris, propelled the A's to a 4-0 win in AL West playoffs opener.
OAK W	000 300 010	4	8	2	**Norris** (9)	Gross (2 on), Murphy	
KC W	000 000 000	0	4	1	**Leonard** (8), Martin (1)		
GAME 2 - OCTOBER 7							Armas drilled a double through Brett's legs to score Murphy in the 8th with the tie-breaking run. McCatty scattered 10 hits.
OAK W	100 000 010	2	10	1	**McCatty** (9)		
KC W	000 010 000	1	6	0	**Jones** (8), Quisenberry (1)		
GAME 3 - OCTOBER 9							Henderson reached base all 4 times and scored three times as the A's swept the series, winning 4-1 behind Langford.
KC W	000 100 000	1	10	3	**Gura** (3.2), Martin (4.1)		
OAK W	101 200 00x	4	7	0	**Langford** (7.1), Underwood (0.1), Beard (1.1) **SV**	McKay	

Team totals

		W	AB	H	2B	3B	HR	R	RBI	BA	BB	SO	ERA
OAK	W	3	99	25	5	0	3	10	9	.253	6	10	0.67
KC	W	0	98	20	1	0	0	2	2	.204	7	11	2.08

Individual Batting

OAKLAND (WEST)

	AB	H	2B	3B	HR	R	RBI	BA
T. Armas, of	11	6	2	0	0	1	3	.545
D. Murphy, of	11	6	1	0	1	4	2	.545
D. McKay, 2b	11	3	0	0	1	1	1	.273
R. Henderson, of	11	2	0	0	0	3	0	.182
M. Heath, c	8	0	0	0	0	0	0	.000
K. Moore, 1b	8	0	0	0	0	0	0	.000
C. Johnson, dh	7	2	1	0	0	0	0	.286
M. Klutts, 3b	7	1	0	0	0	0	0	.143
F. Stanley, ss	6	0	0	0	0	0	0	.000
W. Gross, 3b	5	2	0	0	1	1	3	.400
K. Drumright, dh	4	1	0	0	0	0	0	.250
J. Spencer, 1b	4	1	1	0	0	0	0	.250
R. Picciolo, ss	3	1	0	0	0	0	0	.333
J. Newman, c	3	0	0	0	0	0	0	.000
R. Bosetti, of	0	0	0	0	0	0	0	—

Errors: T. Armas, D. McKay, M. Norris
Stolen Bases: R. Henderson (2)

KANSAS CITY (WEST)

	AB	H	2B	3B	HR	R	RBI	BA
W. Wilson, of	13	4	0	0	0	0	1	.308
G. Brett, 3b	12	2	0	0	0	0	0	.167
A. Otis, of	12	0	0	0	0	0	1	.000
C. Hurdle, of	11	3	0	0	0	0	0	.273
F. White, 2b	11	2	0	0	0	1	0	.182
H. McRae, dh	11	1	1	0	0	0	0	.091
J. Wathan, c	10	3	0	0	0	1	0	.300
W. Aikens, 1b	9	3	0	0	0	0	0	.333
U. Washington, ss	9	2	0	0	0	0	0	.222
C. Geronimo	0	0	0	0	0	0	0	—
L. May, 1b	0	0	0	0	0	0	0	—

Errors: G. Brett, U. Washington, J. Wathan, F. White

Individual Pitching

OAKLAND (WEST)

	W	L	ERA	IP	H	BB	SO	SV
S. McCatty	1	0	1.00	9	6	4	3	0
M. Norris	1	0	0.00	9	4	3	2	0
R. Langford	1	0	1.23	7.1	10	0	3	0
D. Beard	0	0	0.00	1.1	0	0	2	1
T. Underwood	0	0	0.00	0.1	0	0	1	0

KANSAS CITY (WEST)

	W	L	ERA	IP	H	BB	SO	SV
M. Jones	0	1	2.25	8	9	0	2	0
D. Leonard	0	1	1.13	8	7	1	3	0
R. Martin	0	0	0.00	5.1	1	2	2	0
L. Gura	0	1	7.36	3.2	7	3	3	0
D. Quisenberry	0	0	0.00	1	1	0	0	0

1981 AMERICAN LEAGUE CHAMPIONSHIP SERIES

New York (East) defeats Oakland (West) 3 games to 0

LINE SCORES			R	H	E	PITCHERS (innings pitched)	HOME RUNS (men on)	HIGHLIGHTS
GAME 1 - OCTOBER 13								A 3-run double by Nettles in the first inning triggered the Yankees' 3-1 win over the A's. Gossage preserved John's victory.
OAK	**W**	000 010 000	1	8	1	**Norris** (7.1), Underwood (0.2)		
NY	**E**	300 000 00x	3	7	1	**John** (6), Davis (1.1), Gossage (1.2) **SV**		
GAME 2 - OCTOBER 14								Three-run homers by Nettles and Piniella were the most telling blows in the Yankees' 13-3 rout of the A's. Frazier pitched 5.2 innings of shutout relief to gain the victory.
OAK	**W**	001 200 000	3	11	1	**McCatty** (3.1), Beard (0.2), Jones (2), Kingman (0.1), Owchinko (1.2)		
NY	**E**	100 701 40x	13	19	0	May (3.1), **Frazier** (5.2)	Nettles (2 on), Piniella (2 on)	
GAME 3 - OCTOBER 15								Randolph broke up a scoreless duel with a 2-out homer in the 6th inning to back five-hit pitching by Righetti, Davis and Gossage, as the Yankees swept the AL championship.
NY	**E**	000 001 003	4	10	0	**Righetti** (6), Davis (2), Gossage (1)	Randolph	
OAK	**W**	000 000 000	0	5	2	**Keough** (8.1), Underwood (0.2)		

Team totals

		W	AB	H	2B	3B	HR	R	RBI	BA	BB	SO	ERA
NY	**E**	3	107	36	4	0	3	20	20	.336	13	10	1.33
OAK	**W**	0	99	22	4	1	0	4	4	.222	6	23	6.84

Individual Batting

NEW YORK (EAST)

	AB	H	2B	3B	HR	R	RBI	BA
L. Milbourne, ss	13	6	0	0	0	4	1	.462
D. Winfield, of	13	2	1	0	0	2	2	.154
J. Mumphrey, of	12	6	1	0	0	2	0	.500
G. Nettles, 3b	12	6	2	0	1	2	9	.500
W. Randolph, 2b	12	4	0	0	1	2	2	.333
B. Watson, 1b	12	3	0	0	0	0	1	.250
R. Cerone, c	10	1	0	0	0	1	0	.100
O. Gamble, dh, of	6	1	0	0	0	2	1	.167
L. Piniella, dh, of	5	3	0	0	1	2	3	.600
R. Jackson, of	4	0	0	0	0	1	1	.000
B. Murcer, dh	3	1	0	0	0	0	0	.333
D. Revering, 1b	2	1	0	0	0	0	0	.500
B. Brown, of	1	1	0	0	0	2	0	1.000
B. Foote, c	1	1	0	0	0	0	0	1.000
A. Robertson, ss	1	0	0	0	0	0	0	.000
A. Rodriguez, 3b	0	0	0	0	0	0	0	—

Errors: G. Nettles

Stolen Bases: R. Jackson, D. Winfield

OAKLAND (WEST)

	AB	H	2B	3B	HR	R	RBI	BA
T. Armas, of	12	2	0	0	0	0	0	.167
R. Henderson, of	11	4	2	1	0	0	1	.364
D. McKay, 2b	11	3	0	0	0	0	1	.273
K. Moore, 1b	9	2	0	0	0	0	0	.222
D. Murphy, of	8	2	1	0	0	0	1	.250
M. Klutts, 3b	7	3	0	0	0	1	0	.429
M. Heath, c, of	6	2	0	0	0	1	0	.333
C. Johnson, dh	6	0	0	0	0	0	0	.000
R. Picciolo, ss	5	1	0	0	0	1	0	.200
W. Gross, 3b	5	0	0	0	0	0	0	.000
J. Newman, c	5	0	0	0	0	0	0	.000
R. Bosetti, dh, of	4	1	1	0	0	1	0	.250
K. Drumright, dh	4	0	0	0	0	0	0	.000
F. Stanley, ss	3	1	0	0	0	0	1	.333
J. Spencer, 1b	2	0	0	0	0	0	0	.000
M. Davis	1	1	0	0	0	0	0	1.000

Errors: R. Henderson, M. Klutts, D. McKay, R. Picciolo

Stolen Bases: R. Henderson (2)

Individual Pitching

NEW YORK (EAST)

	W	L	ERA	IP	H	BB	SO	SV
T. John	1	0	1.50	6	6	1	3	0
D. Righetti	1	0	0.00	6	4	2	4	0
G. Frazier	1	0	0.00	5.2	5	1	5	0
R. Davis	0	0	0.00	3.1	0	2	4	0
R. May	0	0	8.10	3.1	6	0	5	0
G. Gossage	0	0	0.00	2.2	1	0	2	1

OAKLAND (WEST)

	W	L	ERA	IP	H	BB	SO	SV
M. Keough	0	1	1.08	8.1	7	6	2	0
M. Norris	0	1	3.68	7.1	6	2	4	0
S. McCatty	0	1	13.50	3.1	6	2	2	0
J. Jones	0	0	4.50	2	2	1	0	0
B. Owchinko	0	0	5.40	1.2	3	0	0	0
T. Underwood	0	0	13.50	1.1	4	2	2	0
D. Beard	0	0	40.50	0.2	5	0	0	0
B. Kingman	0	0	81.00	0.1	3	0	0	0

1981 WORLD SERIES

Los Angeles (N.L.) defeats New York (A.L.) 4 games to 2

LINE SCORES			R	H	E	PITCHERS (innings pitched)	HOME RUNS (men on)	HIGHLIGHTS
GAME 1 - OCTOBER 20								Watson homered with two on in the first inning to propel the Yankees to a 5-3 win. Gossage quelled a Dodger rally in the 8th to preserve Guidry's triumph.
LA	N	000 010 020	3	5	0	**Reuss** (2.2), Castillo (1), Goltz (0.1), Niedenfuer (3), Stewart (1)	Yeager	
NY	A	301 100 00x	5	6	0	**Guidry** (7), Davis (0), Gossage (2) **SV**	Watson (2 on)	
GAME 2 - OCTOBER 21								John and Gossage combined to shut out the Dodgers on 4 hits. Watson continued his hot streak with 2 hits and an RBI.
LA	N	000 000 000	0	4	2	**Hooton** (6), Forster (1.0), Howe (0.1), Stewart (0.2)		
NY	A	000 010 02x	3	6	1	**John** (7), Gossage (2) **SV**		
GAME 3 - OCTOBER 23								Cey hit a 3-run homer but the winning run crossed the plate on a double play as the Dodgers came from behind to win 5-4. Valenzuela staggered to victory despite giving up 9 hits and 7 walks.
NY	A	022 000 000	4	9	0	Righetti (2), **Frazier** (2), May (3), Davis (1)	Watson, Cerone (1 on)	
LA	N	300 020 00x	5	11	1	**Valenzuela** (9)	Cey (2 on)	
GAME 4 - OCTOBER 24								A pinch 2-run homer by Johnstone and some shoddy fielding by Yankee outfielders helped the Dodgers score 5 runs in the 7th and 8th innings and overcome a 6-3 deficit. The 8-7 victory tied the Series at 2 games each.
NY	A	211 002 010	7	13	1	Reuschel (3), May (1.1), Davis (1), **Frazier** (0.2), John (2)	Randolph, Jackson	
LA	N	002 013 20x	8	14	2	Welch (0), Goltz (3), Forster (1), Niedenfuer (2), **Howe** (3)	Johnstone (1 on)	
GAME 5 - OCTOBER 25								Seventh inning back-to-back homers by Guerrero and Yeager off Guidry provided the Dodgers with their third straight win over the Yankees. Reuss allowed only 5 hits.
NY	A	010 000 000	1	5	0	**Guidry** (7), Gossage (1)		
LA	N	000 000 20x	2	4	3	**Reuss** (9)	Guerrero, Yeager	
GAME 6 - OCTOBER 28								Guerrero drove in 5 runs as the Dodgers pounded 6 pitchers for 13 hits to win their 4th straight and capture the World Series, 4 games to 2. Frazier, in relief, was charged with his 3rd loss.
LA	N	000 134 010	9	13	1	**Hooton** (5.1), Howe (3.1)	Guerrero	
NY	A	001 001 000	2	7	2	John (4), **Frazier** (1), Davis (0.2), Reuschel (0.2), May (2), LaRoche (1)	Randolph	

Team totals

		W	AB	H	2B	3B	HR	R	RBI	BA	BB	SO	ERA
LA	N	4	198	51	6	1	6	27	26	.258	20	44	3.29
NY	A	2	193	46	8	1	6	22	22	.238	33	24	4.24

Individual Batting

LOS ANGELES (N.L.)

	AB	H	2B	3B	HR	R	RBI	BA
B. Russell, ss	25	6	0	0	0	1	2	.240
S. Garvey, 1b	24	10	1	0	0	3	0	.417
D. Baker, of	24	4	0	0	0	3	1	.167
D. Lopes, 2b	22	5	1	0	0	6	2	.227
P. Guerrero, of	21	7	1	1	2	2	7	.333
R. Cey, 3b	20	7	0	0	1	3	6	.350
S. Yeager, c	14	4	1	0	2	2	4	.286
R. Monday, of	13	3	1	0	0	1	0	.231
D. Thomas, 3b, of, ss	7	0	0	0	0	2	1	.000
K. Landreaux, of	6	1	1	0	0	1	0	.167
M. Scioscia, c	4	1	0	0	0	1	0	.250
B. Hooton, p	4	0	0	0	0	1	0	.000
J. Johnstone	3	2	0	0	1	1	3	.667
J. Reuss, p	3	0	0	0	0	0	0	.000
F. Valenzuela, p	3	0	0	0	0	0	0	.000
R. Smith	2	1	0	0	0	0	0	.500
S. Howe, p	2	0	0	0	0	0	0	.000
S. Sax, 2b	1	0	0	0	0	0	0	.000

Errors: D. Lopes (6), S. Howe, B. Russell, D. Stewart
Stolen Bases: D. Lopes (4), K. Landreaux, B. Russell

NEW YORK (A.L.)

	AB	H	2B	3B	HR	R	RBI	BA
B. Watson, 1b	22	7	1	0	2	2	7	.318
D. Winfield, of	22	1	0	0	0	0	1	.045
R. Cerone, c	21	4	1	0	1	2	3	.190
L. Milbourne, ss	20	5	2	0	0	2	3	.250
W. Randolph, 2b	18	4	1	1	2	5	3	.222
L. Piniella, of	16	7	1	0	0	2	3	.438
J. Mumphrey, of	15	3	0	0	0	2	0	.200
A. Rodriguez, 3b	12	5	0	0	0	1	0	.417
R. Jackson, dh, of	12	4	1	0	1	3	1	.333
G. Nettles, 3b	10	4	1	0	0	1	0	.400
O. Gamble, of	6	2	0	0	0	1	1	.333
R. Guidry, p	5	0	0	0	0	0	0	.000
B. Murcer	3	0	0	0	0	0	0	.000
G. Frazier, p	2	0	0	0	0	0	0	.000
T. John, p	2	0	0	0	0	0	0	.000
R. Reuschel, p	2	0	0	0	0	0	0	.000
B. Brown, of	1	0	0	0	0	1	0	.000
B. Foote	1	0	0	0	0	0	0	.000
G. Gossage, p	1	0	0	0	0	0	0	.000
R. May, p	1	0	0	0	0	0	0	.000
D. Righetti, p	1	0	0	0	0	0	0	.000
A. Robertson	0	0	0	0	0	0	0	—

Errors: L. Milbourne (2), R. Jackson, G. Nettles
Stolen Bases: J. Mumphrey, L. Piniella, W. Randolph, D. Winfield

Individual Pitching

LOS ANGELES (N.L.)

	W	L	ERA	IP	H	BB	SO	SV
J. Reuss	1	1	3.86	11.2	10	3	8	0
B. Hooton	1	1	1.59	11.1	8	9	3	0
F. Valenzuela	1	0	4.00	9	9	7	6	0
S. Howe	1	0	3.86	7	7	1	4	1
T. Niedenfuer	0	0	0.00	5	3	1	0	0
D. Goltz	0	0	5.40	3.1	4	1	2	0
T. Forster	0	0	0.00	2	1	3	0	0
D. Stewart	0	0	0.00	1.2	1	2	1	0
B. Castillo	0	0	9.00	1	0	5	0	0
B. Welch	0	0	∞	0.0	3	1	0	0

NEW YORK (A.L.)

	W	L	ERA	IP	H	BB	SO	SV
R. Guidry	1	1	1.93	14	8	4	15	0
T. John	1	0	0.69	13	11	0	8	0
R. May	0	0	2.84	6.1	5	1	5	0
G. Gossage	0	0	0.00	5	2	2	5	2
G. Frazier	0	3	17.18	3.2	9	3	2	0
R. Reuschel	0	0	4.91	3.2	7	3	2	0
R. Davis	0	0	23.14	2.1	4	5	4	0
D. Righetti	0	0	13.50	2	5	2	1	0
D. LaRoche	0	0	0.00	1	0	0	2	0

1982 NATIONAL LEAGUE CHAMPIONSHIP SERIES

St. Louis (East) defeats Atlanta (West) 3 games to 0

LINE SCORES						PITCHERS (innings pitched)	HOME RUNS (men on)	HIGHLIGHTS
GAME 1 - OCTOBER 7								Game 1 came a day late after rain washed away the previous day's effort with Atlanta leading 1-0 in the fifth. In the game that counted, the Cardinals scored five in the sixth to break open a 1-0 game. Bob Forsch scattered three hits and walked none for the win.
ATL	**W**	000 000 000	0	3	0	**Perez** (5), Bedrosian (0.2), Moore (1.1), Walk (1)		
STL	**E**	001 005 01x	7	13	1	**B. Forsch** (9)		
GAME 2 - OCTOBER 9								Another day of rain allowed Phil Niekro, who pitched in the Game 1 washout, to come back on two days' rest. Niekro left the game with a 3-2 lead, but Garber could not hold it. Ken Oberkfell, 6-for-10 against Garber in the season, singled home the winning run with first base open in the bottom of the ninth.
ATL	**W**	002 010 000	3	6	0	Niekro (6), **Garber** (2.1)		
STL	**E**	100 001 011	4	9	1	Stuper (6), Bair (1), **Sutter** (2)		
GAME 3 - OCTOBER 10								Five Cardinal hits, topped by rookie Willie McGee's triple, led to four runs in the second inning to chase Rick Camp. McGee added a homer in the ninth and Bruce Sutter set down seven straight hitters to nail down the Cardinals' first pennant in fourteen years.
STL	**E**	040 010 001	6	12	0	**Andujar** (6.2), Sutter (2.1) **SV**	McGee	
ATL	**W**	000 000 200	2	6	1	**Camp** (1), Perez (3.2), Moore (1.1), Mahler (1.2), Bedrosian (0.1), Garber (1)		

Team totals

		W	AB	H	2B	3B	HR	R	RBI	BA	BB	SO	ERA
STL	**E**	3	103	34	4	2	1	17	16	.330	12	16	1.33
ATL	**W**	0	89	15	1	0	0	5	3	.169	6	15	6.05

Individual Batting

ST. LOUIS (EAST)

	AB	H	2B	3B	HR	R	RBI	BA
K. Oberkfell, 3b	15	3	0	0	0	1	2	.200
G. Hendrick, of	13	4	0	0	0	2	2	.308
W. McGee, of	13	4	0	2	1	4	5	.308
T. Herr, 2b	13	3	1	0	0	1	0	.231
K. Hernandez, 1b	12	4	0	0	0	3	1	.333
L. Smith, of	11	3	0	0	0	1	1	.273
D. Porter, c	9	5	3	0	0	3	1	.556
O. Smith, ss	9	5	0	0	0	0	3	.556
B. Forsch, p	3	2	0	0	0	1	1	.667
D. Green, of	1	1	0	0	0	1	0	1.000
J. Andujar, p	1	0	0	0	0	0	0	.000
S. Braun	1	0	0	0	0	0	0	.000
J. Stuper, p	1	0	0	0	0	0	0	.000
B. Sutter, p	1	0	0	0	0	0	0	.000

Errors: W. McGee, K. Oberkfell
Stolen Bases: O. Smith

ATLANTA (WEST)

	AB	H	2B	3B	HR	R	RBI	BA
D. Murphy, of	11	3	0	0	0	1	0	.273
R. Ramirez, ss	11	2	0	0	0	1	1	.182
J. Royster, 3b, of	11	2	0	0	0	0	0	.182
B. Horner, 3b	11	1	0	0	0	0	0	.091
C. Chambliss, 1b	10	0	0	0	0	0	0	.000
C. Washington, of	9	3	0	0	0	0	0	.333
G. Hubbard, 2b	9	2	0	0	0	1	1	.222
B. Benedict, c	8	2	1	0	0	1	0	.250
P. Perez, p	3	0	0	0	0	0	0	.000
L. Whisenton	2	0	0	0	0	0	0	.000
B. Butler, of	1	0	0	0	0	0	0	.000
G. Garber, p	1	0	0	0	0	0	0	.000
T. Harper, of	1	0	0	0	0	1	0	.000
B. Pocoroba	1	0	0	0	0	0	0	.000
P. Niekro, p	0	0	0	0	0	0	1	—

Errors: R. Ramirez
Stolen Bases: D. Murphy

Individual Pitching

ST. LOUIS (EAST)

	W	L	ERA	IP	H	BB	SO	SV
B. Forsch	1	0	0.00	9	3	0	6	0
J. Andujar	1	0	2.70	6.2	6	2	4	0
J. Stuper	0	0	3.00	6	4	1	4	0
B. Sutter	1	0	0.00	4.1	0	0	1	1
D. Bair	0	0	0.00	1	2	3	0	0

ATLANTA (WEST)

	W	L	ERA	IP	H	BB	SO	SV
P. Perez	0	1	5.19	8.2	10	2	4	0
P. Niekro	0	0	3.00	6	6	4	5	0
G. Garber	0	1	8.10	3.1	4	1	3	0
D. Moore	0	0	0.00	2.2	2	0	1	0
R. Mahler	0	0	0.00	1.2	3	2	0	0
S. Bedrosian	0	0	18.00	1	3	1	2	0
R. Camp	0	1	36.00	1	4	1	0	0
B. Walk	0	0	9.00	1	2	1	1	0

1982 AMERICAN LEAGUE CHAMPIONSHIP SERIES

Milwaukee (East) defeats California (West) 3 games to 2

LINE SCORES			R	H	E	PITCHERS (innings pitched)	HOME RUNS (men on)	HIGHLIGHTS
GAME 1 - OCTOBER 5								Don Baylor tied a Championship Series record with five RBIs as Tommy John hurled a seven-hitter, shutting out the Brewers over the final six innings.
MIL	**E**	021 000 000	3	7	2	**Caldwell** (3), Slaton (3), Ladd (1), Bernard (1)	Thomas (1 on)	
CAL	**W**	104 210 00x	8	10	0	**John** (9)	Lynn	
GAME 2 - OCTOBER 6								Bruce Kison's five-hitter put the Angels up two games to none. Reggie Jackson's solo homer in the fourth gave California a 4-0 lead before Molitor's homer cut it to 4-2.
MIL	**E**	000 020 000	2	5	0	**Vuckovich** (8)	Molitor (1 on)	
CAL	**W**	021 100 00x	4	6	0	**Kison** (9)	Re. Jackson	
GAME 3 - OCTOBER 8								Don Sutton and the Brewers staved off elimination with a 5-3 victory at home. Paul Molitor's two-run home run provided the margin.
CAL	**W**	000 000 030	3	8	0	**Zahn** (3.2), Witt (3), Hassler (1.1)	Boone	
MIL	**E**	000 300 20x	5	6	0	**Sutton** (7.2), Ladd (1.1) **SV**	Molitor (1 on)	
GAME 4 - OCTOBER 9								Mark Brouhard, a reserve outfielder, had three hits, three RBIs, and four runs scored as the Brewers evened the series.
CAL	**W**	000 001 040	5	5	3	**John** (3.1), Goltz (3.2), Sanchez (1)	Baylor (3 on)	
MIL	**E**	030 301 02x	9	9	2	**Haas** (7.1), Slaton (1.2) **SV**	Brouhard (1 on)	
GAME 5 - OCTOBER 10								Cecil Cooper singled in the tying and winning runs in the seventh to give the Brewers their first AL title. They also became the first team to win a Championship Series after trailing two games to none.
CAL	**W**	101 100 000	3	11	1	Kison (5), **Sanchez** (1.2), Hassler (1.1)		
MIL	**E**	100 100 20x	4	6	4	Vuckovich (6.1), **McClure** (1.2), Ladd (1) **SV**	Oglivie	

Team totals

		W	AB	H	2B	3B	HR	R	RBI	BA	BB	SO	ERA
MIL	**E**	3	151	33	4	0	5	23	20	.219	15	28	4.19
CAL	**W**	2	157	40	8	1	4	23	23	.255	16	34	4.29

Individual Batting

MILWAUKEE (EAST)

	AB	H	2B	3B	HR	R	RBI	BA
C. Cooper, 1b	20	3	2	0	0	1	4	.150
P. Molitor, 3b	19	6	1	0	2	4	5	.316
T. Simmons, c	18	3	0	0	0	3	1	.167
R. Yount, ss	16	4	0	0	0	1	0	.250
J. Gantner, 2b	16	3	0	0	0	1	2	.188
B. Oglivie, of	15	2	0	0	1	1	1	.133
G. Thomas, of	15	1	0	0	1	1	3	.067
C. Moore, of	13	6	0	0	0	3	0	.462
D. Money, dh	11	2	0	0	0	2	1	.182
M. Brouhard, of	4	3	1	0	1	4	3	.750
R. Howell, dh	3	0	0	0	0	0	0	.000
M. Edwards, dh, of	1	0	0	0	0	2	0	.000

Errors: C. Cooper (2), P. Molitor (2), B. Oglivie (2), M. Caldwell, R. Yount

Stolen Bases: M. Edwards, P. Molitor

CALIFORNIA (WEST)

	AB	H	2B	3B	HR	R	RBI	BA
D. DeCinces, 3b	19	6	2	0	0	5	0	.316
B. Downing, of	19	3	1	0	0	4	0	.158
F. Lynn, of	18	11	2	0	1	4	5	.611
R. Jackson, of	18	2	0	0	1	2	2	.111
D. Baylor, dh	17	5	1	1	1	2	10	.294
R. Carew, 1b	17	3	1	0	0	2	0	.176
B. Boone, c	16	4	0	0	1	3	4	.250
T. Foli, ss	16	2	0	0	0	0	1	.125
B. Grich, 2b	15	3	1	0	0	1	1	.200
R. Jackson	1	1	0	0	0	0	0	1.000
R. Wilfong	1	0	0	0	0	0	0	.000
J. Beniquez, of	0	0	0	0	0	0	0	—
B. Clark, of	0	0	0	0	0	0	0	—

Errors: D. DeCinces (3), F. Lynn

Stolen Bases: R. Carew

Individual Pitching

MILWAUKEE (EAST)

	W	L	ERA	IP	H	BB	SO	SV
P. Vuckovich	0	1	4.40	14.1	15	7	8	0
D. Sutton	1	0	3.52	7.2	8	2	9	0
M. Haas	1	0	4.91	7.1	5	5	7	0
J. Slaton	0	0	1.93	4.2	3	1	3	1
P. Ladd	0	0	0.00	3.1	0	0	5	2
M. Caldwell	0	1	15.00	3	7	1	2	0
B. McClure	1	0	0.00	1.2	2	0	0	0
D. Bernard	0	0	0.00	1	0	0	0	0

CALIFORNIA (WEST)

	W	L	ERA	IP	H	BB	SO	SV
B. Kison	1	0	1.93	14	8	3	12	0
T. John	1	1	5.11	12.1	11	6	6	0
D. Goltz	0	0	7.36	3.2	4	2	2	0
G. Zahn	0	1	7.36	3.2	4	1	2	0
M. Witt	0	0	6.00	3	2	2	3	0
A. Hassler	0	0	0.00	2.2	0	0	2	0
L. Sanchez	0	1	6.75	2.2	4	1	1	0

1982 WORLD SERIES

St. Louis (N.L.) defeats Milwaukee (A.L.) 4 games to 3

LINE SCORES						PITCHERS (innings pitched)	HOME RUNS (men on)	HIGHLIGHTS
GAME 1 - OCTOBER 12								Caldwell allowed three hits as Milwaukee hammered four Cardinal pitchers. Molitor had the first five-hit game in World Series history, and Yount added four of his own.
MIL	**A**	200 112 004	10	17	0	**Caldwell** (9)	Simmons	
STL	**N**	000 000 000	0	3	1	**Forsch** (5.2), Kaat (1.1), LaPoint (1.2), Lahti (0.1)		
GAME 2 - OCTOBER 13								Porter doubled in two runs in the sixth and had a key single in the Cards' game-winning rally in the eighth.
MIL	**A**	012 010 000	4	10	1	Sutton (6), **McClure** (1.1), Ladd (0.2)	Simmons	
STL	**N**	002 002 01x	5	8	0	Stuper (4), Kaat (0.2), Bair (2), **Sutter** (2.1)		
GAME 3 - OCTOBER 15								Rookie McGee sparkled with two home runs and a great catch at the wall, driving in four runs and saving another. Andujar was hit on the leg with a line drive, and had to leave the game, leading to an early appearance by relief ace Sutter.
STL	**N**	000 030 201	6	6	1	**Andujar** (6.1), Kaat (0.1), Bair (0), Sutter (2.1) **SV**	McGee (2 on), McGee	
MIL	**A**	000 000 020	2	5	3	**Vuckovich** (8.2), McClure (0.1)	Cooper (1 on)	
GAME 4 - OCTOBER 16								With Sutter unavailable, four Cardinal pitchers could not stop the Brewers from rallying for a 7-5 win after LaPoint's error opened the door in the seventh.
STL	**N**	130 001 000	5	8	1	LaPoint (6.2), **Bair** (0), Kaat (0), Lahti (1.1)		
MIL	**A**	000 010 60x	7	10	2	Haas (5.1), **Slaton** (2), McClure (1.2) **SV**		
GAME 5 - OCTOBER 17								Yount became the first in Series history to have two four-hit games. Caldwell got his second win, McClure his second save.
STL	**N**	001 000 102	4	15	2	**Forsch** (7), Sutter (1)		
MIL	**A**	101 010 12x	6	11	1	**Caldwell** (8.1), McClure (0.2) **SV**	Yount	
GAME 6 - OCTOBER 19								Rookie Stuper earned a complete-game win despite two rain delays totalling more than two and a half hours. Dane Iorg led the way with two doubles and a triple.
MIL	**A**	000 000 001	1	4	4	**Sutton** (4.1), Slaton (0.2), Medich (2), Bernard (1)		
STL	**N**	020 326 00x	13	12	1	**Stuper** (9)	Hernandez (1 on), Porter (1 on)	
GAME 7 - OCTOBER 20								A three-run rally in the sixth, capped by Hendrick's go-ahead single, overcame a 3-1 deficit to give St. Louis the championship.
MIL	**A**	000 012 000	3	7	0	Vuckovich (5.1), **McClure** (0.1), Haas (2), Caldwell (0.1)	Oglivie	
STL	**N**	000 103 02x	6	15	1	**Andujar** (7), Sutter (2) **SV**		

Team totals

		W	AB	H	2B	3B	HR	R	RBI	BA	BB	SO	ERA
STL	**N**	4	245	67	16	3	4	39	34	.273	20	25	3.84
MIL	**A**	3	238	64	12	2	5	33	28	.269	19	28	4.80

Individual Batting

ST. LOUIS (N.L.)

	AB	H	2B	3B	HR	R	RBI	BA
G. Hendrick, of	28	9	0	0	0	5	5	.321
L. Smith, dh, of	28	9	4	1	0	6	1	.321
D. Porter, c	28	8	2	0	1	1	5	.286
K. Hernandez, 1b	27	7	2	0	1	4	8	.259
W. McGee, of	25	6	0	0	2	6	5	.240
T. Herr, 2b	25	4	2	0	0	2	5	.160
K. Oberkfell, 3b	24	7	1	0	0	4	1	.292
O. Smith, ss	24	5	0	0	0	3	1	.208
D. Iorg, dh	17	9	4	1	0	4	1	.529
D. Green, dh, of	10	2	1	1	0	3	0	.200
G. Tenace, dh	6	0	0	0	0	0	0	.000
S. Braun, dh	2	1	0	0	0	0	2	.500
M. Ramsey, 3b	1	0	0	0	0	1	0	.000
G. Brummer, c	0	0	0	0	0	0	0	—

Errors: K. Hernandez (2), J. Andujar, B. Forsch, T. Herr, D. LaPoint, K. Oberkfell

Stolen Bases: W. McGee (2), K. Oberkfell (2), L. Smith (2), O. Smith

MILWAUKEE (A.L.)

	AB	H	2B	3B	HR	R	RBI	BA
P. Molitor, 3b	31	11	0	0	0	5	2	.355
R. Yount, ss	29	12	3	0	1	6	6	.414
C. Cooper, 1b	28	8	1	0	1	3	6	.286
B. Oglivie, of	27	6	0	1	1	4	1	.222
C. Moore, of	26	9	3	0	0	3	2	.346
G. Thomas, of	26	3	0	0	0	0	3	.115
J. Gantner, 2b	24	8	4	1	0	5	4	.333
T. Simmons, c	23	4	0	0	2	2	3	.174
D. Money, dh	13	3	1	0	0	4	1	.231
R. Howell, dh	11	0	0	0	0	1	0	.000
M. Edwards, of	0	0	0	0	0	0	0	—
N. Yost, c	0	0	0	0	0	0	0	—

Errors: J. Gantner (5), R. Yount (3), C. Cooper, B. Oglivie, T. Simmons

Stolen Bases: P. Molitor

Individual Pitching

ST. LOUIS (N.L.)

	W	L	ERA	IP	H	BB	SO	SV
J. Andujar	2	0	1.35	13.1	10	1	4	0
J. Stuper	1	0	3.46	13	10	5	5	0
B. Forsch	0	2	4.97	12.2	18	3	4	0
D. LaPoint	0	0	3.24	8.1	10	2	3	0
B. Sutter	1	0	4.70	7.2	6	3	6	2
J. Kaat	0	0	3.86	2.1	4	2	2	0
D. Bair	0	1	9.00	2	2	2	3	0
J. Lahti	0	0	10.80	1.2	4	1	1	0

MILWAUKEE (A.L.)

	W	L	ERA	IP	H	BB	SO	SV
M. Caldwell	2	0	2.04	17.2	19	3	6	0
P. Vuckovich	0	1	4.50	14	16	5	4	0
D. Sutton	0	1	7.84	10.1	12	1	5	0
M. Haas	0	0	7.36	7.1	8	3	4	0
B. McClure	0	2	4.15	4.1	5	3	5	2
J. Slaton	1	0	0.00	2.2	1	2	1	0
D. Medich	0	0	18.00	2	5	1	0	0
D. Bernard	0	0	0.00	1	0	0	1	0
P. Ladd	0	0	0.00	0.2	1	2	0	0

1983 NATIONAL LEAGUE CHAMPIONSHIP SERIES

Philadelphia (East) defeats Los Angeles (West) 3 games to 1

LINE SCORES			R	H	E	PITCHERS (innings pitched)	HOME RUNS (men on)	HIGHLIGHTS
GAME 1 - OCTOBER 4								Mike Schmidt's first-inning homer accounted for all the scoring, and Al Holland shut down a bases-loaded threat in the eighth to preserve the 1-0 win.
PHI	E	100 000 000	1	5	1	**Carlton** (7.2), Holland (1.1) **SV**	Schmidt	
LA	W	000 000 000	0	7	0	**Reuss** (8), Niedenfuer (1)		
GAME 2 - OCTOBER 5								Two Philadelphia errors and a two-run triple by Pedro Guerrero gave the Dodgers the win behind Valenzuela's and Niedenfuer's seven-hitter.
PHI	E	010 000 000	1	7	2	**Denny** (6), Reed (2)	Matthews	
LA	W	100 020 01x	4	6	1	**Valenzuela** (8), Niedenfuer (1) **SV**		
GAME 3 - OCTOBER 7								Gary Matthews went three-for-three and drove in four runs as rookie Charlie Hudson went the distance for the Phillies.
LA	W	000 200 000	2	4	0	**Welch** (1.1), Pena (2.2), Honeycutt (0.1), Beckwith (1.2), Zachry (2)	Marshall (1 on)	
PHI	E	021 120 10x	7	9	1	**Hudson** (9)	Matthews	
GAME 4 - OCTOBER 8								Gary Matthews's three-run homer in the first and Sixto Lezcano's three hits led the 13-hit attack that gave Steve Carlton his second victory and Philadelphia the National League pennant.
LA	W	000 100 010	2	10	0	**Reuss** (4), Beckwith (0.2), Honeycutt (1.1), Zachry (2)	Baker	
PHI	E	300 022 00x	7	13	1	**Carlton** (6), Reed (1.1), Holland (1.2)	Matthews (2 on), Lezcano (1 on)	

Team totals

		W	AB	H	2B	3B	HR	R	RBI	BA	BB	SO	ERA
PHI	E	3	130	34	4	0	5	16	15	.262	15	22	1.03
LA	W	1	129	27	5	1	2	8	7	.209	11	31	3.97

Individual Batting

PHILADELPHIA (EAST)

	AB	H	2B	3B	HR	R	RBI	BA
P. Rose, 1b	16	6	0	0	0	3	0	.375
M. Schmidt, 3b	15	7	2	0	1	5	2	.467
J. Morgan, 2b	15	1	0	0	0	1	0	.067
G. Matthews, of	14	6	0	0	3	4	8	.429
S. Lezcano, of	13	4	0	0	1	2	2	.308
B. Diaz, c	13	2	1	0	0	0	0	.154
I. DeJesus, ss	12	3	0	0	0	0	1	.250
G. Maddox, of	11	3	1	0	0	0	1	.273
S. Carlton, p	5	1	0	0	0	0	0	.200
G. Gross, of	5	0	0	0	0	1	0	.000
C. Hudson, p	4	0	0	0	0	0	0	.000
V. Hayes, of	2	0	0	0	0	0	0	.000
J. Lefebvre, of	2	0	0	0	0	0	1	.000
T. Perez	1	1	0	0	0	0	0	1.000
J. Denny, p	1	0	0	0	0	0	0	.000
O. Virgil	1	0	0	0	0	0	0	.000
B. Dernier, of	0	0	0	0	0	0	0	—
J. Samuel	0	0	0	0	0	0	0	—

Errors: I. DeJesus (2), S. Lezcano, G. Maddox, M. Schmidt
Stolen Bases: G. Matthews, P. Rose

LOS ANGELES (WEST)

	AB	H	2B	3B	HR	R	RBI	BA
S. Sax, 2b	16	4	0	0	0	0	0	.250
M. Marshall, 1b, of	15	2	1	0	1	1	2	.133
D. Baker, of	14	5	1	0	1	4	1	.357
B. Russell, ss	14	4	0	0	0	1	0	.286
K. Landreaux, of	14	2	0	0	0	0	1	.143
P. Guerrero, 3b	12	3	1	1	0	1	2	.250
D. Thomas, of	9	4	1	0	0	0	0	.444
G. Brock, 1b	9	0	0	0	0	1	0	.000
J. Fimple, c	7	1	0	0	0	0	1	.143
S. Yeager, c	6	1	1	0	0	0	0	.167
J. Reuss, p	3	0	0	0	0	0	0	.000
F. Valenzuela, p	3	0	0	0	0	0	0	.000
R. Landestoy	2	0	0	0	0	0	0	.000
C. Maldonado	2	0	0	0	0	0	0	.000
J. Morales	2	0	0	0	0	0	0	.000
A. Pena, p	1	1	0	0	0	0	0	1.000
R. Monday	0	0	0	0	0	0	0	—

Errors: B. Russell
Stolen Bases: B. Russell, S. Sax, D. Thomas

Individual Pitching

PHILADELPHIA (EAST)

	W	L	ERA	IP	H	BB	SO	SV
S. Carlton	2	0	0.66	13.2	13	5	13	0
C. Hudson	1	0	2.00	9	4	2	9	0
J. Denny	0	1	0.00	6	5	3	3	0
R. Reed	0	0	2.70	3.1	4	1	3	0
A. Holland	0	0	0.00	3	1	0	3	1

LOS ANGELES (WEST)

	W	L	ERA	IP	H	BB	SO	SV
J. Reuss	0	2	4.50	12	14	3	4	0
F. Valenzuela	1	0	1.13	8	7	4	5	0
P. Zachry	0	0	2.25	4	4	2	2	0
A. Pena	0	0	6.75	2.2	4	1	3	0
J. Beckwith	0	0	0.00	2.1	1	2	3	0
T. Niedenfuer	0	0	0.00	2	0	1	3	1
R. Honeycutt	0	0	21.60	1.2	4	0	2	0
B. Welch	0	1	6.75	1.1	0	2	0	0

1983 AMERICAN LEAGUE CHAMPIONSHIP SERIES

Baltimore (East) defeats Chicago (West) 3 games to 1

LINE SCORES					PITCHERS (innings pitched)	HOME RUNS (men on)	HIGHLIGHTS
GAME 1 - OCTOBER 5							Five-hit pitching by LaMarr Hoyt carried the White Sox to victory in Game 1. Rudy Law had three hits and scored a run to pace the Chicago attack.
CHI W	001 001 000	2	7	0	**Hoyt** (9)		
BAL E	000 000 001	1	5	1	**McGregor** (6.2), Stewart (0.1), T. Martinez (2)		
GAME 2 - OCTOBER 6							Mike Boddicker struck out 14 batters in his five-hit shutout effort. Gary Roenicke slammed a two-run homer and scored three runs for the Orioles.
CHI W	000 000 000	0	5	2	**Bannister** (6), Barojas (1), Lamp (1)		
BAL E	010 102 00x	4	6	0	**Boddicker** (9)	Roenicke (1 on)	
GAME 3 - OCTOBER 7							Eddie Murray drove in three runs and scored four as Mike Flanagan and Sammy Stewart combined on a six-hitter. Cal Ripken chipped in with two hits and scored three times.
BAL E	310 020 014	11	8	1	**Flanagan** (5), Stewart (4) **SV**	Murray (2 on)	
CHI W	010 000 000	1	6	1	**Dotson** (5), Tidrow (2), Koosman (0.1), Lamp (0.2)		
GAME 4 - OCTOBER 8							Tito Landrum's tenth-inning homer snapped a scoreless tie and ignited a three-run outburst that gave Baltimore the American League pennant.
BAL E	000 000 000 3	3	9	0	Davis (6), **T. Martinez** (4)	Landrum	
CHI W	000 000 000 0	0	10	0	**Burns** (9.1), Barojas (0), Agosto (0.1), Lamp (0.1)		

Team totals

		W	AB	H	2B	3B	HR	R	RBI	BA	BB	SO	ERA
BAL	**E**	3	129	28	9	0	3	19	17	.217	16	24	0.49
CHI	**W**	1	133	28	4	0	0	3	2	.211	12	26	4.00

Individual Batting

BALTIMORE (EAST)

	AB	H	2B	3B	HR	R	RBI	BA
C. Ripken, ss	15	6	2	0	0	5	1	.400
E. Murray, 1b	15	4	0	0	1	5	3	.267
T. Cruz, 3b	15	2	0	0	0	0	1	.133
R. Dauer, 2b	14	0	0	0	0	0	1	.000
K. Singleton, dh	12	3	2	0	0	0	1	.250
R. Dempsey, c	12	2	0	0	0	1	0	.167
T. Landrum, of	10	2	0	0	1	2	1	.200
J. Shelby, of	9	2	0	0	0	1	0	.222
A. Bumbry, of	8	1	1	0	0	0	1	.125
J. Lowenstein, dh, of	6	1	1	0	0	0	2	.167
D. Ford, dh, of	5	1	1	0	0	0	0	.200
G. Roenicke, of	4	3	1	0	1	4	4	.750
J. Dwyer, of	4	1	1	0	0	1	0	.250
B. Ayala, dh	0	0	0	0	0	0	1	—
J. Nolan	0	0	0	0	0	0	1	—
J. Palmer, dh	0	0	0	0	0	0	0	—

Errors: R. Dempsey, E. Murray
Stolen Bases: E. Murray, J. Shelby

CHICAGO (WEST)

	AB	H	2B	3B	HR	R	RBI	BA
R. Law, of	18	7	1	0	0	1	0	.389
C. Fisk, c	17	3	1	0	0	0	0	.176
T. Paciorek, 1b, of	16	4	0	0	0	1	1	.250
H. Baines, of	16	2	0	0	0	0	0	.125
G. Luzinski, dh	15	2	1	0	0	0	0	.133
J. Cruz, 2b	12	4	0	0	0	0	0	.333
V. Law, 3b	11	2	0	0	0	0	1	.182
R. Kittle, of	7	2	1	0	0	1	0	.286
S. Fletcher, ss	7	0	0	0	0	0	0	.000
J. Dybzinski, ss	4	1	0	0	0	0	0	.250
M. Squires, 1b	4	0	0	0	0	0	0	.000
G. Walker, 1b	3	1	0	0	0	0	0	.333
J. Hairston, of	3	0	0	0	0	0	0	.000
A. Rodriguez, 3b	0	0	0	0	0	0	0	—

Errors: J. Hairston, V. Law, A. Rodriguez
Stolen Bases: J. Cruz (2), R. Law (2)

Individual Pitching

BALTIMORE (EAST)

	W	L	ERA	IP	H	BB	SO	SV
M. Boddicker	1	0	0.00	9	5	3	14	0
S. McGregor	0	1	1.35	6.2	6	3	2	0
S. Davis	0	0	0.00	6	5	2	2	0
T. Martinez	1	0	0.00	6	5	3	5	0
M. Flanagan	1	0	1.80	5	5	0	1	0
S. Stewart	0	0	0.00	4.1	2	1	2	1

CHICAGO (WEST)

	W	L	ERA	IP	H	BB	SO	SV
B. Burns	0	1	0.96	9.1	6	5	8	0
L. Hoyt	1	0	1.00	9	5	0	4	0
F. Bannister	0	1	4.50	6	5	1	5	0
R. Dotson	0	1	10.80	5	6	3	3	0
D. Tidrow	0	0	3.00	3	1	3	3	0
D. Lamp	0	0	0.00	2	0	2	1	0
S. Barojas	0	0	18.00	1	4	0	0	0
J. Agosto	0	0	0.00	0.1	0	0	0	0
J. Koosman	0	0	54.00	0.1	1	2	0	0

1983 WORLD SERIES

Baltimore (A.L.) defeats Philadelphia (N.L.) 4 games to 1

LINE SCORES			R	H	E	PITCHERS (innings pitched)	HOME RUNS (men on)	HIGHLIGHTS
GAME 1 - OCTOBER 11								Homers by Morgan and Maddox offset Dwyer's first-inning shot to give the Phillies a 1-0 lead in the Series.
PHI	N	000 001 010	2	5	0	**Denny** (7.2), Holland (1.2) **SV**	Morgan, Maddox	
BAL	A	100 000 000	1	5	1	**McGregor** (8), Stewart (0.2) T. Martinez (0.1)	Dwyer	
GAME 2 - OCTOBER 12								Boddicker pitched a masterful three-hitter to even the Series. Lowenstein rapped out three hits to lead the Baltimore attack.
PHI	N	000 100 000	1	3	0	**Hudson** (4.1), Hernandez (0.2), Andersen (2), Reed (1)		
BAL	A	000 030 10x	4	9	1	**Boddicker** (9)	Lowenstein	
GAME 3 - OCTOBER 14								DeJesus's error in the seventh let in the game-winning run as the Orioles came back from a 2-0 deficit. Dempsey hit two doubles and shut down the Phils' running game in this pivotal contest.
BAL	A	000 001 200	3	6	1	Flanagan (4), **Palmer** (2), Stewart (2), T. Martinez (1) **SV**	Ford	
PHI	N	011 000 000	2	8	2	**Carlton** (6.2), Holland (2.1)	Matthews, Morgan	
GAME 4 - OCTOBER 15								Dauer broke a 1-for-25 slump with three hits and three RBIs and manager Altobelli used four consecutive pinch-hitters to forge the go-ahead rally in the sixth as Baltimore took a commanding three games to one edge.
BAL	A	000 202 100	5	10	1	**Davis** (5), Stewart (2.1) T. Martinez (1.2) **SV**		
PHI	N	000 120 001	4	10	0	**Denny** (5.1), Hernandez (0.1), Reed (1.1), Andersen (2)		
GAME 5 - OCTOBER 16								McGregor scattered five hits and Murray blasted two homers as the Orioles won their third straight on the road to clinch the Series. Dempsey homered and doubled, and was named the series MVP.
BAL	A	011 210 000	5	5	0	**McGregor** (9)	Murray, Dempsey, Murray (1 on)	
PHI	N	000 000 000	0	5	1	**Hudson** (4.0), Bystrom (1), Hernandez (3)		

Team totals

		W	AB	H	2B	3B	HR	R	RBI	BA	BB	SO	ERA
BAL	A	4	164	35	8	0	6	18	17	.213	10	37	1.60
PHI	N	1	159	31	4	1	4	9	9	.195	7	29	3.48

Individual Batting

BALTIMORE (A.L.)

	AB	H	2B	3B	HR	R	RBI	BA
E. Murray, 1b	20	5	0	0	2	2	3	.250
R. Dauer, 2b, 3b	19	4	1	0	0	2	3	.211
C. Ripken, ss	18	3	0	0	0	2	1	.167
T. Cruz, 3b	16	2	0	0	0	1	0	.125
R. Dempsey, c	13	5	4	0	1	3	2	.385
J. Lowenstein, of	13	5	1	0	1	2	1	.385
D. Ford, of	12	2	0	0	1	1	1	.167
A. Bumbry, of	11	1	1	0	0	0	1	.091
J. Shelby, of	9	4	0	0	0	1	1	.444
J. Dwyer, of	8	3	1	0	1	3	1	.375
G. Roenicke, of	7	0	0	0	0	0	0	.000
S. McGregor, p	5	0	0	0	0	0	0	.000
M. Boddicker, p	3	0	0	0	0	0	1	.000
S. Davis, p	2	0	0	0	0	0	0	.000
J. Nolan, c	2	0	0	0	0	0	0	.000
S. Stewart, p	2	0	0	0	0	0	0	.000
B. Ayala	1	1	0	0	0	1	1	1.000
M. Flanagan, p	1	0	0	0	0	0	0	.000
L. Sakata, 2b	1	0	0	0	0	0	0	.000
K. Singleton	1	0	0	0	0	0	1	.000
T. Landrum, of	0	0	0	0	0	0	0	—

Errors: T. Cruz (2), J. Lowenstein, E. Murray
Stolen Bases: T. Landrum

PHILADELPHIA (N.L.)

	AB	H	2B	3B	HR	R	RBI	BA
M. Schmidt, 3b	20	1	0	0	0	0	0	.050
J. Morgan, 2b	19	5	0	1	2	3	2	.263
P. Rose, 1b, of	16	5	1	0	0	1	1	.313
G. Matthews, of	16	4	0	0	1	1	1	.250
I. DeJesus, ss	16	2	0	0	0	0	0	.125
B. Diaz, c	15	5	1	0	0	1	0	.333
G. Maddox, of	12	3	1	0	1	1	1	.250
T. Perez, 1b	10	2	0	0	0	0	0	.200
S. Lezcano, of	8	1	0	0	0	0	0	.125
G. Gross, of	6	0	0	0	0	0	0	.000
J. Denny, p	5	1	0	0	0	1	1	.200
J. Lefebvre, of	5	1	1	0	0	0	2	.200
S. Carlton, p	3	0	0	0	0	0	0	.000
V. Hayes, of	3	0	0	0	0	0	0	.000
O. Virgil, c	2	1	0	0	0	0	1	.500
C. Hudson, p	2	0	0	0	0	0	0	.000
J. Samuel	1	0	0	0	0	0	0	.000
B. Dernier	0	0	0	0	0	1	0	—

Errors: I. DeJesus, B. Diaz, M. Schmidt
Stolen Bases: J. Morgan

Individual Pitching

BALTIMORE (A.L.)

	W	L	ERA	IP	H	BB	SO	SV
S. McGregor	1	1	1.06	17	9	2	12	0
M. Boddicker	1	0	0.00	9	3	0	6	0
S. Davis	1	0	5.40	5	6	1	3	0
S. Stewart	0	0	0.00	5	2	2	6	0
M. Flanagan	0	0	4.50	4	6	1	1	0
T. Martinez	0	0	3.00	3	3	0	0	2
J. Palmer	1	0	0.00	2	2	1	1	0

PHILADELPHIA (N.L.)

	W	L	ERA	IP	H	BB	SO	SV
J. Denny	1	1	3.46	13	12	3	9	0
C. Hudson	0	2	8.64	8.1	9	1	6	0
S. Carlton	0	1	2.70	6.2	5	3	7	0
L. Andersen	0	0	2.25	4	4	0	1	0
G. Hernandez	0	0	0.00	4	0	1	4	0
A. Holland	0	0	0.00	3.2	1	0	5	1
R. Reed	0	0	2.70	3.1	4	2	4	0
M. Bystrom	0	0	0.00	1	0	0	1	0

1984 NATIONAL LEAGUE CHAMPIONSHIP SERIES

San Diego (West) defeats Chicago (East) 3 games to 2

LINE SCORES			R	H	E	PITCHERS (innings pitched)	HOME RUNS (men on)	HIGHLIGHTS
GAME 1 - OCTOBER 2								In the first playoff appearance for both clubs, the Cubs set NL LCS records for runs, hits, home runs, and total bases in battering the Padres. A strike by major league umpires caused the league to call in college and former pro umps to work the games.
SD	W	000 000 000	0	6	1	**Show** (4), Harris (2), Booker (2)		
CHI	E	203 062 00x	13	16	0	**Sutcliffe** (7), Brusstar (2)	Dernier, Matthews, Sutcliffe, Matthews (2 on), Cey	
GAME 2 - OCTOBER 3								Trout scattered five hits before yielding to Lee Smith, who nailed down the win. Sandberg and Moreland each had two hits for the Cubs.
SD	W	000 101 000	2	5	0	**Thurmond** (3.2), Hawkins (1.1), Dravecky (2), Lefferts (1)		
CHI	E	102 100 00x	4	8	1	**Trout** (8.1), Smith (0.2) **SV**		
GAME 3 - OCTOBER 4								Templeton's two-run double in the fifth gave the Padres their first lead of the series, and McReynolds's homer in the sixth put the game away. Whitson allowed five hits over eight innings to keep San Diego's hopes alive.
CHI	E	010 000 000	1	5	0	**Eckersley** (5.1), Frazier (1.2), Stoddard (1)		
SD	W	000 034 00x	7	11	0	**Whitson** (8), Gossage (1)	McReynolds (2 on)	
GAME 4 - OCTOBER 6								Garvey capped a four-for-five, five RBI game with his two run homer in the bottom of the ninth to win one of the most dramatic LCS games ever played.
CHI	E	000 300 020	5	8	1	Sanderson (4.2), Brusstar (1.1), Stoddard (1), **Smith** (1.1)	Davis (1 on), Durham	
SD	W	002 010 202	7	11	0	Lollar (4.1), Hawkins (0.2), Dravecky (2), Gossage (1), **Lefferts** (1)	Garvey (1 on)	
GAME 5 - OCTOBER 7								The Padres became the first National League team to come back from two games down to win the series. Durham's error allowed Martinez to score the tying run and then three straight singles capped the four run 7th inning rally that won San Diego's first pennant.
CHI	E	210 000 000	3	5	1	**Sutcliffe** (6.1), Trout (0.2), Brusstar (1)	Durham (1 on), Davis	
SD	W	000 002 40x	6	8	0	Show (1.1), Hawkins (1.2), Dravecky (2), **Lefferts** (2), Gossage (2) **SV**		

Team totals

		W	AB	H	2B	3B	HR	R	RBI	BA	BB	SO	ERA
SD	W	3	155	41	5	1	2	22	20	.265	14	22	5.23
CHI	E	2	162	42	11	0	9	26	25	.259	20	28	4.25

Individual Batting

SAN DIEGO (WEST)

	AB	H	2B	3B	HR	R	RBI	BA
S. Garvey, 1b	20	8	1	0	1	1	7	.400
T. Gwynn, of	19	7	3	0	0	6	3	.368
A. Wiggins, 2b	19	6	0	0	0	4	1	.316
T. Kennedy, c	18	4	0	0	0	2	1	.222
C. Martinez, of	17	3	0	0	0	1	0	.176
G. Templeton, ss	15	5	1	0	0	2	2	.333
G. Nettles, 3b	14	2	0	0	0	1	2	.143
K. McReynolds, of	10	3	0	0	1	2	4	.300
L. Salazar, 3b, of	5	1	0	1	0	0	0	.200
B. Brown, of	4	0	0	0	0	1	0	.000
E. Whitson, p	3	0	0	0	0	0	0	.000
T. Flannery	2	1	0	0	0	2	0	.500
K. Bevacqua	2	0	0	0	0	0	0	.000
M. Ramirez	2	0	0	0	0	0	0	.000
C. Summers	2	0	0	0	0	0	0	.000
M. Thurmond, p	1	1	0	0	0	0	0	1.000
T. Lollar, p	1	0	0	0	0	0	0	.000
E. Show, p	1	0	0	0	0	0	0	.000

Errors: G. Templeton
Stolen Bases: B. Brown, G. Templeton

CHICAGO (EAST)

	AB	H	2B	3B	HR	R	RBI	BA
L. Durham, 1b	20	3	0	0	2	2	4	.150
R. Sandberg, 2b	19	7	2	0	0	3	2	.368
R. Cey, 3b	19	3	1	0	1	3	3	.158
J. Davis, c	18	7	2	0	2	3	6	.389
K. Moreland, of	18	6	2	0	0	3	2	.333
B. Dernier, of	17	4	2	0	1	5	1	.235
L. Bowa, ss	15	3	1	0	0	1	1	.200
G. Matthews, of	15	3	0	0	2	4	5	.200
R. Sutcliffe, p	6	3	0	0	1	1	1	.500
S. Trout, p	2	1	0	0	0	0	0	.500
T. Bosley	2	0	0	0	0	0	0	.000
D. Eckersley, p	2	0	0	0	0	0	0	.000
S. Sanderson, p	2	0	0	0	0	0	0	.000
H. Cotto, of	1	1	0	0	0	1	0	1.000
S. Lake, c	1	1	1	0	0	0	0	1.000
W. Brusstar, p	1	0	0	0	0	0	0	.000
R. Hebner	1	0	0	0	0	0	0	.000
D. Lopes, of	1	0	0	0	0	0	0	.000
T. Veryzer, 3b, ss	1	0	0	0	0	0	0	.000
G. Woods, of	1	0	0	0	0	0	0	.000

Errors: L. Durham, R. Sandberg, S. Trout
Stolen Bases: R. Sandberg (3), B. Dernier (2), G. Matthews

Individual Pitching

SAN DIEGO (WEST)

	W	L	ERA	IP	H	BB	SO	SV
E. Whitson	1	0	1.13	8	5	2	6	0
D. Dravecky	0	0	0.00	6	2	0	5	0
E. Show	0	1	13.50	5.1	8	4	2	0
T. Lollar	0	0	6.23	4.1	3	4	3	0
G. Gossage	0	0	4.50	4	5	1	5	1
C. Lefferts	2	0	0.00	4	1	1	1	0
A. Hawkins	0	0	0.00	3.2	0	2	1	0
M. Thurmond	0	1	9.82	3.2	7	2	1	0
G. Booker	0	0	0.00	2	2	1	2	0
G. Harris	0	0	31.50	2	9	3	2	0

CHICAGO (EAST)

	W	L	ERA	IP	H	BB	SO	SV
R. Sutcliffe	1	1	3.38	13.1	9	8	10	0
S. Trout	1	0	2.00	9	5	3	3	0
D. Eckersley	0	1	8.44	5.1	9	0	0	0
W. Brusstar	0	0	0.00	4.2	6	0	1	0
S. Sanderson	0	0	5.79	4.2	6	1	2	0
L. Smith	0	1	9.00	2	3	0	3	1
T. Stoddard	0	0	4.50	2	1	2	2	0
G. Frazier	0	0	10.80	1.2	2	0	1	0

1984 AMERICAN LEAGUE CHAMPIONSHIP SERIES

Detroit (East) defeats Kansas City (West) 3 games to 0

LINE SCORES					PITCHERS (innings pitched)	HOME RUNS (men on)	HIGHLIGHTS
GAME 1 - OCTOBER 2							Trammell led the Detroit attack with three hits, including a triple and a solo homer, and three RBIs to support Morris's five-hitter.
DET E 200 110 121	8	14	0		**Morris** (7), Hernandez (2)	Herndon, Trammell, Parrish	
KC W 000 000 100	1	5	1		**Black** (5), Huismann (2.2), M. Jones (1.1)		
GAME 2 - OCTOBER 3							The Royals rallied from three runs down on RBI pinch hits by Iorg and McRae in the seventh and eighth, but Grubb's two-run double in the eleventh gave the Tigers the victory.
DET E 201 000 000 02	5	8	1		Petry (7), Hernandez (1), **Lopez** (3)	Gibson	
KC W 000 100 110 00	3	10	3		Saberhagen (8), **Quisenberry** (3)		
GAME 3 - OCTOBER 5							Leibrandt allowed just three hits in eight innings, but Wilcox was even better, giving up two before yielding to Hernandez, who locked up Detroit's first pennant in sixteen years.
KC W 000 000 000	0	3	3		**Leibrandt** (8)		
DET E 010 000 00x	1	3	0		**Wilcox** (8), Hernandez (1) **SV**		

Team totals

	W	AB	H	2B	3B	HR	R	RBI	BA	BB	SO	ERA
DET E	3	107	25	4	1	4	14	14	.234	8	17	1.24
KC W	0	106	18	1	1	0	4	4	.170	6	21	3.86

Individual Batting

DETROIT (EAST)

	AB	H	2B	3B	HR	R	RBI	BA
L. Whitaker, 2b	14	2	0	0	0	3	0	.143
C. Lemon, of	13	0	0	0	0	1	0	.000
K. Gibson, of	12	5	1	0	1	2	2	.417
L. Parrish, c	12	3	1	0	1	1	3	.250
A. Trammell, ss	11	4	0	1	1	2	3	.364
D. Evans, 1b, 3b	10	3	1	0	0	1	1	.300
B. Garbey, dh	9	3	0	0	0	1	0	.333
M. Castillo, 3b	8	2	0	0	0	0	2	.250
L. Herndon, of	5	1	0	0	1	1	1	.200
R. Jones, of	5	0	0	0	0	1	0	.000
J. Grubb	4	1	1	0	0	0	2	.250
T. Brookens, 2b, 3b	2	0	0	0	0	0	0	.000
D. Bergman, 1b	1	1	0	0	0	1	0	1.000
R. Kuntz, of	1	0	0	0	0	0	0	.000
D. Baker, ss	0	0	0	0	0	0	0	—

Errors: T. Brookens

Stolen Bases: D. Bergman, M. Castillo, D. Evans, K. Gibson

KANSAS CITY (WEST)

	AB	H	2B	3B	HR	R	RBI	BA
G. Brett, 3b	13	3	0	0	0	0	0	.231
W. Wilson, of	13	2	0	0	0	0	0	.154
D. Motley, of	12	2	0	0	0	0	1	.167
F. White, 2b	12	1	0	0	0	1	0	.083
D. Slaught, c	11	4	0	0	0	0	0	.364
S. Balboni, 1b	10	1	0	0	0	0	0	.100
J. Orta, dh	10	1	0	1	0	1	1	.100
O. Concepcion, ss	7	0	0	0	0	0	0	.000
P. Sheridan, of	6	0	0	0	0	1	0	.000
L. Jones, of	5	1	0	0	0	1	0	.200
H. McRae	2	2	1	0	0	0	1	1.000
D. Iorg	2	1	0	0	0	0	1	.500
B. Biancalana, ss	1	0	0	0	0	0	0	.000
U. Washington	1	0	0	0	0	0	0	.000
J. Wathan	1	0	0	0	0	0	0	.000
G. Pryor, 3b	0	0	0	0	0	0	0	—

Errors: D. Slaught (3), S. Balboni, O. Concepcion, B. Saberhagen, P. Sheridan

Individual Pitching

DETROIT (EAST)

	W	L	ERA	IP	H	BB	SO	SV
M. Wilcox	1	0	0.00	8	2	2	8	0
J. Morris	1	0	1.29	7	5	1	4	0
D. Petry	0	0	2.57	7	4	1	4	0
G. Hernandez	0	0	2.25	4	3	1	3	1
A. Lopez	1	0	0.00	3	4	1	2	0

KANSAS CITY (WEST)

	W	L	ERA	IP	H	BB	SO	SV
C. Leibrandt	0	1	1.13	8	3	4	6	0
B. Saberhagen	0	0	2.25	8	6	1	5	0
B. Black	0	1	7.20	5	7	1	3	0
D. Quisenberry	0	1	3.00	3	2	1	1	0
M. Huismann	0	0	10.13	2.2	6	1	2	0
M. Jones	0	0	6.75	1.1	1	0	0	0

1984 WORLD SERIES

Detroit (A.L.) defeats San Diego (N.L.) 4 games to 1

LINE SCORES			R	H	E	PITCHERS (innings pitched)	HOME RUNS (men on)	HIGHLIGHTS
GAME 1 - OCTOBER 9								
DET	A	100 020 000	3	8	0	Morris (9)	Herndon (1 on)	Herndon's two-run homer in the fifth powered the Tigers to the win. San Diego's best hope to even the score was cut off when Gibson threw Bevacqua out as he tried to stretch a leadoff double into a triple in the seventh.
SD	N	200 000 000	2	8	1	Thurmond (5), Hawkins (2.2), Dravecky (1.1)		
GAME 2 - OCTOBER 10								
DET	A	300 000 000	3	7	3	Petry (4.1), Lopez (0.2), Scherrer (1.1) Bair (0.2), Hernandez (1)		Bevacqua's three-run homer in the fifth brought the Padres back from an early deficit to even the Series. Hawkins allowed one hit in five and a third innings of relief to earn the victory.
SD	N	100 130 00x	5	11	0	Whitson (0.2), Hawkins (5.1), Lefferts (3) SV	Bevacqua (2 on)	
GAME 3 - OCTOBER 12								
SD	N	001 000 100	2	10	0	Lollar (1.2), Booker (1), Harris (5.1)		San Diego pitchers walked eleven Tigers to tie a Series record in a slow-moving, sloppily played contest. Castillo was the surprise hero for Detroit with his two-run homer. Detroit left 14 runners on base, and the Padres stranded 10.
DET	A	041 000 00x	5	7	0	Wilcox (6), Scherrer (0.2), Hernandez (2.1) SV	Castillo (1 on)	
GAME 4 - OCTOBER 13								
SD	N	010 000 001	2	5	2	Show (2.2), Dravecky (3.1), Lefferts (1) Gossage (1)	Kennedy	A pair of two-run homers by Trammell provided Morris with all the scoring he needed to back up his five-hitter.
DET	A	202 000 00x	4	7	0	Morris (9)	Trammell (1 on), Trammell (1 on)	
GAME 5 - OCTOBER 14								
SD	N	001 200 010	4	10	1	Thurmond (0.1), Hawkins (4), Lefferts (2), Gossage (1.2)	Bevacqua	Gibson cracked two homers and drove in five as the Tigers won the Series. He also scored the run that put Detroit ahead to stay in the fifth on a popup fielded by Wiggins in short right field. Detroit battered Padre starters for a 13.94 ERA in the Series as Sparky Anderson became the first to manage a World Series winner in both leagues.
DET	A	300 010 13x	8	11	1	Petry (3.2), Scherrer (1), Lopez (2.1) Hernandez (2) SV	Gibson (1 on), Parrish, Gibson (2 on)	

Team totals

		W	AB	H	2B	3B	HR	R	RBI	BA	BB	SO	ERA
DET	A	4	158	40	4	0	7	23	23	.253	24	27	3.07
SD	N	1	166	44	7	0	3	15	14	.265	11	26	4.71

Individual Batting

DETROIT (A.L.)

	AB	H	2B	3B	HR	R	RBI	BA
A. Trammell, ss	20	9	1	0	2	5	6	.450
K. Gibson, of	18	6	0	0	2	4	7	.333
L. Parrish, c	18	5	1	0	1	3	2	.278
L. Whitaker, 2b	18	5	2	0	0	6	0	.278
C. Lemon, of	17	5	0	0	0	1	1	.294
L. Herndon, of	15	5	0	0	1	1	3	.333
D. Evans, 1b, 3b	15	1	0	0	0	1	1	.067
B. Garbey, dh	12	0	0	0	0	0	0	.000
M. Castillo, 3b	9	3	0	0	1	2	2	.333
D. Bergman, 1b	5	0	0	0	0	0	0	.000
J. Grubb, dh	3	1	0	0	0	0	0	.333
T. Brookens, 3b	3	0	0	0	0	0	0	.000
R. Jones, of	3	0	0	0	0	0	0	.000
H. Johnson	1	0	0	0	0	0	0	.000
R. Kuntz	1	0	0	0	0	0	1	.000

Errors: K. Gibson (2), L. Parrish, A. Trammell

Stolen Bases: K. Gibson (3), C. Lemon (2), L. Parrish, A. Trammell

SAN DIEGO (N.L.)

	AB	H	2B	3B	HR	R	RBI	BA
A. Wiggins, 2b	22	8	1	0	0	2	1	.364
S. Garvey, 1b	20	4	2	0	0	2	2	.200
G. Templeton, ss	19	6	1	0	0	1	0	.316
T. Gwynn, of	19	5	0	0	0	1	0	.263
T. Kennedy, c	19	4	1	0	1	2	3	.211
K. Bevacqua, dh	17	7	2	0	2	4	4	.412
C. Martinez, of	17	3	0	0	0	0	0	.176
B. Brown, of	15	1	0	0	0	1	2	.067
G. Nettles, 3b	12	3	0	0	0	2	2	.250
L. Salazar, 3b, of	3	1	0	0	0	0	0	.333
B. Bochy	1	1	0	0	0	0	0	1.000
T. Flannery, 2b	1	1	0	0	0	0	0	1.000
C. Summers	1	0	0	0	0	0	0	.000
R. Roenicke, of	0	0	0	0	0	0	0	—

Errors: A. Wiggins (2), T. Gwynn, C. Martinez

Stolen Bases: T. Gwynn, A. Wiggins

Individual Pitching

DETROIT (A.L.)

	W	L	ERA	IP	H	BB	SO	SV
J. Morris	2	0	2.00	18	13	3	13	0
D. Petry	0	1	9.00	8	14	5	4	0
M. Wilcox	1	0	1.50	6	7	2	4	0
G. Hernandez	0	0	1.69	5.1	4	0	0	2
A. Lopez	1	0	0.00	3	1	1	4	0
B. Scherrer	0	0	3.00	3	5	0	0	0
D. Bair	0	0	0.00	0.2	0	0	1	0

SAN DIEGO (N.L.)

	W	L	ERA	IP	H	BB	SO	SV
A. Hawkins	1	1	0.75	12	4	6	4	0
C. Lefferts	0	0	0.00	6	2	1	7	1
G. Harris	0	0	0.00	5.1	3	3	5	0
M. Thurmond	0	1	10.13	5.1	12	3	2	0
D. Dravecky	0	0	0.00	4.2	3	1	5	0
G. Gossage	0	0	13.50	2.2	3	1	2	0
E. Show	0	1	10.13	2.2	4	1	2	0
T. Lollar	0	1	21.60	1.2	4	4	0	0
G. Booker	0	0	9.00	1	0	4	0	0
E. Whitson	0	0	40.50	0.2	5	0	0	0

1985 NATIONAL LEAGUE CHAMPIONSHIP SERIES

St. Louis (East) defeats Los Angeles (West) 4 games to 2

LINE SCORES						PITCHERS (innings pitched)	HOME RUNS (men on)	HIGHLIGHTS
GAME 1 - OCTOBER 9								Uncharacteristic Cardinal fielding lapses led to all four Dodger runs as Los Angeles chased St. Louis's ace Tudor, winner of twenty of his last twenty-one decisions.
STL	**E**	000 000 100	1	8	1	**Tudor** (5.2), Dayley (0.1), Campbell (1.0), Worrell (1)		
LA	**W**	000 103 00x	4	8	0	**Valenzuela** (6.1), Niedenfuer (2.2) **SV**		
GAME 2 - OCTOBER 10								Every Dodger starter had at least one hit, battering five Cardinal pitchers to take a 2-0 lead in the series.
STL	**E**	001 000 001	2	8	1	**Andujar** (4.1), Horton (1.1), Campbell (0.1), Dayley (1), Lahti (1)		
LA	**W**	003 212 00x	8	13	1	**Hershiser** (9)	Brock (1 on)	
GAME 3 - OCTOBER 12								The St. Louis running game revived with the move to Busch Stadium's artificial surface; their first three runs were aided by three stolen bases and two errors on pickoff attempts.
LA	**W**	000 100 100	2	7	2	**Welch** (2.2), Honeycutt (1.1), Diaz (2), Howell (2)		
STL	**E**	220 000 00x	4	8	0	**Cox** (6.0), Horton (0.2), Worrell (1.1), Dayley (1) **SV**	Herr	
GAME 4 - OCTOBER 13								The Cardinals sent fourteen men to the plate in the home second, scoring an LCS-record nine runs on eight singles, two walks, and an error.
LA	**W**	000 000 110	2	5	2	**Reuss** (1.2), Honeycutt (0), Castillo (5.1), Diaz (1)	Madlock	
STL	**E**	090 110 01x	12	15	0	**Tudor** (7), Horton (1), Campbell (1)		
GAME 5 - OCTOBER 14								Ozzie Smith's one-out homer in the ninth (his first ever from the left side of the plate) was the game-winning blow.
LA	**W**	000 200 000	2	5	1	Valenzuela (8), **Niedenfuer** (0.1)	Madlock (1 on)	
STL	**E**	200 000 001	3	5	1	Forsch (3.1), Dayley (2.2), Worrell (2), **Lahti** (1)	Smith	
GAME 6 - OCTOBER 16								Marshall's eighth-inning home run gave the Dodgers a 5-4 lead. But with two out in the ninth and runners on second and third, the Dodgers chose to pitch to Jack Clark. Clark's towering homer gave the Cardinals the pennant.
STL	**E**	001 000 303	7	12	1	Andujar (6), **Worrell** (2), Dayley (1) **SV**	Clark (2 on)	
LA	**W**	110 020 010	5	8	0	Hershiser (6.1), **Niedenfuer** (2.2)	Madlock, Marshall	

Team totals

		W	AB	H	2B	3B	HR	R	RBI	BA	BB	SO	ERA
STL	**E**	4	201	56	10	1	3	29	26	.279	30	34	3.46
LA	**W**	2	197	46	12	1	5	23	23	.234	19	31	3.51

Individual Batting

ST. LOUIS (EAST)

	AB	H	2B	3B	HR	R	RBI	BA
W. McGee, of	26	7	1	0	0	6	3	.269
T. Pendleton, 3b	24	5	1	0	0	2	4	.208
O. Smith, ss	23	10	1	1	1	4	3	.435
J. Clark, 1b	21	8	0	0	1	4	4	.381
T. Herr, 2b	21	7	4	0	1	2	6	.333
D. Porter, c	15	4	1	0	0	1	0	.267
T. Landrum, of	14	6	0	0	0	2	4	.429
V. Coleman, of	14	4	0	0	0	2	1	.286
C. Cedeno, of	12	2	1	0	0	2	0	.167
A. Van Slyke, of	11	1	0	0	0	1	1	.091
J. Andujar, p	4	1	1	0	0	1	0	.250
J. Tudor, p	4	0	0	0	0	1	0	.000
T. Nieto, c	3	0	0	0	0	1	0	.000
K. Dayley, p	2	1	0	0	0	0	0	.500
S. Braun	2	0	0	0	0	0	0	.000
D. Cox, p	2	0	0	0	0	0	0	.000
M. Jorgensen	2	0	0	0	0	0	0	.000
B. Harper	1	0	0	0	0	0	0	.000

Errors: J. Andujar (2), T. Pendleton, D. Porter

Stolen Bases: W. McGee (2), V. Coleman, T. Herr, T. Landrum, O. Smith

LOS ANGELES (WEST)

	AB	H	2B	3B	HR	R	RBI	BA
B. Madlock, 3b	24	8	1	0	3	5	7	.333
M. Marshall, of	23	5	2	0	1	1	3	.217
S. Sax, 2b	20	6	3	0	0	1	1	.300
P. Guerrero, of	20	5	1	0	0	2	4	.250
K. Landreaux, of	18	7	3	0	0	4	2	.389
M. Duncan, ss	18	4	2	1	0	2	1	.222
M. Scioscia, c	16	4	0	0	0	2	1	.250
E. Cabell, 1b	13	1	0	0	0	1	0	.077
G. Brock, 1b	12	1	0	0	1	2	2	.083
O. Hershiser, p	7	2	0	0	0	1	1	.286
C. Maldonado, of	7	1	0	0	0	0	1	.143
F. Valenzuela, p	5	1	0	0	0	0	0	.200
D. Anderson, 3b, ss	5	0	0	0	0	1	0	.000
B. Castillo, p	2	0	0	0	0	0	0	.000
S. Yeager, c	2	0	0	0	0	0	0	.000
L. Matuszek, 1b, of	1	1	0	0	0	1	0	1.000
B. Bailor, 3b	1	0	0	0	0	0	0	.000
J. Johnstone	1	0	0	0	0	0	0	.000
T. Niedenfuer, p	1	0	0	0	0	0	0	.000
B. Welch, p	1	0	0	0	0	0	0	.000
T. Whitfield	0	0	0	0	0	0	0	—

Errors: M. Duncan, C. Maldonado, J. Reuss, M. Scioscia, F. Valenzuela, B. Welch

Stolen Bases: P. Guerrero (2), M. Duncan, B. Madlock

Individual Pitching

ST. LOUIS (EAST)

	W	L	ERA	IP	H	BB	SO	SV
J. Tudor	1	1	2.84	12.2	10	3	8	0
J. Andujar	0	1	6.97	10.1	14	4	9	0
T. Worrell	1	0	1.42	6.1	4	2	3	0
D. Cox	1	0	3.00	6	4	5	4	0
K. Dayley	0	0	0.00	6	2	1	3	2
B. Forsch	0	0	5.40	3.1	3	2	0	0
R. Horton	0	0	9.00	3	4	2	1	0
B. Campbell	0	0	0.00	2.1	3	0	2	0
J. Lahti	1	0	0.00	2	2	0	1	0

LOS ANGELES (WEST)

	W	L	ERA	IP	H	BB	SO	SV
O. Hershiser	1	0	3.52	15.1	17	6	5	0
F. Valenzuela	1	0	1.88	14.1	11	10	13	0
T. Niedenfuer	0	2	6.35	5.2	5	2	5	1
B. Castillo	0	0	3.38	5.1	4	2	4	0
C. Diaz	0	0	3.00	3	5	1	2	0
B. Welch	0	1	6.75	2.2	5	6	2	0
K. Howell	0	0	0.00	2	0	0	2	0
J. Reuss	0	1	10.80	1.2	5	1	0	0
R. Honeycutt	0	0	13.50	1.1	4	2	1	0

1985 AMERICAN LEAGUE CHAMPIONSHIP SERIES

Kansas City (West) defeats Toronto (East) 4 games to 3

LINE SCORES					PITCHERS (innings pitched)	HOME RUNS (men on)	HIGHLIGHTS
GAME 1 - OCTOBER 8							Stieb scattered three hits over eight innings, striking out eight, as the Blue Jays took the first ALCS game ever played in Canada.
KC	**W** 000 000 001	1	5	1	**Leibrandt** (2.0), Farr (2), Gubicza (3), Jackson (1)		
TOR	**E** 023 100 00x	6	11	0	**Stieb** (8), Henke (1)		
GAME 2 - OCTOBER 9							The Royals fought back on Sheridan's pinch homer in the ninth and White's disputed single in the tenth. But singles by Fernandez, Moseby and Oliver provided the winning runs.
KC	**W** 002 100 001 1	5	10	3	Black (7), **Quisenberry** (2.2)	Wilson (1 on), Sheridan	
TOR	**E** 000 102 010 2	6	10	0	Key (3.1), Lamp (3.2), Lavelle (0), **Henke** (3)		
GAME 3 - OCTOBER 11							George Brett's extraordinary display (four-for-four, four runs, three RBI, eleven total bases) drove the Royals past the Blue Jays despite a shaky performance by their 20-game winner Saberhagen.
TOR	**E** 000 050 000	5	13	1	Alexander (5.0), Lamp (2), **Clancy** (1)	Barfield (1 on), Mulliniks (1 on)	
KC	**W** 100 112 01x	6	10	1	Saberhagen (4.1), Black (0.1), **Farr** (4.1)	Brett, Brett (1 on), Sundberg	
GAME 4 - OCTOBER 12							Oliver's ninth-inning double drove in the winning runs, as Quisenberry failed to hold the Blue Jays in check for the second time in the series.
TOR	**E** 000 000 003	3	7	0	Stieb (6.2), **Henke** (2.1)		
KC	**W** 000 001 000	1	2	0	**Leibrandt** (8.0), Quisenberry (1)		
GAME 5 - OCTOBER 13							Danny Jackson's eight-hit shutout helped the Royals stave off elimination. Lonnie Smith snapped a 2-for-14 slump with three hits, scoring his first run.
TOR	**E** 000 000 000	0	8	0	**Key** (5.1), Acker (2.2)		
KC	**W** 110 000 00x	2	8	0	**Jackson** (9)		
GAME 6 - OCTOBER 15							Brett's third home run of the series, all of them off Alexander, put the Royals ahead to stay in the fifth to force a seventh game.
KC	**W** 101 012 000	5	8	1	**Gubicza** (5.1), Black (3.1), Quisenberry (0.1) **SV**	Brett	
TOR	**E** 101 001 000	3	8	2	**Alexander** (5.1), Lamp (3.2)		
GAME 7 - OCTOBER 16							Sundberg's bases-loaded triple broke open a 2-1 game and gave the Royals their third straight win and the AL pennant.
KC	**W** 010 104 000	6	8	0	Saberhagen (3), **Leibrandt** (5.1) Quisenberry (0.2)	Sheridan	
TOR	**E** 000 010 001	2	8	1	**Stieb** (5.2), Acker (3.1)		

Team totals

		W	AB	H	2B	3B	HR	R	RBI	BA	BB	SO	ERA
KC	**W**	4	227	51	9	1	7	26	26	.225	22	51	3.16
TOR	**E**	3	242	65	19	0	2	25	23	.269	16	37	3.77

Individual Batting

KANSAS CITY (WEST)

	AB	H	2B	3B	HR	R	RBI	BA
W. Wilson, of	29	9	0	0	1	5	2	.310
L. Smith, of	28	7	2	0	0	2	1	.250
F. White, 2b	25	5	0	0	0	1	3	.200
S. Balboni, 1b	25	3	0	0	0	1	1	.120
J. Sundberg, c	24	4	1	1	1	3	6	.167
G. Brett, 3b	23	8	2	0	3	6	5	.348
H. McRae, dh	23	6	2	0	0	1	3	.261
P. Sheridan, of	20	3	0	0	2	4	3	.150
B. Biancalana, ss	18	4	1	0	0	2	1	.222
J. Orta, dh	5	0	0	0	0	0	0	.000
D. Motley, of	3	1	0	0	0	1	1	.333
D. Iorg	2	1	1	0	0	0	0	.500
O. Concepcion, ss	1	0	0	0	0	0	0	.000
J. Quirk	1	0	0	0	0	0	0	.000
L. Jones, of	0	0	0	0	0	0	0	—

Errors: S. Balboni (2), G. Brett (2), L. Smith, J. Sundberg
Stolen Bases: L. Smith, W. Wilson

TORONTO (EAST)

	AB	H	2B	3B	HR	R	RBI	BA
L. Moseby, of	31	7	1	0	0	5	4	.226
D. Garcia, 2b	30	7	4	0	0	4	1	.233
G. Bell, of	28	9	3	0	0	4	1	.321
W. Upshaw, 1b	26	6	2	0	0	2	1	.231
J. Barfield, of	25	7	1	0	1	3	4	.280
T. Fernandez, ss	24	8	2	0	0	2	2	.333
E. Whitt, c	21	4	1	0	0	1	2	.190
C. Johnson, dh	19	7	2	0	0	1	2	.368
G. Iorg, 3b	15	2	0	0	0	1	0	.133
R. Mulliniks, 3b	11	4	1	0	1	1	3	.364
A. Oliver, dh	8	3	1	0	0	0	3	.375
C. Fielder	3	1	1	0	0	0	0	.333
J. Burroughs	1	0	0	0	0	0	0	.000
J. Hearron, c	0	0	0	0	0	0	0	—
M. Lee, 2b	0	0	0	0	0	0	0	—
L. Thornton	0	0	0	0	0	1	0	—

Errors: T. Fernandez (2), J. Barfield, W. Upshaw
Stolen Bases: J. Barfield, L. Moseby

Individual Pitching

KANSAS CITY (WEST)

	W	L	ERA	IP	H	BB	SO	SV
C. Leibrandt	1	2	5.28	15.1	17	4	6	0
B. Black	0	0	1.69	10.2	11	4	8	0
D. Jackson	1	0	0.00	10	10	1	7	0
M. Gubicza	1	0	3.24	8.1	4	4	4	0
B. Saberhagen	0	0	6.14	7.1	12	2	6	0
S. Farr	1	0	1.42	6.1	4	1	3	0
D. Quisenberry	0	1	3.86	4.2	7	0	3	1

TORONTO (EAST)

	W	L	ERA	IP	H	BB	SO	SV
D. Stieb	1	1	3.10	20.1	11	10	18	0
D. Alexander	0	1	8.71	10.1	14	3	9	0
D. Lamp	0	0	0.00	9.1	2	1	10	0
J. Key	0	1	5.19	8.2	15	2	5	0
T. Henke	2	0	4.26	6.1	5	4	4	0
J. Acker	0	0	0.00	6	2	0	5	0
J. Clancy	0	1	9.00	1	2	1	0	0
G. Lavelle	0	0	—	0.0	0	1	0	0

1985 WORLD SERIES

Kansas City (A.L.) defeats St. Louis (N.L.) 4 games to 3

LINE SCORES			R	H	E	PITCHERS (innings pitched)	HOME RUNS (men on)	HIGHLIGHTS
GAME 1 - OCTOBER 19								St. Louis bunched their seven hits to produce three runs and take game one of the so-called I-70 Series, named for the highway linking the two cities.
STL	N	001 100 001	3	7	1	**Tudor** (6.2), Worrell (2.1) **SV**		
KC	A	010 000 000	1	8	0	**Jackson** (7), Quisenberry (1.2), Black (0.1)		
GAME 2 - OCTOBER 20								Charlie Leibrandt had allowed just two hits in the first eight innings. But two-out hits by Clark, Landrum, and Pendleton, the last a bases-loaded double, gave the Cards four runs and a come-from-behind win.
STL	N	000 000 004	4	6	0	Cox (7), **Dayley** (1), Lahti (1) **SV**		
KC	A	000 200 000	2	9	0	**Leibrandt** (8.2), Quisenberry (0.1)		
GAME 3 - OCTOBER 22								White, batting cleanup in the absence of McRae (no DH this year), drove in three runs with a double and the first home run of the Series.
KC	A	000 220 200	6	11	0	**Saberhagen** (9)	White (1 on)	
STL	N	000 010 000	1	6	0	**Andujar** (4.0), Campbell (1), Horton (2), Dayley (2)		
GAME 4 - OCTOBER 23								Tudor shut out the Royals on five hits, striking out eight while walking one. Cardinal runs scored on solo homers by Landrum and McGee, and a surprise two-strike squeeze bunt by Tom Nieto.
KC	A	000 000 000	0	5	1	**Black** (5), Beckwith (2), Quisenberry (1)		
STL	N	011 010 00x	3	6	0	**Tudor** (9)	Landrum, McGee	
GAME 5 - OCTOBER 24								As he had in game five of the LCS, Jackson gave the Royals a complete-game win to keep them alive. Cardinals rookie Todd Worrell tied a Series record by striking out six straight batters in his perfect two-inning stint for the Cards.
KC	A	130 000 011	6	11	2	**Jackson** (9)		
STL	N	100 000 000	1	5	1	**Forsch** (1.2), Horton (2), Campbell (1.1), Worrell (2), Lahti (2)		
GAME 6 - OCTOBER 26								A disputed play at first, a single, a passed ball, and an intentional pass set up Dane Iorg's two-run pinch single in the ninth that evened the Series.
STL	N	000 000 010	1	5	0	Cox (7), Dayley (1), **Worrell** (0.1)		
KC	A	000 000 002	2	10	0	Leibrandt (7.2), **Quisenberry** (1.1)		
GAME 7 - OCTOBER 27								The Royals romped to their first World Series title in a laugher. They became the sixth team to win after trailing 3-1 in games, and the first to win after losing the first two games at home.
STL	N	000 000 000	0	5	0	**Tudor** (2.1), Campbell (1.2), Lahti (0.2), Horton (0), Andujar (0), Forsch (1.1), Dayley (2)		
KC	A	023 060 00x	11	14	0	**Saberhagen** (9)	Motley (1 on)	

Team totals

		W	AB	H	2B	3B	HR	R	RBI	BA	BB	SO	ERA
KC	A	4	236	68	12	2	2	28	26	.288	28	56	1.89
STL	N	3	216	40	10	1	2	13	13	.185	18	42	3.96

Individual Batting

KANSAS CITY (A.L.)

	AB	H	2B	3B	HR	R	RBI	BA
W. Wilson, of	30	11	0	1	0	2	3	.367
F. White, 2b	28	7	3	0	1	4	6	.250
G. Brett, 3b	27	10	1	0	0	5	1	.370
L. Smith, of	27	9	3	0	0	4	4	.333
S. Balboni, 1b	25	8	0	0	0	2	3	.320
J. Sundberg, c	24	6	2	0	0	6	1	.250
B. Biancalana, ss	18	5	0	0	0	2	2	.278
P. Sheridan, of	18	4	2	0	0	0	1	.222
D. Motley, of	11	4	0	0	1	1	3	.364
B. Saberhagen, p	7	0	0	0	0	1	0	.000
D. Jackson, p	6	0	0	0	0	0	0	.000
C. Leibrandt, p	4	0	0	0	0	0	0	.000
L. Jones, of	3	2	1	1	0	0	0	.667
J. Orta	3	1	0	0	0	0	0	.333
D. Iorg	2	1	0	0	0	0	2	.500
B. Black, p	1	0	0	0	0	0	0	.000
H. McRae	1	0	0	0	0	0	0	.000
J. Wathan	1	0	0	0	0	0	0	.000
O. Concepcion, ss	0	0	0	0	0	1	0	—
G. Pryor, 3b	0	0	0	0	0	0	0	—

Errors: B. Black, G. Brett, D. Jackson
Stolen Bases: W. Wilson (3), L. Smith (2), G. Brett, F. White

ST. LOUIS (N.L.)

	AB	H	2B	3B	HR	R	RBI	BA
W. McGee, of	27	7	2	0	1	2	2	.259
T. Herr, 2b	26	4	2	0	0	2	0	.154
T. Landrum, of	25	9	2	0	1	3	1	.360
J. Clark, 1b	25	6	2	0	0	1	4	.240
T. Pendleton, 3b	23	6	1	1	0	3	3	.261
O. Smith, ss	23	2	0	0	0	1	0	.087
C. Cedeno, of	15	2	1	0	0	1	1	.133
D. Porter, c	15	2	0	0	0	0	0	.133
A. Van Slyke, of	11	1	0	0	0	0	0	.091
T. Nieto, c	5	0	0	0	0	0	1	.000
J. Tudor, p	5	0	0	0	0	0	0	.000
B. Harper	4	1	0	0	0	0	1	.250
D. Cox, p	4	0	0	0	0	0	0	.000
M. Jorgensen, of	3	0	0	0	0	0	0	.000
J. Andujar, p	1	0	0	0	0	0	0	.000
S. Braun	1	0	0	0	0	0	0	.000
I. DeJesus	1	0	0	0	0	0	0	.000
R. Horton, p	1	0	0	0	0	0	0	.000
T. Worrell, p	1	0	0	0	0	0	0	.000
T. Lawless	0	0	0	0	0	0	0	—

Errors: T. Pendleton, O. Smith
Stolen Bases: W. McGee, O. Smith

Individual Pitching

KANSAS CITY (A.L.)

	W	L	ERA	IP	H	BB	SO	SV
B. Saberhagen	2	0	0.50	18	11	1	10	0
C. Leibrandt	0	1	2.76	16.1	10	4	10	0
D. Jackson	1	1	1.69	16	9	5	12	0
B. Black	0	1	5.06	5.1	4	5	4	0
D. Quisenberry	1	0	2.08	4.1	5	3	3	0
J. Beckwith	0	0	0.00	2	1	0	3	0

ST. LOUIS (N.L.)

	W	L	ERA	IP	H	BB	SO	SV
J. Tudor	2	1	3.00	18	15	7	14	0
D. Cox	0	0	1.29	14	14	4	13	0
K. Dayley	1	0	0.00	6	1	3	5	0
T. Worrell	0	1	3.86	4.2	4	2	6	1
J. Andujar	0	1	9.00	4	10	4	3	0
B. Campbell	0	0	2.25	4	4	2	5	0
R. Horton	0	0	6.75	4	4	5	5	0
J. Lahti	0	0	12.27	3.2	10	0	2	1
B. Forsch	0	1	12.00	3	6	1	3	0

1986 NATIONAL LEAGUE CHAMPIONSHIP SERIES

New York (East) defeats Houston (West) 4 games to 2

LINE SCORES						PITCHERS (innings pitched)	HOME RUNS (men on)	HIGHLIGHTS
GAME 1 - OCTOBER 8								Scott struck out 14 to tie an NLCS mark as he shut down the Mets on five hits.
NY	**E**	000 000 000	0	5	0	**Gooden** (7), Orosco (1)		
HOU	**W**	010 000 00x	1	7	1	**Scott** (9)	Davis	
GAME 2 - OCTOBER 9								New York evened the LCS at one game apiece on Ojeda's ten-hitter, backed by RBIs from Carter and Strawberry in the fourth and Hernandez's two-run triple in the fifth.
NY	**E**	000 230 000	5	10	0	**Ojeda** (9)		
HOU	**W**	000 000 100	1	10	2	**Ryan** (5), Andersen (2), Lopez (1.1), Kerfeld (0.2)		
GAME 3 - OCTOBER 11								Trailing 4-0, the Mets rallied for four in the sixth, the big blow coming on Strawberry's homer. Houston took the lead aided by Knight's error in the seventh, but Dykstra's homer won the game in the bottom of the ninth.
HOU	**W**	220 000 100	5	8	1	Knepper (7), Kerfeld (1), **Smith** (0.1)	Doran (1 on)	
NY	**E**	000 004 002	6	10	1	Darling (5), Aguilera (2), **Orosco** (2)	Strawberry (2 on), Dykstra (1 on)	
GAME 4 - OCTOBER 12								Scott stymied the Mets again, this time on three hits, with Houston's runs coming on homers by Ashby and Thon.
HOU	**W**	020 010 000	3	4	1	**Scott** (9)	Ashby (1 on), Thon	
NY	**E**	000 000 010	1	3	0	**Fernandez** (6), McDowell (2), Sisk (1)		
GAME 5 - OCTOBER 14								Carter's single broke a 1-for-21 slump to drive in the winning run in the 12th inning, overshadowing Ryan's nine innings of two-hit, 12-strikeout pitching for the Astros.
HOU	**W**	000 010 000 000	1	9	1	Ryan (9), **Kerfeld** (2.1)		
NY	**E**	000 010 000 001	2	4	0	Gooden (10), **Orosco** (2)	Strawberry	
GAME 6 - OCTOBER 15								New York rallied from three down in the top of the ninth on RBIs by Wilson, Hernandez, and Knight. Backman's single in the 14th put the Mets up a run, but Hatcher's towering homer tied the score. Three in the top of the 16th put the Mets ahead, but the outcome was in doubt until Orosco struck out Bass with two on to clinch the pennant.
NY	**E**	000 000 003 000 010	7	11	0	Ojeda (5), Aguilera (3), McDowell (5), **Orosco** (3)		
HOU	**W**	300 000 000 000 010	6	11	1	Knepper (8.1), Smith (1.2), Andersen (3), **Lopez** (2.0), Calhoun (1)	Hatcher	

Team totals

		W	AB	H	2B	3B	HR	R	RBI	BA	BB	SO	ERA
NY	**E**	4	227	43	4	2	3	21	19	.189	14	57	2.29
HOU	**W**	2	225	49	6	0	5	17	17	.218	17	40	2.87

Individual Batting

NEW YORK (EAST)

	AB	H	2B	3B	HR	R	RBI	BA
G. Carter, c	27	4	1	0	0	1	2	.148
K. Hernandez, 1b	26	7	1	1	0	3	3	.269
M. Wilson, of	26	3	0	0	0	2	1	.115
R. Knight, 3b	24	4	0	0	0	1	2	.167
L. Dykstra, of	23	7	1	1	1	3	3	.304
D. Strawberry, of	22	5	1	0	2	4	5	.227
W. Backman, 2b	21	5	0	0	0	5	2	.238
R. Santana, ss	17	3	0	0	0	0	0	.176
K. Mitchell, of	8	2	0	0	0	1	0	.250
T. Teufel, 2b	6	1	0	0	0	0	0	.167
L. Mazzilli	5	1	0	0	0	0	0	.200
D. Gooden, p	5	0	0	0	0	0	0	.000
B. Ojeda, p	5	0	0	0	0	1	0	.000
D. Heep, of	4	1	0	0	0	0	1	.250
K. Elster, ss	3	0	0	0	0	0	0	.000
H. Johnson	2	0	0	0	0	0	0	.000
R. Darling, p	1	0	0	0	0	0	0	.000
S. Fernandez, p	1	0	0	0	0	0	0	.000
R. McDowell, p	1	0	0	0	0	0	0	.000

Errors: R. Knight
Stolen Bases: W. Backman, L. Dykstra, D. Strawberry, M. Wilson

HOUSTON (WEST)

	AB	H	2B	3B	HR	R	RBI	BA
B. Doran, 2b	27	6	0	0	1	3	3	.222
G. Davis, 1b	26	7	1	0	1	3	3	.269
J. Cruz, of	26	5	0	0	0	0	2	.192
B. Hatcher, of	25	7	0	0	1	4	2	.280
K. Bass, of	24	7	2	0	0	0	0	.292
A. Ashby, c	23	3	1	0	1	2	2	.130
D. Walling, 3b	19	3	1	0	0	1	2	.158
C. Reynolds, ss	12	4	0	0	0	1	0	.333
D. Thon, ss	12	3	0	0	1	1	1	.250
P. Garner, 3b	9	2	1	0	0	1	2	.222
M. Scott, p	6	0	0	0	0	0	0	.000
B. Knepper, p	5	0	0	0	0	0	0	.000
N. Ryan, p	4	0	0	0	0	0	0	.000
T. Puhl	3	2	0	0	0	0	0	.667
D. Lopes	2	0	0	0	0	1	0	.000
J. Pankovits	2	0	0	0	0	0	0	.000

Errors: C. Reynolds (2), K. Bass, G. Davis, B. Hatcher, C. Kerfeld, M. Scott
Stolen Bases: B. Hatcher (3), K. Bass (2), B. Doran (2), T. Puhl

Individual Pitching

NEW YORK (EAST)

	W	L	ERA	IP	H	BB	SO	SV
D. Gooden	0	1	1.06	17	16	5	9	0
B. Ojeda	1	0	2.57	14	15	4	6	0
J. Orosco	3	0	3.38	8	5	2	10	0
R. McDowell	0	0	0.00	7	1	0	3	0
S. Fernandez	0	1	4.50	6	3	1	5	0
R. Aguilera	0	0	0.00	5	2	2	2	0
R. Darling	0	0	7.20	5	6	2	5	0
D. Sisk	0	0	0.00	1	1	1	0	0

HOUSTON (WEST)

	W	L	ERA	IP	H	BB	SO	SV
M. Scott	2	0	0.50	18	8	1	19	0
B. Knepper	0	0	3.52	15.1	13	1	9	0
N. Ryan	0	1	3.86	14	9	1	17	0
L. Andersen	0	0	0.00	5	1	2	3	0
C. Kerfeld	0	1	2.25	4	2	1	4	0
A. Lopez	0	1	8.10	3.1	7	4	3	0
D. Smith	0	1	9.00	2	2	3	2	0
J. Calhoun	0	0	9.00	1	1	1	0	0

1986 AMERICAN LEAGUE CHAMPIONSHIP SERIES

Boston (East) defeats California (West) 4 games to 3

LINE SCORES						PITCHERS (innings pitched)	HOME RUNS (men on)	HIGHLIGHTS
GAME 1 - OCTOBER 7								Witt shut down the Red Sox on five hits as the Angels reached 24-game winner Clemens for four in the second after two were out.
CAL	**W**	041 000 030	8	11	0	**Witt** (9)		
BOS	**E**	000 001 000	1	5	1	**Clemens** (7.1), Sambito (0.1), Stanley (1.1)		
GAME 2 - OCTOBER 8								In a sloppy game played in late afternoon sun, Boston evened the LCS as Grich lost Evans's pop double in the fifth, and three Angel errors led to three Boston runs in the 7th.
CAL	**W**	000 110 000	2	11	3	**McCaskill** (7), Lucas (0.2), Corbett (0.1)	Joyner	
BOS	**E**	110 010 33x	9	13	2	**Hurst** (9)	Rice (1 on)	
GAME 3 - OCTOBER 10								Seventh-inning homers by Schofield and Pettis off Boston starter Boyd lifted the Angels to the win.
BOS	**E**	010 000 020	3	9	1	**Boyd** (6.2), Sambito (0.1), Schiraldi (1)		
CAL	**W**	000 001 31x	5	8	0	**Candelaria** (7), Moore (2) **SV**	Schofield, Pettis (1 on)	
GAME 4 - OCTOBER 11								Schiraldi hit Downing with two out and the bases loaded to force in the tying run in the ninth, and Grich's single in the 11th drove in Narron with the game-winner.
BOS	**E**	000 001 020 00	3	6	1	Clemens (8.1), **Schiraldi** (2)		
CAL	**W**	000 000 003 01	4	11	2	Sutton (6.1), Lucas (0.1), Ruhle (0.2), Finley (0), **Corbett** (3.2)	DeCinces	
GAME 5 - OCTOBER 12								Henderson's dramatic two-out two-run homer with the Red Sox one strike away from elimination gave Boston a 6-5 lead. Wilfong's single tied the game in the bottom of the ninth, but a Henderson sacrifice fly in the 11th proved the winner and sent the LCS back to Boston.
BOS	**E**	020 000 004 01	7	12	0	Hurst (6), Stanley (2.1), Sambito (0) **Crawford** (1.2), Schiraldi (1) **SV**	Gedman (1 on), Baylor (1 on), Henderson (1 on)	
CAL	**W**	001 002 201 00	6	13	0	Witt (8.2), Lucas (0), **Moore** (2), Finley (0.1)	Boone, Grich (1 on)	
GAME 6 - OCTOBER 14								Boston batted around in the third, battering McCaskill for the second time in the LCS. Owen had four hits for Boston, and Barrett had three.
CAL	**W**	200 000 110	4	11	1	**McCaskill** (2.1), Lucas (1.1), Corbett (2.2), Finley (1.2)	Downing	
BOS	**E**	205 010 20x	10	16	1	**Boyd** (7), Stanley (2)		
GAME 7 - OCTOBER 15								Errors by Schofield and Pettis led to seven unearned runs off Candelaria and sealed the victory for Boston, extending Gene Mauch's streak to 25 years of managing without a pennant.
CAL	**W**	000 000 010	1	6	2	**Candelaria** (3.2), Sutton (3.1), Moore (1)		
BOS	**E**	030 400 10x	8	8	1	**Clemens** (7.0), Schiraldi (2)	Rice (2 on), Evans	

Team totals

		W	AB	H	2B	3B	HR	R	RBI	BA	BB	SO	ERA
BOS	**E**	4	254	69	11	2	6	41	35	.272	19	31	3.58
CAL	**W**	3	256	71	11	0	7	30	29	.277	20	44	3.94

Individual Batting

BOSTON (EAST)

	AB	H	2B	3B	HR	R	RBI	BA
J. Rice, of	31	5	1	0	2	8	6	.161
M. Barrett, 2b	30	11	2	0	0	4	5	.367
W. Boggs, 3b	30	7	1	1	0	3	2	.233
R. Gedman, c	28	10	1	0	1	4	6	.357
B. Buckner, 1b	28	6	1	0	0	3	3	.214
D. Evans, of	28	6	1	0	1	2	4	.214
D. Baylor, dh	26	9	3	0	1	6	2	.346
S. Owen, ss	21	9	0	1	0	5	3	.429
T. Armas, of	16	2	1	0	0	1	0	.125
D. Henderson, of	9	1	0	0	1	3	4	.111
D. Stapleton, 1b	3	2	0	0	0	2	0	.667
M. Greenwell	2	1	0	0	0	0	0	.500
E. Romero, ss	2	0	0	0	0	0	0	.000

Errors: S. Owen (5), W. Boggs (2)
Stolen Bases: S. Owen

CALIFORNIA (WEST)

	AB	H	2B	3B	HR	R	RBI	BA
D. DeCinces, 3b	32	9	3	0	1	2	3	.281
D. Schofield, ss	30	9	1	0	1	4	2	.300
B. Downing, of	27	6	0	0	1	2	7	.222
G. Pettis, of	26	9	1	0	1	4	4	.346
R. Jackson, dh	26	5	2	0	0	2	2	.192
B. Grich, 1b, 2b	24	5	0	0	1	1	3	.208
B. Boone, c	22	10	0	0	1	4	2	.455
R. Jones, of	17	3	1	0	0	4	2	.176
R. Wilfong, 2b	13	4	1	0	0	1	2	.308
G. Hendrick, 1b, of	12	1	0	0	0	0	0	.083
W. Joyner, 1b	11	5	2	0	1	3	2	.455
R. Burleson, 2b, dh	11	3	0	0	0	0	0	.273
J. Narron, c	2	1	0	0	0	1	0	.500
D. White, of	2	1	0	0	0	2	0	.500
J. Howell	1	0	0	0	0	0	0	.000

Errors: B. Grich (3), D. DeCinces (2), D. Schofield (2), G. Pettis
Stolen Bases: D. Schofield

Individual Pitching

BOSTON (EAST)

	W	L	ERA	IP	H	BB	SO	SV
R. Clemens	1	1	4.37	22.2	22	7	17	0
B. Hurst	1	0	2.40	15	18	1	8	0
O. Boyd	1	1	4.61	13.2	17	3	8	0
C. Schiraldi	0	1	1.50	6	5	3	9	1
B. Stanley	0	0	4.76	5.2	7	3	1	0
S. Crawford	1	0	0.00	1.2	1	2	1	0
J. Sambito	0	0	0.00	0.2	1	1	0	0

CALIFORNIA (WEST)

	W	L	ERA	IP	H	BB	SO	SV
M. Witt	1	0	2.55	17.2	13	2	8	0
J. Candelaria	1	1	0.84	10.2	11	6	7	0
D. Sutton	0	0	1.86	9.2	6	1	4	0
K. McCaskill	0	2	7.71	9.1	16	5	7	0
D. Corbett	1	0	5.40	6.2	9	2	2	0
D. Moore	0	1	7.20	5	8	2	0	1
G. Lucas	0	0	11.57	2.1	3	1	2	0
C. Finley	0	0	0.00	2	1	0	1	0
V. Ruhle	0	0	13.50	0.2	2	0	0	0

1986 WORLD SERIES

New York (N.L.) defeats Boston (A.L.) 4 games to 3

LINE SCORES			R	H	E	PITCHERS (innings pitched)	HOME RUNS (men on)	HIGHLIGHTS
GAME 1 - OCTOBER 18								A walk to Rice, a wild pitch, and Teufel's error led to the only run of the game as Hurst allowed the Mets just four singles.
BOS	**A**	000 000 100	1	5	0	**Hurst** (8), Schiraldi (1) **SV**		
NY	**N**	000 000 000	0	4	1	**Darling** (7), McDowell (2)		
GAME 2 - OCTOBER 19								Boston exploded for eighteen hits to take a 2-0 lead in the Series, as the much ballyhooed Clemens-Gooden matchup failed to last through the fifth.
BOS	**A**	003 120 201	9	18	0	Clemens (4.1), **Crawford** (1.2), Stanley (3) **SV**	Henderson, Evans (1 on)	
NY	**N**	002 010 000	3	8	1	**Gooden** (5), Aguilera (1.0), Orosco (2), Fernandez (0.1), Sisk (0.2)		
GAME 3 - OCTOBER 21								Dykstra's leadoff homer triggered a four-run outburst in the first. Ojeda earned the win against the team that sent him to the Mets the previous winter.
NY	**N**	400 000 210	7	13	0	**Ojeda** (7), McDowell (2)	Dykstra	
BOS	**A**	001 000 000	1	5	0	**Boyd** (7), Sambito (0), Stanley (2)		
GAME 4 - OCTOBER 22								Carter's two homers, combined with Darling's seven innings of four-hit pitching, helped even the Series at two games apiece.
NY	**N**	000 300 210	6	12	0	**Darling** (7), McDowell (0.2), Orosco (1.1) **SV**	Carter (1 on), Dykstra (1 on), Carter	
BOS	**A**	000 000 020	2	7	1	**Nipper** (6), Crawford (2), Stanley (1)		
GAME 5 - OCTOBER 23								Hurst scattered 10 hits for his second victory, as the Red Sox became the first home team to lead in any game.
NY	**N**	000 000 011	2	10	1	**Gooden** (4.0), Fernandez (4)	Teufel	
BOS	**A**	011 020 00x	4	12	0	**Hurst** (9)		
GAME 6 - OCTOBER 25								With two out and nobody on in the bottom of the tenth, the Mets staged one of the most dramatic comebacks in World Series history. Twice a strike away from elimination, they bunched three singles, a Stanley wild pitch, and a grounder through Buckner's legs for a miraculous come-from-behind victory.
BOS	**A**	110 000 100 2	5	13	3	Clemens (7), **Schiraldi** (2.2), Stanley (0)	Henderson	
NY	**N**	000 020 010 3	6	8	2	Ojeda (6), McDowell (1.2), Orosco (0.1), **Aguilera** (2)		
GAME 7 - OCTOBER 27								Knight's leadoff homer in the seventh proved the game-winning blow as the Mets overcame a 3-0 deficit to win the Series. For Boston, it was the fourth Series appearance since their last win in '18, all seven-game defeats.
BOS	**A**	030 000 020	5	9	0	Hurst (6), **Schiraldi** (0.1), Sambito (0.1), Stanley (0.1), Nipper (0.1), Crawford (0.2)	Evans, Gedman	
NY	**N**	000 003 32x	8	10	0	Darling (3.2), Fernandez (2.1), **McDowell** (1.0), Orosco (2) **SV**	Knight, Strawberry	

Team totals

		W	AB	H	2B	3B	HR	R	RBI	BA	BB	SO	ERA
NY	**N**	4	240	65	6	0	7	32	29	.271	21	43	3.29
BOS	**A**	3	248	69	11	2	5	27	26	.278	28	53	4.31

Individual Batting

NEW YORK (N.L.)

	AB	H	2B	3B	HR	R	RBI	BA
G. Carter, c	29	8	2	0	2	4	9	.276
L. Dykstra, of	27	8	0	0	2	4	3	.296
M. Wilson, of	26	7	1	0	0	3	0	.269
K. Hernandez, 1b	26	6	0	0	0	1	4	.231
D. Strawberry, of	24	5	1	0	1	4	1	.208
R. Knight, 3b	23	9	1	0	1	4	5	.391
R. Santana, ss	20	5	0	0	0	3	2	.250
W. Backman, 2b	18	6	0	0	0	4	1	.333
D. Heep, dh, of	11	1	0	0	0	0	2	.091
T. Teufel, 2b	9	4	1	0	1	1	1	.444
K. Mitchell, dh, of	8	2	0	0	0	1	0	.250
L. Mazzilli, dh, of	5	2	0	0	0	2	0	.400
H. Johnson, 3b, ss	5	0	0	0	0	0	0	.000
R. Darling, p	3	0	0	0	0	0	0	.000
D. Gooden, p	2	1	0	0	0	1	0	.500
B. Ojeda, p	2	0	0	0	0	0	0	.000
J. Orosco, p	1	1	0	0	0	0	1	1.000
K. Elster, ss	1	0	0	0	0	0	0	.000

Errors: K. Elster, K. Hernandez, R. Knight, R. Santana, T. Teufel
Stolen Bases: D. Strawberry (3), M. Wilson (3), W. Backman

BOSTON (A.L.)

	AB	H	2B	3B	HR	R	RBI	BA
B. Buckner, 1b	32	6	0	0	0	2	1	.188
W. Boggs, 3b	31	9	3	0	0	3	3	.290
M. Barrett, 2b	30	13	2	0	0	1	4	.433
R. Gedman, c	30	6	1	0	1	1	1	.200
J. Rice, of	27	9	1	1	0	6	0	.333
D. Evans, of	26	8	2	0	2	4	9	.308
D. Henderson, of	25	10	1	1	2	6	5	.400
S. Owen, ss	20	6	0	0	0	2	2	.300
D. Baylor, dh	11	2	1	0	0	1	1	.182
R. Clemens, p	4	0	0	0	0	1	0	.000
M. Greenwell	3	0	0	0	0	0	0	.000
B. Hurst, p	3	0	0	0	0	0	0	.000
T. Armas	1	0	0	0	0	0	0	.000
S. Crawford, p	1	0	0	0	0	0	0	.000
E. Romero, ss	1	0	0	0	0	0	0	.000
C. Schiraldi, p	1	0	0	0	0	0	0	.000
B. Stanley, p	1	0	0	0	0	0	0	.000
D. Stapleton, 1b	1	0	0	0	0	0	0	.000

Errors: R. Gedman (2), B. Buckner, D. Evans

Individual Pitching

NEW YORK (N.L.)

	W	L	ERA	IP	H	BB	SO	SV
R. Darling	1	1	1.53	17.2	13	10	12	0
B. Ojeda	1	0	2.08	13	13	5	9	0
D. Gooden	0	2	8.00	9	17	4	9	0
R. McDowell	1	0	4.91	7.1	10	6	2	0
S. Fernandez	0	0	1.35	6.2	6	1	10	0
J. Orosco	0	0	0.00	5.2	2	0	6	2
R. Aguilera	1	0	12.00	3	8	1	4	0
D. Sisk	0	0	0.00	0.2	0	1	1	0

BOSTON (A.L.)

	W	L	ERA	IP	H	BB	SO	SV
B. Hurst	2	0	1.96	23	18	6	17	0
R. Clemens	0	0	3.18	11.1	9	6	11	0
O. Boyd	0	1	7.71	7	9	1	3	0
A. Nipper	0	1	7.11	6.1	10	2	2	0
B. Stanley	0	0	0.00	6.1	5	1	4	1
S. Crawford	1	0	6.23	4.1	5	0	4	0
C. Schiraldi	0	2	13.50	4	7	3	2	1
J. Sambito	0	0	27.00	0.1	2	2	0	0

1987 NATIONAL LEAGUE CHAMPIONSHIP SERIES

St. Louis (East) defeats San Francisco (West) 4 games to 3

LINE SCORES			R	H	E	PITCHERS (innings pitched)	HOME RUNS (men on)	HIGHLIGHTS
GAME 1 - OCTOBER 6								Mathews allowed four hits over seven innings and singled in two runs in a three run sixth that gave the Cards a win in the series opener.
SF	**W**	100 100 010	3	7	1	**Reuschel** (6), Lefferts (1), Garrelts (1)	Leonard	
STL	**E**	001 103 00x	5	10	1	**Mathews** (7.1), Worrell (0.1), Dayley (1.1) **SV**		
GAME 2 - OCTOBER 7								Dravecky hurled a two hitter and Will Clark and Jeff Leonard supplied the firepower as the Giants evened the series.
SF	**W**	020 100 020	5	10	0	**Dravecky** (9)	W. Clark (1 on), Leonard	
STL	**E**	000 000 000	0	2	1	**Tudor** (8), Forsch (1)		
GAME 3 - OCTOBER 9								Lindeman drove in three runs with a home run and a sacrifice fly to give the Cards a 2-1 lead in the series. The Cards trailed 4-0 after five innings.
STL	**E**	000 002 400	6	11	1	Magrane (4), **Forsch** (2), Worrell (3) **SV**	Lindeman (1 on)	
SF	**W**	031 000 001	5	7	1	Hammaker (6.0), **Robinson** (0), Lefferts (1), LaCoss (2)	Leonard, Spilman	
GAME 4 - OCTOBER 10								Leonard homered in his fourth consecutive game, his homer coming with one on in the fifth to give the Giants the lead in a 4-2 victory as Mike Krukow went the distance giving up nine hits.
STL	**E**	020 000 000	2	9	0	**Cox** (8)		
SF	**W**	000 120 01x	4	9	2	**Krukow** (9)	Leonard (1 on), Thompson, Brenly	
GAME 5 - OCTOBER 11								Uribe delivered a two run single to highlight a four run fourth inning and Joe Price pitched five innings of one hit shutout relief to earn the victory, giving the Giants a 3-2 lead.
STL	**E**	101 100 000	3	7	0	Mathews (3), **Forsch** (0), Horton (3), Dayley (2)		
SF	**W**	101 400 00x	6	7	1	Reuschel (4), **Price** (5)	Mitchell	
GAME 6 - OCTOBER 13								Pena tripled in the second inning and scored on Oquendo's short sacrfice fly to account for the only run as three Cardinal pitchers combined on a six hitter.
SF	**W**	000 000 000	0	6	0	**Dravecky** (6), Robinson (2)		
STL	**E**	010 000 00x	1	5	0	**Tudor** (7.2), Worrell (1), Dayley (.2) **SV**		
GAME 7 - OCTOBER 14								Cox scattered eight hits and Oquendo belted a three run homer as the Cards captured the NL Pennant in seven games. The Giants were held scoreless over the last 22 innings.
SF	**W**	000 000 000	0	8	1	**Hammaker** (2), Price (0.2), Downs (1.1), Garrelts (1.2), Lefferts (0), LaCoss (1.1), Robinson (1)		
STL	**E**	040 002 00x	6	12	0	**Cox** (9)	Oquendo (2 on)	

Team totals

		W	AB	H	2B	3B	HR	R	RBI	BA	BB	SO	ERA
STL	**E**	4	215	56	4	4	2	23	22	.260	16	42	2.95
SF	**W**	3	226	54	7	1	9	23	20	.239	17	51	3.30

Individual Batting

ST. LOUIS (EAST)

	AB	H	2B	3B	HR	R	RBI	BA
T. Herr, 2b	27	6	0	0	0	0	3	.222
W. McGee, of	26	8	1	1	0	2	2	.308
V. Coleman, of	26	7	1	0	0	3	4	.269
O. Smith, ss	25	5	0	1	0	2	1	.200
T. Pena, c	21	8	0	1	0	5	0	.381
T. Pendleton, 3b	19	4	0	1	0	3	1	.211
J. Lindeman, 1b	13	4	0	0	1	1	3	.308
D. Driessen, 1b	12	3	2	0	0	1	1	.250
J. Oquendo, 3b, of	12	2	0	0	1	3	4	.167
C. Ford, of	9	3	0	0	0	2	0	.333
D. Cox, p	6	2	0	0	0	0	1	.333
T. Lawless, 3b, of	6	2	0	0	0	0	0	.333
J. Tudor, p	4	0	0	0	0	0	0	.000
J. Morris, of	3	0	0	0	0	0	0	.000
G. Mathews, p	2	2	0	0	0	0	2	1.000
J. Clark, 1b	1	0	0	0	0	0	0	.000
J. Magrane, p	1	0	0	0	0	0	0	.000
T. Pagnozzi, c	1	0	0	0	0	0	0	.000
T. Worrell, of, p	1	0	0	0	0	0	0	.000
L. Johnson, of	0	0	0	0	0	1	0	—

Errors: D. Driessen, T. Herr, O. Smith
Stolen Bases: V. Coleman, T. Herr, L. Johnson, T. Pena

SAN FRANCISCO (WEST)

	AB	H	2B	3B	HR	R	RBI	BA
K. Mitchell, 3b	30	8	1	0	1	2	2	.267
J. Uribe, ss	26	7	1	0	0	1	2	.269
W. Clark, 1b	25	9	2	0	1	3	3	.360
J. Leonard, of	24	10	0	0	4	5	5	.417
C. Davis, of	20	3	1	0	0	2	0	.150
R. Thompson, 2b	20	2	0	1	1	4	2	.100
C. Maldonado, of	19	4	1	0	0	2	2	.211
B. Brenly, c	17	4	1	0	1	3	2	.235
M. Aldrete, of	10	1	0	0	0	0	1	.100
B. Melvin, c	7	3	0	0	0	0	0	.429
E. Milner, of	7	1	0	0	0	0	0	.143
D. Dravecky, p	6	1	0	0	0	0	0	.167
C. Speier, 2b	5	0	0	0	0	0	0	.000
A. Hammaker, p	3	0	0	0	0	0	0	.000
H. Spilman, 1b	2	1	0	0	1	1	1	.500
M. Krukow, p	2	0	0	0	0	0	0	.000
R. Reuschel, p	2	0	0	0	0	0	0	.000
J. Price, p	1	0	0	0	0	0	0	.000

Errors: W. Clark, C. Davis, K. Mitchell, R. Reuschel, R. Thompson, J. Uribe
Stolen Bases: R. Thompson (2), W. Clark, K. Mitchell, J. Uribe

Individual Pitching

ST. LOUIS (EAST)

	W	L	ERA	IP	H	BB	SO	SV
D. Cox	1	1	2.12	17	17	3	11	0
J. Tudor	1	1	1.76	15.1	16	5	12	0
G. Mathews	1	0	3.48	10.1	6	3	10	0
T. Worrell	0	0	2.08	4.1	4	1	6	1
K. Dayley	0	0	0.00	4	1	2	4	2
J. Magrane	0	0	9.00	4	4	2	3	0
B. Forsch	1	1	12.00	3	4	1	3	0
R. Horton	0	0	0.00	3	2	0	2	0

SAN FRANCISCO (WEST)

	W	L	ERA	IP	H	BB	SO	SV
D. Dravecky	1	1	0.60	15	7	4	14	0
R. Reuschel	0	1	6.30	10	15	2	2	0
M. Krukow	1	0	2.00	9	9	1	3	0
A. Hammaker	0	1	7.88	8	12	0	7	0
J. Price	1	0	0.00	5.2	3	1	7	0
M. LaCoss	0	0	0.00	3.1	1	3	2	0
D. Robinson	0	1	9.00	3	3	0	3	0
S. Garrelts	0	0	6.75	2.2	2	4	4	0
C. Lefferts	0	0	0.00	2	3	1	0	0
K. Downs	0	0	0.00	1.1	1	0	0	0

1987 AMERICAN LEAGUE CHAMPIONSHIP SERIES

Minnesota (West) defeats Detroit (East) 4 games to 1

LINE SCORES						PITCHERS (innings pitched)	HOME RUNS (men on)	HIGHLIGHTS
GAME 1 - OCTOBER 7								An RBI double by Puckett, a pinch single by Baylor, and a two run double by Brunansky in the eighth inning rallied the Twins to victory. Gaetti homered twice for the winners.
DET	E	001 001 120	5	10	0	**Alexander,** (7.1), Henneman (0), Hernandez (0.1), King (0.1)	Gibson, Heath	
MIN	W	010 030 04x	8	10	0	Viola (7), **Reardon** (2)	Gaetti, Gaetti	
GAME 2 - OCTOBER 8								Laudner and Gladden drove in two runs apiece and Hrbek added a solo home run to give the Twins a 2-0 edge in the series.
DET	E	020 000 010	3	7	1	**Morris** (8)	Lemon (1 on), Whitaker	
MIN	W	030 210 00x	6	6	0	**Blyleven** (7.1), Berenguer (1.2) **SV**	Hrbek	
GAME 3 - OCTOBER 10								The Tigers squandered a 5-0 lead, but won in the eighth on Pat Sheridan's two run homer.
MIN	W	000 202 200	6	8	1	Straker (2.2), Schatzeder (3.1), Berenguer (1), **Reardon** (1)	Gagne, Brunansky (1 on)	
DET	E	005 000 02x	7	7	0	Terrell (6.0), **Henneman** (3)	Sheridan (1 on)	
GAME 4 - OCTOBER 11								Solo homers by Puckett and Gagne powered the Twins to their first victory on the road and a 3-1 series advantage.
MIN	W	001 111 010	5	7	1	**Viola** (5), Atherton (0.1), Berenguer (2.2), Reardon (1) **SV**	Puckett, Gagne	
DET	E	100 011 000	3	7	3	**Tanana** (5.1), Petry (3.1), Thurmond (0.1)		
GAME 5 - OCTOBER 12								Brunansky's two run double and RBI singles by Gladden and Puckett produced four second inning runs that propelled the Twins to their first AL Pennant since 1965.
MIN	W	040 000 113	9	15	1	**Blyleven** (6), Schatzeder (1), Berenguer (0.2), Reardon (1.1) **SV**	Brunansky	
DET	E	000 300 011	5	9	1	**Alexander** (1.2), King (5), Henneman (2), Robinson (0.1)	Lemon, Nokes (1 on)	

Team totals

		W	AB	H	2B	3B	HR	R	RBI	BA	BB	SO	ERA
MIN	W	4	171	46	13	1	8	34	33	.269	20	25	4.50
DET	E	1	167	40	4	0	7	23	21	.240	18	35	6.70

Individual Batting

MINNESOTA (WEST)

	AB	H	2B	3B	HR	R	RBI	BA
K. Puckett, of	24	5	1	0	1	3	3	.208
D. Gladden, of	20	7	2	0	0	5	5	.350
G. Gaetti, 3b	20	6	1	0	2	5	5	.300
K. Hrbek, 1b	20	3	0	0	1	4	1	.150
G. Gagne, ss	18	5	3	0	2	5	3	.278
T. Brunansky, of	17	7	4	0	2	5	9	.412
S. Lombardozzi, 2b	15	4	0	0	0	2	1	.267
T. Laudner, c	14	1	1	0	0	1	2	.071
R. Bush, dh	12	3	0	1	0	4	2	.250
D. Baylor, dh	5	2	0	0	0	0	1	.400
S. Butera, c	3	2	0	0	0	0	0	.667
A. Newman, 2b	2	0	0	0	0	0	0	.000
G. Larkin, of	1	1	1	0	0	0	1	1.000
M. Davidson, of	0	0	0	0	0	0	0	—

Errors: G. Gagne (2), S. Lombardozzi
Stolen Bases: R. Bush (3), K. Puckett

DETROIT (EAST)

	AB	H	2B	3B	HR	R	RBI	BA
K. Gibson, of	21	6	1	0	1	4	4	.286
A. Trammell, ss	20	4	1	0	0	3	2	.200
C. Lemon, of	18	5	0	0	2	4	4	.278
D. Evans, 1b, 3b	17	5	0	0	0	0	0	.294
L. Whitaker, 2b	17	3	0	0	1	4	1	.176
M. Nokes, c, dh	14	2	0	0	1	2	2	.143
T. Brookens, 3b	13	0	0	0	0	0	0	.000
P. Sheridan, of	10	3	1	0	1	2	2	.300
L. Herndon, dh, of	9	3	1	0	0	1	2	.333
J. Grubb, dh	7	4	0	0	0	0	0	.571
M. Heath, c	7	2	0	0	1	1	2	.286
J. Morrison, 3b, dh	5	2	0	0	0	1	0	.400
B. Madlock, dh	5	0	0	0	0	0	0	.000
D. Bergman, 1b, dh	4	1	0	0	0	0	2	.250
J. Morris, p	0	0	0	0	0	1	0	—

Errors: D. Evans (3), L. Herndon, A. Trammell
Stolen Bases: K. Gibson (3), P. Sheridan, L. Whitaker

Individual Pitching

MINNESOTA (WEST)

	W	L	ERA	IP	H	BB	SO	SV
B. Blyleven	2	0	4.05	13.1	12	3	9	0
F. Viola	1	0	5.25	12	14	5	9	0
J. Berenguer	0	0	1.50	6	1	3	6	1
J. Reardon	1	1	5.06	5.1	7	3	5	2
D. Schatzeder	0	0	0.00	4.1	2	0	5	0
L. Straker	0	0	16.88	2.2	3	4	1	0
K. Atherton	0	0	0.00	0.1	1	0	0	0

DETROIT (EAST)

	W	L	ERA	IP	H	BB	SO	SV
D. Alexander	0	2	10.00	9	14	1	5	0
J. Morris	0	1	6.75	8	6	3	7	0
W. Terrell	0	0	9.00	6	7	4	4	0
E. King	0	0	1.69	5.1	3	2	4	0
F. Tanana	0	1	5.06	5.1	6	4	1	0
M. Henneman	1	0	10.80	5	6	6	3	0
D. Petry	0	0	0.00	3.1	1	0	1	0
G. Hernandez	0	0	0.00	0.1	2	0	0	0
J. Robinson	0	0	0.00	0.1	1	0	0	0
M. Thurmond	0	0	0.00	0.1	0	0	0	0

1987 WORLD SERIES

Minnesota (A.L.) defeats St. Louis (N.L.) 4 games to 3

LINE SCORES			R	H	E	PITCHERS (innings pitched)	HOME RUNS (men on)	HIGHLIGHTS
GAME 1 - OCTOBER 17								Gladden highlighted the seven run fourth inning with a grand slam and Viola allowed five hits in eight innings as the Twins won the opener.
STL	**N**	010 000 000	1	5	1	**Magrane** (3.0), Forsch (3), Horton (2)		
MIN	**A**	000 720 10x	10	11	0	**Viola** (8), Atherton (1)	Gladden (3 on), Lombardozzi (1 on)	
GAME 2 - OCTOBER 18								Bush's bases loaded double highlighted a six run fourth inning as the Twins romped to their second straight win.
STL	**N**	000 010 120	4	9	0	**Cox** (3.2), Tunnell (2.1), Dayley (1.1), Worrell (0.2)		
MIN	**A**	010 601 00x	8	10	0	**Blyleven** (7), Berenguer (1), Reardon (1)	Gaetti, Laudner	
GAME 3 - OCTOBER 20								Coleman doubled home two runs as the Cardinals rallied against reliever Berenguer for three runs in the seventh to overcome a 1-0 Twins lead.
MIN	**A**	000 001 000	1	5	1	Straker (6), **Berenguer** (0.1), Schatzeder (1.2)		
STL	**N**	000 000 30x	3	9	1	**Tudor** (7), Worrell (2) **SV**		
GAME 4 - OCTOBER 21								Three run homer by Lawless sparked a six run fourth inning as the Cards evened the Series at 2-2.
MIN	**A**	001 010 000	2	7	1	**Viola** (3.1), Schatzeder (0.2), Niekro (2), Frazier (2)	Gagne	
STL	**N**	001 600 00x	7	10	1	Mathews (3.2), **Forsch** (2.2), Dayley (2.2) **SV**	Lawless (2 on)	
GAME 5 - OCTOBER 22								Ford broke up a scoreless pitching duel between Cox and Blyleven with a bases-loaded single in the sixth inning, giving the Cards a 3-2 Series lead.
MIN	**A**	000 000 020	2	6	1	**Blyleven** (6), Atherton (0.1), Reardon (1.2)		
STL	**N**	000 003 10x	4	10	0	**Cox** (7.1), Dayley (0.1), Worrell (1.1) **SV**		
GAME 6 - OCTOBER 24								Baylor hit a game-tying two run homer in the fifth inning and Hrbek hit a grand slam in the sixth as the Twins tied the Series 3-3.
STL	**N**	110 210 000	5	11	2	**Tudor** (4.0), Horton (1.0), Forsch (0.2), Dayley (0.1), Tunnell (2)	Herr	
MIN	**A**	200 044 01x	11	15	0	Straker (3.0), **Schatzeder** (2), Berenguer (3), Reardon (1)	Baylor (1 on), Hrbek (3 on)	
GAME 7 - OCTOBER 25								Viola pitched a six-hitter for eight innings to post his second Series win and bring the Minnesota Twins their first World Championship.
STL	**N**	020 000 000	2	6	1	Magrane (4.1), **Cox** (0.2), Worrell (3)		
MIN	**A**	010 011 01x	4	10	0	**Viola** (8), Reardon (1) **SV**		

Team totals

		W	AB	H	2B	3B	HR	R	RBI	BA	BB	SO	ERA
MIN	**A**	4	238	64	10	3	7	38	38	.269	29	36	3.75
STL	**N**	3	232	60	8	0	2	26	25	.259	13	44	5.64

Individual Batting

MINNESOTA (A.L.)

	AB	H	2B	3B	HR	R	RBI	BA
D. Gladden, of	31	9	2	1	1	3	7	.290
G. Gagne, ss	30	6	1	0	1	5	3	.200
K. Puckett, of	28	10	1	1	0	5	3	.357
G. Gaetti, 3b	27	7	2	1	1	4	4	.259
T. Brunansky, of	25	5	0	0	0	5	2	.200
K. Hrbek, 1b	24	5	0	0	1	4	6	.208
T. Laudner, c	22	7	1	0	1	4	4	.318
S. Lombardozzi, 2b	17	7	1	0	1	3	4	.412
D. Baylor, dh	13	5	0	0	1	3	3	.385
R. Bush, dh	6	1	1	0	0	1	2	.167
A. Newman, 2b	5	1	0	0	0	0	0	.200
G. Larkin, 1b, dh	3	0	0	0	0	1	0	.000
R. Smalley, ss	2	1	1	0	0	0	0	.500
L. Straker, p	2	0	0	0	0	0	0	.000
B. Blyleven, p	1	0	0	0	0	0	0	.000
M. Davidson, of	1	0	0	0	0	0	0	.000
F. Viola, p	1	0	0	0	0	0	0	.000
S. Butera, c	0	0	0	0	0	0	0	—

Errors: G. Gagne (2), K. Puckett
Stolen Bases: G. Gaetti (2), D. Gladden (2), T. Brunansky, K. Puckett

ST. LOUIS (N.L.)

	AB	H	2B	3B	HR	R	RBI	BA
T. Herr, 2b	28	7	0	0	1	2	1	.250
O. Smith, ss	28	6	0	0	0	3	2	.214
V. Coleman, of	28	4	2	0	0	5	2	.143
W. McGee, of	27	10	2	0	0	2	4	.370
J. Oquendo, 3b, of	24	6	0	0	0	2	2	.250
T. Pena, c, dh	22	9	1	0	0	2	4	.409
J. Lindeman, 1b, of	15	5	1	0	0	3	2	.333
C. Ford, of	13	4	0	0	0	1	2	.308
D. Driessen, 1b	13	3	2	0	0	3	1	.231
T. Lawless, 3b	10	1	0	0	1	1	3	.100
T. Pendleton, dh	7	3	0	0	0	2	1	.429
T. Pagnozzi, dh	4	1	0	0	0	0	0	.250
S. Lake, c	3	1	0	0	0	0	1	.333
D. Cox, p	2	0	0	0	0	0	0	.000
B. Forsch, p	2	0	0	0	0	0	0	.000
J. Morris, of	2	0	0	0	0	0	0	.000
J. Tudor, p	2	0	0	0	0	0	0	.000
K. Dayley, p	1	0	0	0	0	0	0	.000
G. Mathews, p	1	0	0	0	0	0	0	.000
L. Johnson, of	0	0	0	0	0	0	0	—

Errors: J. Lindeman (3), T. Lawless, W. McGee, T. Pena
Stolen Bases: V. Coleman (6), T. Pendleton (2), O. Smith (2), L. Johnson, T. Pena

Individual Pitching

MINNESOTA (A.L.)

	W	L	ERA	IP	H	BB	SO	SV
F. Viola	2	1	3.72	19.1	17	3	16	0
B. Blyleven	1	1	2.77	13	13	2	12	0
L. Straker	0	0	4.00	9	9	3	6	0
J. Reardon	0	0	0.00	4.2	5	0	3	1
J. Berenguer	0	1	10.38	4.1	10	0	1	0
D. Schatzeder	1	0	6.23	4.1	4	3	3	0
G. Frazier	0	0	0.00	2	1	0	2	0
J. Niekro	0	0	0.00	2	1	1	1	0
K. Atherton	0	0	6.75	1.1	0	1	0	0

ST. LOUIS (N.L.)

	W	L	ERA	IP	H	BB	SO	SV
D. Cox	1	2	7.71	11.2	13	8	9	0
J. Tudor	1	1	5.73	11	15	3	8	0
J. Magrane	0	1	8.59	7.1	9	5	5	0
T. Worrell	0	0	1.29	7	6	4	3	2
B. Forsch	1	0	9.95	6.1	8	5	3	0
K. Dayley	0	0	1.93	4.2	2	0	3	1
L. Tunnell	0	0	2.08	4.1	4	2	1	0
G. Mathews	0	0	2.45	3.2	2	2	3	0
R. Horton	0	0	6.00	3	5	0	1	0

1988 NATIONAL LEAGUE CHAMPIONSHIP SERIES

Los Angeles (West) defeats New York (East) 4 games to 3

LINE SCORES			R	H	E	PITCHERS (innings pitched)	HOME RUNS (men on)	HIGHLIGHTS
GAME 1 - OCTOBER 4								New York rallied for three runs in the ninth inning to overcome a 2-0 deficit. Strawberry doubled home the first run against Hershiser, and Carter's 2-out bloop double off Howell plated the tying and winning runs.
NY	**E**	000 000 003	3	8	1	Gooden (7), **Myers** (2)		
LA	**W**	100 000 100	2	4	0	Hershiser (8.1), **Howell** (0.2)		
GAME 2 - OCTOBER 5								Los Angeles jumped to an early 5-0 lead behind the rookie Belcher, who struck out 10. Hernandez homered and drove in all three New York runs.
NY	**E**	000 200 001	3	6	0	**Cone** (2), Aguilera (3), Leach (2), McDowell (1)	Hernandez (1 on)	
LA	**W**	140 010 00x	6	7	0	**Belcher** (8.1), Orosco (0), Pena (0.2) **SV**		
GAME 3 - OCTOBER 8								New York sent 10 men to the plate during a 5 run eighth inning rally in which Dodger reliever Howell was ejected and subsequently suspended for having pine tar in his glove.
LA	**W**	021 000 010	4	7	2	Hershiser (7), Howell (0), **Pena** (0.2), Orosco (0), Horton (0.1)		
NY	**E**	001 002 05x	8	9	2	Darling (6), McDowell (1.2), **Myers** (0.1), Cone (1)		
GAME 4 - OCTOBER 9								Scioscia belted a 2 run homer in the ninth inning off Gooden to tie the game, then Gibson connected off McDowell in the 12th as Los Angeles evened the series 2-2.
LA	**W**	200 000 002 001	5	7	1	Tudor (5), Holton (1), Horton (2), **Pena** (3), Leary (0.1), Orosco (0.1), Hershiser (0.1) **SV**	Scioscia (1 on), Gibson	
NY	**E**	000 301 000 000	4	10	2	Gooden (8.1), Myers (2.1), **McDowel**	Strawberry (1 on), McReynolds	
GAME 5 - OCTOBER 10								Dodgers scored three times in both the fourth and fifth innings and held off Mets to take series lead for the first time. Big blow was Gibson's three run homer which gave Los Angeles a 6-0 lead.
LA	**W**	000 330 001	7	12	0	**Belcher** (7), Horton (0.1), Holton (1.2) **SV**	Gibson (2 on)	
NY	**E**	000 030 010	4	9	1	**Fernandez** (4.0), Leach (1), Aguilera (2), McDowell (2)	Dykstra (2 on)	
GAME 6 - OCTOBER 11								Cone went the distance on a five hitter, while McReynolds went 4 for 4 with a home run and 3 RBI as Mets forced a seventh game.
NY	**E**	101 021 000	5	11	0	**Cone** (9)	McReynolds (1 on)	
LA	**W**	000 010 000	1	5	2	**Leary** (4.0), Holton (1.1), Horton (1.2), Orosco (2)		
GAME 7 - OCTOBER 12								Los Angeles completed upset of heavily favored Mets, who had beaten them 10 times in 11 meetings during the regular season. Series MVP Hershiser pitched a 5 hit shutout to wrap up Dodgers' first flag in seven years.
NY	**E**	000 000 000	0	5	2	**Darling** (1.0), Gooden (3), Leach (2), Aguilera (2)		
LA	**W**	150 000 00x	6	10	0	**Hershiser** (9)		

Team totals

		W	AB	H	2B	3B	HR	R	RBI	BA	BB	SO	ERA
LA	W	4	243	52	7	1	3	31	30	.214	25	54	3.32
NY	E	3	240	58	12	1	5	27	27	.242	28	42	3.94

Individual Batting

LOS ANGELES (WEST)

	AB	H	2B	3B	HR	R	RBI	BA
S. Sax, 2b	30	8	0	0	0	7	3	.267
M. Marshall, of	30	7	1	1	0	3	5	.233
K. Gibson, of	26	4	0	0	2	2	6	.154
A. Griffin, ss	25	4	1	0	0	1	3	.160
J. Shelby, of	24	4	0	0	0	3	3	.167
J. Hamilton, 3b	23	5	0	0	0	2	1	.217
M. Scioscia, c	22	8	1	0	1	3	2	.364
M. Hatcher, 1b, of	21	5	2	0	0	4	3	.238
O. Hershiser, p	9	0	0	0	0	1	1	.000
F. Stubbs, 1b	8	2	0	0	0	0	0	.250
T. Belcher, p	8	1	0	0	0	1	0	.125
R. Dempsey, c	5	2	2	0	0	1	2	.400
T. Woodson, 1b	4	1	0	0	0	0	0	.250
M. Davis	2	0	0	0	0	0	0	.000
J. Tudor, p	2	0	0	0	0	0	0	.000
B. Holton, p	1	1	0	0	0	1	0	1.000
D. Heep	1	0	0	0	0	0	0	.000
T. Leary, p	1	0	0	0	0	0	0	.000
M. Sharperson, 3b, ss	1	0	0	0	0	0	1	.000
J. Gonzalez, of	0	0	0	0	0	2	0	—

Errors: J. Hamilton (2), M. Hatcher (2), K. Gibson

Stolen Bases: S. Sax (5), K. Gibson (2), J. Shelby (2)

NEW YORK (EAST)

	AB	H	2B	3B	HR	R	RBI	BA
D. Strawberry, of	30	9	2	0	1	5	6	.300
K. McReynolds, of	28	7	2	0	2	4	4	.250
G. Jefferies, 3b	27	9	2	0	0	2	1	.333
G. Carter, c	27	6	1	1	0	0	4	.222
K. Hernandez, 1b	26	7	0	0	1	2	5	.269
W. Backman, 2b	22	6	1	0	0	2	2	.273
H. Johnson, 3b, ss	18	1	0	0	0	3	0	.056
L. Dykstra, of	14	6	3	0	1	6	3	.429
M. Wilson, of	13	2	0	0	0	2	1	.154
K. Elster, ss	8	2	1	0	0	1	1	.250
D. Gooden, p	5	1	0	0	0	0	0	.200
M. Sasser, c	5	1	0	0	0	0	0	.200
D. Cone, p	4	0	0	0	0	0	0	.000
R. Darling, p	3	0	0	0	0	0	0	.000
D. Magadan	3	0	0	0	0	0	0	.000
T. Teufel, 2b	3	0	0	0	0	0	0	.000
L. Mazzilli	2	1	0	0	0	0	0	.500
R. Aguilera, p	1	0	0	0	0	0	0	.000
S. Fernandez, p	1	0	0	0	0	0	0	.000

Errors: W. Backman (2), K. Elster (2), K. Hernandez, G. Jefferies, H. Johnson, R. McDowell

Stolen Bases: K. McReynolds (2), W. Backman, K. Hernandez, H. Johnson, L. Mazzilli

Individual Pitching

LOS ANGELES (WEST)

	W	L	ERA	IP	H	BB	SO	SV
O. Hershiser	1	0	1.09	24.2	18	7	15	1
T. Belcher	2	0	4.11	15.1	12	4	16	0
J. Tudor	0	0	7.20	5	8	1	1	0
R. Horton	0	0	0.00	4.1	4	2	3	0
T. Leary	0	1	6.23	4.1	8	3	3	0
A. Pena	1	1	4.15	4.1	1	5	1	1
B. Holton	0	0	2.25	4	2	1	2	1
J. Orosco	0	0	7.71	2.1	4	3	0	0
J. Howell	0	1	27.00	0.2	1	2	1	0

NEW YORK (EAST)

	W	L	ERA	IP	H	BB	SO	SV
D. Gooden	0	0	2.95	18.1	10	8	20	0
D. Cone	1	1	4.50	12	10	5	9	0
R. Aguilera	0	0	1.29	7	3	2	4	0
R. Darling	0	1	7.71	7	11	4	7	0
R. McDowell	0	1	4.50	6	6	2	5	0
T. Leach	0	0	0.00	5	4	1	4	0
R. Myers	2	0	0.00	4.2	1	2	0	0
S. Fernandez	0	1	13.50	4	7	1	5	0

1988 AMERICAN LEAGUE CHAMPIONSHIP SERIES

Oakland (West) defeats Boston (East) 4 games to 0

LINE SCORES						PITCHERS (innings pitched)	HOME RUNS (men on)	HIGHLIGHTS
GAME 1 - OCTOBER 5								Henderson's eighth inning RBI single gave Oakland the series opener. A's scored on Canseco's fourth inning homer, before Boston drew even on sacrifice fly by Boggs in seventh. Hurst pitched a complete game in losing effort for Red Sox.
OAK	**W**	000 100 010	2	6	0	Stewart (6.1), **Honeycutt** (0.2), Eckersley (2) **SV**	Canseco	
BOS	**E**	000 000 100	1	6	0	**Hurst** (9)		
GAME 2 - OCTOBER 6								Oakland posted their second consecutive late inning victory as Weiss singled home winning run in ninth inning. Boston scored twice in sixth to lead 2-0, but Oakland responded an inning later with Canseco's two run homer and McGwire's RBI single off Clemens. Boston tied it in bottom of the seventh on Gedman's homer.
OAK	**W**	000 000 301	4	10	1	Davis (6.1), Caderet (0.1), **Nelson** (1.1), Eckersley (1) **SV**	Canseco (1 on)	
BOS	**E**	000 002 100	3	4	1	Clemens (7), Stanley (0.1), **Smith** (1.2)	Gedman	
GAME 3 - OCTOBER 8								Oakland slammed four homers to charge back from early 5-0 deficit. McGwire's solo shot got Athletics on the board, then Lansford's 2 run homer brought them within a run in the second. Hassey gave them the lead for good an inning later with his two run homer. Henderson added another two run blast in the eighth to close out the scoring.
BOS	**E**	320 000 100	6	12	0	**Boddicker** (2.2), Gardner (4.2), Stanley (0.2)	Greenwell	
OAK	**W**	042 010 12x	10	15	1	Welch (1.2), **Nelson** (3.1), Young (1.1), Plunk (0.1), Honeycutt (0.1), Eckersley (2) **SV**	McGwire, Lansford (1 on), Hassey (1 on), Henderson (1 on)	
GAME 4 - OCTOBER 9								In winning their first pennant since 1974, Oakland became the first team to sweep a best-of-seven League Championship Series. Eckersley saved all 4 games to set a playoff record and win the series MVP award. Canseco hit his third homer of the series to open the scoring.
BOS	**E**	000 001 000	1	4	0	**Hurst** (4), Smithson (2.1), Smith (1.2)		
OAK	**W**	101 000 02x	4	10	1	**Stewart** (7.0), Honeycutt (1), Eckersley (1) **SV**	Canseco	

Team totals

		W	AB	H	2B	3B	HR	R	RBI	BA	BB	SO	ERA
OAK	**W**	4	137	41	8	0	7	20	20	.299	10	35	2.00
BOS	**E**	0	126	26	4	0	2	11	10	.206	18	23	5.29

Individual Batting

OAKLAND (WEST)

	AB	H	2B	3B	HR	R	RBI	BA
C. Lansford, 3b	17	5	1	0	1	4	2	.294
D. Henderson, of	16	6	1	0	1	2	4	.375
J. Canseco, of	16	5	1	0	3	4	4	.313
M. McGwire, 1b	15	5	0	0	1	4	3	.333
W. Weiss, ss	15	5	2	0	0	2	2	.333
D. Parker, dh, of	12	3	1	0	0	1	0	.250
M. Gallego, 2b	12	1	0	0	0	1	0	.083
R. Hassey, c	8	4	1	0	1	2	3	.500
T. Phillips, 2b, of	7	2	1	0	0	0	0	.286
D. Baylor, dh	6	0	0	0	0	0	1	.000
L. Polonia, of	5	2	0	0	0	0	0	.400
S. Javier, of	4	2	0	0	0	0	1	.500
T. Steinbach, c	4	1	0	0	0	0	0	.250

Errors: D. Henderson (2), D. Parker
Stolen Bases: J. Canseco

BOSTON (EAST)

	AB	H	2B	3B	HR	R	RBI	BA
E. Burks, of	17	4	1	0	0	2	1	.235
M. Barrett, 2b	15	1	0	0	0	2	0	.067
R. Gedman, c	14	5	0	0	1	1	1	.357
M. Greenwell, of	14	3	1	0	1	2	3	.214
W. Boggs, 3b	13	5	0	0	0	2	3	.385
J. Rice, dh	13	2	0	0	0	0	1	.154
D. Evans, of	12	2	1	0	0	1	1	.167
J. Reed, ss	11	3	1	0	0	0	0	.273
T. Benzinger, 1b	11	1	0	0	0	0	0	.091
L. Parrish, 1b, dh	6	0	0	0	0	0	0	.000
S. Owen	0	0	0	0	0	0	0	—
E. Romero	0	0	0	0	0	0	0	—
K. Romine	0	0	0	0	0	1	0	—

Errors: R. Clemens

Individual Pitching

OAKLAND (WEST)

	W	L	ERA	IP	H	BB	SO	SV
D. Stewart	1	0	1.35	13.1	9	6	11	0
S. Davis	0	0	0.00	6.1	2	5	4	0
D. Eckersley	0	0	0.00	6	1	2	5	4
G. Nelson	2	0	0.00	4.2	5	1	0	0
R. Honeycutt	1	0	0.00	2	0	2	0	0
B. Welch	0	0	27.00	1.2	6	2	0	0
C. Young	0	0	0.00	1.1	1	0	2	0
G. Cadaret	0	0	27.00	0.1	1	0	0	0
E. Plunk	0	0	0.00	0.1	1	0	1	0

BOSTON (EAST)

	W	L	ERA	IP	H	BB	SO	SV
B. Hurst	0	2	2.77	13	10	5	12	0
R. Clemens	0	0	3.86	7	6	0	8	0
W. Gardner	0	0	5.79	4.2	6	2	8	0
L. Smith	0	1	8.10	3.1	6	1	4	0
M. Boddicker	0	1	20.25	2.2	8	1	2	0
M. Smithson	0	0	0.00	2.1	3	0	1	0
B. Stanley	0	0	9.00	1	2	1	0	0

1988 WORLD SERIES

Los Angeles (N.L.) defeats Oakland (A.L.) 4 games to 1

LINE SCORES			R	H	E	PITCHERS (innings pitched)	HOME RUNS (men on)	HIGHLIGHTS
GAME 1 - OCTOBER 15								Two out, two run pinch homer by Gibson in ninth off relief ace Eckersley gave Dodgers a dramatic Series opening victory. Grand slam by Canseco gave Oakland the lead until Gibson's blast. It was to be injured Gibson's only appearance in the Series.
OAK	**A**	040 000 000	4	7	0	Stewart (8), **Eckersley** (0.2)	Canseco (3 on)	
LA	**N**	200 001 002	5	7	0	Belcher (2), Leary (3), Holton (2), **Pena** (2)	Hatcher (1 on), Gibson (1 on)	
GAME 2 - OCTOBER 16								Hershiser limited Oakland to three hits while collecting three himself, as Los Angeles took a 2-0 Series lead. Dodgers tallied five times in the third inning, capped by Marshall's 3 run homer. Parker had all three Oakland hits off Hershiser.
OAK	**A**	000 000 000	0	3	0	**Davis** (3.1), Nelson (1.2), Young (1), Plunk (1), Honeycutt (1)		
LA	**N**	005 100 00x	6	10	1	**Hershiser** (9)	Marshall (2 on)	
GAME 3 - OCTOBER 18								Ninth inning homer by McGwire powered Athletics to their only victory of the Series. Los Angeles left 10 runners on base and failed to capitalize on a bases loaded, nobody out opportunity in the sixth inning.
LA	**N**	000 010 000	1	8	1	Tudor (1.1), Leary (3.2), Pena (3), **Howell** (0.1)		
OAK	**A**	001 000 001	2	5	0	Welch (5.0), Cadaret (0.1), Nelson (1.2), **Honeycutt** (2)	McGwire	
GAME 4 - OCTOBER 19								Los Angeles took advantage of sloppy fielding by Oakland to take a 3-1 lead in the Series. Errors by infielders Hubbard and Weiss, along with Steinbach's passed ball led to Dodgers' first three runs. Strong relief work by Howell saved win for Belcher.
LA	**N**	201 000 100	4	8	1	**Belcher** (6.2), Howell (2.1) **SV**		
OAK	**A**	100 001 100	3	9	2	**Stewart** (6.1), Cadaret (1.2), Eckersley (1)		
GAME 5 - OCTOBER 20								Injury-riddled Dodgers climaxed a miraculous postseason by defeating Athletics 4 games to 1 to win their second World Championship of the 1980's. Series MVP Hershiser wrapped up the title with a 4 hitter, receiving support from Hatcher and Davis, who each smacked a two run homer.
LA	**N**	200 201 000	5	8	0	**Hershiser** (9)	Hatcher (1 on)	
OAK	**A**	001 000 010	2	4	0	**Davis** (4.2), Cadaret (0), Nelson (3) Honeycutt (0.1), Plunk (0.2), Burns (0.1)	Davis (1 on)	

Team totals

		W	AB	H	2B	3B	HR	R	RBI	BA	BB	SO	ERA
LA	**N**	4	167	41	8	1	5	21	19	.246	13	36	2.05
OAK	**A**	1	158	28	3	0	2	11	11	.177	17	41	3.89

Individual Batting

LOS ANGELES (N.L.)

	AB	H	2B	3B	HR	R	RBI	BA
S. Sax, 2b	20	6	0	0	0	3	0	.300
M. Hatcher, of	19	7	1	0	2	5	5	.368
J. Hamilton, 3b	19	2	0	0	0	1	0	.105
J. Shelby, of	18	4	1	0	0	0	1	.222
F. Stubbs, 1b	17	5	2	0	0	3	2	.294
A. Griffin, ss	16	3	0	0	0	2	0	.188
M. Scioscia, c	14	3	0	0	0	0	1	.214
M. Marshall, of	13	3	0	1	1	2	3	.231
D. Heep, dh, of	8	2	1	0	0	0	0	.250
M. Davis, dh, of	7	1	0	0	1	3	2	.143
R. Dempsey, c	5	1	1	0	0	0	1	.200
T. Woodson, 1b	4	0	0	0	0	0	1	.000
O. Hershiser, p	3	3	2	0	0	1	1	1.000
J. Gonzalez, of	2	0	0	0	0	0	0	.000
K. Gibson	1	1	0	0	1	1	2	1.000
D. Anderson, dh	1	0	0	0	0	0	0	.000

Errors: A. Griffin, J. Hamilton, M. Scioscia
Stolen Bases: M. Davis (2), S. Sax, J. Shelby

OAKLAND (A.L.)

	AB	H	2B	3B	HR	R	RBI	BA
D. Henderson, of	20	6	2	0	0	1	1	.300
J. Canseco, of	19	1	0	0	1	1	5	.053
C. Lansford, 3b	18	3	0	0	0	2	1	.167
M. McGwire, 1b	17	1	0	0	1	1	1	.059
W. Weiss, ss	16	1	0	0	0	1	0	.063
D. Parker, dh, of	15	3	0	0	0	0	0	.200
G. Hubbard, 2b	12	3	0	0	0	2	0	.250
T. Steinbach, c, dh	11	4	1	0	0	0	0	.364
L. Polonia, of	9	1	0	0	0	1	0	.111
R. Hassey, c	8	2	0	0	0	0	1	.250
S. Javier, of	4	2	0	0	0	0	2	.500
T. Phillips, 2b, of	4	1	0	0	0	1	0	.250
D. Stewart, p	3	0	0	0	0	1	0	.000
D. Baylor	1	0	0	0	0	0	0	.000
S. Davis, p	1	0	0	0	0	0	0	.000
M. Gallego, 2b	0	0	0	0	0	0	0	—

Errors: G. Hubbard, W. Weiss
Stolen Bases: J. Canseco, G. Hubbard, W. Weiss

Individual Pitching

LOS ANGELES (N.L.)

	W	L	ERA	IP	H	BB	SO	SV
O. Hershiser	2	0	1.00	18	7	6	17	0
T. Belcher	1	0	6.23	8.2	10	6	10	0
T. Leary	0	0	1.35	6.2	6	2	4	0
A. Pena	1	0	0.00	5	2	1	7	0
J. Howell	0	1	3.38	2.2	3	1	2	1
B. Holton	0	0	0.00	2	0	1	0	0
J. Tudor	0	0	0.00	1.1	0	0	1	0

OAKLAND (A.L.)

	W	L	ERA	IP	H	BB	SO	SV
D. Stewart	0	1	3.14	14.1	12	5	5	0
S. Davis	0	2	11.25	8	14	1	7	0
G. Nelson	0	0	1.42	6.1	4	3	3	0
B. Welch	0	0	1.80	5	6	3	8	0
R. Honeycutt	1	0	0.00	3.1	0	0	5	0
G. Cadaret	0	0	0.00	2	2	0	3	0
D. Eckersley	0	1	10.80	1.2	2	1	2	0
E. Plunk	0	0	0.00	1.2	0	0	3	0
C. Young	0	0	0.00	1	1	0	0	0
T. Burns	0	0	0.00	0.1	0	0	0	0

1989 NATIONAL LEAGUE CHAMPIONSHIP SERIES

San Francisco (West) defeats Chicago (East) 4 games to 1

LINE SCORES				R	H	E	PITCHERS (innings pitched)	HOME RUNS (men on)	HIGHLIGHTS
GAME 1 - OCTOBER 4									Clark went 4-for-4, homered twice and drove in a playoff-record 6 runs to lead Giants. Clark's fourth inning grand slam off Maddux gave Giants an 8-3 lead, breaking open a tight game.
SF	**W**	301 400 030		11	13	0	**Garrelts** (7), Brantley (1), Hammaker (1)	Clark, Clark (3 on), Mitchell (2 on)	
CHI	**E**	201 000 000		3	10	1	**Maddux** (4), Kilgus (3), Wilson (2)	Grace (1 on), Sandberg	
GAME 2 - OCTOBER 5									Chicago evened the series by scoring a playoff-record six runs in the opening inning. Walton singled twice in the frame, scored the first run and drove in the sixth.
SF	**W**	000 200 021		5	10	0	**Reuschel** (0.2), Downs (4.2), Lefferts (0.2), Brantley (1), Bedrosian (1)	Mitchell (1 on), Williams (1 on), Thompson	
CHI	**E**	600 003 00x		9	11	0	Bielecki (4.2), Assenmacher (0.1), **Lancaster** (4)		
GAME 3 - OCTOBER 7									Robby Thompson's two-run homer in seventh inning gave San Francisco a 5-4 victory and the lead in the series. Chicago had taken a 4-3 lead in the top of the seventh on Sandberg's sacrifice fly.
CHI	**E**	200 100 100		4	10	0	Sutcliffe (6), Assenmacher (0.1), **Lancaster** (1.2)		
SF	**W**	300 000 20x		5	8	3	LaCoss (3.0), Brantley (3), **Robinson** (1.2), Lefferts (0.1), Bedrosian (1) **SV**	Thompson	
GAME 4 - OCTOBER 8									Homer by Matt Williams in the fifth inning snapped a 4-4 tie, and strong relief work by Downs and Bedrosian made the lead stand up. Chicago loaded the bases in the ninth inning with two out, but Dawson struck out on three pitches to end the game.
CHI	**E**	110 020 000		4	12	1	Maddux (3.1), **Wilson** (1.2), Sanderson (2.0), Williams (1)	Salazar	
SF	**W**	102 120 00x		6	9	1	Garrelts (4.2), **Downs** (4), Bedrosian (0.1) **SV**	Williams	
GAME 5 - OCTOBER 9									Clark's bases-loaded single in the eighth inning carried Giants to their first pennant since 1962. Bielecki retired the first two Giants in the eighth, but walked the next three. Williams relieved, and Clark singled to center for a 3-1 lead. Chicago's ninth-inning rally fell a run short. Clark, who hit .650 in the five games, was named MVP of the series.
CHI	**E**	001 000 001		2	10	1	**Bielecki** (7.2), Williams (0), Lancaster (0.1)		
SF	**W**	000 000 12x		3	4	1	**Reuschel** (8), Bedrosian (1) **SV**		

Team totals

		W	AB	H	2B	3B	HR	R	RBI	BA	BB	SO	ERA
SF	**W**	4	165	44	6	2	8	30	29	.267	17	29	4.09
CHI	**E**	1	175	53	9	3	3	22	21	.303	16	27	5.57

Individual Batting

SAN FRANCISCO (WEST)

	AB	H	2B	3B	HR	R	RBI	BA
W. Clark, 1b	20	13	3	1	2	8	8	.650
M. Williams, 3b, ss	20	6	1	0	2	2	9	.300
B. Butler, of	19	4	0	0	0	6	0	.211
R. Thompson, 2b	18	5	0	0	2	5	3	.278
K. Mitchell, of	17	6	0	0	2	5	7	.353
J. Uribe, ss	17	4	1	0	0	2	1	.235
T. Kennedy, c	16	3	1	0	0	0	0	.188
P. Sheridan, of	13	2	0	1	0	1	0	.154
S. Garrelts, p	4	0	0	0	0	0	0	.000
K. Oberkfell, 3b	4	0	0	0	0	0	0	.000
K. Downs, p	3	0	0	0	0	0	0	.000
C. Maldonado, of	3	0	0	0	0	1	1	.000
D. Nixon, of	3	0	0	0	0	0	0	.000
K. Manwaring, c	2	0	0	0	0	0	0	.000
R. Reuschel, p	2	0	0	0	0	0	0	.000
G. Litton	1	1	0	0	0	0	0	1.000
B. Bathe	1	0	0	0	0	0	0	.000
M. LaCoss, p	1	0	0	0	0	0	0	.000
E. Riles	1	0	0	0	0	0	0	.000

Errors: J. Uribe (2), M. LaCoss, K. Mitchell, D. Nixon
Stolen Bases: D. Nixon, J. Uribe

CHICAGO (EAST)

	AB	H	2B	3B	HR	R	RBI	BA
J. Walton, of	22	8	0	0	0	4	2	.364
R. Sandberg, 2b	20	8	3	1	1	6	4	.400
L. Salazar, 3b	19	7	0	1	1	2	2	.368
S. Dunston, ss	19	6	0	0	0	2	0	.316
A. Dawson, of	19	2	1	0	0	0	3	.105
M. Grace, 1b	17	11	3	1	1	3	8	.647
D. Smith, of	15	3	1	0	0	2	0	.200
J. Girardi, c	10	1	0	0	0	1	0	.100
M. Wynne, of	6	1	0	0	0	0	0	.167
M. Bielecki, p	5	1	0	0	0	0	2	.200
R. Wrona, c	5	0	0	0	0	0	0	.000
L. McClendon, c, of	3	2	0	0	0	0	0	.667
M. Webster, of	3	1	0	0	0	0	0	.333
V. Law, 3b	3	0	0	0	0	0	0	.000
G. Maddux, p	3	0	0	0	0	1	0	.000
R. Sutcliffe, p	2	1	1	0	0	0	0	.500
C. Wilkerson, 3b	2	1	0	0	0	1	0	.500
L. Lancaster, p	1	0	0	0	0	0	0	.000
D. Ramos	1	0	0	0	0	0	0	.000

Errors: S. Dunston, G. Maddux, L. Salazar
Stolen Bases: S. Dunston, M. Grace, D. Smith

Individual Pitching

SAN FRANCISCO (WEST)

	W	L	ERA	IP	H	BB	SO	SV
S. Garrelts	1	0	5.40	11.2	16	2	8	0
K. Downs	1	0	3.12	8.2	8	6	6	0
R. Reuschel	1	1	5.19	8.2	12	2	5	0
J. Brantley	0	0	0.00	5	1	2	3	0
S. Bedrosian	0	0	2.70	3.1	4	2	2	3
M. LaCoss	0	0	9.00	3	7	0	2	0
D. Robinson	1	0	0.00	1.2	3	0	0	0
A. Hammaker	0	0	0.00	1	1	0	0	0
C. Lefferts	0	0	9.00	1	1	2	1	0

CHICAGO (EAST)

	W	L	ERA	IP	H	BB	SO	SV
M. Bielecki	0	1	3.65	12.1	7	6	11	0
G. Maddux	0	1	13.50	7.1	13	4	5	0
L. Lancaster	1	1	6.00	6	6	1	3	0
R. Sutcliffe	0	0	4.50	6	5	4	2	0
S. Wilson	0	1	4.91	3.2	3	1	4	0
P. Kilgus	0	0	0.00	3	4	1	1	0
S. Sanderson	0	0	0.00	2	2	0	1	0
M. Williams	0	0	0.00	1	1	0	2	0
P. Assenmacher	0	0	13.50	0.2	3	0	0	0

1989 AMERICAN LEAGUE CHAMPIONSHIP SERIES

Oakland (West) defeats Toronto (East) 4 games to 1

LINE SCORES			R	H	E	PITCHERS (innings pitched)	HOME RUNS (men on)	HIGHLIGHTS
GAME 1 - OCTOBER 3								Athletics rallied for three sixth-inning runs to take series opener as Stewart and Eckersley combined on a five-hitter. Liriano's wild throw on attempted double play allowed Oakland to score twice after McGwire's homer tied the game.
TOR	E	020 100 000	3	5	1	**Stieb** (5.1), Acker (1.2), Ward (1)	Whitt	
OAK	W	010 013 02x	7	11	0	**Stewart** (8), Eckersley (1)	D. Henderson, McGwire	
GAME 2 - OCTOBER 4								Rickey Henderson's postseason-record four stolen bases helped Oakland take a 2-0 lead in the series. Trailing 1-0, Athletics scored twice in the fourth inning. Henderson walked, stole second and third, and scored on single by Lansford. McGwire's double drove in the go-ahead run.
TOR	E	001 000 020	3	5	1	**Stottlemyre** (5.0), Acker (0.1), Wells (1), Henke (0.2), Cerutti (1)		
OAK	W	000 203 10x	6	9	1	**Moore** (7), Honeycutt (0), Eckersley (2) **SV**	Parker	
GAME 3 - OCTOBER 6								Toronto tallied four times in the fourth inning to erase 3-0 deficit. Two-run double by Fernandez tied the score, and go-ahead run scored on Whitt's RBI single. Parker homered for Oakland.
OAK	W	101 100 000	3	8	1	**Davis** (6.1), Honeycutt (0), Nelson (1.1), M. Young (0.1)	Parker	
TOR	E	000 400 30x	7	8	0	**Key** (6), Acker (2), Henke (1)		
GAME 4 - OCTOBER 7								Rickey Henderson hit two, two-run homers and Canseco belted a massive shot into the Skydome's upper deck to help Oakland build a 5-1 lead. Jays cut the lead to 6-5 in the eighth inning before Eckersley shut the door.
OAK	W	003 020 100	6	11	1	**Welch** (5.2), Honeycutt (1.2), Eckersley (1.2) **SV**	R. Henderson (1 on), Canseco, R. Henderson (1 on)	
TOR	E	000 101 120	5	13	0	**Flanagan** (4.1), Ward (2.2), Cerutti (1.2), Acker (0.1)		
GAME 5 - OCTOBER 8								Stewart bested Stieb for the second time in the series as Athletics became first team to win back-to-back pennants since 1978 Yankees and Dodgers. Rickey Henderson set a postseason series record with eight stolen bases, and was named series MVP.
OAK	W	101 000 200	4	4	0	**Stewart** (8.0), Eckersley (1) **SV**		
TOR	E	000 000 012	3	9	0	**Stieb** (6.0), Acker (2), Henke (1)	Moseby, Bell	

Team totals

		W	AB	H	2B	3B	HR	R	RBI	BA	BB	SO	ERA
OAK	W	4	158	43	9	1	7	26	23	.272	20	32	3.89
TOR	E	1	165	40	5	0	3	21	19	.242	15	24	5.02

Individual Batting

OAKLAND (WEST)

	AB	H	2B	3B	HR	R	RBI	BA
D. Henderson, of	19	5	3	0	1	4	1	.263
M. McGwire, 1b	18	7	1	0	1	3	3	.389
T. Phillips, 2b, 3b	18	3	1	0	0	1	1	.167
J. Canseco, of	17	5	0	0	1	1	3	.294
D. Parker, dh	16	3	0	0	2	2	3	.188
R. Henderson, of	15	6	1	1	2	8	5	.400
T. Steinbach, c, dh	15	3	0	0	0	0	1	.200
C. Lansford, 3b	11	5	0	0	0	2	4	.455
M. Gallego, 2b, ss	11	3	1	0	0	3	1	.273
W. Weiss, ss	9	1	1	0	0	2	0	.111
R. Hassey, c	6	1	0	0	0	0	1	.167
S. Javier, of	2	0	0	0	0	0	0	.000
K. Phelps	1	1	1	0	0	0	0	1.000
L. Blankenship, 2b	0	0	0	0	0	0	0	—

Errors: J. Canseco, R. Henderson, M. McGwire
Stolen Bases: R. Henderson (8), C. Lansford (2), T. Phillips (2), W. Weiss

TORONTO (EAST)

	AB	H	2B	3B	HR	R	RBI	BA
F. McGriff, 1b	21	3	0	0	0	1	3	.143
T. Fernandez, ss	20	7	3	0	0	6	1	.350
G. Bell, dh, of	20	4	0	0	1	2	2	.200
M. Wilson, of	19	5	0	0	0	2	2	.263
K. Gruber, 3b	17	5	1	0	0	2	1	.294
L. Moseby, of	16	5	0	0	1	4	2	.313
E. Whitt, c	16	2	0	0	1	1	3	.125
J. Felix, of	11	3	1	0	0	0	3	.273
M. Lee, 2b	8	2	0	0	0	2	0	.250
L. Mazzilli, dh	8	0	0	0	0	0	0	.000
N. Liriano, 2b	7	3	0	0	0	1	1	.429
P. Borders, c	1	1	0	0	0	0	1	1.000
R. Mulliniks	1	0	0	0	0	0	0	.000

Errors: N. Liriano, F. McGriff
Stolen Bases: T. Fernandez (5), N. Liriano (3), K. Gruber, L. Moseby, M. Wilson

Individual Pitching

OAKLAND (WEST)

	W	L	ERA	IP	H	BB	SO	SV
D. Stewart	2	0	2.81	16	13	3	9	0
M. Moore	1	0	0.00	7	3	2	3	0
S. Davis	0	1	7.11	6.1	5	2	3	0
D. Eckersley	0	0	1.59	5.2	4	0	2	3
B. Welch	1	0	3.18	5.2	8	1	4	0
R. Honeycutt	0	0	32.40	1.2	6	5	1	0
G. Nelson	0	0	0.00	1.1	1	0	2	0
M. Young	0	0	0.00	0.1	0	2	0	0

TORONTO (EAST)

	W	L	ERA	IP	H	BB	SO	SV
D. Stieb	0	2	6.35	11.1	12	6	10	0
J. Acker	0	0	1.42	6.1	4	1	4	0
J. Key	1	0	4.50	6	7	2	2	0
T. Stottlemyre	0	1	7.20	5	7	2	3	0
M. Flanagan	0	1	10.38	4.1	7	1	3	0
D. Ward	0	0	7.36	3.2	6	3	5	0
J. Cerutti	0	0	0.00	2.2	0	3	1	0
T. Henke	0	0	0.00	2.2	0	0	3	0
D. Wells	0	0	0.00	1	0	2	1	0

1989 WORLD SERIES

Oakland (A.L.) defeats San Francisco (N.L.) 4 games to 0

LINE SCORES			R	H	E	PITCHERS (innings pitched)	HOME RUNS (men on)	HIGHLIGHTS
GAME 1 - OCTOBER 14								Athletics took opener behind Stewart's five-hitter. Oakland jumped out to 3-0 lead in the second inning, and solo homers by Parker and Weiss added to the lead.
SF	**N**	000 000 000	0	5	1	**Garrelts** (4), Hammaker (1.2), Brantley (1.1), LaCoss (1)		
OAK	**A**	031 100 00x	5	11	1	**Stewart** (9)	Parker, Weiss	
GAME 2 - OCTOBER 15								A's broke open a 1-1 game by scoring four times in the fourth inning. Parker's RBI double snapped the tie, then Steinbach followed with a three run homer. Moore pitched seven strong innings as the Giants were held to four hits.
SF	**N**	001 000 000	1	4	0	**Reuschel** (4.0), Downs (2), Lefferts (1), Bedrosian (1)		
OAK	**A**	100 400 00x	5	7	0	**Moore** (7.0), Honeycutt (1.1), Eckersley (1)	Steinbach (2 on)	
GAME 3 - OCTOBER 27								A devastating earthquake hit the Bay Area minutes before the scheduled start of Game 3 on October 17. The Series was then postponed for ten days. When play resumed on October 27, the Athletics hit a record-tying five home runs (2 by Dave Henderson) to take a 3-0 Series lead. The teams combined for seven round-trippers, setting a series record for one game. Stewart became the first pitcher to ever win two games in both the LCS and World Series, and was later named MVP of the Series.
OAK	**A**	200 241 040	13	14	0	**Stewart** (7), Honeycutt (1), Nelson (0.2), Burns (0.1)	D. Henderson, Phillips, Canseco (2 on), D. Henderson, Lansford	
SF	**N**	010 200 004	7	10	3	**Garrelts** (3.1), Downs (1), Brantley (2.2), Hammaker (0.2), Lefferts (1.1)	Williams, Bathe (2 on)	
GAME 4 - OCTOBER 28								Athletics raced out to an 8-0 lead and held off the Giants to sweep the Series and win their first World Championship in fifteen years. Rickey Henderson led off the game with a home run, and winning pitcher Moore doubled home two runs an inning later. Mitchell and Litton homered for San Francisco.
OAK	**A**	130 031 010	9	12	0	**Moore** (6), Nelson (0.1), Honeycutt (0.1), Burns (1.1), Eckersley (1) **SV**	R. Henderson	
SF	**N**	000 002 400	6	9	0	**Robinson** (1.2), LaCoss (3.1), Brantley (1), Downs (1.2), Lefferts (0.1), Bedrosian (1.2)	Mitchell (1 on), Litton (1 on)	

Team totals

		W	AB	H	2B	3B	HR	R	RBI	BA	BB	SO	ERA
OAK	**A**	4	146	44	8	3	9	32	30	.301	18	22	3.50
SF	**N**	0	134	28	4	1	4	14	14	.209	8	27	8.21

Individual Batting

OAKLAND (A.L.)

	AB	H	2B	3B	HR	R	RBI	BA
R. Henderson, of	19	9	1	2	1	4	3	.474
M. McGwire, 1b	17	5	1	0	0	0	1	.294
T. Phillips, 2b, 3b, of	17	4	1	0	1	2	3	.235
C. Lansford, 3b	16	7	1	0	1	5	4	.438
T. Steinbach, c	16	4	0	1	1	3	7	.250
W. Weiss, ss	15	2	0	0	1	3	1	.133
J. Canseco, of	14	5	0	0	1	5	3	.357
D. Henderson, of	13	4	2	0	2	6	4	.308
D. Parker, dh	9	2	1	0	1	2	2	.222
M. Moore, p	3	1	1	0	0	1	2	.333
D. Stewart, p	3	0	0	0	0	0	0	.000
L. Blankenship, 2b	2	1	0	0	0	1	0	.500
M. Gallego, 2b, 3b	1	0	0	0	0	0	0	.000
K. Phelps	1	0	0	0	0	0	0	.000
S. Javier, of	0	0	0	0	0	0	0	—

Errors: D. Stewart
Stolen Bases: R. Henderson (3), J. Canseco

SAN FRANCISCO (N.L.)

	AB	H	2B	3B	HR	R	RBI	BA
K. Mitchell, of	17	5	0	0	1	2	2	.294
W. Clark, 1b	16	4	1	0	0	2	0	.250
M. Williams, 3b, ss	16	2	0	0	1	1	1	.125
B. Butler, of	14	4	1	0	0	1	1	.286
T. Kennedy, c	12	2	0	0	0	1	2	.167
C. Maldonado, of	11	1	0	1	0	1	0	.091
R. Thompson, 2b	11	1	0	0	0	0	2	.091
E. Riles, dh	8	0	0	0	0	0	0	.000
G. Litton, 2b, 3b	6	3	1	0	1	1	3	.500
K. Oberkfell, 3b	6	2	0	0	0	1	0	.333
D. Nixon, of	5	1	0	0	0	1	0	.200
J. Uribe, ss	5	1	0	0	0	1	0	.200
B. Bathe	2	1	0	0	1	1	3	.500
P. Sheridan, of	2	0	0	0	0	0	0	.000
K. Manwaring, c	1	1	1	0	0	1	0	1.000
S. Garrelts, p	1	0	0	0	0	0	0	.000
M. LaCoss, p	1	0	0	0	0	0	0	.000

Errors: T. Kennedy, C. Lefferts, K. Mitchell, K. Oberkfell
Stolen Bases: B. Butler (2)

Individual Pitching

OAKLAND (A.L.)

	W	L	ERA	IP	H	BB	SO	SV
D. Stewart	2	0	1.69	16	10	2	14	0
M. Moore	2	0	2.08	13	9	3	10	0
R. Honeycutt	0	0	6.75	2.2	4	0	2	0
T. Burns	0	0	0.00	1.2	1	1	0	0
D. Eckersley	0	0	0.00	1.2	0	0	0	1
G. Nelson	0	0	54.00	1	4	2	1	0

SAN FRANCISCO (N.L.)

	W	L	ERA	IP	H	BB	SO	SV
S. Garrelts	0	2	9.82	7.1	13	1	8	0
K. Downs	0	0	7.71	4.2	3	2	4	0
J. Brantley	0	0	4.15	4.1	5	3	1	0
M. LaCoss	0	0	6.23	4.1	4	3	2	0
R. Reuschel	0	1	11.25	4	5	4	2	0
S. Bedrosian	0	0	0.00	2.2	0	2	2	0
C. Lefferts	0	0	3.38	2.2	2	2	1	0
A. Hammaker	0	0	15.43	2.1	8	0	2	0
D. Robinson	0	1	21.60	1.2	4	1	0	0

1990 NATIONAL LEAGUE CHAMPIONSHIP SERIES

Cincinnati (West) defeats Pittsburgh (East) 4 games to 2

LINE SCORES						PITCHERS (innings pitched)	HOME RUNS (men on)	HIGHLIGHTS
GAME 1 - OCTOBER 4								Leftfielder Davis misplayed Van Slyke's seventh-inning fly ball into a game-winning double as Pirates rallied from a 3-0 deficit. Bream's two-run homer tied the game in the fourth inning. Cincinnati put runners on first and third in the ninth with nobody out, but were turned back by Power.
PIT	**E**	001 200 100	4	7	1	**Walk** (6), Belinda (2), Patterson (0.1), Power (0.2) **SV**	Bream (1 on)	
CIN	**W**	300 000 000	3	5	0	Rijo (5.1), **Charlton** (2.2), Dibble (1)		
GAME 2 - OCTOBER 5								O'Neill drove in both Cincinnati runs with a single and double against Drabek, while Browning teamed with Dibble and Myers on a six-hitter that evened the series. Lind homered for Pittsburgh's only run.
PIT	**E**	000 010 000	1	6	0	**Drabek** (8)	Lind	
CIN	**W**	100 010 00x	2	5	0	**Browning** (6), Dibble (1.1), Myers (1.2) **SV**		
GAME 3 - OCTOBER 8								Duncan drove in four runs, three of them coming on a fifth-inning homer that put the Reds ahead to stay. Hatcher's two-run homer gave Cincinnati a 2-0 lead before Pirates scored twice in the fourth inning.
CIN	**W**	020 030 001	6	13	1	**Jackson** (5.1), Dibble (1.2), Charlton (1), Myers (1) **SV**	Hatcher (1 on), Duncan (2 on)	
PIT	**E**	000 200 010	3	8	0	**Smith** (5), Landrum (1), Smiley (2), Belinda (1)		
GAME 4 - OCTOBER 9								Two-run homer by Sabo broke a 2-2 tie in the seventh inning. Davis made the defensive play of the game for the Reds by throwing out Bonilla at third base in the eighth inning as he tried to stretch a double into a triple.
CIN	**W**	000 200 201	5	10	1	**Rijo** (7.0), Myers (1), Dibble (1) **SV**	O'Neill, Sabo (1 on)	
PIT	**E**	100 100 010	3	8	0	**Walk** (7), Power (2)	Bell	
GAME 5 - OCTOBER 10								Drabek kept Pittsburgh's hopes alive with a strong performance before Patterson bailed him out of a ninth-inning jam. Reds scored a run in the top of the first, but Pirates scored twice in their half on Van Slyke's RBI triple and a forceout.
CIN	**W**	100 000 010	2	7	0	**Browning** (5), Mahler (1.2), Charlton (0.1), Scudder (1)		
PIT	**E**	200 100 00x	3	6	1	**Drabek** (8.1), Patterson (0.2) **SV**		
GAME 6 - OCTOBER 12								Cincinnati nailed down first pennant since 1976 on the strength of a combined one-hitter by Jackson, Charlton, and Myers. Reds broke a 1-1 tie in the seventh inning as pinch-hitter Quinones singled home Oester. Martinez doubled for Pittsburgh's only hit and run, and was robbed of a possible two-run homer in the ninth on a brilliant catch by Braggs.
PIT	**E**	000 010 000	1	1	3	Power (2.1), **Smith** (4), Belinda (0.2), Landrum (1)		
CIN	**W**	100 000 10x	2	9	0	Jackson (6), **Charlton** (1), Myers (2) **SV**		

Team totals

		W	AB	H	2B	3B	HR	R	RBI	BA	BB	SO	ERA
CIN	**W**	4	192	49	9	0	4	20	20	.255	10	37	2.38
PIT	**E**	2	186	36	9	2	3	15	14	.194	27	49	3.29

Individual Batting

CINCINNATI (WEST)

	AB	H	2B	3B	HR	R	RBI	BA
B. Larkin, ss	23	6	2	0	0	5	1	.261
E. Davis, of	23	4	1	0	0	2	2	.174
C. Sabo, 3b	22	5	0	0	1	1	3	.227
M. Duncan, 2b	20	6	0	0	1	1	4	.300
P. O'Neill, of	17	8	3	0	1	1	4	.471
B. Hatcher, of	15	5	1	0	1	2	2	.333
J. Oliver, c	14	2	0	0	0	1	0	.143
H. Morris, 1b	12	5	1	0	0	3	1	.417
T. Benzinger, 1b	9	3	0	0	0	0	0	.333
H. Winningham, of	7	2	1	0	0	1	1	.286
J. Reed, c	7	0	0	0	0	0	0	.000
G. Braggs, of	5	1	0	0	0	0	0	.200
J. Rijo, p	5	0	0	0	0	0	0	.000
R. Oester, 2b	3	1	0	0	0	1	0	.333
T. Browning, p	3	0	0	0	0	0	0	.000
D. Jackson, p	3	0	0	0	0	0	0	.000
L. Quinones	2	1	0	0	0	1	2	.500
R. Dibble, p	2	0	0	0	0	0	0	.000
B. Bates	0	0	0	0	0	1	0	—

Errors: M. Duncan, B. Larkin
Stolen Bases: B. Larkin (3), P. O'Neill, L. Quinones, H. Winningham

PITTSBURGH (EAST)

	AB	H	2B	3B	HR	R	RBI	BA
A. Van Slyke, of	24	5	1	1	0	3	3	.208
J. Lind, 2b	21	5	1	1	1	1	2	.238
B. Bonilla, 3b, of	21	4	1	0	0	0	1	.190
J. Bell, ss	20	5	1	0	1	3	1	.250
B. Bonds, of	18	3	0	0	0	4	1	.167
D. Slaught, c	11	1	1	0	0	0	1	.091
R. Reynolds, of	10	2	0	0	0	0	0	.200
J. King, 3b	10	1	0	0	0	0	0	.100
S. Bream, 1b	8	4	1	0	1	1	3	.500
C. Martinez, 1b	8	2	2	0	0	0	2	.250
G. Redus, 1b	8	2	0	0	0	1	0	.250
W. Backman, 3b	7	1	1	0	0	1	0	.143
D. Drabek, p	6	1	0	0	0	0	0	.167
M. LaValliere, c	6	0	0	0	0	1	0	.000
B. Walk, p	4	0	0	0	0	0	0	.000
Z. Smith, p	3	0	0	0	0	0	0	.000
T. Power, p	1	0	0	0	0	0	0	.000

Errors: J. Bell, B. Bonilla, D. Drabek, R. Reynolds, D. Slaught
Stolen Bases: B. Bonds (2), W. Backman, G. Redus, R. Reynolds, A. Van Slyke

Individual Pitching

CINCINNATI (WEST)

	W	L	ERA	IP	H	BB	SO	SV
J. Rijo	1	0	4.38	12.1	10	7	15	0
D. Jackson	1	0	2.38	11.1	8	7	8	0
T. Browning	1	1	3.27	11	9	6	5	0
R. Myers	0	0	0.00	5.2	2	3	7	3
N. Charlton	1	1	1.80	5	4	3	3	0
R. Dibble	0	0	0.00	5	0	1	10	1
R. Mahler	0	0	0.00	1.2	2	0	0	0
S. Scudder	0	0	0.00	1	1	0	1	0

PITTSBURGH (EAST)

	W	L	ERA	IP	H	BB	SO	SV
D. Drabek	1	1	1.65	16.1	12	3	13	0
B. Walk	1	1	4.85	13	11	2	8	0
Z. Smith	0	2	6.00	9	14	1	8	0
T. Power	0	0	3.60	5	6	2	3	1
S. Belinda	0	0	2.45	3.2	3	0	4	0
B. Landrum	0	0	0.00	2	0	0	1	0
J. Smiley	0	0	0.00	2	2	0	0	0
B. Patterson	0	0	0.00	1	1	2	0	1

1990 AMERICAN LEAGUE CHAMPIONSHIP SERIES

Oakland (West) defeats Boston (East) 4 games to 0

LINE SCORES			R	H	E	PITCHERS (innings pitched)	HOME RUNS (men on)	HIGHLIGHTS
GAME 1 - OCTOBER 6								Athletics broke open a 2-1 game with seven runs in the ninth inning. After Boggs homered in the fourth inning to give Boston a 1-0 lead, Oakland tied the score in the seventh on Rickey Henderson's sacrifice fly and gained the lead an inning later on an RBI single by Lansford. Stewart pitched a four-hitter over eight innings to pick up the win.
OAK	**W**	000 000 117	9	13	0	**Stewart** (8), Eckersley (1) **SV**		
BOS	**E**	000 100 000	1	5	1	Clemens (6), **Andersen** (1.0), Bolton (0.1), Lamp (0.1), Murphy (0.2)	Boggs	
GAME 2 - OCTOBER 7								Baines drove in three runs to back Welch's strong pitching performance as Oakland took a 2-0 lead in the series. Baines singled home his first run in the fourth to tie the game, drove in the go-ahead run with a grounder in the seventh, and doubled in an insurance run in the ninth.
OAK	**W**	000 100 102	4	13	1	**Welch** (7.1), Honeycutt (0.1), Eckersley (1.1) **SV**		
BOS	**E**	001 000 000	1	6	0	Kiecker (5.2), **Harris** (0.1), Andersen (1.0), Reardon (2)		
GAME 3 - OCTOBER 9								Randolph, filling in for the injured Weiss, hit two RBI singles to lift the Athletics to their third straight win. His first hit gave Oakland a 2-1 leadin the fourth inning, and he drove in their final run in the sixth.
BOS	**E**	010 000 000	1	8	3	**Boddicker** (8)		
OAK	**W**	000 202 00x	4	6	0	**Moore** (6), Nelson (1.2), Honeycutt (0.1), Eckersley (1) **SV**		
GAME 4 - OCTOBER 10								Oakland became the first team to win three consecutive pennants since the Yankees of 1976-77-78 as Stewart and Honeycutt held Boston to four hits. With Oakland leading 1-0 in the second inning, Boston starter Roger Clemens was ejected by plate umpire Terry Cooney. Bolton replaced Clemens and gave up a two-run double to Gallego. Athletics, who became first team to win a playoff series without hitting a home run, held Red Sox to just four runs in the series.
BOS	**E**	000 000 001	1	4	1	**Clemens** (1.2), Bolton (2.2), Gray (2.2), Andersen (1)		
OAK	**W**	030 000 00x	3	6	0	**Stewart** (8.0), Honeycutt (1) **SV**		

Team totals

		W	AB	H	2B	3B	HR	R	RBI	BA	BB	SO	ERA
OAK	**W**	4	127	38	4	0	0	20	18	.299	19	21	1.00
BOS	**E**	0	126	23	5	0	1	4	4	.183	6	16	4.50

Individual Batting

OAKLAND (WEST)

	AB	H	2B	3B	HR	R	RBI	BA
R. Henderson, of	17	5	0	0	0	1	3	.294
C. Lansford, 3b	16	7	1	0	0	2	2	.438
H. Baines, dh	14	5	1	0	0	2	3	.357
M. McGwire, 1b	13	2	0	0	0	2	2	.154
T. Steinbach, c	11	5	0	0	0	2	1	.455
J. Canseco, of	11	2	0	0	0	3	1	.182
M. Gallego, 2b, ss	10	4	1	0	0	1	2	.400
W. McGee, of	9	2	1	0	0	3	0	.222
W. Randolph, 2b	8	3	0	0	0	1	3	.375
W. Weiss, ss	7	0	0	0	0	2	0	.000
D. Henderson, of	6	1	0	0	0	0	1	.167
R. Hassey, c, dh	3	1	0	0	0	0	0	.333
J. Quirk	1	1	0	0	0	0	0	1.000
D. Jennings, of	1	0	0	0	0	0	0	.000
L. Blankenship	0	0	0	0	0	1	0	—

Errors: W. Weiss
Stolen Bases: J. Canseco (2), R. Henderson (2), W. McGee (2), H. Baines, L. Blankenship, D. Henderson

BOSTON (EAST)

	AB	H	2B	3B	HR	R	RBI	BA
W. Boggs, 3b	16	7	1	0	1	1	1	.438
E. Burks, of	15	4	2	0	0	1	0	.267
J. Reed, 2b, ss	15	2	0	0	0	0	1	.133
T. Pena, c	14	3	0	0	0	0	0	.214
M. Greenwell, of	14	0	0	0	0	1	0	.000
D. Evans, dh	13	3	1	0	0	0	0	.231
C. Quintana, 1b	13	0	0	0	0	0	1	.000
T. Brunansky, of	12	1	0	0	0	0	1	.083
L. Rivera, ss	9	2	1	0	0	1	0	.222
M. Marshall	3	1	0	0	0	0	0	.333
D. Heep	2	0	0	0	0	0	0	.000
M. Barrett, 2b	0	0	0	0	0	0	0	—
R. Kutcher	0	0	0	0	0	0	0	—

Errors: M. Boddicker, J. Gray, M. Greenwell, T. Pena, L. Rivera
Stolen Bases: E. Burks

Individual Pitching

OAKLAND (WEST)

	W	L	ERA	IP	H	BB	SO	SV
D. Stewart	2	0	1.13	16	8	2	4	0
B. Welch	1	0	1.23	7.1	6	3	4	0
M. Moore	1	0	1.50	6	4	1	5	0
D. Eckersley	0	0	0.00	3.1	2	0	3	2
R. Honeycutt	0	0	0.00	1.2	0	0	0	1
G. Nelson	0	0	0.00	1.2	3	0	0	0

BOSTON (EAST)

	W	L	ERA	IP	H	BB	SO	SV
M. Boddicker	0	1	2.25	8	6	3	7	0
R. Clemens	0	1	3.52	7.2	7	5	4	0
D. Kiecker	0	0	1.59	5.2	6	1	2	0
J. Gray	0	0	2.70	3.1	4	1	2	0
L. Andersen	0	1	6.00	3	3	3	3	0
T. Bolton	0	0	0.00	3	2	2	3	0
J. Reardon	0	0	9.00	2	3	1	0	0
R. Murphy	0	0	13.50	0.2	2	1	0	0
G. Harris	0	1	27.00	0.1	3	0	0	0
D. Lamp	0	0	108.00	0.1	2	2	0	0

1990 WORLD SERIES

LINE SCORES | **PITCHERS (innings pitched)** | **HOME RUNS (men on)** | **HIGHLIGHTS**

Cincinnati (N.L.) defeats Oakland (A.L.) 4 games to 0

GAME 1 - OCTOBER 16

Team	Lg	Line score	R	H	E	Pitchers (innings pitched)	Home runs (men on)
OAK	**A**	000 000 000	0	9	1	**Stewart** (4), Burns (0.2), Nelson (1.1), Sanderson (1), Eckersley (1)	
CIN	**N**	202 030 00x	7	10	0	**Rijo** (7), Dibble (1), Myers (1)	Davis (1 on)

Cincinnati reached Stewart for four runs in the first three innings to win the Series opener. Two-run homer by Davis opened the scoring in the first inning, and the Reds went on to score twice more in the third and three times in the fifth. Rijo and two relievers kept Oakland off the scoreboard

GAME 2 - OCTOBER 17

Team	Lg	Line score	R	H	E	Pitchers (innings pitched)	Home runs (men on)
OAK	**A**	103 000 000 0	4	10	2	Welch (7.1), Honeycutt (1.2), **Eckersley** (0.1)	Canseco
CIN	**N**	200 100 010 1	5	14	2	Jackson (2.2), Scudder (1.1), Armstrong (3.0), Charlton (1), **Dibble** (2)	

Oliver bounced a single down the leftfield line in the tenth inning to give the Reds a 2-0 lead in the Series. Oakland took a 4-2 lead with three runs in the third inning, but were held scoreless by the Cincinnati bullpen over the last seven frames. Reds' Hatcher went 4-for-4 to set a Series record with seven consecutive hits.

GAME 3 - OCTOBER 19

Team	Lg	Line score	R	H	E	Pitchers (innings pitched)	Home runs (men on)
CIN	**N**	017 000 000	8	14	1	**Browning** (6.0), Dibble (1.2), Myers (1.1)	Sabo, Sabo (1 on)
OAK	**A**	021 000 000	3	7	1	**Moore** (2.2), Sanderson (0.2), Klink (0), Nelson (3.2), Burns (1), Young (1)	Baines (1 on), R. Henderson

Sabo cracked two home runs, including a two-run shot in Cincinnati's seven-run third inning. Sabo's first homer gave the Reds a 1-0 lead before Baines connected with a man on to give Oakland a 2-1 lead. Reds then erupted for seven runs against Moore and Sanderson to take an 8-2 lead.

GAME 4 - OCTOBER 20

Team	Lg	Line score	R	H	E	Pitchers (innings pitched)	Home runs (men on)
CIN	**N**	000 000 020	2	7	1	**Rijo** (8.1), Myers (0.2) **SV**	
OAK	**A**	100 000 000	1	2	1	**Stewart** (9)	

Series MVP Rijo outpitched Stewart for the second time, leading Cincinnati to a sweep over the heavily favored Athletics. Trailing 1-0, the Reds loaded the bases in the eighth inning with nobody out. Braggs drove in the tying run with a ground ball, then a sacrifice fly by Morris plated the winning run. Rijo allowed Oakland's only run in the first inning, then retired 20 straight batters before Myers set down the final two. The championship was Cincinnati's first since 1976.

Team totals

		W	AB	H	2B	3B	HR	R	RBI	BA	BB	SO	ERA
CIN	**N**	4	142	45	9	2	3	22	22	.317	15	9	1.70
OAK	**A**	0	135	28	4	0	3	8	8	.207	12	28	4.33

Individual Batting

CINCINNATI (N.L.)

	AB	H	2B	3B	HR	R	RBI	BA
J. Oliver, c	18	6	3	0	0	2	2	.333
B. Larkin, ss	17	6	1	1	0	3	1	.353
C. Sabo, 3b	16	9	1	0	2	2	5	.563
E. Davis, of	14	4	0	0	1	3	5	.286
M. Duncan, 2b	14	2	0	0	0	1	1	.143
H. Morris, 1b, dh	14	1	0	0	0	0	2	.071
B. Hatcher, of	12	9	4	1	0	6	2	.750
P. O'Neill, of	12	1	0	0	0	2	1	.083
T. Benzinger, 1b	11	2	0	0	0	1	0	.182
H. Winningham, of	4	2	0	0	0	1	0	.500
G. Braggs, of	4	0	0	0	0	0	2	.000
J. Rijo, p	3	1	0	0	0	0	0	.333
B. Bates	1	1	0	0	0	1	0	1.000
R. Oester	1	1	0	0	0	0	1	1.000
D. Jackson, p	1	0	0	0	0	0	0	.000

Errors: J. Oliver (3), D. Jackson
Stolen Bases: M. Duncan, P. O'Neill

OAKLAND (A.L.)

	AB	H	2B	3B	HR	R	RBI	BA
R. Henderson, of	15	5	2	0	1	2	1	.333
C. Lansford, 3b	15	4	0	0	0	0	1	.267
W. Randolph, 2b	15	4	0	0	0	0	0	.267
M. McGwire, 1b	14	3	0	0	0	1	0	.214
D. Henderson, of	13	3	1	0	0	2	0	.231
J. Canseco, of	12	1	0	0	1	1	2	.083
M. Gallego, ss	11	1	0	0	0	0	1	.091
W. McGee, of	10	2	1	0	0	1	0	.200
T. Steinbach, c	8	1	0	0	0	0	0	.125
H. Baines, dh	7	1	0	0	1	1	2	.143
R. Hassey, c	6	2	0	0	0	0	1	.333
J. Quirk, c	3	0	0	0	0	0	0	.000
B. Welch, p	3	0	0	0	0	0	0	.000
D. Jennings	1	1	0	0	0	0	0	1.000
L. Blankenship	1	0	0	0	0	0	0	.000
D. Stewart, p	1	0	0	0	0	0	0	.000
M. Bordick, ss	0	0	0	0	0	0	0	—
R. Honeycutt	0	0	0	0	0	0	0	—

Errors: M. McGwire (2), M. Gallego, R. Hassey, D. Stewart
Stolen Bases: R. Henderson (3), M. Gallego, C. Lansford, W. McGee, W. Randolph

Individual Pitching

CINCINNATI (N.L.)

	W	L	ERA	IP	H	BB	SO	SV
J. Rijo	2	0	0.59	15.1	9	5	14	0
T. Browning	1	0	4.50	6	6	2	2	0
R. Dibble	1	0	0.00	4.2	3	1	4	0
J. Armstrong	0	0	0.00	3	1	0	3	0
R. Myers	0	0	0.00	3	2	0	3	1
D. Jackson	0	0	10.13	2.2	6	2	0	0
N. Charlton	0	0	0.00	1	1	0	0	0

OAKLAND (A.L.)

	W	L	ERA	IP	H	BB	SO	SV
D. Stewart	0	2	3.46	13	10	6	5	0
B. Welch	0	0	4.91	7.1	9	2	2	0
G. Nelson	0	0	0.00	5	3	2	0	0
M. Moore	0	1	6.75	2.2	8	0	1	0
T. Burns	0	0	16.20	1.2	5	2	0	0
R. Honeycutt	0	0	0.00	1.2	2	1	0	0
S. Sanderson	0	0	10.80	1.2	4	1	0	0
D. Eckersley	0	1	6.75	1.1	3	0	1	0
C. Young	0	0	0.00	1	1	0	0	0
J. Klink	0	0	—	0.0	0	1	0	0

1991 NATIONAL LEAGUE CHAMPIONSHIP SERIES

Atlanta (West) defeats Pittsburgh (East) 4 games to 3

LINE SCORES			R	H	E	PITCHERS (innings pitched)	HOME RUNS (men on)	HIGHLIGHTS
GAME 1 - OCTOBER 9								Van Slyke drove in Pirates' first two runs with a homer and a double. Drabek pitched six scoreless innings, but had to leave the game after injuring his hamstring while running the bases.
ATL	**W**	000 000 001	1	5	1	**Glavine** (6), Wohlers (1), Stanton (1)	Justice	
PIT	**E**	102 001 01x	5	8	1	**Drabek** (6), Walk (3) **SV**	Van Slyke	
GAME 2 - OCTOBER 10								Braves evened the series behind the combined shutout pitching of Avery and Pena. Lemke doubled home Justice with the only run of the game in the sixth inning.
ATL	**W**	000 001 000	1	8	0	**Avery** (8.1), Pena (0.2) **SV**		
PIT	**E**	000 000 000	0	6	0	**Smith** (7), Mason (1), Belinda (1)		
GAME 3 - OCTOBER 12								Merced led off the game with a home run, but the Braves answered with four runs in their half, capped by Olson's two-run homer. Atlanta extended their lead to 6-1 by the third inning, and homers by Gant and Bream completed the rout.
PIT	**E**	100 100 100	3	10	2	**Smiley** (2), Landrum (1), Patterson (2), Kipper (2), Rodriguez (1)	Merced, Bell	
ATL	**W**	411 000 13x	10	11	0	**Smoltz** (6.1), Stanton (0.2), Wohlers (0.1), Pena (1.2) **SV**	Olson (1 on), Gant, Bream (2 on)	
GAME 4 - OCTOBER 14								Pinch-hitter LaValliere's RBI single in the tenth inning evened the series for Pittsburgh. Van Slyke led off the decisive frame with a walk and stole second with two out. After Buechele walked, LaValliere delivered Van Slyke with the game-winner.
PIT	**E**	010 010 000 1	3	11	1	Tomlin (6), Walk (2), **Belinda** (2)		
ATL	**W**	200 000 000 0	2	7	1	Leibrandt (6.2), Clancy (0.1), Stanton (2), **Mercker** (0.2), Wohlers (0.1)		
GAME 5 - OCTOBER 14								Zane Smith, who lost the second game of the series 1-0, avenged that defeat by the same score as Pittsburgh took a 3 games to 2 lead. The Pirates scored the game's only run in the fifth inning on a run-scoring single by Lind.
PIT	**E**	000 010 000	1	6	2	**Smith** (7.2), Mason (1.1) **SV**		
ATL	**W**	000 000 000	0	9	1	**Glavine** (8), Pena (1)		
GAME 6 - OCTOBER 16								Avery won his second 1-0 game as he outdueled Drabek. Game was scoreless until the top of the ninth when Gant walked, stole second, and scored on Olson's two-out double.
ATL	**W**	000 000 001	1	7	0	**Avery** (8), Pena (1) **SV**		
PIT	**E**	000 000 000	0	4	0	**Drabek** (9)		
GAME 7 - OCTOBER 17								The Braves won their first pennant since moving to Atlanta in 1966 behind Smoltz, who tossed a six-hit shutout. Braves struck for three runs in the first inning on Gant's sacrifice fly and a two-run homer by Hunter, who added an RBI double in the fifth inning.
ATL	**W**	300 010 000	4	6	1	**Smoltz** (9)	Hunter (1 on)	
PIT	**E**	000 000 000	0	6	0	**Smiley** (0.2), Walk (4.1), Mason (2), Belinda (2)		

Team totals

		W	AB	H	2B	3B	HR	R	RBI	BA	BB	SO	ERA
ATL	**W**	4	229	53	10	1	5	19	19	.231	22	42	1.57
PIT	**E**	3	228	51	10	0	3	12	11	.224	22	57	2.57

Individual Batting

ATLANTA (WEST)

	AB	H	2B	3B	HR	R	RBI	BA
T. Pendleton, 3b	30	5	1	1	0	1	1	.167
R. Gant, of	27	7	1	0	1	4	3	.259
D. Justice, of	25	5	1	0	1	4	2	.200
G. Olson, c	24	8	1	0	1	3	4	.333
L. Smith, of	24	6	3	0	0	3	0	.250
M. Lemke, 2b	20	4	1	0	0	1	1	.200
R. Belliard, ss	19	4	0	0	0	0	1	.211
B. Hunter, 1b	18	6	2	0	1	2	4	.333
S. Bream, 1b	10	3	0	0	1	1	3	.300
S. Avery, p	7	1	0	0	0	0	0	.143
J. Smoltz, p	5	1	0	0	0	0	0	.200
T. Glavine, p	4	1	0	0	0	0	0	.250
T. Gregg	4	1	0	0	0	0	0	.250
K. Mitchell, of	4	0	0	0	0	0	0	.000
J. Treadway, 2b	3	1	0	0	0	0	0	.333
J. Blauser, ss	2	0	0	0	0	0	0	.000
J. Willard	2	0	0	0	0	0	0	.000
C. Leibrandt, p	1	0	0	0	0	0	0	.000

Errors: R. Belliard, J. Blauser, D. Justice, M. Lemke
Stolen Bases: R. Gant (7), G. Olson, L. Smith, J. Smoltz

PITTSBURGH (EAST)

	AB	H	2B	3B	HR	R	RBI	BA
J. Bell, ss	29	12	2	0	1	2	1	.414
B. Bonds, of	27	4	1	0	0	1	0	.148
J. Lind, 2b	25	4	0	0	0	0	3	.160
A. Van Slyke, of	25	4	2	0	1	3	2	.160
B. Bonilla, of	23	7	2	0	0	2	1	.304
S. Buechele, 3b	23	7	2	0	0	2	0	.304
G. Redus, 1b	19	3	0	0	0	1	0	.158
D. Slaught, c	17	4	0	0	0	0	1	.235
O. Merced, 1b	9	2	0	0	1	1	1	.222
M. LaValliere, c	6	2	0	0	0	0	1	.333
D. Drabek, p	5	1	1	0	0	0	1	.200
Z. Smith, p	5	0	0	0	0	0	0	.000
C. Wilkerson	4	0	0	0	0	0	0	.000
G. Varsho	2	1	0	0	0	0	0	.500
C. Espy	2	0	0	0	0	0	0	.000
L. McClendon, 1b	2	0	0	0	0	0	0	.000
R. Tomlin, p	2	0	0	0	0	0	0	.000
B. Walk, p	2	0	0	0	0	0	0	.000
R. Mason, p	1	0	0	0	0	0	0	.000

Errors: G. Redus (2), J. Bell, B. Bonds, J. Lind, O. Merced
Stolen Bases: B. Bonds (3), G. Redus (2), A. Van Slyke

Individual Pitching

ATLANTA (WEST)

	W	L	ERA	IP	H	BB	SO	SV
S. Avery	2	0	0.00	16.1	9	4	17	0
J. Smoltz	2	0	1.76	15.1	14	3	15	0
T. Glavine	0	2	3.21	14	12	6	11	0
C. Leibrandt	0	0	1.35	6.2	8	3	6	0
A. Pena	0	0	0.00	4.1	1	0	4	3
M. Stanton	0	0	2.45	3.2	4	3	3	0
M. Wohlers	0	0	0.00	1.2	3	1	1	0
K. Mercker	0	1	13.50	0.2	0	2	0	0
J. Clancy	0	0	0.00	0.1	0	0	0	0

PITTSBURGH (EAST)

	W	L	ERA	IP	H	BB	SO	SV
D. Drabek	1	1	0.60	15	10	5	10	0
Z. Smith	1	1	0.61	14.2	15	3	10	0
B. Walk	0	0	1.93	9.1	5	3	5	1
R. Tomlin	0	0	3.00	6	6	2	1	0
S. Belinda	1	0	0.00	5	0	3	4	0
R. Mason	0	0	0.00	4.1	3	1	2	1
J. Smiley	0	2	23.63	2.2	8	1	3	0
B. Kipper	0	0	4.50	2	2	0	1	0
B. Patterson	0	0	0.00	2	1	0	3	0
B. Landrum	0	0	9.00	1	2	2	2	0
R. Rodriguez	0	0	27.00	1	1	2	1	0

1991 AMERICAN LEAGUE CHAMPIONSHIP SERIES

Minnesota (West) defeats Toronto (East) 4 games to 1

LINE SCORES						PITCHERS (innings pitched)	HOME RUNS (men on)	HIGHLIGHTS
GAME 1 - OCTOBER 8								The Twins raced to a 5-0 lead after three innings, helped by four stolen bases. The Blue Jays scored three runs in the sixth inning off winning pitcher Morris, but were held scoreless over the final three innings by relievers Willis and Aguilera.
TOR	**E**	000 103 000	4	9	3	**Candiotti** (2.2), Wells (3), Timlin (2.1)		
MIN	**W**	221 000 00x	5	11	0	**Morris** (5.1), Willis (2.1), Aguilera (1.1) **SV**		
GAME 2 - OCTOBER 9								White scored three runs, while Carter and Gruber drove in two runs apiece as Toronto tied the series. Guzman and two relievers limited the Twins to five singles.
TOR	**E**	102 000 200	5	9	0	**Guzman** (5.2), Henke (1.1), Ward (2) **SV**		
MIN	**W**	001 001 000	2	5	1	**Tapani** (6.1), Bedrosian (0.1), Guthrie (2.1)		
GAME 3 - OCTOBER 11								A pinch-hit homer by Pagliarulo in the tenth inning gave Minnesota a come-from-behind victory and a 2-1 lead in the series. Blue Jays opened the scoring with two first-inning runs, including a solo homer by Carter. The Twins rallied with single runs in the fifth and sixth innings.
MIN	**W**	000 011 000 1	3	7	0	Erickson (4.0), West (2.2), Willis (2), **Guthrie** (0.1), Aguilera (1) **SV**	Pagliarulo	
TOR	**E**	200 000 000 0	2	5	1	Key (6), Wells (1.2), Henke (1.1), **Timlin** (1)	Carter	
GAME 4 - OCTOBER 12								Puckett went 3-for-4, including a home run that ignited a four-run fourth inning, giving Morris his second victory of the series. Gladden added three hits and three RBI for Minnesota, while Borders had three hits and drove in two runs for Toronto.
MIN	**W**	000 402 111	9	13	1	**Morris** (8), Bedrosian (1)	Puckett	
TOR	**E**	010 001 001	3	11	2	**Stottlemyre** (3.2), Wells (1.2), Acker (0.2), Timlin (2), MacDonald (1)		
GAME 5 - OCTOBER 13								Series MVP Puckett singled home the tie-breaking run in the eighth inning and the Twins went on to wrap up the A.L. flag with their third consecutive victory at Toronto. Blue Jays led 5-2 until Minnesota scored three times in the sixth inning on an error by Borders and a two-run double by Knoblauch.
MIN	**W**	110 003 030	8	14	2	Tapani (4), **West** (3), Willis (1), Aguilera (1) **SV**	Puckett	
TOR	**E**	003 200 000	5	9	1	Candiotti (5.1), Timlin (0.1), **Ward** (2.1), Wells (1.1)		

Team totals

		W	AB	H	2B	3B	HR	R	RBI	BA	BB	SO	ERA
MIN	**W**	4	181	50	9	1	3	27	25	.276	15	37	3.33
TOR	**E**	1	173	43	6	0	1	19	18	.249	15	30	4.60

Individual Batting

MINNESOTA (WEST)

	AB	H	2B	3B	HR	R	RBI	BA
D. Gladden, of	23	6	0	0	0	4	3	.261
K. Puckett, of	21	9	1	0	2	4	6	.429
K. Hrbek, 1b	21	3	0	0	0	0	3	.143
C. Knoblauch, 2b	20	7	2	0	0	5	3	.350
S. Mack, of	18	6	1	1	0	4	3	.333
B. Harper, c	18	5	2	0	0	1	1	.278
C. Davis, dh	17	5	2	0	0	3	2	.294
G. Gagne, ss	17	4	0	0	0	1	1	.235
M. Pagliarulo, 3b	15	5	1	0	1	4	3	.333
S. Leius, 3b	4	0	0	0	0	0	0	.000
G. Larkin	3	0	0	0	0	0	0	.000
J. Ortiz, c	3	0	0	0	0	0	0	.000
P. Sorrento	1	0	0	0	0	0	0	.000
J. Brown, dh	0	0	0	0	0	1	0	—
A. Newman, 3b, ss	0	0	0	0	0	0	0	—

Errors: G. Gagne (2), B. Harper, S. Mack
Stolen Bases: D. Gladden (3), C. Knoblauch (2), S. Mack (2), C. Davis

TORONTO (EAST)

	AB	H	2B	3B	HR	R	RBI	BA
D. White, of	22	8	1	0	0	5	0	.364
K. Gruber, 3b	21	6	1	0	0	1	4	.286
C. Maldonado, of	20	2	1	0	0	1	1	.100
R. Alomar, 2b	19	9	0	0	0	3	4	.474
P. Borders, c	19	5	1	0	0	0	2	.263
J. Carter, dh, of	19	5	2	0	1	3	4	.263
J. Olerud, 1b	19	3	0	0	0	1	3	.158
M. Lee, ss	16	2	0	0	0	3	0	.125
M. Wilson, of	8	2	0	0	0	1	0	.250
R. Mulliniks, dh	8	1	0	0	0	1	0	.125
R. Ducey, of	1	0	0	0	0	0	0	.000
P. Tabler, dh	1	0	0	0	0	0	0	.000
R. Gonzales, 1b, ss	0	0	0	0	0	0	0	—

Errors: K. Gruber (3), P. Borders (2), M. Lee, M. Timlin
Stolen Bases: D. White (3), R. Alomar (2), K. Gruber, M. Wilson

Individual Pitching

MINNESOTA (WEST)

	W	L	ERA	IP	H	BB	SO	SV
J. Morris	2	0	4.05	13.1	17	1	7	0
K. Tapani	0	1	7.84	10.1	16	3	9	0
D. West	1	0	0.00	5.2	1	4	4	0
C. Willis	0	0	0.00	5.1	2	0	3	0
S. Erickson	0	0	4.50	4	3	5	2	0
R. Aguilera	0	0	0.00	3.1	1	0	3	3
M. Guthrie	1	0	0.00	2.2	0	0	0	0
S. Bedrosian	0	0	0.00	1.1	3	2	2	0

TORONTO (EAST)

	W	L	ERA	IP	H	BB	SO	SV
T. Candiotti	0	1	8.22	7.2	17	2	5	0
D. Wells	0	0	2.35	7.2	6	2	9	0
J. Key	0	0	3.00	6	5	1	1	0
J. Guzman	1	0	3.18	5.2	4	4	2	0
M. Timlin	0	1	3.18	5.2	5	2	5	0
D. Ward	0	1	6.23	4.1	4	1	6	1
T. Stottlemyre	0	1	9.82	3.2	7	1	3	0
T. Henke	0	0	0.00	2.2	0	1	5	0
B. MacDonald	0	0	9.00	1	1	1	0	0
J. Acker	0	0	0.00	0.2	1	0	1	0

1991 WORLD SERIES

Minnesota (A.L.) defeats Atlanta (N.L.) 4 games to 3

LINE SCORES			R	H	E	PITCHERS (innings pitched)	HOME RUNS (men on)	HIGHLIGHTS
GAME 1 - OCTOBER 19								Homers by Gagne and Hrbek carried Morris and the Twins to victory. Gagne slugged a three-run homer in the fifth inning for a 4-0 lead, and Hrbek connected an inning later.
ATL	**N**	000 001 010	2	6	1	**Leibrandt** (4.0), Clancy (2), Wohlers (1), Stanton (1)		
MIN	**A**	001 031 00x	5	9	1	**Morris** (7.0), Guthrie (0.2), Aguilera (1.1) **SV**	Gagne (2 on), Hrbek	
GAME 2 - OCTOBER 20								The Twins again relied on the long ball to take a 2-0 lead in the Series. Davis belted a two-run homer in the first inning, and after the Braves tied the score, the rookie Leius led off the eighth inning with a round-tripper to make a winner of Tapani.
ATL	**N**	010 010 000	2	8	1	**Glavine** (8)		
MIN	**A**	200 000 01x	3	4	1	**Tapani** (8), Aguilera (1) **SV**	Davis (1 on), Leius	
GAME 3 - OCTOBER 22								Lemke singled to score Justice with two outs in the in 12th inning to give Atlanta their first win of the Series. Twins forced extra innings when Davis pinch-hit a two-run homer in the eighth.
MIN	**A**	100 000 120 000	4	10	1	Erickson (4.2), West (0), Leach (0.1), Bedrosian (2), Willis (2), Guthrie (2), **Aguilera** (0.2)	Puckett, Davis (1 on)	
ATL	**N**	010 120 000 001	5	8	2	Avery (7.0), Pena (2), Stanton (2), Wohlers (0.1), Mercker (0.1), **Clancy** (0.1)	Justice, Smith	
GAME 4 - OCTOBER 23								The Braves knotted the Series as pinch-hitter Willard's ninth-inning sacrifice fly scored Lemke, who had tripled, with the winning run. Pendleton and Smith homered for Atlanta's first two runs. Pagliarulo had three hits, including a home run, and drove in both runs for Minnesota.
MIN	**A**	010 000 100	2	7	0	Morris (6), Willis (1.1), **Guthrie** (1), Bedrosian (0.1)	Pagliarulo	
ATL	**N**	001 000 101	3	8	0	Smoltz (7), Wohlers (0.1), **Stanton** (1.2)	Pendleton, Smith	
GAME 5 - OCTOBER 24								Atlanta pounded out 17 hits while scoring the most runs in a Series game since 1960. Justice led the assault by driving in five runs, two coming on a homer in the Braves' four-run fourth inning. Lonnie Smith homered for the third consecutive game, tying a Series record.
MIN	**A**	000 003 011	5	7	1	**Tapani** (4), Leach (2), West (0), Bedrosian (1), Willis (1)		
ATL	**N**	000 400 63x	14	17	1	**Glavine** (5.1), Mercker (0.2), Clancy (2), St. Claire (1)	Justice, Smith (1 on), Hunter	
GAME 6 - OCTOBER 26								Puckett led off the bottom of the 11th with a home run to keep the Twins alive in the Series. Puckett figured in all of Minnesota's scoring with three hits, three RBI, and two runs scored.
ATL	**N**	000 020 100 00	3	9	1	Avery (6), Stanton (2), Pena (2), **Leibrandt** (0)	Pendleton (1 on)	
MIN	**A**	200 010 000 01	4	9	0	Erickson (6.0), Guthrie (0.1), Willis (2.2), **Aguilera** (2)	Puckett	
GAME 7 - OCTOBER 27								The Twins won their second World Championship in five years in dramatic fashion, winning the deciding game 1-0 in ten innings on pinch-hitter Larkin's bases loaded single. Morris pitched ten scoreless innings to pick up his second victory and the Series MVP award. Gladden led off the tenth with a double and was bunted to third base. Following two intentional walks, Larkin lifted a drive over the drawn-in outfield to give Minnesota the championship in a battle of teams that finished last the previous season.
ATL	**N**	000 000 000 0	0	7	0	Smoltz (7.1), Stanton (0.2), **Pena** (1.1)		
MIN	**A**	000 000 000 1	1	10	0	**Morris** (10)		

Team totals

		W	AB	H	2B	3B	HR	R	RBI	BA	BB	SO	ERA
MIN	**A**	4	241	56	8	4	8	24	24	.232	21	48	3.74
ATL	**N**	3	249	63	10	4	8	29	29	.253	26	39	3.17

Individual Batting

MINNESOTA (A.L.)

	AB	H	2B	3B	HR	R	RBI	BA
D. Gladden, of	30	7	2	2	0	5	0	.233
C. Knoblauch, 2b	26	8	1	0	0	3	2	.308
K. Hrbek, 1b	26	3	1	0	1	2	2	.115
K. Puckett, of	24	6	0	1	2	4	4	.250
G. Gagne, ss	24	4	1	0	1	1	3	.167
S. Mack, of	23	3	1	0	0	0	1	.130
B. Harper, c	21	8	2	0	0	2	1	.381
C. Davis, dh, of	18	4	0	0	2	4	4	.222
S. Leius, 3b, ss	14	5	0	0	1	2	2	.357
M. Pagliarulo, 3b	11	3	0	0	1	1	2	.273
J. Ortiz, c	5	1	0	0	0	0	1	.200
G. Larkin, dh	4	2	0	0	0	0	1	.500
R. Bush, of	4	1	0	0	0	0	0	.250
A. Newman, 2b, 3b, ss	2	1	0	1	0	0	1	.500
J. Brown, dh, of	2	0	0	0	0	0	0	.000
J. Morris, p	2	0	0	0	0	0	0	.000
P. Sorrento, 1b	2	0	0	0	0	0	0	.000
R. Aguilera, p	1	0	0	0	0	0	0	.000
S. Erickson, p	1	0	0	0	0	0	0	.000
K. Tapani, p	1	0	0	0	0	0	0	.000

Errors: D. Gladden, B. Harper, C. Knoblauch, S. Leius
Stolen Bases: C. Knoblauch (4), D. Gladden (2), K. Puckett

ATLANTA (N.L.)

	AB	H	2B	3B	HR	R	RBI	BA
T. Pendleton, 3b	30	11	3	0	2	6	3	.367
R. Gant, of	30	8	0	1	0	3	4	.267
D. Justice, of	27	7	0	0	2	5	6	.259
G. Olson, c	27	6	2	0	0	3	1	.222
L. Smith, dh, of	26	6	0	0	3	5	3	.231
M. Lemke, 2b	24	10	1	3	0	4	4	.417
S. Bream, 1b	24	3	2	0	0	0	0	.125
B. Hunter, 1b, of	21	4	1	0	1	2	3	.190
R. Belliard, ss	16	6	1	0	0	0	4	.375
J. Blauser, ss	6	1	0	0	0	0	0	.167
J. Treadway, 2b	4	1	0	0	0	1	0	.250
S. Avery, p	3	0	0	0	0	0	0	.000
T. Gregg	3	0	0	0	0	0	0	.000
T. Glavine, p	2	0	0	0	0	0	0	.000
K. Mitchell, of	2	0	0	0	0	0	0	.000
J. Smoltz, p	2	0	0	0	0	0	0	.000
F. Cabrera, c	1	0	0	0	0	0	0	.000
J. Clancy, p	1	0	0	0	0	0	0	.000
J. Willard	0	0	0	0	0	0	1	—

Errors: T. Pendleton (2), B. Hunter, D. Justice, M. Lemke, J. Treadway
Stolen Bases: D. Justice (2), R. Gant, G. Olson, L. Smith

Individual Pitching

MINNESOTA (A.L.)

	W	L	ERA	IP	H	BB	SO	SV
J. Morris	2	0	1.17	23	18	9	15	0
K. Tapani	1	1	4.50	12	13	2	7	0
S. Erickson	0	0	5.06	10.2	10	4	5	0
C. Willis	0	0	5.14	7	6	2	2	0
R. Aguilera	1	1	1.80	5	6	1	3	2
M. Guthrie	0	1	2.25	4	3	4	3	0
S. Bedrosian	0	0	5.40	3.1	3	0	2	0
T. Leach	0	0	3.86	2.1	2	0	2	0
D. West	0	0	∞	0.0	2	4	0	0

ATLANTA (N.L.)

	W	L	ERA	IP	H	BB	SO	SV
J. Smoltz	0	0	1.26	14.1	13	1	11	0
T. Glavine	1	1	2.70	13.1	8	7	8	0
S. Avery	0	0	3.46	13	10	1	8	0
M. Stanton	1	0	0.00	7.1	5	2	7	0
A. Pena	0	1	3.38	5.1	6	3	7	0
J. Clancy	1	0	4.15	4.1	3	4	2	0
C. Leibrandt	0	2	11.25	4	8	1	3	0
M. Wohlers	0	0	0.00	1.2	2	2	1	0
K. Mercker	0	0	0.00	1	0	0	1	0
R. St. Claire	0	0	9.00	1	1	0	0	0

1992 NATIONAL LEAGUE CHAMPIONSHIP SERIES

Atlanta (West) defeats Pittsburgh (East) 4 games to 3

LINE SCORES						PITCHERS (innings pitched)	HOME RUNS (men on)	HIGHLIGHTS
GAME 1 - OCTOBER 6								Bream had two hits, scored twice, and drove in a run to pace Atlanta's victory. Smoltz held Pittsburgh to just four hits over eight innings, with Lind's home run accounting for their only run. Blauser homered in the fifth inning to give the Braves a 4-0 lead.
PIT	**E**	000 000 010	1	5	1	**Drabek** (4.2), Patterson (1.1), Neagle (1), Cox (1)	Lind	
ATL	**W**	010 210 10x	5	8	0	**Smoltz** (8), Stanton (1)	Blauser	
GAME 2 - OCTOBER 7								Braves knocked out Jackson with a four run second inning on their way to a lopsided victory and a 2-0 lead in the series. Atlanta scored four more times in the fifth inning on Gant's grand slam, and after Pittsburgh rallied for four runs in the seventh inning, Braves finished the rout with five runs in their half of the inning.
PIT	**E**	000 000 410	5	7	0	**Jackson** (1.2), Mason (0.1), Walk (2.2), Tomlin (1.1), Neagle (0.2), Patterson (0.1), Belinda (1)		
ATL	**W**	040 040 50x	13	14	0	**Avery** (6.1), Freeman (0.1), Stanton (0.1), Wohlers (1), Reardon (1)	Gant (3 on)	
GAME 3 - OCTOBER 9								Wakefield outpitched Glavine to lead Pirates to their first win of the series. The rookie knuckleball pitcher went the distance, holding the Braves to five hits. Redus went 3-for-3 for Pittsburgh and scored the deciding run on Van Slyke's sacrifice fly in the seventh inning.
ATL	**W**	000 100 100	2	5	0	**Glavine** (6.1), Stanton (0.2), Wohlers (1)	Bream, Gant	
PIT	**E**	000 011 10x	3	8	1	**Wakefield** (9)	Slaught	
GAME 4 - OCTOBER 10								Nixon went 4-for-5 with two runs scored and two RBIs, and Smoltz gained his second victory as Atlanta took a 3-1 lead in the series.
ATL	**W**	020 022 000	6	11	1	**Smoltz** (6.1), Stanton (1.2), Reardon (1) **SV**		
PIT	**E**	021 000 100	4	6	3	**Drabek** (4.1), Tomlin (1.1), Cox (0.1), Mason (3)		
GAME 5 - OCTOBER 11								Walk limited Braves to three hits, while Pirates knocked out Avery during a four run first inning which included consecutive run scoring doubles by Bonds, King, and McClendon.
ATL	**W**	000 000 010	1	3	0	**Avery** (0.1), P. Smith (3.2), Leibrandt (1.2), Freeman (1.1), Mercker (1)		
PIT	**E**	401 001 10x	7	13	0	**Walk** (9)		
GAME 6 - OCTOBER 13								Pittsburgh erupted for eight runs off Glavine in the second inning as they evened the series. Bonds led off the inning with a home run, and Bell capped the uprising with a three run shot. Wakefield picked up his second complete game victory of the series. Justice homered twice for Atlanta.
PIT	**E**	080 041 000	13	13	1	**Wakefield** (9)	Bonds, Bell (2 on), McClendon	
ATL	**W**	000 100 102	4	9	1	**Glavine** (1.0), Leibrandt (3), Freeman (2), Mercker (2), Wohlers (1)	Justice, Justice (1 on)	
GAME 7 - OCTOBER 14								Pinch-hitter Cabrera's two-out single scored the tying and winning runs as Atlanta scored three times in the bottom of the ninth to win their second consecutive pennant. Drabek, who became the first pitcher to lose three playoff games in one series, carried a 2-0 lead into the ninth, but loaded the bases with nobody out. Belinda relieved him and recorded two outs, including Gant's sacrifice fly, before giving up Cabrera's winning hit.
PIT	**E**	100 001 000	2	7	1	**Drabek** (8.0), Belinda (0.2)		
ATL	**W**	000 000 003	3	7	0	Smoltz (6), Stanton (0.2), P. Smith (0), Avery (1.1), **Reardon** (1)		

Team totals

		W	AB	H	2B	3B	HR	R	RBI	BA	BB	SO	ERA
ATL	**W**	4	234	57	11	2	6	34	32	.244	29	28	4.72
PIT	**E**	3	231	59	20	3	5	35	32	.255	29	42	4.45

Individual Batting

ATLANTA (WEST)

	AB	H	2B	3B	HR	R	RBI	BA
T. Pendleton, 3b	30	7	2	0	0	2	3	.233
O. Nixon, of	28	8	2	0	0	5	2	.286
D. Justice, of	25	7	1	0	2	5	6	.280
J. Blauser, ss	24	5	0	1	1	3	4	.208
D. Berryhill, c	24	4	1	0	0	1	1	.167
S. Bream, 1b	22	6	3	0	1	5	2	.273
R. Gant, of	22	4	0	0	2	5	6	.182
M. Lemke, 2b, 3b	21	7	1	0	0	2	2	.333
J. Smoltz, p	7	2	0	0	0	1	1	.286
L. Smith	6	2	0	1	0	1	1	.333
B. Hunter, 1b	5	1	0	0	0	1	0	.200
D. Sanders, of	5	0	0	0	0	0	0	.000
J. Treadway, 2b	3	2	0	0	0	1	0	.667
F. Cabrera	2	1	0	0	0	0	2	.500
S. Avery, p	2	0	0	0	0	0	1	.000
R. Belliard, 2b, ss	2	0	0	0	0	1	0	.000
T. Glavine, p	2	0	0	0	0	0	0	.000
M. Stanton, p	1	1	1	0	0	1	1	1.000
C. Leibrandt, p	1	0	0	0	0	0	0	.000
J. Lopez, c	1	0	0	0	0	0	0	.000
P. Smith, p	1	0	0	0	0	0	0	.000

Errors: J. Blauser (2)
Stolen Bases: O. Nixon (3), R. Gant, J. Smoltz

PITTSBURGH (EAST)

	AB	H	2B	3B	HR	R	RBI	BA
A. Van Slyke, of	29	8	3	1	0	1	4	.276
J. King, 3b	29	7	4	0	0	4	2	.241
J. Bell, ss	29	5	2	0	1	3	4	.172
J. Lind, 2b	27	6	2	1	1	5	5	.222
B. Bonds, of	23	6	1	0	1	5	2	.261
G. Redus, 1b	16	7	4	1	0	4	3	.438
D. Slaught, c	12	4	1	0	1	5	5	.333
L. McClendon, of	11	8	2	0	1	4	4	.727
A. Cole, of	10	2	0	0	0	2	1	.200
M. LaValliere, c	10	2	0	0	0	1	0	.200
O. Merced, 1b	10	1	1	0	0	0	2	.100
D. Drabek, p	6	0	0	0	0	0	0	.000
T. Wakefield, p	6	0	0	0	0	1	0	.000
B. Walk, p	5	0	0	0	0	0	0	.000
C. Espy, of	3	2	0	0	0	0	0	.667
G. Varsho, of	2	1	0	0	0	0	0	.500
J. Wehner	2	0	0	0	0	0	0	.000
C. Garcia, 2b	1	0	0	0	0	0	0	.000

Errors: J. Lind (2), J. Bell, J. King, O. Merced
Stolen Bases: B. Bonds

Individual Pitching

ATLANTA (WEST)

	W	L	ERA	IP	H	BB	SO	SV
J. Smoltz	2	0	2.66	20.1	14	10	19	0
S. Avery	1	1	9.00	8	13	2	3	0
T. Glavine	0	2	12.27	7.1	13	3	2	0
C. Leibrandt	0	0	1.93	4.2	4	3	3	0
M. Stanton	0	0	0.00	4.1	2	2	5	0
M. Freeman	0	0	14.73	3.2	8	2	1	0
P. Smith	0	0	2.45	3.2	2	3	3	0
K. Mercker	0	0	0.00	3	1	1	1	0
J. Reardon	1	0	0.00	3	0	2	3	1
M. Wohlers	0	0	0.00	3	2	1	2	0

PITTSBURGH (EAST)

	W	L	ERA	IP	H	BB	SO	SV
T. Wakefield	2	0	3.00	18	14	5	7	0
D. Drabek	0	3	3.71	17	18	6	10	0
B. Walk	1	0	3.86	11.2	6	7	6	0
R. Mason	0	0	0.00	3.1	0	2	1	0
R. Tomlin	0	0	6.75	2.2	5	1	0	0
S. Belinda	0	0	0.00	1.2	2	1	2	0
D. Jackson	0	1	21.60	1.2	4	2	0	0
D. Neagle	0	0	27.00	1.2	4	3	0	0
B. Patterson	0	0	5.40	1.2	3	1	1	0
D. Cox	0	0	0.00	1.1	1	1	1	0

1992 AMERICAN LEAGUE CHAMPIONSHIP SERIES

Toronto (East) defeats Oakland (West) 4 games to 2

LINE SCORES			R	H	E	PITCHERS (innings pitched)	HOME RUNS (men on)	HIGHLIGHTS
GAME 1 - OCTOBER 7								Baines homered off Morris leading off the ninth inning to give Oakland the series opener. Toronto had rallied to tie the game in the eighth inning on Olerud's RBI single. Athletics took a 3-0 lead in the second inning as McGwire and Steinbach hit consecutive home runs, before Blue Jays narrowed the lead on homers by Borders and Winfield.
OAK	**W**	030 000 001	4	6	1	Stewart (7.2), **Russell** (0.1), Eckersley (1) **SV**	McGwire (1 on), Steinbach, Baines	
TOR	**E**	000 011 010	3	9	0	**Morris** (9)	Borders, Winfield	
GAME 2 - OCTOBER 8								Two-run homer by Gruber in the fifth inning was all Cone needed to even the series for Toronto. Cone held Oakland scoreless until the final inning, when he was relieved by Henke after allowing a leadoff triple to Sierra. Henke allowed an RBI single to Baines before nailing down the win.
OAK	**W**	000 000 001	1	6	0	**Moore** (7), Corsi (0.2), Parrett (0.1)		
TOR	**E**	000 020 10x	3	4	0	**Cone** (8.0), Henke (1) **SV**	Gruber (1 on)	
GAME 3 - OCTOBER 10								Blue Jays outlasted Athletics in a sloppy game that took three hours and forty minutes to play. Oakland made three errors and was charged with three wild pitches. Maldonado's homer in the fifth inning gave Toronto the lead for good.
TOR	**E**	010 110 211	7	9	1	**Guzman** (6), Ward (1), Timlin (0.1), Henke (1.2) **SV**	Alomar, Maldonado	
OAK	**W**	000 200 210	5	13	3	**Darling** (6), Downs (1), Corsi (0.1), Russell (0.2), Honeycutt (0.2), Eckersley (0.1)		
GAME 4 - OCTOBER 11								Toronto rallied from a five run deficit to grab a dramatic victory in eleven innings. With Blue Jays trailing 6-4 in the ninth inning, Alomar reached Eckersley for a game tying homer. In the eleventh, Borders hit a sacrifice fly to score Bell with the winning run.
TOR	**E**	010 000 032 01	7	17	4	Morris (3.1), Stottlemyre (3.2), Timlin (1), **Ward** (2), Henke (1) **SV**	Olerud, Alomar (1 on)	
OAK	**W**	005 001 000 00	6	12	3	Welch (7.0), Parrett (0), Eckersley (1.2), Corsi (1), **Downs** (1.1)		
GAME 5 - OCTOBER 12								Sierra belted a two run homer in the first inning, and Browne went 4-for-4 as Oakland stayed alive in the series. Stewart went the route on a seven-hitter to get the win. Winfield homered for Toronto's only run.
TOR	**E**	000 100 100	2	7	3	**Cone** (4.0), Key (3), Eichhorn (1)	Winfield	
OAK	**W**	201 030 00x	6	8	0	**Stewart** (9)	Sierra (1 on)	
GAME 6 - OCTOBER 14								The Toronto Blue Jays became the first Canadian team to reach the World Series as they won their first pennant in four trips to the championship series. Carter's two run homer in the first inning got the Blue Jays started, and Maldonado's three run clout in the third gave them a 6-0 lead for Guzman, who won his second game of the series.
OAK	**W**	000 001 010	2	7	1	**Moore** (2.2), Parrett (2), Honeycutt (1.1), Russell (1), Witt (1)		
TOR	**E**	204 010 02x	9	13	0	**Guzman** (7), Ward (1), Henke (1)	Carter (1 on), Maldonado (2 on)	

Team totals

		W	AB	H	2B	3B	HR	R	RBI	BA	BB	SO	ERA
TOR	**E**	4	210	59	8	1	10	31	30	.281	23	29	3.44
OAK	**W**	2	207	52	5	1	4	24	23	.251	24	33	4.50

Individual Batting

TORONTO (EAST)

	AB	H	2B	3B	HR	R	RBI	BA
R. Alomar, 2b	26	11	1	0	2	4	4	.423
J. Carter, 1b, of	26	5	0	0	1	2	3	.192
D. Winfield, dh	24	6	1	0	2	7	3	.250
J. Olerud, 1b	23	8	2	0	1	4	4	.348
D. White, of	23	8	2	0	0	2	2	.348
P. Borders, c	22	7	0	0	1	3	3	.318
C. Maldonado, of	22	6	0	0	2	3	6	.273
K. Gruber, 3b	22	2	1	0	1	3	2	.091
M. Lee, ss	18	5	1	1	0	2	3	.278
E. Sprague	2	1	0	0	0	0	0	.500
A. Griffin, ss	2	0	0	0	0	0	0	.000
D. Bell, of	0	0	0	0	0	1	0	—

Errors: M. Lee (3), P. Borders, J. Carter, D. Cone, K. Gruber, D. White
Stolen Bases: R. Alomar (5), J. Carter (2)

OAKLAND (WEST)

	AB	H	2B	3B	HR	R	RBI	BA
H. Baines, dh	25	11	2	0	1	6	4	.440
R. Sierra, of	24	8	2	1	1	4	7	.333
T. Steinbach, c	24	7	0	0	1	1	5	.292
R. Henderson, of	23	6	0	0	0	5	1	.261
W. Wilson, dh, of	22	5	1	0	0	0	0	.227
M. McGwire, 1b	20	3	0	0	1	1	3	.150
M. Bordick, 2b, ss	19	1	0	0	0	1	0	.053
C. Lansford, 3b	18	3	0	0	0	0	1	.167
L. Blankenship, 2b	13	3	0	0	0	2	0	.231
J. Browne, 3b, of	10	4	0	0	0	3	2	.400
W. Weiss, ss	6	1	0	0	0	1	0	.167
E. Fox, dh, of	1	0	0	0	0	0	0	.000
J. Quirk	1	0	0	0	0	0	0	.000
R. Ready	1	0	0	0	0	0	0	.000

Errors: R. Henderson (3), L. Blankenship (2), C. Lansford, M. McGwire
Stolen Bases: W. Wilson (7), E. Fox (2), R. Henderson (2), W. Weiss (2), L. Blankenship, M. Bordick, R. Sierra

Individual Pitching

TORONTO (EAST)

	W	L	ERA	IP	H	BB	SO	SV
J. Guzman	2	0	2.08	13	12	5	11	0
J. Morris	0	1	6.57	12.1	11	9	6	0
D. Cone	1	1	3.00	12	11	5	9	0
T. Henke	0	0	0.00	4.2	3	2	2	3
D. Ward	1	0	6.75	4	6	1	2	0
T. Stottlemyre	0	0	2.45	3.2	3	0	1	0
J. Key	0	0	0.00	3	2	2	1	0
M. Timlin	0	0	6.75	1.1	4	0	1	0
M. Eichhorn	0	0	0.00	1	0	0	0	0

OAKLAND (WEST)

	W	L	ERA	IP	H	BB	SO	SV
D. Stewart	1	0	2.70	16.2	14	6	7	0
M. Moore	0	2	7.45	9.2	11	5	7	0
B. Welch	0	0	2.57	7	7	1	7	0
R. Darling	0	1	3.00	6	4	2	3	0
D. Eckersley	0	0	6.00	3	8	0	2	1
K. Downs	0	1	3.86	2.1	3	1	0	0
J. Parrett	0	0	11.57	2.1	6	0	1	0
J. Corsi	0	0	0.00	2	2	3	0	0
R. Honeycutt	0	0	0.00	2	0	0	1	0
J. Russell	1	0	9.00	2	2	4	0	0
B. Witt	0	0	18.00	1	2	1	1	0

1992 WORLD SERIES

Toronto (A.L.) defeats Atlanta (N.L.) 4 games to 2

LINE SCORES				R	H	E	PITCHERS (innings pitched)	HOME RUNS (men on)	HIGHLIGHTS
GAME 1 - OCTOBER 17									Berryhill smacked a three run homer off Morris in the sixth inning to lead Glavine and the Braves to victory in the Series opener. Glavine held Toronto to four hits, including a solo homer by Carter, and didn't walk a batter.
TOR	**A**	000 100 000		1	4	0	**Morris** (6), Stottlemyre (1), Wells (1)	Carter	
ATL	**N**	000 003 00x		3	4	0	**Glavine** (9)	Berryhill (2 on)	
GAME 2 - OCTOBER 18									Two run pinch-hit homer by Sprague in the ninth inning off Reardon enabled the Blue Jays to even the Series.
TOR	**A**	000 020 012		5	9	2	Cone (4.1), Wells (1.2), Stottlemyre (1), **Ward** (1), Henke (1) **SV**	Sprague (1 on)	
ATL	**N**	010 120 000		4	5	1	Smoltz (7.1), Stanton (0.1), **Reardon** (1.1)		
GAME 3 - OCTOBER 20									Maldonado's single with the bases loaded gave the Blue Jays their second consecutive ninth inning win. Atlanta took a 2-1 lead on Smith's RBI single in the top of the eighth before Gruber tied the game for Toronto with a home run in the home half of the inning.
ATL	**N**	000 001 010		2	9	0	**Avery** (8.0), Wohlers (0.1), Stanton (0), Reardon (0)		
TOR	**A**	000 100 011		3	6	1	Guzman (8), **Ward** (1)	Carter, Gruber	
GAME 4 - OCTOBER 21									Key held the Braves scoreless until the eighth inning, then received relief help from Ward and Henke to give the Blue Jays their third straight win. Borders homered in the third inning to open the scoring, and White added an RBI single in the seventh.
ATL	**N**	000 000 010		1	5	0	**Glavine** (8)		
TOR	**A**	001 000 10x		2	6	0	**Key** (7.2), Ward (0.1), Henke (1) **SV**	Borders	
GAME 5 - OCTOBER 22									Grand slam home run by Lonnie Smith highlighted a five run fifth inning that sent Morris to his second loss of the Series. Smoltz worked six innings for the victory, with Stanton picking up the save with three scoreless innings. Justice hit a solo homer for the Braves, while Borders drove in both Toronto runs.
ATL	**N**	100 150 000		7	13	0	**Smoltz** (6.0), Stanton (3) **SV**	Justice, L. Smith (3 on)	
TOR	**A**	010 100 000		2	6	0	**Morris** (4.2), Wells (1.1), Timlin (1), Eichhorn (1), Stottlemyre (1)		
GAME 6 - OCTOBER 24									Two run double by Winfield in the eleventh inning carried the Blue Jays to their first World Championship, the first ever won by a Canadian team. With one out in the eleventh, Leibrandt hit White with a pitch, and Alomar followed with a single. Carter flew out for the second out, then Winfield scored the runners with a drive past third base and down the left field line. Braves got a run back in their half of the inning, but Timlin came in to retire Nixon, who had tied the game in the ninth with a two-out single, on a bunt back to the mound for the final out. Atlanta became the first team to lose consecutive World Series since Los Angeles in 1977-78.
TOR	**A**	100 100 000	02	4	14	1	Cone (6), Stottlemyre (0.2), Wells (0.1), Ward (1), Henke (1.1), **Key** (1.1), Timlin (0.1) **SV**	Maldonado	
ATL	**N**	001 000 001	01	3	8	1	Avery (4), P. Smith (3), Stanton (1.2), Wohlers (0.1) **Leibrandt** (2)		

Team totals

		W	AB	H	2B	3B	HR	R	RBI	BA	BB	SO	ERA
TOR	**A**	4	196	45	8	0	6	17	17	.230	18	33	2.78
ATL	**N**	2	200	44	6	0	3	20	19	.220	20	48	2.65

Individual Batting

TORONTO (A.L.)

	AB	H	2B	3B	HR	R	RBI	BA
D. White, of	26	6	1	0	0	2	2	.231
R. Alomar, 2b	24	5	1	0	0	3	0	.208
J. Carter, 1b, of	22	6	2	0	2	2	3	.273
D. Winfield, dh, of	22	5	1	0	0	0	3	.227
P. Borders, c	20	9	3	0	1	2	3	.450
C. Maldonado, of	19	3	0	0	1	1	2	.158
K. Gruber, 3b	19	2	0	0	1	2	1	.105
M. Lee, ss	19	2	0	0	0	1	0	.105
J. Olerud, 1b	13	4	0	0	0	2	0	.308
D. Cone, p	4	2	0	0	0	0	1	.500
E. Sprague, 1b	2	1	0	0	1	1	2	.500
J. Morris, p	2	0	0	0	0	0	0	.000
P. Tabler	2	0	0	0	0	0	0	.000
D. Bell	1	0	0	0	0	1	0	.000
J. Key, p	1	0	0	0	0	0	0	.000
A. Griffin, ss	0	0	0	0	0	0	0	—

Errors: P. Borders, A. Griffin, K. Gruber, M. Lee
Stolen Bases: R. Alomar (3), K. Gruber, D. White

ATLANTA (N.L.)

	AB	H	2B	3B	HR	R	RBI	BA
O. Nixon, of	27	8	1	0	0	3	1	.296
T. Pendleton, 3b	25	6	2	0	0	2	2	.240
J. Blauser, ss	24	6	0	0	0	2	0	.250
D. Berryhill, c	22	2	0	0	1	1	3	.091
M. Lemke, 2b	19	4	0	0	0	0	2	.211
D. Justice, of	19	3	0	0	1	4	3	.158
D. Sanders, of	15	8	2	0	0	4	1	.533
S. Bream, 1b	15	3	0	0	0	1	0	.200
L. Smith, dh	12	2	0	0	1	1	5	.167
R. Gant, of	8	1	1	0	0	2	0	.125
B. Hunter, 1b	5	1	0	0	0	0	2	.200
J. Smoltz, p	3	0	0	0	0	0	0	.000
T. Glavine, p	2	0	0	0	0	0	0	.000
S. Avery, p	1	0	0	0	0	0	0	.000
F. Cabrera	1	0	0	0	0	0	0	.000
P. Smith, p	1	0	0	0	0	0	0	.000
J. Treadway	1	0	0	0	0	0	0	.000
R. Belliard, 2b, ss	0	0	0	0	0	0	0	—

Errors: S. Bream, D. Justice
Stolen Bases: O. Nixon (5), D. Sanders (5), J. Blauser (2), R. Gant (2), D. Justice

Individual Pitching

TORONTO (A.L.)

	W	L	ERA	IP	H	BB	SO	SV
J. Morris	0	2	8.44	10.2	13	6	12	0
D. Cone	0	0	3.48	10.1	9	8	8	0
J. Key	2	0	1.00	9	6	0	6	0
J. Guzman	0	0	1.13	8	8	1	7	0
D. Wells	0	0	0.00	4.1	1	2	3	0
T. Stottlemyre	0	0	0.00	3.2	4	0	4	0
T. Henke	0	0	2.70	3.1	2	2	1	2
D. Ward	2	0	0.00	3.1	1	1	6	0
M. Timlin	0	0	0.00	1.1	0	0	0	1
M. Eichhorn	0	0	0.00	1	0	0	1	0

ATLANTA (N.L.)

	W	L	ERA	IP	H	BB	SO	SV
T. Glavine	1	1	1.59	17	10	4	8	0
J. Smoltz	1	0	2.70	13.1	13	7	12	0
S. Avery	0	1	3.75	12	11	3	11	0
M. Stanton	0	0	0.00	5	3	2	1	1
P. Smith	0	0	0.00	3	3	0	0	0
C. Leibrandt	0	1	9.00	2	3	0	0	0
J. Reardon	0	1	13.50	1.1	2	1	1	0
M. Wohlers	0	0	0.00	0.2	0	1	0	0

1993 NATIONAL LEAGUE CHAMPIONSHIP SERIES

LINE SCORES | **PITCHERS (innings pitched)** | **HOME RUNS (men on)** | **HIGHLIGHTS**

Philadelphia (East) defeats Atlanta (West) 4 games to 2

GAME 1 - OCTOBER 6

Team		Line score	R	H	E	Pitchers (innings pitched)	Home runs (men on)
ATL	W	001 100 001 0	3	9	0	Avery (6), Mercker (2), **McMichael** (1.1)	
PHI	E	100 101 000 1	4	9	1	Schilling (8), **Williams** (2)	Incaviglia

Batiste, a defensive replacement at third base whose error helped Braves tie the game in the ninth inning, redeemed himself with a single in the tenth inning that scored Kruk with the winning run. Philadelphia starter Schilling fanned 10 batters, including an LCS record five at the start of the game.

GAME 2 - OCTOBER 7

Team		Line score	R	H	E	Pitchers (innings pitched)	Home runs (men on)
ATL	W	206 010 041	14	16	0	**Maddux** (7), Stanton (1), Wohlers (1)	McGriff (1 on), Blauser, Berryhill (2 on), Pendleton
PHI	E	000 200 001	3	7	2	**Greene** (2.1), Thigpen (0.2), Rivera (2), Mason (2), West (1), Andersen (1)	Hollins (1 on), Dykstra

Braves slugged four home runs in scoring the most runs ever in an LCS game. McGriff started the assault with a two run homer in the opening inning, and Atlanta broke the contest open with a 6 run third inning featuring a solo homer by Blauser and a three run clout by Berryhill. Pendleton added a solo homer in the fifth, while Philadelphia got home runs by Hollins and Dykstra as the teams combined for a LCS record six roundtrippers.

GAME 3 - OCTOBER 9

Team		Line score	R	H	E	Pitchers (innings pitched)	Home runs (men on)
PHI	E	000 101 011	4	10	1	**Mulholland** (5.0), Mason (1), Andersen (0.1), West (0.2), Thigpen (1)	Kruk
ATL	W	000 005 40x	9	12	0	**Glavine** (7), Mercker (1), McMichael (1)	

Braves scored five runs in the sixth and four more in the seventh to take a 2-1 lead in the series. Kruk had given the Phillies a 2-0 lead with an RBI triple and a solo homer before Mulholland faltered in the sixth, allowing run scoring hits to McGriff and Pendleton and a tiebreaking two run double by Justice.

GAME 4 - OCTOBER 10

Team		Line score	R	H	E	Pitchers (innings pitched)	Home runs (men on)
PHI	E	000 200 000	2	8	1	**Jackson** (7.2), Williams (1.1) **SV**	
ATL	W	010 000 000	1	10	1	**Smoltz** (6.1), Mercker (0.2), Wohlers (2)	

Philadelphia evened the series as Jackson kept the Braves in check and singled home the deciding run in the fourth inning. Leftfielder Thompson made a leaping catch of Lemke's drive with two on and two out in the eighth inning to preserve the victory.

GAME 5 - OCTOBER 11

Team		Line score	R	H	E	Pitchers (innings pitched)	Home runs (men on)
PHI	E	100 100 001 1	4	6	1	Schilling (8.0), **Williams** (1), Andersen (1) **SV**	Daulton, Dykstra
ATL	W	000 000 003 0	3	7	1	Avery (7), Mercker (1), McMichael (1), **Wohlers** (1)	

Dykstra's tenth inning homer off Wohlers won it for the Phillies after the Braves rallied from a 3-0 deficit with three runs in the ninth. Schilling blanked Atlanta for eight innings and was relieved by Williams after a walk and an error by Batiste put the first two batters on in the ninth. McGriff drove in the first run with a single and Justice followed with a sacrifice fly before Cabrera tied the game with a single. Williams then retired Lemke and Pecota with the winning run at third base, setting up Philadelphia's second extra inning victory of the series.

GAME 6 - OCTOBER 13

Team		Line score	R	H	E	Pitchers (innings pitched)	Home runs (men on)
ATL	W	000 010 200	3	5	3	**Maddux** (5.2), Mercker (0.1), McMichael (0.2), Wohlers (1.1)	Blauser (1 on)
PHI	E	002 022 00x	6	7	1	**Greene** (7), West (1), Williams (1) **SV**	Hollins (1 on)

Phillies advanced to the World Series for the first time in ten years with their third straight victory over the Braves. Daulton, Hollins, and Morandini drove in two runs apiece, and Greene rebounded from a poor performance in the second game of the series to pick up the victory. Williams figured in all four Philadelphia victories with two wins and two saves. Blauser hit a two run homer for Atlanta, who failed in their bid for a third consecutive pennant.

Team totals

		W	AB	H	2B	3B	HR	R	RBI	BA	BB	SO	ERA
PHI	E	4	207	47	11	4	7	23	22	.227	26	51	4.75
ATL	W	2	215	59	14	0	5	33	32	.274	22	54	3.15

Individual Batting

PHILADELPHIA (EAST)

	AB	H	2B	3B	HR	R	RBI	BA
L. Dykstra, of	25	7	1	0	2	5	2	.280
J. Kruk, 1b	24	6	2	1	1	4	5	.250
K. Stocker, ss	22	4	1	0	0	0	1	.182
D. Hollins, 3b	20	4	1	0	2	2	4	.200
D. Daulton, c	19	5	1	0	1	2	3	.263
M. Morandini, 2b	16	4	0	1	0	1	2	.250
M. Duncan, 2b	15	4	0	2	0	3	0	.267
J. Eisenreich, of	15	2	1	0	0	0	1	.133
M. Thompson, of	13	3	1	0	0	2	0	.231
P. Incaviglia, of	12	2	0	0	1	2	1	.167
W. Chamberlain, of	11	4	3	0	0	1	1	.364
C. Schilling, p	5	0	0	0	0	0	0	.000
D. Jackson, p	4	1	0	0	0	0	1	.250
T. Mulholland, p	2	0	0	0	0	0	0	.000
K. Batiste, 3b	1	1	0	0	0	0	1	1.000
R. Jordan	1	0	0	0	0	0	0	.000
T. Longmire	1	0	0	0	0	0	0	.000
T. Pratt, c	1	0	0	0	0	0	0	.000
T. Greene, p	0	0	0	0	0	1	0	—

Errors: K. Batiste (2), M. Duncan, M. Morandini, K. Stocker, M. Thompson, M. Williams

Stolen Bases: D. Hollins, M. Morandini

ATLANTA (WEST)

	AB	H	2B	3B	HR	R	RBI	BA
R. Gant, of	27	5	3	0	0	4	3	.185
T. Pendleton, 3b	26	9	1	0	1	4	5	.346
J. Blauser, ss	25	7	1	0	2	5	4	.280
M. Lemke, 2b	24	5	2	0	0	2	4	.208
F. McGriff, 1b	23	10	2	0	1	6	4	.435
O. Nixon, of	23	8	2	0	0	3	4	.348
D. Justice, of	21	3	1	0	0	2	4	.143
D. Berryhill, c	19	4	0	0	1	2	3	.211
S. Avery, p	4	2	1	0	0	1	0	.500
G. Maddux, p	4	1	0	0	0	1	0	.250
F. Cabrera, c	3	2	0	0	0	0	1	.667
G. Olson, c	3	1	1	0	0	0	0	.333
B. Pecota	3	1	0	0	0	1	0	.333
T. Glavine, p	3	0	0	0	0	0	0	.000
D. Sanders, of	3	0	0	0	0	0	0	.000
S. Bream, 1b	1	1	0	0	0	1	0	1.000
R. Belliard, 2b, ss	1	0	0	0	0	1	0	.000
J. Smoltz, p	1	0	0	0	0	0	0	.000
T. Tarasco, of	1	0	0	0	0	0	0	.000

Errors: M. Lemke (2), R. Gant, D. Justice, G. Maddux

Individual Pitching

PHILADELPHIA (EAST)

	W	L	ERA	IP	H	BB	SO	SV
C. Schilling	0	0	1.69	16	11	5	19	0
T. Greene	1	1	9.64	9.1	12	7	7	0
D. Jackson	1	0	1.17	7.2	9	2	6	0
M. Williams	2	0	1.69	5.1	6	2	5	2
T. Mulholland	0	1	7.20	5	9	1	2	0
R. Mason	0	0	0.00	3	1	0	2	0
D. West	0	0	13.50	2.2	5	2	5	0
L. Andersen	0	0	15.43	2.1	4	1	3	1
B. Rivera	0	0	4.50	2	1	1	2	0
B. Thigpen	0	0	5.40	1.2	1	1	3	0

ATLANTA (WEST)

	W	L	ERA	IP	H	BB	SO	SV
S. Avery	0	0	2.77	13	9	6	10	0
G. Maddux	1	1	4.97	12.2	11	7	11	0
T. Glavine	1	0	2.57	7	6	0	5	0
J. Smoltz	0	1	0.00	6.1	8	5	10	0
M. Wohlers	0	1	3.38	5.1	2	3	10	0
K. Mercker	0	0	1.80	5	3	2	4	0
G. McMichael	0	1	6.75	4	7	2	1	0
M. Stanton	0	0	0.00	1	1	1	0	0

1993 AMERICAN LEAGUE CHAMPIONSHIP SERIES

Toronto (East) defeats Chicago (West) 4 games to 2

LINE SCORES						PITCHERS (innings pitched)	HOME RUNS (men on)	HIGHLIGHTS
GAME 1 - OCTOBER 5								Molitor and Sprague had four hits apiece in Toronto's 17-hit attack. Olerud's two run double gave the Jays a 4-3 lead in the fifth inning. Molitor's two run homer in the seventh sealed the victory for Guzman, who walked eight and threw three wild pitches.
TOR	**E**	000 230 200	7	17	1	**Guzman** (6), Cox (2), Ward (1)	Molitor (1 on)	
CHI	**W**	000 300 000	3	6	1	**McDowell** (6.2), DeLeon (1), Radinsky (0.1), McCaskill (1)		
GAME 2 - OCTOBER 6								Blue Jays took advantage of sloppy Chicago fielding and Stewart's clutch pitching to take a 2-0 lead in the series. Errors by Pasqua and Cora led to two of Toronto's runs, and Stewart pitched out of a bases loaded, nobody out jam in the sixth inning to preserve the lead.
TOR	**E**	100 200 000	3	8	0	**Stewart** (6), Leiter (2), Ward (1) **SV**	ÿ	
CHI	**W**	100 000 000	1	7	2	**Fernandez** (8), Hernandez (1)	ÿ	
GAME 3 - OCTOBER 8								Chicago tallied five times in the third inning to gain their first victory of the series. With the bases full and two out, third baseman Sprague couldn't handle Thomas's smash, which went for an infield hit. Burks and Johnson later singled home two runs apiece to give Alvarez all the support he needed to record his complete game victory.
CHI	**W**	005 100 000	6	12	0	**Alvarez** (9)		
TOR	**E**	001 000 000	1	7	1	**Hentgen** (3.0), Cox (3), Eichhorn (2), Castillo (1)		
GAME 4 - OCTOBER 9								Johnson, who hadn't homered during the regular season, hit a two run homer as well as a two run triple to lead the White Sox to a series-tying victory. Johnson's homer off Stottlemyre scored the first runs of the game, but Toronto rallied for three runs and led 3-2 entering the sixth. Chicago tied the game on a homer by Thomas, and Johnson's triple gave the White Sox a 5-3 lead.
CHI	**W**	020 003 101	7	11	0	Bere (2.1), **Belcher** (3.2), McCaskill (1.1), Radinsky (0.2), Hernandez (1) **SV**	Johnson (1 on), Thomas	
TOR	**E**	003 001 000	4	9	0	**Stottlemyre** (6), Leiter (0.2), Timlin (2.1)		
GAME 5 - OCTOBER 10								Blue Jays scored a run in each of the first four innings as they took a 3-2 lead in the series. Guzman allowed just three hits over seven innings for his second victory over McDowell. Burks and Ventura homered for the White Sox.
CHI	**W**	000 010 002	3	5	1	**McDowell** (2.1), DeLeon (3.2), Radinsky (0.1), Hernandez (1.2)	Burks, Ventura (1 on)	
TOR	**E**	111 100 10x	5	14	0	**Guzman** (7), Castillo (1), Ward (1)		
GAME 6 - OCTOBER 12								Stewart ran his LCS record to 8-0 including four pennant clinching victories as he pitched Toronto to their second straight AL flag. Blue Jays took advantage of two errors to take a 3-2 lead in the fourth inning, and added three runs in the ninth on White's homer and a two run triple by Molitor. Newson homered for Chicago.
TOR	**E**	020 100 003	6	10	0	**Stewart** (7.1), Ward (1.2) **SV**	White	
CHI	**W**	002 000 001	3	5	3	**Fernandez** (7), McCaskill (1.1), Radinsky (0.1), Hernandez (0.1)	Newson	

Team totals

		W	AB	H	2B	3B	HR	R	RBI	BA	BB	SO	ERA
TOR	**E**	4	216	65	8	3	2	26	24	.301	21	36	3.67
CHI	**W**	2	194	46	5	1	5	23	22	.237	32	43	3.57

Individual Batting

TORONTO (EAST)

	AB	H	2B	3B	HR	R	RBI	BA
D. White, of	27	12	1	1	1	3	2	.444
J. Carter, of	27	7	0	0	0	2	2	.259
R. Henderson, of	25	3	2	0	0	4	0	.120
R. Alomar, 2b	24	7	1	0	0	3	4	.292
P. Borders, c	24	6	1	0	0	1	3	.250
P. Molitor, dh	23	9	2	1	1	7	5	.391
J. Olerud, 1b	23	8	1	0	0	5	3	.348
T. Fernandez, ss	22	7	0	0	0	1	1	.318
E. Sprague, 3b	21	6	0	1	0	0	4	.286

Errors: R. Henderson, J. Olerud

Stolen Bases: R. Alomar (4), R. Henderson (2), P. Borders

CHICAGO (WEST)

	AB	H	2B	3B	HR	R	RBI	BA
T. Raines, of	27	12	2	0	0	5	1	.444
E. Burks, of	23	7	1	0	1	4	3	.304
L. Johnson, of	23	5	1	1	1	2	6	.217
O. Guillen, ss	22	6	1	0	0	4	2	.273
J. Cora, 2b	22	3	0	0	0	1	1	.136
R. Ventura, 1b, 3b	20	4	0	0	1	2	5	.200
F. Thomas, 1b, dh	17	6	0	0	1	2	3	.353
R. Karkovice, c	15	0	0	0	0	0	0	.000
B. Jackson, dh	10	0	0	0	0	1	0	.000
D. Pasqua, 1b	6	0	0	0	0	1	0	.000
W. Newson, dh	5	1	0	0	1	1	1	.200
M. LaValliere, c	3	1	0	0	0	0	0	.333
C. Grebeck, 3b	1	1	0	0	0	0	0	1.000

Errors: J. Cora (3), J. McDowell, D. Pasqua, S. Radinsky, R. Ventura

Stolen Bases: O. Guillen, L. Johnson, T. Raines

Individual Pitching

TORONTO (EAST)

	W	L	ERA	IP	H	BB	SO	SV
D. Stewart	2	0	2.02	13.1	8	8	8	0
J. Guzman	2	0	2.08	13	8	9	9	0
T. Stottlemyre	0	1	7.50	6	6	4	4	0
D. Cox	0	0	0.00	5	3	2	5	0
D. Ward	0	0	5.79	4.2	4	3	8	2
P. Hentgen	0	1	18.00	3	9	2	3	0
A. Leiter	0	0	3.38	2.2	4	2	2	0
M. Timlin	0	0	3.86	2.1	3	0	2	0
T. Castillo	0	0	0.00	2	0	1	1	0
M. Eichhorn	0	0	0.00	2	1	1	1	0

CHICAGO (WEST)

	W	L	ERA	IP	H	BB	SO	SV
A. Fernandez	0	2	1.80	15	15	6	10	0
W. Alvarez	1	0	1.00	9	7	2	6	0
J. McDowell	0	2	10.00	9	18	5	5	0
J. DeLeon	0	0	1.93	4.2	7	1	6	0
R. Hernandez	0	0	0.00	4	4	0	1	1
T. Belcher	1	0	2.45	3.2	3	3	1	0
K. McCaskill	0	0	0.00	3.2	3	1	3	0
J. Bere	0	0	11.57	2.1	5	2	3	0
S. Radinsky	0	0	10.80	1.2	3	1	1	0

1993 WORLD SERIES

Toronto (A.L.) defeats Philadelphia (N.L.) 4 games to 2

LINE SCORES			R	H	E	PITCHERS (innings pitched)	HOME RUNS (men on)	HIGHLIGHTS
GAME 1 - OCTOBER 16								Home runs by White and Olerud carried the Blue Jays to a come-from-behind victory in the Series opener. Phillies took three leads in the game before White homered to tie the score at 4 in the fifth inning. Olerud's blast an inning later gave Toronto the lead, and they added three more runs in the seventh inning.
PHI	**N**	201 010 001	5	11	1	**Schilling** (6.1), West (0), Andersen (0.2), Mason (1)		
TOR	**A**	021 011 30x	8	10	3	Guzman (5), **Leiter** (2.2), Ward (1.1) **SV**	White, Olerud	
GAME 2 - OCTOBER 17								Three run homer by Eisenreich capped a five run third inning as the Phillies tied the series. RBI singles by Kruk and Hollins scored the first two runs, then Eisenreich connected off Stewart for a 5-0 lead. Carter slammed a two run homer for Toronto, while Dykstra homered for Philadelphia's final run.
PHI	**N**	005 000 100	6	12	0	**Mulholland** (5.2), Mason (1.2), Williams (1.2) **SV**	Eisenreich (2 on), Dykstra	
TOR	**A**	000 201 010	4	8	0	**Stewart** (6), Castillo (1), Eichhorn (0.1), Timlin (1.2)	Carter (1 on)	
GAME 3 - OCTOBER 19								Blue Jays struck for three runs in the first inning folowing a 72 minute rain delay at the start. Molitor tripled home the first two runs and scored the third run on Carter's sacrifice fly. Molitor also homered and singled, while Alomar had 4 hits. Thompson homered for the Phillies.
TOR	**A**	301 001 302	10	13	1	**Hentgen** (6), Cox (2), Ward (1)	Molitor	
PHI	**N**	000 001 101	3	9	0	**Jackson** (5), Rivera (1.1), Thigpen (1.2), Andersen (1)	Thompson	
GAME 4 - OCTOBER 20								White's two run triple off Williams capped a six run eighth inning for Toronto as they outlasted the Phillies in a wild record breaking game. The 29 combined runs easily broke the old record of 22 set in 1936 and the game took 4 hours and 14 minutes to play, making it the longest by time in Series history by one minute over a 12 inning game in 1973. Dykstra homered twice in a losing cause and scored four runs and teammate Thompson drove in five. Fernandez had 5 RBI for the Blue Jays.
TOR	**A**	304 002 060	15	18	0	Stottlemyre (2), Leiter (2.2), **Castillo** (2.1), Timlin (0.2), Ward (1.1) **SV**		
PHI	**N**	420 151 100	14	14	0	Greene (2.1), Mason (2.2), West (1), Andersen (1.1), **Williams** (0.2), Thigpen (1)	Dykstra (1 on), Daulton (1 on), Dykstra (1 on)	
GAME 5 - OCTOBER 21								Schilling pitched a five-hit shutout to cut Toronto's Series lead to 3-2. Phillies scored single runs in the first two innings. Dykstra scored the first run on Kruk's infield out, and double by Stocker scored Daulton in the second.
TOR	**A**	000 000 000	0	5	1	**Guzman** (7), Cox (1)		
PHI	**N**	110 000 00x	2	5	1	**Schilling** (9)		
GAME 6 - OCTOBER 23								Carter lined a three run homer over the left field fence with one out in the bottom of the ninth inning as the Blue Jays became the first team since the 1978 Yankees to repeat as World Series champions. Philadelphia had erased a 5-1 deficit to take the lead with five runs in the seventh inning, three scoring on Dykstra's fourth home run of the Series. In the ninth, Williams walked Henderson and allowed a single to Molitor before yielding Carter's series-winning hit.
PHI	**N**	000 100 500	6	7	0	Mulholland (5), Mason (2.1), West (0), Andersen (0.2), **Williams** (0.1)	Dykstra (2 on)	
TOR	**A**	300 110 003	8	10	2	Stewart (6.0), Cox (0.1), Leiter (1.2), **Ward** (1)	Molitor, Carter (2 on)	

Team totals

		W	AB	H	2B	3B	HR	R	RBI	BA	BB	SO	ERA
TOR	**A**	4	206	64	13	5	6	45	45	.311	25	30	5.77
PHI	**N**	2	212	58	7	2	7	36	35	.274	34	50	7.57

Individual Batting

TORONTO (A.L.)

	AB	H	2B	3B	HR	R	RBI	BA
R. Alomar, 2b	25	12	2	1	0	5	6	.480
J. Carter, of	25	7	1	0	2	6	8	.280
P. Molitor, 1b, 3b, dh	24	12	2	2	2	10	8	.500
D. White, of	24	7	3	2	1	8	7	.292
P. Borders, c	23	7	0	0	0	2	1	.304
R. Henderson, of	22	5	2	0	0	6	2	.227
T. Fernandez, ss	21	7	1	0	0	2	9	.333
J. Olerud, 1b	17	4	1	0	1	5	2	.235
E. Sprague, 1b, 3b	15	1	0	0	0	0	2	.067
P. Hentgen, p	3	0	0	0	0	0	0	.000
R. Butler	2	1	0	0	0	1	0	.500
J. Guzman, p	2	0	0	0	0	0	0	.000
A. Leiter, p	1	1	1	0	0	0	0	1.000
T. Castillo, p	1	0	0	0	0	0	0	.000
D. Cox, p	1	0	0	0	0	0	0	.000
W. Canate	0	0	0	0	0	0	0	—
A. Griffin, 3b	0	0	0	0	0	0	0	—
R. Knorr, c	0	0	0	0	0	0	0	—

Errors: R. Alomar (2), J. Carter (2), E. Sprague (2), P. Borders
Stolen Bases: R. Alomar (4), R. Henderson, P. Molitor, D. White

PHILADELPHIA (N.L.)

	AB	H	2B	3B	HR	R	RBI	BA
M. Duncan, 2b, dh	29	10	0	1	0	5	2	.345
J. Eisenreich, of	26	6	0	0	1	3	7	.231
L. Dykstra, of	23	8	1	0	4	9	8	.348
J. Kruk, 1b	23	8	1	0	0	4	4	.348
D. Hollins, 3b	23	6	1	0	0	5	2	.261
D. Daulton, c	23	5	2	0	1	4	4	.217
K. Stocker, ss	19	4	1	0	0	1	1	.211
M. Thompson, of	16	5	1	1	1	3	6	.313
R. Jordan, dh	10	2	0	0	0	0	0	.200
P. Incaviglia, of	8	1	0	0	0	0	1	.125
M. Morandini, 2b	5	1	0	0	0	1	0	.200
C. Schilling, p	2	1	0	0	0	0	0	.500
W. Chamberlain	2	0	0	0	0	0	0	.000
T. Greene, p	1	1	0	0	0	1	0	1.000
D. Jackson, p	1	0	0	0	0	0	0	.000
R. Mason, p	1	0	0	0	0	0	0	.000
K. Batiste, 3b	0	0	0	0	0	0	0	—

Errors: M. Duncan, M. Thompson
Stolen Bases: L. Dykstra (4), M. Duncan (3)

Individual Pitching

TORONTO (A.L.)

	W	L	ERA	IP	H	BB	SO	SV
J. Guzman	0	1	3.75	12	10	8	12	0
D. Stewart	0	1	6.75	12	10	8	8	0
A. Leiter	1	0	7.71	7	12	2	5	0
P. Hentgen	1	0	1.50	6	5	3	6	0
D. Ward	1	0	1.93	4.2	3	0	7	2
T. Castillo	1	0	8.10	3.1	6	3	1	0
D. Cox	0	0	8.10	3.1	6	5	6	0
M. Timlin	0	0	0.00	2.1	2	0	4	0
T. Stottlemyre	0	0	27.00	2	3	4	1	0
M. Eichhorn	0	0	0.00	0.1	1	1	0	0

PHILADELPHIA (N.L.)

	W	L	ERA	IP	H	BB	SO	SV
C. Schilling	1	1	3.52	15.1	13	5	9	0
T. Mulholland	1	0	6.75	10.2	14	3	5	0
R. Mason	0	0	1.17	7.2	4	1	7	0
D. Jackson	0	1	7.20	5	6	1	1	0
L. Andersen	0	0	12.27	3.2	5	3	3	0
B. Thigpen	0	0	0.00	2.2	1	1	0	0
M. Williams	0	2	20.25	2.2	5	4	1	1
T. Greene	0	0	27.00	2.1	7	4	1	0
B. Rivera	0	0	27.00	1.1	4	2	3	0
D. West	0	0	27.00	1	5	1	0	0

1995 NATIONAL LEAGUE DIVISIONAL PLAYOFFS

Atlanta (East) defeats Colorado (Wild Card) 3 games to 1

LINE SCORES						PITCHERS (innings pitched)	HOME RUNS (men on)	HIGHLIGHTS
GAME 1 - OCTOBER 3								Jones hit his second home run of the game in the ninth inning to win it for Atlanta. Colorado loaded the bases in the bottom of the ninth, but Wohlers fanned Galarraga and Painter to save the game. Rockies had to use Painter, a pitcher, to pinch hit after using all of their regular players.
ATL	**E**	001 002 011	5	12	1	Maddux (7), McMichael (0.1), **Pena** (0.2), Wohlers (1) **SV**	Grissom, Jones, Jones	
CLR	*	000 300 010	4	13	4	Ritz (5.1), Reed (1), Ruffin (0.2), Munoz (0.2), Holmes (0.1), **Leskanic** (1)	Castilla (1 on)	
GAME 2 - OCTOBER 4								Braves pulled out another ninth inning victory by scoring four times. Jones led off the inning with a doubled and scored on McGriff's single to tie it. Holmes came in the retire the next two batters, but yielded singles to Devereaux and Mordecai, the latter hit scoring McGriff with the go-ahead run. Atlanta then padded their lead by scoring two runs on a throwing error by Colorado second baseman Young. Rockies had rallied from a 3-0 deficit, tying the game on Walker's three run homer in the sixth, and they took the lead in the eighth on a run scoring double by Galaragga.
ATL	**E**	101 100 004	7	13	1	Glavine (7), Avery (0.2), **Pena** (0.1), Wohlers (1) **SV**	Grissom	
CLR	*	000 003 010	4	8	2	Painter (5), Reed (1.1), Ruffin (0.2), Leskanic (1), **Munoz** (0.1), Holmes (0.2)	Walker (2 on)	
GAME 3 - OCTOBER 6								Colorado scored twice in the tenth inning after allowing Atlanta to tie the game in the ninth on Polonia's RBI single. After Wohlers retired the first two Rockies in the tenth, Bichette doubled, and after Walker was walked intentionally, Galarraga singled for a 6-5 lead. Castilla followed by singling home Walker with an insurance run.
CLR	*	102 002 000 2	7	9	0	Swift (6.0), Reed (0.1), Munoz (0), Leskanic (1), Ruffin (1), **Holmes** (0.2), Thompson (1) **SV**	Young (1 on), Castilla (1 on)	
ATL	**E**	000 300 101 0	5	11	0	Smoltz (5.2), Clontz (1.1), Borbon (1), McMichael (1), **Wohlers** (0.2), Mercker (0.1)		
GAME 4 - OCTOBER 7								McGriff homered twice and Grissom went 5-for-5 as Atlanta advanced to their fourth consecutive League Championship Series. A three run homer by Bichette gave Colorado the lead in the third, but Atlanta responded in their half of the inning with four runs, capped by McGriff's first homer, a two run shot off Saberhagen. He also hit a solo homer two inning later.
CLR	*	003 001 000	4	11	1	**Saberhagen** (4), Ritz (1.2), Munoz (0.1), Reynoso (1), Ruffin (1)	Bichette (2 on), Castilla	
ATL	**E**	004 213 00x	10	15	0	**Maddux** (7), Pena (2)	McGriff (1 on), McGriff	

Team totals

		W	AB	H	2B	3B	HR	R	RBI	BA	BB	SO	ERA
ATL	**E**	3	154	51	8	0	7	27	24	.331	12	27	4.38
CLR	*	1	143	41	7	0	6	19	18	.287	9	29	5.75

Individual Batting

ATLANTA (EAST)

	AB	H	2B	3B	HR	R	RBI	BA
M. Grissom, of	21	11	2	0	3	5	4	.524
M. Lemke, 2b	19	4	1	0	0	3	1	.211
C. Jones, 3b	18	7	2	0	2	4	4	.389
F. McGriff, 1b	18	6	0	0	2	4	6	.333
R. Klesko, of	15	7	1	0	0	5	1	.467
D. Justice, of	13	3	0	0	0	2	0	.231
J. Lopez, c	9	4	0	0	0	0	3	.444
G. Maddux, p	6	1	0	0	0	1	0	.167
J. Blauser, ss	6	0	0	0	0	0	0	.000
M. Devereaux, of	5	1	0	0	0	1	0	.200
C. O'Brien, c	5	1	0	0	0	0	0	.200
R. Belliard, ss	5	0	0	0	0	1	0	.000
M. Mordecai, ss	3	2	1	0	0	1	2	.667
D. Smith	3	2	1	0	0	0	1	.667
T. Glavine, p	3	1	0	0	0	0	0	.333
L. Polonia	3	1	0	0	0	0	2	.333
J. Smoltz, p	2	0	0	0	0	0	0	.000

Errors: J. Blauser, D. Justice
Stolen Bases: M. Grissom (2), L. Polonia

COLORADO (WILD CARD)

	AB	H	2B	3B	HR	R	RBI	BA
A. Galarraga, 1b	18	5	1	0	0	1	2	.278
D. Bichette, of	17	10	3	0	1	6	3	.588
E. Young, 2b	16	7	1	0	1	3	2	.438
J. Girardi, c	16	2	0	0	0	0	0	.125
V. Castilla, 3b	15	7	1	0	3	3	6	.467
L. Walker, of	14	3	0	0	1	3	3	.214
W. Weiss, ss	12	2	0	0	0	1	0	.167
M. Kingery, of	10	2	0	0	0	1	0	.200
E. Burks, of	6	2	1	0	0	1	2	.333
J. Bates, 2b, 3b	4	1	0	0	0	0	0	.250
J. Vander Wal	4	0	0	0	0	0	0	.000
B. Swift, p	3	0	0	0	0	0	0	.000
T. Hubbard	2	0	0	0	0	0	0	.000
L. Painter, p	2	0	0	0	0	0	0	.000
K. Ritz, p	2	0	0	0	0	0	0	.000
J. Owens, c	1	0	0	0	0	0	0	.000
B. Saberhagen, p	1	0	0	0	0	0	0	.000

Errors: E. Young (3), E. Burks, V. Castilla, J. Girardi, K. Ritz
Stolen Bases: L. Walker, W. Weiss, E. Young

Individual Pitching

ATLANTA (EAST)

	W	L	ERA	IP	H	BB	SO	SV
G. Maddux	1	0	4.50	14	19	2	7	0
T. Glavine	0	0	2.57	7	5	1	3	0
J. Smoltz	0	0	7.94	5.2	5	1	6	0
A. Pena	2	0	0.00	3	3	1	2	0
M. Wohlers	0	1	6.75	2.2	6	2	4	2
B. Clontz	0	0	0.00	1.1	0	0	2	0
G. McMichael	0	0	6.75	1.1	1	2	1	0
P. Borbon	0	0	0.00	1	1	0	3	0
S. Avery	0	0	13.50	0.2	1	0	1	0
K. Mercker	0	0	0.00	0.1	0	0	0	0

COLORADO (WILD CARD)

	W	L	ERA	IP	H	BB	SO	SV
K. Ritz	0	0	7.71	7	12	3	5	0
B. Swift	0	0	6.00	6	7	2	3	0
L. Painter	0	0	5.40	5	5	2	4	0
B. Saberhagen	0	1	11.25	4	7	1	3	0
B. Ruffin	0	0	2.70	3.1	3	2	2	0
C. Leskanic	0	1	6.00	3	3	0	4	0
S. Reed	0	0	0.00	2.2	2	1	3	0
D. Holmes	1	0	0.00	1.2	6	0	2	0
M. Munoz	0	1	13.50	1.1	4	1	1	0
A. Reynoso	0	0	0.00	1	2	0	0	0
M. Thompson	0	0	0.00	1	0	0	0	1

1995 NATIONAL LEAGUE DIVISIONAL PLAYOFFS

LINE SCORES						PITCHERS (innings pitched)	HOME RUNS (men on)	HIGHLIGHTS

Cincinnati (Central) defeats Los Angeles (West) 3 games to 0

GAME 1 - OCTOBER 3								
CIN	C	400 030 000	7	12	0	**Schourek** (7), Jackson (1), Brantley (1)	Santiago (1 on)	Cincinnati struck for four runs off Martinez in the first inning of their series-opening win. Morris doubled home the first two runs, and Santiago belted a two run homer to make it 4-0. Schourek made the lead stand up, as he allowed five hits and struck out five in seven innings to pick up the victory. Piazza homered for Los Angeles.
LA	W	000 011 000	2	8	0	**Martinez** (4.1), Cummings (0.2), Astacio (2), Guthrie (1), Osuna (1)	Piazza	

GAME 2 - OCTOBER 4								
CIN	C	000 200 012	5	6	0	Smiley (6), **Burba** (1), Jackson (1), Brantley (1) **SV**	Sanders (1 on)	Cincinnati overcame a two home run, four RBI performance by Karros to take their second consecutive victory at Los Angeles. Larkin's RBI single in the eighth gave the Reds the lead, and they scored two insurance runs in the ninth. Dodgers stranded 11 baserunners..
LA	W	100 100 002	4	14	2	Valdes (7), **Osuna** (1), Tapani (0.1), Guthrie (0.1), Astacio (0.1)	Karros, Karros (1 on)	

GAME 3 - OCTOBER 6								
LA	W	000 100 000	1	9	1	**Nomo** (5.0), Tapani (0), Guthrie (0), Astacio (1), Cummings (0.2), Osuna (1.1)		Home runs by Gant, Boone, and Mark Lewis powered Cincinnati to their series-clinching win. Lewis hit the first pinch hit grand slam in postseason history to break open the game in the sixth inning. Wells, who struck out 8, picked up the victory, allowing only an unearned run.
CIN	C	002 104 30x	10	11	2	**Wells** (6.1), Jackson (1.2), Brantley (1)	Gant (1 on), Boone, M. Lewis (3 on)	

Team totals

		W	AB	H	2B	3B	HR	R	RBI	BA	BB	SO	ERA
CIN	C	3	104	29	6	0	5	22	22	.279	13	28	2.00
LA	W	0	111	31	2	0	3	7	7	.279	5	17	6.92

Individual Batting

CINCINNATI (CENTRAL)

	AB	H	2B	3B	HR	R	RBI	BA
B. Larkin, ss	13	5	0	0	0	2	1	.385
R. Gant, of	13	3	0	0	1	3	2	.231
R. Sanders, of	13	2	1	0	1	3	2	.154
H. Morris, 1b	10	5	1	0	0	5	2	.500
B. Boone, 2b	10	3	1	0	1	4	1	.300
T. Howard, of	10	1	1	0	0	0	0	.100
B. Santiago, c	9	3	0	0	1	2	3	.333
J. Branson, 3b	7	2	1	0	0	0	2	.286
M. Duncan, 2b	3	2	0	0	0	1	1	.667
D. Wells, p	3	1	0	0	0	0	0	.333
D. Lewis, of	3	0	0	0	0	0	0	.000
J. Walton, of	3	0	0	0	0	0	0	.000
M. Lewis, 3b	2	1	0	0	1	2	5	.500
P. Schourek, p	2	0	0	0	0	0	0	.000
J. Smiley, p	2	0	0	0	0	0	0	.000
M. Jackson, p	1	1	1	0	0	0	3	1.000

Errors: M. Lewis, R. Sanders

Stolen Bases: B. Larkin (4), R. Sanders (2), B. Boone, M. Duncan, H. Morris

LOS ANGELES (WEST)

	AB	H	2B	3B	HR	R	RBI	BA
B. Butler, of	15	4	0	0	0	1	1	.267
M. Piazza, c	14	3	1	0	1	1	1	.214
C. Fonville, ss	12	6	0	0	0	1	0	.500
E. Karros, 1b	12	6	1	0	2	3	4	.500
D. DeShields, 2b	12	3	0	0	0	1	0	.250
T. Wallach, 3b	12	1	0	0	0	0	0	.083
R. Kelly, of	11	4	0	0	0	0	0	.364
R. Mondesi, of	9	2	0	0	0	0	1	.222
D. Hansen	3	2	0	0	0	0	0	.667
I. Valdes, p	3	0	0	0	0	0	0	.000
T. Hollandsworth, of	2	0	0	0	0	0	0	.000
H. Nomo, p	2	0	0	0	0	0	0	.000
M. Webster	2	0	0	0	0	0	0	.000
C. Gwynn	1	0	0	0	0	0	0	.000
R. Martinez, p	1	0	0	0	0	0	0	.000
B. Ashley	0	0	0	0	0	0	0	—
J. Offerman	0	0	0	0	0	0	0	—

Errors: C. Fonville, R. Kelly, A. Osuna

Individual Pitching

CINCINNATI (CENTRAL)

	W	L	ERA	IP	H	BB	SO	SV
P. Schourek	1	0	2.57	7	5	3	5	0
D. Wells	1	0	0.00	6.1	6	1	8	0
J. Smiley	0	0	3.00	6	9	0	1	0
M. Jackson	0	0	0.00	3.2	4	0	1	0
J. Brantley	0	0	6.00	3	5	0	2	1
D. Burba	1	0	0.00	1	2	1	0	0

LOS ANGELES (WEST)

	W	L	ERA	IP	H	BB	SO	SV
I. Valdes	0	0	0.00	7	3	1	6	0
H. Nomo	0	1	9.00	5	7	2	6	0
R. Martinez	0	1	14.54	4.1	10	2	3	0
P. Astacio	0	0	0.00	3.1	1	0	5	0
A. Osuna	0	1	2.70	3.1	3	1	3	0
J. Cummings	0	0	20.25	1.1	3	2	3	0
M. Guthrie	0	0	6.75	1.1	2	1	1	0
K. Tapani	0	0	81.00	0.1	0	4	1	0

1995 NATIONAL LEAGUE CHAMPIONSHIP SERIES

Atlanta (East) defeats Cincinnati (Central) 4 games to 0

LINE SCORES			R	H	E	PITCHERS (innings pitched)	HOME RUNS (men on)	HIGHLIGHTS
GAME 1 - OCTOBER 10								Devereaux lined an RBI single in the eleventh inning to give Atlanta the victory. Braves were handcuffed by Schourek for the first eight innings and trailed 1-0 going into the ninth before tying the game on a run scoring grounder by Justice. Cincinnati put runners on the corners in the bottom of the 11th, but McMichael induced Sanders to ground into a game ending double play.
ATL	**E**	000 000 001 01	2	7	0	Glavine (7), Pena (1), **Wohlers** (2), Clontz (0.1), Avery (0), McMichael (0.2) **SV**		
CIN	**C**	000 100 000 00	1	8	0	Schourek (8.1), Brantley (1.2), **Jackson** (1)		
GAME 2 - OCTOBER 11								Braves scored four in the tenth for their second consecutive extra inning win. Portugal's wild pitch allowed Atlanta to take the lead, then Lopez followed with a three run homer to seal the victory.
ATL	**E**	100 100 000 4	6	11	1	Smoltz (7), Pena (1), **McMichael** (1), Wohlers (1)	Lopez (2 on)	
CIN	**C**	000 020 000 0	2	9	1	Smiley (5), Burba (2), Jackson (1), Brantley (1), **Portugal** (1)		
GAME 3 - OCTOBER 13								O'Brien slammed a three run homer to break the seal on a scoreless game in the sixth inning, and Jones added a two run homer an inning later to make a winner of Maddux.
CIN	**C**	000 000 011	2	8	0	**Wells** (6), Hernandez (0.2), Carrasco (1.1)	O'Brien (2 on), Jones (1 on)	
ATL	**E**	000 003 20x	5	12	1	**Maddux** (8), Wohlers (1)		
GAME 4 - OCTOBER 14								Braves wrapped up the first four game sweep in NLCS history as Avery and three relievers blanked Cincinnati. Atlanta broke open the contest with five seventh inning runs, including a three run homer off the bat of series MVP Devereaux.
CIN	**C**	000 000 000	0	3	1	**Schourek** (6), Jackson (0.1), Burba (1.2)		
ATL	**E**	001 000 50x	6	12	1	**Avery** (6), McMichael (1), Pena (1), Wohlers (1)	Devereaux (2 on)	

Team totals

		W	AB	H	2B	3B	HR	R	RBI	BA	BB	SO	ERA
ATL	**E**	4	149	42	6	1	4	19	17	.282	16	22	1.15
CIN	**C**	0	134	28	5	1	0	5	4	.209	12	31	4.62

Individual Batting

ATLANTA (EAST)

	AB	H	2B	3B	HR	R	RBI	BA
M. Grissom, of	19	5	0	1	0	2	0	.263
M. Lemke, 2b	18	3	0	0	0	2	1	.167
C. Jones, 3b	16	7	0	0	1	3	3	.438
F. McGriff, 1b	16	7	4	0	0	5	0	.438
J. Lopez, c	14	5	1	0	1	2	3	.357
M. Devereaux, of	13	4	1	0	1	2	5	.308
R. Belliard, ss	11	3	0	0	0	1	0	.273
D. Justice, of	11	3	0	0	0	1	1	.273
R. Klesko, of	7	0	0	0	0	0	0	.000
C. O'Brien, c	5	2	0	0	1	1	3	.400
J. Blauser, ss	4	0	0	0	0	0	0	.000
J. Smoltz, p	3	1	0	0	0	0	0	.333
G. Maddux, p	3	0	0	0	0	0	0	.000
S. Avery, p	2	1	0	0	0	0	0	.500
L. Polonia, of	2	1	0	0	0	0	1	.500
M. Mordecai, ss	2	0	0	0	0	0	0	.000
D. Smith	2	0	0	0	0	0	0	.000
T. Glavine, p	1	0	0	0	0	0	0	.000

Errors: R. Belliard, M. Grissom, J. Smoltz
Stolen Bases: C. Jones, J. Smoltz

CINCINNATI (CENTRAL)

	AB	H	2B	3B	HR	R	RBI	BA
B. Larkin, ss	18	7	2	1	0	1	0	.389
R. Gant, of	16	3	0	0	0	1	1	.188
R. Sanders, of	16	2	0	0	0	0	0	.125
B. Boone, 2b	14	3	0	0	0	1	0	.214
B. Santiago, c	13	3	0	0	0	0	0	.231
H. Morris, 1b	12	2	1	0	0	0	1	.167
J. Branson, 3b	9	1	1	0	0	2	0	.111
T. Howard, of	8	2	1	0	0	0	1	.250
J. Walton, of	7	0	0	0	0	0	0	.000
P. Schourek, p	5	0	0	0	0	0	0	.000
M. Lewis, 3b	4	1	0	0	0	0	0	.250
M. Duncan, 1b	3	0	0	0	0	0	0	.000
L. Harris	2	2	0	0	0	0	1	1.000
E. Taubensee, c	2	1	0	0	0	0	0	.500
D. Wells, p	2	1	0	0	0	0	0	.500
E. Anthony	1	0	0	0	0	0	0	.000
D. Lewis, of	1	0	0	0	0	0	0	.000
J. Smiley, p	1	0	0	0	0	0	0	.000

Errors: B. Larkin, R. Sanders
Stolen Bases: J. Branson, L. Harris, B. Larkin, H. Morris

Individual Pitching

ATLANTA (EAST)

	W	L	ERA	IP	H	BB	SO	SV
G. Maddux	1	0	1.13	8	7	2	4	0
T. Glavine	0	0	1.29	7	7	2	5	0
J. Smoltz	0	0	2.57	7	7	2	2	0
S. Avery	1	0	0.00	6	2	4	6	0
M. Wohlers	1	0	1.80	5	2	0	8	0
A. Pena	0	0	0.00	3	2	1	4	0
G. McMichael	1	0	0.00	2.2	0	1	2	1
B. Clontz	0	0	0.00	0.1	1	0	0	0

CINCINNATI (CENTRAL)

	W	L	ERA	IP	H	BB	SO	SV
P. Schourek	0	1	1.26	14.1	14	3	13	0
D. Wells	0	1	4.50	6	8	2	3	0
J. Smiley	0	0	3.60	5	5	0	1	0
D. Burba	0	0	0.00	3.2	3	4	0	0
J. Brantley	0	0	0.00	2.2	0	2	1	0
M. Jackson	0	1	23.14	2.1	5	4	1	0
H. Carrasco	0	0	0.00	1.1	1	0	3	0
M. Portugal	0	1	36.00	1	3	1	0	0
X. Hernandez	0	0	27.00	0.2	3	0	0	0

1995 AMERICAN LEAGUE DIVISIONAL PLAYOFFS

LINE SCORES			R	H	E	PITCHERS (innings pitched)	HOME RUNS (men on)	HIGHLIGHTS

Seattle (West) defeats New York (Wild Card) 3 games to 2

GAME 1 - OCTOBER 3

			R	H	E	Pitchers	Home Runs
SEA	W	000 101 202	6	9	0	Bosio (5.2), **Nelson** (0.1), Ayala (0.1), Risley (0.2), Wells (1)	Griffey, Griffey (1 on)
NY	*	002 002 41x	9	13	0	**Cone** (8), Wetteland (1)	Boggs (1 on), Sierra (1 on)

Two run homer by Sierra capped a four run seventh inning as New York took the series opener. Seattle had tied the score in the top of the inning on Griffey's second roundtripper of the game, a two run shot. Yanks regained the lead 5-4 on an RBI double by Bernie Williams. O'Neill followed with a sacrifice fly before Sierra connected off Ayala.

GAME 2 - OCTOBER 4

			R	H	E	Pitchers	Home Runs
SEA	W	001 001 200 001 000	5	16	2	Benes (5.0), Risley (1), Charlton (4), Nelson (1.1) **Belcher** (3)	Coleman, Griffey
NY	*	000 012 100 001 002	7	11	0	Pettitte (7), Wickman (1.1), Wetteland (3.1), **Rivera** (3.1)	Sierra, Mattingly, O'Neill, Leyritz (1 on)

Leyritz slammed a two run homer to give New York a wild fifteen inning victory in a game that lasted five hours and thirteen minutes. Back-to-back homers by Sierra and Mattingly in the sixth enabled Yanks to take a 3-2 lead, but Seattle tallied twice to regain the lead in the seventh. O'Neill then homered in the bottom of that inning to draw New York even. In the 12th, Griffey homered for Seattle, and New York tied it when Sierra hit a two-out RBI double in which Bernie Williams was thrown out at home attempting to score the winning run.

GAME 3 - OCTOBER 6

			R	H	E	Pitchers	Home Runs
NY	*	000 100 120	4	6	2	**McDowell** (5.1), Howe (0), Wickman (0.2), Hitchcock (0.2), Rivera (1.1)	B. Williams, B. Williams (1 on), Stanley
SEA	W	000 024 10x	7	7	0	**Johnson** (7), Risley (0.2), Charlton (1.1) **SV**	T. Martinez (1 on)

Johnson fanned ten batters over seven innings in pitching Seattle to their first postseason victory. Tino Martinez homered with a man on in the fifth inning to give the Mariners the lead, and they added four runs in the sixth. Bernie Williams homered twice for New York, once from each side of the plate, becoming the first player to perform the feat in a postseason game.

GAME 4 - OCTOBER 7

			R	H	E	Pitchers	Home Runs
NY	*	302 000 012	8	14	1	Kamienicki (5), Hitchcock (1), Wickman (1), **Wetteland** (0), Howe (1)	O'Neill (1 on)
SEA	W	004 011 05x	11	16	0	Bosio (2.0), Nelson (4.0), Belcher (1.1), **Charlton** (0.2), Ayala (0.1), Risley (0.2) **SV**	E. Martinez (2 on), Griffey, E. Martinez (3 on), Buhner

Edgar Martinez homered twice, driving in a postseason record seven runs as Seattle overcame a 5-0 lead to even the series. Martinez homered with two runners on in the third inning to bring the Mariners to within 5-3, then powered a tiebreaking grand slam in the eighth off Wetteland. Buhner added a solo shot two batters later.

GAME 5 - OCTOBER 8

			R	H	E	Pitchers	Home Runs
NY	*	000 202 000 01	5	6	0	Cone (7.2), Rivera (0.2), **McDowell** (1.2)	O'Neill (1 on)
SEA	W	001 100 020 02	6	15	0	Benes (6.2), Charlton (1.1), **Johnson** (3)	Cora, Griffey

Edgar Martinez doubled home the tying and winning runs in the bottom of the eleventh inning as Seattle rebounded to win the series after dropping the first two games. The Game 3 starting pitchers both figured in the decision. Velarde's RBI single off Johnson gave New York a 5-4 lead in the top of the eleventh, but the Mariners rallied against McDowell when Cora beat out a bunt, Griffey singled, and Martinez hit a drive into the leftfield corner to score both runners. Mariners sent the game into extra innings with two eighth inning runs, on Griffey's fifth homer of the series and Strange's bases loaded walk against Cone. The teams combined to hit 22 homers in the series, setting a postseason record.

Team totals

		W	AB	H	2B	3B	HR	R	RBI	BA	BB	SO	ERA
SEA	W	3	200	63	6	1	11	35	33	.315	25	41	5.79
NY	*	2	193	50	12	0	11	33	32	.259	32	43	5.94

Individual Batting

SEATTLE (WEST)

	AB	H	2B	3B	HR	R	RBI	BA
J. Buhner, of	24	11	1	0	1	2	3	.458
K. Griffey, of	23	9	0	0	5	9	7	.391
V. Coleman, of	23	5	0	1	1	6	1	.217
T. Martinez, 1b	22	9	1	0	1	4	5	.409
E. Martinez, dh	21	12	3	0	2	6	10	.571
L. Sojo, ss	20	5	0	0	0	0	3	.250
J. Cora, 2b	19	6	1	0	1	7	1	.316
M. Blowers, 1b, 3b	18	3	0	0	0	0	1	.167
D. Wilson, c	17	2	0	0	0	0	1	.118
D. Strange, 3b	4	0	0	0	0	0	1	.000
A. Diaz, of	3	1	0	0	0	0	0	.333
C. Widger, c	3	0	0	0	0	0	0	.000
F. Fermin, 2b, ss	1	0	0	0	0	0	0	.000
W. Newson	1	0	0	0	0	0	0	.000
A. Rodriguez, ss	1	0	0	0	0	1	0	.000

Errors: J. Cora, L. Sojo
Stolen Bases: V. Coleman, J. Cora, K. Griffey

NEW YORK (WILD CARD)

	AB	H	2B	3B	HR	R	RBI	BA
D. Mattingly, 1b	24	10	4	0	1	3	6	.417
R. Sierra, dh	23	4	2	0	2	2	5	.174
B. Williams, of	21	9	2	0	2	8	5	.429
T. Fernandez, ss	21	5	2	0	0	0	0	.238
W. Boggs, 3b	19	5	2	0	1	4	3	.263
P. O'Neill, of	18	6	0	0	3	5	6	.333
R. Velarde, 2b, 3b, of	17	3	0	0	0	3	1	.176
M. Stanley, c	16	5	0	0	1	2	3	.313
D. James, of	12	1	0	0	0	0	0	.083
J. Leyritz, c	7	1	0	0	1	1	2	.143
R. Davis, 3b	5	1	0	0	0	0	0	.200
G. Williams, of	5	0	0	0	0	1	0	.000
P. Kelly, 2b	3	0	0	0	0	3	1	.000
D. Strawberry	2	0	0	0	0	0	0	.000
J. Posada	0	0	0	0	0	1	0	—

Errors: D. Mattingly, M. Stanley, R. Velarde
Stolen Bases: B. Williams

Individual Pitching

SEATTLE (WEST)

	W	L	ERA	IP	H	BB	SO	SV
A. Benes	0	0	5.40	11.2	10	9	8	0
R. Johnson	2	0	2.70	10	5	6	16	0
C. Bosio	0	0	10.57	7.2	10	4	2	0
N. Charlton	1	0	2.45	7.1	4	3	9	1
J. Nelson	0	1	3.18	5.2	7	3	7	0
T. Belcher	0	1	6.23	4.1	4	5	0	0
B. Risley	0	0	6.00	3	2	0	1	1
B. Wells	0	0	9.00	1	2	1	0	0
B. Ayala	0	0	54.00	0.2	6	1	0	0

NEW YORK (WILD CARD)

	W	L	ERA	IP	H	BB	SO	SV
D. Cone	1	0	4.60	15.2	15	9	14	0
J. McDowell	0	2	9.00	7	8	4	6	0
A. Pettitte	0	0	5.14	7	9	3	0	0
M. Rivera	1	0	0.00	5.1	3	1	8	0
S. Kamieniecki	0	0	7.20	5	9	4	4	0
J. Wetteland	0	1	14.54	4.1	8	2	5	0
B. Wickman	0	0	0.00	3	5	0	3	0
S. Hitchcock	0	0	5.40	1.2	2	2	1	0
S. Howe	0	0	18.00	1	4	0	0	0

1995 AMERICAN LEAGUE DIVISIONAL PLAYOFFS

Cleveland (Central) defeats Boston (East) 3 games to 0

LINE SCORES						PITCHERS (innings pitched)	HOME RUNS (men on)	HIGHLIGHTS
GAME 1 - OCTOBER 3								Pena's thirteenth inning homer at 2:08 in the morning ended a five hour contest that included two rain delays. Boston took a 2-0 lead on Valentin's third ining home run. Cleveland scored three times to take the lead in the sixth, but Alicea, who had four hits, homered in the eighth for Boston to tie the game. Naehring homered to give Boston the lead in the top of the eleventh, but Belle led off the bottom of the inning with a home run for Cleveland to make it 4-4.
BOS	E	002 000 010 010 0	4	11	2	Clemens (7), Cormier (0.1), Belinda (0.1), Stanton (2.1), Aguilera (0.2), Maddux (0.2), **Smith** (1.1)	Valentin (1 on), Alicea, Naehring	
CLE	C	000 003 000 010 1	5	10	2	Martinez (6), Tavarez (1.1), Assenmacher (0.1), Plunk (1.1), Mesa (1), Poole (1.2), **Hill** (1.1)	Belle, Pena	
GAME 2 - OCTOBER 4								Hershiser and three relievers combined on a three-hit shutout for Cleveland. Indians scored on a two run double by Vizquel in the fifth, and Murray's two run homer in the eighth off Hanson, who pitched a complete game in defeat.
BOS	E	000 000 000	0	3	1	**Hanson** (8)		
CLE	C	000 020 02x	4	4	2	**Hershiser** (7.1), Tavarez (0.1), Assenmacher (0.1), Mesa (1)	Murray (1 on)	
GAME 3 - OCTOBER 6								Indians completed a series sweep, winning their first postseason series since 1948. Thome's two run homer gave Cleveland a 2-0 lead in the third inning, and they put the game away with a four run sixth that included a two run single by Vizquel. A key for Cleveland was holding Boston sluggers Canseco and Vaughn hitless in the series as they went a combined 0-for-27.
CLE	C	021 005 000	8	11	2	**Nagy** (7), Tavarez (1), Assenmacher (1)	Thome (1 on)	
BOS	E	000 100 010	2	7	1	**Wakefield** (5.1), Cormier (0.1), Maddux (2.1), Hudson (1)		

Team totals

		W	AB	H	2B	3B	HR	R	RBI	BA	BB	SO	ERA
CLE	C	3	114	25	4	1	4	17	17	.219	13	22	1.74
BOS	E	0	114	21	2	0	3	6	6	.184	11	26	5.16

Individual Batting

CLEVELAND (CENTRAL)

	AB	H	2B	3B	HR	R	RBI	BA
C. Baerga, 2b	14	4	1	0	0	2	1	.286
E. Murray, dh	13	5	0	1	1	3	3	.385
K. Lofton, of	13	2	0	0	0	1	0	.154
J. Thome, 3b	13	2	0	0	1	1	3	.154
O. Vizquel, ss	12	2	1	0	0	2	4	.167
M. Ramirez, of	12	0	0	0	0	1	0	.000
A. Belle, of	11	3	1	0	1	3	3	.273
S. Alomar, c	11	2	1	0	0	1	1	.182
P. Sorrento, 1b	10	3	0	0	0	2	1	.300
T. Pena, c	2	1	0	0	1	1	1	.500
W. Kirby, of	1	1	0	0	0	0	0	1.000
A. Espinoza, 3b	1	0	0	0	0	0	0	.000
H. Perry	1	0	0	0	0	0	0	.000

Errors: K. Lofton (2), P. Sorrento (2), C. Baerga, A. Belle
Stolen Bases: O. Vizquel

BOSTON (EAST)

	AB	H	2B	3B	HR	R	RBI	BA
M. Greenwell, of	15	3	0	0	0	0	0	.200
M. Vaughn, 1b	14	0	0	0	0	0	0	.000
T. Naehring, 3b	13	4	0	0	1	2	1	.308
J. Canseco, dh, of	13	0	0	0	0	0	0	.000
J. Valentin, ss	12	3	1	0	1	1	2	.250
D. Hosey, of	12	0	0	0	0	1	0	.000
L. Alicea, 2b	10	6	1	0	1	1	1	.600
M. Macfarlane, c	9	3	0	0	0	0	1	.333
L. Tinsley, of	5	0	0	0	0	0	0	.000
R. Jefferson, dh	4	1	0	0	0	1	0	.250
W. McGee, of	4	1	0	0	0	0	1	.250
B. Haselman, c	2	0	0	0	0	0	0	.000
M. Stairs	1	0	0	0	0	0	0	.000

Errors: M. Macfarlane (2), L. Alicea, J. Valentin
Stolen Bases: L. Alicea, D. Hosey

Individual Pitching

CLEVELAND (CENTRAL)

	W	L	ERA	IP	H	BB	SO	SV
O. Hershiser	1	0	0.00	7.1	3	2	7	0
C. Nagy	1	0	1.29	7	4	5	6	0
D. Martinez	0	0	3.00	6	5	0	2	0
J. Tavarez	0	0	6.75	2.2	5	0	3	0
J. Mesa	0	0	0.00	2	0	2	0	0
P. Assenmacher	0	0	0.00	1.2	0	0	3	0
J. Poole	0	0	5.40	1.2	2	1	2	0
K. Hill	1	0	0.00	1.1	1	0	2	0
E. Plunk	0	0	0.00	1.1	1	1	1	0

BOSTON (EAST)

	W	L	ERA	IP	H	BB	SO	SV
E. Hanson	0	1	4.50	8	4	4	5	0
R. Clemens	0	0	3.86	7	5	1	5	0
T. Wakefield	0	1	11.81	5.1	5	5	4	0
M. Maddux	0	0	0.00	3	2	1	1	0
M. Stanton	0	0	0.00	2.1	1	0	4	0
Z. Smith	0	1	6.75	1.1	1	0	0	0
J. Hudson	0	0	0.00	1	2	1	0	0
R. Aguilera	0	0	13.50	0.2	3	0	1	0
R. Cormier	0	0	13.50	0.2	2	1	2	0
S. Belinda	0	0	0.00	0.1	0	0	0	0

1995 AMERICAN LEAGUE CHAMPIONSHIP SERIES

Cleveland (Central) defeats Seattle (West) 4 games to 2

LINE SCORES						PITCHERS (innings pitched)	HOME RUNS (men on)	HIGHLIGHTS
GAME 1 - OCTOBER 10								
CLE	**C** 001 000 100	2	10	1		**Martinez** (6.1), Tavarez (1), Assenmacher (0), Plunk (0.2)	Belle	Emergency starter Wolcott, a rookie who was placed on the active roster before the series, pitched seven effective innings as Seattle won on Sojo's tiebreaking double in the seventh inning. Mariners struck first on a two run homer by Blowers in the second, and Cleveland tied it on Belle's solo homer off Wolcott in the seventh.
SEA	**W** 020 000 10x	3	7	0		**Wolcott** (7), Nelson (0.2), Charlton (1.1) **SV**	Blowers (1 on)	
GAME 2 - OCTOBER 11								
CLE	**C** 000 022 010	5	12	0		**Hershiser** (8), Mesa (1)	Ramirez, Ramirez	Ramirez went 4-for-4, including two solo homers to help Cleveland even the series. Hershiser held Seattle to 4 hits over 8 innings to pick up the win. Griffey and Buhner homered for the two Mariner runs.
SEA	**W** 000 001 001	2	6	1		**Belcher** (5.2), Ayala (2.2), Risley (0.2)	Griffey, Buhner	
GAME 3 - OCTOBER 13								
SEA	**W** 011 000 000 03	5	9	1		Johnson (8), **Charlton** (3)	Buhner, Buhner (2 on)	Buhner, who misplayed a fly ball to help Cleveland tie the game, blasted his second homer of the game, a three run shot off Plunk in the eleventh inning to win it for the Mariners. Charlton picked up the victory with three hitless innings in relief.
CLE	**C** 000 100 010 00	2	4	2		Nagy (8), Mesa (1), **Tavarez** (1.0), Assenmacher (0.1), Plunk (0.2)		
GAME 4 - OCTOBER 14								
SEA	**W** 000 000 000	0	6	1		**Benes** (2.1), Wells (3), Ayala (1), Nelson (1.1), Risley (0.1)		Cleveland used the power of Murray and Thome and an outstanding pitching performance by Hill to tie the series 2-2. Murray's two run homer gave the Indians a 3-0 first inning lead, and Thome continued the assault against Benes with a man on in the third to make it 6-0. Hill held Seattle to five hits in seven shutout innings.
CLE	**C** 312 001 00x	7	9	0		**Hill** (7), Poole (1), Ogea (0.2), Embree (0.1)	Murray (1 on), Thome (1 on)	
GAME 5 - OCTOBER 15								
SEA	**W** 001 010 000	2	5	2		**Bosio** (5.1), Nelson (1), Risley (1.2)		With Cleveland trailing 2-1 in the sixth inning, Murray doubled and Thome followed with a home run to give the Indians the lead in the game and the series. Hershiser struck out 8 batters in six innings and clutch bullpen work from Assenmacher held off the Mariners. Seattle threatened in the seventh, putting runners on the corners with one out, but Assenmacher fanned Griffey and Buhner to preserve the lead.
CLE	**C** 100 002 00x	3	10	4		**Hershiser** (6), Tavarez (0.1), Assenmacher (1), Plunk (0.2), Mesa (1) **SV**	Thome (1 on)	
GAME 6 - OCTOBER 17								
CLE	**C** 000 010 030	4	8	0		**Martinez** (7), Tavarez (1), Mesa (1)	Baerga	Indians blanked Seattle to wrap up their first pennant since 1954. Martinez, Tavarez, and Mesa combined to hold the Mariners to four hits, and Cleveland took advantage of sloppy fielding by Seattle to score their first three runs. Cora's two base error allowed Espinoza to reach and eventually score on Lofton's RBI single in the fifth, and two runners scored on Wilson's passed ball in the eighth. Baerga homered for Cleveland's final run.
SEA	**W** 000 000 000	0	4	1		**Johnson** (7.1), Charlton (1.2)		

Team totals

		W	AB	H	2B	3B	HR	R	RBI	BA	BB	SO	ERA
CLE	**C**	4	206	53	6	3	7	23	21	.257	25	37	1.64
SEA	**W**	2	201	37	8	0	5	12	10	.184	15	46	3.33

Individual Batting

CLEVELAND (CENTRAL)

	AB	H	2B	3B	HR	R	RBI	BA
C. Baerga, 2b	25	10	0	0	1	3	4	.400
K. Lofton, of	24	11	0	2	0	4	3	.458
E. Murray, dh	24	6	1	0	1	2	3	.250
O. Vizquel, ss	23	2	1	0	0	2	2	.087
M. Ramirez, of	21	6	0	0	2	2	2	.286
A. Belle, of	18	4	1	0	1	1	1	.222
S. Alomar, c	15	4	1	1	0	0	1	.267
J. Thome, 3b	15	4	0	0	2	2	5	.267
P. Sorrento, 1b	13	2	1	0	0	2	0	.154
A. Espinoza, 3b	8	1	0	0	0	1	0	.125
H. Perry, 1b	8	0	0	0	0	0	0	.000
T. Pena, c	6	2	1	0	0	1	0	.333
W. Kirby, of	5	1	0	0	0	2	0	.200
R. Amaro, dh	1	0	0	0	0	1	0	.000

Errors: A. Belle (2), P. Sorrento (2), S. Alomar, A. Espinoza, J. Thome
Stolen Bases: K. Lofton (5), O. Vizquel (3), W. Kirby

SEATTLE (WEST)

	AB	H	2B	3B	HR	R	RBI	BA
J. Buhner, of	23	7	2	0	3	5	5	.304
J. Cora, 2b	23	4	1	0	0	3	0	.174
E. Martinez, dh	23	2	0	0	0	0	0	.087
T. Martinez, 1b	22	3	0	0	0	1	0	.136
K. Griffey, of	21	7	2	0	1	2	2	.333
L. Sojo, ss	20	5	2	0	0	0	1	.250
V. Coleman, of	20	2	0	0	0	0	0	.100
M. Blowers, 3b	18	4	0	0	1	1	2	.222
D. Wilson, c	16	0	0	0	0	0	0	.000
A. Diaz, of	7	3	1	0	0	0	0	.429
D. Strange, 3b	4	0	0	0	0	0	0	.000
R. Amaral	2	0	0	0	0	0	0	.000
A. Rodriguez	1	0	0	0	0	0	0	.000
C. Widger, c	1	0	0	0	0	0	0	.000
F. Fermin, 2b, ss	0	0	0	0	0	0	0	—

Errors: J. Buhner, J. Cora, K. Griffey, T. Martinez, L. Sojo, D. Wilson
Stolen Bases: V. Coleman (4), J. Cora (2), K. Griffey (2), E. Martinez

Individual Pitching

CLEVELAND (CENTRAL)

	W	L	ERA	IP	H	BB	SO	SV
O. Hershiser	2	0	1.29	14	9	3	15	0
D. Martinez	1	1	2.02	13.1	10	3	7	0
C. Nagy	0	0	1.13	8	5	0	6	0
K. Hill	1	0	0.00	7	5	3	6	0
J. Mesa	0	0	2.25	4	3	1	1	1
J. Tavarez	0	1	2.70	3.1	3	1	2	0
E. Plunk	0	0	9.00	2	1	3	2	0
P. Assenmacher	0	0	0.00	1.1	0	1	2	0
J. Poole	0	0	0.00	1	0	0	2	0
C. Ogea	0	0	0.00	0.2	1	0	2	0
A. Embree	0	0	0.00	0.1	0	0	1	0

SEATTLE (WEST)

	W	L	ERA	IP	H	BB	SO	SV
R. Johnson	0	1	2.35	15.1	12	2	13	0
B. Wolcott	1	0	2.57	7	8	5	2	0
N. Charlton	1	0	0.00	6	1	1	5	1
T. Belcher	0	1	6.35	5.2	9	2	1	0
C. Bosio	0	1	3.38	5.1	7	2	3	0
B. Ayala	0	0	2.45	3.2	3	3	3	0
J. Nelson	0	0	0.00	3	3	5	3	0
B. Wells	0	0	3.00	3	2	2	2	0
B. Risley	0	0	0.00	2.2	2	1	2	0
A. Benes	0	1	23.14	2.1	6	2	3	0

1995 WORLD SERIES

Atlanta (N.L.) defeats Cleveland (A.L.) 4 games to 2

LINE SCORES			R	H	E	PITCHERS (innings pitched)	HOME RUNS (men on)	HIGHLIGHTS
GAME 1 - OCTOBER 21								Maddux pitched a two hitter to outduel Hershiser. Atlanta scored twice in the seventh to break a 1-1 tie. Polonia's grounder scored the lead run, and Belliard followed with a squeeze bunt for a 3-1 lead. Lofton scored the Cleveland runs, which were both unearned.
CLE	A	100 000 001	2	2	0	**Hershiser** (6.0), Assenmacher (0), Tavarez (1.1), Embree (0.2)		
ATL	N	010 000 20x	3	3	2	**Maddux** (9)	McGriff	
GAME 2 - OCTOBER 22								A two run homer by Lopez snapped a 2-2 tie in the sixth inning, and Braves held on to take a 2-0 lead in the Series. Murray homered with a man on in the second to give Cleveland the lead, and Atlanta tied it with a pair of runs in the third.
CLE	A	020 000 100	3	6	2	**Martinez** (5.2), Embree (0.1), Poole (1), Tavarez (1)	Murray (1 on)	
ATL	N	002 002 00x	4	8	2	**Glavine** (6), McMichael (0.2), Pena (1), Wohlers (1.1) **SV**	Lopez (1 on)	
GAME 3 - OCTOBER 24								Murray ripped a single to score the winning run in the bottom of the eleventh to give Cleveland their first win of the Series. Baerga led off the decisive frame with a double off Pena and Belle was intentially walked before Murray delivered pinch runner Espinoza with the game winner. Cleveland had squandered a 4-1 lead and fell behind 6-5 before tying the game in the eighth on Alomar's RBI double. Lofton went 3-for-3 and scored three runs for the Indians, while McGriff and Klesko homered in a losing cause for Atlanta.
ATL	N	100 001 130 00	6	12	1	Smoltz (2.1), Clontz (2.1), Mercker (2), McMichael (0.2), Wohlers (2.2), **Pena** (0)	McGriff, Klesko	
CLE	A	202 000 110 01	7	12	2	Nagy (7.2), Assenmacher (0.1), Tavarez (0.2), **Mesa** (3)		
GAME 4 - OCTOBER 25								Atlanta scored three runs in the seventh inning to break a 1-1 tie. Polonia doubled home the go-ahead run and Justice ripped a two run single to give the Braves a 4-1 lead. The game was scoreless until the teams traded sixth inning home runs by Klesko and Belle.
ATL	N	000 001 301	5	11	1	**Avery** (6), McMichael (2), Wohlers (0), Borbon (1) **SV**	Klesko	
CLE	A	000 001 001	2	6	0	**Hill** (6.1), Assenmacher (0.2), Tavarez (0.2), Embree (1.1)	Belle, Ramirez	
GAME 5 - OCTOBER 26								Hershiser avenged his opening game loss to Maddux by allowing five hits and striking out 6 in eight innings for Cleveland. Thome singled home the go-ahead run in the sixth inning and hit a key homer in the eighth that enabled the Indians to withstand Klesko's two run homer in the ninth. Klesko homered in all three games at Cleveland. The Indians scored first on Belle's two run homer in the first inning before Atlanta tied it on Polonia's solo homer in the fourth and Grissom's RBI infield single in the fifth.
ATL	N	000 110 002	4	7	0	**Maddux** (7), Clontz (1)	Polonia, Klesko (1 on)	
CLE	A	200 002 01x	5	8	1	**Hershiser** (8), Mesa (1) **SV**	Belle (1 on), Thome	
GAME 6 - OCTOBER 28								Glavine and Wohlers pitched the first combined one-hitter in World Series play to give the Braves their first World Championship since moving to Atlanta in 1966. The Braves became the first team to win the World Series representing three cities--Boston in 1914, Milwaukee in 1957, and Atlanta. Justice homered leading off the sixth against Poole for the only run of the game. Cleveland's only hit was a sixth inning signle by Pena.
CLE	A	000 000 000	0	1	1	Martinez (4.2), **Poole** (1.1), Hill (0), Embree (1), Tavarez (0.2), Assenmacher (0.1)		
ATL	N	000 001 00x	1	6	0	**Glavine** (8), Wohlers (1) **SV**	Justice	

Team totals

		W	AB	H	2B	3B	HR	R	RBI	BA	BB	SO	ERA
ATL	**N**	4	193	47	10	0	8	23	23	.244	25	34	2.67
CLE	**A**	2	195	35	7	1	5	19	17	.179	25	37	3.57

Individual Batting

ATLANTA (N.L.)

	AB	H	2B	3B	HR	R	RBI	BA
M. Grissom, of	25	9	1	0	0	3	1	.360
F. McGriff, 1b	23	6	2	0	2	5	3	.261
M. Lemke, 2b	22	6	0	0	0	1	0	.273
C. Jones, 3b	21	6	3	0	0	3	1	.286
D. Justice, of	20	5	1	0	1	3	5	.250
J. Lopez, c	17	3	2	0	1	1	3	.176
R. Klesko, dh, of	16	5	0	0	3	4	4	.313
R. Belliard, ss	16	0	0	0	0	0	1	.000
L. Polonia, of	14	4	1	0	1	3	4	.286
M. Devereaux, dh, of	4	1	0	0	0	0	1	.250
T. Glavine, p	4	0	0	0	0	0	0	.000
M. Mordecai, dh, ss	3	1	0	0	0	0	0	.333
G. Maddux, p	3	0	0	0	0	0	0	.000
C. O'Brien, c	3	0	0	0	0	0	0	.000
D. Smith	2	1	0	0	0	0	0	.500

Errors: R. Belliard (2), M. Devereaux, C. Jones, M. Lemke, F. McGriff
Stolen Bases: M. Grissom (3), F. McGriff, L. Polonia

CLEVELAND (A.L.)

	AB	H	2B	3B	HR	R	RBI	BA
C. Baerga, 2b	26	5	2	0	0	1	4	.192
K. Lofton, of	25	5	1	0	0	6	0	.200
O. Vizquel, ss	23	4	0	1	0	3	1	.174
J. Thome, 3b	19	4	1	0	1	1	2	.211
E. Murray, 1b, dh	19	2	0	0	1	1	3	.105
M. Ramirez, of	18	4	0	0	1	2	2	.222
A. Belle, of	17	4	0	0	2	4	4	.235
S. Alomar, c	15	3	2	0	0	0	1	.200
P. Sorrento, 1b	11	2	1	0	0	0	0	.182
T. Pena, c	6	1	0	0	0	0	0	.167
H. Perry, 1b	5	0	0	0	0	0	0	.000
D. Martinez, p	3	0	0	0	0	0	0	.000
A. Espinoza, 3b	2	1	0	0	0	1	0	.500
R. Amaro, of	2	0	0	0	0	0	0	.000
O. Hershiser, p	2	0	0	0	0	0	0	.000
W. Kirby, of	1	0	0	0	0	0	0	.000
J. Poole, p	1	0	0	0	0	0	0	.000

Errors: C. Baerga, A. Belle, O. Hershiser, D. Martinez, P. Sorrento, J. Thome
Stolen Bases: K. Lofton (6), M. Ramirez, O. Vizquel

Individual Pitching

ATLANTA (N.L.)

	W	L	ERA	IP	H	BB	SO	SV
G. Maddux	1	1	2.25	16	9	3	8	0
T. Glavine	2	0	1.29	14	4	6	11	0
S. Avery	1	0	1.50	6	3	5	3	0
M. Wohlers	0	0	1.80	5	4	3	3	2
B. Clontz	0	0	2.70	3.1	2	0	2	0
G. McMichael	0	0	2.70	3.1	3	2	2	0
J. Smoltz	0	0	15.43	2.1	6	2	4	0
K. Mercker	0	0	4.50	2	1	2	2	0
P. Borbon	0	0	0.00	1	0	0	2	1
A. Pena	0	1	9.00	1	3	2	0	0

CLEVELAND (A.L.)

	W	L	ERA	IP	H	BB	SO	SV
O. Hershiser	1	1	2.57	14	8	4	13	0
D. Martinez	0	1	3.48	10.1	12	8	5	0
C. Nagy	0	0	6.43	7	8	1	4	0
K. Hill	0	1	4.26	6.1	7	4	1	0
J. Tavarez	0	0	0.00	4.1	3	2	1	0
J. Mesa	1	0	4.50	4	5	1	4	1
A. Embree	0	0	2.70	3.1	2	2	2	0
J. Poole	0	1	3.86	2.1	1	0	1	0
P. Assenmacher	0	0	6.75	1.1	1	3	3	0

PART FOURTEEN

All-Star Games

Scores and Highlights of
Every All-Star Game

All-Star Games

Baseball's midsummer classic, the All-Star Game, began in 1933. With the exception of 1959–62, when two games were held yearly, and 1945, when no game was played due to wartime restrictions, the game has been an annual event that features the best talent of the American and National leagues. This section provides information about these games through today. Included are facts about the individual games, the pitchers, home-run hitters, and highlights, which feature key plays, all-time records, and special achievements. Most of the information is self-explanatory. That which may appear unfamiliar is listed below:

Innings Pitched. Pitchers are listed in the order of appearance. In parentheses, following each pitcher's name, are the numberof innings he pitched in the game. For example, J. Doe (2.1) would mean that he pitched 2⅓ innings. J. Doe (2.0) would mean that Doe started a third inning but failed to retire a batter.

Winning and Losing Pitchers. Indicated by boldfaced print.

Save. The relief pitcher who is credited with a save is indicated by the abbreviation SV, which appears in boldfaced print after his innings pitched.

Home Runs. Players are listed in the order their home runs were hit.

LINE SCORES					PITCHERS (innings pitched)	HOME RUNS (men on)	HIGHLIGHTS
1933 - JULY 6 AT CHICAGO							Ruth's third-inning homer with one on gave the American League a 3-0 lead and proved enough of a margin to win the first All-Star Game.
N	000 002 000	2	8	0	**Hallahan** (2), Warneke (4), Hubbell (2)	Frisch	
A	012 001 00x	4	9	1	**Gomez** (3), Crowder (3), Grove (3) **SV**	Ruth (1 on)	
1934 - JULY 10 AT NEW YORK							Hubbell struck out Ruth, Gehrig, Foxx, Simmons, and Cronin consecutively as the National League jumped to a 4-0 lead before the American League exploded for six runs in the fifth. Harder kept the senior circuit in check with one hit through the final five innings and Averill captured the hitting honors with a double, triple, and three RBIs.
A	000 261 000	9	14	1	Gomez (3), Ruffing (1), **Harder** (5)		
N	103 030 000	7	8	1	Hubbell (3), Warneke (1), **Mungo** (1), D. Dean (3), Frankhouse (1)	Frisch, Medwick (2 on)	
1935 - JULY 8 AT CLEVELAND							Foxx drove in three runs with a two-run homer and an RBI single to lead the American League to victory behind Gomez's three-hit six-inning pitching performance.
N	000 100 000	1	4	1	**Walker** (2), Schumacher (4), Derringer (1), D. Dean (1)		
A	210 010 00x	4	8	0	**Gomez** (6), Harder (3) **SV**	Foxx (1 on)	
1936 - JULY 7 AT BOSTON							The National League won for the first time as they jumped out to a 4-0 lead before the American League scored three times in the seventh. Shutout pitching by Dean and Hubbell aided in the victory as Medwick's RBI single in the fifth proved the deciding run.
A	000 000 300	3	7	1	**Grove** (3), Rowe (3), Harder (2)	Gehrig	
N	020 020 00x	4	9	0	**D. Dean** (3), Hubbell (3), Davis (0.2), Warneke (2.1) **SV**	Galan	
1937 - JULY 7 AT WASHINGTON							Led by Gehrig's four RBIs and homer in the third with DiMaggio aboard, the American League easily coasted to a victory. Medwick stroked four hits in the losing cause and Dizzy Dean broke his toe on an Averill line drive which would prove his undoing. He returned too soon after the injury, and by favoring his bad foot, developed a sore arm.
N	000 111 000	3	13	0	**D. Dean** (3), Hubbell (0.2), Blanton (0.1), Grissom (1), Mungo (2), Walters (1)		
A	002 312 00x	8	13	2	**Gomez** (3), Bridges (3), Harder (3) **SV**	Gehrig (1 on)	
1938 - JULY 6 AT CINCINNATI							The National League scored four times before the American League got on the board in the ninth inning to break the shutout. The victory was sparked by the pitching of Vander Meer and Lee. Medwick and Goodman excelled in the field.
A	000 000 001	1	7	4	**Gomez** (3), Allen (3), Grove (2)		
N	100 100 20x	4	8	0	**Vander Meer** (3), Lee (3), Brown (3) **SV**		
1939 - JULY 11 AT NEW YORK							Feller saved the American League's 3-1 lead when he entered the game in the sixth with one out and the bases loaded and forced Vaughan to hit into a double play. Joe DiMaggio's homer in the fifth with the score 2-1 provided an insurance run.
N	001 000 000	1	7	1	Derringer (3), **Lee** (3), Fette (2)		
A	000 210 00x	3	6	1	Ruffing (3), **Bridges** (2.1), Feller (3.2) **SV**	J. DiMaggio	
1940 - JULY 9 AT ST. LOUIS							Before Ruffing could retire a single man, the National League jumped off to a 3-0 lead in the first on West's homer and coasted to the first shutout in All-Star Game history. Manager McKechnie led the Nationals to their mid-summer victory, led the Cincinnati Reds to a World Series championship, and also piloted a National League club to a 2-1 win over the junior circuit in an impromptu All-Star Game held in Tampa, Florida on St. Patrick's Day for the benefit of the Finnish Relief fund.
A	000 000 000	0	3	1	**Ruffing** (3), Newsom (3), Feller (2)		
N	300 000 01x	4	7	0	**Derringer** (2), Walters (2), Wyatt (2), French (2), Hubbell (1) **SV**	West (2 on)	
1941 - JULY 8 AT DETROIT							The American League was losing 5-4 in the bottom of the ninth and only one out away from defeat when Williams delivered a clutch home run with two men aboard to end the game. Vaughan's two home runs set an All-Star Game record.
N	000 001 220	5	10	2	Wyatt (2), Derringer (2), Walters (2), **Passeau** (2.2)	Vaughan (1 on), Vaughan (1 on)	
A	000 101 014	7	11	3	Feller (3), Lee (3), Hudson (1), **E. Smith** (2)	Williams (2 on)	
1942 - JULY 6 AT NEW YORK							Boudreau's homer, followed by Henrich's double and York's homer in the first, carried the American League to an easy victory. Owen's pinch-hit homer in the eighth spoiled the shutout. The next night at Cleveland, in an All-Star Game which took place for the Ball and Bat and Army-Navy relief, the American League handed Mickey Cochrane's Service All-Stars, made up largely of major leaguers in the armed forces, a 5-0 defeat.
A	300 000 000	3	7	0	**Chandler** (4), Benton (5) **SV**	Boudreau, York (1 on)	
N	000 000 010	1	6	1	**M. Cooper** (3), Vander Meer (3), Passeau (2), Walters (1)	Owen	
1943 - JULY 13 AT PHILADELPHIA							Doerr's three-run homer in the second paced the junior circuit in the first night All-Star Game. In the course of losing, Vander Meer tied a record with six strikeouts and Vince DiMaggio had a single, triple, and homer. American fighting men throughout the world heard the game via shortwave radio.
N	100 000 101	3	10	3	**M. Cooper** (2.1), Vander Meer (2.2), Sewell (1), Javery (2)	V. DiMaggio	
A	031 010 00x	5	8	1	**Leonard** (3), Newhouser (3), Hughson (3) **SV**	Doerr (2 on)	
1944 - JULY 11 AT PITTSBURGH							The National League scored four times in the fifth to put the game out of reach. Cavarretta set an All-Star Game record as he reached base five times with a triple, a single, and three walks.
A	010 000 000	1	6	3	Borowy (3), **Hughson** (1.2), Muncrief (1.1), Newhouser (1.2), Newsom (0.1)		
N	000 040 21x	7	12	1	Walters (3), **Raffensberger** (2), Sewell (3), Tobin (1) **SV**		
1945 - NO GAME PLAYED							
1946 - JULY 9 AT BOSTON							The All-Star Game resumed after a one-year wartime interruption as Williams led a one man assault with four hits and five RBIs in the most one-sided midsummer-classic in history. His two home runs tied Vaughan's 1941 record-setting feat, and his five RBIs set a record. In the last three innings, Kramer held the Nationals hitless.
N	000 000 000	0	3	0	**Passeau** (3), Higbe (1.1), Blackwell (2.2), Sewell (1)		
A	200 130 24x	12	14	1	**Feller** (3), Newhouser (3), Kramer (3) **SV**	Keller (1 on), Williams, Williams (2 on)	
1947 - JULY 8 AT CHICAGO							The National League held a 1-0 lead on Mize's home run until the sixth when the American League tied the score on a double-play ball hit by Joe DiMaggio which brought Appling home. Spence singled home Doerr with the deciding run in the next inning after Doerr reached third as the result of a pick-off attempt by Sain that wound up in center field.
A	000 001 100	2	8	0	Newhouser (3), **Shea** (3), Masterson (1.2), Page (1.1) **SV**		
N	000 100 000	1	5	1	Blackwell (3), Brecheen (3), **Sain** (1), Spahn (2)	Mize	
1948 - JULY 13 AT ST. LOUIS							The American League defeated the National League 5-2 despite the absence of DiMaggio, Williams, Kell, and Newhouser. Raschi aided his own cause with a single in the fourth producing two RBIs.
N	200 000 000	2	8	0	Branca (3), **Schmitz** (0.1), Sain (1.2), Blackwell (3)	Musial (1 on)	
A	011 300 00x	5	6	0	Masterson (3), **Raschi** (3), Coleman (3) **SV**	Evers	

LINE SCORES					PITCHERS (innings pitched)	HOME RUNS (men on)	HIGHLIGHTS
1949 - JULY 12 AT BROOKLYN							In a see-saw slugfest, the Americans proved the victor in a game that marked the appearance of Robinson, Newcombe, Campanella, and Doby, the first black playersin All-Star play. The key play of the game came in the second with the bases filled when Williams made a spectacular catch of Newcombe's slicing liner in the left field corner. Raschi's one-hit pitching over the last three innings also aided in checking the Nationals.
A	400 202 300	11	13	1	Parnell (1), **Trucks** (2), Brissie (3), Raschi (3) **SV**		
N	212 002 000	7	12	5	Spahn (1.1), **Newcombe** (2.2), Munger (1), Bickford (1), Pollet (1), Blackwell (1), Roe (1)	Musial (1 on), Kiner (1 on)	
1950 - JULY 11 AT CHICAGO							Kiner's homer in the top of the ninth sent the game into extra innings before Schoendienst settled the contest in the 14th with a home run. Jansen allowed one hit and struck out six in checking the American League for five innings. The contest was marred as Williams broke his elbow while making a catch against the left field wall in the first, and was lost to the Red Sox until the end of the season.
N	020 000 001 000 01	4	10	0	Roberts (3), Newcombe (2), Konstanty (1), Jansen (5), **Blackwell** (3)	Kiner, Schoendienst	
A	001 020 000 000 00	3	8	1	Raschi (3), Lemon (3), Houtteman (3), Reynolds (3), **Gray** (1.1), Feller (0.2)		
1951 - JULY 10 AT DETROIT							Home run records fell as both leagues combined to hit six round trippers. The National League, with four of the home runs, used them to send six runs across and topple the American League in what marked the first back-to-back victories in All-Star play for the senior circuit.
N	100 302 110	8	12	1	Roberts (2), **Maglie** (3), Newcombe (3), Blackwell (1) **SV**	Musial, Elliott (1 on), Kiner, Hodges (1 on)	
A	010 110 000	3	10	2	Garver (3), **Lopat** (1), Hutchinson (3), Parnell (1), Lemon (1)	Wertz, Kell	
1952 - JULY 8 AT PHILADELPHIA							Sauer's homer with Musial aboard in the fourth proved the deciding run in a five-inning game shortened by rain.
A	000 20	2	5	0	Raschi (2), **Lemon** (2), Shantz (1)		
N	100 20	3	3	0	Simmons (3), **Rush** (2)	J. Robinson, Sauer (1 on)	
1953 - JULY 14 AT CINCINNATI							Slaughter's two hits, RBI, two runs, and diving catch of Kuenn's line drive sparked the National League. The American League broke the shutout with two outs in the ninth as Minoso singled home Fain.
A	000 000 001	1	5	0	Pierce (3), **Reynolds** (2), Garcia (2), Paige (1)		
N	000 020 12x	5	10	0	Roberts (3), **Spahn** (2), Simmons (2), Dickson (2) **SV**		
1954 - JULY 13 AT CLEVELAND							Doby's pinch-hit homer in the eighth, followed by Fox's single which sent two runs home, ended the highest scoring All-Star Game in history. The victory broke afour game losing streak for the American League and produced two hit records: 17 for the junior circuit and a combined total of 31 for the game. Rosen's five RBIs and two home runs also tied the All-Star Game record.
N	000 520 020	9	14	0	Roberts (3), Antonelli (2), Spahn (0.2), Grissom (1.1), **Conley** (0.1), Erskine (0.2)	Kluszewski (1 on), Bell (1 on)	
A	004 121 03x	11	17	1	Ford (3), Consuegra (0.1), Lemon (0.2), Porterfield (3), Keegan (0.2), **Stone** (0.1), Trucks (1) **SV**	Rosen (2 on), Boone, Rosen (1 on), Doby	
1955 - JULY 12 AT MILWAUKEE							Conley struck out the side in the 12th and Musial hit a homer to give the National League a victory after being down 5-0. The American League's first inning barrage of four runs featured Mantle's homer with two on.
A	400 001 000 000	5	10	2	Pierce (3), Wynn (3), Ford (1.2), **Sullivan** (3.1)	Mantle (2 on)	
N	000 000 230 00	6	13	1	Roberts (3), Haddix (3), Newcombe (1), Jones (0.2), Nuxhall (3.1), **Conley** (1)	Musial	
1956 - JULY 10 AT WASHINGTON							Three sparkling fielding plays by Ken Boyer, along with his three hits, paced the National League as they score five times before the American League got on the board with back-to-back homers in the sixth by Williams and Mantle.
N	001 211 200	7	11	0	**Friend** (3), Spahn (2), Antonelli (4) **SV**	Mays (1 on), Musial	
A	000 003 000	3	11	0	**Pierce** (3), Ford (1), Wilson (1), Brewer (2), Score (1), Wynn (1)	Williams (1 on), Mantle	
1957 - JULY 9 AT ST. LOUIS							Minoso's running catch of Hodges' line drive with one on and two out in the ninth ended a three-run National League rally and preserved the victory for the American League, who also scored their final three runs in the ninth.
A	020 001 003	6	10	0	**Bunning** (3), Loes (3), Wynn (0.1), Pierce (1.2), Mossi (0.2), Grim (0.1) **SV**		
N	000 000 203	5	9	1	**Simmons** (1), Burdette (4), Sanford (1), Jackson (2), Labine (1)		
1958 - JULY 8 AT BALTIMORE							McDougald's pinch-hit single in the sixth scored Malzone for the deciding run in the first All-Star Game played without an extra base hit. O'Dell pitched perfect ball to check the National League.
N	210 000 000	3	4	2	Spahn (3), **Friend** (2.1), L. Jackson (0.2), Farrell (2)		
A	110 011 00x	4	9	2	Turley (1.2), Narleski (3.1), **Wynn** (1), O'Dell (3) **SV**		
1959 - JULY 7 AT PITTSBURGH							Aaron knocked in the tying run with a single and scored the deciding run as Mays tripled him home in the eighth. Drysdale got the National League off to a good start by pitching perfect ball for three innings.
A	000 100 030	4	8	0	Wynn (3), Duren (3), Bunning (1), **Ford** (0.1), Daley (0.2)	Kaline	
N	100 000 22x	5	9	1	Drysdale (3), Burdette (3), Face (1.2), **Antonelli** (0.1), Elston (1) **SV**	Mathews	
1959 - AUGUST 3 AT LOS ANGELES							Berra's two run homer in the third inning proved decisive in the first All Star Game played in California.
A	012 000 110	5	6	0	**Walker** (3), Wynn (2), Wilhelm (1), O'Dell (1), McLish (2) **SV**	Malzone, Berra (1 on), Colavito	
N	100 010 100	3	6	3	**Drysdale** (3), Conley (2), Jones (2), Face (2)	Robinson, Gilliam	
1960 - JULY 11 AT KANSAS CITY							The National League jumped to a 5-0 lead and held on to win as Mays paced the attack with a single, double, and triple. Face relieved with the bases full in the sixth and retired the side as he forced Aparicio to hit into a double play.
N	311 000 000	5	12	4	**Friend** (3), McCormick (2.1), Face (1.2), Buhl (1.1), Law (0.2) **SV**	Banks (1 on), Crandall	
A	000 001 020	3	6	1	**Monbouquette** (2), Estrada (1), Coates (2), Bell (2), Lary (1), Daley (1)	Kaline (1 on)	
1960 - JULY 13 AT NEW YORK							The game was sparked by Mays's three hits, Musial's pinch-hit homer in the seventh, and the shutout pitching of the National League.
N	021 000 102	6	10	0	**Law** (2), Podres (2), S. Williams (2), Jackson (1), Henry (1), McDaniel (1) **SV**	Mathews (1 on), Mays, Musial, K. Boyer (1 on)	
A	000 000 000	0	8	0	**Ford** (3), Wynn (2), Staley (2), Lary (1), Bell (1)		
1961 - JULY 31 AT BOSTON							The first tie game in All-Star history occured as rain fell after the ninth inning to end the contest and cancel excellent pitching performances. Colavito's homer in the first was the only run scored until White drove in Mathews on a single in the sixth.
N	000 001 000	1	5	1	Purkey (2), Mahaffey (2), Koufax (2), Miller (3)		
A	100 000 000	1	4	0	Bunning (3), Schwall (3), Pascual (3)	Colavito	

LINE SCORES						PITCHERS (innings pitched)	HOME RUNS (men on)	HIGHLIGHTS
1961 - JULY 11 AT SAN FRANCISCO	A	000 001 002 1	4	4	2	Ford (3), Lary (0), Donovan (2), Bunning (2), Fornieles (0.1), **Wilhelm** (1.2)	Killebrew	Clemente hit a game-winning single in the bottom of the tenth after Mays tied the game with a double that drove in Aaron. Seven errors by both sides set an All-Star Game record.
	N	010 100 010 2	5	11	5	Spahn (3), Purkey (2), McCormick (3), Face (0.1), Koufax (0), **Miller** (1.2)	Altman	
1962 - JULY 10 AT WASHINGTON	N	000 002 010	3	8	0	Drysdale (3), **Marichal** (2), Purkey (2), Shaw (2) **SV**		Entering the game in the sixth inning, Wills sparked the National League and scored the first run of the game. In the eighth inning he scored the insurance run. Clemente led the attack with three hits.
	A	000 001 000	1	4	0	Bunning (3), **Pascual** (3), Donovan (2), Pappas (1)		
1962 - JULY 30 AT CHICAGO	A	001 201 302	9	10	0	Stenhouse (2), **Herbert** (3), Aguirre (3), Pappas (1) **SV**	Runnels, Wagner (1 on), Colavito (2 on)	With one man on and one out in the seventh, Moran hit a line drive which umpire Burkhart ruled trapped by Aaron. After Maris tapped a roller to force Moran, Colavito hit a home run to make the score 7-1 and ice the game. Two double plays in the middle of the game also helped to subdue the Nationals.
	N	010 000 111	4	10	4	Podres (2), **Mahaffey** (2), Gibson (2), Farrell (1), Marichal (2)	Roseboro	
1963 - JULY 9 AT CLEVELAND	N	012 010 010	5	6	0	O'Toole (2), **Jackson** (2), Culp (1), Woodeshick (2), Drysdale (2) **SV**		The National League used only six singles to win as Mays led the attack with two RBIs, two runs, two stolen bases, and a catch against the center field fence to rob Pepitone of an extra base hit. Musial's 24th All-Star appearance set a record. A tribute was paid to Mantle as the players named him starting centerfielder even though he was unable to play because of a broken foot.
	A	012 000 000	3	11	1	McBride (3), **Bunning** (2), Bouton (1), Pizarro (1), Radatz (2)		
1964 - JULY 7 AT NEW YORK	A	100 002 100	4	9	1	Chance (3), Wyatt (1), Pascual (2), **Radatz** (2.2)		Mays walked, stole second, and scored in the last of the ninth to tie the game on Cepeda's bloop single before Callison's homer with two on gave the National League a dramatic come-from-behind victory.
	N	000 210 004	7	8	0	Drysdale (3), Bunning (2), Short (1), Farrell (2), **Marichal** (1)	Williams, Boyer, Callison (2 on)	
1965 - JULY 13 AT MINNESOTA	N	320 000 100	6	11	0	Marichal (3), Maloney (1.2), Drysdale (0.1), **Koufax** (1), Farrell (1), Gibson (2) **SV**	Mays, Torre (1 on), Stargell (1 on)	The National League jumped to a 5-0 lead on three homers before McAuliffe and Killebrew hit two-run homers in the fifth to tie the game. Santo's single in the seventh drove in the deciding run. An American League rally was cut off in the eighth as Mays recovered after slipping to make a leaping, backhanded catch of Hall's fly with two men on and two out.
	A	000 140 000	5	8	0	Pappas (1), Grant (2), Richert (2), **McDowell** (2), Fisher (2)	McAuliffe (1 on), Killebrew (1 on)	
1966 - JULY 12 AT ST. LOUIS	A	010 000 000 0	1	6	0	McLain (3), Kaat (2), Stottlemyre (2), Siebert (2), **Richert** (0.1)		A single in the bottom of the tenth by Wills sent McCarver home with the winning run in a game that took place in 105-degree temperature. The victory came in spite of Brooks Robinson's three hits and McLain's three perfect innings. After Aaron lost Robinson's fly in the background of white shirts for a triple in the second, Koufax uncorked a wild pitch to lose the shutout.
	N	000 100 000 1	2	6	0	Koufax (3), Bunning (2), Marichal (3), **Perry** (2)		
1967 - JULY 11 AT CALIFORNIA	N	010 000 000 000 001	2	9	0	Marichal (3), Jenkins (3), Gibson (2), Short (2), Cuellar (2), **Drysdale** (2), Seaver (1) **SV**	Allen, Perez	After Allen's homer in the second and Brooks Robinson's equalizer in the sixth, Perez homered in the 15th inning to end the longest All-Star Game in history. The pitching proved superior as 30 batters go down via the strikeout route. The American League's five pitchers allowed no walks. Jenkins proved the most spectacular of the seven National League pitchers as he equalled the record of Hubbell, Vander Meer, and Jansen by striking out six.
	A	000 001 000 000 000	1	8	0	Chance (3), McGlothlin (2), Peters (3), Downing (2), **Hunter** (5)	B. Robinson	
1968 - JULY 9 AT HOUSTON	A	000 000 000	0	3	1	**Tiant** (2), Odom (2), McLain (2), McDowell (1), Stottlemyre (0.1), John (0.2)		Mays scored on a double-play ball in the first to give the National League mound staff all the support they needed in winning the first 1-0 game in All-Star history. Seaver sparkled with five strikeouts in a game that typified the pitchers' stranglehold on the batters.
	N	100 000 00x	1	5	0	**Drysdale** (3), Marichal (2), Carlton (1), Seaver (2), Reed (0.2), Koosman (0.1) **SV**		
1969 - JULY 23 AT WASHINGTON	N	125 100 000	9	11	0	**Carlton** (3), Gibson (1), Singer (2), Koosman (1.2), Dierker (0.1), Niekro (1) **SV**	Bench (1 on), McCovey, McCovey (1 on)	San Francisco's Willie McCovey became the fourth player in All-Star history to hit two home runs in a game and drove in three runs to lead the National League to its seventh straight victory. Bench of the Reds also homered and knocked in a pair of runs as the winners battered seven American League pitchers for 11 hits in a game played in the nation's capital to help celebrate baseball's 100th anniversary.
	A	011 100 000	3	6	2	**Stottlemyre** (2), Odom (0.1), Knowles (0.2), McLain (1), McNally (2), McDowell (2), Culp (1)	Freehan, Howard	
1970 - JULY 14 AT CINCINNATI	A	000 001 120 000	4	12	0	Palmer (3), McDowell (3), J. Perry (2), Hunter (0.1), Peterson (0), Stottlemyre (1.2), **Wright** (1.2)		The National League, after trailing 4-1 in the ninth, won in the 12th on singles by Rose, Grabarkewitz and Hickman for their eighth straight triumph. The game marked the first time since 1957 that the starters were elected by the fans.
	N	000 000 103 001	5	10	0	Seaver (3), Merritt (2), G. Perry (2), Gibson (2), **Osteen** (3)	Dietz	
1971 - JULY 13 AT DETROIT	N	021 000 010	4	5	0	**Ellis** (3), Marichal (2), Jenkins (1), Wilson (2)	Bench (1 on), Aaron, Clemente	The American League finally snaps the NL's dominance, winning for the first time since 1962 with a power display by Jackson, Frank Robinson and Killebrew. Jackson's homer was an epic shot off the light towers, and Robinson's made him the first to homer for each league. Aaron's homer was his first in All-Star competition.
	A	004 002 00x	6	7	0	**Blue** (3), Palmer (2), Cuellar (2), Lolich (2) **SV**	Jackson (1 on), F. Robinson (1 on), Killebrew (1 on)	
1972 - JULY 25 AT ATLANTA	A	001 000 020 0	3	6	0	Palmer (3), Lolich (2), Perry (2), Wood (2), **McNally** (0.1)	Rojas (1 on)	The seventh extra-inning All-Star game ended in the 10th inning when Colbert walked, was sacrificed to second, and raced home on Morgan's hit to make the National League 7-for-7 in extra-inning games. The most popular hit was Aaron's homer before his home fans.
	N	000 002 001 1	4	8	0	Gibson (2), Blass (1), Sutton (2), Carlton (1), Stoneman (2), **McGraw** (2)	Aaron (1 on)	
1973 - JULY 24 AT KANSAS CITY	N	002 122 000	7	10	0	**Wise** (2), Osteen (2), Sutton (1), Twitchell (1), Giusti (1), Seaver (1), Brewer (1) **SV**	Bonds (1 on), Davis (1 on), Bench	A record 54 players (28 by the National League and 26 by the American) are used as the NL continued to assert its power. Aaron broke a 1-1 tie with his RBI single in third before Bench, Bonds and Davis rap insurance homers.
	A	010 000 000	1	5	0	Hunter (1.1), Holtzman (0.2), **Blyleven** (1), Singer (2), Ryan (2), Lyle (1), Fingers (1)		

LINE SCORES					PITCHERS (innings pitched)	HOME RUNS (men on)	HIGHLIGHTS
1974 - JULY 23 AT PITTSBURGH							Steve Garvey, who was not even listed on the All-Star ballot, was the hero of the National League's victory, hitting a double and single, driving in one run and scoring another. In addition, he made several sparkling defensive plays at first base to give the National League their 11th victory in the last 12 games.
A	002 000 000	2	4	1	Perry (3), **Tiant** (2), Hunter (2), Fingers (1)		
N	010 210 12x	7	10	1	Messersmith (3), **Brett** (2), Matlack (1), McGlothen (1), Marshall (2)	Smith	
1975 - JULY 15 AT MILWAUKEE							A three-run outburst in the ninth inning against Hunter and Gossage snapped a 3-3 tie and gave the NL their 12th victory in 13 games. A single by Madlock with the bases full was the key blow. Yastrzemski accounted for all the AL's runs with a three-run pinch homer.
N	021 000 003	6	13	1	Reuss (3), Sutton (2), Seaver (1), **Matlack** (2), Jones (1)	Garvey, Wynn	
A	000 003 000	3	10	1	Blue (2), Busby (2), Kaat (2), **Hunter** (2), Gossage (1)	Yastrzemski (2 on)	
1976 - JULY 13 AT PHILADELPHIA							Scoring early and often, the NL tagged Fidrych and his 3 successors for 10 hits, including home runs by Foster and Cedeno. The rout was the National League's fifth straight victory, giving them 13 of the last 14.
A	000 100 000	1	5	0	**Fidrych** (2), Hunter (2), Tiant (2), Tanana (2)	Lynn	
N	202 000 03x	7	10	0	**Jones** (3), Seaver (2), Montefusco (2), Rhoden (1), K. Forsch (1)	Foster (1 on), Cedeno (1 on)	
1977 - JULY 19 AT NEW YORK							The NL rocked Palmer for four runs in the first inning, sparked by homers from Morgan and Luzinski, and went on to defeat the AL 7-5 for its sixth straight.
N	401 000 020	7	9	1	**Sutton** (3), Lavelle (2), Seaver (2), R. Reuschel (1), Gossage (1)	Morgan, Garvey, Luzinski (1 on)	
A	000 002 102	5	8	0	**Palmer** (2), Kern (1), Eckersley (2), LaRoche (1), Campbell (1), Lyle (2)	Scott (1 on)	
1978 - JULY 11 AT SAN DIEGO							The NL spotted the AL three runs then came roaring from behind to win on a four-run assault against Gossage in the eighth. Garvey, whose single tied the score in the third, tripled in the tie-breaking run.
A	201 000 000	3	8	1	Palmer (2.2), Keough (0.1), Sorensen (3), Kern (0.2), Guidry (0.1), **Gossage** (1)		
N	003 000 04x	7	10	0	Blue (3), Rogers (2), Fingers (2), **Sutter** (1.2), P. Niekro (0.1)		
1979 - JULY 17 AT SEATTLE							Mazzilli of the Mets hit a game-tying pinch home run in the eighth on his first All-Star at bat, and walked with the bases full in the ninth to give the National League its eighth straight win.
N	211 001 011	7	10	0	Carlton (1), Andujar (2), Rogers (2), Perry (0), Sambito (0.2), LaCoss (1.1), **Sutter** (2)	Mazzilli	
A	302 001 000	6	10	0	Ryan (2), Stanley (2), Clear (2), **Kern** (2.2), Guidry (0.1)	Lynn (1 on)	
1980 - JULY 8 AT LOS ANGELES							Griffey led the National League to its ninth straight victory, 4-2, with a single and a home run as five pitchers held the American League to seven hits. Lynn accounted for the AL's runs with a two-run homer in the fifth that gave the losers a temporary 2-0 lead. It was the NL's 17th win in 18 games.
A	000 020 000	2	7	1	Stone (3), **John** (2.1), Farmer (0.2), Stieb (1), Gossage (1)	Lynn (1 on)	
N	000 012 10x	4	7	0	Richard (2), Welch (3), **Reuss** (1), Bibby (1), Sutter (2) **SV**	Griffey	
1981 - AUGUST 9 AT CLEVELAND							Schmidt hit a 2-run homer off Fingers in the eighth inning to to lift the National League to a 5-4 victory over the American League before 72,086, the largest crowd ever to see an All-Star Game. It was the NL's tenth straight win and the 18th in the last 19 meetings with the AL. The game, held on August 9, was the latest All-Star Game ever held, owing to the ten-week player strike.
N	000 011 120	5	9	1	Valenzuela (1), Seaver (1), Knepper (2), Hooton (1.2), Ruthven (0.1) **Blue** (1), Ryan (1), Sutter (1) **SV**	Carter, Carter, Parker, Schmidt (1 on)	
A	010 003 000	4	11	1	Morris (2), Barker (2), K. Forsch (1), Norris (1), Davis (1), **Fingers** (0.1), Stieb (1.2)	Singleton	
1982 - JULY 13 AT MONTREAL							Led by Concepcion's two-run homer, the National League maintained its mastery over the American, winning its 11th straight. The game was the first All-Star Game played outside the United States.
A	100 000 000	1	8	2	**Eckersley** (3), Clancy (1), Bannister (1), Quisenberry (2), Fingers (1)		
N	021 001 00x	4	8	1	**Rogers** (3), Carlton (2), Soto (2), Valenzuela (0.2), Minton (0.2), Howe (0.1), Hume (0.1) **SV**	Concepcion (1 on)	
1983 - JULY 6 AT CHICAGO							Paced by Fred Lynn's grand slam, the American League tallied seven runs in the third to break the Nationals' winning streak in taking the 50th anniversary game. The game was played at Comiskey Park, site of the first mid-summer classic.
N	100 110 000	3	8	3	**Soto** (2), Hammaker (0.2), Dawley (1.1), Dravecky (2), Perez (0.2), Orosco (0.1), L. Smith (1)		
A	117 000 22x	13	15	2	**Stieb** (3), Honeycutt (2), Stanley (2), Young (1), Quisenberry (1)	Rice, Lynn (3 on)	
1984 - JULY 10 AT SAN FRANCISCO							Pitchers prevailed in the San Francisco twilight, as a nine-inning-record twenty-one strikeouts were recorded. Nineteen-year-old Dwight Gooden, the youngest All-Star ever, combined with Fernando Valenzuela to strike out six consecutive hitters, breaking Carl Hubbell's fifty-year-old mark.
A	010 000 000	1	7	2	**Stieb** (2), Morris (2), Dotson (2), Caudill (1), W. Hernandez (1)	Brett	
N	110 000 01x	3	8	0	**Lea** (2), Valenzuela (2), Gooden (2), Soto (2), Gossage (1) **SV**	Carter, Murphy	
1985 - JULY 16 AT MINNESOTA							Steve Garvey's two-out single in the third inning, which scored Tommy Herr from second base was enough to put the National League ahead to stay. Rickey Henderson scored the lone American League run on George Brett's sacrifice fly in the first inning. The American League managed only five singles. This win made it 21 of the last 23 for the Nationals.
N	011 020 002	6	9	1	**Hoyt** (3), Ryan (3), Valenzuela (1), Reardon (1), Gossage (1)		
A	100 000 000	1	5	0	**Morris** (2.2), Key (0.1), Blyleven (2), Stieb (1), Moore (2), Petry (0.1), Hernandez (0.2)		
1986 - JULY 15 AT HOUSTON							Lou Whitaker's two run homer in the second inning off Dwight Gooden was the key blow for the American League. Frank White added a solo shot for a needed insurance run as the Nationals rallied in the eighth with two runs and left the tying and winning runs on base in the ninth.
A	020 000 100	3	5	0	**Clemens** (3), Higuera (3), Hough (1.2), Righetti (0.2), Aase (0.2) **SV**	Whitaker (1 on), White	
N	000 000 020	2	5	1	**Gooden** (3), Valenzuela (3), Scott (1), Fernandez (1), Krukow (1)		

LINE SCORES					PITCHERS (innings pitched)	HOME RUNS (men on)	HIGHLIGHTS
1987 - JULY 14 AT OAKLAND							Tim Raines, hitless in six previous All-Star contests, hit a two-out triplein the top of the 13th inning to drive home the only runs of the game.
N	000 000 000 000 2	2	8	2	Scott (2), Sutcliffe (2), Hershiser (2), Reuschel (1.1), Franco (0.2), Bedrosian (1), **L. Smith** (3), Fernandez (1) **SV**		
A	000 000 000 000 0	0	6	1	Saberhagen (3), Morris (2), Langston (2), Plesac (1), Righetti (0.1), Henke (2.2), **Howell** (2)		
1988 - JULY 12 AT CINCINNATI							Steinbach's third inning homer and fourth inning sacrifice fly was all the American League needed to turn back the Nationals. It was the A.L.'s second victory in the last three meetings.
A	001 100 000	2	6	2	**Viola** (2), Clemens (1), Gubicza (2), Stieb (1), Russell (1), Jones (0.2), Plesac (0.1), Eckersley (1) **SV**	Steinbach	
N	000 100 000	1	5	0	**Gooden** (3), Knepper (1), Cone (1), Gross (1), Davis (0.2), Walk (0.1), Hershiser (1), Worrell (1)		
1989 - JULY 11 AT CALIFORNIA							All nine A.L. starters hit safely as they won consecutive games for the first time in 31 years. Bo Jackson and Wade Boggs hit back-to-back first inning homers to wipe out a 2-0 deficit. 42-year-old Nolan Ryan became the oldest All-Star winner in the first game played with the designated hitter.
N	200 000 010	3	9	1	Reuschel (1), **Smoltz** (1), Sutcliffe (1), Burke (2), M. Davis (1), Howell (1), Williams (1)		
A	212 000 00x	5	12	0	Stewart (1), **Ryan** (2), Gubicza (1), Moore (1), Swindell (1.2), Russell (1), Plesac (0), Jones (1.1) **SV**	Jackson, Boggs	
1990 - JULY 10 AT CHICAGO							Julio Franco doubled home the only runs of the game in the seventh inning to give the Americans the victory. Nationals could manage only two hits, the lowest total in All-Star history.
A	000 000 200	2	7	0	Welch (2), Stieb (2), **Saberhagen** (2), Thigpen (1), Finley (1), Eckersley (1) **SV**		
N	000 000 000	0	2	1	Armstrong (2), R. Martinez (1), D. Martinez (1), Viola (1), D. Smith (0.2), **Brantley** (0.1), Dibble (1), Myers (1), Franco (1)		
1991 - JULY 9 AT TORONTO							Ripken smacked a three run homer off Dennis Martinez in the third inning as the American League ran their winning streak to four. Tony LaRussa became the first manager to win three consecutive All-Star games.
N	100 100 000	2	10	1	Glavine (2), **Martinez** (2), Viola (1), Harnisch (1), Smiley (0), Dibble (1), Morgan (1)	Dawson	
A	003 001 10x	4	8	0	Morris (2), **Key** (1), Clemens (1), McDowell (2), Reardon (0.2), Aguilera (1.1), Eckersley (1) **SV**	Ripken (2 on)	
1992 - JULY 14 AT SAN DIEGO							Americans set All-Star game records with 19 hits, including seven straight singles in the first inning, while tying the record for most runs. Griffey led the assault with three hits, including a home run, two runs scored and two RBIs.
A	411 004 030	13	19	1	**Brown** (1), McDowell (1), Guzman (1), Clemens (1), Mussina (1), Langston (1), Nagy (1), Montgomery (0.2), Aguilera (0.2), Eckersley (0.2)	Griffey, Sierra (1 on)	
N	000 001 032	6	12	1	**Glavine** (1.2), Maddux (1.1), Cone (1), Tewksbury (1.2), Smoltz (0.1), Martinez (1), Jones (1), Charlton (1)	Clark (2 on)	
1993 - JULY 13 AT BALTIMORE							Americans scored three times in both the fifth and sixth innings to claim their sixth consecutive victory. Sheffield's two-run homer gave the NL a 2-0 lead in the opening inning before AL tied the game on home runs by Puckett and Roberto Alomar. AL grabbed the lead in the fifth inning with run scoring hits by Belle, Griffey, and Puckett against losing pitcher Burkett.
N	200 001 000	3	7	2	Mulholland (2), Benes (2), **Burkett** (0.2), Avery (1), Smoltz (0.1), Beck (1), Harvey (1)	Sheffield (1 on)	
A	011 033 10x	9	11	0	Langston (2), Johnson (2), **McDowell** (1), Key (1), Montgomery (1), Aguilera (1), Ward (1)	R. Alomar, Puckett	
1994 - JULY 12 AT PITTSBURGH							Alou doubled home Gwynn from first base in the tenth inning to give the Nationals their first All-Star game victory in seven years. AL erased deficits of 4-1 and 5-4 to take a 7-5 lead into the ninth inning before pinch-hitter McGriff's tworun homer off Lee Smith tied it up and set the stage for the National's ninth victory in nine extra inning All-Star games.
A	100 003 300 0	7	15	0	Key (2), Cone (2), Mussina (1), Johnson (1), Hentgen (1), Alvarez (1), Smith (1), **Bere** (0)		
N	103 001 002 1	8	12	1	Maddux (3), Hill (2), Drabek (0.2), Hudek (0.2), Jackson (0), Beck (1.2), Myers (1), **Jones** (1)	Grissom, McGriff (1 on)	
1995 - JULY 11 AT TEXAS							Home runs accounted for all the scoring in the National League's victory. After Thomas homered with a man on to give AL a 2-0 lead, NL responded with solo clouts by Biggio, Piazza, and Conine, the NL's only three hits of the game. Conine's pinch homer off Ontiveros in the eighth was the decisive blow.
N	000 001 110	3	3	0	Nomo (2), Smiley (2), Green (1), Neagle (1), Perez (0.1), **Slocumb** (1), Henke (0.2), Myers (1) **SV**	Biggio, Piazza, Conine	
A	000 200 000	2	8	0	Johnson (2), Appier (2), Martinez (2), Rogers (1), **Ontiveros** (0.2), Wells (0.1), Mesa (1)	Thomas (1 on)	

PART FIFTEEN

The All-American Girls Professional Baseball League

The All-American Girls Professional Baseball League

This section presents a summary record of the All-American Girls Professional Baseball League (AAGPBL). Records of this league are extremely sketchy; however, thanks to the research of John Kovach, the Encyclopedia is able to provide an overview of the league: the teams and their nicknames, significant changes in the league's rules, the team standings, and a complete listing of every woman who ever played in the league.

The editorial staff of *The Baseball Encyclopedia* will welcome any additional materials and research on this unique period of baseball history that our readers are able to provide.

About the AAGPBL

In late 1942, World War II threatened the suspension of baseball play in the major leagues. Chicago Cubs owner Philip Wrigley decided to come up with a plan to put baseball in Wrigley Field even if major league play was shut down.

Wrigley, with the help of Cubs assistant general manager Ken Sells, brainstormed and came up with the idea of a women's professional baseball league. The league would be a hybrid version of men's baseball, with shorter pitching distances, shorter basepaths, a mandated underarm pitching delivery, and a ball that, at least at the beginning of the league, resembled a softball more than a standard-sized baseball.

The All-American Girls Professionall Baseball League (AAGPBL) made its debut in 1943 with teams in Racine and Kenosha, Wisconsin; Rockford, Illinois; and South Bend, Indiana. All of the women played in skirts. This was done, according to Wrigley, to show that the players could look feminine while still playing a terrific brand of ball.

Salaries in the AAGPBL ranged from $50 to $125 a week per player. At that time, an average wage earner was making around $40 a week. Fan interest in the league was slow at the start, butby the end of the first season, paid crowds of 3,000 or more were not uncommon. Several former major league players managed in the league, including Jimmie Foxx and Max Carey. Carey even served as league president in the late 1940s.

During the course of its run, the AAGPBL was at home at one time or another in fourteen different midwestern cities. Two of them, Rockford and South Bend, were the only two cities to field teams for the duration of the league (1943–54). In 1948, the league had ten teams that together drew one million paying customers. (At the same time, many men's minor league clubs were having attendance problems.) Several AAGPBL teams set attendance records of more than 100,000 paid fans during a single season.

After the 1944 season, when it appeared that major league play would not be interrupted, Wrigley sold the league to Chicago advertising executive Arthur Meyerhoff. It was under Meyerhoff that expansion and publicity of the AAGPBL reached its zenith.

Changes in ball size, basepath length, pitching distances, and pitching delivery (from underhand to sidearm to overhand) were made during Meyerhoff's tenure. However, after Meyerhoff turned over the franchises' publicity and operations to local team ownership in 1951, the lack of central control was a key factor in the league's ultimate decline.

In 1954, the last game was played in the AAGPBL. The owners decided to suspend play for the 1955 season, and the next season never got off the ground.

—John Kovach

Research Sources: South Bend Tribune, 1943–54; AAGPBL Players Association; AAGPBL Archives, Northern Indiana Historical Society, South Bend, Indiana.

ALL-AMERICAN GIRLS PROFESSIONAL BASEBALL LEAGUE TEAMS, NICKNAMES, SEASONS PLAYED

TEAMS	YEARS PLAYED
Rockford (IL) Peaches	1943–1954
South Bend (IN) Blue Sox	1943–1954
acine (WI) Belles	1943–1950
Kenosha (WI) Comets	1943–1951
Grand Rapids (MI) Chicks	1945–1954
Fort Wayne (IN) Daisies	1945–1954
Muskegon (MI) Lassies	1946–1949
Muskegon Belles	1953
Peoria (IL) Redwings	1946–1951
Kalamazoo (MI) Lassies	1950–1954
Battle Creek (MI) Belles	1951–1952
Milwaukee (WI) Chicks	1944
Minneapolis (MN) Millerettes	1944
Chicago (IL) Colleens	1948
Springfield (IL) Sallies	1948

RULE CHANGES, 1943–1954

YEAR	Ball Size	Basepaths	Pitching Dist.	Delivery
1943	12"	65'	40'	Underhand
1944	11½" (Mid-year)	68' (Mid-year)	40'	Underhand
1945	11½"	68'	42' (Mid-year)	Underhand
1946	11"	72'	43'	Underhand/ Limited Sidearm
1947	11"	72'	43'	Sidearm
1948	10⅜"	72'	50'	Overhand
1949	10"	72'	55' (Mid-year)	Overhand
1950	10"	72'	55'	Overhand
1952	10"	72'	55'	Overhand
1953	10"	75'	56'	Overhand
1954	9"–9¼" (Mid-year)	85'	60'	Overhand

YEARLY STANDINGS AND LEAGUE CHAMPIONS

1943

FIRST HALF	SECOND HALF
Racine, 20–15	Kenosha, 33–21
South Bend, 21–16	South Bend, 30–24
Kenosha, 16–19	Racine, 25–23
Rockford, 15–22	Rockford, 20–34

League Champion: Racine

1944

FIRST HALF	SECOND HALF
Kenosha, 36–23	Milwaukee, 40–19
South Bend, 33–25	South Bend, 31–27
Milwaukee, 31–27	Rockford, 29–28
Racine, 28–32	Racine, 26–31
Rockford, 24–32	Kenosha, 25–32
Minneapolis, 23–36	Minneapolis, 22–36

League Champion: Milwaukee

1945

Rockford, 67–43
Fort Wayne, 62–47
Grand Rapids, 60–50
Racine, 50–60
South Bend, 49–60
Kenosha, 41–69

League Champion: Rockford

1946

Racine, 74–38
Grand Rapids, 71–41
South Bend, 70–42
Rockford, 60–52
Fort Wayne, 52–60
Muskegon, 46–66
Kenosha, 42–70
Peoria, 33–79

League Champion: Racine

1947

Muskegon, 69–43
Grand Rapids, 65–47
Racine, 65–47
South Bend, 57–54
Peoria, 55–57
Rockford, 48–63
Fort Wayne, 45–67
Kenosha, 43–69

League Champion: Grand Rapids

1948

EASTERN DIVISION	WESTERN DIVISION
Grand Rapids, 77–47	Racine, 76–49
Muskegon, 66–57	Rockford, 74–49
South Bend, 57–69	Peoria, 70–55
Fort Wayne, 53–72	Kenosha, 61–64
Chicago, 47–76	Springfield, 41–84

League Champion: Rockford

1949

South Bend, 75–36
Rockford, 75–36*
Grand Rapids, 57–54
Kenosha, 56–55
Fort Wayne, 53–57
Muskegon, 46–66
Racine, 45–65
Peoria, 36–73

League Champion: Grand Rapids

1950

Rockford, 67–44
Fort Wayne, 62–43
Kenosha, 64–46
Grand Rapids, 59–53
South Bend, 55–55
Racine, 50–60

YEARLY STANDINGS AND LEAGUE CHAMPIONS *cont.*

Peoria, 44–63

Kalamazoo, 36–73

League Champion: Rockford

1951

FIRST HALF	**SECOND HALF**
Grand Rapids, 40–13	South Bend, 38–14
Fort Wayne, 34–17	Rockford, 34–15
South Bend, 38–22	Fort Wayne, 34–18
Rockford, 31–26	Grand Rapids, 31–22
Peoria, 28–25	Peoria, 21–31
Kenosha, 21–36	Battle Creek, 19–35
Kalamazoo, 19–38	Kenosha, 15–35
Battle Creek, 11–45	Kalamazoo, 15–37

League Champion: South Bend

1952

Fort Wayne, 67–42

South Bend, 64–45

Rockford, 55–54

Grand Rapids, 50–60

Kalamazoo, 49–60

Battle Creek, 43–67

League Champion: South Bend

1953

Fort Wayne, 66–39

Grand Rapids, 62–44

Kalamazoo, 56–50

Rockford, 51–55

South Bend, 44–62

Muskegon, 38–67

League Champion: Grand Rapids

1954

Fort Wayne, 54–40

South Bend, 48–44

Grand Rapids, 46–45

Kalamazoo, 48–49

Rockford, 37–55

League Champion: Kalamazoo

*Rockford defeated South Bend, four games to zero, in a best-of-seven playoff to be recognized as the divisional winner

ALL-AMERICAN GIRLS PROFESSIONAL BASEBALL LEAGUE PLAYER ROSTER

An asterisk after a player's maiden name indicates played in the league under that name

NAME	Maiden Name	Years Played	NAME	Maiden Name	Years Played	NAME	Maiden Name	Years Played
Abbott, Velma		1946–48	Barney, Edith		1948–49	Borg, Lorraine		1944
Adams, Evelyn		1946	Barr, Doris		1944–46	Born, Ruth		1943
Albright, Eileen		1948	Barringer, Patricia		194750	Boyce, Ethel		1946
Allard, Beatrice		1949	Baskovich, Mary	Beschorner*	1949–50	Bretting, Elizabeth	Fabac*	1946–48
Allen, Agnes		1949–54	Batikis, Anastasia		1945	Briggs, Rita		1947–54
Allen, Doreen Betty	Petryna*	1948–49	Battaglia, Fern		1951	Briggs, Wilma		1948–54
Alspaugh, Melba		1948–50	Baumgart, Jacquelin	Mattson*	1950–51	Brody, Leola		1943
Alvares, Isabel		1949–54	Baumgartner, Mary		1949–54	Brown, Barbara	Berger*	1949–50
Alverson, Noella	Leduc*	1951–54	Beare, Kathryn		1946	Brown, Marnie	Danhauser*	1943–49
Applegren, Amy Irene		1944–53	Becker, Donna		1950–51	Brown, Patricia		1950–51
Armato, Angie		1953	Beckett, Christine	Jewitt*	1948–49	Bryson, Marion		1946
Armstrong, Charlotte		1944–45	Bell, Virginia		1948	Buccor, Katherine		1946
Arnold, Lenna		1946	Bellman, Lois		1949	Buckley, Jean		1950–54
Arnold, Louise		1951–52	Benner, Gertrude	Alderfer*	1949	Bureker, Geraldine		1948–49
Atkinson, Barbara	Tetro*	1948–49	Bennett, Catherine		1943–44	Burkovich, Shirley		1949–51
Badini, Jane	Jacobs*		Berger, Margaret		1944	Butcher, Mary		1945
Bajda, Dolores	Mueller*	1949	Bergmann, Erma		1946–51	Caden, Mary Lou	Studnicka*	1951–53
Baker, Mary		1943–53	Bevis, Muriel		1950	Calacupcio, Aldine		1947
Ballingall, Chris		1953–54	Bird, Nalda		1945	Callow, Eleanor		1948–54
Barbaze, Barbara		1948	Bittner, Jaynne		1947–54	Cameron, Dorothy	Shinen*	1945
Barker, Joan	Lequia	1953	Blair, Maybell		1947–48	Campbell, Georgia		1946
Barker, Lois		1950	Blaski, Alice		1953–54	Campbell, Ruth		1949
Barnett, Charlene		1947–50	Blumetta, Kay		1944–54	Carey, Mary		1946–54

ALL-AMERICAN GIRLS PROFESSIONAL BASEBALL LEAGUE PLAYER ROSTER *cont.*

NAME	Maiden Name	Years Played	NAME	Maiden Name	Years Played	NAME	Maiden Name	Years Played
Carlson, Phyllis		1949	Dunn, Gertrude		1951–54	Heafner, Ruby		1946–51
Carroll, Margaret	Jurgensmeier*	1951	Dusanko, Julie		1944	Healy, Dorothy		1948
Carteaux, Rita	Rehrer*	1946	Dustrude, Beverly		1947	Hershey, Esther		1948
Carver, Virginia		1954	Dwojak, Loretta		1944	Heverly, Ruth	Williams*	1946–53
Carveth, Betty		1945	Earl, Elsie	Wingrove*	1946–47	Hickey, Lillian		1946–47
Cato, Nancy	Mudge*	1950–54	Earp, Mildred		1946–50	Hickson, Irene		1943–51
Chapman, Dorothy	McGuire*	1944–47	Eastman, Jean	Faut*	1946–53	Hill, Betty	Luna*	1944–50
Chester, Bea		1944	Edwards, Geraldine		1951	Hlavaty, Lillian		1951
Chiancola, Joan	Tysver	1950	Eisen, Thelma		1944–52	Hockbein, Violet	Hackbarth*	1946
Chiano, Clara		1944	Elliott, Gloria	Cordes*	1950–54	Hoffman, Nadine		1946
Childress, Cartha	Doyle*	1946–47	Emerson, June		1948–49	Hoffmann, Barbara		1951–52
Childress, Thelma		1946	Emry, Betty		1945–46	Holda, Mary		1943
Christ, Dorothy		1948	English, Madeline		1943–50	Holderness, Joan		1948–51
Cindric, Ann		1948–50	Ewald, Esther			Holgerson, Margaret	Silvestri	1946–52
Cione, Jean		1945–54	Faralla, Lillian		1946–51	Holle, Mable		1943
Clapp, Louise		1953	Fenton, Peggy		1945	Holmes, Agnes	Zurkowski*	1945
Clark, Corrine		1947	Ferguson, Fern		1945	Hood, Marjorie		1943
Coben, Muriel		1943	Ferguson, Sarah Jane	Sands*	1953–54	Hoover, Alice		1948
Colacito, Lucille		1944–45	Figlo, Josephine		1944	Horstman, Catherine		1950–54
Collins, Dorothy	Wiltse*	1944–50	Fisher, Alva Jo		1945–48	Hosbein, Marion		1954
Cook, Clara		1943–44	Fitzgerald, Meryle		1946	Hosted, Ann		1954
Cook, Donna		1946–54	Flaherty, Mary		1948	Huff, Anna	Kunkel*	1950–51
Cook, Doris		1949–53	Florreich, Lois		1943–50	Hundeby, Thelma	Grambo*	1946
Cook, Dorothy		1946	Foss, Anita		1948–51	Hunter, Dorothy		1943–54
Cooke, Penny	O'Brian*	1944–45	Foss, Betty	Weaver	1950–54	Hutchison, Anna May		1944–50
Cooper, Bonnie		1952	Fountain, Betty		1949	Jackson, Lillian		1943–45
Cornett, Betty Jane		1950–51	Fox, Helen	Nicol	1943–54	Jameson, Shirley		1943–48
Corrigan, Rita		1943	Francis, Betty		1949–54	Jamieson, Janet		1948
Courtney, Patricia		1950	Franks, Hermine		1946	Janowsky, Loretta		1951
Cramer, Peggy		1954	Fricker, Marion	Wohlwender*	1943	Janssen, Frances		1948–52
Crawley, Pauline		1946–51	Fritz, Betty Jane		1943–44	Jaykoski, Joan		1952
Crigler, Idona		1947–48	Gacioch, Rose		1944–54	Jenkins, Marilyn		1952–54
Crites, Shirley		1953	Galdonik, Barbara		1950–51	Jinright, Migdalia	Perez*	1948–54
Cryan, Marge	Villa*	1946–50	Gallegos, Luisa		1948–49	Jochum, Betsy		1943–48
D'Angelo, Josephine		1943–44	Gamberdella, Esther	Morrison*	1950	Johnson, Ester		1946
Dabbs, Sarah Mavis		1947	Gascon, Eileen		1949–51	Jones, Doris		1945
Daetweiler, Louella		1944	Gates, Barbara		1953–54	Jones, Margaret	Russo*	1950–54
Dailey, Mary		1950–51	Gentry, Ruth	Middleton*	1950–54	Junor, Daisy		1946–49
Dancer, Faye		1944–50	Georges, Beulah		1948–49	Kabick, Josephine		1944–47
Daniels, Audrey	Haines*	1944–51	Gilcrist, Jean		1946	Kamenshek, Dorothy		1943–53
Danz, Shirley		1949–50	Gilmore, June		1944	Kaufman, Joan E.		1954
Davis, Gladys		1943–47	Glaser, Rose Mary		1944	Kazmierczak, Marie		1944
Davis, Lavonne	Paire*	1944–53	Goldsmith, Bethany		1949–51	Keagle, Merle		1946–47
Davis, Marguerite	Jones*	1944	Gosbee, Ann		1954	Keating, Edythe	Perlick*	1943–49
Dean, Eileen	Burmeister*	1943–44	Grant, Olga		1944	Kelley, Lillian	Decambra*	1947
Dearfield, Norma	Whitney*	1949	Green, Dorothy		1943–53	Kelley, Marie M.	Mansfield*	1950–54
Decambra, Alice		1946–50	Griffin, Viola	Thompson*	1944–47	Kellogg, Vivian		1944–54
Deegan, Mildred		1943–52	Grund, Betty		1946	Kelly, Esther	Lyman*	1946
Deemer, Audrey		1950	Gutz, Julie		1948–50	Kemmerer, Beatrice		1950–51
Degner, Betty		1949	Habben, Carol		1953–54	Keough, Lavina		1946
Delmonico, Lena	Surkowski	1944–48	Haines, Martha		1947	Keppel, Evelyn		1947
Dennert, Pauline		1947	Hammond, Marlene		1954	Kerrar, Adeline		1944
Denoble, Jerre		1947	Hanna, Marjorie		1944	Kerrigan, Marguerite		1950–52
Denton, Mona		1946–47	Hardin, Julia		1946	Kerwin, Irene		1949–50
Deschaine, Alice	Pollit*	1947–53	Harding, Jean	Geissinger*	1951–54	Key, Dorothy	Ferguson*	1945–54
Deyotte, Anne	Surkowski	1945	Hargraves, Johanna	Hageman*	1943–49	Keyes, Erma		1951
Dokish, Wanita		1954	Harmon, Annabelle	Lee*	1944–50	Kidd, Glenna Sue		1949–54
Donahoe, Clara	Schillace*	1943–46	Harnett, Ann		1943–47	Kiely, Helen	Walulik*	1948–50
Donahue, Terry		1946–49	Harney, Elsie		1943–48	Kinney, Ysora	Castillo*	1949–51
Dowler, Jean	Lovell*	1948–54	Hasham, Josephine		1948–54	Kleinhams, Shirley		1948
Downs, Dorothea		1945	Havlish, Jean		1953–54	Klosowski, Delores		1943–44
Doxey, Marilyn	Jones*	1948–54	Hay, Florence		1949	Knebl, Joan	Berger*	1951–54
Doyle, Dorothy	Harrell*	1944–52	Haylett, Alice		1946–49	Kobucsewski, Thersa		1946–47
Dries, Dolores	Lee*	1952–54	Hayslip, Martha		1948	Koehn, Phyllis		1943–49
Dummerth, Edna	Frank*	1944	Headin, Irene		1945	Kolanko, Mary Lou		1950

ALL-AMERICAN GIRLS PROFESSIONAL BASEBALL LEAGUE PLAYER ROSTER *cont.*

NAME	Maiden Name	Years Played
Konalchik, Helen		1945
Konwinski, Dolly	Niemiec*	1949–52
Kotil, Arlene		1949–51
Kotowicz, Irene		1945–50
Krick, Jaynie		1949–52
Kruckel, Marie		1946–49
Kunkel, Karen	Violetta*	1953–54
Kurys, Sophie		1943–52
LaCamera, Helen	Ketola*	1950
Lafser, Audrey	Kissel*	1944
Lang, Margie		1943
Lawson, Mary		1946
Leach, Beverly		1947
Lee, Laurie Ann		1948
Lenard, Jo		1944–53
Lesko, Jeanie	DesCombes*	1953–54
Lessing, Ruth		1944–49
Lester, Mary Louise		1943–44
Liebrich, Barbara		1948–54
Linehan, Rhoda	Leonard*	1946
Lionikas, Kay		1948
Little, Alta		1947–48
Little, Olive		1943–46
Lobrovich, Clara		1947
Lonetto, Sarah		1947–48
Lovett, Frances		1946
Luckey, Lillian		1946
Luhtala, Shirley		1951
Mahon, Elizabeth B.		1944–52
Mahoney, Marie		1947–48
Malach, Kay		1946–47
Mandella, Lenora		1949–51
Manina, Virginia	Ventura	1952–53
Manning, Martha	Rommelaere*	1950
Marks, Gloria		1943–44
Marlowe, Jean		1948–54
(also played as Malanowski)		
Marrero, Mirtha		1948–53
Marsh, Doris		1945
Marshall, Theda		1947–49
Martin, Pauline		1946
Martz, Ruby	Knezovich*	1943–44
Mason, Pat		1950
Matlock, Ruth		1950
Maxwell, Bernadine		
Maxwell, Margaret	Callaghan*	1944–51
Mayer, Alice		1943
Mayer, Charlene	Pryer*	1946–52
Mc Faul, Gene	George*	1948
Mc Kenna, Betty		1951–53
Mc Veigh, Jeannie		
McAuley, Mildred	Warwick*	1943–44
McCloskey, Gloria		1953
McComb, Joanne		1950
McCreary, Ethel		1943
McCulloch, Colleen	Smith*	1949
McDaniel, Kay	Heim*	1943–44
McNaughton, Alice	Holmayer*	1946–50
Meacham, Mildred		1947–49
Meier, Naomi		1946–51
Melin, Berith		1943
Metesch, Bernice		1948–49
Metrolis, Norma		1946–50
Mikelson, Darlene		1943–45
Miller, Pauline		1948
Moczynski, Betty		1943
Moellering, Rita	Meyer*	1946–50
Moffet, Jane		1949–51
Montalbano, Rose		1951–52
Montgomery, Dorothy		1945–47
Moon, Dorothy		1946
Mooney, Georgette	Vincent*	1947–51
Moore, Dolores		1952–54
Moore, Eleanore		1951–52
Moore, Helen		1944
Moore, Mary		1950–52
Moraty, Mary		1946
Moroz, Evelyn	Wawryshyn*	1946–51
Morris, Carolyn		1944–46
Mueller, Dorothy		1947–53
Murk, Janet	Jacobs*	1944–47
Murray, Marge		1948–49
Nahtyk, Liz		1947
Neal, Doris		1948–49
Nearing, Merna		1943
Nobrain, Sally		1947
Noga, Arleene	Johnson*	1945–48
Nordquist, Helen		1951–54
Normine, Cynthia		1950
Norris, Donna		1953–54
O'Brien, Eileen		1946
O'Connor, Patricia		1946
O'Dowd, Anna Mae		1949–53
O'Hara, Janice		1943–50
O'Meara, Mary	Froning*	1951–54
Ogden, Joanne		1953
Olinger, Marilyn		1948–53
Ortman, Dorothy		1944
Overleese M.D., Joanne		1946
Ozburn, Dolly	Vanderlip*	1952–54
Palermo, Toni		1949–50
Palesh, Shirley		1949–50
Panos, Vickie		1944
Parker, Dorothy	Naum*	1946–51
Parrott, Beatrice	Arbour*	1947
Payne, Barbara		1949–51
Pechulis, Katherine		1948
Peppas, June		1948–54
Perkin, Janet	Anderson*	1946
Peters, Marjorie		1943–44
Petras, Ernestine		1944–52
Petrovic, Anna	Meyer*	1944
Pieper, Marge		1946–54
Piersol, Virginia	Carrigy*	1944
Pirok, Pauline		1944–47
Piskula, Grace		1944
Podolski, Bertha		1946
Powell, Rose	Folder	1944
Pratt, Mary		1943–47
Price, LaVerne		1944
Proefrock, Ellen	Ahrndt*	1944
Purdham, Mary Ellen	Kimball*	1948–49
Randall, Maxine	Kline*	1948–54
Rapp, Elizabeth	Farrow*	1944
Redman, Magdalen		1948–54
Reeser, Sara		1946–48
Reid, Dorice		1948–50
Reynolds, Mary		1946–49
Richard, Ruth		1947–54
Richards, Lucille	Stone*	1945
Richardson, Marie		1953
Ricketts, Joyce		1953–54
Rini, Mary		1945–46
Rios, Georgiana		1948
Risinger, Earlene		1948–54
Roach, Marian		1946
Rockwell, Nancy	DeShone*	1948
Rohrer, Kay		1945
Romatowski, Jenny		1946–54
Ross, Lucella	MacLean*	1943–44
Roth, Elaine		194851
Rotvig, Barbara		1948–49
Rountree M.D., Mary		1946–52
Roy, Patricia		1954
Roylance, Juanita		1946
Ruiz, Gloria		1948
Rukavina, Terry		1950–54
Rumsey, Janet		1951–54
Russell, Betty		1946
Rusynyk, Betty Jean	McFadden*	1943
Sams, Doris		1946–53
Sandiford, Helen	Nelson*	1943
Sanvitas, Irene	Ruhnke*	1944–47
Satterfield, Doris		1948–53
Sauer, Louise	Erickson*	1948–50
Savage, Jacquelyn	Kelley*	1947–53
Schachter, Blanche		1948
Schallern, Ellen		1946
Schatz, Joan		1950–52
Scheer, Edna		1950
Schenck, Audrey		1950
Schick, Yolande	Teillet*	1945–47
Schmidt, Marilyn		1952
Schofield, June		1948–49
Schroeder, Dorothy		1943–54
Schuller, Betty	Bayse*	1950
Schulze, Shirley		1944
Schweigerdt, Gloria		1950–52
Scott, Patricia		1948–53
Sears, Janet	Wiley*	1950–51
Seitzinger, Audrey	Bleiler*	1950–51
Shadic, Lillian		1949
Shastal, Mary	Kustra	1944
Sheriffs, Vivian	Anderson*	1943–44
Shively, Twila		1945–50
Shollenberger, Fern		1946–54
Shuman, Amy		1946
Siegfried, Delores		1947
Simmons, Maxine	Drinkwater*	1954
Simpson, Louise		1944
Sindelar, Joan		1949–50
Sloan, Francis		1946
Smith, Charlotte		1943–44
Smith, Helen		1946–47
Smith, Jean		1948–54
Smith, Marjean		1948
Smith, Shirley		1947
Sopkovic, Kay		1945
Sowers, Barbara		1953–54

ALL-AMERICAN GIRLS PROFESSIONAL BASEBALL LEAGUE PLAYER ROSTER *cont.*

NAME	Maiden Name	Years Played
Stagman, Donna		1946
Stanton, Marion	Watson*	1946–47
Starck, Mae		1947
St. Aubin, Helen	Callaghan*	1944–49
Steele, Joyce		1953
Stefani, Margaret		1943–47
Steffes, Helen	Filarski*	1944–50
Stephens, Ruby		1946–50
Steuert, Beverly		1952
Stevens, Lorraine	Fisher*	1947–49
Stevenson, Emily		1944–45
Stevenson, Rosemary		1954
Stocker, Jeanette		1946
Stoll, Jane		1946–54
Stolze, Dorothy		1946–52
Stovroff, Shirley		1948–52
Straka, Sylvia	Wronski*	1944–45
Sutherland, Shirley		1950
Taylor, Eunice		1950–51
Taylor, Mary		1953–54
Taylor, Norma	Berger*	1950
Terkowski, Georgia		1952–53
Terry, Betty		1946
Tesseine, Dolly	Pearson*	1948–54
Tetzlaff, Doris		1944–53
Tezak, Virginia		1948–49
Thomas, Erla		1944
Thomas, Helen		1951
Thomas, Mava Lee		1951
Thompson, Anne Jane		1943–44
Thompson, Barbara		1951–52
Thompson, Beverly	Stuhr*	1949–50
Thompson, Mary		1944
Tipton, Gloria		1946
Tognatti, Alice		1946
Torrison, Loraine		1944
Trezza, Betty		1944–50
Tronnier, Ellen		1943
Tucker, Elizabeth		1946–49
Uselmann, Therese	McKinley*	1949
Van Sant, Helene	Machado*	1946–47
Visich, Gene	Travis*	1948
Volkert, Beverly	Hatzell*	1949–51
Volkov, Kay	Shinen*	1945
Vonderau, Kathryn		1946–53
Voyce, Inez		1946–53
Vukovich, Francis		1950
Wagner, Audrey		1944–48
Wagoner, Betty		1948–54
Walker, Dodie	Nelson*	1947–48
Walker, Nellie Jean		1945
Walmsley, Thelma		1946
Walter, Mary		1946
Wanless, Betty		1953–54
Warfel, Betty		1948
Warner, Elleanor	Moore*	1950–54
Warren, Nancy		1946–54
Weaver, Jean		1950–53
Weaver, Joanne		1951–54
Weddle, Mary		1954
Weeks, Rossey		1947
Wegman, Marie		1947–50
Weierman, Shirley Ann		1953–54
Weise, Gertrude	Ganote*	1944–45
Weiss, Elma	Steck*	1948–49
Weitzman, Violet	Schmidt*	1946
Wenzell, Margaret		1945–53
Westerman, Helen		1944
Westerman, Joyce	Hill*	1945–49
Whalen, Dorothy		1943
Whalen, Ruth		1948
White, Delores	Brumfield*	1947–53
Whiteman, Vera		1946
Whiting, Betty		1944–52
Wicken, Elizabeth	Berthiaume*	1945–46
Wigiser, Margaret		1944–45
Wildfong, Hazel	Measner	1946–47
Williams, Wilma		1953
Wilson, Verna		1946
Wind, Dorothy		1943–44
Winn, Laverne		1950
Winter, Doris	Harrington*	1952
Winter, Joanne		1943–50
Wirth, Senaida		1946–50
Wise, Phyllis	Baker*	1953–54
Wisham, Mary	Nesbitt*	1943–50
Wisniewski, Connie		1944–52
Witiuk, Doris	Shero*	1950
Witzel, Norene	Arnold*	1949
Wolf, Eleanor	Dapkus*	1943–50
Wood, Mary		1946–47
Wood, Trois		1951
Wuethrich, Lorraine		1943–44
Wyatt, Helen	Waddell*	1950–51
Yahr, Betty R.		1946
Young, Barbara	Parks*	1950
Youngberg, Renae		1951–54
Youngen, Lois		1951–54
Zale, Philomena T.	Gianfrancisco*	1945–49
Zeigler, Marie		1953–54
Ziegler, Alma		1944–54
Zillmer, Ruth	Ries*	1952
Zipay, Sue	Parsons*	1953–54
Zonia, Violet		1948
Zoromapa, Marie	Menheer*	1945

Appendixes

A. Sources
B. Decisions of the Special Baseball Records Committee
C. Major Changes in Playing Rules and Scoring Rules

Appendix A
Sources

The following is the list of official documents, private collections, and newspapers that were used during the research of this volume:

Official Records

American League, 1905–present
National League, 1903–present

Collections

Lee Allen   John Tattersall   Files of the National Baseball Hall of Fame and Museum, Cooperstown, N.Y.

Trade Papers

The Sporting Life (1885–1916)   *The Sporting News* (1916–)
The Sporting Times (1890)

Newspapers

Albany, N.Y.	*Argus*
Altoona, Pa.	*Morning Tribune, Times*
Baltimore, Md.	*American, Herald, Sun*
Boston, Mass.	*Globe, Herald, Morning Journal, Post, Daily Advertiser, Evening Transcript*
Brooklyn, N.Y.	*Daily Eagle*
Buffalo, N.Y.	*Courier-Express, Evening News, Times*
Chicago, Ill.	*Daily News, Evening Journal, Evening Mail, Herald Interocean, Record, Record Herald, Times, Tribune*
Cincinnati, Ohio	*Commercial Gazette, Commercial Tribune, Enquirer, Evening Telegram, News Journal, Post, Times-Star*
Cleveland, Ohio	*Evening Herald, Leader, Plain Dealer, World*
Columbus, Ohio	*Dispatch, Evening Post, Evening Press, Ohio State Journal*
Detroit, Mich.	*Evening News, Free Press, Journal, Post and Tribune, Times, Tribune*
Hartford, Conn.	*Courant, Times*
Indianapolis, Ind.	*Journal, News Sentinel, Star*
Kansas City, Mo.	*Journal, Star, Star-Times, Times*
Louisville, Ky.	*Commercial, Courier-Journal*
Milwaukee, Wis.	*Daily News, Evening Wisconsin, Journal, Sentinel*
Newark, N.J.	*Eagle, News, Star-Ledger*
New York, N.Y.	*American, Clipper, Herald, Journal, Mail, News, Post, Press, Sun, Telegram, Times, Tribune, World*
Philadelphia, Pa.	*Evening Bulletin, Inquirer, Item, Ledger, North American, Press, Record, Times*
Pittsburgh, Pa.	*Chronicle-Telegraph, Dispatch, Gazette, Leader, Post, Press, Times*
Providence, R.I.	*Evening Bulletin, Journal, Press, Telegram*
Richmond, Va.	*Dispatch, State, Whig*
Rochester, N.Y.	*Democrat and Chronicle, Herald, Post and Express, Union and Advertiser*
St. Louis, Mo.	*Globe-Democrat, Missouri Republican, Post-Dispatch, Star-Times*
Syracuse, N.Y.	*Courier, Daily Standard, Herald, Journal*
Toledo, Ohio	*Bee, Blade*
Troy, N.Y.	*Press, Telegram, Times*
Washington, D.C.	*Evening Star, Herald, Post, Sunday Chronicle, Sunday Sentinel, Times*
Wilmington, Del.	*Journal Every Evening, Morning News, Star*
Worcester, Mass.	*Evening Gazette, Spy*

The following is the Editorial Staff listing that appeared in the landmark first edition of *The Baseball Encyclopedia,* published in 1969. While considerable work has been done on the Encyclopedia since then, the work of these people formed the foundation on which all subsequent efforts have been based.

Editorial Staff

DAVID S. NEFT
Director of Research, Information Concepts Incorporated

LEE ALLEN
Historian, National Baseball Hall of Fame and Museum

ROBERT MARKEL
Executive Editor, The Macmillan Company

John C. Tattersall
Consulting Editor

Neil R. Armann
Systems Manager

Jordan A. Deutsch
Associate Editor

Research Supervisors

Richard M. Cohen, Donald C. Henry, Roland T. Johnson

Researchers

Gary R. Abram, N. Richard Anderson, Eugene B. Galusha, Irving Moss, Alan Stolowitz

Associate Researchers

William R. Bevilacqua, Stephen Hirdt, John G. Hogrogian, John Liscio, Dennis J. Murphy, William J. Murphy, George A. Shanahan, James M. Taylor, Raymond J. Walsh, Richard Wangeman

Assistant Researchers

Thomas E. Alberto, Charles D. Blatz, John Boyle, Robert F. Brennan, Calvin Clark, Alphonso Cook, Jr., Michael J. Kitson, Mati Kuuskmae, Edward Madera, James C. Madera, Thomas J. Malvey, Philip A. Marino, Robert Re, Ronald J. Riccardi

Programmers

Joanne Cotterill, Senior Programmer

Harriet Cinque, Anselmo O. Clarke, Robert A. Hyslop, R. William Ihrie, Basil M. Jarrett, Lawrence A. Lenczewski

Design and Production

Abe Lerner, Faulkner Lewis

Additional research for the tenth edition has been provided by members of the Society for American Baseball Research, including Robert Anderson, Bob Bailey, Dan Bennett, Joey Beretta, Clarence Blasco, Richard Bozzone, Arnie Braunstein, William Carle, Bob Davids, Harold Dellinger, Dan Dischley, Joe Dittmar, Jack Dougherty, Scott Flatow, Jerry Gregory, Chuck Hershberger, Ralph Horton, Tom Hufford, John Husman, Lou Jacobson, Dr. Jose J. Jimenez, Richard Johnson, Ed Koller, Fred London, Bob McConnell, Andy McCue, Norman Macht, Peter Morris, David Nemec, Joe Overfield, Frank Phelps, Rich Puff, Bob Richardson, John Schwartz, Tom Shrimplin, Joe Simenic, Bill Simpson, Jack Smalling, David Smith, Lyle Spatz, Bob Tholkes, Dick Thompson, Dave Vincent, William Weiss, Walt Wilson, Ralph Winnie, and Dave Zeman.

Appendix B

Decisions of the Special Baseball Records Committee

In 1887 eleven men had batting averages higher than .400. It is an astonishing feat, until one learns that bases on balls were counted as hits in the official averages that year. There are other such records based on definitions which were either incomplete or inconsistent with the rest of baseball history. It was because of these factors that it became necessary to draw up a code of rules governing record-keeping procedures. A group was formed for this purpose and was called the Special Baseball Records Committee.

It should be noted that the Committee's concern was not with laying future ground rules, which is the duty of the Baseball Rules Committee, but rather to establish the rules governing record-keeping procedures that mostly concern past play.

David Grote, director of public relations for the National League, and Robert Holbrook, executive assistant to the president of the American League, served as co-chairmen of the Special Baseball Records Committee.

Other members included Jack Lang, secretary-treasurer of the Baseball Writers Association of America, Joseph Reichler, director of public relations of the office of the Commissioner of Baseball, and Lee Allen, historian of the Baseball Hall of Fame.

The Committee met twice in 1968. At the first meeting, which took place in St. Petersburg, Florida, on March 5, they voted on the issues in question. The Committee met again in New York City on November 14, and reviewed their decisions after they were given an opportunity to see what changes had resulted in the records after much of the research was completed.

Most of the important issues concerned the period before 1920, a time that was somewhat chaotic in baseball record-keeping procedures. The following is a list of the decisions on seventeen issues as voted by the Committee:

1. The following leagues are defined as "major":

National League, 1876 to the present	Federal League, 1914–15
American League, 1901 to the present	Players' League, 1890
American Association, 1882–91	Union Association, 1884

The National Association, 1871–1875, shall not be considered as a "major league" due to its erratic schedule and procedures, but it will continue to be recognized as the first professional baseball league.

2. Major league baseball shall have one set of records, starting in 1876, without any arbitrary division into nineteenth- and twentieth-century data.

3. There shall be no change in rules used in past years governing the minimum appearances necessary for recognition as a league leader for averages (batting average, slugging average, fielding average, earned run average, and pitchers' winning percentage).

4. For all-time single season records, no asterisk or official sign shall be used to indicate the number of games scheduled.

5. Performances in all tie games of five or more innings shall be included in the official averages. (Before 1885 this was not done.)

6. Several games in the National League in 1877, 1879, and 1899 that were subsequently declared "unofficial" for varying reasons, shall now be counted as "official."

7. All appearances by a player in an official game shall be counted as a game played. (Before 1912 many pinch hitters, pinch runners, and substitutes who did not bat were not credited with a game played.)

8. Bases on balls shall always be treated as neither a time at bat nor a hit for the batter. (In 1887 bases on balls were scored as hits and in 1876 bases on balls were scored as outs.)

9. A distinction shall be made in the definition of stolen bases. Before 1898 stolen bases were credited any time a runner advanced an extra base on a hit or out. Since these bases advanced cannot be separated from bases stolen, according to the modern definition, there shall be two sets of records, one starting with 1898 and the other before 1898.

10. Bases on balls, wild pitches, passed balls, balks, and hit batsmen shall not be counted as errors. (These items were frequently scored as errors before 1889.)

11. A pitcher shall not be credited with an assist on a strikeout. (Before 1889 pitchers were usually awarded an assist on a strikeout.)

12. Scoring rules governing won and lost decisions by a pitcher did not become official until 1950. It was decided that all pitching decisions during the period 1901–49 shall stand as they are in the official records, but that for the period 1876–1900 the 1950 ruling shall be in effect. The reason for this was that since 1920 the official scorer did exist, and he had the explicit authority to award the victory based on common practice, which was very close to the rule adopted in 1950. In the pre-1901 period, however, there was no official scoring rule or common practice for wins by a pitcher and for many years no official scorer.

13. The present definition on earned runs, as was established in 1969 by the Baseball Scoring Rules Committee, shall be effective from that date on in defining earned runs. Prior to that date, the 1917 definition of earned runs shall be applied to the years 1876–1911, and to the American League in 1912. (Before 1912 there was a period when there was no official compilation of earned runs, and a time where bases on balls, hit batsmen, and wild pitches were considered errors in the computation of earned runs.)

14. Fractional innings pitched shall be used in the calculation of earned run averages.

15. The earned run average of a pitcher who allowed one or more earned runs during a season without retiring a batter shall be "infinity."

16. 1894 shall be considered the starting date for exempting a man from a time at bat for a sacrifice bunt hit. Before 1894 a batter was credited with a sacrifice hit and charged with a time at bat every time he advanced a runner on any type of out.

17. Sudden Death Home Runs. Before 1920, when the team batting last won the game in the ninth or in an extra inning, the ruling was that the team could not win by more than one run. If a man hit an outside-the-park home run, which, under present rules, would have resulted in a victory by more than one run, he was given credit for a lesser hit and only the winning run counted. The committee originally voted that before 1920 any ball hit outside the park in a sudden death situation should be counted as a home run. However, after the committee had a further opportunity to review their ruling and polled their colleagues on the issue, they reversed their decision on May 5, 1969. The following 40 players lost home runs because of the rulings:

DATE	BATTER	TEAM	LEAGUE	OPP.	HIT
June 17, 1884	Roger Connor	N.Y.	N.L.	Bos.	Single
Sept. 6, 1884	Hardy Richardson	Buf.	N.L.	Bos.	Triple
April 21, 1885	Fred Mann	Pit.	A.A.	Lou.	Double
July 30, 1885	Tommy McCarthy	Bos.	N.L.	Det.	Double
Aug. 20, 1885	Paul Hines	Pro.	N.L.	Bos.	Single
June 5, 1890	Sam Thompson	Phi.	N.L.	Bkn.	Single
July 30, 1890	Al McCauley	Phi.	N.L.	Chi.	Triple
June 17, 1890	Mike Griffin	N.Y.	P.L.	Phi.	Double
May 7, 1891	King Kelly	Cin.	A.A.	Bos.	Single
Sept. 13, 1891	George Wood	Phi.	A.A.	Mil.	Double (first game)
July 7, 1892	Buck Ewing	N.Y.	N.L.	St. L.	Single
May 13, 1893	Lou Bierbauer	Pit.	N.L.	Lou.	Single
Aug. 9, 1893	George Van Haltren	Pit.	N.L.	Chi.	Double
June 20, 1894	Hugh Duffy	Bos.	N.L.	Bal.	Triple
Aug. 27, 1895	Bill Lange	Chi.	N.L.	Was.	Single
Sept. 2, 1895	Mike Tiernan	N.Y.	N.L.	Cle.	Triple
Sept. 27, 1895	Duke Farrell	N.Y.	N.L.	Bal.	Triple
July 27, 1896	Charlie Irwin	Cin.	N.L.	Cle.	Triple
June 4, 1897	Parke Wilson	N.Y.	N.L.	Lou.	Double
July 15, 1899	Jimmy Collins	Bos.	N.L.	Pit.	Single
July 24, 1899	Ginger Beaumont	Pit.	N.L.	Phi.	Triple
July 24, 1900	Jimmy Collins	Bos.	N.L.	St. L.	Single
July 27, 1900	Chick Stahl	Bos.	N.L.	Pit.	Single
May 17, 1901	Bill Coughlin	Was.	A.L.	Phi.	Single
Sept. 1, 1902	Ed Gremminger	Bos.	N.L.	Cin.	Double
June 26, 1903	Pat Moran	Bos.	N.L.	Chi.	Triple
Aug. 31, 1903	Barry McCormick	Was.	A.L.	Bos.	Triple
Sept. 10, 1904	Roger Bresnahan	N.Y.	N.L.	Phi.	Double
May 5, 1906	Sherry Magee	Phi.	N.L.	Bkn.	Triple
June 2, 1906	Tim Jordan	Bkn.	N.L.	Bos.	Double
Apr. 30, 1908	Frank Bowerman	Bos.	N.L.	N.Y.	Double
May 25, 1908	Joe Tinker	Chi.	N.L.	N.Y.	Double
Sept. 28, 1908	Cy Seymour	N.Y.	N.L.	Phi.	Single
April 23, 1910	Doc Crandall	N.Y.	N.L.	Bkn.	Single
Aug. 24, 1911	Tex Erwin	Bkn.	N.L.	Chi.	Triple
June 17, 1914	Sherry Magee	Phi.	N.L.	St. L.	Double
April 19, 1917	Ping Bodie	Phi.	A.L.	Bos.	Triple
July 8, 1918	Babe Ruth	Bos.	A.L.	Cle.	Triple
July 18, 1918 (second game)	Frank Baker	N.Y.	A.L.	Det.	Single
April 19, 1918	Irish Meusel	Phi.	N.L.	Bos.	Triple

Appendix C

Major Changes in Playing Rules and Scoring Rules

Part of the history of major league baseball is the history of playing and scoring rules. This is a continual process of trying to maintain the delicate balance between offense and defense, trying to ensure the fairest possible scoring decisions, and closing obscure loopholes discovered by alert observers. Listed here are the major changes in the rules since 1876 as they have been adopted. Included are scoring practices that were not officially adopted as rules but that were used in the compilation of the official averages. An asterisk (*) before a rule indicates that this scoring rule was affected by a decision of the Special Baseball Records Committee (see Appendix B).

1877 *Time at bat not charged to the batter on a base on balls.

1880 Base on balls on eight balls instead of nine.
Runner out if hit by a batted ball.
Catcher must catch ball on a fly to retire the batter on a strikeout.

1881 Pitcher's box located 50 feet from home plate instead of 45 feet.

1882 Base on balls on seven balls.

1883 *Error charged to the pitcher for a base on balls, wild pitch, hit batter, and balk.
*Error charged to the catcher for a passed ball.
Foul ball caught on the first bounce is no longer an out.

1884 Pitcher's motion limited to a shoulder-high delivery, instead of a delivery where his hand must pass below his hip.
Base on balls on six balls.

1885 *Official averages to include performances in all tie games of five or more innings.
A portion of one side of the bat may be flat instead of round.
Pitcher credited with an assist on batter's strikeout.

1886 Pitcher's box changed to 4 × 7 feet, instead of 6 × 6 feet.
Base on balls on seven balls.
*Stolen base credited to the runner for each base advanced by his own volition (i.e., if the runner advances from first to third on a single, he is credited with a stolen base).

1887 Batter no longer allowed to call for a high or low pitch.
Strike zone defined as the area between the top of the shoulder and the bottom of the knee.
Pitcher's box changed to 4 × 5 1/2 feet.
Batter hit by pitched ball entitled to first base and not charged with the time at bat.
Base on balls on five balls.
*Batter's base on balls credited as a hit, and charged as a time at bat.
No error charged to the catcher on a passed ball.
No error charged to the pitcher for a base on balls, wild pitch, hit batter, and balk.
Strikeout on four strikes instead of three strikes, where the first called third strike did not count.

1888 Batter's base on balls not a hit or a time at bat.
*Error charged to the pitcher for a base on balls, wild pitch, hit batter, and balk.
Batter credited with a hit if the base runner is struck by a batted ball.
Strikeout on three strikes.
Ground rule double instead of a home run if the ball is batted over the fence in fair territory where the fence is less than 210 feet from home plate.
*Error charged to the catcher on a passed ball.

1889 No error charged to the catcher on a passed ball.
No error charged to the pitcher for a base on balls, wild pitch, hit batter, and balk.
Sacrifice bunt recognized, but the batter charged with a time at bat.

Bases on balls on four balls.
Pitcher not credited with an assist for batter's strikeout.

1891 Any player may be substituted during a game, but the player substituted for may not re-enter the game. (Before this, substitutions could be made only in case of an injury or with the permission of the opposing team.)

1892 Ground rule double if the ball is hit over the fence in fair territory where the fence is less than 235 feet from home plate.

1893 Pitching distance lengthened to 60 feet 6 inches, and marked by a rubber slab 12 inches long and 4 inches wide.The bat must be completely round.

1894 *When a bunt results in advancing a base runner and the batter is put out, or could have been put out, the batter is credited with a sacrifice hit and not charged with a time at bat. (This rule was actually adopted in 1893, but was not used at all until 1894 and not uniformly recognized until 1897.)
Batter charged with a strike for hitting a foul bunt.

1895 Pitcher's rubber enlarged to 24 × 6 inches.
Maximum diameter of the bat increased to 2¾ inches from 2½ inches.
Batter automatically out on an infield fly when there is one out and first and second or first, second, and third bases are occupied.
Strike charged to a batter on a foul tip.

1897 *Earned run is a run scored by the aid of hits only.

1898 *Stolen base credited to the base runner whenever he reaches a base he attempted to steal without the aid of battery or fielding errors or a hit by the batter.
Error not charged to the infielder attempting to complete a double play unless the throw is so wild it gives the runner an additional base.
Error not charged against the catcher attempting to prevent a stolen base unless the throw is so wild it gives the runner an additional base.

1900 A pitcher must win at least 15 games to qualify as the league leader in Winning Percentage, instead of appearing in at least 25 games.
Home plate changed from a 12-inch square to a 5-sided figure 17 inches wide.

1901 Infield fly rule changed to be in effect when there are no outs, as well as when there is one out.
Any foul ball not caught on a fly is a strike unless the batter has two strikes on him (National League).

1903 Pitcher's mound must not be higher than 15 inches above the base lines and home plate.
Any foul ball not caught on a fly is a strike unless the batter has two strikes on him (American League).

1907 *All appearances by a player in an official game count as a game played (American League). Before this, pinch hitters, pinch runners, and defensive substitutes often were not credited with a game played.

1908 Batter credited with a sacrifice fly and not charged with a time at bat if he hits a fly ball which is caught, but a runner scores on the catch.

1909 Pitcher or catcher charged with an error if a wild pitch or passed ball on the third strike allows the batter to reach first base.
Stolen base not credited to any runner on an attempted double steal if either runner is thrown out.
Bunt on third strike is a strikeout and the catcher is credited with the put out.

1912 Earned run charged to the pitcher every time a player scores by the aid of safe hits, sacrifice hits, base on balls, hit batters, wild pitches, and balks before fielding chances have been offered to retire the side.
*All appearances by a player in an official game count as a game played (National League). Before this, pinch hitters, pinch runners, and defensive substitutes often were not credited with a game played.

1917 Earned runs also include runs scored by the aid of stolen bases.

1920 The spitball and other unorthodox deliveries abolished. Special provision made to allow each team to name two pitchers as spitball pitchers for the 1920 season and thereafter no spitballers will be allowed.
If the batter hits a home run in the bottom of the ninth or subsequent innings with the winning run on base, all runners, including the batter, shall score, instead of just the winning run, and the batter shall be credited with a home run instead of the number of bases necessary to score the winning run.
A ball hit over the fence will be judged fair or foul in respect to where the ball was when it passed over the fence, instead of where it landed.
If the winning run is on base in the bottom half of the final inning and the batter drives the run home, credit the batter with as many bases as the runner had to take in order to score, instead of the number of bases the batter made before the runner scored.
Stolen base not credited to the runner if no effort is made to put the runner out.
A player must appear in at least 100 games to qualify

1975 In their December 1975 meeting, the American League adopted the designated hitter as a permanent official rule. The National League decided against adopting the designated hitter rule for its use.

The relief pitcher's save rule was amended again. A pitcher shall be credited with a save when he is the finishing but not the winning pitcher and when he qualifies under one of the following conditions: (1) he enters the game with a lead of no more than three runs and pitches for at least one inning; (2) he enters the game with the potential tying run either on base, at bat, or on deck; or (3) he pitches effectively for at least three innings regardless of his team's lead.

1978 On December 5, 1978, at a meeting of the Baseball Playing Rules Committee, several rules changes were adopted. The changes were to be effective with the start of the 1979 season.

The first change alters Playing Rules 4.11 and 4.12 creating, under certain circumstances, suspended games instead of reverting to a prior inning when rain forces the calling of games. In fairness to the visiting team which does not control game conditions, revised section 4.11(d) is amended to read:

(d) A called game ends at the moment the umpire terminates play.
EXCEPTION: If the game is called while an inning is in progress and before it is completed, the game becomes a SUSPENDED GAME in each of the following situations:
(1) The visiting team has scored one or more runs to tie the score and the home team has not scored.
(2) The visiting team has scored one or more runs to take the lead and the home team has not tied the score or retaken the lead.

The change on protested games reads as follows: "Even if it is held that the protested decision violated the rules, no replay of the game will be ordered unless in the opinion of the League President the violation adversely affected the protesting team's chances of winning the game" (4.19). This rule revision will protect a team that won a game convincingly on its merits from being penalized on a technicality.

A victory will not be credited to a relief pitcher who is ineffective in a brief appearance when a succeeding relief pitcher pitches effectively in helping his team maintain the lead. In such cases, the succeeding relief pitcher will be credited with the victory.

A new official statistic has been added: The RBI that gives a club the lead which it never relinquishes.

A pitcher who pitches only one-third of an inning in an entire season will not have his total ERA "rounded off" as is the normal procedure. In such cases, his total for innings pitched will be carried as one-third. Any games played to break a divisional tie shall be included in the statistics for that championship season. Official Scoring Rules will now include the examples that currently appear on the Official Score Sheet.

1982 Earned run average shall be calculated on the basis of a pitcher's total innings pitched, including fractional innings, which are not to be rounded off.

1987 In early December, Commissioner Peter Ueberroth announced a further clarification of the strike zone. Specifically, that the strike zone is that area over home plate, the upper limit of which is a horizontal line at the midpoint between the top of the shoulders and the top of the uniform pants, and the lower level is a line at the top of the knees. The strike zone shall be determined from the batter's stance as the batter is prepared to swing at a pitched ball.

1989 The game-winning RBI has been eliminated as an official statistic.

1991 The commissioner's office determined new scoring guidelines for no-hit games. Under these guidelines, a pitcher must pitch at least nine innings and pitch a complete game and allow no hits in order to qualify as having pitched a no-hit game.

Combined no-hitters. If a game is completed after at least nine full innings without any hit being given up and more than one pitcher has pitched in the game for the team not allowing any hits, this game shall be deemed a no-hitter and shall be identified as a combined no-hitter.

No-hitters of less than nine innings. If a game is ruled to be complete but less than nine innings have been played and no hits have been given up, that game shall not be an official no-hitter but rather shall be identified separately as a game comprised of a certain number of no-hit innings.

No-hitters broken up in extra innings. Games which are completed after more than nine full innings during which no hits were given up by a pitcher until after the ninth inning shall not be no-hitters but shall be identified as "games by pitchers who pitched nine or more hitless innings."

These same rules shall apply to perfect games.

The commissioner's office also determined that Roger Maris's single-season home run record of 61, set in a 162-game season in 1961, would no longer have an asterisk associated with it. However, it should be pointed out that in 1968, a special records committee made up of representatives from the commissioner's office, the Hall of Fame, and the Baseball Writers Association of America had already ruled that no asterisks shall ever be placed next to any single season record (see Appendix B, rule 4).

1996 The strike zone is that area over home plate, the upper limit of which is a horizontal line at the midpoint between the top of the shoulders and the top of the uniform pants, and the lower level is a line at the hallow beneath the knee cap.

Note:

The following were the qualifications used in this volume to determine league leaders in categories where no formal rule has ever been adopted:

A relief pitcher must win at least 8 games in relief to qualify as the league leader in Winning Percentage.

A relief pitcher must pitch at least one-third of an inning in relief for every scheduled game to qualify as the league leader in Earned Run Average and all relief pitching averages other than Winning Percentage.

Pinch Hit Batting Average—A pinch hitter must have at least 30 at bats to qualify as the league leader.

For All Other Batting Averages and Percentages—It is the rule that was used for Batting Average in effect at the time.

For All Other Fielding Averages and Percentages—It is the rule that was used for Fielding Averages at the particular position in effect at the time.

For All Other Pitching Averages and Percentages—It is the rule that was used for Earned Run Averages in effect at the time.